S0-AIQ-617

Presented to

By

On

IN THE BEGINNING WAS THE WORD,
AND THE WORD WAS WITH GOD,
AND THE WORD WAS GOD.

JOHN 1:1

One Solitary Life

AUTHOR UNKNOWN

He was born in an obscure village, the child of a peasant woman. He grew up in another village, where he worked in a carpenter shop until he was thirty. Then for three years he was an itinerant preacher.

He never wrote a book. He never held an office. He never traveled more than two hundred miles from the place where he was born. He did none of the things one usually associates with greatness.

He was only thirty-three when the tide of public opinion turned against him. He was turned over to his enemies and went through the mockery of a trial. He was nailed to a cross between two thieves. When he was dead, he was laid in a borrowed grave.

Nineteen centuries have come and gone, and today he is the central figure of the human race and leader of mankind's progress.

All the armies that ever marched, all the navies that ever sailed, all the kings that ever reigned have not affected the life of man as much as that One Solitary Life.

TOP TEN SURPRISES ABOUT *Jesus*

BY PHILIP YANCEY

Growing up in the church, I learned the name of Jesus as soon as I learned the names of my family members. But now, as I reflect on what I learned in the process of writing *The Jesus I Never Knew*, some childhood impressions have been confirmed, others overturned. I have come up with a "top ten" list of insights that surprised me.

1. JESUS WAS A JEW

I knew that, of course. But the more I studied Jesus, the more I realized that his humanity had receded far away. I knew Christ—"Light of Light, very God of very God, begotten, not made"—but not Jesus, or Rabbi Jeshua bar-Joseph, the Jew from Nazareth.

Jesus' true-blue Jewishness leaps out from Matthew's very first sentence, which introduces him as the son of David, the son of Abraham. Jesus grew up in an era of Jewish pride, when families were adopting names that harked back to the times of the patriarchs and the exodus from Egypt (not unlike ethnic Americans who choose African names for their children). Circumcised as a baby, Jesus attended religious festivals in Jerusalem as a young man, and as an adult he worshiped in the synagogue and temple. Even his controversies with other Jews, such as the Pharisees, underscored the fact that they expected him to share their values and act more like them.

Growing up, I did not know a single Jew. I do now. I know something of their culture: the close ties that keep sacred holidays alive even for families who no longer believe in their meaning; the passionate arguments that at first unsettled me but soon attracted me as a style of personal engagement; the respect, even reverence, for legalism amid a society that mainly values autonomy; the ability to link arms and dance and sing and laugh even when the world offers scant reason for celebration.

This was the culture Jesus grew up in, a Jewish culture. Yes, he changed it, but always from his starting point as a Jew. Now when I find myself wondering what Jesus was like as a teenager, I think of Jewish boys I know in Chicago. When the thought jars me, I remember that in his own day Jesus got the opposite reaction. A Jewish teenager, surely—but the Son of God?

2. YET JESUS DID NOT ACT LIKE A JEW

During Jesus' life society was, in effect, a religious caste system based on steps toward holiness. Rules on washing hands and avoiding defilement were an attempt to make the devoted more acceptable to God. Sinners, menstruating women, the physically deformed, and other undesirables were banned from the temple.

In the midst of this tight religious caste system, Jesus appeared, with no qualms about socializing with children or sinners or even Samaritans. He touched, or was touched by, the "unclean": those with leprosy, the deformed, a hemorrhaging woman, the lunatic and possessed. Although Levitical laws prescribed a day of purification after touching a sick person, Jesus conducted mass healings in which he touched scores; he never concerned himself with the rules of defilement after contact with the sick or even the dead.

Pharisees believed that touching an unclean person polluted the one who touched. Yet when Jesus touched a person with leprosy, Jesus did not become soiled—the leprous became clean. When an immoral woman washed Jesus' feet, *she* went away forgiven and transformed. As Walter Wink puts it, "the contagion of holiness overcomes the contagion of uncleanness." In short, Jesus moved the emphasis from God's holiness (exclusive) to God's mercy (inclusive). Instead of the message "No undesirables allowed," he proclaimed, "In God's kingdom, no one is any longer an undesirable."

Jesus' attitude convicts me today, because I sense a movement in the reverse direction. I hear many calls that we show less mercy and more morality. Stigmatize homosexuals, shame unwed mothers, harass the homeless and punish law-breakers. Christians need to be a moral voice. In doing so, though, we must follow Jesus' example of "loving the sinner while hating the sin." I am struck by the power of mercy as demonstrated by Jesus, who came for the sick and not for the well, for sinners and not for the righteous. I spent half my life rebelling against the legalism of my childhood; when I tasted the first draught of the Living Water offered by Jesus, I knew I was changed forever.

3. JESUS LOST THE "CULTURE WARS"

Not long ago I addressed the topic "Culture Wars" before a large gathering that was tilted toward the liberal Democratic persuasion and included a strong minority of Jews. I had been selected as the token evangelical Christian on a panel that included the presidents of the Disney Channel and Warner Brothers, as well as the president of Wellesley College and Anita Hill's personal attorney.

To prepare for my talk, I went through the Gospels for guidance, only to be reminded how unpolitical Jesus was. Today, each time an election rolls around, Christians debate whether this or that candidate is "God's man" for the White House. Projecting myself back into Jesus' time, I had difficulty imagining him pondering whether Tiberius, Octavius or Julius Caesar was "God's man" for the empire.

I was also struck by what happens when Christians lose the culture wars. (A missionary in Afghanistan told me that after bulldozing the only Christian church in the country, the Afghans dug a huge hole underneath its foundation; they had heard rumors about an underground church!) In waves of persecution during the 1960s and 1970s, for instance, Chinese believers were fined, imprisoned and tortured. Yet, despite the government oppression, a spiritual revival broke out that could well be the largest in the history of the church. As many as fifty million believers gave their allegiance to an invisible kingdom even as the visible kingdom made them suffer for it.

When my turn came to speak, I said that the man I follow, a Palestinian Jew from the first century, had also been involved in a culture war. He went up against a rigid religious establishment and a pagan empire. The two powers, often at odds, conspired together to eliminate him. His response? Not to fight, but to give his life for these his enemies, and to point to that gift as proof of his love. Among the last words he said before his death were, "Father, forgive them, for they do not know what they are doing"(Luke 23:34).

After the panel, a television celebrity came up to me whose name every reader would recognize. "I've got to tell you, what you said stabbed me right in the heart," he said. "I was prepared to dislike you because I dislike all right-wing Christians, and I assumed you were one. I don't follow Jesus—I'm a Jew. But when you told about Jesus forgiving his enemies, I realized how far from that spirit I am. I fight my enemies, especially the right-wingers. I don't forgive them. I have much to learn from the spirit of Jesus."

4. JESUS WAS A POOR SALESMAN

Sometimes I wonder how Jesus would have fared in this day of mass media and high-tech ministry. I can't picture him worrying about the details of running a large organization. I can't see him letting some make-up artist improve his looks before a TV appearance. And I have a hard time imagining the fund-raising letters Jesus might write.

Investigative reporters on television like to do exposés of evangelists who claim powers of supernatural healing with little evidence to back them up. In direct contrast, Jesus, who had manifest supernatural powers, tended to downplay them. Seven times in Mark's Gospel he told a healed person, "Tell no one!" When crowds pressed around him, he fled to solitude or rowed across a lake.

We sometimes use the term "Savior complex" to describe an unhealthy syndrome of obsession over solving others' problems. Ironically, the true Savior seemed remarkably free of such a complex. He had no compulsion to convert the entire world in his lifetime or to cure people who were not ready to be cured.

I never sensed Jesus twisting a person's arm. Rather, he stated the consequences of a choice, then threw the decision back to the other party. For example, he once answered a wealthy man's question with uncompromising words, then let him walk away. Mark pointedly adds this comment about the man who rejected Jesus' advice: "Jesus looked at him and loved him"(Mark 10:21).

In short, Jesus showed an incredible respect for human freedom. Those of us in ministry need the kind of "Savior complex" that Jesus demonstrated. As Elton Trueblood has observed, the major symbols of invitation that Jesus used had a severe, even offensive quality: the yoke of burden, the cup of suffering, the towel of servanthood. "Take up your cross and follow me," he said, in the least manipulative invitation that has ever been given (see Mark 8:34).

5. NO ONE KNOWS WHAT JESUS LOOKED LIKE

John's Gospel records this hyperbolic comment: "Jesus did many other things as well. If every one of them were written down, I suppose that even the whole world would not have room for the books that would be written"(John 21:25). After spending time in seminary libraries browsing through the thousands of books on Jesus, I had the eerie sense that John's prophecy was coming true.

And yet, here is a strange thing: With this preponderance of scholarship, we still lack certain basic information about Jesus. The four Gospels skip over nine-tenths of his life, omitting much that would interest modern readers. We have only one scene from his adolescence and know nothing about his schooling. Details of his family life are so scant that scholars still debate how many brothers and sisters he had. The facts of biography considered essential to modern readers simply did not concern the Gospel writers.

We also know nothing about Jesus' shape, stature or eye color. As a writer, I could not begin where I normally begin in reporting on a person—by describing what he looked like. The first semi-realistic portraits of Jesus did not come until the fifth century, and these were pure speculation; until then, the Greeks had portrayed him as a young, beardless figure resembling the god Apollo.

I once showed to a class several dozen art slides portraying Jesus in a variety of forms—African, Korean, Chinese—and then asked the class to describe what they thought Jesus looked like. Virtually everyone suggested he was tall (unlikely for a first-century Jew), most said handsome, and no one said overweight. I showed a BBC film on the life of Christ that featured a fat actor in the title role, and some in the class found it offensive. We prefer a tall, handsome, and above all, slender Jesus.

One tradition dating back to the second century suggested Jesus was a hunchback. Most Christians today would find this notion repulsive and perhaps heretical. Was he not a perfect specimen of humanity? Yet in all the Bible I can find only one physical description of sorts, a prophecy written hundreds of years before Jesus' birth. Here is Isaiah's portrayal (52:14; 53:2-3), in the midst of a passage that the New Testament applies to the life of Jesus: "Just as there were many who were appalled at him—his appearance was so disfigured beyond that of any man and his form marred beyond human likeness. He had no beauty or majesty to attract us to him, nothing in his appearance that we should desire him. He was despised and rejected by men, a man of sorrows, and familiar with suffering. Like one from whom men hide their faces he was despised, and we esteemed him not."

Evidently our glamorized representations of Jesus say more about us than about him.

6. YOU MIGHT NOT HAVE WANTED JESUS AT YOUR BACKYARD BARBECUE

One impression about Jesus struck me more forcefully than any other: We have tamed him. The Jesus I learned about as a child was sweet and inoffensive, the kind of person whose lap you want to climb on, Mister Rogers with a beard. Indeed, Jesus did have qualities of gentleness and compassion that attracted little children. Mister Rogers, however, he assuredly was not.

I realized this fact when I studied the Sermon on the Mount (see Matthew 5-7). "Blessed are the poor. Blessed are the persecuted. Blessed are those who mourn." These sayings have a soft, proverbial ring to them—unless you happen to know someone poor, persecuted or mourning. The homeless huddling over heating grates in our major cities, the tortured masses in refugee camps, the victims of natural disaster—who would think of calling them blessed, or "lucky"?

In all the movies about Jesus' life, surely the most provocative—and perhaps the most accurate—portrayal of the Sermon on the Mount appears in a low-budget BBC production entitled *Son of Man*. The director, Dennis Potter, sets the Sermon on the Mount against a background of violence and chaos. Roman soldiers have just invaded a Galilean village to exact vengeance for some trespass against the empire. They have strung up Jewish men of fighting age, shoved their hysterical wives to the ground, and even speared babies in order to "teach these Jews a lesson."

Into that tumultuous scene of blood and tears and grieving for the dead strides Jesus with eyes ablaze. "I tell you: Love your enemies and pray for those who persecute you," he shouts above the groans. "Love the man who would kick you and spit at you. Love the soldier who would drive his sword in your belly. Love the brigand who robs and tortures you. Listen to me! Love your enemy! If a Roman soldier hits you on the left cheek, offer him the right one. Listen! I tell you, it is hard to follow me. What I'm saying to you hasn't been said since the world began!" You can imagine the villagers' response to such unwelcome advice. The Sermon on the Mount did not soothe them; it infuriated them.

I came away from my study of Jesus both comforted and terrified. Jesus came to earth "full of grace and truth," said John (John 1:14). His truth comforts my intellectual doubts even as his grace comforts my emotional doubts. And yet, I also encountered a terrifying aspect of Jesus, one that I had never learned about in church school. Did anyone go away from Jesus' presence feeling satisfied about his or her life?

Few people felt comfortable around Jesus; those who did were the type no one else felt comfortable around. The Jesus I met in the Gospels was anything but tame.

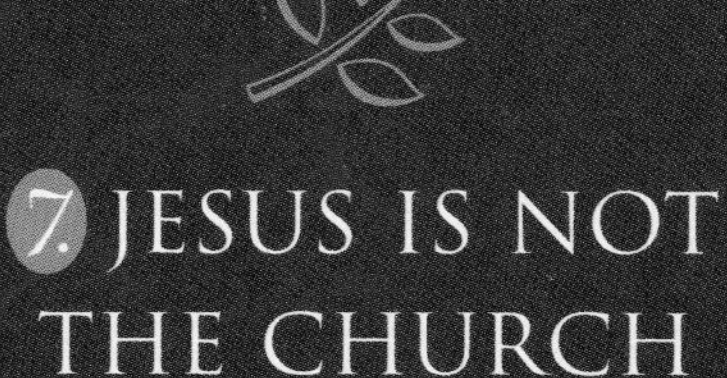

7. JESUS IS NOT THE CHURCH

George Buttrick, former chaplain at Harvard University, recalls that students would come into his office, plop down on a chair and declare, "I don't believe in God." Buttrick would give this disarming reply: "Sit down and tell me what kind of God you don't believe in. I probably don't believe in that God either."

Many people who reject Jesus are rejecting not Jesus, but a distortion of him as presented by the church. To our everlasting shame, the watching world judges Jesus by a church whose history includes the Crusades, the Inquisition, the Conquistadores in Latin America, and a slave ship called the *Good Ship Jesus*.

In order to get to know Jesus, I had to strip away layers of dust and grime applied by the church itself. In my case, the racism, intolerance and petty legalism of a fundamentalist church in the South obscured the image of Jesus. A Russian or a European Catholic confronts a very different restoration process. "For not only dust, but also too much gold can cover up the true figure," wrote Hans Küng about his own search. Many abandon the quest entirely; rebuffed by the church, they never make it to Jesus.

I often wish that we could somehow set aside church history, remove the church's many layers of interpretation and encounter the words of the Gospels for the first time. Not everyone would accept Jesus—they did not in his own day—but at least people would not reject him for the wrong reasons.

Once I was able to cut through the fog still clinging from my own upbringing, my opinion of Jesus changed remarkably. Brilliant, untamed, tender, creative, merciful, clever, loving, irreducible, paradoxically humble—Jesus stands up to scrutiny. He is who I want my God to be.

8. YET THE CHURCH IS JESUS

What I have just longed for, nonetheless, is not only impossible; it is unscriptural. Jesus planned from the beginning to die so that we his church could take his place. ("Once again," as Robert Farrar Capon reminds us, "God was—and still is—throwing sinkers.") He stayed just long enough to gather around him followers who could carry the message to others. Killing Jesus, says Walter Wink, was like trying to destroy a dandelion seed-head by blowing on it.

The church is where God lives. What Jesus brought to a few—healing grace, the good-news message of God's love—the church can now bring to all. "Unless a kernel of wheat falls to the ground and dies," he explained, "it remains only a single seed. But if it dies, it produces many seeds"(John 12:24).

As I worked through the Gospels I concluded that the Ascension represents my greatest struggle of faith—not whether it happened, but why. It challenges me more than belief in the Resurrection and other miracles.

It seems odd to admit such a notion—I have never read a book or article designed to answer doubts about the Ascension—yet for me what has happened since Jesus' departure strikes at the core of my faith. Would it not have been better if Jesus had stayed on earth to direct us?

"It is for your good that I am going away," Jesus told his disciples, who had the same question. "Unless I go away, the Counselor will not come to you"(John 16:7). I find it much easier to accept the fact of God incarnating in Jesus of Nazareth than in the people who attend my local church and in me. Yet that is what we are asked to believe; that is how we are asked to live. Jesus played his part and then left. Now it is up to us, the body of Christ.

9. THE SATURDAY JESUS

The author and preacher Tony Campolo delivers a stirring sermon adapted from an elderly black pastor at his church in Philadelphia. "It's Friday, but Sunday's Comin" is the title of the sermon, and once you know the title you know the whole sermon. In a cadence that increases in tempo and in volume, Campolo contrasts how the world looked on Friday—when the forces of evil won over the forces of good, when every friend and disciple fled in fear, when the Son of God died on a cross—with how it looked on Easter Sunday. The disciples who lived through both days, Friday and Sunday, learned that when God seems most absent he may be closest of all; when God looks most powerless he may be most powerful; when God looks most dead he may be coming back to life. They learned never to count God out.

Campolo's sermon skips one day, though. The other two days, Good Friday and Easter Sunday, are perhaps the most significant days on the entire church calendar, and yet, in a real sense, we live our lives on Saturday, the day in between. Can we trust that Jesus can make something holy and beautiful and good out of a world that includes squalid refugee camps, duplicitous politicians and inner-city ghettos in the richest nation on earth? Human history grinds on, between the time of promise and fulfillment. It's Saturday on planet Earth; will Sunday ever come?

Perhaps that is why the authors of the Gospels devoted so much more space to Jesus' last week than to the several weeks when he was making resurrection appearances. They knew that the history to follow would often resemble Saturday, the in-between day, more than Sunday, the day of rejoicing. It is a good thing to remember that in the cosmic drama, we live our days on Saturday, the day with no name.

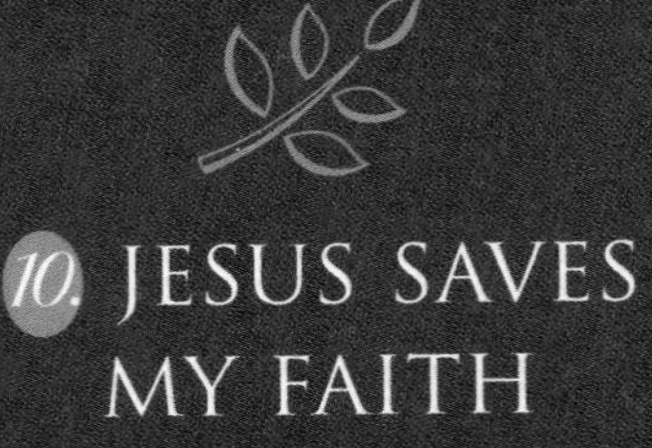

10. JESUS SAVES MY FAITH

"Why am I a Christian?" I sometimes ask myself, and to be perfectly honest, the reasons reduce to two: (1) the lack of good alternatives and (2) Jesus. I tend to spend a lot of time pondering unanswerable questions such as the problem of pain or providence versus free will. Often, when I do so, the fog begins to drift in. But if I look at Jesus, clarity is restored. Jesus gave no philosophical answer to the problem of pain, but he did give an existential answer. I cannot learn from him why bad things occur, but I can learn how God feels about it. I look at how Jesus responds to the sisters of his good friend Lazarus (see John 1), or to a leprosy patient banned from the town gates (see Mark 1:40-45). Jesus gives God a face, and that face is streaked with tears. Why doesn't God answer my prayers? I do not know, but it helps me to realize that Jesus himself knew something of that feeling. He prayed all night over his choice of disciples, and still that list included one named Judas. In Gethsemane, he threw himself on the ground, crying out for some other way, but there was no other way. At its core, Gethsemane depicts, after all, the story of unanswered prayer (see Luke 22:39-46). The cup of suffering was not removed.

Mostly, Jesus corrects my foggy conceptions of God. Jesus reveals a God who comes in search of us, a God who makes room for our freedom even when it costs the Son's life, a God who is vulnerable. Above all, Jesus reveals a God who is love. On our own, would any of us come up with the notion of a God who loves and yearns to be loved? Those raised in a Christian tradition may miss the shock of Jesus' message, but in truth, love has never been a normal way of describing what happens between human beings and their God. Not once does the Quran apply the word *love* to God. Aristotle stated bluntly, "It would be eccentric for anyone to claim that he loved Zeus" or that Zeus loved a human being, for that matter. In dazzling contrast, the Christian Bible affirms that God is love and cites love as the main reason Jesus came to earth: "This is how God showed his love among us: He sent his one and only Son into the world that we might live through him"(1John 4:9).

The story of Jesus is the story of a celebration, a story of love. It involves pain and disappointment, yes, for God as well as for us. But Jesus embodies the promise of a God who will go to any length to get his family back.

Old Testament Prophecies Fulfilled in Christ

OT Text	Subject	NT Text
Ge 3:15	Satan against Jesus	Lk 22:53
Ge 3:15	Jesus' victory over Satan	Heb 2:14; 1 Jn 3:8
Ge 12:3	Gentiles blessed through Christ as the seed of Abraham	Ac 3:25; Gal 3:8
Ge 13:15	Messiah as the seed of Abraham	Gal 3:15–16, 19
Ge 14:18–20	Jesus' priesthood according to the likeness of Melchizedek	Heb 7
Ge 18:18	Gentiles blessed through Christ as the seed of Abraham	Ac 3:25; Gal 3:8
Ge 22:18	Gentiles blessed through Christ as the seed of Abraham	Ac 3:25; Gal 3:8
Ge 26:4	Gentiles blessed through Christ as the seed of Abraham	Ac 3:25; Gal 3:8
Ge 49:10	Coming ruler from Judah	Lk 1:32–33
Ex 12:1—14:46	The Messiah as the Passover Lamb	Jn 19:31–36; 1 Co 5:7; 1 Pe 1:19
Ex 16:4	Messiah to give true bread from heaven	Jn 6:31–33
Ex 24:8	The Messiah's blood to be shed as sacrifice	Heb 9:11–28
Lev 16:15–17	Atoning sacrifice of blood	Ro 3:25; Heb 9:1–14, 24; 1 Jn 2:2
Nu 21:8–9	Life through looking at one on a cross	Jn 3:14–15
Nu 24:17	Coming ruler from Jacob	Lk 1:32–33
Nu 24:17	Coming Star out of Jacob	Rev 22:16
Dt 18:17	Coming prophet sent from God	Jn 6:14; 12:49–50; Ac 3:22–23
Dt 21:23	Messiah cursed for hanging on a tree	Gal 3:13
Dt 30:12–14	Jesus is God's Word near to us	Ro 10:6–8
2Sa 7:14	Messiah to be God's Son	Heb 1:5
2Sa 7:16	David's Son as eternal king	Lk 1:32–33; Rev 19:11–16
1Ch 17:13	Messiah to be God's Son	Heb 1:5
1Ch 17:14	David's Son as eternal king	Lk 1:32–33; Rev 19:11–16
Ps 2:7	God's address to his Son	Mt 3:17; 17:5; Mk 1:11; 9:7; Lk 3:22; 9:35; Ac 13:33; Heb 1:5
Ps 2:9	Messiah to rule the nations with power	Rev 2:27
Ps 8:2	Children to praise God's Son	Mt 21:16
Ps 8:4–5	Jesus lower than the angels	Heb 2:6–9

OT Text	Subject	NT Text
Ps 8:6	Everything subject to God's Son	1Co 15:27–28; Eph 1:22
Ps 16:8–11	David's Son to be raised from the dead	Ac 2:25–32; 13:35–37
Ps 22:1	God-forsaken cry by the Messiah	Mt 27:46; Mk 15:34
Ps 22:7–8	Messiah mocked by a crowd	Mt 27:29, 41–44; Mk 15:18, 29–32; Lk 23:35–39
Ps 22:18	Casting lots for Jesus' clothes	Mt 27:35; Mk 15:24; Lk 23:34; Jn 19:24
Ps 22:22	Jesus to declare his name in the church	Heb 2:12
Ps 31:5	Messiah to commit his spirit to God	Lk 23:46
Ps 34:20	Messiah to have no broken bones	Jn 19:31–36
Ps 35:19	Messiah experiencing hatred for no reason	Jn 15:25
Ps 40:6–8	Messiah to do God's perfect will	Jn 6:48; Heb 10:5–9
Ps 41:9	The Messiah's betrayal by a friend	Jn 13:18
Ps 45:6–7	Characteristics of the coming King	Heb 1:8–9
Ps 68:18	Ascension and giving gifts to humans	Eph 4:7–11
Ps 69:4	Messiah experiencing hatred for no reason	Jn 15:25
Ps 69:9	The Messiah's zeal for God's house	Jn 2:14–22
Ps 69:21	The thirst of the suffering Messiah	Jn 19:29
Ps 69:25	Judgment on the Messiah's persecutor	Ac 1:20
Ps 78:2	Messiah to speak in parables	Mt 13:34–35
Ps 102:25–27	Characteristics of the coming King	Heb 1:10–12
Ps 110:1	Jesus exalted in power at God's right hand	Ac 2:34–35; 1Co 15:25; Eph 1:20–22; Heb 1:13; 10:12–13
Ps 110:1	Jesus as Son and Lord of David	Mt 22:41–45; Mk 12:35–37; Lk 20:41–44
Ps 110:4	Jesus' priesthood after Melchizedek	Heb 5:6; 7:11–22
Ps 118:22–23	Rejected stone to become capstone	Mt 21:42–44; Mk 12:10–12; Lk 20:17–19; Ac 4:10–11; 1Pe 2:7–8
Ps 118:26	Messiah to come in the name of the Lord	Mt 21:9; Mk 11:9; Lk 19:38; Jn 12:13
Isa 6:9–10	Hearts to be closed to the gospel	Mt 13:14–15; Mk 4:12; Lk 8:10; Jn 12:37–41
Isa 7:14	Virgin birth of the Messiah	Mt 1:18–23; Lk 1:26–35
Isa 8:14	A stone on which people stumble	Ro 9:32–33; 1Pe 2:7–8
Isa 9:1–2	Ministry to begin in Galilee	Mt 4:13–16; Mk 1:14–15; Lk 4:14–15
Isa 9:6–7	David's Son as eternal king	Lk 1:32–33

OT Text	Subject	NT Text
Isa 9:7	The Messiah to be God	Jn 1:1, 18
Isa 9:7	The Messiah to be a man of peace	Eph 2:14–17
Isa 11:1–2	Rod of Jesse (David) to receive the Spirit	Mt 3:16; Mk 1:16; Lk 3:21–22
Isa 11:10	Rod of Jesse (David) as coming ruler	Lk 1:32–33
Isa 11:10	Salvation to be available for Gentiles	Ro 15:12
Isa 22:22	Jesus to receive the key of David	Rev 3:7
Isa 25:8	Death to be swallowed up in victory	1Co 15:54
Isa 28:16	Messiah to be the chief cornerstone	Ro 9:32–33; 1Pe 2:6
Isa 35:5–6	Messiah to be a mighty worker of miracles	Mt 11:4–6; Lk 7:22
Isa 40:3–5	Jesus' forerunner, a voice in the desert	Mt 3:3; Mk 1:3; Lk 3:4–6; Jn 1:23
Isa 42:1–4	Messiah as the chosen servant of the Lord	Mt 12:15–21
Isa 45:23	Every knee to bow before the Messiah	Ro 14:11; Php 2:10
Isa 49:6	Messiah as a light to the Gentiles	Ac 13:46–47
Isa 50:6	Beating God's servant	Mt 27:26–30; Mk 14:65; 15:15, 19; Lk 22:63; Jn 19:1, 3
Isa 50:6	Spitting on God's servant	Mt 26:67; Mk 14:65
Isa 53:1	Israel not to believe in the Messiah	Jn 12:38; Ro 10:16
Isa 53:3	Messiah to be rejected by his own people	Jn 1:11
Isa 53:4–5	Healing ministry of God's servant	Mt 8:16–17; Mk 1:32–34; Lk. 4:40–41; 1Pe 2:24
Isa 53:7–8	Suffering Lamb of God	Jn 1:29, 36; Ac 8:30–35; 1Pe 1:19; Rev 5:6, 12
Isa 53:9	The sinless servant of God	Heb 4:15; 1Pe 2:22
Isa 53:9	Messiah to be buried in a rich man's grave	Mt 27:57–60
Isa 53:12	God's servant numbered with transgressors	Mt 27:38; Mk 15:27–28; Lk 22:37; 23:33; Jn 19:18
Isa 55:3	Everlasting covenant through the Messiah	Lk 22:20; 1Co 11:25
Isa 55:3	Blessings of David given to the Messiah	Ac 13:33
Isa 59:20–21	Israel's Deliverer to come from Zion	Ro 11:26–27
Isa 60:1–3	Gentiles coming to worship the Messiah	Mt 2:11; Ro 15:8–12
Isa 61:1–2	The Messiah anointed by the Holy Spirit	Mt 3:16; Mk 1:10; Lk 4:18–21
Isa 65:1	Gentiles would believe in the Messiah	Ro 10:20
Isa 65:2	Israel would reject the Messiah	Ro 10:21
Jer 23:5	David's Son to be a great King	Lk 1:32–33
Jer 23:6	David's Son to be Savior	Mt 1:21

OT Text	Subject	NT Text
Jer 23:6	Messiah to be named "Our Righteousness"	1Co 1:30
Jer 31:5	Rachel weeping for slain children	Mt 2:16–18
Jer 31:31–34	Jesus and the new covenant	Lk 22:20; 1Co 11:25; Heb 8:8–12; 10:15–18
Jer 32:40	Everlasting covenant through the Messiah	Lk 22:20; 1Co 11:25
Jer 33:15	David's Son to be a great King	Lk 1:32–33
Jer 33:16	David's Son to be Savior	Mt 1:21
Jer 33:16	Messiah to be named "Our Righteousness"	1Co 1:30
Eze 21:26–27	A rightful crown for the Messiah	Lk 1:32–33
Eze 34:23–24	The coming good shepherd	Jn 10:11, 14, 16; Heb 13:20; 1Pe 5:4
Eze 37:24–25	Messiah to be David's son and a king	Lk 1:32–33
Eze 37:24–25	The coming good shepherd	Jn 10:11, 14, 16; Heb 13:20; 1Pe 5:4
Eze 37:26	Messiah's everlasting covenant of peace	Lk 22:20; 1Co 11:25
Da 7:13–14	The coming of the Son of Man	Mt 24:30; 26:64; Mk 13:26; 14:62; Lk 21:27; Rev 1:13; 14:14
Da 7:27	The coming everlasting kingdom of the Messiah	Rev 11:15
Da 9:24–26	Timetable for the Messiah's coming	Gal 4:4
Hos 11:1	Jesus to return from Egypt	Mt 2:14–15
Joel 2:28–32	God's Spirit to be poured out	Ac 2:14–21
Am 9:11–12	Gentiles would believe in the Messiah	Ac 15:13–18
Jnh 1:17	Messiah to be three days and nights in grave	Mt 12:39–40
Mic 5:2	The Messiah to be born in Bethlehem	Mt 2:1–6
Mic 5:2	The Messiah as an eternal king	Lk 1:32–33
Mic 5:4	The coming shepherd of God's flock	Jn 10:11, 14
Mic 5:5	The Messiah to be a man of peace	Eph 2:14–17
Zec 9:9	The coming ruler on a donkey	Mt 21:1–9; Mk 11:1–10; Lk 19:28–38; Jn 12:12–16
Zec 11:12–13	Thirty pieces of silver for a potter's field	Mt 27:1–10
Zec 12:10	Looking on the pierced Messiah	Jn 19:37; Rev 1:7
Zec 13:7	Striking the coming shepherd; the sheep flee	Mt 26:31; 26:55–56; Mk 14:27; 14:48–50
Mal 3:1	The forerunner to the Messiah	Mt 11:7–10; Mk 1:2–4; Lk 7:24–27
Mal 4:5–6	The forerunner as Elijah returned	Mt 11:14; 17:11–13; Mk 9:11–13; Lk 1:16–17

NEW INTERNATIONAL VERSION

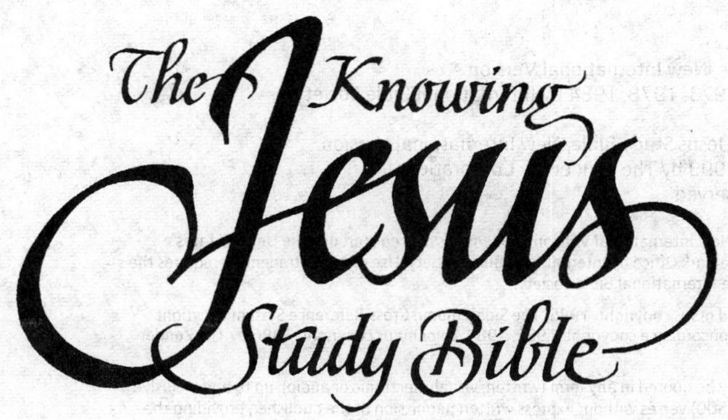

A ONE-YEAR STUDY OF JESUS
IN EVERY BOOK OF THE BIBLE

general editors
Edward Hindson, D.Phil.
and
Edward Dobson, Ed.D.

ZondervanPublishingHouse
Grand Rapids, Michigan, 49530, U.S.A.

Printed in the United States of America

YOU WILL BE PLEASED TO KNOW THAT A PORTION OF THE PURCHASE PRICE OF YOUR NEW NIV BIBLE HAS BEEN PROVIDED TO INTERNATIONAL BIBLE SOCIETY TO HELP SPREAD THE GOSPEL OF JESUS CHRIST TO THE WORLD!

Contents

Old Testament

New Testament

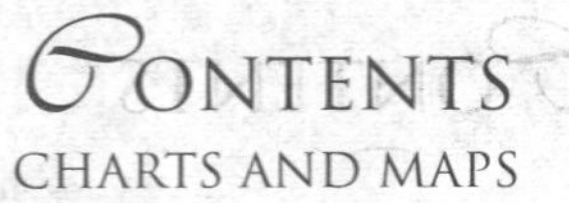

CONTENTS

CHARTS AND MAPS

Note: Maps are *italicized.*

The Greatest Story Ever Told

The story of Jesus is the greatest story ever told. It is about the greatest Person who has ever lived. The portrait of Jesus in the Bible reveals God at work in our lives. We see his power. We hear his voice. We experience his love. Jesus towers above the greatest human beings of all time because he is God.

Jesus looked like a man, but he spoke as God. He lived among men, but he also lived above men. His person, character, wisdom and love outshine those of any other human being who has ever lived. He stands like a beacon of light against the darkness of this world. When we examine his life, we find ourselves irresistibly drawn to him.

As we read the pages of Scripture, we soon discover that Jesus is the theme of the whole Bible. Theologian Michael Horton has observed, "Once we truly grasp the message of the New Testament, it is impossible to read the Old Testament again without seeing Christ on every page, in every story, foreshadowed or anticipated in every event and narrative. The Bible must be read as a whole, beginning with Genesis and ending with Revelation, letting promise and fulfillment guide our expectations for what we will find there."

Our goal in this study Bible is to allow Jesus Christ to shine forth from the pages of Scripture. We have sought to point the reader to every passage, picture, type, illustration, quotation or prophecy that points to him from both the Old Testament and the New Testament. Jesus told his disciples, "Everything must be fulfilled that is written about me in the Law of Moses, the Prophets and the Psalms" (Luke 24:44). Next, Luke told us that Jesus "opened their minds so they could understand the Scriptures" (verse 45).

We have been careful to include every major reference in the Old Testament that clearly points to Jesus. At the same time, we have exercised caution to avoid forcing passages that do not have a specific parallel to him. Our overall purpose is to magnify Jesus as the One whom the Bible is really all about. It is our hope that this study of Jesus in every book of the Bible will illuminate him to each reader's heart and honor the Savior who gave himself for us.

Edward Hindson   Edward G Dobson

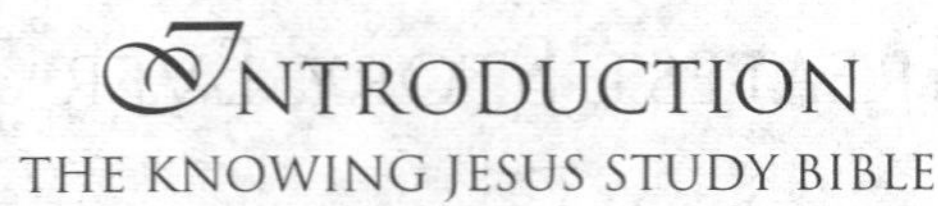

Introduction

THE KNOWING JESUS STUDY BIBLE

DISCOVER

THE LIVING PERSON REVEALED IN EVERY PART OF THE BIBLE

No one has ever demonstrated such compassion for those in need, such goodness, such all-encompassing love, as Jesus. Nearly two millenia after his emergence on the world scene, Jesus Christ remains the focal point, the bright Star in the history of God's dealings with humankind. Truly, Jesus is "the Light of the World." For those who long to know him better and grow closer to him, *The Knowing Jesus Study Bible* will help foster a greater understanding of our Lord and Savior and of what he has done that has so profoundly influenced both world history and countless individual lives.

The Knowing Jesus Study Bible provides a compelling, one-year study that presents Jesus as the theme of the entire Bible. Its 365 full-page studies, called "Discoveries," feature challenging, fresh insights into the person and work of Jesus. More than 200 in-text notes weave together information and application to show how Jesus is revealed in every part of Scripture. With a wealth of insight and commentary accompanying the text of Scripture, this Bible is a resource that readers will consult again and again.

The Knowing Jesus Study Bible is part of Zondervan's **Discovery Series**. A new approach to Bible study, Discovery Bibles offer one-year, in-depth topical studies. The notes are designed to lead to new, personal discoveries and life-changing applications of Scripture.

Quick Take:

HOW TO USE "THE KNOWING JESUS STUDY BIBLE"

To begin a one-year study on the person and presence of Jesus Christ throughout the Scripture, turn to the first "Discovery" on page 3.

Read the "Discovery," as well as the chapter of Scripture immediately preceding it, and spend some time with the "Self-Discovery" question or reflection.

Check the bottom of the page for your next daily reading.

Features

The Word of God — The primary feature of this Bible is the Word of God itself. As you seek to develop a more intimate relationship with Jesus Christ, God's Spirit will guide and direct you through his Word. This Bible features the New International Version text, today's most widely read English translation.

Discoveries — 365 daily "Discoveries," full-page articles sprinkled throughout the text of the Bible, feature intriguing insights into the person and work of Jesus, related to the particular Scripture passage that they address. Each "Discovery" includes a "Self-Discovery"—an open-ended question or invitation to personal reflection related to the topic. At the end of each "Discovery" you will find the page number for the next article.

Jesus Focuses Numerous in-text notes throughout both the Old and the New Testaments relate the text of Scripture to Jesus, the Messiah. Some notes feature helpful factual or background information, some point out Old Testament appearances of the second person of the Trinity, some focus on Old Testament foreshadowings of the promised One, and some comment on Jesus' words or actions in the passage.

JESUS FOCUS
ALWAYS EXISTING
The New Testament shows us clearly that Jesus has always existed as God the Son, the second person of the Trinity. John 1:1–2 says, "In the beginning was the Word, and the Word was with God, and the Word was God. He was with God in the beginning." Even before our Lord was born to a young woman named Mary as Jesus of Nazareth, he existed and was one with God (Genesis 1:1–2). Jesus showed us who God is because he is "the image of the invisible God." The Bible also tells us that he is "over all creation," "before all things" and the "exact representation" of God the Father (Colossians 1:13–19). Jesus is God, showing us the identity of

Jesus and You Similar to the "Jesus Focus" notes, the "Jesus and You" notes relate the Scripture passage to the daily experience of the reader and offer an invitation to personal reflection and application.

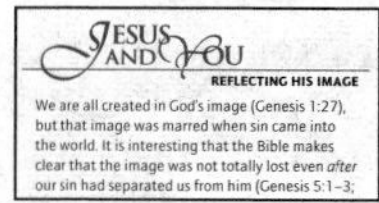

JESUS AND YOU
REFLECTING HIS IMAGE
We are all created in God's image (Genesis 1:27), but that image was marred when sin came into the world. It is interesting that the Bible makes clear that the image was not totally lost even after our sin had separated us from him (Genesis 5:1–3;

Portraits "Portraits" feature brief sketches of individuals who were somehow related to the Messiah, either because of their personal association with Jesus Christ, their place in his lineage, or the fact that events in their lives foreshadowed similar events in the life of Jesus.

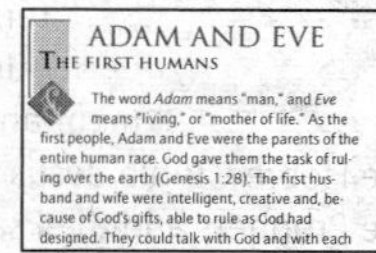

Quotes Brief devotional quotations from various individuals are sprinkled throughout the Bible. These quotes represent a wide variety of individuals, from Puritan and patristic fathers to well-known contemporary figures such as Charles Stanley, Jim Cymbala, Kay Arthur, Jack Hayford or Joni Eareckson Tada.

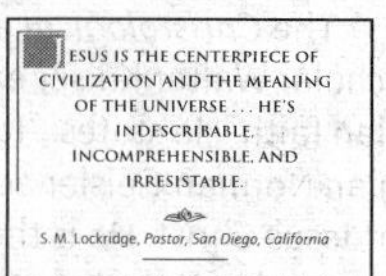

"Jesus In . . . "—Each book of the Bible is prefaced by a brief introductory statement focusing on the presence of Jesus in the book. Alongside the introduction are two or three sidebar questions and answers to pique your interest. Also included is a one-sentence "Jesus Is . . ." statement, drawing on some particular attribute of Jesus that is highlighted in the book.

In-text Maps and Charts—A variety of in-text maps and charts are included (see listing on page iv), dealing with various aspects of Jesus' life and ministry or with prophetic or symbolic themes.

Presentation page—A full-color presentation page is included in the front of the Bible.

"One Solitary Life"—This classic, anonymous poem about Jesus is featured on a full color insert page.

"Top Ten Surprises About Jesus"—Philip Yancey, author of *The Jesus I Never Knew*, has contributed this beautiful and thought-provoking ten-page introductory article, also included in full color.

"Old Testament Prophecies Fulfilled in Christ"—This informative four-page chart is included near the front of the Bible.

Color Inserts throughout the Bible—Coupling beautiful photography with key Bible verses relating to Jesus, these 18 pages are a delightful enhancement to *The Knowing Jesus Study Bible*.

Additional helpful information—A variety of helpful charts and articles are included in the back of the Bible. See the Table of Contents for a complete listing.

NIV Concordance—A New International Version concordance facilitates and enhances serious Bible study.

Two full-color maps—Full-color insert maps of "Jerusalem in Jesus' Time" and "Jesus Ministry" are included at the back of the Bible.

Jesus in the Old Testament

By Edward Hindson, D. Phil.

The story of the Bible is God's story. It is a revelation of his promise in which the end is anticipated from the beginning. The story does not begin with the fulfillment of the promise but with the promise itself. It is the story of God's love for humanity, and it centers on the promised Redeemer.

Jesus is the key personality of the Bible. He is the One God promised in the Old Testament and provided in the New Testament. He is foreseen in the prophecies, types and rituals of the Hebrew Bible. Jesus himself said, "Everything must be fulfilled that is written about me in the Law of Moses, the Prophets and the Psalms" (Luke 24:44). On at least five different occasions Jesus claimed to be the theme of the Old Testament Scriptures (Matthew 5:17; Luke 24:17; Luke 24:44; John 5:39; Hebrews 10:7).

The *Christological* approach to the Bible views Christ as the central theme of Scripture. Old Testament scholar Walter Kaiser explains that this approach is not that of mere imposition on the Biblical text by the Christian faith. He states: "It is rather the claim of the Bible itself . . . strung out on the wash line of history."[1] Theologian Norman Geisler adds: "The inseparable relationship of both Old and New Testaments centers in the person of Jesus Christ. He is the theme of both testaments, and as a result, the personality of Christ is the unity in the plurality of the whole Bible"[2]

The Old Testament in the New

Jesus often quoted the Old Testament to explain and defend his ministry: "Have you never read in the Scriptures . . ?" (e.g., Matthew 21:42). He used the phrases "it is written" (92 times) and "that it might be fulfilled" (33 times) to support his Messianic claims and to emphasize the divine authority of his ministry. This can readily be seen in the incident when John the Baptist asked: "Are you the one who was to come, or should we expect someone else?" Jesus replied, "Report to John . . . The blind receive sight, the lame walk, those who have leprosy are cured, the deaf hear, the dead are raised, and the good news is preached to the poor" (Matthew 11:2–5). The Savior's response was a direct quotation of the Messianic signs as listed by the prophet Isaiah (Isaiah 35:5–6; 61:1).

God had a special relationship with the people of Israel. He appeared to the patriarchs, called Moses, anointed David and established Israel's laws and institutions to point the way to the coming of the promised One. He even strengthened their faith with visible demonstrations of his power. He also sent his prophets to predict the coming Redeemer and to prepare the way for Christ, so that when he came he might be identified by comparing the predictions with their fulfillments.

The relationship of Christ to the Old Testament is based on the conviction that certain ceremonies and historical events were ordained by God to point to a greater reality to come. New Testament examples include references to the tabernacle (Hebrews 8:1–5), the sacrifices (John 1:29), the priesthood (Hebrews 7:14–28), the exodus and the wilderness (1 Corinthians 10:1–11), Noah (1 Peter 3:20–21), Jonah (Matthew 12:39–40), Melchizedek (Hebrews 7:1–3), Hagar and Sarah (Galatians 4:22–26) and Elijah (Matthew 11:14).

In the Old Testament Christ is:	In the New Testament Christ is:
Concealed	Revealed
Anticipated	Acknowledged
Contained	Explained
Promised	Proclaimed
Pictured	Present
Predicted	Fulfilled

THE RELATIONSHIP BETWEEN THE TESTAMENTS

The relationship between the Old and New Testaments tells the story of the continuous history of God's people. The Biblical concepts and themes (e.g., salvation, redemption, sacrifice) of the Old Testament are the basis of New Testament teaching. Old Testament quotations are used to support New Testament truths (e.g., Acts 2:16–21, quoting Joel 2:28–32). But the ultimate connection between the Testaments is in the area of prediction and fulfillment. God himself declared that these prophecies and their fulfillments are verification that the Bible is true (see Isaiah 46:9–10).

Norman Geisler suggests the following outline for the sections of the Old Testament:

Sections of the Old Testament	
The Law:	Foundation for Christ
History:	Preparation for Christ
Poetry:	Aspiration for Christ
Prophecy:	Expectation of Christ

In the Old Testament Jesus Christ is predicted. In the New Testament he is predominant. Jesus is the focus of Biblical truth throughout the entire Bible. God's revelation converges in him in the Old Testament and emerges from him in the New Testament. Every book of the Bible is a progressive revelation of the Person of Jesus Christ and his redeeming love.

[1] Walter Kaiser, *Toward an Old Testament Theology* (Grand Rapids: Zondervan, 1978), p. 42.
[2] Norman Geisler, *Christ: The Theme of the Bible* (Chicago: Moody Press, 1968), p. 3.

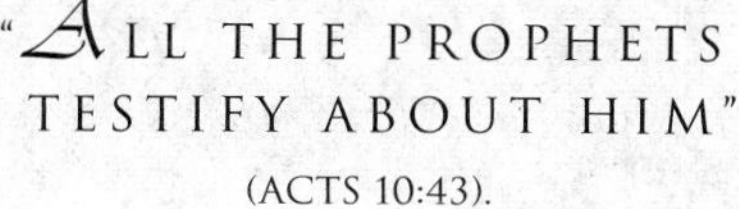
"ALL THE PROPHETS
TESTIFY ABOUT HIM"
(ACTS 10:43).

OLD
TESTAMENT

GENESIS

What is the significance of God's promise to Adam? (Genesis 3:15)

♦ *The offspring of the woman, Eve, would eventually crush the serpent's head, a promise fulfilled in Jesus' victory over Satan—a victory in which all believers will share (Romans 16:20).*

In what way would Abram bless all peoples on earth? (Genesis 12:3)

♦ *God's desire was to redeem humanity from the depths to which it had fallen when Adam sinned. Eventually, through Abram, God would send Jesus to fulfill his plan and offer redemption to the whole world.*

Is there evidence that Abraham foresaw the coming of the Messiah? (see John 8:56)

♦ *While it is impossible to know the extent of Abraham's foreknowledge of this event, the New Testament Scripture referred to indicates that he anticipated Jesus' coming with joy.*

Jesus in Genesis Jesus appears in Genesis as the Promised One whom the Father will send to save us. In this book of beginnings he appears as the eternal Son of God. As God, Jesus was involved in creating the universe. As our Savior, Jesus would one day bring humanity back into fellowship with God. Jesus was one with the Father before the beginning of time (John 1:1) and holds together everything he has created (Colossians 1:17). But he also appears in Genesis as the One who will crush the serpent's head (Genesis 3:15). The first 11 chapters of Genesis cover four major events: the creation, the fall of humanity, the flood and the record of nations that came into existence afterward. The next 39 chapters (Genesis 12—50) provide a close-up view of one family—Abraham and his descendants. God called this family to himself so that through them he might eventually bless all the families of the earth (Genesis 12:2).

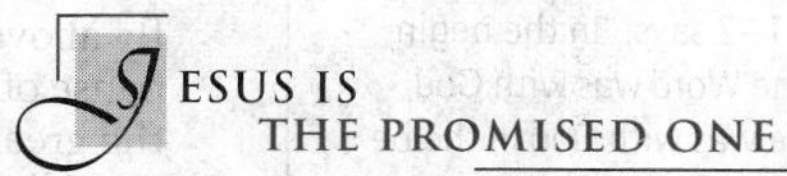

JESUS IS THE PROMISED ONE

The Beginning

1 In the beginning[a] God created
the heavens and the earth.[b] 2 Now
the earth was[a] formless and empty,[c] darkness was over the surface
of the deep, and the Spirit of God[d]
was hovering over the waters.

3 And God said,[e] "Let there be light,"
and there was light.[f] 4 God saw that
the light was good, and he separated the light from the darkness.
5 God called the light "day," and the
darkness he called "night."[g] And
there was evening, and there was
morning—the first day.
6 And God said, "Let there be an expanse[h] between the waters to separate water from water." 7 So God
made the expanse and separated
the water under the expanse from
the water above it.[i] And it was so.
8 God called the expanse "sky." And
there was evening, and there was
morning—the second day.
9 And God said, "Let the water under
the sky be gathered to one place,[j]
and let dry ground appear." And it
was so. 10 God called the dry ground
"land," and the gathered waters he
called "seas." And God saw that it
was good.
11 Then God said, "Let the land
produce vegetation:[k] seed-bearing
plants and trees on the land that
bear fruit with seed in it, according
to their various kinds." And it was
so. 12 The land produced vegetation:
plants bearing seed according to
their kinds and trees bearing fruit
with seed in it according to their
kinds. And God saw that it was
good. 13 And there was evening, and
there was morning—the third day.

1:1 [a] Jn 1:1-2 [b] Job 38:4; Ps 90:2; Isa 42:5; 44:24; 45:12,18; Ac 17:24; Heb 11:3; Rev 4:11
1:2 [c] Jer 4:23 [d] Ps 104:30
1:3 [e] Ps 33:6,9; 148:5; Heb 11:3 [f] 2Co 4:6*
1:5 [g] Ps 74:16
1:6 [h] Jer 10:12
1:7 [i] Job 38:8-11,16; Ps 148:4
1:9 [j] Job 38:8-11; Ps 104:6-9; Pr 8:29; Jer 5:22; 2Pe 3:5
1:11 [k] Ps 65:9-13; 104:14

JESUS FOCUS

ALWAYS EXISTING

The New Testament shows us clearly that Jesus has always existed as God the Son, the second person of the Trinity. John 1:1–2 says, "In the beginning was the Word, and the Word was with God, and the Word was God. He was with God in the beginning." Even before our Lord was born to a young woman named Mary as Jesus of Nazareth, he existed and was one with God (Genesis 1:1–2). Jesus showed us who God is because he is "the image of the invisible God." The Bible also tells us that he is "over all creation," "before all things" and the "exact representation" of God the Father (Colossians 1:13–19). Jesus is God, showing us the identity of the Father both now and in the past (John 1:18; 8:19; 14:6–11). Time as we know it doesn't apply to God. He has always existed, he is now and he will always be alive (Hebrews 1:2; 13:8).

JESUS IS THE CENTERPIECE OF CIVILIZATION AND THE MEANING OF THE UNIVERSE . . . HE'S INDESCRIBABLE, INCOMPREHENSIBLE, AND IRRESISTABLE.

S. M. Lockridge, *Pastor, San Diego, California*

14 And God said, "Let there be lights[l] in
the expanse of the sky to separate
the day from the night, and let them
serve as signs[m] to mark seasons[n]
and days and years, 15 and let them
be lights in the expanse of the sky to
give light on the earth." And it was
so. 16 God made two great lights—
the greater light to govern[o] the day
and the lesser light to govern[p] the
night. He also made the stars.[q]
17 God set them in the expanse of
the sky to give light on the earth,
18 to govern the day and the night,[r]
and to separate light from darkness.
And God saw that it was good.
19 And there was evening, and there
was morning—the fourth day.
20 And God said, "Let the water teem
with living creatures, and let birds
fly above the earth across the expanse of the sky." 21 So God created
the great creatures of the sea and
every living and moving thing with
which the water teems,[s] according
to their kinds, and every winged
bird according to its kind. And God
saw that it was good. 22 God blessed
them and said, "Be fruitful and increase in number and fill the water
in the seas, and let the birds increase on the earth."[t] 23 And there
was evening, and there was morning—the fifth day.

1:14 [l] Ps 74:16 [m] Jer 10:2 [n] Ps 104:19
1:16 [o] Ps 136:8 [p] Ps 136:9 [q] Job 38:7,31-32; Ps 8:3; Isa 40:26
1:18 [r] Jer 33:20,25
1:21 [s] Ps 104:25-26
1:22 [t] ver 28; Ge 8:17

[a] 2 Or possibly *became*

DISCOVERY 1

IN THE BEGINNING . . . GOD

Our universe is not just physical matter shaped by chance. To the contrary, the opening sentence of the Bible tells us that there is a God—a God who works in unimaginably creative ways! God created everything that exists—every molecule—from the smallest single-cell animal to the most complex of his creatures—human beings (Genesis 1). It has been said that everything after the first four words of the Bible, "In the beginning God," is merely commentary.

All three persons in our triune God were involved in that creative process: *God the Father* (Genesis 1:3,27), *God the Son* (see John 1:1–3) and *God the Holy Spirit* (Genesis 1:1–2). God introduced the idea of this *tri-unity* already in the first chapter of the Bible and continued to reinforce the concept throughout Scripture. One of the Hebrew names for God is *Elohim,* a plural noun describing God's incomparable majesty and power revealed in Creation. Through the Scriptures he has revealed more about himself as he has interacted with his people throughout history. Finally, he came in the person of Jesus Christ so that we could get to know him even more intimately (Philippians 2:6–7).

Jesus personifies the *living* Word from God about himself. He is the Word made flesh, the Name above all names. For many the name of Jesus brings extraordinary comfort and hope. But others use his name to express anger, amazement or disgust; to them it is no more than a convenient expletive. The Name that is like no other stirs conflicting emotions in those who hear it, because Jesus is more than just a religious leader and teacher. He is more than simply a figure in world history. He is more than merely a moral influence. Jesus Christ is the Son of God.

Something about Jesus prompts people to take sides. Ultimately, each of us must either be *for* him or *against* him. "For what do righteousness and wickedness have in common? Or what fellowship can light have with darkness?" (2 Corinthians 6:14). Jesus himself declared, "Do not suppose that I have come to bring peace to the earth. I did not come to bring peace, but a sword" (Matthew 10:34). Either we reject him and live life on our own terms, or else we acknowledge him as God and surrender our lives to him, getting to know him and learning to live in the way he intended.

One day each of us will stand before Jesus in heaven, and the choice we have made during our lifetime will be apparent. For Jesus, who was in the beginning, is also forever: "Behold, I am coming soon! My reward is with me, and I will give to everyone according to what he has done. I am the Alpha and the Omega, the First and the Last, the Beginning and the End" (Revelation 22:12–13).

***Self-Discovery:** In what specific ways does your life demonstrate that Jesus is your Creator and Lord?*

GO TO DISCOVERY 2 ON PAGE 7

[24] And God said, "Let the land produce
living creatures according to their
kinds: livestock, creatures that
move along the ground, and wild
animals, each according to its
1:25 kind." And it was so. [25]God made
u Jer 27:5 the wild animals[u] according to
their kinds, the livestock according
to their kinds, and all the creatures
that move along the ground according to their kinds. And God
saw that it was good.
[26]Then God said, "Let us[v] make
1:26 v Ps 100:3 man in our image,[w] in our likeness,
w Ge 9:6; Jas 3:9 and let them rule[x] over the fish of
x Ps 8:6-8 the sea and the birds of the air, over
the livestock, over all the earth,[a]
and over all the creatures that
move along the ground."
1:27 [27] So God created man in his own
y 1Co 11:7 image,[y]
z Ge 5:2; Mt 19:4*; Mk 10:6* in the image of God he created
him;
male and female[z] he created
them.

[28]God blessed them and said to
them, "Be fruitful and increase in
1:28 a Ge 9:1,7; Lev 26:9 number; fill the earth[a] and subdue
it. Rule over the fish of the sea and
the birds of the air and over every
living creature that moves on the
ground."
[29]Then God said, "I give you
every seed-bearing plant on the
face of the whole earth and every
tree that has fruit with seed in it. 1:29 b Ps 104:14
They will be yours for food.[b] [30]And
to all the beasts of the earth and all
the birds of the air and all the creatures that move on the ground—
everything that has the breath of 1:30
life in it—I give every green plant c Ps 104:14,27; 145:15
for food.[c]" And it was so.
[31]God saw all that he had made,[d] 1:31 d Ps 104:24
and it was very good.[e] And there e 1Ti 4:4
was evening, and there was morning—the sixth day.

2 Thus the heavens and the earth
were completed in all their vast
array.
[2] By the seventh day God had finished
the work he had been doing; so on 2:2 f Ex 20:11;
the seventh day he rested[b] from all 31:17; Heb 4:4*
his work.[f] [3] And God blessed the
seventh day and made it holy,[g] be- 2:3 g Lev 23:3;
cause on it he rested from all the Isa 58:13
work of creating that he had done.

Adam and Eve

[4]This is the account of the heavens
and the earth when they were created.

When the LORD God made the earth
and the heavens— [5]and no shrub of the
field had yet appeared on the earth[c] and 2:5
no plant of the field had yet sprung up,[h] h Ge 1:11
for the LORD God had not sent rain on i Ps 65:9-10
the earth[c][i] and there was no man to

[a] *26* Hebrew; Syriac *all the wild animals* [b] *2* Or *ceased*; also in verse 3 [c] *5* Or *land*; also in verse 6

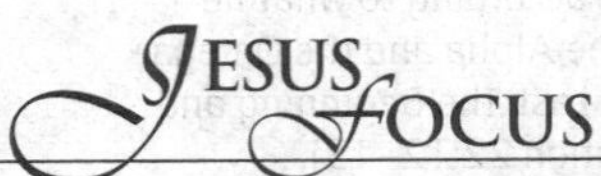

AT WORK IN CREATION

All things—"things in heaven and on earth, visible and invisible"—are made through Jesus (Colossians 1:16), and we can find real meaning for our lives only through a relationship with him (John 1:4). He created all things for his own purposes, so that he could enjoy them. The triune God—God the Father, God the Son and God the Holy Spirit—created the universe (Isaiah 40:12). The Father designed it all, but both the Son and the Spirit were involved in the actual creative process. We know this because God refers to himself as "us" when he talks about creating the world (Genesis 1:26). The Old Testament foreshadows the truth that the one God is three distinct persons, and the New Testament testifies to this truth.

REFLECTING HIS IMAGE

We are all created in God's image (Genesis 1:27), but that image was marred when sin came into the world. It is interesting that the Bible makes clear that the image was not totally lost even *after* our sin had separated us from him (Genesis 5:1–3; 9:6; 1 Corinthians 11:7; James 3:9). His image may have been *defaced*, but it was certainly not *erased* by sin. Even though all of creation has been affected by sin (Romans 8:22–23), through the work of Jesus we have a living hope (Romans 8:24; 1 Peter 1:3–5). When we live in relationship with God, we are being "conformed to the likeness" of Jesus (Romans 8:29). We bring honor to the One who created us by responding in obedience and faith in Jesus.

work the ground, 6but streams[a] came up
from the earth and watered the whole
surface of the ground— 7the LORD God
formed the man[b] from the dust[j] of the
ground[k] and breathed into his nostrils
the breath[l] of life,[m] and the man became
a living being.[n]
8Now the LORD God had planted a
garden in the east, in Eden;[o] and there
he put the man he had formed. 9And the
LORD God made all kinds of trees grow
out of the ground—trees that were
pleasing to the eye and good for food. In
the middle of the garden were the tree of
life[p] and the tree of the knowledge of
good and evil.[q]
10A river watering the garden flowed
from Eden; from there it was separated
into four headwaters. 11The name of the
first is the Pishon; it winds through the
entire land of Havilah, where there is gold.
12(The gold of that land is good; aromatic
resin[c] and onyx are also there.) 13The
name of the second river is the Gihon; it
winds through the entire land of Cush.[d]
14The name of the third river is the Tigris;[r]
it runs along the east side of Asshur. And
the fourth river is the Euphrates.
15The LORD God took the man and
put him in the Garden of Eden to work
it and take care of it. 16And the LORD
God commanded the man, "You are free
to eat from any tree in the garden; 17but
you must not eat from the tree of the
knowledge of good and evil, for when
you eat of it you will surely die."[s]
18The LORD God said, "It is not good
for the man to be alone. I will make a
helper suitable for him."[t]
19Now the LORD God had formed out
of the ground all the beasts of the field[u]
and all the birds of the air. He brought
them to the man to see what he would
name them; and whatever the man
called each living creature,[v] that was its
name. 20So the man gave names to all
the livestock, the birds of the air and all
the beasts of the field.
But for Adam[e] no suitable helper was
found. 21So the LORD God caused the
man to fall into a deep sleep; and while
he was sleeping, he took one of the man's
ribs[f] and closed up the place with flesh.
22Then the LORD God made a woman
from the rib[g][w] he had taken out of the
man, and he brought her to the man.

2:7 [j]Ge 3:19 [k]Ps 103:14 [l]Job 33:4 [m]Ac 17:25 [n]1Co 15:45*
2:8 [o]Ge 3:23,24; Isa 51:3
2:9 [p]Ge 3:22,24; Rev 2:7; 22:2,14, 19 [q]Eze 47:12
2:14 [r]Da 10:4
2:17 [s]Dt 30:15,19; Ro 5:12; 6:23; Jas 1:15
2:18 [t]1Co 11:9
2:19 [u]Ps 8:7 [v]Ge 1:24
2:22 [w]1Co 11:8,9,12

[a]6 Or *mist* [b]7 The Hebrew for *man (adam)* sounds like and may be related to the Hebrew for *ground (adamah)*; it is also the name *Adam* (see Gen. 2:20). [c]12 Or *good; pearls* [d]13 Possibly southeast Mesopotamia [e]20 Or *the man* [f]21 Or *took part of the man's side* [g]22 Or *part*

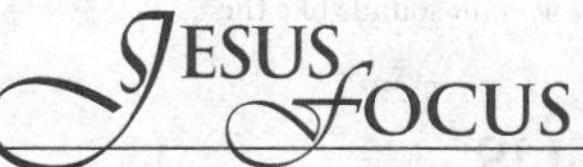

TWO "ADAMS"

The crowning glory of everything God created is humanity (Genesis 2; Psalm 8:5–8). We are completely different from the rest of creation because we are made in God's image and likeness—and we are created to have a relationship with him. God named the first man *Adam*, and the same Hebrew word is used to refer to human beings in general. Adam represented the entire human race, and this means that when he chose to sin, all of humanity suffered the consequences (see Romans 5:12–17). The result of turning away from our Creator was separation from him—both in time, as physical bodies decay and die, and for eternity. But God didn't leave us in that dismal situation. Instead, he himself became a man, Jesus, the "last Adam," who set us free from the penalty and power of sin by dying in our place (Romans 5:12–21; 6:1–23; 1 Corinthians 15:22,45). Jesus then came back to life, illustrating that we can live forever because we have died with him and have been raised to new life with him (Romans 6:1–14).

ADAM AND EVE

THE FIRST HUMANS

The word *Adam* means "man," and *Eve* means "living," or "mother of life." As the first people, Adam and Eve were the parents of the entire human race. God gave them the task of ruling over the earth (Genesis 1:28). The first husband and wife were intelligent, creative and, because of God's gifts, able to rule as God had designed. They could talk with God and with each other in a fellowship that was not corrupted in any way. But first Eve and then Adam chose to turn from God's way, plunging all of humanity into sin along with themselves (Genesis 3). But God didn't leave them irreparably stuck with a broken relationship with himself: In his mercy he stepped into the mess they had created and provided a way to temporarily cover their sin (Genesis 3:21) until the time he would permanently cover it through the finished work of Jesus. Knowing that God makes it possible for us to enjoy a renewed relationship with himself offers bright hope for our future.

[23]The man said,

2:23 [x]Ge 29:14; Eph 5:28-30

"This is now bone of my bones
and flesh of my flesh;[x]
she shall be called 'woman,[a]'
for she was taken out of man."

2:24 [y]Mal 2:15 [z]Mt 19:5*; Mk 10:7-8*; 1Co 6:16*; Eph 5:31*

[24]For this reason a man will leave his father and mother and be united[y] to his
wife, and they will become one flesh.[z]

2:25 [a]Ge 3:7,10-11

[25]The man and his wife were both
naked,[a] and they felt no shame.

The Fall of Man

3:1 [b]2Co 11:3; Rev 12:9; 20:2

3 Now the serpent[b] was more crafty
than any of the wild animals the
LORD God had made. He said to the
woman, "Did God really say, 'You must
not eat from any tree in the garden'?"
[2]The woman said to the serpent, "We
may eat fruit from the trees in the garden, [3]but God did say, 'You must not eat
fruit from the tree that is in the middle
of the garden, and you must not touch
it, or you will die.'"

3:4 [c]Jn 8:44; 2Co 11:3

[4]"You will not surely die," the serpent
said to the woman. [c] [5]"For God knows
that when you eat of it your eyes will be

3:5 [d]Isa 14:14; Eze 28:2

opened, and you will be like God,[d]
knowing good and evil."
[6]When the woman saw that the fruit

3:6 [e]Jas 1:14-15; 1Jn 2:16 [f]1Ti 2:14

of the tree was good for food and pleasing to the eye, and also desirable[e] for
gaining wisdom, she took some and ate
it. She also gave some to her husband,
who was with her, and he ate it.[f] [7]Then
the eyes of both of them were opened,
and they realized they were naked; so
they sewed fig leaves together and made
coverings for themselves.
[8]Then the man and his wife heard the
sound of the LORD God as he was walk- 3:8 [g]Dt 23:14 [h]Job 31:33; Ps 139:7-12; Jer 23:24
ing[g] in the garden in the cool of the day,
and they hid[h] from the LORD God among
the trees of the garden. [9]But the LORD
God called to the man, "Where are you?"
[10]He answered, "I heard you in the
garden, and I was afraid because I was
naked; so I hid."
[11]And he said, "Who told you that you
were naked? Have you eaten from the tree
that I commanded you not to eat from?"
[12]The man said, "The woman you put
here with me—she gave me some fruit
from the tree, and I ate it."
[13]Then the LORD God said to the
woman, "What is this you have done?"
The woman said, "The serpent de- 3:13 [i]2Co 11:3; 1Ti 2:14
ceived me,[i] and I ate."
[14]So the LORD God said to the serpent,
"Because you have done this,

"Cursed[j] are you above all the
livestock 3:14 [j]Dt 28:15-20 [k]Isa 65:25; Mic 7:17
and all the wild animals!
You will crawl on your belly
and you will eat dust[k]
all the days of your life.

[a] 23 The Hebrew for *woman* sounds like the Hebrew for *man.*

JESUS FOCUS

THE CREATION OF WOMAN

It was love at first sight! God created a woman from Adam's rib and brought her to him as his companion (Genesis 2:21–22). The words for "man" and "woman" look very similar in Hebrew: *ish* and *ishah*. While men and women often appear to have more differences than similarities, these two words remind us that they have much in common spiritually. And both are created in God's image. Jesus affirmed the importance of women by including them in his ministry (Luke 8:1–3) and also affirmed the significance of marriage by quoting Genesis 2:23–24 to advocate marital purity (Matthew 19:4–6).

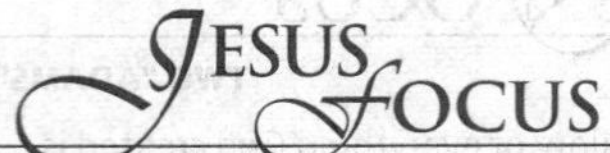

GOOD NEWS PROMISED

Genesis 3:15 is often called the "first gospel" because it represents the first time God suggested that he would send a Messiah to rescue his people from their sins. God promised that one day someone would defeat the power of Satan. This prophecy isn't very clearly stated in Genesis 3, but the passage does look down the corridor of time and foreshadow the day when Jesus would be born as a man to triumph over Satan and his dominion of darkness. The image of the victor stomping the head of the one he will defeat and being injured in the process points ahead to Jesus' own suffering. Jesus endured the most agonizing of deaths and then came back to life—representing God's ultimate victory over the power of Satan (1 Peter 3:18). Even after his people had turned away from him, God gave them hope through the promise of a better day ahead—the day when Jesus would triumph over Satan (Colossians 2:13–15).

DISCOVERY 2

Fellowship Restored

People want to be in charge of their own lives. This theme began to unfold in the Garden of Eden, when humanity first turned away from God. God created a perfect world and placed a man (Adam) and woman (Eve) in the Garden of Eden. In the entire garden there was only one tree whose fruit they were forbidden to eat—the tree of the knowledge of good and evil. God told them that, if they were to eat the fruit from that tree, they would die. Adam and Eve were not innately prone to sinful choices, nor were they surrounded by temptation in an evil environment or victims of dysfunctional backgrounds. They were sinless people in an idyllic environment—and still they chose to disregard God and indulge in sin.

God's judgment against Adam and Eve was immediate and severe. First, he declared that there would be *continual conflict between Satan and the woman and her offspring* (Genesis 3:15). From that point on Eve (and all women after her) would experience pain in childbirth and conflict with her husband (verse 16). Adam (and all men after him) would struggle for survival in a world full of hostility and frustration. And each day would inexorably lead both of them closer to physical death and a return to dust (verses 17–19).

The Bible records the ongoing conflict between God and his archenemy Satan, between good and evil, between human beings and demons. Because God is perfectly holy, he could not tolerate unholiness in his people; he banished Adam and Eve from the perfection of the garden to live in a world contaminated with the effects of their sin. They got what they wanted: to be in charge of their own lives—along with all the hardship that would entail for humankind.

The sons and daughters of Adam and Eve continued to turn away from God. Throughout the story of God's people in the Old Testament we see the pattern repeated: The people fall into sin, God judges them and punishes their sin, then invites his people back into relationship with him. God continued to do whatever was necessary to maintain his requirements for holiness and yet to offer his people his loving mercy, but, like their ancestors they were determined to go their own way. And so it continues . . .

God did not leave humanity hopeless but provided a way to draw people back to himself—a whisper of hope uttered in the same breath as his initial judgment against evil. God pronounced that *the woman's offspring would crush the head of the serpent* (verse 16). The "offspring" God referred to in this promise is Jesus, his own Son. Eventually, Jesus Christ would crush the power of Satan in this world (Galatians 3:16; Hebrews 2:14; Revelation 12:1–5) in order to set us free from the vicious bondage of sin and death. In Christ Jesus, God offers his redemptive grace and makes it possible for us to live in fellowship with him.

Self-Discovery: *Do you frequently find yourself being tempted by the serpent (Satan)? Or are you allowing Jesus to "crush" his influence in your life?*

GO TO DISCOVERY 3 ON PAGE 10

3:15 [l]Jn 8:44; Ac 13:10; 1Jn 3:8 [m]Isa 7:14; Mt 1:23; Rev 12:17 [n]Ro 16:20; Heb 2:14

15 And I will put enmity
between you and the woman,
and between your offspring[a] [l]
and hers;[m]
he will crush[b] your head,[n]
and you will strike his heel."

16 To the woman he said,

"I will greatly increase your pains
in childbearing;
with pain you will give birth to
children.
Your desire will be for your husband,
and he will rule over you.[o]"

3:16 [o]1Co 11:3; Eph 5:22

17 To Adam he said, "Because you listened to your wife and ate from the tree about which I commanded you, 'You must not eat of it,'

"Cursed[p] is the ground because of
you;
through painful toil you will eat
of it
all the days of your life.[q]
18 It will produce thorns and thistles
for you,
and you will eat the plants of the
field.[r]
19 By the sweat of your brow
you will eat your food[s]
until you return to the ground,
since from it you were taken;
for dust you are
and to dust you will return."[t]

3:17 [p]Ge 5:29; Ro 8:20-22 [q]Job 5:7; 14:1; Ecc 2:23

3:18 [r]Ps 104:14

3:19 [s]2Th 3:10 [t]Ge 2:7; Ps 90:3; 104:29; Ecc 12:7

> IF THEY WERE CAST OUT OF PARADISE BECAUSE OF THE TREE AND THE EATING THEREOF, SHALL NOT BELIEVERS NOW ENTER MORE EASILY INTO PARADISE BECAUSE OF THE TREE OF JESUS?
>
> Cyril of Jerusalem, *Early Church Father*

20 Adam[c] named his wife Eve,[d] because she would become the mother of all the living.

21 The LORD God made garments of skin for Adam and his wife and clothed them. 22 And the LORD God said, "The man has now become like one of us, knowing good and evil. He must not be allowed to reach out his hand and take also from the tree of life[u] and eat, and live forever." 23 So the LORD God banished him from the Garden of Eden[v] to work the ground[w] from which he had been taken. 24 After he drove the man out, he placed on the east side[e] of the Garden of Eden cherubim[x] and a flaming sword[y] flashing back and forth to guard the way to the tree of life.[z]

3:22 [u]Rev 22:14

3:23 [v]Ge 2:8 [w]Ge 4:2

3:24 [x]Ex 25:18-22 [y]Ps 104:4 [z]Ge 2:9

Cain and Abel

4 Adam[c] lay with his wife Eve, and she became pregnant and gave birth to Cain.[f] She said, "With the help of the LORD I have brought forth[g] a man." 2 Later she gave birth to his brother Abel.[a]

Now Abel kept flocks, and Cain worked the soil. 3 In the course of time Cain brought some of the fruits of the soil as an offering to the LORD.[b] 4 But Abel brought fat portions[c] from some of the firstborn of his flock.[d] The LORD looked with favor on Abel and his offering,[e] 5 but on Cain and his offering he did not look with favor. So Cain was very angry, and his face was downcast.

6 Then the LORD said to Cain, "Why are you angry? Why is your face downcast? 7 If you do what is right, will you not be accepted? But if you do not do what is right, sin is crouching at your door;[f] it desires to have you, but you must master it.[g]"

8 Now Cain said to his brother Abel, "Let's go out to the field."[h] And while they were in the field, Cain attacked his brother Abel and killed him.[h]

9 Then the LORD said to Cain, "Where is your brother Abel?"

"I don't know," he replied. "Am I my brother's keeper?"

10 The LORD said, "What have you done? Listen! Your brother's blood cries out to me from the ground.[i] 11 Now you are under a curse and driven from the ground, which opened its mouth to receive your brother's blood from your hand. 12 When you work the ground, it will no longer yield its crops for you. You will be a restless wanderer on the earth."

13 Cain said to the LORD, "My punishment is more than I can bear. 14 Today

4:2 [a]Lk 11:51

4:3 [b]Nu 18:12

4:4 [c]Lev 3:16 [d]Ex 13:2,12 [e]Heb 11:4

4:7 [f]Nu 32:23 [g]Ro 6:16

4:8 [h]Mt 23:35; 1Jn 3:12

4:10 [i]Ge 9:5; Nu 35:33; Heb 12:24; Rev 6:9-10

[a] 15 Or *seed* [b] 15 Or *strike* [c] 20,1 Or *The man* [d] 20 *Eve* probably means *living.* [e] 24 Or *placed in front* [f] 1 *Cain* sounds like the Hebrew for *brought forth* or *acquired.* [g] 1 Or *have acquired* [h] 8 Samaritan Pentateuch, Septuagint, Vulgate and Syriac; Masoretic Text does not have *"Let's go out to the field."*

me from the land, and I
you are from your presence;[j] I will
anderer on the earth, and
will be me will kill me."[k]
be LORD said to him, "Not so[a];
kills Cain[l], he will suffer
even times over.[m]" Then the
mark on Cain so that no one
him would kill him. [16]So Cain
from the LORD's presence and
he land of Nod,[b] east of Eden.[n]
lay with his wife, and she be-
egnant and gave birth to Enoch.
as then building a city, and he
it after his son[o] Enoch. [18]To
ch was born Irad, and Irad was the
father of Mehujael, and Mehujael was
the father of Methushael, and Methushael was the father of Lamech.
[19]Lamech married two women, one
named Adah and the other Zillah.
[20]Adah gave birth to Jabal; he was the father of those who live in tents and raise
livestock. [21]His brother's name was Ju-
bal; he was the father of all who play the
harp and flute. [22]Zillah also had a son,
Tubal-Cain, who forged all kinds of tools
out of[c] bronze and iron. Tubal-Cain's sister was Naamah.
[23]Lamech said to his wives,

4:14 [j]2Ki 17:18; Ps 51:11; 139:7-12; Jer 7:15; 52:3 [k]Ge 9:6; Nu 35:19,21,27,33

"Adah and Zillah, listen to me;
wives of Lamech, hear my words.
I have killed[d][p] a man for wounding
me,
a young man for injuring me.
[24]If Cain is avenged[q] seven times,[r]
then Lamech seventy-seven
times."

4:23 [p]Ex 20:13; Lev 19:18
4:24 [q]Dt 32:35 [r]ver 15

[25]Adam lay with his wife again, and
she gave birth to a son and named him
Seth,[e][s] saying, "God has granted me another child in place of Abel, since Cain
killed him."[t] [26]Seth also had a son, and
he named him Enosh.

At that time men began to call on[f] the
name of the LORD.[u]

4:25 [s]Ge 5:3 [t]ver 8
4:26 [u]Ge 12:8; 1Ki 18:24; Ps 116:17; Joel 2:32; Zep 3:9; Ac 2:21; 1Co 1:2

From Adam to Noah

5 This is the written account of
Adam's line.

When God created man, he made
him in the likeness of God.[v] [2]He created
them male and female[w] and blessed
them. And when they were created, he
called them "man.[g]"
[3]When Adam had lived 130 years, he
had a son in his own likeness, in his own
image;[x] and he named him Seth. [4]After
Seth was born, Adam lived 800 years
and had other sons and daughters. [5]Al-
together, Adam lived 930 years, and then
he died.[y]
[6]When Seth had lived 105 years, he
became the father[h] of Enosh. [7]And after
he became the father of Enosh, Seth
lived 807 years and had other sons and
daughters. [8]Altogether, Seth lived 912
years, and then he died.
[9]When Enosh had lived 90 years, he
became the father of Kenan. [10]And after
he became the father of Kenan, Enosh
lived 815 years and had other sons and
daughters. [11]Altogether, Enosh lived 905
years, and then he died.
[12]When Kenan had lived 70 years, he
became the father of Mahalalel. [13]And
after he became the father of Mahalalel,
Kenan lived 840 years and had other
sons and daughters. [14]Altogether, Kenan
lived 910 years, and then he died.

5:1 [v]Ge 1:27; Eph 4:24; Col 3:10
5:2 [w]Ge 1:27; Mt 19:4; Mk 10:6; Gal 3:28
5:3 [x]Ge 1:26; 1Co 15:49
5:5 [y]Ge 3:19

[a] 15 Septuagint, Vulgate and Syriac; Hebrew *Very well* [b] 16 *Nod* means *wandering* (see verses 12 and 14). [c] 22 Or *who instructed all who work in* [d] 23 Or *I will kill* [e] 25 *Seth* probably means *granted.* [f] 26 Or *to proclaim* [g] 2 Hebrew *adam* [h] 6 *Father* may mean *ancestor;* also in verses 7–26.

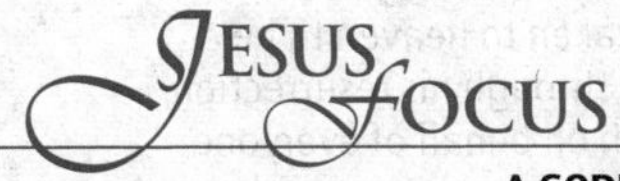

A GODLY FAMILY LINE

After Abel had been killed (Genesis 4), Cain turned away from God and reared a family that refused to recognize the Creator. In fact, Cain's family actually boasted about its sinful and selfish actions. The offspring of Cain's brother Seth, on the other hand, represented the family line from which God's promised Messiah would eventually emerge. The contrast between Cain's ungodly family and Seth's righteous descendants can be seen from the time of Adam to the time of Noah.

The New Testament traces Jesus' family line from Adam through the family of Seth (Luke 3:23–38). God's promise to Adam and Eve (Genesis 3:15) begins to be realized, and we see how God protected the family line so that the Promised One, his beloved Son Jesus the Messiah, could generations later take on our human flesh and walk this earth. God's divine protection of this lineage assures us that he will do whatever is necessary in every generation to keep his promises.

DISCOVERY 3

One Who Pleased God

"And then he died." This is the final statement that can be made about any person's earthly life, and the phrase is repeated throughout the detailed account of Adam's descendants in Genesis 5. In the middle of this list, however, something shocking appears—the account of a man who did *not* die. Instead, God simply took Enoch away. Incredible!

So, unlike every other person before him and almost everyone after him, Enoch did not die. (The Bible mentions only two people who were exempted from death—Enoch and Elijah [see 2 Kings 2:3–5].) Enoch did not "experience death . . . because God had taken him away" (Hebrew 11:5). Two characteristics were true of Enoch's life that made this possible: He took God at his word (he had faith in God), and he chose to listen to those words (he obeyed God). Enoch was "taken from this life" because of his faith, and he was "commended as one who pleased God" (Hebrews 11:5). In fact, Enoch's life illustrates the truth that "without faith it is impossible to please God" (Hebrews 11:6).

Enoch was a prophet, and he warned people that God would judge them for turning away from him. He spoke out against the actions, attitudes and words of the people in his generation who refused to become right with God (Jude 14–15). Enoch's message went against the grain of popular thinking—just as the same message does today. Because of sin in the world and in ourselves, we naturally prefer to do what *we* want instead of what God wants.

But in keeping with his message, Enoch walked with God. The word *walked* connotes a sense of relationship and obedience. To walk in this way involves one's entire life (Colossians 1:9–12). Because Enoch lived this way, he is an example for every believer. Each of us is called to walk—to live our whole lives—in faith (Romans 4:12), in a new life (Romans 6:4), according to the Spirit (Romans 8:4), in wisdom (Ephesians 5:15), in a manner that is pleasing to the Lord (Colossians 1:10) and in the light (1 John 1:7).

Just as Enoch had done before him, Jesus *pleased God*. Jesus said what his Father wanted him to say (John 8:28), honored the Father (John 8:50), did the work of the Father (John 17:4) and submitted to the Father's will (Luke 22:42). Because he walked with God, Enoch was spared death and was taken to heaven to be with God. Jesus, through his resurrection, conquered death on behalf of everyone who would believe in him. Because Jesus sits now at the Father's right hand (Mark 16:19; Luke 24:51), we can, like Enoch, enjoy God's presence forever.

***Self-Discovery:** What final statement would you like to have other people make about your life?*

GO TO DISCOVERY 4 ON PAGE 13

15When Mahalalel had lived 65 years,
he became the father of Jared. 16And after he became the father of Jared, Mahalalel lived 830 years and had other sons
and daughters. 17Altogether, Mahalalel
lived 895 years, and then he died.
5:18 18When Jared had lived 162 years, he
[z] Jude 1:14 became the father of Enoch.[z] 19And after he became the father of Enoch, Jared
lived 800 years and had other sons and
daughters. 20Altogether, Jared lived 962
years, and then he died.
21When Enoch had lived 65 years, he
became the father of Methuselah. 22And
5:22 after he became the father of Methuse-
[a] ver 24; Ge 6:9; 17:1; 48:15; lah, Enoch walked with God[a] 300 years
Mic 6:8; Mal 2:6 and had other sons and daughters. 23Al-
5: together, Enoch lived 365 years. 24Enoch
[b] ver walked with God;[b] then he was no more,
[c] 2Ki 2: Heb because God took him away.[c]
25When Methuselah had lived 187
years, he became the father of Lamech.
26And after he became the father of Lamech, Methuselah lived 782 years and
had other sons and daughters. 27Alto-
gether, Methuselah lived 969 years, and
then he died.
28When Lamech had lived 182 years,
he had a son. 29He named him Noah[a]
and said, "He will comfort us in the la-
5:29 bor and painful toil of our hands caused
[d] Ge 3:17; Ro 8:20 by the ground the LORD has cursed.[d]"
30After Noah was born, Lamech lived
595 years and had other sons and
daughters. 31Altogether, Lamech lived
777 years, and then he died.
32After Noah was 500 years old, he became the father of Shem, Ham and Japheth.

The Flood

6:1 6 When men began to increase in
[e] Ge 1:28 number on the earth[e] and daughters were born to them, 2the sons of God
saw that the daughters of men were
beautiful, and they married any of them
they chose. 3Then the LORD said, "My
6:3 Spirit will not contend with[b] man forev-
[f] Isa 57:16 er,[f] for he is mortal[c];[g] his days will be a
[g] Ps 78:39 hundred and twenty years."
6:4 4The Nephilim[h] were on the earth in
[h] Nu 13:33 those days—and also afterward—when
the sons of God went to the daughters of
men and had children by them. They
were the heroes of old, men of renown.
5The LORD saw how great man's
wickedness on the earth had become,
and that every inclination of the 6:5
thoughts of his heart was only evil all the [i] Ge 8:21; Ps 14:1-3
time.[i] 6The LORD was grieved[j] that he
had made man on the earth, and his 6:6
heart was filled with pain. 7So the LORD [j] 1Sa 15:11,35; Isa 63:10
said, "I will wipe mankind, whom I have
created, from the face of the earth—
men and animals, and creatures that
move along the ground, and birds of the
air—for I am grieved that I have made 6:8
them." 8But Noah found favor in the eyes [k] Ge 19:19; Ex 33:12,13,17;
of the LORD.[k] Lk 1:30; Ac 7:46

9This is the account of Noah. 6:9

Noah was a righteous man, blameless [l] Ge 7:1; Eze 14:14,20;
among the people of his time,[l] and he Heb 11:7;
walked with God.[m] 10Noah had three 2Pe 2:5 [m] Ge 5:22
sons: Shem, Ham and Japheth.[n] 6:10
11Now the earth was corrupt in God's [n] Ge 5:32
sight and was full of violence.[o] 12God
saw how corrupt the earth had become, 6:11 [o] Eze 7:23; 8:17
for all the people on earth had corrupt-
ed their ways.[p] 13So God said to Noah, "I 6:12 [p] Ps 14:1-3
am going to put an end to all people, for
the earth is filled with violence because

[a] 29 *Noah* sounds like the Hebrew for *comfort.* [b] 3 Or *My spirit will not remain in* [c] 3 Or *corrupt*

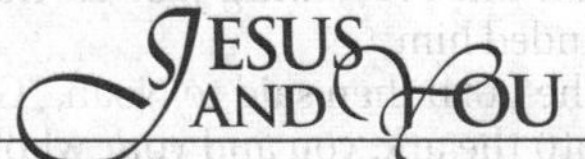

FINDING HIS GRACE

Eventually even the godly line of people suffered a spiritual decline, and God's judgment that accrues to the "ungodly" fell on them as well (Genesis 6:1–8). The "sons of God" married the "daughters of men," and sin ran rampant on the earth. Both God's people and those who had refused him were suffering because of the situation. As sin wreaked more and more havoc, God in his mercy decided to interrupt its relentless spread by sending a flood to cover the whole earth. God's judgment was radical because sin is far more serious than we can conceptualize or comprehend. But God still demonstrated that he loves his people and keeps his promises: Noah and his family were kept safe (verse 8), and God has also provided us with the means for a repaired relationship with himself: The New Testament assures us that Jesus is the way to life and offers us freedom from the penalty and power of sin, just as the ark was God's provision for Noah and his family. Our only hope lies in taking Jesus at his word and turning to him for salvation (Romans 5:6–8).

of them. I am surely going to destroy
6:13 [q] ver 17; Eze 7:2-3 both them and the earth.[q] 14So make
yourself an ark of cypress[a] wood;[r] make
6:14 rooms in it and coat it with pitch[s] inside
[r] Heb 11:7; and out. 15This is how you are to build it:
1Pe 3:20 [s] Ex 2:3 The ark is to be 450 feet long, 75 feet
wide and 45 feet high.[b] 16Make a roof for
it and finish[c] the ark to within 18
inches[d] of the top. Put a door in the side
of the ark and make lower, middle and
upper decks. 17I am going to bring floodwaters on the earth to destroy all life under the heavens, every creature that has
6:17 the breath of life in it. Everything on
[t] Ge 7:4,21-23; 2Pe 2:5 earth will perish.[t] 18But I will establish
6:18 my covenant with you,[u] and you will en-
[u] Ge 9:9-16 ter the ark[v]—you and your sons and
[v] Ge 7:1,7,13 your wife and your sons' wives with you.
19You are to bring into the ark two of all
living creatures, male and female, to
6:20 [w] Ge 7:15 keep them alive with you. 20Two[w] of
every kind of bird, of every kind of ani-
mal and of every kind of creature that
moves along the ground will come to
you to be kept alive. 21You are to take
every kind of food that is to be eaten and
store it away as food for you and for
them."

6:22 [x] Ge 7:5,9,16 22Noah did everything just as God
commanded him.[x]

7:1 [y] Mt 24:38 **7** The LORD then said to Noah, "Go
[z] Ge 6:9; into the ark, you and your whole
Eze 14:14 family,[y] because I have found you righ-
7:2 teous[z] in this generation. 2Take with you
[a] ver 8; Ge 8:20; seven[e] of every kind of clean[a] animal, a
Lev 10:10; 11:1-47 male and its mate, and two of every kind

JESUS FOCUS

A WORLDWIDE FLOOD

Was there really a flood that covered the entire planet (Genesis 6—8)? And did one man and his family actually survive by constructing a boat? Some people believe in the historical accuracy of the story of Noah and the flood, while others do not. However, when Jesus talked about this event, he referred to Noah as a real person and to the flood as an actual historical occurrence (Matthew 24:37–39). Our Lord used the example of the flood to explain what the situation will be like when he comes back for his people (Luke 17:26–27). The flood was "universal" in that it covered the whole planet, and Jesus' return will be universal because it will affect all people to the ends of the earth.

of unclean animal, a male and its mate,
3and also seven of every kind of bird,
male and female, to keep their various
kinds alive throughout the earth. 4Seven
days from now I will send rain on the
earth for forty days and forty nights, and
I will wipe from the face of the earth
every living creature I have made."
5And Noah did all that the LORD com- 7:5
manded him.[b] [b] Ge 6:22
6Noah was six hundred years old
when the floodwaters came on the
earth. 7And Noah and his sons and his
wife and his sons' wives entered the ark
to escape the waters of the flood. 8Pairs
of clean and unclean animals, of birds
and of all creatures that move along the
ground, 9male and female, came to
Noah and entered the ark, as God had
commanded Noah. 10And after the sev-
en days the floodwaters came on the
earth.
11In the six hundredth year of Noah's
life, on the seventeenth day of the second month—on that day all the springs 7:11
of the great deep[c] burst forth, and the [c] Eze 26:19
floodgates of the heavens[d] were opened. [d] Ge 8:2
12And rain fell on the earth forty days 7:12
and forty nights.[e] [e] ver 4
13On that very day Noah and his sons,
Shem, Ham and Japheth, together with
his wife and the wives of his three sons,
entered the ark. 14They had with them
every wild animal according to its kind,
all livestock according to their kinds,
every creature that moves along the
ground according to its kind and every
bird according to its kind, everything
with wings. 15Pairs of all creatures that
have the breath of life in them came to 7:15
Noah and entered the ark.[f] 16The ani- [f] Ge 6:19
mals going in were male and female of
every living thing, as God had commanded Noah. Then the LORD shut
him in.
17For forty days[g] the flood kept com- 7:17
ing on the earth, and as the waters in- [g] ver 4
creased they lifted the ark high above
the earth. 18The waters rose and increased greatly on the earth, and the ark
floated on the surface of the water.

[a] *14* The meaning of the Hebrew for this word is uncertain. [b] *15* Hebrew *300 cubits long, 50 cubits wide and 30 cubits high* (about 140 meters long, 23 meters wide and 13.5 meters high)
[c] *16* Or *Make an opening for light by finishing*
[d] *16* Hebrew *a cubit* (about 0.5 meter) [e] *2* Or *seven pairs;* also in verse 3

DISCOVERY 4

AN ARK OF SAFETY

Noah lived in a culture that was thoroughly wicked. In fact, the people of his day actually *preferred* to do evil (Genesis 6:5). They were corrupt and full of violence. Seeing all the sin in the world hurt God: "His heart was filled with pain" (verse 6). God knew that it was time to pronounce judgment against the whole world, so he asked Noah to construct an ark to protect himself, his family and representatives of each animal species God had created.

The 40-day "voyage" must have been an ordeal for Noah and his family—being trapped in close quarters aboard a boat along with a menagerie of animals. And it must have seemed as though God had shut the door and then abandoned the castaways. But the Lord had not forgotten. When it was safe, God opened the door of the ark, and the small band of survivors stepped out into the blinding light to make a new start. God promised Noah that he would never again destroy the whole earth in the same way, and the rainbow reminds us of that covenant even today.

God exercises judgment against the sins of humanity, but he also offers redemption—that is the "good news" of the gospel! The story of the flood can be thought of as an archetype of the salvation story. First, *God notices sin.* Sometimes it seems as though sin and sinners flourish without intervention. But God is aware of everything that goes on in his creation; *he notices all sin and every sinner*. Second, *God judges every sin and every sinner*, but he also *provides an avenue of escape*. Noah trusted what God said and did what he asked. Finally, *we are saved by God's grace* when we trust what he says. Noah "found favor"—God's spontaneous kindness or grace—with God (verse 8). The writer to the Hebrews reported that, "by faith Noah, when warned about things not yet seen, in holy fear built an ark to save his family. By his faith he condemned the world and became heir of the righteousness that comes by faith" (Hebrews 11:7).

Jesus has told us that the cultural conditions at the end of the world will be similar to those in Noah's day: "As it was in the days of Noah, so it will be at the coming of the Son of Man. For in the days before the flood, people were eating and drinking, marrying and giving in marriage, up to the day Noah entered the ark; and they knew nothing about what would happen until the flood came and took them all away" (Matthew 24:37–39). Just as God's judgment during Noah's life affected all of creation, so his final judgment will be universal in scope. But we have an "ark of safety" in the Lord Jesus Christ, "who gave himself for our sins to rescue us from the present evil age, according to the will of our God and Father, to whom be glory for ever and ever" (Galatians 1:3–5).

Self-Discovery: *What symbol reminds you of God's love and of his gracious promises?*

GO TO DISCOVERY 5 ON PAGE 20

19 They rose greatly on the earth, and all
7:19 the high mountains under the entire
h Ps 104:6 heavens were covered.[h] 20 The waters
rose and covered the mountains to a
depth of more than twenty feet.[a,b]
21 Every living thing that moved on the
earth perished—birds, livestock, wild
7:21 animals, all the creatures that swarm
i Ge 6:7,13 over the earth, and all mankind.[c]
7:22 22 Everything on dry land that had the
j Ge 1:30 breath of life[j] in its nostrils died. 23 Every
living thing on the face of the earth was
7:23 wiped out; men and animals and the
k Mt 24:39; Lk 17:27; creatures that move along the ground
1Pe 3:20; and the birds of the air were wiped from
2Pe 2:5 the earth.[k] Only Noah was left, and
l Heb 11:7 those with him in the ark.[l]
7:24 24 The waters flooded the earth for a
m Ge 8:3 hundred and fifty days.[m]
8:1 **8** But God remembered[n] Noah and
n Ge 9:15; 19:29; all the wild animals and the live-
Ex 2:24; 1Sa 1:11,19 stock that were with him in the ark, and
o Ex 14:21 he sent a wind over the earth,[o] and the
waters receded. 2 Now the springs of the
8:2 p Ge 7:11 deep and the floodgates of the heavens[p]
had been closed, and the rain had
stopped falling from the sky. 3 The water
receded steadily from the earth. At the
end of the hundred and fifty days the
water had gone down, 4 and on the seventeenth day of the seventh month the
ark came to rest on the mountains of
Ararat. 5 The waters continued to recede
until the tenth month, and on the first
day of the tenth month the tops of the
mountains became visible.
6 After forty days Noah opened the
window he had made in the ark 7 and
sent out a raven, and it kept flying back
and forth until the water had dried up
from the earth. 8 Then he sent out a dove
to see if the water had receded from the
surface of the ground. 9 But the dove
could find no place to set its feet because there was water over all the surface of the earth; so it returned to Noah
in the ark. He reached out his hand and
took the dove and brought it back to
himself in the ark. 10 He waited seven
more days and again sent out the dove
from the ark. 11 When the dove returned
to him in the evening, there in its beak
was a freshly plucked olive leaf! Then
Noah knew that the water had receded
from the earth. 12 He waited seven more
days and sent the dove out again, but
this time it did not return to him.

13 By the first day of the first month of
Noah's six hundred and first year, the
water had dried up from the earth. Noah
then removed the covering from the ark
and saw that the surface of the ground
was dry. 14 By the twenty-seventh day of
the second month the earth was completely dry.
15 Then God said to Noah, 16 "Come out
of the ark, you and your wife and your 8:16
sons and their wives.[q] 17 Bring out every q Ge 7:13
kind of living creature that is with you—
the birds, the animals, and all the creatures that move along the ground—so
they can multiply on the earth and be 8:17
fruitful and increase in number upon it."[r] r Ge 1:22
18 So Noah came out, together with his
sons and his wife and his sons' wives.
19 All the animals and all the creatures
that move along the ground and all the
birds—everything that moves on the
earth—came out of the ark, one kind after another.
20 Then Noah built an altar to the 8:20
LORD[s] and, taking some of all the clean s Ge 12:7-8; 13:18; 22:9
animals and clean[t] birds, he sacrificed t Ge 7:8; Lev 11:1-47
burnt offerings[u] on it. 21 The LORD u Ge 22:2,13;
smelled the pleasing aroma[v] and said in Ex 10:25
his heart: "Never again will I curse the 8:21
ground[w] because of man, even though[c] v Lev 1:9,13;
every inclination of his heart is evil from 2Co 2:15 w Ge 3:17
childhood.[x] And never again will I de- x Ge 6:5; Ps 51:5;
stroy all living creatures,[y] as I have done. Jer 17:9 y Ge 9:11,15;

22 "As long as the earth endures, Isa 54:9
seedtime and harvest,
cold and heat,
summer and winter, 8:22
day and night z Ge 1:14;
will never cease."[z] Jer 33:20,25

God's Covenant With Noah

9 Then God blessed Noah and his
sons, saying to them, "Be fruitful
and increase in number and fill the 9:1
earth.[a] 2 The fear and dread of you will a Ge 1:22
fall upon all the beasts of the earth and
all the birds of the air, upon every creature that moves along the ground, and
upon all the fish of the sea; they are giv-
en into your hands. 3 Everything that 9:3
lives and moves will be food for you.[b] b Ge 1:29
Just as I gave you the green plants, I now
give you everything.
4 "But you must not eat meat that has

[a] 20 Hebrew *fifteen cubits* (about 6.9 meters)
[b] 20 Or *rose more than twenty feet, and the mountains were covered*
[c] 21 Or *man, for*

9:4 c Lev 3:17; 17:10-14; Dt 12:16,23-25; 1Sa 14:33 its lifeblood still in it.[c] 5And for your
lifeblood I will surely demand an ac-
counting. I will demand an accounting
from every animal.[d] And from each
9:5 d Ex 21:28-32 e Ge 4:10 man, too, I will demand an accounting
for the life of his fellow man.[e]

9:6 f Ge 4:14; Ex 21:12,14; Lev 24:17; Mt 26:52 g Ge 1:26 6"Whoever sheds the blood of man,
by man shall his blood be shed;[f]
for in the image of God[g]
has God made man.

7As for you, be fruitful and increase in
9:7 h Ge 1:22 number; multiply on the earth and increase upon it."[h]
8Then God said to Noah and to his
9:9 i Ge 6:18 sons with him: 9"I now establish my covenant with you[i] and with your descen-
dants after you 10and with every living
creature that was with you—the birds,
the livestock and all the wild animals, all
those that came out of the ark with
9:11 j ver 16; Isa 24:5 k Ge 8:21; Isa 54:9 you—every living creature on earth. 11I
establish my covenant[j] with you: Never
again will all life be cut off by the waters
of a flood; never again will there be a
flood to destroy the earth.[k]"
9:12 l ver 17; Ge 17:11 12And God said, "This is the sign of
the covenant[l] I am making between me
and you and every living creature with
you, a covenant for all generations to
come: 13I have set my rainbow in the
clouds, and it will be the sign of the covenant between me and the earth.
14Whenever I bring clouds over the
earth and the rainbow appears in the
9:15 m Ex 2:24; Lev 26:42,45; Dt 7:9; Eze 16:60 clouds, 15I will remember my covenant[m]
between me and you and all living crea-
tures of every kind. Never again will the
waters become a flood to destroy all life.

JESUS AND YOU

A PROMISE TO NOAH

Once the rain stopped the waters began to recede. In order to demonstrate his trustworthiness, God set a rainbow in the sky as a visible sign of his promise to Noah's family: God pledged that he would never again flood the entire planet (Genesis 9:12–16) and assured the small cluster of survivors, "I now establish my covenant with you and with your descendants" (verse 9). This *covenant* or agreement between God and humanity is a divine contract. Through Noah God protected the family line of his promised Messiah, Jesus, thereby keeping his promise to all people.

16Whenever the rainbow appears in the
clouds, I will see it and remember the 9:16 n ver 11; Ge 17:7,13,19; 2Sa 7:13; 23:5
everlasting covenant[n] between God and
all living creatures of every kind on the
earth."
17So God said to Noah, "This is the 9:17 o ver 12; Ge 17:11
sign of the covenant[o] I have established
between me and all life on the earth."

The Sons of Noah

18The sons of Noah who came out of
the ark were Shem, Ham and Japheth. 9:18 p ver 25-27; Ge 10:6,15
(Ham was the father of Canaan.)[p]
19These were the three sons of Noah,
and from them came the people who 9:19 q Ge 10:32
were scattered over the earth.[q]
20Noah, a man of the soil, proceeded[a]
to plant a vineyard. 21When he drank
some of its wine, he became drunk and
lay uncovered inside his tent. 22Ham, the
father of Canaan, saw his father's nakedness and told his two brothers outside.
23But Shem and Japheth took a garment
and laid it across their shoulders; then
they walked in backward and covered
their father's nakedness. Their faces
were turned the other way so that they
would not see their father's nakedness.
24When Noah awoke from his wine
and found out what his youngest son
had done to him, 25he said,

"Cursed be Canaan![r] 9:25 r ver 18 s Ge 25:23; Jos 9:23
The lowest of slaves
will he be to his brothers.[s]"

26He also said,

"Blessed be the LORD, the God of
Shem!
May Canaan be the slave of
Shem.[b]
27May God extend the territory of
Japheth[c];
may Japheth live in the tents of
Shem,
and may Canaan be his[d] slave."

28After the flood Noah lived 350 years.
29Altogether, Noah lived 950 years, and
then he died.

The Table of Nations

10 This is the account[t] of Shem, 10:1 t Ge 2:4
Ham and Japheth, Noah's sons,
who themselves had sons after the flood.

[a] 20 Or *soil, was the first* [b] 26 Or *be his slave*
[c] 27 *Japheth* sounds like the Hebrew for *extend.*
[d] 27 Or *their*

The Japhethites

10:2 [2]The sons[a] of Japheth:
u Eze 38:6 Gomer,[u] Magog,[v] Madai, Javan,
v Eze 38:2; Rev 20:8 Tubal,[w] Meshech and Tiras.
w Isa 66:19 [3]The sons of Gomer:
10:3 Ashkenaz,[x] Riphath and Togarmah.[y]
x Jer 51:27 y Eze 27:14; 38:6 [4]The sons of Javan:
10:4 Elishah, Tarshish,[z] the Kittim
z Eze 27:12,25; Jnh 1:3 and the Rodanim.[b] [5](From these
the maritime peoples spread out
into their territories by their
clans within their nations, each
with its own language.)

The Hamites

[6]The sons of Ham:
10:6 Cush, Mizraim,[c] Put and Ca-
a ver 15; Ge 9:18 naan.[a]
[7]The sons of Cush:
Seba, Havilah, Sabtah, Raamah
and Sabteca.
The sons of Raamah:
Sheba and Dedan.

[8]Cush was the father[d] of Nimrod, who
grew to be a mighty warrior on the
earth. [9]He was a mighty hunter before
the LORD; that is why it is said, "Like
Nimrod, a mighty hunter before the
10:10 LORD." [10]The first centers of his kingdom
b Ge 11:9 were Babylon,[b] Erech, Akkad and Cal-
c Ge 11:2 neh, in[e] Shinar.[f c] [11]From that land he
10:11 went to Assyria,[d] where he built Nin-
d Ps 83:8; Mic 5:6 eveh,[e] Rehoboth Ir,[g] Calah [12]and Resen,
e Jnh 1:2; 4:11; Na 1:1 which is between Nineveh and Calah;
that is the great city.

[13]Mizraim was the father of
the Ludites, Anamites, Lehabites, Naphtuhites, [14]Pathrusites,
10:14 Casluhites (from whom the Phi-
f Ge 21:32,34; 26:1,8 listines[f] came) and Caphtorites.
10:15 [15]Canaan[g] was the father of
g ver 6; Ge 9:18 Sidon[h] his firstborn,[h] and of the
h Eze 28:21 i Ge 23:3,20 Hittites,[i] [16]Jebusites,[j] Amorites,
Girgashites, [17]Hivites, Arkites,
10:16 j 1Ch 11:4 Sinites, [18]Arvadites, Zemarites
and Hamathites.

10:18 k Ge 12:6; Ex 13:11 Later the Canaanite[k] clans scattered
10:19 [19]and the borders of Canaan[l] reached
l Ge 11:31; 13:12; 17:8 from Sidon[m] toward Gerar as far as Gaza,
and then toward Sodom, Gomorrah, Ad-
m ver 15 mah and Zeboiim, as far as Lasha.

[20]These are the sons of Ham by their
clans and languages, in their territories
and nations.

The Semites

[21]Sons were also born to Shem, whose 10:21
older brother was[i] Japheth; Shem was n ver 24; Nu 24:24
the ancestor of all the sons of Eber.[n]

[22]The sons of Shem:
Elam,[o] Asshur, Arphaxad,[p] Lud 10:22
and Aram. o Jer 49:34 p Lk 3:36
[23]The sons of Aram:
Uz,[q] Hul, Gether and Meshech.[j] 10:23 q Job 1:1
[24]Arphaxad was the father of[k] Shelah, 10:24
and Shelah the father of Eber.[r] r ver 21
[25]Two sons were born to Eber:
One was named Peleg,[l] because
in his time the earth was divided;
his brother was named Joktan.
[26]Joktan was the father of
Almodad, Sheleph, Hazarmaveth, Jerah, [27]Hadoram, Uzal,
Diklah, [28]Obal, Abimael, Sheba,
[29]Ophir, Havilah and Jobab. All
these were sons of Joktan.
[30]The region where they lived stretched
from Mesha toward Sephar, in the eastern hill country.

[31]These are the sons of Shem by their
clans and languages, in their territories
and nations.

[32]These are the clans of Noah's sons,[s] 10:32
according to their lines of descent, with- s ver 1 t Ge 9:19
in their nations. From these the nations
spread out over the earth[t] after the
flood.

The Tower of Babel

11 Now the whole world had one
language and a common
speech. [2]As men moved eastward,[m] they
found a plain in Shinar[f u] and settled 11:2 u Ge 10:10
there.

[3]They said to each other, "Come, let's 11:3
make bricks[v] and bake them thorough- v Ex 1:14
ly." They used brick instead of stone, and

[a] *2 Sons* may mean *descendants* or *successors* or *nations*; also in verses 3, 4, 6, 7, 20–23, 29 and 31.
[b] *4* Some manuscripts of the Masoretic Text and Samaritan Pentateuch (see also Septuagint and 1 Chron. 1:7); most manuscripts of the Masoretic Text *Dodanim*
[c] *6* That is, Egypt; also in verse 13
[d] *8 Father* may mean *ancestor* or *predecessor* or *founder*; also in verses 13, 15, 24 and 26.
[e] *10* Or *Erech and Akkad—all of them in*
[f] *10* That is, Babylonia
[g] *11* Or *Nineveh with its city squares*
[h] *15* Or *of the Sidonians, the foremost*
[i] *21* Or *Shem, the older brother of*
[j] *23* See Septuagint and 1 Chron. 1:17; Hebrew *Mash*
[k] *24* Hebrew; Septuagint *father of Cainan, and Cainan was the father of*
[l] *25 Peleg* means *division.*
[m] *2* Or *from the east*; or *in the east*

11:3 tar[w] for mortar. 4Then they said, "Come,
w Ge 14:10 let us build ourselves a city, with a tow-
11:4 er that reaches to the heavens,[x] so that
x Dt 1:28; 9:1 y Ge 6:4 we may make a name[y] for ourselves and
z Dt 4:27 not be scattered over the face of the
whole earth."[z]

11:5 5But the LORD came down[a] to see the
a ver 7; Ge 18:21; city and the tower that the men were
Ex 3:8; 19:11,18, 20 building. 6The LORD said, "If as one people speaking the same language they
have begun to do this, then nothing they
plan to do will be impossible for them.
11:7 7Come, let us[b] go down and confuse
b Ge 1:26 c Ge 42:23 their language so they will not understand each other."[c]

8So the LORD scattered them from
11:8 d Ge 9:19; there over all the earth,[d] and they
Lk 1:51 stopped building the city. 9That is why it
11:9 was called Babel[a][e]—because there the
e Ge 10:10 LORD confused the language of the
whole world. From there the LORD scattered them over the face of the whole
earth.

From Shem to Abram

10This is the account of Shem.

Two years after the flood, when Shem
was 100 years old, he became the father[b]
of Arphaxad. 11And after he became the
father of Arphaxad, Shem lived 500
years and had other sons and daughters.

12When Arphaxad had lived 35 years,
he became the father of Shelah.[f] 13And 11:12 f Lk 3:35
after he became the father of Shelah, Arphaxad lived 403 years and had other
sons and daughters.[c]

14When Shelah had lived 30 years, he
became the father of Eber. 15And after he
became the father of Eber, Shelah lived
403 years and had other sons and daughters.

16When Eber had lived 34 years, he became the father of Peleg. 17And after he
became the father of Peleg, Eber lived
430 years and had other sons and daughters.

18When Peleg had lived 30 years, he
became the father of Reu. 19And after he
became the father of Reu, Peleg lived 209
years and had other sons and daughters.

20When Reu had lived 32 years, he be- 11:20 g Lk 3:35
came the father of Serug.[g] 21And after he
became the father of Serug, Reu lived
207 years and had other sons and
daughters.

22When Serug had lived 30 years, he
became the father of Nahor. 23And after
he became the father of Nahor, Serug
lived 200 years and had other sons and
daughters.

24When Nahor had lived 29 years, he 11:24
became the father of Terah.[h] 25And after h Lk 3:34
he became the father of Terah, Nahor
lived 119 years and had other sons and
daughters.

26After Terah had lived 70 years, he 11:26 i Lk 3:34
became the father of Abram,[i] Nahor[j] j Jos 24:2
and Haran.

27This is the account of Terah.

Terah became the father of Abram, 11:27 k ver 31;
Nahor and Haran. And Haran became Ge 12:4; 14:12;
the father of Lot.[k] 28While his father Te- 19:1; 2Pe 2:7
rah was still alive, Haran died in Ur of 11:28
the Chaldeans,[l] in the land of his birth. l ver 31; Ge 15:7
29Abram and Nahor both married. The 11:29
name of Abram's wife was Sarai,[m] and m Ge 17:15
the name of Nahor's wife was Milcah;[n] n Ge 22:20
she was the daughter of Haran, the fa-

[a] 9 That is, Babylon; *Babel* sounds like the Hebrew for *confused*. [b] *10 Father* may mean *ancestor;* also in verses 11–25. [c] *12,13* Hebrew; Septuagint (see also Luke 3:35, 36 and note at Gen. 10:24) *35 years, he became the father of Cainan. 13And after he became the father of Cainan, Arphaxad lived 430 years and had other sons and daughters, and then he died. When Cainan had lived 130 years, he became the father of Shelah. And after he became the father of Shelah, Cainan lived 330 years and had other sons and daughters*

ABRAHAM
FATHER OF FAITH

Abraham's original name was *Abram*, which means "high" or "exalted father." God later changed that name to *Abraham*, meaning "father of many." Abraham was Noah's descendant through his son Shem, and he eventually became a forefather of both the Jews and the Arabs. Before he departed for Haran in Syria, Abram lived in an area called Ur in ancient Sumeria (Mesopotamia). Later he followed God's directions to Canaan, where God promised that his descendants would eventually settle (Genesis 15:1–6). Abraham is known as the father of all believers because he took God at his word and did what was asked of him. The New Testament refers to Abraham as Israel's ancestor and the patriarch of the Messiah's family line (Matthew 1:1). God promised to bless *all* nations through Abraham, and he did just that through Jesus, who is both the Son of God and the son of Abraham (Galatians 3:6–10).

ther of both Milcah and Iscah. [30]Now Sarai was barren; she had no children.[o]
[31]Terah took his son Abram, his
grandson Lot son of Haran, and his
daughter-in-law Sarai, the wife of his
son Abram, and together they set out
from Ur of the Chaldeans[p] to go to Canaan.[q] But when they came to Haran,
they settled there.
[32]Terah lived 205 years, and he died in
Haran.

The Call of Abram

12 The LORD had said to Abram,
"Leave your country, your people and your father's household and go
to the land I will show you.[r]

[2]"I will make you into a great nation[s]
and I will bless you;[t]
I will make your name great,
and you will be a blessing.
[3]I will bless those who bless you,
and whoever curses you I will
curse;[u]
and all peoples on earth
will be blessed through you.[v]"

[4]So Abram left, as the LORD had told
him; and Lot went with him. Abram was

11:30 [o]Ge 16:1; 18:11
11:31 [p]Ge 15:7; Ne 9:7; Ac 7:4 [q]Ge 10:19
12:1 [r]Ac 7:3*; Heb 11:8
12:2 [s]Ge 15:5; 17:2,4; 18:18; 22:17; Dt 26:5 [t]Ge 24:1,35
12:3 [u]Ge 27:29; Ex 23:22; Nu 24:9 [v]Ge 18:18; 22:18; 26:4; Ac 3:25; Gal 3:8*

JESUS FOCUS

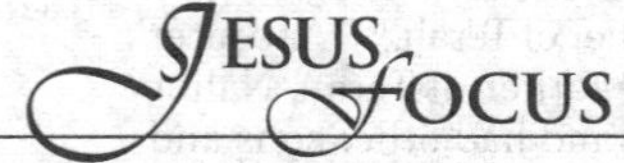

GOD'S CALL

When human beings turned away from God, God focused his attention on one man through whom he chose to make good on his promises. God asked Abram to leave his home and to follow his directions "to the land I will show you" (Genesis 12:1). Then God made a covenant promise that included several aspects. First, he promised to make Abram's name great and to make of his family a mighty nation. God also pledged to bless him and to use him to be a blessing to others, and he made it known that through Abram all people everywhere would have a renewed opportunity to enter into relationship with their Creator—through the work of Jesus (verses 2–3).

God promised that Abram's descendants would settle in Canaan (verse 7), from the "river of Egypt to the great river, the Euphrates" (Genesis 15:18). This promise was fulfilled during David's reign (2 Samuel 8:1–15), and many believe its ultimate fulfillment will occur when Jesus returns to reign on earth for ever and ever (see Luke 1:31–33; Revelation 11:15).

seventy-five years old when he set out
from Haran.[w] [5]He took his wife Sarai, his
nephew Lot, all the possessions they had
accumulated and the people[x] they had
acquired in Haran, and they set out for
the land of Canaan, and they arrived
there.
[6]Abram traveled through the land[y] as
far as the site of the great tree of Moreh[z]
at Shechem. At that time the Canaanites[a] were in the land. [7]The LORD appeared to Abram[b] and said, "To your offspring[a] I will give this land."[c] So he built
an altar there to the LORD,[d] who had appeared to him.
[8]From there he went on toward the
hills east of Bethel[e] and pitched his tent,
with Bethel on the west and Ai on the
east. There he built an altar to the LORD
and called on the name of the LORD.
[9]Then Abram set out and continued toward the Negev.[f]

12:4 [w]Ge 11:31
12:5 [x]Ge 14:14; 17:23
12:6 [y]Heb 11:9 [z]Ge 35:4; Dt 11:30 [a]Ge 10:18
12:7 [b]Ge 17:1; 18:1; Ex 6:3 [c]Ge 13:15,17; 15:18; 17:8; Ps 105:9-11 [d]Ge 13:4
12:8 [e]Ge 13:3
12:9 [f]Ge 13:1,3

JESUS CHRIST IS THE KEY TO BOTH THE INSPIRATION AND INTERPRETATION OF THE BIBLE.

Norman Geisler,
Dean, Southern Evangelical Seminary, Charlotte, North Carolina

Abram in Egypt

[10]Now there was a famine in the land,
and Abram went down to Egypt to live
there for a while because the famine was
severe. [11]As he was about to enter Egypt,
he said to his wife Sarai, "I know what a
beautiful woman you are. [12]When the
Egyptians see you, they will say, 'This is
his wife.' Then they will kill me but will let
you live. [13]Say you are my sister,[g] so that I
will be treated well for your sake and my
life will be spared because of you."
[14]When Abram came to Egypt, the
Egyptians saw that she was a very beautiful woman. [15]And when Pharaoh's officials saw her, they praised her to Pharaoh, and she was taken into his palace.
[16]He treated Abram well for her sake,
and Abram acquired sheep and cattle,
male and female donkeys, menservants
and maidservants, and camels.
[17]But the LORD inflicted serious diseases on Pharaoh and his household[h]

12:13 [g]Ge 20:2; 26:7
12:17 [h]1Ch 16:21

[a]7 Or *seed*

because of Abram's wife Sarai. [18]So Phar-
12:18 aoh summoned Abram. "What have you
[i]Ge 20:9; 26:10 done to me?"[i] he said. "Why didn't you
tell me she was your wife? [19]Why did
you say, 'She is my sister,' so that I took
her to be my wife? Now then, here is
your wife. Take her and go!" [20]Then
Pharaoh gave orders about Abram to his
men, and they sent him on his way, with
his wife and everything he had.

Abram and Lot Separate

13:1 **13** So Abram went up from Egypt
[j]Ge 12:9 to the Negev,[j] with his wife and
everything he had, and Lot went with
him. [2]Abram had become very wealthy
in livestock and in silver and gold.

[3]From the Negev he went from place
13:3 [k]Ge 12:8 to place until he came to Bethel,[k] to the
place between Bethel and Ai where his
13:4 tent had been earlier [4]and where he had
[l]Ge 12:7 first built an altar.[l] There Abram called
on the name of the LORD.

[5]Now Lot, who was moving about
with Abram, also had flocks and herds
and tents. [6]But the land could not support them while they stayed together, for
13:6 their possessions were so great that they
[m]Ge 36:7 were not able to stay together.[m] [7]And
13:7 quarreling[n] arose between Abram's
[n]Ge 26:20,21 [o]Ge 12:6 herdsmen and the herdsmen of Lot. The
Canaanites and Perizzites were also liv-
ing in the land[o] at that time.

13:8 [8]So Abram said to Lot, "Let's not have
[p]Pr 15:18; 20:3 any quarreling between you and me,[p] or
[q]Ps 133:1 between your herdsmen and mine, for
we are brothers.[q] [9]Is not the whole land
before you? Let's part company. If you go
to the left, I'll go to the right; if you go to
the right, I'll go to the left."

[10]Lot looked up and saw that the
13:10 whole plain of the Jordan was well wa-
[r]Ge 2:8-10; Isa 51:3 tered, like the garden of the LORD,[r] like
the land of Egypt, toward Zoar.[s] (This
[s]Ge 19:22,30 [t]Ge 14:8; 19:17-29 was before the LORD destroyed Sodom
and Gomorrah.)[t] [11]So Lot chose for him-
self the whole plain of the Jordan and set
out toward the east. The two men parted company: [12]Abram lived in the land
13:12 [u]Ge 19:17,25,29 of Canaan, while Lot lived among the
[v]Ge 14:12 cities of the plain[u] and pitched his tents
near Sodom.[v] [13]Now the men of Sodom
13:13 [w]Ge 18:20; Eze 16:49-50; 2Pe 2:8 were wicked and were sinning greatly
against the LORD.[w]

[14]The LORD said to Abram after Lot
had parted from him, "Lift up your eyes
from where you are and look north and
south, east and west.[x] [15]All the land that 13:14 [x]Ge 28:14; Dt 3:27
you see I will give to you and your off-
spring[a] forever.[y] [16]I will make your off-
spring like the dust of the earth, so that 13:15 [y]Ge 12:7; Gal 3:16*
if anyone could count the dust, then
your offspring could be counted. [17]Go,
walk through the length and breadth of 13:17 [z]ver 15; Nu 13:17-25
the land,[z] for I am giving it to you."

[18]So Abram moved his tents and went 13:18 [a]Ge 14:13,24; 18:1 [b]Ge 35:27
to live near the great trees of Mamre[a] at
Hebron,[b] where he built an altar to the [c]Ge 8:20
LORD.[c]

Abram Rescues Lot

14 At this time Amraphel king of 14:1
Shinar,[b][d] Arioch king of Ellasar, [d]Ge 10:10
Kedorlaomer king of Elam and Tidal
king of Goiim [2]went to war against Bera
king of Sodom, Birsha king of Gomorrah, Shinab king of Admah, Shemeber
king of Zeboiim,[e] and the king of Bela 14:2 [e]Ge 10:19
(that is, Zoar).[f] [3]All these latter kings [f]Ge 13:10
joined forces in the Valley of Siddim (the 14:3
Salt Sea[c][g]). [4]For twelve years they had [g]Nu 34:3,12; Dt 3:17;
been subject to Kedorlaomer, but in the Jos 3:16; 15:2,5
thirteenth year they rebelled.

[5]In the fourteenth year, Kedorlaomer
and the kings allied with him went out 14:5
and defeated the Rephaites[h] in Ashte- [h]Ge 15:20; Dt 2:11,20
roth Karnaim, the Zuzites in Ham, the [i]Dt 2:10
Emites[i] in Shaveh Kiriathaim [6]and the 14:6
Horites[j] in the hill country of Seir,[k] as far [j]Dt 2:12,22
as El Paran[l] near the desert. [7]Then they [k]Dt 2:1,5,22 [l]Ge 21:21;
turned back and went to En Mishpat Nu 10:12
(that is, Kadesh), and they conquered
the whole territory of the Amalekites, as
well as the Amorites who were living in 14:7 [m]2Ch 20:2
Hazazon Tamar.[m]

[8]Then the king of Sodom, the king of 14:8
Gomorrah,[n] the king of Admah, the king [n]Ge 13:10; 19:17-29
of Zeboiim[o] and the king of Bela (that is, [o]Dt 29:23
Zoar) marched out and drew up their
battle lines in the Valley of Siddim
[9]against Kedorlaomer king of Elam, Tidal king of Goiim, Amraphel king of Shinar and Arioch king of Ellasar—four
kings against five. [10]Now the Valley of
Siddim was full of tar pits, and when the
kings of Sodom and Gomorrah fled,
some of the men fell into them and the 14:10
rest fled to the hills.[p] [11]The four kings [p]Ge 19:17,30
seized all the goods of Sodom and Go-
morrah and all their food; then they
went away. [12]They also carried off

[a] *15* Or *seed;* also in verse 16 [b] *1* That is, Babylonia; also in verse 9 [c] *3* That is, the Dead Sea

DISCOVERY 5

Pursuing the Lost

It's hard to know what to do when someone we love is in trouble. Every day people we know make decisions that culminate in financial crises, health problems, immoral living situations or emotional suffering. These people may simply be in the wrong place at the wrong time, or they may be trapped by sinful lifestyles. Sometimes it's a combination.

Abram knew what it was like to look on in anguished concern. His relative Lot was living in Sodom at the time the city was seized, and he and his family were taken captive. Abram might have rationalized that Lot was experiencing the consequence of his own bad choices. If Lot had not been living in a city known for its unrestrained lifestyle, he would not have found himself in this predicament. Abram might also have left Lot's rescue in the hands of the sovereign God. God surely knew what had happened and was more than capable of delivering Abram's nephew—according to his own timing, of course. Instead, when Abram heard that Lot was in trouble, he went out of his way to help. That choice demanded his personal involvement and resources.

Abram assembled his 318 servants, all of whom were trained to fight, gathered the needed supplies and set off to take back what had been stolen. He was outnumbered, with no guarantee that the rescue attempt would be successful. Even if he were to return with Lot, Lot might choose to place himself at risk again by returning to Sodom.

When we see someone we love making ungodly choices, we are tempted to throw up our hands at the regrettable situation and deplore, "Those are the consequences!" We might even go so far as to pray for that person: "Lord, please help her find the way out." While it is undeniable that there are natural consequences for sin, and it is always good to pray for others, our Lord expects us to love with actions as well as with empathy or prayer. Jesus was explicit: The important thing is to bring back those who are lost and wandering (Matthew 18:12–14; Luke 15). He himself came to save people from sin, not to condemn us for sinning (Luke 19:10; John 3:17).

In Galatians 6:1–2 Paul stated, "Brothers, if someone is caught in a sin, you who are spiritual should restore him gently . . . Carry each other's burdens, and in this way you will fulfill the law of Christ." Every commandment God ever gave finds its fulfillment in the act of loving others just as we love ourselves (John 13:34–35), and sometimes that means going out of our way to lead them back to God.

Our Father in heaven expects no more of us than he was willing to give. When we were completely powerless to reach out to him, he did what was necessary to rescue us from our sins (Romans 5:6–8). Jesus provided us with a model of compassion that leads us to sacrifice our resources and even our security—our pride, money, possessions, time or personal safety. Like Abram, we are called to attempt to retrieve that which has been lost or stolen.

Self-Discovery: When did you last fulfill the law of Jesus Christ by intervening to help someone who was making unwise choices?

GO TO DISCOVERY 6 ON PAGE 26

Abram's nephew Lot and his possessions, since he was living in Sodom.
13 One who had escaped came and reported this to Abram the Hebrew. Now
Abram was living near the great trees of
14:13 [q] ver 24; Ge 13:18
Mamre[q] the Amorite, a brother[a] of Eshcol and Aner, all of whom were allied
with Abram. 14 When Abram heard that
his relative had been taken captive, he
14:14 [r] Ge 15:3 [s] Dt 34:1; Jdg 18:29
called out the 318 trained men born in
his household[r] and went in pursuit as
far as Dan.[s] 15 During the night Abram
divided his men to attack them and he
routed them, pursuing them as far as
Hobah, north of Damascus. 16 He recovered all the goods and brought back his
relative Lot and his possessions, together with the women and the other
people.
17 After Abram returned from defeating Kedorlaomer and the kings allied
with him, the king of Sodom came out
14:17 [t] 2Sa 18:18
to meet him in the Valley of Shaveh (that
is, the King's Valley).[t]
14:18 [u] Ps 110:4; Heb 5:6 [v] Ps 76:2; Heb 7:2
18 Then Melchizedek[u] king of Salem[b][v]
brought out bread and wine. He was
priest of God Most High, 19 and he
blessed Abram,[w] saying,

"Blessed be Abram by God Most
High,
14:19 [w] Heb 7:6 [x] ver 22
Creator[c] of heaven and earth.[x]
14:20 [y] Ge 24:27 [z] Ge 28:22; Dt 26:12; Heb 7:4
20 And blessed be[d] God Most High,[y]
who delivered your enemies into
your hand."

Then Abram gave him a tenth of everything.[z]
21 The king of Sodom said to Abram,
"Give me the people and keep the goods
for yourself."
14:22 [a] Ex 6:8; Da 12:7; Rev 10:5-6 [b] ver 19
22 But Abram said to the king of Sod-
om, "I have raised my hand[a] to the LORD,
God Most High, Creator of heaven and
earth,[b] and have taken an oath 23 that I
14:23 [c] 2Ki 5:16
will accept nothing belonging to you,[c]
not even a thread or the thong of a sandal, so that you will never be able to say,
'I made Abram rich.' 24 I will accept nothing but what my men have eaten and the
share that belongs to the men who went
with me—to Aner, Eshcol and Mamre.
Let them have their share."

God's Covenant With Abram

15:1 [d] Da 10:1 [e] Ge 21:17; 26:24; 46:3; 2Ki 6:16; Ps 27:1; Isa 41:10,13-14 [f] Dt 33:29; 2Sa 22:3,31; Ps 3:3
15 After this, the word of the LORD
came to Abram[d] in a vision:

"Do not be afraid,[e] Abram.
I am your shield,[e][f]
your very great reward.[f]"

2 But Abram said, "O Sovereign LORD,
what can you give me since I remain
15:2 [g] Ac 7:5
childless[g] and the one who will inherit[g]
my estate is Eliezer of Damascus?" 3 And
15:3 [h] Ge 24:2,34
Abram said, "You have given me no children; so a servant[h] in my household will
be my heir."
4 Then the word of the LORD came to
15:4 [i] Gal 4:28
him: "This man will not be your heir, but
a son coming from your own body will
15:5 [j] Ps 147:4; Jer 33:22 [k] Ge 12:2; 22:17; Ex 32:13; Ro 4:18*; Heb 11:12
be your heir."[i] 5 He took him outside and
said, "Look up at the heavens and count
the stars[j]—if indeed you can count
them." Then he said to him, "So shall
your offspring be."[k]
15:6 [l] Ps 106:31; Ro 4:3*,20-24*; Gal 3:6*; Jas 2:23*
6 Abram believed the LORD, and he
credited it to him as righteousness.[l]
7 He also said to him, "I am the LORD,
who brought you out of Ur of the
Chaldeans to give you this land to take
possession of it."

a 13 Or *a relative;* or *an ally* *b* 18 That is, Jerusalem *c* 19 Or *Possessor;* also in verse 22 *d* 20 Or *And praise be to* *e* 1 Or *sovereign* *f* 1 Or *shield; / your reward will be very great* *g* 2 The meaning of the Hebrew for this phrase is uncertain.

JESUS FOCUS

A DIFFERENT KIND OF PRIEST

God frequently uses servants and messengers about whom we know little or nothing. *Melchizedek*, which means "king of righteousness," was one of these. He stepped on to the pages of Scripture without prior introduction and disappeared just as suddenly (Genesis 14:18–20). Melchizedek is referred to as the "king of Salem" and was most likely a local priest in Jerusalem. He obviously believed in *El Elyon*, "God Most High," and lived to please him. Although we know little about him, he appeared in the Bible as a "type" or picture of Jesus Christ.

God's promised Messiah would be like Melchizedek (Psalm 110:4), chosen by God himself to be a priest. Jesus is our high priest, even though he is not from Levi's family line, because, like Melchizedek, he was chosen by God. Some people believe that Melchizedek was actually Jesus himself appearing to his people. Others conclude that God used Melchizedek to show us who the Messiah would be. Regardless of which is true, one thing we know for certain: Both are God's priests, chosen by God himself (Hebrews 7:3).

15:8 8But Abram said, "O Sovereign LORD,
[m]Lk 1:18 how can I know[m] that I will gain possession of it?"
9So the LORD said to him, "Bring me a
heifer, a goat and a ram, each three years
old, along with a dove and a young pigeon."
10Abram brought all these to him, cut
15:10 them in two and arranged the halves op-
[n]ver 17; Jer 34:18 posite each other;[n] the birds, however,
[o]Lev 1:17 he did not cut in half.[o] 11Then birds of
prey came down on the carcasses, but
Abram drove them away.
12As the sun was setting, Abram fell
15:12 [p]Ge 2:21 into a deep sleep,[p] and a thick and
dreadful darkness came over him.
13Then the LORD said to him, "Know for
certain that your descendants will be
15:13 [q]Ex 1:11 strangers in a country not their own,
[r]ver 16; Ex 12:40; Ac 7:6,17 and they will be enslaved[q] and mistreated four hundred years.[r] 14But I will pun-
ish the nation they serve as slaves, and
15:14 [s]Ac 7:7* afterward they will come out[s] with great
[t]Ex 12:32-38 possessions.[t] 15You, however, will go to
15:15 your fathers in peace and be buried at a
[u]Ge 25:8 good old age.[u] 16In the fourth generation
15:16 your descendants will come back here,
[v]1Ki 21:26 for the sin of the Amorites[v] has not yet
reached its full measure."
17When the sun had set and darkness
had fallen, a smoking firepot with a
blazing torch appeared and passed be-
tween the pieces.[w] 18On that day the 15:17 [w]ver 10
LORD made a covenant with Abram and
said, "To your descendants I give this 15:18
land,[x] from the river[a] of Egypt[y] to the [x]Ge 12:7 [y]Nu 34:5
great river, the Euphrates— 19the land of
the Kenites, Kenizzites, Kadmonites,
20Hittites, Perizzites, Rephaites, 21Amo-
rites, Canaanites, Girgashites and Jebusites."

Hagar and Ishmael

16 Now Sarai, Abram's wife, had 16:1
borne him no children.[z] But [z]Ge 11:30; Gal 4:24-25
she had an Egyptian maidservant[a] [a]Ge 21:9
named Hagar; 2so she said to Abram,
"The LORD has kept me from having
children. Go, sleep with my maidservant; perhaps I can build a family 16:2
through her."[b] [b]Ge 30:3-4,9-10
Abram agreed to what Sarai said. 3So
after Abram had been living in Canaan[c] 16:3
ten years, Sarai his wife took her Egyp- [c]Ge 12:5
tian maidservant Hagar and gave her to
her husband to be his wife. 4He slept
with Hagar, and she conceived.
When she knew she was pregnant,
she began to despise her mistress. 5Then
Sarai said to Abram, "You are responsible for the wrong I am suffering. I put
my servant in your arms, and now that

[a]*18* Or *Wadi*

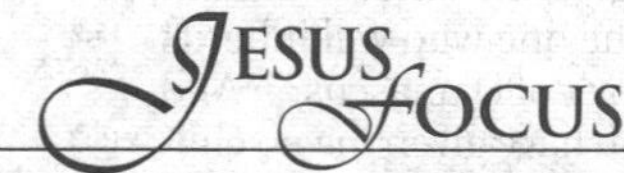

LIVING ON CREDIT

Ten years had passed since Abram had accepted God's promise that he would father a son, but still there was no child. So Abram made a suggestion to God: He proposed adopting his servant Eliezer as his legal heir (Genesis 15:2–3). But God's response was unequivocal. He restated his original promise: "A son coming from your own body will be your heir" (verse 4). The Bible tells us that "Abram believed the LORD, and [God] credited it to him as righteousness" (verse 6). This verse is so significant that it is quoted five times in the New Testament (Romans 4:3,9,22; Galatians 3:6; James 2:23). The concept of crediting something to our account is called *imputation.* God imputes, or credits, righteousness to us because we believe in Jesus and accept his sacrifice on our behalf. That means that, as far as God is concerned, we ourselves are counted as righteous on account of Jesus' death and resurrection (Romans 4:23–24).

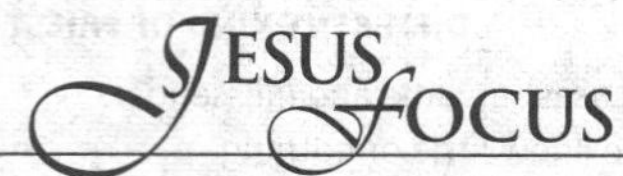

CUTTING A COVENANT

In the ancient Near East men would "cut a covenant" with one another. The concept is not unlike our term *cutting a deal*—but they did it literally! The two parties making the agreement would cut animals in half and lay the remains side by side, leaving a path between the pieces. Then the individuals would join hands and walk together on the path. In this way each was implicitly stating to the other, "I'll keep my half of the bargain if you will keep yours." Such agreements were called *conditional* covenants. In Genesis 15 God himself, represented by the firepot and blazing torch, moved between the pieces alone (verses 17–18). God promised to preserve Abram's family and to bring his descendants back to the promised land. So the covenant with Abram was an *unconditional* promise from God, guaranteeing the land to Abram's descendants, including the Messiah. God's unconditional promise was fulfilled when Jesus came to earth through the line of Abram (see Luke 3).

she knows she is pregnant, she despises
16:5 me. May the LORD judge between you
[d] Ge 31:53 and me."[d]
6"Your servant is in your hands,"
Abram said. "Do with her whatever you
think best." Then Sarai mistreated Hagar; so she fled from her.
16:7 7The angel of the LORD[e] found Hagar
[e] Ge 21:17; 22:11,15; 31:11 near a spring in the desert; it was the
[f] Ge 20:1 spring that is beside the road to Shur.[f]
8And he said, "Hagar, servant of Sarai,
where have you come from, and where
are you going?"
"I'm running away from my mistress
Sarai," she answered.
9Then the angel of the LORD told her,
"Go back to your mistress and submit to
her." 10The angel added, "I will so in-
16:10 crease your descendants that they will
[g] Ge 13:16; 17:20 be too numerous to count."[g]
11The angel of the LORD also said to
her:

"You are now with child
and you will have a son.
You shall name him Ishmael,[a]
16:11 for the LORD has heard of your
[h] Ex 2:24; 3:7,9 misery.[h]
12He will be a wild donkey of a man;
his hand will be against
everyone
and everyone's hand against
him,
and he will live in hostility 16:12
toward[b] all his brothers.[i]" [i] Ge 25:18

13She gave this name to the LORD who
spoke to her: "You are the God who sees
me," for she said, "I have now seen[c] the 16:13 [j] Ge 32:30
One who sees me."[j] 14That is why the
well was called Beer Lahai Roi[d]; it is still
there, between Kadesh and Bered.
15So Hagar bore Abram a son,[k] and 16:15
Abram gave the name Ishmael to the son [k] Gal 4:22
she had borne. 16Abram was eighty-six
years old when Hagar bore him Ishmael.

The Covenant of Circumcision

17 When Abram was ninety-nine
years old, the LORD appeared to
him and said, "I am God Almighty[e];[l] 17:1 [l] Ge 28:3; Ex 6:3
walk before me and be blameless.[m] 2I [m] Dt 18:13
will confirm my covenant between me 17:2
and you[n] and will greatly increase your [n] Ge 15:18
numbers."
3Abram fell facedown, and God said
to him, 4"As for me, this is my covenant 17:4
with you:[o] You will be the father of many [o] Ge 15:18 [p] ver 16;
nations.[p] 5No longer will you be called Ge 12:2; 35:11; 48:19

[a] *11 Ishmael* means *God hears.* [b] *12* Or *live to the east / of* [c] *13* Or *seen the back of* [d] *14 Beer Lahai Roi* means *well of the Living One who sees me.* [e] *1* Hebrew *El-Shaddai*

THE ANGEL OF THE LORD

Angel of the Lord	Activity or Attribute	Jesus
Genesis 16:7,13	Called "LORD"	John 20:28
Genesis 48:15–16	Called "God"	Hebrews 1:8
Exodus 3:2–14	"I AM"	John 8:58
Exodus 23:20–23	Sent from God	John 5:30; 6:38
Joshua 5:13–15	Commander of the Lord's army	Revelation 19:1–14
Judges 13:15–18	Name is "Wonderful"	Isaiah 9:6
Isaiah 63:9	Redeemed his own	Ephesians 5:25

When the "angel of the LORD" appears in the Bible, he is identified with God and yet distinguished from him. He is also referred to as "the angel of his presence" (Isaiah 63:9). The same statements that are made about the nature, character, mission and activities of the angel of the Lord are stated of Jesus. The "angel of the LORD" is thought by many to be God the Son, appearing in human history before Jesus came to earth as a man.

17:5 qver 15; Ne 9:7 Abram[a]; your name will be Abraham,[b][q]
rRo 4:17* for I have made you a father of many na-
17:6 tions.[r] 6 I will make you very fruitful;[s] I
sGe 35:11 will make nations of you, and kings will
tMt 1:6 come from you.[t] 7 I will establish my covenant as an everlasting covenant be-
tween me and you and your descen-
17:7 uEx 29:45,46 dants after you for the generations to
vRo 9:8; Gal 3:16 come, to be your God[u] and the God of
your descendants after you.[v] 8 The whole
17:8 land of Canaan,[w] where you are now an
wPs 105:9,11 alien,[x] I will give as an everlasting pos-
xGe 23:4; 28:4; Ex 6:4 yGe 12:7 session to you and your descendants after you;[y] and I will be their God."
9 Then God said to Abraham, "As for
you, you must keep my covenant, you
and your descendants after you for the
generations to come. 10 This is my cov-
17:10 zver 23; enant with you and your descendants
Ge 21:4; Jn 7:22; after you, the covenant you are to keep:
Ac 7:8; Ro 4:11 Every male among you shall be circum-
17:11 cised.[z] 11 You are to undergo circumci-
aEx 12:48; Dt 10:16 sion,[a] and it will be the sign of the cov-
bRo 4:11 enant[b] between me and you. 12 For the
17:12 generations to come every male among
cLev 12:3; you who is eight days old must be cir-
Lk 2:21 cumcised,[c] including those born in your
household or bought with money from
a foreigner—those who are not your offspring. 13 Whether born in your household or bought with your money, they
must be circumcised. My covenant in
your flesh is to be an everlasting covenant. 14 Any uncircumcised male, who
has not been circumcised in the flesh, 17:14
will be cut off from his people;[d] he has dEx 4:24-26
broken my covenant."
15 God also said to Abraham, "As for
Sarai your wife, you are no longer to call
her Sarai; her name will be Sarah. 16 I will
bless her and will surely give you a son 17:16
by her.[e] I will bless her so that she will be eGe 18:10
the mother of nations;[f] kings of peoples fGe 35:11;
will come from her." Gal 4:31
17 Abraham fell facedown; he laughed[g] 17:17 gGe 18:12; 21:6
and said to himself, "Will a son be born
to a man a hundred years old? Will Sarah bear a child at the age of ninety?"
18 And Abraham said to God, "If only Ishmael might live under your blessing!"
19 Then God said, "Yes, but your wife 17:19
Sarah will bear you a son,[h] and you will hGe 18:14; 21:2
call him Isaac.[c] I will establish my cov- iGe 26:3
enant with him[i] as an everlasting covenant for his descendants after him.
20 And as for Ishmael, I have heard you: I
will surely bless him; I will make him
fruitful and will greatly increase his 17:20
numbers.[j] He will be the father of twelve jGe 16:10
rulers,[k] and I will make him into a great kGe 25:12-16
nation.[l] 21 But my covenant I will estab- lGe 21:18
lish with Isaac, whom Sarah will bear to 17:21
you by this time next year."[m] 22 When he mGe 21:2
had finished speaking with Abraham,
God went up from him.
23 On that very day Abraham took his
son Ishmael and all those born in his
household or bought with his money,
every male in his household, and circumcised them, as God told him.
24 Abraham was ninety-nine years old 17:24
when he was circumcised,[n] 25 and his nRo 4:11
son Ishmael was thirteen; 26 Abraham
and his son Ishmael were both circumcised on that same day. 27 And every
male in Abraham's household, including
those born in his household or bought
from a foreigner, was circumcised with
him.

[a] 5 *Abram* means *exalted father.* [b] 5 *Abraham* means *father of many.* [c] 19 *Isaac* means *he laughs.*

JESUS FOCUS

A BINDING COVENANT

Because God seemed overly slow in fulfilling his promise that Abram would father a son, Abram and his wife Sarai decided to help out by arranging for Abram to have sexual relations with their servant Hagar. Ishmael was born when Abram was 86 years old, and there is no record that God spoke to Abram again until he was 99 years of age (Genesis 17:1). It was then that God restated his promise to Abram—with several dramatic additions. First, God changed Abram's name to *Abraham*, or "father of many." God also referred to the covenant he had made with Abraham as an "everlasting covenant," guaranteeing the land to Abraham's descendants forever (verses 7–8). Third, *circumcision* (cutting away the male foreskin) was the sign that God designated to show that Abraham had accepted God's covenant. Sarai's name was also changed—to *Sarah*, meaning "princess." God promised that she would bear Abraham a son in their old age. When Abraham laughed at what seemed an absurd promise from God, the Lord instructed him to call the baby *Isaac*, or "he laughs." Finally, God made it clear that his covenant would be through the family line of Isaac rather than Ishmael.

The Three Visitors

18 The LORD appeared to Abra-
18:1 ham near the great trees of
[o]Ge 13:18; 14:13 Mamre[o] while he was sitting at the entrance to his tent in the heat of the day.
18:2 2 Abraham looked up and saw three
[p]ver 16,22; Ge 32:24; men[p] standing nearby. When he saw
Jos 5:13; them, he hurried from the entrance of
Jdg 13:6-11; Heb 13:2 his tent to meet them and bowed low to
the ground.
3 He said, "If I have found favor in your
eyes, my lord,[a] do not pass your servant
18:4 by. 4 Let a little water be brought, and
[q]Ge 19:2; 43:24 then you may all wash your feet[q] and
rest under this tree. 5 Let me get you
18:5 something to eat,[r] so you can be re-
[r]Jdg 13:15 freshed and then go on your way—now
that you have come to your servant."
"Very well," they answered, "do as you
say."
6 So Abraham hurried into the tent to
Sarah. "Quick," he said, "get three seahs[b]
of fine flour and knead it and bake some
bread."
7 Then he ran to the herd and selected
a choice, tender calf and gave it to a servant, who hurried to prepare it. 8 He then
brought some curds and milk and the
calf that had been prepared, and set
18:8 these before them.[s] While they ate, he
[s]Ge 19:3 stood near them under a tree.

9 "Where is your wife Sarah?" they
asked him.
"There, in the tent," he said.
10 Then the LORD[c] said, "I will surely
return to you about this time next year, 18:10
and Sarah your wife will have a son."[t] [t]Ro 9:9*
Now Sarah was listening at the en-
trance to the tent, which was behind
him. 11 Abraham and Sarah were already
old and well advanced in years,[u] and Sar- 18:11 [u]Ge 17:17
ah was past the age of childbearing.[v] 12 So [v]Ro 4:19
Sarah laughed[w] to herself as she thought, 18:12
"After I am worn out and my master[d][x] is [w]Ge 17:17; 21:6
old, will I now have this pleasure?" [x]1Pe 3:6
13 Then the LORD said to Abraham,
"Why did Sarah laugh and say, 'Will I
really have a child, now that I am old?' 18:14
14 Is anything too hard for the LORD?[y] I [y]Jer 32:17,27;
will return to you at the appointed time Zec 8:6; Mt 19:26;
next year and Sarah will have a son." Lk 1:37; Ro 4:21
15 Sarah was afraid, so she lied and
said, "I did not laugh."
But he said, "Yes, you did laugh."

Abraham Pleads for Sodom

16 When the men got up to leave, they

[a] *3* Or *O Lord* [b] *6* That is, probably about 20 quarts (about 22 liters) [c] *10* Hebrew *Then he* [d] *12* Or *husband*

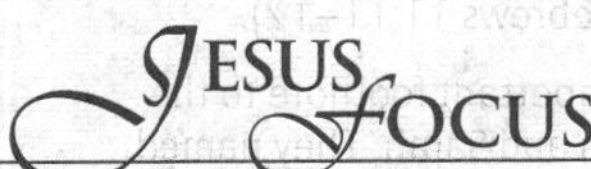

FACE-TO-FACE

There are reasonably clear indications that God the Son appeared from time to time to speak to people in the Old Testament (see the chart on page 23). "Three men" appeared to Abraham as he sat in the shade of his tent. Two of them were angels, but the third was Jesus himself (see Genesis 18:13–22). When this man spoke, the Bible identifies him as "the LORD." After the two angels had gone on their way, Abraham was left standing before the Lord (verse 22). We refer to these appearances of God the Son in a visible form prior to Jesus' birth as divine manifestations (*theophanies* or *christophanies*). The New Testament states that no one has seen God the Father except God the Son and that the Son makes the Father known to his people (John 1:18). When God wanted to make himself known to his people, whether in the Old Testament or the New, it was Jesus who made it possible.

LAUGHING AT GOD

When Sarah overheard God promising Abraham a son (Genesis 18:10), she "laughed to herself" (verse 12) because she knew she was too old, just as Abraham had done when he had first heard the news (Genesis 17:17). The Hebrew Bible uses wording that implies that Sarah had already gone through menopause, so that it would be physically impossible for her to give birth. But God confronted Abraham with a rhetorical question: "Is anything too hard for the LORD?" (Genesis 18:14). God intended to perform a miracle, and he wanted both Sarah and Abraham to know it—even if they couldn't quite believe it. God's plan all along had been to begin the family line of the Messiah with a miracle birth. Later, he completed it with a second miracle birth—the virgin birth of Jesus (compare Isaiah 7:14 with Matthew 1:23). We sometimes denigrate Sarah for laughing at God. However, as incredible as it sounds, laughing at God is not that unusual. We in effect do the same thing every time we read God's words and fail to put them into practice or hear his promises and decide not to believe them.

GOD OF THE IMPOSSIBLE

When God called Abram to leave the familiarity of his country and family, he made several promises to him (Genesis 12:1–3). One of these promises was that Abram and Sarai's descendants would be a "great nation." Abram believed God's promise, even though its fulfillment appeared impossible to him. Years later, however, it seemed as though God had reneged. Sarai (now called Sarah) was well beyond the age of childbearing, and for her to conceive had become a biological impossibility. Hadn't it?

According to the account in Genesis 18, God appeared to Abraham again, this time to make an incredible announcement to Abraham and Sarah: "I will surely return to you about this time next year, and Sarah your wife will have a son" (verse 10). When Sarah overheard this unlikely proposition, she snickered. *After I am worn out and my master is old*, she said to herself, *will I now have this pleasure*? (verse 12). It seemed ridiculous! But God was not laughing, and he asked Sarah a very serious question: "Is anything too hard for the LORD?" (verse 14). He came through on his promise to Abraham and Sarah. The Jewish race began because God intervened in a miraculous way.

Thousands of years later God involved himself once again in the lives of a Jewish couple—Joseph and Mary. God again performed a miracle, and his own son was born in human flesh. Abraham and Sarah were very old; Mary was very young. Abraham and Sarah had a son when they were beyond the age of childbearing; Joseph and Mary had a son apart from the natural way: Jesus was conceived by the Holy Spirit (Matthew 1:18–25). In both cases, the birth of the son occurred because God stepped in and kept his promise to his people through miraculous means.

God's purposes are never frustrated by difficult circumstances, nor are his promises thwarted by our narrow definitions of the possible. In fact, God's promises are always accomplished through his power, which is most clearly demonstrated in "impossible" situations. *Nothing* is too hard for God! The challenge for us is to believe in the same way that Abraham did: "By faith Abraham, even though he was past age—and Sarah herself was barren—was enabled to become a father because he considered him faithful who had made the promise. And so from this one man, and he as good as dead, came descendants as numerous as the stars in the sky and as countless as the sand on the seashore" (Hebrews 11:11–12).

There is an important footnote to the story of Abraham and Sarah. They named their son Isaac, which means "laughter." Sarah's snort of incredulity turned into the laughter of delight when God met her needs more fully than she had ever believed possible.

Self-Discovery: *When did God last surprise you by doing the "impossible" in your life?*

GO TO DISCOVERY 7 ON PAGE 31

looked down toward Sodom, and Abraham walked along with them to see
18:17 them on their way. [17]Then the LORD said,
[z]Am 3:7 “Shall I hide from Abraham[z] what I am
[a]Ge 19:24 about to do?[a] [18]Abraham will surely be-
18:18 come a great and powerful nation,[b] and
[b]Gal 3:8* all nations on earth will be blessed
18:19 through him. [19]For I have chosen him, so
[c]Dt 4:9-10; 6:7 that he will direct his children[c] and his
[d]Jos 24:15; Eph 6:4 household after him to keep the way of
the LORD[d] by doing what is right and
just, so that the LORD will bring about for
Abraham what he has promised him.”
[20]Then the LORD said, “The outcry
against Sodom and Gomorrah is so
18:21 great and their sin so grievous [21]that I
[e]Ge 11:5 will go down[e] and see if what they have
done is as bad as the outcry that has
reached me. If not, I will know.”
[22]The men turned away and went to-
18:22 [f]Ge 19:1 ward Sodom,[f] but Abraham remained
standing before the LORD.[a] [23]Then Abraham approached him and said: “Will
18:23 you sweep away the righteous with the
[g]Nu 16:22 wicked?[g] [24]What if there are fifty righteous people in the city? Will you really
sweep it away and not spare[b] the place
18:24 for the sake of the fifty righteous people
[h]Jer 5:1 in it?[h] [25]Far be it from you to do such a
18:25 thing—to kill the righteous with the
[i]Job 8:3,20; Ps 58:11; 94:2; wicked, treating the righteous and the
Isa 3:10-11; wicked alike. Far be it from you! Will not
Ro 3:6 the Judge[c] of all the earth do right?”[i]
[26]The LORD said, “If I find fifty righ-
18:26 teous people in the city of Sodom, I will
[j]Jer 5:1 spare the whole place for their sake.[j]”
[27]Then Abraham spoke up again:
18:27 “Now that I have been so bold as to
[k]Ge 2:7; 3:19; speak to the Lord, though I am nothing
Job 30:19; 42:6 but dust and ashes,[k] [28]what if the number of the righteous is five less than fifty?
Will you destroy the whole city because
of five people?”
“If I find forty-five there,” he said, “I
will not destroy it.”
[29]Once again he spoke to him, “What
if only forty are found there?”
He said, “For the sake of forty, I will
not do it.”
[30]Then he said, “May the Lord not be
angry, but let me speak. What if only
thirty can be found there?”
He answered, “I will not do it if I find
thirty there.”
[31]Abraham said, “Now that I have
been so bold as to speak to the Lord,
what if only twenty can be found there?”
He said, “For the sake of twenty, I will
not destroy it.”
[32]Then he said, “May the Lord not be
angry, but let me speak just once more.[l] 18:32 [l]Jdg 6:39
What if only ten can be found there?” [m]Jer 5:1
He answered, “For the sake of ten,[m] I
will not destroy it.”
[33]When the LORD had finished speaking with Abraham, he left, and Abraham
returned home.

> **THE TERM CHRISTOPHANY REFERS TO TEMPORARY VISIBLE AND AUDIBLE MANIFESTATIONS OF GOD THE SON IN HUMAN FORM.**
>
> 
>
> James Borland, *Professor, Liberty University, Lynchburg, Virginia*

Sodom and Gomorrah Destroyed

19 The two angels arrived at Sod- 19:1
om[n] in the evening, and Lot was [n]Ge 18:22 [o]Ge 18:1
sitting in the gateway of the city.[o] When
he saw them, he got up to meet them and
bowed down with his face to the ground.
[2]“My lords,” he said, “please turn aside to
your servant’s house. You can wash your 19:2
feet[p] and spend the night and then go on [p]Ge 18:4;
your way early in the morning.” Lk 7:44
“No,” they answered, “we will spend
the night in the square.”
[3]But he insisted so strongly that they
did go with him and entered his house.
He prepared a meal for them, baking 19:3
bread without yeast, and they ate.[q] [4]Be- [q]Ge 18:6
fore they had gone to bed, all the men
from every part of the city of Sodom—
both young and old—surrounded the
house. [5]They called to Lot, “Where are
the men who came to you tonight? 19:5
Bring them out to us so that we can have [r]Jdg 19:22;
sex with them.”[r] Isa 3:9; Ro 1:24-27
[6]Lot went outside to meet them[s] and 19:6
shut the door behind him [7]and said, [s]Jdg 19:23
“No, my friends. Don’t do this wicked
thing. [8]Look, I have two daughters who
have never slept with a man. Let me
bring them out to you, and you can do
what you like with them. But don’t do
anything to these men, for they have 19:8
come under the protection of my roof.”[t] [t]Jdg 19:24
[9]“Get out of our way,” they replied.

[a] *22* Masoretic Text; an ancient Hebrew scribal tradition *but the LORD remained standing before Abraham* [b] *24* Or *forgive*; also in verse 26 [c] *25* Or *Ruler*

And they said, "This fellow came here as
19:9 an alien, and now he wants to play the
u Ex 2:14; judge![u] We'll treat you worse than them."
Ac 7:27 They kept bringing pressure on Lot and
moved forward to break down the door.
10 But the men inside reached out and
pulled Lot back into the house and shut
the door. 11 Then they struck the men
19:11 who were at the door of the house,
v Dt 28:28-29; 2Ki 6:18; young and old, with blindness[v] so that
Ac 13:11 they could not find the door.
12 The two men said to Lot, "Do you
have anyone else here—sons-in-law,
19:12 sons or daughters, or anyone else in the
w Ge 7:1 city who belongs to you?[w] Get them out
of here, 13 because we are going to destroy this place. The outcry to the LORD
19:13 against its people is so great that he has
x 1Ch 21:15 sent us to destroy it."[x]
14 So Lot went out and spoke to his
sons-in-law, who were pledged to marry[a] his daughters. He said, "Hurry and
19:14 get out of this place, because the LORD is
y Nu 16:21 about to destroy the city![y]" But his sons-
z Ex 9:21; Lk 17:28 in-law thought he was joking.[z]
15 With the coming of dawn, the an-
gels urged Lot, saying, "Hurry! Take your
wife and your two daughters who are
19:15 a Nu 16:26 here, or you will be swept away[a] when
b Rev 18:4 the city is punished.[b]"
16 When he hesitated, the men grasped
his hand and the hands of his wife and of
his two daughters and led them safely
out of the city, for the LORD was merciful
to them. 17 As soon as they had brought
them out, one of them said, "Flee for
19:17 c Jer 48:6 your lives![c] Don't look back,[d] and don't
d ver 26 stop anywhere in the plain! Flee to the
mountains or you will be swept away!"
18 But Lot said to them, "No, my
lords,[b] please! 19 Your[c] servant has found
favor in your[c] eyes, and you[c] have shown
great kindness to me in sparing my life.
But I can't flee to the mountains; this disaster will overtake me, and I'll die.
20 Look, here is a town near enough to
run to, and it is small. Let me flee to it—
it is very small, isn't it? Then my life will
be spared."
21 He said to him, "Very well, I will
grant this request too; I will not overthrow the town you speak of. 22 But flee
there quickly, because I cannot do anything until you reach it." (That is why the
town was called Zoar.[d])
23 By the time Lot reached Zoar, the
sun had risen over the land. 24 Then the
LORD rained down burning sulfur on 19:24
Sodom and Gomorrah[e]—from the LORD e Dt 29:23; Isa 1:9; 13:19
out of the heavens.[f] 25 Thus he overthrew f Lk 17:29;
those cities and the entire plain, includ- 2Pe 2:6; Jude 7
ing all those living in the cities—and 19:25
also the vegetation in the land.[g] 26 But g Ps 107:34; Eze 16:48
Lot's wife looked back,[h] and she became
a pillar of salt.[i] 19:26 h ver 17
27 Early the next morning Abraham i Lk 17:32
got up and returned to the place where 19:27
he had stood before the LORD.[j] 28 He j Ge 18:22
looked down toward Sodom and Go-
morrah, toward all the land of the plain,
and he saw dense smoke rising from the 19:28
land, like smoke from a furnace.[k] k Rev 9:2; 18:9
29 So when God destroyed the cities of
the plain, he remembered Abraham, and 19:29
he brought Lot out of the catastrophe[l] l 2Pe 2:7
that overthrew the cities where Lot had
lived.

Lot and His Daughters

30 Lot and his two daughters left Zoar 19:30
and settled in the mountains,[m] for he m ver 19
was afraid to stay in Zoar. He and his
two daughters lived in a cave. 31 One day
the older daughter said to the younger,
"Our father is old, and there is no man
around here to lie with us, as is the custom all over the earth. 32 Let's get our father to drink wine and then lie with him
and preserve our family line through our
father."
33 That night they got their father to
drink wine, and the older daughter went
in and lay with him. He was not aware of
it when she lay down or when she
got up.
34 The next day the older daughter said
to the younger, "Last night I lay with my
father. Let's get him to drink wine again
tonight, and you go in and lie with him
so we can preserve our family line
through our father." 35 So they got their
father to drink wine that night also, and
the younger daughter went and lay with
him. Again he was not aware of it when
she lay down or when she got up.
36 So both of Lot's daughters became
pregnant by their father. 37 The older
daughter had a son, and she named him
Moab[e]; he is the father of the Moabites[n] 19:37 n Dt 2:9
of today. 38 The younger daughter also
had a son, and she named him Ben-

[a] 14 Or *were married to* [b] 18 Or *No, Lord*; or *No, my lord* [c] 19 The Hebrew is singular.
[d] 22 *Zoar* means *small.* [e] 37 *Moab* sounds like the Hebrew for *from father.*

19:38 Ammi[a]; he is the father of the Am-
o Dt 2:19 monites[o] of today.

Abraham and Abimelech

20 Now Abraham moved from
20:1 p Ge 18:1 there[p] into the region of the
q Ge 26:1,6,17 Negev and lived between Kadesh and
Shur. For a while he stayed in Gerar,[q]
[2]and there Abraham said of his wife Sar-
20:2 r ver 12; ah, "She is my sister.[r]" Then Abimelech
Ge 12:13; 26:7 king of Gerar sent for Sarah and took
s Ge 12:15 her.[s]
[3]But God came to Abimelech in a
20:3 t Job 33:15; dream[t] one night and said to him, "You
Mt 27:19 are as good as dead because of the
u Ps 105:14 woman you have taken; she is a married
woman."[u]
[4]Now Abimelech had not gone near
20:4 her, so he said, "Lord, will you destroy an
v Ge 18:25 innocent nation?[v] [5]Did he not say to me,
'She is my sister,' and didn't she also say,
'He is my brother'? I have done this with
a clear conscience and clean hands."
[6]Then God said to him in the dream,
20:6 "Yes, I know you did this with a clear
w 1Sa 25:26,34 conscience, and so I have kept[w] you
from sinning against me. That is why I
did not let you touch her. [7]Now return
20:7 the man's wife, for he is a prophet, and
x ver 17; 1Sa 7:5; he will pray for you[x] and you will live.
Job 42:8 But if you do not return her, you may be
sure that you and all yours will die."
[8]Early the next morning Abimelech
summoned all his officials, and when he
told them all that had happened, they
were very much afraid. [9]Then Abimelech called Abraham in and said,
"What have you done to us? How have I
wronged you that you have brought
such great guilt upon me and my king-
20:9 dom? You have done things to me that
y Ge 12:18; should not be done.[y] [10]And Abimelech
26:10; 34:7 asked Abraham, "What was your reason
for doing this?"
20:11 [11]Abraham replied, "I said to myself,
z Ge 42:18; Ps 36:1 'There is surely no fear of God[z] in this
a Ge 12:12; 26:7 place, and they will kill me because of
my wife.'[a] [12]Besides, she really is my sister, the daughter of my father though
not of my mother; and she became my
wife. [13]And when God had me wander
from my father's household, I said to her,
'This is how you can show your love to
me: Everywhere we go, say of me, "He is
my brother." ' "
[14]Then Abimelech brought sheep and
cattle and male and female slaves and
gave them to Abraham,[b] and he re- 20:14 b Ge 12:16
turned Sarah his wife to him. [15]And
Abimelech said, "My land is before you; 20:15
live wherever you like."[c] c Ge 13:9
[16]To Sarah he said, "I am giving your
brother a thousand shekels[b] of silver.
This is to cover the offense against you
before all who are with you; you are
completely vindicated."
[17]Then Abraham prayed to God,[d] and 20:17
God healed Abimelech, his wife and his d Job 42:9
slave girls so they could have children
again, [18]for the LORD had closed up every
womb in Abimelech's household be- 20:18
cause of Abraham's wife Sarah.[e] e Ge 12:17

The Birth of Isaac

21 Now the LORD was gracious to 21:1 f 1Sa 2:21
Sarah[f] as he had said, and the g Ge 8:1; 17:16,
LORD did for Sarah what he had prom- 21; Gal 4:23
ised.[g] [2]Sarah became pregnant and bore 21:2
a son[h] to Abraham in his old age,[i] at the h Ge 17:19 i Gal 4:22;
very time God had promised him. Heb 11:11
[3]Abraham gave the name Isaac[c][j] to the 21:3
son Sarah bore him. [4]When his son Isaac j Ge 17:19
was eight days old, Abraham circum- 21:4
cised him,[k] as God commanded him. k Ge 17:10,12;
[5]Abraham was a hundred years old Ac 7:8
when his son Isaac was born to him.

[a] *38 Ben-Ammi* means *son of my people.*
[b] *16* That is, about 25 pounds (about 11.5 kilograms)
[c] *3 Isaac* means *he laughs.*

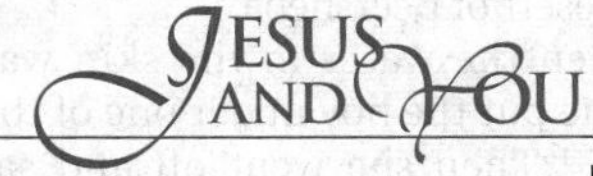

JESUS AND ISAAC

Nowhere in the Bible are we explicitly told that Isaac presents us with an early foreshadowing of Jesus, but the parallels are obvious. Isaac, like Jesus, was the son of God's promise and the apple of his father's eye (Genesis 21). God predicted both births, and both babies were conceived through miracles. God made a covenant with Isaac and promised that it would last forever, just as Jesus embodied God's eternal promise made to all people. Isaac was the only son of Abraham and Sarah, just as Jesus is God's only Son. Both Isaac and Jesus were offered as sacrifices to God, and each carried the wood for the sacrifice himself. Abraham bound Isaac, and Isaac, like Jesus centuries later, did exactly what his father asked of him. Isaac was willing to obey whatever his father asked because he trusted him, and his attitude mirrors Jesus' submission to the will of God the Father (Luke 22:42; Philippians 2:8).

21:6 [l]Ge 17:17; Isa 54:1 6Sarah said, "God has brought me
laughter,[l] and everyone who hears about
this will laugh with me." 7And she added,
"Who would have said to Abraham that
Sarah would nurse children? Yet I have
borne him a son in his old age."

Hagar and Ishmael Sent Away

8The child grew and was weaned, and
on the day Isaac was weaned Abraham
held a great feast. 9But Sarah saw that
21:9 the son whom Hagar the Egyptian had
[m]Ge 16:15 borne to Abraham[m] was mocking,[n]
[n]Gal 4:29 10and she said to Abraham, "Get rid of
that slave woman and her son, for that
21:10 slave woman's son will never share in the
[o]Gal 4:30* inheritance with my son Isaac."[o]
11The matter distressed Abraham
21:11 greatly because it concerned his son.[p]
[p]Ge 17:18 12But God said to him, "Do not be so distressed about the boy and your maid-
servant. Listen to whatever Sarah tells
21:12 you, because it is through Isaac that
[q]Ro 9:7*; Heb 11:18* your offspring[a] will be reckoned.[q] 13I will
make the son of the maidservant into a
21:13 nation[r] also, because he is your off-
[r]ver 18 spring."
14Early the next morning Abraham
took some food and a skin of water and
gave them to Hagar. He set them on her
shoulders and then sent her off with the
21:14 boy. She went on her way and wandered
[s]ver 31,32 in the desert of Beersheba.[s]
15When the water in the skin was
gone, she put the boy under one of the
bushes. 16Then she went off and sat
down nearby, about a bowshot away, for
she thought, "I cannot watch the boy
die." And as she sat there nearby, she[b]
began to sob.
21:17 17God heard the boy crying,[t] and the
[t]Ex 3:7 angel of God called to Hagar from heav-
en and said to her, "What is the matter,
Hagar? Do not be afraid; God has heard
the boy crying as he lies there. 18Lift the
21:18 boy up and take him by the hand, for I
[u]ver 13 will make him into a great nation."[u]
21:19 19Then God opened her eyes[v] and she
[v]Nu 22:31 saw a well of water. So she went and
filled the skin with water and gave the
boy a drink.
21:20 20God was with the boy[w] as he grew
[w]Ge 26:3,24; 28:15; 39:2,21, 23 up. He lived in the desert and became an
archer. 21While he was living in the
21:21 Desert of Paran, his mother got a wife
[x]Ge 24:4,38 for him[x] from Egypt.

The Treaty at Beersheba

22At that time Abimelech and Phicol
the commander of his forces said to
Abraham, "God is with you in everything you do. 23Now swear[y] to me here 21:23
before God that you will not deal falsely [y]ver 31; Jos 2:12
with me or my children or my descen-
dants. Show to me and the country
where you are living as an alien the same
kindness I have shown to you."
24Abraham said, "I swear it."
25Then Abraham complained to
Abimelech about a well of water that 21:25
Abimelech's servants had seized.[z] [z]Ge 26:15,18, 20-22
26But Abimelech said, "I don't know
who has done this. You did not tell me,
and I heard about it only today."
27So Abraham brought sheep and cattle and gave them to Abimelech, and the 21:27
two men made a treaty.[a] 28Abraham set [a]Ge 26:28,31
apart seven ewe lambs from the flock,
29and Abimelech asked Abraham, "What
is the meaning of these seven ewe lambs
you have set apart by themselves?"
30He replied, "Accept these seven 21:30
lambs from my hand as a witness[b] that I [b]Ge 31:44,47, 48,50,52
dug this well."
31So that place was called Beersheba,[c][c] 21:31
because the two men swore an oath [c]Ge 26:33
there.
32After the treaty had been made at
Beersheba, Abimelech and Phicol the
commander of his forces returned to the
land of the Philistines. 33Abraham planted a tamarisk tree in Beersheba, and
there he called upon the name of the 21:33
LORD,[d] the Eternal God.[e] 34And Abra- [d]Ge 4:26 [e]Dt 33:27
ham stayed in the land of the Philistines
for a long time.

Abraham Tested

22 Some time later God tested[f] 22:1
Abraham. He said to him, [f]Dt 8:2,16; Heb 11:17; Jas 1:12-13
"Abraham!"
"Here I am," he replied.
2Then God said, "Take your son[g], your 22:2
only son, Isaac, whom you love, and go [g]ver 12,16; Jn 3:16;
to the region of Moriah.[h] Sacrifice him Heb 11:17;
there as a burnt offering on one of the 1Jn 4:9
mountains I will tell you about." [h]2Ch 3:1
3Early the next morning Abraham got
up and saddled his donkey. He took with
him two of his servants and his son
Isaac. When he had cut enough wood

[a] 12 Or *seed* [b] 16 Hebrew; Septuagint *the child*
[c] 31 *Beersheba* can mean *well of seven* or *well of the oath.*

DISCOVERY 7

THE MOMENT OF TRUTH

Few stories are filled with more pathos than this one: A father and his young son trudge up a mountainside. The father intends to sacrifice the cherished son in obedience to God's command. This event had begun with the terse statement, "Some time later God tested Abraham" (Genesis 22:1). Abraham had been tested before, and he had on more than one occasion failed the test (see Genesis 6, 12 and 20). How would he stand up to this test?

That question creates excruciating tension in Abraham's heart as he and Isaac journey up the mountain toward the sacrificial moment. Abraham laments every step forward with his entire being. The driving passion of his life, the son for whom he had trusted God and upon whom all of his hopes have rested is, it seems, about to be wrenched irrevocably away. But at the same time, unknown to Abraham, a ram is making its sure-footed ascent up the other side of the mountain. For every step Abraham takes toward the top, the ram also takes a step. And it was God's plan all along that they meet in the same place at the same time for the same purpose. Abraham calls the place of the near-sacrifice *Yahweh-yireh* or "The LORD Will Provide" (Genesis 22:14).

God tests each of us so that we too can learn to trust what he says. He often touches areas of our lives that are most precious to us, sometimes even those areas that we want to declare "off limits" even to him. Such a moment of testing is lonely and demands unwavering faith in God. And deliverance may not come until what we perceive to be the last possible moment! We might be scaling the side of a mountain alone, dreading what we might encounter at the summit but knowing there is no turning back. Yet, unknown to us, God's provision is *already* on the way. We may not see it—we may not even know that it exists—but the "ram" will meet us at the top. The Lord will provide!

This Biblical narrative, possibly more than any other, helps us to perceive clearly the Father's own limitless love for his only Son Jesus. Like Abraham, God did not withhold the sacrifice of his only Son (Romans 8:32). And, like Isaac, Jesus willingly obeyed, subjecting his own will to that of his Father (John 10:14–18).

There is, however, one significant difference between the two stories. In Abraham's case, God provided a substitute for Isaac, a ram caught by its horns in the bushes. But there could be no substitute when Jesus offered his life as the sacrifice for the sin of all humanity. On the cross, God's own Son took upon himself the Father's wrath against *all* sin for *all* time. Even in this—at great cost to himself—the Lord provides!

***Self-Discovery:** Identify one "moment of truth" or particular moment of testing that stands out in your memory. How did the Lord provide for your need?*

GO TO DISCOVERY 8 ON PAGE 34

for the burnt offering, he set out for the
place God had told him about. 4On the
third day Abraham looked up and saw
the place in the distance. 5He said to his
servants, "Stay here with the donkey
while I and the boy go over there. We
will worship and then we will come back
to you."
6Abraham took the wood for the
22:6 burnt offering and placed it on his son
iJn 19:17 Isaac,[i] and he himself carried the fire
and the knife. As the two of them went
on together, 7Isaac spoke up and said to
his father Abraham, "Father?"
"Yes, my son?" Abraham replied.
22:7 "The fire and wood are here," Isaac
jLev 1:10 said, "but where is the lamb[j] for the
burnt offering?"
8Abraham answered, "God himself
will provide the lamb for the burnt offering, my son." And the two of them
went on together.
9When they reached the place God
had told him about, Abraham built an
altar there and arranged the wood on it.
He bound his son Isaac and laid him on
22:9 kHeb 11:17-19; the altar,[k] on top of the wood. 10Then he
Jas 2:21 reached out his hand and took the knife
to slay his son. 11But the angel of the
LORD called out to him from heaven,
"Abraham! Abraham!"
"Here I am," he replied.

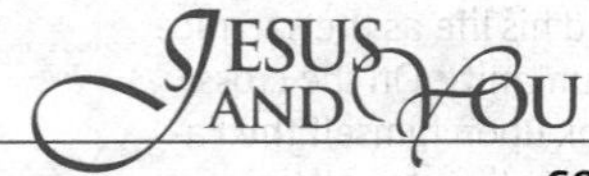

GOD OUR PROVIDER

As the Great Provider God always does whatever is necessary to meet our needs. Abraham assured Isaac that God himself would provide a lamb for the sacrifice on Mount Moriah—and provide one he did! It had never been God's plan to allow Abraham to follow through with the sacrifice, and the "angel of the LORD" (possibly Jesus himself; see page 23) called out to stop him (Genesis 22:11–12). The angel of the Lord prevented Abraham from doing to his son what God the Father would later allow Jesus Christ to do on our behalf. More than two thousand years later God would send Jesus to this same region to become the ultimate and final sacrifice for our sins, to pay the debt and set us free. God the Son would himself become the sacrificial Lamb of God. There has never been anyone else who loves us as he does, and no one else deserves our lives, our love and our unqualified devotion.

12"Do not lay a hand on the boy," he
said. "Do not do anything to him. Now I 22:12
know that you fear God,[l] because you l1Sa 15:22;
have not withheld from me your son, Jas 2:21-22 mver 2; Jn 3:16
your only son.[m]"
13Abraham looked up and there in a
thicket he saw a ram[a] caught by its
horns. He went over and took the ram
and sacrificed it as a burnt offering in- 22:13
stead of his son.[n] 14So Abraham called nRo 8:32
that place The LORD Will Provide. And to
this day it is said, "On the mountain of 22:14
the LORD it will be provided.[o]" over 8
15The angel of the LORD called to
Abraham from heaven a second time
16and said, "I swear by myself,[p] declares 22:16
the LORD, that because you have done pLk 1:73; Heb 6:13
this and have not withheld your son,
your only son, 17I will surely bless you 22:17
and make your descendants[q] as numer- qHeb 6:14*
ous as the stars in the sky[r] and as the rGe 15:5
sand on the seashore.[s] Your descen- sGe 26:24; 32:12 tGe 24:60
dants will take possession of the cities of
their enemies,[t] 18and through your off- 22:18
spring[b] all nations on earth will be uGe 12:2,3; Ac 3:25*;
blessed,[u] because you have obeyed me."[v] Gal 3:8* vver 10
19Then Abraham returned to his ser-
vants, and they set off together for Beersheba. And Abraham stayed in Beersheba.

Nahor's Sons

20Some time later Abraham was told,
"Milcah is also a mother; she has borne 22:20
sons to your brother Nahor:[w] 21Uz the wGe 11:29
firstborn, Buz his brother, Kemuel (the
father of Aram), 22Kesed, Hazo, Pildash,
Jidlaph and Bethuel." 23Bethuel became 22:23
the father of Rebekah.[x] Milcah bore xGe 24:15
these eight sons to Abraham's brother
Nahor. 24His concubine, whose name
was Reumah, also had sons: Tebah, Ga-
ham, Tahash and Maacah.

The Death of Sarah

23 Sarah lived to be a hundred and
twenty-seven years old. 2She 23:2
died at Kiriath Arba[y] (that is, Hebron)[z] yJos 14:15
in the land of Canaan, and Abraham zver 19; Ge 13:18
went to mourn for Sarah and to weep
over her.
3Then Abraham rose from beside his
dead wife and spoke to the Hittites.[c] He

[a] 13 Many manuscripts of the Masoretic Text, Samaritan Pentateuch, Septuagint and Syriac; most manuscripts of the Masoretic Text *a ram behind* ⌊*him*⌋ [b] 18 Or *seed* [c] 3 Or *the sons of Heth*; also in verses 5, 7, 10, 16, 18 and 20

23:4 [a]Ge 17:8; 1Ch 29:15; Ps 105:12; Heb 11:9,13 said, [4]"I am an alien and a stranger[a]
among you. Sell me some property for a
burial site here so I can bury my dead."
[5]The Hittites replied to Abraham,
[6]"Sir, listen to us. You are a mighty
23:6 [b]Ge 14:14-16; 24:35 prince[b] among us. Bury your dead in the
choicest of our tombs. None of us will
refuse you his tomb for burying your
dead."
[7]Then Abraham rose and bowed
down before the people of the land, the
Hittites. [8]He said to them, "If you are
willing to let me bury my dead, then listen to me and intercede with Ephron
23:8 [c]Ge 25:9 son of Zohar[c] on my behalf [9]so he will
sell me the cave of Machpelah, which
belongs to him and is at the end of his
field. Ask him to sell it to me for the full
price as a burial site among you."
[10]Ephron the Hittite was sitting
among his people and he replied to
23:10 [d]Ge 34:20-24; Ru 4:4 Abraham in the hearing of all the Hittites who had come to the gate[d] of his
city. [11]"No, my lord," he said. "Listen to
23:11 [e]2Sa 24:23 me; I give[a][e] you the field, and I give[a] you
the cave that is in it. I give[a] it to you in
the presence of my people. Bury your
dead."
[12]Again Abraham bowed down before
the people of the land [13]and he said to
Ephron in their hearing, "Listen to me, if
you will. I will pay the price of the field.
Accept it from me so I can bury my dead
there."
[14]Ephron answered Abraham, [15]"Listen to me, my lord; the land is worth
23:15 [f]Eze 45:12 four hundred shekels[b] of silver,[f] but
what is that between me and you? Bury
your dead."
[16]Abraham agreed to Ephron's terms
and weighed out for him the price he
23:16 [g]Jer 32:9; Zec 11:12 had named in the hearing of the Hittites: four hundred shekels of silver,[g] ac-
cording to the weight current among
the merchants.
23:17 [h]Ge 25:9; 49:30-32; 50:13; Ac 7:16 [17]So Ephron's field in Machpelah near
Mamre[h]—both the field and the cave in
it, and all the trees within the borders of
the field—was deeded [18]to Abraham as
his property in the presence of all the
Hittites who had come to the gate of the
city. [19]Afterward Abraham buried his
wife Sarah in the cave in the field of
Machpelah near Mamre (which is at Hebron) in the land of Canaan. [20]So the
23:20 [i]Jer 32:10 field and the cave in it were deeded[i] to
Abraham by the Hittites as a burial site.

Isaac and Rebekah

24 Abraham was now old and well
advanced in years, and the 24:1 [j]ver 35
LORD had blessed him in every way.[j] [2]He
said to the chief[c] servant in his house-
hold, the one in charge of all that he 24:2 [k]Ge 39:4-6 [l]ver 9; Ge 47:29
had,[k] "Put your hand under my thigh.[l] [3]I
want you to swear by the LORD, the God
of heaven and the God of earth,[m] that 24:3 [m]Ge 14:19 [n]Ge 28:1; Dt 7:3 [o]Ge 10:15-19
you will not get a wife for my son[n] from
the daughters of the Canaanites,[o]
among whom I am living, [4]but will go to 24:4 [p]Ge 12:1; 28:2
my country and my own relatives[p] and
get a wife for my son Isaac."
[5]The servant asked him, "What if the
woman is unwilling to come back with
me to this land? Shall I then take your
son back to the country you came from?"
[6]"Make sure that you do not take my
son back there," Abraham said. [7]"The
LORD, the God of heaven, who brought
me out of my father's household and my
native land and who spoke to me and
promised me on oath, saying, 'To your 24:7 [q]Gal 3:16* [r]Ge 12:7; 13:15 [s]Ex 23:20,23
offspring[d][q] I will give this land'[r]—he will
send his angel before you[s] so that you
can get a wife for my son from there. [8]If
the woman is unwilling to come back
with you, then you will be released from
this oath of mine. Only do not take my
son back there." [9]So the servant put his

[a] *11* Or *sell* [b] *15* That is, about 10 pounds (about 4.5 kilograms) [c] *2* Or *oldest* [d] *7* Or *seed*

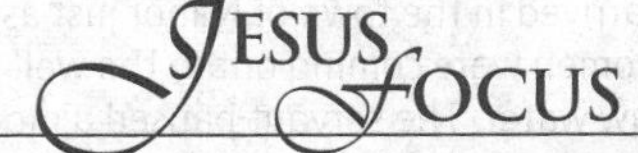

A BRIDE FOR ISAAC

When it was time for Isaac to find a wife, Abraham sent his servant back to Haran to bring back a suitable young woman. The servant asked the natural question: "What if the woman is unwilling?" (Genesis 24:5). But Abraham assured him, "The LORD, the God of heaven . . . will send his angel before you" (verse 7). The servant asked God to lead him to the right woman—and, "before he had finished praying" (verse 15), Rebekah had already arrived in answer to that prayer. When she was asked whether she was willing to go with the servant, Rebekah agreed, seemingly without hesitation. This story provides us with a powerful image of our role as servants in finding a "bride" for Jesus, the Father's Son. God sends us into the world to exemplify Jesus' love for others and to ask them the same question Rebekah was asked: "Will you go with this man?" (verse 58).

DISCOVERY 8

Prayer, Promises and Presence

As Abraham approached the end of his life, one of his overriding concerns was to find a wife for his son Isaac. God had promised that Abraham's family would become a great nation through Isaac—and that wouldn't happen unless Isaac were married. God's kindness and faithfulness were part of his promise to Abraham (Genesis 12:1–3), because *God leads through his promises.* So Abraham sent a servant on a 450-mile journey in search of a suitable bride chosen from among his relatives.

The apostle Peter would later write: "[God's] divine power has given us everything we need for life and godliness through our knowledge of him who called us by his own glory and goodness. Through these he has given us his very great and precious promises, so that through them you may participate in the divine nature and escape the corruption in the world caused by evil desires" (2 Peter 1:3–4).

As God would have it, Abraham's servant arrived in the town of Nahor just as the women were coming out to the well to draw water. The servant paused a moment and asked God for a sign to tell him which young woman to choose: Isaac's future bride would offer him a drink—and then offer to provide water for all ten of his camels. That meant she would have to draw around 250 gallons of water from the deep well! A young woman named Rebekah did in fact make this exceptional offer, and she eventually became Isaac's bride. The servant's task was overwhelming, yet he stopped and asked for God's direction. And all along the way God was in control of even the smallest details. *God leads through prayer.*

The apostle Paul wrote to the Corinthian believers to thank them for their prayers on his behalf: "[God] has delivered us from ... a deadly peril, and he will deliver us. On him we have set our hope that he will continue to deliver us, as you help us by your prayers. Then many will give thanks on our behalf for the gracious favor granted us in answer to the prayers of many" (2 Corinthians 1:10–11).

God traveled with Abraham's servant all along the tortuous journey, but it wasn't until the end of the 450-mile trip that God revealed the bride (Genesis 24:27). *God leads by his presence.*

As Jude expressed so beautifully in verses 24 and 25 of his short letter: "To him who is able to keep you from falling and to present you before his glorious presence without fault and with great joy—to the only God our Savior be glory, majesty, power and authority, through Jesus Christ our Lord."

Whenever we face challenges, we can go back to God's Word to discover and claim his promises. When we take them at face value, we learn to trust him. When we face uncertainty or difficult decisions, the place to start is in conversation with God. But we need to keep walking, working, praying and serving—because he walks at our side and shows us details as we go along.

Our part along the way is to trust, follow and *thank* God. The servant was quick to declare his praise for God (Genesis 24:27) in thanksgiving for a task concluded through God's leading. As we consider how God has led us through many situations, and how he has pursued us with the gift of his Son, we can only do the same thing. We did not pursue a relationship with God through Jesus. Instead, God reached out to us through his Son.

Self-Discovery: *What specific signs help you to identify God's leading in your life?*

GO TO DISCOVERY 9 ON PAGE 41

24:9 t ver 2 hand under the thigh[t] of his master
Abraham and swore an oath to him
concerning this matter.
10 Then the servant took ten of his
master's camels and left, taking with
him all kinds of good things from his
master. He set out for Aram Naharaim[a]
and made his way to the town of Nahor.
24:11 11 He had the camels kneel down near
u Ex 2:15 v ver 13; the well[u] outside the town; it was to-
1Sa 9:11 ward evening, the time the women go
out to draw water.[v]
24:12 12 Then he prayed, "O LORD, God of my
w ver 27,42,48; master Abraham,[w] give me success to-
Ge 26:24; Ex 3:6,15,16 day, and show kindness to my master
Abraham. 13 See, I am standing beside
this spring, and the daughters of the
townspeople are coming out to draw
water. 14 May it be that when I say to a
girl, 'Please let down your jar that I may
have a drink,' and she says, 'Drink, and
I'll water your camels too'—let her be
24:14 the one you have chosen for your ser-
x Jdg 6:17,37 vant Isaac. By this I will know[x] that you
have shown kindness to my master."
24:15 y ver 45 15 Before he had finished praying,[y] Re-
z Ge 22:23 bekah[z] came out with her jar on her
a Ge 22:20 shoulder. She was the daughter of Be-
b Ge 11:29 thuel son of Milcah,[a] who was the wife
of Abraham's brother Nahor.[b] 16 The girl
24:16 c Ge 26:7 was very beautiful,[c] a virgin; no man had
ever lain with her. She went down to the
spring, filled her jar and came up again.
17 The servant hurried to meet her and
said, "Please give me a little water from
your jar."
24:18 18 "Drink,[d] my lord," she said, and
d ver 14 quickly lowered the jar to her hands and
gave him a drink.
19 After she had given him a drink, she
said, "I'll draw water for your camels
24:19 e ver 14 too,[e] until they have finished drinking."
20 So she quickly emptied her jar into the
trough, ran back to the well to draw
more water, and drew enough for all his
camels. 21 Without saying a word, the
man watched her closely to learn
24:21 whether or not the LORD had made his
f ver 12 journey successful.[f]
22 When the camels had finished
drinking, the man took out a gold nose
24:22 g ver 47 ring[g] weighing a beka[b] and two gold
bracelets weighing ten shekels.[c] 23 Then
he asked, "Whose daughter are you?
Please tell me, is there room in your father's house for us to spend the night?"
24 She answered him, "I am the daugh-

ter of Bethuel, the son that Milcah bore 24:24
to Nahor.[h]" 25 And she added, "We have h ver 15
plenty of straw and fodder, as well as
room for you to spend the night."
26 Then the man bowed down and 24:26
worshiped the LORD,[i] 27 saying, "Praise be i ver 48,52;
to the LORD,[j] the God of my master Ex 4:31
Abraham, who has not abandoned his 24:27
kindness and faithfulness[k] to my mas- j Ex 18:10;
ter. As for me, the LORD has led me on Ru 4:14;
the journey[l] to the house of my master's 1Sa 25:32 k ver 49;
relatives."[m] Ge 32:10; Ps 98:3 l ver 21 m ver 12,48
28 The girl ran and told her mother's
household about these things. 29 Now Re- 24:29
bekah had a brother named Laban,[n] and n ver 4; Ge 29:5,
he hurried out to the man at the spring. 12,13
30 As soon as he had seen the nose ring,
and the bracelets on his sister's arms,
and had heard Rebekah tell what the
man said to her, he went out to the man
and found him standing by the camels
near the spring. 31 "Come, you who are
blessed by the LORD,"[o] he said. "Why are 24:31
you standing out here? I have prepared o Ge 26:29; Ru 3:10;
the house and a place for the camels." Ps 115:15
32 So the man went to the house, and
the camels were unloaded. Straw and
fodder were brought for the camels, and
water for him and his men to wash their 24:32
feet.[p] 33 Then food was set before him, p Ge 43:24; Jdg 19:21
but he said, "I will not eat until I have
told you what I have to say."
"Then tell us," ⌞Laban⌟ said.
34 So he said, "I am Abraham's servant.
35 The LORD has blessed my master
abundantly,[q] and he has become 24:35
wealthy. He has given him sheep and q ver 1 r Ge 13:2
cattle, silver and gold, menservants and
maidservants, and camels and donkeys.[r]
36 My master's wife Sarah has borne him
a son in her[d] old age,[s] and he has given 24:36
him everything he owns.[t] 37 And my s Ge 21:2,10 t Ge 25:5
master made me swear an oath, and
said, 'You must not get a wife for my son
from the daughters of the Canaanites, in
whose land I live,[u] 38 but go to my father's 24:37
family and to my own clan, and get a u ver 3
wife for my son.'[v] 24:38
39 "Then I asked my master, 'What if the v ver 4
woman will not come back with me?'[w]
40 "He replied, 'The LORD, before whom 24:39
I have walked, will send his angel with w ver 5
you[x] and make your journey a success,
so that you can get a wife for my son 24:40 x ver 7

[a] *10* That is, Northwest Mesopotamia
[b] *22* That is, about 1/5 ounce (about 5.5 grams)
[c] *22* That is, about 4 ounces (about 110 grams)
[d] *36* Or *his*

from my own clan and from my father's
family. [41]Then, when you go to my clan,
you will be released from my oath even
if they refuse to give her to you—you
will be released from my oath.'[y]
24:41 [y]ver 8 [42]"When I came to the spring today, I
said, 'O LORD, God of my master Abra-
24:42 [z]ver 12 ham, if you will, please grant success[z] to
the journey on which I have come. [43]See,
24:43 [a]ver 13 [b]ver 14 I am standing beside this spring;[a] if a
maiden comes out to draw water and I
say to her, "Please let me drink a little
water from your jar,"[b] [44]and if she says to
me, "Drink, and I'll draw water for your
camels too," let her be the one the LORD
has chosen for my master's son.'
[45]"Before I finished praying in my
24:45 [c]1Sa 1:13 [d]ver 15 [e]ver 17 heart,[c] Rebekah came out, with her jar
on her shoulder.[d] She went down to the
spring and drew water, and I said to her,
'Please give me a drink.'[e]
[46]"She quickly lowered her jar from
her shoulder and said, 'Drink, and I'll
24:46 [f]ver 18-19 water your camels too.'[f] So I drank, and
she watered the camels also.
[47]"I asked her, 'Whose daughter are
24:47 [g]ver 23 [h]ver 24 [i]Eze 16:11-12 you?'[g]
"She said, 'The daughter of Bethuel
son of Nahor, whom Milcah bore to
him.'[h]
"Then I put the ring in her nose and
the bracelets on her arms,[i] [48]and I
24:48 [j]ver 26 [k]ver 27 bowed down and worshiped the LORD.[j] I
praised the LORD, the God of my master
Abraham, who had led me on the right
road to get the granddaughter of my
master's brother for his son.[k] [49]Now if
24:49 [l]Ge 47:29; Jos 2:14 you will show kindness and faithfulness[l]
to my master, tell me; and if not, tell me,
so I may know which way to turn."
[50]Laban and Bethuel answered, "This
24:50 [m]Ps 118:23 [n]Ge 31:7,24,29, 42 is from the LORD;[m] we can say nothing to
you one way or the other.[n] [51]Here is Re-
bekah; take her and go, and let her become the wife of your master's son, as
the LORD has directed."
[52]When Abraham's servant heard
what they said, he bowed down to the
24:52 [o]ver 26 ground before the LORD.[o] [53]Then the servant brought out gold and silver jewelry
and articles of clothing and gave them
24:53 [p]ver 10,22 to Rebekah; he also gave costly gifts[p] to
her brother and to her mother. [54]Then
he and the men who were with him ate
and drank and spent the night there.
When they got up the next morning,
he said, "Send me on my way[q] to my 24:54 [q]ver 56,59
master."
[55]But her brother and her mother
replied, "Let the girl remain with us ten
days or so; then you[a] may go."
[56]But he said to them, "Do not detain
me, now that the LORD has granted success to my journey. Send me on my way
so I may go to my master."
[57]Then they said, "Let's call the girl
and ask her about it." [58]So they called
Rebekah and asked her, "Will you go
with this man?"
"I will go," she said.
[59]So they sent their sister Rebekah on 24:59 [r]Ge 35:8
her way, along with her nurse[r] and
Abraham's servant and his men. [60]And
they blessed Rebekah and said to her,

"Our sister, may you increase 24:60 [s]Ge 17:16 [t]Ge 22:17
to thousands upon thousands;[s]
may your offspring possess
the gates of their enemies."[t]

[61]Then Rebekah and her maids got
ready and mounted their camels and
went back with the man. So the servant
took Rebekah and left.
[62]Now Isaac had come from Beer La- 24:62 [u]Ge 16:14; 25:11 [v]Ge 20:1
hai Roi,[u] for he was living in the Negev.[v]
[63]He went out to the field one evening to
meditate,[b][w] and as he looked up, he saw 24:63 [w]Ps 1:2; 77:12; 119:15,27,48, 97,148; 143:5; 145:5
camels approaching. [64]Rebekah also
looked up and saw Isaac. She got down
from her camel [65]and asked the servant,
"Who is that man in the field coming to
meet us?"
"He is my master," the servant answered. So she took her veil and covered
herself.
[66]Then the servant told Isaac all he
had done. [67]Isaac brought her into the
tent of his mother Sarah, and he married 24:67 [x]Ge 25:20 [y]Ge 29:18,20 [z]Ge 23:1-2
Rebekah.[x] So she became his wife, and
he loved her;[y] and Isaac was comforted
after his mother's death.[z]

The Death of Abraham

25 Abraham took[c] another wife,
whose name was Keturah. [2]She
bore him Zimran, Jokshan, Medan, Mid-
ian, Ishbak and Shuah.[a] [3]Jokshan was 25:2 [a]1Ch 1:32,33
the father of Sheba and Dedan; the de-
scendants of Dedan were the Asshu-
rites, the Letushites and the Leummites.
[4]The sons of Midian were Ephah, Epher,

[a] 55 Or *she* [b] 63 The meaning of the Hebrew for this word is uncertain. [c] 1 Or *had taken*

Hanoch, Abida and Eldaah. All these
were descendants of Keturah.
25:5 5 Abraham left everything he owned
b Ge 24:36 to Isaac.[b] 6 But while he was still living,
25:6 he gave gifts to the sons of his concu-
c Ge 22:24 bines[c] and sent them away from his son
d Ge 21:10,14 Isaac[d] to the land of the east.
7 Altogether, Abraham lived a hun-
dred and seventy-five years. 8 Then
25:8 Abraham breathed his last and died at a
e Ge 15:15 f ver 17; good old age,[e] an old man and full of
Ge 35:29; 49:29, 33 years; and he was gathered to his people.[f] 9 His sons Isaac and Ishmael buried
25:9 g Ge 35:29 him[g] in the cave of Machpelah near
h Ge 50:13 Mamre, in the field of Ephron son of Zo-
25:10 har the Hittite,[h] 10 the field Abraham
i Ge 23:16 had bought from the Hittites.[a][i] There
Abraham was buried with his wife
Sarah. 11 After Abraham's death, God
25:11 blessed his son Isaac, who then lived
j Ge 16:14 near Beer Lahai Roi.[j]

Ishmael's Sons

12 This is the account of Abraham's
25:12 son Ishmael, whom Sarah's maidservant,
k Ge 16:1 l Ge 16:15 Hagar[k] the Egyptian, bore to Abraham.[l]

13 These are the names of the sons of
Ishmael, listed in the order of their
birth: Nebaioth the firstborn of Ishmael, Kedar, Adbeel, Mibsam, 14 Mishma,
Dumah, Massa, 15 Hadad, Tema, Jetur,
Naphish and Kedemah. 16 These were
the sons of Ishmael, and these are the
25:16 m Ge 17:20 names of the twelve tribal rulers[m] according to their settlements and camps.
17 Altogether, Ishmael lived a hundred
and thirty-seven years. He breathed his
last and died, and he was gathered to
25:17 n ver 8 his people.[n] 18 His descendants settled
in the area from Havilah to Shur, near
the border of Egypt, as you go toward
25:18 Asshur. And they lived in hostility to-
o Ge 16:12 ward[b] all their brothers.[o]

Jacob and Esau

19 This is the account of Abraham's
son Isaac.

Abraham became the father of Isaac,
25:20 p ver 26; 20 and Isaac was forty years old[p] when he
Ge 26:34 married Rebekah[q] daughter of Bethuel
q Ge 24:67 r Ge 24:29 the Aramean from Paddan Aram[c] and
sister of Laban[r] the Aramean.
25:21 s 1Ch 5:20; 21 Isaac prayed to the LORD on behalf
2Ch 33:13; of his wife, because she was barren. The
Ezr 8:23; Ps 127:3; LORD answered his prayer,[s] and his wife
Ro 9:10 Rebekah became pregnant. 22 The babies
jostled each other within her, and she
said, "Why is this happening to me?" So 25:22
she went to inquire of the LORD.[t] t 1Sa 9:9; 10:22
23 The LORD said to her,

"Two nations[u] are in your womb, 25:23 u Ge 17:4
and two peoples from within v Ge 27:29,40;
you will be separated; Mal 1:3; Ro 9:11-12*
one people will be stronger than
the other,
and the older will serve the
younger.[v]"

24 When the time came for her to give
birth, there were twin boys in her womb.
25 The first to come out was red, and his 25:25
whole body was like a hairy garment;[w] w Ge 27:11
so they named him Esau.[d] 26 After this,
his brother came out, with his hand
grasping Esau's heel;[x] so he was named 25:26 x Hos 12:3
Jacob.[e][y] Isaac was sixty years old when y Ge 27:36
Rebekah gave birth to them.
27 The boys grew up, and Esau became
a skillful hunter, a man of the open
country,[z] while Jacob was a quiet man, 25:27 z Ge 27:3,5
staying among the tents. 28 Isaac, who
had a taste for wild game,[a] loved Esau, 25:28 a Ge 27:; 19
but Rebekah loved Jacob.[b] b Ge 27:6
29 Once when Jacob was cooking some
stew, Esau came in from the open country, famished. 30 He said to Jacob, "Quick,
let me have some of that red stew! I'm

[a] 10 Or *the sons of Heth* [b] 18 Or *lived to the east of* [c] 20 That is, Northwest Mesopotamia
[d] 25 *Esau* may mean *hairy*; he was also called Edom, which means *red.* [e] 26 *Jacob* means *he grasps the heel* (figuratively, *he deceives*).

JESUS FOCUS

JACOB AND ESAU

God's plan was that the Messiah's lineage would pass through Isaac to his son Jacob—but this would not happen without a struggle. Isaac and Rebekah had a set of nonidentical twins who fought from the day they were born. *Esau* was called "hairy," and *Jacob* was called "he grasps the heel," because God had told Rebekah that "two nations are in your womb" and that "the older will serve the younger" (Genesis 25:23). Typically, in ancient Near Eastern families the eldest son received the *birthright* (the position of leadership and authority) and the *blessing* (twice the amount of the family inheritance that the other sons received). Jacob traded Esau a bowl of stew for the birthright, and he later stole the blessing by deceiving Isaac (see Genesis 27).

famished!" (That is why he was also
called Edom.[a])
31Jacob replied, "First sell me your
birthright."
32"Look, I am about to die," Esau said.
"What good is the birthright to me?"
33But Jacob said, "Swear to me first."
25:33 [c]Ge 27:36; Heb 12:16 So he swore an oath to him, selling his
birthright[c] to Jacob.
34Then Jacob gave Esau some bread
and some lentil stew. He ate and drank,
and then got up and left.
So Esau despised his birthright.

Isaac and Abimelech

26:1 [d]Ge 12:10 [e]Ge 20:1 26 Now there was a famine in the
land[d]—besides the earlier fam-
ine of Abraham's time—and Isaac went
to Abimelech king of the Philistines in
26:2 [f]Ge 12:7; 17:1; 18:1 [g]Ge 12:1 Gerar.[e] 2The LORD appeared[f] to Isaac
and said, "Do not go down to Egypt; live
in the land where I tell you to live.[g] 3Stay
26:3 [h]Ge 20:1; 28:15 [i]Ge 12:2; 22:16-18 [j]Ge 12:7; 13:15; 15:18 in this land for a while,[h] and I will be
with you and will bless you.[i] For to you
and your descendants I will give all
these lands[j] and will confirm the oath I
swore to your father Abraham. 4I will
26:4 [k]Ge 15:5; 22:17; Ex 32:13 [l]Ge 12:3; 22:18; Gal 3:8 make your descendants as numerous as
the stars in the sky[k] and will give them
all these lands, and through your offspring[b] all nations on earth will be
blessed,[l] 5because Abraham obeyed
26:5 [m]Ge 22:16 me[m] and kept my requirements, my
commands, my decrees and my laws."
6So Isaac stayed in Gerar.
7When the men of that place asked
him about his wife, he said, "She is my
26:7 [n]Ge 12:13; 20:2, 12; Pr 29:25 sister,[n]" because he was afraid to say,
"She is my wife." He thought, "The men
of this place might kill me on account of
Rebekah, because she is beautiful."
8When Isaac had been there a long
time, Abimelech king of the Philistines
looked down from a window and saw
Isaac caressing his wife Rebekah. 9So
Abimelech summoned Isaac and said,
"She is really your wife! Why did you say,
'She is my sister'?"
Isaac answered him, "Because I
thought I might lose my life on account
of her."
10Then Abimelech said, "What is this
26:10 [o]Ge 20:9 you have done to us?[o] One of the men
might well have slept with your wife, and
you would have brought guilt upon us."
11So Abimelech gave orders to all the
people: "Anyone who molests[p] this man 26:11 [p]Ps 105:15
or his wife shall surely be put to death."
12Isaac planted crops in that land and
the same year reaped a hundredfold, be- 26:12 [q]ver 3; Job 42:12
cause the LORD blessed him.[q] 13The man
became rich, and his wealth continued 26:13 [r]Pr 10:22
to grow until he became very wealthy.[r]
14He had so many flocks and herds and 26:14 [s]Ge 24:36 [t]Ge 37:11
servants[s] that the Philistines envied
him.[t] 15So all the wells[u] that his father's
servants had dug in the time of his fa- 26:15 [u]Ge 21:30 [v]Ge 21:25
ther Abraham, the Philistines stopped
up,[v] filling them with earth.
16Then Abimelech said to Isaac,
"Move away from us; you have become 26:16 [w]Ex 1:9
too powerful for us.[w]"
17So Isaac moved away from there
and encamped in the Valley of Gerar
and settled there. 18Isaac reopened the 26:18 [x]Ge 21:30
wells[x] that had been dug in the time of
his father Abraham, which the Philistines had stopped up after Abraham
died, and he gave them the same names
his father had given them.
19Isaac's servants dug in the valley and
discovered a well of fresh water there.
20But the herdsmen of Gerar quarreled
with Isaac's herdsmen and said, "The wa- 26:20 [y]Ge 21:25
ter is ours!"[y] So he named the well Esek,[c]
because they disputed with him. 21Then
they dug another well, but they quarreled over that one also; so he named it
Sitnah.[d] 22He moved on from there and
dug another well, and no one quarreled
over it. He named it Rehoboth,[e] saying,
"Now the LORD has given us room and 26:22 [z]Ge 17:6; Ex 1:7
we will flourish[z] in the land."
23From there he went up to Beersheba. 24That night the LORD appeared to
him and said, "I am the God of your fa- 26:24 [a]Ge 24:12; Ex 3:6 [b]Ge 15:1 [c]ver 4 [d]Ge 17:7
ther Abraham.[a] Do not be afraid,[b] for I
am with you; I will bless you and will increase the number of your descendants[c]
for the sake of my servant Abraham."[d]
25Isaac built an altar[e] there and called 26:25 [e]Ge 12:7,8; 13:4,18; Ps 116:17
on the name of the LORD. There he
pitched his tent, and there his servants
dug a well.
26Meanwhile, Abimelech had come to
him from Gerar, with Ahuzzath his personal adviser and Phicol the command-
er of his forces.[f] 27Isaac asked them, 26:26 [f]Ge 21:22
"Why have you come to me, since you
were hostile to me and sent me away?[g]" 26:27 [g]ver 16

[a] 30 *Edom* means *red.* [b] 4 Or *seed* [c] 20 *Esek* means *dispute.* [d] 21 *Sitnah* means *opposition.* [e] 22 *Rehoboth* means *room.*

28They answered, "We saw clearly that
26:28 hGe 21:22 the LORD was with you;[h] so we said,
'There ought to be a sworn agreement
between us'—between us and you. Let
us make a treaty with you 29that you will
do us no harm, just as we did not molest
26:29 you but always treated you well and sent
iGe 24:31; you away in peace. And now you are
Ps 115:15 blessed by the LORD."[i]
26:30 30Isaac then made a feast[j] for them,
jGe 19:3 and they ate and drank. 31Early the next
26:31 morning the men swore an oath[k] to
kGe 21:31 each other. Then Isaac sent them on
their way, and they left him in peace.
32That day Isaac's servants came and
told him about the well they had dug.
They said, "We've found water!" 33He
26:33 called it Shibah,[a] and to this day the
lGe 21:14 name of the town has been Beersheba.[b][l]
34When Esau was forty years old,[m] he
26:34 mGe 25:20 married Judith daughter of Beeri the
nGe 28:9; 36:2 Hittite, and also Basemath daughter of
26:35 Elon the Hittite.[n] 35They were a source
oGe 27:46 of grief to Isaac and Rebekah.[o]

Jacob Gets Isaac's Blessing

27 When Isaac was old and his
eyes were so weak that he could
27:1 pGe 48:10; no longer see,[p] he called for Esau his
1Sa 3:2 older son[q] and said to him, "My son."
qGe 25:25 "Here I am," he answered.
27:2 2Isaac said, "I am now an old man and
rGe 47:29 don't know the day of my death.[r] 3Now
then, get your weapons—your quiver
27:3 and bow—and go out to the open coun-
sGe 25:27 try[s] to hunt some wild game for me.
27:4 4Prepare me the kind of tasty food I like
tver 10,25,31; Ge 49:28; and bring it to me to eat, so that I may
Dt 33:1; give you my blessing[t] before I die."
Heb 11:20 5Now Rebekah was listening as Isaac
spoke to his son Esau. When Esau left
for the open country to hunt game and
27:6 bring it back, 6Rebekah said to her son
uGe 25:28 Jacob,[u] "Look, I overheard your father
say to your brother Esau, 7'Bring me
some game and prepare me some tasty
food to eat, so that I may give you my
blessing in the presence of the LORD before I die.' 8Now, my son, listen carefully
27:8 vver 13,43 and do what I tell you:[v] 9Go out to the
flock and bring me two choice young
goats, so I can prepare some tasty food
for your father, just the way he likes it.
10Then take it to your father to eat, so
that he may give you his blessing before
he dies."
11Jacob said to Rebekah his mother,

"But my brother Esau is a hairy man,[w] 27:11
and I'm a man with smooth skin. wGe 25:25
12What if my father touches me?[x] I 27:12
would appear to be tricking him and xver 22
would bring down a curse on myself
rather than a blessing."
13His mother said to him, "My son, let
the curse fall on me.[y] Just do what I say;[z] 27:13 yMt 27:25
go and get them for me." zver 8
14So he went and got them and
brought them to his mother, and she
prepared some tasty food, just the way
his father liked it. 15Then Rebekah took
the best clothes[a] of Esau her older son, 27:15 aver 27
which she had in the house, and put
them on her younger son Jacob. 16She
also covered his hands and the smooth
part of his neck with the goatskins.
17Then she handed to her son Jacob the
tasty food and the bread she had made.
18He went to his father and said, "My
father."
"Yes, my son," he answered. "Who
is it?"
19Jacob said to his father, "I am Esau
your firstborn. I have done as you told
me. Please sit up and eat some of my
game so that you may give me your 27:19
blessing."[b] bver 4
20Isaac asked his son, "How did you
find it so quickly, my son?"
"The LORD your God gave me suc- 27:20
cess,[c]" he replied. cGe 24:12
21Then Isaac said to Jacob, "Come
near so I can touch you,[d] my son, to 27:21
know whether you really are my son dver 12
Esau or not."
22Jacob went close to his father Isaac,
who touched him and said, "The voice is
the voice of Jacob, but the hands are the
hands of Esau." 23He did not recognize
him, for his hands were hairy like those
of his brother Esau;[e] so he blessed him. 27:23 ever 16
24"Are you really my son Esau?" he asked.
"I am," he replied.
25Then he said, "My son, bring me
some of your game to eat, so that I may 27:25
give you my blessing."[f] fver 4
Jacob brought it to him and he ate;
and he brought some wine and he
drank. 26Then his father Isaac said to
him, "Come here, my son, and kiss me." 27:27
27So he went to him and kissed him[g]. gHeb 11:20

[a] 33 *Shibah* can mean *oath* or *seven*.
[b] 33 *Beersheba* can mean *well of the oath* or *well of seven*.

When Isaac caught the smell of his
27:27 h SS 4:11 clothes,[h] he blessed him and said,
i Ps 65:9-13

"Ah, the smell of my son
is like the smell of a field
that the LORD has blessed.[i]
27:28 j Dt 33:13 28 May God give you of heaven's dew[j]
k ver 39 and of earth's richness[k]—
l Ge 45:18; Nu 18:12; an abundance of grain and new
Dt 33:28 wine.[l]
27:29 29 May nations serve you
m Isa 45:14,23; 49:7,23 and peoples bow down to you.[m]
n Ge 9:25; 25:23; Be lord over your brothers,
37:7 o Ge 12:3; and may the sons of your
Nu 24:9; mother bow down to you.[n]
Zep 2:8 May those who curse you be cursed
and those who bless you be
blessed.[o]"

30 After Isaac finished blessing him
and Jacob had scarcely left his father's
presence, his brother Esau came in from
hunting. 31 He too prepared some tasty
food and brought it to his father. Then
he said to him, "My father, sit up and eat
27:31 some of my game, so that you may give
p ver 4 me your blessing."[p]
27:32 32 His father Isaac asked him, "Who
q ver 18 are you?"[q]

"I am your son," he answered, "your
firstborn, Esau."

33 Isaac trembled violently and said,
"Who was it, then, that hunted game
27:33 and brought it to me? I ate it just before
r ver 29; Ge 28:3, you came and I blessed him—and in-
4; Ro 11:29 deed he will be blessed![r]"
34 When Esau heard his father's words,
27:34 s Heb 12:17 he burst out with a loud and bitter cry[s]
and said to his father, "Bless me—me
too, my father!"
27:35 35 But he said, "Your brother came de-
t Jer 9:4; 12:6 ceitfully[t] and took your blessing."
27:36 36 Esau said, "Isn't he rightly named Ja-
u Ge 25:26 cob[a]?[u] He has deceived me these two
v Ge 25:33 times: He took my birthright,[v] and now
he's taken my blessing!" Then he asked,
"Haven't you reserved any blessing
for me?"

37 Isaac answered Esau, "I have made
him lord over you and have made all his
27:37 relatives his servants, and I have sus-
w ver 28 tained him with grain and new wine.[w]
So what can I possibly do for you, my
son?"

38 Esau said to his father, "Do you have
only one blessing, my father? Bless me
27:38 x Heb 12:17 too, my father!" Then Esau wept aloud.[x]
39 His father Isaac answered him,

"Your dwelling will be
away from the earth's richness, 27:39
away from the dew[y] of heaven y ver 28
above.
40 You will live by the sword 27:40
and you will serve[z] your brother.[a] z 2Sa 8:14 a Ge 25:23
But when you grow restless, b 2Ki 8:20-22
you will throw his yoke
from off your neck.[b]"

Jacob Flees to Laban

41 Esau held a grudge[c] against Jacob[d] 27:41 c Ge 37:4
because of the blessing his father had d Ge 32:11
given him. He said to himself, "The days e Ge 50:4,10
of mourning[e] for my father are near; f Ob 1:10
then I will kill my brother Jacob."[f]
42 When Rebekah was told what her
older son Esau had said, she sent for her
younger son Jacob and said to him,
"Your brother Esau is consoling himself
with the thought of killing you. 43 Now 27:43
then, my son, do what I say:[g] Flee at g ver 8
once to my brother Laban[h] in Haran.[i] h Ge 24:29 i Ge 11:31
44 Stay with him for a while[j] until your 27:44
brother's fury subsides. 45 When your j Ge 31:38,41
brother is no longer angry with you and 27:45
forgets what you did to him,[k] I'll send k ver 35
word for you to come back from there.
Why should I lose both of you in one
day?"
46 Then Rebekah said to Isaac, "I'm
disgusted with living because of these
Hittite women. If Jacob takes a wife
from among the women of this land,
from Hittite women like these, my life 27:46
will not be worth living."[l] l Ge 26:35

28 So Isaac called for Jacob and
blessed[b] him and commanded
him: "Do not marry a Canaanite 28:1
woman.[m] 2 Go at once to Paddan Aram,[c] m Ge 24:3
to the house of your mother's father Be- 28:2
thuel.[n] Take a wife for yourself there, n Ge 25:20
from among the daughters of Laban,
your mother's brother. 3 May God
Almighty[d][o] bless you and make you 28:3 o Ge 17:1
fruitful[p] and increase your numbers un- p Ge 17:6
til you become a community of peoples.
4 May he give you and your descendants 28:4
the blessing given to Abraham,[q] so that q Ge 12:2,3
you may take possession of the land r Ge 17:8
where you now live as an alien,[r] the land
God gave to Abraham." 5 Then Isaac sent
Jacob on his way, and he went to Paddan 28:5
Aram,[s] to Laban son of Bethuel the s Hos 12:12

[a] 36 *Jacob* means *he grasps the heel* (figuratively, *he deceives*). [b] 1 Or *greeted* [c] 2 That is, Northwest Mesopotamia; also in verses 5, 6 and 7
[d] 3 Hebrew *El-Shaddai*

DISCOVERY 9

HEAVEN'S OPEN DOOR

After Jacob had stolen the blessing from his brother Esau, he fled for his life (Genesis 27:41–46). That night as he lay, alone and vulnerable, under the stars, he experienced a remarkable dream—a stairway stretching from earth to heaven, and angels of God ascending and descending (Genesis 28:12). The dream reminded Jacob that the reality of God's presence encompassed much more than what he could see around him. The eternal dimension—heaven—exists as well, and it is closely connected to the life we know. God the Father wants us to be in relationship with him. That connection comes through his Son, Jesus (John 14:6); he is the "ladder" or mediator between God and humanity (1 Timothy 2:5).

In his dream Jacob also saw God standing at the top of the staircase (Genesis 28:13). God designed creation so that he could interact with it. He stands ready and constantly attentive—and even more, he speaks to us: "I will not leave you," he told Jacob. He had made a promise, and God fully intended to fulfill it (verse 15). What welcome words for a man alone, afraid for his life and on the run. Jacob had no family, no home, and yet the God of the universe was promising to accompany him, reminding Jacob that all the promises he'd ever made were still valid. Generations later Jesus would make the same promise to his disciples (Matthew 28:19–20), and it still applies to us as well (Philippians 1:6).

When Jacob awoke from the dream, he knew he had been in the very presence of God (Genesis 28:17), so he renamed the place *Beth-El*, which means "the house of God" (verse 19). Jacob is not the only person with whom God desires to interact. Throughout the Bible heaven "opens," and God is in daily relationship with his creation. God promised to open heaven when his people honored him and to overwhelm them with blessing (Malachi 3:10). Heaven opened again when John baptized Jesus (Mark 1:10) and Jesus used the stairway of Jacob's dream as a metaphor of himself, the stairway to God, predicting that his disciples would "see heaven open, and the angels of God ascending and descending on the Son of Man" (John 1:51). Stephen was the first man to be martyred for believing in Jesus, and we read that heaven opened to receive him (Acts 7:56). When Peter needed a reminder that God's truth was for Gentiles as well as Jews, God opened heaven to show him (Acts 10:11).

Each of us can personally experience what Jacob did—God's undivided attention and awesome presence. There is more to life than what we see with our physical eyes. Above and within all of our circumstances there is God, loving us, speaking to us and promising to stay with us. One day Jesus will return for his own, and heaven's door will be thrown open one last time—to remain open for all eternity (Revelation 19:11).

***Self-Discovery:** What particular experience, dream, memory, book, Scripture passage, song or poem serves to remind you of God's nearness?*

GO TO DISCOVERY 10 ON PAGE 48

28:5 [t]Ge 24:29 Aramean, the brother of Rebekah,[t] who
was the mother of Jacob and Esau.
6Now Esau learned that Isaac had
blessed Jacob and had sent him to Paddan Aram to take a wife from there, and
that when he blessed him he commanded him, "Do not marry a Canaanite
28:6 [u]ver 1 woman,"[u] 7and that Jacob had obeyed
his father and mother and had gone to
28:8 Paddan Aram. 8Esau then realized how
[v]Ge 24:3 displeasing the Canaanite women[v] were
[w]Ge 26:35 to his father Isaac;[w] 9so he went to Ishmael and married Mahalath, the sister
28:9 [x]Ge 25:13 of Nebaioth[x] and daughter of Ishmael
[y]Ge 26:34 son of Abraham, in addition to the wives
he already had.[y]

Jacob's Dream at Bethel

28:10 [z]Ge 11:31 10Jacob left Beersheba and set out for
Haran.[z] 11When he reached a certain
place, he stopped for the night because
the sun had set. Taking one of the stones
there, he put it under his head and lay
28:12 [a]Ge 20:3 down to sleep. 12He had a dream[a] in
[b]Jn 1:51 which he saw a stairway[a] resting on the
earth, with its top reaching to heaven,
and the angels of God were ascending
28:13 [c]Ge 12:7; 35:7, and descending on it.[b] 13There above it[b]
9; 48:3 stood the LORD,[c] and he said: "I am the
[d]Ge 26:24 LORD, the God of your father Abraham
[e]Ge 13:15; 35:12 and the God of Isaac.[d] I will give you and
your descendants the land[e] on which
you are lying. 14Your descendants will be
28:14 [f]Ge 26:4 like the dust of the earth, and you[f] will
[g]Ge 13:14 spread out to the west and to the east, to
the north and to the south.[g] All peoples
on earth will be blessed through you and

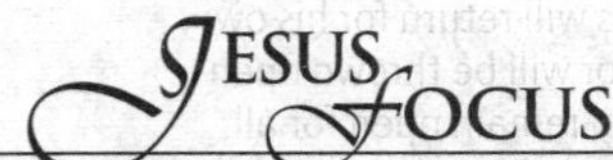

DREAM OF PROMISE

Jacob ran away from his family in order to save his life after his brother Esau had vowed to kill him (Genesis 27:41–43). Traveling north to Haran, he stopped at Luz, a place he renamed *Bethel*, or "house of God." There he met God personally for the first time (Genesis 28:10–15). He dreamed about a stairway that reached into heaven. To people in ancient cultures this kind of stairway symbolized access into God's presence. In the New Testament Jesus later referred to himself as our avenue of access to God. In John 1:51 Jesus used language similar to the Genesis account of Jacob's dream to illustrate his role as the only mediator between God and people (see also 1 Timothy 2:5).

your offspring.[h] 15I am with you[i] and will 28:14
watch over you[j] wherever you go, and I [h]Ge 12:3; 18:18; 22:18; Gal 3:8
will bring you back to this land. I will not
leave you[k] until I have done what I have 28:15
promised you."[l] [i]Ge 26:3; 48:21 [j]Nu 6:24;
16When Jacob awoke from his sleep, Ps 121:5,7-8 [k]Dt 31:6,8
he thought, "Surely the LORD is in this [l]Nu 23:19
place, and I was not aware of it." 17He
was afraid and said, "How awesome is 28:17
this place![m] This is none other than the [m]Ex 3:5;
house of God; this is the gate of heaven." Jos 5:15
18Early the next morning Jacob took
the stone he had placed under his head 28:18
and set it up as a pillar[n] and poured oil [n]Ge 35:14
on top of it.[o] 19He called that place Beth- [o]Lev 8:11
el,[c] though the city used to be called 28:19
Luz.[p] [p]Jdg 1:23,26
20Then Jacob made a vow,[q] saying, "If 28:20
God will be with me and will watch over [q]Ge 31:13; Jdg 11:30;
me[r] on this journey I am taking and will 2Sa 15:8 [r]ver 15
give me food to eat and clothes to wear
21so that I return safely[s] to my father's 28:21 [s]Jdg 11:31
house, then the LORD[d] will be my God[t] [t]Dt 26:17
22and[e] this stone that I have set up as a 28:22
pillar will be God's house,[u] and of all that [u]Ge 35:7,14 [v]Ge 14:20;
you give me I will give you a tenth.[v]" Lev 27:30

Jacob Arrives in Paddan Aram

29 Then Jacob continued on his
journey and came to the land of 29:1
the eastern peoples.[w] 2There he saw a [w]Jdg 6:3,33
well in the field, with three flocks of
sheep lying near it because the flocks
were watered from that well. The stone
over the mouth of the well was large.
3When all the flocks were gathered there,
the shepherds would roll the stone away
from the well's mouth and water the
sheep. Then they would return the stone
to its place over the mouth of the well.
4Jacob asked the shepherds, "My
brothers, where are you from?"
"We're from Haran,[x]" they replied. 29:4 [x]Ge 28:10
5He said to them, "Do you know La-
ban, Nahor's grandson?"
"Yes, we know him," they answered.
6Then Jacob asked them, "Is he well?"
"Yes, he is," they said, "and here comes
his daughter Rachel with the sheep."
7"Look," he said, "the sun is still high;
it is not time for the flocks to be gathered. Water the sheep and take them
back to pasture."
8"We can't," they replied, "until all the

[a] 12 Or *ladder* [b] 13 Or *There beside him* [c] 19 *Bethel* means *house of God.* [d] 20,21 Or *Since God . . . father's house, the* LORD [e] 21,22 Or *house, and the* LORD *will be my God,* 22*then*

flocks are gathered and the stone has
been rolled away from the mouth of the
well. Then we will water the sheep.”
29:9 [9]While he was still talking with them,
[y]Ex 2:16 Rachel came with her father’s sheep,[y] for
she was a shepherdess. [10]When Jacob
saw Rachel daughter of Laban, his
mother’s brother, and Laban’s sheep, he
went over and rolled the stone away
29:10 [z]Ex 2:17 from the mouth of the well and watered
his uncle’s sheep.[z] [11]Then Jacob kissed
29:11 [a]Ge 33:4 Rachel and began to weep aloud.[a] [12]He
had told Rachel that he was a relative[b] of
29:12 [b]Ge 13:8; 14:14, her father and a son of Rebekah. So she
16 [c]Ge 24:28 ran and told her father.[c]
29:13 [13]As soon as Laban[d] heard the news
[d]Ge 24:29 about Jacob, his sister’s son, he hurried
to meet him. He embraced him and
kissed him and brought him to his
29:14 [e]Ge 2:23; home, and there Jacob told him all these
Jdg 9:2; things. [14]Then Laban said to him, “You
2Sa 19:12-13 are my own flesh and blood.”[e]

Jacob Marries Leah and Rachel

After Jacob had stayed with him for a
whole month, [15]Laban said to him, “Just
because you are a relative of mine,
should you work for me for nothing? Tell
me what your wages should be.”
[16]Now Laban had two daughters; the
name of the older was Leah, and the
name of the younger was Rachel. [17]Leah
had weak[a] eyes, but Rachel was lovely in
form, and beautiful. [18]Jacob was in love
with Rachel and said, “I’ll work for you
seven years in return for your younger 29:18
daughter Rachel.”[f] [f]Hos 12:12
[19]Laban said, “It’s better that I give her
to you than to some other man. Stay
here with me.” [20]So Jacob served seven
years to get Rachel, but they seemed like
only a few days to him because of his 29:20 [g]SS 8:7;
love for her.[g] Hos 12:12
[21]Then Jacob said to Laban, “Give me
my wife. My time is completed, and I
want to lie with her.[h]” 29:21 [h]Jdg 15:1
[22]So Laban brought together all the
people of the place and gave a feast.[i] 29:22 [i]Jdg 14:10;
[23]But when evening came, he took his Jn 2:1-2
daughter Leah and gave her to Jacob,
and Jacob lay with her. [24]And Laban gave
his servant girl Zilpah to his daughter as
her maidservant.
[25]When morning came, there was
Leah! So Jacob said to Laban, “What is 29:25 [j]Ge 12:18
this you have done to me?[j] I served you [k]Ge 27:36
for Rachel, didn’t I? Why have you deceived me?[k]”
[26]Laban replied, “It is not our custom
here to give the younger daughter in
marriage before the older one. [27]Finish 29:27
this daughter’s bridal week;[l] then we will [l]Jdg 14:12
give you the younger one also, in return
for another seven years of work.”
[28]And Jacob did so. He finished the
week with Leah, and then Laban gave
him his daughter Rachel to be his wife.
[29]Laban gave his servant girl Bilhah[m] to 29:29
his daughter Rachel as her maidser- [m]Ge 30:3
vant.[n] [30]Jacob lay with Rachel also, and [n]Ge 16:1
he loved Rachel more than Leah.[o] And 29:30 [o]ver 16
he worked for Laban another seven [p]Ge 31:41
years.[p]

Jacob’s Children

[31]When the LORD saw that Leah was 29:31
not loved,[q] he opened her womb,[r] but [q]Dt 21:15-17 [r]Ge 11:30; 30:1;
Rachel was barren. [32]Leah became preg- Ps 127:3
nant and gave birth to a son. She named 29:32
him Reuben,[b] for she said, “It is because [s]Ge 16:11;
the LORD has seen my misery.[s] Surely my 31:42; Ex 4:31;
husband will love me now.” Dt 26:7; Ps 25:18
[33]She conceived again, and when she
gave birth to a son she said, “Because
the LORD heard that I am not loved, he
gave me this one too.” So she named him 29:33
Simeon.[c][t] [t]Ge 34:25; 49:5

[a] 17 Or *delicate* [b] 32 *Reuben* sounds like the Hebrew for *he has seen my misery*; the name means *see, a son.* [c] 33 *Simeon* probably means *one who hears.*

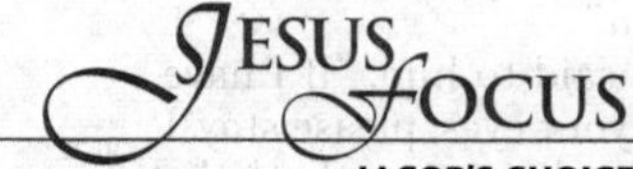

JACOB’S CHOICE. GOD’S CHOICE

While he was in Haran Jacob fell in love with Rachel, the daughter of Laban, his uncle, and asked for permission to marry her (Genesis 29:18). Laban agreed—but only if Jacob would work for him for seven years to pay the marriage dowry. After the seven years, however, Laban deceived his nephew by switching brides, and Leah, Rachel’s sister, married Jacob instead. Jacob, the deceiver, had finally been duped himself! Even though she was not Jacob’s choice, Leah represented God’s choice for Jacob. Despite the fact that Jacob had been tricked into marrying her, Leah became a part of the family line of the promised Messiah: Leah’s son Judah would later receive the birthright and the place of leadership among the 12 sons of Israel (Genesis 49:9–10). In fact, both David and Jesus would be direct descendants of Leah through Judah.

[34]Again she conceived, and when she
gave birth to a son she said, "Now at last
29:34 [u]Ge 30:20; 1Sa 1:2-4 [v]Ge 49:5-7 my husband will become attached to
me,[u] because I have borne him three
sons." So he was named Levi.[a][v]
[35]She conceived again, and when she
gave birth to a son she said, "This time I
29:35 [w]Ge 49:8; Mt 1:2-3 will praise the LORD." So she named him
Judah.[b][w] Then she stopped having chil-
dren.

30 When Rachel saw that she was
not bearing Jacob any chil-
30:1 [x]Ge 29:31; 1Sa 1:5-6 [y]Lev 18:18 dren,[x] she became jealous of her sister.[y]
So she said to Jacob, "Give me children,
or I'll die!"
[2]Jacob became angry with her and
30:2 [z]Ge 16:2; 20:18; 29:31 said, "Am I in the place of God, who has
kept you from having children?"[z]
[3]Then she said, "Here is Bilhah, my
maidservant. Sleep with her so that she
30:3 [a]Ge 16:2 can bear children for me and that
through her I too can build a family."[a]
30:4 [b]ver 9,18 [c]Ge 16:3-4 [4]So she gave him her servant Bilhah
as a wife.[b] Jacob slept with her,[c] [5]and she
became pregnant and bore him a son.
[6]Then Rachel said, "God has vindicated
30:6 [d]Ps 35:24; 43:1; La 3:59 [e]Ge 49:16-17 me;[d] he has listened to my plea and giv-
en me a son." Because of this she named
him Dan.[c][e]
[7]Rachel's servant Bilhah conceived
again and bore Jacob a second son.
[8]Then Rachel said, "I have had a great
30:8 [f]Hos 12:3-4 [g]Ge 49:21 struggle with my sister, and I have won."[f]
So she named him Naphtali.[d][g]
[9]When Leah saw that she had stopped
having children, she took her maidservant Zilpah and gave her to Jacob as a
30:9 [h]ver 4 wife.[h] [10]Leah's servant Zilpah bore Jacob
30:11 [i]Ge 49:19 a son. [11]Then Leah said, "What good fortune!"[e] So she named him Gad.[f][i]
[12]Leah's servant Zilpah bore Jacob a
30:13 [j]Ps 127:3 [k]Pr 31:28; Lk 1:48 [l]Ge 49:20 second son. [13]Then Leah said, "How
happy I am! The women will call me[j]
happy."[k] So she named him Asher.[g][l]
[14]During wheat harvest, Reuben went
30:14 [m]SS 7:13 out into the fields and found some man-
drake plants,[m] which he brought to his
mother Leah. Rachel said to Leah,
"Please give me some of your son's mandrakes."
[15]But she said to her, "Wasn't it
30:15 [n]Nu 16:9,13 enough[n] that you took away my husband? Will you take my son's mandrakes
too?"
"Very well," Rachel said, "he can sleep
with you tonight in return for your son's
mandrakes."
[16]So when Jacob came in from the
fields that evening, Leah went out to
meet him. "You must sleep with me," she
said. "I have hired you with my son's
mandrakes." So he slept with her that
night.
[17]God listened to Leah,[o] and she be- 30:17 [o]Ge 25:21
came pregnant and bore Jacob a fifth
son. [18]Then Leah said, "God has reward-
ed me for giving my maidservant to my 30:18 [p]Ge 49:14
husband." So she named him Issachar.[h][p]
[19]Leah conceived again and bore Jacob a sixth son. [20]Then Leah said, "God
has presented me with a precious gift.
This time my husband will treat me with
honor, because I have borne him six 30:20 [q]Ge 35:23; 49:13; Mt 4:13
sons." So she named him Zebulun.[i][q]
[21]Some time later she gave birth to a
daughter and named her Dinah. 30:22 [r]Ge 8:1; 1Sa 1:19-20 [s]Ge 29:31
[22]Then God remembered Rachel;[r] he
listened to her and opened her womb.[s]
[23]She became pregnant and gave birth 30:23 [t]ver 6 [u]Isa 4:1; Lk 1:25
to a son[t] and said, "God has taken away
my disgrace."[u] [24]She named him Jo-
seph,[j][v] and said, "May the LORD add to 30:24 [v]Ge 35:24; 37:2; 39:1; 49:22-26 [w]Ge 35:17
me another son."[w]

Jacob's Flocks Increase

[25]After Rachel gave birth to Joseph, Ja- 30:25 [x]Ge 24:54
cob said to Laban, "Send me on my way[x]
so I can go back to my own homeland.
[26]Give me my wives and children, for 30:26 [y]Ge 29:20,30; Hos 12:12
whom I have served you,[y] and I will be
on my way. You know how much work
I've done for you."
[27]But Laban said to him, "If I have
found favor in your eyes, please stay. I 30:27 [z]Ge 26:24; 39:3,5
have learned by divination that[k] the
LORD has blessed me because of you."[z]
[28]He added, "Name your wages,[a] and I 30:28 [a]Ge 29:15
will pay them."
[29]Jacob said to him, "You know how I 30:29 [b]Ge 31:6 [c]Ge 31:38-40
have worked for you[b] and how your live-
stock has fared under my care.[c] [30]The
little you had before I came has increased greatly, and the LORD has
blessed you wherever I have been. But
now, when may I do something for my
own household?[d]" 30:30 [d]1Ti 5:8

[a] 34 *Levi* sounds like and may be derived from the Hebrew for *attached.* [b] 35 *Judah* sounds like and may be derived from the Hebrew for *praise.* [c] 6 *Dan* here means *he has vindicated.* [d] 8 *Naphtali* means *my struggle.* [e] 11 Or *"A troop is coming!"* [f] 11 *Gad* can mean *good fortune* or *a troop.* [g] 13 *Asher* means *happy.* [h] 18 *Issachar* sounds like the Hebrew for *reward.* [i] 20 *Zebulun* probably means *honor.* [j] 24 *Joseph* means *may he add.* [k] 27 Or possibly *have become rich and*

31"What shall I give you?" he asked.

"Don't give me anything," Jacob replied. "But if you will do this one thing for me, I will go on tending your flocks and watching over them: 32Let me go through all your flocks today and remove from them every speckled or spotted sheep, every dark-colored lamb and every spotted or speckled goat.[e] They will be my wages. 33And my honesty will testify for me in the future, whenever you check on the wages you have paid me. Any goat in my possession that is not speckled or spotted, or any lamb that is not dark-colored, will be considered stolen."

34"Agreed," said Laban. "Let it be as you have said." 35That same day he removed all the male goats that were streaked or spotted, and all the speckled or spotted female goats (all that had white on them) and all the dark-colored lambs, and he placed them in the care of his sons.[f] 36Then he put a three-day journey between himself and Jacob, while Jacob continued to tend the rest of Laban's flocks.

37Jacob, however, took fresh-cut branches from poplar, almond and plane trees and made white stripes on them by peeling the bark and exposing the white inner wood of the branches. 38Then he placed the peeled branches in all the watering troughs, so that they would be directly in front of the flocks when they came to drink. When the flocks were in heat and came to drink, 39they mated in front of the branches. And they bore young that were streaked or speckled or spotted. 40Jacob set apart the young of the flock by themselves, but made the rest face the streaked and dark-colored animals that belonged to Laban. Thus he made separate flocks for himself and did not put them with Laban's animals. 41Whenever the stronger females were in heat, Jacob would place the branches in the troughs in front of the animals so they would mate near the branches, 42but if the animals were weak, he would not place them there. So the weak animals went to Laban and the strong ones to Jacob. 43In this way the man grew exceedingly prosperous and came to own large flocks, and maidservants and menservants, and camels and donkeys.[g]

30:32 [e] Ge 31:8,12
30:35 [f] Ge 31:1
30:43 [g] ver 30; Ge 12:16; 13:2; 24:35; 26:13-14

Jacob Flees From Laban

31 Jacob heard that Laban's sons were saying, "Jacob has taken everything our father owned and has gained all this wealth from what belonged to our father." 2And Jacob noticed that Laban's attitude toward him was not what it had been.

3Then the LORD said to Jacob, "Go back[h] to the land of your fathers and to your relatives, and I will be with you."[i]

4So Jacob sent word to Rachel and Leah to come out to the fields where his flocks were. 5He said to them, "I see that your father's attitude toward me is not what it was before, but the God of my father has been with me.[j] 6You know that I've worked for your father with all my strength,[k] 7yet your father has cheated me by changing my wages ten times.[l] However, God has not allowed him to harm me.[m] 8If he said, 'The speckled ones will be your wages,' then all the flocks gave birth to speckled young; and if he said, 'The streaked ones will be your wages,'[n] then all the flocks bore streaked young. 9So God has taken away your father's livestock and has given them to me.[o]

10"In breeding season I once had a dream in which I looked up and saw that the male goats mating with the flock were streaked, speckled or spotted. 11The angel of God[p] said to me in the dream, 'Jacob.' I answered, 'Here I am.' 12And he said, 'Look up and see that all the male goats mating with the flock are streaked, speckled or spotted, for I have seen all that Laban has been doing to you.[q] 13I am the God of Bethel,[r] where you anointed a pillar and where you made a vow to me. Now leave this land at once and go back to your native land.[s]' "

14Then Rachel and Leah replied, "Do we still have any share in the inheritance of our father's estate? 15Does he not regard us as foreigners? Not only has he sold us, but he has used up what was paid for us.[t] 16Surely all the wealth that God took away from our father belongs to us and our children. So do whatever God has told you."

17Then Jacob put his children and his wives on camels, 18and he drove all his livestock ahead of him, along with all the goods he had accumulated in Pad-

31:3 [h] ver 13; Ge 32:9 [i] Ge 21:22; 26:3; 28:15
31:5 [j] Ge 21:22; 26:3
31:6 [k] Ge 30:29
31:7 [l] ver 41; Job 19:3 [m] ver 52; Ps 37:28; 105:14
31:8 [n] Ge 30:32
31:9 [o] ver 1,16; Ge 30:42
31:11 [p] Ge 16:7; 48:16
31:12 [q] Ex 3:7
31:13 [r] Ge 28:10-22 [s] ver 3; Ge 32:9
31:15 [t] Ge 29:20

dan Aram,[a] to go to his father Isaac[u] in
the land of Canaan.[v]
19When Laban had gone to shear his
sheep, Rachel stole her father's household gods.[w] 20Moreover, Jacob deceived[x]
Laban the Aramean by not telling him
he was running away.[y] 21So he fled with
all he had, and crossing the River,[b] he
headed for the hill country of Gilead.[z]

Laban Pursues Jacob

22On the third day Laban was told
that Jacob had fled. 23Taking his relatives
with him, he pursued Jacob for seven
days and caught up with him in the hill
country of Gilead. 24Then God came to
Laban the Aramean in a dream at night
and said to him,[a] "Be careful not to say
anything to Jacob, either good or bad."[b]
25Jacob had pitched his tent in the hill
country of Gilead when Laban overtook
him, and Laban and his relatives camped
there too. 26Then Laban said to Jacob,
"What have you done? You've deceived
me,[c] and you've carried off my daughters
like captives in war.[d] 27Why did you run
off secretly and deceive me? Why didn't
you tell me, so I could send you away
with joy and singing to the music of tambourines[e] and harps?[f] 28You didn't even
let me kiss my grandchildren and my
daughters good-by.[g] You have done a
foolish thing. 29I have the power to harm
you;[h] but last night the God of your father[i] said to me, 'Be careful not to say
anything to Jacob, either good or bad.'
30Now you have gone off because you
longed to return to your father's house.
But why did you steal my gods?[j]"
31Jacob answered Laban, "I was afraid,
because I thought you would take your
daughters away from me by force. 32But
if you find anyone who has your gods, he
shall not live.[k] In the presence of our relatives, see for yourself whether there is
anything of yours here with me; and if
so, take it." Now Jacob did not know that
Rachel had stolen the gods.
33So Laban went into Jacob's tent and
into Leah's tent and into the tent of the
two maidservants, but he found nothing.
After he came out of Leah's tent, he entered Rachel's tent. 34Now Rachel had
taken the household gods and put them
inside her camel's saddle and was sitting
on them. Laban searched[l] through everything in the tent but found nothing.

31:18 [u] Ge 35:27 [v] Ge 10:19
31:19 [w] ver 30,32,34-35; Ge 35:2; Jdg 17:5; 1Sa 19:13; Hos 3:4
31:20 [x] Ge 27:36 [y] ver 27
31:21 [z] Ge 37:25
31:24 [a] Ge 20:3; Job 33:15 [b] Ge 24:50
31:26 [c] Ge 27:36 [d] 1Sa 30:2-3
31:27 [e] Ex 15:20 [f] Ge 4:21
31:28 [g] ver 55
31:29 [h] ver 7 [i] ver 53
31:30 [j] ver 19; Jdg 18:24
31:32 [k] Ge 44:9
31:34 [l] ver 37; Ge 44:12

35Rachel said to her father, "Don't be
angry, my lord, that I cannot stand up in
your presence;[m] I'm having my period."
So he searched but could not find the
household gods.
36Jacob was angry and took Laban to
task. "What is my crime?" he asked Laban. "What sin have I committed that
you hunt me down? 37Now that you have
searched through all my goods, what
have you found that belongs to your
household? Put it here in front of your
relatives[n] and mine, and let them judge
between the two of us.
38"I have been with you for twenty
years now. Your sheep and goats have
not miscarried, nor have I eaten rams
from your flocks. 39I did not bring you
animals torn by wild beasts; I bore the
loss myself. And you demanded payment from me for whatever was stolen
by day or night.[o] 40This was my situation: The heat consumed me in the daytime and the cold at night, and sleep fled
from my eyes. 41It was like this for the
twenty years I was in your household. I
worked for you fourteen years for your
two daughters[p] and six years for your
flocks, and you changed my wages ten
times.[q] 42If the God of my father,[r] the
God of Abraham and the Fear of Isaac,[s]
had not been with me,[t] you would surely have sent me away empty-handed.
But God has seen my hardship and the
toil of my hands,[u] and last night he rebuked you."
43Laban answered Jacob, "The women
are my daughters, the children are my
children, and the flocks are my flocks. All
you see is mine. Yet what can I do today
about these daughters of mine, or about
the children they have borne? 44Come
now, let's make a covenant,[v] you and I,
and let it serve as a witness between us."[w]
45So Jacob took a stone and set it up
as a pillar.[x] 46He said to his relatives,
"Gather some stones." So they took
stones and piled them in a heap, and
they ate there by the heap. 47Laban
called it Jegar Sahadutha,[c] and Jacob
called it Galeed.[d]
48Laban said, "This heap is a witness
between you and me today." That is why
it was called Galeed. 49It was also called

31:35 [m] Ex 20:12; Lev 19:3,32
31:37 [n] ver 23
31:39 [o] Ex 22:13
31:41 [p] Ge 29:30 [q] ver 7
31:42 [r] ver 5; Ex 3:15; 1Ch 12:17 [s] ver 53; Isa 8:13 [t] Ps 124:1-2 [u] Ge 29:32
31:44 [v] Ge 21:27; 26:28 [w] Jos 24:27
31:45 [x] Ge 28:18

[a] *18* That is, Northwest Mesopotamia [b] *21* That is, the Euphrates [c] *47* The Aramaic *Jegar Sahadutha* means *witness heap.* [d] *47* The Hebrew *Galeed* means *witness heap.*

31:49 [y]Jdg 11:29; Mizpah,[a][y] because he said, "May the
1Sa 7:5-6 LORD keep watch between you and me
when we are away from each other. [50]If
you mistreat my daughters or if you take
any wives besides my daughters, even
31:50 though no one is with us, remember that
[z]Jer 29:23; 42:5 God is a witness[z] between you and me."

31:51 [51]Laban also said to Jacob, "Here is
[a]Ge 28:18 this heap, and here is this pillar[a] I have
31:52 set up between you and me. [52]This heap
[b]Ge 21:30 is a witness, and this pillar is a witness,[b]
[c]ver 7; Ge 26:29 that I will not go past this heap to your
side to harm you and that you will not
go past this heap and pillar to my side to
31:53 harm me.[c] [53]May the God of Abraham[d]
[d]Ge 28:13 [e]Ge 16:5 and the God of Nahor, the God of their
[f]Ge 21:23,27 father, judge between us."[e]
[g]ver 42 So Jacob took an oath[f] in the name of
the Fear of his father Isaac.[g] [54]He offered
a sacrifice there in the hill country and
invited his relatives to a meal. After they
had eaten, they spent the night there.

[55]Early the next morning Laban
kissed his grandchildren and his daugh-
31:55 [h]ver 28 ters[h] and blessed them. Then he left and
[i]Ge 18:33; 30:25 returned home.[i]

Jacob Prepares to Meet Esau

32:1 [j]Ge 16:11; **32** Jacob also went on his way, and
2Ki 6:16-17; the angels of God[j] met him.
Ps 34:7; 91:11; [2]When Jacob saw them, he said, "This is
Heb 1:14 the camp of God!"[k] So he named that
32:2 [k]Ge 28:17 place Mahanaim.[b][l]
[l]2Sa 2:8,29 [3]Jacob sent messengers ahead of him
32:3 to his brother Esau[m] in the land of Seir,
[m]Ge 27:41-42 the country of Edom.[n] [4]He instructed
[n]Ge 25:30; them: "This is what you are to say to my
36:8,9 master Esau: 'Your servant Jacob says, I
have been staying with Laban and have
remained there till now. [5]I have cattle
and donkeys, sheep and goats, menser-
32:5 vants and maidservants.[o] Now I am
[o]Ge 12:16; 30:43 [p]Ge 33:8, sending this message to my lord, that I
10,15 may find favor in your eyes.[p]' "

[6]When the messengers returned to
Jacob, they said, "We went to your
brother Esau, and now he is coming to
32:6 meet you, and four hundred men are
[q]Ge 33:1 with him."[q]

32:7 [7]In great fear[r] and distress Jacob di-
[r]ver 11 vided the people who were with him
into two groups,[c] and the flocks and
herds and camels as well. [8]He thought,
"If Esau comes and attacks one group,[d]
the group[d] that is left may escape."

[9]Then Jacob prayed, "O God of my fa-
32:9 [s]Ge 28:13; 31:42 ther Abraham, God of my father Isaac,[s]
O LORD, who said to me, 'Go back to
your country and your relatives, and I 32:9
will make you prosper,'[t] [10]I am unworthy [t]Ge 31:13
of all the kindness and faithfulness[u] you 32:10
have shown your servant. I had only my [u]Ge 24:27
staff when I crossed this Jordan, but now
I have become two groups. [11]Save me, I
pray, from the hand of my brother Esau,
for I am afraid he will come and attack 32:11
me,[v] and also the mothers with their [v]Ps 59:2 [w]Ge 27:41
children.[w] [12]But you have said, 'I will
surely make you prosper and will make 32:12
your descendants like the sand[x] of the [x]Ge 22:17 [y]Ge 28:13-15;
sea, which cannot be counted.[y]' " Hos 1:10; Ro 9:27

[13]He spent the night there, and from
what he had with him he selected a gift[z] 32:13
for his brother Esau: [14]two hundred fe- [z]Ge 43:11,15, 25,26; Pr 18:16
male goats and twenty male goats, two
hundred ewes and twenty rams, [15]thirty
female camels with their young, forty
cows and ten bulls, and twenty female
donkeys and ten male donkeys. [16]He put
them in the care of his servants, each
herd by itself, and said to his servants,
"Go ahead of me, and keep some space
between the herds."

[17]He instructed the one in the lead:
"When my brother Esau meets you and
asks, 'To whom do you belong, and
where are you going, and who owns all
these animals in front of you?' [18]then
you are to say, 'They belong to your ser-
vant[a] Jacob. They are a gift sent to my 32:18 [a]Ge 18:3
lord Esau, and he is coming behind us.' "

[19]He also instructed the second, the
third and all the others who followed the
herds: "You are to say the same thing to
Esau when you meet him. [20]And be sure
to say, 'Your servant Jacob is coming behind us.' " For he thought, "I will pacify
him with these gifts I am sending on
ahead; later, when I see him, perhaps he 32:20
will receive me."[b] [21]So Jacob's gifts went [b]Ge 33:10; Pr 21:14
on ahead of him, but he himself spent
the night in the camp.

Jacob Wrestles With God

[22]That night Jacob got up and took his
two wives, his two maidservants and his
eleven sons and crossed the ford of the 32:22
Jabbok.[c] [23]After he had sent them across [c]Dt 2:37; 3:16;
the stream, he sent over all his posses- Jos 12:2
sions. [24]So Jacob was left alone, and a 32:24
man[d] wrestled with him till daybreak. [d]Ge 18:2

[a]49 *Mizpah* means *watchtower.* [b]2 *Mahanaim* means *two camps.* [c]7 Or *camps;* also in verse 10 [d]8 Or *camp*

DISCOVERY 10

Wrestling With God

Jacob had a second amazing dream in which God revealed to him that there is more to life and to God than what we can see around us (see Genesis 28:10–22). And before he was reunited with his brother Esau, Jacob had another unusual experience.

Jacob was afraid to meet his brother: The last time they had been together Esau had threatened to kill him (Genesis 27:41). True, Jacob had been away for 20 years, but had those years mellowed Esau's anger or fueled his grudge into full-blown hatred?

The night before the anticipated reunion a man came and wrestled with Jacob. Jacob struggled with all his strength. He may at first have thought that his unidentified challenger was Esau or someone sent by his brother to murder him under the cover of darkness. But Jacob eventually realized that the "man" was God himself and refused to stop wrestling until God had blessed him. And God did bless him! As part of that blessing God changed Jacob's name to *Israel*, which means "he struggles with God." To this day the Jewish nation retains that name—and it is still a nation that struggles with God.

Jacob's new name also implied a new identity in terms of his relationship with God. God may not change a person's name with every encounter, but there is *always* change. Second Corinthians 5:17 tells us that, when we commit our lives to Jesus, he changes us into someone brand-new: "If anyone is in Christ, he is a new creation; the old has gone, the new has come."

Paul in his letter to Titus referred to such a radical change as the "washing of rebirth": "But when the kindness and love of God our Savior appeared, he saved us, not because of righteous things we had done, but because of his mercy. He saved us through the washing of rebirth and renewal by the Holy Spirit, whom he poured out on us generously through Jesus Christ our Savior, so that, having been justified by his grace, we might become heirs having the hope of eternal life" (Titus 3:4–7).

Jacob was altered forever, so he named the place where he and God had wrestled *Peniel*, which means "face of God" (Genesis 32:30). Each of us needs our own "Peniel," a place to meet with God, wrestle with him and come away changed.

And God has given us just such a place—the Bible. In his Word we can meet him, get to know him and come away forever changed. In the Bible we have the awesome opportunity to meet God face-to-face! He tells us who he is and what he wants from us and even divulges his plan for his creation (Luke 16:27–31).

***Self-Discovery:** When in your life have you "wrestled" with God and come away changed?*

GO TO DISCOVERY 11 ON PAGE 52

25When the man saw that he could not
overpower him, he touched the socket
32:25 e ver 32 of Jacob's hip[e] so that his hip was
wrenched as he wrestled with the man.
26Then the man said, "Let me go, for it is
daybreak."
32:26 But Jacob replied, "I will not let you go
f Hos 12:4 unless you bless me."[f]
27The man asked him, "What is your
name?"
"Jacob," he answered.
32:28 28Then the man said, "Your name will
g Ge 17:5; 35:10; no longer be Jacob, but Israel,[a g] because
1Ki 18:31 you have struggled with God and with
men and have overcome."
32:29 29Jacob said, "Please tell me your
h Jdg 13:17 name."[h]
i Jdg 13:18 But he replied, "Why do you ask my
j Ge 35:9 name?"[i] Then he blessed[j] him there.
32:30 30So Jacob called the place Peniel,[b]
k Ge 16:13; saying, "It is because I saw God face to
Ex 24:11; face,[k] and yet my life was spared."
Nu 12:8; 31The sun rose above him as he
Jdg 6:22; 13:22 passed Peniel,[c] and he was limping because of his hip. 32Therefore to this day
the Israelites do not eat the tendon attached to the socket of the hip, because
the socket of Jacob's hip was touched
near the tendon.

Jacob Meets Esau

33 Jacob looked up and there was
Esau, coming with his four
33:1 l Ge 32:6 hundred men;[l] so he divided the children among Leah, Rachel and the two
maidservants. 2He put the maidservants
and their children in front, Leah and her
children next, and Rachel and Joseph in
33:3 the rear. 3He himself went on ahead and
m Ge 18:2; 42:6 bowed down to the ground[m] seven
times as he approached his brother.
4But Esau ran to meet Jacob and embraced him; he threw his arms around
33:4 his neck and kissed him. And they
n Ge 45:14-15 wept.[n] 5Then Esau looked up and saw
the women and children. "Who are
these with you?" he asked.
Jacob answered, "They are the chil-
33:5 o Ge 48:9; dren God has graciously given your ser-
Ps 127:3; Isa 8:18 vant.[o]"
6Then the maidservants and their
children approached and bowed down.
7Next, Leah and her children came and
bowed down. Last of all came Joseph
and Rachel, and they too bowed down.
33:8 8Esau asked, "What do you mean by
p Ge 32:14-16 all these droves I met?"[p]
"To find favor in your eyes, my lord,"[q] 33:8 q Ge 24:9; 32:5
he said.
9But Esau said, "I already have plenty,
my brother. Keep what you have for
yourself."
10"No, please!" said Jacob. "If I have
found favor in your eyes, accept this gift
from me. For to see your face is like see- 33:10 r Ge 16:13
ing the face of God,[r] now that you have s Ge 32:20
received me favorably.[s] 11Please accept 33:11
the present[t] that was brought to you, for t 1Sa 25:27
God has been gracious to me[u] and I have u Ge 30:43
all I need." And because Jacob insisted,
Esau accepted it.
12Then Esau said, "Let us be on our
way; I'll accompany you."
13But Jacob said to him, "My lord
knows that the children are tender and
that I must care for the ewes and cows
that are nursing their young. If they are
driven hard just one day, all the animals
will die. 14So let my lord go on ahead of
his servant, while I move along slowly at
the pace of the droves before me and
that of the children, until I come to my 33:14
lord in Seir.[v]" v Ge 32:3
15Esau said, "Then let me leave some
of my men with you."
"But why do that?" Jacob asked. "Just 33:15
let me find favor in the eyes of my lord."[w] w Ge 34:11; 47:25; Ru 2:13
16So that day Esau started on his way
back to Seir. 17Jacob, however, went to 33:17
Succoth,[x] where he built a place for him- x Jos 13:27;
self and made shelters for his livestock. Jdg 8:5,6,8,14, 14-16,15,16;
That is why the place is called Succoth.[d] Ps 60:6
18After Jacob came from Paddan 33:18
Aram,[e y] he arrived safely at the[f] city of y Ge 25:20; 28:2
Shechem[z] in Canaan and camped with- z Jos 24:1;
in sight of the city. 19For a hundred Jdg 9:1
pieces of silver,[g] he bought from the sons 33:19
of Hamor, the father of Shechem,[a] the a Jos 24:32
plot of ground[b] where he pitched his b Jn 4:5
tent. 20There he set up an altar and
called it El Elohe Israel.[h]

Dinah and the Shechemites

34 Now Dinah,[c] the daughter Leah 34:1
had borne to Jacob, went out to c Ge 30:21
visit the women of the land. 2When Shechem son of Hamor the Hivite, the ruler

[a] 28 *Israel* means *he struggles with God.*
[b] 30 *Peniel* means *face of God.* [c] 31 Hebrew *Penuel,* a variant of *Peniel* [d] 17 *Succoth* means *shelters.* [e] 18 That is, Northwest Mesopotamia [f] 18 Or *arrived at Shalem, a* [g] 19 Hebrew *hundred kesitahs;* a kesitah was a unit of money of unknown weight and value. [h] 20 *El Elohe Israel* can mean *God, the God of Israel* or *mighty is the God of Israel.*

of that area, saw her, he took her and violated her. 3His heart was drawn to Dinah daughter of Jacob, and he loved the
girl and spoke tenderly to her. 4And Shechem said to his father Hamor, "Get me
this girl as my wife."
5When Jacob heard that his daughter
Dinah had been defiled, his sons were in
the fields with his livestock; so he kept
quiet about it until they came home.
34:6 6Then Shechem's father Hamor went
[d]Jdg 14:2-5 out to talk with Jacob.[d] 7Now Jacob's
sons had come in from the fields as soon
as they heard what had happened. They
34:7 were filled with grief and fury, because
[e]Dt 22:21; Shechem had done a disgraceful thing
Jdg 20:6; in[a] Israel[e] by lying with Jacob's daugh-
2Sa 13:12 [f]Jos 7:15 ter—a thing that should not be done.[f]
8But Hamor said to them, "My son
Shechem has his heart set on your
daughter. Please give her to him as his
wife. 9Intermarry with us; give us your
34:10 daughters and take our daughters for
[g]Ge 47:6,27 yourselves. 10You can settle among us;[g]
the land is open to you.[h] Live in it, trade[b] 34:10 [h]Ge 13:9; 20:15
in it,[i] and acquire property in it." [i]Ge 42:34
11Then Shechem said to Dinah's fa-
ther and brothers, "Let me find favor in
your eyes, and I will give you whatever
you ask. 12Make the price for the bride[j] 34:12 [j]Ex 22:16;
and the gift I am to bring as great as you Dt 22:29;
like, and I'll pay whatever you ask me. 1Sa 18:25
Only give me the girl as my wife."
13Because their sister Dinah had been
defiled, Jacob's sons replied deceitfully
as they spoke to Shechem and his father
Hamor. 14They said to them, "We can't
do such a thing; we can't give our sister 34:14
to a man who is not circumcised.[k] That [k]Ge 17:14;
would be a disgrace to us. 15We will give Jdg 14:3
our consent to you on one condition
only: that you become like us by cir- 34:15
cumcising all your males.[l] 16Then we [l]Ex 12:48
will give you our daughters and take
your daughters for ourselves. We'll settle
among you and become one people with
you. 17But if you will not agree to be circumcised, we'll take our sister[c] and go."
18Their proposal seemed good to Hamor and his son Shechem. 19The young
man, who was the most honored of all
his father's household, lost no time in doing what they said, because he was de- 34:19
lighted with Jacob's daughter.[m] 20So Ha- [m]ver 3
mor and his son Shechem went to the 34:20
gate of their city[n] to speak to their fellow [n]Ru 4:1;
townsmen. 21"These men are friendly to- 2Sa 15:2
ward us," they said. "Let them live in our
land and trade in it; the land has plenty
of room for them. We can marry their
daughters and they can marry ours.
22But the men will consent to live with us
as one people only on the condition that
our males be circumcised, as they themselves are. 23Won't their livestock, their
property and all their other animals become ours? So let us give our consent to
them, and they will settle among us."
24All the men who went out of the city 34:24
gate[o] agreed with Hamor and his son [o]Ge 23:10
Shechem, and every male in the city was
circumcised.
25Three days later, while all of them
were still in pain, two of Jacob's sons,
Simeon and Levi, Dinah's brothers, took 34:25
their swords[p] and attacked the unsus- [p]Ge 49:5
pecting city, killing every male.[q] 26They [q]Ge 49:7
put Hamor and his son Shechem to the
sword and took Dinah from Shechem's

[a] 7 Or *against* [b] 10 Or *move about freely*; also in verse 21 [c] 17 Hebrew *daughter*

JESUS FOCUS

BACK TO BETHEL

Despite their tearful reunion, Jacob did not trust Esau's invitation to travel south with him to Seir (also called Edom). Instead, Jacob went only a few miles to Succoth (Genesis 33:17). Later he moved north to Shechem, where his daughter Dinah was raped. Jacob unwisely allowed his sons to agree to compensation—Dinah in exchange for intermarriage between the pagan family of Hamor the Hivite and the family of Jacob. If such marriages would have taken place, the ancestral line of Jesus would have been jeopardized by means of the introduction of pagan beliefs and practices. So God instructed Jacob to come back to Bethel where he had met God years earlier (see Genesis 28:10–22). This was a spiritual turning point in Jacob's difficult walk with God. He took his family back to Bethel and rebuilt the altar of God, this time calling it *El-Bethel*, or "God of Bethel, the house of God" (Genesis 35). Jacob was making it clear to his family that they were returning to God rather than merely to Jacob's boyhood home. Because Jacob turned back to God and placed his trust in him, God promised that his family would settle in the land. Once again God confirmed the promise he had made to Abraham that the Messiah would emerge from a family line chosen and set apart by God.

27The sons of Jacob came
house ad bodies and looted the
upon eir sister had been defiled.
city l their flocks and herds and
l everything else of theirs in
28 out in the fields. 29They car-
l their wealth and all their
d children, taking as plunder
g in the houses.
Jacob said to Simeon and Levi,
ve brought trouble on me by
me a stench[r] to the Canaanites
rizzites, the people living in this
We are few in number,[t] and if they
orces against me and attack me, I
ny household will be destroyed."
But they replied, "Should he have
eated our sister like a prostitute?"

Jacob Returns to Bethel

35 Then God said to Jacob, "Go up
35:1 [u] Ge 28:19 to Bethel[u] and settle there, and
[v] Ge 27:43 build an altar there to God, who appeared to you when you were fleeing
from your brother Esau."[v]
35:2 [w] Ge 18:19; Jos 24:15 2So Jacob said to his household[w] and
to all who were with him, "Get rid of the
[x] Ge 31:19 foreign gods[x] you have with you, and pu-
[y] Ex 19:10,14 rify yourselves and change your clothes.[y]
3Then come, let us go up to Bethel,
where I will build an altar to God, who
35:3 [z] Ge 32:7 answered me in the day of my distress[z]
[a] Ge 28:15,20-22; 31:3,42 and who has been with me wherever I
have gone."[a] 4So they gave Jacob all the
foreign gods they had and the rings in
35:4 their ears, and Jacob buried them under
[b] Jos 24:25-26 the oak at Shechem.[b] 5Then they set out,
35:5 and the terror of God[c] fell upon the
[c] Ex 15:16; 23:27; Jos 2:9 towns all around them so that no one
pursued them.
35:6 6Jacob and all the people with him
[d] Ge 28:19; 48:3 came to Luz[d] (that is, Bethel) in the land
of Canaan. 7There he built an altar, and
he called the place El Bethel,[b] because it
35:7 was there that God revealed himself to
[e] Ge 28:13 him[e] when he was fleeing from his
brother.
35:8 8Now Deborah, Rebekah's nurse,[f] died
[f] Ge 24:59 and was buried under the oak below
Bethel. So it was named Allon Bacuth.[c]
9After Jacob returned from Paddan
35:9 Aram,[d] God appeared to him again and
[g] Ge 32:29 blessed him.[g] 10God said to him, "Your
35:10 name is Jacob,[e] but you will no longer be
[h] Ge 17:5 called Jacob; your name will be Israel.[f]"[h]
So he named him Israel.
11And God said to him, "I am God

Almighty[g];[i] be fruitful and increase in 35:11 [i] Ge 17:1; Ex 6:3
number. A nation[j] and a community of [j] Ge 28:3; 48:4
nations will come from you, and kings [k] Ge 17:6
will come from your body.[k] 12The land I
gave to Abraham and Isaac I also give to
you, and I will give this land to your de- 35:12 [l] Ge 13:15; 28:13
scendants after you.[l]"[m] 13Then God [m] Ge 12:7; 26:3
went up from him[n] at the place where 35:13
he had talked with him. [n] Ge 17:22
14Jacob set up a stone pillar at the
place where God had talked with him,
and he poured out a drink offering on it; 35:14
he also poured oil on it.[o] 15Jacob called [o] Ge 28:18
the place where God had talked with 35:15
him Bethel.[h][p] [p] Ge 28:19

The Deaths of Rachel and Isaac

16Then they moved on from Bethel.
While they were still some distance
from Ephrath, Rachel began to give
birth and had great difficulty. 17And as
she was having great difficulty in childbirth, the midwife said to her, "Don't be
afraid, for you have another son."[q] 18As 35:17 [q] Ge 30:24
she breathed her last—for she was dy-
ing—she named her son Ben-Oni.[i] But
his father named him Benjamin.[j]
19So Rachel died and was buried on 35:19
the way to Ephrath (that is, Bethlehem[r]). [r] Ge 48:7;
20Over her tomb Jacob set up a pillar, Ru 1:1,19; Mic 5:2; Mt 2:16

[a] 27 Or *because* [b] 7 *El Bethel* means *God of Bethel.* [c] 8 *Allon Bacuth* means *oak of weeping.* [d] 9 That is, Northwest Mesopotamia; also in verse 26 [e] 10 *Jacob* means *he grasps the heel* (figuratively, *he deceives*). [f] 10 *Israel* means *he struggles with God.* [g] 11 Hebrew *El-Shaddai* [h] 15 *Bethel* means *house of God.* [i] 18 *Ben-Oni* means *son of my trouble.* [j] 18 *Benjamin* means *son of my right hand.*

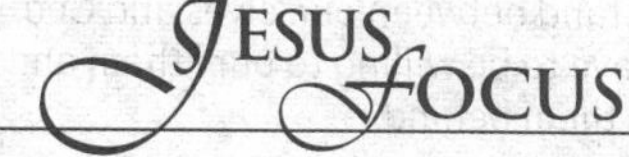

JACOB'S GRIEF

After meeting with God at Bethel, Jacob journeyed south toward Mamre (later called Hebron) to see his father Isaac. On the way Rachel gave birth to a second son, Benjamin, near Ephrath (also called Bethlehem). Rachel died during childbirth—on the way to the very town in which God's promised Messiah, through the line of Rachel's sister Leah, would be born. In fact, both David and Jesus would be born in Bethlehem. It may strike us as ironic that Jacob lost his favorite wife Rachel near the very location at which Leah's descendants would propagate the royal line of Israel's kings, culminating with the birth of the King of kings and Lord of lords (Luke 2:4–7; Revelation 17:14).

DISCOVERY 11

Back to the Basics

Twenty years after Jacob had left Bethel (Genesis 28:10–22) God told him to return to that place where he had been blessed. Like Jacob, we often need to get back to the beginning of our spiritual sojourn, back to the basics.

One of those basics is obedience: "Then God said . . ." (Genesis 35:1). It is easy to get sidetracked by all the things we need to do and all the people with whom we need to interact. But God would rather have our unquestioning obedience than some extravagant action to demonstrate that we believe in him (1 Samuel 15:22). In fact, our willingness to simply do what God asks is the ultimate test of our love for him (John 14:15). Jacob went back to Bethel simply because God asked him to.

Before he went back, though, Jacob had to "get rid of the foreign gods" (Genesis 35:2). Over the years his family had picked up many idols. We do the same thing. We fill our lives with unimportant things that distract us and cloud our focus. Every now and then we need to take inventory of the "gods" we have accumulated—the objects, goals and passions that stand between ourselves and God. We have to be willing to bury them and leave them behind.

When Jacob arrived at Bethel, God confirmed the covenant he had made and blessed Jacob again. He reminded Jacob that he is *El-Shaddai*—"God Almighty"—who keeps his promises (verse 11). This name for God appears in Scripture for the first time when God changed Abram's name to Abraham and repeated his promise of blessing (Genesis 17:1).

Eventually Jacob and his family left Bethel. They had almost reached Ephrath, the ancient name for Bethlehem, when Rachel gave birth to their son. She named him *Ben-Oni*, "son of my sorrow," before she died. Jacob renamed the baby *Benjamin*, or "son of my right hand." Similarly, from Mary's perspective, Jesus, who would also be born in Bethlehem, would be the "son of [her] sorrow" (Luke 2:35; John 19:25), but to God he is the "son of my right hand" (Hebrews 1:3). From the "man of sorrows" (Isaiah 53:3), Jesus was exalted to the "Lord of glory" (1 Corinthians 2:8).

Despite the obstacles that confront us and the griefs that are inherent in each of our lives, God never fails to fulfill his gracious promises—but that fulfillment is often contingent upon our own willingness to trust and obey.

What is your next step in doing what God asks? Of what is he asking you to let go so that you can move ahead? There are "gods" that stand between each of us and God. In order to experience God's blessing and the life that he intends for us, we have to get rid of those encumbrances. Only then can we walk forward with him, not weighed down with unnecessary baggage.

***Self-Discovery:** What "baggage" holds you back from enjoying the most fulfilling possible relationship with God?*

GO TO DISCOVERY 12 ON PAGE 57

35:20 and to this day that pillar marks Rachel's
s 1Sa 10:2 tomb.[s]
21 Israel moved on again and pitched
35:22 his tent beyond Migdal Eder. 22 While Is-
t Ge 49:4; 1Ch 5:1 rael was living in that region, Reuben
u Ge 29:29; went in and slept with his father's con-
Lev 18:8 cubine[t] Bilhah,[u] and Israel heard of it.

Jacob had twelve sons:
35:23 23 The sons of Leah:
v Ge 46:8 Reuben the firstborn[v] of Jacob,
w Ge 29:35 Simeon, Levi, Judah,[w] Issachar
x Ge 30:20 and Zebulun.[x]
35:24 24 The sons of Rachel:
y Ge 30:24 z ver 18 Joseph[y] and Benjamin.[z]
25 The sons of Rachel's maidservant
Bilhah:
35:25 a Ge 30:8 Dan and Naphtali.[a]
26 The sons of Leah's maidservant Zil-
35:26 pah:
b Ge 30:11 c Ge 30:13 Gad[b] and Asher.[c]
These were the sons of Jacob, who
were born to him in Paddan Aram.

35:27 27 Jacob came home to his father Isaac
d Ge 13:18; 18:1 in Mamre,[d] near Kiriath Arba[e] (that is,
e Jos 14:15 Hebron), where Abraham and Isaac had
35:28 stayed. 28 Isaac lived a hundred and
f Ge 25:7,20 eighty years.[f] 29 Then he breathed his last
35:29 and died and was gathered to his peo-
g Ge 25:8; 49:33 ple,[g] old and full of years.[h] And his sons
h Ge 15:15 i Ge 25:9 Esau and Jacob buried him.[i]

Esau's Descendants

36:1 **36** This is the account of Esau
j Ge 25:30 (that is, Edom).[j]

2 Esau took his wives from the
36:2 women of Canaan:[k] Adah daughter
k Ge 28:8-9 of Elon the Hittite,[l] and Oholiba-
l Ge 26:34 m ver 25 mah daughter of Anah[m] and
granddaughter of Zibeon the Hi-
vite— 3 also Basemath daughter of
Ishmael and sister of Nebaioth.
4 Adah bore Eliphaz to Esau, Bas-
36:4 n 1Ch 1:35 emath bore Reuel,[n] 5 and Oholibamah bore Jeush, Jalam and Korah.
These were the sons of Esau, who
were born to him in Canaan.
6 Esau took his wives and sons
and daughters and all the members
of his household, as well as his livestock and all his other animals and
36:6 all the goods he had acquired in
o Ge 12:5 Canaan,[o] and moved to a land
some distance from his brother Jacob. 7 Their possessions were too
great for them to remain together;
the land where they were staying
could not support them both be- 36:7
cause of their livestock.[p] 8 So Esau[q] p Ge 13:6; 17:8; 28:4
(that is, Edom) settled in the hill
country of Seir.[r] 36:8 q Dt 2:4 r Ge 32:3

9 This is the account of Esau the father
of the Edomites in the hill country of
Seir.

10 These are the names of Esau's sons:
Eliphaz, the son of Esau's wife
Adah, and Reuel, the son of
Esau's wife Basemath.
11 The sons of Eliphaz:[s] 36:11
Teman,[t] Omar, Zepho, Gatam s ver 15-16; Job 2:11
and Kenaz. t Am 1:12; Hab 3:3
12 Esau's son Eliphaz also had a
concubine named Timna, who 36:12
bore him Amalek.[u] These were u Ex 17:8,16; Nu 24:20;
grandsons of Esau's wife Adah.[v] 1Sa 15:2 v ver 16
13 The sons of Reuel:
Nahath, Zerah, Shammah and
Mizzah. These were grandsons
of Esau's wife Basemath.
14 The sons of Esau's wife Oholibamah daughter of Anah and granddaughter of Zibeon, whom she
bore to Esau:
Jeush, Jalam and Korah.

15 These were the chiefs[w] among 36:15 w Ex 15:15
Esau's descendants: x Job 2:11
The sons of Eliphaz the firstborn of
Esau:
Chiefs Teman,[x] Omar, Zepho, Ke-
naz, 16 Korah,[a] Gatam and Ama- 36:16 y ver 12
lek. These were the chiefs de-
scended from Eliphaz in Edom;
they were grandsons of Adah.[y]
17 The sons of Esau's son Reuel:[z] 36:17
Chiefs Nahath, Zerah, Shammah z 1Ch 1:37
and Mizzah. These were the
chiefs descended from Reuel in
Edom; they were grandsons of
Esau's wife Basemath.
18 The sons of Esau's wife Oholibamah:
Chiefs Jeush, Jalam and Korah.
These were the chiefs descended
from Esau's wife Oholibamah
daughter of Anah.
19 These were the sons of Esau (that is, 36:19
Edom),[a] and these were their chiefs. a Ge 25:30

20 These were the sons of Seir the Ho- 36:20
rite,[b] who were living in the region: b Ge 14:6;
Lotan, Shobal, Zibeon, Anah, Dt 2:12,22; 1Ch 1:38

[a] 16 Masoretic Text; Samaritan Pentateuch (see also Gen. 36:11 and 1 Chron. 1:36) does not have *Korah.*

21 Dishon, Ezer and Dishan.
These sons of Seir in Edom were
Horite chiefs.
22 The sons of Lotan:
Hori and Homam.[a] Timna was
Lotan's sister.
23 The sons of Shobal:
Alvan, Manahath, Ebal, Shepho
and Onam.
24 The sons of Zibeon:
Aiah and Anah. This is the Anah
who discovered the hot springs[b]
in the desert while he was grazing
the donkeys of his father Zibeon.
25 The children of Anah:
Dishon and Oholibamah daughter of Anah.
26 The sons of Dishon[c]:
Hemdan, Eshban, Ithran and Keran.
27 The sons of Ezer:
Bilhan, Zaavan and Akan.
28 The sons of Dishan:
Uz and Aran.
29 These were the Horite chiefs:
Lotan, Shobal, Zibeon, Anah,
30 Dishon, Ezer and Dishan. These
were the Horite chiefs, according
to their divisions, in the land of
Seir.

The Rulers of Edom

36:31 31 These were the kings who reigned in
[c] Ge 17:6; 1Ch 1:43 Edom before any Israelite king[c] reigned[d]:
32 Bela son of Beor became king of
Edom. His city was named Dinhabah.
36:33 33 When Bela died, Jobab son of Zerah
[d] Jer 49:13,22 from Bozrah[d] succeeded him as
king.
36:34 34 When Jobab died, Husham from
[e] Eze 25:13 the land of the Temanites[e] succeeded him as king.
35 When Husham died, Hadad son of
Bedad, who defeated Midian in
36:35 [f] Ge 19:37; Nu 22:1; Dt 1:5; Ru 1:1,6 the country of Moab,[f] succeeded
him as king. His city was named
Avith.
36 When Hadad died, Samlah from
Masrekah succeeded him as king.
37 When Samlah died, Shaul from Rehoboth on the river[e] succeeded
him as king.
38 When Shaul died, Baal-Hanan son
of Acbor succeeded him as king.
39 When Baal-Hanan son of Acbor
died, Hadad[f] succeeded him as
king. His city was named Pau,
and his wife's name was Mehetabel daughter of Matred, the
daughter of Me-Zahab.

40 These were the chiefs descended
from Esau, by name, according to their
clans and regions:
Timna, Alvah, Jetheth, 41 Oholibamah, Elah, Pinon, 42 Kenaz, Teman, Mibzar, 43 Magdiel and
Iram. These were the chiefs of
Edom, according to their settlements in the land they occupied.

This was Esau the father of the Edomites.

Joseph's Dreams

37 Jacob lived in the land where
his father had stayed,[g] the land 37:1 [g] Ge 17:8
of Canaan.[h] [h] Ge 10:19

2 This is the account of Jacob.

Joseph, a young man of seventeen, was 37:2 [i] Ps 78:71
tending the flocks[i] with his brothers, the [j] Ge 35:25
sons of Bilhah[j] and the sons of Zilpah,[k] [k] Ge 35:26
his father's wives, and he brought their [l] 1Sa 2:24
father a bad report[l] about them.

3 Now Israel loved Joseph more than 37:3
any of his other sons,[m] because he had [m] Ge 25:28
been born to him in his old age;[n] and he [n] Ge 44:20
made a richly ornamented[g] robe[o] for [o] 2Sa 13:18-19
him. 4 When his brothers saw that their
father loved him more than any of them,
they hated him[p] and could not speak a 37:4 [p] Ge 27:41; 49:22-23; Ac 7:9
kind word to him.

5 Joseph had a dream,[q] and when he 37:5
told it to his brothers, they hated him all [q] Ge 20:3; 28:12
the more. 6 He said to them, "Listen to
this dream I had: 7 We were binding
sheaves of grain out in the field when
suddenly my sheaf rose and stood
upright, while your sheaves gathered 37:7 [r] Ge 42:6,9; 43:26,28; 44:14; 50:18
around mine and bowed down to it."[r]

8 His brothers said to him, "Do you intend to reign over us? Will you actually
rule us?"[s] And they hated him all the 37:8 [s] Ge 49:26

[a] 22 Hebrew *Hemam,* a variant of *Homam* (see 1 Chron. 1:39) [b] 24 Vulgate; Syriac *discovered water;* the meaning of the Hebrew for this word is uncertain. [c] 26 Hebrew *Dishan,* a variant of *Dishon* [d] 31 Or *before an Israelite king reigned over them* [e] 37 Possibly the Euphrates [f] 39 Many manuscripts of the Masoretic Text, Samaritan Pentateuch and Syriac (see also 1 Chron. 1:50); most manuscripts of the Masoretic Text *Hadar* [g] 3 The meaning of the Hebrew for *richly ornamented* is uncertain; also in verses 23 and 32.

more bec of his dream and what he
had sa had another dream, and he
9 T is brothers. "Listen," he said,
told her dream, and this time the
"moon and eleven stars were
own to me."
en he told his father as well as
thers,[t] his father rebuked him
aid, "What is this dream you had?
our mother and I and your broth-
ctually come and bow down to the
und before you?"[u] 11His brothers
re jealous of him,[v] but his father kept
e matter in mind.[w]

oseph Sold by His Brothers

12Now his brothers had gone to graze their father's flocks near Shechem, 13and Israel said to Joseph, "As you know, your brothers are grazing the flocks near Shechem. Come, I am going to send you to them."

"Very well," he replied.

14So he said to him, "Go and see if all is well with your brothers and with the flocks, and bring word back to me." Then he sent him off from the Valley of Hebron.[x]

When Joseph arrived at Shechem, 15a man found him wandering around in the fields and asked him, "What are you looking for?"

16He replied, "I'm looking for my brothers. Can you tell me where they are grazing their flocks?"

17"They have moved on from here," the man answered. "I heard them say, 'Let's go to Dothan.[y]' "

So Joseph went after his brothers and found them near Dothan. 18But they saw him in the distance, and before he reached them, they plotted to kill him.[z]

19"Here comes that dreamer!" they said to each other. 20"Come now, let's kill him and throw him into one of these cisterns[a] and say that a ferocious animal devoured him. Then we'll see what comes of his dreams."[b]

21When Reuben heard this, he tried to rescue him from their hands. "Let's not take his life," he said.[c] 22"Don't shed any blood. Throw him into this cistern here in the desert, but don't lay a hand on him." Reuben said this to rescue him from them and take him back to his father.

23So when Joseph came to his brothers, they stripped him of his robe—the richly ornamented robe he was wearing— 24and they took him and threw him into the cistern.[d] Now the cistern was empty; there was no water in it.

25As they sat down to eat their meal, they looked up and saw a caravan of Ishmaelites coming from Gilead. Their camels were loaded with spices, balm and myrrh,[e] and they were on their way to take them down to Egypt.[f]

26Judah said to his brothers, "What will we gain if we kill our brother and cover up his blood?[g] 27Come, let's sell him to the Ishmaelites and not lay our hands on him; after all, he is our brother,[h] our own flesh and blood." His brothers agreed.

28So when the Midianite[i] merchants came by, his brothers pulled Joseph up out of the cistern and sold him for twenty shekels[a] of silver to the Ishmaelites, who took him to Egypt.[j]

29When Reuben returned to the cistern and saw that Joseph was not there,

t ver 5

37:14 x Ge 13:18; 35:27
37:17 y 2Ki 6:13
37:18 z 1Sa 19:1; Mk 14:1; Ac 23:12
37:20 a Jer 38:6,9 b Ge 50:20
37:21 c Ge 42:22
37:24 d Jer 41:7
37:25 e Ge 43:11 f ver 28
37:26 g ver 20; Ge 4:10
37:27 h Ge 42:21
37:28 i Ge 25:2; Jdg 6:1-3 j Ge 45:4-5; Ps 105:17; Ac 7:9

a 28 That is, about 8 ounces (about 0.2 kilogram)

JOSEPH
PRESERVER OF ISRAEL

Joseph, which means "may [God] add," was Jacob's 11th son and the firstborn of his beloved wife Rachel. Joseph was his father's favorite son, a fact that infuriated his halfbrothers. One day when Joseph came to visit them in the fields, the brothers plotted to kill him but instead sold him as a slave to a passing caravan of Ishmaelites on the way to Egypt (Genesis 37). Then they deceived their father, making it appear that Joseph had been killed and eaten by a wild animal. In the meantime, Joseph was taken to Egypt, where he became the slave of Potiphar, captain of Pharaoh's guard. Joseph was later falsely accused by Potiphar's wife of sexual assault and locked up in the royal dungeon. After 13 years of slavery and imprisonment, Joseph was finally released to stand before Pharaoh, the ruler of Egypt, to interpret the king's troublesome dream (Genesis 41:1–40). Because Pharaoh was so impressed with Joseph's wisdom and integrity, he appointed him second-in-command, or prime minister, of the land of Egypt. God used Joseph in this position to spare his family from a famine, once again preserving the ancestral line of the promised Messiah (Genesis 50:20).

37:29 k ver 34; he tore his clothes.[k] 30He went back to
Ge 44:13; his brothers and said, "The boy isn't
Job 1:20 there! Where can I turn now?"[l]
37:30 31Then they got Joseph's robe,[m]
l ver 22; slaughtered a goat and dipped the robe
Ge 42:13,36 in the blood. 32They took the ornament-
37:31 ed robe back to their father and said,
m ver 3,23 "We found this. Examine it to see
37:33 n ver 20 whether it is your son's robe."
o Ge 44:20,28 33He recognized it and said, "It is my
son's robe! Some ferocious animal[n] has
devoured him. Joseph has surely been
torn to pieces."[o]
37:34 34Then Jacob tore his clothes,[p] put on
p ver 29 q 2Sa 3:31 sackcloth[q] and mourned for his son
r Ge 50:3,10,11 many days.[r] 35All his sons and daughters
came to comfort him, but he refused to
be comforted. "No," he said, "in mourn-
37:35 s Ge 42:38; ing will I go down to the grave[a s] to my
44:22,29,31 son." So his father wept for him.
36Meanwhile, the Midianites[b] sold Jo-
37:36 seph in Egypt to Potiphar, one of Phar-
t Ge 39:1 aoh's officials, the captain of the guard.[t]

Judah and Tamar

38 At that time, Judah left his
brothers and went down to stay
with a man of Adullam named Hirah.
2There Judah met the daughter of a
38:2 u 1Ch 2:3 Canaanite man named Shua.[u] He married her and lay with her; 3she became
38:3 v ver 6; pregnant and gave birth to a son, who
Ge 46:12; was named Er.[v] 4She conceived again
Nu 26:19 and gave birth to a son and named him
Onan. 5She gave birth to still another
son and named him Shelah. It was at
Kezib that she gave birth to him.
6Judah got a wife for Er, his firstborn,
38:7 w ver 10; and her name was Tamar. 7But Er, Ju-
Ge 46:12; dah's firstborn, was wicked in the LORD's
1Ch 2:3 sight; so the LORD put him to death.[w]
8Then Judah said to Onan, "Lie with
your brother's wife and fulfill your duty
38:8 x Dt 25:5-6; to her as a brother-in-law to produce
Mt 22:24-28 offspring for your brother."[x] 9But Onan
knew that the offspring would not be
his; so whenever he lay with his brother's
wife, he spilled his semen on the ground
to keep from producing offspring for his
brother. 10What he did was wicked in
38:10 y Ge 46:12; the LORD's sight; so he put him to death
Dt 25:7-10 also.[y]
11Judah then said to his daughter-in-
law Tamar, "Live as a widow in your father's house until my son Shelah grows
38:11 z Ru 1:13 up."[z] For he thought, "He may die too,

just like his brothers." So Ta
live in her father's house.
12After a long time Judah's
daughter of Shua, died. When Ju
recovered from his grief, he wen
Timnah,[a] to the men who were she
his sheep, and his friend Hirah the A
lamite went with him.
13When Tamar was told, "Your fathe
in-law is on his way to Timnah to shear
his sheep," 14she took off her widow's
clothes, covered herself with a veil to
disguise herself, and then sat down at
the entrance to Enaim, which is on the
road to Timnah. For she saw that,
though Shelah[b] had now grown up, she 38:14 b ver 11
had not been given to him as his wife.
15When Judah saw her, he thought she
was a prostitute, for she had covered her
face. 16Not realizing that she was his
daughter-in-law,[c] he went over to her by 38:16 c Lev 18:15;
the roadside and said, "Come now, let 20:12
me sleep with you."
"And what will you give me to sleep
with you?" she asked.
17"I'll send you a young goat[d] from my 38:17 d Eze 16:33
flock," he said. e ver 20
"Will you give me something as a
pledge[e] until you send it?" she asked.
18He said, "What pledge should I give
you?"
"Your seal[f] and its cord, and the staff 38:18
in your hand," she answered. So he gave f ver 25
them to her and slept with her, and she
became pregnant by him. 19After she
left, she took off her veil and put on her 38:19
widow's clothes[g] again. g ver 14
20Meanwhile Judah sent the young
goat by his friend the Adullamite in order to get his pledge back from the
woman, but he did not find her. 21He
asked the men who lived there, "Where 38:21
is the shrine prostitute[h] who was beside h Lev 19:29; Hos 4:14
the road at Enaim?"
"There hasn't been any shrine prostitute here," they said.
22So he went back to Judah and said,
"I didn't find her. Besides, the men who
lived there said, 'There hasn't been any
shrine prostitute here.'"
23Then Judah said, "Let her keep what
she has, or we will become a laughingstock. After all, I did send her this young
goat, but you didn't find her."

[a] 35 Hebrew *Sheol* [b] 36 Samaritan Pentateuch, Septuagint, Vulgate and Syriac (see also verse 28); Masoretic Text *Medanites*

DISCOVERY 12

TAMAR AND GRACE

Life is filled with interruptions. The telephone seems to ring nonstop. An unexpected visitor stops by and devours precious hours. A crisis slams into our routine, and our energies are absorbed with picking up the pieces. We often respond in exasperation and demand to know *why*! And so it feels when Tamar's story appears in the narrative of Joseph's life—bizarre, disconnected, a seeming interruption (Genesis 38). We are puzzled and ask, "What does this have to do with anything?" But God very intentionally included Tamar's story in the Joseph account; from his perspective, it is anything but an interruption.

Joseph's brother Judah had married a Canaanite woman, and the couple had three sons, Er, Onan and Shelah. Er married Tamar but then died without leaving an heir. Verse 7 tells us that God put Er to death because of his wickedness. According to custom, the next brother, Onan, married Tamar. But Onan cheated her by refusing to cooperate in producing an heir for his brother—resulting in his own death. After that Judah decided that "enough was enough" and refused to allow his third son, Shelah, to marry Tamar.

Tamar resorted to deceit: She posed as a prostitute, seduced her father-in-law and became pregnant. Not realizing that he himself was the father, Judah condemned Tamar to be burned to death. However, when the truth was revealed Judah admitted his own sin and rescinded the demand. Tamar gave birth to twins. Perez, meaning "breaking out," emerged as the firstborn, but Zerah, meaning "scarlet," had been tagged by the midwife as the older twin. Again, God had all the particulars under control, and it becomes obvious later what he had in mind. According to Matthew 1:3 Perez, not Zerah, is an ancestor of David—part of the family line God used to keep his promise of a Messiah for his people. This apparent "disruption" in the story of Joseph turns out to be quite significant after all!

In spite of the wickedness of Er and Onan, Tamar's deceitful action of seducing Judah and the unethical behavior of Judah against Tamar, *"the birth of Jesus Christ came about"* (Matthew 1:18). It is easy to become distracted, thinking that God is far removed from the day-to-day occurrences of our lives. But God's favor and blessing are seen in the manner in which he averted a disruption in the Messiah's family line, despite all of the sordid behavior that accompanies the story. His Promised One, Jesus, is proof that God's grace continues, even when we turn away from him.

The "interruption" in the story of Joseph reminds us that the unwelcome breaks in our routines may well be *gracious intrusions* by the God who holds all the details and who does amazing things in spite of our sometimes messy entanglements that seem to threaten to thwart his purpose.

***Self-Discovery:** What seemingly insignificant "interruption" in your life has had unexpected life-changing significance?*

GO TO DISCOVERY 13 ON PAGE 60

24 About three months later Judah was
told, "Your daughter-in-law Tamar is
guilty of prostitution, and as a result she
is now pregnant."
38:24 i Lev 21:9; Dt 22:21,22 Judah said, "Bring her out and have
her burned to death!"[i]
25 As she was being brought out, she
sent a message to her father-in-law. "I
am pregnant by the man who owns
these," she said. And she added, "See if
you recognize whose seal and cord and
38:25 j ver 18 staff these are."[j]
38:26 k 1Sa 24:17 l ver 11 26 Judah recognized them and said,
"She is more righteous than I,[k] since I
wouldn't give her to my son Shelah.[l]"
And he did not sleep with her again.
27 When the time came for her to give
birth, there were twin boys in her
38:27 m Ge 25:24 womb.[m] 28 As she was giving birth, one of
them put out his hand; so the midwife
took a scarlet thread and tied it on his
wrist and said, "This one came out first."
38:29 n Ge 46:12; Nu 26:20,21; Ru 4:12,18; 1Ch 2:4; Mt 1:3 29 But when he drew back his hand, his
brother came out, and she said, "So this
is how you have broken out!" And he was
named Perez.[a][n] 30 Then his brother, who
had the scarlet thread on his wrist, came
38:30 o 1Ch 2:4 out and he was given the name Zerah.[b][o]

Joseph and Potiphar's Wife

39 Now Joseph had been taken
down to Egypt. Potiphar, an
Egyptian who was one of Pharaoh's offi-
39:1 p Ge 37:36 q Ge 37:25; Ps 105:17 cials, the captain of the guard,[p] bought
him from the Ishmaelites who had tak-
en him there.[q]
39:2 r Ge 21:20,22; Ac 7:9 2 The LORD was with Joseph[r] and he
prospered, and he lived in the house of
39:3 s Ge 21:22; 26:28 t Ps 1:3 his Egyptian master. 3 When his master
saw that the LORD was with him[s] and
that the LORD gave him success in everything he did,[t] 4 Joseph found favor in his
eyes and became his attendant. Potiphar
put him in charge of his household, and
39:4 u ver 8,22; Ge 24:2 he entrusted to his care everything he
owned.[u] 5 From the time he put him in
charge of his household and of all that
39:5 v Ge 26:24; 30:27 he owned, the LORD blessed the household of the Egyptian because of Joseph.[v]
The blessing of the LORD was on everything Potiphar had, both in the house
and in the field. 6 So he left in Joseph's
care everything he had; with Joseph in
charge, he did not concern himself with
anything except the food he ate.
39:6 w 1Sa 16:12 Now Joseph was well-built and handsome,[w] 7 and after a while his master's
wife took notice of Joseph and said, 39:7 x 2Sa 13:11; Pr 7:15-18
"Come to bed with me!"[x]
8 But he refused.[y] "With me in charge,"
he told her, "my master does not con- 39:8 y Pr 6:23-24
cern himself with anything in the house;
everything he owns he has entrusted to
my care. 9 No one is greater in this house 39:9 z Ge 41:33,40 a Ge 20:6; 42:18; 2Sa 12:13
than I am.[z] My master has withheld
nothing from me except you, because
you are his wife. How then could I do
such a wicked thing and sin against
God?"[a] 10 And though she spoke to Joseph day after day, he refused to go to
bed with her or even be with her.
11 One day he went into the house to
attend to his duties, and none of the
household servants was inside. 12 She 39:12 b Pr 7:13
caught him by his cloak[b] and said,
"Come to bed with me!" But he left his
cloak in her hand and ran out of the
house.
13 When she saw that he had left his
cloak in her hand and had run out of the
house, 14 she called her household servants. "Look," she said to them, "this
Hebrew has been brought to us to make
sport of us! He came in here to sleep
with me, but I screamed.[c] 15 When he 39:14 c Dt 22:24,27
heard me scream for help, he left his
cloak beside me and ran out of the
house."
16 She kept his cloak beside her until
his master came home. 17 Then she told 39:17 d Ex 23:1,7; Ps 101:5
him this story:[d] "That Hebrew slave you
brought us came to me to make sport of
me. 18 But as soon as I screamed for help,
he left his cloak beside me and ran out
of the house."
19 When his master heard the story his
wife told him, saying, "This is how your 39:19 e Pr 6:34
slave treated me," he burned with anger.[e]
20 Joseph's master took him and put him 39:20 f Ge 40:3; Ps 105:18
in prison,[f] the place where the king's
prisoners were confined.
But while Joseph was there in the
prison, 21 the LORD was with him; he
showed him kindness and granted him
favor in the eyes of the prison warden.[g] 39:21 g Ex 3:21
22 So the warden put Joseph in charge of
all those held in the prison, and he was
made responsible for all that was done 39:22 h ver 4
there.[h] 23 The warden paid no attention
to anything under Joseph's care, because
the LORD was with Joseph and gave him 39:23 i ver 3
success in whatever he did.[i]

[a] 29 *Perez* means *breaking out.* [b] 30 *Zerah* can mean *scarlet* or *brightness.*

The Cupbearer and the Baker

40:1 **40** Some time later, the cupbearer[j]
j Ne 1:11 and the baker of the king of
Egypt offended their master, the king of
40:2 k Pr 16:14,15 Egypt. 2Pharaoh was angry[k] with his two
officials, the chief cupbearer and the
40:3 chief baker, 3and put them in custody in
l Ge 39:20 the house of the captain of the guard,[l] in
the same prison where Joseph was con-
40:4 fined. 4The captain of the guard assigned
m Ge 39:4 them to Joseph,[m] and he attended them.
After they had been in custody for
some time, 5each of the two men—the
cupbearer and the baker of the king of
Egypt, who were being held in prison—
40:5 had a dream the same night, and each
n Ge 41:11 dream had a meaning of its own.[n]
6When Joseph came to them the next
morning, he saw that they were dejected. 7So he asked Pharaoh's officials who
were in custody with him in his master's
40:7 house, "Why are your faces so sad to-
o Ne 2:2 day?"[o]
8"We both had dreams," they answered, "but there is no one to interpret
40:8 them."[p]
p Ge 41:8,15 q Ge 41:16; Then Joseph said to them, "Do not in-
Da 2:22,28,47 terpretations belong to God?[q] Tell me
your dreams."
9So the chief cupbearer told Joseph
his dream. He said to him, "In my dream
I saw a vine in front of me, 10and on the
vine were three branches. As soon as it
budded, it blossomed, and its clusters
ripened into grapes. 11Pharaoh's cup was
in my hand, and I took the grapes,
squeezed them into Pharaoh's cup and
put the cup in his hand."
40:12 r Ge 41:12,15, 12"This is what it means,[r]" Joseph said
25; Da 2:36; to him. "The three branches are three
4:19 days. 13Within three days Pharaoh will
lift up your head and restore you to your
position, and you will put Pharaoh's cup
in his hand, just as you used to do when
40:14 you were his cupbearer. 14But when all
s Lk 23:42 goes well with you, remember me[s] and
t Jos 2:12; show me kindness;[t] mention me to
1Sa 20:14,42; 1Ki 2:7 Pharaoh and get me out of this prison.
40:15 15For I was forcibly carried off from the
u Ge 37:26-28 land of the Hebrews,[u] and even here I
have done nothing to deserve being put
in a dungeon."
16When the chief baker saw that Joseph had given a favorable interpretation, he said to Joseph, "I too had a
dream: On my head were three baskets
of bread.[a] 17In the top basket were all
kinds of baked goods for Pharaoh, but
the birds were eating them out of the
basket on my head."
18"This is what it means," Joseph said. 40:18
"The three baskets are three days.[v] v ver 12
19Within three days Pharaoh will lift off 40:19
your head[w] and hang you on a tree.[b] w ver 13
And the birds will eat away your flesh."
20Now the third day was Pharaoh's 40:20
birthday,[x] and he gave a feast for all his x Mt 14:6-10 y Mk 6:21
officials.[y] He lifted up the heads of the
chief cupbearer and the chief baker in
the presence of his officials: 21He restored the chief cupbearer to his posi- 40:21
tion, so that he once again put the cup z ver 13
into Pharaoh's hand,[z] 22but he hanged[c] 40:22
the chief baker,[a] just as Joseph had said a ver 19
to them in his interpretation.[b] b Ps 105:19
23The chief cupbearer, however, did 40:23
not remember Joseph; he forgot him.[c] c Job 19:14; Ecc 9:15

Pharaoh's Dreams

41 When two full years had 41:1
passed, Pharaoh had a dream:[d] d Ge 20:3
He was standing by the Nile, 2when out
of the river there came up seven cows, 41:2
sleek and fat,[e] and they grazed among e ver 26
the reeds.[f] 3After them, seven other f Isa 19:6
cows, ugly and gaunt, came up out of the
Nile and stood beside those on the riverbank. 4And the cows that were ugly and
gaunt ate up the seven sleek, fat cows.
Then Pharaoh woke up.
5He fell asleep again and had a second
dream: Seven heads of grain, healthy
and good, were growing on a single
stalk. 6After them, seven other heads of
grain sprouted—thin and scorched by
the east wind. 7The thin heads of grain
swallowed up the seven healthy, full
heads. Then Pharaoh woke up; it had
been a dream.
8In the morning his mind was trou- 41:8
bled,[g] so he sent for all the magicians[h] g Da 2:1,3; 4:5,
and wise men of Egypt. Pharaoh told 19 h Ex 7:11,22;
them his dreams, but no one could in- Da 1:20; 2:2,27;
terpret them for him. 4:7
9Then the chief cupbearer said to
Pharaoh, "Today I am reminded of my
shortcomings. 10Pharaoh was once angry 41:10
with his servants,[i] and he imprisoned i Ge 40:2
me and the chief baker in the house of j Ge 39:20
the captain of the guard.[j] 11Each of us
had a dream the same night, and each 41:11
dream had a meaning of its own.[k] 12Now k Ge 40:5

[a] 16 Or *three wicker baskets* [b] 19 Or *and impale you on a pole* [c] 22 Or *impaled*

DISCOVERY 13

JOSEPH AND JESUS

Few people in the Bible suffered more injustice than Joseph. The more he tried to do what was right, the more other people did him wrong! Yet God was at work, orchestrating every detail; decades later Joseph finally realized what God had been doing. God used Joseph to save his entire family during a time of severe famine, thereby preserving the family line from which the Messiah would be born—the future nation of Israel.

There are many parallels between the lives of Joseph and Jesus. Both were rejected. Because Joseph dreamed that he would rule over his brothers and because his father reserved a special love for him, the brothers were inordinately jealous. When Joseph came to visit them in the fields they saw an opportunity to kill him (Genesis 37:5–11,17). Jesus also came to his own people, only to have them turn against him (John 1:11). Jesus knew what it was to be despised and rejected (Isaiah 53:3).

Both Joseph and Jesus were sold for silver. Reuben convinced the brothers to hold Joseph in a pit for a while instead of killing him, intending to rescue him later. But another brother had a different idea. Judah spied a caravan plodding through the area and convinced the other brothers to sell Joseph as a slave. The Ishmaelites paid 20 pieces of silver for Joseph before continuing on toward Egypt (Genesis 37:28). Many years later Judas would receive 30 pieces of silver for turning over Jesus to the religious authorities (Matthew 26:14–16). One significant difference exists, however: While Joseph was sold against his own will, Jesus *chose* to become a servant and die on the cross, paying for our sin with his life (Philippians 2:6–11).

Both Joseph and Jesus forgave. Joseph forgave his brothers for their abominable actions and treated them with kindness, rather than exercising his position and authority to punish them (Genesis 50:11–21). Jesus was ridiculed and tested throughout his ministry and finally scorned, beaten and murdered. But far from holding a grudge, his sole purpose was to offer his perfect life as a sacrifice so that God would not hold our sin against us (2 Corinthians 5:19). Even while he hung dying on the cross he implored, "Father, forgive them . . . they do not know what they are doing" (Luke 23:34).

Finally, God used both Joseph and Jesus to deliver his people. As the years stretched on it must have seemed to Joseph that God had forgotten him, but every nuance of Joseph's situation was in the hands of his Creator. He began his life in Egypt as a slave but eventually became second-in-command to Pharaoh himself, entrusted with the responsibility for distributing the scarce food supply (Genesis 41:39–40). Ultimately, God used Joseph to save his own family from starvation. Hundreds of years later Jesus came to save his people from dying. He came to free us from the one obstacle that stood between us and eternal life with him: sin (Romans 5:1–5).

***Self-Discovery:** Identify a situation in your life in which evil or trouble has ultimately resulted in something good.*

GO TO DISCOVERY 14 ON PAGE 72

a young Hebrew was there with us, a servant of the captain of the guard. We told
him our dreams, and he interpreted
41:12 them for us, giving each man the inter-
l Ge 40:12 pretation of his dream.[l] 13And things
turned out exactly as he interpreted
41:13 them to us: I was restored to my position,
m Ge 40:22 and the other man was hanged.[a m]"
41:14 14So Pharaoh sent for Joseph, and he
n Ps 105:20; was quickly brought from the dungeon.[n]
Da 2:25 When he had shaved and changed his
clothes, he came before Pharaoh.
15Pharaoh said to Joseph, "I had a
dream, and no one can interpret it. But
41:15 I have heard it said of you that when you
o Da 5:16 hear a dream you can interpret it."[o]
16"I cannot do it," Joseph replied to
41:16 Pharaoh, "but God will give Pharaoh the
p Ge 40:8; Da 2:30; answer he desires."[p]
Ac 3:12; 2Co 3:5 17Then Pharaoh said to Joseph, "In my
dream I was standing on the bank of the
Nile, 18when out of the river there came
up seven cows, fat and sleek, and they
grazed among the reeds. 19After them,
seven other cows came up—scrawny
and very ugly and lean. I had never seen
such ugly cows in all the land of Egypt.
20The lean, ugly cows ate up the seven
fat cows that came up first. 21But even
after they ate them, no one could tell
that they had done so; they looked just
as ugly as before. Then I woke up.
22"In my dreams I also saw seven
heads of grain, full and good, growing on
a single stalk. 23After them, seven other
heads sprouted—withered and thin and
scorched by the east wind. 24The thin
heads of grain swallowed up the seven
good heads. I told this to the magicians,
41:24 but none could explain it to me.[q]"
q ver 8 25Then Joseph said to Pharaoh, "The
dreams of Pharaoh are one and the same.
God has revealed to Pharaoh what he is
41:25 about to do.[r] 26The seven good cows[s] are
r Da 2:45 seven years, and the seven good heads of
41:26 grain are seven years; it is one and the
s ver 2 same dream. 27The seven lean, ugly cows
that came up afterward are seven years,
and so are the seven worthless heads of
41:27 grain scorched by the east wind: They are
t Ge 12:10; 2Ki 8:1 seven years of famine.[t]
28"It is just as I said to Pharaoh: God
41:29 has shown Pharaoh what he is about to
u ver 47 do. 29Seven years of great abundance[u]
are coming throughout the land of
41:30 Egypt, 30but seven years of famine[v] will
v ver 54; Ge 47:13 follow them. Then all the abundance in

Egypt will be forgotten, and the famine
will ravage the land.[w] 31The abundance 41:30 w ver 56
in the land will not be remembered, be-
cause the famine that follows it will be
so severe. 32The reason the dream was
given to Pharaoh in two forms is that the 41:32
matter has been firmly decided[x] by God, x Nu 23:19;
and God will do it soon. Isa 46:10-11
33"And now let Pharaoh look for a discerning and wise man[y] and put him in 41:33 y ver 39
charge of the land of Egypt. 34Let Phar-
aoh appoint commissioners over the 41:34
land to take a fifth[z] of the harvest of z 1Sa 8:15
Egypt during the seven years of abun- a ver 48
dance.[a] 35They should collect all the food
of these good years that are coming and
store up the grain under the authority of
Pharaoh, to be kept in the cities for 41:35
food.[b] 36This food should be held in re- b ver 48
serve for the country, to be used during
the seven years of famine that will come
upon Egypt,[c] so that the country may 41:36 c ver 56
not be ruined by the famine."
37The plan seemed good to Pharaoh

[a] 13 Or *impaled*

JOSEPH AND GOD'S SON

Joseph is never mentioned in the New Testament as a foreshadowing of Jesus, but there are striking similarities between the two. There were three distinct periods in Joseph's life: He was the *beloved son*, held in supreme regard by his father; he was the *suffering servant*, rejected by his own brothers; and he was an *exalted savior*, granted a position of princely splendor, majesty and authority. These three descriptions apply to Jesus as well. Both were especially loved by their fathers (Genesis 37:3; Matthew 3:17) but rejected by others (Genesis 37:4–8; John 15:25) Both were stripped and humiliated (Genesis 37:23; Matthew 27:28) and sold for pieces of silver (Genesis 37:28; Matthew 26:15). Each was taken to Egypt at some point in his life (Genesis 37:28; Matthew 2:14–15) and faced the temptation to sin (Genesis 39:7; Matthew 4:1–11). Both Joseph and Jesus lived in relative obscurity until around the age of 30 (Genesis 41:46; Luke 3:23), at which time they rose to great prominence (Genesis 41:40–41; Philippians 2:9–10). Each was associated with two other prisoners (Genesis 40:2–3; Luke 23:32), and each took a Gentile "bride" (Genesis 41:45; Matthew 25:1–6; Ephesians 5:25–32).

41:37 and to all his officials.[d] 38So Pharaoh
d Ge 45:16 asked them, "Can we find anyone like
41:38 this man, one in whom is the spirit of
e Nu 27:18; Job 32:8; Da 4:8, God[a]?"[e]
8-9,18; 5:11,14 39Then Pharaoh said to Joseph, "Since
God has made all this known to you,
there is no one so discerning and wise as
you. 40You shall be in charge of my
palace, and all my people are to submit
41:40 to your orders.[f] Only with respect to the
f Ps 105:21-22; Ac 7:10 throne will I be greater than you."

Joseph in Charge of Egypt

41So Pharaoh said to Joseph, "I hereby
41:41 g Ge 42:6; Da 6:3 put you in charge of the whole land of
41:42 Egypt."[g] 42Then Pharaoh took his signet
h Est 3:10 ring[h] from his finger and put it on Jo-
i Da 5:7,16,29 seph's finger. He dressed him in robes of
41:43 fine linen and put a gold chain around
j Est 6:9 his neck.[i] 43He had him ride in a chariot
as his second-in-command,[b] and men
shouted before him, "Make way[c]!"[j] Thus
he put him in charge of the whole land
of Egypt.
44Then Pharaoh said to Joseph, "I am
Pharaoh, but without your word no one
41:44 k Ps 105:22 will lift hand or foot in all Egypt."[k]
45Pharaoh gave Joseph the name Zaph-
enath-Paneah and gave him Asenath
41:45 daughter of Potiphera, priest of On,[d] to
l ver 50; Ge 46:20,27 be his wife.[l] And Joseph went throughout the land of Egypt.
41:46 m Ge 37:2 46Joseph was thirty years old[m] when
n 1Sa 16:21; he entered the service[n] of Pharaoh king
Da 1:19 of Egypt. And Joseph went out from
Pharaoh's presence and traveled
throughout Egypt. 47During the seven
years of abundance the land produced
plentifully. 48Joseph collected all the
food produced in those seven years of
abundance in Egypt and stored it in the
cities. In each city he put the food grown
in the fields surrounding it. 49Joseph
stored up huge quantities of grain, like
the sand of the sea; it was so much that
he stopped keeping records because it
was beyond measure.
50Before the years of famine came,
two sons were born to Joseph by Ase-
41:50 nath daughter of Potiphera, priest of
o Ge 46:20; 48:5 On.[o] 51Joseph named his firstborn[p] Manasseh[e] and said, "It is because God has
41:51 p Ge 48:14,18,20 made me forget all my trouble and all
41:52 my father's household." 52The second
q Ge 48:1,5; son he named Ephraim[f][q] and said, "It is
50:23 r Ge 17:6; because God has made me fruitful[r] in
28:3; 49:22 the land of my suffering."

53The seven years of abundance in
Egypt came to an end, 54and the seven 41:54
years of famine began,[s] just as Joseph s ver 30;
had said. There was famine in all the Ps 105:11; Ac 7:11
other lands, but in the whole land of
Egypt there was food. 55When all Egypt 41:55
began to feel the famine,[t] the people t Dt 32:24 u ver 41
cried to Pharaoh for food. Then Pharaoh
told all the Egyptians, "Go to Joseph and
do what he tells you."[u]
56When the famine had spread over
the whole country, Joseph opened the
storehouses and sold grain to the Egyptians, for the famine[v] was severe 41:56 v Ge 12:10
throughout Egypt. 57And all the coun-
tries came to Egypt to buy grain from Jo- 41:57
seph,[w] because the famine was severe in w Ge 42:5; 47:15
all the world.

Joseph's Brothers Go to Egypt

42 When Jacob learned that there 42:1
was grain in Egypt,[x] he said to x Ac 7:12
his sons, "Why do you just keep looking
at each other?" 2He continued, "I have
heard that there is grain in Egypt. Go
down there and buy some for us, so that 42:2 y Ge 43:8
we may live and not die."[y]
3Then ten of Joseph's brothers went
down to buy grain from Egypt. 4But Jacob did not send Benjamin, Joseph's
brother, with the others, because he was 42:4
afraid that harm might come to him.[z] z ver 38
5So Israel's sons were among those who 42:5
went to buy grain,[a] for the famine was in a Ge 41:57
the land of Canaan also.[b] b Ge 12:10; Ac 7:11
6Now Joseph was the governor of the 42:6
land,[c] the one who sold grain to all its c Ge 41:41
people. So when Joseph's brothers ar- d Ge 37:7-10
rived, they bowed down to him with
their faces to the ground.[d] 7As soon as
Joseph saw his brothers, he recognized
them, but he pretended to be a stranger 42:7
and spoke harshly to them.[e] "Where do e ver 30
you come from?" he asked.
"From the land of Canaan," they
replied, "to buy food."
8Although Joseph recognized his 42:8
brothers, they did not recognize him.[f] f Ge 37:2
9Then he remembered his dreams[g] 42:9
about them and said to them, "You are g Ge 37:7

[a] 38 Or *of the gods* [b] 43 Or *in the chariot of his second-in-command;* or *in his second chariot* [c] 43 Or *Bow down* [d] 45 That is, Heliopolis; also in verse 50 [e] 51 *Manasseh* sounds like and may be derived from the Hebrew for *forget.* [f] 52 *Ephraim* sounds like the Hebrew for *twice fruitful.*

spies! You have come to see where our
land is unprotected.”
10“No, my lord,” they answered. “Your
servants have come to buy food. 11We
are all the sons of one man. Your servants are honest men, not spies.”
12“No!” he said to them. “You have
come to see where our land is unprotected.”
13But they replied, “Your servants
were twelve brothers, the sons of one
42:13 man, who lives in the land of Canaan.
h Ge 37:30,33; The youngest is now with our father,
44:20 and one is no more.”[h]
14Joseph said to them, “It is just as I
told you: You are spies! 15And this is how
you will be tested: As surely as Pharaoh
42:15 lives,[i] you will not leave this place unless
i 1Sa 17:55 your youngest brother comes here.
16Send one of your number to get your
brother; the rest of you will be kept in
prison, so that your words may be test-
42:16 ed to see if you are telling the truth.[j] If
j ver 11 you are not, then as surely as Pharaoh
42:17 lives, you are spies!” 17And he put them
k Ge 40:4 all in custody[k] for three days.
18On the third day, Joseph said to
42:18 them, “Do this and you will live, for I fear
l Ge 20:11; God:[l] 19If you are honest men, let one of
Lev 25:43 your brothers stay here in prison, while
the rest of you go and take grain back for
your starving households. 20But you
42:20 must bring your youngest brother to
m ver 15,34; me,[m] so that your words may be verified
Ge 43:5; 44:23 and that you may not die.” This they proceeded to do.
21They said to one another, “Surely we
are being punished because of our
42:21 brother.[n] We saw how distressed he was
n Ge 37:26-28 when he pleaded with us for his life, but
o Hos 5:15 we would not listen; that's why this distress[o] has come upon us.”
22Reuben replied, “Didn't I tell you
42:22 not to sin against the boy?[p] But you
p Ge 37:21-22 wouldn't listen! Now we must give an ac-
q Ge 9:5 counting[q] for his blood.”[r] 23They did not
r 1Ki 2:32; realize that Joseph could understand
2Ch 24:22; them, since he was using an interpreter.
Ps 9:12 24He turned away from them and began to weep, but then turned back and
42:24 spoke to them again. He had Simeon
s ver 13; taken from them and bound before their
Ge 43:14,23; eyes.[s]
45:14-15 25Joseph gave orders to fill their bags
42:25 with grain,[t] to put each man's silver back
t Ge 43:2 in his sack,[u] and to give them provisions
u Ge 44:1,8 for their journey.[v] After this was done
v Ro 12:17,20-21
for them, 26they loaded their grain on
their donkeys and left.
27At the place where they stopped for
the night one of them opened his sack to
get feed for his donkey, and he saw his
silver in the mouth of his sack.[w] 28“My 42:27
silver has been returned,” he said to his w Ge 43:21-22
brothers. “Here it is in my sack.”
Their hearts sank and they turned to
each other trembling and said, “What is 42:28
this that God has done to us?”[x] x Ge 43:23
29When they came to their father Jacob in the land of Canaan, they told him
all that had happened to them. They
said, 30“The man who is lord over the 42:30
land spoke harshly to us[y] and treated us y ver 7
as though we were spying on the land.
31But we said to him, ‘We are honest
men; we are not spies.[z] 32We were twelve 42:31 z ver 11
brothers, sons of one father. One is no
more, and the youngest is now with our
father in Canaan.’
33“Then the man who is lord over the
land said to us, ‘This is how I will know
whether you are honest men: Leave one
of your brothers here with me, and take
food for your starving households and

JESUS AND YOU

EVERYTHING IS AGAINST ME!

Jacob endured years of anguish over the loss of Joseph, never realizing that his own sons had deceived him. When Joseph's nine older brothers returned from Egypt without Simeon, whom Joseph had detained as a hostage, Jacob was understandably concerned (Genesis 42:29–36). But when the brothers requested permission to take Benjamin to Egypt so that Simeon might be set free, Jacob vehemently objected. “You have deprived me of my children,” he protested. “Joseph is no more and Simeon is no more, and now you want to take Benjamin. Everything is against me!” (verse 36). But nothing could have been further from the truth. God's sovereign will and loving purpose for Jacob's life were beginning to come together like the movements of a grand symphony. Without Joseph's work in Egypt the lineage of Jesus would have been in jeopardy. When Joseph pointed out to his brothers God's unsurpassed power to work in all circumstances to accomplish his will (Genesis 50:20), his words applied to the future as well as to the past—to the time when God would provide a Messiah for all people through the line of Joseph's brother Judah.

42:33 go.[a] 34But bring your youngest brother
a ver 19,20 to me so I will know that you are not
spies but honest men. Then I will give
42:34 your brother back to you, and you can
b Ge 34:10 trade[a] in the land.[b]' "
35As they were emptying their sacks,
there in each man's sack was his pouch
of silver! When they and their father saw
42:35 the money pouches, they were fright-
c Ge 43:12,15,18 ened.[c] 36Their father Jacob said to them,
"You have deprived me of my children.
Joseph is no more and Simeon is no
42:36 more, and now you want to take Benja-
d Ge 43:14 min.[d] Everything is against me!"
37Then Reuben said to his father, "You
may put both of my sons to death if I do
not bring him back to you. Entrust him
to my care, and I will bring him back."
38But Jacob said, "My son will not go
42:38 down there with you; his brother is
e Ge 37:33 dead[e] and he is the only one left. If harm
f ver 4 g Ge 37:35 comes to him[f] on the journey you are
h Ge 44:29,34 taking, you will bring my gray head
down to the grave[b][g] in sorrow.[h]"

The Second Journey to Egypt

43:1 43 Now the famine was still severe
i Ge 12:10; in the land.[i] 2So when they had
41:56-57 eaten all the grain they had brought
from Egypt, their father said to them,
"Go back and buy us a little more food."
3But Judah said to him, "The man
warned us solemnly, 'You will not see my
face again unless your brother is with
43:3 j Ge 42:15; 44:23 you.'[j] 4If you will send our brother along
with us, we will go down and buy food
for you. 5But if you will not send him, we
will not go down, because the man said
43:5 to us, 'You will not see my face again un-
k Ge 42:15; 2Sa 3:13 less your brother is with you.[k]' "
6Israel asked, "Why did you bring this
trouble on me by telling the man you
had another brother?"
7They replied, "The man questioned
us closely about ourselves and our fam-
43:7 l ver 27 ily. 'Is your father still living?'[l] he asked
m Ge 42:13 us. 'Do you have another brother?'[m] We
simply answered his questions. How
were we to know he would say, 'Bring
your brother down here'?"
8Then Judah said to Israel his father,
"Send the boy along with me and we will
43:8 go at once, so that we and you and our
n Ge 42:2; children may live and not die.[n] 9I myself
Ps 33:18-19 will guarantee his safety; you can hold
me personally responsible for him. If I
do not bring him back to you and set
him here before you, I will bear the 43:9
blame before you all my life.[o] 10As it is, if o Ge 42:37;
we had not delayed, we could have gone 44:32; Phm 1:18-19
and returned twice."
11Then their father Israel said to
them, "If it must be, then do this: Put
some of the best products of the land in
your bags and take them down to the 43:11
man as a gift[p]—a little balm[q] and a lit- p Ge 32:20;
tle honey, some spices[r] and myrrh, some Pr 18:16 q Ge 37:25;
pistachio nuts and almonds. 12Take Jer 8:22 r 1Ki 10:2
double the amount of silver with you, for
you must return the silver that was put
back into the mouths of your sacks.[s] 43:12 s Ge 42:25
Perhaps it was a mistake. 13Take your
brother also and go back to the man at
once. 14And may God Almighty[c][t] grant 43:14
you mercy before the man so that he will t Ge 17:1; 28:3; 35:11 u Ge 42:24
let your other brother and Benjamin v Est 4:16
come back with you.[u] As for me, if I am
bereaved, I am bereaved."[v]
15So the men took the gifts and double the amount of silver, and Benjamin
also. They hurried[w] down to Egypt and 43:15 w Ge 45:9,13
presented themselves[x] to Joseph. x Ge 47:2,7
16When Joseph saw Benjamin with
them, he said to the steward of his 43:16
house,[y] "Take these men to my house, y Ge 44:1,4,12
slaughter an animal and prepare din- z ver 31;
ner;[z] they are to eat with me at noon." Lk 15:23
17The man did as Joseph told him and
took the men to Joseph's house. 18Now
the men were frightened[a] when they 43:18 a Ge 42:35
were taken to his house. They thought,
"We were brought here because of the
silver that was put back into our sacks
the first time. He wants to attack us and
overpower us and seize us as slaves and
take our donkeys."
19So they went up to Joseph's steward
and spoke to him at the entrance to the
house. 20"Please, sir," they said, "we came 43:20
down here the first time to buy food.[b] b Ge 42:3
21But at the place where we stopped for
the night we opened our sacks and each
of us found his silver—the exact
weight—in the mouth of his sack. So we 43:21
have brought it back with us.[c] 22We have c ver 15; Ge 42:27,35
also brought additional silver with us to
buy food. We don't know who put our
silver in our sacks."
23"It's all right," he said. "Don't be
afraid. Your God, the God of your father, 43:23
has given you treasure in your sacks;[d] I d Ge 42:28

[a] 34 Or *move about freely* [b] 38 Hebrew *Sheol*
[c] 14 Hebrew *El-Shaddai*

43:23 received your silver." Then he brought
[e]Ge 42:24 Simeon out to them.[e]
[24]The steward took the men into Jo-
43:24 [f]ver 16 seph's house,[f] gave them water to wash
[g]Ge 18:4; 24:32 their feet[g] and provided fodder for their
donkeys. [25]They prepared their gifts for
Joseph's arrival at noon, because they
had heard that they were to eat there.
[26]When Joseph came home, they pre-
43:26 [h]Mt 2:11 sented to him the gifts[h] they had
[i]Ge 37:7,10 brought into the house, and they bowed
down before him to the ground.[i] [27]He
asked them how they were, and then he
43:27 said, "How is your aged father you told
[j]ver 7 me about? Is he still living?"[j]
[28]They replied, "Your servant our fa-
43:28 ther is still alive and well." And they
[k]Ge 37:7 bowed low to pay him honor.[k]
[29]As he looked about and saw his
brother Benjamin, his own mother's son,
43:29 he asked, "Is this your youngest brother,
[l]Ge 42:13 the one you told me about?"[l] And he
[m]Nu 6:25; Ps 67:1 said, "God be gracious to you,[m] my son."
43:30 [30]Deeply moved[n] at the sight of his
[n]Jn 11:33,38 brother, Joseph hurried out and looked
[o]Ge 42:24; 45:2, 14,15; 46:29 for a place to weep. He went into his private room and wept[o] there.
43:31 [31]After he had washed his face, he
[p]Ge 45:1 came out and, controlling himself,[p] said,
"Serve the food."
[32]They served him by himself, the
brothers by themselves, and the Egyptians who ate with him by themselves,
because Egyptians could not eat with
43:32 [q]Gal 2:12 Hebrews,[q] for that is detestable to Egyp-
[r]Ge 46:34; Ex 8:26 tians.[r] [33]The men had been seated before him in the order of their ages, from
the firstborn to the youngest; and they
looked at each other in astonishment.
[34]When portions were served to them
43:34 from Joseph's table, Benjamin's portion
[s]Ge 37:3; 45:22 was five times as much as anyone else's.[s]
So they feasted and drank freely with
him.

A Silver Cup in a Sack

44 Now Joseph gave these instructions to the steward of his
house: "Fill the men's sacks with as
much food as they can carry, and put
44:1 each man's silver in the mouth of his
[t]Ge 42:25 sack.[t] [2]Then put my cup, the silver one,
in the mouth of the youngest one's sack,
along with the silver for his grain." And
he did as Joseph said.
[3]As morning dawned, the men were
sent on their way with their donkeys.
[4]They had not gone far from the city
when Joseph said to his steward, "Go after those men at once, and when you
catch up with them, say to them, 'Why 44:4
have you repaid good with evil?[u] [5]Isn't [u]Ps 35:12
this the cup my master drinks from and 44:5
also uses for divination?[v] This is a [v]Ge 30:27;
wicked thing you have done.' " Dt 18:10-14
[6]When he caught up with them, he
repeated these words to them. [7]But they
said to him, "Why does my lord say such
things? Far be it from your servants to
do anything like that! [8]We even brought
back to you from the land of Canaan the
silver we found inside the mouths of our 44:8
sacks.[w] So why would we steal silver or [w]Ge 42:25; 43:21
gold from your master's house? [9]If any of
your servants is found to have it, he will 44:9
die;[x] and the rest of us will become my [x]Ge 31:32
lord's slaves."
[10]"Very well, then," he said, "let it be as
you say. Whoever is found to have it will
become my slave; the rest of you will be
free from blame."
[11]Each of them quickly lowered his
sack to the ground and opened it.
[12]Then the steward proceeded to search,
beginning with the oldest and ending
with the youngest. And the cup was 44:12
found in Benjamin's sack.[y] [13]At this, they [y]ver 2
tore their clothes.[z] Then they all loaded 44:13
their donkeys and returned to the city. [z]Ge 37:29; Nu 14:6;
[14]Joseph was still in the house when 2Sa 1:11
Judah and his brothers came in, and
they threw themselves to the ground be- 44:14
fore him.[a] [15]Joseph said to them, "What [a]Ge 37:7,10
is this you have done? Don't you know
that a man like me can find things out 44:15
by divination?[b]" [b]ver 5; Ge 30:27
[16]"What can we say to my lord?" Judah replied. "What can we say? How can

JESUS FOCUS

JUDAH SPEAKS UP

At the most critical moment in Joseph's deliberations with his brothers, Judah spoke up and offered himself as the guarantee for Benjamin's life (Genesis 44:33). Joseph was overwhelmed by this gesture and burst into tears. Judah's sacrificial offer to be a substitute mirrors the actual sacrifice made by Judah's descendant Jesus some 1800 years later. Jesus' sacrifice did more than preserve the life of one person; his death and resurrection saved the lives of all who believe in him.

we prove our innocence? God has uncovered your servants' guilt. We are now
44:16 [c]ver 9; Ge 43:18 [d]ver 2 my lord's slaves[c]—we ourselves and the
one who was found to have the cup.[d]"
17But Joseph said, "Far be it from me
to do such a thing! Only the man who
was found to have the cup will become
my slave. The rest of you, go back to your
father in peace."
18Then Judah went up to him and
said: "Please, my lord, let your servant
speak a word to my lord. Do not be an-
44:18 [e]Ge 18:30; Ex 32:22 gry[e] with your servant, though you are
equal to Pharaoh himself. 19My lord
asked his servants, 'Do you have a father
44:19 [f]Ge 43:7 or a brother?'[f] 20And we answered, 'We
have an aged father, and there is a young
44:20 [g]Ge 37:3 [h]Ge 37:33 [i]Ge 42:13 son born to him in his old age.[g] His
brother is dead,[h] and he is the only one
of his mother's sons left, and his father
loves him.'[i]
21"Then you said to your servants,
'Bring him down to me so I can see him
44:21 [j]Ge 42:15 for myself.'[j] 22And we said to my lord,
'The boy cannot leave his father; if he
44:22 [k]Ge 37:35 leaves him, his father will die.'[k] 23But
you told your servants, 'Unless your
youngest brother comes down with you,
44:23 [l]Ge 43:5 you will not see my face again.'[l] 24When
we went back to your servant my father,
we told him what my lord had said.
25"Then our father said, 'Go back and
44:25 [m]Ge 43:2 buy a little more food.'[m] 26But we said,
'We cannot go down. Only if our
youngest brother is with us will we go.
We cannot see the man's face unless our
youngest brother is with us.'
27"Your servant my father said to us,
44:27 [n]Ge 46:19 'You know that my wife bore me two
sons.[n] 28One of them went away from me,
and I said, "He has surely been torn to **44:28** [o]Ge 37:33
pieces."[o] And I have not seen him since.
29If you take this one from me too and
harm comes to him, you will bring my **44:29** [p]Ge 42:38
gray head down to the grave[a] in misery.'[p]
30"So now, if the boy is not with us
when I go back to your servant my fa-
ther and if my father, whose life is close- **44:30** [q]1Sa 18:1
ly bound up with the boy's life,[q] 31sees
that the boy isn't there, he will die. Your
servants will bring the gray head of our
father down to the grave in sorrow.
32Your servant guaranteed the boy's
safety to my father. I said, 'If I do not
bring him back to you, I will bear the **44:32** [r]Ge 43:9
blame before you, my father, all my life!'[r]
33"Now then, please let your servant **44:33** [s]Ge 43:18 [t]Jn 15:13
remain here as my lord's slave[s] in place
of the boy,[t] and let the boy return with
his brothers. 34How can I go back to my
father if the boy is not with me? No! Do
not let me see the misery that would **44:34** [u]Est 8:6
come upon my father."[u]

Joseph Makes Himself Known

45 Then Joseph could no longer
control himself[v] before all his **45:1** [v]Ge 43:31
attendants, and he cried out, "Have
everyone leave my presence!" So there
was no one with Joseph when he made
himself known to his brothers. 2And he **45:2** [w]Ge 29:11 [x]ver 16; Ge 46:29
wept[w] so loudly that the Egyptians
heard him, and Pharaoh's household
heard about it.[x]
3Joseph said to his brothers, "I am Jo- **45:3** [y]Ac 7:13 [z]ver 15
seph! Is my father still living?"[y] But his
brothers were not able to answer him,[z]
because they were terrified at his presence.
4Then Joseph said to his brothers,
"Come close to me." When they had
done so, he said, "I am your brother Jo- **45:4** [a]Ge 37:28
seph, the one you sold into Egypt![a] 5And
now, do not be distressed[b] and do not be **45:5** [b]Ge 42:21 [c]Ge 42:22 [d]ver 7-8; Ge 50:20; Ps 105:17
angry with yourselves for selling me
here,[c] because it was to save lives that
God sent me ahead of you.[d] 6For two
years now there has been famine in the
land, and for the next five years there **45:7** [e]2Ki 19:4,30,31; Isa 10:20,21; Mic 4:7; Zep 2:7 [f]Ex 15:2; Est 4:14; Isa 25:9
will not be plowing and reaping. 7But
God sent me ahead of you to preserve
for you a remnant[e] on earth and to save
your lives by a great deliverance.[b][f]
8"So then, it was not you who sent me **45:8** [g]Jdg 17:10
here, but God. He made me father[g] to

[a] 29 Hebrew *Sheol;* also in verse 31 [b] 7 Or *save you as a great band of survivors*

JESUS FOCUS

FAMILY TIES

When Leah's son Judah offered to protect Rachel's son Benjamin (Genesis 44:33), a bond of trust in the family, which had been severed for many years by jealousy and betrayal, began to be restored. In this way Judah united the hearts of the 12 brothers, just as his descendant King David would later integrate the 12 tribes of Israel into a cohesive unit (see 2 Samuel 5:1–5). Ultimately, Judah's descendant Jesus would unite all people—Jews and Gentiles—into one church (Romans 10:12–13; Ephesians 2:11–22).

Pharaoh, lord of his entire household
45:8 h Ge 41:41 and ruler of all Egypt.[h] 9Now hurry back
to my father and say to him, 'This is what
your son Joseph says: God has made me
lord of all Egypt. Come down to me;
45:9 i Ge 43:10 don't delay.[i] 10You shall live in the region
45:10 j Ge 46:28,34; 7:1 of Goshen[j] and be near me—you, your
children and grandchildren, your flocks
and herds, and all you have. 11I will pro-
45:11 k Ge 47:12 vide for you there,[k] because five years of
famine are still to come. Otherwise you
and your household and all who belong
to you will become destitute.'
12"You can see for yourselves, and so
can my brother Benjamin, that it is
really I who am speaking to you. 13Tell
my father about all the honor accorded
me in Egypt and about everything you
have seen. And bring my father down
45:13 l Ac 7:14 here quickly.[l]"
14Then he threw his arms around his
brother Benjamin and wept, and Benjamin embraced him, weeping. 15And he
45:15 m Lk 15:20 kissed[m] all his brothers and wept over
them. Afterward his brothers talked with
n ver 3 him.[n]
16When the news reached Pharaoh's
45:16 o Ac 7:13 palace that Joseph's brothers had come,[o]
Pharaoh and all his officials were
pleased. 17Pharaoh said to Joseph, "Tell
your brothers, 'Do this: Load your animals and return to the land of Canaan,
18and bring your father and your fami-
45:18 p Ge 27:28; 46:34; 47:6,11, 27; Nu 18:12,29 lies back to me. I will give you the best of
the land of Egypt[p] and you can enjoy the
q Ps 37:19 fat of the land.'[q]
19"You are also directed to tell them,
45:19 r Ge 46:5 'Do this: Take some carts[r] from Egypt
for your children and your wives, and get
your father and come. 20Never mind
about your belongings, because the best
of all Egypt will be yours.' "
21So the sons of Israel did this. Joseph
gave them carts, as Pharaoh had commanded, and he also gave them provi-
45:21 s Ge 42:25 sions for their journey.[s] 22To each of
them he gave new clothing, but to Ben-
45:22 jamin he gave three hundred shekels[a] of
t Ge 37:3; 43:34 silver and five sets of clothes.[t] 23And this
is what he sent to his father: ten donkeys
loaded with the best things of Egypt,
and ten female donkeys loaded with
grain and bread and other provisions for
his journey. 24Then he sent his brothers
45:24 u Ge 42:21-22 away, and as they were leaving he said to
them, "Don't quarrel on the way!"[u]
25So they went up out of Egypt and
came to their father Jacob in the land of
Canaan. 26They told him, "Joseph is still
alive! In fact, he is ruler of all Egypt." Jacob was stunned; he did not believe 45:26
them.[v] 27But when they told him every- v Ge 44:28
thing Joseph had said to them, and 45:27
when he saw the carts[w] Joseph had sent w ver 19
to carry him back, the spirit of their father Jacob revived. 28And Israel said, "I'm
convinced! My son Joseph is still alive. I
will go and see him before I die."

Jacob Goes to Egypt

46 So Israel set out with all that
was his, and when he reached 46:1
Beersheba,[x] he offered sacrifices to the x Ge 21:14; 28:10 y Ge 26:24;
God of his father Isaac.[y] 28:13; 31:42
2And God spoke to Israel in a vision at 46:2
night[z] and said, "Jacob! Jacob!" z Ge 15:1; Job 33:14-15
"Here I am,"[a] he replied. a Ge 22:1; 31:11
3"I am God, the God of your father,"[b] 46:3
he said. "Do not be afraid to go down to b Ge 28:13
Egypt, for I will make you into a great c Ge 12:2;
nation[c] there.[d] 4I will go down to Egypt Dt 26:5 d Ex 1:7
with you, and I will surely bring you 46:4
back again.[e] And Joseph's own hand will e Ge 28:15; 48:21; Ex 3:8
close your eyes.[f]" f Ge 50:1,24
5Then Jacob left Beersheba, and Israel's sons took their father Jacob and their
children and their wives in the carts[g] 46:5 g Ge 45:19
that Pharaoh had sent to transport him.
6They also took with them their livestock and the possessions they had ac- 46:6
quired in Canaan, and Jacob and all his h Dt 26:5;
offspring went to Egypt.[h] 7He took with Jos 24:4;
him to Egypt his sons and grandsons Ps 105:23; Isa 52:4; Ac 7:15
and his daughters and granddaugh- 46:7
ters—all his offspring.[i] i Ge 45:10

8These are the names of the sons of 46:8
Israel[j] (Jacob and his descendants) who j Ex 1:1; Nu 26:4
went to Egypt:

Reuben the firstborn of Jacob.
9The sons of Reuben:[k] 46:9
Hanoch, Pallu, Hezron and Car- k 1Ch 5:3
mi.
10The sons of Simeon:[l] 46:10
Jemuel,[m] Jamin, Ohad, Jakin, l Ge 29:33; Nu 26:14
Zohar and Shaul the son of a m Ex 6:15
Canaanite woman.
11The sons of Levi:[n] 46:11
Gershon, Kohath and Merari. n Ge 29:34; Nu 3:17
12The sons of Judah:[o] 46:12
Er, Onan, Shelah, Perez and Ze- o Ge 29:35

[a] *22* That is, about 7 1/2 pounds (about 3.5 kilograms)

rah (but Er and Onan had died
46:12 in the land of Canaan).
p 1Ch 2:5; The sons of Perez:[p]
Mt 1:3 Hezron and Hamul.
46:13 13 The sons of Issachar:[q]
q Ge 30:18 Tola, Puah,[a] [r] Jashub[b] and Shim-
r 1Ch 7:1 ron.
46:14 14 The sons of Zebulun:[s]
s Ge 30:20 Sered, Elon and Jahleel.
15 These were the sons Leah bore to Jacob in Paddan Aram,[c] besides his
daughter Dinah. These sons and daughters of his were thirty-three in all.

46:16 16 The sons of Gad:[t]
t Ge 30:11 Zephon,[d] [u] Haggi, Shuni, Ezbon,
u Nu 26:15 Eri, Arodi and Areli.
46:17 17 The sons of Asher:[v]
v Ge 30:13; Imnah, Ishvah, Ishvi and Beriah.
1Ch 7:30-31 Their sister was Serah.
The sons of Beriah:
Heber and Malkiel.
18 These were the children born to Ja-
46:18 cob by Zilpah,[w] whom Laban had given
w Ge 30:10 to his daughter Leah[x]—sixteen in all.
x Ge 29:24

46:19 19 The sons of Jacob's wife Rachel:
y Ge 44:27 Joseph and Benjamin.[y] 20 In
46:20 Egypt, Manasseh[z] and Ephraim[a]
z Ge 41:51 were born to Joseph by Asenath
a Ge 41:52 daughter of Potiphera, priest of
On.[e]
46:21 21 The sons of Benjamin:[b]
b Nu 26:38-41; Bela, Beker, Ashbel, Gera, Naa-
1Ch 7:6-12; 8:1 man, Ehi, Rosh, Muppim, Hup-
pim and Ard.
22 These were the sons of Rachel who
were born to Jacob—fourteen in all.
23 The son of Dan:
Hushim.
24 The sons of Naphtali:
Jahziel, Guni, Jezer and Shillem.
25 These were the sons born to Jacob
46:25 by Bilhah,[c] whom Laban had given to
c Ge 30:8 his daughter Rachel[d]—seven in all.
d Ge 29:29

26 All those who went to Egypt with Jacob—those who were his direct descen-
46:26 dants, not counting his sons' wives—
e ver 5-7; Ex 1:5; numbered sixty-six persons.[e] 27 With the
Dt 10:22 two sons[f] who had been born to Joseph
in Egypt, the members of Jacob's family,
46:27 which went to Egypt, were seventy[g] in
f Ac 7:14 all.[f]

46:28 28 Now Jacob sent Judah ahead of him
g Ge 45:10 to Joseph to get directions to Goshen.[g]
When they arrived in the region of Go-
shen, 29 Joseph had his chariot made
ready and went to Goshen to meet his father Israel. As soon as Joseph appeared
before him, he threw his arms around his 46:29
father[h] and wept for a long time.[h] h Ge 45:14-15; Lk 15:20
30 Israel said to Joseph, "Now I am
ready to die, since I have seen for myself
that you are still alive."
31 Then Joseph said to his brothers
and to his father's household, "I will go
up and speak to Pharaoh and will say to
him, 'My brothers and my father's
household, who were living in the land 46:31
of Canaan, have come to me.[i] 32 The men i Ge 47:1
are shepherds; they tend livestock, and
they have brought along their flocks and
herds and everything they own.' 33 When
Pharaoh calls you in and asks, 'What is 46:33
your occupation?'[j] 34 you should answer, j Ge 47:3
'Your servants have tended livestock
from our boyhood on, just as our fathers
did.' Then you will be allowed to settle in 46:34
the region of Goshen,[k] for all shepherds k Ge 45:10
are detestable to the Egyptians.[l]" l Ge 43:32; Ex 8:26

47 Joseph went and told Pharaoh,
"My father and brothers, with
their flocks and herds and everything
they own, have come from the land of 47:1
Canaan and are now in Goshen."[m] 2 He m Ge 46:31
chose five of his brothers and presented
them before Pharaoh.
3 Pharaoh asked the brothers, "What 47:3
is your occupation?"[n] n Ge 46:33
"Your servants are shepherds," they
replied to Pharaoh, "just as our fathers
were." 4 They also said to him, "We have 47:4
come to live here awhile,[o] because the o Ge 15:13; Dt 26:5
famine is severe in Canaan[p] and your p Ge 43:1
servants' flocks have no pasture. So now, q Ge 46:34
please let your servants settle in Go-
shen."[q]
5 Pharaoh said to Joseph, "Your father
and your brothers have come to you,
6 and the land of Egypt is before you; settle your father and your brothers in the
best part of the land.[r] Let them live in 47:6
Goshen. And if you know of any among r Ge 45:18
them with special ability,[s] put them in s Ex 18:21,25
charge of my own livestock."

[a] 13 Samaritan Pentateuch and Syriac (see also 1 Chron. 7:1); Masoretic Text *Puvah*
[b] 13 Samaritan Pentateuch and some Septuagint manuscripts (see also Num. 26:24 and 1 Chron. 7:1); Masoretic Text *Iob*
[c] 15 That is, Northwest Mesopotamia
[d] 16 Samaritan Pentateuch and Septuagint (see also Num. 26:15); Masoretic Text *Ziphion*
[e] 20 That is, Heliopolis
[f] 27 Hebrew; Septuagint *the nine children*
[g] 27 Hebrew (see also Exodus 1:5 and footnote); Septuagint (see also Acts 7:14) *seventy-five*
[h] 29 Hebrew *around him*

7 Then Joseph brought his father Jacob
47:7 in and presented him before Pharaoh.
[t] ver 10; After Jacob blessed[a] Pharaoh,[t] 8 Pharaoh
2Sa 14:22 asked him, "How old are you?"
9 And Jacob said to Pharaoh, "The
47:9 years of my pilgrimage are a hundred
[u] Ge 25:7 and thirty.[u] My years have been few and
[v] Heb 11:9,13 difficult,[v] and they do not equal the
[w] Ge 35:28 years of the pilgrimage of my fathers.[w]"
47:10 10 Then Jacob blessed[b] Pharaoh[x] and
[x] ver 7 went out from his presence.
11 So Joseph settled his father and his
brothers in Egypt and gave them property in the best part of the land, the dis-
47:11 [y] Ex 1:11; 12:37 trict of Rameses,[y] as Pharaoh directed.
12 Joseph also provided his father and his
brothers and all his father's household
with food, according to the number of
47:12 [z] Ge 45:11 their children.[z]

Joseph and the Famine

13 There was no food, however, in the
whole region because the famine was se-
47:13 [a] Ge 41:30; vere; both Egypt and Canaan wasted
Ac 7:11 away because of the famine.[a] 14 Joseph
collected all the money that was to be
found in Egypt and Canaan in payment
for the grain they were buying, and he
47:14 [b] Ge 41:56 brought it to Pharaoh's palace.[b] 15 When
the money of the people of Egypt and
Canaan was gone, all Egypt came to Joseph and said, "Give us food. Why
47:15 [c] ver 19; Ex 16:3 should we die before your eyes?[c] Our
money is used up."
16 "Then bring your livestock," said Joseph. "I will sell you food in exchange for
your livestock, since your money is
gone." 17 So they brought their livestock
47:17 to Joseph, and he gave them food in ex-
[d] Ex 14:9 change for their horses,[d] their sheep and
goats, their cattle and donkeys. And he
brought them through that year with
food in exchange for all their livestock.
18 When that year was over, they came
to him the following year and said, "We
cannot hide from our lord the fact that
since our money is gone and our livestock belongs to you, there is nothing
left for our lord except our bodies and
our land. 19 Why should we perish before
your eyes—we and our land as well? Buy
us and our land in exchange for food,
and we with our land will be in bondage
to Pharaoh. Give us seed so that we may
live and not die, and that the land may
not become desolate."
20 So Joseph bought all the land in
Egypt for Pharaoh. The Egyptians, one
and all, sold their fields, because the
famine was too severe for them. The
land became Pharaoh's, 21 and Joseph reduced the people to servitude,[c] from one
end of Egypt to the other. 22 However, he
did not buy the land of the priests, because they received a regular allotment
from Pharaoh and had food enough 47:22
from the allotment[e] Pharaoh gave them. [e] Dt 14:28-29;
That is why they did not sell their land. Ezr 7:24
23 Joseph said to the people, "Now that
I have bought you and your land today
for Pharaoh, here is seed for you so you
can plant the ground. 24 But when the 47:24
crop comes in, give a fifth[f] of it to Phar- [f] Ge 41:34
aoh. The other four-fifths you may keep
as seed for the fields and as food for
yourselves and your households and
your children."
25 "You have saved our lives," they said.
"May we find favor in the eyes of our 47:25
lord;[g] we will be in bondage to Pharaoh." [g] Ge 32:5
26 So Joseph established it as a law concerning land in Egypt—still in force today—that a fifth of the produce belongs
to Pharaoh. It was only the land of the 47:26
priests that did not become Pharaoh's.[h] [h] ver 22
27 Now the Israelites settled in Egypt
in the region of Goshen. They acquired 47:27
property there and were fruitful and in- [i] Ge 17:6; 46:3;
creased greatly in number.[i] Ex 1:7
28 Jacob lived in Egypt[j] seventeen 47:28
years, and the years of his life were a [j] Ps 105:23
hundred and forty-seven. 29 When the
time drew near for Israel to die,[k] he 47:29
called for his son Joseph and said to him, [k] Dt 31:14
"If I have found favor in your eyes, put [l] Ge 24:2
your hand under my thigh[l] and promise [m] Ge 24:49
that you will show me kindness and
faithfulness.[m] Do not bury me in Egypt,
30 but when I rest with my fathers, carry 47:30
me out of Egypt and bury me where they [n] Ge 49:29-32;
are buried."[n] 50:5,13;
Ac 7:15-16
"I will do as you say," he said.
31 "Swear to me,"[o] he said. Then Joseph 47:31 [o] Ge 21:23
swore to him,[p] and Israel worshiped as [p] Ge 24:3
he leaned on the top of his staff.[d][q] [q] Heb 11:21 *fn*
1Ki 1:47

Manasseh and Ephraim

48 Some time later Joseph was
told, "Your father is ill." So he
took his two sons Manasseh and Ephra-

[a] 7 Or *greeted* [b] 10 Or *said farewell to*
[c] 21 Samaritan Pentateuch and Septuagint (see also Vulgate); Masoretic Text *and he moved the people into the cities* [d] 31 Or *Israel bowed down at the head of his bed*

48:1 r Ge 41:52 im[r] along with him. 2 When Jacob was
told, "Your son Joseph has come to you,"
Israel rallied his strength and sat up on
the bed.
48:3 s Ge 28:19 t Ge 28:13; 35:9-12 3 Jacob said to Joseph, "God Almighty[a]
appeared to me at Luz[s] in the land of
Canaan, and there he blessed me[t] 4 and
48:4 u Ge 17:6 said to me, 'I am going to make you
fruitful and will increase your numbers.[u]
I will make you a community of peoples,
and I will give this land as an everlasting
possession to your descendants after
you.'
5 "Now then, your two sons born to
48:5 v Ge 41:50-52; 46:20 w 1Ch 5:1; Jos 14:4 you in Egypt[v] before I came to you here
will be reckoned as mine; Ephraim and
Manasseh will be mine,[w] just as Reuben
and Simeon are mine. 6 Any children
born to you after them will be yours; in
the territory they inherit they will be
reckoned under the names of their
brothers. 7 As I was returning from Paddan,[b] to my sorrow Rachel died in the
land of Canaan while we were still on
the way, a little distance from Ephrath.
48:7 x Ge 35:19 So I buried her there beside the road to
Ephrath" (that is, Bethlehem).[x]
8 When Israel saw the sons of Joseph,
he asked, "Who are these?"
48:9 y Ge 33:5 z Ge 27:4 9 "They are the sons God has given me
here,"[y] Joseph said to his father.
Then Israel said, "Bring them to me so
I may bless[z] them."
10 Now Israel's eyes were failing because of old age, and he could hardly
48:10 a Ge 27:1 b Ge 27:27 see.[a] So Joseph brought his sons close to
him, and his father kissed them[b] and
embraced them.
11 Israel said to Joseph, "I never expect-
48:11 c Ge 50:23; Ps 128:6 ed to see your face again, and now God
has allowed me to see your children too."[c]
12 Then Joseph removed them from Israel's knees and bowed down with his
face to the ground. 13 And Joseph took
both of them, Ephraim on his right toward Israel's left hand and Manasseh on
48:13 d Ps 110:1 his left toward Israel's right hand,[d] and
brought them close to him. 14 But Israel
reached out his right hand and put it on
Ephraim's head, though he was the
younger, and crossing his arms, he put
48:14 e Ge 41:51 his left hand on Manasseh's head, even
though Manasseh was the firstborn.[e]
48:15 f Ge 17:1 15 Then he blessed[f] Joseph and said,

"May the God before whom my
fathers
Abraham and Isaac walked,
the God who has been my
shepherd[g] 48:15 g Ge 49:24
all my life to this day,
16 the Angel who has delivered me
from all harm
—may he bless these boys.[h] 48:16 h Heb 11:21 i Ge 28:13
May they be called by my name
and the names of my fathers
Abraham and Isaac,[i]
and may they increase greatly
upon the earth."

17 When Joseph saw his father placing
his right hand on Ephraim's head[j] he was 48:17 j ver 14
displeased; so he took hold of his father's
hand to move it from Ephraim's head to
Manasseh's head. 18 Joseph said to him,
"No, my father, this one is the firstborn;
put your right hand on his head."
19 But his father refused and said, "I
know, my son, I know. He too will be-
come a people, and he too will become 48:19 k Ge 17:20 l Ge 25:23
great.[k] Nevertheless, his younger broth-
er will be greater than he,[l] and his descendants will become a group of nations." 20 He blessed them that day and
said,

"In your[c] name will Israel
pronounce this blessing:
'May God make you like 48:20 m Nu 2:18 n Nu 2:20; Ru 4:11
Ephraim[m] and
Manasseh.[n]'"

So he put Ephraim ahead of Manasseh.
21 Then Israel said to Joseph, "I am 48:21 o Ge 26:3; 46:4 p Ge 28:13; 50:24
about to die, but God will be with you[d][o]
and take you[d] back to the land of your[d]
fathers.[p] 22 And to you, as one who is 48:22 q Ge 37:8 r Jos 24:32; Jn 4:5
over your brothers,[q] I give the ridge of
land[e][r] I took from the Amorites with my
sword and my bow."

Jacob Blesses His Sons

49 Then Jacob called for his sons
and said: "Gather around so I 49:1 s Nu 24:14; Jer 23:20
can tell you what will happen to you in
days to come.[s]

2 "Assemble and listen, sons of Jacob; 49:2 t Ps 34:11
listen to your father Israel.[t]

3 "Reuben, you are my firstborn,[u] 49:3 u Ge 29:32 v Dt 21:17; Ps 78:51
my might, the first sign of my
strength,[v]

a 3 Hebrew *El-Shaddai* *b* 7 That is, Northwest Mesopotamia *c* 20 The Hebrew is singular. *d* 21 The Hebrew is plural. *e* 22 Or *And to you I give one portion more than to your brothers—the portion*

excelling in honor, excelling in
power.

49:4 [w] Isa 57:20 [x] Ge 35:22; Dt 27:20

[4] Turbulent as the waters,[w] you will
no longer excel,
for you went up onto your
father's bed,
onto my couch and defiled it.[x]

[5] "Simeon and Levi are brothers—

49:5 [y] Ge 34:25; Pr 4:17

their swords[a] are weapons of
violence.[y]

49:6 [z] Pr 1:15; Eph 5:11 [a] Ge 34:26

[6] Let me not enter their council,
let me not join their assembly,[z]
for they have killed men in their
anger[a]
and hamstrung oxen as they
pleased.

49:7 [b] Jos 19:1,9; 21:1-42

[7] Cursed be their anger, so fierce,
and their fury, so cruel!
I will scatter them in Jacob
and disperse them in Israel.[b]

[8] "Judah,[b] your brothers will praise
you;
your hand will be on the neck of
your enemies;

49:8 [c] Dt 33:7; 1Ch 5:2

your father's sons will bow down
to you.[c]

49:9 [d] Nu 24:9; Eze 19:5; Mic 5:8 [e] Rev 5:5

[9] You are a lion's[d] cub, O Judah;[e]
you return from the prey, my son.
Like a lion he crouches and lies
down,
like a lioness—who dares to
rouse him?

49:10 [f] Nu 24:17,19; Ps 60:7 [g] Ps 2:9; Isa 42:1,4

[10] The scepter will not depart from
Judah,[f]
nor the ruler's staff from
between his feet,
until he comes to whom it belongs[c]
and the obedience of the nations
is his.[g]

[11] He will tether his donkey to a vine,
his colt to the choicest branch;
he will wash his garments in wine,
his robes in the blood of grapes.

[12] His eyes will be darker than wine,
his teeth whiter than milk.[d]

49:13 [h] Ge 30:20; Dt 33:18-19; Jos 19:10-11

[13] "Zebulun[h] will live by the seashore
and become a haven for ships;
his border will extend toward
Sidon.

49:14 [i] Ge 30:18

[14] "Issachar[i] is a rawboned[e] donkey
lying down between two
saddlebags.[f]

[15] When he sees how good is his
resting place
and how pleasant is his land,
he will bend his shoulder to the
burden
and submit to forced labor.

49:16 [j] Ge 30:6; Dt 33:22; Jdg 18:26-27

[16] "Dan[g][j] will provide justice for his
people
as one of the tribes of Israel.

49:17 [k] Jdg 18:27

[17] Dan[k] will be a serpent by the
roadside,
a viper along the path,
that bites the horse's heels
so that its rider tumbles
backward.

49:18 [l] Ps 119:166,174

[18] "I look for your deliverance,
O LORD.[l]

49:19 [m] Ge 30:11; Dt 33:20; 1Ch 5:18

[19] "Gad[h][m] will be attacked by a band
of raiders,
but he will attack them at their
heels.

49:20 [n] Ge 30:13; Dt 33:24

[20] "Asher's[n] food will be rich;
he will provide delicacies fit for a
king.

[a] *5* The meaning of the Hebrew for this word is uncertain. [b] *8* *Judah* sounds like and may be derived from the Hebrew for *praise.* [c] *10* Or *until Shiloh comes;* or *until he comes to whom tribute belongs* [d] *12* Or *will be dull from wine, / his teeth white from milk* [e] *14* Or *strong* [f] *14* Or *campfires* [g] *16* *Dan* here means *he provides justice.* [h] *19* *Gad* can mean *attack* and *band of raiders.*

JESUS FOCUS

A SON'S BIRTHRIGHT

Jacob's will stipulated that the birthright was to go to Judah (Genesis 49:9–12), although Joseph was to receive the blessing. The birthright generally conferred on the eldest son the position of leadership in the family after the father's death, and the blessing bequeathed to him a portion of his father's inheritance twice that of any other son. Judah's older brothers were passed over because of their negative personal qualities, and Judah was promised the scepter and the ruler's staff—symbols of leadership—until the advent of the One to whom leadership really belonged—in Jacob's words, "until he comes to whom it belongs" (Genesis 49:10). This phrase is almost identical to the one found in Ezekiel 21:27, in which Zedekiah, the last king of Judah, was told to remove his crown until "he comes to whom it rightfully belongs." Bible scholars believe that this phrase refers to Jesus. In this way Jacob prophesied that the promised line of the Messiah would come through Judah.

DISCOVERY 14

In the Place of God?

Imagine yourself in the sandals of one of Joseph's brothers. You've never really liked your younger brother; he always seems to get the best gifts, and Dad spoils him. Then one day he tells you he's had some dreams that signify he's going to be in charge: "I will rule over you," he nonchalantly announces! Finally, you see a chance to get rid of him—and make a little money in the process. So you and your other brothers sell him off and contrive a story for your dad about how a wild animal has mauled him. Your father in anguish buys the story, and you breathe a sigh of relief. That troublesome little brother is out of your hair for good . . . or so you think.

Now, years later, you discover that your brother is more than just alive—he is the second most powerful man in Egypt and holds the ability to save your life! Your stomach churns in indescribable dread: How will he react? Will he exact revenge? He can, you know!

But Joseph has grown into a godly man. He knows that he does not have the moral right to punish the brothers for their heinous crime against him. "Am I in the place of God?" he asks rhetorically (Genesis 50:19). Joseph might be second only to Pharaoh in Egypt, but he cannot begin to challenge God's position in the universe. Ultimately, his brothers will answer to God. His responsibility is to forgive them, allowing God to bring about justice in his own way (Leviticus 19:18; Proverbs 20:22).

Joseph also knows that God's purposes are more encompassing than even the most evil of human intentions. Joseph's brothers probably felt ingenious in their plot to rid their lives of this thorn in their side. However, their actions fit perfectly into God's plan for Joseph's life—and for theirs! The most adverse circumstances, the most repulsive actions, the most clever and evil schemes are no match for the God who *will* achieve his purposes (Isaiah 45:7, Romans 8:28).

Joseph knows that he is being used by God to prevent the deaths of those around him, and he readily acknowledges who is really responsible. He assures his brothers that he isn't going to hurt them. His forgiveness is validated only when he finds within himself the ability to treat them kindly.

God the Son didn't hold a grudge either. While he hung dying on the cross, he appealed to the Father to forgive his tormentors, "for they do not know what they are doing" (Luke 23:34). The religious leaders and Romans thought they could rid their lives of Jesus simply by crucifying him. Instead of ending his influence, his death only reinforced it. Jesus came back to life again, offering to save anyone who would believe in him—even those responsible for his horrible death. The very ones who had snarled "Crucify him!" and thought they were harming him actually helped to complete God's plan—to provide peace, purpose and a way home to God the Father.

Self-Discovery: *As you think about mistakes of your past, listen to the prayer of Jesus asking God to forgive you.*

GO TO DISCOVERY 15 ON PAGE 74

HE IS ALL IN ALL: PATRIARCH AMONG THE PATRIARCHS; LAW IN THE LAWS; CHIEF PRIEST AMONG PRIESTS; RULER AMONG KINGS; THE PROPHET AMONG PROPHETS; THE ANGEL AMONG ANGELS; THE MAN AMONG MEN; SON IN THE FATHER; GOD IN GOD: KING TO ALL ETERNITY.

Irenaeus, *Early Church Father*

49:21 °Ge 30:8; Dt 33:23

21 "Naphtali[o] is a doe set free
that bears beautiful fawns.[a]

49:22 pGe 30:24; Dt 33:13-17

22 "Joseph[p] is a fruitful vine,
a fruitful vine near a spring,
whose branches climb over a
wall.[b]
23 With bitterness archers attacked
him;

49:23 qGe 37:24

they shot at him with hostility.[q]

49:24 rPs 18:34 sPs 132:2,5; Isa 1:24; 41:10 tIsa 28:16

24 But his bow remained steady,
his strong arms[r] stayed[c] limber,
because of the hand of the Mighty
One of Jacob,[s]
because of the Shepherd, the
Rock of Israel,[t]

49:25 uGe 28:13

25 because of your father's God,[u] who
helps you,
because of the Almighty,[d] who
blesses you
with blessings of the heavens above,
blessings of the deep that lies
below,[v]
blessings of the breast and womb.

49:25 vGe 27:28

26 Your father's blessings are greater
than the blessings of the ancient
mountains,
than[e] the bounty of the age-old
hills.
Let all these rest on the head of
Joseph,
on the brow of the prince
among[f] his brothers.[w]

49:26 wDt 33:15-16

27 "Benjamin[x] is a ravenous wolf;
in the morning he devours the
prey,
in the evening he divides the
plunder."

49:27 xGe 35:18; Jdg 20:12-13

28 All these are the twelve tribes of Israel, and this is what their father said to them when he blessed them, giving each the blessing appropriate to him.

The Death of Jacob

29 Then he gave them these instructions:[y] "I am about to be gathered to my people.[z] Bury me with my fathers[a] in the cave in the field of Ephron the Hittite,

49:29 yGe 50:16 zGe 25:8 aGe 15:15; 47:30; 50:13

[a] 21 Or *free; / he utters beautiful words* [b] 22 Or *Joseph is a wild colt, / a wild colt near a spring, / a wild donkey on a terraced hill* [c] 23,24 Or *archers will attack . . . will shoot . . . will remain . . . will stay* [d] 25 Hebrew *Shaddai* [e] 26 Or *of my progenitors, / as great as* [f] 26 Or *the one separated from*

LINE OF THE MESSIAH IN GENESIS

Designation	Quotation	Reference
Human Being	"offspring" of the woman	Genesis 3:15
Line of Seth	"another child in place of Abel"	Genesis 4:25
Descendant of Noah	"But Noah found favor"	Genesis 6:8
Line of Shem	"This is the account of Shem"	Genesis 11:10–32
Descendant of Abraham	"a son coming from your own body"	Genesis 12:1–3; 15:4–6
Son of Sarah	"I . . . will surely give you a son by her"	Genesis 17:16
Descendant of Isaac	"I will establish my covenant with him"	Genesis 17:19
Descendant of Jacob	"All people on earth will be blessed through you"	Genesis 28:14
Tribe of Judah	"The scepter will not depart from Judah"	Genesis 49:9–10

DISCOVERY 15

Judah and Jesus

The blessing of Jacob's sons comprises the longest poem in the book of Genesis. It contains blessings and future predictions for each of the 12 sons. Judah's blessing is of particular interest, because Judah was Jesus' ancestor. In fact Jacob's entire blessing is replete with prophecies about the coming Messiah.

In the blessing Jacob alerts his sons that Judah will be the focus of praise from his brothers. He will conquer his enemies, and his brothers will honor and serve him. Although Judah was Leah's fourth son, he received some of the rights of a firstborn.

Judah is described as a lion, a metaphor symbolic of sovereignty and strength (Genesis 49:9). The nation of Israel is also called a lion (Ezekiel 19:1–7; Micah 5:8), a symbol of the power Israel would hold over her enemies (Numbers 24:5–9). Ultimately, Jesus is referred to as the "Lion of the tribe of Judah" (Revelation 5:5), designating him as the only one who has the strength to overcome our ultimate enemies, sin and death (Revelation 5:9–10).

The scepter referred to in Genesis 49:10 symbolized for God's people a future kingdom—God's kingdom which would one day include the entire world. Balaam referred to this scepter in Numbers 24:17: "I see him, but not now; I behold him, but not near. A star will come out of Jacob; a scepter will rise out of Israel." This blessing meant that one of Judah's descendants (the Messiah) would receive this worldwide scepter and that all the nations would obey him (see Ezekiel 21:26–27). The future kingdom of the Messiah would be unparalleled in splendor (Genesis 49:11–12).

Both vines and wine are often used in the Bible as pictures of abundance, and we are told that in God's future kingdom there will be so many vines that they will be used for hitching posts, and as much wine as there is water to wash in. These words describe the world as God intended it—paradise regained!

Jacob's blessing of Judah is one example of how God reminds us throughout the Bible that he has always been at work to accomplish what he has planned. God's plan—and his promise—from the beginning was to bless Judah's family line with a righteous king to rule the world. One day Jesus will return to fulfill this ancient promise once and for all. He will rule the universe the way God intended it to be ruled—with perfect holiness.

Self-Discovery: *When you think of Jesus as the Lion of the Tribe of Judah, how does this image compare with your perception of the meek and humble Jesus?*

GO TO DISCOVERY 16 ON PAGE 78

49:30 b Ge 23:9 [30]the cave in the field of Machpelah,[b]
c Ge 23:20 near Mamre in Canaan, which Abraham
bought as a burial place from Ephron
49:31 the Hittite, along with the field.[c] [31]There
d Ge 25:9 Abraham[d] and his wife Sarah[e] were
e Ge 23:19 f Ge 35:29 buried, there Isaac and his wife Rebekah[f] were buried, and there I buried Leah.
[32]The field and the cave in it were
bought from the Hittites.[a]"
[33]When Jacob had finished giving instructions to his sons, he drew his feet
49:33 g ver 29; up into the bed, breathed his last and
Ge 25:8; Ac 7:15 was gathered to his people.[g]

50 Joseph threw himself upon his
50:1 father and wept over him and
h Ge 46:4 kissed him.[h] [2]Then Joseph directed the
50:2 physicians in his service to embalm his
i ver 26; father Israel. So the physicians em-
2Ch 16:14 balmed him,[i] [3]taking a full forty days, for
50:3 that was the time required for embalm-
j Ge 37:34; Nu 20:29; ing. And the Egyptians mourned for
Dt 34:8 him seventy days.[j]
[4]When the days of mourning had
passed, Joseph said to Pharaoh's court,
"If I have found favor in your eyes, speak
to Pharaoh for me. Tell him, [5]'My father
50:5 k Ge 47:31 made me swear an oath[k] and said, "I am
l 2Ch 16:14; about to die; bury me in the tomb I dug
Isa 22:16 m Ge 47:31 for myself[l] in the land of Canaan."[m] Now
let me go up and bury my father; then I
will return.' "
[6]Pharaoh said, "Go up and bury your
father, as he made you swear to do."
[7]So Joseph went up to bury his father.
All Pharaoh's officials accompanied
him—the dignitaries of his court and all
the dignitaries of Egypt— [8]besides all
the members of Joseph's household and
his brothers and those belonging to his
father's household. Only their children
and their flocks and herds were left in
Goshen. [9]Chariots and horsemen[b] also
went up with him. It was a very large
company.
[10]When they reached the threshing
50:10 floor of Atad, near the Jordan, they
n 2Sa 1:17; Ac 8:2 lamented loudly and bitterly;[n] and there
o 1Sa 31:13; Joseph observed a seven-day period[o] of
Job 2:13 mourning for his father. [11]When the
Canaanites who lived there saw the
mourning at the threshing floor of Atad,
they said, "The Egyptians are holding a
solemn ceremony of mourning." That is
why that place near the Jordan is called
Abel Mizraim.[c]
[12]So Jacob's sons did as he had commanded them: [13]They carried him to the
land of Canaan and buried him in the
cave in the field of Machpelah, near
Mamre, which Abraham had bought as a
burial place from Ephron the Hittite, 50:13
along with the field.[p] [14]After burying his p Ge 23:20; Ac 7:16
father, Joseph returned to Egypt, togeth-
er with his brothers and all the others
who had gone with him to bury his father.

Joseph Reassures His Brothers

[15]When Joseph's brothers saw that
their father was dead, they said, "What
if Joseph holds a grudge against us and
pays us back for all the wrongs we did to 50:15
him?"[q] [16]So they sent word to Joseph, q Ge 37:28; 42:21-22
saying, "Your father left these instruc-
tions before he died: [17]'This is what you
are to say to Joseph: I ask you to forgive
your brothers the sins and the wrongs
they committed in treating you so badly.' Now please forgive the sins of the servants of the God of your father." When
their message came to him, Joseph wept.
[18]His brothers then came and threw 50:18 r Ge 37:7
themselves down before him.[r] "We are s Ge 43:18
your slaves,"[s] they said.
[19]But Joseph said to them, "Don't be 50:19 t Ro 12:19;
afraid. Am I in the place of God?[t] [20]You in- Heb 10:30
tended to harm me,[u] but God intended[v] 50:20
it for good[w] to accomplish what is now u Ge 37:20
being done, the saving of many lives.[x] [21]So v Mic 4:11-12 w Ro 8:28
then, don't be afraid. I will provide for you x Ge 45:5
and your children.[y]" And he reassured 50:21
them and spoke kindly to them. y Ge 45:11; 47:12

The Death of Joseph

[22]Joseph stayed in Egypt, along with
all his father's family. He lived a hundred 50:22
and ten years[z] [23]and saw the third gen- z Ge 25:7;
eration[a] of Ephraim's children. Also the Jos 24:29
children of Makir[b] son of Manasseh 50:23 a Job 42:16
were placed at birth on Joseph's knees.[d] b Nu 32:39,40
[24]Then Joseph said to his brothers, "I 50:24
am about to die.[c] But God will surely c Ge 48:21
come to your aid[d] and take you up out d Ex 3:16-17 e Ge 15:14
of this land to the land[e] he promised on f Ge 12:7; 26:3;
oath to Abraham, Isaac and Jacob."[f] 28:13; 35:12
[25]And Joseph made the sons of Israel 50:25
swear an oath and said, "God will surely g Ge 47:29-30;
come to your aid, and then you must Ex 13:19; Jos 24:32;
carry my bones up from this place."[g] Heb 11:22
[26]So Joseph died at the age of a hundred and ten. And after they embalmed 50:26
him,[h] he was placed in a coffin in Egypt. h ver 2

[a] 32 Or *the sons of Heth* [b] 9 Or *charioteers*
[c] 11 *Abel Mizraim* means *mourning of the Egyptians.* [d] 23 That is, were counted as his

Exodus

Why did the firstborn of Egypt have to die in the final plague? (Exodus 12:29)

♦ *This tragedy was necessary in order to convince Pharaoh to release Israel from slavery. This event becomes an important part of the Bible's theme of redemption, which refers to buying back or exchanging one life for another. The firstborn among the Israelites were spared because their families had offered lambs as their redemption.*

Why was so much blood needed for worship? (Exodus 29:11–21)

♦ *A just and holy God could not ignore sin. But God allowed a substitute to take the place of the sinner. Anything less than blood would have devalued sin in the eyes of the people. In the New Testament Jesus became the sacrificial Lamb, removing the need for ongoing animal sacrifices.*

Jesus in Exodus The book of Exodus focuses on how God brings his people back to himself again and again. Guiding them out of slavery in Egypt, ordaining the Passover feast as a visible demonstration of his promises, providing the gift of the law and furnishing guidelines for worship at the tabernacle—all of these prefigure what Jesus would later do as our Redeemer and Passover Lamb (Hebrews 9:22–28). God's law was a gift to lead us to Jesus (see Galatians 3:23–24). Even the intricate details of the tabernacle and the sacrificial system point us to the way in which Jesus sets us free from sin when we accept him both as the sacrifice for our sins and our great high priest. By recounting the failures of the Israelites and God's continual love for them, Exodus illustrates how imperfect people can know the God who loves them perfectly and cares for them completely. In Exodus, as later in the gospel record of Jesus' sacrifice, God went to astonishing lengths to reach those he loved.

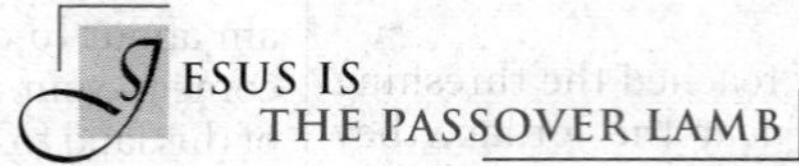

JESUS IS THE PASSOVER LAMB

The Israelites Oppressed

1 These are the names of the sons of
1:1 a Ge 46:8 Israel[a] who went to Egypt with Jacob, each with his family: 2Reuben, Simeon, Levi and Judah; 3Issachar, Zebulun
and Benjamin; 4Dan and Naphtali; Gad
1:5 and Asher. 5The descendants of Jacob
b Ge 46:26 numbered seventy*[a]* in all;[b] Joseph was
already in Egypt.
1:6 6Now Joseph and all his brothers and
c Ge 50:26 all that generation died,[c] 7but the Israel-
1:7 ites were fruitful and multiplied greatly
d Ge 46:3; and became exceedingly numerous,[d] so
Dt 26:5; Ac 7:17 that the land was filled with them.
8Then a new king, who did not know
about Joseph, came to power in Egypt.
9"Look," he said to his people, "the Isra-
1:9 elites have become much too numer-
e Ps 105:24-25 ous[e] for us. 10Come, we must deal
1:10 f Ps 83:3 shrewdly[f] with them or they will become
g Ac 7:17-19 even more numerous and, if war breaks
out, will join our enemies, fight against
us and leave the country."[g]
1:11 11So they put slave masters[h] over
h Ex 3:7 i Ge 15:13; them to oppress them with forced labor,[i]
Ex 2:11; 5:4; 6:6-7 j Ge 47:11 and they built Pithom and Rameses[j] as
k 1Ki 9:19; store cities[k] for Pharaoh. 12But the more
2Ch 8:4 they were oppressed, the more they multiplied and spread; so the Egyptians
came to dread the Israelites 13and
1:13 l Dt 4:20 worked them ruthlessly.[l] 14They made
their lives bitter with hard labor in brick
1:14 m Ex 2:23; 6:9; and mortar and with all kinds of work in
Nu 20:15; the fields; in all their hard labor the
Ps 81:6; Ac 7:19 Egyptians used them ruthlessly.[m]
15The king of Egypt said to the He-
brew midwives, whose names were
Shiphrah and Puah, 16"When you help
the Hebrew women in childbirth and
observe them on the delivery stool, if it
is a boy, kill him; but if it is a girl, let her
1:17 live." 17The midwives, however, feared[n]
n ver 21; Pr 16:6 God and did not do what the king of
o Da 3:16-18; Ac 4:18-20; 5:29 Egypt had told them to do;[o] they let the
boys live. 18Then the king of Egypt sum-
moned the midwives and asked them,
"Why have you done this? Why have you
let the boys live?"
1:19 19The midwives answered Pharaoh,
p Jos 2:4-6; 2Sa 17:20 "Hebrew women are not like Egyptian
women; they are vigorous and give birth
1:20 before the midwives arrive."[p]
q ver 12; 20So God was kind to the midwives[q]
Pr 11:18; Isa 3:10 and the people increased and became
1:21 even more numerous. 21And because the
r 1Sa 2:35; midwives feared God, he gave them fam-
2Sa 7:11,27-29; 1Ki 11:38 ilies[r] of their own.
22Then Pharaoh gave this order to all
his people: "Every boy that is born*[b]* you 1:22 s Ac 7:19
must throw into the Nile, but let every
girl live."[s]

The Birth of Moses

2 Now a man of the house of Levi 2:1
married a Levite woman,[t] 2and t Ex 6:20; Nu 26:59
she became pregnant and gave birth to
a son. When she saw that he was a fine 2:2 u Ac 7:20;
child, she hid him for three months.[u] Heb 11:23
3But when she could hide him no longer,
she got a papyrus basket for him and
coated it with tar and pitch. Then she
placed the child in it and put it among
the reeds along the bank of the Nile. 4His 2:4
sister[v] stood at a distance to see what v Ex 15:20; Nu 26:59
would happen to him.
5Then Pharaoh's daughter went down
to the Nile to bathe, and her attendants 2:5
were walking along the river bank.[w] She w Ex 7:15; 8:20
saw the basket among the reeds and
sent her slave girl to get it. 6She opened
it and saw the baby. He was crying, and
she felt sorry for him. "This is one of the
Hebrew babies," she said.
7Then his sister asked Pharaoh's

a 5 Masoretic Text (see also Gen. 46:27); Dead Sea Scrolls and Septuagint (see also Acts 7:14 and note at Gen. 46:27) *seventy-five* *b 22* Masoretic Text; Samaritan Pentateuch, Septuagint and Targums *born to the Hebrews*

MOSES
LEADER OF THE EXODUS

Moses, meaning "drawn out" (Exodus 2:10), was the younger brother of Miriam and Aaron, Israelites from the family of Jacob's son Levi. Moses was adopted and raised in luxury by Pharaoh's daughter but was later forced to flee to Midian, where he married Zipporah and lived in exile for 40 years. When Moses was 80 years old, God asked him to lead the Israelites out of slavery in Egypt—thus the title of the book detailing the Israelites' journey is *Exodus*, which means a mass exit or flight. Moses continued to lead the Israelites for another 40 years as they traveled and lived in the Sinai desert. During this time he received the tablets of the law and instructions for the tabernacle, the priesthood and the system of sacrifices. In the Bible Moses' name is often used to represent the law itself (John 9:28 and Luke 24:27), and he later appeared with Elijah (who represented God's prophets) at the time of Jesus' transfiguration (Matthew 17:1–8).

At Odds With the World

Nations have tried throughout history to eliminate the Jewish people from the face of the earth. One recent attempt was the Holocaust (1933 to 1945). Under the leadership of Adolf Hitler, the German Nazi regime attempted to eradicate the Jewish race from Europe—and later the entire world. A staggering six million Jews were murdered, including eighty percent of the intellectual and cultural leadership of the European Jewish community. Toward the end of that period, the rate of murder was drastically escalated, so that 10,000 people were killed daily in Hungary.

Hatred of the Jews (called *anti-Semitism*) has been a part of their history from the beginning, and discrimination made their lives nearly unbearable during the later years of the Israelites' stay in Egypt. Because of the famine the Israelites had traded what they had in order to buy grain, so they were indebted to the Egyptian government. Eventually the Egyptians saw the growing community as a threat and reacted by enslaving the Israelites, subjecting them to cruel and back-breaking labor (Exodus 1:11). But God's people continued to thrive (verse 12). Finally, Pharaoh ordered that every Israelite baby boy be drowned in the Nile as a barbaric means of population control (verses 15–16).

God's people have always been targets for hatred. History is replete with examples: the Romans, the Crusaders, the Turks, the Germans and many others. God chose the Jews and set them apart from all other nations as a special people (Romans 9:4). Because of that they are among the primary focuses of God's enemy, the devil, and anti-Semitism is one of his strategies.

In Old Testament times it would also have greatly benefited Satan to destroy the family line through which God's promised Messiah would be born. Even after Jesus' birth we know of two instances in which Satan tried to destroy him. First Herod, motivated by fear of a new "king," decreed that all male babies in Bethlehem and its vicinity be put to death (Matthew 2:13–18). Satan took a more direct approach when Jesus was an adult, trying to induce Jesus to voluntarily turn away from God's plan (Matthew 4:1–11; Mark 1:12–13; Luke 4:1–13).

Whether the reference is to the Jewish people (Israel) or to believers (the church), to be part of God's family means to be at odds with Satan and the world (see Genesis 3:15). Jesus himself emphasized that God's people will be hated (John 15:18–27). Family and friends may mock us because we choose to follow Jesus, but that shouldn't surprise us. It's been that way from the beginning.

***Self-Discovery:** When were you last a target for ridicule or hatred because of your Christian commitment?*

GO TO DISCOVERY 17 ON PAGE 80

daughter, "Shall I go and get one of the
Hebrew women to nurse the baby for
you?"

8"Yes, go," she answered. And the girl
went and got the baby's mother. 9Phar-
aoh's daughter said to her, "Take this baby
and nurse him for me, and I will pay you."
So the woman took the baby and nursed
him. 10When the child grew older, she
took him to Pharaoh's daughter and he
became her son. She named him Moses,[a]
saying, "I drew him out of the water."

Moses Flees to Midian

2:11 11One day, after Moses had grown up,
x Ac 7:23; Heb 11:24-26 he went out to where his own people[x]
were and watched them at their hard la-
bor. He saw an Egyptian beating a Hebrew, one of his own people. 12Glancing
this way and that and seeing no one, he
killed the Egyptian and hid him in the
sand. 13The next day he went out and
saw two Hebrews fighting. He asked the
one in the wrong, "Why are you hitting
2:13 y Ac 7:26 your fellow Hebrew?"[y]

14The man said, "Who made you ruler
2:14 z Ac 7:27* and judge over us?[z] Are you thinking of
killing me as you killed the Egyptian?"
Then Moses was afraid and thought,
"What I did must have become known."

2:15 15When Pharaoh heard of this, he
a Ac 7:29; Heb 11:27 tried to kill Moses, but Moses fled from
Pharaoh and went to live in Midian,[a]
2:16 where he sat down by a well. 16Now a
b Ex 3:1 priest of Midian[b] had seven daughters,
c Ge 24:11 and they came to draw water[c] and fill
the troughs to water their father's flock.
17Some shepherds came along and drove
2:17 them away, but Moses got up and came
d Ge 29:10 to their rescue and watered their flock.[d]
2:18 18When the girls returned to Reuel[e]
e Nu 10:29 their father, he asked them, "Why have
you returned so early today?"

19They answered, "An Egyptian rescued us from the shepherds. He even
drew water for us and watered the flock."

20"And where is he?" he asked his
2:20 daughters. "Why did you leave him? In-
f Ge 31:54 vite him to have something to eat."[f]

2:21 21Moses agreed to stay with the man,
g Ex 18:2 who gave his daughter Zipporah[g] to Mo-
2:22 ses in marriage. 22Zipporah gave birth to
h Ex 18:3-4; a son, and Moses named him Gershom,[b]
Heb 11:13 saying, "I have become an alien[h] in a foreign land."

2:23 23During that long period,[i] the king of
i Ac 7:30 Egypt died. The Israelites groaned in
their slavery and cried out, and their cry[j] 2:23 j Ex 3:7,9; Dt 26:7; Jas 5:4
for help because of their slavery went up
to God. 24God heard their groaning and
he remembered his covenant[k] with 2:24 k Ex 6:5; Ps 105:10,42
Abraham, with Isaac and with Jacob.
25So God looked on the Israelites and 2:25
was concerned[l] about them. l Ex 3:7; 4:31

Moses and the Burning Bush

3 Now Moses was tending the flock 3:1 m Ex 2:18
of Jethro[m] his father-in-law, the n 1Ki 19:8
priest of Midian, and he led the flock to o Ex 18:5
the far side of the desert and came to Horeb,[n] the mountain[o] of God. 2There the 3:2
angel of the LORD[p] appeared to him in p Ge 16:7
flames of fire from within a bush.[q] Moses q Dt 33:16; Mk 12:26;
saw that though the bush was on fire it Ac 7:30
did not burn up. 3So Moses thought, "I
will go over and see this strange sight—
why the bush does not burn up."

4When the LORD saw that he had gone
over to look, God called to him from
within the bush, "Moses! Moses!"

And Moses said, "Here I am."

5"Do not come any closer," God said. 3:5
"Take off your sandals, for the place r Ge 28:17; Jos 5:15;
where you are standing is holy ground."[r] Ac 7:33*
6Then he said, "I am the God of your fa- 3:6
ther, the God of Abraham, the God of s Ex 4:5; Mt 22:32*;
Isaac and the God of Jacob."[s] At this, Mk 12:26*;
Moses hid his face, because he was Lk 20:37*;
afraid to look at God. Ac 7:32*

[a] 10 *Moses* sounds like the Hebrew for *draw out.*
[b] 22 *Gershom* sounds like the Hebrew for *an alien there.*

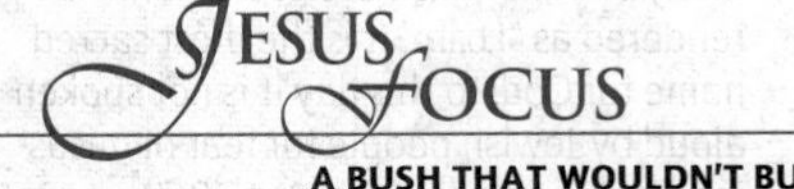

A BUSH THAT WOULDN'T BURN UP

God apparently takes delight in the creative and unusual. From a bush burning in the desert—burning, but not burning up—he showed himself to Moses on Mount Horeb (Exodus 3). The "angel of the LORD" (possibly Jesus himself; see page 23) appeared and called to Moses. When Moses asked his name, God replied, "I AM WHO I AM" and instructed Moses to tell the Israelites, "I AM has sent me to you" (verse 14). This was God's way of saying, "I exist, and I am and always will be with you." In the New Testament Jesus would declare, "Before Abraham was born, I am" (John 8:58). It is no wonder that many of the people wanted to stone Jesus because of this proclamation: They understood that he was claiming to be equal with God, the great I AM of the Old Testament.

DISCOVERY 17

I Am Who I Am

As Moses trudged through the desert one day, he noticed a bush burning in the distance. The unusual thing was that the bush was not being consumed. Moses was drawn to investigate this phenomenon, and what (or rather *who*) he found there changed his life—because he encountered God himself! God informed Moses that he was delegating him to lead the people of Israel out of their bondage to Egypt (Exodus 3:10). Moses voiced a very natural objection: "Suppose I go to the Israelites and say to them, 'The God of your fathers has sent me to you,' and they ask me, 'What is his name?' Then what shall I tell them?" (verse 13). God replied, "I AM WHO I AM. This is what you are to say to the Israelites: 'I AM has sent me to you'" (verse 14).

God's name, *Yahweh*, comes from the Hebrew verb *hayah*, meaning "to be." The name reminds us that God simply *is*—no further description should be necessary. He is the God who transcends time so that past, present and future become irrelevant; he is eternal and unchanging. In many of our English Bibles his name is rendered as "LORD." It is the most sacred name for God; to this day it is not spoken aloud by Jewish people for fear of misusing God's name (see Exodus 20:7).

When Jesus was on earth, he applied this most sacred name of God to himself. In this way he implicitly claimed to be the God who exists, eternal and unchanging. One day, when a Jewish delegation came to talk to him, Jesus told them that their forefather Abraham "rejoiced at the thought of seeing my day" (John 8:56). The men were puzzled because Jesus was so young. How was it that Abraham could have looked forward to Jesus' life? Jesus responded, "I tell you the truth . . . before Abraham was born, I am!" (John 8:58).

Throughout the Gospel of John, Jesus repeatedly used the phrase "I am" in combination with other descriptive words to flesh out our picture of him (see John 6:35; 8:12; 9:5; 10:7,11,14; 11:25; 14:6; 15:1). If Jesus is all that he claims to be—and he is!—we can turn to him for everything. No other person and nothing else in this world can meet our deepest needs. Jesus is the incarnation of all the fullness of God, a God we can know personally. We know the great "I AM"! Every day is a burning-bush day in Jesus Christ!

Self-Discovery: *Jesus called himself "I AM." Think about who he is to you and fill in the blank below with the most meaningful sentence you can think of: Jesus is*

____.

GO TO DISCOVERY 18 ON PAGE 84

7The LORD said, "I have indeed seen
the misery of my people in Egypt. I have
3:7 heard them crying out because of their
t Ex 2:25 slave drivers, and I am concerned[t] about
3:8 their suffering. 8So I have come down[u]
u Ge 50:24 v ver 17; to rescue them from the hand of the
Ex 13:5; Dt 1:25 Egyptians and to bring them up out of
w Ge 15:18-21 that land into a good and spacious land,
a land flowing with milk and honey[v]—
the home of the Canaanites, Hittites,
Amorites, Perizzites, Hivites and Jebusites.[w] 9And now the cry of the Israelites
has reached me, and I have seen the way
3:9 x Ex 1:14; 2:23 the Egyptians are oppressing[x] them.
10So now, go. I am sending you to Phar-
3:10 y Mic 6:4 aoh to bring my people the Israelites out
of Egypt."[y]
3:11 z Ex 6:12,30; 11But Moses said to God, "Who am I,[z]
1Sa 18:18 that I should go to Pharaoh and bring
the Israelites out of Egypt?"
3:12 12And God said, "I will be with you.[a]
a Ge 31:3; Jos 1:5; Ro 8:31 And this will be the sign to you that it is
I who have sent you: When you have
brought the people out of Egypt, you[a]
will worship God on this mountain."
13Moses said to God, "Suppose I go to
the Israelites and say to them, 'The God
of your fathers has sent me to you,' and
they ask me, 'What is his name?' Then
what shall I tell them?"
3:14 b Ex 6:2-3; 14God said to Moses, "I AM WHO I AM.[b]
Jn 8:58; Heb 13:8 This is what you are to say to the Israelites: 'I AM[b] has sent me to you.'"
15God also said to Moses, "Say to the
Israelites, 'The LORD,[c] the God of your fathers—the God of Abraham, the God of
Isaac and the God of Jacob—has sent
3:15 c Ps 135:13; me to you.' This is my name[c] forever, the
Hos 12:5 name by which I am to be remembered
from generation to generation.
3:16 d Ex 4:29 16"Go, assemble the elders[d] of Israel
and say to them, 'The LORD, the God of
your fathers—the God of Abraham,
Isaac and Jacob—appeared to me and
said: I have watched over you and have
seen what has been done to you in Egypt.
17And I have promised to bring you up
3:17 e Ge 15:16; out of your misery in Egypt[e] into the
Jos 24:11 land of the Canaanites, Hittites, Amorites, Perizzites, Hivites and Jebusites—
a land flowing with milk and honey.'
3:18 f Ex 4:1,8,31 18"The elders of Israel will listen[f] to
g Ex 5:1,3 you. Then you and the elders are to go to
the king of Egypt and say to him, 'The
LORD, the God of the Hebrews, has met
with us. Let us take a three-day journey
into the desert to offer sacrifices[g] to the
LORD our God.' 19But I know that the
king of Egypt will not let you go unless a 3:19
mighty hand[h] compels him. 20So I will h Ex 4:21; 5:2
stretch out my hand[i] and strike the 3:20
Egyptians with all the wonders[j] that I i Ex 6:1,6; 9:15 j Dt 6:22;
will perform among them. After that, he Ne 9:10; Ac 7:36
will let you go.[k] k Ex 12:31-33
21"And I will make the Egyptians fa- 3:21
vorably disposed[l] toward this people, so l Ex 12:36
that when you leave you will not go m Ps 105:37
empty-handed.[m] 22Every woman is to
ask her neighbor and any woman living
in her house for articles of silver and 3:22
gold[n] and for clothing, which you will n Ex 11:2
put on your sons and daughters. And so o Eze 39:10
you will plunder[o] the Egyptians."

Signs for Moses

4 Moses answered, "What if they do
not believe me or listen[p] to me and 4:1 p Ex 3:18; 6:30
say, 'The LORD did not appear to you'?"
2Then the LORD said to him, "What is
that in your hand?"
"A staff,"[q] he replied. 4:2 q ver 17,20
3The LORD said, "Throw it on the
ground."
Moses threw it on the ground and it
became a snake, and he ran from it.
4Then the LORD said to him, "Reach out
your hand and take it by the tail." So
Moses reached out and took hold of the
snake and it turned back into a staff in
his hand. 5"This," said the LORD, "is so
that they may believe[r] that the LORD, the 4:5 r Ex 19:9
God of their fathers—the God of Abra-
ham, the God of Isaac and the God of Jacob—has appeared to you."
6Then the LORD said, "Put your hand
inside your cloak." So Moses put his
hand into his cloak, and when he took it 4:6 s Nu 12:10;
out, it was leprous,[d] like snow.[s] 2Ki 5:1,27
7"Now put it back into your cloak," he
said. So Moses put his hand back into 4:7 t Nu 12:13-15;
his cloak, and when he took it out, it was Dt 32:39;
restored,[t] like the rest of his flesh. 2Ki 5:14; Mt 8:3
8Then the LORD said, "If they do not
believe you or pay attention to the first
miraculous sign, they may believe the
second. 9But if they do not believe these
two signs or listen to you, take some water from the Nile and pour it on the dry

a 12 The Hebrew is plural. *b* 14 Or *I WILL BE WHAT I WILL BE* *c* 15 The Hebrew for *LORD* sounds like and may be derived from the Hebrew for *I AM* in verse 14. *d* 6 The Hebrew word was used for various diseases affecting the skin—not necessarily leprosy.

4:9 ground. The water you take from the riv-
u Ex 7:17-21 er will become blood[u] on the ground."
10 Moses said to the LORD, "O Lord, I
have never been eloquent, neither in the
past nor since you have spoken to your
4:10 v Ex 6:12; Jer 1:6 servant. I am slow of speech and
tongue."[v]
4:11 w Ps 94:9; 11 The LORD said to him, "Who gave
Mt 11:5 man his mouth? Who makes him deaf
4:12 or mute? Who gives him sight or makes
x Isa 50:4; him blind?[w] Is it not I, the LORD? 12 Now
Jer 1:9; Mt 10:19-20; go; I will help you speak and will teach
Mk 13:11; you what to say."[x]
Lk 12:12; 21:14-15 13 But Moses said, "O Lord, please
send someone else to do it."
14 Then the LORD's anger burned
against Moses and he said, "What about
your brother, Aaron the Levite? I know
4:14 he can speak well. He is already on his
y ver 27 way to meet[y] you, and his heart will be
4:15 glad when he sees you. 15 You shall speak
z Nu 23:5,12,16 to him and put words in his mouth;[z] I
will help both of you speak and will
teach you what to do. 16 He will speak to
4:16 the people for you, and it will be as if he
a Ex 7:1-2 were your mouth[a] and as if you were
4:17 God to him. 17 But take this staff[b] in your
b ver 2 c Ex 7:9-21 hand so you can perform miraculous
signs[c] with it."

Moses Returns to Egypt

18 Then Moses went back to Jethro his
father-in-law and said to him, "Let me
go back to my own people in Egypt to
see if any of them are still alive."
Jethro said, "Go, and I wish you well."
19 Now the LORD had said to Moses in
4:19 d Ex 2:15 Midian, "Go back to Egypt, for all the
e Ex 2:23 men who wanted to kill[d] you are dead.[e]"
20 So Moses took his wife and sons, put
4:20 them on a donkey and started back to
f Ex 17:9; Nu 20:8-9,11 Egypt. And he took the staff[f] of God in
his hand.
4:21 g Ex 3:19,20 21 The LORD said to Moses, "When you
h Ex 7:3,13; return to Egypt, see that you perform
9:12,35; 14:4,8; before Pharaoh all the wonders[g] I have
Dt 2:30; given you the power to do. But I will
Isa 63:17; Jn 12:40; harden his heart[h] so that he will not let
Ro 9:18 the people go. 22 Then say to Pharaoh,
4:22 'This is what the LORD says: Israel is my
i Isa 63:16; 64:8; Jer 31:9; firstborn son,[i] 23 and I told you, "Let my
Hos 11:1; Ro 9:4 son go,[j] so he may worship me." But you
4:23 refused to let him go; so I will kill your
j Ex 5:1; 7:16 firstborn son.' "[k]
k Ex 11:5; 12:12, 29 24 At a lodging place on the way, the
4:24 LORD met ⌊Moses⌋[a] and was about to
l Nu 22:22 kill[l] him. 25 But Zipporah took a flint
knife, cut off her son's foreskin[m] and 4:25 m Ge 17:14;
touched ⌊Moses'⌋ feet with it.[b] "Surely Jos 5:2,3
you are a bridegroom of blood to me,"
she said. 26 So the LORD let him alone. (At
that time she said "bridegroom of
blood," referring to circumcision.)
27 The LORD said to Aaron, "Go into the
desert to meet Moses." So he met Moses 4:27
at the mountain[n] of God and kissed[o] n Ex 3:1 o ver 14
him. 28 Then Moses told Aaron every- 4:28
thing the LORD had sent him to say,[p] and p ver 8-9,16
also about all the miraculous signs he
had commanded him to perform.
29 Moses and Aaron brought together 4:29
all the elders[q] of the Israelites, 30 and q Ex 3:16
Aaron told them everything the LORD
had said to Moses. He also performed
the signs before the people, 31 and they 4:31
believed.[r] And when they heard that the r ver 8; Ex 3:18
LORD was concerned[s] about them and s Ex 2:25
had seen their misery, they bowed down
and worshiped.

Bricks Without Straw

5 Afterward Moses and Aaron went
to Pharaoh and said, "This is what
the LORD, the God of Israel, says: 'Let my
people go, so that they may hold a festi- 5:1
val[t] to me in the desert.' " t Ex 3:18
2 Pharaoh said, "Who is the LORD,[u] 5:2
that I should obey him and let Israel go? u 2Ki 18:35; Job 21:15
I do not know the LORD and I will not let v Ex 3:19
Israel go."[v]
3 Then they said, "The God of the Hebrews has met with us. Now let us take
a three-day journey into the desert to offer sacrifices to the LORD our God, or he 5:3
may strike us with plagues[w] or with the w Ex 3:18
sword."
4 But the king of Egypt said, "Moses
and Aaron, why are you taking the peo- 5:4
ple away from their labor?[x] Get back to x Ex 1:11
your work!" 5 Then Pharaoh said, "Look,
the people of the land are now numer- 5:5
ous,[y] and you are stopping them from y Ex 1:7,9
working."
6 That same day Pharaoh gave this order to the slave drivers and foremen in
charge of the people: 7 "You are no longer
to supply the people with straw for making bricks; let them go and gather their
own straw. 8 But require them to make
the same number of bricks as before;
don't reduce the quota. They are lazy;
that is why they are crying out, 'Let us go

[a] 24 Or ⌊*Moses' son*⌋; Hebrew *him* [b] 25 Or *and drew near ⌊Moses'⌋ feet*

and sacrifice to our God.' [9]Make the
work harder for the men so that they
keep working and pay no attention to
lies."
[10]Then the slave drivers and the foremen went out and said to the people,
"This is what Pharaoh says: 'I will not
give you any more straw. [11]Go and get
your own straw wherever you can find it,
but your work will not be reduced at
all.' " [12]So the people scattered all over
Egypt to gather stubble to use for straw.
[13]The slave drivers kept pressing them,
saying, "Complete the work required of
you for each day, just as when you had
straw." [14]The Israelite foremen appoint-
5:14 ed by Pharaoh's slave drivers were beat-
[z] Isa 10:24 en[z] and were asked, "Why didn't you
meet your quota of bricks yesterday or
today, as before?"
[15]Then the Israelite foremen went and
appealed to Pharaoh: "Why have you
treated your servants this way? [16]Your
servants are given no straw, yet we are
told, 'Make bricks!' Your servants are being beaten, but the fault is with your
own people."
[17]Pharaoh said, "Lazy, that's what you
5:17 [a] ver 8 are—lazy![a] That is why you keep saying,
'Let us go and sacrifice to the LORD.'
[18]Now get to work. You will not be given
any straw, yet you must produce your
full quota of bricks."
[19]The Israelite foremen realized they
were in trouble when they were told,
"You are not to reduce the number of
bricks required of you for each day."
[20]When they left Pharaoh, they found
Moses and Aaron waiting to meet them,
[21]and they said, "May the LORD look
5:21 upon you and judge you! You have made
[b] Ge 34:30 us a stench[b] to Pharaoh and his officials
[c] Ex 14:11 and have put a sword in their hand to
kill us."[c]

God Promises Deliverance

[22]Moses returned to the LORD and
5:22 said, "O Lord, why have you brought
[d] Nu 11:11 trouble upon this people?[d] Is this why
you sent me? [23]Ever since I went to Pharaoh to speak in your name, he has
5:23 brought trouble upon this people, and
[e] Jer 4:10 you have not rescued[e] your people at all."
6 Then the LORD said to Moses,
"Now you will see what I will do to
6:1 [f] Ex 3:19 Pharaoh: Because of my mighty hand[f] he
[g] Ex 3:20 will let them go;[g] because of my mighty
hand he will drive them out of his coun-
try."[h] **6:1** [h] Ex 12:31,33,39
[2]God also said to Moses, "I am the
LORD. [3]I appeared to Abraham, to Isaac **6:3** [i] Ge 17:1
and to Jacob as God Almighty,[a][i] but by [j] Ps 68:4; 83:18;
my name[j] the LORD[b][k] I did not make Isa 52:6
myself known to them.[c] [4]I also estab- [k] Ex 3:14
lished my covenant[l] with them to give **6:4** [l] Ge 15:18
them the land of Canaan, where they [m] Ge 28:4,13
lived as aliens.[m] [5]Moreover, I have heard **6:5**
the groaning[n] of the Israelites, whom [n] Ex 2:23
the Egyptians are enslaving, and I have
remembered my covenant.
[6]"Therefore, say to the Israelites: 'I am
the LORD, and I will bring you out from
under the yoke of the Egyptians. I will
free you from being slaves to them, and **6:6**
I will redeem[o] you with an outstretched [o] Dt 7:8;
arm[p] and with mighty acts of judgment. 1Ch 17:21 [p] Dt 26:8
[7]I will take you as my own people, and I
will be your God.[q] Then you will know[r] **6:7** [q] Dt 4:20;
that I am the LORD your God, who 2Sa 7:24 [r] Ex 16:12;
brought you out from under the yoke of Isa 41:20
the Egyptians. [8]And I will bring you to **6:8**
the land[s] I swore with uplifted hand[t] to [s] Ge 15:18; 26:3
give to Abraham, to Isaac and to Jacob.[u] [t] Ge 14:22
I will give it to you as a possession. I am [u] Ps 136:21-22
the LORD.' "
[9]Moses reported this to the Israelites,
but they did not listen to him because of
their discouragement and cruel
bondage.
[10]Then the LORD said to Moses, [11]"Go,
tell Pharaoh king of Egypt to let the Israelites go out of his country."
[12]But Moses said to the LORD, "If the
Israelites will not listen to me, why
would Pharaoh listen to me, since I **6:12** [v] ver 30;
speak with faltering lips[d]?"[v] Ex 4:10; Jer 1:6

Family Record of Moses and Aaron

[13]Now the LORD spoke to Moses and
Aaron about the Israelites and Pharaoh
king of Egypt, and he commanded them
to bring the Israelites out of Egypt.

[14]These were the heads of their **6:14**
families[e]:[w] [w] Ge 46:9

The sons of Reuben the firstborn
son of Israel were Hanoch and Pallu, Hezron and Carmi. These were
the clans of Reuben.

[a] 3 Hebrew *El-Shaddai* [b] 3 See note at Exodus 3:15. [c] 3 Or *Almighty, and by my name the LORD did I not let myself be known to them?*
[d] 12 Hebrew *I am uncircumcised of lips*; also in verse 30 [e] 14 The Hebrew for *families* here and in verse 25 refers to units larger than clans.

DISCOVERY 18

Yahweh Is Salvation

For nearly 400 years, while living in Egypt, God's people had watched the Egyptians worship pagan "gods"—birds, insects and other animals. Each god had its own name, its own special significance and its own ceremonies. God asked Moses to infiltrate this society and extricate his people, removing them from a place of slavery to a place of promise.

God's instructions were straightforward: "Tell the Israelites that I am the LORD" (Exodus 6:6). "Tell Pharaoh to let the Israelites go" (verse 11), "then stand back and watch what I am going to do to Pharaoh" (verse 1). But could such a simple plan deliver more than two million people from captivity? We have the advantage of knowing the end of the story—and the answer was a resounding yes!

God is true to his word; he has never lied and has kept every promise he has ever made. Moses continually reminded the people that God would keep his promises to them (Genesis 17:7–8; Exodus 6:4). He had promised to redeem them (Exodus 6:1,6) and to adopt them as his own people, cementing the relationship as permanent and official (verse 7). Similarly, when God adopts us into his family, the arrangement is forever! Finally, God promised to give the Israelites a new home, land that he had long ago promised to Abraham (Numbers 13:21–27).

But there is a poignant note of sadness in this narrative: When Moses told the people that there was a God who had perceived their suffering and wanted to set them free, they refused to believe him. Their bondage had blinded them to hope (Exodus 6:9). Sadly, Jesus would later receive a similar response (John 8:32–36).

The Hebrew name for Jesus is *Yeshua*, which means "*Yahweh* is salvation," "because he will save his people from their sins" (Matthew 1:21). Luke asserted in Acts 4:12 that "salvation is found in no one else, for there is no other name under heaven given to men by which we must be saved."

Like Moses, Jesus was born to set us free from bondage—the bondage of sin. And he waits patiently in the wings for us to acknowledge him as our eternal hope and salvation.

***Self-Discovery:** From what kind of "bondage" is Jesus patiently waiting to set you free? Will you allow him to?*

GO TO DISCOVERY 19 ON PAGE 91

6:15 [x]Ge 46:10; 15The sons of Simeon[x] were Je-
1Ch 4:24 muel, Jamin, Ohad, Jakin, Zohar
and Shaul the son of a Canaanite
woman. These were the clans of
Simeon.
16These were the names of the
6:16 [y]Ge 46:11 sons of Levi according to their
[z]Nu 3:17 records: Gershon,[y] Kohath and Merari.[z] Levi lived 137 years.
17The sons of Gershon, by clans,
6:17 [a]1Ch 6:17 were Libni and Shimei.[a]
6:18 18The sons of Kohath were Am-
[b]1Ch 6:2,18 ram, Izhar, Hebron and Uzziel.[b] Kohath lived 133 years.
6:19 19The sons of Merari were Mahli
[c]Nu 1Ch 6:19; 23:21 and Mushi.[c]
These were the clans of Levi according to their records.
6:20 20Amram married his father's sis-
[d]Ex 2:1-2; Nu 26:59 ter Jochebed, who bore him Aaron
and Moses.[d] Amram lived 137 years.
6:21 21The sons of Izhar[e] were Korah,
[e]1Ch 6:38 Nepheg and Zicri.
6:22 22The sons of Uzziel were Misha-
[f]Lev 10:4; Nu 3:30 el, Elzaphan[f] and Sithri.
23Aaron married Elisheba, daugh-
6:23 [g]Ru 4:19,20 ter of Amminadab[g] and sister of
[h]Lev 10:1 Nahshon, and she bore him Nadab
[i]Nu 3:2,32 [j]Nu 26:60 and Abihu,[h] Eleazar[i] and Ithamar.[j]
6:24 24The sons of Korah[k] were Assir,
[k]Nu 26:11 Elkanah and Abiasaph. These were
the Korahite clans.
6:25 25Eleazar son of Aaron married
[l]Nu 25:7,11; one of the daughters of Putiel, and
Jos 24:33; Ps 106:30 she bore him Phinehas.[l]

These were the heads of the Levite families, clan by clan.
6:26 26It was this same Aaron and Moses
[m]Ex 7:4; 12:17, to whom the LORD said, "Bring the Isra-
41,51 elites out of Egypt by their divisions."[m]
27They were the ones who spoke to
Pharaoh king of Egypt about bringing
the Israelites out of Egypt. It was the
same Moses and Aaron.

Aaron to Speak for Moses

28Now when the LORD spoke to Moses
6:29 in Egypt, 29he said to him, "I am the
[n]ver 11; Ex 7:2 LORD.[n] Tell Pharaoh king of Egypt everything I tell you."
6:30 30But Moses said to the LORD, "Since I
[o]ver 12; Ex 4:10 speak with faltering lips,[o] why would
Pharaoh listen to me?"

7 Then the LORD said to Moses,
7:1 [p]Ex 4:16 "See, I have made you like God[p] to
Pharaoh, and your brother Aaron will be
your prophet. 2You are to say everything
I command you, and your brother Aaron is to tell Pharaoh to let the Israelites
go out of his country. 3But I will harden 7:3
Pharaoh's heart,[q] and though I multiply [q]Ex 4:21; 11:9
my miraculous signs and wonders in
Egypt, 4he will not listen[r] to you. Then I 7:4
will lay my hand on Egypt and with [r]Ex 11:9
mighty acts of judgment[s] I will bring out [s]Ex 3:20; 6:6
my divisions, my people the Israelites.
5And the Egyptians will know that I am 7:5
the LORD[t] when I stretch out my hand[u] [t]ver 17; Ex 8:19,
against Egypt and bring the Israelites 22 [u]Ex 3:20
out of it."
6Moses and Aaron did just as the 7:6
LORD commanded[v] them. 7Moses was [v]ver 2
eighty years old[w] and Aaron eighty- 7:7 [w]Dt 31:2; 34:7;
three when they spoke to Pharaoh. Ac 7:23,30

Aaron's Staff Becomes a Snake

8The LORD said to Moses and Aaron,
9"When Pharaoh says to you, 'Perform a
miracle,[x]' then say to Aaron, 'Take your 7:9 [x]Isa 7:11;
staff and throw it down before Pharaoh,' Jn 2:18
and it will become a snake."[y] [y]Ex 4:2-5
10So Moses and Aaron went to Pharaoh and did just as the LORD commanded. Aaron threw his staff down in front
of Pharaoh and his officials, and it became a snake. 11Pharaoh then summoned wise men and sorcerers, and the 7:11
Egyptian magicians[z] also did the same [z]Ge 41:8;
things by their secret arts:[a] 12Each one 2Ti 3:8 [a]ver 22; Ex 8:7,18
threw down his staff and it became a
snake. But Aaron's staff swallowed up
their staffs. 13Yet Pharaoh's heart[b] be- 7:13
came hard and he would not listen to [b]Ex 4:21
them, just as the LORD had said.

The Plague of Blood

14Then the LORD said to Moses, "Phar- 7:14
aoh's heart is unyielding;[c] he refuses to [c]Ex 8:15,32;
let the people go. 15Go to Pharaoh in the 10:1,20,27
morning as he goes out to the water.
Wait on the bank of the Nile to meet
him, and take in your hand the staff that
was changed into a snake. 16Then say to
him, 'The LORD, the God of the Hebrews,
has sent me to say to you: Let my people
go, so that they may worship[d] me in the 7:16
desert. But until now you have not lis- [d]Ex 3:18; 5:1,3
tened. 17This is what the LORD says: By
this you will know that I am the LORD:[e] 7:17
With the staff that is in my hand I will [e]Ex 5:2 [f]Ex 4:9; Rev 11:6; 16:4
strike the water of the Nile, and it will be
changed into blood.[f] 18The fish in the
Nile will die, and the river will stink; the

7:18 Egyptians will not be able to drink its
g ver 21,24 water.' "[g]
19 The LORD said to Moses, "Tell Aar-
7:19 on, 'Take your staff and stretch out your
h Ex 8:5-6,16; hand[h] over the waters of Egypt—over
9:22; 10:12,21; the streams and canals, over the ponds
14:21 and all the reservoirs'—and they will
turn to blood. Blood will be everywhere
in Egypt, even in the wooden buckets
and stone jars."
20 Moses and Aaron did just as the
LORD had commanded. He raised his
staff in the presence of Pharaoh and his
7:20 officials and struck the water of the
i Ex 17:5 Nile,[i] and all the water was changed into
j Ps 78:44; 105:29 blood.[j] 21 The fish in the Nile died, and
the river smelled so bad that the Egyp-
tians could not drink its water. Blood
was everywhere in Egypt.
22 But the Egyptian magicians did the
7:22 k ver 11 same things by their secret arts,[k] and
Pharaoh's heart became hard; he would
not listen to Moses and Aaron, just as
the LORD had said. 23 Instead, he turned
and went into his palace, and did not
take even this to heart. 24 And all the
Egyptians dug along the Nile to get
drinking water, because they could not
drink the water of the river.

The Plague of Frogs

25 Seven days passed after the LORD
8 struck the Nile. 1 Then the LORD
said to Moses, "Go to Pharaoh and
say to him, 'This is what the LORD says:
8:1 Let my people go, so that they may wor-
l Ex 3:12,18; 4:23 ship[l] me. 2 If you refuse to let them go, I
will plague your whole country with
frogs. 3 The Nile will teem with frogs.
They will come up into your palace and
your bedroom and onto your bed, into
the houses of your officials and on your
8:3 people,[m] and into your ovens and knead-
m Ex 10:6 ing troughs. 4 The frogs will go up on you
and your people and all your officials.' "
5 Then the LORD said to Moses, "Tell
Aaron, 'Stretch out your hand with your
8:5 n Ex 7:19 staff[n] over the streams and canals and
ponds, and make frogs come up on the
land of Egypt.' "
6 So Aaron stretched out his hand over
8:6 the waters of Egypt, and the frogs[o] came
o Ps 78:45; 105:30 up and covered the land. 7 But the magi-
8:7 cians did the same things by their secret
p Ex 7:11 arts;[p] they also made frogs come up on
the land of Egypt.
8 Pharaoh summoned Moses and Aar-
on and said, "Pray[q] to the LORD to take 8:8
the frogs away from me and my people, q ver 28; Ex 9:28; 10:17
and I will let your people go to offer sac- r ver 25
rifices[r] to the LORD."
9 Moses said to Pharaoh, "I leave to
you the honor of setting the time for me
to pray for you and your officials and
your people that you and your houses
may be rid of the frogs, except for those
that remain in the Nile."
10 "Tomorrow," Pharaoh said.
Moses replied, "It will be as you say, so 8:10 s Ex 9:14;
that you may know there is no one like Dt 4:35; 33:26;
the LORD our God.[s] 11 The frogs will leave 2Sa 7:22; 1Ch 17:20;
you and your houses, your officials and Ps 86:8;
your people; they will remain only in the Isa 46:9; Jer 10:6
Nile."
12 After Moses and Aaron left Pharaoh, Moses cried out to the LORD about
the frogs he had brought on Pharaoh.
13 And the LORD did what Moses asked.
The frogs died in the houses, in the
courtyards and in the fields. 14 They were
piled into heaps, and the land reeked of
them. 15 But when Pharaoh saw that 8:15
there was relief, he hardened his heart[t] t Ex 7:14
and would not listen to Moses and Aar-
on, just as the LORD had said.

The Plague of Gnats

16 Then the LORD said to Moses, "Tell
Aaron, 'Stretch out your staff and strike
the dust of the ground,' and throughout
the land of Egypt the dust will become
gnats." 17 They did this, and when Aaron
stretched out his hand with the staff and 8:17
struck the dust of the ground, gnats[u] u Ps 105:31
came upon men and animals. All the
dust throughout the land of Egypt be-
came gnats. 18 But when the magicians[v] 8:18 v Ex 9:11; Da 5:8
tried to produce gnats by their secret w Ex 7:11
arts,[w] they could not. And the gnats
were on men and animals.
19 The magicians said to Pharaoh, 8:19
"This is the finger[x] of God." But Phar- x Ex 7:5; 10:7;
aoh's heart was hard and he would not Ps 8:3; Lk 11:20
listen, just as the LORD had said.

The Plague of Flies

20 Then the LORD said to Moses, "Get 8:20
up early in the morning[y] and confront y Ex 7:15; 9:13
Pharaoh as he goes to the water and say z ver 1; Ex 3:18
to him, 'This is what the LORD says: Let
my people go, so that they may worship[z]
me. 21 If you do not let my people go, I
will send swarms of flies on you and
your officials, on your people and into

your houses. The houses of the Egyptians will be full of flies, and even the
ground where they are.
22" 'But on that day I will deal differ-
8:22 ently with the land of Goshen, where my
[a] Ex 9:4,6,26; people live;[a] no swarms of flies will be
10:23; 11:7 there, so that you will know[b] that I, the
[b] Ex 7:5; 9:29 LORD, am in this land. 23I will make a distinction[a] between my people and your
people. This miraculous sign will occur
tomorrow.' "
24And the LORD did this. Dense
swarms of flies poured into Pharaoh's
8:24 palace and into the houses of his offi-
[c] Ps 78:45; cials, and throughout Egypt the land
105:31 was ruined by the flies.[c]
8:25 25Then Pharaoh summoned[d] Moses
[d] ver 8; Ex 9:27 and Aaron and said, "Go, sacrifice to
your God here in the land."
26But Moses said, "That would not be
right. The sacrifices we offer the LORD
8:26 our God would be detestable to the
[e] Ge 43:32; 46:34 Egyptians.[e] And if we offer sacrifices
that are detestable in their eyes, will they
not stone us? 27We must take a three-
8:27 day journey into the desert to offer sac-
[f] Ex 3:18 rifices[f] to the LORD our God, as he commands us."
28Pharaoh said, "I will let you go to of-
8:28 fer sacrifices to the LORD your God in the
[g] ver 8; Ex 9:28; desert, but you must not go very far.
1Ki 13:6 Now pray[g] for me."
29Moses answered, "As soon as I leave
you, I will pray to the LORD, and tomorrow the flies will leave Pharaoh and his
officials and his people. Only be sure
8:29 that Pharaoh does not act deceitfully[h]
[h] ver 15 again by not letting the people go to offer sacrifices to the LORD."
8:30 30Then Moses left Pharaoh and
[i] ver 12 prayed to the LORD,[i] 31and the LORD did
what Moses asked: The flies left Pharaoh
and his officials and his people; not a fly
8:32 remained. 32But this time also Pharaoh
[j] ver 8,15; hardened his heart[j] and would not let
Ex 4:21 the people go.

The Plague on Livestock

9 Then the LORD said to Moses, "Go
to Pharaoh and say to him, 'This is
what the LORD, the God of the Hebrews,
9:1 says: "Let my people go, so that they may
[k] Ex 8:1 worship[k] me." 2If you refuse to let them
9:3 go and continue to hold them back, 3the
[l] Ex 7:4 hand[l] of the LORD will bring a terrible
plague on your livestock in the field—on
your horses and donkeys and camels
and on your cattle and sheep and goats.
4But the LORD will make a distinction
between the livestock of Israel and that
of Egypt,[m] so that no animal belonging 9:4
to the Israelites will die.' " [m] ver 26; Ex 8:22
5The LORD set a time and said, "Tomorrow the LORD will do this in the
land." 6And the next day the LORD did it:
All the livestock[n] of the Egyptians died,[o] 9:6
but not one animal belonging to the Is- [n] ver 19-21; Ex 11:5
raelites died. 7Pharaoh sent men to in- [o] Ps 78:48-50
vestigate and found that not even one of
the animals of the Israelites had died.
Yet his heart was unyielding and he 9:7
would not let the people go.[p] [p] Ex 7:14; 8:32

The Plague of Boils

8Then the LORD said to Moses and
Aaron, "Take handfuls of soot from a
furnace and have Moses toss it into the
air in the presence of Pharaoh. 9It will
become fine dust over the whole land of 9:9
Egypt, and festering boils[q] will break out [q] Dt 28:27,35;
on men and animals throughout the Rev 16:2
land."
10So they took soot from a furnace
and stood before Pharaoh. Moses tossed
it into the air, and festering boils broke
out on men and animals. 11The magi- 9:11
cians[r] could not stand before Moses be- [r] Ex 8:18
cause of the boils that were on them and
on all the Egyptians. 12But the LORD
hardened Pharaoh's heart[s] and he would 9:12
not listen to Moses and Aaron, just as [s] Ex 4:21
the LORD had said to Moses.

The Plague of Hail

13Then the LORD said to Moses, "Get
up early in the morning, confront Pharaoh and say to him, 'This is what the
LORD, the God of the Hebrews, says: Let
my people go, so that they may worship[t] 9:13
me, 14or this time I will send the full [t] Ex 8:20
force of my plagues against you and
against your officials and your people, so 9:14 [u] Ex 8:10
you may know[u] that there is no one like[v] [v] 2Sa 7:22;
me in all the earth. 15For by now I could 1Ch 17:20; Ps 86:8;
have stretched out my hand and struck Isa 46:9; Jer 10:6
you and your people[w] with a plague that 9:15
would have wiped you off the earth. [w] Ex 3:20
16But I have raised you up[b] for this very 9:16
purpose,[x] that I might show you my [x] Pr 16:4
power[y] and that my name might be pro- [y] Ro 9:17*
claimed in all the earth. 17You still set
yourself against my people and will not

[a] *23* Septuagint and Vulgate; Hebrew *will put a deliverance* [b] *16* Or *have spared you*

let them go. 18Therefore, at this time to-
9:18 [z] ver 23 [a] ver 24 morrow I will send the worst hailstorm[z]
that has ever fallen on Egypt, from the
day it was founded till now.[a] 19Give an
order now to bring your livestock and
everything you have in the field to a
place of shelter, because the hail will fall
on every man and animal that has not
been brought in and is still out in the
field, and they will die.' "
20Those officials of Pharaoh who
9:20 [b] Pr 13:13 feared[b] the word of the LORD hurried to
bring their slaves and their livestock in-
side. 21But those who ignored the word
of the LORD left their slaves and livestock
in the field.
22Then the LORD said to Moses,
"Stretch out your hand toward the sky
so that hail will fall all over Egypt—on
men and animals and on everything
growing in the fields of Egypt." 23When
Moses stretched out his staff toward the
9:23 [c] Ps 18:13 [d] Jos 10:11; Ps 78:47; 105:32; Isa 30:30; Eze 38:22; Rev 8:7; 16:21 sky, the LORD sent thunder[c] and hail,[d]
and lightning flashed down to the
ground. So the LORD rained hail on the
land of Egypt; 24hail fell and lightning
flashed back and forth. It was the worst
storm in all the land of Egypt since it
had become a nation. 25Throughout
Egypt hail struck everything in the
fields—both men and animals; it beat
9:25 [e] Ps 105:32-33 down everything growing in the fields
and stripped every tree.[e] 26The only
9:26 [f] ver 4 [g] Ex 8:22; 10:23; 11:7; 12:13 place it did not hail was the land of Goshen,[f] where the Israelites were.[g]
27Then Pharaoh summoned Moses
9:27 [h] Ex 10:16 [i] 2Ch 12:6; Ps 129:4; La 1:18 and Aaron. "This time I have sinned,"[h] he
said to them. "The LORD is in the right,[i]
and I and my people are in the wrong.
28Pray[j] to the LORD, for we have had
9:28 [j] Ex 10:17 [k] Ex 8:8 enough thunder and hail. I will let you
go;[k] you don't have to stay any longer."
29Moses replied, "When I have gone
9:29 [l] 1Ki 8:22,38; Ps 143:6; Isa 1:15 [m] Ex 19:5; Ps 24:1; 1Co 10:26 out of the city, I will spread out my hands[l]
in prayer to the LORD. The thunder will
stop and there will be no more hail, so
you may know that the earth[m] is the
LORD's. 30But I know that you and your officials still do not fear the LORD God."
9:31 [n] Ru 1:22; 2:23 31(The flax and barley[n] were destroyed, since the barley had headed and
the flax was in bloom. 32The wheat and
spelt, however, were not destroyed, because they ripen later.)
33Then Moses left Pharaoh and went
out of the city. He spread out his hands
toward the LORD; the thunder and hail
stopped, and the rain no longer poured
down on the land. 34When Pharaoh saw
that the rain and hail and thunder had
stopped, he sinned again: He and his officials hardened their hearts. 35So Phar-
aoh's heart[o] was hard and he would not 9:35 [o] Ex 4:21
let the Israelites go, just as the LORD had
said through Moses.

The Plague of Locusts

10 Then the LORD said to Moses,
"Go to Pharaoh, for I have hard-
ened his heart[p] and the hearts of his of- 10:1 [p] Ex 4:21 [q] Ex 7:3
ficials so that I may perform these
miraculous signs[q] of mine among them
2that you may tell your children[r] and 10:2 [r] Ex 12:26-27; 13:8,14; Dt 4:9; Ps 44:1; 78:4,5; Joel 1:3
grandchildren how I dealt harshly with
the Egyptians and how I performed my
signs among them, and that you may
know that I am the LORD."
3So Moses and Aaron went to Pharaoh and said to him, "This is what the
LORD, the God of the Hebrews, says: 10:3 [s] 1Ki 21:29; Jas 4:10; 1Pe 5:6
'How long will you refuse to humble[s]
yourself before me? Let my people go, so
that they may worship me. 4If you refuse
to let them go, I will bring locusts[t] into 10:4 [t] Rev 9:3
your country tomorrow. 5They will cov-
er the face of the ground so that it cannot be seen. They will devour what little
you have left[u] after the hail, including 10:5 [u] Ex 9:32; Joel 1:4
every tree that is growing in your fields.
6They will fill your houses and those of
all your officials and all the Egyptians—
something neither your fathers nor your
forefathers have ever seen from the day
they settled in this land till now.' " Then
Moses turned and left Pharaoh.
7Pharaoh's officials said to him, "How
long will this man be a snare[v] to us? Let 10:7 [v] Ex 23:33; Jos 23:13; 1Sa 18:21; Ecc 7:26 [w] Ex 8:19
the people go, so that they may worship
the LORD their God. Do you not yet realize that Egypt is ruined?"[w]
8Then Moses and Aaron were 10:8 [x] Ex 8:8
brought back to Pharaoh. "Go, worship[x]
the LORD your God," he said. "But just
who will be going?"
9Moses answered, "We will go with
our young and old, with our sons and
daughters, and with our flocks and
herds, because we are to celebrate a festival to the LORD."
10Pharaoh said, "The LORD be with
you—if I let you go, along with your
women and children! Clearly you are
bent on evil.[a] 11No! Have only the men

[a] 10 Or *Be careful, trouble is in store for you!*

go; and worship the LORD, since that's
what you have been asking for." Then
Moses and Aaron were driven out of
Pharaoh's presence.
10:12 12And the LORD said to Moses,
[y]Ex 7:19 "Stretch out your hand[y] over Egypt so
that locusts will swarm over the land
and devour everything growing in the
fields, everything left by the hail."
13So Moses stretched out his staff
over Egypt, and the LORD made an east
wind blow across the land all that day
and all that night. By morning the wind
10:13 [z]Ps 105:34 had brought the locusts;[z] 14they invaded
all Egypt and settled down in every area
of the country in great numbers. Never
10:14 [a]Ps 78:46; before had there been such a plague of
Joel 2:1-11,25 locusts,[a] nor will there ever be again.
10:15 15They covered all the ground until it
[b]ver 5; was black. They devoured[b] all that was
Ps 105:34-35 left after the hail—everything growing
in the fields and the fruit on the trees.
Nothing green remained on tree or plant
in all the land of Egypt.
16Pharaoh quickly summoned Moses
10:16 and Aaron and said, "I have sinned[c]
[c]Ex 9:27 against the LORD your God and against
you. 17Now forgive my sin once more
10:17 [d]Ex 8:8 and pray[d] to the LORD your God to take
this deadly plague away from me."
10:18 18Moses then left Pharaoh and prayed
[e]Ex 8:30 to the LORD.[e] 19And the LORD changed
the wind to a very strong west wind,
which caught up the locusts and carried
them into the Red Sea.[a] Not a locust was
left anywhere in Egypt. 20But the LORD
10:20 [f]Ex 4:21; 11:10 hardened Pharaoh's heart,[f] and he would
not let the Israelites go.

The Plague of Darkness

21Then the LORD said to Moses,
"Stretch out your hand toward the sky
10:21 [g]Dt 28:29 so that darkness[g] will spread over
Egypt—darkness that can be felt." 22So
Moses stretched out his hand toward
10:22 [h]Ps 105:28; the sky, and total darkness[h] covered all
Rev 16:10 Egypt for three days. 23No one could see
anyone else or leave his place for three
days. Yet all the Israelites had light in the
10:23 [i]Ex 8:22 places where they lived.[i]
24Then Pharaoh summoned Moses
10:24 and said, "Go, worship the LORD. Even
[j]ver 8-10 your women and children[j] may go with
you; only leave your flocks and herds behind."
25But Moses said, "You must allow us
to have sacrifices and burnt offerings to
present to the LORD our God. 26Our livestock too must go with us; not a hoof is
to be left behind. We have to use some of
them in worshiping the LORD our God,
and until we get there we will not know
what we are to use to worship the LORD."
27But the LORD hardened Pharaoh's
heart,[k] and he was not willing to let 10:27 [k]ver 20; Ex 4:21
them go. 28Pharaoh said to Moses, "Get
out of my sight! Make sure you do not
appear before me again! The day you see
my face you will die."
29"Just as you say," Moses replied, "I
will never appear[l] before you again." 10:29 [l]Heb 11:27

The Plague on the Firstborn

11 Now the LORD had said to Moses, "I will bring one more
plague on Pharaoh and on Egypt. After
that, he will let you go from here, and
when he does, he will drive you out completely. 2Tell the people that men and
women alike are to ask their neighbors
for articles of silver and gold."[m] 3(The 11:2 [m]Ex 3:21,22
LORD made the Egyptians favorably dis-
posed toward the people, and Moses
himself was highly regarded[n] in Egypt 11:3
by Pharaoh's officials and by the people.) [n]Dt 34:11
4So Moses said, "This is what the 11:4
LORD says: 'About midnight[o] I will go [o]Ex 12:29
throughout Egypt. 5Every firstborn[p] son 11:5
in Egypt will die, from the firstborn son [p]Ex 4:23;
of Pharaoh, who sits on the throne, to Ps 78:51
the firstborn son of the slave girl, who is
at her hand mill, and all the firstborn of
the cattle as well. 6There will be loud 11:6
wailing[q] throughout Egypt—worse than [q]Ex 12:30
there has ever been or ever will be again.
7But among the Israelites not a dog will
bark at any man or animal.' Then you
will know that the LORD makes a dis-
tinction[r] between Egypt and Israel. 8All 11:7 [r]Ex 8:22
these officials of yours will come to me,
bowing down before me and saying,
'Go,[s] you and all the people who follow 11:8 [s]Ex 12:31-33
you!' After that I will leave." Then Moses,
hot with anger, left Pharaoh.
9The LORD had said to Moses, "Phar-
aoh will refuse to listen[t] to you—so that 11:9 [t]Ex 7:4
my wonders may be multiplied in
Egypt." 10Moses and Aaron performed
all these wonders before Pharaoh, but
the LORD hardened Pharaoh's heart,[u] 11:10 [u]Ex 4:21; 10:20,
and he would not let the Israelites go out 27
of his country.

[a] 19 Hebrew *Yam Suph*; that is, Sea of Reeds

The Passover

12 The LORD said to Moses and
Aaron in Egypt, 2"This month
12:2 [v]Ex 13:4; Dt 16:1 is to be for you the first month,[v] the first
month of your year. 3Tell the whole com-
munity of Israel that on the tenth day of
this month each man is to take a lamb[a]
for his family, one for each household. 4If
any household is too small for a whole
lamb, they must share one with their
nearest neighbor, having taken into account the number of people there are.
You are to determine the amount of
lamb needed in accordance with what
each person will eat. 5The animals you
12:5 [w]Lev 22:18-21; Heb 9:14 choose must be year-old males without
defect,[w] and you may take them from
the sheep or the goats. 6Take care of
them until the fourteenth day of the
12:6 [x]Lev 23:5; Nu 9:1-3,5,11 [y]Ex 16:12; Dt 16:4,6 month,[x] when all the people of the community of Israel must slaughter them at
twilight.[y] 7Then they are to take some of
the blood and put it on the sides and
tops of the doorframes of the houses
12:8 [z]Ex 34:25; Nu 9:12 [a]Dt 16:7 [b]Nu 9:11 [c]Dt 16:3-4; 1Co 5:8 where they eat the lambs. 8That same
night[z] they are to eat the meat roasted[a]
over the fire, along with bitter herbs,[b]
and bread made without yeast.[c] 9Do not
eat the meat raw or cooked in water, but
roast it over the fire—head, legs and inner parts. 10Do not leave any of it till
morning;[d] if some is left till morning, 12:10 [d]Ex 23:18; 34:25
you must burn it. 11This is how you are
to eat it: with your cloak tucked into 12:11 [e]Dt 16:3 [f]ver 13,21,27, 43; Dt 16:1
your belt, your sandals on your feet and
your staff in your hand. Eat it in haste;[e]
it is the LORD's Passover.[f]
12"On that same night I will pass 12:12 [g]Ex 11:4; Am 5:17 [h]Nu 33:4 [i]Ex 6:2
through[g] Egypt and strike down every
firstborn—both men and animals—and
I will bring judgment on all the gods[h] of
Egypt. I am the LORD.[i] 13The blood will
be a sign for you on the houses where
you are; and when I see the blood, I will
pass over you. No destructive plague will
touch you when I strike Egypt.
14"This is a day you are to commemo- 12:14 [j]Ex 13:9 [k]ver 17,24; Ex 13:5,10; 2Ki 23:21
rate;[j] for the generations to come you
shall celebrate it as a festival to the
LORD—a lasting ordinance.[k] 15For seven
days you are to eat bread made without
yeast.[l] On the first day remove the yeast 12:15 [l]Ex 13:6-7; 23:15; 34:18; Lev 23:6; Dt 16:3 [m]Ge 17:14; Nu 9:13
from your houses, for whoever eats any-
thing with yeast in it from the first day
through the seventh must be cut off[m]
from Israel. 16On the first day hold a sacred assembly, and another one on the
seventh day. Do no work at all on these
days, except to prepare food for everyone to eat—that is all you may do.
17"Celebrate the Feast of Unleavened
Bread, because it was on this very day
that I brought your divisions out of
Egypt.[n] Celebrate this day as a lasting 12:17 [n]ver 41; Ex 13:3
ordinance for the generations to come.
18In the first month[o] you are to eat bread 12:18 [o]ver 2; Lev 23:5-8; Nu 28:16-25
made without yeast, from the evening of
the fourteenth day until the evening of
the twenty-first day. 19For seven days no
yeast is to be found in your houses. And
whoever eats anything with yeast in it
must be cut off from the community of
Israel, whether he is an alien or native-
born. 20Eat nothing made with yeast.
Wherever you live, you must eat unleavened bread."
21Then Moses summoned all the elders of Israel and said to them, "Go at
once and select the animals for your 12:21 [p]ver 11; Mk 14:12-16
families and slaughter the Passover[p]
lamb. 22Take a bunch of hyssop, dip it
into the blood in the basin and put some 12:22 [q]ver 7; Heb 11:28
of the blood[q] on the top and on both
sides of the doorframe. Not one of you
shall go out the door of his house until
morning. 23When the LORD goes through

[a] 3 The Hebrew word can mean *lamb* or *kid*; also in verse 4.

JESUS FOCUS

GOD'S ANGER PASSED OVER

The Passover is one of the holiest days on the Hebrew calendar. It commemorates the time when the angel of death "passed over" the homes of the Israelites on which lambs' blood had been applied to the doorframes (Exodus 12). On that dreadful night when the firstborn of every Egyptian family died, the Israelites were spared because they were literally "under the blood." On that same night each Israelite family ate a hurried meal of roasted lamb, bitter herbs and bread without yeast. God directed them to celebrate this meal on an annual basis as the Feast of Unleavened Bread, in order to remind them of their relationship with him. In the New Testament Jesus is referred to as "our Passover lamb" (1 Corinthians 5:7), and John the Baptist called him "the Lamb of God, who takes away the sin of the world" (John 1:29). In Revelation Jesus appeared as the Lamb who looked as if he had been slain and as the only One worthy of our full devotion (Revelation 5:6–14).

DISCOVERY 19

The Passover

The Feast of Unleavened Bread began with the Passover meal and marked the beginning of the Jewish religious calendar (Exodus 12:1–2). The first Passover occurred in Egypt. Each household was instructed to select a lamb "without defect" (verse 5) and to kill it and sprinkle its blood on the sides and top of their doorframe. The family was to roast the meat with bitter herbs and eat it along with bread made without yeast (to facilitate a hasty departure).

That night God pronounced judgment on Pharaoh and all of Egypt in the most dramatic manner—every firstborn offspring, from animals to people, was struck dead. However, those who trusted and obeyed were "passed over" and spared. The Israelites ate their meal quickly, ready to leave at a moment's notice (verse 11).

The Passover is still celebrated in the Jewish community. The meal is carefully prepared to remind people of what happened on that memorable night. A bowl of salt water represents the tears shed in Egypt, as well as the salt water of the Red Sea, which the Israelites miraculously crossed on dry ground as they fled Pharaoh's pursuing army. Bitter herbs represent the bitterness of slavery and the hyssop used to smear the lambs' blood on their doorframes. A paste represents the clay the Israelite slaves had used to make bricks. The meal also includes unleavened bread, a roasted lamb and four glasses of wine (symbolic of the four times the term "Pharaoh's glass" is mentioned in Genesis 40; these references are viewed as a symbol of salvation). The family prays, discusses the implications of the meal and sings Passover psalms (Psalms 115—118).

It is significant that this is the very meal that Jesus was celebrating with his disciples on the night he was arrested. And it was during this Passover meal that he instituted the sacrament of Communion, or the Lord's Supper. He picked up the loaf of unleavened bread and broke it into pieces, distributing them among his disciples. "Take and eat; this is my body," he invited. He then picked up a cup of wine and declared, "This is my blood of the covenant" (Matthew 26:26–28).

Jesus was not adding a new dimension to the Passover but was instead establishing a *new* covenant with God's people (1 Corinthians 11:25). The original Passover meal reminded the disciples that a lamb's blood protected them from God's judgment. Jesus let them (and us) know, however, when he initiated this sacrament, that he himself was the unblemished Lamb whose final sacrifice would do infinitely more than protect them—his sacrifice actually *removed* sin and repaired the damage it had caused to our relationship with God (see John 1:29; 1 Corinthians 5:7). Jesus is worthy of all our honor and devotion because he is the Lamb who was slain to set us free from bondage to sin (Revelation 5:12).

Self-Discovery: *When you think of Jesus as the Lamb of God whose blood protects you from God's judgment, removes the stain of sin and repairs the damage sin has caused, are you filled with gratitude? How will you express that gratitude?*

GO TO DISCOVERY 20 ON PAGE 96

the land to strike down the Egyptians,
12:23 [r] Rev 7:3 [s] ver 13 [t] 1Co 10:10; Heb 11:28 he will see the blood[r] on the top and
sides of the doorframe and will pass
over[s] that doorway, and he will not permit the destroyer[t] to enter your houses
and strike you down.
24“Obey these instructions as a lasting
ordinance for you and your descendants.
25When you enter the land that the LORD
will give you as he promised, observe this
12:26 [u] Ex 10:2; 13:8, 14-15; Jos 4:6 ceremony. 26And when your children[u]
ask you, ‘What does this ceremony mean
to you?’ 27then tell them, ‘It is the Pass-
12:27 [v] ver 11 [w] Ex 4:31 over[v] sacrifice to the LORD, who passed
over the houses of the Israelites in Egypt
and spared our homes when he struck
down the Egyptians.’ ” Then the people
bowed down and worshiped.[w] 28The Israelites did just what the LORD commanded Moses and Aaron.
29At midnight[x] the LORD struck down
12:29 [x] Ex 11:4 [y] Ex 4:23; Ps 78:51 [z] Ex 9:6 all the firstborn[y] in Egypt, from the firstborn of Pharaoh, who sat on the throne,
to the firstborn of the prisoner, who was
in the dungeon, and the firstborn of all
the livestock[z] as well. 30Pharaoh and all
his officials and all the Egyptians got up
during the night, and there was loud
12:30 [a] Ex 11:6 wailing[a] in Egypt, for there was not a
house without someone dead.

The Exodus

31During the night Pharaoh summoned Moses and Aaron and said, “Up!
Leave my people, you and the Israelites!
12:31 [b] Ex 8:8 Go, worship[b] the LORD as you have requested. 32Take your flocks and herds,[c] as
12:32 [c] Ex 10:9,26 you have said, and go. And also bless me.”
33The Egyptians urged the people to
12:33 [d] Ps 105:38 hurry and leave[d] the country. “For otherwise,” they said, “we will all die!” 34So
the people took their dough before the
yeast was added, and carried it on their
shoulders in kneading troughs wrapped
in clothing. 35The Israelites did as Moses
12:35 [e] Ex 3:22 instructed and asked the Egyptians for
articles of silver and gold[e] and for clothing. 36The LORD had made the Egyptians
favorably disposed toward the people,
12:36 [f] Ex 3:22 and they gave them what they asked for;
so they plundered[f] the Egyptians.
12:37 [g] Nu 33:3-5 [h] Ex 38:26; Nu 1:46; 11:13, 21 37The Israelites journeyed from Rameses to Succoth.[g] There were about six
hundred thousand men[h] on foot, besides women and children. 38Many oth-
12:38 [i] Nu 11:4 er people[i] went up with them, as well as
large droves of livestock, both flocks and
herds. 39With the dough they had
brought from Egypt, they baked cakes of
unleavened bread. The dough was with-
out yeast because they had been driven 12:39 [j] ver 31-33; Ex 6:1; 11:1
out[j] of Egypt and did not have time to
prepare food for themselves.
40Now the length of time the Israelite 12:40 [k] Ge 15:13; Ac 7:6; Gal 3:17
people lived in Egypt[a] was 430 years.[k]
41At the end of the 430 years, to the very
day, all the LORD's divisions[l] left Egypt.[m] 12:41 [l] ver 17; Ex 6:26 [m] Ex 3:10
42Because the LORD kept vigil that night
to bring them out of Egypt, on this night 12:42 [n] Ex 13:10; Dt 16:1,6
all the Israelites are to keep vigil to hon-
or the LORD for the generations to come.[n]

Passover Restrictions

43The LORD said to Moses and Aaron,
“These are the regulations for the Pass- 12:43 [o] ver 11 [p] ver 48; Nu 9:14
over:[o]
“No foreigner[p] is to eat of it. 44Any
slave you have bought may eat of it after
you have circumcised[q] him, 45but a tem- 12:44 [q] Ge 17:12-13
porary resident and a hired worker[r] may 12:45 [r] Lev 22:10
not eat of it.
46“It must be eaten inside one house; 12:46 [s] Nu 9:12; Jn 19:36*
take none of the meat outside the house.
Do not break any of the bones.[s] 47The
whole community of Israel must celebrate it.
48“An alien living among you who
wants to celebrate the LORD's Passover
must have all the males in his household
circumcised; then he may take part like
one born in the land.[t] No uncircumcised 12:48 [t] Nu 9:14
male may eat of it. 49The same law ap-
plies to the native-born and to the alien[u] 12:49 [u] Nu 15:15-16, 29; Gal 3:28
living among you.”
50All the Israelites did just what the
LORD had commanded Moses and Aaron. 51And on that very day the LORD
brought the Israelites out of Egypt by
their divisions.[v] 12:51 [v] ver 41; Ex 6:26

Consecration of the Firstborn

13 The LORD said to Moses, 2“Con-
secrate to me every firstborn 13:2 [w] ver 12,13,15; Ex 22:29; Nu 3:13; Dt 15:19; Lk 2:23*
male.[w] The first offspring of every womb
among the Israelites belongs to me,
whether man or animal.”
3Then Moses said to the people,
“Commemorate this day, the day you
came out of Egypt, out of the land of
slavery, because the LORD brought you
out of it with a mighty hand.[x] Eat noth- 13:3 [x] Ex 3:20; 6:1 [y] Ex 12:19
ing containing yeast.[y] 4Today, in the

[a] *40* Masoretic Text; Samaritan Pentateuch and Septuagint *Egypt and Canaan*

13:4 [z] Ex 12:2 month of Abib,[z] you are leaving. 5When
the LORD brings you into the land of the
Canaanites, Hittites, Amorites, Hivites
13:5 [a] Ex 3:8 and Jebusites[a]—the land he swore to
[b] Ex 12:25-26 your forefathers to give you, a land flowing with milk and honey—you are to ob-
serve this ceremony[b] in this month: 6For
13:6 seven days eat bread made without yeast
[c] Ex 12:15-20 and on the seventh day hold a festival[c] to
the LORD. 7Eat unleavened bread during
those seven days; nothing with yeast in it
is to be seen among you, nor shall any
yeast be seen anywhere within your bor-
13:8 [d] ver 14; ders. 8On that day tell your son,[d] 'I do
Ex 10:2; this because of what the LORD did for me
Ps 78:5-6 when I came out of Egypt.' 9This obser-
13:9 vance will be for you like a sign on your
[e] ver 16; Dt 6:8; hand and a reminder on your forehead[e]
11:18 that the law of the LORD is to be on your
lips. For the LORD brought you out of
Egypt with his mighty hand. 10You must
13:10 keep this ordinance[f] at the appointed
[f] Ex 12:24-25 time year after year.
11"After the LORD brings you into the
land of the Canaanites and gives it to you,
as he promised on oath to you and your
forefathers, 12you are to give over to the
LORD the first offspring of every womb.
13:12 All the firstborn males of your livestock
[g] Lev 27:26; Lk 2:23* belong to the LORD.[g] 13Redeem with a
lamb every firstborn donkey, but if you
do not redeem it, break its neck.[h] Re- 13:13 [h] Ex 34:20
deem every firstborn among your sons.[i] [i] Nu 18:15
14"In days to come, when your son[j] 13:14
asks you, 'What does this mean?' say to [j] Ex 10:2; 12:26-27; Dt 6:20
him, 'With a mighty hand the LORD [k] ver 3,9
brought us out of Egypt, out of the land
of slavery.[k] 15When Pharaoh stubbornly
refused to let us go, the LORD killed every
firstborn in Egypt, both man and animal. This is why I sacrifice to the LORD
the first male offspring of every womb 13:15
and redeem each of my firstborn sons.'[l] [l] Ex 12:29
16And it will be like a sign on your hand 13:16
and a symbol on your forehead[m] that [m] ver 9
the LORD brought us out of Egypt with
his mighty hand."

Crossing the Sea

17When Pharaoh let the people go,
God did not lead them on the road
through the Philistine country, though
that was shorter. For God said, "If they 13:17
face war, they might change their minds [n] Ex 14:11; Nu 14:1-4;
and return to Egypt."[n] 18So God led[o] the Dt 17:16
people around by the desert road to- 13:18
ward the Red Sea.[a] The Israelites went [o] Ps 136:16
up out of Egypt armed for battle.[p] [p] Jos 1:14
19Moses took the bones of Joseph[q] 13:19
with him because Joseph had made the [q] Jos 24:32;
sons of Israel swear an oath. He had said, Ac 7:16 [r] Ge 50:24-25
"God will surely come to your aid, and
then you must carry my bones up with
you from this place."[b][r]
20After leaving Succoth they camped
at Etham on the edge of the desert.[s] 21By 13:20 [s] Nu 33:6
day the LORD went ahead of them in a 13:21
pillar of cloud[t] to guide them on their [t] Ex 14:19,24;
way and by night in a pillar of fire to give 33:9-10;
them light, so that they could travel by Nu 9:16;
day or night. 22Neither the pillar of cloud Dt 1:33; Ne 9:12,19;
by day nor the pillar of fire by night left Ps 78:14; 99:7; 105:39; Isa 4:5;
its place in front of the people. 1Co 10:1

14 Then the LORD said to Moses,
2"Tell the Israelites to turn back
and encamp near Pi Hahiroth, between
Migdol[u] and the sea. They are to encamp 14:2 [u] Nu 33:7;
by the sea, directly opposite Baal Ze- Jer 44:1
phon. 3Pharaoh will think, 'The Israelites
are wandering around the land in confusion, hemmed in by the desert.' 4And I 14:4
will harden Pharaoh's heart,[v] and he will [v] Ex 4:21
pursue them. But I will gain glory[w] for [w] Ro 9:17,22-23
myself through Pharaoh and all his army,

[a] 18 Hebrew *Yam Suph*; that is, Sea of Reeds
[b] 19 See Gen. 50:25.

JESUS FOCUS

LEAVING EGYPT

The exodus experience (Exodus 12 and 13) is one of the great events in the Old Testament. Not only did God deliver his people from slavery, but he also judged everything represented by the nation of Egypt. In fact, God punished the Egyptians so severely that they were *glad* to see the Israelites go. But the Exodus meant more than deliverance; it entailed allegiance to God as well. The New Testament points out that God's people were in a sense "baptized into Moses" as they followed him through the Red Sea (1 Corinthians 10:1–12). The picture is one of the entire nation becoming unified in submission to the leader whom God had given them. When the Hebrew people demonstrated their trust in God by crossing the Red Sea, the event foreshadowed the sacrament of baptism. Just as the Israelites submitted to Moses as the deliverer and leader God had sent them, so Christian baptism signifies that Jesus is our deliverer and leader, the One to whom we submit as Savior and Lord of our lives.

14:4 and the Egyptians will know that I am
[x]Ex 7:5 the LORD."[x] So the Israelites did this.
5When the king of Egypt was told that
the people had fled, Pharaoh and his officials changed their minds about them
and said, "What have we done? We have
let the Israelites go and have lost their
services!" 6So he had his chariot made
ready and took his army with him. 7He
took six hundred of the best chariots,
along with all the other chariots of
14:8 Egypt, with officers over all of them. 8The
[y]ver 4; Ex 11:10 LORD hardened the heart[y] of Pharaoh
[z]Nu 33:3; king of Egypt, so that he pursued the Is-
Ac 13:17 raelites, who were marching out boldly.[z]
9The Egyptians—all Pharaoh's horses
and chariots, horsemen[a] and troops—
14:9 pursued the Israelites and overtook[a]
[a]Ex 15:9 them as they camped by the sea near Pi
Hahiroth, opposite Baal Zephon.
10As Pharaoh approached, the Israelites looked up, and there were the Egyp-
14:10 tians, marching after them. They were
[b]Jos 24:7; terrified and cried[b] out to the LORD.
Ne 9:9; Ps 34:17 11They said to Moses, "Was it because
there were no graves in Egypt that you
14:11 brought us to the desert to die?[c] What
[c]Ps 106:7-8 have you done to us by bringing us out
of Egypt? 12Didn't we say to you in
Egypt, 'Leave us alone; let us serve the
Egyptians'? It would have been better
for us to serve the Egyptians than to die
in the desert!"
14:13 13Moses answered the people, "Do
[d]Ge 15:1 not be afraid.[d] Stand firm and you will
[e]2Ch 20:17; see[e] the deliverance the LORD will bring
Isa 41:10,13-14 [f]ver 30 you today. The Egyptians you see today
14:14 you will never see[f] again. 14The LORD will
[g]ver 25; fight[g] for you; you need only to be still."[h]
Ex 15:3; Dt 1:30; 3:22; 2Ch 20:29 15Then the LORD said to Moses, "Why
[h]Ps 37:7; 46:10; are you crying out to me? Tell the Israel-
Isa 30:15 ites to move on. 16Raise your staff[i] and
14:16 stretch out your hand over the sea to di-
[i]Ex 4:17; vide the water[j] so that the Israelites can
Nu 20:8-9,11 [j]Isa 10:26 go through the sea on dry ground. 17I
will harden the hearts of the Egyptians
14:17 so that they will go in after them.[k] And I
[k]ver 4 will gain glory through Pharaoh and all
his army, through his chariots and his
horsemen. 18The Egyptians will know
that I am the LORD when I gain glory
through Pharaoh, his chariots and his
horsemen."
19Then the angel of God, who had
been traveling in front of Israel's army,
withdrew and went behind them. The
14:19 [l]Ex 13:21 pillar of cloud[l] also moved from in front
and stood behind them, 20coming be-
tween the armies of Egypt and Israel.
Throughout the night the cloud brought
darkness to the one side and light to the
other side; so neither went near the other all night long.
21Then Moses stretched out his hand
over the sea, and all that night the LORD
drove the sea back with a strong east 14:21
wind[m] and turned it into dry land. The [m]Ex 15:8 [n]Ps 74:13;
waters were divided,[n] 22and the Israel- 114:5; Isa 63:12
ites went through the sea on dry 14:22
ground,[o] with a wall of water on their [o]Ex 15:19;
right and on their left. Ne 9:11; Ps 66:6; Heb 11:29
23The Egyptians pursued them, and
all Pharaoh's horses and chariots and
horsemen followed them into the sea.
24During the last watch of the night the
LORD looked down from the pillar of fire
and cloud[p] at the Egyptian army and 14:24
threw it into confusion. 25He made the [p]Ex 13:21
wheels of their chariots come off[b] so
that they had difficulty driving. And the
Egyptians said, "Let's get away from the 14:25
Israelites! The LORD is fighting[q] for them [q]ver 14
against Egypt."

> THE WHOLE CHRISTIAN FAITH RESTS NOT ON EMULATING CHRIST . . . ITS NOT ABOUT MEN AND WOMEN CLIMBING UP TO GOD. IT'S ABOUT GOD DESCENDING TO SAVE A REBEL RACE.
>
> Michael S. Horton, *American Theologian*

26Then the LORD said to Moses,
"Stretch out your hand over the sea so
that the waters may flow back over the
Egyptians and their chariots and horsemen." 27Moses stretched out his hand
over the sea, and at daybreak the sea
went back to its place.[r] The Egyptians 14:27
were fleeing toward[c] it, and the LORD [r]Jos 4:18
swept them into the sea.[s] 28The water [s]Ex 15:1,21; Ps 78:53; 106:11
flowed back and covered the chariots
and horsemen—the entire army of
Pharaoh that had followed the Israelites
into the sea. Not one of them survived.
29But the Israelites went through the 14:29
sea on dry ground,[t] with a wall of water [t]ver; 22
on their right and on their left. 30That

[a] 9 Or *charioteers*; also in verses 17, 18, 23, 26 and 28 [b] 25 Or *He jammed the wheels of their chariots* (see Samaritan Pentateuch, Septuagint and Syriac) [c] 27 Or *from*

14:30 [u]Ps 106:8,10,21 day the LORD saved[u] Israel from the
hands of the Egyptians, and Israel saw
the Egyptians lying dead on the shore.
31 And when the Israelites saw the great
power the LORD displayed against the
14:31 Egyptians, the people feared the LORD
[v]Ps 106:12; and put their trust[v] in him and in Moses
Jn 2:11 his servant.

The Song of Moses and Miriam

15:1 [w]Rev 15:3 [x]Ps 106:12 **15** Then Moses and the Israelites sang this song[w] to the LORD:

"I will sing[x] to the LORD,
for he is highly exalted.
The horse and its rider
he has hurled into the sea.

15:2 [y]Ps 59:17 [z]Ps 18:2,46; Isa 12:2; Hab 3:18 [a]Ge 28:21 [b]Ex 3:6,15-16; Isa 25:1

2 The LORD is my strength[y] and my song;
he has become my salvation.[z]
He is my God,[a] and I will praise him,
my father's God, and I will exalt[b] him.

15:3 [c]Ex 14:14; Ps 24:8; Rev 19:11 [d]Ex 6:2-3,7-8; Ps 83:18

3 The LORD is a warrior;[c]
the LORD is his name.[d]
4 Pharaoh's chariots and his army[e]
he has hurled into the sea.
The best of Pharaoh's officers
are drowned in the Red Sea.[a]

15:4 [e]Ex 14:6-7

5 The deep waters have covered them;
they sank to the depths like a stone.[f]

15:5 [f]ver 10; Ne 9:11

15:6 [g]Ps 118:15

6 "Your right hand,[g] O LORD,
was majestic in power.
Your right hand, O LORD,
shattered the enemy.
7 In the greatness of your majesty
you threw down those who opposed you.
You unleashed your burning anger;[h]
it consumed them like stubble.

15:7 [h]Ps 78:49-50

15:8 [i]Ex 14:21 [j]Ps 78:13 [k]Ex 14:22

8 By the blast of your nostrils[i]
the waters piled up.[j]
The surging waters stood firm like a wall;[k]
the deep waters congealed in the heart of the sea.

9 "The enemy boasted,
'I will pursue,[l] I will overtake them.
I will divide the spoils;[m]
I will gorge myself on them.
I will draw my sword
and my hand will destroy them.'

15:9 [l]Ex 14:5-9 [m]Jdg 5:30; Isa 53:12

10 But you blew with your breath,
and the sea covered them.
They sank like lead
in the mighty waters.[n]

15:10 [n]ver 5; Ex 14:27-28

11 "Who among the gods is like you,[o] O LORD?
Who is like you—
majestic in holiness,[p]
awesome in glory,[q]
working wonders?

15:11 [o]Ex 8:10; Dt 3:24; Ps 77:13 [p]Isa 6:3; Rev 4:8 [q]Ps 8:1

12 You stretched out your right hand
and the earth swallowed them.

13 "In your unfailing love you will lead[r]
the people you have redeemed.
In your strength you will guide them
to your holy dwelling.[s]

15:13 [r]Ne 9:12; Ps 77:20 [s]Ps 78:54

14 The nations will hear and tremble;[t]
anguish will grip the people of Philistia.

15:14 [t]Dt 2:25

15 The chiefs[u] of Edom will be terrified,
the leaders of Moab will be seized with trembling,[v]
the people[b] of Canaan will melt[w] away;

15:15 [u]Ge 36:15 [v]Nu 22:3 [w]Jos 5:1

16 terror[x] and dread will fall upon them.
By the power of your arm
they will be as still as a stone[y]—
until your people pass by, O LORD,
until the people you bought[c][z] pass by.

15:16 [x]Ex 23:27; Jos 2:9 [y]1Sa 25:37 [z]Ps 74:2

17 You will bring them in and plant[a] them
on the mountain[b] of your inheritance—
the place, O LORD, you made for your dwelling,
the sanctuary, O Lord, your hands established.

15:17 [a]Ps 44:2 [b]Ps 78:54,68

18 The LORD will reign
for ever and ever."

19 When Pharaoh's horses, chariots and
horsemen[d] went into the sea,[c] the LORD 15:19 [c]Ex 14:28
brought the waters of the sea back over [d]Ex 14:22
them, but the Israelites walked through
the sea on dry ground.[d] 20 Then Miriam[e] 15:20 [e]Nu 26:59
the prophetess,[f] Aaron's sister, took a [f]Jdg 4:4
tambourine in her hand, and all the [g]Jdg 11:34; 1Sa 18:6;
women followed her, with tambourines Ps 30:11; 150:4
and dancing.[g] 21 Miriam sang to them:

"Sing to the LORD,
for he is highly exalted.

[a] 4 Hebrew *Yam Suph*; that is, Sea of Reeds; also in verse 22 [b] 15 Or *rulers* [c] 16 Or *created* [d] 19 Or *charioteers*

DISCOVERY 20

Miriam: A Time to Sing and Dance

The crossing of the Red Sea, along with the destruction of Pharaoh's army in the middle of it, stands as a dramatic moment in Jewish history. After this victory Moses led the Israelites in a song celebrating God's power and authority. Miriam sang with him, leading the women in a dance with tambourines (Exodus 15:21).

Moses first acknowledged that the people had escaped from the Egyptians because the right hand of God, "majestic in power," had shattered the enemy (verse 6). God deserved full honor from the people, because he had "hurled" the Egyptian horses and riders into the sea. God's power is incredible and undisputed. He had accomplished this remarkable miracle with a mere breath (verses 8–10).

The song lyrics then move from celebration of God's work in the past to his promise of future protection and salvation. God had delivered the Israelites from the Egyptian army, and he would give them victory as well over those already living in the promised land.

Miriam, who led the women in music and dance, is the first woman in the Bible referred to as a prophetess (see also Judges 4:4; 2 Kings 22:14; Nehemiah 6:14; Isaiah 8:3; Luke 2:36; Acts 21:9). A prophet or prophetess was someone who spoke for God, delivering God's message to his people. In addition to serving as prophetess, Miriam shared the leadership role with her brothers Moses and Aaron. God declared, "I sent Moses to lead you, also Aaron and Miriam" (Micah 6:4). After Moses' initial song of celebration Miriam and the other women repeated the theme: "Sing to the LORD, for he is highly exalted" (Exodus 15:21).

Our circumstances are different, but our God is the same. We have as much to celebrate as the Israelites did. God has set us free from bondage, protected us from potential harm, led us through deep waters and helped us overcome countless obstacles. Every one of those deliverances stands as reason enough to sing and dance! We can "sing with gratitude" in our hearts (Colossians 3:16–17), sing aloud in praise to God for his ultimate gift of salvation in Jesus.

Our liberation is even greater than that of the children of Israel. We have been extricated from the "dominion of darkness" to become a part of God's glorious kingdom—"the kingdom of the Son he loves" (Colossians 1:13).

As the apostle Paul urged us, we who have been saved by the shed blood of Jesus are called to "speak to one another with psalms, hymns and spiritual songs. Sing and make music in your heart to the Lord, always giving thanks to God the Father for everything, in the name of our Lord Jesus Christ" (Ephesians 5:19–20).

Self-Discovery: *How do you celebrate Jesus' deliverance in your life?*

GO TO DISCOVERY 21 ON PAGE 99

The horse and its rider
he has hurled into the sea."[h]

The Waters of Marah and Elim

[22]Then Moses led Israel from the Red Sea and they went into the Desert of Shur. For three days they traveled in the desert without finding water. [23]When they came to Marah, they could not drink its water because it was bitter. (That is why the place is called Marah.[a][i]) [24]So the people grumbled[j] against Moses, saying, "What are we to drink?"

[25]Then Moses cried out[k] to the LORD, and the LORD showed him a piece of wood. He threw it into the water, and the water became sweet.

There the LORD made a decree and a law for them, and there he tested[l] them. [26]He said, "If you listen carefully to the voice of the LORD your God and do what is right in his eyes, if you pay attention to his commands and keep all his decrees,[m] I will not bring on you any of the diseases[n] I brought on the Egyptians, for I am the LORD, who heals[o] you."

[27]Then they came to Elim, where there were twelve springs and seventy palm trees, and they camped[p] there near the water.

Manna and Quail

16 The whole Israelite community set out from Elim and came to the Desert of Sin,[q] which is between Elim and Sinai, on the fifteenth day of the second month after they had come out of Egypt. [2]In the desert the whole community grumbled[r] against Moses and Aaron. [3]The Israelites said to them, "If only we had died by the LORD's hand in Egypt![s] There we sat around pots of meat and ate all the food[t] we wanted, but you have brought us out into this desert to starve this entire assembly to death."

[4]Then the LORD said to Moses, "I will rain down bread from heaven[u] for you. The people are to go out each day and gather enough for that day. In this way I will test them and see whether they will follow my instructions. [5]On the sixth day they are to prepare what they bring in, and that is to be twice[v] as much as they gather on the other days."

[6]So Moses and Aaron said to all the Israelites, "In the evening you will know that it was the LORD who brought you out of Egypt,[w] [7]and in the morning you will see the glory[x] of the LORD, because he has heard your grumbling[y] against him. Who are we, that you should grumble against us?"[z] [8]Moses also said, "You will know that it was the LORD when he gives you meat to eat in the evening and all the bread you want in the morning, because he has heard your grumbling against him. Who are we? You are not grumbling against us, but against the LORD."[a]

[9]Then Moses told Aaron, "Say to the entire Israelite community, 'Come before the LORD, for he has heard your grumbling.'"

[10]While Aaron was speaking to the whole Israelite community, they looked toward the desert, and there was the glory[b] of the LORD appearing in the cloud.[c]

[11]The LORD said to Moses, [12]"I have heard the grumbling[d] of the Israelites. Tell them, 'At twilight you will eat meat, and in the morning you will be filled with bread. Then you will know that I am the LORD your God.'"

[13]That evening quail[e] came and covered the camp, and in the morning there was a layer of dew[f] around the camp. [14]When the dew was gone, thin flakes like frost[g] on the ground appeared on the desert floor. [15]When the Israelites saw it, they said to each other, "What is it?" For they did not know what it was.

Moses said to them, "It is the bread[h] the LORD has given you to eat. [16]This is what the LORD has commanded: 'Each one is to gather as much as he needs. Take an omer[b][i] for each person you have in your tent.'"

[17]The Israelites did as they were told; some gathered much, some little. [18]And when they measured it by the omer, he who gathered much did not have too much, and he who gathered little did not have too little.[j] Each one gathered as much as he needed.

[19]Then Moses said to them, "No one is to keep any of it until morning."[k]

[20]However, some of them paid no attention to Moses; they kept part of it until morning, but it was full of maggots and began to smell. So Moses was angry with them.

[21]Each morning everyone gathered as

15:21 h ver 1; Ex 14:27
15:23 i Nu 33:8
15:24 j Ex 14:12; 16:2
15:25 k Ex 14:10 l Jdg 3:4
15:26 m Dt 7:12 n Dt 28:27,58-60 o Ex 23:25-26
15:27 p Nu 33:9
16:1 q Nu 33:11,12
16:2 r Ex 14:11; 15:24; 1Co 10:10
16:3 s Ex 17:3 t Nu 11:4,34
16:4 u Dt 8:3; Jn 6:31*
16:5 v ver 22
16:6 w Ex 6:6
16:7 x ver 10; Isa 35:2; 40:5 y ver 12; Nu 14:2,27,28 z Nu 16:11
16:8 a 1Sa 8:7; Ro 13:2
16:10 b ver 7; Nu 16:19 c Ex 13:21; 1Ki 8:10
16:12 d ver 7
16:13 e Nu 11:31; Ps 78:27-28; 105:40 f Nu 11:9
16:14 g ver 31; Nu 11:7-9; Ps 105:40
16:15 h ver 4; Jn 6:31
16:16 i ver 32,36
16:18 j 2Co 8:15*
16:19 k ver 23; Ex 12:10; 23:18

[a] 23 *Marah* means *bitter.* [b] 16 That is, probably about 2 quarts (about 2 liters); also in verses 18, 32, 33 and 36

much as he needed, and when the sun grew hot, it melted away. 22 On the sixth day, they gathered twice[l] as much—two omers[a] for each person—and the leaders of the community[m] came and reported this to Moses. 23 He said to them, "This is what the LORD commanded: 'Tomorrow is to be a day of rest, a holy Sabbath[n] to the LORD. So bake what you want to bake and boil what you want to boil. Save whatever is left and keep it until morning.'"

24 So they saved it until morning, as Moses commanded, and it did not stink or get maggots in it. 25 "Eat it today," Moses said, "because today is a Sabbath to the LORD. You will not find any of it on the ground today. 26 Six days you are to gather it, but on the seventh day, the Sabbath,[o] there will not be any."

27 Nevertheless, some of the people went out on the seventh day to gather it, but they found none. 28 Then the LORD said to Moses, "How long will you[b] refuse to keep my commands[p] and my instructions? 29 Bear in mind that the LORD has given you the Sabbath; that is why on the sixth day he gives you bread for two days. Everyone is to stay where he is on the seventh day; no one is to go out." 30 So the people rested on the seventh day.

31 The people of Israel called the bread manna.[c][q] It was white like coriander seed and tasted like wafers made with honey. 32 Moses said, "This is what the LORD has commanded: 'Take an omer of manna and keep it for the generations to come, so they can see the bread I gave you to eat in the desert when I brought you out of Egypt.'"

33 So Moses said to Aaron, "Take a jar and put an omer of manna[r] in it. Then place it before the LORD to be kept for the generations to come."

34 As the LORD commanded Moses, Aaron put the manna in front of the Testimony,[s] that it might be kept. 35 The Israelites ate manna[t] forty years,[u] until they came to a land that was settled; they ate manna until they reached the border of Canaan.[v]

36 (An omer is one tenth of an ephah.)

16:22 [l] ver 5 [m] Ex 34:31
16:23 [n] Ge 2:3; Ex 20:8; 23:12; Lev 23:3
16:26 [o] Ex 20:9-10
16:28 [p] 2Ki 17:14; Ps 78:10; 106:13
16:31 [q] Nu 11:7-9
16:33 [r] Heb 9:4
16:34 [s] Ex 25:16,21,22; 40:20; Nu 17:4,10
16:35 [t] Jn 6:31,49 [u] Ne 9:21 [v] Jos 5:12

Water From the Rock

17 The whole Israelite community set out from the Desert of Sin,[w] traveling from place to place as the LORD commanded. They camped at Rephidim, but there was no water[x] for the people to drink. 2 So they quarreled with Moses and said, "Give us water[y] to drink."

Moses replied, "Why do you quarrel with me? Why do you put the LORD to the test?"[z]

3 But the people were thirsty for water there, and they grumbled[a] against Moses. They said, "Why did you bring us up out of Egypt to make us and our children and livestock die of thirst?"

4 Then Moses cried out to the LORD, "What am I to do with these people? They are almost ready to stone[b] me."

5 The LORD answered Moses, "Walk on ahead of the people. Take with you some of the elders of Israel and take in your hand the staff with which you struck the Nile,[c] and go. 6 I will stand there before you by the rock at Horeb. Strike the rock, and water[d] will come out of it for the people to drink." So Moses did this in the sight of the elders of Israel. 7 And he called the place Massah[d] and Meribah[e][e] because the Israelites quarreled and because they tested the LORD saying, "Is the LORD among us or not?"

The Amalekites Defeated

8 The Amalekites[f] came and attacked the Israelites at Rephidim. 9 Moses said to Joshua, "Choose some of our men and go out to fight the Amalekites. Tomorrow I will stand on top of the hill with the staff[g] of God in my hands."

10 So Joshua fought the Amalekites as Moses had ordered, and Moses, Aaron and Hur[h] went to the top of the hill. 11 As long as Moses held up his hands, the Israelites were winning,[i] but whenever he lowered his hands, the Amalekites were winning. 12 When Moses' hands grew tired, they took a stone and put it under him and he sat on it. Aaron and Hur held his hands up—one on one side, one on the other—so that his hands remained steady till sunset. 13 So Joshua overcame the Amalekite army with the sword.

14 Then the LORD said to Moses, "Write[j] this on a scroll as something to be remembered and make sure that Joshua hears it, because I will completely blot

17:1 [w] Ex 16:1 [x] Nu 33:14
17:2 [y] Nu 20:2 [z] Dt 6:16; Ps 78:18,41; 1Co 10:9
17:3 [a] Ex 15:24; 16:2-3
17:4 [b] Nu 14:10; 1Sa 30:6
17:5 [c] Ex 7:20
17:6 [d] Nu 20:11; Ps 114:8; 1Co 10:4
17:7 [e] Nu 20:13,24; Ps 81:7
17:8 [f] Ge 36:12; Dt 25:17-19
17:9 [g] Ex 4:17
17:10 [h] Ex 24:14
17:11 [i] Jas 5:16
17:14 [j] Ex 24:4; 34:27; Nu 33:2

a 22 That is, probably about 4 quarts (about 4.5 liters) *b 28* The Hebrew is plural. *c 31* *Manna* means *What is it?* (see verse 15). *d 7* *Massah* means *testing.* *e 7* *Meribah* means *quarreling.*

DISCOVERY 21

GOD OUR SOURCE

Backpacking requires careful planning: If you forget something you cannot easily go back for it once you are trekking through the wilderness. Everything you will potentially need must be packed.

The Old Testament Israelites found themselves ill-prepared for their walk through the desert. They had brought many things with them but were unable to carry two key items: food and water. You may be able to get by on a camping trip without a tent, map or compass. But you cannot survive long without adequate food or water: It didn't take long before the hungry and thirsty throng began complaining. Moses talked to God, who provided *manna*—literally "What is it?" (Exodus 16:15). The manna appeared on the ground each morning, and the people simply collected it to grind and make bread. They were instructed not to gather more than they needed for one day, except on the sixth day when they were to collect enough for the Sabbath as well. In a very practical way God taught his people that he alone was their source of everyday sustenance.

The Israelites also lamented to Moses about their lack of water, directing their complaints against God (Exodus 17:1–3). Either they had not learned to trust God or had all too quickly forgotten. Despite the continuing appearance of manna, the urgency of their thirst obscured their vision of God. God was patient with the Israelites in the desert, instructing Moses to strike a rock in order to procure water. That must have seemed a strange thing to do, but when he obeyed the cold refreshment gushed forth (verse 6).

The manna and water from the rock provide us with an early picture of God's promises about his Son Jesus. Jesus compared himself to the manna: "Your forefathers ate the manna in the desert, yet they died. But here is the bread that comes down from heaven, which a man may eat and not die . . . I will give [my life] for the life of the world" (John 6:49–51). Jesus also compared himself to much-needed water, telling the people that anyone who is thirsty should come to him for a drink. Anyone who believes that Jesus is the Son of God will have "streams of living water" flowing from him or her John 7:37–38).

At first glance the Israelites' attitude seems puzzling: After God had given them bread, they complained about not having meat. After God supplied quail to supplement their diet, they complained about lack of drinking water. Time and again they forgot God's promise to care for them. If truth be told, we are not so different. The pressing needs in our own lives often loom so large that we fail to see beyond or around them. The tyranny of the urgent results in repeated memory lapses.

We all endure "desert" experiences, times during which we muster up little hope and find ourselves doubting that God will keep his promises. But when we feel desperate we can learn from the Israelites. We can take time to thank God for what he has already done and trust in him to fulfill our immediate and long-term needs through his Son Jesus.

Self-Discovery: *Are you allowing Jesus to be the all-sufficient bread and water that satisfies the hunger and thirst in your soul?*

GO TO DISCOVERY 22 ON PAGE 102

17:14 out the memory of Amalek[k] from under
k 1Sa 15:3; heaven."
30:17-18 15 Moses built an altar and called it
The LORD is my Banner. 16 He said, "For
hands were lifted up to the throne of the
LORD. The[a] LORD will be at war against
the Amalekites from generation to generation."

Jethro Visits Moses

18 Now Jethro, the priest of Midi-
18:1 an[l] and father-in-law of Moses,
l Ex 2:16; 3:1 heard of everything God had done for
Moses and for his people Israel, and how
the LORD had brought Israel out of
Egypt.
2 After Moses had sent away his wife
18:2 Zipporah,[m] his father-in-law Jethro re-
m Ex 2:21; 4:25 ceived her 3 and her two sons.[n] One son
18:3 was named Gershom,[b] for Moses said, "I
n Ex 4:20; have become an alien in a foreign
Ac 7:29 land";[o] 4 and the other was named Elie-
o Ex 2:22 zer,[c][p] for he said, "My father's God was
18:4 my helper; he saved me from the sword
p 1Ch 23:15 of Pharaoh."
5 Jethro, Moses' father-in-law, together with Moses' sons and wife, came to
him in the desert, where he was camped
18:5 near the mountain[q] of God. 6 Jethro had
q Ex 3:1 sent word to him, "I, your father-in-law
Jethro, am coming to you with your wife
and her two sons."
7 So Moses went out to meet his fa-
18:7 ther-in-law and bowed down[r] and
r Ge 43:28 kissed[s] him. They greeted each other
s Ge 29:13 and then went into the tent. 8 Moses told
his father-in-law about everything the
LORD had done to Pharaoh and the
Egyptians for Israel's sake and about all
18:8 the hardships they had met along the
t Ex 15:6,16; way and how the LORD had saved[t] them.
Ps 81:7 9 Jethro was delighted to hear about all
the good things the LORD had done for
Israel in rescuing them from the hand of
the Egyptians. 10 He said, "Praise be to
18:10 the LORD,[u] who rescued you from the
u Ge 14:20; hand of the Egyptians and of Pharaoh,
Ps 68:19-20 and who rescued the people from the
hand of the Egyptians. 11 Now I know
that the LORD is greater than all other
18:11 gods,[v] for he did this to those who had
v Ex 12:12; treated Israel arrogantly."[w] 12 Then Jeth-
15:11; 2Ch 2:5 ro, Moses' father-in-law, brought a burnt
w Lk 1:51 offering and other sacrifices to God, and
Aaron came with all the elders of Israel
to eat bread with Moses' father-in-law in
18:12 the presence[x] of God.
x Dt 12:7

13 The next day Moses took his seat to
serve as judge for the people, and they
stood around him from morning till
evening. 14 When his father-in-law saw
all that Moses was doing for the people,
he said, "What is this you are doing for
the people? Why do you alone sit as
judge, while all these people stand
around you from morning till evening?"
15 Moses answered him, "Because the 18:15
people come to me to seek God's will.[y] y Nu 9:6,8;
16 Whenever they have a dispute, it is Dt 17:8-13
brought to me, and I decide between the
parties and inform them of God's de- 18:16
crees and laws."[z] z Lev 24:12
17 Moses' father-in-law replied, "What
you are doing is not good. 18 You and
these people who come to you will only
wear yourselves out. The work is too
heavy for you; you cannot handle it 18:18
alone.[a] 19 Listen now to me and I will give a Nu 11:11,14,
you some advice, and may God be with 17
you.[b] You must be the people's represen- 18:19
tative before God and bring their dis- b Ex 3:12
putes[c] to him. 20 Teach them the decrees c Nu 27:5
and laws,[d] and show them the way to 18:20
live[e] and the duties they are to perform.[f] d Dt 5:1
21 But select capable men[g] from all the e Ps 143:8
people—men who fear God, trustwor- f Dt 1:18
thy men who hate dishonest gain[h]—and 18:21
appoint them as officials[i] over thou- g Ac 6:3
sands, hundreds, fifties and tens. 22 Have h Dt 16:19;
them serve as judges for the people at all Ps 15:5;
times, but have them bring every diffi- Eze 18:8
cult case[j] to you; the simple cases they i Dt 1:13,15;
can decide themselves. That will make 2Ch 19:5-10
your load lighter, because they will 18:22
share[k] it with you. 23 If you do this and j Dt 1:17-18
God so commands, you will be able to k Nu 11:17
stand the strain, and all these people
will go home satisfied."
24 Moses listened to his father-in-law
and did everything he said. 25 He chose
capable men from all Israel and made
them leaders of the people, officials over 18:25
thousands, hundreds, fifties and tens.[l] l Dt 1:13-15
26 They served as judges for the people at
all times. The difficult cases they
brought to Moses, but the simple ones 18:26
they decided themselves.[m] m ver 22
27 Then Moses sent his father-in-law
on his way, and Jethro returned to his 18:27
own country.[n] n Nu 10:29-30

a 16 Or *"Because a hand was against the throne of the LORD, the* b 3 *Gershom* sounds like the Hebrew for *an alien there.* c 4 *Eliezer* means *my God is helper.*

At Mount Sinai

19 In the third month after the Israelites left Egypt—on the very
day—they came to the Desert of Sinai.
2 After they set out from Rephidim,[o] they
entered the Desert of Sinai, and Israel
camped there in the desert in front of
the mountain.[p]
3 Then Moses went up to God, and the
LORD called[q] to him from the mountain
and said, "This is what you are to say to
the house of Jacob and what you are to
tell the people of Israel: 4 'You yourselves
have seen what I did to Egypt,[r] and how
I carried you on eagles' wings[s] and
brought you to myself. 5 Now if you obey
me fully[t] and keep my covenant,[u] then
out of all nations you will be my treasured possession.[v] Although the whole
earth[w] is mine, 6 you[a] will be for me a
kingdom of priests[x] and a holy nation.'[y]
These are the words you are to speak to
the Israelites."
7 So Moses went back and summoned
the elders of the people and set before
them all the words the LORD had commanded him to speak. 8 The people all
responded together, "We will do everything the LORD has said."[z] So Moses
brought their answer back to the LORD.
9 The LORD said to Moses, "I am going
to come to you in a dense cloud,[a] so that
the people will hear me speaking[b] with
you and will always put their trust in
you." Then Moses told the LORD what the
people had said.
10 And the LORD said to Moses, "Go to
the people and consecrate[c] them today
and tomorrow. Have them wash their
clothes[d] 11 and be ready by the third day,[e]
because on that day the LORD will come
down on Mount Sinai in the sight of all
the people. 12 Put limits for the people
around the mountain and tell them, 'Be
careful that you do not go up the mountain or touch the foot of it. Whoever
touches the mountain shall surely be
put to death. 13 He shall surely be stoned[f]
or shot with arrows; not a hand is to be
laid on him. Whether man or animal, he
shall not be permitted to live.' Only
when the ram's horn sounds a long blast
may they go up to the mountain."
14 After Moses had gone down the
mountain to the people, he consecrated
them, and they washed their clothes.
15 Then he said to the people, "Prepare
yourselves for the third day. Abstain
from sexual relations."
16 On the morning of the third day
there was thunder and lightning, with a
thick cloud over the mountain, and a
very loud trumpet blast.[g] Everyone in
the camp trembled.[h] 17 Then Moses led
the people out of the camp to meet with
God, and they stood at the foot of the
mountain. 18 Mount Sinai was covered
with smoke,[i] because the LORD descended on it in fire.[j] The smoke billowed up
from it like smoke from a furnace,[k] the
whole mountain[b] trembled[l] violently,
19 and the sound of the trumpet grew
louder and louder. Then Moses spoke
and the voice[m] of God answered[n] him.[c]
20 The LORD descended to the top of
Mount Sinai and called Moses to the top
of the mountain. So Moses went up
21 and the LORD said to him, "Go down
and warn the people so they do not force
their way through to see[o] the LORD and
many of them perish. 22 Even the priests,
who approach[p] the LORD, must consecrate themselves, or the LORD will break
out against them."[q]
23 Moses said to the LORD, "The people
cannot come up Mount Sinai, because
you yourself warned us, 'Put limits[r]
around the mountain and set it apart as
holy.' "
24 The LORD replied, "Go down and
bring Aaron[s] up with you. But the
priests and the people must not force
their way through to come up to the
LORD, or he will break out against them."
25 So Moses went down to the people
and told them.

The Ten Commandments

20 And God spoke all these words:

2 "I am the LORD your God, who
brought you out of Egypt, out
of the land of slavery.[t]
3 "You shall have no other gods before[d] me.[u]
4 "You shall not make for yourself an
idol[v] in the form of anything
in heaven above or on the
earth beneath or in the waters
below. 5 You shall not bow

19:2 [o] Ex 17:1 [p] Ex 3:1
19:3 [q] Ex 3:4; Ac 7:38
19:4 [r] Dt 29:2 [s] Isa 63:9
19:5 [t] Ex 15:26 [u] Dt 5:2 [v] Dt 14:2; Ps 135:4 [w] Ex 9:29; Dt 10:14
19:6 [x] 1Pe 2:5 [y] Dt 7:6; 26:19; Isa 62:12
19:8 [z] Ex 24:3,7; Dt 5:27
19:9 [a] ver 16; Ex 24:15-16 [b] Dt 4:12,36
19:10 [c] Lev 11:44; Heb 10:22 [d] Ge 35:2
19:11 [e] ver 16
19:13 [f] Heb 12:20*
19:16 [g] Heb 12:18-19; Rev 4:1 [h] Heb 12:21
19:18 [i] Ps 104:32 [j] Ex 3:2; 24:17; Dt 4:11; 2Ch 7:1; Ps 18:8; Heb 12:18 [k] Ge 19:28 [l] Jdg 5:5; Ps 68:8; Jer 4:24
19:19 [m] Ne 9:13 [n] Ps 81:7
19:21 [o] Ex 3:5; 1Sa 6:19
19:22 [p] Lev 10:3 [q] 2Sa 6:7
19:23 [r] ver 12
19:24 [s] Ex 24:1,9
20:2 [t] Ex 13:3
20:3 [u] Dt 6:14; Jer 35:15
20:4 [v] Lev 26:1; Dt 4:15-19,23; 27:15

[a] *5,6* Or *possession, for the whole earth is mine. 6You*
[b] *18* Most Hebrew manuscripts; a few Hebrew manuscripts and Septuagint *all the people*
[c] *19* Or *and God answered him with thunder*
[d] *3* Or *besides*

DISCOVERY 22

THE TEN COMMANDMENTS

The Ten Commandments are the laws God gave Moses to pass along to the people. They form the foundation of Jewish life and the basis for our social morality even today, because they serve as an enduring guide for grateful living for Christians in all ages and in all places. The commands are divided into two general categories. The first four deal with our relationship with God, while the final six focus upon our relationships with other people. Many people view the Ten Commandments as a series of negative injunctions, visualizing an irate God thundering *"Thou shalt not!"* However, every time God forbids something, at the heart is a very positive principle or value:

1. Command: You shall have no other gods before me.

   Principle: There is only one Creator—God (Exodus 20:2).

2. Command: You shall not make for yourself an idol.

   Principle: God is a spirit and must be worshiped in spirit and truth (John 4:24).

3. Command: You shall not misuse the name of the LORD your God.

   Principle: God's name reveals his character (Exodus 3:14).

4. Command: Remember the Sabbath day.

   Principle: We need cycles of work and rest in the routine of life (Mark 6:30–31).

5. Command: Honor your father and your mother.

   Principle: Parents are worthy of respect (Ephesians 6:1–2).

6. Command: You shall not murder.

   Principle: Life is a sacred gift from God that must be valued and protected (Psalm 139:13–16).

7. Command: You shall not commit adultery.

   Principle: Sexuality is a gift from God to be practiced within the sanctity and commitment of marriage (1 Corinthians 7:1–7).

8. Command: You shall not steal.

   Principle: God can be trusted to provide what we need (Philippians 4:19).

9. Command: You shall not give false testimony.

   Principle: Honesty in conversation is important (Ephesians 4:25).

10. Command: You shall not covet.

    Principle: We must learn to be content with what we have (1 Timothy 6:6).

God's law reveals his heart and his priorities, but that law cannot save us—because we are unable to keep it! (Romans 3:20). The law itself highlights this inability and points us to Jesus Christ (Galatians 3:24). That doesn't mean that the law is unimportant or that we may give up on obedience. The law reflects God's greatest desire: that we love him and the people he has created (Mark 12:29–31).

***Self-Discovery:** How does the impossibility of keeping God's law help you to appreciate the work of Jesus?*

GO TO DISCOVERY 23 ON PAGE 111

20:5 [w]Isa 44:15,17, 19 [x]Ex 34:14; Dt 4:24 [y]Nu 14:18; Jer 32:18
down to them or worship[w]
them; for I, the LORD your
God, am a jealous God,[x] punishing the children for the sin
of the fathers to the third and
fourth generation[y] of those
20:6 [z]Dt 7:9
who hate me, 6but showing
love to a thousand[z] ⌞genera-
tions⌟ of those who love me
and keep my command-
ments.
7"You shall not misuse the name of
the LORD your God, for the
20:7 [a]Lev 19:12; Mt 5:33
LORD will not hold anyone
guiltless who misuses his
name.[a]
20:8 [b]Ex 31:13-16; Lev 26:2
8"Remember the Sabbath[b] day by
keeping it holy. 9Six days you
20:9 [c]Ex 34:21; Lk 13:14
shall labor and do all your
work,[c] 10but the seventh day is
a Sabbath to the LORD your
God. On it you shall not do
any work, neither you, nor
your son or daughter, nor your
manservant or maidservant,
nor your animals, nor the
alien within your gates. 11For
in six days the LORD made the
heavens and the earth, the
sea, and all that is in them, but
20:11 [d]Ge 2:2
he rested[d] on the seventh day.
Therefore the LORD blessed
the Sabbath day and made it
holy.
12"Honor your father and your moth- 20:12 [e]Mt 15:4*; Mk 7:10*; Eph 6:2
er,[e] so that you may live long
in the land the LORD your God
is giving you.
13"You shall not murder.[f] 20:13 [f]Mt 5:21*; Ro 13:9*
14"You shall not commit adultery.[g] 20:14 [g]Mt 19:18*
15"You shall not steal.[h] 20:15 [h]Lev 19:11,13; Mt 19:18*
16"You shall not give false testimony
against your neighbor.[i] 20:16 [i]Ex 23:1,7; Mt 19:18*
17"You shall not covet[j] your neigh- 20:17 [j]Ro 7:7*; 13:9*; Eph 5:3
bor's house. You shall not cov-
et your neighbor's wife, or his
manservant or maidservant,
his ox or donkey, or anything
that belongs to your neighbor."

18When the people saw the thunder
and lightning and heard the trumpet[k] 20:18 [k]Ex 19:16-19; Heb 12:18-19
and saw the mountain in smoke, they
trembled with fear. They stayed at a distance 19and said to Moses, "Speak to us
yourself and we will listen. But do not 20:19 [l]Dt 5:5,23-27; Gal 3:19
have God speak to us or we will die."[l]
20Moses said to the people, "Do not be
afraid. God has come to test you, so that 20:20 [m]Dt 4:10; Isa 8:13 [n]Pr 16:6
the fear[m] of God will be with you to keep
you from sinning."[n]
21The people remained at a distance,
while Moses approached the thick dark- 20:21 [o]Dt 5:22
ness[o] where God was.

THE TEN COMMANDMENTS

God's Way	Society's Way
Unity of God	Many gods
Spirituality of God	Idolatry
Majesty of God	Profanity
Worship of God	Paganism (false gods)
Sanctity of family	Children rebelling
Sanctity of life	Murder
Sanctity of marriage	Sexual sin
Sanctity of property	Theft
Sanctity of character	Slander
Sanctity of contentment	Covetousness

Idols and Altars

22Then the LORD said to Moses, "Tell
the Israelites this: 'You have seen for
yourselves that I have spoken to you
from heaven:[p] 23Do not make any gods
to be alongside me;[q] do not make for
yourselves gods of silver or gods of gold.[r]
24" 'Make an altar of earth for me and
sacrifice on it your burnt offerings and
fellowship offerings,[a] your sheep and
goats and your cattle. Wherever I cause
my name[s] to be honored, I will come to
you and bless[t] you. 25If you make an altar of stones for me, do not build it with
dressed stones, for you will defile it if
you use a tool[u] on it. 26And do not go up
to my altar on steps, lest your nakedness
be exposed on it.'

20:22 [p] Ne 9:13
20:23 [q] ver 3 [r] Ex 32:4, 8,31
20:24 [s] Dt 12:5; 16:6, 11; 2Ch 6:6 [t] Ge 12:2
20:25 [u] Dt 27:5-6

21 "These are the laws[v] you are to
set before them:

21:1 [v] Dt 4:14

Hebrew Servants

2"If you buy a Hebrew servant, he is to
serve you for six years. But in the seventh year, he shall go free,[w] without paying anything. 3If he comes alone, he is to
go free alone; but if he has a wife when
he comes, she is to go with him. 4If his
master gives him a wife and she bears
him sons or daughters, the woman and
her children shall belong to her master,
and only the man shall go free.
5"But if the servant declares, 'I love my
master and my wife and children and do
not want to go free,'[x] 6then his master
must take him before the judges.[b][y] He
shall take him to the door or the doorpost and pierce his ear with an awl. Then
he will be his servant for life.[z]

21:2 [w] Jer 34:8,14
21:5 [x] Dt 15:16
21:6 [y] Ex 22:8-9 [z] Ne 5:5

7"If a man sells his daughter as a servant, she is not to go free as menservants do. 8If she does not please the
master who has selected her for himself,[c] he must let her be redeemed. He
has no right to sell her to foreigners, because he has broken faith with her. 9If he
selects her for his son, he must grant her
the rights of a daughter. 10If he marries
another woman, he must not deprive
the first one of her food, clothing and
marital rights.[a] 11If he does not provide
her with these three things, she is to go
free, without any payment of money.

21:10 [a] 1Co 7:3-5

Personal Injuries

12"Anyone who strikes a man and kills
him shall surely be put to death.[b] 13How-
ever, if he does not do it intentionally,
but God lets it happen, he is to flee to a
place[c] I will designate. 14But if a man
schemes and kills another man deliberately,[d] take him away from my altar and
put him to death.[e]
15"Anyone who attacks[d] his father or
his mother must be put to death.
16"Anyone who kidnaps another and
either sells[f] him or still has him when he
is caught must be put to death.[g]
17"Anyone who curses his father or
mother must be put to death.[h]
18"If men quarrel and one hits the
other with a stone or with his fist[e] and
he does not die but is confined to bed,
19the one who struck the blow will not
be held responsible if the other gets up
and walks around outside with his staff;
however, he must pay the injured man

21:12 [b] Ge 9:6; Mt 26:52
21:13 [c] Nu 35:10-34; Dt 19:2-13; Jos 20:9; 1Sa 24:4,10,18
21:14 [d] Heb 10:26 [e] Dt 19:11-12; 1Ki 2:28-34
21:16 [f] Ge 37:28 [g] Ex 22:4; Dt 24:7
21:17 [h] Lev 20:9-10; Mt 15:4*; Mk 7:10*

[a] 24 Traditionally *peace offerings* [b] 6 Or *before God* [c] 8 Or *master so that he does not choose her* [d] 15 Or *kills* [e] 18 Or *with a tool*

THE PURPOSE OF THE LAW OF GOD

First Table (Exodus 20:3–12)	Second Table (Exodus 20:13–17)
Spirituality	Morality
Our Relation to God	Our Relation to Others
Love Your God (Matthew 22:37–38)	Love Your Neighbor (Matthew 22:39–40)
Sanctity of character	Slander
Sanctity of contentment	Covetousness

for the loss of his time and see that he is
completely healed.
20“If a man beats his male or female
slave with a rod and the slave dies as a
direct result, he must be punished, 21but
he is not to be punished if the slave gets
21:21 up after a day or two, since the slave is
[i]Lev 25:44-46 his property.[i]
22“If men who are fighting hit a pregnant woman and she gives birth prema-
21:22 turely[a] but there is no serious injury,
[j]ver 30; the offender must be fined whatever the
Dt 22:18-19 woman's husband demands[j] and the
21:23 court allows. 23But if there is serious in-
[k]Lev 24:19; jury, you are to take life for life,[k] 24eye for
Dt 19:21 eye, tooth for tooth,[l] hand for hand, foot
21:24 for foot, 25burn for burn, wound for
[l]Mt 5:38* wound, bruise for bruise.
26“If a man hits a manservant or
maidservant in the eye and destroys it,
he must let the servant go free to compensate for the eye. 27And if he knocks
out the tooth of a manservant or maidservant, he must let the servant go free
to compensate for the tooth.
21:28 28“If a bull gores a man or a woman to
[m]ver 32; Ge 9:5 death, the bull must be stoned to death,[m]
and its meat must not be eaten. But the
owner of the bull will not be held responsible. 29If, however, the bull has had
the habit of goring and the owner has
been warned but has not kept it penned
up and it kills a man or woman, the bull
must be stoned and the owner also must
be put to death. 30However, if payment is
demanded of him, he may redeem his life 21:30
by paying whatever is demanded.[n] 31This [n]ver 22;
law also applies if the bull gores a son or Nu 35:31
daughter. 32If the bull gores a male or female slave, the owner must pay thirty
shekels[b][o] of silver to the master of the 21:32
slave, and the bull must be stoned. [o]Zec 11:12-13; Mt 26:15; 27:3,9
33“If a man uncovers a pit or digs one
and fails to cover it and an ox or a donkey falls into it, 34the owner of the pit
must pay for the loss; he must pay its
owner, and the dead animal will be his.
35“If a man's bull injures the bull of another and it dies, they are to sell the live
one and divide both the money and the
dead animal equally. 36However, if it was
known that the bull had the habit of goring, yet the owner did not keep it penned
up, the owner must pay, animal for animal, and the dead animal will be his.

Protection of Property

22 “If a man steals an ox or a sheep
and slaughters it or sells it, he
must pay back[p] five head of cattle for 22:1
the ox and four sheep for the sheep. [p]2Sa 12:6; Pr 6:31; Lk 19:8
2“If a thief is caught breaking in[q] and is 22:2
struck so that he dies, the defender is not [q]Mt 6:19-20;
guilty of bloodshed;[r] 3but if it happens[c] 24:43 [r]Nu 35:27
after sunrise, he is guilty of bloodshed.
“A thief must certainly make restitu- 22:3
tion, but if he has nothing, he must be [s]Ex 21:2;
sold[s] to pay for his theft. Mt 18:25
4“If the stolen animal is found alive in
his possession—whether ox or donkey 22:4
or sheep—he must pay back double.[t] [t]Ge 43:12
5“If a man grazes his livestock in a
field or vineyard and lets them stray and
they graze in another man's field, he
must make restitution from the best of
his own field or vineyard.
6“If a fire breaks out and spreads into
thornbushes so that it burns shocks of
grain or standing grain or the whole
field, the one who started the fire must
make restitution.
7“If a man gives his neighbor silver or
goods for safekeeping and they are
stolen from the neighbor's house, the
thief, if he is caught, must pay back dou- 22:7
ble.[u] 8But if the thief is not found, the [u]ver 4
owner of the house must appear before

JESUS FOCUS

RESPECTING GOD'S LAW

Jesus always demonstrated the utmost respect for God's law. He himself declared that he didn't come to get rid of the law but to fulfill it (Matthew 5:17). Our Lord did, however, express contempt for anyone who taught God's law but failed to practice it (Matthew 5:19). Godly living involves going beyond the literal demands of the law to focus on its spirit and its deep, underlying principles. Although the law specifies that we may not murder (Exodus 20:13), Jesus took the injunction one step further, stipulating that we should not be angry (Matthew 5:22). The law tells us not to commit adultery (Exodus 20:14), but Jesus specified that we may not lust (Matthew 5:28). We as Christians are called to make God's commands a matter of attitude and heart, of total commitment, rather than treating them merely as a listing of rules to be kept externally.

[a] 22 Or *she has a miscarriage* [b] 32 That is, about 12 ounces (about 0.3 kilogram) [c] 3 Or *if he strikes him*

22:8 [v]Ex 21:6; Dt 17:8-9; 19:17 the judges[a][v] to determine whether he
has laid his hands on the other man's
property. 9 In all cases of illegal possession of an ox, a donkey, a sheep, a garment, or any other lost property about
which somebody says, 'This is mine,'
both parties are to bring their cases be-
22:9 [w]ver 28; Dt 25:1 fore the judges.[w] The one whom the
judges declare[b] guilty must pay back
double to his neighbor.

10 "If a man gives a donkey, an ox, a
sheep or any other animal to his neighbor for safekeeping and it dies or is injured or is taken away while no one is
looking, 11 the issue between them will
22:11 [x]Heb 6:16 be settled by the taking of an oath[x] before the LORD that the neighbor did not
lay hands on the other person's property. The owner is to accept this, and no
restitution is required. 12 But if the animal was stolen from the neighbor, he
must make restitution to the owner. 13 If
it was torn to pieces by a wild animal, he
shall bring in the remains as evidence
22:13 [y]Ge 31:39 and he will not be required to pay for the
torn animal.[y]

14 "If a man borrows an animal from
his neighbor and it is injured or dies
while the owner is not present, he must
make restitution. 15 But if the owner is
with the animal, the borrower will not
have to pay. If the animal was hired, the
money paid for the hire covers the loss.

Social Responsibility

22:16 [z]Dt 22:28 16 "If a man seduces a virgin[z] who is
not pledged to be married and sleeps
with her, he must pay the bride-price,
and she shall be his wife. 17 If her father
22:18 [a]Lev 20:27; Dt 18:11; 1Sa 28:3 absolutely refuses to give her to him, he
must still pay the bride-price for virgins.

18 "Do not allow a sorceress[a] to live.

22:19 [b]Lev 18:23; Dt 27:21 19 "Anyone who has sexual relations
with an animal[b] must be put to death.

22:20 [c]Dt 17:2-5 20 "Whoever sacrifices to any god other than the LORD must be destroyed.[c][c]

22:21 [d]Lev 19:33 [e]Dt 10:19 21 "Do not mistreat an alien[d] or oppress him, for you were aliens[e] in Egypt.

22 "Do not take advantage of a widow
22:22 [f]Dt 24:6,10,12,17 or an orphan.[f] 23 If you do and they cry
out[g] to me, I will certainly hear their
cry.[h] 24 My anger will be aroused, and I
22:23 [g]Lk 18:7 [h]Dt 15:9; Ps 18:6 will kill you with the sword; your wives
will become widows and your children
fatherless.[i]

25 "If you lend money to one of my
22:24 [i]Ps 69:24; 109:9 people among you who is needy, do not
be like a moneylender; charge him no 22:25 [j]Lev 25:35-37; Dt 23:20; Ps 15:5
interest.[d][j] 26 If you take your neighbor's
cloak as a pledge,[k] return it to him by
sunset, 27 because his cloak is the only 22:26 [k]Dt 24:6
covering he has for his body. What else
will he sleep in? When he cries out to 22:27 [l]Ex 34:6
me, I will hear, for I am compassionate.[l]

28 "Do not blaspheme God[e][m] or curse 22:28 [m]Lev 24:11,16 [n]Ecc 10:20; Ac 23:5*
the ruler of your people.[n]

29 "Do not hold back offerings[o] from
your granaries or your vats.[f]

"You must give me the firstborn of 22:29 [o]Ex 23:15,16,19 [p]Ex 13:2
your sons.[p] 30 Do the same with your cat-
tle and your sheep.[q] Let them stay with 22:30 [q]Ex 13:12; Dt 15:19 [r]Lev 22:27
their mothers for seven days, but give
them to me on the eighth day.[r]

31 "You are to be my holy people.[s] So 22:31 [s]Lev 19:2 [t]Eze 4:14
do not eat the meat of an animal torn by
wild beasts;[t] throw it to the dogs.

Laws of Justice and Mercy

23 "Do not spread false reports.[u] 23:1 [u]Ex 20:16; Ps 101:5 [v]Ps 35:11; Ac 6:11
Do not help a wicked man by
being a malicious witness.[v]

2 "Do not follow the crowd in doing
wrong. When you give testimony in a 23:2 [w]Dt 16:19
lawsuit, do not pervert justice[w] by siding
with the crowd, 3 and do not show favoritism to a poor man in his lawsuit.

4 "If you come across your enemy's ox
or donkey wandering off, be sure to take 23:4 [x]Dt 22:1-3
it back to him.[x] 5 If you see the donkey[y]
of someone who hates you fallen down 23:5 [y]Dt 22:4
under its load, do not leave it there; be
sure you help him with it.

6 "Do not deny justice[z] to your poor 23:6 [z]ver 2
people in their lawsuits. 7 Have nothing
to do with a false charge[a] and do not put 23:7 [a]Eph 4:25
an innocent or honest person to death,
for I will not acquit the guilty.

8 "Do not accept a bribe,[b] for a bribe 23:8 [b]Dt 10:17; 16:19; Pr 15:27
blinds those who see and twists the
words of the righteous.

9 "Do not oppress an alien;[c] you your- 23:9 [c]Ex 22:21
selves know how it feels to be aliens, because you were aliens in Egypt.

Sabbath Laws

10 "For six years you are to sow your
fields and harvest the crops, 11 but during the seventh year let the land lie un-

[a] 8 Or *before God*; also in verse 9 [b] 9 Or *whom God declares* [c] 20 The Hebrew term refers to the irrevocable giving over of things or persons to the LORD, often by totally destroying them. [d] 25 Or *excessive interest* [e] 28 Or *Do not revile the judges* [f] 29 The meaning of the Hebrew for this phrase is uncertain.

plowed and unused. Then the poor
among your people may get food from
it, and the wild animals may eat what
they leave. Do the same with your vineyard and your olive grove.
23:12 [12]"Six days do your work,[d] but on the
d Ex 20:9 seventh day do not work, so that your ox
and your donkey may rest and the slave
born in your household, and the alien as
well, may be refreshed.
23:13 [13]"Be careful[e] to do everything I have
e 1Ti 4:16 said to you. Do not invoke the names of
other gods; do not let them be heard on
your lips.

The Three Annual Festivals

23:14 [14]"Three times[f] a year you are to cele-
f Ex 34:23,24 brate a festival to me.
[15]"Celebrate the Feast of Unleavened
23:15 g Ex 12:17 Bread;[g] for seven days eat bread made
h Ex 34:20 without yeast, as I commanded you. Do
this at the appointed time in the month
of Abib, for in that month you came out
of Egypt.
"No one is to appear before me empty-
handed.[h]
23:16 [16]"Celebrate the Feast of Harvest with
i Ex 34:22 the firstfruits[i] of the crops you sow in
j Dt 16:13 your field.
"Celebrate the Feast of Ingathering at
the end of the year, when you gather in
your crops from the field.[j]
23:17 k Dt 16:16 [17]"Three times[k] a year all the men are
to appear before the Sovereign LORD.
[18]"Do not offer the blood of a sacrifice
23:18 to me along with anything containing
l Ex 34:25 m Dt 16:4 yeast.[l]
"The fat of my festival offerings must
not be kept until morning.[m]
23:19 [19]"Bring the best of the firstfruits[n] of
n Ex 22:29; Dt 26:2,10 your soil to the house of the LORD your
o Dt 14:21 God.
"Do not cook a young goat in its
mother's milk.[o]

God's Angel to Prepare the Way

23:20 [20]"See, I am sending an angel[p] ahead
p Ex 14:19; 32:34 q Ex 15:17 of you to guard you along the way and to
bring you to the place I have prepared.[q]
23:21 [21]Pay attention to him and listen[r] to
r Nu 14:11; Dt 18:19 what he says. Do not rebel against him;
s Ps 78:8,40,56 he will not forgive your rebellion,[s] since
my Name is in him. [22]If you listen care-
23:22 fully to what he says and do all that I say,
t Ge 12:3; I will be an enemy[t] to your enemies and
Dt 30:7 will oppose those who oppose you. [23]My
angel will go ahead of you and bring you
into the land of the Amorites, Hittites, 23:23
Perizzites, Canaanites, Hivites and Jebu- u ver 20; Jos 24:8,11
sites,[u] and I will wipe them out. [24]Do not
bow down before their gods or worship[v] 23:24 v Ex 20:5
them or follow their practices.[w] You w Dt 12:30-31
must demolish[x] them and break their sa- x Ex 34:13;
cred stones to pieces. [25]Worship the Nu 33:52
LORD your God,[y] and his blessing[z] will be 23:25
on your food and water. I will take away y Dt 6:13; Mt 4:10
sickness[a] from among you, [26]and none z Dt 7:12-15; 28:1-14
will miscarry or be barren[b] in your land. a Ex 15:26
I will give you a full life span.[c] 23:26
[27]"I will send my terror[d] ahead of you b Dt 7:14;
and throw into confusion[e] every nation Mal 3:11
you encounter. I will make all your ene- c Job 5:26
mies turn their backs and run. [28]I will 23:27
send the hornet[f] ahead of you to drive d Ex 15:14; Dt 2:25
the Hivites, Canaanites and Hittites out e Dt 7:23
of your way. [29]But I will not drive them 23:28
out in a single year, because the land f Dt 7:20;
would become desolate and the wild an- Jos 24:12
imals[g] too numerous for you. [30]Little by 23:29
little I will drive them out before you, g Dt 7:22
until you have increased enough to take
possession of the land.
[31]"I will establish your borders from
the Red Sea[a] to the Sea of the Philistines,[b] and from the desert to the Riv-
er.[c][h] I will hand over to you the people 23:31 h Ge 15:18
who live in the land and you will drive i Jos 21:44;
them out[i] before you. [32]Do not make a 24:12,18

[a] *31* Hebrew *Yam Suph*; that is, Sea of Reeds
[b] *31* That is, the Mediterranean [c] *31* That is, the Euphrates

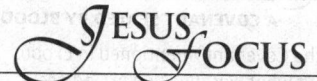

JESUS FOCUS

GUARDIAN ANGEL

God promised to send his angel ahead of his people as they traveled, in order to guard them and lead them to the promised land (Exodus 23:20–33), the place he had prepared for them (see Jesus' similar statement in John 14:2–3). Many people believe that this angel was the "angel of the LORD," Jesus himself. When God stated, "my Name is in him" (verse 21), it seems reasonable to conclude that the reference was to God the Son. To listen to this guide is to listen to God; to rebel against him is to rebel against God. If the people were to believe him, he promised to go ahead of them like a hornet and drive their enemies out of the land. Later on Joshua met the "commander of the army of the LORD" face-to-face and worshiped him as God—even though he did not acknowledge him to be God the Father (Joshua 5:13–15).

23:32 [j]Ex 34:12; Dt 7:2 covenant[j] with them or with their gods.
33Do not let them live in your land, or
they will cause you to sin against me, be-
23:33 [k]Dt 7:16; Ps 106:36 cause the worship of their gods will certainly be a snare[k] to you."

The Covenant Confirmed

24 Then he said to Moses, "Come
up to the LORD, you and Aaron,
24:1 [l]Ex 6:23; Lev 10:1-2 [m]Nu 11:16 Nadab and Abihu,[l] and seventy of the
elders[m] of Israel. You are to worship at a
distance, 2but Moses alone is to approach the LORD; the others must not
come near. And the people may not
come up with him."

3When Moses went and told the peo-
24:3 [n]Ex 19:8; Dt 5:27 ple all the LORD's words and laws, they
responded with one voice, "Everything
the LORD has said we will do."[n] 4Moses
24:4 [o]Dt 31:9 [p]Ge 28:18 then wrote[o] down everything the LORD
had said.

He got up early the next morning and
built an altar at the foot of the mountain
and set up twelve stone pillars[p] representing the twelve tribes of Israel. 5Then
he sent young Israelite men, and they offered burnt offerings and sacrificed
young bulls as fellowship offerings[a] to
24:6 [q]Heb 9:18 the LORD. 6Moses took half of the blood[q]
and put it in bowls, and the other half he
sprinkled on the altar. 7Then he took the

Book of the Covenant[r] and read it to the 24:7 [r]Heb 9:19
people. They responded, "We will do
everything the LORD has said; we will
obey."

8Moses then took the blood, sprinkled it on the people and said, "This is
the blood of the covenant[s] that the LORD 24:8 [s]Heb 9:20*; 1Pe 1:2
has made with you in accordance with
all these words."

9Moses and Aaron, Nadab and Abihu,
and the seventy elders[t] of Israel went up 24:9 [t]ver 1
10and saw[u] the God of Israel. Under his 24:10 [u]Mt 17:2; Jn 1:18; 6:46 [v]Eze 1:26 [w]Rev 4:3
feet was something like a pavement
made of sapphire,[b][v] clear as the sky[w] itself. 11But God did not raise his hand
against these leaders of the Israelites; 24:11 [x]Ge 32:30; Ex 19:21
they saw[x] God, and they ate and drank.

12The LORD said to Moses, "Come up
to me on the mountain and stay here, 24:12 [y]Ex 32:15-16
and I will give you the tablets of stone,[y]
with the law and commands I have written for their instruction."

13Then Moses set out with Joshua[z] his 24:13 [z]Ex 17:9 [a]Ex 3:1
aide, and Moses went up on the moun-
tain[a] of God. 14He said to the elders,
"Wait here for us until we come back to
you. Aaron and Hur are with you, and
anyone involved in a dispute can go to
them."

15When Moses went up on the moun- 24:15 [b]Ex 19:9
tain, the cloud[b] covered it, 16and the glo-
ry[c] of the LORD settled on Mount Sinai. 24:16 [c]Ex 16:10 [d]Ps 99:7
For six days the cloud covered the
mountain, and on the seventh day the
LORD called to Moses from within the
cloud.[d] 17To the Israelites the glory of 24:17 [e]Ex 3:2; Dt 4:36; Heb 12:18,29
the LORD looked like a consuming fire[e]
on top of the mountain. 18Then Moses
entered the cloud as he went on up the 24:18 [f]Dt 9:9 [g]Ex 34:28
mountain. And he stayed on the moun-
tain forty[f] days and forty nights.[g]

Offerings for the Tabernacle

25 The LORD said to Moses, 2"Tell
the Israelites to bring me an
offering. You are to receive the offering
for me from each man whose heart 25:2 [h]Ex 35:21; 1Ch 29:5,7,9; Ezr 2:68; 2Co 8:11-12; 9:7
prompts[h] him to give. 3These are the of-
ferings you are to receive from them:
gold, silver and bronze; 4blue, purple and
scarlet yarn and fine linen; goat hair;
5ram skins dyed red and hides of sea 25:6 [i]Ex 27:20; 30:22-32
cows[c]; acacia wood; 6olive oil[i] for the
light; spices for the anointing oil and for
the fragrant incense; 7and onyx stones

[a] 5 Traditionally *peace offerings* [b] 10 Or *lapis lazuli* [c] 5 That is, dugongs

JESUS FOCUS

A COVENANT SEALED BY BLOOD

"The Book of the Covenant" mentioned in Exodus 24:7 spelled out what was involved in God's covenant, or contract, with Moses. The details are found in Exodus 20:2—23:33. The covenant God made with Moses was a *blood covenant*, signifying that half the blood of a sacrificed animal was sprinkled on the altar and the remaining half sprinkled on the people, thereby binding them to the laws of God. When Jesus introduced the new covenant (or new "testament"), he referred to his blood as the "blood of the covenant" (Mark 14:24; see also 1 Corinthians 11:25). Hebrews 7:22–27 assures us that Jesus is God's guarantee of an even better covenant. Unlike human priests who continually had to make sacrifices both for their own sins and for the sins of the people, Jesus was able to enter the Most Holy Place—the very presence of God—to make a sacrifice "once for all by his own blood" (Hebrews 9:12), thereby mediating the new covenant between God and humanity.

25:7 [j]Ex 28:4,6-14 and other gems to be mounted on the
[k]Ex 28:15-30 ephod[j] and breastpiece.[k]
25:8 8“Then have them make a sanctuary[l]
[l]Ex 36:1-5; for me, and I will dwell[m] among them.
Heb 9:1-2 9Make this tabernacle and all its fur-
[m]Ex 29:45; 1Ki 6:13; nishings exactly like the pattern[n] I will
2Co 6:16; Rev 21:3 show you.

25:9 *The Ark*

[n]ver 40; Ac 7:44; Heb 8:5 10“Have them make a chest[o] of acacia
25:10 wood—two and a half cubits long, a cu-
[o]Dt 10:1-5; bit and a half wide, and a cubit and a
Heb 9:4 half high.[a] 11Overlay it with pure gold,
both inside and out, and make a gold
molding around it. 12Cast four gold rings
for it and fasten them to its four feet,
with two rings on one side and two rings
on the other. 13Then make poles of acacia wood and overlay them with gold.
14Insert the poles into the rings on the
sides of the chest to carry it. 15The poles
25:15 are to remain in the rings of this ark;
[p]1Ki 8:8 they are not to be removed.[p] 16Then put
25:16 in the ark the Testimony,[q] which I will
[q]Dt 31:26; Heb 9:4 give you.
17“Make an atonement cover[b][r] of pure
25:17 [r]Ro 3:25 gold—two and a half cubits long and a
cubit and a half wide.[c] 18And make two
cherubim out of hammered gold at the
ends of the cover. 19Make one cherub on
one end and the second cherub on the
other; make the cherubim of one piece
with the cover, at the two ends. 20The
25:20 cherubim are to have their wings spread
[s]1Ki 8:7; 1Ch 28:18; upward, overshadowing[s] the cover with
Heb 9:5 them. The cherubim are to face each
other, looking toward the cover. 21Place
25:21 [t]Ex 26:34 the cover on top of the ark[t] and put in
[u]ver 16 the ark the Testimony,[u] which I will give
25:22 you. 22There, above the cover between
[v]Nu 7:89; the two cherubim[v] that are over the ark
1Sa 4:4; 2Sa 6:2; 2Ki 19:15; of the Testimony, I will meet[w] with you
Ps 80:1; Isa 37:16 and give you all my commands for the
[w]Ex 29:42-43 Israelites.

The Table

25:23 23“Make a table[x] of acacia wood—two
[x]Heb 9:2 cubits long, a cubit wide and a cubit and
a half high.[d] 24Overlay it with pure gold
and make a gold molding around it.
25Also make around it a rim a handbreadth[e] wide and put a gold molding
on the rim. 26Make four gold rings for
the table and fasten them to the four
corners, where the four legs are. 27The
rings are to be close to the rim to hold
the poles used in carrying the table.

28Make the poles of acacia wood, overlay
them with gold and carry the table with
them. 29And make its plates and dishes
of pure gold, as well as its pitchers and
bowls for the pouring out of offerings.[y] 25:29 [y]Nu 4:7
30Put the bread of the Presence[z] on this 25:30
table to be before me at all times. [z]Lev 24:5-9

The Lampstand

31“Make a lampstand[a] of pure gold 25:31
and hammer it out, base and shaft; its [a]1Ki 7:49; Zec 4:2;
flowerlike cups, buds and blossoms shall Heb 9:2;
be of one piece with it. 32Six branches are Rev 1:12
to extend from the sides of the lamp-
stand—three on one side and three on
the other. 33Three cups shaped like al-

[a] *10* That is, about 3 3/4 feet (about 1.1 meters) long and 2 1/4 feet (about 0.7 meter) wide and high
[b] *17* Traditionally *a mercy seat*
[c] *17* That is, about 3 3/4 feet (about 1.1 meters) long and 2 1/4 feet (about 0.7 meter) wide
[d] *23* That is, about 3 feet (about 0.9 meter) long and 1 1/2 feet (about 0.5 meter) wide and 2 1/4 feet (about 0.7 meter) high
[e] *25* That is, about 3 inches (about 8 centimeters)

ONLY A SHADOW

The *tabernacle*, which literally means “dwelling place” or “tent of meeting,” was a symbol of God’s presence with his people. God himself furnished the details of its pattern (Exodus 25—27), because it was “a copy and shadow of what is in heaven” (Hebrews 8:5). The book of Hebrews goes on to tell us that even God’s law is only a shadow of the good things that God has in store for us (Hebrews 7; 10; see also Exodus 10:1). Jesus is the ultimate fulfillment of what God designed the tabernacle to be. The priests offered sacrifices continually, but Jesus’ sacrifice is far superior because he offered the sacrifice in “heaven itself” (Hebrews 9:23–28).

Tabernacle Types	Descriptions of Jesus
One Entry	“I am the gate” (John 10:9)
Bronze Altar	“Look, the Lamb of God” (John 1:29)
Basin for washing	“Unless I wash you” (John 13:8–10)
Lampstand	“I am the light” (John 8:12)
Bread of the Presence	“I am the bread of life” (John 6:48)
Incense	“I pray for them” (John 17:9)
Curtain	“Through the curtain, that is, his body” (Hebrews 10:20)
Atonement Cover (Mercy Seat)	“Enter the Most Holy Place by the blood of Jesus” (Hebrews 10:19)
Glory of God	“We have seen his glory” (John 1:14)

mond flowers with buds and blossoms
are to be on one branch, three on the
next branch, and the same for all six
branches extending from the lampstand.
34 And on the lampstand there are to be
four cups shaped like almond flowers
with buds and blossoms. 35 One bud shall
be under the first pair of branches extending from the lampstand, a second
bud under the second pair, and a third
bud under the third pair—six branches
in all. 36 The buds and branches shall all
be of one piece with the lampstand,
hammered out of pure gold.

25:37 [b] Ex 27:21; Lev 24:3-4; Nu 8:2

37 "Then make its seven lamps[b] and set
them up on it so that they light the space
in front of it. 38 Its wick trimmers and
trays are to be of pure gold. 39 A talent[a] of
pure gold is to be used for the lampstand
and all these accessories. 40 See that you
make them according to the pattern[c]
shown you on the mountain.

25:40 [c] Ex 26:30; Nu 8:4; Ac 7:44; Heb 8:5*

The Tabernacle

26 "Make the tabernacle with ten
curtains of finely twisted linen
and blue, purple and scarlet yarn, with
cherubim worked into them by a skilled
craftsman. 2 All the curtains are to be the
same size—twenty-eight cubits long
and four cubits wide.[b] 3 Join five of the
curtains together, and do the same with
the other five. 4 Make loops of blue material along the edge of the end curtain
in one set, and do the same with the end
curtain in the other set. 5 Make fifty
loops on one curtain and fifty loops on
the end curtain of the other set, with the
loops opposite each other. 6 Then make
fifty gold clasps and use them to fasten
the curtains together so that the tabernacle is a unit.

7 "Make curtains of goat hair for the
tent over the tabernacle—eleven altogether. 8 All eleven curtains are to be the
same size—thirty cubits long and four
cubits wide.[c] 9 Join five of the curtains together into one set and the other six into
another set. Fold the sixth curtain double at the front of the tent. 10 Make fifty
loops along the edge of the end curtain
in one set and also along the edge of the
end curtain in the other set. 11 Then
make fifty bronze clasps and put them in
the loops to fasten the tent together as a
unit. 12 As for the additional length of the
tent curtains, the half curtain that is left
over is to hang down at the rear of the
tabernacle. 13 The tent curtains will be a
cubit[d] longer on both sides; what is left
will hang over the sides of the tabernacle
so as to cover it. 14 Make for the tent a
covering of ram skins dyed red, and over
that a covering of hides of sea cows.[e][d]

26:14 [d] Ex 36:19; Nu 4:25

15 "Make upright frames of acacia
wood for the tabernacle. 16 Each frame is
to be ten cubits long and a cubit and a
half wide,[f] 17 with two projections set
parallel to each other. Make all the
frames of the tabernacle in this way.
18 Make twenty frames for the south side
of the tabernacle 19 and make forty silver
bases to go under them—two bases for
each frame, one under each projection.
20 For the other side, the north side of the
tabernacle, make twenty frames 21 and
forty silver bases—two under each
frame. 22 Make six frames for the far end,
that is, the west end of the tabernacle,
23 and make two frames for the corners
at the far end. 24 At these two corners
they must be double from the bottom all
the way to the top, and fitted into a single ring; both shall be like that. 25 So
there will be eight frames and sixteen
silver bases—two under each frame.

26 "Also make crossbars of acacia
wood: five for the frames on one side of
the tabernacle, 27 five for those on the
other side, and five for the frames on the
west, at the far end of the tabernacle.
28 The center crossbar is to extend from
end to end at the middle of the frames.
29 Overlay the frames with gold and
make gold rings to hold the crossbars.
Also overlay the crossbars with gold.

30 "Set up the tabernacle according to
the plan[e] shown you on the mountain.

26:30 [e] Ex 25:9,40; Ac 7:44; Heb 8:5

31 "Make a curtain[f] of blue, purple and
scarlet yarn and finely twisted linen,
with cherubim[g] worked into it by a
skilled craftsman. 32 Hang it with gold
hooks on four posts of acacia wood
overlaid with gold and standing on four
silver bases. 33 Hang the curtain from the
clasps and place the ark of the Testimony behind the curtain.[h] The curtain will
separate the Holy Place from the Most

26:31 [f] 2Ch 3:14; Mt 27:51; Heb 9:3 [g] Ex 36:35

26:33 [h] Ex 40:3,21; Lev 16:2

[a] *39* That is, about 75 pounds (about 34 kilograms)
[b] *2* That is, about 42 feet (about 12.5 meters) long and 6 feet (about 1.8 meters) wide
[c] *8* That is, about 45 feet (about 13.5 meters) long and 6 feet (about 1.8 meters) wide
[d] *13* That is, about 1 1/2 feet (about 0.5 meter)
[e] *14* That is, dugongs
[f] *16* That is, about 15 feet (about 4.5 meters) long and 2 1/4 feet (about 0.7 meter) wide

DISCOVERY 23

Living in a Tent

A tent is important when backpacking, because it provides shelter and protection from the elements. However, a tent is too confining and unstable to be suitable for permanent residence. God's people lived in tents while they traveled through the desert, and even today people who live in tents tend to be nomadic. Interestingly, however, the Bible uses the symbol of a tent to describe God's presence among his people.

First of all, God himself lived in a tent called the tabernacle—he gave Moses specific instructions about its construction, because it was to be the place where God's presence would live (Exodus 26:1–29). The tabernacle could be disassembled and carried as the people made their way across the desert toward the land God had promised them. Each time the tabernacle was set up, God's glory would again fill it like a cloud (Exodus 40:34–38). When the people finally settled in the land, the tabernacle would be replaced by the temple. However, while the temple of God was a more permanent structure, it was still only a building.

Second, when God became a man, he lived in another kind of tent—a human body. The apostle John explained it this way: "The Word became flesh and made his dwelling among us. We have seen his glory" (John 1:14). The phrase "made his dwelling" literally means "lived in a tent." God the Son confined his glory to the limitations of a human body, just as God had earlier limited his glory to the confines of the tabernacle and, later on, the temple (Philippians 2:6–11).

Third, we also live in tents—our physical bodies (2 Corinthians 5:1–5). Just as the tabernacle, and later Jesus' physical body, were temporary, so our physical bodies provide only transient dwelling places. They will be made permanent in eternity with God.

The apostle Peter urged Christians to whom he wrote to "make [their] calling and election sure" (2 Peter 1:10), adding: "I think it is right to refresh your memory as long as I live in the tent of this body, because I know that I will soon put it aside, as our Lord Jesus Christ has made clear to me" (2 Peter 1:13–14).

It can be difficult to understand and accept the concept that life on earth is fleeting and that "the real thing" will come later—and last forever. But it feels good to come home after living in a tent for a few days. Imagine the comfort and sense of belonging when we leave this temporary life. While the reality of death can be painful and difficult to accept, our real hope must be in Jesus—and the perfect permanent residence he has prepared for us (John 14:1–4). Settling into heaven will be like coming home and crawling into our own bed after nights spent sleeping in a tent on the hard ground!

Self-Discovery: *Is there a "hard-ground" situation in your life right now that feels permanent? Are you able to find comfort in God's promise both of his presence today and of a permanent eternal home?*

GO TO DISCOVERY 24 ON PAGE 113

26:33 Holy Place.[i] [34]Put the atonement cover[j]
[i]Heb 9:2-3 on the ark of the Testimony in the Most
26:34 Holy Place. [35]Place the table[k] outside the
[j]Ex 25:21; curtain on the north side of the taber-
40:20; Heb 9:5 nacle and put the lampstand[l] opposite
26:35 [k]Heb 9:2 it on the south side.
[l]Ex 40:22,24 [36]"For the entrance to the tent make a
curtain of blue, purple and scarlet yarn
and finely twisted linen—the work of an
embroiderer. [37]Make gold hooks for this
curtain and five posts of acacia wood
overlaid with gold. And cast five bronze
bases for them.

The Altar of Burnt Offering

27:1 **27** "Build an altar[m] of acacia
[m]Eze 43:13 wood, three cubits[a] high; it is to
be square, five cubits long and five cu-
27:2 bits wide.[b] [2]Make a horn[n] at each of the
[n]Ps 118:27 four corners, so that the horns and the
altar are of one piece, and overlay the altar with bronze. [3]Make all its utensils of
bronze—its pots to remove the ashes,
and its shovels, sprinkling bowls, meat
forks and firepans. [4]Make a grating for
it, a bronze network, and make a bronze
ring at each of the four corners of the
network. [5]Put it under the ledge of the
altar so that it is halfway up the altar.
[6]Make poles of acacia wood for the altar
and overlay them with bronze. [7]The
poles are to be inserted into the rings so
they will be on two sides of the altar
when it is carried. [8]Make the altar hol-
27:8 low, out of boards. It is to be made just
[o]Ex 25:9,40 as you were shown[o] on the mountain.

The Courtyard

[9]"Make a courtyard for the tabernacle. The south side shall be a hundred
cubits[c] long and is to have curtains of
finely twisted linen, [10]with twenty posts
and twenty bronze bases and with silver
hooks and bands on the posts. [11]The
north side shall also be a hundred cubits
long and is to have curtains, with twenty posts and twenty bronze bases and
with silver hooks and bands on the
posts.
[12]"The west end of the courtyard shall
be fifty cubits[d] wide and have curtains,
with ten posts and ten bases. [13]On the
east end, toward the sunrise, the courtyard shall also be fifty cubits wide. [14]Cur-
tains fifteen cubits[e] long are to be on
one side of the entrance, with three
posts and three bases, [15]and curtains fifteen cubits long are to be on the other
side, with three posts and three bases.
[16]"For the entrance to the courtyard,
provide a curtain twenty cubits[f] long, of
blue, purple and scarlet yarn and finely
twisted linen—the work of an embroiderer—with four posts and four bases.
[17]All the posts around the courtyard are
to have silver bands and hooks, and
bronze bases. [18]The courtyard shall be a
hundred cubits long and fifty cubits
wide,[g] with curtains of finely twisted
linen five cubits[h] high, and with bronze
bases. [19]All the other articles used in the
service of the tabernacle, whatever their
function, including all the tent pegs for
it and those for the courtyard, are to be
of bronze.

Oil for the Lampstand

[20]"Command the Israelites to bring
you clear oil of pressed olives for the
light so that the lamps may be kept
burning. [21]In the Tent of Meeting,[p] out- 27:21
side the curtain that is in front of the [p]Ex 28:43
Testimony,[q] Aaron and his sons are to [q]Ex 26:31,33 [r]Ex 25:37; 30:8;
keep the lamps[r] burning before the 1Sa 3:3;
LORD from evening till morning. This is 2Ch 13:11 [s]Ex 29:9;
to be a lasting ordinance[s] among the Is- Lev 3:17; 16:34;
raelites for the generations to come. Nu 18:23; 19:21

The Priestly Garments

28 "Have Aaron[t] your brother 28:1
brought to you from among the [t]Heb 5:4 [u]Nu 18:1-7;
Israelites, along with his sons Nadab and Heb 5:1
Abihu, Eleazar and Ithamar, so they may
serve me as priests.[u] [2]Make sacred gar- 28:2
ments[v] for your brother Aaron, to give [v]Ex 29:5,29; 31:10; 39:1;
him dignity and honor. [3]Tell all the Lev 8:7-9,30
skilled men[w] to whom I have given wis- 28:3
dom[x] in such matters that they are to [w]Ex 31:6; 36:1 [x]Ex 31:3
make garments for Aaron, for his conse-
cration, so he may serve me as priest.
[4]These are the garments they are to 28:4
make: a breastpiece,[y] an ephod, a robe,[z] [y]ver 15-30
a woven tunic,[a] a turban and a sash. [z]ver 31-35 [a]ver 39
They are to make these sacred garments
for your brother Aaron and his sons, so
they may serve me as priests. [5]Have

[a] *1* That is, about 4 1/2 feet (about 1.3 meters)
[b] *1* That is, about 7 1/2 feet (about 2.3 meters) long and wide [c] *9* That is, about 150 feet (about 46 meters); also in verse 11 [d] *12* That is, about 75 feet (about 23 meters); also in verse 13 [e] *14* That is, about 22 1/2 feet (about 6.9 meters); also in verse 15 [f] *16* That is, about 30 feet (about 9 meters) [g] *18* That is, about 150 feet (about 46 meters) long and 75 feet (about 23 meters) wide [h] *18* That is, about 7 1/2 feet (about 2.3 meters)

DISCOVERY 24

DRESSED TO MEET OUR LORD

Being one of God's priests was serious business. A priest represented God when he stood in front of the people. Conversely, he represented the people when he stood before God presiding over the religious duties in the tabernacle. Even with regard to the priestly clothing, it was necessary to adhere to detailed instructions from God. When the priests entered the tabernacle, they must be dressed in priestly attire. The high priest's special accoutrements included a breastplate, an ephod, a robe, a woven tunic, a turban and a sash (Exodus 28:4).

If the high priest failed to wear the specified articles of clothing, he was disobeying God and could expect to suffer a severe penalty (verse 43). It may seem petty to us now for God to have been concerned about what the priests wore, but everything about the tabernacle reflected God's holiness. It was a place where the people worshiped him, but it was also a reminder of how sin prevents people from enjoying their intended relationship with God. Even the priestly vestments were a reminder of the importance of purity.

Access to God's presence is never easy or cheap. Repairing the damage sin caused in us came at a high personal price for God—his Son's own life. Jesus acted as the final and perfect sacrifice, removing the barrier of sin from between ourselves and God. Jesus Christ acts as our great high priest, having opened the avenue of access to God through his once-for-all sacrificial offering (Hebrews 9:11–15).

Each of us must be "dressed" appropriately to enter the presence of God. The only way we may approach God is through Jesus, in a sense "wearing" his purifying blood. Nothing we can do ourselves to try to win God's acceptance is any better than wearing filthy rags (Isaiah 64:6). God accepts us solely because Jesus died for our sins, and, ironically, his spilled blood is the only "stain-remover" that allows us to approach God clothed in clean garments (Romans 3:21–24).

Our high priest, Jesus, wore the priestly garments of holiness, blamelessness, purity and sinlessness (Hebrews 7:26). His priestly gown is also described in Revelation 1:13. God also refers to us, his people, as priests (Revelation 1:6), and our priestly garment is the righteousness of Jesus (2 Corinthians 5:21; Galatians 3:27).

Self-Discovery: *If Christian virtues could be associated with particular articles of clothing, in what "outfit" would you be most appropriately dressed to meet Jesus?*

GO TO DISCOVERY 25 ON PAGE 120

them use gold, and blue, purple and
scarlet yarn, and fine linen.

The Ephod

6“Make the ephod of gold, and of blue,
purple and scarlet yarn, and of finely
twisted linen—the work of a skilled
craftsman. 7It is to have two shoulder
pieces attached to two of its corners, so
it can be fastened. 8Its skillfully woven
waistband is to be like it—of one piece
with the ephod and made with gold, and
with blue, purple and scarlet yarn, and
with finely twisted linen.
9“Take two onyx stones and engrave
on them the names of the sons of Israel
10in the order of their birth—six names
on one stone and the remaining six on
the other. 11Engrave the names of the
sons of Israel on the two stones the way
a gem cutter engraves a seal. Then
mount the stones in gold filigree settings 12and fasten them on the shoulder
pieces of the ephod as memorial stones
for the sons of Israel. Aaron is to bear
the names on his shoulders as a memorial before the LORD. 13Make gold filigree
settings 14and two braided chains of
pure gold, like a rope, and attach the
chains to the settings.

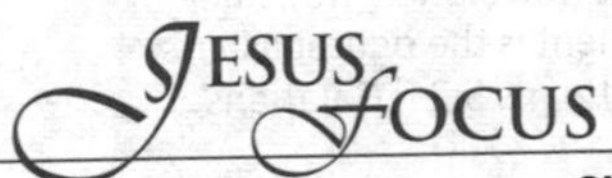

ONE HIGH PRIEST

Jesus is called our “great high priest” in the New Testament (Hebrews 4:14) because he did infinitely more than any human priest could have done (Exodus 28—29). The book of Hebrews clarifies how the sacrificial system foreshadowed what Jesus himself would do for all people.

The Pattern: the high priest	The Perfection: Jesus Christ
Entered earthly tabernacle	Entered heavenly temple (Hebrews 6:19–20)
Entered once a year	Entered once for all (Hebrews 9:25–26)
Went behind the curtain	Tore the curtain (Hebrews 10:20)
Offered many sacrifices	Offered one sacrifice (Hebrews 10:11–12)
Paid for his own sins	Paid for our sins (Hebrews 7:27)
Offered the blood of bulls	Offered his own blood (Hebrews 9:12)

The Breastpiece

15“Fashion a breastpiece for making
decisions—the work of a skilled craftsman. Make it like the ephod: of gold, and
of blue, purple and scarlet yarn, and of
finely twisted linen. 16It is to be square—
a span[a] long and a span wide—and folded double. 17Then mount four rows of
precious stones on it. In the first row
there shall be a ruby, a topaz and a beryl;
18in the second row a turquoise, a sapphire[b] and an emerald; 19in the third row
a jacinth, an agate and an amethyst; 20in
the fourth row a chrysolite, an onyx and
a jasper.[c] Mount them in gold filigree
settings. 21There are to be twelve stones,
one for each of the names of the sons of
Israel, each engraved like a seal with the
name of one of the twelve tribes.
22“For the breastpiece make braided
chains of pure gold, like a rope. 23Make
two gold rings for it and fasten them to
two corners of the breastpiece. 24Fasten
the two gold chains to the rings at the
corners of the breastpiece, 25and the other ends of the chains to the two settings,
attaching them to the shoulder pieces of
the ephod at the front. 26Make two gold
rings and attach them to the other two
corners of the breastpiece on the inside
edge next to the ephod. 27Make two more
gold rings and attach them to the bottom
of the shoulder pieces on the front of the
ephod, close to the seam just above the
waistband of the ephod. 28The rings of
the breastpiece are to be tied to the rings
of the ephod with blue cord, connecting
it to the waistband, so that the breastpiece will not swing out from the ephod.
29“Whenever Aaron enters the Holy 28:29
Place,[b] he will bear the names of the [b] ver 12
sons of Israel over his heart on the
breastpiece of decision as a continuing
memorial before the LORD. 30Also put 28:30
the Urim and the Thummim[c] in the [c] Lev 8:8;
breastpiece, so they may be over Aaron’s Nu 27:21;
heart whenever he enters the presence Dt 33:8;
of the LORD. Thus Aaron will always bear Ezr 2:63;
the means of making decisions for the Ne 7:65
Israelites over his heart before the LORD.

Other Priestly Garments

31“Make the robe of the ephod entirely

[a] *16* That is, about 9 inches (about 22 centimeters) [b] *18* Or *lapis lazuli* [c] *20* The precise identification of some of these precious stones is uncertain.

of blue cloth, 32 with an opening for the
head in its center. There shall be a woven
edge like a collar[a] around this opening, so
that it will not tear. 33 Make pomegranates
of blue, purple and scarlet yarn around
the hem of the robe, with gold bells between them. 34 The gold bells and the
pomegranates are to alternate around
the hem of the robe. 35 Aaron must wear
it when he ministers. The sound of the
bells will be heard when he enters the
Holy Place before the LORD and when he
comes out, so that he will not die.
36 "Make a plate of pure gold and en-
28:36 [d] Zec 14:20 grave on it as on a seal: HOLY TO THE
LORD.[d] 37 Fasten a blue cord to it to attach
it to the turban; it is to be on the front of
28:38 [e] Lev 10:17; 22:9,16; Nu 18:1; Heb 9:28; 1Pe 2:24 the turban. 38 It will be on Aaron's forehead, and he will bear the guilt[e] involved
in the sacred gifts the Israelites consecrate, whatever their gifts may be. It will
be on Aaron's forehead continually so
that they will be acceptable to the LORD.
39 "Weave the tunic of fine linen and
make the turban of fine linen. The sash
is to be the work of an embroiderer.
28:40 [f] ver 4; Ex 39:41 40 Make tunics, sashes and headbands
for Aaron's sons,[f] to give them dignity
28:41 [g] Ex 29:7; Lev 10:7 [h] Ex 29:7-9; 30:30; 40:15; Lev 8:1-36; Heb 7:28 and honor. 41 After you put these clothes
on your brother Aaron and his sons,
anoint[g] and ordain them. Consecrate
them so they may serve me as priests.[h]
42 "Make linen undergarments[i] as a
covering for the body, reaching from the
28:42 [i] Lev 6:10; 16:4, 23; Eze 44:18 waist to the thigh. 43 Aaron and his sons
must wear them whenever they enter
28:43 [j] Ex 27:21 [k] Ex 20:26 [l] Lev 17:7 the Tent of Meeting[j] or approach the altar to minister in the Holy Place, so that
they will not incur guilt and die.[k]
"This is to be a lasting ordinance[l] for
Aaron and his descendants.

Consecration of the Priests

29 "This is what you are to do to
consecrate them, so they may
serve me as priests: Take a young bull
and two rams without defect. 2 And from
fine wheat flour, without yeast, make
29:2 [m] Lev 2:1,4; 6:19-23 bread, and cakes mixed with oil, and
wafers spread with oil.[m] 3 Put them in a
basket and present them in it—along
with the bull and the two rams. 4 Then
29:4 [n] Ex 40:12; Heb 10:22 bring Aaron and his sons to the entrance to the Tent of Meeting and wash
them with water.[n] 5 Take the garments[o]
29:5 [o] Ex 28:2; Lev 8:7 and dress Aaron with the tunic, the robe
of the ephod, the ephod itself and the
breastpiece. Fasten the ephod on him by 29:5 [p] Ex 28:8
its skillfully woven waistband.[p] 6 Put the
turban on his head and attach the sa- 29:6 [q] Lev 8:9
cred diadem[q] to the turban. 7 Take the
anointing oil[r] and anoint him by pour- 29:7 [r] Ex 30:25,30, 31; Lev 8:12; 21:10; Nu 35:25; Ps 133:2
ing it on his head. 8 Bring his sons and
dress them in tunics 9 and put headbands on them. Then tie sashes on Aar-
on and his sons.[b][s] The priesthood is 29:9 [s] Ex 28:40 [t] Ex 40:15; Nu 3:10; 18:7; 25:13; Dt 18:5
theirs by a lasting ordinance.[t] In this
way you shall ordain Aaron and his sons.
10 "Bring the bull to the front of the
Tent of Meeting, and Aaron and his sons
shall lay their hands on its head.
11 Slaughter it in the LORD's presence at
the entrance to the Tent of Meeting.
12 Take some of the bull's blood and put
it on the horns[u] of the altar with your 29:12 [u] Ex 27:2

[a] *32* The meaning of the Hebrew for this word is uncertain. [b] *9* Hebrew; Septuagint *on them*

JESUS FOCUS

OUR PRIEST FOREVER

The system of animal sacrifices and the function of the Old Testament priesthood were intended to be in effect for only a period of time (Exodus 29). The sacrificial system was never intended to remove the people's sins but only to cover sin until God's promised Messiah would come to accomplish once and for all what the Old Testament system could not. The priests were ordinary men with human flaws, men who, like ourselves, needed to be rescued from the effects of sin. At best they could only represent what Jesus would later do perfectly. Jesus is called "a high priest forever, in the order of Melchizedek" (Hebrews 6:20). Melchizedek was introduced as the "priest of God Most High" before Levi's family line had been chosen for the priesthood (Genesis 14:18–20). In the same way, Jesus is our priest—even though he is from the family of Judah—because God specifically chose him. The book of Hebrews explains how Jesus' priesthood takes the place of the Levitical priesthood (Hebrews 7:17–19).

Levi's Priesthood	Jesus as our Priest
Temporary	Eternal (Hebrews 7:21–23)
Fallible	Sinless (Hebrews 7:26)
Changeable	Unchanging (Hebrews 7:24)
Continual	Permanent (Hebrews 9:12,26)
Imperfect	Perfect (Hebrews 2:14–18)
Incomplete	Complete (Hebrews 7:25)
Insufficient	All-sufficient (Hebrews 10:11–12)

finger, and pour out the rest of it at the
29:13 v Lev 3:3,5,9 base of the altar. 13Then take all the fat[v]
around the inner parts, the covering of
the liver, and both kidneys with the fat
on them, and burn them on the altar.
29:14 14But burn the bull's flesh and its hide
w Lev 4:11-12, 21; Heb 13:11 and its offal outside the camp.[w] It is a
sin offering.
15"Take one of the rams, and Aaron
and his sons shall lay their hands on its
head. 16Slaughter it and take the blood
and sprinkle it against the altar on all
sides. 17Cut the ram into pieces and
wash the inner parts and the legs, putting them with the head and the other
pieces. 18Then burn the entire ram on
the altar. It is a burnt offering to the
29:18 x Ge 8:21 LORD, a pleasing aroma,[x] an offering
made to the LORD by fire.
29:19 y ver 3 19"Take the other ram,[y] and Aaron
and his sons shall lay their hands on its
head. 20Slaughter it, take some of its
blood and put it on the lobes of the right
ears of Aaron and his sons, on the
thumbs of their right hands, and on the
big toes of their right feet. Then sprinkle
blood against the altar on all sides.
29:21 z Heb 9:22 21And take some of the blood[z] on the al-
a Ex 30:25,31 tar and some of the anointing oil[a] and
b ver 1 sprinkle it on Aaron and his garments
and on his sons and their garments.
Then he and his sons and their garments will be consecrated.[b]
22"Take from this ram the fat, the fat
tail, the fat around the inner parts, the
covering of the liver, both kidneys with
the fat on them, and the right thigh.
(This is the ram for the ordination.)
23From the basket of bread made without yeast, which is before the LORD, take
a loaf, and a cake made with oil, and a
wafer. 24Put all these in the hands of Aaron and his sons and wave them before
29:24 c Lev 7:30 the LORD as a wave offering.[c] 25Then
take them from their hands and burn
them on the altar along with the burnt
offering for a pleasing aroma to the
LORD, an offering made to the LORD by
fire. 26After you take the breast of the
ram for Aaron's ordination, wave it before the LORD as a wave offering, and it
29:26 d Lev 7:31-34 will be your share.[d]
27"Consecrate those parts of the ordi-
29:27 nation ram that belong to Aaron and his
e Lev 7:31,34; Dt 18:3 sons:[e] the breast that was waved and the
thigh that was presented. 28This is always
to be the regular share from the Israelites
for Aaron and his sons. It is the contribu-
tion the Israelites are to make to the LORD 29:28 f Lev 10:15
from their fellowship offerings.[a][f]
29"Aaron's sacred garments will belong
to his descendants so that they can be 29:29 g Nu 20:26,28
anointed and ordained in them.[g] 30The
son[h] who succeeds him as priest and 29:30 h Nu 20:28
comes to the Tent of Meeting to minis-
ter in the Holy Place is to wear them
seven days.
31"Take the ram for the ordination
and cook the meat in a sacred place. 32At
the entrance to the Tent of Meeting,
Aaron and his sons are to eat the meat 29:32
of the ram and the bread[i] that is in the i Mt 12:4
basket. 33They are to eat these offerings
by which atonement was made for their
ordination and consecration. But no one 29:33
else may eat[j] them, because they are sa- j Lev 10:14; 22:10,13
cred. 34And if any of the meat of the or-
dination ram or any bread is left over till 29:34
morning,[k] burn it up. It must not be eat- k Ex 12:10
en, because it is sacred.
35"Do for Aaron and his sons everything I have commanded you, taking
seven days to ordain them. 36Sacrifice a 29:36
bull each day[l] as a sin offering to make l Heb 10:11
atonement. Purify the altar by making m Ex 40:10
atonement for it, and anoint it to consecrate[m] it. 37For seven days make atonement for the altar and consecrate it.
Then the altar will be most holy, and 29:37 n Ex 30:28-29;
whatever touches it will be holy.[n] 40:10; Mt 23:19
38"This is what you are to offer on the 29:38
altar regularly each day:[o] two lambs a o Nu 28:3-8;
year old. 39Offer one in the morning and 1Ch 16:40;
the other at twilight.[p] 40With the first Da 12:11
lamb offer a tenth of an ephah[b] of fine 29:39
flour mixed with a quarter of a hin[c] of oil p Eze 46:13-15
from pressed olives, and a quarter of a
hin of wine as a drink offering. 41Sacri-
fice the other lamb at twilight with the
same grain offering and its drink offering as in the morning—a pleasing aroma, an offering made to the LORD by fire.
42"For the generations to come[q] this 29:42
burnt offering is to be made regularly at q Ex 30:8
the entrance to the Tent of Meeting be- r Ex 25:22
fore the LORD. There I will meet you and
speak to you;[r] 43there also I will meet
with the Israelites, and the place will be 29:43
consecrated by my glory.[s] s 1Ki 8:11
44"So I will consecrate the Tent of
Meeting and the altar and will conse-

[a] 28 Traditionally *peace offerings* [b] 40 That is, probably about 2 quarts (about 2 liters)
[c] 40 That is, probably about 1 quart (about 1 liter)

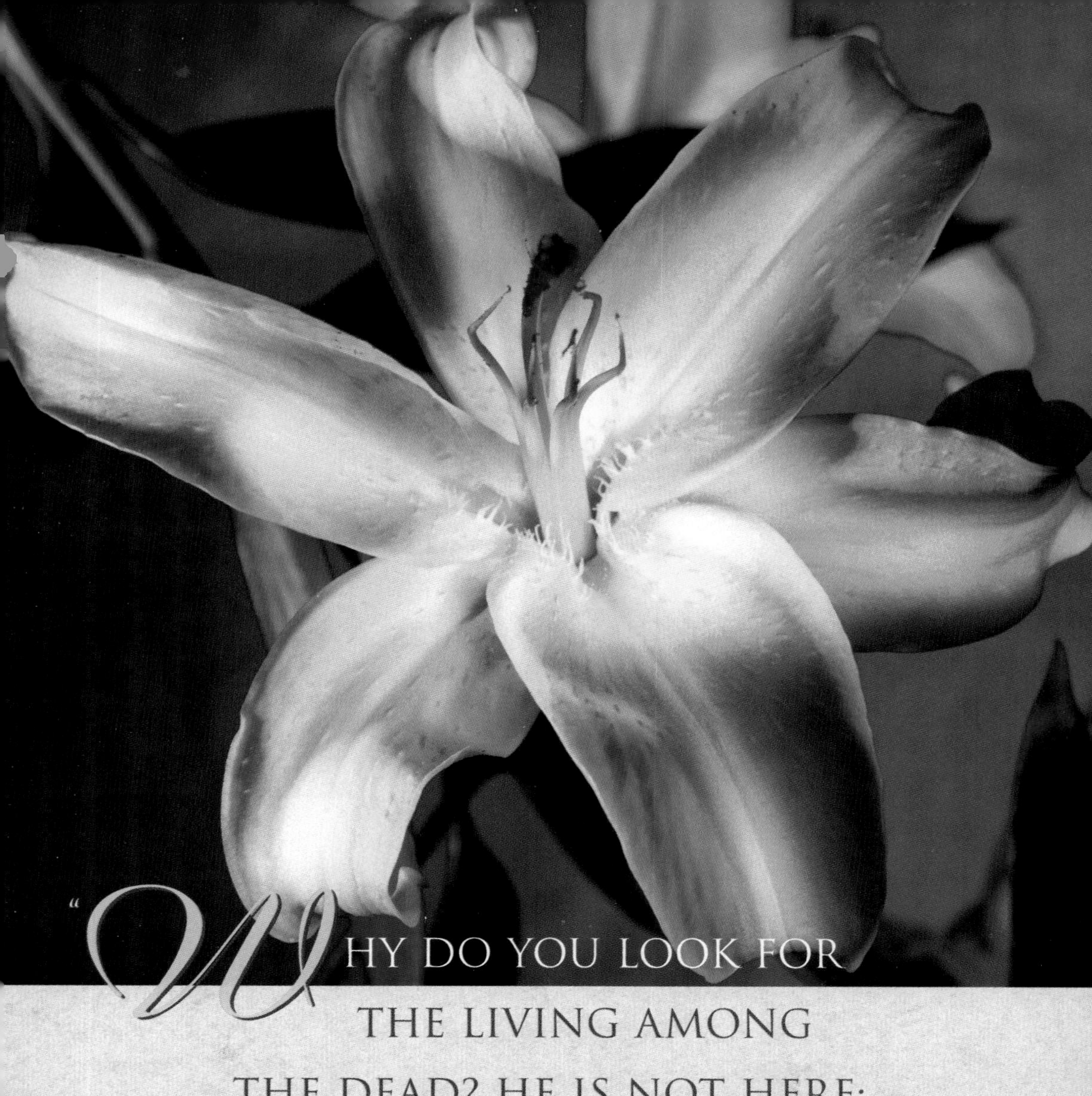

"WHY DO YOU LOOK FOR
THE LIVING AMONG
THE DEAD? HE IS NOT HERE;
he has risen!"

— LUKE 24:5-6 —

"I AM THE GOOD SHEPHERD.
THE *good shepherd* LAYS
DOWN HIS LIFE FOR THE SHEEP."

—JOHN 10:11—

29:44 crate Aaron and his sons to serve me as
t Lev 21:15 priests.[t] 45Then I will dwell[u] among the
29:45 u Ex 25:8; Israelites and be their God.[v] 46They will
Lev 26:12; know that I am the LORD their God, who
Zec 2:10; Jn 14:17 brought them out of Egypt so that I
v 2Co 6:16; might dwell among them. I am the LORD
Rev 21:3 their God.[w]

29:46 w Ex 20:2 *The Altar of Incense*

30:1 x Ex 37:25 30 "Make an altar[x] of acacia wood
y Rev 8:3 for burning incense.[y] 2It is to be
square, a cubit long and a cubit wide,
30:2 and two cubits high[a]—its horns[z] of one
z Ex 27:2 piece with it. 3Overlay the top and all the
sides and the horns with pure gold, and
make a gold molding around it. 4Make
two gold rings for the altar below the
molding—two on opposite sides—to
hold the poles used to carry it. 5Make
the poles of acacia wood and overlay
them with gold. 6Put the altar in front of
the curtain that is before the ark of the
30:6 Testimony—before the atonement cov-
a Ex 25:22; 26:34 er[a] that is over the Testimony—where I
will meet with you.
30:7 7"Aaron must burn fragrant incense[b]
b ver 34-35; Ex 27:21; on the altar every morning when he
1Sa 2:28 tends the lamps. 8He must burn incense
again when he lights the lamps at twilight so incense will burn regularly before the LORD for the generations to
come. 9Do not offer on this altar any
30:9 c Lev 10:1 other incense[c] or any burnt offering or
grain offering, and do not pour a drink
30:10 offering on it. 10Once a year Aaron shall
d Lev 16:18-19, 30 make atonement[d] on its horns. This annual atonement must be made with the
blood of the atoning sin offering for the
generations to come. It is most holy to
the LORD."

Atonement Money

11Then the LORD said to Moses,
30:12 12"When you take a census[e] of the Isra-
e Ex 38:25; Nu 1:2,49; elites to count them, each one must pay
2Sa 24:1 f Nu 31:50; the LORD a ransom[f] for his life at the time
Mt 20:28 he is counted. Then no plague[g] will come
g 2Sa 24:13 on them when you number them. 13Each
one who crosses over to those already
30:13 counted is to give a half shekel,[b] accord-
h Nu 3:47; Mt 17:24 ing to the sanctuary shekel,[h] which
weighs twenty gerahs. This half shekel is
an offering to the LORD. 14All who cross
over, those twenty years old or more, are
to give an offering to the LORD. 15The rich
30:15 i Pr 22:2; are not to give more than a half shekel
Eph 6:9 and the poor are not to give less[i] when
you make the offering to the LORD to
atone for your lives. 16Receive the atonement money from the Israelites and use
it for the service of the Tent of Meeting.[j] 30:16 j Ex 38:25-28
It will be a memorial for the Israelites be-
fore the LORD, making atonement for
your lives."

Basin for Washing

17Then the LORD said to Moses, 30:18
18"Make a bronze basin,[k] with its bronze k Ex 38:8; 40:7, 30
stand, for washing. Place it between the
Tent of Meeting and the altar, and put
water in it. 19Aaron and his sons are to
wash their hands and feet[l] with water[m] 30:19 l Ex 40:31-32;
from it. 20Whenever they enter the Tent Isa 52:11
of Meeting, they shall wash with water so m Ps 26:6
that they will not die. Also, when they approach the altar to minister by presenting an offering made to the LORD by fire,
21they shall wash their hands and feet so
that they will not die. This is to be a last-
ing ordinance[n] for Aaron and his descen- 30:21 n Ex 27:21;
dants for the generations to come." 28:43

Anointing Oil

22Then the LORD said to Moses,
23"Take the following fine spices: 500
shekels[c] of liquid myrrh,[o] half as much 30:23 o Ge 37:25
(that is, 250 shekels) of fragrant cinna-
mon, 250 shekels of fragrant cane, 24500
shekels of cassia[p]—all according to the 30:24 p Ps 45:8
sanctuary shekel—and a hin[d] of olive
oil. 25Make these into a sacred anointing
oil, a fragrant blend, the work of a per- 30:25
fumer.[q] It will be the sacred anointing q Ex 37:29
oil.[r] 26Then use it to anoint[s] the Tent of r Ex 40:9
Meeting, the ark of the Testimony, 27the 30:26 s Ex 40:9;
table and all its articles, the lampstand Lev 8:10; Nu 7:1
and its accessories, the altar of incense,
28the altar of burnt offering and all its
utensils, and the basin with its stand.
29You shall consecrate them so they will
be most holy, and whatever touches 30:29
them will be holy.[t] t Ex 29:37
30"Anoint Aaron and his sons and 30:30
consecrate[u] them so they may serve me u Ex 29:7;
as priests. 31Say to the Israelites, 'This is Lev 8:2,12,30
to be my sacred anointing oil for the
generations to come. 32Do not pour it on
men's bodies and do not make any oil
with the same formula. It is sacred, and

[a] *2* That is, about 1 1/2 feet (about 0.5 meter) long and wide and about 3 feet (about 0.9 meter) high
[b] *13* That is, about 1/5 ounce (about 6 grams); also in verse 15
[c] *23* That is, about 12 1/2 pounds (about 6 kilograms)
[d] *24* That is, probably about 4 quarts (about 4 liters)

32:7 brought up out of Egypt,[b] have become
b ver 4,11 c Ge 6:11-12; corrupt.[c] 8They have been quick to turn
Dt 9:12 away from what I commanded them
32:8 and have made themselves an idol[d] cast
d Ex 20:4 in the shape of a calf. They have bowed
e Ex 22:20 f 1Ki 12:28 down to it and sacrificed[e] to it and have
said, 'These are your gods, O Israel, who
brought you up out of Egypt.'[f]
9"I have seen these people," the LORD
32:9 said to Moses, "and they are a stiff-
g Ex 33:3,5; necked[g] people. 10Now leave me alone
34:9; Isa 48:4; Ac 7:51 so that my anger may burn against them
32:10 and that I may destroy them. Then I will
h Nu 14:12; Dt 9:14 make you into a great nation."[h]
11But Moses sought the favor[i] of the
32:11 LORD his God. "O LORD," he said, "why
i Dt 9:18 j Dt 9:26 should your anger burn against your
people, whom you brought out of Egypt
with great power and a mighty hand?[j]
12Why should the Egyptians say, 'It was
with evil intent that he brought them
out, to kill them in the mountains and
32:12 k Nu 14:13-16; to wipe them off the face of the earth'?[k]
Dt 9:28 Turn from your fierce anger; relent and
32:13 do not bring disaster on your people.
l Ex 2:24 13Remember[l] your servants Abraham,
m Ge 22:16; Heb 6:13 Isaac and Israel, to whom you swore by
n Ge 15:5; 26:4 your own self:[m] 'I will make your de-
o Ge 12:7 scendants as numerous as the stars[n] in
the sky and I will give your descendants
all this land[o] I promised them, and it will
be their inheritance forever.' " 14Then the
32:14 p 2Sa 24:16; LORD relented[p] and did not bring on his
Ps 106:45 people the disaster he had threatened.
15Moses turned and went down the
mountain with the two tablets of the
32:15 q Ex 31:18 Testimony[q] in his hands.[r] They were in-
r Dt 9:15 scribed on both sides, front and back.
16The tablets were the work of God; the
32:16 writing was the writing of God, en-
s Ex 31:18 graved on the tablets.[s]
17When Joshua heard the noise of the
people shouting, he said to Moses,
"There is the sound of war in the camp."
18Moses replied:

"It is not the sound of victory,
it is not the sound of defeat;
it is the sound of singing that I
hear."

19When Moses approached the camp
32:19 t Dt 9:16 and saw the calf[t] and the dancing, his
u Dt 9:17 anger burned and he threw the tablets
out of his hands, breaking them to
pieces[u] at the foot of the mountain.
20And he took the calf they had made
and burned it in the fire; then he ground
it to powder, scattered it on the water[v] 32:20 v Dt 9:21
and made the Israelites drink it.
21He said to Aaron, "What did these
people do to you, that you led them into
such great sin?"
22"Do not be angry, my lord," Aaron answered. "You know how prone these people are to evil.[w] 23They said to me, 'Make 32:22
us gods who will go before us. As for this w Dt 9:24
fellow Moses who brought us up out of
Egypt, we don't know what has happened
to him.'[x] 24So I told them, 'Whoever has 32:23
any gold jewelry, take it off.' Then they x ver 1
gave me the gold, and I threw it into the
fire, and out came this calf!"[y] 32:24 y ver 4
25Moses saw that the people were
running wild and that Aaron had let
them get out of control and so become a
laughingstock to their enemies. 26So he
stood at the entrance to the camp and
said, "Whoever is for the LORD, come to
me." And all the Levites rallied to him.
27Then he said to them, "This is what
the LORD, the God of Israel, says: 'Each
man strap a sword to his side. Go back
and forth through the camp from one
end to the other, each killing his brother 32:27
and friend and neighbor.' "[z] 28The Levites z Nu 25:3,5; Dt 33:9
did as Moses commanded, and that day
about three thousand of the people died.
29Then Moses said, "You have been set
apart to the LORD today, for you were
against your own sons and brothers, and
he has blessed you this day."
30The next day Moses said to the peo-
ple, "You have committed a great sin.[a] 32:30 a 1Sa 12:20
But now I will go up to the LORD; perhaps b Lev 1:4;
I can make atonement[b] for your sin." Nu 25:13
31So Moses went back to the LORD and 32:31
said, "Oh, what a great sin these people c Dt 9:18
have committed![c] They have made them- d Ex 20:23
selves gods of gold.[d] 32But now, please for- 32:32
give their sin—but if not, then blot me[e] e Ro 9:3
out of the book[f] you have written." f Ps 69:28; Da 12:1;
33The LORD replied to Moses, "Who- Php 4:3;
ever has sinned against me I will blot Rev 3:5; 21:27
out[g] of my book. 34Now go, lead the peo- 32:33
ple to the place[h] I spoke of, and my an- g Dt 29:20; Ps 9:5
gel[i] will go before you. However, when
the time comes for me to punish,[j] I will 32:34 h Ex 3:17
punish them for their sin." i Ex 23:20 j Dt 32:35;
35And the LORD struck the people Ps 99:8;
with a plague because of what they did Ro 2:5-6
with the calf[k] Aaron had made. 32:35 k ver 4

33 Then the LORD said to Moses,
"Leave this place, you and the
people you brought up out of Egypt, and

DISCOVERY 25

THE GLORY OF GOD

Without question Moses is one of the most remarkable men in the Bible. God spoke to him "face to face, as a man speaks with his friend" (Exodus 33:11). During one of these conversations, Moses asked the Lord for three things. First, he wanted to know the Lord's intentions for the people of Israel (verses 12–13). God assured him that "My Presence will go with you . . ." (verse 14). Second, Moses pleaded with God not to send the people to the promised land unless God would go with them (verse 15). God reaffirmed his promise not to leave his people. Finally, Moses asked to see God's glory (verse 18).

The "*glory* of God" refers to his beauty and power displayed in a way we can see, a visible manifestation of who he is. Moses asked to see the tangible representation of God's character and presence, which were to accompany his people. God agreed, but only to allow Moses a partial glimpse of his splendor, a fleeting afterglow. Moses would not be allowed a frontal view of God; he could not lay eyes on his "face" but only view his disappearing back. God tucked Moses safely in the cleft of a rock, covered the crack with his hand and then passed by. It was only then that God removed his hand and instructed Moses to look up so he could see God's glory passing by (verses 21–23).

When Moses emerged from the mountain after this incident, his appearance had been radically altered. His face was so radiant that he was forced to cover it with a veil when he spoke to other people. When he spoke to God, he could remove the veil (Exodus 34:29–35).

God has never desired to erect barriers between himself and people. He has wanted from the beginning to relate to us as a loving Creator. So Jesus came into the world to allow God's glory to be universally visible and permanently present with his people: "The Word became flesh and made his dwelling among us. We have seen his glory, the glory of the One and Only, who came from the Father, full of grace and truth" (John 1:14). Jesus reveals God to us. When he met God in the desert, Moses was allowed only to see his back. Hundreds of years later he stood with Elijah on the Mount of Transfiguration and saw Jesus—God the Son—in *all* his glory (Luke 9:28–36). There they were, in "glorious splendor, talking with Jesus" (Luke 9:31)!

As we follow Jesus, we reflect that same glory to other people. "God . . . made his light shine in our hearts to give us the light of the knowledge of the glory of God in the face of Christ" (2 Corinthians 4:6). We are living demonstrations of who God is. That doesn't happen overnight, but he continues to transform us into the likeness of Jesus (2 Corinthians 3:18). When God is in our lives, others will be able to see his presence by the continual changes they observe.

Self-Discovery: *Identify one specific way in which those around you can see God's glory reflected in you.*

GO TO DISCOVERY 26 ON PAGE 126

go up to the land I promised on oath to Abraham, Isaac and Jacob, saying, 'I will give it to your descendants.'[l] 2I will send an angel[m] before you and drive out the Canaanites, Amorites, Hittites, Perizzites, Hivites and Jebusites.[n] 3Go up to the land flowing with milk and honey.[o] But I will not go with you, because you are a stiff-necked[p] people and I might destroy[q] you on the way."

4When the people heard these distressing words, they began to mourn[r] and no one put on any ornaments. 5For the LORD had said to Moses, "Tell the Israelites, 'You are a stiff-necked people. If I were to go with you even for a moment, I might destroy you. Now take off your ornaments and I will decide what to do with you.'" 6So the Israelites stripped off their ornaments at Mount Horeb.

33:1 [l] Ge 12:7
33:2 [m] Ex 32:34 [n] Ex 23:27-31; Jos 24:11
33:3 [o] Ex 3:8 [p] Ex 32:9 [q] Ex 32:10
33:4 [r] Nu 14:39

The Tent of Meeting

7Now Moses used to take a tent and pitch it outside the camp some distance away, calling it the "tent of meeting."[s] Anyone inquiring of the LORD would go to the tent of meeting outside the camp. 8And whenever Moses went out to the tent, all the people rose and stood at the entrances to their tents,[t] watching Moses until he entered the tent. 9As Moses went into the tent, the pillar of cloud[u] would come down and stay at the entrance, while the LORD spoke[v] with Moses. 10Whenever the people saw the pillar of cloud standing at the entrance to the tent, they all stood and worshiped, each at the entrance to his tent. 11The LORD would speak to Moses face to face,[w] as a man speaks with his friend. Then Moses would return to the camp, but his young aide Joshua son of Nun did not leave the tent.

33:7 [s] Ex 29:42-43
33:8 [t] Nu 16:27
33:9 [u] Ex 13:21 [v] Ex 31:18; Ps 99:7
33:11 [w] Nu 12:8; Dt 34:10

A RULE I HAVE HAD FOR YEARS IS: TO TREAT THE LORD JESUS CHRIST AS A PERSONAL FRIEND.

D. L. Moody, *American Evangelist*

Moses and the Glory of the LORD

12Moses said to the LORD, "You have been telling me, 'Lead these people,'[x] but you have not let me know whom you will send with me. You have said, 'I know you by name[y] and you have found favor with me.' 13If you are pleased with me, teach me your ways[z] so I may know you and continue to find favor with you. Remember that this nation is your people."[a]

14The LORD replied, "My Presence[b] will go with you, and I will give you rest."[c]

15Then Moses said to him, "If your Presence does not go with us, do not send us up from here. 16How will anyone know that you are pleased with me and with your people unless you go with us?[d] What else will distinguish me and your people from all the other people on the face of the earth?"[e]

17And the LORD said to Moses, "I will do the very thing you have asked, because I am pleased with you and I know you by name."

18Then Moses said, "Now show me your glory."

19And the LORD said, "I will cause all my goodness to pass in front of you, and I will proclaim my name, the LORD, in your presence. I will have mercy on whom I will have mercy, and I will have compassion on whom I will have com-

33:12 [x] Ex 3:10 [y] ver 17; Jn 10:14-15; 2Ti 2:19
33:13 [z] Ps 25:4; 86:11; 119:33 [a] Ex 34:9; Dt 9:26,29
33:14 [b] Isa 63:9 [c] Jos 21:44; 22:4
33:16 [d] Nu 14:14 [e] Ex 34:10

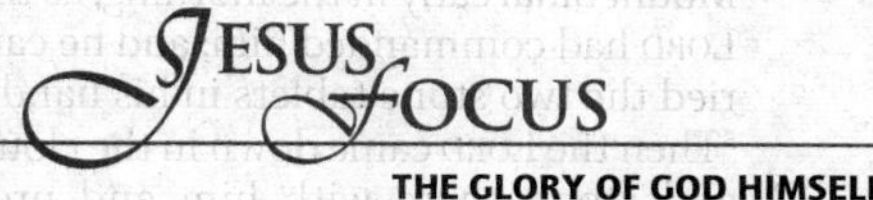

THE GLORY OF GOD HIMSELF

In the Old Testament God demonstrated his presence with his people in a special way—the *shekinah glory.* God promised his people that his very presence would go with them wherever they journeyed (Exodus 33:7–11). Moses wanted to see God's "glory" and asked God to show it to him—and for one brief moment he was allowed to see the reflection of God's glory (verses 18–32). In Exodus 40:34 we read that the "glory of the LORD filled the tabernacle" so that Moses could not even go inside. This glory rested on the ark of the covenant, first in the tabernacle and later on in Solomon's temple, but it departed before the temple was destroyed by the Babylonians (Ezekiel 8:4—11:23). There is no record that the glory of God ever returned—until Jesus came. Matthew recorded that Jesus was "transfigured" when he met with Moses and Elijah atop a mountain, meaning that for a brief time he could be seen in all of his glory (Matthew 17:1–8). Though Moses, who represents the law, and Elijah, who represents the prophets, appeared with him, God reminded the disciples to focus on Jesus, to listen to the One who is infinitely more excellent than either Moses or Elijah.

passion.[f] 20But," he said, "you cannot see my face, for no one may see[g] me and live."

21Then the LORD said, "There is a place near me where you may stand on a rock. 22When my glory passes by, I will put you in a cleft in the rock and cover you with my hand[h] until I have passed by. 23Then I will remove my hand and you will see my back; but my face must not be seen."

The New Stone Tablets

34 The LORD said to Moses, "Chisel out two stone tablets like the first ones, and I will write on them the words that were on the first tablets,[i] which you broke.[j] 2Be ready in the morning, and then come up on Mount Sinai.[k] Present yourself to me there on top of the mountain. 3No one is to come with you or be seen anywhere on the mountain;[l] not even the flocks and herds may graze in front of the mountain."

4So Moses chiseled out two stone tablets like the first ones and went up Mount Sinai early in the morning, as the LORD had commanded him; and he carried the two stone tablets in his hands. 5Then the LORD came down in the cloud and stood there with him and proclaimed his name, the LORD.[m] 6And he passed in front of Moses, proclaiming, "The LORD, the LORD, the compassionate[n] and gracious God, slow to anger,[o] abounding in love[p] and faithfulness,[q] 7maintaining love to thousands,[r] and forgiving wickedness, rebellion and sin.[s] Yet he does not leave the guilty unpunished;[t] he punishes the children and their children for the sin of the fathers to the third and fourth generation."

8Moses bowed to the ground at once and worshiped. 9"O Lord, if I have found favor in your eyes," he said, "then let the Lord go with us.[u] Although this is a stiff-necked people, forgive our wickedness and our sin, and take us as your inheritance."[v]

10Then the LORD said: "I am making a covenant[w] with you. Before all your people I will do wonders never before done in any nation in all the world.[x] The people you live among will see how awesome is the work that I, the LORD, will do for you. 11Obey what I command you today. I will drive out before you the Amorites, Canaanites, Hittites, Perizzites, Hivites and Jebusites.[y] 12Be careful not to make a treaty with those who live in the land where you are going, or they will be a snare[z] among you. 13Break down their altars, smash their sacred stones and cut down their Asherah poles.[a][a] 14Do not worship any other god,[b] for the LORD, whose name is Jealous, is a jealous God.[c]

15"Be careful not to make a treaty with those who live in the land; for when they prostitute[d] themselves to their gods and sacrifice to them, they will invite you and you will eat their sacrifices.[e] 16And when you choose some of their daughters as wives[f] for your sons and those daughters prostitute themselves to their gods,[g] they will lead your sons to do the same.

17"Do not make cast idols.[h]

18"Celebrate the Feast of Unleavened Bread.[i] For seven days eat bread made without yeast,[j] as I commanded you. Do this at the appointed time in the month of Abib,[k] for in that month you came out of Egypt.

19"The first offspring[l] of every womb belongs to me, including all the firstborn males of your livestock, whether from herd or flock. 20Redeem the firstborn donkey with a lamb, but if you do not redeem it, break its neck.[m] Redeem all your firstborn sons.

"No one is to appear before me empty-handed.[n]

21"Six days you shall labor, but on the seventh day you shall rest;[o] even during the plowing season and harvest you must rest.

22"Celebrate the Feast of Weeks with the firstfruits of the wheat harvest, and the Feast of Ingathering[p] at the turn of the year.[b] 23Three times[q] a year all your men are to appear before the Sovereign LORD, the God of Israel. 24I will drive out nations[r] before you and enlarge your territory, and no one will covet your land when you go up three times each year to appear before the LORD your God.

25"Do not offer the blood of a sacrifice to me along with anything containing yeast,[s] and do not let any of the sacrifice from the Passover Feast remain until morning.[t]

26"Bring the best of the firstfruits of

33:19 f Ro 9:15*
33:20 g Ge 32:30; Isa 6:5
33:22 h Ps 91:4
34:1 i Dt 10:2,4 j Ex 32:19
34:2 k Ex 19:11
34:3 l Ex 19:12-13,21
34:5 m Ex 33:19
34:6 n Ps 86:15 o Nu 14:18; Ro 2:4 p Ne 9:17; Ps 103:8; Joel 2:13 q Ps 108:4
34:7 r Ex 20:6 s Ps 103:3; 130:4, 8; Da 9:9; 1Jn 1:9 t Job 10:14; Na 1:3
34:9 u Ex 33:15 v Ps 33:12
34:10 w Dt 5:2-3 x Ex 33:16; Dt 4:32
34:11 y Ex 33:2
34:12 z Ex 23:32-33
34:13 a Ex 23:24; Dt 12:3; 2Ki 18:4
34:14 b Ex 20:3 c Ex 20:5; Dt 4:24
34:15 d Jdg 2:17 e Nu 25:2; 1Co 8:4
34:16 f Dt 7:3 g 1Ki 11:4
34:17 h Ex 32:8
34:18 i Ex 12:17 j Ex 12:15 k Ex 12:2
34:19 l Ex 13:2
34:20 m Ex 13:13,15 n Ex 23:15; Dt 16:16
34:21 o Ex 20:9; Lk 13:14
34:22 p Ex 23:16
34:23 q Ex 23:14
34:24 r Ex 23:28; 33:2; Ps 78:55
34:25 s Ex 23:18 t Ex 12:8,10

a 13 That is, symbols of the goddess Asherah
b 22 That is, in the fall

your soil to the house of the LORD your God.

"Do not cook a young goat in its mother's milk."[u]

27 Then the LORD said to Moses, "Write[v] down these words, for in accordance with these words I have made a covenant with you and with Israel." 28 Moses was there with the LORD forty days and forty nights[w] without eating bread or drinking water. And he wrote on the tablets[x] the words of the covenant—the Ten Commandments.[y]

The Radiant Face of Moses

29 When Moses came down from Mount Sinai with the two tablets of the Testimony in his hands,[z] he was not aware that his face was radiant[a] because he had spoken with the LORD. 30 When Aaron and all the Israelites saw Moses, his face was radiant, and they were afraid to come near him. 31 But Moses called to them; so Aaron and all the leaders of the community came back to him, and he spoke to them. 32 Afterward all the Israelites came near him, and he gave them all the commands[b] the LORD had given him on Mount Sinai.

33 When Moses finished speaking to them, he put a veil[c] over his face. 34 But whenever he entered the LORD's presence to speak with him, he removed the veil until he came out. And when he came out and told the Israelites what he had been commanded, 35 they saw that his face was radiant. Then Moses would put the veil back over his face until he went in to speak with the LORD.

Sabbath Regulations

35

Moses assembled the whole Israelite community and said to them, "These are the things the LORD has commanded[d] you to do: 2 For six days, work is to be done, but the seventh day shall be your holy day, a Sabbath[e] of rest to the LORD. Whoever does any work on it must be put to death. 3 Do not light a fire in any of your dwellings on the Sabbath day.[f]"

Materials for the Tabernacle

4 Moses said to the whole Israelite community, "This is what the LORD has commanded: 5 From what you have, take an offering for the LORD. Everyone who is willing is to bring to the LORD an offering of gold, silver and bronze; 6 blue, purple and scarlet yarn and fine linen; goat hair; 7 ram skins dyed red and hides of sea cows[a]; acacia wood; 8 olive oil for the light; spices for the anointing oil and for the fragrant incense; 9 and onyx stones and other gems to be mounted on the ephod and breastpiece.

10 "All who are skilled among you are to come and make everything the LORD has commanded:[g] 11 the tabernacle[h] with its tent and its covering, clasps, frames, crossbars, posts and bases; 12 the ark[i] with its poles and the atonement cover and the curtain that shields it; 13 the table[j] with its poles and all its articles and the bread of the Presence; 14 the lampstand[k] that is for light with its accessories, lamps and oil for the light; 15 the altar[l] of incense with its poles, the anointing oil[m] and the fragrant incense;[n] the curtain for the doorway at the entrance to the tabernacle; 16 the altar[o] of burnt offering with its bronze grating, its poles and all its utensils; the bronze basin with its stand; 17 the curtains of the courtyard with its posts and bases, and the curtain for the entrance to the courtyard;[p] 18 the tent pegs for the tabernacle and for the courtyard, and their ropes; 19 the woven garments worn for ministering in the sanctuary—both the sacred garments[q] for Aaron the priest and the garments for his sons when they serve as priests."

20 Then the whole Israelite community withdrew from Moses' presence, 21 and everyone who was willing and whose heart moved him came and brought an offering to the LORD for the work on the Tent of Meeting, for all its service, and for the sacred garments. 22 All who were willing, men and women alike, came and brought gold jewelry of all kinds: brooches, earrings, rings and ornaments. They all presented their gold as a wave offering to the LORD. 23 Everyone who had blue, purple or scarlet yarn[r] or fine linen, or goat hair, ram skins dyed red or hides of sea cows brought them. 24 Those presenting an offering of silver or bronze brought it as an offering to the LORD, and everyone who had acacia wood for any part of the work brought it. 25 Every skilled woman[s] spun with her

[a] 7 That is, dugongs; also in verse 23

34:26 u Ex 23:19
34:27 v Ex 17:14; 24:4
34:28 w Ge 7:4; Ex 24:18; Mt 4:2 x ver 1; Ex 31:18 y Dt 4:13; 10:4
34:29 z Ex 32:15 a Ps 34:5; Mt 17:2; 2Co 3:7,13
34:32 b Ex 24:3
34:33 c 2Co 3:13
35:1 d Ex 34:32
35:2 e Ex 20:9-10; 34:21; Lev 23:3
35:3 f Ex 16:23
35:10 g Ex 31:6
35:11 h Ex 26:1-37
35:12 i Ex 25:10-22
35:13 j Ex 25:23-30; Lev 24:5-6
35:14 k Ex 25:31
35:15 l Ex 30:1-6 m Ex 30:25 n Ex 30:34-38
35:16 o Ex 27:1-8
35:17 p Ex 27:9
35:19 q Ex 28:2; 31:10; 39:1
35:23 r 1Ch 29:8
35:25 s Ex 28:3

hands and brought what she had
spun—blue, purple or scarlet yarn or
fine linen. 26And all the women who
were willing and had the skill spun the
35:27 goat hair. 27The leaders[t] brought onyx
t1Ch 29:6; Ezr 2:68 stones and other gems to be mounted
on the ephod and breastpiece. 28They
also brought spices and olive oil for the
35:28 light and for the anointing oil and for
uEx 25:6 the fragrant incense.[u] 29All the Israelite
35:29 men and women who were willing[v]
vver 21; 1Ch 29:9 brought to the LORD freewill offerings[w]
wver 4-9; Ex 25:1-7; 36:3; 2Ki 12:4 for all the work the LORD through Moses
had commanded them to do.

Bezalel and Oholiab

30Then Moses said to the Israelites,
"See, the LORD has chosen Bezalel son of
Uri, the son of Hur, of the tribe of Judah,
31and he has filled him with the Spirit of
God, with skill, ability and knowledge in
35:31 all kinds of crafts[x]— 32to make artistic
xver 35; 2Ch 2:7,14 designs for work in gold, silver and
bronze, 33to cut and set stones, to work
in wood and to engage in all kinds of
artistic craftsmanship. 34And he has giv-
35:34 en both him and Oholiab[y] son of
yEx 31:6 zf2Ch 2:14 Ahisamach, of the tribe of Dan, the ability to teach[z] others. 35He has filled them
35:35 with skill to do all kinds of work[a] as
aver 31; Ex 31:3,6; 1Ki 7:14 craftsmen, designers, embroiderers in
blue, purple and scarlet yarn and fine
linen, and weavers—all of them master

36 craftsmen and designers. 1So
Bezalel, Oholiab and every
36:1 skilled person[b] to whom the LORD has
bEx 28:3 cEx 25:8 given skill and ability to know how to
carry out all the work of constructing
the sanctuary[c] are to do the work just as
the LORD has commanded."

36:2 2Then Moses summoned Bezalel[d]
dEx 31:2 eEx 31:6 and Oholiab[e] and every skilled person to
fEx 25:2; 35:21, 26; 1Ch 29:5 whom the LORD had given ability and
who was willing[f] to come and do the
36:3 work. 3They received from Moses all the
gEx 35:29 offerings[g] the Israelites had brought to
carry out the work of constructing the
sanctuary. And the people continued to
bring freewill offerings morning after
morning. 4So all the skilled craftsmen
who were doing all the work on the
sanctuary left their work 5and said to
Moses, "The people are bringing more
36:5 than enough[h] for doing the work the
h2Ch 24:14; 31:10; 2Co 8:2-3 LORD commanded to be done."
6Then Moses gave an order and they
sent this word throughout the camp:
"No man or woman is to make anything
else as an offering for the sanctuary."
And so the people were restrained from
bringing more, 7because what they al- 36:7
ready had was more[i] than enough to do i1Ki 7:47
all the work.

The Tabernacle

8All the skilled men among the workmen made the tabernacle with ten curtains of finely twisted linen and blue,
purple and scarlet yarn, with cherubim
worked into them by a skilled craftsman. 9All the curtains were the same
size—twenty-eight cubits long and four
cubits wide.[a] 10They joined five of the
curtains together and did the same with
the other five. 11Then they made loops of
blue material along the edge of the end
curtain in one set, and the same was
done with the end curtain in the other
set. 12They also made fifty loops on one
curtain and fifty loops on the end curtain of the other set, with the loops opposite each other. 13Then they made fifty
gold clasps and used them to fasten the
two sets of curtains together so that the 36:13
tabernacle was a unit.[j] jver 18

14They made curtains of goat hair for
the tent over the tabernacle—eleven altogether. 15All eleven curtains were the
same size—thirty cubits long and four
cubits wide.[b] 16They joined five of the
curtains into one set and the other six
into another set. 17Then they made fifty
loops along the edge of the end curtain
in one set and also along the edge of the
end curtain in the other set. 18They
made fifty bronze clasps to fasten the 36:18
tent together as a unit.[k] 19Then they kver 13
made for the tent a covering of ram
skins dyed red, and over that a covering
of hides of sea cows.[c]

20They made upright frames of acacia
wood for the tabernacle. 21Each frame
was ten cubits long and a cubit and a
half wide,[d] 22with two projections set
parallel to each other. They made all the
frames of the tabernacle in this way.
23They made twenty frames for the
south side of the tabernacle 24and made
forty silver bases to go under them—two

[a] *9* That is, about 42 feet (about 12.5 meters) long and 6 feet (about 1.8 meters) wide [b] *15* That is, about 45 feet (about 13.5 meters) long and 6 feet (about 1.8 meters) wide [c] *19* That is, dugongs [d] *21* That is, about 15 feet (about 4.5 meters) long and 2 1/4 feet (about 0.7 meter) wide

bases for each frame, one under each
projection. [25]For the other side, the
north side of the tabernacle, they made
twenty frames [26]and forty silver bases—
two under each frame. [27]They made six
frames for the far end, that is, the west
end of the tabernacle, [28]and two frames
were made for the corners of the tabernacle at the far end. [29]At these two corners the frames were double from the
bottom all the way to the top and fitted
into a single ring; both were made alike.
[30]So there were eight frames and sixteen
silver bases—two under each frame.

[31]They also made crossbars of acacia
wood: five for the frames on one side of
the tabernacle, [32]five for those on the
other side, and five for the frames on the
west, at the far end of the tabernacle.
[33]They made the center crossbar so that
it extended from end to end at the middle of the frames. [34]They overlaid the
frames with gold and made gold rings to
hold the crossbars. They also overlaid
the crossbars with gold.

36:35 [l]Ex 39:38; Mt 27:51; Lk 23:45; Heb 9:3 [35]They made the curtain[l] of blue, purple and scarlet yarn and finely twisted
linen, with cherubim worked into it by a
skilled craftsman. [36]They made four
posts of acacia wood for it and overlaid
them with gold. They made gold hooks
for them and cast their four silver bases.
[37]For the entrance to the tent they made
a curtain of blue, purple and scarlet yarn
and finely twisted linen—the work of an
36:37 [m]Ex 27:16 embroiderer;[m] [38]and they made five
posts with hooks for them. They over-
laid the tops of the posts and their
bands with gold and made their five
bases of bronze.

The Ark

37:1 [n]Ex 31:2 [o]Ex 30:6; 39:35; Dt 10:3 **37** Bezalel[n] made the ark[o] of acacia wood—two and a half cu-
bits long, a cubit and a half wide, and a
37:2 [p]ver 11,26 cubit and a half high.[a] [2]He overlaid it
with pure gold,[p] both inside and out,
and made a gold molding around it. [3]He
cast four gold rings for it and fastened
them to its four feet, with two rings on
one side and two rings on the other.
[4]Then he made poles of acacia wood
and overlaid them with gold. [5]And he
inserted the poles into the rings on the
sides of the ark to carry it.

37:6 [q]Ex 26:34; 31:7; Heb 9:5 [6]He made the atonement cover[q] of
pure gold—two and a half cubits long
and a cubit and a half wide.[b] [7]Then he
made two cherubim[r] out of hammered 37:7 [r]Eze 41:18
gold at the ends of the cover. [8]He made
one cherub on one end and the second
cherub on the other; at the two ends he
made them of one piece with the cover.
[9]The cherubim had their wings spread
upward, overshadowing[s] the cover with 37:9 [s]Heb 9:5
them. The cherubim faced each other, [t]Dt 10:3
looking toward the cover.[t]

The Table

[10]They[c] made the table[u] of acacia 37:10 [u]Heb 9:2
wood—two cubits long, a cubit wide,
and a cubit and a half high.[d] [11]Then they 37:11 [v]ver 2
overlaid it with pure gold[v] and made a
gold molding around it. [12]They also
made around it a rim a handbreadth[e]
wide and put a gold molding on the rim.
[13]They cast four gold rings for the table
and fastened them to the four corners,
where the four legs were. [14]The rings[w] 37:14 [w]ver 27
were put close to the rim to hold the
poles used in carrying the table. [15]The
poles for carrying the table were made
of acacia wood and were overlaid with
gold. [16]And they made from pure gold
the articles for the table—its plates and
dishes and bowls and its pitchers for the
pouring out of drink offerings.

The Lampstand

[17]They made the lampstand[x] of pure 37:17 [x]Heb 9:2; Rev 1:12
gold and hammered it out, base and
shaft; its flowerlike cups, buds and blossoms were of one piece with it. [18]Six
branches extended from the sides of the
lampstand—three on one side and three
on the other. [19]Three cups shaped like
almond flowers with buds and blossoms
were on one branch, three on the next
branch and the same for all six branches
extending from the lampstand. [20]And
on the lampstand were four cups shaped
like almond flowers with buds and blossoms. [21]One bud was under the first pair
of branches extending from the lampstand, a second bud under the second
pair, and a third bud under the third
pair—six branches in all. [22]The buds and
the branches were all of one piece with

[a] *1* That is, about 3 3/4 feet (about 1.1 meters) long and 2 1/4 feet (about 0.7 meter) wide and high
[b] *6* That is, about 3 3/4 feet (about 1.1 meters) long and 2 1/4 feet (about 0.7 meter) wide
[c] *10* Or *He*; also in verses 11–29
[d] *10* That is, about 3 feet (about 0.9 meter) long, 1 1/2 feet (about 0.5 meter) wide, and 2 1/4 feet (about 0.7 meter) high
[e] *12* That is, about 3 inches (about 8 centimeters)

The Ark of the Covenant

Many readers skim over passages like the detailed description of the ark of the covenant in Exodus 37. After all, what's the point? There is purpose in everything God tells us, however, and no detail in the Bible is superfluous.

The ark of the covenant served a distinct purpose. Inside this golden box Moses placed the stone tablets God had given him, the tablets on which the law was written. They were to be a constant reminder that the people were obligated to obey God because of who he is and because of his promises (covenant) to them. The problem with the law, however, is that no one (until Jesus) has ever been able to keep it. In one instance, when some Israelites looked into the ark, they immediately fell down dead, condemned simply by looking at the tablets (1 Samuel 6:19).

What the ark needed was a cover so that the people could approach it without fear of death. The atonement cover protected the priests from God's judgment when they stood in his presence. Two guardian angels called *cherubim* were carved on the lid of the ark facing one another. God spoke to Moses from between the angels, above the cover in the place called "the mercy seat."

While the atonement cover protected people from God's judgment when they confronted the written law, Jesus came to offer permanent protection. He stands as the *mediator* between God and ourselves. It is through Jesus, who on the basis of his sacrificial death negotiates with God on our behalf, that we are able to pray and be in relationship with our Creator. Jesus' blood does more than simply act as a barrier. It completely cleanses us from sin.

The ark of the covenant represented many things God wanted his people to know, but it was still only a temporary fixture. Jesus was born to show us what the ark only symbolized. He alone by his perfect life lived up to *all* the requirements of the law. Because he was the only one ever to do that, he represented in his person the sum and substance of the law (Matthew 5:17–20). In fact, in the New Testament Jesus is called the very Word of God (John 1:1). Jesus is also the embodiment of all God's promises to his people (2 Corinthians 1:20), rendering the ark of the covenant unnecessary in terms of serving as a reminder of those promises.

God expects absolute obedience to all of his commands. We do not have the option of picking and choosing which requirements we want to obey and which we prefer to skip over. We don't have the luxury of following the less painful requirements and ignoring the more demanding mandates. Jesus himself is an example of obedience despite the most difficult circumstances imaginable—beaten, mocked, rejected and betrayed, he still adhered flawlessly to the precepts by which God intended us all to live (Hebrews 4).

Self-Discovery: *Can you recall an instance in which you have acted as a mediator or advocate for someone else? Can you identify a recent situation in which you needed Jesus to intercede for you?*

GO TO DISCOVERY 27 ON PAGE 128

37:22 the lampstand, hammered out of pure
[y] ver 17; Nu 8:4 gold.[y]
37:23 23They made its seven lamps,[z] as well
[z] Ex 40:4,25 as its wick trimmers and trays, of pure
gold. 24They made the lampstand and all
its accessories from one talent[a] of pure
gold.

The Altar of Incense

37:25 [a] Ex 30:34-36; 25They made the altar of incense[a] out
Lk 1:11; of acacia wood. It was square, a cubit
Heb 9:4; Rev 8:3 [b] Ex 27:2; long and a cubit wide, and two cubits
Rev 9:13 high[b]—its horns[b] of one piece with it.
26They overlaid the top and all the sides
and the horns with pure gold, and made
37:27 a gold molding around it. 27They made
[c] ver 14 two gold rings[c] below the molding—two
on opposite sides—to hold the poles
used to carry it. 28They made the poles
37:28 of acacia wood and overlaid them with
[d] Ex 25:13 gold.[d]
29They also made the sacred anointing
37:29 [e] Ex 31:11 oil[e] and the pure, fragrant incense[f]—the
[f] Ex 30:1,25; 39:38 work of a perfumer.

The Altar of Burnt Offering

38 They[c] built the altar of burnt
offering of acacia wood, three
cubits[d] high; it was square, five cubits
long and five cubits wide.[e] 2They made a
horn at each of the four corners, so that
the horns and the altar were of one
38:2 piece, and they overlaid the altar with
[g] 2Ch 1:5 bronze.[g] 3They made all its utensils[h] of
38:3 bronze—its pots, shovels, sprinkling
[h] Ex 31:9 bowls, meat forks and firepans. 4They
made a grating for the altar, a bronze
network, to be under its ledge, halfway
up the altar. 5They cast bronze rings to
hold the poles for the four corners of the
bronze grating. 6They made the poles of
acacia wood and overlaid them with
bronze. 7They inserted the poles into the
rings so they would be on the sides of
the altar for carrying it. They made it
hollow, out of boards.

Basin for Washing

38:8 8They made the bronze basin[i] and its
[i] Ex 30:18; 40:7 bronze stand from the mirrors of the
[j] Dt 23:17; women[j] who served at the entrance to
1Sa 2:22; 1Ki 14:24 the Tent of Meeting.

The Courtyard

9Next they made the courtyard. The
south side was a hundred cubits[f] long
and had curtains of finely twisted linen,
10with twenty posts and twenty bronze
bases, and with silver hooks and bands
on the posts. 11The north side was also a
hundred cubits long and had twenty
posts and twenty bronze bases, with silver hooks and bands on the posts.
12The west end was fifty cubits[g] wide
and had curtains, with ten posts and ten
bases, with silver hooks and bands on
the posts. 13The east end, toward the
sunrise, was also fifty cubits wide. 14Cur-
tains fifteen cubits[h] long were on one
side of the entrance, with three posts
and three bases, 15and curtains fifteen
cubits long were on the other side of the
entrance to the courtyard, with three
posts and three bases. 16All the curtains
around the courtyard were of finely
twisted linen. 17The bases for the posts
were bronze. The hooks and bands on
the posts were silver, and their tops were
overlaid with silver; so all the posts of
the courtyard had silver bands.
18The curtain for the entrance to the
courtyard was of blue, purple and scarlet yarn and finely twisted linen—the
work of an embroiderer. It was twenty
cubits[i] long and, like the curtains of the
courtyard, five cubits[j] high, 19with four
posts and four bronze bases. Their
hooks and bands were silver, and their
tops were overlaid with silver. 20All the
tent pegs[k] of the tabernacle and of the 38:20 [k] Ex 35:18
surrounding courtyard were bronze.

The Materials Used

21These are the amounts of the ma- 38:21
terials used for the tabernacle, the tab- [l] Nu 1:50,53;
ernacle of the Testimony,[l] which were 8:24; 9:15; 10:11; 17:7;
recorded at Moses' command by the Le- 1Ch 23:32;
vites under the direction of Ithamar[m] 2Ch 24:6; Ac 7:44;
son of Aaron, the priest. 22(Bezalel[n] son Rev 15:5
of Uri, the son of Hur, of the tribe of Ju- [m] Nu 4:28,33
dah, made everything the LORD com- 38:22
manded Moses; 23with him was Oholi- [n] Ex 31:2
ab[o] son of Ahisamach, of the tribe of 38:23
Dan—a craftsman and designer, and an [o] Ex 31:6
embroiderer in blue, purple and scarlet

[a] *24* That is, about 75 pounds (about 34 kilograms)
[b] *25* That is, about 1 1/2 feet (about 0.5 meter) long and wide, and about 3 feet (about 0.9 meter) high
[c] *1* Or *He*; also in verses 2–9 [d] *1* That is, about 4 1/2 feet (about 1.3 meters) [e] *1* That is, about 7 1/2 feet (about 2.3 meters) long and wide
[f] *9* That is, about 150 feet (about 46 meters)
[g] *12* That is, about 75 feet (about 23 meters)
[h] *14* That is, about 22 1/2 feet (about 6.9 meters)
[i] *18* That is, about 30 feet (about 9 meters)
[j] *18* That is, about 7 1/2 feet (about 2.3 meters)

THE BRONZE ALTAR

God is a God of details. He gave Moses precise instructions for constructing the tabernacle and all of the items associated with it. He specified precise measurements and particular materials in his instructions for the main part of the tabernacle (Exodus 36:8–38), the ark (Exodus 37:1–9), the table (Exodus 37:10–16), the lampstand (Exodus 37:17–24), the altar of incense (Exodus 37:25–29), the altar of burnt offering (Exodus 38:1–7), the basin (verse 8), the courtyard (verses 9–18) and the priestly garments (Exodus 39:1–31). Why all this attention to detail? Why the emphasis on the color of fabric or the placement of a basin?

For one thing, approaching God in worship is not a casual exercise—we must come to him on his terms, not our own. Whenever a priest entered the tabernacle, the first thing he saw was the altar of burnt offering, also called the *bronze altar*. This was the altar on which animals were sacrificed. It was made of acacia wood overlaid with bronze. It measured seven-and-one-half feet wide by four-and-one-half feet high, with a horn at each of the four corners. It also had bronze rings at the corners, through which poles could be inserted in order to carry it. All utensils associated with sacrifice were also made of bronze.

This altar was a constant reminder that the people could not approach God without a sacrifice. Humankind is separated from God by sin (Genesis 2:16–17; 3:21–22). Because the gravity of sin requires death, only a *blood* sacrifice was acceptable in dealing with the problem: "For the life of a creature is in the blood, and I have given it to you to make atonement for yourselves on the altar; it is the blood that makes atonement for one's life" (Leviticus 17:11).

Every time an individual or priest wanted to approach God an animal sacrifice had to be offered to cover the person's sin. Sacrifices were offered continually on the altar of burnt offering. However, each of these animal sacrifices pointed to the final Sacrifice—Jesus Christ, who died as an atonement for humanity's sin (Hebrews 9:11–15).

When Jesus is portrayed in his exalted and glorified state as the Son of God, his feet are described as "like bronze glowing in a furnace" (Revelation 1:15). There is an interesting connection between the bronze altar in the tabernacle and these New Testament words about Jesus' feet. Under the "old covenant" the fire consumed the sacrifice on the bronze altar, which though marked by the flames was not consumed—and God was pleased. Under the "new covenant" in his Son, the process was reversed: The *Sacrifice* himself consumed the destructive "fire" of God's anger, emerging as the victor over sin and death. Jesus' feet, the foundation of the altar, are like bronze—charred by the process but not destroyed by the fire of God's wrath.

Whenever the circumstances of life cause us to question God's love, we can go back to the cross: Jesus died there for us—because he loves us. And God will never again hold our sin against us, provided we accept Jesus into our lives (Romans 8:31–32).

Self-Discovery: The ability to approach God is an incomparable blessing. In what ways, if any, have you been too casual in your worship?

GO TO DISCOVERY 28 ON PAGE 131

yarn and fine linen.) 24The total amount
38:24 [p]Ex 30:16 [q]Ex 30:13; Lev 27:25; Nu 3:47; 18:16 of the gold from the wave offering used
for all the work on the sanctuary[p] was
29 talents and 730 shekels,[a] according to
the sanctuary shekel.[q]

25The silver obtained from those of the
community who were counted in the
38:25 [r]Ex 30:12 census[r] was 100 talents and 1,775
shekels,[b] according to the sanctuary
shekel— 26one beka per person,[s] that is,
38:26 [s]Ex 30:12 [t]Ex 30:13 [u]Ex 30:14 [v]Ex 12:37; Nu 1:46 half a shekel,[c] according to the sanctuary
shekel,[t] from everyone who had crossed
over to those counted, twenty years old
or more,[u] a total of 603,550 men.[v] 27The
38:27 [w]Ex 26:19 100 talents[d] of silver were used to cast
the bases[w] for the sanctuary and for the
curtain—100 bases from the 100 talents,
one talent for each base. 28They used the
1,775 shekels[e] to make the hooks for the
posts, to overlay the tops of the posts,
and to make their bands.

29The bronze from the wave offering
was 70 talents and 2,400 shekels.[f] 30They
used it to make the bases for the entrance to the Tent of Meeting, the
bronze altar with its bronze grating and
all its utensils, 31the bases for the surrounding courtyard and those for its entrance and all the tent pegs for the tabernacle and those for the surrounding
courtyard.

The Priestly Garments

39:1 [x]Ex 35:23 [y]Ex 35:19 [z]ver 41; Ex 28:2 39 From the blue, purple and scarlet yarn[x] they made woven garments for ministering in the sanctuary.[y]
They also made sacred garments[z] for
Aaron, as the LORD commanded Moses.

The Ephod

2They[g] made the ephod of gold, and of
blue, purple and scarlet yarn, and of
finely twisted linen. 3They hammered
out thin sheets of gold and cut strands
to be worked into the blue, purple and
scarlet yarn and fine linen—the work of
a skilled craftsman. 4They made shoulder pieces for the ephod, which were attached to two of its corners, so it could
be fastened. 5Its skillfully woven waistband was like it—of one piece with the
ephod and made with gold, and with
blue, purple and scarlet yarn, and with
finely twisted linen, as the LORD commanded Moses.

6They mounted the onyx stones in
gold filigree settings and engraved them
like a seal with the names of the sons of
Israel. 7Then they fastened them on the
shoulder pieces of the ephod as memorial[a] stones for the sons of Israel, as the 39:7 [a]Lev 24:7; Jos 4:7
LORD commanded Moses.

The Breastpiece

8They fashioned the breastpiece[b]— 39:8 [b]Lev 8:8
the work of a skilled craftsman. They
made it like the ephod: of gold, and of
blue, purple and scarlet yarn, and of
finely twisted linen. 9It was square—a
span[h] long and a span wide—and folded double. 10Then they mounted four
rows of precious stones on it. In the first
row there was a ruby, a topaz and a
beryl; 11in the second row a turquoise, a
sapphire[i] and an emerald; 12in the third
row a jacinth, an agate and an amethyst;
13in the fourth row a chrysolite, an onyx
and a jasper.[j] They were mounted in
gold filigree settings. 14There were
twelve stones, one for each of the names
of the sons of Israel, each engraved like
a seal with the name of one of the twelve
tribes.[c] 39:14 [c]Rev 21:12

15For the breastpiece they made
braided chains of pure gold, like a rope.
16They made two gold filigree settings
and two gold rings, and fastened the
rings to two of the corners of the breastpiece. 17They fastened the two gold
chains to the rings at the corners of the
breastpiece, 18and the other ends of the
chains to the two settings, attaching
them to the shoulder pieces of the
ephod at the front. 19They made two
gold rings and attached them to the other two corners of the breastpiece on the
inside edge next to the ephod. 20Then
they made two more gold rings and attached them to the bottom of the shoulder pieces on the front of the ephod,
close to the seam just above the waistband of the ephod. 21They tied the rings
of the breastpiece to the rings of the
ephod with blue cord, connecting it to

[a] *24* The weight of the gold was a little over one ton (about 1 metric ton). [b] *25* The weight of the silver was a little over 3 3/4 tons (about 3.4 metric tons). [c] *26* That is, about 1/5 ounce (about 5.5 grams) [d] *27* That is, about 3 3/4 tons (about 3.4 metric tons) [e] *28* That is, about 45 pounds (about 20 kilograms) [f] *29* The weight of the bronze was about 2 1/2 tons (about 2.4 metric tons). [g] *2* Or *He*; also in verses 7, 8 and 22 [h] *9* That is, about 9 inches (about 22 centimeters) [i] *11* Or *lapis lazuli* [j] *13* The precise identification of some of these precious stones is uncertain.

the waistband so that the breastpiece
would not swing out from the ephod—
as the LORD commanded Moses.

Other Priestly Garments

22 They made the robe of the ephod
entirely of blue cloth—the work of a
weaver— 23 with an opening in the center of the robe like the opening of a collar,[a] and a band around this opening, so
that it would not tear. 24 They made
pomegranates of blue, purple and scarlet yarn and finely twisted linen around
the hem of the robe. 25 And they made
bells of pure gold and attached them
around the hem between the pomegranates. 26 The bells and pomegranates
alternated around the hem of the robe
to be worn for ministering, as the LORD
commanded Moses.
39:27 27 For Aaron and his sons, they made
[d]Lev 6:10 tunics of fine linen[d]—the work of a
39:28 weaver— 28 and the turban[e] of fine linen,
[e]Ex 28:4 the linen headbands and the undergarments of finely twisted linen. 29 The sash
was of finely twisted linen and blue, purple and scarlet yarn—the work of an
embroiderer—as the LORD commanded
Moses.
30 They made the plate, the sacred diadem, out of pure gold and engraved on
it, like an inscription on a seal: HOLY TO
THE LORD. 31 Then they fastened a blue
cord to it to attach it to the turban, as
the LORD commanded Moses.

Moses Inspects the Tabernacle

32 So all the work on the tabernacle,
the Tent of Meeting, was completed. The
39:32 Israelites did everything just as the LORD
[f]ver 42-43; commanded Moses.[f] 33 Then they
Ex 25:9 brought the tabernacle to Moses: the
tent and all its furnishings, its clasps,
frames, crossbars, posts and bases; 34 the
covering of ram skins dyed red, the covering of hides of sea cows[b] and the
shielding curtain; 35 the ark of the Testi-
39:35 [g]Ex 30:6 mony[g] with its poles and the atonement
cover; 36 the table with all its articles and
the bread of the Presence; 37 the pure
39:37 gold lampstand[h] with its row of lamps
[h]Ex 25:31 and all its accessories, and the oil for the
39:38 light; 38 the gold altar,[i] the anointing oil,
[i]Ex 30:1-10 the fragrant incense, and the curtain[j] for
[j]Ex 36:35 the entrance to the tent; 39 the bronze altar with its bronze grating, its poles and
all its utensils; the basin with its stand;

40 the curtains of the courtyard with its
posts and bases, and the curtain for the 39:40
entrance to the courtyard;[k] the ropes [k]Ex 27:9-19
and tent pegs for the courtyard; all the
furnishings for the tabernacle, the Tent
of Meeting; 41 and the woven garments
worn for ministering in the sanctuary,
both the sacred garments for Aaron the
priest and the garments for his sons
when serving as priests. 39:42 [l]Ex 25:9
42 The Israelites had done all the work
just as the LORD had commanded Moses.[l] 39:43 [m]Lev 9:22,23;
43 Moses inspected the work and saw that Nu 6:23-27;
they had done it just as the LORD had 2Sa 6:18; 1Ki 8:14,55;
commanded. So Moses blessed[m] them. 2Ch 30:27

Setting Up the Tabernacle

40 Then the LORD said to Moses:
2 "Set up the tabernacle, the 40:2
Tent of Meeting,[n] on the first day of the [n]Nu 1:1
first month.[o] 3 Place the ark[p] of the Tes- [o]ver 17; Ex 12:2
timony in it and shield the ark with the 40:3
curtain. 4 Bring in the table and set out [p]ver 21; Nu 4:5; Ex 26:33
what belongs on it.[q] Then bring in the
lampstand[r] and set up its lamps. 5 Place 40:4 [q]Ex 25:30
the gold altar[s] of incense in front of the [r]ver 22-25;
ark of the Testimony and put the curtain Ex 26:35
at the entrance to the tabernacle. 40:5
6 "Place the altar of burnt offering in [s]ver 26; Ex 30:1
front of the entrance to the tabernacle,
the Tent of Meeting; 7 place the basin[t] 40:7
between the Tent of Meeting and the al- [t]ver 30; Ex 30:18
tar and put water in it. 8 Set up the court-
yard around it and put the curtain at the
entrance to the courtyard.
9 "Take the anointing oil and anoint[u] 40:9
the tabernacle and everything in it; con- [u]Ex 30:26;
secrate it and all its furnishings, and it Lev 8:10
will be holy. 10 Then anoint the altar of
burnt offering and all its utensils; consecrate[v] the altar, and it will be most 40:10
holy. 11 Anoint the basin and its stand [v]Ex 29:36
and consecrate them.
12 "Bring Aaron and his sons to the entrance to the Tent of Meeting and wash 40:12
them with water.[w] 13 Then dress Aaron in [w]Lev 8:1-13
the sacred garments,[x] anoint him and 40:13
consecrate[y] him so he may serve me as [x]Ex 28:41 [y]Lev 8:12
priest. 14 Bring his sons and dress them in
tunics. 15 Anoint them just as you anointed their father, so they may serve me as
priests. Their anointing will be to a
priesthood that will continue for all gen- 40:15
erations to come.[z]" 16 Moses did every- [z]Ex 29:9; Nu 25:13
thing just as the LORD commanded him.

[a] *23* The meaning of the Hebrew for this word is uncertain. [b] *34* That is, dugongs

DISCOVERY 28

The Glory of God's Presence

It was Moses who assembled the pieces of the tabernacle, meticulously following God's instructions to the minutest detail. The Bible states six times that Moses did "as the LORD commanded him" (Exodus 40:16,21,23,25,29,32). Finally the initial phase of the work was completed. Then the Israelites labored, again with precision and accuracy, to complete every detailed component of the tabernacle and its furnishings. After Moses had made the final inspection, the people were blessed (Exodus 39:42–43).

Then it happened! The long-awaited moment of the tabernacle's consecration was at hand (see Exodus 29:44). The cloud of the Lord appeared. This was no ordinary cloud (see Exodus 19:16)—it was *God's* cloud, God's glory made visible and his presence rendered unmistakable. A lot of hard work had gone into the construction, but the majesty and splendor of God the Creator overshadowed it all—the real purpose of the tabernacle was to allow the people to experience the reality of God's company. They could now relax and enjoy the blessings of God's continual presence. Whenever the cloud moved, whether by day or night, the people could confidently forge ahead with their journey.

Generations later, in Bethlehem, it happened again—God's glory came down to be with his people. This time there was only a small band of shepherds to witness its arrival. While not a cloud could be seen, the glory of God was indeed evident, erasing the darkness with its brilliant effulgence as Jesus' birth was announced (Luke 2:8–14). The real glory of God is seen not in a cloud, but in Jesus Christ! John 1:14 tells us that "the Word became flesh and made his dwelling among us. We have seen his glory, the glory of the One and Only, who came from the Father, full of grace and truth."

Today we are God's temple; our bodies are the very places in which God's Spirit takes up residence: "Do you not know that your body is a temple of the Holy Spirit, who is in you, whom you have received from God? You are not your own; you were bought at a price. Therefore honor God with your body" (1 Corinthians 6:19–20). As God's people, we want our lives to reflect that. We want to act in ways that honor God. There may be objects and desires we need to set aside, eliminate or pick up in order to accurately reflect who God is. The way we live our lives, our priorities and our attitudes all exemplify to others that God lives in us—and that he wants nothing more than to live in them as well.

How do we become people who glorify God? Moses' example provides us with a good place to start: First, we listen to God's *very* clear instructions in the Bible. Second, we do our part by walking with God, doing what he asks of us. And finally we let God do his part: He fills our lives with his glory, because that glory no longer resides in a cloud—it dwells in *us*!

Self-Discovery: *We no longer have the benefit of God's cloud to tell us when to move and how far to go—but we do have his Word. Are there ways in which your life is more difficult because of this difference? More fulfilling?*

GO TO DISCOVERY 29 ON PAGE 136

40:17 [a] Nu 7:1 [b] ver 2 17 So the tabernacle[a] was set up on the
first day of the first month[b] in the sec-
ond year. 18 When Moses set up the tabernacle, he put the bases in place, erected the frames, inserted the crossbars
and set up the posts. 19 Then he spread
the tent over the tabernacle and put the
covering over the tent, as the LORD commanded him.
40:20 [c] Ex 16:34; 25:16; Dt 10:5; 1Ki 8:9; Heb 9:4 20 He took the Testimony[c] and placed
it in the ark, attached the poles to the
ark and put the atonement cover over it.
21 Then he brought the ark into the tab-
40:21 [d] Ex 26:33 ernacle and hung the shielding curtain[d]
and shielded the ark of the Testimony, as
the LORD commanded him.
22 Moses placed the table[e] in the Tent
40:22 [e] Ex 26:35 of Meeting on the north side of the tabernacle outside the curtain 23 and set out
40:23 [f] ver 4 the bread[f] on it before the LORD, as the
LORD commanded him.
40:24 [g] Ex 26:35 24 He placed the lampstand[g] in the
Tent of Meeting opposite the table on
the south side of the tabernacle 25 and
set up the lamps[h] before the LORD, as the 40:25 [h] ver 4; Ex 25:37
LORD commanded him.
26 Moses placed the gold altar[i] in the 40:26 [i] ver 5; Ex 30:6
Tent of Meeting in front of the curtain
27 and burned fragrant incense on it, as 40:27 [j] Ex 30:7
the LORD commanded[j] him. 28 Then he
put up the curtain[k] at the entrance to 40:28 [k] Ex 26:36
the tabernacle.
29 He set the altar of burnt offering
near the entrance to the tabernacle, the
Tent of Meeting, and offered on it burnt 40:29 [l] ver 6; Ex 29:38-42
offerings and grain offerings,[l] as the
LORD commanded him.
30 He placed the basin[m] between the 40:30 [m] ver 7
Tent of Meeting and the altar and put
water in it for washing, 31 and Moses and
Aaron and his sons used it to wash their
hands and feet. 32 They washed whenever they entered the Tent of Meeting or
approached the altar,[n] as the LORD com- 40:32 [n] Ex 30:20
manded Moses.
33 Then Moses set up the courtyard[o] 40:33 [o] Ex 27:9 [p] ver 8
around the tabernacle and altar and put
up the curtain[p] at the entrance to the
courtyard. And so Moses finished the
work.

The Glory of the LORD

34 Then the cloud[q] covered the Tent of 40:34 [q] Nu 9:15-23; 1Ki 8:12
Meeting, and the glory of the LORD filled
the tabernacle. 35 Moses could not enter
the Tent of Meeting because the cloud
had settled upon it, and the glory of the 40:35 [r] 1Ki 8:11; 2Ch 5:13-14
LORD filled the tabernacle.[r]
36 In all the travels of the Israelites,
whenever the cloud lifted from above 40:36 [s] Nu 9:17-23; 10:13; Ne 9:19
the tabernacle, they would set out;[s]
37 but if the cloud did not lift, they did
not set out—until the day it lifted. 38 So
the cloud[t] of the LORD was over the tab- 40:38 [t] Ex 13:21; Nu 9:15; 1Co 10:1
ernacle by day, and fire was in the cloud
by night, in the sight of all the house of
Israel during all their travels.

MEETING WITH GOD

Whenever God met with his people in the Old Testament, he displayed his glory, both by who he is in all his personal splendor and by what he did for his people (Exodus 40). Ultimately, however, he wanted to glorify himself through the people he had chosen, in order that his glory might reach people everywhere (see Numbers 14:21). In the New Testament Jesus embodied the glory of God (John 1:14; Hebrews 1:3), and he lives in us through God the Holy Spirit (John 16:13–14). When we live the way he wants us to, we reflect his glory to the world around us (2 Corinthians 3:12–18; 4:4–6). Because the Holy Spirit lives in us, we are to honor God to ensure that his holiness might be seen in our lives (1 Corinthians 11:7)

LEVITICUS

Why would the aroma of a sacrifice be important to God? (Leviticus 1:9)

♦ *The writer probably drew from a human experience—the pleasant smell of cooking meat—to help us to understand God's pleasure with the intent behind an offering. A similar figure of speech is used in Ephesians 5:2, describing Jesus' sacrifice as a fragrant offering, pleasing to God.*

After all other sacrifices, why was a Day of Atonement needed? (Leviticus 16:29–30)

♦ *Sacrifices on the Day of Atonement cleansed the nation even of unknown transgressions. This solemn ceremony reminded the Israelites that their privileged access to God was threatened by sin. Later, Jesus' death became the final atonement for believers, making further sacrifices unnecessary (Hebrews 9:23–28).*

Jesus in Leviticus When Jesus offered himself on the cross as the final sacrifice for the sins of humanity, he fulfilled everything God had intended when he had set up the system of animal sacrifices. Jesus' perfect, one-time self-sacrifice nullified the old sacrificial system. Because of his sacrifice Jesus has become our high priest, representing us before God. He makes us clean from our sinful nature, imputing to us his own holiness and enabling us to approach God personally. The New Testament tells us that Jesus is "holy, blameless, pure, set apart from sinners, exalted above the heavens" (Hebrews 7:26). God the Son has mediated a new covenant between God and people, and God alluded to this covenant in advance through the laws found in Leviticus. While believers today are no longer bound by the strictures of the Old Testament law, we will do well to remember that we are still called to be holy as God is holy.

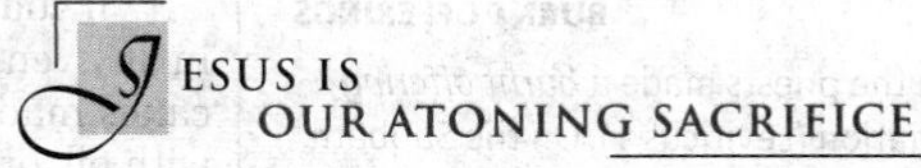

JESUS IS OUR ATONING SACRIFICE

The Burnt Offering

1:1 1 The LORD called to Moses[a] and
[a]Ex 19:3; 25:22 spoke to him from the Tent of
[b]Nu 7:89 Meeting.[b] He said, 2"Speak to the Israelites and say to them: 'When any of you
brings an offering to the LORD, bring as
1:2 your offering an animal from either the
[c]Lev 22:18-19 herd or the flock.[c]
3" 'If the offering is a burnt offering
1:3 from the herd, he is to offer a male with-
[d]Ex 12:5; out defect.[d] He must present it at the
Dt 15:21; Heb 9:14; entrance to the Tent[e] of Meeting so that
1Pe 1:19 [e]Lev 17:9 it[a] will be acceptable to the LORD. 4He is
to lay his hand on the head[f] of the burnt
1:4 offering, and it will be accepted on his
[f]Ex 29:10,15; Lev 3:2 behalf to make atonement[g] for him. 5He
[g]2Ch 29:23-24 is to slaughter[h] the young bull before the
1:5 LORD, and then Aaron's sons the priests
[h]Lev 3:2,8 [i]Heb 12:24; shall bring the blood and sprinkle it
1Pe 1:2 against the altar on all sides[i] at the entrance to the Tent of Meeting. 6He is to
1:6 skin[j] the burnt offering and cut it into
[j]Lev 7:8 pieces. 7The sons of Aaron the priest are
to put fire on the altar and arrange
1:7 [k]Lev 6:12 wood[k] on the fire. 8Then Aaron's sons
1:8 the priests shall arrange the pieces, in-
[l]ver 12 cluding the head and the fat,[l] on the
burning wood that is on the altar. 9He is
to wash the inner parts and the legs with
1:9 water, and the priest is to burn all of it
[m]Ex 29:18 [n]ver 13; on the altar.[m] It is a burnt offering, an of-
Ge 8:21; Nu 15:8-10; fering made by fire, an aroma pleasing
Eph 5:2 to the LORD.[n]
10" 'If the offering is a burnt offering
from the flock, from either the sheep or
1:10 [o]ver 3; Ex 12:5 the goats,[o] he is to offer a male without
defect. 11He is to slaughter it at the north

JESUS FOCUS

BURNT OFFERINGS

Every morning the priests made a *burnt offering* for the entire nation (Leviticus 1). On the Sabbath they offered double burnt offerings, and there were extra offerings on feast days. In addition God's people could voluntarily offer special burnt offerings to express their devotion to God. This sacrifice was a called a *holocaust* offering (from Hebrew words meaning "whole" and "burnt"). The holocaust sacrifice had to be an unblemished male animal, and its blood sacrifice covered over the damage caused by sin in the life of the person making the offering. The burnt offering provides us with a picture of Jesus' ultimate sacrifice for our sin (Hebrews 9:12).

side of the altar before the LORD, and Aaron's sons the priests shall sprinkle its 1:11
blood against the altar on all sides.[p] 12He [p]ver 5
is to cut it into pieces, and the priest shall
arrange them, including the head and the
fat, on the burning wood that is on the altar. 13He is to wash the inner parts and
the legs with water, and the priest is to
bring all of it and burn it on the altar. It is
a burnt offering, an offering made by fire,
an aroma pleasing to the LORD.
14" 'If the offering to the LORD is a
burnt offering of birds, he is to offer a 1:14
dove or a young pigeon.[q] 15The priest [q]Ge 15:9; Lev 5:7; Lk 2:24
shall bring it to the altar, wring off the
head and burn it on the altar; its blood
shall be drained out on the side of the al- 1:15
tar.[r] 16He is to remove the crop with its [r]Lev 5:9
contents[b] and throw it to the east side of
the altar, where the ashes[s] are. 17He shall 1:16 [s]Lev 6:10
tear it open by the wings, not severing it
completely,[t] and then the priest shall 1:17 [t]Ge 15:10
burn it on the wood[u] that is on the fire [u]Lev 5:8
on the altar. It is a burnt offering, an offering made by fire, an aroma pleasing
to the LORD.

The Grain Offering

2 " 'When someone brings a grain 2:1
offering[v] to the LORD, his offering [v]Lev 6:14-18 [w]Nu 15:4
is to be of fine flour. He is to pour oil[w] on
it, put incense on it 2and take it to Aaron's sons the priests. The priest shall 2:2
take a handful of the fine flour[x] and oil, [x]Lev 5:11
together with all the incense,[y] and burn [y]Lev 6:15;
this as a memorial portion[z] on the altar, Isa 66:3 [z]ver 9,
an offering made by fire, an aroma 16; Lev 5:12; 6:15; 24:7;
pleasing to the LORD. 3The rest of the Ac 10:4
grain offering belongs to Aaron and his
sons;[a] it is a most holy part of the offer- 2:3 [a]ver 10;
ings made to the LORD by fire. Lev 6:16; 10:12, 13
4" 'If you bring a grain offering baked
in an oven, it is to consist of fine flour:
cakes made without yeast and mixed
with oil, or[c] wafers made without yeast
and spread with oil.[b] 5If your grain offer- 2:4 [b]Ex 29:2
ing is prepared on a griddle, it is to be
made of fine flour mixed with oil, and
without yeast. 6Crumble it and pour oil
on it; it is a grain offering. 7If your grain 2:7
offering is cooked in a pan,[c] it is to be [c]Lev 7:9
made of fine flour and oil. 8Bring the
grain offering made of these things to
the LORD; present it to the priest, who

[a] 3 Or *he* [b] 16 Or *crop and the feathers*; the meaning of the Hebrew for this word is uncertain. [c] 4 Or *and*

2:9 shall take it to the altar. 9He shall take
d ver 2 out the memorial portion[d] from the
e Ex 29:18; grain offering and burn it on the altar as
Lev 6:15 an offering made by fire, an aroma
pleasing to the LORD.[e] 10The rest of the
2:10 grain offering belongs to Aaron and his
f ver 3 sons;[f] it is a most holy part of the offerings made to the LORD by fire.
11" 'Every grain offering you bring to
2:11 g Ex 23:18; the LORD must be made without yeast,[g]
34:25; Lev 6:16 for you are not to burn any yeast or honey in an offering made to the LORD by
fire. 12You may bring them to the LORD as
2:12 h Lev 7:13; 23:10 an offering of the firstfruits,[h] but they are
not to be offered on the altar as a pleas-
ing aroma. 13Season all your grain offerings with salt. Do not leave the salt of the
2:13 covenant[i] of your God out of your grain
i Nu 18:19; Eze 43:24 offerings; add salt to all your offerings.
2:14 14" 'If you bring a grain offering of
j Lev 23:10 firstfruits[j] to the LORD, offer crushed
heads of new grain roasted in the fire.
15Put oil and incense on it; it is a grain
2:16 offering. 16The priest shall burn the me-
k ver 2 morial portion[k] of the crushed grain
and the oil, together with all the incense,
as an offering made to the LORD by fire.

The Fellowship Offering

3 " 'If someone's offering is a fellow-
3:1 l Lev 7:11-34 ship offering,[a][l] and he offers an
m Lev 1:3; 22:21 animal from the herd, whether male or
female, he is to present before the LORD
an animal without defect.[m] 2He is to lay
3:2 his hand on the head[n] of his offering and
n Ex 29:10,15 o Lev 1:5 slaughter it[o] at the entrance to the Tent
of Meeting. Then Aaron's sons the
priests shall sprinkle the blood against
the altar on all sides. 3From the fellowship offering he is to bring a sacrifice
3:3 made to the LORD by fire: all the fat[p] that
p Ex 29:13 covers the inner parts or is connected to
them, 4both kidneys with the fat on
them near the loins, and the covering of
3:5 the liver, which he will remove with the
q Lev 7:29-34 kidneys. 5Then Aaron's sons[q] are to burn
r Ex 29:13,38-42 it on the altar on top of the burnt offering[r] that is on the burning wood, as an
offering made by fire, an aroma pleasing
to the LORD.
6" 'If he offers an animal from the flock
3:6 s ver 1 as a fellowship offering[s] to the LORD, he is
to offer a male or female without defect.
3:7 7If he offers a lamb, he is to present it be-
t Lev 17:8-9 fore the LORD.[t] 8He is to lay his hand on
3:8 the head of his offering and slaughter it[u]
u ver 2; Lev 1:5 in front of the Tent of Meeting. Then Aaron's sons shall sprinkle its blood against
the altar on all sides. 9From the fellowship offering he is to bring a sacrifice
made to the LORD by fire: its fat, the entire
fat tail cut off close to the backbone, all
the fat that covers the inner parts or is
connected to them, 10both kidneys with
the fat on them near the loins, and the
covering of the liver, which he will remove
with the kidneys. 11The priest shall burn
them on the altar[v] as food,[w] an offering 3:11 v ver 5 w ver 16;
made to the LORD by fire. Lev 21:6,17
12" 'If his offering is a goat, he is to
present it before the LORD. 13He is to lay
his hand on its head and slaughter it in
front of the Tent of Meeting. Then Aar- 3:13
on's sons shall sprinkle[x] its blood against x Ex 24:6
the altar on all sides. 14From what he offers he is to make this offering to the
LORD by fire: all the fat that covers the inner parts or is connected to them,
15both kidneys with the fat on them near
the loins, and the covering of the liver,
which he will remove with the kidneys.
16The priest shall burn them on the altar 3:16
as food, an offering made by fire, a pleas- y 1Sa 2:16
ing aroma. All the fat is the LORD's.[y]
17" 'This is a lasting ordinance for the 3:17 z Lev 6:18; 17:7
generations to come,[z] wherever you live: a Ge 9:4;
You must not eat any fat or any blood.[a]' " Lev 7:25-26; 17:10-16; Dt 12:16; Ac 15:20

The Sin Offering

4 The LORD said to Moses, 2"Say to
the Israelites: 'When anyone sins 4:2 b Lev 5:15-18;
unintentionally[b] and does what is for- Ps 19:12;
bidden in any of the LORD's commands— Heb 9:7

3" 'If the anointed priest sins, bringing
guilt on the people, he must bring to the 4:3
LORD a young bull[c] without defect as a c ver 14;
sin offering[d] for the sin he has commit- Ps 66:15 d Lev 9:2-22;
ted. 4He is to present the bull at the en- Heb 9:13-14
trance to the Tent of Meeting before the
LORD.[e] He is to lay his hand on its head 4:4
and slaughter it before the LORD. 5Then e Lev 1:3
the anointed priest shall take some of
the bull's blood[f] and carry it into the 4:5
Tent of Meeting. 6He is to dip his finger f Lev 16:14
into the blood and sprinkle some of it
seven times before the LORD, in front of
the curtain of the sanctuary. 7The priest
shall then put some of the blood on the
horns of the altar of fragrant incense
that is before the LORD in the Tent of
Meeting. The rest of the bull's blood he 4:7
shall pour out at the base of the altar[g] of g ver 34; Lev 8:15

a 1 Traditionally *peace offering*; also in verses 3, 6 and 9

DISCOVERY 29

The Sin Offering

There were three types of Old Testament sacrifices, and each had its own purpose. The *sin offering* and *burnt offering* each dealt with the issue of sin itself. Both the *burnt* and *grain offerings* had to do with commitment or being set apart for God. Finally, the *fellowship offering* focused on communion between God, the priest and the worshiper.

The basic requirements for God's forgiveness are demonstrated in the sin offering. First of all, there were to be no exceptions. No one could be forgiven apart from sacrifice, and every person had to bring a sin offering. Both the priest and the nation as a whole were obligated to provide a bull (Leviticus 4:3,14), the leaders of the tribes had to bring a male or female goat or lamb (verses 22–23,28,32), every individual was instructed to furnish two birds (Leviticus 5:7) and the very poor were allowed to offer flour (Leviticus 5:11–13). Although God made allowance for differences in economic status, everyone had to bring something.

The sin offering also implied *substitution*. The penalty for sin was death (Genesis 2:15–17). The death of the animal, presented to the Lord at the entrance to the Tent of Meeting, was substituted for the death of each person, in order to cover that person's sin (Leviticus 4:4). Each individual personally identified with the sacrifice by placing his hands on the animal before it was killed. That action represented the transfer of his own guilt to the animal. The person then confessed his sin (Leviticus 5:5), and the animal was killed. Its blood was sprinkled in various places (Leviticus 4:5–7), because God had instructed the Israelites that it was only through the shedding and sprinkling of blood that forgiveness could be made possible (verses 32–35).

The sin offering points us forward to Jesus' sacrifice on the cross. We are all included in the need to be made right with God (Romans 3:23), and there is no way to remove sin except through Jesus Christ (Acts 4:12). It was Jesus, instead of a bull or a sheep, who died in our place. He voluntarily assumed our death penalty (Hebrews 10:8–10).

Because people could not fully relate to the sacrifice, the Sacrifice came down to identify with us. Jesus was born as a man and, as one of us, was in a position to take our sin and guilt upon himself (Philippians 2:6–11). The death of a sinless person was required to pay for sin, and Jesus followed through to the bitter end (1 Peter 1:18–21). When we perceive our sin as God sees it (1 John 1:9) and confess that Jesus is Lord (Romans 10:9–10), his death pays for that sin. In response, we need to thank him continually and determine to put him first in our lives every day.

***Self-Discovery:** Imagine yourself to be an Israelite living during Old Testament times. In what ways would the peace and joy that you experience in Jesus be missing from your life?*

GO TO DISCOVERY 30 ON PAGE 142

4:7 [h] ver 18,30; Lev 5:9; 9:9; 16:18 burnt offering[h] at the entrance to the
Tent of Meeting. 8He shall remove all the
fat[i] from the bull of the sin offering—the
4:8 [i] Lev 3:3-5 fat that covers the inner parts or is connected to them, 9both kidneys with the
fat on them near the loins, and the covering of the liver, which he will remove
4:9 [j] Lev 3:4 with the kidneys[j]— 10just as the fat is removed from the ox[a] sacrificed as a fel-
lowship offering.[b] Then the priest shall
burn them on the altar of burnt offering.
11But the hide of the bull and all its flesh,
4:11 [k] Ex 29:14; Lev 9:11; Nu 19:5 as well as the head and legs, the inner
parts and offal[k]— 12that is, all the rest of
the bull—he must take outside the
4:12 [l] Heb 13:11 [m] Lev 6:11 camp[l] to a place ceremonially clean,[m]
where the ashes are thrown, and burn it
in a wood fire on the ash heap.

4:13 [n] ver 2; Lev 5:2-4,17; Nu 15:24-26 13“ ‘If the whole Israelite community
sins unintentionally[n] and does what is
forbidden in any of the LORD's commands, even though the community is
unaware of the matter, they are guilty.
14When they become aware of the sin
they committed, the assembly must
4:14 [o] ver 3 [p] ver 23, 28 bring a young bull[o] as a sin offering[p] and
present it before the Tent of Meeting.
4:15 [q] Lev 1:4; 8:14, 22; Nu 8:10 15The elders of the community are to lay
their hands on the bull's head[q] before the
LORD, and the bull shall be slaughtered
before the LORD. 16Then the anointed
4:16 [r] ver 5 priest is to take some of the bull's blood[r]
into the Tent of Meeting. 17He shall dip
his finger into the blood and sprinkle it
4:17 [s] ver 6 before the LORD[s] seven times in front of
the curtain. 18He is to put some of the
blood on the horns of the altar that is be-
4:18 [t] ver 7 fore the LORD[t] in the Tent of Meeting.
The rest of the blood he shall pour out at
the base of the altar of burnt offering at
the entrance to the Tent of Meeting. 19He
4:19 [u] ver 8 shall remove all the fat[u] from it and burn
it on the altar, 20and do with this bull just
as he did with the bull for the sin offering. In this way the priest will make
4:20 [v] Heb 10:10-12 [w] Nu 15:25 atonement[v] for them, and they will be
forgiven.[w] 21Then he shall take the bull
outside the camp and burn it as he
4:21 [x] Lev 16:5,15 burned the first bull. This is the sin offering for the community.[x]

4:22 [y] Nu 31:13 [z] ver 2 22“ ‘When a leader[y] sins unintentionally[z] and does what is forbidden in any
of the commands of the LORD his God,
he is guilty. 23When he is made aware of
the sin he committed, he must bring as
his offering a male goat without defect.
24He is to lay his hand on the goat's head
and slaughter it at the place where the
burnt offering is slaughtered before
the LORD. It is a sin offering. 25Then the
priest shall take some of the blood of the
sin offering with his finger and put it on
the horns of the altar of burnt offering
and pour out the rest of the blood at the 4:25 [a] ver 7,18,30,34; Lev 9:9
base of the altar.[a] 26He shall burn all the
fat on the altar as he burned the fat of
the fellowship offering. In this way the
priest will make atonement for the
man's sin, and he will be forgiven.[b] 4:26 [b] Lev 5:10

27“ ‘If a member of the community
sins unintentionally[c] and does what is 4:27 [c] ver 2; Nu 15:27
forbidden in any of the LORD's com-
mands, he is guilty. 28When he is made
aware of the sin he committed, he must
bring as his offering[d] for the sin he com- 4:28 [d] ver 23 [e] ver 3
mitted a female goat[e] without defect.
29He is to lay his hand on the head[f] of 4:29 [f] ver 4,24 [g] Lev 1:4
the sin offering[g] and slaughter it at the
place of the burnt offering. 30Then the
priest is to take some of the blood with
his finger and put it on the horns of the
altar of burnt offering[h] and pour out the 4:30 [h] ver 7
rest of the blood at the base of the altar.
31He shall remove all the fat, just as the
fat is removed from the fellowship offer-

[a] 10 The Hebrew word can include both male and female. [b] 10 Traditionally *peace offering*; also in verses 26, 31 and 35

MADE HOLY THROUGH HIS BLOOD

Blood sacrifices always involved three elements (Leviticus 4). First, the priest, as he presented the sacrifice, had to *submit* himself to what God wanted. Second, the priest had to lay his hands on the animal to *identify* with its death. Finally, the animal had to be *put to death* so that its blood could be sprinkled in front of the curtain or on the atonement cover on the Day of Atonement. Only the fat, the kidneys and part of the liver were burned on the altar; the rest of the carcass was burned outside the camp. The New Testament shows us that Jesus suffered and died as the sacrifice for our sins (John 1:29; Romans 3:25; Ephesians 5:2). Just as the high priest carried the animal's blood into the Most Holy Place, so Jesus carried his own blood into God's presence. The bodies of the animals were burned outside the camp, and Jesus hung on a cross to die outside the city gate so that his people might be made holy (Hebrews 13:11–12).

ing, and the priest shall burn it on the al-
4:31 [i]Ge 8:21 tar as an aroma pleasing to the LORD.[i] In
this way the priest will make atonement
for him, and he will be forgiven.
32“ ‘If he brings a lamb as his sin offering, he is to bring a female without de-
4:32 [j]ver 28 fect.[j] 33He is to lay his hand on its head
and slaughter it for a sin offering at the
place where the burnt offering is slaugh-
4:33 [k]ver 29 tered.[k] 34Then the priest shall take some
of the blood of the sin offering with his
finger and put it on the horns of the altar of burnt offering and pour out the
4:34 [l]ver 7 rest of the blood at the base of the altar.[l]
35He shall remove all the fat, just as the
fat is removed from the lamb of the fellowship offering, and the priest shall
4:35 [m]ver 26,31 burn it on the altar[m] on top of the offerings made to the LORD by fire. In this
way the priest will make atonement for
him for the sin he has committed, and
he will be forgiven.

> I MUST DIE OR GET SOMEBODY TO DIE FOR ME. IF THE BIBLE DOESN'T TEACH THAT, IT DOESN'T TEACH ANYTHING. AND THAT IS WHERE THE ATONEMENT OF JESUS CHRIST COMES IN.
>
> Dwight L. Moody, *American Evangelist*

5 “ ‘If a person sins because he does
not speak up when he hears a pub-
5:1 [n]Pr 29:24 lic charge to testify[n] regarding some-
[o]ver 17 thing he has seen or learned about, he
will be held responsible.[o]
2“ ‘Or if a person touches anything
ceremonially unclean—whether the carcasses of unclean wild animals or of unclean livestock or of unclean creatures
5:2 [p]Lev 11:11,24-40; Dt 14:8 that move along the ground[p]—even
though he is unaware of it, he has be-
come unclean and is guilty.
3“ ‘Or if he touches human unclean-
5:3 [q]Nu 19:11-16 ness[q]—anything that would make him
unclean—even though he is unaware of
it, when he learns of it he will be guilty.
4“ ‘Or if a person thoughtlessly takes
5:4 [r]Nu 30:6,8 an oath[r] to do anything, whether good
or evil—in any matter one might care-
lessly swear about—even though he is
unaware of it, in any case when he learns
5:5 [s]Lev 16:21; 26:40; Nu 5:7; Pr 28:13 of it he will be guilty.
5“ ‘When anyone is guilty in any of
these ways, he must confess[s] in what way
he has sinned 6and, as a penalty for the
sin he has committed, he must bring to
the LORD a female lamb or goat from the
flock as a sin offering;[t] and the priest 5:6 [t]Lev 4:28
shall make atonement for him for his sin.
7“ ‘If he cannot afford[u] a lamb, he is to 5:7 [u]Lev 12:8; 14:21
bring two doves or two young pigeons to
the LORD as a penalty for his sin—one
for a sin offering and the other for a
burnt offering. 8He is to bring them to
the priest, who shall first offer the one
for the sin offering. He is to wring its
head from its neck,[v] not severing it com- 5:8 [v]Lev 1:15
pletely,[w] 9and is to sprinkle some of the [w]Lev 1:17
blood of the sin offering against the side
of the altar; the rest of the blood must be
drained out at the base of the altar.[x] It is 5:9 [x]Lev 4:7,18
a sin offering. 10The priest shall then of-
fer the other as a burnt offering in the
prescribed way[y] and make atonement 5:10 [y]Lev 1:14-17
for him for the sin he has committed, [z]Lev 4:26
and he will be forgiven.[z]
11“ ‘If, however, he cannot afford two
doves or two young pigeons, he is to
bring as an offering for his sin a tenth of
an ephah[a] of fine flour[a] for a sin offering. 5:11 [a]Lev 2:1
He must not put oil or incense on it, be-
cause it is a sin offering. 12He is to bring
it to the priest, who shall take a handful
of it as a memorial portion and burn it
on the altar on top of the offerings made
to the LORD by fire. It is a sin offering. 13In 5:13 [b]Lev 4:26
this way the priest will make atonement[b] [c]Lev 2:3
for him for any of these sins he has committed, and he will be forgiven. The rest
of the offering will belong to the priest,[c]
as in the case of the grain offering.’ ”

The Guilt Offering

14The LORD said to Moses: 15“When a
person commits a violation and sins unintentionally in regard to any of the
LORD's holy things, he is to bring to the
LORD as a penalty[d] a ram[e] from the flock, 5:15 [d]Lev 22:14
one without defect and of the proper [e]Nu 5:8
value in silver, according to the sanctu- [f]Ex 30:13
ary shekel.[b][f] It is a guilt offering. 16He
must make restitution[g] for what he has 5:16 [g]Lev 6:4
failed to do in regard to the holy things, [h]Lev 22:14; Nu 5:7
add a fifth of the value[h] to that and give
it all to the priest, who will make atonement for him with the ram as a guilt offering, and he will be forgiven.
17“If a person sins and does what is

[a] 11 That is, probably about 2 quarts (about 2 liters) [b] 15 That is, about 2/5 ounce (about 11.5 grams)

forbidden in any of the LORD's com-
5:17 mands, even though he does not know
[i]ver 15; Lev 4:2 it,[i] he is guilty and will be held responsible. 18He is to bring to the priest as a guilt
offering a ram from the flock, one without defect and of the proper value. In this
way the priest will make atonement for
him for the wrong he has committed un-
5:18 intentionally, and he will be forgiven.[j] 19It
[j]ver 15 is a guilt offering; he has been guilty of[a]
wrongdoing against the LORD."

6 The LORD said to Moses: 2"If anyone sins and is unfaithful to the
6:2 LORD[k] by deceiving his neighbor[l] about
[k]Nu 5:6; Ac 5:4; Col 3:9 something entrusted to him or left in his
[l]Pr 24:28 [m]Ex 22:7 care[m] or stolen, or if he cheats him, 3or if
he finds lost property and lies about it,[n]
6:3 or if he swears falsely, or if he commits
[n]Dt 22:1-3 any such sin that people may do—
4when he thus sins and becomes guilty,
6:4 he must return[o] what he has stolen or
[o]Lk 19:8 taken by extortion, or what was entrusted to him, or the lost property he found,
5or whatever it was he swore falsely
6:5 about. He must make restitution[p] in full,
[p]Nu 5:7 [q]Lev 5:15 add a fifth of the value to it and give it all
to the owner on the day he presents his
guilt offering.[q] 6And as a penalty he
must bring to the priest, that is, to the
6:6 LORD, his guilt offering,[r] a ram from the
[r]Lev 5:15 flock, one without defect and of the
proper value. 7In this way the priest will
6:7 make atonement[s] for him before the
[s]Lev 4:26 LORD, and he will be forgiven for any of
these things he did that made him
guilty."

The Burnt Offering

8The LORD said to Moses: 9"Give Aaron and his sons this command: 'These
are the regulations for the burnt offering: The burnt offering is to remain on
the altar hearth throughout the night,
till morning, and the fire must be kept
burning on the altar. 10The priest shall
6:10 then put on his linen clothes, with linen
[t]Ex 28:39-42, 43; 39:28 undergarments next to his body,[t] and
shall remove the ashes of the burnt of-
fering that the fire has consumed on the
altar and place them beside the altar.
11Then he is to take off these clothes and
put on others, and carry the ashes outside the camp to a place that is ceremo-
6:11 nially clean.[u] 12The fire on the altar must
[u]Lev 4:12 be kept burning; it must not go out.
Every morning the priest is to add firewood and arrange the burnt offering on
the fire and burn the fat of the fellowship offerings[b] on it. 13The fire must be
kept burning on the altar continuously;
it must not go out.

The Grain Offering

14" 'These are the regulations for the
grain offering:[v] Aaron's sons are to bring 6:14 [v]Lev 2:1; 15:4
it before the LORD, in front of the altar.
15The priest is to take a handful of fine
flour and oil, together with all the incense
on the grain offering,[w] and burn the me- 6:15 [w]Lev 2:9
morial portion[x] on the altar as an aroma [x]Lev 2:2
pleasing to the LORD. 16Aaron and his
sons[y] shall eat the rest[z] of it, but it is to be 6:16 [y]Lev 2:3
eaten without yeast[a] in a holy place;[b] [z]Eze 44:29 [a]Lev 2:11
they are to eat it in the courtyard of the [b]Lev 10:13
Tent of Meeting. 17It must not be baked
with yeast; I have given it as their share of
the offerings made to me by fire. Like the
sin offering and the guilt offering, it is 6:17
most holy.[c] 18Any male descendant of [c]ver 29; Ex 40:10; Nu 18:9,10
Aaron may eat it.[d] It is his regular share
of the offerings made to the LORD by fire 6:18
for the generations to come. Whatever [d]ver 29; Nu 18:9-10
touches them will become holy.[c][e]' " [e]ver 27

19The LORD also said to Moses, 20"This
is the offering Aaron and his sons are to
bring to the LORD on the day he[d] is
anointed: a tenth of an ephah[e][f] of fine 6:20 [f]Ex 16:36
flour as a regular grain offering,[g] half of [g]Ex 29:2
it in the morning and half in the evening.
21Prepare it with oil on a griddle;[h] bring 6:21 [h]Lev 2:5
it well-mixed and present the grain of-
fering broken[f] in pieces as an aroma
pleasing to the LORD. 22The son who is to
succeed him as anointed priest shall prepare it. It is the LORD's regular share and
is to be burned completely. 23Every grain
offering of a priest shall be burned completely; it must not be eaten."

The Sin Offering

24The LORD said to Moses, 25"Say to
Aaron and his sons: 'These are the regulations for the sin offering: The sin offer-
ing is to be slaughtered before the LORD[i] 6:25 [i]Lev 1:3
in the place[j] the burnt offering is slaugh- [j]Lev 1:5,11
tered; it is most holy. 26The priest who
offers it shall eat it; it is to be eaten in a
holy place,[k] in the courtyard[l] of the Tent 6:26 [k]ver 16
of Meeting. 27Whatever touches any of [l]Lev 10:17-18

[a] 19 Or *has made full expiation for his*
[b] 12 Traditionally *peace offerings* [c] 18 Or *Whoever touches them must be holy*; similarly in verse 27 [d] 20 Or *each* [e] 20 That is, probably about 2 quarts (about 2 liters) [f] 21 The meaning of the Hebrew for this word is uncertain.

6:27 the flesh will become holy,[m] and if any of
[m] Ex 29:37 the blood is spattered on a garment, you
must wash it in a holy place. 28The clay
6:28 [n] Lev 11:33; pot[n] the meat is cooked in must be bro-
15:12 ken; but if it is cooked in a bronze pot,
the pot is to be scoured and rinsed with
water. 29Any male in a priest's family
6:29 [o] ver 18 [p] ver 17 may eat it;[o] it is most holy.[p] 30But any sin
offering whose blood is brought into the
6:30 Tent of Meeting to make atonement in
[q] Lev 4:18 the Holy Place[q] must not be eaten; it
[r] Lev 4:12 must be burned.[r]

The Guilt Offering

7 "'These are the regulations for the
7:1 [s] Lev 5:14-6:7 guilt offering,[s] which is most holy:
2The guilt offering is to be slaughtered in
the place where the burnt offering is
slaughtered, and its blood is to be sprinkled against the altar on all sides. 3All its
7:3 [t] Ex 29:13; fat[t] shall be offered: the fat tail and the
Lev 3:4,9 fat that covers the inner parts, 4both
kidneys with the fat on them near the
loins, and the covering of the liver, which
is to be removed with the kidneys. 5The
priest shall burn them on the altar as an
offering made to the LORD by fire. It is a
7:6 guilt offering. 6Any male in a priest's
[u] Lev 6:18; family may eat it,[u] but it must be eaten
Nu 18:9-10 [v] Lev 2:3 in a holy place; it is most holy.[v]
7"'The same law applies to both the
sin offering and the guilt offering: They
7:7 [w] Lev 6:17,26; belong to the priest[w] who makes atone-
1Co 9:13 ment with them. 8The priest who offers
a burnt offering for anyone may keep its
hide for himself. 9Every grain offering
baked in an oven or cooked in a pan or
7:9 [x] Lev 2:5 on a griddle[x] belongs to the priest who
offers it, 10and every grain offering,
whether mixed with oil or dry, belongs
equally to all the sons of Aaron.

The Fellowship Offering

11"'These are the regulations for the
fellowship offering[a] a person may present to the LORD:
12"'If he offers it as an expression of
7:12 thankfulness, then along with this thank
[y] ver 13,15 offering[y] he is to offer cakes of bread
[z] Lev 2:4; made without yeast and mixed with oil,
Nu 6:15 wafers[z] made without yeast and spread
with oil, and cakes of fine flour well-
kneaded and mixed with oil. 13Along
with his fellowship offering of thanksgiving he is to present an offering with
7:13 [a] Lev 23:17; cakes of bread made with yeast.[a] 14He is
Am 4:5 to bring one of each kind as an offering,
a contribution to the LORD; it belongs to
the priest who sprinkles the blood of the
fellowship offerings. 15The meat of his
fellowship offering of thanksgiving must
be eaten on the day it is offered; he must 7:15
leave none of it till morning.[b] [b] Lev 22:30
16"'If, however, his offering is the result of a vow or is a freewill offering, the
sacrifice shall be eaten on the day he offers it, but anything left over may be eat- 7:16
en on the next day.[c] 17Any meat of the [c] Lev 19:5-8
sacrifice left over till the third day must
be burned up. 18If any meat of the fellowship offering is eaten on the third 7:18
day, it will not be accepted.[d] It will not [d] Lev 19:7
be credited[e] to the one who offered it, [e] Nu 18:27
for it is impure; the person who eats any
of it will be held responsible.
19"'Meat that touches anything ceremonially unclean must not be eaten; it
must be burned up. As for other meat,
anyone ceremonially clean may eat it.
20But if anyone who is unclean eats any
meat of the fellowship offering belonging to the LORD, that person must be cut 7:20
off from his people.[f] 21If anyone touches [f] Lev 22:3-7
something unclean[g]—whether human 7:21
uncleanness or an unclean animal or [g] Lev 5:2; 11:24,
any unclean, detestable thing—and 28
then eats any of the meat of the fellowship offering belonging to the LORD, that
person must be cut off from his people.'"

Eating Fat and Blood Forbidden

22The LORD said to Moses, 23"Say to 7:23
the Israelites: 'Do not eat any of the fat [h] Lev 3:17;
of cattle, sheep or goats.[h] 24The fat of an 17:13-14
animal found dead or torn by wild ani-
mals[i] may be used for any other pur- 7:24 [i] Ex 22:31
pose, but you must not eat it. 25Anyone
who eats the fat of an animal from
which an offering by fire may be[b] made
to the LORD must be cut off from his
people. 26And wherever you live, you 7:26 [j] Ge 9:4
must not eat the blood[j] of any bird or
animal. 27If anyone eats blood,[k] that per- 7:27 [k] Lev 17:10-24;
son must be cut off from his people.'" Ac 15:20,29

The Priests' Share

28The LORD said to Moses, 29"Say to
the Israelites: 'Anyone who brings a fellowship offering to the LORD is to bring
part of it as his sacrifice to the LORD.
30With his own hands he is to bring the
offering made to the LORD by fire; he is to

[a] 11 Traditionally *peace offering*; also in verses 13–37 [b] 25 Or *fire is*

bring the fat, together with the breast,
7:30 [l] Ex 29:24; Nu 6:20 and wave the breast before the LORD as a
wave offering.[l] 31The priest shall burn
the fat on the altar, but the breast be-
7:31 [m] ver 34 longs to Aaron and his sons.[m] 32You are
to give the right thigh of your fellowship
7:32 [n] ver 34; Lev 9:21; Nu 6:20 offerings to the priest as a contribution.[n] 33The son of Aaron who offers the
blood and the fat of the fellowship offering shall have the right thigh as his
share. 34From the fellowship offerings of
7:34 [o] Lev 10:15 [p] Ex 29:27; Nu 18:18-19 the Israelites, I have taken the breast
that is waved and the thigh[o] that is pre-
sented and have given them to Aaron
the priest and his sons[p] as their regular
share from the Israelites.' "

35This is the portion of the offerings
made to the LORD by fire that were allotted to Aaron and his sons on the day
they were presented to serve the LORD as
7:36 [q] Ex 40:13,15; Lev 8:12,30 priests. 36On the day they were anointed,[q] the LORD commanded that the Isra-
elites give this to them as their regular
share for the generations to come.

37These, then, are the regulations for
7:37 [r] Lev 6:9 [s] Lev 6:14 [t] ver 1,11 the burnt offering,[r] the grain offering,[s]
the sin offering, the guilt offering, the or-
dination offering[t] and the fellowship offering, 38which the LORD gave Moses on
Mount Sinai on the day he commanded
7:38 [u] Lev 1:2 the Israelites to bring their offerings to
the LORD,[u] in the Desert of Sinai.

The Ordination of Aaron and His Sons

8 The LORD said to Moses, 2"Bring
Aaron and his sons, their gar-
8:2 [v] Ex 30:23-25,30 [w] Ex 29:2-3 ments, the anointing oil,[v] the bull for the
sin offering, the two rams and the bas-
ket containing bread made without
8:3 [x] Nu 8:9 yeast,[w] 3and gather the entire assembly[x]
at the entrance to the Tent of Meeting."
4Moses did as the LORD commanded
him, and the assembly gathered at the
entrance to the Tent of Meeting.

5Moses said to the assembly, "This is
what the LORD has commanded to be
8:6 [y] Ex 29:4; 30:19; Ps 26:6; Ac 22:16; 1Co 6:11; Eph 5:26 done." 6Then Moses brought Aaron and
his sons forward and washed them with
water.[y] 7He put the tunic on Aaron, tied
the sash around him, clothed him with
the robe and put the ephod on him. He
8:7 [z] Ex 28:4 also tied the ephod to him by its skillfully woven waistband; so it was fastened
8:8 [a] Ex 28:30 on him.[z] 8He placed the breastpiece on
him and put the Urim and Thummim[a]
in the breastpiece. 9Then he placed the
turban on Aaron's head and set the gold
plate, the sacred diadem,[b] on the front 8:9 [b] Ex 28:36
of it, as the LORD commanded Moses.

10Then Moses took the anointing oil[c] 8:10 [c] ver 2 [d] Ex 30:26
and anointed[d] the tabernacle and every-
thing in it, and so consecrated them.
11He sprinkled some of the oil on the altar seven times, anointing the altar and
all its utensils and the basin with its
stand, to consecrate them.[e] 12He poured 8:11 [e] Ex 30:29
some of the anointing oil on Aaron's 8:12 [f] Lev 21:10,12 [g] Ex 30:30
head and anointed[f] him to consecrate
him.[g] 13Then he brought Aaron's sons
forward, put tunics on them, tied sashes
around them and put headbands on
them, as the LORD commanded Moses.

14He then presented the bull[h] for the 8:14 [h] Lev 4:3 [i] Ps 66:15; Eze 43:19
sin offering,[i] and Aaron and his sons laid
their hands on its head. 15Moses slaughtered the bull and took some of the blood,
and with his finger he put it on all the
horns of the altar[j] to purify the altar.[k] He 8:15 [j] Lev 4:7 [k] Heb 9:22 [l] Eze 43:20
poured out the rest of the blood at the
base of the altar. So he consecrated it to
make atonement for it.[l] 16Moses also
took all the fat around the inner parts,
the covering of the liver, and both kidneys
and their fat, and burned it on the altar.
17But the bull with its hide and its flesh
and its offal[m] he burned up outside the 8:17 [m] Lev 4:11 [n] Lev 4:12
camp,[n] as the LORD commanded Moses.

18He then presented the ram[o] for the 8:18 [o] ver 2
burnt offering, and Aaron and his sons
laid their hands on its head. 19Then Moses slaughtered the ram and sprinkled
the blood against the altar on all sides.
20He cut the ram into pieces and burned
the head, the pieces and the fat. 21He
washed the inner parts and the legs with
water and burned the whole ram on the
altar as a burnt offering, a pleasing aroma, an offering made to the LORD by fire,
as the LORD commanded Moses.

22He then presented the other ram,
the ram for the ordination,[p] and Aaron 8:22 [p] ver 2
and his sons laid their hands on its
head. 23Moses slaughtered the ram and
took some of its blood and put it on the
lobe of Aaron's right ear, on the thumb
of his right hand and on the big toe of
his right foot. 24Moses also brought Aaron's sons forward and put some of the
blood on the lobes of their right ears, on
the thumbs of their right hands and on
the big toes of their right feet. Then he
sprinkled blood against the altar on
all sides.[q] 25He took the fat, the fat tail, 8:24 [q] Heb 9:18-22
all the fat around the inner parts, the

Jesus Our High Priest

Under the Old Testament system two things were necessary in order to approach God: The worshiper had to bring the appropriate sacrifice, and that sacrifice had to be offered by the appropriate person—the priest. Only the priest was qualified for this function, because he had been chosen by God as a mediator, as one equipped to negotiate between a holy God and sinful people.

The people needed a priest because sin kept them separated from God. In order for the priests to be acceptable mediators they were obligated to adhere to detailed requirements with regard to dress, hygiene, cleansing, life and ministry functions. God takes sin very seriously: Failure to follow his instructions resulted in immediate death for a priest! (Leviticus 8:35).

Because all people are sinful, including the priests, Jesus himself became not only our final sacrifice but also our perfect high priest. The tabernacle affords us an illustration of what Jesus came to do. It had been divided into three main sections—the outer court with the bronze altar, the Holy Place and the Most Holy Place in which the ark of the covenant was placed. Only the high priest himself was allowed to enter the Most Holy Place, and then only once a year on the Day of Atonement (Leviticus 16). Jesus, as our high priest, entered the "Most Holy Place once for all by his own blood" (Hebrews 9:12). Since that time the path to relationship with God has been cleared for everyone (Hebrews 10:19–22). When Jesus died the curtain that protected the Most Holy Place was torn in two (Matthew 27:51), because we no longer needed to fear our holy Creator's judgment!

God appointed Aaron and his descendants to serve as priests for the people both in the tabernacle and later on in the temple (Exodus 29:9). Jesus is unique in that he is *not* a priest from "the order of Aaron." Instead, he comes "in the order of Melchizedek" (Psalm 110:4). Melchizedek, the king of Salem, was a priest whose story is told in Genesis, when Abraham offered him a tithe (Genesis 14:18–20). Melchizedek was specially chosen by God to be a priest, even though he wasn't a member of Aaron's or Levi's family. Melchizedek's name means "king of righteousness." Jesus is the ultimate King of Righteousness and Peace, "holy, blameless, pure, set apart from sinners, exalted above the heavens" (Hebrews 7:26).

All of the priests in the Old Testament offered sacrifices for their *own* sin as well as for the sins of others. The fact that Jesus did not need to offer sacrifices for his own sin makes him unique as a high priest (Hebrews 7:27). And rather than offering animals, he offered *himself* as the final sacrifice for our sins (Hebrews 7:27)—our high priest *became* the sacrifice.

Even now Jesus is our high priest in heaven. He intercedes for us (Romans 8:34; Hebrews 7:25) because he understands our weaknesses from personal experience! (Hebrews 4:14–16). We can approach him with confidence, believing that he knows exactly what we're going through, and we can draw strength from the fact that he never gave in to sin.

Self-Discovery: *Imagine what Jesus' sinless life must have been like. Think about your activities so far today. What might you have done differently if you had possessed the ability always to choose for the right?*

GO TO DISCOVERY 31 ON PAGE 145

covering of the liver, both kidneys and
their fat and the right thigh. 26 Then
from the basket of bread made without
yeast, which was before the LORD, he
took a cake of bread, and one made
with oil, and a wafer; he put these on
the fat portions and on the right thigh.
27 He put all these in the hands of Aaron
and his sons and waved them before the
LORD as a wave offering. 28 Then Moses
took them from their hands and burned
them on the altar on top of the burnt offering as an ordination offering, a pleasing aroma, an offering made to the LORD
by fire. 29 He also took the breast—Mo-
8:29 ses' share of the ordination ram[r]—and
r Lev 7:31-34 waved it before the LORD as a wave offering, as the LORD commanded Moses.
30 Then Moses took some of the
anointing oil and some of the blood
from the altar and sprinkled them on
8:30 Aaron and his garments[s] and on his
s Ex 28:2 sons and their garments. So he conse-
t Nu 3:3 crated[t] Aaron and his garments and his
sons and their garments.
31 Moses then said to Aaron and his
sons, "Cook the meat at the entrance to
the Tent of Meeting and eat it there with
the bread from the basket of ordination
offerings, as I commanded, saying,[a]
'Aaron and his sons are to eat it.' 32 Then
burn up the rest of the meat and the
bread. 33 Do not leave the entrance to the
Tent of Meeting for seven days, until the
days of your ordination are completed,
for your ordination will last seven days.
8:34 34 What has been done today was com-
u Heb 7:16 manded by the LORD[u] to make atonement for you. 35 You must stay at the entrance to the Tent of Meeting day and
8:35 night for seven days and do what the
v Nu 3:7; 9:19; LORD requires,[v] so you will not die; for
Dt 11:1; 1Ki 2:3; that is what I have been commanded."
Eze 48:11 36 So Aaron and his sons did everything
the LORD commanded through Moses.

The Priests Begin Their Ministry

9:1 **9** On the eighth day[w] Moses sum-
w Eze 43:27 moned Aaron and his sons and
the elders of Israel. 2 He said to Aaron,
"Take a bull calf for your sin offering and
a ram for your burnt offering, both without defect, and present them before the
LORD. 3 Then say to the Israelites: 'Take a
male goat for a sin offering, a calf and a
lamb—both a year old and without defect—for a burnt offering, 4 and an ox[b]
and a ram for a fellowship offering[c] to
sacrifice before the LORD, together with
a grain offering mixed with oil. For today
the LORD will appear to you.[x]'" 9:4 x Ex 29:43
5 They took the things Moses com-
manded to the front of the Tent of Meeting, and the entire assembly came near
and stood before the LORD. 6 Then Moses
said, "This is what the LORD has commanded you to do, so that the glory of 9:6 y ver 23;
the LORD[y] may appear to you." Ex 24:16
7 Moses said to Aaron, "Come to the
altar and sacrifice your sin offering and
your burnt offering and make atonement for yourself and the people; sacrifice the offering that is for the people
and make atonement for them, as the 9:7
LORD has commanded.[z]" z Heb 5:1,3; 7:27
8 So Aaron came to the altar and 9:8
slaughtered the calf as a sin offering[a] for a Lev 4:1-12
himself. 9 His sons brought the blood to 9:9
him,[b] and he dipped his finger into the b ver 12,18
blood and put it on the horns of the al- c Lev 4:7
tar; the rest of the blood he poured out
at the base of the altar.[c] 10 On the altar he
burned the fat, the kidneys and the covering of the liver from the sin offering, as
the LORD commanded Moses; 11 the flesh 9:11
and the hide[d] he burned up outside the d Lev 4:11
camp.[e] e Lev 4:12; 8:17
12 Then he slaughtered the burnt offering. His sons handed him the blood,
and he sprinkled it against the altar on
all sides. 13 They handed him the burnt
offering piece by piece, including the
head, and he burned them on the altar.[f] 9:13
14 He washed the inner parts and the legs f Lev 1:8
and burned them on top of the burnt offering on the altar.
15 Aaron then brought the offering
that was for the people.[g] He took the 9:15 g Lev 4:27-31
goat for the people's sin offering and
slaughtered it and offered it for a sin offering as he did with the first one.
16 He brought the burnt offering and 9:16
offered it in the prescribed way.[h] 17 He h Lev 1:1-13
also brought the grain offering, took a
handful of it and burned it on the altar in
addition to the morning's burnt offering.[i] 9:17 i Lev 2:1-2; 3:5
18 He slaughtered the ox and the ram
as the fellowship offering for the people.[j] 9:18 j Lev 3:1-11
His sons handed him the blood, and he
sprinkled it against the altar on all sides.
19 But the fat portions of the ox and the

[a] *31* Or *I was commanded:* [b] *4* The Hebrew word can include both male and female; also in verses 18 and 19. [c] *4* Traditionally *peace offering;* also in verses 18 and 22

ram—the fat tail, the layer of fat, the
kidneys and the covering of the liver—
20 these they laid on the breasts, and
then Aaron burned the fat on the altar.
21 Aaron waved the breasts and the right
9:21 [k] Ex 29:24,26; Lev 7:30-34
thigh before the LORD as a wave offering,[k] as Moses commanded.
22 Then Aaron lifted his hands toward
9:22 [l] Nu 6:23; Dt 21:5; Lk 24:50
the people and blessed them.[l] And having sacrificed the sin offering, the burnt
offering and the fellowship offering, he
stepped down.
23 Moses and Aaron then went into
the Tent of Meeting. When they came
out, they blessed the people; and the glo-
9:23 [m] ver 6
ry of the LORD[m] appeared to all the people. 24 Fire[n] came out from the presence
9:24 [n] Jdg 6:21; 2Ch 7:1 [o] 1Ki 18:39
of the LORD and consumed the burnt offering and the fat portions on the altar.
And when all the people saw it, they
shouted for joy and fell facedown.[o]

The Death of Nadab and Abihu

10:1 [p] Ex 24:1; Nu 3:2-4; 26:61 [q] Lev 16:12 [r] Ex 30:9
10 Aaron's sons Nadab and Abihu[p]
took their censers, put fire in
them[q] and added incense; and they offered unauthorized fire before the LORD,
contrary to his command.[r] 2 So fire came
out from the presence of the LORD and
consumed them,[s] and they died before
10:2 [s] Nu 3:4; 16:35; 26:61
the LORD. 3 Moses then said to Aaron,
"This is what the LORD spoke of when he
said:

10:3 [t] Ex 19:22 [u] Ex 30:29; Lev 21:6; Eze 28:22 [v] Ex Isa; 49:3
" 'Among those who approach me[t]
I will show myself holy;[u]
in the sight of all the people
I will be honored.[v]' "

Aaron remained silent.

4 Moses summoned Mishael and Elza-
10:4 [w] Ex 6:22 [x] Ex 6:18 [y] Ac 5:6,9,10
phan,[w] sons of Aaron's uncle Uzziel,[x] and
said to them, "Come here; carry your
cousins outside the camp,[y] away from
the front of the sanctuary." 5 So they came
10:5 [z] Lev 8:13
and carried them, still in their tunics,[z]
outside the camp, as Moses ordered.
6 Then Moses said to Aaron and his
sons Eleazar and Ithamar, "Do not let
10:6 [a] Lev 21:10 [b] Nu 1:53; 16:22; Jos 7:1; 22:18; 2Sa 24:1
your hair become unkempt,[a][a] and do not
tear your clothes, or you will die and the
LORD will be angry with the whole community.[b] But your relatives, all the house
of Israel, may mourn for those the LORD
has destroyed by fire. 7 Do not leave the
entrance to the Tent of Meeting or you
10:7 [c] Ex 28:41; Lev 21:12
will die, because the LORD's anointing oil[c]
is on you." So they did as Moses said.
8 Then the LORD said to Aaron, 9 "You
10:9 [d] Hos 4:11 [e] Pr 20:1; Isa 28:7; Eze 44:21; Lk 1:15; Eph 5:18; 1Ti 3:3; Tit 1:7
and your sons are not to drink wine[d] or
other fermented drink[e] whenever you
go into the Tent of Meeting, or you will
die. This is a lasting ordinance for the
generations to come. 10 You must distinguish between the holy and the com-
10:10 [f] Lev 11:47; 20:25; Eze 22:26
mon, between the unclean and the
clean,[f] 11 and you must teach[g] the Israel-
10:11 [g] Mal 2:7 [h] Dt 24:8
ites all the decrees the LORD has given
them through Moses.[h]"
12 Moses said to Aaron and his remaining sons, Eleazar and Ithamar, "Take the
grain offering left over from the offerings
10:12 [i] Lev 6:14-18; 21:22
made to the LORD by fire and eat it prepared without yeast beside the altar,[i] for
it is most holy. 13 Eat it in a holy place, because it is your share and your sons' share
of the offerings made to the LORD by fire;
for so I have been commanded. 14 But you
and your sons and your daughters may
eat the breast that was waved and the
10:14 [j] Ex 29:24,26-27; Lev 7:31,34; Nu 18:11
thigh that was presented. Eat them in a
ceremonially clean place;[j] they have been
given to you and your children as your
share of the Israelites' fellowship offer-
10:15 [k] Lev 7:34
ings.[b] 15 The thigh[k] that was presented

[a] 6 Or *Do not uncover your heads*
[b] 14 Traditionally *peace offerings*

GOD'S GLORY CAME DOWN

The Israelites witnessed God's glory from a distance at Mount Sinai (Exodus 19:16–22). But we are told in verse 23 of Leviticus 9 that the majesty and presence of the Lord "appeared to all the people." The glory of the Lord became visible in the very center of their assembly at the Tent of Meeting. This *shekinah glory* was a symbol of God's presence among his people, providing visible reassurance that he was with them personally. But that same glory later left the temple and returned to heaven (see Ezekiel 8—11), and it was only when Jesus arrived on the scene that God's presence and majesty returned. In Jesus, God's promise to be with his people became a physical and tangible reality, and they were once again able to see the glory of God (John 1:14). When the angels announced Jesus' birth, "the glory of the Lord shone" all around (Luke 2:9). A baby had been born (but not just any baby—he was "a Savior . . . Christ the Lord" [Luke 2:11]; "Immanuel . . . God with us" [Matthew 1:23]), and God's presence and majesty had returned to his people in the person of Jesus Christ.

DISCOVERY 31

ONLY ONE WAY

Perhaps no other single statement by Jesus has been perceived as more difficult or even offensive than when he declared, "I am the way and the truth and the life. No one comes to the Father except through me" (John 14:6). As confining as it seems to some people, however, the truth is that Jesus is not one of many ways to heaven; he is the *only* way. He does not represent one of many truths about God; he is the *only* truth. He does not exemplify one way to live among many alternative lifestyles; his is the *only* life. And not one person can come to God the Father unless he or she approaches through Jesus. His sacrifice excludes all other avenues to God. Jesus Christ's gospel may be construed as offensive, because it offers no options.

This narrow focus is not limited to what Jesus said; it is the theme of the entire Bible. God has stipulated very plainly what he wants from us. It is our responsibility to take those commands seriously and to live our lives on his terms rather than our own. Nadab and Abihu, Aaron's sons, learned that lesson the hard way (Leviticus 10:1–3). When the priests brought the fire in a bowl to light the altar in order to burn the sacrifices, they were required to follow specific directions. These two priests offended God by bringing "unauthorized fire," fire that was outside the scope of God's plan. God's response was immediate: "Fire came out from the presence of the LORD and consumed them, and they died before the LORD" (verse 2). Their sin was that they ignored God and dishonored him by doing things their own way.

God is honored when we take his words seriously. We may not light altar fires today, but God still wants us to follow his injunctions. The only way to have a relationship with God the Father is through Jesus, his Son. When we believe that he died for our sins and invite him into our lives, we honor God. And God's expectations for his people have never been options to be obeyed only when we agree with them or find them convenient.

Regardless of what we may think of God's instructions, no matter the potential costs to ourselves, he asks us to obey him. He created us and knows what is best for our lives. To ignore him dishonors him, but to take him seriously demonstrates that we belong to him.

"This is the victory that has overcome the world, even our faith. Who is it that overcomes the world? Only he who believes that Jesus is the Son of God" (1 John 5:4–5).

Self-Discovery: *Has there ever been a time when you have brought "unauthorized fire" into your relationship with God, something you knew full well was outside the scope of his plan?*

GO TO DISCOVERY 32 ON PAGE 154

and the breast that was waved must be
brought with the fat portions of the offerings made by fire, to be waved before
the LORD as a wave offering. This will be
the regular share for you and your children, as the LORD has commanded."
16 When Moses inquired about the
10:16 l Lev 9:3 goat of the sin offering[l] and found that
it had been burned up, he was angry
with Eleazar and Ithamar, Aaron's remaining sons, and asked, 17 "Why didn't
10:17 m Lev 6:24-30 you eat the sin offering[m] in the sanctuary area? It is most holy; it was given to
you to take away the guilt of the community by making atonement for them
before the LORD. 18 Since its blood was
10:18 n Lev 6:26,30 not taken into the Holy Place,[n] you
should have eaten the goat in the sanc-
tuary area, as I commanded."
19 Aaron replied to Moses, "Today they
sacrificed their sin offering and their
10:19 o Lev 9:12 burnt offering[o] before the LORD, but
such things as this have happened to
me. Would the LORD have been pleased
if I had eaten the sin offering today?"
20 When Moses heard this, he was satisfied.

Clean and Unclean Food

11 The LORD said to Moses and
Aaron, 2 "Say to the Israelites: 'Of
all the animals that live on land, these
11:2 p Ac 10:12-14 are the ones you may eat:[p] 3 You may eat
any animal that has a split hoof com-
pletely divided and that chews the cud.
4 " 'There are some that only chew the
cud or only have a split hoof, but you
must not eat them. The camel, though it
chews the cud, does not have a split hoof;
it is ceremonially unclean for you. 5 The
coney,[a] though it chews the cud, does
not have a split hoof; it is unclean for
you. 6 The rabbit, though it chews the
cud, does not have a split hoof; it is un- 11:7
clean for you. 7 And the pig,[q] though it q Isa 65:4; 66:3,
has a split hoof completely divided, does 17
not chew the cud; it is unclean for you.
8 You must not eat their meat or touch 11:8
their carcasses; they are unclean for you.[r] r Isa 52:11; Heb 9:10
9 " 'Of all the creatures living in the wa-
ter of the seas and the streams, you may
eat any that have fins and scales. 10 But
all creatures in the seas or streams that
do not have fins and scales—whether
among all the swarming things or
among all the other living creatures in
the water—you are to detest.[s] 11 And 11:10 s Lev 7:18
since you are to detest them, you must
not eat their meat and you must detest
their carcasses. 12 Anything living in the
water that does not have fins and scales
is to be detestable to you.
13 " 'These are the birds you are to detest and not eat because they are detestable: the eagle, the vulture, the black
vulture, 14 the red kite, any kind of black
kite, 15 any kind of raven, 16 the horned
owl, the screech owl, the gull, any kind
of hawk, 17 the little owl, the cormorant,
the great owl, 18 the white owl, the desert
owl, the osprey, 19 the stork, any kind of
heron, the hoopoe and the bat.[b]
20 " 'All flying insects that walk on all
fours are to be detestable to you.[t] 21 There 11:20 t Ac 10:14
are, however, some winged creatures that
walk on all fours that you may eat: those
that have jointed legs for hopping on the
ground. 22 Of these you may eat any kind
of locust,[u] katydid, cricket or grasshop- 11:22 u Mt 3:4; Mk 1:6
per. 23 But all other winged creatures that
have four legs you are to detest.
24 " 'You will make yourselves unclean
by these; whoever touches their carcasses will be unclean till evening. 25 Whoever picks up one of their carcasses 11:25
must wash his clothes,[v] and he will be v Lev 14:8,47; 15:5 w ver 40;
unclean till evening.[w] Nu 31:24
26 " 'Every animal that has a split hoof
not completely divided or that does not
chew the cud is unclean for you; whoever touches ⌊the carcass of⌋ any of them

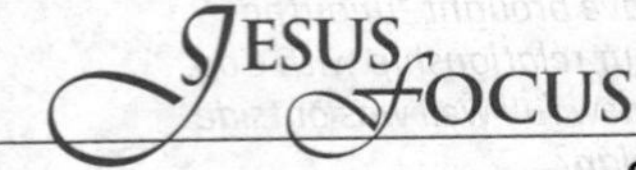

GOD'S HOLINESS

God's holiness is referred to again and again throughout the book of Leviticus. Holiness is often contrasted with the state of being *unclean*. Holiness characterizes God and everything that belongs to him. We are told in Leviticus that God's very name is holy (Leviticus 20:3), and God's people are also called to be holy (Leviticus 11:44–45). Peter quoted this passage to remind us that we are to live lives set apart for God, because Jesus gave his own life to repair the rift in our relationship with God caused by sin (1 Peter 16:19). Without the holiness imputed to us by Jesus himself, we couldn't enjoy fellowship with God (Hebrews 12:10,14).

[a] *5* That is, the hyrax or rock badger [b] *19* The precise identification of some of the birds, insects and animals in this chapter is uncertain.

will be unclean. 27Of all the animals that walk on all fours, those that walk on their paws are unclean for you; whoever touches their carcasses will be unclean till evening. 28Anyone who picks up their carcasses must wash his clothes, and he will be unclean till evening. They are unclean for you.

29" 'Of the animals that move about on the ground, these are unclean for you: the weasel, the rat,[x] any kind of great lizard, 30the gecko, the monitor lizard, the wall lizard, the skink and the chameleon. 31Of all those that move along the ground, these are unclean for you. Whoever touches them when they are dead will be unclean till evening. 32When one of them dies and falls on something, that article, whatever its use, will be unclean, whether it is made of wood, cloth, hide or sackcloth.[y] Put it in water; it will be unclean till evening, and then it will be clean. 33If one of them falls into a clay pot, everything in it will be unclean, and you must break the pot.[z] 34Any food that could be eaten but has water on it from such a pot is unclean, and any liquid that could be drunk from it is unclean. 35Anything that one of their carcasses falls on becomes unclean; an oven or cooking pot must be broken up. They are unclean, and you are to regard them as unclean. 36A spring, however, or a cistern for collecting water remains clean, but anyone who touches one of these carcasses is unclean. 37If a carcass falls on any seeds that are to be planted, they remain clean. 38But if water has been put on the seed and a carcass falls on it, it is unclean for you.

39" 'If an animal that you are allowed to eat dies, anyone who touches the carcass will be unclean till evening. 40Anyone who eats some of the carcass must wash his clothes, and he will be unclean till evening.[a] Anyone who picks up the carcass must wash his clothes, and he will be unclean till evening.

41" 'Every creature that moves about on the ground is detestable; it is not to be eaten. 42You are not to eat any creature that moves about on the ground, whether it moves on its belly or walks on all fours or on many feet; it is detestable. 43Do not defile yourselves by any of these creatures.[b] Do not make yourselves unclean by means of them or be

11:29 [x]Isa 66:17
11:32 [y]Lev 15:12
11:33 [z]Lev 6:28; 15:12
11:40 [a]Lev 17:15; 22:8; Eze 44:31
11:43 [b]Lev 20:25

made unclean by them. 44I am the LORD your God;[c] consecrate yourselves[d] and be holy,[e] because I am holy.[f] Do not make yourselves unclean by any creature that moves about on the ground. 45I am the LORD who brought you up out of Egypt[g] to be your God;[h] therefore be holy, because I am holy.[i]

46" 'These are the regulations concerning animals, birds, every living thing that moves in the water and every creature that moves about on the ground. 47You must distinguish between the unclean and the clean, between living creatures that may be eaten and those that may not be eaten.[j] ' "

Purification After Childbirth

12 The LORD said to Moses, 2"Say to the Israelites: 'A woman who becomes pregnant and gives birth to a son will be ceremonially unclean for seven days, just as she is unclean during her monthly period.[k] 3On the eighth day the boy is to be circumcised.[l] 4Then the woman must wait thirty-three days to be purified from her bleeding. She must not touch anything sacred or go to the sanctuary until the days of her purification are over. 5If she gives birth to a daughter, for two weeks the woman will be unclean, as during her period. Then she must wait sixty-six days to be purified from her bleeding.

6" 'When the days of her purification for a son or daughter are over,[m] she is to bring to the priest at the entrance to the Tent of Meeting a year-old lamb[n] for a

11:44 [c]Ex 6:2,7; Isa 43:3; 51:15 [d]Lev 20:7 [e]Ex 19:6 [f]Lev 19:2; Ps 99:3; Eph 1:4; 1Th 4:7; 1Pe 1:15,16*
11:45 [g]Lev 25:38,55; Ex 6:7; 20:2 [h]Ge 17:7 [i]Ex 19:6; 1Pe 1:16*
11:47 [j]Lev 10:10
12:2 [k]Lev 15:19; 18:19
12:3 [l]Ge 17:12; Lk 1:59; 2:21
12:6 [m]Lk 2:22 [n]Ex 29:38; Lev 23:12; Nu 6:12,14; 7:15

HELP FOR THE POOR

God was very specific about the kinds of offerings the people were to give him under the details of the law, but his grace was manifested in the way he provided alternatives for the poor (Leviticus 12). If a person could not afford a lamb, he or she could offer two doves or two pigeons—one as a burnt offering and one as a sin offering (verse 8). In this way even the poorest people could honor God and receive the benefits of having a new and clean relationship with him. Mary, Jesus' mother, offered this kind of sacrifice after her son's birth (Luke 2:24). Little did she realize then that Jesus would become the ultimate, priceless sacrifice for all sin.

burnt offering and a young pigeon or a
12:6 [o]Lev 5:7 dove for a sin offering.[o] 7He shall offer
them before the LORD to make atone-
ment for her, and then she will be ceremonially clean from her flow of blood.
" 'These are the regulations for the
woman who gives birth to a boy or a girl.
12:8 8If she cannot afford a lamb, she is to
[p]Ge 15:9; Lev 14:22 bring two doves or two young pigeons,[p]
one for a burnt offering and the other for
[q]Lev 5:7; Lk 2:22-24* a sin offering.[q] In this way the priest will
[r]Lev 4:26 make atonement for her, and she will be
clean.[r]' "

Regulations About Infectious Skin Diseases

13 The LORD said to Moses and
Aaron, 2"When anyone has a
13:2 [s]ver 10,19,28,43 [t]ver 4,38,39; Lev 14:56 swelling[s] or a rash or a bright spot[t] on
his skin that may become an infectious
[u]ver 3,9,15; Ex 4:6; Lev 14:3,32; Nu 5:2; Dt 24:8 skin disease,[a][u] he must be brought to
Aaron the priest[v] or to one of his sons[b]
[v]Dt 24:8 who is a priest. 3The priest is to examine
the sore on his skin, and if the hair in the
13:3 sore has turned white and the sore ap-
[w]ver 8,11,20,30; Lev 21:1; Nu 9:6 pears to be more than skin deep,[c] it is an
infectious skin disease. When the priest
examines him, he shall pronounce him
13:4 [x]ver 2 [y]ver 5,21,26,33,46; Lev 14:38; Nu 12:14,15; Dt 24:9 ceremonially unclean.[w] 4If the spot[x] on
his skin is white but does not appear to
be more than skin deep and the hair in
it has not turned white, the priest is to
put the infected person in isolation for
13:5 [z]Lev 14:9 [a]ver 27,32,34,51 seven days.[y] 5On the seventh day[z] the
priest is to examine him,[a] and if he sees
that the sore is unchanged and has not
spread in the skin, he is to keep him in
isolation another seven days. 6On the
seventh day the priest is to examine him
again, and if the sore has faded and has
not spread in the skin, the priest shall
13:6 [b]ver 13,17,23,28,34; Mt 8:3; Lk 5:12-14 pronounce him clean;[b] it is only a rash.
[c]Lev 11:25 The man must wash his clothes,[c] and he
[d]Lev 11:25; 14:8,9,20,48; 15:8; Nu 8:7 will be clean.[d] 7But if the rash does
spread in his skin after he has shown
himself to the priest to be pronounced
clean, he must appear before the priest
13:7 [e]Lk 5:14 again.[e] 8The priest is to examine him,
and if the rash has spread in the skin, he
shall pronounce him unclean; it is an infectious disease.
9"When anyone has an infectious
skin disease, he must be brought to the
priest. 10The priest is to examine him,
and if there is a white swelling in the
skin that has turned the hair white and
if there is raw flesh in the swelling, 11it is

a chronic skin disease[f] and the priest 13:11 [f]Ex 4:6; Lev 14:8; Nu 12:10; Mt 8:2
shall pronounce him unclean. He is not
to put him in isolation, because he is already unclean.
12"If the disease breaks out all over his
skin and, so far as the priest can see, it
covers all the skin of the infected person
from head to foot, 13the priest is to examine him, and if the disease has covered his whole body, he shall pronounce
that person clean. Since it has all turned
white, he is clean. 14But whenever raw
flesh appears on him, he will be unclean.
15When the priest sees the raw flesh, he
shall pronounce him unclean. The raw
flesh is unclean; he has an infectious disease.[g] 16Should the raw flesh change and 13:15 [g]ver 2
turn white, he must go to the priest.
17The priest is to examine him, and if the
sores have turned white, the priest shall
pronounce the infected person clean;[h] 13:17 [h]ver 6
then he will be clean.
18"When someone has a boil[i] on his 13:18 [i]Ex 9:9
skin and it heals, 19and in the place where
the boil was, a white swelling or reddish- 13:19
white[j] spot[k] appears, he must present [j]ver 24,42; Lev 14:37
himself to the priest. 20The priest is to ex- [k]ver 2
amine it, and if it appears to be more
than skin deep and the hair in it has
turned white, the priest shall pronounce
him unclean. It is an infectious skin dis- 13:20
ease[l] that has broken out where the boil [l]ver 2
was. 21But if, when the priest examines it,
there is no white hair in it and it is not
more than skin deep and has faded, then
the priest is to put him in isolation for
seven days. 22If it is spreading in the skin,
the priest shall pronounce him unclean;
it is infectious. 23But if the spot is unchanged and has not spread, it is only a
scar from the boil, and the priest shall 13:23
pronounce him clean.[m] [m]ver 6
24"When someone has a burn on his
skin and a reddish-white or white spot
appears in the raw flesh of the burn,
25the priest is to examine the spot, and if
the hair in it has turned white, and it appears to be more than skin deep, it is an
infectious disease that has broken out in
the burn. The priest shall pronounce
him unclean; it is an infectious skin dis- 13:25
ease.[n] 26But if the priest examines it and [n]ver 11
there is no white hair in the spot and if

[a] 2 Traditionally *leprosy;* the Hebrew word was used for various diseases affecting the skin—not necessarily leprosy; also elsewhere in this chapter.
[b] 2 Or *descendants* [c] 3 Or *be lower than the rest of the skin;* also elsewhere in this chapter

it is not more than skin deep and has
13:26 faded, then the priest is to put him in
o ver 4 isolation for seven days.[o] 27 On the sev-
13:27 enth day the priest is to examine him,[p]
p ver 5 and if it is spreading in the skin, the
priest shall pronounce him unclean; it is
an infectious skin disease. 28 If, however,
the spot is unchanged and has not
spread in the skin but has faded, it is a
swelling from the burn, and the priest
shall pronounce him clean; it is only a
13:28 q ver 2 scar from the burn.[q]
29 "If a man or woman has a sore on
13:29 r ver 43,44 the head[r] or on the chin, 30 the priest is
to examine the sore, and if it appears to
be more than skin deep and the hair in
it is yellow and thin, the priest shall pronounce that person unclean; it is an itch,
an infectious disease of the head or chin.
31 But if, when the priest examines this
kind of sore, it does not seem to be more
than skin deep and there is no black hair
13:31 in it, then the priest is to put the infect-
s ver 4 ed person in isolation for seven days.[s]
13:32 32 On the seventh day the priest is to ex-
t ver 5 amine the sore,[t] and if the itch has not
spread and there is no yellow hair in it
and it does not appear to be more than
skin deep, 33 he must be shaved except
for the diseased area, and the priest is to
keep him in isolation another seven
days. 34 On the seventh day the priest is
13:34 u ver 5 to examine the itch,[u] and if it has not
v Lev 11:25 spread in the skin and appears to be no
more than skin deep, the priest shall
pronounce him clean. He must wash his
clothes, and he will be clean.[v] 35 But if the
itch does spread in the skin after he is
pronounced clean, 36 the priest is to examine him, and if the itch has spread in
the skin, the priest does not need to look
13:36 w ver 30 for yellow hair; the person is unclean.[w]
37 If, however, in his judgment it is unchanged and black hair has grown in it,
the itch is healed. He is clean, and the
priest shall pronounce him clean.
38 "When a man or woman has white
spots on the skin, 39 the priest is to examine them, and if the spots are dull
white, it is a harmless rash that has broken out on the skin; that person is clean.
40 "When a man has lost his hair and is
13:40 x Lev 21:5; bald,[x] he is clean. 41 If he has lost his hair
2Ki 2:23; Isa 3:24; 15:2; from the front of his scalp and has a bald
22:12; forehead, he is clean. 42 But if he has a
Eze 27:31; reddish-white sore on his bald head or
29:18; Am 8:10; Mic 1:16 forehead, it is an infectious disease
breaking out on his head or forehead.
43 The priest is to examine him, and if the
swollen sore on his head or forehead is
reddish-white like an infectious skin disease, 44 the man is diseased and is unclean. The priest shall pronounce him
unclean because of the sore on his head. 13:45
45 "The person with such an infectious y Lev 10:6
disease must wear torn clothes,[y] let his z Eze 24:17,22;
hair be unkempt,[a] cover the lower part Mic 3:7; a Lev 5:2;
of his face[z] and cry out, 'Unclean! Un- La 4:15; Lk 17:12
clean!'[a] 46 As long as he has the infection 13:46
he remains unclean. He must live alone; b Nu 5:1-4;
he must live outside the camp.[b] 12:14; 2Ki 7:3; 15:5; Lk 17:12

Regulations About Mildew

47 "If any clothing is contaminated
with mildew—any woolen or linen
clothing, 48 any woven or knitted material of linen or wool, any leather or anything made of leather— 49 and if the contamination in the clothing, or leather, or
woven or knitted material, or any leather
article, is greenish or reddish, it is a
spreading mildew and must be shown to 13:49
the priest.[c] 50 The priest is to examine the c Mk 1:44
mildew[d] and isolate the affected article 13:50
for seven days. 51 On the seventh day he is d Eze 44:23
to examine it,[e] and if the mildew has 13:51
spread in the clothing, or the woven or e ver 5
knitted material, or the leather, whatev- f Lev 14:44
er its use, it is a destructive mildew; the
article is unclean.[f] 52 He must burn up
the clothing, or the woven or knitted material of wool or linen, or any leather article that has the contamination in it,
because the mildew is destructive; the
article must be burned up.[g] 13:52 g ver 55,57
53 "But if, when the priest examines it,
the mildew has not spread in the clothing, or the woven or knitted material, or
the leather article, 54 he shall order that
the contaminated article be washed.
Then he is to isolate it for another seven
days. 55 After the affected article has
been washed, the priest is to examine it,
and if the mildew has not changed its
appearance, even though it has not
spread, it is unclean. Burn it with fire,
whether the mildew has affected one
side or the other. 56 If, when the priest examines it, the mildew has faded after the
article has been washed, he is to tear the
contaminated part out of the clothing,
or the leather, or the woven or knitted
material. 57 But if it reappears in the

[a] 45 *Or clothes, uncover his head*

clothing, or in the woven or knitted material, or in the leather article, it is spreading, and whatever has the mildew must be burned with fire. 58 The clothing, or the woven or knitted material, or any leather article that has been washed and is rid of the mildew, must be washed again, and it will be clean."

59 These are the regulations concerning contamination by mildew in woolen or linen clothing, woven or knitted material, or any leather article, for pronouncing them clean or unclean.

Cleansing From Infectious Skin Diseases

14 The LORD said to Moses, 2 "These are the regulations for the diseased person at the time of his ceremonial cleansing, when he is brought to the priest:[h] 3 The priest is to go outside the camp and examine him.[i] If the person has been healed of his infectious skin disease,[a] 4 the priest shall order that two live clean birds and some cedar wood, scarlet yarn and hyssop be brought for the one to be cleansed.[j] 5 Then the priest shall order that one of the birds be killed over fresh water in a clay pot. 6 He is then to take the live bird and dip it, together with the cedar wood, the scarlet yarn and the hyssop, into the blood of the bird that was killed over the fresh water.[k] 7 Seven times he shall sprinkle[l] the one to be cleansed of the infectious disease and pronounce him clean. Then he is to release the live bird in the open fields.

8 "The person to be cleansed must wash his clothes,[m] shave off all his hair and bathe with water;[n] then he will be ceremonially clean.[o] After this he may come into the camp,[p] but he must stay outside his tent for seven days. 9 On the seventh day he must shave off all his hair; he must shave his head, his beard, his eyebrows and the rest of his hair. He must wash his clothes and bathe himself with water, and he will be clean.

10 "On the eighth day[q] he must bring two male lambs and one ewe lamb a year old, each without defect, along with three-tenths of an ephah[b] of fine flour mixed with oil for a grain offering,[r] and one log[c] of oil.[s] 11 The priest who pronounces him clean shall present both the one to be cleansed and his offerings before the LORD at the entrance to the Tent of Meeting.

12 "Then the priest is to take one of the male lambs and offer it as a guilt offering,[t] along with the log of oil; he shall wave them before the LORD as a wave offering.[u] 13 He is to slaughter the lamb in the holy place[v] where the sin offering and the burnt offering are slaughtered. Like the sin offering, the guilt offering belongs to the priest;[w] it is most holy. 14 The priest is to take some of the blood of the guilt offering and put it on the lobe of the right ear of the one to be cleansed, on the thumb of his right hand and on the big toe of his right foot.[x] 15 The priest shall then take some of the log of oil, pour it in the palm of his own left hand, 16 dip his right forefinger into the oil in his palm, and with his finger sprinkle some of it before the LORD seven times. 17 The priest is to put some of the oil remaining in his palm on the lobe of the right ear of the one to be cleansed, on the thumb of his right hand and on the big toe of his right foot, on top of the blood of the guilt offering. 18 The rest of the oil in his palm the priest shall put on the head of the one to be cleansed and make atonement for him before the LORD.

19 "Then the priest is to sacrifice the sin offering and make atonement for the one to be cleansed from his uncleanness. After that, the priest shall slaughter the burnt offering 20 and offer it on the altar, together with the grain offering, and make atonement for him, and he will be clean.[y]

21 "If, however, he is poor[z] and cannot afford these,[a] he must take one male lamb as a guilt offering to be waved to make atonement for him, together with a tenth of an ephah[d] of fine flour mixed with oil for a grain offering, a log of oil, 22 and two doves or two young pigeons,[b] which he can afford, one for a sin offering and the other for a burnt offering.

23 "On the eighth day he must bring them for his cleansing to the priest at the entrance to the Tent of Meeting, before the LORD.[c] 24 The priest is to take the

14:2 [h] Mt 8:2-4; Mk 1:40-44; Lk 5:12-14; 17:14
14:3 [i] Lev 13:46
14:4 [j] ver 6,49,51,52; Nu 19:6; Ps 51:7
14:6 [k] ver 4
14:7 [l] 2Ki 5:10,14; Isa 52:15; Eze 36:25
14:8 [m] Lev 11:25; 13:6 [n] ver 9 [o] ver 20 [p] Nu 5:2,3; 12:14,15; 2Ch 26:21
14:10 [q] Mt 8:4; Mk 1:44; Lk 5:14 [r] Lev 2:1 [s] ver 12,15,21, 24
14:12 [t] Lev 5:18; 6:6-7 [u] Ex 29:24
14:13 [v] Ex 29:11 [w] Lev 6:24-30; 7:7
14:14 [x] Ex 29:20; Lev 8:23
14:20 [y] ver 8
14:21 [z] Lev 5:7; 12:8 [a] ver 22,32
14:22 [b] Lev 5:7
14:23 [c] ver 10,11

[a] *3* Traditionally *leprosy*; the Hebrew word was used for various diseases affecting the skin—not necessarily leprosy; also elsewhere in this chapter. [b] *10* That is, probably about 6 quarts (about 6.5 liters) [c] *10* That is, probably about 2/3 pint (about 0.3 liter); also in verses 12, 15, 21 and 24 [d] *21* That is, probably about 2 quarts (about 2 liters)

lamb for the guilt offering,[d] together
with the log of oil,[e] and wave them before the LORD as a wave offering.[f] 25He
shall slaughter the lamb for the guilt offering and take some of its blood and
put it on the lobe of the right ear of the
one to be cleansed, on the thumb of his
right hand and on the big toe of his right
foot.[g] 26The priest is to pour some of the
oil into the palm of his own left hand,[h]
27and with his right forefinger sprinkle
some of the oil from his palm seven
times before the LORD. 28Some of the oil
in his palm he is to put on the same
places he put the blood of the guilt offering—on the lobe of the right ear of
the one to be cleansed, on the thumb of
his right hand and on the big toe of his
right foot. 29The rest of the oil in his
palm the priest shall put on the head of
the one to be cleansed, to make atonement for him before the LORD.[i] 30Then
he shall sacrifice the doves or the young
pigeons, which the person can afford,[j]
31one[a] as a sin offering and the other as
a burnt offering,[k] together with the
grain offering. In this way the priest will
make atonement before the LORD on behalf of the one to be cleansed.[l]"

32These are the regulations for anyone
who has an infectious skin disease[m] and
who cannot afford the regular offerings[n]
for his cleansing.

Cleansing From Mildew

33The LORD said to Moses and Aaron,
34"When you enter the land of Canaan,[o]
which I am giving you as your possession,[p] and I put a spreading mildew in a
house in that land, 35the owner of the
house must go and tell the priest, 'I have
seen something that looks like mildew
in my house.' 36The priest is to order the
house to be emptied before he goes in to
examine the mildew, so that nothing in
the house will be pronounced unclean.
After this the priest is to go in and inspect the house. 37He is to examine the
mildew on the walls, and if it has greenish or reddish[q] depressions that appear
to be deeper than the surface of the wall,
38the priest shall go out the doorway of
the house and close it up for seven days.[r]
39On the seventh day[s] the priest shall return to inspect the house. If the mildew
has spread on the walls, 40he is to order
that the contaminated stones be torn

14:24 [d]Nu 6:14 [e]ver 10 [f]ver 12
14:25 [g]ver 14; Ex 29:20
14:26 [h]ver 15
14:29 [i]ver 18
14:30 [j]Lev 5:7
14:31 [k]ver 22; Lev 5:7; 15:15,30 [l]ver 18,19
14:32 [m]Lev 13:2 [n]ver 21
14:34 [o]Ge 12:5; Ex 6:4; Nu 13:2 [p]Ge 17:8; 48:4; Nu 27:12; 32:22; Dt 3:27; 7:1; 32:49
14:37 [q]Lev 13:19
14:38 [r]Lev 13:4
14:39 [s]Lev 13:5

out and thrown into an unclean place
outside the town.[t] 41He must have all the
inside walls of the house scraped and
the material that is scraped off dumped
into an unclean place outside the town.
42Then they are to take other stones to
replace these and take new clay and
plaster the house.

43"If the mildew reappears in the house
after the stones have been torn out and
the house scraped and plastered, 44the
priest is to go and examine it and, if the
mildew has spread in the house, it is a destructive mildew; the house is unclean.[u]
45It must be torn down—its stones, timbers and all the plaster—and taken out of
the town to an unclean place.

46"Anyone who goes into the house
while it is closed up will be unclean till
evening.[v] 47Anyone who sleeps or eats in
the house must wash his clothes.[w]

48"But if the priest comes to examine
it and the mildew has not spread after
the house has been plastered, he shall
pronounce the house clean,[x] because the
mildew is gone. 49To purify the house he
is to take two birds and some cedar
wood, scarlet yarn and hyssop.[y] 50He
shall kill one of the birds over fresh water
in a clay pot.[z] 51Then he is to take the
cedar wood, the hyssop,[a] the scarlet yarn
and the live bird, dip them into the blood
of the dead bird and the fresh water, and
sprinkle the house seven times.[b] 52He
shall purify the house with the bird's
blood, the fresh water, the live bird, the
cedar wood, the hyssop and the scarlet
yarn. 53Then he is to release the live bird
in the open fields[c] outside the town. In
this way he will make atonement for the
house, and it will be clean.[d]"

54These are the regulations for any infectious skin disease,[e] for an itch, 55for
mildew[f] in clothing or in a house, 56and
for a swelling, a rash or a bright spot,[g]
57to determine when something is clean
or unclean.

These are the regulations for infectious skin diseases and mildew.[h]

Discharges Causing Uncleanness

15 The LORD said to Moses and
Aaron, 2"Speak to the Israelites
and say to them: 'When any man has a
bodily discharge,[i] the discharge is un-

14:40 [t]ver 45
14:44 [u]Lev 13:51
14:46 [v]Lev 11:24
14:47 [w]Lev 11:25
14:48 [x]Lev 13:6
14:49 [y]ver 4; 1Ki 4:33; ver 4
14:50 [z]ver 5
14:51 [a]ver 6; Ps 51:7 [b]ver 4,7
14:53 [c]ver 7 [d]ver 20
14:54 [e]Lev 13:2,30
14:55 [f]Lev 13:47-52
14:56 [g]Lev 13:2
14:57 [h]Lev 10:10
15:2 [i]ver 16,32; Lev 22:4; Nu 5:2; 2Sa 3:29; Mt 9:20

[a] *31* Septuagint and Syriac; Hebrew *31such as the person can afford, one*

clean. 3 Whether it continues flowing from his body or is blocked, it will make him unclean. This is how his discharge will bring about uncleanness:

4 " 'Any bed the man with a discharge lies on will be unclean, and anything he sits on will be unclean. 5 Anyone who touches his bed must wash his clothes[j] and bathe with water,[k] and he will be unclean till evening.[l] 6 Whoever sits on anything that the man with a discharge sat on must wash his clothes and bathe with water, and he will be unclean till evening.

7 " 'Whoever touches the man[m] who has a discharge[n] must wash his clothes and bathe with water, and he will be unclean till evening.

8 " 'If the man with the discharge spits[o] on someone who is clean, that person must wash his clothes and bathe with water, and he will be unclean till evening.

9 " 'Everything the man sits on when riding will be unclean, 10 and whoever touches any of the things that were under him will be unclean till evening; whoever picks up those things[p] must wash his clothes and bathe with water, and he will be unclean till evening.

11 " 'Anyone the man with a discharge touches without rinsing his hands with water must wash his clothes and bathe with water, and he will be unclean till evening.

12 " 'A clay pot[q] that the man touches must be broken, and any wooden article[r] is to be rinsed with water.

13 " 'When a man is cleansed from his discharge, he is to count off seven days[s] for his ceremonial cleansing; he must wash his clothes and bathe himself with fresh water, and he will be clean.[t] 14 On the eighth day he must take two doves or two young pigeons[u] and come before the LORD to the entrance to the Tent of Meeting and give them to the priest. 15 The priest is to sacrifice them, the one for a sin offering[v] and the other for a burnt offering.[w] In this way he will make atonement before the LORD for the man because of his discharge.[x]

16 " 'When a man has an emission of semen,[y] he must bathe his whole body with water, and he will be unclean till evening.[z] 17 Any clothing or leather that has semen on it must be washed with water, and it will be unclean till evening. 18 When a man lies with a woman and there is an emission of semen,[a] both must bathe with water, and they will be unclean till evening.

19 " 'When a woman has her regular flow of blood, the impurity of her monthly period[b] will last seven days, and anyone who touches her will be unclean till evening.

20 " 'Anything she lies on during her period will be unclean, and anything she sits on will be unclean. 21 Whoever touches her bed must wash his clothes and bathe with water, and he will be unclean till evening.[c] 22 Whoever touches anything she sits on must wash his clothes and bathe with water, and he will be unclean till evening. 23 Whether it is the bed or anything she was sitting on, when anyone touches it, he will be unclean till evening.

24 " 'If a man lies with her and her monthly flow[d] touches him, he will be unclean for seven days; any bed he lies on will be unclean.

25 " 'When a woman has a discharge of blood for many days at a time other than her monthly period[e] or has a discharge that continues beyond her period, she will be unclean as long as she has the discharge, just as in the days of her period. 26 Any bed she lies on while her discharge continues will be unclean, as is her bed during her monthly period, and anything she sits on will be unclean, as during her period. 27 Whoever touches them will be unclean; he must wash his clothes and bathe with water, and he will be unclean till evening.

28 " 'When she is cleansed from her discharge, she must count off seven days, and after that she will be ceremonially clean. 29 On the eighth day she must take two doves or two young pigeons[f] and bring them to the priest at the entrance to the Tent of Meeting. 30 The priest is to sacrifice one for a sin offering and the other for a burnt offering. In this way he will make atonement for her before the LORD for the uncleanness of her discharge.[g]

31 " 'You must keep the Israelites separate from things that make them unclean, so they will not die in their uncleanness for defiling my dwelling place,[a][h] which is among them.' "

32 These are the regulations for a man

[a] *31* Or *my tabernacle*

15:5 [j] Lev 11:25 [k] Lev 14:8 [l] Lev 11:24
15:7 [m] ver 19; Lev 22:5 [n] ver 16; Lev 22:4
15:8 [o] Nu 12:14
15:10 [p] Nu 19:10
15:12 [q] Lev 6:28 [r] Lev 11:32
15:13 [s] Lev 8:33 [t] ver 5
15:14 [u] Lev 14:22
15:15 [v] Lev 5:7 [w] Lev 14:31 [x] Lev 14:18,19
15:16 [y] ver 2; Lev 22:4; Dt 23:10 [z] ver 5; Dt 23:11
15:18 [a] 1Sa 21:4
15:19 [b] ver 24; Lev 12:2
15:21 [c] ver 27
15:24 [d] ver 19; Lev 12:2; 18:19; 20:18; Eze 18:6
15:25 [e] Mt 9:20; Mk 5:25; Lk 8:43
15:29 [f] Lev 14:22
15:30 [g] Lev 5:10; 14:20,31; 18:19; 2Sa 11:4; Mk 5:25; Lk 8:43
15:31 [h] Lev 20:3; Nu 5:3; 19:13, 20; 2Sa 15:25; 2Ki 21:7; Ps 33:14; 74:7; 76:2; Eze 5:11; 23:38

with a discharge, for anyone made unclean by an emission of semen,[i] 33 for a woman in her monthly period, for a man or a woman with a discharge, and for a man who lies with a woman who is ceremonially unclean.[j]

The Day of Atonement

16 The LORD spoke to Moses after the death of the two sons of Aaron who died when they approached the LORD.[k] 2 The LORD said to Moses: "Tell your brother Aaron not to come whenever he chooses[l] into the Most Holy Place[m] behind the curtain in front of the atonement cover on the ark, or else he will die, because I appear[n] in the cloud[o] over the atonement cover.

3 "This is how Aaron is to enter the sanctuary area:[p] with a young bull for a sin offering and a ram for a burnt offering. 4 He is to put on the sacred linen tunic, with linen undergarments next to his body; he is to tie the linen sash around him and put on the linen turban.[q] These are sacred garments;[r] so he must bathe himself with water[s] before he puts them on. 5 From the Israelite community[t] he is to take two male goats[u] for a sin offering and a ram for a burnt offering.

6 "Aaron is to offer the bull for his own sin offering to make atonement for himself and his household.[v] 7 Then he is to take the two goats and present them before the LORD at the entrance to the Tent of Meeting. 8 He is to cast lots for the two goats—one lot for the LORD and the other for the scapegoat.[a] 9 Aaron shall bring the goat whose lot falls to the LORD and sacrifice it for a sin offering. 10 But the goat chosen by lot as the scapegoat shall be presented alive before the LORD to be used for making atonement[w] by sending it into the desert as a scapegoat.

11 "Aaron shall bring the bull for his own sin offering to make atonement for himself and his household,[x] and he is to slaughter the bull for his own sin offering. 12 He is to take a censer full of burning coals[y] from the altar before the LORD and two handfuls of finely ground fragrant incense[z] and take them behind the curtain. 13 He is to put the incense on the fire before the LORD, and the smoke of the incense will conceal the atonement cover above the Testimony, so that he will not die.[a] 14 He is to take some of the bull's blood[b] and with his finger sprinkle it on the front of the atonement cover; then he shall sprinkle some of it with his finger seven times before the atonement cover.[c]

15 "He shall then slaughter the goat for the sin offering for the people[d] and take its blood behind the curtain[e] and do with it as he did with the bull's blood: He shall sprinkle it on the atonement cover and in front of it. 16 In this way he will make atonement[f] for the Most Holy Place because of the uncleanness and rebellion of the Israelites, whatever their sins have been. He is to do the same for the Tent of Meeting, which is among them in the midst of their uncleanness. 17 No one is to be in the Tent of Meeting from the time Aaron goes in to make atonement in the Most Holy Place until he comes out, having made atonement for himself, his household and the whole community of Israel.

18 "Then he shall come out to the altar[g] that is before the LORD and make atonement for it. He shall take some of the bull's blood and some of the goat's blood and put it on all the horns of the altar.[h] 19 He shall sprinkle some of the blood on it with his finger seven times to cleanse it and to consecrate it from the uncleanness of the Israelites.[i]

20 "When Aaron has finished making atonement for the Most Holy Place, the Tent of Meeting and the altar, he shall bring forward the live goat. 21 He is to lay both hands on the head of the live goat and confess[j] over it all the wickedness and rebellion of the Israelites—all their sins—and put them on the goat's head. He shall send the goat away into the desert in the care of a man appointed for the task. 22 The goat will carry on itself all their sins[k] to a solitary place; and the man shall release it in the desert.

23 "Then Aaron is to go into the Tent of Meeting and take off the linen garments he put on before he entered the Most Holy Place, and he is to leave them there.[l] 24 He shall bathe himself with water in a holy place and put on his regular garments.[m] Then he shall come out and sacrifice the burnt offering for himself and the burnt offering for the people, to make atonement for himself and for the

[a] 8 That is, the goat of removal; Hebrew *azazel*; also in verses 10 and 26

15:32 [i] ver 2
15:33 [j] ver 19,24,25
16:1 [k] Lev 10:1
16:2 [l] Ex 30:10; Heb 9:7 [m] Heb 9:25; 10:19 [n] Ex 25:22 [o] Ex 40:34
16:3 [p] Heb 9:24,25
16:4 [q] Ex 28:39 [r] Ex 28:42 [s] ver 24; Heb 10:22
16:5 [t] Lev 4:13-21 [u] 2Ch 29:23
16:6 [v] Lev 9:7; Heb 5:3; 7:27; 9:7,12
16:10 [w] Isa 53:4-10; Ro 3:25; 1Jn 2:2
16:11 [x] Heb 7:27; 9:7
16:12 [y] Lev 10:1 [z] Ex 30:34-38
16:13 [a] Ex 28:43; Lev 22:9
16:14 [b] Lev 4:5; Heb 9:7,13,25 [c] Lev 4:6
16:15 [d] Heb 9:7,12 [e] Heb 9:3
16:16 [f] Ex 29:36
16:18 [g] Lev 4:7 [h] Lev 4:25
16:19 [i] Eze 43:20
16:21 [j] Lev 5:5
16:22 [k] Isa 53:12
16:23 [l] Eze 42:14; 44:19
16:24 [m] ver 3-5

DISCOVERY 32

THE DAY OF ATONEMENT

The Day of Atonement (*Yom Kippur*) was the most important day in the Jewish religious calendar. It was the only day of the year on which the high priest could enter the Most Holy Place to sprinkle blood on the ark of the covenant. This symbolic action was intended to cover the sins of the nation, as well as his own sin, by substituting the death of another—in this case an animal. This idea of covering sin through substitution is called *atonement*.

Leviticus 16 delineates in detail the elaborate preparations necessary for this ritual. First, the high priest was to wash himself and put on garments reserved especially for that day. Next, he was to offer a bull as a sacrifice for his own sins and for the sins of the other priests, sprinkling some of the blood in front of the ark in the Most Holy Place. Next, two goats were to be set aside, one to be a sin offering for the collective sins of the people, the other to become the "scapegoat."

The two goats symbolized what Jesus Christ would come to earth to accomplish. The first goat represented Jesus' death and the manner in which his blood would be shed to remove the guilt of our sin. The second goat represented the transference of our sins to Jesus, just as in the Old Testament the sins of the people were symbolically transferred to the goat. This "scapegoat" carried away the people's sins "to a solitary place" (verse 22), while Jesus stood alone in our place as our sin was transferred to him.

Sin is a serious problem for which there was no simple solution. Once the Old Testament sacrificial system was operating, the high priest sacrificed animals as substitutes to appease God's wrath against the sins of people. In the New Testament, however, we learn that Jesus came as the "Lamb of God" to remove our sin *once and for all* (1 Peter 2:24). His sacrificial death was the turning point in all of human history. No longer do animals have to die in our stead, and we are no longer separated from God by an impenetrable barrier.

Unlike the high priest, we can approach God without restriction (Hebrews 4:16). In fact, being in relationship with Jesus means that we can enjoy uninterrupted fellowship with the Father. The high priest's special clothing was removed and left behind in the Most Holy Place after he had offered the sacrifices, highlighting the importance of purity when approaching God. But because Jesus has already paid for our sins, God now perceives us as completely spotless and holy. Jesus made a trade with us—he took upon himself our sin and offered in its place his own righteousness (Romans 3:25–26).

Self-Discovery: *Does the fact that your sins have been transferred to Jesus and his righteousness has been transferred to you (2 Corinthians 5:21) give you confidence in approaching God? Have you thanked him for this amazing substitution?*

GO TO DISCOVERY 33 ON PAGE 157

people. 25 He shall also burn the fat of the
sin offering on the altar.
26 "The man who releases the goat as a
16:26 [n] Lev 11:25 scapegoat must wash his clothes[n] and
bathe himself with water; afterward he
may come into the camp. 27 The bull and
the goat for the sin offerings, whose
blood was brought into the Most Holy
16:27 Place to make atonement, must be tak-
[o] Lev 4:12,21; en outside the camp;[o] their hides, flesh
Heb 13:11 and offal are to be burned up. 28 The man
who burns them must wash his clothes
and bathe himself with water; afterward
he may come into the camp.
29 "This is to be a lasting ordinance for
16:29 you: On the tenth day of the seventh
[p] Lev 23:27,32; month you must deny yourselves[a][p] and
Nu 29:7; not do any work—whether native-born
Isa 58:3 or an alien living among you— 30 because on this day atonement will be
made for you, to cleanse you. Then, be-
16:30 fore the LORD, you will be clean from all
[q] Jer 33:8; your sins.[q] 31 It is a sabbath of rest, and
Eph 5:26 you must deny yourselves;[r] it is a lasting
16:31 ordinance. 32 The priest who is anointed
[r] Isa 58:3,5 and ordained to succeed his father as
16:32 high priest is to make atonement. He is
[s] ver 4; to put on the sacred linen garments[s]
Nu 20:26,28 33 and make atonement for the Most
Holy Place, for the Tent of Meeting and
16:33 the altar, and for the priests and all the
[t] ver 11,16-18 people of the community.[t]
34 "This is to be a lasting ordinance for
you: Atonement is to be made once a
16:34 [u] Heb 9:7,25 year[u] for all the sins of the Israelites."
And it was done, as the LORD com-
manded Moses.

Eating Blood Forbidden

17 The LORD said to Moses,
2 "Speak to Aaron and his sons
and to all the Israelites and say to them:
'This is what the LORD has commanded:
3 Any Israelite who sacrifices an ox,[b] a
lamb or a goat in the camp or outside of
it 4 instead of bringing it to the entrance
to the Tent of Meeting to present it as an
offering to the LORD in front of the tab-
17:4 ernacle of the LORD[v]—that man shall be
[v] Dt 12:5-21 [w] Ge 17:14 considered guilty of bloodshed; he has
shed blood and must be cut off from his
people.[w] 5 This is so the Israelites will
bring to the LORD the sacrifices they are
now making in the open fields. They
must bring them to the priest, that is, to
the LORD, at the entrance to the Tent of
Meeting and sacrifice them as fellowship offerings.[c] 6 The priest is to sprinkle
the blood against the altar of the LORD[x] 17:6 [x] Lev 3:2
at the entrance to the Tent of Meeting [y] Nu 18:17
and burn the fat as an aroma pleasing to
the LORD.[y] 7 They must no longer offer 17:7
any of their sacrifices to the goat idols[d][z] [z] Ex 22:20;
to whom they prostitute themselves.[a] 2Ch 11:15
This is to be a lasting ordinance for [a] Ex 32:8; 34:15; Dt 32:17;
them and for the generations to come.' 1Co 10:20
8 "Say to them: 'Any Israelite or any
alien living among them who offers a
burnt offering or sacrifice 9 and does not
bring it to the entrance to the Tent of
Meeting[b] to sacrifice it to the LORD—that 17:9 [b] ver 4
man must be cut off from his people.
10 " 'Any Israelite or any alien living
among them who eats any blood—I will
set my face against that person who eats 17:10
blood[c] and will cut him off from his peo- [c] Ge 9:4;
ple. 11 For the life of a creature is in the Lev 3:17; Dt 12:16,23;
blood,[d] and I have given it to you to make 1Sa 14:33
atonement for yourselves on the altar; it 17:11
is the blood that makes atonement for [d] ver 14; Ge 9:4
one's life.[e] 12 Therefore I say to the Israel- [e] Heb 9:22
ites, "None of you may eat blood, nor may
an alien living among you eat blood."
13 " 'Any Israelite or any alien living
among you who hunts any animal or
bird that may be eaten must drain out
the blood and cover it with earth,[f] 14 be- 17:13 [f] Lev 7:26;
cause the life of every creature is its Dt 12:16
blood. That is why I have said to the Israelites, "You must not eat the blood of
any creature, because the life of every

[a] 29 Or *must fast*; also in verse 31 [b] 3 The Hebrew word can include both male and female. [c] 5 Traditionally *peace offerings* [d] 7 Or *demons*

KOSHER CODE

One of the *kosher* regulations (the rules about what was acceptable to God) was that God's people were not to eat blood. Blood represented life and was used during sacrifices to repair the damage caused by sin (Leviticus 17). In the same way, Jesus' blood is the ultimate sacrifice for our sins. When he instituted the celebration of the Lord's Supper, Jesus announced, "This cup is the new covenant in my blood, which is poured out for you" (Luke 22:20). The fact that his blood repaired the damage caused by sin is one of the most important truths taught in the New Testament (Romans 3:25–26; 2 Corinthians 5:17,19,21; 1 Peter 1:18–19).

17:14 creature is its blood; anyone who eats it
g ver 11; Ge 9:4 must be cut off."[g]
[15]" 'Anyone, whether native-born or
17:15 alien, who eats anything found dead or
h Ex 22:31; torn by wild animals[h] must wash his
Dt 14:21 clothes and bathe with water, and he will
be ceremonially unclean till evening;
then he will be clean. [16]But if he does not
wash his clothes and bathe himself, he
will be held responsible.' "

Unlawful Sexual Relations

18 The LORD said to Moses,
18:2 [2]"Speak to the Israelites and say
i Ex 6:7; to them: 'I am the LORD your God.[i] [3]You
Lev 11:44; must not do as they do in Egypt, where
Eze 20:5 you used to live, and you must not do as
18:3 they do in the land of Canaan, where I
j ver 24-30; am bringing you. Do not follow their
Ex 23:24; practices.[j] [4]You must obey my laws and
Lev 20:23 be careful to follow my decrees. I am the
18:4 LORD your God.[k] [5]Keep my decrees and
k ver 2 laws, for the man who obeys them will
18:5 live by them.[l] I am the LORD.
l Eze 20:11; [6]" 'No one is to approach any close rel-
Ro 10:5*; ative to have sexual relations. I am the
Gal 3:12* LORD.
18:7 [7]" 'Do not dishonor your father[m] by
m Lev 20:11 having sexual relations with your moth-
n Eze 22:10 er.[n] She is your mother; do not have relations with her.
18:8 [8]" 'Do not have sexual relations with
o 1Co 5:1 your father's wife;[o] that would dishonor
p Lev 20:11 your father.[p]
18:9 [9]" 'Do not have sexual relations with
q Lev 20:17 your sister,[q] either your father's daughter
or your mother's daughter, whether she
was born in the same home or elsewhere.
[10]" 'Do not have sexual relations with
your son's daughter or your daughter's
daughter; that would dishonor you.
[11]" 'Do not have sexual relations with
the daughter of your father's wife, born
to your father; she is your sister.
18:12 [12]" 'Do not have sexual relations with
r Lev 20:19 your father's sister;[r] she is your father's
close relative.
[13]" 'Do not have sexual relations with
your mother's sister, because she is your
mother's close relative.
[14]" 'Do not dishonor your father's
18:14 brother by approaching his wife to have
s Lev 20:20 sexual relations; she is your aunt.[s]
18:15 [15]" 'Do not have sexual relations with
t Lev 20:12 your daughter-in-law.[t] She is your son's
wife; do not have relations with her.
[16]" 'Do not have sexual relations with
your brother's wife;[u] that would dishon- 18:16 u Lev 20:21
or your brother.
[17]" 'Do not have sexual relations with 18:17
both a woman and her daughter.[v] Do not v Lev 20:14
have sexual relations with either her son's
daughter or her daughter's daughter; they
are her close relatives. That is wickedness.
[18]" 'Do not take your wife's sister as a
rival wife and have sexual relations with
her while your wife is living. 18:19
[19]" 'Do not approach a woman to have w Lev 15:24;
sexual relations during the uncleanness 20:18
of her monthly period.[w] 18:20
[20]" 'Do not have sexual relations with x Ex 20:14;
your neighbor's wife[x] and defile yourself Lev 20:10;
with her. Mt 5:27,28; 1Co 6:9;
[21]" 'Do not give any of your children[y] Heb 13:4
to be sacrificed[a] to Molech,[z] for you 18:21 y Dt 12:31
must not profane the name of your z Lev 20:2-5
God.[a] I am the LORD. a Lev 19:12;
[22]" 'Do not lie with a man as one lies 21:6; Eze 36:20
with a woman;[b] that is detestable. 18:22 b Lev 20:13;
[23]" 'Do not have sexual relations with Dt 23:18;
an animal and defile yourself with it. A Ro 1:27
woman must not present herself to an 18:23
animal to have sexual relations with it; c Ex 22:19;
that is a perversion.[c] Lev 20:15; Dt 27:21
[24]" 'Do not defile yourselves in any of
these ways, because this is how the na- 18:24
tions that I am going to drive out before d ver 3,27,30
you[d] became defiled.[e] [25]Even the land e Dt 18:12
was defiled; so I punished it for its sin,[f] 18:25
and the land vomited out its inhabi- f Lev 20:23;
tants.[g] [26]But you must keep my decrees Dt 9:5; 18:12 g ver 28;
and my laws. The native-born and the Lev 20:22
aliens living among you must not do any
of these detestable things, [27]for all these
things were done by the people who
lived in the land before you, and the land
became defiled. [28]And if you defile the
land, it will vomit you out as it vomited
out the nations that were before you.
[29]" 'Everyone who does any of these
detestable things—such persons must
be cut off from their people. [30]Keep my
requirements[h] and do not follow any of 18:30 h Dt 11:1 i ver 2
the detestable customs that were prac-
ticed before you came and do not defile
yourselves with them. I am the LORD
your God.[i]' "

Various Laws

19 The LORD said to Moses,
[2]"Speak to the entire assembly
of Israel and say to them: 'Be holy be- 19:2 j 1Pe 1:16*;
cause I, the LORD your God, am holy.[j] Lev 11:44

[a] 21 Or *to be passed through* ⌞*the fire*⌟

DISCOVERY 33

DECLARED HOLY

God is holy. The Bible emphasizes this throughout its pages but especially in the book of Leviticus. The word *holy* occurs 74 times in this book alone. Every rule and regulation contained in it reflect God's holiness, his essential character. This holy God calls his followers to the same standard of righteousness (Leviticus 11:44–45; 19:1–2; 20:7,26). The word *holy* means "separated." God's holiness implies two things: First, he is absolutely perfect, completely separate from sin and evil (James 1:13). Second, God is separate from and stands above the created order in terms of his majesty and glory (Isaiah 6:1–5).

Leviticus defined for the people what it meant to live a holy life in relationship to a holy God. Chapters 1—16 focus mainly on the worship of our holy God; chapters 17—27 discuss primarily our daily walk with him. Every dimension of life and worship is covered in these instructions! It's interesting to note that while this book is the *first* one studied by Jewish children, it is often the *last* book to be considered by Christians.

No one could possibly keep all of the regulations contained in Leviticus. God knew that, so he provided the Day of Atonement, the "centerpiece" of Leviticus (chapter 16). On this one day the high priest would offer a special annual sacrifice to cover the sin of the people. Failure to keep the smallest detail of God's commands constitutes sin, and the only reparation for sin is the shedding of blood. In addition to the Day of Atonement, people *continually* brought sin offerings to God—because they continually sinned.

God's character has never changed; he is *eternally* holy. While not one of us can meet the standard, he still requires absolute holiness from each of us (Romans 3:23). But despite our sin, God *declares* us holy—completely righteous and justified—in Jesus Christ! His was the sacrifice of atonement; in him we are forgiven and our sin forever removed. When God looks at us, he perceives us in the same way he views Jesus—as perfect and righteous (Romans 3:25; 4:1–2). As we get to know him, God the Holy Spirit works in us to change us so that our lives begin to reflect his holiness (Galatians 5:16–26; James 4:7–10).

"Prepare your minds for action; be self-controlled; set your hope fully on the grace to be given you when Jesus Christ is revealed. As obedient children, do not conform to the evil desires you had when you lived in ignorance. But just as he who called you is holy, so be holy in all you do; for it is written: 'Be holy, because I am holy.'" (1 Peter 1:13–16).

Self-Discovery: *Picture what it means for you to be declared holy in God's sight. What might God see when he looks at your life and declares you blameless because of the sacrifice of Jesus?*

GO TO DISCOVERY 34 ON PAGE 162

19:3 [k]Ex 20:12 [l]Lev 11:44 3“ ‘Each of you must respect his mother and father,[k] and you must observe my
Sabbaths. I am the LORD your God.[l]
19:4 [m]Ex 20:4,23; 34:17; Lev 26:1; Ps 96:5; 115:4-7 4“ ‘Do not turn to idols or make gods
of cast metal for yourselves.[m] I am the
LORD your God.
5“ ‘When you sacrifice a fellowship offering[a] to the LORD, sacrifice it in such a
way that it will be accepted on your behalf. 6It shall be eaten on the day you
sacrifice it or on the next day; anything
left over until the third day must be
burned up. 7If any of it is eaten on the
third day, it is impure and will not be accepted. 8Whoever eats it will be held responsible because he has desecrated
what is holy to the LORD; that person
must be cut off from his people.
9“ ‘When you reap the harvest of your
land, do not reap to the very edges of
your field or gather the gleanings of your
19:9 [n]Lev 23:10,22; Dt 24:19-22 harvest.[n] 10Do not go over your vineyard
a second time or pick up the grapes that
have fallen. Leave them for the poor and
the alien. I am the LORD your God.
19:11 [o]Ex 20:15 [p]Eph 4:25 11“ ‘Do not steal.[o]
“ ‘Do not lie.[p]
“ ‘Do not deceive one another.
19:12 [q]Ex 20:7; Mt 5:33 12“ ‘Do not swear falsely by my name[q]
and so profane the name of your God. I
am the LORD.
19:13 [r]Ex 22:15,25-27 [s]Dt 24:15; Jas 5:4 13“ ‘Do not defraud your neighbor or
rob him.[r]
“ ‘Do not hold back the wages of a
hired man overnight.[s]
14“ ‘Do not curse the deaf or put a
19:14 [t]Dt 27:18 stumbling block in front of the blind,[t]
but fear your God. I am the LORD.
19:15 [u]Ex 23:2,6 [v]Dt 1:17 15“ ‘Do not pervert justice;[u] do not
show partiality[v] to the poor or fa-
voritism to the great, but judge your
neighbor fairly.
19:16 [w]Ps 15:3; Eze 22:9 [x]Ex 23:7 16“ ‘Do not go about spreading slander[w] among your people.
“ ‘Do not do anything that endangers
your neighbor's life.[x] I am the LORD.
19:17 [y]1Jn 2:9; 3:15 [z]Mt 18:15; Lk 17:3 17“ ‘Do not hate your brother in your
heart.[y] Rebuke your neighbor frankly[z]
so you will not share in his guilt.
19:18 [a]Ro 12:19 [b]Ps 103:9 [c]Mt 5:43*; 19:16*; 22:39*; Mk 12:31*; Lk 10:27*; Jn 13:34; Ro 13:9*; Gal 5:14*; Jas 2:8* 18“ ‘Do not seek revenge[a] or bear a
grudge[b] against one of your people, but
love your neighbor as yourself.[c] I am the
LORD.
19“ ‘Keep my decrees.
“ ‘Do not mate different kinds of animals.

“ ‘Do not plant your field with two 19:19 [d]Dt 22:9 [e]Dt 22:11
kinds of seed.[d]
“ ‘Do not wear clothing woven of two
kinds of material.[e]
20“ ‘If a man sleeps with a woman who
is a slave girl promised to another man
but who has not been ransomed or giv-
en her freedom, there must be due punishment. Yet they are not to be put to
death, because she had not been freed.
21The man, however, must bring a ram
to the entrance to the Tent of Meeting 19:21 [f]Lev 5:15
for a guilt offering to the LORD.[f] 22With
the ram of the guilt offering the priest is
to make atonement for him before the
LORD for the sin he has committed, and
his sin will be forgiven.
23“ ‘When you enter the land and
plant any kind of fruit tree, regard its
fruit as forbidden.[b] For three years you
are to consider it forbidden[b]; it must not
be eaten. 24In the fourth year all its fruit
will be holy,[g] an offering of praise to the 19:24 [g]Pr 3:9
LORD. 25But in the fifth year you may eat
its fruit. In this way your harvest will be
increased. I am the LORD your God.
26“ ‘Do not eat any meat with the
blood still in it.[h] 19:26 [h]Lev 17:10 [i]Dt 18:10
“ ‘Do not practice divination or sor-
cery.[i]
27“ ‘Do not cut the hair at the sides of
your head or clip off the edges of your 19:27 [j]Lev 21:5
beard.[j]
28“ ‘Do not cut your bodies for the
dead or put tattoo marks on yourselves.
I am the LORD.
29“ ‘Do not degrade your daughter by
making her a prostitute,[k] or the land will 19:29 [k]Dt 23:18
turn to prostitution and be filled with
wickedness.
30“ ‘Observe my Sabbaths and have rev-
erence for my sanctuary. I am the LORD.[l] 19:30 [l]Lev 26:2
31“ ‘Do not turn to mediums or seek
out spiritists,[m] for you will be defiled by 19:31 [m]Lev 20:6; Isa 8:19
them. I am the LORD your God.
32“ ‘Rise in the presence of the aged,
show respect for the elderly[n] and revere 19:32 [n]1Ti 5:1
your God. I am the LORD.
33“ ‘When an alien lives with you in
your land, do not mistreat him. 34The
alien living with you must be treated as
one of your native-born.[o] Love him as 19:34 [o]Ex 12:48 [p]Dt 10:19
yourself, for you were aliens in Egypt.[p] I
am the LORD your God.
35“ ‘Do not use dishonest standards

[a] 5 Traditionally *peace offering* [b] 23 Hebrew *uncircumcised*

when measuring length, weight or
quantity. 36Use honest scales and honest
weights, an honest ephah[a] and an hon-
19:36 [q]Dt 25:13-15 est hin.[b][q] I am the LORD your God, who
brought you out of Egypt.
37" 'Keep all my decrees and all my
laws and follow them. I am the LORD.' "

Punishments for Sin

20 The LORD said to Moses, 2"Say
to the Israelites: 'Any Israelite or
any alien living in Israel who gives[c] any of
his children to Molech must be put to
death. The people of the community are
to stone him. 3I will set my face against
that man and I will cut him off from his
people; for by giving his children to Mo-
20:3 [r]Lev 15:31 lech, he has defiled my sanctuary[r] and
[s]Lev 18:21 profaned my holy name.[s] 4If the people
of the community close their eyes when
that man gives one of his children to Mo-
20:4 [t]Dt 17:2-5 lech and they fail to put him to death,[t] 5I
will set my face against that man and his
family and will cut off from their people
both him and all who follow him in pros-
tituting themselves to Molech.
6" 'I will set my face against the person who turns to mediums and spiritists
20:6 [u]Lev 19:31 to prostitute himself by following them,
and I will cut him off from his people.[u]
20:7 [v]Eph 1:4; 7" 'Consecrate yourselves and be
1Pe 1:16* holy,[v] because I am the LORD your God.
20:8 [w]Ex 31:13 8Keep my decrees and follow them. I am
the LORD, who makes you holy.[d][w]
20:9 9" 'If anyone curses his father or
[x]Dt 27:16 mother,[x] he must be put to death.[y] He
[y]Ex 21:17; Mt 15:4*; has cursed his father or his mother, and
Mk 7:10* his blood will be on his own head.[z]
[z]ver 11; 2Sa 1:16 10" 'If a man commits adultery with
another man's wife[a]—with the wife of
20:10 [a]Ex 20:14; his neighbor—both the adulterer and
Dt 5:18; 22:22 the adulteress must be put to death.
20:11 11" 'If a man sleeps with his father's
[b]Lev 18:7; Dt 27:23 wife, he has dishonored his father.[b] Both
the man and the woman must be put to
death; their blood will be on their own
heads.
20:12 12" 'If a man sleeps with his daughter-
[c]Lev 18:15 in-law,[c] both of them must be put to
death. What they have done is a perversion; their blood will be on their own
heads.
13" 'If a man lies with a man as one lies
20:13 with a woman, both of them have done
[d]Lev 18:22 what is detestable.[d] They must be put to
death; their blood will be on their own
heads.

14" 'If a man marries both a woman
and her mother,[e] it is wicked. Both he 20:14 [e]Lev 18:17
and they must be burned in the fire, so [f]Dt 27:23
that no wickedness will be among you.[f]
15" 'If a man has sexual relations with
an animal,[g] he must be put to death, and 20:15 [g]Lev 18:23
you must kill the animal.
16" 'If a woman approaches an animal
to have sexual relations with it, kill both
the woman and the animal. They must
be put to death; their blood will be on
their own heads.
17" 'If a man marries his sister[h], the 20:17 [h]Lev 18:9
daughter of either his father or his moth-
er, and they have sexual relations, it is a
disgrace. They must be cut off before the
eyes of their people. He has dishonored
his sister and will be held responsible.
18" 'If a man lies with a woman during
her monthly period[i] and has sexual re- 20:18
lations with her, he has exposed the [i]Lev 15:24; 18:19
source of her flow, and she has also uncovered it. Both of them must be cut off
from their people.
19" 'Do not have sexual relations with
the sister of either your mother or your
father,[j] for that would dishonor a close 20:19
relative; both of you would be held re- [j]Lev 18:12-13
sponsible.
20" 'If a man sleeps with his aunt,[k] he 20:20 [k]Lev 18:14
has dishonored his uncle. They will be
held responsible; they will die childless.
21" 'If a man marries his brother's wife,[l] 20:21 [l]Lev 18:16
it is an act of impurity; he has dishon-
ored his brother. They will be childless.
22" 'Keep all my decrees and laws and
follow them, so that the land[m] where I 20:22
am bringing you to live may not vomit [m]Lev 18:25-28
you out. 23You must not live according 20:23
to the customs of the nations[n] I am go- [n]Lev 18:3
ing to drive out before you.[o] Because [o]Lev 18:24,27, 30
they did all these things, I abhorred
them. 24But I said to you, "You will possess their land; I will give it to you as an
inheritance, a land flowing with milk 20:24
and honey."[p] I am the LORD your God, [p]Ex 3:8; 13:5;
who has set you apart from the nations.[q] 33:3 [q]Ex 33:16
25" 'You must therefore make a dis-
tinction between clean and unclean animals and between unclean and clean
birds.[r] Do not defile yourselves by any 20:25
animal or bird or anything that moves [r]Lev 11:1-47;
along the ground—those which I have Dt 14:3-21
set apart as unclean for you. 26You are to

[a] 36 An ephah was a dry measure. [b] 36 A hin was a liquid measure. [c] 2 Or *sacrifices*; also in verses 3 and 4 [d] 8 Or *who sanctifies you*; or *who sets you apart as holy*

20:26 be holy to me[a] because I, the LORD, am
s Lev 19:2 holy,[s] and I have set you apart from the
nations to be my own.
27“ ‘A man or woman who is a medi-
20:27 um or spiritist among you must be put
t Lev 19:31 to death.[t] You are to stone them; their
blood will be on their own heads.’ ”

Rules for Priests

21 The LORD said to Moses, “Speak
to the priests, the sons of Aaron, and say to them: ‘A priest must not
make himself ceremonially unclean for
21:1 u Eze 44:25 any of his people who die,[u] 2except for a
close relative, such as his mother or fa-
ther, his son or daughter, his brother, 3or
an unmarried sister who is dependent
on him since she has no husband—for
her he may make himself unclean. 4He
must not make himself unclean for people related to him by marriage,[b] and so
defile himself.
5“ ‘Priests must not shave their heads
21:5 v Eze 44:20 or shave off the edges of their beards[v] or
w Lev 19:28; Dt 14:1 cut their bodies.[w] 6They must be holy to
their God and must not profane the
21:6 x Lev 18:21 name of their God.[x] Because they pres-
y Lev 3:11 ent the offerings made to the LORD by
fire,[y] the food of their God, they are to be
holy.
7“ ‘They must not marry women defiled by prostitution or divorced from
21:7 z ver 13,14 their husbands,[z] because priests are
a Eze 44:22 holy to their God.[a] 8Regard them as
21:8 b ver 6 holy,[b] because they offer up the food of
your God. Consider them holy, because
I the LORD am holy—I who make you
holy.[c]
9“ ‘If a priest’s daughter defiles herself
by becoming a prostitute, she disgraces
21:9 c Ge 38:24; Lev 19:29 her father; she must be burned in the
fire.[c]
10“ ‘The high priest, the one among
his brothers who has had the anointing
oil poured on his head and who has been
21:10 d Lev 16:32 ordained to wear the priestly garments,[d]
e Lev 10:6 must not let his hair become unkempt[d]
21:11 or tear his clothes.[e] 11He must not enter
f Nu 19:11,13,14 a place where there is a dead body.[f] He
g Lev 19:28 must not make himself unclean,[g] even
for his father or mother, 12nor leave the
sanctuary of his God or desecrate it, be-
21:12 cause he has been dedicated by the
h Ex 29:6-7; Lev 10:7 anointing oil[h] of his God. I am the LORD.
13“ ‘The woman he marries must be a
21:13 i Eze 44:22 virgin.[i] 14He must not marry a widow, a
divorced woman, or a woman defiled by
prostitution, but only a virgin from his
own people, 15so he will not defile his
offspring among his people. I am the
LORD, who makes him holy.[e]’ ”
16The LORD said to Moses, 17“Say to
Aaron: ‘For the generations to come
none of your descendants who has a de-
fect may come near to offer the food of 21:17 j ver 6
his God.[j] 18No man who has any defect[k]
may come near: no man who is blind or 21:18 k Lev 22:19-25
lame, disfigured or deformed; 19no man
with a crippled foot or hand, 20or who is
hunchbacked or dwarfed, or who has
any eye defect, or who has festering or 21:20 l Dt 23:1;
running sores or damaged testicles.[l] Isa 56:3
21No descendant of Aaron the priest
who has any defect is to come near to
present the offerings made to the LORD
by fire. He has a defect; he must not
come near to offer the food of his God.
22He may eat the most holy food of his 21:22
God,[m] as well as the holy food; 23yet be- m 1Co 9:13
cause of his defect, he must not go near
the curtain or approach the altar, and so
desecrate my sanctuary. I am the LORD,
who makes them holy.[f]’ ”
24So Moses told this to Aaron and his
sons and to all the Israelites.

22 The LORD said to Moses, 2“Tell
Aaron and his sons to treat with
respect the sacred offerings the Israelites
consecrate to me, so they will not profane my holy name. I am the LORD.
3“Say to them: ‘For the generations to
come, if any of your descendants is ceremonially unclean and yet comes near
the sacred offerings that the Israelites
consecrate to the LORD, that person 22:3
must be cut off from my presence.[n] I am n Lev 7:20,21;
the LORD. Nu 19:13
4“ ‘If a descendant of Aaron has an infectious skin disease[g] or a bodily dis- 22:4
charge,[o] he may not eat the sacred offer- o Lev 14:1-32;
ings until he is cleansed. He will also be 15:2-15
unclean if he touches something defiled p Lev 11:24-28,
by a corpse[p] or by anyone who has an 39
emission of semen, 5or if he touches any 22:5
crawling thing[q] that makes him un- q Lev 11:24-28,
clean, or any person[r] who makes him 43 r Lev 15:7
unclean, whatever the uncleanness may

[a] 26 Or *be my holy ones* [b] 4 Or *unclean as a leader among his people* [c] 8 Or *who sanctify you*; or *who set you apart as holy* [d] 10 Or *not uncover his head* [e] 15 Or *who sanctifies him*; or *who sets him apart as holy* [f] 23 Or *who sanctifies them*; or *who sets them apart as holy* [g] 4 Traditionally *leprosy*; the Hebrew word was used for various diseases affecting the skin—not necessarily leprosy.

be. 6 The one who touches any such
thing will be unclean till evening. He
must not eat any of the sacred offerings
unless he has bathed himself with water.
7 When the sun goes down, he will be
22:7 clean, and after that he may eat the sa-
[s] Nu 18:11 cred offerings, for they are his food.[s] 8 He
22:8 must not eat anything found dead[t] or
[t] Lev 11:39 [u] Ex 22:31; torn by wild animals,[u] and so become
Lev 17:15 unclean[v] through it. I am the LORD.
[v] Lev 11:40 9 " 'The priests are to keep my require-
22:9 ments so that they do not become guilty
[w] ver 16; and die[w] for treating them with con-
Ex 28:43 tempt. I am the LORD, who makes them
holy.[a]

10 " 'No one outside a priest's family
may eat the sacred offering, nor may the
guest of a priest or his hired worker eat
it. 11 But if a priest buys a slave with
22:11 money, or if a slave is born in his house-
[x] Ge 17:13; hold, that slave may eat his food.[x] 12 If a
Ex 12:44 priest's daughter marries anyone other
than a priest, she may not eat any of the
sacred contributions. 13 But if a priest's
daughter becomes a widow or is divorced, yet has no children, and she returns to live in her father's house as in
her youth, she may eat of her father's
food. No unauthorized person, however,
may eat any of it.

14 " 'If anyone eats a sacred offering by
mistake, he must make restitution to
22:14 the priest for the offering and add a fifth
[y] Lev 5:15 of the value[y] to it. 15 The priests must not
22:15 desecrate the sacred offerings the Israel-
[z] Nu 18:32 ites present to the LORD[z] 16 by allowing
them to eat the sacred offerings and so
bring upon them guilt requiring pay-
22:16 ment.[a] I am the LORD, who makes them
[a] ver 9 holy.' "

Unacceptable Sacrifices

17 The LORD said to Moses, 18 "Speak to
Aaron and his sons and to all the Israelites and say to them: 'If any of you—either an Israelite or an alien living in Is-
22:18 rael—presents a gift[b] for a burnt
[b] Lev 1:2 offering to the LORD, either to fulfill a
22:19 vow or as a freewill offering, 19 you must
[c] Lev 1:3 present a male without defect[c] from the
22:20 cattle, sheep or goats in order that it
[d] Dt 15:21; 17:1; may be accepted on your behalf. 20 Do
Mal 1:8,14; Heb 9:14; not bring anything with a defect,[d] be-
1Pe 1:19 cause it will not be accepted on your be-
22:21 half. 21 When anyone brings from the
[e] Lev 3:6; herd or flock a fellowship offering[b] [e] to
Nu 15:3,8 the LORD to fulfill a special vow or as a
freewill offering, it must be without defect or blemish to be acceptable. 22 Do
not offer to the LORD the blind, the injured or the maimed, or anything with
warts or festering or running sores. Do
not place any of these on the altar as an
offering made to the LORD by fire. 23 You
may, however, present as a freewill offering an ox[c] or a sheep that is deformed or
stunted, but it will not be accepted in
fulfillment of a vow. 24 You must not offer
to the LORD an animal whose testicles
are bruised, crushed, torn or cut.[f] You 22:24 [f] Lev 21:20
must not do this in your own land, 25 and
you must not accept such animals from
the hand of a foreigner and offer them as
the food of your God.[g] They will not be 22:25 [g] Lev 21:6
accepted on your behalf, because they
are deformed and have defects.' "

26 The LORD said to Moses, 27 "When a
calf, a lamb or a goat is born, it is to re- 22:27
main with its mother for seven days.[h] [h] Ex 22:30
From the eighth day on, it will be acceptable as an offering made to the LORD
by fire. 28 Do not slaughter a cow or a 22:28
sheep and its young on the same day.[i] [i] Dt 22:6,7

29 "When you sacrifice a thank offer- 22:29
ing[j] to the LORD, sacrifice it in such a [j] Lev 7:12;
way that it will be accepted on your be- Ps 107:22
half. 30 It must be eaten that same day; 22:30
leave none of it till morning.[k] I am the [k] Lev 7:15
LORD.

31 "Keep[l] my commands and follow 22:31
them. I am the LORD. 32 Do not profane [l] Dt 4:2,40;
my holy name.[m] I must be acknowl- Ps 105:45
edged as holy by the Israelites.[n] I am the 22:32 [m] Lev 18:21
LORD, who makes[d] you holy[e] 33 and who [n] Lev 10:3
brought you out of Egypt to be your 22:33
God.[o] I am the LORD." [o] Lev 11:45

23 The LORD said to Moses,
2 "Speak to the Israelites and say
to them: 'These are my appointed
feasts,[p] the appointed feasts of the LORD, 23:2
which you are to proclaim as sacred as- [p] ver 4,37,44;
semblies.[q] Nu 29:39 [q] ver 21,27

The Sabbath

3 " 'There are six days when you may 23:3 [r] Ex 20:9
work,[r] but the seventh day is a Sabbath [s] Ex 20:10;
of rest,[s] a day of sacred assembly. You are 31:13-17; Lev 19:3;
not to do any work; wherever you live, it Dt 5:13;
is a Sabbath to the LORD. Heb 4:9,10

[a] 9 Or *who sanctifies them*; or *who sets them apart as holy*; also in verse 16 [b] 21 Traditionally *peace offering* [c] 23 The Hebrew word can include both male and female. [d] 32 Or *made* [e] 32 Or *who sanctifies you*; or *who sets you apart as holy*

THE JEWISH RELIGIOUS CALENDAR

Every aspect of Jewish life centered around the activities of the temple and the related religious celebrations. Each ritual served a dual purpose, reminding God's people of their past and directing their attention to their future hope. The New Testament points to Jesus Christ as the one in whom all of the feasts and festivals find their fulfillment (see Matthew 12:1–14; 26:17; Romans 8:23; 1 Corinthians 15:20–23).

An ongoing celebration is the *Sabbath*. On one day each week God wanted his people to focus their attention exclusively upon him. The Sabbath reminded them that God had created the world and then rested to enjoy his work, recalled the covenant God had made with Moses (Exodus 20:11) and provided a glimpse into the future, when they would be delivered from sin and its consequences (Romans 6:5–8). Only through Jesus' death were we able to experience that deliverance (Hebrews 4:1–11).

Passover is the central Jewish religious feast, reminding the people of God's deliverance from slavery in Egypt (Exodus 12:1–30). Ultimately, Jesus is the One who frees us from our bondage to sin (1 Corinthians 5:7). When he celebrated the Passover with his disciples, our Lord redirected their attention to himself as God's Passover Lamb (Matthew 26:17–30).

The *Feast of Unleavened Bread* (*Matsah*) reminded the people that they had been set apart from Egypt and that God no longer wanted them to associate with that sinful nation (Exodus 13:1–10). It also directed the focus of the people to the fellowship possible with God. In the New Testament we discover that Jesus is God's provision for that intimate relationship with himself (1 John 1:1–4).

The celebration of *Firstfruits* recalled the bountiful harvest God had given the Israelites once they had entered the promised land (Leviticus 23:10). The festival instilled hope for the day on which God would gather his people to himself. Jesus offered eternal life, and Paul described this as the first resurrection harvest (1 Thessalonians 4:13–18).

The *Feast of Weeks* (*Pentecost*) celebrated the firstfruits of the grain harvest (Leviticus 23:16) and pointed to the day on which God would "harvest" the redeemed in Jesus Christ (Acts 2). The *Feast of Trumpets* (*Rosh Hashanah)* marked the beginning of the civil year (Leviticus 23:23–25) and reminded the Israelites of their hope that God would one day regather his people (Ezekiel 37:12–14; 1 Corinthians 15:52). The *Feast of Tabernacles* or *Booths (Succoth)* called to mind the time the people had spent living in the desert (Leviticus 23:43) and reminds us that there will come a day in which we will find our place of belonging in Jesus (Zechariah 14:16; John 7:25–44).

Finally, the *Day of Atonement (Yom Kippur)* was the day of cleansing from national sin (Leviticus 16). It pointed to Jesus' future death in our place to atone for our sins (Hebrews 9:28; 10:19–22; see also Discovery #32 on Page 154).

***Self-Discovery:** How can elements of these different celebrations enrich your worship of Jesus this weekend?*

GO TO DISCOVERY 35 ON PAGE 173

The Passover and Unleavened Bread

4" 'These are the LORD's appointed
feasts, the sacred assemblies you are to
proclaim at their appointed times: 5The
23:5 LORD's Passover begins at twilight on the
[t] Ex 12:18-19; fourteenth day of the first month.[t] 6On
Nu 28:16-17; the fifteenth day of that month the
Dt 16:1-8 LORD's Feast of Unleavened Bread begins; for seven days you must eat bread
made without yeast. 7On the first day
23:7 hold a sacred assembly[u] and do no reg-
[u] ver 3,8 ular work. 8For seven days present an offering made to the LORD by fire. And on
the seventh day hold a sacred assembly
and do no regular work.' "

Firstfruits

9The LORD said to Moses, 10"Speak to
the Israelites and say to them: 'When
you enter the land I am going to give you
23:10 and you reap its harvest, bring to the
[v] Ex 23:16,19; priest a sheaf[v] of the first grain you har-
34:26 vest. 11He is to wave the sheaf before the
23:11 LORD[w] so it will be accepted on your be-
[w] Ex 29:24 half; the priest is to wave it on the day after the Sabbath. 12On the day you wave
the sheaf, you must sacrifice as a burnt
offering to the LORD a lamb a year old
without defect, 13together with its grain
23:13 offering[x] of two-tenths of an ephah[a] of
[x] Lev 2:14-16; fine flour mixed with oil—an offering
6:20 made to the LORD by fire, a pleasing aroma—and its drink offering of a quarter
of a hin[b] of wine. 14You must not eat any
bread, or roasted or new grain, until the
very day you bring this offering to your
23:14 God.[y] This is to be a lasting ordinance
[y] Ex 34:26 [z] Nu 15:21 for the generations to come,[z] wherever
you live.

Feast of Weeks

15" 'From the day after the Sabbath,
the day you brought the sheaf of the
wave offering, count off seven full weeks.
16Count off fifty days up to the day after
23:16 the seventh Sabbath,[a] and then present
[a] Nu 28:26; Ac 2:1 an offering of new grain to the LORD.
17From wherever you live, bring two
loaves made of two-tenths of an ephah
of fine flour, baked with yeast, as a wave
23:17 offering of firstfruits[b] to the LORD. 18Pre-
[b] Ex 34:22; Lev 2:12 sent with this bread seven male lambs,
each a year old and without defect, one
young bull and two rams. They will be a
burnt offering to the LORD, together with
their grain offerings and drink offerings—an offering made by fire, an aroma pleasing to the LORD. 19Then sacrifice one male goat for a sin offering and
two lambs, each a year old, for a fellowship offering.[c] 20The priest is to wave the
two lambs before the LORD as a wave offering, together with the bread of the
firstfruits. They are a sacred offering to
the LORD for the priest. 21On that same
day you are to proclaim a sacred assembly[c] and do no regular work.[d] This is to 23:21
be a lasting ordinance for the genera- [c] ver 2 [d] ver 3
tions to come, wherever you live.

22" 'When you reap the harvest[e] of 23:22
your land, do not reap to the very edges [e] Lev 19:9
of your field or gather the gleanings of [f] Lev 19:10; Dt 24:19-21;
your harvest.[f] Leave them for the poor Ru 2:15
and the alien. I am the LORD your God.' "

Feast of Trumpets

23The LORD said to Moses, 24"Say to
the Israelites: 'On the first day of the seventh month you are to have a day of rest,

a 13 That is, probably about 4 quarts (about 4.5 liters); also in verse 17 *b 13* That is, probably about 1 quart (about 1 liter) *c 19* Traditionally *peace offering*

JESUS FOCUS

RESTING WITH GOD

The seventh day of the week (Saturday) was designated as the Sabbath for God's people (Leviticus 23). It was to be a day of rest, following God's example of resting on the seventh day following the work of creation (Genesis 2:2–3; Deuteronomy 5:14). However, the Jewish religious establishment later developed complicated and rigid rules regarding Sabbath observance. Jesus encountered legalistic attitudes from people who devoted much of their energy to strict adherence to rules. Instead of allowing himself to become buried in sorting through the technicalities of religious life, Jesus defended doing good deeds on the Sabbath because, as he stated, "My Father is always at his work to this very day, and I, too, am working" (John 5:17). The Bible makes it clear that attitude and heart are much more important to God than keeping religious traditions (Isaiah 1:11–15; 58:5–14; Hosea 6:6; Matthew 12:7). In the New Testament, the first day of the week (Sunday) replaced the Sabbath as the day on which most Christians engage in formal worship; this change came about in commemoration of the day of the week on which Jesus arose from the dead (Mark 16:2; Acts 20:7).

a sacred assembly commemorated with trumpet blasts.[g] 25Do no regular work,[h] but present an offering made to the LORD by fire.' "

Day of Atonement

26The LORD said to Moses, 27"The tenth day of this seventh month[i] is the Day of Atonement.[j] Hold a sacred assembly[k] and deny yourselves,[a] and present an offering made to the LORD by fire. 28Do no work on that day, because it is the Day of Atonement, when atonement is made for you before the LORD your God. 29Anyone who does not deny himself on that day must be cut off from his people.[l] 30I will destroy from among his people[m] anyone who does any work on that day. 31You shall do no work at all. This is to be a lasting ordinance for the generations to come, wherever you live. 32It is a sabbath of rest for you, and you must deny yourselves. From the evening of the ninth day of the month until the following evening you are to observe your sabbath."

Feast of Tabernacles

33The LORD said to Moses, 34"Say to the Israelites: 'On the fifteenth day of the seventh month the LORD's Feast of Tabernacles[n] begins, and it lasts for seven days. 35The first day is a sacred assembly; do no regular work. 36For seven days present offerings made to the LORD by fire, and on the eighth day hold a sacred assembly[o] and present an offering made to the LORD by fire. It is the closing assembly; do no regular work.

37(" 'These are the LORD's appointed feasts, which you are to proclaim as sacred assemblies for bringing offerings made to the LORD by fire—the burnt offerings and grain offerings, sacrifices and drink offerings[p] required for each day. 38These offerings are in addition to those for the LORD's Sabbaths[q] and[b] in addition to your gifts and whatever you have vowed and all the freewill offerings you give to the LORD.)

39" 'So beginning with the fifteenth day of the seventh month, after you have gathered the crops of the land, celebrate the festival to the LORD for seven days;[r] the first day is a day of rest, and the eighth day also is a day of rest. 40On the first day you are to take choice fruit from the trees, and palm fronds, leafy branches and poplars,[s] and rejoice before the LORD your God for seven days. 41Celebrate this as a festival to the LORD for seven days each year. This is to be a lasting ordinance for the generations to come; celebrate it in the seventh month. 42Live in booths[t] for seven days: All native-born Israelites are to live in booths 43so your descendants will know[u] that I had the Israelites live in booths when I brought them out of Egypt. I am the LORD your God.' "

44So Moses announced to the Israelites the appointed feasts of the LORD.

Oil and Bread Set Before the LORD

24 The LORD said to Moses, 2"Command the Israelites to bring you clear oil of pressed olives for the light so that the lamps may be kept burning continually. 3Outside the curtain of the Testimony in the Tent of Meeting, Aaron is to tend the lamps before the LORD from evening till morning, continually. This is to be a lasting ordinance for the generations to come. 4The lamps on the pure gold lampstand[v] before the LORD must be tended continually.

5"Take fine flour and bake twelve loaves of bread,[w] using two-tenths of an ephah[c] for each loaf. 6Set them in two rows, six in each row, on the table of pure gold[x] before the LORD. 7Along each row put some pure incense as a memorial portion[y] to represent the bread and to be an offering made to the LORD by fire. 8This bread is to be set out before the LORD regularly,[z] Sabbath after Sabbath,[a] on behalf of the Israelites, as a lasting covenant. 9It belongs to Aaron and his sons,[b] who are to eat it in a holy place, because it is a most holy part of their regular share of the offerings made to the LORD by fire."

A Blasphemer Stoned

10Now the son of an Israelite mother and an Egyptian father went out among the Israelites, and a fight broke out in the camp between him and an Israelite. 11The son of the Israelite woman blasphemed the Name[c] with a curse; so they

[a] 27 Or *and fast;* also in verses 29 and 32 [b] 38 Or *These feasts are in addition to the LORD's Sabbaths, and these offerings are* [c] 5 That is, probably about 4 quarts (about 4.5 liters)

23:24 [g] Lev 25:9; Nu 10:9,10; 29:1
23:25 [h] ver 21
23:27 [i] Lev 16:29 [j] Ex 30:10 [k] Nu 29:7
23:29 [l] Ge 17:14; Nu 5:2
23:30 [m] Lev 20:3
23:34 [n] Ex 23:16; Dt 16:13; Ezr 3:4; Ne 8:14; Zec 14:16; Jn 7:2
23:36 [o] 2Ch 7:9; Ne 8:18; Jn 7:37
23:37 [p] ver 2,4
23:38 [q] Eze 45:17
23:39 [r] Ex 23:16; Dt 16:13
23:40 [s] Ne 8:14-17
23:42 [t] Ne 8:14-16
23:43 [u] Dt 31:13; Ps 78:5
24:4 [v] Ex 25:31; 31:8
24:5 [w] Ex 25:30
24:6 [x] Ex 25:23-30; 1Ki 7:48
24:7 [y] Lev 2:2
24:8 [z] Nu 4:7; 1Ch 9:32; 2Ch 2:4 [a] Mt 12:5
24:9 [b] Lev 8:31; Mt 12:4; Mk 2:26; Lk 6:4
24:11 [c] Ex 3:15

brought him to Moses. (His mother's
name was Shelomith, the daughter of
24:12 Dibri the Danite.) 12They put him in cus-
d Ex 18:16; tody until the will of the LORD should be
Nu 15:34 made clear to them.[d]
13Then the LORD said to Moses:
14"Take the blasphemer outside the
24:14 camp. All those who heard him are to lay
e Lev 20:27; their hands on his head, and the entire
Dt 13:9; 17:5,7; 21:21 assembly is to stone him.[e] 15Say to the
24:15 Israelites: 'If anyone curses his God,[f] he
f Ex 22:28 will be held responsible; 16anyone who
blasphemes the name of the LORD must
24:16 be put to death.[g] The entire assembly
g 1Ki 21:10,13; Mt 26:66 must stone him. Whether an alien or
native-born, when he blasphemes the
Name, he must be put to death.
24:17 17" 'If anyone takes the life of a human
h Ge 9:6; Ex 21:12; being, he must be put to death.[h] 18Any-
Nu 35:30-31; one who takes the life of someone's ani-
Dt 27:24 mal must make restitution[i]—life for life.
24:18 19If anyone injures his neighbor, whatev-
i ver 21 er he has done must be done to him:
24:20 20fracture for fracture, eye for eye, tooth
j Ex 21:24; Mt 5:38* for tooth.[j] As he has injured the other, so
he is to be injured. 21Whoever kills an
24:21 animal must make restitution, but who-
k ver 17 ever kills a man must be put to death.[k]
24:22 22You are to have the same law for the
l Ex 12:49 alien[l] and the native-born.[m] I am the
m Nu 9:14; 15:16 LORD your God.' "
23Then Moses spoke to the Israelites,
and they took the blasphemer outside
the camp and stoned him. The Israelites
did as the LORD commanded Moses.

The Sabbath Year

25 The LORD said to Moses on
Mount Sinai, 2"Speak to the Israelites and say to them: 'When you enter the land I am going to give you, the
land itself must observe a sabbath to the
LORD. 3For six years sow your fields, and
for six years prune your vineyards and
25:3 gather their crops.[n] 4But in the seventh
n Ex 23:10 year the land is to have a sabbath of rest,
a sabbath to the LORD. Do not sow your
fields or prune your vineyards. 5Do not
reap what grows of itself or harvest the
grapes of your untended vines. The land
is to have a year of rest. 6Whatever the
25:6 land yields during the sabbath year[o] will
o ver 20 be food for you—for yourself, your
manservant and maidservant, and the
hired worker and temporary resident
who live among you, 7as well as for your
livestock and the wild animals in your
land. Whatever the land produces may
be eaten.

The Year of Jubilee

8" 'Count off seven sabbaths of
years—seven times seven years—so that
the seven sabbaths of years amount to a
period of forty-nine years. 9Then have 25:9
the trumpet[p] sounded everywhere on p Lev 23:24
the tenth day of the seventh month;
on the Day of Atonement sound the
trumpet throughout your land. 10Conse-
crate the fiftieth year and proclaim lib- 25:10 q Isa 61:1;
erty[q] throughout the land to all its in- Jer 34:8,15,17; Lk 4:19
habitants. It shall be a jubilee[r] for you; r Nu 36:4
each one of you is to return to his fami-
ly property and each to his own clan.
11The fiftieth year shall be a jubilee for
you; do not sow and do not reap what
grows of itself or harvest the untended
vines. 12For it is a jubilee and is to be
holy for you; eat only what is taken directly from the fields.
13" 'In this Year of Jubilee[s] everyone is 25:13
to return to his own property. s ver 10
14" 'If you sell land to one of your
countrymen or buy any from him, do 25:14
not take advantage of each other.[t] 15You t Lev 19:13;
are to buy from your countryman on the 1Sa 12:3,4
basis of the number of years[u] since the 25:15
Jubilee. And he is to sell to you on the u Lev 27:18,23
basis of the number of years left for harvesting crops. 16When the years are
many, you are to increase the price, and 25:16 v ver 27,51,52
when the years are few, you are to de-
crease the price,[v] because what he is 25:17 w Pr 22:22;
really selling you is the number of crops. Jer 7:5,6; 1Th 4:6
17Do not take advantage of each other,[w] x Lev 19:14
but fear your God.[x] I am the LORD your y Lev 19:32
God.[y]
18" 'Follow my decrees and be careful 25:18 z Lev 26:4,5;
to obey my laws, and you will live safely Dt 12:10; Ps 4:8;
in the land.[z] 19Then the land will yield its Jer 23:6
fruit,[a] and you will eat your fill and live 25:19 a Lev 26:4
there in safety. 20You may ask, "What will 25:20
we eat in the seventh year[b] if we do not b ver 4
plant or harvest our crops?" 21I will send
you such a blessing[c] in the sixth year that 25:21 c Dt 28:8,12;
the land will yield enough for three years. Hag 2:19;
22While you plant during the eighth year, Mal 3:10
you will eat from the old crop and will 25:22
continue to eat from it until the harvest d Lev 26:10
of the ninth year comes in.[d]
23" 'The land must not be sold perma- 25:23 e Ex 19:5
nently, because the land is mine[e] and f Ge 23:4; 1Ch 29:15;
you are but aliens[f] and my tenants. Ps 39:12; Heb 11:13;
24Throughout the country that you hold 1Pe 2:11

as a possession, you must provide for
the redemption of the land.
25“ ‘If one of your countrymen be-
25:25 comes poor and sells some of his proper-
g Ru 2:20; Jer 32:7 ty, his nearest relative[g] is to come and re-
h Lev 27:13,19, deem[h] what his countryman has sold.
31; Ru 4:4 26If, however, a man has no one to redeem
it for him but he himself prospers and acquires sufficient means to redeem it, 27he
is to determine the value for the years
since he sold it and refund the balance to
the man to whom he sold it; he can then
go back to his own property. 28But if he
does not acquire the means to repay him,
what he sold will remain in the possession of the buyer until the Year of Jubilee.
25:28 It will be returned in the Jubilee, and he
i ver 10 can then go back to his property.[i]
29“ ‘If a man sells a house in a walled
city, he retains the right of redemption a
full year after its sale. During that time
he may redeem it. 30If it is not redeemed
before a full year has passed, the house in
the walled city shall belong permanently
to the buyer and his descendants. It is
not to be returned in the Jubilee. 31But
houses in villages without walls around
them are to be considered as open country. They can be redeemed, and they are
to be returned in the Jubilee.
32“ ‘The Levites always have the right
to redeem their houses in the Levitical
25:32 j Nu 35:1-8; towns,[j] which they possess. 33So the
Jos 21:2 property of the Levites is redeemable—
that is, a house sold in any town they
hold—and is to be returned in the Jubilee, because the houses in the towns of
the Levites are their property among the
Israelites. 34But the pastureland belong-
25:34 ing to their towns must not be sold; it is
k Nu 35:2-5 their permanent possession.[k]
35“ ‘If one of your countrymen be-
25:35 l Dt 24:14,15 comes poor[l] and is unable to support
m Dt 15:8; himself among you, help him[m] as you
Ps 37:21,26; Lk 6:35 would an alien or a temporary resident,
25:36 so he can continue to live among you.
n Ex 22:25; 36Do not take interest[n] of any kind[a]
Dt 23:19-20 from him, but fear your God, so that
your countryman may continue to live
among you. 37You must not lend him
money at interest or sell him food at a
25:38 profit. 38I am the LORD your God, who
o Ge 17:7; brought you out of Egypt to give you the
Lev 11:45 land of Canaan and to be your God.[o]
25:39 39“ ‘If one of your countrymen be-
p Ex 21:2; Dt 15:12; comes poor among you and sells himself
1Ki 9:22 to you, do not make him work as a slave.[p]
40He is to be treated as a hired worker or
a temporary resident among you; he is to
work for you until the Year of Jubilee.
41Then he and his children are to be released, and he will go back to his own
clan and to the property[q] of his forefa- 25:41 q ver 28
thers. 42Because the Israelites are my servants, whom I brought out of Egypt, they
must not be sold as slaves. 43Do not rule 25:43 r Ex 1:13;
over them ruthlessly,[r] but fear your God. Eze 34:4; Col 4:1
44“ ‘Your male and female slaves are to
come from the nations around you;
from them you may buy slaves. 45You
may also buy some of the temporary residents living among you and members
of their clans born in your country, and
they will become your property. 46You
can will them to your children as inherited property and can make them slaves
for life, but you must not rule over your
fellow Israelites ruthlessly.
47“ ‘If an alien or a temporary resident
among you becomes rich and one of
your countrymen becomes poor and
sells himself to the alien living among
you or to a member of the alien's clan,
48he retains the right of redemption after he has sold himself. One of his rela- 25:48
tives[s] may redeem him: 49An uncle or a s Ne 5:5
cousin or any blood relative in his clan 25:49
may redeem him. Or if he prospers,[t] he t ver 26
may redeem himself. 50He and his buyer
are to count the time from the year he
sold himself up to the Year of Jubilee.
The price for his release is to be based 25:50
on the rate paid to a hired man[u] for that u Job 7:1;
number of years. 51If many years remain, Isa 16:14; 21:16
he must pay for his redemption a larger
share of the price paid for him. 52If only
a few years remain until the Year of Jubilee, he is to compute that and pay for
his redemption accordingly. 53He is to be
treated as a man hired from year to year;
you must see to it that his owner does
not rule over him ruthlessly.
54“ ‘Even if he is not redeemed in any
of these ways, he and his children are to
be released in the Year of Jubilee, 55for
the Israelites belong to me as servants.
They are my servants, whom I brought
out of Egypt. I am the LORD your God.

Reward for Obedience

26 “ ‘Do not make idols[v] or set up 26:1
an image or a sacred stone[w] for v Ex 20:4; Lev 19:4; Dt 5:8
yourselves, and do not place a carved w Ex 23:24

[a] 36 Or *take excessive interest*; similarly in verse 37

stone[x] in your land to bow down before
it. I am the LORD your God.
2“ ‘Observe my Sabbaths and have reverence for my sanctuary.[y] I am the LORD.
3“ ‘If you follow my decrees and are
careful to obey[z] my commands, 4I will
send you rain[a] in its season, and the
ground will yield its crops and the trees
of the field their fruit.[b] 5Your threshing
will continue until grape harvest and the
grape harvest will continue until planting, and you will eat all the food you
want[c] and live in safety in your land.[d]
6“ ‘I will grant peace in the land,[e] and
you will lie down[f] and no one will make
you afraid.[g] I will remove savage beasts[h]
from the land, and the sword will not
pass through your country. 7You will
pursue your enemies, and they will fall
by the sword before you. 8Five of you will
chase a hundred, and a hundred of you
will chase ten thousand, and your enemies will fall by the sword before you.[i]
9“ ‘I will look on you with favor and
make you fruitful and increase your
numbers,[j] and I will keep my covenant[k]
with you. 10You will still be eating last
year’s harvest when you will have to
move it out to make room for the new.[l]
11I will put my dwelling place[a][m] among
you, and I will not abhor you. 12I will
walk[n] among you and be your God, and
you will be my people.[o] 13I am the LORD
your God, who brought you out of Egypt
so that you would no longer be slaves to
the Egyptians; I broke the bars of your
yoke[p] and enabled you to walk with
heads held high.

Punishment for Disobedience

14“ ‘But if you will not listen to me and
carry out all these commands,[q] 15and if
you reject my decrees and abhor my
laws and fail to carry out all my commands and so violate my covenant,
16then I will do this to you: I will bring
upon you sudden terror, wasting diseases and fever[r] that will destroy your
sight and drain away your life.[s] You will
plant seed in vain, because your enemies
will eat it.[t] 17I will set my face[u] against
you so that you will be defeated by your
enemies; those who hate you will rule
over you,[v] and you will flee even when
no one is pursuing you.[w]
18“ ‘If after all this you will not listen
to me, I will punish you for your sins

26:1 x Nu 33:52
26:2 y Lev 19:30
26:3 z Dt 7:12; 11:13, 22; 28:1,9
26:4 a Dt 11:14 b Ps 67:6
26:5 c Dt 11:15; Joel 2:19,26; Am 9:13 d Lev 25:18
26:6 e Ps 29:11; 85:8; 147:14 f Ps 4:8 g Zep 3:13 h ver 22
26:8 i Dt 32:30; Jos 23:10
26:9 j Ge 17:6; Ne 9:23 k Ge 17:7
26:10 l Lev 25:22
26:11 m Ex 25:8; Ps 76:2; Eze 37:27
26:12 n Ge 3:8 o 2Co 6:16*
26:13 p Eze 34:27
26:14 q Dt 28:15-68; Mal 2:2
26:16 r Dt 28:22,35 s 1Sa 2:33 t Job 31:8
26:17 u Lev 17:10 v Ps 106:41 w ver 36,37; Dt 28:7,25; Ps 53:5

seven times over.[x] 19I will break down
your stubborn pride[y] and make the sky
above you like iron and the ground beneath you like bronze.[z] 20Your strength
will be spent in vain,[a] because your soil
will not yield its crops, nor will the trees
of the land yield their fruit.[b]
21“ ‘If you remain hostile toward me
and refuse to listen to me, I will multiply
your afflictions seven times over,[c] as
your sins deserve. 22I will send wild animals[d] against you, and they will rob you
of your children, destroy your cattle and
make you so few in number that your
roads will be deserted.
23“ ‘If in spite of these things you do
not accept my correction[e] but continue
to be hostile toward me, 24I myself will
be hostile toward you and will afflict you
for your sins seven times over. 25And I
will bring the sword upon you to avenge
the breaking of the covenant. When you
withdraw into your cities, I will send a
plague[f] among you, and you will be giv-
en into enemy hands. 26When I cut off
your supply of bread,[g] ten women will be
able to bake your bread in one oven, and
they will dole out the bread by weight.
You will eat, but you will not be satisfied.
27“ ‘If in spite of this you still do not
listen to me but continue to be hostile
toward me, 28then in my anger I will be
hostile toward you, and I myself will
punish you for your sins seven times
over. 29You will eat the flesh of your sons
and the flesh of your daughters.[h] 30I will
destroy your high places,[i] cut down your
incense altars[j] and pile your dead bodies on the lifeless forms of your idols,[k]
and I will abhor you. 31I will turn your
cities into ruins and lay waste your sanctuaries,[l] and I will take no delight in the
pleasing aroma of your offerings. 32I will
lay waste the land,[m] so that your enemies who live there will be appalled. 33I
will scatter you among the nations[n] and
will draw out my sword and pursue you.
Your land will be laid waste, and your
cities will lie in ruins. 34Then the land
will enjoy its sabbath years all the time
that it lies desolate and you are in the
country of your enemies;[o] then the land
will rest and enjoy its sabbaths. 35All the
time that it lies desolate, the land will
have the rest it did not have during the
sabbaths you lived in it.

a 11 Or *my tabernacle*

26:18 x ver 21
26:19 y Isa 25:11 z Dt 28:23
26:20 a Ps 127:1; Isa 17:11 b Dt 11:17
26:21 c ver 18
26:22 d Dt 32:24
26:23 e Jer 2:30; 5:3
26:25 f Nu 14:12; Eze 5:17
26:26 g Ps 105:16; Isa 3:1; Mic 6:14
26:29 h Dt 28:53
26:30 i 2Ch 34:3; Eze 6:3 j Eze 6:6 k Eze 6:13
26:31 l Ps 74:3-7
26:32 m Jer 9:11
26:33 n Dt 4:27; Eze 12:15; 20:23; Zec 7:14
26:34 o ver 43; 2Ch 36:21

36“ ‘As for those of you who are left, I
will make their hearts so fearful in the
lands of their enemies that the sound of
26:36 a windblown leaf will put them to
[p] Eze 21:7 flight.[p] They will run as though fleeing
from the sword, and they will fall, even
though no one is pursuing them. 37They
will stumble over one another as though
fleeing from the sword, even though no
26:37 one is pursuing them. So you will not be
[q] Jos 7:12 able to stand before your enemies.[q]
26:38 38You will perish among the nations; the
[r] Dt 4:26 land of your enemies will devour you.[r]
39Those of you who are left will waste
away in the lands of their enemies be-
26:39 cause of their sins; also because of their
[s] Eze 4:17 fathers' sins they will waste away.[s]
26:40 40“ ‘But if they will confess their sins
[t] Jer 3:12-15; and the sins of their fathers[t]—their
Lk 15:18; treachery against me and their hostility
1Jn 1:9 toward me, 41which made me hostile toward them so that I sent them into the
26:41 land of their enemies—then when their
[u] Eze 44:7,9; uncircumcised hearts[u] are humbled and
Ac 7:51 they pay for their sin, 42I will remember
26:42 my covenant with Jacob[v] and my cov-
[v] Ge 22:15-18; enant with Isaac[w] and my covenant with
28:15 [w] Ge 26:5 Abraham, and I will remember the land.
43For the land will be deserted by them
and will enjoy its sabbaths while it lies
desolate without them. They will pay for
their sins because they rejected my laws
and abhorred my decrees. 44Yet in spite
26:44 of this, when they are in the land of their
[x] Ro 11:2 enemies, I will not reject them or abhor[x]
[y] Dt 4:31; them so as to destroy them completely,[y]
Jer 30:11 breaking my covenant[z] with them. I am
[z] Jer 33:26 the LORD their God. 45But for their sake
26:45 I will remember[a] the covenant with their
[a] Ge 17:7 ancestors whom I brought out of Egypt[b]
[b] Ex 6:8; in the sight of the nations to be their
Lev 25:38 God. I am the LORD.’ ”
46These are the decrees, the laws and
the regulations that the LORD estab-
26:46 lished on Mount Sinai between himself
[c] Lev 7:38; 27:34 and the Israelites through Moses.[c]

Redeeming What Is the LORD's

27 The LORD said to Moses,
2“Speak to the Israelites and say
27:2 to them: ‘If anyone makes a special vow[d]
[d] Nu 6:2 to dedicate persons to the LORD by giving equivalent values, 3set the value of a
27:3 male between the ages of twenty and
[e] Ex 30:13; sixty at fifty shekels[a] of silver, according
Nu 3:47; 18:16 to the sanctuary shekel[b];[e] 4and if it is a
female, set her value at thirty shekels.[c]
5If it is a person between the ages of five
and twenty, set the value of a male at
twenty shekels[d] and of a female at ten
shekels.[e] 6If it is a person between one
month and five years, set the value of a **27:6**
male at five shekels[f][f] of silver and that of [f] Nu 18:16
a female at three shekels[g] of silver. 7If it
is a person sixty years old or more, set
the value of a male at fifteen shekels[h]
and of a female at ten shekels. 8If anyone **27:8**
making the vow is too poor to pay[g] the [g] Lev 5:11
specified amount, he is to present the [h] ver 12,14
person to the priest, who will set the value[h] for him according to what the man
making the vow can afford.
9“ ‘If what he vowed is an animal that
is acceptable as an offering to the LORD,
such an animal given to the LORD becomes holy. 10He must not exchange it
or substitute a good one for a bad one, **27:10**
or a bad one for a good one;[i] if he should [i] ver 33
substitute one animal for another, both
it and the substitute become holy. 11If
what he vowed is a ceremonially unclean animal—one that is not acceptable as an offering to the LORD—the animal must be presented to the priest,
12who will judge its quality as good or

[a] *3* That is, about 1 1/4 pounds (about 0.6 kilogram); also in verse 16 [b] *3* That is, about 2/5 ounce (about 11.5 grams); also in verse 25
[c] *4* That is, about 12 ounces (about 0.3 kilogram)
[d] *5* That is, about 8 ounces (about 0.2 kilogram)
[e] *5* That is, about 4 ounces (about 110 grams); also in verse 7 [f] *6* That is, about 2 ounces (about 55 grams) [g] *6* That is, about 1 1/4 ounces (about 35 grams) [h] *7* That is, about 6 ounces (about 170 grams)

JESUS FOCUS

BOUGHT BACK

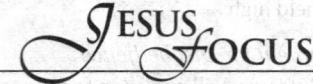

The final chapter of Leviticus emphasizes the importance of paying vows and tithes when they are due. In fact, Leviticus 27 reminds us that there is always a price to pay when buying back someone or something. An article that is purchased back is said to be *redeemed*. That is exactly what God the Son did for us when he died on the cross and came back to life. Jesus referred to his death as a "ransom for many" (Mark 10:45), and God reminds us throughout the New Testament that Jesus died as a payment for our sin. Our Savior paid the price that we could not afford to pay in order to enable us to enjoy a restored relationship with the Father who loves us (Ephesians 1:7; Titus 2:14; 1 Peter 1:18–19).

bad. Whatever value the priest then sets,
that is what it will be. 13If the owner
27:13 [j]ver 15,19; Lev 25:25 wishes to redeem[j] the animal, he must
add a fifth to its value.
14" 'If a man dedicates his house as
something holy to the LORD, the priest
will judge its quality as good or bad.
Whatever value the priest then sets, so
it will remain. 15If the man who dedi-
27:15 [k]ver 13,20 cates his house redeems it,[k] he must add
a fifth to its value, and the house will
again become his.
16" 'If a man dedicates to the LORD
part of his family land, its value is to be
set according to the amount of seed required for it—fifty shekels of silver to a
homer[a] of barley seed. 17If he dedicates
his field during the Year of Jubilee, the
value that has been set remains. 18But if
he dedicates his field after the Jubilee,
the priest will determine the value according to the number of years that re-
27:18 [l]Lev 25:15 main[l] until the next Year of Jubilee, and
its set value will be reduced. 19If the man
who dedicates the field wishes to redeem it, he must add a fifth to its value,
and the field will again become his. 20If,
however, he does not redeem the field, or
if he has sold it to someone else, it can
never be redeemed. 21When the field is
27:21 [m]Lev 25:10 [n]ver 28; Nu 18:14; Eze 44:29 released in the Jubilee,[m] it will become
holy, like a field devoted to the LORD;[n] it
will become the property of the priests.[b]
22" 'If a man dedicates to the LORD a
field he has bought, which is not part of
his family land, 23the priest will determine its value up to the Year of Jubilee,
and the man must pay its value on that
day as something holy to the LORD. 24In
the Year of Jubilee the field will revert to
27:24 [o]Lev 25:28 the person from whom he bought it,[o]
the one whose land it was. 25Every value
is to be set according to the sanctuary 27:25 [p]Ex 30:13; Nu 18:16 [q]Nu 3:47; Eze 45:12
shekel,[p] twenty gerahs[q] to the shekel.
26" 'No one, however, may dedicate the
firstborn of an animal, since the first-
born already belongs to the LORD;[r] 27:26 [r]Ex 13:2,12
whether an ox[c] or a sheep, it is the LORD's.
27If it is one of the unclean animals,[s] he 27:27 [s]ver 11
may buy it back at its set value, adding a
fifth of the value to it. If he does not redeem it, it is to be sold at its set value.
28" 'But nothing that a man owns and 27:28 [t]Nu 18:14; Jos 6:17-19
devotes[d][t] to the LORD—whether man or
animal or family land—may be sold or
redeemed; everything so devoted is
most holy to the LORD.
29" 'No person devoted to destruction[e] may be ransomed; he must be put
to death.
30" 'A tithe[u] of everything from the 27:30 [u]Ge 28:22; 2Ch 31:6; Mal 3:8
land, whether grain from the soil or fruit
from the trees, belongs to the LORD; it is
holy to the LORD. 31If a man redeems any
of his tithe, he must add a fifth of the
value to it. 32The entire tithe of the herd
and flock—every tenth animal that
passes under the shepherd's rod[v]—will 27:32 [v]Jer 33:13; Eze 20:37
be holy to the LORD. 33He must not pick
out the good from the bad or make any
substitution.[w] If he does make a substi- 27:33 [w]ver 10
tution, both the animal and its substi-
tute become holy and cannot be redeemed.' "

34These are the commands the LORD
gave Moses on Mount Sinai for the Isra- 27:34 [x]Lev 26:46; Dt 4:5
elites.[x]

[a] *16* That is, probably about 6 bushels (about 220 liters) [b] *21* Or *priest* [c] *26* The Hebrew word can include both male and female. [d] *28* The Hebrew term refers to the irrevocable giving over of things or persons to the LORD. [e] *29* The Hebrew term refers to the irrevocable giving over of things or persons to the LORD, often by totally destroying them.

Why kill someone who wanted to come close to God? (Numbers 1:51–53)

♦ *A sinner will die in the blazing light and awe-inspiring power of God's holiness except when God makes special provision. God's ultimate provision was Jesus, but here he used the tents of the Levites to form a protective barrier around the tabernacle, preventing any Israelite from accidentally wandering into God's holy presence.*

Why prohibit breaking any bones of the Passover lamb? (Numbers 9:12)

♦ *No reason is given here or elsewhere, but the prohibition against breaking a bone parallels the fact that none of Jesus' bones were broken during the crucifixion (John 19:36). Jesus is the consummate Passover lamb, who sacrificed himself for the sins of the people (John 1:29,36; 1 Corinthians 5:7).*

Jesus in Numbers It is reasonable to conclude that God the Son may have stepped in at a critical time for the young nation of Israel, as it prepared to enter the land of promise. Many scholars believe that Jesus, as the "angel of the LORD," blocked the path before Balaam and his donkey. He confronted the false prophet Balaam, changed Balaam's words and through Balaam blessed the Israelites rather than cursing them (Numbers 22:22–35). In a prophecy that would be fulfilled ultimately in the coming of the Messianic ruler, Balaam predicted that "a star [would] come out of Jacob" (Numbers 24:17).

Be ready while reading Numbers to see a God of mercy, who even in Old Testament times held his arms open wide for those who would turn back to him. Jesus' sacrificial death would later personify that mercy but would also fully satisfy God's demand for justice. Finally, consider that, just as God promised to lead the Israelites into their promised land, Jesus has promised to be with us in our journey toward our own.

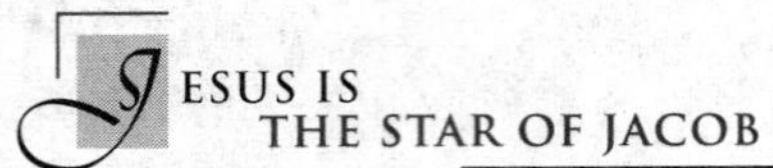

The Census

1:1 **1** The LORD spoke to Moses in the
a Ex 40:2 Tent of Meeting[a] in the Desert of
b Ex 19:1 Sinai[b] on the first day of the second
c Ex 40:17 month[c] of the second year after the Is-
1:2 raelites came out of Egypt. He said:
d Ex 30:11-16; 2"Take a census[d] of the whole Israelite
Nu 26:2 community by their clans and families,
listing every man by name, one by one.
3You and Aaron are to number by their
1:3 divisions all the men in Israel twenty
e Ex 30:14 years old or more[e] who are able to serve
1:4 in the army. 4One man from each tribe,
f ver 16 each the head of his family,[f] is to help
g Ex 18:21; you.[g] 5These are the names of the men
Dt 1:15 who are to assist you:

1:5 from Reuben,[h] Elizur son of Shed-
h Ge 29:32; eur;
Dt 33:6; Rev 7:5 6from Simeon, Shelumiel son of
1:7 Zurishaddai;
i Ge 29:35; 7from Judah,[i] Nahshon son of Am-
Ps 78:68 minadab;[j]
j Ru 4:20; 8from Issachar,[k] Nethanel son of
1Ch 2:10; Zuar;
Lk 3:32
1:8 9from Zebulun,[l] Eliab son of Helon;
k Ge 30:18 10from the sons of Joseph:
1:9 from Ephraim,[m] Elishama son of
l ver 30 Ammihud;
1:10 from Manasseh, Gamaliel son of
m ver 32 Pedahzur;
11from Benjamin, Abidan son of
Gideoni;
1:12
n ver 38 12from Dan,[n] Ahiezer son of Ammishaddai;
1:13
o ver 40 13from Asher,[o] Pagiel son of Ocran;
14from Gad, Eliasaph son of Deuel;[p]
1:14
p Nu 2:14 15from Naphtali,[q] Ahira son of Enan."

16These were the men appointed from
1:15 the community, the leaders[r] of their an-
q ver 42 cestral tribes. They were the heads of the
1:16 clans of Israel.[s]
r Ex 18:25 17Moses and Aaron took these men
s ver 4; Ex 18:21; whose names had been given, 18and they
Nu 7:2 called the whole community together
1:18 on the first day of the second month.[t]
t ver 1 The people indicated their ancestry[u] by
u Ezr 2:59; their clans and families, and the men
Heb 7:3 twenty years old or more were listed by
name, one by one, 19as the LORD commanded Moses. And so he counted
them in the Desert of Sinai:

1:20
v Nu 26:5-11; 20From the descendants of Reuben[v] the
Rev 7:5 firstborn son of Israel:
All the men twenty years old or
more who were able to serve in
the army were listed by name,
one by one, according to the
records of their clans and families. 21The number from the tribe
of Reuben was 46,500.

22From the descendants of Simeon:[w] 1:22
All the men twenty years old or w Nu 26:12-14;
more who were able to serve in Rev 7:7
the army were counted and listed by name, one by one, according to the records of their clans
and families. 23The number from
the tribe of Simeon was 59,300.

24From the descendants of Gad:[x] 1:24
All the men twenty years old or x Ge 30:11;
more who were able to serve in Nu 26:15-18;
the army were listed by name, ac- Rev 7:5
cording to the records of their
clans and families. 25The number
from the tribe of Gad was 45,650.

26From the descendants of Judah:[y] 1:26
All the men twenty years old or y Ge 29:35;
more who were able to serve in Nu 26:19-22;
the army were listed by name, Mt 1:2; Rev 7:5
according to the records of their
clans and families. 27The number from the tribe of Judah was
74,600.

28From the descendants of Issachar:[z] 1:28
All the men twenty years old or z Nu 26:23-25;
more who were able to serve in Rev 7:7
the army were listed by name,
according to the records of their
clans and families. 29The number from the tribe of Issachar
was 54,400.

30From the descendants of Zebulun:[a] 1:30
All the men twenty years old or a Nu 26:26-27;
more who were able to serve in Rev 7:8
the army were listed by name,
according to the records of their
clans and families. 31The number from the tribe of Zebulun
was 57,400.

32From the sons of Joseph:
From the descendants of Ephraim:[b] 1:32
All the men twenty years old or b Nu 26:35-37
more who were able to serve in
the army were listed by name,
according to the records of their
clans and families. 33The number from the tribe of Ephraim
was 40,500. 1:34

34From the descendants of Manasseh:[c] c Nu 26:28-34;
Rev 7:6

All the men twenty years old or
more who were able to serve in
the army were listed by name,
according to the records of their
clans and families. 35 The number from the tribe of Manasseh
was 32,200.
1:36 36 From the descendants of Benjamin:[d]
[d] Nu 26:38-41; All the men twenty years old or
2Ch 17:17; more who were able to serve in
Rev 7:8 the army were listed by name,
according to the records of their
clans and families. 37 The number from the tribe of Benjamin
was 35,400.
1:38 38 From the descendants of Dan:[e]
[e] Ge 30:6; Nu 26:42-43 All the men twenty years old or
more who were able to serve in
the army were listed by name, according to the records of their
clans and families. 39 The number
from the tribe of Dan was 62,700.
1:40 40 From the descendants of Asher:[f]
[f] Nu 26:44-47; All the men twenty years old or
Rev 7:6 more who were able to serve in
the army were listed by name,
according to the records of their
clans and families. 41 The number from the tribe of Asher was
41,500.
1:42 42 From the descendants of Naphtali:[g]
[g] Nu 26:48-50; All the men twenty years old or
Rev 7:6 more who were able to serve in
the army were listed by name,
according to the records of their
clans and families. 43 The number from the tribe of Naphtali
was 53,400.
1:44 44 These were the men counted by
[h] Nu 26:64 Moses and Aaron[h] and the twelve leaders of Israel, each one representing his
family. 45 All the Israelites twenty years
old or more who were able to serve in Is-
1:46 rael's army were counted according to
[i] Ex 12:37; their families. 46 The total number was
38:26; Nu 2:32; 26:51 603,550.[i]
47 The families of the tribe of Levi,[j]
1:47 [j] Nu 2:33; 26:57 however, were not counted[k] along with
[k] Nu 4:3,49 the others. 48 The LORD had said to Moses: 49 "You must not count the tribe of
Levi or include them in the census of the
other Israelites. 50 Instead, appoint the
1:50 Levites to be in charge of the tabernacle
[l] Ex 38:21; Ac 7:44 of the Testimony[l]—over all its furnishings and everything belonging to it.
They are to carry the tabernacle and all
its furnishings; they are to take care of it
and encamp around it. 51 Whenever the
tabernacle is to move, the Levites are to
take it down, and whenever the tabernacle is to be set up, the Levites shall do 1:51
it.[m] Anyone else who goes near it shall [m] Nu 3:38; 4:1-33
be put to death. 52 The Israelites are to
set up their tents by divisions, each man
in his own camp under his own stan- 1:52
dard.[n] 53 The Levites, however, are to set [n] Nu 2:2; Ps 20:5
up their tents around the tabernacle of
the Testimony so that wrath will not
fall[o] on the Israelite community. The Le- 1:53 [o] Lev 10:6;
vites are to be responsible for the care of Nu 16:46; 18:5
the tabernacle of the Testimony.[p]" [p] Nu 18:2-4
54 The Israelites did all this just as the
LORD commanded Moses.

> IF YOU WISH TO BE DISAPPOINTED, LOOK TO OTHERS. IF YOU WISH TO BE DOWNHEARTED, LOOK TO YOURSELF. IF YOU WISH TO BE ENCOURAGED ... LOOK UPON JESUS CHRIST.
>
> Eric Sauer, *Author and Theologian*

The Arrangement of the Tribal Camps

2 The LORD said to Moses and Aaron: 2 "The Israelites are to camp
around the Tent of Meeting some dis-
tance from it, each man under his stan- 2:2 [q] Nu 1:52;
dard[q] with the banners of his family." Ps 74:4; Isa 31:9
3 On the east, toward the sunrise,
the divisions of the camp of Judah
are to encamp under their standard.
The leader of the people of Judah is 2:3
Nahshon son of Amminadab.[r] 4 His [r] Nu 10:14; Ru 4:20;
division numbers 74,600. 1Ch 2:10
5 The tribe of Issachar will camp
next to them. The leader of the people of Issachar is Nethanel son of 2:5
Zuar.[s] 6 His division numbers 54,400. [s] Nu 1:8
7 The tribe of Zebulun will be
next. The leader of the people of 2:7
Zebulun is Eliab son of Helon.[t] 8 His [t] Nu 1:9
division numbers 57,400.
9 All the men assigned to the
camp of Judah, according to their
divisions, number 186,400. They 2:9
will set out first.[u] [u] Nu 10:14
10 On the south will be the

Marching Orders

When you embark on a journey it helps to have an idea not only of *where* you are going but also of *how* you intend to get there. God knew that as his people made their way out of Egypt in search of the promised land, they would need a map. Without clear-cut directions regarding both *where* and *how* to go, the Israelite assembly would soon disintegrate into a disorganized, chaotic mob. They would never reach their destination.

God's map included travel instructions. *Each individual knew his position with relation to his tribe* (Numbers 2:3–33). Every man stood with his family under that family's banner. Also, *each tribe knew its position with relation to the larger community*. While the people were resting, the arrangement was carefully configured according to God's instructions to Moses with three tribes camping on each of the four sides of the Tent of Meeting. Finally, *the whole community knew its position in relation to God*. In the very center of the community the people set up the Tent of Meeting, ensuring that God would remain the central focus of all activity. The people were required to maintain a respectful distance from the Tent of Meeting.

Our own spiritual journey with God is based on two elements: First, we need to have a right relationship with God. Without God at the center of their plans, decisions and community life, the Israelites would have had no hope. God's presence in the middle of the camp promised order, peace and supernatural guidance.

But we just as surely need to have a right relationship with others. Because God positioned the Israelite people, they couldn't quarrel over favored spots. He stipulated marching orders to eliminate disputes over who would lead and who would follow. There would have to have been a commitment to harmony in order for this impressive throng to have reached its final destination.

Every Christian is also on a journey, and it is vital on that journey to have a proper relationship both with God and with each other. As we travel along, Jesus is the person we imitate as we learn what he desires. Jesus came to serve people and to do God's will, and he is our example for both. He brings order to all our relationships. Without his death, burial and resurrection, we would have no hope for reconciliation with the perfect God who created us: "Once you were alienated from God and were enemies in your minds because of your evil behavior. But now he has reconciled you by Christ's physical body through death to present you holy in his sight, without blemish and free from accusation" (Colossians 1:21–22).

Self-Discovery: *How can the work of Jesus help you to repair your relationship either with God or with some other person?*

GO TO DISCOVERY 36 ON PAGE 180

divisions of the camp of Reuben
under their standard. The leader
of the people of Reuben is Elizur
2:10 v Nu 1:5 son of Shedeur.[v] 11His division
numbers 46,500.
12The tribe of Simeon will camp
next to them. The leader of the
2:12 people of Simeon is Shelumiel son
w Nu 1:6 of Zurishaddai.[w] 13His division
numbers 59,300.
14The tribe of Gad will be next.
2:14 The leader of the people of Gad is
x Nu 1:14 Eliasaph son of Deuel.[a] [x] 15His division numbers 45,650.
16All the men assigned to the
2:16 y Nu 10:18 camp of Reuben,[y] according to
their divisions, number 151,450.
They will set out second.

17Then the Tent of Meeting and
2:17 z Nu 1:53; 10:21 the camp of the Levites[z] will set
out in the middle of the camps.
They will set out in the same order
as they encamp, each in his own
place under his standard.

18On the west will be the divi-
2:18 a Ge 48:20; sions of the camp of Ephraim[a] un-
Jer 31:18-20 der their standard. The leader of
b Nu 1:10 the people of Ephraim is Elishama
son of Ammihud.[b] 19His division
numbers 40,500.
20The tribe of Manasseh will be
next to them. The leader of the
2:20 people of Manasseh is Gamaliel
c Nu 1:10 son of Pedahzur.[c] 21His division
numbers 32,200.
22The tribe of Benjamin will be
next. The leader of the people of
2:22 Benjamin is Abidan son of Gideo-
d Nu 1:11; Ps 68:27 ni.[d] 23His division numbers 35,400.
24All the men assigned to the
2:24 e Nu 10:22 camp of Ephraim,[e] according to
f Ps 80:2 their divisions, number 108,100.
They will set out third.[f]

25On the north will be the divisions of the camp of Dan, under
their standard. The leader of the
people of Dan is Ahiezer son of
2:25 g Nu 1:12 Ammishaddai.[g] 26His division
numbers 62,700.
27The tribe of Asher will camp
next to them. The leader of the peo-
2:27 h Nu 1:13 ple of Asher is Pagiel son of Ocran.[h]
28His division numbers 41,500.
29The tribe of Naphtali will be
next. The leader of the people of
Naphtali is Ahira son of Enan.[i] 2:29 i Nu 1:15
30His division numbers 53,400.
31All the men assigned to the
camp of Dan number 157,600. They 2:31
will set out last,[j] under their stan- j Nu 10:25
dards.

32These are the Israelites, counted according to their families. All
those in the camps, by their divi- 2:32 k Ex 38:26;
sions, number 603,550.[k] 33The Le- Nu 1:46
vites, however, were not counted[l] 2:33
along with the other Israelites, as l Nu 1:47; 26:57-62
the LORD commanded Moses.
34So the Israelites did everything the
LORD commanded Moses; that is the
way they encamped under their standards, and that is the way they set out,
each with his clan and family.

The Levites

3 This is the account of the family of 3:1
Aaron and Moses[m] at the time the m Ex 6:27
LORD talked with Moses on Mount Sinai.
2The names of the sons of Aaron were
Nadab the firstborn and Abihu, Eleazar 3:2 n Ex 6:23;
and Ithamar.[n] 3Those were the names of Nu 26:60
Aaron's sons, the anointed priests,[o] who 3:3
were ordained to serve as priests. 4Na- o Ex 28:41
dab and Abihu, however, fell dead before 3:4
the LORD[p] when they made an offering p Lev 10:2
with unauthorized fire before him in the q Lev 10:1
Desert of Sinai.[q] They had no sons; so r 1Ch 24:1
only Eleazar and Ithamar served as
priests during the lifetime of their father
Aaron.[r]
5The LORD said to Moses, 6"Bring the 3:6
tribe of Levi[s] and present them to Aaron s Dt 10:8; 31:9;
the priest to assist him.[t] 7They are to per- 1Ch 15:2 t Nu 8:6-22;
form duties for him and for the whole 18:1-7;
community at the Tent of Meeting by 2Ch 29:11
doing the work[u] of the tabernacle. 8They 3:7
are to take care of all the furnishings of u Lev 8:35; Nu 1:50
the Tent of Meeting, fulfilling the obliga-
tions of the Israelites by doing the work
of the tabernacle. 9Give the Levites to
Aaron and his sons;[v] they are the Israel- 3:9 v Nu 8:19; 18:6
ites who are to be given wholly to him.[b]
10Appoint Aaron and his sons to serve as 3:10
priests;[w] anyone else who approaches w Ex 29:9
the sanctuary must be put to death."[x] x Nu 1:51

[a] *14* Many manuscripts of the Masoretic Text, Samaritan Pentateuch and Vulgate (see also Num. 1:14); most manuscripts of the Masoretic Text *Reuel* [b] *9* Most manuscripts of the Masoretic Text; some manuscripts of the Masoretic Text, Samaritan Pentateuch and Septuagint (see also Num. 8:16) *to me*

3:12 11 The LORD also said to Moses, 12 "I
y Mal 2:4 have taken the Levites[y] from among the
z ver 41; Nu 8:16,18 Israelites in place of the first male off-
a Ex 13:2 spring[z] of every Israelite woman. The
3:13 Levites are mine,[a] 13 for all the firstborn
b Ex 13:12 are mine.[b] When I struck down all the
firstborn in Egypt, I set apart for myself
every firstborn in Israel, whether man or
animal. They are to be mine. I am the
LORD."
3:15 14 The LORD said to Moses in the
c ver 39 Desert of Sinai, 15 "Count[c] the Levites by
d Nu 26:62 their families and clans. Count every
male a month old or more."[d] 16 So Moses
counted them, as he was commanded
by the word of the LORD.

17 These were the names of the sons
3:17 e Ge 46:11 of Levi:[e]
f Ex 6:16 Gershon, Kohath and Merari.[f]
18 These were the names of the Ger-
3:18 shonite clans:
g Ex 6:17 Libni and Shimei.[g]
19 The Kohathite clans:
3:19 Amram, Izhar, Hebron and Uz-
h Ex 6:18 ziel.[h]
3:20 i Ge 46:11 20 The Merarite clans:[i]
j Ex 6:19 Mahli and Mushi.[j]

These were the Levite clans, according to their families.

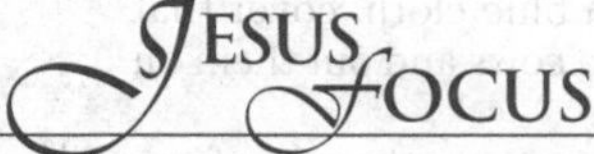

THE FAMILY OF LEVI

Levi's descendants constituted the priestly line and were also a part of the Messiah's lineage through Jacob and Leah (Numbers 3). The Levites were divided into three groups, each identified with one of Levi's sons: the Gershonites, the Kohathites and the Merarites. The Levites were Aaron's assistants, serving in the tabernacle. During the 40 years in the desert the Levites were in charge of the tabernacle and its furnishings. Later they assisted the priests in caring for the temple and in offering sacrifices, as well as functioning as officers, gatekeepers and musicians. The tribe of Levi did not receive any of the land God had promised, because the Levites were to be supported by gifts and tithes from God's people. According to the common practice of naming a son after the founder of the family, one of Jesus' ancestors was named Levi (Luke 3:24). Jesus referred to the Levite priests in Luke 10:32, and his disciple Matthew was also known as Levi. Finally, in the book of Acts, we read that Paul's friend Barnabas was a Levite (Acts 4:36).

21 To Gershon belonged the clans of 3:21
the Libnites and Shimeites;[k] these were k Ex 6:17
the Gershonite clans. 22 The number of
all the males a month old or more who
were counted was 7,500. 23 The Gershonite clans were to camp on the west, behind the tabernacle. 24 The leader of the
families of the Gershonites was Eliasaph
son of Lael. 25 At the Tent of Meeting the
Gershonites were responsible for the 3:25
care of the tabernacle[l] and tent, its cov- l Ex 25:9
erings,[m] the curtain at the entrance[n] to m Ex 26:14
the Tent of Meeting, 26 the curtains of the n Ex 26:36; Nu 4:25
courtyard[o], the curtain at the entrance 3:26
to the courtyard surrounding the taber- o Ex 27:9
nacle and altar, and the ropes[p]—and p Ex 35:18
everything related to their use.

27 To Kohath belonged the clans of the
Amramites, Izharites, Hebronites and
Uzzielites;[q] these were the Kohathite 3:27 q 1Ch 26:23
clans. 28 The number of all the males a
month old or more was 8,600.[a] The Kohathites were responsible for the care of
the sanctuary. 29 The Kohathite clans 3:29
were to camp on the south side[r] of the r Nu 1:53
tabernacle. 30 The leader of the families
of the Kohathite clans was Elizaphan
son of Uzziel. 31 They were responsible 3:31
for the care of the ark,[s] the table,[t] the s Ex 25:10-22
lampstand,[u] the altars,[v] the articles of t Ex 25:23 u Ex 25:31
the sanctuary used in ministering, the v Ex 27:1; 30:1
curtain,[w] and everything related to their w Ex 26:33
use.[x] 32 The chief leader of the Levites x Nu 4:15
was Eleazar son of Aaron, the priest. He
was appointed over those who were responsible for the care of the sanctuary.

33 To Merari belonged the clans of the
Mahlites and the Mushites;[y] these were 3:33 y Ex 6:19
the Merarite clans. 34 The number of all
the males a month old or more who
were counted was 6,200. 35 The leader of
the families of the Merarite clans was
Zuriel son of Abihail; they were to camp 3:35
on the north side of the tabernacle.[z] z Nu 1:53; 2:25
36 The Merarites were appointed[a] to take 3:36
care of the frames of the tabernacle, its a Nu 4:32
crossbars, posts, bases, all its equipment, and everything related to their
use, 37 as well as the posts of the surrounding courtyard with their bases,
tent pegs and ropes.

38 Moses and Aaron and his sons were 3:38
to camp to the east[b] of the tabernacle, b Nu 2:3

[a] 28 Hebrew; some Septuagint manuscripts *8,300*

toward the sunrise, in front of the Tent of
3:38 Meeting.[c] They were responsible for the
c Nu 1:53 d ver 7; care of the sanctuary[d] on behalf of the Is-
Nu 18:5 e ver 10; raelites. Anyone else who approached
Nu 1:51 the sanctuary was to be put to death.[e]

39 The total number of Levites counted at the LORD's command by Moses and
Aaron according to their clans, including every male a month old or more, was
3:39 f Nu 26:62 22,000.[f]

40 The LORD said to Moses, "Count all
the firstborn Israelite males who are a
3:40 g ver 15 month old or more[g] and make a list of
their names. 41 Take the Levites for me in
place of all the firstborn of the Israel-
3:41 h ver 12 ites,[h] and the livestock of the Levites in
place of all the firstborn of the livestock
of the Israelites. I am the LORD."

42 So Moses counted all the firstborn
of the Israelites, as the LORD commanded him. 43 The total number of firstborn
males a month old or more, listed by
3:43 i ver 39 name, was 22,273.[i]

44 The LORD also said to Moses,
45 "Take the Levites in place of all the
firstborn of Israel, and the livestock of
the Levites in place of their livestock.
3:46 The Levites are to be mine. I am the
j Ex 13:13; LORD. 46 To redeem[j] the 273 firstborn Is-
Nu 18:15 raelites who exceed the number of the
3:47 Levites, 47 collect five shekels[a][k] for each
k Lev 27:6 l Ex 30:13 one, according to the sanctuary shekel,[l]
m Lev 27:25 which weighs twenty gerahs.[m] 48 Give the
money for the redemption of the addi-
tional Israelites to Aaron and his sons."

49 So Moses collected the redemption
money from those who exceeded the
number redeemed by the Levites. 50 From
the firstborn of the Israelites he collect-
3:50 n ver 46-48 ed silver weighing 1,365 shekels,[b][n] according to the sanctuary shekel. 51 Moses
gave the redemption money to Aaron
and his sons, as he was commanded by
the word of the LORD.

The Kohathites

4 The LORD said to Moses and Aar-
4:2 o Ex 30:12 on: 2 "Take a census[o] of the Kohathite branch of the Levites by their
clans and families. 3 Count all the men
4:3 p ver 23; from thirty to fifty years of age[p] who
Nu 8:25; come to serve in the work in the Tent of
1Ch 23:3,24,27; Ezr 3:8 Meeting.

4 "This is the work of the Kohathites in
the Tent of Meeting: the care of the most
holy things.[q] 5 When the camp is to 4:4 q ver 19
move, Aaron and his sons are to go in
and take down the shielding curtain[r] 4:5
and cover the ark of the Testimony with r Ex 26:31,33
it.[s] 6 Then they are to cover this with s Ex 25:10,16
hides of sea cows,[c] spread a cloth of sol- 4:6
id blue over that and put the poles[t] in t Ex 25:13-15;
place. 1Ki 8:7; 2Ch 5:8

7 "Over the table of the Presence[u] they 4:7
are to spread a blue cloth and put on it u Ex 25:23,29;
the plates, dishes and bowls, and the jars Lev 24:6 v Ex 25:30
for drink offerings; the bread that is continually there[v] is to remain on it. 8 Over
these they are to spread a scarlet cloth,
cover that with hides of sea cows and
put its poles in place.

9 "They are to take a blue cloth and
cover the lampstand that is for light, together with its lamps, its wick trimmers 4:9
and trays,[w] and all its jars for the oil used w Ex 25:31,37, 38
to supply it. 10 Then they are to wrap it
and all its accessories in a covering of
hides of sea cows and put it on a carrying frame.

11 "Over the gold altar[x] they are to 4:11 x Ex 30:1
spread a blue cloth and cover that with
hides of sea cows and put its poles in
place.

12 "They are to take all the articles
used for ministering in the sanctuary,
wrap them in a blue cloth, cover that
with hides of sea cows and put them on
a carrying frame.

13 "They are to remove the ashes from 4:13
the bronze altar[y] and spread a purple y Ex 27:1-8
cloth over it. 14 Then they are to place on
it all the utensils used for ministering at
the altar, including the firepans, meat 4:14
forks,[z] shovels and sprinkling bowls.[a] z 2Ch 4:16
Over it they are to spread a covering of a Jer 52:18
hides of sea cows and put its poles[b] in b Ex 27:6
place.

15 "After Aaron and his sons have finished covering the holy furnishings and
all the holy articles, and when the camp
is ready to move, the Kohathites are to 4:15
come to do the carrying.[c] But they must c Nu 7:9
not touch the holy things or they will d Nu 1:51;
die.[d] The Kohathites are to carry those 2Sa 6:6,7
things that are in the Tent of Meeting.

16 "Eleazar[e] son of Aaron, the priest, is 4:16
to have charge of the oil for the light,[f] e Lev 10:6
the fragrant incense, the regular grain f Ex 25:6 g Ex 29:41;
offering[g] and the anointing oil. He is to Lev 6:14-23

a 47 That is, about 2 ounces (about 55 grams)
b 50 That is, about 35 pounds (about 15.5 kilograms) *c 6* That is, dugongs; also in verses 8, 10, 11, 12, 14 and 25

be in charge of the entire tabernacle and
everything in it, including its holy furnishings and articles."
[17]The LORD said to Moses and Aaron,
[18]"See that the Kohathite tribal clans are
not cut off from the Levites. [19]So that
4:19 they may live and not die when they
h ver 15 come near the most holy things,[h] do this
for them: Aaron and his sons are to go
into the sanctuary and assign to each
man his work and what he is to carry.
4:20 [20]But the Kohathites must not go in to
i Ex 19:21; look[i] at the holy things, even for a mo-
1Sa 6:19 ment, or they will die."

The Gershonites

[21]The LORD said to Moses, [22]"Take a
census also of the Gershonites by their
4:23 families and clans. [23]Count all the men
j ver 3; 1Ch 23:3, from thirty to fifty years of age[j] who
24,27 come to serve in the work at the Tent of
Meeting.
[24]"This is the service of the Gershonite clans as they work and carry burdens:
4:25 [25]They are to carry the curtains of the
k Ex 27:10-18; tabernacle,[k] the Tent of Meeting,[l] its cov-
Nu 3:26 ering[m] and the outer covering of hides of
l Nu 3:25 sea cows, the curtains for the entrance to
m Ex 26:14 the Tent of Meeting, [26]the curtains of the
courtyard surrounding the tabernacle
and altar, the curtain for the entrance,
the ropes and all the equipment used in
its service. The Gershonites are to do all
that needs to be done with these things.
[27]All their service, whether carrying or
doing other work, is to be done under
the direction of Aaron and his sons. You
shall assign to them as their responsibil-
4:28 ity all they are to carry. [28]This is the ser-
n Nu 7:7 vice of the Gershonite clans[n] at the Tent
of Meeting. Their duties are to be under
the direction of Ithamar son of Aaron,
the priest.

The Merarites

4:29 [29]"Count the Merarites by their clans
o Ge 46:11 and families.[o] [30]Count all the men from
thirty to fifty years of age who come to
serve in the work at the Tent of Meeting.
[31]This is their duty as they perform service at the Tent of Meeting: to carry the
4:31 frames of the tabernacle, its crossbars,
p Nu 3:36 posts and bases,[p] [32]as well as the posts
of the surrounding courtyard with their
bases, tent pegs, ropes, all their equipment and everything related to their
use. Assign to each man the specific
things he is to carry. [33]This is the service
of the Merarite clans as they work at the
Tent of Meeting under the direction of
Ithamar son of Aaron, the priest."

The Numbering of the Levite Clans

[34]Moses, Aaron and the leaders of the
community counted the Kohathites[q] by 4:34
their clans and families. [35]All the men q ver 2
from thirty to fifty years of age who
came to serve in the work in the Tent of
Meeting, [36]counted by clans, were 2,750.
[37]This was the total of all those in the
Kohathite clans[r] who served in the Tent 4:37
of Meeting. Moses and Aaron counted r Nu 3:27
them according to the LORD's command
through Moses.
[38]The Gershonites[s] were counted by 4:38
their clans and families. [39]All the men s Ge 46:11
from thirty to fifty years of age who
came to serve in the work at the Tent of
Meeting, [40]counted by their clans and
families, were 2,630. [41]This was the total
of those in the Gershonite clans who
served at the Tent of Meeting. Moses
and Aaron counted them according to
the LORD's command.
[42]The Merarites were counted by their
clans and families. [43]All the men from
thirty to fifty years of age who came to
serve in the work at the Tent of Meeting,
[44]counted by their clans, were 3,200.
[45]This was the total of those in the Me- 4:45
rarite clans.[t] Moses and Aaron counted t ver 29
them according to the LORD's command
through Moses.
[46]So Moses, Aaron and the leaders of
Israel counted all the Levites by their
clans and families. [47]All the men from 4:47
thirty to fifty years of age[u] who came to u ver 3
do the work of serving and carrying the 4:48
Tent of Meeting [48]numbered 8,580.[v] [49]At v Nu 3:39
the LORD's command through Moses,
each was assigned his work and told
what to carry.
Thus they were counted,[w] as the LORD 4:49
commanded Moses. w Nu 1:47

The Purity of the Camp

5 The LORD said to Moses, [2]"Command the Israelites to send away
from the camp anyone who has an in- 5:2
fectious skin disease[a][x] or a discharge[y] of x Lev 13:46
any kind, or who is ceremonially un- y Lev 15:2; Mt 9:20

[a] 2 Traditionally *leprosy*; the Hebrew word was
used for various diseases affecting the skin—not
necessarily leprosy.

5:2 clean[z] because of a dead body. [3]Send
z Lev 13:3; away male and female alike; send them
Nu 9:6-10 outside the camp so they will not defile
their camp, where I dwell among
5:3 them.[a]" [4]The Israelites did this; they
a Lev 26:12; Nu 35:34; sent them outside the camp. They did
2Co 6:16 just as the LORD had instructed Moses.

Restitution for Wrongs

[5]The LORD said to Moses, [6]"Say to the
Israelites: 'When a man or woman
5:6 wrongs another in any way[a] and so is
b Lev 6:2 unfaithful[b] to the LORD, that person is
c Lev 5:14-6:7 guilty[c] [7]and must confess[d] the sin he has
5:7 committed. He must make full restitu-
d Lev 5:5; 26:40; tion[e] for his wrong, add one fifth to it
Jos 7:19; Lk 19:8 e Lev 6:5 and give it all to the person he has
wronged. [8]But if that person has no
close relative to whom restitution can be
made for the wrong, the restitution belongs to the LORD and must be given to
5:8 the priest, along with the ram with
f Lev 6:6,7; 7:7 which atonement is made for him.[f] [9]All
5:9 the sacred contributions the Israelites
g Lev 6:17; 7:6-14 bring to a priest will belong to him.[g]
[10]Each man's sacred gifts are his own,
5:10 but what he gives to the priest will be-
h Lev 10:13 long to the priest.[h]' "

The Test for an Unfaithful Wife

[11]Then the LORD said to Moses,
[12]"Speak to the Israelites and say to
5:12 them: 'If a man's wife goes astray[i] and is
i Ex 20:14 unfaithful to him [13]by sleeping with an-
5:13 other man,[j] and this is hidden from her
j Lev 18:20; 20:10 husband and her impurity is undetected (since there is no witness against her
and she has not been caught in the act),
5:14 [14]and if feelings of jealousy[k] come over
k Pr 6:34; SS 8:6 her husband and he suspects his wife
and she is impure—or if he is jealous
and suspects her even though she is not
impure— [15]then he is to take his wife to
the priest. He must also take an offering
5:15 of a tenth of an ephah[b][l] of barley flour[m]
l Ex 16:36 m Lev 6:20 on her behalf. He must not pour oil on it
n Eze 29:16 or put incense on it, because it is a grain
offering for jealousy, a reminder[n] offering to draw attention to guilt.
[16]" 'The priest shall bring her and have
her stand before the LORD. [17]Then he
shall take some holy water in a clay jar
and put some dust from the tabernacle
floor into the water. [18]After the priest
has had the woman stand before the
5:18 o Lev 10:6; LORD, he shall loosen her hair[o] and place
1Co 11:6 in her hands the reminder offering, the
grain offering for jealousy, while he himself holds the bitter water that brings a
curse. [19]Then the priest shall put the
woman under oath and say to her, "If no
other man has slept with you and you
have not gone astray[p] and become im- 5:19 p ver 12,29
pure while married to your husband,
may this bitter water that brings a curse
not harm you. [20]But if you have gone
astray[q] while married to your husband 5:20 q ver 12
and you have defiled yourself by sleeping
with a man other than your husband"—
[21]here the priest is to put the woman under this curse of the oath[r]—"may the 5:21 r Jos 6:26;
LORD cause your people to curse and de- 1Sa 14:24;
nounce you when he causes your thigh Ne 10:29
to waste away and your abdomen to
swell.[c] [22]May this water[s] that brings a 5:22 s Ps 109:18
curse[t] enter your body so that your ab- t ver 18
domen swells and your thigh wastes u Dt 27:15
away.[d]"
" 'Then the woman is to say, "Amen.
So be it.[u]"
[23]" 'The priest is to write these curses
on a scroll[v] and then wash them off into 5:23 v Jer 45:1
the bitter water. [24]He shall have the
woman drink the bitter water that
brings a curse, and this water will enter
her and cause bitter suffering. [25]The
priest is to take from her hands the
grain offering for jealousy, wave it before 5:25
the LORD[w] and bring it to the altar. [26]The w Lev 8:27
priest is then to take a handful of the
grain offering as a memorial offering
and burn it on the altar; after that, he is
to have the woman drink the water. [27]If
she has defiled herself and been unfaithful to her husband, then when she
is made to drink the water that brings a
curse, it will go into her and cause bitter
suffering; her abdomen will swell and
her thigh waste away,[e] and she will be- 5:27
come accursed[x] among her people. [28]If, x Isa 43:28;
however, the woman has not defiled her- 65:15; Jer 26:6; 29:18; 42:18;
self and is free from impurity, she will be 44:12,22;
cleared of guilt and will be able to have Zec 8:13
children.
[29]" 'This, then, is the law of jealousy
when a woman goes astray[y] and defiles 5:29
herself while married to her husband, y ver 19
[30]or when feelings of jealousy come over

[a] 6 Or *woman commits any wrong common to mankind* [b] 15 That is, probably about 2 quarts (about 2 liters) [c] 21 Or *causes you to have a miscarrying womb and barrenness* [d] 22 Or *body and cause you to be barren and have a miscarrying womb* [e] 27 Or *suffering; she will have barrenness and a miscarrying womb*

a man because he suspects his wife. The
priest is to have her stand before the
LORD and is to apply this entire law to
her. 31The husband will be innocent of
any wrongdoing, but the woman will
5:31 [z] Lev 5:1; 20:17 bear the consequences[z] of her sin.' "

The Nazirite

6 The LORD said to Moses, 2"Speak
to the Israelites and say to them:
'If a man or woman wants to make a
6:2 [a] Ge 28:20; Ac 21:23 [b] Jdg 13:5; 16:17; Am 2:11,12 special vow[a], a vow of separation to the
LORD as a Nazirite,[b] 3he must abstain
from wine[c] and other fermented drink
and must not drink vinegar[d] made from
6:3 [c] Lk 1:15 [d] Ru 2:14; Ps 69:21; Pr 10:26 wine or from other fermented drink. He
must not drink grape juice or eat grapes
or raisins. 4As long as he is a Nazirite, he
must not eat anything that comes from
the grapevine, not even the seeds or
skins.
5" 'During the entire period of his vow
6:5 [e] Ps 52:2; 57:4; 59:7; Isa 7:20; Eze 5:1 [f] 1Sa 1:11 of separation no razor[e] may be used on
his head.[f] He must be holy until the pe-
riod of his separation to the LORD is over;
he must let the hair of his head grow
long. 6Throughout the period of his separation to the LORD he must not go near
6:6 [g] Lev 21:1-3; Nu 19:11-22 a dead body.[g] 7Even if his own father or
mother or brother or sister dies, he must
6:7 [h] Nu 9:6 not make himself ceremonially unclean[h] on account of them, because the
symbol of his separation to God is on his
head. 8Throughout the period of his separation he is consecrated to the LORD.
9" 'If someone dies suddenly in his
presence, thus defiling the hair he has
6:9 [i] ver 18 [j] Lev 14:9 dedicated,[i] he must shave his head on
the day of his cleansing[j]—the seventh
day. 10Then on the eighth day he must
6:10 [k] Lev 5:7; 14:22 bring two doves or two young pigeons[k]
to the priest at the entrance to the Tent
of Meeting. 11The priest is to offer one as
a sin offering and the other as a burnt
6:11 [l] Ge 8:20 [m] Ex 29:36 offering[l] to make atonement[m] for him
because he sinned by being in the pres-
ence of the dead body. That same day he
is to consecrate his head. 12He must
dedicate himself to the LORD for the period of his separation and must bring a
year-old male lamb as a guilt offering.
The previous days do not count, because
he became defiled during his separation.
13" 'Now this is the law for the Nazirite
when the period of his separation is
6:13 [n] Ac 21:26 over.[n] He is to be brought to the entrance to the Tent of Meeting. 14There he
is to present his offerings to the LORD: a
year-old male lamb without defect for a
burnt offering, a year-old ewe lamb
without defect for a sin offering,[o] a ram 6:14 [o] Lev 14:10; Nu 15:27
without defect for a fellowship offering,[a]
15together with their grain offerings and
drink offerings,[p] and a basket of bread 6:15 [p] Nu 15:1-7 [q] Ex 29:2; Lev 2:4
made without yeast—cakes made of
fine flour mixed with oil, and wafers
spread with oil.[q]
16" 'The priest is to present them before the LORD and make the sin offering
and the burnt offering. 17He is to present
the basket of unleavened bread and is to
sacrifice the ram as a fellowship offering
to the LORD, together with its grain offering and drink offering.
18" 'Then at the entrance to the Tent
of Meeting, the Nazirite must shave off
the hair that he dedicated.[r] He is to take 6:18 [r] ver 9; Ac 21:24
the hair and put it in the fire that is un-
der the sacrifice of the fellowship offering.
19" 'After the Nazirite has shaved off
the hair of his dedication, the priest is to
place in his hands a boiled shoulder of
the ram, and a cake and a wafer from the
basket, both made without yeast. 20The
priest shall then wave them before the
LORD as a wave offering; they are holy
and belong to the priest, together with
the breast that was waved and the thigh
that was presented. After that, the Nazirite may drink wine.[s] 6:20 [s] Ecc 9:7
21" 'This is the law of the Nazirite who
vows his offering to the LORD in accor-
dance with his separation, in addition to 6:23 [t] Dt 21:5; 1Ch 23:13
whatever else he can afford. He must ful-
fill the vow he has made, according to 6:24 [u] Dt 28:3-6; Ps 28:9 [v] 1Sa 2:9; Ps 17:8
the law of the Nazirite.' "

The Priestly Blessing

22The LORD said to Moses, 23"Tell Aar-
on and his sons, 'This is how you are to 6:25 [w] Job 29:24; Ps 31:16; 80:3; 119:135 [x] Ge 43:29; Ps 25:16; 86:16
bless[t] the Israelites. Say to them:

24" ' "The LORD bless you[u]
and keep you;[v] 6:26 [y] Ps 4:6; 44:3 [z] Ps 29:11; 37:11,37; Jn 14:27
25the LORD make his face shine upon
you[w]
and be gracious to you;[x]
26the LORD turn his face[y] toward you
and give you peace.[z]" ' 6:27 [a] Dt 28:10; 2Sa 7:23; 2Ch 7:14; Ne 9:10; Jer 25:29

27"So they will put my name[a] on the
Israelites, and I will bless them."

[a] *14* Traditionally *peace offering*; also in verses 17 and 18

DISCOVERY 36

A Blessing for All Time

As priests, Aaron and his descendants blessed the people of Israel with these words: "The LORD bless you and keep you; the LORD make his face shine upon you and be gracious to you; the LORD turn his face toward you and give you peace" (Numbers 6:24–26).

This blessing identified the Israelites directly and publicly with their God—"so they will put my name on the Israelites" (verse 27). This blessing reminded the people of what God had done and would continue to do for them.

The most important word in the blessing is *LORD*. God is the source of each of the three parts of the blessing. Every time this blessing was pronounced it reminded the people that they were indebted to God for everything they had. This is true in our own lives today. God is the source of every spiritual blessing in Jesus Christ (Ephesians 1:3–14), as well as of every material blessing (James 1:17).

God's people have always been the focal point of God's attention. He makes "his face shine upon" us and turns his face toward us. When you turn toward someone to look at him or her, you are offering your full attention. Essentially, God is saying that his people enjoy the undivided attention of the God of the universe—what a powerful thought! If you are walking with him, this includes you! And he wants to be the center of *your* attention as well.

Numbers 6:24–26 enumerates three blessings we receive from God: He keeps us, he is gracious and he offers peace. The New Testament refers to these same three blessings as coming from Jesus Christ. Our Lord himself stated in John 10:28: "My sheep hear my voice; I know them, and they follow me. I give them eternal life, and they shall never perish; no one can snatch them out of my hand." The apostle Paul professed in Acts 15:11 that we are saved through the grace of our Lord Jesus Christ. And Jesus conferred the gift of peace on his disciples in John 14:27: "Peace I leave with you; my peace I give you. I do not give to you as the world gives. Do not let your hearts be troubled and do not be afraid."

Whatever our circumstances, we are blessed by God. He will keep us safe through every difficulty. He will be gracious to us and fill us with peace in the midst of life's storms.

Self-Discovery: *Select a symbol, such as the sun, to help you visualize God's face shining down on you today. Bask in the warmth and revel in the light. Can you imagine God smiling as he fixes his gaze on you, his beloved child?*

GO TO DISCOVERY 37 ON PAGE 185

Offerings at the Dedication of the Tabernacle

7 When Moses finished setting up
7:1 [b]Ex 40:17 the tabernacle,[b] he anointed it
[c]Ex 40:9 and consecrated it and all its furnish-
[d]ver 84,88; ings.[c] He also anointed and consecrated
Ex 40:10 the altar and all its utensils.[d] 2Then the
7:2 [e]Nu 1:5-16 leaders of Israel,[e] the heads of families
who were the tribal leaders in charge of
those who were counted, made offerings. 3They brought as their gifts before
the LORD six covered carts and twelve
oxen—an ox from each leader and a cart
from every two. These they presented
before the tabernacle.
4The LORD said to Moses, 5"Accept
these from them, that they may be used
in the work at the Tent of Meeting. Give
them to the Levites as each man's work
requires."
6So Moses took the carts and oxen
and gave them to the Levites. 7He gave
two carts and four oxen to the Gershon-
7:7 [f]Nu 4:24-26,28 ites,[f] as their work required, 8and he
gave four carts and eight oxen to the
7:8 [g]Nu 4:31-33 Merarites,[g] as their work required. They
were all under the direction of Ithamar
son of Aaron, the priest. 9But Moses did
not give any to the Kohathites, because
7:9 [h]Nu 4:15 they were to carry on their shoulders[h]
the holy things, for which they were
responsible.
7:10 [i]ver 1 [j]2Ch 7:9 10When the altar was anointed,[i] the
leaders brought their offerings for its
dedication[j] and presented them before
the altar. 11For the LORD had said to Moses, "Each day one leader is to bring his
offering for the dedication of the altar."

12The one who brought his offering on
the first day was Nahshon son of Amminadab of the tribe of Judah.
13His offering was one silver plate
weighing a hundred and thirty
shekels,[a] and one silver sprinkling
7:13 bowl weighing seventy shekels,[b]
[k]Ex 30:13; both according to the sanctuary
Nu 3:47 shekel,[k] each filled with fine flour
[l]Lev 2:1 mixed with oil as a grain offering;[l]
7:14 [m]Ex 30:34 14one gold dish weighing ten
shekels,[c] filled with incense;[m] 15one
7:15 [n]Ex 24:5; 29:3; young bull,[n] one ram and one male
Nu 28:11 lamb a year old, for a burnt offer-
[o]Lev 1:3 ing;[o] 16one male goat for a sin offer-
7:16 [p]Lev 4:3,23 ing;[p] 17and two oxen, five rams, five
male goats and five male lambs a
year old, to be sacrificed as a fel-
lowship offering.[d][q] This was the of- 7:17 [q]Lev 3:1
fering of Nahshon son of Ammin- [r]Nu 1:7
adab.[r]

18On the second day Nethanel son of
Zuar,[s] the leader of Issachar, brought his 7:18 [s]Nu 1:8
offering.
19The offering he brought was one
silver plate weighing a hundred
and thirty shekels, and one silver
sprinkling bowl weighing seventy
shekels, both according to the
sanctuary shekel, each filled with
fine flour mixed with oil as a grain
offering; 20one gold dish[t] weighing 7:20
ten shekels, filled with incense; [t]ver 14
21one young bull, one ram and one
male lamb a year old, for a burnt offering; 22one male goat for a sin offering; 23and two oxen, five rams,
five male goats and five male lambs
a year old, to be sacrificed as a fellowship offering. This was the offering of Nethanel son of Zuar.

24On the third day, Eliab son of Helon,[u] 7:24 [u]Nu 1:9
the leader of the people of Zebulun,
brought his offering.
25His offering was one silver plate
weighing a hundred and thirty
shekels, and one silver sprinkling
bowl weighing seventy shekels,
both according to the sanctuary
shekel, each filled with fine flour
mixed with oil as a grain offering;
26one gold dish weighing ten
shekels, filled with incense; 27one
young bull, one ram and one male
lamb a year old, for a burnt offering; 28one male goat for a sin offering; 29and two oxen, five rams, five
male goats and five male lambs a
year old, to be sacrificed as a fellowship offering. This was the offering of Eliab son of Helon.

30On the fourth day Elizur son of Shede- 7:30
ur,[v] the leader of the people of Reuben, [v]Nu 1:5
brought his offering.
31His offering was one silver plate
weighing a hundred and thirty
shekels, and one silver sprinkling
bowl weighing seventy shekels,

[a] *13* That is, about 3 1/4 pounds (about 1.5 kilograms); also elsewhere in this chapter
[b] *13* That is, about 1 3/4 pounds (about 0.8 kilogram); also elsewhere in this chapter
[c] *14* That is, about 4 ounces (about 110 grams); also elsewhere in this chapter
[d] *17* Traditionally *peace offering*; also elsewhere in this chapter

both according to the sanctuary
shekel, each filled with fine flour
mixed with oil as a grain offering;
32 one gold dish weighing ten
shekels, filled with incense; 33 one
young bull, one ram and one male
lamb a year old, for a burnt offering; 34 one male goat for a sin offering; 35 and two oxen, five rams, five
male goats and five male lambs a
year old, to be sacrificed as a fellowship offering. This was the offering of Elizur son of Shedeur.

36 On the fifth day Shelumiel son of Zuri-
7:36 [w]Nu 1:6 shaddai,[w] the leader of the people of
Simeon, brought his offering.
37 His offering was one silver plate
weighing a hundred and thirty
shekels, and one silver sprinkling
bowl weighing seventy shekels,
both according to the sanctuary
shekel, each filled with fine flour
mixed with oil as a grain offering;
38 one gold dish weighing ten
shekels, filled with incense; 39 one
young bull, one ram and one male
lamb a year old, for a burnt offering;
40 one male goat for a sin offering;
41 and two oxen, five rams, five male
goats and five male lambs a year
old, to be sacrificed as a fellowship
offering. This was the offering of
Shelumiel son of Zurishaddai.

42 On the sixth day Eliasaph son of Deu-
7:42 [x]Nu 1:14 el,[x] the leader of the people of Gad,
brought his offering.
43 His offering was one silver plate
weighing a hundred and thirty
shekels, and one silver sprinkling
bowl weighing seventy shekels,
both according to the sanctuary
shekel, each filled with fine flour
mixed with oil as a grain offering;
44 one gold dish weighing ten
shekels, filled with incense; 45 one
young bull, one ram and one male
lamb a year old, for a burnt offering; 46 one male goat for a sin offering; 47 and two oxen, five rams, five
male goats and five male lambs a
year old, to be sacrificed as a fellowship offering. This was the offering of Eliasaph son of Deuel.

48 On the seventh day Elishama son of
7:48 [y]Nu 1:10 Ammihud,[y] the leader of the people of
Ephraim, brought his offering.
49 His offering was one silver plate
weighing a hundred and thirty
shekels, and one silver sprinkling
bowl weighing seventy shekels,
both according to the sanctuary
shekel, each filled with fine flour
mixed with oil as a grain offering;
50 one gold dish weighing ten
shekels, filled with incense; 51 one
young bull, one ram and one male
lamb a year old, for a burnt offering;
52 one male goat for a sin offering;
53 and two oxen, five rams, five male
goats and five male lambs a year
old, to be sacrificed as a fellowship
offering. This was the offering of 7:53
Elishama son of Ammihud.[z] [z]Nu 1:10

54 On the eighth day Gamaliel son of Pe- 7:54
dahzur,[a] the leader of the people of Ma- [a]Nu 1:10; 2:20
nasseh, brought his offering.
55 His offering was one silver plate
weighing a hundred and thirty
shekels, and one silver sprinkling
bowl weighing seventy shekels,
both according to the sanctuary
shekel, each filled with fine flour
mixed with oil as a grain offering;
56 one gold dish weighing ten
shekels, filled with incense; 57 one
young bull, one ram and one male
lamb a year old, for a burnt offering; 58 one male goat for a sin offering; 59 and two oxen, five rams, five
male goats and five male lambs a
year old, to be sacrificed as a fellowship offering. This was the offering of Gamaliel son of Pedahzur.

60 On the ninth day Abidan son of Gide- 7:60
oni,[b] the leader of the people of Benja- [b]Nu 1:11
min, brought his offering.
61 His offering was one silver plate
weighing a hundred and thirty
shekels, and one silver sprinkling
bowl weighing seventy shekels,
both according to the sanctuary
shekel, each filled with fine flour
mixed with oil as a grain offering;
62 one gold dish weighing ten
shekels, filled with incense; 63 one
young bull, one ram and one male
lamb a year old, for a burnt offering; 64 one male goat for a sin offering; 65 and two oxen, five rams, five
male goats and five male lambs a
year old, to be sacrificed as a fel-

lowship offering. This was the offering of Abidan son of Gideoni.
66 On the tenth day Ahiezer son of Am-
7:66 [c] Nu 1:12; 2:25 mishaddai,[c] the leader of the people of
Dan, brought his offering.
67 His offering was one silver plate
weighing a hundred and thirty
shekels, and one silver sprinkling
bowl weighing seventy shekels,
both according to the sanctuary
shekel, each filled with fine flour
mixed with oil as a grain offering;
68 one gold dish weighing ten
shekels, filled with incense; 69 one
young bull, one ram and one male
lamb a year old, for a burnt offering; 70 one male goat for a sin offering; 71 and two oxen, five rams, five
male goats and five male lambs a
year old, to be sacrificed as a fellowship offering. This was the offering of Ahiezer son of Ammishaddai.
72 On the eleventh day Pagiel son of Oc-
7:72 [d] Nu 1:13 ran,[d] the leader of the people of Asher,
brought his offering.
73 His offering was one silver plate
weighing a hundred and thirty
shekels, and one silver sprinkling
bowl weighing seventy shekels,
both according to the sanctuary
shekel, each filled with fine flour
mixed with oil as a grain offering;
74 one gold dish weighing ten
shekels, filled with incense; 75 one
young bull, one ram and one male
lamb a year old, for a burnt offering; 76 one male goat for a sin offering; 77 and two oxen, five rams, five
male goats and five male lambs a
year old, to be sacrificed as a fellowship offering. This was the offering of Pagiel son of Ocran.
7:78 [e] Nu 1:15; 2:29 78 On the twelfth day Ahira son of Enan,[e]
the leader of the people of Naphtali,
brought his offering.
79 His offering was one silver plate
weighing a hundred and thirty
shekels, and one silver sprinkling
bowl weighing seventy shekels,
both according to the sanctuary
shekel, each filled with fine flour
mixed with oil as a grain offering;
80 one gold dish weighing ten
shekels, filled with incense; 81 one
young bull, one ram and one male
lamb a year old, for a burnt offering; 82 one male goat for a sin offering; 83 and two oxen, five rams, five
male goats and five male lambs a
year old, to be sacrificed as a fellowship offering. This was the offering of Ahira son of Enan.
84 These were the offerings of the Israelite leaders for the dedication of the al-
tar when it was anointed:[f] twelve silver 7:84 [f] ver 1,10
plates, twelve silver sprinkling bowls[g] [g] Nu 4:14
and twelve gold dishes.[h] 85 Each silver [h] ver 14
plate weighed a hundred and thirty
shekels, and each sprinkling bowl seventy shekels. Altogether, the silver dishes
weighed two thousand four hundred
shekels,[a] according to the sanctuary
shekel. 86 The twelve gold dishes filled
with incense weighed ten shekels each,
according to the sanctuary shekel. Altogether, the gold dishes weighed a hundred and twenty shekels.[b] 87 The total
number of animals for the burnt offering came to twelve young bulls, twelve
rams and twelve male lambs a year old,
together with their grain offering.
Twelve male goats were used for the sin
offering. 88 The total number of animals
for the sacrifice of the fellowship offering came to twenty-four oxen, sixty
rams, sixty male goats and sixty male
lambs a year old. These were the offerings for the dedication of the altar after 7:88
it was anointed.[i] [i] ver 1,10
89 When Moses entered the Tent of 7:89
Meeting to speak with the LORD,[j] he [j] Ex 25:21,22;
heard the voice speaking to him from 33:9,11 [k] Ps 80:1; 99:1
between the two cherubim above the
atonement cover[k] on the ark of the Testimony. And he spoke with him.

Setting Up the Lamps

8 The LORD said to Moses, 2 "Speak
to Aaron and say to him, 'When
you set up the seven lamps, they are to
light the area in front of the lamp- 8:2
stand.[l] ' " [l] Ex 25:37; Lev 24:2,4
3 Aaron did so; he set up the lamps so
that they faced forward on the lampstand, just as the LORD commanded Moses. 4 This is how the lampstand was
made: It was made of hammered 8:4
gold[m]—from its base to its blossoms. [m] Ex 25:18,36;
The lampstand was made exactly like 25:18 [n] Ex 25:9
the pattern[n] the LORD had shown Moses.

[a] *85* That is, about 60 pounds (about 28 kilograms)
[b] *86* That is, about 3 pounds (about 1.4 kilograms)

The Setting Apart of the Levites

5 The LORD said to Moses: 6 "Take the
8:6 Levites from among the other Israelites
o Lev 22:2; and make them ceremonially clean.[o] 7 To
Isa 1:16; 52:11 purify them, do this: Sprinkle the water
8:7 of cleansing[p] on them; then have them
p Nu 19:9,17 q Lev 14:9; shave their whole bodies[q] and wash
Dt 21:12 their clothes,[r] and so purify themselves.
r Lev 14:8 8 Have them take a young bull with its
8:8 grain offering of fine flour mixed with
s Lev 2:1; oil;[s] then you are to take a second young
Nu 15:8-10 bull for a sin offering. 9 Bring the Levites
8:9 to the front of the Tent of Meeting[t] and
t Ex 40:12 assemble the whole Israelite communi-
u Lev 8:3 ty.[u] 10 You are to bring the Levites before
the LORD, and the Israelites are to lay
8:10 their hands on them.[v] 11 Aaron is to pre-
v Ac 6:6 sent the Levites before the LORD as a wave
8:11 offering[w] from the Israelites, so that they
w Lev 7:30 may be ready to do the work of the LORD.
12 "After the Levites lay their hands on
8:12 the heads of the bulls,[x] use the one for a
x Ex 29:10 y Ex 29:36 sin offering to the LORD and the other for
a burnt offering, to make atonement[y]
for the Levites. 13 Have the Levites stand
in front of Aaron and his sons and then
present them as a wave offering to the
LORD. 14 In this way you are to set the Le-
8:14 vites apart from the other Israelites, and
z Nu 3:12 the Levites will be mine.[z]
15 "After you have purified the Levites
8:15 a Ex 29:24 and presented them as a wave offering,[a]
they are to come to do their work at the
Tent of Meeting. 16 They are the Israelites
who are to be given wholly to me. I have
taken them as my own in place of the
8:16 b Nu 3:12 firstborn, the first male offspring[b] from
every Israelite woman. 17 Every firstborn
8:17 male in Israel, whether man or animal,[c]
c Ex 4:23 d Ex 13:2; is mine. When I struck down all the
Lk 2:23 firstborn in Egypt, I set them apart for
myself.[d] 18 And I have taken the Levites
in place of all the firstborn sons in Isra-
8:18 e Nu 3:12 el.[e] 19 Of all the Israelites, I have given the
Levites as gifts to Aaron and his sons[f] to
8:19 f Nu 3:9 do the work at the Tent of Meeting on
g Nu 1:53 behalf of the Israelites[g] and to make
h Nu 16:46 atonement for them[h] so that no plague
will strike the Israelites when they go
near the sanctuary."
20 Moses, Aaron and the whole Israelite community did with the Levites just
as the LORD commanded Moses. 21 The
8:21 Levites purified themselves and washed
i ver 7 their clothes.[i] Then Aaron presented
them as a wave offering before the LORD
and made atonement for them to purify
them.[j] 22 After that, the Levites came to 8:21
do their work at the Tent of Meeting un- j ver 12
der the supervision of Aaron and his
sons. They did with the Levites just as
the LORD commanded Moses.
23 The LORD said to Moses, 24 "This applies to the Levites: Men twenty-five
years old or more[k] shall come to take 8:24 k 1Ch 23:3
part in the work at the Tent of Meeting,[l] l Ex 38:21;
25 but at the age of fifty, they must retire Nu 4:3
from their regular service and work no
longer. 26 They may assist their brothers
in performing their duties at the Tent of
Meeting, but they themselves must not
do the work. This, then, is how you are to
assign the responsibilities of the Levites."

The Passover

9 The LORD spoke to Moses in the 9:1
Desert of Sinai in the first month[m] m Ex 40:2
of the second year after they came out of n Nu 1:1
Egypt.[n] He said, 2 "Have the Israelites
celebrate the Passover at the appointed
time. 3 Celebrate it at the appointed
time, at twilight on the fourteenth day of 9:3
this month, in accordance with all its o Ex 12:2-11,43-
rules and regulations.[o]" 49; Lev 23:5-8; Dt 16:1-8
4 So Moses told the Israelites to celebrate the Passover, 5 and they did so in
the Desert of Sinai at twilight on the
fourteenth day of the first month.[p] The 9:5
Israelites did everything just as the LORD p Ex 12:1-13; Jos 5:10
commanded Moses.
6 But some of them could not celebrate the Passover on that day because 9:6
they were ceremonially unclean[q] on ac- q Lev 5:3
count of a dead body. So they came to r Ex 18:15;
Moses and Aaron[r] that same day 7 and Nu 27:2
said to Moses, "We have become unclean because of a dead body, but why
should we be kept from presenting the
LORD's offering with the other Israelites
at the appointed time?"
8 Moses answered them, "Wait until I 9:8
find out what the LORD commands con- s Ex 18:15;
cerning you."[s] Nu 27:5,21; Ps 85:8
9 Then the LORD said to Moses, 10 "Tell
the Israelites: 'When any of you or your
descendants are unclean because of a
dead body or are away on a journey, they 9:10
may still celebrate[t] the LORD's Passover. t 2Ch 30:2
11 They are to celebrate it on the fourteenth day of the second month at twi- 9:11
light. They are to eat the lamb, together u Ex 12:8
with unleavened bread and bitter 9:12
herbs.[u] 12 They must not leave any of it v Ex 12:10,43
till morning[v] or break any of its bones.[w] w Ex 12:46; Jn 19:36*

DISCOVERY 37

Pray and Obey

It was a simple proposition for the Israelites to know what God wanted; he made his intentions crystal clear. When the cloud of his glory settled down to cover the Tent of Meeting, the people stopped, set up camp and stayed put until further notice. When the cloud lifted from the Tent of Meeting, the people pulled up stakes and followed wherever it led them. God made his intentions even more explicit at night, when the hovering cloud appeared like fire. Time for some much-needed rest and relaxation under the cool evening sky.

Although there was no advance warning, no date circled on a calendar, the people of God never had to wonder *when* to go. The cloud might remain in one place for a year, a month, two days or only a few hours (Numbers 9:21–22). God directed his people to stay or forge ahead whenever he chose—and they obeyed, every time.

As straightforward as God's instructions to the Israelites were, understanding his desires today can be fully as simple. He never intended that discovering or doing his will should be a complicated exercise. He gave us his Word, the Bible, as our map and guidebook. God wants us to believe in his Son, Jesus Christ (1 John 3:23). There need be no doubt or guessing game for us any more than there was for the sojourning Israelites. We take God at his word, trusting Jesus to remove the sin from our lives and repair the damage it has done.

Another of God's explicit commands is that we love each other. In the words of Jesus Christ, "My command is this: Love each other as I have loved you. Greater love has no one than this, that he lay down his life for his friends. You are my friends if you do what I command" (John 15:12–14). When we walk in God's love, we do so all of the time: "If anyone obeys his word, God's love is truly made complete in him. This is how we know we are in him: Whoever claims to live in him must walk as Jesus did" (1 John 2:5–6).

No more speculation about whether a cloud will remain stationary or be pushed along by a sudden gust of wind—what a great sense of freedom! We at times express much concern about "finding the will of God," but we can make this quest more complicated than it needs to be. God's will is so clear-cut that we may cloud the issue with all kinds of caveats and extenuating possibilities—instead of simply praying and obeying.

Self-Discovery: *Think about your own experience with "finding the will of God." Do you feel an overall sense of security and well-being when you practice praying and obeying?*

GO TO DISCOVERY 38 ON PAGE 190

When they celebrate the Passover, they
must follow all the regulations. 13But if a
man who is ceremonially clean and not
on a journey fails to celebrate the
Passover, that person must be cut off
9:13 [x]Ge 17:14; from his people[x] because he did not
Ex 12:15 present the LORD's offering at the appointed time. That man will bear the
consequences of his sin.
9:14 [y]Ex 12:48,49 14"'An alien[y] living among you who
wants to celebrate the LORD's Passover
must do so in accordance with its rules
and regulations. You must have the
same regulations for the alien and the
native-born.'"

The Cloud Above the Tabernacle

15On the day the tabernacle, the Tent
9:15 [z]Ex 40:34 of the Testimony, was set up, the cloud[z]
[a]Ex 13:21 covered it. From evening till morning
the cloud above the tabernacle looked
like fire.[a] 16That is how it continued to
be; the cloud covered it, and at night it
looked like fire. 17Whenever the cloud
lifted from above the Tent, the Israelites
set out; wherever the cloud settled, the
9:17 Israelites encamped.[b] 18At the LORD's
[b]Ex 40:36-38; command the Israelites set out, and at
Nu 10:11,12; his command they encamped. As long
1Co 10:1 as the cloud stayed over the tabernacle,
they remained in camp. 19When the
cloud remained over the tabernacle a
long time, the Israelites obeyed the
LORD's order and did not set out.
20Sometimes the cloud was over the
tabernacle only a few days; at the LORD's
command they would encamp, and
then at his command they would set
out. 21Sometimes the cloud stayed only
from evening till morning, and when it
lifted in the morning, they set out.
Whether by day or by night, whenever
the cloud lifted, they set out. 22Whether
the cloud stayed over the tabernacle for
two days or a month or a year, the Israelites would remain in camp and not set
out; but when it lifted, they would set
out. 23At the LORD's command they encamped, and at the LORD's command
they set out. They obeyed the LORD's order, in accordance with his command
through Moses.

The Silver Trumpets

10 The LORD said to Moses: 2"Make
10:2 [c]Ne 12:35; two trumpets[c] of hammered sil-
Ps 47:5 ver, and use them for calling the community[d] together and for having the 10:2 [d]Jer 4:5,19; 6:1;
camps set out. 3When both are sounded, Hos 5:8;
the whole community is to assemble be- Joel 2:1,15;
fore you at the entrance to the Tent of Am 3:6
Meeting. 4If only one is sounded, the 10:4
leaders[e]—the heads of the clans of Isra- [e]Ex 18:21;
el—are to assemble before you. 5When a Nu 1:16; 7:2
trumpet blast is sounded, the tribes 10:5
camping on the east are to set out.[f] 6At [f]ver 14
the sounding of a second blast, the 10:6
camps on the south are to set out.[g] The [g]ver 18
blast will be the signal for setting out. 7To 10:7
gather the assembly, blow the trumpets,[h] [h]Eze 33:3;
but not with the same signal.[i] Joel 2:1 [i]1Co 14:8
8"The sons of Aaron, the priests, are to
blow the trumpets. This is to be a lasting
ordinance for you and the generations to 10:8
come.[j] 9When you go into battle in your [j]Nu 31:6
own land against an enemy who is op- 10:9
pressing you,[k] sound a blast on the [k]Jdg 2:18; 6:9;
trumpets. Then you will be remembered[l] 1Sa 10:18; Ps 106:42
by the LORD your God and rescued from [l]Ge 8:1
your enemies.[m] 10Also at your times of [m]Ps 106:4
rejoicing—your appointed feasts and
New Moon festivals[n]—you are to sound 10:10 [n]Ps 81:3
the trumpets[o] over your burnt offerings [o]Lev 23:24
and fellowship offerings,[a] and they will
be a memorial for you before your God. I
am the LORD your God."

The Israelites Leave Sinai

11On the twentieth day of the second 10:11
month of the second year,[p] the cloud [p]Ex 40:17
lifted[q] from above the tabernacle of the [q]Nu 9:17
Testimony. 12Then the Israelites set out
from the Desert of Sinai and traveled
from place to place until the cloud came
to rest in the Desert of Paran. 13They set
out, this first time, at the LORD's com- 10:13
mand through Moses.[r] [r]Dt 1:6
14The divisions of the camp of Judah
went first, under their standard.[s] Nah- 10:14 [s]Nu 2:3-9
shon son of Amminadab[t] was in com- [t]Nu 1:7
mand. 15Nethanel son of Zuar was over
the division of the tribe of Issachar,
16and Eliab son of Helon was over the division of the tribe of Zebulun. 17Then
the tabernacle was taken down, and the
Gershonites and Merarites, who carried 10:17
it, set out.[u] [u]Nu 4:21-32
18The divisions of the camp of Reuben 10:18
went next, under their standard.[v] Elizur [v]Nu 2:10-16
son of Shedeur was in command. 19She-
lumiel son of Zurishaddai was over the
division of the tribe of Simeon, 20and
Eliasaph son of Deuel was over the divi-

[a] 10 Traditionally *peace offerings*

sion of the tribe of Gad. 21 Then the Ko-
10:21 hathites set out, carrying the holy
[w] Nu 4:20 things.[w] The tabernacle was to be set up
[x] ver 17 before they arrived.[x]
22 The divisions of the camp of Ephra-
10:22 [y] Nu 2:24 im[y] went next, under their standard.
Elishama son of Ammihud was in com-
mand. 23 Gamaliel son of Pedahzur was
over the division of the tribe of Manasseh, 24 and Abidan son of Gideoni was
over the division of the tribe of Benjamin.
10:25 25 Finally, as the rear guard[z] for all the
[z] Nu 2:31; Jos 6:9 units, the divisions of the camp of Dan
set out, under their standard. Ahiezer son
of Ammishaddai was in command. 26 Pagiel son of Ocran was over the division of
the tribe of Asher, 27 and Ahira son of
Enan was over the division of the tribe of
Naphtali. 28 This was the order of march
for the Israelite divisions as they set out.
10:29 [a] Jdg 4:11 29 Now Moses said to Hobab[a] son of
[b] Ex 2:18 Reuel[b] the Midianite, Moses' father-in-
[c] Ex 3:1 law,[c] "We are setting out for the place
[d] Ge 12:7 about which the LORD said, 'I will give it
to you.'[d] Come with us and we will treat
you well, for the LORD has promised
good things to Israel."
10:30 [e] Mt 21:29 30 He answered, "No, I will not go;[e] I
am going back to my own land and my
own people."
31 But Moses said, "Please do not leave
10:31 [f] Job 29:15 us. You know where we should camp in
10:32 the desert, and you can be our eyes.[f] 32 If
[g] Dt 10:18 you come with us, we will share with you[g]
[h] Ps 22:27-31; whatever good things the LORD gives us.[h]"
67:5-7 33 So they set out[i] from the mountain
10:33 [i] ver 12; Dt 1:33 of the LORD and traveled for three days.
[j] Jos 3:3 The ark of the covenant of the LORD[j]
went before them during those three
days to find them a place to rest. 34 The
10:34 cloud of the LORD was over them by day
[k] Nu 9:15-23 when they set out from the camp.[k]
35 Whenever the ark set out, Moses
said,

10:35 "Rise up, O LORD!
[l] Ps 68:1 May your enemies be scattered;[l]
[m] Dt 7:10; 32:41; Ps 68:2; Isa 17:12-14 may your foes flee before you.[m]"

36 Whenever it came to rest, he said,

10:36 [n] Isa 63:17 "Return,[n] O LORD,
[o] Dt 1:10 to the countless thousands of
Israel.[o]"

Fire From the LORD

11 Now the people complained
about their hardships in the
hearing of the LORD, and when he heard
them his anger was aroused. Then fire
from the LORD burned among them[p] 11:1 [p] Lev 10:2
and consumed some of the outskirts of
the camp. 2 When the people cried out to 11:2
Moses, he prayed to the LORD[q] and the [q] Nu 21:7
fire died down. 3 So that place was called 11:3
Taberah,[a][r] because fire from the LORD [r] Dt 9:22
had burned among them.

Quail From the LORD

4 The rabble with them began to crave
other food,[s] and again the Israelites 11:4
started wailing[t] and said, "If only we had [s] Ex 12:38
meat to eat! 5 We remember the fish we [t] Ps 78:18; 1Co 10:6
ate in Egypt at no cost—also the cu-
cumbers, melons, leeks, onions and gar-
lic.[u] 6 But now we have lost our appetite; 11:5
we never see anything but this manna!" [u] Ex 16:3
7 The manna was like coriander seed[v] 11:7 [v] Ex 16:31
and looked like resin.[w] 8 The people went [w] Ge 2:12
around gathering it, and then ground it
in a handmill or crushed it in a mortar.
They cooked it in a pot or made it into
cakes. And it tasted like something
made with olive oil. 9 When the dew[x] set- 11:9
tled on the camp at night, the manna [x] Ex 16:13
also came down.
10 Moses heard the people of every
family wailing, each at the entrance to
his tent. The LORD became exceedingly
angry, and Moses was troubled. 11 He
asked the LORD, "Why have you brought
this trouble on your servant? What have
I done to displease you that you put the 11:11
burden of all these people on me?[y] 12 Did [y] Ex 5:22
I conceive all these people? Did I give
them birth? Why do you tell me to carry
them in my arms, as a nurse carries an 11:12
infant,[z] to the land you promised on [z] Isa 40:11;
oath to their forefathers?[a] 13 Where can I 49:23 [a] Ex 13:5
get meat for all these people?[b] They 11:13
keep wailing to me, 'Give us meat to eat!' [b] Jn 6:5-9
14 I cannot carry all these people by my- 11:14
self; the burden is too heavy for me.[c] 15 If [c] Ex 18:18
this is how you are going to treat me, put 11:15
me to death[d] right now[e]—if I have [d] Ex 32:32
found favor in your eyes—and do not let [e] 1Ki 19:4; Jnh 4:3
me face my own ruin."
16 The LORD said to Moses: "Bring me
seventy of Israel's elders who are known
to you as leaders and officials among the
people. Have them come to the Tent of
Meeting, that they may stand there with
you. 17 I will come down and speak with
you there, and I will take of the Spirit
that is on you and put the Spirit on

[a] 3 *Taberah* means *burning.*

them.[f] They will help you carry the burden of the people so that you will not have to carry it alone.[g]

[18]"Tell the people: 'Consecrate yourselves[h] in preparation for tomorrow, when you will eat meat. The LORD heard you when you wailed,[i] "If only we had meat to eat! We were better off in Egypt!"[j] Now the LORD will give you meat, and you will eat it. [19]You will not eat it for just one day, or two days, or five, ten or twenty days, [20]but for a whole month—until it comes out of your nostrils and you loathe it[k]—because you have rejected the LORD,[l] who is among you, and have wailed before him, saying, "Why did we ever leave Egypt?"'"

[21]But Moses said, "Here I am among six hundred thousand men[m] on foot, and you say, 'I will give them meat to eat for a whole month!' [22]Would they have enough if flocks and herds were slaughtered for them? Would they have enough if all the fish in the sea were caught for them?"[n]

[23]The LORD answered Moses, "Is the LORD's arm too short?[o] You will now see whether or not what I say will come true for you.[p]"

[24]So Moses went out and told the people what the LORD had said. He brought together seventy of their elders and had them stand around the Tent. [25]Then the LORD came down in the cloud[q] and spoke with him,[r] and he took of the Spirit[s] that was on him and put the Spirit on the seventy elders.[t] When the Spirit rested on them, they prophesied,[u] but they did not do so again.[a]

[26]However, two men, whose names were Eldad and Medad, had remained in the camp. They were listed among the elders, but did not go out to the Tent. Yet the Spirit also rested on them, and they prophesied in the camp. [27]A young man ran and told Moses, "Eldad and Medad are prophesying in the camp."

[28]Joshua son of Nun, who had been Moses' aide[v] since youth, spoke up and said, "Moses, my lord, stop them!"[w]

[29]But Moses replied, "Are you jealous for my sake? I wish that all the LORD's people were prophets[x] and that the LORD would put his Spirit on them!" [30]Then Moses and the elders of Israel returned to the camp.

[31]Now a wind went out from the LORD and drove quail[y] in from the sea. It brought them[b] down all around the camp to about three feet[c] above the ground, as far as a day's walk in any direction. [32]All that day and night and all the next day the people went out and gathered quail. No one gathered less than ten homers.[d] Then they spread them out all around the camp. [33]But while the meat was still between their teeth[z] and before it could be consumed, the anger of the LORD burned against the people, and he struck them with a severe plague.[a] [34]Therefore the place was named Kibroth Hattaavah,[e][b] because there they buried the people who had craved other food.

[35]From Kibroth Hattaavah the people traveled to Hazeroth[c] and stayed there.

Miriam and Aaron Oppose Moses

12 Miriam and Aaron began to talk against Moses because of his Cushite wife,[d] for he had married a Cushite. [2]"Has the LORD spoken only through Moses?" they asked. "Hasn't he also spoken through us?"[e] And the LORD heard this.[f]

[3](Now Moses was a very humble man,[g] more humble than anyone else on the face of the earth.)

[4]At once the LORD said to Moses, Aaron and Miriam, "Come out to the Tent of Meeting, all three of you." So the three of them came out. [5]Then the LORD came down in a pillar of cloud;[h] he stood at the entrance to the Tent and summoned Aaron and Miriam. When both of them stepped forward, [6]he said, "Listen to my words:

"When a prophet of the LORD is
among you,
I reveal myself to him in visions,[i]
I speak to him in dreams.[j]
[7]But this is not true of my servant
Moses;[k]
he is faithful in all my house.[l]
[8]With him I speak face to face,
clearly and not in riddles;[m]
he sees the form of the LORD.[n]
Why then were you not afraid

[a]25 Or *prophesied and continued to do so*
[b]31 Or *They flew* [c]31 Hebrew *two cubits* (about 1 meter) [d]32 That is, probably about 60 bushels (about 2.2 kiloliters) [e]34 *Kibroth Hattaavah* means *graves of craving.*

11:17 [f]ver 25,29; 1Sa 10:6; 2Ki 2:9,15; Joel 2:28 [g]Ex 18:18
11:18 [h]Ex 19:10 [i]Ex 16:7 [j]ver 5; Ac 7:39
11:20 [k]Ps 78:29; 106:14,15 [l]Jos 24:27; 1Sa 10:19
11:21 [m]Ex 12:37
11:22 [n]Mt 15:33
11:23 [o]Isa 50:2; 59:1 [p]Nu 23:19; Eze 12:25; 24:14
11:25 [q]Nu 12:5 [r]ver 17 [s]1Sa 10:6 [t]Ac 2:17 [u]1Sa 10:10
11:28 [v]Ex 33:11; Jos 1:1 [w]Mk 9:38-40
11:29 [x]1Co 14:5
11:31 [y]Ex 16:13; Ps 78:26-28
11:33 [z]Ps 78:30 [a]Ps 106:15
11:34 [b]Dt 9:22
11:35 [c]Nu 33:17
12:1 [d]Ex 2:21
12:2 [e]Nu 16:3 [f]Nu 11:1
12:3 [g]Mt 11:29
12:5 [h]Nu 11:25
12:6 [i]Ge 15:1; 46:2 [j]Ge 31:10; 1Ki 3:5; Heb 1:1
12:7 [k]Jos 1:1-2; Ps 105:26 [l]Heb 3:2,5
12:8 [m]Dt 34:10 [n]Ex 20:4; Ps 17:15

to speak against my servant
Moses?"

12:9 ⁹The anger of the LORD burned
against them, and he left them.[o] oGe 17:22
¹⁰When the cloud lifted from above
12:10 the Tent, there stood Miriam—leprous,[a]
pEx 4:6; Dt 24:9 like snow.[p] Aaron turned toward her
q2Ki 5:1,27 and saw that she had leprosy;[q] ¹¹and he
said to Moses, "Please, my lord, do not
12:11 hold against us the sin we have so fool-
r2Sa 19:19; ishly committed.[r] ¹²Do not let her be like
24:10 a stillborn infant coming from its mother's womb with its flesh half eaten away."
12:13 ¹³So Moses cried out to the LORD,
sIsa 30:26; "O God, please heal her![s]"
Jer 17:14 ¹⁴The LORD replied to Moses, "If her fa-
12:14 ther had spit in her face,[t] would she not
tDt 25:9; Job 17:6; 30:9- have been in disgrace for seven days?
10; Isa 50:6 Confine her outside the camp[u] for seven
uLev 13:46; Nu 5:2-3 days; after that she can be brought back."
¹⁵So Miriam was confined outside the
camp for seven days, and the people did
not move on till she was brought back.
12:16 ¹⁶After that, the people left Hazeroth[v]
vNu 11:35 and encamped in the Desert of Paran.

Exploring Canaan

13 The LORD said to Moses, ²"Send
13:2 wDt 1:22 some men to explore[w] the land
of Canaan, which I am giving to the Israelites. From each ancestral tribe send
one of its leaders."
³So at the LORD's command Moses
sent them out from the Desert of Paran.
All of them were leaders of the Israelites.
⁴These are their names:

from the tribe of Reuben, Shammua son of Zaccur;
⁵from the tribe of Simeon, Shaphat
son of Hori;
13:6 ⁶from the tribe of Judah, Caleb son
xver 30; of Jephunneh;[x]
Nu 14:6,24; ⁷from the tribe of Issachar, Igal son
34:19; Jdg 1:12-15 of Joseph;
⁸from the tribe of Ephraim, Hoshea
son of Nun;
⁹from the tribe of Benjamin, Palti
son of Raphu;
¹⁰from the tribe of Zebulun, Gaddiel
son of Sodi;
¹¹from the tribe of Manasseh (a tribe
of Joseph), Gaddi son of Susi;
¹²from the tribe of Dan, Ammiel son
of Gemalli;
¹³from the tribe of Asher, Sethur son
of Michael;
¹⁴from the tribe of Naphtali, Nahbi
son of Vophsi;
¹⁵from the tribe of Gad, Geuel son of
Maki.

¹⁶These are the names of the men Moses
sent to explore the land. (Moses gave 13:16 yver 8
Hoshea son of Nun[y] the name Joshua.)[z] zDt 32:44
¹⁷When Moses sent them to explore
Canaan, he said, "Go up through the 13:17
Negev[a] and on into the hill country.[b] aGe 12:9 bJdg 1:9
¹⁸See what the land is like and whether
the people who live there are strong or
weak, few or many. ¹⁹What kind of land
do they live in? Is it good or bad? What
kind of towns do they live in? Are they
unwalled or fortified? ²⁰How is the soil?
Is it fertile or poor? Are there trees on it
or not? Do your best to bring back some
of the fruit of the land.[c]" (It was the sea- 13:20 cDt 1:25
son for the first ripe grapes.)
²¹So they went up and explored the
land from the Desert of Zin[d] as far as 13:21 dNu 20:1; 27:14;
Rehob,[e] toward Lebo[b] Hamath.[f] ²²They 33:36; Jos 15:1
went up through the Negev and came to eJos 19:28 fJos 13:5
Hebron, where Ahiman, Sheshai and 13:22
Talmai,[g] the descendants of Anak,[h] gJos 15:14
lived. (Hebron had been built seven hJos 15:13
years before Zoan in Egypt.)[i] ²³When iPs 78:12,43; Isa 19:11,13
they reached the Valley of Eshcol,[c] they
cut off a branch bearing a single cluster
of grapes. Two of them carried it on a
pole between them, along with some
pomegranates and figs. ²⁴That place was
called the Valley of Eshcol because of the
cluster of grapes the Israelites cut off
there. ²⁵At the end of forty days they returned from exploring the land.

Report on the Exploration

²⁶They came back to Moses and Aaron and the whole Israelite community at
Kadesh in the Desert of Paran. There
they reported to them[j] and to the whole 13:26 jNu 32:8
assembly and showed them the fruit of
the land. ²⁷They gave Moses this account: "We went into the land to which
you sent us, and it does flow with milk
and honey![k] Here is its fruit.[l] ²⁸But the 13:27 kEx 3:8 lDt 1:25
people who live there are powerful, and
the cities are fortified and very large.[m] 13:28
We even saw descendants of Anak there. mDt 1:28; 9:1,2
²⁹The Amalekites live in the Negev; the
Hittites, Jebusites and Amorites live in

[a] *10* The Hebrew word was used for various diseases affecting the skin—not necessarily leprosy. [b] *21* Or *toward the entrance to*
[c] *23* *Eshcol* means *cluster*; also in verse 24.

DISCOVERY 38

It's All In Who You See

Once the children of Israel reached the borders of the promised land, Moses sent 12 spies, one from each tribe, to scout the land and assess the strength of its people. The spies traveled from the Desert of Zin in the south to Rehob in the north (Numbers 13:21), a distance of approximately 250 miles. Upon their return they reported that they were impressed with the land—"it [did] flow with milk and honey!" just as God had promised—but also that they were discouraged because the inhabitants were very strong (verses 27–28). Ten of the spies conceded that it would be impossible for the Israelites to conquer the land (verses 31–33). But Joshua and Caleb alone were confident that God would give them the land (verse 30)—because he had said he would!

There were 12 spies, all on the same mission, all observing the same sights, but responding with very different conclusions. We can learn from them. First, *it's not what you see but who you see that matters.* All 12 spies noticed the same things—the wealth of the land and the power of the occupants. But Joshua and Caleb perceived something beyond the obvious—they realized that the power of God was greater than that of any enemy. They knew that God would lead them and give them the land because they trusted him (Numbers 14:8). While the other ten spies lamented over the obstacles, Joshua and Caleb expressed enthusiasm about the opportunities. The other ten spies shrank back in consternation in the face of an intimidating enemy, but Joshua and Caleb saw their conquering Lord. In the same way, when we face our battles, we must look beyond the obstacles to God, who is ever present with us (Philippians 4:13).

In the final analysis *faith and obedience are what matter to God.* Because the people had failed to trust God to lead them into the land, God declared that no one over the age of twenty—except Joshua and Caleb—would ever enter the promised land. The entire adult generation would die in the desert, tantalizingly close to their destination. It was *then* that the people almost unanimously decided that they should enter the land after all and do battle with its people! God warned them against this course of action, but they proceeded anyway—and were defeated (Numbers 14:44–45). They missed the point: God honors faith *and* obedience. He had promised to go with them as they conquered the land but had asked them to trust him. Instead, they had refused to trust and tried futilely to achieve the same goal in their own strength.

When Jesus was about to leave his disciples and return to heaven, he knew that their faith and obedience would be tested and so he promised that he would be with them. In the same way, Jesus promises to walk through life at our side and lead us safely into his kingdom: "Surely I am with you always, to the very end of the age" (Matthew 28:20). We need to believe his Word and act on it, to trust and to obey.

***Self-Discovery:** How do the words of Jesus give you courage to see beyond the obstacles in your life to the presence and power of God?*

GO TO DISCOVERY 39 ON PAGE 199

the hill country; and the Canaanites live near the sea and along the Jordan."

30Then Caleb silenced the people before Moses and said, "We should go up and take possession of the land, for we can certainly do it."

31But the men who had gone up with him said, "We can't attack those people; they are stronger than we are."[n] 32And they spread among the Israelites a bad report[o] about the land they had explored. They said, "The land we explored devours[p] those living in it. All the people we saw there are of great size.[q] 33We saw the Nephilim[r] there (the descendants of Anak[s] come from the Nephilim). We seemed like grasshoppers in our own eyes, and we looked the same to them."

The People Rebel

14 That night all the people of the community raised their voices and wept aloud. 2All the Israelites grumbled against Moses and Aaron, and the whole assembly said to them, "If only we had died in Egypt! Or in this desert![t] 3Why is the LORD bringing us to this land only to let us fall by the sword? Our wives and children will be taken as plunder. Wouldn't it be better for us to go back to Egypt?" 4And they said to each other, "We should choose a leader and go back to Egypt.[u]"

5Then Moses and Aaron fell facedown[v] in front of the whole Israelite assembly gathered there. 6Joshua son of Nun and Caleb son of Jephunneh, who were among those who had explored the land, tore their clothes 7and said to the entire Israelite assembly, "The land we passed through and explored is exceedingly good.[w] 8If the LORD is pleased with us,[x] he will lead us into that land, a land flowing with milk and honey,[y] and will give it to us. 9Only do not rebel[z] against the LORD. And do not be afraid of the people of the land,[a] because we will swallow them up. Their protection is gone, but the LORD is with us. Do not be afraid of them."

10But the whole assembly talked about stoning[b] them. Then the glory of the LORD[c] appeared at the Tent of Meeting to all the Israelites. 11The LORD said to Moses, "How long will these people treat me with contempt? How long will they refuse to believe in me,[d] in spite of all the miraculous signs I have performed among them? 12I will strike them down with a plague and destroy them, but I will make you into a nation[e] greater and stronger than they."

13Moses said to the LORD, "Then the Egyptians will hear about it! By your power you brought these people up from among them.[f] 14And they will tell the inhabitants of this land about it. They have already heard[g] that you, O LORD, are with these people and that you, O LORD, have been seen face to face, that your cloud stays over them, and that you go before them in a pillar of cloud by day and a pillar of fire by night.[h] 15If you put these people to death all at one time, the nations who have heard this report about you will say, 16'The LORD was not able to bring these people into the land he promised them on oath; so he slaughtered them in the desert.'[i]

17"Now may the Lord's strength be displayed, just as you have declared: 18'The LORD is slow to anger, abounding in love and forgiving sin and rebellion.[j] Yet he does not leave the guilty unpunished; he punishes the children for the sin of the fathers to the third and fourth generation.'[k] 19In accordance with your great love, forgive[l] the sin of these people,[m] just as you have pardoned them from the time they left Egypt until now."[n]

20The LORD replied, "I have forgiven them,[o] as you asked. 21Nevertheless, as surely as I live[p] and as surely as the glory of the LORD fills the whole earth,[q] 22not one of the men who saw my glory and the miraculous signs I performed in Egypt and in the desert but who disobeyed me and tested me ten times[r]— 23not one of them will ever see the land I promised on oath[s] to their forefathers. No one who has treated me with contempt will ever see it.[t] 24But because my servant Caleb has a different spirit and follows me wholeheartedly,[u] I will bring him into the land he went to, and his descendants will inherit it.[v] 25Since the Amalekites and Canaanites are living in the valleys, turn[w] back tomorrow and set out toward the desert along the route to the Red Sea.[a]"

26The LORD said to Moses and Aaron: 27"How long will this wicked community grumble against me? I have heard the

13:31 [n] Dt 1:28; 9:1; Jos 14:8
13:32 [o] Nu 14:36,37 [p] Eze 36:13,14 [q] Am 2:9
13:33 [r] Ge 6:4 [s] Dt 1:28
14:2 [t] Nu 11:1
14:4 [u] Ne 9:17
14:5 [v] Nu 16:4,22,45
14:7 [w] Nu 13:27; Dt 1:25
14:8 [x] Dt 10:15 [y] Nu 13:27
14:9 [z] Dt 1:26; 9:7,23,24 [a] Dt 1:21; 7:18; 20:1
14:10 [b] Ex 17:4 [c] Lev 9:23
14:11 [d] Ps 78:22; 106:24
14:12 [e] Ex 32:10
14:13 [f] Ex 32:11-14; Ps 106:23
14:14 [g] Ex 15:14 [h] Ex 13:21
14:16 [i] Jos 7:7
14:18 [j] Ex 34:6; Ps 145:8; Jnh 4:2 [k] Ex 20:5
14:19 [l] Ex 34:9 [m] Ps 106:45 [n] Ps 78:38
14:20 [o] Ps 106:23; Mic 7:18-20
14:21 [p] Dt 32:40; Isa 49:18 [q] Ps 72:19; Isa 6:3; Hab 2:14
14:22 [r] Ex 14:11; 32:1; 1Co 10:5
14:23 [s] Nu 32:11 [t] Heb 3:18
14:24 [u] ver 6-9; Jos 14:8,14 [v] Nu 32:12
14:25 [w] Dt 1:40

[a] 25 Hebrew *Yam Suph*; that is, Sea of Reeds

complaints of these grumbling Israel-
14:27 x Ex 16:12 ites.[x] 28So tell them, 'As surely as I live,[y]
declares the LORD, I will do to you the
14:28 y ver 21 very things I heard you say: 29In this
desert your bodies will fall[z]—every one
14:29 z Nu 26:65 of you twenty years old or more[a] who
a Nu 1:45 was counted in the census and who has
grumbled against me. 30Not one of you
will enter the land I swore with uplifted
hand to make your home, except Caleb
son of Jephunneh and Joshua son of
Nun. 31As for your children that you said
would be taken as plunder, I will bring
them in to enjoy the land you have re-
14:31 b Ps 106:24 jected.[b] 32But you—your bodies will fall[c]
14:32 in this desert. 33Your children will be
c 1Co 10:5 shepherds here for forty years, suffering
for your unfaithfulness, until the last of
your bodies lies in the desert. 34For forty
years—one year for each of the forty
14:34 d Nu 13:25 days you explored the land[d]—you will
suffer for your sins and know what it is
like to have me against you.' 35I, the
LORD, have spoken, and I will surely do
these things[e] to this whole wicked com- 14:35 e Nu 23:19
munity, which has banded together
against me. They will meet their end in
this desert; here they will die."
36So the men Moses had sent[f] to ex- 14:36 f Nu 13:4-16
plore the land, who returned and made g Nu 13:32
the whole community grumble against
him by spreading a bad report[g] about
it— 37these men responsible for spread-
ing the bad report[h] about the land were 14:37 h 1Co 10:10
struck down and died of a plague[i] before i Nu 16:49
the LORD. 38Of the men who went to ex-
plore the land, only Joshua son of Nun 14:38
and Caleb son of Jephunneh survived.[j] j Jos 14:6
39When Moses reported this to all the 14:39
Israelites, they mourned[k] bitterly. 40Ear- k Ex 33:4
ly the next morning they went up to-
ward the high hill country. "We have 14:40
sinned[l]," they said. "We will go up to the l Dt 1:41
place the LORD promised."
41But Moses said, "Why are you disobeying the LORD's command? This will
not succeed![m] 42Do not go up, because 14:41 m 2Ch 24:20
the LORD is not with you. You will be de- 14:42
feated by your enemies,[n] 43for the n Dt 1:42
Amalekites and Canaanites will face you
there. Because you have turned away
from the LORD, he will not be with you
and you will fall by the sword."
44Nevertheless, in their presumption
they went up[o] toward the high hill coun- 14:44 o Dt 1:43
try, though neither Moses nor the ark of p Nu 31:6
the LORD's covenant moved from the
camp.[p] 45Then the Amalekites and
Canaanites who lived in that hill coun- 14:45
try came down and attacked them and q Nu 21:3; Dt 1:44;
beat them down all the way to Hormah.[q] Jdg 1:17

Supplementary Offerings

15 The LORD said to Moses,
2"Speak to the Israelites and say
to them: 'After you enter the land I am
giving you[r] as a home 3and you present 15:2 r Lev 23:10
to the LORD offerings made by fire, from
the herd or the flock,[s] as an aroma 15:3 s Lev 1:2
pleasing to the LORD[t]—whether burnt t ver 24; Ge 8:21; Ex 29:18
offerings[u] or sacrifices, for special vows u Nu 28:19,27
or freewill offerings[v] or festival offer- v Lev 22:18,21; Ezr 1:4
ings[w]— 4then the one who brings his of- w Lev 23:1-44
fering shall present to the LORD a grain
offering[x] of a tenth of an ephah[a] of fine 15:4 x Lev 2:1; 6:14
flour mixed with a quarter of a hin[b] of
oil. 5With each lamb for the burnt offer-

a 4 That is, probably about 2 quarts (about 2 liters)
b 4 That is, probably about 1 quart (about 1 liter); also in verse 5

JESUS FOCUS

SHEPHERDS FOR GOD

Numbers 14 is a pivotal chapter in the history of Israel's sojourn in the desert. Instead of listening to the God-fearing spies Joshua and Caleb, the Israelites chose to believe the report of the other ten spies and literally cried aloud in fear of the obstacles and opposition awaiting them in the promised land. They were so afraid, in fact, that they talked about returning to slavery in Egypt. If God had not stepped in, the lineage of the promised Messiah might have been in jeopardy. But God overruled the unbelieving Israelites, condemning the older generation to die in the desert over the next 40 years. God promised that the younger generation (those 19 years old and younger), as well as those who would be born while his people were living in the desert, would be shepherds until they entered the land of promise (verse 33). What began as punishment for the older generation became a blessing for the younger. Shepherding remained very important to God's people, and Jesus used the analogy of a shepherd as an illustration of his tender care for his own. David, the first king in the Messiah's family line, was a shepherd, and Jesus referred to himself as the "good shepherd" (John 10:11–18), a Shepherd who would both lead his sheep and suffer and die for them (Matthew 26:31).

ing or the sacrifice, prepare a quarter of
15:5 y Nu 28:7,14 a hin of wine[y] as a drink offering.
6" 'With a ram[z] prepare a grain offer-
15:6 z Lev 5:15 ing[a] of two-tenths of an ephah[a] of fine
a Nu 28:12 flour mixed with a third of a hin[b] of oil,[b]
b Eze 46:14 7and a third of a hin of wine as a drink
offering. Offer it as an aroma pleasing to
the LORD.
8" 'When you prepare a young bull as
15:8 a burnt offering or sacrifice, for a special
c Lev 1:3; 3:1 vow or a fellowship offering[c c] to the
15:9 LORD, 9bring with the bull a grain offer-
d Lev 14:10 ing of three-tenths of an ephah[d d] of fine
flour mixed with half a hin[e] of oil. 10Also
bring half a hin of wine as a drink offering. It will be an offering made by fire, an
aroma pleasing to the LORD. 11Each bull
or ram, each lamb or young goat, is to be
prepared in this manner. 12Do this for
15:13 each one, for as many as you prepare.
e Lev 16:29 13" 'Everyone who is native-born[e]
must do these things in this way when
he brings an offering made by fire as an
aroma pleasing to the LORD. 14For the
generations to come, whenever an alien
or anyone else living among you presents an offering made by fire as an aroma pleasing to the LORD, he must do exactly as you do. 15The community is to
have the same rules for you and for the
15:15 alien living among you; this is a lasting
f ver 29; Nu 9:14 ordinance for the generations to come.[f]
You and the alien shall be the same be-
fore the LORD: 16The same laws and reg-
15:16 ulations will apply both to you and to
g Nu 9:14 the alien living among you.[g]' "
17The LORD said to Moses, 18"Speak to
the Israelites and say to them: 'When
15:19 you enter the land to which I am taking
h Jos 5:11,12 you 19and you eat the food of the land,[h]
present a portion as an offering to the
15:20 LORD. 20Present a cake from the first of
i Ex 34:26; Lev 23:14; your ground meal[i] and present it as an
Dt 26:2,10 offering from the threshing floor.[j]
j Lev 2:14 21Throughout the generations to come
15:21 you are to give this offering to the LORD
k Ro 11:16 from the first of your ground meal.[k]

Offerings for Unintentional Sins

22" 'Now if you unintentionally fail to
keep any of these commands the LORD
15:22 l Lev 4:2 gave Moses[l]— 23any of the LORD's commands to you through him, from the day
the LORD gave them and continuing
through the generations to come—
24and if this is done unintentionally
without the community being aware of

it,[m] then the whole community is to of- 15:24 m Lev 5:15
fer a young bull for a burnt offering[n] as n Lev 4:14
an aroma pleasing to the LORD, along o Lev 4:3
with its prescribed grain offering and
drink offering, and a male goat for a sin
offering.[o] 25The priest is to make atonement for the whole Israelite community,
and they will be forgiven,[p] for it was not 15:25 p Lev 4:20;
intentional and they have brought to the Ro 3:25;
LORD for their wrong an offering made Heb 2:17
by fire and a sin offering. 26The whole Israelite community and the aliens living
among them will be forgiven, because all
the people were involved in the unin- 15:26
tentional wrong.[q] q ver 24
27" 'But if just one person sins unin- 15:27
tentionally,[r] he must bring a year-old fe- r Lev 4:27
male goat for a sin offering. 28The priest
is to make atonement before the LORD
for the one who erred by sinning unintentionally, and when atonement has
been made for him, he will be forgiven.[s] 15:28
29One and the same law applies to every- s Lev 4:35
one who sins unintentionally, whether
he is a native-born Israelite or an alien.
30" 'But anyone who sins defiantly,[t] 15:30
whether native-born or alien,[u] blas- t Nu 14:40-44; Dt 1:43; 17:13;
phemes the LORD, and that person must Ps 19:13 u ver 14
be cut off from his people. 31Because he 15:31
has despised the LORD's word and broken v 2Sa 12:9;
his commands,[v] that person must sure- Ps 119:126; Pr 13:13
ly be cut off; his guilt remains on him.[w]' " w Lev 5:1; Eze 18:20

The Sabbath-Breaker Put to Death

32While the Israelites were in the
desert, a man was found gathering wood
on the Sabbath day.[x] 33Those who found 15:32 x Ex 31:14,15;
him gathering wood brought him to 35:2,3
Moses and Aaron and the whole assembly, 34and they kept him in custody, because it was not clear what should be 15:34
done to him.[y] 35Then the LORD said to y Nu 9:8
Moses, "The man must die.[z] The whole 15:35
assembly must stone him outside the z Ex 31:14,15;
camp.[a]" 36So the assembly took him out- Dt 21:21 a Lev 20:2;
side the camp and stoned him to death, 24:14; Ac 7:58
as the LORD commanded Moses.

Tassels on Garments

37The LORD said to Moses, 38"Speak
to the Israelites and say to them:

[a] *6* That is, probably about 4 quarts (about 4.5 liters) [b] *6* That is, probably about 1 1/4 quarts (about 1.2 liters); also in verse 7
[c] *8* Traditionally *peace offering* [d] *9* That is, probably about 6 quarts (about 6.5 liters)
[e] *9* That is, probably about 2 quarts (about 2 liters); also in verse 10

'Throughout the generations to come you are to make tassels on the corners of your garments,[b] with a blue cord on each tassel. 39 You will have these tassels to look at and so you will remember[c] all the commands of the LORD, that you may obey them and not prostitute yourselves by going after the lusts of your own hearts and eyes. 40 Then you will remember to obey all my commands and will be consecrated to your God.[d] 41 I am the LORD your God, who brought you out of Egypt to be your God. I am the LORD your God.' "

15:38 [b] Dt 22:12; Mt 23:5
15:39 [c] Dt 4:23; 6:12; Ps 73:27
15:40 [d] Lev 11:44; Ro 12:1; Col 1:22; 1Pe 1:15

Korah, Dathan and Abiram

16 Korah[e] son of Izhar, the son of Kohath, the son of Levi, and certain Reubenites—Dathan and Abiram, sons of Eliab,[f] and On son of Peleth—became insolent[a] 2 and rose up against Moses. With them were 250 Israelite men, well-known community leaders who had been appointed members of the council.[g] 3 They came as a group to oppose Moses and Aaron[h] and said to them, "You have gone too far! The whole community is holy,[i] every one of them, and the LORD is with them.[j] Why then do you set yourselves above the LORD's assembly?"[k]

4 When Moses heard this, he fell facedown.[l] 5 Then he said to Korah and all his followers: "In the morning the LORD will show who belongs to him and who is holy,[m] and he will have that person come near him. The man he chooses[n] he will cause to come near him. 6 You, Korah, and all your followers are to do this: Take censers 7 and tomorrow put fire and incense in them before the LORD. The man the LORD chooses will be the one who is holy. You Levites have gone too far!"

8 Moses also said to Korah, "Now listen, you Levites! 9 Isn't it enough for you that the God of Israel has separated you from the rest of the Israelite community and brought you near himself to do the work at the LORD's tabernacle and to stand before the community and minister to them?[o] 10 He has brought you and all your fellow Levites near himself, but now you are trying to get the priesthood too.[p] 11 It is against the LORD that you and all your followers have banded together. Who is Aaron that you should grumble[q] against him?"[r]

16:1 [e] Jude 1:11 [f] Nu 26:8; Dt 11:6
16:2 [g] Nu 1:16; 26:9
16:3 [h] ver 7; Ps 106:16 [i] Ex 19:6 [j] Nu 14:14 [k] Nu 12:2
16:4 [l] Nu 14:5
16:5 [m] Lev 10:3; 2Ti 2:19* [n] Nu 17:5; Ps 65:4
16:9 [o] Nu 3:6; Dt 10:8
16:10 [p] Nu 3:10; 18:7
16:11 [q] 1Co 10:10 [r] Ex 16:7

12 Then Moses summoned Dathan and Abiram, the sons of Eliab. But they said, "We will not come! 13 Isn't it enough that you have brought us up out of a land flowing with milk and honey to kill us in the desert?[s] And now you also want to lord it over us?[t] 14 Moreover, you haven't brought us into a land flowing with milk and honey[u] or given us an inheritance of fields and vineyards.[v] Will you gouge out the eyes of[b] these men?[w] No, we will not come!"

15 Then Moses became very angry and said to the LORD, "Do not accept their offering. I have not taken so much as a donkey[x] from them, nor have I wronged any of them."

16 Moses said to Korah, "You and all your followers are to appear before the LORD tomorrow—you and they and Aaron.[y] 17 Each man is to take his censer and put incense in it—250 censers in all—and present it before the LORD. You and Aaron are to present your censers also." 18 So each man took his censer, put fire and incense in it, and stood with Moses and Aaron at the entrance to the Tent of Meeting. 19 When Korah had gathered all his followers in opposition to them[z] at the entrance to the Tent of Meeting, the glory of the LORD[a] appeared to the entire assembly. 20 The LORD said to Moses and Aaron, 21 "Separate yourselves from this assembly so I can put an end to them at once."[b]

22 But Moses and Aaron fell facedown[c] and cried out, "O God, God of the spirits of all mankind,[d] will you be angry with the entire assembly when only one man sins?"[e]

23 Then the LORD said to Moses, 24 "Say to the assembly, 'Move away from the tents of Korah, Dathan and Abiram.' "

25 Moses got up and went to Dathan and Abiram, and the elders of Israel followed him. 26 He warned the assembly, "Move back from the tents of these wicked men![f] Do not touch anything belonging to them, or you will be swept away[g] because of all their sins." 27 So they moved away from the tents of Korah, Dathan and Abiram. Dathan and Abiram had come out and were standing with their wives, children and little ones at the entrances to their tents.

16:13 [s] Nu 14:2 [t] Ac 7:27,35
16:14 [u] Lev 20:24 [v] Ex 22:5; 23:11; Nu 20:5 [w] Jdg 16:21; 1Sa 11:2
16:15 [x] 1Sa 12:3
16:16 [y] ver 6
16:19 [z] ver 42 [a] Ex 16:7; Nu 14:10; 20:6
16:21 [b] Ex 32:10
16:22 [c] Nu 14:5 [d] Nu 27:16; Job 12:10; Heb 12:9 [e] Ge 18:23
16:26 [f] Isa 52:11 [g] Ge 19:15

[a] 1 Or *Peleth—took* ⌞*men*⌟ [b] 14 Or *you make slaves of;* or *you deceive*

16:28 [28]Then Moses said, "This is how you
h Ex 3:12; will know that the LORD has sent me[h] to
Jn 5:36; 6:38 do all these things and that it was not
my idea: [29]If these men die a natural
death and experience only what usually
happens to men, then the LORD has not
16:29 sent me.[i] [30]But if the LORD brings about
i Ecc 3:19 something totally new, and the earth
opens its mouth and swallows them,
16:30 with everything that belongs to them,
j ver 33; Ps 55:15 and they go down alive into the grave,[a][j]
then you will know that these men have
treated the LORD with contempt."
16:31 [31]As soon as he finished saying all
k Mic 1:3-4 this, the ground under them split apart[k]
16:32 [32]and the earth opened its mouth and
l Nu 26:11; swallowed them,[l] with their households
Dt 11:6; and all Korah's men and all their posses-
Ps 106:17 sions. [33]They went down alive into the
grave, with everything they owned; the
earth closed over them, and they perished and were gone from the community. [34]At their cries, all the Israelites
around them fled, shouting, "The earth
is going to swallow us too!"
16:35 m Nu 11:1-3; [35]And fire came out from the LORD[m]
26:10 n Lev 10:2 and consumed[n] the 250 men who were
offering the incense.
[36]The LORD said to Moses, [37]"Tell Eleazar son of Aaron, the priest, to take the
censers out of the smoldering remains
and scatter the coals some distance
away, for the censers are holy— [38]the
censers of the men who sinned at the
16:38 o Pr 20:2 cost of their lives.[o] Hammer the censers
p Nu 26:10; into sheets to overlay the altar, for they
Eze 14:8; were presented before the LORD and
2Pe 2:6 have become holy. Let them be a sign[p]
to the Israelites."
[39]So Eleazar the priest collected the
bronze censers brought by those who
had been burned up, and he had them
hammered out to overlay the altar, [40]as
the LORD directed him through Moses.
This was to remind the Israelites that no
one except a descendant of Aaron
16:40 should come to burn incense[q] before the
q Ex 30:7-10; LORD,[r] or he would become like Korah
Nu 1:51 and his followers.[s]
r 2Ch 26:18 s Nu 3:10 [41]The next day the whole Israelite
community grumbled against Moses
and Aaron. "You have killed the LORD's
people," they said.
16:42 [42]But when the assembly gathered in
t ver 19; Nu 20:6 opposition[t] to Moses and Aaron and
turned toward the Tent of Meeting, sud-
denly the cloud covered it and the glory
of the LORD appeared. [43]Then Moses and
Aaron went to the front of the Tent of
Meeting, [44]and the LORD said to Moses,
[45]"Get away from this assembly so I can
put an end to them at once." And they
fell facedown.
[46]Then Moses said to Aaron, "Take
your censer and put incense in it, along
with fire from the altar, and hurry to the
assembly[u] to make atonement[v] for 16:46
them. Wrath has come out from the u Lev 10:6 v Nu 18:5; 25:13;
LORD; the plague[w] has started." [47]So Aar- Dt 9:22 w Nu 8:19;
on did as Moses said, and ran into the Ps 106:29
midst of the assembly. The plague had
already started among the people,[x] but 16:47 x Nu 25:6-8
Aaron offered the incense and made
atonement for them. [48]He stood between the living and the dead, and the 16:48
plague stopped.[y] [49]But 14,700 people y Nu 25:8;
died from the plague, in addition to Ps 106:30
those who had died because of Korah.[z] 16:49 z ver 32
[50]Then Aaron returned to Moses at the
entrance to the Tent of Meeting, for the
plague had stopped.

The Budding of Aaron's Staff

17 [1]The LORD said to Moses,
[2]"Speak to the Israelites and get
twelve staffs from them, one from the
leader of each of their ancestral tribes.
Write the name of each man on his staff.
[3]On the staff of Levi write Aaron's
name,[a] for there must be one staff for 17:3
the head of each ancestral tribe. [4]Place a Nu 1:3
them in the Tent of Meeting in front of 17:4 b ver 7
the Testimony,[b] where I meet with you.[c] c Ex 25:22
[5]The staff belonging to the man I
choose[d] will sprout, and I will rid myself 17:5 d Nu 16:5
of this constant grumbling against you
by the Israelites."
[6]So Moses spoke to the Israelites, and
their leaders gave him twelve staffs, one
for the leader of each of their ancestral
tribes, and Aaron's staff was among
them. [7]Moses placed the staffs before 17:7
the LORD in the Tent of the Testimony.[e] e Ex 38:21;
[8]The next day Moses entered the Tent Ac 7:44
of the Testimony and saw that Aaron's
staff, which represented the house of
Levi, had not only sprouted but had
budded, blossomed and produced al- 17:8
monds.[f] [9]Then Moses brought out all f Eze 17:24;
the staffs from the LORD's presence to all Heb 9:4
the Israelites. They looked at them, and
each man took his own staff.
[10]The LORD said to Moses, "Put back

[a] *30* Hebrew *Sheol*; also in verse 33

Aaron's staff in front of the Testimony, to
17:10 [g]Dt 9:24 be kept as a sign to the rebellious.[g] This
will put an end to their grumbling
against me, so that they will not die."
[11]Moses did just as the LORD commanded him.
[12]The Israelites said to Moses, "We
17:12 [h]Isa 6:5 will die! We are lost, we are all lost![h]
[13]Anyone who even comes near the tab-
17:13 [i]Nu 1:51 ernacle of the LORD will die.[i] Are we all
going to die?"

Duties of Priests and Levites

18 The LORD said to Aaron, "You,
your sons and your father's
family are to bear the responsibility for
18:1 [j]Ex 28:38 offenses against the sanctuary,[j] and you
and your sons alone are to bear the responsibility for offenses against the
priesthood. [2]Bring your fellow Levites
from your ancestral tribe to join you and
assist you when you and your sons min-
18:2 [k]Nu 3:10 ister[k] before the Tent of the Testimony.
[3]They are to be responsible to you and
18:3 [l]Nu 1:51 are to perform all the duties of the Tent,[l]
[m]ver 7; Nu 4:15 but they must not go near the furnishings of the sanctuary or the altar, or both
they and you will die.[m] [4]They are to join
you and be responsible for the care of
the Tent of Meeting—all the work at the
Tent—and no one else may come near
where you are.
[5]"You are to be responsible for the
18:5 [n]Nu 16:46 care of the sanctuary and the altar,[n] so
that wrath will not fall on the Israelites
again. [6]I myself have selected your fellow
Levites from among the Israelites as a
18:6 [o]Nu 3:9 gift to you,[o] dedicated to the LORD to do
the work at the Tent of Meeting. [7]But
only you and your sons may serve as
priests in connection with everything at
18:7 [p]Heb 9:3,6 the altar and inside the curtain.[p] I am
[q]ver 20; Ex 29:9 giving you the service of the priesthood
[r]Nu 3:10 as a gift.[q] Anyone else who comes near
the sanctuary must be put to death.[r]"

Offerings for Priests and Levites

[8]Then the LORD said to Aaron, "I myself have put you in charge of the offerings presented to me; all the holy offerings the Israelites give me I give to you
and your sons as your portion and regu-
18:8 [s]Lev 6:16; 7:6, lar share.[s] [9]You are to have the part of
31-34,36 the most holy offerings that is kept from
18:9 the fire. From all the gifts they bring me
[t]Lev 2:1 as most holy offerings, whether grain[t] or
[u]Lev 6:25 [v]Lev 5:15; 7:7 sin[u] or guilt offerings,[v] that part belongs
to you and your sons. [10]Eat it as some- 18:10
thing most holy; every male shall eat it.[w] [w]Lev 6:16
You must regard it as holy.
[11]"This also is yours: whatever is set
aside from the gifts of all the wave offer- 18:11
ings[x] of the Israelites. I give this to you [x]Ex 29:26
and your sons and daughters as your reg- [y]Lev 22:1-16
ular share. Everyone in your household
who is ceremonially clean[y] may eat it.
[12]"I give you all the finest olive oil and
all the finest new wine and grain they
give the LORD as the firstfruits of their 18:12 [z]Ex 23:19;
harvest.[z] [13]All the land's firstfruits that Ne 10:35
they bring to the LORD will be yours.[a] 18:13
Everyone in your household who is cer- [a]Ex 22:29; 23:19
emonially clean may eat it.
[14]"Everything in Israel that is devot-
ed[a] to the LORD[b] is yours. [15]The first off- 18:14 [b]Lev 27:28
spring of every womb, both man and an-
imal, that is offered to the LORD is 18:15
yours.[c] But you must redeem[d] every [c]Ex 13:2
firstborn son and every firstborn male of [d]Nu 3:46
unclean animals.[e] [16]When they are a [e]Ex 13:13
month old, you must redeem them at 18:16
the redemption price set at five shekels[b][f] [f]Lev 27:6
of silver, according to the sanctuary [g]Ex 30:13
shekel,[g] which weighs twenty gerahs.
[17]"But you must not redeem the firstborn of an ox, a sheep or a goat; they are
holy.[h] Sprinkle their blood[i] on the altar 18:17 [h]Dt 15:19
and burn their fat as an offering made [i]Lev 3:2
by fire, an aroma pleasing to the LORD.
[18]Their meat is to be yours, just as the
breast of the wave offering[j] and the right 18:18
thigh are yours. [19]Whatever is set aside [j]Lev 7:30
from the holy offerings the Israelites
present to the LORD I give to you and
your sons and daughters as your regular
share. It is an everlasting covenant of 18:19
salt[k] before the LORD for both you and [k]Lev 2:13;
your offspring." 2Ch 13:5
[20]The LORD said to Aaron, "You will
have no inheritance in their land, nor 18:20
will you have any share among them;[l] I [l]Dt 12:12
am your share and your inheritance[m] [m]Dt 10:9; 14:27; 18:1-2;
among the Israelites. Jos 13:33; Eze 44:28
[21]"I give to the Levites all the tithes[n]
in Israel as their inheritance[o] in return 18:21
for the work they do while serving at the [n]Dt 14:22;
Tent of Meeting. [22]From now on the Is- Mal 3:8 [o]Lev 27:30-33;
raelites must not go near the Tent of Heb 7:5
Meeting, or they will bear the conse- 18:22
quences of their sin and will die.[p] [23]It is [p]Lev 22:9;
the Levites who are to do the work at the Nu 1:51

[a] *14* The Hebrew term refers to the irrevocable giving over of things or persons to the LORD.
[b] *16* That is, about 2 ounces (about 55 grams)

Tent of Meeting and bear the responsibility for offenses against it. This is a
lasting ordinance for the generations to
18:23 q ver 20 come. They will receive no inheritance[q]
among the Israelites. 24 Instead, I give to
the Levites as their inheritance the
tithes that the Israelites present as an offering to the LORD. That is why I said
concerning them: 'They will have no inheritance among the Israelites.' "
25 The LORD said to Moses, 26 "Speak to
the Levites and say to them: 'When you
18:26 receive from the Israelites the tithe I give
r ver 21 you[r] as your inheritance, you must pre-
s Ne 10:38 sent a tenth of that tithe as the LORD's offering.[s] 27 Your offering will be reckoned
to you as grain from the threshing floor
or juice from the winepress. 28 In this way
you also will present an offering to the
18:28 t Mal 3:8 LORD from all the tithes[t] you receive
from the Israelites. From these tithes
you must give the LORD's portion to Aaron the priest. 29 You must present as the
LORD's portion the best and holiest part
of everything given to you.'
30 "Say to the Levites: 'When you present the best part, it will be reckoned to
you as the product of the threshing floor
18:30 u ver 27 or the winepress.[u] 31 You and your households may eat the rest of it anywhere, for
it is your wages for your work at the Tent
of Meeting. 32 By presenting the best
18:32 v Lev 22:15 part[v] of it you will not be guilty in this
w Lev 19:8 matter; then you will not defile the holy
offerings[w] of the Israelites, and you will
not die.' "

The Water of Cleansing

19 The LORD said to Moses and
Aaron: 2 "This is a requirement
19:2 x Ge 15:9; of the law that the LORD has command-
Heb 9:13 y Lev 22:19-25 ed: Tell the Israelites to bring you a red
z Dt 21:3; 1Sa 6:7 heifer[x] without defect or blemish[y] and
that has never been under a yoke.[z] 3 Give
19:3 it to Eleazar[a] the priest; it is to be taken
a Nu 3:4 outside the camp[b] and slaughtered in
b Lev 4:12,21; Heb 13:11 his presence. 4 Then Eleazar the priest is
to take some of its blood on his finger
19:4 and sprinkle[c] it seven times toward the
c Lev 4:17 front of the Tent of Meeting. 5 While he
19:5 watches, the heifer is to be burned—its
d Ex 29:14 hide, flesh, blood and offal.[d] 6 The priest
19:6 is to take some cedar wood, hyssop[e] and
e ver 18; Ps 51:7 f Lev 14:4 scarlet wool[f] and throw them onto the
burning heifer. 7 After that, the priest
19:7 g Lev 11:25; must wash his clothes and bathe himself
16:26,28; 22:6 with water.[g] He may then come into the
camp, but he will be ceremonially un-
clean till evening. 8 The man who burns
it must also wash his clothes and bathe
with water, and he too will be unclean
till evening.
9 "A man who is clean shall gather up
the ashes of the heifer[h] and put them in 19:9 h Heb 9:13
a ceremonially clean place outside the i ver 13; Nu 8:7
camp. They shall be kept by the Israelite
community for use in the water of
cleansing:[i] it is for purification from sin.
10 The man who gathers up the ashes of
the heifer must also wash his clothes,
and he too will be unclean till evening.
This will be a lasting ordinance both for
the Israelites and for the aliens living
among them.
11 "Whoever touches the dead body[j] of 19:11
anyone will be unclean for seven days.[k] j Lev 21:1; Nu 5:2
12 He must purify himself with the water k Nu 31:19
on the third day and on the seventh 19:12
day;[l] then he will be clean. But if he does l ver 19;
not purify himself on the third and sev- Nu 31:19
enth days, he will not be clean. 13 Who-
ever touches the dead body[m] of anyone 19:13 m Lev 20:3
and fails to purify himself defiles the n Lev 15:31; 2Ch 36:14
LORD's tabernacle.[n] That person must be o Lev 7:20; 22:3
cut off from Israel.[o] Because the water of
cleansing has not been sprinkled on

JESUS FOCUS

THE RED HEIFER

In the middle of describing the sacrificial system, God gave his people a unique provision, the ashes of the *red heifer* (Numbers 19:9). The red heifer was a cow "without defect or blemish" (verse 2). It was slaughtered rather than sacrificed, outside of the camp rather than at the altar. A priest had to be present to sprinkle some of the animal's blood in the direction of the tabernacle, but the rest of the animal was burned to ashes—a ritual unlike any other in the Old Testament. Cedar wood, hyssop and scarlet wool were tossed onto the carcass while it burned, and the ashes were kept outside the camp to mix with the "water of cleansing" used in certain purifying ceremonies. This water was sprinkled on people, tents or furniture that had become "unclean" because of contact with a dead body. In Hebrews 9:12–14, the cleansing power of Jesus' blood is contrasted with the sprinkled water containing the ashes of the red heifer. Once again God provided his people with a foreshadowing of what he himself would one day do for them.

19:13 [p] Hag 2:13 him, he is unclean;[p] his uncleanness remains on him.
14“This is the law that applies when a
person dies in a tent: Anyone who enters
the tent and anyone who is in it will be
unclean for seven days, 15and every open
container without a lid fastened on it
will be unclean.
16“Anyone out in the open who
touches someone who has been killed
with a sword or someone who has died
19:16 [q] Nu 31:19 [r] Mt 23:27 a natural death,[q] or anyone who touches
a human bone or a grave,[r] will be un-
clean for seven days.
17“For the unclean person, put some
19:17 [s] ver 9 ashes[s] from the burned purification offering into a jar and pour fresh water
over them. 18Then a man who is cere-
19:18 [t] ver 6 monially clean is to take some hyssop,[t]
dip it in the water and sprinkle the tent
and all the furnishings and the people
who were there. He must also sprinkle
anyone who has touched a human bone
or a grave or someone who has been
killed or someone who has died a natural death. 19The man who is clean is to
sprinkle the unclean person on the third
and seventh days, and on the seventh
19:19 [u] Eze 36:25; Heb 10:22 day he is to purify him.[u] The person being cleansed must wash his clothes and
bathe with water, and that evening he
will be clean. 20But if a person who is unclean does not purify himself, he must
be cut off from the community, because
he has defiled the sanctuary of the LORD.
The water of cleansing has not been
sprinkled on him, and he is unclean.
21This is a lasting ordinance for them.
“The man who sprinkles the water of
cleansing must also wash his clothes,
and anyone who touches the water of
cleansing will be unclean till evening.
19:22 [v] Lev 5:2; Hag 2:13,14 22Anything that an unclean[v] person
touches becomes unclean, and anyone
who touches it becomes unclean till
evening.”

Water From the Rock

20 In the first month the whole Israelite community arrived at
20:1 [w] Nu 13:21 [x] Nu 33:36 [y] Ex 15:20 the Desert of Zin,[w] and they stayed at
Kadesh.[x] There Miriam[y] died and was
buried.
20:2 [z] Ex 17:1 [a] Nu 16:19 2Now there was no water for the community,[z] and the people gathered in op-
position[a] to Moses and Aaron. 3They
20:3 [b] Ex 17:2 quarreled[b] with Moses and said, “If only
we had died when our brothers fell dead 20:3 [c] Nu 14:2; 16:31-35
before the LORD![c] 4Why did you bring
the LORD’s community into this desert,
that we and our livestock should die 20:4 [d] Ex 14:11; 17:3; Nu 14:3; 16:13
here?[d] 5Why did you bring us up out of
Egypt to this terrible place? It has no
grain or figs, grapevines or pomegran- 20:5 [e] Nu 16:14
ates.[e] And there is no water to drink!”
6Moses and Aaron went from the assembly to the entrance to the Tent of
Meeting and fell facedown,[f] and the glo- 20:6 [f] Nu 14:5 [g] Nu 16:19
ry of the LORD[g] appeared to them. 7The
LORD said to Moses, 8“Take the staff,[h] 20:8 [h] Ex 4:17,20 [i] Ex 17:6; Isa 43:20
and you and your brother Aaron gather
the assembly together. Speak to that
rock before their eyes and it will pour
out its water.[i] You will bring water out of
the rock for the community so they and
their livestock can drink.”
9So Moses took the staff from the
LORD’s presence,[j] just as he commanded 20:9 [j] Nu 17:10
him. 10He and Aaron gathered the as-
sembly together in front of the rock and
Moses said to them, “Listen, you rebels, 20:10 [k] Ps 106:32,33
must we bring you water out of this
rock?”[k] 11Then Moses raised his arm 20:11 [l] Ex 17:6; Dt 8:15; Ps 78:16; Isa 48:2; 1Co 10:4
and struck the rock twice with his staff.
Water[l] gushed out, and the community
and their livestock drank.
12But the LORD said to Moses and Aar-
on, “Because you did not trust in me 20:12 [m] Nu 27:14 [n] ver 24; Dt 1:37; 3:27
enough to honor me as holy[m] in the sight
of the Israelites, you will not bring this
community into the land I give them.”[n]
13These were the waters of Meribah,[a][o] 20:13 [o] Ex 17:7 [p] Dt 33:8; Ps 95:8; 106:32
where the Israelites quarreled[p] with the
LORD and where he showed himself holy
among them.

Edom Denies Israel Passage

14Moses sent messengers from Ka-
desh[q] to the king of Edom,[r] saying: 20:14 [q] Jdg 11:16-17 [r] Dt 2:4 [s] Jos 2:11; 9:9

“This is what your brother Israel
says: You know[s] about all the hardships that have come upon us.
15Our forefathers went down into
Egypt,[t] and we lived there many 20:15 [t] Ge 46:6 [u] Ge 15:13; Ex 12:40 [v] Ex 1:11; Dt 26:6
years.[u] The Egyptians mistreated[v]
us and our fathers, 16but when we
cried out to the LORD, he heard our
cry[w] and sent an angel[x] and 20:16 [w] Ex 2:23; 3:7 [x] Ex 14:19
brought us out of Egypt.
“Now we are here at Kadesh, a
town on the edge of your territory.
17Please let us pass through your

[a] 13 *Meribah* means *quarreling.*

DISCOVERY 39

WATER FROM THE ROCK

Forty years earlier, when the people had complained of thirst, God had instructed Moses to strike a rock with his staff, with the amazing result that water had flowed from that rock (Exodus 17:1–7). Now the Israelites were complaining again about a water shortage. This time God told Moses to simply *speak* to the rock. But Moses was angry, and in the passion of the moment he struck the rock twice. Water did gush forth for the people to drink (Numbers 20:11), but God was displeased with Moses: Because of this seemingly insignificant (and apparently understandable!) lapse of self-control, Moses would not be permitted to lead the people into the land God had promised them.

Similarly, when God gives us instructions he expects us to pay attention to the details. Partial *obedience* may as accurately be defined as partial *disobedience*. Are there areas of our lives in which we are not totally committed to doing what God wants us to do? Has he asked us to do or offer something that we have done or relinquished only in part? If so, we have made the same mistake Moses did: We have *hit* the rock, when God had instructed us to *speak* to it.

There are consequences when we fail to obey God completely. For Moses the penalty seemed severe, but in reality the same is true for us. When we choose not to take God at his word, we voluntarily walk away from the blessings he is waiting for us to claim.

Despite the dire consequence of Moses' disobedience, God did honor the people's request for water to quench their unsatisfied thirst. As with so many passages in the Old Testament, this second incident with Moses and the rock provides us with an early foreshadowing of Jesus. In the New Testament Paul referred to this incident, observing that God's people "drank from the spiritual rock that accompanied them, and that rock was Christ" (1 Corinthians 10:4). They quenched their thirst with water God had provided from the rock, just as we quench our spiritual thirst with "living water" from the real Rock—Jesus Christ.

As we get to know him through his Word, our lives become more conformed to God's holiness: "Husbands, love your wives, just as Christ loved the church and gave himself up for her to make her holy, cleansing her by the washing with water through the word, and to present her to himself as a radiant church, without stain or wrinkle or any other blemish, but holy and blameless" (Ephesians 5:25–27).

God's people in the Old Testament needed water every day to survive in the desert. And so do we. But our source of living water is endless, ever fresh and satisfying. We have Jesus, the *living water*, to sustain us (John 15:1–4).

Self-Discovery: *In what ways have you been "drinking" from the rock of "living water"? Is your soul satisfied with Jesus' love?*

GO TO DISCOVERY 40 ON PAGE 201

country. We will not go through any
field or vineyard, or drink water
from any well. We will travel along
the king's highway and not turn to
the right or to the left until we have
20:17 [y]Nu 21:22 passed through your territory.[y]"

18 But Edom answered:

"You may not pass through here;
if you try, we will march out and attack you with the sword."

19 The Israelites replied:

"We will go along the main road,
20:19 and if we or our livestock[z] drink
[z]Ex 12:38 [a]Dt 2:6,28 any of your water, we will pay for
it.[a] We only want to pass through
on foot—nothing else."

20 Again they answered:

"You may not pass through."

Then Edom came out against them
with a large and powerful army. 21 Since
Edom refused to let them go through
20:21 their territory, Israel turned away from
[b]Dt 2:8; them.[b]
Jdg 11:18

The Death of Aaron

22 The whole Israelite community set
20:22 out from Kadesh and came to Mount
[c]Nu 33:37 Hor.[c] 23 At Mount Hor, near the border of
20:23 Edom,[d] the LORD said to Moses and Aar-
[d]Nu 33:37 on, 24 "Aaron will be gathered to his peo-
20:24 ple.[e] He will not enter the land I give the
[e]Ge 25:8 [f]ver 10 Israelites, because both of you rebelled
against my command[f] at the waters of
20:25 Meribah. 25 Get Aaron and his son Elea-
[g]Nu 33:38 zar and take them up Mount Hor.[g] 26 Remove Aaron's garments and put them on
his son Eleazar, for Aaron will be gath-
20:26 [h]ver 24 ered to his people;[h] he will die there."

27 Moses did as the LORD commanded:
They went up Mount Hor in the sight of
the whole community. 28 Moses removed
Aaron's garments and put them on his
20:28 [i]Ex 29:29 son Eleazar.[i] And Aaron died there[j] on
[j]Nu 33:38; top of the mountain. Then Moses and
Dt 10:6; 32:50 Eleazar came down from the mountain,
29 and when the whole community
20:29 learned that Aaron had died, the entire
[k]Dt 34:8 house of Israel mourned for him[k] thirty
days.

Arad Destroyed

21:1 **21** When the Canaanite king of
[l]Nu 33:40; Jos 12:14 Arad,[l] who lived in the Negev,[m]
[m]Jdg 1:9,16 heard that Israel was coming along the
road to Atharim, he attacked the Israelites and captured some of them. 2 Then
Israel made this vow to the LORD: "If you
will deliver these people into our hands,
we will totally destroy[a] their cities." 3 The
LORD listened to Israel's plea and gave
the Canaanites over to them. They completely destroyed them and their towns;
so the place was named Hormah.[b]

The Bronze Snake

4 They traveled from Mount Hor[n] 21:4 [n]Nu 20:22
along the route to the Red Sea,[c] to go [o]Dt 2:8;
around Edom. But the people grew im- Jdg 11:18
patient on the way;[o] 5 they spoke against
God[p] and against Moses, and said, 21:5 [p]Ps 78:19
"Why have you brought us up out of [q]Nu 14:2,3
Egypt to die in the desert?[q] There is no [r]Nu 11:6
bread! There is no water! And we detest
this miserable food!"[r]

6 Then the LORD sent venomous 21:6
snakes[s] among them; they bit the peo- [s]Dt 8:15; Jer 8:17
ple and many Israelites died.[t] 7 The peo- [t]1Co 10:9
ple came to Moses[u] and said, "We 21:7
sinned when we spoke against the LORD [u]Ps 78:34;
and against you. Pray that the LORD[v] will Hos 5:15 [v]Ex 8:8; Ac 8:24
take the snakes away from us." So Moses [w]Nu 11:2
prayed[w] for the people.

8 The LORD said to Moses, "Make a
snake and put it up on a pole;[x] anyone 21:8 [x]Jn 3:14
who is bitten can look at it and live." 9 So
Moses made a bronze snake[y] and put it 21:9 [y]2Ki 18:4
up on a pole. Then when anyone was [z]Jn 3:14-15
bitten by a snake and looked at the
bronze snake, he lived.[z]

The Journey to Moab

10 The Israelites moved on and
camped at Oboth.[a] 11 Then they set out 21:10 [a]Nu 33:43
from Oboth and camped in Iye Abarim,
in the desert that faces Moab[b] toward 21:11 [b]Nu 33:44
the sunrise. 12 From there they moved on
and camped in the Zered Valley.[c] 13 They 21:12 [c]Dt 2:13,14
set out from there and camped along- 21:13
side the Arnon[d], which is in the desert [d]Nu 22:36;
extending into Amorite territory. The Jdg 11:13,18
Arnon is the border of Moab, between
Moab and the Amorites. 14 That is why
the Book of the Wars of the LORD says:

"... Waheb in Suphah[d] and the
ravines,

[a] *2* The Hebrew term refers to the irrevocable giving over of things or persons to the LORD, often by totally destroying them; also in verse 3.
[b] *3* *Hormah* means *destruction.*
[c] *4* Hebrew *Yam Suph*; that is, Sea of Reeds
[d] *14* The meaning of the Hebrew for this phrase is uncertain.

DISCOVERY 40

Look Up and Be Healed

When God's people complained about the food and water God had provided for them in the desert, he sent an infestation of venomous snakes into the camp. Many of the people became sick or died from the bites. Finally they turned back to God, and he provided a way for them to be saved from the reptiles. Anyone who followed his instructions would be healed (Numbers 21:4–8).

Faith must always be central in our relationship with God. But when we turn away from him and fall into sin, there are inevitable consequences. For the Israelites the consequences took the form of writhing snakes. There was no humanly available antidote for their poison. God told Moses to fashion a bronze snake and raise it on a pole. If the people were to look up at the snake, they would be healed. The remedy seemed like such a simple act, but the surprising fact is that some people simply refused. They knew that they were in desperate need of healing but declined to do something as simple as turning their gaze upward!

Jesus referred to this story to explain the meaning of his own life. A religious leader named Nicodemus came under cover of night to question him about his teachings. To ask people to fix their eyes on a statue in order to accomplish physical healing may have seemed very strange, but Jesus told Nicodemus something fully as unexpected: "No one can see the kingdom of God unless he is born again" (John 3:3). Of course, Nicodemus knew that there was no way for a man to return to his mother's womb and be born again, but Jesus explained that he was talking about spiritual life: "Just as Moses lifted up the snake in the desert, so the Son of Man must be lifted up, that everyone who believes in him may have eternal life" (John 3:14–15).

God the Son knew his purpose, and he knew what was coming. He must soon be "lifted up" to die on a wooden cross, just as the replica of the snake had been lifted up on a wooden pole. By using that analogy, Jesus was explaining the only way to be saved from sin. Salvation is an act of faith. "Everyone who believes" that Jesus died for his or her sins will be saved from the otherwise unavoidable consequence—death.

The writer to the Hebrews urged us as Christians to look up at our risen Lord: "Let us fix our eyes on Jesus, the author and perfecter of our faith, who for the joy set before him endured the cross, scorning its shame, and sat down at the right hand of the throne of God. Consider him who endured such opposition from sinful men, so that you will not grow weary and lose heart" (Hebrews 12:2–3).

Some people today think that putting their faith in Jesus is just as naive as looking to a metal statue for salvation: "All I have to do is *believe*? But that's too simple!" And they are partially right; it is simple—an elemental act of faith. Simple . . . and true.

Self-Discovery: *Why do you think some of the suffering Israelites chose not to look up at the bronze snake? Think back to a time when this same attitude held you back from obeying a simple instruction?*

GO TO DISCOVERY 41 ON PAGE 218

21:15 [e] ver 28; Dt 2:9, 18
the Arnon 15 and[a] the slopes of
the ravines
that lead to the site of Ar[e]
and lie along the border of
Moab."

21:16 [f] Jdg 9:21
16 From there they continued on to Beer,[f]
the well where the LORD said to Moses,
"Gather the people together and I will
give them water."

21:17 [g] Ex 15:1
17 Then Israel sang this song:[g]

"Spring up, O well!
Sing about it,
18 about the well that the princes dug,
that the nobles of the people
sank—
the nobles with scepters and
staffs."

Then they went from the desert to Mattanah, 19 from Mattanah to Nahaliel,
from Nahaliel to Bamoth, 20 and from
Bamoth to the valley in Moab where the
top of Pisgah overlooks the wasteland.

Defeat of Sihon and Og

21:21 [h] Dt 1:4; 2:26-27; Jdg 11:19-21
21 Israel sent messengers to say to Sihon[h] king of the Amorites:

22 "Let us pass through your
country. We will not turn aside into
any field or vineyard, or drink water
from any well. We will travel along
the king's highway until we have
21:22 [i] Nu 20:17
passed through your territory.[i]"

21:23 [j] Nu 20:21 [k] Dt 2:32; Jdg 11:20
23 But Sihon would not let Israel pass
through his territory.[j] He mustered his
entire army and marched out into the
desert against Israel. When he reached
Jahaz,[k] he fought with Israel. 24 Israel,
21:24 [l] Dt 2:33; Ps 135:10-11; Am 2:9 [m] Dt 2:37
however, put him to the sword[l] and took
over his land from the Arnon to the Jabbok, but only as far as the Ammonites,[m]
because their border was fortified. 25 Israel captured all the cities of the Amo-
21:25 [n] Nu 13:29; Jdg 10:11; Am 2:10
rites[n] and occupied them, including
Heshbon and all its surrounding settlements. 26 Heshbon was the city of Sihon[o]
21:26 [o] Dt 29:7; Ps 135:11
king of the Amorites, who had fought
against the former king of Moab and
had taken from him all his land as far as
the Arnon.
27 That is why the poets say:

"Come to Heshbon and let it be
rebuilt;
let Sihon's city be restored.

28 "Fire went out from Heshbon,
a blaze from the city of Sihon.[p] 21:28 [p] Jer 48:45
It consumed Ar[q] of Moab, [q] ver 15
the citizens of Arnon's heights.[r] [r] Nu 22:41; Isa 15:2
29 Woe to you, O Moab![s]
You are destroyed, O people of 21:29 [s] Isa 25:10; Jer 48:46
Chemosh![t] [t] Jdg 11:24; 1Ki 11:7,33; 2Ki 23:13; Jer 48:7,46
He has given up his sons as
fugitives[u] [u] Isa 15:5
and his daughters as captives[v] [v] Isa 16:2
to Sihon king of the Amorites.

30 "But we have overthrown them;
Heshbon is destroyed all the way
to Dibon.[w] 21:30 [w] Nu 32:3; Isa 15:2; Jer 48:18,22
We have demolished them as far as
Nophah,
which extends to Medeba."

31 So Israel settled in the land of the
Amorites.
32 After Moses had sent spies to Jazer,[x] 21:32 [x] Nu 32:1,3,35; Jer 48:32
the Israelites captured its surrounding
settlements and drove out the Amorites
who were there. 33 Then they turned and
went up along the road toward Ba-
shan[y],[z] and Og king of Bashan and his 21:33 [y] Dt 3:3 [z] Dt 3:4
whole army marched out to meet them [a] Dt 1:4; 3:1,10; Jos 13:12,31
in battle at Edrei.[a]
34 The LORD said to Moses, "Do not be
afraid of him, for I have handed him over
to you, with his whole army and his land.
Do to him what you did to Sihon king of
the Amorites, who reigned in Heshbon.[b]" 21:34 [b] Dt 3:2
35 So they struck him down, together
with his sons and his whole army, leaving them no survivors. And they took
possession of his land.

Balak Summons Balaam

22 Then the Israelites traveled to
the plains of Moab and camped
along the Jordan across from Jericho.[b][c] 22:1 [c] Nu 33:48
2 Now Balak son of Zippor[d] saw all
that Israel had done to the Amorites, 22:2 [d] Jdg 11:25
3 and Moab was terrified because there
were so many people. Indeed, Moab was
filled with dread[e] because of the Israel- 22:3 [e] Ex 15:15
ites.
4 The Moabites said to the elders of
Midian, "This horde is going to lick up
everything around us, as an ox licks up
the grass of the field." 22:5 [f] Dt 23:4; Jos 13:22; 24:9; Ne 13:2; Mic 6:5; 2Pe 2:15
So Balak son of Zippor, who was king
of Moab at that time, 5 sent messengers
to summon Balaam son of Beor,[f] who

[a] 14,15 Or *"I have been given from Suphah and the ravines / of the Arnon* 15 *to* [b] 1 Hebrew *Jordan of Jericho*; possibly an ancient name for the Jordan River

was at Pethor, near the River,[a] in his native land. Balak said:

"A people has come out of Egypt;
they cover the face of the land and
have settled next to me. 6Now
22:6 [g] ver 12,17; Nu 23:7,11,13
come and put a curse[g] on these
people, because they are too powerful for me. Perhaps then I will be
able to defeat them and drive them
out of the country. For I know that
those you bless are blessed, and
those you curse are cursed."

7The elders of Moab and Midian left,
22:7 [h] Nu 23:23; 24:1
taking with them the fee for divination.[h]
When they came to Balaam, they told
him what Balak had said.
8"Spend the night here," Balaam said
to them, "and I will bring you back the
22:8 [i] ver 19
answer the LORD gives me.[i]" So the Moabite princes stayed with him.
22:9 [j] Ge 20:3 [k] ver 20
9God came to Balaam[j] and asked,[k]
"Who are these men with you?"
10Balaam said to God, "Balak son of
Zippor, king of Moab, sent me this message: 11'A people that has come out of
Egypt covers the face of the land. Now
come and put a curse on them for me.
Perhaps then I will be able to fight them
and drive them away.' "
12But God said to Balaam, "Do not go
with them. You must not put a curse on
22:12 [l] Ge 12:2; 22:17; Nu 23:20
those people, because they are blessed.[l]"
13The next morning Balaam got up
and said to Balak's princes, "Go back to
your own country, for the LORD has refused to let me go with you."
14So the Moabite princes returned to
Balak and said, "Balaam refused to
come with us."
15Then Balak sent other princes, more
numerous and more distinguished than
the first. 16They came to Balaam and said:

"This is what Balak son of Zippor says: Do not let anything keep
you from coming to me, 17because
22:17 [m] ver 37; Nu 24:11 [n] ver 6
I will reward you handsomely[m] and
do whatever you say. Come and put
a curse[n] on these people for me."

18But Balaam answered them, "Even if
22:18 [o] ver 38; Nu 23:12,26; 24:13; 1Ki 22:14; 2Ch 18:13; Jer 42:4
Balak gave me his palace filled with sil-
ver and gold, I could not do anything
great or small to go beyond the command of the LORD my God.[o] 19Now stay
22:19 [p] ver 8
here tonight as the others did, and I will
find out what else the LORD will tell me.[p]"
20That night God came to Balaam[q]
22:20 [q] Ge 20:3 [r] ver 35,38; Nu 23:5,12,16, 26; 24:13; 2Ch 18:13
and said, "Since these men have come to
summon you, go with them, but do only
what I tell you."[r]

Balaam's Donkey

21Balaam got up in the morning, saddled his donkey and went with the
princes of Moab. 22But God was very an-
22:22 [s] Ex 4:14 [t] Ge 16:7; Ex 23:20; Jdg 13:3,6,13
gry[s] when he went, and the angel of the
LORD[t] stood in the road to oppose him.
Balaam was riding on his donkey, and
his two servants were with him. 23When
the donkey saw the angel of the LORD
standing in the road with a drawn
22:23 [u] Jos 5:13 [v] ver 25,27
sword[u] in his hand, she turned off the
road into a field. Balaam beat her[v] to get
her back on the road.
24Then the angel of the LORD stood in
a narrow path between two vineyards,
with walls on both sides. 25When the
donkey saw the angel of the LORD, she
pressed close to the wall, crushing Balaam's foot against it. So he beat her
again.
26Then the angel of the LORD moved
on ahead and stood in a narrow place
where there was no room to turn, either
to the right or to the left. 27When the
donkey saw the angel of the LORD, she
22:27 [w] Nu 11:1; Jas 1:19
lay down under Balaam, and he was angry[w] and beat her with his staff. 28Then
22:28 [x] 2Pe 2:16
the LORD opened the donkey's mouth,[x]
and she said to Balaam, "What have I

[a] 5 That is, the Euphrates

JESUS FOCUS

LYING PROPHETS

In the New Testament Jesus regularly warned people to be on their guard against false prophets (see Matthew 7:15; 24:4,11,24–25). In his letter to the church at Pergamum (Revelation 2:14) our Lord specifically condemned the teaching of Balaam. Balaam was a pagan prophet and a fitting example of a false teacher. While he claimed to believe in the true God, his actions proved this claim to be untrue (Numbers 22). Balaam's specialty was divination, but he was blind to authentic spiritual truth; even his donkey could perceive the truth that Balaam missed. The "angel of the LORD" who talked with Balaam may have been Jesus himself, who in Old Testament times periodically stepped into human history to bless and defend his people (see page 23).

done to you to make you beat me these
22:28 [y] ver 32 three times?[y]"
29Balaam answered the donkey, "You
22:29 [z] Dt 25:4; have made a fool of me! If I had a sword
Pr 12:10; 27:23- in my hand, I would kill you right now.[z]"
27; Mt 15:19 30The donkey said to Balaam, "Am I
not your own donkey, which you have always ridden, to this day? Have I been in
the habit of doing this to you?"
"No," he said.
31Then the LORD opened Balaam's
22:31 [a] Ge 21:19 eyes,[a] and he saw the angel of the LORD
standing in the road with his sword
drawn. So he bowed low and fell facedown.
32The angel of the LORD asked him,
"Why have you beaten your donkey
these three times? I have come here to
oppose you because your path is a reckless one before me.[a] 33The donkey saw
me and turned away from me these
three times. If she had not turned away,
22:33 I would certainly have killed you by
[b] ver 29 now,[b] but I would have spared her."
34Balaam said to the angel of the LORD,
22:34 [c] Ge 39:9; "I have sinned.[c] I did not realize you were
Nu 14:40; 1Sa 15:24,30; standing in the road to oppose me. Now
2Sa 12:13; if you are displeased, I will go back."
24:10; Job 33:27; 35The angel of the LORD said to Ba-
Ps 51:4 laam, "Go with the men, but speak only
what I tell you." So Balaam went with the
princes of Balak.
36When Balak heard that Balaam was
coming, he went out to meet him at the
22:36 [d] Nu 21:13 Moabite town on the Arnon[d] border, at
the edge of his territory. 37Balak said to
Balaam, "Did I not send you an urgent
summons? Why didn't you come to me?
Am I really not able to reward you?"
38"Well, I have come to you now," Balaam replied. "But can I say just any-
22:38 thing? I must speak only what God puts
[e] Nu 23:5,16,26 in my mouth."[e]
39Then Balaam went with Balak to
Kiriath Huzoth. 40Balak sacrificed cattle
22:40 and sheep,[f] and gave some to Balaam
[f] Nu 23:1,14,29; and the princes who were with him.
Eze 45:23 41The next morning Balak took Balaam
22:41 [g] Nu 21:28 up to Bamoth Baal,[g] and from there he
[h] Nu 23:13 saw part of the people.[h]

Balaam's First Oracle

23 Balaam said, "Build me seven
altars here, and prepare seven
23:1 [i] Nu 22:40 bulls and seven rams[i] for me." 2Balak did
23:2 as Balaam said, and the two of them of-
[j] ver 14,30 fered a bull and a ram on each altar.[j]
3Then Balaam said to Balak, "Stay
here beside your offering while I go
aside. Perhaps the LORD will come to
meet with me.[k] Whatever he reveals to 23:3 [k] ver 15
me I will tell you." Then he went off to a
barren height.
4God met with him,[l] and Balaam said, 23:4 [l] ver 16
"I have prepared seven altars, and on
each altar I have offered a bull and a ram."
5The LORD put a message in Balaam's 23:5 [m] Dt 18:18;
mouth[m] and said, "Go back to Balak and Jer 1:9
give him this message."[n] [n] Nu 22:20
6So he went back to him and found 23:6
him standing beside his offering, with all [o] ver 17
the princes of Moab.[o] 7Then Balaam[p] 23:7 [p] Nu 22:5
uttered his oracle:[q] [q] ver 18;

"Balak brought me from Aram, Nu 24:3,21
the king of Moab from the [r] Nu 22:6;
eastern mountains. Dt 23:4
'Come,' he said, 'curse Jacob for me;
come, denounce Israel.'[r]
8How can I curse
those whom God has not 23:8
cursed?[s] [s] Nu 22:12
How can I denounce
those whom the LORD has not
denounced?
9From the rocky peaks I see them,
from the heights I view them.
I see a people who live apart 23:9
and do not consider themselves [t] Ex 33:16;
one of the nations.[t] Dt 32:8; 33:28
10Who can count the dust of Jacob[u] 23:10 [u] Ge 13:16
or number the fourth part of [v] Ps 116:15;
Israel? Isa 57:1
Let me die the death of the [w] Ps 37:37
righteous,[v]
and may my end be like theirs![w]"

11Balak said to Balaam, "What have
you done to me? I brought you to curse 23:11
my enemies, but you have done nothing [x] Nu 24:10;
but bless them!"[x] Ne 13:2
12He answered, "Must I not speak 23:12
what the LORD puts in my mouth?"[y] [y] Nu 22:20,38

Balaam's Second Oracle

13Then Balak said to him, "Come with
me to another place where you can see
them; you will see only a part but not all
of them. And from there, curse them for
me." 14So he took him to the field of Zo-
phim on the top of Pisgah, and there he
built seven altars and offered a bull and 23:14
a ram on each altar.[z] [z] ver 2

[a] 32 The meaning of the Hebrew for this clause is uncertain.

15 Balaam said to Balak, "Stay here beside your offering while I meet with him over there."

16 The LORD met with Balaam and put a message in his mouth[a] and said, "Go back to Balak and give him this message."

17 So he went to him and found him standing beside his offering, with the princes of Moab. Balak asked him, "What did the LORD say?"

18 Then he uttered his oracle:

"Arise, Balak, and listen;
hear me, son of Zippor.
19 God is not a man,[b] that he should lie,
nor a son of man, that he should change his mind.[c]
Does he speak and then not act?
Does he promise and not fulfill?
20 I have received a command to bless;
he has blessed,[d] and I cannot change it.[e]

21 "No misfortune is seen in Jacob,[f]
no misery observed in Israel.[a][g]
The LORD their God is with them;[h]
the shout of the King[i] is among them.
22 God brought them out of Egypt;[j]
they have the strength of a wild ox.[k]
23 There is no sorcery against Jacob,
no divination[l] against Israel.
It will now be said of Jacob
and of Israel, 'See what God has done!'
24 The people rise like a lioness;[m]
they rouse themselves like a lion[n]
that does not rest till he devours his prey
and drinks the blood of his victims."

25 Then Balak said to Balaam, "Neither curse them at all nor bless them at all!"

26 Balaam answered, "Did I not tell you I must do whatever the LORD says?"

Balaam's Third Oracle

27 Then Balak said to Balaam, "Come, let me take you to another place.[o] Perhaps it will please God to let you curse them for me from there." 28 And Balak took Balaam to the top of Peor,[p] overlooking the wasteland.

29 Balaam said, "Build me seven altars here, and prepare seven bulls and seven rams for me." 30 Balak did as Balaam had said, and offered a bull and a ram on each altar.

24 Now when Balaam saw that it pleased the LORD to bless Israel, he did not resort to sorcery[q] as at other times, but turned his face toward the desert.[r] 2 When Balaam looked out and saw Israel encamped tribe by tribe, the Spirit of God came upon him[s] 3 and he uttered his oracle:

"The oracle of Balaam son of Beor,
the oracle of one whose eye sees clearly,
4 the oracle of one who hears the words of God,[t]
who sees a vision from the Almighty,[b][u]
who falls prostrate, and whose eyes are opened:

5 "How beautiful are your tents, O Jacob,
your dwelling places, O Israel!

6 "Like valleys they spread out,
like gardens beside a river,
like aloes[v] planted by the LORD,
like cedars beside the waters.[w]
7 Water will flow from their buckets;
their seed will have abundant water.

"Their king will be greater than Agag;[x]
their kingdom will be exalted.[y]

8 "God brought them out of Egypt;
they have the strength of a wild ox.
They devour hostile nations
and break their bones in pieces;[z]
with their arrows they pierce them.[a]
9 Like a lion they crouch and lie down,
like a lioness[b]—who dares to rouse them?

"May those who bless you be blessed
and those who curse you be cursed!"[c]

10 Then Balak's anger burned against Balaam. He struck his hands together[d] and said to him, "I summoned you to

[a] 21 Or *He has not looked on Jacob's offenses / or on the wrongs found in Israel.* [b] 4 Hebrew *Shaddai;* also in verse 16

23:16 [a] Nu 22:38
23:19 [b] Isa 55:9; Hos 11:9 [c] 1Sa 15:29; Mal 3:6; Tit 1:2; Jas 1:17
23:20 [d] Ge 22:17; Nu 22:12 [e] Isa 43:13
23:21 [f] Ps 32:2,5; Ro 4:7-8 [g] Isa 40:2; Jer 50:20 [h] Ex 29:45,46; Ps 145:18 [i] Dt 33:5; Ps 89:15-18
23:22 [j] Nu 24:8 [k] Dt 33:17; Job 39:9
23:23 [l] Nu 24:1; Jos 13:22
23:24 [m] Na 2:11 [n] Ge 49:9
23:27 [o] ver 13
23:28 [p] Ps 106:28
24:1 [q] Nu 23:23 [r] Nu 23:28
24:2 [s] Nu 11:25,26; 1Sa 10:10; 19:20; 2Ch 15:1
24:4 [t] Nu 22:20 [u] Ge 15:1
24:6 [v] Ps 45:8 [w] Ps 1:3; 104:16
24:7 [x] 2Sa 15:8 [y] 2Sa 5:12; 1Ch 14:2; Ps 145:11-13
24:8 [z] Ps 2:9; Jer 50:17 [a] Ps 45:5
24:9 [b] Ge 49:9; Nu 23:24 [c] Ge 12:3
24:10 [d] Eze 21:14

curse my enemies, but you have blessed
24:10 [e]Nu 23:11 them[e] these three times.[f] 11 Now leave at
[f]Ne 13:2 once and go home! I said I would reward
24:11 [g]Nu 22:17 you handsomely,[g] but the LORD has kept
you from being rewarded."
12 Balaam answered Balak, "Did I not
24:12 [h]Nu 22:18 tell the messengers you sent me,[h]
13 'Even if Balak gave me his palace filled
with silver and gold, I could not do any-
24:13 [i]Nu 22:18 thing of my own accord, good or bad, to
[j]Nu 22:20 go beyond the command of the LORD[i]—
and I must say only what the LORD
says'?[j] 14 Now I am going back to my peo-
24:14 [k]Ge 49:1; Nu 31:8,16; Da 2:28; Mic 6:5 ple, but come, let me warn you of what
this people will do to your people in days
to come."[k]

Balaam's Fourth Oracle

15 Then he uttered his oracle:

"The oracle of Balaam son of Beor,
the oracle of one whose eye sees
clearly,
16 the oracle of one who hears the
words of God,
who has knowledge from the
Most High,
who sees a vision from the
Almighty,
who falls prostrate, and whose
eyes are opened:

17 "I see him, but not now;
24:17 [l]Rev 1:7 I behold him, but not near.[l]
[m]Mt 2:2 A star will come out of Jacob;[m]
24:17 [n]Ge 49:10 a scepter will rise out of Israel.[n]
[o]Nu 21:29; Isa 15:1-16:14 He will crush the foreheads of
Moab,[o]
the skulls[a] of[b] all the sons of
Sheth.[c]
18 Edom[p] will be conquered; 24:18 [p]Am 9:12
Seir, his enemy, will be conquered,
but Israel will grow strong.
19 A ruler will come out of Jacob[q] 24:19 [q]Ge 49:10; Mic 5:2
and destroy the survivors of the
city."

Balaam's Final Oracles

20 Then Balaam saw Amalek[r] and ut- 24:20 [r]Ex 17:14
tered his oracle:

"Amalek was first among the
nations,
but he will come to ruin at last."

21 Then he saw the Kenites[s] and ut- 24:21 [s]Ge 15:19
tered his oracle:

"Your dwelling place is secure,
your nest is set in a rock;
22 yet you Kenites will be destroyed 24:22 [t]Ge 10:22
when Asshur[t] takes you captive."

23 Then he uttered his oracle:

"Ah, who can live when God does
this?[d]
24 Ships will come from the shores 24:24 [u]Ge 10:4
of Kittim;[u] [v]Ge 10:21
they will subdue Asshur and Eber,[v] [w]ver 20
but they too will come to ruin.[w]"

25 Then Balaam[x] got up and returned 24:25 [x]Nu 31:8
home and Balak went his own way.

Moab Seduces Israel

25 While Israel was staying in 25:1 [y]Jos 2:1;
Shittim,[y] the men began to in- Mic 6:5
dulge in sexual immorality[z] with Moab- [z]1Co 10:8; Rev 2:14
ite women,[a] 2 who invited them to the [a]Nu 31:16
sacrifices[b] to their gods.[c] The people ate 25:2 [b]Ex 34:15
and bowed down before these gods. 3 So [c]Ex 20:5;
Israel joined in worshiping the Baal of Dt 32:38;
Peor.[d] And the LORD's anger burned 1Co 10:20
against them.
4 The LORD said to Moses, "Take all the 25:3 [d]Ps 106:28; Hos 9:10
leaders of these people, kill them and ex-
pose them in broad daylight before the 25:4 [e]Dt 4:3
LORD,[e] so that the LORD's fierce anger[f] [f]Dt 13:17
may turn away from Israel."

[a] *17* Samaritan Pentateuch (see also Jer. 48:45); the meaning of the word in the Masoretic Text is uncertain. [b] *17* Or possibly *Moab, / batter* [c] *17* Or *all the noisy boasters* [d] *23* Masoretic Text; with a different word division of the Hebrew *A people will gather from the north.*

STAR OF JACOB

Balaam's fourth prophecy, recorded in Numbers 24, was inspired by "the Spirit of God" (verse 2). God used this pagan prophet to proclaim the truth, and Balaam correctly predicted that "a star [would] come out of Jacob; a scepter [would] rise out of Israel" (verse 17). This prophecy was initially fulfilled by David but was ultimately realized in the birth and ministry of Jesus. The reference to the scepter, a symbol of royalty, is similar to Jacob's prediction in Genesis 49:10: "The scepter will not depart from Judah." And the reference to the star may have influenced the Magi who would search generations later for the newborn "king of the Jews" (Matthew 2:2). Balaam's prophecy stipulated that the one whom Balaam foresaw was "not now" and "not near," indicating that ultimate fulfillment might be expected in the distant future.

5 So Moses said to Israel's judges, "Each of you must put to death[g] those of your men who have joined in worshiping the Baal of Peor."

6 Then an Israelite man brought to his family a Midianite woman right before the eyes of Moses and the whole assembly of Israel while they were weeping at the entrance to the Tent of Meeting. 7 When Phinehas son of Eleazar, the son of Aaron, the priest, saw this, he left the assembly, took a spear in his hand 8 and followed the Israelite into the tent. He drove the spear through both of them—through the Israelite and into the woman's body. Then the plague against the Israelites was stopped;[h] 9 but those who died in the plague[i] numbered 24,000.[j]

10 The LORD said to Moses, 11 "Phinehas son of Eleazar, the son of Aaron, the priest, has turned my anger away from the Israelites;[k] for he was as zealous as I am for my honor[l] among them, so that in my zeal I did not put an end to them. 12 Therefore tell him I am making my covenant of peace[m] with him. 13 He and his descendants will have a covenant of a lasting priesthood,[n] because he was zealous for the honor of his God and made atonement[o] for the Israelites."

14 The name of the Israelite who was killed with the Midianite woman was Zimri son of Salu, the leader of a Simeonite family. 15 And the name of the Midianite woman who was put to death was Cozbi[p] daughter of Zur, a tribal chief of a Midianite family.[q]

16 The LORD said to Moses, 17 "Treat the Midianites[r] as enemies and kill them, 18 because they treated you as enemies when they deceived you in the affair of Peor[s] and their sister Cozbi, the daughter of a Midianite leader, the woman who was killed when the plague came as a result of Peor."

The Second Census

26 After the plague the LORD said to Moses and Eleazar son of Aaron, the priest, 2 "Take a census[t] of the whole Israelite community by families—all those twenty years old or more who are able to serve in the army[u] of Israel." 3 So on the plains of Moab[v] by the Jordan across from Jericho,[a][w] Moses and Eleazar the priest spoke with them and said,

25:5 [g] Ex 32:27
25:8 [h] Nu 16:46-48; Ps 106:30
25:9 [i] Nu 14:37; 1Co 10:8 [j] Nu 31:16
25:11 [k] Ps 106:30 [l] Ex 20:5; Dt 32:16,21; Ps 78:58
25:12 [m] Isa 54:10; Eze 34:25; Mal 2:4,5
25:13 [n] Ex 29:9 [o] Nu 16:46
25:15 [p] ver 18 [q] Nu 31:8; Jos 13:21
25:17 [r] Nu 31:1-3
25:18 [s] Nu 31:16
26:2 [t] Ex 30:11-16; 38:25-26; Nu 1:2 [u] Nu 1:3
26:3 [v] Nu 33:48 [w] Nu 22:1

4 "Take a census of the men twenty years old or more, as the LORD commanded Moses."

These were the Israelites who came out of Egypt:

5 The descendants of Reuben, the firstborn son of Israel, were:
through Hanoch,[x] the Hanochite clan;
through Pallu,[y] the Palluite clan;
6 through Hezron, the Hezronite clan;
through Carmi, the Carmite clan.
7 These were the clans of Reuben; those numbered were 43,730.

8 The son of Pallu was Eliab, 9 and the sons of Eliab[z] were Nemuel, Dathan and Abiram. The same Dathan and Abiram were the community[a] officials who rebelled against Moses and Aaron and were among Korah's followers when they rebelled against the LORD.[b] 10 The earth opened its mouth and swallowed them along with Korah, whose followers died when the fire devoured the 250 men. And they served as a warning sign.[c] 11 The line of Korah,[d] however, did not die out.[e]

12 The descendants of Simeon by their clans were:
through Nemuel, the Nemuelite clan;
through Jamin,[f] the Jaminite clan;
through Jakin, the Jakinite clan;
13 through Zerah,[g] the Zerahite clan;
through Shaul, the Shaulite clan.
14 These were the clans of Simeon; there were 22,200 men.[h]

15 The descendants of Gad by their clans were:
through Zephon,[i] the Zephonite clan;
through Haggi, the Haggite clan;
through Shuni, the Shunite clan;
16 through Ozni, the Oznite clan;
through Eri, the Erite clan;
17 through Arodi,[b] the Arodite clan;
through Areli, the Arelite clan.
18 These were the clans of Gad;[j] those numbered were 40,500.

19 Er and Onan were sons of Judah, but they died[k] in Canaan.

26:5 [x] Ge 46:9 [y] 1Ch 5:3
26:9 [z] Nu 16:1 [a] Nu 1:16 [b] Nu 16:2
26:10 [c] Nu 16:35,38
26:11 [d] Ex 6:24 [e] Nu 16:33; Dt 24:16
26:12 [f] 1Ch 4:24
26:13 [g] Ge 46:10
26:14 [h] Nu 1:23
26:15 [i] Ge 46:16
26:18 [j] Nu 1:25; Jos 13:24-28
26:19 [k] Ge 38:2-10; 46:12

[a] 3 Hebrew *Jordan of Jericho*; possibly an ancient name for the Jordan River; also in verse 63
[b] 17 Samaritan Pentateuch and Syriac (see also Gen. 46:16); Masoretic Text *Arod*

20 The descendants of Judah by their clans were:
26:20 through Shelah,[l] the Shelanite clan;
[l] 1Ch 2:3 through Perez, the Perezite clan;
[m] Jos 7:17 through Zerah, the Zerahite clan.[m]
21 The descendants of Perez were:
26:21 [n] Ru 4:19; 1Ch 2:9 through Hezron,[n] the Hezronite clan;
through Hamul, the Hamulite clan.
26:22 [o] Nu 1:27 22 These were the clans of Judah;[o] those numbered were 76,500.

23 The descendants of Issachar by their clans were:
26:23 [p] Ge 46:13; 1Ch 7:1 through Tola,[p] the Tolaite clan;
through Puah, the Puite[a] clan;
24 through Jashub,[q] the Jashubite clan;
26:24 [q] Ge 46:13 through Shimron, the Shimronite clan.
26:25 [r] Nu 1:29 25 These were the clans of Issachar;[r] those numbered were 64,300.

26 The descendants of Zebulun by their clans were:
through Sered, the Seredite clan;
through Elon, the Elonite clan;
through Jahleel, the Jahleelite clan.
26:27 [s] Nu 1:31 27 These were the clans of Zebulun;[s] those numbered were 60,500.

28 The descendants of Joseph by their clans through Manasseh and Ephraim were:

29 The descendants of Manasseh:
26:29 [t] Jos 17:1 through Makir,[t] the Makirite clan
[u] Jdg 11:1 (Makir was the father of Gilead[u]);
through Gilead, the Gileadite clan.
30 These were the descendants of Gilead:
26:30 [v] Jos 17:2; Jdg 6:11 through Iezer,[v] the Iezerite clan;
through Helek, the Helekite clan;
31 through Asriel, the Asrielite clan;
through Shechem, the Shechemite clan;
32 through Shemida, the Shemidaite clan;
through Hepher, the Hepherite clan.
26:33 [w] Nu 27:1 [x] Nu 36:11 33 (Zelophehad[w] son of Hepher had no sons; he had only daughters, whose names were Mahlah, Noah, Hoglah, Milcah and Tirzah.)[x]
26:34 [y] Nu 1:35 34 These were the clans of Manasseh; those numbered were 52,700.[y]

35 These were the descendants of Ephraim by their clans:
through Shuthelah, the Shuthelahite clan;
through Beker, the Bekerite clan;
through Tahan, the Tahanite clan.
36 These were the descendants of Shuthelah:
through Eran, the Eranite clan.
37 These were the clans of Ephraim;[z] those numbered were 32,500. 26:37 [z] Nu 1:33

These were the descendants of Joseph by their clans.

38 The descendants of Benjamin[a] by their clans were: 26:38 [a] Ge 46:21; 1Ch 7:6
through Bela, the Belaite clan;
through Ashbel, the Ashbelite clan;
through Ahiram, the Ahiramite clan;
39 through Shupham,[b] the Shuphamite clan;
through Hupham, the Huphamite clan.
40 The descendants of Bela through Ard[b] and Naaman were: 26:40 [b] Ge 46:21; 1Ch 8:3
through Ard,[c] the Ardite clan;
through Naaman, the Naamite clan.
41 These were the clans of Benjamin;[c] those numbered were 45,600. 26:41 [c] Nu 1:37

42 These were the descendants of Dan by their clans: 26:42 [d] Ge 46:23
through Shuham,[d] the Shuhamite clan.
These were the clans of Dan: 43 All of them were Shuhamite clans; and those numbered were 64,400.

44 The descendants of Asher by their clans were:
through Imnah, the Imnite clan;
through Ishvi, the Ishvite clan;
through Beriah, the Beriite clan;
45 and through the descendants of Beriah:
through Heber, the Heberite clan;
through Malkiel, the Malkielite clan.
46 (Asher had a daughter named Serah.)
47 These were the clans of Asher;[e] those numbered were 53,400. 26:47 [e] Nu 1:41

a 23 Samaritan Pentateuch, Septuagint, Vulgate and Syriac (see also 1 Chron. 7:1); Masoretic Text *through Puvah, the Punite* *b 39* A few manuscripts of the Masoretic Text, Samaritan Pentateuch, Vulgate and Syriac (see also Septuagint); most manuscripts of the Masoretic Text *Shephupham* *c 40* Samaritan Pentateuch and Vulgate (see also Septuagint); Masoretic Text does not have *through Ard.*

26:48 [f] Ge 46:24; 1Ch 7:13

48 The descendants of Naphtali[f] by their clans were:

through Jahzeel, the Jahzeelite clan;
through Guni, the Gunite clan;
49 through Jezer, the Jezerite clan;
through Shillem, the Shillemite clan.

26:50 [g] Nu 1:43

50 These were the clans of Naphtali;[g] those numbered were 45,400.

26:51 [h] Ex 12:37; 38:26; Nu 1:46; 11:21

51 The total number of the men of Israel was 601,730.[h]

52 The LORD said to Moses, 53 "The land is to be allotted to them as an inheritance

26:53 [i] Jos 11:23; 14:1; Eze 45:8

based on the number of names.[i] 54 To a larger group give a larger inheritance, and to a smaller group a smaller one; each is to receive its inheritance according to the

26:54 [j] Nu 33:54

number[j] of those listed. 55 Be sure that the

26:55 [k] Nu 34:14

land is distributed by lot.[k] What each group inherits will be according to the names for its ancestral tribe. 56 Each inheritance is to be distributed by lot among the larger and smaller groups."

26:57 [l] Ge 46:11; Ex 6:16-19

57 These were the Levites[l] who were counted by their clans:

through Gershon, the Gershonite clan;
through Kohath, the Kohathite clan;
through Merari, the Merarite clan.

58 These also were Levite clans:

the Libnite clan,
the Hebronite clan,
the Mahlite clan,
the Mushite clan,
the Korahite clan.

26:58 [m] Ex 6:20

26:59 [n] Ex 2:1 [o] Ex 6:20

(Kohath was the forefather of Amram;[m] 59 the name of Amram's wife was Jochebed,[n] a descendant of Levi, who was born to the Levites[a] in Egypt. To Amram she bore Aaron, Moses[o] and their sister Miriam.

26:60 [p] Nu 3:2

60 Aaron was the father of Nadab and Abihu, Eleazar and Ithamar.[p]

26:61 [q] Lev 10:1-2 [r] Nu 3:4

61 But Nadab and Abihu[q] died when they made an offering before the LORD with unauthorized fire.)[r]

26:62 [s] Nu 3:39 [t] Nu 1:47 [u] Nu 18:23 [v] Nu 2:33; Dt 10:9

62 All the male Levites a month old or more numbered 23,000.[s] They were not counted[t] along with the other Israelites because they received no inheritance[u] among them.[v]

26:63 [w] ver 3

63 These are the ones counted by Moses and Eleazar the priest when they counted the Israelites on the plains of Moab[w] by the Jordan across from Jericho.

26:64 [x] Nu 14:29; Dt 2:14-15; Heb 3:17

64 Not one of them was among those counted[x] by Moses and Aaron the priest when they counted the Israelites in the Desert of Sinai.

26:65 [y] Nu 14:28; 1Co 10:5 [z] Jos 14:6-10

65 For the LORD had told those Israelites they would surely die in the desert,[y] and not one of them was left except Caleb son of Jephunneh and Joshua son of Nun.[z]

Zelophehad's Daughters

27:1 [a] Nu 26:33 [b] Jos 17:2,3 [c] Nu 36:1

27 The daughters of Zelophehad[a] son of Hepher,[b] the son of Gilead, the son of Makir,[c] the son of Manasseh, belonged to the clans of Manasseh son of Joseph. The names of the daughters were Mahlah, Noah, Hoglah, Milcah and Tirzah. They approached 2 the entrance to the Tent of Meeting and stood before Moses, Eleazar the priest, the leaders and the whole assembly, and

27:3 [d] Nu 26:65 [e] Nu 16:2 [f] Nu 26:33

said, 3 "Our father died in the desert.[d] He was not among Korah's followers, who banded together against the LORD,[e] but he died for his own sin and left no sons.[f] 4 Why should our father's name disappear from his clan because he had no son? Give us property among our father's relatives."

27:5 [g] Ex 18:19 [h] Nu 9:8

5 So Moses brought their case[g] before the LORD[h] 6 and the LORD said to him, 7 "What Zelophehad's daughters are saying is right. You must certainly give

27:7 [i] Job 42:15 [j] Jos 17:4

them property as an inheritance[i] among their father's relatives and turn their father's inheritance over to them.[j]

8 "Say to the Israelites, 'If a man dies and leaves no son, turn his inheritance over to his daughter. 9 If he has no daughter, give his inheritance to his brothers. 10 If he has no brothers, give his inheritance to his father's brothers. 11 If his father had no brothers, give his inheritance to the nearest relative in his clan, that he may possess it. This is to be

27:11 [k] Nu 35:29

a legal requirement[k] for the Israelites, as the LORD commanded Moses.' "

Joshua to Succeed Moses

27:12 [l] Nu 33:47; Jer 22:20 [m] Dt 3:23-27; 32:48-52

12 Then the LORD said to Moses, "Go up this mountain in the Abarim range[l] and see the land[m] I have given the Israelites.

27:13 [n] Nu 31:2 [o] Nu 20:28

13 After you have seen it, you too will be gathered to your people,[n] as your brother Aaron[o] was, 14 for when the

[a] 59 Or *Jochebed, a daughter of Levi, who was born to Levi*

community rebelled at the waters in the Desert of Zin, both of you disobeyed my command to honor me as holy[p] before their eyes." (These were the waters of Meribah[q] Kadesh, in the Desert of Zin.)

[15]Moses said to the LORD, [16]"May the LORD, the God of the spirits of all mankind,[r] appoint a man over this community [17]to go out and come in before them, one who will lead them out and bring them in, so the LORD's people will not be like sheep without a shepherd."[s]

[18]So the LORD said to Moses, "Take Joshua son of Nun, a man in whom is the spirit,[a][t] and lay your hand on him.[u] [19]Have him stand before Eleazar the priest and the entire assembly and commission him[v] in their presence.[w] [20]Give him some of your authority so the whole Israelite community will obey him.[x] [21]He is to stand before Eleazar the priest, who will obtain decisions for him by inquiring[y] of the Urim[z] before the LORD. At his command he and the entire community of the Israelites will go out, and at his command they will come in."

[22]Moses did as the LORD commanded him. He took Joshua and had him stand before Eleazar the priest and the whole assembly. [23]Then he laid his hands on him and commissioned him, as the LORD instructed through Moses.

Daily Offerings

28 The LORD said to Moses, [2]"Give this command to the Israelites and say to them: 'See that you present to me at the appointed time the food[a] for my offerings made by fire, as an aroma pleasing to me.' [3]Say to them: 'This is the offering made by fire that you are to present to the LORD: two lambs a year old without defect, as a regular burnt offering each day.[b] [4]Prepare one lamb in the morning and the other at twilight, [5]together with a grain offering of a tenth of an ephah[*b*] of fine flour mixed with a quarter of a hin[*c*] of oil[c] from pressed olives. [6]This is the regular burnt offering instituted at Mount Sinai[d] as a pleasing aroma, an offering made to the LORD by fire. [7]The accompanying drink offering[e] is to be a quarter of a hin of fermented drink with each lamb. Pour out the drink offering to the LORD at the sanctuary.[f] [8]Prepare the second lamb at twilight, along with the same kind of grain offering and drink offering that you prepare in the morning. This is an offering made by fire, an aroma pleasing to the LORD.[g]

Sabbath Offerings

[9]" 'On the Sabbath[h] day, make an offering of two lambs a year old without defect, together with its drink offering and a grain offering of two-tenths of an ephah[*d*][i] of fine flour mixed with oil. [10]This is the burnt offering for every Sabbath, in addition to the regular burnt offering[j] and its drink offering.

Monthly Offerings

[11]" 'On the first of every month,[k] present to the LORD a burnt offering of two young bulls, one ram and seven male lambs a year old, all without defect.[l] [12]With each bull there is to be a grain offering[m] of three-tenths of an ephah[*e*][n] of fine flour mixed with oil; with the ram, a grain offering of two-tenths of an ephah of fine flour mixed with oil; [13]and with each lamb, a grain offering[o] of a tenth of an ephah of fine flour mixed with oil. This is for a burnt offering, a pleasing aroma, an offering made to the LORD by fire. [14]With each bull there is to be a drink offering[p] of half a hin[*f*] of wine; with the ram, a third of a hin[*g*]; and with each lamb, a quarter of a hin. This is the monthly burnt offering to be made at each new moon[q] during the year. [15]Besides the regular burnt offering[r] with its drink offering, one male goat is to be presented to the LORD as a sin offering.[s]

The Passover

[16]" 'On the fourteenth day of the first month the LORD's Passover[t] is to be held. [17]On the fifteenth day of this month there is to be a festival; for seven days[u] eat bread made without yeast.[v] [18]On the first day hold a sacred assembly and do no regular work.[w] [19]Present to the LORD an offering made by fire, a burnt offering of two young bulls, one ram and seven male lambs a year old, all without defect.

27:14 [p]Nu 20:12 [q]Ex 17:7; Dt 32:51; Ps 106:32
27:16 [r]Nu 16:22
27:17 [s]Dt 31:2; 1Ki 22:17; Eze 34:5; Zec 10:2; Mt 9:36; Mk 6:34
27:18 [t]Ge 41:38; Nu 11:25-29 [u]ver 23; Dt 34:9
27:19 [v]Dt 3:28; 31:14, 23 [w]Dt 31:7
27:20 [x]Jos 1:16,17
27:21 [y]Jos 9:14 [z]Ex 28:30
28:2 [a]Lev 3:11
28:3 [b]Ex 29:38
28:5 [c]Lev 2:1; Nu 15:4
28:6 [d]Ex 19:3
28:7 [e]Ex 29:41 [f]Lev 3:7
28:8 [g]Lev 1:9
28:9 [h]Ex 20:10 [i]Lev 23:13
28:10 [j]ver 3
28:11 [k]Nu 10:10 [l]Lev 1:3
28:12 [m]Nu 15:6 [n]Nu 15:9
28:13 [o]Lev 6:14
28:14 [p]Nu 15:7 [q]Ezr 3:5
28:15 [r]ver 3,23,24 [s]Lev 4:3
28:16 [t]Ex 12:6,18; Lev 23:5; Dt 16:1
28:17 [u]Ex 12:19 [v]Ex 23:15; 34:18; Lev 23:6; Dt 16:3-8
28:18 [w]Ex 12:16; Lev 23:7

a 18 Or *Spirit* *b 5* That is, probably about 2 quarts (about 2 liters); also in verses 13, 21 and 29 *c 5* That is, probably about 1 quart (about 1 liter); also in verses 7 and 14 *d 9* That is, probably about 4 quarts (about 4.5 liters); also in verses 12, 20 and 28 *e 12* That is, probably about 6 quarts (about 6.5 liters); also in verses 20 and 28 *f 14* That is, probably about 2 quarts (about 2 liters) *g 14* That is, probably about 1 1/4 quarts (about 1.2 liters)

28:20 20With each bull prepare a grain offering
x Lev 14:10 of three-tenths of an ephah[x] of fine flour
mixed with oil; with the ram, two-
tenths; 21and with each of the seven
28:22 lambs, one-tenth. 22Include one male
y Ro 8:3 goat as a sin offering[y] to make atone-
z Nu 15:28 ment for you.[z] 23Prepare these in addition to the regular morning burnt offering. 24In this way prepare the food for
the offering made by fire every day for
seven days as an aroma pleasing to the
LORD; it is to be prepared in addition to
the regular burnt offering and its drink
offering. 25On the seventh day hold a sacred assembly and do no regular work.

Feast of Weeks

28:26 26" 'On the day of firstfruits,[a] when
a Ex 34:22 you present to the LORD an offering of
b Ex 23:16 new grain during the Feast of Weeks,[b]
c ver 18; hold a sacred assembly and do no regu-
Dt 16:10 lar work.[c] 27Present a burnt offering of
two young bulls, one ram and seven
male lambs a year old as an aroma
pleasing to the LORD. 28With each bull
there is to be a grain offering of three-
tenths of an ephah of fine flour mixed
with oil; with the ram, two-tenths; 29and
28:29 with each of the seven lambs, one-
d ver 13 tenth.[d] 30Include one male goat to make
atonement for you. 31Prepare these to-
28:31 gether with their drink offerings, in ad-
e ver 3,19 dition to the regular burnt offering[e] and
its grain offering. Be sure the animals
are without defect.

Feast of Trumpets

29 " 'On the first day of the seventh
29:1 month hold a sacred assembly
f Lev 23:24 and do no regular work.[f] It is a day for
29:2 you to sound the trumpets. 2As an aro-
g Nu 28:2 ma pleasing to the LORD,[g] prepare a
h Nu 28:3 burnt offering of one young bull, one
ram and seven male lambs a year old, all
without defect.[h] 3With the bull prepare
a grain offering of three-tenths of an
ephah[a] of fine flour mixed with oil; with
the ram, two-tenths[b]; 4and with each of
29:5 the seven lambs, one-tenth.[c] 5Include
i Nu 28:15 one male goat[i] as a sin offering to make
29:6 atonement for you. 6These are in addi-
j Nu 28:11 tion to the monthly[j] and daily burnt of-
k Nu 28:3 ferings[k] with their grain offerings and
drink offerings as specified. They are offerings made to the LORD by fire—a
pleasing aroma.

Day of Atonement

7" 'On the tenth day of this seventh
month hold a sacred assembly. You 29:7
must deny yourselves[d][l] and do no l Ac 27:9
work.[m] 8Present as an aroma pleasing to m Ex 31:15;
the LORD a burnt offering of one young Lev 16:29;
bull, one ram and seven male lambs a 23:26-32
year old, all without defect. 9With the
bull prepare a grain offering[n] of three- 29:9
tenths of an ephah of fine flour mixed n ver 3,18
with oil; with the ram, two-tenths; 10and
with each of the seven lambs, one-
tenth.[o] 11Include one male goat as a sin 29:10
offering, in addition to the sin offering o Nu 28:13
for atonement and the regular burnt of- 29:11
fering[p] with its grain offering, and their p Lev 16:3;
drink offerings. Nu 28:3

Feast of Tabernacles

12" 'On the fifteenth day of the sev- 29:12
enth[q] month,[r] hold a sacred assembly q 1Ki 8:2
and do no regular work. Celebrate a fes- r Lev 23:24
tival to the LORD for seven days. 13Pre-
sent an offering made by fire as an aroma pleasing to the LORD, a burnt
offering of thirteen young bulls, two
rams and fourteen male lambs a year
old, all without defect. 14With each of
the thirteen bulls prepare a grain offer- 29:14
ings[s] of three-tenths of an ephah of fine s ver 3
flour mixed with oil; with each of the
two rams, two-tenths; 15and with each of
the fourteen lambs, one-tenth. 16Include
one male goat as a sin offering, in addition to the regular burnt offering with 29:16
its grain offering and drink offering.[t] t ver 6
17" 'On the second day[u] prepare 29:17
twelve young bulls, two rams and four- u Lev 23:36
teen male lambs a year old, all without v Nu 28:3
defect.[v] 18With the bulls, rams and
lambs, prepare their grain offerings[w] 29:18
and drink offerings[x] according to the w ver 9 x Nu 28:7 y Nu 15:4-12
number specified.[y] 19Include one male 29:19
goat as a sin offering,[z] in addition to the z Nu 28:15
regular burnt offering with its grain offering, and their drink offerings.
20" 'On the third day prepare eleven
bulls, two rams and fourteen male 29:20
lambs a year old, all without defect.[a] a ver 17
21With the bulls, rams and lambs, prepare their grain offerings and drink offerings according to the number speci-

[a] *3* That is, probably about 6 quarts (about 6.5 liters); also in verses 9 and 14 [b] *3* That is, probably about 4 quarts (about 4.5 liters); also in verses 9 and 14 [c] *4* That is, probably about 2 quarts (about 2 liters); also in verses 10 and 15 [d] *7* Or *must fast*

29:21 fied.[b] [22]Include one male goat as a sin of-
[b] ver 18 fering, in addition to the regular burnt
offering with its grain offering and drink
offering.
[23]" 'On the fourth day prepare ten
bulls, two rams and fourteen male
lambs a year old, all without defect.
[24]With the bulls, rams and lambs, prepare their grain offerings and drink offerings according to the number specified. [25]Include one male goat as a sin
offering, in addition to the regular burnt
offering with its grain offering and drink
offering.
[26]" 'On the fifth day prepare nine bulls,
two rams and fourteen male lambs a
year old, all without defect. [27]With the
bulls, rams and lambs, prepare their
grain offerings and drink offerings according to the number specified. [28]In-
clude one male goat as a sin offering, in
addition to the regular burnt offering
with its grain offering and drink offering.
[29]" 'On the sixth day prepare eight
bulls, two rams and fourteen male
lambs a year old, all without defect.
[30]With the bulls, rams and lambs, prepare their grain offerings and drink offerings according to the number specified. [31]Include one male goat as a sin
offering, in addition to the regular burnt
offering with its grain offering and drink
offering.
[32]" 'On the seventh day prepare seven
bulls, two rams and fourteen male
lambs a year old, all without defect.
[33]With the bulls, rams and lambs, prepare their grain offerings and drink offerings according to the number specified. [34]Include one male goat as a sin
offering, in addition to the regular burnt
offering with its grain offering and drink
offering.
[35]" 'On the eighth day hold an assem-
29:35 bly[c] and do no regular work. [36]Present an
[c] Lev 23:36 offering made by fire as an aroma pleas-
29:36 ing to the LORD,[d] a burnt offering of one
[d] Lev 1:9 [e] ver 2 bull, one ram and seven male lambs a
year old,[e] all without defect. [37]With the
bull, the ram and the lambs, prepare
their grain offerings and drink offerings
according to the number specified. [38]In-
clude one male goat as a sin offering, in
addition to the regular burnt offering
with its grain offering and drink offering.
29:39 [39]" 'In addition to what you vow[f] and
[f] Nu 6:2 your freewill offerings, prepare these for
the LORD at your appointed feasts:[g] your 29:39
burnt offerings,[h] grain offerings, drink [g] Lev 23:2
offerings and fellowship offerings.[a] ' " [h] Lev 1:3; 1Ch 23:31; 2Ch 31:3
[40]Moses told the Israelites all that the
LORD commanded him.

Vows

30 Moses said to the heads of the 30:1
tribes of Israel:[i] "This is what [i] Nu 1:4
the LORD commands: [2]When a man 30:2
makes a vow to the LORD or takes an [j] Dt 23:21-23;
oath to obligate himself by a pledge, he Jdg 11:35;
must not break his word but must do Job 22:27;
everything he said.[j] Ps 22:25; 50:14; 116:14;
[3]"When a young woman still living in Pr 20:25;
her father's house makes a vow to the Ecc 5:4,5;
LORD or obligates herself by a pledge Jnh 1:16
[4]and her father hears about her vow or
pledge but says nothing to her, then all
her vows and every pledge by which she
obligated herself will stand.[k] [5]But if her 30:4
father forbids her when he hears about [k] ver 7
it, none of her vows or the pledges by
which she obligated herself will stand;
the LORD will release her because her father has forbidden her.
[6]"If she marries after she makes a 30:6
vow[l] or after her lips utter a rash prom- [l] Lev 5:4
ise by which she obligates herself [7]and
her husband hears about it but says
nothing to her, then her vows or the
pledges by which she obligated herself
will stand. [8]But if her husband[m] forbids 30:8
her when he hears about it, he nullifies [m] Ge 3:16
the vow that obligates her or the rash
promise by which she obligates herself,
and the LORD will release her.
[9]"Any vow or obligation taken by a
widow or divorced woman will be binding on her.
[10]"If a woman living with her husband
makes a vow or obligates herself by a
pledge under oath [11]and her husband
hears about it but says nothing to her
and does not forbid her, then all her vows
or the pledges by which she obligated
herself will stand. [12]But if her husband
nullifies them when he hears about
them, then none of the vows or pledges 30:12
that came from her lips will stand.[n] Her [n] Eph 5:22;
husband has nullified them, and the Col 3:18
LORD will release her. [13]Her husband may
confirm or nullify any vow she makes or
any sworn pledge to deny herself. [14]But if
her husband says nothing to her about it
from day to day, then he confirms all her

[a] 39 Traditionally *peace offerings*

vows or the pledges binding on her. He
confirms them by saying nothing to her
when he hears about them. 15If, however,
he nullifies them some time after he
hears about them, then he is responsible
for her guilt."
16These are the regulations the LORD
gave Moses concerning relationships
between a man and his wife, and between a father and his young daughter
still living in his house.

Vengeance on the Midianites

31:2 **31** The LORD said to Moses, 2"Take
o Ge 25:2 vengeance on the Midianites[o]
p Nu 20:26; for the Israelites. After that, you will be
27:13 gathered to your people.[p]"
3So Moses said to the people, "Arm
some of your men to go to war against
31:3 the Midianites and to carry out the
q Jdg 11:36; LORD's vengeance[q] on them. 4Send into
1Sa 24:12; battle a thousand men from each of the
2Sa 4:8; 22:48; tribes of Israel." 5So twelve thousand
Ps 94:1; 149:7 men armed for battle, a thousand from
each tribe, were supplied from the clans
of Israel. 6Moses sent them into battle, a
thousand from each tribe, along with
Phinehas son of Eleazar, the priest, who
31:6 r Nu 14:44 took with him articles from the sanctu-
s Nu 10:9 ary[r] and the trumpets[s] for signaling.
7They fought against Midian, as the
31:7 t Dt 20:13; LORD commanded Moses, and killed
Jdg 21:11; every man.[t] 8Among their victims were
1Ki 11:15,16 Evi, Rekem, Zur, Hur and Reba[u]—the five
31:8 kings of Midian.[v] They also killed Balaam
u Jos 13:21 son of Beor with the sword.[w] 9The Israel-
v Nu 25:15 ites captured the Midianite women and
w Jos 13:22 children and took all the Midianite herds,
31:10 flocks and goods as plunder. 10They
x Ge 25:16; burned all the towns where the Midian-
1Ch 6:54; Ps 69:25; ites had settled, as well as all their
Eze 25:4 camps.[x] 11They took all the plunder and
31:11 spoils, including the people and animals,[y]
y Dt 20:14 12and brought the captives, spoils and
31:12 plunder to Moses and Eleazar the priest
z Nu 27:2 and the Israelite assembly[z] at their camp
on the plains of Moab, by the Jordan
across from Jericho.[a]
13Moses, Eleazar the priest and all the
leaders of the community went to meet
31:14 them outside the camp. 14Moses was an-
a ver 48; gry with the officers of the army[a]—the
Ex 18:21; commanders of thousands and com-
Dt 1:15 manders of hundreds—who returned
from the battle.
15"Have you allowed all the women to
live?" he asked them. 16"They were the
ones who followed Balaam's advice[b] and 31:16
were the means of turning the Israelites b 2Pe 2:15; Rev 2:14
away from the LORD in what happened at c Nu 25:1-9
Peor,[c] so that a plague struck the LORD's
people. 17Now kill all the boys. And kill
every woman who has slept with a man,[d] 31:17
18but save for yourselves every girl who d Dt 7:2; 20:16-18; Jdg 21:11
has never slept with a man.
19"All of you who have killed anyone or
touched anyone who was killed[e] must 31:19 e Nu 19:16
stay outside the camp seven days. On f Nu 19:12
the third and seventh days you must purify yourselves[f] and your captives. 20Pu-
rify every garment[g] as well as everything 31:20
made of leather, goat hair or wood." g Nu 19:19
21Then Eleazar the priest said to the
soldiers who had gone into battle, "This
is the requirement of the law that the
LORD gave Moses: 22Gold, silver, bronze, 31:22
iron,[h] tin, lead 23and anything else that h Jos 6:19; 22:8
can withstand fire must be put through
the fire,[i] and then it will be clean. But it 31:23
must also be purified with the water of i 1Co 3:13
cleansing.[j] And whatever cannot with- j Nu 19:9,17
stand fire must be put through that wa-
ter. 24On the seventh day wash your 31:24
clothes and you will be clean.[k] Then you k Lev 11:25
may come into the camp."

Dividing the Spoils

25The LORD said to Moses, 26"You and
Eleazar the priest and the family heads of
the community are to count all the peo- 31:26
ple[l] and animals that were captured. l Nu 1:19
27Divide[m] the spoils between the soldiers 31:27
who took part in the battle and the rest of m Jos 22:8; 1Sa 30:24
the community. 28From the soldiers who
fought in the battle, set apart as tribute 31:28
for the LORD[n] one out of every five hun- n Nu 18:21
dred, whether persons, cattle, donkeys,
sheep or goats. 29Take this tribute from
their half share and give it to Eleazar the
priest as the LORD's part. 30From the Israelites' half, select one out of every fifty,
whether persons, cattle, donkeys, sheep,
goats or other animals. Give them to the
Levites, who are responsible for the care
of the LORD's tabernacle.[o]" 31So Moses 31:30 o Nu 3:7; 18:3
and Eleazar the priest did as the LORD
commanded Moses.
32The plunder remaining from the
spoils that the soldiers took was 675,000
sheep, 33 72,000 cattle, 34 61,000 donkeys
35and 32,000 women who had never slept
with a man.

a 12 Hebrew *Jordan of Jericho*; possibly an ancient name for the Jordan River

36 The half share of those who fought
in the battle was:
337,500 sheep, 37 of which the trib-
31:37 p ver 38-41 ute for the LORD[p] was 675;
38 36,000 cattle, of which the tribute
for the LORD was 72;
39 30,500 donkeys, of which the tribute for the LORD was 61;
40 16,000 people, of which the tribute
for the LORD was 32.

41 Moses gave the tribute to Eleazar
31:41 q Nu 5:9; 18:8 the priest as the LORD's part,[q] as the
LORD commanded Moses.

42 The half belonging to the Israelites,
which Moses set apart from that of the
fighting men— 43 the community's
half—was 337,500 sheep, 44 36,000 cattle,
45 30,500 donkeys 46 and 16,000 people.
47 From the Israelites' half, Moses selected one out of every fifty persons and animals, as the LORD commanded him, and
gave them to the Levites, who were responsible for the care of the LORD's tabernacle.

48 Then the officers who were over the
units of the army—the commanders of
thousands and commanders of hundreds—went to Moses 49 and said to
him, "Your servants have counted the
31:49 soldiers under our command, and not
r Jer 23:4 one is missing.[r] 50 So we have brought as
an offering to the LORD the gold articles
each of us acquired—armlets, bracelets,
31:50 signet rings, earrings and necklaces—to
s Ex 30:16 make atonement for ourselves[s] before
the LORD."

51 Moses and Eleazar the priest accepted from them the gold—all the
crafted articles. 52 All the gold from the
commanders of thousands and commanders of hundreds that Moses and
Eleazar presented as a gift to the LORD
weighed 16,750 shekels.[a] 53 Each soldier
31:53 had taken plunder[t] for himself. 54 Moses
t Dt 20:14 and Eleazar the priest accepted the gold
from the commanders of thousands and
commanders of hundreds and brought
31:54 it into the Tent of Meeting as a memori-
u Ex 28:12 al[u] for the Israelites before the LORD.

The Transjordan Tribes

32 The Reubenites and Gadites,
who had very large herds and
32:1 v Nu 21:32 flocks, saw that the lands of Jazer[v] and
w Ex 12:38 Gilead were suitable for livestock.[w] 2 So
they came to Moses and Eleazar the
priest and to the leaders of the commu- 32:3
nity, and said, 3 "Ataroth,[x] Dibon, Jazer, x ver 34 y ver 36
Nimrah,[y] Heshbon, Elealeh,[z] Sebam, z ver 37; Isa 15:4; 16:9;
Nebo and Beon[a]— 4 the land the LORD Jer 48:34
subdued[b] before the people of Israel— a ver 38; Jos 13:17;
are suitable for livestock,[c] and your ser- Eze 25:9
vants have livestock. 5 If we have found
favor in your eyes," they said, "let this 32:4 b Nu 21:34
land be given to your servants as our c Ex 12:38
possession. Do not make us cross the
Jordan."

6 Moses said to the Gadites and Reubenites, "Shall your countrymen go to
war while you sit here? 7 Why do you discourage the Israelites from going over
into the land the LORD has given them?[d] 32:7 d Nu 13:27-14:4
8 This is what your fathers did when I
sent them from Kadesh Barnea to look 32:8 e Nu 13:3,26;
over the land.[e] 9 After they went up to Dt 1:19-25
the Valley of Eshcol[f] and viewed the
land, they discouraged the Israelites 32:9 f Nu 13:23;
from entering the land the LORD had giv- Dt 1:24
en them. 10 The LORD's anger was 32:10 g Nu 11:1
aroused[g] that day and he swore this
oath: 11 'Because they have not followed
me wholeheartedly, not one of the men
twenty years old or more[h] who came up 32:11 h Ex 30:14
out of Egypt will see the land I promised i Nu 14:23
on oath[i] to Abraham, Isaac and Jacob[j]— j Nu 14:28-30
12 not one except Caleb son of Jephun-
neh the Kenizzite and Joshua son of
Nun, for they followed the LORD whole- 32:12 k Nu 14:24,30;
heartedly.'[k] 13 The LORD's anger burned Dt 1:36; Ps 63:8
against Israel[l] and he made them wan-
der in the desert forty years, until the 32:13 l Ex 4:14
whole generation of those who had done m Nu 14:28-35; 26:64,65
evil in his sight was gone.[m]

14 "And here you are, a brood of sinners, standing in the place of your fathers and making the LORD even more 32:14 n ver 10;
angry with Israel.[n] 15 If you turn away Dt 1:34; Ps 78:59
from following him, he will again leave
all this people in the desert, and you will 32:15 o Dt 30:17-18;
be the cause of their destruction.[o]" 2Ch 7:20

16 Then they came up to him and said,
"We would like to build pens here for our 32:16 p Ex 12:38;
livestock[p] and cities for our women and Dt 3:19
children. 17 But we are ready to arm our-
selves and go ahead of the Israelites[q] un- 32:17 q Jos 4:12,13
til we have brought them to their place.[r] r Nu 22:4; Dt 3:20
Meanwhile our women and children will
live in fortified cities, for protection from
the inhabitants of the land. 18 We will not
return to our homes until every Israelite 32:18
has received his inheritance.[s] 19 We will s Jos 22:1-4

[a] 52 That is, about 420 pounds (about 190 kilograms)

not receive any inheritance with them
on the other side of the Jordan, because
32:19 our inheritance has come to us on the
tJos 12:1 east side of the Jordan."[t]
20Then Moses said to them, "If you
32:20 will do this—if you will arm yourselves
uDt 3:18 before the LORD for battle,[u] 21and if all of
you will go armed over the Jordan before
the LORD until he has driven his enemies
out before him— 22then when the land
32:22 is subdued before the LORD, you may re-
vJos 22:4 turn[v] and be free from your obligation to
wDt 3:18-20 the LORD and to Israel. And this land will
be your possession before the LORD.[w]
23"But if you fail to do this, you will be
32:23 xGe 4:7; 44:16; sinning against the LORD; and you may
Isa 59:12 be sure that your sin will find you out.[x]
32:24 24Build cities for your women and chil-
yver 1,16 dren, and pens for your flocks,[y] but do
zNu 30:2 what you have promised.[z]"
25The Gadites and Reubenites said to
Moses, "We your servants will do as our
lord commands. 26Our children and
wives, our flocks and herds will remain
32:26 aJos 1:14 here in the cities of Gilead.[a] 27But your
servants, every man armed for battle,
will cross over to fight before the LORD,
just as our lord says."
32:28 28Then Moses gave orders about
bDt 3:18-20; them[b] to Eleazar the priest and Joshua
Jos 1:13 son of Nun and to the family heads of
the Israelite tribes. 29He said to them, "If
the Gadites and Reubenites, every man
armed for battle, cross over the Jordan
with you before the LORD, then when the
land is subdued before you, give them
the land of Gilead as their possession.
30But if they do not cross over with you
armed, they must accept their possession with you in Canaan."
31The Gadites and Reubenites an-
32:31 swered, "Your servants will do what the
cver 29 LORD has said.[c] 32We will cross over before the LORD into Canaan armed, but
the property we inherit will be on this
side of the Jordan."
32:33 33Then Moses gave to the Gadites,[d]
dJos 13:24-28; the Reubenites and the half-tribe of Ma-
1Sa 13:7 eDt 2:26 nasseh son of Joseph the kingdom of Si-
fNu 21:24; hon king of the Amorites[e] and the king-
Jos 12:6 dom of Og king of Bashan—the whole
32:34 gDt 2:36; land with its cities and the territory
Jdg 11:26 around them.[f]
32:35 34The Gadites built up Dibon, Ata-
hver 3 roth, Aroer,[g] 35Atroth Shophan, Jazer,[h]
32:36 Jogbehah, 36Beth Nimrah[i] and Beth Ha-
iver 3 ran as fortified cities, and built pens for

their flocks. 37And the Reubenites rebuilt Heshbon, Elealeh and Kiriathaim,
38as well as Nebo[j] and Baal Meon (these 32:38
names were changed) and Sibmah. They jver 3; Isa 15:2;
gave names to the cities they rebuilt. Jer 48:1,22
39The descendants of Makir[k] son of 32:39
Manasseh went to Gilead, captured it kGe 50:23
and drove out the Amorites who were
there. 40So Moses gave Gilead to the 32:40 lDt 3:15;
Makirites,[l] the descendants of Manas- Jos 17:1
seh, and they settled there. 41Jair, a de- 32:41
scendant of Manasseh, captured their mDt 3:14;
settlements and called them Havvoth Jos 13:30;
Jair.[a][m] 42And Nobah captured Kenath Jdg 10:4; 1Ch 2:23
and its surrounding settlements and 32:42
called it Nobah after himself.[n] n2Sa 18:18; Ps 49:11

Stages in Israel's Journey

33 Here are the stages in the journey of the Israelites when they
came out of Egypt[o] by divisions under 33:1
the leadership of Moses and Aaron.[p] 2At oMic 6:4 pPs 77:20
the LORD's command Moses recorded
the stages in their journey. This is their
journey by stages:

3The Israelites set out from Rameses on the fifteenth day of the first
month, the day after the Passover.[q] 33:3
They marched out boldly[r] in full qEx 13:4 rEx 14:8
view of all the Egyptians, 4who were
burying all their firstborn, whom
the LORD had struck down among
them; for the LORD had brought 33:4
judgment on their gods.[s] sEx 12:12
5The Israelites left Rameses and 33:5
camped at Succoth.[t] tEx 12:37
6They left Succoth and camped 33:6
at Etham, on the edge of the desert.[u] uEx 13:20
7They left Etham, turned back to 33:7
Pi Hahiroth, to the east of Baal Ze- vEx 14:9
phon,[v] and camped near Migdol.[w] wEx 14:2
8They left Pi Hahiroth[b] and 33:8
passed through the sea[x] into the xEx 14:22
desert, and when they had traveled yEx 15:23
for three days in the Desert of
Etham, they camped at Marah.[y]
9They left Marah and went to
Elim, where there were twelve
springs and seventy palm trees, 33:9
and they camped[z] there. zEx 15:27
10They left Elim and camped by
the Red Sea.[c]

[a] *41* Or *them the settlements of Jair* [b] *8* Many manuscripts of the Masoretic Text, Samaritan Pentateuch and Vulgate; most manuscripts of the Masoretic Text *left from before Hahiroth*
[c] *10* Hebrew *Yam Suph*; that is, Sea of Reeds; also in verse 11

33:11 11 They left the Red Sea and
a Ex 16:1 camped in the Desert of Sin.[a]
12 They left the Desert of Sin and
camped at Dophkah.
13 They left Dophkah and
camped at Alush.
14 They left Alush and camped at
Rephidim, where there was no water for the people to drink.
33:15 15 They left Rephidim[b] and
b Ex 17:1 c Ex 19:1 camped in the Desert of Sinai.[c]
33:16 16 They left the Desert of Sinai
d Nu 11:34 and camped at Kibroth Hattaavah.[d]
33:17 17 They left Kibroth Hattaavah
e Nu 11:35 and camped at Hazeroth.[e]
18 They left Hazeroth and
camped at Rithmah.
19 They left Rithmah and camped
at Rimmon Perez.
33:20 20 They left Rimmon Perez and
f Jos 10:29 camped at Libnah.[f]
21 They left Libnah and camped
at Rissah.
22 They left Rissah and camped at
Kehelathah.
23 They left Kehelathah and
camped at Mount Shepher.
24 They left Mount Shepher and
camped at Haradah.
25 They left Haradah and camped
at Makheloth.
26 They left Makheloth and
camped at Tahath.
27 They left Tahath and camped
at Terah.
28 They left Terah and camped at
Mithcah.
29 They left Mithcah and camped
at Hashmonah.
33:30 30 They left Hashmonah and
g Dt 10:6 camped at Moseroth.[g]
31 They left Moseroth and
camped at Bene Jaakan.
32 They left Bene Jaakan and
camped at Hor Haggidgad.
33:33 33 They left Hor Haggidgad and
h Dt 10:7 camped at Jotbathah.[h]
34 They left Jotbathah and
camped at Abronah.
33:35 i Dt 2:8; 35 They left Abronah and camped
1Ki 9:26; 22:48 at Ezion Geber.[i]
36 They left Ezion Geber and
33:36 camped at Kadesh, in the Desert of
j Nu 20:1 Zin.[j]
37 They left Kadesh and camped
33:37 k Nu 20:22 at Mount Hor,[k] on the border of
l Nu 20:16; 21:4 Edom.[l] 38 At the LORD's command

Aaron the priest went up Mount 33:38
Hor, where he died[m] on the first day m Dt 10:6
of the fifth month of the fortieth n Nu 20:25-28
year after the Israelites came out of
Egypt.[n] 39 Aaron was a hundred and
twenty-three years old when he
died on Mount Hor.
40 The Canaanite king of Arad,[o] 33:40 o Nu 21:1
who lived in the Negev of Canaan,
heard that the Israelites were
coming.
41 They left Mount Hor and
camped at Zalmonah.
42 They left Zalmonah and
camped at Punon.
43 They left Punon and camped 33:43
at Oboth.[p] p Nu 21:10
44 They left Oboth and camped at
Iye Abarim, on the border of Moab.[q] 33:44 q Nu 21:11
45 They left Iyim[a] and camped at
Dibon Gad.
46 They left Dibon Gad and
camped at Almon Diblathaim.
47 They left Almon Diblathaim
and camped in the mountains of 33:47
Abarim,[r] near Nebo. r Nu 27:12
48 They left the mountains of Abarim and camped on the plains of
Moab by the Jordan across from 33:48
Jericho.[b][s] 49 There on the plains of s Nu 22:1
Moab they camped along the Jor-
dan from Beth Jeshimoth to Abel 33:49
Shittim.[t] t Nu 25:1

50 On the plains of Moab by the Jordan
across from Jericho the LORD said to Moses, 51 "Speak to the Israelites and say to
them: 'When you cross the Jordan into 33:51
Canaan,[u] 52 drive out all the inhabitants u Jos 3:17
of the land before you. Destroy all their
carved images and their cast idols, and 33:52 v Ex 23:24;
demolish all their high places.[v] 53 Take 34:13; Lev 26:1;
possession of the land and settle in it, for Dt 7:2,5; 12:3;
I have given you the land to possess.[w] Jos 11:12;
54 Distribute the land by lot, according to Ps 106:34-36
your clans.[x] To a larger group give a larg- 33:53 w Dt 11:31;
er inheritance, and to a smaller group a Jos 21:43
smaller one. Whatever falls to them by 33:54
lot will be theirs. Distribute it according x Nu 26:54
to your ancestral tribes.
55 " 'But if you do not drive out the inhabitants of the land, those you allow to
remain will become barbs in your eyes 33:55
and thorns[y] in your sides. They will give y Jos 23:13;
you trouble in the land where you will Jdg 2:3; Ps 106:36

[a] 45 That is, Iye Abarim [b] 48 Hebrew *Jordan of Jericho*; possibly an ancient name for the Jordan River; also in verse 50

live. 56 And then I will do to you what I plan to do to them.’ ”

Boundaries of Canaan

34 The LORD said to Moses, 2 “Command the Israelites and say to them: ‘When you enter Canaan, the land that will be allotted to you as an inheritance[z] will have these boundaries:[a]

3 “ ‘Your southern side will include some of the Desert of Zin[b] along the border of Edom. On the east, your southern boundary will start from the end of the Salt Sea,[a][c] 4 cross south of Scorpion[b] Pass,[d] continue on to Zin and go south of Kadesh Barnea.[e] Then it will go to Hazar Addar and over to Azmon, 5 where it will turn, join the Wadi of Egypt[f] and end at the Sea.[c]

6 “ ‘Your western boundary will be the coast of the Great Sea. This will be your boundary on the west.

7 “ ‘For your northern boundary,[g] run a line from the Great Sea to Mount Hor 8 and from Mount Hor to Lebo[d] Hamath.[h] Then the boundary will go to Zedad, 9 continue to Ziphron and end at Hazar Enan. This will be your boundary on the north.

10 “ ‘For your eastern boundary, run a line from Hazar Enan to Shepham. 11 The boundary will go down from Shepham to Riblah[i] on the east side of Ain and continue along the slopes east of the Sea of Kinnereth.[e][j] 12 Then the boundary will go down along the Jordan and end at the Salt Sea.

“ ‘This will be your land, with its boundaries on every side.’ ”

13 Moses commanded the Israelites: “Assign this land by lot as an inheritance.[k] The LORD has ordered that it be given to the nine and a half tribes, 14 because the families of the tribe of Reuben, the tribe of Gad and the half-tribe of Manasseh have received their inheritance.[l] 15 These two and a half tribes have received their inheritance on the east side of the Jordan of Jericho,[f] toward the sunrise.”

16 The LORD said to Moses, 17 “These are the names of the men who are to assign the land for you as an inheritance: Eleazar the priest and Joshua[m] son of Nun. 18 And appoint one leader from each tribe to help[n] assign the land. 19 These are their names:

34:2 [z] Ge 17:8; Dt 1:7-8; Ps 78:54-55 [a] Eze 47:15
34:3 [b] Jos 15:1-3 [c] Ge 14:3
34:4 [d] Jos 15:3 [e] Nu 32:8
34:5 [f] Ge 15:18; Jos 15:4
34:7 [g] Eze 47:15-17
34:8 [h] Nu 13:21; Jos 13:5
34:11 [i] 2Ki 23:33; Jer 39:5 [j] Dt 3:17; Jos 11:2; 13:27
34:13 [k] Jos 14:1-5
34:14 [l] Nu 32:33; Jos 14:3
34:17 [m] Jos 14:1
34:18 [n] Nu 1:4,16

Caleb[o] son of Jephunneh,
from the tribe of Judah;[p]
20 Shemuel son of Ammihud,
from the tribe of Simeon;[q]
21 Elidad son of Kislon,
from the tribe of Benjamin;[r]
22 Bukki son of Jogli,
the leader from the tribe of Dan;
23 Hanniel son of Ephod,
the leader from the tribe of Manasseh son of Joseph;
24 Kemuel son of Shiphtan,
the leader from the tribe of Ephraim son of Joseph;
25 Elizaphan son of Parnach,
the leader from the tribe of Zebulun;
26 Paltiel son of Azzan,
the leader from the tribe of Issachar;
27 Ahihud son of Shelomi,
the leader from the tribe of Asher;[s]
28 Pedahel son of Ammihud,
the leader from the tribe of Naphtali.”

29 These are the men the LORD commanded to assign the inheritance to the Israelites in the land of Canaan.

Towns for the Levites

35 On the plains of Moab by the Jordan across from Jericho,[g] the LORD said to Moses, 2 “Command the Israelites to give the Levites towns to live in[t] from the inheritance the Israelites will possess. And give them pasturelands around the towns. 3 Then they will have towns to live in and pasturelands for their cattle, flocks and all their other livestock.

4 “The pasturelands around the towns that you give the Levites will extend out fifteen hundred feet[h] from the town wall. 5 Outside the town, measure three thousand feet[i] on the east side, three thousand on the south side, three thousand on the west and three thousand on the north, with the town in the center.

34:19 [o] Nu 26:65 [p] Ge 29:35; Dt 33:7
34:20 [q] Ge 49:5
34:21 [r] Ge 49:27; Ps 68:27
34:27 [s] Nu 1:40
35:2 [t] Lev 25:32-34; Jos 14:3,4

[a] *3* That is, the Dead Sea; also in verse 12
[b] *4* Hebrew *Akrabbim*
[c] *5* That is, the Mediterranean; also in verses 6 and 7
[d] *8* Or *to the entrance to*
[e] *11* That is, Galilee
[f] *15* *Jordan of Jericho* was possibly an ancient name for the Jordan River.
[g] *1* Hebrew *Jordan of Jericho*; possibly an ancient name for the Jordan River
[h] *4* Hebrew *a thousand cubits* (about 450 meters)
[i] *5* Hebrew *two thousand cubits* (about 900 meters)

DISCOVERY 41

CITIES OF REFUGE

When God divided the promised land among the 12 tribes, 48 cities were given to the Levites. Six of these were called "cities of refuge." Three (Kadesh, Shechem and Hebron) were on the western side of the Jordan River, with three (Golan, Ramoth and Bezer) on the eastern side. A city of refuge was designated as a place to which a person could flee for safety if he or she had accidentally killed someone, thereby escaping from the victim's relatives. Life is sacred to God, and the law he gave to Moses reflected that (Exodus 20:13). The penalty specified for murder was death (Exodus 21:12), and this punishment was often carried out by the victim's family. However, if the murder was unintentional, the person could flee to a city of refuge and receive a public trial (Numbers 35:12), which was held to ensure that anyone who had killed intentionally would not escape the death penalty. As long as the person stayed in the city, he was protected. When the high priest died, he was free to go home (verses 25,28).

God's laws are very specific when it comes to protecting human life. Capital punishment for murder required more than one witness (verse 30). No one could offer a sum of money to free a murderer, and the death sentence for an intentional murder had to be carried out (verse 31).

The cities of refuge served as ancient illustrations of the Good News about Jesus. We are all guilty of turning away from God. Because of that, each of us is under a death sentence. God informed humanity from the very beginning that turning away from him would result in death (Genesis 2:16–17), and we see the consequences of that sentence throughout history (Romans 6:23).

But Jesus is our refuge, our only safety net against death and God's judgment. Jesus himself assumed the death penalty for us (1 Peter 3:18), and when we choose to put our hope in him we become a part of God's family (John 1:12). In Jesus Christ, our supreme city of refuge, we are safe forever from God's righteous judgment: "There is now no condemnation for those who are in Christ Jesus, because through Christ Jesus the law of the Spirit of life set me free from the law of sin and death" (Romans 8:1–2).

In ancient times the six cities of refuge provided protection, but a person had to make it to the city first in order to be safe. It was not enough to know *about* the city or to *want* to go there. It was not enough to pitch a tent just outside the gates. A person had to be within the city walls in order to be protected. In the same way, it is not enough to know *about* Jesus or *want* to meet him. It is not enough to be somewhere *near* to a saving belief. We must choose to be "in Jesus"—accepting his payment for our sin—in order to be rescued from the death penalty: "If anyone is in Christ, he is a new creation; the old has gone, the new has come!" (2 Corinthians 5:17).

Self-Discovery: How is Jesus a "city of refuge" for you? Where can you go to spend time alone with the Lord in total safety and security?

GO TO DISCOVERY 42 ON PAGE 225

They will have this area as pastureland
for the towns.

Cities of Refuge

6“Six of the towns you give the Levites
35:6 will be cities of refuge, to which a person
[u]Jos 20:7-9; who has killed someone may flee.[u] In
21:3,13 addition, give them forty-two other
towns. 7In all you must give the Levites
forty-eight towns, together with their
pasturelands. 8The towns you give the
Levites from the land the Israelites possess are to be given in proportion to the
35:8 inheritance of each tribe: Take many
[v]Nu 26:54; towns from a tribe that has many, but
33:54; Jos 21:1- few from one that has few.”[v]
42 9Then the LORD said to Moses:
10“Speak to the Israelites and say to
35:10 them: ‘When you cross the Jordan into
[w]Jos 20:2 Canaan,[w] 11select some towns to be your
cities of refuge, to which a person who
35:11 has killed someone[x] accidentally[y] may
[x]ver 22-25 [y]Ex 21:13; flee. 12They will be places of refuge from
Dt 19:1-13 the avenger,[z] so that a person accused of
35:12 murder may not die before he stands tri-
[z]Dt 19:6; al before the assembly. 13These six towns
Jos 20:3 you give will be your cities of refuge.
14Give three on this side of the Jordan
and three in Canaan as cities of refuge.
15These six towns will be a place of
refuge for Israelites, aliens and any other people living among them, so that
anyone who has killed another accidentally can flee there.
16“ ‘If a man strikes someone with an
iron object so that he dies, he is a mur-
35:16 derer; the murderer shall be put to
[a]Ex 21:12; Lev 24:17 death.[a] 17Or if anyone has a stone in his
hand that could kill, and he strikes
someone so that he dies, he is a murderer; the murderer shall be put to death.
18Or if anyone has a wooden object in
his hand that could kill, and he hits
someone so that he dies, he is a murderer; the murderer shall be put to death.
19The avenger of blood shall put the
35:19 murderer to death; when he meets him,
[b]ver 21 he shall put him to death.[b] 20If anyone
35:20 with malice aforethought shoves anoth-
[c]Ge 4:8; Ex 21:14; er or throws something at him inten-
Dt 19:11; 2Sa 3:27; 20:10 tionally[c] so that he dies 21or if in hostility he hits him with his fist so that he
dies, that person shall be put to death;
he is a murderer. The avenger of blood
shall put the murderer to death when he
meets him.
22“ ‘But if without hostility someone
suddenly shoves another or throws
something at him unintentionally[d] 23or, 35:22 [d]ver 11;
without seeing him, drops a stone on Ex 21:13
him that could kill him, and he dies,
then since he was not his enemy and he
did not intend to harm him, 24the as- 35:24
sembly[e] must judge between him and [e]ver 12; Jos 20:6
the avenger of blood according to these
regulations. 25The assembly must protect the one accused of murder from the
avenger of blood and send him back to
the city of refuge to which he fled. He
must stay there until the death of the
high priest, who was anointed with the 35:25
holy oil.[f] [f]Ex 29:7
26“ ‘But if the accused ever goes outside the limits of the city of refuge to
which he has fled 27and the avenger of
blood finds him outside the city, the
avenger of blood may kill the accused
without being guilty of murder. 28The accused must stay in his city of refuge until the death of the high priest; only after
the death of the high priest may he return to his own property.
29“ ‘These are to be legal requirements[g] for you throughout the genera- 35:29
tions to come, wherever you live. [g]Nu 27:11
30“ ‘Anyone who kills a person is to be 35:30
put to death as a murderer only on the [h]ver 16;
testimony of witnesses. But no one is to Dt 17:6; 19:15;
be put to death on the testimony of only Mt 18:16; Jn 7:51;
one witness.[h] 2Co 13:1; Heb 10:28
31“ ‘Do not accept a ransom for the life
of a murderer, who deserves to die. He
must surely be put to death.
32“ ‘Do not accept a ransom for anyone
who has fled to a city of refuge and so allow him to go back and live on his own
land before the death of the high priest.
33“ ‘Do not pollute the land where you
are. Bloodshed pollutes the land,[i] and 35:33
atonement cannot be made for the land [i]Ge 9:6; Ps 106:38;
on which blood has been shed, except by Mic 4:11
the blood of the one who shed it. 34Do
not defile the land[j] where you live and 35:34
where I dwell,[k] for I, the LORD, dwell [j]Lev 18:24,25 [k]Ex 29:45
among the Israelites.’ ”

Inheritance of Zelophehad’s Daughters

36 The family heads of the clan of 36:1
Gilead[l] son of Makir, the son of [l]Nu 26:29 [m]Nu 27:2
Manasseh, who were from the clans of
the descendants of Joseph, came and
spoke before Moses and the leaders,[m]
the heads of the Israelite families. 2They

said, "When the LORD commanded my
lord to give the land as an inheritance to
the Israelites by lot, he ordered you to
36:2 give the inheritance of our brother
[n] Nu 26:33; Zelophehad[n] to his daughters. 3Now
27:1,7 suppose they marry men from other Israelite tribes; then their inheritance will
be taken from our ancestral inheritance
and added to that of the tribe they marry into. And so part of the inheritance
36:4 allotted to us will be taken away. 4When
[o] Lev 25:10 the Year of Jubilee[o] for the Israelites
comes, their inheritance will be added
to that of the tribe into which they marry, and their property will be taken from
the tribal inheritance of our forefathers."
5Then at the LORD's command Moses
gave this order to the Israelites: "What
the tribe of the descendants of Joseph is
saying is right. 6This is what the LORD
commands for Zelophehad's daughters:
They may marry anyone they please as
36:7 long as they marry within the tribal clan
[p] 1Ki 21:3 of their father. 7No inheritance[p] in Israel is to pass from tribe to tribe, for every
Israelite shall keep the tribal land inherited from his forefathers. 8Every daughter who inherits land in any Israelite
tribe must marry someone in her fa-
ther's tribal clan,[q] so that every Israelite 36:8
will possess the inheritance of his fa- [q] 1Ch 23:22
thers. 9No inheritance may pass from
tribe to tribe, for each Israelite tribe is to
keep the land it inherits."
10So Zelophehad's daughters did as
the LORD commanded Moses. 11Zelo-
phehad's daughters—Mahlah, Tirzah,
Hoglah, Milcah and Noah[r]—married 36:11
their cousins on their father's side. [r] Nu 26:33; 27:1
12They married within the clans of the
descendants of Manasseh son of Joseph,
and their inheritance remained in their
father's clan and tribe.
13These are the commands and regu- 36:13
lations the LORD gave through Moses[s] to [s] Lev 26:46;
the Israelites on the plains of Moab by 27:34 [t] Nu 22:1
the Jordan across from Jericho.[a][t]

[a] 13 Hebrew *Jordan of Jericho*; possibly an ancient name for the Jordan River

DEUTERONOMY

Did God love Israel more than other nations? (Deuteronomy 4:33)

♦*God gave Israel his special attention at this point in history so that he could use the Israelites as a means to bring his blessings to the whole world (Genesis 12:2–3) and as a witness to testify to other nations about him. The ultimate expression of God's love—for Israel and the world—was that he sent his Son to die (John 3:16).*

What is the significance of the clause, anyone who is hung on a tree is under God's curse? (Deuteronomy 21:23)

♦*Any person executed for breaking one of God's commands was cursed by God. The corpse hanging on a tree was a public exhibition of judgment. Jesus willingly took this curse upon himself by hanging on the cross (Galatians 3:13).*

Jesus in Deuteronomy God promised that a prophet would appear "from among [the Israelites'] own brothers" and that his purpose would be to finish what God had begun through Moses (Deuteronomy 18:15). Moses predicted a future prophet with divine authority, and God promised to put his own words into the mouth of that prophet (Deuteronomy 18:18). God's people anticipated the Promised One for centuries and were still looking for him at the time Jesus entered human history as a baby. John the Baptist denied that he himself was that prophet (John 1:21,25) but pointed to the "one who comes after me," referring to Jesus as the "Lamb of God, who takes away the sin of the world" (John 1:29). Nathanael and Philip each recognized that Jesus was the long-awaited prophet (John 1:45,49), and both Peter and Stephen quoted Deuteronomy 18:15 in reference to Jesus (Acts 3:22–26; 7:37).

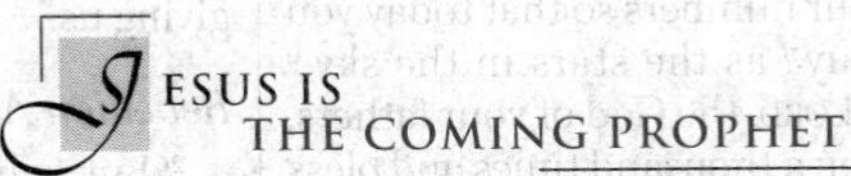

JESUS IS THE COMING PROPHET

The Command to Leave Horeb

1 These are the words Moses spoke
to all Israel in the desert east of
the Jordan—that is, in the Arabah—opposite Suph, between Paran and Tophel,
Laban, Hazeroth and Dizahab. 2(It takes 1:2 [a]Ex 3:1 [b]Nu 13:26; Dt 9:23
eleven days to go from Horeb[a] to Kadesh
Barnea[b] by the Mount Seir road.)
3In the fortieth year,[c] on the first day 1:3 [c]Nu 33:38 [d]Dt 4:1-2
of the eleventh month, Moses pro-
claimed[d] to the Israelites all that the
LORD had commanded him concerning
them. 4This was after he had defeated 1:4 [e]Nu 21:21-26 [f]Nu 21:25 [g]Nu 21:33-35; Jos 13:12
Sihon[e] king of the Amorites, who
reigned in Heshbon,[f] and at Edrei had
defeated Og[g] king of Bashan, who
reigned in Ashtaroth.
5East of the Jordan in the territory of
Moab, Moses began to expound this law,
saying:

6The LORD our God said to us[h] at Ho- 1:6 [h]Nu 10:13 [i]Ex 3:1
reb,[i] "You have stayed long enough at
this mountain. 7Break camp and advance into the hill country of the Amorites; go to all the neighboring peoples in
the Arabah, in the mountains, in the
western foothills, in the Negev[j] and 1:7 [j]Jos 10:40 [k]Dt 11:24
along the coast, to the land of the
Canaanites and to Lebanon,[k] as far as
the great river, the Euphrates. 8See, I
have given you this land. Go in and take
possession of the land that the LORD
swore[l] he would give to your fathers—to 1:8 [l]Ge 12:7; 15:18; 17:7-8; 26:4; 28:13
Abraham, Isaac and Jacob—and to their
descendants after them."

The Appointment of Leaders

9At that time I said to you, "You are
too heavy a burden for me to carry 1:9 [m]Ex 18:18
alone.[m] 10The LORD your God has in-
creased your numbers so that today you 1:10 [n]Ge 15:5 [o]Dt 10:22; 28:62
are as many[n] as the stars in the sky.[o]
11May the LORD, the God of your fathers,
increase you a thousand times and bless
you as he has promised![p] 12But how can 1:11 [p]Ge 22:17; Ex 32:13
I bear your problems and your burdens
and your disputes all by myself?
13Choose some wise, understanding and
respected men[q] from each of your 1:13 [q]Ex 18:21
tribes, and I will set them over you."
14You answered me, "What you propose to do is good."
15So I took[r] the leading men of your 1:15 [r]Ex 18:25
tribes, wise and respected men, and appointed them to have authority over
you—as commanders of thousands, of
hundreds, of fifties and of tens and as
tribal officials. 16And I charged your
judges at that time: Hear the disputes
between your brothers and judge fairly,[s] 1:16 [s]Dt 16:18; Jn 7:24 [t]Lev 24:22
whether the case is between brother Is-
raelites or between one of them and an
alien.[t] 17Do not show partiality[u] in judg- 1:17 [u]Lev 19:15; Dt 16:19; Pr 24:23; Jas 2:1 [v]2Ch 19:6 [w]Ex 18:26
ing; hear both small and great alike. Do
not be afraid of any man,[v] for judgment
belongs to God. Bring me any case too
hard for you, and I will hear it.[w] 18And at
that time I told you everything you were
to do.

Spies Sent Out

19Then, as the LORD our God commanded us, we set out from Horeb and
went toward the hill country of the Amorites through all that vast and dreadful
desert[x] that you have seen, and so we 1:19 [x]Dt 8:15; Jer 2:2,6 [y]ver 2; Nu 13:26
reached Kadesh Barnea.[y] 20Then I said
to you, "You have reached the hill country of the Amorites, which the LORD our
God is giving us. 21See, the LORD your
God has given you the land. Go up and
take possession of it as the LORD, the
God of your fathers, told you. Do not be 1:21 [z]Jos 1:6,9,18
afraid;[z] do not be discouraged."
22Then all of you came to me and said,
"Let us send men ahead to spy out the
land for us and bring back a report
about the route we are to take and the
towns we will come to."
23The idea seemed good to me; so I se-
lected[a] twelve of you, one man from 1:23 [a]Nu 13:1-3
each tribe. 24They left and went up into
the hill country, and came to the Valley
of Eshcol[b] and explored it. 25Taking with 1:24 [b]Nu 13:21-25
them some of the fruit of the land, they
brought it down to us and reported,[c] "It 1:25 [c]Nu 13:27
is a good land that the LORD our God is
giving us."

Rebellion Against the LORD

26But you were unwilling to go up;[d] 1:26 [d]Nu 14:1-4
you rebelled against the command of the
LORD your God. 27You grumbled[e] in your 1:27 [e]Dt 9:28; Ps 106:25
tents and said, "The LORD hates us; so he
brought us out of Egypt to deliver us into
the hands of the Amorites to destroy us.
28Where can we go? Our brothers have
made us lose heart. They say, 'The people
are stronger and taller[f] than we are; the 1:28 [f]Nu 13:32 [g]Nu 13:33; Dt 9:1-3
cities are large, with walls up to the sky.
We even saw the Anakites[g] there.' "
29Then I said to you, "Do not be terrified; do not be afraid of them. 30The

1:30 [h] Ex 14:14; Dt 3:22; Ne 4:20 LORD your God, who is going before you,
will fight[h] for you, as he did for you in
Egypt, before your very eyes, 31and in the
1:31 [i] Dt 32:10-12; Isa 46:3-4; 63:9; Hos 11:3; Ac 13:18 desert. There you saw how the LORD
your God carried[i] you, as a father carries
his son, all the way you went until you
reached this place."
1:32 [j] Ps 106:24; Jude 1:5 32In spite of this, you did not trust[j] in
the LORD your God, 33who went ahead of
you on your journey, in fire by night and
1:33 [k] Ex 13:21; Ps 78:14 [l] Nu 10:33 in a cloud by day,[k] to search[l] out places
for you to camp and to show you the
way you should go.
1:34 [m] Nu 14:23,28-30 34When the LORD heard what you
said, he was angry and solemnly swore:[m]
35"Not a man of this evil generation shall
1:35 [n] Ps 95:11 see the good land[n] I swore to give your
forefathers, 36except Caleb son of Je-
phunneh. He will see it, and I will give
him and his descendants the land he set
1:36 [o] Nu 14:24; Jos 14:9 his feet on, because he followed the
LORD wholeheartedly.[o]"
37Because of you the LORD became an-
1:37 [p] Dt 3:26; 4:21 [q] Nu 20:12 gry[p] with me also and said, "You shall
not enter[q] it, either. 38But your assistant,
1:38 [r] Nu 14:30 [s] Dt 31:7 [t] Dt 3:28 Joshua[r] son of Nun, will enter it. Encourage[s] him, because he will lead[t] Isra-
el to inherit it. 39And the little ones that
1:39 [u] Nu 14:3 [v] Isa 7:15-16 you said would be taken captive,[u] your
children who do not yet know[v] good
from bad—they will enter the land. I will
give it to them and they will take possession of it. 40But as for you, turn
1:40 [w] Nu 14:25 around and set out toward the desert
along the route to the Red Sea.[a w]"
41Then you replied, "We have sinned
against the LORD. We will go up and
fight, as the LORD our God commanded
us." So every one of you put on his
weapons, thinking it easy to go up into
the hill country.
42But the LORD said to me, "Tell them,
'Do not go up and fight, because I will
not be with you. You will be defeated by
1:42 [x] Nu 14:41-43 your enemies.' "[x]
43So I told you, but you would not listen. You rebelled against the LORD's
command and in your arrogance you
marched up into the hill country. 44The
Amorites who lived in those hills came
1:44 [y] Ps 118:12 out against you; they chased you like a
swarm of bees[y] and beat you down from
Seir all the way to Hormah. 45You came
back and wept before the LORD, but he
paid no attention to your weeping and
turned a deaf ear to you. 46And so you
stayed in Kadesh[z] many days—all the 1:46 [z] Nu 20:1; Jdg 11:17
time you spent there.

Wanderings in the Desert

2 Then we turned back and set out
toward the desert along the route
to the Red Sea,[a a] as the LORD had direct- 2:1 [a] Nu 21:4
ed me. For a long time we made our way
around the hill country of Seir.
2Then the LORD said to me, 3"You have
made your way around this hill country
long enough; now turn north. 4Give the
people these orders:[b] 'You are about to 2:4 [b] Nu 20:14-21
pass through the territory of your broth-
ers the descendants of Esau, who live in
Seir. They will be afraid of you, but be
very careful. 5Do not provoke them to
war, for I will not give you any of their
land, not even enough to put your foot
on. I have given Esau the hill country of
Seir as his own.[c] 6You are to pay them in 2:5 [c] Ge 36:8; Jos 24:4
silver for the food you eat and the water
you drink.' "
7The LORD your God has blessed you
in all the work of your hands. He has
watched[d] over your journey through 2:7 [d] Dt 8:2-4
this vast desert. These forty years the
LORD your God has been with you, and
you have not lacked anything.
8So we went on past our brothers the
descendants of Esau, who live in Seir. We
turned from the Arabah road, which 2:8 [e] 1Ki 9:26 [f] Jdg 11:18
comes up from Elath and Ezion Geber,[e]
and traveled along the desert road of
Moab.[f]
9Then the LORD said to me, "Do not
harass the Moabites or provoke them to
war, for I will not give you any part of
their land. I have given Ar[g] to the de- 2:9 [g] Nu 21:15 [h] Ge 19:36-38
scendants of Lot[h] as a possession."
10(The Emites[i] used to live there—a 2:10 [i] Ge 14:5 [j] Nu 13:22,33
people strong and numerous, and as tall
as the Anakites.[j] 11Like the Anakites,
they too were considered Rephaites, but
the Moabites called them Emites. 12Ho-
rites used to live in Seir, but the descendants of Esau drove them out. They destroyed the Horites from before them
and settled in their place, just as Israel
did[k] in the land the LORD gave them as 2:12 [k] ver 22
their possession.)
13And the LORD said, "Now get up and
cross the Zered Valley." So we crossed
the valley.
14Thirty-eight years passed from the
time we left Kadesh Barnea[l] until we 2:14 [l] Nu 13:26

[a] 40,1 Hebrew *Yam Suph*; that is, Sea of Reeds

crossed the Zered Valley. By then, that
2:14 m Nu 14:29-35 entire generation[m] of fighting men had
n Dt 1:34-35 perished from the camp, as the LORD had
sworn to them.[n] 15 The LORD's hand was
2:15 o Ps 106:26 against them until he had completely
eliminated[o] them from the camp.
16 Now when the last of these fighting
men among the people had died, 17 the
LORD said to me, 18 "Today you are to
pass by the region of Moab at Ar.
2:19 p Ge 19:38 19 When you come to the Ammonites,[p]
q ver 9 do not harass them or provoke them to
war, for I will not give you possession of
any land belonging to the Ammonites. I
have given it as a possession to the descendants of Lot.[q]"
20 (That too was considered a land of
the Rephaites, who used to live there;
but the Ammonites called them Zam-
zummites. 21 They were a people strong
and numerous, and as tall as the Ana-
2:21 r ver 10 kites.[r] The LORD destroyed them from
before the Ammonites, who drove them
out and settled in their place. 22 The
LORD had done the same for the descen-
2:22 s Ge 36:8 dants of Esau, who lived in Seir,[s] when
he destroyed the Horites from before
them. They drove them out and have
2:23 lived in their place to this day. 23 And as
t Jos 13:3 for the Avvites[t] who lived in villages as
u Ge 10:14 far as Gaza, the Caphtorites[u] coming
v Am 9:7 out from Caphtor[a v] destroyed them and
settled in their place.)

Defeat of Sihon King of Heshbon

24 "Set out now and cross the Arnon
2:24 w Nu 21:13-14; Gorge.[w] See, I have given into your hand
Jdg 11:13,18 Sihon the Amorite, king of Heshbon,
and his country. Begin to take possession of it and engage him in battle.
2:25 25 This very day I will begin to put the
x Dt 11:25 terror[x] and fear[y] of you on all the na-
y Jos 2:9,11 tions under heaven. They will hear re-
z Ex 15:14-16 ports of you and will tremble[z] and be in
anguish because of you."
26 From the desert of Kedemoth I sent
messengers to Sihon king of Heshbon
offering peace and saying, 27 "Let us pass
through your country. We will stay on
2:27 the main road; we will not turn aside to
a Nu 21:21-22 the right or to the left.[a] 28 Sell us food to
eat and water to drink for their price in
silver. Only let us pass through on
2:28 b Nu 20:19 foot[b]— 29 as the descendants of Esau,
who live in Seir, and the Moabites, who
live in Ar, did for us—until we cross the
Jordan into the land the LORD our God is
giving us." 30 But Sihon king of Heshbon
refused to let us pass through. For the 2:30
LORD[c] your God had made his spirit c Jos 11:20
stubborn[d] and his heart obstinate in or- d Ex 4:21; Nu 21:23;
der to give him into your hands, as he Ro 9:18
has now done.
31 The LORD said to me, "See, I have begun to deliver Sihon and his country
over to you. Now begin to conquer and 2:31
possess his land."[e] e Dt 1:8
32 When Sihon and all his army came
out to meet us in battle[f] at Jahaz, 33 the 2:32 f Nu 21:23
LORD our God delivered him over to us 2:33
and we struck him down,[g] together with g Dt 29:7
his sons and his whole army. 34 At that
time we took all his towns and com- 2:34
pletely destroyed[b h] them—men, women h Dt 3:6; 7:2
and children. We left no survivors. 35 But
the livestock and the plunder from the
towns we had captured we carried off 2:36
for ourselves. 36 From Aroer[i] on the rim i Dt 3:12; 4:48;
of the Arnon Gorge, and from the town Jos 13:9 j Ps 44:3
in the gorge, even as far as Gilead, not
one town was too strong for us. The
LORD our God gave[j] us all of them. 37 But
in accordance with the command of the 2:37
LORD our God,[k] you did not encroach on k ver 18-19
any of the land of the Ammonites,[l] nei- l Nu 21:24
ther the land along the course of the m Ge 32:22; Dt 3:16
Jabbok[m] nor that around the towns in
the hills.

Defeat of Og King of Bashan

3 Next we turned and went up
along the road toward Bashan,
and Og king of Bashan with his whole
army marched out to meet us in battle 3:1
at Edrei.[n] 2 The LORD said to me, "Do not n Nu 21:33
be afraid[o] of him, for I have handed him 3:2
over to you with his whole army and his o Nu 21:34
land. Do to him what you did to Sihon
king of the Amorites, who reigned in
Heshbon."
3 So the LORD our God also gave into
our hands Og king of Bashan and all his
army. We struck them down, leaving no
survivors.[p] 4 At that time we took all his 3:3
cities. There was not one of the sixty cit- p Nu 21:35
ies that we did not take from them—the
whole region of Argob, Og's kingdom in
Bashan.[q] 5 All these cities were fortified 3:4
with high walls and with gates and q 1Ki 4:13
bars, and there were also a great many
unwalled villages. 6 We completely

a 23 That is, Crete *b* 34 The Hebrew term refers to the irrevocable giving over of things or persons to the LORD, often by totally destroying them.

When God Says No

When God's people arrived at the border of the promised land, Moses pleaded with God for permission to "go over and see the good land" (Deuteronomy 3:25). In many instances Moses was granted what he asked of God. But this time God not only refused but even appeared annoyed with Moses for pressing the issue: "That is enough . . . Do not speak to me anymore about this matter" (verse 26).

God had already informed Moses that he could not enter the land with the people, but he did make the concession of allowing Moses to view the land from a distance (verse 27). While voicing our requests and concerns to God is critically important, God will sometimes say no, just as he did to Moses.

Twice in the New Testament we read of prayers to which God responded with a resounding *no.* In one case the apostle Paul was struggling with a chronic physical ailment he described as a "thorn in the flesh" (2 Corinthians 12:1–10). Paul pleaded with God to remove the "thorn" and heal him (2 Corinthians 12:8), but God refused. Instead, God promised that he would be with Paul and grant him the strength to endure.

Another prayer that God declined to answer in the affirmative was voiced by his own Son Jesus, when he asked (undoubtedly already knowing the answer) whether there was any way to avoid the suffering that loomed ahead (Mark 14:32–36). But no other sacrifice could have bridged the chasm of sin that separated humankind from God. The Father was unwilling to exempt his Son from the ordeal to come, and Jesus graciously accepted the inevitable.

God often has overarching plans that transcend our desire for temporary relief from our own personal pain. In fact, our discomfort may actually serve to strengthen our resolve and further his goals. Through his own disability Paul learned firsthand about God's power, presence and grace. And Jesus, by yielding to his Father's larger purpose, paid the death penalty for our sin. Even in Moses' case God had a master plan. Although Moses had failed to follow God's instructions and was compelled to pay the consequences, God used a new leader, Joshua, after Moses' death to lead the people into the land.

It's all too easy to fixate on our own personal comfort and lose sight of what God might be planning. He always has our best in mind, however, and never rejects our requests out of a spirit of indifference or cruelty. When he says *no* or *enough*, we should prepare ourselves—chances are, something better is on the way!

The apostle Paul spoke words of comfort to the believers in Rome, words that still reverberate in our souls: "We know that in all things God works for the good of those who love him, who have been called according to his purpose . . . What, then, shall we say in response to this? If God is for us, who can be against us? He who did not spare his own Son, but gave him up for us all—how will he not also, along with him, graciously give us all things?" (Romans 8:28,31–32).

Self-Discovery: *Think about a time in your life when God replied to your request with an emphatic no. How did you feel at the time? Looking back, are you able to see evidence of God's gentle hand nudging you in a different direction?*

GO TO DISCOVERY 43 ON PAGE 231

3:6 destroyed[a] them, as we had done with Si-
[r]Dt 2:24,34 hon king of Heshbon, destroying[a r] every
city—men, women and children. 7But all
the livestock and the plunder from their
cities we carried off for ourselves.

8So at that time we took from these
two kings of the Amorites the territory
east of the Jordan, from the Arnon
Gorge as far as Mount Hermon. 9(Her-
3:9 [s]Dt 4:48; mon is called Sirion[s] by the Sidonians;
Ps 29:6 the Amorites call it Senir.)[t] 10We took all
[t]1Ch 5:23 the towns on the plateau, and all Gilead,
3:10 and all Bashan as far as Salecah[u] and
[u]Jos 13:11 Edrei, towns of Og's kingdom in Bashan.
11(Only Og king of Bashan was left of the
3:11 remnant of the Rephaites.[v] His bed[b] was
[v]Ge 14:5 [w]2Sa 12:26; made of iron and was more than thir-
Jer 49:2 teen feet long and six feet wide.[c] It is still
in Rabbah[w] of the Ammonites.)

Division of the Land

12Of the land that we took over at that
time, I gave the Reubenites and the Gad-
3:12 ites the territory north of Aroer[x] by the
[x]Nu 32:32-38; Arnon Gorge, including half the hill
Dt 2:36; country of Gilead, together with its
Jos 13:8-13 towns. 13The rest of Gilead and also all of
Bashan, the kingdom of Og, I gave to the
half tribe of Manasseh. (The whole region of Argob in Bashan used to be
3:14 known as a land of the Rephaites. 14Jair,[y]
[y]Nu 32:41; a descendant of Manasseh, took the
1Ch 2:22 whole region of Argob as far as the border of the Geshurites and the Maac-
athites; it was named after him, so that
to this day Bashan is called Havvoth
Jair.[d]) 15And I gave Gilead to Makir.[z] 3:15 [z]Nu 32:39-40
16But to the Reubenites and the Gadites
I gave the territory extending from Gilead down to the Arnon Gorge (the middle
of the gorge being the border) and out to 3:16
the Jabbok River,[a] which is the border of [a]Nu 21:24
the Ammonites. 17Its western border was 3:17
the Jordan in the Arabah, from Kinne- [b]Nu 34:11;
reth[b] to the Sea of the Arabah (the Salt Jos 13:27 [c]Ge 14:3;
Sea[e c]), below the slopes of Pisgah. Jos 12:3
18I commanded you at that time: "The
LORD your God has given you this land
to take possession of it. But all your
able-bodied men, armed for battle, must
cross over ahead of your brother Israel- 3:18
ites.[d] 19However, your wives, your chil- [d]Nu 32:17
dren and your livestock (I know you
have much livestock) may stay in the
towns I have given you, 20until the LORD
gives rest to your brothers as he has to
you, and they too have taken over the
land that the LORD your God is giving
them, across the Jordan. After that, each
of you may go back to the possession I
have given you."

Moses Forbidden to Cross the Jordan

21At that time I commanded Joshua:
"You have seen with your own eyes all
that the LORD your God has done to
these two kings. The LORD will do the
same to all the kingdoms over there
where you are going. 22Do not be afraid[e] 3:22
of them; the LORD your God himself will [e]Dt 1:29 [f]Ex 14:14;
fight[f] for you." Dt 20:4
23At that time I pleaded with the
LORD: 24"O Sovereign LORD, you have begun to show to your servant your great- 3:24
ness[g] and your strong hand. For what [g]Dt 11:2
god[h] is there in heaven or on earth who [h]Ex 15:11; Ps 86:8
can do the deeds and mighty works[i] you [i]Ps 71:16,19
do?[j] 25Let me go over and see the good [j]2Sa 7:22
land[k] beyond the Jordan—that fine hill 3:25
country and Lebanon." [k]Dt 4:22
26But because of you the LORD was an-
gry[l] with me and would not listen to me. 3:26 [l]Dt 1:37; 31:2
"That is enough," the LORD said. "Do not
speak to me anymore about this matter.

[a] *6* The Hebrew term refers to the irrevocable giving over of things or persons to the LORD, often by totally destroying them. [b] *11* Or *sarcophagus* [c] *11* Hebrew *nine cubits long and four cubits wide* (about 4 meters long and 1.8 meters wide) [d] *14* Or *called the settlements of Jair* [e] *17* That is, the Dead Sea

JESUS FOCUS

OUTSIDE THE PROMISED LAND

Because Moses in anger had struck the rock twice after God had instructed him merely to speak to it, he was not allowed to accompany the people into the promised land (Numbers 20:7–12), although he was able to view it from the top of Mount Pisgah (Deuteronomy 3:27). Moses later died on Mount Nebo in Moab, across from Jericho on the east bank of the Jordan River (Deuteronomy 34:1). Interestingly, Elijah would be taken to heaven from the same location as Moses—from the east bank of the Jordan River, across from Jericho (2 Kings 2:4–15). In the New Testament Moses would appear with Elijah at the time of Jesus' transfiguration (Luke 9:28–36). Moses represented God's law and Elijah God's prophets. Their presence on the Mount of Transfiguration testified to the superiority of Jesus over even these great heroes of Israel's past (see Hebrews 1:1; 3:1–6).

[27]Go up to the top of Pisgah and look west and north and south and east. Look at the land with your own eyes, since you are not going to cross this Jordan.[m] [28]But commission[n] Joshua, and encourage and strengthen him, for he will lead this people across[o] and will cause them to inherit the land that you will see." [29]So we stayed in the valley near Beth Peor.[p]

Obedience Commanded

4 Hear now, O Israel, the decrees and laws I am about to teach you. Follow them so that you may live[q] and may go in and take possession of the land that the LORD, the God of your fathers, is giving you. [2]Do not add[r] to what I command you and do not subtract from it, but keep the commands of the LORD your God that I give you.

[3]You saw with your own eyes what the LORD did at Baal Peor.[s] The LORD your God destroyed from among you everyone who followed the Baal of Peor, [4]but all of you who held fast to the LORD your God are still alive today.

[5]See, I have taught you decrees and laws as the LORD my God commanded me, so that you may follow them in the land you are entering to take possession of it. [6]Observe them carefully, for this will show your wisdom[t] and understanding to the nations, who will hear about all these decrees and say, "Surely this great nation is a wise and understanding people."[u] [7]What other nation is so great[v] as to have their gods near[w] them the way the LORD our God is near us whenever we pray to him? [8]And what other nation is so great as to have such righteous decrees and laws as this body of laws I am setting before you today?

[9]Only be careful,[x] and watch yourselves closely so that you do not forget the things your eyes have seen or let them slip from your heart as long as you live. Teach[y] them to your children[z] and to their children after them. [10]Remember the day you stood before the LORD your God at Horeb,[a] when he said to me, "Assemble the people before me to hear my words so that they may learn to revere me as long as they live in the land and may teach them to their children." [11]You came near and stood at the foot of the mountain while it blazed with fire[b] to the very heavens, with black clouds and deep darkness. [12]Then the LORD spoke[c] to you out of the fire. You heard the sound of words but saw no form; there was only a voice. [13]He declared to you his covenant,[d] the Ten Commandments,[e] which he commanded you to follow and then wrote them on two stone tablets. [14]And the LORD directed me at that time to teach you the decrees and laws you are to follow in the land that you are crossing the Jordan to possess.

Idolatry Forbidden

[15]You saw no form[f] of any kind the day the LORD spoke to you at Horeb out of the fire. Therefore watch yourselves very carefully,[g] [16]so that you do not become corrupt and make for yourselves an idol,[h] an image of any shape, whether formed like a man or a woman, [17]or like any animal on earth or any bird that flies in the air, [18]or like any creature that moves along the ground or any fish in the waters below. [19]And when you look up to the sky and see the sun,[i] the moon and the stars—all the heavenly array[j]—do not be enticed into bowing down to them and worshiping things the LORD your God has apportioned to all the nations under heaven. [20]But as for you, the LORD took you and brought you out of the iron-smelting furnace,[k] out of Egypt, to be the people of his inheritance,[l] as you now are.

[21]The LORD was angry with me[m] because of you, and he solemnly swore that I would not cross the Jordan and enter the good land the LORD your God is giving you as your inheritance. [22]I will die in this land; I will not cross the Jordan; but you are about to cross over and take possession of that good land.[n] [23]Be careful not to forget the covenant[o] of the LORD your God that he made with you; do not make for yourselves an idol[p] in the form of anything the LORD your God has forbidden. [24]For the LORD your God is a consuming fire,[q] a jealous God.

[25]After you have had children and grandchildren and have lived in the land a long time—if you then become corrupt and make any kind of idol, doing evil[r] in the eyes of the LORD your God and provoking him to anger, [26]I call heaven and earth as witnesses against you[s] this day that you will quickly perish

3:27 [m]Nu 27:12
3:28 [n]Nu 27:18-23 [o]Dt 31:3,23
3:29 [p]Dt 4:46; 34:6
4:1 [q]Dt 5:33; 8:1; 16:20; 30:15-20; Eze 20:11; Ro 10:5
4:2 [r]Dt 12:32; Jos 1:7; Rev 22:18-19
4:3 [s]Nu 25:1-9; Ps 106:28
4:6 [t]Dt 30:19-20; Ps 19:7; Pr 1:7 [u]Job 28:28
4:7 [v]2Sa 7:23 [w]Ps 46:1; Isa 55:6
4:9 [x]Pr 4:23 [y]Ge 18:19; Eph 6:4 [z]Ps 78:5-6
4:10 [a]Ex 19:9,16
4:11 [b]Ex 19:18; Heb 12:18-19
4:12 [c]Ex 20:22; Dt 5:4,22
4:13 [d]Dt 9:9,11 [e]Ex 24:12; 31:18; 34:28
4:15 [f]Isa 40:18 [g]Jos 23:11
4:16 [h]Ex 20:4-5; 32:7; Dt 5:8; Ro 1:23
4:19 [i]Dt 17:3; Job 31:26 [j]2Ki 17:16; 21:3; Ro 1:25
4:20 [k]1Ki 8:51; Jer 11:4 [l]Ex 19:5; Dt 9:29
4:21 [m]Nu 20:12; Dt 1:37
4:22 [n]Dt 3:25
4:23 [o]ver 9,16 [p]Ex 20:4
4:24 [q]Ex 24:17; Dt 9:3; Heb 12:29
4:25 [r]2Ki 17:2,17
4:26 [s]Dt 30:18-19; Isa 1:2; Mic 6:2

from the land that you are crossing the Jordan to possess. You will not live there long but will certainly be destroyed. 27 The LORD will scatter[t] you among the peoples, and only a few of you will survive among the nations to which the LORD will drive you. 28 There you will worship man-made gods[u] of wood and stone, which cannot see or hear or eat or smell.[v] 29 But if from there you seek[w] the LORD your God, you will find him if you look for him with all your heart[x] and with all your soul.[y] 30 When you are in distress and all these things have happened to you, then in later days[z] you will return to the LORD your God and obey him. 31 For the LORD your God is a merciful[a] God; he will not abandon or destroy you or forget the covenant with your forefathers, which he confirmed to them by oath.

The LORD Is God

32 Ask[b] now about the former days, long before your time, from the day God created man on the earth;[c] ask from one end of the heavens to the other.[d] Has anything so great as this ever happened, or has anything like it ever been heard of? 33 Has any other people heard the voice of God[*a*] speaking out of fire, as you have, and lived?[e] 34 Has any god ever tried to take for himself one nation out of another nation,[f] by testings, by miraculous signs[g] and wonders,[h] by war, by a mighty hand and an outstretched arm,[i] or by great and awesome deeds,[j] like all the things the LORD your God did for you in Egypt before your very eyes?

35 You were shown these things so that you might know that the LORD is God; besides him there is no other.[k] 36 From heaven he made you hear his voice[l] to discipline you. On earth he showed you his great fire, and you heard his words from out of the fire. 37 Because he loved[m] your forefathers and chose their descendants after them, he brought you out of Egypt by his Presence and his great strength,[n] 38 to drive out before you nations greater and stronger than you and to bring you into their land to give it to you for your inheritance,[o] as it is today.

39 Acknowledge and take to heart this day that the LORD is God in heaven above and on the earth below. There is no other.[p] 40 Keep[q] his decrees and commands, which I am giving you today, so that it may go well[r] with you and your children after you and that you may live long[s] in the land the LORD your God gives you for all time.

Cities of Refuge

41 Then Moses set aside three cities east of the Jordan, 42 to which anyone who had killed a person could flee if he had unintentionally killed his neighbor without malice aforethought. He could flee into one of these cities and save his life. 43 The cities were these: Bezer in the desert plateau, for the Reubenites; Ramoth in Gilead, for the Gadites; and Golan in Bashan, for the Manassites.

Introduction to the Law

44 This is the law Moses set before the Israelites. 45 These are the stipulations, decrees and laws Moses gave them when they came out of Egypt 46 and were in the valley near Beth Peor east of the Jordan, in the land of Sihon[t] king of the Amorites, who reigned in Heshbon and was defeated by Moses and the Israelites as they came out of Egypt. 47 They took possession of his land and the land of Og king of Bashan, the two Amorite kings east of the Jordan. 48 This land extended from Aroer[u] on the rim of the Arnon Gorge to Mount Siyon[*b*][v] (that is, Hermon), 49 and included all the Arabah east of the Jordan, as far as the Sea of the Arabah,[*c*] below the slopes of Pisgah.

The Ten Commandments

5 Moses summoned all Israel and said:

Hear, O Israel, the decrees and laws I declare in your hearing today. Learn them and be sure to follow them. 2 The LORD our God made a covenant[w] with us at Horeb. 3 It was not with our fathers that the LORD made this covenant, but with us, with all of us who are alive here today.[x] 4 The LORD spoke[y] to you face to face out of the fire on the mountain. 5 (At that time I stood between[z] the LORD and you to declare to you the word of the LORD, because you were afraid[a] of the fire and did not go up the mountain.) And he said:

a 33 Or *of a god* *b* 48 Hebrew; Syriac (see also Deut. 3:9) *Sirion* *c* 49 That is, the Dead Sea

4:27 [t] Lev 26:33; Dt 28:36,64; Ne 1:8
4:28 [u] Dt 28:36,64; 1Sa 26:19; Jer 16:13 [v] Ps 115:4-8; 135:15-18
4:29 [w] 2Ch 15:4; Isa 55:6 [x] Jer 29:13 [y] Dt 30:1-3,10
4:30 [z] Dt 31:29; Jer 23:20; Hos 3:5
4:31 [a] 2Ch 30:9; Ne 9:31; Ps 116:5; Jnh 4:2
4:32 [b] Dt 32:7; Job 8:8 [c] Ge 1:27 [d] Mt 24:31
4:33 [e] Ex 20:22; Dt 5:24-26
4:34 [f] Ex 6:6 [g] Ex 7:3 [h] Dt 7:19; 26:8 [i] Ex 13:3 [j] Dt 34:12
4:35 [k] Dt 32:39; 1Sa 2:2; Isa 45:5,18
4:36 [l] Ex 19:9,19
4:37 [m] Dt 10:15 [n] Ex 13:3,9,14
4:38 [o] Dt 7:1; 9:5
4:39 [p] ver 35; Jos 2:11
4:40 [q] Lev 22:31; Dt 5:33 [r] Dt 5:16 [s] Dt 6:3,18; Eph 6:2-3
4:46 [t] Nu 21:26; Dt 3:29
4:48 [u] Dt 2:36 [v] Dt 3:9
5:2 [w] Ex 19:5
5:3 [x] Heb 8:9
5:4 [y] Dt 4:12,33,36
5:5 [z] Gal 3:19 [a] Ex 20:18,21

6 "I am the LORD your God, who
brought you out of Egypt, out
of the land of slavery.
7 "You shall have no other gods before[a] me.
8 "You shall not make for yourself an
idol in the form of anything in
heaven above or on the earth
beneath or in the waters below. 9 You shall not bow down
to them or worship them; for
I, the LORD your God, am a
jealous God, punishing the
children for the sin of the fathers to the third and fourth
5:9 generation of those who hate
b Ex 34:7 me,[b] 10 but showing love to a
thousand ⌞generations⌟ of
5:10 those who love me and keep
c Jer 32:18 my commandments.[c]
11 "You shall not misuse the name of
the LORD your God, for the
5:11 LORD will not hold anyone
d Lev 19:12; Mt 5:33-37 guiltless who misuses his
name.[d]
5:12 12 "Observe the Sabbath day by keep-
e Ex 20:8 ing it holy,[e] as the LORD your
God has commanded you.
13 Six days you shall labor and
5:14 do all your work, 14 but the sev-
f Ge 2:2; Heb 4:4 enth day[f] is a Sabbath to the
LORD your God. On it you shall
not do any work, neither you,
nor your son or daughter, nor
your manservant or maidservant, nor your ox, your donkey
or any of your animals, nor the
alien within your gates, so that
your manservant and maid-
servant may rest, as you do.
15 Remember that you were
slaves in Egypt and that the
LORD your God brought you
out of there with a mighty
5:15 hand and an outstretched
g Dt 4:34 arm.[g] Therefore the LORD your
5:16 God has commanded you to
h Ex 20:12; observe the Sabbath day.
Lev 19:3; 16 "Honor your father and your moth-
Dt 27:16; er,[h] as the LORD your God has
Eph 6:2-3*; Col 3:20 commanded you, so that you
i Dt 4:40 may live long[i] and that it may
5:17 go well with you in the land the
j Mt 5:21-22* LORD your God is giving you.
5:18 17 "You shall not murder.[j]
k Mt 5:27-30; Lk 18:20*; 18 "You shall not commit adultery.[k]
Jas 2:11* 19 "You shall not steal.

20 "You shall not give false testimony
against your neighbor.
21 "You shall not covet your neighbor's wife. You shall not set
your desire on your neighbor's
house or land, his manservant
or maidservant, his ox or donkey, or anything that belongs 5:21
to your neighbor."[l] l Ro 7:7*; 13:9*
22 These are the commandments the
LORD proclaimed in a loud voice to your
whole assembly there on the mountain
from out of the fire, the cloud and the
deep darkness; and he added nothing
more. Then he wrote them on two stone 5:22
tablets[m] and gave them to me. m Ex 24:12; 31:18; Dt 4:13
23 When you heard the voice out of the
darkness, while the mountain was
ablaze with fire, all the leading men of
your tribes and your elders came to me.
24 And you said, "The LORD our God has
shown us his glory and his majesty, and
we have heard his voice from the fire. Today we have seen that a man can live
even if God speaks with him.[n] 25 But now, 5:24
why should we die? This great fire will n Ex 19:19
consume us, and we will die if we hear
the voice of the LORD our God any
longer.[o] 26 For what mortal man has ever 5:25
heard the voice of the living God speak- o Dt 18:16
ing out of fire, as we have, and sur-
vived?[p] 27 Go near and listen to all that 5:26 p Dt 4:33
the LORD our God says. Then tell us
whatever the LORD our God tells you. We
will listen and obey."
28 The LORD heard you when you
spoke to me and the LORD said to me, "I
have heard what this people said to you. 5:28
Everything they said was good.[q] 29 Oh, q Dt 18:17
that their hearts would be inclined to 5:29
fear me[r] and keep all my commands[s] al- r Ps 81:8,13
ways, so that it might go well with them s Dt 11:1; Isa 48:18
and their children forever![t] t Dt 4:1,40
30 "Go, tell them to return to their tents.
31 But you stay here[u] with me so that I 5:31
may give you all the commands, decrees u Ex 24:12
and laws you are to teach them to follow
in the land I am giving them to possess."
32 So be careful to do what the LORD
your God has commanded you; do not 5:32
turn aside to the right or to the left.[v] v Dt 17:11,20; 28:14; Jos 1:7;
33 Walk in all the way that the LORD your 23:6; Pr 4:27
God has commanded you,[w] so that you
may live and prosper and prolong your 5:33 w Jer 7:23
days[x] in the land that you will possess. x Dt 4:40

a 7 Or *besides*

Love the LORD Your God

6 These are the commands, decrees
and laws the LORD your God directed me to teach you to observe in the
land that you are crossing the Jordan to
possess, 2so that you, your children and
6:2 their children after them may fear[y] the
y Ex 20:20; Dt 10:12-13 LORD your God as long as you live by
keeping all his decrees and commands
that I give you, and so that you may enjoy long life. 3Hear, O Israel, and be careful to obey so that it may go well with
6:3 z Dt 5:33 you and that you may increase greatly[z]
a Ex 3:8 in a land flowing with milk and honey,[a]
just as the LORD, the God of your fathers,
promised you.
6:4 4Hear, O Israel: The LORD our God, the
b Mk 12:29*; 1Co 8:4 LORD is one.[a][b] 5Love[c] the LORD your God
with all your heart and with all your soul
6:5 and with all your strength.[d] 6These com-
c Mt 22:37*; Mk 12:30*; mandments that I give you today are to
Lk 10:27* be upon your hearts.[e] 7Impress them on
d Dt 10:12 your children. Talk about them when you
6:6 sit at home and when you walk along the
e Dt 11:18 road, when you lie down and when you
get up.[f] 8Tie them as symbols on your 6:7 f Dt 4:9; 11:19;
hands and bind them on your foreheads.[g] Eph 6:4
9Write them on the doorframes of your 6:8
houses and on your gates.[h] g Ex 13:9,16; Dt 11:18
10When the LORD your God brings you
into the land he swore to your fathers, to 6:9
Abraham, Isaac and Jacob, to give you— h Dt 11:20
a land with large, flourishing cities you 6:10
did not build,[i] 11houses filled with all i Jos 24:13
kinds of good things you did not pro-
vide, wells you did not dig, and vineyards and olive groves you did not
plant—then when you eat and are satis-
fied,[j] 12be careful that you do not forget 6:11 j Dt 8:10
the LORD, who brought you out of Egypt,
out of the land of slavery.
13Fear the LORD[k] your God, serve him 6:13
only[l] and take your oaths in his name. k Dt 10:20 l Mt 4:10*;
14Do not follow other gods, the gods of Lk 4:8*
the peoples around you; 15for the LORD
your God[m], who is among you, is a jeal- 6:15
ous God and his anger will burn against m Dt 4:24
you, and he will destroy you from the
face of the land. 16Do not test the LORD 6:16
your God[n] as you did at Massah. 17Be n Ex 17:7;
sure to keep the commands of the LORD Mt 4:7*; Lk 4:12*
your God and the stipulations and de-
crees he has given you.[o] 18Do what is 6:17 o Dt 11:22;
right and good in the LORD's sight, so Ps 119:4
that it may go well[p] with you and you 6:18
may go in and take over the good land p Dt 4:40
that the LORD promised on oath to your
forefathers, 19thrusting out all your enemies before you, as the LORD said.

a 4 Or *The LORD our God is one LORD;* or *The LORD is our God, the LORD is one;* or *The LORD is our God, the LORD alone*

JESUS FOCUS

GOD IS ONE

The *Shema,* meaning "hear," in Deuteronomy 6:4–5 emphasizes God's unity. This passage states that there can be only one all-powerful, infinite, limitless and perfect God. Because God has revealed himself to us, we are able to identify the God of the Bible as that one true God. Christians believe that God is a tri-unity, or Trinity—one being expressed in three persons: God the Father, God the Son and God the Holy Spirit. Jesus, God the Son, is identified with Yahweh (or "the LORD"), God the Father, in both the Old Testament and the New.

Yahweh (the LORD)	Title or Act	Jesus
Genesis 1:1	Creator	John 1:3
Isaiah 45:22	Savior	John 4:42
Joel 3:12	Judge	John 5:27
Exodus 3:14	"I AM"	John 8:58
Isaiah 60:19–20	Light	John 8:12
Psalm 23:1	Shepherd	John 10:11
Hosea 13:14	Redeemer	Revelation 5:9
Deuteronomy 32:4	Rock	1 Corinthians 10:4
Jeremiah 31:34	Forgiver of Sins	Mark 2:7–10
Isaiah 45:23–24	Lord Who Is to Be Worshiped	Philippians 2:10–11

TESTING GOD

When Satan tempted Jesus (Matthew 4:1–11), our Lord's response on several occasions was to quote from the book of Deuteronomy. First, when Satan suggested that Jesus turn stones into bread and violate his fast, Jesus quoted Deuteronomy 8:3: "Man does not live on bread alone but on every word that comes from the mouth of the LORD." In response to Satan's suggestion that Jesus throw himself from the highest point of the temple, Jesus quoted Deuteronomy 6:16: "Do not test the LORD your God." Finally, when Satan suggested that Jesus honor him rather than the Father, Jesus repeated Deuteronomy 6:13: "Fear the LORD your God, serve him only."

DISCOVERY 43

Loving God, Loving Each Other

Before we can commit our lives to God, we have to accept the truth *about* him, and he wants us to acknowledge one truth above all else: He is God, and there is no other. The statement, "The LORD our God, the LORD is one" is called the *shema* from the Hebrew word meaning "to hear" (Deuteronomy 6:4). This was the most basic statement of truth for God's people in ancient Israel, and it is still the core confession for Jewish people today. In fact these words are recited every morning and evening by orthodox Jews. This statement reminded God's people that they did not worship many different gods, like the people of the countries around them, but instead followed the one true God.

In many places, like this one, the word for "God" is plural, which seems to indicate that God is more than one person. At the same time, the Bible is very clear that there is only one true God. This may be one way God chose to help his people understand that he is "triune"—Father, Son and Holy Spirit. Also, the Hebrew language sometimes uses the plural form of a word to connote majesty and greatness. There are many places in the Bible in which God is referred to in the plural but yet is clearly acknowledged as one God (Psalm 2:7; Isaiah 48:16; Matthew 3:13–17).

However, there is more to knowing God than simply adhering to an intellectual truth about him: God wants us to live out his truth. The *shema* is followed by an exhortation to "Love the LORD your God with all your heart and with all your soul and with all your strength" (Deuteronomy 6:5). This command summarizes all of the rest: We are to love him above anything else and also to love the people he has created (Matthew 22:37–39; Romans 13:9; Galatians 5:14). Seekers often ask what rules they will have to follow if they give their lives to Jesus. The answer is, "Just one—love God and others!" God repeats that many times in Deuteronomy (see Deuteronomy 7:9; 10:12; 11:1,13; 13:3; 19:9; 30:6,16,20).

What exactly does it mean to love God? Well, first of all, love implies commitment; it is a decision we make about who or what we'll be devoted to. But love is essentially something we do rather than something we have (like a feeling). Love is a noun, but it is also a verb. Essentially, because it is something we do, *love means obedience*. It is agreeing with God's demands on our lives. Jesus said that what is manifested in our lives is the true test of our love for him (John 14:15). If we claim to love God but don't live life the way he asks us to, we are lying to God, ourselves and others (1 John 2:4–6). Love is something we demonstrate rather than merely verbalize: "Let us not love with words or tongue but with actions and in truth" (1 John 3:18).

Self-Discovery: *Does the summary of God's law (the command to love God and others) make obedience easier or more difficult for you? If you find that your love for God and others is less than it should be, does it help to consider Christ's love for you? (1 John 4:19).*

GO TO DISCOVERY 44 ON PAGE 236

[20]In the future, when your son asks
6:20 [q]Ex 13:14 you,[q] "What is the meaning of the stipulations, decrees and laws the LORD our
God has commanded you?" [21]tell him:
"We were slaves of Pharaoh in Egypt, but
the LORD brought us out of Egypt with a
mighty hand. [22]Before our eyes the LORD
sent miraculous signs and wonders—
great and terrible—upon Egypt and
Pharaoh and his whole household. [23]But
he brought us out from there to bring us
in and give us the land that he promised
on oath to our forefathers. [24]The LORD
commanded us to obey all these decrees
6:24 [r]Dt 10:12; Jer 32:39 [s]Ps 41:2 and to fear the LORD our God,[r] so that
we might always prosper and be kept
alive, as is the case today.[s] [25]And if we
are careful to obey all this law before the
6:25 [t]Dt 24:13; Ro 10:3,5 LORD our God, as he has commanded us,
that will be our righteousness.[t]"

Driving Out the Nations

7 When the LORD your God brings
you into the land you are entering
to possess and drives out before you
7:1 [u]Dt 31:3; Ac 13:19 many nations[u]—the Hittites, Girgashites, Amorites, Canaanites, Perizzites,
Hivites and Jebusites, seven nations
larger and stronger than you— [2]and
when the LORD your God has delivered
them over to you and you have defeated
them, then you must destroy them to-
7:2 [v]Ex 23:32 [w]Dt 13:8 tally.[a] Make no treaty[v] with them, and
show them no mercy.[w] [3]Do not inter-
7:3 [x]Ex 34:15-16; Ezr 9:2 marry with them.[x] Do not give your
daughters to their sons or take their
daughters for your sons, [4]for they will
turn your sons away from following me
to serve other gods, and the LORD's anger
will burn against you and will quickly
7:4 [y]Dt 6:15 destroy[y] you. [5]This is what you are to do
to them: Break down their altars, smash
their sacred stones, cut down their
7:5 [z]Ex 23:24; Dt 12:2-3 Asherah poles[b] and burn their idols in
the fire.[z] [6]For you are a people holy[a] to
7:6 [a]Ex 19:5-6; 1Pe 2:9 [b]Ps 50:5; Jer 2:3 [c]Dt 14:2 the LORD your God.[b] The LORD your God
has chosen[c] you out of all the peoples on
the face of the earth to be his people, his
treasured possession.

[7]The LORD did not set his affection on
you and choose you because you were
more numerous than other peoples, for
7:7 [d]Dt 10:22 you were the fewest of all peoples.[d] [8]But
it was because the LORD loved[e] you and
7:8 [e]Dt 10:15 [f]Ex 32:13 kept the oath he swore[f] to your forefathers that he brought you out with a
mighty hand and redeemed you from
the land of slavery,[g] from the power of 7:8 [g]Ex 13:14
Pharaoh king of Egypt. [9]Know therefore
that the LORD your God is God;[h] he is the 7:9 [h]Dt 4:35 [i]1Co 1:9; 2Ti 2:13 [j]Ne 1:5; Da 9:4
faithful God,[i] keeping his covenant of
love[j] to a thousand generations of those
who love him and keep his commands.
[10]But

those who hate him he will repay
to their face by destruction;
he will not be slow to repay to
their face those who hate
him.

[11]Therefore, take care to follow the commands, decrees and laws I give you today.

[12]If you pay attention to these laws
and are careful to follow them, then the 7:12 [k]Lev 26:3-13; Dt 28:1-14; Ps 105:8-9
LORD your God will keep his covenant of
love with you, as he swore to your forefa-
thers.[k] [13]He will love you and bless you[l] 7:13 [l]Jn 14:21 [m]Dt 28:4
and increase your numbers. He will bless
the fruit of your womb, the crops of your
land—your grain, new wine and oil—the
calves of your herds and the lambs of
your flocks in the land that he swore to
your forefathers to give you.[m] [14]You will
be blessed more than any other people;
none of your men or women will be
childless, nor any of your livestock with- 7:14 [n]Ex 23:26
out young.[n] [15]The LORD will keep you free
from every disease.[o] He will not inflict on 7:15 [o]Ex 15:26
you the horrible diseases you knew in
Egypt, but he will inflict them on all who
hate you. [16]You must destroy all the peoples the LORD your God gives over to you.
Do not look on them with pity[p] and do 7:16 [p]ver 2; Ex 23:33 [q]Jdg 8:27
not serve their gods, for that will be a
snare[q] to you.

[17]You may say to yourselves, "These
nations are stronger than we are. How 7:17 [r]Nu 33:53
can we drive them out?"[r] [18]But do not be
afraid[s] of them; remember well what the 7:18 [s]Dt 31:6 [t]Ps 105:5
LORD your God did to Pharaoh and to all
Egypt.[t] [19]You saw with your own eyes the
great trials, the miraculous signs and
wonders, the mighty hand and outstretched arm, with which the LORD your
God brought you out. The LORD your
God will do the same to all the peoples 7:19 [u]Dt 4:34
you now fear.[u] [20]Moreover, the LORD your
God will send the hornet[v] among them 7:20 [v]Ex 23:28; Jos 24:12
until even the survivors who hide from
you have perished. [21]Do not be terrified

[a] *2* The Hebrew term refers to the irrevocable giving over of things or persons to the LORD, often by totally destroying them; also in verse 26.
[b] *5* That is, symbols of the goddess Asherah; here and elsewhere in Deuteronomy

by them, for the LORD your God, who is
among you,[w] is a great and awesome
God.[x] 22The LORD your God will drive out
those nations before you, little by little.[y]
You will not be allowed to eliminate
them all at once, or the wild animals will
multiply around you. 23But the LORD
your God will deliver them over to you,
throwing them into great confusion until they are destroyed. 24He will give their
kings into your hand, and you will wipe
out their names from under heaven. No
one will be able to stand up against you;[z]
you will destroy them. 25The images of
their gods you are to burn[a] in the fire. Do
not covet[b] the silver and gold on them,
and do not take it for yourselves, or you
will be ensnared[c] by it, for it is detestable[d] to the LORD your God. 26Do not
bring a detestable thing into your house
or you, like it, will be set apart for destruction.[e] Utterly abhor and detest it,
for it is set apart for destruction.

Do Not Forget the LORD

8 Be careful to follow every command I am giving you today, so
that you may live[f] and increase and may
enter and possess the land that the LORD
promised on oath to your forefathers.
2Remember how the LORD your God led[g]
you all the way in the desert these forty
years, to humble you and to test you in
order to know what was in your heart,
whether or not you would keep his commands. 3He humbled you, causing you
to hunger and then feeding you with
manna,[h] which neither you nor your fathers had known, to teach you that man
does not live on bread alone but on
every word that comes from the mouth
of the LORD.[i] 4Your clothes did not wear
out and your feet did not swell during
these forty years.[j] 5Know then in your
heart that as a man disciplines his son,
so the LORD your God disciplines you.[k]
6Observe the commands of the LORD
your God, walking in his ways and re-
vering him.[l] 7For the LORD your God is
bringing you into a good land—a land
with streams and pools of water, with
springs flowing in the valleys and hills;[m]
8a land with wheat and barley, vines and
fig trees, pomegranates, olive oil and
honey; 9a land where bread will not be
scarce and you will lack nothing; a land

7:21 [w] Jos 3:10 [x] Dt 10:17; Ne 9:32
7:22 [y] Ex 23:28-30
7:24 [z] Jos 23:9
7:25 [a] Ex 32:20; 1Ch 14:12 [b] Jos 7:21 [c] Jdg 8:27 [d] Dt 17:1
7:26 [e] Lev 27:28-29
8:1 [f] Dt 4:1
8:2 [g] Am 2:10
8:3 [h] Ex 16:12,14,35 [i] Ex 16:2-3; Mt 4:4*; Lk 4:4*
8:4 [j] Dt 29:5; Ne 9:21
8:5 [k] 2Sa 7:14; Pr 3:11-12; Heb 12:5-11; Rev 3:19
8:6 [l] Dt 5:33
8:7 [m] Dt 11:9-12

where the rocks are iron and you can dig
copper out of the hills.
10When you have eaten and are satisfied,[n] praise the LORD your God for the
good land he has given you. 11Be careful
that you do not forget the LORD your
God, failing to observe his commands,
his laws and his decrees that I am giving
you this day. 12Otherwise, when you eat
and are satisfied, when you build fine
houses and settle down,[o] 13and when
your herds and flocks grow large and
your silver and gold increase and all you
have is multiplied, 14then your heart will
become proud and you will forget[p] the
LORD your God, who brought you out of
Egypt, out of the land of slavery. 15He led
you through the vast and dreadful
desert,[q] that thirsty and waterless land,
with its venomous snakes[r] and scorpions. He brought you water out of hard
rock.[s] 16He gave you manna to eat in the
desert, something your fathers had never known,[t] to humble and to test you so
that in the end it might go well with you.
17You may say to yourself,[u] "My power
and the strength of my hands have produced this wealth for me." 18But remember the LORD your God, for it is he who
gives you the ability to produce wealth,[v]
and so confirms his covenant, which he
swore to your forefathers, as it is today.
19If you ever forget the LORD your God
and follow other gods and worship and
bow down to them, I testify against you
today that you will surely be destroyed.[w]
20Like the nations the LORD destroyed
before you, so you will be destroyed for
not obeying the LORD your God.

Not Because of Israel's Righteousness

9 Hear, O Israel. You are now about
to cross the Jordan to go in and
dispossess nations greater and stronger
than you,[x] with large cities that have
walls up to the sky.[y] 2The people are
strong and tall—Anakites! You know
about them and have heard it said:
"Who can stand up against the Anakites?"[z] 3But be assured today that the
LORD your God is the one who goes
across ahead of you[a] like a devouring
fire.[b] He will destroy them; he will subdue them before you. And you will drive
them out and annihilate them quickly,[c]
as the LORD has promised you.
4After the LORD your God has driven

8:10 [n] Dt 6:10-12
8:12 [o] Hos 13:6
8:14 [p] Ps 106:21
8:15 [q] Jer 2:6 [r] Nu 21:6 [s] Nu 20:11; Ps 78:15; 114:8
8:16 [t] Ex 16:15
8:17 [u] Dt 9:4,7,24
8:18 [v] Pr 10:22; Hos 2:8
8:19 [w] Dt 4:26; 30:18
9:1 [x] Dt 4:38; 11:23, 31 [y] Dt 1:28
9:2 [z] Nu 13:22,28, 32-33
9:3 [a] Dt 31:3; Jos 3:11 [b] Dt 4:24; Heb 12:29 [c] Ex 23:31; Dt 7:23-24

them out before you, do not say to yourself,[d] "The LORD has brought me here to take possession of this land because of my righteousness." No, it is on account of the wickedness of these nations[e] that the LORD is going to drive them out before you. [5]It is not because of your righteousness or your integrity[f] that you are going in to take possession of their land; but on account of the wickedness of these nations, the LORD your God will drive them out before you, to accomplish what he swore[g] to your fathers, to Abraham, Isaac and Jacob. [6]Understand, then, that it is not because of your righteousness that the LORD your God is giving you this good land to possess, for you are a stiff-necked people.[h]

The Golden Calf

[7]Remember this and never forget how you provoked the LORD your God to anger in the desert. From the day you left Egypt until you arrived here, you have been rebellious against the LORD. [8]At Horeb you aroused the LORD's wrath so that he was angry enough to destroy you.[i] [9]When I went up on the mountain to receive the tablets of stone, the tablets of the covenant that the LORD had made with you, I stayed on the mountain forty days and forty nights; I ate no bread and drank no water.[j] [10]The LORD gave me two stone tablets inscribed by the finger of God.[k] On them were all the commandments the LORD proclaimed to you on the mountain out of the fire, on the day of the assembly.

[11]At the end of the forty days and forty nights, the LORD gave me the two stone tablets, the tablets of the covenant. [12]Then the LORD told me, "Go down from here at once, because your people whom you brought out of Egypt have become corrupt.[l] They have turned away quickly[m] from what I commanded them and have made a cast idol for themselves."

[13]And the LORD said to me, "I have seen this people[n], and they are a stiff-necked people indeed! [14]Let me alone,[o] so that I may destroy them and blot out[p] their name from under heaven. And I will make you into a nation stronger and more numerous than they."

[15]So I turned and went down from the mountain while it was ablaze with fire. And the two tablets of the covenant were in my hands.[a][q] [16]When I looked, I saw that you had sinned against the LORD your God; you had made for yourselves an idol cast in the shape of a calf.[r] You had turned aside quickly from the way that the LORD had commanded you. [17]So I took the two tablets and threw them out of my hands, breaking them to pieces before your eyes.

[18]Then once again I fell[s] prostrate before the LORD for forty days and forty nights; I ate no bread and drank no water, because of all the sin you had committed, doing what was evil in the LORD's sight and so provoking him to anger. [19]I feared the anger and wrath of the LORD, for he was angry enough with you to destroy you.[t] But again the LORD listened to me.[u] [20]And the LORD was angry enough with Aaron to destroy him, but at that time I prayed for Aaron too. [21]Also I took that sinful thing of yours, the calf you had made, and burned it in the fire. Then I crushed it and ground it to powder as fine as dust and threw the dust into a stream that flowed down the mountain.[v]

[22]You also made the LORD angry at Taberah,[w] at Massah[x] and at Kibroth Hattaavah.[y]

[23]And when the LORD sent you out from Kadesh Barnea, he said, "Go up and take possession of the land I have given you." But you rebelled against the command of the LORD your God. You did not trust[z] him or obey him. [24]You have been rebellious against the LORD ever since I have known you.[a]

[25]I lay prostrate before the LORD those forty days and forty nights because the LORD had said he would destroy you.[b] [26]I prayed to the LORD and said, "O Sovereign LORD, do not destroy your people, your own inheritance that you redeemed by your great power and brought out of Egypt with a mighty hand.[c] [27]Remember your servants Abraham, Isaac and Jacob. Overlook the stubbornness of this people, their wickedness and their sin. [28]Otherwise, the country from which you brought us will say, 'Because the LORD was not able to take them into the land he had promised them, and because he hated them, he brought them out to put them to death in the desert.'[d] [29]But they are your

[a] 15 Or *And I had the two tablets of the covenant with me, one in each hand*

9:4 d Dt 8:17; e Lev 18:21,24-30; Dt 18:9-14
9:5 f Tit 3:5; g Ge 12:7; 13:15; 15:7; 17:8; 26:4
9:6 h ver 13; Ex 32:9; Dt 31:27
9:8 i Ex 32:7-10; Ps 106:19
9:9 j Ex 24:12,15,18; 34:28
9:10 k Ex 31:18; Dt 4:13
9:12 l Ex 32:7-8; Dt 31:29; m Jdg 2:17
9:13 n ver 6; Ex 32:9; Dt 10:16
9:14 o Ex 32:10; p Nu 14:12; Dt 29:20
9:15 q Ex 19:18; 32:15
9:16 r Ex 32:19
9:18 s Ex 34:28
9:19 t Ex 32:10-11,14; u Dt 10:10
9:21 v Ex 32:20
9:22 w Nu 11:3; x Ex 17:7; y Nu 11:34
9:23 z Ps 106:24
9:24 a ver 7; Dt 31:27
9:25 b ver 18
9:26 c Ex 32:11
9:28 d Ex 32:12; Nu 14:16

9:29 e Dt 4:20; people, your inheritance[e] that you
1Ki 8:51 f Dt 4:34; brought out by your great power and
Ne 1:10 your outstretched arm.[f]"

Tablets Like the First Ones

10 At that time the LORD said
10:1 to me, "Chisel out two stone
g Ex 25:10; tablets[g] like the first ones and come up
34:1-2 to me on the mountain. Also make a
wooden chest.[a] 2I will write on the
tablets the words that were on the first
10:2 h Ex 25:16,21; tablets, which you broke. Then you are
Dt 4:13 to put them in the chest."[h]
10:3 3So I made the ark out of acacia wood[i]
i Ex 25:5,10; and chiseled[j] out two stone tablets like
37:1-9 j Ex 34:4 the first ones, and I went up on the
mountain with the two tablets in my
hands. 4The LORD wrote on these tablets
what he had written before, the Ten
10:4 k Ex 20:1 Commandments he had proclaimed[k] to
you on the mountain, out of the fire, on
the day of the assembly. And the LORD
gave them to me. 5Then I came back
10:5 l Ex 34:29 down the mountain[l] and put the tablets
m Ex 40:20 in the ark[m] I had made, as the LORD com-
n 1Ki 8:9 manded me, and they are there now.[n]
10:6 6(The Israelites traveled from the wells
o Nu 33:30-31, of the Jaakanites to Moserah.[o] There
38 p Nu 20:25-28 Aaron died and was buried, and Eleazar
his son succeeded him as priest.[p] 7From
there they traveled to Gudgodah and on
10:7 to Jotbathah, a land with streams of wa-
q Nu 33:32-34 ter.[q] 8At that time the LORD set apart the
tribe of Levi[r] to carry the ark of the cov-
10:8 r Nu 3:6 enant of the LORD, to stand before the
s Dt 18:5 LORD to minister[s] and to pronounce
t Dt 21:5 blessings[t] in his name, as they still do to-
10:9 day. 9That is why the Levites have no
u Nu 18:20; share or inheritance among their broth-
Dt 18:1-2; ers; the LORD is their inheritance,[u] as the
Eze 44:28 LORD your God told them.)
10Now I had stayed on the mountain
forty days and nights, as I did the first
time, and the LORD listened to me at this
10:10 time also. It was not his will to destroy
v Ex 33:17; you.[v] 11"Go," the LORD said to me, "and
34:28; Dt 9:18- lead the people on their way, so that they
19,25 may enter and possess the land that I
swore to their fathers to give them."

Fear the LORD

10:12 12And now, O Israel, what does the
w Mic 6:8 LORD your God ask of you[w] but to fear
x Dt 5:33; 6:13; the LORD your God, to walk in all his
Mt 22:37 ways, to love him,[x] to serve the LORD
y Dt 6:5 your God with all your heart[y] and with
all your soul, 13and to observe the LORD's
commands and decrees that I am giving
you today for your own good?
14To the LORD your God belong the
heavens, even the highest heavens,[z] 10:14
the earth and everything in it.[a] 15Yet the z 1Ki 8:27
LORD set his affection on your forefa- a Ex 19:5
thers and loved[b] them, and he chose 10:15 b Dt 4:37
you, their descendants, above all the nations, as it is today. 16Circumcise[c] your 10:16
hearts, therefore, and do not be stiff- c Jer 4:4 d Dt 9:6
necked[d] any longer. 17For the LORD your
God is God of gods[e] and Lord of lords, 10:17
the great God, mighty and awesome, e Jos 22:22; Da 2:47
who shows no partiality[f] and accepts no f Ac 10:34;
bribes. 18He defends the cause of the fa- Ro 2:11; Eph 6:9
therless and the widow,[g] and loves the 10:18
alien, giving him food and clothing. g Ps 68:5
19And you are to love those who are
aliens, for you yourselves were aliens in 10:19
Egypt.[h] 20Fear the LORD your God and h Lev 19:34
serve him.[i] Hold fast[j] to him and take 10:20 i Mt 4:10
your oaths in his name.[k] 21He is your j Dt 11:22
praise;[l] he is your God, who performed k Ps 63:11
for you those great and awesome won- 10:21
ders[m] you saw with your own eyes. l Ex 15:2;
22Your forefathers who went down into Jer 17:14 m Ps 106:21-22
Egypt were seventy in all,[n] and now the 10:22
LORD your God has made you as numer- n Ge 46:26-27
ous as the stars in the sky.[o] o Ge 15:5; Dt 1:10

Love and Obey the LORD

11 Love[p] the LORD your God and 11:1
keep his requirements, his de- p Dt 10:12
crees, his laws and his commands al- q Zec 3:7
ways.[q] 2Remember today that your children were not the ones who saw and
experienced the discipline of the LORD
your God:[r] his majesty, his mighty hand, 11:2 r Dt 5:24; 8:5
his outstretched arm; 3the signs he per-
formed and the things he did in the
heart of Egypt, both to Pharaoh king of
Egypt and to his whole country; 4what
he did to the Egyptian army, to its
horses and chariots, how he overwhelmed them with the waters of the
Red Sea[b][s] as they were pursuing you, 11:4 s Ex 14:27
and how the LORD brought lasting ruin
on them. 5It was not your children who
saw what he did for you in the desert until you arrived at this place, 6and what he 11:6
did[t] to Dathan and Abiram, sons of Eli- t Nu 16:1-35
ab the Reubenite, when the earth
opened its mouth right in the middle of
all Israel and swallowed them up with
their households, their tents and every

[a] *1* That is, an ark [b] *4* Hebrew *Yam Suph*; that is, Sea of Reeds

What God Wants

God's expectations for his people are clear, and they are reiterated throughout his Word. Few passages capture the essence of these expectations, however, as succinctly as Moses' question: "And now, O Israel, what does the LORD your God ask of you but to fear the LORD your God, to walk in all his ways, to love him, to serve the LORD your God with all your heart and with all your soul, and to observe the LORD's commands and decrees that I am giving you today for your own good?" (Deuteronomy 10:12–13). What does he expect? *Action*. Look at the verbs he uses:

1. God wants us to *fear* him. Fearing God means that we understand how great he is when we compare ourselves to him. He is the God of the highest heavens (verse 14), and we are to revere him and tremble before him because he is an awesome God.

2. God wants us to *walk* in his ways. Walking describes an entire lifestyle—how we conduct ourselves at home and at work, in worship and in recreation. Our walk includes every aspect of our lives, not just the activities and areas we consider spiritual.

3. God wants us to *love* him. Loving God is the essence of his entire law. Jesus told us that adherence to the rest of the commandments follows when we keep the first one: Have no other god before him (Deuteronomy 5:7; Matthew 22:37).

4. God wants us to *serve* him—with our whole hearts. Service is not an obligation, complying with what he says because we have to. Rather, we are to serve with passion—we devote ourselves to him because we want to, because we cannot conceive of any other appropriate response.

5. God wants us to *observe* his commands, to obey the rules for right living he has given to us.

There is great benefit in devoting our lives to knowing God. We don't do it because *he* needs this devotion. Without question, he deserves all honor because he is God. But he asks us to live his way because all these things are for *our* own good (Deuteronomy 10:13). We were created for communion with God and can find our true purpose only when we live our lives in praise of his glory.

Jesus was the perfect example of this: "Father, the time has come. Glorify your Son, that your Son may glorify you . . . I have brought you glory on earth by completing the work you gave me to do" (John 17:1,4). Moses' words comprise an excellent mission statement for every believer, and Jesus provides us the model to follow as we get to know God. We can return to them again and again as we evaluate our lives. They form the basis for our relationship with God.

***Self-Discovery:** Today, before making any significant decisions, ask yourself, "What would Jesus do?"*

GO TO DISCOVERY 45 ON PAGE 240

living thing that belonged to them. 7But
it was your own eyes that saw all these
great things the LORD has done.
8Observe therefore all the commands
I am giving you today, so that you may
have the strength to go in and take over
11:8 the land that you are crossing the Jordan
u Jos 1:7 to possess,[u] 9and so that you may live
long[v] in the land that the LORD swore[w]
11:9 to your forefathers to give to them and
v Dt 4:40; Pr 10:27 their descendants, a land flowing with
w Dt 9:5 x Ex 3:8 milk and honey.[x] 10The land you are entering to take over is not like the land of
Egypt, from which you have come,
where you planted your seed and irrigated it by foot as in a vegetable garden.
11But the land you are crossing the Jordan to take possession of is a land of
mountains and valleys that drinks rain
11:11 y Dt 8:7 from heaven.[y] 12It is a land the LORD
your God cares for; the eyes[z] of the LORD
11:12 z 1Ki 9:3 your God are continually on it from the
beginning of the year to its end.
11:13 a Dt 6:17 13So if you faithfully obey[a] the commands I am giving you today—to love[b]
b Dt 10:12 the LORD your God and to serve him
with all your heart and with all your
11:14 soul— 14then I will send rain[c] on your
c Lev 26:4; Dt 28:12 land in its season, both autumn and
d Joel 2:23; Jas 5:7 spring rains,[d] so that you may gather in
your grain, new wine and oil. 15I will provide grass[e] in the fields for your cattle,
11:15 e Ps 104:14 f Dt 6:11 and you will eat and be satisfied.[f]
16Be careful, or you will be enticed to
11:16 turn away and worship other gods and
g Dt 8:19; 29:18; Job 31:9,27 bow down to them.[g] 17Then the LORD's
anger[h] will burn against you, and he will
11:17 shut[i] the heavens so that it will not rain
h Dt 6:15 and the ground will yield no produce,
i 1Ki 8:35; 2Ch 6:26 and you will soon perish[j] from the good
j Dt 4:26 land the LORD is giving you. 18Fix these
words of mine in your hearts and minds;
11:18 tie them as symbols on your hands and
k Dt 6:6-8 bind them on your foreheads.[k] 19Teach
them to your children,[l] talking about
11:19 l Dt 6:7 them when you sit at home and when
m Dt 4:9-10 you walk along the road, when you lie
down and when you get up.[m] 20Write
them on the doorframes of your houses
11:20 n Dt 6:9 and on your gates,[n] 21so that your days
and the days of your children may be
11:21 o Pr 3:2; 4:10 many[o] in the land that the LORD swore
p Ps 72:5 to give your forefathers, as many as the
days that the heavens are above the
earth.[p]
11:22 q Dt 6:17 22If you carefully observe[q] all these
commands I am giving you to follow—to

love the LORD your God, to walk in all his
ways and to hold fast[r] to him— 23then 11:22 r Dt 10:20
the LORD will drive out all these nations
before you, and you will dispossess nations larger and stronger than you.[s] 11:23 s Dt 4:38; 9:1
24Every place where you set your foot will
be yours:[t] Your territory will extend from 11:24 t Ge 15:18;
the desert to Lebanon, and from the Euphrates River to the western sea.[a] 25No Ex 23:31; Jos 1:3; 14:9
man will be able to stand against you.
The LORD your God, as he promised you,
will put the terror and fear of you on the 11:25 u Ex 23:27;
whole land, wherever you go.[u] Dt 7:24
26See, I am setting before you today a
blessing and a curse[v]— 27the blessing[w] if 11:26 v Dt 30:1,15,19
you obey the commands of the LORD
your God that I am giving you today; 11:27 w Dt 28:1-14
28the curse if you disobey[x] the commands of the LORD your God and turn 11:28 x Dt 28:15
from the way that I command you today
by following other gods, which you have
not known. 29When the LORD your God
has brought you into the land you are entering to possess, you are to proclaim on
Mount Gerizim the blessings, and on
Mount Ebal the curses.[y] 30As you know, 11:29 y Dt 27:12-13; Jos 8:33
these mountains are across the Jordan,
west of the road,[b] toward the setting sun,
near the great trees of Moreh,[z] in the territory of those Canaanites living in the 11:30 z Ge 12:6 a Jos 4:19
Arabah in the vicinity of Gilgal.[a] 31You
are about to cross the Jordan to enter
and take possession[b] of the land the 11:31 b Dt 9:1; Jos 1:11
LORD your God is giving you. When you
have taken it over and are living there,
32be sure that you obey all the decrees
and laws I am setting before you today.

The One Place of Worship

12 These are the decrees and laws
you must be careful to follow in
the land that the LORD, the God of your
fathers, has given you to possess—as
long as you live in the land.[c] 2Destroy 12:1 c Dt 4:9-10; 1Ki 8:40
completely all the places on the high
mountains and on the hills and under
every spreading tree[d] where the nations 12:2 d 2Ki 16:4; 17:10
you are dispossessing worship their
gods. 3Break down their altars, smash[e] 12:3 e Nu 33:52;
their sacred stones and burn their Asherah poles in the fire; cut down the idols Dt 7:5; Jdg 2:2
of their gods and wipe out their names
from those places.
4You must not worship the LORD your
God in their way. 5But you are to seek

[a] 24 That is, the Mediterranean [b] 30 Or *Jordan, westward*

the place the LORD your God will choose
from among all your tribes to put his
12:5 Name there for his dwelling.[f] To that
f ver 11,13; place you must go; 6there bring your
2Ch 7:12,16 burnt offerings and sacrifices, your
12:6 g Dt 14:22-23 tithes[g] and special gifts, what you have
vowed to give and your freewill offer-
ings, and the firstborn of your herds and
flocks. 7There, in the presence of the
LORD your God, you and your families
12:7 h ver 12,18; shall eat and shall rejoice[h] in everything
Lev 23:40; you have put your hand to, because the
Dt 14:26 LORD your God has blessed you.
8You are not to do as we do here today, everyone as he sees fit, 9since you
have not yet reached the resting place
and the inheritance the LORD your God
is giving you. 10But you will cross the Jordan and settle in the land the LORD your
12:10 God is giving[i] you as an inheritance, and
i Dt 11:31 he will give you rest from all your enemies around you so that you will live in
safety. 11Then to the place the LORD your
God will choose as a dwelling for his
Name[j]—there you are to bring every- 12:11 j ver 5; Dt 15:20;
thing I command you: your burnt offer- 16:2
ings and sacrifices, your tithes and special gifts, and all the choice possessions
you have vowed to the LORD. 12And there 12:12
rejoice[k] before the LORD your God, you, k ver 7 l Dt 10:9;
your sons and daughters, your menser- 14:29
vants and maidservants, and the Levites
from your towns, who have no allotment
or inheritance[l] of their own. 13Be careful
not to sacrifice your burnt offerings anywhere you please. 14Offer them only at
the place the LORD will choose[m] in one of 12:14 m ver 11
your tribes, and there observe every-
thing I command you.
15Nevertheless, you may slaughter
your animals in any of your towns and
eat as much of the meat as you want, as
if it were gazelle or deer,[n] according to 12:15
the blessing the LORD your God gives n ver 20-23;
you. Both the ceremonially unclean and Dt 14:5; 15:22
the clean may eat it. 16But you must not 12:16
eat the blood;[o] pour it out on the ground o Ge 9:4;
like water.[p] 17You must not eat in your Lev 7:26; 17:10-
own towns the tithe of your grain and 12 p Dt 15:23
new wine and oil, or the firstborn of your
herds and flocks, or whatever you have
vowed to give, or your freewill offerings
or special gifts. 18Instead, you are to eat[q] 12:18
them in the presence of the LORD your q Dt 14:23
God at the place the LORD your God will r ver 5 s ver 7,12
choose[r]—you, your sons and daughters,
your menservants and maidservants,
and the Levites from your towns—and
you are to rejoice[s] before the LORD your
God in everything you put your hand to. 12:19
19Be careful not to neglect the Levites[t] as t Dt 14:27
long as you live in your land.
20When the LORD your God has en- 12:20
larged your territory[u] as he promised[v] u Dt 19:8
you, and you crave meat and say, "I v Ge 15:18;
would like some meat," then you may eat Dt 11:24
as much of it as you want. 21If the place
where the LORD your God chooses to put
his Name is too far away from you, you
may slaughter animals from the herds
and flocks the LORD has given you, as I
have commanded you, and in your own
towns you may eat as much of them as
you want. 22Eat them as you would
gazelle or deer.[w] Both the ceremonially 12:22
unclean and the clean may eat. 23But be w ver 15
sure you do not eat the blood,[x] because 12:23 x ver 16; Ge 9:4;
the blood is the life, and you must not Lev 17:11,14

JESUS FOCUS

A PLACE FOR GOD

God commanded the Israelites to destroy the high places of pagan religion in the new land (Deuteronomy 12:2). He then informed them that he would lead them to "the place the LORD your God will choose . . . to put his Name there for his dwelling" (verse 5). At this location they would find a "resting place . . . inheritance . . . [and] safety" (verse 9–10). In response to God's promises the Israelites first set up the tabernacle at Shiloh. Later, when David captured Jerusalem, he made that city his capital and brought the ark of the covenant there in preparation for the construction of a temple for God—which was actually completed years later by his son Solomon (1 Kings 5—6). The Samaritans later challenged the idea of a "proper" place to honor God and, in 400 B.C., built a rival temple on Mount Gerizim. This point of contention became a subject for discussion when Jesus spoke with the Samaritan woman at the well at Sychar (John 4:19–24). In response to the woman's inquiry about the correct place to worship, Jesus replied, "Salvation is from the Jews"—meaning that God had chosen Israel to reach all of humanity with his love and salvation (Luke 2:30–32). But Jesus also stated that God desires people to "worship [him] in spirit and in truth," regardless of location, implying that the place of worship is less important than the attitude of the worshiper (John 4:21–24).

eat the life with the meat. 24You must
not eat the blood; pour it out on the
ground like water. 25Do not eat it, so that
12:25 y Dt 4:40; Isa 3:10 it may go well[y] with you and your children after you, because you will be doing
z Ex 15:26; Dt 13:18; 1Ki 11:38 what is right[z] in the eyes of the LORD.
26But take your consecrated things
12:26 a ver 17; Nu 5:9-10 and whatever you have vowed to give,[a]
and go to the place the LORD will choose.
27Present your burnt offerings[b] on the
12:27 b Lev 1:5,9,13 altar of the LORD your God, both the
meat and the blood. The blood of your
sacrifices must be poured beside the altar of the LORD your God, but you may
eat the meat. 28Be careful to obey all
these regulations I am giving you, so
12:28 c ver 25; Dt 4:40 that it may always go well[c] with you and
your children after you, because you will
be doing what is good and right in the
eyes of the LORD your God.
12:29 d Jos 23:4 29The LORD your God will cut off[d] before you the nations you are about to in-
vade and dispossess. But when you have
driven them out and settled in their
land, 30and after they have been destroyed before you, be careful not to be
ensnared by inquiring about their gods,
saying, "How do these nations serve
their gods? We will do the same." 31You
must not worship the LORD your God in
their way, because in worshiping their
12:31 e Dt 9:5 f Dt 18:10; Jer 32:35 gods, they do all kinds of detestable
things the LORD hates.[e] They even burn
their sons[f] and daughters in the fire as
sacrifices to their gods.
12:32 g Dt 4:2; Jos 1:7; Rev 22:18-19 32See that you do all I command you;
do not add[g] to it or take away from it.

Worshiping Other Gods

13:1 h Mt 24:24; Mk 13:22; 2Th 2:9 13 If a prophet,[h] or one who foretells by dreams, appears among
you and announces to you a miraculous
sign or wonder, 2and if the sign or wonder of which he has spoken takes place,
13:2 i ver 6,13 and he says, "Let us follow other gods"[i]
(gods you have not known) "and let us
worship them," 3you must not listen to
the words of that prophet or dreamer.
13:3 j Dt 8:2,16 The LORD your God is testing[j] you to
find out whether you love him with all
your heart and with all your soul. 4It is
13:4 k 2Ki 23:3; 2Ch 34:31 l Dt 10:20 the LORD your God you must follow,[k]
and him you must revere. Keep his com-
mands and obey him; serve him and
hold fast[l] to him. 5That prophet or
dreamer must be put to death, because
he preached rebellion against the LORD
your God, who brought you out of Egypt
and redeemed you from the land of slavery; he has tried to turn you from the
way the LORD your God commanded
you to follow. You must purge the evil[m] 13:5 m Dt 17:7,12; 1Co 5:13
from among you.
6If your very own brother, or your son
or daughter, or the wife you love, or your
closest friend secretly entices[n] you, say- 13:6 n Dt 17:2-7; 29:18
ing, "Let us go and worship other gods"
(gods that neither you nor your fathers
have known, 7gods of the peoples
around you, whether near or far, from
one end of the land to the other), 8do not
yield[o] to him or listen to him. Show him 13:8 o Pr 1:10
no pity. Do not spare him or shield him.
9You must certainly put him to death.[p] 13:9 p Dt 17:5,7
Your hand must be the first in putting
him to death, and then the hands of all
the people. 10Stone him to death, because he tried to turn you away from the
LORD your God, who brought you out of
Egypt, out of the land of slavery. 11Then
all Israel will hear and be afraid,[q] and no 13:11 q Dt 19:20
one among you will do such an evil thing
again.
12If you hear it said about one of the
towns the LORD your God is giving you
to live in 13that wicked men[r] have arisen 13:13 r ver 2,6; 1Jn 2:19
among you and have led the people of
their town astray, saying, "Let us go and
worship other gods" (gods you have not
known), 14then you must inquire, probe
and investigate it thoroughly. And if it is
true and it has been proved that this detestable thing has been done among
you, 15you must certainly put to the
sword all who live in that town. Destroy
it completely,[a] both its people and its
livestock. 16Gather all the plunder of the
town into the middle of the public
square and completely burn the town
and all its plunder as a whole burnt of-
fering to the LORD your God.[s] It is to re- 13:16 s Jos 6:24 t Jos 8:28; Jer 49:2
main a ruin[t] forever, never to be rebuilt.
17None of those condemned things[a]
shall be found in your hands, so that the
LORD will turn from his fierce anger;[u] he 13:17 u Nu 25:4 v Dt 30:3 w Dt 7:13 x Ge 22:17; 26:4, 24; 28:14
will show you mercy, have compassion[v]
on you, and increase your numbers,[w] as
he promised[x] on oath to your forefathers, 18because you obey the LORD your
God, keeping all his commands that I

a 15,17 The Hebrew term refers to the irrevocable giving over of things or persons to the LORD, often by totally destroying them.

The High Cost of Rebellion

God's people needed to know how to tell the difference between one of God's prophets and a false prophet. The book of Deuteronomy lists three tests. First, every prediction of a true prophet comes true (Deuteronomy 18:21–22). There are numerous examples in the Gospels to illustrate that Jesus met this criterion (see, for example, Matthew 16:21–26; Mark 9:30–32; 10:32–34; Luke 19:41–44; 22:31–38). Second, signs and wonders from God accompany the message (Deuteronomy 13:2; see also Mark 1:40–45). And third, God's prophet will always call people to follow the one true God (Deuteronomy 13:2–3; see also John 4:34; 6:38; 10:37–38; 12:49–50; 17:1–5). If a prophet's message failed any of these tests, he was to be rejected. Even today God's true spokesmen and women will always encourage his people to follow, revere, obey, serve and cling to him alone (Deuteronomy 13:4). This was so important to God that he demanded that false prophets be executed (verses 5,10,15).

There are several reasons for so severe a penalty. For one, false prophets who did not encourage people to follow God were in effect preaching rebellion *against* the command to "have no other gods before [him]" (Exodus 20:3) and against acceptance of the reality of God's provision and the truth of God's deliverance from slavery (Exodus 20:5). In God's eyes turning away from him is as serious a sin as worshiping Satan himself or practicing the occult (1 Samuel 15:23).

The second reason is that God requires purity from his people: "You must purge the evil from among you," he said (Deuteronomy 13:5). Sin contaminates, and "just a little" evil among his people will eventually corrupt the entire community. Sin and those who promote it must be removed from among God's people (1 Corinthians 5:13).

The third reason for the harsh penalty is that false prophets are used by Satan to accomplish his work. They are referred to as "wicked men" (Deuteronomy 13:13); the word used has its root in *belial*, which is later used by Paul as a name for Satan (2 Corinthians 6:15).

Finally, the punishment was so uncompromising because God wanted to preserve his people. If false prophets were allowed to speak unchecked, they could lead God's people into false religion and marriages with ungodly partners. As a result, the nation of Israel would lose her identity as God's covenant people. Preservation of the family line of God's promised Messiah would be in jeopardy. God planned to use the Jewish people to bring all of humanity back into a relationship with him. Any threat to their unique identity and existence as a people had to be eradicated.

All of us need to be careful who we are listening to. When we love God, we must be willing to do whatever it takes to eliminate the false influences from our lives—no matter what measures may be involved.

Self-Discovery: *Think of one instance in which a "little" sin has had big consequences in your life or in the life of someone you love.*

GO TO DISCOVERY 46 ON PAGE 244

13:18 am giving you today and doing what is
[y]Dt 12:25,28 right[y] in his eyes.

Clean and Unclean Food

14:1 **14** You are the children[z] of the
[z]Lev 19:28; 21:5; Jer 16:6; 41:5; Ro 8:14; 9:8; Gal 3:26 LORD your God. Do not cut
yourselves or shave the front of your
heads for the dead, 2for you are a people
14:2 holy to the LORD your God.[a] Out of all
[a]Lev 20:26 [b]Dt 7:6; 26:18-19 the peoples on the face of the earth, the
LORD has chosen you to be his treasured
possession.[b]
14:3 3Do not eat any detestable thing.[c]
[c]Eze 4:14 4These are the animals you may eat:[d] the
14:4 ox, the sheep, the goat, 5the deer, the
[d]Lev 11:2-45; Ac 10:14 gazelle, the roe deer, the wild goat,
the ibex, the antelope and the mountain
sheep.[a] 6You may eat any animal that
has a split hoof divided in two and
that chews the cud. 7However, of those
that chew the cud or that have a split
hoof completely divided you may not
eat the camel, the rabbit or the coney.[b]
Although they chew the cud, they do
not have a split hoof; they are ceremonially unclean for you. 8The pig is also unclean; although it has a split hoof, it does
14:8 not chew the cud. You are not to eat
[e]Lev 11:26-27 their meat or touch their carcasses.[e]

> JESUS WAS AN INCISIVE THINKER. HE GAVE NEW LIFE AND MEANING TO MUCH THAT WAS MERELY TRADITIONAL.
>
> Clifford Wilson, *Australian Scholar*

9Of all the creatures living in the water, you may eat any that has fins and
scales. 10But anything that does not have
fins and scales you may not eat; for you
it is unclean.
11You may eat any clean bird. 12But
these you may not eat: the eagle, the vulture, the black vulture, 13the red kite, the
black kite, any kind of falcon, 14any kind
of raven, 15the horned owl, the screech
owl, the gull, any kind of hawk, 16the little owl, the great owl, the white owl, 17the
desert owl, the osprey, the cormorant,
18the stork, any kind of heron, the hoopoe and the bat.
19All flying insects that swarm are unclean to you; do not eat them. 20But any
winged creature that is clean you may
eat.

21Do not eat anything you find al-
ready dead.[f] You may give it to an alien 14:21
living in any of your towns, and he may [f]Lev 17:15; 22:8 [g]ver 2
eat it, or you may sell it to a foreigner. [h]Ex 23:19; 34:26
But you are a people holy to the LORD
your God.[g]
Do not cook a young goat in its mother's milk.[h]

Tithes

22Be sure to set aside a tenth[i] of all 14:22
that your fields produce each year. 23Eat [i]Lev 27:30; Dt 12:6,17; Ne 10:37
the tithe of your grain, new wine and oil,
and the firstborn of your herds and
flocks in the presence of the LORD your
God at the place he will choose as a
dwelling for his Name,[j] so that you may 14:23 [j]Dt 12:5
learn[k] to revere the LORD your God al- [k]Dt 4:10
ways. 24But if that place is too distant
and you have been blessed by the LORD
your God and cannot carry your tithe
(because the place where the LORD will
choose to put his Name is so far away),
25then exchange your tithe for silver, and
take the silver with you and go to the
place the LORD your God will choose.
26Use the silver to buy whatever you like:
cattle, sheep, wine or other fermented
drink, or anything you wish. Then you
and your household shall eat there in the
presence of the LORD your God and re- 14:26
joice.[l] 27And do not neglect the Levites[m] [l]Dt 12:7-8
living in your towns, for they have no al- 14:27 [m]Dt 12:19
lotment or inheritance of their own.[n] [n]Nu 18:20
28At the end of every three years,
bring all the tithes of that year's produce
and store it in your towns,[o] 29so that the 14:28
Levites (who have no allotment[p] or in- [o]Dt 26:12
heritance of their own) and the aliens,[q] 14:29
the fatherless and the widows who live [p]ver 27 [q]Dt 26:12
in your towns may come and eat and be [r]Dt 15:10; Mal 3:10
satisfied, and so that the LORD your God
may bless[r] you in all the work of your
hands.

The Year for Canceling Debts

15 At the end of every seven years 15:1
you must cancel debts.[s] 2This is [s]Dt 31:10
how it is to be done: Every creditor shall
cancel the loan he has made to his fellow
Israelite. He shall not require payment
from his fellow Israelite or brother, because the LORD's time for canceling
debts has been proclaimed. 3You may re-

[a] *5* The precise identification of some of the birds and animals in this chapter is uncertain.
[b] *7* That is, the hyrax or rock badger

15:3 quire payment from a foreigner,[t] but you
t Dt 23:20 must cancel any debt your brother owes
you. 4However, there should be no poor
among you, for in the land the LORD your
God is giving you to possess as your in-
15:4 heritance, he will richly bless[u] you, 5if
u Dt 28:8 only you fully obey the LORD your God
15:5 and are careful to follow[v] all these com-
v Dt 28:1 mands I am giving you today. 6For the
LORD your God will bless you as he has
promised, and you will lend to many nations but will borrow from none. You
15:6 will rule over many nations but none
w Dt 28:12-13, 44 will rule over you.[w]
7If there is a poor man among your
brothers in any of the towns of the land
that the LORD your God is giving you, do
15:7 not be hardhearted or tightfisted[x] to-
x 1Jn 3:17 ward your poor brother. 8Rather be
15:8 openhanded[y] and freely lend him what-
y Mt 5:42; Lk 6:34 ever he needs. 9Be careful not to harbor
this wicked thought: "The seventh year,
15:9 the year for canceling debts,[z] is near," so
z ver 1 a Mt 20:15 that you do not show ill will[a] toward
b Dt 24:15 your needy brother and give him nothing. He may then appeal to the LORD
against you, and you will be found guilty
of sin.[b] 10Give generously to him and do
15:10 so without a grudging heart;[c] then be-
c 2Co 9:5 d Dt 14:29; 24:19 cause of this the LORD your God will
bless[d] you in all your work and in every-
thing you put your hand to. 11There will
always be poor people in the land.
Therefore I command you to be open-
15:11 handed toward your brothers and to-
e Mt 26:11; Mk 14:7; Jn 12:8 ward the poor and needy in your land.[e]

Freeing Servants

12If a fellow Hebrew, a man or a
woman, sells himself to you and serves
you six years, in the seventh year you
15:12 must let him go free.[f] 13And when you
f Ex 21:2; Lev 25:39; Jer 34:14 release him, do not send him away empty-handed. 14Supply him liberally from
your flock, your threshing floor and your
winepress. Give to him as the LORD your
God has blessed you. 15Remember that
15:15 you were slaves[g] in Egypt and the LORD
g Dt 5:15 h Dt 16:12 your God redeemed you.[h] That is why I
give you this command today.
16But if your servant says to you, "I do
not want to leave you," because he loves
you and your family and is well off with
you, 17then take an awl and push it
through his ear lobe into the door, and
he will become your servant for life. Do
the same for your maidservant.
18Do not consider it a hardship to set
your servant free, because his service to
you these six years has been worth twice
as much as that of a hired hand. And the
LORD your God will bless you in everything you do.

The Firstborn Animals

19Set apart for the LORD your God
every firstborn male[i] of your herds and 15:19 i Ex 13:2
flocks. Do not put the firstborn of your
oxen to work, and do not shear the firstborn of your sheep. 20Each year you and
your family are to eat them in the presence of the LORD your God at the place
he will choose.[j] 21If an animal has a de- 15:20 j Dt 12:5-7,17, 18; 14:23
fect, is lame or blind, or has any serious
flaw, you must not sacrifice it to the 15:21
LORD your God.[k] 22You are to eat it in k Lev 22:19-25
your own towns. Both the ceremonially
unclean and the clean may eat it, as if it 15:22
were gazelle or deer.[l] 23But you must not l Dt 12:15,22
eat the blood; pour it out on the ground 15:23
like water.[m] m Dt 12:16

Passover

16 Observe the month of Abib[n] 16:1
and celebrate the Passover of n Ex 12:2; 13:4
the LORD your God, because in the
month of Abib he brought you out of
Egypt by night. 2Sacrifice as the Passover to the LORD your God an animal
from your flock or herd at the place the
LORD will choose as a dwelling for his 16:2
Name.[o] 3Do not eat it with bread made o Dt 12:5,26
with yeast, but for seven days eat un- 16:3
leavened bread, the bread of affliction,[p] p Ex 12:8,39; 34:18
because you left Egypt in haste[q]—so q Ex 12:11,15,19
that all the days of your life you may re- r Ex 13:3,6-7
member the time of your departure
from Egypt.[r] 4Let no yeast be found in
your possession in all your land for sev-
en days. Do not let any of the meat you
sacrifice on the evening of the first day 16:4
remain until morning.[s] s Ex 12:10; 34:25
5You must not sacrifice the Passover
in any town the LORD your God gives you
6except in the place he will choose as a
dwelling for his Name. There you must
sacrifice the Passover in the evening, 16:6
when the sun goes down, on the an- t Ex 12:6;
niversary[a][t] of your departure from Dt 12:5
Egypt. 7Roast[u] it and eat it at the place 16:7
the LORD your God will choose. Then in u Ex 12:8; 2Ch 35:13
the morning return to your tents. 8For
six days eat unleavened bread and on

[a] 6 Or *down, at the time of day*

16:8 [v]Ex 12:16; 13:6; the seventh day hold an assembly[v] to
Lev 23:8 the LORD your God and do no work.

Feast of Weeks

16:9 [w]Ex 34:22; 9Count off seven weeks[w] from the
Lev 23:15 time you begin to put the sickle to the
[x]Ex 23:16; standing grain.[x] 10Then celebrate
Nu 28:26 the Feast of Weeks to the LORD your God
by giving a freewill offering in proportion to the blessings the LORD your God
16:11 [y]Dt 12:7 has given you. 11And rejoice[y] before the
[z]Dt 12:12 LORD your God at the place he will
choose as a dwelling for his Name—you,
your sons and daughters, your menservants and maidservants, the Levites[z] in
your towns, and the aliens, the fatherless
and the widows living among you. 12Re-
16:12 [a]Dt 15:15 member that you were slaves in Egypt,[a]
and follow carefully these decrees.

Feast of Tabernacles

13Celebrate the Feast of Tabernacles
16:13 [b]Lev 23:34 for seven days after you have gathered
[c]Ex 23:16 the produce of your threshing floor[b] and
your winepress.[c] 14Be joyful[d] at your
16:14 [d]ver 11 Feast—you, your sons and daughters,
your menservants and maidservants,
and the Levites, the aliens, the fatherless
and the widows who live in your towns.
15For seven days celebrate the Feast to
the LORD your God at the place the LORD
will choose. For the LORD your God will
16:15 [e]Lev 23:39 bless you in all your harvest and in all
the work of your hands, and your joy[e]
will be complete.
16Three times a year all your men
must appear before the LORD your God
at the place he will choose: at the Feast
16:16 of Unleavened Bread, the Feast of Weeks
[f]Ex 23:14,16 and the Feast of Tabernacles.[f] No man
[g]Ex 34:20 should appear before the LORD empty-
handed:[g] 17Each of you must bring a gift
in proportion to the way the LORD your
God has blessed you.

Judges

16:18 [h]Dt 1:16 18Appoint judges[h] and officials for
each of your tribes in every town the
LORD your God is giving you, and they
16:19 shall judge the people fairly. 19Do not
[i]Ex 23:2,8 pervert justice[i] or show partiality.[j] Do
[j]Lev 19:15; Dt 1:17 not accept a bribe,[k] for a bribe blinds
[k]Ecc 7:7 the eyes of the wise and twists the words
of the righteous. 20Follow justice and
justice alone, so that you may live and
possess the land the LORD your God is
giving you.

Worshiping Other Gods

21Do not set up any wooden Asherah 16:21 [l]Dt 7:5
pole[a][l] beside the altar you build to the [m]Ex 34:13; 2Ki 17:16; 21:3;
LORD your God,[m] 22and do not erect a sa- 2Ch 33:3
cred stone,[n] for these the LORD your God
hates. 16:22 [n]Lev 26:1

17 Do not sacrifice to the LORD
your God an ox or a sheep that
has any defect[o] or flaw in it, for that 17:1 [o]Mal 1:8,13
would be detestable to him.[p] [p]Dt 15:21
2If a man or woman living among you
in one of the towns the LORD gives you is 17:2 [q]Dt 13:6-11
found doing evil in the eyes of the LORD
your God in violation of his covenant,[q]
3and contrary to my command[r] has 17:3 [r]Jer 7:22-23
worshiped other gods, bowing down to [s]Job 31:26
them or to the sun[s] or the moon or the
stars of the sky, 4and this has been
brought to your attention, then you
must investigate it thoroughly. If it is 17:4
true and it has been proved that this de- [t]Dt 13:12-14
testable thing has been done in Israel,[t]
5take the man or woman who has done 17:5 [u]Lev 24:14
this evil deed to your city gate and stone
that person to death.[u] 6On the testimo- 17:6 [v]Nu 35:30;
ny of two or three witnesses a man shall Dt 19:15;
be put to death, but no one shall be put Jos 7:25; Mt 18:16;
to death on the testimony of only one Jn 8:17; 2Co 13:1;
witness.[v] 7The hands of the witnesses 1Ti 5:19;
must be the first in putting him to Heb 10:28

[a] 21 Or *Do not plant any tree dedicated to Asherah*

JESUS AND YOU

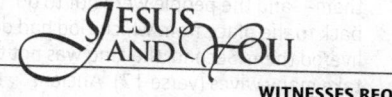

WITNESSES REQUIRED

One provision of the law God gave his people through Moses stipulated that no one could be condemned based on the testimony of a single witness (Deuteronomy 17:6–7). Jesus would later use this same principle to teach us how to deal with someone who has sinned against us (Matthew 18:15–20). He explained three steps to follow in order to resolve personal conflicts. Initially, the confrontation should be *personal*, "just between the two of you" (Matthew 18:15). If the issue cannot be resolved in this way, the discussion should become *plural*, involving two or three witnesses (verse 16). Finally, in the event of a continuing impasse, the confrontation should be made *public*: "Tell it to the church" (verse 17). Both Israel and the church are viewed in Scripture as God's community of people, and he wants us to respect and love one another with the same attitude of compassion that he has shown to us.

DISCOVERY 46

So You Want to Be King!

Long before Israel had her first king, God specified instructions about the kind of king the nation should have. First, God himself wanted to choose the king (Deuteronomy 17:15). Israel was not a democracy but a *theocracy*, a system of government in which God was the leader—the One who in a direct manner deputized human appointees to lead the people his way. God used his prophets to reveal to the people who their king should be (1 Samuel 9—12; 16; 1 Kings 1). Second, the king had to be Jewish; the issue was not one of race but of spiritual devotion (Deuteronomy 17:15).

With regard to future kings, God issued a warning with three components. First, the king was not to accumulate a large number of horses (verse 16). God wanted the king and his army to be dependent on *him* rather than on their own military strength. Acquiring horses would also entail returning to Egypt to purchase them—and the people were not to go back to the place from which God had delivered them. Second, the king was not to take many wives (verse 17). Ancient kings often acquired wives from the surrounding nations to seal political alliances. God prohibited this because he wanted the Israelites to depend on *him* rather than on their own political savvy. These foreign wives might also lead the king's heart toward other gods, which in fact they later often did. Finally, the king was not to accumulate large amounts of wealth, lest he be tempted to rely on his riches instead of on his God (Deuteronomy 17:17; Proverbs 30:8–9).

The king whom God chose was to be given his own copy of the Mosaic law, and he should "read it all the days of his life so that he may learn to revere the LORD his God and follow carefully all the words of this law" (Deuteronomy 17:19). Although he would be the leader of the nation, the king would never be exempt from the law. If anything, he would need to be an even more careful student of and obedient servant to that law, so that he could lead God's people in God's way.

In all the history of Israel, not one of the kings kept the law flawlessly—until God sent the final, perfect King: Jesus Christ. He was chosen by God himself, depended on him alone and followed the Father's desires in every detail.

Every person who walks with God is a leader in some way. God wants each of us to live in a manner that will cause others to want to know him. Just as the Old Testament kings were to function as servants on behalf of the people, so we are to surrender our wills and live lives of thankful service to Jesus and other people (Deuteronomy 17:20; Mark 10:42–45).

Each of us as a believer in Jesus fills a kingly role (2 Timothy 2:12), but we are always in the service of the King of kings. Walking humbly with Jesus and loving others comprise God's prescription for leading a life that honors and pleases our glorious King. In the words of the apostle Paul, "Now to the King [Jesus] eternal, immortal, invisible, the only God, be honor and glory for ever and ever. Amen" (1 Timothy 1:17).

***Self-Discovery:** How does it affect your daily life to acknowledge Jesus as King?*

GO TO DISCOVERY 47 ON PAGE 247

17:7 death, and then the hands of all the peo-
[w] Dt 13:5,9 ple. You must purge the evil[w] from
among you.

Law Courts

8 If cases come before your courts that
are too difficult for you to judge—
17:8 whether bloodshed, lawsuits or as-
[x] 2Ch 19:10 saults[x]—take them to the place the
[y] Dt 12:5; Hag 2:11 LORD your God will choose.[y] 9 Go to the
17:9 priests, who are Levites, and to the judge
[z] Dt 19:17; who is in office at that time. Inquire of
Eze 44:24 them and they will give you the verdict.[z]
10 You must act according to the deci-
sions they give you at the place the LORD
will choose. Be careful to do everything
they direct you to do. 11 Act according to
the law they teach you and the decisions
they give you. Do not turn aside from
17:11 what they tell you, to the right or to the
[a] Dt 25:1 left.[a] 12 The man who shows contempt[b]
17:12 for the judge or for the priest who stands
[b] Nu 15:30 ministering there to the LORD your God
must be put to death. You must purge
the evil from Israel. 13 All the people will
17:13 hear and be afraid, and will not be con-
[c] Dt 13:11; 19:20 temptuous again.[c]

The King

14 When you enter the land the LORD
your God is giving you and have taken
17:14 possession of it and settled in it, and you
[d] Dt 11:31; say, "Let us set a king over us like all the
1Sa 8:5,19-20 nations around us,"[d] 15 be sure to appoint
over you the king the LORD your God
17:15 chooses. He must be from among your
[e] Jer 30:21 own brothers.[e] Do not place a foreigner
over you, one who is not a brother Israelite. 16 The king, moreover, must not ac-
17:16 quire great numbers of horses for him-
[f] 1Ki 4:26; 10:26 self[f] or make the people return to Egypt[g]
[g] Isa 31:1; to get more of them,[h] for the LORD has
Hos 11:5 told you, "You are not to go back that
[h] 1Ki 10:28; Eze 17:15 way again."[i] 17 He must not take many
[i] Ex 13:17 wives,[j] or his heart will be led astray. He
17:17 must not accumulate large amounts of
[j] 1Ki 11:3 silver and gold.
17:18 18 When he takes the throne of his
[k] Dt 31:22,24 kingdom, he is to write[k] for himself on a
scroll a copy of this law, taken from that
of the priests, who are Levites. 19 It is to
17:19 be with him, and he is to read it all the
[l] Jos 1:8 days of his life[l] so that he may learn to
revere the LORD his God and follow carefully all the words of this law and these
decrees 20 and not consider himself better than his brothers and turn from the
law[m] to the right or to the left.[n] Then he 17:20
and his descendants will reign a long [m] 1Ki 15:5
time over his kingdom in Israel. [n] Dt 5:32

Offerings for Priests and Levites

18 The priests, who are Levites—
indeed the whole tribe of
Levi—are to have no allotment or inheritance with Israel. They shall live on the
offerings made to the LORD by fire, for
that is their inheritance.[o] 2 They shall 18:1
have no inheritance among their broth- [o] Dt 10:9;
ers; the LORD is their inheritance, as he 1Co 9:13
promised them.

3 This is the share due the priests from
the people who sacrifice a bull or a
sheep: the shoulder, the jowls and the inner parts.[p] 4 You are to give them the 18:3
firstfruits of your grain, new wine and [p] Lev 7:28-34
oil, and the first wool from the shearing 18:4
of your sheep,[q] 5 for the LORD your God [q] Ex 22:29;
has chosen them[r] and their descendants Nu 18:12 18:5
out of all your tribes to stand and min- [r] Ex 28:1
ister[s] in the LORD's name always. [s] Dt 10:8

6 If a Levite moves from one of your
towns anywhere in Israel where he is living, and comes in all earnestness to the
place the LORD will choose,[t] 7 he may 18:6
minister in the name of the LORD his [t] Nu 35:2-3
God like all his fellow Levites who serve
there in the presence of the LORD. 8 He is
to share equally in their benefits, even
though he has received money from the 18:8
sale of family possessions.[u] [u] 2Ch 31:4; Ne 12:44,47

Detestable Practices

9 When you enter the land the LORD
your God is giving you, do not learn to 18:9
imitate[v] the detestable ways of the na- [v] Dt 12:29-31
tions there. 10 Let no one be found
among you who sacrifices his son or
daughter in[a] the fire, who practices div- 18:10
ination[w] or sorcery, interprets omens, [w] Dt 12:31
engages in witchcraft,[x] 11 or casts spells, [x] Lev 19:31
or who is a medium or spiritist or who
consults the dead. 12 Anyone who does
these things is detestable to the LORD,
and because of these detestable practices the LORD your God will drive out 18:12
those nations before you.[y] 13 You must be [y] Lev 18:24;
blameless before the LORD your God. Dt 9:4

The Prophet

14 The nations you will dispossess listen to those who practice sorcery or div-

[a] 10 *Or who makes his son or daughter pass through*

ination. But as for you, the LORD your God has not permitted you to do so. 15 The LORD your God will raise up for you a prophet like me from among your own brothers.[z] You must listen to him. 16 For this is what you asked of the LORD your God at Horeb on the day of the assembly when you said, "Let us not hear the voice of the LORD our God nor see this great fire anymore, or we will die."[a]

17 The LORD said to me: "What they say is good. 18 I will raise up for them a prophet like you from among their brothers; I will put my words[b] in his mouth, and he will tell them everything I command him.[c] 19 If anyone does not listen to my words that the prophet speaks in my name, I myself will call him to account.[d] 20 But a prophet who presumes to speak in my name anything I have not commanded him to say, or a prophet who speaks in the name of other gods,[e] must be put to death."[f]

21 You may say to yourselves, "How can we know when a message has not been spoken by the LORD?" 22 If what a prophet proclaims in the name of the LORD does not take place or come true, that is a message the LORD has not spoken.[g] That prophet has spoken presumptuously.[h] Do not be afraid of him.

18:15 [z] Jn 1:21; Ac 3:22*; 7:37*
18:16 [a] Ex 20:19; Dt 5:23-27
18:18 [b] Isa 51:16; Jn 17:8 [c] Jn 4:25-26; 8:28; 12:49-50
18:19 [d] Ac 3:23*
18:20 [e] Jer 14:14 [f] Dt 13:1-5
18:22 [g] Jer 28:9 [h] ver 20

> FOR JESUS CHRIST TO ME IS THE OUTSTANDING PERSONALITY OF ALL TIME . . . EVERYTHING HE EVER SAID OR DID HAS VALUE FOR US TODAY, AND THAT IS SOMETHING YOU CAN SAY OF NO OTHER MAN, ALIVE OR DEAD.
>
> Sholem Asck, *Jewish Author*

Cities of Refuge

19 When the LORD your God has destroyed the nations whose land he is giving you, and when you have driven them out and settled in their towns and houses,[i] 2 then set aside for yourselves three cities centrally located in the land the LORD your God is giving you to possess. 3 Build roads to them and divide into three parts the land the LORD your God is giving you as an inheritance, so that anyone who kills a man may flee there.

19:1 [i] Dt 12:29

4 This is the rule concerning the man who kills another and flees there to save his life—one who kills his neighbor unintentionally, without malice aforethought. 5 For instance, a man may go into the forest with his neighbor to cut wood, and as he swings his ax to fell a tree, the head may fly off and hit his neighbor and kill him. That man may flee to one of these cities and save his life. 6 Otherwise, the avenger of blood[j] might pursue him in a rage, overtake him if the distance is too great, and kill him even though he is not deserving of death, since he did it to his neighbor without malice aforethought. 7 This is why I command you to set aside for yourselves three cities.

8 If the LORD your God enlarges your territory, as he promised on oath to your forefathers, and gives you the whole land he promised them, 9 because you carefully follow all these laws I command you today—to love the LORD your God and to walk always in his ways[k]—then you are to set aside three more cities. 10 Do this so that innocent blood will not be shed in your land, which the LORD your God is giving you as your inheritance, and so that you will not be guilty of bloodshed.[l]

11 But if a man hates his neighbor and lies in wait for him, assaults and kills him,[m] and then flees to one of these cities, 12 the elders of his town shall send for him, bring him back from the city, and hand him over to the avenger of blood to die. 13 Show him no pity.[n] You must purge from Israel the guilt of shedding innocent blood,[o] so that it may go well with you.

14 Do not move your neighbor's boundary stone set up by your predecessors in the inheritance you receive in the land the LORD your God is giving you to possess.[p]

Witnesses

15 One witness is not enough to convict a man accused of any crime or offense he may have committed. A matter must be established by the testimony of two or three witnesses.[q]

16 If a malicious witness[r] takes the stand to accuse a man of a crime, 17 the two men involved in the dispute must stand in the presence of the LORD before the priests and the judges[s] who are in

19:6 [j] Nu 35:12
19:9 [k] Jos 20:7-8
19:10 [l] Nu 35:33; Dt 21:1-9
19:11 [m] Nu 35:16
19:13 [n] Dt 7:2 [o] 1Ki 2:31
19:14 [p] Dt 27:17; Pr 22:28; Hos 5:10
19:15 [q] Nu 35:30; Dt 17:6; Mt 18:16*; Jn 8:17; 2Co 13:1*; 1Ti 5:19; Heb 10:28
19:16 [r] Ex 23:1; Ps 27:12
19:17 [s] Dt 17:9

THE TRUE PROPHET

Many people wish that God would speak to them in the same way we talk to one another—face-to-face so that they would know exactly what he wants from them. But when God spoke directly to his people in the Old Testament, the encounter was more than they could handle, and they asked God instead to communicate with them through prophets. Exodus 20:19 records the terrified response of the Israelites after they had witnessed God's fearsome display of power from Mount Sinai, when they implored Moses, "Speak to us yourself and we will listen. But do not have God speak to us or we will die."

God had already given them Moses as their first spokesperson, and he represented the beginning of a long succession of men and women whose lives would be dedicated to speaking God's truth. But one future prophet would do more than speak for God. This coming prophet would himself be God—we know that this prophet did come, that he was God incarnate (in the flesh) and that his name was Jesus.

This promised future prophet would surpass all others in several ways. God would choose, anoint and guide him in a unique manner. This prophet would have no need to declare himself as a prophet of God; God himself would make the announcement. The prophet would speak only the words God would give him (Deuteronomy 18:18). Other prophets would be fallible, except when they were communicating God's words directly, but Jesus would be completely sinless—because he is God the Son. Throughout history many people have claimed to speak for God, but few of their predictions have become reality. When God sends a true prophet, his people cannot escape responsibility for listening to him (verse 19).

God's plan was to speak to his people through his prophets, and their number includes Jesus, his final Word (John 1:1–5). He still expects us to listen to and follow that Word every day, thereby living life the way he intended it to be lived.

The writer to the Hebrews opened his book with a beautiful statement of this truth: "In the past God spoke to our forefathers through the prophets at many times and in various ways, but in these last days he has spoken to us by his Son, whom he appointed heir of all things, and through whom he made the universe" (Hebrews 1:1–2).

Self-Discovery: *Have you ever experienced Jesus speaking with you so intimately that you felt that you were having a face-to-face exchange? What causes this experience to stand out in your memory? Were there life-changing consequences?*

GO TO DISCOVERY 48 ON PAGE 253

office at the time. 18The judges must
make a thorough investigation, and if the
witness proves to be a liar, giving false tes-
19:19 t Pr 19:5,9 timony against his brother, 19then do to
him as he intended to do to his brother.[t]
19:20 u Dt 17:13; 21:21 You must purge the evil from among you.
20The rest of the people will hear of this
19:21 v ver 13 w Ex 21:24; Lev 24:20; Mt 5:38* and be afraid,[u] and never again will such
an evil thing be done among you. 21Show
no pity:[v] life for life, eye for eye, tooth for
tooth, hand for hand, foot for foot.[w]

Going to War

20 When you go to war against
your enemies and see horses
and chariots and an army greater than
20:1 x Ps 20:7; Isa 31:1 y Dt 31:6,8 z 2Ch 32:7-8 yours,[x] do not be afraid[y] of them,[z] because the LORD your God, who brought
you up out of Egypt, will be with you.
2When you are about to go into battle,
the priest shall come forward and address the army. 3He shall say: "Hear, O Israel, today you are going into battle
against your enemies. Do not be faint-
20:3 a Jos 23:10 hearted[a] or afraid; do not be terrified or
give way to panic before them. 4For the
LORD your God is the one who goes with
20:4 b Dt 1:30; 3:22; Jos 23:10 you to fight[b] for you against your enemies to give you victory."
5The officers shall say to the army:
"Has anyone built a new house and not
20:5 c Ne 12:27 dedicated[c] it? Let him go home, or he
may die in battle and someone else may
dedicate it. 6Has anyone planted a vineyard and not begun to enjoy it? Let him
go home, or he may die in battle and
someone else enjoy it. 7Has anyone become pledged to a woman and not married her? Let him go home, or he may die
20:7 d Dt 24:5 in battle and someone else marry her.[d]"
8Then the officers shall add, "Is any man
afraid or fainthearted? Let him go home
so that his brothers will not become dis-
20:8 e Jdg 7:3 heartened too."[e] 9When the officers have
finished speaking to the army, they shall
appoint commanders over it.
10When you march up to attack a city,
20:10 f Lk 14:31-32 make its people an offer of peace.[f] 11If
they accept and open their gates, all the
people in it shall be subject to forced la-
20:11 g 1Ki 9:21 bor[g] and shall work for you. 12If they refuse to make peace and they engage you
in battle, lay siege to that city. 13When
the LORD your God delivers it into your
20:13 h Nu 31:7 hand, put to the sword all the men in it.[h]
14As for the women, the children, the
20:14 i Jos 8:2; 22:8 livestock[i] and everything else in the city,
you may take these as plunder for your-
selves. And you may use the plunder the
LORD your God gives you from your enemies. 15This is how you are to treat all
the cities that are at a distance from you
and do not belong to the nations nearby.
16However, in the cities of the nations
the LORD your God is giving you as an
inheritance, do not leave alive anything 20:16 j Ex 23:31-33; Nu 21:2-3; Dt 7:2; Jos 11:14
that breathes.[j] 17Completely destroy[a]
them—the Hittites, Amorites, Canaanites, Perizzites, Hivites and Jebusites—
as the LORD your God has commanded
you. 18Otherwise, they will teach you to 20:18 k Ex 34:16; Dt 7:4; 12:30-31 l Ex 23:33
follow all the detestable things they do
in worshiping their gods,[k] and you will
sin[l] against the LORD your God.
19When you lay siege to a city for a
long time, fighting against it to capture
it, do not destroy its trees by putting an
ax to them, because you can eat their
fruit. Do not cut them down. Are the
trees of the field people, that you should
besiege them?[b] 20However, you may cut
down trees that you know are not fruit
trees and use them to build siege works
until the city at war with you falls.

Atonement for an Unsolved Murder

21 If a man is found slain, lying in
a field in the land the LORD your
God is giving you to possess, and it is
not known who killed him, 2your elders
and judges shall go out and measure the
distance from the body to the neighboring towns. 3Then the elders of the town
nearest the body shall take a heifer that
has never been worked and has never
worn a yoke 4and lead her down to a valley that has not been plowed or planted
and where there is a flowing stream.
There in the valley they are to break the
heifer's neck. 5The priests, the sons of
Levi, shall step forward, for the LORD
your God has chosen them to minister 21:5 m 1Ch 23:13 n Dt 17:8-11
and to pronounce blessings[m] in the
name of the LORD and to decide all cases
of dispute and assault.[n] 6Then all the
elders of the town nearest the body shall
wash their hands[o] over the heifer whose 21:6 o Mt 27:24
neck was broken in the valley, 7and they
shall declare: "Our hands did not shed
this blood, nor did our eyes see it done.

a 17 The Hebrew term refers to the irrevocable giving over of things or persons to the LORD, often by totally destroying them. *b 19* Or *down to use in the siege, for the fruit trees are for the benefit of man.*

8 Accept this atonement for your people
Israel, whom you have redeemed,
O LORD, and do not hold your people
21:8 guilty of the blood of an innocent man."
p Nu 35:33-34 And the bloodshed will be atoned for.[p]
21:9 9 So you will purge[q] from yourselves the
q Dt 19:13 guilt of shedding innocent blood, since
you have done what is right in the eyes
of the LORD.

Marrying a Captive Woman

10 When you go to war against your
enemies and the LORD your God delivers
21:10 them into your hands[r] and you take
r Jos 21:44 captives, 11 if you notice among the captives a beautiful woman and are attract-
ed to her, you may take her as your wife.
12 Bring her into your home and have her
21:12 shave her head,[s] trim her nails 13 and put
s Lev 14:9; Nu 6:9 aside the clothes she was wearing when
captured. After she has lived in your
house and mourned her father and
21:13 t Ps 45:10 mother for a full month,[t] then you may
go to her and be her husband and she
shall be your wife. 14 If you are not
pleased with her, let her go wherever she
wishes. You must not sell her or treat her
21:14 as a slave, since you have dishonored
u Ge 34:2 her.[u]

The Right of the Firstborn

15 If a man has two wives, and he loves
one but not the other, and both bear
him sons but the firstborn is the son of
21:15 the wife he does not love,[v] 16 when he
v Ge 29:33 wills his property to his sons, he must
not give the rights of the firstborn to the
son of the wife he loves in preference to
21:16 his actual firstborn, the son of the wife
w 1Ch 26:10 he does not love.[w] 17 He must acknowledge the son of his unloved wife as the
firstborn by giving him a double share of
21:17 all he has. That son is the first sign of his
x Ge 49:3 father's strength.[x] The right of the first-
y Ge 25:31 born belongs to him.[y]

A Rebellious Son

18 If a man has a stubborn and rebellious son who does not obey his father
21:18 and mother[z] and will not listen to them
z Pr 1:8; Isa 30:1; when they discipline him, 19 his father
Eph 6:1-3 and mother shall take hold of him and
bring him to the elders at the gate of his
town. 20 They shall say to the elders,
"This son of ours is stubborn and rebellious. He will not obey us. He is a profli-
gate and a drunkard." 21 Then all the men
of his town shall stone him to death. You 21:21
must purge the evil[a] from among you. a Dt 19:19; 1Co 5:13*
All Israel will hear of it and be afraid.[b] b Dt 13:11

Various Laws

22 If a man guilty of a capital offense[c] 21:22
is put to death and his body is hung on c Dt 22:26;
a tree, 23 you must not leave his body on Mk 14:64; Ac 23:29
the tree overnight.[d] Be sure to bury him 21:23
that same day, because anyone who is d Jos 8:29; 10:27;
hung on a tree is under God's curse.[e] You Jn 19:31 e Gal 3:13*
must not desecrate[f] the land the LORD f Lev 18:25;
your God is giving you as an inheritance. Nu 35:34

22 If you see your brother's ox or
sheep straying, do not ignore it 22:1
but be sure to take it back to him.[g] 2 If g Ex 23:4-5
the brother does not live near you or if
you do not know who he is, take it home
with you and keep it until he comes
looking for it. Then give it back to him.
3 Do the same if you find your brother's
donkey or his cloak or anything he loses.
Do not ignore it.
4 If you see your brother's donkey[h] or 22:4
his ox fallen on the road, do not ignore h Ex 23:5
it. Help him get it to its feet.
5 A woman must not wear men's
clothing, nor a man wear women's clothing, for the LORD your God detests anyone who does this.
6 If you come across a bird's nest beside the road, either in a tree or on the
ground, and the mother is sitting on
the young or on the eggs, do not take the 22:6
mother with the young.[i] 7 You may take i Lev 22:28
the young, but be sure to let the mother
go, so that it may go well with you and 22:7
you may have a long life.[j] j Dt 4:40
8 When you build a new house, make a
parapet around your roof so that you may
not bring the guilt of bloodshed on your
house if someone falls from the roof.
9 Do not plant two kinds of seed in
your vineyard;[k] if you do, not only the 22:9
crops you plant but also the fruit of the k Lev 19:19
vineyard will be defiled.[a]
10 Do not plow with an ox and a don- 22:10
key yoked together.[l] l 2Co 6:14
11 Do not wear clothes of wool and 22:11 m Lev 19:19
linen woven together.[m]
12 Make tassels on the four corners of 22:12 n Nu 15:37-41;
the cloak you wear.[n] Mt 23:5

Marriage Violations

13 If a man takes a wife and, after lying
with her[o], dislikes her 14 and slanders her 22:13 o Dt 24:1

[a] 9 Or *be forfeited to the sanctuary*

and gives her a bad name, saying, "I
married this woman, but when I approached her, I did not find proof of her
virginity," 15then the girl's father and
mother shall bring proof that she was a
virgin to the town elders at the gate.
16The girl's father will say to the elders, "I
gave my daughter in marriage to this
man, but he dislikes her. 17Now he has
slandered her and said, 'I did not find
your daughter to be a virgin.' But here is
the proof of my daughter's virginity."
Then her parents shall display the cloth
22:18 before the elders of the town, 18and the
pEx 18:21 elders[p] shall take the man and punish
him. 19They shall fine him a hundred
shekels of silver[a] and give them to the
girl's father, because this man has given
an Israelite virgin a bad name. She shall
continue to be his wife; he must not divorce her as long as he lives.
20If, however, the charge is true and no
proof of the girl's virginity can be found,
21she shall be brought to the door of her
father's house and there the men of her
town shall stone her to death. She has
22:21 qGe 34:7; done a disgraceful thing[q] in Israel by be-
Dt 13:5; 23:17- ing promiscuous while still in her fa-
18; Jdg 20:6; 2Sa 13:12 ther's house. You must purge the evil
from among you.
22If a man is found sleeping with another man's wife, both the man who
22:22 rLev 20:10; slept with her and the woman must die.[r]
Jn 8:5 You must purge the evil from Israel.
23If a man happens to meet in a town
a virgin pledged to be married and he
sleeps with her, 24you shall take both of
them to the gate of that town and stone
them to death—the girl because she was
in a town and did not scream for help,
22:24 and the man because he violated anoth-
sver 21-22; er man's wife. You must purge the evil
1Co 5:13* from among you.[s]
25But if out in the country a man happens to meet a girl pledged to be married and rapes her, only the man who
has done this shall die. 26Do nothing to
the girl; she has committed no sin deserving death. This case is like that of
someone who attacks and murders his
neighbor, 27for the man found the girl
out in the country, and though the betrothed girl screamed, there was no one
to rescue her.
28If a man happens to meet a virgin
22:28 who is not pledged to be married and
tEx 22:16 rapes her and they are discovered,[t] 29he

shall pay the girl's father fifty shekels of
silver.[b] He must marry the girl, for he has
violated her. He can never divorce her as
long as he lives. 22:30
30A man is not to marry his father's uLev 18:8;
wife; he must not dishonor his father's 20:11; 18:8;
bed.[u] Dt 27:20; 1Co 5:1

Exclusion From the Assembly

23 No one who has been emascu-
lated by crushing or cutting
may enter the assembly of the LORD.
2No one born of a forbidden marriage[c] nor any of his descendants may
enter the assembly of the LORD, even
down to the tenth generation.
3No Ammonite or Moabite or any of
his descendants may enter the assembly
of the LORD, even down to the tenth gen- 23:3
eration.[v] 4For they did not come to meet vNe 13:2
you with bread and water on your way
when you came out of Egypt, and they 23:4
hired Balaam[w] son of Beor from Pethor wNu 22:5-6;
in Aram Naharaim[d] to pronounce a 23:7; 2Pe 2:15
curse on you. 5However, the LORD your
God would not listen to Balaam but 23:5
turned the curse[x] into a blessing for you, xPr 26:2
because the LORD your God loves you.
6Do not seek a treaty of friendship with 23:6
them as long as you live.[y] yEzr 9:12
7Do not abhor an Edomite, for he is 23:7
your brother.[z] Do not abhor an Egyp- zGe 25:26;
tian, because you lived as an alien in his Ob 1:10,12
country.[a] 8The third generation of chil- aEx 22:21; 23:9;
dren born to them may enter the assem- Lev 19:34; Dt 10:19
bly of the LORD.

Uncleanness in the Camp

9When you are encamped against
your enemies, keep away from everything impure. 10If one of your men is unclean because of a nocturnal emission,
he is to go outside the camp and stay 23:10
there.[b] 11But as evening approaches he is bLev 15:16
to wash himself, and at sunset he may
return to the camp.
12Designate a place outside the camp
where you can go to relieve yourself. 13As
part of your equipment have something
to dig with, and when you relieve yourself, dig a hole and cover up your excre- 23:14
ment. 14For the LORD your God moves[c] cLev 26:12
about in your camp to protect you and
to deliver your enemies to you. Your

[a] *19* That is, about 2 1/2 pounds (about 1 kilogram)
[b] *29* That is, about 1 1/4 pounds (about 0.6 kilogram)
[c] *2* Or *one of illegitimate birth*
[d] *4* That is, Northwest Mesopotamia

23:14 [d]Ex 3:5 camp must be holy,[d] so that he will not
see among you anything indecent and
turn away from you.

Miscellaneous Laws

23:15 [e]1Sa 30:15 15 If a slave has taken refuge with you,
do not hand him over to his master.[e]
16 Let him live among you wherever he
23:16 likes and in whatever town he chooses.
[f]Ex 22:21 Do not oppress[f] him.
23:17 17 No Israelite man[g] or woman is to
[g]Ge 19:25; 2Ki 23:7 become a shrine prostitute.[h] 18 You must
[h]Lev 19:29; Dt 22:21 not bring the earnings of a female prostitute or of a male prostitute[a] into the
house of the LORD your God to pay any
vow, because the LORD your God detests
them both.
19 Do not charge your brother interest,
23:19 [i]Ex 22:25; whether on money or food or anything
Lev 25:35-37 else that may earn interest.[i] 20 You may
charge a foreigner interest, but not a
brother Israelite, so that the LORD your
23:20 God may bless[j] you in everything you
[j]Dt 15:10; 28:12 put your hand to in the land you are entering to possess.
21 If you make a vow to the LORD your
God, do not be slow to pay it, for the
23:21 LORD your God will certainly demand it
[k]Nu 30:1-2; of you and you will be guilty of sin.[k]
Ecc 5:4-5; Mt 5:33 22 But if you refrain from making a vow,
you will not be guilty. 23 Whatever your
lips utter you must be sure to do, because you made your vow freely to the
LORD your God with your own mouth.
24 If you enter your neighbor's vineyard, you may eat all the grapes you
want, but do not put any in your basket.
25 If you enter your neighbor's grainfield,
you may pick kernels with your hands,
23:25 but you must not put a sickle to his
[l]Mt 12:1; Mk 2:23; Lk 6:1 standing grain.[l]

24:1 **24** If a man marries a woman who
[m]Dt 22:13 becomes displeasing to him[m]
[n]Mt 5:31*; 19:7-9; because he finds something indecent
Mk 10:4-5 about her, and he writes her a certificate
of divorce,[n] gives it to her and sends her
from his house, 2 and if after she leaves
his house she becomes the wife of another man, 3 and her second husband
dislikes her and writes her a certificate
of divorce, gives it to her and sends her
from his house, or if he dies, 4 then her
first husband, who divorced her, is not
allowed to marry her again after she has
been defiled. That would be detestable
in the eyes of the LORD. Do not bring sin
upon the land the LORD[o] your God is giv- 24:4
ing you as an inheritance. [o]Jer 3:1
5 If a man has recently married, he
must not be sent to war or have any other duty laid on him. For one year he is to
be free to stay at home and bring happi- 24:5
ness to the wife he has married.[p] [p]Dt 20:7
6 Do not take a pair of millstones—
not even the upper one—as security for
a debt, because that would be taking a
man's livelihood as security.
7 If a man is caught kidnapping one of
his brother Israelites and treats him as a
slave or sells him, the kidnapper must
die.[q] You must purge the evil from 24:7 [q]Ex 21:16
among you.
8 In cases of leprous[b] diseases be very
careful to do exactly as the priests, who
are Levites, instruct you. You must follow carefully what I have commanded 24:8
them.[r] 9 Remember what the LORD your [r]Lev 13:1-46; 14:2
God did to Miriam along the way after 24:9
you came out of Egypt.[s] [s]Nu 12:10
10 When you make a loan of any kind
to your neighbor, do not go into his
house to get what he is offering as a
pledge. 11 Stay outside and let the man to
whom you are making the loan bring
the pledge out to you. 12 If the man is
poor, do not go to sleep with his pledge
in your possession. 13 Return his cloak to 24:13
him by sunset[t] so that he may sleep in it. [t]Ex 22:26

[a] 18 Hebrew *of a dog* [b] 8 The Hebrew word was used for various diseases affecting the skin—not necessarily leprosy.

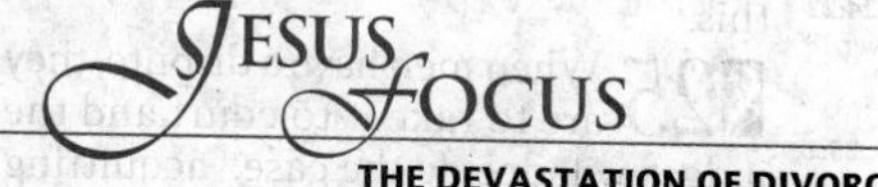

THE DEVASTATION OF DIVORCE

In the Old Testament divorce was under some circumstances permitted, but it was never advocated or promoted (Leviticus 21:7,14; Numbers 30:9; Deuteronomy 24:1–4). Jesus would later clarify God's view of divorce, referring to the higher law of creation "at the beginning" (Matthew 19:3–12). Our Lord pointed out that Moses permitted divorce among the Israelites because "[their] hearts were hard" and that permission for divorce was granted only in the event the marriage hadn't been kept pure. Jesus based his statements regarding divorce on the provisions of God's law recorded in Deuteronomy 24, but he introduced his own comments with the phrase, "I tell you." By adding his own interpretation of the law, Jesus was exercising his authority as the Son of God.

Then he will thank you, and it will be regarded as a righteous act in the sight of
the LORD your God.[u]
14 Do not take advantage of a hired
man who is poor and needy, whether he
is a brother Israelite or an alien living in
one of your towns.[v] 15 Pay him his wages
each day before sunset, because he is
poor[w] and is counting on it.[x] Otherwise
he may cry to the LORD against you, and
you will be guilty of sin.[y]
16 Fathers shall not be put to death for
their children, nor children put to death
for their fathers; each is to die for his own
sin.[z]
17 Do not deprive the alien or the fatherless of justice,[a] or take the cloak of
the widow as a pledge. 18 Remember that
you were slaves in Egypt and the LORD
your God redeemed you from there.
That is why I command you to do this.
19 When you are harvesting in your
field and you overlook a sheaf, do not go
back to get it.[b] Leave it for the alien, the
fatherless and the widow, so that the
LORD your God may bless[c] you in all the
work of your hands. 20 When you beat
the olives from your trees, do not go over
the branches a second time.[d] Leave
what remains for the alien, the fatherless
and the widow. 21 When you harvest the
grapes in your vineyard, do not go over
the vines again. Leave what remains for
the alien, the fatherless and the widow.
22 Remember that you were slaves in
Egypt. That is why I command you to do
this.[e]

25 When men have a dispute, they
are to take it to court and the
judges will decide the case,[f] acquitting
the innocent and condemning the
guilty.[g] 2 If the guilty man deserves to be
beaten,[h] the judge shall make him lie
down and have him flogged in his presence with the number of lashes his
crime deserves, 3 but he must not give
him more than forty lashes.[i] If he is
flogged more than that, your brother
will be degraded in your eyes.[j]
4 Do not muzzle an ox while it is
treading out the grain.[k]
5 If brothers are living together and
one of them dies without a son, his widow must not marry outside the family.
Her husband's brother shall take her and
marry her and fulfill the duty of a brother-in-law to her.[l] 6 The first son she bears

24:13 u Dt 6:25; Da 4:27
24:14 v Lev 25:35-43; Dt 15:12-18
24:15 w Jer 22:13 x Lev 19:13 y Dt 15:9; Jas 5:4
24:16 z 2Ki 14:6; 2Ch 25:4; Jer 31:29-30; Eze 18:20
24:17 a Dt 1:17; 10:17-18; 16:19
24:19 b Lev 19:9; 23:22 c Pr 19:17
24:20 d Lev 19:10
24:22 e ver 18
25:1 f Dt 19:17 g Dt 1:16-17
25:2 h Lk 12:47-48
25:3 i 2Co 11:24 j Job 18:3
25:4 k Pr 12:10; 1Co 9:9*; 1Ti 5:18*
25:5 l Mt 22:24; Mk 12:19; Lk 20:28

shall carry on the name of the dead
brother so that his name will not be
blotted out from Israel.[m]
7 However, if a man does not want to
marry his brother's wife, she shall go to
the elders at the town gate and say, "My
husband's brother refuses to carry on his
brother's name in Israel. He will not fulfill the duty of a brother-in-law to me."[n]
8 Then the elders of his town shall summon him and talk to him. If he persists
in saying, "I do not want to marry her,"
9 his brother's widow shall go up to him
in the presence of the elders, take off one
of his sandals,[o] spit in his face and say,
"This is what is done to the man who
will not build up his brother's family
line." 10 That man's line shall be known in
Israel as The Family of the Unsandaled.
11 If two men are fighting and the wife
of one of them comes to rescue her husband from his assailant, and she reaches
out and seizes him by his private parts,
12 you shall cut off her hand. Show her no
pity.[p]
13 Do not have two differing weights in
your bag—one heavy, one light.[q] 14 Do
not have two differing measures in your
house—one large, one small. 15 You must
have accurate and honest weights and
measures, so that you may live long[r] in
the land the LORD your God is giving
you. 16 For the LORD your God detests
anyone who does these things, anyone
who deals dishonestly.[s]
17 Remember what the Amalekites[t]
did to you along the way when you came
out of Egypt. 18 When you were weary
and worn out, they met you on your
journey and cut off all who were lagging
behind; they had no fear of God.[u]
19 When the LORD your God gives you
rest from all the enemies around you in
the land he is giving you to possess as an
inheritance, you shall blot out the memory of Amalek[v] from under heaven. Do
not forget!

Firstfruits and Tithes

26 When you have entered the
land the LORD your God is giving you as an inheritance and have tak-
en possession of it and settled in it, 2 take
some of the firstfruits[w] of all that you
produce from the soil of the land the
LORD your God is giving you and put
them in a basket. Then go to the place

25:6 m Ge 38:9; Ru 4:5,10
25:7 n Ru 4:1-2,5-6
25:9 o Ru 4:7-8,11
25:12 p Dt 19:13
25:13 q Lev 19:35-37; Pr 11:1; Eze 45:10; Mic 6:11
25:15 r Ex 20:12
25:16 s Pr 11:1
25:17 t Ex 17:8
25:18 u Ps 36:1; Ro 3:18
25:19 v 1Sa 15:2-3
26:2 w Ex 22:29; 23:16,19; Nu 18:13; Pr 3:9

Offering the Firstfruits

When God's people entered the land he had promised them, he asked that they take the first portion of the harvest (called the *firstfruits*) and offer it to him in worship and celebration. First each Israelite had to place the produce in a basket and take the basket to the tabernacle (Deuteronomy 26:2). Then he would lay it in front of the altar and recite a blessing, including in the recitation a brief but detailed history of what God had done for his people (verses 4–10). Finally each individual was to bow down in worship and thank God for all the good things he had given his children (verses 10–11).

The instructions in Deuteronomy 26 seem to relate to a one-time offering to celebrate the arrival in the land God had promised, but God also wanted his people to offer him their firstfruits on an annual basis (see Leviticus 23:10–11). In so doing the people declared that God was good and that they trusted him to oversee the rest of the harvest.

Offering the firstfruits had a purpose beyond demonstrating thankfulness, however. This practice provides an early picture of Jesus, who is "the firstfruits of those who have fallen asleep" (1 Corinthians 15:20). He died on the cross to pay the penalty for our sin but then came back to life to prove that death would not ultimately prevail. The offering of the firstfruits in the Old Testament represented the harvest to follow, just as Jesus' resurrection guarantees the future resurrection of all of God's people. "As in Adam all die, so in Christ all will be made alive. But each in his own turn: Christ, the firstfruits; then, when he comes, those who belong to him" (1 Corinthians 15:23).

Jesus is our firstfruits in another way. In the Old Testament God's people celebrated the fact that God had set them free from slavery and led them to the place of blessing he had promised. Because Jesus died in our place, we celebrate that God has freed us from the slavery and oppression of sin. He has rescued us from "the dominion of darkness" and brought us into "the kingdom of the Son he loves" (Colossians 1:13).

In response to God's amazing goodness we must give him the first and the best of everything—the best of what we have and of who we are. We must also tell others about his goodness to us and demonstrate our devotion by submitting every aspect of our lives to him. The writer to the Hebrews invited us, through Jesus, to "continually offer to God a sacrifice of praise—the fruit of lips that confess his name" (Hebrews 13:15).

Self-Discovery: *What "firstfruits" can you offer to God? Does your gift involve money, time, talent or some other sacrifice?*

GO TO DISCOVERY 49 ON PAGE 255

the LORD your God will choose as a
26:2 [x]Dt 12:5 dwelling for his Name[x] 3and say to the
priest in office at the time, "I declare today to the LORD your God that I have
come to the land the LORD swore to our
forefathers to give us." 4The priest shall
take the basket from your hands and set
it down in front of the altar of the LORD
your God. 5Then you shall declare before
26:5 the LORD your God: "My father was a
[y]Hos 12:12 wandering Aramean,[y] and he went
[z]Ge 43:1-2; 45:7,11; 46:27; Dt 10:22 down into Egypt with a few people[z] and
lived there and became a great nation,
powerful and numerous. 6But the Egyp-
26:6 [a]Ex 1:11,14 tians mistreated us and made us suffer,[a]
putting us to hard labor. 7Then we cried
out to the LORD, the God of our fathers,
26:7 [b]Ex 2:23-25 [c]Ex 3:9 and the LORD heard our voice[b] and saw[c]
our misery, toil and oppression. 8So the
LORD brought us out of Egypt with a
mighty hand and an outstretched arm,
with great terror and with miraculous
26:8 [d]Dt 4:34 signs and wonders.[d] 9He brought us to
this place and gave us this land, a land
26:9 [e]Ex 3:8 flowing with milk and honey;[e] 10and
now I bring the firstfruits of the soil that
you, O LORD, have given me." Place the
basket before the LORD your God and
bow down before him. 11And you and
26:11 [f]Dt 12:7 [g]Dt 16:11 the Levites[f] and the aliens among you
shall rejoice[g] in all the good things the
LORD your God has given to you and
your household.
12When you have finished setting
26:12 [h]Lev 27:30 [i]Nu 18:24; Dt 14:28-29; Heb 7:5,9 aside a tenth[h] of all your produce in the
third year, the year of the tithe,[i] you shall
give it to the Levite, the alien, the fatherless and the widow, so that they may
eat in your towns and be satisfied.
13Then say to the LORD your God: "I have
removed from my house the sacred portion and have given it to the Levite, the
alien, the fatherless and the widow, according to all you commanded. I have
not turned aside from your commands
26:13 [j]Ps 119:141,153, 176 nor have I forgotten any of them.[j] 14I
have not eaten any of the sacred portion
while I was in mourning, nor have I re-
26:14 [k]Lev 7:20; Hos 9:4 moved any of it while I was unclean,[k]
nor have I offered any of it to the dead. I
have obeyed the LORD my God; I have
26:15 [l]Isa 63:15; Zec 2:13 done everything you commanded me.
15Look down from heaven,[l] your holy
dwelling place, and bless your people Israel and the land you have given us as
you promised on oath to our forefathers,
a land flowing with milk and honey."

Follow the LORD's Commands

16The LORD your God commands you
this day to follow these decrees and
laws; carefully observe them with all
your heart and with all your soul.[m] 17You 26:16 [m]Dt 4:29
have declared this day that the LORD is
your God and that you will walk in his
ways, that you will keep his decrees,
commands and laws, and that you will
obey him. 18And the LORD has declared
this day that you are his people, his 26:18
treasured possession[n] as he promised, [n]Ex 6:7; 19:5; Dt 7:6; 14:2; 28:9
and that you are to keep all his com-
mands. 19He has declared that he will set
you in praise, fame and honor high 26:19
above all the nations[o] he has made and [o]Dt 4:7-8; 28:1, 13,44 [p]Ex 19:6; Dt 7:6; 1Pe 2:9
that you will be a people holy[p] to the
LORD your God, as he promised.

The Altar on Mount Ebal

27 Moses and the elders of Israel
commanded the people: "Keep
all these commands that I give you today. 2When you have crossed the Jordan
into the land the LORD your God is giving you, set up some large stones and
coat them with plaster.[q] 3Write on them 27:2 [q]Jos 8:31
all the words of this law when you have
crossed over to enter the land the LORD
your God is giving you, a land flowing
with milk and honey,[r] just as the LORD, 27:3 [r]Dt 26:9
the God of your fathers, promised you.
4And when you have crossed the Jordan,
set up these stones on Mount Ebal,[s] as I 27:4 [s]Dt 11:29
command you today, and coat them
with plaster. 5Build there an altar[t] to the 27:5 [t]Jos 8:31 [u]Ex 20:25
LORD your God, an altar of stones. Do
not use any iron tool[u] upon them. 6Build
the altar of the LORD your God with
fieldstones and offer burnt offerings on
it to the LORD your God. 7Sacrifice fellowship offerings[a] there, eating them
and rejoicing in the presence of the LORD
your God. 8And you shall write very
clearly all the words of this law on these
stones you have set up."

Curses From Mount Ebal

9Then Moses and the priests, who are
Levites, said to all Israel, "Be silent, O Israel, and listen! You have now become 27:9
the people of the LORD your God.[v] 10Obey [v]Dt 26:18
the LORD your God and follow his com-
mands and decrees that I give you today."
11On the same day Moses commanded the people:

[a] 7 Traditionally *peace offerings*

DISCOVERY 49

The Mountain of Consequences

We sometimes tend to focus on God's blessings and forget that he is a God of both blessings and curses. From the beginning God made himself clear: If we live the way he wants us to, he will bless us, but if we turn and go our own way, we will suffer dreadful consequences (Genesis 1:28; 2:15–17).

Deuteronomy 27 and 28 describe how God's people reminded themselves of this fact. Moses divided the 12 tribes into two groups. Six of the tribes gathered at the foot of Mount Gerizim and the other six at the foot of Mount Ebal. Those at Mount Gerizim called out a recitation of God's blessings, while those on the other side cited the consequences for failure to follow his precepts (Deuteronomy 27:11–14). The Levites stood in the valley between the two mountains shouting a reminder of their own: "Be silent, O Israel, and listen! You have now become the people of the LORD your God. Obey the LORD your God and follow his commands and decrees that I give you today" (verses 9–10).

God promised his people many things if they would only choose to take him at his word. He would give them a land of their own, and every aspect of their lives would be touched by his love (Deuteronomy 28:1–14). However, if they opted to turn away from him, they would be overwhelmed by defeat, disease and destruction.

But how can a loving God *curse* anyone? For one thing, the very consequences for walking away from God demonstrate that what we do matters to him. A God who ignored what we did or overlooked sin would be a God who didn't take us seriously, didn't attribute value to us. But the fact is that God does care; he holds us accountable because we are of infinite worth in his sight.

That there are consequences for turning away from him also means that God keeps his word. We may not relish the idea of God's judgment, but God cannot permit evil to go unpunished—he knows too well the damage it causes, and such a course of action would be inconsistent with who he is. In fact, when we see the effects of sin on the world around us, as well as in our own lives, we should thank God for promising to get rid of it once and for all!

And that is just what he has done. Though we still live with the effects of evil, God himself did what was necessary to take care of the sin problem in order that we could receive his blessing. All of humanity starts its journey at the foot of Mount Ebal, so to speak, the mountain of consequences. We have all broken God's law and have become separated from him (Galatians 3:10). But the good news is that Jesus has "redeemed us from the curse of the law by becoming a curse for us" (Galatians 3:13). Jesus is the only One who can lead us from Mount Ebal to Mount Gerizim, the place of blessing. And when we are with Jesus, we are blessed "with *every* spiritual blessing" (Ephesians 1:3).

Self-Discovery: *Envision yourself standing on Mount Gerizim, the place of blessing. How do you feel? Take time to thank Jesus for leading you on your journey from Mount Ebal to Mount Gerizim.*

GO TO DISCOVERY 50 ON PAGE 263

12 When you have crossed the Jordan, these tribes shall stand on Mount Gerizim[w] to bless the people: Simeon, Levi, Judah, Issachar, Joseph and Benjamin.[x] 13 And these tribes shall stand on Mount Ebal to pronounce curses: Reuben, Gad, Asher, Zebulun, Dan and Naphtali.

27:12 [w] Dt 11:29 [x] Jos 8:35

14 The Levites shall recite to all the people of Israel in a loud voice:

15 "Cursed is the man who carves an image or casts an idol[y]—a thing detestable to the LORD, the work of the craftsman's hands—and sets it up in secret."

Then all the people shall say, "Amen!"

27:15 [y] Ex 20:4; 34:17; Lev 19:4; 26:1; Dt 4:16,23; 5:8; Isa 44:9

16 "Cursed is the man who dishonors his father or his mother."[z]

Then all the people shall say, "Amen!"

27:16 [z] Ex 20:12; 21:17; Lev 19:3; 20:9

17 "Cursed is the man who moves his neighbor's boundary stone."[a]

Then all the people shall say, "Amen!"

27:17 [a] Dt 19:14; Pr 22:28

18 "Cursed is the man who leads the blind astray on the road."[b]

Then all the people shall say, "Amen!"

27:18 [b] Lev 19:14

19 "Cursed is the man who withholds justice from the alien,[c] the fatherless or the widow."[d]

Then all the people shall say, "Amen!"

27:19 [c] Ex 22:21; Dt 24:19 [d] Dt 10:18

20 "Cursed is the man who sleeps with his father's wife, for he dishonors his father's bed."[e]

Then all the people shall say, "Amen!"

27:20 [e] Lev 18:7; Dt 22:30

21 "Cursed is the man who has sexual relations with any animal."[f]

Then all the people shall say, "Amen!"

27:21 [f] Lev 18:23

22 "Cursed is the man who sleeps with his sister, the daughter of his father or the daughter of his mother."[g]

Then all the people shall say, "Amen!"

27:22 [g] Lev 18:9; 20:17

23 "Cursed is the man who sleeps with his mother-in-law."[h]

Then all the people shall say, "Amen!"

27:23 [h] Lev 20:14

24 "Cursed is the man who kills[i] his neighbor secretly."

Then all the people shall say, "Amen!"

27:24 [i] Lev 24:17; Nu 35:31

25 "Cursed is the man who accepts a bribe to kill an innocent person."[j]

Then all the people shall say, "Amen!"

27:25 [j] Ex 23:7-8; Dt 10:17; Eze 22:12

26 "Cursed is the man who does not uphold the words of this law by carrying them out."[k]

Then all the people shall say, "Amen!"

27:26 [k] Jer 11:3; Gal 3:10*

Blessings for Obedience

28 If you fully obey the LORD your God and carefully follow all his commands[l] I give you today, the LORD your God will set you high above all the nations on earth.[m] 2 All these blessings will come upon you[n] and accompany you if you obey the LORD your God:

28:1 [l] Ex 15:26; Lev 26:3; Dt 7:12-26 [m] Dt 26:19

28:2 [n] Zec 1:6

3 You will be blessed[o] in the city and blessed in the country.[p]

28:3 [o] Ps 128:1,4 [p] Ge 39:5

4 The fruit of your womb will be blessed, and the crops of your land and the young of your livestock—the calves of your herds and the lambs of your flocks.[q]

28:4 [q] Ge 49:25; Pr 10:22

5 Your basket and your kneading trough will be blessed.

6 You will be blessed when you come in and blessed when you go out.[r]

28:6 [r] Ps 121:8

7 The LORD will grant that the enemies who rise up against you will be defeated before you. They will come at you from one direction but flee from you in seven.[s]

28:7 [s] Lev 26:8,17

8 The LORD will send a blessing on your barns and on everything you put your hand to. The LORD your God will bless you in the land he is giving you.

9 The LORD will establish you as his holy people,[t] as he promised you on oath, if you keep the commands of the LORD your God and walk in his ways. 10 Then all the peoples on earth will see that you are called by the name[u] of the LORD, and they will fear you. 11 The LORD will grant you abundant prosperity—in the fruit of your womb, the young of your livestock and the crops of your ground—in the land he swore to your forefathers to give you.[v]

28:9 [t] Ex 19:6; Dt 7:6

28:10 [u] 2Ch 7:14

28:11 [v] Dt 30:9; Pr 10:22

12 The LORD will open the heavens, the storehouse of his bounty, to send rain[w] on your land in season and to bless all the work of your hands. You will lend to many nations but will borrow from none.[x] 13 The LORD will make you the

28:12 [w] Lev 26:4 [x] Dt 15:3,6

head, not the tail. If you pay attention to
the commands of the LORD your God
that I give you this day and carefully follow them, you will always be at the top,
never at the bottom. [14]Do not turn aside
28:14 [y]Dt 5:32 from any of the commands I give you today, to the right or to the left,[y] following
other gods and serving them.

Curses for Disobedience

28:15 [z]Lev 26:14 [a]Jos 23:15; Da 9:11; Mal 2:2 [15]However, if you do not obey[z] the
LORD your God and do not carefully fol-
low all his commands and decrees I am
giving you today, all these curses will
come upon you and overtake you:[a]

[16]You will be cursed in the city
and cursed in the country.
[17]Your basket and your kneading
trough will be cursed.
[18]The fruit of your womb will be
cursed, and the crops of your land,
and the calves of your herds and
the lambs of your flocks.
[19]You will be cursed when you
come in and cursed when you go
out.

28:20 [b]Mal 2:2 [c]Isa 51:20; 66:15 [d]Dt 4:26 [20]The LORD will send on you curses,[b]
confusion and rebuke[c] in everything
you put your hand to, until you are destroyed and come to sudden ruin[d] because of the evil you have done in for-
saking him.[a] [21]The LORD will plague you 28:21 [e]Lev 26:25; Jer 24:10
with diseases until he has destroyed you
from the land you are entering to possess.[e] [22]The LORD will strike you with
wasting disease, with fever and inflam-
mation, with scorching heat and
drought,[f] with blight and mildew, which 28:22 [f]Lev 26:16
will plague you until you perish.[g] [23]The [g]Am 4:9
sky over your head will be bronze, the
ground beneath you iron.[h] [24]The LORD 28:23 [h]Lev 26:19
will turn the rain of your country into
dust and powder; it will come down
from the skies until you are destroyed.

[25]The LORD will cause you to be defeated before your enemies. You will
come at them from one direction but
flee from them in seven,[i] and you will 28:25 [i]Isa 30:17
become a thing of horror to all the king- [j]Jer 15:4; 24:9; Eze 23:46
doms on earth.[j] [26]Your carcasses will be
food for all the birds of the air and the
beasts of the earth, and there will be no
one to frighten them away.[k] [27]The LORD 28:26 [k]Jer 7:33; 16:4; 34:20
will afflict you with the boils of Egypt[l]
and with tumors, festering sores and the
itch, from which you cannot be cured. 28:27 [l]ver 60-61; 1Sa 5:6
[28]The LORD will afflict you with mad-
ness, blindness and confusion of mind.
[29]At midday you will grope[m] about like a 28:29 [m]Job 5:14; Isa 59:10
blind man in the dark. You will be un-
successful in everything you do; day
after day you will be oppressed and
robbed, with no one to rescue you.

[30]You will be pledged to be married to
a woman, but another will take her and
ravish her.[n] You will build a house, but 28:30 [n]Job 31:10; Jer 8:10
you will not live in it.[o] You will plant a [o]Am 5:11
vineyard, but you will not even begin to [p]Jer 12:13
enjoy its fruit.[p] [31]Your ox will be slaughtered before your eyes, but you will eat
none of it. Your donkey will be forcibly
taken from you and will not be returned.
Your sheep will be given to your enemies,
and no one will rescue them. [32]Your sons
and daughters will be given to another
nation,[q] and you will wear out your eyes 28:32 [q]ver 41
watching for them day after day, power-
less to lift a hand. [33]A people that you do
not know will eat what your land and labor produce, and you will have nothing
but cruel oppression all your days.[r] [34]The 28:33 [r]Jer 5:15-17
sights you see will drive you mad. [35]The
LORD will afflict your knees and legs with
painful boils[s] that cannot be cured, 28:35 [s]ver 27
spreading from the soles of your feet to
the top of your head.

[36]The LORD will drive you and the

[a] 20 Hebrew *me*

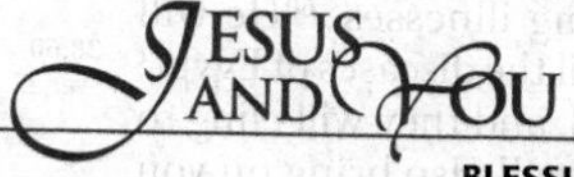

BLESSINGS AND CURSES

Typical of many ancient Near Eastern covenants, the one in Deuteronomy 28 includes a listing of blessings for those who would choose to obey (verses 3–6), as well as an enumeration of curses for those who would refuse to do so (verses 16–19). In fact, the Old Testament closes with a reminder of what would happen if Israel did not repent: "... Or else I will come and strike the land with a curse" (Malachi 4:6). By contrast, Jesus' ministry began with the teaching known as the Beatitudes: "Blessed are ..." (Matthew 5:3–12). Like the blessings stipulated in Deuteronomy 28, the blessings specified by Jesus are spiritual, personal and temporal. If we as human beings were to receive what we deserve, the curses would far outnumber the blessings. But Jesus took the curse of the law upon himself by dying in our place so that we can experience the blessings that derive from a right relationship with God (Galatians 3:13).

king[t] you set over you to a nation unknown to you or your fathers.[u] There you will worship other gods, gods of wood and stone.[v] 37You will become a thing of horror and an object of scorn and ridicule to all the nations where the LORD will drive you.[w]

38You will sow much seed in the field but you will harvest little,[x] because locusts will devour[y] it. 39You will plant vineyards and cultivate them but you will not drink the wine or gather the grapes, because worms will eat them.[z] 40You will have olive trees throughout your country but you will not use the oil, because the olives will drop off.[a] 41You will have sons and daughters but you will not keep them, because they will go into captivity.[b] 42Swarms of locusts will take over all your trees and the crops of your land.

43The alien who lives among you will rise above you higher and higher, but you will sink lower and lower.[c] 44He will lend to you, but you will not lend to him.[d] He will be the head, but you will be the tail.[e]

45All these curses will come upon you. They will pursue you and overtake you until you are destroyed,[f] because you did not obey the LORD your God and observe the commands and decrees he gave you. 46They will be a sign and a wonder to you and your descendants forever.[g] 47Because you did not serve[h] the LORD your God joyfully and gladly[i] in the time of prosperity, 48therefore in hunger and thirst, in nakedness and dire poverty, you will serve the enemies the LORD sends against you. He will put an iron yoke[j] on your neck until he has destroyed you.

49The LORD will bring a nation against you from far away, from the ends of the earth,[k] like an eagle[l] swooping down, a nation whose language you will not understand, 50a fierce-looking nation without respect for the old[m] or pity for the young. 51They will devour the young of your livestock and the crops of your land until you are destroyed. They will leave you no grain, new wine or oil, nor any calves of your herds or lambs of your flocks until you are ruined.[n] 52They will lay siege to all the cities throughout your land until the high fortified walls in which you trust fall down. They will besiege all the cities throughout the land the LORD your God is giving you.[o]

28:36 [t] 2Ki 17:4,6; 24:12,14; 25:7, 11 [u] Jer 16:13 [v] Dt 4:28
28:37 [w] Jer 24:9
28:38 [x] Mic 6:15; Hag 1:6,9 [y] Joel 1:4
28:39 [z] Isa 5:10; 17:10-11
28:40 [a] Mic 6:15
28:41 [b] ver 32
28:43 [c] ver 13
28:44 [d] ver 12 [e] ver 13
28:45 [f] ver 15
28:46 [g] Isa 8:18; Eze 14:8
28:47 [h] Dt 32:15 [i] Ne 9:35
28:48 [j] Jer 28:13-14
28:49 [k] Jer 5:15; 6:22 [l] La 4:19; Hos 8:1
28:50 [m] Isa 47:6
28:51 [n] ver 33

53Because of the suffering that your enemy will inflict on you during the siege, you will eat the fruit of the womb, the flesh of the sons and daughters the LORD your God has given you.[p] 54Even the most gentle and sensitive man among you will have no compassion on his own brother or the wife he loves or his surviving children, 55and he will not give to one of them any of the flesh of his children that he is eating. It will be all he has left because of the suffering your enemy will inflict on you during the siege of all your cities. 56The most gentle and sensitive[q] woman among you—so sensitive and gentle that she would not venture to touch the ground with the sole of her foot—will begrudge the husband she loves and her own son or daughter 57the afterbirth from her womb and the children she bears. For she intends to eat them secretly during the siege and in the distress that your enemy will inflict on you in your cities.

58If you do not carefully follow all the words of this law, which are written in this book, and do not revere[r] this glorious and awesome name[s]—the LORD your God— 59the LORD will send fearful plagues on you and your descendants, harsh and prolonged disasters, and severe and lingering illnesses. 60He will bring upon you all the diseases of Egypt[t] that you dreaded, and they will cling to you. 61The LORD will also bring on you every kind of sickness and disaster not recorded in this Book of the Law, until you are destroyed.[u] 62You who were as numerous as the stars in the sky[v] will be left but few in number, because you did not obey the LORD your God. 63Just as it pleased[w] the LORD to make you prosper and increase in number, so it will please[x] him to ruin and destroy you. You will be uprooted[y] from the land you are entering to possess.

64Then the LORD will scatter[z] you among all nations,[a] from one end of the earth to the other. There you will worship other gods—gods of wood and stone, which neither you nor your fathers have known. 65Among those nations you will find no repose, no resting place for the sole of your foot. There the LORD will give you an anxious mind, eyes

28:52 [o] Jer 10:18; Zep 1:14-16,17
28:53 [p] Lev 26:29; 2Ki 6:28-29; Jer 19:9; La 2:20; 4:10
28:56 [q] ver 54
28:58 [r] Mal 1:14 [s] Ex 6:3
28:60 [t] ver 27
28:61 [u] Dt 4:25-26
28:62 [v] Dt 4:27; 10:22; Ne 9:23
28:63 [w] Jer 32:41 [x] Pr 1:26 [y] Jer 12:14; 45:4
28:64 [z] Lev 26:33; Dt 4:27 [a] Ne 1:8

28:65 weary with longing, and a despairing
b Lev 26:16,36 heart.[b] 66You will live in constant suspense, filled with dread both night and
day, never sure of your life. 67In the
morning you will say, "If only it were
evening!" and in the evening, "If only it
were morning!"—because of the terror
28:67 that will fill your hearts and the sights
c ver 34; Job 7:4 that your eyes will see.[c] 68The LORD will
send you back in ships to Egypt on a
journey I said you should never make
again. There you will offer yourselves for
sale to your enemies as male and female
slaves, but no one will buy you.

Renewal of the Covenant

29 These are the terms of the covenant the LORD commanded
Moses to make with the Israelites in
29:1 Moab, in addition to the covenant he
d Dt 5:2-3 had made with them at Horeb.[d]
2Moses summoned all the Israelites
and said to them:

Your eyes have seen all that the LORD
29:2 did in Egypt to Pharaoh, to all his offi-
e Ex 19:4 cials and to all his land.[e] 3With your own
29:3 eyes you saw those great trials, those
f Dt 4:34; 7:19 miraculous signs and great wonders.[f]
4But to this day the LORD has not given
29:4 you a mind that understands or eyes
g Isa 6:10; that see or ears that hear.[g] 5During the
Ac 28:26-27; Ro 11:8*; forty years that I led you through the
Eph 4:18 desert, your clothes did not wear out,
29:5 nor did the sandals on your feet.[h] 6You
h Dt 8:4 ate no bread and drank no wine or other fermented drink. I did this so that you
29:6 might know that I am the LORD your
i Dt 8:3 God.[i]
29:7 7When you reached this place, Sihon[j]
j Dt 2:32; 3:1 king of Heshbon and Og king of Bashan
k Nu 21:21-24, 33-35 came out to fight against us, but we defeated them.[k] 8We took their land and
29:8 gave it as an inheritance to the Reuben-
l Nu 32:33; ites, the Gadites and the half-tribe of
Dt 3:12-13 Manasseh.[l]
29:9 9Carefully follow[m] the terms of this
m Dt 4:6; Jos 1:7 covenant, so that you may prosper in
n 1Ki 2:3 everything you do.[n] 10All of you are
standing today in the presence of the
LORD your God—your leaders and chief
men, your elders and officials, and all
the other men of Israel, 11together with
your children and your wives, and the
aliens living in your camps who chop
29:11 your wood and carry your water.[o] 12You
o Jos 9:21,23,27 are standing here in order to enter into
a covenant with the LORD your God, a
covenant the LORD is making with you
this day and sealing with an oath, 13to 29:13
confirm you this day as his people,[p] that p Dt 28:9
he may be your God[q] as he promised q Ge 17:7; Ex 6:7
you and as he swore to your fathers,
Abraham, Isaac and Jacob. 14I am mak- 29:14
ing this covenant,[r] with its oath, not r Jer 31:31
only with you 15who are standing here
with us today in the presence of the
LORD our God but also with those who 29:15
are not here today.[s] s Ac 2:39
16You yourselves know how we lived in
Egypt and how we passed through the
countries on the way here. 17You saw
among them their detestable images and
idols of wood and stone, of silver and
gold.[t] 18Make sure there is no man or 29:17
woman, clan or tribe among you today t Dt 28:36
whose heart turns away from the LORD
our God to go and worship the gods of
those nations; make sure there is no root 29:18
among you that produces such bitter u Dt 11:16;
poison.[u] Heb 12:15
19When such a person hears the
words of this oath, he invokes a blessing
on himself and therefore thinks, "I will
be safe, even though I persist in going
my own way." This will bring disaster on
the watered land as well as the dry.[a]
20The LORD will never be willing to for- 29:20
give him; his wrath and zeal[v] will burn[w] v Eze 23:25
against that man. All the curses written w Ps 74:1; 79:5
in this book will fall upon him, and the x Ex 32:33; Dt 9:14
LORD will blot[x] out his name from under
heaven. 21The LORD will single him out
from all the tribes of Israel for disaster,
according to all the curses of the covenant written in this Book of the Law.
22Your children who follow you in later generations and foreigners who come
from distant lands will see the calamities that have fallen on the land and the
diseases with which the LORD has af- 29:22
flicted it.[y] 23The whole land will be a y Jer 19:8
burning waste[z] of salt[a] and sulfur— 29:23
nothing planted, nothing sprouting, no z Isa 34:9
vegetation growing on it. It will be like a Jer 17:6
the destruction of Sodom and Gomor- b Ge 19:24,25;
rah,[b] Admah and Zeboiim, which the Zep 2:9
LORD overthrew in fierce anger. 24All the
nations will ask: "Why has the LORD
done this to this land?[c] Why this fierce, 29:24 c 1Ki 9:8;
burning anger?" Jer 22:8-9
25And the answer will be: "It is because this people abandoned the covenant of the LORD, the God of their fa-

[a] 19 Or *way, in order to add drunkenness to thirst.*

thers, the covenant he made with them
when he brought them out of Egypt.
26They went off and worshiped other
gods and bowed down to them, gods
they did not know, gods he had not giv-
en them. 27Therefore the LORD's anger
burned against this land, so that he
brought on it all the curses written in
this book.[d] 28In furious anger and in
great wrath the LORD uprooted[e] them
from their land and thrust them into
another land, as it is now."
29The secret things belong to the LORD
our God, but the things revealed belong
to us and to our children forever, that we
may follow all the words of this law.

Prosperity After Turning to the LORD

30 When all these blessings and
curses[f] I have set before you
come upon you and you take them to
heart wherever the LORD your God disperses you among the nations,[g] 2and
when you and your children return[h] to
the LORD your God and obey him with
all your heart and with all your soul according to everything I command you
today, 3then the LORD your God will restore your fortunes[a][i] and have compassion on you and gather[j] you again from
all the nations where he scattered you.[k]
4Even if you have been banished to the
most distant land under the heavens,
from there the LORD your God will gather you and bring you back.[l] 5He will
bring[m] you to the land that belonged to
your fathers, and you will take possession of it. He will make you more prosperous and numerous than your fathers.
6The LORD your God will circumcise
your hearts and the hearts of your descendants,[n] so that you may love him
with all your heart and with all your
soul, and live. 7The LORD your God will
put all these curses on your enemies
who hate and persecute you.[o] 8You will
again obey the LORD and follow all his
commands I am giving you today. 9Then
the LORD your God will make you most
prosperous in all the work of your hands
and in the fruit of your womb, the young
of your livestock and the crops of your
land.[p] The LORD will again delight in you
and make you prosperous, just as he delighted in your fathers, 10if you obey the
LORD your God and keep his commands
and decrees that are written in this

29:27 [d] Da 9:11,13,14
29:28 [e] 1Ki 14:15; 2Ch 7:20; Ps 52:5; Pr 2:22
30:1 [f] ver 15,19; Dt 11:26 [g] Lev 26:40-45; Dt 28:64; 29:28; 1Ki 8:47
30:2 [h] Dt 4:30; Ne 1:9
30:3 [i] Ps 126:4 [j] Ps 147:2; Jer 32:37; Eze 34:13 [k] Jer 29:14
30:4 [l] Ne 1:8-9; Isa 43:6
30:5 [m] Jer 29:14
30:6 [n] Dt 10:16; Jer 32:39
30:7 [o] Dt 7:15
30:9 [p] Dt 28:11; Jer 31:28; 32:41

Book of the Law and turn to the LORD
your God with all your heart and with all
your soul.[q]

The Offer of Life or Death

11Now what I am commanding you today is not too difficult for you or beyond
your reach.[r] 12It is not up in heaven, so
that you have to ask, "Who will ascend
into heaven to get it and proclaim it to us
so we may obey it?"[s] 13Nor is it beyond
the sea, so that you have to ask, "Who
will cross the sea to get it and proclaim it
to us so we may obey it?" 14No, the word
is very near you; it is in your mouth and
in your heart so you may obey it.
15See, I set before you today life and
prosperity, death and destruction.[t] 16For
I command you today to love the LORD
your God, to walk in his ways, and to
keep his commands, decrees and laws;
then you will live and increase, and the
LORD your God will bless you in the land
you are entering to possess.
17But if your heart turns away and you
are not obedient, and if you are drawn
away to bow down to other gods and
worship them, 18I declare to you this day
that you will certainly be destroyed.[u]
You will not live long in the land you are
crossing the Jordan to enter and possess.
19This day I call heaven and earth as
witnesses against you[v] that I have set
before you life and death, blessings and
curses.[w] Now choose life, so that you
and your children may live 20and that
you may love[x] the LORD your God, listen
to his voice, and hold fast to him. For the
LORD is your life,[y] and he will give you
many years in the land he swore to give
to your fathers, Abraham, Isaac and
Jacob.

Joshua to Succeed Moses

31 Then Moses went out and
spoke these words to all Israel:
2"I am now a hundred and twenty years
old[z] and I am no longer able to lead you.[a]
The LORD has said to me, 'You shall not
cross the Jordan.'[b] 3The LORD your God
himself will cross[c] over ahead of you.[d] He
will destroy these nations before you,
and you will take possession of their
land. Joshua also will cross[e] over ahead
of you, as the LORD said. 4And the LORD
will do to them what he did to Sihon and

[a] 3 Or *will bring you back from captivity*

30:10 [q] Dt 4:29
30:11 [r] Isa 45:19,23
30:12 [s] Ro 10:6*
30:15 [t] Dt 11:26
30:18 [u] Dt 8:19
30:19 [v] Dt 4:26 [w] ver 1
30:20 [x] Dt 6:5; 10:20 [y] Ps 27:1; Jn 11:25
31:2 [z] Dt 34:7 [a] Nu 27:17; 1Ki 3:7 [b] Dt 3:23,26
31:3 [c] Nu 27:18 [d] Dt 9:3 [e] Dt 3:28

Og, the kings of the Amorites, whom he
31:5 destroyed along with their land. 5The
[f]Dt 7:2 LORD will deliver[f] them to you, and you
must do to them all that I have com-
31:6 manded you. 6Be strong and coura-
[g]Jos 10:25; 1Ch 22:13 geous.[g] Do not be afraid or terrified[h] be-
[h]Dt 7:18 cause of them, for the LORD your God
[i]Dt 1:29; 20:4 [j]Jos 1:5 goes with you;[i] he will never leave you[j]
[k]Heb 13:5* nor forsake[k] you."
31:7 7Then Moses summoned Joshua and
[l]Dt 1:38; 3:28 said[l] to him in the presence of all Israel,
"Be strong and courageous, for you must
go with this people into the land that
the LORD swore to their forefathers to
give them, and you must divide it
among them as their inheritance. 8The
31:8 LORD himself goes before you and will be
[m]Ex 13:21; with you;[m] he will never leave you nor
33:14 forsake you. Do not be afraid; do not be
discouraged."

The Reading of the Law

9So Moses wrote down this law and
31:9 gave it to the priests, the sons of Levi,
[n]ver 25; who carried[n] the ark of the covenant of
Nu 4:15; Jos 3:3 the LORD, and to all the elders of Israel.
10Then Moses commanded them: "At
31:10 the end of every seven years, in the year
[o]Dt 15:1 for canceling debts,[o] during the Feast of
[p]Lev 23:34 Tabernacles,[p] 11when all Israel comes to
31:11 appear[q] before the LORD your God at the
[q]Dt 16:16 place he will choose, you shall read this
[r]Jos 8:34-35; 2Ki 23:2 law[r] before them in their hearing. 12As-
semble the people—men, women and
31:12 children, and the aliens living in your
[s]Dt 4:10 towns—so they can listen and learn[s] to
fear the LORD your God and follow care-
31:13 fully all the words of this law. 13Their
[t]Dt 11:2; children,[t] who do not know this law,
Ps 78:6-7 must hear it and learn to fear the LORD
your God as long as you live in the land
you are crossing the Jordan to possess."

Israel's Rebellion Predicted

31:14 14The LORD said to Moses, "Now the
[u]Nu 27:13; day of your death[u] is near. Call Joshua
Dt 32:49-50 and present yourselves at the Tent of
Meeting, where I will commission him."
So Moses and Joshua came and presented themselves at the Tent of Meeting.
15Then the LORD appeared at the Tent
31:15 in a pillar of cloud, and the cloud stood
[v]Ex 33:9 over the entrance to the Tent.[v] 16And the
LORD said to Moses: "You are going to
rest with your fathers, and these people
31:16 will soon prostitute[w] themselves to the
[w]Jdg 2:12 foreign gods of the land they are entering. They will forsake[x] me and break the 31:16
covenant I made with them. 17On that [x]Jdg 10:6,13
day I will become angry[y] with them and 31:17
forsake[z] them; I will hide[a] my face from [y]Jdg 2:14,20
them, and they will be destroyed. Many [z]Jdg 6:13; 2Ch 15:2
disasters and difficulties will come upon [a]Dt 32:20;
them, and on that day they will ask, Isa 1:15; 8:17 [b]Nu 14:42
'Have not these disasters come upon us
because our God is not with us?'[b] 18And
I will certainly hide my face on that day
because of all their wickedness in turning to other gods.
19"Now write down for yourselves this
song and teach it to the Israelites and
have them sing it, so that it may be a witness for me against them. 20When I have
brought them into the land flowing with
milk and honey, the land I promised on
oath to their forefathers,[c] and when they 31:20 [c]Dt 6:10-12
eat their fill and thrive, they will turn to [d]Dt 32:15-17
other gods[d] and worship them, rejecting [e]ver 16
me and breaking my covenant.[e] 21And
when many disasters and difficulties 31:21
come upon them,[f] this song will testify [f]ver 17
against them, because it will not be for- [g]Hos 5:3
gotten by their descendants. I know
what they are disposed to do,[g] even before I bring them into the land I promised them on oath." 22So Moses wrote[h] 31:22
down this song that day and taught it to [h]ver 19
the Israelites.
23The LORD gave this command[i] to 31:23
Joshua son of Nun: "Be strong and [i]ver 7 [j]Jos 1:6
courageous,[j] for you will bring the Israelites into the land I promised them on
oath, and I myself will be with you."
24After Moses finished writing in a
book the words of this law from beginning to end, 25he gave this command to
the Levites who carried the ark of the
covenant of the LORD: 26"Take this Book
of the Law and place it beside the ark of
the covenant of the LORD your God.
There it will remain as a witness against 31:26
you.[k] 27For I know how rebellious and [k]ver 19
stiff-necked[l] you are. If you have been re- 31:27
bellious against the LORD while I am still [l]Ex 32:9; Dt 9:6, 24
alive and with you, how much more will
you rebel after I die! 28Assemble before
me all the elders of your tribes and all
your officials, so that I can speak these
words in their hearing and call heaven 31:28
and earth to testify against them.[m] 29For [m]Dt 4:26; 30:19;
I know that after my death you are sure 32:1
to become utterly corrupt[n] and to turn 31:29
from the way I have commanded you. In [n]Dt 32:5; Jdg 2:19
days to come, disaster[o] will fall upon you [o]Dt 28:15

because you will do evil in the sight of the LORD and provoke him to anger by what your hands have made."

The Song of Moses

30 And Moses recited the words of this song from beginning to end in the hearing of the whole assembly of Israel:

32 Listen, O heavens,[p] and I will speak;
hear, O earth, the words of my mouth.
2 Let my teaching fall like rain
and my words descend like dew,[q]
like showers[r] on new grass,
like abundant rain on tender plants.
3 I will proclaim the name of the LORD.[s]
Oh, praise the greatness[t] of our God!
4 He is the Rock,[u] his works are perfect,[v]
and all his ways are just.
A faithful God[w] who does no wrong,
upright and just is he.
5 They have acted corruptly toward him;
to their shame they are no longer his children,
but a warped and crooked generation.[a][x]
6 Is this the way you repay[y] the LORD,
O foolish and unwise people?[z]
Is he not your Father,[a] your Creator,[b]
who made you and formed you?[b]
7 Remember the days of old;
consider the generations long past.
Ask your father and he will tell you,
your elders, and they will explain to you.[c]
8 When the Most High gave the nations their inheritance,
when he divided all mankind,[d]
he set up boundaries for the peoples
according to the number of the sons of Israel.[c]
9 For the LORD's portion[e] is his people,
Jacob his allotted inheritance.[f]

32:1 p Isa 1:2
32:2 q Isa 55:11 r Ps 72:6
32:3 s Ex 33:19 t Dt 3:24
32:4 u ver 15,18,30 v 2Sa 22:31 w Dt 7:9
32:5 x Dt 31:29
32:6 y Ps 116:12 z Ps 74:2 a Dt 1:31; Isa 63:16 b ver 15
32:7 c Ex 13:14
32:8 d Ge 11:8; Ac 17:26
32:9 e Jer 10:16 f 1Ki 8:51,53

10 In a desert[g] land he found him,
in a barren and howling waste.
He shielded him and cared for him;
he guarded him as the apple of his eye,[h]
11 like an eagle that stirs up its nest
and hovers over its young,[i]
that spreads its wings to catch them
and carries them on its pinions.
12 The LORD alone led him;
no foreign god was with him.[j]
13 He made him ride on the heights[k] of the land
and fed him with the fruit of the fields.
He nourished him with honey from the rock,
and with oil[l] from the flinty crag,
14 with curds and milk from herd and flock
and with fattened lambs and goats,
with choice rams of Bashan
and the finest kernels of wheat.[m]
You drank the foaming blood of the grape.[n]
15 Jeshurun[d] grew fat[o] and kicked;
filled with food, he became heavy and sleek.
He abandoned[p] the God who made him
and rejected the Rock[q] his Savior.
16 They made him jealous[r] with their foreign gods
and angered[s] him with their detestable idols.
17 They sacrificed to demons, which are not God—
gods they had not known,[t]
gods that recently appeared,[u]
gods your fathers did not fear.
18 You deserted the Rock, who fathered you;
you forgot[v] the God who gave you birth.
19 The LORD saw this and rejected them[w]
because he was angered by his sons and daughters.[x]

32:10 g Jer 2:6 h Ps 17:8; Zec 2:8
32:11 i Ex 19:4
32:12 j ver 39
32:13 k Isa 58:14 l Job 29:6
32:14 m Ps 81:16; 147:14 n Ge 49:11
32:15 o Dt 31:20 p ver 6; Isa 1:4, 28 q ver 4
32:16 r 1Co 10:22 s Ps 78:58
32:17 t Dt 28:64 u Jdg 5:8
32:18 v Isa 17:10
32:19 w Jer 44:21-23 x Ps 106:40

[a] 5 Or *Corrupt are they and not his children, / a generation warped and twisted to their shame* [b] 6 Or *Father, who bought you* [c] 8 Masoretic Text; Dead Sea Scrolls (see also Septuagint) *sons of God* [d] 15 *Jeshurun* means *the upright one,* that is, Israel.

DISCOVERY 50

The Song of Moses

Moses gave Israel her first national anthem, a song to be memorized by every child in each succeeding generation. It is a powerful ballad of epic proportions describing the history, feelings and failings of the nation of Israel, the "apple of God's eye" (Deuteronomy 32:10; Zechariah 2:8). God gave his people this song as a constant reminder that he is faithful and just, the One who keeps his promises and always does what is right. But the song was also a painful reminder that God's people were corrupt and foolish when they rejected the wonderful things God wanted to give them.

We might say that this was the first and only "rock" song in the Bible. The theme is clear: God is the Rock, the only One solid enough for us to count on. God is the main character of the song, and the opening lyrics describe him as great, steadfast and perfect (Deuteronomy 32:4). Moses went on to refer to God as Father, Creator and Most High.

The middle section of this song reminded the people of how they as a nation had responded to God. After all the great things he had done to protect and provide for them, they had turned their hearts against him. They had suffered a kind of spiritual amnesia and had forgotten what he had done. Because they had been selfish and stubborn, they had rejected the Rock (verse 15) and deserted him (verse 18).

The final section of the song pointed the people to one very important fact: No "rock" about which any other nation might boast could *ever* compare to the Rock of Israel: "For their rock is not like our Rock, as even our enemies concede" (verse 31). This hymn resounds with chords of love and redemption, showing that God wants to save his people and show them mercy—no matter how they have responded in the past.

This song carries a theme that is familiar to us from both the Old and the New Testaments, for they point to another Rock who was rejected (Psalm 118:22; Matthew 21:42; 1 Peter 2:7). The Bible reminds us that we need to "come to [Jesus], the living Stone—rejected by men but chosen by God and precious to him" (1 Peter 2:4). And though it has been more than 3,000 years since Moses wrote *his* song, we often voice the same refrain of spiritual forgetfulness. God has done so much for us, yet how often don't we reject his offer of grace and abandon his careful plan for our lives in order to do our own thing!

Peter didn't allow us to wallow in our failure; instead, he moved on to encourage us to sing a new song of praise to Jesus the Rock: "Declare the praises of him who called you out of darkness into his wonderful light" (1 Peter 2:9). Now that is a song worth singing!

Self-Discovery: *Think about the qualities of a rock, particularly of a large and protecting rock. In what ways is Jesus a rock for you?*

GO TO DISCOVERY 51 ON PAGE 267

20 "I will hide my face[y] from them," he said,
"and see what their end will be;
for they are a perverse generation,[z]
children who are unfaithful.
21 They made me jealous[a] by what is no god
and angered me with their worthless idols.[b]
I will make them envious by those who are not a people;
I will make them angry by a nation that has no understanding.[c]
22 For a fire has been kindled by my wrath,
one that burns to the realm of death[a] below.[d]
It will devour the earth and its harvests
and set afire the foundations of the mountains.
23 "I will heap calamities[e] upon them
and spend my arrows[f] against them.
24 I will send wasting famine against them,
consuming pestilence[g] and deadly plague;[h]
I will send against them the fangs of wild beasts,[i]
the venom of vipers[j] that glide in the dust.
25 In the street the sword will make them childless;
in their homes terror will reign.[k]
Young men and young women will perish,
infants and gray-haired men.[l]
26 I said I would scatter[m] them
and blot out their memory from mankind,[n]
27 but I dreaded the taunt of the enemy,
lest the adversary misunderstand
and say, 'Our hand has triumphed;
the LORD has not done all this.' "[o]

28 They are a nation without sense,
there is no discernment in them.
29 If only they were wise and would understand this[p]
and discern what their end will be!
30 How could one man chase a thousand,
or two put ten thousand to flight,[q]
unless their Rock had sold them,
unless the LORD had given them up?[r]
31 For their rock is not like our Rock,
as even our enemies concede.
32 Their vine comes from the vine of Sodom
and from the fields of Gomorrah.
Their grapes are filled with poison,
and their clusters with bitterness.
33 Their wine is the venom of serpents,
the deadly poison of cobras.[s]
34 "Have I not kept this in reserve
and sealed it in my vaults?[t]
35 It is mine to avenge; I will repay.[u]
In due time their foot will slip;[v]
their day of disaster is near
and their doom rushes upon them.[w]"
36 The LORD will judge his people
and have compassion on his servants[x]
when he sees their strength is gone
and no one is left, slave or free.
37 He will say: "Now where are their gods,
the rock they took refuge in,[y]
38 the gods who ate the fat of their sacrifices
and drank the wine of their drink offerings?
Let them rise up to help you!
Let them give you shelter!
39 "See now that I myself am He![z]
There is no god besides me.[a]
I put to death and I bring to life,[b]
I have wounded and I will heal,[c]
and no one can deliver out of my hand.[d]
40 I lift my hand to heaven and declare:
As surely as I live forever,
41 when I sharpen my flashing sword[e]
and my hand grasps it in judgment,
I will take vengeance on my adversaries
and repay those who hate me.[f]

[a] 22 Hebrew *to Sheol*

32:20 y Dt 31:17,29 z ver 5
32:21 a 1Co 10:22 b 1Ki 16:13,26 c Ro 10:19*
32:22 d Ps 18:7-8; Jer 15:14; La 4:11
32:23 e Dt 29:21 f Ps 7:13; Eze 5:16
32:24 g Dt 28:22 h Ps 91:6 i Lev 26:22 j Am 5:18-19
32:25 k Eze 7:15 l 2Ch 36:17; La 2:21
32:26 m Dt 4:27 n Ps 34:16
32:27 o Isa 10:13
32:29 p Dt 5:29; Ps 81:13
32:30 q Lev 26:8 r Ps 44:12
32:33 s Ps 58:4
32:34 t Jer 2:22; Hos 13:12
32:35 u Ro 12:19*; Heb 10:30* v Jer 23:12 w Eze 7:8-9
32:36 x Dt 30:1-3; Ps 135:14; Joel 2:14
32:37 y Jdg 10:14; Jer 2:28
32:39 z Isa 41:4 a Isa 45:5 b 1Sa 2:6; Ps 68:20 c Hos 6:1 d Ps 50:22
32:41 e Isa 34:6; 66:16; Eze 21:9-10 f Jer 50:29

32:42 [g] ver 23 [h] Jer 46:10,14

42 I will make my arrows drunk with
blood,[g]
while my sword devours flesh:[h]
the blood of the slain and the
captives,
the heads of the enemy leaders."

32:43 [i] Ro 15:10* [j] 2Ki 9:7 [k] Ps 65:3; 85:1; Rev 19:2

43 Rejoice,[i] O nations, with his
people,[a,b]
for he will avenge the blood of
his servants;[j]
he will take vengeance on his
enemies
and make atonement for his
land and people.[k]

32:44 [l] Nu 13:8,16

44 Moses came with Joshua[c][l] son of
Nun and spoke all the words of this song
in the hearing of the people. 45 When
Moses finished reciting all these words
to all Israel, 46 he said to them, "Take to
heart all the words I have solemnly de-

32:46 [m] Eze 40:4

clared to you this day,[m] so that you may
command your children to obey carefully all the words of this law. 47 They are
not just idle words for you—they are

32:47 [n] Dt 30:20

your life.[n] By them you will live long in
the land you are crossing the Jordan to
possess."

Moses to Die on Mount Nebo

48 On that same day the LORD told Mo-

32:49 [o] Nu 27:12

ses, 49 "Go up into the Abarim[o] Range to
Mount Nebo in Moab, across from Jericho, and view Canaan, the land I am giving the Israelites as their own possession. 50 There on the mountain that you

32:50 [p] Ge 25:8

have climbed you will die[p] and be gathered to your people, just as your brother
Aaron died on Mount Hor and was
gathered to his people. 51 This is because
both of you broke faith with me in the
presence of the Israelites at the waters of

32:51 [q] Nu 20:11-13 [r] Nu 27:14

Meribah Kadesh in the Desert of Zin[q]
and because you did not uphold my holiness among the Israelites.[r] 52 Therefore,
you will see the land only from a dis-

32:52 [s] Dt 34:1-3 [t] Dt 1:37

tance;[s] you will not enter[t] the land I am
giving to the people of Israel."

Moses Blesses the Tribes

33:1 [u] Jos 14:6

33 This is the blessing that Moses
the man of God[u] pronounced
on the Israelites before his death. 2 He
said:

33:2 [v] Ex 19:18; Ps 68:8 [w] Jdg 5:4

"The LORD came from Sinai[v]
and dawned over them from
Seir;[w]

33:2 [x] Hab 3:3 [y] Da 7:10; Ac 7:53; Rev 5:11

he shone forth from Mount
Paran.[x]
He came with[d] myriads of holy
ones[y]
from the south, from his
mountain slopes.[e]

33:3 [z] Hos 11:1 [a] Dt 14:2 [b] Lk 10:39

3 Surely it is you who love[z] the
people;
all the holy ones are in your
hand.[a]
At your feet they all bow down,[b]
and from you receive
instruction,

33:4 [c] Jn 1:17 [d] Ps 119:111

4 the law that Moses gave us,[c]
the possession of the assembly
of Jacob.[d]
5 He was king over Jeshurun[f]
when the leaders of the people
assembled,
along with the tribes of Israel.

6 "Let Reuben live and not die,
nor[g] his men be few."

33:7 [e] Ge 49:10

7 And this he said about Judah:[e]

"Hear, O LORD, the cry of Judah;
bring him to his people.
With his own hands he defends his
cause.
Oh, be his help against his foes!"

8 About Levi he said:

33:8 [f] Ex 28:30 [g] Ex 17:7

"Your Thummim and Urim[f] belong
to the man you favored.
You tested him at Massah;
you contended with him at the
waters of Meribah.[g]

33:9 [h] Ex 32:26-29 [i] Mal 2:5

9 He said of his father and mother,[h]
'I have no regard for them.'
He did not recognize his brothers
or acknowledge his own children,
but he watched over your word
and guarded your covenant.[i]

33:10 [j] Lev 10:11; Dt 31:9-13 [k] Ps 51:19

10 He teaches your precepts to Jacob
and your law to Israel.[j]
He offers incense before you
and whole burnt offerings on
your altar.[k]

33:11 [l] 2Sa 24:23

11 Bless all his skills, O LORD,
and be pleased with the work of
his hands.[l]

[a] 43 Or *Make his people rejoice, O nations*
[b] 43 Masoretic Text; Dead Sea Scrolls (see also Septuagint) *people, / and let all the angels worship him /*
[c] 44 Hebrew *Hoshea,* a variant of *Joshua*
[d] 2 Or *from*
[e] 2 The meaning of the Hebrew for this phrase is uncertain.
[f] 5 *Jeshurun* means *the upright one,* that is, Israel; also in verse 26.
[g] 6 Or *but let*

Smite the loins of those who rise
up against him;
strike his foes till they rise no
more."

[12]About Benjamin he said:

"Let the beloved of the LORD rest
secure in him,[m]
for he shields him all day long,
and the one the LORD loves rests
between his shoulders.[n]"

33:12 [m] Dt 12:10 [n] Ex 28:12

[13]About Joseph[o] he said:

"May the LORD bless his land
with the precious dew from
heaven above
and with the deep waters that lie
below;[p]
[14]with the best the sun brings forth
and the finest the moon can
yield;
[15]with the choicest gifts of the
ancient mountains[q]
and the fruitfulness of the
everlasting hills;
[16]with the best gifts of the earth and
its fullness
and the favor of him who dwelt
in the burning bush.[r]
Let all these rest on the head of
Joseph,
on the brow of the prince
among[a] his brothers.
[17]In majesty he is like a firstborn bull;
his horns are the horns of a wild
ox.[s]
With them he will gore[t] the
nations,
even those at the ends of the
earth.
Such are the ten thousands of
Ephraim;
such are the thousands of
Manasseh."

33:13 [o] Ge 49:25 [p] Ge 27:28
33:15 [q] Hab 3:6
33:16 [r] Ex 3:2
33:17 [s] Nu 23:22 [t] 1Ki 22:11; Ps 44:5

[18]About Zebulun[u] he said:

"Rejoice, Zebulun, in your going
out,
and you, Issachar, in your tents.
[19]They will summon peoples to the
mountain[v]
and there offer sacrifices of
righteousness;[w]
they will feast on the abundance of
the seas,[x]
on the treasures hidden in the
sand."

33:18 [u] Ge 49:13-15
33:19 [v] Ex 15:17; Isa 2:3 [w] Ps 4:5 [x] Isa 60:5,11

[20]About Gad[y] he said:

"Blessed is he who enlarges Gad's
domain!
Gad lives there like a lion,
tearing at arm or head.
[21]He chose the best land for himself;[z]
the leader's portion was kept for
him.
When the heads of the people
assembled,
he carried out the LORD's
righteous will,[a]
and his judgments concerning
Israel."

33:20 [y] Ge 49:19
33:21 [z] Nu 32:1-5,31-32 [a] Jos 4:12; 22:1-3

[22]About Dan[b] he said:

"Dan is a lion's cub,
springing out of Bashan."

33:22 [b] Ge 49:16

[23]About Naphtali he said:

"Naphtali is abounding with the
favor of the LORD
and is full of his blessing;
he will inherit southward to the
lake."

[24]About Asher[c] he said:

"Most blessed of sons is Asher;
let him be favored by his
brothers,
and let him bathe his feet in oil.[d]
[25]The bolts of your gates will be iron
and bronze,
and your strength will equal
your days.[e]

[26]"There is no one like the God of
Jeshurun,[f]
who rides on the heavens to help
you[g]
and on the clouds in his majesty.
[27]The eternal God is your refuge,[h]
and underneath are the
everlasting arms.
He will drive out your enemy
before you,[i]
saying, 'Destroy him!'[j]
[28]So Israel will live in safety alone;[k]
Jacob's spring is secure
in a land of grain and new wine,
where the heavens drop dew.[l]
[29]Blessed are you, O Israel![m]
Who is like you,[n]
a people saved by the LORD?[o]
He is your shield and helper[p]
and your glorious sword.

33:24 [c] Ge 49:21 [d] Ge 49:20; Job 29:6
33:25 [e] Dt 4:40; 32:47
33:26 [f] Ex 15:11 [g] Ps 104:3
33:27 [h] Ps 90:1 [i] Jos 24:18 [j] Dt 7:2
33:28 [k] Nu 23:9; Jer 23:6 [l] Ge 27:28
33:29 [m] Ps 144:15 [n] Ps 18:44 [o] 2Sa 7:23 [p] Ps 115:9-11

[a] 16 Or *of the one separated from*

DISCOVERY 51

THE GOD OF SECOND CHANCES

God used Moses to lead his people out of bondage in Egypt, through the desert wasteland and to the borders of the land he had promised to give them. But Moses was not perfect. When the people needed water and God instructed Moses to speak to a rock to obtain it, Moses instead struck the rock twice with his staff. (See also Discovery #39 on page 199.) The people enjoyed the cool refreshment they needed, but Moses had dishonored God by doing things his own way. Because of his disobedience Moses would not be permitted to enter the promised land (Numbers 20:1–13).

Before the people took possession of the land, however, God invited Moses to the top of Mount Nebo. From this vantage point God revealed a panoramic view of the land in which the people would settle (Deuteronomy 34:1). Receiving this satisfaction that God was going to keep his promise, Moses died. Though an old man, he was still strong and filled with potential (verse 7), but because of his lack of trust that potential was cut short; he was unable to finish the monumental task of leading the people triumphantly to their final destination.

That tragedy is often repeated in our own lives. Because we fail to follow God's instructions, we suffer the consequences of our choices, and our potential is unachieved. We end up grieving over what could have been.

But the example of Moses' life also inspires hope in us. God is always the God of second chances, and Moses' story doesn't end on Mount Nebo. Matthew recorded an epilogue in Matthew 17:1–3: "After six days Jesus took with him Peter, James and John the brother of James and led them up a high mountain by themselves. There he was transfigured before them. His face shone like the sun, and his clothes became as white as the light. Just then there appeared before them Moses and Elijah, talking with Jesus." Moses had disobeyed God, and that lapse had cost him dearly. But his relationship with God had not been severed. In God's mercy Moses was the man God had called him to be on into eternity.

Disobedience has a cost, but God is still working on the story of our lives. Moses suffered loss but was given a future. And that future was far brighter than anything he could ever have dreamed!

In the final analysis, the simple, yet unfathomable beauty of the salvation story may be summed up in a few powerful words: "God demonstrated his own love for us in this: While we were still sinners, Christ died for us" (Romans 5:8). Our God is truly the God of second chances!

Self-Discovery: *Has there ever been a time in which you failed to achieve your full potential because of your lack of obedience? Jesus is able to forgive and erase past mistakes and give you another chance.*

GO TO DISCOVERY 52 ON PAGE 271

Your enemies will cower before
you,
and you will trample down their
33:29 q Dt 32:13 high places.[a][q]"

The Death of Moses

34 Then Moses climbed Mount
Nebo from the plains of Moab
to the top of Pisgah, across from Jeri-
34:1 cho.[r] There the LORD showed[s] him the
r Dt 32:49 whole land—from Gilead to Dan, [2]all of
s Dt 32:52 Naphtali, the territory of Ephraim and
Manasseh, all the land of Judah as far as
34:2 the western sea,[b][t] [3]the Negev and the
t Dt 11:24 whole region from the Valley of Jericho,
34:3 the City of Palms,[u] as far as Zoar. [4]Then
u Jdg 1:16; 3:13; 2Ch 28:15 the LORD said to him, "This is the land I
promised on oath[v] to Abraham, Isaac
34:4 and Jacob when I said, 'I will give it[w] to
v Ge 28:13 w Ge 12:7 your descendants.' I have let you see it
x Dt 3:27 with your eyes, but you will not cross[x]
over into it."
34:5 [5]And Moses the servant of the LORD[y]
y Nu 12:7 z Dt 32:50; died[z] there in Moab, as the LORD had
Jos 1:1-2 said. [6]He buried him[c] in Moab, in the
valley opposite Beth Peor,[a] but to this 34:6 a Dt 3:29
day no one knows where his grave is.[b] b Jude 1:9
[7]Moses was a hundred and twenty years 34:7
old[c] when he died, yet his eyes were not c Dt 31:2
weak[d] nor his strength gone. [8]The Isra- d Ge 27:1
elites grieved for Moses in the plains of 34:8
Moab thirty days, until the time of e Ge 50:3,10; 2Sa 11:27
weeping and mourning[e] was over.
[9]Now Joshua son of Nun was filled 34:9
with the spirit[d] of wisdom[f] because Mo- f Ge 41:38;
ses had laid his hands on him.[g] So the Is- Isa 11:2; Da 6:3
raelites listened to him and did what the g Nu 27:18,23
LORD had commanded Moses.
[10]Since then, no prophet has risen in 34:10
Israel like Moses,[h] whom the LORD knew h Dt 18:15,18
face to face,[i] [11]who did all those miracu- i Ex 33:11;
lous signs and wonders[j] the LORD sent Nu 12:6,8; Dt 5:4
him to do in Egypt—to Pharaoh and to 34:11
all his officials[k] and to his whole land. j Dt 4:34
[12]For no one has ever shown the mighty k Dt 7:19
power or performed the awesome deeds
that Moses did in the sight of all Israel.

[a] 29 Or *will tread upon their bodies* [b] 2 That is, the Mediterranean [c] 6 Or *He was buried*
[d] 9 Or *Spirit*

Do God's promises to Joshua and Israel apply to us? (Joshua 1:9)

♦ *God made two kinds of promises to Joshua and Israel—physical and spiritual. Both look back to God's pledge to give Abraham land, posterity and spiritual blessings (Genesis 12:2–3). The promise of spiritual blessing extends to all believers in Jesus (Abraham's heirs—see Galatians 3:29).*

Why did God speak as though victory had already come? (Joshua 6:2)

♦ *Old Testament Hebrew sometimes stated predictions about the future in the present or even the past tense. Prophecies about Jesus' suffering in Isaiah 53 are a good example. In this instance God was guaranteeing that he had resolved absolutely to give Jericho over to the Israelites.*

Jesus in Joshua In Hebrew the names *Joshua* and *Jesus* are the same—*Yeshua,* which means "The LORD saves." Both Joshua and Jesus were used by God at different times in history to bring deliverance to his people, but the Bible does record an instance where many Bible students believe the two worked together. When the "commander of the army of the LORD" appeared to Joshua, Joshua fell on his face in reverence (Joshua 5:14). Many have concluded that this heavenly visitor was not merely *representing* God: This visitor was God the Son, stepping into the situation in human form at a critical moment in human history.

Though the Israelites had failed to enter the promised land the first time and had wasted 40 years for their failure, God gave them another chance. So too in our own spiritual life, God offers redemption through the shed blood of Jesus for our wasted years—our wilderness wanderings. Joshua records the good news of the success of the Israelites the second time around.

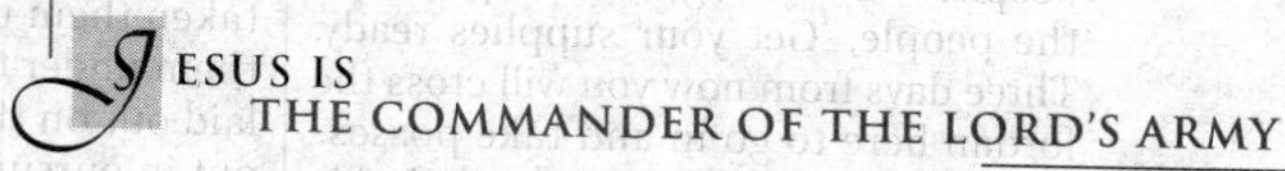

JESUS IS
THE COMMANDER OF THE LORD'S ARMY

The LORD Commands Joshua

1 After the death of Moses the ser-
1:1 aNu 12:7; Dt 34:5 bEx 24:13; Dt 1:38 vant of the LORD,[a] the LORD said to
Joshua[b] son of Nun, Moses' aide: 2"Mo-
ses my servant is dead. Now then, you
and all these people, get ready to cross
1:2 cver 11 the Jordan River[c] into the land I am
about to give to them—to the Israelites.
3I will give you every place where you set
1:3 dDt 11:24 your foot,[d] as I promised Moses. 4Your
territory will extend from the desert to
Lebanon, and from the great river, the
1:4 eGe 15:18 fNu 34:2-12 Euphrates[e]—all the Hittite country—to
the Great Sea[a] on the west.[f] 5No one will
be able to stand up against you[g] all the
1:5 gDt 7:24 hJos 3:7; 6:27 iDt 31:6-8 days of your life. As I was with[h] Moses,
so I will be with you; I will never leave
you nor forsake[i] you.

JESUS IS THE GREATEST LEADER
THE WORLD HAS EVER SEEN.

John Maxwell, *Leadership Expert*

6"Be strong and courageous, because
you will lead these people to inherit the
1:6 jDt 31:23 land I swore to their forefathers[j] to give
them. 7Be strong and very courageous.
Be careful to obey all the law my servant
Moses gave you; do not turn from it to
1:7 kDt 5:32; 28:14 lJos 11:15 the right or to the left,[k] that you may be
successful wherever you go.[l] 8Do not let
this Book of the Law depart from your
mouth; meditate on it day and night, so
that you may be careful to do everything
written in it. Then you will be prosper-
1:8 mDt 29:9; Ps 1:1-3 ous and successful.[m] 9Have I not commanded you? Be strong and courageous.
1:9 nPs 27:1 over 7; Dt 31:7-8; Jer 1:8 Do not be terrified;[n] do not be discouraged, for the LORD your God will be with
you wherever you go."[o]
10So Joshua ordered the officers of the
people: 11"Go through the camp and tell
the people, 'Get your supplies ready.
Three days from now you will cross the
Jordan here to go in and take posses-
1:11 pJoel 3:2 sion[p] of the land the LORD your God is
giving you for your own.' "
12But to the Reubenites, the Gadites
1:12 qNu 32:20-22 and the half-tribe of Manasseh,[q] Joshua
said, 13"Remember the command that
Moses the servant of the LORD gave you:
1:13 rDt 3:18-20 'The LORD your God is giving you rest[r]
and has granted you this land.' 14Your
wives, your children and your livestock
may stay in the land that Moses gave
you east of the Jordan, but all your fighting men, fully armed, must cross over
ahead of your brothers. You are to help
your brothers 15until the LORD gives
them rest, as he has done for you, and
until they too have taken possession of
the land that the LORD your God is giving them. After that, you may go back
and occupy your own land, which Moses
the servant of the LORD gave you east of 1:15 sJos 22:1-4
the Jordan toward the sunrise."[s]
16Then they answered Joshua, "Whatever you have commanded us we will do,
and wherever you send us we will go.
17Just as we fully obeyed Moses, so we
will obey you.[t] Only may the LORD your 1:17 tver 5,9
God be with you as he was with Moses.
18Whoever rebels against your word and
does not obey your words, whatever you
may command them, will be put to
death. Only be strong and courageous!"

Rahab and the Spies

2 Then Joshua son of Nun secretly 2:1 uJas 2:25 vNu 25:1; Jos 3:1 wHeb 11:31
sent two spies[u] from Shittim.[v]
"Go, look over the land," he said, "especially Jericho." So they went and entered
the house of a prostitute[b] named Rahab[w] and stayed there.
2The king of Jericho was told, "Look!
Some of the Israelites have come here
tonight to spy out the land." 3So the king
of Jericho sent this message to Rahab:
"Bring out the men who came to you
and entered your house, because they
have come to spy out the whole land."
4But the woman had taken the two 2:4 x2Sa 17:19-20
men and hidden them.[x] She said, "Yes,
the men came to me, but I did not know
where they had come from. 5At dusk,
when it was time to close the city gate,
the men left. I don't know which way
they went. Go after them quickly. You
may catch up with them." 6(But she had
taken them up to the roof and hidden
them under the stalks of flax[y] she had 2:6 yJas 2:25 zEx 1:17,19; 2Sa 17:19
laid out on the roof.)[z] 7So the men set
out in pursuit of the spies on the road
that leads to the fords of the Jordan, and
as soon as the pursuers had gone out,
the gate was shut.
8Before the spies lay down for the
night, she went up on the roof 9and said 2:9 aGe 35:5; Ex 23:27; Dt 2:25
to them, "I know that the LORD has given
this land to you and that a great fear[a] of

[a] *4* That is, the Mediterranean [b] *1* Or possibly *an innkeeper*

DISCOVERY 52

Joshua: Yahweh Saves

God's people lived in the desert for 40 years, traveling from place to place as he directed them. After Moses died, they were ready under Joshua's leadership to enter the land God had promised them. Joshua had been a slave in Egypt and knew from firsthand experience that God could be counted on to deliver his people. He had already led the Israelite army to victory over the Amalekites (Exodus 17:8–13) and had traveled with Moses up Mount Sinai when God had given him the law (Exodus 24:13–14). Joshua was also one of the two spies who had believed that God would indeed give his people the land he had promised (Numbers 14:26–34). Joshua was a man in "whom is the spirit" (Numbers 27:18).

God had promised Moses that the people would conquer the land (Joshua 1:3), the same promise he had earlier made to Abraham and to his descendants (Genesis 12:2–3; 17:19–21). Even the boundaries of that land had been identified for Abraham (Genesis 15:18–21). The story of Joshua reveals the manner in which God would keep that promise generations later.

In many ways Joshua's life and leadership illustrate what Jesus would do for God's people. Even their names are similar. Joshua's original name was *Hoshea*, which means "salvation." Moses later changed his name to Joshua, meaning "the LORD saves" (Numbers 13:16). In Greek, the language of the New Testament, the name *Joshua* is the same as *Jesus*, which also means "savior." God's angel instructed Mary to name her son Jesus, because "he [would] save his people from their sins" (Matthew 1:21).

Joshua and Jesus carried out similar roles in God's plan. Joshua led God's people into the land God had promised them, ushering them into the long-awaited place of rest. Jesus died on the cross and came back again to life so that we could know God, and he offers our souls the rest we crave (Hebrews 4:8–11). Like the Israelites, many of us are wandering in a wilderness of unmet hopes and failures. Jesus will lead us into the promised land where we can rest in the faithfulness of God and in the completed work of Christ.

Our rest is letting Jesus live through us by his Holy Spirit. Just as Joshua helped God's people defeat their enemies, so Jesus gives us victory over our enemies—sin and Satan and his evil plans (Hebrews 2:14–16). When the nation sinned and was in consequence defeated in battle, Joshua prayed to God for the people (Joshua 7:6–9), and in the same way Jesus continually speaks to God on our behalf (Hebrews 7:25). Jesus is indeed our true Savior.

Self-Discovery: *In what ways are you wandering in a wilderness of unmet hopes and failures? Will you allow Jesus to lead you into the peace and rest found only through faith in him?*

GO TO DISCOVERY 53 ON PAGE 273

you has fallen on us, so that all who live
in this country are melting in fear because of you. 10We have heard how the
2:10 [b]Ex 14:21 LORD dried up[b] the water of the Red Sea[a]
[c]Nu 23:22 for you when you came out of Egypt,[c]
[d]Nu 21:21,24, and what you did to Sihon and Og,[d] the
34-35 two kings of the Amorites east of the
Jordan, whom you completely destroyed.[b] 11When we heard of it, our
hearts melted and everyone's courage
2:11 [e]Ex 15:14; failed because of you,[e] for the LORD your
Jos 5:1; 7:5; God is God in heaven above and on the
Ps 22:14; earth[f] below. 12Now then, please swear
Isa 13:7 [f]Dt 4:39 to me by the LORD that you will show
kindness to my family, because I have
shown kindness to you. Give me a sure
2:12 [g]ver 18 sign[g] 13that you will spare the lives of my
father and mother, my brothers and sis-
ters, and all who belong to them, and
that you will save us from death."

14"Our lives for your lives!" the men
assured her. "If you don't tell what we are
2:14 doing, we will treat you kindly and faith-
[h]Jdg 1:24; Mt 5:7 fully[h] when the LORD gives us the land."

15So she let them down by a rope
2:15 [i]Ac 9:25 through the window,[i] for the house she
lived in was part of the city wall. 16Now
she had said to them, "Go to the hills so
the pursuers will not find you. Hide
2:16 [j]Jas 2:25 yourselves there three days[j] until they
[k]Heb 11:31 return, and then go on your way."[k]

2:17 [l]Ge 24:8 17The men said to her, "This oath[l] you
made us swear will not be binding on us
18unless, when we enter the land, you
have tied this scarlet cord in the window
through which you let us down, and unless you have brought your father and
mother, your brothers and all your fami-
2:18 [m]ver 12; ly[m] into your house. 19If anyone goes out-
Jos 6:23 side your house into the street, his blood
will be on his own head;[n] we will not be
2:19 responsible. As for anyone who is in the
[n]Eze 33:4 [o]Mt 27:25 house with you, his blood will be on our
head[o] if a hand is laid on him. 20But if
you tell what we are doing, we will be released from the oath you made us swear."

21"Agreed," she replied. "Let it be as
you say." So she sent them away and they
departed. And she tied the scarlet cord
in the window.

22When they left, they went into the
hills and stayed there three days, until
the pursuers had searched all along the
road and returned without finding
them. 23Then the two men started back.
They went down out of the hills, forded
the river and came to Joshua son of Nun
and told him everything that had happened to them. 24They said to Joshua,
"The LORD has surely given the whole 2:24
land into our hands;[p] all the people are [p]ver 9; Jos 6:2
melting in fear because of us."

Crossing the Jordan

3 Early in the morning Joshua and
all the Israelites set out from
Shittim[q] and went to the Jordan, where 3:1 [q]Jos 2:1
they camped before crossing over. 2After
three days the officers went throughout 3:2
the camp,[r] 3giving orders to the people: [r]Jos 1:11
"When you see the ark of the covenant[s] 3:3
of the LORD your God, and the priests,[t] [s]Nu 10:33
who are Levites, carrying it, you are to [t]Dt 31:9
move out from your positions and fol-
low it. 4Then you will know which way
to go, since you have never been this way
before. But keep a distance of about a
thousand yards[c] between you and the
ark; do not go near it."

5Joshua told the people, "Consecrate 3:5 [u]Ex 19:10,14;
yourselves,[u] for tomorrow the LORD will Lev 20:7;
do amazing things among you." Jos 7:13; 1Sa 16:5;

6Joshua said to the priests, "Take up Joel 2:16
the ark of the covenant and pass on
ahead of the people." So they took it up
and went ahead of them.

[a] *10* Hebrew *Yam Suph*; that is, Sea of Reeds
[b] *10* The Hebrew term refers to the irrevocable giving over of things or persons to the LORD, often by totally destroying them.
[c] *4* Hebrew *about two thousand cubits* (about 900 meters)

JESUS FOCUS

STEPPING OUT

In two separate instances God enabled his people to cross bodies of water on dry land: the Red Sea (Exodus 14) and the Jordan River (Joshua 3). On both occasions God used Israel's human leader to show his own incredible power, proving that God himself had chosen that man to lead the people. When the Israelites crossed the Red Sea "the angel of God," thought by many to be Jesus himself, protected them from the Egyptians (Exodus 14:19–20). As they crossed the Jordan River the ark of the covenant, the sacred symbol of the Lord's presence and majesty, led the way. In the New Testament Jesus displayed an equally great manifestation of God's power when he walked on top of the water on the Sea of Galilee (John 6:19). In each case God demonstrated his power over the forces of nature and indicated that the human leader involved was acting with his blessing and approval.

Rahab's Scarlet Rope

Before Joshua led the people into the land, he sent two spies ahead to gather information. They paid special attention to Jericho, because it was the key city in the Jordan valley. When the spies arrived in Jericho, they were invited to stay with a prostitute named Rahab. The king of the city soon learned of their presence and dispatched soldiers to Rahab's house. She hid the spies on her rooftop and told the soldiers that they had left just before dark to investigate the rest of the land. After the soldiers had gone, Rahab lowered the spies over the city wall in a large basket. Before they left, they asked her to dangle a scarlet rope out of her window so that she and anyone else in her house might be spared when Israel conquered Jericho.

Rahab was a most unlikely candidate as an individual to be used by God. Yet, in spite of her low position in society, God used *this* prostitute because she believed in him. Before she lowered the spies over the wall, she told them, "I know that the LORD has given this land to you and that a great fear of you has fallen on us, so that all who live in this country are melting in fear because of you. We have heard how the LORD dried up the water of the Red Sea . . . When we heard of it, our hearts melted and everyone's courage failed because of you, for the LORD your God is God in heaven above and on the earth below" (Joshua 2:9–11).

Rahab believed two things: that God had given the land to his people and that he had demonstrated his power on their behalf. And based on those two beliefs she came to an important conclusion: The God of Israel is the only true God, the God of all heaven and earth. Because she believed that God was who he said he was, she and her family were spared when the city was destroyed.

Rahab put that faith into practice immediately. She protected the spies, putting her own life at risk. She could have turned them over to the soldiers and been rewarded by the king, but she knew the spies had been sent by the one true God.

Besides having a place in the family line of Jesus, Rahab is mentioned two other times in the New Testament. First, she is listed among the heroes of the faith in Hebrews 11:31. James also cites her as an example of a person who acted upon what she believed: "In the same way, was not even Rahab the prostitute considered righteous for what she did when she gave lodging to the spies and sent them off in a different direction?" (James 2:25). Many people down through the years have seen a connection between the scarlet rope she hung from her window and the shed blood of Jesus. Rahab was saved because of the scarlet rope, and we are saved by believing that Jesus shed his blood and gave his life on the cross to atone for our sin.

Self-Discovery: *In your home or office are there any objects that indicate to others that you are trusting in Jesus Christ for your salvation?*

GO TO DISCOVERY 54 ON PAGE 275

7And the LORD said to Joshua, "Today I will begin to exalt you[v] in the eyes of all Israel, so they may know that I am with you as I was with Moses.[w] 8Tell the priests[x] who carry the ark of the covenant: 'When you reach the edge of the Jordan's waters, go and stand in the river.' "

9Joshua said to the Israelites, "Come here and listen to the words of the LORD your God. 10This is how you will know that the living God[y] is among you and that he will certainly drive out before you the Canaanites, Hittites, Hivites, Perizzites, Girgashites, Amorites and Jebusites.[z] 11See, the ark of the covenant of the Lord of all the earth[a] will go into the Jordan ahead of you. 12Now then, choose twelve men[b] from the tribes of Israel, one from each tribe. 13And as soon as the priests who carry the ark of the LORD—the Lord of all the earth[c]—set foot in the Jordan, its waters flowing downstream[d] will be cut off and stand up in a heap.[e]"

14So when the people broke camp to cross the Jordan, the priests carrying the ark of the covenant[f] went ahead[g] of them. 15Now the Jordan is at flood stage[h] all during harvest. Yet as soon as the priests who carried the ark reached the Jordan and their feet touched the water's edge, 16the water from upstream stopped flowing.[i] It piled up in a heap a great distance away, at a town called Adam in the vicinity of Zarethan,[j] while the water flowing down[k] to the Sea of the Arabah[l] (the Salt Sea[a][m]) was completely cut off. So the people crossed over opposite Jericho. 17The priests who carried the ark of the covenant of the LORD stood firm on dry ground in the middle of the Jordan, while all Israel passed by until the whole nation had completed the crossing on dry ground.[n]

4 When the whole nation had finished crossing the Jordan,[o] the LORD said to Joshua, 2"Choose twelve men[p] from among the people, one from each tribe, 3and tell them to take up twelve stones[q] from the middle of the Jordan from right where the priests stood and to carry them over with you and put them down at the place where you stay tonight.[r]"

4So Joshua called together the twelve men he had appointed from the Israelites, one from each tribe, 5and said to them, "Go over before the ark of the LORD your God into the middle of the Jordan. Each of you is to take up a stone on his shoulder, according to the number of the tribes of the Israelites, 6to serve as a sign among you. In the future, when your children ask you, 'What do these stones mean?'[s] 7tell them that the flow of the Jordan was cut off[t] before the ark of the covenant of the LORD. When it crossed the Jordan, the waters of the Jordan were cut off. These stones are to be a memorial[u] to the people of Israel forever."

8So the Israelites did as Joshua commanded them. They took twelve stones from the middle of the Jordan, according to the number of the tribes of the Israelites, as the LORD had told Joshua;[v] and they carried them over with them to their camp, where they put them down. 9Joshua set up the twelve stones[w] that had been[b] in the middle of the Jordan at the spot where the priests who carried the ark of the covenant had stood. And they are there to this day.

10Now the priests who carried the ark remained standing in the middle of the Jordan until everything the LORD had commanded Joshua was done by the people, just as Moses had directed Joshua. The people hurried over, 11and as soon as all of them had crossed, the ark of the LORD and the priests came to the other side while the people watched. 12The men of Reuben, Gad and the half-tribe of Manasseh crossed over, armed, in front of the Israelites,[x] as Moses had directed them. 13About forty thousand armed for battle crossed over before the LORD to the plains of Jericho for war.

14That day the LORD exalted[y] Joshua in the sight of all Israel; and they revered him all the days of his life, just as they had revered Moses.

15Then the LORD said to Joshua, 16"Command the priests carrying the ark of the Testimony[z] to come up out of the Jordan."

17So Joshua commanded the priests, "Come up out of the Jordan."

18And the priests came up out of the river carrying the ark of the covenant of the LORD. No sooner had they set their feet on the dry ground than the waters

3:7 [v] Jos 4:14; 1Ch 29:25 [w] Jos 1:5
3:8 [x] ver 3
3:10 [y] Dt 5:26; 1Sa 17:26,36; 2Ki 19:4,16; Hos 1:10; Mt 16:16; 1Th 1:9 [z] Ex 33:2; Dt 7:1
3:11 [a] ver 13; Job 41:11; Zec 6:5
3:12 [b] Jos 4:2,4
3:13 [c] ver 11 [d] ver 16 [e] Ex 15:8; Ps 78:13
3:14 [f] Ps 132:8 [g] Ac 7:44-45
3:15 [h] Jos 4:18; 1Ch 12:15
3:16 [i] Ps 66:6; 74:15 [j] 1Ki 4:12; 7:46 [k] ver 13 [l] Dt 1:1 [m] Ge 14:3
3:17 [n] Ex 14:22,29
4:1 [o] Dt 27:2
4:2 [p] Jos 3:12
4:3 [q] ver 20 [r] ver 19
4:6 [s] ver 21; Ex 12:26; 13:14
4:7 [t] Jos 3:13 [u] Ex 12:14
4:8 [v] ver 20
4:9 [w] Ge 28:18; Jos 24:26; 1Sa 7:12
4:12 [x] Nu 32:27
4:14 [y] Jos 3:7
4:16 [z] Ex 25:22

[a] *16* That is, the Dead Sea [b] *9* Or *Joshua also set up twelve stones*

DISCOVERY 54

Stones of Remembrance

We are all familiar with the famous and dramatic Red Sea crossing (Exodus 14). With the Egyptians in hot pursuit, God parted the waters and allowed his people to cross the sea on dry land. Then God used the same water to engulf and destroy the Egyptian army.

But we may not be as familiar with the story of another miraculous water crossing—the day on which the Israelites crossed the Jordan River on their way into Canaan while the river was at flood stage (Joshua 3:7–17). The Israelites did not know where they were going, but Joshua and the priests assured them that the ark of the covenant would guide them. As the first Israelites gingerly approached the riverbank, Joshua and the leaders stepped into the water. And, reminiscent of the Red Sea adventure, the river at once stopped flowing! Fifteen miles upriver the water "piled up." All of the water below the point at which they stood also stopped flowing.

We face similar kinds of situations in our own lives. It is frequently at those junctures at which we don't know where to turn next that God demonstrates his power most dramatically. Each new day we live brings us to a place we have never been before. There are new choices to be made, directions to be followed, fears to be conquered—and the solutions are all too often anything but obvious. When we are willing to take God at his word, however, he directs our course. Sometimes he requires that we take a first step before he will make anything happen. But we have God's promise that he will always guide and protect us (Isaiah 43:2–5).

There is one important object lesson from this second miraculous crossing. After the entire nation had finished crossing the Jordan, God instructed Joshua to select 12 men and to direct them to go back into the middle of the Jordan and to pick up one stone apiece for Joshua to use for erecting a monument to God (Joshua 4:1–3). As we look back, each of us can pinpoint moments in our lives when God has done something unusual, something to protect us, something too improbable to be a coincidence, something to alter our perception of him forever. We, like the Israelites, can recollect those times as memory "stones." Not only will they remind us of how God has been with us all along, but we can also tell other people about our experiences so that they too can see the power of God at work.

Remembering is important because it highlights the power of God. Even Jesus set up a "stone" of remembrance, but his was unlike any other. He explained the significance of his death and resurrection and instructed the disciples to keep the tradition of the Passover feast as a way to remember him (Luke 22:14–20). Each time we partake of the bread and the cup in communion, we are reminded of the love and faithfulness of Christ. Every day in small ways God is at work to change us into the kind of people he wants us to be, and it is through the miracle of Jesus dying for our sins and rising again to new life that we see the consummate manifestation of God's power.

Self-Discovery: *What memory "stones" do you cherish in your life?*

GO TO DISCOVERY 55 ON PAGE 283

of the Jordan returned to their place and
4:18 [a]Jos 3:15 ran at flood stage[a] as before.
[19]On the tenth day of the first month
4:19 the people went up from the Jordan and
[b]Jos 5:9 camped at Gilgal[b] on the eastern border
of Jericho. [20]And Joshua set up at Gilgal
4:20 the twelve stones[c] they had taken out
[c]ver 3,8 of the Jordan. [21]He said to the Israelites,
"In the future when your descendants
4:21 ask their fathers, 'What do these stones
[d]ver 6 mean?'[d] [22]tell them, 'Israel crossed the
Jordan on dry ground.'[e] [23]For the LORD
4:22 [e]Jos 3:17 your God dried up the Jordan before you
until you had crossed over. The LORD
your God did to the Jordan just what he
had done to the Red Sea[a] when he dried
4:23 it up before us until we had crossed
[f]Ex 14:21 over.[f] [24]He did this so that all the peoples
4:24 of the earth might know[g] that the hand
[g]1Ki 8:42-43; of the LORD is powerful[h] and so that you
2Ki 19:19; might always fear the LORD your God.[i]"
Ps 106:8; Jer 10:7 [h]Ex 15:16; 1Ch 29:12; Ps 89:13 [i]Ex 14:31

Circumcision at Gilgal

5 Now when all the Amorite kings
west of the Jordan and all the
5:1 Canaanite kings along the coast[j] heard
[j]Nu 13:29 how the LORD had dried up the Jordan
before the Israelites until we had crossed 5:1
over, their hearts melted[k] and they no [k]Jos 2:9-11
longer had the courage to face the Israelites.
[2]At that time the LORD said to Joshua, 5:2
"Make flint knives[l] and circumcise the [l]Ex 4:25
Israelites again." [3]So Joshua made flint
knives and circumcised the Israelites at
Gibeath Haaraloth.[b]
[4]Now this is why he did so: All those
who came out of Egypt—all the men of
military age—died in the desert on the 5:4
way after leaving Egypt.[m] [5]All the people [m]Dt 2:14
that came out had been circumcised,
but all the people born in the desert during the journey from Egypt had not.
[6]The Israelites had moved about in the
desert forty years[n] until all the men who 5:6 [n]Dt 2:7
were of military age when they left [o]Nu 14:23,29-
Egypt had died, since they had not 35; Dt 2:14
obeyed the LORD. For the LORD had [p]Ex 3:8
sworn to them that they would not see
the land that he had solemnly promised
their fathers to give us,[o] a land flowing
with milk and honey.[p] [7]So he raised up
their sons in their place, and these were
the ones Joshua circumcised. They were
still uncircumcised because they had
not been circumcised on the way. [8]And

[a] 23 Hebrew *Yam Suph*; that is, Sea of Reeds
[b] 3 *Gibeath Haaraloth* means *hill of foreskins.*

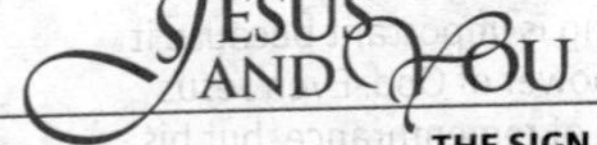

THE SIGN OF THE PROMISE

Although it was the sign of the first promise God had made to humans through Abraham (Genesis 17:9–14), the rite of circumcision was not practiced for a period of time after the Israelites had refused to follow God into the promised land (Numbers 14). When they finally did enter the land, however, the Lord commanded Joshua to circumcise all males who had not received this rite during their time in the desert (Joshua 5:1–8). Apparently God had not allowed the Israelites to dedicate their children to him while they themselves were unwilling to place their trust in him.

Centuries later parents still dedicated their male children to God in the same way. When Jesus was born Mary and Joseph brought him to the temple to be circumcised when he was eight days old, just as God's law required (Luke 2:21). Later Jesus pointed out that although some of the people objected to his healing on the Sabbath, they did allow baby boys to be circumcised on the seventh day in keeping with the law (John 7:22–23). He accused them of being more concerned about outward appearances than they were about being the kind of people God wanted them to be.

JESUS FOCUS

COMMANDER OF THE LORD'S ARMY

In the view of many Bible students Jesus himself appeared in the book of Joshua as the "commander of the army of the LORD" with a sword in his hand (Joshua 5:13–15). This "commander" is thought be God the Son for a number of reasons. First, he accepted the honor Joshua gave him (an ordinary angel would never have done so). The visitor also informed Joshua that he was standing in a "holy" place" (Joshua 5:15), implying that he was in God's very presence. Finally, Scripture indicates that it was the Lord himself who spoke: "Then the LORD said . . . " (Joshua 6:2). It is reasonable to conclude that this visitor was the same person who had led God's people out of Egypt and protected them while they lived in the desert (Exodus 14:19; 1 Corinthians 10:4). Now that the people were on the verge of conquering the land God had promised them, the preincarnate Jesus appeared once again and reminded Joshua who was really in charge of the battle.

after the whole nation had been circum-
5:8 cised, they remained where they were in
[q] Ge 34:25 camp until they were healed.[q]
9Then the LORD said to Joshua, "Today
I have rolled away the reproach of Egypt
from you." So the place has been called
Gilgal[a] to this day.
5:10 10On the evening of the fourteenth day
[r] Ex 12:6 of the month,[r] while camped at Gilgal on
the plains of Jericho, the Israelites celebrated the Passover. 11The day after the
5:11 Passover, that very day, they ate some of
[s] Nu 15:19 the produce of the land:[s] unleavened
[t] Lev 23:14 bread and roasted grain.[t] 12The manna
stopped the day after[b] they ate this food
from the land; there was no longer any
5:12 manna for the Israelites, but that year
[u] Ex 16:35 they ate of the produce of Canaan.[u]

The Fall of Jericho

13Now when Joshua was near Jericho,
5:13 he looked up and saw a man[v] standing in
[v] Ge 18:2; 32:24 front of him with a drawn sword[w] in his
[w] Nu 22:23 hand. Joshua went up to him and asked,
"Are you for us or for our enemies?"
14"Neither," he replied, "but as commander of the army of the LORD I have
5:14 now come." Then Joshua fell facedown[x]
[x] Ge 17:3 to the ground in reverence, and asked
him, "What message does my Lord[c]
have for his servant?"
15The commander of the LORD's army
5:15 replied, "Take off your sandals, for the
[y] Ex 3:5; Ac 7:33 place where you are standing is holy."[y]
And Joshua did so.

6:1 6 Now Jericho[z] was tightly shut up
[z] Jos 24:11 because of the Israelites. No one
went out and no one came in.
2Then the LORD said to Joshua, "See, I
6:2 have delivered[a] Jericho into your hands,
[a] Dt 7:24; Jos 2:9,24; 8:1 along with its king and its fighting men.
3March around the city once with all the
armed men. Do this for six days. 4Have
seven priests carry trumpets of rams'
horns in front of the ark. On the seventh
day, march around the city seven times,
6:4 with the priests blowing the trumpets.[b]
[b] Lev 25:9; Nu 10:8 5When you hear them sound a long
6:5 blast[c] on the trumpets, have all the peo-
[c] Ex 19:13 ple give a loud shout;[d] then the wall of
[d] ver 20; 1Sa 4:5; Ps 42:4; Isa 42:13 the city will collapse and the people will
go up, every man straight in."
6So Joshua son of Nun called the
priests and said to them, "Take up the
ark of the covenant of the LORD and have
seven priests carry trumpets in front of
it." 7And he ordered the people, "Advance[e]! March around the city, with the 6:7
armed guard going ahead of the ark of [e] Ex 14:15
the LORD."
8When Joshua had spoken to the people, the seven priests carrying the seven
trumpets before the LORD went forward,
blowing their trumpets, and the ark of
the LORD's covenant followed them. 9The
armed guard marched ahead of the
priests who blew the trumpets, and the
rear guard[f] followed the ark. All this 6:9
time the trumpets were sounding. 10But [f] ver 13; Isa 52:12
Joshua had commanded the people, "Do
not give a war cry, do not raise your
voices, do not say a word until the day I
tell you to shout. Then shout![g]" 11So he 6:10 [g] ver 20
had the ark of the LORD carried around
the city, circling it once. Then the people
returned to camp and spent the night
there.
12Joshua got up early the next morning and the priests took up the ark of the
LORD. 13The seven priests carrying the
seven trumpets went forward, marching
before the ark of the LORD and blowing
the trumpets. The armed men went
ahead of them and the rear guard followed the ark of the LORD, while the
trumpets kept sounding. 14So on the
second day they marched around
the city once and returned to the camp.
They did this for six days.
15On the seventh day, they got up at
daybreak and marched around the city
seven times in the same manner, except
that on that day they circled the city sev-
en times.[h] 16The seventh time around, 6:15
when the priests sounded the trumpet [h] 1Ki 18:44
blast, Joshua commanded the people,
"Shout! For the LORD has given you the
city! 17The city and all that is in it are to 6:17
be devoted[d][i] to the LORD. Only Rahab [i] Lev 27:28;
the prostitute[e] and all who are with her Dt 20:17
in her house shall be spared, because she [j] Jos 2:4
hid[j] the spies we sent. 18But keep away 6:18
from the devoted things,[k] so that you [k] Jos 7:1
will not bring about your own destruc- [l] Jos 7:12
tion by taking any of them. Otherwise [m] Jos 7:25,26
you will make the camp of Israel liable to
destruction[l] and bring trouble[m] on it.
19All the silver and gold and the articles

[a] 9 *Gilgal* sounds like the Hebrew for *roll.*
[b] 12 Or *the day*
[c] 14 Or *lord*
[d] 17 The Hebrew term refers to the irrevocable giving over of things or persons to the LORD, often by totally destroying them; also in verses 18 and 21.
[e] 17 Or possibly *innkeeper*; also in verses 22 and 25

6:19 [n]ver 24; of bronze and iron[n] are sacred to the
Nu 31:22 LORD and must go into his treasury."
20 When the trumpets sounded,[o] the
6:20 [o]Jdg 6:34; people shouted, and at the sound of the
Jer 4:21; Am 2:2 trumpet, when the people gave a loud
[p]ver 5 shout,[p] the wall collapsed; so every man
[q]Heb 11:30 charged straight in, and they took the
6:21 city.[q] 21 They devoted the city to the LORD
[r]Dt 20:16 and destroyed[r] with the sword every living thing in it—men and women, young
and old, cattle, sheep and donkeys.
22 Joshua said to the two men who had
spied out the land, "Go into the prostitute's house and bring her out and all
who belong to her, in accordance with
6:22 your oath to her."[s] 23 So the young men
[s]Jos 2:14; Heb 11:31 who had done the spying went in and
brought out Rahab, her father and
mother and brothers and all who be-
6:23 longed to her.[t] They brought out her en-
[t]Jos 2:13 tire family and put them in a place outside the camp of Israel.
24 Then they burned the whole city
and everything in it, but they put the silver and gold and the articles of bronze
6:24 [u]ver 19 and iron[u] into the treasury of the LORD's
6:25 house. 25 But Joshua spared Rahab the
[v]Heb 11:31 prostitute,[v] with her family and all who
belonged to her, because she hid the
men Joshua had sent as spies to Jeri- 6:25
cho[w]—and she lives among the Israel- [w]Jos 2:6
ites to this day.
26 At that time Joshua pronounced
this solemn oath: "Cursed before the
LORD is the man who undertakes to rebuild this city, Jericho:

"At the cost of his firstborn son
will he lay its foundations;
at the cost of his youngest
will he set up its gates."[x] 6:26 [x]1Ki 16:34

27 So the LORD was with Joshua,[y] and 6:27 [y]Ge 39:2; Jos 1:5
his fame spread[z] throughout the land. [z]Jos 9:1

Achan's Sin

7 But the Israelites acted unfaithfully in regard to the devoted
things[a];[a] Achan son of Carmi, the son of 7:1 [a]Jos 6:18
Zimri,[b] the son of Zerah,[b] of the tribe of [b]Jos 22:20
Judah, took some of them. So the LORD's
anger burned against Israel.
2 Now Joshua sent men from Jericho to
Ai, which is near Beth Aven[c] to the east 7:2 [c]Jos 18:12;
of Bethel, and told them, "Go up and spy 1Sa 13:5; 14:23
out the region." So the men went up and
spied out Ai.
3 When they returned to Joshua, they
said, "Not all the people will have to go
up against Ai. Send two or three thousand men to take it and do not weary all
the people, for only a few men are there."
4 So about three thousand men went up; 7:4
but they were routed by the men of Ai,[d] [d]Lev 26:17;
5 who killed about thirty-six of them. Dt 28:25
They chased the Israelites from the city
gate as far as the stone quarries[c] and 7:5
struck them down on the slopes. At this [e]Lev 26:36; Jos 2:9,11;
the hearts of the people melted[e] and be- Eze 21:7; Na 2:10
came like water.
6 Then Joshua tore his clothes[f] and fell 7:6 [f]Ge 37:29
facedown to the ground before the ark of [g]1Sa 4:12;
the LORD, remaining there till evening. 2Sa 13:19;
The elders of Israel did the same, and Ne 9:1; Job 2:12;
sprinkled dust[g] on their heads. 7 And La 2:10;
Joshua said, "Ah, Sovereign LORD, why did Rev 18:19
you ever bring this people across the Jordan to deliver us into the hands of the 7:7
Amorites to destroy us?[h] If only we had [h]Ex 5:22
been content to stay on the other side of
the Jordan! 8 O Lord, what can I say, now
that Israel has been routed by its ene-

a 1 The Hebrew term refers to the irrevocable giving over of things or persons to the LORD, often by totally destroying them; also in verses 11, 12, 13 and 15. *b 1* See Septuagint and 1 Chron. 2:6; Hebrew *Zabdi*; also in verses 17 and 18. *c 5* Or *as far as Shebarim*

JESUS FOCUS

MERCY FOR A SINNER

When Joshua sent spies into Jericho, two of them met a prostitute named Rahab. Because she helped them to escape, they promised to warn her family before the city was conquered (Joshua 2:12–14). Joshua honored that promise (Joshua 6:25). At first Rahab's family stayed outside the Israelite camp (verse 23), but later they were integrated into the community. Even though she and her family were technically God's "enemies" because they had been living in the city God had commanded his people to conquer, Rahab found a welcome among his people. Rahab's extraordinary faith is twice noted in the New Testament as a stirring example for others (Hebrews 11:31; James 2:25). And Rahab is listed in Jesus' genealogy as the mother of Boaz, although it is probable that there were actually several generations between the two (Matthew 1:5). Tamar, Rahab, Ruth and Bathsheba—all women whose backgrounds or reputations were unfamiliar or unsavory—are listed in Jesus' family tree, and God's grace is powerfully evidenced by the inclusion of these names.

mies? 9The Canaanites and the other
people of the country will hear about
7:9 this and they will surround us and wipe
[i]Ex 32:12; out our name from the earth.[i] What then
Dt 9:28 will you do for your own great name?"
10The LORD said to Joshua, "Stand up!
What are you doing down on your face?
7:11 11Israel has sinned; they have violated
[j]Jos 6:17-19 my covenant,[j] which I commanded
[k]Ac 5:1-2 them to keep. They have taken some of
the devoted things; they have stolen,
they have lied,[k] they have put them with
their own possessions. 12That is why the
7:12 Israelites cannot stand against their en-
[l]Nu 14:45; emies;[l] they turn their backs and run be-
Jdg 2:14 cause they have been made liable to de-
[m]Jos 6:18 struction.[m] I will not be with you
anymore unless you destroy whatever
among you is devoted to destruction.
13"Go, consecrate the people. Tell
7:13 them, 'Consecrate yourselves[n] in prepa-
[n]Jos 3:5; 6:18 ration for tomorrow; for this is what the
LORD, the God of Israel, says: That which
is devoted is among you, O Israel. You
cannot stand against your enemies until you remove it.
14" 'In the morning, present yourselves tribe by tribe. The tribe that the
7:14 LORD takes[o] shall come forward clan by
[o]Pr 16:33 clan; the clan that the LORD takes shall
come forward family by family; and the
family that the LORD takes shall come
forward man by man. 15He who is
caught with the devoted things shall be
7:15 destroyed by fire, along with all that be-
[p]1Sa 14:39 longs to him.[p] He has violated the cov-
[q]ver 11 enant[q] of the LORD and has done a dis-
[r]Ge 34:7 graceful thing in Israel!' "[r]
16Early the next morning Joshua had
Israel come forward by tribes, and Judah
7:17 was taken. 17The clans of Judah came
[s]Nu 26:20 forward, and he took the Zerahites.[s] He
had the clan of the Zerahites come for-
ward by families, and Zimri was taken.
18Joshua had his family come forward
man by man, and Achan son of Carmi,
the son of Zimri, the son of Zerah, of the
tribe of Judah, was taken.
19Then Joshua said to Achan, "My son,
7:19 give glory[t] to the LORD,[a] the God of Isra-
[t]1Sa 6:5; el, and give him the praise.[b] Tell[u] me
Jer 13:16; Jn 9:24* what you have done; do not hide it
[u]1Sa 14:43 from me."
20Achan replied, "It is true! I have
sinned against the LORD, the God of Israel. This is what I have done: 21When I saw
in the plunder a beautiful robe from
Babylonia,[c] two hundred shekels[d] of silver and a wedge of gold weighing fifty 7:21
shekels,[e] I coveted[v] them and took them. [v]Dt 7:25;
They are hidden in the ground inside my Eph 5:5;
tent, with the silver underneath." 1Ti 6:10
22So Joshua sent messengers, and they
ran to the tent, and there it was, hidden
in his tent, with the silver underneath.
23They took the things from the tent,
brought them to Joshua and all the Israelites and spread them out before the
LORD.
24Then Joshua, together with all Israel,
took Achan son of Zerah, the silver, the
robe, the gold wedge, his sons and
daughters, his cattle, donkeys and sheep,
his tent and all that he had, to the Valley 7:24
of Achor.[w] 25Joshua said, "Why have you [w]ver 26;
brought this trouble[x] on us? The LORD Jos 15:7
will bring trouble on you today." 7:25
Then all Israel stoned him,[y] and after [x]Jos 6:18
they had stoned the rest, they burned [y]Dt 17:5
them. 26Over Achan they heaped up a
large pile of rocks, which remains to this 7:26
day. Then the LORD turned from his [z]Nu 25:4;
fierce anger.[z] Therefore that place has Dt 13:17
been called the Valley of Achor[f][a] ever [a]ver 24; Isa 65:10;
since. Hos 2:15

Ai Destroyed

8 Then the LORD said to Joshua, "Do
not be afraid;[b] do not be discour- 8:1
aged.[c] Take the whole army[d] with you, [b]Dt 31:6
and go up and attack Ai. For I have de- [c]Dt 1:21; 7:18; Jos 1:9 [d]Jos 10:7
livered[e] into your hands the king of Ai, [e]Jos 6:2
his people, his city and his land. 2You
shall do to Ai and its king as you did to
Jericho and its king, except that you may
carry off their plunder and livestock for 8:2
yourselves.[f] Set an ambush behind the [f]ver 27;
city." Dt 20:14
3So Joshua and the whole army moved
out to attack Ai. He chose thirty thousand of his best fighting men and sent
them out at night 4with these orders:
"Listen carefully. You are to set an ambush behind the city. Don't go very far
from it. All of you be on the alert. 5I and
all those with me will advance on the
city, and when the men come out against
us, as they did before, we will flee from
them. 6They will pursue us until we have
lured them away from the city, for they

[a] 19 A solemn charge to tell the truth [b] 19 Or *and confess to him* [c] 21 Hebrew *Shinar*
[d] 21 That is, about 5 pounds (about 2.3 kilograms)
[e] 21 That is, about 1 1/4 pounds (about 0.6 kilogram) [f] 26 *Achor* means *trouble.*

will say, 'They are running away from us
as they did before.' So when we flee from
them, 7you are to rise up from ambush
8:7 and take the city. The LORD your God will
[g] Jdg 7:7; give it into your hand.[g] 8When you have
1Sa 23:4 taken the city, set it on fire.[h] Do what the
8:8 LORD has commanded.[i] See to it; you
[h] Jdg 20:29-38 have my orders."
[i] ver 19 9Then Joshua sent them off, and they
8:9 went to the place of ambush[j] and lay in
[j] 2Ch 13:13 wait between Bethel and Ai, to the west
of Ai—but Joshua spent that night with
the people.
8:10 10Early the next morning[k] Joshua
[k] Ge 22:3 [l] Jos 7:6 mustered his men, and he and the leaders of Israel[l] marched before them to Ai.
11The entire force that was with him
marched up and approached the city
and arrived in front of it. They set up
camp north of Ai, with the valley between them and the city. 12Joshua had
taken about five thousand men and set
them in ambush between Bethel and Ai,
to the west of the city. 13They had the
soldiers take up their positions—all
those in the camp to the north of the
city and the ambush to the west of it.
That night Joshua went into the valley.
14When the king of Ai saw this, he
and all the men of the city hurried out
early in the morning to meet Israel in
8:14 battle at a certain place overlooking the
[m] Dt 1:1 Arabah.[m] But he did not know[n] that an
[n] Jdg 20:34 ambush had been set against him be-
8:15 hind the city. 15Joshua and all Israel let
[o] Jdg 20:36 themselves be driven back[o] before them,
[p] Jos 15:61; 16:1; 18:12 and they fled toward the desert.[p] 16All
the men of Ai were called to pursue
8:16 them, and they pursued Joshua and
[q] Jdg 20:31 were lured away[q] from the city. 17Not a
man remained in Ai or Bethel who did
not go after Israel. They left the city
open and went in pursuit of Israel.
8:18 18Then the LORD said to Joshua, "Hold
[r] Job 41:26; out toward Ai the javelin[r] that is in your
Ps 35:3 [s] Ex 4:2; hand,[s] for into your hand I will deliver
14:16; 17:9-12 the city." So Joshua held out his javelin[t]
[t] ver 26 toward Ai. 19As soon as he did this, the
8:19 men in the ambush rose quickly[u] from
[u] Jdg 20:33 their position and rushed forward. They
[v] ver 8 entered the city and captured it and
quickly set it on fire.[v]
20The men of Ai looked back and saw
8:20 the smoke of the city rising against the
[w] Jdg 20:40 sky,[w] but they had no chance to escape
in any direction, for the Israelites who
had been fleeing toward the desert had
turned back against their pursuers.
21For when Joshua and all Israel saw that
the ambush had taken the city and that
smoke was going up from the city, they
turned around and attacked the men of
Ai. 22The men of the ambush also came
out of the city against them, so that they
were caught in the middle, with Israelites on both sides. Israel cut them down,
leaving them neither survivors nor fugi- 8:22 [x] Dt 7:2; Jos 10:1
tives.[x] 23But they took the king of Ai
alive[y] and brought him to Joshua. 8:23 [y] 1Sa 15:8
24When Israel had finished killing all
the men of Ai in the fields and in the
desert where they had chased them, and
when every one of them had been put to
the sword, all the Israelites returned to
Ai and killed those who were in it.
25Twelve thousand men and women fell
that day—all the people of Ai.[z] 26For 8:25 [z] Dt 20:16-18
Joshua did not draw back the hand that
held out his javelin until he had de- 8:26
stroyed[a][a] all who lived in Ai.[b] 27But Isra- [a] Nu 21:2 [b] Ex 17:12
el did carry off for themselves the live- 8:27
stock and plunder of this city, as the [c] ver 2
LORD had instructed Joshua.[c]
28So Joshua burned[d] Ai[e] and made it 8:28
a permanent heap of ruins,[f] a desolate [d] Nu 31:10 [e] Jos 7:2; Jer 49:3
place to this day.[g] 29He hung the king of [f] Dt 13:16;
Ai on a tree and left him there until Jos 10:1
evening. At sunset,[h] Joshua ordered [g] Ge 35:20
them to take his body from the tree and 8:29
throw it down at the entrance of the city [h] Dt 21:23; Jn 19:31
gate. And they raised a large pile of [i] 2Sa 18:17
rocks[i] over it, which remains to this day.

The Covenant Renewed at Mount Ebal

30Then Joshua built on Mount Ebal[j] 8:30 [j] Dt 11:29
an altar[k] to the LORD, the God of Israel, [k] Ex 20:24
31as Moses the servant of the LORD had
commanded the Israelites. He built it
according to what is written in the Book
of the Law of Moses—an altar of uncut 8:31
stones, on which no iron tool[l] had been [l] Ex 20:25
used. On it they offered to the LORD [m] Dt 27:6-7
burnt offerings and sacrificed fellowship
offerings.[b][m] 32There, in the presence of
the Israelites, Joshua copied on stones 8:32
the law of Moses, which he had written.[n] [n] Dt 27:8
33All Israel, aliens and citizens[o] alike, 8:33
with their elders, officials and judges, [o] Lev 16:29
were standing on both sides of the ark of

a 26 The Hebrew term refers to the irrevocable giving over of things or persons to the LORD, often by totally destroying them. *b 31* Traditionally *peace offerings*

the covenant of the LORD, facing those
8:33 who carried it—the priests, who were
pDt 31:12 Levites.[p] Half of the people stood in
qDt 11:29; front of Mount Gerizim and half of them
27:11-14 in front of Mount Ebal,[q] as Moses the
servant of the LORD had formerly commanded when he gave instructions to
bless the people of Israel.
34 Afterward, Joshua read all the words
of the law—the blessings and the
curses—just as it is written in the Book
8:34 rDt 28:61; of the Law.[r] 35 There was not a word of all
31:11; Jos 1:8 that Moses had commanded that Joshua
8:35 did not read to the whole assembly of Is-
sEx 12:38; rael, including the women and children,
Dt 31:12 and the aliens who lived among them.[s]

The Gibeonite Deception

9 Now when all the kings west of
the Jordan heard about these
things—those in the hill country, in the
western foothills, and along the entire
9:1 tNu 34:6 coast of the Great Sea[a][t] as far as Leba-
uEx 3:17; non (the kings of the Hittites, Amorites,
Jos 3:10 Canaanites, Perizzites, Hivites and Jebusites)[u]— 2 they came together to make
war against Joshua and Israel.
9:3 3 However, when the people of Gibe-
vver 17; on[v] heard what Joshua had done to Jeri-
Jos 10:2; 2Sa 2:12; cho and Ai, 4 they resorted to a ruse:
2Ch 1:3; They went as a delegation whose don-
Isa 28:21 keys were loaded[b] with worn-out sacks
and old wineskins, cracked and mend-
ed. 5 The men put worn and patched
sandals on their feet and wore old
clothes. All the bread of their food sup-
9:6 ply was dry and moldy. 6 Then they went
wJos 5:10 to Joshua in the camp at Gilgal[w] and
said to him and the men of Israel, "We
have come from a distant country; make
a treaty with us."
9:7 xver 1; Jos 11:19 7 The men of Israel said to the Hivites,[x]
yEx 23:32; "But perhaps you live near us. How then
Dt 7:2 can we make a treaty[y] with you?"
9:8 8 "We are your servants,[z]" they said to
zDt 20:11; 2Ki 10:5 Joshua.
But Joshua asked, "Who are you and
where do you come from?"
9:9 9 They answered: "Your servants have
aDt 20:15 come from a very distant country[a] be-
bver 24; Jos 2:9 cause of the fame of the LORD your God.
For we have heard reports[b] of him: all
that he did in Egypt, 10 and all that he did
to the two kings of the Amorites east of
the Jordan—Sihon king of Heshbon, and
9:10 cNu 21:33 Og king of Bashan,[c] who reigned in Ash-
dNu 21:24,35 taroth.[d] 11 And our elders and all those
living in our country said to us, 'Take
provisions for your journey; go and meet
them and say to them, "We are your servants; make a treaty with us." ' 12 This
bread of ours was warm when we
packed it at home on the day we left to
come to you. But now see how dry and
moldy it is. 13 And these wineskins that
we filled were new, but see how cracked
they are. And our clothes and sandals
are worn out by the very long journey."
14 The men of Israel sampled their pro-
visions but did not inquire[e] of the LORD. 9:14 eNu 27:21
15 Then Joshua made a treaty of peace[f] 9:15
with them to let them live, and the lead- fEx 23:32;
ers of the assembly ratified it by oath. Jos 11:19; 2Sa 21:2
16 Three days after they made the
treaty with the Gibeonites, the Israelites
heard that they were neighbors, living
near them. 17 So the Israelites set out and
on the third day came to their cities:
Gibeon, Kephirah, Beeroth[g] and Kiriath 9:17
Jearim.[h] 18 But the Israelites did not at- gJos 18:25 h1Sa 7:1-2
tack them, because the leaders of the as-
sembly had sworn an oath[i] to them by 9:18 iPs 15:4
the LORD, the God of Israel. jEx 15:24
The whole assembly grumbled[j]
against the leaders, 19 but all the leaders
answered, "We have given them our oath
by the LORD, the God of Israel, and we
cannot touch them now. 20 This is what
we will do to them: We will let them live,
so that wrath will not fall on us for breaking the oath we swore to them." 21 They
continued, "Let them live,[k] but let them 9:21
be woodcutters and water carriers[l] for kver 15 lDt 29:11
the entire community." So the leaders'
promise to them was kept.
22 Then Joshua summoned the
Gibeonites and said, "Why did you deceive us by saying, 'We live a long way[m] 9:22
from you,' while actually you live near[n] mver 6 nver 16
us? 23 You are now under a curse:[o] You 9:23
will never cease to serve as woodcutters oGe 9:25
and water carriers for the house of my
God."
24 They answered Joshua, "Your servants were clearly told[p] how the LORD 9:24
your God had commanded his servant pver 9
Moses to give you the whole land and to
wipe out all its inhabitants from before
you. So we feared for our lives because of
you, and that is why we did this. 25 We

[a] *1* That is, the Mediterranean [b] *4* Most Hebrew manuscripts; some Hebrew manuscripts, Vulgate and Syriac (see also Septuagint) *They prepared provisions and loaded their donkeys*

9:25 [q]Ge 16:6 are now in your hands.[q] Do to us whatever seems good and right to you."
26So Joshua saved them from the Israelites, and they did not kill them. 27That
day he made the Gibeonites woodcutters and water carriers for the community and for the altar of the LORD at the
9:27 [r]Dt 12:5 place the LORD would choose.[r] And that
is what they are to this day.

The Sun Stands Still

10 Now Adoni-Zedek king of Jerusalem[s] heard that Joshua had
10:1 [s]Jdg 1:7 [t]Jos 8:1 [u]Dt 20:16; Jos 8:22 [v]Jos 9:15 taken Ai[t] and totally destroyed[a u] it, doing to Ai and its king as he had done to
Jericho and its king, and that the people
of Gibeon had made a treaty of peace[v]
with Israel and were living near them.
2He and his people were very much
alarmed at this, because Gibeon was an
important city, like one of the royal cities; it was larger than Ai, and all its men
were good fighters. 3So Adoni-Zedek
king of Jerusalem appealed to Hoham
10:3 [w]Ge 13:18 [x]2Ch 11:9; 25:27; Ne 11:30; Isa 36:2; 37:8; Jer 34:7; Mic 1:13 king of Hebron,[w] Piram king of Jarmuth,
Japhia king of Lachish[x] and Debir king
of Eglon. 4"Come up and help me attack
Gibeon," he said, "because it has made
peace[y] with Joshua and the Israelites."
10:4 [y]Jos 9:15 5Then the five kings of the Amorites[z]—the kings of Jerusalem, Hebron,
10:5 [z]Nu 13:29 Jarmuth, Lachish and Eglon—joined
forces. They moved up with all their
troops and took up positions against
Gibeon and attacked it.
6The Gibeonites then sent word to
Joshua in the camp at Gilgal: "Do not
abandon your servants. Come up to us
quickly and save us! Help us, because all
the Amorite kings from the hill country
have joined forces against us."
7So Joshua marched up from Gilgal
10:7 [a]Jos 8:1 with his entire army,[a] including all the
best fighting men. 8The LORD said to
10:8 [b]Dt 3:2; Jos 1:9 Joshua, "Do not be afraid[b] of them; I have
given them into your hand. Not one of
them will be able to withstand you."
9After an all-night march from Gilgal,
Joshua took them by surprise. 10The
LORD threw them into confusion before
10:10 [c]Dt 7:23 [d]Jos 16:3,5 [e]Jos 15:35 Israel,[c] who defeated them in a great victory at Gibeon. Israel pursued them
along the road going up to Beth Horon[d]
and cut them down all the way to Azekah[e] and Makkedah. 11As they fled before Israel on the road down from Beth
Horon to Azekah, the LORD hurled large
hailstones[f] down on them from the sky, 10:11 [f]Ps 18:12; Isa 28:2,17
and more of them died from the hail-
stones than were killed by the swords of
the Israelites.
12On the day the LORD gave the Amo-
rites[g] over to Israel, Joshua said to the 10:12 [g]Am 2:9 [h]Jdg 1:35; 12:12
LORD in the presence of Israel:

"O sun, stand still over Gibeon,
O moon, over the Valley of
Aijalon.[h]"
13So the sun stood still,[i] 10:13 [i]Hab 3:11 [j]2Sa 1:18 [k]Isa 38:8
and the moon stopped,
till the nation avenged itself on[b]
its enemies,

as it is written in the Book of Jashar.[j]
The sun stopped[k] in the middle of the
sky and delayed going down about a full
day. 14There has never been a day like it 10:14 [l]ver 42; Ex 14:14; Dt 1:30; Ps 106:43; 136:24
before or since, a day when the LORD lis-
tened to a man. Surely the LORD was
fighting[l] for Israel!
15Then Joshua returned with all Israel 10:15 [m]ver 43
to the camp at Gilgal.[m]

Five Amorite Kings Killed

16Now the five kings had fled and hidden in the cave at Makkedah. 17When
Joshua was told that the five kings had
been found hiding in the cave at Makkedah, 18he said, "Roll large rocks up to
the mouth of the cave, and post some
men there to guard it. 19But don't stop!
Pursue your enemies, attack them from
the rear and don't let them reach their
cities, for the LORD your God has given
them into your hand."
20So Joshua and the Israelites de-
stroyed them completely[n]—almost to 10:20 [n]Dt 20:16
a man—but the few who were left
reached their fortified cities. 21The
whole army then returned safely to Joshua in the camp at Makkedah, and no
one uttered a word against the Israelites.
22Joshua said, "Open the mouth of the
cave and bring those five kings out to
me." 23So they brought the five kings out
of the cave—the kings of Jerusalem, Hebron, Jarmuth, Lachish and Eglon.
24When they had brought these kings to
Joshua, he summoned all the men of Israel and said to the army commanders
who had come with him, "Come here
and put your feet[o] on the necks of these 10:24 [o]Mal 4:3

[a] *1* The Hebrew term refers to the irrevocable giving over of things or persons to the LORD, often by totally destroying them; also in verses 28, 35, 37, 39 and 40. [b] *13* Or *nation triumphed over*

DISCOVERY 55

THE DAY THE SUN STOOD STILL

Joshua was a brilliant military leader. In all of his battles he assumed an offensive stance, attacking enemy armies and often employing the element of surprise. When the enemy was scattered, "he totally destroyed all who breathed, just as the LORD, the God of Israel, had commanded" (Joshua 10:40).

Joshua may have been a gifted strategist, but all victory ultimately comes from God. In one incident Joshua asked God to keep the sun from setting so that his army might have more time to defeat the enemy. God agreed, and "the sun stopped in the middle of the sky and delayed going down about a full day" (verse 13). Somehow the God of the universe chose to slow down the rotation of the earth! This is amazing in and of itself, but what heightens its impact is that the primary "gods" worshiped by the enemy were the sun and the moon. God directed a blow at the very essence of their belief system. As a result they conceded, "Surely the LORD was fighting for Israel" (verse 14).

In the New Testament we read of another day when God altered the earth's rotation: This time, though, he chose *not* to listen to the cries of a man—and the sun was darkened. When Jesus implored, "My God, my God, why have you forsaken me?" (Matthew 27:46), God turned his back on his only Son. During that long afternoon, the sun was darkened for three hours—and the greatest victory of all time, the victory over sin and death, was fought and won. The apostle Paul stated the glorious truth in this way: "He has rescued us from the dominion of darkness and brought us into the kingdom of the Son he loves, in whom we have redemption, the forgiveness of sins" (Colossians 1:13–14). In the words of a well-loved hymn of the faith:

Sun of my soul, Thou Savior dear,
It is not night if Thou be near;
O may no earthborn cloud arise
To hide Thee from Thy servant's eyes.

The God we serve has the power to intervene in the natural order of things to accomplish his purposes—and sometimes that intervention comes in the form of a miracle. Ours is indeed the God of supernatural power.

Self-Discovery: *Imagine as best you can how Jesus must have felt knowing that his Father had turned his back on him in his hour of extremity. If you have been a Christian for most of your life, try to imagine how you would feel if you didn't have the assurance that God is walking with you through every step of your life. Does this exercise intensify your desire to reach out to the lost?*

GO TO DISCOVERY 56 ON PAGE 288

10:24 kings." So they came forward and placed
pPs 110:1 their feet[p] on their necks.
[25]Joshua said to them, "Do not be
10:25 afraid; do not be discouraged. Be strong
qDt 31:6 and courageous.[q] This is what the LORD
will do to all the enemies you are going
to fight." [26]Then Joshua struck and killed
the kings and hung them on five trees,
and they were left hanging on the trees
until evening.
10:27 [27]At sunset[r] Joshua gave the order
rDt 21:23; and they took them down from the trees
Jos 8:9,29 and threw them into the cave where
they had been hiding. At the mouth of
the cave they placed large rocks, which
are there to this day.
[28]That day Joshua took Makkedah. He
put the city and its king to the sword
10:28 and totally destroyed everyone in it. He
sDt 20:16 left no survivors.[s] And he did to the king
tJos 6:21 of Makkedah as he had done to the king
of Jericho.[t]

Southern Cities Conquered

[29]Then Joshua and all Israel with him
moved on from Makkedah to Libnah
and attacked it. [30]The LORD also gave
that city and its king into Israel's hand.
The city and everyone in it Joshua put to
the sword. He left no survivors there.
And he did to its king as he had done to
the king of Jericho.
[31]Then Joshua and all Israel with him
moved on from Libnah to Lachish; he
took up positions against it and attacked it. [32]The LORD handed Lachish
over to Israel, and Joshua took it on the
second day. The city and everyone in it
he put to the sword, just as he had done
10:33 to Libnah. [33]Meanwhile, Horam king of
uJos 16:3,10; Gezer[u] had come up to help Lachish,
Jdg 1:29; 1Ki 9:15 but Joshua defeated him and his army—
until no survivors were left.
[34]Then Joshua and all Israel with him
moved on from Lachish to Eglon; they
took up positions against it and attacked it. [35]They captured it that same
day and put it to the sword and totally
destroyed everyone in it, just as they had
done to Lachish.
10:36 [36]Then Joshua and all Israel with him
vJos 14:13; went up from Eglon to Hebron[v] and at-
15:13; Jdg 1:10 tacked it. [37]They took the city and put it
to the sword, together with its king, its
villages and everyone in it. They left no
survivors. Just as at Eglon, they totally
destroyed it and everyone in it.
[38]Then Joshua and all Israel with him 10:38
turned around and attacked Debir.[w] wJos 15:15;
[39]They took the city, its king and its vil- Jdg 1:11
lages, and put them to the sword. Every-
one in it they totally destroyed. They left
no survivors. They did to Debir and its
king as they had done to Libnah and its
king and to Hebron.
[40]So Joshua subdued the whole region,
including the hill country, the Negev,[x] 10:40 xGe 12:9;
the western foothills and the mountain Jos 12:8 yDt 1:7
slopes,[y] together with all their kings.[z] He zDt 7:24
left no survivors. He totally destroyed all aDt 20:16-17
who breathed, just as the LORD, the God
of Israel, had commanded.[a] [41]Joshua
subdued them from Kadesh Barnea[b] to 10:41 bGe 14:7
Gaza[c] and from the whole region of Go- cGe 10:19
shen[d] to Gibeon. [42]All these kings and dJos 11:16;
their lands Joshua conquered in one 15:51
campaign, because the LORD, the God of 10:42
Israel, fought[e] for Israel. ever 14
[43]Then Joshua returned with all Israel 10:43
to the camp at Gilgal.[f] fver 15; Jos 5:9

Northern Kings Defeated

11 When Jabin[g] king of Hazor[h] 11:1
heard of this, he sent word to gJdg 4:2,7,23
Jobab king of Madon, to the kings of hver 10; 1Sa 12:9
Shimron[i] and Acshaph, [2]and to the iJos 19:15
northern kings who were in the moun- 11:2
tains, in the Arabah[j] south of Kinne- jJos 12:3
reth,[k] in the western foothills and in kNu 34:11
Naphoth Dor[a][l] on the west; [3]to the lJos 17:11; Jdg 1:27;
Canaanites in the east and west; to the 1Ki 4:11
Amorites, Hittites, Perizzites and Jebusites in the hill country; and to the Hi- 11:3
vites[m] below Hermon in the region of mDt 7:1;
Mizpah.[n] [4]They came out with all their Jdg 3:3,5; 1Ki 9:20
troops and a large number of horses and nGe 31:49;
chariots—a huge army, as numerous as Jos 15:38; 18:26
the sand on the seashore.[o] [5]All these 11:4
kings joined forces[p] and made camp to- oJdg 7:12;
gether at the Waters of Merom, to fight 1Sa 13:5
against Israel. 11:5
[6]The LORD said to Joshua, "Do not be pJdg 5:19
afraid of them, because by this time tomorrow I will hand all of them over[q] to 11:6 qJos 10:8
Israel, slain. You are to hamstring[r] their r2Sa 8:4
horses and burn their chariots."
[7]So Joshua and his whole army came
against them suddenly at the Waters of
Merom and attacked them, [8]and the
LORD gave them into the hand of Israel.
They defeated them and pursued them
all the way to Greater Sidon, to Misre- 11:8
photh Maim,[s] and to the Valley of Miz- sJos 13:6

[a] 2 Or *in the heights of Dor*

pah on the east, until no survivors were
left. 9 Joshua did to them as the LORD had
directed: He hamstrung their horses and
burned their chariots.
10 At that time Joshua turned back and
captured Hazor and put its king to the
sword. (Hazor had been the head of all
these kingdoms.) 11 Everyone in it they
put to the sword. They totally destroyed[a]
11:11 them, not sparing anything that
[t] Dt 20:16-17 breathed,[t] and he burned up Hazor itself.
12 Joshua took all these royal cities and
their kings and put them to the sword.
11:12 He totally destroyed them, as Moses the
[u] Nu 33:50-52; servant of the LORD had commanded.[u]
Dt 7:2 13 Yet Israel did not burn any of the cities
built on their mounds—except Hazor,
which Joshua burned. 14 The Israelites
carried off for themselves all the plunder
and livestock of these cities, but all the
people they put to the sword until they
11:14 completely destroyed them, not sparing
[v] Nu 31:11-12 anyone that breathed.[v] 15 As the LORD
commanded his servant Moses, so Mo-
ses commanded Joshua, and Joshua did
11:15 it; he left nothing undone of all that the
[w] Ex 34:11; Jos 1:7 LORD commanded Moses.[w]
16 So Joshua took this entire land: the
11:16 hill country, all the Negev, the whole re-
[x] Jos 10:41 gion of Goshen, the western foothills,[x]
the Arabah and the mountains of Israel
with their foothills, 17 from Mount Halak,
11:17 which rises toward Seir, to Baal Gad in
[y] Jos 12:7 the Valley of Lebanon[y] below Mount
[z] Dt 7:24 Hermon. He captured all their kings and
struck them down, putting them to
death.[z] 18 Joshua waged war against all
these kings for a long time. 19 Except for
11:19 the Hivites living in Gibeon,[a] not one
[a] Jos 9:3 city made a treaty of peace with the Israelites, who took them all in battle.
20 For it was the LORD himself who hard-
11:20 ened their hearts[b] to wage war against
[b] Ex 14:17; Israel, so that he might destroy them to-
Ro 9:18 tally, exterminating them without mer-
[c] Dt 7:16; Jdg 14:4 cy, as the LORD had commanded Moses.[c]
21 At that time Joshua went and de-
11:21 stroyed the Anakites[d] from the hill
[d] Nu 13:22,33; Dt 9:2 country: from Hebron, Debir and Anab,
11:22 from all the hill country of Judah, and
[e] 1Sa 17:4; from all the hill country of Israel. Joshua
1Ki 2:39; totally destroyed them and their towns.
1Ch 8:13 22 No Anakites were left in Israelite terri-
[f] 1Sa 5:1; Isa 20:1 tory; only in Gaza, Gath[e] and Ashdod[f]
11:23 did any survive. 23 So Joshua took the en-
[g] Jos 21:43-45 tire land,[g] just as the LORD had directed
[h] Dt 1:38; 12:9-10; 25:19 Moses, and he gave it as an inheritance[h]
to Israel according to their tribal divi- 11:23
sions.[i] [i] Nu 26:53
Then the land had rest from war.[j] [j] Jos 14:15

List of Defeated Kings

12 These are the kings of the land
whom the Israelites had defeated and whose territory they took over
east of the Jordan, from the Arnon
Gorge to Mount Hermon,[k] including all 12:1
the eastern side of the Arabah: [k] Dt 3:8

2 Sihon king of the Amorites,
who reigned in Heshbon. He ruled
from Aroer on the rim of the Arnon
Gorge—from the middle of the
gorge—to the Jabbok River, which
is the border of the Ammonites.
This included half of Gilead.[l] 3 He 12:2 [l] Dt 2:36
also ruled over the eastern Arabah 12:3
from the Sea of Kinnereth[b][m] to the [m] Jos 11:2
Sea of the Arabah (the Salt Sea[c]), to [n] Jos 13:20
Beth Jeshimoth,[n] and then south-
ward below the slopes of Pisgah.

4 And the territory of Og king of Ba- 12:4
shan,[o] [o] Nu 21:21,33; Dt 3:11 [p] Dt 1:4
one of the last of the Rephaites,
who reigned in Ashtaroth[p] and Edrei. 5 He ruled over Mount Hermon,
Salecah,[q] all of Bashan to the bor- 12:5 [q] Dt 3:10
der of the people of Geshur[r] and [r] 1Sa 27:8
Maacah,[s] and half of Gilead to the [s] Dt 3:14
border of Sihon king of Heshbon.

6 Moses, the servant of the LORD, and
the Israelites conquered them. And Moses the servant of the LORD gave their
land to the Reubenites, the Gadites and
the half-tribe of Manasseh to be their 12:6
possession.[t] [t] Nu 32:29,33; Jos 13:8
7 These are the kings of the land that
Joshua and the Israelites conquered on
the west side of the Jordan, from Baal
Gad in the Valley of Lebanon[u] to Mount 12:7 [u] Jos 11:17
Halak, which rises toward Seir (their
lands Joshua gave as an inheritance to
the tribes of Israel according to their
tribal divisions— 8 the hill country,
the western foothills, the Arabah, the
mountain slopes, the desert and the
Negev[v]—the lands of the Hittites, Amo- 12:8
rites, Canaanites, Perizzites, Hivites and [v] Jos 11:16
Jebusites):

[a] *11* The Hebrew term refers to the irrevocable giving over of things or persons to the LORD, often by totally destroying them; also in verses 12, 20 and 21. [b] *3* That is, Galilee [c] *3* That is, the Dead Sea

12:9 [w]Jos 6:2 [x]Jos 8:29
9 the king of Jericho[w] one
the king of Ai[x] (near Bethel) one
12:10 [y]Jos 10:23
10 the king of Jerusalem[y] one
the king of Hebron one
11 the king of Jarmuth one
the king of Lachish one
12 the king of Eglon one
12:12 [z]Jos 10:33
the king of Gezer[z] one
13 the king of Debir one
the king of Geder one
14 the king of Hormah one
12:14 [a]Nu 21:1
the king of Arad[a] one
15 the king of Libnah one
the king of Adullam one
16 the king of Makkedah one
12:16 [b]Jos 7:2
the king of Bethel[b] one
17 the king of Tappuah one
12:17 [c]1Ki 4:10
the king of Hepher[c] one
12:18 [d]Jos 13:4
18 the king of Aphek[d] one
the king of Lasharon one
19 the king of Madon one
the king of Hazor one
20 the king of Shimron Meron one
12:20 [e]Jos 11:1
the king of Acshaph[e] one
21 the king of Taanach one
the king of Megiddo one
12:22 [f]Jos 19:37; 20:7; 21:32 [g]1Sa 15:12
22 the king of Kedesh[f] one
the king of Jokneam in Carmel[g] one
12:23 [h]Jos 11:2
23 the king of Dor (in Naphoth Dor[a][h]) one
the king of Goyim in Gilgal one
12:24 [i]Ps 135:11; Dt 7:24
24 the king of Tirzah one
thirty-one kings in all.[i]

Land Still to Be Taken

13:1 [j]Ge 24:1; Jos 14:10
13 When Joshua was old and well advanced in years,[j] the LORD
said to him, "You are very old, and there
are still very large areas of land to be
taken over.

2 "This is the land that remains: all
the regions of the Philistines and
13:3 [k]Jer 2:18 [l]Jdg 1:18 [m]Jdg 3:3 [n]Dt 2:23
Geshurites: 3 from the Shihor River[k]
on the east of Egypt to the territory of Ekron[l] on the north, all of it
counted as Canaanite (the territory of the five Philistine rulers[m] in
Gaza, Ashdod, Ashkelon, Gath and
13:4 [o]Jos 12:18; 19:30 [p]Am 2:10
Ekron—that of the Avvites);[n] 4 from
the south, all the land of the
Canaanites, from Arah of the Sidonians as far as Aphek,[o] the region
13:5 [q]1Ki 5:18; Ps 83:7; Eze 27:9 [r]Jos 12:7
of the Amorites,[p] 5 the area of the
Gebalites[b];[q] and all Lebanon[r] to
the east, from Baal Gad below
Mount Hermon to Lebo[c] Hamath.

6 "As for all the inhabitants of the
mountain regions from Lebanon to Misrephoth Maim,[s] that is, all the Sidonians, I myself will drive them out before
13:6 [s]Jos 11:8 [t]Nu 33:54
the Israelites. Be sure to allocate this
land to Israel for an inheritance, as I
have instructed you,[t] 7 and divide it as an
13:7 [u]Jos 11:23; Ps 78:55
inheritance[u] among the nine tribes and
half of the tribe of Manasseh."

Division of the Land East of the Jordan

8 The other half of Manasseh,[d] the Reubenites and the Gadites had received the
inheritance that Moses had given them
east of the Jordan, as he, the servant of
13:8 [v]Jos 12:6
the LORD, had assigned[v] it to them.

13:9 [w]ver 16; Jdg 11:26 [x]Jer 48:8,21 [y]Nu 21:30
9 It extended from Aroer[w] on the
rim of the Arnon Gorge, and from
the town in the middle of the gorge,
and included the whole plateau[x] of
Medeba as far as Dibon,[y] 10 and all
the towns of Sihon king of the Amorites, who ruled in Heshbon, out
13:10 [z]Nu 21:24
to the border of the Ammonites.[z]
11 It also included Gilead, the territory of the people of Geshur and
Maacah, all of Mount Hermon and
13:11 [a]Jos 12:5
all Bashan as far as Salecah[a]—
13:12 [b]Dt 3:11 [c]Jos 12:4 [d]Ge 14:5
12 that is, the whole kingdom of Og
in Bashan,[b] who had reigned in
Ashtaroth[c] and Edrei and had survived as one of the last of the Rephaites.[d] Moses had defeated them
and taken over their land. 13 But the
Israelites did not drive out the peo-
13:13 [e]Jos 12:5 [f]Dt 3:14
ple of Geshur[e] and Maacah,[f] so
they continue to live among the Israelites to this day.

14 But to the tribe of Levi he gave no
inheritance, since the offerings made by
13:14 [g]ver 33; Dt 18:1-2
fire to the LORD, the God of Israel, are
their inheritance, as he promised them.[g]

15 This is what Moses had given to the
tribe of Reuben, clan by clan:

13:16 [h]ver 9; Jos 12:2 [i]Nu 21:30
16 The territory from Aroer[h] on the
rim of the Arnon Gorge, and from
the town in the middle of the gorge,
and the whole plateau past Medeba[i]

[a] 23 Or *in the heights of Dor* [b] 5 That is, the area of Byblos [c] 5 Or *to the entrance to* [d] 8 Hebrew *With it* (that is, with the other half of Manasseh)

13:17 [j]Nu 32:3 17to Heshbon and all its towns on
[k]1Ch 5:8 the plateau, including Dibon,[j] Bamoth Baal, Beth Baal Meon,[k] 18Ja-
13:18 [l]Nu 21:23 haz,[l] Kedemoth, Mephaath,[m] 19Kir-
[m]Jer 48:21 iathaim,[n] Sibmah, Zereth Shahar on
13:19 the hill in the valley, 20Beth Peor,[o]
[n]Nu 32:37 the slopes of Pisgah, and Beth Jeshi-
13:20 moth 21—all the towns on the pla-
[o]Dt 3:29 teau and the entire realm of Sihon
king of the Amorites, who ruled at
Heshbon. Moses had defeated him
13:21 [p]Nu 25:15 and the Midianite chiefs,[p] Evi, Re-
[q]Nu 31:8 kem, Zur, Hur and Reba[q]—princes
allied with Sihon—who lived in that
country. 22In addition to those slain
13:22 in battle, the Israelites had put to
[r]Nu 22:5; 31:8 the sword Balaam son of Beor,[r] who
practiced divination. 23The bound-
ary of the Reubenites was the bank
of the Jordan. These towns and their
villages were the inheritance of the
Reubenites, clan by clan.

24This is what Moses had given to the
tribe of Gad, clan by clan:

13:25 25The territory of Jazer,[s] all the
[s]Nu 21:32; Jos 21:39 towns of Gilead and half the Ammonite country as far as Aroer,
13:26 near Rabbah; 26and from Heshbon[t]
[t]Nu 21:25; Jer 49:3 to Ramath Mizpah and Betonim,
[u]Jos 10:3 and from Mahanaim to the territory of Debir;[u] 27and in the valley,
Beth Haram, Beth Nimrah, Suc-
13:27 [v]Ge 33:17 coth[v] and Zaphon with the rest of
[w]Nu 34:11 the realm of Sihon king of Heshbon
(the east side of the Jordan, the territory up to the end of the Sea of
Kinnereth[a w]). 28These towns and
13:28 their villages were the inheritance
[x]Nu 32:33 of the Gadites,[x] clan by clan.

29This is what Moses had given to the
half-tribe of Manasseh, that is, to half
the family of the descendants of Manasseh, clan by clan:

30The territory extending from Ma-
13:30 hanaim[y] and including all of Ba-
[y]Ge 32:2 [z]Nu 32:41 shan, the entire realm of Og king of
Bashan—all the settlements of
Jair[z] in Bashan, sixty towns, 31half
of Gilead, and Ashtaroth and Edrei
(the royal cities of Og in Bashan).
This was for the descendants of
13:31 [a]Ge 50:23 Makir[a] son of Manasseh—for half
of the sons of Makir, clan by clan.

32This is the inheritance Moses had
given when he was in the plains of Moab
across the Jordan east of Jericho. 33But to
the tribe of Levi, Moses had given no inheritance; the LORD, the God of Israel, is 13:33
their inheritance,[b] as he promised them.[c] [b]Nu 18:20 [c]ver 14; Jos 18:7

Division of the Land West of the Jordan

14 Now these are the areas the Israelites received as an inheritance in the land of Canaan, which Eleazar the priest, Joshua son of Nun and
the heads of the tribal clans of Israel allotted to them.[d] 2Their inheritances 14:1 [d]Nu 34:17-18
were assigned by lot[e] to the nine-and-a-
half tribes, as the LORD had commanded 14:2 [e]Nu 26:55
through Moses. 3Moses had granted the
two-and-a-half tribes their inheritance
east of the Jordan[f] but had not granted 14:3 [f]Nu 32:33
the Levites an inheritance among the [g]Jos 13:14
rest,[g] 4for the sons of Joseph had become
two tribes—Manasseh and Ephraim.[h] 14:4 [h]Ge 41:52; 48:5
The Levites received no share of the land
but only towns to live in, with pasturelands for their flocks and herds. 5So the
Israelites divided the land, just as the 14:5 [i]Nu 34:13; 35:2;
LORD had commanded Moses.[i] Jos 21:2

Hebron Given to Caleb

6Now the men of Judah approached
Joshua at Gilgal, and Caleb son of Je-
phunneh[j] the Kenizzite said to him, 14:6 [j]Nu 13:6; 14:30
"You know what the LORD said to Moses [k]Nu 13:26
the man of God at Kadesh Barnea[k]
about you and me. 7I was forty years old
when Moses the servant of the LORD
sent me from Kadesh Barnea to explore
the land.[l] And I brought him back a re- 14:7 [l]Nu 13:17
port according to my convictions,[m] 8but [m]Nu 13:30;
my brothers who went up with me made 14:6-9
the hearts of the people melt with fear.[n] 14:8 [n]Nu 13:31
I, however, followed the LORD my God [o]Nu 14:24
wholeheartedly.[o] 9So on that day Moses
swore to me, 'The land on which your
feet have walked will be your inheri-
tance and that of your children[p] forever, 14:9 [p]Nu 14:24;
because you have followed the LORD my Dt 1:36
God wholeheartedly.'[b]

10"Now then, just as the LORD prom-
ised,[q] he has kept me alive for forty-five 14:10 [q]Nu 14:30
years since the time he said this to Mo-
ses, while Israel moved about in the
desert. So here I am today, eighty-five
years old! 11I am still as strong[r] today as 14:11 [r]Dt 34:7
the day Moses sent me out; I'm just as
vigorous to go out to battle now as I was
then. 12Now give me this hill country

[a] 27 That is, Galilee [b] 9 Deut. 1:36

DISCOVERY 56

CALEB—A MAN OF CONVICTION

The reading of a will is always serious business—how much more momentous the reading of God's "will"! God divided the promised land among his children. Each of the 12 tribes would receive the particular inheritance God intended to provide (see Deuteronomy 32:8). Surprisingly, each tribe discovered its allotted portion by the casting of lots. This "lottery," strange as it may seem to us, comprised God's chosen method of communication, and the people accepted this system with a respectful attitude and decorum.

The aged Caleb, however, came forward with an interesting proposition (Joshua 14:6–12). Instead of waiting for the dice to be thrown, he requested a special piece of property—Hebron, the place to which he and Joshua had been sent as spies some 40 years earlier. This was the location at which they had seen the luscious fruit of a land so fertile that the Bible describes it as "flowing with milk and honey." True, there would be a few giants to contend with, but their presence did not constitute an obstacle in Caleb's mind (Numbers 13:26–28). He must have been fantasizing about a return to that bountiful land for half his life!

But why did Joshua grant Caleb's request? Joshua knew that Caleb had been the only person in Israel besides himself who had believed God's promise that he would give the land to his people. Caleb's focus was right on target—centered on God's Word—and he followed the Lord wholeheartedly.

Caleb was a man of obedience, but more than that, he was a man of conviction (Joshua 14:7). He kept his eye on the best God had to offer and refused to let go of the dream—even after 40 long years. So Joshua granted Caleb's request on behalf of the tribe of Judah—and the description given of the land is incredible (Joshua 15). Even today, the property that was allotted to Judah comprises some of the most verdant land in all of Israel and contains some of the wealthiest mineral deposits in the world. What a fitting reward for wholehearted faithfulness!

Caleb's courage is a reflection of Jesus' courage as he climbed the hill of Calvary. There on the cross Jesus destroyed "him who holds the power of death—that is the devil—and [set] free those who all their lives were held in slavery by their fear of death" (Hebrews 2:14–15). "And having disarmed the powers and authorities, he made a public spectacle of them, triumphing over them by the cross" (Colossians 2:15). We have a choice, just as the people of Israel did: Either we turn back in fear of the giants or we enter the land God has promised to those who walk with him. But there is no rolling of the dice; we simply take God at his word, continue on our journey with him and boldly speak out for him, just as Caleb did.

When we are willing to trust him, God confers on us our inheritance through Jesus—our sin is removed and our relationship with God eternally secured!

Self-Discovery: *What are the giants in your life that cause you to want to turn around and flee? Ask Jesus to help you overcome your fear.*

GO TO DISCOVERY 57 ON PAGE 298

14:12 that the LORD promised me that day. You
[s]Nu 13:33 yourself heard then that the Anakites[s]
[t]Nu 13:28 were there and their cities were large
and fortified,[t] but, the LORD helping me,
14:13 I will drive them out just as he said."
[u]Jos 22:6,7 [13]Then Joshua blessed[u] Caleb son of
[v]Jos 10:36 Jephunneh and gave him Hebron[v] as his
[w]Jdg 1:20; 1Ch 6:56 inheritance.[w] [14]So Hebron has belonged
to Caleb son of Jephunneh the Kenizzite
ever since, because he followed the
LORD, the God of Israel, wholeheartedly.
14:15 [15](Hebron used to be called Kiriath
[x]Ge 23:2 Arba[x] after Arba,[y] who was the greatest
[y]Jos 15:13 man among the Anakites.)
[z]Jos 11:23 Then the land had rest[z] from war.

Allotment for Judah

15 The allotment for the tribe of
Judah, clan by clan, extended
15:1 down to the territory of Edom,[a] to the
[a]Nu 34:3 [b]Nu 33:36 Desert of Zin[b] in the extreme south.
[2]Their southern boundary start-
ed from the bay at the southern
15:3 end of the Salt Sea,[a] [3]crossed south
[c]Nu 34:4 of Scorpion[b] Pass,[c] continued on to
Zin and went over to the south of
Kadesh Barnea. Then it ran past
Hezron up to Addar and curved
15:4 around to Karka. [4]It then passed
[d]Nu 34:5 along to Azmon[d] and joined the
[e]Ge 15:18 Wadi of Egypt,[e] ending at the sea.
This is their[c] southern boundary.
15:5 [5]The eastern boundary[f] is the
[f]Nu 34:10 [g]Jos 18:15-19 Salt Sea as far as the mouth of the
Jordan.
The northern boundary[g] started
from the bay of the sea at the
15:6 mouth of the Jordan, [6]went up to
[h]Jos 18:19,21 Beth Hoglah[h] and continued north
[i]Jos 18:17 of Beth Arabah to the Stone of Bohan[i] son of Reuben. [7]The boundary
then went up to Debir from the Val-
15:7 ley of Achor[j] and turned north to
[j]Jos 7:24 [k]2Sa 17:17; 1Ki 1:9 Gilgal, which faces the Pass of
Adummim south of the gorge. It
continued along to the waters of En
Shemesh and came out at En Rogel.[k] [8]Then it ran up the Valley of
Ben Hinnom along the southern
15:8 slope of the Jebusite[l] city (that is, Je-
[l]ver 63; Jos 18:16,28; Jdg 1:21; 19:10 rusalem). From there it climbed to
the top of the hill west of the Hin-
nom Valley at the northern end of
the Valley of Rephaim. [9]From the
hilltop the boundary headed to-
15:9 ward the spring of the waters of
[m]Jos 18:15 Nephtoah,[m] came out at the towns
of Mount Ephron and went down
toward Baalah[n] (that is, Kiriath Jea- 15:9 [n]1Ch 13:6
rim). [10]Then it curved westward
from Baalah to Mount Seir, ran
along the northern slope of Mount
Jearim (that is, Kesalon), continued
down to Beth Shemesh and crossed 15:10
to Timnah.[o] [11]It went to the north- [o]Ge 38:12; Jdg 14:1
ern slope of Ekron, turned toward
Shikkeron, passed along to Mount 15:11
Baalah and reached Jabneel.[p] The [p]Jos 19:33
boundary ended at the sea.
[12]The western boundary is the 15:12
coastline of the Great Sea.[d] [q] [q]Nu 34:6
These are the boundaries around the
people of Judah by their clans.
[13]In accordance with the LORD's command to him, Joshua gave to Caleb son of
Jephunneh a portion in Judah—Kiriath
Arba, that is, Hebron. (Arba was the fore- 15:13
father of Anak.)[r] [14]From Hebron Caleb [r]Jos 14:13-15
drove out the three Anakites[s]—Sheshai, 15:14
Ahiman and Talmai[t]—descendants of [s]Nu 13:33
Anak.[u] [15]From there he marched against [t]Nu 13:22 [u]Jdg 1:10,20
the people living in Debir (formerly
called Kiriath Sepher). [16]And Caleb said,
"I will give my daughter Acsah[v] in mar- 15:16 [v]Jdg 1:12
riage to the man who attacks and cap-
tures Kiriath Sepher." [17]Othniel[w] son of 15:17 [w]Jdg 3:9,11
Kenaz, Caleb's brother, took it; so Caleb
gave his daughter Acsah to him in marriage.
[18]One day when she came to Othniel,
she urged him[e] to ask her father for a
field. When she got off her donkey, Caleb asked her, "What can I do for you?"
[19]She replied, "Do me a special favor.
Since you have given me land in the Negev, give me also springs of water." So Caleb gave her the upper and lower springs.
[20]This is the inheritance of the tribe of
Judah, clan by clan:

[21]The southernmost towns of the tribe
of Judah in the Negev toward the boundary of Edom were:

Kabzeel, Eder,[x] Jagur, [22]Kinah, Di- 15:21
monah, Adadah, [23]Kedesh, Hazor, [x]Ge 35:21
Ithnan, [24]Ziph,[y] Telem, Bealoth, 15:24
[25]Hazor Hadattah, Kerioth Hezron [y]1Sa 23:14
(that is, Hazor), [26]Amam, Shema, 15:26
Moladah,[z] [27]Hazar Gaddah, Hesh- [z]1Ch 4:28

[a] *2* That is, the Dead Sea; also in verse 5
[b] *3* Hebrew *Akrabbim* [c] *4* Hebrew *your*
[d] *12* That is, the Mediterranean; also in verse 47
[e] *18* Hebrew and some Septuagint manuscripts; other Septuagint manuscripts (see also note at Judges 1:14) *Othniel, he urged her*

15:28 mon, Beth Pelet, [28]Hazar Shual,
a Ge 21:31 Beersheba,[a] Biziothiah, [29]Baalah,[b]
15:29 Iim, Ezem, [30]Eltolad,[c] Kesil, Hor-
b ver 9 mah, [31]Ziklag,[d] Madmannah, San-
15:30 sannah, [32]Lebaoth, Shilhim, Ain
c Jos 19:4 and Rimmon[e]—a total of twenty-
15:31 nine towns and their villages.
d 1Sa 27:6
[33]In the western foothills:
15:32 Eshtaol,[f] Zorah, Ashnah, [34]Za-
e Jdg 20:45 noah,[g] En Gannim, Tappuah,
15:33 f Jdg 13:25; Enam, [35]Jarmuth,[h] Adullam,[i] So-
16:31 coh, Azekah, [36]Shaaraim, Adithaim
15:34 and Gederah[j] (or Gederothaim)[a]—
g 1Ch 4:18; fourteen towns and their villages.
Ne 3:13 [37]Zenan, Hadashah, Migdal Gad,
15:35 [38]Dilean, Mizpah, Joktheel,[k] [39]La-
h Jos 10:3 chish,[l] Bozkath,[m] Eglon, [40]Cabbon,
i 1Sa 22:1 Lahmas, Kitlish, [41]Gederoth, Beth
15:36 Dagon, Naamah and Makkedah[n]—
j 1Ch 12:4 sixteen towns and their villages.
15:38 [42]Libnah, Ether, Ashan,[o] [43]Iph-
k 2Ki 14:7 tah, Ashnah, Nezib, [44]Keilah, Ac-
15:39 zib[p] and Mareshah[q]—nine towns
l Jos 10:3; 2Ki 14:19 and their villages.
m 2Ki 22:1 [45]Ekron, with its surrounding
settlements and villages; [46]west of
15:41 n Jos 10:10 Ekron, all that were in the vicinity
of Ashdod, together with their vil-
15:42 o 1Sa 30:30 lages; [47]Ashdod,[r] its surrounding
settlements and villages; and Gaza,
15:44 p Jdg 1:31 its settlements and villages, as far
q Mic 1:15 as the Wadi of Egypt[s] and the
15:47 coastline of the Great Sea.[t]
r Jos 11:22
s ver 4 t Nu 34:6 [48]In the hill country:
15:48 Shamir, Jattir,[u] Socoh, [49]Dannah,
u 1Sa 30:27 Kiriath Sannah (that is, Debir[v]),
15:49 [50]Anab, Eshtemoh,[w] Anim, [51]Go-
v Jos 10:3 shen,[x] Holon and Giloh—eleven
15:50 towns and their villages.
w Jos 21:14 [52]Arab, Dumah,[y] Eshan, [53]Janim,
15:51 Beth Tappuah, Aphekah, [54]Hum-
x Jos 10:41; tah, Kiriath Arba (that is, Hebron)
11:16 and Zior—nine towns and their
15:52 villages.
y Ge 25:14 [55]Maon, Carmel,[z] Ziph, Juttah,
15:55 [56]Jezreel,[a] Jokdeam, Zanoah, [57]Kain,
z Jos 12:22 Gibeah[b] and Timnah—ten towns
15:56 and their villages.
a Jos 17:16 [58]Halhul, Beth Zur,[c] Gedor, [59]Ma-
15:57 arath, Beth Anoth and Eltekon—
b Jos 18:28; six towns and their villages.
Jdg 19:12 [60]Kiriath Baal (that is, Kiriath Je-
15:58 arim[d]) and Rabbah[e]—two towns
c 1Ch 2:45 and their villages.
15:60 [61]In the desert:
d Jos 18:14 e Dt 3:11 Beth Arabah, Middin, Secacah,

[62]Nibshan, the City of Salt and En
Gedi[f]—six towns and their villages. 15:62 f 1Sa 23:29
[63]Judah could not[g] dislodge the Jebu- 15:63
sites[h], who were living in Jerusalem; to g Jdg 1:21
this day the Jebusites live there with the h 2Sa 5:6
people of Judah.

Allotment for Ephraim and Manasseh

16 The allotment for Joseph
began at the Jordan of Jer-
icho,[b] east of the waters of Jericho,
and went up from there through 16:1
the desert[i] into the hill country of i Jos 8:15; 18:12
Bethel. [2]It went on from Bethel 16:2
(that is, Luz[j]),[c] crossed over to the j Jos 18:13
territory of the Arkites in Ataroth,
[3]descended westward to the terri-
tory of the Japhletites as far as the 16:3 k 2Ch 8:5
region of Lower Beth Horon[k] and l Jos 10:33;
on to Gezer,[l] ending at the sea. 1Ki 9:15
[4]So Manasseh and Ephraim, the descen-
dants of Joseph, received their inheri- 16:4 m Jos 17:14
tance.[m]

[5]This was the territory of Ephraim, clan
by clan:
The boundary of their inheri- 16:5
tance went from Ataroth Addar[n] in n Jos 18:13
the east to Upper Beth Horon [6]and
continued to the sea. From Micme-
thath[o] on the north it curved east- 16:6 o Jos 17:7
ward to Taanath Shiloh, passing by
it to Janoah on the east. [7]Then it
went down from Janoah to Ata-
roth[p] and Naarah, touched Jericho 16:7 p 1Ch 7:28
and came out at the Jordan. [8]From
Tappuah the border went west to 16:8
the Kanah Ravine[q] and ended at q Jos 17:9
the sea. This was the inheritance of
the tribe of the Ephraimites, clan by
clan. [9]It also included all the towns
and their villages that were set aside
for the Ephraimites within the inheritance of the Manassites.
[10]They did not dislodge the Canaanites
living in Gezer; to this day the Canaan- 16:10
ites live among the people of Ephraim r Jos 17:13;
but are required to do forced labor.[r] Jdg 1:28-29; 1Ki 9:16

17 This was the allotment for the
tribe of Manasseh as Joseph's 17:1
firstborn,[s] that is, for Makir,[t] Manasseh's s Ge 41:51
firstborn. Makir was the ancestor of the t Ge 50:23
Gileadites, who had received Gilead and
Bashan because the Makirites were

[a] 36 Or *Gederah and Gederothaim* [b] 1 *Jordan of Jericho* was possibly an ancient name for the Jordan River. [c] 2 Septuagint; Hebrew *Bethel to Luz*

great soldiers. [2]So this allotment was for
17:2 the rest of the people of Manasseh—the
[u]Nu 26:30; clans of Abiezer,[u] Helek, Asriel, She-
1Ch 7:18 chem, Hepher and Shemida. These are
the other male descendants of Manasseh son of Joseph by their clans.
17:3 [3]Now Zelophehad son of Hepher,[v] the
[v]Nu 27:1 son of Gilead, the son of Makir, the son
[w]Nu 26:33 of Manasseh, had no sons but only
daughters,[w] whose names were Mahlah,
Noah, Hoglah, Milcah and Tirzah. [4]They
went to Eleazar the priest, Joshua son of
Nun, and the leaders and said, "The
LORD commanded Moses to give us an
inheritance among our brothers." So
Joshua gave them an inheritance along
17:4 with the brothers of their father, accord-
[x]Nu 27:5-7 ing to the LORD's command.[x] [5]Manas-
seh's share consisted of ten tracts of land
besides Gilead and Bashan east of the
Jordan, [6]because the daughters of the
tribe of Manasseh received an inheritance among the sons. The land of Gilead belonged to the rest of the descendants of Manasseh.
[7]The territory of Manasseh extended from Asher to Micme-
17:7 thath[y] east of Shechem.[z] The
[y]Jos 16:6 boundary ran southward from
[z]Ge 12:6; there to include the people living at
Jos 21:21 En Tappuah. [8](Manasseh had the
17:8 land of Tappuah, but Tappuah[a] it-
[a]Jos 16:8 self, on the boundary of Manasseh,
belonged to the Ephraimites.)
17:9 [9]Then the boundary continued
[b]Jos 16:8 south to the Kanah Ravine.[b] There
were towns belonging to Ephraim
lying among the towns of Manasseh, but the boundary of Manasseh
was the northern side of the ravine
and ended at the sea. [10]On the
south the land belonged to Ephraim, on the north to Manasseh. The
territory of Manasseh reached the
sea and bordered Asher on the
17:10 north and Issachar[c] on the east.
[c]Ge 30:18 [11]Within Issachar and Asher,
17:11 [d]1Sa 31:10; Manasseh also had Beth Shan,[d] Ib-
1Ki 4:12; leam and the people of Dor,[e] En-
1Ch 7:29 [e]Jos 11:2 dor,[f] Taanach and Megiddo,[g] to-
[f]1Sa 28:7; gether with their surrounding
Ps 83:10 settlements (the third in the list is
[g]1Ki 9:15 Naphoth[a]).
17:12 [12]Yet the Manassites were not able[h] to
[h]Jdg 1:27 occupy these towns, for the Canaanites
were determined to live in that region.
[13]However, when the Israelites grew

stronger, they subjected the Canaanites
to forced labor but did not drive them 17:13
out completely.[i] [i]Jos 16:10
[14]The people of Joseph said to Joshua,
"Why have you given us only one allotment and one portion for an inheritance? We are a numerous people and
the LORD has blessed us abundantly."[j] 17:14
[15]"If you are so numerous," Joshua an- [j]Nu 26:28-37
swered, "and if the hill country of Ephra-
im is too small for you, go up into the
forest and clear land for yourselves there
in the land of the Perizzites and Reph- 17:15
aites.[k]" [k]Ge 14:5
[16]The people of Joseph replied, "The
hill country is not enough for us, and all
the Canaanites who live in the plain
have iron chariots,[l] both those in Beth 17:16
Shan and its settlements and those in [l]Jdg 1:19; 4:3,13
the Valley of Jezreel."
[17]But Joshua said to the house of Joseph—to Ephraim and Manasseh—
"You are numerous and very powerful.
You will have not only one allotment
[18]but the forested hill country as well.
Clear it, and its farthest limits will be
yours; though the Canaanites have iron 17:18
chariots[m] and though they are strong, [m]ver 16
you can drive them out."

Division of the Rest of the Land

18 The whole assembly of the Isra- 18:1
elites gathered at Shiloh[n] and [n]Jos 19:51; 21:2;
set up the Tent of Meeting[o] there. The Jdg 18:31; 21:12,
country was brought under their con- 19; 1Sa 1:3; 4:3;
trol, [2]but there were still seven Israelite Jer 7:12; 26:6
tribes who had not yet received their in- [o]Ex 27:21
heritance.
[3]So Joshua said to the Israelites: "How
long will you wait before you begin to
take possession of the land that the
LORD, the God of your fathers, has given
you? [4]Appoint three men from each
tribe. I will send them out to make a survey of the land and to write a description of it, according to the inheritance of 18:4
each.[p] Then they will return to me. [5]You [p]Mic 2:5
are to divide the land into seven parts.
Judah is to remain in its territory on the 18:5
south[q] and the house of Joseph in its ter- [q]Jos 15:1
ritory on the north.[r] [6]After you have [r]Jos 16:1-4
written descriptions of the seven parts
of the land, bring them here to me and I 18:6
will cast lots[s] for you in the presence of [s]Jos 14:2
the LORD our God. [7]The Levites, howev-
er, do not get a portion among you, be-

[a] *11* That is, Naphoth Dor

cause the priestly service of the LORD is
18:7 their inheritance.[t] And Gad, Reuben
[t]Jos 13:33 and the half-tribe of Manasseh have al-
[u]Jos 13:8 ready received their inheritance on the
east side of the Jordan. Moses the servant of the LORD gave it to them.[u]"
8 As the men started on their way to
map out the land, Joshua instructed
them, "Go and make a survey of the land
and write a description of it. Then return to me, and I will cast lots for you
18:8 here at Shiloh[v] in the presence of the
[v]ver 1 LORD." 9 So the men left and went
through the land. They wrote its description on a scroll, town by town, in
seven parts, and returned to Joshua in
the camp at Shiloh. 10 Joshua then cast
18:10 lots[w] for them in Shiloh in the presence[x]
[w]Nu 34:13 of the LORD, and there he distributed the
[x]ver 1; Jer 7:12 [y]Nu 33:54; land to the Israelites according to their
Jos 19:51 tribal divisions.[y]

Allotment for Benjamin

11 The lot came up for the tribe of Benjamin, clan by clan. Their allotted territory lay between the tribes of Judah and
Joseph:
12 On the north side their boundary began at the Jordan, passed the
northern slope of Jericho and head-
18:12 ed west into the hill country, com-
[z]Jos 16:1 [a]Jos 7:2 ing out at the desert[z] of Beth Aven.[a]
13 From there it crossed to the south
18:13 slope of Luz[b] (that is, Bethel[c]) and
[b]Ge 28:19 went down to Ataroth Addar[d] on
[c]Jdg 1:23 [d]Jos 16:5 the hill south of Lower Beth Horon.
18:14 14 From the hill facing Beth Ho-
[e]Jos 10:10 ron[e] on the south the boundary
turned south along the western
side and came out at Kiriath Baal
(that is, Kiriath Jearim), a town of
the people of Judah. This was the
western side.
15 The southern side began at the
outskirts of Kiriath Jearim on the
west, and the boundary came out at
the spring of the waters of Nephto-
18:15 ah.[f] 16 The boundary went down to
[f]Jos 15:9 the foot of the hill facing the Valley
of Ben Hinnom, north of the Valley
of Rephaim. It continued down the
18:16 Hinnom Valley[g] along the southern
[g]Jos 15:8; 2Ki 23:10 slope of the Jebusite city and so to
[h]Jos 15:7 En Rogel.[h] 17 It then curved north,
went to En Shemesh, continued to
Geliloth, which faces the Pass of
Adummim, and ran down to the

Stone of Bohan[i] son of Reuben. 18 It 18:17 [i]Jos 15:6
continued to the northern slope of
Beth Arabah[a][j] and on down into 18:18 [j]Jos 15:6
the Arabah. 19 It then went to the
northern slope of Beth Hoglah and
came out at the northern bay of the 18:19
Salt Sea,[b][k] at the mouth of the Jor- [k]Ge 14:3
dan in the south. This was the
southern boundary.
20 The Jordan formed the boundary on the eastern side.
These were the boundaries that marked 18:20
out the inheritance of the clans of Ben- [l]Jos 21:4,17;
jamin on all sides.[l] 1Sa 9:1

21 The tribe of Benjamin, clan by clan,
had the following cities:
Jericho, Beth Hoglah, Emek Ke- 18:22
ziz, 22 Beth Arabah, Zemaraim, [m]Jos 16:1
Bethel,[m] 23 Avvim, Parah, Ophrah,
24 Kephar Ammoni, Ophni and 18:24 [n]Isa 10:29
Geba[n]—twelve towns and their villages. 18:25
25 Gibeon,[o] Ramah,[p] Beeroth,[q] [o]Jos 9:3 [p]Jdg 4:5 [q]Jos 9:17
26 Mizpah,[r] Kephirah, Mozah, 27 Re-
kem, Irpeel, Taralah, 28 Zelah,[s] Hae- 18:26 [r]Jos 11:3
leph, the Jebusite city[t] (that is, Jerusalem[u]), Gibeah[v] and Kiriath— 18:28 [s]2Sa 21:14
fourteen towns and their villages. [t]Jos 15:8
This was the inheritance of Benjamin [u]Jos 10:1
for its clans. [v]Jos 15:57

Allotment for Simeon

19 The second lot came out for the
tribe of Simeon, clan by clan.
Their inheritance lay within the territo- 19:1
ry of Judah.[w] 2 It included: [w]ver 9; Ge 49:7
Beersheba[x] (or Sheba),[c] Mola- 19:2
dah, 3 Hazar Shual, Balah, Ezem, [x]Ge 21:14; 1Ki 19:3
4 Eltolad, Bethul, Hormah, 5 Ziklag,
Beth Marcaboth, Hazar Susah,
6 Beth Lebaoth and Sharuhen—
thirteen towns and their villages;
7 Ain, Rimmon, Ether and 19:7
Ashan[y]—four towns and their vil- [y]Jos 15:42
lages— 8 and all the villages around
these towns as far as Baalath Beer 19:8
(Ramah in the Negev).[z] [z]Jos 10:40
This was the inheritance of the tribe of
the Simeonites, clan by clan. 9 The inheritance of the Simeonites was taken from 19:9
the share of Judah,[a] because Judah's por- [a]Ge 49:7
tion was more than they needed. So the [b]Eze 48:24
Simeonites received their inheritance
within the territory of Judah.[b]

[a] *18* Septuagint; Hebrew *slope facing the Arabah*
[b] *19* That is, the Dead Sea [c] *2* Or *Beersheba, Sheba*; 1 Chron. 4:28 does not have *Sheba.*

Allotment for Zebulun

19:10 [c]Jos 21:7,34 10The third lot came up for Zebulun,[c]
clan by clan:
The boundary of their inheritance went as far as Sarid. 11Going
west it ran to Maralah, touched
19:11 [d]Jos 12:22 Dabbesheth, and extended to the
ravine near Jokneam.[d] 12It turned
east from Sarid toward the sunrise
to the territory of Kisloth Tabor
and went on to Daberath and up to
Japhia. 13Then it continued east-
19:13 [e]Jos 15:32 ward to Gath Hepher and Eth Ka-
zin; it came out at Rimmon[e] and
turned toward Neah. 14There the
boundary went around on the
north to Hannathon and ended at
the Valley of Iphtah El. 15Included
19:15 [f]Ge 35:19 were Kattath, Nahalal, Shimron, Id-
alah and Bethlehem.[f] There were
twelve towns and their villages.
19:16 [g]ver 10; Jos 21:7 [h]Eze 48:26 16These towns and their villages were
the inheritance of Zebulun,[g] clan by
clan.[h]

Allotment for Issachar

19:17 [i]Ge 30:18 17The fourth lot came out for Issachar,[i]
19:18 [j]Jos 15:56 [k]1Sa 28:4; 2Ki 4:8 clan by clan. 18Their territory included:
Jezreel,[j] Kesulloth, Shunem,[k]
19Hapharaim, Shion, Anaharath,
20Rabbith, Kishion, Ebez, 21Remeth,
En Gannim, En Haddah and Beth
19:22 [l]Jdg 4:6,12; Ps 89:12 [m]Jos 15:10 Pazzez. 22The boundary touched
Tabor,[l] Shahazumah and Beth She-
mesh,[m] and ended at the Jordan.
There were sixteen towns and their
villages.
19:23 [n]Jos 17:10 [o]Ge 49:15; Eze 48:25 23These towns and their villages were
the inheritance of the tribe of Issachar,[n]
clan by clan.[o]

Allotment for Asher

19:24 [p]Jos 17:7 24The fifth lot came out for the tribe of
Asher,[p] clan by clan. 25Their territory included:
Helkath, Hali, Beten, Acshaph,
26Allammelech, Amad and Mishal.
On the west the boundary touched
19:26 [q]Jos 12:22 Carmel[q] and Shihor Libnath. 27It
then turned east toward Beth Da-
19:27 [r]ver 10 [s]1Ki 9:13 gon, touched Zebulun[r] and the Valley of Iphtah El, and went north to
Beth Emek and Neiel, passing Cabul[s] on the left. 28It went to Ab-
19:28 [t]Jdg 1:31 [u]1Ch 6:76 [v]Ge 10:19; Jos 11:8 don,[a] Rehob,[t] Hammon[u] and Kanah, as far as Greater Sidon.[v] 29The
boundary then turned back toward
Ramah[w] and went to the fortified 19:29 [w]Jos 18:25
city of Tyre,[x] turned toward Hosah [x]2Sa 5:11; 24:7; Isa 23:1; Jer 25:22; Eze 26:2
and came out at the sea in the re-
gion of Aczib,[y] 30Ummah, Aphek [y]Jdg 1:31
and Rehob. There were twenty-two
towns and their villages.
31These towns and their villages were 19:31 [z]Ge 30:13; Eze 48:2
the inheritance of the tribe of Asher,[z]
clan by clan.

Allotment for Naphtali

32The sixth lot came out for Naphtali,
clan by clan:
33Their boundary went from He-
leph and the large tree in Zaanan-
nim, passing Adami Nekeb and
Jabneel to Lakkum and ending at
the Jordan. 34The boundary ran
west through Aznoth Tabor and
came out at Hukkok. It touched
Zebulun on the south, Asher on the
west and the Jordan[b] on the east.
35The fortified cities were Ziddim,
Zer, Hammath, Rakkath, Kinne- 19:35 [a]Jos 11:2
reth,[a] 36Adamah, Ramah,[b] Hazor,[c]
37Kedesh, Edrei,[d] En Hazor, 38Iron, 19:36 [b]Jos 18:25 [c]Jos 11:1
Migdal El, Horem, Beth Anath and
Beth Shemesh. There were nine-
teen towns and their villages. 19:37 [d]Nu 21:33
39These towns and their villages were 19:39 [e]Dt 33:23; Eze 48:3
the inheritance of the tribe of Naphtali,
clan by clan.[e]

Allotment for Dan

40The seventh lot came out for the tribe
of Dan, clan by clan. 41The territory of
their inheritance included:
Zorah, Eshtaol, Ir Shemesh,
42Shaalabbin, Aijalon,[f] Ithlah, 19:42 [f]Jdg 1:35
43Elon, Timnah,[g] Ekron, 44Eltekeh,
Gibbethon, Baalath, 45Jehud, Bene 19:43 [g]Ge 38:12
Berak, Gath Rimmon,[h] 46Me Jarkon
and Rakkon, with the area facing 19:45 [h]Jos 21:24; 1Ch 6:69
Joppa.[i]
47(But the Danites had difficulty tak- 19:46 [i]2Ch 2:16; Jnh 1:3
ing possession of their territory,[j] so they
went up and attacked Leshem[k], took it,
put it to the sword and occupied it. They 19:47 [j]Jdg 18:1 [k]Jdg 18:7,14 [l]Jdg 18:27,29
settled in Leshem and named it Dan af-
ter their forefather.)[l]
48These towns and their villages were 19:48 [m]Ge 30:6
the inheritance of the tribe of Dan,[m]
clan by clan.

[a] 28 Some Hebrew manuscripts (see also Joshua 21:30); most Hebrew manuscripts *Ebron*
[b] 34 Septuagint; Hebrew *west, and Judah, the Jordan,*

Allotment for Joshua

49When they had finished dividing
the land into its allotted portions, the Israelites gave Joshua son of Nun an inheritance among them, 50as the LORD
had commanded. They gave him the
19:50 [n]Jos 24:30 town he asked for—Timnath Serah[a][n] in
the hill country of Ephraim. And he
built up the town and settled there.
51These are the territories that Eleazar the priest, Joshua son of Nun and the
heads of the tribal clans of Israel assigned by lot at Shiloh in the presence of
the LORD at the entrance to the Tent of
19:51 [o]Jos 14:1; 18:10; Meeting. And so they finished dividing
Ac 13:19 the land.[o]

Cities of Refuge

20 Then the LORD said to Joshua:
2"Tell the Israelites to designate
the cities of refuge, as I instructed you
through Moses, 3so that anyone who
kills a person accidentally and uninten-
20:3 [p]Lev 4:2 tionally[p] may flee there and find protec-
[q]Nu 35:12 tion from the avenger of blood.[q]
4"When he flees to one of these cities,
he is to stand in the entrance of the city
20:4 [r]Ru 4:1; Jer 38:7 gate[r] and state his case before the el-
[s]Jos 7:6 ders[s] of that city. Then they are to admit
him into their city and give him a place
to live with them. 5If the avenger of
blood pursues him, they must not surrender the one accused, because he
killed his neighbor unintentionally and
without malice aforethought. 6He is to
stay in that city until he has stood trial
20:6 [t]Nu 35:12 before the assembly[t] and until the death
of the high priest who is serving at that
time. Then he may go back to his own
home in the town from which he fled."
20:7 [u]Jos 21:32; 7So they set apart Kedesh[u] in Galilee
1Ch 6:76 in the hill country of Naphtali, She-
[v]Ge 12:6 chem[v] in the hill country of Ephraim,
[w]Jos 10:36; and Kiriath Arba (that is, Hebron[w]) in
21:11 [x]Lk 1:39 the hill country of Judah.[x] 8On the east
side of the Jordan of Jericho[b] they desig-
20:8 nated Bezer[y] in the desert on the pla-
[y]Jos 21:36; teau in the tribe of Reuben, Ramoth in
1Ch 6:78 [z]Jos 12:2 Gilead[z] in the tribe of Gad, and Golan in
Bashan in the tribe of Manasseh. 9Any of
the Israelites or any alien living among
them who killed someone accidentally
could flee to these designated cities and
20:9 [a]Ex 21:13; not be killed by the avenger of blood pri-
Nu 35:15 or to standing trial before the assembly.[a]

Towns for the Levites

21 Now the family heads of the Levites approached Eleazar the
priest, Joshua son of Nun, and the heads
of the other tribal families of Israel[b] 2at 21:1 [b]Jos 14:1
Shiloh[c] in Canaan and said to them,
"The LORD commanded through Moses 21:2 [c]Jos 18:1
that you give us towns to live in, with [d]Nu 35:2-3
pasturelands for our livestock."[d] 3So, as
the LORD had commanded, the Israelites
gave the Levites the following towns and
pasturelands out of their own inheritance:
4The first lot came out for the Kohathites, clan by clan. The Levites who
were descendants of Aaron the priest
were allotted thirteen towns from the
tribes of Judah, Simeon and Benjamin.[e] 21:4 [e]ver 19
5The rest of Kohath's descendants were
allotted ten towns from the clans of the
tribes of Ephraim, Dan and half of Ma- 21:5
nasseh.[f] [f]ver 26
6The descendants of Gershon were allotted thirteen towns from the clans of 21:6
the tribes of Issachar,[g] Asher, Naphtali [g]Ge 30:18
and the half-tribe of Manasseh in Ba-
shan.
7The descendants of Merari,[h] clan by 21:7
clan, received twelve towns from the [h]Ex 6:16
tribes of Reuben, Gad and Zebulun.[i] [i]Jos 19:10
8So the Israelites allotted to the Levites these towns and their pasturelands, as the LORD had commanded
through Moses.

9From the tribes of Judah and Simeon
they allotted the following towns by
name 10(these towns were assigned to
the descendants of Aaron who were
from the Kohathite clans of the Levites,
because the first lot fell to them):
11They gave them Kiriath Arba 21:11
(that is, Hebron[j]), with its sur- [j]Jos 15:13; 1Ch 6:55
rounding pastureland, in the hill
country of Judah. (Arba was the
forefather of Anak.) 12But the fields 21:13
and villages around the city they [k]Jos 15:42;
had given to Caleb son of Jephun- 1Ch 6:57
neh as his possession.
13So to the descendants of Aaron 21:14
the priest they gave Hebron (a city [l]Jos 15:48 [m]Jos 15:50
of refuge for one accused of mur-
der), Libnah,[k] 14Jattir,[l] Eshtemoa,[m] 21:15 [n]Jos 15:51
15Holon,[n] Debir, 16Ain, Juttah[o] and 21:16 [o]Jos 15:55
Beth Shemesh,[p] together with their [p]Jos 15:10

[a] 50 Also known as *Timnath Heres* (see Judges 2:9)
[b] 8 *Jordan of Jericho* was possibly an ancient name for the Jordan River.

pasturelands—nine towns from
these two tribes.
21:17 17 And from the tribe of Benja-
q Jos 18:24 min they gave them Gibeon, Geba,[q]
18 Anathoth and Almon, together
with their pasturelands—four
towns.
19 All the towns for the priests, the descendants of Aaron, were thirteen, together with their pasturelands.
20 The rest of the Kohathite clans of the
Levites were allotted towns from the
tribe of Ephraim:
21:21 21 In the hill country of Ephraim
r Jos 17:7; 20:7 they were given Shechem[r] (a city of
refuge for one accused of murder)
21:22 and Gezer, 22 Kibzaim and Beth Ho-
s Jos 10:10 ron,[s] together with their pasture-
t 1Sa 1:1 lands—four towns.[t]
23 Also from the tribe of Dan they
21:24 received Eltekeh, Gibbethon, 24 Ai-
u Jos 19:45 jalon and Gath Rimmon,[u] together
with their pasturelands—four
towns.
25 From half the tribe of Manasseh they received Taanach and
Gath Rimmon, together with their
pasturelands—two towns.
26 All these ten towns and their pasturelands were given to the rest of the Kohathite clans.
27 The Levite clans of the Gershonites
were given:
from the half-tribe of Manasseh,
21:27 v Jos 12:5 Golan in Bashan[v] (a city of refuge
w Nu 35:6 for one accused of murder[w]) and
Be Eshtarah, together with their
pasturelands—two towns;
21:28 28 from the tribe of Issachar,[x]
x Ge 30:18 Kishion, Daberath, 29 Jarmuth and
En Gannim, together with their
pasturelands—four towns;
21:30 30 from the tribe of Asher,[y]
y Jos 17:7 Mishal, Abdon, 31 Helkath and Rehob, together with their pasturelands—four towns;
32 from the tribe of Naphtali,
21:32 Kedesh[z] in Galilee (a city of refuge
z Jos 12:22 for one accused of murder[a]), Ham-
a Nu 35:6; Jos 20:7 moth Dor and Kartan, together
with their pasturelands—three
21:33 towns.
b ver 6 33 All the towns of the Gershonite[b] clans
were thirteen, together with their pasturelands.

34 The Merarite clans (the rest of the Levites) were given: 21:34
from the tribe of Zebulun,[c] c Jos 19:10;
Jokneam, Kartah, 35 Dimnah and 1Ch 6:77
Nahalal, together with their pasturelands—four towns;
36 from the tribe of Reuben,
Bezer,[d] Jahaz, 37 Kedemoth and 21:36
Mephaath, together with their pas- d Jos 20:8
turelands—four towns;
38 from the tribe of Gad,
Ramoth[e] in Gilead (a city of refuge 21:38
for one accused of murder), Maha- e Dt 4:43
naim,[f] 39 Heshbon and Jazer, to- f Ge 32:2
gether with their pasturelands—
four towns in all.
40 All the towns allotted to the Merarite
clans, who were the rest of the Levites,
were twelve.
41 The towns of the Levites in the territory held by the Israelites were forty-
eight in all, together with their pasturelands.[g] 42 Each of these towns had 21:41
pasturelands surrounding it; this was g Nu 35:7
true for all these towns.

43 So the LORD gave Israel all the land
he had sworn to give their forefathers,[h] 21:43
and they took possession[i] of it and set- h Dt 34:4 i Dt 11:31
tled there.[j] 44 The LORD gave them rest[k] j Dt 17:14
on every side, just as he had sworn to 21:44
their forefathers. Not one of their ene- k Ex 33:14; Jos 1:13
mies[l] withstood them; the LORD handed l Dt 6:19 m Ex 23:31
all their enemies[m] over to them.[n] 45 Not n Dt 7:24; 21:10
one of all the LORD's good promises[o] to 21:45
the house of Israel failed; every one was o Jos 23:14;
fulfilled. Ne 9:8

Eastern Tribes Return Home

22 Then Joshua summoned the
Reubenites, the Gadites and
the half-tribe of Manasseh 2 and said to
them, "You have done all that Moses the
servant of the LORD commanded,[p] and 22:2
you have obeyed me in everything I p Nu 32:25
commanded. 3 For a long time now—to
this very day—you have not deserted
your brothers but have carried out the
mission the LORD your God gave you.
4 Now that the LORD your God has given
your brothers rest as he promised, return to your homes[q] in the land that 22:4
Moses the servant of the LORD gave you q Nu 32:22; Dt 3:20
on the other side of the Jordan.[r] 5 But be r Nu 32:18; Jos 1:13-15
very careful to keep the commandment[s]
and the law that Moses the servant of 22:5
the LORD gave you: to love the LORD your s Isa 43:22
God, to walk in all his ways, to obey his

commands,[t] to hold fast to him and to
serve him with all your heart and all
your soul.[u]"
6Then Joshua blessed[v] them and sent
them away, and they went to their homes.
7(To the half-tribe of Manasseh Moses
had given land in Bashan,[w] and to the
other half of the tribe Joshua gave land on
the west side[x] of the Jordan with their
brothers.) When Joshua sent them home,
he blessed them, 8saying, "Return to your
homes with your great wealth—with
large herds of livestock,[y] with silver, gold,
bronze and iron, and a great quantity of
clothing—and divide[z] with your brothers
the plunder[a] from your enemies."
9So the Reubenites, the Gadites and
the half-tribe of Manasseh left the Israelites at Shiloh in Canaan to return to
Gilead,[b] their own land, which they had
acquired in accordance with the command of the LORD through Moses.
10When they came to Geliloth near
the Jordan in the land of Canaan, the
Reubenites, the Gadites and the half-
tribe of Manasseh built an imposing altar there by the Jordan. 11And when the
Israelites heard that they had built the

22:5 [t] Dt 5:29 [u] Dt 6:6,17
22:6 [v] Ex 39:43
22:7 [w] Nu 32:33; Jos 12:5 [x] Jos 17:2,5
22:8 [y] Dt 20:14 [z] Nu 31:27 [a] Ge 49:27; 1Sa 30:16; Isa 9:3
22:9 [b] Nu 32:26,29

JESUS FOCUS

FAITHFUL WITNESS

As the tribes of Reuben, Gad and half of Manasseh prepared to recross the Jordan River to the land that had been allotted to them on the eastern slope, they constructed an imposing altar to demonstrate their loyalty to God (Joshua 22). The tribes who were to remain on the west bank, however, protested the altar, presuming that it had been constructed for the purpose of offering sacrifices (the only altar allowed for sacrifices was the one in the tabernacle); they even went so far as to propose war against their brothers. When the east bank tribes assured their countrymen that the altar was simply a memorial or witness for succeeding generations, it was accepted (verses 28,34). In the New Testament Jesus is referred to as the "faithful witness" (Revelation 1:5): More than an altar, he is God's personal testimony of his love and grace to every person. The altar of witness on the banks of the Jordan River reminded the people that "the LORD is God" (Joshua 22:34), while Jesus, as the eternal and all-powerful Son of God, reminds us that God is Lord of all.

altar on the border of Canaan at Geliloth
near the Jordan on the Israelite side,
12the whole assembly of Israel gathered
at Shiloh[c] to go to war against them.
13So the Israelites sent Phinehas[d] son
of Eleazar,[e] the priest, to the land of Gilead—to Reuben, Gad and the half-tribe
of Manasseh. 14With him they sent ten
of the chief men, one for each of the
tribes of Israel, each the head of a family division among the Israelite clans.[f]
15When they went to Gilead—to Reuben, Gad and the half-tribe of Manasseh—they said to them: 16"The whole assembly of the LORD says: 'How could you
break faith[g] with the God of Israel like
this? How could you turn away from the
LORD and build yourselves an altar in rebellion[h] against him now? 17Was not the
sin of Peor[i] enough for us? Up to this
very day we have not cleansed ourselves
from that sin, even though a plague fell
on the community of the LORD! 18And are
you now turning away from the LORD?
" 'If you rebel against the LORD today,
tomorrow he will be angry with the
whole community[j] of Israel. 19If the land
you possess is defiled, come over to the
LORD's land, where the LORD's tabernacle
stands, and share the land with us. But
do not rebel against the LORD or against
us by building an altar for yourselves,
other than the altar of the LORD our God.
20When Achan son of Zerah acted
unfaithfully regarding the devoted
things,[a][k] did not wrath[l] come upon the
whole community of Israel? He was not
the only one who died for his sin.' "[m]
21Then Reuben, Gad and the half-tribe
of Manasseh replied to the heads of the
clans of Israel: 22"The Mighty One, God,
the LORD! The Mighty One, God,[n] the
LORD![o] He knows![p] And let Israel know! If
this has been in rebellion or disobedience to the LORD, do not spare us this
day. 23If we have built our own altar to
turn away from the LORD and to offer
burnt offerings and grain offerings,[q] or
to sacrifice fellowship offerings[b] on it,
may the LORD himself call us to account.[r]
24"No! We did it for fear that some day
your descendants might say to ours,
'What do you have to do with the LORD,
the God of Israel? 25The LORD has made

22:12 [c] Jos 18:1
22:13 [d] Nu 25:7 [e] Nu 3:32; Jos 24:33
22:14 [f] Nu 1:4
22:16 [g] Dt 13:14 [h] Dt 12:13-14
22:17 [i] Nu 25:1-9
22:18 [j] Lev 10:6; Nu 16:22
22:20 [k] Jos 7:1 [l] Ps 7:11 [m] Jos 7:5
22:22 [n] Dt 10:17 [o] Ps 50:1 [p] 1Ki 8:39; Job 10:7; Ps 44:21; Jer 17:10
22:23 [q] Jer 41:5 [r] Dt 12:11; 18:19; 1Sa 20:16

[a] *20* The Hebrew term refers to the irrevocable giving over of things or persons to the LORD, often by totally destroying them. [b] *23* Traditionally *peace offerings*; also in verse 27

the Jordan a boundary between us and
you—you Reubenites and Gadites! You
have no share in the LORD.' So your descendants might cause ours to stop fearing the LORD.
26"That is why we said, 'Let us get
ready and build an altar—but not for
burnt offerings or sacrifices.' 27On the
22:27 [s] Ge 21:30; contrary, it is to be a witness[s] between
Jos 24:27 us and you and the generations that fol-
[t] Dt 12:6 low, that we will worship the LORD at his
sanctuary with our burnt offerings, sacrifices and fellowship offerings.[t] Then in
the future your descendants will not be
able to say to ours, 'You have no share in
the LORD.'
28"And we said, 'If they ever say this to
us, or to our descendants, we will answer: Look at the replica of the LORD's altar, which our fathers built, not for burnt
offerings and sacrifices, but as a witness
between us and you.'
22:29 [u] Jos 24:16 29"Far be it from us to rebel[u] against
[v] Dt 12:13-14 the LORD and turn away from him today
by building an altar for burnt offerings,
grain offerings and sacrifices, other than
the altar of the LORD our God that
stands before his tabernacle.[v]"
30When Phinehas the priest and the
leaders of the community—the heads of
the clans of the Israelites—heard what
Reuben, Gad and Manasseh had to say,
they were pleased. 31And Phinehas son of
Eleazar, the priest, said to Reuben, Gad
22:31 and Manasseh, "Today we know that the
[w] Lev 26:11-12; LORD is with us,[w] because you have not
2Ch 15:2 acted unfaithfully toward the LORD in
this matter. Now you have rescued the Israelites from the LORD's hand."
32Then Phinehas son of Eleazar, the
priest, and the leaders returned to Canaan from their meeting with the Reubenites and Gadites in Gilead and reported to the Israelites. 33They were glad
22:33 [x] 1Ch 29:20; to hear the report and praised God.[x]
Da 2:19; Lk 2:28 And they talked no more about going to
war against them to devastate the coun-
try where the Reubenites and the Gadites lived.
34And the Reubenites and the Gadites
22:34 gave the altar this name: A Witness[y] Be-
[y] Ge 21:30 tween Us that the LORD is God.

Joshua's Farewell to the Leaders

23 After a long time had passed
23:1 [z] Dt 12:9; and the LORD had given Israel
Jos 21:44 rest[z] from all their enemies around
them, Joshua, by then old and well ad- 23:1
vanced in years,[a] 2summoned all Isra- [a] Jos 13:1
el—their elders,[b] leaders, judges and of- 23:2
ficials[c]—and said to them: "I am old and [b] Jos 7:6
well advanced in years. 3You yourselves [c] Jos 24:1
have seen everything the LORD your God
has done to all these nations for your
sake; it was the LORD your God who
fought for you.[d] 4Remember how I have 23:3 [d] Ex 14:14
allotted[e] as an inheritance for your 23:4
tribes all the land of the nations that re- [e] Jos 19:51
main—the nations I conquered—be- [f] Nu 34:6
tween the Jordan and the Great Sea[a][f] in
the west. 5The LORD your God himself
will drive them out of your way. He will
push them out before you, and you will
take possession of their land, as the 23:5 [g] Ex 23:30;
LORD your God promised you.[g] Nu 33:53
6"Be very strong; be careful to obey all
that is written in the Book of the Law of
Moses, without turning aside to the 23:6
right or to the left.[h] 7Do not associate [h] Dt 5:32;
with these nations that remain among Jos 1:7
you; do not invoke the names of their 23:7
gods or swear[i] by them. You must not [i] Ex 23:13;
serve them or bow down[j] to them. 8But Ps 16:4; Jer 5:7 [j] Ex 20:5
you are to hold fast to the LORD[k] your
God, as you have until now. 23:8 [k] Dt 10:20
9"The LORD has driven out before you
great and powerful nations;[l] to this day 23:9 [l] Dt 11:23
no one has been able to withstand you.[m] [m] Dt 7:24
10One of you routs a thousand,[n] because 23:10
the LORD your God fights for you,[o] just [n] Lev 26:8
as he promised. 11So be very careful to [o] Ex 14:14; Dt 3:22
love the LORD[p] your God.
12"But if you turn away and ally your- 23:11
selves with the survivors of these na- [p] Jos 22:5
tions that remain among you and if you
intermarry with them[q] and associate 23:12 [q] Dt 7:3
with them,[r] 13then you may be sure that [r] Ex 34:16;
the LORD your God will no longer drive Ps 106:34-35
out these nations before you. Instead,
they will become snares[s] and traps for 23:13 [s] Ex 23:33
you, whips on your backs and thorns in [t] Nu 33:55
your eyes,[t] until you perish from this
good land, which the LORD your God has
given you.
14"Now I am about to go the way of all
the earth.[u] You know with all your heart 23:14 [u] 1Ki 2:2
and soul that not one of all the good [v] Jos 21:45
promises the LORD your God gave you
has failed. Every promise has been fulfilled; not one has failed.[v] 15But just as
every good promise of the LORD your
God has come true, so the LORD will
bring on you all the evil he has threat-

[a] *4* That is, the Mediterranean

DISCOVERY 57

FAMOUS LAST WORDS

When Joshua came to the end of his life, he assembled all the people to hear his farewell address. His words sounded very similar to those of Moses in the book of Deuteronomy. Both men reminded the people to focus on God and his covenant with them.

Joshua reminded the people of several things. First, God had been good to them. He had fought their battles and given them great success. With God at their side, they were a thousand times stronger than their enemies (Joshua 23:10). The Lord had kept all of his promises to the children of Israel (verse 14). Because of that, the people owed him everything. God wanted them to put his commands into practice (verse 6), to be devoted to him in every area of their lives (verse 11), to fear him and to serve him (Joshua 24:14).

But the decision was theirs: They would have to choose between the gods of the Canaanites around them and the Lord God who had chosen them. On this point Joshua was adamant: Whatever the rest of Israel did, he and his family had already determined to serve the Lord (Joshua 24:15). Joshua's final speech concludes with a stern warning. If the people were to turn away from God they would experience disaster. The promise God had made to them was replete with blessings—available only if they would accept it and follow him.

Joshua's ultimatum to God's people in the Old Testament sounds very similar to what Jesus said in the New Testament. God the Son reminded his people of his love and commitment to them. Jesus is our Shepherd, the One who "lays down his life for the sheep" (John 10:1–21). He has given us everything we need to live life to the fullest. We have received every spiritual and material blessing, including eternal salvation (Ephesians 1:3). But the choice is ours: We can either walk in company with Jesus or choose a different course.

From the beginning God has desired a relationship with each of us that is not contaminated by sin. He wants our total commitment. Paul summed it up well: "I urge you, brothers, in view of God's mercy, to offer your bodies as living sacrifices, holy and pleasing to God—this is your spiritual act of worship" (Romans 12:1).

Jesus too is remembered for his famous last words, which we recall as the Great Commision: "All authority in heaven and on earth has been given to me. Therefore go and make disciples of all nations, baptizing them in the name of the Father and of the Son and of the Holy Spirit, and teaching them to obey everything I have commanded you. And surely I am with you always, to the very end of the age" (Matthew 28:18–20).

Self-Discovery: *Can you truthfully declare with Joshua, "As for me and my household, we will serve the LORD" (Joshua 24:15)? In what concrete way does that faith commitment come to expression in your relationships?*

GO TO DISCOVERY 58 ON PAGE 304

23:15 ened, until he has destroyed you from
w Lev 26:17; this good land he has given you.[w] 16If
Dt 28:15 you violate the covenant of the LORD
your God, which he commanded you,
and go and serve other gods and bow
down to them, the LORD's anger will
burn against you, and you will quickly
23:16 perish from the good land he has given
x Dt 4:25-26 you.[x]"

The Covenant Renewed at Shechem

24 Then Joshua assembled all the
tribes of Israel at Shechem. He
24:1 summoned the elders, leaders, judges
y Jos 23:2 and officials of Israel,[y] and they presented themselves before God.
2Joshua said to all the people, "This is
what the LORD, the God of Israel, says:
'Long ago your forefathers, including Terah the father of Abraham and Nahor,
24:2 lived beyond the River[a] and worshiped
z Ge 11:32 other gods.[z] 3But I took your father
Abraham from the land beyond the Riv-
24:3 a Ge 12:1 er and led him throughout Canaan[a] and
b Ge 15:5 gave him many descendants.[b] I gave him
c Ge 21:3 Isaac,[c] 4and to Isaac I gave Jacob and
24:4 Esau.[d] I assigned the hill country of Seir[e]
d Ge 25:26 e Dt 2:5 to Esau, but Jacob and his sons went
f Ge 46:5-6 down to Egypt.[f]
5" 'Then I sent Moses and Aaron,[g] and
24:5 g Ex 3:10 I afflicted the Egyptians by what I did
there, and I brought you out. 6When I
brought your fathers out of Egypt, you
came to the sea, and the Egyptians pur-
24:6 sued them with chariots and horse-
h Ex 14:9 men[b][h] as far as the Red Sea.[c] 7But they
24:7 cried to the LORD for help, and he put
i Ex 14:20 darkness[i] between you and the Egyp-
j Ex 14:28 k Dt 1:46 tians; he brought the sea over them and
covered them.[j] You saw with your own
eyes what I did to the Egyptians. Then
you lived in the desert for a long time.[k]
8" 'I brought you to the land of the
Amorites who lived east of the Jordan.
They fought against you, but I gave
them into your hands. I destroyed them
24:8 from before you, and you took posses-
l Nu 21:31 sion of their land.[l] 9When Balak son of
24:9 Zippor,[m] the king of Moab, prepared to
m Nu 22:2 fight against Israel, he sent for Balaam
n Nu 22:6 son of Beor to put a curse on you.[n] 10But
24:10 I would not listen to Balaam, so he
o Nu 23:11; blessed you[o] again and again, and I de-
Dt 23:5 livered you out of his hand.
24:11 11" 'Then you crossed the Jordan[p] and
p Jos 3:16-17 came to Jericho.[q] The citizens of Jericho
q Jos 6:1 fought against you, as did also the Amorites, Perizzites, Canaanites, Hittites,
Girgashites, Hivites and Jebusites, but I 24:11
gave them into your hands.[r] 12I sent the r Ex 23:23;
hornet[s] ahead of you, which drove them Dt 7:1
out before you—also the two Amorite 24:12
kings. You did not do it with your own s Ex 23:28; Dt 7:20; Ps 44:3,
sword and bow. 13So I gave you a land on 6-7
which you did not toil and cities you did
not build; and you live in them and eat
from vineyards and olive groves that you 24:13
did not plant.'[t] t Dt 6:10-11
14"Now fear the LORD and serve him 24:14
with all faithfulness.[u] Throw away the u Dt 10:12;
gods[v] your forefathers worshiped be- 18:13; 1Sa 12:24;
yond the River and in Egypt,[w] and serve 2Co 1:12
the LORD. 15But if serving the LORD v ver 23
seems undesirable to you, then choose w Eze 23:3
for yourselves this day whom you will
serve, whether the gods your forefathers
served beyond the River, or the gods of
the Amorites,[x] in whose land you are liv- 24:15 x Jdg 6:10;
ing. But as for me and my household, we Ru 1:15
will serve the LORD."[y] y Ru 1:16; 1Ki 18:21
16Then the people answered, "Far be
it from us to forsake the LORD to serve
other gods! 17It was the LORD our God
himself who brought us and our fathers
up out of Egypt, from that land of slavery, and performed those great signs before our eyes. He protected us on our entire journey and among all the nations
through which we traveled. 18And the
LORD drove out before us all the nations,
including the Amorites, who lived in the
land. We too will serve the LORD, because he is our God."
19Joshua said to the people, "You are
not able to serve the LORD. He is a holy
God;[z] he is a jealous God.[a] He will not 24:19
forgive your rebellion[b] and your sins. 20If z Lev 19:2; 20:26 a Ex 20:5
you forsake the LORD[c] and serve foreign b Ex 23:21
gods, he will turn[d] and bring disaster on 24:20
you and make an end of you,[e] after he c 1Ch 28:9,20 d Ac 7:42
has been good to you." e Jos 23:15
21But the people said to Joshua, "No!
We will serve the LORD."
22Then Joshua said, "You are witnesses against yourselves that you have 24:22
chosen[f] to serve the LORD." f Ps 119:30,173
"Yes, we are witnesses," they replied.
23"Now then," said Joshua, "throw 24:23
away the foreign gods[g] that are among g ver 14
you and yield your hearts[h] to the LORD, h 1Ki 8:58;
the God of Israel." Ps 119:36; 141:4

[a] 2 That is, the Euphrates; also in verses 3, 14 and 15 [b] 6 Or *charioteers* [c] 6 Hebrew *Yam Suph*; that is, Sea of Reeds

24And the people said to Joshua, "We
will serve the LORD our God and obey
him."[i]

25On that day Joshua made a covenant[j] for the people, and there at Shechem he drew up for them decrees and
laws.[k] 26And Joshua recorded these
things in the Book of the Law of God.[l]
Then he took a large stone[m] and set it
up there under the oak near the holy
place of the LORD.

27"See!" he said to all the people. "This
stone will be a witness[n] against us. It has
heard all the words the LORD has said to
us. It will be a witness against you if you
are untrue to your God."

Buried in the Promised Land

28Then Joshua sent the people away,
each to his own inheritance.

29After these things, Joshua son of
Nun, the servant of the LORD, died at the
age of a hundred and ten.[o] 30And they
buried him in the land of his inheritance, at Timnath Serah[a][p] in the hill
country of Ephraim, north of Mount Gaash.

31Israel served the LORD throughout
the lifetime of Joshua and of the elders[q]
who outlived him and who had experienced everything the LORD had done for
Israel.

32And Joseph's bones, which the Israelites had brought up from Egypt,[r] were
buried at Shechem in the tract of land[s]
that Jacob bought for a hundred pieces
of silver[b] from the sons of Hamor, the father of Shechem. This became the inheritance of Joseph's descendants.

33And Eleazar son of Aaron[t] died and
was buried at Gibeah, which had been
allotted to his son Phinehas[u] in the hill
country of Ephraim.

[a] *30* Also known as *Timnath Heres* (see Judges 2:9)
[b] *32* Hebrew *hundred kesitahs*; a kesitah was a unit of money of unknown weight and value.

24:24 [i] Ex 19:8; 24:3,7; Dt 5:27
24:25 [j] Ex 24:8 [k] Ex 15:25
24:26 [l] Dt 31:24 [m] Ge 28:18
24:27 [n] Jos 22:27
24:29 [o] Jdg 2:8
24:30 [p] Jos 19:50
24:31 [q] Jdg 2:7
24:32 [r] Ge 50:25; Ex 13:19 [s] Ge 33:19; Jn 4:5; Ac 7:16
24:33 [t] Jos 22:13 [u] Ex 6:25

JUDGES

What impact might the repeated pattern of evil, idolatry, covenant-breaking and repentance portrayed in Judges have had on its readers?

♦ *Readers of Judges, particularly during and after the Babylonian exile, saw the hope of a new David who would teach Israel to keep her covenant with the Lord. This expectation was fulfilled in the coming of Jesus.*

Can we determine God's will by "putting out a fleece"? (Judges 6:37–40)

♦ *"Putting out a fleece" seems to indicate a lack of faith and courage on Gideon's part. Similarly, we don't need extraordinary signs to discover God's will. Christian living is a walk of faith, not sight (Hebrews 11:1; 2 Corinthians 5:7), and Jesus commended those who believe without seeing (John 20:29).*

Jesus in Judges After Joshua had died the people turned away from God, but they soon learned that without God's protection they would inevitably suffer at the hands of their enemies. In the young nation's most desperate moments God provided judges who would act as his human representatives to save his people from chaos and destruction. According to many Bible scholars, it was the preincarnate Jesus who himself appeared personally to Gideon as the "angel of the LORD" to summon him to lead in Israel's defense (Judges 6:11–16).

Judges records God's faithfulness in repeatedly providing a new beginning for the Israelites by sending a new judge to rescue them. As we read through these accounts we can observe the striking contrast between human sin and divine, unrelenting love. We can then allow our thoughts to turn to God's definitive gesture of unrelenting love—the sacrifice of his own Son to wipe the slate clean for those who will believe!

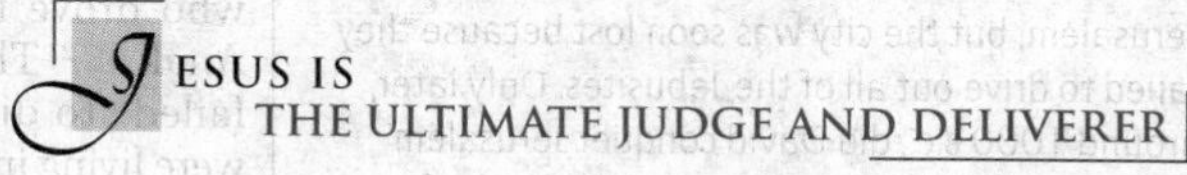
JESUS IS
THE ULTIMATE JUDGE AND DELIVERER

Israel Fights the Remaining Canaanites

1:1 1 After the death[a] of Joshua, the Is-
a Jos 24:29 b Nu 27:21 raelites asked the LORD, "Who will
c ver 27; be the first[b] to go up and fight for us
Jdg 3:1-6 against the Canaanites?[c]"
1:2 2 The LORD answered, "Judah[d] is to go;
d Ge 49:8 e ver 4; Jdg 3:28 I have given the land into their hands.[e]"
3 Then the men of Judah said to the
Simeonites their brothers, "Come up
with us into the territory allotted to us,
to fight against the Canaanites. We in
turn will go with you into yours." So the
1:3 f ver 17 Simeonites[f] went with them.
1:4 4 When Judah attacked, the LORD gave
g Ge 13:7; the Canaanites and Perizzites[g] into their
Jos 3:10 hands and they struck down ten thou-
h 1Sa 11:8 sand men at Bezek.[h] 5 It was there that
they found Adoni-Bezek and fought
against him, putting to rout the Canaanites and Perizzites. 6 Adoni-Bezek fled,
but they chased him and caught him,
and cut off his thumbs and big toes.
7 Then Adoni-Bezek said, "Seventy
kings with their thumbs and big toes cut
off have picked up scraps under my
1:7 i Lev 24:19 table. Now God has paid me back[i] for
what I did to them." They brought him
to Jerusalem, and he died there.
8 The men of Judah attacked Jerusa-
1:8 j ver 21; lem[j] also and took it. They put the city
Jos 15:63 to the sword and set it on fire.

JESUS FOCUS

THE TRIBE OF JUDAH

After Joshua's death the leadership responsibility fell on Judah's family, just as Jacob's prophecy had indicated that it would (Genesis 49:10; Judges 1). Because the Messiah would come from Judah's family line, members of this tribe were chosen to lead at the time God set up the system of judges. At first they were successful and took control of Jerusalem, but the city was soon lost because they failed to drive out all of the Jebusites. Only later, around 1000 B.C., did David conquer Jerusalem (2 Samuel 5:6–10). By the end of the book of Judges none of the tribes had godly leaders. A recurring refrain throughout this dismal book is that "Israel had no king." The frustration of living in a lawless society left God's people looking for the promised king he would one day send, initially fulfilled in the person of David and ultimately in the person of Jesus, the Messiah, the consummate Judge and Deliverer.

9 After that, the men of Judah went
down to fight against the Canaanites liv- 1:9
ing in the hill country,[k] the Negev[l] and k Nu 13:17
the western foothills. 10 They advanced l Nu 21:1
against the Canaanites living in Hebron[m] 1:10
(formerly called Kiriath Arba[n]) and de- m Ge 13:18 n Ge 35:27
feated Sheshai, Ahiman and Talmai.[o] o Jos 15:14
11 From there they advanced against 1:11
the people living in Debir[p] (formerly p Jos 15:15
called Kiriath Sepher). 12 And Caleb said,
"I will give my daughter Acsah in marriage to the man who attacks and cap-
tures Kiriath Sepher." 13 Othniel son of
Kenaz, Caleb's younger brother, took it;
so Caleb gave his daughter Acsah to him
in marriage.
14 One day when she came to Othniel,
she urged him[a] to ask her father for a
field. When she got off her donkey, Caleb asked her, "What can I do for you?"
15 She replied, "Do me a special favor.
Since you have given me land in the
Negev, give me also springs of water."
Then Caleb gave her the upper and lower springs.
16 The descendants of Moses' father- 1:16
in-law,[q] the Kenite,[r] went up from the q Nu 10:29
City of Palms[b][s] with the men of Judah to r Ge 15:19; Jdg 4:11
live among the people of the Desert of s Dt 34:3;
Judah in the Negev near Arad.[t] Jdg 3:13 t Nu 21:1
17 Then the men of Judah went with
the Simeonites[u] their brothers and at- 1:17 u ver 3 v Nu 21:3
tacked the Canaanites living in Zephath,
and they totally destroyed[c] the city.
Therefore it was called Hormah.[d][v] 18 The 1:18
men of Judah also took[e] Gaza,[w] Ashke- w Jos 11:22
lon and Ekron—each city with its terri-
tory.
19 The LORD was with[x] the men of Ju- 1:19 x ver 2
dah. They took possession of the hill y Jos 17:16
country, but they were unable to drive
the people from the plains, because they
had iron chariots.[y] 20 As Moses had 1:20
promised, Hebron[z] was given to Caleb, z Jos 14:9; 15:13-
who drove from it the three sons of 14 a ver 10; Jos 14:13
Anak.[a] 21 The Benjamites, however, 1:21
failed[b] to dislodge the Jebusites, who b Jos 15:63
were living in Jerusalem;[c] to this day the c ver 8
Jebusites live there with the Benjamites.
22 Now the house of Joseph attacked
Bethel, and the LORD was with them.

[a] 14 Hebrew; Septuagint and Vulgate *Othniel, he urged her* [b] 16 That is, Jericho [c] 17 The Hebrew term refers to the irrevocable giving over of things or persons to the LORD, often by totally destroying them. [d] 17 *Hormah* means *destruction.* [e] 18 Hebrew; Septuagint *Judah did not take*

1:23 23 When they sent men to spy out Bethel
d Ge 28:19 (formerly called Luz),[d] 24 the spies saw a
man coming out of the city and they
said to him, "Show us how to get into
the city and we will see that you are
1:24 e Jos 2:12,14 treated well.[e]" 25 So he showed them, and
they put the city to the sword but
1:25 f Jos 6:25 spared[f] the man and his whole family.
26 He then went to the land of the Hit-
tites, where he built a city and called it
Luz, which is its name to this day.
27 But Manasseh did not drive out the
people of Beth Shan or Taanach or Dor
1:27 g Jos 17:11 or Ibleam[g] or Megiddo and their sur-
h ver 1 rounding settlements, for the Canaanites[h] were determined to live in that
land. 28 When Israel became strong, they
pressed the Canaanites into forced labor
but never drove them out completely.
29 Nor did Ephraim drive out the Ca-
1:29 i 1Ki 9:16 naanites living in Gezer,[i] but the Ca-
j Jos 16:10 naanites continued to live there among
them.[j] 30 Neither did Zebulun drive out
the Canaanites living in Kitron or Naha-
lol, who remained among them; but they
did subject them to forced labor. 31 Nor
did Asher drive out those living in Acco
1:31 k Jdg 10:6 or Sidon or Ahlab or Aczib[k] or Helbah or
Aphek or Rehob, 32 and because of this
the people of Asher lived among the
Canaanite inhabitants of the land. 33 Neither did Naphtali drive out those living
in Beth Shemesh or Beth Anath[l]; but the
1:33 l Jos 19:38 Naphtalites too lived among the
Canaanite inhabitants of the land, and
those living in Beth Shemesh and Beth
Anath became forced laborers for them.
1:34 m Ex 3:17 34 The Amorites[m] confined the Danites
to the hill country, not allowing them to
come down into the plain. 35 And the
Amorites were determined also to hold
out in Mount Heres, Aijalon[n] and Shaal-
1:35 n Jos 19:42 bim, but when the power of the house of
Joseph increased, they too were pressed
into forced labor. 36 The boundary of the
1:36 o Jos 15:3 Amorites was from Scorpion[a] Pass[o] to
Sela and beyond.

The Angel of the LORD at Bokim

2:1 p Jdg 6:11 q ver 5 2 The angel of the LORD[p] went up
r Ex 20:2 from Gilgal to Bokim[q] and said, "I
s Ge 17:8 brought you up out of Egypt[r] and led
t Lev 26:42-44; Dt 7:9 you into the land that I swore to give to
your forefathers.[s] I said, 'I will never
break my covenant with you,[t] 2 and you
2:2 u Ex 23:32; 34:12; Dt 7:2 shall not make a covenant with the people of this land,[u] but you shall break
down their altars.[v] Yet you have dis- 2:2 v Ex 34:13
obeyed me. Why have you done this?
3 Now therefore I tell you that I will not
drive them out before you;[w] they will be 2:3 w Jos 23:13
⌞thorns⌟[x] in your sides and their gods x Nu 33:55
will be a snare[y] to you." y Dt 7:16; Jdg 3:6; Ps 106:36
4 When the angel of the LORD had spo-
ken these things to all the Israelites, the
people wept aloud, 5 and they called that
place Bokim.[b] There they offered sacrifices to the LORD.

Disobedience and Defeat

6 After Joshua had dismissed the Israelites, they went to take possession of the
land, each to his own inheritance. 7 The
people served the LORD throughout the
lifetime of Joshua and of the elders who
outlived him and who had seen all the
great things the LORD had done for Israel.
8 Joshua son of Nun, the servant of the
LORD, died at the age of a hundred and
ten. 9 And they buried him in the land of
his inheritance, at Timnath Heres[c][z] in 2:9 z Jos 19:50

[a] 36 Hebrew *Akrabbim* [b] 5 *Bokim* means *weepers.* [c] 9 Also known as *Timnath Serah* (see Joshua 19:50 and 24:30)

JESUS AND YOU

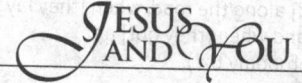

LOSERS, WEEPERS

The "angel of the LORD" (thought by many to be the preincarnate Jesus) came from the place of victory (Gilgal) to meet God's people at Bokim, the place of defeat (Judges 2:1–5). Even the name *Bokim* (meaning "weepers") furnishes a clue about Israel's desolate situation. The "angel of the LORD" assured the people that God would not break his promise with them, even though the situation appeared bleak at the moment. But because of Israel's disobedience, God would no longer help his people to defeat their enemies. Although the current generation had been born in the land of promise, the people had turned away from God again and again.

It might appear as though God was playing mind games with his people, continually vacillating in his methods and intentions. But it was really God's people who were playing games with him. The tragedy is that the Israelites had turned to Canaanite gods—the very idols they had once fought to eradicate from the land. The same can be true of us: When we turn away from God we often return to the very habits and temptations from which we had been set free.

DISCOVERY 58

SECOND-GENERATION FAITH

After Joshua and his generation had died, the succeeding generation turned away from God. Incredibly, they did not know God or recall what he had done for their parents and grandparents. In only one generation, the people had turned their backs on the God who had led them into the land of promise.

Any generation is only one step away from this potential tragedy. How can we prevent this cycle from recurring? Part of the responsibility for the Israelites lay with the parents—those who knew God and remembered what he had done. God had made it clear that parents were to "impress" his precepts upon their children. They were to "talk about them when [they sat] at home and when [they walked] along the road, when [they lay] down and when [they got] up" (Deuteronomy 6:7).

Parents had been instructed to reminisce aloud about the things God had done in their personal lives, to ensure that these memories might be passed along to future generations (Deuteronomy 6:20–25). Apparently this injunction had not been followed; somehow an entire generation had grown up ignorant of the incredible things God had done so recently for his people. Christian parents still today are concerned about their children walking with God. They don't want to see them follow the pattern of Joshua's day. Our responsibility as parents is still to rear our children in the "training and instruction of the Lord" (Ephesians 6:4).

Once the people had turned away from the Lord they began to worship the idols they had adopted from the surrounding culture (Judges 2:12). God had promised them blessing if they would only walk with him but bitter consequences if they refused (Joshua 23:14–16). God's goal, however, has always been to draw his people back to himself. Time and again he sent leaders—the judges and prophets—to remind the Israelites of who he was and what he had done.

What we see happening to Israel during the time of the judges is truly a warning for us. In the New Testament one church stands out as an example similar to that of Israel. Paul's letter to the Ephesians makes it clear that at one time the church in Ephesus had been vibrant and mature (Ephesians 2:1–7). But within a generation that had changed. The first step toward bringing up a generation that does not know God is to lose the passion of our love for Jesus (Revelation 2:1–6). Paul's letter to the church in Ephesus is pointed and direct. The Ephesian Christians had lost their first love, had strayed from their focus—Jesus! The first step away from God for any of us is a step away from our center. And the distance only widens with each succeeding step. But our confidence rests in this joyous truth: When we turn away, Jesus himself lovingly pursues us!

Self-Discovery: *If you are a parent, a teacher or someone otherwise involved with children or young people, identify a few specific ways in which you can "impress" on them the importance of loving and living for Jesus.*

GO TO DISCOVERY 59 ON PAGE 307

the hill country of Ephraim, north of
Mount Gaash.
10After that whole generation had
been gathered to their fathers, another
generation grew up, who knew neither
2:10 [a] Ex 5:2; the LORD nor what he had done for Isra-
1Sa 2:12; el.[a] 11Then the Israelites did evil in the
1Ch 28:9; Gal 4:8 eyes of the LORD[b] and served the Baals.[c]
12They forsook the LORD, the God of their
2:11 [b] Jdg 3:12; 4:1; fathers, who had brought them out of
6:1; 10:6 [c] Jdg 3:7; 8:33 Egypt. They followed and worshiped various gods[d] of the peoples around them.[e]
2:12 They provoked the LORD to anger 13be-
[d] Ps 106:36 [e] Dt 31:16; cause they forsook him and served Baal
Jdg 10:6 and the Ashtoreths.[f] 14In his anger[g]
2:13 against Israel the LORD handed them
[f] Jdg 10:6 over[h] to raiders who plundered them. He
2:14 sold them[i] to their enemies all around,
[g] Dt 31:17 whom they were no longer able to resist.[j]
[h] Ps 106:41 [i] Dt 32:30; 15Whenever Israel went out to fight, the
Jdg 3:8 hand of the LORD was against them to
[j] Dt 28:25 defeat them, just as he had sworn to
them. They were in great distress.
2:16 [k] Ac 13:20 16Then the LORD raised up judges,[a][k]
[l] Ps 106:43 who saved[l] them out of the hands of
2:17 these raiders. 17Yet they would not listen
[m] Ex 34:15 [n] ver 7 to their judges but prostituted[m] themselves to other gods and worshiped
them. Unlike their fathers, they quickly
turned from the way in which their fathers had walked, the way of obedience
to the LORD's commands.[n] 18Whenever
the LORD raised up a judge for them, he
was with the judge and saved them out
of the hands of their enemies as long as
the judge lived; for the LORD had com-
2:18 passion[o] on them as they groaned[p] un-
[o] Dt 32:36; Jos 1:5 der those who oppressed and afflicted
[p] Ps 106:44 them. 19But when the judge died, the
people returned to ways even more cor-
2:19 rupt[q] than those of their fathers, follow-
[q] Jdg 3:12 [r] Jdg 4:1; 8:33 ing other gods and serving and worshiping them.[r] They refused to give up their
evil practices and stubborn ways.
2:20 20Therefore the LORD was very angry[s]
[s] ver 14; Jos 23:16 with Israel and said, "Because this nation has violated the covenant that I laid
down for their forefathers and has not
listened to me, 21I will no longer drive
2:21 [t] Jos 23:13 out[t] before them any of the nations
Joshua left when he died. 22I will use
2:22 [u] Dt 8:2,16; them to test[u] Israel and see whether
Jdg 3:1,14 they will keep the way of the LORD and
walk in it as their forefathers did." 23The
LORD had allowed those nations to remain; he did not drive them out at once
by giving them into the hands of Joshua.

3 These are the nations the LORD left 3:1
to test[v] all those Israelites who had [v] Jdg 2:21-22
not experienced any of the wars in Ca-
naan 2(he did this only to teach warfare
to the descendants of the Israelites who
had not had previous battle experience):
3the five[w] rulers of the Philistines, all the 3:3
Canaanites, the Sidonians, and the Hi- [w] Jos 13:3
vites living in the Lebanon mountains
from Mount Baal Hermon to Lebo[b] Ha- 3:4
math. 4They were left to test[x] the Israel- [x] Dt 8:2;
ites to see whether they would obey the Jdg 2:22
LORD's commands, which he had given
their forefathers through Moses.
5The Israelites lived[y] among the 3:5 [y] Ps 106:35
Canaanites, Hittites, Amorites, Perizzites, Hivites and Jebusites. 6They took
their daughters in marriage and gave
their own daughters to their sons, and 3:6 [z] Ex 34:16;
served their gods.[z] Dt 7:3-4

Othniel

7The Israelites did evil in the eyes of 3:7
the LORD; they forgot the LORD[a] their [a] Dt 4:9
God and served the Baals and the Ashe- [b] Ex 34:13; Jdg 2:11,13
rahs.[b] 8The anger of the LORD burned
against Israel so that he sold[c] them into 3:8
the hands of Cushan-Rishathaim king of [c] Jdg 2:14
Aram Naharaim,[c] to whom the Israelites
were subject for eight years. 9But when 3:9
they cried out[d] to the LORD, he raised up [d] ver 15; Jdg 6:6,
for them a deliverer, Othniel[e] son of Ke- 7; 10:10; Ps 106:44
naz, Caleb's younger brother, who saved [e] Jdg 1:13
them. 10The Spirit of the LORD came 3:10
upon him,[f] so that he became Israel's [f] Nu 11:25,29;
judge[d] and went to war. The LORD gave 24:2; Jdg 6:34;
Cushan-Rishathaim king of Aram into 11:29; 13:25;
the hands of Othniel, who overpowered 14:6,19; 1Sa 11:6
him. 11So the land had peace for forty
years, until Othniel son of Kenaz died.

Ehud

12Once again the Israelites did evil in 3:12
the eyes of the LORD,[g] and because they [g] Jdg 2:11,14
did this evil the LORD gave Eglon king of [h] 1Sa 12:9
Moab[h] power over Israel. 13Getting the
Ammonites and Amalekites to join him,
Eglon came and attacked Israel, and
they took possession of the City of 3:13
Palms.[e][i] 14The Israelites were subject to [i] Jdg 1:16
Eglon king of Moab for eighteen years.
15Again the Israelites cried out to the 3:15
LORD, and he gave them a deliverer[j]— [j] ver 9; Ps 78:34;
Ehud, a left-handed man, the son of 107:13

[a] *16* Or *leaders*; similarly in verses 17–19 [b] *3* Or *to the entrance to* [c] *8* That is, Northwest Mesopotamia [d] *10* Or *leader* [e] *13* That is, Jericho

Gera the Benjamite. The Israelites sent
him with tribute to Eglon king of Moab.
16Now Ehud had made a double-edged
sword about a foot and a half[a] long,
which he strapped to his right thigh under his clothing. 17He presented the
3:17 tribute to Eglon king of Moab, who was
k ver 12 a very fat man.[k] 18After Ehud had presented the tribute, he sent on their way
the men who had carried it. 19At the
idols[b] near Gilgal he himself turned
back and said, "I have a secret message
for you, O king."

The king said, "Quiet!" And all his attendants left him.

20Ehud then approached him while he
was sitting alone in the upper room of his
summer palace[c] and said, "I have a message from God for you." As the king rose
from his seat, 21Ehud reached with his left
hand, drew the sword from his right
thigh and plunged it into the king's belly.
22Even the handle sank in after the blade,
which came out his back. Ehud did not
pull the sword out, and the fat closed in
over it. 23Then Ehud went out to the
porch[d]; he shut the doors of the upper
room behind him and locked them.

24After he had gone, the servants
came and found the doors of the upper
3:24 room locked. They said, "He must be re-
l 1Sa 24:3 lieving himself[l] in the inner room of the
3:25 house." 25They waited to the point of
m 2Ki 2:17; 8:11 embarrassment,[m] but when he did not
open the doors of the room, they took a
key and unlocked them. There they saw
their lord fallen to the floor, dead.

26While they waited, Ehud got away.
He passed by the idols and escaped to Se-
irah. 27When he arrived there, he blew a
3:27 trumpet[n] in the hill country of Ephraim,
n Jdg 6:34; 1Sa 13:3 and the Israelites went down with him
from the hills, with him leading them.

28"Follow me," he ordered, "for the
LORD has given Moab, your enemy, into
3:28 your hands.[o]" So they followed him
o Jdg 7:9,15 p Jos 2:7; down and, taking possession of the
Jdg 7:24; 12:5 fords of the Jordan[p] that led to Moab,
they allowed no one to cross over. 29At
that time they struck down about ten
thousand Moabites, all vigorous and
strong; not a man escaped. 30That day
3:30 Moab was made subject to Israel, and
q ver 11 the land had peace[q] for eighty years.

Shamgar

31After Ehud came Shamgar son of
Anath,[r] who struck down six hundred[s] 3:31 r Jdg 5:6
Philistines with an oxgoad. He too saved s Jos 23:10
Israel.

Deborah

4 After Ehud died, the Israelites 4:1
once again did evil[t] in the eyes of t Jdg 2:19
the LORD. 2So the LORD sold them into
the hands of Jabin, a king of Canaan,
who reigned in Hazor.[u] The command- 4:2 u Jos 11:1
er of his army was Sisera,[v] who lived in v ver 13,16;
Harosheth Haggoyim. 3Because he had 1Sa 12:9; Ps 83:9
nine hundred iron chariots[w] and had
cruelly oppressed[x] the Israelites for 4:3 w Jdg 1:19
twenty years, they cried to the LORD for x Ps 106:42
help.

4Deborah, a prophetess, the wife of
Lappidoth, was leading[e] Israel at that
time. 5She held court under the Palm of
Deborah between Ramah and Bethel[y] in 4:5 y Ge 35:8
the hill country of Ephraim, and the Israelites came to her to have their disputes decided. 6She sent for Barak son of
Abinoam[z] from Kedesh in Naphtali and 4:6 z Heb 11:32
said to him, "The LORD, the God of Isra-
el, commands you: 'Go, take with you
ten thousand men of Naphtali and Zebulun and lead the way to Mount Tabor.
7I will lure Sisera, the commander of Jabin's army, with his chariots and his
troops to the Kishon River[a] and give him 4:7 a Ps 83:9
into your hands.' "

8Barak said to her, "If you go with me,
I will go; but if you don't go with me, I
won't go."

9"Very well," Deborah said, "I will go
with you. But because of the way you are
going about this,[f] the honor will not be
yours, for the LORD will hand Sisera over
to a woman." So Deborah went with Bar- 4:9
ak to Kedesh,[b] 10where he summoned[c] b ver 21; Jdg 2:14
Zebulun and Naphtali. Ten thousand
men followed him, and Deborah also 4:10 c ver 14;
went with him. Jdg 5:15,18

11Now Heber the Kenite had left 4:11
the other Kenites,[d] the descendants of d Jdg 1:16
Hobab,[e] Moses' brother-in-law,[g] and e Nu 10:29
pitched his tent by the great tree in Za- f Jos 19:33
anannim[f] near Kedesh.

12When they told Sisera that Barak
son of Abinoam had gone up to Mount

a *16* Hebrew *a cubit* (about 0.5 meter) b *19* Or *the stone quarries*; also in verse 26 c *20* The meaning of the Hebrew for this phrase is uncertain. d *23* The meaning of the Hebrew for this word is uncertain. e *4* Traditionally *judging* f *9* Or *But on the expedition you are undertaking* g *11* Or *father-in-law*

DISCOVERY 59

Deborah and Barak

There is no gratification in being conquered, overthrown, crushed or mastered—especially if the setback is our own fault: a bad choice, poor judgment or failure to have done the right thing when we knew we should. Israel had once again failed miserably (Judges 4:1). Because they did not believe God, the people "did evil in the eyes of the LORD"—marrying idol-worshipers and indulging in immoral and unethical practices. The result was 20 years of oppression. Living conditions became almost unbearable (Judges 5:6–8). The economy was in ruin, crime and conflict were rampant, and leading a "normal" life was impossible. Israel groaned in the agony of defeat.

At that point God sent two people to help the nation turn its focus back on himself. Deborah was a prophetess and Barak a military strategist. God used them both to set his people free from their oppression, and for the next 40 years Israel exulted in the thrill of victory. Judges 4 describes how God set the people free, and chapter 5 reiterates the theme in poetic language.

Defeat can come in many forms: a broken marriage, substance abuse or addiction, financial chaos, spiritual bankruptcy, uncontrolled anger, familial tensions, the disappointment of a broken promise, death or a debilitating disease. And there is always agony in defeat, whether or not it is our own fault.

But God did something to stop the cycle: "The deliverer will come from Zion" (Romans 11:26). We no longer have to live lives marred by failure, and we are no longer ultimately enslaved to Satan and his schemes: "We are more than conquerors through him who loved us" (Romans 8:37). In this life we *will* have trouble; we will have obstacles that simply can't be overcome, at least by our human power or effort. But, says Jesus, "Take heart! I have overcome the world" (John 16:33).

In addition, God often sends a Deborah or a Barak into our lives—people who can empathize with us, encourage us and help to see us through. In fact, the Bible tells us that God often uses brokenness in our lives to enable us to assist other broken people along the way. His design is to use each of us as a Deborah or a Barak for someone else.

"Encourage one another daily," urged the writer to the Hebrews, "as long as it is called Today, so that none of you may be hardened by sin's deceitfulness. We have come to share in Christ if we hold firmly till the end the confidence we had at first" (Hebrews 3:13–14).

Self-Discovery: *In what specific ways are you "more than a conqueror" because of Jesus' work in your life? How can you use your experience to help others find victory through him?*

GO TO DISCOVERY 60 ON PAGE 311

Tabor, 13Sisera gathered together his
4:13 g ver 3 nine hundred iron chariots[g] and all the
men with him, from Harosheth Hag-
goyim to the Kishon River.
14Then Deborah said to Barak, "Go!
This is the day the LORD has given Sisera
into your hands. Has not the LORD gone
4:14 h Dt 9:3; 2Sa 5:24; Ps 68:7 ahead[h] of you?" So Barak went down
Mount Tabor, followed by ten thousand
men. 15At Barak's advance, the LORD
4:15 i Jos 10:10; Ps 83:9-10 routed[i] Sisera and all his chariots and
army by the sword, and Sisera aban-
doned his chariot and fled on foot. 16But
Barak pursued the chariots and army as
far as Harosheth Haggoyim. All the
troops of Sisera fell by the sword; not a
4:16 j Ps 83:9 man was left.[j]
17Sisera, however, fled on foot to the
tent of Jael, the wife of Heber the Kenite,
because there were friendly relations between Jabin king of Hazor and the clan
of Heber the Kenite.
18Jael went out to meet Sisera and said
to him, "Come, my lord, come right in.
Don't be afraid." So he entered her tent,
and she put a covering over him.
19"I'm thirsty," he said. "Please give me
4:19 k Jdg 5:25 some water." She opened a skin of milk,[k]
gave him a drink, and covered him up.
20"Stand in the doorway of the tent,"
he told her. "If someone comes by and
asks you, 'Is anyone here?' say 'No.' "
21But Jael, Heber's wife, picked up a
tent peg and a hammer and went quietly to him while he lay fast asleep, exhausted. She drove the peg through his
4:21 l Jdg 5:26 temple into the ground, and he died.[l]
22Barak came by in pursuit of Sisera,
and Jael went out to meet him. "Come,"
she said, "I will show you the man you're
looking for." So he went in with her, and
there lay Sisera with the tent peg
through his temple—dead.
4:23 m Ne 9:24; Ps 18:47 23On that day God subdued[m] Jabin, the
Canaanite king, before the Israelites.
24And the hand of the Israelites grew
stronger and stronger against Jabin, the
Canaanite king, until they destroyed him.

The Song of Deborah

5:1 n Ex 15:1 **5** On that day Deborah and Barak
son of Abinoam sang this song:[n]

2"When the princes in Israel take
the lead,
5:2 o 2Ch 17:16; Ps 110:3 p ver 9 when the people willingly offer[o]
themselves—
praise the LORD![p]

3"Hear this, you kings! Listen, you
rulers!
I will sing to[a] the LORD, I will
sing;
I will make music to[b] the LORD, 5:3 q Ps 27:6
the God of Israel.[q]

4"O LORD, when you went out from
Seir,[r] 5:4 r Dt 33:2 s Ps 68:8
when you marched from the
land of Edom,
the earth shook, the heavens
poured,
the clouds poured down water.[s]
5The mountains quaked[t] before the 5:5 t Ex 19:18; Ps 68:8; 97:5; Isa 64:3
LORD, the One of Sinai,
before the LORD, the God of Israel.

6"In the days of Shamgar son of 5:6 u Jdg 3:31 v Jdg 4:17 w Isa 33:8
Anath,[u]
in the days of Jael,[v] the roads[w]
were abandoned;
travelers took to winding paths.
7Village life[c] in Israel ceased,
ceased until I,[d] Deborah, arose,
arose a mother in Israel.
8When they chose new gods,[x] 5:8 x Dt 32:17
war came to the city gates,
and not a shield or spear was seen
among forty thousand in Israel.
9My heart is with Israel's princes,
with the willing volunteers[y] 5:9 y ver 2
among the people.
Praise the LORD!

10"You who ride on white donkeys,[z] 5:10 z Jdg 10:4; 12:14
sitting on your saddle blankets,
and you who walk along the road,
consider 11the voice of the singers[e]
at the watering places.
They recite the righteous acts[a] 5:11 a 1Sa 12:7; Mic 6:5 b ver 8
of the LORD,
the righteous acts of his
warriors[f] in Israel.
"Then the people of the LORD
went down to the city gates.[b]
12'Wake up,[c] wake up, Deborah! 5:12 c Ps 57:8 d Ps 68:18; Eph 4:8
Wake up, wake up, break out in
song!
Arise, O Barak!
Take captive your captives,[d]
O son of Abinoam.'

13"Then the men who were left
came down to the nobles;

[a] 3 Or *of* [b] 3 Or / *with song I will praise* [c] 7 Or *Warriors* [d] 7 Or *you* [e] 11 Or *archers*; the meaning of the Hebrew for this word is uncertain. [f] 11 Or *villagers*

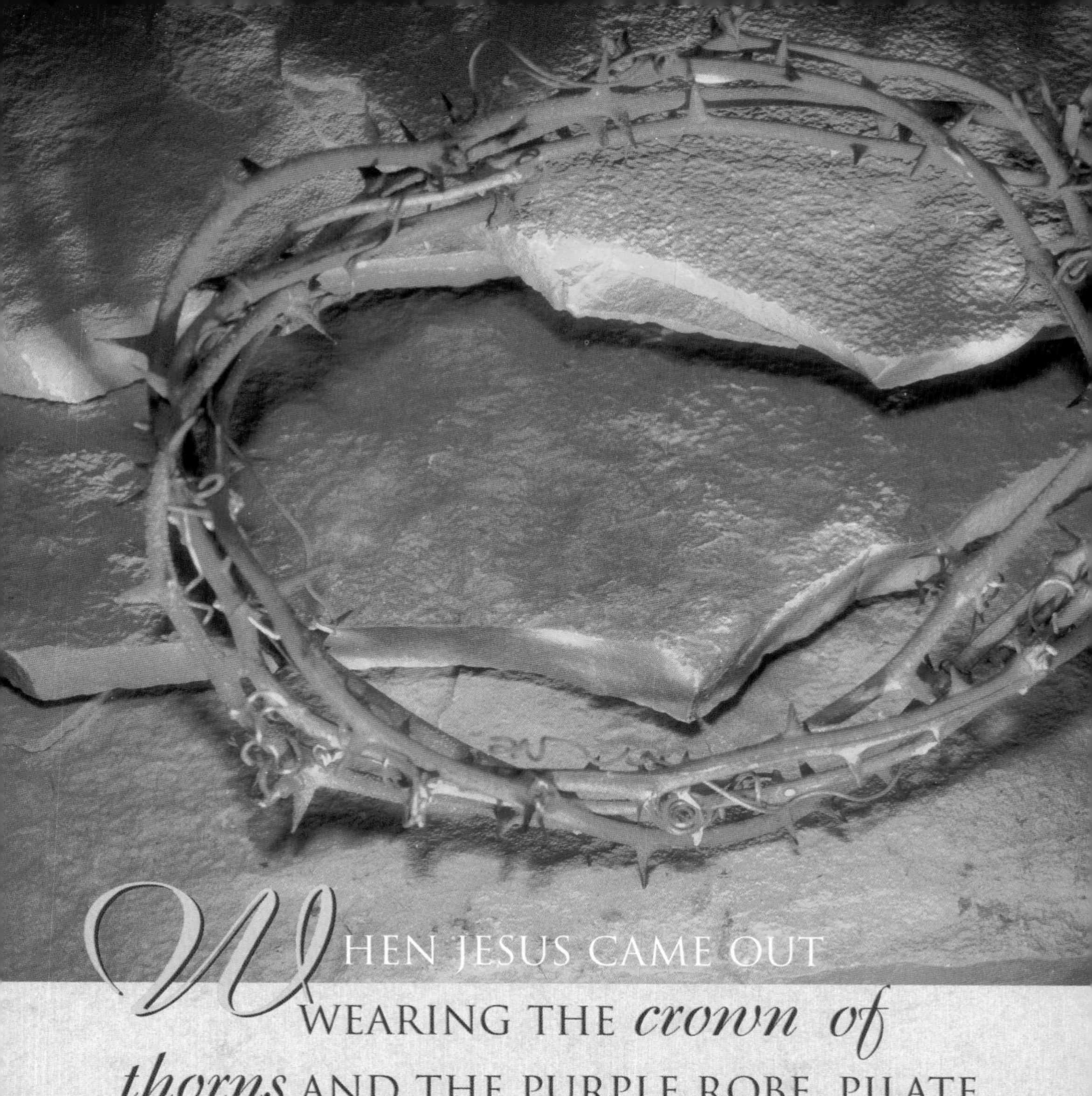

WHEN JESUS CAME OUT WEARING THE *crown of thorns* AND THE PURPLE ROBE, PILATE SAID TO THEM, "HERE IS THE MAN!"

— JOHN 19:5 —

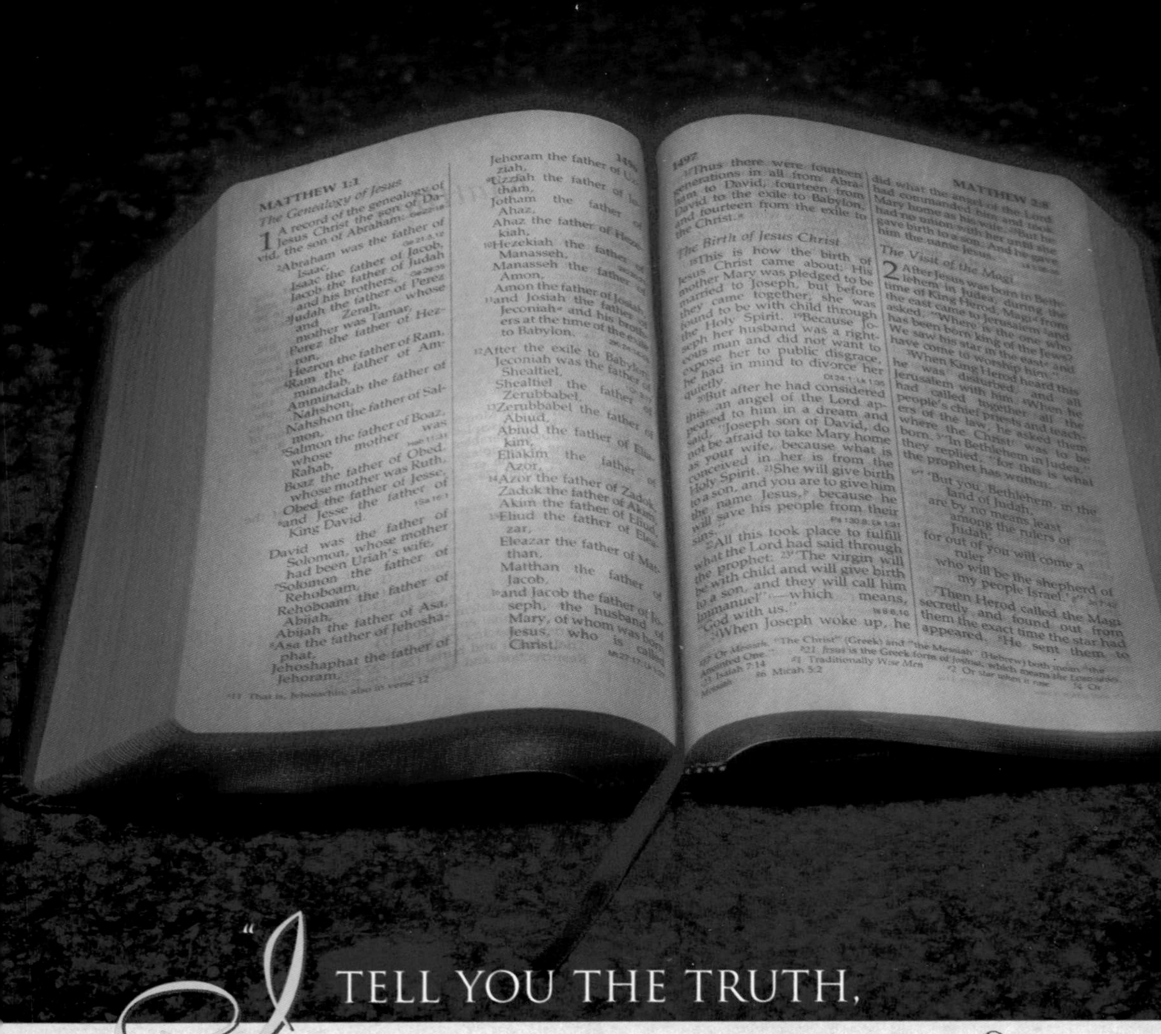

"I TELL YOU THE TRUTH,
WHOEVER HEARS *my word*
AND BELIEVES HIM WHO SENT ME HAS
eternal life AND WILL NOT BE
CONDEMNED; HE HAS CROSSED OVER
FROM DEATH TO LIFE."

—JOHN 5:24—

the people of the LORD
came to me with the mighty.
14 Some came from Ephraim, whose
5:14 [e] Jdg 3:13 roots were in Amalek;[e]
Benjamin was with the people
who followed you.
From Makir captains came down,
from Zebulun those who bear a
commander's staff.
15 The princes of Issachar were with
5:15 [f] Jdg 4:10 Deborah;[f]
yes, Issachar was with Barak,
rushing after him into the valley.
In the districts of Reuben
there was much searching of
heart.
16 Why did you stay among the
campfires[a]
5:16 to hear the whistling for the
[g] Nu 32:1 flocks?[g]
In the districts of Reuben
there was much searching of
heart.
17 Gilead stayed beyond the Jordan.
And Dan, why did he linger by
5:17 the ships?
[h] Jos 19:29 Asher remained on the coast[h]
and stayed in his coves.
18 The people of Zebulun risked their
very lives;
so did Naphtali on the heights of
5:18 the field.[i]
[i] Jdg 4:6,10
5:19 19 "Kings came[j], they fought;
[j] Jos 11:5; Jdg 4:13 the kings of Canaan fought
[k] Jdg 1:27 at Taanach by the waters of
[l] ver 30 Megiddo,[k]
but they carried off no silver, no
plunder.[l]
5:20
[m] Jos 10:11 20 From the heavens[m] the stars fought,
from their courses they fought
against Sisera.
5:21 21 The river Kishon[n] swept them
[n] Jdg 4:7 away,
the age-old river, the river
Kishon.
March on, my soul; be strong!
22 Then thundered the horses'
hoofs—
galloping, galloping go his
mighty steeds.
rse Meroz,' said the angel of the
LORD.
rse its people bitterly,
e they did not come to help
he LORD,
the LORD against the
ghty.'

5:24 24 "Most blessed of women be Jael,[o]
[o] Jdg 4:17 the wife of Heber the Kenite,
most blessed of tent-dwelling
women.
5:25 25 He asked for water, and she gave
[p] Jdg 4:19 him milk;[p]
in a bowl fit for nobles she
brought him curdled milk.
26 Her hand reached for the tent peg,
her right hand for the workman's
hammer.
She struck Sisera, she crushed his
head,
she shattered and pierced his
5:26 temple.[q]
[q] Jdg 4:21
27 At her feet he sank,
he fell; there he lay.
At her feet he sank, he fell;
where he sank, there he fell—
dead.
28 "Through the window peered
Sisera's mother;
5:28 behind the lattice she cried out,[r]
[r] Pr 7:6 'Why is his chariot so long in
coming?
Why is the clatter of his chariots
delayed?'
29 The wisest of her ladies answer her;
indeed, she keeps saying to
herself,
5:30 30 'Are they not finding and dividing
[s] Ex 15:9; 1Sa 30:24 the spoils:[s]
a girl or two for each man,
colorful garments as plunder for
Sisera,
colorful garments embroidered,
highly embroidered garments
for my neck—
all this as plunder?'
31 "So may all your enemies perish,
O LORD!
But may they who love you be
5:31 like the sun[t]
[t] 2Sa 23:4; Ps 19:4; 89:36 when it rises in its strength."
[u] Jdg 3:11
Then the land had peace[u] forty years.

Gideon

6:1 **6** Again the Israelites did evil in the
[v] Jdg 2:11 eyes of the LORD,[v] and for seven
[w] Nu 25:15-18; 31:1-3 years he gave them into the hands of the
Midianites.[w] 2 Because the power of
6:2 Midian was so oppressive,[x] the Israelites
[x] 1Sa 13:6; Isa 8:21 prepared shelters for themselves in
[y] Heb 11:38 mountain clefts, caves and strongholds.[y]

[a] 16 Or *saddlebags*

3 Whenever the Israelites planted their
6:3 [z]Jdg 3:13 crops, the Midianites, Amalekites[z] and
other eastern peoples invaded the coun-
6:4 try. 4 They camped on the land and ru-
[a]Lev 26:16; ined the crops[a] all the way to Gaza and
Dt 28:30,51 did not spare a living thing for Israel,
neither sheep nor cattle nor donkeys.
5 They came up with their livestock and
6:5 their tents like swarms of locusts.[b] It
[b]Jdg 7:12 [c]Jdg 8:10 was impossible to count the men and
their camels;[c] they invaded the land to
6:6 ravage it. 6 Midian so impoverished the
[d]Jdg 3:9 Israelites that they cried out[d] to the
LORD for help.
7 When the Israelites cried to the LORD
because of Midian, 8 he sent them a
prophet, who said, "This is what the
LORD, the God of Israel, says: I brought
6:8 [e]Jdg 2:1 you up out of Egypt,[e] out of the land of
slavery. 9 I snatched you from the power
of Egypt and from the hand of all your
oppressors. I drove them from before
6:9 [f]Ps 44:2 you and gave you their land.[f] 10 I said to
6:10 you, 'I am the LORD your God; do not
[g]2Ki 17:35 worship[g] the gods of the Amorites,[h] in
[h]Jer 10:2 whose land you live.' But you have not
listened to me."
6:11 11 The angel of the LORD[i] came and sat
[i]Ge 16:7 down under the oak in Ophrah that be-
[j]Jos 17:2 [k]Heb 11:32 longed to Joash the Abiezrite,[j] where his
son Gideon[k] was threshing wheat in a
winepress to keep it from the Midianites. 12 When the angel of the LORD ap- 6:12
peared to Gideon, he said, "The LORD is [l]Jos 1:5;
with you,[l] mighty warrior." Jdg 13:3; Lk 1:11,28
13 "But sir," Gideon replied, "if the LORD
is with us, why has all this happened to
us? Where are all his wonders that our
fathers told[m] us about when they said, 6:13 [m]Ps 44:1
'Did not the LORD bring us up out of [n]2Ch 15:2
Egypt?' But now the LORD has aban-
doned[n] us and put us into the hand of
Midian."
14 The LORD turned to him and said,
"Go in the strength you have[o] and save 6:14 [o]Heb 11:34
Israel out of Midian's hand. Am I not
sending you?"
15 "But Lord,[a]" Gideon asked, "how
can I save Israel? My clan is the weakest
in Manasseh, and I am the least in my 6:15 [p]Ex 3:11;
family.[p]" 1Sa 9:21
16 The LORD answered, "I will be with 6:16
you[q], and you will strike down all the [q]Ex 3:12;
Midianites together." Jos 1:5
17 Gideon replied, "If now I have found
favor in your eyes, give me a sign[r] that it 6:17 [r]ver 36-37;
is really you talking to me. 18 Please do Ge 24:14;
not go away until I come back and bring Isa 38:7-8
my offering and set it before you."
And the LORD said, "I will wait until
you return."
19 Gideon went in, prepared a young
goat, and from an ephah[b] of flour he
made bread without yeast. Putting the
meat in a basket and its broth in a pot,
he brought them out and offered them
to him under the oak.[s] 6:19 [s]Ge 18:7-8
20 The angel of God said to him, "Take
the meat and the unleavened bread, 6:20
place them on this rock,[t] and pour [t]Jdg 13:19
out the broth." And Gideon did so.
21 With the tip of the staff that was in his
hand, the angel of the LORD touched the 6:21
meat and the unleavened bread.[u] Fire [u]Lev 9:24
flared from the rock, consuming the
meat and the bread. And the angel of the
LORD disappeared. 22 When Gideon real- 6:22 [v]Jdg 13:16,21
ized[v] that it was the angel of the LORD, he [w]Ge 32:30;
exclaimed, "Ah, Sovereign LORD! I have Ex 33:20;
seen the angel of the LORD face to face!"[w] Jdg 13:22
23 But the LORD said to him, "Peace! Do
not be afraid.[x] You are not going to die." 6:23 [x]Da 10:19
24 So Gideon built an altar to the LORD
there and called[y] it The LORD is Peace. To 6:24 [y]Ge 22:14
this day it stands in Ophrah[z] of the [z]Jdg 8:32
Abiezrites.

[a] 15 Or *sir* [b] 19 That is, probably about 3/5 bushel (about 22 liters)

JESUS FOCUS

FROM COWARD TO CONQUERER

The situation had deteriorated badly for Israel by the time the "angel of the LORD" called Gideon to be a "mighty warrior" (Judges 6:12). Interestingly, Gideon himself was something of a coward. God found him threshing wheat in a winepress, hiding from the Midianites. The Lord demonstrated his sense of the ironic when he instructed the timorous Gideon to "go in the strength you have and save Israel" (verse 14). Gideon realized the identity of the "angel" and made the assumption that he was destined to die because he had seen God face-to-face. Instead the "Spirit of the LORD" strengthened him, and he rallied a massive army against the Midianites (verses 34–35). God pared down the army until it consisted of Gideon and a mere 300 men. But because this tiny band believed God's word, the soldiers were able to stand against the enemy (Judges 7:16–22). Once again the "angel of the LORD" had stepped in to ensure the continuation of the family line of the Messiah.

DISCOVERY 60

An Unlikely Hero

For seven years God's people had been oppressed by the Midianites. But finally they turned back to God, and he sent a leader named Gideon to liberate them. The Bible tells us more about Gideon than about any other person in the book of Judges.

It all started when Gideon was secretly threshing wheat—terrified that the Midianites would catch him and confiscate the precious grain. The angel of the Lord (thought by many to be Jesus himself; see page 23) appeared to him. The angel addressed Gideon as a mighty warrior (Judges 6:12). Ironically, Gideon, the intimidated farmer trying to scratch out a living in constant fear of marauding enemies, was at this time anything but a mighty warrior! The angel's greeting does not even seem to make sense. But the angel saw unrealized potential in Gideon. He knew what Gideon was *intended* to be, what he could become with God's help. The same is true in our lives. God sees beyond who we are at any given moment, beyond the limits imposed by our fear and self-doubt. Instead, he looks forward to helping us become all that he intends us to be.

The angel commanded Gideon to go and save Israel "in the strength you have" (verse 14). Gideon objected: "My clan is the weakest in Manasseh, and I am the least in my family" (verse 15). Even so, Gideon did obey, and 32,000 Israelites showed up to fight against the Midianites. But at this juncture God surprised Gideon: "You have too many men for me to deliver Midian into their hands" (Judges 7:2). God's intention was to ensure that the people would maintain focus and realize afterward that they had not saved themselves by their own strength. Eventually God pared the army down to a mere 300 valiant men—all of whom believed in God. And with that handful of men, plus Gideon, *plus God himself*, the Midianites were defeated.

Throughout history we see God using the least likely individuals to accomplish his purposes; because of this, people will be able to see beyond the person to the God who wants to be known (1 Corinthians 1:26–31). In the New Testament the apostle Paul felt the same way as Gideon about his place among God's people. He described himself as "the least of the apostles" (1 Corinthians 15:9), yet God selected Paul to be one of the most important figures in the early church. And when God determined to take on flesh and blood and save the human race from its sin, he arrived as a baby—in the most helpless and vulnerable of human states. Instead of making his debut in the corridors of power with pomp and fanfare, God the Son entered the world in a rude stable and slept in a feeding trough.

We all experience times during which we feel inadequate to accomplish what the Lord asks. Sometimes we think that other people are more talented or better suited for a given job. But Jesus knows what's involved, and he identifies the right person for the task. If he is asking *you* to do it, then *you're* the perfect choice! Refuse to give in to fear and stand prepared with the resources he has provided: You plus the Lord Jesus form a mighty army capable of great things!

Self-Discovery: *How would you respond if Jesus were to ask you to do something great "in the strength you have"?*

GO TO DISCOVERY 61 ON PAGE 318

25That same night the LORD said to
6:25 him, "Take the second bull from your fa-
[a]Ex 34:13; ther's herd, the one seven years old.[a]
Dt 7:5 Tear down your father's altar to Baal and
cut down the Asherah pole[b][a] beside it.
26Then build a proper kind of[c] altar to
the LORD your God on the top of this
height. Using the wood of the Asherah
pole that you cut down, offer the second[d] bull as a burnt offering."
27So Gideon took ten of his servants
and did as the LORD told him. But because he was afraid of his family and the
men of the town, he did it at night rather
than in the daytime.
28In the morning when the men of the
6:28 [b]1Ki 16:32 town got up, there was Baal's altar,[b] demolished, with the Asherah pole beside
it cut down and the second bull sacrificed on the newly built altar!
29They asked each other, "Who did
this?"
When they carefully investigated,
they were told, "Gideon son of Joash
did it."
30The men of the town demanded of
Joash, "Bring out your son. He must die,
because he has broken down Baal's altar
and cut down the Asherah pole beside it."
31But Joash replied to the hostile
crowd around him, "Are you going to
plead Baal's cause? Are you trying to
save him? Whoever fights for him shall
be put to death by morning! If Baal really
is a god, he can defend himself when
someone breaks down his altar." 32So
6:32 that day they called Gideon "Jerub-
[c]Jdg 7:1; 8:29, Baal,[e][c]" saying, "Let Baal contend with
35; 1Sa 12:11 him," because he broke down Baal's altar.
33Now all the Midianites, Amalekites
6:33 and other eastern peoples[d] joined forces
[d]ver 3 and crossed over the Jordan and
[e]Jos 17:16 camped in the Valley of Jezreel.[e] 34Then
6:34 the Spirit of the LORD came upon[f] Gide-
[f]Jdg 3:10; on, and he blew a trumpet,[g] summoning
1Ch 12:18; 2Ch 24:20 the Abiezrites to follow him. 35He sent
[g]Jdg 3:27 messengers throughout Manasseh, calling them to arms, and also into Asher,
6:35 [h]Jdg 4:6 Zebulun and Naphtali,[h] so that they too
went up to meet them.
36Gideon said to God, "If you will save[i]
6:36 [i]ver 14 Israel by my hand as you have promised— 37look, I will place a wool fleece
6:37 on the threshing floor.[j] If there is dew
[j]Ex 4:3-7 only on the fleece and all the ground is
[k]Ge 24:14 dry, then I will know[k] that you will save
Israel by my hand, as you said." 38And
that is what happened. Gideon rose early the next day; he squeezed the fleece
and wrung out the dew—a bowlful of
water.
39Then Gideon said to God, "Do not
be angry with me. Let me make just one 6:39
more request.[l] Allow me one more test [l]Ge 18:32
with the fleece. This time make the
fleece dry and the ground covered with
dew." 40That night God did so. Only the
fleece was dry; all the ground was covered with dew.

Gideon Defeats the Midianites

7 Early in the morning, Jerub-Baal[m] 7:1 [m]Jdg 6:32
(that is, Gideon) and all his men [n]Ge 12:6
camped at the spring of Harod. The
camp of Midian was north of them in
the valley near the hill of Moreh.[n] 2The
LORD said to Gideon, "You have too
many men for me to deliver Midian into
their hands. In order that Israel may not
boast against me that her own strength[o] 7:2 [o]Dt 8:17;
has saved her, 3announce now to the 2Co 4:7
people, 'Anyone who trembles with fear
may turn back and leave Mount Gile-
ad.[p]' " So twenty-two thousand men left, 7:3 [p]Dt 20:8
while ten thousand remained.
4But the LORD said to Gideon, "There
are still too many[q] men. Take them down 7:4
to the water, and I will sift them for you [q]1Sa 14:6
there. If I say, 'This one shall go with you,'
he shall go; but if I say, 'This one shall not
go with you,' he shall not go."
5So Gideon took the men down to the
water. There the LORD told him, "Separate those who lap the water with their
tongues like a dog from those who kneel
down to drink." 6Three hundred men
lapped with their hands to their mouths.
All the rest got down on their knees to
drink.
7The LORD said to Gideon, "With the
three hundred men that lapped I will
save you and give the Midianites into
your hands. Let all the other men go, 7:7
each to his own place."[r] 8So Gideon sent [r]1Sa 14:6
the rest of the Israelites to their tents
but kept the three hundred, who took
over the provisions and trumpets of the
others.
Now the camp of Midian lay below

[a] 25 Or *Take a full-grown, mature bull from your father's herd* [b] 25 That is, a symbol of the goddess Asherah; here and elsewhere in Judges [c] 26 Or *build with layers of stone an* [d] 26 Or *full-grown*; also in verse 28 [e] 32 *Jerub-Baal* means *let Baal contend.*

him in the valley. 9During that night the
LORD said to Gideon, "Get up, go down
7:9 s Jos 2:24; 10:8; 11:6 against the camp, because I am going to
give it into your hands.[s] 10If you are
afraid to attack, go down to the camp
with your servant Purah 11and listen to
what they are saying. Afterward, you will
be encouraged to attack the camp." So he
and Purah his servant went down to the
7:12 outposts of the camp. 12The Midianites,
t Jdg 8:10 the Amalekites[t] and all the other eastern
u Jdg 6:5 v Jer 49:29 peoples had settled in the valley, thick as
w Jos 11:4 locusts.[u] Their camels[v] could no more be
counted than the sand on the seashore.[w]
13Gideon arrived just as a man was
telling a friend his dream. "I had a
dream," he was saying. "A round loaf of
barley bread came tumbling into the
Midianite camp. It struck the tent with
such force that the tent overturned and
collapsed."
14His friend responded, "This can be
nothing other than the sword of Gideon
son of Joash, the Israelite. God has given
the Midianites and the whole camp into
his hands."
7:15 15When Gideon heard the dream and
x 1Sa 15:31 its interpretation, he worshiped God.[x]
He returned to the camp of Israel and
called out, "Get up! The LORD has given
7:16 the Midianite camp into your hands."
y Ge 14:15 16Dividing the three hundred men[y] into
z 2Sa 18:2 three companies,[z] he placed trumpets
and empty jars in the hands of all of
them, with torches inside.
17"Watch me," he told them. "Follow
my lead. When I get to the edge of the
camp, do exactly as I do. 18When I and
7:18 a Jdg 3:27 all who are with me blow our trumpets,[a]
then from all around the camp blow
yours and shout, 'For the LORD and for
Gideon.' "
19Gideon and the hundred men with
him reached the edge of the camp at the
beginning of the middle watch, just after
they had changed the guard. They blew
their trumpets and broke the jars that
were in their hands. 20The three companies blew the trumpets and smashed the
jars. Grasping the torches in their left
hands and holding in their right hands
7:20 the trumpets they were to blow, they
b ver 14 shouted, "A sword[b] for the LORD and for
Gideon!" 21While each man held his po-
7:21 sition around the camp, all the Midian-
c 2Ki 7:7 ites ran, crying out as they fled.[c]
22When the three hundred trumpets
sounded,[d] the LORD caused the men 7:22
throughout the camp to turn on each d Jos 6:20
other[e] with their swords. The army fled e 1Sa 14:20; 2Ch 20:23
to Beth Shittah toward Zererah as far as f 1Ki 4:12; 19:16
the border of Abel Meholah[f] near Tab-
bath. 23Israelites from Naphtali, Asher 7:23
and all Manasseh were called out,[g] and g Jdg 6:35
they pursued the Midianites. 24Gideon
sent messengers throughout the hill
country of Ephraim, saying, "Come
down against the Midianites and seize
the waters of the Jordan[h] ahead of them 7:24
as far as Beth Barah." h Jdg 3:28
So all the men of Ephraim were called
out and they took the waters of the Jordan as far as Beth Barah. 25They also
captured two of the Midianite leaders,
Oreb and Zeeb[i]. They killed Oreb at the 7:25
rock of Oreb,[j] and Zeeb at the winepress i Jdg 8:3; Ps 83:11
of Zeeb. They pursued the Midianites j Isa 10:26
and brought the heads of Oreb and Zeeb k Jdg 8:4
to Gideon, who was by the Jordan.[k]

Zebah and Zalmunna

8 Now the Ephraimites asked Gideon, "Why have you treated us like
this? Why didn't you call us when you
went to fight Midian?"[l] And they criti- 8:1
cized him sharply.[m] l Jdg 12:1 m 2Sa 19:41
2But he answered them, "What have I
accomplished compared to you? Aren't
the gleanings of Ephraim's grapes better
than the full grape harvest of Abiezer? 8:3
3God gave Oreb and Zeeb,[n] the Midian- n Jdg 7:25;
ite leaders, into your hands. What was I Pr 15:1
able to do compared to you?" At this,
their resentment against him subsided.
4Gideon and his three hundred men,
exhausted yet keeping up the pursuit,
came to the Jordan[o] and crossed it. 5He 8:4 o Jdg 7:25
said to the men of Succoth,[p] "Give my
troops some bread; they are worn out, 8:5
and I am still pursuing Zebah and Zal- p Ge 33:17 q Ps 83:11
munna,[q] the kings of Midian."
6But the officials of Succoth said, "Do
you already have the hands of Zebah
and Zalmunna in your possession? Why 8:6
should we give bread[r] to your troops?"[s] r 1Sa 25:11 s ver 15
7Then Gideon replied, "Just for that,
when the LORD has given Zebah and Zal-
munna[t] into my hand, I will tear your 8:7 t Jdg 7:15
flesh with desert thorns and briers."
8From there he went up to Peniel[a][u] 8:8 u Ge 32:30;
and made the same request of them, but 1Ki 12:25
they answered as the men of Succoth

[a] 8 Hebrew *Penuel*, a variant of *Peniel*; also in verses 9 and 17

had. 9 So he said to the men of Peniel,
8:9 [v]ver 17 "When I return in triumph, I will tear
down this tower."[v]
10 Now Zebah and Zalmunna were in
Karkor with a force of about fifteen
thousand men, all that were left of the
armies of the eastern peoples; a hundred
8:10 [w]Jdg 6:5; 7:12; Isa 9:4 and twenty thousand swordsmen had
fallen.[w] 11 Gideon went up by the route of
8:11 [x]Nu 32:42 [y]Nu 32:35 the nomads east of Nobah[x] and Jogbehah[y] and fell upon the unsuspecting
army. 12 Zebah and Zalmunna, the two
kings of Midian, fled, but he pursued
them and captured them, routing their
entire army.
13 Gideon son of Joash then returned
from the battle by the Pass of Heres. 14 He
caught a young man of Succoth and
questioned him, and the young man
wrote down for him the names of the
seventy-seven officials of Succoth, the
elders of the town. 15 Then Gideon came
and said to the men of Succoth, "Here
are Zebah and Zalmunna, about whom
you taunted me by saying, 'Do you already have the hands of Zebah and Zalmunna in your possession? Why should
8:15 [z]ver 6 we give bread to your exhausted men?[z]' "
16 He took the elders of the town and
8:16 [a]ver 7 taught the men of Succoth a lesson[a] by
punishing them with desert thorns and
briers. 17 He also pulled down the tower
of Peniel and killed the men of the
8:17 [b]ver 9 town.[b]
18 Then he asked Zebah and Zalmun-
8:18 [c]Jos 19:22; Jdg 4:6 na, "What kind of men did you kill at Tabor?[c]"
"Men like you," they answered, "each
one with the bearing of a prince."
19 Gideon replied, "Those were my
brothers, the sons of my own mother. As
surely as the LORD lives, if you had
spared their lives, I would not kill you."
20 Turning to Jether, his oldest son, he
said, "Kill them!" But Jether did not draw
his sword, because he was only a boy
and was afraid.
21 Zebah and Zalmunna said, "Come,
do it yourself. 'As is the man, so is his
strength.' " So Gideon stepped forward
8:21 [d]ver 26; Ps 83:11 and killed them, and took the ornaments[d] off their camels' necks.

Gideon's Ephod

22 The Israelites said to Gideon, "Rule
over us—you, your son and your grandson—because you have saved us out of
the hand of Midian."
23 But Gideon told them, "I will not
rule over you, nor will my son rule over 8:23
you. The LORD will rule[e] over you." 24 And [e]Ex 16:8; 1Sa 8:7; 10:19; 12:12
he said, "I do have one request, that each
of you give me an earring from your
share of the plunder." (It was the custom 8:24
of the Ishmaelites[f] to wear gold ear- [f]Ge 25:13
rings.)
25 They answered, "We'll be glad to
give them." So they spread out a garment, and each man threw a ring from
his plunder onto it. 26 The weight of the
gold rings he asked for came to seventeen hundred shekels,[a] not counting the
ornaments, the pendants and the purple
garments worn by the kings of Midian
or the chains that were on their camels'
necks. 27 Gideon made the gold into an 8:27
ephod,[g] which he placed in Ophrah, his [g]Jdg 17:5; 18:14
town. All Israel prostituted themselves [h]Dt 7:16; Ps 106:39
by worshiping it there, and it became a
snare[h] to Gideon and his family.

Gideon's Death

28 Thus Midian was subdued before
the Israelites and did not raise its head
again. During Gideon's lifetime, the land 8:28 [i]Jdg 5:31
enjoyed peace[i] forty years.
29 Jerub-Baal[j] son of Joash went back 8:29 [j]Jdg 7:1
home to live. 30 He had seventy sons[k] of
his own, for he had many wives. 31 His 8:30 [k]Jdg 9:2,5,18,24
concubine, who lived in Shechem, also
bore him a son, whom he named Abim- 8:31 [l]Jdg 9:1
elech.[l] 32 Gideon son of Joash died at a
good old age[m] and was buried in the 8:32 [m]Ge 25:8
tomb of his father Joash in Ophrah of
the Abiezrites.
33 No sooner had Gideon died than the
Israelites again prostituted themselves 8:33 [n]Jdg 2:11,13,19
to the Baals.[n] They set up Baal-Berith[o] [o]Jdg 9:4
as their god[p] and 34 did not remember[q] [p]Jdg 9:27,46
the LORD their God, who had rescued 8:34
them from the hands of all their enemies [q]Jdg 3:7; Dt 4:9; Ps 78:11,42
on every side. 35 They also failed to show
kindness to the family of Jerub-Baal
(that is, Gideon) for all the good things 8:35
he had done for them.[r] [r]Jdg 9:16

Abimelech

9 Abimelech[s] son of Jerub-Baal 9:1 [s]Jdg 8:31
went to his mother's brothers in
Shechem and said to them and to all his
mother's clan, 2 "Ask all the citizens of

[a] 26 That is, about 43 pounds (about 19.5 kilograms)

Shechem, 'Which is better for you: to
have all seventy of Jerub-Baal's sons rule
9:2 [t] Ge 29:14; over you, or just one man?' Remember, I
Jdg 8:30 am your flesh and blood.[t]"
3When the brothers repeated all this
to the citizens of Shechem, they were inclined to follow Abimelech, for they said,
"He is our brother." 4They gave him seventy shekels[a] of silver from the temple of
9:4 [u] Jdg 8:33 Baal-Berith,[u] and Abimelech used it to
[v] Jdg 11:3; hire reckless adventurers,[v] who became
2Ch 13:7 his followers. 5He went to his father's
home in Ophrah and on one stone mur-
9:5 [w] ver 2; Jdg 8:30 dered his seventy brothers,[w] the sons of
[x] 2Ki 11:2 Jerub-Baal. But Jotham, the youngest
son of Jerub-Baal, escaped by hiding.[x]
6Then all the citizens of Shechem and
Beth Millo gathered beside the great tree
at the pillar in Shechem to crown Abimelech king.
7When Jotham was told about this, he
9:7 climbed up on the top of Mount Geri-
[y] Dt 11:29; zim[y] and shouted to them, "Listen to me,
27:12; Jn 4:20 citizens of Shechem, so that God may listen to you. 8One day the trees went out
to anoint a king for themselves. They
said to the olive tree, 'Be our king.'
9"But the olive tree answered, 'Should
I give up my oil, by which both gods and
men are honored, to hold sway over the
trees?'
10"Next, the trees said to the fig tree,
'Come and be our king.'
11"But the fig tree replied, 'Should I
give up my fruit, so good and sweet, to
hold sway over the trees?'
12"Then the trees said to the vine,
'Come and be our king.'
9:13 13"But the vine answered, 'Should I
[z] Ecc 2:3 give up my wine,[z] which cheers both
gods and men, to hold sway over the
trees?'
14"Finally all the trees said to the
thornbush, 'Come and be our king.'
15"The thornbush said to the trees, 'If
you really want to anoint me king over
9:15 [a] Isa 30:2 you, come and take refuge in my shade;[a]
[b] ver 20 but if not, then let fire come out[b] of the
[c] Isa 2:13 thornbush and consume the cedars of
Lebanon!'[c]
16"Now if you have acted honorably
and in good faith when you made Abimelech king, and if you have been fair to
Jerub-Baal and his family, and if you
have treated him as he deserves— 17and
to think that my father fought for you,
risked his life to rescue you from the
hand of Midian 18(but today you have revolted against my father's family, mur-
dered his seventy sons[d] on a single 9:18 [d] ver 5-6;
stone, and made Abimelech, the son of Jdg 8:30
his slave girl, king over the citizens of
Shechem because he is your brother)—
19if then you have acted honorably and
in good faith toward Jerub-Baal and his
family today, may Abimelech be your
joy, and may you be his, too! 20But if you 9:20
have not, let fire come out[e] from Abim- [e] ver 15
elech and consume you, citizens of Shechem and Beth Millo, and let fire come
out from you, citizens of Shechem and
Beth Millo, and consume Abimelech!"
21Then Jotham fled, escaping to Beer,
and he lived there because he was afraid
of his brother Abimelech.
22After Abimelech had governed Isra-
el three years, 23God sent an evil spirit[f] 9:23
between Abimelech and the citizens of [f] 1Sa 16:14,23; 18:10;
Shechem, who acted treacherously 1Ki 22:22;
against Abimelech. 24God did this in or- Isa 19:14; 33:1
der that the crime against Jerub-Baal's
seventy sons, the shedding[g] of their 9:24 [g] Nu 35:33;
blood, might be avenged[h] on their 1Ki 2:32
brother Abimelech and on the citizens [h] ver 56-57 [i] Dt 27:25
of Shechem, who had helped him[i] mur-
der his brothers. 25In opposition to him
these citizens of Shechem set men on
the hilltops to ambush and rob everyone
who passed by, and this was reported to
Abimelech.
26Now Gaal son of Ebed moved with
his brothers into Shechem, and its citizens put their confidence in him. 27After
they had gone out into the fields and
gathered the grapes and trodden[j] them, 9:27 [j] Am 9:13
they held a festival in the temple of their [k] Jdg 8:33
god.[k] While they were eating and drink-
ing, they cursed Abimelech. 28Then Gaal
son of Ebed said, "Who[l] is Abimelech, 9:28
and who is Shechem, that we should be [l] 1Sa 25:10;
subject to him? Isn't he Jerub-Baal's son, 1Ki 12:16 [m] Ge 34:2,6
and isn't Zebul his deputy? Serve the
men of Hamor,[m] Shechem's father! Why 9:29
should we serve Abimelech? 29If only this [n] 2Sa 15:4
people were under my command![n] Then
I would get rid of him. I would say to
Abimelech, 'Call out your whole army!' "[b]
30When Zebul the governor of the city
heard what Gaal son of Ebed said, he
was very angry. 31Under cover he sent
messengers to Abimelech, saying, "Gaal

[a] 4 That is, about 1 3/4 pounds (about 0.8 kilogram) [b] 29 Septuagint; Hebrew *him." Then he said to Abimelech, "Call out your whole army!"*

son of Ebed and his brothers have come
to Shechem and are stirring up the city
against you. 32Now then, during the
night you and your men should come
9:32 [o]Jos 8:2 and lie in wait[o] in the fields. 33In the
morning at sunrise, advance against the
city. When Gaal and his men come out
9:33 against you, do whatever your hand
[p]1Sa 10:7 finds to do.[p]"
34So Abimelech and all his troops set
out by night and took up concealed positions near Shechem in four companies.
35Now Gaal son of Ebed had gone out
and was standing at the entrance to the
9:35 city gate just as Abimelech and his sol-
[q]Ps 32:7; Jer 49:10 diers came out from their hiding place.[q]
36When Gaal saw them, he said to Ze-
bul, "Look, people are coming down
from the tops of the mountains!"
Zebul replied, "You mistake the shadows of the mountains for men."
37But Gaal spoke up again: "Look, people are coming down from the center of
the land, and a company is coming from
the direction of the soothsayers' tree."
38Then Zebul said to him, "Where is
your big talk now, you who said, 'Who is
Abimelech that we should be subject to
him?' Aren't these the men you rid-
9:38 [r]ver 28-29 iculed?[r] Go out and fight them!"
39So Gaal led out[a] the citizens of Shechem and fought Abimelech. 40Abim-
elech chased him, and many fell wounded in the flight—all the way to the
entrance to the gate. 41Abimelech stayed
in Arumah, and Zebul drove Gaal and
his brothers out of Shechem.
42The next day the people of Shechem
went out to the fields, and this was reported to Abimelech. 43So he took his
men, divided them into three compa-
9:43 [s]Jdg 7:16 nies[s] and set an ambush in the fields.
When he saw the people coming out of
the city, he rose to attack them. 44Abim-
elech and the companies with him
rushed forward to a position at the entrance to the city gate. Then two companies rushed upon those in the fields
and struck them down. 45All that day
Abimelech pressed his attack against
the city until he had captured it and
killed its people. Then he destroyed the
9:45 [t]ver 20; 2Ki 3:25 [u]Dt 29:23 city[t] and scattered salt[u] over it.
46On hearing this, the citizens in the
tower of Shechem went into the strong-
9:46 [v]Jdg 8:33 hold of the temple[v] of El-Berith. 47When
Abimelech heard that they had assem-
bled there, 48he and all his men went up 9:48
Mount Zalmon.[w] He took an ax and cut [w]Ps 68:14
off some branches, which he lifted to his
shoulders. He ordered the men with
him, "Quick! Do what you have seen me
do!" 49So all the men cut branches and
followed Abimelech. They piled them
against the stronghold and set it on fire
over the people inside. So all the people
in the tower of Shechem, about a thousand men and women, also died.
50Next Abimelech went to Thebez[x] 9:50 [x]2Sa 11:21
and besieged it and captured it. 51Inside
the city, however, was a strong tower, to
which all the men and women—all the
people of the city—fled. They locked
themselves in and climbed up on the
tower roof. 52Abimelech went to the tower and stormed it. But as he approached
the entrance to the tower to set it on fire,
53a woman dropped an upper millstone 9:53
on his head and cracked his skull.[y] [y]2Sa 11:21
54Hurriedly he called to his armor-
bearer, "Draw your sword and kill me,[z] 9:54 [z]1Sa 31:4;
so that they can't say, 'A woman killed 2Sa 1:9
him.'" So his servant ran him through,
and he died. 55When the Israelites saw
that Abimelech was dead, they went
home.
56Thus God repaid the wickedness
that Abimelech had done to his father
by murdering his seventy brothers.
57God also made the men of Shechem 9:57
pay for all their wickedness.[a] The curse [a]ver 20
of Jotham son of Jerub-Baal came on
them.

Tola

10 After the time of Abimelech a 10:1
man of Issachar,[b] Tola son of [b]Ge 30:18
Puah,[c] the son of Dodo, rose to save[d] Is- [c]Ge 46:13 [d]Jdg 2:16; 6:14
rael. He lived in Shamir, in the hill coun-
try of Ephraim. 2He led[b] Israel twenty-
three years; then he died, and was
buried in Shamir.

Jair

3He was followed by Jair of Gilead,
who led Israel twenty-two years. 4He had
thirty sons, who rode thirty donkeys.
They controlled thirty towns in Gilead,
which to this day are called Havvoth
Jair.[c][e] 5When Jair died, he was buried in 10:4 [e]Nu 32:41
Kamon.

[a] 39 Or *Gaal went out in the sight of*
[b] 2 Traditionally *judged*; also in verse 3 [c] 4 Or *called the settlements of Jair*

Jephthah

6Again the Israelites did evil in the eyes of the LORD.[f] They served the Baals and the Ashtoreths,[g] and the gods of Aram, the gods of Sidon, the gods of Moab, the gods of the Ammonites and the gods of the Philistines.[h] And because the Israelites forsook the LORD[i] and no longer served him, 7he became angry[j] with them. He sold them[k] into the hands of the Philistines and the Ammonites, 8who that year shattered and crushed them. For eighteen years they oppressed all the Israelites on the east side of the Jordan in Gilead, the land of the Amorites. 9The Ammonites also crossed the Jordan to fight against Judah, Benjamin and the house of Ephraim; and Israel was in great distress. 10Then the Israelites cried out to the LORD, "We have sinned against you, forsaking our God and serving the Baals."[l]

11The LORD replied, "When the Egyptians,[m] the Amorites, the Ammonites,[n] the Philistines,[o] 12the Sidonians, the Amalekites and the Maonites[a] oppressed you[p] and you cried to me for help, did I not save you from their hands? 13But you have forsaken me and served other gods, so I will no longer save you. 14Go and cry out to the gods you have chosen. Let them save you when you are in trouble![q]"

15But the Israelites said to the LORD, "We have sinned. Do with us whatever you think best,[r] but please rescue us now." 16Then they got rid of the foreign gods among them and served the LORD.[s] And he could bear Israel's misery[t] no longer.[u]

17When the Ammonites were called to arms and camped in Gilead, the Israelites assembled and camped at Mizpah.[v] 18The leaders of the people of Gilead said to each other, "Whoever will launch the attack against the Ammonites will be the head[w] of all those living in Gilead."

11 Jephthah[x] the Gileadite was a mighty warrior.[y] His father was Gilead; his mother was a prostitute. 2Gilead's wife also bore him sons, and when they were grown up, they drove Jephthah away. "You are not going to get any inheritance in our family," they said, "because you are the son of another woman." 3So Jephthah fled from his brothers and settled in the land of Tob,[z] where a group of adventurers[a] gathered around him and followed him.

4Some time later, when the Ammonites[b] made war on Israel, 5the elders of Gilead went to get Jephthah from the land of Tob. 6"Come," they said, "be our commander, so we can fight the Ammonites."

7Jephthah said to them, "Didn't you hate me and drive me from my father's house?[c] Why do you come to me now, when you're in trouble?"

8The elders of Gilead said to him, "Nevertheless, we are turning to you now; come with us to fight the Ammonites, and you will be our head[d] over all who live in Gilead."

9Jephthah answered, "Suppose you take me back to fight the Ammonites and the LORD gives them to me—will I really be your head?"

10The elders of Gilead replied, "The LORD is our witness;[e] we will certainly do as you say." 11So Jephthah went with the elders of Gilead, and the people made him head and commander over them. And he repeated all his words before the LORD in Mizpah.[f]

12Then Jephthah sent messengers to the Ammonite king with the question: "What do you have against us that you have attacked our country?"

13The king of the Ammonites answered Jephthah's messengers, "When Israel came up out of Egypt, they took away my land from the Arnon to the Jabbok,[g] all the way to the Jordan. Now give it back peaceably."

14Jephthah sent back messengers to the Ammonite king, 15saying:

> "This is what Jephthah says: Israel did not take the land of Moab[h] or the land of the Ammonites.[i] 16But when they came up out of Egypt, Israel went through the desert to the Red Sea[b][j] and on to Kadesh.[k] 17Then Israel sent messengers[l] to the king of Edom, saying, 'Give us permission to go through your country,'[m] but the king of Edom would not listen. They sent also to the king of Moab, and he refused.[n] So Israel stayed at Kadesh.

[a] *12* Hebrew; some Septuagint manuscripts *Midianites* [b] *16* Hebrew *Yam Suph*; that is, Sea of Reeds

10:6 [f] Jdg 2:11 [g] Jdg 2:13 [h] Jdg 2:12 [i] Dt 32:15
10:7 [j] Dt 31:17 [k] Dt 32:30; Jdg 2:14; 1Sa 12:9
10:10 [l] 1Sa 12:10
10:11 [m] Ex 14:30 [n] Nu 21:21; Jdg 3:13 [o] Jdg 3:31
10:12 [p] Ps 106:42
10:14 [q] Dt 32:37
10:15 [r] 1Sa 3:18; 2Sa 15:26
10:16 [s] Jos 24:23; Jer 18:8 [t] Isa 63:9 [u] Dt 32:36; Ps 106:44-45
10:17 [v] Ge 31:49; Jdg 11:29
10:18 [w] Jdg 11:8,9
11:1 [x] Heb 11:32 [y] Jdg 6:12
11:3 [z] 2Sa 10:6,8 [a] Jdg 9:4
11:4 [b] Jdg 10:9
11:7 [c] Ge 26:27
11:8 [d] Jdg 10:18
11:10 [e] Ge 31:50; Jer 42:5
11:11 [f] Jos 11:3; Jdg 10:17; 20:1; 1Sa 10:17
11:13 [g] Ge 32:22; Nu 21:24
11:15 [h] Dt 2:9 [i] Dt 2:19
11:16 [j] Nu 14:25; Dt 1:40 [k] Nu 20:1
11:17 [l] Nu 20:14 [m] Nu 20:18,21 [n] Jos 24:9

DISCOVERY 61

THE LORD AS JUDGE

Throughout the period of Israel's judges, God raised up leaders who would deliver the Israelites from their enemies. During the lifetime of each judge the land was secure. Jephthah had a dispute with the Ammonites over some land, and he sent a lengthy message to their king outlining the reasons for his contention that the land belonged to Israel. Jephthah appealed to God: "Let the LORD, the Judge, decide the dispute" (Judges 11:27).

The Lord is the Judge of all the people of the earth (Genesis 18:25). Each one of us is accountable to him and will stand one day before him. In the New Testament we learn that God the Father gave the ultimate responsibility for judgment to his Son, Jesus (John 5:22). There are at least two different kinds of judgment mentioned in the Bible, and each demonstrates God's holiness.

First, there is judgment against unbelievers, against people who have refused to recognize Jesus as God's Son. Their judgment is referred to as the judgment before the great white throne (Revelation 20:11–15). All of the deeds of every human being are recorded in the books of heaven. Because such individuals have refused to accept the reality of Jesus' death and his offer of eternal life, they will be compelled to suffer the penalty for their own sin. They will be judged according to the manner in which they have lived their lives, down to the minutest detail. Not one of us is perfect (Romans 3:23), and the just penalty for all sin is severe—eternal death. Those who refuse God's gracious offer will spend eternity without him in the "lake of fire" (Revelation 20:14–15).

But there is also judgment for believers. The apostle Paul refers to the judgment seat of Christ (2 Corinthians 5:10). Our judgment will not be a time for God to judge us for our *sin*. Once we have accepted Jesus' sacrifice for our sin, God no longer holds that sin against us—our slate has been wiped clean. Instead, he will reward us for the way in which we have served him. Everything we have done will be "revealed with fire." God uses that word picture to describe the manner by which the worth of what we have done will be determined. Gold, silver and other costly stones are often purified by fire. They come out glinting more brilliantly than before. But wood, hay and straw leave behind only a pile of ashes. Ultimately, there is no value in these consumable materials (1 Corinthians 3:12–14). God will reward each of us based on the quality of our devotion to him (2 Timothy 4:6–8).

If we were to stand today before Jesus, our Righteous Judge, what kind of residue would our lives leave behind? If we have not chosen to invite Jesus into our lives, the flames of judgment will bring only agony. If we believe in him, we should desire the quality of our lives to reflect that faith. And one day he will reward us beyond anything we can imagine.

Self-Discovery: Picture yourself as being a nugget of dazzling gold that has been refined by fire. Then envision God looking at you in the same light. How does this picture make you feel?

GO TO DISCOVERY 62 ON PAGE 324

18“Next they traveled through
11:18 the desert, skirted the lands of
o Nu 21:4 Edom[o] and Moab, passed along the
p Dt 2:8 eastern side[p] of the country of
q Nu 21:13 Moab, and camped on the other
side of the Arnon.[q] They did not
enter the territory of Moab, for the
Arnon was its border.
19“Then Israel sent messengers
to Sihon king of the Amorites, who
ruled in Heshbon, and said to him,
11:19 ‘Let us pass through your country
r Nu 21:21-22; to our own place.’[r] 20Sihon, howev-
Dt 2:26-27 er, did not trust Israel[a] to pass
11:20 through his territory. He mustered
s Nu 21:23; all his men and encamped at Jahaz
Dt 2:32 and fought with Israel.[s]
21“Then the LORD, the God of Israel, gave Sihon and all his men
into Israel’s hands, and they defeated them. Israel took over all the
land of the Amorites who lived in
that country, 22capturing all of it
from the Arnon to the Jabbok and
11:22 from the desert to the Jordan.[t]
t Dt 2:36 23“Now since the LORD, the God
of Israel, has driven the Amorites
out before his people Israel, what
right have you to take it over?
11:24 24Will you not take what your god
u Nu 21:29; Chemosh[u] gives you? Likewise,
Jos 3:10; whatever the LORD our God has giv-
1Ki 11:7 en us, we will possess. 25Are you
11:25 better than Balak son of Zippor,[v]
v Nu 22:2 king of Moab? Did he ever quarrel
w Jos 24:9 with Israel or fight with them?[w]
26For three hundred years Israel oc-
11:26 cupied[x] Heshbon, Aroer, the sur-
x Nu 21:25 rounding settlements and all the
towns along the Arnon. Why didn’t
you retake them during that time?
27I have not wronged you, but you
are doing me wrong by waging war
11:27 against me. Let the LORD, the
y Ge 18:25 Judge,[b][y] decide[z] the dispute this
z Ge 16:5; 31:53; day between the Israelites and the
1Sa 24:12,15 Ammonites.”

28The king of Ammon, however, paid no
attention to the message Jephthah sent
him.
11:29 29Then the Spirit[a] of the LORD came
a Nu 11:25; upon Jephthah. He crossed Gilead and
Jdg 3:10; 6:34; Manasseh, passed through Mizpah of
14:6,19; 15:14; Gilead, and from there he advanced
1Sa 11:6; 16:13; Isa 11:2 against the Ammonites. 30And Jephthah
11:30 made a vow[b] to the LORD: “If you give the
b Ge 28:20 Ammonites into my hands, 31whatever
comes out of the door of my house to
meet me when I return in triumph from
the Ammonites will be the LORD’s, and I
will sacrifice it as a burnt offering.”
32Then Jephthah went over to fight
the Ammonites, and the LORD gave
them into his hands. 33He devastated
twenty towns from Aroer to the vicinity 11:33
of Minnith,[c] as far as Abel Keramim. c Eze 27:17
Thus Israel subdued Ammon.
34When Jephthah returned to his
home in Mizpah, who should come out
to meet him but his daughter, dancing
to the sound of tambourines![d] She was 11:34
an only child. Except for her he had nei- d Ex 15:20;
ther son nor daughter. 35When he saw Jer 31:4
her, he tore his clothes and cried, “Oh!
My daughter! You have made me miserable and wretched, because I have made 11:35
a vow to the LORD that I cannot break.[e]” e Nu 30:2;
36“My father,” she replied, “you have Ecc 5:2,4,5
given your word to the LORD. Do to me 11:36
just as you promised,[f] now that the LORD f Lk 1:38
has avenged you of your enemies,[g] the g 2Sa 18:19
Ammonites. 37But grant me this one request,” she said. “Give me two months to
roam the hills and weep with my friends,
because I will never marry.”
38“You may go,” he said. And he let her
go for two months. She and the girls
went into the hills and wept because she
would never marry. 39After the two
months, she returned to her father and
he did to her as he had vowed. And she
was a virgin.
From this comes the Israelite custom
40that each year the young women of Israel go out for four days to commemorate the daughter of Jephthah the Gileadite.

Jephthah and Ephraim

12 The men of Ephraim called out
their forces, crossed over to Zaphon and said to Jephthah, “Why did
you go to fight the Ammonites without
calling us to go with you?[h] We’re going 12:1
to burn down your house over your h Jdg 8:1
head.”
2Jephthah answered, “I and my people
were engaged in a great struggle with
the Ammonites, and although I called,
you didn’t save me out of their hands.
3When I saw that you wouldn’t help, I 12:3
took my life in my hands[i] and crossed i 1Sa 19:5; 28:21; Job 13:14

[a] 20 Or *however, would not make an agreement for Israel* [b] 27 Or *Ruler*

over to fight the Ammonites, and the
LORD gave me the victory over them.
Now why have you come up today to
fight me?"
4Jephthah then called together the
men of Gilead and fought against
Ephraim. The Gileadites struck them
down because the Ephraimites had said,
"You Gileadites are renegades from
12:5 Ephraim and Manasseh." 5The Gilea-
j Jos 22:11; dites captured the fords of the Jordan[j]
Jdg 3:28 leading to Ephraim, and whenever a survivor of Ephraim said, "Let me cross
over," the men of Gilead asked him, "Are
you an Ephraimite?" If he replied, "No,"
6they said, "All right, say 'Shibboleth.' " If
he said, "Sibboleth," because he could
not pronounce the word correctly, they
seized him and killed him at the fords of
the Jordan. Forty-two thousand Ephraimites were killed at that time.
7Jephthah led[a] Israel six years. Then
Jephthah the Gileadite died, and was
buried in a town in Gilead.

Ibzan, Elon and Abdon

8After him, Ibzan of Bethlehem led Israel. 9He had thirty sons and thirty
daughters. He gave his daughters away in
marriage to those outside his clan, and
for his sons he brought in thirty young
women as wives from outside his clan.
Ibzan led Israel seven years. 10Then Ibzan died, and was buried in Bethlehem.
11After him, Elon the Zebulunite led
Israel ten years. 12Then Elon died, and
was buried in Aijalon in the land of Zebulun.
13After him, Abdon son of Hillel, from
Pirathon, led Israel. 14He had forty sons
12:14 and thirty grandsons,[k] who rode on sev-
k Jdg 10:4 l Jdg 5:10 enty donkeys.[l] He led Israel eight years.
15Then Abdon son of Hillel died, and
12:15 was buried at Pirathon in Ephraim, in
m Jdg 5:14 the hill country of the Amalekites.[m]

The Birth of Samson

13 Again the Israelites did evil in
the eyes of the LORD, so the
13:1 LORD delivered them into the hands of
n Jdg 2:11; 1Sa 12:9 the Philistines[n] for forty years.
2A certain man of Zorah,[o] named Ma-
13:2 o Jos 15:33; noah, from the clan of the Danites, had a
19:41 wife who was sterile and remained child-
13:3 less. 3The angel of the LORD[p] appeared to
p ver 6,8; her[q] and said, "You are sterile and child-
Jdg 6:12 q ver 10 less, but you are going to conceive and
have a son.[r] 4Now see to it that you drink 13:3 r Lk 1:13
no wine or other fermented drink and
that you do not eat anything unclean,[s] 13:4 s ver 14;
5because you will conceive and give birth Nu 6:2-4;
to a son. No razor[t] may be used on his Lk 1:15
head, because the boy is to be a Nazi-
rite,[u] set apart to God from birth, and he 13:5 t Nu 6:5; 1Sa 1:11
will begin[v] the deliverance of Israel from u Nu 6:2,13
the hands of the Philistines." v 1Sa 7:13
6Then the woman went to her hus-
band and told him, "A man of God[w] 13:6 w ver 8;
came to me. He looked like an angel of 1Sa 2:27; 9:6
God,[x] very awesome. I didn't ask him x ver 17-18; Mt 28:3
where he came from, and he didn't tell
me his name. 7But he said to me, 'You
will conceive and give birth to a son.
Now then, drink no wine or other fermented drink and do not eat anything
unclean, because the boy will be a Nazirite of God from birth until the day of his
death.' "
8Then Manoah prayed to the LORD:
"O Lord, I beg you, let the man of God
you sent to us come again to teach us
how to bring up the boy who is to be
born."
9God heard Manoah, and the angel of
God came again to the woman while she
was out in the field; but her husband
Manoah was not with her. 10The woman
hurried to tell her husband, "He's here!
The man who appeared to me the other
day!"
11Manoah got up and followed his
wife. When he came to the man, he said,
"Are you the one who talked to my wife?"
"I am," he said.
12So Manoah asked him, "When your
words are fulfilled, what is to be the rule
for the boy's life and work?"
13The angel of the LORD answered,
"Your wife must do all that I have told
her. 14She must not eat anything that
comes from the grapevine, nor drink any 13:14
wine or other fermented drink[y] nor eat y Nu 6:4 z ver 4
anything unclean.[z] She must do every-
thing I have commanded her."
15Manoah said to the angel of the
LORD, "We would like you to stay until 13:15
we prepare a young goat[a] for you." a ver 3; Jdg 6:19
16The angel of the LORD replied, "Even
though you detain me, I will not eat any
of your food. But if you prepare a burnt 13:16
offering,[b] offer it to the LORD." (Manoah b Jdg 6:20
did not realize that it was the angel of
the LORD.)

[a] 7 Traditionally *judged*; also in verses 8–14

13:17 17Then Manoah inquired of the angel
c Ge 32:29 of the LORD, "What is your name,[c] so
that we may honor you when your word
comes true?"
13:18 d Isa 9:6 18He replied, "Why do you ask my
name?[d] It is beyond understanding.[a]"
19Then Manoah took a young goat, to-
13:19 e Jdg 6:20 gether with the grain offering, and sacrificed it on a rock[e] to the LORD. And the
LORD did an amazing thing while Mano-
13:20 f Lev 9:24 g 1Ch 21:16; Eze 1:28; Mt 17:6 ah and his wife watched: 20As the flame[f]
blazed up from the altar toward heaven,
the angel of the LORD ascended in the
flame. Seeing this, Manoah and his wife
fell with their faces to the ground.[g]
21When the angel of the LORD did not
13:21 h ver 16; Jdg 6:22 show himself again to Manoah and his
wife, Manoah realized[h] that it was the
angel of the LORD.
13:22 i Dt 5:26 j Ge 32:30; Jdg 6:22 22"We are doomed[i] to die!" he said to
his wife. "We have seen[j] God!"
23But his wife answered, "If the LORD
had meant to kill us, he would not have
accepted a burnt offering and grain of-
13:23 k Ps 25:14 fering from our hands, nor shown us all
these things or now told us this."[k]
13:24 l Heb 11:32 m 1Sa 3:19 n Lk 1:80 24The woman gave birth to a boy and
named him Samson.[l] He grew[m] and the
LORD blessed him,[n] 25and the Spirit of
the LORD began to stir[o] him while he was
13:25 o Jdg 3:10 p Jdg 18:12 in Mahaneh Dan,[p] between Zorah and
Eshtaol.

Samson's Marriage

14:1 q Ge 38:12 14 Samson went down to Timnah[q] and saw there a young
Philistine woman. 2When he returned,
he said to his father and mother, "I have
14:2 r Ge 21:21; 34:4 seen a Philistine woman in Timnah;
now get her for me as my wife."[r]
3His father and mother replied, "Isn't
there an acceptable woman among your
14:3 s Ge 24:4 t Dt 7:3 u Ex 34:16 relatives or among all our people?[s] Must
you go to the uncircumcised[t] Philistines
to get a wife?[u]"
But Samson said to his father, "Get
her for me. She's the right one for me."
4(His parents did not know that this was
from the LORD, who was seeking an oc-
14:4 v Jos 11:20 w Jdg 13:1 casion to confront the Philistines;[v] for at
that time they were ruling over Israel.)[w]
5Samson went down to Timnah together with his father and mother. As they
approached the vineyards of Timnah,
suddenly a young lion came roaring to-
14:6 x Jdg 3:10; 13:25 ward him. 6The Spirit of the LORD came
upon him in power[x] so that he tore the
lion apart with his bare hands as he
might have torn a young goat. But he
told neither his father nor his mother
what he had done. 7Then he went down
and talked with the woman, and he
liked her.
8Some time later, when he went back
to marry her, he turned aside to look at
the lion's carcass. In it was a swarm of
bees and some honey, 9which he scooped
out with his hands and ate as he went
along. When he rejoined his parents, he
gave them some, and they too ate it. But
he did not tell them that he had taken
the honey from the lion's carcass.
10Now his father went down to see the
woman. And Samson made a feast there,
as was customary for bridegrooms.
11When he appeared, he was given thirty
companions.
12"Let me tell you a riddle,[y]" Samson 14:12 y 1Ki 10:1; Eze 17:2 z Ge 29:27 a Ge 45:22; 2Ki 5:5
said to them. "If you can give me the an-
swer within the seven days of the feast,[z]
I will give you thirty linen garments and
thirty sets of clothes.[a] 13If you can't tell
me the answer, you must give me thirty
linen garments and thirty sets of
clothes."
"Tell us your riddle," they said. "Let's
hear it."
14He replied,

"Out of the eater, something to eat;
out of the strong, something
sweet."

For three days they could not give the
answer.
15On the fourth[b] day, they said to 14:15 b Jdg 16:5; Ecc 7:26 c Jdg 15:6
Samson's wife, "Coax[b] your husband
into explaining the riddle for us, or we
will burn you and your father's household to death.[c] Did you invite us here to
rob us?"
16Then Samson's wife threw herself on
him, sobbing, "You hate me! You don't
really love me.[d] You've given my people 14:16 d Jdg 16:15
a riddle, but you haven't told me the an-
swer."
"I haven't even explained it to my father or mother," he replied, "so why
should I explain it to you?" 17She cried
the whole seven days[e] of the feast. So on 14:17 e Est 1:5
the seventh day he finally told her, be-
cause she continued to press him. She in
turn explained the riddle to her people.

[a] *18* Or *is wonderful* [b] *15* Some Septuagint manuscripts and Syriac; Hebrew *seventh*

Samson and Delilah

16 One day Samson went to Gaza,
where he saw a prostitute. He
went in to spend the night with her. 2The
people of Gaza were told, "Samson is
here!" So they surrounded the place and
16:2 lay in wait for him all night at the city
[t] 1Sa 23:26; gate.[t] They made no move during the
Ps 118:10-12; Ac 9:24 night, saying, "At dawn we'll kill him."
3But Samson lay there only until the
middle of the night. Then he got up and
took hold of the doors of the city gate,
together with the two posts, and tore
them loose, bar and all. He lifted them to
his shoulders and carried them to the
16:3 [u] Jos 10:36 top of the hill that faces Hebron.[u]
16:4 4Some time later, he fell in love[v] with a
[v] Ge 24:67 woman in the Valley of Sorek whose
name was Delilah. 5The rulers of the Phi-
16:5 [w] Jos 13:3 listines[w] went to her and said, "See if you
[x] Ex 10:7; can lure[x] him into showing you the se-
Jdg 14:15 [y] ver 18 cret of his great strength and how we can
overpower him so we may tie him up
and subdue him. Each one of us will give
you eleven hundred shekels[a] of silver."[y]
6So Delilah said to Samson, "Tell me
the secret of your great strength and
how you can be tied up and subdued."
7Samson answered her, "If anyone ties
me with seven fresh thongs[b] that have
not been dried, I'll become as weak as
any other man."
8Then the rulers of the Philistines
brought her seven fresh thongs that had
not been dried, and she tied him with
16:9 them. 9With men hidden in the room,[z]
[z] ver 12 she called to him, "Samson, the Philistines are upon you!" But he snapped the
thongs as easily as a piece of string
snaps when it comes close to a flame. So
the secret of his strength was not discovered.
16:10 10Then Delilah said to Samson, "You
[a] ver 13 have made a fool of me;[a] you lied to me.
Come now, tell me how you can be tied."
11He said, "If anyone ties me securely
16:11 with new ropes[b] that have never been
[b] Jdg 15:13 used, I'll become as weak as any other
man."
12So Delilah took new ropes and tied
him with them. Then, with men hidden
in the room, she called to him, "Samson,
the Philistines are upon you!" But he
snapped the ropes off his arms as if they
were threads.
13Delilah then said to Samson, "Until
now, you have been making a fool of me

> **It is possible to know Bible stories, yet miss the Bible story . . . the story of Jesus.**
>
> Edmund P. Clowney,
> *President, Westminster Theological Seminary, Philadelphia, Pennsylvania*

and lying to me. Tell me how you can be
tied."
He replied, "If you weave the seven
braids of my head into the fabric ⌞on the
loom⌟ and tighten it with the pin, I'll become as weak as any other man." So
while he was sleeping, Delilah took the
seven braids of his head, wove them into
the fabric 14and[c] tightened it with the
pin.
Again she called to him, "Samson, the 16:14
Philistines are upon you!"[c] He awoke [c] ver 9,20
from his sleep and pulled up the pin and
the loom, with the fabric.
15Then she said to him, "How can you
say, 'I love you,'[d] when you won't confide 16:15 [d] Jdg 14:16
in me? This is the third time[e] you have [e] Nu 24:10
made a fool of me and haven't told me [f] ver 5
the secret of your great strength.[f]"
16With such nagging she prodded him
day after day until he was tired to death.
17So he told her everything.[g] "No ra- 16:17 [g] Mic 7:5
zor has ever been used on my head," he [h] Nu 6:2,5;
said, "because I have been a Nazirite[h] set Jdg 13:5
apart to God since birth. If my head were
shaved, my strength would leave me,
and I would become as weak as any other man."
18When Delilah saw that he had told
her everything, she sent word to the
rulers of the Philistines[i], "Come back 16:18
once more; he has told me everything." [i] Jos 13:3; 1Sa 5:8
So the rulers of the Philistines returned
with the silver in their hands. 19Having
put him to sleep on her lap, she called a
man to shave off the seven braids of his
hair, and so began to subdue him.[d] And 16:19
his strength left him.[j] [j] Pr 7:26-27
20Then she called, "Samson, the Philistines are upon you!"
He awoke from his sleep and thought,

[a] *5* That is, about 28 pounds (about 13 kilograms)
[b] *7* Or *bowstrings*; also in verses 8 and 9
[c] *13,14* Some Septuagint manuscripts; Hebrew *"⌞I can⌟ if you weave the seven braids of my head into the fabric ⌞on the loom⌟." 14So she*
[d] *19* Hebrew; some Septuagint manuscripts *and he began to weaken*

LORD, REMEMBER ME

The story of Samson is among the best known in the Bible. The angel of the Lord informed Samson's mother that she would bear a special son, who would be born to take the Nazirite vow (Judges 13:5). As an adult Samson would be renowned for his almost superhuman strength, the secret of which lay in a particular clause of his Nazirite vow; his hair, which must never be cut, symbolized the presence of the Spirit of the Lord within him.

God sent Samson to free Israel after the people had been in bondage to the Philistines for 40 years. Samson once killed a thousand Philistines with a donkey's jawbone (Judges 15:15–16). People recognized far and wide that he was able to perform spectacular feats because the Spirit of the Lord was with him (Judges 14:6,19; 15:14).

But Samson demonstrated some serious character flaws. He was careless about adhering to the details of the vow he had made to God. For example, he once scooped honey out of a lion's carcass, violating his promise not to touch the body of a dead animal. Samson also revealed his lack of self-control by indulging his weakness for women. At least once he spent the night with a prostitute (Judges 16:1) and later fell in love with a Philistine woman named Delilah (verse 4).

Eventually Delilah tricked Samson into divulging the secret behind his great strength. She immediately revealed the information to waiting Philistine men, who proceeded to shave Samson's head. Because Samson had broken his vow to the Lord, the Spirit of the Lord left him and the Philistines were able to capture him. They gouged out his eyes and forced him to grind corn in prison. The powerful Samson had been defeated because he had turned away from God (Galatians 6:7–8).

One day the Philistines decided as a diversion to bring the fallen hero to a party. Samson stood between the pillars that supported the temple and pleaded with God for one final favor: "LORD, remember me . . . strengthen me just once more" (Judges 16:28). God answered that prayer by giving back Samson's strength for one final task. Samson pushed with all his might against the pillars, and the temple came crashing down. Through this final sacrificial deed, Samson killed more of the enemy through his death than he had during his lifetime.

Jesus didn't display the physical strength of Samson, but he did display God's power in overcoming sin, disease and demons. "He was crucified in weakness, yet he lives to God's power" (2 Corinthians 13:4). Like Samson, just when his enemies thought they had conquered him, Jesus turned the tables and through his death overcame Satan, sin and all the powers of darkness. Then he rose from the dead through the mighty power of God.

Self-Discovery: *Do you ever feel that the power of darkness is winning in your life? In what ways does the promise of Jesus to "overcome the world" afford you hope?*

GO TO DISCOVERY 63 ON PAGE 330

"I'll go out as before and shake myself
free." But he did not know that the LORD
had left him.[k]
21 Then the Philistines[l] seized him,
gouged out his eyes[m] and took him
down to Gaza. Binding him with bronze
shackles, they set him to grinding[n] in the
prison. 22 But the hair on his head began
to grow again after it had been shaved.

The Death of Samson

23 Now the rulers of the Philistines assembled to offer a great sacrifice to Dagon[o] their god and to celebrate, saying,
"Our god has delivered Samson, our enemy, into our hands."
24 When the people saw him, they
praised their god,[p] saying,

"Our god has delivered our enemy
into our hands,[q]
the one who laid waste our land
and multiplied our slain."

25 While they were in high spirits,[r]
they shouted, "Bring out Samson to entertain us." So they called Samson out of
the prison, and he performed for them.
When they stood him among the pillars, 26 Samson said to the servant who
held his hand, "Put me where I can feel
the pillars that support the temple, so
that I may lean against them." 27 Now the
temple was crowded with men and
women; all the rulers of the Philistines
were there, and on the roof[s] were about
three thousand men and women watching Samson perform. 28 Then Samson
prayed to the LORD,[t] "O Sovereign LORD,
remember me. O God, please strength-
en me just once more, and let me with
one blow get revenge[u] on the Philistines
for my two eyes." 29 Then Samson
reached toward the two central pillars
on which the temple stood. Bracing
himself against them, his right hand on
the one and his left hand on the other,
30 Samson said, "Let me die with the Philistines!" Then he pushed with all his
might, and down came the temple on
the rulers and all the people in it. Thus
he killed many more when he died than
while he lived.
31 Then his brothers and his father's
whole family went down to get him.
They brought him back and buried him
between Zorah and Eshtaol in the tomb
of Manoah[v] his father. He had led[a][w] Israel twenty years.[x]

16:20 [k] Nu 14:42; Jos 7:12; 1Sa 16:14; 18:12; 28:15
16:21 [l] Jer 47:1 [m] Nu 16:14 [n] Job 31:10; Isa 47:2
16:23 [o] 1Sa 5:2; 1Ch 10:10
16:24 [p] Da 5:4 [q] 1Sa 31:9; 1Ch 10:9
16:25 [r] Jdg 9:27; Ru 3:7; Est 1:10
16:27 [s] Dt 22:8; Jos 2:8
16:28 [t] Jdg 15:18 [u] Jer 15:15
16:31 [v] Jdg 13:2 [w] Ru 1:1; 1Sa 4:18 [x] Jdg 15:20

Micah's Idols

17 Now a man named Micah[y]
from the hill country of Ephra-
im 2 said to his mother, "The eleven hundred shekels[b] of silver that were taken
from you and about which I heard you
utter a curse—I have that silver with me;
I took it."
Then his mother said, "The LORD
bless you,[z] my son!"
3 When he returned the eleven hundred shekels of silver to his mother, she
said, "I solemnly consecrate my silver to
the LORD for my son to make a carved
image and a cast idol.[a] I will give it back
to you."
4 So he returned the silver to his mother, and she took two hundred shekels[c] of
silver and gave them to a silversmith,
who made them into the image and the
idol.[b] And they were put in Micah's
house.
5 Now this man Micah had a shrine,[c]
and he made an ephod[d] and some idols[e]
and installed[f] one of his sons as his
priest.[g] 6 In those days Israel had no
king;[h] everyone did as he saw fit.[i]
7 A young Levite from Bethlehem in
Judah,[j] who had been living within the
clan of Judah, 8 left that town in search of
some other place to stay. On his way[d] he
came to Micah's house in the hill country of Ephraim.
9 Micah asked him, "Where are you
from?"
"I'm a Levite from Bethlehem in Judah," he said, "and I'm looking for a place
to stay."
10 Then Micah said to him, "Live with
me and be my father and priest,[k] and I'll
give you ten shekels[e] of silver a year, your
clothes and your food." 11 So the Levite
agreed to live with him, and the young
man was to him like one of his sons.
12 Then Micah installed[l] the Levite, and
the young man became his priest and
lived in his house. 13 And Micah said,
"Now I know that the LORD will be good
to me, since this Levite has become my
priest."

17:1 [y] Jdg 18:2,13
17:2 [z] Ru 2:20; 1Sa 15:13; 2Sa 2:5
17:3 [a] Ex 20:4,23; 34:17; Lev 19:4
17:4 [b] Ex 32:4; Isa 17:8
17:5 [c] Isa 44:13; Eze 8:10 [d] Jdg 8:27 [e] Ge 31:19; Jdg 18:14 [f] Nu 16:10 [g] Ex 29:9; Jdg 18:24
17:6 [h] Jdg 18:1; 19:1; 21:25 [i] Dt 12:8
17:7 [j] Jdg 19:1; Ru 1:1-2; Mic 5:2; Mt 2:1
17:10 [k] Jdg 18:19
17:12 [l] Nu 16:10

[a] 31 Traditionally *judged* [b] 2 That is, about 28 pounds (about 13 kilograms) [c] 4 That is, about 5 pounds (about 2.3 kilograms) [d] 8 Or *To carry on his profession* [e] 10 That is, about 4 ounces (about 110 grams)

Danites Settle in Laish

18:1 m Jdg 17:6; 19:1 **18** In those days Israel had no
n Jos 19:47 king.[m]
And in those days the tribe of the
Danites was seeking a place of their own
where they might settle, because they
had not yet come into an inheritance
18:2 among the tribes of Israel.[n] 2So the Dan-
o Jdg 13:25 ites[o] sent five warriors from Zorah and
p Jos 2:1 Eshtaol to spy out the land and explore
q Jdg 17:1 it. These men represented all their clans.
They told them, "Go, explore the land."[p]
The men entered the hill country of
Ephraim and came to the house of Micah,[q] where they spent the night. 3When
they were near Micah's house, they recognized the voice of the young Levite; so
they turned in there and asked him,
"Who brought you here? What are you
doing in this place? Why are you here?"
4He told them what Micah had done
for him, and said, "He has hired me and
18:4 r Jdg 17:12 I am his priest.[r]"
5Then they said to him, "Please in-
18:5 s 1Ki 22:5 quire of God[s] to learn whether our journey will be successful."
6The priest answered them, "Go in
18:6 t 1Ki 22:6 peace[t]. Your journey has the LORD's approval."
7So the five men left and came to La-
18:7 u Jos 19:47 ish,[u] where they saw that the people
v ver 28 were living in safety, like the Sidonians,
unsuspecting and secure. And since
their land lacked nothing, they were
prosperous.[a] Also, they lived a long way
from the Sidonians[v] and had no relationship with anyone else.[b]
8When they returned to Zorah and
Eshtaol, their brothers asked them,
"How did you find things?"
9They answered, "Come on, let's attack them! We have seen that the land is
very good. Aren't you going to do something? Don't hesitate to go there and
18:9 take it over.[w] 10When you get there, you
w Nu 13:30; 1Ki 22:3 will find an unsuspecting people and a
18:10 spacious land that God has put into
x ver 7,27; your hands, a land that lacks nothing[x]
Dt 8:9 whatever.[y]"
y 1Ch 4:40 11Then six hundred men[z] from the
18:11 clan of the Danites,[a] armed for battle,
z ver 16,17 set out from Zorah and Eshtaol. 12On
a Jdg 13:2 their way they set up camp near Kiriath
Jearim in Judah. This is why the place
18:12 west of Kiriath Jearim is called Mahaneh
b Jdg 13:25 Dan[c][b] to this day. 13From there they

went on to the hill country of Ephraim
and came to Micah's house.
14Then the five men who had spied
out the land of Laish said to their brothers, "Do you know that one of these
houses has an ephod, other household
gods, a carved image and a cast idol?[c] 18:14
c Ge 31:19;
Now you know what to do." 15So they Jdg 17:5
turned in there and went to the house of
the young Levite at Micah's place and
greeted him. 16The six hundred Dan-
ites,[d] armed for battle, stood at the en- 18:16 d ver 11
trance to the gate. 17The five men who
had spied out the land went inside and
took the carved image, the ephod, the
other household gods[e] and the cast idol 18:17
while the priest and the six hundred e Ge 31:19;
armed men stood at the entrance to the Mic 5:13
gate.
18When these men went into Micah's
house and took[f] the carved image, the 18:18 f Isa 46:2;
ephod, the other household gods and Jer 43:11;
the cast idol, the priest said to them, Hos 10:5
"What are you doing?"
19They answered him, "Be quiet![g] 18:19
Don't say a word. Come with us, and be g Job 21:5; 29:9;
40:4; Mic 7:16
our father and priest.[h] Isn't it better that h Jdg 17:10
you serve a tribe and clan in Israel as
priest rather than just one man's household?" 20Then the priest was glad. He
took the ephod, the other household
gods and the carved image and went
along with the people. 21Putting their little children, their livestock and their
possessions in front of them, they
turned away and left.
22When they had gone some distance
from Micah's house, the men who lived
near Micah were called together and
overtook the Danites. 23As they shouted
after them, the Danites turned and said
to Micah, "What's the matter with you
that you called out your men to fight?"
24He replied, "You took the gods I
made, and my priest, and went away.
What else do I have? How can you ask,
'What's the matter with you?' "
25The Danites answered, "Don't argue
with us, or some hot-tempered men will
attack you, and you and your family will
lose your lives." 26So the Danites went
their way, and Micah, seeing that they
were too strong for him,[i] turned around 18:26
and went back home. i Ps 18:17; 35:10

[a] 7 The meaning of the Hebrew for this clause is uncertain. [b] 7 Hebrew; some Septuagint manuscripts *with the Arameans* [c] 12 *Mahaneh Dan* means *Dan's camp.*

27Then they took what Micah had
made, and his priest, and went on to La-
18:27 ish, against a peaceful and unsuspecting
[j] ver 7,10 people.[j] They attacked them with the
[k] Ge 49:17; Jos 19:47 sword and burned down their city.[k]
28There was no one to rescue them be-
18:28 [l] ver 7 cause they lived a long way from Sidon[l]
[m] Nu 13:21; 2Sa 10:6 and had no relationship with anyone
else. The city was in a valley near Beth
Rehob.[m]
The Danites rebuilt the city and set-
18:29 [n] Ge 14:14 tled there. 29They named it Dan[n] after
[o] Jos 19:47; 1Ki 15:20 their forefather Dan, who was born to Israel—though the city used to be called
Laish.[o] 30There the Danites set up for
18:30 themselves the idols, and Jonathan son
[p] Ex 2:22; Jdg 17:3,5 of Gershom,[p] the son of Moses,[a] and his
sons were priests for the tribe of Dan
until the time of the captivity of the
18:31 land. 31They continued to use the idols
[q] Jdg 19:18 Micah had made, all the time the house
[r] Jos 18:1; Jer 7:14 of God[q] was in Shiloh.[r]

A Levite and His Concubine

19 In those days Israel had no
king.
Now a Levite who lived in a remote
19:1 [s] Jdg 18:1 area in the hill country of Ephraim[s] took
[t] Ru 1:1 a concubine from Bethlehem in Judah.[t]
2But she was unfaithful to him. She left
him and went back to her father's house
in Bethlehem, Judah. After she had been
there four months, 3her husband went
to her to persuade her to return. He had
with him his servant and two donkeys.
She took him into her father's house,
and when her father saw him, he gladly
welcomed him. 4His father-in-law, the
girl's father, prevailed upon him to stay;
so he remained with him three days, eat-
19:4 [u] Ex 32:6 ing and drinking,[u] and sleeping there.
5On the fourth day they got up early
and he prepared to leave, but the girl's
father said to his son-in-law, "Refresh
19:5 [v] ver 8; Ge 18:5 yourself[v] with something to eat; then
you can go." 6So the two of them sat
down to eat and drink together. Afterward the girl's father said, "Please stay
19:6 [w] ver 9,22; tonight and enjoy yourself."[w] 7And when
Jdg 16:25 the man got up to go, his father-in-law
persuaded him, so he stayed there that
night. 8On the morning of the fifth day,
when he rose to go, the girl's father said,
"Refresh yourself. Wait till afternoon!"
So the two of them ate together.
9Then when the man, with his concubine and his servant, got up to leave, his
father-in-law, the girl's father, said, "Now
look, it's almost evening. Spend the
night here; the day is nearly over. Stay
and enjoy yourself. Early tomorrow
morning you can get up and be on your
way home." 10But, unwilling to stay another night, the man left and went to-
ward Jebus[x] (that is, Jerusalem), with his 19:10 [x] Ge 10:16;
two saddled donkeys and his concubine. Jos 15:8; 1Ch 11:4-5
11When they were near Jebus and the
day was almost gone, the servant said to
his master, "Come, let's stop at this city 19:11
of the Jebusites[y] and spend the night." [y] Jos 3:10
12His master replied, "No. We won't
go into an alien city, whose people are
not Israelites. We will go on to Gibeah."
13He added, "Come, let's try to reach
Gibeah or Ramah[z] and spend the night 19:13
in one of those places." 14So they went [z] Jos 18:25
on, and the sun set as they neared Gibe-
ah in Benjamin.[a] 15There they stopped 19:14
to spend the night. They went and sat in [a] 1Sa 10:26; Isa 10:29
the city square,[b] but no one took them 19:15
into his home for the night. [b] Ge 19:2
16That evening[c] an old man from the 19:16
hill country of Ephraim,[d] who was living [c] Ps 104:23
in Gibeah (the men of the place were [d] ver 1
Benjamites), came in from his work in
the fields. 17When he looked and saw
the traveler in the city square, the old
man asked, "Where are you going? 19:17
Where did you come from?"[e] [e] Ge 29:4
18He answered, "We are on our way
from Bethlehem in Judah to a remote
area in the hill country of Ephraim
where I live. I have been to Bethlehem in
Judah and now I am going to the house
of the LORD.[f] No one has taken me into 19:18 [f] Jdg 18:31
his house. 19We have both straw and
fodder[g] for our donkeys and bread and 19:19 [g] Ge 24:25
wine[h] for ourselves your servants—me, [h] Ge 14:18
your maidservant, and the young man
with us. We don't need anything."
20"You are welcome at my house," the
old man said. "Let me supply whatever
you need. Only don't spend the night in
the square." 21So he took him into his
house and fed his donkeys. After they
had washed their feet, they had some- 19:21
thing to eat and drink.[i] [i] Ge 24:32-33; Lk 7:44
22While they were enjoying them- 19:22
selves,[j] some of the wicked men[k] of the [j] Jdg 16:25
city surrounded the house. Pounding on [k] Dt 13:13
the door, they shouted to the old man

[a] *30* An ancient Hebrew scribal tradition, some Septuagint manuscripts and Vulgate; Masoretic Text *Manasseh*

who owned the house, "Bring out the
19:22 [l] Ge 19:4-5; Jdg 20:5; Ro 1:26-27
man who came to your house so we can
have sex with him.[l]"
23 The owner of the house went out-
19:23 [m] Ge 19:6 [n] Ge 34:7; Lev 19:29; Dt 22:21; Jdg 20:6; 2Sa 13:12; Ro 1:27
side[m] and said to them, "No, my friends,
don't be so vile. Since this man is my
guest, don't do this disgraceful thing.[n]
24 Look, here is my virgin daughter,[o] and
his concubine. I will bring them out to
you now, and you can use them and do
19:24 [o] Ge 19:8; Dt 21:14
to them whatever you wish. But to this
man, don't do such a disgraceful thing."
25 But the men would not listen to
him. So the man took his concubine and
sent her outside to them, and they raped
19:25 [p] 1Sa 31:4
her and abused her[p] throughout the
night, and at dawn they let her go. 26 At
daybreak the woman went back to the
house where her master was staying, fell
down at the door and lay there until
daylight.
27 When her master got up in the
morning and opened the door of the
house and stepped out to continue on
his way, there lay his concubine, fallen in
the doorway of the house, with her
hands on the threshold. 28 He said to her,
"Get up; let's go." But there was no answer. Then the man put her on his donkey and set out for home.
29 When he reached home, he took a
19:29 [q] Ge 22:6 [r] Jdg 20:6; 1Sa 11:7
knife[q] and cut up his concubine, limb by
limb, into twelve parts and sent them
into all the areas of Israel.[r] 30 Everyone
who saw it said, "Such a thing has never
19:30 [s] Hos 9:9 [t] Jdg 20:7; Pr 13:10
been seen or done, not since the day the
Israelites came up out of Egypt.[s] Think
about it! Consider it! Tell us what to do![t]"

Israelites Fight the Benjamites

20 Then all the Israelites[u] from
20:1 [u] Jdg 21:5 [v] 1Sa 3:20; 2Sa 3:10; 1Ki 4:25 [w] 1Sa 11:7 [x] 1Sa 7:5
Dan to Beersheba[v] and from
the land of Gilead came out as one
man[w] and assembled[x] before the LORD
in Mizpah. 2 The leaders of all the people
of the tribes of Israel took their places in
the assembly of the people of God, four
20:2 [y] Jdg 8:10
hundred thousand soldiers[y] armed with
swords. 3 (The Benjamites heard that the
Israelites had gone up to Mizpah.) Then
the Israelites said, "Tell us how this awful thing happened."
4 So the Levite, the husband of the
murdered woman, said, "I and my con-
20:4 [z] Jos 15:57 [a] Jdg 19:15
cubine came to Gibeah[z] in Benjamin to
spend the night.[a] 5 During the night the
men of Gibeah came after me and sur-
rounded the house, intending to kill 20:5 [b] Jdg 19:22 [c] Jdg 19:25-26
me.[b] They raped my concubine, and she
died.[c] 6 I took my concubine, cut her into
pieces and sent one piece to each region 20:6 [d] Jdg 19:29 [e] Jos 7:15; Jdg 19:23
of Israel's inheritance,[d] because they
committed this lewd and disgraceful
act[e] in Israel. 7 Now, all you Israelites, 20:7 [f] Jdg 19:30
speak up and give your verdict.[f]"
8 All the people rose as one man, saying, "None of us will go home. No, not
one of us will return to his house. 9 But
now this is what we'll do to Gibeah: 20:9 [g] Lev 16:8
We'll go up against it as the lot directs.[g]
10 We'll take ten men out of every hundred from all the tribes of Israel, and a
hundred from a thousand, and a thousand from ten thousand, to get provisions for the army. Then, when the army
arrives at Gibeah[a] in Benjamin, it can
give them what they deserve for all this
vileness done in Israel." 11 So all the men
of Israel got together and united as one 20:11 [h] ver 1
man[h] against the city.
12 The tribes of Israel sent men
throughout the tribe of Benjamin, saying, "What about this awful crime that
was committed among you? 13 Now sur-
render those wicked men[i] of Gibeah so 20:13 [i] Dt 13:13; Jdg 19:22 [j] Dt 17:12
that we may put them to death and
purge the evil from Israel.[j]"
But the Benjamites would not listen
to their fellow Israelites. 14 From their
towns they came together at Gibeah to
fight against the Israelites. 15 At once the
Benjamites mobilized twenty-six thousand swordsmen from their towns, in
addition to seven hundred chosen men
from those living in Gibeah. 16 Among all
these soldiers there were seven hundred 20:16 [k] Jdg 3:15; 1Ch 12:2
chosen men who were left-handed,[k]
each of whom could sling a stone at a
hair and not miss.
17 Israel, apart from Benjamin, mustered four hundred thousand swordsmen, all of them fighting men.
18 The Israelites went up to Bethel[b] 20:18 [l] ver 26-27; Nu 27:21 [m] ver 23,28
and inquired of God.[l] They said, "Who
of us shall go first to fight[m] against the
Benjamites?"
The LORD replied, "Judah shall go
first."
19 The next morning the Israelites got
up and pitched camp near Gibeah. 20 The
men of Israel went out to fight the Ben-

[a] *10* One Hebrew manuscript; most Hebrew manuscripts *Geba,* a variant of *Gibeah* [b] *18* Or *to the house of God*; also in verse 26

jamites and took up battle positions
against them at Gibeah. 21The Ben-
20:21 jamites came out of Gibeah and cut
[n]ver 25 down twenty-two thousand Israelites[n]
on the battlefield that day. 22But the men
of Israel encouraged one another and
again took up their positions where they
had stationed themselves the first day.
23The Israelites went up and wept before
20:23 the LORD until evening,[o] and they in-
[o]Jos 7:6 [p]ver 18 quired of the LORD. They said, "Shall we
go up again to battle[p] against the Ben-
jamites, our brothers?"

The LORD answered, "Go up against
them."

24Then the Israelites drew near to
Benjamin the second day. 25This time,
when the Benjamites came out from
Gibeah to oppose them, they cut down
20:25 another eighteen thousand Israelites,[q]
[q]ver 21 all of them armed with swords.

26Then the Israelites, all the people,
went up to Bethel, and there they sat
20:26 weeping before the LORD.[r] They fasted
[r]ver 23
[s]Jdg 21:4 that day until evening and presented
burnt offerings and fellowship offerings[a] to the LORD.[s] 27And the Israelites
inquired of the LORD. (In those days the
20:27 ark of the covenant of God[t] was there,
[t]Jos 18:1 28with Phinehas son of Eleazar,[u] the son
20:28 of Aaron, ministering before it.)[v] They
[u]Jos 24:33
[v]Dt 18:5 asked, "Shall we go up again to battle
[w]Jdg 7:9 with Benjamin our brother, or not?"

The LORD responded, "Go, for tomorrow I will give them into your hands.[w]"

20:29 29Then Israel set an ambush[x] around
[x]Jos 8:2,4 Gibeah. 30They went up against the Benjamites on the third day and took up positions against Gibeah as they had done
before. 31The Benjamites came out to
20:31 meet them and were drawn away[y] from
[y]Jos 8:16 the city. They began to inflict casualties
on the Israelites as before, so that about
thirty men fell in the open field and on
the roads—the one leading to Bethel
and the other to Gibeah.

32While the Benjamites were saying,
20:32 "We are defeating them as before,"[z] the
[z]ver 39 Israelites were saying, "Let's retreat and
draw them away from the city to the
roads."

33All the men of Israel moved from
their places and took up positions at
Baal Tamar, and the Israelite ambush
20:33 charged out of its place[a] on the west[b] of
[a]Jos 8:19 Gibeah.[c] 34Then ten thousand of Israel's
finest men made a frontal attack on
Gibeah. The fighting was so heavy that
the Benjamites did not realize[b] how 20:34
near disaster was.[c] 35The LORD defeated [b]Jos 8:14 [c]Isa 47:11
Benjamin[d] before Israel, and on that day
the Israelites struck down 25,100 Ben- 20:35 [d]1Sa 9:21
jamites, all armed with swords. 36Then
the Benjamites saw that they were beat-
en.

Now the men of Israel had given way[e] 20:36
before Benjamin, because they relied on [e]Jos 8:15
the ambush they had set near Gibeah.
37The men who had been in ambush
made a sudden dash into Gibeah, spread 20:37
out and put the whole city to the sword.[f] [f]Jos 8:19
38The men of Israel had arranged with
the ambush that they should send up a
great cloud of smoke[g] from the city, 20:38 [g]Jos 8:20
39and then the men of Israel would turn
in the battle.

The Benjamites had begun to inflict
casualties on the men of Israel (about
thirty), and they said, "We are defeating
them as in the first battle."[h] 40But when 20:39
the column of smoke began to rise from [h]ver 32
the city, the Benjamites turned and
saw the smoke of the whole city going
up into the sky.[i] 41Then the men of Isra- 20:40
el turned on them, and the men of Ben- [i]Jos 8:20
jamin were terrified, because they realized that disaster had come upon them.
42So they fled before the Israelites in the
direction of the desert, but they could
not escape the battle. And the men of Israel who came out of the towns cut
them down there. 43They surrounded
the Benjamites, chased them and easily[d]
overran them in the vicinity of Gibeah
on the east. 44Eighteen thousand Ben-
jamites fell, all of them valiant fighters.[j] 20:44 [j]Ps 76:5
45As they turned and fled toward the
desert to the rock of Rimmon,[k] the Isra- 20:45 [k]Jos 15:32;
elites cut down five thousand men along Jdg 21:13
the roads. They kept pressing after the
Benjamites as far as Gidom and struck
down two thousand more.

46On that day twenty-five thousand
Benjamite swordsmen fell, all of them
valiant fighters. 47But six hundred men
turned and fled into the desert to the
rock of Rimmon, where they stayed four
months. 48The men of Israel went back
to Benjamin and put all the towns to
the sword, including the animals and

[a] 26 Traditionally *peace offerings* [b] 33 Some Septuagint manuscripts and Vulgate; the meaning of the Hebrew for this word is uncertain.
[c] 33 Hebrew *Geba,* a variant of *Gibeah* [d] 43 The meaning of the Hebrew for this word is uncertain.

DISCOVERY 63

OUR OWN THING

Israel failed to recognize the all-faithful, almighty and all-loving God as her king, and this rejection must have broken God's heart. Israel was a nation blessed by God, enjoying the good fruit of the promised land. But the people determined that they no longer required divine intervention in their lives (see Judges 17:6; 18:1; 19:1).

Israel had been familiar with many kings, so why would God's chosen people refuse to acknowledge God as their King? They knew firsthand what it was to be governed by ungodly, even cruel, kings—the pharaoh of Egypt, the king of Jericho, the kings of the Philistine nations and many more. Thoughts of these kings brought only horrible memories of war, death and captivity. God Almighty, the Most High (Deuteronomy 32:8), was so different: He was their Protector, their Provider and the ultimate Promise Keeper. But in return for his blessings the people responded with a nonchalant "No thanks, God; we will do it our own way." And they did just that, worshiping idols and deteriorating into an adulterous nation (see Judges 17—20).

Israel without God acted like a house bursting with 12 young children with no parents or other authority figures in attendance: "Everyone did as he saw fit" (Judges 21:25). Imagine living in a community like that—what a nightmare! No law or order, no justice or concern for others. The confusion and pandemonium boded disaster for everyone.

Human beings have always wanted to direct their own course, but throughout the ages God has had a better plan. Even though he had reluctantly allowed Israel her own human king (Deuteronomy 17:14–15), God has always desired to reign over his chosen people (1 Samuel 12:12–15). So after the downfall of all of the human kings and kingdoms, God sent his Son Jesus to be the King of Israel. Jesus entered Jerusalem astride a donkey, indicating that he was coming as the gentle King of peace. Shortly thereafter, however, King Jesus was beaten and crucified by his own people. His rightful title was even used as a mockery when his enemies hung a sign above his head: "THIS IS JESUS, THE KING OF THE JEWS" (Matthew 27:37–44).

Why would people reject Jesus? After all, he had performed miracles, taught the truth of God and proven that he was God's Promised One by fulfilling all of the prophecies concerning the Messiah. The answer is simple: The people still wanted to do as they saw fit. The same answer applies when we reject God's word to us. We so often prefer to do our own thing, even if the result is chaos in our lives—and we are breaking God's heart. Will we have the courage to call an end to pursuing our own will and seek to do God's will?

***Self-Discovery:** When did you last advise the Lord in effect that, although you were thankful for his offer to help, you were perfectly capable of handling the problem yourself? Looking back, did you feel good about yourself because of your tenacity and self-sufficiency? How do you feel about that same situation now?*

GO TO DISCOVERY 64 ON PAGE 335

20:48 everything else they found. All the
[l]Jdg 21:23 towns they came across they set on fire.[l]

Wives for the Benjamites

21:1 21 The men of Israel had taken an
[m]Jos 9:18 oath[m] at Mizpah:[n] "Not one of
[n]Jdg 20:1 us will give[o] his daughter in marriage to
[o]ver 7,18 a Benjamite."
2The people went to Bethel,[a] where
they sat before God until evening, raising their voices and weeping bitterly.
3"O LORD, the God of Israel," they cried,
"why has this happened to Israel? Why
should one tribe be missing from Israel
today?"
21:4 4Early the next day the people built an
[p]Jdg 20:26; altar and presented burnt offerings and
2Sa 24:25 fellowship offerings.[b][p]
21:5 5Then the Israelites asked, "Who from
[q]Jdg 5:23; 20:1 all the tribes of Israel[q] has failed to assemble before the LORD?" For they had
taken a solemn oath that anyone who
failed to assemble before the LORD at
Mizpah should certainly be put to death.
6Now the Israelites grieved for their
brothers, the Benjamites. "Today one
tribe is cut off from Israel," they said.
7"How can we provide wives for those
21:7 who are left, since we have taken an
[r]ver 1 oath[r] by the LORD not to give them any
of our daughters in marriage?" 8Then
they asked, "Which one of the tribes of
Israel failed to assemble before the LORD
21:8 at Mizpah?" They discovered that no
[s]1Sa 11:1; 31:11 one from Jabesh Gilead[s] had come to
the camp for the assembly. 9For when
they counted the people, they found
that none of the people of Jabesh Gilead
were there.
10So the assembly sent twelve thousand fighting men with instructions to
go to Jabesh Gilead and put to the sword
those living there, including the women
and children. 11"This is what you are to
21:11 do," they said. "Kill every male and every
[t]Nu 31:17-18 woman who is not a virgin.[t]" 12They
found among the people living in Jabesh
Gilead four hundred young women who
21:12 had never slept with a man, and they
[u]Jos 18:1 took them to the camp at Shiloh[u] in Canaan.

13Then the whole assembly sent an of-
fer of peace[v] to the Benjamites at the 21:13 [v]Dt 20:10
rock of Rimmon.[w] 14So the Benjamites [w]Jdg 20:47
returned at that time and were given the
women of Jabesh Gilead who had been
spared. But there were not enough for all
of them.
15The people grieved for Benjamin,[x] 21:15
because the LORD had made a gap in the [x]ver 6
tribes of Israel. 16And the elders of the
assembly said, "With the women of Benjamin destroyed, how shall we provide
wives for the men who are left? 17The
Benjamite survivors must have heirs,"
they said, "so that a tribe of Israel will
not be wiped out. 18We can't give them
our daughters as wives, since we Israelites have taken this oath: 'Cursed be
anyone who gives[y] a wife to a Benjamite.' 21:18
19But look, there is the annual festival of [y]ver 1
the LORD in Shiloh,[z] to the north of 21:19
Bethel, and east of the road that goes [z]Jos 18:1; Jdg 18:31;
from Bethel to Shechem, and to the 1Sa 1:3
south of Lebonah."
20So they instructed the Benjamites,
saying, "Go and hide in the vineyards
21and watch. When the girls of Shiloh
come out to join in the dancing,[a] then 21:21 [a]Ex 15:20;
rush from the vineyards and each of you Jdg 11:34
seize a wife from the girls of Shiloh and
go to the land of Benjamin. 22When their
fathers or brothers complain to us, we
will say to them, 'Do us a kindness by
helping them, because we did not get
wives for them during the war, and you
are innocent, since you did not give[b] 21:22
your daughters to them.' " [b]ver 1,18
23So that is what the Benjamites did.
While the girls were dancing, each man
caught one and carried her off to be his
wife. Then they returned to their inheritance and rebuilt the towns and settled 21:23
in them.[c] [c]Jdg 20:48
24At that time the Israelites left that
place and went home to their tribes and
clans, each to his own inheritance.
25In those days Israel had no king; 21:25 [d]Dt 12:8;
everyone did as he saw fit.[d] Jdg 17:6; 18:1; 19:1

[a]2 Or *to the house of God* [b]4 Traditionally *peace offerings*

Jesus in Ruth Understanding the role of the kinsman-redeemer is key to understanding the book of Ruth. The concept of a redeemer paying a ransom for someone's life is mentioned 23 times. A kinsman-redeemer was an influential relative to whom members of the extended family could turn for help in time of need. In the event of the death of a married man in the family, the closest relative was given the opportunity to purchase back any family property that had changed ownership and to marry the widow in order to raise children in the name of her dead husband. The same word translated "kinsman-redeemer" was also used to prophesy the coming of the Messiah: "The Redeemer will come to Zion" (Isaiah 59:20). Jesus is our close relative who came to buy us back into God's family. In the New Testament the concept is reflected in the various words for *redeem*, which suggest paying a ransom, making a purchase or saving from loss (Luke 1:68; Galatians 3:13–14; Ephesians 1:7–8; Titus 2:14; 1 Peter 1:18–21).

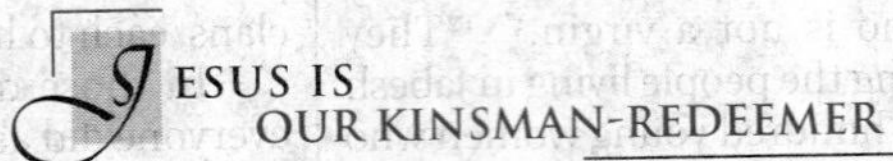

Why might Matthew have included just four mothers, Tamar, Rabab, Ruth and Bathsheba, in his genealogy of Jesus? (Matthew 1:3–6)

♦ *All four of these women were, from a Jewish standpoint, foreigners. Matthew was probably highlighting the fact that Jesus had Gentile blood, an early implication that the promise of salvation was universal in scope.*

In what way was Ruth, a Moabitess, qualified for participation in the coming kingdom of God?

♦ *Ruth strikingly exemplifies the truth that participation in the coming kingdom of God is decided, not by blood and birth, but by the conformity of one's life to the will of God through the "obedience that comes from faith" (Romans 1:5). Her place in the ancestry of David signifies that all nations will be represented in the kingdom of David's greater Son.*

Naomi and Ruth

1 In the days when the judges ruled,[a][a] there was a famine in the land,[b] and a man from Bethlehem in Judah, together with his wife and two sons, went to live for a while in the country of Moab.[c] 2The man's name was Elimelech, his wife's name Naomi, and the names of his two sons were Mahlon and Kilion. They were Ephrathites from Bethlehem,[d] Judah. And they went to Moab and lived there.

3Now Elimelech, Naomi's husband, died, and she was left with her two sons. 4They married Moabite women, one named Orpah and the other Ruth.[e] After they had lived there about ten years, 5both Mahlon and Kilion also died, and Naomi was left without her two sons and her husband.

6When she heard in Moab that the LORD had come to the aid of his people[f] by providing food[g] for them, Naomi and her daughters-in-law prepared to return home from there. 7With her two daughters-in-law she left the place where she had been living and set out on the road that would take them back to the land of Judah.

8Then Naomi said to her two daughters-in-law, "Go back, each of you, to your mother's home. May the LORD show kindness[h] to you, as you have shown to your dead[i] and to me. 9May the LORD grant that each of you will find rest[j] in the home of another husband."

Then she kissed them and they wept aloud 10and said to her, "We will go back with you to your people."

11But Naomi said, "Return home, my daughters. Why would you come with me? Am I going to have any more sons, who could become your husbands?[k] 12Return home, my daughters; I am too old to have another husband. Even if I thought there was still hope for me—even if I had a husband tonight and then gave birth to sons— 13would you wait until they grew up? Would you remain unmarried for them? No, my daughters. It is more bitter for me than for you, because the LORD's hand has gone out against me![l]"

14At this they wept again. Then Orpah kissed her mother-in-law[m] good-by, but Ruth clung to her.[n]

15"Look," said Naomi, "your sister-in-law is going back to her people and her gods.[o] Go back with her."

16But Ruth replied, "Don't urge me to leave you[p] or to turn back from you. Where you go I will go, and where you stay I will stay. Your people will be my people and your God my God.[q] 17Where you die I will die, and there I will be buried. May the LORD deal with me, be it ever so severely,[r] if anything but death separates you and me." 18When Naomi realized that Ruth was determined to go with her, she stopped urging her.[s]

19So the two women went on until they came to Bethlehem. When they arrived in Bethlehem, the whole town was stirred[t] because of them, and the women exclaimed, "Can this be Naomi?"

20"Don't call me Naomi,[b]" she told them. "Call me Mara,[c] because the Almighty[d][u] has made my life very bitter.[v] 21I went away full, but the LORD has brought me back empty.[w] Why call me Naomi? The LORD has afflicted[e] me; the Almighty has brought misfortune upon me."

22So Naomi returned from Moab accompanied by Ruth the Moabitess, her daughter-in-law, arriving in Bethlehem as the barley harvest[x] was beginning.[y]

Ruth Meets Boaz

2 Now Naomi had a relative[z] on her husband's side, from the clan of Elimelech,[a] a man of standing, whose name was Boaz.[b]

2And Ruth the Moabitess said to Naomi, "Let me go to the fields and pick up the leftover grain[c] behind anyone in whose eyes I find favor."

Naomi said to her, "Go ahead, my daughter." 3So she went out and began to glean in the fields behind the harvesters. As it turned out, she found herself working in a field belonging to Boaz, who was from the clan of Elimelech.

4Just then Boaz arrived from Bethlehem and greeted the harvesters, "The LORD be with you![d]"

"The LORD bless you![e]" they called back.

5Boaz asked the foreman of his harvesters, "Whose young woman is that?"

6The foreman replied, "She is the Mo-

1:1 [a]Jdg 2:16-18 [b]Ge 12:10; Ps 105:16 [c]Jdg 3:30
1:2 [d]Ge 35:19
1:4 [e]Mt 1:5
1:6 [f]Ex 4:31; Jer 29:10; Zep 2:7 [g]Ps 132:15; Mt 6:11
1:8 [h]Ru 2:20; 2Ti 1:16 [i]ver 5
1:9 [j]Ru 3:1
1:11 [k]Ge 38:11; Dt 25:5
1:13 [l]Jdg 2:15; Job 4:5; 19:21; Ps 32:4
1:14 [m]Ru 2:11 [n]Pr 17:17; 18:24
1:15 [o]Jos 24:14; Jdg 11:24
1:16 [p]2Ki 2:2 [q]Ru 2:11,12
1:17 [r]1Sa 3:17; 25:22; 2Sa 19:13; 2Ki 6:31
1:18 [s]Ac 21:14
1:19 [t]Mt 21:10
1:20 [u]Ex 6:3 [v]ver 13; Job 6:4
1:21 [w]Job 1:21
1:22 [x]Ex 9:31; Ru 2:23 [y]2Sa 21:9
2:1 [z]Ru 3:2,12 [a]Ru 1:2 [b]Ru 4:21
2:2 [c]ver 7; Lev 19:9; 23:22; Dt 24:19
2:4 [d]Jdg 6:12; Lk 1:28; 2Th 3:16 [e]Ps 129:7-8

[a] *1* Traditionally *judged* [b] *20* *Naomi* means *pleasant*; also in verse 21. [c] *20* *Mara* means *bitter.* [d] *20* Hebrew *Shaddai*; also in verse 21 [e] *21* Or *has testified against*

2:6 abitess[f] who came back from Moab with
f Ru 1:22 Naomi. 7 She said, 'Please let me glean
and gather among the sheaves behind
the harvesters.' She went into the field
and has worked steadily from morning
till now, except for a short rest in the
shelter."
8 So Boaz said to Ruth, "My daughter,
listen to me. Don't go and glean in another field and don't go away from here.
Stay here with my servant girls. 9 Watch
the field where the men are harvesting,
and follow along after the girls. I have
told the men not to touch you. And
whenever you are thirsty, go and get a
drink from the water jars the men have
filled."
10 At this, she bowed down with her
2:10 g 1Sa 25:23 face to the ground.[g] She exclaimed,
h Ps 41:1 "Why have I found such favor in your
i Dt 15:3 eyes that you notice me[h]—a foreigner?[i]"
11 Boaz replied, "I've been told all
about what you have done for your
2:11 mother-in-law[j] since the death of your
j Ru 1:14 k Ru 1:16-17 husband—how you left your father and
mother and your homeland and came to
live with a people you did not know before.[k] 12 May the LORD repay you for what
2:12 you have done. May you be richly re-
l 1Sa 24:19 warded by the LORD,[l] the God of Israel,
m Ps 17:8; 36:7; 57:1; 61:4; 63:7; under whose wings[m] you have come to
91:4 n Ru 1:16 take refuge.[n]"

13 "May I continue to find favor in your
eyes, my lord," she said. "You have given
me comfort and have spoken kindly to
your servant—though I do not have the
standing of one of your servant girls."
14 At mealtime Boaz said to her,
"Come over here. Have some bread and
dip it in the wine vinegar."
When she sat down with the harvesters, he offered her some roasted
grain. She ate all she wanted and had
some left over.[o] 15 As she got up to glean, 2:14 o ver 18
Boaz gave orders to his men, "Even if she
gathers among the sheaves, don't em-
barrass her. 16 Rather, pull out some stalks
for her from the bundles and leave them
for her to pick up, and don't rebuke her."
17 So Ruth gleaned in the field until
evening. Then she threshed the barley
she had gathered, and it amounted to
about an ephah.[a] 18 She carried it back to
town, and her mother-in-law saw how
much she had gathered. Ruth also
brought out and gave her what she had
left over[p] after she had eaten enough. 2:18 p ver 14
19 Her mother-in-law asked her,
"Where did you glean today? Where did
you work? Blessed be the man who took
notice of you![q]" 2:19 q ver 10; Ps 41:1
Then Ruth told her mother-in-law
about the one at whose place she had
been working. "The name of the man I
worked with today is Boaz," she said.
20 "The LORD bless him!" Naomi said to
her daughter-in-law. "He has not
stopped showing his kindness[r] to the 2:20 r Ru 3:10; 2Sa 2:5; Pr 17:17
living and the dead." She added, "That
man is our close relative; he is one of our s Ru 3:9,12; 4:1, 14
kinsman-redeemers.[s]"
21 Then Ruth the Moabitess said, "He
even said to me, 'Stay with my workers
until they finish harvesting all my grain.' "
22 Naomi said to Ruth her daughter-in-
law, "It will be good for you, my daughter,
to go with his girls, because in someone
else's field you might be harmed."
23 So Ruth stayed close to the servant
girls of Boaz to glean until the barley
and wheat harvests[t] were finished. And 2:23 t Dt 16:9
she lived with her mother-in-law.

Ruth and Boaz at the Threshing Floor

3 One day Naomi her mother-in-
law said to her, "My daughter,
should I not try to find a home[b][u] for you, 3:1 u Ru 1:9

a 17 That is, probably about 3/5 bushel (about 22 liters) *b 1* Hebrew *find rest* (see Ruth 1:9)

JESUS AND YOU

JUST WHEN WE NEED HIM

Ruth met Boaz, and the "romance of redemption" began (Ruth 2). Ruth, desperately poor, gathered what was left in the fields after the grain had been harvested. Boaz noticed her and learned from his foreman that she had come back from Moab with Naomi, her mother-in-law. He invited Ruth to continue coming to his field rather than gleaning in another one. Overwhelmed by his kindness, Ruth commented twice on the "favor" (or grace) Boaz had extended to her. Boaz then instructed his farmhands to deliberately drop some stalks for her from their bundles of grain. The manner in which Boaz treated Ruth depicts for us how our Redeemer, Jesus, meets us in life. We grasp at the scraps offered by the world, but he truly meets our needs and offers so much more than we could ever have imagined through the display of his grace in and through us (2 Corinthians 9:7–11; Ephesians 2:4–10).

DISCOVERY 64

THE KINSMAN-REDEEMER

One of the great love stories in the Bible is that of Ruth—an unlikely subject because she was not an Israelite but an immigrant from Moab. But God chose her to become a part of his family. In fact, she became the great-grandmother of King David and part of Jesus' family line.

Ruth's story actually begins when a family from Israel—Elimelech, his wife Naomi and their two sons—emigrated to Moab during a famine. Elimelech died there, and the two sons married Moabitesses named Orpah and Ruth. Eventually the two sons also died and Naomi decided to return to Bethlehem. Ruth insisted on accompanying her mother-in-law and would accept no argument to the contrary (Ruth 1:16–17).

Naomi and Ruth arrived in Bethlehem destitute, which meant that Ruth would be compelled to glean leftover grain during the harvest so that they would have something to eat. While she was laboring in his field she met Boaz, who praised her strong character: "May the LORD repay you for what you have done. May you be richly rewarded by the LORD, the God of Israel, under whose wings you have come to take refuge" (Ruth 2:12). Boaz, apparently quite taken with Ruth, began in secret to help her.

In that society the law provided an opportunity for a man's possessions and land to be passed down to his widow, provided the dead husband's nearest relative would purchase the estate and agree to marry her. If the nearest relative could not or would not "buy back" the widow, then another close relative could exercise this right. Such a person was known as a "kinsman-redeemer." Boaz was Naomi's close relative but not the closest, so he called a meeting with the relative having the first option to be the kinsman-redeemer. This relative had no desire to reclaim the property, so Boaz was free to act. He purchased all of Elimelech's property and married Ruth. Later they had a son named Obed, who in turn fathered Jesse, who had a son named David—God's chosen king for his people (Ruth 4:18–22). As the great-grandparents of David, Boaz and Ruth became a vital link in the line of the Messiah.

The word *redemption*, which refers to the process of buying back something as one's own when a debt is owed, appears 23 times in the book of Ruth. The story of Boaz provides an early picture of the salvation God was planning to provide for the human race through his promised Messiah. Jesus Christ identified with us by assuming our humanity, just as Boaz claimed Ruth as his own. And, like Boaz, Jesus paid a heavy price for our redemption: "He has rescued us from the dominion of darkness and brought us into the kingdom of the Son he loves, in whom we have redemption, the forgiveness of sins" (Colossians 1:13–14). The grand theme of the Bible is captured in this awesome statement: God redeemed our fallen race through his own sacrifice—Jesus, his Son. He is our kinsman-redeemer.

Self-Discovery: *Think about Jesus' sacrifice on the cross and about the incredible price he paid for your salvation. Then honestly answer the question, based on what God has clearly told you in his Word: "How much am I really worth to God?"*

GO TO DISCOVERY 65 ON PAGE 337

where you will be well provided for? 2Is
3:2 v Dt 25:5-10; Ru 2:1 not Boaz, with whose servant girls you
have been, a kinsman[v] of ours? Tonight
he will be winnowing barley on the
threshing floor. 3Wash and perfume
3:3 w 2Sa 14:2 yourself,[w] and put on your best clothes.
Then go down to the threshing floor, but
don't let him know you are there until he
has finished eating and drinking. 4When
he lies down, note the place where he is
lying. Then go and uncover his feet and
lie down. He will tell you what to do."
3:5 x Eph 6:1; Col 3:20 5"I will do whatever you say,"[x] Ruth
answered. 6So she went down to the
threshing floor and did everything her
mother-in-law told her to do.
7When Boaz had finished eating and
3:7 y Jdg 19:6,9,22; 2Sa 13:28; 1Ki 21:7; Est 1:10 drinking and was in good spirits,[y] he
went over to lie down at the far end of
the grain pile. Ruth approached quietly,
uncovered his feet and lay down. 8In the
middle of the night something startled
the man, and he turned and discovered
a woman lying at his feet.
9"Who are you?" he asked.
"I am your servant Ruth," she said.
3:9 z Eze 16:8 a ver 12; Ru 2:20 "Spread the corner of your garment[z] over
me, since you are a kinsman-redeemer.[a]"
10"The LORD bless you, my daughter,"
he replied. "This kindness is greater
than that which you showed earlier: You
have not run after the younger men,
whether rich or poor. 11And now, my
daughter, don't be afraid. I will do for
you all you ask. All my fellow townsmen
know that you are a woman of noble
3:11 b Pr 12:4; 31:10 character.[b] 12Although it is true that I
am near of kin, there is a kinsman-re-
3:12 c ver 9 d Ru 4:1 deemer[c] nearer than[d] I. 13Stay here for
the night, and in the morning if he
3:13 e Dt 25:5; Ru 4:5; Mt 22:24 f Jdg 8:19; Jer 4:2 wants to redeem,[e] good; let him redeem.
But if he is not willing, as surely as the
LORD lives[f] I will do it. Lie here until
morning."
14So she lay at his feet until morning,
but got up before anyone could be recognized; and he said, "Don't let it be
known that a woman came to the
3:14 g Ro 14:16; 2Co 8:21 threshing floor."[g]
15He also said, "Bring me the shawl
you are wearing and hold it out." When
she did so, he poured into it six measures of barley and put it on her. Then
he[a] went back to town.
16When Ruth came to her mother-in-
law, Naomi asked, "How did it go, my
daughter?"

Then she told her everything Boaz
had done for her 17and added, "He gave
me these six measures of barley, saying,
'Don't go back to your mother-in-law
empty-handed.'"
18Then Naomi said, "Wait, my daughter, until you find out what happens. For
the man will not rest until the matter is 3:18 h Ps 37:3-5
settled today."[h]

Boaz Marries Ruth

4 Meanwhile Boaz went up to the
town gate and sat there. When
the kinsman-redeemer he had men- 4:1 i Ru 3:12
tioned[i] came along, Boaz said, "Come
over here, my friend, and sit down." So
he went over and sat down.
2Boaz took ten of the elders[j] of the 4:2 j 1Ki 21:8; Pr 31:23
town and said, "Sit here," and they did
so. 3Then he said to the kinsman-
redeemer, "Naomi, who has come back
from Moab, is selling the piece of land
that belonged to our brother Elimelech.
4I thought I should bring the matter to
your attention and suggest that you buy
it in the presence of these seated here
and in the presence of the elders of my
people. If you will redeem it, do so. But if
you[b] will not, tell me, so I will know. For 4:4 k Lev 25:25; Jer 32:7-8
no one has the right to do it except you,[k]
and I am next in line."
"I will redeem it," he said.
5Then Boaz said, "On the day you buy
the land from Naomi and from Ruth the
Moabitess, you acquire[c] the dead man's 4:5 l Ge 38:8; Dt 25:5-6; Ru 3:13; Mt 22:24
widow, in order to maintain the name of
the dead with his property."[l]
6At this, the kinsman-redeemer said,
"Then I cannot redeem[m] it because I 4:6 m Lev 25:25; Ru 3:13
might endanger my own estate. You re-
deem it yourself. I cannot do it."
7(Now in earlier times in Israel, for the
redemption and transfer of property to
become final, one party took off his sandal and gave it to the other. This was the
method of legalizing transactions in Is- 4:7 n Dt 25:7-9
rael.)[n]
8So the kinsman-redeemer said to
Boaz, "Buy it yourself." And he removed
his sandal.
9Then Boaz announced to the elders
and all the people, "Today you are

a 15 Most Hebrew manuscripts; many Hebrew manuscripts, Vulgate and Syriac *she* *b 4* Many Hebrew manuscripts, Septuagint, Vulgate and Syriac; most Hebrew manuscripts *he*
c 5 Hebrew; Vulgate and Syriac *Naomi, you acquire Ruth the Moabitess,*

DISCOVERY 65

All Peoples Will Be Blessed

From the beginning God had selected the nation of Israel as his own people, not because the Israelites deserved this honor (see Deuteronomy 7:6–10) but simply because God was exercising his prerogative to choose (Romans 9:10–15). But by electing Israel he was not rejecting every other nation. It has always been God's plan that his own people would introduce him to others so that all of humanity would have an opportunity to know the God of love.

The Jewish people trace their lineage back to Abraham and God's covenant with him. God promised that Israel would inherit land and become a great nation. Those who blessed Abraham and his descendants would be blessed by God, while any who cursed Abraham and his descendants would be cursed by God. And God promised that "all peoples on earth will be blessed through you" (Genesis 12:1–3).

In the New Testament Jesus said essentially the same thing. He referred to himself as the good shepherd (John 10:14) who cares for his sheep—those who put their trust in him and learn to walk with him. And then he said something remarkable: "I have other sheep that are not of this sheep pen. I must bring them also. They too will listen to my voice, and there shall be one flock and one shepherd" (John 10:16). The sheep pen referred to the Jewish people, but Jesus was telling his listeners that he would bring in non-Jews as well to form a new, all-encompassing family, the church.

The apostle Paul was a devout Jew, yet he understood that God was calling him to bring the Good News of Jesus to others. God announced that "this man [Paul] is my chosen instrument to carry my name before the Gentiles and their kings and before the people of Israel" (Acts 9:15; Galatians 1:11–17). Anyone who believes in Jesus becomes engrafted into God's family. Just as Boaz married a Gentile bride (Ruth 4), so Jesus' bride, the church, embraces Gentile believers. Both Jews and Gentiles who trust him are included in God's blessing: "There is neither Jew nor Greek, slave nor free, male nor female, for you are all one in Christ Jesus. If you belong to Christ, then you are Abraham's seed, and heirs according to the promise" (Galatians 3:28–29).

Jesus himself stated this truth in simple, straightforward language in John 3:16–17: "For God so loved the world that he gave his one and only Son, that whoever believes in him shall not perish but have eternal life. For God did not send his Son into the world to condemn the world, but to save the world through him."

Self-Discovery: *Try to picture yourself as a "chosen instrument" to carry God's name to others. You are, you know! Are there some specific ways you can share the love of Jesus with those God chooses to place in your path this week?*

GO TO DISCOVERY 66 ON PAGE 342

witnesses that I have bought from Naomi all the property of Elimelech, Kilion
and Mahlon. 10I have also acquired Ruth
the Moabitess, Mahlon's widow, as my
wife, in order to maintain the name of
the dead with his property, so that his
name will not disappear from among his
4:10 [o]Dt 25:6 family or from the town records.[o] Today
you are witnesses!"
4:11 11Then the elders and all those at the
[p]Dt 25:9 gate said, "We are witnesses.[p] May the
[q]Ps 127:3; 128:3 [r]Ge 35:16 LORD make the woman who is coming
into your home like Rachel and Leah,[q]
who together built up the house of Israel. May you have standing in Ephrathah[r]
and be famous in Bethlehem. 12Through
the offspring the LORD gives you by this
4:12 young woman, may your family be like
[s]ver 18; Ge 38:29 that of Perez,[s] whom Tamar bore to Judah."

The Genealogy of David

13So Boaz took Ruth and she became
4:13 [t]Ge 29:31; 33:5; Ru 3:11 his wife. Then he went to her, and the
LORD enabled her to conceive,[t] and she
gave birth to a son. 14The women[u] said 4:14 [u]Lk 1:58
to Naomi: "Praise be to the LORD, who
this day has not left you without a kinsman-redeemer. May he become famous
throughout Israel! 15He will renew your
life and sustain you in your old age. For
your daughter-in-law, who loves you and 4:15
who is better to you than seven sons,[v] [v]Ru 1:16-17; 2:11-12; 1Sa 1:8
has given him birth."

16Then Naomi took the child, laid him
in her lap and cared for him. 17The
women living there said, "Naomi has a 4:17
son." And they named him Obed. He was [w]ver 22; 1Sa 16:1,18;
the father of Jesse,[w] the father of David. 1Ch 2:12,13

18This, then, is the family line of 4:18
Perez[x]: [x]Mt 1:3-6

Perez was the father of Hezron,
19 Hezron the father of Ram, 4:19
Ram the father of Amminadab,[y] [y]Ex 6:23
20 Amminadab the father of Nahshon,
Nahshon the father of Salmon,[a]
21 Salmon the father of Boaz,[z] 4:21 [z]Ru 2:1
Boaz the father of Obed,
22 Obed the father of Jesse,
and Jesse the father of David.

[a] 20 A few Hebrew manuscripts, some Septuagint manuscripts and Vulgate (see also verse 21 and Septuagint of 1 Chron. 2:11); most Hebrew manuscripts *Salma*

JESUS FOCUS

TEN GENERATIONS LATER

The book of Ruth ends with the account of the birth of her son, Obed, and lists the ten generations from Perez (the illegitimate son of Judah and Tamar, see Genesis 38:1–30) to David (Ruth 4:18–22). Although God had promised that the Messiah would come from Judah's family (Genesis 49:9–10), the law did not allow the descendant of an illegitimate child to lead God's people until the tenth generation (Deuteronomy 23:2). This record of the family line would answer any objection that might have been raised regarding David's rightful claim to the throne. Jesus issued from the same family line, and both Tamar and Ruth are mentioned in his genealogy (Matthew 1:3,5). Jesus, God's only Son, was sinless, yet God the Father used sinful, ordinary people to carry on the family line into which he would one day be born as the great "Son of David" (Matthew 1:2) who would fulfill all prophecy and redeem his people from bondage to sin.

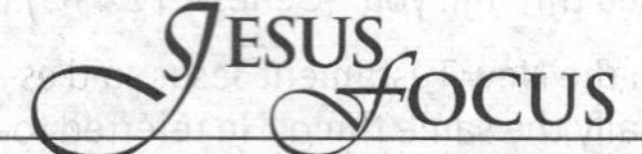

LITTLE TOWN OF BETHLEHEM

Bethlehem ("house of bread") was a small and unremarkable Judean village five miles south of Jerusalem. But it is one of the most significant loactions in the Old Testament. Jacob's wife Rachel died in Bethlehem (Genesis 35:19). Ruth and Boaz met there and became parents in the line of the Messiah. David, their great-grandson, was born there (1 Samuel 16:1), and Micah, the prophet, predicted that the Messiah would be born there (Micah 5:2). Both Matthew 2 and Luke 2 record the spectacular events related to Jesus' birth when that prediction was fulfilled. It was in the little town with such a rich history that the events of the Christmas story had their origin a thousand years before the time of Christ.

1 SAMUEL

Does God's Spirit leave people today as he left Saul? (1 Samuel 16:14; see 1 Samuel 10:10)

- *The presence of the Holy Spirit in Old Testament times had nothing to do with salvation, only indicating that a person had been empowered for service. Today, the Spirit lives in everyone who believes in Jesus. He dwells permanently, according to some (John 14:17); conditionally, according to others (Hebrews 6:4–6).*

Why did David lie to the priest? (1 Samuel 21:2)

- *David's life was on the line, and he may have been trying to protect Ahimelech from any accusation of involvement in his escape from Saul. His desire to preserve another human life took precedence over the commitment to tell the truth. It is interesting that Jesus later cited the incident of David's request for bread (verse 3) to illustrate the principle that human need takes priority over ceremonial law (Luke 6:3–4).*

Jesus in 1 Samuel The book of 1 Samuel teaches us what it means to be the "LORD's anointed" (1 Samuel 16:6). Anointing of priests, kings and prophets suggested that they had been consecrated by God for a special function and endowed by him with power to carry out that task. Essentially, the act of anointing someone implied that God had chosen, blessed and approved the person for special service. The three offices of prophet, priest and king come together in the Messiah, who embodied the fulfillment of a long succession of anointed prophets, priests and kings.

David was anointed by God as Israel's king, and "the Spirit of the LORD came upon [him] in power" (1 Samuel 16:13). As the first king in the Messiah's family line, David furnished an early picture of Jesus. Jesus Christ is the One whom God anointed—his promised Messiah, filled with the empowerment of the Holy Spirit to carry out his ministry (Luke 4:18–21), destined to reign on David's throne forever (see Luke 1:32).

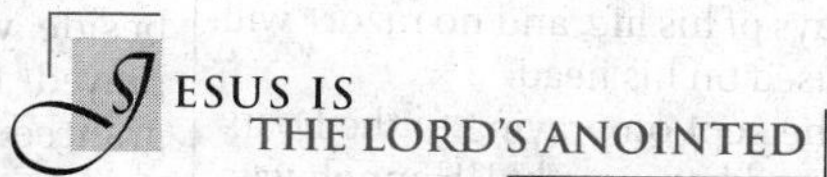
JESUS IS
THE LORD'S ANOINTED

The Birth of Samuel

1 There was a certain man from Ramathaim, a Zuphite[a] from the hill country[a] of Ephraim, whose name was Elkanah[b] son of Jeroham, the son of Elihu, the son of Tohu, the son of Zuph, an Ephraimite. 2 He had two wives;[c] one was called Hannah and the other Peninnah. Peninnah had children, but Hannah had none.

3 Year after year[d] this man went up from his town to worship[e] and sacrifice to the LORD Almighty at Shiloh,[f] where Hophni and Phinehas, the two sons of Eli, were priests of the LORD. 4 Whenever the day came for Elkanah to sacrifice,[g] he would give portions of the meat to his wife Peninnah and to all her sons and daughters. 5 But to Hannah he gave a double portion because he loved her, and the LORD had closed her womb.[h] 6 And because the LORD had closed her womb, her rival kept provoking her in order to irritate her.[i] 7 This went on year after year. Whenever Hannah went up to the house of the LORD, her rival provoked her till she wept and would not eat. 8 Elkanah her husband would say to her, "Hannah, why are you weeping? Why don't you eat? Why are you downhearted? Don't I mean more to you than ten sons?[j]"

9 Once when they had finished eating and drinking in Shiloh, Hannah stood up. Now Eli the priest was sitting on a chair by the doorpost of the LORD's temple.[b k] 10 In bitterness of soul[l] Hannah wept much and prayed to the LORD. 11 And she made a vow, saying, "O LORD Almighty, if you will only look upon your servant's misery and remember[m] me, and not forget your servant but give her a son, then I will give him to the LORD for all the days of his life, and no razor[n] will ever be used on his head."

12 As she kept on praying to the LORD, Eli observed her mouth. 13 Hannah was praying in her heart, and her lips were moving but her voice was not heard. Eli thought she was drunk 14 and said to her, "How long will you keep on getting drunk? Get rid of your wine."

15 "Not so, my lord," Hannah replied, "I am a woman who is deeply troubled. I have not been drinking wine or beer; I was pouring[o] out my soul to the LORD. 16 Do not take your servant for a wicked woman; I have been praying here out of my great anguish and grief."

17 Eli answered, "Go in peace,[p] and may the God of Israel grant you what you have asked of him.[q]"

18 She said, "May your servant find favor in your eyes.[r]" Then she went her way and ate something, and her face was no longer downcast.[s]

19 Early the next morning they arose and worshiped before the LORD and then went back to their home at Ramah. Elkanah lay with Hannah his wife, and the LORD remembered[t] her. 20 So in the course of time Hannah conceived and gave birth to a son. She named[u] him Samuel,[c] saying, "Because I asked the LORD for him."

Hannah Dedicates Samuel

21 When the man Elkanah went up with all his family to offer the annual[v] sacrifice to the LORD and to fulfill his vow,[w] 22 Hannah did not go. She said to her husband, "After the boy is weaned, I will take him and present[x] him before the LORD, and he will live there always."

23 "Do what seems best to you," Elkanah her husband told her. "Stay here until you have weaned him; only may the LORD make good[y] his[d] word." So the woman stayed at home and nursed her son until she had weaned him.

24 After he was weaned, she took the boy with her, young as he was, along with a three-year-old bull,[e z] an ephah[f] of flour and a skin of wine, and brought him to the house of the LORD at Shiloh. 25 When they had slaughtered the bull, they brought the boy to Eli, 26 and she said to him, "As surely as you live, my lord, I am the woman who stood here beside you praying to the LORD. 27 I prayed[a] for this child, and the LORD has granted me what I asked of him. 28 So now I give him to the LORD. For his whole life[b] he will be given over to the LORD." And he worshiped the LORD there.

1:1 [a] Jos 17:17-18 [b] 1Ch 6:27,34
1:2 [c] Dt 21:15-17; Lk 2:36
1:3 [d] ver 21; Ex 23:14; 34:23; Lk 2:41 [e] Dt 12:5-7 [f] Jos 18:1
1:4 [g] Dt 12:17-18
1:5 [h] Ge 16:1; 30:2
1:6 [i] Job 24:21
1:8 [j] Ru 4:15
1:9 [k] 1Sa 3:3
1:10 [l] Job 7:11
1:11 [m] Ge 8:1; 28:20; 29:32 [n] Nu 6:1-21; Jdg 13:5
1:15 [o] Ps 42:4; 62:8; La 2:19
1:17 [p] Jdg 18:6; 1Sa 25:35; 2Ki 5:19; Mk 5:34 [q] Ps 20:3-5
1:18 [r] Ru 2:13 [s] Ecc 9:7; Ro 15:13
1:19 [t] Ge 4:1; 30:22
1:20 [u] Ge 41:51-52; Ex 2:10,22; Mt 1:21
1:21 [v] ver 3 [w] Dt 12:11
1:22 [x] ver 11,28; Lk 2:22
1:23 [y] ver 17; Nu 30:7
1:24 [z] Nu 15:8-10; Dt 12:5; Jos 18:1
1:27 [a] ver 11-13; Ps 66:19-20
1:28 [b] ver 11,22; Ge 24:26,52

[a] *1* Or *from Ramathaim Zuphim* [b] *9* That is, tabernacle [c] *20* *Samuel* sounds like the Hebrew for *heard of God.* [d] *23* Masoretic Text; Dead Sea Scrolls, Septuagint and Syriac *your* [e] *24* Dead Sea Scrolls, Septuagint and Syriac; Masoretic Text *with three bulls* [f] *24* That is, probably about 3/5 bushel (about 22 liters)

Hannah's Prayer

2:1 [c] Lk 1:46-55 [d] Ps 9:14; 13:5 [e] Ps 89:17,24; 92:10; Isa 12:2-3

2 Then Hannah prayed and said:[c]

"My heart rejoices[d] in the LORD;
in the LORD my horn[a][e] is lifted high.
My mouth boasts over my enemies,
for I delight in your deliverance.

2:2 [f] Ex 15:11; Lev 19:2 [g] Dt 32:30-31; 2Sa 22:2,32

2 "There is no one holy[b][f] like the LORD;
there is no one besides you;
there is no Rock[g] like our God.

2:3 [h] Pr 8:13 [i] 1Sa 16:7; 1Ki 8:39 [j] Pr 16:2; 24:11-12

3 "Do not keep talking so proudly
or let your mouth speak such arrogance,[h]
for the LORD is a God who knows,
and by him deeds[i] are weighed.[j]

2:4 [k] Ps 37:15

4 "The bows of the warriors are broken,[k]
but those who stumbled are armed with strength.
5 Those who were full hire themselves out for food,
but those who were hungry hunger no more.

2:5 [l] Ps 113:9; Jer 15:9

She who was barren[l] has borne seven children,
but she who has had many sons pines away.

2:6 [m] Dt 32:39 [n] Isa 26:19

6 "The LORD brings death and makes alive;[m]
he brings down to the grave[c] and raises up.[n]

2:7 [o] Dt 8:18 [p] Job 5:11; Ps 75:7

7 The LORD sends poverty and wealth;[o]
he humbles and he exalts.[p]

2:8 [q] Ps 113:7-8 [r] Job 36:7 [s] Job 38:4

8 He raises[q] the poor from the dust
and lifts the needy from the ash heap;
he seats them with princes
and has them inherit a throne of honor.[r]

"For the foundations[s] of the earth are the LORD's;
upon them he has set the world.

2:9 [t] Ps 91:12 [u] Mt 8:12 [v] Ps 33:16-17

9 He will guard the feet[t] of his saints,
but the wicked will be silenced in darkness.[u]

"It is not by strength[v] that one prevails;

2:10 [w] Ps 2:9 [x] Ps 18:13 [y] Ps 96:13 [z] Ps 21:1 [a] Ps 89:24

10 those who oppose the LORD will be shattered.[w]
He will thunder[x] against them from heaven;
the LORD will judge[y] the ends of the earth.

"He will give strength[z] to his king
and exalt the horn[a] of his anointed."

2:11 [b] ver 18; 1Sa 3:1

11 Then Elkanah went home to Ramah, but the boy ministered[b] before the
LORD under Eli the priest.

Eli's Wicked Sons

2:12 [c] Jer 2:8; 9:6

2:13 [d] Lev 7:29-34

12 Eli's sons were wicked men; they
had no regard[c] for the LORD. 13 Now it
was the practice of the priests with the
people that whenever anyone offered a
sacrifice and while the meat[d] was being
boiled, the servant of the priest would
come with a three-pronged fork in his
hand. 14 He would plunge it into the pan
or kettle or caldron or pot, and the
priest would take for himself whatever
the fork brought up. This is how they
treated all the Israelites who came to
Shiloh. 15 But even before the fat was
burned, the servant of the priest would
come and say to the man who was

[a] 1 *Horn* here symbolizes strength; also in verse 10.
[b] 2 Or *no Holy One* [c] 6 Hebrew *Sheol*

SAMUEL
GOD'S CHOSEN PROPHET

Samuel, which means "heard of God," was the son of Elkanah and Hannah. He was one of God's prophets in the twelfth century B.C., and he had a profound impact on the nation of Israel. Samuel served in the tabernacle in Shiloh under Eli's supervision. Later, he lived in Ramah and traveled in a circuit that included Bethel, Gilgal and Mizpah in order to meet the needs of God's people. God used Samuel to move Israel from rule by judges to rule by kings. Samuel anointed Saul as king of Israel, but Saul refused to follow God. As a result, Samuel anointed David instead. In this manner the Messiah's family line also became the line of royalty. Samuel was the only individual mentioned in the Old Testament who was at one and the same time a prophet (1 Samuel 3:20), a priest (1 Samuel 7:9) and a judge (1 Samuel 7:6,15). His role among God's people is a symbol of what the role of the Messiah would be when Jesus came to earth. Jesus is God's ultimate Prophet (Matthew 21:11; John 7:40), ultimate Priest (Hebrews 9:11), and ultimate King and Judge (Philippians 2:9–11).

Moments to Remember

Life is filled with unforgettable moments: the first day of school, procuring a first driver's license, a first date, graduation, a new job, marriage, a new house, retirement. But few other moments compare with the ecstasy that surrounds the birth of a child!

Hannah was a woman who had been unable to conceive a child. For years she had lived with this galling disappointment, exacerbated by the jeers of the rival wife Peninnah, who flaunted her growing brood. But Hannah never stopped praying (see 1 Samuel 1), and God finally granted her a son. She named him *Samuel*, which means "heard of God." Since God had granted her request, she relinquished Samuel back to the Lord. Hannah's joy at doing so is recorded in 1 Samuel 2:1: "My heart rejoices in the LORD; in the LORD my horn is lifted high." From the time he was a small child Samuel was devoted to God's service, and later in life he became a great leader.

Hannah's story reminds us of another incident that took place generations later . . . another moment to remember. A young woman named Mary was given an incredible message by an angel: "You have found favor with God. You will . . . give birth to a son, and you are to give him the name Jesus" (Luke 1:30–31). Samuel's birth was important because he was to play a significant role in Israel's history, but Jesus' birth was the ultimate miracle—God the Son in human flesh. The angel promised," He will be great and will be called the Son of the Most High. The Lord will give him the throne of his father David, and he will reign over the house of Jacob forever; his kingdom will never end" (Luke 1:32–33).

Mary responded in the same way Hannah had done so long before: She praised God with all her heart (compare Hannah's prayer in 1 Samuel 2:1–10 with Mary's song in Luke1:46–55): "My soul glorifies the Lord and my spirit rejoices in God my Savior, for he has been mindful of the humble state of his servant. From now on all generations will call me blessed" (Luke 1:46–48).

The most important milestone for any of us is the day we ask Jesus into our life. As we get to know him better, there will be many other memorable moments—to relish now and for all eternity.

***Self-Discovery:** Picture God telling you directly that he has heard your cries and that you have found favor with him. Does this incredible declaration cause you to desire to live a life of thankful service? What will you do for Jesus today?*

GO TO DISCOVERY 67 ON PAGE 344

sacrificing, "Give the priest some meat to roast; he won't accept boiled meat from you, but only raw."

16 If the man said to him, "Let the fat be burned up first, and then take whatever you want," the servant would then answer, "No, hand it over now; if you don't, I'll take it by force."

17 This sin of the young men was very great in the LORD's sight, for they[a] were treating the LORD's offering with contempt.[e]

18 But Samuel was ministering[f] before the LORD—a boy wearing a linen ephod.[g] 19 Each year his mother made him a little robe and took it to him when she went up with her husband to offer the annual[h] sacrifice. 20 Eli would bless Elkanah and his wife, saying, "May the LORD give you children by this woman to take the place of the one she prayed[i] for and gave to the LORD." Then they would go home. 21 And the LORD was gracious to Hannah;[j] she conceived and gave birth to three sons and two daughters. Meanwhile, the boy Samuel grew[k] up in the presence of the LORD.

22 Now Eli, who was very old, heard about everything his sons were doing to all Israel and how they slept with the women[l] who served at the entrance to the Tent of Meeting. 23 So he said to them, "Why do you do such things? I hear from all the people about these wicked deeds of yours. 24 No, my sons; it is not a good report that I hear spreading among the LORD's people. 25 If a man sins against another man, God[b] may mediate for him; but if a man sins against the LORD, who will[m] intercede[n] for him?" His sons, however, did not listen to their father's rebuke, for it was the LORD's will to put them to death.

26 And the boy Samuel continued to grow[o] in stature and in favor with the LORD and with men.

Prophecy Against the House of Eli

27 Now a man of God[p] came to Eli and said to him, "This is what the LORD says: 'Did I not clearly reveal myself to your father's house when they were in Egypt under Pharaoh? 28 I chose[q] your father out of all the tribes of Israel to be my priest, to go up to my altar, to burn incense, and to wear an ephod[r] in my presence. I also gave your father's house

2:17 [e] Mal 2:7-9
2:18 [f] ver 11; 1Sa 3:1 [g] ver 28
2:19 [h] 1Sa 1:3
2:20 [i] 1Sa 1:11,27-28; Lk 2:34
2:21 [j] Ge 21:1 [k] ver 26; Jdg 13:24; 1Sa 3:19; Lk 2:40
2:22 [l] Ex 38:8
2:25 [m] Nu 15:30; Jos 11:20 [n] Dt 1:17; 1Sa 3:14; Heb 10:26
2:26 [o] ver 21; Lk 2:52
2:27 [p] Ex 4:14-16; 1Ki 13:1
2:28 [q] Ex 28:1 [r] Lev 8:7-8

all the offerings made with fire by the Israelites. 29 Why do you[c] scorn my sacrifice and offering[s] that I prescribed for my dwelling?[t] Why do you honor your sons more than me by fattening yourselves on the choice parts of every offering made by my people Israel?'

30 "Therefore the LORD, the God of Israel, declares: 'I promised that your house and your father's house would minister before me forever.[u]' But now the LORD declares: 'Far be it from me! Those who honor me I will honor,[v] but those who despise[w] me will be disdained. 31 The time is coming when I will cut short your strength and the strength of your father's house, so that there will not be an old man in your family line[x] 32 and you will see distress in my dwelling. Although good will be done to Israel, in your family line there will never be an old man.[y] 33 Every one of you that I do not cut off from my altar will be spared only to blind your eyes with tears and to grieve your heart, and all your descendants will die in the prime of life.

34 " 'And what happens to your two sons, Hophni and Phinehas, will be a sign to you—they will both die[z] on the same day.[a] 35 I will raise up for myself a faithful priest,[b] who will do according to what is in my heart and mind. I will firmly establish his house, and he will minister before my anointed[c] one always. 36 Then everyone left in your family line will come and bow down before him for a piece of silver and a crust of bread and plead, "Appoint me to some priestly office so I can have food to eat.[d]" ' "

The LORD Calls Samuel

3 The boy Samuel ministered[e] before the LORD under Eli. In those days the word of the LORD was rare;[f] there were not many visions.[g]

2 One night Eli, whose eyes[h] were becoming so weak that he could barely see, was lying down in his usual place. 3 The lamp[i] of God had not yet gone out, and Samuel was lying down in the temple[d] of the LORD, where the ark of God was. 4 Then the LORD called Samuel.

Samuel answered, "Here I am.[j]" 5 And he ran to Eli and said, "Here I am; you called me."

2:29 [s] ver 12-17 [t] Dt 12:5; Mt 10:37
2:30 [u] Ex 29:9 [v] Ps 50:23; 91:15 [w] Mal 2:9
2:31 [x] 1Sa 4:11-18; 22:16-20
2:32 [y] 1Ki 2:26-27; Zec 8:4
2:34 [z] 1Sa 4:11 [a] 1Ki 13:3
2:35 [b] 1Sa 12:3; 1Ki 2:35 [c] 1Sa 16:13; 2Sa 7:11,27; 1Ki 11:38
2:36 [d] 1Ki 2:27
3:1 [e] 1Sa 2:11 [f] Ps 74:9 [g] Am 8:11
3:2 [h] 1Sa 4:15
3:3 [i] Lev 24:1-4
3:4 [j] Isa 6:8

[a] 17 Or *men* [b] 25 Or *the judges* [c] 29 The Hebrew is plural. [d] 3 That is, tabernacle

DISCOVERY 67

Your Servant Is Listening

As a boy Samuel served as assistant to the high priest Eli. One night Samuel heard someone calling his name, so he got up to ask what Eli wanted. But Eli had not called. This happened three times. Finally Eli realized that God was calling Samuel and instructed the child to answer, "Speak, LORD, for your servant is listening" (1 Samuel 3:9). God did call again, and this time Samuel responded. God informed young Samuel that Eli and his family were about to suffer the consequences for disobeying God.

Samuel was the man God would use to move his people from leadership by judges to rule by a king. Samuel grew up to become a judge, priest and prophet in Israel, and he anointed both Saul and David as kings. The Bible tells us that "the LORD was with Samuel as he grew up, and he let none of his words fall to the ground" (verse 19).

Samuel began obeying God very early in life with his simple invitation, "Speak, LORD, for your servant is listening." When we believe God, we make the same commitment to listen and obey. But God's messages don't always seem as clear to us as they did to Samuel. It can be difficult to decipher what God is saying unless we know how to go about it. The first thing we can do is to study and put into practice the words recorded in the Bible. In his Book God spells out what he expects of us, and he will continue to reveal his will and intentions to those who seek him.

We also listen to God through his Holy Spirit. When we give our lives to Jesus, God the Spirit takes up residence in our hearts. Gradually we learn to identify the Spirit's inner voice; we become attuned to his quiet promptings and reminders as we go through our day. The better we know him, the more sensitive we are to that voice. When we ignore what the Holy Spirit is saying, we cause him grief (Ephesians 4:30).

Third, we learn lessons through our own personal experiences. God works in everything that happens in our lives to accomplish what he has in mind—mainly, he is building character in us so that we become more like Jesus (Romans 8:28–29). No matter what our situation we need to ask, "Lord, what can I learn about *you* in this?"

We can also learn from gifted teachers. God bestows varying gifts so that his people can learn from one another. As we learn more about him, we become more and more transformed into the image of his Son (Ephesians 4:11–16).

Finally, we listen to God by talking with him. When we pray, we talk to God about our needs and concerns, our happiness and our pain. But prayer is more than monologue. As Samuel discovered, prayer involves being still and listening to God. Even when his answer is no, God is still speaking to us—and he always gives his best!

Self-Discovery: *In what ways can you become "tuned in" to God's frequency so that you can pick up his signals throughout the course of your day? What can you do today to open yourself up to becoming more Christlike, more conformed to his image?*

GO TO DISCOVERY 68 ON PAGE 349

But Eli said, "I did not call; go back
and lie down." So he went and lay down.
6 Again the LORD called, "Samuel!"
And Samuel got up and went to Eli and
said, "Here I am; you called me."
"My son," Eli said, "I did not call; go
back and lie down."
7 Now Samuel did not yet know the
3:7 LORD: The word of the LORD had not yet
k Ac 19:12 been revealed[k] to him.
8 The LORD called Samuel a third time,
and Samuel got up and went to Eli and
said, "Here I am; you called me."
Then Eli realized that the LORD was
calling the boy. 9 So Eli told Samuel, "Go
and lie down, and if he calls you, say,
'Speak, LORD, for your servant is listening.' " So Samuel went and lay down in
his place.
10 The LORD came and stood there,
calling as at the other times, "Samuel!
Samuel!"
Then Samuel said, "Speak, for your
servant is listening."
11 And the LORD said to Samuel: "See, I
am about to do something in Israel that
will make the ears of everyone who hears
3:11 of it tingle.[l] 12 At that time I will carry out
l 2Ki 21:12; Jer 19:3 against Eli everything[m] I spoke against
3:12 his family—from beginning to end. 13 For
m 1Sa 2:27-36 I told him that I would judge his family
forever because of the sin he knew
3:13 about; his sons made themselves con-
n 1Sa 2:12,17,22,29-31 temptible,[a] and he failed to restrain[n]
them. 14 Therefore, I swore to the house
3:14 of Eli, 'The guilt of Eli's house will never
o Lev 15:30-31; 1Sa 2:25; Isa 22:14 be atoned[o] for by sacrifice or offering.' "
15 Samuel lay down until morning and
then opened the doors of the house of
the LORD. He was afraid to tell Eli the vision, 16 but Eli called him and said, "Samuel, my son."
Samuel answered, "Here I am."
17 "What was it he said to you?" Eli
asked. "Do not hide it from me. May
God deal with you, be it ever so severe-
3:17 ly,[p] if you hide from me anything he told
p Ru 1:17; 2Sa 3:35 you." 18 So Samuel told him everything,
hiding nothing from him. Then Eli said,
3:18 "He is the LORD; let him do what is good
q Job 2:10; Isa 39:8 in his eyes."[q]
19 The LORD was with[r] Samuel as he
3:19 grew[s] up, and he let none[t] of his words
r Ge 21:22; 39:2 s 1Sa 2:21 t 1Sa 9:6 fall to the ground. 20 And all Israel from
Dan to Beersheba[u] recognized that
3:20 Samuel was attested as a prophet of the
u Jdg 20:1 LORD. 21 The LORD continued to appear at
Shiloh, and there he revealed[v] himself to 3:21 v ver 10
Samuel through his word.

4 And Samuel's word came to all Israel.

The Philistines Capture the Ark

Now the Israelites went out to fight
against the Philistines. The Israelites
camped at Ebenezer,[w] and the Philis- 4:1 w 1Sa 7:12
tines at Aphek.[x] 2 The Philistines de- x Jos 12:18; 1Sa 29:1
ployed their forces to meet Israel, and as
the battle spread, Israel was defeated by
the Philistines, who killed about four
thousand of them on the battlefield.
3 When the soldiers returned to camp,
the elders of Israel asked, "Why[y] did the 4:3 y Jos 7:7
LORD bring defeat upon us today before z Nu 10:35;
the Philistines? Let us bring the ark[z] of Jos 6:7
the LORD's covenant from Shiloh, so that
it[b] may go with us and save us from the
hand of our enemies."
4 So the people sent men to Shiloh,
and they brought back the ark of the
covenant of the LORD Almighty, who is
enthroned between the cherubim.[a] And 4:4 a Ex 25:22;
Eli's two sons, Hophni and Phinehas, 2Sa 6:2
were there with the ark of the covenant
of God.
5 When the ark of the LORD's covenant
came into the camp, all Israel raised
such a great shout[b] that the ground 4:5 b Jos 6:5,10
shook. 6 Hearing the uproar, the Philistines asked, "What's all this shouting in
the Hebrew camp?"
When they learned that the ark of the
LORD had come into the camp, 7 the Philistines were afraid.[c] "A god has come 4:7 c Ex 15:14
into the camp," they said. "We're in trouble! Nothing like this has happened before. 8 Woe to us! Who will deliver us
from the hand of these mighty gods?
They are the gods who struck the Egyptians with all kinds of plagues in the
desert. 9 Be strong, Philistines! Be men,
or you will be subject to the Hebrews, as 4:9
they[d] have been to you. Be men, and d Jdg 13:1;
fight!" 1Co 16:13
10 So the Philistines fought, and the Israelites were defeated[e] and every man 4:10
fled to his tent. The slaughter was very e ver 2; Dt 28:25;
great; Israel lost thirty thousand foot 2Sa 18:17; 2Ki 14:12
soldiers. 11 The ark of God was captured,
and Eli's two sons, Hophni and Phine- 4:11
has, died.[f] f 1Sa 2:34; Ps 78:61,64

a 13 Masoretic Text; an ancient Hebrew scribal tradition and Septuagint *sons blasphemed God*
b 3 Or *he*

Death of Eli

12 That same day a Benjamite ran from
the battle line and went to Shiloh, his
4:12 gJos 7:6; 2Sa 1:2; 15:32; Ne 9:1; Job 2:12 clothes torn and dust[g] on his head.
13 When he arrived, there was Eli[h] sitting
on his chair by the side of the road,
4:13 hver 18; 1Sa 1:9 watching, because his heart feared for
the ark of God. When the man entered
the town and told what had happened,
the whole town sent up a cry.

14 Eli heard the outcry and asked,
"What is the meaning of this uproar?"

The man hurried over to Eli, 15 who
was ninety-eight years old and whose
4:15 i1Sa 3:2 eyes[i] were set so that he could not see.
16 He told Eli, "I have just come from the
battle line; I fled from it this very day."

Eli asked, "What happened, my son?"

17 The man who brought the news
replied, "Israel fled before the Philistines, and the army has suffered heavy
losses. Also your two sons, Hophni and
Phinehas, are dead, and the ark of God
has been captured."

18 When he mentioned the ark of God,
Eli fell backward off his chair by the side
of the gate. His neck was broken and he
died, for he was an old man and heavy.
4:18 jver 13 He had led[a][j] Israel forty years.

19 His daughter-in-law, the wife of
Phinehas, was pregnant and near the
time of delivery. When she heard the
news that the ark of God had been captured and that her father-in-law and her
husband were dead, she went into labor
and gave birth, but was overcome by her
labor pains. 20 As she was dying, the
women attending her said, "Don't despair; you have given birth to a son." But
she did not respond or pay any attention.

21 She named the boy Ichabod,[b][k] say-
4:21 kGe 35:18 lPs 26:8; Jer 2:11 ing, "The glory[l] has departed from Israel"—because of the capture of the ark of
God and the deaths of her father-in-law
and her husband. 22 She said, "The glory
has departed from Israel, for the ark of
God has been captured."

The Ark in Ashdod and Ekron

5 After the Philistines had captured
5:1 m1Sa 4:1; 7:12 nJos 13:3 the ark of God, they took it from
Ebenezer[m] to Ashdod.[n] 2 Then they car-
ried the ark into Dagon's temple and set
5:2 oJdg 16:23 it beside Dagon.[o] 3 When the people of
Ashdod rose early the next day, there
5:3 pIsa 19:1; 46:7 was Dagon, fallen[p] on his face on the
ground before the ark of the LORD! They
took Dagon and put him back in his
place. 4 But the following morning when
they rose, there was Dagon, fallen on his
face on the ground before the ark of the
LORD! His head and hands had been bro- 5:4 qEze 6:6; Mic 1:7
ken[q] off and were lying on the threshold;
only his body remained. 5 That is why to
this day neither the priests of Dagon nor
any others who enter Dagon's temple at
Ashdod step on the threshold.[r] 5:5 rZep 1:9

6 The LORD's hand[s] was heavy upon 5:6 sver 7; Ex 9:3; Ps 32:4; Ac 13:11 tver 11; Ps 78:66 uDt 28:27; 1Sa 6:5
the people of Ashdod and its vicinity; he
brought devastation[t] upon them and afflicted them with tumors.[c][u] 7 When the
men of Ashdod saw what was happening, they said, "The ark of the god of Israel must not stay here with us, because
his hand is heavy upon us and upon Dagon our god." 8 So they called together all
the rulers of the Philistines and asked
them, "What shall we do with the ark of
the god of Israel?"

They answered, "Have the ark of the
god of Israel moved to Gath.[v]" So they 5:8 vver 11
moved the ark of the God of Israel.

9 But after they had moved it, the
LORD's hand was against that city, throw-
ing it into a great panic.[w] He afflicted 5:9 wver 6,11; Dt 2:15; 1Sa 7:13; Ps 78:66
the people of the city, both young and
old, with an outbreak of tumors.[d] 10 So
they sent the ark of God to Ekron.

As the ark of God was entering Ekron,
the people of Ekron cried out, "They
have brought the ark of the god of Israel
around to us to kill us and our people."
11 So they called together all the rulers[x] 5:11 xver 6,8-9
of the Philistines and said, "Send the ark
of the god of Israel away; let it go back to
its own place, or it[e] will kill us and our
people." For death had filled the city
with panic; God's hand was very heavy
upon it. 12 Those who did not die were afflicted with tumors, and the outcry of
the city went up to heaven.

The Ark Returned to Israel

6 When the ark of the LORD had
been in Philistine territory seven
months, 2 the Philistines called for the 6:2 yGe 41:8; Ex 7:11; Isa 2:6
priests and the diviners[y] and said,
"What shall we do with the ark of the

[a] 18 Traditionally *judged* [b] 21 *Ichabod* means *no glory.* [c] 6 Hebrew; Septuagint and Vulgate *tumors. And rats appeared in their land, and death and destruction were throughout the city* [d] 9 Or *with tumors in the groin* (see Septuagint) [e] 11 Or *he*

LORD? Tell us how we should send it back to its place."

3 They answered, "If you return the ark of the god of Israel, do not send it away empty,[z] but by all means send a guilt offering[a] to him. Then you will be healed, and you will know why his hand[b] has not been lifted from you."

4 The Philistines asked, "What guilt offering should we send to him?"

They replied, "Five gold tumors and five gold rats, according to the number[c] of the Philistine rulers, because the same plague has struck both you and your rulers. 5 Make models of the tumors[d] and of the rats that are destroying the country, and pay honor[e] to Israel's god. Perhaps he will lift his hand from you and your gods and your land. 6 Why do you harden[f] your hearts as the Egyptians and Pharaoh did? When he[a] treated them harshly, did they[g] not send the Israelites out so they could go on their way?

7 "Now then, get a new cart[h] ready, with two cows that have calved and have never been yoked.[i] Hitch the cows to the cart, but take their calves away and pen them up. 8 Take the ark of the LORD and put it on the cart, and in a chest beside it put the gold objects you are sending back to him as a guilt offering. Send it on its way, 9 but keep watching it. If it goes up to its own territory, toward Beth Shemesh,[j] then the LORD has brought this great disaster on us. But if it does not, then we will know that it was not his hand that struck us and that it happened to us by chance."

10 So they did this. They took two such cows and hitched them to the cart and penned up their calves. 11 They placed the ark of the LORD on the cart and along with it the chest containing the gold rats and the models of the tumors. 12 Then the cows went straight up toward Beth Shemesh, keeping on the road and lowing all the way; they did not turn to the right or to the left. The rulers of the Philistines followed them as far as the border of Beth Shemesh.

13 Now the people of Beth Shemesh were harvesting their wheat in the valley, and when they looked up and saw the ark, they rejoiced at the sight. 14 The cart came to the field of Joshua of Beth Shemesh, and there it stopped beside a large rock. The people chopped up the wood of the cart and sacrificed the cows as a burnt offering[k] to the LORD. 15 The Levites[l] took down the ark of the LORD, together with the chest containing the gold objects, and placed them on the large rock. On that day the people of Beth Shemesh offered burnt offerings and made sacrifices to the LORD. 16 The five rulers of the Philistines saw all this and then returned that same day to Ekron.

17 These are the gold tumors the Philistines sent as a guilt offering to the LORD—one each[m] for Ashdod, Gaza, Ashkelon, Gath and Ekron. 18 And the number of the gold rats was according to the number of Philistine towns belonging to the five rulers—the fortified towns with their country villages. The large rock, on which[b] they set the ark of the LORD, is a witness to this day in the field of Joshua of Beth Shemesh.

19 But God struck down[n] some of the men of Beth Shemesh, putting seventy[c] of them to death because they had looked[o] into the ark of the LORD. The people mourned because of the heavy blow the LORD had dealt them, 20 and the men of Beth Shemesh asked, "Who can stand[p] in the presence of the LORD, this holy[q] God? To whom will the ark go up from here?"

21 Then they sent messengers to the people of Kiriath Jearim,[r] saying, "The Philistines have returned the ark of the LORD. Come down and take it up to your

7 place." 1 So the men of Kiriath Jearim came and took up the ark of the LORD. They took it to Abinadab's[s] house on the hill and consecrated Eleazar his son to guard the ark of the LORD.

Samuel Subdues the Philistines at Mizpah

2 It was a long time, twenty years in all, that the ark remained at Kiriath Jearim, and all the people of Israel mourned and sought after the LORD. 3 And Samuel said to the whole house of Israel, "If you are returning[t] to the LORD with all your hearts, then rid[u] yourselves of the foreign gods and the Ashtoreths[v] and commit[w] yourselves to the LORD and serve him only,[x] and he will deliver you out of

a 6 That is, God *b 18* A few Hebrew manuscripts (see also Septuagint); most Hebrew manuscripts *villages as far as Greater Abel, where* *c 19* A few Hebrew manuscripts; most Hebrew manuscripts and Septuagint *50,070*

6:3 [z] Ex 23:15; Dt 16:16 [a] Lev 5:15 [b] ver 9
6:4 [c] ver 17-18; Jos 13:3; Jdg 3:3
6:5 [d] 1Sa 5:6-11 [e] Jos 7:19; Isa 42:12; Jn 9:24; Rev 14:7
6:6 [f] Ex 7:13; 8:15; 9:34; 14:17 [g] Ex 12:31,33
6:7 [h] 2Sa 6:3 [i] Nu 19:2
6:9 [j] ver 3; Jos 15:10; 21:16
6:14 [k] 2Sa 24:22; 1Ki 19:21
6:15 [l] Jos 3:3
6:17 [m] ver 4
6:19 [n] 2Sa 6:7 [o] Ex 19:21; Nu 4:5,15,20
6:20 [p] 2Sa 6:9; Mal 3:2; Rev 6:17 [q] Lev 11:45
6:21 [r] Jos 9:17; 15:9, 60; 1Ch 13:5-6
7:1 [s] 2Sa 6:3
7:3 [t] Dt 30:10; Isa 55:7; Hos 6:1 [u] Ge 35:2; Jos 24:14 [v] Jdg 2:12-13; 1Sa 31:10 [w] Joel 2:12 [x] Dt 6:13; Mt 4:10; Lk 4:8

the hand of the Philistines." 4So the Israelites put away their Baals and Ashtoreths, and served the LORD only.
5Then Samuel said, "Assemble all Is-
7:5 rael at Mizpah[y] and I will intercede with
y Jdg 20:1 the LORD for you." 6When they had assembled at Mizpah, they drew water
7:6 and poured[z] it out before the LORD. On
z Ps 62:8; that day they fasted and there they con-
La 2:19 a Jdg 10:10; fessed, "We have sinned against the
Ne 9:1; Ps 106:6 LORD." And Samuel was leader[a][a] of Israel at Mizpah.
7When the Philistines heard that Israel had assembled at Mizpah, the rulers
of the Philistines came up to attack
them. And when the Israelites heard of
7:7 b 1Sa 17:11 it, they were afraid[b] because of the Philistines. 8They said to Samuel, "Do not
7:8 stop crying[c] out to the LORD our God for
c 1Sa 12:19,23; us, that he may rescue us from the hand
Isa 37:4; Jer 15:1 of the Philistines." 9Then Samuel[d] took a
7:9 d Ps 99:6 suckling lamb and offered it up as a
e Jer 15:1 whole burnt offering to the LORD. He
cried out to the LORD on Israel's behalf,
and the LORD answered him.[e]
10While Samuel was sacrificing the
burnt offering, the Philistines drew near
to engage Israel in battle. But that day
7:10 f 1Sa 2:10; the LORD thundered[f] with loud thunder
2Sa 22:14-15 against the Philistines and threw them
g Jos 10:10 into such a panic[g] that they were routed
before the Israelites. 11The men of Israel
rushed out of Mizpah and pursued the
Philistines, slaughtering them along the
way to a point below Beth Car.
7:12 12Then Samuel took a stone[h] and set
h Ge 35:14; it up between Mizpah and Shen. He
Jos 4:9 named it Ebenezer,[b] saying, "Thus far
7:13 has the LORD helped us." 13So the Philis-
i Jdg 13:1,5; tines were subdued[i] and did not invade
1Sa 13:5 Israelite territory again.
Throughout Samuel's lifetime, the
hand of the LORD was against the Philistines. 14The towns from Ekron to Gath
that the Philistines had captured from Israel were restored to her, and Israel delivered the neighboring territory from the
power of the Philistines. And there was
peace between Israel and the Amorites.
7:15 15Samuel[j] continued as judge over Is-
j ver 6; 1Sa 12:11 rael all the days of his life. 16From year to
year he went on a circuit from Bethel to
Gilgal to Mizpah, judging Israel in all
those places. 17But he always went back
7:17 k 1Sa 1:19; 8:4 to Ramah,[k] where his home was, and
l Jdg 21:4 there he also judged Israel. And he built
an altar[l] there to the LORD.

Israel Asks for a King

8 When Samuel grew old, he ap- 8:1
pointed[m] his sons as judges for Is- m Dt 16:18-19
rael. 2The name of his firstborn was Joel
and the name of his second was Abijah, 8:2
and they served at Beersheba.[n] 3But his n Ge 22:19;
sons did not walk in his ways. They 1Ki 19:3; Am 5:4-5
turned aside after dishonest gain and
accepted bribes[o] and perverted justice. 8:3
4So all the elders of Israel gathered to- o Ex 23:8; Dt 16:19;
gether and came to Samuel at Ramah.[p] Ps 15:5
5They said to him, "You are old, and your 8:4
sons do not walk in your ways; now ap- p 1Sa 7:17
point a king[q] to lead[c] us, such as all the 8:5
other nations have." q Dt 17:14-20
6But when they said, "Give us a king 8:6
to lead us," this displeased[r] Samuel; so r 1Sa 15:11
he prayed to the LORD. 7And the LORD
told him: "Listen to all that the people
are saying to you; it is not you they have
rejected, but they have rejected me as 8:7
their king.[s] 8As they have done from the s Ex 16:8; 1Sa 10:19
day I brought them up out of Egypt un-
til this day, forsaking me and serving
other gods, so they are doing to you.
9Now listen to them; but warn them 8:9
solemnly and let them know[t] what the t ver 11-18;
king who will reign over them will do." 1Sa 10:25
10Samuel told all the words of the
LORD to the people who were asking him
for a king. 11He said, "This is what the
king who will reign over you will do: He 8:11
will take[u] your sons and make them u 1Sa 10:25;
serve with his chariots and horses, and 14:52 v Dt 17:16;
they will run in front of his chariots.[v] 2Sa 15:1
12Some he will assign to be command- 8:12
ers[w] of thousands and commanders of w 1Sa 22:7
fifties, and others to plow his ground
and reap his harvest, and still others to
make weapons of war and equipment
for his chariots. 13He will take your
daughters to be perfumers and cooks
and bakers. 14He will take the best of
your[x] fields and vineyards[y] and olive 8:14 x Eze 46:18
groves and give them to his attendants. y 1Ki 21:7,15
15He will take a tenth of your grain and
of your vintage and give it to his officials
and attendants. 16Your menservants and
maidservants and the best of your cattle[d] and donkeys he will take for his own
use. 17He will take a tenth of your flocks,
and you yourselves will become his
slaves. 18When that day comes, you will

[a] 6 Traditionally *judge* [b] 12 *Ebenezer* means *stone of help.* [c] 5 Traditionally *judge*; also in verses 6 and 20 [d] 16 Septuagint; Hebrew *young men*

DISCOVERY 68

ALL IN HIS TIME

Not only do God's people need to accept his answers, but we also need to embrace his timing. When the Israelites insisted on having a king, they ignored both God's answer *and* his timing. God knew that by choosing a man as their king they would be turning their backs on his own kingship (1 Samuel 8:7). Saul was not God's first choice, but the people insisted on going ahead with their plan instead of waiting for God.

The entire nation loved Samuel, and when the people insisted on appointing a king, he warned them of the consequences. "He will take everything from you," he cautioned. The prophet went on to specify that a king would claim their sons (verse 11), their daughters (verse 13), their best fields (verse 14), and their servants and animals (verse 16). But the people were insistent: "We want a king over us. Then we will be like all the other nations, with a king to lead us and to go out before us and fight our battles" (verses 19–20).

The same scenario is often true of us today. Though we love God and desire to trust him, we are sometimes more concerned about conforming to our culture. We choose to forget that we have been set apart for God, and we grow tired of being different! We need to remember that we "fit in" with Someone infinitely more worthy of our attention: God has chosen us to be in his family! Just like the nation of Israel, we too are a "chosen people, a royal priesthood, a holy nation, a people belonging to God" (1 Peter 2:9). Our focus needs to be on getting to know God and learning to trust him rather than on striving for assimilation into the world around us (see Romans 12:1–2).

We are like Israel in another way: We often demand to have things our own way. God may allow this to happen, even though the detail may not mesh with his perfect plan. But there are always consequences. Whatever we ask of God needs to be submitted to his will and timing. Even Jesus conceded to his Father in Gethsemene, "If it is not possible for this cup to be taken away . . . may your will be done" (Matthew 26:42).

God knows what's best for us, and fighting his promptings only leads to pain and frustration—both for ourselves and for God (Psalm 78:40–55). But for those who obey, Jesus promises the blessings of his presence. In John 14:23 Jesus said, "If anyone loves me, he will obey my teaching. My Father will love him, and we will come to him and make our home with him."

The apostle Paul addressed both of these issues (our desire to conform to the norms of the culture in which we find ourselves and our propensity to run ahead of God): "Do not conform any longer to the pattern of this world, but be transformed by the renewing of your mind. Then you will be able to test and approve what God's will is—his good, pleasing and perfect will" (Romans 12:2).

Self-Discovery: *Looking back, can you identify a situation in which God withheld a particular blessing for which you had been praying because the timing wasn't yet right?*

GO TO DISCOVERY 69 ON PAGE 354

8:18 cry out for relief from the king you have
z Pr 1:28; chosen, and the LORD will not answer[z]
Isa 1:15; Mic 3:4 you in that day."
8:19 19But the people refused[a] to listen to
a Isa 66:4; Samuel. "No!" they said. "We want a king
Jer 44:16 over us. 20Then we will be like all the
8:20 other nations,[b] with a king to lead us
b ver 5 and to go out before us and fight our
battles."
21When Samuel heard all that the
8:21 people said, he repeated[c] it before the
c Jdg 11:11 LORD. 22The LORD answered, "Listen[d] to
8:22 them and give them a king."
d ver 7 Then Samuel said to the men of Israel, "Everyone go back to his town."

> FOR THIS REASON TOO THE PROPHETS WERE CALLED SEERS, BECAUSE THEY SAW HIM WHO OTHERS DID NOT SEE.
>
> Jerome, *Early Church Father*

Samuel Anoints Saul

9:1 9 There was a Benjamite, a man of
e 1Sa 14:51; standing, whose name was Kish[e]
1Ch 8:33; 9:39 son of Abiel, the son of Zeror, the son of
Becorath, the son of Aphiah of Benja-
9:2 min. 2He had a son named Saul, an im-
f 1Sa 10:24 pressive young man without equal[f]
g 1Sa 10:23 among the Israelites—a head taller[g]
than any of the others.
3Now the donkeys belonging to Saul's
father Kish were lost, and Kish said to
his son Saul, "Take one of the servants
with you and go and look for the don-
9:4 keys." 4So he passed through the hill[h]
h Jos 24:33 country of Ephraim and through the
i 2Ki 4:42 area around Shalisha,[i] but they did not
find them. They went on into the dis-
trict of Shaalim, but the donkeys were
not there. Then he passed through the
territory of Benjamin, but they did not
find them.
5When they reached the district of
9:5 Zuph,[j] Saul said to the servant who was
j 1Sa 1:1 with him, "Come, let's go back, or my fa-
k 1Sa 10:2 ther will stop thinking about the donkeys and start worrying[k] about us."
9:6 6But the servant replied, "Look, in this
l Dt 33:1; town there is a man of God;[l] he is high-
1Ki 13:1 ly respected, and everything[m] he says
m 1Sa 3:19 comes true. Let's go there now. Perhaps
he will tell us what way to take."
7Saul said to his servant, "If we go,
what can we give the man? The food in 9:7
our sacks is gone. We have no gift[n] to n 1Ki 14:3;
take to the man of God. What do we 2Ki 5:5,15; 8:8
have?"
8The servant answered him again.
"Look," he said, "I have a quarter of a
shekel[a] of silver. I will give it to the man
of God so that he will tell us what way to
take." 9(Formerly in Israel, if a man went
to inquire of God, he would say, "Come, 9:9
let us go to the seer," because the proph- o 2Sa 24:11;
et of today used to be called a seer.)[o] 2Ki 17:13;
10"Good," Saul said to his servant. 1Ch 9:22; 26:28;
"Come, let's go." So they set out for the 29:29; Isa 30:10;
town where the man of God was. Am 7:12
11As they were going up the hill to the
town, they met some girls coming out to
draw[p] water, and they asked them, "Is 9:11
the seer here?" p Ge 24:11,13
12"He is," they answered. "He's ahead
of you. Hurry now; he has just come to
our town today, for the people have a 9:12
sacrifice[q] at the high place.[r] 13As soon as q Nu 28:11-15;
you enter the town, you will find him be- 1Sa 7:17
fore he goes up to the high place to eat. r Ge 31:54;
The people will not begin eating until he 1Sa 10:5;
comes, because he must bless the sacri- 1Ki 3:2
fice; afterward, those who are invited
will eat. Go up now; you should find him
about this time."
14They went up to the town, and as
they were entering it, there was Samuel,
coming toward them on his way up to
the high place.
15Now the day before Saul came, the
LORD had revealed this to Samuel:
16"About this time tomorrow I will send
you a man from the land of Benjamin. 9:16
Anoint[s] him leader over my people Isra- s 1Sa 10:1
el; he will deliver[t] my people from the t Ex 3:7-9
hand of the Philistines. I have looked
upon my people, for their cry has
reached me."
17When Samuel caught sight of Saul, 9:17
the LORD said to him, "This[u] is the man u 1Sa 16:12
I spoke to you about; he will govern my
people."
18Saul approached Samuel in the
gateway and asked, "Would you please
tell me where the seer's house is?"
19"I am the seer," Samuel replied. "Go
up ahead of me to the high place, for today you are to eat with me, and in the
morning I will let you go and will tell you
all that is in your heart. 20As for the don- 9:20
keys[v] you lost three days ago, do not v ver 3

[a] 8 That is, about 1/10 ounce (about 3 grams)

9:20 worry about them; they have been
w 1Sa 8:5; 12:13 found. And to whom is all the desire[w] of
Israel turned, if not to you and all your
father's family?"
21Saul answered, "But am I not a Ben-
9:21 x 1Sa 15:17 jamite, from the smallest tribe[x] of Israel,
y Jdg 20:35,46 and is not my clan the least of all the
clans of the tribe of Benjamin?[y] Why do
you say such a thing to me?"
22Then Samuel brought Saul and his
servant into the hall and seated them at
the head of those who were invited—
about thirty in number. 23Samuel said to
the cook, "Bring the piece of meat I gave
you, the one I told you to lay aside."
24So the cook took up the leg[z] with
9:24 z Lev 7:32-34; Nu 18:18 what was on it and set it in front of Saul.
Samuel said, "Here is what has been
kept for you. Eat, because it was set
aside for you for this occasion, from the
time I said, 'I have invited guests.' " And
Saul dined with Samuel that day.
25After they came down from the high
place to the town, Samuel talked with
9:25 a Dt 22:8; Ac 10:9 Saul on the roof[a] of his house. 26They
rose about daybreak and Samuel called
to Saul on the roof, "Get ready, and I will
send you on your way." When Saul got
ready, he and Samuel went outside together. 27As they were going down to the
edge of the town, Samuel said to Saul,
"Tell the servant to go on ahead of us"—
and the servant did so—"but you stay
here awhile, so that I may give you a
message from God."

10:1 b 1Sa 16:13; 2Ki 9:1,3,6 **10** Then Samuel took a flask[b] of oil
and poured it on Saul's head
c Ps 2:12 and kissed him, saying, "Has not the
d Dt 32:9; Ps 78:62,71 LORD anointed[c] you leader over his inheritance?[a] [d] 2When you leave me today,
10:2 you will meet two men near Rachel's
e Ge 35:20 tomb,[e] at Zelzah on the border of Benja-
f 1Sa 9:4 min. They will say to you, 'The donkeys[f]
g 1Sa 9:5 you set out to look for have been found.
And now your father has stopped thinking about them and is worried[g] about
you. He is asking, "What shall I do about
my son?" '
3"Then you will go on from there until you reach the great tree of Tabor.
10:3 h Ge 28:22; 35:7-8 Three men going up to God at Bethel[h]
will meet you there. One will be carrying
three young goats, another three loaves
of bread, and another a skin of wine.
4They will greet you and offer you two
loaves of bread, which you will accept
from them.

5"After that you will go to Gibeah of
God, where there is a Philistine outpost.[i] 10:5 i 1Sa 13:3
As you approach the town, you will meet j 1Sa 9:12
a procession of prophets coming down k 2Ki 3:15
from the high place[j] with lyres, tam- l 1Sa 19:20; 1Co 14:1
bourines, flutes and harps[k] being played
before them, and they will be prophesy-
ing.[l] 6The Spirit[m] of the LORD will come 10:6 m ver 10;
upon you in power, and you will proph- Nu 11:25;
esy with them; and you will be changed 1Sa 19:23-24
into a different person. 7Once these 10:7
signs are fulfilled, do whatever[n] your n Ecc 9:10
hand finds to do, for God is with[o] you. o Jos 1:5; Jdg 6:12; Heb 13:5
8"Go down ahead of me to Gilgal.[p] I
will surely come down to you to sacrifice 10:8
burnt offerings and fellowship offer- p 1Sa 11:14-15

[a] 1 Hebrew; Septuagint and Vulgate *over his people Israel? You will reign over the LORD's people and save them from the power of their enemies round about. And this will be a sign to you that the LORD has anointed you leader over his inheritance:*

JESUS FOCUS

A TRUE PROPHET

It was uncommon for Saul to speak as God's representative, so when the Spirit of God temporarily came upon him and he "prophesied" (1 Samuel 10:10–12), people were shocked, querying, "Is Saul also among the prophets?" Eventually, however, this question became a national joke because Saul proved to be anything but God's prophet. God's people, and especially their leaders, must be completely devoted to him. Saul's personal character didn't demonstrate that devotion, and the people quickly lost respect for his leadership.

Jesus was everything Saul was not. Throughout his time on earth our precious Lord demonstrated that he was devoted to God by his unwavering commitment to doing God's will (Luke 22:42; John 4:34; 6:38; 9:4; 14:30–31; 17:4). Nathanael was one individual who scoffed at the idea that Jesus of Nazareth could be the prophet about whom Moses had written. Philip found Nathanael and related to him that he, along with Andrew and Peter, had "found the one Moses wrote about in the Law [see Deuteronomy 18:14–22], and about whom the prophets also wrote" (John 1:45). Nathanael responded with a sneer: "Nazareth! Can anything good come from there?" (John 1:46). But later on Nathanael met Jesus in person, and then he recognized without a doubt that Jesus was God's promised Messiah. This time Nathanael's response was a ringing testimony: "You are the Son of God" (John 1:49).

ings,[a] but you must wait seven days until I come to you and tell you what you
are to do."

Saul Made King

10:9 9 As Saul turned to leave Samuel, God
q ver 6 changed[q] Saul's heart, and all these
signs were fulfilled that day. 10 When
they arrived at Gibeah, a procession of
prophets met him; the Spirit of God
came upon him in power, and he joined
10:10 r ver 5-6; in their prophesying.[r] 11 When all those
1Sa 19:20 who had formerly known him saw him
10:11 prophesying with the prophets, they
s Mt 13:54; asked each other, "What is this[s] that has
Jn 7:15 happened to the son of Kish? Is Saul also
t 1Sa 19:24 among the prophets?"[t]
12 A man who lived there answered,
"And who is their father?" So it became
a saying: "Is Saul also among the prophets?" 13 After Saul stopped prophesying,
he went to the high place.
10:14 14 Now Saul's uncle[u] asked him and
u 1Sa 14:50 his servant, "Where have you been?"
"Looking for the donkeys," he said.
"But when we saw they were not to be
found, we went to Samuel."
15 Saul's uncle said, "Tell me what
Samuel said to you."
16 Saul replied, "He assured us that the
10:16 donkeys[v] had been found." But he did
v 1Sa 9:20 not tell his uncle what Samuel had said
about the kingship.
17 Samuel summoned the people of Is-
10:17 rael to the LORD at Mizpah[w] 18 and said
w Jdg 20:1; to them, "This is what the LORD, the God
1Sa 7:5 of Israel, says: 'I brought Israel up out of
Egypt, and I delivered you from the
power of Egypt and all the kingdoms
10:18 x Jdg 6:8-9 that oppressed[x] you.' 19 But you have now
rejected your God, who saves you out of
all your calamities and distresses. And
10:19 you have said, 'No, set a king[y] over us.' So
y 1Sa 8:5-7; 12:12 z Jos 7:14; now present[z] yourselves before the LORD
24:1 by your tribes and clans."
20 When Samuel brought all the tribes
of Israel near, the tribe of Benjamin was
chosen. 21 Then he brought forward the
tribe of Benjamin, clan by clan, and Ma-
tri's clan was chosen. Finally Saul son of
Kish was chosen. But when they looked
for him, he was not to be found. 22 So
10:22 they inquired[a] further of the LORD, "Has
a 1Sa 23:2,4,9-11 the man come here yet?"
And the LORD said, "Yes, he has hidden himself among the baggage."
23 They ran and brought him out, and
as he stood among the people he was a
head taller[b] than any of the others. 10:23 b 1Sa 9:2
24 Samuel said to all the people, "Do you
see the man the LORD has chosen?[c] 10:24 c Dt 17:15;
There is no one like him among all the 2Sa 21:6
people." d 1Ki 1:25,34,39
Then the people shouted, "Long live[d]
the king!"
25 Samuel explained to the people the
regulations[e] of the kingship. He wrote 10:25 e Dt 17:14-20;
them down on a scroll and deposited it 1Sa 8:11-18
before the LORD. Then Samuel dismissed
the people, each to his own home.
26 Saul also went to his home in Gibe-
ah,[f] accompanied by valiant men whose 10:26 f 1Sa 11:4
hearts God had touched. 27 But some
troublemakers[g] said, "How can this fel- 10:27 g Dt 13:13
low save us?" They despised him and h 1Ki 10:25;
brought him no gifts.[h] But Saul kept 2Ch 17:5
silent.

Saul Rescues the City of Jabesh

11 Nahash[i] the Ammonite went 11:1 i 1Sa 12:12
up and besieged Jabesh Gilead.[j] j Jdg 21:8
And all the men of Jabesh said to him, k 1Ki 20:34;
"Make a treaty[k] with us, and we will be Eze 17:13
subject to you."
2 But Nahash the Ammonite replied, "I
will make a treaty with you only on the 11:2
condition that I gouge[l] out the right eye l Nu 16:14
of every one of you and so bring dis- m 1Sa 17:26
grace[m] on all Israel."
3 The elders of Jabesh said to him,
"Give us seven days so we can send messengers throughout Israel; if no one
comes to rescue us, we will surrender to
you."
4 When the messengers came to Gibe-
ah[n] of Saul and reported these terms to 11:4 n 1Sa 10:5,26;
the people, they all wept[o] aloud. 5 Just 15:34 o Jdg 2:4;
then Saul was returning from the fields, 1Sa 30:4
behind his oxen, and he asked, "What is
wrong with the people? Why are they
weeping?" Then they repeated to him
what the men of Jabesh had said.
6 When Saul heard their words, the
Spirit[p] of God came upon him in power, 11:6 p Jdg 3:10; 6:34;
and he burned with anger. 7 He took a 13:25; 14:6;
pair of oxen, cut them into pieces, and 1Sa 10:10; 16:13
sent the pieces by messengers through-
out Israel,[q] proclaiming, "This is what 11:7 q Jdg 19:29
will be done to the oxen of anyone[r] who r Jdg 21:5
does not follow Saul and Samuel." Then
the terror of the LORD fell on the people,
and they turned out as one man. 8 When 11:8
Saul mustered[s] them at Bezek,[t] the men s Jdg 20:2 t Jdg 1:4

[a] 8 Traditionally *peace offerings*

of Israel numbered three hundred thousand and the men of Judah thirty thousand.
9They told the messengers who had
come, "Say to the men of Jabesh Gilead,
'By the time the sun is hot tomorrow,
you will be delivered.' " When the messengers went and reported this to the
men of Jabesh, they were elated. 10They
11:10 said to the Ammonites, "Tomorrow we
u ver 3 will surrender[u] to you, and you can do to
us whatever seems good to you."
11The next day Saul separated his
11:11 men into three divisions;[v] during the
v Jdg 7:16 last watch of the night they broke into
the camp of the Ammonites and slaughtered them until the heat of the day.
Those who survived were scattered, so
that no two of them were left together.

Saul Confirmed as King

12The people then said to Samuel,
11:12 "Who[w] was it that asked, 'Shall Saul
w 1Sa 10:27; Lk 19:27 reign over us?' Bring these men to us
and we will put them to death."

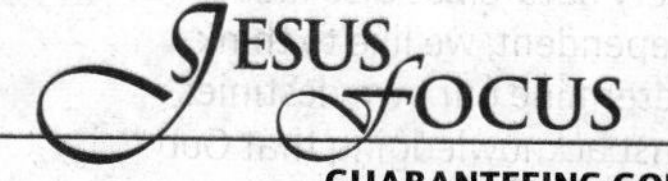

GUARANTEEING GOD'S KINGDOM

God directed Samuel to give the people the kind of king they were demanding, so Samuel reluctantly anointed Saul (1 Samuel 11:12–15). The people traveled to Gilgal, the former site of Joshua's battle camp (see Joshua 4:19—5:11), to renew their loyalty to the Lord. Samuel was worried that serving as the subjects of an earthly king might detract from the people's commitment to God. The prophet was primarily concerned about *God's* kingdom, not Saul's. So when Saul and the Israelites celebrated the advent of their new form of government, Samuel reminded them that their loyalty must always remain thoroughly directed toward God (1 Samuel 12:12–25).

Because the kings of Israel did not always remain committed to God, the people would continually yearn for the day when God would restore his kingdom once and for all. In the New Testament Jesus' disciples recognized him as God's promised Messiah-King, and they asked, "Are you at this time going to restore the kingdom to Israel?" (Acts 1:6). Jesus' answer was that they should not worry about the time but instead focus on God's kingdom, the kingdom that is not of this world (John 18:36) and tell others the good news about him (Acts 1:7–8).

13But Saul said, "No one shall be put 11:13 x 2Sa 19:22
to death today,[x] for this day the LORD y Ex 14:13;
has rescued[y] Israel." 1Sa 19:5
14Then Samuel said to the people,
"Come, let us go to Gilgal[z] and there 11:14 z 1Sa 10:8
reaffirm the kingship.[a]" 15So all the peo- a 1Sa 10:25
ple went to Gilgal[b] and confirmed Saul 11:15
as king in the presence of the LORD. b 1Sa 10:8,17
There they sacrificed fellowship offerings[a] before the LORD, and Saul and all
the Israelites held a great celebration.

Samuel's Farewell Speech

12 Samuel said to all Israel, "I have
listened[c] to everything you said 12:1 c 1Sa 8:7
to me and have set a king[d] over you. d 1Sa 10:24; 11:15
2Now you have a king as your leader.[e] As
for me, I am old and gray, and my sons 12:2
are here with you. I have been your e 1Sa 8:5
leader from my youth until this day.
3Here I stand. Testify against me in the 12:3
presence of the LORD and his anointed.[f] f 1Sa 10:1; 24:6;
Whose ox have I taken? Whose donkey[g] 2Sa 1:14
have I taken? Whom have I cheated? g Nu 16:15 h Dt 16:19
Whom have I oppressed? From whose i Ac 20:33
hand have I accepted a bribe[h] to make
me shut my eyes? If I have done[i] any of
these, I will make it right."
4"You have not cheated or oppressed
us," they replied. "You have not taken
anything from anyone's hand."
5Samuel said to them, "The LORD is
witness against you, and also his anointed is witness this day, that you have not 12:5
found anything[j] in my hand.[k]" j Ac 23:9; 24:20
"He is witness," they said. k Ex 22:4
6Then Samuel said to the people, "It is
the LORD who appointed Moses and 12:6
Aaron and brought[l] your forefathers up l Ex 6:26;
out of Egypt. 7Now then, stand here, be- Mic 6:4
cause I am going to confront[m] you with 12:7
evidence before the LORD as to all the m Isa 1:18;
righteous acts performed by the LORD Mic 6:1-5
for you and your fathers.
8"After Jacob entered Egypt, they
cried[n] to the LORD for help, and the LORD 12:8 n Ex 2:23
sent[o] Moses and Aaron, who brought o Ex 3:10; 4:16
your forefathers out of Egypt and settled
them in this place.
9"But they forgot[p] the LORD their God; 12:9 p Jdg 3:7
so he sold them into the hand of Sisera,[q] q Jdg 4:2
the commander of the army of Hazor, r Jdg 10:7; 13:1
and into the hands of the Philistines[r] s Jdg 3:12
and the king of Moab,[s] who fought
against them. 10They cried out to the
LORD and said, 'We have sinned; we have

[a] 15 Traditionally *peace offerings*

In Awe of God

What a way to end a speech! After he had informed the people that they had sinned by demanding a king, Samuel predicted that God would send a storm to wash away their crops. The prophet then *asked* God to do just that, and he did—that very day! (1 Samuel 12:16–17). The people realized the ramifications of turning away from God and were badly frightened. While God doesn't want his people to live in terror, he does desire that we be aware of his awesome power.

There are many reasons to stand in awe of God. For one thing, he controls the entire universe. He created *everything* simply by speaking and continues to rule over all (Job 25:2). We can also be in wonder because of the wisdom he grants to us (1 Kings 3:28) and because of his laws, which reflect his perfection and holiness (Psalm 119:120). God has amazing power worthy of our deepest respect (Ecclesiastes 5:1–7). His very name should cause us to reflect on who he is and the scope of what he has done for us (Malachi 2:5).

When the disciples saw the awesome power of Jesus over the wind and water, they responded with a new level of respect for him. "In fear and amazement they asked one another, 'Who is this? Even the wind and the waves obey him!' " (Mark 4:41).

Why is it so easy then for us to neglect to give God the respect he so deserves? Fear that comes from a recognition of our sin is a natural reaction—but fear is uncomfortable, and it is easy for us to avoid the issue altogether! When we remember that Jesus died for our sins, however, we realize that we have no reason to be afraid of him. Instead, we can rest in our new standing as beloved children of God, brothers and sisters of our Savior (Romans 8:1–2).

The apostle John had beautiful words to say about the incompatibility of loving God and fearing him (in the sense of being afraid of his response to our sinful condition): "If anyone acknowledges that Jesus is the Son of God, God lives in him and he in God . . . Whoever lives in love lives in God, and God in him . . . There is no fear in love. But perfect love drives out fear, because fear has to do with punishment. The one who fears is not made perfect in love" (1 John 4:15–16,18).

Sin by its very nature has also made us fiercely independent; we like to think that we can determine our own destinies and balk against acknowledging that God is ultimately in control. As we get to know him, though, we learn that Jesus is on our side. We cannot change the fact that he is God, but we can relax in the truth that he is good, that he loves us and that he knows what he's doing.

Maybe we need to spend less time analyzing *why* Jesus does what he does and more time simply learning to love and trust him. When we truly grasp what he has in store for us in the future, we will desire nothing else but to fall to our knees in awe!

Self-Discovery: *Have you ever felt afraid of Jesus because of past mistakes? How do his words recorded in the Bible help you to overcome this unhealthy kind of fear?*

GO TO DISCOVERY 70 ON PAGE 360

12:10 t Jdg 10:10,15 forsaken[t] the LORD and served the Baals
u Jdg 2:13 and the Ashtoreths.[u] But now deliver us
from the hands of our enemies, and we
12:11 will serve you.' 11Then the LORD sent Jer-
v Jdg 6:14,32 w Jdg 4:6 ub-Baal,[a v] Barak,[b w] Jephthah[x] and Sam-
x Jdg 11:1 uel,[c] and he delivered you from the
hands of your enemies on every side, so
that you lived securely.
12:12 12"But when you saw that Nahash[y]
y 1Sa 11:1 z 1Sa 8:5 king[z] of the Ammonites was moving
a Jdg 8:23; against you, you said to me, 'No, we
1Sa 8:6,19 want a king to rule[a] over us'—even
though the LORD your God was your
12:13 b 1Sa 8:5; king. 13Now here is the king[b] you have
Hos 13:11 c 1Sa 10:24 chosen, the one you asked[c] for; see, the
LORD has set a king over you. 14If you
12:14 fear[d] the LORD and serve and obey him
d Jos 24:14 and do not rebel against his commands,
and if both you and the king who reigns
over you follow the LORD your God—
good! 15But if you do not obey the LORD,
12:15 e ver 9; and if you rebel against[e] his commands,
Jos 24:20; Isa 1:20 his hand will be against you, as it was
against your fathers.
12:16 16"Now then, stand still and see[f] this
f Ex 14:13 great thing the LORD is about to do be-
12:17 fore your eyes! 17Is it not wheat harvest[g]
g 1Sa 7:9-10 h Jas 5:18 now? I will call[h] upon the LORD to send
i Pr 26:1 thunder and rain.[i] And you will realize
j 1Sa 8:6-7 what an evil[j] thing you did in the eyes of
the LORD when you asked for a king."
18Then Samuel called upon the LORD,
and that same day the LORD sent thunder and rain. So all the people stood in
12:18 k Ex 14:31 awe[k] of the LORD and of Samuel.
12:19 19The people all said to Samuel, "Pray[l]
l ver 23; Ex 9:28; to the LORD your God for your servants
Jas 5:18; so that we will not die, for we have
1Jn 5:16 added to all our other sins the evil of
12:21 asking for a king."
m Isa 41:24,29; 20"Do not be afraid," Samuel replied.
Jer 16:19; Hab 2:18 "You have done all this evil; yet do not
n Dt 11:16 turn away from the LORD, but serve the
12:22 LORD with all your heart. 21Do not turn
o Ps 106:8 away after useless[m] idols.[n] They can do
p Jos 7:9 q 1Ki 6:13 you no good, nor can they rescue you,
r Dt 7:7; 1Pe 2:9 because they are useless. 22For the sake[o]
12:23 of his great name[p] the LORD will not re-
s Ro 1:9-10; ject[q] his people, because the LORD was
Col 1:9; 2Ti 1:3 pleased to make[r] you his own. 23As for
t 1Ki 8:36; Ps 34:11; me, far be it from me that I should sin
Pr 4:11 against the LORD by failing to pray[s] for
12:24 you. And I will teach[t] you the way that is
u Ecc 12:13 good and right. 24But be sure to fear[u] the
v Isa 5:12 w Dt 10:21 LORD and serve him faithfully with all
12:25 your heart; consider[v] what great[w] things
x 1Sa 31:1-5 he has done for you. 25Yet if you persist[x]
in doing evil, both you and your king will 12:25 y Jos 24:20
be swept[y] away."

Samuel Rebukes Saul

13 Saul was ⌊thirty⌋[d] years old
when he became king, and he
reigned over Israel ⌊forty-⌋[e] two years.
2Saul[f] chose three thousand men
from Israel; two thousand were with him
at Micmash and in the hill country of
Bethel, and a thousand were with Jona-
than at Gibeah[z] in Benjamin. The rest of 13:2 z 1Sa 10:26
the men he sent back to their homes.
3Jonathan attacked the Philistine out- 13:3
post[a] at Geba, and the Philistines heard a 1Sa 10:5
about it. Then Saul had the trumpet

[a] 11 Also called *Gideon* [b] 11 Some Septuagint manuscripts and Syriac; Hebrew *Bedan* [c] 11 Hebrew; some Septuagint manuscripts and Syriac *Samson* [d] 1 A few late manuscripts of the Septuagint; Hebrew does not have *thirty.* [e] 1 See the round number in Acts 13:21; Hebrew does not have *forty-*. [f] 1,2 Or *and when he had reigned over Israel two years, 2he*

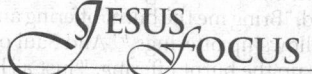

JESUS FOCUS

KING OR PRIEST?

Saul had concluded that Samuel was taking too long in coming to Gilgal to offer a pre-battle sacrifice, so he himself stepped into the role of priest to make the offering (1 Samuel 13:8–9). Saul had panicked because the Philistines had formed a huge army to stand in opposition to the Israelites and the people had begun to flee. Saul rationalized his action away by presenting what he perceived to be a valid excuse for his disobedience: "I thought, 'Now the Philistines will come down against me . . . and I have not sought the LORD's favor.' So I felt compelled to offer the burnt offering" (verse 12). The only problem was that God had not appointed Saul as a priest, nor was it his role to make a sacrifice—only a *true* priest of God could do that. Saul's disregard for God's commands eventually cost him his position as king and led to the prediction that God would find "a man after his own heart" to replace Saul (verse 14). While the offices of priest and king were traditionally filled by different people in Bible times, Jesus, the promised Messiah, is both King and Priest (Hebrews 9:11–15). As believers in Jesus, we now share in his anointing, and so we present ourselves to him as living sacrifices of gratitude (Romans 12:1; 1 Peter 2:5,9) and will someday reign with Jesus over all creation for all eternity (Matthew 25:34; 2 Timothy 2:12).

blown throughout the land and said,
"Let the Hebrews hear!" 4So all Israel
heard the news: "Saul has attacked the
Philistine outpost, and now Israel has
13:4 become a stench[b] to the Philistines."
b Ge 34:30 And the people were summoned to join
Saul at Gilgal.
5The Philistines assembled to fight Israel, with three thousand[a] chariots, six
13:5 thousand charioteers, and soldiers as
c Jos 11:4 numerous as the sand[c] on the seashore.
They went up and camped at Micmash,
east of Beth Aven. 6When the men of Israel saw that their situation was critical
and that their army was hard pressed,
they hid in caves and thickets, among
13:6 the rocks, and in pits and cisterns.[d]
d Jdg 6:2 7Some Hebrews even crossed the Jordan
13:7 to the land of Gad[e] and Gilead.
e Nu 32:33 Saul remained at Gilgal, and all the
troops with him were quaking with fear.
13:8 8He waited seven[f] days, the time set by
f 1Sa 10:8 Samuel; but Samuel did not come to Gilgal, and Saul's men began to scatter. 9So
he said, "Bring me the burnt offering and
the fellowship offerings.[b]" And Saul of-
13:9 fered[g] up the burnt offering. 10Just as he
g 2Sa 24:25; 1Ki 3:4 finished making the offering, Samuel[h]
13:10 arrived, and Saul went out to greet him.
h 1Sa 15:13 11"What have you done?" asked Samuel.
Saul replied, "When I saw that the men
were scattering, and that you did not
come at the set time, and that the Philis-
13:11 tines were assembling at Micmash,[i] 12I
i ver 2,5,16,23 thought, 'Now the Philistines will come
down against me at Gilgal, and I have not
13:12 sought the LORD's favor.'[j] So I felt com-
j Jer 26:19 pelled to offer the burnt offering."
13:13 13"You acted foolishly,[k]" Samuel said.
k 2Ch 16:9 l 1Sa 15:23,24 "You have not kept[l] the command the
LORD your God gave you; if you had, he
would have established your kingdom
over Israel for all time. 14But now your
13:14 kingdom[m] will not endure; the LORD has
m 1Sa 15:28 n Ac 7:46; 13:22 sought out a man after his own heart[n]
o 2Sa 6:21 and appointed[o] him leader of his people,
because you have not kept the LORD's
command."
15Then Samuel left Gilgal[c] and went
13:15 p 1Sa 14:2 up to Gibeah[p] in Benjamin, and Saul
counted the men who were with him.
They numbered about six hundred.

Israel Without Weapons

16Saul and his son Jonathan and the
men with them were staying in Gibeah[d]
in Benjamin, while the Philistines
13:17 camped at Micmash. 17Raiding[q] parties q 1Sa 14:15
went out from the Philistine camp in r Jos 18:23
three detachments. One turned toward
Ophrah[r] in the vicinity of Shual, 18an-
other toward Beth Horon,[s] and the third 13:18 s Jos 18:13-14
toward the borderland overlooking the t Ne 11:34
Valley of Zeboim[t] facing the desert.
19Not a blacksmith[u] could be found in 13:19 u 2Ki 24:14;
the whole land of Israel, because the Phi- Jer 24:1
listines had said, "Otherwise the Hebrews will make swords or spears!" 20So
all Israel went down to the Philistines to
have their plowshares, mattocks, axes
and sickles[e] sharpened. 21The price was
two thirds of a shekel[f] for sharpening
plowshares and mattocks, and a third of
a shekel[g] for sharpening forks and axes
and for repointing goads.
22So on the day of the battle not a sol- 13:22
dier with Saul and Jonathan[v] had a v 1Ch 9:39
sword or spear[w] in his hand; only Saul w Jdg 5:8
and his son Jonathan had them.

Jonathan Attacks the Philistines

23Now a detachment of Philistines 13:23
had gone out to the pass[x] at Micmash. x 1Sa 14:4

14 1One day Jonathan son of Saul
said to the young man bearing
his armor, "Come, let's go over to the
Philistine outpost on the other side." But
he did not tell his father.
2Saul was staying on the outskirts of 14:2
Gibeah[y] under a pomegranate tree in y 1Sa 13:15
Migron.[z] With him were about six hun- z Isa 10:28
dred men, 3among whom was Ahijah,
who was wearing an ephod. He was a 14:3
son of Ichabod's[a] brother Ahitub[b] son of a 1Sa 4:21 b 1Sa 22:11,20
Phinehas, the son of Eli,[c] the LORD's c 1Sa 2:28
priest in Shiloh. No one was aware that
Jonathan had left.
4On each side of the pass[d] that Jona- 14:4
than intended to cross to reach the d 1Sa 13:23
Philistine outpost was a cliff; one was
called Bozez, and the other Seneh. 5One
cliff stood to the north toward Micmash,
the other to the south toward Geba.
6Jonathan said to his young armor-

a 5 Some Septuagint manuscripts and Syriac; Hebrew *thirty thousand* *b* 9 Traditionally *peace offerings* *c* 15 Hebrew; Septuagint *Gilgal and went his way; the rest of the people went after Saul to meet the army, and they went out of Gilgal*
d 16 Two Hebrew manuscripts; most Hebrew manuscripts *Geba,* a variant of *Gibeah*
e 20 Septuagint; Hebrew *plowshares*
f 21 Hebrew *pim*; that is, about 1/4 ounce (about 8 grams) *g* 21 That is, about 1/8 ounce (about 4 grams)

14:6 [e] 1Sa 17:26,36; Jer 9:26 [f] Heb 11:34 [g] Jdg 7:4 [h] 1Sa 17:46-47

bearer, "Come, let's go over to the outpost of those uncircumcised[e] fellows.
Perhaps the LORD will act in our behalf.
Nothing[f] can hinder the LORD from saving, whether by many[g] or by few.[h]"
7 "Do all that you have in mind," his armor-bearer said. "Go ahead; I am with
you heart and soul."
8 Jonathan said, "Come, then; we will
cross over toward the men and let them
see us. 9 If they say to us, 'Wait there until we come to you,' we will stay where we
are and not go up to them. 10 But if they
say, 'Come up to us,' we will climb up, because that will be our sign[i] that the LORD
has given them into our hands."

14:10 [i] Ge 24:14; Jdg 6:36-37

11 So both of them showed themselves
to the Philistine outpost. "Look!" said
the Philistines. "The Hebrews are crawling out of the holes they were hiding[j] in."
12 The men of the outpost shouted to
Jonathan and his armor-bearer, "Come
up to us and we'll teach you a lesson.[k]"

14:11 [j] 1Sa 13:6
14:12 [k] 1Sa 17:43-44 [l] 2Sa 5:24

So Jonathan said to his armor-bearer,
"Climb up after me; the LORD has given
them into the hand[l] of Israel."
13 Jonathan climbed up, using his
hands and feet, with his armor-bearer
right behind him. The Philistines fell before Jonathan, and his armor-bearer followed and killed behind him. 14 In that
first attack Jonathan and his armor-
bearer killed some twenty men in an
area of about half an acre.[a]

Israel Routs the Philistines

14:15 [m] Ge 35:5; 2Ki 7:5-7 [n] 1Sa 13:17

15 Then panic[m] struck the whole
army—those in the camp and field, and
those in the outposts and raiding[n] parties—and the ground shook. It was a
panic sent by God.[b]
16 Saul's lookouts[o] at Gibeah in Benjamin saw the army melting away in all directions. 17 Then Saul said to the men
who were with him, "Muster the forces
and see who has left us." When they did,
it was Jonathan and his armor-bearer
who were not there.

14:16 [o] 2Sa 18:24

18 Saul said to Ahijah, "Bring[p] the ark
of God." (At that time it was with the Israelites.)[c] 19 While Saul was talking to the
priest, the tumult in the Philistine camp
increased more and more. So Saul said to
the priest,[q] "Withdraw your hand."
20 Then Saul and all his men assembled and went to the battle. They found
the Philistines in total confusion, strik-

14:18 [p] 1Sa 30:7
14:19 [q] Nu 27:21

ing[r] each other with their swords.
21 Those Hebrews who had previously
been with the Philistines and had gone
up with them to their camp went[s] over
to the Israelites who were with Saul and
Jonathan. 22 When all the Israelites who
had hidden[t] in the hill country of Ephraim heard that the Philistines were on the
run, they joined the battle in hot pursuit.
23 So the LORD rescued[u] Israel that day,
and the battle moved on beyond Beth
Aven.[v]

14:20 [r] Jdg 7:22; 2Ch 20:23
14:21 [s] 1Sa 29:4
14:22 [t] 1Sa 13:6
14:23 [u] Ex 14:30; Ps 44:6-7 [v] 1Sa 13:5

Jonathan Eats Honey

24 Now the men of Israel were in distress that day, because Saul had bound
the people under an oath,[w] saying,
"Cursed be any man who eats food before evening comes, before I have
avenged myself on my enemies!" So
none of the troops tasted food.
25 The entire army[d] entered the woods,
and there was honey on the ground.
26 When they went into the woods, they
saw the honey oozing out, yet no one put
his hand to his mouth, because they
feared the oath. 27 But Jonathan had not
heard that his father had bound the people with the oath, so he reached out the
end of the staff that was in his hand and
dipped it into the honeycomb.[x] He
raised his hand to his mouth, and his
eyes brightened.[e] 28 Then one of the soldiers told him, "Your father bound the
army under a strict oath, saying, 'Cursed
be any man who eats food today!' That is
why the men are faint."

14:24 [w] Jos 6:26
14:27 [x] ver 43; 1Sa 30:12

29 Jonathan said, "My father has made
trouble[y] for the country. See how my
eyes brightened[f] when I tasted a little of
this honey. 30 How much better it would
have been if the men had eaten today
some of the plunder they took from their
enemies. Would not the slaughter of the
Philistines have been even greater?"
31 That day, after the Israelites had
struck down the Philistines from Micmash to Aijalon,[z] they were exhausted.
32 They pounced on the plunder[a] and,
taking sheep, cattle and calves, they
butchered them on the ground and ate

14:29 [y] Jos 7:25; 1Ki 18:18
14:31 [z] Jos 10:12
14:32 [a] 1Sa 15:19

[a] 14 Hebrew *half a yoke*; a "yoke" was the land plowed by a yoke of oxen in one day. [b] 15 Or *a terrible panic* [c] 18 Hebrew; Septuagint *"Bring the ephod." (At that time he wore the ephod before the Israelites.)* [d] 25 Or *Now all the people of the land* [e] 27 Or *his strength was renewed* [f] 29 Or *my strength was renewed*

14:32 b Ge 9:4; them, together with the blood.[b] 33 Then
Lev 3:17; 7:26; someone said to Saul, "Look, the men
17:10-14; 19:26; are sinning against the LORD by eating
Dt 12:16,23-24 meat that has blood in it."
"You have broken faith," he said. "Roll
a large stone over here at once." 34 Then
he said, "Go out among the men and tell
them, 'Each of you bring me your cattle
and sheep, and slaughter them here and
eat them. Do not sin against the LORD by
eating meat with blood still in it.' "
So everyone brought his ox that night
and slaughtered it there. 35 Then Saul
14:35 built an altar[c] to the LORD; it was the
c 1Sa 7:17 first time he had done this.
36 Saul said, "Let us go down after the
Philistines by night and plunder them
till dawn, and let us not leave one of
them alive."
"Do whatever seems best to you," they
replied.
But the priest said, "Let us inquire of
God here."
37 So Saul asked God, "Shall I go down
after the Philistines? Will you give them
into Israel's hand?" But God did not an-
14:37 d 1Sa 10:22; swer[d] him that day.
28:6,15 38 Saul therefore said, "Come here, all
you who are leaders of the army, and let
us find out what sin has been commit-
14:38 e Jos 7:11; ted[e] today. 39 As surely as the LORD who
1Sa 10:19 rescues Israel lives,[f] even if it lies with
14:39 my son Jonathan, he must die." But not
f 2Sa 12:5 one of the men said a word.
40 Saul then said to all the Israelites,
"You stand over there; I and Jonathan
my son will stand over here."
"Do what seems best to you," the men
replied.
41 Then Saul prayed to the LORD, the
14:41 God of Israel, "Give[g] me the right[h] an-
g Ac 1:24 h Pr 16:33 swer."[a] And Jonathan and Saul were tak-
en by lot, and the men were cleared.
42 Saul said, "Cast the lot between me
and Jonathan my son." And Jonathan
was taken.
43 Then Saul said to Jonathan, "Tell me
what you have done."[i]
So Jonathan told him, "I merely tast-
14:43 ed a little honey[j] with the end of my
i Jos 7:19 j ver 27 staff. And now must I die?"
14:44 44 Saul said, "May God deal with me,
k Ru 1:17 be it ever so severely,[k] if you do not die,
l ver 39 Jonathan.[l]"
45 But the men said to Saul, "Should
Jonathan die—he who has brought
about this great deliverance in Israel?

Never! As surely as the LORD lives, not a 14:45
hair[m] of his head will fall to the ground, m 1Ki 1:52;
for he did this today with God's help." So Lk 21:18;
the men rescued[n] Jonathan, and he was Ac 27:34 n 2Sa 14:11
not put to death.
46 Then Saul stopped pursuing the
Philistines, and they withdrew to their
own land.
47 After Saul had assumed rule over Israel, he fought against their enemies on 14:47
every side: Moab, the Ammonites,[o] o 1Sa 11:1-13
Edom, the kings[b] of Zobah,[p] and the Phi- p ver 52;
listines. Wherever he turned, he inflict- 2Sa 10:6
ed punishment on them.[c] 48 He fought 14:48
valiantly and defeated the Amalekites,[q] q 1Sa 15:2,7
delivering Israel from the hands of those
who had plundered them.

Saul's Family

49 Saul's sons were Jonathan, Ishvi and 14:49
Malki-Shua.[r] The name of his older r 1Sa 31:2;
daughter was Merab, and that of the 1Ch 8:33
younger was Michal.[s] 50 His wife's name s 1Sa 18:17-20
was Ahinoam daughter of Ahimaaz. The
name of the commander of Saul's army
was Abner son of Ner, and Ner was Saul's 14:51
uncle. 51 Saul's father Kish[t] and Abner's t 1Sa 9:1
father Ner were sons of Abiel.
52 All the days of Saul there was bitter
war with the Philistines, and whenever
Saul saw a mighty or brave man, he 14:52
took[u] him into his service. u 1Sa 8:11

The LORD Rejects Saul as King

15 Samuel said to Saul, "I am the 15:1
one the LORD sent to anoint[v] v 1Sa 9:16
you king over his people Israel; so listen
now to the message from the LORD.
2 This is what the LORD Almighty says: 'I 15:2
will punish the Amalekites[w] for what w Ex 17:8-14;
they did to Israel when they waylaid Nu 24:20;
them as they came up from Egypt. 3 Now Dt 25:17-19
go, attack the Amalekites and totally[x] 15:3
destroy[d] everything that belongs to x Nu 24:20;
them. Do not spare them; put to death Dt 20:16-18;
men and women, children and infants, Jos 6:17;
cattle and sheep, camels and donkeys.' " 1Sa 22:19
4 So Saul summoned the men and
mustered them at Telaim—two hundred

a 41 Hebrew; Septuagint *"Why have you not answered your servant today? If the fault is in me or my son Jonathan, respond with Urim, but if the men of Israel are at fault, respond with Thummim."*
b 47 Masoretic Text; Dead Sea Scrolls and Septuagint *king* *c 47* Hebrew; Septuagint *he was victorious* *d 3* The Hebrew term refers to the irrevocable giving over of things or persons to the LORD, often by totally destroying them; also in verses 8, 9, 15, 18, 20 and 21.

thousand foot soldiers and ten thousand men from Judah. 5Saul went to the
city of Amalek and set an ambush in the

15:6 [y] Ex 18:10,19; Nu 10:29-32; 24:22; Jdg 1:16; 4:1

ravine. 6Then he said to the Kenites,[y]
"Go away, leave the Amalekites so that I
do not destroy you along with them; for
you showed kindness to all the Israelites
when they came up out of Egypt." So the
Kenites moved away from the Amalekites.

15:7 [z] 1Sa 14:48 [a] Ge 16:7; 25:17-18; Ex 15:22

7Then Saul attacked the Amalekites[z]
all the way from Havilah to Shur,[a] to the
east of Egypt. 8He took Agag king of the

15:8 [b] 1Sa 30:1

Amalekites alive,[b] and all his people he
totally destroyed with the sword. 9But

15:9 [c] ver 3,15

Saul and the army spared[c] Agag and the
best of the sheep and cattle, the fat
calves[a] and lambs—everything that was
good. These they were unwilling to destroy completely, but everything that
was despised and weak they totally destroyed.

15:11 [d] Ge 6:6; 2Sa 24:16 [e] Jos 22:16 [f] 1Sa 13:13; 1Ki 9:6-7 [g] ver 35

10Then the word of the LORD came to
Samuel: 11"I am grieved[d] that I have
made Saul king, because he has turned[e]
away from me and has not carried out
my instructions."[f] Samuel was troubled,[g] and he cried out to the LORD all
that night.

15:12 [h] Jos 15:55

12Early in the morning Samuel got up
and went to meet Saul, but he was told,
"Saul has gone to Carmel.[h] There he has
set up a monument in his own honor
and has turned and gone on down to
Gilgal."
13When Samuel reached him, Saul
said, "The LORD bless you! I have carried
out the LORD's instructions."
14But Samuel said, "What then is this
bleating of sheep in my ears? What is
this lowing of cattle that I hear?"
15Saul answered, "The soldiers
brought them from the Amalekites; they
spared the best of the sheep and cattle
to sacrifice to the LORD your God, but we
totally destroyed the rest."
16"Stop!" Samuel said to Saul. "Let me
tell you what the LORD said to me last
night."
"Tell me," Saul replied.

15:17 [i] 1Sa 9:21

17Samuel said, "Although you were
once small[i] in your own eyes, did you
not become the head of the tribes of Israel? The LORD anointed you king over
Israel. 18And he sent you on a mission,
saying, 'Go and completely destroy
those wicked people, the Amalekites;
make war on them until you have wiped
them out.' 19Why did you not obey the
LORD? Why did you pounce on the plun-

15:19 [j] 1Sa 14:32

der[j] and do evil in the eyes of the LORD?"

15:20 [k] ver 13

20"But I did obey[k] the LORD," Saul said.
"I went on the mission the LORD assigned me. I completely destroyed the
Amalekites and brought back Agag
their king. 21The soldiers took sheep and
cattle from the plunder, the best of what
was devoted to God, in order to sacrifice
them to the LORD your God at Gilgal."
22But Samuel replied:

"Does the LORD delight in burnt
offerings and sacrifices
as much as in obeying the voice
of the LORD?

15:22 [l] Ps 40:6-8; 51:16; Isa 1:11-15; Jer 7:22; Hos 6:6; Mic 6:6-8; Mt 12:7; Mk 12:33; Heb 10:6-9

To obey is better than sacrifice,[l]
and to heed is better than the fat
of rams.
23For rebellion is like the sin of
divination,[m]
and arrogance like the evil of
idolatry.

15:23 [m] Dt 18:10 [n] 1Sa 13:13

Because you have rejected[n] the
word of the LORD,
he has rejected you as king."

15:24 [o] 2Sa 12:13 [p] Pr 29:25; Isa 51:12-13

24Then Saul said to Samuel, "I have
sinned.[o] I violated the LORD's command
and your instructions. I was afraid[p] of
the people and so I gave in to them.

15:25 [q] Ex 10:17

25Now I beg you, forgive[q] my sin and
come back with me, so that I may worship the LORD."
26But Samuel said to him, "I will not

15:26 [r] 1Sa 13:14

go back with you. You have rejected[r] the
word of the LORD, and the LORD has rejected you as king over Israel!"
27As Samuel turned to leave, Saul
caught hold of the hem of his robe, and

15:27 [s] 1Ki 11:11,31

it tore.[s] 28Samuel said to him, "The LORD

15:28 [t] 1Sa 28:17; 1Ki 11:31

has torn[t] the kingdom of Israel from you
today and has given it to one of your
neighbors—to one better than you. 29He

15:29 [u] 1Ch 29:11; Tit 1:2 [v] Nu 23:19; Eze 24:14

who is the Glory of Israel does not lie[u] or
change[v] his mind; for he is not a man,
that he should change his mind."
30Saul replied, "I have sinned. But

15:30 [w] Isa 29:13; Jn 5:44; 12:43

please honor[w] me before the elders of
my people and before Israel; come back
with me, so that I may worship the LORD
your God." 31So Samuel went back with
Saul, and Saul worshiped the LORD.

[a] 9 Or *the grown bulls*; the meaning of the Hebrew for this phrase is uncertain.

DISCOVERY 70

Obedience, Not Sacrifice

God directed Saul to attack the Amalekites and "totally destroy everything that belongs to them" (1 Samuel 15:3), because the Amalekites had attacked God's people after they had fled from Egypt (Exodus 17:14). This judgment might seem harsh, but we need to remember that, although the Amalekites would have to suffer the consequences for attacking the Israelites, God had waited several hundreds of years before acting. He had given that nation more than enough time to turn to him, but the Amalekites had refused. At this juncture Saul went to war and defeated them, but, contrary to God's explicit instructions, he spared King Agag and the best of the livestock. Saul followed God's instructions only partially. To make matters worse, he erected an altar to honor *himself*! (1 Samuel 15:12).

Following God only in part often leads to thinking too highly of ourselves. Samuel confronted Saul about his actions, and Saul laid the blame on his soldiers, claiming that they had kept the livestock in order to offer animal sacrifices to God. Samuel saw right through that excuse: "Does the LORD delight in burnt offerings and sacrifices as much as in obeying the voice of the LORD? To obey is better than sacrifice, and to heed is better than the fat of rams" (verse 22). Then came the final blow: "Because you have rejected the word of the LORD, he has rejected you as king" (verse 23).

Samuel's words are worth remembering, because they clarify for us what God wants. He desires that we do what he says more than he wants us to make elaborate sacrifices for him. Even if Saul had really kept the animals to give them to God, he would not have understood God's desire. God wanted only Saul's total, uncompromising and unquestioning obedience.

Thinking too highly of ourselves is tantamount to worshiping another god. When we choose to follow our own course of action, aware that we are acting contrary to God's desire and instruction, we are in effect setting up an altar to honor ourselves. And doing only part of what God asks implies turning away from the other part—and living with the consequences.

We can learn a great deal from Saul's disobedience, but we can learn even more from God's perfect example in his Son Jesus. As God's promised Messiah, Jesus reigns as King of the universe. He acted exactly as God wanted him to (Philippians 2:6–11), to the extent of dying on the cross to atone for our sins (Hebrews 10:5–10). Unlike Saul, who obeyed God to a degree, Jesus complied completely with the Father's will—and because of his flawless obedience our disobedience has been forgiven.

Self-Discovery: *In what ways have you set up an altar in your own honor? Have you dealt with this issue in prayer before the Lord?*

GO TO DISCOVERY 71 ON PAGE 362

32Then Samuel said, "Bring me Agag
king of the Amalekites."
Agag came to him confidently,[a]
thinking, "Surely the bitterness of death
is past."
33But Samuel said,

"As your sword has made women
childless,
15:33 so will your mother be childless
x Ge 9:6; Jdg 1:7 among women."[x]

And Samuel put Agag to death before
the LORD at Gilgal.
15:34 34Then Samuel left for Ramah,[y] but
y 1Sa 7:17 z 1Sa 11:4 Saul went up to his home in Gibeah[z] of
15:35 Saul. 35Until the day Samuel[a] died, he
a 1Sa 19:24 did not go to see Saul again, though
b 1Sa 16:1 Samuel mourned[b] for him. And the
LORD was grieved that he had made Saul
king over Israel.

Samuel Anoints David

16:1 16 The LORD said to Samuel, "How
c 1Sa 15:35 long will you mourn[c] for Saul,
d 1Sa 15:23 since I have rejected[d] him as king over
e 2Ki 9:1 Israel? Fill your horn with oil[e] and be on
f Ru 4:17; 1Sa 9:16 your way; I am sending you to Jesse[f] of
g Ps 78:70; Ac 13:22 Bethlehem. I have chosen[g] one of his
sons to be king."
2But Samuel said, "How can I go? Saul
will hear about it and kill me."
The LORD said, "Take a heifer with you
and say, 'I have come to sacrifice to the
16:3 LORD.' 3Invite Jesse to the sacrifice, and I
h Ex 4:15 will show[h] you what to do. You are to
i Dt 17:15; 1Sa 9:16 anoint[i] for me the one I indicate."
4Samuel did what the LORD said. When
16:4 j Ge 48:7; Lk 2:4 he arrived at Bethlehem,[j] the elders of the
k 1Ki 2:13; 2Ki 9:17 town trembled when they met him. They
asked, "Do you come in peace?[k]"
5Samuel replied, "Yes, in peace; I have
come to sacrifice to the LORD. Conse-
16:5 l Ex 19:10,22 crate[l] yourselves and come to the sacrifice with me." Then he consecrated Jes-
se and his sons and invited them to the
sacrifice.
6When they arrived, Samuel saw Eli-
16:6 m 1Sa 17:13 ab[m] and thought, "Surely the LORD's
anointed stands here before the LORD."
7But the LORD said to Samuel, "Do not
consider his appearance or his height,
16:7 for I have rejected him. The LORD does
n Ps 147:10 not look at the things man looks at. Man
o 1Ki 8:39; 1Ch 28:9; looks at the outward appearance,[n] but
Isa 55:8 the LORD looks at the heart."[o]
16:8 8Then Jesse called Abinadab[p] and had
p 1Sa 17:13 him pass in front of Samuel. But Samuel
said, "The LORD has not chosen this one
either." 9Jesse then had Shammah pass
by, but Samuel said, "Nor has the LORD
chosen this one." 10Jesse had seven of his
sons pass before Samuel, but Samuel
said to him, "The LORD has not chosen 16:11
these." 11So he asked Jesse, "Are these all[q] q 1Sa 17:12
the sons you have?"
"There is still the youngest," Jesse answered, "but he is tending the sheep."
Samuel said, "Send for him; we will
not sit down[b] until he arrives."
12So he[r] sent and had him brought in. 16:12
He was ruddy, with a fine appearance r 1Sa 9:17 s Ge 39:6;
and handsome[s] features. 1Sa 17:42
Then the LORD said, "Rise and anoint
him; he is the one."
13So Samuel took the horn of oil and
anointed him in the presence of his
brothers, and from that day on the Spirit

a 32 Or *him trembling, yet* *b* 11 Some Septuagint manuscripts; Hebrew *not gather around*

JESUS FOCUS

GOD'S ANOINTED ONE

The word *messiah* means "anointed one" and refers to a priest or king set apart by God for a high position of service. 1 Samuel 16 tells us how God chose David to be Israel's king after Saul's refusal to remain true to God. Each priest or king was anointed with oil during a ceremony, a sign that he was deserving of reverence and respect from God's people. Moses anointed Aaron and his sons as God's priests (Exodus 30:22–30). Even David, knowing that he had been chosen by God to replace Saul as Israel's king, refused to harm Saul because Saul was "the LORD's anointed" (1 Samuel 24:6). David knew that the role of king was temporary but that God would someday send an ultimate and final King.

Both the psalms and the prophets point ahead to the Messiah, referring to him as David's "son" (Isaiah 9:6–7), the "root of Jesse" (Isaiah 11:10), "the righteous Branch" (Jeremiah 32:5) and the servant of the Lord (Isaiah 42; 49; 50; 52—53). God's people looked forward to the salvation Jesus would bring through his personal suffering and death, recognizing also that he would eventually rule over the nations (Zechariah 9:9–10; Romans 15:12). In the New Testament Jesus is clearly recognized as that Messiah, and he himself claimed to be God's anointed one (John 1:41–42; 4:25–26; 20:31).

DISCOVERY 71

GOD'S X-RAY VISION

One evening the pastor's oldest son arrived at the Wednesday night service right after high school football practice. His hair was tousled and his clothes mud-stained. The music leader, who was dressed immaculately, sat down next to the young man and remarked with a smile, "I see you've come to terms with the principle that God does not look on the outward appearance!"

People have always been surprised by God's choices, because God does not see things as we do. We tend to base our opinions on what we *see*, while God judges us on our inner character. God sent Samuel to the house of Jesse in Bethlehem to anoint Israel's future king. When Samuel saw Eliab, he immediately assumed that this strapping, handsome oldest son was the man of God's choice. But God informed him otherwise: "I have rejected him. The LORD does not look at the things man looks at . . . the LORD looks at the heart" (1 Samuel 16:7). After inspecting seven of Jesse's sons and being instructed by God to reject them all, Samuel finally met the youngest, David. "He is the one," God told him immediately (verse 12).

As God's Son, Jesus based his opinions of people on the same criterion as his Father: sincerity of devotion. What did Jesus look like? Was he tall or short? Did he have olive skin or a pale complexion? What color was his hair? Did he have a slight build, or was he heavyset? Countless artistic renditions of Jesus are available, but no one except an eyewitness from his own day would recognize him in a crowd. Sometimes we think of Jesus as the ultimate human being with a perfect physical appearance. But the prophet Isaiah told us that Jesus "had no beauty or majesty to attract us to him, nothing in his appearance that we should desire him" (Isaiah 53:2). Jesus was not the kind of person everyone noticed on the basis of his physical appearance. In fact, he may have been just the opposite!

Jesus warned people against judging one another based on outward physique or attractiveness. His most pointed condemnation was directed at highly religious but hypocritical people: "You are like whitewashed tombs, which look beautiful on the outside but on the inside are full of dead men's bones and everything unclean. In the same way, on the outside you appear to people as righteous but on the inside you are full of hypocrisy and wickedness" (Matthew 23:27–28).

This principle of *not* judging people based on appearance ought to be our guide in relating to others. And we must reject the idea that our own worth is in any way connected with how we look. Our true value is rooted in the fact that we were created by a loving God and reflect his image—whatever our size, ethnicity or degree of physical beauty. Just because people look religious, talk religious and dress religious, we cannot assume that their hearts are right with God. And when people don't look religious on the outside, we cannot assume that they do not know God. Only God's searching eyes can pierce through our facades for an unobstructed view of our hearts.

Self-Discovery: *How do you feel in the presence of a particularly handsome man or beautiful woman? In the presence of a homely or disagreeable person? What kinds of prejudgments, positive or negative, do you tend to make about people based on their appearance alone?*

GO TO DISCOVERY 72 ON PAGE 368

of the LORD[t] came upon David in power.[u]
Samuel then went to Ramah.

David in Saul's Service

14 Now the Spirit of the LORD had departed[v] from Saul, and an evil[a] spirit[w]
from the LORD tormented him.
15 Saul's attendants said to him, "See,
an evil spirit from God is tormenting
you. 16 Let our lord command his servants here to search for someone who
can play the harp.[x] He will play when the
evil spirit from God comes upon you,
and you will feel better."
17 So Saul said to his attendants, "Find
someone who plays well and bring him
to me."
18 One of the servants answered, "I
have seen a son of Jesse of Bethlehem
who knows how to play the harp. He is a
brave man and a warrior. He speaks well
and is a fine-looking man. And the LORD
is with[y] him."
19 Then Saul sent messengers to Jesse
and said, "Send me your son David, who
is with the sheep." 20 So Jesse took a donkey loaded with bread,[z] a skin of wine
and a young goat and sent them with his
son David to Saul.
21 David came to Saul and entered his
service.[a] Saul liked him very much, and
David became one of his armor-bearers.
22 Then Saul sent word to Jesse, saying,
"Allow David to remain in my service, for
I am pleased with him."
23 Whenever the spirit from God came
upon Saul, David would take his harp
and play. Then relief would come to
Saul; he would feel better, and the evil
spirit[b] would leave him.

David and Goliath

17 Now the Philistines gathered
their forces for war and assembled[c] at Socoh in Judah. They pitched
camp at Ephes Dammim, between Socoh[d] and Azekah. 2 Saul and the Israelites assembled and camped in the Valley
of Elah[e] and drew up their battle line to
meet the Philistines. 3 The Philistines occupied one hill and the Israelites another, with the valley between them.
4 A champion named Goliath,[f] who
was from Gath, came out of the Philistine camp. He was over nine feet[b] tall.
5 He had a bronze helmet on his head
and wore a coat of scale armor of bronze
weighing five thousand shekels[c]; 6 on his
legs he wore bronze greaves, and a
bronze javelin[g] was slung on his back.
7 His spear shaft was like a weaver's rod,[h]
and its iron point weighed six hundred
shekels.[d] His shield bearer[i] went ahead
of him.
8 Goliath stood and shouted to the
ranks of Israel, "Why do you come out
and line up for battle? Am I not a Philistine, and are you not the servants of
Saul? Choose[j] a man and have him
come down to me. 9 If he is able to fight
and kill me, we will become your subjects; but if I overcome him and kill him,
you will become our subjects and serve
us." 10 Then the Philistine said, "This day
I defy[k] the ranks of Israel! Give me a man
and let us fight each other." 11 On hearing
the Philistine's words, Saul and all the Israelites were dismayed and terrified.
12 Now David was the son of an
Ephrathite named Jesse,[l] who was from
Bethlehem[m] in Judah. Jesse had eight[n]
sons, and in Saul's time he was old and
well advanced in years. 13 Jesse's three
oldest sons had followed Saul to the war:

16:13 [t] Nu 27:18; Jdg 11:29 [u] 1Sa 10:1,6,9-10; 11:6
16:14 [v] Jdg 16:20 [w] Jdg 9:23; 1Sa 18:10
16:16 [x] ver 23; 1Sa 18:10; 19:9; 2Ki 3:15
16:18 [y] 1Sa 3:19; 17:32-37
16:20 [z] 1Sa 10:27; Pr 18:16
16:21 [a] Ge 41:46; Pr 22:29
16:23 [b] ver 14-16
17:1 [c] 1Sa 13:5 [d] Jos 15:35; 2Ch 28:18
17:2 [e] 1Sa 21:9
17:4 [f] Jos 11:21-22; 2Sa 21:19
17:6 [g] ver 45
17:7 [h] 2Sa 21:19 [i] ver 41
17:8 [j] 1Sa 8:17
17:10 [k] ver 26,45; 2Sa 21:21
17:12 [l] Ru 4:17; 1Ch 2:13-15 [m] Ge 35:19 [n] 1Sa 16:11

[a] *14* Or *injurious;* also in verses 15, 16 and 23
[b] *4* Hebrew *was six cubits and a span* (about 3 meters)
[c] *5* That is, about 125 pounds (about 57 kilograms)
[d] *7* That is, about 15 pounds (about 7 kilograms)

DAVID
AFTER GOD'S OWN HEART

David, whose name means "beloved," was Israel's second king and the ruler ruled over Judah from its capital in Hebron for seven years. Then he moved the capital to Jerusalem and ruled from that city for 33 years. David was born in Bethlehem and was the great-grandson of Ruth and Boaz (Ruth 4:22) and the son of Jesse. He had become popular with the people after he had slain Goliath the Philistine giant, and he had then become the court musician and armor-bearer for Saul. David ruled for 40 years and became known as Israel's greatest king. In the New Testament people called Jesus the "Son of David" because they recognized that he was the Messiah (Matthew 9:27). Both records of Jesus' family history confirm that he was a direct descendant of David (Matthew 1:6; Luke 3:31). Jesus made it clear, however, that he was at the same time both David's "son" and David's "Lord" (Matthew 22:41–46).

17:13 The firstborn was Eliab;[o] the second,
o 1Sa 16:6 Abinadab; and the third, Shammah.[p]
p 1Sa 16:9 14David was the youngest. The three oldest followed Saul, 15but David went back
and forth from Saul to tend his father's
17:15 sheep[q] at Bethlehem.
q 1Sa 16:19 16For forty days the Philistine came
forward every morning and evening and
took his stand.
17Now Jesse said to his son David,
17:17 "Take this ephah[a] of roasted grain[r] and
r 1Sa 25:18 these ten loaves of bread for your brothers and hurry to their camp. 18Take along
these ten cheeses to the commander of
17:18 s Ge 37:14 their unit.[b] See how your brothers[s] are
and bring back some assurance[c] from
them. 19They are with Saul and all the
men of Israel in the Valley of Elah, fighting against the Philistines."
20Early in the morning David left the
flock with a shepherd, loaded up and set
out, as Jesse had directed. He reached
the camp as the army was going out to
its battle positions, shouting the war
cry. 21Israel and the Philistines were
drawing up their lines facing each other.
22David left his things with the keeper of
supplies, ran to the battle lines and
greeted his brothers. 23As he was talking
with them, Goliath, the Philistine cham-
17:23 pion from Gath, stepped out from his
t ver 8-10 lines and shouted his usual[t] defiance,
and David heard it. 24When the Israelites
saw the man, they all ran from him in
great fear.
25Now the Israelites had been saying,
"Do you see how this man keeps coming
out? He comes out to defy Israel. The
king will give great wealth to the man
who kills him. He will also give him his
17:25 daughter[u] in marriage and will exempt
u Jos 15:16; 1Sa 18:17 his father's family from taxes in Israel."
26David asked the men standing near
him, "What will be done for the man
who kills this Philistine and removes this
17:26 disgrace[v] from Israel? Who is this uncir-
v 1Sa 11:2 w 1Sa 14:6 cumcised[w] Philistine that he should
x ver 10 y Dt 5:26 defy[x] the armies of the living[y] God?"
27They repeated to him what they had
been saying and told him, "This is what
will be done for the man who kills him."
28When Eliab, David's oldest brother,
heard him speaking with the men, he
17:28 z Ge 37:4,8,11; burned with anger[z] at him and asked,
Pr 18:19; "Why have you come down here? And
Mt 10:36 with whom did you leave those few
sheep in the desert? I know how conceited you are and how wicked your
heart is; you came down only to watch
the battle."
29"Now what have I done?" said David.
"Can't I even speak?" 30He then turned
away to someone else and brought up
the same matter, and the men answered
him as before. 31What David said was
overheard and reported to Saul, and
Saul sent for him.
32David said to Saul, "Let no one lose
heart[a] on account of this Philistine; your 17:32 a Dt 20:3;
servant will go and fight him." 1Sa 16:18
33Saul replied,[b] "You are not able to go 17:33
out against this Philistine and fight him; b Nu 13:31
you are only a boy, and he has been a
fighting man from his youth."
34But David said to Saul, "Your servant has been keeping his father's sheep.
When a lion[c] or a bear came and carried 17:34 c Jer 49:19;
off a sheep from the flock, 35I went after Am 3:12
it, struck it and rescued the sheep from
its mouth. When it turned on me, I
seized it by its hair, struck it and killed
it. 36Your servant has killed both the lion
and the bear; this uncircumcised Philistine will be like one of them, because he
has defied the armies of the living God.
37The LORD who delivered[d] me from the 17:37 d 2Co 1:10
paw of the lion[e] and the paw of the bear e 2Ti 4:17
will deliver me from the hand of this f 1Sa 20:13; 1Ch 22:11,16
Philistine."

Saul said to David, "Go, and the LORD
be with[f] you."
38Then Saul dressed David in his own
tunic. He put a coat of armor on him
and a bronze helmet on his head. 39Da-
vid fastened on his sword over the tunic
and tried walking around, because he
was not used to them.
"I cannot go in these," he said to Saul,
"because I am not used to them." So he
took them off. 40Then he took his staff in
his hand, chose five smooth stones from
the stream, put them in the pouch of his
shepherd's bag and, with his sling in his
hand, approached the Philistine.
41Meanwhile, the Philistine, with his
shield bearer in front of him, kept com- 17:42
ing closer to David. 42He looked David g 1Sa 16:12 h Ps 123:3-4;
over and saw that he was only a boy, Pr 16:18
ruddy and handsome,[g] and he despised[h] 17:43
him. 43He said to David, "Am I a dog,[i] i 1Sa 24:14; 2Sa 3:8; 9:8;
that you come at me with sticks?" And 2Ki 8:13

[a] *17* That is, probably about 3/5 bushel (about 22 liters) [b] *18* Hebrew *thousand* [c] *18* Or *some token*; or *some pledge of spoils*

the Philistine cursed David by his gods.
44“Come here,” he said, “and I’ll give your
17:44 flesh to the birds of the air and the
j 1Ki 20:10-11 beasts of the field![j]”
45David said to the Philistine, “You
come against me with sword and spear
and javelin, but I come against you in the
17:45 k 2Sa 22:33,35; 2Ch 32:8; Ps 124:8; Heb 11:32-34 l ver 10 name[k] of the LORD Almighty, the God of
the armies of Israel, whom you have de-
fied.[l] 46This day the LORD will hand you
over to me, and I’ll strike you down and
17:46 m Dt 28:26 n Jos 4:24; 1Ki 8:43; Isa 52:10 o 1Ki 18:36; 2Ki 19:19; Isa 37:20 cut off your head. Today I will give the
carcasses[m] of the Philistine army to the
birds of the air and the beasts of the
earth, and the whole world[n] will know
that there is a God in Israel.[o] 47All those
gathered here will know that it is not by
17:47 p Hos 1:7; Zec 4:6 q 1Sa 14:6; 2Ch 14:11 r 2Ch 20:15; Ps 44:6-7 sword[p] or spear that the LORD saves;[q] for
the battle[r] is the LORD’s, and he will give
all of you into our hands.”
48As the Philistine moved closer to attack him, David ran quickly toward the
battle line to meet him. 49Reaching into
his bag and taking out a stone, he slung
it and struck the Philistine on the forehead. The stone sank into his forehead,
and he fell facedown on the ground.
50So David triumphed over the Philis-
17:50 s 2Sa 23:21 tine with a sling[s] and a stone; without a
sword in his hand he struck down the
Philistine and killed him.
51David ran and stood over him. He
took hold of the Philistine’s sword and

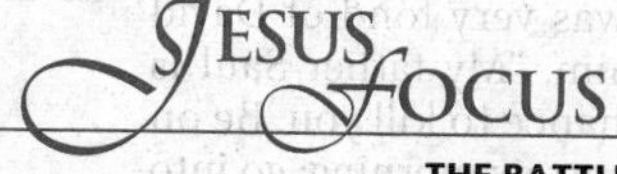

THE BATTLE IS THE LORD’S

David was the victor in his showdown with Goliath the Philistine, not because he relied on his skill with a sling but because he believed in God (1 Samuel 17). God used David’s victory as a dramatic introduction to his chosen future king. David’s hometown was only 15 miles from the Valley of Elah, where the confrontation took place. If the Israelites had been defeated, the Philistines might easily have captured Bethlehem. But God preserved the Messiah’s family line by sending David, the first king in that line, into direct confrontation with the individual who most intimidated the Israelite army. David trusted God in a very personal way and was convinced that God was in control of all the details of life (verse 45–47). Even when Israel faced one of its times of greatest crisis, David cried out with the utmost of confidence, “The battle is the LORD’s” (verse 47).

drew it from the scabbard. After he killed 17:51
him, he cut[t] off his head with the sword.[u] t Heb 11:34 u 1Sa 21:9
When the Philistines saw that their
hero was dead, they turned and ran.
52Then the men of Israel and Judah
surged forward with a shout and pursued the Philistines to the entrance of
Gath[a] and to the gates of Ekron.[v] Their 17:52 v Jos 15:11
dead were strewn along the Shaaraim[w] w Jos 15:36
road to Gath and Ekron. 53When the Israelites returned from chasing the Philistines, they plundered their camp.
54David took the Philistine’s head and
brought it to Jerusalem, and he put the
Philistine’s weapons in his own tent.
55As Saul watched David[x] going out to 17:55 x 1Sa 16:21
meet the Philistine, he said to Abner,
commander of the army, “Abner, whose
son is that young man?”
Abner replied, “As surely as you live,
O king, I don’t know.”
56The king said, “Find out whose son
this young man is.”
57As soon as David returned from
killing the Philistine, Abner took him
and brought him before Saul, with David
still holding the Philistine’s head.
58“Whose son are you, young man?”
Saul asked him.
David said, “I am the son of your ser- 17:58
vant Jesse[y] of Bethlehem.” y ver 12

Saul’s Jealousy of David

18 After David had finished talking with Saul, Jonathan became
one in spirit with David, and he loved[z] 18:1
him as himself.[a] 2From that day Saul z 2Sa 1:26
kept David with him and did not let him a Ge 44:30
return to his father’s house. 3And Jonathan made a covenant[b] with David be- 18:3
cause he loved him as himself. 4Jonathan b 1Sa 20:8,16,17,42
took off the robe[c] he was wearing and 18:4
gave it to David, along with his tunic, c Ge 41:42
and even his sword, his bow and his belt.
5Whatever Saul sent him to do, David
did it so successfully[b] that Saul gave him
a high rank in the army. This pleased all
the people, and Saul’s officers as well.
6When the men were returning home
after David had killed the Philistine, the
women came out from all the towns of
Israel to meet King Saul with singing 18:6
and dancing,[d] with joyful songs and d Ex 15:20 e Jdg 11:34; Ps 68:25
with tambourines[e] and lutes. 7As they
danced, they sang:[f] 18:7 f Ex 15:21

[a] 52 Some Septuagint manuscripts; Hebrew *a valley* [b] 5 Or *wisely*

"Saul has slain his thousands,
and David his tens[g] of
thousands."

8Saul was very angry; this refrain
galled him. "They have credited David
with tens of thousands," he thought,
"but me with only thousands. What
more can he get but the kingdom?[h]"
9And from that time on Saul kept a jealous eye on David.
10The next day an evil[a] spirit[i] from
God came forcefully upon Saul. He was
prophesying in his house, while David
was playing the harp, as he usually[j] did.
Saul had a spear in his hand 11and he
hurled it, saying to himself,[k] "I'll pin David to the wall." But David eluded[l] him
twice.
12Saul was afraid[m] of David, because
the LORD[n] was with[o] David but had left
Saul. 13So he sent David away from him
and gave him command over a thousand
men, and David led[p] the troops in their
campaigns.[q] 14In everything he did he
had great success,[b r] because the LORD
was with[s] him. 15When Saul saw how
successful[c] he was, he was afraid of him.
16But all Israel and Judah loved David,
because he led them in their campaigns.[t]
17Saul said to David, "Here is my older
daughter[u] Merab. I will give her to you in
marriage; only serve me bravely and
fight the battles[v] of the LORD." For Saul
said to himself,[w] "I will not raise a hand
against him. Let the Philistines do that!"
18But David said to Saul, "Who am I,[x]
and what is my family or my father's clan
in Israel, that I should become the king's
son-in-law?[y]" 19So[d] when the time came
for Merab,[z] Saul's daughter, to be given
to David, she was given in marriage to
Adriel of Meholah.[a]
20Now Saul's daughter Michal[b] was in
love with David, and when they told Saul
about it, he was pleased. 21"I will give her
to him," he thought, "so that she may be a
snare[c] to him and so that the hand of the
Philistines may be against him." So Saul
said to David, "Now you have a second
opportunity to become my son-in-law."
22Then Saul ordered his attendants:
"Speak to David privately and say, 'Look,
the king is pleased with you, and his attendants all like you; now become his
son-in-law.'"
23They repeated these words to David.
But David said, "Do you think it is a
small matter to become the king's son-
in-law? I'm only a poor man and little
known."
24When Saul's servants told him what
David had said, 25Saul replied, "Say to
David, 'The king wants no other price[d]
for the bride than a hundred Philistine
foreskins, to take revenge on his enemies.'" Saul's plan[e] was to have David
fall by the hands of the Philistines.
26When the attendants told David
these things, he was pleased to become
the king's son-in-law. So before the allotted time elapsed, 27David and his men
went out and killed two hundred Philistines. He brought their foreskins and
presented the full number to the king so
that he might become the king's son-in-
law. Then Saul gave him his daughter
Michal[f] in marriage.
28When Saul realized that the LORD
was with David and that his daughter
Michal loved David, 29Saul became still
more afraid of him, and he remained his
enemy the rest of his days.
30The Philistine commanders continued to go out to battle, and as often as
they did, David met with more success[e g]
than the rest of Saul's officers, and his
name became well known.

Saul Tries to Kill David

19 Saul told his son Jonathan[h] and
all the attendants to kill[i] David.
But Jonathan was very fond of David
2and warned him, "My father Saul is
looking for a chance to kill you. Be on
your guard tomorrow morning; go into
hiding and stay there. 3I will go out and
stand with my father in the field where
you are. I'll speak[j] to him about you and
will tell you what I find out."
4Jonathan spoke[k] well of David to
Saul his father and said to him, "Let not
the king do wrong[l] to his servant David;
he has not wronged you, and what he
has done has benefited you greatly. 5He
took his life in his hands when he killed
the Philistine. The LORD won a great victory[m] for all Israel, and you saw it and
were glad. Why then would you do
wrong to an innocent[n] man like David
by killing him for no reason?"
6Saul listened to Jonathan and took

18:7 g 1Sa 21:11; 29:5
18:8 h 1Sa 15:8
18:10 i 1Sa 16:14 j 1Sa 19:7
18:11 k 1Sa 20:7,33 l 1Sa 19:10
18:12 m ver 15,29 n 1Sa 16:13 o 1Sa 28:15
18:13 p ver 16; Nu 27:17 q 2Sa 5:2
18:14 r Ge 39:3 s Ge 39:2,23; Jos 6:27; 1Sa 16:18
18:16 t ver 5
18:17 u 1Sa 17:25 v Nu 21:14; 1Sa 25:28 w ver 25
18:18 x 1Sa 9:21; 2Sa 7:18 y ver 23
18:19 z 2Sa 21:8 a Jdg 7:22
18:20 b ver 28
18:21 c ver 17,26
18:25 d Ge 34:12; Ex 22:17; 1Sa 14:24 e ver 17
18:27 f ver 13; 2Sa 3:14
18:30 g ver 5; 2Sa 11:1
19:1 h 1Sa 18:1 i 1Sa 18:9
19:3 j 1Sa 20:12
19:4 k 1Sa 20:32; Pr 31:8,9; Jer 18:20 l Ge 42:22; Pr 17:13
19:5 m 1Sa 11:13; 17:49-50; 1Ch 11:14 n Dt 19:10-13; 1Sa 20:32; Mt 27:4

a 10 Or *injurious* b 14 Or *he was very wise* c 15 Or *wise* d 19 Or *However,* e 30 Or *David acted more wisely*

this oath: "As surely as the LORD lives,
David will not be put to death."
7So Jonathan called David and told
him the whole conversation. He brought
19:7 [o] 1Sa 16:21; 18:2,13 him to Saul, and David was with Saul as
before.[o]
8Once more war broke out, and David
went out and fought the Philistines. He
struck them with such force that they
fled before him.
19:9 [p] 1Sa 16:14; 18:10-11 9But an evil[a] spirit[p] from the LORD
came upon Saul as he was sitting in his
house with his spear in his hand. While
David was playing the harp, 10Saul tried
to pin him to the wall with his spear, but
19:10 [q] 1Sa 18:11 David eluded[q] him as Saul drove the
spear into the wall. That night David
made good his escape.
11Saul sent men to David's house to
19:11 [r] Ps 59 Title watch[r] it and to kill him in the morning.
But Michal, David's wife, warned him, "If
you don't run for your life tonight, tomorrow you'll be killed." 12So Michal let
19:12 [s] Jos 2:15; Ac 9:25 David down through a window,[s] and he
fled and escaped. 13Then Michal took an
idol[b] and laid it on the bed, covering it
with a garment and putting some goats'
hair at the head.
14When Saul sent the men to capture
19:14 [t] Jos 2:4 David, Michal said,[t] "He is ill."
15Then Saul sent the men back to see
David and told them, "Bring him up to
me in his bed so that I may kill him."
16But when the men entered, there was
the idol in the bed, and at the head was
some goats' hair.
17Saul said to Michal, "Why did you
deceive me like this and send my enemy
away so that he escaped?"
Michal told him, "He said to me, 'Let
me get away. Why should I kill you?' "
18When David had fled and made his
19:18 [u] 1Sa 7:17 escape, he went to Samuel at Ramah[u]
and told him all that Saul had done to
him. Then he and Samuel went to Naioth and stayed there. 19Word came to
Saul: "David is in Naioth at Ramah"; 20so
he sent men to capture him. But when
19:20 [v] ver 11,14; Jn 7:32,45 [w] Nu 11:25 [x] 1Sa 10:5; Joel 2:28 they saw a group of prophets[v] prophesying, with Samuel standing there as their
leader, the Spirit of God came upon[w]
Saul's men and they also prophesied.[x]
21Saul was told about it, and he sent
more men, and they prophesied too.
Saul sent men a third time, and they also
prophesied. 22Finally, he himself left for
Ramah and went to the great cistern at
Secu. And he asked, "Where are Samuel
and David?"
"Over in Naioth at Ramah," they said.
23So Saul went to Naioth at Ramah.
But the Spirit of God came even upon
him, and he walked along prophesying[y] 19:23 [y] 1Sa 10:13
until he came to Naioth. 24He stripped[z]
off his robes and also prophesied in 19:24 [z] 2Sa 6:20; Isa 20:2; Mic 1:8 [a] 1Sa 10:11
Samuel's presence. He lay that way all
that day and night. This is why people
say, "Is Saul also among the prophets?"[a]

David and Jonathan

20 Then David fled from Naioth at
Ramah and went to Jonathan
and asked, "What have I done? What is
my crime? How have I wronged[b] your 20:1 [b] 1Sa 24:9
father, that he is trying to take my life?"
2"Never!" Jonathan replied. "You are
not going to die! Look, my father doesn't
do anything, great or small, without
confiding in me. Why would he hide this
from me? It's not so!"
3But David took an oath[c] and said, 20:3 [c] Dt 6:13
"Your father knows very well that I have
found favor in your eyes, and he has said
to himself, 'Jonathan must not know
this or he will be grieved.' Yet as surely as
the LORD lives and as you live, there is
only a step between me and death."
4Jonathan said to David, "Whatever
you want me to do, I'll do for you."
5So David said, "Look, tomorrow is
the New Moon festival,[d] and I am sup- 20:5 [d] Nu 10:10; 28:11 [e] 1Sa 19:2
posed to dine with the king; but let me
go and hide[e] in the field until the
evening of the day after tomorrow. 6If
your father misses me at all, tell him,
'David earnestly asked my permission to
hurry to Bethlehem,[f] his hometown, be- 20:6 [f] 1Sa 17:58 [g] Dt 12:5
cause an annual[g] sacrifice is being made
there for his whole clan.' 7If he says, 'Very
well,' then your servant is safe. But if he
loses his temper,[h] you can be sure that 20:7 [h] 1Sa 25:17
he is determined to harm me. 8As for
you, show kindness to your servant, for
you have brought him into a covenant[i] 20:8 [i] 1Sa 18:3; 23:18 [j] 2Sa 14:32
with you before the LORD. If I am guilty,
then kill[j] me yourself! Why hand me
over to your father?"
9"Never!" Jonathan said. "If I had the
least inkling that my father was determined to harm you, wouldn't I tell you?"
10David asked, "Who will tell me if
your father answers you harshly?"

[a] 9 Or *injurious* [b] 13 Hebrew *teraphim*; also in verse 16

DISCOVERY 72

Two Are Better Than One

David and Jonathan enjoyed one of the most remarkable friendships of all time. Jonathan was King Saul's son. God had rejected Saul and selected David as the future king of Israel. For years Saul reacted with fury against David, attempting repeatedly to kill him. And yet Jonathan, the son who would not ascend to the throne, and David remained the closest of friends.

One day Saul invited David to a feast. David, fearing the possibility of a trap, spoke with Jonathan about his father's anger, asking him to investigate the situation and find out what his father was really thinking. David did not attend the feast, but Jonathan did. The young men realized that if Saul missed David at the celebration, it would be safe for him to show up. But if Saul expressed anger because David had failed to appear, David's life was still in jeopardy.

In fact Saul did express indignation that David had apparently scorned his invitation. Jonathan met with David in secret to divulge the bad news. Jonathan found himself in a delicate position: His father, whom he respected, intended to murder his best friend. Saul seemed in fact to blame everything that had ever gone wrong in his life on David! The two friends parted company with Jonathan's blessing: "Go in peace, for we have sworn friendship with each other in the name of the LORD" (1 Samuel 20:42).

Each of us needs a good friend. Being completely alone is not good for us (Genesis 2:18). We need assurance that others empathize with our pain and love us no matter what life choices we have made. And we often need help. As expressed years later by David's son Solomon, "Two are better than one" because "if one falls down, his friend can help him up" (Ecclesiastes 4:9–10).

In addition to the human friends in our lives, we possess the friendship of Jesus himself. Jesus befriended the most unlikely people—tax collectors and sinners—and he longs for intimacy with each of us as well (Matthew 11:19). John recorded the following words of Jesus in his Gospel: "Greater love has no one than this, that he lay down his life for his friends. You are my friends if you do what I command. I no longer call you servants, because a servant does not know his master's business. Instead, I have called you friends, for everything that I learned from my Father I have made known to you."

Proverbs also reminds us that, while we might have many friends among our peers, there is a divine friend who is closer than a brother (Proverbs 18:24). We are never alone, forsaken or abandoned. Jesus is truly a friend for life.

Self-Discovery: *How does it make you feel when you envision Jesus as being closer than a brother? Do you experience close ties with your own family members? What could you do to enhance those ties?*

GO TO DISCOVERY 73 ON PAGE 374

11“Come,” Jonathan said, “let’s go out into the field.” So they went there together.

12Then Jonathan said to David: “By the LORD, the God of Israel, I will surely sound out my father by this time the day after tomorrow! If he is favorably disposed toward you, will I not send you word and let you know? 13But if my father is inclined to harm you, may the LORD deal with me, be it ever so severely,[k] if I do not let you know and send you away safely. May the LORD be with[l] you as he has been with my father. 14But show me unfailing kindness like that of the LORD as long as I live, so that I may not be killed, 15and do not ever cut off your kindness from my family[m]—not even when the LORD has cut off every one of David’s enemies from the face of the earth.”

20:13 [k] Ru 1:17; 1Sa 3:17 [l] Jos 1:5; 1Sa 17:37; 18:12; 1Ch 22:11,16
20:15 [m] 2Sa 9:7

16So Jonathan made a covenant[n] with the house of David, saying, “May the LORD call David’s enemies to account.” 17And Jonathan had David reaffirm his oath[o] out of love for him, because he loved him as he loved himself.

20:16 [n] 1Sa 25:22
20:17 [o] 1Sa 18:3

18Then Jonathan said to David: “Tomorrow is the New Moon festival. You will be missed, because your seat will be empty.[p] 19The day after tomorrow, toward evening, go to the place where you hid[q] when this trouble began, and wait by the stone Ezel. 20I will shoot three arrows to the side of it, as though I were shooting at a target. 21Then I will send a boy and say, ‘Go, find the arrows.’ If I say to him, ‘Look, the arrows are on this side of you; bring them here,’ then come, because, as surely as the LORD lives, you are safe; there is no danger. 22But if I say to the boy, ‘Look, the arrows are beyond[r] you,’ then you must go, because the LORD has sent you away. 23And about the matter you and I discussed—remember, the LORD is witness[s] between you and me forever.”

20:18 [p] ver 5,25
20:19 [q] 1Sa 19:2
20:22 [r] ver 37
20:23 [s] ver 14-15; Ge 31:50

24So David hid in the field, and when the New Moon festival came, the king sat down to eat. 25He sat in his customary place by the wall, opposite Jonathan,[a] and Abner sat next to Saul, but David’s place was empty.[t] 26Saul said nothing that day, for he thought, “Something must have happened to David to make him ceremonially unclean—surely he is unclean.[u]” 27But the next day, the second day of the month, David’s place was empty again. Then Saul said to his son Jonathan, “Why hasn’t the son of Jesse come to the meal, either yesterday or today?”

20:25 [t] ver 18
20:26 [u] Lev 7:20-21; 15:5; 1Sa 16:5

28Jonathan answered, “David earnestly asked me for permission[v] to go to Bethlehem. 29He said, ‘Let me go, because our family is observing a sacrifice in the town and my brother has ordered me to be there. If I have found favor in your eyes, let me get away to see my brothers.’ That is why he has not come to the king’s table.”

20:28 [v] ver 6

30Saul’s anger flared up at Jonathan and he said to him, “You son of a perverse and rebellious woman! Don’t I know that you have sided with the son of Jesse to your own shame and to the shame of the mother who bore you? 31As long as the son of Jesse lives on this earth, neither you nor your kingdom will be established. Now send and bring him to me, for he must die!”

32“Why[w] should he be put to death? What[x] has he done?” Jonathan asked his father. 33But Saul hurled his spear at him to kill him. Then Jonathan knew that his father intended[y] to kill David.

20:32 [w] 1Sa 19:4; Mt 27:23 [x] Ge 31:36; Lk 23:22
20:33 [y] ver 7; 1Sa 18:11,17

34Jonathan got up from the table in fierce anger; on that second day of the month he did not eat, because he was grieved at his father’s shameful treatment of David.

35In the morning Jonathan went out to the field for his meeting with David. He had a small boy with him, 36and he said to the boy, “Run and find the arrows I shoot.” As the boy ran, he shot an arrow beyond him. 37When the boy came to the place where Jonathan’s arrow had fallen, Jonathan called out after him, “Isn’t the arrow beyond[z] you?” 38Then he shouted, “Hurry! Go quickly! Don’t stop!” The boy picked up the arrow and returned to his master. 39(The boy knew nothing of all this; only Jonathan and David knew.) 40Then Jonathan gave his weapons to the boy and said, “Go, carry them back to town.”

20:37 [z] ver 22

41After the boy had gone, David got up from the south side ⌊of the stone⌋ and bowed down before Jonathan three times, with his face to the ground. Then they kissed each other and wept together—but David wept the most.

[a] *25* Septuagint; Hebrew *wall. Jonathan arose*

20:42 [a]ver 22; 1Sa 1:17 [b]2Sa 1:26; Pr 18:24
42Jonathan said to David, "Go in
peace,[a] for we have sworn friendship[b]
with each other in the name of the LORD,
saying, 'The LORD is witness between
you and me, and between your descendants and my descendants forever.' "
Then David left, and Jonathan went
back to the town.

David at Nob

21:1 [c]1Sa 14:3; 22:9, 19; Ne 11:32; Isa 10:32 [d]1Sa 16:4
21 David went to Nob,[c] to Ahim-
elech the priest. Ahimelech
trembled[d] when he met him, and asked,
"Why are you alone? Why is no one with
you?"
2David answered Ahimelech the
priest, "The king charged me with a certain matter and said to me, 'No one is to
know anything about your mission and
your instructions.' As for my men, I have
told them to meet me at a certain place.
3Now then, what do you have on hand?
Give me five loaves of bread, or whatever you can find."
21:4 [e]Lev 24:8-9 [f]Ex 25:30; Mt 12:4 [g]Ex 19:15
4But the priest answered David, "I
don't have any ordinary bread[e] on hand;
however, there is some consecrated[f]
bread here—provided the men have
kept[g] themselves from women."
5David replied, "Indeed women have
21:5 [h]1Th 4:4
been kept from us, as usual whenever[a] I
set out. The men's things[b] are holy[h] even
on missions that are not holy. How
much more so today!" 6So the priest 21:6 [i]Lev 24:8-9; Mt 12:3-4; Mk 2:25-28; Lk 6:1-5
gave him the consecrated bread,[i] since
there was no bread there except the
bread of the Presence that had been removed from before the LORD and replaced by hot bread on the day it was
taken away.
7Now one of Saul's servants was there
that day, detained before the LORD; he 21:7 [j]1Sa 22:9,22 [k]1Sa 14:47; Ps 52 Title
was Doeg[j] the Edomite,[k] Saul's head
shepherd.
8David asked Ahimelech, "Don't you
have a spear or a sword here? I haven't
brought my sword or any other weapon,
because the king's business was urgent."
9The priest replied, "The sword[l] of 21:9 [l]1Sa 17:51 [m]1Sa 17:2
Goliath the Philistine, whom you killed
in the Valley of Elah,[m] is here; it is
wrapped in a cloth behind the ephod. If
you want it, take it; there is no sword
here but that one."
David said, "There is none like it; give
it to me."

David at Gath

10That day David fled from Saul and
went[n] to Achish king of Gath. 11But the 21:10 [n]1Sa 27:2
servants of Achish said to him, "Isn't
this David, the king of the land? Isn't he
the one they sing about in their dances:

" 'Saul has slain his thousands,
and David his tens of 21:11 [o]1Sa 18:7; 29:5; Ps 56 Title
thousands'?"[o]

12David took these words to heart and
was very much afraid of Achish king of
Gath. 13So he pretended to be insane[p] in 21:13 [p]Ps 34 Title
their presence; and while he was in their
hands he acted like a madman, making
marks on the doors of the gate and letting saliva run down his beard.
14Achish said to his servants, "Look at
the man! He is insane! Why bring him to
me? 15Am I so short of madmen that you
have to bring this fellow here to carry on
like this in front of me? Must this man
come into my house?"

David at Adullam and Mizpah

22 David left Gath and escaped to
the cave[q] of Adullam. When his 22:1 [q]2Sa 23:13; Ps 57 Title; 142 Title
brothers and his father's household
heard about it, they went down to him
there. 2All those who were in distress or

[a]5 Or *from us in the past few days since* [b]5 Or *bodies*

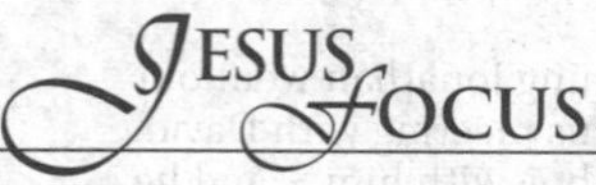

A HIGHER LAW

By the time David reached Nob he was in desperate straits. So the priest Ahimelech allowed him and his men to eat the holy bread, or "consecrated bread," of the tabernacle (1 Samuel 21:4), bread that had been set apart for consumption by the priests alone (Leviticus 24:5–9).

A thousand years later, when Jesus was criticized for allowing his disciples to pick grain on the Sabbath, he referred back to this episode to illustrate his point to his hearers. He challenged them to focus on what is of vital importance: seeking God and his mercy rather than keeping ritual laws. Jesus even went so far as to identify himself as "greater than the temple" and the "Lord of the Sabbath" (Matthew 12:3–8). While rituals are replete with meaning and value as a way to express our devotion to God, he is far more interested in a passionate love relationship with us than in traditions carried out by an apathetic heart.

22:2 [r] 1Sa 23:13; in debt or discontented gathered[r]
25:13; 2Sa 15:20 around him, and he became their leader.
About four hundred men were with him.
3From there David went to Mizpah in
Moab and said to the king of Moab,
"Would you let my father and mother
come and stay with you until I learn
what God will do for me?" 4So he left
them with the king of Moab, and they
stayed with him as long as David was in
the stronghold.
22:5 [s] 2Sa 24:11; 5But the prophet Gad[s] said to David,
1Ch 21:9; 29:29; "Do not stay in the stronghold. Go into
2Ch 29:25 the land of Judah." So David left and
went to the forest of Hereth.

Saul Kills the Priests of Nob

6Now Saul heard that David and his
men had been discovered. And Saul,
22:6 [t] Jdg 4:5 spear in hand, was seated[t] under the
[u] Ge 21:33 tamarisk[u] tree on the hill at Gibeah,
with all his officials standing around
him. 7Saul said to them, "Listen, men of
Benjamin! Will the son of Jesse give all of
you fields and vineyards? Will he make
22:7 [v] 1Sa 8:14 all of you commanders[v] of thousands
and commanders of hundreds? 8Is that
why you have all conspired against me?
No one tells me when my son makes a
22:8 [w] 1Sa 18:3; covenant[w] with the son of Jesse. None of
20:16 you is concerned[x] about me or tells me
[x] 1Sa 23:21 that my son has incited my servant to lie
in wait for me, as he does today."
22:9 9But Doeg[y] the Edomite, who was
[y] 1Sa 21:7; Ps 52 standing with Saul's officials, said, "I saw
Title [z] 1Sa 21:1 the son of Jesse come to Ahimelech son
of Ahitub at Nob.[z] 10Ahimelech in-
22:10 [a] Nu 27:21; quired[a] of the LORD for him; he also gave
1Sa 10:22 [b] 1Sa 21:6 him provisions[b] and the sword of Goliath the Philistine."
11Then the king sent for the priest
Ahimelech son of Ahitub and his father's whole family, who were the priests
at Nob, and they all came to the king.
12Saul said, "Listen now, son of Ahitub."
"Yes, my lord," he answered.
13Saul said to him, "Why have you
22:13 [c] ver 8 conspired[c] against me, you and the son
of Jesse, giving him bread and a sword
and inquiring of God for him, so that he
has rebelled against me and lies in wait
for me, as he does today?"
14Ahimelech answered the king,
22:14 [d] 1Sa 19:4 "Who[d] of all your servants is as loyal as
David, the king's son-in-law, captain of
your bodyguard and highly respected in
your household? 15Was that day the first
time I inquired of God for him? Of
course not! Let not the king accuse your
servant or any of his father's family, for
your servant knows nothing at all about
this whole affair."
16But the king said, "You will surely
die, Ahimelech, you and your father's
whole family."
17Then the king ordered the guards at
his side: "Turn and kill the priests of the
LORD, because they too have sided with
David. They knew he was fleeing, yet
they did not tell me."
But the king's officials were not will-
ing[e] to raise a hand to strike the priests 22:17 [e] Ex 1:17
of the LORD.
18The king then ordered Doeg, "You
turn and strike down the priests." So
Doeg the Edomite turned and struck
them down. That day he killed eighty-
five men who wore the linen ephod.[f] 22:18 [f] 1Sa 2:18,31
19He also put to the sword[g] Nob, the
town of the priests, with its men and 22:19 [g] 1Sa 15:3
women, its children and infants, and its
cattle, donkeys and sheep.
20But Abiathar,[h] a son of Ahimelech 22:20
son of Ahitub, escaped and fled to join [h] 1Sa 23:6,9;
David.[i] 21He told David that Saul had 30:7; 1Ki 2:22,
killed the priests of the LORD. 22Then Da- 26,27 [i] 1Sa 2:32
vid said to Abiathar: "That day, when
Doeg[j] the Edomite was there, I knew he 22:22 [j] 1Sa 21:7
would be sure to tell Saul. I am responsi-
ble for the death of your father's whole
family. 23Stay with me; don't be afraid;
the man who is seeking your life[k] is seek- 22:23
ing mine also. You will be safe with me." [k] 1Ki 2:26

David Saves Keilah

23 When David was told, "Look,
the Philistines are fighting 23:1
against Keilah[l] and are looting the [l] Jos 15:44
threshing floors," 2he inquired[m] of the 23:2
LORD, saying, "Shall I go and attack these [m] ver 4,12;
Philistines?" 1Sa 30:8;
2Sa 5:19,23
The LORD answered him, "Go, attack
the Philistines and save Keilah."
3But David's men said to him, "Here in
Judah we are afraid. How much more,
then, if we go to Keilah against the
Philistine forces!"
4Once again David inquired of the
LORD, and the LORD answered him, "Go
down to Keilah, for I am going to give
the Philistines into your hand.[n]" 5So Da- 23:4
vid and his men went to Keilah, fought [n] Jos 8:7; Jdg 7:7
the Philistines and carried off their live-
stock. He inflicted heavy losses on the

23:6 [o] 1Sa 22:20 Philistines and saved the people of Keilah. 6(Now Abiathar[o] son of Ahimelech
had brought the ephod down with him
when he fled to David at Keilah.)

Saul Pursues David

7Saul was told that David had gone to
Keilah, and he said, "God has handed
him over to me, for David has imprisoned himself by entering a town with
gates and bars." 8And Saul called up all
his forces for battle, to go down to Keilah to besiege David and his men.
9When David learned that Saul was
plotting against him, he said to Abia-
23:9 [p] ver 6; 1Sa 22:20; 30:7 thar[p] the priest, "Bring the ephod." 10Da-
vid said, "O LORD, God of Israel, your ser-
vant has heard definitely that Saul plans
to come to Keilah and destroy the town
on account of me. 11Will the citizens of
Keilah surrender me to him? Will Saul
come down, as your servant has heard?
O LORD, God of Israel, tell your servant."
And the LORD said, "He will."
12Again David asked, "Will the citi-
23:12 [q] ver 20 zens of Keilah surrender[q] me and my
men to Saul?"
And the LORD said, "They will."
23:13 [r] 1Sa 22:2; 25:13 13So David and his men,[r] about six
hundred in number, left Keilah and kept
moving from place to place. When Saul
was told that David had escaped from
Keilah, he did not go there.
14David stayed in the desert strongholds and in the hills of the Desert of
23:14 [s] Jos 15:24,55 [t] Ps 54:3-4 [u] Ps 32:7 Ziph.[s] Day after day Saul searched[t] for
him, but God did not[u] give David into
his hands.
15While David was at Horesh in the
Desert of Ziph, he learned that Saul had
come out to take his life. 16And Saul's
son Jonathan went to David at Horesh
23:16 [v] 1Sa 30:6 and helped him find strength[v] in God.
17"Don't be afraid," he said. "My father
Saul will not lay a hand on you. You will
23:17 [w] 1Sa 20:31; 24:20 be king[w] over Israel, and I will be second
to you. Even my father Saul knows this."
23:18 [x] 1Sa 18:3; 20:16,42; 2Sa 9:1; 21:7 18The two of them made a covenant[x] before the LORD. Then Jonathan went
home, but David remained at Horesh.
19The Ziphites[y] went up to Saul at
23:19 [y] 1Sa 26:1 [z] Ps 54 Title [a] 1Sa 26:3 Gibeah and said, "Is not David hiding
among us[z] in the strongholds at Horesh,
on the hill of Hakilah,[a] south of Jeshimon? 20Now, O king, come down whenever it pleases you to do so, and we will
be responsible for handing[b] him over to 23:20 [b] ver 12
the king."
21Saul replied, "The LORD bless you for
your concern[c] for me. 22Go and make 23:21 [c] 1Sa 22:8
further preparation. Find out where Da-
vid usually goes and who has seen him
there. They tell me he is very crafty.
23Find out about all the hiding places he
uses and come back to me with definite
information.[a] Then I will go with you; if
he is in the area, I will track him down
among all the clans of Judah."
24So they set out and went to Ziph
ahead of Saul. Now David and his men
were in the Desert of Maon,[d] in the Ara- 23:24 [d] Jos 15:55; 1Sa 25:2
bah south of Jeshimon. 25Saul and his
men began the search, and when David
was told about it, he went down to the
rock and stayed in the Desert of Maon.
When Saul heard this, he went into the
Desert of Maon in pursuit of David.
26Saul[e] was going along one side of 23:26 [e] Ps 17:9
the mountain, and David and his men
were on the other side, hurrying to get
away from Saul. As Saul and his forces
were closing in on David and his men to
capture them, 27a messenger came to
Saul, saying, "Come quickly! The Philistines are raiding the land." 28Then Saul
broke off his pursuit of David and went
to meet the Philistines. That is why they
call this place Sela Hammahlekoth.[b]
29And David went up from there and 23:29 [f] 2Ch 20:2
lived in the strongholds of En Gedi.[f]

David Spares Saul's Life

24 After Saul returned from pursuing the Philistines, he was
told, "David is in the Desert of En
Gedi.[g]" 2So Saul took three thousand 24:1 [g] 1Sa 23:28-29
chosen men from all Israel and set out to
look[h] for David and his men near the 24:2 [h] 1Sa 26:2
Crags of the Wild Goats.
3He came to the sheep pens along the
way; a cave[i] was there, and Saul went in 24:3 [i] Ps 57 Title; 142 Title [j] Jdg 3:24
to relieve[j] himself. David and his men
were far back in the cave. 4The men said,
"This is the day the LORD spoke[k] of when 24:4 [k] 1Sa 25:28-30 [l] 1Sa 23:17; 26:8
he said[c] to you, 'I will give your enemy
into your hands for you to deal with as
you wish.' "[l] Then David crept up unnoticed and cut off a corner of Saul's robe.
5Afterward, David was conscience-
stricken[m] for having cut off a corner of 24:5 [m] 2Sa 24:10

[a] 23 Or *me at Nacon* [b] 28 *Sela Hammahlekoth* means *rock of parting.* [c] 4 Or *"Today the LORD is saying*

his robe. 6He said to his men, "The LORD
24:6 forbid that I should do such a thing to
n 1Sa 26:11 my master, the LORD's anointed,[n] or lift
my hand against him; for he is the
anointed of the LORD." 7With these
words David rebuked his men and did
not allow them to attack Saul. And Saul
left the cave and went his way.
8Then David went out of the cave and
called out to Saul, "My lord the king!"
When Saul looked behind him, David
24:8 bowed down and prostrated himself
o 1Sa 25:23-24 with his face to the ground.[o] 9He said to
Saul, "Why do you listen when men say,
'David is bent on harming you'? 10This
day you have seen with your own eyes
how the LORD delivered you into my
hands in the cave. Some urged me to kill
you, but I spared you; I said, 'I will not
lift my hand against my master, because
he is the LORD's anointed.' 11See, my father, look at this piece of your robe in my
hand! I cut off the corner of your robe
24:11 but did not kill you. Now understand
p Ps 7:3 and recognize that I am not guilty[p] of
q 1Sa 23:14,23; wrongdoing or rebellion. I have not
1Sa 26:20 wronged you, but you are hunting[q] me
24:12 down to take my life. 12May the LORD
r Ge 16:5; 31:53; judge[r] between you and me. And may
Job 5:8 the LORD avenge[s] the wrongs you have
s Jdg 11:27; 1Sa 26:10 done to me, but my hand will not touch
24:13 you. 13As the old saying goes, 'From evil-
t Mt 7:20 doers come evil deeds,[t]' so my hand will
not touch you.
14"Against whom has the king of Isra-
24:14 el come out? Whom are you pursuing?
u 1Sa 17:43; A dead dog?[u] A flea?[v] 15May the LORD be
2Sa 9:8 v 1Sa 26:20 our judge[w] and decide between us. May
24:15 he consider my cause and uphold[x] it;
w ver 12 may he vindicate[y] me by delivering[z] me
x Ps 35:1,23; Mic 7:9 y Ps 43:1 from your hand."
z Ps 119:134,154 16When David finished saying this,
24:16 Saul asked, "Is that your voice,[a] David
a 1Sa 26:17 my son?" And he wept aloud. 17"You are
24:17 more righteous than I,"[b] he said. "You
b Ge 38:26; have treated me well,[c] but I have treated
1Sa 26:21 c Mt 5:44 you badly. 18You have just now told me
of the good you did to me; the LORD de-
24:18 livered[d] me into your hands, but you did
d 1Sa 26:23 not kill me. 19When a man finds his enemy, does he let him get away un-
harmed? May the LORD reward you well
24:20 for the way you treated me today. 20I
e 1Sa 23:17 know that you will surely be king[e] and
f 1Sa 13:14 that the kingdom[f] of Israel will be es-
24:21 tablished in your hands. 21Now swear[g]
g Ge 21:23; 2Sa 21:1-9 to me by the LORD that you will not cut
off my descendants or wipe out my
name from my father's family.[h]" 24:21 h 1Sa 20:14-15
22So David gave his oath to Saul. Then
Saul returned home, but David and his 24:22
men went up to the stronghold.[i] i 1Sa 23:29

David, Nabal and Abigail

25 Now Samuel died,[j] and all Isra- 25:1
el assembled and mourned[k] for j 1Sa 28:3 k Nu 20:29;
him; and they buried him at his home in Dt 34:8 l Ge 21:21;
Ramah.[l] 2Ch 33:20
Then David moved down into the
Desert of Maon.[a] 2A certain man in
Maon,[m] who had property there at Car- 25:2
mel, was very wealthy. He had a thou- m Jos 15:55; 1Sa 23:24
sand goats and three thousand sheep,
which he was shearing in Carmel. 3His
name was Nabal and his wife's name was
Abigail.[n] She was an intelligent and 25:3
beautiful woman, but her husband, a n Pr 31:10
Calebite,[o] was surly and mean in his o Jos 15:13
dealings.
4While David was in the desert, he
heard that Nabal was shearing sheep.
5So he sent ten young men and said to
them, "Go up to Nabal at Carmel and
greet him in my name. 6Say to him:
'Long life to you! Good health[p] to you 25:6 p Ps 122:7;
and your household! And good health to Lk 10:5
all that is yours![q] q 1Ch 12:18
7" 'Now I hear that it is sheep-shearing
time. When your shepherds were with
us, we did not mistreat[r] them, and the 25:7
whole time they were at Carmel nothing r ver 15
of theirs was missing. 8Ask your own
servants and they will tell you. Therefore
be favorable toward my young men,
since we come at a festive time. Please
give your servants and your son David
whatever[s] you can find for them.' " 25:8 s Ne 8:10
9When David's men arrived, they gave
Nabal this message in David's name.
Then they waited.
10Nabal answered David's servants,
"Who[t] is this David? Who is this son of 25:10 t Jdg 9:28
Jesse? Many servants are breaking away
from their masters these days. 11Why
should I take my bread[u] and water, and 25:11 u Jdg 8:6
the meat I have slaughtered for my
shearers, and give it to men coming
from who knows where?"
12David's men turned around and
went back. When they arrived, they reported every word. 13David said to his
men, "Put on your swords!" So they put
on their swords, and David put on his.

a 1 Some Septuagint manuscripts; Hebrew *Paran*

DISCOVERY 73

ABIGAIL: A WOMAN OF INTERCESSION

The story of Nabal, Abigail and David incorporates many of the elements of a classic fairy tale—a foolish man, a wise woman, a gracious king and an unexpected marriage—although the narrative is, of course, based on an actual event. Nabal was a wealthy man who lived near the foot of Mount Carmel with his beautiful and intelligent wife, Abigail. David and his men were camping in the same area and providing protection for Nabal's shepherds and flocks.

One day David dispatched ten men to Nabal to ask for food and water. David based this legitimate request on the fact that he and his men were affording protection to Nabal. But Nabal reacted with sarcasm: "Who is this David? Who is this son of Jesse?" (1 Samuel 25:10). When David heard of Nabal's retorts, his response was immediate: "Put on your swords!" (verse 13). David intended to kill Nabal, as well as every male in his household (verse 22).

When a servant informed Abigail of what her husband had done, she realized that her entire household was in danger. She collected enough food for all of David's men, loaded up the donkeys and rode out to meet David personally. When she saw David, she bowed low to the ground and offered to rectify the situation on behalf of her wicked husband.

Abigail demonstrated a godly character in the way she spoke to David. First she agreed with David that her husband had acted without forethought—as was his custom: "My lord, let the blame be on me alone . . . Let my lord pay no attention to that wicked man Nabal," she said. "He is just like his name—his name is Fool" (verses 24–25). She then asked David to forgive the offense, reminding him that revenge would not resolve the problem (verse 28). If David were to kill Nabal and the other men, he would live with "the staggering burden of needless bloodshed" on his conscience (verse 31).

David was so affected by Abigail's words and actions that he sent her home in peace. Ten days later Nabal died, and David and Abigail were later married (verses 40–42).

There are many parallels between this story and our own lives. Each of us, like Nabal, has foolishly rejected God's goodness and stood in danger of his righteous judgment. Like David, God holds us accountable for our sin. Abigail demonstrates for us how Jesus bridged the gap between God and ourselves, interceding on our behalf and accepting the penalty for our sin so that we might be forgiven. On the basis of that forgiveness we collectively become the bride of Christ, his church on earth, entering into an incredible and unanticipated royal marriage relationship.

Self-Discovery: *Think about a time when you have prevented a major blowup by your tactful intervention. How did God bless you for the part you played?*

GO TO DISCOVERY 74 ON PAGE 377

25:13 v 1Sa 23:13 About four hundred men went[v] up with
w 1Sa 30:24 David, while two hundred stayed with
the supplies.[w]
14One of the servants told Nabal's wife
Abigail: "David sent messengers from
25:14 the desert to give our master his greet-
x 1Sa 13:10 ings,[x] but he hurled insults at them.
25:15 15Yet these men were very good to us.
y ver 7 z ver 21 They did not mistreat[y] us, and the whole
time we were out in the fields near them
25:16 nothing was missing.[z] 16Night and day
a Ex 14:22; they were a wall[a] around us all the time
Job 1:10 we were herding our sheep near them.
17Now think it over and see what you
can do, because disaster is hanging over
25:17 our master and his whole household. He
b 1Sa 20:7 is such a wicked[b] man that no one can
talk to him."
18Abigail lost no time. She took two
hundred loaves of bread, two skins of
wine, five dressed sheep, five seahs[a] of
25:18 c 1Ch 12:40 roasted grain, a hundred cakes of raisins[c]
d 2Sa 16:1 and two hundred cakes of pressed figs,
25:19 and loaded them on donkeys.[d] 19Then
e Ge 32:20 she told her servants, "Go on ahead;[e] I'll
follow you." But she did not tell her husband Nabal.
20As she came riding her donkey into
a mountain ravine, there were David and
his men descending toward her, and she
met them. 21David had just said, "It's
been useless—all my watching over this
25:21 fellow's property in the desert so that
f Ps 109:5 nothing of his was missing. He has paid[f]
25:22 me back evil for good. 22May God deal
g 1Sa 3:17; 20:13 with David,[b] be it ever so severely,[g] if by
h 1Ki 14:10; morning I leave alive one male[h] of all
21:21; 2Ki 9:8 who belong to him!"
23When Abigail saw David, she quickly got off her donkey and bowed down
25:23 before David with her face to the
i 1Sa 20:41 ground.[i] 24She fell at his feet and said:
"My lord, let the blame be on me alone.
Please let your servant speak to you;
hear what your servant has to say. 25May
my lord pay no attention to that wicked
25:25 man Nabal. He is just like his name—his
j Pr 14:16 name is Fool,[j] and folly goes with him.
But as for me, your servant, I did not see
the men my master sent.
26"Now since the LORD has kept you,
25:26 k ver 33 my master, from bloodshed[k] and from
l Heb 10:30 avenging[l] yourself with your own hands,
m 2Sa 18:32 as surely as the LORD lives and as you
25:27 live, may your enemies and all who in-
n Ge 33:11; tend to harm my master be like Nabal.[m]
1Sa 30:26 27And let this gift,[n] which your servant

has brought to my master, be given to
the men who follow you. 28Please for- 25:28
give[o] your servant's offense, for the LORD o ver 24
will certainly make a lasting[p] dynasty p 2Sa 7:11,26
for my master, because he fights the q 1Sa 18:17 r 1Sa 24:11
LORD's battles.[q] Let no wrongdoing[r] be
found in you as long as you live. 29Even
though someone is pursuing you to take
your life, the life of my master will be
bound securely in the bundle of the living by the LORD your God. But the lives
of your enemies he will hurl[s] away as 25:29 s Jer 10:18
from the pocket of a sling. 30When the
LORD has done for my master every good
thing he promised concerning him and
has appointed him leader[t] over Israel, 25:30 t 1Sa 13:14
31my master will not have on his con-
science the staggering burden of needless bloodshed or of having avenged
himself. And when the LORD has
brought my master success, remember[u] 25:31 u Ge 40:14
your servant."
32David said to Abigail, "Praise[v] be to 25:32 v Ge 24:27;
the LORD, the God of Israel, who has sent Ex 18:10;
you today to meet me. 33May you be Lk 1:68
blessed for your good judgment and for
keeping me from bloodshed[w] this day 25:33 w ver 26
and from avenging myself with my own
hands. 34Otherwise, as surely as the
LORD, the God of Israel, lives, who has
kept me from harming you, if you had
not come quickly to meet me, not one
male belonging to Nabal would have
been left alive by daybreak."
35Then David accepted from her hand
what she had brought him and said, "Go 25:35
home in peace. I have heard your words x Ge 19:21;
and granted[x] your request." 1Sa 20:42;
36When Abigail went to Nabal, he was 2Ki 5:19
in the house holding a banquet like that
of a king. He was in high[y] spirits and 25:36 y 2Sa 13:23
very drunk.[z] So she told[a] him nothing z Pr 20:1;
until daybreak. 37Then in the morning, Isa 5:11,22; Hos 4:11
when Nabal was sober, his wife told him a ver 19
all these things, and his heart failed him
and he became like a stone. 38About ten
days later, the LORD struck[b] Nabal and 25:38 b 1Sa 26:10;
he died. 2Sa 6:7
39When David heard that Nabal was
dead, he said, "Praise be to the LORD,
who has upheld my cause against Nabal
for treating me with contempt. He has
kept his servant from doing wrong and

a 18 That is, probably about a bushel (about 37 liters) *b 22* Some Septuagint manuscripts; Hebrew *with David's enemies*

has brought Nabal's wrongdoing down
on his own head."
Then David sent word to Abigail, asking her to become his wife. 40His servants went to Carmel and said to Abigail, "David has sent us to you to take
you to become his wife."
41She bowed down with her face to
the ground and said, "Here is your maidservant, ready to serve you and wash the
25:42 feet of my master's servants." 42Abigail[c]
c Ge 24:61-67 quickly got on a donkey and, attended
by her five maids, went with David's
messengers and became his wife. 43Da-
25:43 d Jos 15:56 vid had also married Ahinoam[d] of Jezre-
e 1Sa 27:3; 30:5 el, and they both were his wives.[e] 44But
Saul had given his daughter Michal, Da-
25:44 vid's wife, to Paltiel[a] [f] son of Laish, who
f 2Sa 3:15 g Isa 10:30 was from Gallim.[g]

David Again Spares Saul's Life

26:1 h 1Sa 23:19 **26** The Ziphites[h] went to Saul at
i Ps 54 Title Gibeah and said, "Is not David
hiding[i] on the hill of Hakilah, which
faces Jeshimon?"
2So Saul went down to the Desert of
26:2 Ziph, with his three thousand chosen
j 1Sa 13:2; 24:2 men of Israel, to search[j] there for David.
3Saul made his camp beside the road on
the hill of Hakilah facing Jeshimon, but
David stayed in the desert. When he saw
that Saul had followed him there, 4he
sent out scouts and learned that Saul
had definitely arrived.[b]
5Then David set out and went to the
place where Saul had camped. He saw
26:5 k 1Sa 14:50; where Saul and Abner[k] son of Ner, the
17:55 commander of the army, had lain down.
Saul was lying inside the camp, with the
army encamped around him.
26:6 6David then asked Ahimelech the Hit-
l Jdg 7:10-11; tite and Abishai son of Zeruiah,[l] Joab's
1Ch 2:16 brother, "Who will go down into the
camp with me to Saul?"
"I'll go with you," said Abishai.
7So David and Abishai went to the
army by night, and there was Saul, lying
asleep inside the camp with his spear
stuck in the ground near his head. Abner and the soldiers were lying around
him.
8Abishai said to David, "Today God
has delivered your enemy into your
hands. Now let me pin him to the
ground with one thrust of my spear; I
won't strike him twice."
9But David said to Abishai, "Don't destroy him! Who can lay a hand on the 26:9
LORD's anointed[m] and be guiltless?[n] 10As m 2Sa 1:14
surely as the LORD lives," he said, "the n 1Sa 24:5
LORD himself will strike[o] him; either his 26:10
time[p] will come and he will die,[q] or he o 1Sa 25:38;
will go into battle and perish. 11But the Ro 12:19 p Ge 47:29;
LORD forbid that I should lay a hand on Dt 31:14;
the LORD's anointed. Now get the spear Ps 37:13 q 1Sa 31:6;
and water jug that are near his head, and 2Sa 1:1
let's go."
12So David took the spear and water
jug near Saul's head, and they left. No one
saw or knew about it, nor did anyone
wake up. They were all sleeping, because 26:12
the LORD had put them into a deep sleep.[r] r Ge 2:21; 15:12
13Then David crossed over to the oth-
er side and stood on top of the hill some
distance away; there was a wide space
between them. 14He called out to the
army and to Abner son of Ner, "Aren't
you going to answer me, Abner?"
Abner replied, "Who are you who
calls to the king?"
15David said, "You're a man, aren't
you? And who is like you in Israel? Why
didn't you guard your lord the king?
Someone came to destroy your lord the
king. 16What you have done is not good.
As surely as the LORD lives, you and your
men deserve to die, because you did not
guard your master, the LORD's anointed.
Look around you. Where are the king's
spear and water jug that were near his
head?"
17Saul recognized David's voice and 26:17
said, "Is that your voice,[s] David my son?" s 1Sa 24:16
David replied, "Yes it is, my lord the
king." 18And he added, "Why is my lord
pursuing his servant? What have I done, 26:18
and what wrong[t] am I guilty of? 19Now t 1Sa 24:9,11-14
let my lord the king listen to his ser-
vant's words. If the LORD has incited you
against me, then may he accept an of- 26:19
fering.[u] If, however, men have done it, u 2Sa 16:11
may they be cursed before the LORD! v 2Sa 14:16
They have now driven me from my share
in the LORD's inheritance[v] and have said,
'Go, serve other gods.' 20Now do not let
my blood fall to the ground far from the
presence of the LORD. The king of Israel 26:20
has come out to look for a flea[w]—as one w 1Sa 24:14
hunts a partridge in the mountains."
21Then Saul said, "I have sinned.[x] 26:21 x Ex 9:27;
Come back, David my son. Because you 1Sa 15:24
considered my life precious[y] today, I will y 1Sa 24:17

a 44 Hebrew *Palti*, a variant of *Paltiel* b 4 Or *had come to Nacon*

DISCOVERY 74

Repentance Requires Action

Saul wanted David dead—more than anything else. He viewed David's success and popularity as a threat to his kingdom and wanted the younger man out of the way. Saul pursued David for years, fully intending to kill him. By the end of Saul's life his vengeance had driven him nearly insane.

On one occasion Saul was asleep outdoors, surrounded by his bodyguards. David and his servant Abishai were able to tiptoe past the guards undetected and steal Saul's spear and water jug. David was quicker and brighter than Saul and his bodyguards. He and his servant outwitted Saul, placing the king of Israel in a most humiliating position. Saul responded much like a six-year-old who has just been caught with his hand in the cookie jar, by trying to talk himself out of trouble by saying all the right words. Saul referred to David as "my son" and spoke with apparent affection. He promised David that he would never again try to harm him and even admitted that he had acted like a fool! (1 Samuel 26:17,21,25).

But David was understandably skeptical (1 Samuel 27:1). Life experience has taught us too that we can't always believe words that sound remorseful. Oh, we would *like* to believe them, but we need to assume a wait-and-see stance to find out whether the words will translate into action. And we ourselves have been guilty of apologizing and then failing to follow through on the promise to change our attitudes and ways.

The words *I'm sorry* are empty unless they are backed up by changed behavior. Paul wrote that people should "turn to God and prove their repentance by their deeds" (Acts 26:20). *Repentance* simply means turning around and walking in another direction. That is not accomplished by words, no matter how eloquent, sincere or convincing. Real repentance requires action.

Repentance is God's idea, certainly not our own! Our idea is to walk away from God and ignore our sin, to keep on trying to prove how strong we are and how well we are able to handle our own struggles. Our concept is that "nice guys finish strong," and we tend to sugarcoat our sinful nature. But Jesus knows better. He began his ministry by preaching, "Repent, for the kingdom of heaven is near" (Matthew 4:17). Turning to God and following Jesus are the genuine demonstrations of a new life.

We should experience great sorrow and remorse for our sin—because sin breaks the heart of the Jesus we claim to love—and very likely it hurts other people in the process. Sorrow is not enough, however, unless it leads to repentance (2 Corinthians 7:10). Genuine sorrow for our sin *compels* us to make a change (Matthew 16:24).

Self-Discovery: *Think about a time when you were unable to bring yourself to say those words "I'm sorry." Why were you reluctant? Are there certain sins in your life that have control over you? What might it take for you to bow before Jesus in repentance and seek his power to change your behavior and attitudes?*

GO TO DISCOVERY 75 ON PAGE 388

not try to harm you again. Surely I have
acted like a fool and have erred greatly."
22"Here is the king's spear," David answered. "Let one of your young men
come over and get it. 23The LORD re-
26:23 [z] Ps 62:12 [a] Ps 7:8; 18:20, 24
wards[z] every man for his righteousness[a]
and faithfulness. The LORD delivered you
into my hands today, but I would not lay
a hand on the LORD's anointed. 24As
surely as I valued your life today, so may
26:24 [b] Ps 54:7
the LORD value my life and deliver[b] me
from all trouble."
25Then Saul said to David, "May you
be blessed, my son David; you will do
great things and surely triumph."
So David went on his way, and Saul returned home.

David Among the Philistines

27 But David thought to himself,
"One of these days I will be destroyed by the hand of Saul. The best
thing I can do is to escape to the land of
the Philistines. Then Saul will give up
searching for me anywhere in Israel, and
I will slip out of his hand."
27:2 [c] 1Sa 25:13 [d] 1Sa 21:10 [e] 1Ki 2:39
2So David and the six hundred men[c]
with him left and went[d] over to Achish[e]
son of Maoch king of Gath. 3David and
his men settled in Gath with Achish.
27:3 [f] 1Sa 25:43; 30:3
Each man had his family with him, and
David had his two wives:[f] Ahinoam of
Jezreel and Abigail of Carmel, the widow
of Nabal. 4When Saul was told that David had fled to Gath, he no longer
searched for him.
5Then David said to Achish, "If I have
found favor in your eyes, let a place be
assigned to me in one of the country
towns, that I may live there. Why should
your servant live in the royal city with
you?"
27:6 [g] Jos 15:31; 19:5; Ne 11:28
6So on that day Achish gave him Ziklag,[g] and it has belonged to the kings of
27:7 [h] 1Sa 29:3
Judah ever since. 7David lived[h] in Philistine territory a year and four months.
27:8 [i] Jos 13:2,13 [j] Ex 17:8; 1Sa 15:7-8 [k] Ex 15:22
8Now David and his men went up and
raided the Geshurites,[i] the Girzites and
the Amalekites.[j] (From ancient times
these peoples had lived in the land extending to Shur[k] and Egypt.) 9Whenever
27:9 [l] 1Sa 15:3
David attacked an area, he did not leave
a man or woman alive,[l] but took sheep
and cattle, donkeys and camels, and
clothes. Then he returned to Achish.
10When Achish asked, "Where did
you go raiding today?" David would say,
27:10 [m] 1Sa 30:29; 1Ch 2:9,25 [n] Jdg 1:16
"Against the Negev of Judah" or "Against
the Negev of Jerahmeel[m]" or "Against the
Negev of the Kenites.[n]" 11He did not
leave a man or woman alive to be
brought to Gath, for he thought, "They
might inform on us and say, 'This is
what David did.'" And such was his
practice as long as he lived in Philistine
territory. 12Achish trusted David and
said to himself, "He has become so odi-
ous to his people, the Israelites, that he
will be my servant forever."

Saul and the Witch of Endor

28:1 [o] 1Sa 29:1
28 In those days the Philistines
gathered[o] their forces to fight
against Israel. Achish said to David,
"You must understand that you and
your men will accompany me in the
army."
2David said, "Then you will see for
yourself what your servant can do."
Achish replied, "Very well, I will make
you my bodyguard for life."
28:3 [p] 1Sa 25:1 [q] 1Sa 7:17 [r] Ex 22:18; Lev 19:31; 20:27; Dt 18:10-11; 1Sa 15:23
3Now Samuel was dead,[p] and all Isra-
el had mourned for him and buried him
in his own town of Ramah.[q] Saul had expelled the mediums and spiritists[r] from
the land.
4The Philistines assembled and came
28:4 [s] Jos 19:18; 2Ki 4:8 [t] 1Sa 31:1,3
and set up camp at Shunem,[s] while Saul
gathered all the Israelites and set up
camp at Gilboa.[t] 5When Saul saw the
Philistine army, he was afraid; terror
28:6 [u] 1Sa 14:37; 1Ch 10:13-14; Pr 1:28 [v] Nu 12:6 [w] Ex 28:30; Nu 27:21
filled his heart. 6He inquired[u] of the
LORD, but the LORD did not answer him
by dreams[v] or Urim[w] or prophets. 7Saul
then said to his attendants, "Find me a
woman who is a medium,[x] so I may go
28:7 [x] Ac 16:16 [y] Jos 17:11
and inquire of her."
"There is one in Endor,[y]" they said.
28:8 [z] 2Ch 18:29; 35:22 [a] Dt 18:10-11; 1Ch 10:13; Isa 8:19
8So Saul disguised[z] himself, putting
on other clothes, and at night he and
two men went to the woman. "Consult[a]
a spirit for me," he said, "and bring up for
me the one I name."
9But the woman said to him, "Surely
28:9 [b] ver 3
you know what Saul has done. He has
cut off[b] the mediums and spiritists from
the land. Why have you set a trap for my
life to bring about my death?"
10Saul swore to her by the LORD, "As
surely as the LORD lives, you will not be
punished for this."
11Then the woman asked, "Whom
shall I bring up for you?"
"Bring up Samuel," he said.

12When the woman saw Samuel, she
cried out at the top of her voice and said
to Saul, "Why have you deceived me?
You are Saul!"
13The king said to her, "Don't be
afraid. What do you see?"
The woman said, "I see a spirit[a] coming up out of the ground."
28:14 14"What does he look like?" he asked.
[c] 1Sa 15:27; 24:8 "An old man wearing a robe[c] is coming up," she said.
Then Saul knew it was Samuel, and
he bowed down and prostrated himself
with his face to the ground.
15Samuel said to Saul, "Why have you
disturbed me by bringing me up?"
"I am in great distress," Saul said. "The
28:15 [d] ver 6; Philistines are fighting against me, and
1Sa 18:12 God has turned[d] away from me. He no
longer answers me, either by prophets
or by dreams. So I have called on you to
tell me what to do."
16Samuel said, "Why do you consult
me, now that the LORD has turned away
from you and become your enemy?
17The LORD has done what he predicted
28:17 through me. The LORD has torn[e] the
[e] 1Sa 15:28 kingdom out of your hands and given it
28:18 to one of your neighbors—to David.
[f] 1Sa 15:20 18Because you did not obey[f] the LORD or
[g] 1Ki 20:42 carry out his fierce wrath[g] against the
Amalekites, the LORD has done this to
you today. 19The LORD will hand over
both Israel and you to the Philistines,
28:19 and tomorrow you and your sons[h] will
[h] 1Sa 31:2 be with me. The LORD will also hand over
the army of Israel to the Philistines."
20Immediately Saul fell full length on
the ground, filled with fear because of
Samuel's words. His strength was gone,
for he had eaten nothing all that day and
night.
21When the woman came to Saul and
saw that he was greatly shaken, she said,
28:21 "Look, your maidservant has obeyed
[i] Jdg 12:3; you. I took my life[i] in my hands and did
1Sa 19:5; what you told me to do. 22Now please lis-
Job 13:14 ten to your servant and let me give you
some food so you may eat and have the
strength to go on your way."
28:23 23He refused[j] and said, "I will not eat."
[j] 2Ki 5:13 But his men joined the woman in urging him, and he listened to them. He got
up from the ground and sat on the
couch.
24The woman had a fattened calf at
the house, which she butchered at once.
She took some flour, kneaded it and
baked bread without yeast. 25Then she
set it before Saul and his men, and they
ate. That same night they got up and
left.

Achish Sends David Back to Ziklag

29 The Philistines gathered[k] all 29:1
their forces at Aphek,[l] and Isra- [k] 1Sa 28:1
el camped by the spring in Jezreel.[m] 2As [l] Jos 12:18; 1Sa 4:1
the Philistine rulers marched with their [m] 2Ki 9:30
units of hundreds and thousands, David 29:2
and his men were marching at the rear[n] [n] 1Sa 28:2
with Achish. 3The commanders of the
Philistines asked, "What about these
Hebrews?"
Achish replied, "Is this not David,
who was an officer of Saul king of Israel?
He has already been with me for over a
year,[o] and from the day he left Saul until 29:3 [o] 1Sa 27:7;
now, I have found no fault in him." Da 6:5
4But the Philistine commanders were
angry with him and said, "Send[p] the 29:4 [p] 1Ch 12:19
man back, that he may return to the [q] 1Sa 14:21
place you assigned him. He must not go
with us into battle, or he will turn[q]
against us during the fighting. How better could he regain his master's favor
than by taking the heads of our own
men? 5Isn't this the David they sang
about in their dances:

" 'Saul has slain his thousands,
and David his tens of 29:5
thousands'?"[r] [r] 1Sa 18:7; 21:11

6So Achish called David and said to
him, "As surely as the LORD lives, you
have been reliable, and I would be
pleased to have you serve with me in the
army. From the day[s] you came to me un- 29:6
til now, I have found no fault in you, but [s] 1Sa 27:8-12
the rulers[t] don't approve of you. 7Turn [t] ver 3
back and go in peace; do nothing to displease the Philistine rulers."
8"But what have I done?" asked David.
"What have you found against your servant from the day I came to you until
now? Why can't I go and fight against
the enemies of my lord the king?"
9Achish answered, "I know that you
have been as pleasing in my eyes as an 29:9
angel[u] of God; nevertheless, the Philis- [u] 2Sa 14:17,20;
tine commanders[v] have said, 'He must 19:27 [v] ver 4
not go up with us into battle.' 10Now get
up early, along with your master's servants who have come with you, and

[a] *13* Or *see spirits*; or *see gods*

leave[w] in the morning as soon as it is light."

11 So David and his men got up early in the morning to go back to the land of the Philistines, and the Philistines went up to Jezreel.

David Destroys the Amalekites

30 David and his men reached Ziklag[x] on the third day. Now the Amalekites[y] had raided the Negev and Ziklag. They had attacked Ziklag and burned it, 2 and had taken captive the women and all who were in it, both young and old. They killed none of them, but carried them off as they went on their way.

3 When David and his men came to Ziklag, they found it destroyed by fire and their wives and sons and daughters taken captive. 4 So David and his men wept aloud until they had no strength left to weep. 5 David's two wives[z] had been captured—Ahinoam of Jezreel and Abigail, the widow of Nabal of Carmel. 6 David was greatly distressed because the men were talking of stoning[a] him; each one was bitter in spirit because of his sons and daughters. But David found strength[b] in the LORD his God.

7 Then David said to Abiathar[c] the priest, the son of Ahimelech, "Bring me the ephod.[d]" Abiathar brought it to him, 8 and David inquired[e] of the LORD, "Shall I pursue this raiding party? Will I overtake them?"

"Pursue them," he answered. "You will certainly overtake them and succeed[f] in the rescue."

9 David and the six hundred men[g] with him came to the Besor Ravine, where some stayed behind, 10 for two hundred men were too exhausted[h] to cross the ravine. But David and four hundred men continued the pursuit.

11 They found an Egyptian in a field and brought him to David. They gave him water to drink and food to eat— 12 part of a cake of pressed figs and two cakes of raisins. He ate and was revived,[i] for he had not eaten any food or drunk any water for three days and three nights.

13 David asked him, "To whom do you belong, and where do you come from?"

He said, "I am an Egyptian, the slave of an Amalekite. My master abandoned me when I became ill three days ago. 14 We raided the Negev of the Kerethites[j] and the territory belonging to Judah and the Negev of Caleb.[k] And we burned[l] Ziklag."

15 David asked him, "Can you lead me down to this raiding party?"

He answered, "Swear to me before God that you will not kill me or hand me over to my master, and I will take you down to them."

16 He led David down, and there they were, scattered over the countryside, eating, drinking and reveling[m] because of the great amount of plunder[n] they had taken from the land of the Philistines and from Judah. 17 David fought[o] them from dusk until the evening of the next day, and none of them got away, except four hundred young men who rode off on camels and fled.[p] 18 David recovered[q] everything the Amalekites had taken, including his two wives. 19 Nothing was missing: young or old, boy or girl, plunder or anything else they had taken. David brought everything back. 20 He took all the flocks and herds, and his men drove them ahead of the other livestock, saying, "This is David's plunder."

21 Then David came to the two hundred men who had been too exhausted[r] to follow him and who were left behind at the Besor Ravine. They came out to meet David and the people with him. As David and his men approached, he greeted them. 22 But all the evil men and troublemakers among David's followers said, "Because they did not go out with us, we will not share with them the plunder we recovered. However, each man may take his wife and children and go."

23 David replied, "No, my brothers, you must not do that with what the LORD has given us. He has protected us and handed over to us the forces that came against us. 24 Who will listen to what you say? The share of the man who stayed with the supplies is to be the same as that of him who went down to the battle. All will share alike.[s]" 25 David made this a statute and ordinance for Israel from that day to this.

26 When David arrived in Ziklag, he sent some of the plunder to the elders of Judah, who were his friends, saying, "Here is a present for you from the plunder of the LORD's enemies."

29:10 [w] 1Ch 12:19
30:1 [x] 1Sa 29:4,11 [y] 1Sa 15:7; 27:8
30:5 [z] 1Sa 25:43; 2Sa 2:2
30:6 [a] Ex 17:4; Jn 8:59 [b] Ps 27:14; 56:3-4,11; Ro 4:20
30:7 [c] 1Sa 22:20 [d] 1Sa 23:9
30:8 [e] 1Sa 23:2 [f] ver 18
30:9 [g] 1Sa 27:2
30:10 [h] ver 9,21
30:12 [i] Jdg 15:19
30:14 [j] 2Sa 8:18; 1Ki 1:38,44; Eze 25:16; Zep 2:5 [k] ver 16; Jos 14:13; 15:13 [l] ver 1
30:16 [m] Lk 12:19 [n] ver 14
30:17 [o] 1Sa 11:11 [p] 1Sa 15:3
30:18 [q] Ge 14:16
30:21 [r] ver 10
30:24 [s] Nu 31:27; Jos 22:8

27 He sent it to those who were in
Bethel,[t] Ramoth[u] Negev and Jattir;[v] 28 to
those in Aroer,[w] Siphmoth, Eshtemoa[x]
29 and Racal; to those in the towns of the
Jerahmeelites[y] and the Kenites;[z] 30 to
those in Hormah,[a] Bor Ashan,[b] Athach
31 and Hebron;[c] and to those in all the
other places where David and his men
had roamed.

Saul Takes His Life

31 Now the Philistines fought
against Israel; the Israelites fled
before them, and many fell slain on
Mount Gilboa.[d] 2 The Philistines pressed
hard after Saul and his sons, and they
killed his sons Jonathan, Abinadab and
Malki-Shua. 3 The fighting grew fierce
around Saul, and when the archers overtook him, they wounded[e] him critically.
4 Saul said to his armor-bearer, "Draw
your sword and run me through,[f] or
these uncircumcised[g] fellows will come
and run me through and abuse me."
But his armor-bearer was terrified
and would not do it; so Saul took his
own sword and fell on it. 5 When the armor-bearer saw that Saul was dead, he
too fell on his sword and died with him.
6 So Saul and his three sons and his armor-bearer and all his men died together that same day.
7 When the Israelites along the valley
and those across the Jordan saw that the
Israelite army had fled and that Saul and
his sons had died, they abandoned their
towns and fled. And the Philistines
came and occupied them.
8 The next day, when the Philistines
came to strip the dead, they found Saul
and his three sons fallen on Mount Gilboa. 9 They cut off his head and stripped
off his armor, and they sent messengers
throughout the land of the Philistines to
proclaim the news[h] in the temple of
their idols and among their people.[i]
10 They put his armor in the temple of
the Ashtoreths[j] and fastened his body to
the wall of Beth Shan.[k]
11 When the people of Jabesh Gilead[l]
heard of what the Philistines had done
to Saul, 12 all their valiant men journeyed through the night to Beth Shan.
They took down the bodies of Saul and
his sons from the wall of Beth Shan and
went to Jabesh, where they burned[m]
them. 13 Then they took their bones[n]
and buried them under a tamarisk[o]
tree at Jabesh, and they fasted[p] seven
days.[q]

30:27 [t] Jos 7:2 [u] Jos 19:8 [v] Jos 15:48
30:28 [w] Jos 13:16 [x] Jos 15:50
30:29 [y] 1Sa 27:10 [z] Jdg 1:16; 1Sa 15:6
30:30 [a] Nu 14:45; Jdg 1:17 [b] Jos 15:42
30:31 [c] Jos 14:13; 2Sa 2:1,4
31:1 [d] 1Sa 28:4; 1Ch 10:1-12
31:3 [e] 2Sa 1:6
31:4 [f] Jdg 9:54; 2Sa 1:6,10 [g] 1Sa 14:6
31:9 [h] 2Sa 1:20 [i] Jdg 16:24
31:10 [j] Jdg 2:12-13; 1Sa 7:3 [k] Jos 17:11; 2Sa 21:12
31:11 [l] 1Sa 11:1
31:12 [m] 2Sa 2:4-7; 2Ch 16:14; Am 6:10
31:13 [n] 2Sa 21:12-14 [o] 1Sa 22:6 [p] 2Sa 1:12 [q] Ge 50:10

2 SAMUEL

What effect might the words of 2 Samuel 7:12–13 have had on the Jews living at the time of Jesus' birth?

♦ *This promise spoken by the prophet Nathan of a redeemer from the line of David was a source of hope to the Jewish people, despite the tragedy of the exile and the centuries of silence that preceded Jesus' birth.*

How have David's house and kingdom endured forever? (2 Samuel 7:16)

♦ *All 20 of the kings who ruled in Jerusalem after David were his descendants. Ultimately, Jesus represents the fulfillment of the promise. It is a beautiful irony that David, who wanted to build a house for God, instead received a promise that God would build him a house—the dynasty of kings from which the Messiah would come.*

Jesus in 2 Samuel David's heart was truly devoted to God. But this complicated and passionate man was by no means perfect. The book of 2 Samuel allows us to glimpse his struggles as he faced greater and greater responsibility, as well as his sorrow as he attempted to conceal his own sin. But this book also showcases God's persistent love as it reaches out to him to draw him back to God. As we think about the parallels in our own stories, we can wonder anew at God's infinite grace, seen both in terms of the atoning sacrifice of his Son and his redeeming work of sanctification that turns lives driven by sin into lives directed toward love and service. David's life shows us that no matter how great our triumphs, we cannot turn away from our precious Lord in pride and self-centeredness, and that no matter how deep our despair, God's love will always be there to pick us up.

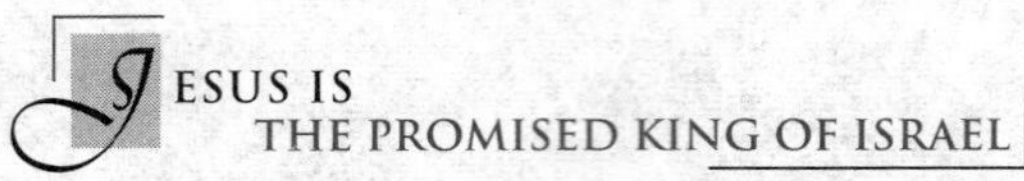

JESUS IS THE PROMISED KING OF ISRAEL

David Hears of Saul's Death

1 After the death[a] of Saul, David returned from defeating[b] the Amalekites and stayed in Ziklag two days. [2]On the third day a man[c] arrived from Saul's camp, with his clothes torn and with dust on his head.[d] When he came to David, he fell to the ground to pay him honor.

[3]"Where have you come from?" David asked him.

He answered, "I have escaped from the Israelite camp."

[4]"What happened?" David asked. "Tell me."

He said, "The men fled from the battle. Many of them fell and died. And Saul and his son Jonathan are dead."

[5]Then David said to the young man who brought him the report, "How do you know that Saul and his son Jonathan are dead?"

[6]"I happened to be on Mount Gilboa,[e]" the young man said, "and there was Saul, leaning on his spear, with the chariots and riders almost upon him. [7]When he turned around and saw me, he called out to me, and I said, 'What can I do?'

[8]"He asked me, 'Who are you?'

" 'An Amalekite,[f] I answered.

[9]"Then he said to me, 'Stand over me and kill me! I am in the throes of death, but I'm still alive.'

[10]"So I stood over him and killed him, because I knew that after he had fallen he could not survive. And I took the crown[g] that was on his head and the band on his arm and have brought them here to my lord."

[11]Then David and all the men with him took hold of their clothes and tore[h] them. [12]They mourned and wept and fasted till evening for Saul and his son Jonathan, and for the army of the LORD and the house of Israel, because they had fallen by the sword.

[13]David said to the young man who brought him the report, "Where are you from?"

"I am the son of an alien, an Amalekite,[i]" he answered.

[14]David asked him, "Why were you not afraid to lift your hand to destroy the LORD's anointed?[j]"

[15]Then David called one of his men and said, "Go, strike him down!"[k] So he struck him down, and he died.[l] [16]For David had said to him, "Your blood be on your own head.[m] Your own mouth testified against you when you said, 'I killed the LORD's anointed.' "

David's Lament for Saul and Jonathan

[17]David took up this lament[n] concerning Saul and his son Jonathan, [18]and ordered that the men of Judah be taught this lament of the bow (it is written in the Book of Jashar):[o]

[19]"Your glory, O Israel, lies slain on
your heights.
How the mighty have fallen![p]

[20]"Tell it not in Gath,[q]
proclaim it not in the streets of
Ashkelon,
lest the daughters of the
Philistines[r] be glad,
lest the daughters of the
uncircumcised rejoice.[s]

[21]"O mountains of Gilboa,[t]
may you have neither dew nor
rain,
nor fields that yield offerings[u]
⌞of grain⌟.
For there the shield of the mighty
was defiled,
the shield of Saul—no longer
rubbed with oil.[v]

[22]From the blood[w] of the slain,
from the flesh of the mighty,
the bow[x] of Jonathan did not turn
back,
the sword of Saul did not return
unsatisfied.

[23]"Saul and Jonathan—
in life they were loved and
gracious,
and in death they were not
parted.
They were swifter than eagles,[y]
they were stronger than lions.[z]

[24]"O daughters of Israel,
weep for Saul,
who clothed you in scarlet and
finery,
who adorned your garments
with ornaments of gold.

[25]"How the mighty have fallen in
battle!
Jonathan lies slain on your
heights.

1:1 a 1Sa 31:6 b 1Sa 30:17
1:2 c 2Sa 4:10 d 1Sa 4:12
1:6 e 1Sa 28:4; 31:2-4
1:8 f 1Sa 15:2; 30:13, 17
1:10 g Jdg 9:54; 2Ki 11:12
1:11 h Ge 37:29; 2Sa 3:31; 13:31
1:13 i ver 8
1:14 j 1Sa 24:6; 26:9
1:15 k 2Sa 4:12
1:15 l 2Sa 4:10
1:16 m Lev 20:9; 2Sa 3:28-29; 1Ki 2:32; Mt 27:24-25; Ac 18:6
1:17 n 2Ch 35:25
1:18 o Jos 10:13; 1Sa 31:3
1:19 p ver 27
1:20 q Mic 1:10 r 1Sa 31:8 s Ex 15:20; 1Sa 18:6
1:21 t ver 6; 1Sa 31:1 u Eze 31:15 v Isa 21:5
1:22 w Isa 34:3,7 x Dt 32:42; 1Sa 18:4
1:23 y Dt 28:49; Jer 4:13 z Jdg 14:18

1:26 26I grieve for you, Jonathan my
a 1Sa 20:42 brother;[a]
b 1Sa 18:1 you were very dear to me.
Your love for me was wonderful,[b]
more wonderful than that of
women.

27"How the mighty have fallen!
1:27 The weapons of war have
c ver 19,25; 1Sa 2:4 perished!"[c]

David Anointed King Over Judah

2 In the course of time, David in-
2:1 quired[d] of the LORD. "Shall I go up
d 1Sa 23:2,11-12 e Ge 13:18; 1Sa 30:31 to one of the towns of Judah?" he asked.
The LORD said, "Go up."
David asked, "Where shall I go?"
"To Hebron,"[e] the LORD answered.
2:2 2So David went up there with his two
f 1Sa 25:43; 30:5 wives,[f] Ahinoam of Jezreel and Abigail,[g]
g 1Sa 25:42 the widow of Nabal of Carmel. 3David
2:3 also took the men who were with him,[h]
h 1Sa 27:2; 30:9 each with his family, and they settled in
Hebron and its towns. 4Then the men of
2:4 Judah came to Hebron[i] and there they
i 1Sa 30:31 j 1Sa 2:35; 2Sa 5:3-5 anointed[j] David king over the house of
k 1Sa 31:11-13 Judah.
When David was told that it was the
men of Jabesh Gilead[k] who had buried

JESUS FOCUS

A KING FOR ISRAEL

After Saul's death the men of Judah heralded David as their king, anointing him at Hebron, the capital of Judah (2 Samuel 2). David ruled there for seven-and-one-half years. After Saul's son Ish-Bosheth had died the remaining tribes came to Hebron to anoint David as king over all of Israel. Shortly thereafter David conquered Jerusalem, the Jebusite stronghold, and began calling it the "City of David." He constructed a royal palace there and started planning the first temple. David's kingdom stretched from the borders of Egypt in the south to Lebanon in the north and bordered the Mediterranean Sea on the west and the Euphrates River on the east (2 Samuel 8:1–15). Under David's rule the kingdom finally reached all the way to the borders of the land God had promised his people (see Joshua 1:3–4). David's life foreshadowed what Jesus would do for God's people. In fact the angel who appeared when Jesus was born announced, "He will be great and will be called the Son of the Most High. The Lord God will give him the throne of his father David" (Luke 1:32).

Saul, 5he sent messengers to the men of
Jabesh Gilead to say to them, "The LORD 2:5
bless[l] you for showing this kindness to l 1Sa 23:21
Saul your master by burying him. 6May
the LORD now show you kindness and 2:6
faithfulness,[m] and I too will show you the m Ex 34:6; 1Ti 1:16
same favor because you have done this.
7Now then, be strong and brave, for Saul
your master is dead, and the house of Judah has anointed me king over them."

War Between the Houses of David and Saul

8Meanwhile, Abner[n] son of Ner, the 2:8
commander of Saul's army, had taken n 1Sa 14:50 o Ge 32:2
Ish-Bosheth son of Saul and brought
him over to Mahanaim.[o] 9He made him 2:9
king over Gilead,[p] Ashuri[a][q] and Jezreel, p Nu 32:26 q Jdg 1:32
and also over Ephraim, Benjamin and all r 1Ch 12:29
Israel.[r]
10Ish-Bosheth son of Saul was forty
years old when he became king over Israel, and he reigned two years. The
house of Judah, however, followed David.
11The length of time David was king in
Hebron over the house of Judah was sev- 2:11
en years and six months.[s] s 2Sa 5:5
12Abner son of Ner, together with the
men of Ish-Bosheth son of Saul, left Ma- 2:12
hanaim and went to Gibeon.[t] 13Joab[u] t Jos 18:25
son of Zeruiah and David's men went 2:13
out and met them at the pool of Gibeon. u 2Sa 8:16;
One group sat down on one side of the 1Ch 2:16; 11:6
pool and one group on the other side.
14Then Abner said to Joab, "Let's have
some of the young men get up and fight
hand to hand in front of us."
"All right, let them do it," Joab said.
15So they stood up and were counted
off—twelve men for Benjamin and Ish-Bosheth son of Saul, and twelve for David. 16Then each man grabbed his opponent by the head and thrust his dagger
into his opponent's side, and they fell
down together. So that place in Gibeon
was called Helkath Hazzurim.[b]
17The battle that day was very fierce,
and Abner and the men of Israel were 2:17
defeated[v] by David's men. v 2Sa 3:1
18The three sons of Zeruiah[w] were 2:18
there: Joab,[x] Abishai[y] and Asahel.[z] Now w 2Sa 3:39 x 2Sa 3:30
Asahel was as fleet-footed as a wild y 1Sa 26:6 z 1Ch 2:16
gazelle.[a] 19He chased Abner, turning nei- a 1Ch 12:8
ther to the right nor to the left as he pur-

[a] 9 Or *Asher* [b] 16 *Helkath Hazzurim* means *field of daggers* or *field of hostilities.*

sued him. 20 Abner looked behind him
and asked, "Is that you, Asahel?"
"It is," he answered.
21 Then Abner said to him, "Turn
aside to the right or to the left; take on
one of the young men and strip him of
his weapons." But Asahel would not stop
chasing him.
22 Again Abner warned Asahel, "Stop
chasing me! Why should I strike you
2:22 down? How could I look your brother
b 2Sa 3:27 Joab in the face?"[b]
23 But Asahel refused to give up the
2:23 pursuit; so Abner thrust the butt of his
c 2Sa 3:27; 4:6 spear into Asahel's stomach,[c] and the
d 2Sa 20:12 spear came out through his back. He fell
there and died on the spot. And every
man stopped when he came to the place
where Asahel had fallen and died.[d]
24 But Joab and Abishai pursued Abner,
and as the sun was setting, they came to
the hill of Ammah, near Giah on the way
to the wasteland of Gibeon. 25 Then the
men of Benjamin rallied behind Abner.
They formed themselves into a group
and took their stand on top of a hill.
2:26 26 Abner called out to Joab, "Must the
e Dt 32:42; sword devour[e] forever? Don't you realize
Jer 46:10,14 that this will end in bitterness? How
long before you order your men to stop
pursuing their brothers?"
27 Joab answered, "As surely as God
lives, if you had not spoken, the men
would have continued the pursuit of
their brothers until morning.[a]"
2:28 28 So Joab[f] blew the trumpet,[g] and all
f 2Sa 18:16 g Jdg 3:27 the men came to a halt; they no longer
pursued Israel, nor did they fight any-
more.
29 All that night Abner and his men
marched through the Arabah. They
crossed the Jordan, continued through
2:29 the whole Bithron[b] and came to Maha-
h ver 8 naim.[h]
30 Then Joab returned from pursuing
Abner and assembled all his men. Besides Asahel, nineteen of David's men
were found missing. 31 But David's men
had killed three hundred and sixty Benjamites who were with Abner. 32 They
2:32 took Asahel and buried him in his fa-
i Ge 49:29 ther's tomb[i] at Bethlehem. Then Joab
and his men marched all night and arrived at Hebron by daybreak.

3 The war between the house of
3:1 Saul and the house of David last-
j 1Ki 14:30 ed a long time.[j] David grew stronger and
stronger,[k] while the house of Saul grew 3:1
weaker and weaker.[l] k 2Sa 5:10
2 Sons were born to David in Hebron: l 2Sa 2:17
His firstborn was Amnon the 3:2
son of Ahinoam[m] of Jezreel; m 1Sa 25:43;
3 his second, Kileab the son of Ab- 1Ch 3:1-3
igail[n] the widow of Nabal of Car- 3:3
mel; n 1Sa 25:42
the third, Absalom[o] the son of o 2Sa 13:1,28 p 1Sa 27:8;
Maacah daughter of Talmai king 2Sa 13:37;
of Geshur;[p] 14:32; 15:8
4 the fourth, Adonijah[q] the son of 3:4
Haggith; q 1Ki 1:5,11
the fifth, Shephatiah the son of
Abital;
5 and the sixth, Ithream the son of
David's wife Eglah.
These were born to David in Hebron.

Abner Goes Over to David

6 During the war between the house of
Saul and the house of David, Abner had
been strengthening his own position in
the house of Saul. 7 Now Saul had had a
concubine[r] named Rizpah[s] daughter of 3:7 r 2Sa 16:21-22
Aiah. And Ish-Bosheth said to Abner, s 2Sa 21:8-11
"Why did you sleep with my father's
concubine?"
8 Abner was very angry because of
what Ish-Bosheth said and he answered,
"Am I a dog's head[t]—on Judah's side? 3:8 t 1Sa 24:14;
This very day I am loyal to the house of 2Sa 9:8; 16:9
your father Saul and to his family and
friends. I haven't handed you over to David. Yet now you accuse me of an offense
involving this woman! 9 May God deal
with Abner, be it ever so severely, if I do
not do for David what the LORD promised[u] him on oath 10 and transfer the 3:9
kingdom from the house of Saul and es- u 1Sa 15:28; 1Ki 19:2
tablish David's throne over Israel and Ju-
dah from Dan to Beersheba."[v] 11 Ish-Bo- 3:10
sheth did not dare to say another word v Jdg 20:1;
to Abner, because he was afraid of him. 1Sa 3:20
12 Then Abner sent messengers on his
behalf to say to David, "Whose land is it?
Make an agreement with me, and I will
help you bring all Israel over to you."
13 "Good," said David. "I will make an
agreement with you. But I demand one
thing of you: Do not come into my pres-

[a] 27 Or *spoken this morning, the men would not have taken up the pursuit of their brothers*; or *spoken, the men would have given up the pursuit of their brothers by morning* [b] 29 Or *morning*; or *ravine*; the meaning of the Hebrew for this word is uncertain.

ence unless you bring Michal daughter
3:13 [w]Ge 43:5; of Saul when you come to see me."[w]
1Sa 18:20 14Then David sent messengers to Ish-
Bosheth son of Saul, demanding, "Give
3:14 [x]1Sa 18:27 me my wife Michal,[x] whom I betrothed
to myself for the price of a hundred
Philistine foreskins."
15So Ish-Bosheth gave orders and had
3:15 [y]Dt 24:1-4 her taken away from her husband[y] Palti-
[z]1Sa 25:44 el[z] son of Laish. 16Her husband, however,
went with her, weeping behind her all the
3:16 way to Bahurim.[a] Then Abner said to
[a]2Sa 16:5; 19:16 him, "Go back home!" So he went back.
3:17 17Abner conferred with the elders[b] of
[b]Jdg 11:11 Israel and said, "For some time you have
wanted to make David your king. 18Now
do it! For the LORD promised David, 'By
my servant David I will rescue my peo-
3:18 ple Israel from the hand of the Philis-
[c]1Sa 9:16 tines[c] and from the hand of all their en-
[d]1Sa 15:28; 2Sa 8:6 emies.[d]' "
19Abner also spoke to the Benjamites
in person. Then he went to Hebron to
tell David everything that Israel and the
3:19 whole house of Benjamin[e] wanted to do.
[e]1Sa 10:20-21; 1Ch 12:2,16,29 20When Abner, who had twenty men
with him, came to David at Hebron, Da-
vid prepared a feast for him and his
men. 21Then Abner said to David, "Let
me go at once and assemble all Israel for
my lord the king, so that they may make
3:21 [f]ver 10,12 a compact[f] with you, and that you may
[g]1Ki 11:37 rule over all that your heart desires."[g] So
David sent Abner away, and he went in
peace.

Joab Murders Abner

22Just then David's men and Joab returned from a raid and brought with
them a great deal of plunder. But Abner
was no longer with David in Hebron, because David had sent him away, and he
had gone in peace. 23When Joab and all
the soldiers with him arrived, he was
told that Abner son of Ner had come to
the king and that the king had sent him
away and that he had gone in peace.
24So Joab went to the king and said,
"What have you done? Look, Abner
came to you. Why did you let him go?
Now he is gone! 25You know Abner son
of Ner; he came to deceive you and observe your movements and find out
everything you are doing."
26Joab then left David and sent messengers after Abner, and they brought
him back from the well of Sirah. But Da-
vid did not know it. 27Now when Abner[h] 3:27 [h]2Sa 2:8
returned to Hebron, Joab took him aside [i]2Sa 2:22; 20:9-10; 1Ki 2:5
into the gateway, as though to speak
with him privately. And there, to avenge
the blood of his brother Asahel, Joab
stabbed him in the stomach, and he
died.[i]
28Later, when David heard about this,
he said, "I and my kingdom are forever
innocent[j] before the LORD concerning 3:28 [j]ver 37; Dt 21:9
the blood of Abner son of Ner. 29May his
blood[k] fall upon the head of Joab and 3:29 [k]Lev 20:9
upon all his father's house![l] May Joab's [l]1Ki 2:31-33
house never be without someone who [m]Lev 15:2
has a running sore[m] or leprosy[a] or who
leans on a crutch or who falls by the
sword or who lacks food."
30(Joab and his brother Abishai murdered Abner because he had killed their
brother Asahel in the battle at Gibeon.)
31Then David said to Joab and all the
people with him, "Tear your clothes and
put on sackcloth[n] and walk in mourn- 3:31 [n]2Sa 1:2,11;
ing[o] in front of Abner." King David him- Ps 30:11; Isa 20:2
self walked behind the bier. 32They [o]Ge 37:34
buried Abner in Hebron, and the king
wept[p] aloud at Abner's tomb. All the 3:32 [p]Nu 14:1;
people wept also. Pr 24:17
33The king sang this lament[q] for Ab- 3:33 [q]2Sa 1:17
ner:

> "Should Abner have died as the
> lawless die?
> 34 Your hands were not bound,
> your feet were not fettered.
> You fell as one falls before wicked
> men."

And all the people wept over him
again.
35Then they all came and urged David
to eat something while it was still day;
but David took an oath, saying, "May
God deal with me, be it ever so severely,[r] 3:35 [r]Ru 1:17; 1Sa 3:17
if I taste bread[s] or anything else before [s]1Sa 31:13;
the sun sets!" 2Sa 1:12; 12:17;
36All the people took note and were Jer 16:7
pleased; indeed, everything the king did
pleased them. 37So on that day all the
people and all Israel knew that the king
had no part[t] in the murder of Abner son 3:37 [t]ver 28
of Ner.
38Then the king said to his men, "Do
you not realize that a prince and a great
man has fallen[u] in Israel this day? 39And 3:38 [u]2Sa 1:19

[a] *29* The Hebrew word was used for various diseases affecting the skin—not necessarily leprosy.

3:39 [v]2Sa 2:18 [w]2Sa 19:5-7 [x]1Ki 2:5-6,33-34; Ps 41:10; 101:8 today, though I am the anointed king, I
am weak, and these sons of Zeruiah[v] are
too strong for me.[w] May the LORD repay[x]
the evildoer according to his evil deeds!"

Ish-Bosheth Murdered

4:1 [y]2Sa 3:27; Ezr 4:4 4 When Ish-Bosheth son of Saul
heard that Abner[y] had died in Hebron,
he lost courage, and all Israel became alarmed.
2Now Saul's son had two
men who were leaders of raiding bands.
One was named Baanah and the other
Recab; they were sons of Rimmon the
Beerothite from the tribe of Benjamin—
4:2 [z]Jos 9:17; 18:25 Beeroth[z] is considered part of Benjamin,
4:3 [a]Ne 11:33 3because the people of Beeroth fled to
Gittaim[a] and have lived there as aliens
to this day.
4:4 [b]1Sa 18:1 [c]1Sa 31:1-4 [d]Lev 21:18 [e]2Sa 9:3,6; 1Ch 8:34; 9:40 4(Jonathan[b] son of Saul had a son
who was lame in both feet. He was five
years old when the news[c] about Saul
and Jonathan came from Jezreel. His
nurse picked him up and fled, but as she
hurried to leave, he fell and became crippled.[d]
His name was Mephibosheth.)[e]
5Now Recab and Baanah, the sons of
Rimmon the Beerothite, set out for the
4:5 [f]2Sa 2:8 house of Ish-Bosheth,[f] and they arrived
there in the heat of the day while he was
taking his noonday rest. 6They went into
4:6 [g]2Sa 2:23 the inner part of the house as if to get
some wheat, and they stabbed[g] him in
the stomach. Then Recab and his brother
Baanah slipped away.
7They had gone into the house while
he was lying on the bed in his bedroom.
After they stabbed and killed him, they
cut off his head. Taking it with them,
they traveled all night by way of the Arabah.
8They brought the head of Ish-Bosheth
to David at Hebron and said to the
king, "Here is the head of Ish-Bosheth
4:8 [h]1Sa 24:4; 25:29 son of Saul,[h] your enemy, who tried to
take your life. This day the LORD has
avenged my lord the king against Saul
and his offspring."
9David answered Recab and his
brother Baanah, the sons of Rimmon
the Beerothite, "As surely as the LORD
4:9 [i]Ge 48:16; 1Ki 1:29 lives, who has delivered[i] me out of all
trouble, 10when a man told me, 'Saul is
dead,' and thought he was bringing good
news, I seized him and put him to death
4:10 [j]2Sa 1:2-16 in Ziklag.[j] That was the reward I gave
him for his news! 11How much more—
when wicked men have killed an innocent
man in his own house and on his
own bed—should I not now demand his
blood[k] from your hand and rid the earth 4:11 [k]Ge 9:5; Ps 9:12
of you!"
12So David gave an order to his men,
and they killed them.[l] They cut off their 4:12 [l]2Sa 1:15
hands and feet and hung the bodies by
the pool in Hebron. But they took the
head of Ish-Bosheth and buried it in Abner's
tomb at Hebron.

David Becomes King Over Israel

5 All the tribes of Israel[m] came to 5:1 [m]2Sa 19:43 [n]1Ch 11:1
David at Hebron and said, "We are
your own flesh and blood.[n] 2In the past,
while Saul was king over us, you were
the one who led Israel on their military
campaigns.[o] And the LORD said to you, 5:2 [o]1Sa 18:5,13,16 [p]1Sa 16:1; 2Sa 7:7 [q]1Sa 25:30
'You will shepherd[p] my people Israel,
and you will become their ruler.[q]' "
3When all the elders of Israel had
come to King David at Hebron, the king
made a compact[r] with them at Hebron 5:3 [r]2Sa 3:21 [s]2Sa 2:4
before the LORD, and they anointed[s] David
king over Israel.
4David was thirty years old[t] when he 5:4 [t]Lk 3:23 [u]1Ki 2:11; 1Ch 3:4 [v]1Ch 26:31; 29:27
became king, and he reigned[u] forty[v]
years. 5In Hebron he reigned over Judah
seven years and six months,[w] and in Jerusalem
he reigned over all Israel and Judah 5:5 [w]2Sa 2:11; 1Ch 3:4
thirty-three years.

David Conquers Jerusalem

6The king and his men marched to Jerusalem[x]
to attack the Jebusites,[y] who 5:6 [x]Jdg 1:8 [y]Jos 15:8
lived there. The Jebusites said to David,
"You will not get in here; even the blind
and the lame can ward you off." They
thought, "David cannot get in here."
7Nevertheless, David captured the fortress 5:7 [z]2Sa 6:12,16; 1Ki 2:10
of Zion, the City of David.[z]
8On that day, David said, "Anyone who
conquers the Jebusites will have to use
the water shaft[a] to reach those 'lame
and blind' who are David's enemies.[b]"
That is why they say, "The 'blind and
lame' will not enter the palace."
9David then took up residence in the
fortress and called it the City of David.
He built up the area around it, from the
supporting terraces[c][a] inward. 10And he 5:9 [a]ver 7; 1Ki 9:15, 24
became more and more powerful,[b] because 5:10 [b]2Sa 3:1
the LORD God Almighty was with
him.
11Now Hiram[c] king of Tyre sent messengers 5:11 [c]1Ki 5:1,18; 1Ch 14:1
to David, along with cedar logs

[a] 8 Or *use scaling hooks* [b] 8 Or *are hated by David* [c] 9 Or *the Millo*

DISCOVERY 75

A Nation, a City and a King

Of all of the cities in the world only one is called "holy." Jerusalem, in Biblical times, was the center of both political authority and religious ceremony for the Israelites, and it remains vital today to the Jewish people as a symbol of national identity and religious activity. Second Samuel 5 is a significant chapter, because it describes how David became God's chosen king, how he conquered and claimed Jerusalem as his own and how he ruled over the nation of Israel from the holy city as God had intended.

People have always talked about "going up" to Jerusalem. The city is built atop a steep hill. The Hinnom Valley on the west and the Kidron Valley on the east join south of the city. Jerusalem is an excellent fortress, because these steep valleys afford natural defenses on three sides. The city also enjoys an excellent water supply from the Gihon spring. Even when under siege Jerusalem can sustain itself for a very long time. When David conquered the city, he constructed terraces on the north end to protect it from attack from that direction. Because of David's military success, and because Jerusalem was his capital city, it became known as the *City of David.*

But Jerusalem is significant for another reason as well. God himself chose the city as the site for his people to build the temple, and hence Jerusalem became known as the *City of God*. With God's presence, his chosen king on the throne and the capital secure and fortified, Israel prospered (verses 9–10).

Generations later Jerusalem would become even more significant. God had promised that "David's son" would reign in Israel forever (2 Samuel 7:12–13). Over the course of years, while the people were scattered and David's family line threatened, God still preserved the royal line so that his promised Messiah would be born. Jesus was not born in Jerusalem, but in many ways his life centered around the city. His parents dedicated him at the temple (Luke 2:22), and Simeon, an elderly resident of Jerusalem, prophesied: "My eyes have seen your salvation, which you have prepared in the sight of all people, a light for revelation to the Gentiles and for glory to your people Israel" (Luke 2:30–32). Jerusalem was also the stage for the final few days of Jesus' life, including his crucifixion just outside the city. Our Lord was arrested, tried and executed in the City of God, and it was also there that he was raised again to life (Matthew 26—28).

The holy city will play an important role in the future as well. The Bible refers to "the new Jerusalem," a place in which God's presence will be with his people forever (Revelation 3:12; 21:2). In that day the purposes of the City of God and the City of David will finally merge. Jesus, the Son of God, will reign forever as God's chosen King.

***Self-Discovery:** In what context can you, along with Simeon, say to God, "My eyes have seen your salvation"?*

GO TO DISCOVERY 76 ON PAGE 391

and carpenters and stonemasons, and they built a palace for David. 12And David knew that the LORD had established him as king over Israel and had exalted his kingdom for the sake of his people Israel.

13After he left Hebron, David took more concubines and wives[d] in Jerusalem, and more sons and daughters were born to him. 14These are the names of the children born to him there:[e] Shammua, Shobab, Nathan, Solomon, 15Ibhar, Elishua, Nepheg, Japhia, 16Elishama, Eliada and Eliphelet.

David Defeats the Philistines

17When the Philistines heard that David had been anointed king over Israel, they went up in full force to search for him, but David heard about it and went down to the stronghold.[f] 18Now the Philistines had come and spread out in the Valley of Rephaim;[g] 19so David inquired[h] of the LORD, "Shall I go and attack the Philistines? Will you hand them over to me?"

The LORD answered him, "Go, for I will surely hand the Philistines over to you."

20So David went to Baal Perazim, and there he defeated them. He said, "As waters break out, the LORD has broken out against my enemies before me." So that place was called Baal Perazim.[a][i] 21The Philistines abandoned their idols there, and David and his men carried them off.[j]

22Once more the Philistines came up and spread out in the Valley of Rephaim; 23so David inquired of the LORD, and he answered, "Do not go straight up, but circle around behind them and attack them in front of the balsam trees. 24As soon as you hear the sound[k] of marching in the tops of the balsam trees, move quickly, because that will mean the LORD has gone out in front[l] of you to strike the Philistine army." 25So David did as the LORD commanded him, and he struck down the Philistines all the way from Gibeon[b][m] to Gezer.[n]

The Ark Brought to Jerusalem

6 David again brought together out of Israel chosen men, thirty thousand in all. 2He and all his men set out from Baalah[o] of Judah[c] to bring up from there the ark[p] of God, which is called by the Name,[d][q] the name of the LORD Almighty, who is enthroned[r] between the cherubim[s] that are on the ark. 3They set the ark of God on a new cart[t] and brought it from the house of Abinadab, which was on the hill. Uzzah and Ahio, sons of Abinadab, were guiding the new cart 4with the ark of God on it,[e] and Ahio was walking in front of it. 5David and the whole house of Israel were celebrating with all their might before the LORD, with songs[f] and with harps, lyres, tambourines, sistrums and cymbals.[u]

6When they came to the threshing floor of Nacon, Uzzah reached out and took hold of[v] the ark of God, because the oxen stumbled. 7The LORD's anger burned against Uzzah because of his irreverent act;[w] therefore God struck him down[x] and he died there beside the ark of God.

8Then David was angry because the LORD's wrath[y] had broken out against Uzzah, and to this day that place is called Perez Uzzah.[g][z]

9David was afraid of the LORD that day and said, "How[a] can the ark of the LORD ever come to me?" 10He was not willing to take the ark of the LORD to be with him in the City of David. Instead, he took it aside to the house of Obed-Edom[b] the Gittite. 11The ark of the LORD remained in the house of Obed-Edom the Gittite for three months, and the LORD blessed him and his entire household.[c]

12Now King David[d] was told, "The LORD has blessed the household of Obed-Edom and everything he has, because of the ark of God." So David went down and brought up the ark of God from the house of Obed-Edom to the City of David with rejoicing. 13When those who were carrying the ark of the LORD had taken six steps, he sacrificed[e] a bull and a fattened calf. 14David, wearing a linen ephod,[f] danced[g] before the LORD with all his might, 15while he and the entire house of Israel brought up the

5:13 [d] Dt 17:17; 1Ch 3:9
5:14 [e] 1Ch 3:5
5:17 [f] 2Sa 23:14; 1Ch 11:16
5:18 [g] Jos 15:8; 17:15; 18:16
5:19 [h] 1Sa 23:2; 2Sa 2:1
5:20 [i] Isa 28:21
5:21 [j] Dt 7:5; 1Ch 14:12; Isa 46:2
5:24 [k] 2Ki 7:6 [l] Jdg 4:14
5:25 [m] Isa 28:21 [n] 1Ch 14:16
6:2 [o] Jos 15:9 [p] 1Sa 4:4; 7:1 [q] Lev 24:16; Isa 63:14
6:2 [r] Ps 99:1 [s] Ex 25:22; 1Ch 13:5-6
6:3 [t] Nu 7:4-9; 1Sa 6:7
6:5 [u] 1Sa 18:6-7; Ezr 3:10; Ps 150:5
6:6 [v] Nu 4:15,19-20; 1Ch 13:9
6:7 [w] 1Ch 15:13-15 [x] Ex 19:22; 1Sa 6:19
6:8 [y] Ps 7:11 [z] Ge 38:29
6:9 [a] Ps 119:120
6:10 [b] 1Ch 13:13; 26:4-5
6:11 [c] Ge 30:27; 39:5
6:12 [d] 1Ki 8:1; 1Ch 15:25
6:13 [e] 1Ki 8:5,62
6:14 [f] Ex 19:6; 1Sa 2:18 [g] Ex 15:20

[a] 20 *Baal Perazim* means *the lord who breaks out.* [b] 25 Septuagint (see also 1 Chron. 14:16); Hebrew *Geba* [c] 2 That is, Kiriath Jearim; Hebrew *Baale Judah,* a variant of *Baalah of Judah* [d] 2 Hebrew; Septuagint and Vulgate do not have *the Name.* [e] 3,4 Dead Sea Scrolls and some Septuagint manuscripts; Masoretic Text *cart* [4]*and they brought it with the ark of God from the house of Abinadab, which was on the hill* [f] 5 See Dead Sea Scrolls, Septuagint and 1 Chronicles 13:8; Masoretic Text *celebrating before the LORD with all kinds of instruments made of pine.* [g] 8 *Perez Uzzah* means *outbreak against Uzzah.*

ark of the LORD with shouts and the
6:15 h Ps 47:5; 98:6 sound of trumpets.[h]
16 As the ark of the LORD was entering
6:16 i 2Sa 5:7 the City of David,[i] Michal daughter of
Saul watched from a window. And when
she saw King David leaping and dancing
before the LORD, she despised him in her
heart.
17 They brought the ark of the LORD
and set it in its place inside the tent that
6:17 j 1Ch 15:1; David had pitched for it,[j] and David sac-
2Ch 1:4 rificed burnt offerings[k] and fellowship
k Lev 1:1-17; offerings[a] before the LORD. 18 After he
1Ki 8:62-64 had finished sacrificing[l] the burnt offer-
6:18 l 1Ki 8:22 ings and fellowship offerings, he blessed
the people in the name of the LORD
Almighty. 19 Then he gave a loaf of bread,
6:19 m Hos 3:1 a cake of dates and a cake of raisins[m] to
n Ne 8:10 each person in the whole crowd of Israelites, both men and women.[n] And all
the people went to their homes.
20 When David returned home to bless
his household, Michal daughter of Saul
came out to meet him and said, "How
the king of Israel has distinguished him-
6:20 o ver 14,16 self today, disrobing[o] in the sight of the
slave girls of his servants as any vulgar
fellow would!"
21 David said to Michal, "It was before
the LORD, who chose me rather than
your father or anyone from his house
6:21 p 1Sa 13:14; when he appointed[p] me ruler over the
15:28 LORD's people Israel—I will celebrate before the LORD. 22 I will become even more
undignified than this, and I will be humiliated in my own eyes. But by these
slave girls you spoke of, I will be held in
honor."
23 And Michal daughter of Saul had no
children to the day of her death.

God's Promise to David

7 After the king was settled in his
7:1 q 1Ch 17:1 palace[q] and the LORD had given
him rest from all his enemies around
him, 2 he said to Nathan the prophet,
7:2 r 2Sa 5:11 "Here I am, living in a palace[r] of cedar,
s Ex 26:1; while the ark of God remains in a tent."[s]
Ac 7:45-46 3 Nathan replied to the king, "Whatever you have in mind, go ahead and do
it, for the LORD is with you."
4 That night the word of the LORD
came to Nathan, saying:
5 "Go and tell my servant David,
7:5 'This is what the LORD says: Are
t 1Ki 8:19; you[t] the one to build me a house to
1Ch 22:8 u 1Ki 5:3-5 dwell in?[u] 6 I have not dwelt in a
house from the day I brought the Is-
raelites up out of Egypt to this day.
I have been moving from place to 7:6
place with a tent[v] as my dwelling.[w] v Ex 40:18,34
7 Wherever I have moved with all w 1Ki 8:16
the Israelites,[x] did I ever say to any 7:7
of their rulers whom I commanded x Dt 23:14
to shepherd[y] my people Israel, y 2Sa 5:2 z Lev 26:11-12
"Why have you not built me a
house of cedar?[z]"'
8 "Now then, tell my servant David, 'This is what the LORD
Almighty says: I took you from the
pasture and from following the 7:8
flock[a] to be ruler[b] over my people a 1Sa 16:11
Israel.[c] 9 I have been with you wher- b 2Sa 6:21
ever you have gone,[d] and I have cut c Ps 78:70-72;
off all your enemies from before 2Co 6:18*
you.[e] Now I will make your name 7:9 d 2Sa 5:10
great, like the names of the greatest e Ps 18:37-42
men of the earth. 10 And I will pro-
vide a place for my people Israel 7:10
and will plant[f] them so that they f Ex 15:17;
can have a home of their own and Isa 5:1-7 g Ps 89:22-23
no longer be disturbed. Wicked[g] h Isa 60:18
people will not oppress them anymore,[h] as they did at the beginning
11 and have done ever since the time 7:11
I appointed leaders[b][i] over my peo- i Jdg 2:16;
ple Israel. I will also give you rest 1Sa 12:9-11 j ver 1
from all your enemies.[j] k 1Sa 25:28
"'The LORD declares to you that l ver 27
the LORD himself will establish[k] a
house[l] for you: 12 When your days 7:12
are over and you rest[m] with your fa- m 1Ki 2:1
thers, I will raise up your offspring n Ps 132:11-12
to succeed you, who will come
from your own body,[n] and I will establish his kingdom. 13 He is the one
who will build a house for my
Name,[o] and I will establish the 7:13 o 1Ki 5:5; 8:19,
throne of his kingdom forever.[p] 14 I 29 p Isa 9:7
will be his father, and he will be my 7:14
son.[q] When he does wrong, I will q Ps 89:26;
punish him with the rod[r] of men, Heb 1:5*
with floggings inflicted by men. r Ps 89:30-33
15 But my love will never be taken
away from him, as I took it away 7:15
from Saul,[s] whom I removed from s 1Sa 15:23,28
before you. 16 Your house and your
kingdom will endure forever before
me[c]; your throne[t] will be estab- 7:16 t Ps 89:36-37
lished forever.[u]'" u ver 13

a 17 Traditionally *peace offerings*; also in verse 18
b 11 Traditionally *judges* *c* 16 Some Hebrew manuscripts and Septuagint; most Hebrew manuscripts *you*

DISCOVERY 76

LEADING GOD'S SHEEP

Before David had learned of his selection as Israel's future king, he had spent his days in the fields, watching over his father's sheep. In 2 Samuel 7:8 God spoke to David through the prophet Nathan: "I took you from the pasture and from following the flock to be ruler over my people Israel." What possible connection could there be between shepherding a flock and ruling a nation? Yet God uses the picture of a shepherd to describe himself—and points out that we have more in common with sheep than we might want to admit. A shepherd ensures that the sheep are fed, watered, cared for and protected from danger. And part of God's plan has always been that his chosen leaders look after the needs of his people in much the same way.

God urges his leaders to be good shepherds over his flock, because they have been entrusted with the well-being of the sheep. When those in positions of authority in the church injure or endanger the flock or scatter the sheep, God promises to replace them with others who will lead responsibly and demonstrate genuine concern (Jeremiah 23:1–4). In God's church the elders are entrusted with the care of church members, much as a shepherd oversees the activity of the flock. The elders' daily lives must reflect Jesus' love—for they will answer to the Chief Shepherd, Jesus himself (1 Peter 5:1–4).

God is unconditionally committed to each of us. David's "Shepherd Psalm" (Psalm 23) is perhaps the best-known chapter in the Bible. We take comfort in the knowledge that our faithful shepherd is there for us in all seasons and conditions and that our well-being is his primary concern. No matter how bleak or blustery the night, he pledges his presence. He protects us and leads us on in paths of celebration and hope.

Jesus is God's ultimate expression of shepherding. Jesus Christ knows each of us intimately. And when God calls people into leadership positions, he is calling them to serve under this shepherding model. As we serve like this we reflect to the world the love of Jesus and introduce him to others as the great Shepherd of the sheep.

Jesus himself stated, "I am the good shepherd. The good shepherd lays down his life for the sheep. The hired hand is not the shepherd who owns the sheep. So when he sees the wolf coming, he abandons the sheep and runs away. Then the wolf attacks the flock and scatters it. The man runs away because he is a hired hand and cares nothing for the sheep. I am the good shepherd; I know my sheep and my sheep know me—just as the Father knows me and I know the Father—and I lay down my life for the sheep" (John 10:11–15).

Self-Discovery: *In what ways are you like a sheep? In what specific ways have you interacted with Jesus as a sheep to a shepherd?*

GO TO DISCOVERY 77 ON PAGE 394

17Nathan reported to David all the
words of this entire revelation.

David's Prayer

18Then King David went in and sat before the LORD, and he said:

7:18 [v]Ex 3:11; "Who am I,[v] O Sovereign LORD,
1Sa 18:18 and what is my family, that you
have brought me this far? 19And as
if this were not enough in your
sight, O Sovereign LORD, you have
also spoken about the future of the
house of your servant. Is this your
7:19 [w]Isa 55:8-9 usual way of dealing with man,[w]
O Sovereign LORD?

7:20 20"What more can David say to
[x]Jn 21:17 you? For you know[x] your servant,[y]
[y]1Sa 16:7 O Sovereign LORD. 21For the sake of
your word and according to your
will, you have done this great thing
and made it known to your servant.

> JESUS IS A GENUINE JEWISH PERSONALITY . . . THE BEST THAT WAS AND IS IN JUDAISM.
>
> Leo Baeck, *Jewish Author*

7:22 22"How great[z] you are,[a] O Sover-
[z]Ps 48:1; 86:10; Jer 10:6 eign LORD! There is no one like you,
[a]Dt 3:24 and there is no God[b] but you, as we
[b]Ex 15:11 have heard with our own ears.[c]
[c]Ex 10:2; Ps 44:1 23And who is like your people Isra-
7:23 el[d]—the one nation on earth that
[d]Dt 4:32-38 God went out to redeem as a peo-
[e]Dt 10:21 ple for himself, and to make a
[f]Dt 9:26; 15:15 name for himself, and to perform
great and awesome wonders[e] by
driving out nations and their gods
from before your people, whom
you redeemed[f] from Egypt?[a] 24You
7:24 have established your people Israel
[g]Dt 26:18 as your very own[g] forever, and you,
[h]Ex 6:6-7; Ps 48:14 O LORD, have become their God.[h]
25"And now, LORD God, keep for-
ever the promise you have made
concerning your servant and his
house. Do as you promised, 26so
that your name will be great forever. Then men will say, 'The LORD
Almighty is God over Israel!' And
the house of your servant David
will be established before you.
27"O LORD Almighty, God of Israel, you have revealed this to your
servant, saying, 'I will build a house
for you.' So your servant has found
courage to offer you this prayer. 28O
Sovereign LORD, you are God! Your
words are trustworthy,[i] and you 7:28
have promised these good things to [i]Ex 34:6; Jn 17:17
your servant. 29Now be pleased to
bless the house of your servant,
that it may continue forever in your
sight; for you, O Sovereign LORD,
have spoken, and with your bless-
ing[j] the house of your servant will 7:29 [j]Nu 6:23-27
be blessed forever."

David's Victories

8 In the course of time, David defeated the Philistines and subdued them, and he took Metheg Ammah from the control of the Philistines.
2David also defeated the Moabites.[k] 8:2
He made them lie down on the ground [k]Ge 19:37; Nu 24:17
and measured them off with a length of
cord. Every two lengths of them were
put to death, and the third length was
allowed to live. So the Moabites became
subject to David and brought tribute.
3Moreover, David fought Hadadezer[l] 8:3 [l]2Sa 10:16,19
son of Rehob, king of Zobah,[m] when he [m]1Sa 14:47
went to restore his control along the Euphrates River. 4David captured a thousand of his chariots, seven thousand
charioteers[b] and twenty thousand foot
soldiers. He hamstrung[n] all but a hun- 8:4
dred of the chariot horses. [n]Jos 11:9
5When the Arameans of Damascus[o] 8:5 [o]1Ki 11:24
came to help Hadadezer king of Zobah,
David struck down twenty-two thousand of them. 6He put garrisons in the
Aramean kingdom of Damascus, and
the Arameans became subject to him 8:6
and brought tribute. The LORD gave Da- [p]ver 14;
vid victory wherever he went.[p] 2Sa 3:18; 7:9
7David took the gold shields[q] that be- 8:7
longed to the officers of Hadadezer and [q]1Ki 10:16
brought them to Jerusalem. 8From
Tebah[c] and Berothai,[r] towns that be- 8:8
longed to Hadadezer, King David took a [r]Eze 47:16
great quantity of bronze.
9When Tou[d] king of Hamath[s] heard 8:9 [s]1Ki 8:65;
that David had defeated the entire army 2Ch 8:4

[a] *23* See Septuagint and 1 Chron. 17:21; Hebrew *wonders for your land and before your people, whom you redeemed from Egypt, from the nations and their gods.* [b] *4* Septuagint (see also Dead Sea Scrolls and 1 Chron. 18:4); Masoretic Text *captured seventeen hundred of his charioteers* [c] *8* See some Septuagint manuscripts (see also 1 Chron. 18:8); Hebrew *Betah.* [d] *9* Hebrew *Toi,* a variant of *Tou;* also in verse 10

of Hadadezer, 10he sent his son Joram[a] to
King David to greet him and congratulate him on his victory in battle over
Hadadezer, who had been at war with
Tou. Joram brought with him articles of
silver and gold and bronze.
8:11 [t] 1Ki 7:51; 1Ch 26:26 11King David dedicated[t] these articles
to the LORD, as he had done with the sil-
ver and gold from all the nations he had
8:12 [u] ver 2 subdued: 12Edom[b] and Moab,[u] the Am-
[v] 2Sa 10:14 monites[v] and the Philistines,[w] and Am-
[w] 2Sa 5:25 [x] 1Sa 27:8 alek.[x] He also dedicated the plunder
taken from Hadadezer son of Rehob,
king of Zobah.
8:13 13And David became famous[y] after he
[y] 2Sa 7:9 [z] 2Ki 14:7; 1Ch 18:12 returned from striking down eighteen
thousand Edomites[c] in the Valley of Salt.[z]
8:14 14He put garrisons throughout Edom,
[a] Nu 24:17-18 and all the Edomites[a] became subject to
[b] Ge 27:29,37-40 [c] ver 6 David.[b] The LORD gave David victory
wherever he went.[c]

8:16 [d] 2Sa 19:13; 1Ch 11:6 [e] 2Sa 20:24; 1Ki 4:3 *David's Officials*

15David reigned over all Israel, doing
what was just and right for all his people. 16Joab[d] son of Zeruiah was over the
8:17 [f] 2Sa 15:24,29; 1Ch 16:39; 24:3 army; Jehoshaphat[e] son of Ahilud was
recorder; 17Zadok[f] son of Ahitub and
[g] 1Ki 4:3; 2Ki 12:10 Ahimelech son of Abiathar were priests;
Seraiah was secretary;[g] 18Benaiah[h] son
8:18 [h] 2Sa 20:23; 1Ki 1:8,38; 1Ch 18:17 of Jehoiada was over the Kerethites[i] and
Pelethites; and David's sons were royal
[i] 1Sa 30:14 advisers.[d]

David and Mephibosheth

9 David asked, "Is there anyone still
left of the house of Saul to whom
9:1 [j] 1Sa 20:14-17, 42 I can show kindness for Jonathan's
sake?"[j]
2Now there was a servant of Saul's
9:2 [k] 2Sa 16:1-4; 19:17,26,29 household named Ziba.[k] They called
him to appear before David, and the
king said to him, "Are you Ziba?"
"Your servant," he replied.
3The king asked, "Is there no one still
left of the house of Saul to whom I can
show God's kindness?"
Ziba answered the king, "There is still
9:3 [l] 1Sa 20:14 [m] 2Sa 4:4 a son of Jonathan;[l] he is crippled[m] in
both feet."
4"Where is he?" the king asked.
Ziba answered, "He is at the house of
9:4 [n] 2Sa 17:27-29 Makir[n] son of Ammiel in Lo Debar."
5So King David had him brought from
Lo Debar, from the house of Makir son
of Ammiel.
6When Mephibosheth son of Jonathan, the son of Saul, came to David, he
bowed down to pay him honor.[o] 9:6 [o] 2Sa 16:4; 19:24-30
David said, "Mephibosheth!"
"Your servant," he replied.
7"Don't be afraid," David said to him,
"for I will surely show you kindness for
the sake of your father Jonathan. I will
restore to you all the land that belonged 9:7 [p] ver 1,3;
to your grandfather Saul, and you will al- 2Sa 12:8; 19:28;
ways eat at my table.[p]" 1Ki 2:7; 2Ki 25:29
8Mephibosheth bowed down and
said, "What is your servant, that you
should notice a dead dog[q] like me?" 9:8 [q] 2Sa 16:9
9Then the king summoned Ziba,
Saul's servant, and said to him, "I have
given your master's grandson everything
that belonged to Saul and his family.
10You and your sons and your servants
are to farm the land for him and bring in
the crops, so that your master's grand-
son[r] may be provided for. And Mephib- 9:10 [r] ver 7,11,13;
osheth, grandson of your master, will al- 2Sa 19:28
ways eat at my table." (Now Ziba had
fifteen sons and twenty servants.)
11Then Ziba said to the king, "Your
servant will do whatever my lord the
king commands his servant to do." So
Mephibosheth ate at David's[e] table like 9:11 [s] Job 36:7;
one of the king's sons.[s] Ps 113:8
12Mephibosheth had a young son
named Mica, and all the members of
Ziba's household were servants of Mephibosheth.[t] 13And Mephibosheth lived 9:12 [t] 1Ch 8:34
in Jerusalem, because he always ate at
the king's table, and he was crippled in
both feet.

David Defeats the Ammonites

10 In the course of time, the king
of the Ammonites died, and his
son Hanun succeeded him as king. 2Da-
vid thought, "I will show kindness to Ha-
nun son of Nahash,[u] just as his father 10:2 [u] 1Sa 11:1
showed kindness to me." So David sent
a delegation to express his sympathy to
Hanun concerning his father.
When David's men came to the
land of the Ammonites, 3the Ammonite
nobles said to Hanun their lord, "Do
you think David is honoring your father by sending men to you to express

[a] *10* A variant of *Hadoram* [b] *12* Some Hebrew manuscripts, Septuagint and Syriac (see also 1 Chron. 18:11); most Hebrew manuscripts *Aram* [c] *13* A few Hebrew manuscripts, Septuagint and Syriac (see also 1 Chron. 18:12); most Hebrew manuscripts *Aram* (that is, Arameans) [d] *18* Or *were priests* [e] *11* Septuagint; Hebrew *my*

DISCOVERY 77

As Good as Our Word

Nearly all business arrangements today involve binding legal contracts. If one party violates the terms of the written contract we have recourse through the judicial system. Such contracts go a long way toward guaranteeing that people will keep their word. But there was a time when a person's word was as good as a signed document; such was the case with King David.

David and Jonathan were the best of friends (see Discovery #72, page 368). The two had pledged undying kindness to one another and to each other's descendants (1 Samuel 20:14–15). Years had passed following this verbal agreement. But even though Jonathan was no longer alive, David kept his word, asking himself, "Is there anyone still left of the house of Saul to whom I can show kindness for Jonathan's sake?" (2 Samuel 9:1).

After consulting Saul's former servant Ziba, David discovered that one of Jonathan's sons, a young man named Mephibosheth who had been crippled from an accident at an early age, was still living. David offered Mephibosheth the land that had belonged to his grandfather Saul and invited him to eat at his own table. He in effect adopted Mephibosheth into his royal family (verse 11). How extraordinary! In ancient cultures the reigning king generally perceived all living relatives of a former king as a threat, and it was common practice to annihilate the entire family.

But David was a man "after God's own heart" (1 Samuel 13:14). The kindness he demonstrated to Jonathan's surviving son is a picture of God's adoption of each of us, despite the fact that we had been God's enemies because of our sin (Colossians 1:21). God provided for us a way out of our dilemma, and that "way" is Jesus, his Son (Romans 8:14–17). Like Mephibosheth, God invites us to commune with him at his own table. As brothers and sisters of Jesus, we share in the incredible inheritance of God's gracious blessings.

Much as King David showed his kindness to Mephibosheth for Jonathan's sake, so God shows his kindness to us for Jesus' sake. And as David restored to Mephibosheth all the land of Saul (2 Samuel 9:7), so God will restore to us all of the blessings which Adam enjoyed before the fall, including fellowship with himself, paradise and the tree of life (see Revelation 22:2).

As stated by the apostle Paul, "The creation waits in eager expectation for the sons of God to be revealed. For the creation was subjected to frustration, not by its own choice, but by the will of the one who subjected it, in hope that the creation itself will be liberated from its bondage to decay and brought into the glorious freedom of the children of God" (Romans 8:19–21).

Self-Discovery: *Have you ever kept a promise or repaid a debt long after anyone else would have known or even cared? What was your motivation?*

GO TO DISCOVERY 78 ON PAGE 396

sympathy? Hasn't David sent them to you to explore the city and spy it out and overthrow it?" [4]So Hanun seized David's men, shaved off half of each man's beard,[v] cut off their garments in the middle at the buttocks,[w] and sent them away.

10:4
[v]Lev 19:27; Isa 15:2; Jer 48:37
[w]Isa 20:4

[5]When David was told about this, he sent messengers to meet the men, for they were greatly humiliated. The king said, "Stay at Jericho till your beards have grown, and then come back."

[6]When the Ammonites realized that they had become a stench[x] in David's nostrils, they hired twenty thousand Aramean[y] foot soldiers from Beth Rehob[z] and Zobah, as well as the king of Maacah[a] with a thousand men, and also twelve thousand men from Tob.

10:6
[x]Ge 34:30
[y]2Sa 8:5
[z]Jdg 18:28
[a]Dt 3:14

[7]On hearing this, David sent Joab out with the entire army of fighting men. [8]The Ammonites came out and drew up in battle formation at the entrance to their city gate, while the Arameans of Zobah and Rehob and the men of Tob and Maacah were by themselves in the open country.

[9]Joab saw that there were battle lines in front of him and behind him; so he selected some of the best troops in Israel and deployed them against the Arameans. [10]He put the rest of the men under the command of Abishai his brother and deployed them against the Ammonites. [11]Joab said, "If the Arameans are too strong for me, then you are to come to my rescue; but if the Ammonites are too strong for you, then I will come to rescue you. [12]Be strong[b] and let us fight bravely for our people and the cities of our God. The LORD will do what is good in his sight."[c]

10:12
[b]Dt 31:6; 1Co 16:13; Eph 6:10
[c]Jdg 10:15; 1Sa 3:18; Ne 4:14

[13]Then Joab and the troops with him advanced to fight the Arameans, and they fled before him. [14]When the Ammonites saw that the Arameans were fleeing, they fled before Abishai and went inside the city. So Joab returned from fighting the Ammonites and came to Jerusalem.

[15]After the Arameans saw that they had been routed by Israel, they regrouped. [16]Hadadezer had Arameans brought from beyond the River[a]; they went to Helam, with Shobach the commander of Hadadezer's army leading them.

[17]When David was told of this, he gathered all Israel, crossed the Jordan and went to Helam. The Arameans formed their battle lines to meet David and fought against him. [18]But they fled before Israel, and David killed seven hundred of their charioteers and forty thousand of their foot soldiers.[b] He also struck down Shobach the commander of their army, and he died there. [19]When all the kings who were vassals of Hadadezer saw that they had been defeated by Israel, they made peace with the Israelites and became subject[d] to them.

So the Arameans[e] were afraid to help the Ammonites anymore.

10:19
[d]2Sa 8:6
[e]1Ki 11:25; 2Ki 5:1

David and Bathsheba

11 In the spring,[f] at the time when kings go off to war, David sent Joab[g] out with the king's men and the whole Israelite army.[h] They destroyed the Ammonites and besieged Rabbah.[i] But David remained in Jerusalem.

11:1
[f]1Ki 20:22,26
[g]2Sa 2:18
[h]1Ch 20:1
[i]2Sa 12:26-28

[2]One evening David got up from his bed and walked around on the roof[j] of the palace. From the roof he saw[k] a woman bathing. The woman was very beautiful, [3]and David sent someone to find out about her. The man said, "Isn't this Bathsheba,[l] the daughter of Eliam[m] and the wife of Uriah[n] the Hittite?" [4]Then David sent messengers to get her.[o] She came to him, and he slept[p] with her. (She had purified herself from her uncleanness.)[q] Then[c] she went back home. [5]The woman conceived and sent word to David, saying, "I am pregnant."

11:2
[j]Dt 22:8; Jos 2:8
[k]Mt 5:28

11:3
[l]1Ch 3:5
[m]2Sa 23:34
[n]2Sa 23:39

11:4
[o]Lev 20:10; Ps 51 Title; Jas 1:14-15
[p]Dt 22:22
[q]Lev 15:25-30; 18:19

[6]So David sent this word to Joab: "Send me Uriah[r] the Hittite." And Joab sent him to David. [7]When Uriah came to him, David asked him how Joab was, how the soldiers were and how the war was going. [8]Then David said to Uriah, "Go down to your house and wash your feet."[s] So Uriah left the palace, and a gift from the king was sent after him. [9]But Uriah slept at the entrance to the palace with all his master's servants and did not go down to his house.

11:6
[r]1Ch 11:41

11:8
[s]Ge 18:4; 43:24; Lk 7:44

[10]When David was told, "Uriah did not go home," he asked him, "Haven't you just come from a distance? Why didn't you go home?"

[a] *16* That is, the Euphrates [b] *18* Some Septuagint manuscripts (see also 1 Chron. 19:18); Hebrew *horsemen* [c] *4* Or *with her. When she purified herself from her uncleanness,*

DISCOVERY 78

Beauty From Tragedy

David was one of Israel's greatest kings. He led the people in spectacular victories and brought prosperity to the nation in the process. But despite his successes on the battlefield David's personality reflected a softer, poetic side; he is the author of many of the psalms.

But David was far from perfect. Although he loved and served the Lord with fervor, he demonstrated incredible blindness in several situations and failed utterly in his illicit relationship with Bathsheba. David discovered the hard way what so many of us have to learn: Once we step off God's narrow path we begin a downward slide that can end up producing an avalanche. In David's case, he got into trouble when he went where is shouldn't have gone and did what he shouldn't have done. Rather than leading his army into battle, David elected to stay at home, delegating Joab to lead in his place (2 Samuel 11:1). And so today, when we are not where God asks us to be or not doing what God asks us to do, we have taken our first step down the slippery slope.

David also used his position and power to attain what he coveted—one night alone with Bathsheba (verse 4). David knew that Bathsheba would be powerless against the advances of the king; at the slightest whim he could make her a victim of sexual manipulation, harassment or even abuse. Afterward, when Bathsheba discovered that she was pregnant, she informed David. But instead of acting honorably toward Bathsheba and her husband Uriah, David immediately set a cover-up plan into motion.

David dispatched Uriah back to the battlefield with a message for Joab: "Put Uriah in the front line where the fighting is fiercest. Then withdraw from him so he will be struck down and die" (verse 15). Joab did as he was told, Uriah was killed and David eventually married Bathsheba. For David, the sin that had begun with negligence escalated into adultery, manipulation and murder.

In the beginning, very few people knew about what David had done. God had seen, however, and that was all that mattered (verse 27). David did turn back to God (see Psalm 51), but he also had to live with the consequences of his choice: Bathsheba's baby died. And throughout his life David experienced family tragedies.

As Christians, however, we know that God often brings beauty and blessing from tragic situations and bad choices. We know little about Bathsheba herself. Some people conjecture that she was as willing a partner as David, while others speculate that David acted against her will. What we *do* know is that eventually David and Bathsheba were blessed with a son named Solomon—the wisest and wealthiest king who had ever lived. In spite of the sin of his parents, at his birth the Lord sent a message letting everyone know that he loved this little baby (2 Samuel 12:25). And Jesus demonstrated this same forgiving love when his disciple, Peter, denied him three times (John 20:15–18). Jesus hates our sin, but he always loves us.

Self-Discovery: *Can you think of specific ways you can follow Christ's example by expressing his love to someone who has failed?*

GO TO DISCOVERY 79 ON PAGE 403

11:11 11Uriah said to David, "The ark[t] and
[t] 2Sa 7:2 Israel and Judah are staying in tents, and
my master Joab and my lord's men are
camped in the open fields. How could I
go to my house to eat and drink and lie
with my wife? As surely as you live, I will
not do such a thing!"
12Then David said to him, "Stay here
one more day, and tomorrow I will send
you back." So Uriah remained in Jerusalem that day and the next. 13At David's
invitation, he ate and drank with him,
and David made him drunk. But in the
evening Uriah went out to sleep on his
mat among his master's servants; he did
not go home.
14In the morning David wrote a let-
11:14 [u] 1Ki 21:8 ter[u] to Joab and sent it with Uriah. 15In it
he wrote, "Put Uriah in the front line
where the fighting is fiercest. Then with-
11:15 draw from him so he will be struck
[v] 2Sa 12:9 [w] 2Sa 12:12 down[v] and die.[w]"
16So while Joab had the city under
siege, he put Uriah at a place where he
knew the strongest defenders were.
17When the men of the city came out
and fought against Joab, some of the
men in David's army fell; moreover, Uriah the Hittite died.
18Joab sent David a full account of the
battle. 19He instructed the messenger:
"When you have finished giving the king
this account of the battle, 20the king's
anger may flare up, and he may ask you,
'Why did you get so close to the city to
fight? Didn't you know they would shoot
11:21 arrows from the wall? 21Who killed
[x] Jdg 8:31 Abimelech[x] son of Jerub-Besheth[a]?
[y] Jdg 9:50-54 Didn't a woman throw an upper millstone on him from the wall,[y] so that he
died in Thebez? Why did you get so
close to the wall?' If he asks you this,
then say to him, 'Also, your servant Uriah the Hittite is dead.'"
22The messenger set out, and when he
arrived he told David everything Joab
had sent him to say. 23The messenger
said to David, "The men overpowered us
and came out against us in the open, but
we drove them back to the entrance to
the city gate. 24Then the archers shot arrows at your servants from the wall, and
some of the king's men died. Moreover,
your servant Uriah the Hittite is dead."
25David told the messenger, "Say this
to Joab: 'Don't let this upset you; the
sword devours one as well as another.
Press the attack against the city and destroy it.' Say this to encourage Joab."
26When Uriah's wife heard that her
husband was dead, she mourned for
him. 27After the time of mourning was
over, David had her brought to his
house, and she became his wife and bore
him a son. But the thing David had done **11:27** [z] 2Sa 12:9;
displeased[z] the LORD. Ps 51:4-5

Nathan Rebukes David

12 The LORD sent Nathan[a] to Da- **12:1** [a] 2Sa 7:2;
vid.[b] When he came to him,[c] he 1Ki 20:35-41
said, "There were two men in a certain [b] Ps 51 Title
town, one rich and the other poor. 2The [c] 2Sa 14:4
rich man had a very large number of
sheep and cattle, 3but the poor man had
nothing except one little ewe lamb he
had bought. He raised it, and it grew up
with him and his children. It shared his
food, drank from his cup and even slept
in his arms. It was like a daughter to him.
4"Now a traveler came to the rich
man, but the rich man refrained from
taking one of his own sheep or cattle to
prepare a meal for the traveler who had
come to him. Instead, he took the ewe
lamb that belonged to the poor man and
prepared it for the one who had come to
him."
5David[d] burned with anger against **12:5**
the man and said to Nathan, "As surely [d] 1Ki 20:40
as the LORD lives, the man who did this
deserves to die! 6He must pay for that **12:6**
lamb four times over,[e] because he did [e] Ex 22:1;
such a thing and had no pity." Lk 19:8
7Then Nathan said to David, "You are
the man! This is what the LORD, the God **12:7**
of Israel, says: 'I anointed[f] you[g] king over [f] 1Sa 16:13
Israel, and I delivered you from the hand [g] 1Ki 20:42
of Saul. 8I gave your master's house to
you,[h] and your master's wives into your **12:8** [h] 2Sa 9:7
arms. I gave you the house of Israel and
Judah. And if all this had been too little,
I would have given you even more. 9Why
did you despise[i] the word of the LORD by **12:9** [i] Nu 15:31;
doing what is evil in his eyes? You struck 1Sa 15:19
down[j] Uriah the Hittite with the sword [j] 2Sa 11:15
and took his wife to be your own. You
killed him with the sword of the Am-
monites. 10Now, therefore, the sword[k] **12:10** [k] 2Sa 13:28;
will never depart from your house, be- 18:14-15;
cause you despised me and took the wife 1Ki 2:25
of Uriah the Hittite to be your own.'
11"This is what the LORD says: 'Out of
your own household I am going to bring

[a] 21 Also known as *Jerub-Baal* (that is, Gideon)

12:11 [l] Dt 28:30; 2Sa 16:21-22 calamity upon you.[l] Before your very
eyes I will take your wives and give them
to one who is close to you, and he will lie
12:12 [m] 2Sa 11:4-15 [n] 2Sa 16:22 with your wives in broad daylight. 12 You
did it in secret,[m] but I will do this thing
in broad daylight[n] before all Israel.'"
12:13 [o] Ge 13:13; Nu 22:34; 1Sa 15:24; 2Sa 24:10 [p] Ps 32:1-5; 51:1, 9; 103:12; Zec 3:4,9 [q] Pr 28:13; Mic 7:18-19 [r] Lev 20:10; 24:17 13 Then David said to Nathan, "I have
sinned[o] against the LORD."
Nathan replied, "The LORD has taken
away[p] your sin.[q] You are not going to
die.[r] 14 But because by doing this you
have made the enemies of the LORD
show utter contempt,[a][s] the son born to
you will die."
15 After Nathan had gone home, the
12:14 [s] Isa 52:5; Ro 2:24 LORD struck[t] the child that Uriah's wife
had borne to David, and he became ill.
12:15 [t] 1Sa 25:38 16 David pleaded with God for the child.
He fasted and went into his house and
12:16 [u] 2Sa 13:31; Ps 5:7 spent the nights lying[u] on the ground.
17 The elders of his household stood be-
side him to get him up from the ground,
12:17 [v] 2Sa 3:35 but he refused, and he would not eat any
food with them.[v]
18 On the seventh day the child died.
David's servants were afraid to tell him
that the child was dead, for they thought,
"While the child was still living, we spoke
to David but he would not listen to us.
How can we tell him the child is dead?
He may do something desperate."
19 David noticed that his servants were
whispering among themselves and he
realized the child was dead. "Is the child
dead?" he asked.
"Yes," they replied, "he is dead."
20 Then David got up from the ground.
After he had washed,[w] put on lotions 12:20 [w] Mt 6:17
and changed his clothes,[x] he went into [x] Job 1:20
the house of the LORD and worshiped.
Then he went to his own house, and at
his request they served him food, and he
ate.
21 His servants asked him, "Why are
you acting this way? While the child was
alive, you fasted and wept,[y] but now that 12:21 [y] Jdg 20:26
the child is dead, you get up and eat!"
22 He answered, "While the child was
still alive, I fasted and wept. I thought, 12:22 [z] Jnh 3:9
'Who knows?[z] The LORD may be gra- [a] Isa 38:1-5
cious to me and let the child live.'[a] 23 But
now that he is dead, why should I fast? 12:23 [b] Ge 37:35
Can I bring him back again? I will go to [c] 1Sa 31:13; 2Sa 13:39;
him,[b] but he will not return to me."[c] Job 7:10; 10:21
24 Then David comforted his wife
Bathsheba,[d] and he went to her and lay 12:24 [d] 1Ki 1:11
with her. She gave birth to a son, and [e] 1Ki 1:10; 1Ch 22:9; 28:5;
they named him Solomon.[e] The LORD Mt 1:6
loved him; 25 and because the LORD loved
him, he sent word through Nathan the 12:25
prophet to name him Jedidiah.[b][f] [f] Ne 13:26
26 Meanwhile Joab fought against Rab- 12:26
bah[g] of the Ammonites and captured [g] Dt 3:11; 1Ch 20:1-3
the royal citadel. 27 Joab then sent mes-
sengers to David, saying, "I have fought
against Rabbah and taken its water supply. 28 Now muster the rest of the troops
and besiege the city and capture it. Otherwise I will take the city, and it will be
named after me."
29 So David mustered the entire army
and went to Rabbah, and attacked and 12:30
captured it. 30 He took the crown[h] from [h] 1Ch 20:2;
the head of their king[c]—its weight was Est 8:15;
a talent[d] of gold, and it was set with pre- Ps 21:3; 132:18
cious stones—and it was placed on Da-
vid's head. He took a great quantity of
plunder from the city 31 and brought out
the people who were there, consigning
them to labor with saws and with iron
picks and axes, and he made them work

DAVID'S FINEST MOMENT

David had sinned against God—and he was certainly aware of this even before the prophet Nathan had confronted him (2 Samuel 12). As king he wielded absolute power in the nation, and he could have exercised his prerogative to have Nathan exiled or even executed for daring to accuse him. But David knew that Nathan was a true prophet who spoke for God himself. The king showed himself to be a man after God's own heart when he admitted both to Nathan and to himself, "I have sinned against the LORD" (verse 13). Although he was the king of Israel, David was not above humbling himself before the King of kings (see also Psalm 51).

David was subject to temptation as all people are, but when David confessed his sin to God and asked for forgiveness, God was merciful. God not only forgave David but also restored him into fellowship with himself. And even though David and Bathsheba had sinned against the Lord, God conferred on them a great blessing: They became the parents of Solomon and ancestors to the Messiah (see 2 Samuel 12:24; Matthew 1:6).

[a] *14* Masoretic Text; an ancient Hebrew scribal tradition *this you have shown utter contempt for the LORD* [b] *25 Jedidiah* means *loved by the LORD.* [c] *30* Or *of Milcom* (that is, Molech) [d] *30* That is, about 75 pounds (about 34 kilograms)

13:31 at brickmaking.[a] He did this to all the
[i] 1Sa 14:47 Ammonite[i] towns. Then David and his
entire army returned to Jerusalem.

Amnon and Tamar

13:1 **13** In the course of time, Amnon[j]
[j] 2Sa 3:2 son of David fell in love with Ta-
[k] 2Sa 14:27; mar,[k] the beautiful sister of Absalom[l]
1Ch 3:9 [l] 2Sa 3:3 son of David.
2 Amnon became frustrated to the
point of illness on account of his sister
Tamar, for she was a virgin, and it
seemed impossible for him to do anything to her.
3 Now Amnon had a friend named
13:3 [m] 1Sa 16:9 Jonadab son of Shimeah,[m] David's
brother. Jonadab was a very shrewd
man. 4 He asked Amnon, "Why do you,
the king's son, look so haggard morning
after morning? Won't you tell me?"
Amnon said to him, "I'm in love with
Tamar, my brother Absalom's sister."
5 "Go to bed and pretend to be ill," Jonadab said. "When your father comes to
see you, say to him, 'I would like my sister Tamar to come and give me something to eat. Let her prepare the food in
my sight so I may watch her and then
eat it from her hand.' "
6 So Amnon lay down and pretended
to be ill. When the king came to see him,
Amnon said to him, "I would like my sister Tamar to come and make some special bread in my sight, so I may eat from
her hand."
7 David sent word to Tamar at the
palace: "Go to the house of your brother
Amnon and prepare some food for him."
8 So Tamar went to the house of her
brother Amnon, who was lying down.
She took some dough, kneaded it, made
the bread in his sight and baked it.
9 Then she took the pan and served him
the bread, but he refused to eat.
13:9 "Send everyone out of here,"[n] Amnon
[n] Ge 45:1 said. So everyone left him. 10 Then Amnon said to Tamar, "Bring the food here
into my bedroom so I may eat from your
hand." And Tamar took the bread she
had prepared and brought it to her
brother Amnon in his bedroom. 11 But
13:11 when she took it to him to eat, he
[o] Ge 39:12 grabbed[o] her and said, "Come to bed
[p] Ge 38:16 with me, my sister."[p]
12 "Don't, my brother!" she said to him.
13:12 "Don't force me. Such a thing should not
[q] Lev 20:17; Jdg 20:6 be done in Israel![q] Don't do this wicked
thing.[r] 13 What about me?[s] Where could 13:12
I get rid of my disgrace? And what about [r] Ge 34:7;
you? You would be like one of the Jdg 19:23
wicked fools in Israel. Please speak to 13:13
the king; he will not keep me from being [s] Ge 20:12;
married to you." 14 But he refused to lis- Lev 18:9; Dt 22:21,23-24
ten to her, and since he was stronger 13:14
than she, he raped her.[t] [t] Ge 34:2;
15 Then Amnon hated her with in- Dt 22:25;
tense hatred. In fact, he hated her more Eze 22:11
than he had loved her. Amnon said to
her, "Get up and get out!"
16 "No!" she said to him. "Sending me
away would be a greater wrong than
what you have already done to me."
But he refused to listen to her. 17 He
called his personal servant and said,
"Get this woman out of here and bolt
the door after her." 18 So his servant put
her out and bolted the door after her.
She was wearing a richly ornamented[b]
robe,[u] for this was the kind of garment 13:18
the virgin daughters of the king wore. [u] Ge 37:23; Jdg 5:30
19 Tamar put ashes[v] on her head and tore 13:19
the ornamented[c] robe she was wearing. [v] Jos 7:6;
She put her hand on her head and went 1Sa 4:12; 2Sa 1:2; Est 4:1;
away, weeping aloud as she went. Da 9:3
20 Her brother Absalom said to her,
"Has that Amnon, your brother, been
with you? Be quiet now, my sister; he is
your brother. Don't take this thing to
heart." And Tamar lived in her brother
Absalom's house, a desolate woman.
21 When King David heard all this, he
was furious.[w] 22 Absalom never said a 13:21 [w] Ge 34:7
word to Amnon, either good or bad;[x] he 13:22
hated[y] Amnon because he had dis- [x] Ge 31:24
graced his sister Tamar. [y] Lev 19:17-18; 1Jn 2:9-11

Absalom Kills Amnon

23 Two years later, when Absalom's
sheepshearers[z] were at Baal Hazor near 13:23
the border of Ephraim, he invited all the [z] 1Sa 25:7
king's sons to come there. 24 Absalom
went to the king and said, "Your servant
has had shearers come. Will the king
and his officials please join me?"
25 "No, my son," the king replied. "All of
us should not go; we would only be a
burden to you." Although Absalom
urged him, he still refused to go, but
gave him his blessing.
26 Then Absalom said, "If not, please
let my brother Amnon come with us."

[a] *31* The meaning of the Hebrew for this clause is uncertain. [b] *18* The meaning of the Hebrew for this phrase is uncertain. [c] *19* The meaning of the Hebrew for this word is uncertain.

The king asked him, "Why should he go with you?" 27But Absalom urged him, so he sent with him Amnon and the rest of the king's sons.

28Absalom[a] ordered his men, "Listen! When Amnon is in high[b] spirits from drinking wine and I say to you, 'Strike Amnon down,' then kill him. Don't be afraid. Have not I given you this order? Be strong and brave.[c]" 29So Absalom's men did to Amnon what Absalom had ordered. Then all the king's sons got up, mounted their mules and fled.

30While they were on their way, the report came to David: "Absalom has struck down all the king's sons; not one of them is left." 31The king stood up, tore[d] his clothes and lay down on the ground; and all his servants stood by with their clothes torn.

32But Jonadab son of Shimeah, David's brother, said, "My lord should not think that they killed all the princes; only Amnon is dead. This has been Absalom's expressed intention ever since the day Amnon raped his sister Tamar. 33My lord the king should not be concerned about the report that all the king's sons are dead. Only Amnon is dead."

34Meanwhile, Absalom had fled.

Now the man standing watch looked up and saw many people on the road west of him, coming down the side of the hill. The watchman went and told the king, "I see men in the direction of Horonaim, on the side of the hill."*[a]*

35Jonadab said to the king, "See, the king's sons are here; it has happened just as your servant said."

36As he finished speaking, the king's sons came in, wailing loudly. The king, too, and all his servants wept very bitterly.

37Absalom fled and went to Talmai[e] son of Ammihud, the king of Geshur. But King David mourned for his son every day.

38After Absalom fled and went to Geshur, he stayed there three years. 39And the spirit of the king*[b]* longed to go to Absalom,[f] for he was consoled[g] concerning Amnon's death.

Absalom Returns to Jerusalem

14 Joab[h] son of Zeruiah knew that the king's heart longed for Absalom. 2So Joab sent someone to Tekoa[i] and had a wise woman[j] brought from there. He said to her, "Pretend you are in mourning. Dress in mourning clothes, and don't use any cosmetic lotions.[k] Act like a woman who has spent many days grieving for the dead. 3Then go to the king and speak these words to him." And Joab[l] put the words in her mouth.

4When the woman from Tekoa went*[c]* to the king, she fell with her face to the ground to pay him honor, and she said, "Help me, O king!"

5The king asked her, "What is troubling you?"

She said, "I am indeed a widow; my husband is dead. 6I your servant had two sons. They got into a fight with each other in the field, and no one was there to separate them. One struck the other and killed him. 7Now the whole clan has risen up against your servant; they say, 'Hand over the one who struck his brother down, so that we may put him to death[m] for the life of his brother whom he killed; then we will get rid of the heir[n] as well.' They would put out the only burning coal I have left,[o] leaving my husband neither name nor descendant on the face of the earth."

8The king said to the woman, "Go home,[p] and I will issue an order in your behalf."

9But the woman from Tekoa said to him, "My lord the king, let the blame[q] rest on me and on my father's family,[r] and let the king and his throne be without guilt.[s]"

10The king replied, "If anyone says anything to you, bring him to me, and he will not bother you again."

11She said, "Then let the king invoke the LORD his God to prevent the avenger[t] of blood from adding to the destruction, so that my son will not be destroyed."

"As surely as the LORD lives," he said, "not one hair[u] of your son's head will fall to the ground.[v]"

12Then the woman said, "Let your servant speak a word to my lord the king."

"Speak," he replied.

13The woman said, "Why then have you devised a thing like this against the

13:28 [a] 2Sa 3:3 [b] Jdg 19:6,9,22; Ru 3:7; 1Sa 25:36 [c] 2Sa 12:10
13:31 [d] Nu 14:6; 2Sa 1:11; 12:16
13:37 [e] ver 34; 2Sa 3:3; 14:23,32
13:39 [f] 2Sa 14:13 [g] 2Sa 12:19-23
14:1 [h] 2Sa 2:18
14:2 [i] 2Ch 11:6; Ne 3:5; Jer 6:1; Am 1:1

14:2 [j] 2Sa 20:16 [k] Ru 3:3; 2Sa 12:20; Isa 1:6
14:3 [l] ver 19
14:7 [m] Nu 35:19 [n] Mt 21:38 [o] Dt 19:10-13
14:8 [p] 1Sa 25:35
14:9 [q] 1Sa 25:24 [r] Mt 27:25 [s] 1Sa 25:28; 1Ki 2:33
14:11 [t] Nu 35:12,21 [u] Mt 10:30 [v] 1Sa 14:45

[a] 34 Septuagint; Hebrew does not have this sentence. *[b]* 39 Dead Sea Scrolls and some Septuagint manuscripts; Masoretic Text *But ⌊the spirit of⌋ David the king* *[c]* 4 Many Hebrew manuscripts, Septuagint, Vulgate and Syriac; most Hebrew manuscripts *spoke*

people of God? When the king says this, does he not convict himself,[w] for the king has not brought back his banished son?[x] 14 Like water[y] spilled on the ground, which cannot be recovered, so we must die.[z] But God does not take away life; instead, he devises ways so that a banished person[a] may not remain estranged from him.

15 "And now I have come to say this to my lord the king because the people have made me afraid. Your servant thought, 'I will speak to the king; perhaps he will do what his servant asks. 16 Perhaps the king will agree to deliver his servant from the hand of the man who is trying to cut off both me and my son from the inheritance[b] God gave us.'

17 "And now your servant says, 'May the word of my lord the king bring me rest, for my lord the king is like an angel[c] of God in discerning[d] good and evil. May the LORD your God be with you.' "

18 Then the king said to the woman, "Do not keep from me the answer to what I am going to ask you."

"Let my lord the king speak," the woman said.

19 The king asked, "Isn't the hand of Joab[e] with you in all this?"

The woman answered, "As surely as you live, my lord the king, no one can turn to the right or to the left from anything my lord the king says. Yes, it was your servant Joab who instructed me to do this and who put all these words into the mouth of your servant. 20 Your servant Joab did this to change the present situation. My lord has wisdom[f] like that of an angel of God—he knows everything that happens in the land.[g]"

21 The king said to Joab, "Very well, I will do it. Go, bring back the young man Absalom."

22 Joab fell with his face to the ground to pay him honor, and he blessed the king.[h] Joab said, "Today your servant knows that he has found favor in your eyes, my lord the king, because the king has granted his servant's request."

23 Then Joab went to Geshur and brought Absalom back to Jerusalem. 24 But the king said, "He must go to his own house; he must not see my face." So Absalom went to his own house and did not see the face of the king.

25 In all Israel there was not a man so highly praised for his handsome appearance as Absalom. From the top of his head to the sole of his foot there was no blemish in him. 26 Whenever he cut the hair of his head[i]—he used to cut his hair from time to time when it became too heavy for him—he would weigh it, and its weight was two hundred shekels[a] by the royal standard.

27 Three sons[j] and a daughter were born to Absalom. The daughter's name was Tamar,[k] and she became a beautiful woman.

28 Absalom lived two years in Jerusalem without seeing the king's face. 29 Then Absalom sent for Joab in order to send him to the king, but Joab refused to come to him. So he sent a second time, but he refused to come. 30 Then he said to his servants, "Look, Joab's field is next to mine, and he has barley[l] there. Go and set it on fire." So Absalom's servants set the field on fire.

31 Then Joab did go to Absalom's house and he said to him, "Why have your servants set my field on fire?[m]"

32 Absalom said to Joab, "Look, I sent word to you and said, 'Come here so I can send you to the king to ask, "Why have I come from Geshur?[n] It would be better for me if I were still there!" ' Now then, I want to see the king's face, and if I am guilty of anything, let him put me to death."[o]

33 So Joab went to the king and told him this. Then the king summoned Absalom, and he came in and bowed down with his face to the ground before the king. And the king kissed[p] Absalom.

Absalom's Conspiracy

15 In the course of time,[q] Absalom provided himself with a chariot[r] and horses and with fifty men to run ahead of him. 2 He would get up early and stand by the side of the road leading to the city gate.[s] Whenever anyone came with a complaint to be placed before the king for a decision, Absalom would call out to him, "What town are you from?" He would answer, "Your servant is from one of the tribes of Israel." 3 Then Absalom would say to him, "Look, your claims are valid and proper, but there is no representative of the king to hear you."[t] 4 And Absalom would add,

[a] 26 That is, about 5 pounds (about 2.3 kilograms)

14:13 w 2Sa 12:7; 1Ki 20:40 x 2Sa 13:38-39
14:14 y Job 14:11; Ps 58:7; Isa 19:5 z Job 10:8; 17:13; 30:23; Ps 22:15; Heb 9:27 a Nu 35:15,25-28; Job 34:15
14:16 b Ex 34:9; 1Sa 26:19
14:17 c ver 20; 1Sa 29:9; 2Sa 19:27 d 1Ki 3:9; Da 2:21
14:19 e ver 3
14:20 f 1Ki 3:12,28; Isa 28:6 g ver 17; 2Sa 18:13; 19:27
14:22 h Ge 47:7
14:26 i 2Sa 18:9; Eze 44:20
14:27 j 2Sa 18:18 k 2Sa 13:1
14:30 l Ex 9:31
14:31 m Jdg 15:5
14:32 n 2Sa 3:3 o 1Sa 20:8
14:33 p Ge 33:4; Lk 15:20
15:1 q 2Sa 12:11 r 1Sa 8:11; 1Ki 1:5
15:2 s Ge 23:10; 2Sa 19:8
15:3 t Pr 12:2

15:4 "If only I were appointed judge in the
u Jdg 9:29 land![u] Then everyone who has a complaint or case could come to me and I
would see that he gets justice."
5 Also, whenever anyone approached
him to bow down before him, Absalom
would reach out his hand, take hold of
him and kiss him. 6 Absalom behaved in
this way toward all the Israelites who
15:6 came to the king asking for justice, and
v Ro 16:18 so he stole the hearts[v] of the men of Israel.
7 At the end of four[a] years, Absalom
said to the king, "Let me go to Hebron
and fulfill a vow I made to the LORD.
15:8 8 While your servant was living at Ge-
w 2Sa 3:3; 13:37- shur[w] in Aram, I made this vow:[x] 'If the
38 x Ge 28:20 LORD takes me back to Jerusalem, I will
worship the LORD in Hebron.[b]' "
9 The king said to him, "Go in peace."
So he went to Hebron.
10 Then Absalom sent secret messengers throughout the tribes of Israel to
say, "As soon as you hear the sound of
15:10 y 1Ki 1:34,39; the trumpets,[y] then say, 'Absalom is king
2Ki 9:13 in Hebron.' " 11 Two hundred men from
Jerusalem had accompanied Absalom.
They had been invited as guests and
went quite innocently, knowing nothing
about the matter. 12 While Absalom was
15:12 offering sacrifices, he also sent for
z ver 31,34; Ahithophel[z] the Gilonite, David's coun-
2Sa 16:15,23; 1Ch 27:33 selor,[a] to come from Giloh,[b] his home-
a Job 19:14; Ps 41:9; 55:13; town. And so the conspiracy gained
Jer 9:4 b Jos 15:51 strength, and Absalom's following kept
c Ps 3:1 on increasing.[c]

David Flees

13 A messenger came and told David,
"The hearts of the men of Israel are with
Absalom."
14 Then David said to all his officials
who were with him in Jerusalem, "Come!
15:14 d 2Sa 12:11; We must flee,[d] or none of us will escape
1Ki 2:26; from Absalom.[e] We must leave immedi-
Ps 132:1; Ps 3 ately, or he will move quickly to overtake
Title e 2Sa 19:9 us and bring ruin upon us and put the
city to the sword."
15 The king's officials answered him,
"Your servants are ready to do whatever
our lord the king chooses."
16 The king set out, with his entire
household following him; but he left ten
15:16 concubines[f] to take care of the palace.
f 2Sa 16:21-22; 20:3 17 So the king set out, with all the people
following him, and they halted at a place
some distance away. 18 All his men
marched past him, along with all the 15:18
Kerethites[g] and Pelethites; and all the six g 1Sa 30:14;
hundred Gittites who had accompanied 2Sa 8:18; 20:7, 23; 1Ki 1:38,44;
him from Gath marched before the king. 1Ch 18:17
19 The king said to Ittai[h] the Gittite,
"Why should you come along with us? 15:19 h 2Sa 18:2
Go back and stay with King Absalom. i Ge 31:15
You are a foreigner,[i] an exile from your
homeland. 20 You came only yesterday.
And today shall I make you wander[j] 15:20 j 1Sa 23:13
about with us, when I do not know k 2Sa 2:6
where I am going? Go back, and take
your countrymen. May kindness and
faithfulness[k] be with you."
21 But Ittai replied to the king, "As
surely as the LORD lives, and as my lord
the king lives, wherever my lord the king 15:21
may be, whether it means life or death, l Ru 1:16-17;
there will your servant be."[l] Pr 17:17
22 David said to Ittai, "Go ahead,
march on." So Ittai the Gittite marched
on with all his men and the families that
were with him.
23 The whole countryside wept aloud
as all the people passed by. The king also
crossed the Kidron Valley,[m] and all the 15:23 m 2Ch 29:16
people moved on toward the desert.
24 Zadok[n] was there, too, and all the 15:24 n 2Sa 8:17
Levites who were with him were carry- o Nu 4:15
ing the ark[o] of the covenant of God. p 1Sa 22:20
They set down the ark of God, and Abiathar[p] offered sacrifices[c] until all the
people had finished leaving the city.
25 Then the king said to Zadok, "Take
the ark of God back into the city. If I find
favor in the LORD's eyes, he will bring me
back and let me see it and his dwelling
place[q] again. 26 But if he says, 'I am not 15:25 q Ex 15:13;
pleased with you,' then I am ready; let Ps 43:3;
him do to me whatever seems good to Jer 25:30
him.[r]" 15:26
27 The king also said to Zadok the r 1Sa 3:18;
priest, "Aren't you a seer?[s] Go back to 2Sa 22:20;
the city in peace, with your son Ahima- 1Ki 10:9
az and Jonathan[t] son of Abiathar. You 15:27 s 1Sa 9:9
and Abiathar take your two sons with t 2Sa 17:17
you. 28 I will wait at the fords[u] in the 15:28
desert until word comes from you to in- u 2Sa 17:16
form me." 29 So Zadok and Abiathar took
the ark of God back to Jerusalem and
stayed there.
30 But David continued up the Mount 15:30
of Olives, weeping[v] as he went; his head[w] v 2Sa 19:4; Ps 126:6
was covered and he was barefoot. All the w Est 6:12; Isa 20:2-4

[a] *7* Some Septuagint manuscripts, Syriac and Josephus; Hebrew *forty* [b] *8* Some Septuagint manuscripts; Hebrew does not have *in Hebron.* [c] *24* Or *Abiathar went up*

The Weeping King

Everyone has a mental picture of what a king should look like and how he should conduct himself. We usually visualize a king as confident, strong, articulate—the kind of person who instinctively knows what to do in any situation. Perhaps most of all we want to assume that a king will remain calm and in control under pressure. The two greatest kings in the Bible, however, contradicted the stereotype. In 2 Samuel 15:30 David wept as he escaped from his palace up the Mount of Olives. Why would such a powerful warrior shed tears?

Because David was not only a king but first and foremost a man, he had many reasons to cry. It broke his heart when his son Absalom turned against him. David also wept because one of his closest friends and advisers deserted him to join forces with Absalom (2 Samuel 15:31; 16:23). Although David still represented God's choice, "the hearts of the men of Israel [were] with Absalom" (2 Samuel 15:13). Finally, David grieved because he knew that those who remained loyal to him would face difficult days. Their only hope would be to flee the city to the desert where they could hide in caves. These faithful followers would live as fugitives as Absalom's men relentlessly hunted them down and attempted to kill them.

Hundreds of years later another King rode down the Mount of Olives into the same city from which David had fled. Just like David, Jesus cried as he thought about the people who were so enthusiastically welcoming him (Matthew 21:9). One reason he wept was his awareness that many people still rejected him. Most of the people failed to understand that Jesus had come to bring a kind of peace that would prove far more lasting and significant than the peace of a nation; he had come to instill peace in their souls. Because Jesus Christ did not conform to their mental image of who and what a king should be, they refused to trust him (Luke 19:41).

Jesus also grieved because he knew that the same people who were welcoming him would prove fickle in their loyalties and turn against him when the circumstances were no longer favorable. One of his ostensibly close friends would in fact turn him over to the religious leaders (Matthew 27:1–5). And Jesus lamented because the city he loved would be destroyed and because his own people had failed to recognize that God himself had come to dwell with them (Luke 19:44). Finally, Jesus sobbed because he knew that those who would continue to follow him would have to endure unspeakably hard times (see, for example, the story of Stephen's martyrdom in Acts 7:54–60).

As Jesus' followers, we live at odds with the world around us. Standing up for God can be painful, lonely, even devastating. But our hope still rests in this reality: Jesus is King of all and will one day come back to rule over his divine kingdom (Revelation 11:15–17). He asks us to carry on what he started—to continue to promote his kingdom among his people. As he lives in us, we will be moved by the circumstances that moved him. But we must be moved beyond tears to action, reaching out to people trapped and lost in their sin.

Self-Discovery: *When you read about Jesus crying, do you feel uncomfortable? embarrassed? touched? How would you likely have reacted had you been present at the time?*

GO TO DISCOVERY 80 ON PAGE 412

people with him covered their heads too
and were weeping as they went up.
15:31 31 Now David had been told, "Ahithophel[x]
x ver 12; is among the conspirators with Absa-
2Sa 16:23; lom." So David prayed, "O LORD, turn
17:14,23 Ahithophel's counsel into foolishness."
32 When David arrived at the summit,
15:32 where people used to worship God, Hu-
y Jos 16:2 shai the Arkite[y] was there to meet him,
z 2Sa 1:2 his robe torn and dust[z] on his head.
33 David said to him, "If you go with me,
15:33 a 2Sa 19:35 you will be a burden[a] to me. 34 But if you
return to the city and say to Absalom, 'I
will be your servant, O king; I was your
father's servant in the past, but now I
15:34 will be your servant,'[b] then you can help
b 2Sa 16:19 me by frustrating Ahithophel's advice.
35 Won't the priests Zadok and Abiathar
be there with you? Tell them anything
15:35 you hear in the king's palace.[c] 36 Their
c 2Sa 17:15-16 two sons, Ahimaaz son of Zadok and
15:36 Jonathan[d] son of Abiathar, are there
d ver 27; with them. Send them to me with any-
2Sa 17:17 thing you hear."
37 So David's friend Hushai[e] arrived at
15:37 e 2Sa 16:16-17; Jerusalem as Absalom[f] was entering the
1Ch 27:33 city.
f 2Sa 16:15

David and Ziba

16 When David had gone a short
16:1 distance beyond the summit,
g 2Sa 9:1-13 there was Ziba,[g] the steward of Mephib-
h 1Sa 25:18 osheth, waiting to meet him. He had a
string of donkeys saddled and loaded
with two hundred loaves of bread, a
hundred cakes of raisins, a hundred
cakes of figs and a skin of wine.[h]
2 The king asked Ziba, "Why have you
brought these?"
Ziba answered, "The donkeys are for
the king's household to ride on, the
bread and fruit are for the men to eat,
16:2 and the wine is to refresh[i] those who be-
i 2Sa 17:27-29 come exhausted in the desert."
3 The king then asked, "Where is your
16:3 master's grandson?"[j]
j 2Sa 9:9-10; 19:26-27 Ziba said to him, "He is staying in Jerusalem, because he thinks, 'Today the
house of Israel will give me back my
grandfather's kingdom.' "
4 Then the king said to Ziba, "All that
belonged to Mephibosheth is now yours."
"I humbly bow," Ziba said. "May I find
favor in your eyes, my lord the king."

Shimei Curses David

16:5 k 2Sa 3:16 5 As King David approached Bahurim,[k]
a man from the same clan as Saul's fam-
ily came out from there. His name was 16:5
Shimei[l] son of Gera, and he cursed[m] as l 2Sa 19:16-23;
he came out. 6 He pelted David and all 1Ki 2:8-9,36,44 m Ex 22:28
the king's officials with stones, though all
the troops and the special guard were on
David's right and left. 7 As he cursed,
Shimei said, "Get out, get out, you man
of blood, you scoundrel! 8 The LORD has
repaid you for all the blood you shed in
the household of Saul, in whose place
you have reigned.[n] The LORD has handed 16:8
the kingdom over to your son Absalom. n 2Sa 21:9
You have come to ruin because you are a
man of blood!"
9 Then Abishai[o] son of Zeruiah said to 16:9
the king, "Why should this dead dog o 2Sa 9:8
curse my lord the king? Let me go over p Ex 22:28; Lk 9:54
and cut off his head."[p]
10 But the king said, "What do you and
I have in common, you sons of Zeruiah?[q] If he is cursing because the LORD 16:10
said to him, 'Curse David,' who can ask, q 2Sa 19:22
'Why do you do this?' "[r] r Ro 9:20
11 David then said to Abishai and all
his officials, "My son,[s] who is of my own 16:11
flesh, is trying to take my life. How s 2Sa 12:11
much more, then, this Benjamite! Leave t Ge 45:5
him alone; let him curse, for the LORD
has told him to.[t] 12 It may be that the
LORD will see my distress[u] and repay me 16:12
with good[v] for the cursing I am receiv- u Ps 4:1; 25:18
ing today.[w]" v Dt 23:5; Ro 8:28
13 So David and his men continued w Ps 109:28
along the road while Shimei was going
along the hillside opposite him, cursing
as he went and throwing stones at him
and showering him with dirt. 14 The king
and all the people with him arrived at
their destination exhausted.[x] And there 16:14
he refreshed himself. x 2Sa 17:2

The Advice of Hushai and Ahithophel

15 Meanwhile, Absalom[y] and all the
men of Israel came to Jerusalem, and 16:15
Ahithophel[z] was with him. 16 Then Hu- y 2Sa 15:37 z 2Sa 15:12
shai[a] the Arkite, David's friend, went to 16:16
Absalom and said to him, "Long live the a 2Sa 15:37
king! Long live the king!"
17 Absalom asked Hushai, "Is this the
love you show your friend? Why didn't
you go with your friend?"[b] 16:17
18 Hushai said to Absalom, "No, the b 2Sa 19:25
one chosen by the LORD, by these people,
and by all the men of Israel—his I will
be, and I will remain with him. 19 Furthermore, whom should I serve? Should

16:19 [c]2Sa 15:34

I not serve the son? Just as I served your
father, so I will serve you."[c]
20 Absalom said to Ahithophel, "Give
us your advice. What should we do?"
21 Ahithophel answered, "Lie with
your father's concubines whom he left to
take care of the palace. Then all Israel
will hear that you have made yourself a
stench in your father's nostrils, and the
hands of everyone with you will be
strengthened." 22 So they pitched a tent
for Absalom on the roof, and he lay with
his father's concubines in the sight of all
Israel.[d]

16:22 [d]2Sa 12:11-12; 15:16

23 Now in those days the advice[e]
Ahithophel gave was like that of one
who inquires of God. That was how both
David[f] and Absalom regarded all of
Ahithophel's advice.

16:23 [e]2Sa 17:14,23 [f]2Sa 15:12

17

17 Ahithophel said to Absalom, "I
would[a] choose twelve thou-
sand men and set out tonight in pursuit
of David. 2 I would[b] attack him while he
is weary and weak.[g] I would[b] strike him
with terror, and then all the people with
him will flee. I would[b] strike down only
the king[h] 3 and bring all the people back
to you. The death of the man you seek
will mean the return of all; all the people
will be unharmed." 4 This plan seemed
good to Absalom and to all the elders of
Israel.

17:2 [g]2Sa 16:14 [h]1Ki 22:31; Zec 13:7

5 But Absalom said, "Summon also
Hushai[i] the Arkite, so we can hear what
he has to say." 6 When Hushai came to
him, Absalom said, "Ahithophel has giv-
en this advice. Should we do what he
says? If not, give us your opinion."
7 Hushai replied to Absalom, "The advice Ahithophel has given is not good
this time. 8 You know your father and his
men; they are fighters, and as fierce as a
wild bear robbed of her cubs.[j] Besides,
your father is an experienced fighter;[k]
he will not spend the night with the
troops. 9 Even now, he is hidden in a cave
or some other place.[l] If he should attack
your troops first,[c] whoever hears about
it will say, 'There has been a slaughter
among the troops who follow Absalom.'
10 Then even the bravest soldier, whose
heart is like the heart of a lion,[m] will
melt[n] with fear, for all Israel knows that
your father is a fighter and that those
with him are brave.[o]
11 "So I advise you: Let all Israel, from
Dan to Beersheba[p]—as numerous as the
sand[q] on the seashore—be gathered to
you, with you yourself leading them into
battle. 12 Then we will attack him wherever he may be found, and we will fall on
him as dew settles on the ground. Neither he nor any of his men will be left
alive. 13 If he withdraws into a city, then
all Israel will bring ropes to that city, and
we will drag it down to the valley[r] until
not even a piece of it can be found."

17:5 [i]2Sa 15:32

17:8 [j]Hos 13:8 [k]1Sa 16:18

17:9 [l]Jer 41:9

17:10 [m]1Ch 12:8 [n]Jos 2:9,11; Eze 21:15 [o]2Sa 23:8; 1Ch 11:11

17:11 [p]Jdg 20:1

17:11 [q]Ge 12:2; 22:17; Jos 11:4

17:13 [r]Mic 1:6

14 Absalom and all the men of Israel
said, "The advice[s] of Hushai the Arkite
is better than that of Ahithophel."[t] For
the LORD had determined to frustrate[u]
the good advice of Ahithophel in order
to bring disaster[v] on Absalom.[w]

17:14 [s]2Sa 16:23 [t]2Sa 15:12 [u]2Sa 15:34; Ne 4:15 [v]Ps 9:16 [w]2Ch 10:8

15 Hushai told Zadok and Abiathar, the
priests, "Ahithophel has advised Absalom and the elders of Israel to do such
and such, but I have advised them to do
so and so. 16 Now send a message immediately and tell David, 'Do not spend the
night at the fords in the desert;[x] cross
over without fail, or the king and all the
people with him will be swallowed up.[y]'"

17:16 [x]2Sa 15:28 [y]2Sa 15:35

17 Jonathan[z] and Ahimaaz were staying at En Rogel.[a] A servant girl was to go
and inform them, and they were to go
and tell King David, for they could not
risk being seen entering the city. 18 But a
young man saw them and told Absalom.
So the two of them left quickly and went
to the house of a man in Bahurim.[b] He
had a well in his courtyard, and they
climbed down into it. 19 His wife took a
covering and spread it out over the
opening of the well and scattered grain
over it. No one knew anything about it.[c]

17:17 [z]2Sa 15:27,36 [a]Jos 15:7; 18:16

17:18 [b]2Sa 3:16; 16:5

17:19 [c]Jos 2:6

20 When Absalom's men came to the
woman[d] at the house, they asked,
"Where are Ahimaaz and Jonathan?"
The woman answered them, "They
crossed over the brook."[d] The men
searched but found no one, so they returned to Jerusalem.

17:20 [d]Ex 1:19; Jos 2:3-5; 1Sa 19:12-17

21 After the men had gone, the two
climbed out of the well and went to inform King David. They said to him, "Set
out and cross the river at once;
Ahithophel has advised such and such
against you." 22 So David and all the people with him set out and crossed the Jordan. By daybreak, no one was left who
had not crossed the Jordan.

[a] 1 Or *Let me* [b] 2 Or *will* [c] 9 Or *When some of the men fall at the first attack* [d] 20 Or *"They passed by the sheep pen toward the water."*

23When Ahithophel saw that his advice[e] had not been followed, he saddled
his donkey and set out for his house in
his hometown. He put his house in order[f] and then hanged himself. So he died
and was buried in his father's tomb.
24David went to Mahanaim,[g] and Absalom crossed the Jordan with all the
men of Israel. 25Absalom had appointed
Amasa[h] over the army in place of Joab.
Amasa was the son of a man named Jether,[a][i] an Israelite[b] who had married Abigail,[c] the daughter of Nahash and sister
of Zeruiah the mother of Joab. 26The Israelites and Absalom camped in the
land of Gilead.
27When David came to Mahanaim,
Shobi son of Nahash[j] from Rabbah[k] of
the Ammonites, and Makir[l] son of Ammiel from Lo Debar, and Barzillai[m] the
Gileadite[n] from Rogelim 28brought bed-
ding and bowls and articles of pottery.
They also brought wheat and barley,
flour and roasted grain, beans and
lentils,[d] 29honey and curds, sheep, and
cheese from cows' milk for David and his
people to eat.[o] For they said, "The people have become hungry and tired and
thirsty in the desert.[p]"

Absalom's Death

18 David mustered the men who
were with him and appointed
over them commanders of thousands
and commanders of hundreds. 2David
sent the troops out[q]—a third under the
command of Joab, a third under Joab's
brother Abishai[r] son of Zeruiah, and a
third under Ittai[s] the Gittite. The king
told the troops, "I myself will surely
march out with you."
3But the men said, "You must not go
out; if we are forced to flee, they won't
care about us. Even if half of us die, they
won't care; but you are worth ten[t] thousand of us.[e] It would be better now for
you to give us support from the city."[u]
4The king answered, "I will do whatever seems best to you."
So the king stood beside the gate
while all the men marched out in units
of hundreds and of thousands. 5The
king commanded Joab, Abishai and Ittai, "Be gentle with the young man Absalom for my sake." And all the troops
heard the king giving orders concerning
Absalom to each of the commanders.

17:23 e 2Sa 15:12; 16:23 f 2Ki 20:1; Mt 27:5
17:24 g Ge 32:2; 2Sa 2:8
17:25 h 2Sa 19:13; 20:4,9-12; 1Ki 2:5,32; 1Ch 12:18 i 1Ch 2:13-17
17:27 j 1Sa 11:1 k Dt 3:11; 2Sa 10:1-2; 12:26,29 l 2Sa 9:4 m 2Sa 19:31-39; 1Ki 2:7 n 2Sa 19:31; Ezr 2:61
17:29 o 1Ch 12:40 p 2Sa 16:2; Ro 12:13
18:2 q Jdg 7:16; 1Sa 11:11 r 1Sa 26:6 s 2Sa 15:19
18:3 t 1Sa 18:7 u 2Sa 21:17

6The army marched into the field to
fight Israel, and the battle took place in
the forest[v] of Ephraim. 7There the army
of Israel was defeated by David's men,
and the casualties that day were great—
twenty thousand men. 8The battle
spread out over the whole countryside,
and the forest claimed more lives that
day than the sword.
9Now Absalom happened to meet David's men. He was riding his mule, and as
the mule went under the thick branches
of a large oak, Absalom's head[w] got
caught in the tree. He was left hanging
in midair, while the mule he was riding
kept on going.
10When one of the men saw this, he
told Joab, "I just saw Absalom hanging
in an oak tree."
11Joab said to the man who had told
him this, "What! You saw him? Why
didn't you strike[x] him to the ground
right there? Then I would have had to
give you ten shekels[f] of silver and a warrior's belt.[y]"
12But the man replied, "Even if a
thousand shekels[g] were weighed out
into my hands, I would not lift my hand
against the king's son. In our hearing the
king commanded you and Abishai and
Ittai, 'Protect the young man Absalom
for my sake.[h]' 13And if I had put my life
in jeopardy[i]—and nothing is hidden
from the king[z]—you would have kept
your distance from me."
14Joab[a] said, "I'm not going to wait
like this for you." So he took three
javelins in his hand and plunged them
into Absalom's heart while Absalom was
still alive in the oak tree. 15And ten of
Joab's armor-bearers surrounded Absalom, struck him and killed him.[b]
16Then Joab[c] sounded the trumpet,
and the troops stopped pursuing Israel,
for Joab halted them. 17They took Absa-

18:6 v Jos 17:18
18:9 w 2Sa 14:26
18:11 x 2Sa 3:39 y 1Sa 18:4
18:13 z 2Sa 14:19-20
18:14 a 2Sa 2:18; 14:30
18:15 b 2Sa 12:10
18:16 c 2Sa 2:28; 20:22

[a] *25* Hebrew *Ithra,* a variant of *Jether*
[b] *25* Hebrew and some Septuagint manuscripts; other Septuagint manuscripts (see also 1 Chron. 2:17) *Ishmaelite* or *Jezreelite*
[c] *25* Hebrew *Abigal,* a variant of *Abigail*
[d] *28* Most Septuagint manuscripts and Syriac; Hebrew *lentils, and roasted grain*
[e] *3* Two Hebrew manuscripts, some Septuagint manuscripts and Vulgate; most Hebrew manuscripts *care; for now there are ten thousand like us*
[f] *11* That is, about 4 ounces (about 115 grams)
[g] *12* That is, about 25 pounds (about 11 kilograms)
[h] *12* A few Hebrew manuscripts, Septuagint, Vulgate and Syriac; most Hebrew manuscripts may be translated *Absalom, whoever you may be.*
[i] *13* Or *Otherwise, if I had acted treacherously toward him*

18:17 lom, threw him into a big pit in the for-
d Jos 7:26 est and piled up[d] a large heap of rocks[e]
e Jos 8:29 over him. Meanwhile, all the Israelites
fled to their homes.
18 During his lifetime Absalom had
18:18 taken a pillar and erected it in the King's
f Ge 14:17 Valley[f] as a monument[g] to himself, for
g Ge 50:5; Nu 32:42; he thought, "I have no son[h] to carry on
1Sa 15:12 h 2Sa 14:27 the memory of my name." He named the
pillar after himself, and it is called Absa-
lom's Monument to this day.

David Mourns

18:19 19 Now Ahimaaz[i] son of Zadok said,
i 2Sa 15:36 "Let me run and take the news to the
j ver 31; Jdg 11:36 king that the LORD has delivered him
from the hand of his enemies."[j]
20 "You are not the one to take the
news today," Joab told him. "You may
take the news another time, but you
must not do so today, because the king's
son is dead."
21 Then Joab said to a Cushite, "Go, tell
the king what you have seen." The Cushite bowed down before Joab and ran off.
22 Ahimaaz son of Zadok again said to
Joab, "Come what may, please let me run
behind the Cushite."
But Joab replied, "My son, why do you
want to go? You don't have any news
that will bring you a reward."
23 He said, "Come what may, I want to
run."
So Joab said, "Run!" Then Ahimaaz
ran by way of the plain[a] and outran the
Cushite.
24 While David was sitting between
the inner and outer gates, the watch-
18:24 k 1Sa 14:16; man[k] went up to the roof of the gateway
2Sa 19:8; by the wall. As he looked out, he saw a
2Ki 9:17; Jer 51:12 man running alone. 25 The watchman
called out to the king and reported it.
The king said, "If he is alone, he must
have good news." And the man came
closer and closer.
26 Then the watchman saw another
man running, and he called down to the
gatekeeper, "Look, another man running alone!"
18:26 l 1Ki 1:42; The king said, "He must be bringing
Isa 52:7; 61:1 good news,[l] too."
18:27 27 The watchman said, "It seems to me
m 2Ki 9:20 that the first one runs like[m] Ahimaaz
son of Zadok."
"He's a good man," the king said. "He
comes with good news."
28 Then Ahimaaz called out to the
king, "All is well!" He bowed down before
the king with his face to the ground and
said, "Praise be to the LORD your God! He
has delivered up the men who lifted
their hands against my lord the king."
29 The king asked, "Is the young man
Absalom safe?"
Ahimaaz answered, "I saw great confusion just as Joab was about to send the
king's servant and me, your servant, but
I don't know what it was."
30 The king said, "Stand aside and wait
here." So he stepped aside and stood
there.
31 Then the Cushite arrived and said,
"My lord the king, hear the good news!
The LORD has delivered you today from
all who rose up against you."
32 The king asked the Cushite, "Is the
young man Absalom safe?"
The Cushite replied, "May the enemies
of my lord the king and all who rise up to
harm you be like that young man."[n] 18:32
33 The king was shaken. He went up to n Jdg 5:31; 1Sa 25:26
the room over the gateway and wept. As
he went, he said: "O my son Absalom!
My son, my son Absalom! If only I had 18:33
died[o] instead of you—O Absalom, my o Ex 32:32 p Ge 43:14;
son, my son!"[p] 2Sa 19:4; Ro 9:3

19 Joab was told, "The king is
weeping and mourning for Ab-
salom." 2 And for the whole army the victory that day was turned into mourning,
because on that day the troops heard it
said, "The king is grieving for his son."
3 The men stole into the city that day as
men steal in who are ashamed when
they flee from battle. 4 The king covered
his face and cried aloud, "O my son Absalom! O Absalom, my son, my son!"

[a] 23 That is, the plain of the Jordan

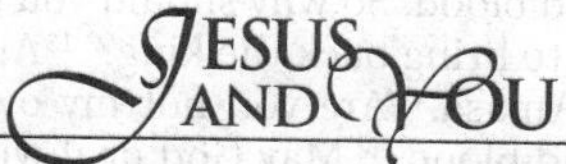

ABSALOM, ABSALOM!

One of the more tragic and heartbreaking images in the Bible is that of David weeping for Absalom (2 Samuel 18:33). David won the military victory against his son but was crushed by the reality of Absalom's death. Jesus experienced similar heartache when he faced rejection by God's people in Jerusalem (Matthew 23:37; Luke 19:41–44). He too understood the tragedy of human pride and the destructive consequences of deliberately rejecting God's anointed King.

5Then Joab went into the house to the
king and said, "Today you have humiliated all your men, who have just saved
your life and the lives of your sons and
daughters and the lives of your wives
and concubines. 6You love those who
hate you and hate those who love you.
You have made it clear today that the
commanders and their men mean nothing to you. I see that you would be
pleased if Absalom were alive today and
all of us were dead. 7Now go out and encourage your men. I swear by the LORD
that if you don't go out, not a man will
be left with you by nightfall. This will be
worse for you than all the calamities
19:7 that have come upon you from your
q Pr 14:28 youth till now."[q]
8So the king got up and took his seat
in the gateway. When the men were told,
19:8 r 2Sa 15:2 "The king is sitting in the gateway,[r]"
they all came before him.

David Returns to Jerusalem

Meanwhile, the Israelites had fled to
their homes. 9Throughout the tribes of
Israel, the people were all arguing with
each other, saying, "The king delivered
us from the hand of our enemies; he is
19:9 the one who rescued us from the hand of
s 2Sa 8:1-14 the Philistines.[s] But now he has fled the
t 2Sa 15:14 country because of Absalom;[t] 10and Absalom, whom we anointed to rule over
us, has died in battle. So why do you say
nothing about bringing the king back?"
11King David sent this message to Za-
19:11 u 2Sa 15:24 dok[u] and Abiathar, the priests: "Ask the
elders of Judah, 'Why should you be the
last to bring the king back to his palace,
since what is being said throughout Israel has reached the king at his quarters? 12You are my brothers, my own
flesh and blood. So why should you be
the last to bring back the king?' 13And
19:13 v 2Sa 17:25 say to Amasa,[v] 'Are you not my own
w Ge 29:14 flesh and blood?[w] May God deal with
x Ru 1:17; 1Ki 19:2; 8:16 me, be it ever so severely,[x] if from now
y 2Sa 2:13 on you are not the commander of my
army in place of Joab.[y]'"
14He won over the hearts of all the
men of Judah as though they were one
man. They sent word to the king, "Return, you and all your men." 15Then the
king returned and went as far as the Jordan.
19:15 z Jos 5:9; Now the men of Judah had come to
1Sa 11:15 Gilgal[z] to go out and meet the king and
bring him across the Jordan. 16Shimei[a] 19:16 a 2Sa 16:5-13;
son of Gera, the Benjamite from Bahu- 1Ki 2:8
rim, hurried down with the men of Judah to meet King David. 17With him
were a thousand Benjamites, along with 19:17
Ziba,[b] the steward of Saul's household,[c] b 2Sa 9:2; 16:1-2
and his fifteen sons and twenty servants. c Ge 43:16
They rushed to the Jordan, where the
king was. 18They crossed at the ford to
take the king's household over and to do
whatever he wished.
When Shimei son of Gera crossed the
Jordan, he fell prostrate before the king
19and said to him, "May my lord not hold
me guilty. Do not remember how your
servant did wrong on the day my lord 19:19
the king left Jerusalem.[d] May the king d 1Sa 22:15;
put it out of his mind. 20For I your ser- 2Sa 16:6-8
vant know that I have sinned, but today
I have come here as the first of the whole
house of Joseph to come down and meet
my lord the king."
21Then Abishai[e] son of Zeruiah said, 19:21 e 1Sa 26:6
"Shouldn't Shimei be put to death for f Ex 22:28
this? He cursed[f] the LORD's anointed."[g] g 1Sa 12:3; 26:9;
22David replied, "What do you and I 2Sa 16:7-8
have in common, you sons of Zeruiah?[h] 19:22 h 2Sa 2:18; 16:10
This day you have become my adver- i 1Sa 11:13
saries! Should anyone be put to death in
Israel today?[i] Do I not know that today
I am king over Israel?" 23So the king said
to Shimei, "You shall not die." And the
king promised him on oath.[j] 19:23 j 1Ki 2:8,42
24Mephibosheth,[k] Saul's grandson,
also went down to meet the king. He 19:24 k 2Sa 4:4; 9:6-10
had not taken care of his feet or
trimmed his mustache or washed his
clothes from the day the king left until
the day he returned safely. 25When he
came from Jerusalem to meet the king,
the king asked him, "Why didn't you go
with me,[l] Mephibosheth?" 19:25 l 2Sa 16:17
26He said, "My lord the king, since I
your servant am lame,[m] I said, 'I will 19:26 m Lev 21:18
have my donkey saddled and will ride on n 2Sa 9:2
it, so I can go with the king.' But Ziba[n]
my servant betrayed me. 27And he has
slandered your servant to my lord the
king. My lord the king is like an angel[o] of 19:27
God; so do whatever pleases you. 28All o 1Sa 29:9;
my grandfather's descendants deserved 2Sa 14:17,20
nothing but death[p] from my lord the 19:28
king, but you gave your servant a place p 2Sa 16:8;
among those who eat at your table.[q] So 21:6-9 q 2Sa 9:7,
what right do I have to make any more 13
appeals to the king?"
29The king said to him, "Why say

more? I order you and Ziba to divide the
fields."
30 Mephibosheth said to the king, "Let
him take everything, now that my lord
19:31 the king has arrived home safely."
r 2Sa 17:27-29, 31 Barzillai[r] the Gileadite also came
27; 1Ki 2:7 down from Rogelim to cross the Jordan
with the king and to send him on his
way from there. 32 Now Barzillai was a
very old man, eighty years of age. He had
19:32 provided for the king during his stay in
s 1Sa 25:2; Mahanaim, for he was a very wealthy[s]
2Sa 17:27 man. 33 The king said to Barzillai, "Cross
over with me and stay with me in Jerusalem, and I will provide for you."
34 But Barzillai answered the king,
"How many more years will I live, that I
19:35 should go up to Jerusalem with the king?
t Ps 90:10 35 I am now eighty[t] years old. Can I tell the
u 2Ch 35:25; Ezr 2:65; difference between what is good and
Ecc 2:8; 12:1; what is not? Can your servant taste what
Isa 5:11-12 he eats and drinks? Can I still hear the
v 2Sa 15:33 voices of men and women singers?[u] Why
should your servant be an added[v] burden
to my lord the king? 36 Your servant will
cross over the Jordan with the king for a
short distance, but why should the king
reward me in this way? 37 Let your servant
return, that I may die in my own town
19:37 near the tomb of my father[w] and mother.
w Ge 49:29; 1Ki 2:7 x ver 40; But here is your servant Kimham.[x] Let
Jer 41:17 him cross over with my lord the king. Do
for him whatever pleases you."
38 The king said, "Kimham shall cross
over with me, and I will do for him whatever pleases you. And anything you desire from me I will do for you."
39 So all the people crossed the Jordan,
and then the king crossed over. The king
kissed Barzillai and gave him his bless-
19:39 y Ge 31:55; ing,[y] and Barzillai returned to his home.
Ge 47:7 40 When the king crossed over to Gil-
gal, Kimham crossed with him. All the
troops of Judah and half the troops of Israel had taken the king over.
41 Soon all the men of Israel were coming to the king and saying to him, "Why
did our brothers, the men of Judah, steal
the king away and bring him and his
19:41 household across the Jordan, together
z Jdg 8:1; 12:1 with all his men?"[z]
42 All the men of Judah answered the
men of Israel, "We did this because the
king is closely related to us. Why are you
angry about it? Have we eaten any of the
king's provisions? Have we taken anything for ourselves?"

43 Then the men of Israel[a] answered 19:43
the men of Judah, "We have ten shares in a 2Sa 5:1
the king; and besides, we have a greater
claim on David than you have. So why
do you treat us with contempt? Were we
not the first to speak of bringing back
our king?"
But the men of Judah responded even
more harshly than the men of Israel.

Sheba Rebels Against David

20 Now a troublemaker named
Sheba son of Bicri, a Benjamite,
happened to be there. He sounded the
trumpet and shouted,

"We have no share[b] in David,[c] 20:1 b Ge 31:14
no part in Jesse's son![d] c Ge 29:14; 1Ki 12:16
Every man to his tent, O Israel!" d 1Sa 22:7-8;

2 So all the men of Israel deserted Da- 2Ch 10:16
vid to follow Sheba son of Bicri. But the
men of Judah stayed by their king all the
way from the Jordan to Jerusalem.
3 When David returned to his palace
in Jerusalem, he took the ten concu- 20:3
bines[e] he had left to take care of the e 2Sa 15:16;
palace and put them in a house under 16:21-22
guard. He provided for them, but did not
lie with them. They were kept in con-
finement till the day of their death, living as widows.
4 Then the king said to Amasa,[f] "Sum- 20:4
mon the men of Judah to come to me f 2Sa 17:25;
within three days, and be here yourself." 19:13
5 But when Amasa went to summon Ju-
dah, he took longer than the time the
king had set for him.
6 David said to Abishai,[g] "Now Sheba 20:6
son of Bicri will do us more harm than g 2Sa 21:17
Absalom did. Take your master's men
and pursue him, or he will find fortified
cities and escape from us." 7 So Joab's
men and the Kerethites[h] and Pelethites 20:7
and all the mighty warriors went out un- h 1Sa 30:14;
der the command of Abishai. They 2Sa 8:18; 15:18; 1Ki 1:38
marched out from Jerusalem to pursue
Sheba son of Bicri.
8 While they were at the great rock in
Gibeon,[i] Amasa came to meet them. 20:8
Joab[j] was wearing his military tunic, and i Jos 9:3 j 2Sa 2:18
strapped over it at his waist was a belt
with a dagger in its sheath. As he
stepped forward, it dropped out of its
sheath.
9 Joab said to Amasa, "How are you,
my brother?" Then Joab took Amasa by
the beard with his right hand to kiss

him. 10 Amasa was not on his guard
20:10 [k] Jdg 3:21; against the dagger[k] in Joab's[l] hand, and
2Sa 2:23; 3:27 Joab plunged it into his belly, and his in-
[l] 1Ki 2:5 testines spilled out on the ground. Without being stabbed again, Amasa died.
Then Joab and his brother Abishai pursued Sheba son of Bicri.
11 One of Joab's men stood beside Amasa and said, "Whoever favors Joab, and
whoever is for David, let him follow
Joab!" 12 Amasa lay wallowing in his
blood in the middle of the road, and the
man saw that all the troops came to a
20:12 [m] 2Sa 2:23 halt[m] there. When he realized that
everyone who came up to Amasa
stopped, he dragged him from the road
into a field and threw a garment over
him. 13 After Amasa had been removed
from the road, all the men went on with
Joab to pursue Sheba son of Bicri.
14 Sheba passed through all the tribes
of Israel to Abel Beth Maacah[a] and
20:14 [n] Nu 21:16 through the entire region of the Berites,[n]
who gathered together and followed
him. 15 All the troops with Joab came and
20:15 [o] 1Ki 15:20; besieged Sheba in Abel Beth Maacah.[o]
2Ki 15:29 They built a siege ramp[p] up to the city,
[p] 2Ki 19:32; and it stood against the outer fortifica-
Isa 37:33; tions. While they were battering the wall
Jer 6:6; 32:24 to bring it down, 16 a wise woman[q] called
20:16 [q] 2Sa 14:2 from the city, "Listen! Listen! Tell Joab to
come here so I can speak to him." 17 He
went toward her, and she asked, "Are you
Joab?"
"I am," he answered.
She said, "Listen to what your servant
has to say."
"I'm listening," he said.
18 She continued, "Long ago they used
to say, 'Get your answer at Abel,' and
20:19 that settled it. 19 We are the peaceful[r]
[r] Dt 2:26 [s] 1Sa 26:19; and faithful in Israel. You are trying to
2Sa 21:3 destroy a city that is a mother in Israel.
Why do you want to swallow up the
LORD's inheritance?"[s]
20 "Far be it from me!" Joab replied,
"Far be it from me to swallow up or destroy! 21 That is not the case. A man
named Sheba son of Bicri, from the hill
country of Ephraim, has lifted up his
hand against the king, against David.
Hand over this one man, and I'll withdraw from the city."
20:21 [t] 2Sa 4:8 The woman said to Joab, "His head[t]
will be thrown to you from the wall."
22 Then the woman went to all the
20:22 [u] Ecc 9:13 people with her wise advice,[u] and they

cut off the head of Sheba son of Bicri
and threw it to Joab. So he sounded the
trumpet, and his men dispersed from
the city, each returning to his home. And 20:23
Joab went back to the king in Jerusalem. [v] 2Sa 2:28; 8:16-18; 24:2
23 Joab[v] was over Israel's entire army;
Benaiah son of Jehoiada was over the 20:24
Kerethites and Pelethites; 24 Adoniram[b][w] [w] 1Ki 4:6; 5:14;
was in charge of forced labor; Jehosha- 12:18; 2Ch 10:18
phat[x] son of Ahilud was recorder; 25 She- [x] 2Sa 8:16;
va was secretary; Zadok[y] and Abiathar 1Ki 4:3
were priests; 26 and Ira the Jairite was Da- 20:25 [y] 1Sa 2:35;
vid's priest. 2Sa 8:17

The Gibeonites Avenged

21 During the reign of David, there 21:1
was a famine[z] for three succes- [z] Ge 12:10;
sive years; so David sought[a] the face of Dt 32:24
the LORD. The LORD said, "It is on ac- [a] Ex 32:11
count of Saul and his blood-stained
house; it is because he put the Gibeonites to death."
2 The king summoned the Gibeonites[b] 21:2 [b] Jos 9:15
and spoke to them. (Now the Gibeonites
were not a part of Israel but were survivors of the Amorites; the Israelites had
sworn to ⌊spare⌋ them, but Saul in his
zeal for Israel and Judah had tried to annihilate them.) 3 David asked the
Gibeonites, "What shall I do for you?
How shall I make amends so that you 21:3 [c] 1Sa 26:19;
will bless the LORD's inheritance?"[c] 2Sa 20:19
4 The Gibeonites answered him, "We
have no right to demand silver or gold
from Saul or his family, nor do we have
the right to put anyone in Israel to 21:4
death."[d] [d] Nu 35:33-34
"What do you want me to do for
you?" David asked.
5 They answered the king, "As for the
man who destroyed us and plotted
against us so that we have been deci-
mated and have no place anywhere in
Israel, 6 let seven of his male descendants 21:6
be given to us to be killed and exposed[e] [e] Nu 25:4
before the LORD at Gibeah of Saul—the [f] 1Sa 10:24
LORD's chosen[f] one."
So the king said, "I will give them to
you." 21:7
7 The king spared Mephibosheth[g] son [g] 2Sa 4:4
of Jonathan, the son of Saul, because of [h] 1Sa 18:3; 20:8,
the oath[h] before the LORD between Da- 15; 2Sa 9:7
vid and Jonathan son of Saul. 8 But the
king took Armoni and Mephibosheth,

[a] 14 Or *Abel, even Beth Maacah*; also in verse 15
[b] 24 Some Septuagint manuscripts (see also 1 Kings 4:6 and 5:14); Hebrew *Adoram*

21:8 i 2Sa 3:7 the two sons of Aiah's daughter Rizpah,[i]
j 1Sa 18:19 whom she had borne to Saul, together
with the five sons of Saul's daughter Merab,[a] whom she had borne to Adriel son
of Barzillai the Meholathite.[j] 9He handed them over to the Gibeonites, who
killed and exposed them on a hill before
the LORD. All seven of them fell together;
21:9 k 2Sa 16:8 they were put to death[k] during the first
l Ru 1:22 days of the harvest, just as the barley
harvest was beginning.[l]

10Rizpah daughter of Aiah took sackcloth and spread it out for herself on a
rock. From the beginning of the harvest
till the rain poured down from the heavens on the bodies, she did not let the
21:10 birds of the air touch them by day or the
m ver 8; wild animals by night.[m] 11When David
Dt 21:23; was told what Aiah's daughter Rizpah,
1Sa 17:44 Saul's concubine, had done, 12he went
21:12 and took the bones of Saul[n] and his son
n 1Sa 31:11-13 Jonathan from the citizens of Jabesh Gil-
o Jos 17:11 ead. (They had taken them secretly from
p 1Sa 31:10 the public square at Beth Shan,[o] where
the Philistines had hung[p] them after
they struck Saul down on Gilboa.) 13Da-
vid brought the bones of Saul and his
son Jonathan from there, and the bones
of those who had been killed and exposed were gathered up.

14They buried the bones of Saul and
his son Jonathan in the tomb of Saul's fa-
21:14 q Jos 18:28 ther Kish, at Zela[q] in Benjamin, and did
r Jos 7:26 everything the king commanded. After
s 2Sa 24:25 that,[r] God answered prayer[s] in behalf of
the land.

Wars Against the Philistines

15Once again there was a battle be-
21:15 t 2Sa 5:25 tween the Philistines[t] and Israel. David
went down with his men to fight against
the Philistines, and he became exhausted. 16And Ishbi-Benob, one of the descendants of Rapha, whose bronze
spearhead weighed three hundred
shekels[b] and who was armed with a new
⌞sword⌟, said he would kill David. 17But
21:17 u 2Sa 20:6 Abishai[u] son of Zeruiah came to David's
v 1Ki 11:36 rescue; he struck the Philistine down
w 2Sa 18:3 and killed him. Then David's men swore
to him, saying, "Never again will you go
out with us to battle, so that the lamp[v]
of Israel will not be extinguished.[w]"

18In the course of time, there was an-
21:18 x 1Ch 11:29; other battle with the Philistines, at Gob.
20:4; 27:11 At that time Sibbecai[x] the Hushathite
killed Saph, one of the descendants of
Rapha.

19In another battle with the Philistines at Gob, Elhanan son of Jaare-Ore-
gim[c] the Bethlehemite killed Goliath[d]
the Gittite, who had a spear with a shaft 21:19
like a weaver's rod.[y] y 1Sa 17:7

20In still another battle, which took
place at Gath, there was a huge man
with six fingers on each hand and six
toes on each foot—twenty-four in all. He
also was descended from Rapha.
21When he taunted Israel, Jonathan son 21:21
of Shimeah,[z] David's brother, killed him. z 1Sa 16:9

22These four were descendants of Rapha in Gath, and they fell at the hands of
David and his men.

David's Song of Praise

22 David sang[a] to the LORD the 22:1 a Ex 15:1;
words of this song when the Jdg 5:1; Ps 18:2-
LORD delivered him from the hand of all 50
his enemies and from the hand of Saul.
2He said:

"The LORD is my rock,[b] my 22:2 b Dt 32:4;
fortress[c] and my deliverer;[d] Ps 71:3
3 my God is my rock, in whom I c Ps 31:3; 91:2
take refuge,[e] d Ps 144:2
my shield[f] and the horn[eg] of my 22:3 e Dt 32:37;
salvation. Jer 16:19
He is my stronghold,[h] my refuge f Ge 15:1
and my savior— g Lk 1:69
from violent men you save me. h Ps 9:9
4 I call to the LORD, who is worthy[i] of 22:4 i Ps 48:1; 96:4
praise,
and I am saved from my enemies.

5 "The waves[j] of death swirled about 22:5 j Ps 69:14-15;
me; 93:4; Jnh 2:3
the torrents of destruction
overwhelmed me.
6 The cords of the grave[f][k] coiled 22:6 k Ps 116:3
around me;
the snares of death confronted
me.
7 In my distress[l] I called[m] to the LORD; 22:7 l Ps 120:1
I called out to my God. m Ps 34:6,15;
From his temple he heard my voice; 116:4
my cry came to his ears. 22:8 n Jdg 5:4; Ps 97:4
8 "The earth[n] trembled and quaked,[o] o Ps 77:18

[a] *8* Two Hebrew manuscripts, some Septuagint manuscripts and Syriac (see also 1 Samuel 18:19); most Hebrew and Septuagint manuscripts *Michal*
[b] *16* That is, about 7 1/2 pounds (about 3.5 kilograms)
[c] *19* Or *son of Jair the weaver*
[d] *19* Hebrew and Septuagint; 1 Chron. 20:5 *son of Jair killed Lahmi the brother of Goliath*
[e] *3* *Horn* here symbolizes strength.
[f] *6* Hebrew *Sheol*

DISCOVERY 80

What Matters in the End

When it comes to our relationship with God, we often experience precisely what we have been anticipating. If we expect God to scowl and plant himself as an obstacle in our path, we will blame him for everything bad that happens. If we expect him to be on our side, however, we will look for his purpose and thank him for guiding us. David recognized that every success he had ever experienced had come as a direct gift from God (2 Samuel 22:18–29). David certainly wasn't perfect, but he was godly—a man after God's own heart (1 Samuel 13:14). And he continued to learn as he walked through life just what it meant to be a man of God.

One way to define godliness is to say that it entails allowing God to change us so that the way we live may be in line with God's character. Life is not easy for anyone. We can choose to muddle through on our own, or we can opt to learn to trust God as we walk with him. David's last song and many of Jesus' words in the New Testament reveal that both lived with the assurance that God was on their side (2 Samuel 22:28; John 17:11) and both trusted God in everything (2 Samuel 22:29–30; John 14:1,27).

There are many times when life seems dark. We can't discern what's ahead, and what's behind is replete with pain and mistakes. But whatever the situation, God is a lamp who "turns [our] darkness into light" (2 Samuel 22:29). David knew that he could turn to God—whether or not he knew what God was doing—and he believed that his heavenly Father would light the darkness before his feet. Our Savior stated in John 8:12 that he himself is the embodiment of that light: "I am the light of the world. Whoever follows me will never walk in darkness, but will have the light of life."

Life can be an uphill battle. But we can learn as David did that "with [God's] help [we] can advance against a troop" (2 Samuel 22:30). This seasoned king had led his army into many battles and had personally faced mortal combat. Through it all David had been aware that, in order to persevere, he would need to trust in God. And Jesus asserted that when we trust God, our enemies will be defeated (John 14:27–30; 15:18–25). We may not be able to envision a way out of our predicament, but when we keep turning to God, he will give us victory.

Finally, David knew that "with my God I can scale a wall" (2 Samuel 22:30). No matter what obstacle seemed to stand in his way, he was confident that God would lead him beyond it. Paul declared in Ephesians 2:14 that Jesus Christ has destroyed another barrier, the dividing wall of hostility between ourselves and God. We face obstacles every day. We can either give up and turn back or trust God to show us a way over, under, around or through the barriers (2 Samuel 22:31,36–37). When God chooses the destination, nothing will stand in our way!

***Self-Discovery:** Identify a time in which you have received from God exactly what you expected—no more and no less. Is it possible that you may have missed out on greater blessings because of your lack of trust?*

GO TO DISCOVERY 81 ON PAGE 423

22:8 [p] Job 26:11

the foundations[p] of the heavens[a]
shook;
they trembled because he was
angry.
9 Smoke rose from his nostrils;

22:9 [q] Ps 97:3; Heb 12:29

consuming fire[q] came from his
mouth,
burning coals blazed out of it.
10 He parted the heavens and came
down;

22:10 [r] 1Ki 8:12; Na 1:3

dark clouds[r] were under his feet.
11 He mounted the cherubim and flew;
he soared[b] on the wings of the
wind.[s]

22:11 [s] Ps 104:3

12 He made darkness his canopy
around him—
the dark[c] rain clouds of the sky.
13 Out of the brightness of his
presence

22:13 [t] ver 9

bolts of lightning[t] blazed forth.
14 The LORD thundered[u] from heaven;

22:14 [u] 1Sa 2:10

the voice of the Most High
resounded.
15 He shot arrows[v] and scattered ⌊the
enemies⌋,

22:15 [v] Dt 32:23

bolts of lightning and routed
them.
16 The valleys of the sea were exposed
and the foundations of the earth
laid bare
at the rebuke[w] of the LORD,

22:16 [w] Na 1:4

at the blast of breath from his
nostrils.

22:17 [x] Ps 144:7 [y] Ex 2:10

17 "He reached down from on high[x]
and took hold of me;
he drew[y] me out of deep waters.
18 He rescued me from my powerful
enemy,
from my foes, who were too
strong for me.
19 They confronted me in the day of
my disaster,
but the LORD was my support.[z]

22:19 [z] Ps 23:4

20 He brought me out into a
spacious[a] place;
he rescued[b] me because he
delighted[c] in me.[d]

22:20 [a] Ps 31:8 [b] Ps 118:5 [c] Ps 22:8 [d] 2Sa 15:26

21 "The LORD has dealt with me
according to my
righteousness;[e]
according to the cleanness of my
hands[f] he has rewarded me.

22:21 [e] 1Sa 26:23 [f] Ps 24:4

22 For I have kept[g] the ways of the
LORD;
I have not done evil by turning
from my God.

22:22 [g] Ge 18:19; Ps 128:1; Pr 8:32

23 All his laws are before me;[h]
I have not turned[i] away from his
decrees.

22:23 [h] Dt 6:4-9; Ps 119:30-32 [i] Ps 119:102

24 I have been blameless[j] before him
and have kept myself from sin.

22:24 [j] Ge 6:9; Eph 1:4

25 The LORD has rewarded me
according to my
righteousness,[k]
according to my cleanness[d] in
his sight.

22:25 [k] ver 21

26 "To the faithful you show yourself
faithful,
to the blameless you show
yourself blameless,
27 to the pure[l] you show yourself pure,
but to the crooked you show
yourself shrewd.[m]

22:27 [l] Mt 5:8 [m] Lev 26:23-24

28 You save the humble,[n]
but your eyes are on the haughty
to bring them low.[o]

22:28 [n] Ex 3:8; Ps 72:12-13 [o] Isa 2:12,17; 5:15

29 You are my lamp,[p] O LORD;
the LORD turns my darkness into
light.

22:29 [p] Ps 27:1

30 With your help I can advance
against a troop[e];
with my God I can scale a wall.

31 "As for God, his way is perfect;[q]
the word of the LORD is flawless.[r]
He is a shield
for all who take refuge in him.

22:31 [q] Dt 32:4; Mt 5:48 [r] Ps 12:6; 119:140; Pr 30:5-6

32 For who is God besides the LORD?
And who is the Rock[s] except our
God?

22:32 [s] 1Sa 2:2

33 It is God who arms me with
strength[f]
and makes my way perfect.
34 He makes my feet like the feet of a
deer;[t]
he enables me to stand on the
heights.[u]

22:34 [t] Hab 3:19 [u] Dt 32:13

35 He trains my hands[v] for battle;
my arms can bend a bow of
bronze.

22:35 [v] Ps 144:1

36 You give me your shield[w] of
victory;
you stoop down to make me
great.

22:36 [w] Eph 6:16

[a] 8 Hebrew; Vulgate and Syriac (see also Psalm 18:7) *mountains* [b] 11 Many Hebrew manuscripts (see also Psalm 18:10); most Hebrew manuscripts *appeared* [c] 12 Septuagint and Vulgate (see also Psalm 18:11); Hebrew *massed* [d] 25 Hebrew; Septuagint and Vulgate (see also Psalm 18:24) *to the cleanness of my hands* [e] 30 Or *can run through a barricade* [f] 33 Dead Sea Scrolls, some Septuagint manuscripts, Vulgate and Syriac (see also Psalm 18:32); Masoretic Text *who is my strong refuge*

37 You broaden the path[x] beneath me,
so that my ankles do not turn.
38 "I pursued my enemies and
crushed them;
I did not turn back till they were
destroyed.
39 I crushed[y] them completely, and
they could not rise;
they fell beneath my feet.
40 You armed me with strength for
battle;
you made my adversaries bow at
my feet.[z]
41 You made my enemies turn their
backs[a] in flight,
and I destroyed my foes.
42 They cried for help,[b] but there was
no one to save them—[c]
to the LORD, but he did not
answer.
43 I beat them as fine as the dust of
the earth;
I pounded and trampled[d] them
like mud[e] in the streets.
44 "You have delivered[f] me from the
attacks of my people;
you have preserved[g] me as the
head of nations.
People[h] I did not know are subject
to me,
45 and foreigners come cringing[i] to
me;
as soon as they hear me, they
obey me.
46 They all lose heart;
they come trembling[a][j] from
their strongholds.
47 "The LORD lives! Praise be to my
Rock!
Exalted be God, the Rock, my
Savior![k]
48 He is the God who avenges me,[l]
who puts the nations under me,
49 who sets me free from my
enemies.[m]
You exalted me above my foes;
from violent men you rescued
me.
50 Therefore I will praise you, O LORD,
among the nations;
I will sing praises to your name.[n]
51 He gives his king great victories;[o]
he shows unfailing kindness to
his anointed,[p]
to David[q] and his descendants
forever."[r]

22:37 [x] Pr 4:11
22:39 [y] Mal 4:3
22:40 [z] Ps 44:5
22:41 [a] Ex 23:27
22:42 [b] Isa 1:15 [c] Ps 50:22
22:43 [d] Mic 7:10 [e] Isa 10:6; Mic 7:10
22:44 [f] 2Sa 3:1 [g] Dt 28:13 [h] 2Sa 8:1-14; Isa 55:3-5
22:45 [i] Ps 66:3; 81:15
22:46 [j] Mic 7:17
22:47 [k] Ps 89:26
22:48 [l] Ps 94:1; 144:2; 1Sa 25:39
22:49 [m] Ps 140:1,4
22:50 [n] Ro 15:9*
22:51 [o] Ps 144:9-10 [p] Ps 89:20 [q] 2Sa 7:13 [r] Ps 89:24,29

The Last Words of David

23 These are the last words of David:

"The oracle of David son of Jesse,
the oracle of the man exalted[s] by
the Most High,
the man anointed[t] by the God of
Jacob,
Israel's singer of songs[b]:
2 "The Spirit[u] of the LORD spoke
through me;
his word was on my tongue.
3 The God of Israel spoke,
the Rock[v] of Israel said to me:
'When one rules over men in
righteousness,[w]
when he rules in the fear of God,[x]
4 he is like the light of morning at
sunrise[y]
on a cloudless morning,
like the brightness after rain
that brings the grass from the
earth.'
5 "Is not my house right with God?
Has he not made with me an
everlasting covenant,[z]
arranged and secured in every
part?
Will he not bring to fruition my
salvation
and grant me my every desire?
6 But evil men are all to be cast aside
like thorns,[a]
which are not gathered with the
hand.
7 Whoever touches thorns
uses a tool of iron or the shaft of
a spear;
they are burned up where they
lie."

23:1 [s] 2Sa 7:8-9; Ps 78:70-71; 89:27 [t] 1Sa 16:12-13; Ps 89:20
23:2 [u] Mt 22:43; 2Pe 1:21
23:3 [v] Dt 32:4; 2Sa 22:2,32 [w] Ps 72:3 [x] 2Ch 19:7,9; Isa 11:1-5
23:4 [y] Jdg 5:31; Ps 89:36
23:5 [z] Ps 89:29; Isa 55:3
23:6 [a] Mt 13:40-41

David's Mighty Men

8 These are the names of David's
mighty men:
Josheb-Basshebeth,[c] a Tahkemonite,[d]
was chief of the Three; he raised his
spear against eight hundred men, whom
he killed[e] in one encounter.

[a] *46* Some Septuagint manuscripts and Vulgate (see also Psalm 18:45); Masoretic Text *they arm themselves.* [b] *1* Or *Israel's beloved singer* [c] *8* Hebrew; some Septuagint manuscripts suggest *Ish-Bosheth,* that is, *Esh-Baal* (see also 1 Chron. 11:11 *Jashobeam*). [d] *8* Probably a variant of *Hacmonite* (see 1 Chron. 11:11) [e] *8* Some Septuagint manuscripts (see also 1 Chron. 11:11); Hebrew and other Septuagint manuscripts *Three; it was Adino the Eznite who killed eight hundred men*

23:9 [b]1Ch 27:4 9Next to him was Eleazar son of Do-
[c]1Ch 8:4 dai[b] the Ahohite.[c] As one of the three
mighty men, he was with David when
they taunted the Philistines gathered ⌊at
Pas Dammim⌋[a] for battle. Then the men
of Israel retreated, 10but he stood his
ground and struck down the Philistines
till his hand grew tired and froze to the
sword. The LORD brought about a great
victory that day. The troops returned to
Eleazar, but only to strip the dead.
11Next to him was Shammah son of
Agee the Hararite. When the Philistines
banded together at a place where there
was a field full of lentils, Israel's troops
fled from them. 12But Shammah took
his stand in the middle of the field. He
defended it and struck the Philistines
down, and the LORD brought about a
great victory.
13During harvest time, three of the
23:13 thirty chief men came down to David at
[d]1Sa 22:1 the cave of Adullam,[d] while a band of
[e]2Sa 5:18 Philistines was encamped in the Valley
23:14 of Rephaim.[e] 14At that time David was in
[f]1Sa 22:4-5 the stronghold,[f] and the Philistine garri-
[g]Ru 1:19 son was at Bethlehem.[g] 15David longed
for water and said, "Oh, that someone
would get me a drink of water from the
well near the gate of Bethlehem!" 16So
the three mighty men broke through the
Philistine lines, drew water from the
well near the gate of Bethlehem and carried it back to David. But he refused to
23:16 drink it; instead, he poured[h] it out be-
[h]Ge 35:14 fore the LORD. 17"Far be it from me,
23:17 O LORD, to do this!" he said. "Is it not the
[i]Lev 17:10-12 blood[i] of men who went at the risk of
their lives?" And David would not
drink it.

Such were the exploits of the three
mighty men.
23:18 18Abishai[j] the brother of Joab son of
[j]2Sa 10:10,14; 1Ch 11:20 Zeruiah was chief of the Three.[b] He
raised his spear against three hundred
men, whom he killed, and so he became
as famous as the Three. 19Was he not
held in greater honor than the Three? He
became their commander, even though
23:20 he was not included among them.
[k]2Sa 8:18; 20:23 20Benaiah[k] son of Jehoiada was a
[l]Jos 15:21 valiant fighter from Kabzeel,[l] who performed great exploits. He struck down
two of Moab's best men. He also went
down into a pit on a snowy day and
killed a lion. 21And he struck down a
huge Egyptian. Although the Egyptian

> WE BELIEVE THAT THE HISTORY OF THE WORLD IS BUT THE HISTORY OF HIS INFLUENCE AND THAT THE CENTER OF THE WHOLE UNIVERSE IS THE CROSS OF CALVARY.
>
> Alexander MacLaren, *Scottish Theologian*

had a spear in his hand, Benaiah went
against him with a club. He snatched
the spear from the Egyptian's hand and
killed him with his own spear. 22Such
were the exploits of Benaiah son of Jehoiada; he too was as famous as the
three mighty men. 23He was held in
greater honor than any of the Thirty, but
he was not included among the Three.
And David put him in charge of his
bodyguard.

24 Among the Thirty were:
Asahel[m] the brother of Joab, 23:24 [m]2Sa 2:18
Elhanan son of Dodo from Beth-
lehem,
25 Shammah the Harodite,[n] 23:25 [n]Jdg 7:1; 1Ch 11:27
Elika the Harodite,
26 Helez[o] the Paltite, 23:26 [o]1Ch 27:10
Ira son of Ikkesh from Tekoa,
27 Abiezer from Anathoth,[p] 23:27 [p]Jos 21:18
Mebunnai[c] the Hushathite,
28 Zalmon the Ahohite, 23:28 [q]1Ch 27:13
Maharai[q] the Netophathite,[r] [r]2Ki 25:23; Ne 7:26
29 Heled[d] son of Baanah the Ne-
tophathite,
Ithai son of Ribai from Gibeah[s] 23:29 [s]Jos 15:57
in Benjamin,
30 Benaiah the Pirathonite,[t] 23:30 [t]Jdg 12:13
Hiddai[e] from the ravines of Ga- [u]Jos 24:30
ash,[u]
31 Abi-Albon the Arbathite,
Azmaveth the Barhumite,[v] 23:31 [v]2Sa 3:16
32 Eliahba the Shaalbonite,
the sons of Jashen,
Jonathan 33son of[f] Shammah the
Hararite,

[a] *9* See 1 Chron. 11:13; Hebrew *gathered there.*
[b] *18* Most Hebrew manuscripts (see also 1 Chron. 11:20); two Hebrew manuscripts and Syriac *Thirty*
[c] *27* Hebrew; some Septuagint manuscripts (see also 1 Chron. 11:29) *Sibbecai*
[d] *29* Some Hebrew manuscripts and Vulgate (see also 1 Chron. 11:30); most Hebrew manuscripts *Heleb*
[e] *30* Hebrew; some Septuagint manuscripts (see also 1 Chron. 11:32) *Hurai*
[f] *33* Some Septuagint manuscripts (see also 1 Chron. 11:34); Hebrew does not have *son of.*

Ahiam son of Sharar[a] the Hararite,
34 Eliphelet son of Ahasbai the
23:34 Maacathite,
w 2Sa 11:3 Eliam[w] son of Ahithophel[x] the
x 2Sa 15:12 Gilonite,
23:35 35 Hezro the Carmelite,[y]
y Jos 12:22 Paarai the Arbite,
23:36 36 Igal son of Nathan from Zobah,[z]
z 1Sa 14:47 the son of Hagri,[b]
37 Zelek the Ammonite,
Naharai the Beerothite, the armor-bearer of Joab son of Zer-
23:38 uiah,
a 2Sa 20:26; 38 Ira the Ithrite,[a]
1Ch 2:53 Gareb the Ithrite
23:39 39 and Uriah[b] the Hittite.
b 2Sa 11:3 There were thirty-seven in all.

David Counts the Fighting Men

24:1 **24** Again[c] the anger of the LORD
c Jos 9:15 burned against Israel, and he
d 1Ch 27:23 incited David against them, saying, "Go
and take a census of[d] Israel and Judah."

24:2 2 So the king said to Joab[e] and the
e 2Sa 20:23 army commanders[c] with him, "Go
f Jdg 20:1; throughout the tribes of Israel from Dan
2Sa 3:10 to Beersheba[f] and enroll the fighting
men, so that I may know how many
there are."

3 But Joab replied to the king, "May the
24:3 LORD your God multiply the troops a
g Dt 1:11 hundred times over,[g] and may the eyes of
my lord the king see it. But why does my
lord the king want to do such a thing?"

4 The king's word, however, overruled
Joab and the army commanders; so they
left the presence of the king to enroll the
fighting men of Israel.

5 After crossing the Jordan, they
24:5 camped near Aroer,[h] south of the town
h Dt 2:36; in the gorge, and then went through Gad
Jos 13:9
i Nu 21:32 and on to Jazer.[i] 6 They went to Gilead
24:6 and the region of Tahtim Hodshi, and on
j Ge 10:19; to Dan Jaan and around toward Sidon.[j]
Jos 19:28; 7 Then they went toward the fortress of
Jdg 1:31 Tyre[k] and all the towns of the Hivites
24:7
k Jos 19:29 and Canaanites. Finally, they went on to
l Ge 21:22-33 Beersheba[l] in the Negev[m] of Judah.
m Dt 1:7;
Jos 11:3 8 After they had gone through the entire land, they came back to Jerusalem at
the end of nine months and twenty days.

9 Joab reported the number of the
fighting men to the king: In Israel there
24:9 were eight hundred thousand able-bod-
n Nu 1:44-46; ied men who could handle a sword, and
1Ch 21:5 in Judah five hundred thousand.[n]

10 David was conscience-stricken[o] af- 24:10 o 1Sa 24:5
ter he had counted the fighting men, p 2Sa 12:13
and he said to the LORD, "I have sinned[p] q Nu 12:11;
greatly in what I have done. Now, 1Sa 13:13
O LORD, I beg you, take away the guilt of
your servant. I have done a very foolish
thing.[q]"

11 Before David got up the next morning, the word of the LORD had come to
Gad[r] the prophet, David's seer:[s] 12 "Go 24:11 r 1Sa 22:5
and tell David, 'This is what the LORD s 1Sa 9:9;
says: I am giving you three options. 1Ch 29:29
Choose one of them for me to carry out
against you.' "

13 So Gad went to David and said to
him, "Shall there come upon you three[d]
years of famine[t] in your land? Or three 24:13 t Dt 28:38-42,
months of fleeing from your enemies 48; Eze 14:21
while they pursue you? Or three days of u Lev 26:25
plague[u] in your land? Now then, think it
over and decide how I should answer the
one who sent me."

14 David said to Gad, "I am in deep distress. Let us fall into the hands of the 24:14
LORD, for his mercy[v] is great; but do not v Ne 9:28;
let me fall into the hands of men." Ps 51:1; 103:8,

15 So the LORD sent a plague on Israel 13; 130:4
from that morning until the end of the
time designated, and seventy thousand
of the people from Dan to Beersheba
died.[w] 16 When the angel stretched out 24:15
his hand to destroy Jerusalem, the LORD w 1Ch 27:24
was grieved[x] because of the calamity 24:16
and said to the angel who was afflicting x Ge 6:6;
the people, "Enough! Withdraw your 1Sa 15:11
hand." The angel of the LORD[y] was then y Ex 12:23;
at the threshing floor of Araunah the Ac 12:23
Jebusite.

17 When David saw the angel who was
striking down the people, he said to the
LORD, "I am the one who has sinned and
done wrong. These are but sheep.[z] What 24:17 z Ps 74:1
have they done? Let your hand fall upon a Jnh 1:12
me and my family."[a]

David Builds an Altar

18 On that day Gad went to David and
said to him, "Go up and build an altar to
the LORD on the threshing floor of Araunah the Jebusite." 19 So David went up, as
the LORD had commanded through Gad.

[a] *33* Hebrew; some Septuagint manuscripts (see also 1 Chron. 11:35) *Sacar* [b] *36* Some Septuagint manuscripts (see also 1 Chron. 11:38); Hebrew *Haggadi* [c] *2* Septuagint (see also verse 4 and 1 Chron. 21:2); Hebrew *Joab the army commander* [d] *13* Septuagint (see also 1 Chron. 21:12); Hebrew *seven*

20 When Araunah looked and saw the
king and his men coming toward him,
he went out and bowed down before the
king with his face to the ground.
21 Araunah said, "Why has my lord the
king come to his servant?"
"To buy your threshing floor," David
answered, "so I can build an altar to the
24:21 LORD, that the plague on the people may
[b] Nu 16:44-50 be stopped."[b]
22 Araunah said to David, "Let my lord
24:22 the king take whatever pleases him and
[c] 1Sa 6:14; offer it up. Here are oxen[c] for the burnt
1Ki 19:21 offering, and here are threshing sledges
24:23 and ox yokes for the wood. 23 O king,
[d] Eze 20:40-41 Araunah gives[d] all this to the king."
Araunah also said to him, "May the LORD
your God accept you."
24 But the king replied to Araunah,
"No, I insist on paying you for it. I will
not sacrifice to the LORD my God burnt
offerings that cost me nothing."[e] 24:24
So David bought the threshing floor [e] Mal 1:13-14
and the oxen and paid fifty shekels[a] of 24:25
silver for them. 25 David built an altar[f] to [f] 1Sa 7:17
the LORD there and sacrificed burnt of- [g] 2Sa 21:14
ferings and fellowship offerings.[b] Then
the LORD answered prayer[g] in behalf of
the land, and the plague on Israel was
stopped.

[a] *24* That is, about 1 1/4 pounds (about 0.6 kilogram) [b] *25* Traditionally *peace offerings*

1 KINGS

Jesus in 1 Kings The book of 1 Kings begins well, recording King Solomon's godly reign and the construction of the temple. However, it ends with the nation divided against itself and in rebellion against God. We can see Jesus in 1 Kings in two ways. First, Jesus, like Solomon, is the wise King of Israel. Second, Jesus is present in 1 Kings as the Lord of the temple who appeared to Solomon (1 Samuel 9:2).

Note as you read that these historical books set the stage for the rest of the Old Testament. Isaiah, Jeremiah, Hosea and Amos all prophesied during this time. Their prophetic admonitions—occasionally heeded, but often dismissed—were graphic warnings of the tragedy toward which both kingdoms were inexorably hurtling. At the same time, however, their beautiful word pictures of the coming Messiah held out the hope of salvation to all who would listen.

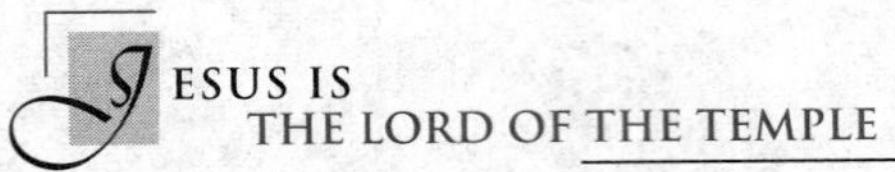
JESUS IS
THE LORD OF THE TEMPLE

Does it matter where we pray? (1 Kings 8:29–30)

- *The Lord hears our prayers no matter where we are, but talking with God in certain places or positions can have a positive effect on our prayers. Solomon's dedication of the temple as a place of prayer reminds us that holy places enrich our worship. An example is the garden of Gethsemane, where Jesus wrestled with the prospect of suffering and death (Matthew 26:36).*

What is the significance of the term "lamp before me"? (1 Kings 11:36)

- *The lamp was symbolic of God's living presence. God had promised David that he would always have a living representative on the throne in Jerusalem. This was a Messianic promise, ultimately fulfilled by Jesus. Several passages use this metaphor in connection with David and his house (1 Kings 15:4; 2 Kings 8:19; 2 Samuel 21:17).*

Adonijah Sets Himself Up as King

1 When King David was old and well advanced in years, he could not keep warm even when they put covers over him. 2So his servants said to him, "Let us look for a young virgin to attend the king and take care of him. She can lie beside him so that our lord the king may keep warm."

3Then they searched throughout Israel for a beautiful girl and found Abishag, a Shunammite,[a] and brought her to the king. 4The girl was very beautiful; she took care of the king and waited on him, but the king had no intimate relations with her.

5Now Adonijah,[b] whose mother was Haggith, put himself forward and said, "I will be king." So he got chariots[c] and horses[a] ready, with fifty men to run ahead of him. 6(His father had never interfered[d] with him by asking, "Why do you behave as you do?" He was also very handsome and was born next after Absalom.)

7Adonijah conferred with Joab[e] son of Zeruiah and with Abiathar[f] the priest, and they gave him their support. 8But Zadok[g] the priest, Benaiah[h] son of Jehoiada, Nathan[i] the prophet, Shimei[j] and Rei[b] and David's special guard[k] did not join Adonijah.

9Adonijah then sacrificed sheep, cattle and fattened calves at the Stone of Zoheleth near En Rogel.[l] He invited all his brothers, the king's sons, and all the men of Judah who were royal officials, 10but he did not invite Nathan the prophet or Benaiah or the special guard or his brother Solomon.[m]

11Then Nathan asked Bathsheba,[n] Solomon's mother, "Have you not heard that Adonijah,[o] the son of Haggith, has become king without our lord David's knowing it? 12Now then, let me advise[p] you how you can save your own life and the life of your son Solomon. 13Go in to King David and say to him, 'My lord the king, did you not swear[q] to me your servant: "Surely Solomon your son shall be king after me, and he will sit on my throne"? Why then has Adonijah become king?' 14While you are still there talking to the king, I will come in and confirm what you have said."

15So Bathsheba went to see the aged king in his room, where Abishag[r] the Shunammite was attending him. 16Bathsheba bowed low and knelt before the king.

"What is it you want?" the king asked.

17She said to him, "My lord, you yourself swore[s] to me your servant by the LORD your God: 'Solomon your son shall be king after me, and he will sit on my throne.' 18But now Adonijah has become king, and you, my lord the king, do not know about it. 19He has sacrificed[t] great numbers of cattle, fattened calves, and sheep, and has invited all the king's sons, Abiathar the priest and Joab the commander of the army, but he has not invited Solomon your servant. 20My lord the king, the eyes of all Israel are on you, to learn from you who will sit on the throne of my lord the king after him. 21Otherwise, as soon as my lord the king is laid to rest[u] with his fathers, I and my son Solomon will be treated as criminals."

22While she was still speaking with the king, Nathan the prophet arrived. 23And they told the king, "Nathan the prophet is here." So he went before the king and bowed with his face to the ground.

24Nathan said, "Have you, my lord the king, declared that Adonijah shall be king after you, and that he will sit on your throne? 25Today he has gone down and sacrificed great numbers of cattle, fattened calves, and sheep. He has invited all the king's sons, the commanders of the army and Abiathar the priest. Right now they are eating and drinking with him and saying, 'Long live King Adonijah!' 26But me your servant, and Zadok the priest, and Benaiah son of Jehoiada, and your servant Solomon he did not invite.[v] 27Is this something my lord the king has done without letting his servants know who should sit on the throne of my lord the king after him?"

David Makes Solomon King

28Then King David said, "Call in Bathsheba." So she came into the king's presence and stood before him.

29The king then took an oath: "As surely as the LORD lives, who has delivered me out of every trouble,[w] 30I will surely carry out today what I swore[x] to you by the LORD, the God of Israel: Solomon your son shall be king after me, and he will sit on my throne in my place."

1:3 [a]Jos 19:18
1:5 [b]2Sa 3:4 [c]2Sa 15:1
1:6 [d]2Sa 3:3-4
1:7 [e]1Ki 2:22,28; 1Ch 11:6 [f]1Sa 22:20; 2Sa 20:25
1:8 [g]2Sa 20:25 [h]2Sa 8:18 [i]2Sa 12:1 [j]1Ki 4:18 [k]2Sa 23:8
1:9 [l]2Sa 17:17
1:10 [m]2Sa 12:24
1:11 [n]2Sa 12:24 [o]2Sa 3:4
1:12 [p]Pr 15:22
1:13 [q]ver 30; 1Ch 22:9-13
1:15 [r]ver 1
1:17 [s]ver 13,30
1:19 [t]ver 9
1:21 [u]Dt 31:16; 1Ki 2:10
1:26 [v]ver 8,10
1:29 [w]2Sa 4:9
1:30 [x]ver 13,17

[a] 5 Or *charioteers* [b] 8 Or *and his friends*

31Then Bathsheba bowed low with
her face to the ground and, kneeling before the king, said, "May my lord King
David live forever!"
32King David said, "Call in Zadok the
priest, Nathan the prophet and Benaiah
son of Jehoiada." When they came before the king, 33he said to them: "Take
your lord's servants with you and set
Solomon my son on my own mule[y] and
take him down to Gihon.[z] 34There have
Zadok the priest and Nathan the prophet anoint[a] him king over Israel. Blow the
trumpet[b] and shout, 'Long live King Solomon!' 35Then you are to go up with
him, and he is to come and sit on my
throne and reign in my place. I have appointed him ruler over Israel and Judah."
36Benaiah son of Jehoiada answered
the king, "Amen! May the LORD, the God
of my lord the king, so declare it. 37As
the LORD was with my lord the king, so
may he be with[c] Solomon to make his
throne even greater[d] than the throne of
my lord King David!"
38So Zadok[e] the priest, Nathan the
prophet, Benaiah son of Jehoiada, the
Kerethites[f] and the Pelethites went
down and put Solomon on King David's
mule and escorted him to Gihon.[g] 39Za-
dok the priest took the horn of oil[h] from
the sacred tent and anointed Solomon.
Then they sounded the trumpet and all
the people shouted,[i] "Long live King Solomon!" 40And all the people went up after him, playing flutes and rejoicing
greatly, so that the ground shook with
the sound.
41Adonijah and all the guests who
were with him heard it as they were finishing their feast. On hearing the sound
of the trumpet, Joab asked, "What's the
meaning of all the noise in the city?"
42Even as he was speaking, Jonathan[j]
son of Abiathar the priest arrived. Adonijah said, "Come in. A worthy man like
you must be bringing good news."[k]
43"Not at all!" Jonathan answered.
"Our lord King David has made Solomon king. 44The king has sent with him
Zadok the priest, Nathan the prophet,
Benaiah son of Jehoiada, the Kerethites
and the Pelethites, and they have put
him on the king's mule, 45and Zadok the
priest and Nathan the prophet have
anointed him king at Gihon. From there
they have gone up cheering, and the city

1:33 [y] 2Sa 20:6-7 [z] 2Ch 32:30; 33:14
1:34 [a] 1Sa 10:1; 16:3, 12; 1Ki 19:16; 2Ki 9:3,13 [b] ver 25; 2Sa 5:3; 15:10
1:37 [c] Jos 1:5,17; 1Sa 20:13 [d] ver 47
1:38 [e] ver 8 [f] 2Sa 8:18 [g] ver 33
1:39 [h] Ex 30:23-32; Ps 89:20 [i] ver 34; 1Sa 10:24
1:42 [j] 2Sa 15:27,36 [k] 2Sa 18:26

resounds[l] with it. That's the noise you
hear. 46Moreover, Solomon has taken his
seat on the royal throne. 47Also, the royal officials have come to congratulate
our lord King David, saying, 'May your
God make Solomon's name more famous than yours and his throne
greater[m] than yours!' And the king
bowed in worship on his bed 48and said,
'Praise be to the LORD, the God of Israel,
who has allowed my eyes to see a successor[n] on my throne today.'"
49At this, all Adonijah's guests rose in
alarm and dispersed. 50But Adonijah, in
fear of Solomon, went and took hold of
the horns[o] of the altar. 51Then Solomon
was told, "Adonijah is afraid of King Solomon and is clinging to the horns of the
altar. He says, 'Let King Solomon swear
to me today that he will not put his servant to death with the sword.'"
52Solomon replied, "If he shows himself to be a worthy man, not a hair[p] of his
head will fall to the ground; but if evil is
found in him, he will die." 53Then King
Solomon sent men, and they brought
him down from the altar. And Adonijah
came and bowed down to King Solomon,
and Solomon said, "Go to your home."

David's Charge to Solomon

2 When the time drew near for David to die,[q] he gave a charge to Solomon his son.
2"I am about to go the way of all the
earth,"[r] he said. "So be strong,[s] show
yourself a man, 3and observe[t] what the
LORD your God requires: Walk in his
ways, and keep his decrees and commands, his laws and requirements, as
written in the Law of Moses, so that you
may prosper[u] in all you do and wherever you go, 4and that the LORD may keep
his promise[v] to me: 'If your descendants
watch how they live, and if they walk
faithfully[w] before me with all their heart
and soul, you will never fail to have a
man on the throne of Israel.'
5"Now you yourself know what Joab[x]
son of Zeruiah did to me—what he did
to the two commanders of Israel's armies, Abner[y] son of Ner and Amasa[z] son
of Jether. He killed them, shedding their
blood in peacetime as if in battle, and
with that blood stained the belt around
his waist and the sandals on his feet.
6Deal with him according to your wis-

1:45 [l] ver 40
1:47 [m] ver 37; Ge 47:31
1:48 [n] 2Sa 7:12; 1Ki 3:6
1:50 [o] 1Ki 2:28
1:52 [p] 1Sa 14:45; 2Sa 14:11
2:1 [q] Ge 47:29; Dt 31:14
2:2 [r] Jos 23:14 [s] Dt 31:7,23; Jos 1:6
2:3 [t] Dt 17:14-20; Jos 1:7 [u] 1Ch 22:13
2:4 [v] 2Sa 7:13,25; 1Ki 8:25 [w] 2Ki 20:3; Ps 132:12
2:5 [x] 2Sa 2:18; 18:5, 12,14 [y] 2Sa 3:27 [z] 2Sa 20:10

2:6 a ver 9 dom,[a] but do not let his gray head go
down to the grave[a] in peace.
2:7 7"But show kindness to the sons of
b 2Sa 17:27; Barzillai[b] of Gilead and let them be
19:31-39 among those who eat at your table.[c]
c 2Sa 9:7 They stood by me when I fled from your
brother Absalom.
2:8 8"And remember, you have with you
d 2Sa 16:5-13 Shimei[d] son of Gera, the Benjamite from
e 2Sa 19:18-23 Bahurim, who called down bitter curses
on me the day I went to Mahanaim.
When he came down to meet me at the
Jordan, I swore[e] to him by the LORD: 'I
will not put you to death by the sword.'
9But now, do not consider him innocent.
2:9 f ver 6 You are a man of wisdom;[f] you will know
what to do to him. Bring his gray head
down to the grave in blood."
2:10 10Then David rested with his fathers
g Ac 2:29; 13:36
h 2Sa 5:7 and was buried[g] in the City of David.[h]
11He had reigned[i] forty years over Isra-
2:11 i 2Sa 5:4,5 el—seven years in Hebron and thirty-
three in Jerusalem. 12So Solomon sat on
2:12 j 1Ch 29:23 the throne[j] of his father David, and his
k 2Ch 1:1 rule was firmly established.[k]

Solomon's Throne Established

13Now Adonijah, the son of Haggith,
went to Bathsheba, Solomon's mother.
Bathsheba asked him, "Do you come
2:13 l 1Sa 16:4 peacefully?"[l]
He answered, "Yes, peacefully." 14Then
he added, "I have something to say to
you."
"You may say it," she replied.
15"As you know," he said, "the kingdom was mine. All Israel looked to me
as their king. But things changed, and
the kingdom has gone to my brother; for
it has come to him from the LORD. 16Now
I have one request to make of you. Do
not refuse me."
"You may make it," she said.
17So he continued, "Please ask King
Solomon—he will not refuse you—to
2:17 m 1Ki 1:3 give me Abishag[m] the Shunammite as
my wife."
18"Very well," Bathsheba replied, "I
will speak to the king for you."
19When Bathsheba went to King Solomon to speak to him for Adonijah, the
king stood up to meet her, bowed down
to her and sat down on his throne. He
had a throne brought for the king's
2:19 n 1Ki 15:13 mother,[n] and she sat down at his right
o Ps 45:9 hand.[o]

20"I have one small request to make of
you," she said. "Do not refuse me."
The king replied, "Make it, my mother; I will not refuse you."
21So she said, "Let Abishag[p] the Shu- 2:21
nammite be given in marriage to your p 1Ki 1:3
brother Adonijah."
22King Solomon answered his mother,
"Why do you request Abishag[q] the Shu- 2:22 q 2Sa 12:8;
nammite for Adonijah? You might as 1Ki 1:3 r 1Ch 3:2
well request the kingdom for him—after
all, he is my older brother[r]—yes, for him
and for Abiathar the priest and Joab son
of Zeruiah!"
23Then King Solomon swore by the
LORD: "May God deal with me, be it ever
so severely,[s] if Adonijah does not pay 2:23 s Ru 1:17
with his life for this request! 24And now,
as surely as the LORD lives—he who has
established me securely on the throne of
my father David and has founded a dy-
nasty for me as he promised[t]—Adonijah 2:24 t 2Sa 7:11;
shall be put to death today!" 25So King 1Ch 22:10
Solomon gave orders to Benaiah[u] son of 2:25
Jehoiada, and he struck down Adonijah u 2Sa 8:18
and he died.
26To Abiathar[v] the priest the king said, 2:26
"Go back to your fields in Anathoth.[w] v 1Sa 22:20
You deserve to die, but I will not put you w Jos 21:18
to death now, because you carried the x 2Sa 15:24
ark[x] of the Sovereign LORD before my fa- y 1Sa 23:6
ther David and shared all my father's
hardships."[y] 27So Solomon removed Abiathar from the priesthood of the LORD,
fulfilling[z] the word the LORD had spoken 2:27
at Shiloh about the house of Eli. z 1Sa 2:27-36
28When the news reached Joab, who
had conspired with Adonijah though
not with Absalom, he fled to the tent of
the LORD and took hold of the horns[a] of 2:28
the altar. 29King Solomon was told that a 1Ki 1:7,50
Joab had fled to the tent of the LORD and
was beside the altar. Then Solomon ordered Benaiah[b] son of Jehoiada, "Go, 2:29
strike him down!" b ver 25
30So Benaiah entered the tent of the
LORD and said to Joab, "The king says, 2:30
'Come out!'[c]" c Ex 21:14
But he answered, "No, I will die here."
Benaiah reported to the king, "This is
how Joab answered me."
31Then the king commanded Benaiah, "Do as he says. Strike him down and
bury him, and so clear me and my father's house of the guilt of the innocent 2:31
blood[d] that Joab shed. 32The LORD will d Nu 35:33;
Dt 19:13; 21:8-9

[a] 6 Hebrew *Sheol*; also in verse 9

repay[e] him for the blood he shed,[f] because without the knowledge of my father David he attacked two men and killed them with the sword. Both of them—Abner son of Ner, commander of Israel's army, and Amasa[g] son of Jether, commander of Judah's army—were better[h] men and more upright than he. 33May the guilt of their blood rest on the head of Joab and his descendants forever. But on David and his descendants, his house and his throne, may there be the LORD's peace forever."

34So Benaiah son of Jehoiada went up and struck down Joab and killed him, and he was buried on his own land[a] in the desert. 35The king put Benaiah[i] son of Jehoiada over the army in Joab's position and replaced Abiathar with Zadok[j] the priest.

36Then the king sent for Shimei[k] and said to him, "Build yourself a house in Jerusalem and live there, but do not go anywhere else. 37The day you leave and cross the Kidron Valley,[l] you can be sure you will die; your blood will be on your own head."[m]

38Shimei answered the king, "What you say is good. Your servant will do as my lord the king has said." And Shimei stayed in Jerusalem for a long time.

39But three years later, two of Shimei's slaves ran off to Achish[n] son of Maacah, king of Gath, and Shimei was told, "Your slaves are in Gath." 40At this, he saddled his donkey and went to Achish at Gath in search of his slaves. So Shimei went away and brought the slaves back from Gath.

41When Solomon was told that Shimei had gone from Jerusalem to Gath and had returned, 42the king summoned Shimei and said to him, "Did I not make you swear by the LORD and warn you, 'On the day you leave to go anywhere else, you can be sure you will die'? At that time you said to me, 'What you say is good. I will obey.' 43Why then did you not keep your oath to the LORD and obey the command I gave you?"

44The king also said to Shimei, "You know in your heart all the wrong[o] you did to my father David. Now the LORD will repay you for your wrongdoing. 45But King Solomon will be blessed, and David's throne will remain secure[p] before the LORD forever."

46Then the king gave the order to Benaiah son of Jehoiada, and he went out and struck Shimei down and killed him.

The kingdom was now firmly established[q] in Solomon's hands.

2:32 [e] Jdg 9:57; Ps 7:16 [f] Jdg 9:24 [g] 2Sa 3:27; 20:10 [h] 2Ch 21:13
2:35 [i] 1Ki 4:4 [j] ver 27; 1Ch 29:22
2:36 [k] ver 8; 2Sa 16:5
2:37 [l] 2Sa 15:23 [m] Lev 20:9; Jos 2:19; 2Sa 1:16
2:39 [n] 1Sa 27:2
2:44 [o] 1Sa 25:39; 2Sa 16:5-13; Eze 17:19
2:45 [p] 2Sa 7:13; Pr 25:5
2:46 [q] ver 12; 2Ch 1:1

Solomon Asks for Wisdom

3 Solomon made an alliance with Pharaoh king of Egypt and married[r] his daughter.[s] He brought her to the City of David[t] until he finished building his palace[u] and the temple of the LORD, and the wall around Jerusalem. 2The people, however, were still sacrificing at the high places,[v] because a temple had not yet been built for the Name of the LORD. 3Solomon showed his love[w] for the LORD by walking according to the statutes[x] of his father David, except that he offered sacrifices and burned incense on the high places.

4The king went to Gibeon[y] to offer sacrifices, for that was the most important high place, and Solomon offered a thousand burnt offerings on that altar. 5At Gibeon the LORD appeared[z] to Solomon during the night in a dream,[a] and God said, "Ask for whatever you want me to give you."

6Solomon answered, "You have shown great kindness to your servant, my father David, because he was faithful[b] to you and righteous and upright in heart. You have continued this great kindness to him and have given him a son[c] to sit on his throne this very day.

7"Now, O LORD my God, you have made your servant king in place of my father David. But I am only a little child[d] and do not know how to carry out my duties. 8Your servant is here among the people you have chosen,[e] a great people, too numerous to count or number.[f] 9So give your servant a discerning[g] heart to govern your people and to distinguish[h] between right and wrong. For who is able[i] to govern this great people of yours?"

10The Lord was pleased that Solomon had asked for this. 11So God said to him, "Since you have asked[j] for this and not for long life or wealth for yourself, nor have asked for the death of your enemies but for discernment in administering justice, 12I will do what you have asked.[k] I will give you a wise[l] and discerning heart, so that there will never have been

3:1 [r] 1Ki 7:8 [s] 1Ki 9:24 [t] 2Sa 5:7 [u] 1Ki 7:1; 9:15, 19
3:2 [v] Lev 17:3-5; Dt 12:2,4-5; 1Ki 22:43
3:3 [w] Dt 6:5; Ps 31:23; 1Co 8:3 [x] 1Ki 2:3; 9:4; 11:4,6,38
3:4 [y] 1Ch 16:39
3:5 [z] 1Ki 9:2 [a] Nu 12:6; Mt 1:20
3:6 [b] 1Ki 2:4; 9:4 [c] 1Ki 1:48
3:7 [d] Nu 27:17; 1Ch 29:1
3:8 [e] Dt 7:6 [f] Ge 15:5
3:9 [g] 2Sa 14:17; Jas 1:5 [h] Pr 2:3-9; Heb 5:14 [i] Ps 72:1-2
3:11 [j] Jas 4:3
3:12 [k] 1Jn 5:14-15 [l] 1Ki 4:29,30,31; 5:12; 10:23; Ecc 1:16

[a] 34 Or *buried in his tomb*

DISCOVERY 81

More Profitable Than Silver

Sometimes we dream about what it would be like to win the lottery. What would we do with a sudden windfall of millions of dollars? Build a dream house ... purchase the ultimate sports car ... give the money away ... move to another location ... quit our job ... or maybe all of the above? We dream, but most of us will never experience firsthand such an abrupt change in status.

But King Solomon was given that chance. In a sense he won God's "lottery" when God invited him to "ask for whatever you want me to give you" (1 Kings 3:5). What an opportunity! God made this unlimited offer—*God*, who owns *everything* in the entire universe.

In light of the possibilities Solomon's request was remarkable: "Give your servant a discerning heart to govern your people and to distinguish between right and wrong" (verse 9). He could have had anything at all, yet Solomon asked for wisdom. And God was delighted to give it to him—along with the honor and riches Solomon had not requested. God also offered Solomon a long life, provided he would take God's words seriously (verse 14).

Wisdom is essentially the insight we need to live life the way God intended. It implies doing what is *right*, not just what is comfortable or pleasant. Solomon would later write about the wisdom God had granted him: "Blessed is the man who finds wisdom, the man who gains understanding, for she is more profitable than silver and yields better returns than gold (Proverbs 3:13–14). Solomon possessed both understanding and riches, and he knew which was the more valuable overall.

There is more to life than that which is temporary. Trusting God's Word and living for him are the wisest courses of action anyone can take. These commitments are more important than money, power, prestige, even a long life. In the New Testament Paul took up the same theme when he reminded us that God's wisdom is primary—and that Jesus is the embodiment of that wisdom (1 Corinthians 1:30).

God's wisdom was Solomon's first priority, and the same must be true for us. Having Jesus in our lives—knowing that he died for our sins and is present to help us live life as he intends it to be lived—is better than anything else we can imagine. Paul expressed this with exuberance in Ephesians 1:3: "Praise be to the God and Father of our Lord Jesus Christ, who has blessed us in the heavenly realms with every spiritual blessing in Christ."

***Self-Discovery:** How do you judge the priorities in your life? Where on your scale would the priorities of wisdom and faith in Jesus fall?*

GO TO DISCOVERY 82 ON PAGE 427

anyone like you, nor will there ever be. 13 Moreover, I will give you what you have not[m] asked for—both riches and honor[n]—so that in your lifetime you will have no equal[o] among kings. 14 And if you walk[p] in my ways and obey my statutes and commands as David your father did, I will give you a long life."[q] 15 Then Solomon awoke[r]—and he realized it had been a dream.

He returned to Jerusalem, stood before the ark of the Lord's covenant and sacrificed burnt offerings[s] and fellowship offerings.[a][t] Then he gave a feast[u] for all his court.

3:13 [m] Mt 6:33; Eph 3:20 [n] 1Ki 4:21-24; Pr 3:1-2,16 [o] 1Ki 10:23
3:14 [p] ver 6; Pr 3:1-2, 16 [q] Ps 61:6; 91:16
3:15 [r] Ge 41:7 [s] 1Ki 8:65 [t] Mk 6:21 [u] Est 1:3,9; Da 5:1

A Wise Ruling

16 Now two prostitutes came to the king and stood before him. 17 One of them said, "My lord, this woman and I live in the same house. I had a baby while she was there with me. 18 The third day after my child was born, this woman also had a baby. We were alone; there was no one in the house but the two of us.

19 "During the night this woman's son died because she lay on him. 20 So she got up in the middle of the night and took my son from my side while I your servant was asleep. She put him by her breast and put her dead son by my breast. 21 The next morning, I got up to nurse my son—and he was dead! But when I looked at him closely in the morning light, I saw that it wasn't the son I had borne."

22 The other woman said, "No! The living one is my son; the dead one is yours."

But the first one insisted, "No! The dead one is yours; the living one is mine." And so they argued before the king.

23 The king said, "This one says, 'My son is alive and your son is dead,' while that one says, 'No! Your son is dead and mine is alive.' "

24 Then the king said, "Bring me a sword." So they brought a sword for the king. 25 He then gave an order: "Cut the living child in two and give half to one and half to the other."

26 The woman whose son was alive was filled with compassion[v] for her son and said to the king, "Please, my lord, give her the living baby! Don't kill him!"

But the other said, "Neither I nor you shall have him. Cut him in two!"

27 Then the king gave his ruling: "Give the living baby to the first woman. Do not kill him; she is his mother."

28 When all Israel heard the verdict the king had given, they held the king in awe, because they saw that he had wisdom[w] from God to administer justice.

3:26 [v] Ge 43:30; Isa 49:15; Jer 31:20; Hos 11:8
3:28 [w] ver 9,11-12; Col 2:3

Solomon's Officials and Governors

4 So King Solomon ruled over all Israel. 2 And these were his chief officials:

Azariah[x] son of Zadok—the priest;
3 Elihoreph and Ahijah, sons of Shisha—secretaries;
Jehoshaphat[y] son of Ahilud—recorder;
4 Benaiah[z] son of Jehoiada—commander in chief;
Zadok[a] and Abiathar—priests;
5 Azariah son of Nathan—in charge of the district officers;
Zabud son of Nathan—a priest and personal adviser to the king;
6 Ahishar—in charge of the palace;
Adoniram son of Abda—in charge of forced labor.

7 Solomon also had twelve district governors over all Israel, who supplied provisions for the king and the royal household. Each one had to provide

4:2 [x] 1Ch 6:10
4:3 [y] 2Sa 8:16
4:4 [z] 1Ki 2:35 [a] 1Ki 2:27

[a] 15 Traditionally *peace offerings*

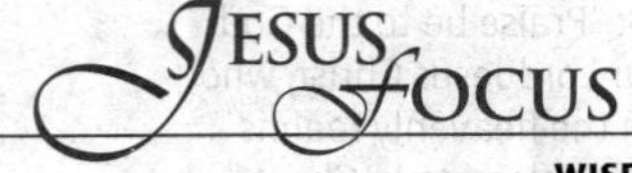

WISDOM FROM GOD

Solomon asked God for the wisdom he would need to rule Israel, and God honored his request (1 Kings 3:2–15), promising to give him "a wise and discerning heart" (verse 12). God also promised that Solomon's wealth and greatness would exceed that of any other king in the world. Eventually Solomon's empire stretched from Egypt to Babylonia. He ruled in peace and prosperity for 40 years and is said to have been wiser than any of the Egyptians or Babylonians ("men of the East", 1 Kings 4:30). Solomon is credited with 3,000 proverbs and 1,005 songs (1 Kings 4:32). In the book of Proverbs Solomon explained the nature of true wisdom: essentially, "God letting us know his mind" (see Proverbs 2:5–11; 3:5–6). That is exactly the quality that sets Jesus apart from other men: As God himself, the Son knows the mind and heart of the Father (see John 7:16–18; 14:9–14,23–24).

supplies for one month in the year.
8 These are their names:

4:8 [b] Jos 24:33

Ben-Hur—in the hill country[b] of
Ephraim;

4:9 [c] Jdg 1:35 [d] Jos 21:16

9 Ben-Deker—in Makaz, Shaalbim,[c]
Beth Shemesh[d] and Elon Beth-
hanan;

4:10 [e] Jos 15:35 [f] Jos 12:17

10 Ben-Hesed—in Arubboth (Socoh[e]
and all the land of Hepher[f] were
his);

4:11 [g] Jos 11:2

11 Ben-Abinadab—in Naphoth Dor[a][g]
(he was married to Taphath
daughter of Solomon);

4:12 [h] Jos 17:11; Jdg 5:19 [i] Jos 3:16 [j] 1Ki 19:16 [k] 1Ch 6:68

12 Baana son of Ahilud—in Taanach
and Megiddo, and in all of Beth
Shan[h] next to Zarethan[i] below
Jezreel, from Beth Shan to Abel
Meholah[j] across to Jokmeam;[k]

4:13 [l] Nu 32:41 [m] Dt 3:4

13 Ben-Geber—in Ramoth Gilead
(the settlements of Jair[l] son of
Manasseh in Gilead were his, as
well as the district of Argob in
Bashan and its sixty large walled
cities[m] with bronze gate bars);

4:14 [n] Jos 13:26

14 Ahinadab son of Iddo—in Mahanaim;[n]

4:15 [o] 2Sa 15:27

15 Ahimaaz[o]—in Naphtali (he had
married Basemath daughter of
Solomon);

4:16 [p] 2Sa 15:32

16 Baana son of Hushai[p]—in Asher
and in Aloth;
17 Jehoshaphat son of Paruah—in Issachar;

4:18 [q] 1Ki 1:8

18 Shimei[q] son of Ela—in Benjamin;
19 Geber son of Uri—in Gilead (the
country of Sihon king of the Am-

4:19 [r] Dt 3:8-10

orites and the country of Og[r]
king of Bashan). He was the only
governor over the district.

Solomon's Daily Provisions

4:20 [s] Ge 22:17; 32:12; 1Ki 3:8

20 The people of Judah and Israel were
as numerous as the sand[s] on the seashore; they ate, they drank and they were

4:21 [t] 2Ch 9:26; Ps 72:11 [u] Jos 1:4; Ps 72:8 [v] Ge 15:18 [w] Ps 68:29

happy. 21 And Solomon ruled[t] over all the
kingdoms from the River[b][u] to the land of
the Philistines, as far as the border of
Egypt.[v] These countries brought tribute[w]
and were Solomon's subjects all his life.
22 Solomon's daily provisions were
thirty cors[c] of fine flour and sixty cors[d]
of meal, 23 ten head of stall-fed cattle,
twenty of pasture-fed cattle and a hundred sheep and goats, as well as deer, gazelles, roebucks and choice fowl. 24 For

4:24 [x] Ps 72:11

he ruled over all the kingdoms west of
the River, from Tiphsah[x] to Gaza, and

4:24 [y] 1Ch 22:9

had peace[y] on all sides. 25 During Solomon's lifetime Judah and Israel, from

4:25 [z] Jdg 20:1 [a] Jer 23:6 [b] Mic 4:4; Zec 3:10

Dan to Beersheba,[z] lived in safety,[a] each
man under his own vine and fig tree.[b]
26 Solomon had four[e] thousand stalls
for chariot horses,[c] and twelve thousand
horses.[f]

4:26 [c] 1Ki 10:26; 2Ch 1:14

27 The district officers,[d] each in his
month, supplied provisions for King Sol-

4:27 [d] ver 7

omon and all who came to the king's
table. They saw to it that nothing was
lacking. 28 They also brought to the proper place their quotas of barley and straw
for the chariot horses and the other
horses.

> **NO ONE ELSE—NOT KING, DICTATOR, SCIENTIST, EDUCATOR, OR MILITARY LEADER—HAS MADE A GREATER CONTRIBUTION TO WORLD HISTORY THAN JESUS HAS.**
>
> Tim LaHaye, *Christian Author*

Solomon's Wisdom

29 God gave Solomon wisdom[e] and

4:29 [e] 1Ki 3:12

very great insight, and a breadth of understanding as measureless as the sand
on the seashore. 30 Solomon's wisdom
was greater than the wisdom of all the
men of the East,[f] and greater than all

4:30 [f] Ge 25:6 [g] Ac 7:22

the wisdom of Egypt.[g] 31 He was wiser[h]
than any other man, including Ethan

4:31 [h] 1Ki 3:12; 1Ch 2:6; 6:33; 15:19; Ps 89 Title

the Ezrahite—wiser than Heman, Calcol and Darda, the sons of Mahol. And
his fame spread to all the surrounding
nations. 32 He spoke three thousand

4:32 [i] Pr 1:1; Ecc 12:9 [j] SS 1:1

proverbs[i] and his songs[j] numbered a
thousand and five. 33 He described plant
life, from the cedar of Lebanon to the
hyssop that grows out of walls. He also
taught about animals and birds, reptiles
and fish. 34 Men of all nations came to

4:34 [k] 1Ki 10:1; 2Ch 9:23

listen to Solomon's wisdom, sent by all
the kings[k] of the world, who had heard
of his wisdom.

Preparations for Building the Temple

5:1 [l] ver 10,18; 2Sa 5:11; 1Ch 14:1

5 When Hiram[l] king of Tyre heard
that Solomon had been anointed

[a] *11* Or *in the heights of Dor* [b] *21* That is, the Euphrates; also in verse 24 [c] *22* That is, probably about 185 bushels (about 6.6 kiloliters) [d] *22* That is, probably about 375 bushels (about 13.2 kiloliters) [e] *26* Some Septuagint manuscripts (see also 2 Chron. 9:25); Hebrew *forty* [f] *26* Or *charioteers*

king to succeed his father David, he sent
his envoys to Solomon, because he had
always been on friendly terms with David. [2]Solomon sent back this message to
Hiram:

5:3 [3]"You know that because of the
m 1Ch 22:8; 28:3 wars[m] waged against my father David from all sides, he could not
build a temple for the Name of the
LORD his God until the LORD put his
enemies under his feet. [4]But now
5:4 the LORD my God has given me
n 1Ki 4:24; rest[n] on every side, and there is no
1Ch 22:9 adversary or disaster. [5]I intend,
5:5 therefore, to build a temple[o] for the
o 1Ch 17:12 Name of the LORD my God, as the
p 2Sa 7:13; LORD told my father David, when he
1Ch 22:10 said, 'Your son whom I will put on
the throne in your place will build
the temple for my Name.'[p]

[6]"So give orders that cedars of
Lebanon be cut for me. My men
will work with yours, and I will pay
you for your men whatever wages
you set. You know that we have no
one so skilled in felling timber as
the Sidonians."

[7]When Hiram heard Solomon's message, he was greatly pleased and said,
"Praise be to the LORD today, for he has
given David a wise son to rule over this
great nation."

[8]So Hiram sent word to Solomon:

"I have received the message you
sent me and will do all you want in
providing the cedar and pine logs.
5:9 [9]My men will haul them down from
q Ezr 3:7 Lebanon to the sea[q], and I will float
r Eze 27:17; Ac 12:20 them in rafts by sea to the place you
specify. There I will separate them
and you can take them away. And
you are to grant my wish by providing food[r] for my royal household."

[10]In this way Hiram kept Solomon
supplied with all the cedar and pine logs
he wanted, [11]and Solomon gave Hiram
twenty thousand cors[a] of wheat as food
for his household, in addition to twenty
thousand baths[b,c] of pressed olive oil.
Solomon continued to do this for Hiram
5:12 year after year. [12]The LORD gave Solomon
s 1Ki 3:12 wisdom,[s] just as he had promised him.
t Am 1:9 There were peaceful relations between
Hiram and Solomon, and the two of
them made a treaty.[t]

[13]King Solomon conscripted labor- 5:13
ers[u] from all Israel—thirty thousand u 1Ki 9:15
men. [14]He sent them off to Lebanon in
shifts of ten thousand a month, so that
they spent one month in Lebanon and 5:14
two months at home. Adoniram[v] was in v 1Ki 4:6;
charge of the forced labor. [15]Solomon 2Ch 10:18
had seventy thousand carriers and
eighty thousand stonecutters in the
hills, [16]as well as thirty-three hundred[d] 5:16
foremen[w] who supervised the project w 1Ki 9:23
and directed the workmen. [17]At the
king's command they removed from the
quarry[x] large blocks of quality stone[y] to 5:17 x 1Ki 6:7
provide a foundation of dressed stone y 1Ch 22:2
for the temple. [18]The craftsmen of Solo- 5:18
mon and Hiram and the men of Gebal[e] [z] z Jos 13:5
cut and prepared the timber and stone
for the building of the temple.

Solomon Builds the Temple

6 In the four hundred and eightieth[f]
year after the Israelites had come
out of Egypt, in the fourth year of Solomon's reign over Israel, in the month of
Ziv, the second month, he began to 6:1
build the temple of the LORD.[a] a Ac 7:47

[2]The temple[b] that King Solomon built 6:2
for the LORD was sixty cubits long, twen- b Eze 41:1
ty wide and thirty high.[g] [3]The portico at
the front of the main hall of the temple
extended the width of the temple, that is
twenty cubits,[h] and projected ten cubits[i]
from the front of the temple. [4]He made 6:4
narrow clerestory windows[c] in the tem- c Eze 40:16;
ple. [5]Against the walls of the main hall 41:16
and inner sanctuary he built a structure
around the building, in which there were 6:5
side rooms.[d] [6]The lowest floor was five d ver 16,19-21;
cubits[j] wide, the middle floor six cubits[k] Eze 41:5-6
and the third floor seven.[l] He made off-
set ledges around the outside of the
temple so that nothing would be inserted into the temple walls.

[7]In building the temple, only blocks

[a] *11* That is, probably about 125,000 bushels (about 4,400 kiloliters) [b] *11* Septuagint (see also 2 Chron. 2:10); Hebrew *twenty cors* [c] *11* That is, about 115,000 gallons (about 440 kiloliters)
[d] *16* Hebrew; some Septuagint manuscripts (see also 2 Chron. 2:2,18) *thirty-six hundred*
[e] *18* That is, Byblos [f] *1* Hebrew; Septuagint *four hundred and fortieth* [g] *2* That is, about 90 feet (about 27 meters) long and 30 feet (about 9 meters) wide and 45 feet (about 13.5 meters) high
[h] *3* That is, about 30 feet (about 9 meters)
[i] *3* That is, about 15 feet (about 4.5 meters)
[j] *6* That is, about 7 1/2 feet (about 2.3 meters); also in verses 10 and 24 [k] *6* That is, about 9 feet (about 2.7 meters) [l] *6* That is, about 10 1/2 feet (about 3.1 meters)

DISCOVERY 82

GOD AMONG US

The temple that Solomon built was patterned after the tabernacle. It had three major sections: the outer courtyard, the Holy Place and the Most Holy Place (Exodus 26:15–30; 36:20–34). The temple was built next to the king's palace and served as Israel's center of worship. God told Solomon, "I have consecrated this temple . . . by putting my Name there forever" (1 Kings 9:3). The temple became the place where the God of Israel "lived."

God vowed to keep the promises he had made to David. He covenanted with his people that he would be with them and continue to live among them as long as they would remain devoted to him (1 Kings 6:11–13). His promise to be with them was conditional, however, beginning with the word *if*. God's presence is always associated with our obedience. If we are walking with him, he is near; when we turn and go our own way, he distances himself (Isaiah 59:1–2).

The building and dedication of the temple constituted one of the most important events in Jewish history. After the ark of the covenant had been brought to the temple and placed in the Holy Place, "the cloud filled the temple of the LORD. And the priests could not perform their service because of the cloud, for the glory of the LORD filled his temple" (1 Kings 8:10–11). God came down and lived among the Israelites. Long before, after Adam and Eve had first sinned, God had gone looking for them in the garden and talked to them. Later, his glory filled first the tabernacle (Exodus 40:34–35) and then the temple, letting the people know that he was still with them.

The ultimate proof that God wants to be present with his people is his Son. Jesus, the Word of God, was born as a human and lived among us (John 1:14). Even when it was time for God the Son to return to heaven, he assured his disciples that he was not abandoning them and soon afterward sent his Holy Spirit to take up residence in the heart of every believer (John 14:15–17). Even today we are God's "temple" (both collectively, as his church, and individually) because of the Holy Spirit living in us. The apostle Paul expressed it this way: "We are the temple of the living God. As God has said, 'I will live with them and walk among them, and I will be their God, and they will be my people' . . . Since we have these promises, dear friends, let us purify ourselves from everything that contaminates body and spirit, perfecting holiness out of reverence for God" (2 Corinthians 6:16; 7:1).

And when God lives within and among his people we are not abandoned.

Self-Discovery: *Try to describe what it is like to have God's Holy Spirit living in your heart. Can you envision a particular symbol that helps you to focus in on this marvelous reality? In what ways might this knowledge change the way you live your life?*

GO TO DISCOVERY 83 ON PAGE 432

dressed[e] at the quarry were used, and no hammer, chisel or any other iron tool[f] was heard at the temple site while it was being built.

8 The entrance to the lowest[a] floor was on the south side of the temple; a stairway led up to the middle level and from there to the third. 9 So he built the temple and completed it, roofing it with beams and cedar[g] planks. 10 And he built the side rooms all along the temple. The height of each was five cubits, and they were attached to the temple by beams of cedar.

11 The word of the LORD came to Solomon: 12 "As for this temple you are building, if you follow my decrees, carry out my regulations and keep all my commands and obey them, I will fulfill through you the promise[h] I gave to David your father. 13 And I will live among the Israelites and will not abandon[i] my people Israel."

14 So Solomon built the temple and completed[j] it. 15 He lined its interior walls with cedar boards, paneling them from the floor of the temple to the ceiling,[k] and covered the floor of the temple with planks of pine. 16 He partitioned off twenty cubits[b] at the rear of the temple with cedar boards from floor to ceiling to form within the temple an inner sanctuary, the Most Holy Place.[l] 17 The main hall in front of this room was forty cubits[c] long. 18 The inside of the temple was cedar,[m] carved with gourds and open flowers. Everything was cedar; no stone was to be seen.

19 He prepared the inner sanctuary[n] within the temple to set the ark of the covenant[o] of the LORD there. 20 The inner sanctuary[p] was twenty cubits long, twenty wide and twenty high.[d] He overlaid the inside with pure gold, and he also overlaid the altar of cedar. 21 Solomon covered the inside of the temple with pure gold, and he extended gold chains across the front of the inner sanctuary, which was overlaid with gold. 22 So he overlaid the whole interior with gold. He also overlaid with gold the altar that belonged to the inner sanctuary.

23 In the inner sanctuary he made a pair of cherubim[q] of olive wood, each ten cubits[e] high. 24 One wing of the first cherub was five cubits long, and the other wing five cubits—ten cubits from wing tip to wing tip. 25 The second cherub also measured ten cubits, for the two cherubim were identical in size and shape. 26 The height of each cherub was ten cubits. 27 He placed the cherubim[r] inside the innermost room of the temple, with their wings spread out. The wing of one cherub touched one wall, while the wing of the other touched the other wall, and their wings touched each other in the middle of the room. 28 He overlaid the cherubim with gold.

29 On the walls all around the temple, in both the inner and outer rooms, he carved cherubim,[s] palm trees and open flowers. 30 He also covered the floors of both the inner and outer rooms of the temple with gold.

31 For the entrance of the inner sanctuary he made doors of olive wood with five-sided jambs. 32 And on the two olive wood doors he carved cherubim, palm trees and open flowers, and overlaid the cherubim and palm trees with beaten gold. 33 In the same way he made four-sided jambs of olive wood for the entrance to the main hall. 34 He also made two pine doors, each having two leaves that turned in sockets. 35 He carved cherubim, palm trees and open flowers on them and overlaid them with gold hammered evenly over the carvings.

36 And he built the inner courtyard of three courses[t] of dressed stone and one course of trimmed cedar beams.

37 The foundation of the temple of the LORD was laid in the fourth year, in the month of Ziv. 38 In the eleventh year in the month of Bul, the eighth month, the temple was finished in all its details according to its specifications.[u] He had spent seven years building it.

Solomon Builds His Palace

7 It took Solomon thirteen years, however, to complete the construction of his palace.[v] 2 He built the Palace[w] of the Forest of Lebanon[x] a hundred cubits long, fifty wide and thirty high,[f] with four rows of cedar columns supporting trimmed cedar beams. 3 It

6:7 [e] Ex 20:25 [f] Dt 27:5
6:9 [g] ver 14,38
6:12 [h] 2Sa 7:12-16; 1Ki 2:4; 9:5
6:13 [i] Ex 25:8; Lev 26:11; Dt 31:6; Heb 13:5
6:14 [j] ver 9,38
6:15 [k] 1Ki 7:7
6:16 [l] Ex 26:33; Lev 16:2; 1Ki 8:6
6:18 [m] 1Ki 7:24; Ps 74:6
6:19 [n] 1Ki 8:6 [o] 1Sa 3:3
6:20 [p] Eze 41:3-4
6:23 [q] Ex 37:1-9
6:27 [r] Ex 25:20; 37:9; 1Ki 8:7; 2Ch 5:8
6:29 [s] ver 32,35
6:36 [t] 1Ki 7:12; Ezr 6:4
6:38 [u] Heb 8:5
7:1 [v] 1Ki 9:10; 2Ch 8:1
7:2 [w] 2Sa 7:2 [x] 1Ki 10:17; 2Ch 9:16

[a] *8* Septuagint; Hebrew *middle*
[b] *16* That is, about 30 feet (about 9 meters)
[c] *17* That is, about 60 feet (about 18 meters)
[d] *20* That is, about 30 feet (about 9 meters) long, wide and high
[e] *23* That is, about 15 feet (about 4.5 meters)
[f] *2* That is, about 150 feet (about 46 meters) long, 75 feet (about 23 meters) wide and 45 feet (about 13.5 meters) high

was roofed with cedar above the beams
that rested on the columns—forty-five
beams, fifteen to a row. 4 Its windows
were placed high in sets of three, facing
each other. 5 All the doorways had rec-
tangular frames; they were in the front
part in sets of three, facing each other.[a]
6 He made a colonnade fifty cubits
long and thirty wide.[b] In front of it was
a portico, and in front of that were pillars and an overhanging roof.
7:7 7 He built the throne hall, the Hall of
[y] Ps 122:5; Pr 20:8 Justice, where he was to judge,[y] and he
[z] 1Ki 6:15 covered it with cedar from floor to ceiling.[c z] 8 And the palace in which he was
to live, set farther back, was similar in
design. Solomon also made a palace like
7:8 this hall for Pharaoh's daughter, whom
[a] 1Ki 3:1; 2Ch 8:11 he had married.[a]
9 All these structures, from the outside
to the great courtyard and from foundation to eaves, were made of blocks of
high-grade stone cut to size and
trimmed with a saw on their inner and
outer faces. 10 The foundations were laid
with large stones of good quality, some
measuring ten cubits[d] and some eight.[e]
11 Above were high-grade stones, cut to
size, and cedar beams. 12 The great
courtyard was surrounded by a wall of
7:12 [b] 1Ki 6:36 three courses[b] of dressed stone and one
course of trimmed cedar beams, as was
the inner courtyard of the temple of the
LORD with its portico.

The Temple's Furnishings

13 King Solomon sent to Tyre and
7:13 [c] 2Ch 2:13 brought Huram,[f c] 14 whose mother was a
widow from the tribe of Naphtali and
whose father was a man of Tyre and a
craftsman in bronze. Huram was highly
7:14 [d] Ex 31:2-5; 35:31; 36:1; 2Ch 2:14 skilled[d] and experienced in all kinds of
bronze work. He came to King Solomon
[e] 2Ch 4:11,16 and did all[e] the work assigned to him.
15 He cast two bronze pillars,[f] each
7:15 [f] 2Ki 25:17; 2Ch 3:15; 4:12; 52:17,21 eighteen cubits high and twelve cubits
around,[g] by line. 16 He also made two cap-
itals[g] of cast bronze to set on the tops of
7:16 [g] 2Ki 25:17 the pillars; each capital was five cubits[h]
high. 17 A network of interwoven chains
festooned the capitals on top of the pillars, seven for each capital. 18 He made
pomegranates in two rows[i] encircling
each network to decorate the capitals on
top of the pillars.[j] He did the same for
each capital. 19 The capitals on top of the
pillars in the portico were in the shape of
lilies, four cubits[k] high. 20 On the capitals
of both pillars, above the bowl-shaped
part next to the network, were the two
hundred pomegranates[h] in rows all 7:20 [h] 2Ch 3:16; 4:13; Jer 52:23
around. 21 He erected the pillars at the
portico of the temple. The pillar to the
south he named Jakin[l] and the one to the
north Boaz.[m i] 22 The capitals on top were 7:21 [i] 1Ki 6:3; 2Ch 3:17
in the shape of lilies. And so the work on
the pillars was completed.
23 He made the Sea[j] of cast metal, cir- 7:23 [j] 2Ki 25:13; 1Ch 18:8; Jer 52:17
cular in shape, measuring ten cubits[d]
from rim to rim and five cubits high. It
took a line of thirty cubits[n] to measure
around it. 24 Below the rim, gourds encircled it—ten to a cubit. The gourds were
cast in two rows in one piece with the
Sea.
25 The Sea stood on twelve bulls,[k] three 7:25 [k] 2Ch 4:4-5; Jer 52:20
facing north, three facing west, three fac-
ing south and three facing east. The Sea
rested on top of them, and their hindquarters were toward the center. 26 It was
a handbreadth[o] in thickness, and its rim
was like the rim of a cup, like a lily blossom. It held two thousand baths.[p]
27 He also made ten movable stands[l] 7:27 [l] ver 38; 2Ch 4:14
of bronze; each was four cubits long,
four wide and three high.[q] 28 This is how
the stands were made: They had side
panels attached to uprights. 29 On the
panels between the uprights were lions,
bulls and cherubim—and on the uprights as well. Above and below the lions
and bulls were wreaths of hammered
work. 30 Each stand[m] had four bronze 7:30 [m] 2Ki 16:17
wheels with bronze axles, and each had
a basin resting on four supports, cast

[a] *5* The meaning of the Hebrew for this verse is uncertain. [b] *6* That is, about 75 feet (about 23 meters) long and 45 feet (about 13.5 meters) wide [c] *7* Vulgate and Syriac; Hebrew *floor* [d] *10,23* That is, about 15 feet (about 4.5 meters) [e] *10* That is, about 12 feet (about 3.6 meters) [f] *13* Hebrew *Hiram,* a variant of *Huram;* also in verses 40 and 45 [g] *15* That is, about 27 feet (about 8.1 meters) high and 18 feet (about 5.4 meters) around [h] *16* That is, about 7 1/2 feet (about 2.3 meters); also in verse 23 [i] *18* Two Hebrew manuscripts and Septuagint; most Hebrew manuscripts *made the pillars, and there were two rows* [j] *18* Many Hebrew manuscripts and Syriac; most Hebrew manuscripts *pomegranates* [k] *19* That is, about 6 feet (about 1.8 meters); also in verse 38 [l] *21* *Jakin* probably means *he establishes.* [m] *21* *Boaz* probably means *in him is strength.* [n] *23* That is, about 45 feet (about 13.5 meters) [o] *26* That is, about 3 inches (about 8 centimeters) [p] *26* That is, probably about 11,500 gallons (about 44 kiloliters); the Septuagint does not have this sentence. [q] *27* That is, about 6 feet (about 1.8 meters) long and wide and about 4 1/2 feet (about 1.3 meters) high

with wreaths on each side. 31On the inside of the stand there was an opening
that had a circular frame one cubit[a]
deep. This opening was round, and with
its basework it measured a cubit and a
half.[b] Around its opening there was engraving. The panels of the stands were
square, not round. 32The four wheels
were under the panels, and the axles of
the wheels were attached to the stand.
The diameter of each wheel was a cubit
and a half. 33The wheels were made like
chariot wheels; the axles, rims, spokes
and hubs were all of cast metal.
34Each stand had four handles, one on
each corner, projecting from the stand.
35At the top of the stand there was a circular band half a cubit[c] deep. The supports and panels were attached to the
top of the stand. 36He engraved cherubim, lions and palm trees on the sur-
faces of the supports and on the panels,
in every available space, with wreaths all
around. 37This is the way he made the
ten stands. They were all cast in the
same molds and were identical in size
7:38 and shape.
n Ex 30:18; 38He then made ten bronze basins,[n]
2Ch 4:6 each holding forty baths[d] and measuring
four cubits across, one basin to go on
each of the ten stands. 39He placed five of
the stands on the south side of the temple and five on the north. He placed the
Sea on the south side, at the southeast
corner of the temple. 40He also made the
basins and shovels and sprinkling bowls.
So Huram finished all the work he
had undertaken for King Solomon in the
temple of the LORD:

41the two pillars;
the two bowl-shaped capitals on
top of the pillars;
the two sets of network decorating
the two bowl-shaped capitals on
top of the pillars;
42the four hundred pomegranates for
the two sets of network (two
rows of pomegranates for each
network, decorating the bowl-
7:42 o ver 20 shaped capitals[o] on top of the
pillars);
43the ten stands with their ten basins;
44the Sea and the twelve bulls under it;
45the pots, shovels and sprinkling
7:45 p Ex 27:3 bowls.[p]

All these objects that Huram made
for King Solomon for the temple of the
LORD were of burnished bronze. 46The 7:46
king had them cast in clay molds in the q 2Ch 4:17
plain[q] of the Jordan between Succoth[r] r Ge 33:17; Jos 13:27
and Zarethan.[s] 47Solomon left all these s Jos 3:16
things unweighed,[t] because there were 7:47
so many; the weight of the bronze was t 1Ch 22:3
not determined.
48Solomon also made all the furnishings that were in the LORD's temple:

the golden altar; 7:48
the golden table[u] on which was the u Ex 37:10
bread of the Presence;[v] v Ex 25:30
49the lampstands[w] of pure gold (five 7:49
on the right and five on the left, w Ex 25:31-38
in front of the inner sanctuary);
the gold floral work and lamps and
tongs;
50the pure gold basins, wick trimmers, sprinkling bowls, dishes 7:50
and censers;[x] x 2Ki 25:13
and the gold sockets for the doors
of the innermost room, the Most
Holy Place, and also for the
doors of the main hall of the
temple.

51When all the work King Solomon
had done for the temple of the LORD was
finished, he brought in the things his father David had dedicated[y]—the silver 7:51 y 2Sa 8:11
and gold and the furnishings—and he
placed them in the treasuries of the
LORD's temple.

The Ark Brought to the Temple

8 Then King Solomon summoned
into his presence at Jerusalem the
elders of Israel, all the heads of the tribes 8:1
and the chiefs[z] of the Israelite families, z Nu 7:2
to bring up the ark[a] of the LORD's cov- a 2Sa 6:17
enant from Zion, the City of David.[b] 2All b 2Sa 5:7
the men of Israel came together to King 8:2
Solomon at the time of the festival[c] in c 2Ch 7:8
the month of Ethanim, the seventh d Lev 23:34
month.[d]
3When all the elders of Israel had ar- 8:3
rived, the priests[e] took up the ark, 4and e Nu 7:9; Jos 3:3
they brought up the ark of the LORD and 8:4
the Tent of Meeting[f] and all the sacred f 1Ki 3:4;
furnishings in it. The priests and Levites 2Ch 1:3
carried them up, 5and King Solomon

[a] 31 That is, about 1 1/2 feet (about 0.5 meter)
[b] 31 That is, about 2 1/4 feet (about 0.7 meter); also in verse 32
[c] 35 That is, about 3/4 foot (about 0.2 meter)
[d] 38 That is, about 230 gallons (about 880 liters)

and the entire assembly of Israel that
had gathered about him were before the
8:5 [g]2Sa 6:13 ark, sacrificing[g] so many sheep and cattle that they could not be recorded or
counted.
8:6 6 The priests then brought the ark of
[h]2Sa 6:17 [i]1Ki 6:19,27 the LORD's covenant[h] to its place in the
inner sanctuary of the temple, the Most
Holy Place, and put it beneath the wings
of the cherubim.[i] 7 The cherubim spread
their wings over the place of the ark and
overshadowed the ark and its carrying
poles. 8 These poles were so long that
their ends could be seen from the Holy
Place in front of the inner sanctuary, but
8:8 not from outside the Holy Place; and
[j]Ex 25:13-15 they are still there today.[j] 9 There was
nothing in the ark except the two stone
8:9 [k]Ex 24:7-8; 25:21; 40:20; Dt 10:2-5; Heb 9:4 tablets[k] that Moses had placed in it at
Horeb, where the LORD made a covenant
with the Israelites after they came out of
Egypt.
8:10 [l]Ex 40:34-35; 2Ch 7:1-2 10 When the priests withdrew from
the Holy Place, the cloud[l] filled the tem-
ple of the LORD. 11 And the priests could
not perform their service because of the
cloud, for the glory of the LORD filled his
temple.
12 Then Solomon said, "The LORD has
8:12 [m]Ps 18:11; 97:2 said that he would dwell in a dark
cloud;[m] 13 I have indeed built a magnifi-
8:13 [n]Ex 15:17; 2Sa 7:13; Ps 132:13 cent temple for you, a place for you to
dwell[n] forever."
14 While the whole assembly of Israel
was standing there, the king turned
8:14 [o]2Sa 6:18 around and blessed[o] them. 15 Then he
said:

8:15 [p]2Sa 7:12-13; 1Ch 29:10,20; Ne 9:5; Lk 1:68 "Praise be to the LORD,[p] the God
of Israel, who with his own hand
has fulfilled what he promised with
his own mouth to my father David.
For he said, 16 'Since the day I
brought my people Israel out of
Egypt, I have not chosen a city in
any tribe of Israel to have a temple
8:16 [q]Dt 12:5 [r]1Sa 16:1 [s]2Sa 7:4-6,8 built for my Name[q] to be there, but
I have chosen[r] David[s] to rule my
people Israel.'
17 "My father David had it in his
8:17 [t]2Sa 7:2; 1Ch 17:1 heart to build a temple[t] for the
Name of the LORD, the God of Isra-
el. 18 But the LORD said to my father
David, 'Because it was in your heart
to build a temple for my Name, you
did well to have this in your heart.
8:19 [u]2Sa 7:5 19 Nevertheless, you[u] are not the
one to build the temple, but your
son, who is your own flesh and
blood—he is the one who will build 8:19 [v]2Sa 7:13; 1Ki 5:3,5
the temple for my Name.'[v]
20 "The LORD has kept the promise he made: I have succeeded David my father and now I sit on the
throne of Israel, just as the LORD
promised, and I have built[w] the 8:20 [w]1Ch 28:6
temple for the Name of the LORD,
the God of Israel. 21 I have provided
a place there for the ark, in which is
the covenant of the LORD that he
made with our fathers when he
brought them out of Egypt."

> **JESUS CHRIST TURNS LIFE RIGHT-SIDE UP, AND HEAVEN OUTSIDE IN.**
>
> Carl F. H. Henry, *American Theologian*

Solomon's Prayer of Dedication

22 Then Solomon stood before the altar of the LORD in front of the whole as-
sembly of Israel, spread out his hands[x] 8:22 [x]Ex 9:29; Ezr 9:5
toward heaven 23 and said:

"O LORD, God of Israel, there is no
God like[y] you in heaven above or on 8:23 [y]1Sa 2:2; 2Sa 7:22 [z]Dt 7:9,12; Ne 1:5; 9:32; Da 9:4
earth below—you who keep your
covenant of love[z] with your servants who continue wholeheartedly in your way. 24 You have kept your
promise to your servant David my
father; with your mouth you have
promised and with your hand you
have fulfilled it—as it is today.
25 "Now LORD, God of Israel, keep
for your servant David my father
the promises[a] you made to him 8:25 [a]1Ki 2:4
when you said, 'You shall never fail
to have a man to sit before me on
the throne of Israel, if only your
sons are careful in all they do to
walk before me as you have done.'
26 And now, O God of Israel, let your
word that you promised[b] your ser- 8:26 [b]2Sa 7:25
vant David my father come true.
27 "But will God really dwell[c] on 8:27 [c]Ac 7:48 [d]2Ch 2:6; Ps 139:7-16; Isa 66:1; Jer 23:24
earth? The heavens, even the high-
est heaven, cannot contain[d] you.
How much less this temple I have
built! 28 Yet give attention to your
servant's prayer and his plea for
mercy, O LORD my God. Hear the
cry and the prayer that your servant

DISCOVERY 83

Dedication of the Temple

How do we gain an audience with God? Men and women have always asked such questions as *Will God hear me? Is he too busy? Does he even care about my daily issues? How often may I come to God? How do I know if he hears me, let alone understands?*

God has always wanted to listen to and communicate with his people. That is why he told Solomon to build a temple. The temple was constructed of brick and mortar, but it was by no means an ordinary building. The building itself was magnificent, the furnishings indescribable! Inside were golden altars and exquisite basins, bowls and dishes. There were gold sockets for the doors, a golden table and golden lampstands. Very impressive indeed!

When he dedicated the temple, however, Solomon seemed unconcerned about the structure itself or the beautiful things within. He was consumed with God's presence and activity, and his focus was entirely on God himself (1 Kings 8). He realized that God was not living in the temple as a man would live. If the entire universe cannot contain God, certainly he could not be confined to a temple! (see also 2 Chronicles 2:6; Acts 7:48–50). Solomon asked God to listen to the people when they came to worship him, to consider their situations and to forgive them. God had promised to be with his people, and Solomon trusted that he would not go back on his word.

Solomon blessed the people, aware that part of the blessing would entail rest and peace. The God of Israel would never renege on his promise or forsake his people. After the blessing the time had come for the sacrifices and offerings, followed by a two-week celebration. Because Solomon had been faithful, God made a special promise to him: His royal throne would be established forever.

This first temple was built by man. Today, however, God's presence is with his people in a very different way—in a "temple" that human hands did not fashion. When Jesus referred to a temple in Jerusalem that would be destroyed and raised again in three days, he was not talking about a building. He was speaking about his own body (John 2:19–21).

Solomon's temple was built hundreds of years before Jesus' birth, but it functioned as a "shadow" of the real thing (Hebrews 9:24). In the temple the people could approach God through the priests, but in Jesus we have direct access to the Father (Ephesians 1:6). The Israelites had to offer sacrifices continually in order to cover their sins, but the debt for our sin was completely paid when Jesus died on the cross (Ephesians 1:7).

"Will God really dwell on earth?" Solomon asked (1 Kings 8:27). The answer is a resounding yes! Solomon knew that God could not really live in the building he had constructed, but God wants to be among his people—and that residence became permanent when God the Son came to earth (John 1:14; Revelation 21:22) and the Holy Spirit came to live with us and in us (John 14:16–17).

Self-Discovery: *Have you ever asked yourself whether you matter to God? Have you ever doubted his care for you? Have your doubts been resolved, so that they are no longer an issue?*

GO TO DISCOVERY 84 ON PAGE 438

is praying in your presence this day. [29]May your eyes be open[e] toward[f] this temple night and day, this place of which you said, 'My Name[g] shall be there,' so that you will hear the prayer your servant prays toward this place. [30]Hear the supplication of your servant and of your people Israel when they pray toward this place. Hear from heaven, your dwelling place, and when you hear, forgive.[h]

[31]"When a man wrongs his neighbor and is required to take an oath and he comes and swears the oath[i] before your altar in this temple, [32]then hear from heaven and act. Judge between your servants, condemning the guilty and bringing down on his own head what he has done. Declare the innocent not guilty, and so establish his innocence.[j]

[33]"When your people Israel have been defeated[k] by an enemy because they have sinned[l] against you, and when they turn back to you and confess your name, praying and making supplication to you in this temple, [34]then hear from heaven and forgive the sin of your people Israel and bring them back to the land you gave to their fathers.

[35]"When the heavens are shut up and there is no rain[m] because your people have sinned against you, and when they pray toward this place and confess your name and turn from their sin because you have afflicted them, [36]then hear from heaven and forgive the sin of your servants, your people Israel. Teach[n] them the right way[o] to live, and send rain on the land you gave your people for an inheritance.

[37]"When famine[p] or plague comes to the land, or blight[q] or mildew, locusts or grasshoppers, or when an enemy besieges them in any of their cities, whatever disaster or disease may come, [38]and when a prayer or plea is made by any of your people Israel—each one aware of the afflictions of his own heart, and spreading out his hands toward this temple—[39]then hear from heaven, your dwelling place. Forgive and act; deal with each man according to all he does, since you know[r] his heart (for you alone know the hearts of all men), [40]so that they will fear[s] you all the time they live in the land you gave our fathers.

[41]"As for the foreigner who does not belong to your people Israel but has come from a distant land because of your name—[42]for men will hear of your great name and your mighty hand[t] and your outstretched arm—when he comes and prays toward this temple, [43]then hear from heaven, your dwelling place, and do whatever the foreigner asks of you, so that all the peoples of the earth may know[u] your name and fear[v] you, as do your own people Israel, and may know that this house I have built bears your Name.

[44]"When your people go to war against their enemies, wherever you send them, and when they pray to the LORD toward the city you have chosen and the temple I have built for your Name, [45]then hear from heaven their prayer and their plea, and uphold their cause.

[46]"When they sin against you—for there is no one who does not sin[w]—and you become angry with them and give them over to the enemy, who takes them captive[x] to his own land, far away or near; [47]and if they have a change of heart in the land where they are held captive, and repent and plead[y] with you in the land of their conquerors and say, 'We have sinned, we have done wrong, we have acted wickedly';[z] [48]and if they turn back to you with all their heart[a] and soul in the land of their enemies who took them captive, and pray[b] to you toward the land you gave their fathers, toward the city you have chosen and the temple[c] I have built for your Name; [49]then from heaven, your dwelling place, hear their prayer and their plea, and uphold their cause. [50]And forgive your people, who have sinned against you; forgive all the offenses they have committed against you, and cause

8:29 [e]2Ch 7:15; Ne 1:6 [f]Da 6:10 [g]Dt 12:11
8:30 [h]Ps 85:2
8:31 [i]Ex 22:11
8:32 [j]Dt 25:1
8:33 [k]Lev 26:17; Dt 28:25 [l]Lev 26:39
8:35 [m]Lev 26:19; Dt 28:24
8:36 [n]1Sa 12:23; Ps 25:4; 94:12 [o]Ps 5:8; 27:11; Jer 6:16
8:37 [p]Lev 26:26 [q]Dt 28:22
8:39 [r]1Sa 16:7; 1Ch 28:9; Ps 11:4; Jer 17:10; Jn 2:24; Ac 1:24
8:40 [s]Ps 130:4
8:42 [t]Dt 3:24
8:43 [u]1Sa 17:46; 2Ki 19:19 [v]Ps 102:15
8:46 [w]Pr 20:9; Ecc 7:20; Ro 3:9; 1Jn 1:8-10 [x]Lev 26:33-39; Dt 28:64
8:47 [y]Lev 26:40; Ne 1:6 [z]Ps 106:6; Da 9:5
8:48 [a]Dt 4:29; Jer 29:12-14 [b]Da 6:10 [c]Jnh 2:4

8:50 [d] 2Ch 30:9; Ps 106:46 their conquerors to show them
mercy;[d] 51for they are your people
and your inheritance,[e] whom you
8:51 [e] Dt 4:20; 9:29; Ne 1:10 [f] Jer 11:4 brought out of Egypt, out of that
iron-smelting furnace.[f]
52"May your eyes be open to your
servant's plea and to the plea of
your people Israel, and may you listen to them whenever they cry out
to you. 53For you singled them out
from all the nations of the world to
8:53 [g] Ex 19:5; Dt 9:26-29 be your own inheritance,[g] just as
you declared through your servant
Moses when you, O Sovereign
LORD, brought our fathers out of
Egypt."

54When Solomon had finished all
these prayers and supplications to the
LORD, he rose from before the altar of the
LORD, where he had been kneeling with
8:55 [h] ver 14; 2Sa 6:18 his hands spread out toward heaven.
55He stood and blessed[h] the whole as-
sembly of Israel in a loud voice, saying:

8:56 [i] Dt 12:10 [j] Jos 21:45; 23:15 56"Praise be to the LORD, who has
given rest[i] to his people Israel just
as he promised. Not one word has
failed of all the good promises[j] he
gave through his servant Moses.
57May the LORD our God be with us
as he was with our fathers; may he
8:57 [k] Dt 31:6; Jos 1:5; Heb 13:5 never leave us nor forsake[k] us.
58May he turn our hearts[l] to him, to
walk in all his ways and to keep the
8:58 [l] Ps 119:36 commands, decrees and regulations he gave our fathers. 59And
may these words of mine, which I
have prayed before the LORD, be
near to the LORD our God day and
night, that he may uphold the cause
of his servant and the cause of his
people Israel according to each
day's need, 60so that all the peo-
8:60 [m] Jos 4:24; 1Sa 17:46 [n] Dt 4:35; 1Ki 18:39; Jer 10:10-12 ples[m] of the earth may know that
the LORD is God and that there is no
other.[n] 61But your hearts must be
fully committed[o] to the LORD our
8:61 [o] 1Ki 11:4; 15:3, 14; 2Ki 20:3 God, to live by his decrees and obey
his commands, as at this time."

The Dedication of the Temple

62Then the king and all Israel with
him offered sacrifices before the LORD.
63Solomon offered a sacrifice of fellowship offerings[a] to the LORD: twenty-two
thousand cattle and a hundred and
twenty thousand sheep and goats. So
the king and all the Israelites dedicated
the temple of the LORD.
64On that same day the king consecrated the middle part of the courtyard
in front of the temple of the LORD, and
there he offered burnt offerings, grain
offerings and the fat of the fellowship offerings, because the bronze altar[p] before 8:64 [p] 2Ch 4:1
the LORD was too small to hold the burnt
offerings, the grain offerings and the fat
of the fellowship offerings.
65So Solomon observed the festival[q] 8:65 [q] ver 2; Lev 23:34 [r] Nu 34:8; Jos 13:5; Jdg 3:3; 2Ki 14:25 [s] Ge 15:18
at that time, and all Israel with him—a
vast assembly, people from Lebo[b] Hamath[r] to the Wadi of Egypt.[s] They celebrated it before the LORD our God for
seven days and seven days more, fourteen days in all. 66On the following day
he sent the people away. They blessed
the king and then went home, joyful and
glad in heart for all the good things the
LORD had done for his servant David and
his people Israel.

The LORD Appears to Solomon

9 When Solomon had finished[t] 9:1 [t] 1Ki 7:1; 2Ch 8:6
building the temple of the LORD
and the royal palace, and had achieved
all he had desired to do, 2the LORD ap- 9:2 [u] 1Ki 3:5
peared[u] to him a second time, as he had
appeared to him at Gibeon. 3The LORD
said to him:

[a] 63 Traditionally *peace offerings;* also in verse 64
[b] 65 Or *from the entrance to*

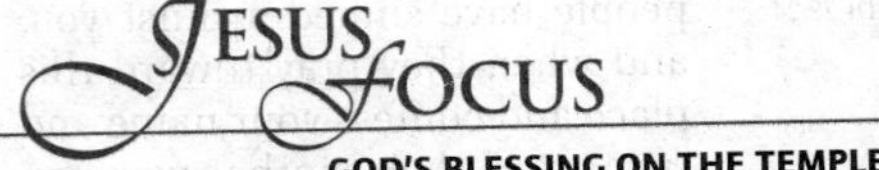

GOD'S BLESSING ON THE TEMPLE

The Lord appeared to Solomon for the first time in a dream at Gibeon (1 Kings 3:5), offering to grant Solomon one request. Solomon humbly opted for wisdom to rule his kingdom, and, because of his unselfish choice, God promised to bless him with peace and prosperity as well (1 Kings 3:13). When Solomon dedicated the temple, the Lord met with him a second time (1 Kings 9:1–9). Since God the Father is unseen (John 1:18), there are many who believe that it was the preincarnate Jesus who actually appeared to people in the Old Testament. So here in 1 Kings 9 it may have been Jesus himself who appeared to Solomon to advise him that God had heard his prayer and had blessed the temple. Little wonder that Jesus in his ministry on earth would have been zealous with regard to the temple and expelled those who were defiling it (Mark 11:15).

9:3 [v]2Ki 20:5; Ps 10:17 [w]Dt 11:12; 1Ki 8:29
"I have heard[v] the prayer and
plea you have made before me; I
have consecrated this temple,
which you have built, by putting
my Name there forever. My eyes[w]
and my heart will always be there.
4"As for you, if you walk before
9:4 [x]Ge 17:1 [y]1Ki 15:5
me in integrity of heart[x] and uprightness, as David[y] your father
did, and do all I command and observe my decrees and laws, 5I will
9:5 [z]1Ch 22:10 [a]2Sa 7:15; 1Ki 2:4
establish[z] your royal throne over Israel forever, as I promised David
your father when I said, 'You shall
never fail[a] to have a man on the
throne of Israel.'
9:6 [b]2Sa 7:14
6"But if you[a] or your sons turn
away[b] from me and do not observe
the commands and decrees I have
given you[a] and go off to serve oth-
9:7 [c]2Ki 17:23; 25:21 [d]Jer 7:14 [e]Ps 44:14 [f]Dt 28:37
er gods and worship them, 7then I
will cut off Israel from the land[c] I
have given them and will reject this
temple I have consecrated for my
Name.[d] Israel will then become a
byword[e] and an object of ridicule[f]
among all peoples. 8And though
this temple is now imposing, all
who pass by will be appalled and
will scoff and say, 'Why has the
9:8 [g]Dt 29:24; Jer 22:8-9
LORD done such a thing to this land
and to this temple?'[g] 9People will
answer, 'Because they have forsak-
en the LORD their God, who
brought their fathers out of Egypt,
and have embraced other gods,
worshiping and serving them—
that is why the LORD brought all
this disaster on them.'"

Solomon's Other Activities

10At the end of twenty years, during
which Solomon built these two buildings—the temple of the LORD and the
royal palace— 11King Solomon gave
twenty towns in Galilee to Hiram king of
Tyre, because Hiram had supplied him
9:11 [h]2Ch 8:2
with all the cedar and pine and gold[h] he
wanted. 12But when Hiram went from
Tyre to see the towns that Solomon had
given him, he was not pleased with
them. 13"What kind of towns are these
you have given me, my brother?" he
9:13 [i]Jos 19:27
asked. And he called them the Land of
Cabul,[b][i] a name they have to this day.
14Now Hiram had sent to the king 120
talents[c] of gold.

15Here is the account of the forced la-
bor King Solomon conscripted[j] to build 9:15 [j]Jos 16:10; 1Ki 5:13 [k]ver 24; 2Sa 5:9 [l]Jos 19:36 [m]Jos 17:11
the LORD's temple, his own palace, the
supporting terraces,[d][k] the wall of Jerusalem, and Hazor,[l] Megiddo and Gezer.[m]
16(Pharaoh king of Egypt had attacked
and captured Gezer. He had set it on fire.
He killed its Canaanite inhabitants and
then gave it as a wedding gift to his
daughter, Solomon's wife. 17And Solo-
mon rebuilt Gezer.) He built up Lower 9:17 [n]Jos 16:3; 2Ch 8:5
Beth Horon,[n] 18Baalath,[o] and Tadmor[e]
in the desert, within his land, 19as well as 9:18 [o]Jos 19:44
all his store cities[p] and the towns for his
chariots[q] and for his horses[f]—whatever 9:19 [p]ver 1 [q]1Ki 4:26
he desired to build in Jerusalem, in Leb-
anon and throughout all the territory he
ruled.
20All the people left from the Amorites, Hittites, Perizzites, Hivites and
Jebusites (these peoples were not Israel-
ites), 21that is, their descendants[r] re- 9:21 [r]Ge 9:25-26
maining in the land, whom the Israelites

[a]6 The Hebrew is plural. [b]13 *Cabul* sounds like the Hebrew for *good-for-nothing.* [c]14 That is, about 4 1/2 tons (about 4 metric tons) [d]15 Or *the Millo*; also in verse 24 [e]18 The Hebrew may also be read *Tamar.* [f]19 Or *charioteers*

JESUS AND YOU

GOOD FOR NOTHING

Solomon gave 20 towns in Galilee to King Hiram, a foreigner, to pay for his services (1 Kings 9:10–13). The northern tribes resented losing part of the land God had promised them, and Hiram wasn't particularly impressed with the towns. In fact, he went so far as to call them *Cabul*, or "good-for-nothing." In New Testament times the resentment on both sides was still strong, and many people still considered the area around the Sea of Galilee to be of little worth. Some of Jesus' critics even refused to believe that he was the Messiah because he had come from that area (John 1:46; 7:41). But Isaiah had predicted that God's promised One would "honor Galilee of the Gentiles" and that a "great light" would appear to them (Isaiah 9:1–2). Most of Jesus' ministry was centered in Galilee—in the very area that Hiram had deemed to be of little value. In his typical fashion God worked with something (in this case, a region) that others called "nothing" and transformed it into something of great value. He can do the same thing with our lives when we place our trust in him.

9:21 [s]Jos 15:63; could not exterminate[a][s]—these Solo-
17:12; Jdg 1:21, mon conscripted for his slave labor
27,29 [t]Ezr 2:55, force,[t] as it is to this day. 22But Solomon
58 did not make slaves[u] of any of the Isra-
9:22 elites; they were his fighting men, his
[u]Lev 25:39 government officials, his officers, his
captains, and the commanders of
9:23 his chariots and charioteers. 23They
[v]1Ki 5:16 were also the chief officials[v] in charge of
Solomon's projects—550 officials super-
vising the men who did the work.
9:24 24After Pharaoh's daughter[w] had
[w]1Ki 3:1; 7:8 [x]2Sa 5:9; come up from the City of David to the
1Ki 11:27; palace Solomon had built for her, he
2Ch 32:5 constructed the supporting terraces.[x]
9:25 25Three[y] times a year Solomon sacri-
[y]Ex 23:14; ficed burnt offerings and fellowship of-
2Ch 8:12-13,16 ferings[b] on the altar he had built for the
LORD, burning incense before the LORD
along with them, and so fulfilled the
9:26 temple obligations.
[z]1Ki 22:48 26King Solomon also built ships[z] at
[a]Nu 33:35; Ezion Geber,[a] which is near Elath in
Dt 2:8 Edom, on the shore of the Red Sea.[c]
9:27 [b]1Ki 10:11; 27And Hiram sent his men—sailors[b] who
Eze 27:8 knew the sea—to serve in the fleet with
9:28 Solomon's men. 28They sailed to Ophir[c]
[c]1Ch 29:4 and brought back 420 talents[d] of gold,
which they delivered to King Solomon.

The Queen of Sheba Visits Solomon

10:1 **10** When the queen of Sheba[d]
[d]Ge 10:7,28; heard about the fame of Solo-
Mt 12:42; mon and his relation to the name of the
Lk 11:31 LORD, she came to test him with hard
[e]Jdg 14:12 questions.[e] 2Arriving at Jerusalem with
a very great caravan—with camels car-
rying spices, large quantities of gold, and
precious stones—she came to Solomon
and talked with him about all that she
had on her mind. 3Solomon answered all
her questions; nothing was too hard for
the king to explain to her. 4When the
queen of Sheba saw all the wisdom of
10:5 Solomon and the palace he had built,
[f]1Ch 26:16 5the food on his table,[f] the seating of his
officials, the attending servants in their
robes, his cupbearers, and the burnt offerings he made at[e] the temple of the
LORD, she was overwhelmed.
6She said to the king, "The report I
heard in my own country about your
achievements and your wisdom is true.
7But I did not believe these things until I
came and saw with my own eyes. In-
10:7 deed, not even half was told me; in wis-
[g]1Ch 29:25 dom and wealth[g] you have far exceeded
the report I heard. 8How happy your
men must be! How happy your officials,
who continually stand before you and 10:8
hear[h] your wisdom! 9Praise[i] be to the [h]Pr 8:34
LORD your God, who has delighted in
you and placed you on the throne of Is- 10:9
rael. Because of the LORD's eternal love [i]1Ki 5:7 [j]2Sa 8:15;
for Israel, he has made you king, to Ps 33:5; 72:2
maintain justice[j] and righteousness."
10And she gave the king 120 talents[f] 10:10
of gold,[k] large quantities of spices, and [k]ver 2
precious stones. Never again were so
many spices brought in as those the
queen of Sheba gave to King Solomon.
11(Hiram's ships brought gold from 10:11
Ophir;[l] and from there they brought [l]Ge 10:29;
great cargoes of almugwood[g] and pre- 1Ki 9:27-28
cious stones. 12The king used the almugwood to make supports for the temple of
the LORD and for the royal palace, and to
make harps and lyres for the musicians.
So much almugwood has never been imported or seen since that day.)
13King Solomon gave the queen of
Sheba all she desired and asked for, besides what he had given her out of his
royal bounty. Then she left and returned
with her retinue to her own country.

Solomon's Splendor

14The weight of the gold[m] that Solo- 10:14
mon received yearly was 666 talents,[h] [m]1Ki 9:28
15not including the revenues from merchants and traders and from all the Ara-
bian kings and the governors of the land.
16King Solomon made two hundred 10:16
large shields[n] of hammered gold; six [n]1Ki 14:26-28
hundred bekas[i] of gold went into each
shield. 17He also made three hundred
small shields of hammered gold, with
three minas[j] of gold in each shield. The
king put them in the Palace of the For- 10:17
est of Lebanon.[o] [o]1Ki 7:2
18Then the king made a great throne
inlaid with ivory and overlaid with fine
gold. 19The throne had six steps, and its
back had a rounded top. On both sides

[a] *21* The Hebrew term refers to the irrevocable giving over of things or persons to the LORD, often by totally destroying them. [b] *25* Traditionally *peace offerings* [c] *26* Hebrew *Yam Suph*; that is, Sea of Reeds [d] *28* That is, about 16 tons (about 14.5 metric tons) [e] *5* Or *the ascent by which he went up to* [f] *10* That is, about 4 1/2 tons (about 4 metric tons) [g] *11* Probably a variant of *algumwood*; also in verse 12 [h] *14* That is, about 25 tons (about 23 metric tons) [i] *16* That is, about 7 1/2 pounds (about 3.5 kilograms) [j] *17* That is, about 3 3/4 pounds (about 1.7 kilograms)

of the seat were armrests, with a lion
standing beside each of them. 20 Twelve
lions stood on the six steps, one at either
end of each step. Nothing like it had ever
been made for any other kingdom. 21 All
King Solomon's goblets were gold, and
all the household articles in the Palace
of the Forest of Lebanon were pure gold.
Nothing was made of silver, because silver was considered of little value in Solomon's days. 22 The king had a fleet of
10:22 p 1Ki 9:26 trading ships[a][p] at sea along with the
ships of Hiram. Once every three years it
returned, carrying gold, silver and ivory,
and apes and baboons.
10:23 q 1Ki 3:13 23 King Solomon was greater in riches[q]
r 1Ki 4:30 and wisdom[r] than all the other kings of
the earth. 24 The whole world sought audience with Solomon to hear the wis-
10:24 s 1Ki 3:9,12,28 dom[s] God had put in his heart. 25 Year after year, everyone who came brought a
gift—articles of silver and gold, robes,
weapons and spices, and horses and
mules.
10:26 t Dt 17:16; 1Ki 4:26; 9:19; 2Ch 1:14; 9:25 26 Solomon accumulated chariots and
horses;[t] he had fourteen hundred chari-
ots and twelve thousand horses,[b] which
he kept in the chariot cities and also
with him in Jerusalem. 27 The king made
10:27 u Dt 17:17 silver as common[u] in Jerusalem as
stones, and cedar as plentiful as sycamore-fig trees in the foothills. 28 Solomon's horses were imported from
Egypt[c] and from Kue[d]—the royal merchants purchased them from Kue.
29 They imported a chariot from Egypt
for six hundred shekels[e] of silver, and a
horse for a hundred and fifty.[f] They also
exported them to all the kings of the 10:29
Hittites[v] and of the Arameans. v 2Ki 7:6-7

Solomon's Wives

11 King Solomon, however, loved 11:1
many foreign women[w] besides w Dt 17:17; Ne 13:26
Pharaoh's daughter—Moabites, Am-
monites, Edomites, Sidonians and Hittites. 2 They were from nations about
which the LORD had told the Israelites, 11:2
"You must not intermarry[x] with them, x Ex 34:16; Dt 7:3-4
because they will surely turn your hearts
after their gods." Nevertheless, Solomon
held fast to them in love. 3 He had seven
hundred wives of royal birth and three
hundred concubines, and his wives led
him astray. 4 As Solomon grew old, his
wives turned his heart after other gods, 11:4
and his heart was not fully devoted[y] to y 1Ki 8:61; 9:4
the LORD his God, as the heart of David
his father had been. 5 He followed Ashto-
reth[z] the goddess of the Sidonians, and 11:5 z ver 33; Jdg 2:13; 2Ki 23:13
Molech[g][a] the detestable god of the Am- a ver 7
monites. 6 So Solomon did evil in the eyes
of the LORD; he did not follow the LORD
completely, as David his father had done.
7 On a hill east[b] of Jerusalem, Solomon 11:7 b 2Ki 23:13
built a high place for Chemosh[c] the de- c Nu 21:29; Jdg 11:24
testable god of Moab, and for Molech[d] d Lev 20:2-5; Ac 7:43
the detestable god of the Ammonites.
8 He did the same for all his foreign
wives, who burned incense and offered
sacrifices to their gods.
9 The LORD became angry with Solomon because his heart had turned away
from the LORD, the God of Israel, who 11:9
had appeared[e] to him twice. 10 Although e ver 2-3; 1Ki 3:5; 9:2
he had forbidden Solomon to follow
other gods,[f] Solomon did not keep the 11:10 f 1Ki 9:6
LORD's command.[g] 11 So the LORD said to g 1Ki 6:12
Solomon, "Since this is your attitude
and you have not kept my covenant and
my decrees, which I commanded you, I
will most certainly tear[h] the kingdom 11:11 h ver 31; 1Ki 12:15-16; 2Ki 17:21
away from you and give it to one of your
subordinates. 12 Nevertheless, for the
sake of David your father, I will not do it
during your lifetime. I will tear it out of
the hand of your son. 13 Yet I will not tear

[a] 22 Hebrew *of ships of Tarshish* [b] 26 Or *charioteers* [c] 28 Or possibly *Muzur*, a region in Cilicia; also in verse 29 [d] 28 Probably *Cilicia* [e] 29 That is, about 15 pounds (about 7 kilograms) [f] 29 That is, about 3 3/4 pounds (about 1.7 kilograms) [g] 5 Hebrew *Milcom*; also in verse 33

JESUS AND YOU

SOLOMON'S SPLENDOR

Solomon's wealth was unequaled in the entire ancient world, and his was the "golden age" of Israel. But despite his influence and affluence Solomon struggled to come to terms with the purpose of his existence (see the book of Ecclesiastes). Jesus commented on Solomon's riches in the Sermon on the Mount: "See how the lilies of the field grow. They do not labor or spin. Yet I tell you that not even Solomon in all his splendor was dressed like one of these" (Matthew 6:28–29). However, our Lord went on to focus our attention on God's tender care for us rather than on our own prosperity. Our priority, he emphasized, should be to seek "first his kingdom and his righteousness, and all [other things necessary] will be given to [us] as well" (Matthew 6:33).

DISCOVERY 84

Solomon: A Wise Fool

Solomon is considered to be the wisest person who has ever lived. He was given his wisdom by God, and it was greater than "all the men of the East" (1 Kings 4:29–34). He authored 3,000 proverbs and composed 1,005 songs. His pithy nuggets of insight are recorded in Ecclesiastes, Song of Songs and Proverbs. But Solomon's actions contradicted his own sagacity!

In the book of Proverbs Solomon had a great deal to say about the dangers of sexual immorality. He pointed out that adultery is the way of death and that it leads only to destruction (see Proverbs 5:1–12). Betraying one's wife in such a way, he emphasized, is like trapping a beautiful deer and then cruelly slaughtering it (Proverbs 7:22–23). Being enticed by a prostitute is like scooping fire into your own lap or walking on hot coals (Proverbs 6:27–28). His advice to husbands is clear: "May you rejoice in the wife of your youth. A loving doe, a graceful deer—may her breasts satisfy you always, may you ever be captivated by her love" (Proverbs 5:18–19).

Solomon was right on target with his warnings. Hopefully he learned from his own mistakes, however, because he unfortunately failed to follow his own advice. He married 700 wives and had 300 concubines. Eventually Solomon was enticed by his wives away from the one true God of Israel and even constructed a pagan altar on a hill east of Jerusalem. One of the gods he worshiped was Ashtoreth, goddess of sex and fertility (1 Kings 11:1–6). Solomon turned sexuality into a religion! Despite his wisdom, Solomon had become the ultimate fool.

God had established the general standard for human sexuality when he had prohibited adultery (Exodus 20:14), and Solomon warned against the devastating consequences of violating God's command. But Jesus went to the heart of the matter—our inner lusts: "Anyone who looks at a woman lustfully has already committed adultery with her in his heart" (Matthew 5:28). Lust is serious. If allowed to go unchecked, it can lead us into sinful acts beyond our wildest imaginations.

Jesus exaggerated to make his point: "If your right eye causes you to sin, gouge it out" (Matthew 5:29). We have to be willing to deal with sinful desires using serious disciplinary measures. Solomon was wise enough to know right from wrong, but he was foolish enough at times to disregard this knowledge. Solomon was a wise fool. Distinguishing right from wrong is a start, but doing what is right and refusing to do what is wrong are disciplines critical to a godly lifestyle.

Self-Discovery: *How do you think Solomon could have plummeted from being the wisest man on earth to the ultimate fool? In your own life, do you consider wisdom a gift from God, and, if so, to what degree do you feel it must be cultivated and exercised to remain strong?*

GO TO DISCOVERY 85 ON PAGE 447

11:13 the whole kingdom from him, but will
[i] 1Ki 12:20 give him one tribe[i] for the sake[j] of David
[j] 2Sa 7:15 my servant and for the sake of Jerusa-
[k] Dt 12:11 lem, which I have chosen."[k]

Solomon's Adversaries

14 Then the LORD raised up against Solomon an adversary, Hadad the Edomite,
from the royal line of Edom. 15 Earlier
when David was fighting with Edom,
Joab the commander of the army, who
11:15 had gone up to bury the dead, had struck
[l] Dt 20:13; down all the men in Edom.[l] 16 Joab and
2Sa 8:14; all the Israelites stayed there for six
1Ch 18:12 months, until they had destroyed all the
men in Edom. 17 But Hadad, still only a
boy, fled to Egypt with some Edomite of-
11:18 ficials who had served his father. 18 They
[m] Nu 10:12 set out from Midian and went to Paran.[m]
Then taking men from Paran with them,
they went to Egypt, to Pharaoh king of
Egypt, who gave Hadad a house and land
and provided him with food.

19 Pharaoh was so pleased with Hadad
that he gave him a sister of his own wife,
Queen Tahpenes, in marriage. 20 The sister of Tahpenes bore him a son named
Genubath, whom Tahpenes brought up
in the royal palace. There Genubath
lived with Pharaoh's own children.

21 While he was in Egypt, Hadad heard
that David rested with his fathers and
that Joab the commander of the army
was also dead. Then Hadad said to Pharaoh, "Let me go, that I may return to my
own country."

22 "What have you lacked here that
you want to go back to your own country?" Pharaoh asked.

"Nothing," Hadad replied, "but do let
me go!"

23 And God raised up against Solomon
11:23 another adversary,[n] Rezon son of Eliada,
[n] ver 14
[o] 2Sa 8:3 who had fled from his master, Hadadezer[o] king of Zobah. 24 He gathered men
around him and became the leader of a
band of rebels when David destroyed the
11:24 forces[a] ⌞of Zobah⌟; the rebels went to Da-
[p] 2Sa 8:5; 10:8, mascus,[p] where they settled and took
18 control. 25 Rezon was Israel's adversary as
long as Solomon lived, adding to the
11:25 trouble caused by Hadad. So Rezon ruled
[q] 2Sa 10:19 in Aram[q] and was hostile toward Israel.

11:26 *Jeroboam Rebels Against Solomon*

[r] 2Sa 20:21; 1Ki 12:2; 26 Also, Jeroboam son of Nebat re-
2Ch 13:6 belled[r] against the king. He was one of
Solomon's officials, an Ephraimite from
Zeredah, and his mother was a widow
named Zeruah.

27 Here is the account of how he rebelled against the king: Solomon had
built the supporting terraces[b] [s] and had 11:27
filled in the gap in the wall of the city of [s] 1Ki 9:24
David his father. 28 Now Jeroboam was a
man of standing,[t] and when Solomon 11:28 [t] Ru 2:1
saw how well[u] the young man did his [u] Pr 22:29
work, he put him in charge of the whole
labor force of the house of Joseph.

29 About that time Jeroboam was go-
ing out of Jerusalem, and Ahijah[v] the 11:29 [v] 1Ki 12:15;
prophet of Shiloh met him on the way, 14:2; 2Ch 9:29
wearing a new cloak. The two of them
were alone out in the country, 30 and
Ahijah took hold of the new cloak he
was wearing and tore[w] it into twelve 11:30
pieces. 31 Then he said to Jeroboam, [w] 1Sa 15:27
"Take ten pieces for yourself, for this is
what the LORD, the God of Israel, says:
'See, I am going to tear[x] the kingdom 11:31
out of Solomon's hand and give you ten [x] ver 11
tribes. 32 But for the sake of my servant
David and the city of Jerusalem, which I
have chosen out of all the tribes of Israel, he will have one tribe. 33 I will do this
because they have[c] forsaken me and
worshiped[y] Ashtoreth the goddess of 11:33
the Sidonians, Chemosh the god of the [y] ver 5-7 [z] 1Ki 3:3
Moabites, and Molech the god of the
Ammonites, and have not walked in my
ways, nor done what is right in my eyes,
nor kept my statutes[z] and laws as David,
Solomon's father, did.

34 " 'But I will not take the whole kingdom out of Solomon's hand; I have made
him ruler all the days of his life for the
sake of David my servant, whom I chose
and who observed my commands and
statutes. 35 I will take the kingdom from
his son's hands and give you ten tribes.
36 I will give one tribe[a] to his son so that 11:36 [a] ver 13;
David my servant may always have a 1Ki 12:17
lamp[b] before me in Jerusalem, the city [b] 1Ki 15:4;
where I chose to put my Name. 37 How- 2Ki 8:19
ever, as for you, I will take you, and you
will rule over all that your heart desires;[c] 11:37
you will be king over Israel. 38 If you do [c] 2Sa 3:21
whatever I command you and walk in
my ways and do what is right in my eyes 11:38
by keeping my statutes[d] and com- [d] Dt 17:19
mands, as David my servant did, I will be

[a] 24 Hebrew *destroyed them* [b] 27 Or *the Millo*
[c] 33 Hebrew; Septuagint, Vulgate and Syriac *because he has*

11:38 [e]Jos 1:5; 2Sa 7:11,27 with you. I will build you a dynasty[e] as
enduring as the one I built for David and
will give Israel to you. 39I will humble David's descendants because of this, but
not forever.' "
40Solomon tried to kill Jeroboam, but
11:40 [f]2Ch 12:2 Jeroboam fled to Egypt, to Shishak[f] the
king, and stayed there until Solomon's
death.

Solomon's Death

41As for the other events of Solomon's
reign—all he did and the wisdom he displayed—are they not written in the
book of the annals of Solomon? 42Solo-
mon reigned in Jerusalem over all Israel
forty years. 43Then he rested with his fathers and was buried in the city of David
11:43 [g]1Ki 14:21; Mt 1:7 his father. And Rehoboam[g] his son succeeded him as king.

Israel Rebels Against Rehoboam

12 Rehoboam went to Shechem,
for all the Israelites had gone
there to make him king. 2When Jeroboam son of Nebat heard this (he was still
12:2 [h]1Ki 11:40 in Egypt, where he had fled[h] from King
Solomon), he returned from[a] Egypt. 3So
they sent for Jeroboam, and he and the
whole assembly of Israel went to Rehoboam and said to him: 4"Your father put
12:4 [i]1Sa 8:11-18; 1Ki 4:20-28 a heavy yoke[i] on us, but now lighten the
harsh labor and the heavy yoke he put
on us, and we will serve you."
5Rehoboam answered, "Go away for
three days and then come back to me."
So the people went away.
6Then King Rehoboam consulted the
12:6 [j]1Ki 4:2 elders[j] who had served his father Solomon during his lifetime. "How would
you advise me to answer these people?"
he asked.
7They replied, "If today you will be a
12:7 [k]Pr 15:1 servant to these people and serve them
and give them a favorable answer,[k] they
will always be your servants."
8But Rehoboam rejected the advice
the elders gave him and consulted the
young men who had grown up with him
and were serving him. 9He asked them,
"What is your advice? How should we
answer these people who say to me,
'Lighten the yoke your father put
on us'?"
10The young men who had grown up
with him replied, "Tell these people who
have said to you, 'Your father put a heavy
yoke on us, but make our yoke lighter'—
tell them, 'My little finger is thicker than
my father's waist. 11My father laid on you
a heavy yoke; I will make it even heavier.
My father scourged you with whips; I
will scourge you with scorpions.' "
12Three days later Jeroboam and all
the people returned to Rehoboam, as the
king had said, "Come back to me in three
days." 13The king answered the people
harshly. Rejecting the advice given him
by the elders, 14he followed the advice of
the young men and said, "My father
made your yoke heavy; I will make it
even heavier. My father scourged[l] you 12:14 [l]Ex 1:14; 5:5-9, 16-18
with whips; I will scourge you with scor-
pions." 15So the king did not listen to the
people, for this turn of events was from
the LORD,[m] to fulfill the word the LORD 12:15 [m]ver 24; Dt 2:30; Jdg 14:4; 2Ch 22:7; 25:20
had spoken to Jeroboam son of Nebat
through Ahijah[n] the Shilonite. [n]1Ki 11:29
16When all Israel saw that the king refused to listen to them, they answered
the king:

"What share do we have in David,
what part in Jesse's son?
To your tents, O Israel![o] 12:16 [o]2Sa 20:1
Look after your own house,
O David!"

[a] 2 Or *he remained in*

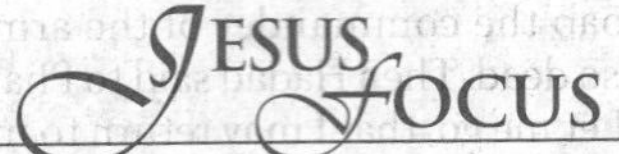

A HOUSE DIVIDED

Jeroboam's rebellion and Rehoboam's stubbornness caused the nation to split in two—ten tribes to the north (referred to as Israel, with Jeroboam as king) and two tribes to the south (called Judah, with Rehoboam as king). This division would in itself bring about national and political calamity, but the real tragedy was that the people of the northern kingdom rejected God's plan: "What share do we have in David, what part in Jesse's son?" (1 Kings 12:16). Israel not only rejected Rehoboam, David's grandson, but by extension the family line of God's promised Messiah as well. Jeroboam set up worship centers at Bethel and Dan—complete with golden calves, the very thing to which Moses had objected in Exodus 32. Later the northern tribes would establish their own capital at Samaria (1 Kings 16:23–24), setting the stage for the bitterness between Israelites and Samaritans that would continue into Jesus' day (Luke 9:51–56; John 4:4–9,20–26).

So the Israelites went home. 17But as for
the Israelites who were living in the
12:17 p 1Ki 11:13,36 towns of Judah,[p] Rehoboam still ruled
over them.
12:18 18King Rehoboam sent out Adoni-
q 2Sa 20:24; ram,[a][q] who was in charge of forced la-
1Ki 4:6; 5:14 bor, but all Israel stoned him to death.
King Rehoboam, however, managed to
get into his chariot and escape to Jerusalem. 19So Israel has been in rebellion
12:19 r 2Ki 17:21 against the house of David[r] to this day.
20When all the Israelites heard that
Jeroboam had returned, they sent and
called him to the assembly and made
him king over all Israel. Only the tribe of
12:20 Judah remained loyal to the house of
s 1Ki 11:13,32 David.[s]

21When Rehoboam arrived in Jerusalem, he mustered the whole house of Judah and the tribe of Benjamin—a hun-
12:21 dred and eighty thousand fighting
t 2Ch 11:1 men—to make war[t] against the house
of Israel and to regain the kingdom for
Rehoboam son of Solomon.
12:22 22But this word of God came to She-
u 2Ch 12:5-7 maiah[u] the man of God: 23"Say to Rehoboam son of Solomon king of Judah, to
the whole house of Judah and Benjamin,
and to the rest of the people, 24'This is
what the LORD says: Do not go up to
fight against your brothers, the Israelites. Go home, every one of you, for this
is my doing.'" So they obeyed the word
of the LORD and went home again, as the
LORD had ordered.

Golden Calves at Bethel and Dan

12:25 25Then Jeroboam fortified Shechem[v]
v Jdg 9:45 w Jdg 8:8,17 in the hill country of Ephraim and lived
there. From there he went out and built
up Peniel.[b][w]

26Jeroboam thought to himself, "The
kingdom will now likely revert to the
house of David. 27If these people go up to
offer sacrifices at the temple of the LORD
12:27 x Dt 12:5-6 in Jerusalem,[x] they will again give their
allegiance to their lord, Rehoboam king
of Judah. They will kill me and return to
King Rehoboam."

28After seeking advice, the king made
12:28 y Ex 32:4; two golden calves.[y] He said to the peo-
2Ki 10:29; 17:16 ple, "It is too much for you to go up to Je-
z Ex 32:8 rusalem. Here are your gods, O Israel,
who brought you up out of Egypt."[z]
12:29 29One he set up in Bethel,[a] and the oth-
a Ge 28:19 b Jdg 18:27-31 er in Dan.[b] 30And this thing became a
sin;[c] the people went even as far as Dan 12:30 c 1Ki 13:34;
to worship the one there. 2Ki 17:21
31Jeroboam built shrines[d] on high
places and appointed priests[e] from all 12:31 d 1Ki 13:32
sorts of people, even though they were e Nu 3:10;
not Levites. 32He instituted a festival on 1Ki 13:33;
the fifteenth day of the eighth[f] month, 2Ki 17:32;
like the festival held in Judah, and of- 2Ch 11:14-15; 13:9
fered sacrifices on the altar. This he did 12:32
in Bethel, sacrificing to the calves he had f Lev 23:33-34;
made. And at Bethel he also installed Nu 29:12
priests at the high places he had made.
33On the fifteenth day of the eighth
month, a month of his own choosing, he
offered sacrifices on the altar he had
built at Bethel.[g] So he instituted the fes- 12:33 g Nu 15:39;
tival for the Israelites and went up to the 1Ki 13:1;
altar to make offerings. Am 7:13

The Man of God From Judah

13 By the word of the LORD a man
of God[h] came from Judah to 13:1 h 2Ki 23:17
Bethel,[i] as Jeroboam was standing by i 1Ki 12:32-33
the altar to make an offering. 2He cried
out against the altar by the word of the
LORD: "O altar, altar! This is what the
LORD says: 'A son named Josiah[j] will be 13:2
born to the house of David. On you he j 2Ki 23:15-16, 20
will sacrifice the priests of the high
places who now make offerings here,
and human bones will be burned on
you.'" 3That same day the man of God 13:3
gave a sign:[k] "This is the sign the LORD k Jdg 6:17;
has declared: The altar will be split apart Isa 7:14; Jn 2:11;
and the ashes on it will be poured out." 1Co 1:22
4When King Jeroboam heard what
the man of God cried out against the altar at Bethel, he stretched out his hand
from the altar and said, "Seize him!" But
the hand he stretched out toward the
man shriveled up, so that he could not
pull it back. 5Also, the altar was split
apart and its ashes poured out according to the sign given by the man of God
by the word of the LORD.
6Then the king said to the man of
God, "Intercede[l] with the LORD your God 13:6
and pray for me that my hand may be re- l Ex 8:8; 9:28;
stored." So the man of God interceded 10:17; Lk 6:27-28; Ac 8:24;
with the LORD, and the king's hand was Jas 5:16
restored and became as it was before.
7The king said to the man of God,
"Come home with me and have some- 13:7
thing to eat, and I will give you a gift."[m] m 1Sa 9:7;
8But the man of God answered the 2Ki 5:15

[a] *18* Some Septuagint manuscripts and Syriac (see also 1 Kings 4:6 and 5:14); Hebrew *Adoram*
[b] *25* Hebrew *Penuel,* a variant of *Peniel*

king, "Even if you were to give me half
13:8 [n] Nu 22:18; your possessions,[n] I would not go with
24:13 [o] ver 16 you, nor would I eat bread[o] or drink water here. 9For I was commanded by the
word of the LORD: 'You must not eat
bread or drink water or return by the
way you came.' " 10So he took another
road and did not return by the way he
had come to Bethel.

11Now there was a certain old prophet living in Bethel, whose sons came and
told him all that the man of God had
done there that day. They also told their
father what he had said to the king.
12Their father asked them, "Which way
did he go?" And his sons showed him
which road the man of God from Judah
had taken. 13So he said to his sons, "Saddle the donkey for me." And when they
had saddled the donkey for him, he
mounted it 14and rode after the man of
God. He found him sitting under an oak
tree and asked, "Are you the man of God
who came from Judah?"

"I am," he replied.

15So the prophet said to him, "Come
home with me and eat."

16The man of God said, "I cannot turn
back and go with you, nor can I eat
13:16 [p] ver 8 bread[p] or drink water with you in this
place. 17I have been told by the word of
the LORD: 'You must not eat bread or
drink water there or return by the way
you came.' "

18The old prophet answered, "I too
am a prophet, as you are. And an angel
said to me by the word of the LORD:
'Bring him back with you to your house
so that he may eat bread and drink wa-
13:18 [q] Dt 13:3 ter.' " (But he was lying[q] to him.) 19So the
man of God returned with him and ate
and drank in his house.

20While they were sitting at the table,
the word of the LORD came to the old
prophet who had brought him back.
21He cried out to the man of God who
had come from Judah, "This is what the
13:21 [r] ver 26 LORD says: 'You have defied[r] the word of
the LORD and have not kept the com-
mand the LORD your God gave you.
22You came back and ate bread and
drank water in the place where he told
you not to eat or drink. Therefore your
body will not be buried in the tomb of
your fathers.' "

23When the man of God had finished
eating and drinking, the prophet who
had brought him back saddled his donkey for him. 24As he went on his way, a
lion[s] met him on the road and killed 13:24 [s] 1Ki 20:36
him, and his body was thrown down on
the road, with both the donkey and the
lion standing beside it. 25Some people
who passed by saw the body thrown
down there, with the lion standing beside the body, and they went and reported it in the city where the old prophet
lived.

26When the prophet who had brought
him back from his journey heard of it, he
said, "It is the man of God who defied
the word of the LORD. The LORD has giv-
en him over to the lion, which has
mauled him and killed him, as the word
of the LORD had warned him."

27The prophet said to his sons, "Saddle the donkey for me," and they did so.
28Then he went out and found the body
thrown down on the road, with the donkey and the lion standing beside it. The
lion had neither eaten the body nor
mauled the donkey. 29So the prophet
picked up the body of the man of God,
laid it on the donkey, and brought it
back to his own city to mourn for him
and bury him. 30Then he laid the body in
his own tomb, and they mourned over
him and said, "Oh, my brother!"[t] 13:30 [t] Jer 22:18

31After burying him, he said to his
sons, "When I die, bury me in the grave
where the man of God is buried; lay my
bones[u] beside his bones. 32For the mes- 13:31 [u] 2Ki 23:18
sage he declared by the word of the LORD
against the altar in Bethel and against 13:32 [v] ver 2;
all the shrines on the high places[v] in the Lev 26:30
towns of Samaria[w] will certainly come [w] 1Ki 16:24,28
true."[x] [x] 2Ki 23:16

33Even after this, Jeroboam did not
change his evil ways, but once more ap-
pointed priests for the high places from 13:33 [y] 1Ki 12:31;
all sorts[y] of people. Anyone who wanted 2Ch 11:15; 13:9
to become a priest he consecrated for
the high places. 34This was the sin[z] of 13:34 [z] 1Ki 12:30
the house of Jeroboam that led to its [a] 1Ki 14:10
downfall and to its destruction[a] from
the face of the earth.

Ahijah's Prophecy Against Jeroboam

14 At that time Abijah son of Jeroboam became ill, 2and Jerobo-
am said to his wife, "Go, disguise your-
self, so you won't be recognized as the 14:2 [b] 1Sa 28:8;
wife of Jeroboam. Then go to Shiloh. 2Sa 14:2;
Ahijah[b] the prophet is there—the one 1Ki 11:29

who told me I would be king over this people. 3 Take ten loaves of bread[c] with you, some cakes and a jar of honey, and go to him. He will tell you what will happen to the boy." 4 So Jeroboam's wife did what he said and went to Ahijah's house in Shiloh.

Now Ahijah could not see; his sight was gone because of his age. 5 But the LORD had told Ahijah, "Jeroboam's wife is coming to ask you about her son, for he is ill, and you are to give her such and such an answer. When she arrives, she will pretend to be someone else."

6 So when Ahijah heard the sound of her footsteps at the door, he said, "Come in, wife of Jeroboam. Why this pretense? I have been sent to you with bad news. 7 Go, tell Jeroboam that this is what the LORD, the God of Israel, says: 'I raised you up from among the people and made you a leader[d] over my people Israel. 8 I tore[e] the kingdom away from the house of David and gave it to you, but you have not been like my servant David, who kept my commands and followed me with all his heart, doing only what was right[f] in my eyes. 9 You have done more evil than all who lived before you. You have made for yourself other gods, idols[g] made of metal; you have provoked me to anger and thrust me behind your back.[h]

10 " 'Because of this, I am going to bring disaster on the house of Jeroboam. I will cut off from Jeroboam every last male in Israel—slave or free.[i] I will burn up the house of Jeroboam as one burns dung, until it is all gone.[j] 11 Dogs[k] will eat those belonging to Jeroboam who die in the city, and the birds of the air will feed on those who die in the country. The LORD has spoken!'

12 "As for you, go back home. When you set foot in your city, the boy will die. 13 All Israel will mourn for him and bury him. He is the only one belonging to Jeroboam who will be buried, because he is the only one in the house of Jeroboam in whom the LORD, the God of Israel, has found anything good.[l]

14 "The LORD will raise up for himself a king over Israel who will cut off the family of Jeroboam. This is the day! What? Yes, even now.[a] 15 And the LORD will strike Israel, so that it will be like a reed swaying in the water. He will uproot[m] Israel from this good land that he gave to their forefathers and scatter them beyond the River,[b] because they provoked[n] the LORD to anger by making Asherah[o] poles.[c] 16 And he will give Israel up because of the sins[p] Jeroboam has committed and has caused Israel to commit."

17 Then Jeroboam's wife got up and left and went to Tirzah.[q] As soon as she stepped over the threshold of the house, the boy died. 18 They buried him, and all Israel mourned for him, as the LORD had said through his servant the prophet Ahijah.

19 The other events of Jeroboam's reign, his wars and how he ruled, are written in the book of the annals of the kings of Israel. 20 He reigned for twenty-two years and then rested with his fathers. And Nadab his son succeeded him as king.

Rehoboam King of Judah

21 Rehoboam son of Solomon was king in Judah. He was forty-one years old when he became king, and he reigned seventeen years in Jerusalem, the city the LORD had chosen out of all the tribes of Israel in which to put his Name. His mother's name was Naamah; she was an Ammonite.[r]

22 Judah[s] did evil in the eyes of the LORD. By the sins they committed they stirred up his jealous anger[t] more than their fathers had done. 23 They also set up for themselves high places, sacred stones[u] and Asherah poles on every high hill and under every spreading tree.[v] 24 There were even male shrine prostitutes[w] in the land; the people engaged in all the detestable practices of the nations the LORD had driven out before the Israelites.

25 In the fifth year of King Rehoboam, Shishak king of Egypt attacked[x] Jerusalem. 26 He carried off the treasures of the temple[y] of the LORD and the treasures of the royal palace. He took everything, including all the gold shields[z] Solomon had made. 27 So King Rehoboam made bronze shields to replace them and assigned these to the commanders of the guard on duty at the entrance to the royal palace. 28 Whenever the king went to the LORD's temple, the guards bore the

a 14 The meaning of the Hebrew for this sentence is uncertain. *b 15* That is, the Euphrates
c 15 That is, symbols of the goddess Asherah; here and elsewhere in 1 Kings

14:3 c 1Sa 9:7
14:7 d 2Sa 12:7-8; 1Ki 16:2
14:8 e 1Ki 11:31,33, 38 f 1Ki 15:5
14:9 g Ex 34:17; 1Ki 12:28; 2Ch 11:15 h Ne 9:26; Ps 50:17; Eze 23:35
14:10 i Dt 32:36; 1Ki 21:21; 2Ki 9:8-9; 14:26 j 1Ki 15:29
14:11 k 1Ki 16:4; 21:24
14:13 l 2Ch 12:12; 19:3
14:15 m Dt 29:28; 2Ki 15:29; 17:6; Ps 52:5
14:15 n Jos 23:15-16 o Ex 34:13; Dt 12:3
14:16 p 1Ki 12:30; 13:34; 15:30,34; 16:2
14:17 q ver 12; 1Ki 15:33; 16:6-9
14:21 r ver 31; 1Ki 11:1; 2Ch 12:13
14:22 s 2Ch 12:1 t Dt 32:21; Ps 78:58; 1Co 10:22
14:23 u Dt 16:22; 2Ki 17:9-10; Eze 16:24-25 v Dt 12:2; Isa 57:5
14:24 w Dt 23:17; 1Ki 15:12; 2Ki 23:7
14:25 x 1Ki 11:40; 2Ch 12:2
14:26 y 1Ki 15:15,18 z 1Ki 10:17

shields, and afterward they returned
them to the guardroom.
29 As for the other events of Rehoboam's reign, and all he did, are they not
written in the book of the annals of the
kings of Judah? 30 There was continual
14:30 warfare[a] between Rehoboam and Jero-
a 1Ki 12:21; 15:6 boam. 31 And Rehoboam rested with his
fathers and was buried with them in the
14:31 City of David. His mother's name was
b ver 21; Naamah; she was an Ammonite.[b] And
2Ch 12:16 Abijah[a] his son succeeded him as king.

Abijah King of Judah

15 In the eighteenth year of the
reign of Jeroboam son of Nebat,
Abijah[b] became king of Judah, 2 and he
reigned in Jerusalem three years. His
15:2 mother's name was Maacah[c] daughter
c 2Ch 11:20; 13:2 of Abishalom.[c]
3 He committed all the sins his father
had done before him; his heart was not
15:3 fully devoted[d] to the LORD his God, as
d 1Ki 11:4; Ps 119:80 the heart of David his forefather had
been. 4 Nevertheless, for David's sake the
15:4 LORD his God gave him a lamp[e] in Jeru-
e 2Sa 21:17; 1Ki 11:36; salem by raising up a son to succeed him
2Ch 21:7 and by making Jerusalem strong. 5 For
David had done what was right in the
eyes of the LORD and had not failed to
15:5 keep[f] any of the LORD's commands all
f 1Ki 9:4; 14:8 the days of his life—except in the case of
g 2Sa 11:2-27; 12:9 Uriah[g] the Hittite.
15:6 6 There was war[h] between Rehoboam[d]
h 1Ki 14:30 and Jeroboam throughout ⌞Abijah's⌟ lifetime. 7 As for the other events of Abijah's
reign, and all he did, are they not written
in the book of the annals of the kings of
Judah? There was war between Abijah
and Jeroboam. 8 And Abijah rested with
his fathers and was buried in the City of
David. And Asa his son succeeded him
as king.

Asa King of Judah

9 In the twentieth year of Jeroboam
king of Israel, Asa became king of Judah,
10 and he reigned in Jerusalem forty-one
years. His grandmother's name was Ma-
15:10 acah[i] daughter of Abishalom.
i ver 2 11 Asa did what was right in the eyes of
the LORD, as his father David had done.
12 He expelled the male shrine prosti-
15:12 tutes[j] from the land and got rid of all the
j 1Ki 14:24; 22:46 idols his fathers had made. 13 He even deposed his grandmother Maacah from
her position as queen mother, because
she had made a repulsive Asherah pole. 15:13
Asa cut the pole down[k] and burned it in k Ex 32:20
the Kidron Valley. 14 Although he did not
remove the high places, Asa's heart was 15:14
fully committed[l] to the LORD all his life. l ver 3; 1Ki 8:61; 22:43
15 He brought into the temple of the
LORD the silver and gold and the articles
that he and his father had dedicated.[m] 15:15 m 1Ki 7:51
16 There was war[n] between Asa and
Baasha king of Israel throughout their 15:16 n ver 32
reigns. 17 Baasha king of Israel went up
against Judah and fortified Ramah[o] to 15:17 o Jos 18:25;
prevent anyone from leaving or entering 1Ki 12:27
the territory of Asa king of Judah.
18 Asa then took all the silver and gold
that was left in the treasuries of the 15:18
LORD's temple[p] and of his own palace. p ver 15; 1Ki 14:26
He entrusted it to his officials and sent[q] q 2Ki 12:18
them to Ben-Hadad[r] son of Tabrimmon, r 1Ki 11:23-24
the son of Hezion, the king of Aram,
who was ruling in Damascus. 19 "Let
there be a treaty between me and you,"
he said, "as there was between my father
and your father. See, I am sending you a
gift of silver and gold. Now break your
treaty with Baasha king of Israel so he
will withdraw from me."
20 Ben-Hadad agreed with King Asa
and sent the commanders of his forces
against the towns of Israel. He con- 15:20
quered[s] Ijon, Dan, Abel Beth Maacah s Jdg 18:29;
and all Kinnereth in addition to Naph- 2Sa 20:14; 2Ki 15:29
tali. 21 When Baasha heard this, he
stopped building Ramah and withdrew
to Tirzah. 22 Then King Asa issued an order to all Judah—no one was exempt—
and they carried away from Ramah the
stones and timber Baasha had been using there. With them King Asa built up 15:22
Geba[t] in Benjamin, and also Mizpah. t Jos 18:24; 21:17
23 As for all the other events of Asa's
reign, all his achievements, all he did
and the cities he built, are they not written in the book of the annals of the kings
of Judah? In his old age, however, his feet
became diseased. 24 Then Asa rested
with his fathers and was buried with
them in the city of his father David. And
Jehoshaphat[u] his son succeeded him as 15:24 u Mt 1:8
king.

a 31 Some Hebrew manuscripts and Septuagint (see also 2 Chron. 12:16); most Hebrew manuscripts *Abijam* *b 1* Some Hebrew manuscripts and Septuagint (see also 2 Chron. 12:16); most Hebrew manuscripts *Abijam*; also in verses 7 and 8 *c 2* A variant of *Absalom*; also in verse 10 *d 6* Most Hebrew manuscripts; some Hebrew manuscripts and Syriac *Abijam* (that is, Abijah)

Nadab King of Israel

25 Nadab son of Jeroboam became king of Israel in the second year of Asa king of Judah, and he reigned over Israel two years. 26 He did evil in the eyes of the LORD, walking in the ways of his father[v] and in his sin, which he had caused Israel to commit.

27 Baasha son of Ahijah of the house of Issachar plotted against him, and he struck him down[w] at Gibbethon,[x] a Philistine town, while Nadab and all Israel were besieging it. 28 Baasha killed Nadab in the third year of Asa king of Judah and succeeded him as king.

29 As soon as he began to reign, he killed Jeroboam's whole family.[y] He did not leave Jeroboam anyone that breathed, but destroyed them all, according to the word of the LORD given through his servant Ahijah the Shilonite— 30 because of the sins[z] Jeroboam had committed and had caused Israel to commit, and because he provoked the LORD, the God of Israel, to anger.

31 As for the other events of Nadab's reign, and all he did, are they not written in the book of the annals of the kings of Israel? 32 There was war[a] between Asa and Baasha king of Israel throughout their reigns.

Baasha King of Israel

33 In the third year of Asa king of Judah, Baasha son of Ahijah became king of all Israel in Tirzah, and he reigned twenty-four years. 34 He did evil[b] in the eyes of the LORD, walking in the ways of Jeroboam and in his sin, which he had caused Israel to commit.

16 Then the word of the LORD came to Jehu[c] son of Hanani[d] against Baasha: 2 "I lifted you up from the dust[e] and made you leader[f] of my people Israel, but you walked in the ways of Jeroboam and caused[g] my people Israel to sin and to provoke me to anger by their sins. 3 So I am about to consume Baasha and his house,[h] and I will make your house like that of Jeroboam son of Nebat. 4 Dogs[i] will eat those belonging to Baasha who die in the city, and the birds of the air will feed on those who die in the country."

5 As for the other events of Baasha's reign, what he did and his achievements, are they not written in the book of the annals[j] of the kings of Israel? 6 Baasha rested with his fathers and was buried in Tirzah.[k] And Elah his son succeeded him as king.

7 Moreover, the word of the LORD came[l] through the prophet Jehu[m] son of Hanani to Baasha and his house, because of all the evil he had done in the eyes of the LORD, provoking him to anger by the things he did, and becoming like the house of Jeroboam—and also because he destroyed it.

Elah King of Israel

8 In the twenty-sixth year of Asa king of Judah, Elah son of Baasha became king of Israel, and he reigned in Tirzah two years.

9 Zimri, one of his officials, who had command of half his chariots, plotted against him. Elah was in Tirzah at the time, getting drunk[n] in the home of Arza, the man in charge[o] of the palace at Tirzah. 10 Zimri came in, struck him down and killed him in the twenty-seventh year of Asa king of Judah. Then he succeeded him as king.

11 As soon as he began to reign and was seated on the throne, he killed off Baasha's whole family.[p] He did not spare a single male, whether relative or friend. 12 So Zimri destroyed the whole family of Baasha, in accordance with the word of the LORD spoken against Baasha through the prophet Jehu— 13 because of all the sins Baasha and his son Elah had committed and had caused Israel to commit, so that they provoked the LORD, the God of Israel, to anger by their worthless idols.[q]

14 As for the other events of Elah's reign, and all he did, are they not written in the book of the annals of the kings of Israel?

Zimri King of Israel

15 In the twenty-seventh year of Asa king of Judah, Zimri reigned in Tirzah seven days. The army was encamped near Gibbethon,[r] a Philistine town. 16 When the Israelites in the camp heard that Zimri had plotted against the king and murdered him, they proclaimed Omri, the commander of the army, king over Israel that very day there in the camp. 17 Then Omri and all the Israelites with him withdrew from Gibbethon and

15:26 [v] 1Ki 12:30; 14:16
15:27 [w] 1Ki 14:14 [x] Jos 19:44; 21:23
15:29 [y] 1Ki 14:10,14
15:30 [z] 1Ki 14:9,16
15:32 [a] ver 16
15:34 [b] ver 26; 1Ki 12:28-29; 13:33; 14:16
16:1 [c] ver 7; 2Ch 19:2; 20:34 [d] 2Ch 16:7
16:2 [e] 1Sa 2:8 [f] 1Ki 14:7-9 [g] 1Ki 15:34
16:3 [h] ver 11; 1Ki 14:10; 15:29; 21:22
16:4 [i] 1Ki 14:11
16:5 [j] 1Ki 14:19; 15:31
16:6 [k] 1Ki 14:17; 15:33
16:7 [l] 1Ki 15:27,29 [m] ver 1
16:9 [n] 2Ki 9:30-33 [o] 1Ki 18:3
16:11 [p] ver 3
16:13 [q] Dt 32:21; 1Sa 12:21; Isa 41:29
16:15 [r] Jos 19:44; 1Ki 15:27

laid siege to Tirzah. 18 When Zimri saw
that the city was taken, he went into the
citadel of the royal palace and set the
palace on fire around him. So he died,
19 because of the sins he had committed,
doing evil in the eyes of the LORD and
walking in the ways of Jeroboam and in
the sin he had committed and had
caused Israel to commit.
20 As for the other events of Zimri's
reign, and the rebellion he carried out,
are they not written in the book of the
annals of the kings of Israel?

Omri King of Israel

21 Then the people of Israel were split
into two factions; half supported Tibni
son of Ginath for king, and the other
half supported Omri. 22 But Omri's followers proved stronger than those of
Tibni son of Ginath. So Tibni died and
Omri became king.
23 In the thirty-first year of Asa king of
Judah, Omri became king of Israel, and
he reigned twelve years, six of them in
Tirzah.[s] 24 He bought the hill of Samaria
from Shemer for two talents[a] of silver
and built a city on the hill, calling it
Samaria,[t] after Shemer, the name of the
former owner of the hill.
25 But Omri did evil[u] in the eyes of the
LORD and sinned more than all those before him. 26 He walked in all the ways of
Jeroboam son of Nebat and in his sin,
which he had caused[v] Israel to commit,
so that they provoked the LORD, the God
of Israel, to anger by their worthless
idols.[w]
27 As for the other events of Omri's
reign, what he did and the things he
achieved, are they not written in the
book of the annals of the kings of Israel?
28 Omri rested with his fathers and was
buried in Samaria. And Ahab his son
succeeded him as king.

Ahab Becomes King of Israel

29 In the thirty-eighth year of Asa king
of Judah, Ahab son of Omri became king
of Israel, and he reigned in Samaria over
Israel twenty-two years. 30 Ahab son of
Omri did more[x] evil in the eyes of the
LORD than any of those before him. 31 He
not only considered it trivial to commit
the sins of Jeroboam son of Nebat, but
he also married[y] Jezebel daughter[z] of
Ethbaal king of the Sidonians, and began to serve Baal[a] and worship him.
32 He set up an altar for Baal in the temple[b] of Baal that he built in Samaria.
33 Ahab also made an Asherah pole[c] and
did more[d] to provoke the LORD, the God
of Israel, to anger than did all the kings
of Israel before him.
34 In Ahab's time, Hiel of Bethel rebuilt
Jericho. He laid its foundations at the
cost of his firstborn son Abiram, and he
set up its gates at the cost of his
youngest son Segub, in accordance with
the word of the LORD spoken by Joshua
son of Nun.[e]

Elijah Fed by Ravens

17 Now Elijah[f] the Tishbite, from
Tishbe[b] in Gilead,[g] said to
Ahab, "As the LORD, the God of Israel,
lives, whom I serve, there will be neither
dew nor rain[h] in the next few years except at my word."
2 Then the word of the LORD came to
Elijah: 3 "Leave here, turn eastward and
hide in the Kerith Ravine, east of the
Jordan. 4 You will drink from the brook,
and I have ordered the ravens[i] to feed
you there."
5 So he did what the LORD had told
him. He went to the Kerith Ravine, east
of the Jordan, and stayed there. 6 The
ravens brought him bread and meat in
the morning[j] and bread and meat in the
evening, and he drank from the brook.

The Widow at Zarephath

7 Some time later the brook dried up
because there had been no rain in the
land. 8 Then the word of the LORD came
to him: 9 "Go at once to Zarephath[k] of Sidon and stay there. I have commanded
a widow[l] in that place to supply you
with food." 10 So he went to Zarephath.
When he came to the town gate, a widow was there gathering sticks. He called
to her and asked, "Would you bring me
a little water in a jar so I may have a
drink?"[m] 11 As she was going to get it, he
called, "And bring me, please, a piece of
bread."
12 "As surely as the LORD your God
lives," she replied, "I don't have any
bread—only a handful of flour in a jar
and a little oil[n] in a jug. I am gathering a
few sticks to take home and make a

a 24 That is, about 150 pounds (about 70 kilograms) *b 1* Or *Tishbite, of the settlers*

16:23 s 1Ki 15:21
16:24 t 1Ki 13:32; Jn 4:4
16:25 u Dt 4:25; Mic 6:16
16:26 v ver 19 w Dt 32:21
16:30 x ver 25; 1Ki 14:9
16:31 y Dt 7:3; 1Ki 11:2 z Jdg 18:7; 2Ki 9:34
16:31 a 2Ki 10:18; 17:16
16:32 b 2Ki 10:21,27; 11:18
16:33 c 2Ki 13:6 d ver 29,30; 1Ki 14:9; 21:25
16:34 e Jos 6:26
17:1 f Mal 4:5; Jas 5:17 g Jdg 12:4 h Dt 10:8; 1Ki 18:1; 2Ki 3:14; Lk 4:25
17:4 i Ge 8:7
17:6 j Ex 16:8
17:9 k Ob 1:20 l Lk 4:26
17:10 m Ge 24:17; Jn 4:7
17:12 n ver 1; 2Ki 4:2

DISCOVERY 85

GOD OF THE OUTSIDER

Elijah had predicted three years of drought in Israel (1 Kings 17:1). During the initial phase of this drought he had slept by the Kerith Ravine, and the ravens had supplied him with food. But when the brook finally dried up, God sent his prophet to stay with a widow in Zarephath, a coastal town situated between Tyre and Sidon.

Although there were many widows in Israel, God chose a destitute pagan widow to accomplish his purpose. When Elijah met the widow, she was gathering sticks for a fire in preparation for cooking one final meal for herself and her son. After that her food supply would be exhausted, and she assumed that she and her son would die. Even so, she asked the prophet to share their meager meal.

Elijah made the incredible promise to her that "the jar of flour will not be used up and the jug of oil will not run dry until the day the LORD gives rain on the land" (verse 14). Every day they ate, but the flour supply was never depleted and the jug of oil never ran dry—a daily miracle.

In much the same way that Elijah with God's help provided for the physical nourishment of this impoverished widow and her son, our Lord expressed concern about the spiritual thirst of a Gentile woman from Samaria (John 4; see Discovery #275, Page 1415). Like the widow of Zarephath, the woman at the well seemed an unlikely candidate for attention from Jesus. Both were outside the circle of God's own people, the Jews, and each lived within the lower echelon of her own society. Interestingly, the initial encounters began in a similar manner: a request, first from Elijah and later from Jesus, for a drink of water (1 Kings 17:10; John 4:7).

The Samaritan woman, though amazed that Jesus was able to reveal her past, mistakenly assumed that he was a prophet (John 4:18). Still skeptical, she become involved in a theological discussion with Jesus, finally stating that she knew that the Messiah would be coming and that he would explain everything (John 4:25). Jesus' response was simple: "I who speak to you am he" (John 4:26). John told us that the woman left her water jar and returned to her home, urging the townspeople to "come, see a man who told me everything I ever did. Could this be the Christ?" (John 4:29).

God has from the beginning desired to embrace all of humanity with his love, to satisfy the hunger and thirst of every person he has created. Both the Old and New Testaments are replete with examples of God and his people holding out "food" and "water" to outsiders from the faith. And frequently these acts of kindness have resulted in ready and eager acceptance.

Self-Discovery: *How has Jesus expressed his care for you and his desire to meet your deepest needs? What specific actions could you take to bring the cup of cold water to someone in his name today?*

GO TO DISCOVERY 86 ON PAGE 451

meal for myself and my son, that we may
eat it—and die."
13Elijah said to her, "Don't be afraid.
Go home and do as you have said. But
first make a small cake of bread for me
from what you have and bring it to me,
and then make something for yourself
and your son. 14For this is what the
LORD, the God of Israel, says: 'The jar of
flour will not be used up and the jug of
oil will not run dry until the day the
LORD gives rain on the land.'"
15She went away and did as Elijah had
told her. So there was food every day for
Elijah and for the woman and her family. 16For the jar of flour was not used up
and the jug of oil did not run dry, in
keeping with the word of the LORD spoken by Elijah.
17Some time later the son of the
woman who owned the house became
ill. He grew worse and worse, and finally stopped breathing. 18She said to Eli-
17:18 [o] 2Ki 3:13; Lk 5:8 jah, "What do you have against me, man
of God? Did you come to remind me of
my sin[o] and kill my son?"

ELIJAH

GOD'S CHOSEN PROPHET

Elijah, whose name means "the LORD is my God," was a prophet from Tishbe in Gilead during the ninth century B.C. (1 Kings 17). He, along with Moses and Elisha, was one of God's leading defenders and great miracle workers of Old Testament times. Elijah's eight recorded miracles are among the most spectacular in the Bible—including the raising of a dead boy (verses 19–23) and the calling down of fire from heaven on Mount Carmel, each in response to his simple and earnest prayer (1 Kings 18:36–38; see also 2 Kings 1:10–12 for another instance). Elijah never experienced death; instead, God simply took him up to heaven in a whirlwind (2 Kings 2:11–12), and Elijah passed along his ministry to his successor, Elisha (2 Kings 2:9–13). Malachi 4:5–6 predicted that an "Elijah" would return before the "great and dreadful day of the LORD," and in the New Testament Jesus identified John the Baptist as the one who had fulfilled this prophecy (Matthew 17:9–13). Elijah was such a prominent person in the Bible that he is mentioned nearly 30 times in the New Testament, and he appeared with Moses on the mountain at the time of Jesus' transfiguration (Matthew 17:3).

19"Give me your son," Elijah replied.
He took him from her arms, carried him
to the upper room where he was staying,
and laid him on his bed. 20Then he cried
out to the LORD, "O LORD my God, have
you brought tragedy also upon this widow I am staying with, by causing her son
to die?" 21Then he stretched[p] himself 17:21 [p] 2Ki 4:34;
out on the boy three times and cried to Ac 20:10
the LORD, "O LORD my God, let this boy's
life return to him!"
22The LORD heard Elijah's cry, and the
boy's life returned to him, and he lived.
23Elijah picked up the child and carried
him down from the room into the
house. He gave him to his mother and
said, "Look, your son is alive!"
24Then the woman said to Elijah, 17:24
"Now I know[q] that you are a man of God [q] Jn 3:2; 16:30
and that the word of the LORD from your [r] Ps 119:43;
mouth is the truth."[r] Jn 17:17

Elijah and Obadiah

18 After a long time, in the third[s] 18:1 [s] 1Ki 17:1;
year, the word of the LORD came Lk 4:25; Jas 5:17
to Elijah: "Go and present yourself to [t] Dt 28:12
Ahab, and I will send rain[t] on the land."
2So Elijah went to present himself to
Ahab.
Now the famine was severe in
Samaria, 3and Ahab had summoned 18:3
Obadiah, who was in charge[u] of his [u] 1Ki 16:9
palace. (Obadiah was a devout believer[v] [v] Ne 7:2
in the LORD. 4While Jezebel[w] was killing 18:4
off the LORD's prophets, Obadiah had [w] 2Ki 9:7
taken a hundred prophets and hidden[x] [x] ver 13; Isa 16:3
them in two caves, fifty in each, and had
supplied them with food and water.)
5Ahab had said to Obadiah, "Go through
the land to all the springs and valleys.
Maybe we can find some grass to keep
the horses and mules alive so we will not
have to kill any of our animals." 6So they
divided the land they were to cover,
Ahab going in one direction and Obadiah in another.
7As Obadiah was walking along, Eli- 18:7
jah met him. Obadiah recognized[y] him, [y] 2Ki 1:8
bowed down to the ground, and said, "Is
it really you, my lord Elijah?"
8"Yes," he replied. "Go tell your master,
'Elijah is here.'"
9"What have I done wrong," asked
Obadiah, "that you are handing your servant over to Ahab to be put to death?
10As surely as the LORD your God lives,
there is not a nation or kingdom where

18:10 my master has not sent someone to
z 1Ki 17:3 look[z] for you. And whenever a nation or
kingdom claimed you were not there, he
made them swear they could not find
you. 11But now you tell me to go to my
18:12 master and say, 'Elijah is here.' 12I don't
a 2Ki 2:16; Eze 3:14; know where the Spirit[a] of the LORD may
Ac 8:39 carry you when I leave you. If I go and tell
Ahab and he doesn't find you, he will kill
me. Yet I your servant have worshiped
the LORD since my youth. 13Haven't you
heard, my lord, what I did while Jezebel
was killing the prophets of the LORD? I
hid a hundred of the LORD's prophets in
two caves, fifty in each, and supplied
them with food and water. 14And now
you tell me to go to my master and say,
'Elijah is here.' He will kill me!"
15Elijah said, "As the LORD Almighty
18:15 lives, whom I serve, I will surely present[b]
b 1Ki 17:1 myself to Ahab today."

Elijah on Mount Carmel

16So Obadiah went to meet Ahab and
told him, and Ahab went to meet Elijah.
18:17 c Jos 7:25; 17When he saw Elijah, he said to him, "Is
1Ki 21:20; that you, you troubler[c] of Israel?"
Ac 16:20 18"I have not made trouble for Israel,"
18:18 Elijah replied. "But you[d] and your fa-
d 1Ki 16:31,33; ther's family have. You have abandoned[e]
21:25 e 2Ch 15:2 the LORD's commands and have followed
the Baals. 19Now summon the people
18:19 from all over Israel to meet me on
f Jos 19:26 Mount Carmel.[f] And bring the four hundred and fifty prophets of Baal and the
four hundred prophets of Asherah, who
eat at Jezebel's table."
20So Ahab sent word throughout all
Israel and assembled the prophets on
Mount Carmel. 21Elijah went before the
18:21 people and said, "How long will you wa-
g Jos 24:15; 2Ki 17:41; ver[g] between two opinions? If the LORD
Mt 6:24 is God, follow him; but if Baal is God, follow him."
But the people said nothing.
18:22 22Then Elijah said to them, "I am the
h 1Ki 19:10 only one of the LORD's prophets left,[h] but
i ver 19 Baal has four hundred and fifty prophets.[i] 23Get two bulls for us. Let them
choose one for themselves, and let them
cut it into pieces and put it on the wood
but not set fire to it. I will prepare the
other bull and put it on the wood but
not set fire to it. 24Then you call on the
name of your god, and I will call on the
18:24 name of the LORD. The god who answers
j ver 38; 1Ch 21:26 by fire[j]—he is God."

Then all the people said, "What you
say is good."
25Elijah said to the prophets of Baal,
"Choose one of the bulls and prepare it
first, since there are so many of you. Call
on the name of your god, but do not
light the fire." 26So they took the bull giv-
en them and prepared it.
Then they called on the name of Baal
from morning till noon. "O Baal, answer
us!" they shouted. But there was no re- 18:26
sponse;[k] no one answered. And they k Ps 115:4-5; Jer 10:5;
danced around the altar they had made. 1Co 8:4; 12:2
27At noon Elijah began to taunt them.
"Shout louder!" he said. "Surely he is a
god! Perhaps he is deep in thought, or
busy, or traveling. Maybe he is sleeping 18:27
and must be awakened."[l] 28So they l Hab 2:19
shouted louder and slashed[m] them- 18:28
selves with swords and spears, as was m Lev 19:28;
their custom, until their blood flowed. Dt 14:1
29Midday passed, and they continued
their frantic prophesying until the time 18:29
for the evening sacrifice.[n] But there was n Ex 29:41
no response, no one answered, no one o ver 26
paid attention.[o]
30Then Elijah said to all the people,
"Come here to me." They came to him,
and he repaired the altar[p] of the LORD, 18:30
which was in ruins. 31Elijah took twelve p 1Ki 19:10
stones, one for each of the tribes descended from Jacob, to whom the word
of the LORD had come, saying, "Your 18:31
name shall be Israel."[q] 32With the stones q Ge 32:28; 35:10; 2Ki 17:34
he built an altar in the name[r] of the
LORD, and he dug a trench around it 18:32
large enough to hold two seahs[a] of seed. r Col 3:17
33He arranged[s] the wood, cut the bull 18:33 s Ge 22:9;
into pieces and laid it on the wood. Then Lev 1:6-8
he said to them, "Fill four large jars with
water and pour it on the offering and on
the wood."
34"Do it again," he said, and they did it
again.
"Do it a third time," he ordered, and
they did it the third time. 35The water
ran down around the altar and even
filled the trench.
36At the time of sacrifice, the prophet
Elijah stepped forward and prayed: 18:36
"O LORD, God of Abraham,[t] Isaac and Is- t Ex 3:6;
rael, let it be known[u] today that you are Mt 22:32 u 1Ki 8:43;
God in Israel and that I am your servant 2Ki 19:19
and have done all these things at your v Nu 16:28
command.[v] 37Answer me, O LORD, an-

a 32 That is, probably about 13 quarts (about 15 liters)

swer me, so these people will know that
you, O LORD, are God, and that you are
turning their hearts back again."
38 Then the fire[w] of the LORD fell and
burned up the sacrifice, the wood, the
stones and the soil, and also licked up
the water in the trench.
39 When all the people saw this, they
fell prostrate and cried, "The LORD—he
is God! The LORD—he is God!"[x]
40 Then Elijah commanded them,
"Seize the prophets of Baal. Don't let
anyone get away!" They seized them,
and Elijah had them brought down to
the Kishon Valley[y] and slaughtered[z]
there.
41 And Elijah said to Ahab, "Go, eat
and drink, for there is the sound of a
heavy rain." 42 So Ahab went off to eat
and drink, but Elijah climbed to the top
of Carmel, bent down to the ground and
put his face between his knees.[a]
43 "Go and look toward the sea," he
told his servant. And he went up and
looked.
"There is nothing there," he said.
Seven times Elijah said, "Go back."
44 The seventh time the servant reported, "A cloud[b] as small as a man's
hand is rising from the sea."
So Elijah said, "Go and tell Ahab,
'Hitch up your chariot and go down before the rain stops you.'"
45 Meanwhile, the sky grew black with
clouds, the wind rose, a heavy rain came
on and Ahab rode off to Jezreel. 46 The
power[c] of the LORD came upon Elijah
and, tucking his cloak into his belt,[d] he
ran ahead of Ahab all the way to Jezreel.

Elijah Flees to Horeb

19 Now Ahab told Jezebel everything Elijah had done and how
he had killed[e] all the prophets with the
sword. 2 So Jezebel sent a messenger to
Elijah to say, "May the gods deal with
me, be it ever so severely,[f] if by this time
tomorrow I do not make your life like
that of one of them."
3 Elijah was afraid[a] and ran[g] for his
life. When he came to Beersheba in Judah, he left his servant there, 4 while he
himself went a day's journey into the
desert. He came to a broom tree, sat
down under it and prayed that he might
die. "I have had enough, LORD," he said.
"Take my life;[h] I am no better than my

18:38 [w] Lev 9:24; Jdg 6:21; 1Ch 21:26; 2Ch 7:1; Job 1:16
18:39 [x] ver 24
18:40 [y] Jdg 4:7 [z] Dt 13:5; 18:20; 2Ki 10:24-25
18:42 [a] ver 19-20; Jas 5:18
18:44 [b] Lk 12:54
18:46 [c] 2Ki 3:15 [d] 2Ki 4:29; 9:1
19:1 [e] 1Ki 18:40
19:2 [f] 1Ki 20:10; 2Ki 6:31; Ru 1:17
19:3 [g] Ge 31:21
19:4 [h] Nu 11:15; Jer 20:18; Jnh 4:8

ancestors." 5 Then he lay down under the
tree and fell asleep.[i]
All at once an angel touched him and
said, "Get up and eat." 6 He looked
around, and there by his head was a
cake of bread baked over hot coals, and
a jar of water. He ate and drank and then
lay down again.
7 The angel of the LORD came back a
second time and touched him and said,
"Get up and eat, for the journey is too
much for you." 8 So he got up and ate and
drank. Strengthened by that food, he
traveled forty[j] days and forty nights until he reached Horeb,[k] the mountain of
God. 9 There he went into a cave[l] and
spent the night.

The LORD Appears to Elijah

And the word of the LORD came to
him: "What are you doing here, Elijah?"
10 He replied, "I have been very zealous[m] for the LORD God Almighty. The Israelites have rejected your covenant,
broken down your altars, and put your
prophets to death with the sword. I am
the only one left,[n] and now they are trying to kill me too."
11 The LORD said, "Go out and stand on
the mountain[o] in the presence of the
LORD, for the LORD is about to pass by."
Then a great and powerful wind[p] tore
the mountains apart and shattered the
rocks before the LORD, but the LORD was
not in the wind. After the wind there
was an earthquake, but the LORD was
not in the earthquake. 12 After the earthquake came a fire, but the LORD was not
in the fire. And after the fire came a gentle whisper.[q] 13 When Elijah heard it, he
pulled his cloak over his face[r] and went
out and stood at the mouth of the cave.
Then a voice said to him, "What are
you doing here, Elijah?"
14 He replied, "I have been very zealous
for the LORD God Almighty. The Israelites have rejected your covenant, broken
down your altars, and put your prophets
to death with the sword. I am the only
one left,[s] and now they are trying to kill
me too."
15 The LORD said to him, "Go back the
way you came, and go to the Desert of
Damascus. When you get there, anoint
Hazael[t] king over Aram. 16 Also, anoint[u]
Jehu son of Nimshi king over Israel, and

[a] 3 Or *Elijah saw*

19:5 [i] Ge 28:11
19:8 [j] Ex 24:18; 34:28; Dt 9:9-11,18; Mt 4:2 [k] Ex 3:1
19:9 [l] Ex 33:22
19:10 [m] Nu 25:13 [n] 1Ki 18:4,22; Ro 11:3*
19:11 [o] Ex 24:12 [p] Eze 1:4; 37:7
19:12 [q] Job 4:16; Zec 4:6
19:13 [r] ver 9; Ex 3:6
19:14 [s] ver 10
19:15 [t] 2Ki 8:7-15
19:16 [u] 2Ki 9:1-3,6

DISCOVERY 86

When God Whispers

How many times have you exclaimed in frustration, "I can't believe this is happening to me!" Very likely Elijah entertained similar thoughts. The prophet experienced numerous intense emotions within just a few short hours. First he challenged the prophets of Baal on Mount Carmel, calling down fire from heaven to consume the pagan altar. Next he single-handedly killed 450 of Baal's prophets. Immediately after that, he experienced a demonstration of God's power as the lengthy drought and famine came to an abrupt end. Finally, running for his life from the murderous queen Jezebel, Elijah suffered sudden burnout and plunged into depression (1 Kings 19:3–5).

Elijah's emotions had run the gamut—from the extraordinary thrill of victory to the chilling fear of impending death, from the apex of euphoria to the depths of depression. It was at this point that the Lord intervened. Elijah took cover in a cave as God began an awesome demonstration of his power. First a rock-splitting wind tore against the mountainside. Then the earth shook with a rumbling earthquake, followed by a raging fire. But God was not present in any of those mighty forces. Finally Elijah's ringing ears detected a gentle whisper. Elijah stepped out of the cave and heard the voice of God; in soft undertones God demonstrated his true power.

The truth Elijah learned that day may be experienced by all of God's people. God—and only God—can turn injustice and evil into praise and victory. Unless we are focused on God's will, we can easily miss his manifestations of power. He can shatter mountains, shake the very foundation of the earth and rain down fire from heaven, but often he speaks to his beloved in a soft, lilting, lover's whisper.

Jesus knew what it was to trust God completely, no matter what evil was swirling around him. While he slept peacefully in a boat, a life-threatening storm on the Sea of Galilee panicked his disciples. They woke the Master, shrieking in their terror, but Jesus simply stood and rebuked the surging waves with one authoritative word, "Quiet!" (Mark 4:39). Instant and perfect peace ensued. When God the Father wanted to teach Elijah about his nature, he spoke in a tranquil voice through a gentle breeze. When God the Son wanted to teach his disciples who he was, he quieted the raging wind.

During the storms of life we need to listen for that same barely audible whisper. We may have to struggle through many difficult days before we quiet down and begin to really hear and understand what God is saying. When we get past the events that drain our energy, we are in a good place to slow down and reflect on what we have just been through. As we sit in quiet meditation and try to make sense of our lives, we meet God (Psalm 46:10). Within our noisy culture we often act as though we detest quietness, filling our lives with any and every nerve-jangling distraction. But if we want to hear God when he speaks, we must slow down, stop talking, sit quietly and listen.

Self-Discovery: *When did you last experience emotional or spiritual "burnout" shortly after a particularly intense or exhilarating experience? How have you dealt with this situation? Have you been able to quiet yourself enough to hear Jesus whisper to you?*

GO TO DISCOVERY 87 ON PAGE 456

19:16 v ver 21; 2Ki 2:9, anoint Elisha[v] son of Shaphat from Abel
15 Meholah to succeed you as prophet.
17Jehu will put to death any who escape
19:17 w 2Ki 8:12,29; the sword of Hazael,[w] and Elisha will put
9:14; 13:3,7,22 to death any who escape the sword of
19:18 Jehu. 18Yet I reserve[x] seven thousand in
x Ro 11:4* Israel—all whose knees have not bowed
y Hos 13:2 down to Baal and all whose mouths
have not kissed[y] him."

The Call of Elisha

19So Elijah went from there and found
Elisha son of Shaphat. He was plowing
with twelve yoke of oxen, and he himself
was driving the twelfth pair. Elijah went
19:19 z 2Ki 2:8,14 up to him and threw his cloak[z] around
him. 20Elisha then left his oxen and ran
19:20 after Elijah. "Let me kiss my father and
a Mt 8:21-22; mother good-by,"[a] he said, "and then I
Lk 9:61 will come with you."

"Go back," Elijah replied. "What have
I done to you?"

21So Elisha left him and went back. He
19:21 b 2Sa 24:22 took his yoke of oxen[b] and slaughtered
c ver 16 them. He burned the plowing equip-
ment to cook the meat and gave it to the
people, and they ate. Then he set out to
follow Elijah and became his attendant.[c]

Ben-Hadad Attacks Samaria

20:1 d 1Ki 15:18; 20 Now Ben-Hadad[d] king of Aram
22:31; 2Ki 6:24 mustered his entire army. Accompanied by thirty-two kings with
their horses and chariots, he went up
and besieged Samaria and attacked it.
2He sent messengers into the city to
Ahab king of Israel, saying, "This is what
Ben-Hadad says: 3'Your silver and gold
are mine, and the best of your wives and
children are mine.' "

4The king of Israel answered, "Just as
you say, my lord the king. I and all I have
are yours."

5The messengers came again and
said, "This is what Ben-Hadad says: 'I
sent to demand your silver and gold,
your wives and your children. 6But
about this time tomorrow I am going to
send my officials to search your palace
and the houses of your officials. They
will seize everything you value and carry it away.' "

7The king of Israel summoned all the
elders of the land and said to them, "See
20:7 e 2Ki 5:7 how this man is looking for trouble![e]
When he sent for my wives and my chil-

ALL KINGS WHEN THEY DIE HAVE THEIR POWER EXTINGUISHED WITH THEIR LIFE: BUT CHRIST CRUCIFIED IS WORSHIPPED BY THE WHOLE WORLD. WE PROCLAIM THE CRUCIFIED, AND THE DEVILS TREMBLE.

Cyril of Jerusalem, *Early Church Father*

dren, my silver and my gold, I did not refuse him."

8The elders and the people all answered, "Don't listen to him or agree to
his demands."

9So he replied to Ben-Hadad's messengers, "Tell my lord the king, 'Your
servant will do all you demanded the
first time, but this demand I cannot
meet.' " They left and took the answer
back to Ben-Hadad.

10Then Ben-Hadad sent another message to Ahab: "May the gods deal with 20:10
me, be it ever so severely, if enough dust[f] f 2Sa 22:43;
remains in Samaria to give each of my 1Ki 19:2
men a handful."

11The king of Israel answered, "Tell
him: 'One who puts on his armor should 20:11
not boast[g] like one who takes it off.' " g Pr 27:1;
12Ben-Hadad heard this message Jer 9:23
while he and the kings were drinking[h] in 20:12
their tents,[a] and he ordered his men: h ver 16;
"Prepare to attack." So they prepared to 1Ki 16:9
attack the city.

Ahab Defeats Ben-Hadad

13Meanwhile a prophet came to Ahab
king of Israel and announced, "This is
what the LORD says: 'Do you see this vast
army? I will give it into your hand today, 20:13
and then you will know[i] that I am the i ver 28; Ex 6:7
LORD.' "

14"But who will do this?" asked Ahab.
The prophet replied, "This is what the
LORD says: 'The young officers of the
provincial commanders will do it.' "

"And who will start[j] the battle?" he 20:14 j Jdg 1:1
asked.

The prophet answered, "You will."

15So Ahab summoned the young officers of the provincial commanders, 232
men. Then he assembled the rest of the
Israelites, 7,000 in all. 16They set out at

[a] 12 Or *in Succoth*; also in verse 16

noon while Ben-Hadad and the 32 kings
allied with him were in their tents getting drunk.[k] 17 The young officers of the
provincial commanders went out first.

20:16 [k] ver 12; 1Ki 16:9

Now Ben-Hadad had dispatched
scouts, who reported, "Men are advancing from Samaria."
18 He said, "If they have come out for
peace, take them alive; if they have come
out for war, take them alive."
19 The young officers of the provincial
commanders marched out of the city
with the army behind them 20 and each
one struck down his opponent. At that,
the Arameans fled, with the Israelites in
pursuit. But Ben-Hadad king of Aram
escaped on horseback with some of his
horsemen. 21 The king of Israel advanced
and overpowered the horses and chariots and inflicted heavy losses on the Arameans.
22 Afterward, the prophet[l] came to the
king of Israel and said, "Strengthen your
position and see what must be done, because next spring[m] the king of Aram will
attack you again."

20:22 [l] ver 13 [m] ver 26; 2Sa 11:1

23 Meanwhile, the officials of the king
of Aram advised him, "Their gods are
gods[n] of the hills. That is why they were
too strong for us. But if we fight them on
the plains, surely we will be stronger
than they. 24 Do this: Remove all the
kings from their commands and replace
them with other officers. 25 You must
also raise an army like the one you
lost—horse for horse and chariot for
chariot—so we can fight Israel on the
plains. Then surely we will be stronger
than they." He agreed with them and
acted accordingly.

20:23 [n] 1Ki 14:23; Ro 1:21-23

26 The next spring[o] Ben-Hadad mustered the Arameans and went up to
Aphek[p] to fight against Israel. 27 When
the Israelites were also mustered and
given provisions, they marched out to
meet them. The Israelites camped opposite them like two small flocks of
goats, while the Arameans covered the
countryside.[q]

20:26 [o] ver 22 [p] 2Ki 13:17

20:27 [q] Jdg 6:6; 1Sa 13:6

28 The man of God came up and told
the king of Israel, "This is what the LORD
says: 'Because the Arameans think the
LORD is a god of the hills and not a god[r]
of the valleys, I will deliver this vast army
into your hands, and you will know[s] that
I am the LORD.' "
29 For seven days they camped oppo-

20:28 [r] ver 23 [s] ver 13

site each other, and on the seventh day
the battle was joined. The Israelites inflicted a hundred thousand casualties
on the Aramean foot soldiers in one day.
30 The rest of them escaped to the city of
Aphek,[t] where the wall collapsed on
twenty-seven thousand of them. And
Ben-Hadad fled to the city and hid[u] in
an inner room.

20:30 [t] ver 26 [u] 1Ki 22:25; 2Ch 18:24

31 His officials said to him, "Look, we
have heard that the kings of the house of
Israel are merciful. Let us go to the king
of Israel with sackcloth[v] around our
waists and ropes around our heads. Perhaps he will spare your life."

20:31 [v] Ge 37:34

32 Wearing sackcloth around their
waists and ropes around their heads,
they went to the king of Israel and said,
"Your servant Ben-Hadad says: 'Please
let me live.' "
The king answered, "Is he still alive?
He is my brother."
33 The men took this as a good sign
and were quick to pick up his word. "Yes,
your brother Ben-Hadad!" they said.
"Go and get him," the king said. When
Ben-Hadad came out, Ahab had him
come up into his chariot.
34 "I will return the cities[w] my father
took from your father," Ben-Hadad offered. "You may set up your own market
areas in Damascus,[x] as my father did in
Samaria."
⌊Ahab said,⌋ "On the basis of a treaty[y]
I will set you free." So he made a treaty
with him, and let him go.

20:34 [w] 1Ki 15:20 [x] Jer 49:23-27 [y] Ex 23:32

A Prophet Condemns Ahab

35 By the word of the LORD one of the
sons of the prophets said to his companion, "Strike me with your weapon,"
but the man refused.[z]
36 So the prophet said, "Because you
have not obeyed the LORD, as soon as
you leave me a lion[a] will kill you." And
after the man went away, a lion found
him and killed him.

20:35 [z] 1Ki 13:21; 2Ki 2:3-7

20:36 [a] 1Ki 13:24

37 The prophet found another man
and said, "Strike me, please." So the man
struck him and wounded him. 38 Then
the prophet went and stood by the road
waiting for the king. He disguised himself with his headband down over his
eyes. 39 As the king passed by, the prophet called out to him, "Your servant went
into the thick of the battle, and someone
came to me with a captive and said,

'Guard this man. If he is missing, it will
20:39 [b] 2Ki 10:24 be your life for his life,[b] or you must pay
a talent[a] of silver.' 40While your servant
was busy here and there, the man disappeared."

"That is your sentence," the king of Israel said. "You have pronounced it yourself."

41Then the prophet quickly removed
the headband from his eyes, and the
king of Israel recognized him as one of
the prophets. 42He said to the king,
"This is what the LORD says: 'You have
20:42 set free a man I had determined should
[c] Jer 48:10 die.[b][c] Therefore it is your life for his life,[d]
[d] ver 39; Jos 2:14; 1Ki 22:31-37 your people for his people.' " 43Sullen and
angry,[e] the king of Israel went to his
20:43 [e] 1Ki 21:4 palace in Samaria.

Naboth's Vineyard

21 Some time later there was an
21:1 [f] 2Ki 9:21 incident involving a vineyard
[g] 1Ki 18:45-46 belonging to Naboth[f] the Jezreelite. The
vineyard was in Jezreel,[g] close to the
palace of Ahab king of Samaria. 2Ahab
said to Naboth, "Let me have your vineyard to use for a vegetable garden, since
it is close to my palace. In exchange I will
give you a better vineyard or, if you prefer, I will pay you whatever it is worth."

3But Naboth replied, "The LORD for-
21:3 [h] Lev 25:23; Nu 36:7; Eze 46:18 bid that I should give you the inheritance[h] of my fathers."

4So Ahab went home, sullen and an-
21:4 [i] 1Ki 20:43 gry[i] because Naboth the Jezreelite had
said, "I will not give you the inheritance
of my fathers." He lay on his bed sulking
and refused to eat.

5His wife Jezebel came in and asked
him, "Why are you so sullen? Why won't
you eat?"

6He answered her, "Because I said to
Naboth the Jezreelite, 'Sell me your vineyard; or if you prefer, I will give you another vineyard in its place.' But he said,
'I will not give you my vineyard.' "

7Jezebel his wife said, "Is this how you
act as king over Israel? Get up and eat!
21:7 [j] 1Sa 8:14 Cheer up. I'll get you the vineyard[j] of Naboth the Jezreelite."

8So she wrote letters in Ahab's name,
21:8 [k] Ge 38:18; Est 3:12; 8:8,10 placed his seal[k] on them, and sent them
to the elders and nobles who lived in Na-
both's city with him. 9In those letters she
wrote:

"Proclaim a day of fasting and
seat Naboth in a prominent place
among the people. 10But seat two
scoundrels[l] opposite him and have 21:10 [l] Ac 6:11
them testify that he has cursed[m] [m] Ex 22:28; Lev 24:15-16
both God and the king. Then take
him out and stone him to death."

11So the elders and nobles who lived
in Naboth's city did as Jezebel directed in
the letters she had written to them.
12They proclaimed a fast[n] and seated 21:12 [n] Isa 58:4
Naboth in a prominent place among the
people. 13Then two scoundrels came
and sat opposite him and brought
charges against Naboth before the people, saying, "Naboth has cursed both
God and the king." So they took him
outside the city and stoned him to
death.[o] 14Then they sent word to Jezebel: 21:13 [o] 2Ki 9:26
"Naboth has been stoned and is dead."

15As soon as Jezebel heard that Naboth had been stoned to death, she said
to Ahab, "Get up and take possession of
the vineyard[p] of Naboth the Jezreelite 21:15 [p] 1Sa 8:14
that he refused to sell you. He is no
longer alive, but dead." 16When Ahab
heard that Naboth was dead, he got up
and went down to take possession of
Naboth's vineyard.

17Then the word of the LORD came to
Elijah the Tishbite: 18"Go down to meet
Ahab king of Israel, who rules in
Samaria. He is now in Naboth's vineyard,
where he has gone to take possession of
it. 19Say to him, 'This is what the LORD
says: Have you not murdered a man and
seized his property?' Then say to him,
'This is what the LORD says: In the place
where dogs licked up Naboth's blood,[q] 21:19 [q] 2Ki 9:26; Ps 9:12; Isa 14:20
dogs[r] will lick up your blood—yes, [r] 1Ki 22:38
yours!' "

20Ahab said to Elijah, "So you have
found me, my enemy!"[s] 21:20 [s] 1Ki 18:17

"I have found you," he answered, "be- [t] ver 25; 2Ki 17:17; Ro 7:14
cause you have sold[t] yourself to do evil
in the eyes of the LORD. 21'I am going to
bring disaster on you. I will consume
your descendants and cut off from Ahab
every last male[u] in Israel—slave or free. 21:21 [u] 1Ki 14:10; 2Ki 9:8
22I will make your house[v] like that of Jer-
oboam son of Nebat and that of Baasha
son of Ahijah, because you have pro- 21:22 [v] 1Ki 15:29; 16:3
voked me to anger and have caused Is- [w] 1Ki 12:30
rael to sin.'[w]

23"And also concerning Jezebel the

[a] 39 That is, about 75 pounds (about 34 kilograms)
[b] 42 The Hebrew term refers to the irrevocable giving over of things or persons to the LORD, often by totally destroying them.

21:23 LORD says: 'Dogs[x] will devour Jezebel by
x 2Ki 9:10,34-36 the wall of[a] Jezreel.'
21:24 24"Dogs[y] will eat those belonging to
y 1Ki 14:11; 16:4 Ahab who die in the city, and the birds of
the air will feed on those who die in the
21:25 country."
z ver 20; 25(There was never[z] a man like Ahab,
1Ki 16:33 who sold himself to do evil in the eyes of
the LORD, urged on by Jezebel his wife.
21:26 a Ge 15:16; 26He behaved in the vilest manner by go-
Lev 18:25-30; ing after idols, like the Amorites[a] the
2Ki 21:11 LORD drove out before Israel.)
21:27 27When Ahab heard these words, he
b Ge 37:34; 2Sa 3:31; tore his clothes, put on sackcloth[b] and
2Ki 6:30 fasted. He lay in sackcloth and went
around meekly.
28Then the word of the LORD came to
Elijah the Tishbite: 29"Have you noticed
how Ahab has humbled himself before
me? Because he has humbled himself, I
will not bring this disaster in his day, but
21:29 I will bring it on his house in the days of
c 2Ki 9:26 his son."[c]

Micaiah Prophesies Against Ahab

22 For three years there was no
war between Aram and Israel.
2But in the third year Jehoshaphat king
of Judah went down to see the king of Israel. 3The king of Israel had said to his
22:3 officials, "Don't you know that Ramoth
d Dt 4:43; Gilead[d] belongs to us and yet we are do-
Jos 21:38 ing nothing to retake it from the king of
Aram?"
4So he asked Jehoshaphat, "Will you
22:4 e 2Ki 3:7 go with me to fight[e] against Ramoth Gilead?"
Jehoshaphat replied to the king of Israel, "I am as you are, my people as your
people, my horses as your horses." 5But
Jehoshaphat also said to the king of Is-
22:5 f Ex 33:7; rael, "First seek the counsel[f] of the
2Ki 3:11 LORD."
6So the king of Israel brought together the prophets—about four hundred
men—and asked them, "Shall I go to
war against Ramoth Gilead, or shall I refrain?"
22:6 "Go,"[g] they answered, "for the Lord
g 1Ki 18:19 will give it into the king's hand."
7But Jehoshaphat asked, "Is there not
22:7 a prophet[h] of the LORD here whom we
h 2Ki 3:11 can inquire of?"
8The king of Israel answered Jehoshaphat, "There is still one man through
22:8 whom we can inquire of the LORD, but I
i Am 5:10 hate[i] him because he never prophesies
anything good[j] about me, but always 22:8
bad. He is Micaiah son of Imlah." j Isa 5:20
"The king should not say that," Jehoshaphat replied.
9So the king of Israel called one of his
officials and said, "Bring Micaiah son of
Imlah at once."
10Dressed in their royal robes, the
king of Israel and Jehoshaphat king of
Judah were sitting on their thrones at 22:10
the threshing floor[k] by the entrance of k ver 6
the gate of Samaria, with all the prophets prophesying before them. 11Now
Zedekiah son of Kenaanah had made 22:11
iron horns[l] and he declared, "This is l Dt 33:17;
what the LORD says: 'With these you will Zec 1:18-21
gore the Arameans until they are destroyed.' "
12All the other prophets were prophesying the same thing. "Attack Ramoth
Gilead and be victorious," they said, "for
the LORD will give it into the king's
hand."
13The messenger who had gone to
summon Micaiah said to him, "Look, as
one man the other prophets are predicting success for the king. Let your word
agree with theirs, and speak favorably."
14But Micaiah said, "As surely as the
LORD lives, I can tell him only what the 22:14
LORD tells me."[m] m Nu 22:18; 24:13;
15When he arrived, the king asked 1Ki 18:10,15
him, "Micaiah, shall we go to war
against Ramoth Gilead, or shall I refrain?"
"Attack and be victorious," he answered, "for the LORD will give it into the
king's hand."
16The king said to him, "How many
times must I make you swear to tell me
nothing but the truth in the name of the
LORD?"
17Then Micaiah answered, "I saw all
Israel scattered on the hills like sheep 22:17
without a shepherd,[n] and the LORD said, n ver 34-36; Nu 27:17;
'These people have no master. Let each Mt 9:36
one go home in peace.' "
18The king of Israel said to Jehoshaphat, "Didn't I tell you that he never
prophesies anything good about me, but
only bad?"
19Micaiah continued, "Therefore hear 22:19 o Isa 6:1;
the word of the LORD: I saw the LORD sit- Eze 1:26; Da 7:9
ting on his throne[o] with all the host[p] of p Job 1:6; 2:1;
Ps 103:20-21; Mt 18:10; Heb 1:7,14

[a] 23 Most Hebrew manuscripts; a few Hebrew manuscripts, Vulgate and Syriac (see also 2 Kings 9:26) *the plot of ground at*

DISCOVERY 87

Full of Compassion and Mercy

Ahab was the wicked king of Israel, and Jehoshaphat was the good king of Judah. The two agreed to fight together against the king of Aram to reclaim Ramoth Gilead for Israel. Before they went to battle, Jehoshaphat was determined to find out what God wanted (1 King 22:5). Ahab didn't mind seeking God's counsel either, as long as he liked what he heard.

False prophets will usually say exactly what the inquirer wants to hear. Ahab called together his 400 prophets and asked them whether or not they should go to war. "Go," they answered, "for the Lord will give [Ramoth Gilead] into the king's hand" (verse 6).

Then Jehoshaphat insisted that they call on God's prophet Micaiah. Ahab knew in advance that he would dislike whatever Micaiah might have to say, because "he never prophesies anything good about me" (verse 8). Before Micaiah met with the two kings, he was counseled by the messenger to agree with the other prophets and predict success. "I can tell [Ahab] only what the LORD tells me," he protested (verse 14).

At first Micaiah did say precisely what the king expected to hear, but in so doing he was mocking the other prophets. Ahab was apparently able to see through this ruse and demanded the truth. Micaiah's immediate response was indirect and, upon first reading, even sounds irrelevant: "I saw all Israel scattered on the hills like sheep without a shepherd, and the LORD said, 'These people have no master' " (verse 17). The prophet then informed the two kings that the Lord had decreed disaster for Ahab (verse 23), predicting that the armies of Israel and Judah would be defeated and that King Ahab would be killed. Ahab and Jehoshaphat did ride off into battle—and Ahab was killed by a "randomly" shot arrow (verse 34).

Matthew in his Gospel account used words virtually identical to Micaiah's: "When Jesus saw the crowds, he had compassion on them, because they were harassed and helpless, like sheep without a shepherd" (Matthew 9:36). Micaiah's vision from the Lord did not involve only Ahab. The prophet's first words after Ahab had impatiently demanded the truth referred not to the king but to the people, the hapless victims of his rash decisions and lack of moral values.

A hired hand, Jesus told a group of Pharisees, cares nothing about a flock of sheep and will, in the face of a wolf, run away and abandon the flock. By contrast, Jesus identified himself as the good shepherd who "lays down his life for the sheep" (John 10:11–14).

Beyond being our Good Shepherd, Jesus is indeed the Lord and Master for whom the masses so desperately long. Like the ten lepers in Luke 17:13, we can call out to him, "Jesus, Master, have pity on us!" And we may be assured that he will hear us, because our "Lord is full of compassion and mercy" (James 5:11).

Self-Discovery: *Are you open to constructive criticism, or do you want to hear only good reports about your attitude or the quality of your work? How does the fact that Jesus cares for you make a difference in how you receive his call on your life to follow him and obey his commands?*

GO TO DISCOVERY 88 ON PAGE 462

heaven standing around him on his
right and on his left. 20And the LORD
said, 'Who will entice Ahab into attacking Ramoth Gilead and going to his
death there?'
"One suggested this, and another
that. 21Finally, a spirit came forward,
stood before the LORD and said, 'I will
entice him.'
22:22 [q] Jdg 9:23; 1Sa 16:14; 18:10; 19:9; Eze 14:9; 2Th 2:11 22" 'By what means?' the LORD asked.
" 'I will go out and be a lying[q] spirit in
the mouths of all his prophets,' he said.
" 'You will succeed in enticing him,'
said the LORD. 'Go and do it.'
23"So now the LORD has put a lying
22:23 [r] Eze 14:9 spirit in the mouths of all these prophets[r] of yours. The LORD has decreed di-
22:24 [s] ver 11 [t] Ac 23:2 saster for you."
24Then Zedekiah[s] son of Kenaanah
went up and slapped[t] Micaiah in the
face. "Which way did the spirit from[a]
the LORD go when he went from me to
speak to you?" he asked.
25Micaiah replied, "You will find out
22:25 [u] 1Ki 20:30 on the day you go to hide[u] in an inner
room."
26The king of Israel then ordered,
"Take Micaiah and send him back to
Amon the ruler of the city and to Joash
the king's son 27and say, 'This is what the
22:27 [v] 2Ch 16:10 king says: Put this fellow in prison[v] and
give him nothing but bread and water
until I return safely.' "
28Micaiah declared, "If you ever re-
22:28 [w] Dt 18:22 turn safely, the LORD has not spoken[w]
through me." Then he added, "Mark my
words, all you people!"

Ahab Killed at Ramoth Gilead

29So the king of Israel and Jehoshaphat king of Judah went up to Ramoth
Gilead. 30The king of Israel said to Jehoshaphat, "I will enter the battle in dis-
22:30 [x] 2Ch 35:32 guise,[x] but you wear your royal robes."
So the king of Israel disguised himself
and went into battle.
31Now the king of Aram had ordered
his thirty-two chariot commanders, "Do
22:31 [y] 2Sa 17:2 not fight with anyone, small or great, except the king[y] of Israel." 32When the
chariot commanders saw Jehoshaphat,
they thought, "Surely this is the king of
Israel." So they turned to attack him, but
when Jehoshaphat cried out, 33the chariot commanders saw that he was not the
22:34 [z] 2Ch 35:23 king of Israel and stopped pursuing him.
34But someone drew his bow[z] at ran-
dom and hit the king of Israel between
the sections of his armor. The king told
his chariot driver, "Wheel around and
get me out of the fighting. I've been
wounded." 35All day long the battle
raged, and the king was propped up in
his chariot facing the Arameans. The
blood from his wound ran onto the floor
of the chariot, and that evening he died.
36As the sun was setting, a cry spread
through the army: "Every man to his 22:36 [a] 2Ki 14:12
town; everyone to his land!"[a]
37So the king died and was brought to
Samaria, and they buried him there.
38They washed the chariot at a pool in
Samaria (where the prostitutes bathed),[b] 22:38 [b] 1Ki 21:19
and the dogs[b] licked up his blood, as the
word of the LORD had declared.
39As for the other events of Ahab's
reign, including all he did, the palace he
built and inlaid with ivory,[c] and the cit- 22:39 [c] 2Ch 9:17; Am 3:15
ies he fortified, are they not written in
the book of the annals of the kings of Israel? 40Ahab rested with his fathers. And
Ahaziah his son succeeded him as king.

Jehoshaphat King of Judah

41Jehoshaphat son of Asa became
king of Judah in the fourth year of Ahab
king of Israel. 42Jehoshaphat was thirty-
five years old when he became king, and
he reigned in Jerusalem twenty-five
years. His mother's name was Azubah
daughter of Shilhi. 43In everything he 22:43 [d] 2Ch 17:3 [e] 1Ki 3:2; 15:14; 2Ki 12:3
walked in the ways of his father Asa[d]
and did not stray from them; he did
what was right in the eyes of the LORD.
The high places,[e] however, were not removed, and the people continued to offer sacrifices and burn incense there.
44Jehoshaphat was also at peace with the
king of Israel.
45As for the other events of Jehoshaphat's reign, the things he achieved and
his military exploits, are they not written in the book of the annals of the kings
of Judah? 46He rid the land of the rest of 22:46 [f] Dt 23:17; 1Ki 14:24; 15:12
the male shrine prostitutes[f] who re-
mained there even after the reign of his
father Asa. 47There was then no king[g] in 22:47 [g] 2Sa 8:14; 2Ki 3:9; 8:20
Edom; a deputy ruled.
48Now Jehoshaphat built a fleet of 22:48 [h] 1Ki 9:26; 10:22
trading ships[c][h] to go to Ophir for gold,
but they never set sail—they were
wrecked at Ezion Geber. 49At that time

[a] 24 Or *Spirit of the weapons* [b] 38 Or *Samaria and cleaned* [c] 48 Hebrew *of ships of Tarshish*

Ahaziah son of Ahab said to Jehoshaphat, "Let my men sail with your men,"
but Jehoshaphat refused.
[50]Then Jehoshaphat rested with his
fathers and was buried with them in the
city of David his father. And Jehoram his
son succeeded him.

Ahaziah King of Israel

[51]Ahaziah son of Ahab became king
of Israel in Samaria in the seventeenth
year of Jehoshaphat king of Judah, and
he reigned over Israel two years. [52]He did
evil[i] in the eyes of the LORD, because he
walked in the ways of his father and
mother and in the ways of Jeroboam son
of Nebat, who caused Israel to sin. [53]He
served and worshiped Baal[j] and provoked the LORD, the God of Israel, to
anger, just as his father[k] had done.

22:52 [i] 1Ki 15:26; 21:25

22:53 [j] Jdg 2:11 [k] 1Ki 16:30-32

2 KINGS

Jesus in 2 Kings As Israel and Judah slipped farther away from God, his commitment to his promise of the coming of the Messiah seemed to fade into the background. The ministries of the prophets Elijah and Elisha called the people back to God, but only for a while. Revivals under Hezekiah and Josiah briefly raised the spiritual hopes of the nation, but the renewed interest in the things of God was again short-lived. In the end the angel of the Lord (possibly Jesus himself) preserved the Messiah's family line when the Assyrians invaded during the days of Hezekiah (2 Kings 19:35). When the situation seemed bleakest and the people assumed that God would be unable to keep his promise, Jesus himself made certain that the Messiah's family line would continue so that he himself could one day be born as Israel's ultimate King.

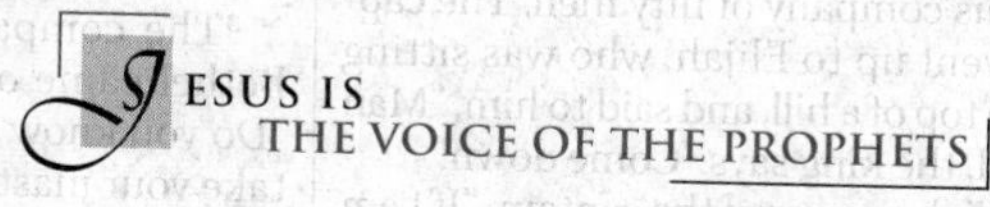
JESUS IS
THE VOICE OF THE PROPHETS

What is the historical focus of the author of 1 and 2 Kings?

- *The focus is covenantal rather than historical or political. The kings who receive the most attention are those during whose reigns there was either notable deviation from or affirmation of the covenant. The author also recognized the far-reaching historical significance of the Davidic covenant, which promised that David's dynasty would endure forever in, through and because of Jesus Christ, son of David (Matthew 1:1) and Son of God (Matthew 3:17).*

Why did prophets wear eccentric clothes? (2 Kings 1:8)

- *Elijah's coarse garments demonstrated the unvarnished toughness of his godly character. He may have intended that his uncomfortable clothing symbolize his sorrow over the people's unfaithfulness. John the Baptist, the forerunner and herald of Jesus, similarly wore rough, animal-skin garments.*

The LORD's Judgment on Ahaziah

1 After Ahab's death, Moab[a] rebelled against Israel. 2Now Ahaziah had fallen through the lattice of his
upper room in Samaria and injured
himself. So he sent messengers,[b] saying
to them, "Go and consult Baal-Zebub,[c]
the god of Ekron,[d] to see if I will recover[e] from this injury."
3But the angel[f] of the LORD said to Elijah[g] the Tishbite, "Go up and meet the
messengers of the king of Samaria and
ask them, 'Is it because there is no God in
Israel[h] that you are going off to consult
Baal-Zebub, the god of Ekron?' 4There-
fore this is what the LORD says: 'You will
not leave[i] the bed you are lying on. You
will certainly die!' " So Elijah went.
5When the messengers returned to
the king, he asked them, "Why have you
come back?"
6"A man came to meet us," they
replied. "And he said to us, 'Go back to
the king who sent you and tell him,
"This is what the LORD says: Is it because
there is no God in Israel that you are
sending men to consult Baal-Zebub, the
god of Ekron? Therefore you will not
leave the bed you are lying on. You will
certainly die!" ' "
7The king asked them, "What kind of
man was it who came to meet you and
told you this?"
8They replied, "He was a man with a
garment of hair[j] and with a leather belt
around his waist."
The king said, "That was Elijah the
Tishbite."
9Then he sent[k] to Elijah a captain[l]
with his company of fifty men. The captain went up to Elijah, who was sitting
on the top of a hill, and said to him, "Man
of God, the king says, 'Come down!' "
10Elijah answered the captain, "If I am
a man of God, may fire come down from
heaven and consume you and your fifty
men!" Then fire[m] fell from heaven and
consumed the captain and his men.
11At this the king sent to Elijah another captain with his fifty men. The captain
said to him, "Man of God, this is what
the king says, 'Come down at once!' "
12"If I am a man of God," Elijah replied,
"may fire come down from heaven and
consume you and your fifty men!" Then
the fire of God fell from heaven and consumed him and his fifty men.

1:1 [a] Ge 19:37; 2Sa 8:2; 2Ki 3:5
1:2 [b] ver 16 [c] Mk 3:22 [d] 1Sa 6:2; Isa 2:6; 14:29; Mt 10:25 [e] Jdg 18:5; 2Ki 8:7-10
1:3 [f] ver 15; Ge 16:7 [g] 1Ki 17:1 [h] 1Sa 28:8
1:4 [i] ver 6,16; Ps 41:8
1:8 [j] 1Ki 18:7; Zec 13:4; Mt 3:4; Mk 1:6
1:9 [k] 2Ki 6:14 [l] Ex 18:25; Isa 3:3
1:10 [m] 1Ki 18:38; Lk 9:54; Rev 11:5; 13:13

13So the king sent a third captain with
his fifty men. This third captain went up
and fell on his knees before Elijah. "Man
of God," he begged, "please have respect
for my life[n] and the lives of these fifty
men, your servants! 14See, fire has fallen
from heaven and consumed the first two
captains and all their men. But now
have respect for my life!"
15The angel[o] of the LORD said to Elijah, "Go down with him; do not be
afraid[p] of him." So Elijah got up and
went down with him to the king.
16He told the king, "This is what the
LORD says: Is it because there is no God
in Israel for you to consult that you have
sent messengers[q] to consult Baal-Zebub, the god of Ekron? Because you have
done this, you will never leave[r] the bed
you are lying on. You will certainly die!"
17So he died,[s] according to the word of
the LORD that Elijah had spoken.
Because Ahaziah had no son, Joram[a][t]
succeeded him as king in the second
year of Jehoram son of Jehoshaphat king
of Judah. 18As for all the other events of
Ahaziah's reign, and what he did, are
they not written in the book of the annals of the kings of Israel?

Elijah Taken Up to Heaven

2 When the LORD was about to
take[u] Elijah up to heaven in a
whirlwind,[v] Elijah and Elisha[w] were on
their way from Gilgal.[x] 2Elijah said to
Elisha, "Stay here;[y] the LORD has sent me
to Bethel."
But Elisha said, "As surely as the LORD
lives and as you live, I will not leave
you."[z] So they went down to Bethel.
3The company[a] of the prophets at
Bethel came out to Elisha and asked,
"Do you know that the LORD is going to
take your master from you today?"
"Yes, I know," Elisha replied, "but do
not speak of it."
4Then Elijah said to him, "Stay here,
Elisha; the LORD has sent me to Jericho.[b]"
And he replied, "As surely as the LORD
lives and as you live, I will not leave you."
So they went to Jericho.
5The company[c] of the prophets at Jericho went up to Elisha and asked him,
"Do you know that the LORD is going to
take your master from you today?"

1:13 [n] 1Sa 26:21; Ps 72:14
1:15 [o] ver 3 [p] Isa 51:12; 57:11; Jer 1:17; Eze 2:6
1:16 [q] ver 2 [r] ver 4
1:17 [s] 2Ki 8:15; Jer 20:6; 28:17 [t] 2Ki 3:1; 8:16
2:1 [u] Ge 5:24; Heb 11:5 [v] ver 11; 1Ki 19:11; Isa 5:28; 66:15; Jer 4:13; Na 1:3 [w] 1Ki 19:16,21 [x] Dt 11:30; 2Ki 4:38
2:2 [y] ver 6 [z] Ru 1:16; 1Sa 1:26; 2Ki 4:30
2:3 [a] 1Sa 10:5; 2Ki 4:1,38
2:4 [b] Jos 3:16; 6:26
2:5 [c] ver 3

[a] *17* Hebrew *Jehoram,* a variant of *Joram*

"Yes, I know," he replied, "but do not
speak of it."
2:6 [d]ver 2 [e]Jos 3:15 6Then Elijah said to him, "Stay here;[d]
[f]Ru 1:16 the LORD has sent me to the Jordan."[e]
And he replied, "As surely as the LORD
lives and as you live, I will not leave
you."[f] So the two of them walked on.
7Fifty men of the company of the
prophets went and stood at a distance,
facing the place where Elijah and Elisha
2:8 [g]1Ki 19:19 had stopped at the Jordan. 8Elijah took
[h]ver 14 his cloak,[g] rolled it up and struck[h] the
[i]Ex 14:21 water with it. The water divided[i] to the
[j]Ex 14:22,29 right and to the left, and the two of them
crossed over on dry[j] ground.
9When they had crossed, Elijah said
to Elisha, "Tell me, what can I do for you
before I am taken from you?"
2:9 [k]Dt 21:17 "Let me inherit a double[k] portion of
[l]Nu 11:17 your spirit,"[l] Elisha replied.
10"You have asked a difficult thing,"
Elijah said, "yet if you see me when I am
taken from you, it will be yours—otherwise not."
11As they were walking along and
2:11 [m]2Ki 6:17; talking together, suddenly a chariot of
Ps 68:17; 104:3, fire[m] and horses of fire appeared and
4; Isa 66:15; separated the two of them, and Elijah
Hab 3:8; Zec 6:1 [n]Ge 5:24 [o]ver 1 went up to heaven[n] in a whirlwind.[o]
2:12 12Elisha saw this and cried out, "My fa-
[p]2Ki 6:17; 13:14 ther! My father! The chariots[p] and
horsemen of Israel!" And Elisha saw him
no more. Then he took hold of his own
clothes and tore[q] them apart. 2:12 [q]Ge 37:29
13He picked up the cloak that had
fallen from Elijah and went back and
stood on the bank of the Jordan. 14Then
he took the cloak[r] that had fallen from 2:14 [r]1Ki 19:19
him and struck[s] the water with it. [s]ver 8
"Where now is the LORD, the God of Elijah?" he asked. When he struck the water, it divided to the right and to the left,
and he crossed over.
15The company[t] of the prophets from 2:15 [t]ver 7; 1Sa 10:5
Jericho, who were watching, said, "The [u]Nu 11:17
spirit[u] of Elijah is resting on Elisha." And
they went to meet him and bowed to the
ground before him. 16"Look," they said,
"we your servants have fifty able men.
Let them go and look for your master.
Perhaps the Spirit[v] of the LORD has 2:16 [v]1Ki 18:12
picked him up[w] and set him down on [w]Ac 8:39
some mountain or in some valley."
"No," Elisha replied, "do not send
them."
17But they persisted until he was too 2:17
ashamed[x] to refuse. So he said, "Send [x]2Ki 8:11
them." And they sent fifty men, who
searched for three days but did not find
him. 18When they returned to Elisha,
who was staying in Jericho, he said to
them, "Didn't I tell you not to go?"

Healing of the Water

19The men of the city said to Elisha,
"Look, our lord, this town is well situated,

JESUS FOCUS

TAKEN TO HEAVEN

Elijah's powerful prophetic ministry came to a dramatic close when God carried him up into heaven by a whirlwind (2 Kings 2:11–12). At the time of Jesus' second coming believers who are still alive will be, like Elijah and Enoch before him (Genesis 5:24), "caught up" to meet Jesus in the air (1 Thessalonians 4:17).

The prophet Malachi predicted that "Elijah" would return before the Messiah entered the scene (Malachi 4:5), and the angel who announced the birth of John the Baptist proclaimed, "He will go on before the Lord, in the spirit and power of Elijah" (Luke 1:17). Jesus himself clarified that when Malachi had mentioned Elijah, he had been referring to John the Baptist (Matthew 17:9–13). The similarities between Elijah and John the Baptist are unmistakable. Both lived in the desert, confronted kings and leaders, and challenged the people to turn back to God.

ELISHA
ELIJAH'S SUCCESSOR

Elisha, whose name means "my God is salvation," was the one appointed to be Elijah's successor after God had taken Elijah to heaven (1 Kings 19:16). Elisha was younger than Elijah and may have felt inadequate in comparison to the aged prophet, because he asked for a "double portion" of Elijah's spirit in order to carry on the work Elijah had begun (2 Kings 2:9). God granted Elisha's request, and Elijah left his cloak behind as a symbol of authority for the young prophet (verse 13). Elisha's work included training other prophets, meeting the needs of the common people and functioning as an instrument through whom God worked to heal many people through miracles. In the New Testament Jesus referred to the incident of the healing of Naaman the Syrian during Elisha's ministry as an example of reaching out to non-Israelites (Luke 4:25–27).

Passing the Mantle

As far as job descriptions are concerned, serving as a prophet was about as rough as it got in ancient Israel. A prophet traveled constantly for little or no pay, and the benefits plan didn't take effect until after death! Despite these drawbacks, many men and women over the years have answered the call to proclaim God's Word to people who as often as not have shown little inclination to hear it. Elijah, after completing many years of prophetic service, knew that the time had come to pass along his long, loose cloak or mantle to his protégé Elisha.

Elisha, a faithful friend, was more than equipped for the task. When Elijah attempted to persuade Elisha to stay behind for Elijah's final journey, the younger man refused (2 Kings 2:1–6). Like Elijah, Elisha was obedient to God, eager to follow in the footsteps of his mentor. The Spirit of God was with him, and Elisha was given the ability to perform miracles.

Old Testament law stipulated that the older, favored brother was to receive a double share of his father's inheritance (Deuteronomy 21:17). Elisha was the "favored son" with respect to the ministry of Elijah, and, when he asked God for a double portion of Elijah's spirit, this unusual request was honored.

Hundreds of years later, also along the banks of the Jordan River, another far more significant "passing of the mantle" took place. Jesus was baptized by John the Baptist, signaling the beginning of Jesus' public ministry (Matthew 3:13–17). As God's own Son, Jesus more than met the requirements for the task. He was and remains faithful, never wavering from his mission of doing the Father's will. He was totally committed to the task that God had given him (John 17:4) and performed it perfectly to the minutest detail. If there was anyone who did *not* need a baptism of repentance, it was Jesus! Even so, he obeyed God's command to be baptized (Matthew 3:15).

At Jesus' baptism the Holy Spirit came down from heaven in the form of a dove to demonstrate to the people that everything Jesus was doing was with the approval and power of the Spirit (Matthew 3:16). During his ministry years Jesus performed numerous miracles, proving that he was indeed God's favored Son (Matthew 3:17; 4:23).

God always endows us with the ability to accomplish what he has asked of us. Whatever God asks, however formidable the task may appear, he promises to provide us with the resources we will need to complete the work.

***Self-Discovery:** Identify an incident in your life in which someone has passed a mantle on to you? Did you feel adequate to the task? Did you rely on Jesus' help as you became familiar with your new responsibilities?*

GO TO DISCOVERY 89 ON PAGE 467

as you can see, but the water is bad and
the land is unproductive.”
20“Bring me a new bowl,” he said, “and
put salt in it.” So they brought it to him.
2:21 21Then he went out to the spring and
y Ex 15:25; threw[y] the salt into it, saying, “This is
2Ki 4:41; 6:6 what the LORD says: ‘I have healed this
water. Never again will it cause death or
2:22 make the land unproductive.’ ” 22And
z Ex 15:25 the water has remained wholesome[z] to
this day, according to the word Elisha
had spoken.

Elisha Is Jeered

23From there Elisha went up to Beth-
2:23 el. As he was walking along the road,
a Ex 22:28; some youths came out of the town and
2Ch 36:16; Job 19:18; jeered[a] at him. “Go on up, you bald-
Ps 31:18 head!” they said. “Go on up, you bald-
2:24 head!” 24He turned around, looked at
b Ge 4:11; Ne 13:25-27 them and called down a curse[b] on them
c Dt 18:19 in the name[c] of the LORD. Then two
bears came out of the woods and
2:25 mauled forty-two of the youths. 25And
d 1Ki 18:20; he went on to Mount Carmel[d] and from
2Ki 4:25 there returned to Samaria.

Moab Revolts

3:1 e 2Ki 1:17 3 Joram[a][e] son of Ahab became king
of Israel in Samaria in the eigh-
teenth year of Jehoshaphat king of Judah, and he reigned twelve years. 2He
3:2 f 1Ki 15:26 did evil[f] in the eyes of the LORD, but not
g 1Ki 16:30-32 as his father[g] and mother had done. He
h Ex 23:24; 2Ki 10:18,26-28 got rid of the sacred stone[h] of Baal that
his father had made. 3Nevertheless he
3:3 i 1Ki 12:28-32; 14:9,16 clung to the sins[i] of Jeroboam son of Nebat, which he had caused Israel to com-
mit; he did not turn away from them.
3:4 j Ge 19:37; 4Now Mesha king of Moab[j] raised
2Ki 1:1 k Ezr 7:17; sheep, and he had to supply the king of
Isa 16:1 Israel with a hundred thousand lambs[k]
and with the wool of a hundred thousand rams. 5But after Ahab died, the
3:5 l 2Ki 1:1 king of Moab rebelled[l] against the king
of Israel. 6So at that time King Joram set
out from Samaria and mobilized all Israel. 7He also sent this message to Jehoshaphat king of Judah: “The king of
Moab has rebelled against me. Will you
3:7 m 1Ki 22:4 go with me to fight[m] against Moab?”
“I will go with you,” he replied. “I am
as you are, my people as your people, my
horses as your horses.”
8“By what route shall we attack?” he
asked.

“Through the Desert of Edom,” he answered.
9So the king of Israel set out with the
king of Judah and the king of Edom.[n] Af- 3:9 n 1Ki 22:47
ter a roundabout march of seven days,
the army had no more water for themselves or for the animals with them.
10“What!” exclaimed the king of Israel. “Has the LORD called us three kings
together only to hand us over to Moab?”
11But Jehoshaphat asked, “Is there no
prophet of the LORD here, that we may 3:11
inquire[o] of the LORD through him?” o Ge 25:22;
An officer of the king of Israel an- 1Ki 22:7
swered, “Elisha[p] son of Shaphat is here. p Ge 20:7 q 1Ki 19:16
He used to pour water on the hands of
Elijah.[b][q]”
12Jehoshaphat said, “The word[r] of the 3:12 r Nu 11:17
LORD is with him.” So the king of Israel
and Jehoshaphat and the king of Edom
went down to him.
13Elisha said to the king of Israel,
“What do we have to do with each other? Go to the prophets of your father
and the prophets of your mother.”
“No,” the king of Israel answered, “because it was the LORD who called us
three kings together to hand us over to
Moab.”
14Elisha said, “As surely as the LORD
Almighty lives, whom I serve, if I did not
have respect for the presence of Jehoshaphat king of Judah, I would not look at
you or even notice you. 15But now bring 3:15
me a harpist.”[s] s 1Sa 16:23
While the harpist was playing, the t Jer 15:17;
hand[t] of the LORD came upon Elisha Eze 1:3
16and he said, “This is what the LORD
says: Make this valley full of ditches.
17For this is what the LORD says: You will
see neither wind nor rain, yet this valley 3:17
will be filled with water,[u] and you, your u Ps 107:35;
cattle and your other animals will drink. Isa 32:2; 35:6; 41:18
18This is an easy[v] thing in the eyes of the 3:18
LORD; he will also hand Moab over to you. v Ge 18:14;
19You will overthrow every fortified city 2Ki 20:10; Isa 49:6;
and every major town. You will cut down Jer 32:17,27; Mk 10:27
every good tree, stop up all the springs,
and ruin every good field with stones.”
20The next morning, about the time[w] 3:20
for offering the sacrifice, there it was— w Ex 29:39-40
water flowing from the direction of x Ex 17:6
Edom! And the land was filled with
water.[x]

[a] *1* Hebrew *Jehoram*, a variant of *Joram*; also in verse 6 [b] *11* That is, he was Elijah's personal servant.

21Now all the Moabites had heard that
the kings had come to fight against
them; so every man, young and old, who
could bear arms was called up and stationed on the border. 22When they got
up early in the morning, the sun was
shining on the water. To the Moabites
across the way, the water looked red—
like blood. 23"That's blood!" they said.
"Those kings must have fought and
slaughtered each other. Now to the plunder, Moab!"
24But when the Moabites came to the
camp of Israel, the Israelites rose up and
fought them until they fled. And the Israelites invaded the land and slaughtered the Moabites. 25They destroyed
the towns, and each man threw a stone
on every good field until it was covered.
They stopped up all the springs and cut
down every good tree. Only Kir Hareseth[y] was left with its stones in place,
but men armed with slings surrounded
it and attacked it as well.

3:25 [y] ver 19; Isa 15:1; 16:7; Jer 48:31,36

26When the king of Moab saw that the
battle had gone against him, he took
with him seven hundred swordsmen to
break through to the king of Edom, but
they failed. 27Then he took his firstborn[z]
son, who was to succeed him as king,
and offered him as a sacrifice on the city
wall. The fury against Israel was great;
they withdrew and returned to their
own land.

3:27 [z] Dt 12:31; 2Ki 16:3; 21:6; 2Ch 28:3; Ps 106:38; Jer 19:4-5; Am 2:1; Mic 6:7

The Widow's Oil

4 The wife of a man from the company[a] of the prophets cried out to
Elisha, "Your servant my husband is
dead, and you know that he revered the
LORD. But now his creditor[b] is coming to
take my two boys as his slaves."
2Elisha replied to her, "How can I help
you? Tell me, what do you have in your
house?"
"Your servant has nothing there at
all," she said, "except a little oil."[c]
3Elisha said, "Go around and ask all
your neighbors for empty jars. Don't ask
for just a few. 4Then go inside and shut
the door behind you and your sons. Pour
oil into all the jars, and as each is filled,
put it to one side."
5She left him and afterward shut the
door behind her and her sons. They
brought the jars to her and she kept
pouring. 6When all the jars were full, she
said to her son, "Bring me another one."
But he replied, "There is not a jar left."
Then the oil stopped flowing.
7She went and told the man of God,[d]
and he said, "Go, sell the oil and pay your
debts. You and your sons can live on
what is left."

4:1 [a] 1Sa 10:5; 2Ki 2:3 [b] Ex 22:26; Lev 25:39-43; Ne 5:3-5; Job 22:6; 24:9

4:2 [c] 1Ki 17:12

4:7 [d] 1Ki 12:22

The Shunammite's Son Restored to Life

8One day Elisha went to Shunem.[e]
And a well-to-do woman was there, who
urged him to stay for a meal. So whenever he came by, he stopped there to eat.
9She said to her husband, "I know that
this man who often comes our way is a
holy man of God. 10Let's make a small
room on the roof and put in it a bed and
a table, a chair and a lamp for him. Then
he can stay[f] there whenever he comes
to us."
11One day when Elisha came, he went
up to his room and lay down there. 12He
said to his servant Gehazi, "Call the Shunammite."[g] So he called her, and she
stood before him. 13Elisha said to him,
"Tell her, 'You have gone to all this trouble for us. Now what can be done for
you? Can we speak on your behalf to the
king or the commander of the army?'"

4:8 [e] Jos 19:18

4:10 [f] Mt 10:41; Ro 12:13

4:12 [g] 2Ki 8:1

JESUS FOCUS

ELISHA'S MIRACLES

A situation in which God steps in and acts in a way that transcends the ordinary laws of nature is defined as a miracle. As an instrument of the Sovereign God, Elisha performed twice as many miracles as Elijah, having received a "double portion" of Elijah's spirit, just as he had requested (2 Kings 2:9). Elisha's miracles included multiplying a widow's oil so that she could continue to bake bread, raising a Shunammite woman's son from the dead, feeding 100 men with only 20 loaves of bread, healing Naaman's leprosy and causing an axhead to float (2 Kings 4—6). Each of Elisha's miracles directly benefited the person who had asked for this special intervention. Jesus' miracles were very similar to Elisha's, and they demonstrate God's tender mercy for ordinary people. God uses miracles to catch our attention, but they do not always cause people to turn to him. In fact, it is quite possible to witness a miracle and go away completely unmoved—as countless people have done (see John 6:26; 10:31–38).

She replied, "I have a home among my
own people."
14"What can be done for her?" Elisha
asked.
Gehazi said, "Well, she has no son and
her husband is old."
15Then Elisha said, "Call her." So he
called her, and she stood in the door-
4:16 way. 16"About this time[h] next year," Eli-
[h] Ge 18:10 sha said, "you will hold a son in your
arms."
"No, my lord," she objected. "Don't
mislead your servant, O man of God!"
17But the woman became pregnant,
and the next year about that same time
she gave birth to a son, just as Elisha had
told her.
18The child grew, and one day he went
4:18 out to his father, who was with the
[i] Ru 2:3 reapers.[i] 19"My head! My head!" he said
to his father.
His father told a servant, "Carry him
to his mother." 20After the servant had
lifted him up and carried him to his
mother, the boy sat on her lap until
4:21 noon, and then he died. 21She went up
[j] ver 32 and laid him on the bed[j] of the man of
God, then shut the door and went out.
22She called her husband and said,
"Please send me one of the servants and
a donkey so I can go to the man of God
quickly and return."
4:23 23"Why go to him today?" he asked.
[k] Nu 10:10; 1Ch 23:31; Ps 81:3 "It's not the New Moon[k] or the Sabbath."
"It's all right," she said.
24She saddled the donkey and said to
her servant, "Lead on; don't slow down
for me unless I tell you." 25So she set out
4:25 and came to the man of God at Mount
[l] 1Ki 18:20; 2Ki 2:25 Carmel.[l]
When he saw her in the distance, the
man of God said to his servant Gehazi,
"Look! There's the Shunammite! 26Run
to meet her and ask her, 'Are you all
right? Is your husband all right? Is your
child all right?' "
"Everything is all right," she said.
27When she reached the man of God
at the mountain, she took hold of his
feet. Gehazi came over to push her away,
but the man of God said, "Leave her
4:27 alone! She is in bitter distress,[m] but the
[m] 1Sa 1:15 LORD has hidden it from me and has not
told me why."
28"Did I ask you for a son, my lord?"
she said. "Didn't I tell you, 'Don't raise
my hopes'?"

29Elisha said to Gehazi, "Tuck your
cloak into your belt,[n] take my staff[o] in 4:29
your hand and run. If you meet anyone, [n] 1Ki 18:46; 2Ki 2:8,14; 9:1
do not greet him, and if anyone greets [o] Ex 4:2; 7:19; 14:16
you, do not answer. Lay my staff on the
boy's face."
30But the child's mother said, "As surely as the LORD lives and as you live, I will
not leave you." So he got up and followed
her.
31Gehazi went on ahead and laid the
staff on the boy's face, but there was no
sound or response. So Gehazi went back
to meet Elisha and told him, "The boy
has not awakened."
32When Elisha reached the house,
there was the boy lying dead on his 4:32
couch.[p] 33He went in, shut the door on [p] ver 21
the two of them and prayed[q] to the 4:33
LORD. 34Then he got on the bed and lay [q] 1Ki 17:20; Mt 6:6
upon the boy, mouth to mouth, eyes to
eyes, hands to hands. As he stretched[r] 4:34
himself out upon him, the boy's body [r] 1Ki 17:21; Ac 20:10
grew warm. 35Elisha turned away and
walked back and forth in the room and
then got on the bed and stretched out
upon him once more. The boy sneezed 4:35
seven times[s] and opened his eyes.[t] [s] Jos 6:15 [t] 2Ki 8:5
36Elisha summoned Gehazi and said,
"Call the Shunammite." And he did.
When she came, he said, "Take your
son."[u] 37She came in, fell at his feet and 4:36
bowed to the ground. Then she took her [u] Heb 11:35
son and went out.

Death in the Pot

38Elisha returned to Gilgal[v] and there 4:38
was a famine[w] in that region. While the [v] 2Ki 2:1
company of the prophets was meeting [w] Lev 26:26; 2Ki 8:1
with him, he said to his servant, "Put on
the large pot and cook some stew for
these men."
39One of them went out into the fields
to gather herbs and found a wild vine.
He gathered some of its gourds and
filled the fold of his cloak. When he returned, he cut them up into the pot of
stew, though no one knew what they
were. 40The stew was poured out for the
men, but as they began to eat it, they
cried out, "O man of God, there is death
in the pot!" And they could not eat it.
41Elisha said, "Get some flour." He put
it into the pot and said, "Serve it to the
people to eat." And there was nothing 4:41
harmful in the pot.[x] [x] Ex 15:25; 2Ki 2:21

Feeding of a Hundred

4:42 y 1Sa 9:4 42 A man came from Baal Shalishah,[y]
z Mt 14:17; bringing the man of God twenty loaves[z]
15:36 a 1Sa 9:7 of barley bread[a] baked from the first ripe
grain, along with some heads of new
grain. "Give it to the people to eat," Elisha said.
43 "How can I set this before a hundred
men?" his servant asked.
4:43 But Elisha answered, "Give it to the
b Lk 9:13 people to eat.[b] For this is what the LORD
c Mt 14:20; says: 'They will eat and have some left
Jn 6:12 over.[c]' " 44 Then he set it before them, and
they ate and had some left over, accord-
ing to the word of the LORD.

Naaman Healed of Leprosy

5 Now Naaman was commander of
5:1 d Ge 10:22; the army of the king of Aram.[d]
2Sa 10:19 He was a great man in the sight of his
e Ex 4:6; master and highly regarded, because
Nu 12:10; through him the LORD had given victo-
Lk 4:27 ry to Aram. He was a valiant soldier, but
he had leprosy.[a][e]
5:2 2 Now bands[f] from Aram had gone out
f 2Ki 6:23; 13:20; and had taken captive a young girl from
24:2 Israel, and she served Naaman's wife.
3 She said to her mistress, "If only my
5:3 master would see the prophet[g] who is in
g Ge 20:7 Samaria! He would cure him of his leprosy."
4 Naaman went to his master and told
him what the girl from Israel had said.
5 "By all means, go," the king of Aram
replied. "I will send a letter to the king of
Israel." So Naaman left, taking with him
ten talents[b] of silver, six thousand
5:5 shekels[c] of gold and ten sets of cloth-
h ver 22; ing.[h] 6 The letter that he took to the king
Ge 24:53; of Israel read: "With this letter I am
Jdg 14:12; sending my servant Naaman to you so
1Sa 9:7 that you may cure him of his leprosy."
7 As soon as the king of Israel read the
5:7 i 2Ki 19:14 letter,[i] he tore his robes and said, "Am I
j Ge 30:2 God?[j] Can I kill and bring back to life?[k]
k Dt 32:39; Why does this fellow send someone to
1Sa 2:6 me to be cured of his leprosy? See how
l 1Ki 20:7 he is trying to pick a quarrel[l] with me!"
8 When Elisha the man of God heard
that the king of Israel had torn his robes,
he sent him this message: "Why have
you torn your robes? Have the man
come to me and he will know that there
5:8 m 1Ki 22:7 is a prophet[m] in Israel." 9 So Naaman
went with his horses and chariots and
stopped at the door of Elisha's house.
10 Elisha sent a messenger to say to him,

"Go, wash[n] yourself seven times[o] in the 5:10 n Jn 9:7
Jordan, and your flesh will be restored o Ge 33:3;
and you will be cleansed." Lev 14:7
11 But Naaman went away angry and
said, "I thought that he would surely
come out to me and stand and call on
the name of the LORD his God, wave his
hand[p] over the spot and cure me of my 5:11 p Ex 7:19
leprosy. 12 Are not Abana and Pharpar,
the rivers of Damascus, better than any
of the waters[q] of Israel? Couldn't I wash 5:12 q Isa 8:6
in them and be cleansed?" So he turned r Pr 14:17,29;
and went off in a rage.[r] 19:11; 29:11
13 Naaman's servants went to him and
said, "My father,[s] if the prophet had told 5:13 s 2Ki 6:21; 13:14
you to do some great thing, would you
not have done it? How much more, then,
when he tells you, 'Wash and be
cleansed'!" 14 So he went down and
dipped himself in the Jordan seven 5:14 t Ge 33:3;
times,[t] as the man of God had told him, Lev 14:7;
and his flesh was restored[u] and became Jos 6:15 u Ex 4:7
clean like that of a young boy.[v] v Job 33:25; Lk 4:27
15 Then Naaman and all his atten-
dants went back to the man of God[w]. He 5:15 w Jos 2:11
stood before him and said, "Now I x Jos 4:24;
know[x] that there is no God in all the 1Sa 17:46;
world except in Israel. Please accept Da 2:47
now a gift[y] from your servant." y 1Sa 9:7; 25:27
16 The prophet answered, "As surely as
the LORD lives, whom I serve, I will not
accept a thing." And even though Naa- 5:16 z ver 20,26;
man urged him, he refused.[z] Ge 14:23; Da 5:17
17 "If you will not," said Naaman,
"please let me, your servant, be given as
much earth[a] as a pair of mules can car- 5:17 a Ex 20:24
ry, for your servant will never again
make burnt offerings and sacrifices to
any other god but the LORD. 18 But may
the LORD forgive your servant for this
one thing: When my master enters the
temple of Rimmon to bow down and he
is leaning[b] on my arm and I bow there 5:18 b 2Ki 7:2
also—when I bow down in the temple of
Rimmon, may the LORD forgive your servant for this."
19 "Go in peace,"[c] Elisha said. 5:19 c 1Sa 1:17; Ac 15:33
After Naaman had traveled some dis-
tance, 20 Gehazi, the servant of Elisha the
man of God, said to himself, "My master
was too easy on Naaman, this Aramean,
by not accepting from him what he 5:20 d Ex 20:7
brought. As surely as the LORD[d] lives, I

[a] 1 The Hebrew word was used for various diseases affecting the skin—not necessarily leprosy; also in verses 3, 6, 7, 11 and 27. [b] 5 That is, about 750 pounds (about 340 kilograms) [c] 5 That is, about 150 pounds (about 70 kilograms)

VOLUNTARY SERVITUDE?

Although Naaman was the commander of Aram's army and a valiant soldier, he was also a leper. Despite Naaman's dreaded illness, however, he was not shunned. In fact, we are told that he was still held in high regard by the king of Aram for his military exploits. Interestingly, the writer of 2 Kings credited Aram's success to God: Naaman was victorious, he stated, "because through him the LORD had given victory to Aram" (2 Kings 5:1).

Although Israel had negotiated a peace treaty with the Arameans during the reign of Ahab (1 Kings 20:34), minor border skirmishes continued between the two states in the aftermath of the battle for control of Ramoth Gilead, a battle in which Ahab had been killed (see Discovery #87, page 456). Marauding bands from Aram would apparently swoop down into Israelite territory and take captives as trophies. In one such raid they had captured a young Israelite girl and had carried her into Aram and given her to Naaman's wife as a personal slave. We can surmise from this that she was probably a particularly capable and talented young lady.

This slave girl was also a true worshiper of God. Far from having become embittered as a result of this tragic turn of events in her life, she retained her sweet spirit and did her best to serve her mistress well. She was apparently distraught because of Naaman's illness and made an unsolicited suggestion to her mistress. The opening words of her short statement are revealing: *If only* carries a suggestion of yearning or pathos. This young slave saw her master's suffering and wanted to do what she could to alleviate his pain, so much so that she felt comfortable expressing her proposal: "If only my master would see the prophet who is in Samaria! He would cure him of his leprosy" (2 Kings 5:2).

Our Lord Jesus proposed a radical approach in Mark 10:44–45, one of voluntary servitude: "Whoever wants to become great among you must be your servant, and whoever wants to be first must be slave of all. For even the Son of Man did not come to be served, but to serve, and to give his life as a ransom for many." Obviously, the girl from Israel had not offered herself as a slave to the Aramean raiders, but she had of her own volition offered faithful service.

The apostle Paul expressed a similar sentiment: "Though I am free and belong to no man, I make myself a slave to everyone, to win as many as possible . . . I have become all things to all men so that by all possible means I might save some. I do this all for the sake of the gospel, that I may share in its blessings" (1 Corinthians 9:19,22–23).

Paul had Good News to share, and he was not above following the example of his Master, Jesus Christ. The slave girl in Aram had good news as well—news of a God in Israel who could heal the sick and broken. God calls each of us to the same level of service, no matter what our calling or station in life. We too have a message to share, and we too can point others to Jesus as the Great Physician.

Self-Discovery: *Have you ever been legitimately concerned about the well-being of someone who had not treated you particularly well? If so, how did your attitude change the dynamics of the situation?*

GO TO DISCOVERY 90 ON PAGE 469

will run after him and get something
from him."
21So Gehazi hurried after Naaman.
When Naaman saw him running toward
him, he got down from the chariot to
meet him. "Is everything all right?" he
asked.
22"Everything is all right," Gehazi answered. "My master sent me to say, 'Two
young men from the company of the
prophets have just come to me from the
hill country of Ephraim. Please give
5:22 them a talent[a] of silver and two sets of
e ver 5; Ge 45:22 clothing.' "[e]
23"By all means, take two talents," said
Naaman. He urged Gehazi to accept
them, and then tied up the two talents
of silver in two bags, with two sets of
clothing. He gave them to two of his servants, and they carried them ahead of
Gehazi. 24When Gehazi came to the hill,
he took the things from the servants and
put them away in the house. He sent the
men away and they left. 25Then he went
in and stood before his master Elisha.
"Where have you been, Gehazi?" Elisha asked.
"Your servant didn't go anywhere,"
Gehazi answered.
26But Elisha said to him, "Was not my
spirit with you when the man got down
from his chariot to meet you? Is this the
5:26 time[f] to take money, or to accept
f ver 16 g Jer 45:5 clothes, olive groves, vineyards, flocks,
5:27 herds, or menservants and maidser-
h Nu 12:10; vants?[g] 27Naaman's leprosy[h] will cling to
2Ki 15:5 you and to your descendants forever."
i Col 3:5 j Ex 4:6 Then Gehazi[i] went from Elisha's presence and he was leprous, as white as
snow.[j]

An Axhead Floats

6:1 **6** The company[k] of the prophets
k 1Sa 10:5; 2Ki 4:38 said to Elisha, "Look, the place
where we meet with you is too small for
us. 2Let us go to the Jordan, where each
of us can get a pole; and let us build a
place there for us to live."
And he said, "Go."
3Then one of them said, "Won't you
please come with your servants?"
"I will," Elisha replied. 4And he went
with them.
They went to the Jordan and began to
cut down trees. 5As one of them was
cutting down a tree, the iron axhead fell
into the water. "Oh, my lord," he cried
out, "it was borrowed!"
6The man of God asked, "Where did it
fall?" When he showed him the place, 6:6
Elisha cut a stick and threw[l] it there, l Ex 15:25;
and made the iron float. 7"Lift it out," he 2Ki 2:21
said. Then the man reached out his
hand and took it.

Elisha Traps Blinded Arameans

8Now the king of Aram was at war
with Israel. After conferring with his officers, he said, "I will set up my camp in
such and such a place."
9The man of God sent word to the 6:9
king[m] of Israel: "Beware of passing that m ver 12
place, because the Arameans are going
down there." 10So the king of Israel
checked on the place indicated by the
man of God. Time and again Elisha 6:10
warned[n] the king, so that he was on his n Jer 11:18
guard in such places.
11This enraged the king of Aram. He
summoned his officers and demanded
of them, "Will you not tell me which of
us is on the side of the king of Israel?"
12"None of us, my lord the king[o]," said 6:12
one of his officers, "but Elisha, the o ver 9
prophet who is in Israel, tells the king of
Israel the very words you speak in your
bedroom."
13"Go, find out where he is," the king
ordered, "so I can send men and capture 6:13
him." The report came back: "He is in p Ge 37:17
Dothan."[p] 14Then he sent[q] horses and 6:14
chariots and a strong force there. They q 2Ki 1:9
went by night and surrounded the city.
15When the servant of the man of
God got up and went out early the next
morning, an army with horses and chariots had surrounded the city. "Oh, my
lord, what shall we do?" the servant
asked. 6:16
16"Don't be afraid,"[r] the prophet an- r Ge 15:1
swered. "Those who are with us are s 2Ch 32:7; Ps 55:18;
more[s] than those who are with them." Ro 8:31; 1Jn 4:4
17And Elisha prayed, "O LORD, open
his eyes so he may see." Then the LORD
opened the servant's eyes, and he looked
and saw the hills full of horses and char- 6:17
iots[t] of fire all around Elisha. t 2Ki 2:11,12;
18As the enemy came down toward Ps 68:17;
him, Elisha prayed to the LORD, "Strike Zec 6:1-7
these people with blindness."[u] So he 6:18
struck them with blindness, as Elisha u Ge 19:11; Ac 13:11
had asked.

[a] 22 That is, about 75 pounds (about 34 kilograms)

DISCOVERY 90

Horses and Chariots of Fire

The king of Aram was at war with the king of Israel. Every time Aram's army moved, Elisha warned Israel's king and told him exactly where the enemy had relocated. This happened again and again until the king of Aram finally discovered that Elisha was telling the Israelite king "the very words" spoken in his bedroom (2 Kings 6:12). The king of Aram sent a mighty army to Dothan, surrounding the city and intending to capture Elisha.

The next morning when Elisha's servant observed the enemy camped around the city, he was stunned. Then Elisha reminded him that "those who are with us are more than those who are with them" (verse 16). Elisha asked God to open the servant's eyes—and the servant was even more astonished! All the surrounding hills were "full of horses and chariots of fire" (verse 17). When the enemy began its attack, Elisha asked God to do the very opposite of what he had asked him to do for his servant—to strike the soldiers with blindness—and God complied. The prophet himself went out to inform the invading army that they were at the wrong city, even agreeing to lead them to the right location. Elisha led the enemy troops to Samaria, the capital of Israel at the time. Israel's king, rather than killing the soldiers, prepared a feast in their honor and sent them home.

Like Elisha and his servant, we are never alone, although we may be "surrounded" by many enemies and there may appear to be no way to extricate ourselves from life's trying circumstances.

When we place our trust in God, however, his angel "encamps" around us and rescues us (Psalm 34:7). God will command his angels not only to protect us but also to lead us out of danger when the time is right (Psalm 91:11).

Besides the protection of unseen angels, Jesus himself promised that he will be with us forever: "All authority in heaven and on earth has been given to me. Therefore go and make disciples of all nations, baptizing them in the name of the Father and of the Son and of the Holy Spirit, and teaching them to obey everything I have commanded you. And surely I am with you always, to the very end of the age" (Matthew 28:18–20). When Jesus Christ returned to heaven, he left behind his Holy Spirit to remain with us, offering comfort and counsel (John 16:5–16). In spite of threatening forces of darkness, we can have confidence. The apostle John encouraged the early believers, who faced mounting persecution and the aggressive work of Satan, saying, "You, dear children, are from God and have overcome them, because the one [Jesus] who is in you is greater than the one [Satan] who is in the world" (1 John 4:4).

Self-Discovery: *Stop to think about the very real presence of Jesus in your heart and of his angels all around you. In what specific ways does that reality afford you comfort?*

GO TO DISCOVERY 91 ON PAGE 475

19 Elisha told them, “This is not the
road and this is not the city. Follow me,
and I will lead you to the man you are
looking for.” And he led them to Samaria.
20 After they entered the city, Elisha
said, “LORD, open the eyes of these men
so they can see.” Then the LORD opened
their eyes and they looked, and there
they were, inside Samaria.
21 When the king of Israel saw them,
6:21 he asked Elisha, “Shall I kill them, my fa-
v 2Ki 5:13 ther?[v] Shall I kill them?”
22 “Do not kill them,” he answered.
6:22 “Would you kill men you have cap-
w Dt 20:11; tured[w] with your own sword or bow? Set
2Ch 28:8-15; food and water before them so that they
Ro 12:20 may eat and drink and then go back to
their master.” 23 So he prepared a great
feast for them, and after they had finished eating and drinking, he sent them
away, and they returned to their master.
6:23 So the bands[x] from Aram stopped raid-
x 2Ki 5:2 ing Israel’s territory.

Famine in Besieged Samaria

6:24 24 Some time later, Ben-Hadad[y] king
y 1Ki 15:18; 20:1; 2Ki 8:7 of Aram mobilized his entire army and
z Dt 28:52 marched up and laid siege[z] to Samaria.
6:25 25 There was a great famine[a] in the city;
a Lev 26:26; Ru 1:1 the siege lasted so long that a donkey’s
b Isa 36:12 head sold for eighty shekels[a] of silver,
and a quarter of a cab[b] of seed pods[c][b] for
five shekels.[d]
26 As the king of Israel was passing by
on the wall, a woman cried to him,
“Help me, my lord the king!”
27 The king replied, “If the LORD does
not help you, where can I get help for
you? From the threshing floor? From the
winepress?” 28 Then he asked her,
“What’s the matter?”
She answered, “This woman said to
me, ‘Give up your son so we may eat him
today, and tomorrow we’ll eat my son.’
6:29 29 So we cooked my son and ate[c] him.
c Lev 26:29; Dt 28:53-55 The next day I said to her, ‘Give up your
son so we may eat him,’ but she had hid-
den him.”
6:30 30 When the king heard the woman’s
d 2Ki 18:37; Isa 22:15 words, he tore[d] his robes. As he went
e Ge 37:34; 1Ki 21:27 along the wall, the people looked, and
there, underneath, he had sackcloth[e] on
his body. 31 He said, “May God deal with
me, be it ever so severely, if the head of
Elisha son of Shaphat remains on his
shoulders today!”
32 Now Elisha was sitting in his house,
and the elders[f] were sitting with him. 6:32
The king sent a messenger ahead, but f Eze 8:1; 14:1; 20:1 g 1Ki 18:4
before he arrived, Elisha said to the eld- h ver 31
ers, “Don’t you see how this murderer[g] is
sending someone to cut off my head?[h]
Look, when the messenger comes, shut
the door and hold it shut against him. Is
not the sound of his master’s footsteps
behind him?”
33 While he was still talking to them,
the messenger came down to him. And
⌞the king⌟ said, “This disaster is from 6:33
the LORD. Why should I wait[i] for the i Lev 24:11; Job 2:9; 14:14;
LORD any longer?” Isa 40:31
7 Elisha said, “Hear the word of the
LORD. This is what the LORD says:
About this time tomorrow, a seah[e] of
flour will sell for a shekel[f] and two seahs[g]
of barley for a shekel[j] at the gate of 7:1 j ver 16
Samaria.”
2 The officer on whose arm the king 7:2
was leaning[k] said to the man of God, k 2Ki 5:18
“Look, even if the LORD should open the l ver 19; Ge 7:11;
floodgates[l] of the heavens, could this Ps 78:23;
happen?” Mal 3:10 m ver 17
“You will see it with your own eyes,”
answered Elisha, “but you will not eat[m]
any of it!”

The Siege Lifted

3 Now there were four men with lep- 7:3
rosy[h][n] at the entrance of the city gate. n Lev 13:45-46; Nu 5:1-4
They said to each other, “Why stay here
until we die? 4 If we say, ‘We’ll go into the
city’—the famine is there, and we will
die. And if we stay here, we will die. So
let’s go over to the camp of the Arameans and surrender. If they spare us, we
live; if they kill us, then we die.”
5 At dusk they got up and went to the
camp of the Arameans. When they
reached the edge of the camp, not a man
was there, 6 for the Lord had caused the 7:6
Arameans to hear the sound[o] of chariots o Ex 14:24;
and horses and a great army, so that they 2Sa 5:24; Eze 1:24
said to one another, “Look, the king of p 2Sa 10:6;
Israel has hired[p] the Hittite[q] and Egyp- Jer 46:21
tian kings to attack us!” 7 So they got up q Nu 13:29

[a] *25* That is, about 2 pounds (about 1 kilogram) [b] *25* That is, probably about 1/2 pint (about 0.3 liter) [c] *25* Or *of dove’s dung* [d] *25* That is, about 2 ounces (about 55 grams) [e] *1* That is, probably about 7 quarts (about 7.3 liters); also in verses 16 and 18 [f] *1* That is, about 2/5 ounce (about 11 grams); also in verses 16 and 18 [g] *1* That is, probably about 13 quarts (about 15 liters); also in verses 16 and 18 [h] *3* The Hebrew word is used for various diseases affecting the skin—not necessarily leprosy; also in verse 8.

7:7 [r]Jdg 7:21; Ps 48:4-6; Pr 28:1; Isa 30:17
and fled[r] in the dusk and abandoned
their tents and their horses and donkeys. They left the camp as it was and
ran for their lives.
7:8 [s]Isa 33:23; 35:6
[8]The men who had leprosy[s] reached
the edge of the camp and entered one of
the tents. They ate and drank, and carried away silver, gold and clothes, and
went off and hid them. They returned
and entered another tent and took some
things from it and hid them also.
[9]Then they said to each other, "We're
not doing right. This is a day of good
news and we are keeping it to ourselves.
If we wait until daylight, punishment
will overtake us. Let's go at once and report this to the royal palace."
[10]So they went and called out to the
city gatekeepers and told them, "We
went into the Aramean camp and not a
man was there—not a sound of anyone—only tethered horses and donkeys,
and the tents left just as they were."
[11]The gatekeepers shouted the news,
and it was reported within the palace.
[12]The king got up in the night and
said to his officers, "I will tell you what
the Arameans have done to us. They
7:12 [t]Jos 8:4; 2Ki 6:25-29
know we are starving; so they have left
the camp to hide[t] in the countryside,
thinking, 'They will surely come out, and

SHARING GOOD NEWS

Samaria was under siege by the Arameans, and the people were starving to death. Then four men with leprosy decided to take action (2 Kings 7). "Why stay here until we die?" they asked each other (verse 3), and they resolved to surrender to the Arameans and hope for mercy. But God had another plan. As the four made their way toward the enemy forces, God magnified the sound of their shuffling feet and frightened the Arameans so badly that they retreated! As the four men raided the enemy's tents, they remembered the starving people in Samaria. "We're not doing right," they conceded. "This is a day of good news and we are keeping it to ourselves" (verse 9). In the New Testament we read that giving our lives to Jesus entails taking on a whole new identity that we don't want to keep to ourselves (2 Corinthians 5:17,19). Jesus came to set us free from sin, and we want others to share in the Good News as well (Galatians 5:1; 1 Peter 2:9).

then we will take them alive and get into
the city.' "
[13]One of his officers answered, "Have
some men take five of the horses that
are left in the city. Their plight will be
like that of all the Israelites left here—
yes, they will only be like all these Israelites who are doomed. So let us send
them to find out what happened."
[14]So they selected two chariots with
their horses, and the king sent them after the Aramean army. He commanded
the drivers, "Go and find out what has
happened." [15]They followed them as far
as the Jordan, and they found the whole
road strewn with the clothing and
equipment the Arameans had thrown
away in their headlong flight. So the
messengers returned and reported to
the king. [16]Then the people went out
and plundered[u] the camp of the Arame- 7:16 [u]Isa 33:4,23
ans. So a seah of flour sold for a shekel, [v]ver 1
and two seahs of barley sold for a
shekel,[v] as the LORD had said.
[17]Now the king had put the officer on
whose arm he leaned in charge of the
gate, and the people trampled him in 7:17
the gateway, and he died,[w] just as the [w]ver 2; 2Ki 6:32
man of God had foretold when the king
came down to his house. [18]It happened
as the man of God had said to the king:
"About this time tomorrow, a seah of
flour will sell for a shekel and two seahs
of barley for a shekel at the gate of
Samaria."
[19]The officer had said to the man of
God, "Look, even if the LORD should
open the floodgates[x] of the heavens, 7:19 [x]ver 2
could this happen?" The man of God
had replied, "You will see it with your
own eyes, but you will not eat any of it!"
[20]And that is exactly what happened to
him, for the people trampled him in the
gateway, and he died.

The Shunammite's Land Restored

8 Now Elisha had said to the 8:1
woman[y] whose son he had re- [y]2Ki 4:8-37
stored to life, "Go away with your family [z]Lev 26:26;
and stay for a while wherever you can, Dt 28:22; Ru 1:1 [a]Ge 12:10;
because the LORD has decreed a famine[z] Ps 105:16;
in the land that will last seven years."[a] Hag 1:11
[2]The woman proceeded to do as the
man of God said. She and her family
went away and stayed in the land of the
Philistines seven years.
[3]At the end of the seven years she

came back from the land of the Philistines and went to the king to beg for her
house and land. 4The king was talking to
Gehazi, the servant of the man of God,
and had said, "Tell me about all the great
things Elisha has done." 5Just as Gehazi
8:5 was telling the king how Elisha had re-
b 2Ki 4:35 stored[b] the dead to life, the woman
whose son Elisha had brought back to
life came to beg the king for her house
and land.

Gehazi said, "This is the woman, my
lord the king, and this is her son whom
Elisha restored to life." 6The king asked
the woman about it, and she told him.

Then he assigned an official to her
case and said to him, "Give back everything that belonged to her, including all
the income from her land from the day
she left the country until now."

Hazael Murders Ben-Hadad

8:7 7Elisha went to Damascus,[c] and Ben-
c 2Sa 8:5; 1Ki 11:24 Hadad[d] king of Aram was ill. When the
d 2Ki 6:24 king was told, "The man of God has
8:8 come all the way up here," 8he said to
e 1Ki 19:15 Hazael,[e] "Take a gift[f] with you and go to
f Ge 32:20; 1Sa 9:7; 2Ki 1:2 meet the man of God. Consult[g] the LORD
g Jdg 18:5 through him; ask him, 'Will I recover
from this illness?' "

9Hazael went to meet Elisha, taking
with him as a gift forty camel-loads of all
the finest wares of Damascus. He went
in and stood before him, and said, "Your
son Ben-Hadad king of Aram has sent
me to ask, 'Will I recover from this illness?' "

8:10 10Elisha answered, "Go and say to
h Isa 38:1 him, 'You will certainly recover';[h] but[a]
the LORD has revealed to me that he will
in fact die." 11He stared at him with a
8:11 fixed gaze until Hazael felt ashamed.[i]
i Jdg 3:25 j Lk 19:41 Then the man of God began to weep.[j]

12"Why is my lord weeping?" asked
Hazael.

8:12 "Because I know the harm[k] you will
k 1Ki 19:17; 2Ki 10:32; 12:17; 13:3,7 do to the Israelites," he answered. "You
will set fire to their fortified places, kill
l Ps 137:9; Isa 13:16; Hos 13:16; Na 3:10; Lk 19:44 their young men with the sword, dash[l]
their little children[m] to the ground, and
rip open[n] their pregnant women."
m Ge 34:29 13Hazael said, "How could your ser-
n 2Ki 15:16; Am 1:13 vant, a mere dog,[o] accomplish such a
feat?"

8:13 "The LORD has shown me that you
o 1Sa 17:43; 2Sa 3:8 will become king[p] of Aram," answered
p 1Ki 19:15 Elisha.

14Then Hazael left Elisha and returned to his master. When Ben-Hadad
asked, "What did Elisha say to you?"
Hazael replied, "He told me that you
would certainly recover." 15But the next
day he took a thick cloth, soaked it in
water and spread it over the king's face,
so that he died.[q] Then Hazael succeed- 8:15 q 2Ki 1:17
ed him as king.

Jehoram King of Judah

16In the fifth year of Joram[r] son of 8:16 r 2Ki 1:17; 3:1
Ahab king of Israel, when Jehoshaphat s 2Ch 21:1-4
was king of Judah, Jehoram[s] son of Jehoshaphat began his reign as king of Judah. 17He was thirty-two years old when
he became king, and he reigned in Jerusalem eight years. 18He walked in the
ways of the kings of Israel, as the house
of Ahab had done, for he married a 8:18
daughter[t] of Ahab. He did evil in the t ver 26; 2Ki 11:1
eyes of the LORD. 19Nevertheless, for the
sake of his servant David, the LORD was 8:19
not willing to destroy[u] Judah. He had u Ge 6:13
promised to maintain a lamp[v] for David v 2Sa 21:17; 7:13; 1Ki 11:36; Rev 21:23
and his descendants forever.

20In the time of Jehoram, Edom rebelled against Judah and set up its own 8:20
king.[w] 21So Jehoram[b] went to Zair with w 1Ki 22:47
all his chariots. The Edomites surround-
ed him and his chariot commanders,
but he rose up and broke through by
night; his army, however, fled back
home. 22To this day Edom has been in 8:22
rebellion[x] against Judah. Libnah[y] revolt- x Ge 27:40 y Nu 33:20;
ed at the same time. Jos 21:13; 2Ki 19:8

23As for the other events of Jehoram's
reign, and all he did, are they not written
in the book of the annals of the kings of
Judah? 24Jehoram rested with his fathers
and was buried with them in the City of
David. And Ahaziah his son succeeded
him as king.

Ahaziah King of Judah

25In the twelfth[z] year of Joram son of 8:25 z 2Ki 9:29
Ahab king of Israel, Ahaziah son of Je-
horam king of Judah began to reign.
26Ahaziah was twenty-two years old
when he became king, and he reigned 8:26
in Jerusalem one year. His mother's a ver 18
name was Athaliah,[a] a granddaughter of b 1Ki 16:23
Omri[b] king of Israel. 27He walked in the 8:27 c 1Ki 16:30
ways of the house of Ahab[c] and did evil[d] d 1Ki 15:26

[a] *10* The Hebrew may also be read *Go and say, 'You will certainly not recover,' for.* [b] *21* Hebrew *Joram,* a variant of *Jehoram;* also in verses 23 and 24

in the eyes of the LORD, as the house of
Ahab had done, for he was related by
marriage to Ahab's family.
28 Ahaziah went with Joram son of
Ahab to war against Hazael king of
Aram at Ramoth Gilead.[e] The Arameans
wounded Joram; 29 so King Joram returned to Jezreel[f] to recover from the
wounds the Arameans had inflicted on
him at Ramoth[a] in his battle with Hazael[g] king of Aram.
Then Ahaziah son of Jehoram king of
Judah went down to Jezreel to see Joram
son of Ahab, because he had been
wounded.

Jehu Anointed King of Israel

9 The prophet Elisha summoned a
man from the company[h] of the
prophets and said to him, "Tuck your
cloak into your belt,[i] take this flask of
oil[j] with you and go to Ramoth Gilead.[k]
2 When you get there, look for Jehu son
of Jehoshaphat, the son of Nimshi. Go to
him, get him away from his companions
and take him into an inner room. 3 Then
take the flask and pour the oil[l] on his
head and declare, 'This is what the LORD
says: I anoint you king over Israel.' Then
open the door and run; don't delay!"
4 So the young man, the prophet, went
to Ramoth Gilead. 5 When he arrived, he
found the army officers sitting together.
"I have a message for you, commander,"
he said.
"For which of us?" asked Jehu.
"For you, commander," he replied.
6 Jehu got up and went into the house.
Then the prophet poured the oil[m] on
Jehu's head and declared, "This is what
the LORD, the God of Israel, says: 'I anoint
you king over the LORD's people Israel.
7 You are to destroy the house of Ahab
your master, and I will avenge[n] the blood
of my servants[o] the prophets and the
blood of all the LORD's servants shed by
Jezebel.[p] 8 The whole house[q] of Ahab will
perish. I will cut off from Ahab every last
male[r] in Israel—slave or free. 9 I will
make the house of Ahab like the house of
Jeroboam[s] son of Nebat and like the
house of Baasha[t] son of Ahijah. 10 As for
Jezebel, dogs[u] will devour her on the plot
of ground at Jezreel, and no one will bury
her.'" Then he opened the door and ran.
11 When Jehu went out to his fellow officers, one of them asked him, "Is every-

8:28 [e] Dt 4:43; 1Ki 22:3,29
8:29 [f] 2Ki 9:15 [g] 1Ki 19:15,17
9:1 [h] 1Sa 10:5 [i] 2Ki 4:29 [j] 1Sa 10:1 [k] 2Ki 8:28
9:3 [l] 1Ki 19:16
9:6 [m] 1Ki 19:16; 2Ch 22:7
9:7 [n] Ge 4:24; Rev 6:10 [o] Dt 32:43 [p] 1Ki 18:4; 21:15
9:8 [q] 2Ki 10:17 [r] Dt 32:36; 1Sa 25:22; 1Ki 21:21; 2Ki 14:26
9:9 [s] 1Ki 14:10; 15:29; 16:3,11 [t] 1Ki 16:3
9:10 [u] ver 35-36; 1Ki 21:23

thing all right? Why did this madman[v]
come to you?"
"You know the man and the sort of
things he says," Jehu replied.
12 "That's not true!" they said. "Tell us."
Jehu said, "Here is what he told me:
'This is what the LORD says: I anoint you
king over Israel.'"
13 They hurried and took their cloaks
and spread[w] them under him on the
bare steps. Then they blew the trumpet[x]
and shouted, "Jehu is king!"

Jehu Kills Joram and Ahaziah

14 So Jehu son of Jehoshaphat, the son
of Nimshi, conspired against Joram.
(Now Joram and all Israel had been defending Ramoth Gilead[y] against Hazael
king of Aram, 15 but King Joram[b] had returned to Jezreel to recover[z] from the
wounds the Arameans had inflicted on
him in the battle with Hazael king of
Aram.) Jehu said, "If this is the way you
feel, don't let anyone slip out of the city
to go and tell the news in Jezreel." 16 Then
he got into his chariot and rode to Jezreel, because Joram was resting there and
Ahaziah[a] king of Judah had gone down
to see him.
17 When the lookout[b] standing on the
tower in Jezreel saw Jehu's troops approaching, he called out, "I see some
troops coming."
"Get a horseman," Joram ordered.
"Send him to meet them and ask, 'Do
you come in peace?[c]'"
18 The horseman rode off to meet Jehu
and said, "This is what the king says: 'Do
you come in peace?'"
"What do you have to do with peace?"
Jehu replied. "Fall in behind me."
The lookout reported, "The messenger has reached them, but he isn't coming back."
19 So the king sent out a second horseman. When he came to them he said,
"This is what the king says: 'Do you
come in peace?'"
Jehu replied, "What do you have to do
with peace? Fall in behind me."
20 The lookout reported, "He has
reached them, but he isn't coming back
either. The driving is like[d] that of Jehu son
of Nimshi—he drives like a madman."

[a] 29 Hebrew *Ramah,* a variant of *Ramoth*
[b] 15 Hebrew *Jehoram,* a variant of *Joram;* also in verses 17 and 21–24

9:11 [v] Jer 29:26; Jn 10:20; Ac 26:24
9:13 [w] Mt 21:8; Lk 19:36 [x] 2Sa 15:10; 1Ki 1:34,39
9:14 [y] Dt 4:43; 2Ki 8:28
9:15 [z] 2Ki 8:29
9:16 [a] 2Ch 22:7
9:17 [b] Isa 21:6 [c] 1Sa 16:4
9:20 [d] 2Sa 18:27

21"Hitch up my chariot," Joram ordered. And when it was hitched up, Joram king of Israel and Ahaziah king of
Judah rode out, each in his own chariot,
9:21 to meet Jehu. They met him at the plot
e ver 26; of ground that had belonged to Naboth[e]
1Ki 21:1-7,15-19 the Jezreelite. 22When Joram saw Jehu he
asked, "Have you come in peace, Jehu?"
9:22 "How can there be peace," Jehu replied,
f 1Ki 16:30-33; "as long as all the idolatry and witchcraft
18:19; 2Ch 21:13; of your mother Jezebel[f] abound?"
Rev 2:20 23Joram turned about and fled, calling
9:23 out to Ahaziah, "Treachery,[g] Ahaziah!"
g 2Ki 11:14 24Then Jehu drew his bow[h] and shot
9:24 Joram between the shoulders. The arrow
h 1Ki 22:34 pierced his heart and he slumped down
in his chariot. 25Jehu said to Bidkar, his
chariot officer, "Pick him up and throw
him on the field that belonged to Naboth the Jezreelite. Remember how you
and I were riding together in chariots
behind Ahab his father when the LORD
9:25 made this prophecy[i] about him: 26'Yes-
i 1Ki 21:19-22, 24-29 terday I saw the blood of Naboth[j] and
the blood of his sons, declares the LORD,
9:26 and I will surely make you pay for it on
j 1Ki 21:19 k 1Ki 21:29 this plot of ground, declares the LORD.'[a]
Now then, pick him up and throw him
on that plot, in accordance with the
word of the LORD."[k]
27When Ahaziah king of Judah saw
what had happened, he fled up the road
to Beth Haggan.[b] Jehu chased him,
shouting, "Kill him too!" They wounded
him in his chariot on the way up to Gur
9:27 near Ibleam,[l] but he escaped to Megid-
l Jdg 1:27 m 2Ki 23:29 do[m] and died there. 28His servants took
9:28 him by chariot[n] to Jerusalem and buried
n 2Ki 14:20; him with his fathers in his tomb in the
23:30 City of David. 29(In the eleventh[o] year of
9:29 Joram son of Ahab, Ahaziah had be-
o 2Ki 8:25 come king of Judah.)

Jezebel Killed

9:30 30Then Jehu went to Jezreel. When
p Jer 4:30; Eze 23:40 Jezebel heard about it, she painted[p] her
eyes, arranged her hair and looked out
of a window. 31As Jehu entered the gate,
she asked, "Have you come in peace,
9:31 Zimri,[q] you murderer of your master?"[c]
q 1Ki 16:9-10 32He looked up at the window and
called out, "Who is on my side? Who?"
Two or three eunuchs looked down at
him. 33"Throw her down!" Jehu said. So
they threw her down, and some of her
blood spattered the wall and the horses
9:33 r Ps 7:5 as they trampled her underfoot.[r]

34Jehu went in and ate and drank.
"Take care of that cursed woman," he
said, "and bury her, for she was a king's 9:34
daughter."[s] 35But when they went out to s 1Ki 16:31;
bury her, they found nothing except her 21:25
skull, her feet and her hands. 36They
went back and told Jehu, who said, "This
is the word of the LORD that he spoke
through his servant Elijah the Tishbite: 9:36
On the plot of ground at Jezreel dogs[t] t Ps 68:23;
will devour Jezebel's flesh.[d u] 37Jezebel's Jer 15:3 u 1Ki 21:23
body will be like refuse[v] on the ground 9:37
in the plot at Jezreel, so that no one will v Ps 83:10;
be able to say, 'This is Jezebel.'" Isa 5:25; Jer 8:2; 9:22; 16:4; 25:33; Zep 1:17

Ahab's Family Killed

10 Now there were in Samaria[w] 10:1 w 1Ki 13:32
seventy sons[x] of the house of x Jdg 8:30
Ahab. So Jehu wrote letters and sent y 1Ki 21:1 z ver 5
them to Samaria: to the officials of
Jezreel,[e y] to the elders and to the
guardians[z] of Ahab's children. He said,
2"As soon as this letter reaches you, since
your master's sons are with you and you
have chariots and horses, a fortified city
and weapons, 3choose the best and most
worthy of your master's sons and set
him on his father's throne. Then fight for
your master's house."
4But they were terrified and said, "If
two kings could not resist him, how
can we?"
5So the palace administrator, the city
governor, the elders and the guardians
sent this message to Jehu: "We are your 10:5
servants[a] and we will do anything you a Jos 9:8;
say. We will not appoint anyone as king; 1Ki 20:4,32
you do whatever you think best."
6Then Jehu wrote them a second letter, saying, "If you are on my side and
will obey me, take the heads of your
master's sons and come to me in Jezreel
by this time tomorrow."
Now the royal princes, seventy of
them, were with the leading men of the
city, who were rearing them. 7When the
letter arrived, these men took the 10:7
princes and slaughtered all seventy[b] of b 1Ki 21:21
them. They put their heads[c] in baskets c 2Sa 4:8
and sent them to Jehu in Jezreel. 8When
the messenger arrived, he told Jehu,
"They have brought the heads of the
princes."

a 26 See 1 Kings 21:19. b 27 Or *fled by way of the garden house* c 31 Or *"Did Zimri have peace, who murdered his master?"* d 36 See 1 Kings 21:23. e 1 Hebrew; some Septuagint manuscripts and Vulgate *of the city*

DISCOVERY 91

As Good as His Word

The telephone rang. He assured her, "I'm leaving now. I'll be home in an hour." Two-and-one-half hours later, he appeared in the doorway. No remorse, no apology, no explanation. Not a man of his word!

She guaranteed delivery of the product by 12 o'clock noon on Monday. Monday arrived; noon came and went; night fell; Tuesday morning dawned. Finally, at 3:15 on Wednesday afternoon the package arrived. No notification, no regret, no legitimate reason offered for the delay. Not a business that kept its word.

The scenario is repeated all too often: broken commitments in marriage, broken promises to children, broken contracts in business, broken agreements over property. Talk can be cheap.

But when God tells us he'll do something, he *will*. God through Elijah had promised wicked King Ahab that "because you have sold yourself to do evil in the eyes of the LORD . . . I am going to bring disaster on you" (1 Kings 21:20–21).

That negative promise was fulfilled in gruesome detail. Under the direction of Jehu, a personal bodyguard to Ahab who was to succeed him as king, Ahab's entire family was annihilated. Even though King Jehu was not consistently reliable, not always faithful and rarely honorable, he was designated as God's "instrument of execution"—and God kept his word (2 Kings 10:17).

God always tells the unambiguous truth—no half-truths and no white lies. He doesn't manipulate information to make people feel good or practice deceit to convince his hearers. Instead, he is *genuine* in all that he says (John 17:3; 1 John 5:20).

God likens his words to rain and snow: Both fall on the earth and do not return to the sky as evaporation without first having watered the land. The earth in turn flourishes and produces sustenance for us. God's words also accomplish his intended purpose—even if that intention is not always immediately clear (Isaiah 55:10–11).

God has made many promises to us. When he declares, "Never will I leave you," we may rest assured that *he won't* (Hebrews 13:5). When he affirms that his arms are always underneath us, we know that *he is there* to support us (Deuteronomy 33:27). He promises that nothing can separate us from his love, and *it can't* (Romans 8:37). He assures us that he will forgive our sin when we confess it to him, and *he will* (1 John 1:9). We *can* overcome any obstacle through his strength (Romans 8:38; Philippians 2:13; 4:13); he *will* sustain us when we feel weary (Psalm 55:22); we *are* safe in his hands (John 10:29). And when Jesus pledges to come back for us one day, we know that *he will* (1 Thessalonians 4:17).

The list is lengthy, but more significantly each promise is *true*. Jesus never changes, and his Word stands true (Hebrews 13:8). It can be no other way (Titus 1:2).

Self-Discovery: *Jesus kept his promises to us in spite of the terrible cost involved. How does his faithfulness inspire you to keep your promises to others?*

GO TO DISCOVERY 92 ON PAGE 485

Then Jehu ordered, "Put them in two
piles at the entrance of the city gate until morning."
9The next morning Jehu went out. He
stood before all the people and said,
"You are innocent. It was I who conspired against my master and killed
him, but who killed all these? 10Know
then, that not a word the LORD has spo-
10:10 ken against the house of Ahab will fail.
d 2Ki 9:7-10 The LORD has done what he promised[d]
e 1Ki 21:29 through his servant Elijah."[e] 11So Jehu[f]
10:11 killed everyone in Jezreel who remained
f Hos 1:4 of the house of Ahab, as well as all his
g ver 14; chief men, his close friends and his
Job 18:19 priests, leaving him no survivor.[g]
12Jehu then set out and went toward
Samaria. At Beth Eked of the Shepherds,
13he met some relatives of Ahaziah king
of Judah and asked, "Who are you?"
10:13 They said, "We are relatives of Ahazi-
h 2Ki 8:24,29; 2Ch 22:8 ah,[h] and we have come down to greet
the families of the king and of the queen
i 1Ki 2:19 mother.[i]"
14"Take them alive!" he ordered. So
they took them alive and slaughtered
them by the well of Beth Eked—forty-
two men. He left no survivor.
10:15 15After he left there, he came upon Je-
j Jer 35:6,14-19 honadab[j] son of Recab,[k] who was on his
k 1Ch 2:55; Jer 35:2 way to meet him. Jehu greeted him and
l Ezr 10:19; said, "Are you in accord with me, as I am
Eze 17:18 with you?"
"I am," Jehonadab answered.
"If so," said Jehu, "give me your hand."[l]
So he did, and Jehu helped him up into
10:16 the chariot. 16Jehu said, "Come with me
m Nu 25:13; and see my zeal[m] for the LORD." Then he
1Ki 19:10 had him ride along in his chariot.
17When Jehu came to Samaria, he
10:17 killed all who were left there of Ahab's
n 2Ki 9:8 family;[n] he destroyed them, according
to the word of the LORD spoken to Elijah.

Ministers of Baal Killed

10:18 18Then Jehu brought all the people to-
o Jdg 2:11; gether and said to them, "Ahab served[o]
1Ki 16:31-32 Baal a little; Jehu will serve him much.
10:19 p 1Ki 18:19; 22:6 19Now summon[p] all the prophets of
Baal, all his ministers and all his priests.
See that no one is missing, because I am
going to hold a great sacrifice for Baal.
Anyone who fails to come will no longer
live." But Jehu was acting deceptively in
order to destroy the ministers of Baal.
10:20 q Ex 32:5; 20Jehu said, "Call an assembly[q] in hon-
Joel 1:14 or of Baal." So they proclaimed it. 21Then
he sent word throughout Israel, and all
the ministers of Baal came; not one
stayed away. They crowded into the
temple of Baal until it was full from one
end to the other. 22And Jehu said to the
keeper of the wardrobe, "Bring robes for
all the ministers of Baal." So he brought
out robes for them.
23Then Jehu and Jehonadab son of Recab went into the temple of Baal. Jehu
said to the ministers of Baal, "Look
around and see that no servants of the
LORD are here with you—only ministers
of Baal." 24So they went in to make sacrifices and burnt offerings. Now Jehu
had posted eighty men outside with this
warning: "If one of you lets any of the
men I am placing in your hands escape, 10:24
it will be your life for his life."[r] r 1Ki 20:39
25As soon as Jehu had finished mak- 10:25
ing the burnt offering, he ordered the s Ex 22:20;
guards and officers: "Go in and kill[s] 2Ki 11:18
them; let no one escape."[t] So they cut t 1Ki 18:40
them down with the sword. The guards
and officers threw the bodies out and
then entered the inner shrine of the
temple of Baal. 26They brought the sa- 10:26
cred stone[u] out of the temple of Baal u 1Ki 14:23
and burned it. 27They demolished the
sacred stone of Baal and tore down the
temple[v] of Baal, and people have used it 10:27 v 1Ki 16:32
for a latrine to this day.
28So Jehu[w] destroyed Baal worship in 10:28
Israel. 29However, he did not turn away w 1Ki 19:17
from the sins[x] of Jeroboam son of Nebat, 10:29 x 1Ki 12:30
which he had caused Israel to commit— y 1Ki 12:28-29
the worship of the golden calves[y] at z 1Ki 12:32
Bethel[z] and Dan.
30The LORD said to Jehu, "Because you
have done well in accomplishing what is
right in my eyes and have done to the
house of Ahab all I had in mind to do,
your descendants will sit on the throne 10:30 a ver 35;
of Israel to the fourth generation."[a] 31Yet 2Ki 15:12
Jehu was not careful[b] to keep the law of 10:31
the LORD, the God of Israel, with all his b Pr 4:23
heart. He did not turn away from the c 1Ki 12:30
sins[c] of Jeroboam, which he had caused
Israel to commit.
32In those days the LORD began to re- 10:32
duce[d] the size of Israel. Hazael[e] over- d 2Ki 13:25
powered the Israelites throughout their e 1Ki 19:17;
territory 33east of the Jordan in all the 2Ki 8:12
land of Gilead (the region of Gad, Reu- 10:33
ben and Manasseh), from Aroer[f] by the f Nu 32:34;
Arnon Gorge through Gilead to Bashan. Dt 2:36; Jdg 11:26;
34As for the other events of Jehu's Isa 17:2

reign, all he did, and all his achievements, are they not written in the book of the annals[g] of the kings of Israel? 35 Jehu rested with his fathers and was buried in Samaria. And Jehoahaz his son succeeded him as king. 36 The time that Jehu reigned over Israel in Samaria was twenty-eight years.

10:34 [g] 1Ki 15:31

Athaliah and Joash

11 When Athaliah[h] the mother of Ahaziah saw that her son was dead, she proceeded to destroy the whole royal family. 2 But Jehosheba, the daughter of King Jehoram[a] and sister of Ahaziah, took Joash[i] son of Ahaziah and stole him away from among the royal princes, who were about to be murdered. She put him and his nurse in a bedroom to hide him from Athaliah; so he was not killed.[j] 3 He remained hidden with his nurse at the temple of the LORD for six years while Athaliah ruled the land.

11:1 [h] 2Ki 8:18
11:2 [i] ver 21; 2Ki 12:1 [j] Jdg 9:5

4 In the seventh year Jehoiada sent for the commanders of units of a hundred, the Carites[k] and the guards and had them brought to him at the temple of the LORD. He made a covenant with them and put them under oath at the temple of the LORD. Then he showed them the king's son. 5 He commanded them, saying, "This is what you are to do: You who are in the three companies that are going on duty on the Sabbath[l]—a third of you guarding the royal palace,[m] 6 a third at the Sur Gate, and a third at the gate behind the guard, who take turns guarding the temple— 7 and you who are in the other two companies that normally go off Sabbath duty are all to guard the temple for the king. 8 Station yourselves around the king, each man with his weapon in his hand. Anyone who approaches your ranks[b] must be put to death. Stay close to the king wherever he goes."

11:4 [k] ver 19
11:5 [l] 1Ch 9:25 [m] 1Ki 14:27

9 The commanders of units of a hundred did just as Jehoiada the priest ordered. Each one took his men—those who were going on duty on the Sabbath and those who were going off duty—and came to Jehoiada the priest. 10 Then he gave the commanders the spears and shields[n] that had belonged to King David and that were in the temple of the LORD. 11 The guards, each with his weapon in his hand, stationed themselves around the king—near the altar and the temple, from the south side to the north side of the temple.

11:10 [n] 2Sa 8:7; 1Ch 18:7

12 Jehoiada brought out the king's son and put the crown on him; he presented him with a copy of the covenant[o] and proclaimed him king. They anointed[p] him, and the people clapped their hands[q] and shouted, "Long live the king!"[r]

11:12 [o] Ex 25:16; 2Ki 23:3 [p] 1Sa 9:16; 1Ki 1:39 [q] Ps 47:1; 98:8; Isa 55:12 [r] 1Sa 10:24

13 When Athaliah heard the noise made by the guards and the people, she went to the people at the temple of the LORD. 14 She looked and there was the king, standing by the pillar,[s] as the custom was. The officers and the trumpeters were beside the king, and all the people of the land were rejoicing and blowing trumpets.[t] Then Athaliah tore[u] her robes and called out, "Treason! Treason!"[v]

11:14 [s] 1Ki 7:15; 2Ki 23:3; 2Ch 34:31 [t] 1Ki 1:39 [u] Ge 37:29 [v] 2Ki 9:23

15 Jehoiada the priest ordered the commanders of units of a hundred, who were in charge of the troops: "Bring her out between the ranks[c] and put to the sword anyone who follows her." For the priest had said, "She must not be put to death in the temple[w] of the LORD." 16 So they seized her as she reached the place where the horses enter[x] the palace grounds, and there she was put to death.[y]

11:15 [w] 1Ki 2:30
11:16 [x] Ne 3:28; Jer 31:40 [y] Ge 4:14

17 Jehoiada then made a covenant[z] between the LORD and the king and people that they would be the LORD's people. He also made a covenant between the king and the people.[a] 18 All the people of the

11:17 [z] Ex 24:8; 2Sa 5:3; 2Ch 15:12; 23:3; 29:10; 34:31; Ezr 10:3 [a] 2Ki 23:3; Jer 34:8

[a] 2 Hebrew *Joram,* a variant of *Jehoram* [b] 8 Or *approaches the precincts* [c] 15 Or *out from the precincts*

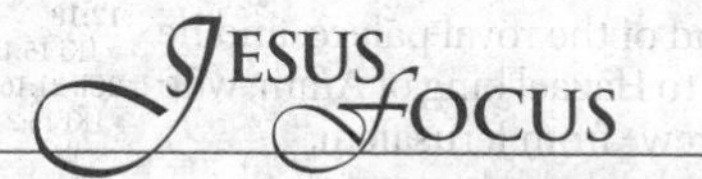

PROTECTING THE FAMILY LINE

The wicked Queen Athaliah was determined to wipe out David's royal line—and she came within one baby of doing just that (2 Kings 11). Had she succeeded, the family line of God's promised Messiah would have been severed. God's entire plan to bring his people back into a restored relationship with himself rested at this point in history on the intervention of one courageous woman—Jehosheba, who hid Joash from Athaliah. Our own contributions may at times seem insignificant, but only God is able to view the big picture. A single act of selfless service can have far-reaching implications.

land went to the temple[b] of Baal and tore it down. They smashed[c] the altars and idols to pieces and killed Mattan the priest[d] of Baal in front of the altars.

Then Jehoiada the priest posted guards at the temple of the LORD. 19 He took with him the commanders of hundreds, the Carites,[e] the guards and all the people of the land, and together they brought the king down from the temple of the LORD and went into the palace, entering by way of the gate of the guards. The king then took his place on the royal throne, 20 and all the people of the land rejoiced.[f] And the city was quiet, because Athaliah had been slain with the sword at the palace.

21 Joash[a] was seven years old when he began to reign.

Joash Repairs the Temple

12 In the seventh year of Jehu, Joash[b][g] became king, and he reigned in Jerusalem forty years. His mother's name was Zibiah; she was from Beersheba. 2 Joash did what was right in the eyes of the LORD all the years Jehoiada the priest instructed him. 3 The high places,[h] however, were not removed; the people continued to offer sacrifices and burn incense there.

4 Joash said to the priests, "Collect[i] all the money that is brought as sacred offerings[j] to the temple of the LORD—the money collected in the census,[k] the money received from personal vows and the money brought voluntarily[l] to the temple. 5 Let every priest receive the money from one of the treasurers, and let it be used to repair whatever damage is found in the temple."

6 But by the twenty-third year of King Joash the priests still had not repaired the temple. 7 Therefore King Joash summoned Jehoiada the priest and the other priests and asked them, "Why aren't you repairing the damage done to the temple? Take no more money from your treasurers, but hand it over for repairing the temple." 8 The priests agreed that they would not collect any more money from the people and that they would not repair the temple themselves.

9 Jehoiada the priest took a chest and bored a hole in its lid. He placed it beside the altar, on the right side as one enters the temple of the LORD. The priests who guarded the entrance[m] put into the chest all the money[n] that was brought to the temple of the LORD. 10 Whenever they saw that there was a large amount of money in the chest, the royal secretary[o] and the high priest came, counted the money that had been brought into the temple of the LORD and put it into bags. 11 When the amount had been determined, they gave the money to the men appointed to supervise the work on the temple. With it they paid those who worked on the temple of the LORD—the carpenters and builders, 12 the masons and stonecutters.[p] They purchased timber and dressed stone for the repair of the temple of the LORD, and met all the other expenses of restoring the temple.

13 The money brought into the temple was not spent for making silver basins, wick trimmers, sprinkling bowls, trumpets or any other articles of gold[q] or silver for the temple of the LORD; 14 it was paid to the workmen, who used it to repair the temple. 15 They did not require an accounting from those to whom they gave the money to pay the workers, because they acted with complete honesty.[r] 16 The money from the guilt offerings[s] and sin offerings[t] was not brought into the temple of the LORD; it belonged[u] to the priests.

17 About this time Hazael[v] king of Aram went up and attacked Gath and captured it. Then he turned to attack Jerusalem. 18 But Joash king of Judah took all the sacred objects dedicated by his fathers—Jehoshaphat, Jehoram and Ahaziah, the kings of Judah—and the gifts he himself had dedicated and all the gold found in the treasuries of the temple of the LORD and of the royal palace, and he sent[w] them to Hazael king of Aram, who then withdrew[x] from Jerusalem.

19 As for the other events of the reign of Joash, and all he did, are they not written in the book of the annals of the kings of Judah? 20 His officials[y] conspired against him and assassinated[z] him at Beth Millo,[a] on the road down to Silla. 21 The officials who murdered him were Jozabad son of Shimeath and Jehozabad son of Shomer. He died and was buried with his fathers in the City of David. And Amaziah his son succeeded him as king.

[a] *21* Hebrew *Jehoash,* a variant of *Joash*
[b] *1* Hebrew *Jehoash,* a variant of *Joash;* also in verses 2, 4, 6, 7 and 18

11:18 [b] 1Ki 16:32 [c] Dt 12:3 [d] 1Ki 18:40; 2Ki 10:25; 23:20
11:19 [e] ver 4
11:20 [f] Pr 11:10; 28:12; 29:2
12:1 [g] 2Ki 11:2
12:3 [h] 1Ki 3:3; 2Ki 14:4; 15:35; 18:4
12:4 [i] 2Ki 22:4 [j] Ex 35:5 [k] Ex 30:12 [l] Ex 35:29; 1Ch 29:3-9
12:9 [m] Jer 35:4 [n] 2Ch 24:8; Mk 12:41; Lk 21:1
12:10 [o] 2Sa 8:17
12:12 [p] 2Ki 22:5-6
12:13 [q] 1Ki 7:48-51; 2Ch 24:14
12:15 [r] 2Ki 22:7; 1Co 4:2
12:16 [s] Lev 5:14-19; Nu 18:9 [t] Lev 4:1-35 [u] Lev 7:7
12:17 [v] 2Ki 8:12
12:18 [w] 1Ki 15:18; 2Ch 21:16-17 [x] 1Ki 15:21
12:20 [y] 2Ki 14:5 [z] 2Ch 24:25 [a] Jdg 9:6

Jehoahaz King of Israel

13 In the twenty-third year of Joash son of Ahaziah king of Judah, Jehoahaz son of Jehu became king
of Israel in Samaria, and he reigned sev-
13:2 enteen years. 2He did evil[b] in the eyes of
b 1Ki 12:26-33 the LORD by following the sins of Jeroboam son of Nebat, which he had caused
13:3 Israel to commit, and he did not turn
c Dt 31:17; away from them. 3So the LORD's anger[c]
Jdg 2:14 burned against Israel, and for a long
d 1Ki 8:12; 12:17; 19:17 time he kept them under the power[d] of
e ver 24 Hazael king of Aram and Ben-Hadad[e]
13:4 his son.
f Dt 4:29; 4Then Jehoahaz sought[f] the LORD's fa-
Ps 78:34 vor, and the LORD listened to him, for he
g Ex 3:7; Dt 26:7 saw[g] how severely the king of Aram was
h 2Ki 14:26 oppressing[h] Israel. 5The LORD provided
13:5 a deliverer[i] for Israel, and they escaped
i ver 25; 2Ki 14:25,27 from the power of Aram. So the Israelites lived in their own homes as they
13:6 had before. 6But they did not turn away
j 1Ki 12:30 from the sins[j] of the house of Jeroboam,
k 1Ki 16:33 which he had caused Israel to commit;
they continued in them. Also, the Asherah pole[a][k] remained standing in Sa-
13:7 maria.
l 2Ki 10:32-33 7Nothing had been left[l] of the army of
m 2Sa 22:43 Jehoahaz except fifty horsemen, ten
chariots and ten thousand foot soldiers,
for the king of Aram had destroyed the
rest and made them like the dust[m] at
threshing time.
8As for the other events of the reign of
Jehoahaz, all he did and his achievements, are they not written in the book
of the annals of the kings of Israel? 9Je-
hoahaz rested with his fathers and was
buried in Samaria. And Jehoash[b] his son
succeeded him as king.

Jehoash King of Israel

10In the thirty-seventh year of Joash
king of Judah, Jehoash son of Jehoahaz
became king of Israel in Samaria, and he
reigned sixteen years. 11He did evil in the
eyes of the LORD and did not turn away
from any of the sins of Jeroboam son of
Nebat, which he had caused Israel to
commit; he continued in them.
12As for the other events of the reign
of Jehoash, all he did and his achieve-
13:12 ments, including his war against Ama-
n 2Ki 14:15 ziah[n] king of Judah, are they not written
o 1Ki 15:31 in the book of the annals[o] of the kings of
13:13 Israel? 13Jehoash rested with his fathers,
p 2Ki 14:23; Hos 1:1 and Jeroboam[p] succeeded him on the
throne. Jehoash was buried in Samaria
with the kings of Israel.
14Now Elisha was suffering from the
illness from which he died. Jehoash king
of Israel went down to see him and wept
over him. "My father! My father!" he
cried. "The chariots[q] and horsemen of 13:14
Israel!" q 2Ki 2:12
15Elisha said, "Get a bow and some ar- 13:15
rows," [r] and he did so. 16"Take the bow in r 1Sa 20:20
your hands," he said to the king of Israel.
When he had taken it, Elisha put his
hands on the king's hands.
17"Open the east window," he said,
and he opened it. "Shoot!"[s] Elisha said, 13:17
and he shot. "The LORD's arrow of victo- s Jos 8:18
ry, the arrow of victory over Aram!" Eli- t 1Ki 20:26
sha declared. "You will completely de-
stroy the Arameans at Aphek."[t]
18Then he said, "Take the arrows," and
the king took them. Elisha told him,
"Strike the ground." He struck it three
times and stopped. 19The man of God
was angry with him and said, "You
should have struck the ground five or six
times; then you would have defeated
Aram and completely destroyed it. But
now you will defeat it only three times."[u] 13:19
20Elisha died and was buried. u ver 25
Now Moabite raiders[v] used to enter 13:20 v 2Ki 3:7; 24:2
the country every spring. 21Once while
some Israelites were burying a man,
suddenly they saw a band of raiders; so
they threw the man's body into Elisha's
tomb. When the body touched Elisha's
bones, the man came to life[w] and stood 13:21
up on his feet. w Mt 27:52
22Hazael king of Aram oppressed[x] Is- 13:22
rael throughout the reign of Jehoahaz. x 1Ki 19:17; 2Ki 8:12
23But the LORD was gracious to them
and had compassion and showed concern for them because of his covenant[y] 13:23
with Abraham, Isaac and Jacob. To this y Ge 13:16-17; Ex 2:24
day he has been unwilling to destroy[z] z Dt 29:20
them or banish them from his pres- a Ex 33:15; 2Ki 14:27;
ence.[a] 17:18; 24:3,20
24Hazael king of Aram died, and Ben-
Hadad[b] his son succeeded him as king. 13:24
25Then Jehoash son of Jehoahaz recap- b ver 3
tured from Ben-Hadad son of Hazael
the towns he had taken in battle from
his father Jehoahaz. Three times[c] Jeho- 13:25
ash defeated him, and so he recovered[d] c ver 18,19
the Israelite towns. d 2Ki 10:32

a 6 That is, a symbol of the goddess Asherah; here and elsewhere in 2 Kings b 9 Hebrew *Joash*, a variant of *Jehoash*; also in verses 12–14 and 25

Amaziah King of Judah

14 In the second year of Jehoash[a]
son of Jehoahaz king of Israel,
Amaziah son of Joash king of Judah began to reign. 2He was twenty-five years
old when he became king, and he
reigned in Jerusalem twenty-nine years.
His mother's name was Jehoaddin; she
was from Jerusalem. 3He did what was
right in the eyes of the LORD, but not as
his father David had done. In everything
he followed the example of his father Joash. 4The high places,[e] however, were
not removed; the people continued to
offer sacrifices and burn incense there.
5After the kingdom was firmly in his
grasp, he executed[f] the officials[g] who
had murdered his father the king. 6Yet
he did not put the sons of the assassins
to death, in accordance with what is
written in the Book of the Law[h] of Moses where the LORD commanded: "Fathers shall not be put to death for their
children, nor children put to death for
their fathers; each is to die for his own
sins."[b][i]
7He was the one who defeated ten
thousand Edomites in the Valley of Salt[j]
and captured Sela[k] in battle, calling it
Joktheel, the name it has to this day.
8Then Amaziah sent messengers to
Jehoash son of Jehoahaz, the son of Jehu,
king of Israel, with the challenge: "Come,
meet me face to face."
9But Jehoash king of Israel replied to
Amaziah king of Judah: "A thistle[l] in
Lebanon sent a message to a cedar in
Lebanon, 'Give your daughter to my son
in marriage.' Then a wild beast in Lebanon came along and trampled the thistle underfoot. 10You have indeed defeated Edom and now you are arrogant.[m]
Glory in your victory, but stay at home!
Why ask for trouble and cause your own
downfall and that of Judah also?"
11Amaziah, however, would not listen,
so Jehoash king of Israel attacked. He
and Amaziah king of Judah faced each
other at Beth Shemesh[n] in Judah. 12Ju-
dah was routed by Israel, and every man
fled to his home.[o] 13Jehoash king of Israel captured Amaziah king of Judah, the
son of Joash, the son of Ahaziah, at Beth
Shemesh. Then Jehoash went to Jerusalem and broke down the wall[p] of Jerusalem from the Ephraim Gate[q] to the Corner Gate[r]—a section about six hundred
feet long.[c] 14He took all the gold and silver and all the articles found in the temple of the LORD and in the treasuries of
the royal palace. He also took hostages
and returned to Samaria.
15As for the other events of the reign
of Jehoash, what he did and his achievements, including his war[s] against Amaziah king of Judah, are they not written
in the book of the annals of the kings of
Israel? 16Jehoash rested with his fathers
and was buried in Samaria with the
kings of Israel. And Jeroboam his son
succeeded him as king.
17Amaziah son of Joash king of Judah
lived for fifteen years after the death of
Jehoash son of Jehoahaz king of Israel.
18As for the other events of Amaziah's
reign, are they not written in the book of
the annals of the kings of Judah?
19They conspired[t] against him in Jerusalem, and he fled to Lachish,[u] but
they sent men after him to Lachish and
killed him there. 20He was brought back
by horse[v] and was buried in Jerusalem
with his fathers, in the City of David.
21Then all the people of Judah took
Azariah,[d][w] who was sixteen years old,
and made him king in place of his father
Amaziah. 22He was the one who rebuilt
Elath[x] and restored it to Judah after Amaziah rested with his fathers.

Jeroboam II King of Israel

23In the fifteenth year of Amaziah son
of Joash king of Judah, Jeroboam[y] son of
Jehoash king of Israel became king in
Samaria, and he reigned forty-one
years. 24He did evil in the eyes of the
LORD and did not turn away from any of
the sins of Jeroboam son of Nebat,
which he had caused Israel to commit.[z]
25He was the one who restored the
boundaries of Israel from Lebo[e] Hamath[a] to the Sea of the Arabah,[f][b] in accordance with the word of the LORD, the
God of Israel, spoken through his servant Jonah[c] son of Amittai, the prophet
from Gath Hepher.
26The LORD had seen how bitterly
everyone in Israel, whether slave or
free,[d] was suffering;[e] there was no one to
help them.[f] 27And since the LORD had

14:4 e 2Ki 12:3; 16:4
14:5 f 2Ki 21:24 g 2Ki 12:20
14:6 h Dt 28:61 i Nu 26:11; Job 21:20; Jer 31:30; 44:3; Eze 18:4,20
14:7 j 2Sa 8:13; 2Ch 25:11 k Jdg 1:36
14:9 l Jdg 9:8-15
14:10 m Dt 8:14; 2Ch 26:16; 32:25
14:11 n Jos 15:10
14:12 o 2Sa 18:17
14:13 p 1Ki 3:1; 2Ch 33:14; 36:19; Jer 39:2 q Ne 8:16; 12:39 r 2Ch 25:23; Jer 31:38; Zec 14:10
14:15 s 2Ki 13:12
14:19 t 2Ki 12:20 u Jos 10:3; 2Ki 18:14,17
14:20 v 2Ki 9:28
14:21 w 2Ki 15:1; 2Ch 26:23
14:22 x 1Ki 9:26; 2Ki 16:6
14:23 y 2Ki 13:13
14:24 z 1Ki 15:30
14:25 a Nu 13:21; 1Ki 8:65 b Dt 3:17 c Jnh 1:1; Mt 12:39
14:26 d Dt 32:36 e 2Ki 13:4 f Ps 18:41; 22:11; 72:12; 107:12; Isa 63:5; La 1:7

a 1 Hebrew *Joash,* a variant of *Jehoash;* also in verses 13, 23 and 27 *b 6* Deut. 24:16
c 13 Hebrew *four hundred cubits* (about 180 meters) *d 21* Also called *Uzziah* *e 25* Or *from the entrance to* *f 25* That is, the Dead Sea

14:27 g 2Ki 13:23 not said he would blot out[g] the name of
h Jdg 6:14 Israel from under heaven, he saved[h]
them by the hand of Jeroboam son of Jehoash.
28 As for the other events of Jeroboam's
reign, all he did, and his military
14:28 i 2Sa 8:5; achievements, including how he recov-
1Ki 11:24 ered for Israel both Damascus[i] and Ha-
j 2Ch 8:3 k 1Ki 15:31 math,[j] which had belonged to Yaudi,[a]
are they not written in the book of the
annals[k] of the kings of Israel? 29 Jeroboam rested with his fathers, the kings of
Israel. And Zechariah his son succeeded
him as king.

Azariah King of Judah

15 In the twenty-seventh year of
Jeroboam king of Israel, Azari-
15:1 l ver 32; ah[l] son of Amaziah king of Judah began
2Ki 14:21 to reign. 2 He was sixteen years old when
he became king, and he reigned in Jerusalem fifty-two years. His mother's
name was Jecoliah; she was from Jerusalem. 3 He did what was right in the
eyes of the LORD, just as his father Amaziah had done. 4 The high places, however, were not removed; the people continued to offer sacrifices and burn
incense there.
15:5 5 The LORD afflicted[m] the king with
m Ge 12:17 n Lev 13:46 leprosy[b] until the day he died, and he
o 2Ch 27:1 lived in a separate house.[c][n] Jotham[o] the
p Ge 41:40 king's son had charge of the palace[p] and
governed the people of the land.
6 As for the other events of Azariah's
reign, and all he did, are they not written
in the book of the annals of the kings of
15:7 Judah? 7 Azariah rested[q] with his fathers
q Isa 6:1; 14:28 and was buried near them in the City of
r ver 5 David. And Jotham[r] his son succeeded
him as king.

Zechariah King of Israel

8 In the thirty-eighth year of Azariah
king of Judah, Zechariah son of Jeroboam became king of Israel in Samaria,
15:9 and he reigned six months. 9 He did evil[s]
s 1Ki 15:26 in the eyes of the LORD, as his fathers had
done. He did not turn away from the
sins of Jeroboam son of Nebat, which he
had caused Israel to commit.
10 Shallum son of Jabesh conspired
against Zechariah. He attacked him in
15:10 front of the people,[d] assassinated[t] him
t 2Ki 12:20 and succeeded him as king. 11 The other
15:11 events of Zechariah's reign are written in
u 1Ki 15:31 the book of the annals[u] of the kings of
Israel. 12 So the word of the LORD spoken
to Jehu was fulfilled:[v] "Your descendants 15:12 v 2Ki 10:30
will sit on the throne of Israel to the
fourth generation."[e]

Shallum King of Israel

13 Shallum son of Jabesh became king
in the thirty-ninth year of Uzziah king of
Judah, and he reigned in Samaria[w] one 15:13 w ver 1,8
month. 14 Then Menahem son of Gadi 15:14
went from Tirzah[x] up to Samaria. He at- x 1Ki 14:17
tacked Shallum son of Jabesh in Samaria, y 2Ki 12:20
assassinated[y] him and succeeded him as
king.
15 The other events of Shallum's reign,
and the conspiracy he led, are written in
the book of the annals[z] of the kings of 15:15 z 1Ki 15:31
Israel.
16 At that time Menahem, starting out
from Tirzah, attacked Tiphsah[a] and 15:16 a 1Ki 4:24
everyone in the city and its vicinity, be- b 2Ki 8:12;
cause they refused to open[b] their gates. Hos 13:16
He sacked Tiphsah and ripped open all
the pregnant women.

Menahem King of Israel

17 In the thirty-ninth year of Azariah
king of Judah, Menahem son of Gadi became king of Israel, and he reigned in
Samaria ten years. 18 He did evil in the
eyes of the LORD. During his entire reign
he did not turn away from the sins of
Jeroboam son of Nebat, which he had
caused Israel to commit.
19 Then Pul[f][c] king of Assyria invaded 15:19
the land, and Menahem gave him a c 1Ch 5:6,26
thousand talents[g] of silver to gain his
support and strengthen his own hold on
the kingdom. 20 Menahem exacted this
money from Israel. Every wealthy man
had to contribute fifty shekels[h] of silver
to be given to the king of Assyria. So the
king of Assyria withdrew[d] and stayed in 15:20 d 2Ki 12:18
the land no longer.
21 As for the other events of Menahem's reign, and all he did, are they not
written in the book of the annals of the
kings of Israel? 22 Menahem rested with
his fathers. And Pekahiah his son succeeded him as king.

[a] *28* Or *Judah* [b] *5* The Hebrew word was used for various diseases affecting the skin—not necessarily leprosy. [c] *5* Or *in a house where he was relieved of responsibility* [d] *10* Hebrew; some Septuagint manuscripts *in Ibleam* [e] *12* 2 Kings 10:30 [f] *19* Also called *Tiglath-Pileser* [g] *19* That is, about 37 tons (about 34 metric tons) [h] *20* That is, about 1 1/4 pounds (about 0.6 kilogram)

Pekahiah King of Israel

23 In the fiftieth year of Azariah king of
Judah, Pekahiah son of Menahem became king of Israel in Samaria, and he
reigned two years. 24 Pekahiah did evil in
the eyes of the LORD. He did not turn
away from the sins of Jeroboam son of
Nebat, which he had caused Israel to
15:25 commit. 25 One of his chief officers, Pe-
[e] 2Ch 28:6; kah[e] son of Remaliah, conspired against
Isa 7:1 him. Taking fifty men of Gilead with
[f] 2Ki 12:20 him, he assassinated[f] Pekahiah, along
with Argob and Arieh, in the citadel of
the royal palace at Samaria. So Pekah
killed Pekahiah and succeeded him as
king.
26 The other events of Pekahiah's reign,
and all he did, are written in the book of
the annals of the kings of Israel.

Pekah King of Israel

15:27 [g] 2Ch 28:6; 27 In the fifty-second year of Azariah
Isa 7:1 [h] Isa 7:4 king of Judah, Pekah[g] son of Remaliah[h]
became king of Israel in Samaria, and he
reigned twenty years. 28 He did evil in the
eyes of the LORD. He did not turn away
15:29 from the sins of Jeroboam son of Nebat,
[i] 2Ki 16:7; 17:6; which he had caused Israel to commit.
1Ch 5:26; 2Ch 28:20; 29 In the time of Pekah king of Israel,
Jer 50:17 Tiglath-Pileser[i] king of Assyria came
[j] 1Ki 15:20 [k] 2Ki 16:9; and took Ijon,[j] Abel Beth Maacah, Jano-
17:24; 2Ch 16:4; ah, Kedesh and Hazor. He took Gilead
Isa 9:1 [l] 2Ki 24:14-16; and Galilee, including all the land of
1Ch 5:22; Naphtali,[k] and deported[l] the people to
Isa 14:6,17; Assyria. 30 Then Hoshea[m] son of Elah
36:17; 45:13 conspired against Pekah son of Remali-
15:30 [m] 2Ki 17:1 ah. He attacked and assassinated[n] him,
[n] 2Ki 12:20 and then succeeded him as king in the
twentieth year of Jotham son of Uzziah.
31 As for the other events of Pekah's
reign, and all he did, are they not written
in the book of the annals of the kings of
Israel?

Jotham King of Judah

15:32 32 In the second year of Pekah son of
[o] 1Ch 5:17 Remaliah king of Israel, Jotham[o] son of
Uzziah king of Judah began to reign.
33 He was twenty-five years old when he
became king, and he reigned in Jerusalem sixteen years. His mother's name
15:34 was Jerusha daughter of Zadok. 34 He did
[p] ver 3; 1Ki 14:8; what was right[p] in the eyes of the LORD,
2Ch 26:4-5 just as his father Uzziah had done. 35 The
15:35 high places,[q] however, were not re-
[q] 2Ki 12:3 moved; the people continued to offer
sacrifices and burn incense there. Jo-
tham rebuilt the Upper Gate[r] of the 15:35 [r] 2Ch 23:20
temple of the LORD.
36 As for the other events of Jotham's
reign, and what he did, are they not written in the book of the annals of the kings
of Judah? 37 (In those days the LORD be- 15:37
gan to send Rezin[s] king of Aram and Pe- [s] 2Ki 16:5;
kah son of Remaliah against Judah.) Isa 7:1
38 Jotham rested with his fathers and was
buried with them in the City of David,
the city of his father. And Ahaz his son
succeeded him as king.

Ahaz King of Judah

16 In the seventeenth year of Pe- 16:1
kah son of Remaliah, Ahaz[t] son [t] Isa 1:1; 14:28
of Jotham king of Judah began to reign.
2 Ahaz was twenty years old when he became king, and he reigned in Jerusalem
sixteen years. Unlike David his father, he 16:2
did not do what was right[u] in the eyes of [u] 1Ki 14:8
the LORD his God. 3 He walked in the
ways of the kings of Israel and even sac- 16:3
rificed his son[v] in[a] the fire, following the [v] Lev 18:21;
detestable[w] ways of the nations the 2Ki 21:6 [w] Lev 18:3;
LORD had driven out before the Israel- Dt 9:4; 12:31
ites. 4 He offered sacrifices and burned
incense at the high places, on the hill- 16:4
tops and under every spreading tree.[x] [x] Dt 12:2; Eze 6:13
5 Then Rezin[y] king of Aram and Pekah
son of Remaliah king of Israel marched 16:5 [y] 2Ki 15:37;
up to fight against Jerusalem and be- Isa 7:1,4
sieged Ahaz, but they could not over- 16:6
power him. 6 At that time, Rezin[z] king of [z] Isa 9:12
Aram recovered Elath[a] for Aram by driv- [a] 2Ki 14:22;
ing out the men of Judah. Edomites then 2Ch 26:2
moved into Elath and have lived there to
this day.
7 Ahaz sent messengers to say to Tig- 16:7 [b] 2Ki 15:29
lath-Pileser[b] king of Assyria, "I am your [c] Isa 2:6;
servant and vassal. Come up and save[c] Jer 2:18; Eze 16:28;
me out of the hand of the king of Aram Hos 10:6
and of the king of Israel, who are attacking me." 8 And Ahaz took the silver and
gold found in the temple of the LORD
and in the treasuries of the royal palace 16:8
and sent it as a gift[d] to the king of As- [d] 2Ki 12:18
syria. 9 The king of Assyria complied by 16:9
attacking Damascus[e] and capturing it. [e] 2Ki 15:29 [f] Isa 22:6;
He deported its inhabitants to Kir[f] and Am 1:5; 9:7
put Rezin to death.
10 Then King Ahaz went to Damascus
to meet Tiglath-Pileser king of Assyria.
He saw an altar in Damascus and sent to
Uriah[g] the priest a sketch of the altar, 16:10
with detailed plans for its construction. [g] Isa 8:2

[a] 3 Or *even made his son pass through*

11 So Uriah the priest built an altar in accordance with all the plans that King Ahaz had sent from Damascus and finished it before King Ahaz returned. 12 When the king came back from Damascus and saw the altar, he approached it and presented offerings[a][h] on it. 13 He offered up his burnt offering[i] and grain offering, poured out his drink offering, and sprinkled the blood of his fellowship offerings[b][j] on the altar. 14 The bronze altar[k] that stood before the LORD he brought from the front of the temple—from between the new altar and the temple of the LORD—and put it on the north side of the new altar.

15 King Ahaz then gave these orders to Uriah the priest: "On the large new altar, offer the morning[l] burnt offering and the evening grain offering, the king's burnt offering and his grain offering, and the burnt offering of all the people of the land, and their grain offering and their drink offering. Sprinkle on the altar all the blood of the burnt offerings and sacrifices. But I will use the bronze altar for seeking guidance."[m] 16 And Uriah the priest did just as King Ahaz had ordered.

17 King Ahaz took away the side panels and removed the basins from the movable stands. He removed the Sea from the bronze bulls that supported it and set it on a stone base.[n] 18 He took away the Sabbath canopy[c] that had been built at the temple and removed the royal entryway outside the temple of the LORD, in deference to the king of Assyria.[o]

19 As for the other events of the reign of Ahaz, and what he did, are they not written in the book of the annals of the kings of Judah? 20 Ahaz rested with his fathers and was buried with them in the City of David. And Hezekiah his son succeeded him as king.

Hoshea Last King of Israel

17 In the twelfth year of Ahaz king of Judah, Hoshea[p] son of Elah became king of Israel in Samaria, and he reigned nine years. 2 He did evil in the eyes of the LORD, but not like the kings of Israel who preceded him.

3 Shalmaneser[q] king of Assyria came up to attack Hoshea, who had been Shalmaneser's vassal and had paid him tribute. 4 But the king of Assyria discovered that Hoshea was a traitor, for he had sent envoys to So[d] king of Egypt, and he no longer paid tribute to the king of Assyria, as he had done year by year. Therefore Shalmaneser seized him and put him in prison. 5 The king of Assyria invaded the entire land, marched against Samaria and laid siege[r] to it for three years. 6 In the ninth year of Hoshea, the king of Assyria captured Samaria[s] and deported[t] the Israelites to Assyria. He settled them in Halah, in Gozan[u] on the Habor River and in the towns of the Medes.

16:12 h 2Ch 26:16
16:13 i Lev 6:8-13; j Lev 7:11-21
16:14 k 2Ch 4:1
16:15 l Ex 29:38-41; m 1Sa 9:9
16:17 n 1Ki 7:27
16:18 o Eze 16:28
17:1 p 2Ki 15:30
17:3 q 2Ki 18:9-12; Hos 10:14

Israel Exiled Because of Sin

7 All this took place because the Israelites had sinned[v] against the LORD their God, who had brought them up out of Egypt[w] from under the power of Pharaoh king of Egypt. They worshiped other gods 8 and followed the practices of the nations[x] the LORD had driven out before them, as well as the practices that the kings of Israel had introduced. 9 The Israelites secretly did things against the LORD their God that were not right. From watchtower to fortified city[y] they built themselves high places in all their towns. 10 They set up sacred stones and Asherah poles[z] on every high hill and under every spreading tree.[a] 11 At every high place they burned incense, as the nations whom the LORD had driven out before them had done. They did wicked things that provoked the LORD to anger. 12 They worshiped idols,[b] though the LORD had said, "You shall not do this."[e] 13 The LORD warned Israel and Judah through all his prophets and seers:[c] "Turn from your evil ways.[d] Observe my commands and decrees, in accordance with the entire Law that I commanded your fathers to obey and that I delivered to you through my servants the prophets."

14 But they would not listen and were as stiff-necked[e] as their fathers, who did not trust in the LORD their God. 15 They rejected his decrees and the covenant[f] he had made with their fathers and the warnings he had given them. They followed worthless idols[g] and themselves became worthless. They imitated the nations[h] around them although the LORD had ordered them, "Do not do as

17:5 r Hos 13:16
17:6 s Hos 13:16; t Dt 28:36,64; 2Ki 18:10-11; u 1Ch 5:26
17:7 v Jos 23:16; Jdg 6:10; w Ex 14:15-31
17:8 x Lev 18:3; Dt 18:9; 2Ki 16:3
17:9 y 2Ki 18:8
17:10 z Ex 34:13; Mic 5:14; a 1Ki 14:23
17:12 b Ex 20:4
17:13 c 1Sa 9:9; d Jer 18:11; 25:5; 35:15
17:14 e Ex 32:9; Dt 31:27; Ac 7:51
17:15 f Dt 29:25; g Dt 32:21; Ro 1:21-23; h Dt 12:30-31

a 12 Or *and went up* b 13 Traditionally *peace offerings* c 18 Or *the dais of his throne* (see Septuagint) d 4 Or *to Sais, to the; So* is possibly an abbreviation for *Osorkon.* e 12 Exodus 20:4,5

they do," and they did the things the
LORD had forbidden them to do.
16They forsook all the commands of
17:16 the LORD their God and made for them-
i 1Ki 12:28 selves two idols cast in the shape of
j 1Ki 14:15,23 calves,[i] and an Asherah[j] pole. They
k 2Ki 21:3 bowed down to all the starry hosts,[k] and
l 1Ki 16:31 17:17 they worshiped Baal.[l] 17They sacrificed[m]
m Dt 18:10-12; their sons and daughters in[a] the fire.
2Ki 16:3 They practiced divination and sorcery[n]
n Lev 19:26 o 1Ki 21:20 and sold[o] themselves to do evil in the
eyes of the LORD, provoking him to anger.
18So the LORD was very angry with Israel and removed them from his presence. Only the tribe of Judah was left,
19and even Judah did not keep the commands of the LORD their God. They fol-
17:19 lowed the practices Israel had intro-
p 1Ki 14:22-23; 2Ki 16:3 duced.[p] 20Therefore the LORD rejected all
the people of Israel; he afflicted them
17:20 and gave them into the hands of plun-
q 2Ki 15:29 derers,[q] until he thrust them from his
presence.
17:21 21When he tore[r] Israel away from the
r 1Ki 11:11 s 1Ki 12:20 house of David, they made Jeroboam
son of Nebat their king.[s] Jeroboam en-
ticed Israel away from following the
LORD and caused them to commit a
great sin. 22The Israelites persisted in all
the sins of Jeroboam and did not turn
away from them 23until the LORD removed them from his presence, as he
had warned through all his servants the
prophets. So the people of Israel were
taken from their homeland into exile in
Assyria, and they are still there.

Samaria Resettled

17:24 24The king of Assyria[t] brought people
t Ezr 4:2,10 u 2Ki 18:34 from Babylon, Cuthah, Avva, Hamath
and Sepharvaim[u] and settled them in
the towns of Samaria to replace the Israelites. They took over Samaria and
lived in its towns. 25When they first lived
there, they did not worship the LORD; so
17:25 he sent lions[v] among them and they
v Ge 37:20 killed some of the people. 26It was reported to the king of Assyria: "The people you deported and resettled in the
towns of Samaria do not know what the
god of that country requires. He has sent
lions among them, which are killing
them off, because the people do not
know what he requires."
27Then the king of Assyria gave this
order: "Have one of the priests you took
captive from Samaria go back to live
there and teach the people what the god
of the land requires." 28So one of the
priests who had been exiled from
Samaria came to live in Bethel and
taught them how to worship the LORD.
29Nevertheless, each national group 17:29
made its own gods in the several towns[w] w Jer 2:28
where they settled, and set them up in x 1Ki 12:31
the shrines[x] the people of Samaria had y Mic 4:5
made at the high places.[y] 30The men
from Babylon made Succoth Benoth, the
men from Cuthah made Nergal, and the
men from Hamath made Ashima; 31the
Avvites made Nibhaz and Tartak, and
the Sepharvites burned their children in
the fire as sacrifices to Adrammelech[z] 17:31 z 2Ki 19:37
and Anammelech, the gods of Sephar- a ver 24
vaim.[a] 32They worshiped the LORD, but 17:32
they also appointed all sorts[b] of their b 1Ki 12:31
own people to officiate for them as
priests in the shrines at the high places.
33They worshiped the LORD, but they also
served their own gods in accordance
with the customs of the nations from
which they had been brought.
34To this day they persist in their former practices. They neither worship the
LORD nor adhere to the decrees and ordinances, the laws and commands that the
LORD gave the descendants of Jacob, 17:34
whom he named Israel.[c] 35When the c Ge 32:28; 35:10; 1Ki 18:31
LORD made a covenant with the Israel-
ites, he commanded them: "Do not wor- 17:35
ship[d] any other gods or bow down to d Ex 20:5;
them, serve them or sacrifice to them. Jdg 6:10
36But the LORD, who brought you up out
of Egypt with mighty power and out- 17:36
stretched arm,[e] is the one you must wor- e Ex 3:20; 6:6; Ps 136:12
ship. To him you shall bow down and to
him offer sacrifices. 37You must always 17:37
be careful[f] to keep the decrees and ordi- f Dt 5:32
nances, the laws and commands he
wrote for you. Do not worship other
gods. 38Do not forget[g] the covenant I 17:38 g Dt 4:23; 6:12
have made with you, and do not worship
other gods. 39Rather, worship the LORD
your God; it is he who will deliver you
from the hand of all your enemies."
40They would not listen, however, but
persisted in their former practices.
41Even while these people were worship- 17:41
ing the LORD,[h] they were serving their h ver 32-33;
idols. To this day their children and 1Ki 18:21;
grandchildren continue to do as their fa- Mt 6:24
thers did.

[a] 17 Or *They made their sons and daughters pass through*

DISCOVERY 92

THE SLIPPERY SLOPE OF REJECTING GOD

When the children of Israel were wandering in the desert, God confirmed his covenant with them. He promised them blessings if they would obey his laws but curses if they chose to disregard them. In fact, God's dire predictions were specific: "The LORD will bring a nation against you from far away . . . a fierce-looking nation without respect for the old or pity for the young. They will devour . . . your land until you are destroyed" (Deuteronomy 28:49–51).

This prophecy was fulfilled through the king of Assyria. He captured Samaria, Israel's capital city, and deported the Israelites to his own country (2 Kings 17:6). God allowed this staggering defeat because Israel had turned away from him in a variety of ways (verses 7–12). For one thing, the people refused to acknowledge how God had delivered them in the past: how he had miraculously rescued them from slavery in Egypt and led them to the land of promise, how he had on a daily basis provided for them and cared for them. Instead the Israelites offered their allegiance to other "gods." They sinned in exactly the same manner as their forefathers during the days of the judges (Judges 2:10).

Second, the Israelites overtly disregarded God's clear commandments. God had never been ambiguous about what he expected, but his chosen people opted for deliberate disobedience (2 Kings 17:16).

Finally, they sinned by ignoring God's warnings given through the prophets. God would have been perfectly justified had he judged the Israelites immediately after they had become enmeshed in idolatry. But he is patient, and he sent one prophet after another to warn them.

Rather than listening, however, the Israelites "were as stiff-necked as their fathers, who did not trust the LORD (verses 13–14).

Each of us should take some time to compare our own lives with those of the Israelites. We should recall daily that Jesus died for our sins and delivered us from the trappings of sin. We must pay very close attention to what God asks of us in the Bible, putting his words into practice rather than simply mouthing them. And we should listen to the messengers God sends to proclaim them. If we choose to reject those words, we will inevitably suffer the consequences.

The apostle Paul, referring to his Israelite forefathers and the consequences which they had faced on account of their disobedience, had this to say: "These things happened to them as examples and were written down as warnings for us, on whom the fulfillment of the ages has come. So, if you think you are standing firm, be careful that you don't fall. No temptation has seized you except what is common to man. And God is faithful; he will not let you be tempted beyond what you can bear. But when you are tempted, he will also provide a way out so that you can stand up under it" (1 Corinthians 10:11–13).

Self-Discovery: *Why do you think it is so easy to forget or ignore the daily blessings that you receive from God? Take a moment and list some of the blessings you have enjoyed so far today, and then stop to thank God for them.*

GO TO DISCOVERY 93 ON PAGE 487

Hezekiah King of Judah

18:1 [i] Isa 1:1; 2Ch 28:27 — 18 In the third year of Hoshea son
of Elah king of Israel, Hezekiah[i]
son of Ahaz king of Judah began to
reign. 2He was twenty-five years old
18:2 [j] Isa 38:5 — when he became king, and he reigned in
Jerusalem twenty-nine years.[j] His moth-
er's name was Abijah[a] daughter of
Zechariah. 3He did what was right in the
18:3 [k] Isa 38:5 — eyes of the LORD, just as his father David[k] had done. 4He removed[l] the high
18:4 [l] 2Ch 31:1 [m] Ex 23:24 [n] Nu 21:9 — places, smashed the sacred stones[m] and
cut down the Asherah poles. He broke
into pieces the bronze snake[n] Moses
had made, for up to that time the Israelites had been burning incense to it. (It
was called[b] Nehushtan.[c])
18:5 [o] 2Ki 19:10; 23:25 — 5Hezekiah trusted[o] in the LORD, the
God of Israel. There was no one like him
among all the kings of Judah, either be-
18:6 [p] Dt 10:20; Jos 23:8; Dt — fore him or after him. 6He held fast[p] to
the LORD and did not cease to follow
him; he kept the commands the LORD
had given Moses. 7And the LORD was
18:7 [q] Ge 39:3; 1Sa 18:14 [r] 2Ki 16:7 — with him; he was successful[q] in whatever he undertook. He rebelled[r] against
the king of Assyria and did not serve
18:8 [s] 2Ki 17:9; Isa 14:29 — him. 8From watchtower to fortified city,[s]
he defeated the Philistines, as far as
Gaza and its territory.
18:9 [t] Isa 1:1 — 9In King Hezekiah's fourth year,[t]
which was the seventh year of Hoshea
son of Elah king of Israel, Shalmaneser
king of Assyria marched against Samaria
and laid siege to it. 10At the end of three
years the Assyrians took it. So Samaria
was captured in Hezekiah's sixth year,
which was the ninth year of Hoshea king
18:11 [u] Isa 37:12 — of Israel. 11The king[u] of Assyria deported
Israel to Assyria and settled them in Ha-
lah, in Gozan on the Habor River and in
towns of the Medes. 12This happened because they had not obeyed the LORD their
18:12 [v] 2Ki 17:15 [w] Da 9:6,10 [x] 1Ki 9:6 — God, but had violated his covenant[v]—all
that Moses the servant of the LORD com-
manded.[w] They neither listened to the
commands[x] nor carried them out.
13In the fourteenth year of King Hez-
18:13 [y] 2Ch 32:1; Isa 1:7; Mic 1:9 — ekiah's reign, Sennacherib king of Assyria attacked all the fortified cities of Ju-
dah[y] and captured them. 14So Hezekiah
king of Judah sent this message to the
king of Assyria at Lachish: "I have done
18:14 [z] Isa 24:5 — wrong.[z] Withdraw from me, and I will
pay whatever you demand of me." The
king of Assyria exacted from Hezekiah
king of Judah three hundred talents[d] of
silver and thirty talents[e] of gold. 15So — 18:15 [a] 1Ki 15:18; 2Ki 16:8
Hezekiah gave[a] him all the silver that
was found in the temple of the LORD and
in the treasuries of the royal palace.
16At this time Hezekiah king of Judah
stripped off the gold with which he had
covered the doors and doorposts of the
temple of the LORD, and gave it to the
king of Assyria.

Sennacherib Threatens Jerusalem

17The king of Assyria sent his supreme
commander,[b] his chief officer and his — 18:17 [b] Isa 20:1 [c] 2Ki 20:20; 2Ch 32:4,30; Isa 7:3
field commander with a large army, from
Lachish to King Hezekiah at Jerusalem.
They came up to Jerusalem and stopped
at the aqueduct of the Upper Pool,[c] on
the road to the Washerman's Field.
18They called for the king; and Eliakim[d] — 18:18 [d] 2Ki 19:2; Isa 22:20 [e] Isa 22:15
son of Hilkiah the palace administrator,
Shebna[e] the secretary, and Joah son of
Asaph the recorder went out to them.
19The field commander said to them,
"Tell Hezekiah:

" 'This is what the great king, the
king of Assyria, says: On what are
you basing this confidence of yours?
20You say you have strategy and military strength—but you speak only
empty words. On whom are you depending, that you rebel against me?
21Look now, you are depending on
Egypt,[f] that splintered reed of a — 18:21 [f] Isa 20:5; Eze 29:6 [g] Isa 30:5,7
staff,[g] which pierces a man's hand
and wounds him if he leans on it!
Such is Pharaoh king of Egypt to all
who depend on him. 22And if you
say to me, "We are depending on the
LORD our God"—isn't he the one
whose high places and altars Hezekiah removed, saying to Judah and
Jerusalem, "You must worship before this altar in Jerusalem"?
23" 'Come now, make a bargain
with my master, the king of Assyria: I will give you two thousand
horses—if you can put riders on
them! 24How can you repulse one
officer[h] of the least of my master's — 18:24 [h] Isa 10:8
officials, even though you are de-
pending on Egypt for chariots and
horsemen[f]? 25Furthermore, have I

[a] *2* Hebrew *Abi*, a variant of *Abijah* [b] *4* Or *He called it* [c] *4* *Nehushtan* sounds like the Hebrew for *bronze* and *snake* and *unclean thing*.
[d] *14* That is, about 11 tons (about 10 metric tons)
[e] *14* That is, about 1 ton (about 1 metric ton)
[f] *24* Or *charioteers*

DISCOVERY 93

DON'T FORGET THE SOURCE

Remember the bronze snake? The Israelites had complained about the water and food, and God in direct response had sent poisonous snakes that bit many of them. But God had provided an antidote to the venom: Anyone willing to look up at the bronze snake that Moses had lifted up on a pole would be allowed to recover. Astonishingly, many people refused to glance upward and died from the snakebites. This experience was a painful lesson in faith for the Israelites (Numbers 21:4–9).

Centuries later Hezekiah became Judah's king. Hezekiah is remembered as a godly king who brought revival to the land (2 Kings 18:4,6). One of his first actions was to destroy all the pagan worship centers and idols—including the bronze snake. God's people had rejected God and had begun to worship the very snake he had graciously provided for their deliverance.

The Israelites had made two basic mistakes. First, they had attempted to merge worship of the one true God with the standard religious practices of their day. Worship of snakes was common among the surrounding peoples, and the Israelites adopted their own snake as an accommodation to this practice. Their second mistake was to worship God's gift rather than God himself. While the bronze snake was only a symbol, a means for blessing and power, God himself is the source of all goodness.

It's easy for any of us to fall into the same trap. We adapt our faith to the ungodly practices of the world around us. When we begin to assimilate some of the patterns of this world, we've taken a dangerous step in the wrong direction: "I urge you, brothers, in view of God's mercy, to offer your bodies as living sacrifices, holy and pleasing to God—this is your spiritual act of worship. Do not conform any longer to the pattern of this world, but be transformed by the renewing of your mind. Then you will be able to test and approve what God's will is—his good, pleasing and perfect will" (Romans 12:1–2). God wants his people to be "a holy nation . . . aliens and strangers in the world" (1 Peter 2:9–12).

Rather than focusing on what God has given us or on the means by which he has chosen to heal us, we must fix our gaze on God himself. Jesus warns us about the danger of worshiping God for *what he does* rather than for *who he is*, about forgetting the true Source of joy and peace. Jesus well understood the inclinations of human hearts: "You are looking for me . . . because you ate the loaves and had your fill" (John 6:26). When we try to get close to Jesus in order to have our selfish needs satisfied, we are getting to know him for the wrong reasons. He deserves our honor and total devotion solely because he is the Son of God.

Self-Discovery: *Are you ever tempted to merge worship of God with the accepted cultural practices of today? Can you identify a time when you may have forgotten who is your true source of joy and peace?*

GO TO DISCOVERY 94 ON PAGE 492

come to attack and destroy this
place without word from the
18:25 LORD?[i] The LORD himself told me to
i 2Ki 19:6,22 march against this country and destroy it.' "
26Then Eliakim son of Hilkiah, and
Shebna and Joah said to the field commander, "Please speak to your servants
18:26 in Aramaic,[j] since we understand it.
j Ezr 4:7 Don't speak to us in Hebrew in the hearing of the people on the wall."
27But the commander replied, "Was it
only to your master and you that my
master sent me to say these things, and
not to the men sitting on the wall—who,
like you, will have to eat their own filth
and drink their own urine?"
28Then the commander stood and
called out in Hebrew: "Hear the word of
the great king, the king of Assyria! 29This
is what the king says: Do not let Hezeki-
18:29 ah deceive[k] you. He cannot deliver you
k 2Ki 19:10 from my hand. 30Do not let Hezekiah
persuade you to trust in the LORD when
he says, 'The LORD will surely deliver us;
this city will not be given into the hand
of the king of Assyria.'
31"Do not listen to Hezekiah. This is
what the king of Assyria says: Make
18:31 peace with me and come out to me.
l Nu 13:23; Then every one of you will eat from his
1Ki 4:25 own vine and fig tree[l] and drink water
m Jer 14:3; from his own cistern,[m] 32until I come
La 4:4 and take you to a land like your own, a
land of grain and new wine, a land of
18:32 bread and vineyards, a land of olive trees
n Dt 8:7-9; 30:19 and honey. Choose life[n] and not death!
"Do not listen to Hezekiah, for he is
misleading you when he says, 'The LORD
18:33 o 2Ki 19:12; will deliver us.' 33Has the god[o] of any na-
Isa 10:10-11 tion ever delivered his land from the
hand of the king of Assyria? 34Where are
18:34 the gods of Hamath[p] and Arpad?[q]
p 2Ki 17:24; 19:13 q Isa 10:9 Where are the gods of Sepharvaim,
Hena and Ivvah? Have they rescued
Samaria from my hand? 35Who of all the
gods of these countries has been able to
save his land from me? How then can
18:35 the LORD deliver Jerusalem from my
r Ps 2:1-2 hand?"[r]
36But the people remained silent and
said nothing in reply, because the king
had commanded, "Do not answer him."
37Then Eliakim son of Hilkiah the
palace administrator, Shebna the secretary and Joah son of Asaph the recorder
went to Hezekiah, with their clothes
torn,[s] and told him what the field com- 18:37 s 2Ki 6:30
mander had said.

Jerusalem's Deliverance Foretold

19 When King Hezekiah heard 19:1 t Ge 37:34;
this, he tore[t] his clothes and 1Ki 21:27;
put on sackcloth and went into the tem- 2Ch 32:20-22
ple of the LORD. 2He sent Eliakim the
palace administrator, Shebna the secretary and the leading priests, all wearing 19:2
sackcloth, to the prophet Isaiah[u] son of u Isa 1:1
Amoz. 3They told him, "This is what
Hezekiah says: This day is a day of distress and rebuke and disgrace, as when
children come to the point of birth and
there is no strength to deliver them. 4It
may be that the LORD your God will hear
all the words of the field commander,
whom his master, the king of Assyria, 19:4
has sent to ridicule[v] the living God, and v 2Ki 18:35
that he will rebuke[w] him for the words w 2Sa 16:12
the LORD your God has heard. Therefore
pray for the remnant that still survives."
5When King Hezekiah's officials came
to Isaiah, 6Isaiah said to them, "Tell your
master, 'This is what the LORD says: Do
not be afraid of what you have heard—
those words with which the underlings 19:6
of the king of Assyria have blasphemed[x] x 2Ki 18:25
me. 7Listen! I am going to put such a
spirit in him that when he hears a certain report, he will return to his own
country, and there I will have him cut 19:7
down with the sword.[y]' " y ver 37
8When the field commander heard
that the king of Assyria had left La- 19:8
chish,[z] he withdrew and found the king z 2Ki 18:14
fighting against Libnah.
9Now Sennacherib received a report
that Tirhakah, the Cushite[a] king ⌞of
Egypt⌟, was marching out to fight
against him. So he again sent messengers to Hezekiah with this word: 10"Say
to Hezekiah king of Judah: Do not let the 19:10
god you depend[a] on deceive[b] you when a 2Ki 18:5
he says, 'Jerusalem will not be handed b 2Ki 18:29
over to the king of Assyria.' 11Surely you
have heard what the kings of Assyria
have done to all the countries, destroying them completely. And will you be
delivered? 12Did the gods of the nations
that were destroyed by my forefathers 19:12
deliver[c] them: the gods of Gozan,[d] Ha- c 2Ki 18:33
ran,[e] Rezeph and the people of Eden d 2Ki 17:6 e Ge 11:31
who were in Tel Assar? 13Where is the
king of Hamath, the king of Arpad, the

[a] 9 That is, from the upper Nile region

king of the city of Sepharvaim, or of
Hena or Ivvah?"[f]

Hezekiah's Prayer

14 Hezekiah received the letter from
the messengers and read it. Then he
went up to the temple of the LORD and
spread it out before the LORD. 15 And Hezekiah prayed to the LORD: "O LORD, God
of Israel, enthroned between the cherubim,[g] you alone are God over all the
kingdoms of the earth. You have made
heaven and earth. 16 Give ear,[h] O LORD,
and hear;[i] open your eyes,[j] O LORD, and
see; listen to the words Sennacherib has
sent to insult the living God.

17 "It is true, O LORD, that the Assyrian
kings have laid waste these nations and
their lands. 18 They have thrown their
gods into the fire and destroyed them,
for they were not gods[k] but only wood
and stone, fashioned by men's hands.[l]
19 Now, O LORD our God, deliver us from
his hand, so that all kingdoms[m] on earth
may know[n] that you alone, O LORD, are
God."

Isaiah Prophesies Sennacherib's Fall

20 Then Isaiah son of Amoz sent a message to Hezekiah: "This is what the LORD,
the God of Israel, says: I have heard[o] your
prayer concerning Sennacherib king of
Assyria. 21 This is the word that the LORD
has spoken against him:

" 'The Virgin Daughter[p] of Zion
despises you and mocks[q] you.
The Daughter of Jerusalem
tosses her head[r] as you flee.
22 Who is it you have insulted and
blasphemed?
Against whom have you raised
your voice
and lifted your eyes in pride?
Against the Holy One[s] of Israel!
23 By your messengers
you have heaped insults on the
Lord.
And you have said,[t]
"With my many chariots[u]
I have ascended the heights of the
mountains,
the utmost heights of Lebanon.
I have cut down its tallest cedars,
the choicest of its pines.
I have reached its remotest parts,
the finest of its forests.
24 I have dug wells in foreign lands
and drunk the water there.
With the soles of my feet
I have dried up all the streams of
Egypt."
25 " 'Have you not heard?[v]
Long ago I ordained it.
In days of old I planned[w] it;
now I have brought it to pass,
that you have turned fortified cities
into piles of stone.[x]
26 Their people, drained of power,
are dismayed[y] and put to shame.
They are like plants in the field,
like tender green shoots,[z]
like grass sprouting on the roof,
scorched[a] before it grows up.
27 " 'But I know[b] where you stay
and when you come and go
and how you rage against me.
28 Because you rage against me
and your insolence has reached
my ears,
I will put my hook[c] in your nose
and my bit[d] in your mouth,
and I will make you return[e]
by the way you came.'

29 "This will be the sign[f] for you,
O Hezekiah:

"This year you will eat what grows
by itself,[g]
and the second year what
springs from that.
But in the third year sow and reap,
plant vineyards[h] and eat their
fruit.
30 Once more a remnant of the house
of Judah
will take root[i] below and bear
fruit above.
31 For out of Jerusalem will come a
remnant,
and out of Mount Zion a band of
survivors.
The zeal[j] of the LORD Almighty will accomplish this.

32 "Therefore this is what the LORD
says concerning the king of Assyria:

"He will not enter this city
or shoot an arrow here.
He will not come before it with
shield
or build a siege ramp against it.
33 By the way that he came he will
return;[k]

19:13 f 2Ki 18:34
19:15 g Ex 25:22
19:16 h Ps 31:2 i 1Ki 8:29 j ver 4; 2Ch 6:40
19:18 k Isa 44:9-11; Jer 10:3-10 l Ps 115:4; Ac 17:29
19:19 m 1Ki 8:43 n Ps 83:18
19:20 o 2Ki 20:5
19:21 p Jer 14:17; La 2:13 q Ps 22:7-8 r Job 16:4; Ps 109:25
19:22 s Ps 71:22; Isa 5:24
19:23 t Isa 10:18 u Ps 20:7
19:25 v Isa 40:21,28 w Isa 10:5; 45:7 x Mic 1:6
19:26 y Ps 6:10 z Isa 4:2 a Ps 129:6
19:27 b Ps 139:1-4
19:28 c Eze 19:9; 29:4 d Isa 30:28 e ver 33
19:29 f 2Ki 20:8-9; Lk 2:12 g Lev 25:5 h Ps 107:37
19:30 i 2Ch 32:22-23
19:31 j Isa 9:7
19:33 k ver 28

he will not enter this city,
declares the LORD.
19:34 34 I will defend[l] this city and save it,
l 2Ki 20:6 for my sake and for the sake of
m 1Ki 11:12-13 David[m] my servant."
19:35 35 That night the angel of the LORD[n]
n Ex 12:23 went out and put to death a hundred
o Job 24:24 and eighty-five thousand men in the Assyrian camp. When the people got up
the next morning—there were all the
dead bodies![o] 36 So Sennacherib king of
19:36 Assyria broke camp and withdrew. He
p Ge 10:11; Jnh 1:2 returned to Nineveh[p] and stayed there.
37 One day, while he was worshiping in
the temple of his god Nisroch, his sons
19:37 Adrammelech and Sharezer cut him
q ver 7 r Ge 8:4 down with the sword,[q] and they escaped
s Ezr 4:2 to the land of Ararat.[r] And Esarhaddon[s]
his son succeeded him as king.

Hezekiah's Illness

20 In those days Hezekiah became
ill and was at the point of
death. The prophet Isaiah son of Amoz
went to him and said, "This is what the
LORD says: Put your house in order, because you are going to die; you will not
recover."
20:3 2 Hezekiah turned his face to the wall
t Ne 13:22 and prayed to the LORD, 3 "Remember,[t]
u 2Ki 18:3-6 O LORD, how I have walked before you
faithfully[u] and with wholehearted devotion and have done what is good in your
eyes." And Hezekiah wept bitterly.
4 Before Isaiah had left the middle
court, the word of the LORD came to
him: 5 "Go back and tell Hezekiah, the
leader of my people, 'This is what the
20:5 LORD, the God of your father David, says:
v 1Sa 9:16; 1Ki 9:3; I have heard[v] your prayer and seen your
2Ki 19:20 tears;[w] I will heal you. On the third day
w Ps 39:12; 56:8 from now you will go up to the temple of
the LORD. 6 I will add fifteen years to your
life. And I will deliver you and this city
from the hand of the king of Assyria. I
20:6 x 2Ki 19:34 will defend[x] this city for my sake and for
the sake of my servant David.'"
7 Then Isaiah said, "Prepare a poultice
of figs." They did so and applied it to the
20:7 y Isa 38:21 boil,[y] and he recovered.
8 Hezekiah had asked Isaiah, "What
will be the sign that the LORD will heal
me and that I will go up to the temple of
the LORD on the third day from now?"
9 Isaiah answered, "This is the LORD's
20:9 sign[z] to you that the LORD will do what
z Dt 13:2; Jer 44:29 he has promised: Shall the shadow go
forward ten steps, or shall it go back ten
steps?"
10 "It is a simple matter for the shadow
to go forward ten steps," said Hezekiah.
"Rather, have it go back ten steps."
11 Then the prophet Isaiah called upon
the LORD, and the LORD made the shad- 20:11
ow go back[a] the ten steps it had gone a Jos 10:13
down on the stairway of Ahaz.

Envoys From Babylon

12 At that time Merodach-Baladan
son of Baladan king of Babylon sent
Hezekiah letters and a gift, because he
had heard of Hezekiah's illness. 13 Hezekiah received the messengers and
showed them all that was in his storehouses—the silver, the gold, the spices
and the fine oil—his armory and everything found among his treasures. There
was nothing in his palace or in all his
kingdom that Hezekiah did not show
them.
14 Then Isaiah the prophet went to
King Hezekiah and asked, "What did
those men say, and where did they come
from?"
"From a distant land," Hezekiah
replied. "They came from Babylon."
15 The prophet asked, "What did they
see in your palace?"
"They saw everything in my palace,"
Hezekiah said. "There is nothing among
my treasures that I did not show them."
16 Then Isaiah said to Hezekiah, "Hear
the word of the LORD: 17 The time will
surely come when everything in your
palace, and all that your fathers have 20:17
stored up until this day, will be carried b 2Ki 24:13;
off to Babylon.[b] Nothing will be left, says 25:13; 2Ch 36:10;
the LORD. 18 And some of your descen- Jer 27:22; 52:17-23
dants,[c] your own flesh and blood, that
will be born to you, will be taken away, 20:18
and they will become eunuchs in the c 2Ki 24:15; 2Ch 33:11;
palace of the king of Babylon." Da 1:3
19 "The word of the LORD you have
spoken is good," Hezekiah replied. For
he thought, "Will there not be peace and
security in my lifetime?"
20 As for the other events of Hezekiah's
reign, all his achievements and how he 20:20
made the pool[d] and the tunnel by which d Ne 3:16
he brought water into the city, are they
not written in the book of the annals of
the kings of Judah? 21 Hezekiah rested
with his fathers. And Manasseh his son
succeeded him as king.

Manasseh King of Judah

21 Manasseh was twelve years old
when he became king, and he
21:1 reigned in Jerusalem fifty-five years. His
e Isa 62:4 mother's name was Hephzibah.[e] 2He did
21:2 evil[f] in the eyes of the LORD, following
f Jer 15:4 g 2Ki 16:3 the detestable practices[g] of the nations
the LORD had driven out before the Isra-
21:3 h 2Ki 18:4 elites. 3He rebuilt the high places[h] his fa-
i Jdg 6:28; ther Hezekiah had destroyed; he also
1Ki 16:32 j Dt 17:3; erected altars to Baal[i] and made an
2Ki 17:16 Asherah pole, as Ahab king of Israel had
done. He bowed down to all the starry
21:4 hosts[j] and worshiped them. 4He built al-
k Jer 32:34 l 2Sa 7:13; tars[k] in the temple of the LORD, of which
1Ki 8:29 the LORD had said, "In Jerusalem I will
put my Name."[l] 5In both courts[m] of the
21:5 m 1Ki 7:12; temple of the LORD, he built altars to all
2Ki 23:12 the starry hosts. 6He sacrificed his own
21:6 son[n] in[a] the fire, practiced sorcery and
n Lev 18:21; Dt 18:10; divination, and consulted mediums and
2Ki 16:3; 17:17 spiritists.[o] He did much evil in the eyes
o Lev 19:31 of the LORD, provoking him to anger.
21:7 7He took the carved Asherah pole[p] he
p Dt 16:21; had made and put it in the temple, of
2Ki 23:4 q 2Sa 7:13; which the LORD had said to David and to
1Ki 8:29; 9:3; his son Solomon, "In this temple and in
2Ki 23:27; Jer 32:34 Jerusalem, which I have chosen out of all
the tribes of Israel, I will put my Name[q]
21:8 r 2Sa 7:10 forever. 8I will not again[r] make the feet
s 2Ki 18:12 of the Israelites wander from the land I
gave their forefathers, if only they will be
careful to do everything I commanded
them and will keep the whole Law that
my servant Moses[s] gave them." 9But the
21:9 people did not listen. Manasseh led
t Pr 29:12 them astray, so that they did more evil[t]
u Dt 9:4 than the nations[u] the LORD had destroyed before the Israelites.
10The LORD said through his servants
the prophets: 11"Manasseh king of Judah
21:11 v 2Ki 24:3-4 has committed these detestable sins. He
w Ge 15:16; 1Ki 21:26 has done more evil[v] than the Amorites[w]
who preceded him and has led Judah
into sin with his idols. 12Therefore this is
21:12 x 2Ki 23:26; what the LORD, the God of Israel, says: I
24:3; Jer 15:4 am going to bring such disaster[x] on Je-
y 1Sa 3:11; rusalem and Judah that the ears of
Jer 19:3 everyone who hears of it will tingle.[y] 13I
will stretch out over Jerusalem the
21:13 z Isa 34:11; measuring line used against Samaria
La 2:8; and the plumb line[z] used against the
Am 7:7-9 house of Ahab. I will wipe[a] out Jerusa-
a 2Ki 23:27 lem as one wipes a dish, wiping it and
21:14 b Ps 78:58-60 turning it upside down. 14I will forsake[b]
c 2Ki 19:4; the remnant[c] of my inheritance and
Mic 2:12 hand them over to their enemies. They
will be looted and plundered by all their
foes, 15because they have done evil[d] in 21:15 d Ex 32:22
my eyes and have provoked[e] me to anger e Jer 25:7
from the day their forefathers came out
of Egypt until this day."
16Moreover, Manasseh also shed so
much innocent blood[f] that he filled Jeru- 21:16 f 2Ki 24:4
salem from end to end—besides the sin
that he had caused Judah to commit, so
that they did evil in the eyes of the LORD.
17As for the other events of Manasseh's reign, and all he did, including the
sin he committed, are they not written
in the book of the annals of the kings of
Judah? 18Manasseh rested with his fathers and was buried in his palace gar-
den,[g] the garden of Uzza. And Amon his 21:18 g ver 26
son succeeded him as king.

Amon King of Judah

19Amon was twenty-two years old
when he became king, and he reigned in
Jerusalem two years. His mother's name
was Meshullemeth daughter of Haruz;
she was from Jotbah. 20He did evil[h] in 21:20 h ver 2-6
the eyes of the LORD, as his father Ma-
nasseh had done. 21He walked in all the
ways of his father; he worshiped the
idols his father had worshiped, and
bowed down to them. 22He forsook the
LORD, the God of his fathers, and did not 21:22
walk[i] in the way of the LORD. i 1Ki 11:33
23Amon's officials conspired against 21:23
him and assassinated[j] the king in his j 2Ki 12:20; 2Ch 33:24-25
palace. 24Then the people of the land
killed[k] all who had plotted against King 21:24 k 2Ki 14:5
Amon, and they made Josiah his son
king in his place.
25As for the other events of Amon's
reign, and what he did, are they not written in the book of the annals of the kings
of Judah? 26He was buried in his grave in 21:26
the garden[l] of Uzza. And Josiah his son l ver 18
succeeded him as king.

The Book of the Law Found

22 Josiah was eight years old when
he became king, and he reigned
in Jerusalem thirty-one years. His mother's name was Jedidah daughter of Ada- 22:1
iah; she was from Bozkath.[m] 2He did m Jos 15:39
what was right[n] in the eyes of the LORD 22:2
and walked in all the ways of his father n Dt 17:19
David, not turning aside to the right[o] or o Dt 5:32
to the left.
3In the eighteenth year of his reign,

[a] 6 Or *He made his own son pass through*

DISCOVERY 94

STEPS TOWARD REVIVAL

Josiah was eight years of age when he became king of Judah. During his 31-year reign he led the nation back to God and to his truth. The historical record of Josiah's reign shows us important principles for spiritual growth.

First, we have to begin with a *personal commitment*. Josiah was only a little boy at the time of his coronation, but he was already determined to do right in God's eyes. The Bible says that he "walked in all the ways of his father David, not turning aside to the right or to the left" (2 Kings 22:2). If we are to experience a growing relationship with God, we too must resolve to do what we know to be right—whatever the consequences.

We also have to *pay careful attention* to God's Word. Over the course of years the Book of the Law had been lost. Hilkiah, Josiah's secretary, recovered the missing volume, and the king listened attentively to the entire book (verses 8–10). We grow spiritually when we take God's words seriously, but we can "lose" God's Word through neglect—by failure to read it or to follow its mandates.

When Josiah heard the Book of the Law read, he immediately realized that the people had "not acted in accordance with all that is written there concerning us" (verse 13). The young king was so grieved that he tore his clothes to demonstrate remorse over his own sin and that of the nation. And he vowed to follow God's law from that moment forward. Confessing our sin and turning away from it are critical steps on the path of spiritual growth.

Josiah then assembled all the leaders of Judah in Jerusalem so that they as well could listen to the Book of the Law. This *public proclamation* of God's Word is vital when we are serious about walking with God. After that corporate reading each individual leader renewed his commitment to the God of Israel (2 Kings 23:3).

Finally, Josiah ordered an aggressive campaign to rid the land of idols. If we, like the nation of Israel, are to experience revival, we must be willing to rid our lives of the clutter that gets in the way.

During the time Jesus was on earth, God's Word had become hidden under the "clutter" of years of tradition. Religious leaders set aside the commands of God in order to observe their human traditions (Mark 7:8–9). Jesus had to recover the truth of the Scripture for his generation and call people to repentance.

God promises that he will always hear his people when they give up their sinful ways and turn back to him (2 Chronicles 7:14). And Jesus promised his disciples the same thing: "If anyone would come after me, he must deny himself and take up his cross and follow me. For whoever wants to save his life will lose it, but whoever loses his life for me will find it" (Matthew 16:24–25).

***Self-Discovery:** Give some thought to your personal "quiet time" habits. Evaluate how consistently you spend time in prayer and in Bible reading. Are there some actions you could take to move you forward on your path of spiritual growth?*

GO TO DISCOVERY 95 ON PAGE 497

22:3 King Josiah sent the secretary, Shaphan[p]
[p] 2Ch 34:20; son of Azaliah, the son of Meshullam, to
Jer 39:14 the temple of the LORD. He said: 4"Go up
to Hilkiah the high priest and have him
get ready the money that has been
22:4 brought into the temple of the LORD,
[q] 2Ki 12:4-5 which the doorkeepers have collected[q]
from the people. 5Have them entrust it
to the men appointed to supervise the
22:5 work on the temple. And have these
[r] 2Ki 12:5,11-14 men pay the workers who repair[r] the
temple of the LORD— 6the carpenters,
the builders and the masons. Also have
22:6 them purchase timber and dressed
[s] 2Ki 12:11-12 stone to repair the temple.[s] 7But they
need not account for the money en-
22:7 trusted to them, because they are acting
[t] 2Ki 12:15 faithfully."[t]
8Hilkiah the high priest said to Shaphan the secretary, "I have found the
22:8 Book of the Law[u] in the temple of the
[u] Dt 31:24 LORD." He gave it to Shaphan, who read it.
9Then Shaphan the secretary went to the
king and reported to him: "Your officials
have paid out the money that was in the
temple of the LORD and have entrusted it
to the workers and supervisors at the
temple." 10Then Shaphan the secretary
informed the king, "Hilkiah the priest
22:10 has given me a book." And Shaphan read
[v] Jer 36:21 from it in the presence of the king.[v]
11When the king heard the words of
the Book of the Law, he tore his robes.
12He gave these orders to Hilkiah the
22:12 priest, Ahikam[w] son of Shaphan, Acbor
[w] 2Ki 25:22; Jer 26:24 son of Micaiah, Shaphan the secretary
and Asaiah the king's attendant: 13"Go
and inquire of the LORD for me and for
the people and for all Judah about what
22:13 is written in this book that has been
[x] Dt 29:24-28; 31:17 found. Great is the LORD's anger[x] that
burns against us because our fathers
have not obeyed the words of this book;
they have not acted in accordance with
all that is written there concerning us."
14Hilkiah the priest, Ahikam, Acbor,
Shaphan and Asaiah went to speak to
the prophetess Huldah, who was the wife
of Shallum son of Tikvah, the son of Harhas, keeper of the wardrobe. She lived in
Jerusalem, in the Second District.
15She said to them, "This is what the
LORD, the God of Israel, says: Tell the man
22:16 who sent you to me, 16'This is what the
[y] Dt 31:29; Jos 23:15 LORD says: I am going to bring disaster[y]
[z] Dt 29:27; Da 9:11 on this place and its people, according to
everything written in the book[z] the king
of Judah has read. 17Because they have 22:17
forsaken[a] me and burned incense to oth- [a] Dt 29:25-27
er gods and provoked me to anger by all
the idols their hands have made,[a] my
anger will burn against this place and
will not be quenched.' 18Tell the king of 22:18
Judah, who sent you to inquire[b] of the [b] 2Ch 34:26;
LORD, 'This is what the LORD, the God of Jer 21:2
Israel, says concerning the words you
heard: 19Because your heart was responsive and you humbled[c] yourself before 22:19
the LORD when you heard what I have [c] Ex 10:3; 1Ki 21:29;
spoken against this place and its people, Ps 51:17; Isa 57:15;
that they would become accursed[d] and Mic 6:8
laid waste,[e] and because you tore your [d] Jer 26:6 [e] Lev 26:31
robes and wept in my presence, I have
heard you, declares the LORD. 20Therefore
I will gather you to your fathers, and you 22:20
will be buried in peace.[f] Your eyes will [f] Isa 57:1
not see all the disaster I am going to
bring on this place.' "
So they took her answer back to the
king.

Josiah Renews the Covenant

23 Then the king called together
all the elders of Judah and Jerusalem. 2He went up to the temple of the
LORD with the men of Judah, the people
of Jerusalem, the priests and the prophets—all the people from the least to the
greatest. He read[g] in their hearing all the 23:2
words of the Book of the Covenant, [g] Dt 31:11; 2Ki 22:8
which had been found in the temple of
the LORD. 3The king stood by the pillar
and renewed the covenant[h] in the pres- 23:3
ence of the LORD—to follow[i] the LORD [h] 2Ki 11:14,17
and keep his commands, regulations [i] Dt 13:4
and decrees with all his heart and all his
soul, thus confirming the words of the
covenant written in this book. Then all
the people pledged themselves to the
covenant.
4The king ordered Hilkiah the high
priest, the priests next in rank and the
doorkeepers[j] to remove[k] from the tem- 23:4
ple of the LORD all the articles made for [j] 2Ki 25:18 [k] 2Ki 21:7
Baal and Asherah and all the starry
hosts. He burned them outside Jerusalem in the fields of the Kidron Valley and
took the ashes to Bethel. 5He did away
with the pagan priests appointed by the
kings of Judah to burn incense on the
high places of the towns of Judah and on
those around Jerusalem—those who
burned incense to Baal, to the sun and

[a] 17 Or *by everything they have done*

23:5 moon, to the constellations and to all
l 2Ki 21:3; the starry hosts.[l] 6He took the Asherah
Jer 8:2 pole from the temple of the LORD to the
Kidron Valley outside Jerusalem and
burned it there. He ground it to powder
23:6 and scattered the dust over the graves of
m Jer 26:23 the common people.[m] 7He also tore
23:7 down the quarters of the male shrine
n 1Ki 14:24; prostitutes,[n] which were in the temple
15:12; Eze 16:16 of the LORD and where women did weav-
ing for Asherah.
8Josiah brought all the priests from
23:8 the towns of Judah and desecrated the
o 1Ki 15:22 high places, from Geba[o] to Beersheba,
where the priests had burned incense.
He broke down the shrines[a] at the
gates—at the entrance to the Gate of
Joshua, the city governor, which is on the
23:9 left of the city gate. 9Although the
p Eze 44:10-14 priests of the high places did not serve[p]
at the altar of the LORD in Jerusalem,
they ate unleavened bread with their fellow priests.
23:10 10He desecrated Topheth,[q] which was
q Isa 30:33; Jer 7:31,32; 19:6 in the Valley of Ben Hinnom,[r] so no one
r Jos 15:8 could use it to sacrifice his son[s] or
s Lev 18:21; Dt 18:10 daughter in[b] the fire to Molech. 11He removed from the entrance to the temple
of the LORD the horses that the kings of
Judah had dedicated to the sun. They
were in the court near the room of an official named Nathan-Melech. Josiah
23:11 then burned the chariots dedicated to
t Dt 4:19 the sun.[t]
23:12 u Jer 19:13; 12He pulled down the altars the kings
Zep 1:5 of Judah had erected on the roof[u] near
v 2Ki 21:5 the upper room of Ahaz, and the altars
Manasseh had built in the two courts[v] of
the temple of the LORD. He removed
them from there, smashed them to
pieces and threw the rubble into the
Kidron Valley. 13The king also desecrated the high places that were east of Jeru-
23:13 salem on the south of the Hill of Cor-
w 1Ki 11:7 ruption—the ones Solomon[w] king of
Israel had built for Ashtoreth the vile
goddess of the Sidonians, for Chemosh
the vile god of Moab, and for Molech[c]
the detestable god of the people of Am-
23:14 x Ex 23:24; mon. 14Josiah smashed[x] the sacred
Dt 7:5,25 stones and cut down the Asherah poles
and covered the sites with human
bones.
23:15 y 1Ki 13:1-3 15Even the altar[y] at Bethel, the high
z 1Ki 12:33 place made by Jeroboam[z] son of Nebat,
who had caused Israel to sin—even that
altar and high place he demolished. He
burned the high place and ground it to
powder, and burned the Asherah pole
also. 16Then Josiah[a] looked around, and 23:16
when he saw the tombs that were there a 1Ki 13:2
on the hillside, he had the bones removed from them and burned on the altar to defile it, in accordance with the
word of the LORD proclaimed by the man
of God who foretold these things.
17The king asked, "What is that tomb-
stone I see?"
The men of the city said, "It marks the
tomb of the man of God who came from
Judah and pronounced against the altar
of Bethel the very things you have done
to it."
18"Leave it alone," he said. "Don't let 23:18
anyone disturb his bones[b]." So they b 1Ki 13:31
spared his bones and those of the
prophet who had come from Samaria.
19Just as he had done at Bethel, Josiah
removed and defiled all the shrines at
the high places that the kings of Israel
had built in the towns of Samaria that
had provoked the LORD to anger. 20Josiah 23:20
slaughtered[c] all the priests of those high c Ex 22:20;
places on the altars and burned human 2Ki 10:25; 11:18
bones[d] on them. Then he went back to d 1Ki 13:2
Jerusalem.
21The king gave this order to all the 23:21
people: "Celebrate the Passover[e] to the e Ex 12:11;
LORD your God, as it is written in this Nu 9:2;
Book of the Covenant." 22Not since the Dt 16:1-8
days of the judges who led Israel, nor
throughout the days of the kings of Israel and the kings of Judah, had any such
Passover been observed. 23But in the
eighteenth year of King Josiah, this Passover was celebrated to the LORD in Jerusalem.
24Furthermore, Josiah got rid of the 23:24
mediums and spiritists,[f] the household f Lev 19:31;
gods,[g] the idols and all the other de- Dt 18:11;
testable things seen in Judah and Jerusa- 2Ki 21:6
lem. This he did to fulfill the require- g Ge 31:19
ments of the law written in the book
that Hilkiah the priest had discovered in
the temple of the LORD. 25Neither before
nor after Josiah was there a king like him
who turned[h] to the LORD as he did— 23:25 h 2Ki 18:5
with all his heart and with all his soul
and with all his strength, in accordance
with all the Law of Moses.
26Nevertheless, the LORD did not turn
away from the heat of his fierce anger,

[a] 8 Or *high places* [b] 10 Or *to make his son or daughter pass through* [c] 13 Hebrew *Milcom*

23:26 [i]2Ki 21:12; Jer 15:4
which burned against Judah because of
all that Manasseh[i] had done to provoke
him to anger. 27So the LORD said, "I will
23:27 [j]2Ki 21:13 [k]2Ki 18:11
remove[j] Judah also from my presence[k]
as I removed Israel, and I will reject Jerusalem, the city I chose, and this temple,
about which I said, 'There shall my
Name be.'[a]"
28As for the other events of Josiah's
reign, and all he did, are they not written
in the book of the annals of the kings of
Judah?
23:29 [l]Jer 46:2 [m]Zec 12:11
29While Josiah was king, Pharaoh
Neco[l] king of Egypt went up to the Euphrates River to help the king of Assyria. King Josiah marched out to meet him
in battle, but Neco faced him and killed
23:30 [n]2Ki 9:28
him at Megiddo.[m] 30Josiah's servants
brought his body in a chariot[n] from Megiddo to Jerusalem and buried him in
his own tomb. And the people of the
land took Jehoahaz son of Josiah and
anointed him and made him king in
place of his father.

Jehoahaz King of Judah

23:31 [o]1Ch 3:15; Jer 22:11 [p]2Ki 24:18
31Jehoahaz[o] was twenty-three years
old when he became king, and he
reigned in Jerusalem three months. His
mother's name was Hamutal[p] daughter
of Jeremiah; she was from Libnah. 32He
did evil in the eyes of the LORD, just as
23:33 [q]2Ki 25:6 [r]1Ki 8:65
his fathers had done. 33Pharaoh Neco
put him in chains at Riblah[q] in the land
of Hamath[b][r] so that he might not reign
in Jerusalem, and he imposed on Judah
a levy of a hundred talents[c] of silver and
23:34 [s]1Ch 3:15; 2Ch 36:5-8 [t]Jer 22:12; Eze 19:3-4
a talent[d] of gold. 34Pharaoh Neco made
Eliakim[s] son of Josiah king in place of
his father Josiah and changed Eliakim's
name to Jehoiakim. But he took Jehoahaz and carried him off to Egypt, and
there he died.[t] 35Jehoiakim paid Pharaoh
Neco the silver and gold he demanded.
In order to do so, he taxed the land and
exacted the silver and gold from the
23:35 [u]ver 33
people of the land according to their as-
sessments.[u]

Jehoiakim King of Judah

23:36 [v]Jer 26:1
36Jehoiakim[v] was twenty-five years
old when he became king, and he
reigned in Jerusalem eleven years. His
mother's name was Zebidah daughter of
Pedaiah; she was from Rumah. 37And he
did evil in the eyes of the LORD, just as
his fathers had done.

24:1 [w]Jer 25:1,9; Da 1:1
24 During Jehoiakim's reign, Nebuchadnezzar[w] king of Babylon
invaded the land, and Jehoiakim became his vassal for three years. But then
he changed his mind and rebelled
24:2 [x]Jer 35:11 [y]Jer 25:9
against Nebuchadnezzar. 2The LORD
sent Babylonian,[e] Aramean,[x] Moabite
and Ammonite raiders against him. He
sent them to destroy[y] Judah, in accordance with the word of the LORD proclaimed by his servants the prophets.
24:3 [z]2Ki 18:25 [a]2Ki 21:12; 23:26
3Surely these things happened to Judah
according to the LORD's command,[z] in
order to remove them from his presence
because of the sins of Manasseh[a] and all
he had done, 4including the shedding of
24:4 [b]2Ki 21:16
innocent blood.[b] For he had filled Jerusalem with innocent blood, and the
LORD was not willing to forgive.
5As for the other events of Jehoiakim's
reign, and all he did, are they not written
in the book of the annals of the kings of
24:6 [c]Jer 22:19
Judah? 6Jehoiakim rested[c] with his fathers. And Jehoiachin his son succeeded
him as king.
24:7 [d]Ge 15:18 [e]Jer 37:5-7; 46:2
7The king of Egypt[d] did not march
out from his own country again, because the king of Babylon[e] had taken all
his territory, from the Wadi of Egypt to
the Euphrates River.

Jehoiachin King of Judah

24:8 [f]1Ch 3:16
8Jehoiachin[f] was eighteen years old
when he became king, and he reigned in
Jerusalem three months. His mother's
name was Nehushta daughter of Elnathan; she was from Jerusalem. 9He did
evil in the eyes of the LORD, just as his father had done.
24:10 [g]Da 1:1
10At that time the officers of Nebuchadnezzar[g] king of Babylon advanced
on Jerusalem and laid siege to it, 11and
Nebuchadnezzar himself came up to the
city while his officers were besieging it.
24:12 [h]2Ki 25:27; Jer 22:24-30; 24:1; 25:1; 29:2; 52:28
12Jehoiachin king of Judah, his mother,
his attendants, his nobles and his officials all surrendered[h] to him.
In the eighth year of the reign of the
king of Babylon, he took Jehoiachin pris-
24:13 [i]2Ki 20:17 [j]2Ki 25:15; Isa 39:6
oner. 13As the LORD had declared,[i] Nebuchadnezzar removed all the treasures[j]
from the temple of the LORD and from
the royal palace, and took away all the

[a] 27 1 Kings 8:29 [b] 33 Hebrew; Septuagint (see also 2 Chron. 36:3) *Neco at Riblah in Hamath removed him* [c] 33 That is, about 3 3/4 tons (about 3.4 metric tons) [d] 33 That is, about 75 pounds (about 34 kilograms) [e] 2 Or *Chaldean*

24:13 k2Ki 25:14; Jer 20:5 l1Ki 7:51
gold articles[k] that Solomon[l] king of Israel had made for the temple of the
LORD. 14He carried into exile[m] all Jerusa-
24:14 mJer 24:1; 52:28 n2Ki 25:12; Jer 40:7; 52:16
lem: all the officers and fighting men,
and all the craftsmen and artisans—a
total of ten thousand. Only the poorest[n]
people of the land were left.
15Nebuchadnezzar took Jehoiachin
24:15 oJer 22:24-28 pEst 2:6; Eze 17:12-14
captive to Babylon. He also took from Jerusalem to Babylon the king's mother,[o]
his wives, his officials and the leading
men[p] of the land. 16The king of Babylon
also deported to Babylon the entire force
of seven thousand fighting men, strong
24:16 qJer 52:28
and fit for war, and a thousand craftsmen and artisans.[q] 17He made Mattani-
24:17 r1Ch 3:15; 2Ch 36:11; Jer 37:1
ah, Jehoiachin's uncle, king in his place
and changed his name to Zedekiah.[r]

Zedekiah King of Judah

24:18 sJer 52:1 t2Ki 23:31
18Zedekiah[s] was twenty-one years old
when he became king, and he reigned in
Jerusalem eleven years. His mother's
name was Hamutal[t] daughter of Jeremiah; she was from Libnah. 19He did evil in
the eyes of the LORD, just as Jehoiakim
had done. 20It was because of the LORD's
anger that all this happened to Jerusa-
24:20 uDt 4:26; 29:27
lem and Judah, and in the end he thrust[u]
them from his presence.

The Fall of Jerusalem

Now Zedekiah rebelled against the
king of Babylon.

25 So in the ninth year of Zedeki-
25:1 vJer 34:1-7 wEze 24:2
ah's reign, on the tenth day of
the tenth month, Nebuchadnezzar[v]
king of Babylon marched against Jerusalem with his whole army. He encamped
outside the city and built siege works[w]
all around it. 2The city was kept under
siege until the eleventh year of King
Zedekiah. 3By the ninth day of the
25:3 xJer 14:18; La 4:9
⌞fourth⌟[a] month the famine[x] in the city
had become so severe that there was no
food for the people to eat. 4Then the city
25:4 yEze 33:21 zJer 4:17
wall was broken through,[y] and the
whole army fled at night through
the gate between the two walls near the
king's garden, though the Babylonians[b]
were surrounding[z] the city. They fled toward the Arabah,[c] 5but the Babylonian[d]
army pursued the king and overtook
25:5 aEze 12:14
him in the plains of Jericho. All his soldiers were separated from him and scat-
25:6 bJer 34:21-22 c2Ki 23:33
tered,[a] 6and he was captured.[b] He was
taken to the king of Babylon at Riblah,[c]
where sentence was pronounced on
him. 7They killed the sons of Zedekiah
before his eyes. Then they put out his
eyes, bound him with bronze shackles
25:7 dJer 21:7; 32:4-5; Eze 12:11
and took him to Babylon.[d]
8On the seventh day of the fifth
month, in the nineteenth year of Nebuchadnezzar king of Babylon, Nebuzaradan commander of the imperial guard,
an official of the king of Babylon, came
25:9 eIsa 60:7 fPs 74:3-8; Jer 2:15; Am 2:5; Mic 3:12
to Jerusalem. 9He set fire[e] to the temple
of the LORD, the royal palace and all the
houses of Jerusalem. Every important
building he burned down.[f] 10The whole
Babylonian army, under the commander of the imperial guard, broke down the
25:10 gNe 1:3
walls[g] around Jerusalem. 11Nebuzaradan
25:11 h2Ki 24:14 i2Ki 24:1
the commander of the guard carried
into exile[h] the people who remained in
the city, along with the rest of the populace and those who had gone over to the
25:12 j2Ki 24:14
king of Babylon.[i] 12But the commander
left behind some of the poorest people[j]

[a]3 See Jer. 52:6. [b]4 Or *Chaldeans*; also in verses 13, 25 and 26 [c]4 Or *the Jordan Valley* [d]5 Or *Chaldean*; also in verses 10 and 24

JERUSALEM FALLS

While good kings like Hezekiah and Josiah temporarily slowed Judah's decline, Zedekiah speeded her fall (2 Kings 25). Zedekiah had entered into a contract with Nebuchadnezzar, king of Babylon (Ezekiel 17:13) but then rebelled against the Babylonian king (2 Kings 25:1; Jeremiah 52:3), even though God's prophet Jeremiah had warned him that this action was contrary to God's desire (2 Chronicles 36:12; Jeremiah 38:17–18). The king ignored Jeremiah, and Jerusalem paid dearly for Zedekiah's rebellion. In 586 B.C. the Babylonians destroyed the city and God's temple along with it. The people of Judah were carried into captivity in Babylon, Jerusalem lay in ashes and once more any hope that God would send his promised Messiah seemed to vanish in the smoke of the ruins. But Jehoiachin, Zedekiah's nephew and the king of Judah, survived (2 Kings 25:27–30)—and once more the family line of the Messiah was spared (see Matthew 1:11). Even after his chosen city had been destroyed and his chosen people forced to go into slavery in a foreign land, God remained in control of Israel's destiny. His redemptive plan would not, could not, be thwarted.

DISCOVERY 95

Jerusalem—City of the King

Every well-known city throughout the world has its "claim to fame"—as well as some stain in its background that would qualify it for the "Hall of Shame." What specific pictures come to mind when you hear the name London—or Chicago, Moscow, Calcutta, Paris, Madrid, New York or Geneva? But no city in the world has a more spectacular history than that of Jerusalem. This remarkable city has been a place of prosperity, intrigue, conflict, power and infamy for centuries. Jerusalem has seen it all!

The events recorded in 2 Kings 25 describe the desperate conditions in Judah and Jerusalem immediately before their citizens were carried away into Babylonian captivity. Jerusalem was under siege and choked by famine. King Zedekiah was captured in a failed escape attempt and was subjected to the most inhumane treatment. The temple, the palace and all of the houses in the city were demolished. Religious leaders were killed and the temple furnishings destroyed. As some people fled in terror for their lives, others were brutally murdered. The entire nation of Judah was captured. It must have appeared to God's people that their city with its sacred temple had been hopelessly ravaged, never again to thrive.

Wrong! To be sure, even today the history of Jerusalem is subject to a continual ebb and flow: peace and tension, prosperity and calamity, unity and division. But think for a moment about the noteworthy events that have occurred in this famous city, especially during Jesus' lifetime—and about the Bible's glorious predictions for its future. Mary and Joseph brought Jesus to the temple in Jerusalem to present him to God the Father as the law required (Luke 2:22–32). When he was twelve years old Jesus returned to the temple and amazed the teachers with his precocious knowledge (Luke 2:41–50). It was in Jerusalem that Satan tempted Jesus to follow him instead of the Father, and it was here that the Son of God triumphed over Satan's wicked schemes (Luke 4:9–13). Jesus spent a great deal of time in Jerusalem ministering to people in need (John 7:12). In Jerusalem Jesus purified the temple from money-making schemes (Matthew 21:12–13). There he was arrested, tried and crucified—and there he rose victorious from the grave (John 20:1–2).

That's not the end of the story, though. It is to Jerusalem that Jesus will return to reign forever: "His feet will stand on the Mount of Olives, east of Jerusalem" (Zechariah 14:1–9).

Jerusalem is significant—in Israel's history, in Jesus' life and in the future. Jesus felt very deeply for the city (Matthew 23:37–39), and in the same way he commiserates with each of us in our difficulties: "He had compassion on them, because they were harassed and helpless, like sheep without a shepherd" (Matthew 9:36).

Sometimes the future appears bleak; always it is uncertain. But our hope is centered in God's promise of resurrection. Jesus returned from the grave, and one day he will come back and take his own to be with him forever (John 14:1–3).

***Self-Discovery:** Now that the Gentiles have been offered salvation through Jesus Christ, do you still view the Jews as God's chosen people? If so, what does that position of honor mean in practical terms today?*

GO TO DISCOVERY 96 ON PAGE 501

of the land to work the vineyards and fields.

13 The Babylonians broke up the bronze pillars, the movable stands and the bronze Sea that were at the temple of the LORD and they carried the bronze to Babylon. 14 They also took away the pots, shovels, wick trimmers, dishes and all the bronze articles[k] used in the temple service. 15 The commander of the imperial guard took away the censers and sprinkling bowls—all that were made of pure gold or silver.

25:14 [k] Ex 27:3; 1Ki 7:47-50

16 The bronze from the two pillars, the Sea and the movable stands, which Solomon had made for the temple of the LORD, was more than could be weighed. 17 Each pillar[l] was twenty-seven feet[a] high. The bronze capital on top of one pillar was four and a half feet[b] high and was decorated with a network and pomegranates of bronze all around. The other pillar, with its network, was similar.

25:17 [l] 1Ki 7:15-22

18 The commander of the guard took as prisoners Seraiah[m] the chief priest, Zephaniah[n] the priest next in rank and the three doorkeepers. 19 Of those still in the city, he took the officer in charge of the fighting men and five royal advisers. He also took the secretary who was chief officer in charge of conscripting the people of the land and sixty of his men who were found in the city. 20 Nebuzaradan the commander took them all and brought them to the king of Babylon at Riblah. 21 There at Riblah, in the land of Hamath, the king had them executed.

25:18 [m] 1Ch 6:14; Ezr 7:1; Ne 11:11 [n] Jer 21:1; 29:25

So Judah went into captivity, away from her land.[o]

25:21 [o] Ge 12:7; Dt 28:64; Jos 23:13; 2Ki 23:27

22 Nebuchadnezzar king of Babylon appointed Gedaliah[p] son of Ahikam, the son of Shaphan, to be over the people he had left behind in Judah. 23 When all the army officers and their men heard that the king of Babylon had appointed Gedaliah as governor, they came to Gedaliah at Mizpah—Ishmael son of Nethaniah, Johanan son of Kareah, Seraiah son of Tanhumeth the Netophathite, Jaazaniah the son of the Maacathite, and their men. 24 Gedaliah took an oath to reassure them and their men. "Do not be afraid of the Babylonian officials," he said. "Settle down in the land and serve the king of Babylon, and it will go well with you."

25:22 [p] Jer 39:14; 40:5,7

25 In the seventh month, however, Ishmael son of Nethaniah, the son of Elishama, who was of royal blood, came with ten men and assassinated Gedaliah and also the men of Judah and the Babylonians who were with him at Mizpah. 26 At this, all the people from the least to the greatest, together with the army officers, fled to Egypt[q] for fear of the Babylonians.

25:26 [q] Isa 30:2; Jer 43:7

Jehoiachin Released

27 In the thirty-seventh year of the exile of Jehoiachin king of Judah, in the year Evil-Merodach[c] became king of Babylon, he released Jehoiachin[r] from prison on the twenty-seventh day of the twelfth month. 28 He spoke kindly to him and gave him a seat of honor[s] higher than those of the other kings who were with him in Babylon. 29 So Jehoiachin put aside his prison clothes and for the rest of his life ate regularly at the king's table.[t] 30 Day by day the king gave Jehoiachin a regular allowance as long as he lived.[u]

25:27 [r] 2Ki 24:12; Jer 52:31-34
25:28 [s] Ezr 5:5; Ne 2:1; Da 2:48
25:29 [t] 2Sa 9:7
25:30 [u] Est 2:9; Jer 28:4

[a] 17 Hebrew *eighteen cubits* (about 8.1 meters)
[b] 17 Hebrew *three cubits* (about 1.3 meters)
[c] 27 Also called *Amel-Marduk*

1 CHRONICLES

Why did David wear an ephod? (1 Chronicles 15:27)

♦*David, though not a priest, may have worn an ephod to show his devotion to God. Some think that the king clothed in a priestly ephod was a picture of the coming Christ who would be both priest and king (Psalm 110; Zechariah 6:12–13; Hebrews 7).*

Why did God decide to change his dwelling from a tent to a temple? (1 Chronicles 17:5–6,12)

♦*Some think that the portable tabernacle was replaced with a permanent temple after Israel had become firmly established in the promised land. Others suggest a symbolic view—that the temple, established firmly on a foundation, pointed forward to the coming Messiah—the Rock of salvation (2 Samuel 22:2–4,32,47; 1 Corinthians 10:4).*

Jesus in 1 Chronicles The books of 1 and 2 Chronicles focus on the family line of David, Israel's greatest king. David provides us with an early picture or "type" of Jesus, the ultimate "son of David" (Matthew1:1) and God's chosen King. God promised the people a Savior and protected the family line so that he could be born at the right time (Galatians 4:4–5).

There is a universal need to belong, to feel connected to others. The book of 1 Chronicles addressed this need for the returning Israelite exiles as it revealed their connection with their ancestors and with God—the opening chapters of 1 Chronicles consist of long lists of names. Think about *your* own status in God's family, not based on the inclusion of your name in a genealogical record but on your position as God's adopted son or daughter (Romans 8:12–25; Galatians 3:26—4:7), grafted into his family on the basis of the redemptive work of your "brother" Jesus (Hebrews 2:10–18).

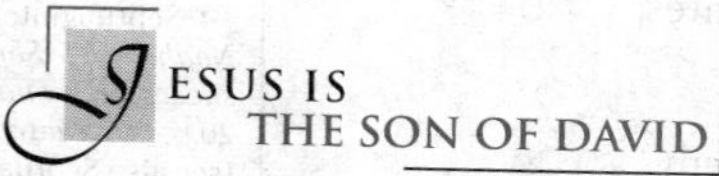
JESUS IS
THE SON OF DAVID

Historical Records From Adam to Abraham

To Noah's Sons

1:1 [a]Ge 5:1-32; Lk 3:36-38

1 Adam,[a] Seth, Enosh, 2 Kenan,[b]
Mahalalel,[c] Jared,[d] 3 Enoch,[e] Methuselah,[f] Lamech,[g] Noah.[h]

1:2 [b]Ge 5:9 [c]Ge 5:12 [d]Ge 5:15

4 The sons of Noah:[a] [i]
Shem, Ham and Japheth.[j]

1:3 [e]Ge 5:18; Jude 1:14 [f]Ge 5:21 [g]Ge 5:25 [h]Ge 5:29

1:4 [i]Ge 6:10; 10:1 [j]Ge 5:32

The Japhethites

5 The sons[b] of Japheth:
Gomer, Magog, Madai, Javan, Tubal, Meshech and Tiras.
6 The sons of Gomer:
Ashkenaz, Riphath[c] and Togarmah.
7 The sons of Javan:
Elishah, Tarshish, the Kittim and the Rodanim.

The Hamites

8 The sons of Ham:
Cush, Mizraim,[d] Put and Canaan.
9 The sons of Cush:
Seba, Havilah, Sabta, Raamah and Sabteca.
The sons of Raamah:
Sheba and Dedan.
10 Cush was the father[e] of
Nimrod, who grew to be a mighty warrior on earth.
11 Mizraim was the father of
the Ludites, Anamites, Lehabites, Naphtuhites, 12 Pathrusites,
Casluhites (from whom the Philistines came) and Caphtorites.
13 Canaan was the father of
Sidon his firstborn,[f] and of the Hittites, 14 Jebusites, Amorites,
Girgashites, 15 Hivites, Arkites,
Sinites, 16 Arvadites, Zemarites and Hamathites.

The Semites

17 The sons of Shem:
Elam, Asshur, Arphaxad, Lud and Aram.
The sons of Aram[g]:
Uz, Hul, Gether and Meshech.
18 Arphaxad was the father of Shelah,
and Shelah the father of Eber.
19 Two sons were born to Eber:
One was named Peleg,[h] because in his time the earth was divided; his brother was named Joktan.
20 Joktan was the father of
Almodad, Sheleph, Hazarmaveth, Jerah, 21 Hadoram, Uzal,
Diklah, 22 Obal,[i] Abimael, Sheba,
23 Ophir, Havilah and Jobab. All these were sons of Joktan.

1:24 [k]Ge 10:21-25; Lk 3:34-36

24 Shem,[k] Arphaxad,[j] Shelah,
25 Eber, Peleg, Reu,
26 Serug, Nahor, Terah
27 and Abram (that is, Abraham).

The Family of Abraham

28 The sons of Abraham:
Isaac and Ishmael.

Descendants of Hagar

29 These were their descendants:
Nebaioth the firstborn of Ishmael, Kedar, Adbeel, Mibsam,
30 Mishma, Dumah, Massa, Hadad, Tema, 31 Jetur, Naphish and
Kedemah. These were the sons of Ishmael.

Descendants of Keturah

1:32 [l]Ge 22:24 [m]Ge 10:7

32 The sons born to Keturah, Abraham's concubine:[l]
Zimran, Jokshan, Medan, Midian, Ishbak and Shuah.
The sons of Jokshan:
Sheba and Dedan.[m]
33 The sons of Midian:
Ephah, Epher, Hanoch, Abida and Eldaah.
All these were descendants of Keturah.

Descendants of Sarah

1:34 [n]Lk 3:34 [o]Ge 21:2-3; Mt 1:2; Ac 7:8 [p]Ge 17:5; 25:25-26

34 Abraham[n] was the father of Isaac.[o]
The sons of Isaac:
Esau and Israel.[p]

[a] 4 Septuagint; Hebrew does not have *The sons of Noah:* [b] 5 *Sons* may mean *descendants* or *successors* or *nations*; also in verses 6–10, 17 and 20. [c] 6 Many Hebrew manuscripts and Vulgate (see also Septuagint and Gen. 10:3); most Hebrew manuscripts *Diphath* [d] 8 That is, Egypt; also in verse 11 [e] 10 *Father* may mean *ancestor* or *predecessor* or *founder*; also in verses 11, 13, 18 and 20. [f] 13 Or *of the Sidonians, the foremost* [g] 17 One Hebrew manuscript and some Septuagint manuscripts (see also Gen. 10:23); most Hebrew manuscripts do not have this line. [h] 19 *Peleg* means *division.* [i] 22 Some Hebrew manuscripts and Syriac (see also Gen. 10:28); most Hebrew manuscripts *Ebal* [j] 24 Hebrew; some Septuagint manuscripts *Arphaxad, Cainan* (see also note at Gen. 11:10)

"I AM THE *light of the world*. WHOEVER FOLLOWS ME WILL NEVER WALK IN DARKNESS, BUT WILL HAVE THE *light of life*."

—JOHN 8:12—

JOHN [THE BAPTIST] SAW JESUS
COMING TOWARD HIM
AND SAID, "LOOK, THE *Lamb of God*,
WHO TAKES AWAY THE SIN
OF THE WORLD!"
—JOHN 1:29—

WHY GENEALOGIES?

The first nine chapters of 1 Chronicles contain many genealogies: of the patriarchs, of the tribe of Judah, of the tribe of Levi, of the six northern tribes, of the tribe of Benjamin, of the citizens of Jerusalem and of Saul. Why does the Bible devote so much space to such seemingly insignificant lists of people?

Well, for one thing the genealogies remind us that the Bible is about the *real* God working with *real* people who lived in *real* places and faced *real* circumstances. A great fish *literally* swallowed a man named Jonah (Jonah 1:17). Peter *actually* walked on the Sea of Galilee during a storm (Matthew 14:22–33). Jesus did *in fact* die on a very *real* cross and did *indeed* come back to life again (Matthew 27:45–56; 28:2–10).

These family trees also trace Jesus' ancestral line, confirming that he is God's promised Messiah. There are many prophecies concerning Jesus' coming, and one of the most significant specifies that he would be David's descendant (Isaiah 9:6–7). The genealogies in both the Old and New Testaments (see Matthew 1:1–17) furnish historical evidence. God has worked throughout history to execute every detail of the word he had given to the prophets.

Another benefit to reading the genealogies is that they can provide us with encouragement. Most of us will never be famous, and it can be difficult to relate to spiritual "giants" like Abraham, Deborah or Peter. We will most likely never cross the Red Sea on dry ground, walk on water or travel around the world planting churches. Instead, our lives will be consumed by the mundane details of work and family, and relatively few people will know our names during our lifetimes, let alone 50 years after our deaths. In fact, we will be as anonymous as Onam, Shammai, Jada, Nadab, Abishur or Molid. These and others like them are the names that take up most of the space in the genealogies; these are the unpretentious individuals who together form an ongoing chain that ultimately leads to Jesus—the final "link."

No matter how insignificant our lives may appear, God forgets no one, and he is vitally interested in ordinary folk. You may go unnoticed by most of the world, but you are known intimately by Jesus if your name is written in the genealogy of God—the book of life (Revelation 20:15). That is the only significance any of us really needs!

Self-Discovery: *How much do you know about the lives of your great-grandparents? Has anyone shared anecdotes about ancestors farther removed than that? If the Christian heritage has been passed from generation to generation in your particular family, you might want to pause and thank God for that legacy.*

GO TO DISCOVERY 97 ON PAGE 509

Esau's Sons

1:35 [q] Ge 36:19 [r] Ge 36:4
35 The sons of Esau:[q]
Eliphaz, Reuel,[r] Jeush, Jalam and Korah.
36 The sons of Eliphaz:
Teman, Omar, Zepho,[a] Gatam and Kenaz;
1:36 [s] Ex 17:14
by Timna: Amalek.[b][s]
37 The sons of Reuel:[t]
1:37 [t] Ge 36:17
Nahath, Zerah, Shammah and Mizzah.

The People of Seir in Edom

38 The sons of Seir:
Lotan, Shobal, Zibeon, Anah, Dishon, Ezer and Dishan.
39 The sons of Lotan:
Hori and Homam. Timna was Lotan's sister.
40 The sons of Shobal:
Alvan,[c] Manahath, Ebal, Shepho and Onam.
The sons of Zibeon:
1:40 [u] Ge 36:2
Aiah and Anah.[u]
41 The son of Anah:
Dishon.
The sons of Dishon:
Hemdan,[d] Eshban, Ithran and Keran.
42 The sons of Ezer:
Bilhan, Zaavan and Akan.[e]
The sons of Dishan[f]:
Uz and Aran.

The Rulers of Edom

43 These were the kings who reigned in Edom before any Israelite king reigned[g]:
Bela son of Beor, whose city was named Dinhabah.
44 When Bela died, Jobab son of Zerah from Bozrah succeeded him as king.
1:45 [v] Ge 36:11
45 When Jobab died, Husham from the land of the Temanites[v] succeeded him as king.
46 When Husham died, Hadad son of Bedad, who defeated Midian in the country of Moab, succeeded him as king. His city was named Avith.
47 When Hadad died, Samlah from Masrekah succeeded him as king.
48 When Samlah died, Shaul from Rehoboth on the river[h] succeeded him as king.
49 When Shaul died, Baal-Hanan son of Acbor succeeded him as king.
50 When Baal-Hanan died, Hadad succeeded him as king. His city was named Pau,[i] and his wife's name was Mehetabel daughter of Matred, the daughter of Me-Zahab. 51 Hadad also died.

The chiefs of Edom were:
Timna, Alvah, Jetheth, 52 Oholibamah, Elah, Pinon, 53 Kenaz, Teman, Mibzar, 54 Magdiel and Iram.
These were the chiefs of Edom.

Israel's Sons

2 These were the sons of Israel:
Reuben, Simeon, Levi, Judah, Issachar, Zebulun, 2 Dan, Joseph, Benjamin, Naphtali, Gad and Asher.

[a] *36* Many Hebrew manuscripts, some Septuagint manuscripts and Syriac (see also Gen. 36:11); most Hebrew manuscripts *Zephi* [b] *36* Some Septuagint manuscripts (see also Gen. 36:12); Hebrew *Gatam, Kenaz, Timna and Amalek* [c] *40* Many Hebrew manuscripts and some Septuagint manuscripts (see also Gen. 36:23); most Hebrew manuscripts *Alian* [d] *41* Many Hebrew manuscripts and some Septuagint manuscripts (see also Gen. 36:26); most Hebrew manuscripts *Hamran* [e] *42* Many Hebrew and Septuagint manuscripts (see also Gen. 36:27); most Hebrew manuscripts *Zaavan, Jaakan* [f] *42* Hebrew *Dishon,* a variant of *Dishan* [g] *43* Or *before an Israelite king reigned over them* [h] *48* Possibly the Euphrates [i] *50* Many Hebrew manuscripts, some Septuagint manuscripts, Vulgate and Syriac (see also Gen. 36:39); most Hebrew manuscripts *Pai*

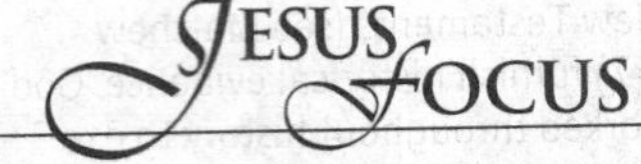

REAL PEOPLE

Together 1 and 2 Chronicles comprise a record of God's people from Adam through the time of David. These books are not intended to be a complete history of Israel. Rather, these genealogies demonstrate that God's hand was on the nation from the beginning of human history. The Gospels complete the record that begins here. The book of Matthew traces Jesus' lineage back to Abraham (Matthew 1:1–16), while Luke follows the trail all the way back to Adam (Luke 3:23–38). Many of the names in the genealogies are unfamiliar to the average reader, but they remind us that God works in the lives of the real, ordinary people who walk with him. These records of family history also highlight for us the true humanity of Jesus the Messiah, God's one and only Son.

Judah

To Hezron's Sons

3 The sons of Judah:[w]
Er, Onan and Shelah.[x] These three were born to him by a Canaanite woman, the daughter of Shua.[y] Er, Judah's firstborn, was wicked in the LORD's sight; so the LORD put him to death.[z]
4 Tamar,[a] Judah's daughter-in-law,[b] bore him Perez[c] and Zerah. Judah had five sons in all.

5 The sons of Perez:[d]
Hezron[e] and Hamul.
6 The sons of Zerah:
Zimri, Ethan, Heman, Calcol and Darda[a]—five in all.
7 The son of Carmi:
Achar,[b][f] who brought trouble on Israel by violating the ban on taking devoted things.[c][g]
8 The son of Ethan:
Azariah.
9 The sons born to Hezron[h] were:
Jerahmeel, Ram and Caleb.[d]

From Ram Son of Hezron

10 Ram[i] was the father of
Amminadab[j], and Amminadab the father of Nahshon,[k] the leader of the people of Judah. 11 Nahshon was the father of Salmon,[e] Salmon the father of Boaz, 12 Boaz[l] the father of Obed and Obed the father of Jesse.[m]
13 Jesse[n] was the father of
Eliab[o] his firstborn; the second son was Abinadab, the third Shimea, 14 the fourth Nethanel, the fifth Raddai, 15 the sixth Ozem and the seventh David. 16 Their sisters were Zeruiah[p] and Abigail. Zeruiah's[q] three sons were Abishai, Joab[r] and Asahel. 17 Abigail was the mother of Amasa,[s] whose father was Jether the Ishmaelite.

Caleb Son of Hezron

18 Caleb son of Hezron had children by his wife Azubah (and by Jerioth). These were her sons: Jesher, Shobab and Ardon. 19 When Azubah died, Caleb[t] married Ephrath, who bore him Hur. 20 Hur was the father of Uri, and Uri the father of Bezalel.[u]
21 Later, Hezron lay with the daughter of Makir the father of Gilead[v] (he had married her when he was sixty years old), and she bore him Segub. 22 Segub was the father of Jair, who controlled twenty-three towns in Gilead. 23 (But Geshur and Aram captured Havvoth Jair,[f][w] as well as Kenath[x] with its surrounding settlements—sixty towns.) All these were descendants of Makir the father of Gilead.

24 After Hezron died in Caleb Ephrathah, Abijah the wife of Hezron bore him Ashhur[y] the father[g] of Tekoa.

Jerahmeel Son of Hezron

25 The sons of Jerahmeel the firstborn of Hezron:
Ram his firstborn, Bunah, Oren, Ozem and[h] Ahijah. 26 Jerahmeel had another wife, whose name was Atarah; she was the mother of Onam.
27 The sons of Ram the firstborn of Jerahmeel:
Maaz, Jamin and Eker.
28 The sons of Onam:
Shammai and Jada.
The sons of Shammai:
Nadab and Abishur.
29 Abishur's wife was named Abihail, who bore him Ahban and Molid.
30 The sons of Nadab:
Seled and Appaim. Seled died without children.
31 The son of Appaim:
Ishi, who was the father of Sheshan.
Sheshan was the father of Ahlai.
32 The sons of Jada, Shammai's brother:

a 6 Many Hebrew manuscripts, some Septuagint manuscripts and Syriac (see also 1 Kings 4:31); most Hebrew manuscripts *Dara* *b 7* *Achar* means *trouble*; *Achar* is called *Achan* in Joshua. *c 7* The Hebrew term refers to the irrevocable giving over of things or persons to the LORD, often by totally destroying them. *d 9* Hebrew *Kelubai*, a variant of *Caleb* *e 11* Septuagint (see also Ruth 4:21); Hebrew *Salma* *f 23* Or *captured the settlements of Jair* *g 24* *Father* may mean *civic leader* or *military leader*; also in verses 42, 45, 49–52 and possibly elsewhere. *h 25* Or *Oren and Ozem, by*

2:3 w Ge 29:35; 38:2-10 x Ge 38:5 y Ge 38:2 z Nu 26:19
2:4 a Ge 38:11-30 b Ge 11:31 c Ge 38:29
2:5 d Ge 46:12 e Nu 26:21
2:7 f Jos 7:1 g Jos 6:18
2:9 h Nu 26:21
2:10 i Lk 3:32-33 j Ex 6:23 k Nu 1:7
2:12 l Ru 2:1 m Ru 4:17
2:13 n Ru 4:17 o 1Sa 16:6
2:16 p 1Sa 26:6 q 2Sa 2:18 r 2Sa 2:13
2:17 s 2Sa 17:25
2:19 t ver 42,50
2:20 u Ex 31:2
2:21 v Nu 27:1
2:23 w Nu 32:41; Dt 3:14; Jos 13:30 x Nu 32:42
2:24 y 1Ch 4:5

Jether and Jonathan. Jether died
without children.
33 The sons of Jonathan:
Peleth and Zaza.
These were the descendants of Jerahmeel.
34 Sheshan had no sons—only daughters.
He had an Egyptian servant
named Jarha. 35 Sheshan gave his
daughter in marriage to his
servant Jarha, and she bore him
Attai.
36 Attai was the father of Nathan,
Nathan the father of Zabad,[z]
37 Zabad the father of Ephlal,
Ephlal the father of Obed,
38 Obed the father of Jehu,
Jehu the father of Azariah,
39 Azariah the father of Helez,
Helez the father of Eleasah,
40 Eleasah the father of Sismai,
Sismai the father of Shallum,
41 Shallum the father of Jekamiah,
and Jekamiah the father of Elishama.

2:36 [z]1Ch 11:41

The Clans of Caleb

42 The sons of Caleb[a] the brother of
Jerahmeel:
Mesha his firstborn, who was the
father of Ziph, and his son Mareshah,[a] who was the father of Hebron.
43 The sons of Hebron:
Korah, Tappuah, Rekem and
Shema. 44 Shema was the father
of Raham, and Raham the father
of Jorkeam. Rekem was the father of Shammai. 45 The son of
Shammai was Maon[b], and Maon
was the father of Beth Zur.[c]
46 Caleb's concubine Ephah was the
mother of Haran, Moza and Ga-
zez. Haran was the father of Ga-
zez.
47 The sons of Jahdai:
Regem, Jotham, Geshan, Pelet,
Ephah and Shaaph.
48 Caleb's concubine Maacah was the
mother of Sheber and Tirhanah.
49 She also gave birth to Shaaph
the father of Madmannah[d] and
to Sheva the father of Macbenah
and Gibea. Caleb's daughter was
Acsah.[e] 50 These were the descendants of Caleb.

2:42 [a]ver 19
2:45 [b]Jos 15:55 [c]Jos 15:58
2:49 [d]Jos 15:31 [e]Jos 15:16

The sons of Hur[f] the firstborn of
Ephrathah:
Shobal the father of Kiriath Jearim,[g] 51 Salma the father of Bethlehem, and Hareph the father of
Beth Gader.
52 The descendants of Shobal the father of Kiriath Jearim were:
Haroeh, half the Manahathites,
53 and the clans of Kiriath Jearim:
the Ithrites,[h] Puthites, Shumath-
ites and Mishraites. From these
descended the Zorathites and
Eshtaolites.
54 The descendants of Salma:
Bethlehem, the Netophathites,[i]
Atroth Beth Joab, half the Manahathites, the Zorites, 55 and
the clans of scribes[b] who lived at
Jabez: the Tirathites, Shimeath-
ites and Sucathites. These are
the Kenites[j] who came from
Hammath,[k] the father of the
house of Recab.[c][l]

2:50 [f]1Ch 4:4 [g]ver 19
2:53 [h]2Sa 23:38
2:54 [i]Ezr 2:22; Ne 7:26; 12:28
2:55 [j]Ge 15:19; Jdg 1:16; Jdg 4:11 [k]Jos 19:35 [l]2Ki 10:15,23; Jer 35:2-19

The Sons of David

3 These were the sons of David[m]
born to him in Hebron:
The firstborn was Amnon the
son of Ahinoam of Jezreel;[n]
the second, Daniel the son of
Abigail[o] of Carmel;
2 the third, Absalom the son of
Maacah daughter of Talmai king
of Geshur;
the fourth, Adonijah[p] the son of
Haggith;
3 the fifth, Shephatiah the son of
Abital;
and the sixth, Ithream, by his
wife Eglah.
4 These six were born to David in
Hebron,[q] where he reigned sev-
en years and six months.[r]
David reigned in Jerusalem thirty-three
years, 5 and these were the children born
to him there:
Shammua,[d] Shobab, Nathan and
Solomon. These four were by
Bathsheba[e][s] daughter of Ammiel. 6 There were also Ibhar, Eli-

3:1 [m]1Ch 14:3; 28:5 [n]Jos 15:56 [o]1Sa 25:42
3:2 [p]1Ki 2:22
3:4 [q]2Sa 5:4; 1Ch 29:27 [r]2Sa 2:11; 5:5
3:5 [s]2Sa 11:3; 12:24

[a] *42* The meaning of the Hebrew for this phrase is uncertain. [b] *55* Or *of the Sopherites* [c] *55* Or *father of Beth Recab* [d] *5* Hebrew *Shimea,* a variant of *Shammua* [e] *5* One Hebrew manuscript and Vulgate (see also Septuagint and 2 Samuel 11:3); most Hebrew manuscripts *Bathshua*

shua,[a] Eliphelet, 7Nogah, Nepheg, Japhia, 8Elishama, Eliada and Eliphelet—nine in all. 9All these were the sons of David, besides his sons by his concubines. And Tamar[t] was their sister.[u]

The Kings of Judah

10Solomon's son was Rehoboam,[v]
Abijah his son,
Asa his son,
Jehoshaphat[w] his son,
11Jehoram[b x] his son,
Ahaziah[y] his son,
Joash[z] his son,
12Amaziah[a] his son,
Azariah his son,
Jotham[b] his son,
13Ahaz[c] his son,
Hezekiah[d] his son,
Manasseh[e] his son,
14Amon[f] his son,
Josiah[g] his son.

15The sons of Josiah:
Johanan the firstborn,
Jehoiakim[h] the second son,
Zedekiah[i] the third,
Shallum[j] the fourth.

16The successors of Jehoiakim:
Jehoiachin[c k] his son,
and Zedekiah.[l]

The Royal Line After the Exile

17The descendants of Jehoiachin the captive:
Shealtiel[m] his son, 18Malkiram, Pedaiah, Shenazzar,[n] Jekamiah, Hoshama and Nedabiah.[o]

19The sons of Pedaiah:
Zerubbabel[p] and Shimei.
The sons of Zerubbabel:
Meshullam and Hananiah.
Shelomith was their sister.

20There were also five others:
Hashubah, Ohel, Berekiah, Hasadiah and Jushab-Hesed.

21The descendants of Hananiah:
Pelatiah and Jeshaiah, and the sons of Rephaiah, of Arnan, of Obadiah and of Shecaniah.

22The descendants of Shecaniah:
Shemaiah and his sons:
Hattush,[q] Igal, Bariah, Neariah and Shaphat—six in all.

23The sons of Neariah:
Elioenai, Hizkiah and Azrikam—three in all.

24The sons of Elioenai:
Hodaviah, Eliashib, Pelaiah, Akkub, Johanan, Delaiah and Anani—seven in all.

Other Clans of Judah

4 The descendants of Judah:[r]
Perez, Hezron,[s] Carmi, Hur and Shobal.

2Reaiah son of Shobal was the father of Jahath, and Jahath the father of Ahumai and Lahad. These were the clans of the Zorathites.

3These were the sons[d] of Etam:
Jezreel, Ishma and Idbash. Their sister was named Hazzelelponi. 4Penuel was the father of Gedor, and Ezer the father of Hushah.
These were the descendants of Hur,[t] the firstborn of Ephrathah and father[e] of Bethlehem.[u]

5Ashhur[v] the father of Tekoa had two wives, Helah and Naarah.

6Naarah bore him Ahuzzam, Hepher, Temeni and Haahashtari. These were the descendants of Naarah.

7The sons of Helah:
Zereth, Zohar, Ethnan, 8and Koz, who was the father of Anub and Hazzobebah and of the clans of Aharhel son of Harum.

9Jabez was more honorable than his
brothers. His mother had named him Jabez,[f] saying, "I gave birth to him in pain."
10Jabez cried out to the God of Israel,
"Oh, that you would bless me and enlarge my territory! Let your hand be with me, and keep me from harm so that I will be free from pain." And God granted his request.

11Kelub, Shuhah's brother, was the father of Mehir, who was the father of Eshton. 12Eshton was the father of Beth Rapha, Paseah and Tehinnah the father of Ir Nahash.[g] These were the men of Recah.

[a] *6* Two Hebrew manuscripts (see also 2 Samuel 5:15 and 1 Chron. 14:5); most Hebrew manuscripts *Elishama* [b] *11* Hebrew *Joram,* a variant of *Jehoram* [c] *16* Hebrew *Jeconiah,* a variant of *Jehoiachin;* also in verse 17 [d] *3* Some Septuagint manuscripts (see also Vulgate); Hebrew *father* [e] *4* *Father* may mean *civic leader* or *military leader;* also in verses 12, 14, 17, 18 and possibly elsewhere. [f] *9* *Jabez* sounds like the Hebrew for *pain.* [g] *12* Or *of the city of Nahash*

3:9 [t] 2Sa 13:1 [u] 1Ch 14:4
3:10 [v] 1Ki 11:43; 14:21-31; 2Ch 12:16 [w] 2Ch 17:1-21:3
3:11 [x] 2Ki 8:16-24; 2Ch 21:1 [y] 2Ch 22:1-10 [z] 2Ki 11:1-12:21
3:12 [a] 2Ki 14:1-22; 2Ch 25:1-28 [b] Isa 1:1; Hos 1:1; Mic 1:1
3:13 [c] 2Ki 16:1-20; 2Ch 28:1; Isa 7:1 [d] 2Ki 18:1-20:21; 2Ch 29:1; Jer 26:19 [e] 2Ch 33:1
3:14 [f] 2Ki 21:19-26; 2Ch 33:21; Zep 1:1 [g] 2Ch 34:1; Jer 1:2; 3:6; 25:3
3:15 [h] 2Ki 23:34 [i] Jer 37:1 [j] 2Ki 23:31
3:16 [k] 2Ki 24:6,8; Mt 1:11 [l] 2Ki 24:18
3:17 [m] Ezr 3:2
3:18 [n] Ezr 1:8; 5:14 [o] Jer 22:30
3:19 [p] Ezr 2:2; 3:2; 5:2; Ne 7:7; 12:1; Hag 1:1; 2:2; Zec 4:6
3:22 [q] Ezr 8:2-3
4:1 [r] Ge 29:35; 46:12; 1Ch 2:3 [s] Nu 26:21
4:4 [t] 1Ch 2:50 [u] Ru 1:19
4:5 [v] 1Ch 2:24

4:13 13 The sons of Kenaz:
[w]Jos 15:17 Othniel[w] and Seraiah.
The sons of Othniel:
Hathath and Meonothai.[a] 14 Meonothai was the father of Ophrah.
Seraiah was the father of Joab,
the father of Ge Harashim.[b] It
was called this because its people were craftsmen.
15 The sons of Caleb son of Jephunneh:
Iru, Elah and Naam.
The son of Elah:
Kenaz.
16 The sons of Jehallelel:
Ziph, Ziphah, Tiria and Asarel.
17 The sons of Ezrah:
Jether, Mered, Epher and Jalon.
4:17 One of Mered's wives gave birth
[x]Ex 15:20 to Miriam,[x] Shammai and Ish-
bah the father of Eshtemoa.
18 (His Judean wife gave birth to
Jered the father of Gedor, Heber
4:18 the father of Soco, and Jekuthiel
[y]Jos 15:34 the father of Zanoah.[y]) These
were the children of Pharaoh's
daughter Bithiah, whom Mered
had married.
19 The sons of Hodiah's wife, the sister
of Naham:
4:19 the father of Keilah[z] the Gar-
[z]Jos 15:44 [a]Dt 3:14 mite, and Eshtemoa the Maacathite.[a]
20 The sons of Shimon:
Amnon, Rinnah, Ben-Hanan
and Tilon.
The descendants of Ishi:
Zoheth and Ben-Zoheth.
4:21 [b]Ge 38:5 21 The sons of Shelah[b] son of Judah:
Er the father of Lecah, Laadah
the father of Mareshah and the
clans of the linen workers at
Beth Ashbea, 22 Jokim, the men
of Cozeba, and Joash and Saraph,
who ruled in Moab and Jashubi
Lehem. (These records are from
ancient times.) 23 They were the
potters who lived at Netaim and
Gederah; they stayed there and
worked for the king.

Simeon

4:24 24 The descendants of Simeon:[c]
[c]Ge 29:33 [d]Nu 26:12 Nemuel, Jamin, Jarib,[d] Zerah and
Shaul;
25 Shallum was Shaul's son, Mibsam his son and Mishma his son.
26 The descendants of Mishma:
Hammuel his son, Zaccur his
son and Shimei his son.
27 Shimei had sixteen sons and six
daughters, but his brothers did not have
many children; so their entire clan did
not become as numerous as the people 4:28
of Judah. 28 They lived in Beersheba,[e] [e]Ge 21:14
Moladah,[f] Hazar Shual, 29 Bilhah, Ezem,[g] [f]Jos 15:26
Tolad, 30 Bethuel, Hormah,[h] Ziklag, 4:29
31 Beth Marcaboth, Hazar Susim, Beth [g]Jos 15:29
Biri and Shaaraim.[i] These were their 4:30
towns until the reign of David. 32 Their [h]Nu 14:45
surrounding villages were Etam, Ain,[j] 4:31
Rimmon, Token and Ashan[k]—five [i]Jos 15:36
towns— 33 and all the villages around 4:32
these towns as far as Baalath.[c] These [j]Nu 34:11
were their settlements. And they kept a [k]Jos 15:42
genealogical record.

34 Meshobab, Jamlech, Joshah son of
Amaziah, 35 Joel, Jehu son of Joshi-
biah, the son of Seraiah, the son of
Asiel, 36 also Elioenai, Jaakobah,
Jeshohaiah, Asaiah, Adiel, Jesimiel,
Benaiah, 37 and Ziza son of Shiphi,
the son of Allon, the son of Jedaiah,
the son of Shimri, the son of Shemaiah.

38 The men listed above by name were
leaders of their clans. Their families increased greatly, 39 and they went to the 4:39
outskirts of Gedor[l] to the east of the val- [l]Jos 15:58
ley in search of pasture for their flocks.
40 They found rich, good pasture, and the 4:40
land was spacious, peaceful and quiet.[m] [m]Jdg 18:7-10
Some Hamites had lived there formerly.
41 The men whose names were listed
came in the days of Hezekiah king of Judah. They attacked the Hamites in their 4:41
dwellings and also the Meunites[n] who [n]2Ch 20:1; 26:7
were there and completely destroyed[d]
them, as is evident to this day. Then they
settled in their place, because there was
pasture for their flocks. 42 And five hundred of these Simeonites, led by Pelatiah, Neariah, Rephaiah and Uzziel, the 4:42
sons of Ishi, invaded the hill country of [o]Ge 14:6
Seir.[o] 43 They killed the remaining 4:43
Amalekites[p] who had escaped, and they [p]1Sa 15:8;
have lived there to this day. 30:17; 2Sa 8:12;
Est 3:1; 9:16

[a] *13* Some Septuagint manuscripts and Vulgate; Hebrew does not have *and Meonothai.*
[b] *14* *Ge Harashim* means *valley of craftsmen.*
[c] *33* Some Septuagint manuscripts (see also Joshua 19:8); Hebrew *Baal*
[d] *41* The Hebrew term refers to the irrevocable giving over of things or persons to the LORD, often by totally destroying them.

Reuben

5 The sons of Reuben[q] the firstborn
of Israel (he was the firstborn, but
when he defiled his father's marriage
bed,[r] his rights as firstborn were given to
the sons of Joseph[s] son of Israel;[t] so he
could not be listed in the genealogical
record in accordance with his birthright,[u] 2and though Judah[v] was the
strongest of his brothers and a ruler[w]
came from him, the rights of the firstborn[x] belonged to Joseph)— 3the sons of
Reuben[y] the firstborn of Israel:
Hanoch, Pallu,[z] Hezron and Carmi.
4 The descendants of Joel:
Shemaiah his son, Gog his son,
Shimei his son, 5Micah his son,
Reaiah his son, Baal his son,
6 and Beerah his son, whom Tiglath-Pileser[a][a] king of Assyria
took into exile. Beerah was a
leader of the Reubenites.

5:1 q Ge 29:32 r Ge 35:22; 49:4 s Ge 48:16,22; 49:26 t Ge 48:5 u 1Ch 26:10
5:2 v Ge 49:10,12 w 1Sa 9:16; 12:12; 2Sa 6:21; 1Ch 11:2; 2Ch 7:18; Ps 60:7; Mic 5:2; Mt 2:6 x Ge 25:31
5:3 y Ge 29:32; 46:9; Ex 6:14; Nu 26:5-11 z Nu 26:5
5:6 a ver 26; 2Ki 15:19; 16:10; 2Ch 28:20

JESUS FOCUS

SELECTIVE HISTORY

The author of 1 and 2 Chronicles focused particularly on two of the 12 tribes of Israel—Judah, the royal line, and Levi, the priestly line (see 1 Chronicles 3:10—4:23; 6). It is entirely possible that these two books, originally written as one, were penned by a priest, possibly Ezra, because the records focus on the relationship between the royal line and the temple, its worship and its priests. The Chronicles provide a very selective history of God's people, omitting many of the unsavory incidents recorded in 1 and 2 Samuel and 1 and 2 Kings—such as those involving Bathsheba, Absalom and Tamar. The Chronicles do not deny anything we read in the other history books of the Bible; they simply exclude it. The Gospels present a different sort of history, revealing the weaknesses and foibles of men and women and pointing out that we all need God's grace in our lives. From Zacchaeus the tax collector (Luke 19:1–10) to the Samaritan woman at the well (John 4:1–30), from Judas the betrayer (Matthew 26:47–50; 27:1–10) to the impetuous Peter (Matthew 26:69–75; John 21:15–23), we glimpse brief vignettes of ourselves, ordinary people in desperate need of salvation that comes through the redeeming work of our precious Savior and Lord Jesus Christ (Romans 3:21–26; Colossians 1:13–14; Titus 2:11–14).

7 Their relatives by clans,[b] listed according to their genealogical records:
Jeiel the chief, Zechariah, 8and
Bela son of Azaz, the son of Shema, the son of Joel. They settled
in the area from Aroer[c] to Nebo
and Baal Meon. 9To the east they
occupied the land up to the edge
of the desert that extends to the
Euphrates River, because their
livestock had increased in Gilead.[d]
10During Saul's reign they waged
war against the Hagrites[e], who
were defeated at their hands; they
occupied the dwellings of the Hagrites throughout the entire region
east of Gilead.

Gad

11 The Gadites[f] lived next to them in
Bashan, as far as Salecah:[g]
12 Joel was the chief, Shapham the
second, then Janai and Shaphat,
in Bashan.
13 Their relatives, by families, were:
Michael, Meshullam, Sheba, Jo-
rai, Jacan, Zia and Eber—seven
in all.
14 These were the sons of Abihail
son of Huri, the son of Jaroah,
the son of Gilead, the son of Michael, the son of Jeshishai, the
son of Jahdo, the son of Buz.
15 Ahi son of Abdiel, the son of
Guni, was head of their family.
16 The Gadites lived in Gilead, in Bashan and its outlying villages,
and on all the pasturelands of
Sharon as far as they extended.
17 All these were entered in the genealogical records during the reigns of
Jotham[h] king of Judah and Jeroboam[i]
king of Israel.
18The Reubenites, the Gadites and the
half-tribe of Manasseh had 44,760 men
ready for military service[j]—able-bodied
men who could handle shield and
sword, who could use a bow, and who
were trained for battle. 19They waged
war against the Hagrites, Jetur,[k] Naphish
and Nodab. 20They were helped[l] in fighting them, and God handed the Hagrites
and all their allies over to them, because

5:7 b ver 17
5:8 c Nu 32:34
5:9 d Nu 32:26; Jos 22:9
5:10 e ver 18-21
5:11 f Jos 13:24-28 g Dt 3:10; Jos 13:11
5:17 h 2Ki 15:32 i 2Ki 14:16,28
5:18 j Nu 1:3
5:19 k ver 10; Ge 25:15; 1Ch 1:31
5:20 l Ps 37:40

[a] 6 Hebrew *Tilgath-Pilneser,* a variant of *Tiglath-Pileser*; also in verse 26

they cried[m] out to him during the battle. He answered their prayers, because they trusted[n] in him. 21 They seized the livestock of the Hagrites—fifty thousand camels, two hundred fifty thousand sheep and two thousand donkeys. They also took one hundred thousand people captive, 22 and many others fell slain, because the battle[o] was God's. And they occupied the land until the exile.[p]

The Half-Tribe of Manasseh

23 The people of the half-tribe of Manasseh were numerous; they settled in the land from Bashan to Baal Hermon, that is, to Senir (Mount Hermon).[q]

24 These were the heads of their families: Epher, Ishi, Eliel, Azriel, Jeremiah, Hodaviah and Jahdiel. They were brave warriors, famous men, and heads of their families. 25 But they were unfaithful[r] to the God of their fathers and prostituted[s] themselves to the gods of the peoples of the land, whom God had destroyed before them. 26 So the God of Israel stirred up the spirit of Pul[t] king of Assyria (that is, Tiglath-Pileser[u] king of Assyria), who took the Reubenites, the Gadites and the half-tribe of Manasseh into exile. He took them to Halah,[v] Habor, Hara and the river of Gozan, where they are to this day.

Levi

6 The sons of Levi:[w]
Gershon, Kohath and Merari.

2 The sons of Kohath:
Amram, Izhar, Hebron and Uzziel.

3 The children of Amram:
Aaron, Moses and Miriam.

The sons of Aaron:
Nadab, Abihu,[x] Eleazar and Ithamar.

4 Eleazar was the father of Phinehas,
Phinehas the father of Abishua,
5 Abishua the father of Bukki,
Bukki the father of Uzzi,
6 Uzzi the father of Zerahiah,
Zerahiah the father of Meraioth,
7 Meraioth the father of Amariah,
Amariah the father of Ahitub,
8 Ahitub the father of Zadok,[y]
Zadok the father of Ahimaaz,
9 Ahimaaz the father of Azariah,
Azariah the father of Johanan,
10 Johanan the father of Azariah[z]
(it was he who served as priest in the temple Solomon built in Jerusalem),
11 Azariah the father of Amariah,
Amariah the father of Ahitub,
12 Ahitub the father of Zadok,
Zadok the father of Shallum,
13 Shallum the father of Hilkiah,[a]
Hilkiah the father of Azariah,
14 Azariah the father of Seraiah,[b]
and Seraiah the father of Jehozadak.

15 Jehozadak[c] was deported when the LORD sent Judah and Jerusalem into exile by the hand of Nebuchadnezzar.

16 The sons of Levi:[d]
Gershon,[a] Kohath and Merari.[e]

17 These are the names of the sons of Gershon:
Libni and Shimei.

18 The sons of Kohath:
Amram, Izhar, Hebron and Uzziel.

19 The sons of Merari:[f]
Mahli and Mushi.

These are the clans of the Levites listed according to their fathers:

20 Of Gershon:
Libni his son, Jehath his son,
Zimmah his son, 21 Joah his son,
Iddo his son, Zerah his son
and Jeatherai his son.

22 The descendants of Kohath:
Amminadab his son, Korah[g] his son,
Assir his son, 23 Elkanah his son,
Ebiasaph his son, Assir his son,
24 Tahath his son, Uriel[h] his son,
Uzziah his son and Shaul his son.

25 The descendants of Elkanah:
Amasai, Ahimoth,
26 Elkanah his son,[b] Zophai his son,
Nahath his son, 27 Eliab his son,
Jeroham his son, Elkanah[i] his son
and Samuel[j] his son.[c]

28 The sons of Samuel:
Joel[d][k] the firstborn

a 16 Hebrew *Gershom*, a variant of *Gershon*; also in verses 17, 20, 43, 62 and 71 *b* 26 Some Hebrew manuscripts, Septuagint and Syriac; most Hebrew manuscripts *Ahimoth* 26*and Elkanah. The sons of Elkanah:* *c* 27 Some Septuagint manuscripts (see also 1 Samuel 1:19,20 and 1 Chron. 6:33,34); Hebrew does not have *and Samuel his son.*
d 28 Some Septuagint manuscripts and Syriac (see also 1 Samuel 8:2 and 1 Chron. 6:33); Hebrew does not have *Joel.*

5:20 m 1Ki 8:44; 2Ch 13:14; 14:11; Ps 20:7-9; 22:5 n Ps 26:1; Da 6:23
5:22 o 2Ch 32:8 p 2Ki 15:29; 17:6
5:23 q Dt 3:8,9; SS 4:8
5:25 r Dt 32:15-18; 2Ki 17:7; 1Ch 9:1; 2Ch 26:16 s Ex 34:15
5:26 t 2Ki 15:19 u 2Ki 15:29 v 2Ki 17:6; 18:11
6:1 w Ge 46:11; Ex 6:16; Nu 26:57; 1Ch 23:6
6:3 x Lev 10:1
6:8 y 2Sa 8:17; 15:27; Ezr 7:2
6:10 z 1Ki 4:2; 6:1; 2Ch 3:1; 26:17-18
6:13 a 2Ki 22:1-20; 2Ch 34:9; 35:8
6:14 b 2Ki 25:18; Ezr 2:2; Ne 11:11
6:15 c 2Ki 25:18; Ne 12:1; Hag 1:1,14; 2:2, 4; Zec 6:11
6:16 d Ge 29:34; Ex 6:16; Nu 3:17-20 e Nu 26:57
6:19 f Ge 46:11; 1Ch 23:21; 24:26
6:22 g Ex 6:24
6:24 h 1Ch 15:5
6:27 i 1Sa 1:1 j 1Sa 1:20
6:28 k ver 33; 1Sa 8:2

DISCOVERY 97

Music and Musicians

Without a doubt, music enhances the worship experience of God's people. In Exodus 15 Moses and the people of Israel sang to the Lord, and musical instruments were a regular component of praising God (Exodus 15:1,20–21). The prophets also recognized the significance of music. When Samuel was preparing Saul for his leadership role, he instructed him to "go to Gibeah of God . . . [and] you will meet a procession of prophets coming down from the high place with lyres, tambourines, flutes and harps being played before them, and they will be prophesying" (1 Samuel 10:5–6).

Of the tribes in charge of temple duties, three assigned one musician each from among their number to full-time temple service; Heman, Asaph and Ethan were selected because they were musically gifted and trained (1 Chronicles 6:31–47). These "ministers of music" employed singing and instrumentation to direct the people in their worship.

Over the centuries many things have changed—so many, in fact, that God's people often fail to agree on the specifics. Some Christians prefer music that is formal and reverent; others relate to a loud and jubilant style. Some consider hymns to be outdated; others feel that contemporary worship choruses are too modern and insubstantial. There have been many variations and changes, both throughout the centuries and from place to place within the same time period: from highly liturgical to impromptu worship structure, from organ to percussion, from monotone chants to songs in an upbeat tempo, from simple to sophisticated arrangements. What has not changed, however, are the role of the musician and the function of music—because music is emotive and pleasurable and helps God's people pay attention to him.

Christian music is many things. It may be a declaration of praise, a backdrop for a statement about our Creator or a venue for prayer. It may be the expression of solemn, heartfelt thanksgiving or rollicking celebration, but it is all intended to honor the Lord.

Many of the best-loved songs sung in churches everywhere direct our attention to Jesus. The apostle Paul enjoins us to "sing and make music in [our] heart to the Lord, always giving thanks to God the Father for everything, in the name of our Lord Jesus Christ" (Ephesians 5:20).

There are several hymns of praise included in the New Testament. For example, the poetic form of Philippians 2:6–11 has led many Bible scholars to regard it as part of the early Christian hymnal. Imagine Paul and the first-century Christians praising God as they sang these words: "God exalted [Jesus] to the highest place and gave him the name that is above every name, that at the name of Jesus every knee should bow, in heaven and on earth and under the earth, and every tongue confess that Jesus Christ is Lord, to the glory of God the Father" (Philippians 2:9–11).

Self-Discovery: *What kind of Christian music moves you most? What style makes you least comfortable? Are you able to look at the different musical forms objectively and make an informed decision about whether or not each honors the triune God—Father, Son and Holy Spirit?*

GO TO DISCOVERY 98 ON PAGE 517

and Abijah the second son.
29 The descendants of Merari:
Mahli, Libni his son,
Shimei his son, Uzzah his son,
30 Shimea his son, Haggiah his son
and Asaiah his son.

The Temple Musicians

31 These are the men[l] David put in charge of the music[m] in the house of the LORD after the ark came to rest there. 32 They ministered with music before the tabernacle, the Tent of Meeting, until Solomon built the temple of the LORD in Jerusalem. They performed their duties according to the regulations laid down for them.

6:31 [l] 1Ch 25:1; 2Ch 29:25-26; Ne 12:45 [m] 1Ch 9:33; 15:19; Ezr 3:10; Ps 68:25

33 Here are the men who served, together with their sons:
From the Kohathites:
Heman,[n] the musician,
the son of Joel,[o] the son of Samuel,
34 the son of Elkanah,[p] the son of Jeroham,
the son of Eliel, the son of Toah,
35 the son of Zuph, the son of Elkanah,
the son of Mahath, the son of Amasai,
36 the son of Elkanah, the son of Joel,
the son of Azariah, the son of Zephaniah,
37 the son of Tahath, the son of Assir,
the son of Ebiasaph, the son of Korah,[q]
38 the son of Izhar,[r] the son of Kohath,
the son of Levi, the son of Israel;
39 and Heman's associate Asaph,[s]
who served at his right hand:
Asaph son of Berekiah, the son of Shimea,[t]
40 the son of Michael, the son of Baaseiah,[a]
the son of Malkijah, 41 the son of Ethni,
the son of Zerah, the son of Adaiah,
42 the son of Ethan, the son of Zimmah,
the son of Shimei, 43 the son of Jahath,
the son of Gershon, the son of Levi;

6:33 [n] 1Ki 4:31; 1Ch 15:17; 25:1 [o] ver 28
6:34 [p] 1Sa 1:1
6:37 [q] Ex 6:24
6:38 [r] Ex 6:21
6:39 [s] 1Ch 25:1,9; 2Ch 29:13; Ne 11:17 [t] 1Ch 15:17

44 and from their associates, the Merarites, at his left hand:
Ethan son of Kishi, the son of Abdi,
the son of Malluch, 45 the son of Hashabiah,
the son of Amaziah, the son of Hilkiah,
46 the son of Amzi, the son of Bani,
the son of Shemer, 47 the son of Mahli,
the son of Mushi, the son of Merari,
the son of Levi.

48 Their fellow Levites[u] were assigned to all the other duties of the tabernacle, the house of God. 49 But Aaron and his descendants were the ones who presented offerings on the altar[v] of burnt offering and on the altar of incense[w] in connection with all that was done in the Most Holy Place, making atonement for Israel, in accordance with all that Moses the servant of God had commanded.

6:48 [u] 1Ch 23:32
6:49 [v] Ex 27:1-8 [w] Ex 30:1-7,10; 2Ch 26:18

50 These were the descendants of Aaron:
Eleazar his son, Phinehas his son,
Abishua his son, 51 Bukki his son,
Uzzi his son, Zerahiah his son,
52 Meraioth his son, Amariah his son,
Ahitub his son, 53 Zadok[x] his son
and Ahimaaz his son.

6:53 [x] 2Sa 8:17

54 These were the locations of their settlements[y] allotted as their territory (they were assigned to the descendants of Aaron who were from the Kohathite clan, because the first lot was for them):

55 They were given Hebron in Judah with its surrounding pasturelands. 56 But the fields and villages around the city were given to Caleb son of Jephunneh.[z]

57 So the descendants of Aaron were given Hebron (a city of refuge), and Libnah,[b][a] Jattir,[b] Eshtemoa, 58 Hilen, Debir,[c] 59 Ashan,[d] Juttah[c] and Beth Shemesh, together with their pasturelands. 60 And from the tribe of Benjamin they

6:54 [y] Nu 31:10
6:56 [z] Jos 14:13; 15:13
6:57 [a] Nu 33:20 [b] Jos 15:48
6:58 [c] Jos 10:3
6:59 [d] Jos 15:42

[a] *40* Most Hebrew manuscripts; some Hebrew manuscripts, one Septuagint manuscript and Syriac *Maaseiah* [b] *57* See Joshua 21:13; Hebrew *given the cities of refuge: Hebron, Libnah.* [c] *59* Syriac (see also Septuagint and Joshua 21:16); Hebrew does not have *Juttah.*

6:60 e Jer 1:1 were given Gibeon,[a] Geba, Alemeth
and Anathoth,[e] together with their
pasturelands.
These towns, which were distributed among the Kohathite
clans, were thirteen in all.
[61] The rest of Kohath's descendants
were allotted ten towns from the clans
of half the tribe of Manasseh.
[62] The descendants of Gershon, clan
by clan, were allotted thirteen towns
from the tribes of Issachar, Asher and
Naphtali, and from the part of the tribe
of Manasseh that is in Bashan.
[63] The descendants of Merari, clan by
clan, were allotted twelve towns from
the tribes of Reuben, Gad and Zebulun.
6:64 [64] So the Israelites gave the Levites
f Nu 35:1-8; Jos 21:3,41-42 these towns[f] and their pasturelands.
[65] From the tribes of Judah, Simeon and
Benjamin they allotted the previously
named towns.
[66] Some of the Kohathite clans were
given as their territory towns from the
tribe of Ephraim.
[67] In the hill country of Ephraim
6:67 they were given Shechem (a city of
g Jos 10:33 refuge), and Gezer,[b g] [68] Jokmeam,[h]
6:68 Beth Horon,[i] [69] Aijalon[j] and Gath
h 1Ki 4:12 Rimmon,[k] together with their pas-
i Jos 10:10 turelands.
6:69 [70] And from half the tribe of Ma-
j Jos 10:12 k Jos 19:45 nasseh the Israelites gave Aner and
Bileam, together with their pas-
turelands, to the rest of the Kohathite clans.
6:71 l 1Ch 23:7 m Jos 20:8 [71] The Gershonites[l] received the following:
From the clan of the half-tribe of
Manasseh
they received Golan in Bashan[m]
and also Ashtaroth, together
with their pasturelands;
[72] from the tribe of Issachar
6:72 n Jos 19:12 they received Kedesh, Daberath,[n]
[73] Ramoth and Anem, together
with their pasturelands;
6:74 o Jos 19:28 [74] from the tribe of Asher
they received Mashal, Abdon,[o]
6:75 p Jos 19:34 [75] Hukok[p] and Rehob,[q] together
q Nu 13:21 with their pasturelands;
[76] and from the tribe of Naphtali
6:76 r Jos 19:28 they received Kedesh in Galilee,
s Nu 32:37 Hammon[r] and Kiriathaim,[s] together with their pasturelands.

[77] The Merarites (the rest of the Levites) received the following:
From the tribe of Zebulun
they received Jokneam, Kartah,[c]
Rimmono and Tabor, together
with their pasturelands;
[78] from the tribe of Reuben across the
Jordan east of Jericho
they received Bezer[t] in the 6:78 t Jos 20:8
desert, Jahzah, [79] Kedemoth[u] and
Mephaath, together with their 6:79 u Dt 2:26
pasturelands;
[80] and from the tribe of Gad
they received Ramoth in Gilead,[v] 6:80 v Jos 20:8
Mahanaim,[w] [81] Heshbon and Ja- w Ge 32:2
zer,[x] together with their pasture- 6:81 x Nu 21:32
lands.[y] y 2Ch 11:14

Issachar

7 The sons of Issachar:[z] 7:1 z Ge 30:18; Nu 26:23
Tola, Puah,[a] Jashub and Shim- a Ge 46:13
ron—four in all.
[2] The sons of Tola:
Uzzi, Rephaiah, Jeriel, Jahmai, Ib-
sam and Samuel—heads of their
families. During the reign of David, the descendants of Tola listed as fighting men in their genealogy numbered 22,600.
[3] The son of Uzzi:
Izrahiah.
The sons of Izrahiah:
Michael, Obadiah, Joel and Isshiah. All five of them were chiefs.
[4] According to their family genealogy, they had 36,000 men
ready for battle, for they had
many wives and children.
[5] The relatives who were fighting
men belonging to all the clans of
Issachar, as listed in their genealogy, were 87,000 in all.

Benjamin

[6] Three sons of Benjamin:[b] 7:6 b Ge 46:21;
Bela, Beker and Jediael. Nu 26:38;
[7] The sons of Bela: 1Ch 8:1-40
Ezbon, Uzzi, Uzziel, Jerimoth
and Iri, heads of families—five in
all. Their genealogical record
listed 22,034 fighting men.
[8] The sons of Beker:
Zemirah, Joash, Eliezer, Elioenai,

[a] 60 See Joshua 21:17; Hebrew does not have *Gibeon.* [b] 67 See Joshua 21:21; Hebrew *given the cities of refuge: Shechem, Gezer.* [c] 77 See Septuagint and Joshua 21:34; Hebrew does not have *Jokneam, Kartah.*

Omri, Jeremoth, Abijah, Anathoth and Alemeth. All these
were the sons of Beker. 9 Their genealogical record listed the
heads of families and 20,200
fighting men.

10 The son of Jediael:
Bilhan.
The sons of Bilhan:
Jeush, Benjamin, Ehud, Kenaanah, Zethan, Tarshish and
Ahishahar. 11 All these sons of
Jediael were heads of families.
There were 17,200 fighting men
ready to go out to war.

12 The Shuppites and Huppites were
the descendants of Ir, and the
Hushites the descendants of
Aher.

7:13 [c] Ge 30:8; 46:24

Naphtali

13 The sons of Naphtali:[c]
Jahziel, Guni, Jezer and Shillem[a]—the descendants of Bilhah.

Manasseh

7:14 [d] Ge 41:51; Jos 17:1; 1Ch 5:23 [e] Nu 26:30

14 The descendants of Manasseh:[d]
Asriel was his descendant
through his Aramean concubine.
She gave birth to Makir the father of
Gilead.[e] 15 Makir took a wife from
among the Huppites and Shuppites.
His sister's name was Maacah.

7:15 [f] Nu 26:33; 36:1-12

Another descendant was named
Zelophehad,[f] who had only daughters.
16 Makir's wife Maacah gave birth
to a son and named him Peresh. His
brother was named Sheresh, and
his sons were Ulam and Rakem.

17 The son of Ulam:
Bedan.

7:17 [g] Nu 26:30; 1Sa 12:11

These were the sons of Gilead[g] son
of Makir, the son of Manasseh.
18 His sister Hammoleketh gave
birth to Ishhod, Abiezer[h] and
Mahlah.

7:18 [h] Jos 17:2

19 The sons of Shemida were:
Ahian, Shechem, Likhi and Aniam.

Ephraim

7:20 [i] Ge 41:52; Nu 1:33; 26:35

20 The descendants of Ephraim:[i]
Shuthelah, Bered his son,
Tahath his son, Eleadah his son,
Tahath his son, 21 Zabad his son
and Shuthelah his son.

> THE SAGES AND HEROES OF HISTORY ARE RECEDING FROM US, . . . BUT TIME HAS NO POWER OVER THE NAME AND DEEDS AND WORDS OF JESUS CHRIST.

W. E. Channing, *Unitarian Abolitionist*

Ezer and Elead were killed by the
native-born men of Gath, when
they went down to seize their livestock. 22 Their father Ephraim
mourned for them many days, and
his relatives came to comfort him.
23 Then he lay with his wife again,
and she became pregnant and gave
birth to a son. He named him Beriah,[b] because there had been misfortune in his family. 24 His daughter was Sheerah, who built Lower
and Upper Beth Horon[j] as well as 7:24 [j] Jos 10:10; 16:3,5
Uzzen Sheerah.

25 Rephah was his son, Resheph his
son,[c]
Telah his son, Tahan his son,
26 Ladan his son, Ammihud his
son,
Elishama his son, 27 Nun his son
and Joshua his son.

28 Their lands and settlements included Bethel and its surrounding villages,
Naaran to the east, Gezer[k] and its villages to the west, and Shechem and its 7:28 [k] Jos 10:33; 16:7
villages all the way to Ayyah and its villages. 29 Along the borders of Manasseh 7:29 [l] Jos 17:11 [m] Jos 11:2
were Beth Shan,[l] Taanach, Megiddo and
Dor,[m] together with their villages. The
descendants of Joseph son of Israel lived
in these towns.

Asher

7:30 [n] Ge 46:17; Nu 1:40; 26:44

30 The sons of Asher:[n]
Imnah, Ishvah, Ishvi and Beriah.
Their sister was Serah.

31 The sons of Beriah:
Heber and Malkiel, who was the
father of Birzaith.

32 Heber was the father of Japhlet,
Shomer and Hotham and of
their sister Shua.

a 13 Some Hebrew and Septuagint manuscripts (see also Gen. 46:24 and Num. 26:49); most Hebrew manuscripts *Shallum* *b* 23 *Beriah* sounds like the Hebrew for *misfortune.* *c* 25 Some Septuagint manuscripts; Hebrew does not have *his son.*

33 The sons of Japhlet:
Pasach, Bimhal and Ashvath.
These were Japhlet's sons.
34 The sons of Shomer:
Ahi, Rohgah,[a] Hubbah and Aram.
35 The sons of his brother Helem:
Zophah, Imna, Shelesh and Amal.
36 The sons of Zophah:
Suah, Harnepher, Shual, Beri,
Imrah, 37 Bezer, Hod, Shamma,
Shilshah, Ithran[b] and Beera.
38 The sons of Jether:
Jephunneh, Pispah and Ara.
39 The sons of Ulla:
Arah, Hanniel and Rizia.
40 All these were descendants of Asher—heads of families, choice men, brave warriors and outstanding leaders. The number of men ready for battle, as listed in their genealogy, was 26,000.

The Genealogy of Saul the Benjamite

8 Benjamin[o] was the father of Bela his firstborn,
Ashbel the second son, Aharah the third,
2 Nohah the fourth and Rapha the fifth.
3 The sons of Bela were:
Addar,[p] Gera, Abihud,[c] 4 Abishua,
Naaman, Ahoah,[q] 5 Gera, Shephuphan and Huram.
6 These were the descendants of Ehud,[r] who were heads of families of those living in Geba and were deported to Manahath:
7 Naaman, Ahijah, and Gera, who deported them and who was the father of Uzza and Ahihud.
8 Sons were born to Shaharaim in Moab after he had divorced his wives Hushim and Baara.
9 By his wife Hodesh he had Jobab, Zibia, Mesha, Malcam,
10 Jeuz, Sakia and Mirmah. These were his sons, heads of families.
11 By Hushim he had Abitub and Elpaal.
12 The sons of Elpaal:
Eber, Misham, Shemed (who built Ono[s] and Lod with its surrounding villages),
13 and Beriah and Shema, who were heads of families of those living in Aijalon[t] and who drove out the inhabitants of Gath.[u]
14 Ahio, Shashak, Jeremoth,
15 Zebadiah, Arad, Eder,
16 Michael, Ishpah and Joha were the sons of Beriah.
17 Zebadiah, Meshullam, Hizki, Heber,
18 Ishmerai, Izliah and Jobab were the sons of Elpaal.
19 Jakim, Zicri, Zabdi,
20 Elienai, Zillethai, Eliel,
21 Adaiah, Beraiah and Shimrath were the sons of Shimei.
22 Ishpan, Eber, Eliel,
23 Abdon, Zicri, Hanan,
24 Hananiah, Elam, Anthothijah,
25 Iphdeiah and Penuel were the sons of Shashak.
26 Shamsherai, Shehariah, Athaliah,
27 Jaareshiah, Elijah and Zicri were the sons of Jeroham.
28 All these were heads of families, chiefs as listed in their genealogy, and they lived in Jerusalem.
29 Jeiel[d] the father[e] of Gibeon lived in Gibeon.[v]
His wife's name was Maacah,
30 and his firstborn son was Abdon, followed by Zur, Kish, Baal, Ner,[f] Nadab,
31 Gedor, Ahio, Zeker
32 and Mikloth, who was the father of Shimeah. They too lived near their relatives in Jerusalem.
33 Ner[w] was the father of Kish,[x] Kish the father of Saul[y], and Saul the father of Jonathan, Malki-Shua, Abinadab and Esh-Baal.[g][z]
34 The son of Jonathan:[a]
Merib-Baal,[h][b] who was the father of Micah.
35 The sons of Micah:
Pithon, Melech, Tarea and Ahaz.
36 Ahaz was the father of Jehoaddah, Jehoaddah was the father of Alemeth, Azmaveth and Zimri, and Zimri was the father of Moza.
37 Moza was the father of Binea; Raphah was his son, Eleasah his son and Azel his son.
38 Azel had six sons, and these were their names:
Azrikam, Bokeru, Ishmael, She-

8:1 [o] Ge 46:21; 1Ch 7:6
8:3 [p] Ge 46:21
8:4 [q] 2Sa 23:9
8:6 [r] Jdg 3:12-30; 1Ch 2:52
8:12 [s] Ezr 2:33; Ne 6:2; 7:37; 11:35
8:13 [t] Jos 10:12 [u] Jos 11:22
8:29 [v] Jos 9:3
8:33 [w] 1Sa 28:19 [x] 1Sa 9:1 [y] 1Sa 14:49 [z] 2Sa 2:8
8:34 [a] 2Sa 9:12 [b] 2Sa 4:4

[a] 34 Or *of his brother Shomer: Rohgah*
[b] 37 Possibly a variant of *Jether*
[c] 3 Or *Gera the father of Ehud*
[d] 29 Some Septuagint manuscripts (see also 1 Chron. 9:35); Hebrew does not have *Jeiel.*
[e] 29 *Father* may mean *civic leader* or *military leader.*
[f] 30 Some Septuagint manuscripts (see also 1 Chron. 9:36); Hebrew does not have *Ner.*
[g] 33 Also known as *Ish-Bosheth*
[h] 34 Also known as *Mephibosheth*

ariah, Obadiah and Hanan. All these were the sons of Azel.

39 The sons of his brother Eshek:

Ulam his firstborn, Jeush the second son and Eliphelet the third. 40 The sons of Ulam were brave warriors who could handle the bow. They had many sons and grandsons—150 in all.

All these were the descendants of Benjamin.[c]

9 All Israel was listed in the genealogies recorded in the book of the kings of Israel.

The People in Jerusalem

The people of Judah were taken captive to Babylon because of their unfaithfulness.[d] 2 Now the first to resettle on their own property in their own towns[e] were some Israelites, priests, Levites and temple servants.[f]

3 Those from Judah, from Benjamin, and from Ephraim and Manasseh who lived in Jerusalem were:

4 Uthai son of Ammihud, the son of Omri, the son of Imri, the son of Bani, a descendant of Perez son of Judah.[g]

5 Of the Shilonites:

Asaiah the firstborn and his sons.

6 Of the Zerahites:

Jeuel.

The people from Judah numbered 690.

7 Of the Benjamites:

Sallu son of Meshullam, the son of Hodaviah, the son of Hassenuah;

8 Ibneiah son of Jeroham; Elah son of Uzzi, the son of Micri; and Meshullam son of Shephatiah, the son of Reuel, the son of Ibnijah.

9 The people from Benjamin, as listed in their genealogy, numbered 956. All these men were heads of their families.

10 Of the priests:

Jedaiah; Jehoiarib; Jakin;

11 Azariah son of Hilkiah, the son of Meshullam, the son of Zadok, the son of Meraioth, the son of Ahitub, the official in charge of the house of God;

12 Adaiah son of Jeroham, the son of Pashhur,[h] the son of Malkijah; and Maasai son of Adiel, the son of Jahzerah, the son of Meshullam, the son of Meshillemith, the son of Immer.

13 The priests, who were heads of families, numbered 1,760. They were able men, responsible for ministering in the house of God.

14 Of the Levites:

Shemaiah son of Hasshub, the son of Azrikam, the son of Hashabiah, a Merarite; 15 Bakbakkar, Heresh, Galal and Mattaniah[i] son of Mica, the son of Zicri, the son of Asaph; 16 Obadiah son of Shemaiah, the son of Galal, the son of Jeduthun; and Berekiah son of Asa, the son of Elkanah, who lived in the villages of the Netophathites.[j]

17 The gatekeepers:[k]

Shallum, Akkub, Talmon, Ahiman and their brothers, Shallum their chief 18 being stationed at the King's Gate[l] on the east, up to the present time. These were the gatekeepers belonging to the camp of the Levites. 19 Shallum[m] son of Kore, the son of Ebiasaph, the son of Korah, and his fellow gatekeepers from his family (the Korahites) were responsible for guarding the thresholds of the Tent[a] just as their fathers had been responsible for guarding the entrance to the dwelling of the LORD. 20 In earlier times Phinehas[n] son of Eleazar was in charge of the gatekeepers, and the LORD was with him. 21 Zechariah[o] son of Meshelemiah was the gatekeeper at the entrance to the Tent of Meeting.

22 Altogether, those chosen to be gatekeepers[p] at the thresholds numbered 212. They were registered by genealogy in their villages. The gatekeepers had been assigned to their positions of trust by David and Samuel the seer.[q] 23 They and their descendants were in charge of guarding the gates of the house of the LORD—the house called the Tent. 24 The gatekeepers were on the four sides: east, west, north and south. 25 Their brothers in their villages had to come from time to time and share their duties for seven-day[r] periods. 26 But the four principal

a 19 That is, the temple; also in verses 21 and 23

8:40 c Nu 26:38
9:1 d 1Ch 5:25
9:2 e Jos 9:27; Ezr 2:70 f Ezr 2:43,58; 8:20; Ne 7:60
9:4 g Ge 38:29; 46:12
9:12 h Ezr 2:38; 10:22; Ne 10:3; Jer 21:1; 38:1
9:15 i 2Ch 20:14; Ne 11:22
9:16 j Ne 12:28
9:17 k ver 22; 1Ch 26:1; 2Ch 8:14; 31:14; Ezr 2:42; Ne 7:45
9:18 l 1Ch 26:14; Eze 43:1; 46:1
9:19 m Jer 35:4
9:20 n Nu 25:7-13
9:21 o 1Ch 26:2,14
9:22 p ver 17; 1Ch 26:1-2; 2Ch 31:15,18 q 1Sa 9:9
9:25 r 2Ki 11:5; 2Ch 23:8

gatekeepers, who were Levites, were en-
9:26 trusted with the responsibility for the
s 1Ch 26:22 rooms and treasuries[s] in the house of
9:27 God. 27 They would spend the night sta-
t Nu 3:38; tioned around the house of God,[t] be-
1Ch 23:30-32 cause they had to guard it; and they had
u Isa 22:22 charge of the key[u] for opening it each
morning.

28 Some of them were in charge of the
articles used in the temple service; they
counted them when they were brought
in and when they were taken out. 29 Others were assigned to take care of the fur-
9:29 nishings and all the other articles of the
v Nu 3:28; sanctuary,[v] as well as the flour and wine,
1Ch 23:29 and the oil, incense and spices. 30 But
9:30 some[w] of the priests took care of mixing
w Ex 30:23-25 the spices. 31 A Levite named Mattithiah,
the firstborn son of Shallum the Korah-
ite, was entrusted with the responsibility for baking the offering bread. 32 Some
9:32 of their Kohathite brothers were in
x Lev 24:5-8; charge of preparing for every Sabbath
1Ch 23:29; the bread set out on the table.[x]
2Ch 13:11 33 Those who were musicians,[y] heads
9:33 of Levite families, stayed in the rooms of
y 1Ch 6:31; 25:1- the temple and were exempt from other
31 z Ps 134:1 duties because they were responsible for
the work day and night.[z]

34 All these were heads of Levite families, chiefs as listed in their genealogy,
and they lived in Jerusalem.

The Genealogy of Saul

9:35 a 1Ch 8:29 35 Jeiel[a] the father[a] of Gibeon lived in
Gibeon.
His wife's name was Maacah,
36 and his firstborn son was Abdon, followed by Zur, Kish, Baal,
Ner, Nadab, 37 Gedor, Ahio,
Zechariah and Mikloth. 38 Mikloth was the father of Shimeam.
They too lived near their rela-
9:39 tives in Jerusalem.
b 1Ch 8:33 39 Ner[b] was the father of Kish,[c] Kish
c 1Sa 9:1 d 1Sa 13:22 the father of Saul, and Saul the
e 2Sa 2:8 father of Jonathan,[d] Malki-Shua,
Abinadab and Esh-Baal.[b][e]
40 The son of Jonathan:
9:40 f 2Sa 4:4 Merib-Baal,[c][f] who was the father
of Micah.
41 The sons of Micah:
Pithon, Melech, Tahrea and
Ahaz.[d]
42 Ahaz was the father of Jadah, Jadah[e] was the father of Alemeth,
Azmaveth and Zimri, and Zimri
was the father of Moza. 43 Moza
was the father of Binea; Rephaiah was his son, Eleasah his son
and Azel his son.
44 Azel had six sons, and these were
their names:
Azrikam, Bokeru, Ishmael, She-
ariah, Obadiah and Hanan.
These were the sons of Azel.

Saul Takes His Life

10 Now the Philistines fought
against Israel; the Israelites fled
before them, and many fell slain on
Mount Gilboa. 2 The Philistines pressed
hard after Saul and his sons, and they
killed his sons Jonathan, Abinadab and
Malki-Shua. 3 The fighting grew fierce
around Saul, and when the archers overtook him, they wounded him.

4 Saul said to his armor-bearer, "Draw
your sword and run me through, or
these uncircumcised fellows will come
and abuse me."

But his armor-bearer was terrified
and would not do it; so Saul took his
own sword and fell on it. 5 When the armor-bearer saw that Saul was dead, he
too fell on his sword and died. 6 So Saul
and his three sons died, and all his house
died together.

7 When all the Israelites in the valley
saw that the army had fled and that Saul
and his sons had died, they abandoned
their towns and fled. And the Philistines
came and occupied them.

8 The next day, when the Philistines
came to strip the dead, they found Saul
and his sons fallen on Mount Gilboa.
9 They stripped him and took his head
and his armor, and sent messengers
throughout the land of the Philistines to
proclaim the news among their idols
and their people. 10 They put his armor
in the temple of their gods and hung up 10:10
his head in the temple of Dagon.[g] g Jdg 16:23

11 When all the inhabitants of Jabesh 10:11
Gilead[h] heard of everything the Philis- h Jdg 21:8
tines had done to Saul, 12 all their valiant
men went and took the bodies of Saul
and his sons and brought them to Ja-

[a] *35 Father* may mean *civic leader* or *military leader.* [b] *39* Also known as *Ish-Bosheth* [c] *40* Also known as *Mephibosheth* [d] *41* Vulgate and Syriac (see also Septuagint and 1 Chron. 8:35); Hebrew does not have *and Ahaz.* [e] *42* Some Hebrew manuscripts and Septuagint (see also 1 Chron. 8:36); most Hebrew manuscripts *Jarah, Jarah*

besh. Then they buried their bones under the great tree in Jabesh, and they
10:13 fasted seven days.
i 2Sa 1:1 13Saul died[i] because he was unfaith-
j 1Sa 15:23; 1Ch 5:25 ful[j] to the LORD; he did not keep[k] the
k 1Sa 13:13 word of the LORD and even consulted a
l Lev 19:31; 20:6; Dt 18:9-14; 1Sa 28:7 medium[l] for guidance, 14and did not inquire of the LORD. So the LORD put him
10:14 to death and turned[m] the kingdom[n]
m 1Ch 12:23 n 1Sa 13:14; 15:28 over to David son of Jesse.

David Becomes King Over Israel

11:1 o 1Ch 9:1 **11** All Israel[o] came together to Da-
p Ge 13:18; 23:19 vid at Hebron[p] and said, "We
are your own flesh and blood. 2In the
past, even while Saul was king, you were
11:2 the one who led Israel on their military
q 1Sa 18:5,16 campaigns.[q] And the LORD your God
r Ps 78:71; Mt 2:6 s 1Ch 5:2 said to you, 'You will shepherd[r] my people Israel, and you will become their
ruler.[s]' "
3When all the elders of Israel had
come to King David at Hebron, he made
11:3 a compact with them at Hebron before
t 1Sa 16:1-13 the LORD, and they anointed[t] David king
over Israel, as the LORD had promised
through Samuel.

David Conquers Jerusalem

4David and all the Israelites marched
11:4 u Ge 10:16; to Jerusalem (that is, Jebus). The Jebu-
15:18-21; sites[u] who lived there 5said to David,
Jos 3:10; 15:8; Jdg 1:21; 19:10 "You will not get in here." Nevertheless,
David captured the fortress of Zion, the
City of David.
6David had said, "Whoever leads the
11:6 attack on the Jebusites will become
v 2Sa 2:13; 8:16 commander-in-chief." Joab[v] son of Zeruiah went up first, and so he received
the command.
7David then took up residence in the
fortress, and so it was called the City of
David. 8He built up the city around it, 11:8
from the supporting terraces[a][w] to the w 2Sa 5:9; 2Ch 32:5
surrounding wall, while Joab restored
the rest of the city. 9And David became 11:9
more and more powerful,[x] because the x 2Sa 3:1; Est 9:4
LORD Almighty was with him.

David's Mighty Men

10These were the chiefs of David's
mighty men—they, together with all Is- 11:10
rael,[y] gave his kingship strong support y ver 1 z ver 3; 1Ch 12:23
to extend it over the whole land, as the
LORD had promised[z]— 11this is the list of 11:11
David's mighty men:[a] a 2Sa 17:10
Jashobeam,[b] a Hacmonite, was chief
of the officers[c]; he raised his spear
against three hundred men, whom he
killed in one encounter.
12Next to him was Eleazar son of Dodai the Ahohite, one of the three mighty
men. 13He was with David at Pas Dammim when the Philistines gathered
there for battle. At a place where there
was a field full of barley, the troops fled
from the Philistines. 14But they took
their stand in the middle of the field.
They defended it and struck the Philistines down, and the LORD brought about 11:14
a great victory.[b] b Ex 14:30; 1Sa 11:13
15Three of the thirty chiefs came
down to David to the rock at the cave of
Adullam, while a band of Philistines was 11:15
encamped in the Valley[c] of Rephaim. c 1Ch 14:9; Isa 17:5
16At that time David was in the strong-
hold,[d] and the Philistine garrison was at 11:16 d 2Sa 5:17
Bethlehem. 17David longed for water
and said, "Oh, that someone would get
me a drink of water from the well near
the gate of Bethlehem!" 18So the Three
broke through the Philistine lines, drew
water from the well near the gate of
Bethlehem and carried it back to David.
But he refused to drink it; instead, he 11:18
poured[e] it out before the LORD. 19"God e Dt 12:16
forbid that I should do this!" he said.
"Should I drink the blood of these men
who went at the risk of their lives?" Because they risked their lives to bring it
back, David would not drink it.

WHO IS YOUR KING?

After Saul's death David was acknowledged as Israel's king (1 Chronicles 11:3). He immediately captured Jerusalem, which had been a Jebusite city, and made it his national capital. This was the first step in the establishment of Jerusalem for a significant role in history. About a thousand years later, Jesus rode into Jerusalem astride a donkey and was hailed by some as the "Son of David" (Matthew 21:1–11), only to become the target of shouts of "Crucify him" a few days later (Mark 15:9–15). Is it any wonder that Jesus wept for Jerusalem, knowing that the city of God was about to reject its rightful King? (Luke 19:41–44).

[a] 8 Or *the Millo* [b] 11 Possibly a variant of *Jashob-Baal* [c] 11 Or *Thirty*; some Septuagint manuscripts *Three* (see also 2 Samuel 23:8)

DISCOVERY 98

SAUL AND DAVID

Saul literally lost everything because he turned away from God to do things his own way. In fact, God gave Israel's throne to David's family after Saul's death because of Saul's refusal to follow him (1 Chronicles 10:13–14).

First of all, Saul was unfaithful. He failed to destroy the Amalekites as God had directed (1 Samuel 15:1–23). Later, rather than listening to God Saul consulted a medium before going into his final battle with the Philistines (1 Samuel 28:1–25). The king sought "wisdom" for winning the battle, but God had been explicit: Anyone who claims to believe in him must do just that—trust *him* for guidance.

Another of Saul's mistakes was that he did not consult God before acting. In his early days as king Saul walked with God and listened to his words. But by the end of his life he habitually ignored God and tried to forge his own path through the situations he faced.

In Saul's case God had allowed the people to choose their own king because of their demand to be like the other nations—with a man to rule over them. David, on the other hand, was God's personal choice as king (1 Chronicles 11:2).

Unlike Saul, David prospered throughout his reign. After he was anointed king he marched into Jerusalem and conquered it. He constructed his palace there, and the city became known as the "city of David." David became "more and more powerful, because the LORD Almighty was with him" (verse 9).

The difference between Saul and David may be compared with that between Adam and Jesus. Adam listened to Satan's influence rather than to God's clear instructions, and as a direct result sin and death made their debut in the world (Genesis 3). Jesus, called the "second Adam," was God's choice to correct the damage caused by the disobedience of the first Adam (Romans 5:12–21).

Saul and David summarize for us the story of humanity: Saul reminds us of our own sin, while David points us ahead to Jesus, who lived to please the Father—which included dying for our sins to enable us to be restored to a right relationship with God. As stated by the apostle Paul, "For just as through the disobedience of the one man [Adam] the many were made sinners, so through the obedience of the one man [Jesus] the many will be made righteous" (Romans 5:19).

Self-Discovery: *In what ways do you "demand to be like the other nations" or capitulate to the culture around you? Have you made concessions for yourself that could adversely affect future generations? Or will your decision to obey Jesus bless future family members?*

GO TO DISCOVERY 99 ON PAGE 523

Such were the exploits of the three
mighty men.
11:20 [f] 1Sa 26:6 20 Abishai[f] the brother of Joab was
chief of the Three. He raised his spear
against three hundred men, whom he
killed, and so he became as famous as
the Three. 21 He was doubly honored
above the Three and became their commander, even though he was not included among them.
11:22 [g] Jos 15:21 [h] 1Sa 17:36 22 Benaiah son of Jehoiada was a
valiant fighter from Kabzeel,[g] who performed great exploits. He struck down
two of Moab's best men. He also went
down into a pit on a snowy day and
killed a lion.[h] 23 And he struck down an
Egyptian who was seven and a half feet[a]
tall. Although the Egyptian had a spear
11:23 [i] 1Sa 17:7 like a weaver's rod[i] in his hand, Benaiah
went against him with a club. He
snatched the spear from the Egyptian's
hand and killed him with his own spear.
24 Such were the exploits of Benaiah son
of Jehoiada; he too was as famous as the
three mighty men. 25 He was held in
greater honor than any of the Thirty, but
he was not included among the Three.
And David put him in charge of his
bodyguard.

26 The mighty men were:
11:26 [j] 2Sa 2:18 Asahel[j] the brother of Joab,
Elhanan son of Dodo from Bethlehem,
11:27 [k] 1Ch 27:8 27 Shammoth[k] the Harorite,
Helez the Pelonite,
28 Ira son of Ikkesh from Tekoa,
11:28 [l] 1Ch 27:12 Abiezer[l] from Anathoth,
11:29 [m] 2Sa 21:18 29 Sibbecai[m] the Hushathite,
Ilai the Ahohite,
30 Maharai the Netophathite,
Heled son of Baanah the Netophathite,
31 Ithai son of Ribai from Gibeah in Benjamin,
11:31 [n] 1Ch 27:14 [o] Jdg 12:13 Benaiah[n] the Pirathonite,[o]
32 Hurai from the ravines of Gaash,
Abiel the Arbathite,
33 Azmaveth the Baharumite,
Eliahba the Shaalbonite,
34 the sons of Hashem the Gizonite,
Jonathan son of Shagee the Hararite,
35 Ahiam son of Sacar the Hararite,
Eliphal son of Ur,
36 Hepher the Mekerathite,
Ahijah the Pelonite,
37 Hezro the Carmelite,
Naarai son of Ezbai,
38 Joel the brother of Nathan,
Mibhar son of Hagri,
39 Zelek the Ammonite,
Naharai the Berothite, the armor-bearer of Joab son of Zeruiah,
40 Ira the Ithrite,
Gareb the Ithrite,
41 Uriah[p] the Hittite, 11:41 [p] 2Sa 11:6
Zabad[q] son of Ahlai, [q] 1Ch 2:36
42 Adina son of Shiza the Reubenite, who was chief of the Reubenites, and the thirty with him,
43 Hanan son of Maacah,
Joshaphat the Mithnite,
44 Uzzia the Ashterathite,[r] 11:44 [r] Dt 1:4
Shama and Jeiel the sons of Hotham the Aroerite,
45 Jediael son of Shimri,
his brother Joha the Tizite,
46 Eliel the Mahavite,
Jeribai and Joshaviah the sons of Elnaam,
Ithmah the Moabite,
47 Eliel, Obed and Jaasiel the Mezobaite.

Warriors Join David

12 These were the men who came
to David at Ziklag,[s] while he 12:1 [s] Jos 15:31;
was banished from the presence of Saul 1Sa 27:2-6
son of Kish (they were among the warriors who helped him in battle; 2 they
were armed with bows and were able to
shoot arrows or to sling stones right-handed or left-handed;[t] they were kins- 12:2 [t] Jdg 3:15; 20:16
men of Saul[u] from the tribe of Benja- [u] 2Sa 3:19
min):

3 Ahiezer their chief and Joash the
sons of Shemaah the Gibeathite; Jeziel and Pelet the sons of Azmaveth;
Beracah, Jehu the Anathothite,
4 and Ishmaiah the Gibeonite, a
mighty man among the Thirty, who
was a leader of the Thirty; Jeremiah,
Jahaziel, Johanan, Jozabad the Ge- 12:4
derathite,[v] 5 Eluzai, Jerimoth, Beali- [v] Jos 15:36
ah, Shemariah and Shephatiah the
Haruphite; 6 Elkanah, Isshiah, Azarel, Joezer and Jashobeam the Korahites; 7 and Joelah and Zebadiah 12:7
the sons of Jeroham from Gedor.[w] [w] Jos 15:58

8 Some Gadites[x] defected to David at 12:8 [x] Ge 30:11
his stronghold in the desert. They were
brave warriors, ready for battle and able

[a] 23 Hebrew *five cubits* (about 2.3 meters)

12:8 to handle the shield and spear. Their
y 2Sa 17:10 faces were the faces of lions,[y] and they
z 2Sa 2:18 were as swift as gazelles[z] in the mountains.

[9] Ezer was the chief,
Obadiah the second in command,
Eliab the third,
[10] Mishmannah the fourth, Jeremiah the fifth,
[11] Attai the sixth, Eliel the seventh,
[12] Johanan the eighth, Elzabad the ninth,
[13] Jeremiah the tenth and Macbannai the eleventh.

[14] These Gadites were army com-
12:14 manders; the least was a match for a
a Lev 26:8 hundred,[a] and the greatest for a thou-
b Dt 32:30 sand.[b] [15] It was they who crossed the Jordan in the first month when it was over-
12:15 flowing all its banks,[c] and they put to
c Jos 3:15 flight everyone living in the valleys, to
12:16 the east and to the west.
d 2Sa 3:19 [16] Other Benjamites[d] and some men
from Judah also came to David in his
stronghold. [17] David went out to meet
them and said to them, "If you have
come to me in peace, to help me, I am
ready to have you unite with me. But if
you have come to betray me to my enemies when my hands are free from violence, may the God of our fathers see it
12:18 and judge you."
e Jdg 3:10; 6:34; [18] Then the Spirit[e] came upon Amas-
1Ch 28:12; ai,[f] chief of the Thirty, and he said:
2Ch 15:1; 20:14;
24:20 f 2Sa 17:25 "We are yours, O David!
g 1Sa 25:5-6 We are with you, O son of Jesse!
Success,[g] success to you,
and success to those who help you,
for your God will help you."

So David received them and made
them leaders of his raiding bands.
[19] Some of the men of Manasseh defected to David when he went with the
Philistines to fight against Saul. (He and
his men did not help the Philistines because, after consultation, their rulers
sent him away. They said, "It will cost us
12:19 our heads if he deserts to his master
h 1Sa 29:2-11 Saul.")[h] [20] When David went to Ziklag,[i]
12:20 these were the men of Manasseh who
i 1Sa 27:6 defected to him: Adnah, Jozabad, Jediael, Michael, Jozabad, Elihu and Zillethai,
leaders of units of a thousand in Manasseh. [21] They helped David against raiding
bands, for all of them were brave warriors, and they were commanders in his
army. [22] Day after day men came to help
David, until he had a great army, like the
army of God.[a]

Others Join David at Hebron

[23] These are the numbers of the men
armed for battle who came to David at 12:23
Hebron[j] to turn[k] Saul's kingdom over to j 2Sa 2:3-4
him, as the LORD had said:[l] k 1Ch 10:14 l 1Sa 16:1;

[24] men of Judah, carrying shield and spear—6,800 armed for battle; 1Ch 11:10
[25] men of Simeon, warriors ready for battle—7,100;
[26] men of Levi—4,600, [27] including Jehoiada, leader of the family of
Aaron, with 3,700 men, [28] and 12:28
Zadok,[m] a brave young warrior, m 2Sa 8:17;
with 22 officers from his family; 1Ch 6:8; 15:11; 16:39; 27:17
[29] men of Benjamin,[n] Saul's kins- 12:29
men—3,000, most[o] of whom n 2Sa 3:19
had remained loyal to Saul's o 2Sa 2:8-9
house until then;
[30] men of Ephraim, brave warriors, famous in their own clans—20,800;
[31] men of half the tribe of Manasseh, designated by name to come and make David king—18,000;
[32] men of Issachar, who understood the times and knew what Israel
should do[p]—200 chiefs, with all 12:32
their relatives under their command; p Est 1:13
[33] men of Zebulun, experienced soldiers prepared for battle with every type of weapon, to help David with undivided loyalty—50,000;
[34] men of Naphtali—1,000 officers, together with 37,000 men carrying shields and spears;
[35] men of Dan, ready for battle—28,600;
[36] men of Asher, experienced soldiers prepared for battle—40,000;
[37] and from east of the Jordan, men of Reuben, Gad and the half-tribe of Manasseh, armed with every type of weapon—120,000.

[38] All these were fighting men who
volunteered to serve in the ranks. They
came to Hebron fully determined to 12:38
make David king over all Israel.[q] All the q 2Sa 5:1-3;
rest of the Israelites were also of one 1Ch 9:1
mind to make David king. [39] The men
spent three days there with David, eat-

[a] 22 Or *a great and mighty army*

12:39 r2Sa 3:20; ing and drinking,[r] for their families had
Isa 25:6-8 supplied provisions for them. 40Also,
their neighbors from as far away as Issachar, Zebulun and Naphtali came bring-
12:40 ing food on donkeys, camels, mules and
s2Sa 16:1; 17:29 oxen. There were plentiful supplies[s] of
t1Sa 25:18 flour, fig cakes, raisin[t] cakes, wine, oil,
u1Ch 29:22 cattle and sheep, for there was joy[u] in Israel.

Bringing Back the Ark

13 David conferred with each of
his officers, the commanders of
thousands and commanders of hundreds. 2He then said to the whole assembly of Israel, "If it seems good to you
and if it is the will of the LORD our God,
let us send word far and wide to the rest
of our brothers throughout the territories of Israel, and also to the priests and
Levites who are with them in their
towns and pasturelands, to come and
13:3 join us. 3Let us bring the ark of our God
v1Sa 7:1-2 back to us,[v] for we did not inquire[w] of[a]
w2Ch 1:5 it[b] during the reign of Saul." 4The whole
assembly agreed to do this, because it
seemed right to all the people.
13:5 5So David assembled all the Israel-
x1Ch 11:1; 15:3 yJos 13:3 ites,[x] from the Shihor River[y] in Egypt to
zNu 13:21 Lebo[c] Hamath,[z] to bring the ark of God
a1Sa 6:21; 7:2 from Kiriath Jearim.[a] 6David and all the
13:6 Israelites with him went to Baalah[b] of
bJos 15:9; 2Sa 6:2 Judah (Kiriath Jearim) to bring up from
cEx 25:22; there the ark of God the LORD, who is en-
2Ki 19:15 throned between the cherubim[c]—the
ark that is called by the Name.
13:7 7They moved the ark of God from
dNu 4:15; Abinadab's[d] house on a new cart, with
1Sa 7:1 Uzzah and Ahio guiding it. 8David and
all the Israelites were celebrating with all
13:8 their might before God, with songs and
e2Sa 6:5; with harps, lyres, tambourines, cymbals
1Ch 15:16,19, and trumpets.[e]
24; 2Ch 5:12; Ps 92:3 9When they came to the threshing
floor of Kidon, Uzzah reached out his
hand to steady the ark, because the oxen
13:10 stumbled. 10The LORD's anger[f] burned
f1Ch 15:13,15 gLev 10:2 against Uzzah, and he struck him down[g]
because he had put his hand on the ark.
So he died there before God.
11Then David was angry because the
LORD's wrath had broken out against Uz-
13:11 zah, and to this day that place is called
h1Ch 15:13; Perez Uzzah.[d][h]
Ps 7:11 12David was afraid of God that day
and asked, "How can I ever bring the ark
of God to me?" 13He did not take the ark

to be with him in the City of David. Instead, he took it aside to the house of 13:13
Obed-Edom[i] the Gittite. 14The ark of i1Ch 15:18,24;
God remained with the family of Obed- 16:38; 26:4-5,15
Edom in his house for three months,
and the LORD blessed his household[j] and 13:14 j2Sa 6:11;
everything he had. 1Ch 26:4-5

David's House and Family

14 Now Hiram king of Tyre sent
messengers to David, along 14:1
with cedar logs,[k] stonemasons and car- k2Ch 2:3;
penters to build a palace for him. 2And Ezr 3:7
David knew that the LORD had established him as king over Israel and that 14:2
his kingdom had been highly exalted[l] lNu 24:7;
for the sake of his people Israel. Dt 26:19
3In Jerusalem David took more wives 14:3
and became the father of more sons[m] m1Ch 3:1
and daughters. 4These are the names of 14:4
the children born to him there:[n] Sham- n1Ch 3:9
mua, Shobab, Nathan, Solomon, 5Ibhar,
Elishua, Elpelet, 6Nogah, Nepheg, Japhia,
7Elishama, Beeliada[e] and Eliphelet.

David Defeats the Philistines

8When the Philistines heard that David had been anointed king over all Isra- 14:8
el,[o] they went up in full force to search o1Ch 11:1
for him, but David heard about it and
went out to meet them. 9Now the Philis- 14:9
tines had come and raided the Valley[p] of pver 13;
Rephaim; 10so David inquired of God: Jos 15:8; 1Ch 11:15
"Shall I go and attack the Philistines?
Will you hand them over to me?"
The LORD answered him, "Go, I will
hand them over to you."
11So David and his men went up to 14:11
Baal Perazim,[q] and there he defeated qIsa 28:21
them. He said, "As waters break out, God
has broken out against my enemies by
my hand." So that place was called Baal
Perazim.[f] 12The Philistines had abandoned their gods there, and David gave 14:12
orders to burn[r] them in the fire.[s] rEx 32:20
13Once more the Philistines raided sJos 7:15
the valley;[t] 14so David inquired of God 14:13
again, and God answered him, "Do not tver 9
go straight up, but circle around them
and attack them in front of the balsam
trees. 15As soon as you hear the sound of
marching in the tops of the balsam
trees, move out to battle, because that
will mean God has gone out in front of

[a] 3 Or *we neglected* [b] 3 Or *him* [c] 5 Or *to the entrance to* [d] 11 *Perez Uzzah* means *outbreak against Uzzah.* [e] 7 A variant of *Eliada*
[f] 11 *Baal Perazim* means *the lord who breaks out.*

you to strike the Philistine army." 16 So David did as God commanded him, and they struck down the Philistine army, all the way from Gibeon[u] to Gezer.[v]

17 So David's fame[w] spread throughout every land, and the LORD made all the nations fear[x] him.

14:16 [u] Jos 9:3 [v] Jos 10:33
14:17 [w] Jos 6:27; 2Ch 26:8 [x] Ex 15:14-16; Dt 2:25

The Ark Brought to Jerusalem

15 After David had constructed buildings for himself in the City of David, he prepared[y] a place for the ark of God and pitched[z] a tent for it. 2 Then David said, "No one but the Levites[a] may carry[b] the ark of God, because the LORD chose them to carry the ark of the LORD and to minister[c] before him forever."

3 David assembled all Israel[d] in Jerusalem to bring up the ark of the LORD to the place he had prepared for it. 4 He called together the descendants of Aaron and the Levites:

5 From the descendants of Kohath,
Uriel the leader and 120 relatives;
6 from the descendants of Merari,
Asaiah the leader and 220 relatives;
7 from the descendants of Gershon,[a]
Joel the leader and 130 relatives;
8 from the descendants of Elizaphan,[e]
Shemaiah the leader and 200 relatives;
9 from the descendants of Hebron,[f]
Eliel the leader and 80 relatives;
10 from the descendants of Uzziel,
Amminadab the leader and 112 relatives.

15:1 [y] Ps 132:1-18 [z] 1Ch 16:1; 17:1
15:2 [a] Nu 4:15; Dt 10:8; 2Ch 5:5 [b] Dt 31:9 [c] 1Ch 23:13
15:3 [d] 1Ki 8:1; 1Ch 13:5
15:8 [e] Ex 6:22
15:9 [f] Ex 6:18

11 Then David summoned Zadok[g] and Abiathar[h] the priests, and Uriel, Asaiah, Joel, Shemaiah, Eliel and Amminadab the Levites. 12 He said to them, "You are the heads of the Levitical families; you and your fellow Levites are to consecrate[i] yourselves and bring up the ark of the LORD, the God of Israel, to the place I have prepared for it. 13 It was because you, the Levites,[j] did not bring it up the first time that the LORD our God broke out in anger against us.[k] We did not inquire of him about how to do it in the prescribed way." 14 So the priests and Levites consecrated themselves in order to bring up the ark of the LORD, the God of Israel. 15 And the Levites carried the ark of God with the poles on their shoulders, as Moses had commanded[l] in accordance with the word of the LORD.

15:11 [g] 1Ch 12:28 [h] 1Sa 22:20
15:12 [i] Ex 19:14-15; Lev 11:44; 2Ch 35:6
15:13 [j] 1Ki 8:4 [k] 2Sa 6:3; 1Ch 13:7-10
15:15 [l] Ex 25:14; Nu 4:5,15

16 David told the leaders of the Levites to appoint their brothers as singers[m] to sing joyful songs, accompanied by musical instruments: lyres, harps and cymbals.[n]

17 So the Levites appointed Heman[o] son of Joel; from his brothers, Asaph[p] son of Berekiah; and from their brothers the Merarites,[q] Ethan son of Kushaiah; 18 and with them their brothers next in rank: Zechariah,[b] Jaaziel, Shemiramoth, Jehiel, Unni, Eliab, Benaiah, Maaseiah, Mattithiah, Eliphelehu, Mikneiah, Obed-Edom[r] and Jeiel,[c] the gatekeepers.

19 The musicians Heman,[s] Asaph and Ethan were to sound the bronze cymbals; 20 Zechariah, Aziel, Shemiramoth, Jehiel, Unni, Eliab, Maaseiah and Benaiah were to play the lyres according to *alamoth*,[d] 21 and Mattithiah, Eliphelehu, Mikneiah, Obed-Edom, Jeiel and Azaziah were to play the harps, directing according to *sheminith*.[d] 22 Kenaniah the head Levite was in charge of the singing;

15:16 [m] Ps 68:25 [n] 1Ch 13:8; 25:1; Ne 12:27,36
15:17 [o] 1Ch 6:33 [p] 1Ch 6:39 [q] 1Ch 6:44
15:18 [r] 1Ch 26:4-5
15:19 [s] 1Ch 25:6

[a] 7 Hebrew *Gershom*, a variant of *Gershon*
[b] 18 Three Hebrew manuscripts and most Septuagint manuscripts (see also verse 20 and 1 Chron. 16:5); most Hebrew manuscripts *Zechariah son and* or *Zechariah, Ben and*
[c] 18 Hebrew; Septuagint (see also verse 21) *Jeiel and Azaziah*
[d] 20,21 Probably a musical term

JESUS FOCUS

A GLORIOUS DAY

It was a momentous day when David brought the ark of the covenant to Jerusalem! The account in 1 Chronicles 15 sweeps us up in the exuberance of praise and honor. The ark of the covenant was the symbol of God's presence among his people, and the *shekinah glory* that rested on it was God's way of making himself visible to his own. The day David brought the ark to Jerusalem was the day when God's glory—his presence and power—came to the city of God for the first time.

In the New Testament, when the infant Jesus was brought to the temple by his parents, Simeon praised God and said, "My eyes have seen your salvation . . . a light for revelation to the Gentiles and for glory to your people Israel" (Luke 2:30,32). When Jesus was born, God's glory came down to humanity once again—this time in the form of a person (John 1:14), the beloved Son of God himself (Matthew 3:13–17).

that was his responsibility because he
was skillful at it.
23 Berekiah and Elkanah were to be
doorkeepers for the ark. 24 Shebaniah,
Joshaphat, Nethanel, Amasai, Zechari-
15:24 ah, Benaiah and Eliezer the priests were
[t] ver 28; to blow trumpets[t] before the ark of God.
1Ch 16:6; 2Ch 7:6 Obed-Edom and Jehiah were also to be
doorkeepers for the ark.
25 So David and the elders of Israel and
the commanders of units of a thousand
15:25 went to bring up the ark[u] of the cov-
[u] 1Ch 13:13; 2Ch 1:4 enant of the LORD from the house of
Obed-Edom, with rejoicing. 26 Because
God had helped the Levites who were
carrying the ark of the covenant of the
15:26 [v] Nu 23:1-4,29 LORD, seven bulls and seven rams[v] were
sacrificed. 27 Now David was clothed in a
robe of fine linen, as were all the Levites
who were carrying the ark, and as were
the singers, and Kenaniah, who was in
charge of the singing of the choirs. David also wore a linen ephod. 28 So all Israel brought up the ark of the covenant of
15:28 the LORD with shouts, with the sounding
[w] 1Ch 13:8 of rams' horns[w] and trumpets, and of
cymbals, and the playing of lyres and
harps.
29 As the ark of the covenant of the
LORD was entering the City of David, Michal daughter of Saul watched from a
window. And when she saw King David
dancing and celebrating, she despised
him in her heart.

16 They brought the ark of God
16:1 and set it inside the tent that
[x] 1Ch 15:1 David had pitched[x] for it, and they presented burnt offerings and fellowship
offerings[a] before God. 2 After David had
finished sacrificing the burnt offerings
16:2 and fellowship offerings, he blessed[y] the
[y] Ex 39:43 people in the name of the LORD. 3 Then
he gave a loaf of bread, a cake of dates
and a cake of raisins to each Israelite
man and woman.
16:4 4 He appointed some of the Levites to
[z] 1Ch 15:2 minister[z] before the ark of the LORD, to
make petition, to give thanks, and
to praise the LORD, the God of Israel:
5 Asaph was the chief, Zechariah second,
then Jeiel, Shemiramoth, Jehiel, Mattithiah, Eliab, Benaiah, Obed-Edom and
Jeiel. They were to play the lyres and
harps, Asaph was to sound the cymbals,
6 and Benaiah and Jahaziel the priests
were to blow the trumpets regularly before the ark of the covenant of God.

David's Psalm of Thanks

7 That day David first committed to
Asaph and his associates this psalm[a] of 16:7 [a] 2Sa 23:1
thanks to the LORD:

8 Give thanks[b] to the LORD, call on 16:8 [b] ver 34;
his name; Ps 136:1
make known among the [c] 2Ki 19:19
nations[c] what he has done.
9 Sing to him, sing praise[d] to him; 16:9 [d] Ex 15:1
tell of all his wonderful acts.
10 Glory in his holy name;
let the hearts of those who seek
the LORD rejoice.
11 Look to the LORD and his strength; 16:11 [e] 1Ch 28:9;
seek[e] his face always. 2Ch 7:14;
12 Remember[f] the wonders he has Ps 24:6; 119:2,
done, 58
his miracles,[g] and the judgments 16:12 [f] Ps 77:11
he pronounced, [g] Ps 78:43
13 O descendants of Israel his
servant,
O sons of Jacob, his chosen ones.

a 1 Traditionally *peace offerings*; also in verse 2

JESUS FOCUS

TWO TABERNACLES

For a number of years Israel apparently had *two* tabernacles: David constructed a new tent for the ark of the covenant when he moved it to Jerusalem (1 Chronicles 16:1), and in the meantime the old tabernacle—either from Moses' time or from after the destruction of Shiloh (Psalm 78:60; Jeremiah 7:12)—remained at Gibeon (1 Chronicles 16:39–40). During David's reign priests were assigned to both locations (verses 37–42), and during Solomon's reign the temple was built on Mount Moriah in Jerusalem, replacing the tabernacles (1 Kings 6). So the question arose: Where should God's people worship? This issue was a continuous point of conflict in Israel—and rival locations later included Dan, Bethel and Samaria.

In the New Testament Jesus discussed that same question with a woman from Samaria (John 4:19–26). After God the Son had come to earth the location of the temple was no longer relevant. Jesus informed the woman that "a time . . . has now come when the true worshipers will worship the Father in spirit and truth" (John 4:23). The spirit of a person's worship is more important than the location. Because Jesus died for our sins, we can have a relationship with God the Father—no matter where we are.

A Simple Expression of Thanks

As king of Israel David followed God's instructions carefully. He defeated the Philistines and brought back to Jerusalem the ark of the covenant, the sign of God's presence and power. King David built a tent for the ark (1 Chronicles 15). The arduous journey was finally over, and the long-awaited moment for God's people had arrived; the ark rested in its intended and permanent place of honor.

What David did next is so basic that it strikes us as profound: David first blessed God's people, then fed them and appointed other leaders. The blessing implies that he respected the Israelites for who they were—the people of God—and that he was reminding them to serve God. Next he cared for their most basic needs, because David was committed to individual lives. Finally the king demonstrated his support for those called by God as servants in ministry. He appointed certain people to do the things that needed to be done—just as God had instructed (1 Chronicles 15:13–16).

When David experienced the power and presence of God, he *didn't* build a temple of marble and stone. He didn't initiate a strategy of organization or unveil a well-articulated plan to change the world. Instead he did a very unpretentious thing: He directed the other leaders to pray and thank God (1 Chronicles 16:4), and then *he* expressed his thanks (verses 7–36)—nothing less and nothing more.

Jesus regularly thanked the Father, and he did just this the last time he was with his disciples before his arrest. He didn't erect a monument or unfold a plan for his followers to carry on their missionary endeavors. Instead he simply shared bread and wine and thanked God for his power and presence (Matthew 26:26–29). Even though he faced the most difficult aspect of his ministry, Jesus was able to reflect back on what the Father had done throughout his life on earth and to express his gratitude.

Every day of our life entails one leg of a unique journey with Christ. Sometimes it is a joyful journey; on other days a relentless, uphill struggle. But no matter what our circumstances, we can respond like David and Jesus, thanking Jesus for being there with us and intervening on our behalf. The apostle Paul reminds us to voice our appreciation to God in every situation (1 Thessalonians 5:18). We may not be able to thank him *for* the situation itself, but we can always acknowledge him as the One who is with us, guiding us and loving us—and as the One who is our sovereign God.

Self-Discovery: *How significant a role does daily thanksgiving play in your prayer life? Does taking the time to thank Jesus on a daily basis make a difference in how you feel about prayer?*

GO TO DISCOVERY 100 ON PAGE 526

14 He is the LORD our God;
his judgments[h] are in all the earth.

16:14 [h] Isa 26:9

15 He remembers[a] his covenant forever,
the word he commanded, for a thousand generations,
16 the covenant[i] he made with Abraham,
the oath he swore to Isaac.

16:16 [i] Ge 12:7; 15:18; 17:2; 22:16-18; 26:3; 28:13; 35:11

17 He confirmed it to Jacob[j] as a decree,
to Israel as an everlasting covenant:

16:17 [j] Ge 35:9-12

18 "To you I will give the land of Canaan[k]
as the portion you will inherit."

16:18 [k] Ge 13:14-17

19 When they were but few in number,[l]
few indeed, and strangers in it,

16:19 [l] Ge 34:30; Dt 7:7

20 they[b] wandered from nation to nation,
from one kingdom to another.
21 He allowed no man to oppress them;
for their sake he rebuked kings:[m]

16:21 [m] Ge 12:17; 20:3; Ex 7:15-18

22 "Do not touch my anointed ones;
do my prophets[n] no harm."

16:22 [n] Ge 20:7

23 Sing to the LORD, all the earth;
proclaim his salvation day after day.
24 Declare his glory among the nations,
his marvelous deeds among all peoples.
25 For great is the LORD and most worthy of praise;[o]
he is to be feared[p] above all gods.[q]

16:25 [o] Ps 48:1 [p] Ps 76:7; 89:7 [q] Dt 32:39

26 For all the gods of the nations are idols,
but the LORD made the heavens.[r]

16:26 [r] Lev 19:4; Ps 102:25

27 Splendor and majesty are before him;
strength and joy in his dwelling place.
28 Ascribe to the LORD, O families of nations,
ascribe to the LORD glory and strength,[s]

16:28 [s] Ps 29:1-2

29 ascribe to the LORD the glory due his name.
Bring an offering and come before him;
worship the LORD in the splendor of his[c] holiness.[t]

16:29 [t] Ps 29:1-2

30 Tremble[u] before him, all the earth!
The world is firmly established;
it cannot be moved.

16:30 [u] Ps 114:7

31 Let the heavens rejoice, let the earth be glad;[v]
let them say among the nations,
"The LORD reigns!"[w]

16:31 [v] Isa 44:23; 49:13 [w] Ps 93:1

32 Let the sea resound, and all that is in it;[x]
let the fields be jubilant, and everything in them!

16:32 [x] Ps 98:7

33 Then the trees[y] of the forest will sing,
they will sing for joy before the LORD,
for he comes to judge[z] the earth.

16:33 [y] Isa 55:12 [z] Ps 96:10; 98:9

34 Give thanks[a] to the LORD, for he is good;[b]
his love endures forever.[c]

16:34 [a] ver 8 [b] Na 1:7 [c] 2Ch 5:13; 7:3; Ezr 3:11; Ps 136:1-26; Jer 33:11

35 Cry out, "Save us, O God our Savior;[d]
gather us and deliver us from the nations,
that we may give thanks to your holy name,
that we may glory in your praise."

16:35 [d] Mic 7:7

36 Praise be to the LORD, the God of Israel,[e]
from everlasting to everlasting.

16:36 [e] Dt 27:15; 1Ki 8:15; Ps 72:18-19

Then all the people said "Amen" and "Praise the LORD."

37 David left Asaph and his associates
before the ark of the covenant of the
LORD to minister there regularly, according to each day's requirements.[f] 38 He
also left Obed-Edom[g] and his sixty-eight
associates to minister with them. Obed-
Edom son of Jeduthun, and also Hosah,[h]
were gatekeepers.

16:37 [f] 2Ch 8:14

16:38 [g] 1Ch 13:13 [h] 1Ch 26:10

39 David left Zadok[i] the priest and his
fellow priests before the tabernacle of
the LORD at the high place in Gibeon[j]
40 to present burnt offerings to the LORD
on the altar of burnt offering regularly,
morning and evening, in accordance
with everything written in the Law[k] of
the LORD, which he had given Israel.
41 With them were Heman[l] and Jeduthun and the rest of those chosen and
designated by name to give thanks to
the LORD, "for his love endures forever."

16:39 [i] 2Sa 8:17; 1Ch 15:11 [j] 1Ki 3:4; 2Ch 1:3

16:40 [k] Ex 29:38; Nu 28:1-8

16:41 [l] 1Ch 6:33; 25:1-6; 2Ch 5:13

[a] *15* Some Septuagint manuscripts (see also Psalm 105:8); Hebrew *Remember* [b] *18–20* One Hebrew manuscript, Septuagint and Vulgate (see also Psalm 105:12); most Hebrew manuscripts *inherit, / 19 though you are but few in number, / few indeed, and strangers in it." / 20 They* [c] *29* Or *LORD with the splendor of*

42 Heman and Jeduthun were responsible
for the sounding of the trumpets and
16:42 cymbals and for the playing of the other
m 2Ch 7:6 instruments for sacred song.[m] The sons
of Jeduthun were stationed at the gate.
43 Then all the people left, each for his
own home, and David returned home to
bless his family.

God's Promise to David

17 After David was settled in his
palace, he said to Nathan the
prophet, "Here I am, living in a palace of
17:1 cedar, while the ark of the covenant of
n 1Ch 15:1 the LORD is under a tent.[n]"
2 Nathan replied to David, "Whatever
17:2 o 2Ch 6:7 you have in mind,[o] do it, for God is with
you."
3 That night the word of God came to
Nathan, saying:
4 "Go and tell my servant David,
17:4 p 1Ch 28:3 'This is what the LORD says: You[p]
are not the one to build me a house
to dwell in. 5 I have not dwelt in a
house from the day I brought Israel
up out of Egypt to this day. I have
moved from one tent site to another, from one dwelling place to another. 6 Wherever I have moved
with all the Israelites, did I ever say
to any of their leaders[a] whom I
commanded to shepherd my people, "Why have you not built me a
house of cedar?" '
7 "Now then, tell my servant David, 'This is what the LORD Almighty
says: I took you from the pasture and
from following the flock, to be ruler[q] 17:7 q 2Sa 6:21
over my people Israel. 8 I have been
with you wherever you have gone,
and I have cut off all your enemies
from before you. Now I will make
your name like the names of the
greatest men of the earth. 9 And I will
provide a place for my people Israel
and will plant them so that they can
have a home of their own and no
longer be disturbed. Wicked people
will not oppress them anymore, as
they did at the beginning 10 and have
done ever since the time I appointed 17:10
leaders[r] over my people Israel. I will r Jdg 2:16
also subdue all your enemies.
" 'I declare to you that the LORD
will build a house for you: 11 When
your days are over and you go to be
with your fathers, I will raise up
your offspring to succeed you, one
of your own sons, and I will establish his kingdom. 12 He is the one 17:12
who will build[s] a house for me, and s 1Ki 5:5
I will establish his throne forever.[t] t 2Ch 7:18
13 I will be his father,[u] and he will be 17:13
my son.[v] I will never take my love u 2Co 6:18
away from him, as I took it away v Lk 1:32; Heb 1:5*
from your predecessor. 14 I will set
him over my house and my king- 17:14
dom forever; his throne[w] will be es- w 1Ki 2:12; 1Ch 28:5
tablished forever.[x]' " x Ps 132:11; Jer 33:17
15 Nathan reported to David all the
words of this entire revelation.

David's Prayer

16 Then King David went in and sat before the LORD, and he said:
"Who am I, O LORD God, and
what is my family, that you have
brought me this far? 17 And as if this
were not enough in your sight,
O God, you have spoken about the
future of the house of your servant.
You have looked on me as though I
were the most exalted of men,
O LORD God.
18 "What more can David say to
you for honoring your servant? For
you know your servant. 19 O LORD,
For the sake[y] of your servant and 17:19 y 2Sa 7:16-17; 2Ki 20:6; Isa 9:7; 37:35; 55:3
according to your will, you have
done this great thing and made z 2Sa 7:25
known all these great promises.[z]

TRUE HUMILITY

Despite David's success as a warrior, he was truly humble. He never forgot his modest background as a shepherd and credited his victories to God rather than to his own military prowess. Even when the prophet Nathan informed David that God wanted one of his sons to build the temple (1 Chronicles 17), the king graciously submitted to God's will—despite his lifelong dream of building a place to honor the God of Israel (1 Chronicles 22:6–10; Acts 7:46). David accepted God's will and believed his promises, including the promise to keep the royal family line safe. This promise was ultimately fulfilled in David's "son" (Matthew 1:1), Jesus, the true and eternal King of Israel (Luke 1:32–33).

[a] 6 Traditionally *judges*; also in verse 10

DISCOVERY 100

The Shepherd King

God reminded King David of his humble beginnings as a young shepherd in the hills outside Bethlehem. Speaking through the prophet Nathan, God used an interesting play on words, literally pointing out to David that he had taken him "from being in front of the sheep" (Hebrew *neged*) to being "in front of God's people" (Hebrew *nagid*) (1 Chronicles 17:7). In God's eyes there is little difference, and in fact there are obvious similarities, between being a shepherd and being a king.

For one thing both sheep and people need *guidance*. Left on their own, individual sheep tend to wander away, and the flock quickly scatters. Even today shepherds often carry an oxgoad—a sharp-pointed stick—to prod and poke the errant sheep back toward the flock. In much the same way people need a leader to help them focus and stay on track. The entire book of Judges describes the repercussions when people lack a godly leader (see Judges 21:25). A leader who stays close to God can use his Word as an oxgoad, reminding the people to stay centered and preventing the church from splintering.

Both sheep and people need *protection*. In 1 Samuel 17 David employed his shepherding experience to convince Saul that he knew how to protect those under his care: When wild animals threatened his sheep, he killed them (1 Samuel 17:34–37). This instinct to protect the flock was second nature for David, and when he became king he led the people in many battles to protect Israel from her enemies. In fact, one of David's greatest accomplishments as king was securing peace for the nation.

Furthermore, both sheep and people need to be *fed*. A shepherd pays close attention to the flock's diet. He knows when the sheep are hungry, when they are glutted from overeating, what they need to eat and when to move them on to new pastures. In the same way we need a steady diet of God's truth in order to remain spiritually healthy. And David could undoubtedly perceive when the people were in danger of spiritual entrenchment; he could sense those stagnant periods when new ideas, new "pastures," were needed to revitalize the flock.

Jesus referred to himself many times as a shepherd. "I am the good shepherd," he told us in John 10:11. In this capacity he too guides us (John 10:3–4), protects us (John 10:15) and feeds us (John 10:10). The apostle John in his "revelation of Jesus Christ" referred repeatedly to Jesus as "the Lamb" but went on to describe him also as the shepherd of those who "have washed their robes and made them white in the blood of the Lamb" (Revelation 7:14): "Never again will they hunger; never again will they thirst. The sun will not beat upon them, nor any scorching heat. For the Lamb at the center of the throne will be their shepherd; he will lead them to springs of living water. And God will wipe away every tear from their eyes" (Revelation 7:16–17).

Self-Discovery: *Is there an area in which your heart has wandered away from your Good Shepherd? Ask Jesus to empower you to move beyond this plateau into fresh, new pastures of intimacy with him.*

GO TO DISCOVERY 101 ON PAGE 539

JESUS, WHOSE NAME IS NOT
SO MUCH WRITTEN AS
PLOUGHED INTO THE HISTORY
OF THIS WORLD.

Ralph Waldo Emerson, *American Philosopher*

20"There is no one like you,
O LORD, and there is no God but
17:20 [a]Ex 8:10; 9:14; 15:11; Isa 44:6; 46:9 you,[a] as we have heard with our
own ears. 21And who is like your
people Israel—the one nation on
earth whose God went out to re-
17:21 [b]Ex 6:6 deem[b] a people for himself, and to
make a name for yourself, and to
perform great and awesome wonders by driving out nations from
before your people, whom you redeemed from Egypt? 22You made
your people Israel your very own
17:22 [c]Ex 19:5-6 forever,[c] and you, O LORD, have become their God.
23"And now, LORD, let the prom-
17:23 [d]1Ki 8:25 ise[d] you have made concerning
your servant and his house be established forever. Do as you promised, 24so that it will be established
and that your name will be great
forever. Then men will say, 'The
LORD Almighty, the God over Israel,
is Israel's God!' And the house of
your servant David will be established before you.
25"You, my God, have revealed to
your servant that you will build a
house for him. So your servant has
found courage to pray to you.
26O LORD, you are God! You have
promised these good things to your
servant. 27Now you have been
pleased to bless the house of your
17:27 [e]Ps 16:11; 21:6 servant, that it may continue forever in your sight;[e] for you, O LORD,
have blessed it, and it will be
blessed forever."

David's Victories

18 In the course of time, David defeated the Philistines and subdued them, and he took Gath and its
surrounding villages from the control of
the Philistines.
18:2 [f]Nu 21:29 2David also defeated the Moabites,[f]
and they became subject to him and
brought tribute.

3Moreover, David fought Hadadezer
king of Zobah,[g] as far as Hamath, when 18:3 [g]1Ch 19:6
he went to establish his control along [h]Ge 2:14
the Euphrates River.[h] 4David captured a
thousand of his chariots, seven thousand charioteers and twenty thousand
foot soldiers. He hamstrung[i] all but a 18:4 [i]Ge 49:6
hundred of the chariot horses.
5When the Arameans of Damascus[j] 18:5 [j]2Ki 16:9; 1Ch 19:6
came to help Hadadezer king of Zobah,
David struck down twenty-two thousand of them. 6He put garrisons in the
Aramean kingdom of Damascus, and
the Arameans became subject to him
and brought tribute. The LORD gave David victory everywhere he went.
7David took the gold shields carried
by the officers of Hadadezer and
brought them to Jerusalem. 8From
Tebah[a] and Cun, towns that belonged to
Hadadezer, David took a great quantity
of bronze, which Solomon used to make
the bronze Sea,[k] the pillars and various 18:8 [k]1Ki 7:23; 2Ch 4:12,15-16
bronze articles.
9When Tou king of Hamath heard
that David had defeated the entire army
of Hadadezer king of Zobah, 10he sent
his son Hadoram to King David to greet
him and congratulate him on his victory
in battle over Hadadezer, who had been
at war with Tou. Hadoram brought all
kinds of articles of gold and silver and
bronze.
11King David dedicated these articles
to the LORD, as he had done with the silver and gold he had taken from all these
nations: Edom[l] and Moab, the Ammon- 18:11 [l]Nu 24:18
ites and the Philistines, and Amalek.[m] [m]Nu 24:20
12Abishai son of Zeruiah struck down
eighteen thousand Edomites[n] in the 18:12 [n]1Ki 11:15
Valley of Salt. 13He put garrisons in
Edom, and all the Edomites became
subject to David. The LORD gave David
victory everywhere he went.

David's Officials

14David reigned[o] over all Israel,[p] doing 18:14 [o]1Ch 29:26
what was just and right for all his peo- [p]1Ch 11:1
ple. 15Joab[q] son of Zeruiah was over the
army; Jehoshaphat son of Ahilud was 18:15 [q]2Sa 5:6-8; 1Ch 11:6
recorder; 16Zadok[r] son of Ahitub and
Ahimelech[b][s] son of Abiathar were
priests; Shavsha was secretary; 17Bena- 18:16 [r]2Sa 8:17; 1Ch 6:8
iah son of Jehoiada was over the Kereth- [s]1Ch 24:6

[a] *8* Hebrew *Tibhath,* a variant of *Tebah*
[b] *16* Some Hebrew manuscripts, Vulgate and Syriac (see also 2 Samuel 8:17); most Hebrew manuscripts *Abimelech*

18:17 [t] 1Sa 30:14; ites and Pelethites;[t] and David's sons
2Sa 8:18; 15:18 were chief officials at the king's side.

The Battle Against the Ammonites

19:1 **19** In the course of time, Nahash
[u] Ge 19:38; king of the Ammonites[u] died,
Jdg 10:17-11:33; and his son succeeded him as king. 2Da-
2Ch 20:1-2; vid thought, "I will show kindness to Ha-
Zep 2:8-11 nun son of Nahash, because his father
showed kindness to me." So David sent
a delegation to express his sympathy to
Hanun concerning his father.

When David's men came to Hanun in
the land of the Ammonites to express
sympathy to him, 3the Ammonite nobles said to Hanun, "Do you think David
is honoring your father by sending men
to you to express sympathy? Haven't his
19:3 men come to you to explore and spy
[v] Nu 21:32 out[v] the country and overthrow it?" 4So
Hanun seized David's men, shaved
them, cut off their garments in the middle at the buttocks, and sent them away.

5When someone came and told David
about the men, he sent messengers to
meet them, for they were greatly humiliated. The king said, "Stay at Jericho till
your beards have grown, and then come
back."

6When the Ammonites realized that
19:6 [w] Ge 34:30 they had become a stench[w] in David's
[x] 1Ch 18:3,5,9 nostrils, Hanun and the Ammonites
sent a thousand talents[a] of silver to hire
chariots and charioteers from Aram Naharaim,[b] Aram Maacah and Zobah.[x]
7They hired thirty-two thousand chari-
19:7 ots and charioteers, as well as the king
[y] Nu 21:30; of Maacah with his troops, who came
Jos 13:9,16 and camped near Medeba,[y] while the
Ammonites were mustered from their
towns and moved out for battle.

8On hearing this, David sent Joab out
with the entire army of fighting men.
9The Ammonites came out and drew up
in battle formation at the entrance to
their city, while the kings who had come
were by themselves in the open country.

10Joab saw that there were battle lines
in front of him and behind him; so he selected some of the best troops in Israel
and deployed them against the Arameans. 11He put the rest of the men under
19:11 [z] 1Sa 26:6 the command of Abishai[z] his brother,
and they were deployed against the Am-
monites. 12Joab said, "If the Arameans
are too strong for me, then you are to
rescue me; but if the Ammonites are too
strong for you, then I will rescue you.
13Be strong and let us fight bravely for
our people and the cities of our God.
The LORD will do what is good in his
sight."

14Then Joab and the troops with him
advanced to fight the Arameans, and
they fled before him. 15When the Ammonites saw that the Arameans were
fleeing, they too fled before his brother
Abishai and went inside the city. So Joab
went back to Jerusalem.

16After the Arameans saw that they
had been routed by Israel, they sent
messengers and had Arameans brought
from beyond the River,[c] with Shophach
the commander of Hadadezer's army
leading them.

17When David was told of this, he 19:17
gathered all Israel[a] and crossed the Jor- [a] 1Ch 9:1
dan; he advanced against them and
formed his battle lines opposite them.
David formed his lines to meet the Arameans in battle, and they fought against
him. 18But they fled before Israel, and
David killed seven thousand of their
charioteers and forty thousand of their
foot soldiers. He also killed Shophach
the commander of their army.

19When the vassals of Hadadezer saw
that they had been defeated by Israel,
they made peace with David and became subject to him.

So the Arameans were not willing to
help the Ammonites anymore.

The Capture of Rabbah

20 In the spring, at the time when
kings go off to war, Joab led out
the armed forces. He laid waste the land 20:1
of the Ammonites and went to Rabbah[b] [b] Dt 3:11;
and besieged it, but David remained in 2Sa 12:26
Jerusalem. Joab attacked Rabbah and [c] Am 1:13-15
left it in ruins.[c] 2David took the crown
from the head of their king[d]—its weight
was found to be a talent[e] of gold, and it
was set with precious stones—and it
was placed on David's head. He took a
great quantity of plunder from the city
3and brought out the people who were
there, consigning them to labor with 20:3
saws and with iron picks and axes.[d] Da- [d] Dt 29:11
vid did this to all the Ammonite towns.

[a] *6* That is, about 37 tons (about 34 metric tons)
[b] *6* That is, Northwest Mesopotamia [c] *16* That is, the Euphrates [d] *2* Or *of Milcom,* that is, Molech [e] *2* That is, about 75 pounds (about 34 kilograms)

Then David and his entire army returned to Jerusalem.

War With the Philistines

20:4 4In the course of time, war broke out
e Jos 10:33 with the Philistines, at Gezer.[e] At that
f Ge 14:5 time Sibbecai the Hushathite killed Sip-
pai, one of the descendants of the Rephaites,[f] and the Philistines were subjugat-
ed.
5In another battle with the Philistines,
Elhanan son of Jair killed Lahmi the
20:5 brother of Goliath the Gittite, who had a
g 1Sa 17:7 spear with a shaft like a weaver's rod.[g]
6In still another battle, which took
place at Gath, there was a huge man
with six fingers on each hand and six
toes on each foot—twenty-four in all. He
also was descended from Rapha. 7When
he taunted Israel, Jonathan son of Shimea, David's brother, killed him.
8These were descendants of Rapha in
Gath, and they fell at the hands of David
and his men.

David Numbers the Fighting Men

21:1
h 2Ch 18:21; 21 Satan[h] rose up against Israel
Ps 109:6 and incited David to take a cen-
i 2Ch 14:8; 25:5 sus[i] of Israel. 2So David said to Joab and
21:2 the commanders of the troops, "Go and
j 1Ch 27:23-24 count[j] the Israelites from Beersheba to
Dan. Then report back to me so that I
may know how many there are."
21:3 3But Joab replied, "May the LORD mul-
k Dt 1:11 tiply his troops a hundred times over.[k]
My lord the king, are they not all my
lord's subjects? Why does my lord want
to do this? Why should he bring guilt on
Israel?"
4The king's word, however, overruled
Joab; so Joab left and went throughout
Israel and then came back to Jerusalem.
21:5 5Joab reported the number of the fight-
l 1Ch 9:1 ing men to David: In all Israel[l] there
were one million one hundred thousand
men who could handle a sword, including four hundred and seventy thousand
in Judah.
6But Joab did not include Levi and
Benjamin in the numbering, because
the king's command was repulsive to
him. 7This command was also evil in the
sight of God; so he punished Israel.
8Then David said to God, "I have
sinned greatly by doing this. Now, I beg
you, take away the guilt of your servant.
I have done a very foolish thing."

9The LORD said to Gad,[m] David's seer,[n] 21:9
10"Go and tell David, 'This is what the m 1Sa 22:5
LORD says: I am giving you three options. n 1Sa 9:9
Choose one of them for me to carry out
against you.'"
11So Gad went to David and said to
him, "This is what the LORD says: 'Take
your choice: 12three years of famine,[o] 21:12 o Dt 32:24
three months of being swept away[a] be- p Eze 30:25
fore your enemies, with their swords q Ge 19:13
overtaking you, or three days of the
sword[p] of the LORD[q]—days of plague in
the land, with the angel of the LORD ravaging every part of Israel.' Now then, decide how I should answer the one who
sent me."
13David said to God, "I am in deep distress. Let me fall into the hands of the 21:13
LORD, for his mercy[r] is very great; but do r Ps 6:4; 86:15;
not let me fall into the hands of men." 130:4,7
14So the LORD sent a plague on Israel,
and seventy thousand men of Israel fell 21:14
dead.[s] 15And God sent an angel[t] to de- s 1Ch 27:24
stroy Jerusalem.[u] But as the angel was 21:15
doing so, the LORD saw it and was t Ge 32:1
grieved[v] because of the calamity and u Ps 125:2 v Ge 6:6;
said to the angel who was destroying[w] Ex 32:14 w Ge 19:13
the people, "Enough! Withdraw your
hand." The angel of the LORD was then
standing at the threshing floor of Araunah[b] the Jebusite.
16David looked up and saw the angel
of the LORD standing between heaven
and earth, with a drawn sword in his
hand extended over Jerusalem. Then
David and the elders, clothed in sack- 21:16
cloth, fell facedown.[x] x Nu 14:5; Jos 7:6
17David said to God, "Was it not I who
ordered the fighting men to be counted?
I am the one who has sinned and done 21:17
wrong. These are but sheep.[y] What have y 2Sa 7:8; Ps 74:1
they done? O LORD my God, let your z Jnh 1:12
hand fall upon me and my family,[z] but
do not let this plague remain on your
people."
18Then the angel of the LORD ordered
Gad to tell David to go up and build an 21:18
altar to the LORD on the threshing floor[a] a 2Ch 3:1
of Araunah the Jebusite. 19So David went
up in obedience to the word that Gad
had spoken in the name of the LORD.
20While Araunah was threshing
wheat,[b] he turned and saw the angel; his 21:20
four sons who were with him hid them- b Jdg 6:11

[a] *12* Hebrew; Septuagint and Vulgate (see also 2 Samuel 24:13) *of fleeing* [b] *15* Hebrew *Ornan,* a variant of *Araunah;* also in verses 18–28

selves. 21Then David approached, and
when Araunah looked and saw him, he
left the threshing floor and bowed down
before David with his face to the ground.
22David said to him, "Let me have the
site of your threshing floor so I can build
an altar to the LORD, that the plague on
the people may be stopped. Sell it to me
at the full price."
23Araunah said to David, "Take it! Let
my lord the king do whatever pleases
him. Look, I will give the oxen for the
burnt offerings, the threshing sledges for
the wood, and the wheat for the grain
offering. I will give all this."
24But King David replied to Araunah,
"No, I insist on paying the full price. I
will not take for the LORD what is yours,
or sacrifice a burnt offering that costs
me nothing."
25So David paid Araunah six hundred
shekels[a] of gold for the site. 26David built
an altar to the LORD there and sacrificed
burnt offerings and fellowship offer-
21:26 ings.[b] He called on the LORD, and the
[c] Lev 9:24; LORD answered him with fire[c] from
Jdg 6:21 heaven on the altar of burnt offering.
27Then the LORD spoke to the angel,
and he put his sword back into its
sheath. 28At that time, when David saw
that the LORD had answered him on the
threshing floor of Araunah the Jebusite,
he offered sacrifices there. 29The tabernacle of the LORD, which Moses had
made in the desert, and the altar of
21:29 burnt offering were at that time on the
[d] 1Ki 3:4; high place at Gibeon.[d] 30But David could
1Ch 16:39 not go before it to inquire of God, because he was afraid of the sword of the
angel of the LORD.

22:1 22 Then David said, "The house of
[e] Ge 28:17; the LORD God[e] is to be here, and
1Ch 21:18-29; 2Ch 3:1 also the altar of burnt offering for Israel."

Preparations for the Temple

2So David gave orders to assemble the
22:2 [f] 1Ki 9:21; aliens[f] living in Israel, and from among
Isa 56:6 them he appointed stonecutters[g] to pre-
[g] 1Ki 5:17-18 pare dressed stone for building the
house of God. 3He provided a large
amount of iron to make nails for the
doors of the gateways and for the fit-
22:3 tings, and more bronze than could be
[h] ver 14; weighed.[h] 4He also provided more cedar
1Ki 7:47; logs[i] than could be counted, for the
1Ch 29:2-5 Sidonians and Tyrians had brought large
22:4 [i] 1Ki 5:6 numbers of them to David.

5David said, "My son Solomon is **22:5**
young[j] and inexperienced, and the [j] 1Ki 3:7;
house to be built for the LORD should be 1Ch 29:1
of great magnificence and fame and
splendor in the sight of all the nations.
Therefore I will make preparations for
it." So David made extensive preparations before his death.
6Then he called for his son Solomon **22:6**
and charged him to build[k] a house for [k] Ac 7:47
the LORD, the God of Israel. 7David said to
Solomon: "My son, I had it in my heart[l] **22:7** [l] 1Ch 17:2
to build[m] a house for the Name[n] of the [m] 2Sa 7:2;
LORD my God. 8But this word of the LORD 1Ki 8:17 [n] Dt 12:5,11
came to me: 'You have shed much blood
and have fought many wars.[o] You are not **22:8** [o] 1Ki 5:3
to build a house for my Name,[p] because [p] 1Ch 28:3
you have shed much blood on the earth
in my sight. 9But you will have a son who **22:9**
will be a man of peace[q] and rest, and I [q] 1Ki 5:4
will give him rest from all his enemies on [r] 2Sa 12:24
every side. His name will be Solomon,[c][r] [s] 1Ki 4:20
and I will grant Israel peace and quiet[s]
during his reign. 10He is the one who will **22:10**
build a house for my Name.[t] He will be [t] 1Ch 17:12
my son,[u] and I will be his father. And I [u] 2Sa 7:13
will establish the throne of his kingdom [v] 2Sa 7:14;
over Israel forever.'[v] 2Ch 6:15
11"Now, my son, the LORD be with[w] **22:11** [w] ver 16
you, and may you have success and
build the house of the LORD your God, as
he said you would. 12May the LORD give **22:12**
you discretion and understanding[x] [x] 1Ki 3:9-12;
when he puts you in command over Is- 2Ch 1:10
rael, so that you may keep the law of the
LORD your God. 13Then you will have
success if you are careful to observe the **22:13** [y] 1Ch 28:7
decrees and laws[y] that the LORD gave [z] Dt 31:6;
Moses for Israel. Be strong and coura- Jos 1:6-9;
geous.[z] Do not be afraid or discouraged. 1Ch 28:20
14"I have taken great pains to provide
for the temple of the LORD a hundred
thousand talents[d] of gold, a million talents[e] of silver, quantities of bronze and
iron too great to be weighed, and wood **22:14**
and stone. And you may add to them.[a] [a] ver 3;
15You have many workmen: stonecut- 1Ch 29:2-5,19
ters, masons and carpenters, as well as
men skilled in every kind of work 16in
gold and silver, bronze and iron—crafts- **22:16**
men[b] beyond number. Now begin the [b] ver 11; 2Ch 2:7
work, and the LORD be with you."

[a] *25* That is, about 15 pounds (about 7 kilograms)
[b] *26* Traditionally *peace offerings* [c] *9* *Solomon* sounds like and may be derived from the Hebrew for *peace.* [d] *14* That is, about 3,750 tons (about 3,450 metric tons) [e] *14* That is, about 37,500 tons (about 34,500 metric tons)

22:17 [c] 1Ch 28:1-6
17 Then David ordered[c] all the leaders
of Israel to help his son Solomon. 18 He
said to them, "Is not the LORD your God
22:18 [d] ver 9; 1Ch 23:25 [e] 2Sa 7:1
with you? And has he not granted you
rest[d] on every side?[e] For he has handed
the inhabitants of the land over to me,
and the land is subject to the LORD and
22:19 [f] ver 7; 1Ki 8:6; 1Ch 28:9; 2Ch 5:7; 7:14
to his people. 19 Now devote your heart
and soul to seeking the LORD your God.[f]
Begin to build the sanctuary of the LORD
God, so that you may bring the ark of
the covenant of the LORD and the sacred
articles belonging to God into the temple
that will be built for the Name of the
LORD."

The Levites

23:1 [g] 1Ki 1:33-39; 1Ch 28:5 [h] 1Ki 1:30; 1Ch 29:28
23 When David was old and full of
years, he made his son Solomon[g]
king over Israel.[h]
2 He also gathered together all the
leaders of Israel, as well as the priests
23:3 [i] ver 24; Nu 8:24 [j] Nu 4:3-49
and Levites. 3 The Levites thirty years old
or more[i] were counted, and the total
number of men was thirty-eight thousand.[j]
23:4 [k] Ezr 3:8 [l] 1Ch 26:29; 2Ch 19:8
4 David said, "Of these, twenty-four
thousand are to supervise[k] the
work of the temple of the LORD and six
thousand are to be officials and judges.[l]
5 Four thousand are to be gatekeepers
23:5 [m] 1Ch 15:16 [n] Ne 12:45
and four thousand are to praise the
LORD with the musical instruments[m] I
have provided for that purpose."[n]
23:6 [o] 2Ch 8:14; 29:25
6 David divided[o] the Levites into
groups corresponding to the sons of
Levi: Gershon, Kohath and Merari.

Gershonites

7 Belonging to the Gershonites:
Ladan and Shimei.
8 The sons of Ladan:
Jehiel the first, Zetham and
Joel—three in all.
9 The sons of Shimei:
Shelomoth, Haziel and Haran—
three in all.
These were the heads of the families
of Ladan.
10 And the sons of Shimei:
Jahath, Ziza,[a] Jeush and Beriah.
These were the sons of Shimei—
four in all.
11 Jahath was the first and Ziza the
second, but Jeush and Beriah did
not have many sons; so they
were counted as one family with
one assignment.

Kohathites

12 The sons of Kohath:[p] 23:12 [p] Ex 6:18
Amram, Izhar, Hebron and Uzziel—four in all.
13 The sons of Amram:[q] 23:13 [q] Ex 6:20; 28:1 [r] Ex 30:7-10; Dt 21:5 [s] Nu 6:23
Aaron and Moses.
Aaron was set apart,[r] he and his
descendants forever, to consecrate
the most holy things, to offer
sacrifices before the LORD, to
minister before him and to pronounce
blessings[s] in his name
forever. 14 The sons of Moses the
man[t] of God were counted as 23:14 [t] Dt 33:1
part of the tribe of Levi.
15 The sons of Moses:
Gershom and Eliezer.[u] 23:15 [u] Ex 18:4
16 The descendants of Gershom:[v] 23:16 [v] 1Ch 26:24-28
Shubael was the first.
17 The descendants of Eliezer:
Rehabiah was the first.
Eliezer had no other sons, but
the sons of Rehabiah were very
numerous.
18 The sons of Izhar:
Shelomith was the first.
19 The sons of Hebron:[w] 23:19 [w] 1Ch 24:23
Jeriah the first, Amariah the second,
Jahaziel the third and Jekameam
the fourth.
20 The sons of Uzziel:
Micah the first and Isshiah the
second.

Merarites

21 The sons of Merari:[x] 23:21 [x] 1Ch 24:26
Mahli and Mushi.
The sons of Mahli:
Eleazar and Kish.
22 Eleazar died without having
sons: he had only daughters.
Their cousins, the sons of Kish,
married them.
23 The sons of Mushi:
Mahli, Eder and Jerimoth—
three in all.

24 These were the descendants of Levi
by their families—the heads of families
as they were registered under their
names and counted individually, that is,
the workers twenty years old or more[y] 23:24 [y] Nu 4:3; 10:17, 21
who served in the temple of the LORD.
25 For David had said, "Since the LORD,
the God of Israel, has granted rest[z] to his 23:25 [z] 1Ch 22:9

[a] *10* One Hebrew manuscript, Septuagint and Vulgate (see also verse 11); most Hebrew manuscripts *Zina*

people and has come to dwell in Jerusalem forever, 26 the Levites no longer need to carry the tabernacle or any of the articles used in its service."[a] 27 According to the last instructions of David, the Levites were counted from those twenty years old or more.

28 The duty of the Levites was to help Aaron's descendants in the service of the temple of the LORD: to be in charge of the courtyards, the side rooms, the purification[b] of all sacred things and the performance of other duties at the house of God. 29 They were in charge of the bread set out on the table,[c] the flour for the grain offerings,[d] the unleavened wafers, the baking and the mixing, and all measurements of quantity and size.[e] 30 They were also to stand every morning to thank and praise the LORD. They were to do the same in the evening[f] 31 and whenever burnt offerings were presented to the LORD on Sabbaths and at New Moon[g] festivals and at appointed feasts.[h] They were to serve before the LORD regularly in the proper number and in the way prescribed for them.

32 And so the Levites[i] carried out their responsibilities for the Tent of Meeting,[j] for the Holy Place and, under their brothers the descendants of Aaron, for the service of the temple of the LORD.[k]

The Divisions of Priests

24 These were the divisions[l] of the sons of Aaron:[m]

The sons of Aaron were Nadab, Abihu, Eleazar and Ithamar.[n] 2 But Nadab and Abihu died before their father did,[o] and they had no sons; so Eleazar and Ithamar served as the priests. 3 With the help of Zadok[p] a descendant of Eleazar and Ahimelech a descendant of Ithamar, David separated them into divisions for their appointed order of ministering. 4 A larger number of leaders were found among Eleazar's descendants than among Ithamar's, and they were divided accordingly: sixteen heads of families from Eleazar's descendants and eight heads of families from Ithamar's descendants. 5 They divided them impartially by drawing lots,[q] for there were officials of the sanctuary and officials of God among the descendants of both Eleazar and Ithamar.

6 The scribe Shemaiah son of Nethanel, a Levite, recorded their names in the presence of the king and of the officials: Zadok the priest, Ahimelech[r] son of Abiathar and the heads of families of the priests and of the Levites—one family being taken from Eleazar and then one from Ithamar.

7 The first lot fell to Jehoiarib,
the second to Jedaiah,[s]
8 the third to Harim,[t]
the fourth to Seorim,
9 the fifth to Malkijah,
the sixth to Mijamin,
10 the seventh to Hakkoz,
the eighth to Abijah,[u]
11 the ninth to Jeshua,
the tenth to Shecaniah,
12 the eleventh to Eliashib,
the twelfth to Jakim,
13 the thirteenth to Huppah,
the fourteenth to Jeshebeab,
14 the fifteenth to Bilgah,
the sixteenth to Immer,[v]
15 the seventeenth to Hezir,[w]
the eighteenth to Happizzez,
16 the nineteenth to Pethahiah,
the twentieth to Jehezkel,
17 the twenty-first to Jakin,
the twenty-second to Gamul,
18 the twenty-third to Delaiah
and the twenty-fourth to Maaziah.

19 This was their appointed order of ministering when they entered the temple of the LORD, according to the regulations prescribed for them by their forefather Aaron, as the LORD, the God of Israel, had commanded him.

The Rest of the Levites

20 As for the rest of the descendants of Levi:[x]

from the sons of Amram: Shubael;
from the sons of Shubael: Jehdeiah.
21 As for Rehabiah,[y] from his sons:
Isshiah was the first.
22 From the Izharites: Shelomoth;
from the sons of Shelomoth: Jahath.
23 The sons of Hebron:[z] Jeriah the first,[a] Amariah the second, Jahaziel the third and Jekameam the fourth.

[a] 23 Two Hebrew manuscripts and some Septuagint manuscripts (see also 1 Chron. 23:19); most Hebrew manuscripts *The sons of Jeriah:*

23:26 [a] Nu 4:5,15; 7:9; Dt 10:8
23:28 [b] 2Ch 29:15; Ne 13:9; Mal 3:3
23:29 [c] Ex 25:30 [d] Lev 2:4-7; 6:20-23 [e] Lev 19:35-36; 1Ch 9:29,32
23:30 [f] 1Ch 9:33; Ps 134:1
23:31 [g] 2Ki 4:23 [h] Lev 23:4; Nu 28:9-29:39; Isa 1:13-14; Col 2:16
23:32 [i] Nu 1:53; 1Ch 6:48 [j] Nu 3:6-8,38 [k] 2Ch 23:18; 31:2; Eze 44:14
24:1 [l] 1Ch 23:6; 28:13; 2Ch 5:11; 8:14; 23:8; 31:2; 35:4,5; Ezr 6:18 [m] Nu 3:2-4 [n] Ex 6:23
24:2 [o] Lev 10:1-2; Nu 3:4
24:3 [p] 2Sa 8:17
24:5 [q] ver 31; 1Ch 25:8
24:6 [r] 1Ch 18:16
24:7 [s] Ezr 2:36; Ne 12:6
24:8 [t] Ezr 2:39; Ne 10:5
24:10 [u] Ne 12:4,17; Lk 1:5
24:14 [v] Jer 20:1
24:15 [w] Ne 10:20
24:20 [x] 1Ch 23:6
24:21 [y] 1Ch 23:17
24:23 [z] 1Ch 23:19

[24] The son of Uzziel: Micah;
from the sons of Micah: Shamir.
[25] The brother of Micah: Isshiah;
from the sons of Isshiah: Zechariah.

24:26 [a] 1Ch 6:19; 23:21

[26] The sons of Merari:[a] Mahli and Mushi.
The son of Jaaziah: Beno.
[27] The sons of Merari:
from Jaaziah: Beno, Shoham, Zaccur and Ibri.
[28] From Mahli: Eleazar, who had no sons.
[29] From Kish: the son of Kish:
Jerahmeel.
[30] And the sons of Mushi: Mahli, Eder and Jerimoth.

24:31 [b] ver 5

These were the Levites, according to their families. [31] They also cast lots,[b] just as their brothers the descendants of Aaron did, in the presence of King David and of Zadok, Ahimelech, and the heads of families of the priests and of the Levites. The families of the oldest brother were treated the same as those of the youngest.

The Singers

25:1 [c] 1Ch 6:39 [d] 1Ch 6:33 [e] 1Ch 16:41,42; Ne 11:17 [f] 1Sa 10:5; 2Ki 3:15 [g] 1Ch 15:16 [h] 1Ch 6:31 [i] 2Ch 5:12; 8:14; 34:12; 35:15; Ezr 3:10

25 David, together with the commanders of the army, set apart some of the sons of Asaph,[c] Heman[d] and Jeduthun[e] for the ministry of prophesying,[f] accompanied by harps, lyres and cymbals.[g] Here is the list of the men[h] who performed this service:[i]

[2] From the sons of Asaph:
Zaccur, Joseph, Nethaniah and Asarelah. The sons of Asaph were under the supervision of Asaph, who prophesied under the king's supervision.

25:3 [j] 1Ch 16:41-42 [k] Ge 4:21; Ps 33:2

[3] As for Jeduthun, from his sons:[j]
Gedaliah, Zeri, Jeshaiah, Shimei,[a] Hashabiah and Mattithiah, six in all, under the supervision of their father Jeduthun, who prophesied, using the harp[k] in thanking and praising the LORD.
[4] As for Heman, from his sons:
Bukkiah, Mattaniah, Uzziel, Shubael and Jerimoth; Hananiah, Hanani, Eliathah, Giddalti and Romamti-Ezer; Joshbekashah, Mallothi, Hothir and Mahazioth. [5] All these were sons of Heman the king's seer. They were given him through the promises of God to exalt him.[b] God gave Heman fourteen sons and three daughters.

25:6 [l] 1Ch 15:16 [m] 1Ch 15:19 [n] 2Ch 23:18; 29:25

[6] All these men were under the supervision of their fathers[l] for the music of the temple of the LORD, with cymbals, lyres and harps, for the ministry at the house of God. Asaph, Jeduthun and Heman[m] were under the supervision of the king.[n] [7] Along with their relatives—all of them trained and skilled in music for the LORD—they numbered 288. [8] Young and old alike, teacher as well as student, cast lots[o] for their duties.

25:8 [o] 1Ch 26:13

25:9 [p] 1Ch 6:39

[9] The first lot, which was for Asaph,[p] fell to Joseph,
his sons and relatives,[c] 12[d]
the second to Gedaliah,
he and his relatives and sons, 12
[10] the third to Zaccur,
his sons and relatives, 12
[11] the fourth to Izri,[e]
his sons and relatives, 12
[12] the fifth to Nethaniah,
his sons and relatives, 12
[13] the sixth to Bukkiah,
his sons and relatives, 12
[14] the seventh to Jesarelah,[f]
his sons and relatives, 12
[15] the eighth to Jeshaiah,
his sons and relatives, 12
[16] the ninth to Mattaniah,
his sons and relatives, 12
[17] the tenth to Shimei,
his sons and relatives, 12
[18] the eleventh to Azarel,[g]
his sons and relatives, 12
[19] the twelfth to Hashabiah,
his sons and relatives, 12
[20] the thirteenth to Shubael,
his sons and relatives, 12
[21] the fourteenth to Mattithiah,
his sons and relatives, 12
[22] the fifteenth to Jerimoth,
his sons and relatives, 12
[23] the sixteenth to Hananiah,
his sons and relatives, 12
[24] the seventeenth to Joshbekashah,

[a] 3 One Hebrew manuscript and some Septuagint manuscripts (see also verse 17); most Hebrew manuscripts do not have *Shimei.* [b] 5 Hebrew *exalt the horn* [c] 9 See Septuagint; Hebrew does not have *his sons and relatives.* [d] 9 See the total in verse 7; Hebrew does not have *twelve.* [e] 11 A variant of *Zeri* [f] 14 A variant of *Asarelah* [g] 18 A variant of *Uzziel*

his sons and relatives, 12
25 the eighteenth to Hanani,
his sons and relatives, 12
26 the nineteenth to Mallothi,
his sons and relatives, 12
27 the twentieth to Eliathah,
his sons and relatives, 12
28 the twenty-first to Hothir,
his sons and relatives, 12
29 the twenty-second to Giddalti,
his sons and relatives, 12
30 the twenty-third to Mahazioth,
his sons and relatives, 12
31 the twenty-fourth to Romamti-
Ezer,
his sons and relatives, 12[q]

25:31 q 1Ch 9:33

The Gatekeepers

26 The divisions of the gatekeepers:[r]

26:1 r 1Ch 9:17

From the Korahites: Meshelemiah
son of Kore, one of the sons of
Asaph.
2 Meshelemiah had sons:
Zechariah[s] the firstborn,
Jediael the second,
Zebadiah the third,
Jathniel the fourth,
3 Elam the fifth,
Jehohanan the sixth
and Eliehoenai the seventh.

26:2 s 1Ch 9:21

4 Obed-Edom also had sons:
Shemaiah the firstborn,
Jehozabad the second,
Joah the third,
Sacar the fourth,
Nethanel the fifth,
5 Ammiel the sixth,
Issachar the seventh
and Peullethai the eighth.
(For God had blessed Obed-
Edom.[t])

26:5 t 2Sa 6:10; 1Ch 13:13; 16:38

6 His son Shemaiah also had sons,
who were leaders in their father's
family because they were very
capable men. 7 The sons of Shemaiah: Othni, Rephael, Obed
and Elzabad; his relatives Elihu
and Semakiah were also able
men. 8 All these were descendants of Obed-Edom; they and
their sons and their relatives
were capable men with the
strength to do the work—descendants of Obed-Edom, 62 in
all.
9 Meshelemiah had sons and relatives, who were able men—18 in
all.
10 Hosah the Merarite had sons:
Shimri the first (although he was
not the firstborn, his father had
appointed him the first),[u] 11 Hilkiah the second, Tabaliah the
third and Zechariah the fourth.
The sons and relatives of Hosah
were 13 in all.

26:10 u Dt 21:16; 1Ch 5:1

12 These divisions of the gatekeepers,
through their chief men, had duties for
ministering[v] in the temple of the LORD,
just as their relatives had. 13 Lots[w] were
cast for each gate, according to their
families, young and old alike.
14 The lot for the East Gate[x] fell to
Shelemiah.[a] Then lots were cast for his
son Zechariah,[y] a wise counselor, and
the lot for the North Gate fell to him.
15 The lot for the South Gate fell to Obed-
Edom,[z] and the lot for the storehouse
fell to his sons. 16 The lots for the West
Gate and the Shalleketh Gate on the upper road fell to Shuppim and Hosah.
Guard was alongside of guard: 17 There
were six Levites a day on the east, four a
day on the north, four a day on the south
and two at a time at the storehouse. 18 As
for the court to the west, there were four
at the road and two at the court itself.
19 These were the divisions of the
gatekeepers who were descendants of
Korah and Merari.[a]

26:12 v 1Ch 9:22
26:13 w 1Ch 24:5,31; 25:8
26:14 x 1Ch 9:18 y 1Ch 9:21
26:15 z 1Ch 13:13; 2Ch 25:24
26:19 a 2Ch 35:15; Ne 7:1; Eze 44:11

The Treasurers and Other Officials

20 Their fellow Levites[b] were[b] in
charge of the treasuries of the house of
God and the treasuries for the dedicated things.[c]
21 The descendants of Ladan, who
were Gershonites through Ladan and
who were heads of families belonging to
Ladan the Gershonite,[d] were Jehieli,
22 the sons of Jehieli, Zetham and his
brother Joel. They were in charge of the
treasuries[e] of the temple of the LORD.
23 From the Amramites, the Izharites,
the Hebronites and the Uzzielites:[f]

26:20 b 2Ch 24:5 c 1Ch 28:12
26:21 d 1Ch 23:7; 29:8
26:22 e 1Ch 9:26
26:23 f Nu 3:27

24 Shubael,[g] a descendant of Gershom
son of Moses, was the officer in
charge of the treasuries. 25 His

26:24 g 1Ch 23:16

[a] 14 A variant of *Meshelemiah* [b] 20 Septuagint; Hebrew *As for the Levites, Ahijah was*

relatives through Eliezer: Rehabiah his son, Jeshaiah his son, Jo-
26:25 ram his son, Zicri his son and
h 1Ch 23:18 Shelomith[h] his son. 26 Shelomith
and his relatives were in charge
26:26 of all the treasures for the things
i 2Sa 8:11 dedicated[i] by King David, by the
heads of families who were the
commanders of thousands and
commanders of hundreds, and
by the other army commanders.
27 Some of the plunder taken in
battle they dedicated for the repair of the temple of the LORD.
26:28 28 And everything dedicated by
j 1Sa 9:9 Samuel the seer[j] and by Saul son
of Kish, Abner son of Ner and
Joab son of Zeruiah, and all the
other dedicated things were in
the care of Shelomith and his relatives.
29 From the Izharites: Kenaniah and
his sons were assigned duties
26:29 away from the temple, as offi-
k Dt 17:8-13; 1Ch 23:4; cials and judges[k] over Israel.
Ne 11:16 30 From the Hebronites: Hashabiah[l]
26:30 and his relatives—seventeen
l 1Ch 27:17 hundred able men—were responsible in Israel west of the
Jordan for all the work of the
26:31 LORD and for the king's service.
m 1Ch 23:19 31 As for the Hebronites,[m] Jeriah
n 2Sa 5:4 was their chief according to the
genealogical records of their
families. In the fortieth[n] year of
David's reign a search was made
in the records, and capable men
among the Hebronites were
found at Jazer in Gilead. 32 Jeriah
had twenty-seven hundred relatives, who were able men and
heads of families, and King David put them in charge of the
Reubenites, the Gadites and the
half-tribe of Manasseh for every
matter pertaining to God and
for the affairs of the king.

Army Divisions

27 This is the list of the Israelites—heads of families, commanders of thousands and commanders of hundreds, and their officers, who
served the king in all that concerned the
army divisions that were on duty month
by month throughout the year. Each division consisted of 24,000 men.

2 In charge of the first division, for the
first month, was Jashobeam[o] son of 27:2 o 2Sa 23:8;
Zabdiel. There were 24,000 men in 1Ch 11:11
his division. 3 He was a descendant
of Perez and chief of all the army
officers for the first month.
4 In charge of the division for the second month was Dodai[p] the Aho- 27:4 p 2Sa 23:9
hite; Mikloth was the leader of his
division. There were 24,000 men in
his division.
5 The third army commander, for the 27:5
third month, was Benaiah[q] son of q 2Sa 23:20
Jehoiada the priest. He was chief
and there were 24,000 men in his
division. 6 This was the Benaiah
who was a mighty man among the
Thirty and was over the Thirty. His
son Ammizabad was in charge of
his division.
7 The fourth, for the fourth month, was
Asahel[r] the brother of Joab; his son 27:7 r 2Sa 2:18;
Zebadiah was his successor. There 1Ch 11:26
were 24,000 men in his division.
8 The fifth, for the fifth month, was the
commander Shamhuth[s] the Izra- 27:8 s 1Ch 11:27
hite. There were 24,000 men in his
division.
9 The sixth, for the sixth month, was
Ira[t] the son of Ikkesh the Tekoite. 27:9 t 2Sa 23:26;
There were 24,000 men in his divi- 1Ch 11:28
sion.
10 The seventh, for the seventh month,
was Helez[u] the Pelonite, an 27:10 u 2Sa 23:26;
Ephraimite. There were 24,000 men 1Ch 11:27
in his division.
11 The eighth, for the eighth month, was
Sibbecai[v] the Hushathite, a Zera- 27:11 v 2Sa 21:18
hite. There were 24,000 men in his
division.
12 The ninth, for the ninth month, was
Abiezer[w] the Anathothite, a Ben- 27:12 w 2Sa 23:27;
jamite. There were 24,000 men in 1Ch 11:28
his division.
13 The tenth, for the tenth month, was
Maharai[x] the Netophathite, a Zera- 27:13 x 2Sa 23:28;
hite. There were 24,000 men in his 1Ch 11:30
division.
14 The eleventh, for the eleventh month,
was Benaiah[y] the Pirathonite, an 27:14 y 1Ch 11:31
Ephraimite. There were 24,000 men
in his division.
15 The twelfth, for the twelfth month, 27:15
was Heldai[z] the Netophathite, from z 2Sa 23:29
the family of Othniel.[a] There were a Jos 15:17
24,000 men in his division.

Officers of the Tribes

16 The officers over the tribes of Israel:

over the Reubenites: Eliezer son of Zicri;

over the Simeonites: Shephatiah son of Maacah;

27:17 [b] 1Ch 26:30 [c] 2Sa 8:17; 1Ch 12:28

17 over Levi: Hashabiah[b] son of Kemuel;

over Aaron: Zadok;[c]

18 over Judah: Elihu, a brother of David;

over Issachar: Omri son of Michael;

19 over Zebulun: Ishmaiah son of Obadiah;

over Naphtali: Jerimoth son of Azriel;

20 over the Ephraimites: Hoshea son of Azaziah;

over half the tribe of Manasseh: Joel son of Pedaiah;

21 over the half-tribe of Manasseh in Gilead: Iddo son of Zechariah;

over Benjamin: Jaasiel son of Abner;

22 over Dan: Azarel son of Jeroham.

These were the officers over the tribes of Israel.

27:23 [d] 1Ch 21:2-5 [e] Ge 15:5

23 David did not take the number of the men twenty years old or less,[d] because the LORD had promised to make Israel as numerous as the stars[e] in the sky.

27:24 [f] 2Sa 24:15; 1Ch 21:7

24 Joab son of Zeruiah began to count the men but did not finish. Wrath came on Israel on account of this numbering,[f] and the number was not entered in the book[a] of the annals of King David.

The King's Overseers

25 Azmaveth son of Adiel was in charge of the royal storehouses.

Jonathan son of Uzziah was in charge of the storehouses in the outlying districts, in the towns, the villages and the watchtowers.

26 Ezri son of Kelub was in charge of the field workers who farmed the land.

27 Shimei the Ramathite was in charge of the vineyards.

Zabdi the Shiphmite was in charge of the produce of the vineyards for the wine vats.

27:28 [g] 1Ki 10:27; 2Ch 1:15

28 Baal-Hanan the Gederite was in charge of the olive and sycamore-fig[g] trees in the western foothills.

Joash was in charge of the supplies of olive oil.

29 Shitrai the Sharonite was in charge of the herds grazing in Sharon. Shaphat son of Adlai was in charge of the herds in the valleys.

30 Obil the Ishmaelite was in charge of the camels.

Jehdeiah the Meronothite was in charge of the donkeys.

27:31 [h] 1Ch 5:10

31 Jaziz the Hagrite[h] was in charge of the flocks.

All these were the officials in charge of King David's property.

32 Jonathan, David's uncle, was a counselor, a man of insight and a scribe. Jehiel son of Hacmoni took care of the king's sons.

27:33 [i] 2Sa 15:12 [j] 2Sa 15:37

33 Ahithophel[i] was the king's counselor.

Hushai[j] the Arkite was the king's friend.

27:34 [k] 1Ki 1:7 [l] 1Ch 11:6

34 Ahithophel was succeeded by Jehoiada son of Benaiah and by Abiathar.[k]

Joab[l] was the commander of the royal army.

David's Plans for the Temple

28:1 [m] 1Ch 11:10; 27:1-31

28 David summoned all the officials[m] of Israel to assemble at Jerusalem: the officers over the tribes, the commanders of the divisions in the service of the king, the commanders of thousands and commanders of hundreds, and the officials in charge of all the property and livestock belonging to the king and his sons, together with the palace officials, the mighty men and all the brave warriors.

28:2 [n] 1Ch 17:2 [o] Ps 99:5; 132:7

2 King David rose to his feet and said: "Listen to me, my brothers and my people. I had it in my heart[n] to build a house as a place of rest for the ark of the covenant of the LORD, for the footstool[o] of our God, and I made plans to build it.

28:3 [p] 2Sa 7:5 [q] 1Ch 22:8 [r] 1Ki 5:3; 1Ch 17:4

3 But God said to me,[p] 'You are not to build a house for my Name,[q] because you are a warrior and have shed blood.'[r]

28:4 [s] 1Ch 17:23,27; 2Ch 6:6 [t] 1Sa 16:1-13 [u] Ge 49:10; 1Ch 5:2

4 "Yet the LORD, the God of Israel, chose me[s] from my whole family[t] to be king over Israel forever. He chose Judah[u] as leader, and from the house of Judah he chose my family, and from my father's sons he was pleased to make me king over all Israel.

28:5 [v] 1Ch 3:1 [w] 1Ch 22:9; 23:1

5 Of all my sons—and the LORD has given me many[v]—he has chosen my son Solomon[w] to sit on the throne of the kingdom of the LORD over Israel.

6 He said to me: 'Solomon your son

[a] 24 Septuagint; Hebrew *number*

is the one who will build my house and my courts, for I have chosen him to be my son,[x] and I will be his father. 7 I will establish his kingdom forever if he is unswerving in carrying out my commands and laws,[y] as is being done at this time.'

28:6 [x] 2Sa 7:13; 1Ch 22:9-10
28:7 [y] 1Ch 22:13

8 "So now I charge you in the sight of all Israel and of the assembly of the LORD, and in the hearing of our God: Be careful to follow all the commands[z] of the LORD your God, that you may possess this good land and pass it on as an inheritance to your descendants forever.[a]

28:8 [z] Dt 6:1 [a] Dt 4:1

9 "And you, my son Solomon, acknowledge the God of your father, and serve him with wholehearted devotion[b] and with a willing mind, for the LORD searches every heart[c] and understands every motive behind the thoughts. If you seek him,[d] he will be found by you; but if you forsake[e] him, he will reject[f] you forever. 10 Consider now, for the LORD has chosen you to build a temple as a sanctuary. Be strong and do the work."

28:9 [b] 1Ch 29:19 [c] 1Sa 16:7; Ps 7:9 [d] Ps 40:16; Jer 29:13 [e] Jos 24:20; 2Ch 15:2 [f] Ps 44:23

11 Then David gave his son Solomon the plans[g] for the portico of the temple, its buildings, its storerooms, its upper parts, its inner rooms and the place of atonement. 12 He gave him the plans of all that the Spirit[h] had put in his mind for the courts of the temple of the LORD and all the surrounding rooms, for the treasuries of the temple of God and for the treasuries for the dedicated things.[i] 13 He gave him instructions for the divisions[j] of the priests and Levites, and for all the work of serving in the temple of the LORD, as well as for all the articles to be used in its service. 14 He designated the weight of gold for all the gold articles to be used in various kinds of service, and the weight of silver for all the silver articles to be used in various kinds of service: 15 the weight of gold for the gold lampstands[k] and their lamps, with the weight for each lampstand and its lamps; and the weight of silver for each silver lampstand and its lamps, according to the use of each lampstand; 16 the weight of gold for each table[l] for consecrated bread; the weight of silver for the silver tables; 17 the weight of pure gold for the forks, sprinkling bowls[m] and pitchers; the weight of gold for each gold dish; the weight of silver for each silver dish; 18 and the weight of the refined gold for the altar of incense.[n] He also gave him the plan for the chariot,[o] that is, the cherubim of gold that spread their wings and shelter[p] the ark of the covenant of the LORD.

28:11 [g] Ex 25:9
28:12 [h] 1Ch 12:18 [i] 1Ch 26:20
28:13 [j] 1Ch 24:1
28:15 [k] Ex 25:31
28:16 [l] Ex 25:23
28:17 [m] Ex 27:3
28:18 [n] Ex 30:1-10 [o] Ex 25:18-22 [p] Ex 25:20

19 "All this," David said, "I have in writing from the hand of the LORD upon me, and he gave me understanding in all the details[q] of the plan.[r]"

28:19 [q] 1Ki 6:38 [r] Ex 25:9

20 David also said to Solomon his son, "Be strong and courageous,[s] and do the work. Do not be afraid or discouraged, for the LORD God, my God, is with you. He will not fail you or forsake[t] you until all the work for the service of the temple of the LORD is finished.[u] 21 The divisions of the priests and Levites are ready for all the work on the temple of God, and every willing man skilled[v] in any craft will help you in all the work. The officials and all the people will obey your every command."

28:20 [s] Dt 31:6; 1Ch 22:13; 2Ch 19:11; Hag 2:4 [t] Dt 4:31; Jos 24:20 [u] 1Ki 6:14; 2Ch 7:11
28:21 [v] Ex 35:25-36:5

Gifts for Building the Temple

29 Then King David said to the whole assembly: "My son Solomon, the one whom God has chosen, is young and inexperienced.[w] The task is

29:1 [w] 1Ki 3:7; 1Ch 22:5; 2Ch 13:7

JESUS FOCUS

GOD'S FOOTSTOOL

David realized that a mere building could never house the eternal, all-powerful God of the universe, but he planned to build the temple as a "footstool" for God (1 Chronicles 28:2)—as well as a specific place for the people to connect with God and as a visible symbol of their devotion to him. When David stated during the dedication celebration that "Yours, O LORD, is the kingdom" (1 Chronicles 29:11), he was saying that the temple would focus the people's attention on the fact that God was in control of everything. David recognized that constructing a temple for God was a feeble human attempt to declare the incomparable greatness, power and majesty of our Creator. Later on that same temple, as well as a second one, would be destroyed because the people had turned away from God. Only in the person of Jesus—*Immanuel*, or "God with us"—did God finally come to dwell with us forever (Isaiah 7:14; Matthew 1:22–23). Jesus Christ died on the cross to pay the penalty for sin in our place, and he came back to life again so that we might enjoy a never-ending relationship with God.

great, because this palatial structure is
not for man but for the LORD God. 2With
all my resources I have provided for the
29:2 x ver 7,14,16; temple of my God—gold[x] for the gold
Ezr 1:4; 6:5; work, silver for the silver, bronze for the
Hag 2:8 y Isa 54:11 bronze, iron for the iron and wood for
z 1Ch 22:2-5 the wood, as well as onyx for the settings, turquoise,[a y] stones of various colors, and all kinds of fine stone and marble—all of these in large quantities.[z]
3Besides, in my devotion to the temple
of my God I now give my personal treasures of gold and silver for the temple of
my God, over and above everything I
29:3 a 2Ch 24:10; have provided[a] for this holy temple:
31:3; 35:8 4three thousand talents[b] of gold (gold of
29:4 Ophir)[b] and seven thousand talents[c] of
b Ge 10:29 refined silver,[c] for the overlaying of the
c 1Ch 22:14 walls of the buildings, 5for the gold work
and the silver work, and for all the work
to be done by the craftsmen. Now, who
is willing to consecrate himself today to
the LORD?"
6Then the leaders of families, the officers of the tribes of Israel, the commanders of thousands and commanders of
29:6 d 1Ch 27:1; 28:1 hundreds, and the officials[d] in charge of
e ver 9; the king's work gave willingly.[e] 7They[f]
Ex 25:1-8; 35:20-29; 36:2; gave toward the work on the temple of
2Ch 24:10; God five thousand talents[d] and ten
Ezr 7:15 thousand darics[e] of gold, ten thousand
29:7 f Ex 25:2; talents[f] of silver, eighteen thousand tal-
Ne 7:70-71 ents[g] of bronze and a hundred thousand
talents[h] of iron. 8Any who had precious
29:8 g Ex 35:27 stones[g] gave them to the treasury of the
h 1Ch 26:21 temple of the LORD in the custody of Jehiel the Gershonite.[h] 9The people rejoiced at the willing response of their
leaders, for they had given freely and
29:9 i 1Ki 8:61; wholeheartedly[i] to the LORD. David the
2Co 9:7 king also rejoiced greatly.

David's Prayer

10David praised the LORD in the presence of the whole assembly, saying,

"Praise be to you, O LORD,
God of our father Israel,
from everlasting to everlasting.
29:11 11Yours, O LORD, is the greatness and
j Ps 24:8; 59:17; 62:11 k Ps 89:11 the power[j]
l Rev 5:12-13 and the glory and the majesty
and the splendor,
for everything in heaven and
earth is yours.[k]
Yours, O LORD, is the kingdom;
29:12 you are exalted as head over all.[l]
m 2Ch 1:12 12Wealth and honor[m] come from you;
you are the ruler[n] of all things. 29:12 n 2Ch 20:6;
In your hands are strength and Ro 11:36
power
to exalt and give strength to all.
13Now, our God, we give you thanks,
and praise your glorious name.

14"But who am I, and who are my people, that we should be able to give as
generously as this? Everything comes
from you, and we have given you only
what comes from your hand. 15We are 29:15
aliens and strangers[o] in your sight, as o Ps 39:12;
were all our forefathers. Our days on Heb 11:13
earth are like a shadow,[p] without hope. p Job 14:2
16O LORD our God, as for all this abundance that we have provided for building you a temple for your Holy Name, it
comes from your hand, and all of it belongs to you. 17I know, my God, that you 29:17
test the heart[q] and are pleased with in- q Ps 139:23; Pr 15:11; 17:3;
tegrity. All these things have I given will- Jer 11:20; 17:10
ingly and with honest intent. And now I r 1Ch 28:9; Ps 15:1-5
have seen with joy how willingly your
people who are here have given to you.[r]
18O LORD, God of our fathers Abraham,
Isaac and Israel, keep this desire in the
hearts of your people forever, and keep
their hearts loyal to you. 19And give my
son Solomon the wholehearted devo- 29:19
tion[s] to keep your commands, require- s 1Ch 28:9 t Ps 72:1
ments and decrees[t] and to do every- u 1Ch 22:14
thing to build the palatial structure for
which I have provided."[u]
20Then David said to the whole assembly, "Praise the LORD your God." So
they all praised the LORD, the God of
their fathers; they bowed low and fell
prostrate before the LORD and the king.

Solomon Acknowledged as King

21The next day they made sacrifices to
the LORD and presented burnt offerings 29:21
to him:[v] a thousand bulls, a thousand v 1Ki 8:62
rams and a thousand male lambs, together with their drink offerings, and
other sacrifices in abundance for all Is- 29:22
rael. 22They ate and drank with great joy[w] w 1Ch 23:1
in the presence of the LORD that day.
Then they acknowledged Solomon

a 2 The meaning of the Hebrew for this word is uncertain. *b* 4 That is, about 110 tons (about 100 metric tons) *c* 4 That is, about 260 tons (about 240 metric tons) *d* 7 That is, about 190 tons (about 170 metric tons) *e* 7 That is, about 185 pounds (about 84 kilograms)
f 7 That is, about 375 tons (about 345 metric tons)
g 7 That is, about 675 tons (about 610 metric tons)
h 7 That is, about 3,750 tons (about 3,450 metric tons)

DISCOVERY 101

True Worship Is . . .

What does it really mean to worship? Worship is a vital component of our faith. We seem to talk about it all the time: We conduct worship services, appoint worship leaders, sing worship choruses and enjoy worship experiences. But what does it really mean to worship our God? Essentially, worship means giving to God, whether that be material gifts or the offering of our praise or our talents. It means expressing how much he is worth to us.

When King David was near death he called the people of Israel together and reminded them of the implications of their status as God's people. He encouraged them to build a temple for God and confirmed that his son Solomon would be their next king. In order to facilitate the work of building the temple David contributed his own personal treasure, and the people responded by donating whatever they had "freely and wholeheartedly" (1 Chronicles 29:2–6,9).

In the New Testament Paul reminded the church in Rome that offering our very bodies to the service of Jesus Christ constitutes our "spiritual act of worship" (Romans 12:1–2). Elsewhere Paul stated it this way: "Become blameless and pure, children of God without fault in a crooked and depraved generation, in which you shine like stars in the universe as you hold out the word of life" (Philippians 2:15–16). The choices we make about what we do should show the world that we honor God and take his Word seriously.

Worship also includes praise, the act of declaring God's greatness to other people and to God himself, just as David did: "Yours, O Lord, is the greatness and the power and the glory and the majesty and the splendor, for everything in heaven and earth is yours" (1 Chronicles 29:11). But true praise involves our lives as well as our lips. Peter wrote in his first letter: "If anyone serves, he should do it with the strength God provides, so that in all things God may be praised through Jesus Christ" (1 Peter 4:11).

Finally, worship entails commitment. David asked the Lord to keep the hearts of the people devoted to God (1 Chronicles 29:18) and particularly to help his son Solomon to retain his focus and to serve God wholeheartedly (verse 19).

God wants his people to live with integrity; he desires a "wholeness," a seamless quality between what we profess to believe and the way we live our lives (verse 17). As we get to know God more intimately, we can't help but compare ourselves to him. We are Jesus' beloved, and as we learn to love him more deeply we will desire increasingly to please him in every area of our lives (Luke 11:28; John 14:15,23–24). He gives us the awesome privilege of joining all of creation in honoring him. If we don't take him up on the offer, he'll cause the very rocks to burst forth in songs of praise (Luke 6:40). If even the rocks want to get involved, how can we pass up the opportunity?

Self-Discovery: *Picture yourself shining like a star in the universe as you hold out the word of life. Is this image simply pious rhetoric, typical of the literature of the time, or is the picture helpful? Is it necessary to maintain a highly visible profile in order to be an effective Christian witness? Why or why not?*

GO TO DISCOVERY 102 ON PAGE 545

son of David as king a second time,
29:22 anointing him before the LORD to be
x 1Ki 1:33-39 ruler and Zadok[x] to be priest. 23 So Solo-
29:23 mon sat on the throne[y] of the LORD as
y 1Ki 2:12 king in place of his father David. He
prospered and all Israel obeyed him.
24 All the officers and mighty men, as
well as all of King David's sons, pledged
their submission to King Solomon.
25 The LORD highly exalted Solomon
29:25 in the sight of all Israel and bestowed
z 2Ch 1:1,12 on him royal splendor[z] such as no king
a 1Ki 3:13; Ecc 2:9 over Israel ever had before.[a]

The Death of David

29:26 b 1Ch 18:14 26 David son of Jesse was king[b] over all
Israel. 27 He ruled over Israel forty
years—seven in Hebron and thirty-three 29:27
in Jerusalem.[c] 28 He died[d] at a good old c 2Sa 5:4-5;
age, having enjoyed long life, wealth and 1Ki 2:11;
honor. His son Solomon succeeded him 1Ch 3:4
as king.[e] 29:28 d Ge 15:15;
29 As for the events of King David's Ac 13:36
reign, from beginning to end, they e 1Ch 23:1
are written in the records of Samuel 29:29
the seer,[f] the records of Nathan[g] the f 1Sa 9:9 g 2Sa 7:2
prophet and the records of Gad[h] the h 1Sa 22:5
seer, 30 together with the details of his
reign and power, and the circumstances that surrounded him and Israel and the kingdoms of all the other
lands.

How is the theme in both 1 and 2 Chronicles of the people of God being heirs to God's covenant promises fulfilled in Jesus?

♦ *All followers of Jesus, whether Jew or Gentile, are included in this promise. At the end of time God will unite all his elect ("the Israel of God" in Galatians 6:16) under the lordship of his Son.*

What is the New Testament significance of the temple? (2 Chronicles 3:3–17)

♦ *(1) Our worship must be centralized, focused on Jesus. (2) Just as Solomon spared no expense to build the temple, we should hold nothing back in our commitment to God. (3) The temple was God's means of meeting with his people, just as he now meets with us through the death and resurrection of Jesus. (4) The temple was used in the New Testament to illustrate Jesus himself—where we meet God (John 2:19; 14:6–10).*

Jesus in 2 Chronicles In the Hebrew Bible the book of 2 Chronicles closes the Old Testament. It records the history of God's people from creation to the Babylonian captivity, with a particular focus on David's family line and the kings of Judah. The book of 2 Chronicles is an important one for us as well, providing us with a sense of how the Lord brought revival to his people.

Peace and prosperity take a front seat as the author stresses the blessings that come from worshiping the true God. Examine Jewish history from the perspective that if a nation honors God it will see success. Then think about the teachings of Jesus, particularly in the Gospel of Matthew, which was directed toward a primarily Jewish audience. In what ways was Jesus a product of his Jewish culture and background? Read and compare the companion passages in 1 and 2 Kings. What does 2 Chronicles consistently highlight? Look beyond the names and circumstances to pinpoint the few successful kings. Why were they successful? What can you learn from their experiences?

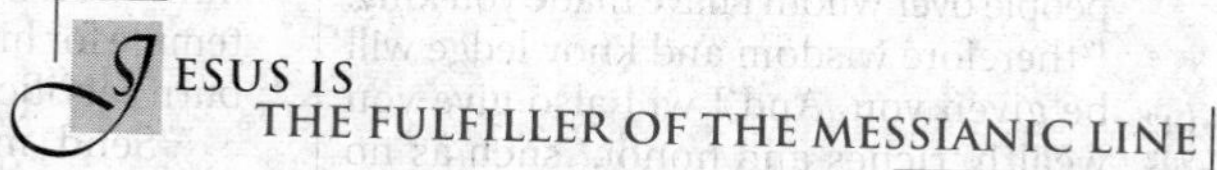

JESUS IS
THE FULFILLER OF THE MESSIANIC LINE

Solomon Asks for Wisdom

1 Solomon son of David established[a] himself firmly over his kingdom, for the LORD his God was with[b] him and made him exceedingly great.[c]

2 Then Solomon spoke to all Israel[d]—to the commanders of thousands and commanders of hundreds, to the judges and to all the leaders in Israel, the heads of families— 3 and Solomon and the whole assembly went to the high place at Gibeon, for God's Tent of Meeting[e] was there, which Moses[f] the LORD's servant had made in the desert. 4 Now David had brought up the ark[g] of God from Kiriath Jearim to the place he had prepared for it, because he had pitched a tent[h] for it in Jerusalem. 5 But the bronze altar[i] that Bezalel[j] son of Uri, the son of Hur, had made was in Gibeon in front of the tabernacle of the LORD; so Solomon and the assembly inquired[k] of him there. 6 Solomon went up to the bronze altar before the LORD in the Tent of Meeting and offered a thousand burnt offerings on it.

7 That night God appeared[l] to Solomon and said to him, "Ask for whatever you want me to give you."

8 Solomon answered God, "You have shown great kindness to David my father and have made me[m] king in his place. 9 Now, LORD God, let your promise[n] to my father David be confirmed, for you have made me king over a people who are as numerous as the dust of the earth.[o] 10 Give me wisdom and knowledge, that I may lead[p] this people, for who is able to govern this great people of yours?"

11 God said to Solomon, "Since this is your heart's desire and you have not asked for wealth,[q] riches or honor, nor for the death of your enemies, and since you have not asked for a long life but for wisdom and knowledge to govern my people over whom I have made you king, 12 therefore wisdom and knowledge will be given you. And I will also give you wealth, riches and honor,[r] such as no king who was before you ever had and none after you will have.[s]"

13 Then Solomon went to Jerusalem from the high place at Gibeon, from before the Tent of Meeting. And he reigned over Israel.

14 Solomon accumulated chariots[t] and horses; he had fourteen hundred chariots and twelve thousand horses,[*a*] which he kept in the chariot cities and also with him in Jerusalem. 15 The king made silver and gold[u] as common in Jerusalem as stones, and cedar as plentiful as sycamore-fig trees in the foothills. 16 Solomon's horses were imported from Egypt[*b*] and from Kue[*c*]—the royal merchants purchased them from Kue. 17 They imported a chariot[v] from Egypt for six hundred shekels[*d*] of silver, and a horse for a hundred and fifty.[*e*] They also exported them to all the kings of the Hittites and of the Arameans.

Preparations for Building the Temple

2 Solomon gave orders to build a temple[w] for the Name of the LORD and a royal palace for himself.[x] 2 He conscripted seventy thousand men as carriers and eighty thousand as stonecutters in the hills and thirty-six hundred as foremen over them.[y]

3 Solomon sent this message to Hiram[*f*][z] king of Tyre:

"Send me cedar logs[a] as you did for my father David when you sent him cedar to build a palace to live in. 4 Now I am about to build a temple[b] for the Name of the LORD my God and to dedicate it to him for burning fragrant incense[c] before him, for setting out the consecrated bread[d] regularly, and for making burnt offerings[e] every morning and evening and on Sabbaths[f] and New Moons and at the appointed feasts of the LORD our God. This is a lasting ordinance for Israel.

5 "The temple I am going to build will be great,[g] because our God is greater than all other gods.[h] 6 But who is able to build a temple for him, since the heavens, even the highest heavens, cannot contain him?[i] Who then am I[j] to build a temple for him, except as a place to burn sacrifices before him?

7 "Send me, therefore, a man skilled to work in gold and silver, bronze and iron, and in purple, crimson and blue yarn, and experi-

---

1:1 [a] 1Ki 2:12,26; 2Ch 12:1 [b] Ge 21:22; 39:2; Nu 14:43 [c] 1Ch 29:25
1:2 [d] 1Ch 9:1; 28:1
1:3 [e] Ex 36:8 [f] Ex 40:18
1:4 [g] 2Sa 6:2; 1Ch 15:25 [h] 2Sa 6:17; 1Ch 15:1
1:5 [i] Ex 38:2 [j] Ex 31:2 [k] 1Ch 13:3
1:7 [l] 2Ch 7:12
1:8 [m] 1Ch 23:1; 28:5
1:9 [n] 2Sa 7:25; 1Ki 8:25 [o] Ge 12:2
1:10 [p] Nu 27:17; 2Sa 5:2; Pr 8:15-16
1:11 [q] Dt 17:17
1:12 [r] 1Ch 29:12 [s] 1Ch 29:25; 2Ch 9:22; Ne 13:26
1:14 [t] 1Sa 8:11; 1Ki 4:26; 9:19
1:15 [u] 1Ki 9:28; Isa 60:5
1:17 [v] SS 1:9
2:1 [w] Dt 12:5 [x] Ecc 2:4
2:2 [y] ver 18; 2Ch 10:4
2:3 [z] 2Sa 5:11 [a] 1Ch 14:1
2:4 [b] ver 1; Dt 12:5 [c] Ex 30:7 [d] Ex 25:30 [e] Ex 29:42; 2Ch 13:11 [f] Nu 28:9-10
2:5 [g] 1Ch 22:5; Ps 135:5 [h] 1Ch 16:25
2:6 [i] 1Ki 8:27; 2Ch 6:18; Jer 23:24 [j] Ex 3:11

---

a 14 Or *charioteers* *b* 16 Or possibly *Muzur,* a region in Cilicia; also in verse 17 *c* 16 Probably Cilicia *d* 17 That is, about 15 pounds (about 7 kilograms) *e* 17 That is, about 3 3/4 pounds (about 1.7 kilograms) *f* 3 Hebrew *Huram,* a variant of *Hiram;* also in verses 11 and 12

enced in the art of engraving, to
2:7 k ver 13-14; Ex 35:31; 1Ch 22:16 work in Judah and Jerusalem with
my skilled craftsmen,[k] whom my
father David provided.
8"Send me also cedar, pine and
algum[a] logs from Lebanon, for I
know that your men are skilled in
cutting timber there. My men will
work with yours 9to provide me
with plenty of lumber, because the
temple I build must be large and
magnificent. 10I will give your servants, the woodsmen who cut the
timber, twenty thousand cors[b] of
ground wheat, twenty thousand
cors of barley, twenty thousand
2:10 l Ezr 3:7 baths[c] of wine and twenty thousand baths of olive oil.[l]"
11Hiram king of Tyre replied by letter
to Solomon:
2:11 m 1Ki 10:9; 2Ch 9:8 "Because the LORD loves[m] his
people, he has made you their king."
12And Hiram added:
"Praise be to the LORD, the God
2:12 n Ne 9:6; Ps 8:3; 33:6; 102:25 of Israel, who made heaven and
earth![n] He has given King David a
wise son, endowed with intelligence and discernment, who will
build a temple for the LORD and a
palace for himself.
2:13 o 1Ki 7:13 13"I am sending you Huram-Abi,[o]
2:14 p Ex 31:6 q Ex 35:31 r Ex 35:35 a man of great skill, 14whose mother was from Dan[p] and whose father
was from Tyre. He is trained[q] to
work in gold and silver, bronze and
iron, stone and wood, and with purple and blue[r] and crimson yarn and
fine linen. He is experienced in all
kinds of engraving and can execute
any design given to him. He will
work with your craftsmen and with
those of my lord, David your father.
15"Now let my lord send his servants the wheat and barley and the
2:15 s ver 10; Ezr 3:7 olive oil[s] and wine he promised,
16and we will cut all the logs from
Lebanon that you need and will
2:16 t Jos 19:46; Jnh 1:3 float them in rafts by sea down to
Joppa.[t] You can then take them up
to Jerusalem."
2:17 u 1Ch 22:2 v 2Sa 24:2 17Solomon took a census of all the
aliens[u] who were in Israel, after the cen-
2:18 w ver 2; 1Ch 22:2; 2Ch 8:8 sus[v] his father David had taken; and
they were found to be 153,600. 18He as-
signed[w] 70,000 of them to be carriers
and 80,000 to be stonecutters in the
hills, with 3,600 foremen over them to
keep the people working.

Solomon Builds the Temple

3 Then Solomon began to build[x] 3:1 x Ac 7:47
the temple of the LORD[y] in Jerusa- y Ge 28:17
lem on Mount Moriah, where the LORD z 2Sa 24:18; 1Ch 21:18
had appeared to his father David. It was
on the threshing floor of Araunah[d][z] the
Jebusite, the place provided by David.
2He began building on the second day of
the second month in the fourth year of 3:2
his reign.[a] a Ezr 5:11
3The foundation Solomon laid for
building the temple of God was sixty cu- 3:3
bits long and twenty cubits wide[e][b] (us- b Eze 41:2
ing the cubit of the old standard). 4The
portico at the front of the temple was
twenty cubits[f] long across the width of
the building and twenty cubits[g] high.
He overlaid the inside with pure gold.
5He paneled the main hall with pine and
covered it with fine gold and decorated
it with palm tree[c] and chain designs. 3:5 c Eze 40:16
6He adorned the temple with precious
stones. And the gold he used was gold of
Parvaim. 7He overlaid the ceiling beams,
doorframes, walls and doors of the tem- 3:7
ple with gold, and he carved cherubim[d] d Ge 3:24; 1Ki 6:29-35; Eze 41:18
on the walls.
8He built the Most Holy Place,[e] its
length corresponding to the width of the 3:8 e Ex 26:33
temple—twenty cubits long and twenty
cubits wide. He overlaid the inside with
six hundred talents[h] of fine gold. 9The
gold nails[f] weighed fifty shekels.[i] He also 3:9 f Ex 26:32
overlaid the upper parts with gold.
10In the Most Holy Place he made a
pair[g] of sculptured cherubim and over- 3:10 g Ex 25:18
laid them with gold. 11The total wing-
span of the cherubim was twenty cubits.
One wing of the first cherub was five cubits[j] long and touched the temple wall,
while its other wing, also five cubits
long, touched the wing of the other

a *8* Probably a variant of *almug*; possibly juniper
b *10* That is, probably about 125,000 bushels (about 4,400 kiloliters)
c *10* That is, probably about 115,000 gallons (about 440 kiloliters)
d *1* Hebrew *Ornan*, a variant of *Araunah*
e *3* That is, about 90 feet (about 27 meters) long and 30 feet (about 9 meters) wide
f *4* That is, about 30 feet (about 9 meters); also in verses 8, 11 and 13
g *4* Some Septuagint and Syriac manuscripts; Hebrew *and a hundred and twenty*
h *8* That is, about 23 tons (about 21 metric tons)
i *9* That is, about 1 1/4 pounds (about 0.6 kilogram)
j *11* That is, about 7 1/2 feet (about 2.3 meters); also in verse 15

cherub. 12Similarly one wing of the second cherub was five cubits long and
touched the other temple wall, and its
other wing, also five cubits long,
3:13 touched the wing of the first cherub.
h Ex 25:18 13The wings of these cherubim[h] extended twenty cubits. They stood on their
3:14 feet, facing the main hall.[a]
i Ex 26:31,33; 14He made the curtain[i] of blue, purple
Heb 9:3 and crimson yarn and fine linen, with
j Ge 3:24 cherubim[j] worked into it.
3:15 15In the front of the temple he made
k 1Ki 7:15; two pillars,[k] which ⌊together⌋ were thir-
Rev 3:12 l 1Ki 7:22 ty-five cubits[b] long, each with a capital[l]
on top measuring five cubits. 16He made
3:16 m 1Ki 7:17 interwoven chains[c][m] and put them on
n 1Ki 7:20 top of the pillars. He also made a hundred pomegranates[n] and attached them
to the chains. 17He erected the pillars in
the front of the temple, one to the south
and one to the north. The one to the
south he named Jakin[d] and the one to
the north Boaz.[e]

The Temple's Furnishings

4:1 o Ex 20:24; 4 He made a bronze altar[o] twenty
27:1-2; 40:6; cubits long, twenty cubits wide
1Ki 8:64; 2Ki 16:14 and ten cubits high.[f] 2He made the Sea[p]
of cast metal, circular in shape, measur-
4:2 p Rev 4:6; 15:2 ing ten cubits from rim to rim and five
cubits[g] high. It took a line of thirty cu-
bits[h] to measure around it. 3Below the
rim, figures of bulls encircled it—ten to
a cubit.[i] The bulls were cast in two rows
in one piece with the Sea.
4The Sea stood on twelve bulls, three
facing north, three facing west, three 4:4 q Nu 2:3-25;
facing south and three facing east.[q] The Eze 48:30-34;
Sea rested on top of them, and their Rev 21:13
hindquarters were toward the center. 5It
was a handbreadth[j] in thickness, and its
rim was like the rim of a cup, like a lily
blossom. It held three thousand baths.[k]
6He then made ten basins[r] for wash- 4:6 r Ex 30:18
ing and placed five on the south side s Ne 13:5,9; Eze 40:38
and five on the north. In them the things
to be used for the burnt offerings[s] were
rinsed, but the Sea was to be used by the
priests for washing.
7He made ten gold lampstands[t] ac- 4:7 t Ex 25:31
cording to the specifications[u] for them u Ex 25:40
and placed them in the temple, five on
the south side and five on the north.
8He made ten tables[v] and placed 4:8 v Ex 25:23
them in the temple, five on the south w Nu 4:14
side and five on the north. He also made
a hundred gold sprinkling bowls.[w]
9He made the courtyard[x] of the 4:9 x 1Ki 6:36;
priests, and the large court and the doors 2Ki 21:5;
for the court, and overlaid the doors with 2Ch 33:5
bronze. 10He placed the Sea on the south
side, at the southeast corner.
11He also made the pots and shovels
and sprinkling bowls. 4:11
So Huram finished[y] the work he had y 1Ki 7:14
undertaken for King Solomon in the
temple of God:

12 the two pillars;
the two bowl-shaped capitals on
top of the pillars;
the two sets of network decorating
the two bowl-shaped capitals on
top of the pillars;
13 the four hundred pomegranates for
the two sets of network (two
rows of pomegranates for each
network, decorating the bowl-
shaped capitals on top of the pillars);

[a] 13 Or *facing inward* [b] 15 That is, about 52 feet (about 16 meters) [c] 16 Or possibly *made chains in the inner sanctuary*; the meaning of the Hebrew for this phrase is uncertain. [d] 17 *Jakin* probably means *he establishes.* [e] 17 *Boaz* probably means *in him is strength.* [f] 1 That is, about 30 feet (about 9 meters) long and wide, and about 15 feet (about 4.5 meters) high [g] 2 That is, about 7 1/2 feet (about 2.3 meters) [h] 2 That is, about 45 feet (about 13.5 meters) [i] 3 That is, about 1 1/2 feet (about 0.5 meter) [j] 5 That is, about 3 inches (about 8 centimeters) [k] 5 That is, about 17,500 gallons (about 66 kiloliters)

JESUS FOCUS

SEPARATED FROM GOD

In both the tabernacle and the temple a curtain separated the Holy Place from the Most Holy Place (2 Chronicles 3:14; see also Exodus 26:33). This curtain was symbolic of the division between God and his people. Even the priests themselves were forbidden to go beyond that curtain into the place of God's presence—with only one exception—because humans were separated from God by their sin. Once each year the high priest was to enter the Most Holy Place on the Day of Atonement to make a special sin offering (Leviticus 16).

When Jesus died on the cross to pay the debt owed to God for our sins, the temple curtain was torn from top to bottom, revealing the previously sacred room (Mark 15:38). This act of God represented the fact that Jesus' sacrifice had made it possible for us to approach God freely (Hebrews 9:7–12; 10:19–22).

DISCOVERY 102

LIVING MOUNT MORIAHS

Mount Moriah was a sacred piece of real estate in Israel; it is very significant in both the Old and New Testaments and continues to be a focal point of conflict today. This mountain was a place of sacrifice from the beginning. It was upon Mount Moriah that Abraham was prepared to offer Isaac as a sacrifice to God (Genesis 22:2). We recall that, just as Abraham was about to plunge the knife into the son of promise, God intervened and provided a ram as a substitute. Abraham called this place "the LORD will provide" (Genesis 22:14).

Mount Moriah was purchased by King David. Although Araunah the Jebusite (1 Chronicles 21:18–30) offered to give it to David, the king replied, "I will not take for the LORD what is yours, or sacrifice a burnt offering that costs me nothing" (1 Chronicles 21:24). In fact, this was the place David designated as the location for the future temple. Later, when King Solomon did build the temple, Mount Moriah became the most sacred place for God's people (2 Chronicles 3). Solomon understood the importance of this impressive edifice: "I have built a magnificent temple for [God], a place for [him] to dwell forever" (2 Chronicles 6:2).

When Jesus died on the cross on Golgotha, Mount Moriah was involved once again. Jesus Christ was crucified outside the gates of the city across the valley from the temple. When he died, the veil in the temple that separated the Most Holy Place was torn in two from top to bottom (Mark 15:38). Jesus' death removed that which separated us from God, thereby enabling us to approach the Father directly. As expressed by the writer to the Hebrews: "Since we have confidence to enter the Most Holy Place by the blood of Jesus, by a new and living way opened for us through the curtain, that is, his body, and since we have a great priest over the house of God, let us draw near to God with a sincere heart in full assurance of faith, having our hearts sprinkled to cleanse us from a guilty conscience and having our bodies washed with pure water" (Hebrews 10:19–22).

Mount Moriah has always been the place where God "lived." Once his Son became flesh and was born of Mary, God was physically present among his people as one of them. And when Jesus returned to heaven, God's Holy Spirit took up residence *within* his people (1 Corinthians 6:19–20). Now, as God's Spirit lives in us, we are living monuments to him—living Mount Moriahs! We are "being built together to become a dwelling in which God lives by his Spirit" (Ephesians 2:22).

Self-Discovery: *Have you ever thought of yourself as a living monument to God? Imagine the presence of God descending and resting in your heart. Does this picture cause you to feel pressured, or does it infuse you with energy?*

GO TO DISCOVERY 103 ON PAGE 550

4:14 14 the stands[z] with their basins;
z 1Ki 7:27-30 15 the Sea and the twelve bulls under it;
16 the pots, shovels, meat forks and all
related articles.

4:16 a 1Ki 7:13 All the objects that Huram-Abi[a]
made for King Solomon for the temple
of the LORD were of polished bronze.
17 The king had them cast in clay molds
4:17 in the plain of the Jordan between Suc-
b Ge 33:17 coth[b] and Zarethan.[a] 18 All these things
4:18 that Solomon made amounted to so
c 1Ki 7:23 much that the weight of the bronze[c] was
not determined.
19 Solomon also made all the furnishings that were in God's temple:

4:19 the golden altar;
d Ex 25:23,30 the tables[d] on which was the bread
4:20 of the Presence;
e Ex 25:31 20 the lampstands[e] of pure gold with
their lamps, to burn in front of
the inner sanctuary as prescribed;
21 the gold floral work and lamps and
tongs (they were solid gold);
4:22 22 the pure gold wick trimmers, sprin-
f Nu 7:14 kling bowls, dishes[f] and censers;[g]
g Lev 10:1 and the gold doors of the temple:
the inner doors to the Most Holy
Place and the doors of the main
hall.

5 When all the work Solomon had
5:1 done for the temple of the LORD
h 1Ki 6:14 was finished,[h] he brought in the things
i 2Sa 8:11 his father David had dedicated[i]—the silver and gold and all the furnishings—
and he placed them in the treasuries of
God's temple.

The Ark Brought to the Temple

2 Then Solomon summoned to Jerusalem the elders of Israel, all the heads of
the tribes and the chiefs of the Israelite
5:2 j Nu 3:31; families, to bring up the ark[j] of the
2Sa 6:12; LORD's covenant from Zion, the City of
1Ch 15:25 David. 3 And all the men of Israel[k] came
5:3 together to the king at the time of the
k 1Ch 9:1; 2Ch 7:8-10 festival in the seventh month.
4 When all the elders of Israel had arrived, the Levites took up the ark, 5 and
they brought up the ark and the Tent of
5:5 Meeting and all the sacred furnishings
l Nu 3:31; in it. The priests, who were Levites,[l] car-
1Ch 15:2 ried them up; 6 and King Solomon and
the entire assembly of Israel that had
gathered about him were before the ark,
sacrificing so many sheep and cattle
that they could not be recorded or
counted. 5:7
7 The priests then brought the ark[m] of m Rev 11:19
the LORD's covenant to its place in the
inner sanctuary of the temple, the Most
Holy Place, and put it beneath the wings 5:8
of the cherubim. 8 The cherubim[n] spread n Ge 3:24
their wings over the place of the ark and
covered the ark and its carrying poles.
9 These poles were so long that their
ends, extending from the ark, could be
seen from in front of the inner sanctuary, but not from outside the Holy Place;
and they are still there today. 10 There 5:10
was nothing in the ark except[o] the two o Heb 9:4
tablets[p] that Moses had placed in it at p Ex 16:34; Dt 10:2
Horeb, where the LORD made a covenant
with the Israelites after they came out of
Egypt.
11 The priests then withdrew from the 5:11
Holy Place. All the priests who were q 1Ch 24:1
there had consecrated themselves, re- 5:12
gardless of their divisions.[q] 12 All the Le- r 1Ki 10:12; 1Ch 25:1;
vites who were musicians[r]—Asaph, He- Ps 68:25

a 17 Hebrew *Zeredatha,* a variant of *Zarethan*

THE COVENANT PROVED

God had long before instructed the Israelites to build a reminder of his treaty, or "covenant," with them—the ark of the covenant (Exodus 25:10–22). The ark was the most sacred piece of furniture in all Israel, and it resided in the inner sanctuary of the tabernacle and later the temple (2 Chronicles 5:7). The ark was eventually lost or hidden, however, and has not been recovered to this day. God's presence and power, his "glory," departed with the ark on account of Israel's sin (1 Samuel 4:21–22; Ezekiel 8–10). Without God's presence the Most Holy Place was for all intents and purposes empty, and the ark had become nothing more than a piece of furniture.

The New Testament teaches that Jesus is the embodiment of God's "glory" (John 1:14; Philippians 2:5–11). When we know Jesus as our Savior and Lord, taking him at his word and learning to live life the way he wants us to, his Spirit—the very presence of God—lives within us. Our bodies become "a temple of the Holy Spirit" (1 Corinthians 6:19), and *we* have become the place where God chooses to be! Because of this great mystery, we become a reflection for the world of who God is (2 Corinthians 3:18).

man, Jeduthun and their sons and relatives—stood on the east side of the altar, dressed in fine linen and playing cymbals, harps and lyres. They were accompanied by 120 priests sounding trumpets.[s] 13 The trumpeters and singers joined in unison, as with one voice, to give praise and thanks to the LORD. Accompanied by trumpets, cymbals and other instruments, they raised their voices in praise to the LORD and sang:

"He is good;
his love endures forever."[t]

Then the temple of the LORD was filled with a cloud, 14 and the priests could not perform[u] their service because of the cloud,[v] for the glory[w] of the LORD filled the temple of God.

6 Then Solomon said, "The LORD has said that he would dwell in a dark cloud;[x] 2 I have built a magnificent temple for you, a place for you to dwell forever.[y]"

3 While the whole assembly of Israel was standing there, the king turned around and blessed them. 4 Then he said:

"Praise be to the LORD, the God of Israel, who with his hands has fulfilled what he promised with his mouth to my father David. For he said, 5 'Since the day I brought my people out of Egypt, I have not chosen a city in any tribe of Israel to have a temple built for my Name to be there, nor have I chosen anyone to be the leader over my people Israel. 6 But now I have chosen Jerusalem[z] for my Name[a] to be there, and I have chosen David[b] to rule my people Israel.'

7 "My father David had it in his heart[c] to build a temple for the Name of the LORD, the God of Israel. 8 But the LORD said to my father David, 'Because it was in your heart to build a temple for my Name, you did well to have this in your heart. 9 Nevertheless, you are not the one to build the temple, but your son, who is your own flesh and blood—he is the one who will build the temple for my Name.'

10 "The LORD has kept the promise he made. I have succeeded David my father and now I sit on the throne of Israel, just as the LORD promised, and I have built the temple for the Name of the LORD, the God of Israel. 11 There I have placed the ark, in which is the covenant[d] of the LORD that he made with the people of Israel."

Solomon's Prayer of Dedication

12 Then Solomon stood before the altar of the LORD in front of the whole assembly of Israel and spread out his hands. 13 Now he had made a bronze platform,[e] five cubits[a] long, five cubits wide and three cubits[b] high, and had placed it in the center of the outer court. He stood on the platform and then knelt down[f] before the whole assembly of Israel and spread out his hands toward heaven. 14 He said:

"O LORD, God of Israel, there is no God like you[g] in heaven or on earth—you who keep your covenant of love[h] with your servants who continue wholeheartedly in your way. 15 You have kept your promise to your servant David my father; with your mouth you have promised[i] and with your hand you have fulfilled it—as it is today.

16 "Now LORD, God of Israel, keep for your servant David my father the promises you made to him when you said, 'You shall never fail[j] to have a man to sit before me on the throne of Israel, if only your sons are careful in all they do to walk before me according to my law,[k] as you have done.' 17 And now, O LORD, God of Israel, let your word that you promised your servant David come true.

18 "But will God really dwell[l] on earth with men? The heavens,[m] even the highest heavens, cannot contain you. How much less this temple I have built! 19 Yet give attention to your servant's prayer and his plea for mercy, O LORD my God. Hear the cry and the prayer that your servant is praying in your presence. 20 May your eyes[n] be open toward this temple day and night, this place of which you said you would put your Name[o] there. May you hear[p] the prayer your servant prays toward this place. 21 Hear the

[a] 13 That is, about 7 1/2 feet (about 2.3 meters)
[b] 13 That is, about 4 1/2 feet (about 1.3 meters)

5:12 [s] 1Ch 13:8; 15:24
5:13 [t] 1Ch 16:34,41; 2Ch 7:3; 20:21; Ezr 3:11; Ps 100:5; 136:1; Jer 33:11
5:14 [u] Ex 40:35; Rev 15:8 [v] Ex 19:16 [w] Ex 29:43; 2Ch 7:2
6:1 [x] Ex 19:9; 1Ki 8:12-50
6:2 [y] Ezr 6:12; 7:15; Ps 135:21
6:6 [z] Dt 12:5; Isa 14:1 [a] Ex 20:24; 2Ch 12:13 [b] 1Ch 28:4
6:7 [c] 1Sa 10:7; 1Ch 17:2; 28:2; Ac 7:46
6:11 [d] Dt 10:2; 2Ch 5:10; Ps 25:10; 50:5
6:13 [e] Ne 8:4 [f] Ps 95:6
6:14 [g] Ex 8:10; 15:11 [h] Dt 7:9
6:15 [i] 1Ch 22:10
6:16 [j] 2Sa 7:13,15; 1Ki 2:4; 2Ch 7:18; 23:3 [k] Ps 132:12
6:18 [l] Rev 21:3 [m] 2Ch 2:6; Ps 11:4; Isa 40:22; 66:1; Ac 7:49
6:20 [n] Ex 3:16; Ps 34:15 [o] Dt 12:11 [p] 2Ch 7:14; 30:20

supplications of your servant and
of your people Israel when they
pray toward this place. Hear from
heaven, your dwelling place; and
when you hear, forgive.[q]
22 “When a man wrongs his
neighbor and is required to take an
oath[r] and he comes and swears the
oath before your altar in this temple,
23 then hear from heaven and act.
Judge between your servants, repaying[s] the guilty by bringing down on
his own head what he has done. Declare the innocent not guilty and so
establish his innocence.
24 “When your people Israel have
been defeated[t] by an enemy because they have sinned against you
and when they turn back and confess your name, praying and making
supplication before you in this temple, 25 then hear from heaven and
forgive the sin of your people Israel
and bring them back to the land you
gave to them and their fathers.
26 “When the heavens are shut up
and there is no rain[u] because your
people have sinned against you,
and when they pray toward this
place and confess your name and
turn from their sin because you
have afflicted them, 27 then hear
from heaven and forgive[v] the sin of
your servants, your people Israel.
Teach them the right way to live,
and send rain on the land you gave
your people for an inheritance.
28 “When famine[w] or plague
comes to the land, or blight or mildew, locusts or grasshoppers, or
when enemies besiege them in any
of their cities, whatever disaster or
disease may come, 29 and when a
prayer or plea is made by any of
your people Israel—each one
aware of his afflictions and pains,
and spreading out his hands toward this temple— 30 then hear
from heaven, your dwelling place.
Forgive,[x] and deal with each man
according to all he does, since you
know his heart (for you alone know
the hearts of men),[y] 31 so that they
will fear you[z] and walk in your
ways all the time they live in the
land you gave our fathers.
32 “As for the foreigner who does

6:21 [q] Ps 51:1; Isa 33:24; 40:2; 43:25; 44:22; 55:7; Mic 7:18
6:22 [r] Ex 22:11
6:23 [s] Isa 3:11; 65:6; Mt 16:27
6:24 [t] Lev 26:17
6:26 [u] Lev 26:19; Dt 11:17; 28:24; 2Sa 1:21; 1Ki 17:1
6:27 [v] ver 30,39; 2Ch 7:14
6:28 [w] 2Ch 20:9
6:30 [x] ver 27 [y] 1Sa 16:7; 1Ch 28:9; Ps 7:9; 44:21; Pr 16:2; 17:3
6:31 [z] Ps 103:11,13; Pr 8:13

not belong to your people Israel but
has come[a] from a distant land because of your great name and your
mighty hand[b] and your outstretched arm—when he comes
and prays toward this temple,
33 then hear from heaven, your
dwelling place, and do whatever
the foreigner[c] asks of you, so that
all the peoples of the earth may
know your name and fear you, as
do your own people Israel, and may
know that this house I have built
bears your Name.
34 “When your people go to war
against their enemies,[d] wherever
you send them, and when they
pray[e] to you toward this city you
have chosen and the temple I have
built for your Name, 35 then hear
from heaven their prayer and their
plea, and uphold their cause.
36 “When they sin against you—
for there is no one who does not
sin[f]—and you become angry with
them and give them over to the enemy, who takes them captive[g] to a
land far away or near; 37 and if they
have a change of heart[h] in the land
where they are held captive, and repent and plead with you in the land
of their captivity and say, ‘We have
sinned, we have done wrong and
acted wickedly’; 38 and if they turn
back to you with all their heart and
soul in the land of their captivity
where they were taken, and pray toward the land you gave their fathers,
toward the city you have chosen and
toward the temple I have built for
your Name; 39 then from heaven,
your dwelling place, hear their
prayer and their pleas, and uphold
their cause. And forgive your people, who have sinned against you.
40 “Now, my God, may your eyes
be open and your ears attentive[i] to
the prayers offered in this place.

41 “Now arise,[j] O LORD God, and
come to your resting
place,[k]
you and the ark of your might.
May your priests,[l] O LORD God,
be clothed with
salvation,
may your saints rejoice in
your goodness.[m]

6:32 [a] 2Ch 9:6; Jn 12:20; Ac 8:27 [b] Ex 3:19,20
6:33 [c] 2Ch 7:14
6:34 [d] Dt 28:7 [e] 1Ch 5:20
6:36 [f] Job 15:14; Ps 143:2; Ecc 7:20; Jer 17:9; Jas 3:1; 1Jn 1:8-10 [g] Lev 26:44
6:37 [h] 2Ch 7:14; 33:12,19,23; Jer 29:13
6:40 [i] 2Ch 7:15; Ne 1:6,11; Ps 17:1,6
6:41 [j] Isa 33:10 [k] 1Ch 28:2 [l] Ps 132:16 [m] Ps 116:12

6:42 [n] Ps 89:24,28; Isa 55:3
42 O LORD God, do not reject your
anointed one.
Remember the great love[n]
promised to David your
servant."

The Dedication of the Temple

7:1 [o] Lev 9:24; 1Ki 18:38 [p] Ex 16:10 [q] Ps 26:8
7 When Solomon finished praying,
fire[o] came down from heaven and
consumed the burnt offering and the
sacrifices, and the glory of the LORD
7:2 [r] 1Ki 8:11 [s] Ex 29:43; 40:35; 2Ch 5:14
filled[p] the temple.[q] 2 The priests could
not enter[r] the temple of the LORD because the glory[s] of the LORD filled it.
3 When all the Israelites saw the fire
coming down and the glory of the LORD
above the temple, they knelt on the
pavement with their faces to the ground,
and they worshiped and gave thanks to
the LORD, saying,

7:3 [t] 1Ch 16:34; 2Ch 5:13; 20:21
"He is good;
his love endures forever."[t]

4 Then the king and all the people offered sacrifices before the LORD. 5 And
King Solomon offered a sacrifice of
twenty-two thousand head of cattle and
a hundred and twenty thousand sheep
and goats. So the king and all the people
dedicated the temple of God. 6 The
7:6 [u] 1Ch 15:16 [v] 2Ch 5:12
priests took their positions, as did the
Levites[u] with the LORD's musical instruments,[v] which King David had made for
praising the LORD and which were used
when he gave thanks, saying, "His love
endures forever." Opposite the Levites,
the priests blew their trumpets, and all
the Israelites were standing.
7 Solomon consecrated the middle
part of the courtyard in front of the temple of the LORD, and there he offered
burnt offerings and the fat of the fellowship offerings,[a] because the bronze altar
he had made could not hold the burnt
offerings, the grain offerings and the fat
portions.
7:8 [w] 2Ch 30:26 [x] Ge 15:18
8 So Solomon observed the festival[w] at
that time for seven days, and all Israel
with him—a vast assembly, people from
Lebo[b] Hamath to the Wadi of Egypt.[x]
9 On the eighth day they held an assembly, for they had celebrated the dedica-
7:9 [y] Lev 23:36
tion of the altar for seven days and the
festival[y] for seven days more. 10 On the
twenty-third day of the seventh month
he sent the people to their homes, joyful
and glad in heart for the good things the
LORD had done for David and Solomon
and for his people Israel.

The LORD Appears to Solomon

11 When Solomon had finished the
temple of the LORD and the royal palace,
and had succeeded in carrying out all he
had in mind to do in the temple of the
LORD and in his own palace, 12 the LORD
appeared to him at night and said:

7:12 [z] Dt 12:5
"I have heard your prayer and
have chosen this place for myself[z]
as a temple for sacrifices.
7:13 [a] 2Ch 6:26-28; Am 4:7
13 "When I shut up the heavens
so that there is no rain,[a] or command locusts to devour the land or
send a plague among my people,
7:14 [b] Lev 26:41; 2Ch 6:37; Jas 4:10 [c] 1Ch 16:11 [d] Isa 55:7; Zec 1:4 [e] 2Ch 6:27 [f] 2Ch 30:20; Isa 30:26; 57:18
14 if my people, who are called by
my name, will humble[b] themselves
and pray and seek my face[c] and
turn[d] from their wicked ways, then
will I hear from heaven and will forgive[e] their sin and will heal[f] their
land. 15 Now my eyes will be open
and my ears attentive to the

[a] 7 Traditionally *peace offerings* [b] 8 Or *from the entrance to*

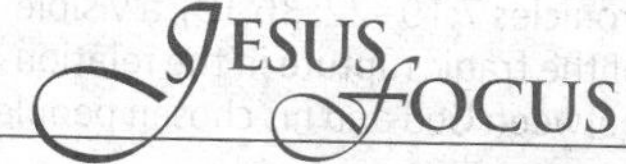

A PROMISED REVIVAL

When the temple was completed and dedicated, the occasion was marked by fire from heaven (2 Chronicles 7:1). God's glory—his presence and power—filled the building. This dramatic scene was unique to Solomon's temple; it did not happen again, not even when the second temple was built. This event marked the high point of Israel's national religious life and experience, as well as the peak of Solomon's reign. God responded to Solomon's prayer by promising to turn the people back to himself if they would "humble themselves and pray and seek my face and turn from their wicked ways" (verse 14).

In the New Testament Jesus became passionately angry when the focus of temple activity moved away from fostering a right relationship with God. He overturned tables and evicted people who were treating the temple as something other than a "house of prayer" (Matthew 21:12–13; Mark 11:15–18). Throughout history God himself has helped his people to refocus when they have gotten off track—and today he still reminds us to walk with him (Micah 6:8).

DISCOVERY 103

A Promise Fulfilled

When the temple was dedicated, Solomon reminded the people of a promise that God had made to his father David. In 2 Samuel 7 the Lord had promised that David's son would build a place for God to dwell with his people. He had also promised to love David and to establish his kingdom forever. Solomon cited himself as proof that God had kept his promise.

The promise had also contained a warning, however. If David's son were to turn his back on God, he would be punished. Eventually Solomon and the people did turn from God into all kinds of sin. This resulted in a succession of wars, hatred and captivity—recorded all the way through the book of Malachi. The most devastating punishment was the fact that Israel's enemies destroyed the temple (2 Chronicles 7:19–22; 36:19), a visible sign of the tragic rupture in the relationship between God and his chosen people.

God punished the Israelites severely, but his promise of eternal love stood firm. Over and over the prophets reassured God's people that God would send a Savior through the royal line of David. Jeremiah announced: " 'The days are coming,' declares the LORD, 'when I will raise up to David a righteous Branch, a King who will reign wisely and do what is just and right in the land. In his days Judah will be saved and Israel will live in safety. This is the name by which he will be called: The LORD Our Righteousness' " (Isaiah 11:1; Jeremiah 23:5–6). This Promised One would come as a child and restore David's "fallen tent," ruling forever (Amos 9:11).

Even though the Israelites could once again be identified as a nation at the time the New Testament opens, they were still a captive people. A temple stood in Jerusalem, but it was a rebuilt temple, not the magnificent structure built by Solomon. Floundering in sin and subject to a brutal nation, God's people were still yearning for the fulfillment of his promise of eternal love through David's family.

Matthew made it perfectly clear that Jesus is that "son of David, the son of Abraham" (Matthew 1:1), and during Jesus' ministry the people asked repeatedly whether he was the One whom God had promised to send for their salvation (see Matthew 12:22–23). But Jesus didn't save the Jews in the manner they were expecting; they anticipated political emancipation, but Jesus came to offer something infinitely greater—spiritual salvation from the bondage of sin.

The apostle Paul expressed this truth in his discourse in Pisidian Antioch: "I want you to know that through Jesus the forgiveness of sin is proclaimed to you. Through him everyone who believes is justified from everything you could not be justified from by the law of Moses" (Acts 13:38–39).

Self-Discovery: *Evaluate the kinds of sins and addictions that hold you in bondage. What kind of freedom are you longing for today? What will it take for you to enjoy the freedom that Jesus wants to give you?*

GO TO DISCOVERY 104 ON PAGE 553

7:15 [g]2Ch 6:40 prayers offered in this place.[g] 16I
have chosen[h] and consecrated this
7:16 temple so that my Name may be
[h]ver 12; 2Ch 6:6 there forever. My eyes and my heart
will always be there.
7:17 17"As for you, if you walk before
[i]1Ki 9:4 me[i] as David your father did, and
do all I command, and observe my
decrees and laws, 18I will establish
your royal throne, as I covenanted
7:18 with David your father when I said,
[j]2Ch 6:16 'You shall never fail to have a man[j]
[k]2Sa 7:13; 2Ch 13:5 to rule over Israel.'[k]
19"But if you[a] turn away[l] and for-
7:19 [l]Dt 28:15 sake[m] the decrees and commands
[m]Lev 26:14,33 I have given you[a] and go off to
serve other gods and worship
7:20 them, 20then I will uproot[n] Israel
[n]Dt 29:28 from my land,[o] which I have given
[o]1Ki 14:15 them, and will reject this temple I
[p]Dt 28:37 have consecrated for my Name. I
will make it a byword and an object
of ridicule[p] among all peoples.
21And though this temple is now so
7:21 imposing, all who pass by will be
[q]Dt 29:24 appalled and say,[q] 'Why has the
LORD done such a thing to this land
and to this temple?' 22People will
answer, 'Because they have forsak-
en the LORD, the God of their fathers, who brought them out of
Egypt, and have embraced other
gods, worshiping and serving
them—that is why he brought all
this disaster on them.' "

Solomon's Other Activities

8 At the end of twenty years, during
which Solomon built the temple
of the LORD and his own palace, 2Solo-
mon rebuilt the villages that Hiram[b] had
given him, and settled Israelites in them.
3Solomon then went to Hamath Zobah
and captured it. 4He also built up Tadmor in the desert and all the store cities
8:5 he had built in Hamath. 5He rebuilt Up-
[r]1Ch 7:24; 2Ch 14:7 per Beth Horon[r] and Lower Beth Horon
as fortified cities, with walls and with
gates and bars, 6as well as Baalath and
all his store cities, and all the cities for
his chariots and for his horses[c]—whatever he desired to build in Jerusalem, in
Lebanon and throughout all the territory he ruled.
7All the people left from the Hittites,
8:7 Amorites, Perizzites, Hivites and Jebu-
[s]Ge 10:16 sites[s] (these peoples were not Israelites),
8that is, their descendants remaining in
the land, whom the Israelites had not de- 8:8
stroyed—these Solomon conscripted[t] [t]1Ki 4:6; 9:21
for his slave labor force, as it is to this
day. 9But Solomon did not make slaves of
the Israelites for his work; they were his
fighting men, commanders of his captains, and commanders of his chariots
and charioteers. 10They were also King
Solomon's chief officials—two hundred
and fifty officials supervising the men.
11Solomon brought Pharaoh's daugh- 8:11
ter[u] up from the City of David to the [u]1Ki 3:1; 7:8
palace he had built for her, for he said,
"My wife must not live in the palace of
David king of Israel, because the places
the ark of the LORD has entered are holy." 8:12
12On the altar[v] of the LORD that he [v]1Ki 8:64; 2Ch 4:1; 15:8
had built in front of the portico, Solo-
mon sacrificed burnt offerings to the
LORD, 13according to the daily require- 8:13
ment[w] for offerings commanded by Mo- [w]Ex 29:38; Nu 28:3
ses for Sabbaths,[x] New Moons and the [x]Nu 28:9

[a]19 The Hebrew is plural. [b]2 Hebrew *Huram,* a variant of *Hiram;* also in verse 18 [c]6 Or *charioteers*

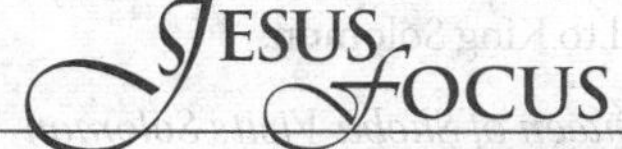

INCONSISTENT LEGALISM

In devotion to God, Solomon adhered strictly to some of God's laws. For example, he carefully kept Pharaoh's daughter, a Gentile, away from the sacred places (2 Chronicles 8:11). Yet at the same time Solomon did not keep other laws. He married foreign wives, and their foreign gods eventually led him astray. He married many of his wives in keeping with the provisions of treaties with other nations—despite the fact that God had specifically instructed his people not to do so (see Exodus 34:15–16; 1 Kings 11:1–4). Solomon allowed his foreign wives to bring their idols and altars with them into Israel, and the practice of worshiping false gods greatly undermined the spiritual vitality of the nation in the end. Solomon took seriously only selected parts of God's law, and this pattern has been repeated throughout history. In the New Testament Jesus faced similar attitudes. In fact, some of his harshest words were aimed at the religious leaders, the Pharisees. While they were meticulous about some of the minute details involved in keeping the law, they too often ignored the spirit of that law—a servant attitude and a heart truly dedicated to God (Matthew 12:1–14; Luke 11:37–54).

8:13 three[y] annual feasts—the Feast of Un-
y Ex 23:14; Dt 16:16 leavened Bread, the Feast of Weeks[z] and
z Ex 23:16 the Feast of Tabernacles. 14In keeping
8:14 with the ordinance of his father David,
a 1Ch 24:1 he appointed the divisions[a] of the
b 1Ch 25:1 c 1Ch 9:17; 26:1 priests for their duties, and the Levites[b]
d Ne 12:24,36 to lead the praise and to assist the
e 1Ch 23:6; Ne 12:45 priests according to each day's requirement. He also appointed the gatekeep-
ers[c] by divisions for the various gates,
because this was what David the man of
God[d] had ordered.[e] 15They did not deviate from the king's commands to the
priests or to the Levites in any matter,
including that of the treasuries.
16All Solomon's work was carried out,
from the day the foundation of the temple of the LORD was laid until its completion. So the temple of the LORD was
finished.
17Then Solomon went to Ezion Geber
and Elath on the coast of Edom. 18And
Hiram sent him ships commanded by
his own officers, men who knew the sea.
These, with Solomon's men, sailed to
Ophir and brought back four hundred
8:18 f 2Ch 9:9 and fifty talents*[a]* of gold,[f] which they delivered to King Solomon.

The Queen of Sheba Visits Solomon

9:1 g Ge 10:7; **9** When the queen of Sheba[g] heard
Eze 23:42; of Solomon's fame, she came to Je-
Mt 12:42; Lk 11:31 rusalem to test him with hard questions.
Arriving with a very great caravan—
with camels carrying spices, large quantities of gold, and precious stones—she
came to Solomon and talked with him
about all she had on her mind. 2Solomon
answered all her questions; nothing was
too hard for him to explain to her.
9:3 3When the queen of Sheba saw the wis-
h 1Ki 5:12 dom of Solomon,[h] as well as the palace
he had built, 4the food on his table, the
seating of his officials, the attending servants in their robes, the cupbearers in
their robes and the burnt offerings he
made at*[b]* the temple of the LORD, she
was overwhelmed.
5She said to the king, "The report I
heard in my own country about your
achievements and your wisdom is true.
9:6 6But I did not believe what they said un-
i 2Ch 6:32 til I came[i] and saw with my own eyes.
Indeed, not even half the greatness of
your wisdom was told me; you have far
exceeded the report I heard. 7How happy your men must be! How happy your
officials, who continually stand before
you and hear your wisdom! 8Praise be to
the LORD your God, who has delighted in
you and placed you on his throne[j] as 9:8 j 1Ki 2:12;
king to rule for the LORD your God. Be- 1Ch 17:14; 28:5;
cause of the love of your God for Israel 29:23; 2Ch 13:8 k 2Ch 2:11
and his desire to uphold them forever, he
has made you king[k] over them, to maintain justice and righteousness."
9Then she gave the king 120 talents*[c]* 9:9
of gold,[l] large quantities of spices, and l 2Ch 8:18
precious stones. There had never been
such spices as those the queen of Sheba
gave to King Solomon.
10(The men of Hiram and the men of 9:10
Solomon brought gold from Ophir;[m] m 2Ch 8:18
they also brought algumwood*[d]* and precious stones. 11The king used the algumwood to make steps for the temple
of the LORD and for the royal palace, and
to make harps and lyres for the musicians. Nothing like them had ever been
seen in Judah.)
12King Solomon gave the queen of

a 18 That is, about 17 tons (about 16 metric tons)
b 4 Or *the ascent by which he went up to*
c 9 That is, about 4 1/2 tons (about 4 metric tons)
d 10 Probably a variant of *almugwood*

JESUS FOCUS

QUEEN OF SHEBA

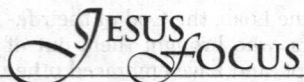

Sheba was located in Arabia (see Genesis 10:28–30) at a place where it was able to control most of the trade between India and Africa. The queen of that region had heard rumors about Solomon's wisdom and wealth, so she decided to go see for herself (2 Chronicles 9). What she discovered was that she had heard only half the story! Solomon was far wiser and more prosperous than his reputation, and the queen recognized that his blessings were a direct result of his relationship with the God of Israel.

In the New Testament Jesus referred back to the queen's famous visit to speak words of condemnation to his own generation. He emphasized that the queen had come from far away—the "ends of the earth"—to listen to and learn from Solomon's wisdom. But "now one greater than Solomon is here," he declared, and the people were refusing to listen (Luke 11:31). The precious Son of God himself was walking among the people, but they were turning away from him, the One who is infinitely greater than Solomon and any other human who has ever walked the earth!

DISCOVERY 104

Rich Toward God

The writer of 2 Chronicles tells us that "when the queen of Sheba heard of Solomon's fame, she came to Jerusalem to test him with hard questions" (2 Chronicles 9:1). The word choice in the second clause of this statement is intriguing. The foreign queen did not come with an intention of cementing a strategic alliance with a wealthy and influential king, nor did she arrive as a spy to substantiate rumors or even to evaluate Israel's strength in the light of a possible conquest. She didn't come on a vacation jaunt, expecting to be wined and dined by opulent fellow royalty. No, it would appear that the queen was on a personal, perhaps even a spiritual, quest. Verses 1 and 2 state further that she talked with Solomon about all that she had on her mind and that Solomon was able to answer all of her questions.

When the queen observed Solomon's incredible wealth firsthand, she was "overwhelmed" by his insight, his palace, the food on his table, the organization of his staff and his devotion to the God of Israel (verses 3–4). She responded in awe of Solomon's God: "Praise be to the LORD your God, who has delighted in you and placed you on his throne as king to rule for the LORD your God . . . He has made you king over them, to maintain justice and righteousness" (verse 8).

It is interesting to recall that when God had offered the young Solomon anything his heart desired (1 Kings 3:5), Solomon had opted for spiritual, as opposed to material, wealth: "I am only a little child and do not know how to carry out my duties . . . So give your servant a discerning heart to govern your people and to distinguish between right and wrong" (1 Kings 3:9).

The queen of Sheba was fabulously wealthy herself, and she demonstrated no jealousy or greed, instead showering Solomon with gifts prior to her departure (2 Chronicles 9:9). It is interesting to note that as she listed in verses 3 and 4 the qualities and possessions that most impressed her about Solomon, "the wisdom of Solomon" was mentioned before "the palace he had built." This foreign dignitary seems to have understood the priority of wisdom and rightly afforded it the highest position.

Jesus told a parable in Luke 12 of a wealthy landowner who stored up grain in ever bigger barns in preparation for kicking back and enjoying the good life. God, however, called him a fool and advised him that his life would that very night be demanded of him. Jesus summarized the lesson with these words: "This is how it will be with anyone who stores up things for himself but is not rich toward God" (Luke 12:21). The queen of Sheba assessed Solomon's great riches and went away satisfied, having verified for herself that this great king was indeed "rich toward God." May that ever be our goal as well!

Self-Discovery: *Jesus has promised to share his wisdom and wealth with you. In what specific ways have you "cashed in" on his offer by faith?*

GO TO DISCOVERY 105 ON PAGE 555

Sheba all she desired and asked for; he
gave her more than she had brought to
him. Then she left and returned with her
retinue to her own country.

Solomon's Splendor

13The weight of the gold that Solomon received yearly was 666 talents,[a]
14not including the revenues brought in
9:14 n2Ch 17:11; Isa 21:13; Jer 25:24; Eze 27:21; 30:5 by merchants and traders. Also all the
kings of Arabia[n] and the governors of
the land brought gold and silver to Solomon.
15King Solomon made two hundred
large shields of hammered gold; six hundred bekas[b] of hammered gold went
into each shield. 16He also made three
9:16 o2Ch 12:9 p1Ki 7:2 hundred small shields[o] of hammered
gold, with three hundred bekas[c] of gold
in each shield. The king put them in the
Palace of the Forest of Lebanon.[p]
17Then the king made a great throne
9:17 q1Ki 22:39 inlaid with ivory[q] and overlaid with pure
gold. 18The throne had six steps, and a
footstool of gold was attached to it. On
both sides of the seat were armrests,
with a lion standing beside each of
them. 19Twelve lions stood on the six
steps, one at either end of each step.
Nothing like it had ever been made for
any other kingdom. 20All King Solomon's
goblets were gold, and all the household
articles in the Palace of the Forest of
Lebanon were pure gold. Nothing was
made of silver, because silver was considered of little value in Solomon's day.
21The king had a fleet of trading ships[d]
manned by Hiram's[e] men. Once every
three years it returned, carrying gold, silver and ivory, and apes and baboons.
22King Solomon was greater in riches
9:22 r1Ki 3:13; 2Ch 1:12 and wisdom than all the other kings of
the earth.[r] 23All the kings[s] of the earth
sought audience with Solomon to hear
9:23 s1Ki 4:34 the wisdom God had put in his heart.
24Year after year, everyone who came
9:24 t2Ch 32:23; Ps 45:12; 68:29; 72:10; Isa 18:7 brought a gift[t]—articles of silver and
gold, and robes, weapons and spices,
and horses and mules.
25Solomon had four thousand stalls
9:25 u1Sa 8:11; 1Ki 4:26 for horses and chariots,[u] and twelve
thousand horses,[f] which he kept in the
chariot cities and also with him in Jeru-
9:26 v1Ki 4:21 wPs 72:8-9 xGe 15:18-21 salem. 26He ruled[v] over all the kings
from the River[g][w] to the land of the Phi-
listines, as far as the border of Egypt.[x]
27The king made silver as common in Jerusalem as stones, and cedar as plentiful as sycamore-fig trees in the foothills.
28Solomon's horses were imported from
Egypt[h] and from all other countries.

Solomon's Death

29As for the other events of Solomon's
reign, from beginning to end, are they 9:29 y2Sa 7:2; 1Ch 29:29 z1Ki 11:29 a2Ch 10:2
not written in the records of Nathan[y]
the prophet, in the prophecy of Ahijah[z]
the Shilonite and in the visions of Iddo
the seer concerning Jeroboam[a] son of
Nebat? 30Solomon reigned in Jerusalem
over all Israel forty years. 31Then he rested with his fathers and was buried in the 9:31 b1Ki 2:10
city of David[b] his father. And Rehoboam
his son succeeded him as king.

Israel Rebels Against Rehoboam

10 Rehoboam went to Shechem,
for all the Israelites had gone
there to make him king. 2When Jerobo- 10:2 c2Ch 9:29 d1Ki 11:40
am[c] son of Nebat heard this (he was in
Egypt, where he had fled[d] from King
Solomon), he returned from Egypt. 3So
they sent for Jeroboam, and he and all 10:3 e1Ch 9:1
Israel[e] went to Rehoboam and said to
him: 4"Your father put a heavy yoke on 10:4 f2Ch 2:2
us,[f] but now lighten the harsh labor and
the heavy yoke he put on us, and we will
serve you."
5Rehoboam answered, "Come back to
me in three days." So the people went
away.
6Then King Rehoboam consulted the 10:6 gJob 8:8-9; 12:12; 15:10; 32:7
elders[g] who had served his father Solo-
mon during his lifetime. "How would
you advise me to answer these people?"
he asked.
7They replied, "If you will be kind to
these people and please them and give 10:7 hPr 15:1
them a favorable answer,[h] they will always be your servants." 10:8 i2Sa 17:14 jPr 13:20
8But Rehoboam rejected[i] the advice
the elders[j] gave him and consulted the
young men who had grown up with him
and were serving him. 9He asked them,
"What is your advice? How should we
answer these people who say to me,
'Lighten the yoke your father put on us'?"
10The young men who had grown up

[a] *13* That is, about 25 tons (about 23 metric tons)
[b] *15* That is, about 7 1/2 pounds (about 3.5 kilograms)
[c] *16* That is, about 3 3/4 pounds (about 1.7 kilograms)
[d] *21* Hebrew *of ships that could go to Tarshish*
[e] *21* Hebrew *Huram,* a variant of *Hiram*
[f] *25* Or *charioteers*
[g] *26* That is, the Euphrates
[h] *28* Or possibly *Muzur,* a region in Cilicia

DISCOVERY 105

Listening to the Wrong Voice

Shortly after Solomon's death his kingdom was divided in two, just as God had said it would be (1 Kings 11:26–40). Rehoboam, Solomon's son, had his coronation in Shechem and, following a rift between the northern and southern tribes, ruled only the southern kingdom (Judah). God had promised that Jeroboam, who had fled to Egypt to escape Solomon's anger, would eventually become king over the northern kingdom (Israel).

On behalf of the northern tribes Jeroboam had approached the new king Rehoboam, asking for relief from taxes. If Rehoboam would agree, Jeroboam indicated, the people from the north would be his loyal subjects. Before responding Rehoboam consulted his many advisers. First he presented the proposal to the elders who had served under his father Solomon. They advised him to listen to the people: "Ease their burden and they will serve you" (see 2 Chronicles 10:7). Next he discussed the situation with his peers. Their advice was exactly the opposite: "Don't give in to their whining; show them that you're even more powerful than your father was. *Increase* the taxes" (see verses 10–11). Rehoboam opted to listen to his younger advisers.

When the northern tribes learned of Rehoboam's intention, they responded, "What share do we have in David, what part in Jesse's son?" (verse 16). The northern residents turned against David's family and resolved to look out for themselves. That decision to secede was the beginning of the end for Israel. The northern kingdom eventually fell, and its citizens were dragged away into captivity, never to return to their land. Part of the reason for this harsh judgment was the fact that the people had rejected David's line as their rightful rulers. They had forgotten that God's promised Messiah was to come through David's family. By rejecting David they were ultimately rejecting God—even though their complaint against Rehoboam was legitimate.

When Jesus was on earth, some of his messages were referred to as "hard teaching" (John 6:60). Many of his disciples were so offended that they no longer followed him. Their complaint was not based on his unrealistic demands; Jesus identified the problem as a lack of spiritual insight: "The Spirit gives life; the flesh counts for nothing. The words I have spoken to you are spirit and they are life. Yet there are some of you who do not believe" (John 6:63–64). The 12 disciples remained loyal, not because they understood what their Lord had said but because they understood who he was. Peter, as was so often the case, acted as spokesman for the group: "We believe and know that you are the Holy One of God" (John 6:69).

We still have to guard against the same kind of mistake Rehoboam made. There are so many perspectives and opinions on such a wide variety of issues that we can easily become confused by listening to the wrong voices—and it is often difficult to discern whose voice is the *right* one! But God has given us his Word so that we might know clearly what he expects, and he has sent his Son Jesus to be our guide. Like sheep, we can train our ears to listen for the distinctive voice of our Shepherd (John 10:1–3).

Self-Discovery: *Have you ever struggled with the "hard teachings" of Jesus? When you remember who he is, how does it change your reaction to what he has said?*

GO TO DISCOVERY 106 ON PAGE 564

with him replied, "Tell the people who
have said to you, 'Your father put a heavy
yoke on us, but make our yoke lighter'—
tell them, 'My little finger is thicker than
my father's waist. 11My father laid on you
a heavy yoke; I will make it even heavier.
My father scourged you with whips; I
will scourge you with scorpions.' "
12Three days later Jeroboam and all
the people returned to Rehoboam, as
the king had said, "Come back to me in
three days." 13The king answered them
harshly. Rejecting the advice of the elders, 14he followed the advice of the
young men and said, "My father made
your yoke heavy; I will make it even
heavier. My father scourged you with
whips; I will scourge you with scorpions." 15So the king did not listen to the
people, for this turn of events was from
10:15 k2Ch 11:4; God,[k] to fulfill the word the LORD had
25:16-20 spoken to Jeroboam son of Nebat
l1Ki 11:29 through Ahijah the Shilonite.[l]
10:16 16When all Israel[m] saw that the king
m1Ch 9:1 refused to listen to them, they answered
n ver 19; 2Sa 20:1 the king:

"What share do we have in David,[n]
what part in Jesse's son?
To your tents, O Israel!
Look after your own house,
O David!"

So all the Israelites went home. 17But as
for the Israelites who were living in the
towns of Judah, Rehoboam still ruled
over them.
10:18 18King Rehoboam sent out Adoni-
o1Ki 5:14 ram,[a][o] who was in charge of forced labor, but the Israelites stoned him to
death. King Rehoboam, however, managed to get into his chariot and escape
to Jerusalem. 19So Israel has been in rebellion against the house of David to
this day.

11 When Rehoboam arrived in Je-
11:1 rusalem,[p] he mustered the
p1Ki 12:21 house of Judah and Benjamin—a hundred and eighty thousand fighting
men—to make war against Israel and to
regain the kingdom for Rehoboam.
11:2 2But this word of the LORD came to
q2Ch 12:5-7,15 Shemaiah[q] the man of God: 3"Say to Rehoboam son of Solomon king of Judah
and to all the Israelites in Judah and
Benjamin, 4'This is what the LORD says:
11:4 Do not go up to fight against your broth-
r2Ch 28:8-11 ers.[r] Go home, every one of you, for this
is my doing.' " So they obeyed the words
of the LORD and turned back from
marching against Jeroboam.

Rehoboam Fortifies Judah

5Rehoboam lived in Jerusalem and
built up towns for defense in Judah:
6Bethlehem, Etam, Tekoa, 7Beth Zur,
Soco, Adullam, 8Gath, Mareshah, Ziph,
9Adoraim, Lachish, Azekah, 10Zorah, Aijalon and Hebron. These were fortified
cities in Judah and Benjamin. 11He
strengthened their defenses and put
commanders in them, with supplies of
food, olive oil and wine. 12He put shields
and spears in all the cities, and made
them very strong. So Judah and Benjamin were his.
13The priests and Levites from all
their districts throughout Israel sided
with him. 14The Levites[s] even aban- 11:14 sNu 35:2-5
doned their pasturelands and property,[t] t2Ch 13:9
and came to Judah and Jerusalem be-
cause Jeroboam and his sons had rejected them as priests of the LORD. 15And he 11:15
appointed[u] his own priests[v] for the high u1Ki 13:33 v1Ki 12:31
places and for the goat[w] and calf[x] idols wLev 17:7
he had made. 16Those from every tribe x1Ki 12:28; 2Ch 13:8
of Israel[y] who set their hearts on seeking 11:16
the LORD, the God of Israel, followed the y2Ch 15:9
Levites to Jerusalem to offer sacrifices to
the LORD, the God of their fathers. 11:17
17They strengthened[z] the kingdom of z2Ch 12:1
Judah and supported Rehoboam son of
Solomon three years, walking in the
ways of David and Solomon during this
time.

Rehoboam's Family

18Rehoboam married Mahalath, who
was the daughter of David's son Jerimoth
and of Abihail, the daughter of Jesse's son
Eliab. 19She bore him sons: Jeush, Shemariah and Zaham. 20Then he married 11:20
Maacah[a] daughter of Absalom, who bore a1Ki 15:2
him Abijah,[b] Attai, Ziza and Shelomith. b2Ch 13:2
21Rehoboam loved Maacah daughter of
Absalom more than any of his other
wives and concubines. In all, he had 11:21
eighteen wives[c] and sixty concubines, cDt 17:17
twenty-eight sons and sixty daughters. 11:22
22Rehoboam appointed Abijah[d] son dDt 21:15-17
of Maacah to be the chief prince among
his brothers, in order to make him king.
23He acted wisely, dispersing some of his
sons throughout the districts of Judah

a 18 Hebrew *Hadoram,* a variant of *Adoniram*

and Benjamin, and to all the fortified
cities. He gave them abundant provisions and took many wives for them.

Shishak Attacks Jerusalem

12:1 e ver 13 **12** After Rehoboam's position as
f 2Ch 11:17 king was established[e] and he
had become strong,[f] he and all Israel[a]
with him abandoned the law of the
12:2 LORD. 2Because they had been unfaith-
g 1Ki 14:22-24 ful[g] to the LORD, Shishak[h] king of Egypt
h 1Ki 11:40 attacked Jerusalem in the fifth year of
King Rehoboam. 3With twelve hundred
chariots and sixty thousand horsemen
12:3 and the innumerable troops of Libyans,
i 2Ch 16:8; Sukkites and Cushites[b][i] that came with
Na 3:9 him from Egypt, 4he captured the forti-
12:4 j 2Ch 11:10 fied cities[j] of Judah and came as far as
Jerusalem.
12:5 k 2Ch 11:2 5Then the prophet Shemaiah[k] came
l Dt 28:15; to Rehoboam and to the leaders of Ju-
2Ch 15:2 dah who had assembled in Jerusalem for
fear of Shishak, and he said to them,
"This is what the LORD says, 'You have
abandoned me; therefore, I now abandon[l] you to Shishak.' "
6The leaders of Israel and the king
12:6 humbled themselves and said, "The
m Ex 9:27; Da 9:14 LORD is just."[m]
7When the LORD saw that they humbled themselves, this word of the LORD
came to Shemaiah: "Since they have
humbled themselves, I will not destroy
12:7 them but will soon give them deliver-
n 1Ki 21:29; Ps 78:38 ance.[n] My wrath will not be poured out
on Jerusalem through Shishak. 8They
12:8 o Dt 28:48 will, however, become subject[o] to him,
so that they may learn the difference between serving me and serving the kings
of other lands."
9When Shishak king of Egypt attacked Jerusalem, he carried off the treasures of the temple of the LORD and the
treasures of the royal palace. He took
12:9 everything, including the gold shields[p]
p 2Ch 9:16 Solomon had made. 10So King Rehoboam made bronze shields to replace them
and assigned these to the commanders
of the guard on duty at the entrance to
the royal palace. 11Whenever the king
went to the LORD's temple, the guards
went with him, bearing the shields, and
afterward they returned them to the
guardroom.
12Because Rehoboam humbled himself, the LORD's anger turned from him,
and he was not totally destroyed. In-
deed, there was some good[q] in Judah. 12:12 q 1Ki 14:13;
13King Rehoboam established himself 2Ch 19:3
firmly in Jerusalem and continued as
king. He was forty-one years old when
he became king, and he reigned seventeen years in Jerusalem, the city the
LORD had chosen out of all the tribes of
Israel in which to put his Name.[r] His 12:13 r Dt 12:5;
mother's name was Naamah; she was an 2Ch 6:6
Ammonite. 14He did evil because he had
not set his heart on seeking the LORD.
15As for the events of Rehoboam's
reign, from beginning to end, are they 12:15
not written in the records of Shemaiah[s] s 2Ch 9:29; 11:2
the prophet and of Iddo the seer that
deal with genealogies? There was continual warfare between Rehoboam and
Jeroboam. 16Rehoboam rested with his
fathers and was buried in the City of Da- 12:16
vid. And Abijah[t] his son succeeded him t 2Ch 11:20
as king.

Abijah King of Judah

13 In the eighteenth year of the
reign of Jeroboam, Abijah became king of Judah, 2and he reigned in
Jerusalem three years. His mother's
name was Maacah,[c] a daughter[d] of Uriel
of Gibeah.
There was war between Abijah[u] and 13:2 u 2Ch 11:20
Jeroboam.[v] 3Abijah went into battle with v 1Ki 15:6
a force of four hundred thousand able
fighting men, and Jeroboam drew up a
battle line against him with eight hundred thousand able troops.
4Abijah stood on Mount Zemaraim,[w] 13:4 w Jos 18:22
in the hill country of Ephraim, and said, x 1Ch 11:1
"Jeroboam and all Israel,[x] listen to me!
5Don't you know that the LORD, the God
of Israel, has given the kingship of Israel
to David and his descendants forever[y] 13:5 y 2Sa 7:13
by a covenant of salt?[z] 6Yet Jeroboam z Lev 2:13;
son of Nebat, an official of Solomon son Nu 18:19
of David, rebelled[a] against his master. 13:6 a 1Ki 11:26
7Some worthless scoundrels[b] gathered
around him and opposed Rehoboam 13:7 b Jdg 9:4
son of Solomon when he was young and
indecisive and not strong enough to resist them.
8"And now you plan to resist the kingdom of the LORD, which is in the hands of
David's descendants. You are indeed a

[a] 1 That is, Judah, as frequently in 2 Chronicles
[b] 3 That is, people from the upper Nile region
[c] 2 Most Septuagint manuscripts and Syriac (see also 2 Chron. 11:20 and 1 Kings 15:2); Hebrew *Micaiah* [d] 2 Or *granddaughter*

vast army and have with you the golden calves[c] that Jeroboam made to be your gods. 9 But didn't you drive out the priests of the LORD,[d] the sons of Aaron, and the Levites, and make priests of your own as the peoples of other lands do? Whoever comes to consecrate himself with a young bull[e] and seven rams may become a priest of what are not gods.[f]

10 "As for us, the LORD is our God, and we have not forsaken him. The priests who serve the LORD are sons of Aaron, and the Levites assist them. 11 Every morning and evening[g] they present burnt offerings and fragrant incense to the LORD. They set out the bread on the ceremonially clean table[h] and light the lamps on the gold lampstand every evening. We are observing the requirements of the LORD our God. But you have forsaken him. 12 God is with us; he is our leader. His priests with their trumpets will sound the battle cry against you.[i] Men of Israel, do not fight against the LORD,[j] the God of your fathers, for you will not succeed."

13 Now Jeroboam had sent troops around to the rear, so that while he was in front of Judah the ambush[k] was behind them. 14 Judah turned and saw that they were being attacked at both front and rear. Then they cried out[l] to the LORD. The priests blew their trumpets 15 and the men of Judah raised the battle cry. At the sound of their battle cry, God routed Jeroboam and all Israel[m] before Abijah and Judah. 16 The Israelites fled before Judah, and God delivered[n] them into their hands. 17 Abijah and his men inflicted heavy losses on them, so that there were five hundred thousand casualties among Israel's able men. 18 The men of Israel were subdued on that occasion, and the men of Judah were victorious because they relied[o] on the LORD, the God of their fathers.

19 Abijah pursued Jeroboam and took from him the towns of Bethel, Jeshanah and Ephron, with their surrounding villages. 20 Jeroboam did not regain power during the time of Abijah. And the LORD struck him down and he died.

21 But Abijah grew in strength. He married fourteen wives and had twenty-two sons and sixteen daughters.

22 The other events of Abijah's reign, what he did and what he said, are written in the annotations of the prophet Iddo.

13:8 c 1Ki 12:28; 2Ch 11:15
13:9 d 2Ch 11:14-15 e Ex 29:35-36 f Jer 2:11
13:11 g Ex 29:39; 2Ch 2:4 h Lev 24:5-9
13:12 i Nu 10:8-9 j Ac 5:39
13:13 k Jos 8:9
13:14 l 2Ch 14:11
13:15 m 2Ch 14:12
13:16 n 2Ch 16:8
13:18 o 1Ch 5:20; 2Ch 14:11; Ps 22:5

14 And Abijah rested with his fathers and was buried in the City of David. Asa his son succeeded him as king, and in his days the country was at peace for ten years.

Asa King of Judah

2 Asa did what was good and right in the eyes of the LORD his God. 3 He removed the foreign altars and the high places, smashed the sacred stones and cut down the Asherah poles.[a][p] 4 He commanded Judah to seek the LORD, the God of their fathers, and to obey his laws and commands. 5 He removed the high places and incense altars[q] in every town in Judah, and the kingdom was at peace under him. 6 He built up the fortified cities of Judah, since the land was at peace. No one was at war with him during those years, for the LORD gave him rest.[r]

7 "Let us build up these towns," he said to Judah, "and put walls around them, with towers, gates and bars. The land is still ours, because we have sought the LORD our God; we sought him and he has given us rest on every side." So they built and prospered.

8 Asa had an army of three hundred thousand men from Judah, equipped with large shields and with spears, and two hundred and eighty thousand from Benjamin, armed with small shields and with bows. All these were brave fighting men.

9 Zerah the Cushite[s] marched out against them with a vast army[b] and three hundred chariots, and came as far as Mareshah.[t] 10 Asa went out to meet him, and they took up battle positions in the Valley of Zephathah near Mareshah.

11 Then Asa called[u] to the LORD his God and said, "LORD, there is no one like you to help the powerless against the mighty. Help us, O LORD our God, for we rely[v] on you, and in your name[w] we have come against this vast army. O LORD, you are our God; do not let man prevail[x] against you."

12 The LORD struck down[y] the Cushites before Asa and Judah. The Cushites fled, 13 and Asa and his army pursued

14:3 p Ex 34:13; Dt 7:5; 1Ki 15:12-14
14:5 q 2Ch 34:4,7
14:6 r 1Ch 22:9; 2Ch 15:15
14:9 s 2Ch 12:3; 16:8 t 2Ch 11:8
14:11 u 2Ch 13:14 v 2Ch 13:18 w 1Sa 17:45 x 1Sa 14:6; Ps 9:19
14:12 y 2Ch 13:15

a 3 That is, symbols of the goddess Asherah; here and elsewhere in 2 Chronicles *b* 9 Hebrew *with an army of a thousand thousands* or *with an army of thousands upon thousands*

14:13 [z]Ge 10:19 them as far as Gerar.[z] Such a great number of Cushites fell that they could not
recover; they were crushed before the
LORD and his forces. The men of Judah
carried off a large amount of plunder.
14:14 14They destroyed all the villages around
[a]Ge 35:5; Gerar, for the terror[a] of the LORD had
2Ch 17:10 fallen upon them. They plundered all
these villages, since there was much
booty there. 15They also attacked the
camps of the herdsmen and carried off
droves of sheep and goats and camels.
Then they returned to Jerusalem.

Asa's Reform

15:1 **15** The Spirit of God came upon[b]
[b]Nu 11:25,26; 24:2; 2Ch 20:14; Azariah son of Oded. 2He went
24:20 out to meet Asa and said to him, "Listen
15:2 to me, Asa and all Judah and Benjamin.
[c]ver 4,15; The LORD is with you[c] when you are with
2Ch 20:17 [d]Jas 4:8 him.[d] If you seek[e] him, he will be found
[e]Jer 29:13 [f]1Ch 28:9; by you, but if you forsake him, he will
2Ch 24:20 forsake you.[f] 3For a long time Israel was
without the true God, without a priest
15:3 [g]Lev 10:11 to teach[g] and without the law.[h] 4But in
[h]2Ch 17:9; their distress they turned to the LORD,
La 2:9 the God of Israel, and sought him,[i] and
15:4 [i]Dt 4:29 he was found by them. 5In those days it
was not safe to travel about,[j] for all the
15:5 [j]Jdg 5:6 inhabitants of the lands were in great
turmoil. 6One nation was being crushed
15:6 [k]Mt 24:7 by another and one city by another,[k] because God was troubling them with
15:7 every kind of distress. 7But as for you, be
[l]Jos 1:7,9 [m]Ps 58:11 strong[l] and do not give up, for your work
will be rewarded."[m]
8When Asa heard these words and
the prophecy of Azariah son of[a] Oded
the prophet, he took courage. He removed the detestable idols from the
15:8 whole land of Judah and Benjamin and
[n]2Ch 13:19 from the towns he had captured[n] in the
[o]2Ch 8:12 hills of Ephraim. He repaired the altar[o]
of the LORD that was in front of the portico of the LORD's temple.
9Then he assembled all Judah and
Benjamin and the people from Ephraim,
15:9 Manasseh and Simeon who had settled
[p]2Ch 11:16-17 among them, for large numbers[p] had
come over to him from Israel when they
saw that the LORD his God was with him.
10They assembled at Jerusalem in the
third month of the fifteenth year of Asa's
reign. 11At that time they sacrificed to
the LORD seven hundred head of cattle
15:11 and seven thousand sheep and goats
[q]2Ch 14:13 from the plunder[q] they had brought

back. 12They entered into a covenant[r] to 15:12
seek the LORD,[s] the God of their fathers, [r]2Ki 11:17;
with all their heart and soul. 13All who 2Ch 23:16;
would not seek the LORD, the God of Is- 34:31 [s]1Ch 16:11
rael, were to be put to death,[t] whether 15:13
small or great, man or woman. 14They [t]Ex 22:20; Dt 13:9-16
took an oath to the LORD with loud ac-
clamation, with shouting and with
trumpets and horns. 15All Judah rejoiced
about the oath because they had sworn
it wholeheartedly. They sought God[u] ea- 15:15 [u]Dt 4:29
gerly, and he was found by them. So the [v]1Ch 22:9;
LORD gave them rest[v] on every side. 2Ch 14:7
16King Asa also deposed his grandmother Maacah from her position as
queen mother, because she had made a 15:16
repulsive Asherah pole.[w] Asa cut the [w]Ex 34:13;
pole down, broke it up and burned it in 2Ch 14:2-5
the Kidron Valley. 17Although he did not
remove the high places from Israel, Asa's
heart was fully committed ⌞to the LORD⌟
all his life. 18He brought into the temple
of God the silver and gold and the articles that he and his father had dedicated.
19There was no more war until the
thirty-fifth year of Asa's reign.

Asa's Last Years

16 In the thirty-sixth year of Asa's 16:1
reign Baasha[x] king of Israel [x]Jer 41:9
went up against Judah and fortified Ramah to prevent anyone from leaving or
entering the territory of Asa king of Judah.
2Asa then took the silver and gold out
of the treasuries of the LORD's temple
and of his own palace and sent it to Ben-
Hadad king of Aram, who was ruling in
Damascus. 3"Let there be a treaty[y] be- 16:3
tween me and you," he said, "as there [y]2Ch 20:35
was between my father and your father.
See, I am sending you silver and gold.
Now break your treaty with Baasha king
of Israel so he will withdraw from me."
4Ben-Hadad agreed with King Asa
and sent the commanders of his forces
against the towns of Israel. They conquered Ijon, Dan, Abel Maim[b] and all
the store cities of Naphtali. 5When Baasha heard this, he stopped building Ramah and abandoned his work. 6Then
King Asa brought all the men of Judah,
and they carried away from Ramah the
stones and timber Baasha had been us-

[a] 8 Vulgate and Syriac (see also Septuagint and verse 1); Hebrew does not have *Azariah son of.*
[b] 4 Also known as *Abel Beth Maacah*

ing. With them he built up Geba and
16:7 Mizpah.
z 1Ki 16:1 7 At that time Hanani[z] the seer came
to Asa king of Judah and said to him:
"Because you relied on the king of Aram
and not on the LORD your God, the army
of the king of Aram has escaped from
16:8 a 2Ch 12:3; 14:9 your hand. 8 Were not the Cushites[a][a] and
b 2Ch 13:16 Libyans a mighty army with great num-
bers of chariots and horsemen[b]? Yet
when you relied on the LORD, he delivered[b] them into your hand. 9 For the
16:9 c Pr 15:3; eyes[c] of the LORD range throughout the
Jer 16:17; earth to strengthen those whose hearts
Zec 4:10 d 1Sa 13:13 are fully committed to him. You have
done a foolish[d] thing, and from now on
you will be at war."
10 Asa was angry with the seer because
of this; he was so enraged that he put
him in prison. At the same time Asa
brutally oppressed some of the people.
11 The events of Asa's reign, from beginning to end, are written in the book
of the kings of Judah and Israel. 12 In the
thirty-ninth year of his reign Asa was afflicted with a disease in his feet. Though
16:12 his disease was severe, even in his illness
e Jer 17:5-6 he did not seek help from the LORD,[e] but
only from the physicians. 13 Then in the
forty-first year of his reign Asa died and
rested with his fathers. 14 They buried
him in the tomb that he had cut out for
himself in the City of David. They laid
16:14 him on a bier covered with spices and
f Ge 50:2; Jn 19:39-40 various blended perfumes,[f] and they
g 2Ch 21:19; Jer 34:5 made a huge fire[g] in his honor.

Jehoshaphat King of Judah

17 Jehoshaphat his son succeeded
him as king and strengthened
himself against Israel. 2 He stationed
troops in all the fortified cities of Judah
and put garrisons in Judah and in the
17:2 towns of Ephraim that his father Asa
h 2Ch 15:8 had captured.[h]
3 The LORD was with Jehoshaphat because in his early years he walked in the
17:3 i 1Ki 22:43 ways his father David[i] had followed. He
did not consult the Baals 4 but sought[j]
17:4 j 1Ki 12:28; the God of his father and followed his
2Ch 22:9 commands rather than the practices of
Israel. 5 The LORD established the king-
17:5 dom under his control; and all Judah
k 1Sa 10:27 brought gifts[k] to Jehoshaphat, so that
l 2Ch 18:1 he had great wealth and honor.[l] 6 His
17:6 m 1Ki 8:61; heart was devoted[m] to the ways of the
2Ch 15:17 LORD; furthermore, he removed the high

places[n] and the Asherah poles[o] from Ju- 17:6 n 1Ki 15:14;
dah.[p] 2Ch 19:3; 20:33
7 In the third year of his reign he sent o Ex 34:13
his officials Ben-Hail, Obadiah, Zechari- p 2Ch 21:12
ah, Nethanel and Micaiah to teach[q] in 17:7
the towns of Judah. 8 With them were cer- q Lev 10:11;
tain Levites[r]—Shemaiah, Nethaniah, Dt 6:4-9; 2Ch 15:3; 35:3
Zebadiah, Asahel, Shemiramoth, Je- 17:8
honathan, Adonijah, Tobijah and Tob- r 2Ch 19:8;
Adonijah—and the priests Elishama and Ne 8:7-8
Jehoram. 9 They taught throughout Judah,
taking with them the Book of the Law[s] of 17:9 s Dt 6:4-9; 28:61
the LORD; they went around to all the
towns of Judah and taught the people.
10 The fear[t] of the LORD fell on all the 17:10 t Ge 35:5;
kingdoms of the lands surrounding Ju- Dt 2:25;
dah, so that they did not make war with 2Ch 14:14
Jehoshaphat. 11 Some Philistines brought
Jehoshaphat gifts and silver as tribute, 17:11
and the Arabs[u] brought him flocks:[v] sev- u 2Ch 9:14; 26:8
en thousand seven hundred rams and v 2Ch 21:16
seven thousand seven hundred goats.
12 Jehoshaphat became more and
more powerful; he built forts and store
cities in Judah 13 and had large supplies
in the towns of Judah. He also kept experienced fighting men in Jerusalem. 17:14
14 Their enrollment[w] by families was as w 2Sa 24:2
follows:

From Judah, commanders of units
of 1,000:
Adnah the commander, with
300,000 fighting men;
15 next, Jehohanan the commander, with 280,000;
16 next, Amasiah son of Zicri, who 17:16
volunteered[x] himself for the x Jdg 5:9;
service of the LORD, with 1Ch 29:9
200,000.
17 From Benjamin:[y] 17:17
Eliada, a valiant soldier, with y Nu 1:36
200,000 men armed with bows
and shields;
18 next, Jehozabad, with 180,000
men armed for battle.

19 These were the men who served the
king, besides those he stationed in the 17:19
fortified cities[z] throughout Judah.[a] z 2Ch 11:10 a 2Ch 25:5

Micaiah Prophesies Against Ahab

18 Now Jehoshaphat had great 18:1
wealth and honor,[b] and he al- b 2Ch 17:5
lied[c] himself with Ahab[d] by marriage. c 2Ch 19:1-3; 22:3 d 2Ch 21:6
2 Some years later he went down to visit

a 8 That is, people from the upper Nile region
b 8 Or *charioteers*

Ahab in Samaria. Ahab slaughtered
many sheep and cattle for him and the
people with him and urged him to attack Ramoth Gilead. 3 Ahab king of Israel asked Jehoshaphat king of Judah,
"Will you go with me against Ramoth
Gilead?"
Jehoshaphat replied, "I am as you are,
and my people as your people; we will
join you in the war." 4 But Jehoshaphat
also said to the king of Israel, "First seek
the counsel of the LORD."
5 So the king of Israel brought together
the prophets—four hundred men—and
asked them, "Shall we go to war against
Ramoth Gilead, or shall I refrain?"
"Go," they answered, "for God will give
it into the king's hand."
6 But Jehoshaphat asked, "Is there not
a prophet of the LORD here whom we can
inquire of?"

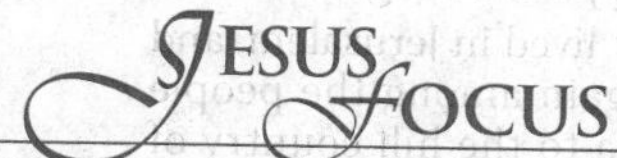

TRUE OR FALSE?

There were many prophets in ancient Israel. Unfortunately, many of them were "false" prophets who did not speak God's truth. Micaiah was one true prophet of God who was committed to telling Ahab the truth, whether the king liked it or not (2 Chronicles 18:7). Ahab wanted to make his own decisions, and at the same time he wanted God to approve! Micaiah reminded the king that in order to please God, he had to live God's way—and Micaiah's honesty nearly cost him his life.

In the New Testament Jesus came as God's ultimate and final prophet (Matthew 21:11; John 6:14; 7:40; Acts 3:22–26). Many people, especially in Jesus' hometown of Nazareth, refused to accept what he said, even though God had given them clear guidelines for how to determine whether or not someone was indeed God's prophet (Deuteronomy 18:17–22). Instead, they questioned Jesus' right to be called a prophet, and Jesus knew that they did not honor him for who he was (Matthew 13:57). By contrast, when a woman from Samaria met Jesus, she was ready to take him at his word and readily affirmed, "I can see that you are a prophet" (John 4:19). As followers of Jesus Christ we share in his prophetic anointing as those who confess his name (Matthew 10:32; Romans 10:9–10; Hebrews 13:15) and lovingly spread everywhere "the fragrance of the knowledge of him" (2 Corinthians 2:14).

7 The king of Israel answered Jehoshaphat, "There is still one man through
whom we can inquire of the LORD, but I
hate him because he never prophesies
anything good about me, but always
bad. He is Micaiah son of Imlah."
"The king should not say that," Jehoshaphat replied.
8 So the king of Israel called one of his
officials and said, "Bring Micaiah son of
Imlah at once."
9 Dressed in their royal robes, the king
of Israel and Jehoshaphat king of Judah
were sitting on their thrones at the
threshing floor by the entrance to the
gate of Samaria, with all the prophets
prophesying before them. 10 Now Zedekiah son of Kenaanah had made iron
horns, and he declared, "This is what the
LORD says: 'With these you will gore the
Arameans until they are destroyed.' "
11 All the other prophets were prophesying the same thing. "Attack Ramoth
Gilead[e] and be victorious," they said, "for 18:11 [e] 2Ch 22:5
the LORD will give it into the king's
hand."
12 The messenger who had gone to
summon Micaiah said to him, "Look, as
one man the other prophets are predicting success for the king. Let your word
agree with theirs, and speak favorably."
13 But Micaiah said, "As surely as the
LORD lives, I can tell him only what my 18:13
God says."[f] [f] Nu 22:18,20,35
14 When he arrived, the king asked
him, "Micaiah, shall we go to war against
Ramoth Gilead, or shall I refrain?"
"Attack and be victorious," he answered, "for they will be given into your
hand."
15 The king said to him, "How many
times must I make you swear to tell me
nothing but the truth in the name of the
LORD?"
16 Then Micaiah answered, "I saw all 18:16
Israel[g] scattered on the hills like sheep [g] 1Ch 9:1
without a shepherd,[h] and the LORD said, [h] Nu 27:17; Eze 34:5-8
'These people have no master. Let each
one go home in peace.' "
17 The king of Israel said to Jehoshaphat, "Didn't I tell you that he never
prophesies anything good about me, but
only bad?"
18 Micaiah continued, "Therefore hear
the word of the LORD: I saw the LORD sit- 18:18
ting on his throne[i] with all the host of [i] Da 7:9
heaven standing on his right and on his

left. 19 And the LORD said, 'Who will entice Ahab king of Israel into attacking Ramoth Gilead and going to his death there?'

"One suggested this, and another that. 20 Finally, a spirit came forward, stood before the LORD and said, 'I will entice him.'

"'By what means?' the LORD asked.

21 "'I will go and be a lying spirit[j] in the mouths of all his prophets,' he said.

18:21 [j] 1Ch 21:1; Job 1:6; Zec 3:1; Jn 8:44

"'You will succeed in enticing him,' said the LORD. 'Go and do it.'

22 "So now the LORD has put a lying spirit in the mouths of these prophets of yours.[k] The LORD has decreed disaster for you."

18:22 [k] Job 12:16; Isa 19:14; Eze 14:9

23 Then Zedekiah son of Kenaanah went up and slapped[l] Micaiah in the face. "Which way did the spirit from[a] the LORD go when he went from me to speak to you?" he asked.

18:23 [l] Jer 20:2; Mk 14:65; Ac 23:2

24 Micaiah replied, "You will find out on the day you go to hide in an inner room."

25 The king of Israel then ordered, "Take Micaiah and send him back to Amon the ruler of the city and to Joash the king's son, 26 and say, 'This is what the king says: Put this fellow in prison[m] and give him nothing but bread and water until I return safely.'"

18:26 [m] 2Ch 16:10; Heb 11:36

27 Micaiah declared, "If you ever return safely, the LORD has not spoken through me." Then he added, "Mark my words, all you people!"

Ahab Killed at Ramoth Gilead

28 So the king of Israel and Jehoshaphat king of Judah went up to Ramoth Gilead. 29 The king of Israel said to Jehoshaphat, "I will enter the battle in disguise, but you wear your royal robes." So the king of Israel disguised[n] himself and went into battle.

18:29 [n] 1Sa 28:8

30 Now the king of Aram had ordered his chariot commanders, "Do not fight with anyone, small or great, except the king of Israel." 31 When the chariot commanders saw Jehoshaphat, they thought, "This is the king of Israel." So they turned to attack him, but Jehoshaphat cried out,[o] and the LORD helped him. God drew them away from him, 32 for when the chariot commanders saw that he was not the king of Israel, they stopped pursuing him.

18:31 [o] 2Ch 13:14

33 But someone drew his bow at random and hit the king of Israel between the sections of his armor. The king told the chariot driver, "Wheel around and get me out of the fighting. I've been wounded." 34 All day long the battle raged, and the king of Israel propped himself up in his chariot facing the Arameans until evening. Then at sunset he died.[p]

18:34 [p] 2Ch 22:5

19 When Jehoshaphat king of Judah returned safely to his palace in Jerusalem, 2 Jehu[q] the seer, the son of Hanani, went out to meet him and said to the king, "Should you help the wicked[r] and love[b] those who hate the LORD?[s] Because of this, the wrath[t] of the LORD is upon you. 3 There is, however, some good[u] in you, for you have rid the land of the Asherah poles[v] and have set your heart on seeking God.[w]"

19:2 [q] 1Ki 16:1 [r] 2Ch 16:2-9 [s] Ps 139:21-22 [t] 2Ch 24:18; 32:25; Ps 7:11

19:3 [u] 1Ki 14:13; 2Ch 12:12 [v] 2Ch 17:6 [w] 2Ch 18:1; 20:35; 25:7; Ezr 7:10

Jehoshaphat Appoints Judges

4 Jehoshaphat lived in Jerusalem, and he went out again among the people from Beersheba to the hill country of Ephraim and turned them back to the LORD, the God of their fathers. 5 He appointed judges[x] in the land, in each of the fortified cities of Judah. 6 He told them, "Consider carefully what you do,[y] because you are not judging for man[z] but for the LORD, who is with you whenever you give a verdict. 7 Now let the fear of the LORD be upon you. Judge carefully, for with the LORD our God there is no injustice[a] or partiality[b] or bribery."

19:5 [x] Ge 47:6; Ex 18:26

19:6 [y] Lev 19:15 [z] Dt 1:17; 16:18-20; 17:8-13

19:7 [a] Ge 18:25; Dt 32:4 [b] Dt 10:17; Job 34:19; Ro 2:11; Col 3:25

8 In Jerusalem also, Jehoshaphat appointed some of the Levites, priests and heads of Israelite families to administer[c] the law of the LORD and to settle disputes. And they lived in Jerusalem. 9 He gave them these orders: "You must serve faithfully and wholeheartedly in the fear of the LORD. 10 In every case that comes before you from your fellow countrymen who live in the cities—whether bloodshed or other concerns of the law, commands, decrees or ordinances—you are to warn them not to sin against the LORD;[d] otherwise his wrath will come on you and your brothers. Do this, and you will not sin.

19:8 [c] 2Ch 17:8-9

19:10 [d] Dt 17:8-13

11 "Amariah the chief priest will be over you in any matter concerning the LORD, and Zebadiah son of Ishmael, the

[a] 23 Or *Spirit of* [b] 2 Or *and make alliances with*

leader of the tribe of Judah, will be over
you in any matter concerning the king,
19:11 and the Levites will serve as officials be-
e 1Ch 28:20 fore you. Act with courage,[e] and may the
LORD be with those who do well."

Jehoshaphat Defeats Moab and Ammon

20 After this, the Moabites and
20:1 Ammonites with some of the
f 1Ch 4:41 Meunites[a][f] came to make war on Jehoshaphat.
2 Some men came and told Jehoshaphat, "A vast army is coming against you
20:2 from Edom,[b] from the other side of the
g Ge 14:7 Sea.[c] It is already in Hazazon Tamar[g]"
(that is, En Gedi). 3 Alarmed, Jehosha-
20:3 phat resolved to inquire of the LORD, and
h 1Sa 7:6; he proclaimed a fast[h] for all Judah. 4 The
2Ch 19:3; people of Judah came together to seek
Ezr 8:21; help from the LORD; indeed, they came
Jer 36:9; Jnh 3:5,7 from every town in Judah to seek him.
5 Then Jehoshaphat stood up in
the assembly of Judah and Jerusalem at
the temple of the LORD in the front of the
new courtyard 6 and said:

20:6 i Mt 6:9 j Dt 4:39 k 1Ch 29:11-12 "O LORD, God of our fathers,[i] are
you not the God who is in heaven?[j]
You rule over all the kingdoms[k] of
the nations. Power and might are
in your hand, and no one can withstand you. 7 O our God, did you not
drive out the inhabitants of this
land before your people Israel and
20:7 give it forever to the descendants of
l Isa 41:8; Abraham your friend?[l] 8 They have
Jas 2:23 lived in it and have built in it a
20:8 sanctuary[m] for your Name, saying,
m 2Ch 6:20 9 'If calamity comes upon us,
whether the sword of judgment, or
20:9 plague or famine,[n] we will stand in
n 2Ch 6:28 your presence before this temple
that bears your Name and will cry
out to you in our distress, and you
will hear us and save us.'

10 "But now here are men from
Ammon, Moab and Mount Seir,
whose territory you would not al-
20:10 low Israel to invade when they
o Nu 20:14-21; came from Egypt;[o] so they turned
Dt 2:4-6,9,18-19 away from them and did not destroy them. 11 See how they are re-
20:11 paying us by coming to drive us out
p Ps 83:1-12 of the possession[p] you gave us as
20:12 an inheritance. 12 O our God, will
q Jdg 11:27 you not judge them?[q] For we have
no power to face this vast army
that is attacking us. We do not
know what to do, but our eyes are 20:12
upon you.[r]" r Ps 25:15; 121:1-2

13 All the men of Judah, with their
wives and children and little ones, stood
there before the LORD.
14 Then the Spirit[s] of the LORD came 20:14 s 2Ch 15:1
upon Jahaziel son of Zechariah, the son
of Benaiah, the son of Jeiel, the son of
Mattaniah, a Levite and descendant of
Asaph, as he stood in the assembly.
15 He said: "Listen, King Jehoshaphat
and all who live in Judah and Jerusalem!
This is what the LORD says to you: 'Do
not be afraid or discouraged[t] because of 20:15 t 2Ch 32:7
this vast army. For the battle[u] is not u Ex 14:13-14;
yours, but God's. 16 Tomorrow march 1Sa 17:47
down against them. They will be climbing up by the Pass of Ziz, and you will
find them at the end of the gorge in the
Desert of Jeruel. 17 You will not have to
fight this battle. Take up your positions; 20:17
stand firm and see[v] the deliverance the v Ex 14:13;
LORD will give you, O Judah and Jerusa- 2Ch 15:2
lem. Do not be afraid; do not be discouraged. Go out to face them tomorrow, and the LORD will be with you.' "
18 Jehoshaphat bowed[w] with his face 20:18 w Ex 4:31
to the ground, and all the people of Ju-
dah and Jerusalem fell down in worship
before the LORD. 19 Then some Levites
from the Kohathites and Korahites
stood up and praised the LORD, the God
of Israel, with very loud voice.
20 Early in the morning they left for the
Desert of Tekoa. As they set out, Jehoshaphat stood and said, "Listen to me, Ju- 20:20
dah and people of Jerusalem! Have faith[x] x Isa 7:9
in the LORD your God and you will be up- y Ge 39:3;
held; have faith in his prophets and you Pr 16:3
will be successful.[y]" 21 After consulting
the people, Jehoshaphat appointed men
to sing to the LORD and to praise him for
the splendor of his[d] holiness[z] as they 20:21
went out at the head of the army, saying: z 1Ch 16:29; Ps 29:2

"Give thanks to the LORD, a 2Ch 5:13;
for his love endures forever."[a] Ps 136:1

22 As they began to sing and praise, the 20:22
LORD set ambushes[b] against the men of b Jdg 7:22;
Ammon and Moab and Mount Seir who 2Ch 13:13
were invading Judah, and they were

[a] *1* Some Septuagint manuscripts; Hebrew *Ammonites* [b] *2* One Hebrew manuscript; most Hebrew manuscripts, Septuagint and Vulgate *Aram* [c] *2* That is, the Dead Sea [d] *21* Or *him with the splendor of*

ABRAHAM: FRIEND OF GOD

How can human beings be friends with Almighty God? On the surface such a relationship seems impossible—until we read the Bible. In 2 Chronicles 20:7 we hear from King Jehoshaphat that his ancestor Abraham had been God's friend. What a magnificent tribute to any godly individual! We remember Abraham as a stalwart patriarch, a pillar of godliness. He is referred to as "Father Abraham," a man of unwavering faith who had been handpicked by God himself to be the founder of a mighty nation. Beyond that honor God would send his promised Messiah through Abraham's family line so that all of humankind might have the opportunity for an eternal relationship with their Creator.

Abraham was the first human being whom God referred to as his "friend," and God never explained his choice. We do know the character traits that God values in a friend, because he talks about friendship in his Word. A friend loves us at all times (Proverbs 17:17; 27:10). A friend sticks with us, sometimes closer than a family member (Proverbs 18:24). A friend is honest (Proverbs 27:6) and encourages us to be the best that we can be (Proverbs 27:9).

Abraham loved and trusted God without reservation and was wholly committed to walking with him. He never withheld anything from God—to the point that he was willing even to relinquish his only son (Genesis 22:1–19). And Abraham never held back from telling God how he felt (Genesis 17:17–18).

God's friendship with Abraham we can at least partially understand; the patriarch was an upstanding and respected citizen of Israel. But in the New Testament Jesus' choice of companions doesn't always make sense to us. Jesus was criticized for being friendly with tax collectors and "sinners" (Matthew 11:19). In Jesus' day, tax collectors were among the most despised people in the country—stereotyped as manipulative, deceitful, selfish. Yet Jesus offered friendship based on his own character, not on the worthiness of the other person. Jesus epitomizes the friend described in Proverbs: unconditional in his love, offering honest encouragement and promising his presence in every situation. Similarly, God did not choose Abraham because of who *Abraham* was; he chose Abraham because of who *he* is.

Jesus offers his friendship to you, and he yearns for you to reciprocate. In John 15:14 he said, "You are my friends if you do what I command." And what he asks is that we love each other (John 15:17). You can be his friend because he took the initiative and first extended his love to you. The apostle John expressed this truth in unforgettable words: "This is how God showed his love among us: He sent his one and only Son into the world that we might live through him. This is love: not that we loved God, but that he loved us and sent his Son as an atoning sacrifice for our sins" (1 John 4:9–10).

Self-Discovery: *Do you consider yourself to be a friend of Jesus? If Jesus did not already know your heart, would he see evidence of your friendship based on your actions?*

GO TO DISCOVERY 107 ON PAGE 573

20:23 [c] Ge 19:38 [d] 2Ch 21:8 [e] Jdg 7:22; 1Sa 14:20; Eze 38:21

defeated. 23The men of Ammon[c] and Moab rose up against the men from Mount Seir[d] to destroy and annihilate them. After they finished slaughtering the men from Seir, they helped to destroy one another.[e]

24When the men of Judah came to the place that overlooks the desert and looked toward the vast army, they saw only dead bodies lying on the ground; no one had escaped. 25So Jehoshaphat and his men went to carry off their plunder, and they found among them a great amount of equipment and clothing[a] and also articles of value—more than they could take away. There was so much plunder that it took three days to collect it. 26On the fourth day they assembled in the Valley of Beracah, where they praised the LORD. This is why it is called the Valley of Beracah[b] to this day.

27Then, led by Jehoshaphat, all the men of Judah and Jerusalem returned joyfully to Jerusalem, for the LORD had given them cause to rejoice over their enemies. 28They entered Jerusalem and went to the temple of the LORD with harps and lutes and trumpets.

20:29 [f] Ge 35:5; Dt 2:25; 2Ch 14:14; 17:10 [g] Ex 14:14

20:30 [h] 1Ch 22:9; 2Ch 14:6-7; 15:15

29The fear[f] of God came upon all the kingdoms of the countries when they heard how the LORD had fought[g] against the enemies of Israel. 30And the kingdom of Jehoshaphat was at peace, for his God had given him rest[h] on every side.

The End of Jehoshaphat's Reign

31So Jehoshaphat reigned over Judah. He was thirty-five years old when he became king of Judah, and he reigned in Jerusalem twenty-five years. His mother's name was Azubah daughter of Shilhi. 32He walked in the ways of his father Asa and did not stray from them; he did what was right in the eyes of the LORD.

20:33 [i] 2Ch 17:6; 19:3

33The high places,[i] however, were not removed, and the people still had not set their hearts on the God of their fathers.

20:34 [j] 1Ki 16:1

34The other events of Jehoshaphat's reign, from beginning to end, are written in the annals of Jehu[j] son of Hanani, which are recorded in the book of the kings of Israel.

20:35 [k] 2Ch 16:3 [l] 2Ch 19:1-3

20:37 [m] 1Ki 9:26; 2Ch 9:21

35Later, Jehoshaphat king of Judah made an alliance[k] with Ahaziah king of Israel, who was guilty of wickedness.[l] 36He agreed with him to construct a fleet of trading ships.[c] After these were built at Ezion Geber, 37Eliezer son of Dodavahu of Mareshah prophesied against Jehoshaphat, saying, "Because you have made an alliance with Ahaziah, the LORD will destroy what you have made." The ships[m] were wrecked and were not able to set sail to trade.[d]

21:1 [n] 1Ch 3:11

21:3 [o] 2Ch 11:23 [p] 2Ch 11:10

21 Then Jehoshaphat rested with his fathers and was buried with them in the City of David. And Jehoram[n] his son succeeded him as king. 2Jehoram's brothers, the sons of Jehoshaphat, were Azariah, Jehiel, Zechariah, Azariahu, Michael and Shephatiah. All these were sons of Jehoshaphat king of Israel.[e] 3Their father had given them many gifts[o] of silver and gold and articles of value, as well as fortified cities[p] in Judah, but he had given the kingdom to Jehoram because he was his firstborn son.

Jehoram King of Judah

21:4 [q] 1Ki 2:12 [r] Jdg 9:5

21:6 [s] 1Ki 12:28-30 [t] 2Ch 18:1; 22:3

21:7 [u] 2Sa 7:13 [v] 2Sa 7:15; 2Ch 23:3 [w] 2Sa 21:17; 1Ki 11:36

21:8 [x] 2Ch 20:22-23

4When Jehoram established[q] himself firmly over his father's kingdom, he put all his brothers[r] to the sword along with some of the princes of Israel. 5Jehoram was thirty-two years old when he became king, and he reigned in Jerusalem eight years. 6He walked in the ways of the kings of Israel,[s] as the house of Ahab had done, for he married a daughter of Ahab.[t] He did evil in the eyes of the LORD. 7Nevertheless, because of the covenant the LORD had made with David,[u] the LORD was not willing to destroy the house of David.[v] He had promised to maintain a lamp[w] for him and his descendants forever.

8In the time of Jehoram, Edom[x] rebelled against Judah and set up its own king. 9So Jehoram went there with his officers and all his chariots. The Edomites surrounded him and his chariot commanders, but he rose up and broke through by night. 10To this day Edom has been in rebellion against Judah.

21:10 [y] Nu 33:20

Libnah[y] revolted at the same time, because Jehoram had forsaken the LORD, the God of his fathers. 11He had also built high places on the hills of Judah and had caused the people of Jerusalem to prostitute themselves and had led Judah astray.

[a] 25 Some Hebrew manuscripts and Vulgate; most Hebrew manuscripts *corpses* [b] 26 *Beracah* means *praise.* [c] 36 Hebrew *of ships that could go to Tarshish* [d] 37 Hebrew *sail for Tarshish*
[e] 2 That is, Judah, as frequently in 2 Chronicles

12Jehoram received a letter from Eli-
21:12 [z]2Ki 1:16-17 [a]2Ch 17:3-6 [b]2Ch 14:2
jah[z] the prophet, which said:

"This is what the LORD, the God of
your father[a] David, says: 'You have
not walked in the ways of your father Jehoshaphat or of Asa[b] king of
Judah. 13But you have walked in the
ways of the kings of Israel, and you
have led Judah and the people of Jerusalem to prostitute themselves,
21:13 [c]ver 6,11; 1Ki 16:29-33 [d]ver 4; 1Ki 2:32
just as the house of Ahab did.[c] You
have also murdered your own
brothers, members of your father's
house, men who were better[d] than
you. 14So now the LORD is about to
strike your people, your sons, your
wives and everything that is yours,
with a heavy blow. 15You yourself
will be very ill with a lingering dis-
21:15 [e]ver 18-19; Nu 12:10
ease[e] of the bowels, until the disease
causes your bowels to come out.'"

16The LORD aroused against Jehoram
the hostility of the Philistines and of the
21:16 [f]2Ch 17:10-11; 22:1; 26:7
Arabs[f] who lived near the Cushites.
17They attacked Judah, invaded it and
carried off all the goods found in the
king's palace, together with his sons and
wives. Not a son was left to him except
21:17 [g]2Ki 12:18; 2Ch 22:1; 25:23; Joel 3:5
Ahaziah,[a] the youngest.[g]
18After all this, the LORD afflicted Jehoram with an incurable disease of the
bowels. 19In the course of time, at the
end of the second year, his bowels came
out because of the disease, and he died
in great pain. His people made no fire in
21:19 [h]2Ch 16:14
his honor,[h] as they had for his fathers.
20Jehoram was thirty-two years old
when he became king, and he reigned in
21:20 [i]2Ch 24:25; 28:27; 33:20; Jer 22:18,28
Jerusalem eight years. He passed away,
to no one's regret, and was buried[i] in the
City of David, but not in the tombs of
the kings.

Ahaziah King of Judah

22:1 [j]2Ch 33:25; 36:1 [k]2Ch 23:20-21; 26:1 [l]2Ch 21:16-17
22 The people[j] of Jerusalem[k] made
Ahaziah, Jehoram's youngest
son, king in his place, since the raiders,[l]
who came with the Arabs into the camp,
had killed all the older sons. So Ahaziah
son of Jehoram king of Judah began to
reign.
2Ahaziah was twenty-two[b] years old
when he became king, and he reigned in
Jerusalem one year. His mother's name
was Athaliah, a granddaughter of Omri.
22:3 [m]2Ch 18:1
3He too walked[m] in the ways of the
22:3 [n]2Ch 21:6
house of Ahab,[n] for his mother encouraged him in doing wrong. 4He did evil in
the eyes of the LORD, as the house of
Ahab had done, for after his father's
death they became his advisers, to his
undoing. 5He also followed their counsel
when he went with Joram[c] son of Ahab
22:5 [o]2Ch 18:11,34
king of Israel to war against Hazael king
of Aram at Ramoth Gilead.[o] The Arameans wounded Joram; 6so he returned
to Jezreel to recover from the wounds
22:6 [p]1Ki 19:15; 2Ki 8:13-15; 9:15
they had inflicted on him at Ramoth[d] in
his battle with Hazael[p] king of Aram.
Then Ahaziah[e] son of Jehoram king of
Judah went down to Jezreel to see Joram
son of Ahab because he had been
wounded.
22:7 [q]2Ki 9:16; 2Ch 10:15
7Through Ahaziah's[q] visit to Joram,
God brought about Ahaziah's downfall.
When Ahaziah arrived, he went out
with Joram to meet Jehu son of Nimshi,
whom the LORD had anointed to destroy
22:8 [r]2Ki 10:13
the house of Ahab. 8While Jehu was executing judgment on the house of Ahab,[r]
he found the princes of Judah and the
sons of Ahaziah's relatives, who had
been attending Ahaziah, and he killed
them. 9He then went in search of Ahazi-
22:9 [s]Jdg 9:5 [t]2Ch 17:4
ah, and his men captured him while he
was hiding[s] in Samaria. He was brought
to Jehu and put to death. They buried
him, for they said, "He was a son of Jehoshaphat, who sought[t] the LORD with
all his heart." So there was no one in the
house of Ahaziah powerful enough to
retain the kingdom.

Athaliah and Joash

10When Athaliah the mother of Ahaziah saw that her son was dead, she proceeded to destroy the whole royal family
of the house of Judah. 11But Jehosheba,[f]
the daughter of King Jehoram, took Joash son of Ahaziah and stole him away
from among the royal princes who were
about to be murdered and put him and
his nurse in a bedroom. Because Jehosheba,[f] the daughter of King Jehoram
and wife of the priest Jehoiada, was Ahaziah's sister, she hid the child from Atha-

[a] *17* Hebrew *Jehoahaz,* a variant of *Ahaziah*
[b] *2* Some Septuagint manuscripts and Syriac (see also 2 Kings 8:26); Hebrew *forty-two*
[c] *5* Hebrew *Jehoram,* a variant of *Joram;* also in verses 6 and 7
[d] *6* Hebrew *Ramah,* a variant of *Ramoth*
[e] *6* Some Hebrew manuscripts, Septuagint, Vulgate and Syriac (see also 2 Kings 8:29); most Hebrew manuscripts *Azariah*
[f] *11* Hebrew *Jehoshabeath,* a variant of *Jehosheba*

liah so she could not kill him. 12He remained hidden with them at the temple
of God for six years while Athaliah ruled
the land.

23 In the seventh year Jehoiada
showed his strength. He made
a covenant with the commanders of
units of a hundred: Azariah son of Jeroham, Ishmael son of Jehohanan, Azariah son of Obed, Maaseiah son of Adaiah,
and Elishaphat son of Zicri. 2They went
23:2 throughout Judah and gathered the Le-
[u] Nu 35:2-5 vites[u] and the heads of Israelite families
from all the towns. When they came to
Jerusalem, 3the whole assembly made a
23:3 [v] 2Ki 11:17 covenant[v] with the king at the temple of
[w] 2Sa 7:12; God.
1Ki 2:4; Jehoiada said to them, "The king's son
2Ch 6:16; 7:18; shall reign, as the LORD promised con-
21:7 cerning the descendants of David.[w]
4Now this is what you are to do: A third
of you priests and Levites who are going
on duty on the Sabbath are to keep
watch at the doors, 5a third of you at the
royal palace and a third at the Foundation Gate, and all the other men are to
be in the courtyards of the temple of the
LORD. 6No one is to enter the temple of
the LORD except the priests and Levites
on duty; they may enter because they
23:6 are consecrated, but all the other men
[x] 1Ch 23:28-29; are to guard[x] what the LORD has as-
Zec 3:7 signed to them.[a] 7The Levites are to station themselves around the king, each
man with his weapons in his hand. Anyone who enters the temple must be put
to death. Stay close to the king wherever he goes."
8The Levites and all the men of Judah
23:8 [y] 2Ki 11:9 did just as Jehoiada the priest ordered.[y]
[z] 1Ch 24:1 Each one took his men—those who were
going on duty on the Sabbath and those
who were going off duty—for Jehoiada
the priest had not released any of the divisions.[z] 9Then he gave the commanders
of units of a hundred the spears and the
large and small shields that had belonged to King David and that were in
the temple of God. 10He stationed all the
men, each with his weapon in his hand,
around the king—near the altar and the
temple, from the south side to the north
side of the temple.
11Jehoiada and his sons brought out
23:11 the king's son and put the crown on
[a] Ex 25:16; him; they presented him with a copy[a] of
Dt 17:18; 1Sa 10:24 the covenant and proclaimed him king.
They anointed him and shouted, "Long
live the king!"
12When Athaliah heard the noise of
the people running and cheering the
king, she went to them at the temple of
the LORD. 13She looked, and there was 23:13
the king,[b] standing by his pillar[c] at the [b] 1Ki 1:41
entrance. The officers and the trum- [c] 1Ki 7:15
peters were beside the king, and all the
people of the land were rejoicing and
blowing trumpets, and singers with musical instruments were leading the
praises. Then Athaliah tore her robes
and shouted, "Treason! Treason!"
14Jehoiada the priest sent out the
commanders of units of a hundred, who
were in charge of the troops, and said to
them: "Bring her out between the ranks[b]
and put to the sword anyone who follows her." For the priest had said, "Do
not put her to death at the temple of the
LORD." 15So they seized her as she 23:15
reached the entrance of the Horse Gate[d] [d] Ne 3:28;
on the palace grounds, and there they Jer 31:40
put her to death.
16Jehoiada then made a covenant[e] 23:16
that he and the people and the king[c] [e] 2Ch 29:10;
would be the LORD's people. 17All the 34:31; Ne 9:38
people went to the temple of Baal and
tore it down. They smashed the altars
and idols and killed[f] Mattan the priest 23:17 [f] Dt 13:6-9
of Baal in front of the altars.
18Then Jehoiada placed the oversight
of the temple of the LORD in the hands of
the priests, who were Levites,[g] to whom 23:18
David had made assignments in the [g] 1Ch 23:28-32;
temple,[h] to present the burnt offerings 2Ch 5:5
of the LORD as written in the Law of Mo- [h] 1Ch 23:6; 25:6
ses, with rejoicing and singing, as David
had ordered. 19He also stationed door- 23:19
keepers[i] at the gates of the LORD's tem- [i] 1Ch 9:22
ple so that no one who was in any way
unclean might enter.
20He took with him the commanders
of hundreds, the nobles, the rulers of the
people and all the people of the land and
brought the king down from the temple
of the LORD. They went into the palace 23:20
through the Upper Gate[j] and seated the [j] 2Ki 15:35
king on the royal throne, 21and all the
people of the land rejoiced. And the city
was quiet, because Athaliah had been 23:21
slain with the sword.[k] [k] 2Ch 22:1

[a] 6 Or *to observe the LORD's command* ⌞*not to enter*⌟
[b] 14 Or *out from the precincts* [c] 16 Or *covenant between* ⌞*the LORD*⌟ *and the people and the king that they* (see 2 Kings 11:17)

Joash Repairs the Temple

24 Joash was seven years old when he became king, and he reigned in Jerusalem forty years. His mother's name was Zibiah; she was from Beersheba. 2 Joash did what was right in the eyes of the LORD[l] all the years of Jehoiada the priest. 3 Jehoiada chose two wives for him, and he had sons and daughters.

4 Some time later Joash decided to restore the temple of the LORD. 5 He called together the priests and Levites and said to them, "Go to the towns of Judah and collect the money[m] due annually from all Israel,[n] to repair the temple of your God. Do it now." But the Levites[o] did not act at once.

6 Therefore the king summoned Jehoiada the chief priest and said to him, "Why haven't you required the Levites to bring in from Judah and Jerusalem the tax imposed by Moses the servant of the LORD and by the assembly of Israel for the Tent of the Testimony?"[p]

7 Now the sons of that wicked woman Athaliah had broken into the temple of God and had used even its sacred objects for the Baals.

8 At the king's command, a chest was made and placed outside, at the gate of the temple of the LORD. 9 A proclamation was then issued in Judah and Jerusalem that they should bring to the LORD the tax that Moses the servant of God had required of Israel in the desert. 10 All the officials and all the people brought their contributions gladly,[q] dropping them into the chest until it was full. 11 Whenever the chest was brought in by the Levites to the king's officials and they saw that there was a large amount of money, the royal secretary and the officer of the chief priest would come and empty the chest and carry it back to its place. They did this regularly and collected a great amount of money. 12 The king and Jehoiada gave it to the men who carried out the work required for the temple of the LORD. They hired[r] masons and carpenters to restore the LORD's temple, and also workers in iron and bronze to repair the temple.

13 The men in charge of the work were diligent, and the repairs progressed under them. They rebuilt the temple of God according to its original design and reinforced it. 14 When they had finished, they brought the rest of the money to the king and Jehoiada, and with it were made articles for the LORD's temple: articles for the service and for the burnt offerings, and also dishes and other objects of gold and silver. As long as Jehoiada lived, burnt offerings were presented continually in the temple of the LORD.

15 Now Jehoiada was old and full of years, and he died at the age of a hundred and thirty. 16 He was buried with the kings in the City of David, because of the good he had done in Israel for God and his temple.

The Wickedness of Joash

17 After the death of Jehoiada, the officials of Judah came and paid homage to the king, and he listened to them. 18 They abandoned[s] the temple of the LORD, the God of their fathers, and worshiped Asherah poles and idols.[t] Because of their guilt, God's anger[u] came upon Judah and Jerusalem. 19 Although the LORD sent prophets to the people to bring them back to him, and though they testified against them, they would not listen.[v]

20 Then the Spirit[w] of God came upon Zechariah[x] son of Jehoiada the priest. He stood before the people and said, "This is what God says: 'Why do you disobey the LORD's commands? You will not prosper.[y] Because you have forsaken the LORD, he has forsaken[z] you.' "

21 But they plotted against him, and by order of the king they stoned[a] him to death[b] in the courtyard of the LORD's temple.[c] 22 King Joash did not remember the kindness Zechariah's father Jehoiada had shown him but killed his son, who said as he lay dying, "May the LORD see this and call you to account."[d]

23 At the turn of the year,[a] the army of Aram marched against Joash; it invaded Judah and Jerusalem and killed all the leaders of the people.[e] They sent all the plunder to their king in Damascus. 24 Although the Aramean army had come with only a few men,[f] the LORD delivered into their hands a much larger army.[g] Because Judah had forsaken the LORD, the God of their fathers, judgment was executed on Joash. 25 When the Arameans withdrew, they left Joash severely wounded. His officials conspired against him for murdering the son of Jehoiada

24:2 [l] 2Ch 25:2; 26:5
24:5 [m] Ex 30:16; Ne 10:32-33; Mt 17:24 [n] 1Ch 11:1 [o] 1Ch 26:20
24:6 [p] Ex 30:12-16; Nu 1:50
24:10 [q] Ex 25:2; 1Ch 29:3,6,9
24:12 [r] 2Ch 34:11
24:18 [s] ver 4; Jos 24:20; 2Ch 7:19 [t] Ex 34:13; 1Ki 14:23; 2Ch 33:3; Jer 17:2 [u] Jos 22:20; 2Ch 19:2
24:19 [v] Nu 11:29; Jer 7:25; Zec 1:4
24:20 [w] Jdg 3:10; 1Ch 12:18; 2Ch 20:14 [x] Mt 23:35; Lk 11:51 [y] Nu 14:41 [z] Dt 31:17; 2Ch 15:2
24:21 [a] Jos 7:25; Ac 7:58-59 [b] Ne 9:26; Jer 26:21 [c] Jer 20:2; Mt 23:35
24:22 [d] Ge 9:5
24:23 [e] 2Ki 12:17-18
24:24 [f] 2Ch 14:9; 16:8; 20:2,12 [g] Lev 26:23-25; Dt 28:25

a 23 Probably in the spring

24:25 the priest, and they killed him in his bed.
h 2Ch 21:20 So he died and was buried[h] in the City of
David, but not in the tombs of the kings.
26Those who conspired against him
were Zabad,[a] son of Shimeath an Am-
24:26 monite woman, and Jehozabad, son of
i 2Ki 12:21 Shimrith[b][i] a Moabite woman.[j] 27The ac-
j Ru 1:4 count of his sons, the many prophecies
about him, and the record of the restoration of the temple of God are written in
the annotations on the book of the
kings. And Amaziah his son succeeded
him as king.

Amaziah King of Judah

25 Amaziah was twenty-five years
old when he became king, and
he reigned in Jerusalem twenty-nine
years. His mother's name was Jehoaddin[c]; she was from Jerusalem. 2He
25:2 did what was right in the eyes of the
k ver 14; LORD, but not wholeheartedly.[k] 3After
1Ki 8:61; the kingdom was firmly in his control,
2Ch 24:2 he executed the officials who had murdered his father the king. 4Yet he did not
put their sons to death, but acted in ac-
25:4 cordance with what is written in the
l Dt 28:61 Law, in the Book of Moses,[l] where the
m Nu 26:11; Dt 24:16 LORD commanded: "Fathers shall not be
put to death for their children, nor chil-
dren put to death for their fathers; each
is to die for his own sins."[d][m]
5Amaziah called the people of Judah
together and assigned them according
to their families to commanders of
thousands and commanders of hun-
25:5 dreds for all Judah and Benjamin. He
n 2Sa 24:2 then mustered[n] those twenty years old[o]
o Ex 30:14 or more and found that there were three
p Nu 1:3; 1Ch 21:1; 2Ch 17:14-19 hundred thousand men ready for military service,[p] able to handle the spear
and shield. 6He also hired a hundred
thousand fighting men from Israel for a
hundred talents[e] of silver.
25:7 7But a man of God came to him and
q 2Ch 16:2-9; 19:1-3 said, "O king, these troops from Israel[q]
must not march with you, for the LORD is
not with Israel—not with any of the people of Ephraim. 8Even if you go and fight
courageously in battle, God will over-
25:8 throw you before the enemy, for God has
r 2Ch 14:11; 20:6 the power to help or to overthrow."[r]
9Amaziah asked the man of God, "But
what about the hundred talents I paid
25:9 for these Israelite troops?"
s Dt 8:18; The man of God replied, "The LORD
Pr 10:22 can give you much more than that."[s]

10So Amaziah dismissed the troops
who had come to him from Ephraim and
sent them home. They were furious with
Judah and left for home in a great rage.[t] 25:10
11Amaziah then marshaled his t ver 13
strength and led his army to the Valley
of Salt, where he killed ten thousand
men of Seir. 12The army of Judah also
captured ten thousand men alive, took
them to the top of a cliff and threw them 25:12
down so that all were dashed to pieces.[u] u Ps 141:6;
13Meanwhile the troops that Amazi- Ob 1:3
ah had sent back and had not allowed to
take part in the war raided Judean
towns from Samaria to Beth Horon.
They killed three thousand people and
carried off great quantities of plunder.
14When Amaziah returned from
slaughtering the Edomites, he brought
back the gods of the people of Seir. He set 25:14
them up as his own gods,[v] bowed down v Ex 20:3;
to them and burned sacrifices to them. 2Ch 28:23;
15The anger of the LORD burned against Isa 44:15
Amaziah, and he sent a prophet to him,
who said, "Why do you consult this peo- 25:15
ple's gods, which could not save[w] their w Ps 96:5;
own people from your hand?" Isa 36:20
16While he was still speaking, the king
said to him, "Have we appointed you an
adviser to the king? Stop! Why be struck
down?"
So the prophet stopped but said, "I
know that God has determined to destroy you, because you have done this
and have not listened to my counsel."
17After Amaziah king of Judah consulted his advisers, he sent this challenge to Jehoash[f] son of Jehoahaz, the
son of Jehu, king of Israel: "Come, meet
me face to face."
18But Jehoash king of Israel replied to
Amaziah king of Judah: "A thistle[x] in 25:18
Lebanon sent a message to a cedar in x Jdg 9:8-15
Lebanon, 'Give your daughter to my son
in marriage.' Then a wild beast in Lebanon came along and trampled the thistle
underfoot. 19You say to yourself that you
have defeated Edom, and now you are
arrogant and proud. But stay at home!
Why ask for trouble and cause your own
downfall and that of Judah also?"
20Amaziah, however, would not listen,

[a] *26* A variant of *Jozabad* [b] *26* A variant of *Shomer* [c] *1* Hebrew *Jehoaddan,* a variant of *Jehoaddin* [d] *4* Deut. 24:16 [e] *6* That is, about 3 3/4 tons (about 3.4 metric tons); also in verse 9 [f] *17* Hebrew *Joash,* a variant of *Jehoash;* also in verses 18, 21, 23 and 25

for God so worked that he might hand
25:20 them over to ⌞Jehoash⌟, because they
y 1Ki 12:15; sought the gods of Edom.[y] 21 So Jehoash
2Ch 10:15; 22:7 king of Israel attacked. He and Amaziah
king of Judah faced each other at Beth
Shemesh in Judah. 22 Judah was routed
by Israel, and every man fled to his
home. 23 Jehoash king of Israel captured
Amaziah king of Judah, the son of Joash,
the son of Ahaziah,[a] at Beth Shemesh.
Then Jehoash brought him to Jerusalem
25:23 and broke down the wall of Jerusalem
z 2Ki 14:13; from the Ephraim Gate[z] to the Corner
Ne 8:16; 12:39 Gate[a]—a section about six hundred
a 2Ch 26:9; Jer 31:38 feet[b] long. 24 He took all the gold and silver and all the articles found in the tem-
25:24 ple of God that had been in the care of
b 1Ch 26:15 Obed-Edom,[b] together with the palace
treasures and the hostages, and returned to Samaria.

25 Amaziah son of Joash king of Judah
lived for fifteen years after the death of
Jehoash son of Jehoahaz king of Israel.
26 As for the other events of Amaziah's
reign, from beginning to end, are they
not written in the book of the kings of
Judah and Israel? 27 From the time that
Amaziah turned away from following
25:27 the LORD, they conspired against him in
c Jos 10:3 Jerusalem and he fled to Lachish[c], but
they sent men after him to Lachish and
killed him there. 28 He was brought back
by horse and was buried with his fathers
in the City of Judah.

Uzziah King of Judah

26:1 **26** Then all the people of Judah[d]
d 2Ch 22:1 took Uzziah,[c] who was sixteen
years old, and made him king in place of
his father Amaziah. 2 He was the one who
rebuilt Elath and restored it to Judah after Amaziah rested with his fathers.

3 Uzziah was sixteen years old when
he became king, and he reigned in Jerusalem fifty-two years. His mother's name
was Jecoliah; she was from Jerusalem.
4 He did what was right in the eyes of the
LORD, just as his father Amaziah had
done. 5 He sought God during the days of
26:5 Zechariah, who instructed him in the
e 2Ch 15:2; 24:2; fear[d] of God.[e] As long as he sought the
Da 1:17 f 2Ch 27:6 LORD, God gave him success.[f]

6 He went to war against the Philis-
26:6 tines[g] and broke down the walls of Gath,
g Isa 2:6; 11:14; 14:29; Jer 25:20 Jabneh and Ashdod.[h] He then rebuilt
h Am 1:8; 3:9 towns near Ashdod and elsewhere
among the Philistines. 7 God helped him
against the Philistines and against the 26:7 i 2Ch 21:16
Arabs[i] who lived in Gur Baal and against j 2Ch 20:1
the Meunites.[j] 8 The Ammonites[k] 26:8
brought tribute to Uzziah, and his fame k Ge 19:38;
spread as far as the border of Egypt, be- 2Ch 17:11
cause he had become very powerful.

9 Uzziah built towers in Jerusalem at 26:9
the Corner Gate,[l] at the Valley Gate[m] l 2Ki 14:13; 2Ch 25:23
and at the angle of the wall, and he for- m Ne 2:13; 3:13
tified them. 10 He also built towers in the
desert and dug many cisterns, because
he had much livestock in the foothills
and in the plain. He had people working
his fields and vineyards in the hills and
in the fertile lands, for he loved the soil.

11 Uzziah had a well-trained army,
ready to go out by divisions according to
their numbers as mustered by Jeiel the
secretary and Maaseiah the officer under
the direction of Hananiah, one of the
royal officials. 12 The total number of
family leaders over the fighting men
was 2,600. 13 Under their command was
an army of 307,500 men trained for war,
a powerful force to support the king
against his enemies. 14 Uzziah provided
shields, spears, helmets, coats of armor,
bows and slingstones for the entire 26:14
army.[n] 15 In Jerusalem he made machines n Jer 46:4
designed by skillful men for use on the
towers and on the corner defenses to
shoot arrows and hurl large stones. His
fame spread far and wide, for he was
greatly helped until he became powerful.

16 But after Uzziah became powerful, 26:16
his pride[o] led to his downfall.[p] He was o 2Ki 14:10
unfaithful[q] to the LORD his God, and en- p Dt 32:15;
tered the temple of the LORD to burn in- 2Ch 25:19 q 1Ch 5:25
cense[r] on the altar of incense. 17 Azariah[s] r 2Ki 16:12
the priest with eighty other courageous 26:17
priests of the LORD followed him in. s 1Ki 4:2; 1Ch 6:10
18 They confronted him and said, "It is
not right for you, Uzziah, to burn incense to the LORD. That is for the 26:18
priests,[t] the descendants[u] of Aaron,[v] t Nu 16:39
who have been consecrated to burn in- u Nu 18:1-7
cense.[w] Leave the sanctuary, for you v Ex 30:7 w 1Ch 6:49
have been unfaithful; and you will not be
honored by the LORD God."

19 Uzziah, who had a censer in his hand
ready to burn incense, became angry.
While he was raging at the priests in
their presence before the incense altar in

a 23 Hebrew *Jehoahaz,* a variant of *Ahaziah*
b 23 Hebrew *four hundred cubits* (about 180 meters)
c 1 Also called *Azariah*
d 5 Many Hebrew manuscripts, Septuagint and Syriac; other Hebrew manuscripts *vision*

26:19 [x]Nu 12:10; 2Ki 5:25-27
the LORD's temple, leprosy[a][x] broke out on
his forehead. 20When Azariah the chief
priest and all the other priests looked at
him, they saw that he had leprosy on his
forehead, so they hurried him out. Indeed, he himself was eager to leave, because the LORD had afflicted him.
21King Uzziah had leprosy until the
26:21 [y]Ex 4:6; Lev 13:46; 14:8; Nu 5:2; 19:12
day he died. He lived in a separate
house[b][y]—leprous, and excluded from
the temple of the LORD. Jotham his son
had charge of the palace and governed
the people of the land.
22The other events of Uzziah's reign,
26:22 [z]2Ki 15:1; Isa 1:1; 6:1
from beginning to end, are recorded by
the prophet Isaiah[z] son of Amoz. 23Uzzi-
ah[a] rested with his fathers and was
26:23 [a]Isa 1:1; 6:1 [b]2Ki 14:21; 15:7; Am 1:1
buried near them in a field for burial
that belonged to the kings, for people
said, "He had leprosy." And Jotham his
son succeeded him as king.[b]

Jotham King of Judah

27:1 [c]2Ki 15:5,32; 1Ch 3:12
27 Jotham[c] was twenty-five years
old when he became king, and
he reigned in Jerusalem sixteen years.
His mother's name was Jerusha daughter
of Zadok. 2He did what was right in the
eyes of the LORD, just as his father Uzziah had done, but unlike him he did not
enter the temple of the LORD. The people,
however, continued their corrupt practices. 3Jotham rebuilt the Upper Gate of
27:3 [d]2Ch 33:14; Ne 3:26
the temple of the LORD and did extensive
work on the wall at the hill of Ophel.[d]
4He built towns in the Judean hills and
forts and towers in the wooded areas.
5Jotham made war on the king of the
27:5 [e]Ge 19:38
Ammonites[e] and conquered them. That
year the Ammonites paid him a hundred talents[c] of silver, ten thousand
cors[d] of wheat and ten thousand cors of
barley. The Ammonites brought him the
same amount also in the second and
third years.
27:6 [f]2Ch 26:5
6Jotham grew powerful[f] because he
walked steadfastly before the LORD his
God.
7The other events in Jotham's reign,
including all his wars and the other
things he did, are written in the book of
the kings of Israel and Judah. 8He was
twenty-five years old when he became
king, and he reigned in Jerusalem sixteen
years. 9Jotham rested with his fathers
and was buried in the City of David. And
Ahaz his son succeeded him as king.

Ahaz King of Judah

28 Ahaz[g] was twenty years old 28:1 [g]1Ch 3:13; Isa 1:1
when he became king, and he
reigned in Jerusalem sixteen years. Unlike David his father, he did not do what
was right in the eyes of the LORD. 2He
walked in the ways of the kings of Israel
and also made cast idols[h] for worshiping 28:2 [h]Ex 34:17; 2Ch 22:3
the Baals. 3He burned sacrifices in the
Valley of Ben Hinnom[i] and sacrificed his 28:3 [i]Jos 15:8; 2Ki 23:10 [j]Lev 18:21; 2Ki 3:27; 2Ch 33:6; Eze 20:26 [k]Dt 18:9; 2Ch 33:2
sons[j] in the fire, following the de-
testable[k] ways of the nations the LORD
had driven out before the Israelites. 4He
offered sacrifices and burned incense at
the high places, on the hilltops and under every spreading tree.
5Therefore the LORD his God handed
him over to the king of Aram.[l] The Ara- 28:5 [l]Isa 7:1
means defeated him and took many of
his people as prisoners and brought
them to Damascus.
He was also given into the hands of
the king of Israel, who inflicted heavy 28:6 [m]2Ki 15:25,27 [n]ver 8; Isa 9:21; 11:13
casualties on him. 6In one day Pekah[m]
son of Remaliah killed a hundred and
twenty thousand soldiers in Judah[n]—
because Judah had forsaken the LORD,
the God of their fathers. 7Zicri, an
Ephraimite warrior, killed Maaseiah the
king's son, Azrikam the officer in charge
of the palace, and Elkanah, second to
the king. 8The Israelites took captive
from their kinsmen[o] two hundred thou- 28:8 [o]Dt 28:25-41; 2Ch 11:4 [p]2Ch 29:9
sand wives, sons and daughters. They
also took a great deal of plunder, which
they carried back to Samaria.[p]
9But a prophet of the LORD named
Oded was there, and he went out to
meet the army when it returned to
Samaria. He said to them, "Because the
LORD, the God of your fathers, was an-
gry[q] with Judah, he gave them into your 28:9 [q]2Ch 25:15; Isa 10:6; 47:6; Zec 1:15 [r]Ezr 9:6; Rev 18:5
hand. But you have slaughtered them in
a rage that reaches to heaven.[r] 10And
now you intend to make the men and
women of Judah and Jerusalem your
slaves.[s] But aren't you also guilty of sins 28:10 [s]Lev 25:39-46
against the LORD your God? 11Now listen
to me! Send back your fellow country-
men you have taken as prisoners, for the 28:11 [t]2Ch 11:4; Jas 2:13
LORD's fierce anger rests on you.[t]"

[a] *19* The Hebrew word was used for various diseases affecting the skin—not necessarily leprosy; also in verses 20, 21 and 23. [b] *21* Or *in a house where he was relieved of responsibilities*
[c] *5* That is, about 3 3/4 tons (about 3.4 metric tons)
[d] *5* That is, probably about 62,000 bushels (about 2,200 kiloliters)

12Then some of the leaders in Ephraim—Azariah son of Jehohanan, Berekiah son of Meshillemoth, Jehizkiah son of
Shallum, and Amasa son of Hadlai—
confronted those who were arriving
from the war. 13"You must not bring
those prisoners here," they said, "or we
will be guilty before the LORD. Do you intend to add to our sin and guilt? For our
guilt is already great, and his fierce anger
rests on Israel."
14So the soldiers gave up the prisoners
and plunder in the presence of the officials and all the assembly. 15The men
designated by name took the prisoners,
and from the plunder they clothed all
who were naked. They provided them
with clothes and sandals, food and
28:15 u 2Ki 6:22; Pr 25:21-22 v Dt 34:3; Jdg 1:16 drink,[u] and healing balm. All those who
were weak they put on donkeys. So they
took them back to their fellow countrymen at Jericho, the City of Palms,[v] and
returned to Samaria.
16At that time King Ahaz sent to the
28:16 w 2Ki 16:7 king[a] of Assyria[w] for help. 17The Edom-
28:17 x Ps 137:7; Isa 34:5 y 2Ch 29:9 ites[x] had again come and attacked Judah and carried away prisoners,[y] 18while
the Philistines[z] had raided towns in the
foothills and in the Negev of Judah. They
28:18 z Eze 16:27,57 a Jos 10:12 captured and occupied Beth Shemesh,
Aijalon[a] and Gederoth, as well as Soco,
Timnah and Gimzo, with their surrounding villages. 19The LORD had humbled Judah because of Ahaz king of Israel,[b] for he had promoted wickedness in
28:19 b 2Ch 21:2 Judah and had been most unfaithful[b] to
the LORD. 20Tiglath-Pileser[c][c] king of As-
28:20 c 2Ki 15:29; 1Ch 5:6 d 2Ki 16:7 syria came to him, but he gave him trouble instead of help.[d] 21Ahaz took some of
the things from the temple of the LORD
and from the royal palace and from the
princes and presented them to the king
of Assyria, but that did not help him.
22In his time of trouble King Ahaz be-
28:22 e Jer 5:3 came even more unfaithful[e] to the LORD.
23He offered sacrifices to the gods[f] of
28:23 f 2Ch 25:14 g Jer 44:17-18 Damascus, who had defeated him; for he
thought, "Since the gods of the kings of
Aram have helped them, I will sacrifice
to them so they will help me."[g] But they
were his downfall and the downfall of all
Israel.
24Ahaz gathered together the furnish-
28:24 h 2Ki 16:18 i 2Ch 29:7 j 2Ch 30:14 ings from the temple of God[h] and took
them away.[d] He shut the doors[i] of the
LORD's temple and set up altars[j] at every
street corner in Jerusalem. 25In every
town in Judah he built high places to
burn sacrifices to other gods and provoked the LORD, the God of his fathers,
to anger.
26The other events of his reign and all
his ways, from beginning to end, are
written in the book of the kings of Judah
and Israel. 27Ahaz rested[k] with his fa- **28:27** k Isa 14:28-32 l 2Ch 21:20; 24:25
thers and was buried[l] in the city of Jeru-
salem, but he was not placed in the
tombs of the kings of Israel. And Hezekiah his son succeeded him as king.

Hezekiah Purifies the Temple

29 Hezekiah[m] was twenty-five **29:1** m 1Ch 3:13
years old when he became king,
and he reigned in Jerusalem twenty-nine
years. His mother's name was Abijah
daughter of Zechariah. 2He did what
was right in the eyes of the LORD, just as **29:2** n 2Ch 28:1; 34:2
his father David[n] had done.
3In the first month of the first year of
his reign, he opened the doors of the **29:3** o 2Ch 28:24
temple of the LORD and repaired[o] them.
4He brought in the priests and the Levites, assembled them in the square on
the east side 5and said: "Listen to me, **29:5** p 2Ch 35:6
Levites! Consecrate[p] yourselves now
and consecrate the temple of the LORD,
the God of your fathers. Remove all de-
filement from the sanctuary. 6Our fa- **29:6** q Ps 106:6-47; Jer 2:27 r 1Ch 5:25; Eze 8:16
thers[q] were unfaithful;[r] they did evil in
the eyes of the LORD our God and forsook him. They turned their faces away
from the LORD's dwelling place and
turned their backs on him. 7They also
shut the doors of the portico and put
out the lamps. They did not burn incense or present any burnt offerings at
the sanctuary to the God of Israel.
8Therefore, the anger of the LORD has
fallen on Judah and Jerusalem; he has
made them an object of dread and hor- **29:8** s Dt 28:25; 2Ch 24:18 t Jer 18:16; 19:8; 25:9,18
ror[s] and scorn,[t] as you can see with your
own eyes. 9This is why our fathers have
fallen by the sword and why our sons
and daughters and our wives are in cap- **29:9** u 2Ch 28:5-8,17
tivity.[u] 10Now I intend to make a cov-
enant[v] with the LORD, the God of Israel, **29:10** v 2Ch 15:12; 23:16
so that his fierce anger will turn away
from us. 11My sons, do not be negligent
now, for the LORD has chosen you to

a 16 One Hebrew manuscript, Septuagint and Vulgate (see also 2 Kings 16:7); most Hebrew manuscripts *kings* *b 19* That is, Judah, as frequently in 2 Chronicles *c 20* Hebrew *Tilgath-Pilneser,* a variant of *Tiglath-Pileser* *d 24* Or *and cut them up*

DISCOVERY 107

THE LEGACY OF FAITH

Chronicles devotes more space to Hezekiah's life than to that of any other king after Solomon. Hezekiah was significant because God used him to bring the nation of Judah back to himself. Hezekiah accomplished several things to make that reversal possible.

First, he restored temple worship. The people of Israel had offered their allegiance to other gods and had stopped burning incense in the temple. In fact, they had gone so far as to lock the doors of the temple. Within the first month of his reign Hezekiah repaired and reopened the doors. He then assembled all of the Levites, instructing them to purify the temple so that the people could once again worship the one true God. After the temple premises had been purified, Hezekiah and his officials offered sacrifices to God for "a sin offering to atone for all Israel, because the king had ordered the burnt offering and the sin offering for all Israel" (2 Chronicles 29:24).

Then Hezekiah summoned all the people together to honor and thank God. He provided the Levites with musical instruments of all kinds: cymbals, harps, lyres, trumpets (verses 25–26). Everyone "bowed in worship, while the singers sang and the trumpeters played . . . They sang praises with gladness and bowed their heads" (verses 28,30).

After the people had dedicated themselves to the Lord, Hezekiah directed them to bring special sacrifices and offerings to the temple (verse 31)—after which they celebrated their return to God (verse 36). The people of Judah ended their festivities by observing the Passover corporately—for the first time in many years. The author of Chronicles records that "there was great joy in Jerusalem" (2 Chronicles 30:26).

What Hezekiah did to inspire a revival among God's people reminds us of the potential importance of a single life when that person is wholly committed to walking with God. The record of Hezekiah's life begins with a summary statement: "He did what was right in the eyes of the LORD, just as his father David had done" (2 Chronicles 29:2). David had died many years earlier, but his legacy lived on, and his faith stood out as an example for Hezekiah.

In the New Testament Jesus spelled out for us God's ultimate standard and example (John 13:15; 1 Peter 2:21). As Paul stated so beautifully, the quality of our own obedience can only be measured against the yardstick of Jesus' perfect submission to the will of his Father: "Your attitude should be the same as that of Christ Jesus: Who, being in very nature God, did not consider equality with God something to be grasped, but made himself nothing, taking the very nature of a servant, being made in human likeness. And being found in appearance as a man, he humbled himself and became obedient to death—even death on a cross!" (Philippians 2:5–8). If we follow Jesus' example, the kind of legacy we leave for our families, our friends, our nation, even our world, will serve as a standard for future generations (1 Peter 2:21).

Self-Discovery: *What kind of legacy would you want to leave for your loved ones and for the broader community of which you are a part? Identify some specific action plans for imitating Jesus' attitude of self-sacrificing humility and love for others.*

GO TO DISCOVERY 108 ON PAGE 583

29:11 [w]Nu 3:6; 8:6,14 stand before him and serve him,[w] to
[x]1Ch 15:2 minister[x] before him and to burn incense."

29:12 [y]Nu 3:17-20 12 Then these Levites[y] set to work:
[z]2Ch 31:15 from the Kohathites,
Mahath son of Amasai and Joel
son of Azariah;
from the Merarites,
Kish son of Abdi and Azariah
son of Jehallelel;
from the Gershonites,
Joah son of Zimmah and Eden[z]
son of Joah;
13 from the descendants of Elizaphan,
Shimri and Jeiel;
29:13 [a]1Ch 6:39 from the descendants of Asaph,[a]
Zechariah and Mattaniah;
14 from the descendants of Heman,
Jehiel and Shimei;
from the descendants of Jeduthun,
Shemaiah and Uzziel.

15 When they had assembled their
29:15 brothers and consecrated themselves,
[b]ver 5; they went in to purify[b] the temple of the
1Ch 23:28; LORD, as the king had ordered, following
2Ch 30:12 the word of the LORD. 16 The priests went
into the sanctuary of the LORD to purify
it. They brought out to the courtyard of
the LORD's temple everything unclean
that they found in the temple of the
LORD. The Levites took it and carried it 29:16
out to the Kidron Valley.[c] 17 They began [c]2Sa 15:23
the consecration on the first day of the
first month, and by the eighth day of the
month they reached the portico of the
LORD. For eight more days they consecrated the temple of the LORD itself, finishing on the sixteenth day of the first
month.

18 Then they went in to King Hezekiah
and reported: "We have purified the entire temple of the LORD, the altar of
burnt offering with all its utensils, and
the table for setting out the consecrated
bread, with all its articles. 19 We have pre- 29:19
pared and consecrated all the articles[d] [d]2Ch 28:24
that King Ahaz removed in his unfaithfulness while he was king. They are now
in front of the LORD's altar."

20 Early the next morning King Hezekiah gathered the city officials together
and went up to the temple of the LORD.
21 They brought seven bulls, seven rams,
seven male lambs and seven male goats 29:21
as a sin offering[e] for the kingdom, for [e]Lev 4:13-14
the sanctuary and for Judah. The king
commanded the priests, the descendants of Aaron, to offer these on the altar of the LORD. 22 So they slaughtered
the bulls, and the priests took the blood
and sprinkled it on the altar; next they
slaughtered the rams and sprinkled
their blood on the altar; then they
slaughtered the lambs and sprinkled 29:22
their blood[f] on the altar. 23 The goats for [f]Lev 4:18
the sin offering were brought before the
king and the assembly, and they laid 29:23
their hands[g] on them. 24 The priests then [g]Lev 4:15
slaughtered the goats and presented
their blood on the altar for a sin offering 29:24
to atone[h] for all Israel, because the king [h]Ex 29:36;
had ordered the burnt offering and the Lev 4:26
sin offering for all Israel.

25 He stationed the Levites in the temple of the LORD with cymbals, harps and 29:25
lyres in the way prescribed by David[i] [i]1Ch 25:6;
and Gad[j] the king's seer and Nathan the 2Ch 8:14
prophet; this was commanded by the [j]1Sa 22:5;
LORD through his prophets. 26 So the Le- 2Sa 24:11
vites stood ready with David's instru-
ments,[k] and the priests with their trum- 29:26 [k]1Ch 15:16
pets.[l] [l]1Ch 15:24; 23:5; 2Ch 5:12

27 Hezekiah gave the order to sacrifice
the burnt offering on the altar. As the offering began, singing to the LORD began
also, accompanied by trumpets and the

GREAT REFORMERS

A handful of Judah's kings were good rulers who used their power and influence to further God's cause. Asa assembled God's people for a great celebration at Jerusalem to demonstrate that they were turning back to God (2 Chronicles 15:9). After the Book of the Law had been discovered, Jehoshaphat sent his officials to educate the people with respect to God's ways (2 Chronicles 17:9). Joash repaired the temple and restored the practice of public worship (2 Chronicles 24:4,13–14). Hezekiah reminded the people of the need to return to God and led a celebration more elaborate than any since the days of Solomon some three hundred years earlier (2 Chronicles 29:10; 30:21–27). Josiah rededicated himself to God in the company of all the people, openly weeping as the priests read aloud the newly rediscovered Book of the Law (2 Chronicles 34:27,30). In the New Testament Jesus called the nation to turn back to God (Matthew 4:17; John 6:29). Although many of the religious leaders rejected him, many people did in fact respond to his teachings (Matthew 21:42).

29:27 [m] 2Ch 23:18 instruments[m] of David king of Israel.
28 The whole assembly bowed in wor-
ship, while the singers sang and the
trumpeters played. All this continued
until the sacrifice of the burnt offering
was completed.
29 When the offerings were finished,
29:29 [n] 2Ch 20:18 the king and everyone present with him
knelt down and worshiped.[n] 30 King Hez-
ekiah and his officials ordered the Levites to praise the LORD with the words
of David and of Asaph the seer. So they
sang praises with gladness and bowed
their heads and worshiped.
31 Then Hezekiah said, "You have now
29:31 [o] Heb 13:15-16 [p] Ex 25:2; 35:22 dedicated yourselves to the LORD. Come
and bring sacrifices[o] and thank offer-
ings to the temple of the LORD." So the
assembly brought sacrifices and thank
offerings, and all whose hearts were willing[p] brought burnt offerings.
32 The number of burnt offerings the
assembly brought was seventy bulls, a
hundred rams and two hundred male
lambs—all of them for burnt offerings
to the LORD. 33 The animals consecrated
as sacrifices amounted to six hundred
bulls and three thousand sheep and
29:34 [q] 2Ch 35:11 [r] 2Ch 30:3,15 goats. 34 The priests, however, were too
few to skin all the burnt offerings;[q] so
their kinsmen the Levites helped them
until the task was finished and until
other priests had been consecrated,[r] for
the Levites had been more conscientious in consecrating themselves than
the priests had been. 35 There were burnt
29:35 [s] Ex 29:13; Lev 3:16 [t] Lev 7:11-21 [u] Nu 15:5-10 offerings in abundance, together with
the fat[s] of the fellowship offerings[a][t]
and the drink offerings[u] that accompanied the burnt offerings.
So the service of the temple of the
LORD was reestablished. 36 Hezekiah and
all the people rejoiced at what God had
brought about for his people, because it
was done so quickly.

Hezekiah Celebrates the Passover

30 Hezekiah sent word to all Israel and Judah and also wrote let-
30:1 [v] Ge 41:52 [w] Ex 12:11; Nu 28:16 ters to Ephraim and Manasseh,[v] inviting
them to come to the temple of the LORD
in Jerusalem and celebrate the Passover[w] to the LORD, the God of Israel.
2 The king and his officials and the whole
assembly in Jerusalem decided to cele-
30:2 [x] Nu 9:10 brate[x] the Passover in the second
month. 3 They had not been able to celebrate it at the regular time because not
enough priests had consecrated[y] them- 30:3 [y] 2Ch 29:34
selves and the people had not assembled
in Jerusalem. 4 The plan seemed right
both to the king and to the whole assembly. 5 They decided to send a proclamation throughout Israel, from Beer- 30:5 [z] Jdg 20:1
sheba to Dan,[z] calling the people to
come to Jerusalem and celebrate the
Passover to the LORD, the God of Israel.
It had not been celebrated in large numbers according to what was written.
6 At the king's command, couriers
went throughout Israel and Judah with
letters from the king and from his officials, which read:

"People of Israel, return to the
LORD, the God of Abraham, Isaac
and Israel, that he may return to
you who are left, who have escaped
from the hand of the kings of As-
syria. 7 Do not be like your fathers[a] 30:7 [a] Ps 78:8,57; 106:6; Eze 20:18 [b] 2Ch 29:8
and brothers, who were unfaithful
to the LORD, the God of their fathers, so that he made them an object of horror,[b] as you see. 8 Do not
be stiff-necked,[c] as your fathers 30:8 [c] Ex 32:9 [d] Nu 25:4; 2Ch 29:10
were; submit to the LORD. Come to
the sanctuary, which he has consecrated forever. Serve the LORD your
God, so that his fierce anger[d] will
turn away from you. 9 If you return[e] 30:9 [e] Dt 30:2-5; Isa 1:16; 55:7 [f] 1Ki 8:50; Ps 106:46 [g] Ex 34:6-7; Dt 4:31; Mic 7:18
to the LORD, then your brothers and
your children will be shown compassion[f] by their captors and will
come back to this land, for the LORD
your God is gracious and compassionate.[g] He will not turn his face
from you if you return to him."

10 The couriers went from town to
town in Ephraim and Manasseh, as far
as Zebulun, but the people scorned and
ridiculed[h] them. 11 Nevertheless, some 30:10 [h] 2Ch 36:16
men of Asher, Manasseh and Zebulun
humbled themselves and went to Jeru-
salem.[i] 12 Also in Judah the hand of God 30:11 [i] ver 25
was on the people to give them unity[j] of 30:12 [j] Jer 32:39; Eze 11:19; Php 2:13
mind to carry out what the king and his
officials had ordered, following the word
of the LORD.

13 A very large crowd of people assem-
bled in Jerusalem to celebrate the Feast 30:13 [k] Nu 28:16
of Unleavened Bread[k] in the second
month. 14 They removed the altars[l] in Je- 30:14 [l] 2Ch 28:24
rusalem and cleared away the incense

[a] 35 Traditionally *peace offerings*

30:14 altars and threw them into the Kidron
m 2Sa 15:23 Valley.[m]
15They slaughtered the Passover lamb
on the fourteenth day of the second
30:15 month. The priests and the Levites were
n 2Ch 29:34 ashamed and consecrated[n] themselves
and brought burnt offerings to the tem-
30:16 ple of the LORD. 16Then they took up
o 2Ch 35:10 their regular positions[o] as prescribed in
the Law of Moses the man of God. The
priests sprinkled the blood handed to
them by the Levites. 17Since many in the
30:17 crowd had not consecrated themselves,
p 2Ch 29:34 the Levites had to kill[p] the Passover
lambs for all those who were not ceremonially clean and could not consecrate
⌊their lambs⌋ to the LORD. 18Although
most of the many people who came
30:18 from Ephraim, Manasseh, Issachar and
q Ex 12:43-49; Zebulun had not purified themselves,[q]
Nu 9:6-10 yet they ate the Passover, contrary to
what was written. But Hezekiah prayed
for them, saying, "May the LORD, who is
good, pardon everyone 19who sets his
heart on seeking God—the LORD, the
God of his fathers—even if he is not
30:20 clean according to the rules of the sanc-
r 2Ch 6:20 tuary." 20And the LORD heard[r] Hezekiah
s 2Ch 7:14; Mal 4:2 and healed[s] the people.[t]
t Jas 5:16 21The Israelites who were present in Je-
30:21 rusalem celebrated the Feast of Unleav-
u Ex 12:15,17; ened Bread[u] for seven days with great re-
13:6 joicing, while the Levites and priests sang
to the LORD every day, accompanied by
the LORD's instruments of praise.[a]
22Hezekiah spoke encouragingly to all
the Levites, who showed good understanding of the service of the LORD. For
the seven days they ate their assigned
portion and offered fellowship offerings[b]
and praised the LORD, the God of their
fathers.
23The whole assembly then agreed to
30:23 v 1Ki 8:65; celebrate[v] the festival seven more days;
2Ch 7:9 so for another seven days they celebrat-
30:24 ed joyfully. 24Hezekiah king of Judah
w 1Ki 8:5; provided[w] a thousand bulls and seven
2Ch 29:34; 35:7; thousand sheep and goats for the as-
Ezr 6:17; 8:35 sembly, and the officials provided them
with a thousand bulls and ten thousand
sheep and goats. A great number of
priests consecrated themselves. 25The
entire assembly of Judah rejoiced, along
with the priests and Levites and all who
30:25 x ver 11 had assembled from Israel[x], including
the aliens who had come from Israel and
those who lived in Judah. 26There was
great joy in Jerusalem, for since the days 30:26
of Solomon[y] son of David king of Israel y 2Ch 7:8
there had been nothing like this in Jerusalem. 27The priests and the Levites 30:27
stood to bless[z] the people, and God z Ex 39:43;
heard them, for their prayer reached Nu 6:23; Dt 26:15;
heaven, his holy dwelling place. 2Ch 23:18; Ps 68:5

31 When all this had ended, the Israelites who were there went
out to the towns of Judah, smashed the 31:1
sacred stones and cut down[a] the Ashe- a 2Ki 18:4;
rah poles. They destroyed the high 2Ch 32:12; Isa 36:7
places and the altars throughout Judah
and Benjamin and in Ephraim and Manasseh. After they had destroyed all of
them, the Israelites returned to their
own towns and to their own property.

Contributions for Worship

31:2
2Hezekiah[b] assigned the priests and b 2Ch 29:9
Levites to divisions[c]—each of them ac- c 1Ch 24:1
cording to their duties as priests or Le- d 1Ch 15:2
vites—to offer burnt offerings and fel- e Ps 7:17; 9:2; 47:6; 71:22
lowship offerings,[b] to minister,[d] to give f 1Ch 23:28-32
thanks and to sing praises[e] at the gates
of the LORD's dwelling.[f] 3The king con- 31:3
tributed[g] from his own possessions for g 1Ch 29:3;
the morning and evening burnt offer- 2Ch 35:7;
ings and for the burnt offerings on the Eze 45:17 h Nu 28:1-29:40
Sabbaths, New Moons and appointed
feasts as written in the Law of the
LORD.[h] 4He ordered the people living in 31:4
Jerusalem to give the portion[i] due the i Nu 18:8;
priests and Levites so they could devote Dt 18:8; Ne 13:10;
themselves to the Law of the LORD. 5As Mal 2:7
soon as the order went out, the Israelites 31:5
generously gave the firstfruits[j] of their j Nu 18:12,24;
grain, new wine,[k] oil and honey and all Ne 13:12; Eze 44:30
that the fields produced. They brought a k Dt 12:17
great amount, a tithe of everything. 6The
men of Israel and Judah who lived in the
towns of Judah also brought a tithe[l] of 31:6 l Lev 27:30;
their herds and flocks and a tithe of the Ne 13:10-12 m Dt 14:28;
holy things dedicated to the LORD their Ru 3:7
God, and they piled them in heaps.[m]
7They began doing this in the third
month and finished in the seventh 31:7 n Ex 23:16
month.[n] 8When Hezekiah and his officials came and saw the heaps, they 31:8
praised the LORD and blessed[o] his peo- o Ps 144:13-15
ple Israel.
9Hezekiah asked the priests and Levites about the heaps; 10and Azariah the 31:10
chief priest, from the family of Zadok,[p] p 2Sa 8:17

a 21 Or *priests praised the LORD every day with resounding instruments belonging to the LORD*
b 22,2 Traditionally *peace offerings*

answered, "Since the people began to
bring their contributions to the temple
of the LORD, we have had enough to eat
and plenty to spare, because the LORD
31:10 [q] Ex 36:5; Eze 44:30; Mal 3:10-12 has blessed his people, and this great
amount is left over."[q]
11Hezekiah gave orders to prepare
storerooms in the temple of the LORD,
and this was done. 12Then they faithful-
31:12 [r] 2Ch 35:9 ly brought in the contributions, tithes
and dedicated gifts. Conaniah,[r] a Levite,
was in charge of these things, and his
brother Shimei was next in rank. 13Jehi-
31:13 [s] 2Ch 35:9 el, Azaziah, Nahath, Asahel, Jerimoth,
Jozabad,[s] Eliel, Ismakiah, Mahath and
Benaiah were supervisors under Conaniah and Shimei his brother, by appointment of King Hezekiah and Azariah the
official in charge of the temple of God.
14Kore son of Imnah the Levite, keeper of the East Gate, was in charge of the
freewill offerings given to God, distributing the contributions made to the LORD
31:15 [t] 2Ch 29:12 [u] Jos 21:9-19 and also the consecrated gifts. 15Eden,[t]
Miniamin, Jeshua, Shemaiah, Amariah
and Shecaniah assisted him faithfully in
the towns[u] of the priests, distributing to
their fellow priests according to their divisions, old and young alike.
16In addition, they distributed to the
males three years old or more whose
31:16 [v] 1Ch 23:3; Ezr 3:4 names were in the genealogical records[v]
—all who would enter the temple of the
LORD to perform the daily duties of their
various tasks, according to their responsibilities and their divisions. 17And they
distributed to the priests enrolled by
their families in the genealogical records
and likewise to the Levites twenty years
old or more, according to their responsibilities and their divisions. 18They included all the little ones, the wives, and
the sons and daughters of the whole
community listed in these genealogical
records. For they were faithful in consecrating themselves.
19As for the priests, the descendants
of Aaron, who lived on the farm lands
31:19 [w] ver 12-15; Lev 25:34; Nu 35:2-5 around their towns or in any other
towns,[w] men were designated by name
to distribute portions to every male
among them and to all who were recorded in the genealogies of the Levites.
20This is what Hezekiah did throughout Judah, doing what was good and
31:20 [x] 2Ki 20:3; 22:2 right and faithful[x] before the LORD his
God. 21In everything that he undertook
in the service of God's temple and in
obedience to the law and the commands, he sought his God and worked
wholeheartedly. And so he prospered.[y] 31:21 [y] Dt 29:9

Sennacherib Threatens Jerusalem

32 After all that Hezekiah had so 32:1 [z] 2Ki 18:13-19; Isa 36:1; 37:9, 17,37
faithfully done, Sennacherib[z]
king of Assyria came and invaded Judah.
He laid siege to the fortified cities,
thinking to conquer them for himself.
2When Hezekiah saw that Sennacherib
had come and that he intended to make 32:2 [a] Isa 22:7; Jer 1:15
war on Jerusalem,[a] 3he consulted with
his officials and military staff about
blocking off the water from the springs
outside the city, and they helped him. 4A
large force of men assembled, and they 32:4 [b] 2Ki 18:17; 20:20; Isa 22:9, 11; Na 3:14
blocked all the springs[b] and the stream
that flowed through the land. "Why
should the kings[a] of Assyria come and
find plenty of water?" they said. 5Then
he worked hard repairing all the broken 32:5 [c] 2Ch 25:23; Isa 22:10 [d] 1Ki 9:24; 1Ch 11:8 [e] Isa 22:8
sections of the wall[c] and building tow-
ers on it. He built another wall outside
that one and reinforced the supporting
terraces[b][d] of the City of David. He also
made large numbers of weapons[e] and
shields.
6He appointed military officers over
the people and assembled them before
him in the square at the city gate and en-
couraged them with these words: 7"Be 32:7 [f] Dt 31:6; 1Ch 22:13 [g] 2Ch 20:15 [h] Nu 14:9; 2Ki 6:16
strong and courageous.[f] Do not be afraid
or discouraged[g] because of the king of
Assyria and the vast army with him, for
there is a greater power with us than
with him.[h] 8With him is only the arm of 32:8 [i] Job 40:9; Isa 52:10; Jer 17:5; 32:21 [j] Dt 3:22; 1Sa 17:45; 2Ch 13:12 [k] 1Ch 5:22; 2Ch 20:17; Ps 20:7; Isa 28:6
flesh,[i] but with us[j] is the LORD our God to
help us and to fight our battles."[k] And
the people gained confidence from what
Hezekiah the king of Judah said.
9Later, when Sennacherib king of Assyria and all his forces were laying siege
to Lachish,[l] he sent his officers to Jeru- 32:9 [l] Jos 10:3,31
salem with this message for Hezekiah
king of Judah and for all the people of Judah who were there:

10"This is what Sennacherib king
of Assyria says: On what are you
basing your confidence,[m] that you 32:10 [m] Eze 29:16
remain in Jerusalem under siege?
11When Hezekiah says, 'The LORD
our God will save us from the hand
of the king of Assyria,' he is mis-

[a] 4 Hebrew; Septuagint and Syriac *king* [b] 5 Or *the Millo*

leading[n] you, to let you die of hunger and thirst. 12 Did not Hezekiah himself remove this god's high places and altars, saying to Judah and Jerusalem, 'You must worship before one altar[o] and burn sacrifices on it'?

13 "Do you not know what I and my fathers have done to all the peoples of the other lands? Were the gods of those nations ever able to deliver their land from my hand?[p] 14 Who of all the gods of these nations that my fathers destroyed has been able to save his people from me? How then can your god deliver you from my hand? 15 Now do not let Hezekiah deceive[q] you and mislead you like this. Do not believe him, for no god of any nation or kingdom has been able to deliver[r] his people from my hand or the hand of my fathers.[s] How much less will your god deliver you from my hand!"

16 Sennacherib's officers spoke further against the LORD God and against his servant Hezekiah. 17 The king also wrote letters[t] insulting[u] the LORD, the God of Israel, and saying this against him: "Just as the gods[v] of the peoples of the other lands did not rescue their people from my hand, so the god of Hezekiah will not rescue his people from my hand." 18 Then they called out in Hebrew to the people of Jerusalem who were on the wall, to terrify them and make them afraid in order to capture the city. 19 They spoke about the God of Jerusalem as they did about the gods of the other peoples of the world—the work of men's hands.[w]

20 King Hezekiah and the prophet Isaiah son of Amoz cried out in prayer to heaven about this. 21 And the LORD sent an angel,[x] who annihilated all the fighting men and the leaders and officers in the camp of the Assyrian king. So he withdrew to his own land in disgrace. And when he went into the temple of his god, some of his sons cut him down with the sword.[y]

22 So the LORD saved Hezekiah and the people of Jerusalem from the hand of Sennacherib king of Assyria and from the hand of all others. He took care of them[a] on every side. 23 Many brought offerings to Jerusalem for the LORD and valuable gifts[z] for Hezekiah king of Judah. From then on he was highly regarded by all the nations.

Hezekiah's Pride, Success and Death

24 In those days Hezekiah became ill and was at the point of death. He prayed to the LORD, who answered him and gave him a miraculous sign. 25 But Hezekiah's heart was proud[a] and he did not respond to the kindness shown him; therefore the LORD's wrath[b] was on him and on Judah and Jerusalem. 26 Then Hezekiah repented[c] of the pride of his heart, as did the people of Jerusalem; therefore the LORD's wrath did not come upon them during the days of Hezekiah.[d]

27 Hezekiah had very great riches and honor,[e] and he made treasuries for his silver and gold and for his precious stones, spices, shields and all kinds of valuables. 28 He also made buildings to store the harvest of grain, new wine and oil; and he made stalls for various kinds of cattle, and pens for the flocks. 29 He built villages and acquired great numbers of flocks and herds, for God had given him very great riches.[f]

30 It was Hezekiah who blocked[g] the upper outlet of the Gihon[h] spring and channeled the water down to the west side of the City of David. He succeeded in everything he undertook. 31 But when envoys were sent by the rulers of Babylon[i] to ask him about the miraculous sign[j] that had occurred in the land, God left him to test[k] him and to know everything that was in his heart.

32 The other events of Hezekiah's reign and his acts of devotion are written in the vision of the prophet Isaiah son of Amoz in the book of the kings of Judah and Israel. 33 Hezekiah rested with his fathers and was buried on the hill where the tombs of David's descendants are. All Judah and the people of Jerusalem honored him when he died. And Manasseh his son succeeded him as king.

Manasseh King of Judah

33 Manasseh[l] was twelve years old when he became king, and he reigned in Jerusalem fifty-five years. 2 He did evil in the eyes of the LORD,[m] following the detestable[n] practices of the na-

a 22 Hebrew; Septuagint and Vulgate *He gave them rest*

32:11 n Isa 37:10
32:12 o 2Ch 31:1
32:13 p ver 15
32:15 q Isa 37:10; r Da 3:15; s Ex 5:2
32:17 t Isa 37:14; u Ps 74:22; Isa 37:4,17; v 2Ki 19:12
32:19 w 2Ki 19:18; Ps 115:4,4-8; Isa 2:8; 17:8
32:21 x Ge 19:13; y 2Ki 19:7
32:23 z 2Ch 9:24; 17:5; Isa 45:14; Zec 14:16-17
32:25 a 2Ki 14:10; 2Ch 26:16; b 2Ch 19:2; 24:18
32:26 c Jer 26:18-19; d 2Ch 34:27,28; Isa 39:8
32:27 e 1Ch 29:12
32:29 f 1Ch 29:12
32:30 g 2Ki 18:17; h 1Ki 1:33
32:31 i Isa 39:1; j ver 24; Isa 38:7; k Ge 22:1; Dt 8:16
33:1 l 1Ch 3:13
33:2 m Jer 15:4; n Dt 18:9; 2Ch 28:3

tions the LORD had driven out before the
Israelites. 3He rebuilt the high places his
father Hezekiah had demolished; he also
33:3 erected altars to the Baals and made
[o]Dt 16:21-22 Asherah poles.[o] He bowed down[p] to all
[p]Dt 17:3; 2Ch 31:1 the starry hosts and worshiped them.
4He built altars in the temple of the
33:4 LORD, of which the LORD had said, "My
[q]2Ch 7:16 Name[q] will remain in Jerusalem forever."
5In both courts of the temple of the
33:5 [r]2Ch 4:9 LORD,[r] he built altars to all the starry
hosts. 6He sacrificed his sons[s] in[a] the
33:6 [s]Lev 18:21; fire in the Valley of Ben Hinnom, prac-
Dt 18:10; 2Ch 28:3 ticed sorcery, divination and witchcraft,
[t]Lev 19:31 and consulted mediums[t] and spiritists.[u]
[u]1Sa 28:13 He did much evil in the eyes of the LORD,
provoking him to anger.
7He took the carved image he had
33:7 [v]2Ch 7:16 made and put it in God's temple,[v] of
which God had said to David and to his
son Solomon, "In this temple and in Jerusalem, which I have chosen out of all
the tribes of Israel, I will put my Name
forever. 8I will not again make the feet of
33:8 [w]2Sa 7:10 the Israelites leave the land[w] I assigned
to your forefathers, if only they will be
careful to do everything I commanded
them concerning all the laws, decrees
and ordinances given through Moses."
9But Manasseh led Judah and the people
of Jerusalem astray, so that they did
33:9 more evil than the nations the LORD had
[x]Jer 15:4 destroyed before the Israelites.[x]
10The LORD spoke to Manasseh and
his people, but they paid no attention.
11So the LORD brought against them the
33:11 army commanders of the king of Assyr-
[y]Dt 28:36 ia, who took Manasseh prisoner,[y] put a
[z]Ps 149:8 hook in his nose, bound him with
bronze shackles[z] and took him to Babylon. 12In his distress he sought the favor
33:12 [a]2Ch 6:37; of the LORD his God and humbled[a] him-
32:26; 1Pe 5:6 self greatly before the God of his fathers.
13And when he prayed to him, the LORD
was moved by his entreaty and listened
to his plea; so he brought him back to Jerusalem and to his kingdom. Then Manasseh knew that the LORD is God.
33:14 14Afterward he rebuilt the outer wall
[b]1Ki 1:33 [c]Ne 3:3; 12:39; of the City of David, west of the Gihon[b]
Zep 1:10 spring in the valley, as far as the en-
[d]2Ch 27:3; Ne 3:26 trance of the Fish Gate[c] and encircling
the hill of Ophel;[d] he also made it much
higher. He stationed military commanders in all the fortified cities in Judah.
33:15 15He got rid of the foreign gods and
[e]ver 3-7; 2Ki 23:12 removed[e] the image from the temple of
the LORD, as well as all the altars he had
built on the temple hill and in Jerusalem;
and he threw them out of the city.
16Then he restored the altar of the LORD
and sacrificed fellowship offerings[b] and
thank offerings[f] on it, and told Judah to 33:16
serve the LORD, the God of Israel. 17The [f]Lev 7:11-18
people, however, continued to sacrifice
at the high places, but only to the LORD
their God.
18The other events of Manasseh's
reign, including his prayer to his God
and the words the seers spoke to him in
the name of the LORD, the God of Israel,
are written in the annals of the kings of
Israel.[c] 19His prayer and how God was
moved by his entreaty, as well as all his
sins and unfaithfulness, and the sites
where he built high places and set up 33:19
Asherah poles and idols before he hum- [g]2Ch 6:37
bled[g] himself—all are written in the [h]2Ki 21:17
records of the seers.[d][h] 20Manasseh rest- 33:20
ed with his fathers and was buried[i] in [i]2Ki 21:18; 2Ch 21:20

[a] 6 Or *He made his sons pass through*
[b] 16 Traditionally *peace offerings*
[c] 18 That is, Judah, as frequently in 2 Chronicles
[d] 19 One Hebrew manuscript and Septuagint; most Hebrew manuscripts *of Hozai*

NEVER TOO LATE

The books of 1 and 2 Chronicles record the major events in the lives of God's people. One of the most amazing is the story of King Manasseh (2 Chronicles 33). Although he was Hezekiah's son, he was one of Judah's worst kings. Manasseh ruled for 52 years—the longest reign of any king in either Israel or Judah. During his reign all of Hezekiah's work in turning the hearts of the people back to God was undone, and the people turned back to idols. Manasseh was captured by the Assyrians and deported, a man defeated and humiliated, to Babylon for a time. In his distress Manasseh humbled himself and prayed to God, and God "was moved by his entreaty and listened to his plea" (verse 13). Manasseh returned to Jerusalem a different man as he turned back to the true God of Israel, and the people followed their king's example and recommitted themselves to God. Manasseh is listed as one of Jesus' descendants (Matthew 1:10). What an honor for a king who had done so much evil! But God takes delight still today in bringing people back to himself and giving them a place in the family of Jesus.

his palace. And Amon his son succeeded him as king.

Amon King of Judah

33:21 21 Amon[j] was twenty-two years old
j 1Ch 3:14 when he became king, and he reigned in
Jerusalem two years. 22 He did evil in the
eyes of the LORD, as his father Manasseh
had done. Amon worshiped and offered
33:23 sacrifices to all the idols Manasseh had
k ver 12; Ex 10:3; made. 23 But unlike his father Manasseh,
2Ch 7:14; he did not humble[k] himself before the
Ps 18:27; 147:6; Pr 3:34 LORD; Amon increased his guilt.
24 Amon's officials conspired against
33:25 him and assassinated him in his palace.
l 2Ch 22:1 25 Then the people[l] of the land killed all
who had plotted against King Amon,
and they made Josiah his son king in his
place.

Josiah's Reforms

34:1 34 Josiah[m] was eight years old
m 1Ch 3:14 n Zep 1:1 when he became king,[n] and he
reigned in Jerusalem thirty-one years.
2 He did what was right in the eyes of the
LORD and walked in the ways of his fa-
34:2 o 2Ch 29:2 ther David,[o] not turning aside to the
right or to the left.
3 In the eighth year of his reign, while
34:3 he was still young, he began to seek the
p 1Ki 13:2; God[p] of his father David. In his twelfth
1Ch 16:11; year he began to purge Judah and Jeru-
2Ch 15:2; 33:17, 22 salem of high places, Asherah poles,
carved idols and cast images. 4 Under his
direction the altars of the Baals were
torn down; he cut to pieces the incense
altars that were above them, and
34:4 q Ex 34:13 smashed the Asherah poles,[q] the idols
r Ex 32:20; and the images. These he broke to
Lev 26:30; pieces and scattered over the graves of
2Ki 23:11; Mic 1:5 those who had sacrificed to them.[r] 5 He
34:5 burned[s] the bones of the priests on their
s 1Ki 13:2 altars, and so he purged Judah and Jerusalem. 6 In the towns of Manasseh,
Ephraim and Simeon, as far as Naphtali,
and in the ruins around them, 7 he tore
down the altars and the Asherah poles
34:7 and crushed the idols to powder[t] and
t Ex 32:20; 2Ch 31:1 cut to pieces all the incense altars
throughout Israel. Then he went back to
Jerusalem.
8 In the eighteenth year of Josiah's
reign, to purify the land and the temple,
he sent Shaphan son of Azaliah and Maaseiah the ruler of the city, with Joah son
of Joahaz, the recorder, to repair the
temple of the LORD his God.

9 They went to Hilkiah[u] the high priest 34:9
and gave him the money that had been u 1Ch 6:13; 2Ch 35:8
brought into the temple of God, which
the Levites who were the doorkeepers
had collected from the people of Manasseh, Ephraim and the entire remnant
of Israel and from all the people of Judah
and Benjamin and the inhabitants of Jerusalem. 10 Then they entrusted it to the
men appointed to supervise the work on
the LORD's temple. These men paid the
workers who repaired and restored 34:11
the temple. 11 They also gave money[v] to v 2Ch 24:12
the carpenters and builders to purchase w 2Ch 33:4-7
dressed stone, and timber for joists and
beams for the buildings that the kings of
Judah had allowed to fall into ruin.[w] 34:12
12 The men did the work faithfully.[x] x 2Ki 12:15 y 1Ch 25:1
Over them to direct them were Jahath
and Obadiah, Levites descended from
Merari, and Zechariah and Meshullam,
descended from Kohath. The Levites—
all who were skilled in playing musical
instruments—[y] 13 had charge of the la- 34:13
borers[z] and supervised all the workers z 1Ch 23:4
from job to job. Some of the Levites were
secretaries, scribes and doorkeepers.

The Book of the Law Found

14 While they were bringing out the
money that had been taken into the
temple of the LORD, Hilkiah the priest
found the Book of the Law of the LORD
that had been given through Moses.
15 Hilkiah said to Shaphan the secretary, 34:15
"I have found the Book of the Law[a] in a 2Ki 22:8;
the temple of the LORD." He gave it to Ezr 7:6; Ne 8:1
Shaphan.
16 Then Shaphan took the book to the
king and reported to him: "Your officials
are doing everything that has been committed to them. 17 They have paid out
the money that was in the temple of the
LORD and have entrusted it to the supervisors and workers." 18 Then Shaphan the
secretary informed the king, "Hilkiah
the priest has given me a book." And
Shaphan read from it in the presence of
the king.
19 When the king heard the words of 34:19 b Dt 28:3-68
the Law,[b] he tore[c] his robes. 20 He gave c Jos 7:6;
these orders to Hilkiah, Ahikam son of Isa 36:22; 37:1
Shaphan[d], Abdon son of Micah,[a] Sha- 34:20
phan the secretary and Asaiah the king's d 2Ki 22:3
attendant: 21 "Go and inquire of the LORD
for me and for the remnant in Israel and

[a] 20 Also called *Acbor son of Micaiah*

Judah about what is written in this book
34:21 that has been found. Great is the LORD's
e 2Ch 29:8; anger that is poured out[e] on us because
La 2:4; 4:11; our fathers have not kept the word of
Eze 36:18 the LORD; they have not acted in accordance with all that is written in this
book."
[22]Hilkiah and those the king had sent
34:22 with him[a] went to speak to the prophet-
f Ex 15:20; ess[f] Huldah, who was the wife of Shal-
Ne 6:14 lum son of Tokhath,[b] the son of Hasrah,[c]
keeper of the wardrobe. She lived in Jerusalem, in the Second District.
[23]She said to them, "This is what the
LORD, the God of Israel, says: Tell the
34:24 man who sent you to me, [24]'This is what
g Pr 16:4; the LORD says: I am going to bring disas-
Isa 3:9; Jer 40:2; 42:10; 44:2,11 ter[g] on this place and its people[h]—all
h 2Ch 36:14-20 the curses[i] written in the book that has
i Dt 28:15-68 been read in the presence of the king of
34:25 Judah. [25]Because they have forsaken me[j]
j 2Ch 33:3-6; and burned incense to other gods and
Jer 22:9 provoked me to anger by all that their
hands have made,[d] my anger will be
poured out on this place and will not be
quenched.' [26]Tell the king of Judah, who
sent you to inquire of the LORD, 'This is
what the LORD, the God of Israel, says
34:27 concerning the words you heard: [27]Be-
k 2Ch 12:7; cause your heart was responsive[k] and
32:26 l Ex 10:3; you humbled[l] yourself before God when
2Ch 6:37 you heard what he spoke against this
place and its people, and because you
humbled yourself before me and tore
your robes and wept in my presence, I
34:28 have heard you, declares the LORD.
m 2Ch 35:20-25 [28]Now I will gather you to your fathers,[m]
n 2Ch 32:26 and you will be buried in peace. Your
eyes will not see all the disaster I am going to bring on this place and on those
who live here.' "[n]
So they took her answer back to the
king.
[29]Then the king called together all the
elders of Judah and Jerusalem. [30]He went
34:30 o 2Ki 23:2; up to the temple of the LORD[o] with the
Ne 8:1-3 men of Judah, the people of Jerusalem,
the priests and the Levites—all the people from the least to the greatest. He
read in their hearing all the words of the
Book of the Covenant, which had been
34:31 found in the temple of the LORD. [31]The
p 1Ki 7:15; king stood by his pillar[p] and renewed
2Ki 11:14 q 2Ki 11:17; the covenant[q] in the presence of the
2Ch 23:16; LORD—to follow[r] the LORD and keep his
29:10 r Dt 13:4 commands, regulations and decrees
with all his heart and all his soul, and to
obey the words of the covenant written
in this book.
[32]Then he had everyone in Jerusalem
and Benjamin pledge themselves to it;
the people of Jerusalem did this in accordance with the covenant of God, the
God of their fathers.
[33]Josiah removed all the detestable[s] 34:33 s ver 3-7;
idols from all the territory belonging to Dt 18:9
the Israelites, and he had all who were
present in Israel serve the LORD their
God. As long as he lived, they did not fail
to follow the LORD, the God of their fathers.

Josiah Celebrates the Passover

35 Josiah celebrated the Passover[t] 35:1 t Ex 12:1-30;
to the LORD in Jerusalem, and Nu 9:3; 28:16
the Passover lamb was slaughtered on
the fourteenth day of the first month.
[2]He appointed the priests to their duties
and encouraged them in the service of
the LORD's temple. [3]He said to the Le- 35:3
vites, who instructed[u] all Israel and who u Dt 33:10; 1Ch 23:26;
had been consecrated to the LORD: "Put 2Ch 5:7; 17:7
the sacred ark in the temple that Solo-
mon son of David king of Israel built. It
is not to be carried about on your shoulders. Now serve the LORD your God and
his people Israel. [4]Prepare yourselves by 35:4
families in your divisions,[v] according to v ver 10;
the directions written by David king of 1Ch 9:10-13; 24:1; 2Ch 8:14;
Israel and by his son Solomon. Ezr 6:18
[5]"Stand in the holy place with a group
of Levites for each subdivision of the
families of your fellow countrymen, the
lay people. [6]Slaughter the Passover 35:6
lambs, consecrate yourselves[w] and pre- w Lev 11:44; 2Ch 29:5,15
pare ⌞the lambs⌟ for your fellow coun-
trymen, doing what the LORD commanded through Moses."
[7]Josiah provided for all the lay people
who were there a total of thirty thousand
sheep and goats for the Passover offer- 35:7
ings,[x] and also three thousand cattle— x 2Ch 30:24
all from the king's own possessions.[y] y 2Ch 31:3
[8]His officials also contributed[z] volun- 35:8
tarily to the people and the priests and z 1Ch 29:3;
Levites. Hilkiah,[a] Zechariah and Jehiel, 2Ch 29:31-36 a 1Ch 6:13
the administrators of God's temple, gave
the priests twenty-six hundred Passover
offerings and three hundred cattle. [9]Also 35:9
Conaniah[b] along with Shemaiah and b 2Ch 31:12

[a] *22* One Hebrew manuscript, Vulgate and Syriac; most Hebrew manuscripts do not have *had sent with him.* [b] *22* Also called *Tikvah* [c] *22* Also called *Harhas* [d] *25* Or *by everything they have done*

35:9 Nethanel, his brothers, and Hashabiah,
[c]2Ch 31:13 Jeiel and Jozabad,[c] the leaders of the Levites, provided five thousand Passover
offerings and five hundred head of cattle for the Levites.
10The service was arranged and the
35:10 priests stood in their places with the Le-
[d]ver 4; Ezr 6:18 vites in their divisions[d] as the king had
[e]2Ch 30:16 ordered.[e] 11The Passover lambs were
35:11 slaughtered,[f] and the priests sprinkled
[f]2Ch 29:22,34; 30:17 the blood handed to them, while the Levites skinned the animals. 12They set
aside the burnt offerings to give them to
the subdivisions of the families of the
people to offer to the LORD, as is written
in the Book of Moses. They did the same
with the cattle. 13They roasted the
Passover animals over the fire as pre-
35:13 scribed,[g] and boiled the holy offerings in
[g]Ex 12:2-11; Lev 6:25; 1Sa 2:13-15 pots, caldrons and pans and served
them quickly to all the people. 14After
this, they made preparations for themselves and for the priests, because the
priests, the descendants of Aaron, were
sacrificing the burnt offerings and the
35:14 fat portions[h] until nightfall. So the Le-
[h]Ex 29:13 vites made preparations for themselves
and for the Aaronic priests.
35:15 15The musicians,[i] the descendants of
[i]1Ch 25:1; 26:12-19; 2Ch 29:30; Ne 12:46; Ps 68:25 Asaph, were in the places prescribed by
David, Asaph, Heman and Jeduthun the
king's seer. The gatekeepers at each gate
did not need to leave their posts, because their fellow Levites made the
preparations for them.
16So at that time the entire service of
the LORD was carried out for the celebration of the Passover and the offering
of burnt offerings on the altar of the
LORD, as King Josiah had ordered. 17The
Israelites who were present celebrated
the Passover at that time and observed
the Feast of Unleavened Bread for seven
days. 18The Passover had not been observed like this in Israel since the days of
the prophet Samuel; and none of the
kings of Israel had ever celebrated such
a Passover as did Josiah, with the priests,
the Levites and all Judah and Israel who
were there with the people of Jerusalem.
19This Passover was celebrated in the
eighteenth year of Josiah's reign.

The Death of Josiah

20After all this, when Josiah had set
35:20 [j]Isa 10:9; Jer 46:2 the temple in order, Neco king of Egypt
went up to fight at Carchemish[j] on the
Euphrates,[k] and Josiah marched out to 35:20 [k]Ge 2:14
meet him in battle. 21But Neco sent messengers to him, saying, "What quarrel is
there between you and me, O king of Judah? It is not you I am attacking at this
time, but the house with which I am at 35:21
war. God has told[l] me to hurry; so stop [l]1Ki 13:18; 2Ki 18:25
opposing God, who is with me, or he will
destroy you."
22Josiah, however, would not turn 35:22
away from him, but disguised[m] himself [m]Jdg 5:19; 1Sa 28:8; 2Ch 18:29
to engage him in battle. He would not
listen to what Neco had said at God's
command but went to fight him on the
plain of Megiddo.
23Archers[n] shot King Josiah, and he 35:23
told his officers, "Take me away; I am [n]1Ki 22:34
badly wounded." 24So they took him out
of his chariot, put him in the other chariot he had and brought him to Jerusalem, where he died. He was buried in the
tombs of his fathers, and all Judah and
Jerusalem mourned for him.
25Jeremiah composed laments for Josiah, and to this day all the men and
women singers commemorate Josiah in 35:25
the laments.[o] These became a tradition [o]Jer 22:10,15-16
in Israel and are written in the Laments.
26The other events of Josiah's reign
and his acts of devotion, according to
what is written in the Law of the LORD—
27all the events, from beginning to end,
are written in the book of the kings of
Israel and Judah.

36

1And the peo-
ple of the land took Jehoahaz
son of Josiah and made him king in Jerusalem in place of his father.

Jehoahaz King of Judah

2Jehoahaz[a] was twenty-three years
old when he became king, and he
reigned in Jerusalem three months. 3The
king of Egypt dethroned him in Jerusalem and imposed on Judah a levy of a
hundred talents[b] of silver and a talent[c]
of gold. 4The king of Egypt made Eliakim, a brother of Jehoahaz, king over Judah and Jerusalem and changed Elia- 36:4
kim's name to Jehoiakim. But Neco[p] [p]Jer 22:10-12
took Eliakim's brother Jehoahaz and carried him off to Egypt.

Jehoiakim King of Judah

36:5
5Jehoiakim[q] was twenty-five years old [q]Jer 22:18; 26:1; 35:1

[a] 2 Hebrew *Joahaz,* a variant of *Jehoahaz;* also in verse 4 [b] 3 That is, about 3 3/4 tons (about 3.4 metric tons) [c] 3 That is, about 75 pounds (about 34 kilograms)

DISCOVERY 108

NEVER FORSAKEN

Occasionally we hear of small children who have been left to fend for themselves for extended periods of time. Abandoned by their parents, they subsist in squalid conditions, with insufficient food and little or no protection or guidance. We decry the injustice, because deep in our souls we understand what it is to feel abandoned—and we fear and loathe it. The mere mention of such a word can trigger a pervasive sense of hopelessness. To abandon someone is to wash our hands of all responsibility, to turn our backs and walk away.

Many times in Israel's history as a nation the people might well have concluded that God had forsaken them—usually after the people had first turned from God's way. In 2 Chronicles 36 Judah failed to follow God's instruction, and consequently Jerusalem fell into enemy hands. The temple was first ransacked and then burned, and the city wall was smashed. Many of the people died, and the survivors were taken captive and exiled to Babylon. Where was God in all of this? Had he given up on his chosen people? Had God reneged on his promise that he would not reject his own? (Psalm 94:14).

By no means!

God allowed Judah to experience the consequences of turning away from him—but he ultimately rescued his people! He raised up (literally "stirred up") Cyrus, the king of Persia. Cyrus did not worship the one true God of Israel, but God still used him to clear the way for the people to return to their land and rebuild their temple (2 Chronicles 36:23; Ezra 1:1–4).

There are times when we all experience the desolation of feeling that God has left us completely alone. Even though we've given our lives to him and committed ourselves to walking with him, there may be circumstances in our lives that leave us feeling as though we've been left to fend for ourselves, to muddle through without help, protection or care. At times we pray but hear only silence in return. We expect God, always compassionate, to intervene—but nothing happens.

Jesus experienced this sense of desolation on the cross and cried out, "My God, My God, why have you forsaken me?" (Matthew 27:46). Our Savior felt the anguish we feel. Unlike the situation with the people of Israel, there was nothing he had done to cause God to forsake him. But God allowed his own Son, as our substitute, to be forsaken, in order that we might never be forsaken.

Even in our most tragic moments we can believe what God has promised: "Never will I leave you; never will I forsake you" (Hebrews 13:5) and "[Nothing] will be able to separate us from the love of God that is in Christ Jesus our Lord" (Romans 8:39). It may appear that God is nowhere to be found, but as we get to know him more intimately we will find out that we *can* take him at his Word—because he always keep his promises.

Self-Discovery: *Take a moment to envision a number of things that might separate two people (disagreement, divorce, distance, a language barrier, prison bars, a cultural taboo, lack of transportation, death—whatever!). Then repeat to yourself that nothing can separate you from the love of God in Christ Jesus your Lord!*

GO TO DISCOVERY 109 ON PAGE 588

when he became king, and he reigned in Jerusalem eleven years. He did evil in the eyes of the LORD his God. **6**Nebuchadnezzar[r] king of Babylon attacked him and bound him with bronze shackles to take him to Babylon.[s] **7**Nebuchadnezzar also took to Babylon articles from the temple of the LORD and put them in his temple[a] there.[t]

8The other events of Jehoiakim's reign, the detestable things he did and all that was found against him, are written in the book of the kings of Israel and Judah. And Jehoiachin his son succeeded him as king.

Jehoiachin King of Judah

9Jehoiachin[u] was eighteen[b] years old when he became king, and he reigned in Jerusalem three months and ten days. He did evil in the eyes of the LORD. **10**In the spring, King Nebuchadnezzar sent for him and brought him to Babylon,[v] together with articles of value from the temple of the LORD, and he made Jehoiachin's uncle,[c] Zedekiah, king over Judah and Jerusalem.

Zedekiah King of Judah

11Zedekiah[w] was twenty-one years old when he became king, and he reigned in Jerusalem eleven years. **12**He did evil in the eyes of the LORD[x] his God and did not humble[y] himself before Jeremiah the prophet, who spoke the word of the LORD. **13**He also rebelled against King Nebuchadnezzar, who had made him take an oath[z] in God's name. He became stiff-necked[a] and hardened his heart and would not turn to the LORD, the God of Israel. **14**Furthermore, all the leaders of the priests and the people became more and more unfaithful,[b] following all the detestable practices of the nations and defiling the temple of the LORD, which he had consecrated in Jerusalem.

The Fall of Jerusalem

15The LORD, the God of their fathers, sent word to them through his messengers[c] again and again,[d] because he had pity on his people and on his dwelling place. **16**But they mocked God's messengers, despised his words and scoffed[e] at his prophets until the wrath[f] of the LORD was aroused against his people and there was no remedy.[g] **17**He brought up against them the king of the Babylonians,[d] who killed their young men with the sword in the sanctuary, and spared neither young man[h] nor young woman, old man or aged. God handed all of them over to Nebuchadnezzar.[i] **18**He carried to Babylon all the articles[j] from the temple of God, both large and small, and the treasures of the LORD's temple and the treasures of the king and his officials. **19**They set fire[k] to God's temple[l] and broke down the wall[m] of Jerusalem; they burned all the palaces and destroyed[n] everything of value there.[o]

20He carried into exile[p] to Babylon the remnant, who escaped from the sword, and they became servants[q] to him and his sons until the kingdom of Persia came to power. **21**The land enjoyed its sabbath rests;[r] all the time of its desolation it rested,[s] until the seventy years[t] were completed in fulfillment of the word of the LORD spoken by Jeremiah.

22In the first year of Cyrus[u] king of Persia, in order to fulfill the word of the LORD spoken by Jeremiah, the LORD moved the heart of Cyrus king of Persia to make a proclamation throughout his realm and to put it in writing:

23"This is what Cyrus king of Persia says:

"'The LORD, the God of heaven, has given me all the kingdoms of the earth and he has appointed[v] me to build a temple for him at Jerusalem in Judah. Anyone of his people among you—may the LORD his God be with him, and let him go up.'"

[a] 7 Or *palace* [b] 9 One Hebrew manuscript, some Septuagint manuscripts and Syriac (see also 2 Kings 24:8); most Hebrew manuscripts *eight* [c] 10 Hebrew *brother,* that is, relative (see 2 Kings 24:17) [d] 17 Or *Chaldeans*

36:6 r Jer 25:9; 27:6; Eze 29:18 s 2Ch 33:11; Eze 19:9; Da 1:1
36:7 t 2Ki 24:13; Ezr 1:7; Da 1:2
36:9 u Jer 22:24-28; 52:31
36:10 v ver 18; 2Ki 20:17; Ezr 1:7; Jer 22:25; 24:1; 29:1; 37:1; Eze 17:12
36:11 w 2Ki 24:17; Jer 27:1; 28:1
36:12 x Jer 37:1-39:18 y Dt 8:3; 2Ch 7:14; 2Ch 33:23; Jer 21:3-7
36:13 z Eze 17:13 a 2Ki 17:14; 2Ch 30:8
36:14 b 1Ch 5:25
36:15 c Isa 5:4; 44:26; Jer 7:25; Hag 1:13; Zec 1:4; Mal 2:7; 3:1 d Jer 7:13,25; 25:3-4; 35:14,15; 44:4-6
36:16 e 2Ki 2:23; Pr 1:25; Jer 5:13 f Ezr 5:12; Pr 1:30-31 g 2Ch 30:10; Pr 29:1; Zec 1:2
36:17 h Jer 6:11 i Ezr 5:12; Jer 32:28
36:18 j ver 7,10
36:19 k Jer 11:16; 17:27; 21:10,14; 22:7; 32:29; 39:8; La 4:11; Eze 20:47; Am 2:5; Zec 11:1 l 1Ki 9:8-9 m 2Ki 14:13 n La 2:6 o Ps 79:1-3
36:20 p Lev 26:44; 2Ki 24:14; Ezr 2:1; Ne 7:6 q Jer 27:7
36:21 r Lev 25:4; 26:34 s 1Ch 22:9 t Jer 1:1; 25:11; 27:22; 29:10; 40:1; Da 9:2; Zec 1:12; 7:5
36:22 u Isa 44:28; 45:1,13; Jer 25:12; 29:10; Da 1:21; 6:28; 10:1
36:23 v Jdg 4:10

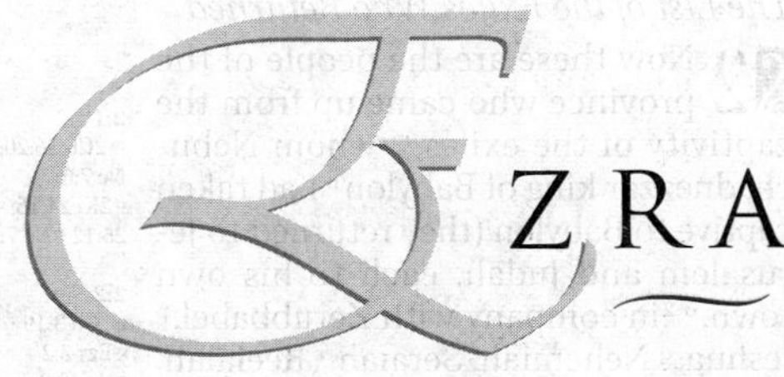

EZRA

What is the significance of genealogies such as those found in Ezra 2 and 8?

♦*Jewish genealogies were important as a means of establishing entitlement to belong within an exclusive community. Jesus was not born into a vacuum. His roots authenticated his place within the society of his birth. While the Gospels exemplify Jesus' uniqueness, Matthew also anchored him firmly within the Jewish community and tradition.*

What was Zerubbabel's place in the Messianic line? (Ezra 5:2)

♦*The name Zerubbabel meant "offspring of Babylon," referring to his birth in exile. He was the grandson of Jehoiachin (1 Chronicles 3:17), the next-to-last king of Judah. Zerubbabel was the last of the Davidic line to be entrusted with political authority by the occupying powers. He was also at ancestor of Jesus (Matthew 1:12–13; Luke 3:27).*

Jesus in Ezra The book of Ezra offers great encouragement for ordinary people looking for a way to fit into God's plan. Quoting official documents, letters and lists, Ezra seems on the surface to be a dull, even perplexing book. Yet hidden within Ezra is a reminder for readers to focus on the team effort of the returning exiles. With careful study and imagination, we can find these heroes coming to life and giving us a glimpse of what they saw as they returned to their homeland. We too can become "heroes" of the faith as we strive to follow Jesus and conform to his will, even in the repetitive tasks and mundane details of our lives. We too can catch a glimpse of a homeland and find renewed purpose as we channel our energies toward the goal of helping others to rebuild lives enslaved to sin.

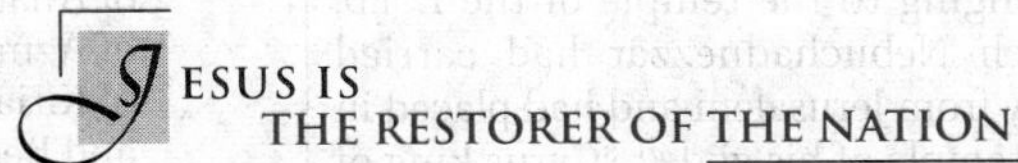

JESUS IS THE RESTORER OF THE NATION

Cyrus Helps the Exiles to Return

1 In the first year of Cyrus king of Persia, in order to fulfill the word of the LORD spoken by Jeremiah,[a] the LORD moved the heart[b] of Cyrus king of Persia to make a proclamation throughout his realm and to put it in writing:

2"This is what Cyrus king of Persia says:

" 'The LORD, the God of heaven, has given me all the kingdoms of the earth and he has appointed[c] me to build[d] a temple for him at Jerusalem in Judah. 3Anyone of his people among you—may his God be with him, and let him go up to Jerusalem in Judah and build the temple of the LORD, the God of Israel, the God who is in Jerusalem. 4And the people of any place where survivors[e] may now be living are to provide him with silver and gold, with goods and livestock, and with freewill offerings[f] for the temple of God in Jerusalem.' "[g]

5Then the family heads of Judah and Benjamin,[h] and the priests and Levites—everyone whose heart God had moved[i]—prepared to go up and build the house[j] of the LORD in Jerusalem. 6All their neighbors assisted them with articles of silver and gold, with goods and livestock, and with valuable gifts, in addition to all the freewill offerings. 7Moreover, King Cyrus brought out the articles belonging to the temple of the LORD, which Nebuchadnezzar had carried away from Jerusalem and had placed in the temple of his god.[a][k] 8Cyrus king of Persia had them brought by Mithredath the treasurer, who counted them out to Sheshbazzar[l] the prince of Judah.

9This was the inventory:

gold dishes	30
silver dishes	1,000
silver pans[b]	29
10gold bowls	30
matching silver bowls	410
other articles	1,000

11In all, there were 5,400 articles of gold and of silver. Sheshbazzar brought all these along when the exiles came up from Babylon to Jerusalem.

1:1 [a] Jer 25:11-12; 29:10-14 [b] 2Ch 36:22,23
1:2 [c] Isa 44:28; 45:13 [d] Ezr 5:13
1:4 [e] Isa 10:20-22 [f] Nu 15:3; Ps 50:14; 54:6; 116:17 [g] Ezr 4:3; 5:13; 6:3,14
1:5 [h] Ezr 4:1; Ne 11:4 [i] ver 1; Ex 35:20-22; 2Ch 36:22; Hag 1:14; Php 2:13 [j] Ps 127:1
1:7 [k] 2Ki 24:13; 2Ch 36:7,10; Ezr 5:14; 6:5
1:8 [l] Ezr 5:14

The List of the Exiles Who Returned

2 Now these are the people of the province who came up from the captivity of the exiles,[m] whom Nebuchadnezzar king of Babylon[n] had taken captive to Babylon (they returned to Jerusalem and Judah, each to his own town,[o] 2in company with Zerubbabel,[p] Jeshua,[q] Nehemiah, Seraiah,[r] Reelaiah, Mordecai, Bilshan, Mispar, Bigvai, Rehum and Baanah):

The list of the men of the people of Israel:

3the descendants of Parosh[s]	2,172
4of Shephatiah	372
5of Arah	775
6of Pahath-Moab (through the line of Jeshua and Joab)	2,812
7of Elam	1,254
8of Zattu	945
9of Zaccai	760
10of Bani	642
11of Bebai	623
12of Azgad	1,222
13of Adonikam[t]	666
14of Bigvai	2,056
15of Adin	454
16of Ater (through Hezekiah)	98
17of Bezai	323
18of Jorah	112
19of Hashum	223
20of Gibbar	95
21the men of Bethlehem[u]	123
22of Netophah	56
23of Anathoth	128
24of Azmaveth	42
25of Kiriath Jearim,[c] Kephirah and Beeroth	743
26of Ramah[v] and Geba	621
27of Micmash	122
28of Bethel and Ai[w]	223
29of Nebo	52
30of Magbish	156
31of the other Elam	1,254
32of Harim	320
33of Lod, Hadid and Ono	725
34of Jericho[x]	345
35of Senaah	3,630

36The priests:

the descendants of Jedaiah[y]

2:1 [m] 2Ch 36:20; Ne 7:6 [n] 2Ki 24:16; 25:12 [o] Ne 7:73
2:2 [p] 1Ch 3:19 [q] Ezr 3:2 [r] Ne 10:2
2:3 [s] Ezr 8:3
2:13 [t] Ezr 8:13
2:21 [u] Mic 5:2
2:26 [v] Jos 18:25
2:28 [w] Ge 12:8
2:34 [x] 1Ki 16:34; 2Ch 28:15
2:36 [y] 1Ch 24:7

[a] *7* Or *gods* [b] *9* The meaning of the Hebrew for this word is uncertain. [c] *25* See Septuagint (see also Neh. 7:29); Hebrew *Kiriath Arim.*

(through the family
of Jeshua) 973
37 of Immer[z] 1,052
38 of Pashhur[a] 1,247
39 of Harim[b] 1,017

40 The Levites:[c]

the descendants of Jeshua[d] and
Kadmiel (through the line of
Hodaviah) 74

41 The singers:[e]

the descendants of Asaph 128

42 The gatekeepers[f] of the temple:

the descendants of
Shallum, Ater, Talmon,
Akkub, Hatita and Shobai 139

43 The temple servants:[g]

the descendants of
Ziha, Hasupha, Tabbaoth,
44 Keros, Siaha, Padon,
45 Lebanah, Hagabah, Akkub,
46 Hagab, Shalmai, Hanan,
47 Giddel, Gahar, Reaiah,
48 Rezin, Nekoda, Gazzam,
49 Uzza, Paseah, Besai,
50 Asnah, Meunim, Nephussim,
51 Bakbuk, Hakupha, Harhur,
52 Bazluth, Mehida, Harsha,
53 Barkos, Sisera, Temah,
54 Neziah and Hatipha

55 The descendants of the servants
of Solomon:

the descendants of
Sotai, Hassophereth, Peruda,
56 Jaala, Darkon, Giddel,
57 Shephatiah, Hattil,
Pokereth-Hazzebaim and Ami

58 The temple servants[h] and the
descendants of the servants
of Solomon 392

59 The following came up from
the towns of Tel Melah, Tel Harsha,
Kerub, Addon and Immer, but they
could not show that their families
were descended[i] from Israel:

60 The descendants of
Delaiah, Tobiah and
Nekoda 652

61 And from among the priests:

The descendants of
Hobaiah, Hakkoz and
Barzillai (a man who had
married a daughter of
Barzillai the Gileadite[j] and
was called by that name).

62 These searched for their family records, but they could not find
them and so were excluded from
the priesthood[k] as unclean. 63 The
governor ordered them not to eat
any of the most sacred food[l] until
there was a priest ministering with
the Urim and Thummim.[m]

64 The whole company numbered
42,360, 65 besides their 7,337 menservants and maidservants; and
they also had 200 men and women
singers.[n] 66 They had 736 horses,[o]
245 mules, 67 435 camels and 6,720
donkeys.

68 When they arrived at the house of
the LORD in Jerusalem, some of the
heads of the families[p] gave freewill offerings toward the rebuilding of the
house of God on its site. 69 According to
their ability they gave to the treasury for
this work 61,000 drachmas[a] of gold,
5,000 minas[b] of silver and 100 priestly
garments.

70 The priests, the Levites, the singers,
the gatekeepers and the temple servants
settled in their own towns, along with
some of the other people, and the rest of
the Israelites settled in their towns.[q]

Rebuilding the Altar

3 When the seventh month came
and the Israelites had settled in
their towns,[r] the people assembled[s] as
one man in Jerusalem. 2 Then Jeshua[t]
son of Jozadak[u] and his fellow priests
and Zerubbabel son of Shealtiel[v] and his
associates began to build the altar of the
God of Israel to sacrifice burnt offerings
on it, in accordance with what is written
in the Law of Moses[w] the man of God.
3 Despite their fear[x] of the peoples
around them, they built the altar on its
foundation and sacrificed burnt offerings on it to the LORD, both the morning
and evening sacrifices.[y] 4 Then in accordance with what is written, they celebrated the Feast of Tabernacles[z] with
the required number of burnt offerings

2:37 z 1Ch 24:14
2:38 a 1Ch 9:12
2:39 b 1Ch 24:8
2:40 c Ge 29:34; Nu 3:9; Dt 18:6-7; 1Ch 16:4; Ezr 7:7; 8:15; Ne 12:24 d Ezr 3:9
2:41 e 1Ch 15:16
2:42 f 1Sa 3:15; 1Ch 9:17
2:43 g 1Ch 9:2; Ne 11:21
2:58 h 1Ki 9:21; 1Ch 9:2
2:59 i Nu 1:18
2:61 j 2Sa 17:27
2:62 k Nu 3:10; 16:39-40
2:63 l Lev 2:3,10 m Ex 28:30; Nu 27:21
2:65 n 2Sa 19:35
2:66 o Isa 66:20
2:68 p Ex 25:2
2:70 q ver 1; 1Ch 9:2; Ne 11:3-4
3:1 r Ne 7:73; 8:1 s Lev 23:24
3:2 t Ezr 2:2; Ne 12:1,8; Hag 2:2 u Hag 1:1; Zec 6:11 v 1Ch 3:17 w Ex 20:24; Dt 12:5-6
3:3 x Ezr 4:4; Da 9:25 y Ex 29:39; Nu 28:1-8
3:4 z Ex 23:16; Nu 29:12-38; Ne 8:14-18; Zec 14:16-19

[a] 69 That is, about 1,100 pounds (about 500 kilograms) [b] 69 That is, about 3 tons (about 2.9 metric tons)

Rebuilding the Temple

The book of Ezra recounts the story of how God provided for his people as he led them out of captivity in Babylon and back to Jerusalem to rebuild the temple. The prophet Jeremiah had predicted that God's people would return (Jeremiah 29:1–23), and when the time came God "moved the heart of Cyrus" (Ezra 1:1), king of Persia, to issue a proclamation: "The LORD, the God of heaven, has given me all the kingdoms of the earth and he has appointed me to build a temple for him at Jerusalem in Judah. Anyone of his people among you—may his God be with him, and let him go up to Jerusalem in Judah and build the temple of the LORD, the God of Israel, the God who is in Jerusalem. And the people of any place where survivors may now be living are to provide him with silver and gold, with goods and livestock, and with freewill offerings for the temple of God in Jerusalem" (verses 2–4).

It is tempting to despair when government leaders take stances that appear to be in direct opposition to God and to his will. But God is always in control, no matter who seems to be in the driver's seat. Proverbs 21:1 states that "the king's heart is in the hand of the LORD; he directs it like a watercourse wherever he pleases." God can and often does use people who have no interest in him to accomplish his purposes. Several people in the New Testament stand as perfect examples. Judas lived with and learned from Jesus for three years, and yet his heart wasn't in it. He turned Jesus over to the authorities, and the Son of God was executed. Pilate thought that he was in charge of Jesus' trial. In frustration he asked Jesus, " 'Don't you realize I have power either to free you or to crucify you?' Jesus answered, 'You would have no power over me if it were not given to you from above' " (John 19:10–11). It had always been God's plan for the Messiah to die for the sin of humanity. Judas and Pilate, however, had no notion that they were instrumental in helping God to fulfill his plan of redemption.

God also moves in the hearts of his own people. After Cyrus had made his proclamation, "everyone whose heart God had moved" prepared to go back to Jerusalem in order to rebuild the temple (Ezra 1:5). Some volunteered to work on the rebuilding project, and others gave what they had to the cause. Once the foundation had been laid and the walls put in place, the people celebrated: "[God] is good; his love to Israel endures forever" (Ezra 3:11).

Our heavenly Father never coerces. Instead, he changes our hearts to accommodate his purposes. The better we get to know him, the more we will see him at work to accomplish his perfect will—no matter who or what may seem to stand in the way!

***Self-Discovery:** Can you recall an instance in recent history in which a nonbelieving government official, whether in your own or in a foreign country, has unwittingly acted in a manner that has furthered the cause of the gospel? What has this example taught you about the providence of God?*

GO TO DISCOVERY 110 ON PAGE 596

prescribed for each day. 5After that, they presented the regular burnt offerings, the New Moon[a] sacrifices and the sacrifices for all the appointed sacred feasts of the LORD,[b] as well as those brought as freewill offerings to the LORD. 6On the first day of the seventh month they began to offer burnt offerings to the LORD, though the foundation of the LORD's temple had not yet been laid.

Rebuilding the Temple

7Then they gave money to the masons and carpenters, and gave food and drink and oil to the people of Sidon and Tyre, so that they would bring cedar logs[c] by sea from Lebanon[d] to Joppa, as authorized by Cyrus[e] king of Persia.

8In the second month of the second year after their arrival at the house of God in Jerusalem, Zerubbabel[f] son of Shealtiel, Jeshua son of Jozadak and the rest of their brothers (the priests and the Levites and all who had returned from the captivity to Jerusalem) began the work, appointing Levites twenty[g] years of age and older to supervise the building of the house of the LORD. 9Jeshua[h] and his sons and brothers and Kadmiel and his sons (descendants of Hodaviah[a]) and the sons of Henadad and their sons and brothers—all Levites—joined together in supervising those working on the house of God.

10When the builders laid[i] the foundation of the temple of the LORD, the priests in their vestments and with trumpets,[j] and the Levites (the sons of Asaph) with cymbals, took their places to praise[k] the LORD, as prescribed by David[l] king of Israel.[m] 11With praise and thanksgiving they sang to the LORD:

"He is good;
his love to Israel endures
forever."[n]

And all the people gave a great shout[o] of praise to the LORD, because the foundation of the house of the LORD was laid. 12But many of the older priests and Levites and family heads, who had seen the former temple,[p] wept aloud when they saw the foundation of this temple being laid, while many others shouted for joy. 13No one could distinguish the sound of the shouts of joy[q] from the sound of weeping, because the people made so much noise. And the sound was heard far away.

3:5 [a] Nu 28:3,11,14; Col 2:16 [b] Lev 23:1-44; Nu 29:39
3:7 [c] 1Ch 14:1 [d] Isa 35:2 [e] Ezr 1:2-4; 6:3
3:8 [f] Zec 4:9 [g] 1Ch 23:24
3:9 [h] Ezr 2:40
3:10 [i] Ezr 5:16 [j] Nu 10:2; 1Ch 16:6 [k] 1Ch 25:1 [l] 1Ch 6:31 [m] Zec 6:12
3:11 [n] 1Ch 16:34,41; 2Ch 7:3; Ps 107:1; 118:1 [o] Ne 12:24
3:12 [p] Hag 2:3,9
3:13 [q] Job 8:21; Ps 27:6; Isa 16:9

Opposition to the Rebuilding

4 When the enemies of Judah and Benjamin heard that the exiles were building a temple for the LORD, the God of Israel, 2they came to Zerubbabel and to the heads of the families and said, "Let us help you build because, like you, we seek your God and have been sacrificing to him since the time of Esarhaddon[r] king of Assyria, who brought us here."[s]

3But Zerubbabel, Jeshua and the rest of the heads of the families of Israel answered, "You have no part with us in building a temple to our God. We alone will build it for the LORD, the God of Israel, as King Cyrus, the king of Persia, commanded us."[t]

4Then the peoples around them set out to discourage the people of Judah and make them afraid to go on building.[b][u] 5They hired counselors to work against them and frustrate their plans during the entire reign of Cyrus king of Persia and down to the reign of Darius king of Persia.

Later Opposition Under Xerxes and Artaxerxes

6At the beginning of the reign of Xerxes,[c][v] they lodged an accusation against the people of Judah and Jerusalem.[w]

7And in the days of Artaxerxes[x] king of Persia, Bishlam, Mithredath, Tabeel and the rest of his associates wrote a letter to Artaxerxes. The letter was written in Aramaic script and in the Aramaic[y] language.[d,e]

8Rehum the commanding officer and Shimshai the secretary wrote a letter against Jerusalem to Artaxerxes the king as follows:

9Rehum the commanding officer and Shimshai the secretary, together with the rest of their associates[z]—the judges and officials over the men from Tripolis, Persia,[f] Erech and Babylon, the Elamites of Susa, 10and the other people whom

4:2 [r] 2Ki 17:24; 19:37 [s] 2Ki 17:41
4:3 [t] Ezr 1:1-4; Ne 2:20
4:4 [u] Ezr 3:3
4:6 [v] Est 1:1; Da 9:1 [w] Est 3:13; 9:5
4:7 [x] Ezr 7:1; Ne 2:1 [y] 2Ki 18:26; Isa 36:11; Da 2:4
4:9 [z] Ezr 5:6; 6:6,13

[a] 9 Hebrew *Yehudah,* probably a variant of *Hodaviah* [b] 4 Or *and troubled them as they built* [c] 6 Hebrew *Ahasuerus,* a variant of Xerxes' Persian name [d] 7 Or *written in Aramaic and translated* [e] 7 The text of Ezra 4:8—6:18 is in Aramaic. [f] 9 Or *officials, magistrates and governors over the men from*

the great and honorable Ashurbanipal[a] deported and settled in the city of Samaria and elsewhere in Trans-Euphrates.[a]

4:10 [a] ver 17; Ne 4:2

11(This is a copy of the letter they sent him.)

To King Artaxerxes,

From your servants, the men of Trans-Euphrates:

12The king should know that the Jews who came up to us from you have gone to Jerusalem and are rebuilding that rebellious and wicked city. They are restoring the walls and repairing the foundations.[b]

4:12 [b] Ezr 5:3,9

13Furthermore, the king should know that if this city is built and its walls are restored, no more taxes, tribute or duty[c] will be paid, and the royal revenues will suffer. 14Now since we are under obligation to the palace and it is not proper for us to see the king dishonored, we are sending this message to inform the king, 15so that a search may be made in the archives[d] of your predecessors. In these records you will find that this city is a rebellious city, troublesome to kings and provinces, a place of rebellion from ancient times. That is why this city was destroyed.[e] 16We inform the king that if this city is built and its walls are restored, you will be left with nothing in Trans-Euphrates.

4:13 [c] Ezr 7:24; Ne 5:4

4:15 [d] Ezr 5:17; 6:1 [e] Est 3:8

17The king sent this reply:

To Rehum the commanding officer, Shimshai the secretary and the rest of their associates living in Samaria and elsewhere in Trans-Euphrates:[f]

4:17 [f] ver 10

Greetings.

18The letter you sent us has been read and translated in my presence. 19I issued an order and a search was made, and it was found that this city has a long history of revolt[g] against kings and has been a place of rebellion and sedition. 20Jerusalem has had powerful kings ruling over the whole of Trans-Euphrates,[h] and taxes, tribute and duty were paid to them. 21Now issue an order to these men to stop work, so that this city will not be rebuilt until I so order. 22Be careful not to neglect this matter. Why let this threat grow, to the detriment of the royal interests?[i]

4:19 [g] 2Ki 18:7

4:20 [h] Ge 15:18-21; Ex 23:31; Jos 1:4; 1Ki 4:21; 1Ch 18:3; Ps 72:8-11

4:22 [i] Da 6:2

23As soon as the copy of the letter of King Artaxerxes was read to Rehum and Shimshai the secretary and their associates,[j] they went immediately to the Jews in Jerusalem and compelled them by force to stop.

4:23 [j] ver 9

24Thus the work on the house of God in Jerusalem came to a standstill until the second year of the reign of Darius[k] king of Persia.

4:24 [k] Ne 2:1-8; Da 9:25; Hag 1:1,15; Zec 1:1

Tattenai's Letter to Darius

5 Now Haggai[l] the prophet and Zechariah[m] the prophet, a descendant of Iddo, prophesied[n] to the Jews in Judah and Jerusalem in the name of the God of Israel, who was over them. 2Then Zerubbabel[o] son of Shealtiel and Jeshua[p] son of Jozadak set to work[q] to rebuild the house of God in Jerusalem. And the prophets of God were with them, helping them.

5:1 [l] Ezr 6:14; Hag 1:1,3,12; 2:1,10,20 [m] Zec 1:1; 7:1 [n] Hag 1:14-2:9; Zec 4:9-10; 8:9

5:2 [o] 1Ch 3:19; Hag 1:14; 2:21; Zec 4:6-10 [p] Ezr 2:2; 3:2 [q] ver 8; Hag 2:2-5

3At that time Tattenai,[r] governor of Trans-Euphrates, and Shethar-Bozenai[s] and their associates went to them and asked, "Who authorized you to rebuild this temple and restore this structure?"[t] 4They also asked, "What are the names of the men constructing this building?"[b] 5But the eye of their God[u] was watching over the elders of the Jews, and they were not stopped until a report could go to Darius and his written reply be received.

5:3 [r] Ezr 6:6 [s] Ezr 6:6 [t] ver 9; Ezr 1:3; 4:12

5:5 [u] 2Ki 25:28; Ezr 7:6,9,28; 8:18,22,31; Ne 2:8,18; Ps 33:18; Isa 66:14

6This is a copy of the letter that Tattenai, governor of Trans-Euphrates, and Shethar-Bozenai and their associates, the officials of Trans-Euphrates, sent to King Darius. 7The report they sent him read as follows:

To King Darius:

Cordial greetings.

8The king should know that we went to the district of Judah, to the temple of the great God. The people are building it with large stones

[a] 10 Aramaic *Osnappar,* a variant of *Ashurbanipal*
[b] 4 See Septuagint; Aramaic *⁴We told them the names of the men constructing this building.*

5:8 and placing the timbers in the
v ver 2 walls. The work[v] is being carried on
with diligence and is making rapid
progress under their direction.
[9]We questioned the elders and
asked them, "Who authorized you
5:9 to rebuild this temple and restore
w Ezr 4:12 this structure?"[w] [10]We also asked
them their names, so that we could
write down the names of their
leaders for your information.
[11]This is the answer they gave us:

"We are the servants of the God
5:11 of heaven and earth, and we are re-
x 1Ki 6:1; building the temple[x] that was built
2Ch 3:1-2 many years ago, one that a great
5:12 king of Israel built and finished.
y 2Ch 36:16 [12]But because our fathers angered[y]
z Dt 21:10; the God of heaven, he handed them
28:36; 2Ki 24:1; over to Nebuchadnezzar the Chal-
25:8,9,11; dean, king of Babylon, who de-
Jer 1:3 stroyed this temple and deported
the people to Babylon.[z]
[13]"However, in the first year of Cy-
5:13 rus king of Babylon, King Cyrus is-
a Ezr 1:1 sued a decree[a] to rebuild this house
of God. [14]He even removed from the
temple[a] of Babylon the gold and silver articles of the house of God,
which Nebuchadnezzar had taken
5:14 from the temple in Jerusalem and
b Ezr 1:7; 6:5; brought to the temple[a] in Babylon.[b]
Da 5:2 "Then King Cyrus gave them to
c 1Ch 3:18 a man named Sheshbazzar,[c] whom
he had appointed governor, [15]and
he told him, 'Take these articles
and go and deposit them in the
temple in Jerusalem. And rebuild
the house of God on its site.' [16]So
5:16 this Sheshbazzar came and laid the
d Ezr 3:10; 6:15 foundations of the house of God[d]
in Jerusalem. From that day to the
present it has been under construction but is not yet finished."

[17]Now if it pleases the king, let a
5:17 search be made in the royal ar-
e Ezr 4:15; 6:1,2 chives[e] of Babylon to see if King
Cyrus did in fact issue a decree to
rebuild this house of God in Jerusalem. Then let the king send us his
decision in this matter.

The Decree of Darius

6 King Darius then issued an order,
6:1 and they searched in the archives[f]
f Ezr 4:15; 5:17 stored in the treasury at Babylon. [2]A
scroll was found in the citadel of Ecbat-
ana in the province of Media, and this
was written on it:

Memorandum:

[3]In the first year of King Cyrus,
the king issued a decree concerning the temple of God in Jerusalem:

Let the temple be rebuilt as a
place to present sacrifices, and let 6:3
its foundations be laid.[g] It is to be g Ezr 3:10;
ninety feet[b] high and ninety feet Hag 2:3
wide, [4]with three courses[h] of large 6:4
stones and one of timbers. The h 1Ki 6:36
costs are to be paid by the royal i ver 8; Ezr 7:20
treasury.[i] [5]Also, the gold[j] and silver 6:5 j 1Ch 29:2
articles of the house of God, which k Ezr 1:7; 5:14
Nebuchadnezzar took from the
temple in Jerusalem and brought to
Babylon, are to be returned to their
places in the temple in Jerusalem;
they are to be deposited in the
house of God.[k]

[6]Now then, Tattenai,[l] governor 6:6 l Ezr 5:3
of Trans-Euphrates, and Shethar- m Ezr 5:3
Bozenai[m] and you, their fellow officials of that province, stay away
from there. [7]Do not interfere with
the work on this temple of God. Let
the governor of the Jews and the
Jewish elders rebuild this house of
God on its site.
[8]Moreover, I hereby decree what
you are to do for these elders of the
Jews in the construction of this
house of God:

The expenses of these men are
to be fully paid out of the royal 6:8
treasury,[n] from the revenues[o] of n ver 4 o 1Sa 9:20
Trans-Euphrates, so that the work
will not stop. [9]Whatever is needed—young bulls, rams, male lambs
for burnt offerings[p] to the God of 6:9
heaven, and wheat, salt, wine and p Lev 1:3,10
oil, as requested by the priests in Jerusalem—must be given them daily without fail, [10]so that they may
offer sacrifices pleasing to the God
of heaven and pray for the well-be- 6:10
ing of the king and his sons.[q] q Ezr 7:23;
[11]Furthermore, I decree that if 1Ti 2:1-2
anyone changes this edict, a beam 6:11
is to be pulled from his house and r Dt 21:22-23; Est 2:23; 5:14;
he is to be lifted up and impaled[r] 9:14

[a] 14 Or *palace* [b] 3 Aramaic *sixty cubits* (about 27 meters)

on it. And for this crime his house is to be made a pile of rubble.[s] 12 May God, who has caused his Name to dwell there,[t] overthrow any king or people who lifts a hand to change this decree or to destroy this temple in Jerusalem.

I Darius[u] have decreed it. Let it be carried out with diligence.

Completion and Dedication of the Temple

13 Then, because of the decree King Darius had sent, Tattenai, governor of Trans-Euphrates, and Shethar-Bozenai and their associates[v] carried it out with diligence. 14 So the elders of the Jews continued to build and prosper under the preaching[w] of Haggai the prophet and Zechariah, a descendant of Iddo. They finished building the temple according to the command of the God of Israel and the decrees of Cyrus,[x] Darius[y] and Artaxerxes,[z] kings of Persia. 15 The temple was completed on the third day of the month Adar, in the sixth year of the reign of King Darius.[a]

16 Then the people of Israel—the priests, the Levites and the rest of the exiles—celebrated the dedication[b] of the house of God with joy. 17 For the dedication of this house of God they offered[c] a hundred bulls, two hundred rams, four hundred male lambs and, as a sin offering for all Israel, twelve male goats, one for each of the tribes of Israel. 18 And they installed the priests in their divisions[d] and the Levites in their groups[e] for the service of God at Jerusalem, according to what is written in the Book of Moses.[f]

The Passover

19 On the fourteenth day of the first month, the exiles celebrated the Passover.[g] 20 The priests and Levites had purified themselves and were all ceremonially clean. The Levites slaughtered[h] the Passover lamb for all the exiles, for their brothers the priests and for themselves. 21 So the Israelites who had returned from the exile ate it, together with all who had separated themselves[i] from the unclean practices[j] of their Gentile neighbors in order to seek the LORD,[k] the God of Israel. 22 For seven days they celebrated with joy the Feast of Unleavened Bread,[l] because the LORD had filled them with joy by changing the attitude[m] of the king of Assyria, so that he assisted them in the work on the house of God, the God of Israel.

Ezra Comes to Jerusalem

7 After these things, during the reign of Artaxerxes[n] king of Persia, Ezra son of Seraiah, the son of Azariah, the son of Hilkiah,[o] 2 the son of Shallum, the son of Zadok,[p] the son of Ahitub,[q] 3 the son of Amariah, the son of Azariah, the son of Meraioth, 4 the son of Zerahiah, the son of Uzzi, the son of Bukki, 5 the son of Abishua, the son of Phinehas, the son of Eleazar, the son of Aaron the chief priest— 6 this Ezra[r] came up from Babylon. He was a teacher well versed in the Law of Moses, which the LORD, the God of Israel, had given. The king had granted him everything he asked, for the hand of the LORD his God was on him.[s] 7 Some of the Israelites, including priests, Levites, singers, gatekeepers and temple servants, also came up to Jerusalem in the seventh year of King Artaxerxes.[t]

8 Ezra arrived in Jerusalem in the fifth month of the seventh year of the king. 9 He had begun his journey from Babylon on the first day of the first month, and he arrived in Jerusalem on the first day of the fifth month, for the gracious hand of his God was on him.[u] 10 For Ezra had devoted himself to the study and observance of the Law of the LORD, and to teaching[v] its decrees and laws in Israel.

King Artaxerxes' Letter to Ezra

11 This is a copy of the letter King Artaxerxes had given to Ezra the priest and teacher, a man learned in matters concerning the commands and decrees of the LORD for Israel:

> 12[a] Artaxerxes, king of kings,[w]
> To Ezra the priest, a teacher of the Law of the God of heaven:
>
> Greetings.
>
> 13 Now I decree that any of the Israelites in my kingdom, including priests and Levites, who wish to go to Jerusalem with you, may go. 14 You are sent by the king and his

[a] 12 The text of Ezra 7:12–26 is in Aramaic.

6:11 [s] Ezr 7:26; Da 2:5; 3:29
6:12 [t] Ex 20:24; Dt 12:5; 1Ki 9:3; 2Ch 6:2 [u] ver 14
6:13 [v] Ezr 4:9
6:14 [w] Ezr 5:1 [x] Ezr 1:1-4 [y] ver 12 [z] Ezr 7:1; Ne 2:1
6:15 [a] Zec 1:1; 4:9
6:16 [b] 1Ki 8:63; 2Ch 7:5
6:17 [c] 2Sa 6:13; 2Ch 29:21; 30:24; Ezr 8:35
6:18 [d] 1Ch 23:6; 2Ch 35:4; Lk 1:5 [e] 1Ch 24:1 [f] Nu 3:6-9; 8:9-11; 18:1-32
6:19 [g] Ex 12:11; Nu 28:16
6:20 [h] 2Ch 30:15,17; 35:11
6:21 [i] Ezr 9:1; Ne 9:2 [j] Dt 18:9; Ezr 9:11; Eze 36:25 [k] 1Ch 22:19; Ps 14:2
6:22 [l] Ex 12:17 [m] Ezr 1:1
7:1 [n] Ezr 4:7; 6:14; Ne 2:1 [o] 2Ki 22:4
7:2 [p] 1Ki 1:8; 1Ch 6:8 [q] Ne 11:11
7:6 [r] Ne 12:36 [s] Ezr 5:5; Isa 41:20
7:7 [t] Ezr 8:1
7:9 [u] ver 6
7:10 [v] ver 25; Dt 33:10; Ne 8:1-8
7:12 [w] Eze 26:7; Da 2:37

7:14 x Est 1:14 seven advisers[x] to inquire about Judah and Jerusalem with regard to
the Law of your God, which is in
your hand. [15]Moreover, you are to
take with you the silver and gold
7:15 y 1Ch 29:6 z 1Ch 29:6,9; 2Ch 6:2 that the king and his advisers have
freely given[y] to the God of Israel,
whose dwelling[z] is in Jerusalem,
7:16 a Ezr 8:25 b Zec 6:10 [16]together with all the silver and
gold[a] you may obtain from the
province of Babylon, as well as the
freewill offerings of the people and
priests for the temple of their God
in Jerusalem.[b] [17]With this money
7:17 c 2Ki 3:4 d Nu 15:5-12 e Dt 12:5-11 be sure to buy bulls, rams and male
lambs,[c] together with their grain
offerings and drink offerings,[d] and
sacrifice[e] them on the altar of the
temple of your God in Jerusalem.
[18]You and your brother Jews may
then do whatever seems best with
the rest of the silver and gold, in ac-
7:19 f Ezr 5:14; Jer 27:22 cordance with the will of your God.
[19]Deliver[f] to the God of Jerusalem
all the articles entrusted to you for
worship in the temple of your God.
[20]And anything else needed for the
temple of your God that you may
7:20 g Ezr 6:4 have occasion to supply, you may
provide from the royal treasury.[g]
[21]Now I, King Artaxerxes, order
all the treasurers of Trans-Euphrates to provide with diligence whatever Ezra the priest, a teacher of
the Law of the God of heaven, may
ask of you— [22]up to a hundred talents[a] of silver, a hundred cors[b] of
wheat, a hundred baths[c] of wine, a
hundred baths[c] of olive oil, and salt
without limit. [23]Whatever the God
of heaven has prescribed, let it be
done with diligence for the temple
of the God of heaven. Why should
7:23 h Ezr 6:10 there be wrath against the realm of
the king and of his sons?[h] [24]You are
also to know that you have no au-
7:24 i Ezr 4:13 j Ezr 8:36 thority to impose taxes, tribute or
duty[i] on any of the priests, Levites,
singers, gatekeepers, temple servants or other workers at this
house of God.[j]
[25]And you, Ezra, in accordance
7:25 k Ex 18:21,26; Dt 16:18 with the wisdom of your God,
which you possess, appoint[k] mag-
istrates and judges to administer
justice to all the people of Trans-
Euphrates—all who know the laws
of your God. And you are to teach[l] 7:25 l ver 10; Lev 10:11
any who do not know them.
[26]Whoever does not obey the law of
your God and the law of the king
must surely be punished by death,
banishment, confiscation of prop- 7:26 m Ezr 6:11
erty, or imprisonment.[m]

[27]Praise be to the LORD, the God of our
fathers, who has put it into the king's 7:27 n Ezr 1:1; 6:22 o 1Ch 29:12
heart[n] to bring honor[o] to the house of
the LORD in Jerusalem in this way [28]and
who has extended his good favor[p] to me 7:28 p 2Ki 25:28 q Ezr 5:5; 9:9
before the king and his advisers and all
the king's powerful officials. Because the
hand of the LORD my God was on me,[q] I
took courage and gathered leading men
from Israel to go up with me.

List of the Family Heads Returning With Ezra

8 These are the family heads and
those registered with them who
came up with me from Babylon during 8:1 r Ezr 7:7
the reign of King Artaxerxes:[r]

[2]of the descendants of Phinehas,
Gershom;
of the descendants of Ithamar,
Daniel;
of the descendants of David, Hat-
tush [3]of the descendants of 8:3 s 1Ch 3:22 t Ezr 2:3
Shecaniah;[s]
of the descendants of Parosh,[t]
Zechariah, and with him were
registered 150 men;
[4]of the descendants of Pahath-
Moab,[u] Eliehoenai son of Zera- 8:4 u Ezr 2:6
hiah, and with him 200 men;
[5]of the descendants of Zattu,[d]
Shecaniah son of Jahaziel, and
with him 300 men;
[6]of the descendants of Adin,[v] Ebed 8:6 v Ezr 2:15; Ne 7:20; 10:16
son of Jonathan, and with him 50
men;
[7]of the descendants of Elam, Jeshaiah son of Athaliah, and with
him 70 men;
[8]of the descendants of Shephatiah,
Zebadiah son of Michael, and
with him 80 men;
[9]of the descendants of Joab, Obadi-

a 22 That is, about 3 3/4 tons (about 3.4 metric tons) *b 22* That is, probably about 600 bushels (about 22 kiloliters) *c 22* That is, probably about 600 gallons (about 2.2 kiloliters) *d 5* Some Septuagint manuscripts (also 1 Esdras 8:32); Hebrew does not have *Zattu.*

ah son of Jehiel, and with him
218 men;
10 of the descendants of Bani,[a] Shelomith son of Josiphiah, and
with him 160 men;
11 of the descendants of Bebai, Zechariah son of Bebai, and with him
28 men;
12 of the descendants of Azgad, Johanan son of Hakkatan, and with
him 110 men;
13 of the descendants of Adonikam,[w]
the last ones, whose names were
Eliphelet, Jeuel and Shemaiah,
and with them 60 men;
14 of the descendants of Bigvai, Uthai
and Zaccur, and with them 70
men.

The Return to Jerusalem

15 I assembled them at the canal that
flows toward Ahava,[x] and we camped
there three days. When I checked among
the people and the priests, I found no Levites[y] there. 16 So I summoned Eliezer,
Ariel, Shemaiah, Elnathan, Jarib, Elnathan, Nathan, Zechariah and Meshullam, who were leaders, and Joiarib and
Elnathan, who were men of learning,
17 and I sent them to Iddo, the leader in
Casiphia. I told them what to say to Iddo
and his kinsmen, the temple servants[z] in
Casiphia, so that they might bring attendants to us for the house of our God.
18 Because the gracious hand of our God
was on us,[a] they brought us Sherebiah, a
capable man, from the descendants of
Mahli son of Levi, the son of Israel, and
Sherebiah's sons and brothers, 18 men;
19 and Hashabiah, together with Jeshaiah
from the descendants of Merari, and his
brothers and nephews, 20 men. 20 They
also brought 220 of the temple servants[b]—a body that David and the officials had established to assist the Levites.
All were registered by name.
21 There, by the Ahava Canal,[c] I proclaimed a fast, so that we might humble
ourselves before our God and ask him
for a safe journey[d] for us and our children, with all our possessions. 22 I was
ashamed to ask the king for soldiers[e]
and horsemen to protect us from enemies on the road, because we had told
the king, "The gracious hand of our God
is on everyone[f] who looks to him, but
his great anger is against all who forsake

8:13 [w] Ezr 2:13
8:15 [x] ver 21,31 [y] Ezr 2:40; 7:7
8:17 [z] Ezr 2:43
8:18 [a] Ezr 5:5
8:20 [b] 1Ch 9:2; Ezr 2:43
8:21 [c] ver 15; 2Ch 20:3 [d] Ps 5:8; 107:7
8:22 [e] Ne 2:9; Ezr 7:6, 9,28 [f] Ezr 5:5

him.[g]" 23 So we fasted[h] and petitioned
our God about this, and he answered
our prayer.
24 Then I set apart twelve of the leading priests, together with Sherebiah,[i]
Hashabiah and ten of their brothers,
25 and I weighed out[j] to them the offering of silver and gold and the articles
that the king, his advisers, his officials
and all Israel present there had donated
for the house of our God. 26 I weighed out
to them 650 talents[b] of silver, silver articles weighing 100 talents,[c] 100 talents[c]
of gold, 27 20 bowls of gold valued at
1,000 darics,[d] and two fine articles of
polished bronze, as precious as gold.
28 I said to them, "You as well as these
articles are consecrated to the LORD.[k]
The silver and gold are a freewill offering
to the LORD, the God of your fathers.
29 Guard them carefully until you weigh
them out in the chambers of the house
of the LORD in Jerusalem before the leading priests and the Levites and the family heads of Israel." 30 Then the priests
and Levites received the silver and gold
and sacred articles that had been
weighed out to be taken to the house of
our God in Jerusalem.
31 On the twelfth day of the first
month we set out from the Ahava Canal[l]
to go to Jerusalem. The hand of our God
was on us, and he protected us from enemies and bandits along the way. 32 So
we arrived in Jerusalem, where we rested three days.[m]
33 On the fourth day, in the house of
our God, we weighed out the silver and
gold and the sacred articles into the
hands of Meremoth[n] son of Uriah, the
priest. Eleazar son of Phinehas was with
him, and so were the Levites Jozabad
son of Jeshua and Noadiah son of Binnui.[o] 34 Everything was accounted for by
number and weight, and the entire
weight was recorded at that time.
35 Then the exiles who had returned
from captivity sacrificed burnt offerings
to the God of Israel: twelve bulls for all
Israel, ninety-six rams, seventy-seven
male lambs and, as a sin offering, twelve
male goats.[p] All this was a burnt offer-

a 10 Some Septuagint manuscripts (also 1 Esdras 8:36); Hebrew does not have *Bani.* *b 26* That is, about 25 tons (about 22 metric tons) *c 26* That is, about 3 3/4 tons (about 3.4 metric tons) *d 27* That is, about 19 pounds (about 8.5 kilograms)

8:22 [g] Dt 31:17; 2Ch 15:2
8:23 [h] 2Ch 20:3; 33:13
8:24 [i] ver 18
8:25 [j] ver 33; Ezr 7:15,16
8:28 [k] Lev 21:6; 22:2-3
8:31 [l] ver 15
8:32 [m] Ge 40:13; Ne 2:11
8:33 [n] Ne 3:4,21 [o] Ne 3:24
8:35 [p] 2Ch 29:21; Ezr 6:17

8:36 [q] Ezr 7:21-24 [r] Est 9:3

ing to the LORD. 36 They also delivered the
king's orders[q] to the royal satraps and to
the governors of Trans-Euphrates, who
then gave assistance to the people and
to the house of God.[r]

Ezra's Prayer About Intermarriage

9 After these things had been done,
the leaders came to me and said,
"The people of Israel, including the
9:1 [s] Ezr 6:21; Ne 9:2 [t] Ge 19:38 [u] Ex 13:5
priests and the Levites, have not kept
themselves separate[s] from the neighboring peoples with their detestable
practices, like those of the Canaanites,
Hittites, Perizzites, Jebusites, Ammonites,[t] Moabites, Egyptians and Am-
9:2 [v] Ex 34:16 [w] Ex 22:31 [x] Ezr 10:2
orites.[u] 2 They have taken some of their
daughters[v] as wives for themselves and
their sons, and have mingled the holy
race[w] with the peoples around them.
And the leaders and officials have led
the way in this unfaithfulness."[x]
3 When I heard this, I tore my tunic
and cloak, pulled hair from my head and
beard and sat down appalled. 4 Then
9:4 [y] Ezr 10:3
everyone who trembled[y] at the words of
the God of Israel gathered around me
because of this unfaithfulness of the exiles. And I sat there appalled until the
evening sacrifice.
9:5 [z] Ex 29:41
5 Then, at the evening sacrifice,[z] I rose
from my self-abasement, with my tunic
and cloak torn, and fell on my knees
with my hands spread out to the LORD
my God 6 and prayed:

"O my God, I am too ashamed
and disgraced to lift up my face to
you, my God, because our sins are
9:6 [a] 2Ch 28:9; Job 42:6; Ps 38:4; Rev 18:5
higher than our heads and our guilt
has reached to the heavens.[a] 7 From
the days of our forefathers[b] until
9:7 [b] 2Ch 29:6 [c] Eze 21:1-32 [d] Dt 28:64 [e] Dt 28:37
now, our guilt has been great. Be-
cause of our sins, we and our kings
and our priests have been subjected to the sword[c] and captivity,[d] to
pillage and humiliation[e] at the
hand of foreign kings, as it is today.
8 "But now, for a brief moment,
9:8 [f] Ps 25:16; Isa 33:2 [g] Ge 45:7 [h] Ecc 12:11; Isa 22:23 [i] Ps 13:3
the LORD our God has been gra-
cious[f] in leaving us a remnant[g] and
giving us a firm place[h] in his sanctuary, and so our God gives light to
our eyes[i] and a little relief in our
9:9 [j] Ex 1:14; Ne 9:36 [k] Ezr 7:28
bondage. 9 Though we are slaves,[j]
our God has not deserted us in our
bondage. He has shown us kindness[k] in the sight of the kings of
Persia: He has granted us new life
to rebuild the house of our God and
repair its ruins,[l] and he has given 9:9 [l] Ps 69:35; Isa 43:1; Jer 32:44
us a wall of protection in Judah and
Jerusalem.
10 "But now, O our God, what can
we say after this? For we have dis- 9:10 [m] Dt 11:8; Isa 1:19-20
regarded the commands[m] 11 you
gave through your servants the
prophets when you said: 'The land
you are entering to possess is a
land polluted[n] by the corruption of 9:11 [n] Lev 18:25-28 [o] Dt 9:4
its peoples. By their detestable
practices[o] they have filled it with
their impurity from one end to the
other. 12 Therefore, do not give your
daughters in marriage to their sons
or take their daughters for your
sons. Do not seek a treaty of friend-
ship with them[p] at any time, that 9:12 [p] Ex 34:15; Dt 7:3; 23:6
you may be strong and eat the good
things of the land and leave it to
your children as an everlasting inheritance.'
13 "What has happened to us is a
result of our evil deeds and our
great guilt, and yet, our God, you
have punished us less than our sins 9:13 [q] Job 11:6; Ps 103:10
have deserved[q] and have given us a
remnant like this. 14 Shall we again
break your commands and inter-
marry[r] with the peoples who com- 9:14 [r] Ne 13:27 [s] Dt 9:8 [t] Dt 9:14
mit such detestable practices?
Would you not be angry enough
with us to destroy us,[s] leaving us no
remnant[t] or survivor? 15 O LORD, 9:15 [u] Ge 18:25; Ps 51:4; Jer 12:1; Da 9:7 [v] Ne 9:33; Ps 130:3; Mal 3:2 [w] 1Ki 8:47
God of Israel, you are righteous![u]
We are left this day as a remnant.
Here we are before you in our guilt,
though because of it not one of us
can stand[v] in your presence.[w]"

The People's Confession of Sin

10 While Ezra was praying and 10:1 [x] 2Ch 20:9; Da 9:20
confessing,[x] weeping and
throwing himself down before the house
of God, a large crowd of Israelites—men,
women and children—gathered around
him. They too wept bitterly. 2 Then
Shecaniah son of Jehiel, one of the de-
scendants of Elam, said to Ezra, "We 10:2 [y] Ezr 9:2; Ne 13:27 [z] Dt 30:8-10
have been unfaithful[y] to our God by
marrying foreign women from the peoples around us. But in spite of this, there
is still hope for Israel.[z] 3 Now let us make 10:3 [a] 2Ch 34:31 [b] Ex 34:16; Dt 7:2-3; Ezr 9:4
a covenant[a] before our God to send
away[b] all these women and their

DISCOVERY 110

When God Demanded Divorce

It is God's intention that a marriage relationship remain intact until one of the partners has died. The institution of marriage began already in the Garden of Eden when God created one woman for one man. When God gave his law to Moses, he included instructions that permitted divorce under certain circumstances (Deuteronomy 24:1–4). God hates divorce (Malachi 2:16), yet he commanded the Israelite men to terminate their relationships with the foreign wives they had married while in Babylon. Why would God command his people to do something contrary to his own stated principle?

The problem was that some of the Israelite men had joined in marriage with wives who did not follow God and had thus "mingled the holy race with the people around them" (Ezra 9:2). Ezra was appalled by this development—so much so that he tore his clothes and pulled hair from his head and beard as a public sign of repentance. After that Ezra prayed, confessing the sin of the people and promising God that they would turn back to him: "What has happened to us is a result of our evil deeds and our great guilt, and yet, our God, you have punished us less than our sins have deserved and have given us a remnant like this" (verse 13).

After this prayer Shecaniah, an adviser to Ezra, suggested that those who had married foreign wives legally divorce them: "Let us make a covenant before our God to send away all these women and their children" (Ezra 10:3). While this forced breakage of family ties strikes us as wrenchingly cruel, the action was taken according to the law of Moses. This incident marks the only time in the Bible in which divorce was mandated. The reason was that the holy line of the Messiah was being jeopardized. If the people had continued to intermarry with foreigners, they would have lost their identity as God's people and turned permanently from serving the one true God. The critical nature of the problem demanded an exceptional and radical solution.

God calls his children today to cultivate relationships in which we share common devotion and values. Paul urged the Corinthian Christians not to "be yoked together with unbelievers" (2 Corinthians 6:14–15). Notice that Paul was not advocating divorce. He was not even talking about divorce. The critical stage in a relationship comes long before divorce, long before separation, long before marital conflict, long before marriage itself or even engagement. Accepting the offer of a casual date with an unbeliever can even in some instances be the first tiny step along a road of conflict and regret.

It is certainly true that "unequally yoked" couples can share deep love and fellowship, as well as many common interests. But Jesus wants us to share our very souls and spirits, and he stated that two people in a marriage relationship "become one flesh" (Matthew 19:5). Paul pointed out that our bodies are living "temple[s] of the Holy Spirit" (1 Corinthians 6:19) and "members of Christ himself" (1 Corinthians 6:15) and later stated that "he who unites himself with the Lord is one with him in spirit" (1 Corinthians 6:17). If we are truly to become one in marriage, then, that Spirit of Christ must be the glue that binds us together.

Self-Discovery: *Are you acquainted with couples who are struggling with the issue of being "unequally yoked"? What impact has this division caused in their lives? In the lives of their children?*

GO TO DISCOVERY 111 ON PAGE 601

children, in accordance with the counsel of my lord and of those who fear the
commands of our God. Let it be done
according to the Law. [4]Rise up; this matter is in your hands. We will support you,
so take courage and do it."
[5]So Ezra rose up and put the leading
10:5 priests and Levites and all Israel under
c Ne 5:12; 13:25 oath[c] to do what had been suggested.
And they took the oath. [6]Then Ezra
withdrew from before the house of God
and went to the room of Jehohanan son
10:6 of Eliashib. While he was there, he ate
d Ex 34:28; Dt 9:18 no food and drank no water,[d] because he
continued to mourn over the unfaith-
fulness of the exiles.
[7]A proclamation was then issued
throughout Judah and Jerusalem for all
the exiles to assemble in Jerusalem.
[8]Anyone who failed to appear within
three days would forfeit all his property,
in accordance with the decision of the
officials and elders, and would himself
be expelled from the assembly of the exiles.
10:9 [9]Within the three days, all the men of
e Ezr 1:5 Judah and Benjamin[e] had gathered in Jerusalem. And on the twentieth day of
the ninth month, all the people were sitting in the square before the house of
God, greatly distressed by the occasion
and because of the rain. [10]Then Ezra the
priest stood up and said to them, "You
have been unfaithful; you have married
foreign women, adding to Israel's guilt.
[11]Now make confession to the LORD, the
God of your fathers, and do his will. Separate yourselves from the peoples
10:11 around you and from your foreign
f ver 3; Dt 24:1; Ne 9:2; Mal 2:10-16 wives."[f]
[12]The whole assembly responded with
10:12 a loud voice:[g] "You are right! We must do
g Jos 6:5 as you say. [13]But there are many people
here and it is the rainy season; so we
cannot stand outside. Besides, this matter cannot be taken care of in a day or
two, because we have sinned greatly in
this thing. [14]Let our officials act for the
whole assembly. Then let everyone in
our towns who has married a foreign
woman come at a set time, along with
10:14 the elders and judges[h] of each town, un-
h Dt 16:18 til the fierce anger[i] of our God in this
i Nu 25:4; 2Ch 29:10; 30:8 matter is turned away from us." [15]Only
Jonathan son of Asahel and Jahzeiah son
10:15 of Tikvah, supported by Meshullam and
j Ne 11:16 Shabbethai[j] the Levite, opposed this.

[16]So the exiles did as was proposed.
Ezra the priest selected men who were
family heads, one from each family division, and all of them designated by
name. On the first day of the tenth
month they sat down to investigate the
cases, [17]and by the first day of the first
month they finished dealing with all the
men who had married foreign women.

Those Guilty of Intermarriage

[18]Among the descendants of the
priests, the following had mar- 10:18
ried foreign women:[k] k Jdg 3:6 l Ezr 2:2

From the descendants of Jeshua[l]
son of Jozadak, and his brothers:
Maaseiah, Eliezer, Jarib and Gedaliah. [19](They all gave their
hands[m] in pledge to put away 10:19 m 2Ki 10:15
their wives, and for their guilt n Lev 5:15; 6:6
they each presented a ram from
the flock as a guilt offering.)[n]
[20]From the descendants of Immer:[o] 10:20 o 1Ch 24:14
Hanani and Zebadiah.

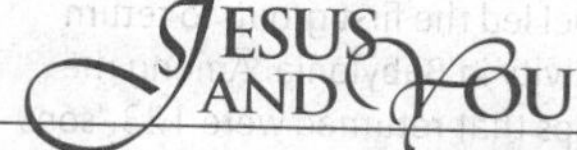

TURNING BACK TO GOD

Ezra, like the prophets, grieved over Israel's sin and compromise. But while the prophets often called God's people to repentance, rarely did their pleas elicit the kind of response Ezra witnessed as he prayed and confessed with high emotion. The returned exiles wept bitterly as they realized the extent of their disobedience (Ezra 10:1). The years in exile must have broken their stubborn pride and softened their hearts. Returning to their God-given homeland must have filled them with a new awe for their God, who had made their homecoming possible. As Ezra obeyed God's instructions, God rejuvenated the passion and devotion of the people who had gathered in Jerusalem. As Ezra had called God's people to turn back to him, so Jesus right from the very outset of his ministry called people to repent because the reign of God had drawn near in and through him (Matthew 4:17). Jesus urged the people of his day to turn away from their sinful way of living and turn to God's way of living—a pattern of life so beautifully summarized in Jesus' Sermon on the Mount (Matthew 5:1—7:29). May our hearts be softened, as in Ezra's day, to hear and respond to God's call to come home—home to the heart of the triune God—Father, Son and Holy Spirit.

10:21 p 1Ch 24:8
[21] From the descendants of Harim:[p]
Maaseiah, Elijah, Shemaiah, Jehiel and Uzziah.

10:22 q 1Ch 9:12
[22] From the descendants of Pashhur:[q]
Elioenai, Maaseiah, Ishmael, Nethanel, Jozabad and Elasah.

10:23 r Ne 8:7; 9:4
[23] Among the Levites:[r]

Jozabad, Shimei, Kelaiah (that is, Kelita), Pethahiah, Judah and Eliezer.

10:24 s Ne 3:1; 12:10; 13:7,28
[24] From the singers:
Eliashib.[s]

From the gatekeepers:
Shallum, Telem and Uri.

[25] And among the other Israelites:

10:25 t Ezr 2:3
From the descendants of Parosh:[t]
Ramiah, Izziah, Malkijah, Mijamin, Eleazar, Malkijah and Benaiah.

ZERUBBABEL
A key link in Jesus' line

Zerubbabel led the first group to return from captivity in Babylonia. Among the many family groups that returned were 123 "sons of Bethlehem" (Ezra 2:21). This brief notation reminds us that, even through the exile, God preserved the family line of his promised Messiah. In fact, Zerubbabel was the grandson of King Jehoiachin (also called Jeconiah) of Judah and an ancestor of Jesus through David's family line (see Matthew 1:12–13 and Luke 3:27). Zerubbabel was a key link in the line of Jesus Christ: God used him to help the Israelites return and rebuild the temple. In addition to its significance as the place for God's people to worship their God, Jesus would later minister in this same temple. The names that appear in Ezra 2 remind us that the nation of Israel did not lose its unique identity or the hope for seeing God's promise fulfilled—even during the years of exile. God himself preserved his people to serve his purposes.

[26] From the descendants of Elam:[u] 10:26 u ver 2
Mattaniah, Zechariah, Jehiel, Abdi, Jeremoth and Elijah.

[27] From the descendants of Zattu:
Elioenai, Eliashib, Mattaniah, Jeremoth, Zabad and Aziza.

[28] From the descendants of Bebai:
Jehohanan, Hananiah, Zabbai and Athlai.

[29] From the descendants of Bani:
Meshullam, Malluch, Adaiah, Jashub, Sheal and Jeremoth.

[30] From the descendants of Pahath-Moab:
Adna, Kelal, Benaiah, Maaseiah, Mattaniah, Bezalel, Binnui and Manasseh.

[31] From the descendants of Harim:
Eliezer, Ishijah, Malkijah, Shemaiah, Shimeon,
[32] Benjamin, Malluch and Shemariah.

[33] From the descendants of Hashum:
Mattenai, Mattattah, Zabad, Eliphelet, Jeremai, Manasseh and Shimei.

[34] From the descendants of Bani:
Maadai, Amram, Uel,
[35] Benaiah, Bedeiah, Keluhi,
[36] Vaniah, Meremoth, Eliashib,
[37] Mattaniah, Mattenai and Jaasu.

[38] From the descendants of Binnui:[a]
Shimei,
[39] Shelemiah, Nathan, Adaiah,
[40] Macnadebai, Shashai, Sharai,
[41] Azarel, Shelemiah, Shemariah,
[42] Shallum, Amariah and Joseph.

[43] From the descendants of Nebo:
Jeiel, Mattithiah, Zabad, Zebina, Jaddai, Joel and Benaiah.

[44] All these had married foreign women, and some of them had children by these wives.[b]

[a] *37,38* See Septuagint (also 1 Esdras 9:34); Hebrew *Jaasu [38] and Bani and Binnui,* [b] *44* Or *and they sent them away with their children*

NEHEMIAH

What spiritual lesson can we learn from the challenges surrounding this building project? (Nehemiah 3:1–32)

♦ *Now, as then, physical situations can affect our spiritual well-being. Limited resources or direct opposition can challenge the plans of Christians today as surely as opponents challenged the Jews of Nehemiah's time. The details of the Jews' encounter offer examples for us of how to meet and overcome such obstacles (Romans 15:4).*

Why did the people weep during the reading of the law? (Nehemiah 8:9–11)

♦ *They were probably grieved to realize how they had failed God. But in a beautiful example of God's grace, already exhibited at this point prior to the birth of Jesus, their leaders exhorted them to stop weeping, not because they weren't sinful, but because "the joy of the LORD is your strength." They could delight in the joy of the Lord because he is a forgiving God, "gracious and compassionate" (Nehemiah 9:17).*

Jesus in Nehemiah Nehemiah was yet another man of God in Bible times who foreshadowed Jesus Christ. God called Nehemiah to lead the returning exiles from Babylonia in rebuilding Jerusalem's city walls—stone by stone. In the New Testament Jesus is referred to as "the stone the builders rejected" (Mark 12:10; 1 Peter 2:7), yet he became the "chief cornerstone" in God's "spiritual house," the church (Ephesians 2:20; 1 Peter 2:5). Just as Nehemiah built a "new" Jerusalem, so Jesus will present a new Jerusalem when he comes back for his people (Revelation 21).

If you've ever faced an overwhelming task, you'll be able to identify with Nehemiah. Together with Ezra, Nehemiah worked to help the returning exiles rebuild their country. Nehemiah struggled with issues still with us today as we attempt to follow Jesus and build on his foundation: maintaining our motivation, overcoming fatigue, dealing with criticism. At the same time Nehemiah also offers inspiration and vision to help us keep our eyes fixed on Jesus and on his eternal city, "the city with foundations, whose architect and builder is God" (Hebrews 11:10).

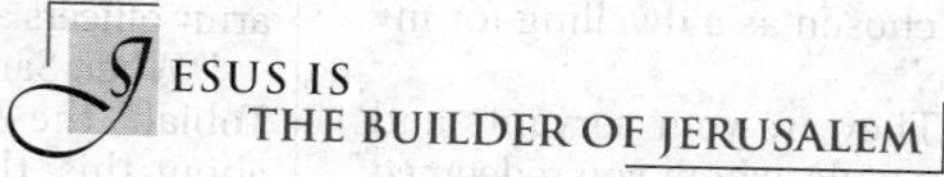

JESUS IS THE BUILDER OF JERUSALEM

Nehemiah's Prayer

1 The words of Nehemiah son of
Hacaliah:

1:1 a Ne 10:1; In the month of Kislev[a] in the twenti-
Zec 7:1 eth year, while I was in the citadel of
1:2 Susa, 2Hanani,[b] one of my brothers,
b Ne 7:2 came from Judah with some other men,
c Jer 52:28 and I questioned them about the Jewish
remnant[c] that survived the exile, and
also about Jerusalem.
3They said to me, "Those who survived the exile and are back in the province are in great trouble and disgrace.
The wall of Jerusalem is broken down,
1:3 and its gates have been burned with
d 2Ki 25:10; fire.[d]"
Ne 2:3,13,17 4When I heard these things, I sat
1:4 down and wept.[e] For some days I
e Ps 137:1 f Ezr 9:4 mourned and fasted[f] and prayed before
the God of heaven. 5Then I said:

"O LORD, God of heaven, the
1:5 great and awesome God,[g] who
g Dt 7:21; Ne 4:14 keeps his covenant of love[h] with
h Ex 20:6; Da 9:4 those who love him and obey his
commands, 6let your ear be atten-
1:6 i 1Ki 8:29 tive and your eyes open to hear[i] the
j Da 9:17 prayer[j] your servant is praying before you day and night for your servants, the people of Israel. I confess
the sins we Israelites, including
myself and my father's house, have
1:7 committed against you. 7We have
k Dt 28:14-15; acted very wickedly[k] toward you.
Ps 106:6 We have not obeyed the commands, decrees and laws you gave
your servant Moses.
1:8 8"Remember[l] the instruction
l 2Ki 20:3 m Lev 26:33 you gave your servant Moses, saying, 'If you are unfaithful, I will
scatter[m] you among the nations,
9but if you return to me and obey
my commands, then even if your
exiled people are at the farthest ho-
1:9 n Dt 30:4 rizon, I will gather[n] them from
o 1Ki 8:48; there and bring them to the place I
Jer 29:14 have chosen as a dwelling for my
Name.'[o]
10"They are your servants and
your people, whom you redeemed
1:10 by your great strength and your
p Ex 32:11; Dt 9:29 mighty hand.[p] 11O Lord, let your
1:11 ear be attentive[q] to the prayer of
q ver this your servant and to the prayer
of your servants who delight in re-
vering your name. Give your servant success today by granting him
favor in the presence of this man."

I was cupbearer[r] to the king. 1:11 r Ge 40:1

Artaxerxes Sends Nehemiah to Jerusalem

2 In the month of Nisan in the twen- 2:1
tieth year of King Artaxerxes,[s] s Ezr 7:1
when wine was brought for him, I took
the wine and gave it to the king. I had not
been sad in his presence before; 2so the
king asked me, "Why does your face look
so sad when you are not ill? This can be
nothing but sadness of heart."
I was very much afraid, 3but I said to 2:3
the king, "May the king live forever![t] t 1Ki 1:31;
Why should my face not look sad when Da 2:4; 5:10; 6:6,
the city[u] where my fathers are buried 21 u Ps 137:6
lies in ruins, and its gates have been de- v Ne 1:3
stroyed by fire?[v]"
4The king said to me, "What is it you
want?"
Then I prayed to the God of heaven,
5and I answered the king, "If it pleases
the king and if your servant has found
favor in his sight, let him send me to the
city in Judah where my fathers are
buried so that I can rebuild it." 2:6
6Then the king[w], with the queen sit- w Ne 5:14; 13:6
ting beside him, asked me, "How long
will your journey take, and when will
you get back?" It pleased the king to
send me; so I set a time.
7I also said to him, "If it pleases the
king, may I have letters to the governors 2:7
of Trans-Euphrates,[x] so that they will x Ezr 8:36
provide me safe-conduct until I arrive in
Judah? 8And may I have a letter to Asaph,
keeper of the king's forest, so he will give
me timber to make beams for the gates of 2:8
the citadel[y] by the temple and for the city y Ne 7:2 z ver 18;
wall and for the residence I will occupy?" Ezr 5:5; 7:6
And because the gracious hand of my
God was upon me,[z] the king granted my
requests. 9So I went to the governors of
Trans-Euphrates and gave them the
king's letters. The king had also sent 2:9
army officers and cavalry[a] with me. a Ezr 8:22
10When Sanballat[b] the Horonite and 2:10
Tobiah[c] the Ammonite official heard b ver 19; Ne 4:1,
about this, they were very much dis- 7 c Ne 4:3;
turbed that someone had come to pro- 13:4-7 d Est 10:3
mote the welfare of the Israelites.[d]

Nehemiah Inspects Jerusalem's Walls

11I went to Jerusalem, and after staying 2:11
there three days[e] 12I set out during the e Ge 40:13

DISCOVERY 111

Beauty From Rubble

Imagine that you were to return to your hometown and find that all of the places that had once been so important in your life have been reduced to rubble. That is exactly what happened to God's people. In the first three chapters of Nehemiah we read that the captive Israelites longed to go back to Jerusalem. And God did eventually allow the return of a band of his people, delegating Nehemiah to lead them and help them rebuild the city walls; with God's help Nehemiah planned for, prayed for and orchestrated the whole undertaking. In this story we glimpse a powerful portrayal of God's forgiveness and the restoration that takes place in the lives of his people when they are willing to renew their commitment to him.

God's first action was to reacquaint his people with his expectations for them. God had been very explicit from the beginning: If the Israelites lived the way he intended, he would bless them, but if they decided to approach life on their own terms they would be conquered and compelled to live in captivity (Deuteronomy 28:1–2). The Israelites knew both God's intentions for them and the consequences for going their own way. God had reminded them over and over throughout the years (compare 1 Kings 9 with the verses in Deuteronomy 28).

At the same time, God has never coerced his children; from the beginning he has allowed each of us to choose whether or not we will follow him. But the Israelites had opted for the same course of action that often tempts us—to turn their backs on God and assimilate themselves into their pagan culture.

The historical backdrop for the book of Nehemiah should have rendered Nehemiah's reminder unnecessary. In 930 B.C. God had followed through on his repeated warning, and the kingdom of Israel had been split in two because of the continued sin of the people. Over the next several hundred years both the northern and southern kingdoms had been conquered by their enemies and many of God's people carried away into captivity. The ray of hope even in this dismal situation was God's pledge to his people that if they would turn from their sin back to him, he would restore their nation and bring them back—back to their homeland and back into restored fellowship with himself (Deuteronomy 30).

Each of us is prone to doing just what God's people, the Israelites, had done. We decide that we can make better choices for our own lives than God can. But no matter where we end up in the process, no matter how far away from home we may wander, no matter who we may find ourselves serving, God promises that he will raise something strong and beautiful from the rubble—and he does that through his Son Jesus Christ. Jesus told the story of the lost son to demonstrate that those who make bad choices can still find forgiveness and restoration through himself (Luke 15:11–32). When we place our trust in him as the One who died for our sin, he will receive us and recreate us as new people.

Self-Discovery: *Think back to a time when you made a choice that was contrary to the Lord's expressed will. What consequences did you experience? Have you returned to Jesus?*

GO TO DISCOVERY 112 ON PAGE 605

night with a few men. I had not told anyone what my God had put in my heart to
do for Jerusalem. There were no mounts
with me except the one I was riding on.
2:13 f 2Ch 26:9 g Ne 3:13 h Ne 1:3 13By night I went out through the Valley Gate[f] toward the Jackal[a] Well and
the Dung Gate,[g] examining the walls[h] of
Jerusalem, which had been broken
down, and its gates, which had been destroyed by fire. 14Then I moved on to-
2:14 i Ne 3:15 j 2Ki 18:17 ward the Fountain Gate[i] and the King's
Pool,[j] but there was not enough room
for my mount to get through; 15so I went
up the valley by night, examining the
wall. Finally, I turned back and reentered
through the Valley Gate. 16The officials
did not know where I had gone or what
I was doing, because as yet I had said
nothing to the Jews or the priests or nobles or officials or any others who would
be doing the work.
17Then I said to them, "You see the
trouble we are in: Jerusalem lies in ruins,
and its gates have been burned with
2:17 k Ne 1:3 l Ps 102:16; Isa 30:13; 58:12 m Eze 5:14 fire.[k] Come, let us rebuild the wall[l] of Jerusalem, and we will no longer be in dis-
grace.[m]" 18I also told them about the
gracious hand of my God upon me[n] and
2:18 n 2Sa 2:7 what the king had said to me.
They replied, "Let us start rebuilding."
So they began this good work.
19But when Sanballat the Horonite,
Tobiah the Ammonite official and Ge-
2:19 o Ne 6:1,2,6 p Ps 44:13-16 shem[o] the Arab heard about it, they
mocked and ridiculed us.[p] "What is this
you are doing?" they asked. "Are you rebelling against the king?"
20I answered them by saying, "The
God of heaven will give us success. We
his servants will start rebuilding, but as
2:20 q Ezr 4:3 for you, you have no share[q] in Jerusalem
or any claim or historic right to it."

Builders of the Wall

3:1 r Ezr 10:24 s Isa 58:12 t ver 32; Ne 12:39 u Ne 12:39; Jer 31:38; Zec 14:10 3 Eliashib[r] the high priest and his
fellow priests went to work and
rebuilt[s] the Sheep Gate.[t] They dedicated
it and set its doors in place, building as
far as the Tower of the Hundred, which
they dedicated, and as far as the Tower
3:2 v Ne 7:36 of Hananel.[u] 2The men of Jericho[v] built
the adjoining section, and Zaccur son of
Imri built next to them.

3:3 w 2Ch 33:14; Ne 12:39 3The Fish Gate[w] was rebuilt by the
sons of Hassenaah. They laid its beams
and put its doors and bolts and bars in
place. 4Meremoth son of Uriah, the son
of Hakkoz, repaired the next section.
Next to him Meshullam son of Berekiah,
the son of Meshezabel, made repairs,
and next to him Zadok son of Baana
also made repairs. 5The next section was 3:5
repaired by the men of Tekoa,[x] but their x 2Sa 14:2
nobles would not put their shoulders to
the work under their supervisors.[b]

6The Jeshanah[c] Gate[y] was repaired by 3:6 y Ne 12:39
Joiada son of Paseah and Meshullam son
of Besodeiah. They laid its beams and
put its doors and bolts and bars in place.
7Next to them, repairs were made by 3:7
men from Gibeon[z] and Mizpah—Mela- z Jos 9:3; Ne 2:7
tiah of Gibeon and Jadon of Meronoth—
places under the authority of the governor of Trans-Euphrates. 8Uzziel son of
Harhaiah, one of the goldsmiths, repaired the next section; and Hananiah,
one of the perfume-makers, made repairs next to that. They restored[d] Jerusa- 3:8
lem as far as the Broad Wall.[a] 9Rephaiah a Ne 12:38
son of Hur, ruler of a half-district of Jerusalem, repaired the next section. 10Ad-
joining this, Jedaiah son of Harumaph
made repairs opposite his house, and
Hattush son of Hashabneiah made repairs next to him. 11Malkijah son of Harim and Hasshub son of Pahath-Moab
repaired another section and the Tower 3:11
of the Ovens.[b] 12Shallum son of Hallo- b Ne 12:38
hesh, ruler of a half-district of Jerusalem,
repaired the next section with the help
of his daughters.

13The Valley Gate[c] was repaired by 3:13 c 2Ch 26:9
Hanun and the residents of Zanoah.[d] d Jos 15:34
They rebuilt it and put its doors and e Ne 2:13
bolts and bars in place. They also repaired five hundred yards[e] of the wall as
far as the Dung Gate.[e]

14The Dung Gate was repaired by Malkijah son of Recab, ruler of the district of 3:14
Beth Hakkerem.[f] He rebuilt it and put its f Jer 6:1
doors and bolts and bars in place.

15The Fountain Gate was repaired by
Shallun son of Col-Hozeh, ruler of the
district of Mizpah. He rebuilt it, roofing
it over and putting its doors and bolts
and bars in place. He also repaired the 3:15
wall of the Pool of Siloam,[f][g] by the King's g Isa 8:6; Jn 9:7
Garden, as far as the steps going down

[a] 13 Or *Serpent* or *Fig* [b] 5 Or *their Lord* or *the governor* [c] 6 Or *Old* [d] 8 Or *They left out part of* [e] 13 Hebrew *a thousand cubits* (about 450 meters) [f] 15 Hebrew *Shelah,* a variant of *Shiloah,* that is, Siloam

from the City of David. 16Beyond him,
3:16 h Jos 15:58 i Ac 2:29 Nehemiah son of Azbuk, ruler of a half-district of Beth Zur,[h] made repairs up to
a point opposite the tombs[a][i] of David, as
far as the artificial pool and the House of
the Heroes.

17Next to him, the repairs were made
by the Levites under Rehum son of Bani.
Beside him, Hashabiah, ruler of half the
3:17 j Jos 15:44 district of Keilah,[j] carried out repairs for
his district. 18Next to him, the repairs
were made by their countrymen under
Binnui[b] son of Henadad, ruler of the
other half-district of Keilah. 19Next to
him, Ezer son of Jeshua, ruler of Mizpah,
repaired another section, from a point
facing the ascent to the armory as far as
the angle. 20Next to him, Baruch son of
Zabbai zealously repaired another section, from the angle to the entrance of
the house of Eliashib the high priest.
3:21 k Ezr 8:33 21Next to him, Meremoth[k] son of Uriah,
the son of Hakkoz, repaired another section, from the entrance of Eliashib's
house to the end of it.

22The repairs next to him were made
by the priests from the surrounding region. 23Beyond them, Benjamin and
Hasshub made repairs in front of their
house; and next to them, Azariah son of
Maaseiah, the son of Ananiah, made repairs beside his house. 24Next to him,
Binnui[l] son of Henadad repaired another section, from Azariah's house to the 3:24 l Ezr 8:33
angle and the corner, 25and Palal son of
Uzai worked opposite the angle and the
tower projecting from the upper palace
near the court of the guard.[m] Next to 3:25 m Jer 32:2; 37:21; 39:14 n Ezr 2:3
him, Pedaiah son of Parosh[n] 26and the
temple servants[o] living on the hill of
Ophel[p] made repairs up to a point op- 3:26 o Ne 7:46; 11:21 p 2Ch 33:14 q Ne 8:1,3,16; 12:37
posite the Water Gate[q] toward the east
and the projecting tower. 27Next to
them, the men of Tekoa[r] repaired another section, from the great projecting 3:27 r ver 5 s Ps 48:12
tower[s] to the wall of Ophel.

28Above the Horse Gate,[t] the priests 3:28 t 2Ki 11:16; 2Ch 23:15; Jer 31:40
made repairs, each in front of his own
house. 29Next to them, Zadok son of Immer made repairs opposite his house.
Next to him, Shemaiah son of Shecaniah,
the guard at the East Gate, made repairs.
30Next to him, Hananiah son of Shelemiah, and Hanun, the sixth son of Zalaph,
repaired another section. Next to them,
Meshullam son of Berekiah made repairs
opposite his living quarters. 31Next to
him, Malkijah, one of the goldsmiths,
made repairs as far as the house of the
temple servants and the merchants, opposite the Inspection Gate, and as far as
the room above the corner; 32and between the room above the corner and 3:32 u ver 1; Jn 5:2
the Sheep Gate[u] the goldsmiths and
merchants made repairs.

Opposition to the Rebuilding

4:1 v Ne 2:10
4 When Sanballat[v] heard that we
were rebuilding the wall, he became angry and was greatly incensed.
He ridiculed the Jews, 2and in the pres- 4:2 w Ezr 4:9-10 x Ps 79:1; Jer 26:18
ence of his associates[w] and the army of
Samaria, he said, "What are those feeble
Jews doing? Will they restore their wall?
Will they offer sacrifices? Will they finish in a day? Can they bring the stones
back to life from those heaps of
rubble[x]—burned as they are?"

3Tobiah[y] the Ammonite, who was at 4:3 y Ne 2:10 z Job 13:12; 15:3
his side, said, "What they are building—
if even a fox climbed up on it, he would
break down their wall of stones!"[z]

4Hear us, O our God, for we are de- 4:4 a Ps 44:13; 79:12; 123:3-4; Jer 33:24
spised.[a] Turn their insults back on their
own heads. Give them over as plunder in

[a] *16* Hebrew; Septuagint, some Vulgate manuscripts and Syriac *tomb* [b] *18* Two Hebrew manuscripts and Syriac (see also Septuagint and verse 24); most Hebrew manuscripts *Bavvai*

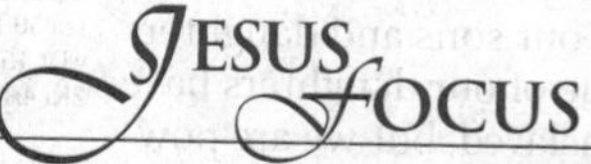

REBUILDING THE WALLS

In order to survive, God's people had to rebuild the walls of Jerusalem; without the city walls the people would have been defenseless against their enemies. If the city had not survived, the family line of the Messiah would have been cut off. By the time God sent his promised Messiah, Jerusalem had again become one of the great cities of the ancient world. Because Israel's cultural identity was constantly threatened by outside forces, the people of God preserved detailed records of their family histories. David's descendants were especially careful to maintain such lists, because his family was the one God had chosen for the Messiah. Because of these meticulous records we have access to a complete and accurate genealogy of Jesus (see Matthew 1:1–17; Luke 3:23–38). Time and again, even throughout the difficult years after the Babylonian exile, God preserved Jesus' ancestral line.

4:5 [b] Isa 2:9; La 1:22 [c] 2Ki 14:27; Ps 51:1; 69:27-28; 109:14; Jer 18:23
a land of captivity. 5 Do not cover up
their guilt[b] or blot out their sins from
your sight,[c] for they have thrown insults
in the face of[a] the builders.

6 So we rebuilt the wall till all of it
reached half its height, for the people
worked with all their heart.

4:7 [d] Ne 2:10
7 But when Sanballat, Tobiah,[d] the
Arabs, the Ammonites and the men of
Ashdod heard that the repairs to Jerusalem's walls had gone ahead and that the
gaps were being closed, they were very
4:8 [e] Ps 2:2; 83:1-18
angry. 8 They all plotted together[e] to
come and fight against Jerusalem and
stir up trouble against it. 9 But we prayed
to our God and posted a guard day and
night to meet this threat.

10 Meanwhile, the people in Judah
4:10 [f] 1Ch 23:4
said, "The strength of the laborers[f] is
giving out, and there is so much rubble
that we cannot rebuild the wall."

11 Also our enemies said, "Before they
know it or see us, we will be right there
among them and will kill them and put
an end to the work."

12 Then the Jews who lived near them
came and told us ten times over, "Wherever you turn, they will attack us."

13 Therefore I stationed some of the
people behind the lowest points of the
wall at the exposed places, posting them
by families, with their swords, spears and
bows. 14 After I looked things over, I stood
up and said to the nobles, the officials
4:14 [g] Ge 28:15; Nu 14:9; Dt 1:29 [h] Ne 1:8 [i] Ne 1:5 [j] 2Sa 10:12
and the rest of the people, "Don't be
afraid[g] of them. Remember[h] the Lord,
who is great and awesome,[i] and fight[j] for
your brothers, your sons and your
daughters, your wives and your homes."

15 When our enemies heard that we
were aware of their plot and that God
4:15 [k] 2Sa 17:14; Job 5:12
had frustrated it,[k] we all returned to the
wall, each to his own work.

16 From that day on, half of my men
did the work, while the other half were
equipped with spears, shields, bows and
armor. The officers posted themselves
behind all the people of Judah 17 who
were building the wall. Those who carried materials did their work with one
4:17 [l] Ps 149:6
hand and held a weapon[l] in the other,
18 and each of the builders wore his
sword at his side as he worked. But the
4:18 [m] Nu 10:2
man who sounded the trumpet[m] stayed
with me.

19 Then I said to the nobles, the officials and the rest of the people, "The
work is extensive and spread out, and
we are widely separated from each other
4:20 [n] Eze 33:3 [o] Ex 14:14; Dt 1:30; 20:4; Jos 10:14
along the wall. 20 Wherever you hear the
sound of the trumpet,[n] join us there.
Our God will fight[o] for us!"

21 So we continued the work with half
the men holding spears, from the first
light of dawn till the stars came out. 22 At
that time I also said to the people, "Have
every man and his helper stay inside Jerusalem at night, so they can serve us as
guards by night and workmen by day."
23 Neither I nor my brothers nor my men
nor the guards with me took off our
clothes; each had his weapon, even
when he went for water.[b]

Nehemiah Helps the Poor

5 Now the men and their wives
raised a great outcry against their
Jewish brothers. 2 Some were saying, "We
and our sons and daughters are numerous; in order for us to eat and stay alive,
we must get grain."

5:3 [p] Ps 109:11 [q] Ge 47:23
3 Others were saying, "We are mort-
gaging our fields,[p] our vineyards and our
homes to get grain during the famine."[q]

4 Still others were saying, "We have
5:4 [r] Ezr 4:13
had to borrow money to pay the king's
tax[r] on our fields and vineyards. 5 Al-
5:5 [s] Ge 29:14 [t] Lev 25:39-43, 47; 2Ki 4:1; Isa 50:1 [u] Dt 15:7-11; 2Ki 4:1
though we are of the same flesh and
blood[s] as our countrymen and though
our sons are as good as theirs, yet we
have to subject our sons and daughters
to slavery.[t] Some of our daughters have
already been enslaved, but we are powerless, because our fields and our vineyards belong to others."[u]

6 When I heard their outcry and these
charges, I was very angry. 7 I pondered
them in my mind and then accused the
5:7 [v] Ex 22:25-27; Lev 25:35-37; Dt 23:19-20; 24:10-13
nobles and officials. I told them, "You
are exacting usury[v] from your own
countrymen!" So I called together a large
meeting to deal with them 8 and said: "As
5:8 [w] Lev 25:47 [x] Jer 34:8
far as possible, we have bought[w] back
our Jewish brothers who were sold to the
Gentiles. Now you are selling your
brothers, only for them to be sold back
to us!" They kept quiet, because they
could find nothing to say.[x]

9 So I continued, "What you are doing
5:9 [y] Isa 52:5
is not right. Shouldn't you walk in the
fear of our God to avoid the reproach[y] of

[a] 5 Or *have provoked you to anger before*
[b] 23 The meaning of the Hebrew for this clause is uncertain.

DISCOVERY 112

GOOD NEWS FOR THE POOR

During Nehemiah's life the rich were becoming richer and the poor increasingly destitute. There had been a famine, and people were being forced to mortgage their fields, vineyards and homes simply to subsist, as well as to borrow money to pay their taxes (Nehemiah 5:3–4). Some were forced to use their own family members as collateral for borrowed money—and in the event the borrower could not repay the debt, the family member would be forced into slavery by the lender.

Nehemiah's response was immediate and passionate: "When I heard their outcry and these charges, I was very angry" (verse 6). He informed the people that the reason they were comfortable with enslaving their own brothers was that they no longer feared God (verse 9). The Israelites listened to Nehemiah and turned back to God, restoring the property they had taken and ceasing the practice of charging interest on money loaned to their countrymen.

But Nehemiah went further. As governor of Judah he was entitled to tax the people so that his own personal needs might be met. But Nehemiah refused to take any land from the people and never demanded from them the portion of food allotted to him as governor. Instead he devoted himself to rebuilding the city wall. Nehemiah understood that he would ultimately answer to God rather than to society. Throughout the Bible God clearly demonstrates his concern for people who lack basic necessities, and he warns that anyone who takes advantage of an individual in need will suffer the consequences (James 5:1–6).

Jesus' attention was always focused on the needy. In fact, when he was asked whether he was indeed God's promised Messiah, Jesus pointed to this very concern for them: "The blind receive sight, the lame walk, those who have leprosy are cured, the deaf hear, the dead are raised, and the good news is preached to the poor" (Matthew 11:4–5). He also announced that God's Spirit was on him, "because he has anointed me to preach good news to the poor. He has sent me to proclaim freedom for the prisoners and recovery of sight for the blind, to release the oppressed" (Luke 4:18).

We see Jesus at work in our own lives when we are paying attention to the underprivileged. Many times we think only in terms of food or clothing, but human lives consist of far more than what we eat or wear. There may be people you know who need a friend to listen to or encourage them or even enjoy recreation with them. There may be an individual who requires a ride to a doctor appointment. Maybe someone stands in need of intercessory prayer, a hot meal for his family during an illness or a visit to her jail cell. None of us can change the world or meet the needs of everyone with whom we cross paths. But we can learn to see the need in another's life—and Jesus asks us simply to reach out to one person at a time.

***Self-Discovery:** When was the last time you reached out to someone in need? What was your motivation? Think of ways you can serve Jesus by serving "the least" of Jesus' brothers and sisters (Matthew 25:40).*

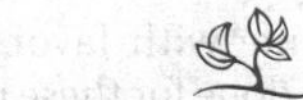

GO TO DISCOVERY 113 ON PAGE 609

our Gentile enemies? 10I and my brothers and my men are also lending the
5:10 people money and grain. But let the ex-
[z]Ex 22:25 acting of usury stop![z] 11Give back to
them immediately their fields, vine-
5:11 yards, olive groves and houses, and also
[a]Isa 58:6 the usury[a] you are charging them—the
hundredth part of the money, grain, new
wine and oil."

12"We will give it back," they said.
"And we will not demand anything more
from them. We will do as you say."

Then I summoned the priests and
made the nobles and officials take an
5:12 [b]Ezr 10:5 oath[b] to do what they had promised. 13I
also shook[c] out the folds of my robe and
5:13 [c]Mt 10:14; Ac 18:6 said, "In this way may God shake out of
his house and possessions every man
[d]Dt 27:15-26 who does not keep this promise. So may
such a man be shaken out and emptied!"

At this the whole assembly said,
"Amen,"[d] and praised the LORD. And the
people did as they had promised.

14Moreover, from the twentieth year
5:14 [e]Ne 2:6; 13:6 of King Artaxerxes,[e] when I was ap-
[f]Ge 42:6; pointed to be their governor[f] in the land
Ezr 6:7; Jer 40:7; Hag 1:1 of Judah, until his thirty-second year—
twelve years—neither I nor my brothers
ate the food allotted to the governor.
15But the earlier governors—those preceding me—placed a heavy burden on
the people and took forty shekels[a] of silver from them in addition to food and
wine. Their assistants also lorded it over
the people. But out of reverence for
5:15 [g]Ge 20:11 God[g] I did not act like that. 16Instead,[h] I
devoted myself to the work on this wall.
5:16 [h]2Th 3:7-10 All my men were assembled there for
the work; we[b] did not acquire any land.

17Furthermore, a hundred and fifty
Jews and officials ate at my table, as well
as those who came to us from the surrounding nations. 18Each day one ox, six
5:18 [i]1Ki 4:23 choice sheep and some poultry[i] were
prepared for me, and every ten days an
abundant supply of wine of all kinds. In
spite of all this, I never demanded the
food allotted to the governor, because
the demands were heavy on these people.

5:19 [j]Ge 8:1; 19Remember[j] me with favor, O my
2Ki 20:3; Ne 1:8; 13:14,22,31 God, for all I have done for these people.

Further Opposition to the Rebuilding

6:1 [k]Ne 2:10 6 When word came to Sanballat,
[l]Ne 2:19 Tobiah,[k] Geshem[l] the Arab and
the rest of our enemies that I had rebuilt
the wall and not a gap was left in it—
though up to that time I had not set the
doors in the gates— 2Sanballat and Geshem sent me this message: "Come, let
us meet together in one of the villages[c] 6:2
on the plain of Ono.[m]" [m]1Ch 8:12

But they were scheming to harm me;
3so I sent messengers to them with this
reply: "I am carrying on a great project
and cannot go down. Why should the
work stop while I leave it and go down to
you?" 4Four times they sent me the same
message, and each time I gave them the
same answer.

5Then, the fifth time, Sanballat[n] sent 6:5 [n]Ne 2:10
his aide to me with the same message,
and in his hand was an unsealed letter
6in which was written:

"It is reported among the na-
tions—and Geshem[d][o] says it is 6:6 [o]Ne 2:19
true—that you and the Jews are
plotting to revolt, and therefore
you are building the wall. Moreover,
according to these reports you are
about to become their king 7and
have even appointed prophets to
make this proclamation about you
in Jerusalem: 'There is a king in Judah!' Now this report will get back
to the king; so come, let us confer
together."

8I sent him this reply: "Nothing like
what you are saying is happening; you
are just making it up out of your head."

9They were all trying to frighten us,
thinking, "Their hands will get too weak
for the work, and it will not be completed."

⌊But I prayed,⌋ "Now strengthen my
hands."

10One day I went to the house of Shemaiah son of Delaiah, the son of
Mehetabel, who was shut in at his home.
He said, "Let us meet in the house of
God, inside the temple[p], and let us close 6:10 [p]Nu 18:7
the temple doors, because men are com-
ing to kill you—by night they are coming to kill you."

11But I said, "Should a man like me
run away? Or should one like me go into
the temple to save his life? I will not go!"
12I realized that God had not sent him,

[a] *15* That is, about 1 pound (about 0.5 kilogram)
[b] *16* Most Hebrew manuscripts; some Hebrew manuscripts, Septuagint, Vulgate and Syriac *I*
[c] *2* Or *in Kephirim*
[d] *6* Hebrew *Gashmu,* a variant of *Geshem*

6:12 [q]Eze 13:22-23 but that he had prophesied against me[q]
[r]Ne 2:10 because Tobiah and Sanballat[r] had hired
him. 13 He had been hired to intimidate
me so that I would commit a sin by do-
6:13 ing this, and then they would give me a
[s]Jer 20:10 bad name to discredit me.[s]

6:14 [t]Ne 1:8 14 Remember[t] Tobiah and Sanballat,[u]
[u]Ne 2:10 O my God, because of what they have
[v]Ex 15:20; Eze 13:17-23; done; remember also the prophetess[v]
Ac 21:9; Rev 2:20 Noadiah and the rest of the prophets[w]
[w]Ne 13:29; Jer 23:9-40; who have been trying to intimidate me.
Zec 13:2-3

The Completion of the Wall

15 So the wall was completed on the
twenty-fifth of Elul, in fifty-two days.
16 When all our enemies heard about
this, all the surrounding nations were
afraid and lost their self-confidence, because they realized that this work had
been done with the help of our God.

17 Also, in those days the nobles of Judah were sending many letters to Tobiah, and replies from Tobiah kept coming
to them. 18 For many in Judah were under
oath to him, since he was son-in-law to
Shecaniah son of Arah, and his son Jehohanan had married the daughter of Meshullam son of Berekiah. 19 Moreover,
they kept reporting to me his good deeds
and then telling him what I said. And Tobiah sent letters to intimidate me.

7:1 [x]1Ch 9:27; 7 After the wall had been rebuilt and
26:12-19; I had set the doors in place, the
Ne 6:1,15 gatekeepers[x] and the singers[y] and the
[y]Ps 68:25 [z]Ne 8:9 Levites[z] were appointed. 2 I put in charge
of Jerusalem my brother Hanani,[a] along
7:2 [a]Ne 1:2 with[a] Hananiah[b] the commander of the
[b]Ne 10:23 citadel,[c] because he was a man of in-
[c]Ne 2:8 tegrity and feared[d] God more than most
[d]1Ki 18:3 men do. 3 I said to them, "The gates of Jerusalem are not to be opened until the
sun is hot. While the gatekeepers are still
on duty, have them shut the doors and
bar them. Also appoint residents of Jerusalem as guards, some at their posts and
some near their own houses."

The List of the Exiles Who Returned

4 Now the city was large and spacious,
7:4 [e]Ne 11:1 but there were few people in it,[e] and the
houses had not yet been rebuilt. 5 So my
God put it into my heart to assemble the
nobles, the officials and the common
people for registration by families. I
found the genealogical record of those
who had been the first to return. This is
what I found written there:

6 These are the people of the province who came up from the captivi-
ty of the exiles[f] whom Nebuchad- 7:6 [f]2Ch 36:20;
nezzar king of Babylon had taken Ezr 2:1-70;
captive (they returned to Jerusalem Ne 1:2
and Judah, each to his own town, 7 in
company with Zerubbabel,[g] Jeshua, 7:7 [g]1Ch 3:19;
Nehemiah, Azariah, Raamiah, Na- Ezr 2:2
hamani, Mordecai, Bilshan, Mispe-
reth, Bigvai, Nehum and Baanah):

The list of the men of Israel:

8 the descendants of Parosh 2,172
9 of Shephatiah 372
10 of Arah 652
11 of Pahath-Moab (through
the line of Jeshua and
Joab) 2,818
12 of Elam 1,254
13 of Zattu 845
14 of Zaccai 760
15 of Binnui 648
16 of Bebai 628
17 of Azgad 2,322
18 of Adonikam 667
19 of Bigvai 2,067
20 of Adin[h] 655 7:20 [h]Ezr 8:6
21 of Ater (through Hezekiah) 98
22 of Hashum 328
23 of Bezai 324
24 of Hariph 112
25 of Gibeon 95

26 the men of Bethlehem and
Netophah[i] 188 7:26 [i]2Sa 23:28; 1Ch 2:54
27 of Anathoth[j] 128
28 of Beth Azmaveth 42 7:27 [j]Jos 21:18
29 of Kiriath Jearim, Kephirah[k]
and Beeroth[l] 743 7:29 [k]Jos 18:26
30 of Ramah and Geba 621 [l]Jos 18:25
31 of Micmash 122
32 of Bethel and Ai[m] 123 7:32 [m]Ge 12:8
33 of the other Nebo 52
34 of the other Elam 1,254
35 of Harim 320
36 of Jericho[n] 345
37 of Lod, Hadid and Ono[o] 721 7:36 [n]Ne 3:2
38 of Senaah 3,930 7:37 [o]1Ch 8:12

39 The priests:

the descendants of Jedaiah
(through the family
of Jeshua) 973
40 of Immer 1,052
41 of Pashhur 1,247
42 of Harim 1,017

[a] 2 Or *Hanani, that is,*

43 The Levites:

the descendants of Jeshua
(through Kadmiel through
the line of Hodaviah) 74

44 The singers:[p]

the descendants of Asaph 148

45 The gatekeepers:[q]

the descendants of
Shallum, Ater, Talmon,
Akkub, Hatita and
Shobai 138

46 The temple servants:[r]

the descendants of
Ziha, Hasupha, Tabbaoth,
47 Keros, Sia, Padon,
48 Lebana, Hagaba, Shalmai,
49 Hanan, Giddel, Gahar,
50 Reaiah, Rezin, Nekoda,
51 Gazzam, Uzza, Paseah,
52 Besai, Meunim, Nephussim,
53 Bakbuk, Hakupha, Harhur,
54 Bazluth, Mehida, Harsha,
55 Barkos, Sisera, Temah,
56 Neziah and Hatipha

57 The descendants of the servants of Solomon:

the descendants of
Sotai, Sophereth, Perida,
58 Jaala, Darkon, Giddel,
59 Shephatiah, Hattil,
Pokereth-Hazzebaim and
Amon

60 The temple servants and the
descendants of the servants
of Solomon[s] 392

61 The following came up from the towns of Tel Melah, Tel Harsha, Kerub, Addon and Immer, but they could not show that their families were descended from Israel:

62 the descendants of
Delaiah, Tobiah and
Nekoda 642

63 And from among the priests:

the descendants of
Hobaiah, Hakkoz and
Barzillai (a man who had
married a daughter of
Barzillai the Gileadite and
was called by that name).

7:44 [p] Ne 11:23
7:45 [q] 1Ch 9:17
7:46 [r] Ne 3:26
7:60 [s] 1Ch 9:2

64 These searched for their family records, but they could not find them and so were excluded from the priesthood as unclean. 65 The governor, therefore, ordered them not to eat any of the most sacred food until there should be a priest ministering with the Urim and Thummim.[t]

66 The whole company numbered 42,360, 67 besides their 7,337 menservants and maidservants; and they also had 245 men and women singers. 68 There were 736 horses, 245 mules,[a] 69 435 camels and 6,720 donkeys.

70 Some of the heads of the families contributed to the work. The governor gave to the treasury 1,000 drachmas[b] of gold, 50 bowls and 530 garments for priests. 71 Some of the heads of the families[u] gave to the treasury for the work 20,000 drachmas[c] of gold and 2,200 minas[d] of silver. 72 The total given by the rest of the people was 20,000 drachmas of gold, 2,000 minas[e] of silver and 67 garments for priests.[v]

73 The priests, the Levites, the gatekeepers, the singers and the temple servants,[w] along with certain of the people and the rest of the Israelites, settled in their own towns.[x]

Ezra Reads the Law

When the seventh month came and the Israelites had settled in their towns,[y]

8 1 all the people assembled as one man in the square before the Water Gate.[z] They told Ezra the scribe to bring out the Book of the Law of Moses,[a] which the LORD had commanded for Israel.

2 So on the first day of the seventh month[b] Ezra the priest brought the Law[c] before the assembly, which was made up of men and women and all who were able to understand. 3 He read it aloud from daybreak till noon as he

[a] *68* Some Hebrew manuscripts (see also Ezra 2:66); most Hebrew manuscripts do not have this verse. [b] *70* That is, about 19 pounds (about 8.5 kilograms) [c] *71* That is, about 375 pounds (about 170 kilograms); also in verse 72 [d] *71* That is, about 1 1/3 tons (about 1.2 metric tons)
[e] *72* That is, about 1 1/4 tons (about 1.1 metric tons)

7:65 [t] Ex 28:30; Ne 8:9
7:71 [u] 1Ch 29:7
7:72 [v] Ex 25:2
7:73 [w] Ne 1:10; Ps 34:22; 103:21; 113:1; 135:1 [x] Ezr 3:1; Ne 11:1 [y] Ezr 3:1
8:1 [z] Ne 3:26 [a] Dt 28:61; 2Ch 34:15; Ezr 7:6
8:2 [b] Lev 23:23-25; Nu 29:1-6 [c] Dt 31:11

DISCOVERY 113

REVIVAL AT THE WATER GATE

After the Israelites had recommitted themselves to God they met together at the Water Gate. There Ezra "praised the LORD, the great God; and all the people lifted their hands and responded 'Amen! Amen!' " (Nehemiah 8:6).

The immediate cause for this revival was Ezra's public reading and explanation of God's law. First he constructed a wooden platform where he and 13 other men, most likely priests, stood. Ezra started reading at dawn and didn't stop until noon. In addition to Ezra's reading, a number of Levites assisted by explaining to the people what the words meant (verse 8).

When Ezra opened the book to begin reading, the people rose to their feet in respect (verse 5). They paid close attention to what Ezra was reading. As the people listened, they were struck by how far their lives had drifted from God's intended course. In genuine remorse they wept together (verse 9), then raised their hands and shouted "Amen! Amen!," showing that they were again reaching out to God and agreeing with everything they had heard from his Word (verse 6). After the people had renewed their commitment to God, Ezra directed them to go home and celebrate (verse 12).

As followers of Jesus we can gather at our own "Water Gate"—the place where we listen to the Word of God. The apostle Paul praised the noble character of the Berean Christians, "for they received the message with great eagerness and examined the Scriptures every day to see if what Paul said was true" (Acts 17:11). Although it is not explicitly stated, the implication seems to be that the Bereans met regularly in an early version of Bible study groups. Paul also encouraged Timothy: "Until I come, devote yourself to the public reading of Scripture, to preaching and to teaching" (1 Timothy 4:13–14). It is difficult for even the most well-intentioned believers to survive without the fellowship of other Christians. While a private devotional time, during which an individual believer meets with Jesus alone, is critical to spiritual well-being, it should not replace regular attendance at worship services, where God's Word is read and explained and our response of praise and worship is offered.

In Matthew 18:12 Jesus spoke of the shepherd who leaves his flock in search of one sheep that has wandered off. Jesus Christ is our shepherd, and he knows the dangers that lurk in the shadows for those who leave the flock in search of "greener pastures." In spite of difficulties, Jesus wants us to join God's people regularly for worship and instruction. If we are offended, he teaches how to resolve the conflicts (Matthew 18:15–17). The writer to the Hebrews urged believers not to "give up meeting together, as some are in the habit of doing" but rather to "encourage one another—and all the more as you see the Day approaching" (Hebrews 10:25).

Self-Discovery: *Think about the last time a believer from your fellowship reached out to you with an encouraging word or even a simple expression of interest. Make it a point this week to encourage a fellow brother or sister in Jesus.*

GO TO DISCOVERY 114 ON PAGE 620

8:3 faced the square before the Water Gate[d]
d Ne 3:26 in the presence of the men, women and
others who could understand. And all
the people listened attentively to the
Book of the Law.
8:4 4Ezra the scribe stood on a high
e 2Ch 6:13 wooden platform[e] built for the occasion.
Beside him on his right stood Mattithi-
ah, Shema, Anaiah, Uriah, Hilkiah and
Maaseiah; and on his left were Pedaiah,
Mishael, Malkijah, Hashum, Hashbad-
danah, Zechariah and Meshullam.
5Ezra opened the book. All the people
8:5 could see him because he was standing[f]
f Jdg 3:20 above them; and as he opened it, the
people all stood up. 6Ezra praised the
8:6 LORD, the great God; and all the people
g Ex 4:31; lifted their hands[g] and responded,
Ezr 9:5; 1Ti 2:8 "Amen! Amen!" Then they bowed down
and worshiped the LORD with their faces
to the ground.
8:7 7The Levites[h]—Jeshua, Bani, Sherebi-
h Ezr 10:23 ah, Jamin, Akkub, Shabbethai, Hodiah,
i Lev 10:11; 2Ch 17:7 Maaseiah, Kelita, Azariah, Jozabad, Hanan and Pelaiah—instructed[i] the people
in the Law while the people were standing there. 8They read from the Book of
the Law of God, making it clear[a] and giving the meaning so that the people could
understand what was being read.
8:9 9Then Nehemiah the governor, Ezra
j Ne 7:1,65,70 the priest and scribe, and the Levites[j]
k Dt 12:7,12; 16:14-15 who were instructing the people said to
them all, "This day is sacred to the LORD
your God. Do not mourn or weep."[k] For
all the people had been weeping as they
listened to the words of the Law.
10Nehemiah said, "Go and enjoy
choice food and sweet drinks, and send
8:10 some to those who have nothing[l] pre-
l 1Sa 25:8; Lk 14:12-14 pared. This day is sacred to our Lord. Do
m Lev 23:40; Dt 12:18; 16:11, 14-15 not grieve, for the joy[m] of the LORD is
your strength."
11The Levites calmed all the people,
saying, "Be still, for this is a sacred day.
Do not grieve."
12Then all the people went away to eat
8:12 and drink, to send portions of food and
n Est 9:22 to celebrate with great joy,[n] because they
now understood the words that had
been made known to them.
13On the second day of the month, the
heads of all the families, along with the
priests and the Levites, gathered around
Ezra the scribe to give attention to the
words of the Law. 14They found written
in the Law, which the LORD had commanded through Moses, that the Israelites were to live in booths during the
feast of the seventh month 15and that
they should proclaim this word and
spread it throughout their towns and in
Jerusalem: "Go out into the hill country
and bring back branches from olive and
wild olive trees, and from myrtles, palms
and shade trees, to make booths"—as it
is written.[b]
16So the people went out and brought
back branches and built themselves
booths on their own roofs, in their
courtyards, in the courts of the house of
God and in the square by the Water
Gate and the one by the Gate of Ephra- 8:16
im.[o] 17The whole company that had re- o 2Ki 14:13;
turned from exile built booths and lived Ne 12:39
in them. From the days of Joshua son of
Nun until that day, the Israelites had not
celebrated[p] it like this. And their joy was 8:17 p 2Ch 7:8; 8:13;
very great. 30:21
18Day after day, from the first day to 8:18
the last, Ezra read[q] from the Book of the q Dt 31:11
Law of God. They celebrated the feast r Lev 23:36,40;
for seven days, and on the eighth day, in Nu 29:35
accordance with the regulation,[r] there
was an assembly.

The Israelites Confess Their Sins

9 On the twenty-fourth day of the
same month, the Israelites gath-
ered together, fasting and wearing sack- 9:1
cloth and having dust on their heads.[s] s Jos 7:6;
2Those of Israelite descent had separat- 1Sa 4:12
ed themselves from all foreigners.[t] They 9:2
stood in their places and confessed their t Ne 13:3,30
sins and the wickedness of their fa- u Ezr 10:11;
thers.[u] 3They stood where they were and Ps 106:6
read from the Book of the Law of the
LORD their God for a quarter of the day,
and spent another quarter in confession
and in worshiping the LORD their God.
4Standing on the stairs were the Le-
vites[v]—Jeshua, Bani, Kadmiel, Shebani- 9:4 v Ezr 10:23
ah, Bunni, Sherebiah, Bani and Kena-
ni—who called with loud voices to the
LORD their God. 5And the Levites—Jeshua, Kadmiel, Bani, Hashabneiah, Sherebiah, Hodiah, Shebaniah and Pethahiah—said: "Stand up and praise the LORD 9:5
your God,[w] who is from everlasting to w Ps 78:4
everlasting.[c]"

"Blessed be your glorious name,
and may it be exalted above all

[a] 8 Or *God, translating it* [b] 15 See Lev. 23:37-40.
[c] 5 Or *God for ever and ever*

blessing and praise. 6 You alone are the LORD.[x] You made the heavens,[y] even the highest heavens, and all their starry host, the earth[z] and all that is on it, the seas[a] and all that is in them.[b] You give life to everything, and the multitudes of heaven worship you.

7 "You are the LORD God, who chose Abram and brought him out of Ur of the Chaldeans[c] and named him Abraham.[d] 8 You found his heart faithful to you, and you made a covenant with him to give to his descendants the land of the Canaanites, Hittites, Amorites, Perizzites, Jebusites and Girgashites.[e] You have kept your promise[f] because you are righteous.[g]

9 "You saw the suffering of our forefathers in Egypt;[h] you heard their cry at the Red Sea.[a][i] 10 You sent miraculous signs[j] and wonders against Pharaoh, against all his officials and all the people of his land, for you knew how arrogantly the Egyptians treated them. You made a name[k] for yourself, which remains to this day. 11 You divided the sea before them,[l] so that they passed through it on dry ground, but you hurled their pursuers into the depths, like a stone into mighty waters.[m] 12 By day you led[n] them with a pillar of cloud,[o] and by night with a pillar of fire to give them light on the way they were to take.

13 "You came down on Mount Sinai;[p] you spoke[q] to them from heaven. You gave them regulations and laws that are just[r] and right, and decrees and commands that are good.[s] 14 You made known to them your holy Sabbath[t] and gave them commands, decrees and laws through your servant Moses. 15 In their hunger you gave them bread from heaven[u] and in their thirst you brought them water from the rock;[v] you told them to go in and take possession of the land you had sworn with uplifted hand to give them.[w]

16 "But they, our forefathers, became arrogant and stiff-necked, and did not obey your commands.[x] 17 They refused to listen and failed to remember[y] the miracles you performed among them. They became stiff-necked and in their rebellion appointed a leader in order to return to their slavery.[z] But you are a forgiving God, gracious and compassionate, slow to anger[a] and abounding in love.[b] Therefore you did not desert them,[c] 18 even when they cast for themselves an image of a calf[d] and said, 'This is your god, who brought you up out of Egypt,' or when they committed awful blasphemies.

19 "Because of your great compassion you did not abandon them in the desert. By day the pillar of cloud did not cease to guide them on their path, nor the pillar of fire by night to shine on the way they were to take. 20 You gave your good Spirit[e] to instruct them. You did not withhold your manna[f] from their mouths, and you gave them water[g] for their thirst. 21 For forty

9:6 [x] Dt 6:4 [y] 2Ki 19:15 [z] Ge 1:1; Isa 37:16 [a] Ps 95:5 [b] Dt 10:14
9:7 [c] Ge 11:31 [d] Ge 17:5
9:8 [e] Ge 15:18-21 [f] Jos 21:45 [g] Ge 15:6; Ezr 9:15
9:9 [h] Ex 3:7 [i] Ex 14:10-30
9:10 [j] Ex 10:1
9:10 [k] Jer 32:20; Da 9:15
9:11 [l] Ex 14:21; Ps 78:13 [m] Ex 15:4-5,10; Heb 11:29
9:12 [n] Ex 15:13 [o] Ex 13:21
9:13 [p] Ex 19:11 [q] Ex 19:19 [r] Ps 119:137 [s] Ex 20:1
9:14 [t] Ge 2:3; Ex 20:8-11
9:15 [u] Ex 16:4; Jn 6:31 [v] Ex 17:6; Nu 20:7-13 [w] Dt 1:8,21
9:16 [x] Dt 1:26-33; 31:29
9:17 [y] Ps 78:42 [z] Nu 14:1-4 [a] Ex 34:6 [b] Nu 14:17-19 [c] Ps 78:11
9:18 [d] Ex 32:4
9:20 [e] Nu 11:17; Isa 63:11,14 [f] Ex 16:15 [g] Ex 17:6

[a] 9 Hebrew *Yam Suph*; that is, Sea of Reeds

JESUS AND YOU

STARTING OVER

Nehemiah 9 consists of an awe-inspiring prayer that reminded the people of how their God had cared for them in the past. God had been at work among his people through all the centuries of human history, guiding them, protecting them and continually calling them to walk with him. This prayer undoubtedly helped the people to place their current experiences in proper perspective—to measure them against God's eternal purposes. Although they were in a very real sense starting over, they could still point to an unchanging hope for the future. God had never reneged on his promises, and they could take him at his word about those promises yet unfulfilled. God had promised an Anointed One (Messiah), and he would keep that promise. Stephen's sermon in Acts 7 had a similar emphasis, tracing the hand of God in the history of Israel from the time of the patriarchs until Jesus—"the Righteous One"—had come to his people (Acts 7:52). Just as God's people throughout history have needed gentle reminders of his faithfulness, so we need to recall that the God who has been there all along can still be counted on in our lives today (1 Corinthians 1:8–9; 1 Thessalonians 5:23–24; Hebrews 10:23).

9:21 years you sustained them in the
h Dt 2:7 i Dt 8:4 desert; they lacked nothing,[h] their
clothes did not wear out nor did
their feet become swollen.[i]
22 "You gave them kingdoms and
nations, allotting to them even the
9:22 remotest frontiers. They took over
j Nu 21:21 the country of Sihon[a][j] king of
k Nu 21:33 Heshbon and the country of Og
king of Bashan.[k] 23 You made their
sons as numerous as the stars in
the sky, and you brought them into
the land that you told their fathers
to enter and possess. 24 Their sons
9:24 went in and took possession of the
l Jos 11:23 land.[l] You subdued before them the
Canaanites, who lived in the land;
you handed the Canaanites over to
them, along with their kings and
the peoples of the land, to deal with
them as they pleased. 25 They captured
fortified cities and fertile
land; they took possession of
houses filled with all kinds of good
things, wells already dug, vineyards,
olive groves and fruit trees in abundance.
9:25 dance. They ate to the full and were
m Dt 6:10-12 well-nourished;[m] they reveled in
n Nu 13:27; your great goodness.[n]
Dt 32:12-15 26 "But they were disobedient
9:26 and rebelled against you; they put
o 1Ki 14:9 your law behind their backs.[o] They
p Mt 21:35-36 killed your prophets,[p] who had ad-
q Jdg 2:12-13 monished them in order to turn
them back to you; they committed
9:27 awful blasphemies.[q] 27 So you hand-
r Jdg 2:14 ed them over to their enemies,[r]
s Ps 106:45 who oppressed them. But when
they were oppressed they cried out
to you. From heaven you heard
them, and in your great compassion[s]
you gave them deliverers, who
rescued them from the hand of
their enemies.
28 "But as soon as they were at
rest, they again did what was evil in
your sight. Then you abandoned
them to the hand of their enemies
so that they ruled over them. And
when they cried out to you again,
9:28 you heard from heaven, and in your
t Ps 106:43 compassion you delivered them[t]
time after time.
29 "You warned them to return to
9:29 your law, but they became arro-
u Ps 5:5; gant[u] and disobeyed your com-
Isa 2:11; Jer 43:2 mands. They sinned against your
ordinances, by which a man will 9:29
live if he obeys them.[v] Stubbornly v Dt 30:16
they turned their backs on you, be- w Zec 7:11-12
came stiff-necked and refused to
listen.[w] 30 For many years you were
patient with them. By your Spirit
you admonished them through 9:30
your prophets.[x] Yet they paid no at- x 2Ki 17:13-18;
tention, so you handed them over 2Ch 36:16
to the neighboring peoples. 31 But
in your great mercy you did not put
an end[y] to them or abandon them, 9:31
for you are a gracious and merciful y Isa 48:9;
God. Jer 4:27
32 "Now therefore, O our God, the 9:32
great, mighty[z] and awesome God, z Ps 24:8 a Dt 7:9
who keeps his covenant of love,[a] do
not let all this hardship seem tri-
fling in your eyes—the hardship
that has come upon us, upon our
kings and leaders, upon our priests
and prophets, upon our fathers and
all your people, from the days of
the kings of Assyria until today.
33 In all that has happened to us, 9:33
you have been just;[b] you have acted b Ge 18:25
faithfully, while we did wrong.[c] c Jer 44:3;
34 Our kings,[d] our leaders, our Da 9:7-8,14
priests and our fathers[e] did not fol- 9:34
low your law; they did not pay at- d 2Ki 23:11 e Jer 44:17
tention to your commands or the
warnings you gave them. 35 Even
while they were in their kingdom,
enjoying your great goodness[f] to 9:35
them in the spacious and fertile f Isa 63:7
land you gave them, they did not g Dt 28:45-48
serve you[g] or turn from their evil
ways.
36 "But see, we are slaves[h] today, 9:36 h Dt 28:48;
slaves in the land you gave our fore- Ezr 9:9
fathers so they could eat its fruit
and the other good things it produces. 37 Because of our sins, its
abundant harvest goes to the kings
you have placed over us. They rule
over our bodies and our cattle as 9:37
they please. We are in great dis- i Dt 28:33;
tress.[i] La 5:5

The Agreement of the People

38 "In view of all this, we are making a 9:38
binding agreement,[j] putting it in writ- j 2Ch 23:16
ing,[k] and our leaders, our Levites and k Isa 44:5
our priests are affixing their seals to it."

[a] 22 One Hebrew manuscript and Septuagint; most Hebrew manuscripts *Sihon, that is, the country of the*

10 Those who sealed it were:

Nehemiah the governor, the son of Hacaliah.

10:2 [l]Ezr 2:2
Zedekiah, 2Seraiah,[l] Azariah, Jeremiah,
10:3 [m]1Ch 9:12
3Pashhur,[m] Amariah, Malkijah,
4Hattush, Shebaniah, Malluch,
10:5 [n]1Ch 24:8
5Harim,[n] Meremoth, Obadiah,
6Daniel, Ginnethon, Baruch,
7Meshullam, Abijah, Mijamin,
8Maaziah, Bilgai and Shemaiah.
These were the priests.

10:9 [o]Ne 12:1
9The Levites:[o]

Jeshua son of Azaniah, Binnui of the sons of Henadad, Kadmiel,
10and their associates: Shebaniah, Hodiah, Kelita, Pelaiah, Hanan,
11Mica, Rehob, Hashabiah,
12Zaccur, Sherebiah, Shebaniah,
13Hodiah, Bani and Beninu.

14The leaders of the people:

Parosh, Pahath-Moab, Elam, Zattu, Bani,
15Bunni, Azgad, Bebai,
10:16 [p]Ezr 8:6
16Adonijah, Bigvai, Adin,[p]
17Ater, Hezekiah, Azzur,
18Hodiah, Hashum, Bezai,
19Hariph, Anathoth, Nebai,
10:20 [q]1Ch 24:15
20Magpiash, Meshullam, Hezir,[q]
21Meshezabel, Zadok, Jaddua,
22Pelatiah, Hanan, Anaiah,
10:23 [r]Ne 7:2
23Hoshea, Hananiah,[r] Hasshub,
24Hallohesh, Pilha, Shobek,
25Rehum, Hashabnah, Maaseiah,
26Ahiah, Hanan, Anan,
27Malluch, Harim and Baanah.

28"The rest of the people—
10:28 [s]Ps 135:1 [t]2Ch 6:26; Ne 9:2
priests, Levites, gatekeepers,
singers, temple servants[s] and all
who separated themselves from the
neighboring peoples[t] for the sake
of the Law of God, together with
their wives and all their sons and
daughters who are able to understand— 29all these now join their
brothers the nobles, and bind
10:29 [u]Nu 5:21; Ps 119:106
themselves with a curse and an
oath[u] to follow the Law of God giv-
en through Moses the servant of
God and to obey carefully all the
commands, regulations and decrees of the LORD our Lord.
30"We promise not to give our
daughters in marriage to the peoples around us or take their daugh-
ters for our sons.[v] 10:30 [v]Ex 34:16; Dt 7:3; Ne 13:23
31"When the neighboring peo-
ples bring merchandise or grain to
sell on the Sabbath,[w] we will not 10:31 [w]Ne 13:16,18; Jer 17:27; Eze 23:38; Am 8:5 [x]Ex 23:11; Lev 25:1-7 [y]Dt 15:1
buy from them on the Sabbath or
on any holy day. Every seventh year
we will forgo working the land[x] and
will cancel all debts.[y]
32"We assume the responsibility
for carrying out the commands to
give a third of a shekel[a] each year
for the service of the house of our
God: 33for the bread set out on the
table;[z] for the regular grain offer- 10:33 [z]Lev 24:6 [a]Nu 10:10; Ps 81:3; Isa 1:14 [b]2Ch 24:5
ings and burnt offerings; for the of-
ferings on the Sabbaths, New
Moon[a] festivals and appointed
feasts; for the holy offerings; for sin
offerings to make atonement for Israel; and for all the duties of the
house of our God.[b]
34"We—the priests, the Levites
and the people—have cast lots[c] to 10:34 [c]Lev 16:8 [d]Ne 13:31
determine when each of our fami-
lies is to bring to the house of our
God at set times each year a contribution of wood[d] to burn on the altar of the LORD our God, as it is
written in the Law.
35"We also assume responsibility
for bringing to the house of the
LORD each year the firstfruits[e] of 10:35 [e]Ex 22:29; 23:19; Nu 18:12 [f]Dt 26:1-11
our crops and of every fruit tree.[f]
36"As it is also written in the Law,
we will bring the firstborn[g] of our 10:36 [g]Ex 13:2; Nu 18:14-16 [h]Ne 13:31
sons and of our cattle, of our herds
and of our flocks to the house of
our God, to the priests ministering
there.[h]
37"Moreover, we will bring to the
storerooms of the house of our
God, to the priests, the first of our
ground meal, of our ⌊grain⌋ offerings, of the fruit of all our trees and
of our new wine and oil.[i] And we 10:37 [i]Lev 23:17; Nu 18:12 [j]Lev 27:30; Nu 18:21 [k]Dt 14:22-29 [l]Eze 44:30
will bring a tithe[j] of our crops to
the Levites,[k] for it is the Levites
who collect the tithes in all the
towns where we work.[l] 38A priest
descended from Aaron is to accompany the Levites when they receive the tithes, and the Levites are
to bring a tenth of the tithes[m] up to 10:38 [m]Nu 18:26
the house of our God, to the store-

[a] *32* That is, about 1/8 ounce (about 4 grams)

rooms of the treasury. 39The people
of Israel, including the Levites, are
to bring their contributions of
grain, new wine and oil to the
storerooms where the articles for
the sanctuary are kept and where
the ministering priests, the gatekeepers and the singers stay.

10:39 [n] Dt 12:6; Ne 13:11,12

"We will not neglect the house of
our God."[n]

The New Residents of Jerusalem

11 Now the leaders of the people
settled in Jerusalem, and the

11:1 [o] Ne 7:4 [p] ver 18; Isa 48:2; 52:1; 64:10; Zec 14:20-21 [q] Ne 7:73

rest of the people cast lots to bring one
out of every ten to live in Jerusalem,[o] the
holy city,[p] while the remaining nine were
to stay in their own towns.[q] 2The people
commended all the men who volunteered to live in Jerusalem.

3These are the provincial leaders who
settled in Jerusalem (now some Israelites, priests, Levites, temple servants
and descendants of Solomon's servants

11:3 [r] 1Ch 9:2-3; Ezr 2:1

lived in the towns of Judah, each on his
own property in the various towns,[r]
4while other people from both Judah

11:4 [s] Ezr 1:5 [t] Ezr 2:70

and Benjamin[s] lived in Jerusalem):[t]

From the descendants of Judah:

Athaiah son of Uzziah, the son of
Zechariah, the son of Amariah, the
son of Shephatiah, the son of Mahalalel, a descendant of Perez; 5and
Maaseiah son of Baruch, the son of
Col-Hozeh, the son of Hazaiah, the
son of Adaiah, the son of Joiarib,
the son of Zechariah, a descendant
of Shelah. 6The descendants of Perez who lived in Jerusalem totaled
468 able men.

7From the descendants of Benjamin:

Sallu son of Meshullam, the son of
Joed, the son of Pedaiah, the son of
Kolaiah, the son of Maaseiah, the
son of Ithiel, the son of Jeshaiah,
8and his followers, Gabbai and Sal-
lai—928 men. 9Joel son of Zicri was
their chief officer, and Judah son of
Hassenuah was over the Second
District of the city.

10From the priests:

Jedaiah; the son of Joiarib; Jakin;

11:11 [u] 2Ki 25:18; Ezr 2:2

11Seraiah[u] son of Hilkiah, the son of
Meshullam, the son of Zadok, the
son of Meraioth, the son of Ahitub,[v] supervisor in the house of

11:11 [v] Ezr 7:2

God, 12and their associates, who
carried on work for the temple—
822 men; Adaiah son of Jeroham,
the son of Pelaliah, the son of Amzi,
the son of Zechariah, the son of
Pashhur, the son of Malkijah, 13and
his associates, who were heads of
families—242 men; Amashsai son
of Azarel, the son of Ahzai, the son
of Meshillemoth, the son of Immer,
14and his[a] associates, who were
able men—128. Their chief officer
was Zabdiel son of Haggedolim.

15From the Levites:

Shemaiah son of Hasshub, the son
of Azrikam, the son of Hashabiah,

11:16 [w] Ezr 10:15 [x] Ezr 8:33

the son of Bunni; 16Shabbethai[w]
and Jozabad,[x] two of the heads of
the Levites, who had charge of the
outside work of the house of God;

11:17 [y] 1Ch 9:15; Ne 12:8 [z] 2Ch 5:12 [a] 1Ch 25:1

17Mattaniah[y] son of Mica, the son
of Zabdi, the son of Asaph,[z] the director who led in thanksgiving and
prayer; Bakbukiah, second among
his associates; and Abda son of
Shammua, the son of Galal, the son

11:18 [b] Rev 21:2

of Jeduthun.[a] 18The Levites in the
holy city[b] totaled 284.

19The gatekeepers:

Akkub, Talmon and their associates, who kept watch at the gates—
172 men.

20The rest of the Israelites, with the
priests and Levites, were in all the towns
of Judah, each on his ancestral property.

11:21 [c] Ezr 2:43; Ne 3:26

21The temple servants[c] lived on the
hill of Ophel, and Ziha and Gishpa were
in charge of them.

22The chief officer of the Levites in Je-

11:22 [d] 1Ch 9:15

rusalem was Uzzi son of Bani, the son of
Hashabiah, the son of Mattaniah,[d] the
son of Mica. Uzzi was one of Asaph's descendants, who were the singers responsible for the service of the house of

11:23 [e] Ne 7:44

God. 23The singers[e] were under the
king's orders, which regulated their daily activity.

11:24 [f] Ge 38:30

24Pethahiah son of Meshezabel, one of
the descendants of Zerah[f] son of Judah,
was the king's agent in all affairs relating
to the people.

[a] 14 Most Septuagint manuscripts; Hebrew *their*

25 As for the villages with their fields, some of the people of Judah lived in Kiriath Arba[g] and its surrounding settlements, in Dibon[h] and its settlements, in Jekabzeel and its villages, 26 in Jeshua, in Moladah, in Beth Pelet,[i] 27 in Hazar Shual, in Beersheba[j] and its settlements, 28 in Ziklag,[k] in Meconah and its settlements, 29 in En Rimmon, in Zorah,[l] in Jarmuth,[m] 30 Zanoah, Adullam[n] and their villages, in Lachish[o] and its fields, and in Azekah[p] and its settlements. So they were living all the way from Beersheba[q] to the Valley of Hinnom.

31 The descendants of the Benjamites from Geba[r] lived in Micmash,[s] Aija, Bethel and its settlements, 32 in Anathoth,[t] Nob[u] and Ananiah, 33 in Hazor,[v] Ramah and Gittaim,[w] 34 in Hadid, Zeboim[x] and Neballat, 35 in Lod and Ono,[y] and in the Valley of the Craftsmen.

36 Some of the divisions of the Levites of Judah settled in Benjamin.

11:25 g Ge 35:27; Jos 14:15 h Nu 21:30
11:26 i Jos 15:27
11:27 j Ge 21:14
11:28 k 1Sa 27:6
11:29 l Jos 15:33 m Jos 10:3
11:30 n Jos 15:35 o Jos 10:3 p Jos 10:10 q Jos 15:28
11:31 r Jos 21:17; Isa 10:29 s 1Sa 13:2
11:32 t Jos 21:18; Isa 10:30 u 1Sa 21:1
11:33 v Jos 11:1 w 2Sa 4:3
11:34 x 1Sa 13:18
11:35 y 1Ch 8:12

Priests and Levites

12 These were the priests[z] and Levites who returned with Zerubbabel[a] son of Shealtiel and with Jeshua:[b]

Seraiah,[c] Jeremiah, Ezra,
2 Amariah, Malluch, Hattush,
3 Shecaniah, Rehum, Meremoth,
4 Iddo,[d] Ginnethon,[a] Abijah,[e]
5 Mijamin,[b] Moadiah, Bilgah,
6 Shemaiah, Joiarib, Jedaiah,[f]
7 Sallu, Amok, Hilkiah and Jedaiah.

These were the leaders of the priests and their associates in the days of Jeshua.

8 The Levites were Jeshua, Binnui, Kadmiel, Sherebiah, Judah, and also Mattaniah,[g] who, together with his associates, was in charge of the songs of thanksgiving. 9 Bakbukiah and Unni, their associates, stood opposite them in the services.

10 Jeshua was the father of Joiakim, Joiakim the father of Eliashib,[h] Eliashib the father of Joiada, 11 Joiada the father of Jonathan, and Jonathan the father of Jaddua.

12 In the days of Joiakim, these were the heads of the priestly families:

of Seraiah's family, Meraiah;
of Jeremiah's, Hananiah;
13 of Ezra's, Meshullam;
of Amariah's, Jehohanan;
14 of Malluch's, Jonathan;
of Shecaniah's,[c] Joseph;
15 of Harim's, Adna;
of Meremoth's,[d] Helkai;
16 of Iddo's,[i] Zechariah;
of Ginnethon's, Meshullam;
17 of Abijah's, Zicri;
of Miniamin's and of Moadiah's, Piltai;
18 of Bilgah's, Shammua;
of Shemaiah's, Jehonathan;
19 of Joiarib's, Mattenai;
of Jedaiah's, Uzzi;
20 of Sallu's, Kallai;
of Amok's, Eber;
21 of Hilkiah's, Hashabiah;
of Jedaiah's, Nethanel.

22 The family heads of the Levites in the days of Eliashib, Joiada, Johanan and Jaddua, as well as those of the priests, were recorded in the reign of Darius the Persian. 23 The family heads among the descendants of Levi up to the time of Johanan son of Eliashib were recorded in the book of the annals. 24 And the leaders of the Levites[j] were Hashabiah, Sherebiah, Jeshua son of Kadmiel, and their associates, who stood opposite them to give praise and thanksgiving, one section responding to the other, as prescribed by David the man of God.

25 Mattaniah, Bakbukiah, Obadiah, Meshullam, Talmon and Akkub were gatekeepers who guarded the storerooms at the gates. 26 They served in the days of Joiakim son of Jeshua, the son of Jozadak, and in the days of Nehemiah the governor and of Ezra the priest and scribe.

12:1 z Ne 10:1-8 a 1Ch 3:19 b Ezr 2:2 c Ezr 2:2
12:4 d Zec 1:1 e Lk 1:5
12:6 f 1Ch 24:7
12:8 g Ne 11:17
12:10 h Ezr 10:24
12:16 i ver 4
12:24 j Ezr 2:40

Dedication of the Wall of Jerusalem

27 At the dedication[k] of the wall of Jerusalem, the Levites were sought out from where they lived and were brought to Jerusalem to celebrate joyfully the dedication with songs of thanksgiving and with the music of cymbals,[l] harps and lyres.[m] 28 The singers also were brought together from the region around Jerusalem—from the villages of the Netophathites,[n] 29 from Beth Gilgal, and from the area of Geba and Azmaveth, for the singers had built villages for

12:27 k Dt 20:5 l 2Sa 6:5 m 1Ch 15:16,28; 25:6; Ps 92:3
12:28 n 1Ch 2:54; 9:16

a *4* Many Hebrew manuscripts and Vulgate (see also Neh. 12:16); most Hebrew manuscripts *Ginnethoi* *b* *5* A variant of *Miniamin*
c *14* Very many Hebrew manuscripts, some Septuagint manuscripts and Syriac (see also Neh. 12:3); most Hebrew manuscripts *Shebaniah's*
d *15* Some Septuagint manuscripts (see also Neh. 12:3); Hebrew *Meraioth's*

themselves around Jerusalem. [30]When
the priests and Levites had purified
12:30 themselves ceremonially, they purified
[o]Ex 19:10; Job 1:5 the people,[o] the gates and the wall.
[31]I had the leaders of Judah go up on
top[a] of the wall. I also assigned two large
choirs to give thanks. One was to pro-
12:31 ceed on top[b] of the wall to the right, to-
[p]Ne 2:13 ward the Dung Gate.[p] [32]Hoshaiah and
half the leaders of Judah followed them,
[33]along with Azariah, Ezra, Meshullam,
12:34 [34]Judah, Benjamin,[q] Shemaiah, Jeremi-
[q]Ezr 1:5 ah, [35]as well as some priests with trum-
12:35 pets,[r] and also Zechariah son of Jona-
[r]Ezr 3:10 than, the son of Shemaiah, the son of
Mattaniah, the son of Micaiah, the son
of Zaccur, the son of Asaph, [36]and his associates—Shemaiah, Azarel, Milalai,
12:36 Gilalai, Maai, Nethanel, Judah and Ha-
[s]1Ch 15:16 nani—with musical instruments[s] ⌞pre-
[t]2Ch 8:14 scribed by⌟ David the man of God.[t]
[u]Ezr 7:6 Ezra[u] the scribe led the procession. [37]At
12:37 the Fountain Gate[v] they continued di-
[v]Ne 2:14; 3:15 [w]Ne 3:26 rectly up the steps of the City of David
on the ascent to the wall and passed
above the house of David to the Water
Gate[w] on the east.
[38]The second choir proceeded in the
opposite direction. I followed them on
top[c] of the wall, together with half the
12:38 people—past the Tower of the Ovens[x] to
[x]Ne 3:11 [y]Ne 3:8 the Broad Wall,[y] [39]over the Gate of
12:39 Ephraim,[z] the Jeshanah[d] Gate,[a] the Fish
[z]2Ki 14:13; Ne 8:16 [a]Ne 3:6 Gate,[b] the Tower of Hananel[c] and the
[b]2Ch 33:14; Ne 3:3 [c]Ne 3:1 Tower of the Hundred,[d] as far as the
[d]Ne 3:1 [e]Ne 3:1 Sheep Gate.[e] At the Gate of the Guard
they stopped.
[40]The two choirs that gave thanks
then took their places in the house of
God; so did I, together with half the officials, [41]as well as the priests—Eliakim,
Maaseiah, Miniamin, Micaiah, Elioenai,
Zechariah and Hananiah with their
trumpets— [42]and also Maaseiah, Shemaiah, Eleazar, Uzzi, Jehohanan, Malkijah, Elam and Ezer. The choirs sang under the direction of Jezrahiah. [43]And on
that day they offered great sacrifices, rejoicing because God had given them
great joy. The women and children also
rejoiced. The sound of rejoicing in Jerusalem could be heard far away.
[44]At that time men were appointed to
12:44 be in charge of the storerooms[f] for the
[f]Ne 13:4,13 [g]Lev 27:30 contributions, firstfruits and tithes.[g]
From the fields around the towns they
were to bring into the storerooms the
portions required by the Law for the
priests and the Levites, for Judah was
pleased with the ministering priests and 12:44
Levites.[h] [45]They performed the service [h]Dt 18:8
of their God and the service of purification, as did also the singers and gatekeepers, according to the commands of 12:45
David[i] and his son Solomon.[j] [46]For long [i]1Ch 25:1; 2Ch 8:14
ago, in the days of David and Asaph,[k] [j]1Ch 6:31; 23:5
there had been directors for the singers 12:46
and for the songs of praise[l] and thanks- [k]2Ch 35:15
giving to God. [47]So in the days of Zerub- [l]2Ch 29:27; Ps 137:4
babel and of Nehemiah, all Israel con-
tributed the daily portions for the
singers and gatekeepers. They also set
aside the portion for the other Levites,
and the Levites set aside the portion for 12:47
the descendants of Aaron.[m] [m]Nu 18:21; Dt 18:8

Nehemiah's Final Reforms

13 On that day the Book of Moses
was read aloud in the hearing
of the people and there it was found
written that no Ammonite or Moabite
should ever be admitted into the assem- 13:1
bly of God,[n] [2]because they had not met [n]ver 23; Dt 23:3
the Israelites with food and water but 13:2
had hired Balaam[o] to call a curse down [o]Nu 22:3-11
on them.[p] (Our God, however, turned [p]Nu 23:7; Dt 23:3
the curse into a blessing.)[q] [3]When the [q]Nu 23:11; Dt 23:4-5
people heard this law, they excluded
from Israel all who were of foreign de- 13:3
scent.[r] [r]ver 23; Ne 9:2
[4]Before this, Eliashib the priest had 13:4
been put in charge of the storerooms[s] of [s]Ne 12:44
the house of our God. He was closely as- [t]Ne 2:10
sociated with Tobiah,[t] [5]and he had provided him with a large room formerly
used to store the grain offerings and incense and temple articles, and also the 13:5
tithes[u] of grain, new wine and oil pre- [u]Lev 27:30; Nu 18:21
scribed for the Levites, singers and gate-
keepers, as well as the contributions for
the priests.
[6]But while all this was going on, I was
not in Jerusalem, for in the thirty-sec- 13:6
ond year of Artaxerxes[v] king of Babylon [v]Ne 2:6; 5:14
I had returned to the king. Some time
later I asked his permission [7]and came
back to Jerusalem. Here I learned about 13:7
the evil thing Eliashib[w] had done in pro- [w]Ezr 10:24
viding Tobiah a room in the courts of
the house of God. [8]I was greatly dis- 13:8
pleased and threw all Tobiah's house- [x]Mt 21:12-13;
hold goods out of the room.[x] [9]I gave or- Jn 2:13-16

[a] 31 Or *go alongside* [b] 31 Or *proceed alongside*
[c] 38 Or *them alongside* [d] 39 Or *Old*

13:9 [y]1Ch 23:28; 2Ch 29:5 ders to purify the rooms,[y] and then I put
back into them the equipment of the
house of God, with the grain offerings
and the incense.
10I also learned that the portions as-
13:10 [z]Dt 12:19 signed to the Levites had not been given
to them,[z] and that all the Levites and
singers responsible for the service had
gone back to their own fields. 11So I re-
13:11 [a]Ne 10:37-39; Hag 1:1-9 buked the officials and asked them,
"Why is the house of God neglected?"[a]
Then I called them together and stationed them at their posts.
13:12 [b]2Ch 31:6 [c]1Ki 7:51; Ne 10:37-39; Mal 3:10 12All Judah brought the tithes[b] of
grain, new wine and oil into the store-
rooms.[c] 13I put Shelemiah the priest, Zadok the scribe, and a Levite named Pedaiah in charge of the storerooms and
made Hanan son of Zaccur, the son of
Mattaniah, their assistant, because
these men were considered trustworthy.
13:13 [d]Ne 12:44; Ac 6:1-5 They were made responsible for distributing the supplies to their brothers.[d]

13:14 [e]Ge 8:1 14Remember[e] me for this, O my God,
and do not blot out what I have so faithfully done for the house of my God and
its services.

15In those days I saw men in Judah
treading winepresses on the Sabbath
and bringing in grain and loading it on
donkeys, together with wine, grapes, figs
and all other kinds of loads. And they
13:15 [f]Ex 20:8-11; 34:21; Dt 5:12-15; Ne 10:31 were bringing all this into Jerusalem on
the Sabbath.[f] Therefore I warned them
against selling food on that day. 16Men
from Tyre who lived in Jerusalem were
bringing in fish and all kinds of merchandise and selling them in Jerusalem
13:16 [g]Ne 10:31 on the Sabbath[g] to the people of Judah.
17I rebuked the nobles of Judah and said
to them, "What is this wicked thing you
are doing—desecrating the Sabbath
day? 18Didn't your forefathers do the
same things, so that our God brought all
this calamity upon us and upon this
city? Now you are stirring up more
13:18 [h]Ne 10:31; Jer 17:21-23 wrath against Israel by desecrating the
Sabbath."[h]
19When evening shadows fell on the
13:19 [i]Lev 23:32 gates of Jerusalem before the Sabbath,[i] I
ordered the doors to be shut and not
opened until the Sabbath was over. I stationed some of my own men at the gates
so that no load could be brought in on
the Sabbath day. 20Once or twice the
merchants and sellers of all kinds of
goods spent the night outside Jerusalem. 21But I warned them and said,
"Why do you spend the night by the
wall? If you do this again, I will lay hands
on you." From that time on they no
longer came on the Sabbath. 22Then I
commanded the Levites to purify themselves and go and guard the gates in order to keep the Sabbath day holy.

Remember[j] me for this also, O my 13:22 [j]Ge 8:1; Ne 12:30
God, and show mercy to me according
to your great love.

23Moreover, in those days I saw men 13:23 [k]Ezr 9:1-2; Mal 2:11 [l]ver 1; Ne 10:30
of Judah who had married[k] women from
Ashdod, Ammon and Moab.[l] 24Half of
their children spoke the language of
Ashdod or the language of one of the
other peoples, and did not know how to
speak the language of Judah. 25I rebuked
them and called curses down on them. I
beat some of the men and pulled out 13:25 [m]Ezr 10:5
their hair. I made them take an oath[m] in
God's name and said: "You are not to
give your daughters in marriage to their
sons, nor are you to take their daughters
in marriage for your sons or for yourselves. 26Was it not because of marriages
like these that Solomon king of Israel
sinned? Among the many nations there 13:26 [n]1Ki 3:13; 2Ch 1:12 [o]2Sa 12:25 [p]1Ki 11:3
was no king like him.[n] He was loved by
his God,[o] and God made him king over
all Israel, but even he was led into sin by
foreign women.[p] 27Must we hear now 13:27 [q]Ezr 9:14; 10:2
that you too are doing all this terrible
wickedness and are being unfaithful to
our God by marrying[q] foreign women?"
28One of the sons of Joiada son of Eli- 13:28 [r]Ezr 10:24 [s]Ne 2:10
ashib[r] the high priest was son-in-law to
Sanballat[s] the Horonite. And I drove
him away from me.

29Remember[t] them, O my God, be- 13:29 [t]Ne 6:14
cause they defiled the priestly office and
the covenant of the priesthood and of
the Levites.

30So I purified the priests and the Le-
vites of everything foreign,[u] and as- 13:30 [u]Ne 10:30
signed them duties, each to his own
task. 31I also made provision for contri-
butions of wood[v] at designated times, 13:31 [v]Ne 10:34 [w]ver 14,22; Ge 8:1
and for the firstfruits.

Remember[w] me with favor, O my God.

ESTHER

Jesus in Esther The book of Esther, like much of the Bible, tells the story of God's involvement with his people. Unlike the rest of the Bible, however, this book shows God's work indirectly. In fact, God's name is not mentioned once, although his influence fills the narrative. Look for the indirect allusions to God's involvement in the lives of his people. Note Esther's revelations of God's character, his faithfulness and his provision for those who trust him, even through events most of us would see as tragic. The book of Esther clearly demonstrates how God works deliverance in the lives of his people, both in Old Testament times and today.

In much the same way that Esther functioned as an advocate for her people, so our Lord Jesus acts as our mediator with God the Father. In the words of Paul to Timothy, "There is one God and one mediator between God and men, the man Christ Jesus, who gave himself as a ransom for all men" (1 Timothy 2:5–6).

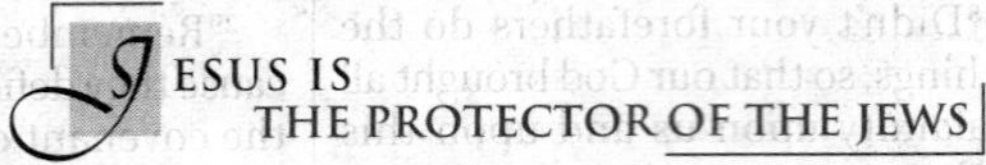
JESUS IS
THE PROTECTOR OF THE JEWS

Is the book of Esther "Godless"? (Esther 4:16)

♦ *Had the events in this book not occurred, the Jewish people would have been annihilated and the chain of redemptive events leading up to the birth of Jesus broken. The question remains, however, as to whether God was deliberately edited out of the story. The author may have been employing the literary device of understatement to emphasize that nothing short of divine intervention could explain the outcome. It is also possible that he didn't want to risk having the book destroyed by the Persian government.*

Is there significance to the series of ironic reversals of fortune and situational contrasts included in the book of Esther?

♦ *Throughout history God has frequently used such reversals and seeming coincidences to reveal his hand in the salvation history of his people. Consider the stories of the exodus, the Babylonian exile, and the crucifixion and resurrection of Jesus.*

Queen Vashti Deposed

1:1 [a]Ezr 4:6; Da 9:1 [b]Est 9:30; Da 3:2; 6:1 [c]Est 8:9 **1** This is what happened during the
time of Xerxes,[a][a] the Xerxes who
ruled over 127 provinces[b] stretching
from India to Cush[b]:[c] 2At that time King
1:2 [d]Ezr 4:9; Ne 1:1; Est 2:8 Xerxes reigned from his royal throne in
the citadel of Susa,[d] 3and in the third
year of his reign he gave a banquet[e] for
1:3 [e]1Ki 3:15; Est 2:18 all his nobles and officials. The military
leaders of Persia and Media, the princes,
and the nobles of the provinces were
present.
4For a full 180 days he displayed the
vast wealth of his kingdom and the
splendor and glory of his majesty.
5When these days were over, the king
1:5 [f]Jdg 14:17 [g]2Ki 21:18; Est 7:7-8 gave a banquet, lasting seven days,[f] in
the enclosed garden[g] of the king's
palace, for all the people from the least
to the greatest, who were in the citadel
of Susa. 6The garden had hangings of
white and blue linen, fastened with
cords of white linen and purple materi-
1:6 [h]Est 7:8; Eze 23:41; Am 3:12; 6:4 al to silver rings on marble pillars. There
were couches[h] of gold and silver on a
mosaic pavement of porphyry, marble,
mother-of-pearl and other costly stones.
7Wine was served in goblets of gold,
each one different from the other, and
1:7 [i]Est 2:18; Da 5:2 the royal wine was abundant, in keeping
with the king's liberality.[i] 8By the king's
command each guest was allowed to
drink in his own way, for the king instructed all the wine stewards to serve
each man what he wished.
1:9 [j]1Ki 3:15 9Queen Vashti also gave a banquet[j]
for the women in the royal palace of
King Xerxes.
1:10 [k]Jdg 16:25; Ru 3:7 [l]Ge 14:18; Est 3:15; 5:6; 7:2; Pr 31:4-7; Da 5:1-4 [m]Est 7:9 10On the seventh day, when King Xerxes was in high spirits[k] from wine,[l] he
commanded the seven eunuchs who
served him—Mehuman, Biztha, Harbona,[m] Bigtha, Abagtha, Zethar and Car-
cas— 11to bring[n] before him Queen
1:11 [n]SS 2:4 [o]Ps 45:11; Eze 16:14 Vashti, wearing her royal crown, in order
to display her beauty[o] to the people and
nobles, for she was lovely to look at.
12But when the attendants delivered the
1:12 [p]Ge 39:19; Est 2:21; 7:7; Pr 19:12 king's command, Queen Vashti refused
to come. Then the king became furious
and burned with anger.[p]
13Since it was customary for the king
to consult experts in matters of law and
1:13 [q]1Ch 12:32; er 10:7; Da 2:12 justice, he spoke with the wise men who
understood the times[q] 14and were clos-
est to the king—Carshena, Shethar, Ad-
matha, Tarshish, Meres, Marsena and
Memucan, the seven nobles[r] of Persia 1:14 [r]2Ki 25:19; Ezr 7:14
and Media who had special access to the
king and were highest in the kingdom.
15"According to law, what must be
done to Queen Vashti?" he asked. "She
has not obeyed the command of King
Xerxes that the eunuchs have taken to
her."
16Then Memucan replied in the presence of the king and the nobles, "Queen
Vashti has done wrong, not only against
the king but also against all the nobles
and the peoples of all the provinces of
King Xerxes. 17For the queen's conduct
will become known to all the women,
and so they will despise their husbands
and say, 'King Xerxes commanded
Queen Vashti to be brought before him,
but she would not come.' 18This very day
the Persian and Median women of the
nobility who have heard about the
queen's conduct will respond to all the
king's nobles in the same way. There will
be no end of disrespect and discord.[s] 1:18 [s]Pr 19:13; 27:15
19"Therefore, if it pleases the king,[t] let
him issue a royal decree and let it be 1:19 [t]Ecc 8:4 [u]Est 8:8; Da 6:8, 12
written in the laws of Persia and Media,
which cannot be repealed,[u] that Vashti is
never again to enter the presence of King
Xerxes. Also let the king give her royal
position to someone else who is better
than she. 20Then when the king's edict is
proclaimed throughout all his vast
realm, all the women will respect their
husbands, from the least to the greatest."
21The king and his nobles were
pleased with this advice, so the king did
as Memucan proposed. 22He sent dispatches to all parts of the kingdom, to
each province in its own script and to
each people in its own language,[v] pro-
claiming in each people's tongue that 1:22 [v]Ne 13:24; Est 8:9; Eph 5:22-24; 1Ti 2:12
every man should be ruler over his own
household.

Esther Made Queen

2 Later when the anger of King Xerxes had subsided,[w] he remem-
bered Vashti and what she had done and 2:1 [w]Est 1:19-20; 7:10
what he had decreed about her. 2Then
the king's personal attendants proposed, "Let a search be made for beautiful young virgins for the king. 3Let the
king appoint commissioners in every

[a] *1* Hebrew *Ahasuerus,* a variant of Xerxes' Persian name; here and throughout Esther [b] *1* That is, the upper Nile region

God of the Impossible

God's fingerprints are all over the book of Esther, but his name is not mentioned even once. Through the courage of one woman God supernaturally protected his people from annihilation and extinction. Esther reminds us that God is constantly at work behind-the-scenes to deliver his own.

The story begins when Esther, a beautiful young Jewish émigré, is chosen by the Persian King Xerxes as his new queen (Xerxes is unaware at this point of her Jewish heritage). The wicked Haman, second-in-command of the Persian empire, plots to have all of the Jews killed as revenge for the refusal of Mordecai, Esther's cousin and former guardian, as well as a high-ranking government official, to bow down to him. Haman convinces Xerxes that this mass extermination will be in the empire's best interest, and the execution is scheduled for a particular day according to a decree from the king himself. The date is chosen by casting lots, or *purim*. Even today, the Jewish people celebrate the Feast of Purim to commemorate God's deliverance from Haman.

Mordecai asks Queen Esther to become involved, and she courageously reveals her heritage and exposes the plot to the king. Because of her love for her people, Esther risks her life by going against the king's law, saying, "If I perish, I perish" (Esther 4:19). The king has mercy on her and grants her request, and eventually Haman is hanged on the very gallows he has erected for Mordecai.

Esther's decision is similar to the one Jesus would make years later. Motivated by his love for us, our Savior became our representative in the courtroom of a holy God. It cost his life to save us from perishing (John 3:16). It seemed impossible for fallen humanity to gain a pardon from an offended God, but Jesus accomplished just that and then rose from the dead to prove it. Just as Haman was publicly humiliated and destroyed, so Jesus "disarmed the powers and authorities" of his enemy, Satan. "He made a public spectacle of them, triumphing over them by the cross" (Colossians 2:15).

That which appears to be a futile cause for human beings is never unattainable for God. In fact, God specializes in the "impossible" as a means for demonstrating who he is. Many people throughout history have scoffed at God's seemingly improbable plans and methods. When he had informed one elderly couple that they were going to have a son, they laughed—until the miracle birth took place (Genesis 18:13–14). And when Mary learned that she had been chosen to give birth to God's Son, she very logically inquired, "How will this be ... since I am a virgin?" (Luke 1:34). God's angel messenger reminded her that "nothing is impossible with God" (Luke 1:37). And even in Persia God was watching out for his people, quietly setting all the pieces in place for their deliverance. Government edicts and all the antipathy Haman could muster could not foil God's plan.

Self-Discovery: *Can you identify a time in which God put all of the pieces in place for an "impossible" dream to come true? What did it teach you about his sovereignty over all things?*

GO TO DISCOVERY 115 ON PAGE 623

province of his realm to bring all these
beautiful girls into the harem at the
citadel of Susa. Let them be placed under the care of Hegai, the king's eunuch,
who is in charge of the women; and let
beauty treatments be given to them.
4Then let the girl who pleases the king
be queen instead of Vashti." This advice
appealed to the king, and he followed it.
5Now there was in the citadel of Susa
a Jew of the tribe of Benjamin, named
Mordecai son of Jair, the son of Shimei,
the son of Kish,[x] 6who had been carried
into exile from Jerusalem by Nebuchadnezzar king of Babylon, among those
taken captive with Jehoiachin[a][y] king of
Judah.[z] 7Mordecai had a cousin named
Hadassah, whom he had brought up because she had neither father nor mother. This girl, who was also known as Esther,[a] was lovely[b] in form and features,
and Mordecai had taken her as his own
daughter when her father and mother
died.
8When the king's order and edict had
been proclaimed, many girls were
brought to the citadel of Susa[c] and put
under the care of Hegai. Esther also was
taken to the king's palace and entrusted
to Hegai, who had charge of the harem.
9The girl pleased him and won his favor.[d] Immediately he provided her with
her beauty treatments and special food.[e]
He assigned to her seven maids selected
from the king's palace and moved her
and her maids into the best place in the
harem.
10Esther had not revealed her nationality and family background, because
Mordecai had forbidden her to do so.[f]
11Every day he walked back and forth
near the courtyard of the harem to find
out how Esther was and what was happening to her.
12Before a girl's turn came to go in to
King Xerxes, she had to complete twelve
months of beauty treatments prescribed
for the women, six months with oil of
myrrh and six with perfumes[g] and cos-
metics. 13And this is how she would go
to the king: Anything she wanted was
given her to take with her from the harem to the king's palace. 14In the evening
she would go there and in the morning
return to another part of the harem to
the care of Shaashgaz, the king's eunuch
who was in charge of the concubines.[h]

2:5 [x] 1Sa 9:1; Est 3:2
2:6 [y] 2Ki 24:6,15; 2Ch 36:10,20 [z] Da 1:1-5; 5:13
2:7 [a] Ge 41:45 [b] Ge 39:6
2:8 [c] ver 3,15; Ne 1:1; Est 1:2; Da 8:2
2:9 [d] Ge 39:21 [e] ver 3,12; Ge 37:3; 1Sa 9:22-24; 2Ki 25:30; Eze 16:9-13; Da 1:5
2:10 [f] ver 20
2:12 [g] Pr 27:9; SS 1:3; Isa 3:24
2:14 [h] 1Ki 11:3; SS 6:8; Da 5:2

She would not return to the king unless
he was pleased with her and summoned
her by name.[i]
15When the turn came for Esther (the
girl Mordecai had adopted, the daughter
of his uncle Abihail[j]) to go to the king,[k]
she asked for nothing other than what
Hegai, the king's eunuch who was in
charge of the harem, suggested. And Esther won the favor[l] of everyone who saw
her. 16She was taken to King Xerxes in
the royal residence in the tenth month,
the month of Tebeth, in the seventh year
of his reign.
17Now the king was attracted to Esther more than to any of the other
women, and she won his favor and approval more than any of the other virgins. So he set a royal crown on her head
and made her queen[m] instead of Vashti.
18And the king gave a great banquet,[n]
Esther's banquet, for all his nobles and
officials.[o] He proclaimed a holiday
throughout the provinces and distributed gifts with royal liberality.[p]

Mordecai Uncovers a Conspiracy

19When the virgins were assembled a
second time, Mordecai was sitting at the
king's gate.[q] 20But Esther had kept secret her family background and nationality just as Mordecai had told her to do,
for she continued to follow Mordecai's
instructions as she had done when he
was bringing her up.[r]
21During the time Mordecai was sitting at the king's gate, Bigthana[b] and Teresh, two of the king's officers[s] who
guarded the doorway, became angry[t]
and conspired to assassinate King Xerxes. 22But Mordecai found out about the
plot and told Queen Esther, who in turn
reported it to the king, giving credit to
Mordecai. 23And when the report was
investigated and found to be true, the
two officials were hanged[u] on a gallows.[c]
All this was recorded in the book of the
annals[v] in the presence of the king.

Haman's Plot to Destroy the Jews

3 After these events, King Xerxes
honored Haman son of Hamme-
datha, the Agagite,[w] elevating him and
giving him a seat of honor higher than

2:14 [i] Est 4:11
2:15 [j] Est 9:29 [k] Ps 45:14 [l] Ge 18:3; 30:27; Est 5:8
2:17 [m] Est 1:11; Eze 16:9-13
2:18 [n] 1Ki 3:15; Est 1:3 [o] Ge 40:20 [p] Est 1:7
2:19 [q] ver 21; Est 3:2; 4:2; 5:13
2:20 [r] ver 10
2:21 [s] Ge 40:2; Est 6:2 [t] Est 1:12; 3:5; 5:9; 7:7
2:23 [u] Ge 40:19; Ps 7:14-16; Pr 26:27 [v] Est 6:1; 10:2
3:1 [w] ver 10; Ex 17:8-16; Nu 24:7; Dt 25:17-19; 1Sa 14:48; Est 5:11

[a] 6 Hebrew *Jeconiah*, a variant of *Jehoiachin*
[b] 21 Hebrew *Bigthan*, a variant of *Bigthana*
[c] 23 Or *were hung* (or *impaled*) *on poles*; similarly elsewhere in Esther

that of all the other nobles. 2All the royal officials at the king's gate knelt down
and paid honor to Haman, for the king
had commanded this concerning him.
But Mordecai would not kneel down or
pay him honor.
3Then the royal officials at the king's
3:3 gate asked Mordecai, "Why do you dis-
x Est 5:9; obey the king's command?"[x] 4Day after
Da 3:12 day they spoke to him but he refused to
3:4 comply.[y] Therefore they told Haman
y Ge 39:10 about it to see whether Mordecai's behavior would be tolerated, for he had
told them he was a Jew.
5When Haman saw that Mordecai
3:5 would not kneel down or pay him honor,
z Est 2:21; 5:9 he was enraged.[z] 6Yet having learned
who Mordecai's people were, he scorned
3:6 the idea of killing only Mordecai. Instead
a Pr 16:25 Haman looked for a way[a] to destroy[b] all
b Ps 74:8; 83:4 Mordecai's people, the Jews,[c] throughout
c Est 9:24 the whole kingdom of Xerxes.
7In the twelfth year of King Xerxes, in
3:7 the first month, the month of Nisan,
d Est 9:24,26 they cast the *pur*[d] (that is, the lot[e]) in the
e Lev 16:8; 1Sa 10:21 presence of Haman to select a day and
f ver 13; Ezr 6:15; month. And the lot fell on[a] the twelfth
Est 9:19 month, the month of Adar.[f]
8Then Haman said to King Xerxes,
"There is a certain people dispersed and
scattered among the peoples in all the
provinces of your kingdom whose cus-
3:8 toms[g] are different from those of all oth-
g Ac 16:20-21 er people and who do not obey[h] the
h Jer 29:7; Da 6:13 king's laws; it is not in the king's best in-
i Ezr 4:15 terest to tolerate them.[i] 9If it pleases the
king, let a decree be issued to destroy
them, and I will put ten thousand talents[b] of silver into the royal treasury for
3:9 the men who carry out this business."[j]
j Est 7:4 10So the king took his signet ring[k]
3:10 from his finger and gave it to Haman
k Ge 41:42; son of Hammedatha, the Agagite, the
Est 7:6; 8:2 enemy of the Jews. 11"Keep the money,"
the king said to Haman, "and do with
the people as you please."
12Then on the thirteenth day of the
first month the royal secretaries were
3:12 summoned. They wrote out in the script
l Ne 13:24 of each province and in the language[l] of
m Ge 38:18; 1Ki 21:8; each people all Haman's orders to the
Est 8:8-10 king's satraps, the governors of the various provinces and the nobles of the various peoples. These were written in the
name of King Xerxes himself and
sealed[m] with his own ring. 13Dispatches
were sent by couriers to all the king's
provinces with the order to destroy, kill 3:13
and annihilate all the Jews[n]—young and n 1Sa 15:3; Ezr 4:6;
old, women and little children—on a Est 8:10-14 o ver 7
single day, the thirteenth day of the p Est 8:11; 9:10
twelfth month, the month of Adar,[o] and
to plunder[p] their goods. 14A copy of the
text of the edict was to be issued as law
in every province and made known to
the people of every nationality so they 3:14
would be ready for that day.[q] q Est 8:8; 9:1
15Spurred on by the king's command,
the couriers went out, and the edict was 3:15
issued in the citadel of Susa.[r] The king r Est 8:14
and Haman sat down to drink,[s] but the s Est 1:10
city of Susa was bewildered.[t] t Est 8:15

Mordecai Persuades Esther to Help

4 When Mordecai learned of all
that had been done, he tore his 4:1
clothes,[u] put on sackcloth and ashes,[v] u Nu 14:6 v 2Sa 13:19;
and went out into the city, wailing[w] Eze 27:30-31;
loudly and bitterly. 2But he went only as Jnh 3:5-6 w Ex 11:6;
far as the king's gate,[x] because no one Ps 30:11
clothed in sackcloth was allowed to en- 4:2
ter it. 3In every province to which the x Est 2:19
edict and order of the king came, there
was great mourning among the Jews,
with fasting, weeping and wailing. Many
lay in sackcloth and ashes.
4When Esther's maids and eunuchs
came and told her about Mordecai, she
was in great distress. She sent clothes for
him to put on instead of his sackcloth,
but he would not accept them. 5Then
Esther summoned Hathach, one of the
king's eunuchs assigned to attend her,
and ordered him to find out what was
troubling Mordecai and why.
6So Hathach went out to Mordecai in
the open square of the city in front of the
king's gate. 7Mordecai told him everything that had happened to him, including the exact amount of money Haman
had promised to pay into the royal trea- 4:7
sury for the destruction of the Jews.[y] 8He y Est 3:9; 7:4
also gave him a copy of the text of the
edict for their annihilation, which had
been published in Susa, to show to Esther and explain it to her, and he told
him to urge her to go into the king's
presence to beg for mercy and plead
with him for her people.
9Hathach went back and reported to
Esther what Mordecai had said. 10Then

[a] 7 Septuagint; Hebrew does not have *And the lot fell on.* [b] 9 That is, about 375 tons (about 345 metric tons)

God Protects His People

When God makes a promise, we know that we can trust him simply because at the very core of his nature he is faithful. That means that he keeps his Word: "He is the Rock . . . a faithful God who does no wrong" (Deuteronomy 32:4). Each of us has been afraid at one time or another. In those times of fear it is easy to forget that God is still in control and promises to rescue us.

God's people have always known persecution, because we live in a world where so many oppose God and his purposes (John 15:18–21). One of the more recent examples of persecution is World War II, but that was by no means the first incident in which a national leader had attempted to annihilate an entire population of God's people. In the book of Esther we catch a behind-the-scenes glimpse of an incident in which the survival of the entire Jewish nation was threatened. In Esther's story we see clearly that God cares about his chosen people and controls the events of history.

Queen Esther played a vital role in saving the Jews. God could have saved his people with or without Esther's help. He had promised that the nation would never be completely annihilated (2 Kings 19:31; Ezra 9:8). But Esther was God's chosen tool, and her cousin Mordecai believed that God had allowed her marriage to the Persian king in order to enable her to be an instrument in stopping the massacre (Esther 4:12–14).

In the New Testament Jesus recognized that choosing to follow him would not be an easy option for us. He minced no words: "If anyone would come after me, he must deny himself and take up his cross and follow me" (Mark 8:34). The cross implied death, and Jesus didn't want anyone to miss the point: "I tell you the truth . . . no one who has left home or brothers or sisters or mother or father or children or fields for me and the gospel will fail to receive a hundred times as much in this present age (homes, brothers, sisters, mothers, children and fields—and with them, persecutions) and in the age to come, eternal life. But many who are first will be last, and the last first" (Mark 10:29–31)

The next time you are afraid for any reason, think about who God is: He is good, he loves you and he is in control, even when you can't see him at work. You may lose a loved one, suffer from chronic illness or experience no relief from agonizing emotional pain. The painful reality of life is this: "In this world you will have trouble." But Jesus told yet another truth: "I have overcome the world" (John 16:33). Comfort is ours, because Jesus has won the victory. And those who belong to him are safe and secure, because "no one can snatch them out of [his] Father's hand" (John 10:29).

Self-Discovery: *Picture yourself as a baby bird held firmly but gently in the hands of Jesus. At first your little heart beats wildly, but finally you begin to relax. From what particular dangers do you feel secure?*

GO TO DISCOVERY 116 ON PAGE 626

she instructed him to say to Mordecai, 11 “All the king’s officials and the people of the royal provinces know that for any man or woman who approaches the king in the inner court without being summoned[z] the king has but one law:[a] that he be put to death. The only exception to this is for the king to extend the gold scepter[b] to him and spare his life. But thirty days have passed since I was called to go to the king.”

12 When Esther’s words were reported to Mordecai, 13 he sent back this answer: “Do not think that because you are in the king’s house you alone of all the Jews will escape. 14 For if you remain silent[c] at this time, relief[d] and deliverance[e] for the Jews will arise from another place, but you and your father’s family will perish. And who knows but that you have come to royal position for such a time as this?”[f]

15 Then Esther sent this reply to Mordecai: 16 “Go, gather together all the Jews who are in Susa, and fast[g] for me. Do not eat or drink for three days, night or day. I and my maids will fast as you do. When this is done, I will go to the king, even though it is against the law. And if I perish, I perish.”[h]

17 So Mordecai went away and carried out all of Esther’s instructions.

Esther’s Request to the King

5 On the third day Esther put on her royal robes[i] and stood in the inner court of the palace, in front of the king’s[j] hall. The king was sitting on his royal throne in the hall, facing the entrance. 2 When he saw Queen Esther standing in the court, he was pleased with her and held out to her the gold scepter that was in his hand. So Esther approached and touched the tip of the scepter.[k]

3 Then the king asked, “What is it, Queen Esther? What is your request? Even up to half the kingdom,[l] it will be given you.”

4 “If it pleases the king,” replied Esther, “let the king, together with Haman, come today to a banquet I have prepared for him.”

5 “Bring Haman at once,” the king said, “so that we may do what Esther asks.”

So the king and Haman went to the banquet Esther had prepared. 6 As they were drinking wine,[m] the king again asked Esther, “Now what is your petition? It will be given you. And what is your request? Even up to half the kingdom,[n] it will be granted.”[o]

7 Esther replied, “My petition and my request is this: 8 If the king regards me with favor[p] and if it pleases the king to grant my petition and fulfill my request, let the king and Haman come tomorrow to the banquet[q] I will prepare for them. Then I will answer the king’s question.”

Haman’s Rage Against Mordecai

9 Haman went out that day happy and in high spirits. But when he saw Mordecai at the king’s gate and observed that he neither rose nor showed fear in his presence, he was filled with rage[r] against Mordecai.[s] 10 Nevertheless, Haman restrained himself and went home.

Calling together his friends and Zeresh,[t] his wife, 11 Haman boasted[u] to them about his vast wealth, his many sons,[v] and all the ways the king had honored him and how he had elevated him above the other nobles and officials. 12 “And that’s not all,” Haman added. “I’m the only person[w] Queen Esther invited to accompany the king to the banquet she gave. And she has invited me along with the king tomorrow. 13 But all this gives me no satisfaction as long as I see that Jew Mordecai sitting at the king’s gate.[x]”

14 His wife Zeresh and all his friends said to him, “Have a gallows built, seventy-five feet[a] high,[y] and ask the king in the morning to have Mordecai hanged[z] on it. Then go with the king to the dinner and be happy.” This suggestion delighted Haman, and he had the gallows built.

Mordecai Honored

6 That night the king could not sleep;[a] so he ordered the book of the chronicles,[b] the record of his reign, to be brought in and read to him. 2 It was found recorded there that Mordecai had exposed Bigthana and Teresh, two of the king’s officers who guarded the doorway, who had conspired to assassinate King Xerxes.

3 “What honor and recognition has Mordecai received for this?” the king asked.

“Nothing has been done for him,”[c] his attendants answered.

[a] 14 Hebrew *fifty cubits* (about 23 meters)

4:11 [z] Est 2:14 [a] Da 2:9 [b] Est 5:1,2; 8:4
4:14 [c] Ecc 3:7; Isa 62:1; Am 5:13 [d] Est 9:16,22 [e] Ge 45:7; Dt 28:29 [f] Ge 50:20
4:16 [g] 2Ch 20:3; Est 9:31 [h] Ge 43:14
5:1 [i] Est 4:16; Eze 16:13 [j] Est 6:4; Pr 21:1
5:2 [k] Est 4:11; 8:4; Pr 21:1
5:3 [l] Est 7:2; Da 5:16; Mk 6:23
5:6 [m] Est 1:10
5:6 [n] Mk 6:23 [o] Est 7:2; 9:12
5:8 [p] Est 2:15; 7:3; 8:5 [q] 1Ki 3:15; Est 6:14
5:9 [r] Est 2:21; Pr 14:17 [s] Est 3:3,5
5:10 [t] Est 6:13
5:11 [u] Pr 13:16 [v] Est 9:7-10,13
5:12 [w] Job 22:29; Pr 16:18; 29:23
5:13 [x] Est 2:19
5:14 [y] Est 7:9 [z] Ezr 6:11; Est 6:4
6:1 [a] Da 2:1; 6:18 [b] Est 2:23; 10:2
6:3 [c] Ecc 9:13-16

4The king said, "Who is in the court?"
Now Haman had just entered the outer
court of the palace to speak to the king
about hanging Mordecai on the gallows
he had erected for him.
5His attendants answered, "Haman is
standing in the court."
"Bring him in," the king ordered.
6When Haman entered, the king
asked him, "What should be done for
the man the king delights to honor?"
Now Haman thought to himself,
"Who is there that the king would rather
honor than me?" 7So he answered the
king, "For the man the king delights to
6:8 [d] Ge 41:42; honor, 8have them bring a royal robe[d] the
Isa 52:1 king has worn and a horse[e] the king has
[e] 1Ki 1:33 ridden, one with a royal crest placed on
its head. 9Then let the robe and horse be
entrusted to one of the king's most noble
princes. Let them robe the man the king
delights to honor, and lead him on the
horse through the city streets, proclaiming before him, 'This is what is done for
6:9 [f] Ge 41:43 the man the king delights to honor!'[f]"
10"Go at once," the king commanded
Haman. "Get the robe and the horse and
do just as you have suggested for Mordecai the Jew, who sits at the king's gate.
Do not neglect anything you have rec-
ommended."
6:11 [g] Ge 41:42 11So Haman got[g] the robe and the
horse. He robed Mordecai, and led him
on horseback through the city streets,
proclaiming before him, "This is what is
done for the man the king delights to
honor!"
12Afterward Mordecai returned to the
6:12 [h] 2Sa 15:30; king's gate. But Haman rushed home,
Jer 14:3,4; with his head covered[h] in grief, 13and
Mic 3:7 told Zeresh[i] his wife and all his friends
6:13 [i] Est 5:10 everything that had happened to him.
[j] Ps 57:6; His advisers and his wife Zeresh said
Pr 26:27; 28:18 to him, "Since Mordecai, before whom
your downfall[j] has started, is of Jewish
origin, you cannot stand against him—
you will surely come to ruin!" 14While
they were still talking with him, the
6:14 [k] 1Ki 3:15; king's eunuchs arrived and hurried Ha-
Est 5:8 man away to the banquet[k] Esther had
prepared.

Haman Hanged

7:1 [l] Ge 40:20-22; **7** So the king and Haman went to
Mt 22:1-14 dine[l] with Queen Esther, 2and as
they were drinking wine[m] on that sec-
7:2 [m] Est 1:10 ond day, the king again asked, "Queen
Esther, what is your petition? It will be
given you. What is your request? Even up 7:2
to half the kingdom,[n] it will be granted.[o]" [n] Est 5:3
3Then Queen Esther answered, "If I [o] Est 9:12
have found favor[p] with you, O king, and 7:3
if it pleases your majesty, grant me my [p] Est 2:15
life—this is my petition. And spare my
people—this is my request. 4For I and
my people have been sold for destruction and slaughter and annihilation.[q] If 7:4
we had merely been sold as male and fe- [q] Est 3:9
male slaves, I would have kept quiet, because no such distress would justify disturbing the king.[a]"
5King Xerxes asked Queen Esther,
"Who is he? Where is the man who has
dared to do such a thing?"
6Esther said, "The adversary and enemy is this vile Haman."
Then Haman was terrified before the
king and queen. 7The king got up in a 7:7
rage,[r] left his wine and went out into the [r] Ge 34:7;
palace garden.[s] But Haman, realizing Est 1:12;
that the king had already decided his Pr 19:12; 20:1-2 [s] 2Ki 21:18
fate,[t] stayed behind to beg Queen Esther [t] Est 6:13
for his life.
8Just as the king returned from the
palace garden to the banquet hall, Ha- 7:8
man was falling on the couch[u] where [u] Est 1:6
Esther was reclining.[v] [v] Ge 39:14 [w] Ge 34:7
The king exclaimed, "Will he even [x] Est 6:12
molest the queen while she is with me in
the house?"[w]
As soon as the word left the king's
mouth, they covered Haman's face.[x] 7:9
9Then Harbona,[y] one of the eunuchs at- [y] Est 1:10
tending the king, said, "A gallows seven- [z] Est 5:14 [a] Ps 7:14-16;
ty-five feet[b] high[z] stands by Haman's 9:16; Pr 11:5-6;
house. He had it made for Mordecai, 26:27; Mt 7:2
who spoke up to help the king."
The king said, "Hang him on it!"[a] 10So 7:10
they hanged Haman[b] on the gallows[c] he [b] Pr 10:28
had prepared for Mordecai.[d] Then the [c] Est 9:25 [d] Da 6:24
king's fury subsided.[e] [e] Est 2:1

The King's Edict in Behalf of the Jews

8 That same day King Xerxes gave
Queen Esther the estate of Ha- 8:1
man,[f] the enemy of the Jews. And Mor- [f] Est 2:7; 7:6;
decai came into the presence of the Pr 22:22-23
king, for Esther had told how he was related to her. 2The king took off his signet 8:2
ring,[g] which he had reclaimed from Ha- [g] Ge 41:42;
man, and presented it to Mordecai. And Est 3:10

[a] 4 Or *quiet, but the compensation our adversary offers cannot be compared with the loss the king would suffer* [b] 9 Hebrew *fifty cubits* (about 23 meters)

8:2 h Pr 13:22; Esther appointed him over Haman's es-
Da 2:48 tate.[h]
3Esther again pleaded with the king,
falling at his feet and weeping. She
begged him to put an end to the evil
plan of Haman the Agagite, which he
had devised against the Jews. 4Then the
8:4 i Est 4:11; 5:2 king extended the gold scepter[i] to Esther and she arose and stood before him.
5"If it pleases the king," she said, "and
if he regards me with favor and thinks it
the right thing to do, and if he is pleased
with me, let an order be written overrul-
ing the dispatches that Haman son of
Hammedatha, the Agagite, devised and
wrote to destroy the Jews in all the king's
provinces. 6For how can I bear to see di-
8:6 saster fall on my people? How can I bear
j Est 7:4; 9:1 to see the destruction of my family?"[j]
7King Xerxes replied to Queen Esther
and to Mordecai the Jew, "Because Haman attacked the Jews, I have given his
estate to Esther, and they have hanged
8:8 him on the gallows. 8Now write another
k Est 3:12-14 decree[k] in the king's name in behalf of
l Ge 41:42 the Jews as seems best to you, and seal it
m Est 1:19; Da 6:15 with the king's signet ring[l]—for no document written in the king's name and
sealed with his ring can be revoked."[m]
9At once the royal secretaries were
summoned—on the twenty-third day of
the third month, the month of Sivan.
They wrote out all Mordecai's orders to
the Jews, and to the satraps, governors
8:9 and nobles of the 127 provinces stretch-
n Est 1:1 ing from India to Cush.[a][n] These orders
o Est 1:22 were written in the script of each province and the language of each people
and also to the Jews in their own script
and language.[o] 10Mordecai wrote in the
name of King Xerxes, sealed the dispatches with the king's signet ring, and
sent them by mounted couriers, who
rode fast horses especially bred for the
king.
11The king's edict granted the Jews in
every city the right to assemble and protect themselves; to destroy, kill and annihilate any armed force of any nationality or province that might attack them
8:11 and their women and children; and to
p Est 9:10,15,16 plunder[p] the property of their enemies.
12The day appointed for the Jews to do
this in all the provinces of King Xerxes
was the thirteenth day of the twelfth
8:12 q Est 3:13; 9:1 month, the month of Adar.[q] 13A copy of
the text of the edict was to be issued as
law in every province and made known
to the people of every nationality so that
the Jews would be ready on that day[r] to 8:13
avenge themselves on their enemies. r Est 3:14
14The couriers, riding the royal horses,
raced out, spurred on by the king's command. And the edict was also issued in
the citadel of Susa.
15Mordecai[s] left the king's presence 8:15 s Est 9:4
wearing royal garments of blue and t Ge 41:42
white, a large crown of gold and a purple u Est 3:15
robe of fine linen.[t] And the city of Susa
held a joyous celebration.[u] 16For the 8:16
Jews it was a time of happiness and joy,[v] v Ps 97:10-12
gladness and honor.[w] 17In every province w Ps 112:4
and in every city, wherever the edict of
the king went, there was joy[x] and glad- 8:17 x Est 9:19,27;
ness among the Jews, with feasting and Ps 35:27;
celebrating. And many people of other Pr 11:10
nationalities became Jews because fear[y] y Ex 15:14,16; Dt 11:25
of the Jews had seized them.[z] z Est 9:3

Triumph of the Jews

9 On the thirteenth day of the
twelfth month, the month of
Adar,[a] the edict commanded by the king 9:1 a Est 8:12
was to be carried out. On this day the b Jer 29:4-7
enemies of the Jews had hoped to over- c Est 3:12-14;
power them, but now the tables were Pr 22:22-23
turned and the Jews got the upper
hand[b] over those who hated them.[c] 2The
Jews assembled in their cities[d] in all the 9:2 d ver 15-18
provinces of King Xerxes to attack those e Est 8:11,17;
seeking their destruction. No one could Ps 71:13,24
stand against them,[e] because the people
of all the other nationalities were afraid
of them. 3And all the nobles of the
provinces, the satraps, the governors
and the king's administrators helped the 9:3
Jews,[f] because fear of Mordecai had f Ezr 8:36
seized them. 4Mordecai was prominent[g] 9:4
in the palace; his reputation spread g Ex 11:3
throughout the provinces, and he be- h 2Sa 3:1;
came more and more powerful.[h] 1Ch 11:9
5The Jews struck down all their enemies with the sword, killing and de-
stroying them,[i] and they did what they 9:5 i Ezr 4:6
pleased to those who hated them. 6In
the citadel of Susa, the Jews killed and
destroyed five hundred men. 7They also
killed Parshandatha, Dalphon, Aspatha,
8Poratha, Adalia, Aridatha, 9Parmashta,
Arisai, Aridai and Vaizatha, 10the ten 9:10
sons[j] of Haman son of Hammedatha, j Est 5:11
the enemy of the Jews. But they did not k Ge 14:23;
lay their hands on the plunder.[k] 1Sa 14:32; Est 3:13; 8:11

[a] 9 That is, the upper Nile region

11 The number of those slain in the
citadel of Susa was reported to the king
that same day. 12 The king said to Queen
Esther, "The Jews have killed and destroyed five hundred men and the ten
sons of Haman in the citadel of Susa.
What have they done in the rest of the
king's provinces? Now what is your petition? It will be given you. What is your
9:12 request? It will also be granted."[l]
[l] Est 5:6; 7:2 13 "If it pleases the king," Esther answered, "give the Jews in Susa permis-
sion to carry out this day's edict tomor-
9:13 row also, and let Haman's ten sons[m] be
[m] Est 5:11 [n] Dt 21:22-23 hanged[n] on gallows."
14 So the king commanded that this be
done. An edict was issued in Susa, and
9:14 they hanged[o] the ten sons of Haman.
[o] Ezr 6:11 15 The Jews in Susa came together on the
fourteenth day of the month of Adar,
and they put to death in Susa three hun-
9:15 dred men, but they did not lay their
[p] Ge 14:23; Est 8:11 hands on the plunder.[p]
16 Meanwhile, the remainder of the
Jews who were in the king's provinces
also assembled to protect themselves
9:16 and get relief[q] from their enemies.[r] They
[q] Est 4:14 [r] Dt 25:19 killed seventy-five thousand of them[s]
[s] 1Ch 4:43 but did not lay their hands on the plunder. 17 This happened on the thirteenth
day of the month of Adar, and on the
fourteenth they rested and made it a day 9:17
of feasting[t] and joy. [t] 1Ki 3:15

Purim Celebrated

18 The Jews in Susa, however, had assembled on the thirteenth and fourteenth, and then on the fifteenth they
rested and made it a day of feasting and
joy.
19 That is why rural Jews—those living
in villages—observe the fourteenth of 9:19
the month of Adar[u] as a day of joy and [u] Est 3:7
feasting, a day for giving presents to [v] ver 22; Dt 16:11,14;
each other.[v] Ne 8:10,12; Est 2:9;
20 Mordecai recorded these events, Rev 11:10
and he sent letters to all the Jews
throughout the provinces of King Xerxes, near and far, 21 to have them celebrate annually the fourteenth and fifteenth days of the month of Adar 22 as 9:22
the time when the Jews got relief[w] [w] Est 4:14
from their enemies, and as the month [x] Ne 8:12; Ps 30:11-12
when their sorrow was turned into joy [y] 2Ki 25:30
and their mourning into a day of celebration.[x] He wrote them to observe the
days as days of feasting and joy and giving presents of food[y] to one another and
gifts to the poor.
23 So the Jews agreed to continue the
celebration they had begun, doing what
Mordecai had written to them. 24 For Haman son of Hammedatha, the Agagite,[z] 9:24
the enemy of all the Jews, had plotted [z] Ex 17:8-16
against the Jews to destroy them and [a] Est 3:7
had cast the *pur*[a] (that is, the lot[b]) for [b] Lev 16:8
their ruin and destruction. 25 But when
the plot came to the king's attention,[a]
he issued written orders that the evil
scheme Haman had devised against the
Jews should come back onto his own 9:25
head,[c] and that he and his sons should [c] Ps 7:16
be hanged[d] on the gallows.[e] 26 (Therefore [d] Dt 21:22-23 [e] Est 7:10
these days were called Purim, from the 9:26
word *pur*.[f]) Because of everything writ- [f] ver 20; Est 3:7
ten in this letter and because of what
they had seen and what had happened
to them, 27 the Jews took it upon themselves to establish the custom that they
and their descendants and all who join
them should without fail observe these
two days every year, in the way prescribed and at the time appointed.
28 These days should be remembered and
observed in every generation by every

[a] 25 Or *when Esther came before the king*

JESUS FOCUS

A DAY TO REMEMBER

Christians recall the Christmas story each December, reading it, singing about it and reenacting it in plays and pageants; in the same way, contemporary Jews still commemorate their deliverance from Haman's devious plot with their annual Feast of Purim (Esther 9:18–32). This festival derives its name from the casting of lots (Hebrew, *purim*) to select the date on which the Jews were to have been killed (Esther 3:7). The gamble backfired on Haman, however, and he was the one executed. During the modern Feast of Purim, Jewish families read the book of Esther and act out the drama it portrays. There is a significant connection between the Jewish commemoration of Purim and our own Christmas celebration: If there had not been the cause for celebration of a Feast of Purim, there would never have been a Christmas. If God had not delivered his people from Haman's edict to destroy the Jews, Jesus would never have been born. Once again we see clearly that God has always had one resolute purpose: to prepare the world for the coming Savior.

family, and in every province and in
every city. And these days of Purim
should never cease to be celebrated by
the Jews, nor should the memory of
them die out among their descendants.
9:29 [29]So Queen Esther, daughter of Abi-
g Est 2:15 hail,[g] along with Mordecai the Jew,
wrote with full authority to confirm this
second letter concerning Purim. [30]And
9:30 Mordecai sent letters to all the Jews in
h Est 1:1 the 127 provinces[h] of the kingdom of
Xerxes—words of goodwill and assur-
ance— [31]to establish these days of Purim at their designated times, as Mordecai the Jew and Queen Esther had
decreed for them, and as they had es-
9:31 tablished for themselves and their de-
i Est 4:16 scendants in regard to their times of
j Est 4:1-3 fasting[i] and lamentation.[j] [32]Esther's decree confirmed these regulations about
Purim, and it was written down in the
records.

The Greatness of Mordecai

10 King Xerxes imposed tribute
throughout the empire, to its 10:1
distant shores.[k] [2]And all his acts of pow- k Ps 72:10; 97:1; Isa 24:15
er and might, together with a full ac-
count of the greatness of Mordecai[l] to 10:2 l Est 8:15; 9:4
which the king had raised him,[m] are m Ge 41:44
they not written in the book of the an- n Est 2:23
nals[n] of the kings of Media and Persia? 10:3
[3]Mordecai the Jew was second[o] in rank[p] o Da 5:7 p Ge 41:43
to King Xerxes,[q] preeminent among the q Ge 41:40
Jews, and held in high esteem by his r Ne 2:10; Jer 29:4-7;
many fellow Jews, because he worked for Da 6:3
the good of his people and spoke up for
the welfare of all the Jews.[r]

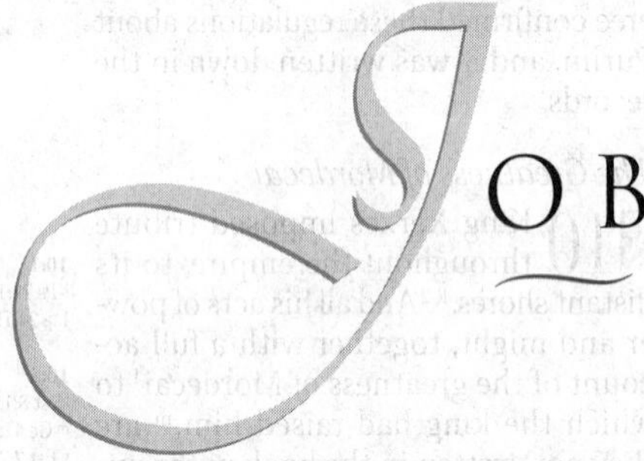

Why did Job long for a mediator between himself and God? (Job 9:33–35)

♦*Confident of his clear conscience but seemingly unable to gain a hearing from God, Job longed for an arbitrator to decide his case with God. Job knew there was no one who could make an appeal to God on his behalf. Yet his desire for an advocate is a powerful example of our need for a Savior.*

What hope is there for the discouraged or depressed? (Job 17:15)

♦*That we are not alone. God is present with us even in the depths of our despair (Psalm 139). Our ultimate hope, though, lies in Jesus, who promises one day to wipe away every tear (Revelation 21:4).*

How is death the great equalizer? (Job 21:23–26)

♦*Everyone will eventually die. But although the physical fate of all may be the same, there is no parity after death in the spiritual realm. Faith in Jesus makes the difference between eternal death and eternal life (Matthew 25:46).*

Jesus in Job First-time readers may find the book of Job difficult to understand. Read the first two chapters and the last chapter of the book to see things that Job and his friends did not see. The chapters that come between these three are the observations of Job and his friends about the circumstances of Job's life. Job's friends made some profounc statements, but they also made some colossal errors in judgment. Remember that people in Job's time were impressed by speakers who used flowery language rather than point-by-point logic. As a result, watch for a wide range of literary techniques in this book: dialogue, poetry, proverbs, riddles, laments, curses and word pictures.

With God's permission, Satan pulled out all the stops in his attempt to force Job to sin, but even under this tremendous pressure Job did not fold. Compare this remark able story to that of Satan's temptation of Jesus in the desert (Matthew 4:1–11). How will you respond when Satan aims his arsenal in your direction?

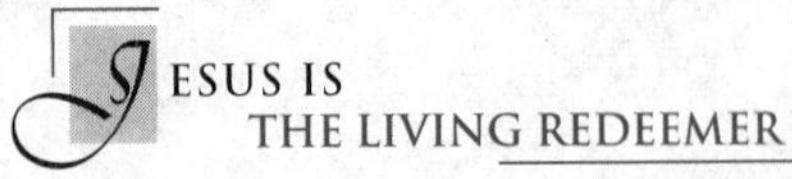

Prologue

1:1 **1** In the land of Uz[a] there lived a
[a]Jer 25:20 man whose name was Job.[b] This
[b]Eze 14:14,20; Jas 5:11 [c]Ge 6:9; man was blameless[c] and upright; he
17:1 [d]Ge 22:12; feared God[d] and shunned evil. 2He had
Ex 18:21 seven sons and three daughters,[e] 3and
1:2 he owned seven thousand sheep, three
[e]Job 42:13 thousand camels, five hundred yoke of
oxen and five hundred donkeys, and had
a large number of servants. He was the
1:3 greatest man[f] among all the people of
[f]Job 29:25 the East.
4His sons used to take turns holding
feasts in their homes, and they would invite their three sisters to eat and drink
with them. 5When a period of feasting
had run its course, Job would send and
1:5 have them purified. Early in the morn-
[g]Ge 8:20; ing he would sacrifice a burnt offering[g]
Job 42:8 for each of them, thinking, "Perhaps my
[h]Job 8:4 [i]1Ki 21:10,13 children have sinned[h] and cursed God[i]
in their hearts." This was Job's regular
custom.

Job's First Test

1:6 6One day the angels[a][j] came to present
[j]Job 38:7 [k]Job 2:1 themselves before the LORD, and Satan[b]
also came with them.[k] 7The LORD said to
Satan, "Where have you come from?"
Satan answered the LORD, "From
1:7 roaming through the earth and going
[l]1Pe 5:8 back and forth in it."[l]
1:8 8Then the LORD said to Satan, "Have
[m]Jos 1:7; you considered my servant Job?[m] There
Job 42:7-8 is no one on earth like him; he is blame-
[n]ver 1 less and upright, a man who fears God
and shuns evil."[n]
1:9 9"Does Job fear God for nothing?"[o]
[o]1Ti 6:5 Satan replied. 10"Have you not put a
1:10 hedge around him and his household
[p]Ps 34:7 [q]ver 3; and everything he has?[p] You have
Job 29:6; 31:25; Ps 128:1-2 blessed the work of his hands, so that
his flocks and herds are spread
throughout the land.[q] 11But stretch out
your hand and strike everything he
1:11 has,[r] and he will surely curse you to
[r]Job 19:21 [s]Job 2:5 your face."[s]
12The LORD said to Satan, "Very well,
then, everything he has is in your hands,
but on the man himself do not lay a
finger."
Then Satan went out from the presence of the LORD.
13One day when Job's sons and daughters were feasting and drinking wine at
the oldest brother's house, 14a messenger came to Job and said, "The oxen
were plowing and the donkeys were 1:15
grazing nearby, 15and the Sabeans[t] at- [t]Ge 10:7;
tacked and carried them off. They put Job 6:19
the servants to the sword, and I am the
only one who has escaped to tell you!"
16While he was still speaking, another messenger came and said, "The fire of
God fell from the sky[u] and burned up 1:16 [u]Ge 19:24
the sheep and the servants,[v] and I am [v]Lev 10:2;
the only one who has escaped to tell Nu 11:1-3
you!"
17While he was still speaking, another messenger came and said, "The 1:17
Chaldeans[w] formed three raiding par- [w]Ge 11:28,31
ties and swept down on your camels and
carried them off. They put the servants
to the sword, and I am the only one who
has escaped to tell you!"
18While he was still speaking, yet another messenger came and said, "Your
sons and daughters were feasting and
drinking wine at the oldest brother's 1:19
house, 19when suddenly a mighty wind[x] [x]Jer 4:11; 13:24

[a] 6 Hebrew *the sons of God* [b] 6 *Satan* means *accuser.*

THE LIMITS OF SATAN'S POWER

Job's story alerts us to the fact that Satan possesses supernatural power to oppress people, even God's people (Job 1). This idea might trouble us, because it opens the door to the idea that Satan can wreak havoc in anyone's life at any time. But we need to remember that his power is limited by God's permission and is subject to God's incomparable power (Job 1:12). "Satan can only go to the end of his chain," as John Newton, the writer of the great hymn "Amazing Grace," put it.

In the New Testament we are given other examples of Satan testing God's people. Satan tempted Jesus, only to find that Jesus would not yield (Luke 4:3–13). We also find that Satan asked permission to "sift [Peter] as wheat," but Jesus reassured Peter by telling him that he had prayed "that your faith may not fail" (Luke 22:31–32). Every person who walks with God can take comfort from the same source of encouragement: God will not let us be tempted beyond what we can bear—and when we are tempted he promises to provide a way out (1 Corinthians 10:13). Furthermore, our precious Jesus stands ready to give us compassionate help when we are tempted, for he is able to sympathize with our weaknesses as One who experienced temptation yet did not yield (Hebrews 4:14–16).

DISCOVERY 117

How About Job?

In an ancient century Satan was on the prowl, seeking a prey to tear apart. Finally he confronted God with shocking arrogance: "I can get anyone to leave you and follow me!" And God responded: "Really? What about my servant Job?"

Who was this man Job whom God singled out for Satan's attention? God said there was no one quite like him (Job 1:1,8). Though no human being, with the exception of Jesus Christ, has ever been without sin, Job was "blameless" in the sense that habitual or flagrant sin had not characterized his life or sullied his reputation. Job was "upright" in the eyes of God; he "feared God" and worshiped him with reverence and devotion. He literally "shunned evil," doing everything possible to avoid sin and to eradicate any thought or action that was inappropriate in the life of one who walks with God.

Indeed, there was no one quite like Job, and Satan had his work cut out for him.

God gave Satan permission to attack anything in Job's life in any way he could—with the single exception that he could not touch Job personally. After ravaging Job's family, fortune and health, there was nothing left for Satan to do. At this extremity most of us would have caved in and cursed God or at least nursed deep-seated bitterness toward him. But not Job. When he learned that all of his children had been taken from him, Job fell flat on his face to honor God (verse 20). What an extraordinary response to nearly inconceivable anguish and seeming injustice. Job knew that God had not deserted him, and he made the choice to trust him—no matter what the outcome.

Satan is very predictable. He is our avowed adversary and always attacks at our point of greatest weakness. He would later use the same tactic with God's Son himself (Matthew 4:4–11). After Jesus' physical and emotional reserves had been depleted from having fasted in the desert for 40 days, Satan attempted to lure him into rejecting God's plan. The devil again employed his full arsenal with suggestions involving food, power and wealth. But Jesus resisted every ploy, using God's own words as his source of strength to form a wall of defense. At each point of attack Jesus demonstrated that he was blameless and upright and that he feared and loved the Father and refused to indulge in sin. Jesus would not allow himself to honor Satan by giving in to his enticements. Instead he challenged Satan: "Worship the Lord your God, and serve him only" (Matthew 4:10). Even when responding to a direct frontal attack, Jesus remained loyal to his Father and to his earthly mission.

The situation hasn't changed much over the centuries. Satan remains "[our] enemy the devil [who] prowls around like a roaring lion looking for someone to devour" (1 Peter 5:8). But we can stand firm with God's help through any temptation by remaining "self-controlled and alert . . . Resist him, standing firm in the faith" (1 Peter 5:8–9)—just as Job and Jesus did.

***Self-Discovery:** At what point of weakness are you most vulnerable to Satan's attacks? Gain strength from the example of Jesus.*

GO TO DISCOVERY 118 ON PAGE 635

swept in from the desert and struck the
four corners of the house. It collapsed
on them and they are dead, and I am
the only one who has escaped to tell
you!"
1:20 [20]At this, Job got up and tore his robe[y]
y Ge 37:29 and shaved his head. Then he fell to the
z 1Pe 5:6 ground in worship[z] [21]and said:

"Naked I came from my mother's
1:21 womb,
a Ecc 5:15; and naked I will depart.[a a]
1Ti 6:7 b 1Sa 2:7 The LORD gave and the LORD has
c Job 2:10; taken away;[b]
Eph 5:20; 1Th 5:18 may the name of the LORD be
praised."[c]

1:22 [22]In all this, Job did not sin by charg-
d Job 2:10 ing God with wrongdoing.[d]

Job's Second Test

2:1 **2** On another day the angels[b] came
e Job 1:6 to present themselves before the
LORD, and Satan also came with them[e]
to present himself before him. [2]And the
LORD said to Satan, "Where have you
come from?"
Satan answered the LORD, "From
roaming through the earth and going
back and forth in it."
[3]Then the LORD said to Satan, "Have
you considered my servant Job? There is
no one on earth like him; he is blameless
2:3 and upright, a man who fears God and
f Job 1:1,8 shuns evil.[f] And he still maintains his in-
g Job 27:6 tegrity,[g] though you incited me against
h Job 9:17 him to ruin him without any reason."[h]
[4]"Skin for skin!" Satan replied. "A man
will give all he has for his own life. [5]But
2:5 stretch out your hand and strike his
i Job 19:20 flesh and bones,[i] and he will surely curse
j Job 1:11 you to your face."[j]
[6]The LORD said to Satan, "Very well,
2:6 then, he is in your hands; but you must
k Job 1:12 spare his life."[k]
[7]So Satan went out from the presence
2:7 of the LORD and afflicted Job with
l Dt 28:35; painful sores from the soles of his feet to
Job 7:5 the top of his head.[l] [8]Then Job took a
2:8 piece of broken pottery and scraped
m Job 42:6; himself with it as he sat among the
Jer 6:26; ashes.[m]
Eze 27:30; [9]His wife said to him, "Are you still
Mt 11:21 holding on to your integrity? Curse God
and die!"
2:10 [10]He replied, "You are talking like a
n Job 1:21 foolish[c] woman. Shall we accept good
from God, and not trouble?"[n]

In all this, Job did not sin in what he 2:10
said.[o] o Job 1:22; Ps 39:1; Jas 1:12; 5:11

Job's Three Friends

[11]When Job's three friends, Eliphaz the 2:11
Temanite,[p] Bildad the Shuhite[q] and Zo- p Ge 36:11; Jer 49:7
phar the Naamathite, heard about all the q Ge 25:2
troubles that had come upon him, they r Job 42:11; Ro 12:15
set out from their homes and met to-
gether by agreement to go and sympathize with him and comfort him.[r]
[12]When they saw him from a distance,
they could hardly recognize him; they
began to weep aloud, and they tore their 2:12
robes and sprinkled dust on their heads.[s] s Jos 7:6; Ne 9:1; La 2:10;
[13]Then they sat on the ground with him Eze 27:30
for seven days and seven nights.[t] No one 2:13
said a word to him, because they saw t Ge 50:10;
how great his suffering was. Eze 3:15

[a] *21* Or *will return there* [b] *1* Hebrew *the sons of God* [c] *10* The Hebrew word rendered *foolish* denotes moral deficiency.

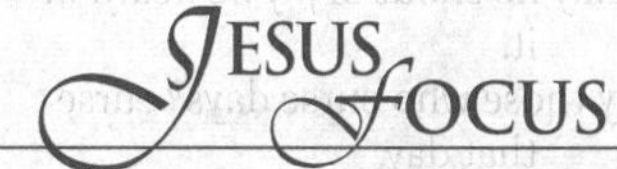

WHEN GOD DOESN'T ANSWER

Job's suffering was so intense that his friends sat and commiserated with him in silence for a full week before finally speaking (Job 2:13). Shared grief and silent empathy are often the best help we can offer. When Job's friends finally did speak, however, they only added to his suffering by blaming him for the catastrophes and trying to entice him to question God. Sometimes God's people wonder why God seems to ignore their cries for help. But it may be that his silence reflects the very shared grief that is so often our only recourse in dealing with a hurting friend or loved one. While Jesus was suffering the cruel agony of the cross, the experience of God's silence must have seemed excruciating—so much so that Jesus cried out in despair: "My God, my God, why have you forsaken me?" (Matthew 27:46). But God's silence is never a rejection of his people. In Jesus' case, as in our own situations, God the Father knew exactly where he was and what he was doing: He was making it possible for us to have a relationship with him. The abandonment that Jesus *felt* was precisely what we *deserved*. In those awful moments when Jesus took our place and accepted the punishment for our sins, God the Father was right there with him in the middle of the pain. At the most crucial moment in history God may have been silent—but he was at work!

Job Speaks

3 After this, Job opened his mouth and cursed the day of his birth. [2]He said:

[3]"May the day of my birth perish,
and the night it was said, 'A boy is born!'[u]
[4]That day—may it turn to darkness;
may God above not care about it;
may no light shine upon it.
[5]May darkness and deep shadow[a][v]
claim it once more;
may a cloud settle over it;
may blackness overwhelm its light.
[6]That night—may thick darkness[w] seize it;
may it not be included among the days of the year
nor be entered in any of the months.
[7]May that night be barren;
may no shout of joy be heard in it.
[8]May those who curse days[b] curse that day,
those who are ready to rouse Leviathan.[x]
[9]May its morning stars become dark;
may it wait for daylight in vain
and not see the first rays of dawn,[y]
[10]for it did not shut the doors of the womb on me
to hide trouble from my eyes.

[11]"Why did I not perish at birth,
and die as I came from the womb?[z]
[12]Why were there knees to receive me[a]
and breasts that I might be nursed?
[13]For now I would be lying down[b] in peace;
I would be asleep and at rest[c]
[14]with kings and counselors of the earth,[d]
who built for themselves places now lying in ruins,[e]
[15]with rulers[f] who had gold,
who filled their houses with silver.[g]
[16]Or why was I not hidden in the ground like a stillborn child,[h]
like an infant who never saw the light of day?
[17]There the wicked cease from turmoil,
and there the weary are at rest.[i]
[18]Captives also enjoy their ease;
they no longer hear the slave driver's shout.[j]
[19]The small and the great are there,
and the slave is freed from his master.

[20]"Why is light given to those in misery,
and life to the bitter of soul,[k]
[21]to those who long for death that does not come,[l]
who search for it more than for hidden treasure,[m]
[22]who are filled with gladness
and rejoice when they reach the grave?
[23]Why is life given to a man
whose way is hidden,
whom God has hedged in?[n]
[24]For sighing comes to me instead of food;[o]
my groans pour out like water.[p]
[25]What I feared has come upon me;
what I dreaded[q] has happened to me.
[26]I have no peace, no quietness;
I have no rest,[r] but only turmoil."

HE WHO HAS REALLY GRASPED WHAT JESUS SAID CAN APPRECIATE HIS SILENCE.

Ignatius, *Early Church Father*

Eliphaz

4 Then Eliphaz the Temanite replied:

[2]"If someone ventures a word with you, will you be impatient?
But who can keep from speaking?[s]
[3]Think how you have instructed many,
how you have strengthened feeble hands.[t]
[4]Your words have supported those who stumbled;

3:3 [u]Job 10:18-19; Jer 20:14-18
3:5 [v]Job 10:21,22; Ps 23:4; Jer 2:6; 13:16
3:6 [w]Job 23:17
3:8 [x]Job 41:1,8,10, 25
3:9 [y]Job 41:18
3:11 [z]Job 10:18
3:12 [a]Ge 30:3; Isa 66:12
3:13 [b]Job 17:13 [c]Job 7:8-10,21; 10:22; 14:10-12; 19:27; 21:13,23
3:14 [d]Job 12:17 [e]Job 15:28
3:15 [f]Job 12:21 [g]Job 27:17
3:16 [h]Ps 58:8; Ecc 6:3
3:17 [i]Job 17:16
3:18 [j]Job 39:7
3:20 [k]1Sa 1:10; Jer 20:18; Eze 27:30-31
3:21 [l]Rev 9:6 [m]Pr 2:4
3:23 [n]Job 19:6,8,12; Ps 88:8; La 3:7
3:24 [o]Job 6:7; 33:20 [p]Ps 42:3,4
3:25 [q]Job 30:15
3:26 [r]Job 7:4,14
4:2 [s]Job 32:20
4:3 [t]Isa 35:3; Heb 12:12

[a] 5 Or *and the shadow of death* [b] 8 Or *the sea*

DISCOVERY 118

Facing the Dark Night of Your Soul

All the power in the universe amounts to a mere spark when compared to God's infinite strength. He can do anything, and yet he allows innocent people to suffer—sometimes for a very long time under agonizing circumstances. If he is so powerful, why doesn't he do something to rectify the situation? The question appears again and again not only throughout history but daily in the lives of people all around us. The book of Job describes one such struggle.

In a matter of just a few days Job lost his children, his health and his wealth. The situation seemed so intolerable that his wife counseled him to "curse God and die" just to get the suffering over with (Job 2:9). Job described his traumatic series of tragedies as a "darkness" and even went so far as to express a wish that the day of his birth be cursed (Job 3:1–4).

Job knew what it was to endure intense grief: "Sighing comes to me instead of food; my groans pour out like water. What I feared has come upon me; what I dreaded has happened to me. I have no peace, no quietness; I have no rest, but only turmoil" (verses 24–26). The frustrating element in Job's story is that no answers were offered in response to the questions. Instead God simply pointed Job toward a new way to interpret the suffering—from God's own perspective.

The first point this book drives home is that Satan is alive and well. It was Satan, not God, who brought about Job's suffering. Sometimes human suffering is Satan's fault. He is the one who accuses God's people and tries to destroy us by tempting us to reject God (Revelation 12:10). But even though Satan caused the tragedies in Job's life, God put limits on what his enemy could do (Job 1:12; 2:6). Nothing ever happens to God's people without God's permission—including the trials brought about as a result of Satan's direct assaults.

If God controls the boundaries of suffering, why does he allow it at all? For one thing God is patient. If he were to pronounce immediate judgment upon every injustice in the world caused by sin, all sinners would of necessity be destroyed. Instead God uses suffering to teach us to turn to him for strength and guidance and to bolster our faith: "Consider it pure joy . . . whenever you face trials of many kinds, because you know that the testing of your faith develops perseverance" (James 1:2–3). Thinking about the sufferings of Jesus can bring us the encouragement we need to endure. The writer to the Hebrews invites us to "fix our eyes on Jesus, the author and perfecter of our faith, who for the joy set before him endured the cross, scorning its shame, and sat down at the right hand of the throne of God. Consider him who endured such opposition from sinful men, so that you will not grow weary and lose heart" (Hebrews 12:2–3).

Self-Discovery: *Are you willing to pray honestly, even in a difficult situation, that God's will might be done? If so, are you willing to accept the outcome one way or the other?*

GO TO DISCOVERY 119 ON PAGE 641

you have strengthened faltering
knees.[u]
5 But now trouble comes to you, and
you are discouraged;
it strikes[v] you, and you are
dismayed.[w]
6 Should not your piety be your
confidence[x]
and your blameless[y] ways your
hope?

7 "Consider now: Who, being
innocent, has ever
perished?[z]
Where were the upright ever
destroyed?[a]
8 As I have observed, those who
plow evil[b]
and those who sow trouble reap
it.[c]
9 At the breath of God[d] they are
destroyed;
at the blast of his anger they
perish.[e]
10 The lions may roar and growl,
yet the teeth of the great lions
are broken.[f]
11 The lion perishes for lack of prey,[g]
and the cubs of the lioness are
scattered.

12 "A word was secretly brought to
me,
my ears caught a whisper[h] of it.[i]
13 Amid disquieting dreams in the
night,
when deep sleep falls on men,[j]
14 fear and trembling seized me
and made all my bones shake.[k]
15 A spirit glided past my face,
and the hair on my body stood
on end.
16 It stopped,
but I could not tell what it was.
A form stood before my eyes,
and I heard a hushed voice:
17 'Can a mortal be more righteous
than God?[l]
Can a man be more pure than
his Maker?[m]
18 If God places no trust in his
servants,
if he charges his angels with
error,[n]
19 how much more those who live in
houses of clay,[o]
whose foundations[p] are in the
dust,[q]

4:4 [u] Isa 35:3; Heb 12:12
4:5 [v] Job 19:21 [w] Job 6:14
4:6 [x] Pr 3:26 [y] Job 1:1
4:7 [z] Job 36:7 [a] Job 8:20; Ps 37:25
4:8 [b] Job 15:35 [c] Pr 22:8; Hos 10:13; Gal 6:7-8
4:9 [d] Job 15:30; Isa 30:33; 2Th 2:8 [e] Job 40:13
4:10 [f] Job 5:15; Ps 58:6
4:11 [g] Job 27:14; Ps 34:10
4:12 [h] Job 26:14 [i] Job 33:14
4:13 [j] Job 33:15
4:14 [k] Jer 23:9; Hab 3:16
4:17 [l] Job 9:2 [m] Job 35:10
4:18 [n] Job 15:15
4:19 [o] Job 10:9 [p] Job 22:16 [q] Ge 2:7

who are crushed more readily
than a moth!
20 Between dawn and dusk they are
broken to pieces;
unnoticed, they perish forever.[r]
21 Are not the cords of their tent
pulled up,[s]
so that they die without
wisdom?'[a][t]

5 "Call if you will, but who will
answer you?
To which of the holy ones[u] will
you turn?
2 Resentment kills a fool,
and envy slays the simple.[v]

4:20 [r] Job 14:2,20; 20:7; Ps 90:5-6
4:21 [s] Job 8:22 [t] Job 18:21; 36:12
5:1 [u] Job 15:15
5:2 [v] Pr 12:16

[a] *21* Some interpreters end the quotation after verse 17.

JESUS AND YOU

MISGUIDED JUDGMENT

Job's friends wrongly assumed that his pain was a direct punishment for some misdeed on his part; their long, eloquent speeches implied that he needed to submit to God's discipline (Job 5:17). We too are often quick to judge someone else's actions and motivations when the walls appear to be crashing in all around him or her. But just as we often do, Job's friends were starting from an invalid premise. In reality, God was not disciplining Job; he was using Job's situation and response as a lesson to Satan—and ultimately as an example for us. Jesus referred to two events in New Testament times as object lessons to teach people the truths found in Job. In the first instance, Pilate had apparently made arrangements for certain Galileans to be executed while they were offering sacrifices in the temple (Luke 13:1–3). In the second instance 18 people were crushed to death when a tower in Siloam collapsed. "Do you think they were more guilty than all the others living in Jerusalem?" (Luke 13:4), Jesus asked, responding immediately and emphatically to his own rhetorical question: "I tell you, no!" (Luke 13:5). Whether something bad happens by accident or because someone has done something wrong, God remains in control. Jesus was quick to refocus the attitudes of his listeners, encouraging people to look at their own lives rather than trying to determine what sin someone else had done that would bring tragedy into his or her life. No matter what happens in life or what other people choose to do, we can opt for placing our trust in God's perfect plan and provision.

5:3 [w]Ps 37:35; Jer 12:2 [x]Job 24:18

3 I myself have seen a fool taking
root,[w]
but suddenly his house was
cursed.[x]

5:4 [y]Job 4:11 [z]Am 5:12

4 His children are far from safety,[y]
crushed in court[z] without a
defender.

5:5 [a]Job 18:8-10

5 The hungry consume his harvest,[a]
taking it even from among
thorns,
and the thirsty pant after his
wealth.
6 For hardship does not spring from
the soil,
nor does trouble sprout from the
ground.

5:7 [b]Job 14:1

7 Yet man is born to trouble[b]
as surely as sparks fly upward.

8 "But if it were I, I would appeal to
God;

5:8 [c]Ps 35:23; 50:15

I would lay my cause before him.[c]

5:9 [d]Job 42:3; Ps 40:5

9 He performs wonders that cannot
be fathomed,[d]
miracles that cannot be counted.
10 He bestows rain on the earth;

5:10 [e]Job 36:28

he sends water upon the
countryside.[e]

5:11 [f]Ps 113:7-8

11 The lowly he sets on high,[f]
and those who mourn are lifted
to safety.

5:12 [g]Ne 4:15; Ps 33:10

12 He thwarts the plans[g] of the crafty,
so that their hands achieve no
success.

5:13 [h]1Co 3:19*

13 He catches the wise in their
craftiness,[h]
and the schemes of the wily are
swept away.

5:14 [i]Job 12:25 [j]Dt 28:29

14 Darkness[i] comes upon them in the
daytime;
at noon they grope as in the
night.[j]

5:15 [k]Ps 35:10 [l]Job 4:10

15 He saves the needy[k] from the
sword in their mouth;
he saves them from the clutches
of the powerful.[l]

5:16 [m]Ps 107:42

16 So the poor have hope,
and injustice shuts its mouth.[m]

5:17 [n]Jas 1:12 [o]Ps 94:12; Pr 3:11 [p]Heb 12:5-11

17 "Blessed is the man whom God
corrects;[n]
so do not despise the discipline[o]
of the Almighty.[a][p]

5:18 [q]Isa 30:26 [r]1Sa 2:6

18 For he wounds, but he also binds
up;[q]
he injures, but his hands also
heal.[r]

19 From six calamities he will rescue
you;

5:19 [s]Ps 34:19; 91:10

in seven no harm will befall you.[s]

5:20 [t]Ps 33:19 [u]Ps 144:10

20 In famine[t] he will ransom you from
death,
and in battle from the stroke of
the sword.[u]

5:21 [v]Ps 31:20 [w]Ps 91:5

21 You will be protected from the lash
of the tongue,[v]
and need not fear[w] when
destruction comes.
22 You will laugh at destruction and
famine,
and need not fear the beasts of

5:22 [x]Ps 91:13; Eze 34:25

the earth.[x]
23 For you will have a covenant with

5:23 [y]Ps 91:12 [z]Isa 11:6-9

the stones[y] of the field,
and the wild animals will be at
peace with you.[z]
24 You will know that your tent is
secure;
you will take stock of your
property and find nothing

5:24 [a]Job 8:6

missing.[a]

5:25 [b]Ps 112:2 [c]Ps 72:16; Isa 44:3-4

25 You will know that your children
will be many,[b]
and your descendants like the
grass of the earth.[c]

5:26 [d]Ge 15:15

26 You will come to the grave in full
vigor,[d]
like sheaves gathered in season.
27 "We have examined this, and it is
true.
So hear it and apply it to yourself."

Job

6 Then Job replied:

2 "If only my anguish could be
weighed
and all my misery be placed on

6:2 [e]Job 31:6

the scales![e]

6:3 [f]Pr 27:3 [g]Job 23:2

3 It would surely outweigh the sand[f]
of the seas—
no wonder my words have been
impetuous.[g]

6:4 [h]Ps 38:2 [i]Job 16:12,13 [j]Job 21:20 [k]Job 30:15 [l]Ps 88:15-18

4 The arrows[h] of the Almighty are in
me,[i]
my spirit drinks[j] in their poison;
God's terrors[k] are marshaled
against me.[l]
5 Does a wild donkey bray when it
has grass,
or an ox bellow when it has
fodder?

[a] 17 Hebrew *Shaddai*; here and throughout Job

6 Is tasteless food eaten without salt,
or is there flavor in the white of
an egg[a]?
7 I refuse to touch it;
such food makes me ill.[m]
8 "Oh, that I might have my request,
that God would grant what I
hope for,[n]
9 that God would be willing to crush
me,
to let loose his hand and cut me
off![o]
10 Then I would still have this
consolation—
my joy in unrelenting pain—
that I had not denied the words[p]
of the Holy One.[q]
11 "What strength do I have, that I
should still hope?
What prospects, that I should be
patient?[r]
12 Do I have the strength of stone?
Is my flesh bronze?
13 Do I have any power to help myself,[s]
now that success has been
driven from me?
14 "A despairing man[t] should have the
devotion[u] of his friends,
even though he forsakes the fear
of the Almighty.
15 But my brothers are as
undependable as
intermittent streams,[v]

6:7 [m]Job 3:24
6:8 [n]Job 14:13
6:9 [o]Nu 11:15; 1Ki 19:4
6:10 [p]Job 22:22; 23:12 [q]Lev 19:2; Isa 57:15
6:11 [r]Job 21:4
6:13 [s]Job 26:2
6:14 [t]Job 4:5 [u]Job 15:4
6:15 [v]Ps 38:11; Jer 15:18

WHY KEEP LIVING?

Job's wife counseled him to "curse God and die!" (Job 2:9). Job didn't take her advice, but he did curse the day he was born (Job 3:1–10). His suffering was so intense that he pleaded with God for a quick death (Job 6:8–9). His speeches contain some of the most profound expressions of pain and despair in all of literature. But God did not grant Job's request. Even when circumstances were so desperate that Job wanted to die, God was still at work in his life, doing what he knew was best. God taught Job a new perspective on pain and suffering and used Job's situation and response to teach Satan a lesson about the depth of God's grace and the tenacity of this man's faith. It is tempting to focus on pleasures and comfort as our ultimate purpose in life, but Jesus reminds us that *he* alone must be our reason for living (John 14:6).

as the streams that overflow
16 when darkened by thawing ice
and swollen with melting snow,
17 but that cease to flow in the dry
season,
and in the heat[w] vanish from
their channels.
18 Caravans turn aside from their
routes;
they go up into the wasteland
and perish.
19 The caravans of Tema[x] look for
water,
the traveling merchants of Sheba
look in hope.
20 They are distressed, because they
had been confident;
they arrive there, only to be
disappointed.[y]
21 Now you too have proved to be of
no help;
you see something dreadful and
are afraid.[z]
22 Have I ever said, 'Give something
on my behalf,
pay a ransom for me from your
wealth,
23 deliver me from the hand of the
enemy,
ransom me from the clutches of
the ruthless'?
24 "Teach me, and I will be quiet;[a]
show me where I have been
wrong.
25 How painful are honest words![b]
But what do your arguments
prove?
26 Do you mean to correct what I say,
and treat the words of a
despairing man as wind?[c]
27 You would even cast lots[d] for the
fatherless
and barter away your friend.
28 "But now be so kind as to look at
me.
Would I lie to your face?[e]
29 Relent, do not be unjust;
reconsider, for my integrity is at
stake.[b][f]
30 Is there any wickedness on my lips?[g]
Can my mouth not discern[h]
malice?

7

"Does not man have hard
service[i] on earth?[j]

6:17 [w]Job 24:19
6:19 [x]Ge 25:15; Isa 21:14
6:20 [y]Jer 14:3
6:21 [z]Ps 38:11
6:24 [a]Ps 39:1
6:25 [b]Ecc 12:11
6:26 [c]Job 8:2; 15:3
6:27 [d]Joel 3:3; Na 3:10; 2Pe 2:3
6:28 [e]Job 27:4; 33:1, 3; 36:3,4
6:29 [f]Job 23:7,10; 34:5,36; 42:6
6:30 [g]Job 27:4 [h]Job 12:11
7:1 [i]Job 14:14; Isa 40:2 [j]Job 5:7

[a]6 The meaning of the Hebrew for this phrase is uncertain. [b]29 Or *my righteousness still stands*

Are not his days like those of a
hired man?[k]
2 Like a slave longing for the evening
shadows,
or a hired man waiting eagerly
for his wages,[l]
3 so I have been allotted months of
futility,
and nights of misery have been
assigned to me.[m]
4 When I lie down I think, 'How long
before I get up?'[n]
The night drags on, and I toss till
dawn.
5 My body is clothed with worms[o]
and scabs,
my skin is broken and festering.

6 "My days are swifter than a
weaver's shuttle,[p]
and they come to an end
without hope.[q]
7 Remember, O God, that my life is
but a breath;[r]
my eyes will never see happiness
again.[s]
8 The eye that now sees me will see
me no longer;
you will look for me, but I will be
no more.[t]
9 As a cloud vanishes and is gone,
so he who goes down to the
grave[a][u] does not return.[v]
10 He will never come to his house
again;
his place[w] will know him no
more.[x]

11 "Therefore I will not keep silent;[y]
I will speak out in the anguish of
my spirit,
I will complain in the bitterness
of my soul.[z]
12 Am I the sea, or the monster of the
deep,[a]
that you put me under guard?
13 When I think my bed will comfort
me
and my couch will ease my
complaint,[b]
14 even then you frighten me with
dreams
and terrify[c] me with visions,
15 so that I prefer strangling and
death,[d]
rather than this body of mine.
16 I despise my life;[e] I would not live
forever.

7:1 [k] Job 14:6
7:2 [l] Lev 19:13
7:3 [m] Job 16:7; Ps 6:6
7:4 [n] Dt 28:67
7:5 [o] Job 17:14; Isa 14:11
7:6 [p] Job 9:25 [q] Job 13:15; 17:11,15
7:7 [r] Ps 78:39; Jas 4:14 [s] Job 9:25
7:8 [t] Job 20:7,9,21
7:9 [u] Job 11:8 [v] 2Sa 12:23; Job 30:15
7:10 [w] Job 27:21,23 [x] Job 8:18
7:11 [y] Ps 40:9 [z] 1Sa 1:10
7:12 [a] Eze 32:2-3
7:13 [b] Job 9:27
7:14 [c] Job 9:34
7:15 [d] 1Ki 19:4
7:16 [e] Job 9:21; 10:1

Let me alone; my days have no
meaning.
17 "What is man that you make so
much of him,
that you give him so much
attention,[f]
18 that you examine him every
morning
and test him every moment?[g]
19 Will you never look away from me,
or let me alone even for an
instant?[h]
20 If I have sinned, what have I done
to you,[i]
O watcher of men?
Why have you made me your
target?[j]
Have I become a burden to you?[b]
21 Why do you not pardon my
offenses
and forgive my sins?[k]
For I will soon lie down in the dust;[l]
you will search for me, but I will
be no more."

Bildad

8 Then Bildad the Shuhite replied:

2 "How long will you say such things?
Your words are a blustering
wind.[m]
3 Does God pervert justice?[n]
Does the Almighty pervert what
is right?[o]
4 When your children sinned against
him,
he gave them over to the penalty
of their sin.[p]
5 But if you will look to God
and plead[q] with the Almighty,
6 if you are pure and upright,
even now he will rouse himself
on your behalf[r]
and restore you to your rightful
place.[s]
7 Your beginnings will seem humble,
so prosperous[t] will your future
be.

8 "Ask the former generations[u]
and find out what their fathers
learned,
9 for we were born only yesterday
and know nothing,[v]

7:17 [f] Ps 8:4; 144:3; Heb 2:6
7:18 [g] Job 14:3
7:19 [h] Job 9:18
7:20 [i] Job 35:6 [j] Job 16:12
7:21 [k] Job 10:14 [l] Job 10:9; Ps 104:29
8:2 [m] Job 6:26
8:3 [n] Dt 32:4; 2Ch 19:7; Ro 3:5 [o] Ge 18:25
8:4 [p] Job 1:19
8:5 [q] Job 11:13
8:6 [r] Ps 7:6 [s] Job 5:24
8:7 [t] Job 42:12
8:8 [u] Dt 4:32; 32:7; Job 15:18
8:9 [v] Ge 47:9

[a] 9 Hebrew *Sheol* [b] 20 A few manuscripts of the Masoretic Text, an ancient Hebrew scribal tradition and Septuagint; most manuscripts of the Masoretic Text *I have become a burden to myself.*

and our days on earth are but a
shadow.[w]
10 Will they not instruct you and tell
you?
Will they not bring forth words
from their understanding?
11 Can papyrus grow tall where there
is no marsh?
Can reeds thrive without water?
12 While still growing and uncut,
they wither more quickly than
grass.[x]
13 Such is the destiny of all who forget
God;[y]
so perishes the hope of the
godless.[z]
14 What he trusts in is fragile[a];
what he relies on is a spider's
web.[a]
15 He leans on his web,[b] but it gives
way;
he clings to it, but it does not
hold.[c]
16 He is like a well-watered plant in
the sunshine,
spreading its shoots[d] over the
garden;[e]
17 it entwines its roots around a pile
of rocks
and looks for a place among the
stones.
18 But when it is torn from its spot,
that place disowns it and says, 'I
never saw you.'[f]
19 Surely its life withers[g] away,
and[b] from the soil other plants
grow.[h]
20 "Surely God does not reject a
blameless[i] man
or strengthen the hands of
evildoers.[j]
21 He will yet fill your mouth with
laughter[k]
and your lips with shouts of joy.[l]
22 Your enemies will be clothed in
shame,[m]
and the tents of the wicked will
be no more."[n]

Job

9

Then Job replied:

2 "Indeed, I know that this is true.
But how can a mortal be
righteous before God?[o]
3 Though one wished to dispute
with him,
he could not answer him one
time out of a thousand.[p]
4 His wisdom[q] is profound, his
power is vast.[r]
Who has resisted him and come
out unscathed?[s]
5 He moves mountains without their
knowing it
and overturns them in his anger.[t]
6 He shakes the earth[u] from its place
and makes its pillars tremble.[v]
7 He speaks to the sun and it does
not shine;
he seals off the light of the stars.[w]
8 He alone stretches out the heavens[x]
and treads on the waves of the
sea.[y]
9 He is the Maker of the Bear and
Orion,
the Pleiades and the
constellations of the south.[z]
10 He performs wonders[a] that cannot
be fathomed,
miracles that cannot be counted.[b]
11 When he passes me, I cannot see
him;
when he goes by, I cannot
perceive him.[c]
12 If he snatches away, who can stop
him?[d]
Who can say to him, 'What are
you doing?'[e]

a 14 The meaning of the Hebrew for this word is uncertain. *b 19* Or *Surely all the joy it has / is that*

8:9 [w] 1Ch 29:15; Job 7:6
8:12 [x] Ps 129:6; Jer 17:6
8:13 [y] Ps 9:17 [z] Job 11:20; 13:16; 15:34; Pr 10:28
8:14 [a] Isa 59:5
8:15 [b] Job 27:18 [c] Ps 49:11
8:16 [d] Ps 80:11 [e] Ps 37:35; Jer 11:16
8:18 [f] Job 7:8; Ps 37:36
8:19 [g] Job 20:5 [h] Ecc 1:4
8:20 [i] Job 1:1 [j] Job 21:30
8:21 [k] Job 5:22 [l] Ps 126:2; 132:16
8:22 [m] Ps 35:26; 109:29; 132:18 [n] Job 18:6,14,21
9:2 [o] Job 4:17; Ps 143:2; Ro 3:20
9:3 [p] Job 10:2; 40:2
9:4 [q] Job 11:6 [r] Job 36:5 [s] 2Ch 13:12
9:5 [t] Mic 1:4
9:6 [u] Isa 2:21; Hag 2:6; Heb 12:26 [v] Job 26:11
9:7 [w] Isa 13:10; Eze 32:8
9:8 [x] Ge 1:6; Ps 104:2-3 [y] Job 38:16; Ps 77:19
9:9 [z] Ge 1:16; Job 38:31; Am 5:8
9:10 [a] Ps 71:15 [b] Job 5:9
9:11 [c] Job 23:8-9; 35:14
9:12 [d] Job 11:10 [e] Isa 45:9; Ro 9:20

ARMS TOO SHORT

A gospel musical from some years ago based on the book of Job was titled "Arms Too Short to Box With God." Job knew that he didn't stand a chance if he was going to box with God, for God is just so incomparably great (Job 9:1–20; see also Isaiah 59:1). Because of the boundless, unfathomable distance Job perceived between God and humanity, Job pled for an arbitrator to intercede on his behalf, but none was available (Job 9:33–35). What Job longed for, what we long for, Jesus provides. The New Testament describes Jesus as the "one mediator between God and men" (1 Timothy 2:5). Whenever we feel as though we are unable to reach God or to obtain a fair hearing from him, we can remember that Jesus speaks directly to God the Father on our behalf (Hebrews 7:25; 1 John 2:1).

Righteous Before God?

People will attempt just about anything in order to present themselves in a favorable light before others whose opinions they value. We often do the same thing with God. We presume that he will be pleased if we are kind enough, "religious" enough or willing to sacrifice enough. If we work hard enough, maybe that will suit him, or maybe we can charm him if we do enough to help our neighbors. Perhaps we can become sufficiently accomplished in some area to impress him once and for all.

But again and again God reminds us that there is nothing we can do to persuade him to love us more than he already does, to be more supportive and encouraging than he already is. Job came to terms with this reality in chapter 9:1, where he asked rhetorically, "How can a mortal be righteous before God?"

The apostle Paul made the same mistake we often do. For years he had lived under the presupposition that his list of merits was quite impressive to God (Philippians 3:5–6). He defended the "purity" of the Jewish faith with obsessive passion, even to the point of "breathing out murderous threats against the Lord's disciples" (Acts 9:1).

When measured against the lives of most other people, whether religious or not, Paul's credentials were indeed imposing. Then one day he learned through a dramatic encounter with the risen Jesus that all of his self-congratulation meant nothing when compared to God's purity. He realized that God is one hundred percent holy, that he can tolerate nothing less than absolute perfection.

Since the beginning of time not one person except Jesus Christ has been able to exhibit the faultlessness God's very nature demands of us. Hebrews 4:15 reminds us that "we do not have a high priest who is unable to sympathize with our weaknesses, but we have one who has been tempted in every way, just as we are—yet was without sin." And the writer to the Hebrews took up the same theme in Hebrews 7:26: "Such a high priest meets our need—one who is holy, blameless, pure, set apart from sinners, exalted above the heavens."

This desperate state of affairs is precisely why Jesus, God's sinless Son, was born as a human. He died on the cross in our place and then rose from the dead to prove that the dire situation brought about by our sinfulness need not prove terminal. We can choose life with God or death separated from him by an impenetrable gulf. When we make the decision to accept Jesus as Savior we become God's beloved children. God no longer sees the chasm of sin that has separated us from himself; instead he views us just as he sees Jesus—as pure and untarnished: "God made him who had no sin to be sin for us, so that in him we might become the righteousness of God" (2 Corinthians 5:21).

Self-Discovery: *Are you sometimes tempted to congratulate yourself because you think your own credentials for salvation are so impressive? If someone else has congratulated you for something you have accomplished for the Lord, did you make it a point to give God the glory?*

GO TO DISCOVERY 120 ON PAGE 651

9:13 [f]Job 26:12; Ps 89:10; Isa 30:7; 51:9

13 God does not restrain his anger;
even the cohorts of Rahab[f]
cowered at his feet.

14 "How then can I dispute with him?
How can I find words to argue
with him?

9:15 [g]Job 10:15 [h]Job 8:5

15 Though I were innocent, I could
not answer him;[g]
I could only plead[h] with my
Judge for mercy.
16 Even if I summoned him and he
responded,
I do not believe he would give
me a hearing.

9:17 [i]Job 16:12 [j]Job 30:22 [k]Job 16:14 [l]Job 2:3

17 He would crush me[i] with a storm[j]
and multiply[k] my wounds for no
reason.[l]
18 He would not let me regain my
breath
but would overwhelm me with
misery.[m]

9:18 [m]Job 7:19; 27:2

19 If it is a matter of strength, he is
mighty!
And if it is a matter of justice,
who will summon him*[a]*?
20 Even if I were innocent, my mouth
would condemn me;
if I were blameless, it would
pronounce me guilty.

9:21 [n]Job 1:1 [o]Job 7:16

21 "Although I am blameless,[n]
I have no concern for myself;
I despise my own life.[o]

9:22 [p]Job 10:8; Ecc 9:2,3; Eze 21:3

22 It is all the same; that is why I say,
'He destroys both the blameless
and the wicked.'[p]

9:23 [q]Heb 11:36 [r]Job 24:1,12

23 When a scourge[q] brings sudden
death,
he mocks the despair of the
innocent.[r]

9:24 [s]Job 10:3; 16:11 [t]Job 12:6

24 When a land falls into the hands of
the wicked,[s]
he blindfolds its judges.[t]
If it is not he, then who is it?

9:25 [u]Job 7:6

25 "My days are swifter than a runner;[u]
they fly away without a glimpse
of joy.

9:26 [v]Isa 18:2 [w]Hab 1:8

26 They skim past like boats of
papyrus,[v]
like eagles swooping down on
their prey.[w]

9:27 [x]Job 7:11

27 If I say, 'I will forget my complaint,[x]
I will change my expression, and
smile,'

9:28 [y]Job 3:25; Ps 119:120 [z]Job 7:21

28 I still dread[y] all my sufferings,
for I know you will not hold me
innocent.[z]

9:29 [a]Ps 37:33

29 Since I am already found guilty,
why should I struggle in vain?[a]

9:30 [b]Job 31:7 [c]Jer 2:22

30 Even if I washed myself with soap*[b]*
and my hands[b] with washing
soda,[c]
31 you would plunge me into a slime
pit
so that even my clothes would
detest me.

9:32 [d]Ro 9:20 [e]Ps 143:2; Ecc 6:10

32 "He is not a man like me that I
might answer him,[d]
that we might confront each
other in court.[e]

9:33 [f]1Sa 2:25

33 If only there were someone to
arbitrate between us,[f]
to lay his hand upon us both,

9:34 [g]Job 13:21; Ps 39:10

34 someone to remove God's rod from
me,[g]
so that his terror would frighten
me no more.
35 Then I would speak up without
fear of him,
but as it now stands with me, I
cannot.[h]

9:35 [h]Job 13:21

10:1 [i]1Ki 19:4 [j]Job 7:11

10 "I loathe my very life;[i]
therefore I will give free rein to
my complaint
and speak out in the bitterness
of my soul.[j]
2 I will say to God: Do not condemn
me,
but tell me what charges[k] you
have against me.

10:2 [k]Job 9:29

10:3 [l]Job 9:22 [m]Job 14:15; Ps 138:8; Isa 64:8 [n]Job 21:16; 22:18

3 Does it please you to oppress me,[l]
to spurn the work of your
hands,[m]
while you smile on the schemes
of the wicked?[n]

10:4 [o]1Sa 16:7

4 Do you have eyes of flesh?
Do you see as a mortal sees?[o]

10:5 [p]Ps 90:2,4; 2Pe 3:8

5 Are your days like those of a mortal
or your years like those of a
man,[p]

10:6 [q]Job 14:16

6 that you must search out my faults
and probe after my sin[q]—
7 though you know that I am not
guilty
and that no one can rescue me
from your hand?

10:8 [r]Ps 119:73

8 "Your hands shaped[r] me and made
me.
Will you now turn and destroy
me?

a 19 See Septuagint; Hebrew *me.* *b* 30 Or *snow*

[9] Remember that you molded me
like clay.[s]
Will you now turn me to dust
again?[t]
[10] Did you not pour me out like milk
and curdle me like cheese,
[11] clothe me with skin and flesh
and knit me together[u] with
bones and sinews?
[12] You gave me life[v] and showed me
kindness,
and in your providence watched
over my spirit.

[13] "But this is what you concealed in
your heart,
and I know that this was in your
mind:[w]
[14] If I sinned, you would be watching
me
and would not let my offense go
unpunished.[x]
[15] If I am guilty—woe to me![y]
Even if I am innocent, I cannot
lift my head,[z]
for I am full of shame
and drowned in[a] my affliction.
[16] If I hold my head high, you stalk
me like a lion[a]
and again display your awesome
power against me.[b]
[17] You bring new witnesses against
me[c]
and increase your anger toward
me;[d]
your forces come against me
wave upon wave.

[18] "Why then did you bring me out of
the womb?[e]
I wish I had died before any eye
saw me.
[19] If only I had never come into being,
or had been carried straight
from the womb to the
grave!
[20] Are not my few days[f] almost over?[g]
Turn away from me[h] so I can
have a moment's joy
[21] before I go to the place of no
return,[i]
to the land of gloom and deep
shadow,[b][j]
[22] to the land of deepest night,
of deep shadow and disorder,
where even the light is like
darkness."

10:9 [s] Isa 64:8 [t] Ge 2:7
10:11 [u] Ps 139:13,15
10:12 [v] Job 33:4
10:13 [w] Job 23:13
10:14 [x] Job 7:21
10:15 [y] Job 9:13; Isa 3:11 [z] Job 9:15
10:16 [a] Isa 38:13; La 3:10 [b] Job 5:9
10:17 [c] Job 16:8 [d] Ru 1:21
10:18 [e] Job 3:11
10:20 [f] Job 14:1 [g] Job 7:19 [h] Job 7:16
10:21 [i] 2Sa 12:23; Job 3:13; 16:22 [j] Ps 23:4; 88:12

Zophar

11 Then Zophar the Naamathite
replied:

[2] "Are all these words to go
unanswered?[k]
Is this talker to be vindicated?
[3] Will your idle talk reduce men to
silence?
Will no one rebuke you when
you mock?[l]
[4] You say to God, 'My beliefs are
flawless[m]
and I am pure[n] in your sight.'
[5] Oh, how I wish that God would
speak,
that he would open his lips
against you
[6] and disclose to you the secrets of
wisdom,[o]
for true wisdom has two sides.
Know this: God has even
forgotten some of your sin.[p]

[7] "Can you fathom[q] the mysteries of
God?
Can you probe the limits of the
Almighty?
[8] They are higher than the heavens[r]—
what can you do?
They are deeper than the depths
of the grave[c]—what can
you know?
[9] Their measure is longer than the
earth
and wider than the sea.

[10] "If he comes along and confines
you in prison
and convenes a court, who can
oppose him?[s]
[11] Surely he recognizes deceitful men;
and when he sees evil, does he
not take note?[t]
[12] But a witless man can no more
become wise
than a wild donkey's colt can be
born a man.[d]

[13] "Yet if you devote your heart[u] to him
and stretch out your hands to
him,[v]
[14] if you put away the sin that is in
your hand
and allow no evil[w] to dwell in
your tent,[x]

11:2 [k] Job 8:2
11:3 [l] Job 17:2; 21:3
11:4 [m] Job 6:10 [n] Job 10:7
11:6 [o] Job 9:4 [p] Ezr 9:13; Job 15:5
11:7 [q] Ecc 3:11; Ro 11:33
11:8 [r] Job 22:12
11:10 [s] Job 9:12; Rev 3:7
11:11 [t] Job 34:21-25; Ps 10:14
11:13 [u] 1Sa 7:3; Ps 78:8 [v] Ps 88:9
11:14 [w] Ps 101:4 [x] Job 22:23

[a] 15 Or *and aware of* [b] 21 Or *and the shadow of death*; also in verse 22 [c] 8 Hebrew *than Sheol* [d] 12 Or *wild donkey can be born tame*

11:15 [y] Job 22:26; 1Jn 3:21

[15] then you will lift up your face[y]
without shame;
you will stand firm and without
fear.

11:16 [z] Isa 65:16 [a] Job 22:11

[16] You will surely forget your trouble,[z]
recalling it only as waters gone
by.[a]

11:17 [b] Job 22:28; Ps 37:6; Isa 58:8,10

[17] Life will be brighter than
noonday,[b]
and darkness will become like
morning.

11:18 [c] Ps 3:5 [d] Lev 26:6; Pr 3:24

[18] You will be secure, because there is
hope;
you will look about you and take
your rest[c] in safety.[d]

11:19 [e] Lev 26:6 [f] Isa 45:14

[19] You will lie down, with no one to
make you afraid,[e]
and many will court your favor.[f]

11:20 [g] Dt 28:65; Job 17:5 [h] Job 27:22; 34:22 [i] Job 8:13

[20] But the eyes of the wicked will fail,[g]
and escape will elude them;[h]
their hope will become a dying
gasp."[i]

Job

12 Then Job replied:

12:2 [j] Job 17:10

[2] "Doubtless you are the people,
and wisdom will die with you![j]
[3] But I have a mind as well as you;
I am not inferior to you.
Who does not know all these
things?[k]

12:3 [k] Job 13:2

12:4 [l] Job 21:3 [m] Ps 91:15 [n] Job 6:29

[4] "I have become a laughingstock[l] to
my friends,
though I called upon God and he
answered[m]—
a mere laughingstock, though
righteous and blameless![n]
[5] Men at ease have contempt for
misfortune
as the fate of those whose feet
are slipping.

12:6 [o] Job 22:18 [p] Job 9:24; 21:9

[6] The tents of marauders are
undisturbed,[o]
and those who provoke God are
secure[p]—
those who carry their god in
their hands.[a]
[7] "But ask the animals, and they will
teach you,
or the birds of the air, and they
will tell you;
[8] or speak to the earth, and it will
teach you,
or let the fish of the sea inform
you.

12:9 [q] Isa 41:20

[9] Which of all these does not know
that the hand of the LORD has
done this?[q]

12:10 [r] Job 27:3; 33:4; Ac 17:28

[10] In his hand is the life of every
creature
and the breath of all mankind.[r]

12:11 [s] Job 34:3

[11] Does not the ear test words
as the tongue tastes food?[s]

12:12 [t] Job 15:10 [u] Job 32:7,9

[12] Is not wisdom found among the
aged?[t]
Does not long life bring
understanding?[u]

12:13 [v] Job 11:6 [w] Job 9:4 [x] Job 32:8; 38:36

[13] "To God belong wisdom[v] and
power;[w]
counsel and understanding are
his.[x]

12:14 [y] Job 19:10 [z] Job 37:7; Isa 25:2

[14] What he tears down[y] cannot be
rebuilt;[z]
the man he imprisons cannot be
released.

12:15 [a] 1Ki 8:35 [b] 1Ki 17:1 [c] Ge 7:11

[15] If he holds back the waters,[a] there
is drought;[b]
if he lets them loose, they
devastate the land.[c]

12:16 [d] Job 13:7,9

[16] To him belong strength and
victory;
both deceived and deceiver are
his.[d]

12:17 [e] Job 19:9 [f] Job 3:14

[17] He leads counselors away stripped[e]
and makes fools of judges.[f]

12:18 [g] Ps 116:16

[18] He takes off the shackles[g] put on
by kings
and ties a loincloth[b] around
their waist.

12:19 [h] Job 24:12,22; 34:20,28; 35:9

[19] He leads priests away stripped
and overthrows men long
established.[h]

12:20 [i] Job 32:9

[20] He silences the lips of trusted
advisers
and takes away the discernment
of elders.[i]
[21] He pours contempt on nobles
and disarms the mighty.

12:22 [j] 1Co 4:5 [k] Job 3:5 [l] Da 2:22

[22] He reveals the deep things of
darkness[j]
and brings deep shadows[k] into
the light.[l]

12:23 [m] Jer 25:9 [n] Ps 107:38; Isa 9:3; 26:15

[23] He makes nations great, and
destroys them;[m]
he enlarges nations,[n] and
disperses them.

12:24 [o] Ps 107:40

[24] He deprives the leaders of the earth
of their reason;
he sends them wandering
through a trackless waste.[o]

[a] 6 Or *secure / in what God's hand brings them*
[b] 18 Or *shackles of kings / and ties a belt*

[25] They grope in darkness with no light;[p]
he makes them stagger like drunkards.[q]

12:25 [p] Job 5:14 [q] Ps 107:27; Isa 24:20

13 "My eyes have seen all this,
my ears have heard and understood it.
[2] What you know, I also know;
I am not inferior to you.[r]
[3] But I desire to speak to the Almighty
and to argue my case with God.[s]
[4] You, however, smear me with lies;[t]
you are worthless physicians, all of you!
[5] If only you would be altogether silent!
For you, that would be wisdom.[u]
[6] Hear now my argument;
listen to the plea of my lips.
[7] Will you speak wickedly on God's behalf?
Will you speak deceitfully for him?[v]
[8] Will you show him partiality?[w]
Will you argue the case for God?
[9] Would it turn out well if he examined you?
Could you deceive him as you might deceive men?[x]
[10] He would surely rebuke you
if you secretly showed partiality.
[11] Would not his splendor[y] terrify you?
Would not the dread of him fall on you?
[12] Your maxims are proverbs of ashes;
your defenses are defenses of clay.

13:2 [r] Job 12:3
13:3 [s] Job 23:3-4
13:4 [t] Ps 119:69; Jer 23:32
13:5 [u] Pr 17:28
13:7 [v] Job 36:4
13:8 [w] Lev 19:15
13:9 [x] Job 12:16; Gal 6:7
13:11 [y] Job 31:23

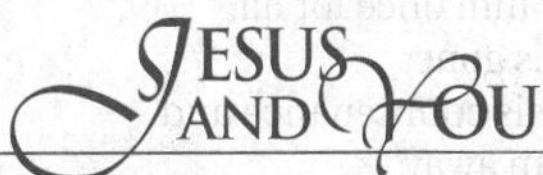

DISCIPLESHIP COSTS

Job's words in Job 13:15 demonstrate just how serious he was about trusting God: "Though he slay me, yet will I hope in him." In fact, Job's faith was more important to him than his own life. He questioned God, yearning to get to know him even better, but he also believed what God said. We are given the same choice that Job faced: No matter what happens in life, we have to be willing to trust and obey. Jesus reminded his followers that the sacrifice for following him can at times be demanding (Luke 9:23–27; 14:26–27). But the result far outweighs the difficulty along the way—it is a blessed relationship with God that will last through all eternity.

[13] "Keep silent and let me speak;
then let come to me what may.
[14] Why do I put myself in jeopardy
and take my life in my hands?
[15] Though he slay me, yet will I hope[z] in him;[a]
I will surely[a] defend my ways to his face.[b]
[16] Indeed, this will turn out for my deliverance,[c]
for no godless man would dare come before him!
[17] Listen carefully to my words;[d]
let your ears take in what I say.
[18] Now that I have prepared my case,[e]
I know I will be vindicated.
[19] Can anyone bring charges against me?[f]
If so, I will be silent and die.[g]

[20] "Only grant me these two things, O God,
and then I will not hide from you:
[21] Withdraw your hand[h] far from me,
and stop frightening me with your terrors.
[22] Then summon me and I will answer,[i]
or let me speak, and you reply.[j]
[23] How many wrongs and sins have I committed?[k]
Show me my offense and my sin.
[24] Why do you hide your face[l]
and consider me your enemy?[m]
[25] Will you torment a windblown leaf?[n]
Will you chase after dry chaff?[o]
[26] For you write down bitter things against me
and make me inherit the sins of my youth.[p]
[27] You fasten my feet in shackles;[q]
you keep close watch on all my paths
by putting marks on the soles of my feet.

[28] "So man wastes away like something rotten,
like a garment eaten by moths.[r]

14 "Man born of woman
is of few days and full of trouble.[s]
[2] He springs up like a flower[t] and withers away;[u]

13:15 [z] Job 7:6 [a] Ps 23:4; Pr 14:32 [b] Job 27:5
13:16 [c] Isa 12:1
13:17 [d] Job 21:2
13:18 [e] Job 23:4
13:19 [f] Job 40:4; Isa 50:8 [g] Job 10:8
13:21 [h] Ps 39:10
13:22 [i] Job 14:15 [j] Job 9:16
13:23 [k] 1Sa 26:18
13:24 [l] Dt 32:20; Ps 13:1; Isa 8:17 [m] Job 19:11; La 2:5
13:25 [n] Lev 26:36 [o] Job 21:18; Isa 42:3
13:26 [p] Ps 25:7
13:27 [q] Job 33:11
13:28 [r] Isa 50:9; Jas 5:2
14:1 [s] Job 5:7; Ecc 2:23
14:2 [t] Jas 1:10 [u] Ps 90:5-6

[a] 15 Or *He will surely slay me; I have no hope — / yet I will*

like a fleeting shadow,[v] he does
not endure.
3 Do you fix your eye on such a one?[w]
Will you bring him[a] before you
for judgment?[x]
4 Who can bring what is pure[y] from
the impure?[z]
No one![a]
5 Man's days are determined;
you have decreed the number of
his months[b]
and have set limits he cannot
exceed.
6 So look away from him and let him
alone,[c]
till he has put in his time like a
hired man.[d]

7 "At least there is hope for a tree:
If it is cut down, it will sprout
again,
and its new shoots will not fail.
8 Its roots may grow old in the ground
and its stump die in the soil,

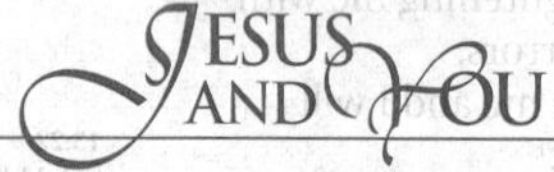

WORTH IT ALL

Temporary or unstable hope for the future is not enough—our hope must be permanent and unchangeable. Job understood that truth, and when he questioned God he wasn't just asking whether life was worth living. Behind each question was his single overriding concern: "If a man dies, will he live again?" (Job 14:14). Faced with his own mortality, Job was asking whether there is more to come, or whether this life is all there is. Only that which lasts forever will ultimately satisfy the ache in our hearts. Job, like most people who suffer, looked beyond himself into the realm of eternity for the answer. The hopeful statement in the last part of verse 14 ("I will wait for my renewal to come") is reaffirmed in Job 19:25–26, where Job declares with confidence, "in my flesh I will see God." We were created by God to enjoy an unending relationship with him (Ecclesiastes 3:11), but sin stands in our way. Something deep within us cries out against that separation, and we want to believe there is more to life than what we're seeing in the here and now. God's ultimate answer to our longing for eternal life is the precious gift of his own Son. Jesus gave us all the assurance we will ever need for this life and the life to come: "I am the resurrection and the life. He who believes in me will live" (John 11:25).

9 yet at the scent of water it will bud
and put forth shoots like a plant.
10 But man dies and is laid low;
he breathes his last and is no
more.[e]
11 As water disappears from the sea
or a riverbed becomes parched
and dry,[f]
12 so man lies down and does not rise;
till the heavens are no more,[g]
men will not awake
or be roused from their sleep.[h]

13 "If only you would hide me in the
grave[b]
and conceal me till your anger
has passed![i]
If only you would set me a time
and then remember me!
14 If a man dies, will he live again?
All the days of my hard service
I will wait for my renewal[c] to
come.
15 You will call and I will answer you;[j]
you will long for the creature
your hands have made.
16 Surely then you will count my steps[k]
but not keep track of my sin.[l]
17 My offenses will be sealed up in a
bag;[m]
you will cover over my sin.[n]

18 "But as a mountain erodes and
crumbles
and as a rock is moved from its
place,
19 as water wears away stones
and torrents wash away the soil,
so you destroy man's hope.[o]
20 You overpower him once for all,
and he is gone;
you change his countenance and
send him away.
21 If his sons are honored, he does not
know it;
if they are brought low, he does
not see it.[p]
22 He feels but the pain of his own
body
and mourns only for himself."

Eliphaz

15 Then Eliphaz the Temanite replied:

2 "Would a wise man answer with
empty notions

14:2 [v]Job 8:9
14:3 [w]Ps 8:4; 144:3 [x]Ps 143:2
14:4 [y]Ps 51:10 [z]Eph 2:1-3 [a]Jn 3:6; Ro 5:12
14:5 [b]Job 21:21
14:6 [c]Job 7:19 [d]Job 7:1,2; Ps 39:13
14:10 [e]Job 13:19
14:11 [f]Isa 19:5
14:12 [g]Rev 20:11; 21:1 [h]Ac 3:21
14:13 [i]Isa 26:20
14:15 [j]Job 13:22
14:16 [k]Ps 139:1-3; Pr 5:21; Jer 32:19 [l]Job 10:6
14:17 [m]Dt 32:34 [n]Hos 13:12
14:19 [o]Job 7:6
14:21 [p]Ecc 9:5; Isa 63:16

[a] 3 Septuagint, Vulgate and Syriac; Hebrew *me*
[b] 13 Hebrew *Sheol*
[c] 14 Or *release*

or fill his belly with the hot east
wind?[q]
[3] Would he argue with useless words,
with speeches that have no value?
[4] But you even undermine piety
and hinder devotion to God.
[5] Your sin prompts your mouth;
you adopt the tongue of the
crafty.[r]
[6] Your own mouth condemns you,
not mine;
your own lips testify against you.[s]

[7] "Are you the first man ever born?[t]
Were you brought forth before
the hills?[u]
[8] Do you listen in on God's council?[v]
Do you limit wisdom to
yourself?
[9] What do you know that we do not
know?
What insights do you have that
we do not have?[w]
[10] The gray-haired and the aged[x] are
on our side,
men even older than your father.
[11] Are God's consolations[y] not
enough for you,
words[z] spoken gently to you?[a]
[12] Why has your heart[b] carried you
away,
and why do your eyes flash,
[13] so that you vent your rage against
God
and pour out such words from
your mouth?

[14] "What is man, that he could be pure,
or one born of woman,[c] that he
could be righteous?[d]
[15] If God places no trust in his holy
ones,
if even the heavens are not pure
in his eyes,[e]
[16] how much less man, who is vile
and corrupt,[f]
who drinks up evil like water![g]

[17] "Listen to me and I will explain to
you;
let me tell you what I have seen,
[18] what wise men have declared,
hiding nothing received from
their fathers[h]
[19] (to whom alone the land was given
when no alien passed among
them):
[20] All his days the wicked man suffers
torment,
the ruthless through all the years
stored up for him.[i]
[21] Terrifying sounds fill his ears;[j]
when all seems well, marauders
attack him.[k]
[22] He despairs of escaping the
darkness;
he is marked for the sword.[l]
[23] He wanders about[m]—food for
vultures[a];
he knows the day of darkness is
at hand.[n]
[24] Distress and anguish fill him with
terror;
they overwhelm him, like a king
poised to attack,
[25] because he shakes his fist at God
and vaunts himself against the
Almighty,[o]
[26] defiantly charging against him
with a thick, strong shield.

[27] "Though his face is covered with
fat
and his waist bulges with flesh,[p]
[28] he will inhabit ruined towns
and houses where no one lives,[q]
houses crumbling to rubble.[r]
[29] He will no longer be rich and his
wealth will not endure,[s]
nor will his possessions spread
over the land.
[30] He will not escape the darkness;[t]
a flame[u] will wither his shoots,
and the breath of God's mouth[v]
will carry him away.
[31] Let him not deceive himself by
trusting what is worthless,[w]
for he will get nothing in return.
[32] Before his time[x] he will be paid in
full,[y]
and his branches will not
flourish.[z]
[33] He will be like a vine stripped of its
unripe grapes,[a]
like an olive tree shedding its
blossoms.
[34] For the company of the godless will
be barren,
and fire will consume the tents
of those who love bribes.[b]
[35] They conceive trouble and give
birth to evil;[c]
their womb fashions deceit."

a 23 Or *about, looking for food*

15:2 [q] Job 6:26
15:5 [r] Job 5:13
15:6 [s] Lk 19:22
15:7 [t] Job 38:21 [u] Ps 90:2; Pr 8:25
15:8 [v] Ro 11:34; 1Co 2:11
15:9 [w] Job 13:2
15:10 [x] Job 32:6-7
15:11 [y] 2Co 1:3-4 [z] Zec 1:13 [a] Job 36:16
15:12 [b] Job 11:13
15:14 [c] Job 14:4; 25:4 [d] Pr 20:9; Ecc 7:20
15:15 [e] Job 4:18; 25:5
15:16 [f] Ps 14:1 [g] Job 34:7; Pr 19:28
15:18 [h] Job 8:8
15:20 [i] Job 24:1; 27:13-23
15:21 [j] Job 18:11; 20:25 [k] Job 27:20; 1Th 5:3
15:22 [l] Job 19:29; 27:14
15:23 [m] Ps 59:15; 109:10 [n] Job 18:12
15:25 [o] Job 36:9
15:27 [p] Ps 17:10
15:28 [q] Isa 5:9 [r] Job 3:14
15:29 [s] Job 27:16-17
15:30 [t] Job 5:14 [u] Job 22:20 [v] Job 4:9
15:31 [w] Isa 59:4
15:32 [x] Ecc 7:17 [y] Job 22:16; Ps 55:23 [z] Job 18:16
15:33 [a] Hab 3:17
15:34 [b] Job 8:22
15:35 [c] Ps 7:14; Isa 59:4; Hos 10:13

Job

16 Then Job replied:

[2] "I have heard many things like these;
miserable comforters are you all![d]
[3] Will your long-winded speeches never end?
What ails you that you keep on arguing?[e]
[4] I also could speak like you,
if you were in my place;
I could make fine speeches against you
and shake my head[f] at you.
[5] But my mouth would encourage you;
comfort from my lips would bring you relief.

[6] "Yet if I speak, my pain is not relieved;
and if I refrain, it does not go away.
[7] Surely, O God, you have worn me out;[g]
you have devastated my entire household.
[8] You have bound me—and it has become a witness;
my gauntness[h] rises up and testifies against me.[i]
[9] God assails me and tears[j] me in his anger
and gnashes his teeth at me;[k]
my opponent fastens on me his piercing eyes.[l]
[10] Men open their mouths[m] to jeer at me;
they strike my cheek[n] in scorn
and unite together against me.[o]
[11] God has turned me over to evil men
and thrown me into the clutches of the wicked.[p]
[12] All was well with me, but he shattered me;
he seized me by the neck and crushed me.[q]
He has made me his target;[r]
[13] his archers surround me.
Without pity, he pierces[s] my kidneys
and spills my gall on the ground.
[14] Again and again[t] he bursts upon me;
he rushes at me like a warrior.[u]

[15] "I have sewed sackcloth[v] over my skin
and buried my brow in the dust.
[16] My face is red with weeping,
deep shadows ring my eyes;
[17] yet my hands have been free of violence[w]
and my prayer is pure.

[18] "O earth, do not cover my blood;[x]
may my cry never be laid to rest![y]
[19] Even now my witness[z] is in heaven;
my advocate is on high.
[20] My intercessor is my friend[a]
as my eyes pour out[a] tears to God;
[21] on behalf of a man he pleads[b] with God
as a man pleads for his friend.

[22] "Only a few years will pass
before I go on the journey of no return.[c]

17 [1] My spirit is broken,
my days are cut short,
the grave awaits me.[d]

a 20 Or *My friends treat me with scorn*

16:2 [d] Job 13:4
16:3 [e] Job 6:26
16:4 [f] Ps 22:7; 109:25; La 2:15; Zep 2:15; Mt 27:39
16:7 [g] Job 7:3
16:8 [h] Job 19:20 [i] Job 10:17
16:9 [j] Hos 6:1 [k] Ps 35:16; La 2:16; Ac 7:54 [l] Job 13:24
16:10 [m] Ps 22:13 [n] Isa 50:6; La 3:30; Mic 5:1; Ac 23:2 [o] Ps 35:15
16:11 [p] Job 1:15,17
16:12 [q] Job 9:17 [r] La 3:12
16:13 [s] Job 20:24
16:14 [t] Job 9:17 [u] Joel 2:7
16:15 [v] Ge 37:34
16:17 [w] Isa 59:6; Jnh 3:8
16:18 [x] Isa 26:21 [y] Ps 66:18-19
16:19 [z] Ge 31:50; Ro 1:9; 1Th 2:5
16:20 [a] La 2:19
16:21 [b] Ps 9:4
16:22 [c] Ecc 12:5
17:1 [d] Ps 88:3-4

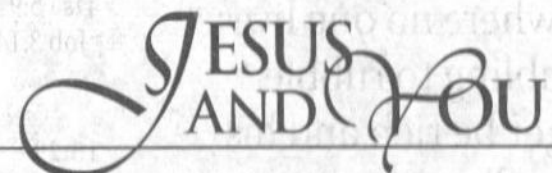

IS GOD ANGRY?

Somewhere deep inside himself Job knew that he had done nothing to deserve the kind of pain he was suffering. But he still had an uncomfortable feeling that God was angry with him (Job 16:9). Many of us feel the same way when we suffer for no apparent reason. We might begin to question everything in our lives—God, others and ourselves. However, God himself has already rectified the problem in the relationship between human beings and himself. Jesus is his answer, and we can choose to live life in a way that shows that we have staked our future on him. The New Testament reminds us that for those who willfully reject Jesus "it is a dreadful thing to fall into the hands of the living God" (Hebrews 10:31). There will inevitably be times in each of our lives when we feel as though God is so angry with us that he has turned and walked away. But we can take great comfort from God's Word that "God did not appoint us to suffer wrath but to receive salvation through our Lord Jesus Christ" (1 Thessalonians 5:9). Because of God's great love for us he places us in a new position in relationship to him: Jesus' blood stands between us and God's anger (Romans 5:9; Ephesians 2:3–10).

17:2 e 1Sa 1:6-7 — 2 Surely mockers[e] surround me;
my eyes must dwell on their
hostility.

17:3 f Ps 119:122 — 3 "Give me, O God, the pledge you
g Pr 6:1 — demand.[f]
h Isa 38:14 — Who else will put up security[g]
for me?[h]
4 You have closed their minds to
understanding;
therefore you will not let them
triumph.
5 If a man denounces his friends for
17:5 — reward,
i Job 11:20 — the eyes of his children will fail.[i]

17:6 j Job 30:9 — 6 "God has made me a byword[j] to
everyone,
a man in whose face people spit.
17:7 k Job 16:8 — 7 My eyes have grown dim with grief;[k]
my whole frame is but a shadow.
17:8 l Job 22:19 — 8 Upright men are appalled at this;
the innocent are aroused[l]
against the ungodly.
17:9 m Pr 4:18 — 9 Nevertheless, the righteous[m] will
n Job 22:30 — hold to their ways,
and those with clean hands[n] will
grow stronger.

10 "But come on, all of you, try again!
17:10 o Job 12:2 — I will not find a wise man among
you.[o]
11 My days have passed, my plans are
shattered,
17:11 p Job 7:6 — and so are the desires of my
heart.[p]
12 These men turn night into day;
in the face of darkness they say,
'Light is near.'
17:13 q Job 3:13 — 13 If the only home I hope for is the
grave,[a][q]
if I spread out my bed in
darkness,
17:14 r Job 13:28; 30:28,30; Ps 16:10 — 14 if I say to corruption,[r] 'You are my
father,'
s Job 21:26 — and to the worm,[s] 'My mother'
or 'My sister,'
17:15 t Job 7:6 — 15 where then is my hope?[t]
Who can see any hope for me?
17:16 u Job 3:17-19; Jnh 2:6 — 16 Will it go down to the gates of
death[a]?[u]
Will we descend together into
the dust?"

Bildad

18 Then Bildad the Shuhite replied:

2 "When will you end these speeches?
Be sensible, and then we can talk.
3 Why are we regarded as cattle
and considered stupid in your — 18:3 v Ps 73:22
sight?[v]
4 You who tear yourself[w] to pieces in — 18:4 w Job 13:14
your anger,
is the earth to be abandoned for
your sake?
Or must the rocks be moved
from their place?

5 "The lamp of the wicked is snuffed — 18:5 x Job 21:17; Pr 13:9; 20:20; 24:20
out;[x]
the flame of his fire stops
burning.
6 The light in his tent becomes dark;
the lamp beside him goes out. — 18:7
7 The vigor of his step is weakened;[y] — y Pr 4:12
his own schemes[z] throw him — z Job 5:13
down.[a] — a Job 15:6
8 His feet thrust him into a net[b] — 18:8 b Job 22:10; Ps 9:15; 35:7
and he wanders into its mesh.
9 A trap seizes him by the heel;
a snare holds him fast.
10 A noose is hidden for him on the
ground;
a trap lies in his path.
11 Terrors startle him on every side[c] — 18:11 c Job 15:21; Jer 6:25; 20:3
and dog[d] his every step. — d Job 20:8
12 Calamity is hungry[e] for him;
disaster is ready for him when — 18:12 e Isa 8:21
he falls.
13 It eats away parts of his skin;
death's firstborn devours his — 18:13 f Zec 14:12
limbs.[f]
14 He is torn from the security of his — 18:14 g Job 8:22
tent[g]
and marched off to the king of
terrors.
15 Fire resides[b] in his tent; — 18:15 h Ps 11:6
burning sulfur[h] is scattered over
his dwelling.
16 His roots dry up below[i] — 18:16 i Isa 5:24; Hos 9:1-16; Am 2:9
and his branches wither above.[j] — j Job 15:30; Mal 4:1
17 The memory of him perishes from
the earth;
he has no name in the land.[k] — 18:17 k Ps 34:16; Pr 2:22; 10:7
18 He is driven from light into
darkness[l] — 18:18 l Job 5:14
and is banished from the world.
19 He has no offspring[m] or — 18:19 m Jer 22:30
descendants[n] among his — n Isa 14:22
people, — o Job 27:14-15
no survivor where once he lived.[o]
20 Men of the west are appalled at his — 18:20 p Ps 37:13; Jer 50:27,31
fate;[p]

[a] 13,16 Hebrew *Sheol* [b] 15 Or *Nothing he had remains*

men of the east are seized with
horror.
21 Surely such is the dwelling[q] of an
evil man;
such is the place of one who
knows not God."[r]

18:21 [q]Job 21:28 [r]Jer 9:3; 1Th 4:5

Job

19 Then Job replied:

2 "How long will you torment me
and crush me with words?
3 Ten times now you have
reproached me;
shamelessly you attack me.
4 If it is true that I have gone astray,
my error[s] remains my concern
alone.
5 If indeed you would exalt
yourselves above me[t]
and use my humiliation against
me,
6 then know that God has wronged
me[u]
and drawn his net[v] around me.
7 "Though I cry, 'I've been wronged!'
I get no response;[w]
though I call for help, there is no
justice.[x]
8 He has blocked my way so I cannot
pass;[y]
he has shrouded my paths in
darkness.[z]
9 He has stripped[a] me of my honor
and removed the crown from my
head.[b]
10 He tears me down[c] on every side
till I am gone;
he uproots my hope[d] like a tree.[e]
11 His anger[f] burns against me;
he counts me among his
enemies.[g]
12 His troops advance in force;[h]
they build a siege ramp[i] against
me
and encamp around my tent.
13 "He has alienated my brothers[j]
from me;
my acquaintances are completely
estranged from me.[k]
14 My kinsmen have gone away;
my friends have forgotten me.
15 My guests and my maidservants
count me a stranger;
they look upon me as an alien.
16 I summon my servant, but he does
not answer,
though I beg him with my own
mouth.
17 My breath is offensive to my wife;
I am loathsome to my own
brothers.
18 Even the little boys[l] scorn me;
when I appear, they ridicule me.
19 All my intimate friends[m] detest
me;[n]
those I love have turned against
me.
20 I am nothing but skin and bones;[o]
I have escaped with only the
skin of my teeth.[a]
21 "Have pity on me, my friends, have
pity,
for the hand of God has struck
me.
22 Why do you pursue[p] me as God
does?
Will you never get enough of my
flesh?[q]
23 "Oh, that my words were recorded,
that they were written on a
scroll,[r]
24 that they were inscribed with an
iron tool on[b] lead,
or engraved in rock forever!
25 I know that my Redeemer[c][s] lives,[t]
and that in the end he will stand
upon the earth.[d]

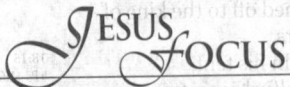

19:4 [s]Job 6:24
19:5 [t]Ps 35:26; 38:16; 55:12
19:6 [u]Job 27:2 [v]Job 18:8
19:7 [w]Job 30:20 [x]Job 9:24; Hab 1:2-4
19:8 [y]Job 3:23; La 3:7 [z]Job 30:26
19:9 [a]Job 12:17 [b]Ps 89:39,44; La 5:16
19:10 [c]Job 12:14 [d]Job 7:6 [e]Job 24:20
19:11 [f]Job 16:9 [g]Job 13:24
19:12 [h]Job 16:13 [i]Job 30:12
19:13 [j]Ps 69:8 [k]Job 16:7; Ps 88:8
19:18 [l]2Ki 2:23
19:19 [m]Ps 55:12-13 [n]Ps 38:11
19:20 [o]Job 33:21; Ps 102:5
19:22 [p]Job 13:25; 16:11 [q]Ps 69:26
19:23 [r]Isa 30:8
19:25 [s]Ps 78:35; Pr 23:11; Isa 43:14; Jer 50:34 [t]Job 16:19

[a] 20 Or *only my gums* [b] 24 Or *and* [c] 25 Or *defender* [d] 25 Or *upon my grave*

JESUS FOCUS

THERE IS HOPE

In the midst of all of his agony Job never lost faith in God. In one grand outburst of hope and confidence, he declared, "I know that my Redeemer lives!" (Job 19:25). Job may have felt at times as though God was absent or unconcerned, but in his heart of hearts he knew that God hadn't gone anywhere, that God was continually at work in his life to vindicate him despite his circumstances. Job also recognized that this life is not the end. The New Testament reminds us that we too have the hope of eternal life because of Jesus' glorious resurrection from the dead (1 Peter 1:3). Jesus is our living Savior, our eternal Redeemer—and the One we can ultimately depend on to vindicate us on the basis of his shed blood on the cross (1 Timothy 2:5–6; Hebrews 8:6; 9:15; 12:24).

DISCOVERY 120

My Redeemer Lives

Job never received the answers to all of his questions about why God was allowing him to suffer, but he did learn some very important lessons. He learned that God is indeed alive and involved in our lives. Even when we do not understand why life can be so difficult or why he doesn't do something to alleviate our pain, God is with us (Lamentations 3:55–57).

Beyond this, the God of the universe desires an individual relationship with each one of us. Job acknowledged God as "my Redeemer" rather than perceiving him as a detached and unconcerned force of energy. Given Job's limited understanding of God's salvation plan, his confession is indeed remarkable: "I know that my Redeemer lives, and that in the end he will stand upon the earth" (Job 19:25). Job knew where true security lay, and Jesus reminded us of the same thing: "I give them eternal life, and they shall never perish; no one can snatch them out of my hand" (John 10:28).

Job also learned that there is more to life than this physical, temporal existence. In the midst of unspeakable anguish Job set his sights beyond what was happening at the moment, eagerly anticipating the day he would finally be with God: "After my skin has been destroyed; yet in my flesh will I see God; I myself will see him with my own eyes—I, and not another. How my heart yearns within me!" (Job 19:26–27).

This life is all we know, but it is not all there is! While our earthly circumstances may bring indescribable agony, we know that if we accept Jesus as Savior our present life is only the very beginning of our story: "Our present sufferings are not worth comparing with the glory that will be revealed in us" (Romans 8:18). Many of us can at one time or another relate to Paul's sentiment that he wanted to leave this life to be with God, "which is better by far" (Philippians 1:23). God's people ache to be with him. Job described this desire by saying that his heart yearned to see God (Job 19:27), and Paul noted that we "groan inwardly as we wait eagerly for our adoption as sons, the redemption of our bodies" (Romans 8:23).

In the midst of our suffering we can remember that God is on our side even as we live in a world full of sin—but that one day we will be with him in heaven, and sin will be banished forever. Like Job, we know that our Redeemer, Jesus Christ, is vibrantly alive and vitally involved in our day-by-day affairs, and that in the end he will stand upon the earth. We too will see him with our own eyes. How our hearts yearn for that day of days!

Self-Discovery: *Do you look forward to your future life with your precious Lord in heaven, or is it difficult to set your sights beyond this world's enticements? What would it mean to you to live as one who has been raised up with Christ and seated with him in the heavenly realms (Ephesians 2:6)?*

GO TO DISCOVERY 121 ON PAGE 657

JESUS IS A MESSIAH WHO WINS HIS PEOPLE BACK BY REDEMPTION, RATHER THAN AN ENLIGHTENED PHILOSOPHER WHO, BY HIS THERAPEUTIC WISDOM, GUIDES US TO HIGHER AND HAPPIER LIVING.

Michael Horton, *American Theologian*

[26] And after my skin has been
destroyed,
yet[a] in[b] my flesh I will see God;[u]
[27] I myself will see him
with my own eyes—I, and not
another.
How my heart yearns[v] within me!
[28] "If you say, 'How we will hound him,
since the root of the trouble lies
in him,[c]'
[29] you should fear the sword
yourselves;
for wrath will bring punishment
by the sword,[w]
and then you will know that
there is judgment.[d]"[x]

19:26 [u] Ps 17:15; Mt 5:8; 1Co 13:12; 1Jn 3:2
19:27 [v] Ps 73:26
19:29 [w] Job 15:22 [x] Job 22:4; Ps 1:5; 9:7

Zophar

20 Then Zophar the Naamathite replied:

[2] "My troubled thoughts prompt me
to answer
because I am greatly disturbed.
[3] I hear a rebuke[y] that dishonors me,
and my understanding inspires
me to reply.

[4] "Surely you know how it has been
from of old,
ever since man[e] was placed on
the earth,
[5] that the mirth of the wicked is brief,
the joy of the godless lasts but a
moment.[z]
[6] Though his pride reaches to the
heavens
and his head touches the clouds,[a]
[7] he will perish forever,[b] like his own
dung;
those who have seen him will
say, 'Where is he?'[c]
[8] Like a dream[d] he flies away,[e] no
more to be found,
banished[f] like a vision of the
night.[g]
[9] The eye that saw him will not see
him again;
his place will look on him no
more.[h]
[10] His children[i] must make amends
to the poor;
his own hands must give back
his wealth.[j]
[11] The youthful vigor[k] that fills his
bones
will lie with him in the dust.[l]

[12] "Though evil is sweet in his mouth
and he hides it under his tongue,
[13] though he cannot bear to let it go
and keeps it in his mouth,[m]
[14] yet his food will turn sour in his
stomach;
it will become the venom of
serpents within him.
[15] He will spit out the riches he
swallowed;
God will make his stomach
vomit them up.
[16] He will suck the poison[n] of
serpents;
the fangs of an adder will kill
him.[o]
[17] He will not enjoy the streams,
the rivers flowing with honey[p]
and cream.[q]
[18] What he toiled for he must give
back uneaten;
he will not enjoy the profit from
his trading.
[19] For he has oppressed the poor and
left them destitute;[r]
he has seized houses he did not
build.

[20] "Surely he will have no respite from
his craving;[s]
he cannot save himself by his
treasure.
[21] Nothing is left for him to devour;
his prosperity will not endure.[t]
[22] In the midst of his plenty, distress
will overtake him;
the full force of misery will come
upon him.
[23] When he has filled his belly,
God will vent his burning anger
against him

20:3 [y] Job 19:3
20:5 [z] Job 8:12; Ps 37:35-36; 73:19
20:6 [a] Isa 14:13-14; Ob 1:3-4
20:7 [b] Job 4:20 [c] Job 7:10; 8:18
20:8 [d] Ps 73:20 [e] Job 27:21-23 [f] Job 18:18 [g] Ps 90:5
20:9 [h] Job 7:8
20:10 [i] Job 5:4 [j] Job 27:16-17
20:11 [k] Job 13:26 [l] Job 21:26
20:13 [m] Nu 11:18-20
20:16 [n] Dt 32:32 [o] Dt 32:24
20:17 [p] Dt 32:13 [q] Job 29:6
20:19 [r] Job 24:4,14; 35:9
20:20 [s] Ecc 5:12-14
20:21 [t] Job 15:29

[a] 26 Or *And after I awake, / though this ⸤body⸥ has been destroyed, / then* [b] 26 Or */ apart from* [c] 28 Many Hebrew manuscripts, Septuagint and Vulgate; most Hebrew manuscripts *me* [d] 29 Or */ that you may come to know the Almighty* [e] 4 Or *Adam*

20:23 [u]Ps 78:30-31
and rain down his blows upon
him.[u]
20:24 [v]Isa 24:18; Am 5:19
24 Though he flees[v] from an iron
weapon,
a bronze-tipped arrow pierces
him.
25 He pulls it out of his back,
the gleaming point out of his
liver.
20:25 [w]Job 18:11 [x]Job 16:13
Terrors[w] will come over him;[x]
26 total darkness[y] lies in wait for
his treasures.
20:26 [y]Job 18:18 [z]Ps 21:9
A fire unfanned will consume him[z]
and devour what is left in his
tent.
27 The heavens will expose his guilt;
the earth will rise up against
him.[a]
20:27 [a]Dt 31:28
28 A flood will carry off his house,[b]
20:28 [b]Dt 28:31 [c]Job 21:17,20, 30
rushing waters[a] on the day of
God's wrath.[c]
29 Such is the fate God allots the
wicked,
the heritage appointed for them
20:29 [d]Job 27:13
by God."[d]

Job

21 Then Job replied:

2 "Listen carefully to my words;
let this be the consolation you
give me.
3 Bear with me while I speak,
and after I have spoken, mock
21:3 [e]Job 16:10
on.[e]
21:4 [f]Job 6:11
4 "Is my complaint directed to man?
Why should I not be impatient?[f]
21:5 [g]Jdg 18:19; Job 29:9; 40:4
5 Look at me and be astonished;
clap your hand over your mouth.[g]
6 When I think about this, I am
terrified;
trembling seizes my body.
7 Why do the wicked live on,
21:7 [h]Job 12:6; Ps 73:3; Jer 12:1; Hab 1:13
growing old and increasing in
power?[h]
8 They see their children established
21:8 [i]Ps 17:14
around them,
their offspring before their eyes.[i]
21:9 [j]Ps 73:5
9 Their homes are safe and free from
fear;[j]
the rod of God is not upon them.
10 Their bulls never fail to breed;
their cows calve and do not
21:10 [k]Ex 23:26
miscarry.[k]
11 They send forth their children as a
flock;
their little ones dance about.
12 They sing to the music of
tambourine and harp;
they make merry to the sound of
21:12 [l]Ps 81:2
the flute.[l]
13 They spend their years in
21:13 [m]Job 36:11
prosperity[m]
and go down to the grave[b] in
peace.[c]
14 Yet they say to God, 'Leave us
21:14 [n]Job 22:17 [o]Pr 1:29
alone![n]
We have no desire to know your
ways.[o]
15 Who is the Almighty, that we
should serve him?
21:15 [p]Ex 5:2; Job 34:9; Mal 3:14
What would we gain by praying
to him?'[p]
16 But their prosperity is not in their
own hands,
so I stand aloof from the counsel
of the wicked.

17 "Yet how often is the lamp of the
21:17 [q]Job 18:5
wicked snuffed out?[q]
How often does calamity come
upon them,
the fate God allots in his anger?
21:18 [r]Job 13:25; Ps 1:4
18 How often are they like straw
before the wind,
like chaff[r] swept away by a gale?
21:19 [s]Ex 20:5; Jer 31:29; Eze 18:2
19 It is said, 'God stores up a man's
punishment for his sons.'[s]

[a] 28 Or *The possessions in his house will be carried off, / washed away* [b] 13 Hebrew *Sheol* [c] 13 Or *in an instant*

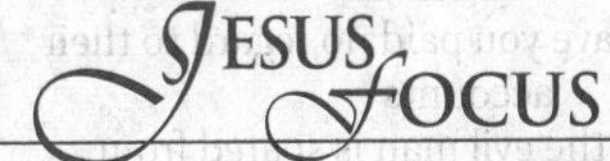

THE WICKED PROSPER

Job was aware that evil people often suffer punishment in this life. But he also recognized that the wicked sometimes seem to prosper even more than those who trust in God (Job 21:7–13). How could a just God allow the innocent to suffer while the wicked flourish? This question still haunts us today. Interestingly enough, however, it is a question that Jesus rarely addressed. Our Lord looked at all of life in light of its eventual outcome rather than merely in terms of the here and now (Luke 18:29–30). "Blessed are those who mourn," Jesus stated, "for they will be comforted" (Matthew 5:4). Life is frequently difficult and painful, but Jesus reminded us of the lesson Job had learned: We can live life with contentment and hope because we know that our reward will be eternal life with God (Matthew 5:12; John 5:24).

Let him repay the man himself,
so that he will know it!
20 Let his own eyes see his
destruction;
let him drink[t] of the wrath of the
Almighty.[a][u]

21:20 [t] Ps 75:8; Isa 51:17 [u] Jer 25:15; Rev 14:10

21 For what does he care about the
family he leaves behind
when his allotted months[v] come
to an end?

21:21 [v] Job 14:5

22 "Can anyone teach knowledge to
God,[w]
since he judges even the
highest?[x]

21:22 [w] Job 35:11; 36:22; Isa 40:13-14; Ro 11:34 [x] Ps 82:1

23 One man dies in full vigor,
completely secure and at ease,
24 his body[b] well nourished,
his bones rich with marrow.[y]

21:24 [y] Pr 3:8

25 Another man dies in bitterness of
soul,
never having enjoyed anything
good.
26 Side by side they lie in the dust,
and worms cover them both.[z]

21:26 [z] Job 24:20; Ecc 9:2-3; Isa 14:11

27 "I know full well what you are
thinking,
the schemes by which you would
wrong me.
28 You say, 'Where now is the great
man's[a] house,
the tents where wicked men
lived?'[b]

21:28 [a] Job 1:3; 12:21; 31:37 [b] Job 8:22

29 Have you never questioned those
who travel?
Have you paid no regard to their
accounts—
30 that the evil man is spared from
the day of calamity,[c]
that he is delivered from[c] the
day of wrath?[d]

21:30 [c] Pr 16:4 [d] Job 20:22,28; 2Pe 2:9

31 Who denounces his conduct to his
face?
Who repays him for what he has
done?
32 He is carried to the grave,
and watch is kept over his tomb.
33 The soil in the valley is sweet to
him;[e]
all men follow after him,
and a countless throng goes[d]
before him.[f]

21:33 [e] Job 3:22; 17:16; 24:24 [f] Job 3:19

34 "So how can you console me[g] with
your nonsense?
Nothing is left of your answers
but falsehood!"

21:34 [g] Job 16:2

Eliphaz

22 Then Eliphaz the Temanite replied:

2 "Can a man be of benefit to God?[h]
Can even a wise man benefit him?
3 What pleasure would it give the
Almighty if you were
righteous?
What would he gain if your ways
were blameless?

22:2 [h] Lk 17:10

4 "Is it for your piety that he rebukes
you
and brings charges against you?[i]
5 Is not your wickedness great?
Are not your sins[j] endless?
6 You demanded security[k] from your
brothers for no reason;
you stripped men of their
clothing, leaving them
naked.
7 You gave no water to the weary
and you withheld food from the
hungry,[l]
8 though you were a powerful man,
owning land—
an honored man,[m] living on it.
9 And you sent widows away empty-
handed[n]
and broke the strength of the
fatherless.
10 That is why snares are all around
you,
why sudden peril terrifies you,
11 why it is so dark[o] you cannot see,
and why a flood of water covers
you.[p]

22:4 [i] Job 14:3; 19:29; Ps 143:2
22:5 [j] Job 11:6; 15:5
22:6 [k] Ex 22:26; Dt 24:6,17; Eze 18:12,16
22:7 [l] Job 31:17,21,31
22:8 [m] Isa 3:3; 9:15
22:9 [n] Job 24:3,21
22:11 [o] Job 5:14 [p] Ps 69:1-2; 124:4-5; La 3:54

TO TIE JESUS CHRIST TO THE VERY BEST HUMAN SYSTEM IS TO TIE A STAR, LIGHT YEARS DISTANT, TO A DEAD HORSE HERE ON EARTH. NEITHER STAR NOR CHRIST WILL THUS BE BOUND.

Joe Bayly, *American Author*

12 "Is not God in the heights of
heaven?[q]
And see how lofty are the
highest stars!

22:12 [q] Job 11:8

[a] *17–20* Verses 17 and 18 may be taken as exclamations and 19 and 20 as declarations.
[b] *24* The meaning of the Hebrew for this word is uncertain.
[c] *30* Or *man is reserved for the day of calamity, / that he is brought forth to*
[d] *33* Or / *as a countless throng went*

[13] Yet you say, 'What does God know?[r]
Does he judge through such
darkness?[s]
[14] Thick clouds[t] veil him, so he does
not see us
as he goes about in the vaulted
heavens.'
[15] Will you keep to the old path
that evil men have trod?
[16] They were carried off before their
time,[u]
their foundations washed away
by a flood.[v]
[17] They said to God, 'Leave us alone!
What can the Almighty do to
us?'[w]
[18] Yet it was he who filled their
houses with good things,[x]
so I stand aloof from the counsel
of the wicked.[y]

[19] "The righteous see their ruin and
rejoice;[z]
the innocent mock[a] them,
saying,
[20] 'Surely our foes are destroyed,
and fire[b] devours their wealth.'

[21] "Submit to God and be at peace
with him;
in this way prosperity will come
to you.[c]
[22] Accept instruction from his mouth
and lay up his words in your
heart.
[23] If you return[d] to the Almighty, you
will be restored:[e]
If you remove wickedness far
from your tent[f]
[24] and assign your nuggets to the
dust,
your gold of Ophir to the rocks
in the ravines,[g]
[25] then the Almighty will be your gold,
the choicest silver for you.[h]
[26] Surely then you will find delight in
the Almighty[i]
and will lift up your face to God.
[27] You will pray to him,[j] and he will
hear you,
and you will fulfill your vows.
[28] What you decide on will be done,
and light will shine on your ways.
[29] When men are brought low and
you say, 'Lift them up!'
then he will save the downcast.[k]
[30] He will deliver even one who is not
innocent,

22:13 [r] Ps 10:11; Isa 29:15 [s] Eze 8:12
22:14 [t] Job 26:9
22:16 [u] Job 15:32 [v] Job 14:19; Mt 7:26-27
22:17 [w] Job 21:15
22:18 [x] Job 12:6 [y] Job 21:16
22:19 [z] Ps 58:10; 107:42 [a] Ps 52:6
22:20 [b] Job 15:30
22:21 [c] Ps 34:8-10
22:23 [d] Job 8:5; Isa 31:6; Zec 1:3 [e] Isa 19:22; Ac 20:32 [f] Job 11:14
22:24 [g] Job 31:25
22:25 [h] Isa 33:6
22:26 [i] Job 27:10; Isa 58:14
22:27 [j] Job 33:26; 34:28; Isa 58:9
22:29 [k] Mt 23:12; 1Pe 5:5

who will be delivered through the
cleanness of your hands."[l]

Job

23 Then Job replied:

[2] "Even today my complaint[m] is
bitter;[n]
his hand[a] is heavy in spite of[b]
my groaning.
[3] If only I knew where to find him;
if only I could go to his dwelling!
[4] I would state my case[o] before him
and fill my mouth with
arguments.
[5] I would find out what he would
answer me,
and consider what he would say.
[6] Would he oppose me with great
power?[p]
No, he would not press charges
against me.
[7] There an upright man could
present his case before
him,[q]
and I would be delivered forever
from my judge.

[8] "But if I go to the east, he is not
there;
if I go to the west, I do not find
him.
[9] When he is at work in the north, I
do not see him;
when he turns to the south, I
catch no glimpse of him.[r]
[10] But he knows the way that I take;
when he has tested me,[s] I will
come forth as gold.[t]
[11] My feet have closely followed his
steps;[u]
I have kept to his way without
turning aside.[v]
[12] I have not departed from the
commands of his lips;[w]
I have treasured the words of his
mouth more than my daily
bread.[x]

[13] "But he stands alone, and who can
oppose him?
He does whatever he pleases.[y]
[14] He carries out his decree against
me,
and many such plans he still has
in store.[z]

[a] 2 Septuagint and Syriac; Hebrew / *the hand on me* [b] 2 Or *heavy on me in*

22:30 [l] Job 42:7-8
23:2 [m] Job 7:11 [n] Job 6:3
23:4 [o] Job 13:18
23:6 [p] Job 9:4
23:7 [q] Job 13:3
23:9 [r] Job 9:11
23:10 [s] Ps 66:10; 139:1-3 [t] 1Pe 1:7
23:11 [u] Ps 17:5 [v] Ps 44:18
23:12 [w] Job 6:10 [x] Jn 4:32,34
23:13 [y] Ps 115:3
23:14 [z] 1Th 3:3

15 That is why I am terrified before
him;
when I think of all this, I fear
him.
16 God has made my heart faint;[a]
the Almighty[b] has terrified me.
17 Yet I am not silenced by the
darkness,[c]
by the thick darkness that
covers my face.

24 "Why does the Almighty not
set times for judgment?[d]
Why must those who know him
look in vain for such days?[e]
2 Men move boundary stones;[f]
they pasture flocks they have
stolen.
3 They drive away the orphan's
donkey
and take the widow's ox in
pledge.[g]
4 They thrust the needy from the
path
and force all the poor[h] of the
land into hiding.[i]
5 Like wild donkeys in the desert,
the poor go about their labor[j] of
foraging food;
the wasteland provides food for
their children.
6 They gather fodder in the fields
and glean in the vineyards of the
wicked.
7 Lacking clothes, they spend the
night naked;
they have nothing to cover
themselves in the cold.[k]
8 They are drenched by mountain
rains
and hug[l] the rocks for lack of
shelter.
9 The fatherless[m] child is snatched
from the breast;
the infant of the poor is seized
for a debt.
10 Lacking clothes, they go about
naked;
they carry the sheaves, but still
go hungry.
11 They crush olives among the
terraces[a];
they tread the winepresses, yet
suffer thirst.
12 The groans of the dying rise from
the city,
and the souls of the wounded
cry out for help.[n]

23:16 [a] Dt 20:3; Ps 22:14; Jer 51:46 [b] Job 27:2
23:17 [c] Job 19:8
24:1 [d] Jer 46:10 [e] Ac 1:7
24:2 [f] Dt 19:14; 27:17; Pr 23:10
24:3 [g] Dt 24:6,10,12, 17; Job 22:6
24:4 [h] Job 29:12; 30:25; Ps 41:1 [i] Pr 28:28
24:5 [j] Ps 104:23
24:7 [k] Ex 22:27; Job 22:6
24:8 [l] La 4:5
24:9 [m] Dt 24:17
24:12 [n] Eze 26:15

But God charges no one with
wrongdoing.[o]

13 "There are those who rebel against
the light,[p]
who do not know its ways
or stay in its paths.[q]
14 When daylight is gone, the
murderer rises up
and kills the poor and needy;
in the night he steals forth like a
thief.[r]
15 The eye of the adulterer watches
for dusk;[s]
he thinks, 'No eye will see me,'[t]
and he keeps his face concealed.
16 In the dark, men break into houses,[u]
but by day they shut themselves
in;
they want nothing to do with
the light.[v]
17 For all of them, deep darkness is
their morning[b];
they make friends with the
terrors of darkness.[c]

18 "Yet they are foam[w] on the surface
of the water;[x]
their portion of the land is
cursed,
so that no one goes to the
vineyards.
19 As heat and drought snatch away
the melted snow,[y]
so the grave[d][z] snatches away
those who have sinned.
20 The womb forgets them,
the worm feasts on them;
evil men are no longer remembered[a]
but are broken like a tree.[b]
21 They prey on the barren and
childless woman,
and to the widow show no
kindness.[c]
22 But God drags away the mighty by
his power;
though they become established,
they have no assurance of
life.[d]
23 He may let them rest in a feeling of
security,[e]
but his eyes are on their ways.[f]
24 For a little while they are exalted,
and then they are gone;[g]

24:12 [o] Job 9:23
24:13 [p] Jn 3:19-20 [q] Isa 5:20
24:14 [r] Ps 10:9
24:15 [s] Pr 7:8-9 [t] Ps 10:11
24:16 [u] Ex 22:2; Mt 6:19 [v] Jn 3:20
24:18 [w] Job 9:26 [x] Job 22:16
24:19 [y] Job 6:17 [z] Job 21:13
24:20 [a] Job 18:17; Pr 10:7 [b] Ps 31:12; Da 4:14
24:21 [c] Job 22:9
24:22 [d] Dt 28:66
24:23 [e] Job 12:6 [f] Job 11:11
24:24 [g] Job 14:21; Ps 37:10

[a] *11* Or *olives between the millstones*; the meaning of the Hebrew for this word is uncertain. [b] *17* Or *them, their morning is like the shadow of death* [c] *17* Or *of the shadow of death* [d] *19* Hebrew *Sheol*

DISCOVERY 121

When God Seems Distant

Job's situation was so devastating that several friends came to offer comfort. They sat and grieved with him for a full week before saying anything (see Job 1:11–13). Then began a long conversation. Job's happy life had disintegrated, and everybody seemed to have an opinion about why this had happened. Job remained convinced that God is just and yearned to dialogue with him about the reversals he was experiencing. He expressed frustration because he could not determine where to find God. And in exasperation Job asked, "Why does the Almighty not set times for judgment?" (Job 24:1). Essentially he was asking why God doesn't seem to be available to discuss things when it seems that the circumstances have spun out of control.

But God isn't silent when faced with injustice. While the Bible isn't God's answer book for all of our agonizing questions, it is his revelation to us about who he is and how we can get to know him. And God assures us that he sees everything, that he is not blind to our pain or to the injustices we suffer, that he is not insensitive to our needs or our desires (Matthew 6:8). More important, *we* are the ones obligated to answer to God, because he created us; God is not accountable to explain himself to his creatures (Matthew 22:37–40; Romans 12:19).

God has a plan, even though we can't always decipher it. He never acts randomly (Isaiah 50:8), and his plan is so all-encompassing that it stretches throughout all eternity—and only he can see the whole picture from start to finish. He is concerned with teaching us and changing us to be more like Jesus, and it is his good pleasure to concentrate more on the beauty he is fashioning into our lives than on the amount of time the process requires. When God says that he is at work, we need to take him at his word (Philippians 1:6; 2:13).

While we yearn for justice in the world, God himself longs for it even more. He created a perfect world, only to see it destroyed by sin. So he himself did what was needed to reverse the effects of sin. God the Father had one answer to the problem of inequity and evil in the world: Jesus. And one day he'll take the final steps to ensure that justice will reign forever. Once Jesus has established his kingdom on the earth, all that is right and fair will prevail (Isaiah 65:17–25; Revelation 21:1–5). Until that day, we can do nothing better than to hold fast to his promises.

Job wished that "there were someone to arbitrate between [himself and God]" (Job 9:33), and his friend Elihu picked up the same thread in Job 33:23–24, where he expressed his desire for an angelic mediator who could represent Job before God. Thank God that we do have One who represents us: "For there is one God and one mediator between God and men, the man Jesus Christ, who gave himself as a ransom for all men" (1 Timothy 2:5–6).

Self-Discovery: *When a friend or acquaintance is suffering, are you quick to come forward with advice, or do you offer empathy and encouragement whether or not you know the "right" words to say? Take a moment to list some of the ways the Lord is at work in your life to change you to be more like Jesus.*

GO TO DISCOVERY 122 ON PAGE 664

they are brought low and
gathered up like all others;
they are cut off like heads of
grain.[h]
25 “If this is not so, who can prove me
false
and reduce my words to
nothing?”[i]

24:24 [h] Isa 17:5
24:25 [i] Job 6:28; 27:4

Bildad

25

Then Bildad the Shuhite replied:

2 “Dominion and awe belong to God;[j]
he establishes order in the
heights of heaven.
3 Can his forces be numbered?
Upon whom does his light not
rise?[k]
4 How then can a man be righteous
before God?
How can one born of woman be
pure?[l]
5 If even the moon[m] is not bright
and the stars are not pure in his
eyes,[n]
6 how much less man, who is but a
maggot—
a son of man,[o] who is only a
worm!”[p]

25:2 [j] Job 9:4; Rev 1:6
25:3 [k] Jas 1:17
25:4 [l] Job 4:17; 14:4
25:5 [m] Job 31:26 [n] Job 15:15
25:6 [o] Job 7:17 [p] Ps 22:6

Job

26

Then Job replied:

2 “How you have helped the
powerless![q]
How you have saved the arm
that is feeble![r]
3 What advice you have offered to
one without wisdom!
And what great insight you have
displayed!
4 Who has helped you utter these
words?
And whose spirit spoke from
your mouth?

5 “The dead are in deep anguish,[s]
those beneath the waters and all
that live in them.
6 Death[a][t] is naked before God;
Destruction[b] lies uncovered.[u]
7 He spreads out the northern
⌊skies⌋[v] over empty space;
he suspends the earth over
nothing.
8 He wraps up the waters[w] in his
clouds,[x]
yet the clouds do not burst
under their weight.
9 He covers the face of the full moon,
spreading his clouds[y] over it.
10 He marks out the horizon on the
face of the waters[z]
for a boundary between light
and darkness.[a]
11 The pillars of the heavens quake,
aghast at his rebuke.
12 By his power he churned up the
sea;[b]
by his wisdom[c] he cut Rahab to
pieces.
13 By his breath the skies became fair;
his hand pierced the gliding
serpent.[d]
14 And these are but the outer fringe
of his works;
how faint the whisper we hear of
him!
Who then can understand the
thunder of his power?”[e]

26:2 [q] Job 6:12 [r] Ps 71:9
26:5 [s] Ps 88:10
26:6 [t] Ps 139:8 [u] Job 41:11; Pr 15:11; Heb 4:13
26:7 [v] Job 9:8
26:8 [w] Pr 30:4 [x] Job 37:11
26:9 [y] Job 22:14; Ps 97:2
26:10 [z] Pr 8:27,29 [a] Job 38:8-11
26:12 [b] Ex 14:21; Isa 51:15; Jer 31:35 [c] Job 12:13
26:13 [d] Isa 27:1
26:14 [e] Job 36:29

27

And Job continued his discourse:[f]

2 “As surely as God lives, who has
denied me justice,[g]
the Almighty, who has made me
taste bitterness of soul,[h]
3 as long as I have life within me,
the breath of God[i] in my nostrils,
4 my lips will not speak wickedness,
and my tongue will utter no
deceit.[j]
5 I will never admit you are in the
right;
till I die, I will not deny my
integrity.[k]
6 I will maintain my righteousness
and never let go of it;
my conscience will not reproach
me as long as I live.[l]

7 “May my enemies be like the
wicked,
my adversaries like the unjust!
8 For what hope has the godless[m]
when he is cut off,
when God takes away his life?[n]
9 Does God listen to his cry
when distress comes upon him?[o]
10 Will he find delight in the
Almighty?[p]
Will he call upon God at all
times?

27:1 [f] Job 29:1
27:2 [g] Job 34:5 [h] Job 9:18
27:3 [i] Job 32:8; 33:4
27:4 [j] Job 6:28
27:5 [k] Job 2:9; 13:15
27:6 [l] Job 2:3
27:8 [m] Job 8:13 [n] Job 11:20; Lk 12:20
27:9 [o] Job 35:12; Pr 1:28; Isa 1:15; Jer 14:12; Mic 3:4
27:10 [p] Job 22:26

[a] 6 Hebrew *Sheol* [b] 6 Hebrew *Abaddon*

[11] "I will teach you about the power
of God;
the ways of the Almighty I will
not conceal.
[12] You have all seen this yourselves.
Why then this meaningless talk?

[13] "Here is the fate God allots to the
wicked,
the heritage a ruthless man
receives from the
Almighty:[q]
[14] However many his children, their
fate is the sword;[r]
his offspring will never have
enough to eat.[s]
[15] The plague will bury those who
survive him,
and their widows will not weep
for them.[t]
[16] Though he heaps up silver like dust
and clothes like piles of clay,[u]
[17] what he lays up the righteous will
wear,[v]
and the innocent will divide his
silver.
[18] The house he builds is like a moth's
cocoon,[w]
like a hut[x] made by a watchman.
[19] He lies down wealthy, but will do
so no more;[y]
when he opens his eyes, all is
gone.
[20] Terrors overtake him like a flood;[z]
a tempest snatches him away in
the night.[a]
[21] The east wind carries him off, and
he is gone;
it sweeps him out of his place.[b]
[22] It hurls itself against him without
mercy[c]
as he flees headlong from its
power.[d]
[23] It claps its hands in derision
and hisses him out of his place.[e]

28 "There is a mine for silver
and a place where gold is
refined.
[2] Iron is taken from the earth,
and copper is smelted from ore.[f]
[3] Man puts an end to the darkness;[g]
he searches the farthest recesses
for ore in the blackest darkness.
[4] Far from where people dwell he
cuts a shaft,
in places forgotten by the foot of
man;
far from men he dangles and
sways.
[5] The earth, from which food comes,[h]
is transformed below as by fire;
[6] sapphires[a] come from its rocks,
and its dust contains nuggets of
gold.
[7] No bird of prey knows that hidden
path,
no falcon's eye has seen it.
[8] Proud beasts do not set foot on it,
and no lion prowls there.
[9] Man's hand assaults the flinty rock
and lays bare the roots of the
mountains.
[10] He tunnels through the rock;
his eyes see all its treasures.
[11] He searches[b] the sources of the
rivers
and brings hidden things to light.

[12] "But where can wisdom be found?[i]
Where does understanding
dwell?
[13] Man does not comprehend its
worth;[j]
it cannot be found in the land of
the living.
[14] The deep says, 'It is not in me';
the sea says, 'It is not with me.'
[15] It cannot be bought with the finest
gold,
nor can its price be weighed in
silver.[k]
[16] It cannot be bought with the gold
of Ophir,
with precious onyx or sapphires.
[17] Neither gold nor crystal can
compare with it,
nor can it be had for jewels of
gold.[l]
[18] Coral and jasper are not worthy of
mention;
the price of wisdom is beyond
rubies.[m]
[19] The topaz of Cush cannot compare
with it;
it cannot be bought with pure
gold.[n]

[20] "Where then does wisdom come
from?
Where does understanding
dwell?[o]

27:13 [q] Job 15:20; 20:29
27:14 [r] Dt 28:41; Job 15:22; Hos 9:13 [s] Job 20:10
27:15 [t] Ps 78:64
27:16 [u] Zec 9:3
27:17 [v] Pr 28:8; Ecc 2:26
27:18 [w] Job 8:14 [x] Isa 1:8
27:19 [y] Job 7:8
27:20 [z] Job 15:21 [a] Job 20:8
27:21 [b] Job 7:10; 21:18
27:22 [c] Jer 13:14; Eze 5:11; 24:14 [d] Job 11:20
27:23 [e] Job 18:18
28:2 [f] Dt 8:9
28:3 [g] Ecc 1:13
28:5 [h] Ps 104:14
28:12 [i] Ecc 7:24
28:13 [j] Pr 3:15; Mt 13:44-46
28:15 [k] Pr 3:13-14; 8:10-11; 16:16
28:17 [l] Pr 16:16
28:18 [m] Pr 3:15
28:19 [n] Pr 8:19
28:20 [o] ver 23,28

[a] *6* Or *lapis lazuli;* also in verse 16
[b] *11* Septuagint, Aquila and Vulgate; Hebrew *He dams up*

[21] It is hidden from the eyes of every
living thing,
concealed even from the birds of
the air.
[22] Destruction[a][p] and Death say,
'Only a rumor of it has reached
our ears.'

28:22 [p]Job 26:6

[23] God understands the way to it
and he alone knows where it
dwells,[q]

28:23 [q]Pr 8:22-31

[24] for he views the ends of the earth[r]
and sees everything under the
heavens.[s]

28:24 [r]Ps 33:13-14 [s]Pr 15:3

[25] When he established the force of
the wind
and measured out the waters,[t]

28:25 [t]Job 12:15; Ps 135:7

[26] when he made a decree for the rain
and a path for the thunderstorm,[u]

28:26 [u]Job 37:3,8,11; 38:25,27

[27] then he looked at wisdom and
appraised it;
he confirmed it and tested it.
[28] And he said to man,
'The fear of the Lord—that is
wisdom,
and to shun evil is
understanding.[v]'"

28:28 [v]Dt 4:6; Ps 111:10; Pr 1:7; 9:10

29 Job continued his discourse:[w]

29:1 [w]Job 13:12; 27:1

[2] "How I long for the months gone by,
for the days when God watched
over me,[x]

29:2 [x]Jer 31:28

[3] when his lamp shone upon my head
and by his light I walked
through darkness![y]

29:3 [y]Job 11:17

[4] Oh, for the days when I was in my
prime,
when God's intimate friendship
blessed my house,[z]

29:4 [z]Ps 25:14; Pr 3:32

[5] when the Almighty was still with me
and my children were around me,
[6] when my path was drenched with
cream[a]
and the rock[b] poured out for me
streams of olive oil.[c]

29:6 [a]Job 20:17 [b]Ps 81:16 [c]Dt 32:13

[7] "When I went to the gate[d] of the
city
and took my seat in the public
square,

29:7 [d]Job 31:21

[8] the young men saw me and
stepped aside
and the old men rose to their
feet;
[9] the chief men refrained from
speaking
and covered their mouths with
their hands;[e]

29:9 [e]Job 21:5

[10] the voices of the nobles were
hushed,
and their tongues stuck to the
roof of their mouths.[f]

29:10 [f]Ps 137:6

[11] Whoever heard me spoke well of
me,
and those who saw me
commended me,
[12] because I rescued the poor[g] who
cried for help,
and the fatherless[h] who had
none to assist him.[i]

29:12 [g]Job 24:4 [h]Job 31:17,21 [i]Ps 72:12; Pr 21:13

[13] The man who was dying blessed
me;[j]
I made the widow's[k] heart sing.

29:13 [j]Job 31:20 [k]Job 22:9

[14] I put on righteousness[l] as my
clothing;
justice was my robe and my
turban.

29:14 [l]Job 27:6; Ps 132:9; Isa 59:17; 61:10; Eph 6:14

[15] I was eyes[m] to the blind
and feet to the lame.

29:15 [m]Nu 10:31

[16] I was a father to the needy;[n]
I took up the case of the stranger.

29:16 [n]Job 24:4; Pr 29:7

[17] I broke the fangs of the wicked
and snatched the victims from
their teeth.[o]

29:17 [o]Ps 3:7

[18] "I thought, 'I will die in my own
house,
my days as numerous as the
grains of sand.[p]

29:18 [p]Ps 30:6

[19] My roots will reach to the water,[q]
and the dew will lie all night on
my branches.

29:19 [q]Job 18:16; Jer 17:8

[20] My glory will remain fresh in me,
the bow[r] ever new in my hand.'[s]

29:20 [r]Ps 18:34 [s]Ge 49:24

[21] "Men listened to me expectantly,
waiting in silence for my counsel.
[22] After I had spoken, they spoke no
more;
my words fell gently on their
ears.[t]

29:22 [t]Dt 32:2

[23] They waited for me as for showers
and drank in my words as the
spring rain.
[24] When I smiled at them, they
scarcely believed it;
the light of my face was precious
to them.[b]
[25] I chose the way for them and sat as
their chief;
I dwelt as a king[u] among his
troops;
I was like one who comforts
mourners.[v]

29:25 [u]Job 1:3; 31:37 [v]Job 4:4

[a] *22* Hebrew *Abaddon* [b] *24* The meaning of the Hebrew for this clause is uncertain.

30:1 [w]Job 12:4

30

"But now they mock me,[w]
men younger than I,
whose fathers I would have
disdained
to put with my sheep dogs.
2 Of what use was the strength of
their hands to me,
since their vigor had gone from
them?
3 Haggard from want and hunger,
they roamed[a] the parched land
in desolate wastelands at night.
4 In the brush they gathered salt
herbs,
and their food[b] was the root of
the broom tree.
5 They were banished from their
fellow men,
shouted at as if they were thieves.
6 They were forced to live in the dry
stream beds,
among the rocks and in holes in
the ground.
7 They brayed among the bushes
and huddled in the undergrowth.
8 A base and nameless brood,
they were driven out of the land.

30:9 [x]Ps 69:11 [y]Job 12:4; La 3:14,63 [z]Job 17:6

9 "And now their sons mock me[x] in
song;[y]
I have become a byword[z] among
them.

30:10 [a]Nu 12:14; Dt 25:9; Isa 50:6; Mt 26:67

10 They detest me and keep their
distance;
they do not hesitate to spit in
my face.[a]

30:11 [b]Ru 1:21 [c]Ps 32:9

11 Now that God has unstrung my
bow and afflicted me,[b]
they throw off restraint[c] in my
presence.

30:12 [d]Ps 140:4-5 [e]Job 19:12

12 On my right the tribe[c] attacks;
they lay snares for my feet,[d]
they build their siege ramps
against me.[e]

30:13 [f]Isa 3:12

13 They break up my road;[f]
they succeed in destroying me—
without anyone's helping them.[d]
14 They advance as through a gaping
breach;
amid the ruins they come rolling
in.

30:15 [g]Job 31:23; Ps 55:4-5 [h]Job 3:25; Hos 13:3

15 Terrors overwhelm me;[g]
my dignity is driven away as by
the wind,
my safety vanishes like a cloud.[h]

30:16 [i]Job 3:24; Ps 22:14; 42:4

16 "And now my life ebbs away;[i]
days of suffering grip me.
17 Night pierces my bones;
my gnawing pains never rest.
18 In his great power ⌊God⌋ becomes
like clothing to me[e];
he binds me like the neck of my
garment.

30:19 [j]Ps 69:2,14

19 He throws me into the mud,[j]
and I am reduced to dust and
ashes.

30:20 [k]Job 19:7

20 "I cry out to you, O God, but you do
not answer;[k]
I stand up, but you merely look
at me.

30:21 [l]Job 19:6,22 [m]Job 16:9,14 [n]Job 10:3

21 You turn on me ruthlessly;[l]
with the might of your hand[m]
you attack me.[n]

30:22 [o]Job 27:21 [p]Job 9:17

22 You snatch me up and drive me
before the wind;[o]
you toss me about in the storm.[p]

30:23 [q]Job 9:22; 10:8 [r]Job 3:19

23 I know you will bring me down to
death,[q]
to the place appointed for all the
living.[r]

30:24 [s]Job 19:7

24 "Surely no one lays a hand on a
broken man
when he cries for help in his
distress.[s]

30:25 [t]Job 24:4; Ps 35:13-14; Ro 12:15

25 Have I not wept for those in
trouble?
Has not my soul grieved for the
poor?[t]

30:26 [u]Job 3:25-26; 19:8; Jer 8:15

26 Yet when I hoped for good, evil
came;
when I looked for light, then
came darkness.[u]

30:27 [v]La 2:11

27 The churning inside me never
stops;[v]
days of suffering confront me.

30:28 [w]Ps 38:6; 42:9; 43:2 [x]Job 19:7

28 I go about blackened,[w] but not by
the sun;
I stand up in the assembly and
cry for help.[x]

30:29 [y]Ps 44:19 [z]Ps 102:6; Mic 1:8

29 I have become a brother of jackals,[y]
a companion of owls.[z]

30:30 [a]La 4:8 [b]Ps 102:3

30 My skin grows black and peels;[a]
my body burns with fever.[b]

30:31 [c]Isa 24:8

31 My harp is tuned to mourning,[c]
and my flute to the sound of
wailing.

31:1 [d]Mt 5:28

31

"I made a covenant with my
eyes
not to look lustfully at a girl.[d]

[a] 3 Or *gnawed* [b] 4 Or *fuel* [c] 12 The meaning of the Hebrew for this word is uncertain.
[d] 13 Or *me. / 'No one can help him,' ⌊they say⌋.*
[e] 18 Hebrew; Septuagint ⌊*God*⌋ *grasps my clothing*

2 For what is man's lot from God
above,
his heritage from the Almighty
on high?[e]
3 Is it not ruin[f] for the wicked,
disaster for those who do
wrong?[g]
4 Does he not see my ways[h]
and count my every step?[i]

5 "If I have walked in falsehood
or my foot has hurried after
deceit[j]—
6 let God weigh me in honest scales[k]
and he will know that I am
blameless—
7 if my steps have turned from the
path,[l]
if my heart has been led by my
eyes,
or if my hands[m] have been
defiled,
8 then may others eat what I have
sown,[n]
and may my crops be uprooted.[o]

9 "If my heart has been enticed[p] by a
woman,
or if I have lurked at my
neighbor's door,
10 then may my wife grind another
man's grain,
and may other men sleep with
her.[q]
11 For that would have been shameful,
a sin to be judged.[r]
12 It is a fire[s] that burns to
Destruction[a];[t]
it would have uprooted my
harvest.[u]

13 "If I have denied justice to my
menservants and
maidservants
when they had a grievance
against me,[v]
14 what will I do when God confronts
me?
What will I answer when called
to account?
15 Did not he who made me in the
womb make them?
Did not the same one form us
both within our mothers?[w]

16 "If I have denied the desires of the
poor[x]
or let the eyes of the widow[y]
grow weary,
17 if I have kept my bread to myself,
not sharing it with the
fatherless[z]—
18 but from my youth I reared him as
would a father,
and from my birth I guided the
widow—
19 if I have seen anyone perishing for
lack of clothing,[a]
or a needy[b] man without a
garment,
20 and his heart did not bless me
for warming him with the fleece
from my sheep,
21 if I have raised my hand against the
fatherless,[c]
knowing that I had influence in
court,
22 then let my arm fall from the
shoulder,
let it be broken off at the joint.[d]
23 For I dreaded destruction from
God,
and for fear of his splendor[e] I
could not do such things.

24 "If I have put my trust in gold[f]
or said to pure gold, 'You are my
security,'[g]
25 if I have rejoiced over my great
wealth,[h]
the fortune my hands had
gained,
26 if I have regarded the sun[i] in its
radiance
or the moon moving in splendor,
27 so that my heart was secretly
enticed
and my hand offered them a kiss
of homage,
28 then these also would be sins to be
judged,[j]
for I would have been unfaithful
to God on high.

29 "If I have rejoiced at my enemy's
misfortune[k]
or gloated over the trouble that
came to him[l]—
30 I have not allowed my mouth to sin
by invoking a curse against his
life—
31 if the men of my household have
never said,
'Who has not had his fill of Job's
meat?'[m]—

[a] 12 Hebrew *Abaddon*

31:2 [e] Job 20:29
31:3 [f] Job 21:30 [g] Job 34:22
31:4 [h] 2Ch 16:9 [i] Pr 5:21
31:5 [j] Mic 2:11
31:6 [k] Job 6:2; 27:5-6
31:7 [l] Job 23:11 [m] Job 9:30
31:8 [n] Lev 26:16; Job 20:18 [o] Mic 6:15
31:9 [p] Job 24:15
31:10 [q] Dt 28:30; Jer 8:10
31:11 [r] Ge 38:24; Lev 20:10; Dt 22:22-24
31:12 [s] Job 15:30 [t] Job 26:6 [u] Job 20:28
31:13 [v] Dt 24:14-15
31:15 [w] Job 10:3
31:16 [x] Job 5:16; 20:19 [y] Job 22:9
31:17 [z] Job 22:7; 29:12
31:19 [a] Job 22:6 [b] Job 24:4
31:21 [c] Job 22:9
31:22 [d] Job 38:15
31:23 [e] Job 13:11
31:24 [f] Job 22:25 [g] Mt 6:24; Mk 10:24
31:25 [h] Ps 62:10
31:26 [i] Eze 8:16
31:28 [j] Dt 17:2-7
31:29 [k] Ob 1:12 [l] Pr 17:5; 24:17-18
31:31 [m] Job 22:7

32 but no stranger had to spend the
night in the street,
31:32 [n]Ge 19:2-3; Ro 12:13
for my door was always open to
the traveler[n]—
33 if I have concealed[o] my sin as men
31:33 [o]Pr 28:13 [p]Ge 3:8
do,[a]
by hiding[p] my guilt in my heart
34 because I so feared the crowd[q]
31:34 [q]Ex 23:2
and so dreaded the contempt of
the clans
that I kept silent and would not
go outside
35 ("Oh, that I had someone to hear
31:35 [r]Job 19:7; 30:28 [s]Job 27:7; 35:14
me![r]
I sign now my defense—let the
Almighty answer me;
let my accuser[s] put his
indictment in writing.
36 Surely I would wear it on my
shoulder,
I would put it on like a crown.
37 I would give him an account of my
every step;
31:37 [t]Job 1:3; 29:25
like a prince[t] I would approach
him.)—
31:38 [u]Ge 4:10
38 "if my land cries out against me[u]
and all its furrows are wet with
tears,
31:39 [v]1Ki 21:19 [w]Lev 19:13; Jas 5:4
39 if I have devoured its yield without
payment[v]
or broken the spirit of its
tenants,[w]
31:40 [x]Ge 3:18
40 then let briers[x] come up instead of
wheat
and weeds instead of barley."

The words of Job are ended.

Elihu

32 So these three men stopped an-
32:1 [y]Job 10:7; 33:9
swering Job, because he was
righteous in his own eyes.[y] 2 But Elihu son
32:2 [z]Ge 22:21 [a]Job 27:5; 30:21
of Barakel the Buzite,[z] of the family of
Ram, became very angry with Job for justifying himself rather than God.[a] 3 He was
also angry with the three friends, because
they had found no way to refute Job, and
yet had condemned him.[b] 4 Now Elihu
had waited before speaking to Job because they were older than he. 5 But when
he saw that the three men had nothing
more to say, his anger was aroused.
6 So Elihu son of Barakel the Buzite
said:

"I am young in years,
32:6 [b]Job 15:10
and you are old;[b]
that is why I was fearful,
not daring to tell you what I
know.
7 I thought, 'Age should speak;
advanced years should teach
wisdom.'
8 But it is the spirit[c] in a man,
32:8 [c]Job 27:3; 33:4 [d]Pr 2:6
the breath of the Almighty,[c] that
gives him understanding.[d]
9 It is not only the old[d] who are wise,[e]
32:9 [e]1Co 1:26
not only the aged who
understand what is right.
10 "Therefore I say: Listen to me;
I too will tell you what I know.
11 I waited while you spoke,
I listened to your reasoning;
while you were searching for words,
12 I gave you my full attention.
But not one of you has proved Job
wrong;
none of you has answered his
arguments.
13 Do not say, 'We have found
32:13 [f]Jer 9:23
wisdom;[f]
let God refute him, not man.'
14 But Job has not marshaled his
words against me,
and I will not answer him with
your arguments.
15 "They are dismayed and have no
more to say;
words have failed them.
16 Must I wait, now that they are silent,
now that they stand there with
no reply?
17 I too will have my say;
I too will tell what I know.
18 For I am full of words,
and the spirit within me
compels me;
19 inside I am like bottled-up wine,
like new wineskins ready to burst.
20 I must speak and find relief;
I must open my lips and reply.
21 I will show partiality[g] to no one,[h]
32:21 [g]Lev 19:15; Job 13:10 [h]Mt 22:16
nor will I flatter any man;
22 for if I were skilled in flattery,
my Maker would soon take me
away.

33 "But now, Job, listen to my
words;
33:1 [i]Job 13:6
pay attention to everything I say.[i]

[a] 33 Or *as Adam did* [b] 3 Masoretic Text; an ancient Hebrew scribal tradition *Job, and so had condemned God* [c] 8 Or *Spirit*; also in verse 18 [d] 9 Or *many*; or *great*

DISCOVERY 122

THE DANGER OF SELF-RIGHTEOUSNESS

Job's three friends, Eliphaz, Bildad and Zophar, employed every argument they could think of to convince Job that all of the tragedy in his life was due to the fact that he had sinned in some way. But Job refused to acknowledge this: "I will maintain my righteousness and never let go of it; my conscience will not reproach me as long as I live" (Job 27:6). And in chapter 32 a fourth companion, Elihu, "became very angry with Job for justifying himself rather than God" (verse 2).

But Job was right. Intuitively he knew that his suffering was not the result of some specific sin but that God was in some way using the tragedies in his life to verify that Job did indeed put his faith in God. While Job's assessment of the situation was correct to the extent that his immediate suffering was not the result of his own sin, however, he was in no way stating that his life was blameless. With the one exception of Jesus Christ, no person who has ever lived can claim perfection (see Hebrews 14:5). From God's perspective every one of us has fallen short of his expectation for our lives (Romans 3:9–18).

God has different criteria from our own—he sees beyond a person's façade into his or her heart. Jesus warns us about an attitude of complacency based upon our own righteousness (Luke 18:9–14) by relating a story about two men. The first man Jesus described was a religious leader. This man exclaimed, "God, I thank you that I am not like other men—robbers, evildoers, adulterers—or even like this tax collector! I fast twice a week and give a tenth of all I get" (Luke 18:11–12). In his own mind this prominent citizen assumed that he and God were on the best of terms because of all the "good" things he had accomplished. He recognized sin in other people but was blind to its presence in his own life.

But this man's demeanor is contrasted with the attitude of another, a despised tax collector. At that time tax collectors were considered as among the worst of all possible sinners, because they habitually took advantage of ordinary people in order to pad their own pocketbooks. This man, though, was different. He would not even permit himself to look up toward heaven. Instead he beat his breast, a sign of intense sorrow and regret, and admitted to God that he was a sinner in need of mercy (Luke 18:13).

After comparing the prayers of the two men, Jesus came to a shocking conclusion: The tax collector went home justified (Luke 18:14). The second man was honest with himself and with God. He knew both that he had failed to live the way God wanted him to and that God would forgive him. Becoming right with God is never based on what we do, how good or kind we are or how favorably we may compare ourselves with others. It does depend on agreeing with God's assessment of our sinful nature, accepting his wonderful offer of forgiveness and committing our lives to him.

***Self-Discovery:** Do you identify more closely with the religious leader or with the tax collector in Jesus' story? Or is your stance in prayer somewhere in between?*

GO TO DISCOVERY 123 ON PAGE 674

2 I am about to open my mouth;
my words are on the tip of my tongue.
3 My words come from an upright heart;
my lips sincerely speak what I know.[j]
4 The Spirit of God has made me;[k]
the breath of the Almighty[l] gives me life.
5 Answer me[m] then, if you can;
prepare[n] yourself and confront me.
6 I am just like you before God;
I too have been taken from clay.[o]
7 No fear of me should alarm you,
nor should my hand be heavy upon you.[p]

8 "But you have said in my hearing—
I heard the very words—
9 'I am pure[q] and without sin;[r]
I am clean and free from guilt.
10 Yet God has found fault with me;
he considers me his enemy.[s]
11 He fastens my feet in shackles;[t]
he keeps close watch on all my paths.'[u]

12 "But I tell you, in this you are not right,
for God is greater than man.[v]
13 Why do you complain to him[w]
that he answers none of man's words[a]?
14 For God does speak[x]—now one way, now another—
though man may not perceive it.
15 In a dream,[y] in a vision of the night,
when deep sleep falls on men
as they slumber in their beds,
16 he may speak[z] in their ears
and terrify them with warnings,
17 to turn man from wrongdoing
and keep him from pride,
18 to preserve his soul from the pit,[b][a]
his life from perishing by the sword.[c][b]
19 Or a man may be chastened on a bed of pain
with constant distress in his bones,[c]
20 so that his very being finds food[d] repulsive
and his soul loathes the choicest meal.[e]
21 His flesh wastes away to nothing,
and his bones, once hidden, now stick out.[f]
22 His soul draws near to the pit,[d]
and his life to the messengers of death.[e][g]
23 "Yet if there is an angel on his side
as a mediator, one out of a thousand,
to tell a man what is right for him,[h]
24 to be gracious to him and say,
'Spare him from going down to the pit[f];[i]
I have found a ransom for him'—
25 then his flesh is renewed like a child's;
it is restored as in the days of his youth.[j]
26 He prays to God and finds favor with him,[k]
he sees God's face and shouts for joy;[l]
he is restored by God to his righteous state.[m]
27 Then he comes to men and says,
'I sinned,[n] and perverted what was right,[o]
but I did not get what I deserved.[p]
28 He redeemed my soul from going down to the pit,[g]
and I will live to enjoy the light.'[q]
29 "God does all these things to a man[r]—
twice, even three times—
30 to turn back his soul from the pit,[h]
that the light of life[s] may shine on him.

31 "Pay attention, Job, and listen to me;
be silent, and I will speak.
32 If you have anything to say, answer me;
speak up, for I want you to be cleared.
33 But if not, then listen to me;
be silent, and I will teach you wisdom.[t]"

34 Then Elihu said:

2 "Hear my words, you wise men;

[a] 13 *Or that he does not answer for any of his actions* [b] 18 *Or preserve him from the grave* [c] 18 *Or from crossing the River* [d] 22 *Or He draws near to the grave* [e] 22 *Or to the dead* [f] 24 *Or grave* [g] 28 *Or redeemed me from going down to the grave* [h] 30 *Or turn him back from the grave*

33:3 [j] Job 6:28; 27:4; 36:4
33:4 [k] Ge 2:7; Job 10:3 [l] Job 27:3
33:5 [m] ver 32 [n] Job 13:18
33:6 [o] Job 4:19
33:7 [p] Job 9:34; 13:21; 2Co 2:4
33:9 [q] Job 10:7 [r] Job 13:23; 16:17
33:10 [s] Job 13:24
33:11 [t] Job 13:27 [u] Job 14:16
33:12 [v] Ecc 7:20
33:13 [w] Job 40:2; Isa 45:9
33:14 [x] Ps 62:11
33:15 [y] Job 4:13
33:16 [z] Job 36:10,15
33:18 [a] ver 22,24,28, 30 [b] Job 15:22
33:19 [c] Job 30:17
33:20 [d] Ps 107:18 [e] Job 3:24; 6:6
33:21 [f] Job 16:8; 19:20
33:22 [g] Ps 88:3
33:23 [h] Mic 6:8
33:24 [i] Isa 38:17
33:25 [j] 2Ki 5:14
33:26 [k] Job 34:28 [l] Job 22:26 [m] Ps 50:15; 51:12
33:27 [n] 2Sa 12:13 [o] Lk 15:21 [p] Ro 6:21
33:28 [q] Job 22:28
33:29 [r] 1Co 12:6; Eph 1:11; Php 2:13
33:30 [s] Ps 56:13
33:33 [t] Ps 34:11

listen to me, you men of learning.
[3] For the ear tests words
as the tongue tastes food.[u]
[4] Let us discern for ourselves what is right;
let us learn together what is good.[v]

[5] "Job says, 'I am innocent,[w]
but God denies me justice.[x]
[6] Although I am right,
I am considered a liar;
although I am guiltless,
his arrow inflicts an incurable wound.'[y]
[7] What man is like Job,
who drinks scorn like water?[z]
[8] He keeps company with evildoers;
he associates with wicked men.[a]
[9] For he says, 'It profits a man nothing
when he tries to please God.'[b]

[10] "So listen to me, you men of understanding.
Far be it from God to do evil,[c]
from the Almighty to do wrong.[d]
[11] He repays a man for what he has done;[e]
he brings upon him what his conduct deserves.[f]
[12] It is unthinkable that God would do wrong,
that the Almighty would pervert justice.[g]
[13] Who appointed him over the earth?
Who put him in charge of the whole world?[h]
[14] If it were his intention
and he withdrew his spirit[a] and breath,[i]
[15] all mankind would perish together
and man would return to the dust.[j]

[16] "If you have understanding, hear this;
listen to what I say.
[17] Can he who hates justice govern?[k]
Will you condemn the just and mighty One?[l]
[18] Is he not the One who says to kings, 'You are worthless,'
and to nobles, 'You are wicked,'[m]
[19] who shows no partiality[n] to princes
and does not favor the rich over the poor,[o]
for they are all the work of his hands?[p]
[20] They die in an instant, in the middle of the night;[q]
the people are shaken and they pass away;
the mighty are removed without human hand.[r]

[21] "His eyes are on the ways of men;
he sees their every step.[s]
[22] There is no dark place,[t] no deep shadow,[u]
where evildoers can hide.
[23] God has no need to examine men further,
that they should come before him for judgment.[v]
[24] Without inquiry he shatters the mighty[w]
and sets up others in their place.[x]
[25] Because he takes note of their deeds,
he overthrows them in the night and they are crushed.
[26] He punishes them for their wickedness
where everyone can see them,
[27] because they turned from following him[y]
and had no regard for any of his ways.[z]
[28] They caused the cry of the poor to come before him,
so that he heard the cry of the needy.[a]
[29] But if he remains silent, who can condemn him?
If he hides his face, who can see him?
Yet he is over man and nation alike,
[30] to keep a godless man from ruling,
from laying snares for the people.[b]

[31] "Suppose a man says to God,
'I am guilty but will offend no more.
[32] Teach me what I cannot see;[c]
if I have done wrong, I will not do so again.'[d]
[33] Should God then reward you on your terms,
when you refuse to repent?[e]
You must decide, not I;
so tell me what you know.

[a] 14 Or *Spirit*

34:3 [u] Job 12:11
34:4 [v] 1Th 5:21
34:5 [w] Job 33:9 [x] Job 27:2
34:6 [y] Job 6:4
34:7 [z] Job 15:16
34:8 [a] Job 22:15; Ps 50:18
34:9 [b] Job 21:15; 35:3
34:10 [c] Ge 18:25 [d] Dt 32:4; Job 8:3; Ro 9:14
34:11 [e] Ps 62:12; Mt 16:27; Ro 2:6; 2Co 5:10 [f] Jer 32:19; Eze 33:20
34:12 [g] Job 8:3
34:13 [h] Job 38:4,6
34:14 [i] Ps 104:29
34:15 [j] Ge 3:19; Job 9:22
34:17 [k] 2Sa 23:3-4 [l] Job 40:8
34:18 [m] Ex 22:28
34:19 [n] Dt 10:17; Ac 10:34 [o] Lev 19:15 [p] Job 10:3
34:20 [q] Ex 12:29 [r] Job 12:19
34:21 [s] Job 31:4; Pr 15:3
34:22 [t] Ps 139:12 [u] Am 9:2-3
34:23 [v] Job 11:11
34:24 [w] Job 12:19 [x] Da 2:21
34:27 [y] Ps 28:5; Isa 5:12 [z] 1Sa 15:11
34:28 [a] Ex 22:23; Job 35:9; Jas 5:4
34:30 [b] Pr 29:2-12
34:32 [c] Job 35:11; Ps 25:4 [d] Job 33:27
34:33 [e] Job 41:11

[34]"Men of understanding declare,
wise men who hear me say to me,
[35]'Job speaks without knowledge;[f]
his words lack insight.'
[36]Oh, that Job might be tested to the utmost
for answering like a wicked man![g]
[37]To his sin he adds rebellion;
scornfully he claps his hands[h] among us
and multiplies his words against God."[i]

34:35 [f]Job 35:16; 38:2
34:36 [g]Job 22:15
34:37 [h]Job 27:23 [i]Job 23:2

35

Then Elihu said:

[2]"Do you think this is just?
You say, 'I will be cleared by God.[a]'
[3]Yet you ask him, 'What profit is it to me,[b]
and what do I gain by not sinning?'[j]

[4]"I would like to reply to you
and to your friends with you.
[5]Look up at the heavens[k] and see;
gaze at the clouds so high above you.[l]
[6]If you sin, how does that affect him?
If your sins are many, what does that do to him?[m]
[7]If you are righteous, what do you give to him,[n]
or what does he receive[o] from your hand?[p]
[8]Your wickedness affects only a man like yourself,
and your righteousness only the sons of men.

[9]"Men cry out[q] under a load of oppression;
they plead for relief from the arm of the powerful.[r]
[10]But no one says, 'Where is God my Maker,[s]
who gives songs in the night,[t]
[11]who teaches[u] more to us than to[c] the beasts of the earth
and makes us wiser than[d] the birds of the air?'
[12]He does not answer[v] when men cry out
because of the arrogance of the wicked.
[13]Indeed, God does not listen to their empty plea;
the Almighty pays no attention to it.[w]
[14]How much less, then, will he listen
when you say that you do not see him,[x]
that your case[y] is before him
and you must wait for him,
[15]and further, that his anger never punishes
and he does not take the least notice of wickedness.[e]
[16]So Job opens his mouth with empty talk;
without knowledge he multiplies words."[z]

35:3 [j]Job 9:29-31; 34:9
35:5 [k]Ge 15:5 [l]Job 22:12
35:6 [m]Pr 8:36
35:7 [n]Ro 11:35 [o]Pr 9:12 [p]Job 22:2-3; Lk 17:10
35:9 [q]Ex 2:23 [r]Job 12:19
35:10 [s]Job 27:10; Isa 51:13 [t]Ps 42:8; 149:5; Ac 16:25
35:11 [u]Ps 94:12
35:12 [v]Pr 1:28
35:13 [w]Job 27:9; Pr 15:29; Isa 1:15; Jer 11:11
35:14 [x]Job 9:11 [y]Ps 37:6
35:16 [z]Job 34:35,37

36

Elihu continued:

[2]"Bear with me a little longer and I will show you
that there is more to be said in God's behalf.
[3]I get my knowledge from afar;
I will ascribe justice to my Maker.[a]
[4]Be assured that my words are not false;[b]
one perfect in knowledge[c] is with you.

[5]"God is mighty, but does not despise men;[d]
he is mighty, and firm in his purpose.[e]
[6]He does not keep the wicked alive[f]
but gives the afflicted their rights.[g]
[7]He does not take his eyes off the righteous;[h]
he enthrones them with kings[i]
and exalts them forever.
[8]But if men are bound in chains,[j]
held fast by cords of affliction,
[9]he tells them what they have done—
that they have sinned arrogantly.[k]
[10]He makes them listen[l] to correction
and commands them to repent of their evil.[m]
[11]If they obey and serve him,[n]
they will spend the rest of their days in prosperity
and their years in contentment.
[12]But if they do not listen,
they will perish by the sword[f][o]
and die without knowledge.[p]

36:3 [a]Job 8:3; 37:23
36:4 [b]Job 33:3 [c]Job 37:5,16,23
36:5 [d]Ps 22:24 [e]Job 12:13
36:6 [f]Job 8:22 [g]Job 5:15
36:7 [h]Ps 33:18 [i]Ps 113:8
36:8 [j]Ps 107:10,14
36:9 [k]Job 15:25
36:10 [l]Job 33:16 [m]2Ki 17:13
36:11 [n]Isa 1:19
36:12 [o]Job 15:22 [p]Job 4:21

[a]2 Or *My righteousness is more than God's* [b]3 Or *you* [c]11 Or *teaches us by* [d]11 Or *us wise by* [e]15 Symmachus, Theodotion and Vulgate; the meaning of the Hebrew for this word is uncertain. [f]12 Or *will cross the River*

36:13 [q]Ro 2:5
13 "The godless in heart[q] harbor resentment;
even when he fetters them, they do not cry for help.
36:14 [r]Dt 23:17
14 They die in their youth,
among male prostitutes of the shrines.[r]
15 But those who suffer he delivers in their suffering;
he speaks to them in their affliction.
36:16 [s]Hos 2:14 [t]Ps 23:5
16 "He is wooing[s] you from the jaws of distress
to a spacious place free from restriction,
to the comfort of your table[t] laden with choice food.
17 But now you are laden with the judgment due the wicked;
judgment and justice have taken hold of you.[u]
36:17 [u]Job 22:11
18 Be careful that no one entices you by riches;
36:18 [v]Job 34:33
do not let a large bribe turn you aside.[v]
19 Would your wealth
or even all your mighty efforts
sustain you so you would not be in distress?
36:20 [w]Job 34:20,25
20 Do not long for the night,[w]
to drag people away from their homes.[a]
36:21 [x]Ps 66:18 [y]Heb 11:25
21 Beware of turning to evil,[x]
which you seem to prefer to affliction.[y]
36:22 [z]Isa 40:13; 1Co 2:16
22 "God is exalted in his power.
Who is a teacher like him?[z]
36:23 [a]Job 34:13 [b]Job 8:3
23 Who has prescribed his ways for him,[a]
or said to him, 'You have done wrong'?[b]
36:24 [c]Ps 92:5; 138:5 [d]Ps 59:16; Rev 15:3
24 Remember to extol his work,[c]
which men have praised in song.[d]
25 All mankind has seen it;
men gaze on it from afar.
36:26 [e]1Co 13:12 [f]Job 10:5; Ps 90:2; 102:24; Heb 1:12
26 How great is God—beyond our understanding![e]
The number of his years is past finding out.[f]
36:27 [g]Job 38:28; Ps 147:8
27 "He draws up the drops of water,
which distill as rain to the streams[b];[g]
36:28 [h]Job 5:10
28 the clouds pour down their moisture
and abundant showers fall on mankind.[h]
36:29 [i]Job 26:14; 37:16
29 Who can understand how he spreads out the clouds,
how he thunders from his pavilion?[i]
30 See how he scatters his lightning about him,
bathing the depths of the sea.
36:31 [j]Job 37:13 [k]Ps 136:25; Ac 14:17
31 This is the way he governs[c] the nations[j]
and provides food in abundance.[k]
36:32 [l]Job 37:12,15
32 He fills his hands with lightning
and commands it to strike its mark.[l]
33 His thunder announces the coming storm;
even the cattle make known its approach.[d]

37

"At this my heart pounds
and leaps from its place.
37:2 [m]Ps 29:3-9
2 Listen! Listen to the roar of his voice,
to the rumbling that comes from his mouth.[m]
3 He unleashes his lightning beneath the whole heaven
and sends it to the ends of the earth.
4 After that comes the sound of his roar;
he thunders with his majestic voice.
When his voice resounds,
he holds nothing back.
37:5 [n]Job 5:9
5 God's voice thunders in marvelous ways;
he does great things beyond our understanding.[n]
37:6 [o]Job 38:22 [p]Job 36:27
6 He says to the snow,[o] 'Fall on the earth,'
and to the rain shower, 'Be a mighty downpour.'[p]
37:7 [q]Job 12:14
7 So that all men he has made may know his work,
he stops every man from his labor.[e][q]
37:8 [r]Job 38:40; Ps 104:22
8 The animals take cover;
they remain in their dens.[r]
9 The tempest comes out from its chamber,
the cold from the driving winds.
10 The breath of God produces ice,

[a] *20* The meaning of the Hebrew for verses 18–20 is uncertain. [b] *27* Or *distill from the mist as rain* [c] *31* Or *nourishes* [d] *33* Or *announces his coming— / the One zealous against evil* [e] *7* Or / *he fills all men with fear by his power*

and the broad waters become
frozen.[s]
11 He loads the clouds with moisture;
he scatters his lightning through
them.[t]
12 At his direction they swirl around
over the face of the whole earth
to do whatever he commands
them.[u]
13 He brings the clouds to punish
men,[v]
or to water his earth[a] and show
his love.[w]

14 "Listen to this, Job;
stop and consider God's wonders.
15 Do you know how God controls
the clouds
and makes his lightning flash?
16 Do you know how the clouds hang
poised,
those wonders of him who is
perfect in knowledge?[x]
17 You who swelter in your clothes
when the land lies hushed under
the south wind,
18 can you join him in spreading out
the skies,[y]
hard as a mirror of cast bronze?

19 "Tell us what we should say to him;
we cannot draw up our case
because of our darkness.
20 Should he be told that I want to
speak?
Would any man ask to be
swallowed up?
21 Now no one can look at the sun,
bright as it is in the skies
after the wind has swept them
clean.
22 Out of the north he comes in
golden splendor;
God comes in awesome majesty.
23 The Almighty is beyond our reach
and exalted in power;[z]
in his justice[a] and great
righteousness, he does not
oppress.[b]
24 Therefore, men revere him,[c]
for does he not have regard for
all the wise[d] in heart?[b]"

37:10 [s] Job 38:29-30; Ps 147:17
37:11 [t] Job 36:27,29
37:12 [u] Ps 148:8
37:13 [v] 1Sa 12:17 [w] Ex 9:18; 1Ki 18:45; Job 38:27
37:16 [x] Job 36:4
37:18 [y] Job 9:8; Ps 104:2; Isa 44:24
37:23 [z] Job 9:4; 36:4; 1Ti 6:16 [a] Job 8:3 [b] Isa 63:9; Eze 18:23,32
37:24 [c] Mt 10:28 [d] Mt 11:25

The LORD Speaks

38 Then the LORD answered Job
out of the storm.[e] He said:

2 "Who is this that darkens my
counsel
with words without knowledge?[f]
3 Brace yourself like a man;
I will question you,
and you shall answer me.[g]

4 "Where were you when I laid the
earth's foundation?[h]
Tell me, if you understand.
5 Who marked off its dimensions?[i]
Surely you know!
Who stretched a measuring line
across it?
6 On what were its footings set,
or who laid its cornerstone[j]—
7 while the morning stars sang
together
and all the angels[c] shouted for
joy?

8 "Who shut up the sea behind
doors[k]
when it burst forth from the
womb,[l]
9 when I made the clouds its garment
and wrapped it in thick
darkness,
10 when I fixed limits for it[m]
and set its doors and bars in
place,[n]
11 when I said, 'This far you may
come and no farther;
here is where your proud waves
halt'?[o]

12 "Have you ever given orders to the
morning,
or shown the dawn its place,
13 that it might take the earth by the
edges
and shake the wicked[p] out of it?
14 The earth takes shape like clay
under a seal;
its features stand out like those
of a garment.
15 The wicked are denied their light,[q]
and their upraised arm is
broken.[r]

16 "Have you journeyed to the springs
of the sea
or walked in the recesses of the
deep?[s]
17 Have the gates of death[t] been
shown to you?
Have you seen the gates of the
shadow of death[d]?

38:1 [e] Job 40:6
38:2 [f] Job 35:16; 42:3; 1Ti 1:7
38:3 [g] Job 40:7
38:4 [h] Ps 104:5; Pr 8:29
38:5 [i] Pr 8:29; Isa 40:12
38:6 [j] Job 26:7
38:8 [k] Jer 5:22 [l] Ge 1:9-10
38:10 [m] Ps 33:7; 104:9 [n] Job 26:10
38:11 [o] Ps 89:9
38:13 [p] Ps 104:35
38:15 [q] Job 18:5 [r] Ps 10:15
38:16 [s] Ps 77:19
38:17 [t] Ps 9:13

[a] 13 Or *to favor them* [b] 24 Or *for he does not have regard for any who think they are wise.*
[c] 7 Hebrew *the sons of God* [d] 17 Or *gates of deep shadows*

38:18 [u] Job 28:24

[18] Have you comprehended the vast
expanses of the earth?[u]
Tell me, if you know all this.

[19] "What is the way to the abode of
light?
And where does darkness
reside?

38:20 [v] Job 26:10

[20] Can you take them to their places?
Do you know the paths[v] to their
dwellings?

38:21 [w] Job 15:7

[21] Surely you know, for you were
already born![w]
You have lived so many years!

38:22 [x] Job 37:6

[22] "Have you entered the storehouses
of the snow[x]
or seen the storehouses of the
hail,

38:23 [y] Isa 30:30; Eze 13:11 [z] Ex 9:18; Jos 10:11; Rev 16:21

[23] which I reserve for times of
trouble,[y]
for days of war and battle?[z]
[24] What is the way to the place where
the lightning is dispersed,
or the place where the east
winds are scattered over
the earth?
[25] Who cuts a channel for the
torrents of rain,
and a path for the
thunderstorm,[a]

38:25 [a] Job 28:26

38:26 [b] Job 36:27

[26] to water[b] a land where no man
lives,
a desert with no one in it,

38:27 [c] Ps 104:14; 107:35

[27] to satisfy a desolate wasteland
and make it sprout with grass?[c]

38:28 [d] Ps 147:8; Jer 14:22

[28] Does the rain have a father?[d]
Who fathers the drops of dew?

38:29 [e] Ps 147:16-17

[29] From whose womb comes the ice?
Who gives birth to the frost
from the heavens[e]
[30] when the waters become hard as
stone,
when the surface of the deep is
frozen?[f]

38:30 [f] Job 37:10

[31] "Can you bind the beautiful[a]
Pleiades?
Can you loose the cords of
Orion?[g]

38:31 [g] Job 9:9; Am 5:8

[32] Can you bring forth the
constellations in their
seasons[b]
or lead out the Bear[c] with its
cubs?

38:33 [h] Ps 148:6; Jer 31:36

[33] Do you know the laws[h] of the
heavens?
Can you set up ⌞God's[d]⌟
dominion over the earth?

[34] "Can you raise your voice to the
clouds
and cover yourself with a flood
of water?[i]

38:34 [i] Job 22:11; 36:27-28

38:35 [j] Job 36:32; 37:3

[35] Do you send the lightning bolts on
their way?[j]
Do they report to you, 'Here we
are'?

38:36 [k] Job 9:4 [l] Job 32:8; Ps 51:6; Ecc 2:26

[36] Who endowed the heart[e] with
wisdom[k]
or gave understanding[l] to the
mind[f]?
[37] Who has the wisdom to count the
clouds?
Who can tip over the water jars
of the heavens
[38] when the dust becomes hard
and the clods of earth stick
together?

[39] "Do you hunt the prey for the
lioness
and satisfy the hunger of the
lions[m]

38:39 [m] Ps 104:21

38:40 [n] Job 37:8

[40] when they crouch in their dens[n]
or lie in wait in a thicket?

38:41 [o] Lk 12:24 [p] Ps 147:9; Mt 6:26

[41] Who provides food for the raven[o]
when its young cry out to God
and wander about for lack of
food?[p]

39:1 [q] Dt 14:5

39

"Do you know when the
mountain goats[q] give birth?
Do you watch when the doe
bears her fawn?
[2] Do you count the months till they
bear?
Do you know the time they give
birth?
[3] They crouch down and bring forth
their young;
their labor pains are ended.
[4] Their young thrive and grow
strong in the wilds;
they leave and do not return.

39:5 [r] Job 6:5; 11:12; 24:5

[5] "Who let the wild donkey[r] go free?
Who untied his ropes?

39:6 [s] Job 24:5; Ps 107:34; Jer 2:24 [t] Hos 8:9

[6] I gave him the wasteland[s] as his
home,
the salt flats as his habitat.[t]

39:7 [u] Job 3:18

[7] He laughs at the commotion in the
town;
he does not hear a driver's shout.[u]

[a] *31* Or *the twinkling*; or *the chains of the* [b] *32* Or *the morning star in its season* [c] *32* Or *out Leo* [d] *33* Or *his*; or *their* [e] *36* The meaning of the Hebrew for this word is uncertain. [f] *36* The meaning of the Hebrew for this word is uncertain.

[8]He ranges the hills for his pasture
and searches for any green thing.

39:9 [v]Nu 23:22; Dt 33:17

[9]"Will the wild ox[v] consent to serve
you?
Will he stay by your manger at
night?
[10]Can you hold him to the furrow
with a harness?
Will he till the valleys behind
you?
[11]Will you rely on him for his great
strength?
Will you leave your heavy work
to him?
[12]Can you trust him to bring in your
grain
and gather it to your threshing
floor?

[13]"The wings of the ostrich flap
joyfully,
but they cannot compare with
the pinions and feathers of
the stork.
[14]She lays her eggs on the ground
and lets them warm in the sand,
[15]unmindful that a foot may crush
them,
that some wild animal may
trample them.

39:16 [w]La 4:3

[16]She treats her young harshly,[w] as if
they were not hers;
she cares not that her labor was
in vain,

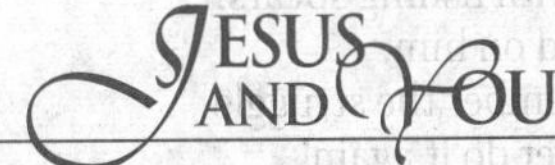

WHEN GOD SPEAKS

Job experienced more tragedy in just a few days than most people do in a lifetime. But when he needed God most, his Creator spoke "out of the storm" (Job 38:1). The same is true for us: God often reveals himself best when we are at our worst. He may allow us to suffer for a season (1 Peter 1:6; 5:10), but we have his promise that he will never put more *on* us than he has already put *in* us to help us to endure (1 Corinthians 10:13). The greatest resource he provides for us is himself (Philippians 2:13). Our Lord Jesus suffered unfairly for our sins—in order that we might have a relationship with his Father (2 Corinthians 5:17–21). This is a free gift offered to us by God with no strings attached (Romans 5:6,8). Jesus is "the righteous [who died] for the unrighteous, to bring you to God" (1 Peter 3:18).

[17]for God did not endow her with
wisdom
or give her a share of good sense.[x]

39:17 [x]Job 35:11

[18]Yet when she spreads her feathers
to run,
she laughs at horse and rider.

[19]"Do you give the horse his strength
or clothe his neck with a flowing
mane?
[20]Do you make him leap like a locust,[y]
striking terror with his proud
snorting?[z]

39:20 [y]Joel 2:4-5 [z]Jer 8:16

[21]He paws fiercely, rejoicing in his
strength,
and charges into the fray.[a]

39:21 [a]Jer 8:6

[22]He laughs at fear, afraid of nothing;
he does not shy away from the
sword.
[23]The quiver rattles against his side,
along with the flashing spear
and lance.
[24]In frenzied excitement he eats up
the ground;
he cannot stand still when the
trumpet sounds.[b]

39:24 [b]Jer 4:5,19; Eze 7:14; Am 3:6

[25]At the blast of the trumpet[c] he
snorts, 'Aha!'
He catches the scent of battle
from afar,
the shout of commanders and
the battle cry.[d]

39:25 [c]Jos 6:5 [d]Am 1:14; 2:2

[26]"Does the hawk take flight by your
wisdom
and spread his wings toward the
south?
[27]Does the eagle soar at your
command
and build his nest on high?[e]

39:27 [e]Jer 49:16; Ob 1:4

[28]He dwells on a cliff and stays there
at night;
a rocky crag is his stronghold.
[29]From there he seeks out his food;[f]
his eyes detect it from afar.

39:29 [f]Job 9:26

[30]His young ones feast on blood,
and where the slain are, there is
he."[g]

39:30 [g]Mt 24:28; Lk 17:37

40

The LORD said to Job:[h]

40:1 [h]Job 10:2; 13:3; 23:4; 31:35; 33:13

[2]"Will the one who contends with
the Almighty correct him?
Let him who accuses God
answer him!"

[3]Then Job answered the LORD:

[4]"I am unworthy[i]—how can I reply
to you?

40:4 [i]Job 42:6

I put my hand over my mouth.[j]
5 I spoke once, but I have no answer[k]—
twice, but I will say no more."[l]

6 Then the LORD spoke to Job out of
the storm:[m]

7 "Brace yourself like a man;
I will question you,
and you shall answer me.[n]
8 "Would you discredit my justice?[o]
Would you condemn me to justify yourself?
9 Do you have an arm like God's,[p]
and can your voice thunder like his?[q]
10 Then adorn yourself with glory and splendor,
and clothe yourself in honor and majesty.[r]
11 Unleash the fury of your wrath,[s]
look at every proud man and bring him low,[t]
12 look at every proud man and humble him,[u]
crush[v] the wicked where they stand.
13 Bury them all in the dust together;
shroud their faces in the grave.
14 Then I myself will admit to you
that your own right hand can save you.[w]

15 "Look at the behemoth,[a]
which I made along with you
and which feeds on grass like an ox.
16 What strength he has in his loins,
what power in the muscles of his belly!
17 His tail[b] sways like a cedar;
the sinews of his thighs are close-knit.
18 His bones are tubes of bronze,
his limbs like rods of iron.
19 He ranks first among the works of God,[x]
yet his Maker can approach him with his sword.
20 The hills bring him their produce,[y]
and all the wild animals play[z] nearby.
21 Under the lotus plants he lies,
hidden among the reeds in the marsh.
22 The lotuses conceal him in their shadow;
the poplars by the stream[a] surround him.
23 When the river rages, he is not alarmed;
he is secure, though the Jordan should surge against his mouth.
24 Can anyone capture him by the eyes,[c]
or trap him and pierce his nose?[b]

41 "Can you pull in the leviathan[d][c] with a fishhook
or tie down his tongue with a rope?
2 Can you put a cord through his nose
or pierce his jaw with a hook?[d]
3 Will he keep begging you for mercy?
Will he speak to you with gentle words?
4 Will he make an agreement with you
for you to take him as your slave for life?[e]
5 Can you make a pet of him like a bird
or put him on a leash for your girls?
6 Will traders barter for him?
Will they divide him up among the merchants?
7 Can you fill his hide with harpoons
or his head with fishing spears?
8 If you lay a hand on him,
you will remember the struggle and never do it again!
9 Any hope of subduing him is false;
the mere sight of him is overpowering.
10 No one is fierce enough to rouse him.[f]
Who then is able to stand against me?[g]
11 Who has a claim against me that I must pay?[h]
Everything under heaven belongs to me.[i]

12 "I will not fail to speak of his limbs,
his strength and his graceful form.
13 Who can strip off his outer coat?

[a] 15 Possibly the hippopotamus or the elephant
[b] 17 Possibly trunk [c] 24 Or *by a water hole*
[d] 1 Possibly the crocodile

40:4 j Job 29:9
40:5 k Job 9:3 l Job 9:15
40:6 m Job 38:1
40:7 n Job 38:3; 42:4
40:8 o Job 27:2; Ro 3:3
40:9 p 2Ch 32:8 q Job 37:5; Ps 29:3-4
40:10 r Ps 93:1; 104:1
40:11 s Isa 42:25; Na 1:6 t Isa 2:11, 12,17; Da 4:37
40:12 u 1Sa 2:7 v Isa 13:11; 63:2-3,6
40:14 w Ps 20:6; 60:5; 108:6
40:19 x Job 41:33
40:20 y Ps 104:14 z Ps 104:26
40:22 a Isa 44:4
40:24 b Job 41:2,7,26
41:1 c Job 3:8; Ps 104:26; Isa 27:1
41:2 d Isa 37:29
41:4 e Ex 21:6
41:10 f Job 3:8 g Jer 50:44
41:11 h Ro 11:35 i Ex 19:5; Dt 10:14; Ps 24:1; 50:12; 1Co 10:26

Who would approach him with
a bridle?
14 Who dares open the doors of his
mouth,
ringed about with his fearsome
teeth?
15 His back has[a] rows of shields
tightly sealed together;
16 each is so close to the next
that no air can pass between.
17 They are joined fast to one
another;
they cling together and cannot
be parted.
18 His snorting throws out flashes of
light;
his eyes are like the rays of
dawn.[j]
19 Firebrands stream from his mouth;
sparks of fire shoot out.
20 Smoke pours from his nostrils
as from a boiling pot over a fire
of reeds.
21 His breath[k] sets coals ablaze,
and flames dart from his
mouth.[l]
22 Strength resides in his neck;
dismay goes before him.
23 The folds of his flesh are tightly
joined;
they are firm and immovable.
24 His chest is hard as rock,
hard as a lower millstone.
25 When he rises up, the mighty are
terrified;
they retreat before his thrashing.
26 The sword that reaches him has no
effect,
nor does the spear or the dart or
the javelin.
27 Iron he treats like straw
and bronze like rotten wood.
28 Arrows do not make him flee;
slingstones are like chaff to him.
29 A club seems to him but a piece of
straw;
he laughs at the rattling of the
lance.
30 His undersides are jagged
potsherds,
leaving a trail in the mud like a
threshing sledge.[m]
31 He makes the depths churn like a
boiling caldron
and stirs up the sea like a pot of
ointment.

41:18 [j] Job 3:9
41:21 [k] Isa 40:7 [l] Ps 18:8
41:30 [m] Isa 41:15

IN THE HEART OF LONDON CITY, MID THE DWELLINGS OF THE POOR, THESE BRIGHT, GOLDEN WORDS WERE UTTERED, "I HAVE CHRIST! WHAT WANT I MORE?"

Anonymous

32 Behind him he leaves a glistening
wake;
one would think the deep had
white hair.
33 Nothing on earth is his equal[n]—
a creature without fear.
34 He looks down on all that are
haughty;
he is king over all that are
proud."[o]

Job

42 Then Job replied to the LORD:

2 "I know that you can do all things;[p]
no plan of yours can be
thwarted.[q]
3 ⌞You asked,⌟ 'Who is this that
obscures my counsel
without knowledge?'[r]
Surely I spoke of things I did not
understand,
things too wonderful for me to
know.[s]

4 ⌞"You said,⌟ 'Listen now, and I will
speak;
I will question you,
and you shall answer me.'[t]
5 My ears had heard of you[u]
but now my eyes have seen you.[v]
6 Therefore I despise myself[w]
and repent in dust and ashes."[x]

Epilogue

7 After the LORD had said these things
to Job, he said to Eliphaz the Temanite, "I
am angry with you and your two
friends,[y] because you have not spoken of
me what is right, as my servant Job has.
8 So now take seven bulls and seven
rams[z] and go to my servant Job and sacrifice a burnt offering[a] for yourselves. My
servant Job will pray for you, and I will
accept his prayer[b] and not deal with you
according to your folly.[c] You have not

41:33 [n] Job 40:19
41:34 [o] Job 28:8
42:2 [p] Ge 18:14; Mt 19:26 [q] 2Ch 20:6
42:3 [r] Job 38:2 [s] Ps 40:5; 131:1; 139:6
42:4 [t] Job 38:3; 40:7
42:5 [u] Job 26:14; Ro 10:17 [v] Jdg 13:22; Isa 6:5; Eph 1:17-18
42:6 [w] Job 40:4 [x] Ezr 9:6
42:7 [y] Job 32:3
42:8 [z] Nu 23:1,29 [a] Job 1:5 [b] Ge 20:17; Jas 5:15-16; 1Jn 5:16 [c] Job 22:30

[a] 15 Or *His pride is his*

DISCOVERY 123

Nursing a Grudge

Job's friends assumed that they were doing him a favor and apparently believed that they were correctly reflecting God's perspective. But God was unhappy with their positions (Job 42:7). Eliphaz, Bildad and Zophar could not accept the premise that an innocent man could suffer to such an extent as Job. The best "support" they seemed able to offer was an attempt to help Job to determine what he had done to deserve such punishment. The three wanted appropriately to defend God's character, but in so doing they placed the full blame on Job.

Even when we set out to help our friends we may in fact hurt them if our advice fails to correctly interpret the facts. We need to be cautious about what we say to a hurting brother or sister. And when others offer us advice, we need to weigh their conclusions against what God tells us in his Word. Because of the misguided counsel of these three purported friends, a major rift occurred in Job's relationship with them.

Each of us suffers daily hurts of many kinds: People betray us, "the system" makes us feel insignificant and circumstances frequently appear unbalanced or unfair. When we find ourselves feeling isolated or defeated, we need to talk to God about it. Even when he was dying on the cross, Jesus refused to nurse a grudge, instead asking the Father to forgive his accusers (Luke 23:34). God works through his Holy Spirit to produce his own character in us (Galatians 5:22–23). He shows kindness that is infinitely beyond what his enemies deserve or expect, and he wants us to follow his lead (Luke 6:36), reflecting the traits of kindness, compassion and forgiveness in our dealings with others (Ephesians 4:32).

Many times it feels as though our forgiveness equates to "giving in" to the system or to some person who has hurt us. But the reality is that when we choose to offer our forgiveness, whether or not it is deserved, God blesses us beyond what we have experienced before—we enjoy a greater peace, a steadier pattern of growth, a growing love for God and others, and a stronger determination to trust in him.

Jesus always did exactly what his Father asked of him, to the point of enduring excruciating physical, spiritual and emotional pain. But when the testing was over the Father blessed him with a "name that is above every name" (Philippians 2:7–11)—a reward that would not have been possible had Jesus opted to hold a grudge or do things his own way. No matter what situations we may face, God wants us to hang on through the trial. And he is there waiting, holding out his eternal promise of one day making all things right (James 1:12)—and of pouring out on us blessings beyond what we can possibly imagine (1 Corinthians 2:9; Ephesians 3:20).

Self-Discovery: *Can you recall praying for someone who had wronged you? Have you ever asked Jesus for the grace to enable you to forgive?*

GO TO DISCOVERY 124 ON PAGE 678

spoken of me what is right, as my servant
Job has." 9So Eliphaz the Temanite, Bildad the Shuhite and Zophar the Naamathite did what the LORD told them; and
the LORD accepted Job's prayer.
42:10 10After Job had prayed for his friends,
[d] Dt 30:3; the LORD made him prosperous again[d]
Ps 14:7 [e] Job 1:3; and gave him twice as much as he had
Ps 85:1-3; 126:5-6 before.[e] 11All his brothers and sisters
42:11 and everyone who had known him be-
[f] Job 19:13 fore[f] came and ate with him in his
house. They comforted and consoled
him over all the trouble the LORD had
brought upon him, and each one gave
him a piece of silver[a] and a gold ring.
12The LORD blessed the latter part of
Job's life more than the first. He had
fourteen thousand sheep, six thousand
camels, a thousand yoke of oxen and a
thousand donkeys. 13And he also had
seven sons and three daughters. 14The
first daughter he named Jemimah, the
second Keziah and the third Keren-
Happuch. 15Nowhere in all the land were
there found women as beautiful as Job's
daughters, and their father granted
them an inheritance along with their
brothers.
16After this, Job lived a hundred and
forty years; he saw his children and their
children to the fourth generation. 17And 42:17 [g] Ge 15:15; 25:8
so he died, old and full of years.[g]

[a] *11* Hebrew *him a kesitah*; a kesitah was a unit of money of unknown weight and value.

PSALMS

Does God help us out of all our troubles? (Psalm 34:17)

- *Not exactly—as life's sorrows and heartaches easily demonstrate. But the Lord does not promise so much to remove our difficulties as to see us through them. God can use even trouble to accomplish his purposes; Jesus was made perfect through suffering (Hebrews 2:10). The bottom line is that God changes something—if not our troubles, then he changes us.*

What did redemption mean in the Old Testament? (Psalm 130:7–8)

- *God redeemed his people from Egyptian slavery and later from Babylonian captivity. In both cases redemption was applied to the entire nation, not to individuals. But there were hints of individual responsibility for sin (Ezekiel 18:14–20, for example). The understanding of redemption continued to develop through Old Testament history, culminating in Jesus.*

Jesus in Psalms Many of the psalms express the fervent hope of God's people for the coming Messiah. At least 36 of the 150 psalms point ahead to Jesus Christ. These are often called "Messianic Psalms," because they predict something about the coming Savior. Songs that begin as poems about David find their ultimate fulfillment in the King of kings, the One whom God had promised to send. Jesus himself stated that "everything must be fulfilled that is written about me in the Law of Moses, the Prophets and the Psalms" (Luke 24:44). The Messianic psalms describe Jesus in a variety of ways and point to many of the sufferings our Lord would experience: He was God the Son (Psalm 2), the One chosen by God (Psalm 45), a teacher of parables (Psalm 78) and a priest forever (Psalm 110). He was betrayed by a friend (Psalm 41), lied about (Psalm 35), mocked and eventually crucified (Psalm 22). But the story doesn't stop there. This long-awaited Savior came back to life (Psalm 16) and returned to heaven to reign with the Father (Psalm 68). He will come again to rule over the new heaven and the new earth forever (Psalm 72).

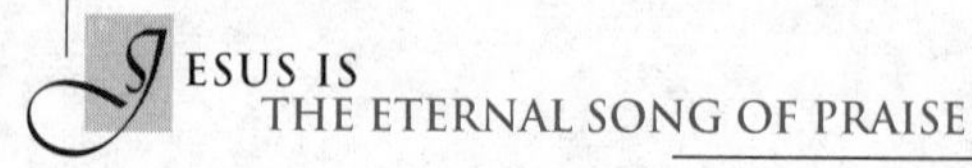

JESUS IS
THE ETERNAL SONG OF PRAISE

BOOK I

Psalms 1–41

PSALM 1

1:1 [a]Pr 4:14 [b]Ps 26:4; Jer 15:17

[1]Blessed is the man
who does not walk[a] in the
counsel of the wicked
or stand in the way of sinners
or sit[b] in the seat of mockers.

1:2 [c]Ps 119:16,35 [d]Ps 119:1 [e]Jos 1:8

[2]But his delight[c] is in the law of the
LORD,[d]
and on his law he meditates[e] day
and night.

1:3 [f]Ps 128:3 [g]Jer 17:8 [h]Eze 47:12 [i]Ge 39:3

[3]He is like a tree[f] planted by
streams of water,[g]
which yields its fruit[h] in
season
and whose leaf does not wither.
Whatever he does prospers.[i]

1:4 [j]Job 21:18; Isa 17:13

[4]Not so the wicked!
They are like chaff[j]
that the wind blows away.

1:5 [k]Ps 5:5 [l]Ps 9:7-8,16

[5]Therefore the wicked will not
stand[k] in the judgment,[l]
nor sinners in the assembly of
the righteous.

1:6 [m]Ps 37:18; 2Ti 2:19 [n]Ps 9:6

[6]For the LORD watches over[m] the
way of the righteous,
but the way of the wicked will
perish.[n]

PSALM 2

[1]Why do the nations conspire[a]
and the peoples plot[o] in vain?
[2]The kings[p] of the earth take their
stand
and the rulers gather together
against the LORD
and against his Anointed[q] One.[b][r]
[3]"Let us break their chains," they say,
"and throw off their fetters."[s]

2:1 [o]Ps 21:11
2:2 [p]Ps 48:4 [q]Jn 1:41 [r]Ps 74:18,23; Ac 4:25-26*
2:3 [s]Jer 5:5

[4]The One enthroned in heaven
laughs;[t]
the Lord scoffs at them.
[5]Then he rebukes them in his anger
and terrifies them in his wrath,[u]
saying,
[6]"I have installed my King[c]
on Zion, my holy hill."

2:4 [t]Ps 37:13; 59:8; Pr 1:26
2:5 [u]Ps 21:9; 78:49-50

[7]I will proclaim the decree of the
LORD:
He said to me, "You are my Son[d];
today I have become your
Father.[e][v]
[8]Ask of me,
and I will make the nations your
inheritance,
the ends of the earth[w] your
possession.

2:7 [v]Ac 13:33*; Heb 1:5*
2:8 [w]Ps 22:27

[a] *1* Hebrew; Septuagint *rage* [b] *2* Or *anointed one* [c] *6* Or *king* [d] *7* Or *son;* also in verse 12 [e] *7* Or *have begotten you*

JESUS FOCUS

COMPLETE HAPPINESS

When we hear the word *beatitude*, we tend to think of Jesus' Sermon on the Mount in the New Testament (Matthew 5:3–12). The book of Psalms also begins with a *beatitude*, a word meaning "blessed." Psalm 1 is a preface to the entire collection of songs. It defines true happiness and stipulates the way to attain it, and it does so by talking about the ways of a person who trusts in God and walks with him. The emphasis is on the spiritual nature of those people who are truly blessed by God. The word *blessed* can be read in Psalm 1 as "how very happy!" and the same holds true for Jesus' beatitudes. Jesus, like the psalmist, emphasized that only those who seek God and display a certain disposition before him are truly joyful and distinctively blessed.

SONGS OF THE MESSIAH

The psalms are filled with prophecies about the Messiah God had promised to send to his people. These "Messianic psalms" often describe the experiences of Israel's kings, but at the same time they point beyond the present to the eventual and final King of kings, God's Anointed One. Psalm 2 specifies that the Messiah is the Son of God who will ultimately rule the nations on behalf of God the Father. The phrase "kiss the Son" in verse 12 invites us to make peace with God through his Promised One, Jesus. Psalm 2 is quoted frequently in the New Testament as referring to Jesus (see, for example, Acts 13:33; Hebrews 1:5; Revelation 19:15). Almost one-third (112 of 360) of the quotations in the New Testament from the Hebrew Bible are taken from the psalms—and all of them point us ultimately to the Savior.

Jesus: The Anointed One

Originally composed for the coronation of a new king, Psalm 2 warns surrounding nations that the Lord himself has selected and anointed Israel's king. The song invites Israel's neighbors to turn to God and submit themselves to the rule of his chosen king (referred to as "the Son"). But this psalm also points to a future King—God's promised Savior.

The word used for "anointed one" is the Hebrew *Messiah*. Psalm 2 predicts that God's anointed one will come to his people. In the New Testament Peter and John were arrested and forced to testify before the Sanhedrin, the highest religious counsel. The Sanhedrin instructed these disciples to stop teaching about Jesus, but they refused, citing Psalm 2 as their basis: "Why do the nations rage and the peoples plot in vain . . . against the Lord and against his Anointed One?" (Acts 4:25–26). Peter and John realized that those who were opposing them were ultimately resisting God and his promised Messiah, Jesus "the Christ."

This psalm also reveals something about the relationship between God and his promised One: It is the relationship between a father and a son (Psalm 2:7). And this relationship places Jesus far above every created being—including the angels. The writer to the Hebrews quoted verse 7 when he asked the question, "To which of the angels did God ever say, 'You are my Son; today I have become your Father'?"(Hebrews 1:5). Paul referred to this paternal tie when he was teaching about Jesus in the synagogue in Pisidian Antioch: "We tell you the good news: What God promised our fathers he has fulfilled for us, their children, by raising up Jesus. As it is written in the second Psalm: 'You are my Son; today I have become your Father'" (Acts 13:32–33).

How are we to know that Jesus is God's anointed One, the One before whom we are to bow? Paul pointed out in Romans 1:3 that the proof is found in the resurrection of Jesus Christ: "Through the Spirit of holiness [Jesus] was declared with power to be the Son of God by his resurrection from the dead." Paul's confirmation of this truth in Acts 13 also centers around Jesus' resurrection from the dead. Unlike other human beings, including David, God did not allow the body of Jesus, his Holy One, to decay in the grave (Acts 13:35). Through Jesus' death and resurrection, declared Paul, everyone who believes is justified (Acts 13:39). Paul's admonitions in Acts 13:40–41 sound very much like those of David in Psalm 2: "Take care that what the prophets have said does not happen to you: 'Look, you scoffers, wonder and perish, for I am going to do something in your days that you would never believe, even if someone told you.' "

Finally, this psalm offers hope for the future. One day the Messiah will rule a worldwide kingdom: "Ask of me, and I will make the nations your inheritance" (Psalm 2:8). God was promising his people that his Messiah would represent him in a way no other could, by representing his very nature and character, and that because of this we should desire to be devoted to him completely: "Serve the Lord with fear and rejoice with trembling" (verse 11).

***Self-Discovery:** When you envision Jesus as your King, what associations or descriptive words come to mind? How will you respond to his presence?*

GO TO DISCOVERY 125 ON PAGE 682

THE MESSIAH IS THE HOPE OF THE WORLD AND THE PSALMS ARE THE MEDIUM OF HIS DIVINE REVELATION AND MISSION.

W. Graham Scroggie, *British Theologian*

2:9 [x]Rev 12:5 [y]Ps 89:23 [z]Rev 2:27*

9 You will rule them with an iron
scepter[a];[x]
you will dash them to pieces[y]
like pottery.[z]"

10 Therefore, you kings, be wise;
be warned, you rulers of the earth.

2:11 [a]Heb 12:28 [b]Ps 119:119-120

11 Serve the LORD with fear
and rejoice[a] with trembling.[b]

2:12 [c]Jn 5:23 [d]Rev 6:16 [e]Ps 34:8; Ro 9:33

12 Kiss the Son,[c] lest he be angry
and you be destroyed in your way,
for his wrath[d] can flare up in a
moment.
Blessed are all who take refuge[e]
in him.

PSALM 3

A psalm of David. When he fled from his son Absalom.[f]

3:1 [f]2Sa 15:14

1 O LORD, how many are my foes!
How many rise up against me!

3:2 [g]Ps 71:11

2 Many are saying of me,
"God will not deliver him.[g]"
Selah[b]

3:3 [h]Ge 15:1; Ps 28:7 [i]Ps 27:6

3 But you are a shield[h] around me,
O LORD;
you bestow glory on me and lift[c]
up my head.[i]

3:4 [j]Ps 2:6

4 To the LORD I cry aloud,
and he answers me from his holy
hill.[j] *Selah*

3:5 [k]Lev 26:6; Pr 3:24

5 I lie down and sleep;[k]
I wake again, because the LORD
sustains me.

3:6 [l]Ps 27:3

6 I will not fear[l] the tens of thousands
drawn up against me on every
side.

3:7 [m]Ps 7:6 [n]Ps 6:4 [o]Job 16:10 [p]Ps 58:6

7 Arise,[m] O LORD!
Deliver me,[n] O my God!
Strike[o] all my enemies on the jaw;
break the teeth[p] of the wicked.

3:8 [q]Isa 43:3,11

8 From the LORD comes deliverance.[q]
May your blessing be on your
people. *Selah*

PSALM 4

For the director of music. With stringed instruments. A psalm of David.

4:1 [r]Ps 25:16 [s]Ps 17:6

1 Answer me when I call to you,
O my righteous God.
Give me relief from my distress;
be merciful[r] to me and hear my
prayer.[s]

4:2 [t]Ps 31:6

2 How long, O men, will you turn my
glory into shame[d]?
How long will you love delusions
and seek false gods[e]?[t] *Selah*

4:3 [u]Ps 31:23 [v]Ps 6:8

3 Know that the LORD has set apart
the godly[u] for himself;
the LORD will hear[v] when I call to
him.

4:4 [w]Eph 4:26* [x]Ps 77:6

4 In your anger do not sin;[w]
when you are on your beds,[x]
search your hearts and be silent.
Selah

4:5 [y]Dt 33:19; Ps 37:3

5 Offer right sacrifices
and trust in the LORD.[y]

[a] 9 Or *will break them with a rod of iron* [b] 2 A word of uncertain meaning, occurring frequently in the Psalms; possibly a musical term [c] 3 Or *LORD, / my Glorious One, who lifts* [d] 2 Or *you dishonor my Glorious One* [e] 2 Or *seek lies*

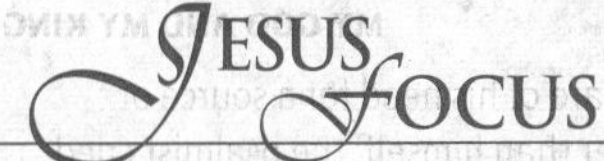

SONGS OF WAR

Many people are puzzled or distressed by psalms that express a desire for other people to be harmed. Words of praise for God are often woven together with pleas for God's wrath to fall on others (Psalm 3). These appeals seem to fly in the face of God's command to love our enemies. How could these so-called "war psalms" (or "cursing psalms") belong to the Prince of Peace? The answer is that they represent the desire of the writer for God to exercise justice in this fallen world—to judge those who have turned away from God and to defend those who are walking with him. Such psalms reflect God's own desire for justice. They are, in fact, not the emotional petitions of angry men but the war cries of the Prince of Peace himself. Jesus himself quoted a couple of these psalms in the New Testament (Psalm 35:19; 69:4; John 15:25). Jesus, God's promised Messiah and King, will come with justice to judge and make war when he returns to set things right at the end of time (Revelation 19:11–15).

6 Many are asking, "Who can show
us any good?"
4:6 [z] Nu 6:25 Let the light of your face shine
upon us,[z] O LORD.
4:7 [a] Ac 14:17 [b] Isa 9:3 7 You have filled my heart[a] with
greater joy[b]
than when their grain and new
wine abound.
4:8 [c] Ps 3:5 [d] Lev 25:18 8 I will lie down and sleep[c] in peace,
for you alone, O LORD,
make me dwell in safety.[d]

PSALM 5

For the director of music. For flutes.
A psalm of David.

1 Give ear to my words, O LORD,
consider my sighing.
5:2 [e] Ps 3:4 [f] Ps 84:3 2 Listen to my cry for help,[e]
my King and my God,[f]
for to you I pray.
5:3 [g] Ps 88:13 3 In the morning,[g] O LORD, you hear
my voice;
in the morning I lay my requests
before you
and wait in expectation.
4 You are not a God who takes
pleasure in evil;
with you the wicked[h] cannot 5:4 [h] Ps 11:5; 92:15
dwell.
5 The arrogant[i] cannot stand[j] in 5:5 [i] Ps 73:3 [j] Ps 1:5 [k] Ps 11:5
your presence;
you hate[k] all who do wrong.
6 You destroy those who tell lies;[l] 5:6 [l] Ps 55:23; Rev 21:8
bloodthirsty and deceitful men
the LORD abhors.

7 But I, by your great mercy,
will come into your house;
in reverence will I bow down[m] 5:7 [m] Ps 138:2
toward your holy temple.
8 Lead me, O LORD, in your 5:8 [n] Ps 31:1 [o] Ps 27:11
righteousness[n]
because of my enemies—
make straight your way[o] before
me.

9 Not a word from their mouth can
be trusted;
their heart is filled with
destruction.
Their throat is an open grave;[p] 5:9 [p] Lk 11:44 [q] Ro 3:13*
with their tongue they speak
deceit.[q]
10 Declare them guilty, O God!
Let their intrigues be their
downfall.
Banish them for their many sins,[r] 5:10 [r] Ps 9:16 [s] Ps 107:11
for they have rebelled[s] against
you.

11 But let all who take refuge in you
be glad;
let them ever sing for joy.[t] 5:11 [t] Ps 2:12 [u] Ps 69:36 [v] Isa 65:13
Spread your protection over them,
that those who love your name[u]
may rejoice in you.[v]
12 For surely, O LORD, you bless the
righteous;
you surround them[w] with your 5:12 [w] Ps 32:7
favor as with a shield.

MY GOD AND MY KING

Continually aware of his need for a source of strength greater than himself, the psalmist cried out to the One he addressed as "my King and my God," begging God to mete out true justice in the world (Psalm 5:2). And even though it appeared that evil was gaining the upper hand, the songwriter still trusted his King and God with his eternal soul, because he believed in God's great mercy. Jesus is Lord and God to all who believe that he is the Son of God (1 John 4:13–16; 51–5) and trust in him for their salvation. In fact, after Jesus died and came back to life, he visited his disciples. Thomas, who had doubted that Jesus had actually returned, fell on his knees and cried out, "My Lord and my God!" (John 20:28). Like the psalmist, Thomas recognized Jesus' true identity as God's promised Messiah. We all face times that are especially trying, but even when life is flowing smoothly we need someone greater than ourselves to help us overcome the challenges we face. Like so many of God's people who have gone before us, we can cry out to our Lord and our God, who waits to hear from us so that he may once again reveal himself to us in his grace and in his tender power.

PSALM 6

For the director of music. With stringed
instruments. According to *sheminith*.[a]
A psalm of David.

1 O LORD, do not rebuke me in your 6:1 [x] Ps 38:1
anger[x]
or discipline me in your wrath.

[a] Title: Probably a musical term

[2] Be merciful to me, LORD, for I am
faint;
O LORD, heal me,[y] for my bones
are in agony.[z]
[3] My soul is in anguish.[a]
How long,[b] O LORD, how long?

[4] Turn, O LORD, and deliver me;
save me because of your
unfailing love.[c]
[5] No one remembers you when he is
dead.
Who praises you from the
grave[a]?[d]

[6] I am worn out[e] from groaning;
all night long I flood my bed
with weeping
and drench my couch with tears.[f]
[7] My eyes grow weak[g] with sorrow;
they fail because of all my foes.

[8] Away from me,[h] all you who do
evil,[i]
for the LORD has heard my
weeping.
[9] The LORD has heard my cry for
mercy;[j]
the LORD accepts my prayer.
[10] All my enemies will be ashamed
and dismayed;
they will turn back in sudden
disgrace.[k]

PSALM 7

A *shiggaion*[b] of David, which he sang to the LORD concerning Cush, a Benjamite.

[1] O LORD my God, I take refuge in
you;
save and deliver me from all who
pursue me,[l]
[2] or they will tear me like a lion[m]
and rip me to pieces with no one
to rescue[n] me.

[3] O LORD my God, if I have done this
and there is guilt on my hands[o]—
[4] if I have done evil to him who is at
peace with me
or without cause have robbed
my foe—
[5] then let my enemy pursue and
overtake me;
let him trample my life to the
ground
and make me sleep in the dust.
Selah

[6] Arise,[p] O LORD, in your anger;
rise up against the rage of my
enemies.[q]
Awake,[r] my God; decree justice.
[7] Let the assembled peoples gather
around you.
Rule over them from on high;
[8] let the LORD judge the peoples.
Judge me, O LORD, according to my
righteousness,[s]
according to my integrity,
O Most High.
[9] O righteous God,[t]
who searches minds and hearts,[u]
bring to an end the violence of the
wicked
and make the righteous secure.[v]

[10] My shield[c] is God Most High,
who saves the upright in heart.[w]
[11] God is a righteous judge,[x]
a God who expresses his wrath
every day.
[12] If he does not relent,
he[d] will sharpen his sword;[y]
he will bend and string his bow.
[13] He has prepared his deadly
weapons;
he makes ready his flaming
arrows.

[14] He who is pregnant with evil
and conceives trouble gives
birth[z] to disillusionment.
[15] He who digs a hole and scoops it out
falls into the pit he has made.[a]
[16] The trouble he causes recoils on
himself;
his violence comes down on his
own head.

[17] I will give thanks to the LORD
because of his
righteousness[b]
and will sing praise[c] to the name
of the LORD Most High.

PSALM 8

For the director of music. According to *gittith*.[e] A psalm of David.

[1] O LORD, our Lord,
how majestic is your name in all
the earth!

[a] *5* Hebrew *Sheol* [b] Title: Probably a literary or musical term [c] *10* Or *sovereign* [d] *12* Or *If a man does not repent, / God* [e] Title: Probably a musical term

6:2 [y] Hos 6:1 [z] Ps 22:14; 31:10
6:3 [a] Jn 12:27 [b] Ps 90:13
6:4 [c] Ps 17:13
6:5 [d] Ps 30:9; 88:10-12; Ecc 9:10; Isa 38:18
6:6 [e] Ps 69:3 [f] Ps 42:3
6:7 [g] Ps 31:9
6:8 [h] Ps 119:115 [i] Mt 7:23; Lk 13:27
6:9 [j] Ps 116:1
6:10 [k] Ps 71:24; 73:19
7:1 [l] Ps 31:15
7:2 [m] Isa 38:13 [n] Ps 50:22
7:3 [o] 1Sa 24:11; Isa 59:3
7:6 [p] Ps 94:2 [q] Ps 138:7 [r] Ps 44:23
7:8 [s] Ps 18:20; 96:13
7:9 [t] Jer 11:20 [u] 1Ch 28:9; Ps 26:2; Rev 2:23 [v] Ps 37:23
7:10 [w] Ps 125:4
7:11 [x] Ps 50:6
7:12 [y] Dt 32:41
7:14 [z] Job 15:35; Isa 59:4; Jas 1:15
7:15 [a] Job 4:8
7:17 [b] Ps 71:15-16 [c] Ps 9:2

DISCOVERY 125

A Song of Praise

"[The Lord] is worthy of praise," David exulted with utmost confidence (Psalm 18:3). To *praise* someone means to boast about that person—about who he is or what she does. There are many abstract reasons to boast about God—he is totally good, completely wise and perfectly just—but this recitation of facts can somehow fail to influence our day-to-day lives. We learn who God is not just by knowing his attributes but also by observing him in action, and that is how we are moved to adore him.

Psalm 8 recounts some concrete and specific things God has done, introducing us to the Creator-Artist responsible for our remarkable cosmos. The breathtaking beauty and awesome variety in nature cause us to marvel at the wisdom, power and continuing providence of the One who created the universe. Anything that humankind designs or accomplishes pales by comparison! Part of our worship experience is the acknowledgment deep within ourselves of how infinitely greater God is than we are. This kind of recognition requires a humble and trusting heart—the heart of a child.

In the Gospel accounts children frequently recognized Jesus for who he was. In one instance they called him the "Son of David," apparently without having been coached (Matthew 21:15). Based simply on his words and actions they perceived intuitively that he was God's promised Messiah. Not so with the religious leaders. Those same words and deeds exasperated them, and they challenged Jesus to intervene. Instead Jesus quoted Psalm 8:2: "From the lips of children and infants you have ordained praise." Jesus gratefully accepted the children's homage.

When we gaze at the starry night sky and contemplate the power of the Creator we may well contrast that might with our own limited abilities and view ourselves as puny and insignificant. Can our individual lives mean anything to the Designer of such a spectacular creation? Psalm 8 affirms the answer: God is indeed "mindful" of us, reaching out to his cherished creatures with compassion and tenderness.

Furthermore, God often chooses to use the inconsequential, weak or powerless things to reflect his character and to silence those who have come to a wrong conclusion (1 Corinthians 1:26–31). Humanity is dwarfed by the vast expanse of the universe, but we as individuals are of infinite importance to God. Our Lord proved this when his only Son entered the human race as a helpless infant for the purpose of eventually dying in our place. But the story remains incomplete until we acknowledge that Jesus Christ also rose from the dead and now sits in the place of honor alongside God the Father.

While nature speaks eloquently about God, nowhere is he more clearly seen than in Jesus. The psalmist referred to our Savior's incarnation in Psalm 8:5–6, and the writer to the Hebrews applied this passage to Jesus, who is "the radiance of God's glory and the exact representation of his being" (Hebrews 1:3) and who will someday "rule over the works of [God's] hands" and have "everything [placed] under his feet" (Psalm 8:6).

Self-Discovery: *Identify one particular scene in nature that is most likely to move you to adoration? What has God been doing in your life of late that would cause you to marvel at his greatness and his goodness?*

GO TO DISCOVERY 126 ON PAGE 687

You have set your glory
  above the heavens.[d]

8:1 [d] Ps 57:5; 113:4; 148:13

[2] From the lips of children and
    infants
  you have ordained praise[a][e]
because of your enemies,
  to silence the foe[f] and the
    avenger.

8:2 [e] Mt 21:16* [f] Ps 44:16; 1Co 1:27

[3] When I consider your heavens,[g]
  the work of your fingers,
the moon and the stars,[h]
  which you have set in place,
[4] what is man that you are mindful
    of him,
  the son of man that you care for
    him?[i]

8:3 [g] Ps 89:11 [h] Ps 136:9

8:4 [i] Job 7:17; Ps 144:3; Heb 2:6

[5] You made him a little lower than
    the heavenly beings[b]
  and crowned him with glory and
    honor.[j]

8:5 [j] Ps 21:5; 103:4

[6] You made him ruler[k] over the
    works of your hands;
  you put everything under his
    feet:[l][m]
[7] all flocks and herds,
  and the beasts of the field,
[8] the birds of the air,
  and the fish of the sea,
  all that swim the paths of the
    seas.

8:6 [k] Ge 1:28 [l] Heb 2:6-8* [m] 1Co 15:25, 27*; Eph 1:22

[9] O LORD, our Lord,
  how majestic is your name in all
    the earth![n]

8:9 [n] ver 1

CHILDREN SING PRAISE

Children can teach us a great deal about taking God at his word because they are naturally trusting (Psalm 8:2). Such ingenuous confidence can literally shut the mouths of God's enemies. There is no effective action that can counteract childlike trust and humble praise. Jesus included children in his ministry, insisting that the disciples allow them to approach him unimpeded (Matthew 18:3; Mark 10:14). During our Lord's triumphal entry into Jerusalem, it was the children who shouted, "Hosanna to the Son of David" (Matthew 21:15). When the religious leaders objected to the fact that the children were referring to Jesus as the Messiah, Jesus quoted Psalm 8:2. He reminded these leaders that God wants us, like the children, to offer our childlike trust and to worship him with a humble and open spirit.

PSALM 9[c]

For the director of music. To ⌞the tune of⌟ "The Death of the Son." A psalm of David.

[1] I will praise you, O LORD, with all
    my heart;[o]
  I will tell of all your wonders.[p]
[2] I will be glad and rejoice[q] in you;
  I will sing praise to your name,[r]
    O Most High.

9:1 [o] Ps 86:12 [p] Ps 26:7

9:2 [q] Ps 5:11 [r] Ps 92:1; 83:18

[3] My enemies turn back;
  they stumble and perish before
    you.
[4] For you have upheld my right and
    my cause;[s]
  you have sat on your throne,
    judging righteously.[t]

9:4 [s] Ps 140:12 [t] 1Pe 2:23

[5] You have rebuked the nations and
    destroyed the wicked;
  you have blotted out their
    name[u] for ever and ever.

9:5 [u] Pr 10:7

[6] Endless ruin has overtaken the
    enemy,
  you have uprooted their cities;
  even the memory of them[v] has
    perished.

9:6 [v] Ps 34:16

[7] The LORD reigns forever;
  he has established his throne[w]
    for judgment.

9:7 [w] Ps 89:14

[8] He will judge the world in
    righteousness;[x]
  he will govern the peoples with
    justice.

9:8 [x] Ps 96:13

[9] The LORD is a refuge for the
    oppressed,
  a stronghold in times of
    trouble.[y]

9:9 [y] Ps 32:7

[10] Those who know your name[z] will
    trust in you,
  for you, LORD, have never
    forsaken[a] those who seek
    you.

9:10 [z] Ps 91:14 [a] Ps 37:28

[11] Sing praises to the LORD, enthroned
    in Zion;[b]
  proclaim among the nations[c]
    what he has done.[d]

9:11 [b] Ps 76:2 [c] Ps 107:22 [d] Ps 105:1

[12] For he who avenges blood[e]
    remembers;
  he does not ignore the cry of the
    afflicted.

9:12 [e] Ge 9:5

[a] 2 Or *strength* [b] 5 Or *than God* [c] Psalms 9 and 10 may have been originally a single acrostic poem, the stanzas of which begin with the successive letters of the Hebrew alphabet. In the Septuagint they constitute one psalm.

9:13 [f]Ps 38:19 13 O LORD, see how my enemies[f]
persecute me!
Have mercy and lift me up from
9:14 the gates of death,
[g]Ps 106:2 14 that I may declare your praises[g]
[h]Ps 13:5; 51:12 in the gates of the Daughter of
Zion
and there rejoice in your
salvation.[h]
15 The nations have fallen into the pit
9:15 [i]Ps 7:15-16 they have dug;[i]
[j]Ps 35:8; 57:6 their feet are caught in the net
they have hidden.[j]
16 The LORD is known by his justice;
the wicked are ensnared by the
work of their hands.
Higgaion.[a] *Selah*
9:17 17 The wicked return to the grave,[b][k]
[k]Ps 49:14 all the nations that forget God.[l]
[l]Job 8:13; Ps 50:22 18 But the needy will not always be
forgotten,
9:18 [m]Ps 71:5; Pr 23:18 nor the hope[m] of the afflicted[n]
[n]Ps 12:5 ever perish.

19 Arise, O LORD, let not man triumph;
let the nations be judged in your
presence.
20 Strike them with terror, O LORD;
9:20 [o]Ps 62:9; Isa 31:3 let the nations know they are but
men.[o] *Selah*

PSALM 10[c]

10:1 [p]Ps 22:1,11 1 Why, O LORD, do you stand far off?[p]
[q]Ps 13:1 Why do you hide yourself[q] in
times of trouble?

2 In his arrogance the wicked man
hunts down the weak,
who are caught in the schemes
he devises.
10:3 [r]Ps 94:4 3 He boasts[r] of the cravings of his
heart;
he blesses the greedy and reviles
the LORD.
4 In his pride the wicked does not
seek him;
10:4 in all his thoughts there is no
[s]Ps 14:1; 36:1 room for God.[s]
5 His ways are always prosperous;
he is haughty and your laws are
far from him;
he sneers at all his enemies.
6 He says to himself, "Nothing will
shake me;
10:6 [t]Rev 18:7 I'll always be happy[t] and never
have trouble."

7 His mouth is full of curses[u] and lies 10:7 [u]Ro 3:14*
and threats;[v] [v]Ps 73:8
trouble and evil are under his [w]Ps 140:3
tongue.[w]
8 He lies in wait near the villages;
from ambush he murders the 10:8
innocent,[x] [x]Ps 94:6
watching in secret for his victims.
9 He lies in wait like a lion in cover;
he lies in wait to catch the 10:9
helpless;[y] [y]Ps 17:12; 59:3; 140:5
he catches the helpless and
drags them off in his net.
10 His victims are crushed, they
collapse;
they fall under his strength.
11 He says to himself, "God has 10:11
forgotten;[z] [z]Job 22:13
he covers his face and never sees."

12 Arise, LORD! Lift up your hand,[a] 10:12 [a]Ps 17:7;
O God. Mic 5:9
Do not forget the helpless.[b] [b]Ps 9:12
13 Why does the wicked man revile
God?
Why does he say to himself,
"He won't call me to account"? 10:14
14 But you, O God, do see trouble[c] [c]Ps 22:11
and grief; [d]Ps 37:5 [e]Ps 68:5
you consider it to take it in
hand.
The victim commits himself to
you;[d]
you are the helper[e] of the
fatherless.
15 Break the arm of the wicked and 10:15
evil man;[f] [f]Ps 37:17
call him to account for his
wickedness
that would not be found out.

16 The LORD is King for ever and 10:16
ever;[g] [g]Ps 29:10
the nations[h] will perish from his [h]Dt 8:20
land.
17 You hear, O LORD, the desire of the 10:17
afflicted;[i] [i]1Ch 29:18; Ps 34:15
you encourage them, and you
listen to their cry, 10:18
18 defending the fatherless[j] and the [j]Ps 82:3 [k]Ps 9:9
oppressed,[k]
in order that man, who is of the
earth, may terrify no more.

[a] 16 Or *Meditation*; possibly a musical notation
[b] 17 Hebrew *Sheol* [c] Psalms 9 and 10 may have been originally a single acrostic poem, the stanzas of which begin with the successive letters of the Hebrew alphabet. In the Septuagint they constitute one psalm.

PSALM 11

For the director of music. Of David.

11:1 [l] Ps 56:11 — 1 In the LORD I take refuge.[l]
How then can you say to me:
"Flee like a bird to your
mountain.
2 For look, the wicked bend their
bows;
11:2 [m] Ps 7:13 [n] Ps 64:3-4 — they set their arrows[m] against
the strings
to shoot from the shadows
at the upright in heart.[n]
11:3 [o] Ps 82:5 — 3 When the foundations[o] are being
destroyed,
what can the righteous do[a]?"
11:4 [p] Ps 18:6 [q] Ps 103:19 [r] Ps 33:13 [s] Ps 34:15-16 — 4 The LORD is in his holy temple;[p]
the LORD is on his heavenly
throne.[q]
He observes the sons of men;[r]
his eyes examine[s] them.
11:5 [t] Ge 22:1; Jas 1:12 [u] Ps 5:5 — 5 The LORD examines the righteous,[t]
but the wicked[b] and those who
love violence
his soul hates.[u]
6 On the wicked he will rain
11:6 [v] Eze 38:22 [w] Jer 4:11-12 — fiery coals and burning sulfur;[v]
a scorching wind[w] will be their
lot.
11:7 [x] Ps 7:9,11; 45:7 [y] Ps 33:5 [z] Ps 17:15 — 7 For the LORD is righteous,[x]
he loves justice;[y]
upright men will see his face.[z]

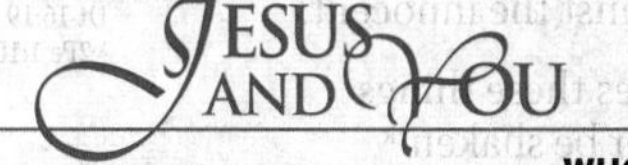

WHO NEEDS GOD?

Although he was called a "man after [God's] own heart" (1 Samuel 13:14). David recognized the painful reality that no human being is completely good (Psalm 14:3). The apostle Paul later quoted Psalm 14 as an apt description for humanity's bondage to sin (Romans 3:10–12). If we are left to our own devices, we will remain lost in our sins. Psalms 10—14 focus on how foolish it is to stay trapped in our pride and not open our hearts to the Lord's gentle touch. A person who doesn't want to follow God's teachings "struts about" (Psalm 12:8) and rationalizes, "God has forgotten . . . he won't call me to account" (Psalm 10:11–13). Jesus also talked about how utterly foolish it is to ignore God. He told a story about a rich young man who had made present and future plans without any thought for God (Luke 12:20). In the end, Jesus emphasized, we cannot plot out a future without relinquishing control of our lives to the God who created us, because he alone controls the future. Jesus reminds us, just as the psalmists do, to dedicate our lives to God and to live wisely, realizing that God holds the key to that which lies ahead.

PSALM 12

For the director of music. According to *sheminith.*[c] A psalm of David.

12:1 [a] Isa 57:1 — 1 Help, LORD, for the godly are no
more;[a]
the faithful have vanished from
among men.
2 Everyone lies to his neighbor;
12:2 [b] Ps 10:7; 41:6; 55:21; Ro 16:18 — their flattering lips speak with
deception.[b]
3 May the LORD cut off all flattering
lips
12:3 [c] Da 7:8; Rev 13:5 — and every boastful tongue[c]
4 that says, "We will triumph with
our tongues;
we own our lips[d]—who is our
master?"
5 "Because of the oppression of the
weak
and the groaning of the needy,
I will now arise," says the LORD.
12:5 [d] Ps 10:18; 34:6 — "I will protect them[d] from those
who malign them."
12:6 [e] 2Sa 22:31; Ps 18:30; Pr 30:5 — 6 And the words of the LORD are
flawless,[e]
like silver refined in a furnace of
clay,
purified seven times.
7 O LORD, you will keep us safe
12:7 [f] Ps 37:28 — and protect us from such people
forever.[f]
12:8 [g] Ps 55:10-11 — 8 The wicked freely strut[g] about
when what is vile is honored
among men.

PSALM 13

For the director of music. A psalm of David.

1 How long, O LORD? Will you forget
me forever?

[a] 3 Or *what is the Righteous One doing* [b] 5 Or *The LORD, the Righteous One, examines the wicked, /* [c] Title: Probably a musical term [d] 4 Or */ our lips are our plowshares*

13:1 [h]Job 13:24; Ps 44:24

How long will you hide your
face[h] from me?

13:2 [i]Ps 42:4 [j]Ps 42:9

[2] How long must I wrestle with my
thoughts[i]
and every day have sorrow in my
heart?
How long will my enemy
triumph over me?[j]

13:3 [k]Ps 5:1 [l]Ezr 9:8 [m]Jer 51:39

[3] Look on me and answer,[k] O LORD
my God.
Give light to my eyes,[l] or I will
sleep in death;[m]

13:4 [n]Ps 25:2

[4] my enemy will say, "I have
overcome him,[n]"
and my foes will rejoice when I
fall.

13:5 [o]Ps 52:8 [p]Ps 9:14

[5] But I trust in your unfailing love;[o]
my heart rejoices in your
salvation.[p]

13:6 [q]Ps 116:7

[6] I will sing[q] to the LORD,
for he has been good to me.

PSALM 14

For the director of music. Of David.

14:1 [r]Ps 10:4

[1] The fool[a] says in his heart,
"There is no God."[r]
They are corrupt, their deeds are
vile;
there is no one who does good.

14:2 [s]Ps 33:13 [t]Ps 92:6

[2] The LORD looks down from heaven[s]
on the sons of men
to see if there are any who
understand,[t]
any who seek God.

14:3 [u]Ps 58:3 [v]Ps 143:2 [w]Ro 3:10-12*

[3] All have turned aside,
they have together become
corrupt;[u]
there is no one who does good,[v]
not even one.[w]

14:4 [x]Ps 82:5 [y]Ps 27:2 [z]Ps 79:6; Isa 64:7

[4] Will evildoers never learn—[x]
those who devour my people[y] as
men eat bread
and who do not call on the LORD?[z]
[5] There they are, overwhelmed with
dread,
for God is present in the
company of the righteous.
[6] You evildoers frustrate the plans of
the poor,
but the LORD is their refuge.[a]

14:6 [a]Ps 9:9; 40:17

[7] Oh, that salvation for Israel would
come out of Zion!
When the LORD restores the
fortunes[b] of his people,
let Jacob rejoice and Israel be
glad!

14:7 [b]Ps 53:6

PSALM 15

A psalm of David.

15:1 [c]Ps 27:5-6 [d]Ps 24:3-5

[1] LORD, who may dwell in your
sanctuary?[c]
Who may live on your holy hill?[d]

15:2 [e]Ps 24:4; Zec 8:3,16; Eph 4:25

[2] He whose walk is blameless
and who does what is righteous,
who speaks the truth[e] from his
heart

15:3 [f]Ex 23:1

[3] and has no slander[f] on his
tongue,
who does his neighbor no wrong
and casts no slur on his
fellowman,

15:4 [g]Ac 28:10 [h]Jdg 11:35

[4] who despises a vile man
but honors[g] those who fear the
LORD,
who keeps his oath[h]
even when it hurts,

15:5 [i]Ex 22:25 [j]Ex 23:8; Dt 16:19 [k]2Pe 1:10

[5] who lends his money without usury[i]
and does not accept a bribe[j]
against the innocent.

He who does these things
will never be shaken.[k]

PSALM 16

A *miktam*[b] of David.

16:1 [l]Ps 17:8 [m]Ps 7:1

[1] Keep me safe,[l] O God,
for in you I take refuge.[m]

16:2 [n]Ps 73:25

[2] I said to the LORD, "You are my
Lord;
apart from you I have no good
thing."[n]

16:3 [o]Ps 101:6

[3] As for the saints who are in the
land,[o]
they are the glorious ones in
whom is all my delight.[c]

16:4 [p]Ps 32:10 [q]Ps 106:37-38

[4] The sorrows[p] of those will increase
who run after other gods.[q]
I will not pour out their libations of
blood

[a] *1* The Hebrew words rendered *fool* in Psalms denote one who is morally deficient. [b] Title: Probably a literary or musical term [c] *3* Or *As for the pagan priests who are in the land / and the nobles in whom all delight, I said:*

DISCOVERY 126

Bridging the Gap

The bad news is that we have all been separated from God by sin and cannot under our own power make that relationship right again. The real tragedy is that sin has produced such an unbreachable divide that most of the time we don't even *want* to turn back to God. But there is unimaginable good news as well—God himself has designed a way to bridge the gap. The only hope for humanity is God himself, and the psalmist realized that his help would come from "Zion," where God dwells.

There are many ways we can deny God, either completely or in part. The Bible declares that only a foolish person claims that God does not exist or that he isn't interested in the decisions we make. When we deny God in any area of life, we will make ungodly decisions. It all begins with an attitude: "The fool says in his heart, 'There is no God' " (Psalm 14:1). If we do not believe that God exists or that he cares about a certain issue in our lives, we quickly conclude that we are on our own and are free to live in whatever manner we choose.

This problem is common to all of humanity: "All have turned aside, they have together become corrupt; there is no one who does good, not even one" (verse 3). In the New Testament Paul cited this verse to describe how all people have turned away from God (Romans 3:9–18), and the apostle expressed a similar sentiment in his letter to Titus: "At one time we too were foolish, disobedient, deceived and enslaved by all kinds of passions and pleasures . . . But when the kindness and love of God our Savior appeared, he saved us, not because of righteous things we had done, but because of his mercy" (Titus 3:3–5).

God is the only One who can repair the damage brought about by sin and rebuild a relationship with each one of us. He wants us to know that he hasn't abandoned us, that he is still "present in the company of the righteous" (Psalm 14:5). Being right with God is not a state we can work toward or bring about; it is something that happens only when we accept that Jesus died for our sin. Righteousness results not from our innate goodness but from our belief in God and our decision to walk with him (Romans 3:21–31).

God is a refuge, a place of safety and a shelter from danger. This image recurs again and again in Scripture, and especially in the psalms (see Psalm 46:1; 61:3; 62:7–8; 71:7; 73:28; 91:2,9). When the problems of life seem overwhelming, when we are afraid or in need of comfort, we can turn to God: "Salvation for Israel [comes] out of Zion" (Psalm 14:7), the city of Jerusalem (Zechariah 8:3). Centuries after this psalm was written, Jesus died on a cross outside Jerusalem. His death paid the debt for our sin, and he came back to life again so we too could live forever with him (Romans 6:1–14).

Self-Discovery: *Have you ever thanked the Lord for giving you the grace to want to live for him? Can you remember back to when you first felt this desire? What were some of the specific commitments you made at the time, both in terms of behavior and attitude, that expressed your desire to live a life of gratitude?*

GO TO DISCOVERY 127 ON PAGE 689

THE WARDERS OF HELL TREMBLED WHEN THEY SAW HIM.

Hippolytus, *Early Church Father*

16:4 [r] Ex 23:13 or take up their names[r] on my
lips.

16:5 [s] Ps 73:26 [t] Ps 23:5 [5] LORD, you have assigned me my
portion[s] and my cup;[t]
you have made my lot secure.
[6] The boundary lines have fallen for
me in pleasant places;
16:6 [u] Ps 78:55; Jer 3:19 surely I have a delightful
inheritance.[u]

[7] I will praise the LORD, who counsels
16:7 [v] Ps 73:24 [w] Ps 77:6 me;[v]
even at night[w] my heart
instructs me.
[8] I have set the LORD always before
me.
16:8 [x] Ps 73:23 Because he is at my right hand,[x]
I will not be shaken.

16:9 [y] Ps 4:7; 30:11 [z] Ps 4:8 [9] Therefore my heart is glad[y] and my
tongue rejoices;
my body also will rest secure,[z]
[10] because you will not abandon me
to the grave,[a]
16:10 [a] Ac 13:35* nor will you let your Holy One[b]
see decay.[a]
16:11 [b] Mt 7:14 [11] You have made[c] known to me the
path of life;[b]

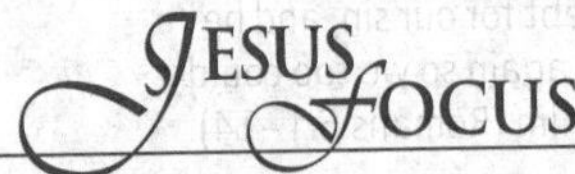

NEW LIFE

Because we were made for eternity, the things of time cannot fully and permanently satisfy. We seem to have an innate sense that there is more to life than what we experience in the here and now. In Psalm 16:10 David indicated that he believed he would enjoy eternal life. Both Peter and Paul quoted this psalm in the New Testament, referring to it as a prediction of Jesus' death and resurrection (Acts 2:25–28; 13:35–37). The psalm itself centers around the security and confidence in which God's people can rest as they face death. While David's words proclaim his complete confidence that not even the grave can rob him of life, ultimately they point us to Jesus, the quintessential "Holy One," who would come back to life again after he had died for our sins (Matthew 28:6; Mark 16:6; 1 Corinthians 15:20).

you will fill me with joy in your 16:11 [c] Ac 2:25-28*
presence,[c] [d] Ps 36:7-8
with eternal pleasures[d] at your
right hand.

PSALM 17

A prayer of David.

[1] Hear, O LORD, my righteous plea; 17:1
listen to my cry.[e] [e] Ps 61:1
Give ear to my prayer— [f] Isa 29:13
it does not rise from deceitful
lips.[f]
[2] May my vindication come from you;
may your eyes see what is right.
[3] Though you probe my heart and
examine me at night,
though you test me,[g] you will 17:3 [g] Ps 26:2; 66:10
find nothing;[h] [h] Job 23:10; Jer 50:20
I have resolved that my mouth [i] Ps 39:1
will not sin.[i]
[4] As for the deeds of men—
by the word of your lips
I have kept myself
from the ways of the violent.
[5] My steps have held to your paths;[j] 17:5 [j] Ps 44:18; 119:133
my feet have not slipped.[k] [k] Ps 18:36
[6] I call on you, O God, for you will 17:6
answer me;[l] [l] Ps 86:7
give ear to me[m] and hear my [m] Ps 116:2
prayer.[n] [n] Ps 88:2
[7] Show the wonder of your great 17:7
love,[o] [o] Ps 31:21
you who save by your right [p] Ps 20:6
hand[p]
those who take refuge in you
from their foes.
[8] Keep me as the apple of your eye;[q] 17:8 [q] Dt 32:10
hide me in the shadow of your
wings
[9] from the wicked who assail me,
from my mortal enemies who
surround me.[r] 17:9 [r] Ps 31:20; 109:3
[10] They close up their callous hearts,[s] 17:10 [s] Ps 73:7
and their mouths speak with [t] 1Sa 2:3
arrogance.[t]
[11] They have tracked me down, they 17:11
now surround me,[u] [u] Ps 37:14; 88:17
with eyes alert, to throw me to
the ground.
[12] They are like a lion[v] hungry for 17:12 [v] Ps 7:2; 10:9
prey,

a 10 Hebrew *Sheol* *b 10* Or *your faithful one*
c 11 Or *You will make*

DISCOVERY 127

HOPE FOR *TODAY*

For the individual who walks with God by means of a personal relationship with Jesus Christ, Psalm 16:11 offers a sense of peace, hope and immeasurable comfort. These words afford us something to which we can cling when the burdens of life seem unbearable. We can rest secure (verse 9) because we have the assurance that the God who loves us will never abandon us. That promise was sealed when Jesus came back to life after his crucifixion (note the word picture in verse 10). Our greatest hope for the future is not simply that we will live forever—but that we will live eternally *with Jesus*.

Sometimes the fulfillment of God's promises can appear to be so far in the future that we have a difficult time comprehending that those promises apply right now. While it is reassuring to know that things will work out "someday," we cannot help but ask the poignant question, *But what about today*? Psalm 16 is a *Messianic* psalm: It looks forward in time to God's promised Messiah, Jesus. In it we can glimpse something of the perspective of the promised One. And when we view our situation through Jesus' eyes, we perceive a strong and sure hope for *today*.

First of all we are invited to keep our eyes on God the Father (verses 1–2), the One who keeps us safe today and will continue to do so in the future. He is our place of refuge, a secure retreat to whom we can flee when we face attack or injury. Secondly, God wants us to know that we are a delight to him. In Matthew 17:5 God identified Jesus as his Son, in whom he was "well pleased," and, now that we have been given the righteousness of Jesus (2 Corinthians 5:21) God takes the same delight in us.

Thirdly, we have the assurance that the circumstances of our lives are carefully assigned to us by our loving heavenly Father (Psalm 16:5–6). In Romans 8:28–29 we learn that God is working through all of the events in our lives to conform us "to the likeness of his Son."

Fourthly, there is a significant difference in outlook between God's people and those who disown him. We can learn from others who know God and gain perspective on life's situations from them. When we keep our focus on our loving Lord we will not be shaken by the changes and trials of life. This unique vantage point helps us to carry on in the present *and* look forward to the future.

As we live a God-centered life, we respond to truth in three ways: We delight in our God-given inheritance (Psalm 16:5–6), we thank God for being with us and guiding us each hour of each day (verses 7–8), and we celebrate *constantly*—because our hope in the One who raised our precious Savior Jesus Christ from the dead will last today, tomorrow and forever (verses 9–11).

Self-Discovery: *If you have been a Christian for a long time, try to imagine the sense of hopelessness the unbeliever must feel when facing a crisis situation. What difference does your faith in Jesus make, both in good times and in bad?*

GO TO DISCOVERY 128 ON PAGE 693

THERE IS SOMETHING WRONG WITH A CHRISTIANITY WHICH REJECTS THE OLD TESTAMENT, OR EVEN IMAGINES THAT WE ARE ESSENTIALLY DIFFERENT FROM OLD TESTAMENT SAINTS.

Martyn Lloyd-Jones, *Pastor, London, England*

like a great lion crouching in
cover.
[13] Rise up, O LORD, confront them,
bring them down;[w]
rescue me from the wicked by
your sword.
[14] O LORD, by your hand save me from
such men,
from men of this world[x] whose
reward is in this life.
You still the hunger of those you
cherish;
their sons have plenty,
and they store up wealth[y] for
their children.
[15] And I—in righteousness I will see
your face;
when I awake, I will be satisfied
with seeing your likeness.[z]

17:13 [w] Ps 7:12; 22:20; 73:18
17:14 [x] Lk 16:8 [y] Ps 73:3-7
17:15 [z] Nu 12:8; Ps 4:6-7; 16:11; 1Jn 3:2

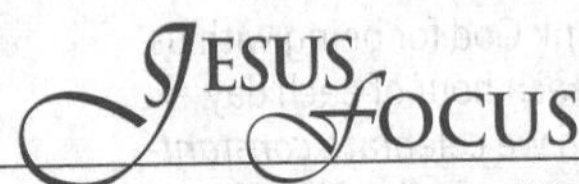

SEEING GOD'S FACE

The Bible tells us that God is a safe place to whom we can run (Psalm 16:1; 17:7–8), and we understand this idea better as we get to know him and learn to trust him. We want to draw close enough to God to see his face (Psalm 17:15), to read his expression. To see God's face is to know him personally. This concept is similar to that of being granted the great honor of an audience with the King. The book of Revelation points out our ability one day to approach the throne of God and Jesus (the Lamb of God) in the Holy City, the new Jerusalem: "[We] will see his face" (Revelation 22:4). Everyone who places his or her trust in Jesus Christ belongs to God's family—and we will one day enjoy a permanent audience with the King. Even today, however, we can look for opportunities to glimpse the face of God as we learn to walk more closely with him and allow his light to shine in our hearts and in our lives (2 Corinthians 4:6).

PSALM 18

For the director of music. Of David the servant of the LORD. He sang to the LORD the words of this song when the LORD delivered him from the hand of all his enemies and from the hand of Saul. He said:

[1] I love you, O LORD, my strength.

[2] The LORD is my rock,[a] my fortress
and my deliverer;
my God is my rock, in whom I
take refuge.
He is my shield[b] and the horn[a]
of my salvation,[c] my
stronghold.
[3] I call to the LORD, who is worthy of
praise,[d]
and I am saved from my enemies.

[4] The cords of death[e] entangled me;
the torrents[f] of destruction
overwhelmed me.
[5] The cords of the grave[b] coiled
around me;
the snares of death[g] confronted
me.
[6] In my distress I called to the LORD;
I cried to my God for help.
From his temple he heard my voice;[h]
my cry came before him, into his
ears.

[7] The earth trembled and quaked,[i]
and the foundations of the
mountains shook;
they trembled because he was
angry.[j]
[8] Smoke rose from his nostrils;
consuming fire[k] came from his
mouth,
burning coals blazed out of it.
[9] He parted the heavens and came
down;[l]
dark clouds were under his feet.
[10] He mounted the cherubim[m] and
flew;
he soared on the wings of the
wind.[n]
[11] He made darkness his covering,[o]
his canopy around him—
the dark rain clouds of the sky.
[12] Out of the brightness of his
presence[p] clouds advanced,
with hailstones and bolts of
lightning.[q]

18:2 [a] Ps 19:14 [b] Ps 59:11 [c] Ps 75:10
18:3 [d] Ps 48:1
18:4 [e] Ps 116:3 [f] Ps 124:4
18:5 [g] Ps 116:3
18:6 [h] Ps 34:15
18:7 [i] Jdg 5:4 [j] Ps 68:7-8
18:8 [k] Ps 50:3
18:9 [l] Ps 144:5
18:10 [m] Ps 80:1 [n] Ps 104:3
18:11 [o] Dt 4:11; Ps 97:2
18:12 [p] Ps 104:2 [q] Ps 97:3

[a] 2 *Horn* here symbolizes strength. [b] 5 Hebrew *Sheol*

13 The LORD thundered[r] from heaven;
the voice of the Most High
resounded.[a]
14 He shot his arrows and scattered
⌊the enemies⌋,
great bolts of lightning and
routed them.[s]
15 The valleys of the sea were exposed
and the foundations of the earth
laid bare
at your rebuke,[t] O LORD,
at the blast of breath from your
nostrils.

16 He reached down from on high and
took hold of me;
he drew me out of deep waters.[u]
17 He rescued me from my powerful
enemy,
from my foes, who were too
strong for me.[v]
18 They confronted me in the day of
my disaster,
but the LORD was my support.[w]
19 He brought me out into a spacious
place;[x]
he rescued me because he
delighted in me.[y]

20 The LORD has dealt with me
according to my
righteousness;
according to the cleanness of my
hands[z] he has rewarded me.
21 For I have kept the ways of the
LORD;[a]
I have not done evil by turning[b]
from my God.
22 All his laws are before me;[c]
I have not turned away from his
decrees.
23 I have been blameless before him
and have kept myself from sin.
24 The LORD has rewarded me
according to my
righteousness,[d]
according to the cleanness of my
hands in his sight.

25 To the faithful[e] you show yourself
faithful,
to the blameless you show
yourself blameless,
26 to the pure you show yourself pure,
but to the crooked you show
yourself shrewd.[f]
27 You save the humble
but bring low those whose eyes
are haughty.[g]

18:13 [r] Ps 29:3; 104:7
18:14 [s] Ps 144:6
18:15 [t] Ps 76:6; 106:9
18:16 [u] Ps 144:7
18:17 [v] Ps 35:10
18:18 [w] Ps 59:16
18:19 [x] Ps 31:8 [y] Ps 118:5
18:20 [z] Ps 24:4
18:21 [a] 2Ch 34:33 [b] Ps 119:102
18:22 [c] Ps 119:30
18:24 [d] 1Sa 26:23
18:25 [e] 1Ki 8:32; Ps 62:12; Mt 5:7
18:26 [f] Pr 3:34
18:27 [g] Pr 6:17

28 You, O LORD, keep my lamp burning;
my God turns my darkness into
light.[h]
29 With your help[i] I can advance
against a troop[b];
with my God I can scale a wall.

30 As for God, his way is perfect;[j]
the word of the LORD is flawless.[k]
He is a shield
for all who take refuge[l] in him.
31 For who is God besides the LORD?[m]
And who is the Rock[n] except our
God?
32 It is God who arms me with
strength[o]
and makes my way perfect.
33 He makes my feet like the feet of a
deer;[p]
he enables me to stand on the
heights.[q]
34 He trains my hands for battle;[r]
my arms can bend a bow of
bronze.
35 You give me your shield of victory,
and your right hand sustains[s]
me;
you stoop down to make me
great.
36 You broaden the path beneath me,
so that my ankles do not turn.

37 I pursued my enemies[t] and
overtook them;
I did not turn back till they were
destroyed.
38 I crushed them so that they could
not rise;[u]
they fell beneath my feet.[v]
39 You armed me with strength for
battle;
you made my adversaries bow at
my feet.
40 You made my enemies turn their
backs[w] in flight,
and I destroyed[x] my foes.
41 They cried for help, but there was
no one to save them[y]—
to the LORD, but he did not
answer.[z]
42 I beat them as fine as dust borne
on the wind;
I poured them out like mud in
the streets.

[a] *13* Some Hebrew manuscripts and Septuagint (see also 2 Samuel 22:14); most Hebrew manuscripts *resounded, / amid hailstones and bolts of lightning* [b] *29* Or *can run through a barricade*

18:28 [h] Job 18:6; 29:3
18:29 [i] Heb 11:34
18:30 [j] Dt 32:4; Rev 15:3 [k] Ps 12:6 [l] Ps 17:7
18:31 [m] Dt 32:39; 86:8; Isa 45:5,6,14,18,21 [n] Dt 32:31; 1Sa 2:2
18:32 [o] Isa 45:5
18:33 [p] Hab 3:19 [q] Dt 32:13
18:34 [r] Ps 144:1
18:35 [s] Ps 119:116
18:37 [t] Ps 37:20; 44:5
18:38 [u] Ps 36:12 [v] Ps 47:3
18:40 [w] Ps 21:12 [x] Ps 94:23
18:41 [y] Ps 50:22 [z] Job 27:9; Pr 1:28

18:43 [a] 2Sa 8:1-14 [b] Isa 52:15; 55:5
18:44 [c] Ps 66:3
18:45 [d] Mic 7:17
18:46 [e] Ps 51:14
18:47 [f] Ps 47:3
18:48 [g] Ps 59:1
18:49 [h] Ps 108:1 [i] Ro 15:9*
18:50 [j] Ps 144:10 [k] Ps 89:4

43 You have delivered me from the
attacks of the people;
you have made me the head of
nations;[a]
people I did not know[b] are
subject to me.
44 As soon as they hear me, they obey
me;
foreigners[c] cringe before me.
45 They all lose heart;
they come trembling from their
strongholds.[d]

46 The LORD lives! Praise be to my
Rock!
Exalted be God my Savior![e]
47 He is the God who avenges me,
who subdues nations[f] under me,
48 who saves[g] me from my
enemies.
You exalted me above my foes;
from violent men you rescued me.
49 Therefore I will praise you among
the nations, O LORD;
I will sing[h] praises to your name.[i]
50 He gives his king great victories;
he shows unfailing kindness to
his anointed,
to David[j] and his descendants
forever.[k]

PSALM 19

For the director of music. A psalm of David.

19:1 [l] Isa 40:22 [m] Ps 50:6; Ro 1:19
19:2 [n] Ps 74:16
19:4 [o] Ro 10:18* [p] Ps 104:2

1 The heavens[l] declare[m] the glory of
God;
the skies proclaim the work of
his hands.
2 Day after day they pour forth
speech;
night after night they display
knowledge.[n]
3 There is no speech or language
where their voice is not heard.*[a]*
4 Their voice*[b]* goes out into all the
earth,
their words to the ends of the
world.[o]
In the heavens he has pitched a
tent[p] for the sun,
5 which is like a bridegroom
coming forth from his
pavilion,
like a champion rejoicing to run
his course.

19:6 [q] Ps 113:3; Ecc 1:5
19:7 [r] Ps 23:3 [s] Ps 93:5; 111:7 [t] Ps 119:98-100
19:8 [u] Ps 12:6; 119:128
19:9 [v] Ps 119:138,142
19:10 [w] Pr 8:10
19:12 [x] Ps 51:2; 90:8; 139:6
19:14 [y] Ps 104:34 [z] Ps 18:2 [a] Isa 47:4

6 It rises at one end of the heavens
and makes its circuit to the
other;[q]
nothing is hidden from its heat.

7 The law of the LORD is perfect,
reviving the soul.[r]
The statutes of the LORD are
trustworthy,[s]
making wise the simple.[t]
8 The precepts of the LORD are
right,[u]
giving joy to the heart.
The commands of the LORD are
radiant,
giving light to the eyes.
9 The fear of the LORD is pure,
enduring forever.
The ordinances of the LORD are
sure
and altogether righteous.[v]
10 They are more precious than gold,[w]
than much pure gold;
they are sweeter than honey,
than honey from the comb.
11 By them is your servant warned;
in keeping them there is great
reward.

12 Who can discern his errors?
Forgive my hidden faults.[x]
13 Keep your servant also from willful
sins;
may they not rule over me.
Then will I be blameless,
innocent of great transgression.
14 May the words of my mouth and
the meditation of my heart
be pleasing[y] in your sight,
O LORD, my Rock[z] and my
Redeemer.[a]

PSALM 20

For the director of music. A psalm of David.

20:1 [b] Ps 46:7,11 [c] Ps 91:14
20:2 [d] Ps 3:4

1 May the LORD answer you when
you are in distress;
may the name of the God of
Jacob[b] protect you.[c]
2 May he send you help from the
sanctuary[d]
and grant you support from
Zion.

a 3 Or *They have no speech, there are no words; / no sound is heard from them* *b* 4 Septuagint, Jerome and Syriac; Hebrew *line*

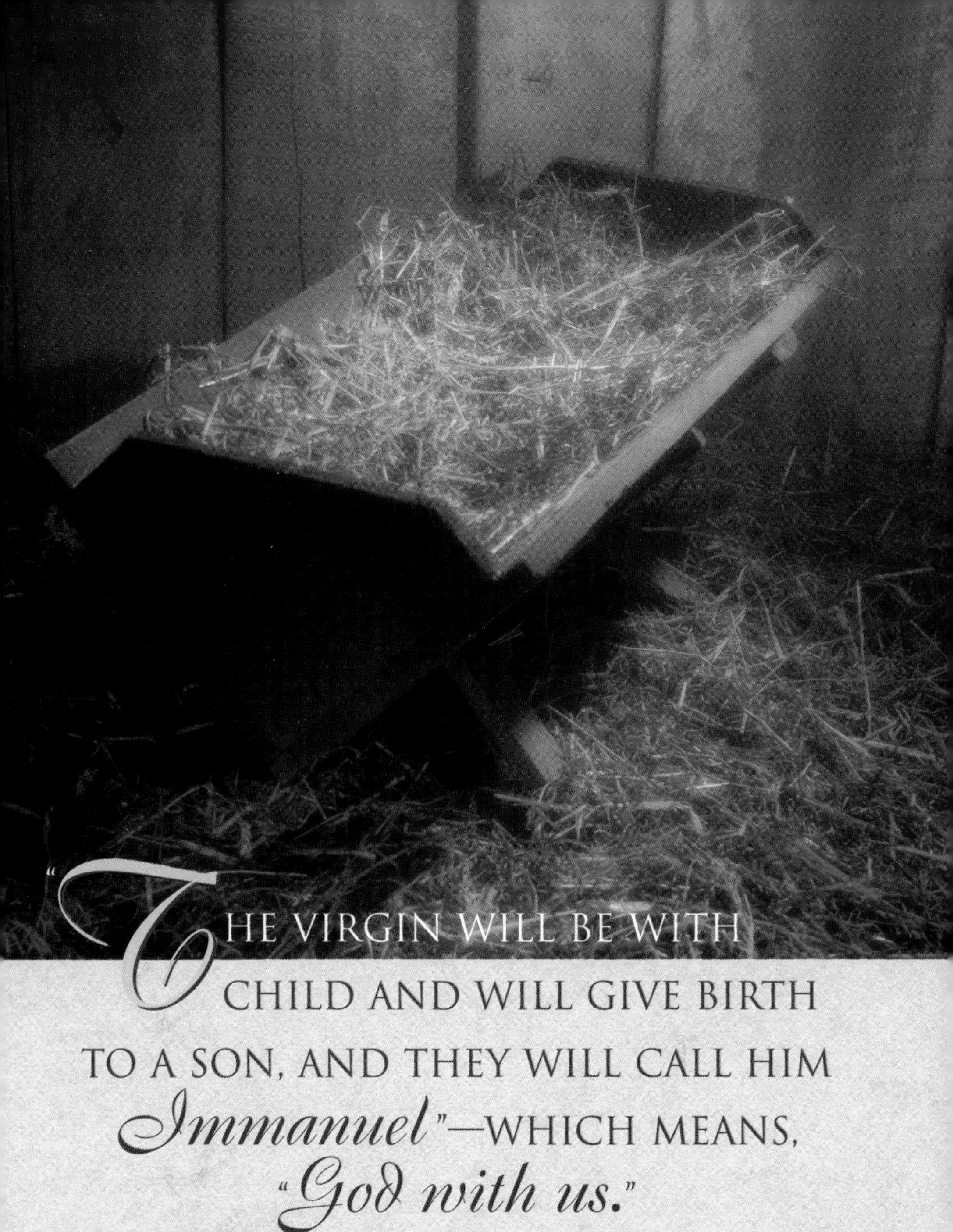

"THE VIRGIN WILL BE WITH CHILD AND WILL GIVE BIRTH TO A SON, AND THEY WILL CALL HIM *Immanuel*"—WHICH MEANS, "*God with us.*"

—MATTHEW 1:23—

*H*E WAS *pierced* FOR OUR TRANSGRESSIONS, HE WAS CRUSHED FOR OUR INIQUITIES; THE PUNISHMENT THAT BROUGHT US *peace* WAS UPON HIM, AND BY HIS WOUNDS WE ARE *healed*.

— ISAIAH 53:5 —

DISCOVERY 128

GETTING ACQUAINTED WITH GOD

Since God is spirit, we cannot see him, and it is sometimes difficult to imagine that we can become intimately involved with him. God is so powerful, so infinite, and we are so small, so insignificant—can he even be aware of us? As God of the universe, he must be very busy. It doesn't seem possible that he could devote time to the minute details of every individual life. The Bible declares emphatically, however, that we *can* get to know God.

What God has created reveals to us something of what he is like. Verses 1 and 2 of Psalm 19 affirm that all of nature points us skyward. As the sovereign Creator and Ruler of the cosmos, God deserves all honor. In creation we perceive glimpses both of God's power and of his ability to preserve and maintain what he has created. His beauty, perfection and wisdom are manifested in the cycles of nature and the amazing ecological balance in the world around us. We can deduce something of God's nature as we gaze in wonder at the mountains, oceans and cloud formations. Romans 1:20 concludes, "Since the creation of the world God's invisible qualities—his eternal power and divine nature—have been clearly seen, being understood from what has been made, so that men are without excuse."

Creation, however, can only provide general, inductive knowledge about God. How can we experience him more intimately, get to know him "up close and personal"? Through his Word—both his written Word and Jesus, the Living Word. In fact, Jesus took on himself our human flesh so that we could relate to God very personally. Throughout history God had used the prophets, his spokespersons, to *tell* his people what he was like, but at the appointed time he sent his Son down to earth to *show* us in person (Hebrews 1:1–3).

In the New Testament Philip implored Jesus to "show us the Father and that will be enough for us" (John 14:8). Jesus replied, "Anyone who has seen me has seen the Father" (John 14:9). He was reinforcing what he had already said: "The Son can do nothing by himself; he can do only what he sees the Father doing, because whatever the Father does the Son also does" (John 5:19).

We *can* know God. We become acquainted with him by reading his Word and seeing his love in action through Jesus' compassion for people (Matthew 14:14). Hebrews 4:15–16 reminds us that "we do not have a high priest who is unable to sympathize with our weaknesses, but we have one who has been tempted in every way, just as we are—yet without sin. Let us then approach the throne of grace with confidence, so that we may receive mercy and find grace to help us in our time of need." Jesus mirrored for us God's holiness and power (John 9:1–12), and we know that our relationship with the Father is secure when we accept the Son into our lives. Jesus said, "the Father himself loves you because you have loved me and have believed that I came from God" (John 16:27).

Self-Discovery: *Have you ever felt reluctant to bring a minor problem to God's attention, assuming he must be busy dealing with more urgent issues? What might it take for you to experience Jesus as the One who loves you passionately, as a Bridegroom cherishes his bride?*

GO TO DISCOVERY 129 ON PAGE 696

20:3 [e] Ac 10:4 [f] Ps 51:19
3 May he remember[e] all your
sacrifices
and accept your burnt offerings.[f]
Selah

20:4 [g] Ps 21:2; 145:16,19
4 May he give you the desire of your
heart[g]
and make all your plans
succeed.
5 We will shout for joy when you are
victorious

20:5 [h] Ps 9:14; 60:4 [i] 1Sa 1:17
and will lift up our banners[h] in
the name of our God.
May the LORD grant all your
requests.[i]

20:6 [j] Ps 28:8; 41:11; Isa 58:9
6 Now I know that the LORD saves his
anointed;[j]
he answers him from his holy
heaven
with the saving power of his
right hand.

20:7 [k] Ps 33:17; Isa 31:1 [l] 2Ch 32:8
7 Some trust in chariots and some in
horses,[k]
but we trust in the name of the
LORD our God.[l]
8 They are brought to their knees
and fall,

20:8 [m] Mic 7:8 [n] Ps 37:23
but we rise up[m] and stand firm.[n]

20:9 [o] Ps 3:7; 17:6
9 O LORD, save the king!
Answer[a] us[o] when we call!

PSALM 21

For the director of music. A psalm of David.

1 O LORD, the king rejoices in your
strength.
How great is his joy in the

21:1 [p] Ps 59:16-17
victories you give![p]

21:2 [q] Ps 37:4
2 You have granted him the desire of
his heart[q]
and have not withheld the
request of his lips.
Selah
3 You welcomed him with rich
blessings

21:3 [r] 2Sa 12:30
and placed a crown of pure gold[r]
on his head.
4 He asked you for life, and you gave
it to him—

21:4 [s] Ps 61:5-6; 91:16; 133:3
length of days, for ever and ever.[s]

21:5 [t] Ps 18:50
5 Through the victories[t] you gave,
his glory is great;
you have bestowed on him
splendor and majesty.
6 Surely you have granted him
eternal blessings

21:6 [u] Ps 43:4 [v] 1Ch 17:27
and made him glad with the joy[u]
of your presence.[v]
7 For the king trusts in the LORD;
through the unfailing love of the
Most High
he will not be shaken.

21:8 [w] Isa 10:10
8 Your hand will lay hold[w] on all your
enemies;
your right hand will seize your
foes.
9 At the time of your appearing
you will make them like a fiery
furnace.
In his wrath the LORD will swallow
them up,

21:9 [x] Ps 50:3; La 2:2; Mal 4:1
and his fire will consume
them.[x]
10 You will destroy their descendants
from the earth,

21:10 [y] Dt 28:18; Ps 37:28
their posterity from mankind.[y]

21:11 [z] Ps 2:1 [a] Ps 10:2
11 Though they plot evil[z] against you
and devise wicked schemes,[a]
they cannot succeed;

21:12 [b] Ps 7:12-13; 18:40
12 for you will make them turn their
backs[b]
when you aim at them with
drawn bow.
13 Be exalted, O LORD, in your
strength;
we will sing and praise your
might.

[a] 9 Or *save! / O King, answer*

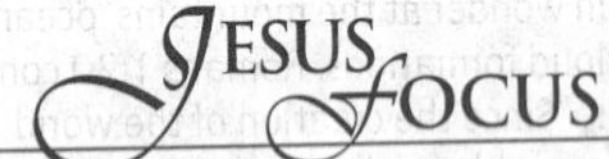

ROYAL SONGS

Psalms that point ahead to the consummate King promised by God are called "royal psalms" (see Psalms 2, 18, 20, 21, 45, 61, 72, 89 and 110). These songs celebrate the entire line of Davidic kings but ultimately point to the Messiah himself. David was acutely aware of his role as a representative of God's kingdom on earth. Because of this responsibility David understood that he must depend on God for help in ruling the kingdom in the way God wanted (Psalm 21:1–2,6–7). David's reference to the victory crown of gold (verse 3) is alluded to in Revelation 14:14, where it refers to Jesus. David and the kings who followed in his family line foreshadowed Jesus, the only One who could fulfill the prophecies and the only One whose "kingdom truly will endure forever" (2 Samuel 7:16; Psalm 89:3–4; Luke 1:33).

PSALM 22

For the director of music. To ⌞the tune of⌟ "The Doe of the Morning." A psalm of David.

22:1 [c] Mt 27:46*; Mk 15:34* [d] Ps 10:1
1 My God, my God, why have you
forsaken me?[c]
Why are you so far[d] from saving
me,
so far from the words of my
groaning?
2 O my God, I cry out by day, but you
do not answer,
22:2 [e] Ps 42:3
by night,[e] and am not silent.
3 Yet you are enthroned as the Holy
22:3 [f] Ps 99:9 [g] Dt 10:21
One;[f]
you are the praise[g] of Israel.[a]
4 In you our fathers put their trust;
they trusted and you delivered
them.
5 They cried to you and were saved;
22:5 [h] Isa 49:23
in you they trusted and were not
disappointed.[h]
22:6 [i] Job 25:6; Isa 41:14 [j] Ps 31:11 [k] Isa 49:7; 53:3
6 But I am a worm[i] and not a man,
scorned by men[j] and despised[k]
by the people.
7 All who see me mock me;
22:7 [l] Mt 27:39,44 [m] Mk 15:29
they hurl insults,[l] shaking their
heads:[m]
22:8 [n] Ps 91:14 [o] Mt 27:43
8 "He trusts in the LORD;
let the LORD rescue him.[n]
Let him deliver him,
since he delights[o] in him."

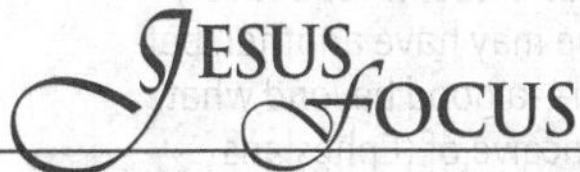

DEATH ON A CROSS

Psalm 22 has been called the "Song of the Cross." There is no way to deny the fact that it points to God's promised Messiah. The psalm even predicts Jesus' precise words from the cross: "My God, my God, why have you forsaken me?" (verse 1; see also Matthew 27:46; Mark 15:34). David vividly described the excruciating pain of the crucifixion, down to the minute details: the piercing of Jesus' hands and feet (verse 16), the taunting by the crowd (verses 7–13) and the soldiers gambling for his robe (verse 18). The New Testament explicitly interprets this psalm as referring to Jesus (Matthew 27:35–36,46; Luke 23:35; John 19:23–28). David penned these prophetic words more than a thousand years before Jesus' birth in Bethlehem (Luke 2:1–7).

22:9 [p] Ps 71:6
9 Yet you brought me out of the
womb;[p]
you made me trust in you
even at my mother's breast.
22:10 [q] Isa 46:3
10 From birth[q] I was cast upon you;
from my mother's womb you
have been my God.
11 Do not be far from me,
for trouble is near
22:11 [r] Ps 72:12
and there is no one to help.[r]
22:12 [s] Ps 68:30 [t] Dt 32:14
12 Many bulls[s] surround me;
strong bulls of Bashan[t] encircle
me.
22:13 [u] Ps 17:12 [v] Ps 35:21
13 Roaring lions[u] tearing their prey
open their mouths wide[v] against
me.
14 I am poured out like water,
22:14 [w] Ps 31:10 [x] Job 30:16; Da 5:6
and all my bones are out of
joint.[w]
My heart has turned to wax;
it has melted away[x] within me.
15 My strength is dried up like a
potsherd,
22:15 [y] Ps 38:10; Jn 19:28 [z] Ps 104:29
and my tongue sticks to the roof
of my mouth;[y]
you lay me[b] in the dust[z] of death.
16 Dogs[a] have surrounded me;
22:16 [a] Ps 59:6 [b] Isa 53:5; Zec 12:10; Jn 19:34
a band of evil men has encircled
me,
they have pierced[c][b] my hands
and my feet.
22:17 [c] Lk 23:35 [d] Lk 23:27
17 I can count all my bones;
people stare[c] and gloat over me.[d]
18 They divide my garments among
22:18 [e] Mt 27:35*; Lk 23:34; Jn 19:24*
them
and cast lots[e] for my clothing.
19 But you, O LORD, be not far off;
22:19 [f] Ps 70:5
O my Strength, come quickly[f] to
help me.
20 Deliver my life from the sword,
22:20 [g] Ps 35:17
my precious life[g] from the power
of the dogs.
21 Rescue me from the mouth of the
lions;
save[d] me from the horns of the
wild oxen.

22 I will declare your name to my
22:22 [h] Heb 2:12*
brothers;
22:23 [i] Ps 86:12; 135:19
in the congregation I will praise
you.[h]
23 You who fear the LORD, praise him![i]

[a] 3 Or *Yet you are holy, / enthroned on the praises of Israel* [b] 15 Or */ I am laid* [c] 16 Some Hebrew manuscripts, Septuagint and Syriac; most Hebrew manuscripts */ like the lion,* [d] 21 Or */ you have heard*

NEVER ABANDONED

Centuries before crucifixion had become a common method of execution, Psalm 22 described death on a cross in more detail than any other Old Testament passage. The psalm opens with the very words Jesus would utter as he surrendered his spirit: "My God, my God, why have you forsaken me?" (Mark 15:34). There is a sense in which it means exactly that—God the Father abandoning his Son to serve as the atonement for sin so that we would ultimately never be abandoned.

We often reflect on the physical torture Jesus endured during his ordeal, but he also suffered excruciating emotional and spiritual anguish—and this type of pain can sometimes be the most difficult to bear. Jesus cried out to God to deliver him, but God had leveled the full fury of his wrath against sin on Jesus, on whom was laid "the iniquity of us all" (Isaiah 53:6).Throughout his entire ministry Jesus had been dismissed, ridiculed and accused of unspeakable evil. As the hour of his death was approaching, one of his closest companions sold him to the enemy, and the rest of his intimate band of followers scattered when the demands become too hard. But like the psalmist Jesus knew that his Father was with him every step along the way (Psalm 22:9–11).

Psalm 22 also describes the physical torture to which Jesus would be subjected. Both his hands and feet were pierced with huge nails in order to suspend him securely from the wooden cross (verse 16). He was "poured out like water," meaning that his physical strength was entirely depleted. Even his bones were wrenched out of joint (verse 14). He was so thirsty that his tongue stuck to the roof of his mouth (verse 15). Historians agree that crucifixion was one of the least humane methods of execution, and Jesus felt the searing pain of every breath.

But his suffering was not pointless. God desired to gather his own into his forever family (verses 25–26). His people can experience firsthand that he is the one true and glorious God (verse 27). This yearning for his people to enter into relationship with him stretched beyond the generation living at the time the psalm was composed, beyond the first century A.D. when Jesus cried out with the identical words with which the psalm begins. God's longing for relationship applied "to a people yet unborn" (verse 31), and that includes all of us.

There are times in life when we too want to cry out, "My God, my God, why have you forsaken me?" The experiences of life can be so fraught with pain that it feels as though God has turned his back on us. Yet this is the truth we can hold on to: Though God may elect not to deliver us from the difficult circumstances, he promises that he will never stop loving us. He will be with us in the midst of every situation, and he may have another, better plan in mind—a good beyond what we can even conceive of (Ephesians 3:20). As Paul stated so eloquently in 1 Corinthians 2:9, "No eye has seen, no ear has heard, no mind has conceived what God has prepared for those who love him."

Self-Discovery: *Think back to the most painful ordeal of your life. Was the anguish primarily physical, emotional or spiritual? How does it help to know that Jesus understands your pain?*

GO TO DISCOVERY 130 ON PAGE 699

All you descendants of Jacob,
honor him!
22:23 [j]Ps 33:8 Revere him,[j] all you descendants
of Israel!
24 For he has not despised or
disdained
the suffering of the afflicted one;
22:24 [k]Ps 69:17 [l]Heb 5:7 he has not hidden his face[k] from
him
but has listened to his cry for
help.[l]
25 From you comes the theme of my
praise in the great
22:25 [m]Ps 35:18 [n]Ecc 5:4 assembly;[m]
before those who fear you[a] will I
fulfill my vows.[n]
22:26 [o]Ps 107:9 [p]Ps 40:16 26 The poor will eat[o] and be
satisfied;
they who seek the LORD will
praise him—[p]
may your hearts live forever!
22:27 [q]Ps 2:8 [r]Ps 86:9 27 All the ends of the earth[q]
will remember and turn to the
LORD,
and all the families of the nations
will bow down before him,[r]
22:28 [s]Ps 47:7-8 28 for dominion belongs to the
LORD[s]
and he rules over the nations.
22:29 [t]Ps 45:12 [u]Isa 26:19 29 All the rich[t] of the earth will feast
and worship;
all who go down to the dust[u] will
kneel before him—
those who cannot keep
themselves alive.
22:30 [v]Ps 102:28 30 Posterity[v] will serve him;
future generations will be told
about the Lord.
31 They will proclaim his
righteousness
22:31 [w]Ps 78:6 to a people yet unborn[w]—
for he has done it.

PSALM 23

A psalm of David.

23:1 [x]Isa 40:11; Jn 10:11; 1Pe 2:25 [y]Php 4:19 1 The LORD is my shepherd,[x] I shall
not be in want.[y]
2 He makes me lie down in green
pastures,
23:2 [z]Eze 34:14; Rev 7:17 he leads me beside quiet waters,[z]
3 he restores my soul.[a]
He guides me in paths of
23:3 [a]Ps 19:7 [b]Ps 5:8; 85:13 righteousness[b]
for his name's sake.

JESUS IS A FRIEND OF MINE. HE WALKED THROUGH THE VALLEY OF HELL WITH ME AND SAW ME THROUGH IT.

Aaron Nevill, *Grammy Award-winning Singer*

4 Even though I walk
23:4 [c]Job 10:21-22 [d]Ps 3:6; 27:1 [e]Isa 43:2 through the valley of the shadow
of death,[b][c]
I will fear no evil,[d]
for you are with me;[e]
your rod and your staff,
they comfort me.
5 You prepare a table before me
in the presence of my enemies.
23:5 [f]Ps 92:10 [g]Ps 16:5 You anoint my head with oil;[f]
my cup[g] overflows.
6 Surely goodness and love will
follow me
all the days of my life,
and I will dwell in the house of the
LORD
forever.

[a] 25 Hebrew *him* [b] 4 Or *through the darkest valley*

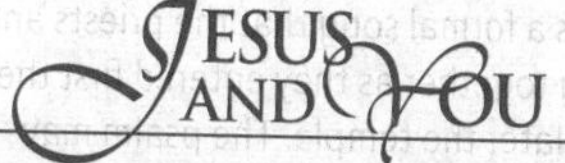

MY SHEPHERD

Psalm 23, perhaps the best-loved of all the psalms, describes Jesus as our heavenly Shepherd-King. This image of God as our Shepherd constitutes perhaps the most intimate word picture in the book of Psalms. A shepherd lives directly with his sheep, aware of their every move and their every error in judgment—loving, guiding and protecting them. The relationship between the shepherd and his sheep is a wonderful picture of God's love for his cherished people, and it was an example that the people of ancient Israel could immediately understand.

In the New Testament Jesus referred to himself as the "good shepherd" (John 10:11); he used that image to express his undying love and compassion for his own, promising to one day lay down his very life for us, his sheep (John 10:15). When we give control of our lives to Jesus, he receives us as a gentle Shepherd and answers us that we "will dwell in the house of the LORD forever" (Psalm 23:6).

PSALM 24

Of David. A psalm.

24:1 [h] Ex 9:29; Job 41:11; Ps 89:11 [i] 1Co 10:26*

[1] The earth is the LORD's,[h] and
everything in it,
the world, and all who live in it;[i]
[2] for he founded it upon the seas
and established it upon the
waters.

24:3 [j] Ps 2:6 [k] Ps 15:1; 65:4

[3] Who may ascend the hill[j] of the
LORD?
Who may stand in his holy
place?[k]

24:4 [l] Job 17:9 [m] Mt 5:8

[4] He who has clean hands[l] and a
pure heart,[m]
who does not lift up his soul to
an idol
or swear by what is false.[a]
[5] He will receive blessing from the
LORD
and vindication from God his
Savior.

JESUS FOCUS

OPEN THE GATES

Psalm 24 celebrates the Lord's entrance into Zion, his holy city. It is a formal song that the priests and the people sang together as they entered first the tabernacle and later the temple. The psalm may actually have been written at the time David was bringing the ark of the covenant to Jerusalem for the very first time (see 2 Samuel 6). It culminates in the King of glory being welcomed by his people in a victory parade.

Some people believe that Psalm 24 anticipates the time when Jesus would ascend to the heavenly Jerusalem to his place of glory at the right hand of the Father (Acts 2:33; Philippians 2:9; see also Psalm 47:5). Others believe it points to Jesus' final triumph over evil, his second coming when he will take his people with him into eternity (Revelation 21—22). As the eternal Son of God, Jesus is the "King of kings and Lord of lords" (1 Timothy 6:15; Revelation 19:16; see also Revelation 17:14). The Bible tells us that when the King of glory returns to earth, he will come into the royal city of the kingdom of God as the victorious conqueror, the "king over the whole earth (Zechariah 14:1–9; see also Ezekiel 43:1–5; Acts 1:11–12). This anthem of praise might well be sung when that glorious event occurs.

24:6 [n] Ps 27:8

[6] Such is the generation of those
who seek him,
who seek your face,[n] O God of
Jacob.[b] *Selah*

24:7 [o] Isa 26:2 [p] Ps 97:6; 1Co 2:8

[7] Lift up your heads, O you gates;[o]
be lifted up, you ancient doors,
that the King of glory[p] may
come in.
[8] Who is this King of glory?
The LORD strong and mighty,
the LORD mighty in battle.[q]

24:8 [q] Ps 76:3-6

[9] Lift up your heads, O you gates;
lift them up, you ancient doors,
that the King of glory may
come in.
[10] Who is he, this King of glory?
The LORD Almighty—
he is the King of glory. *Selah*

PSALM 25[c]

Of David.

25:1 [r] Ps 86:4
25:2 [s] Ps 41:11

[1] To you, O LORD, I lift up my soul;[r]
[2] in you I trust,[s] O my God.
Do not let me be put to shame,
nor let my enemies triumph over
me.

25:3 [t] Isa 49:23

[3] No one whose hope is in you
will ever be put to shame,[t]
but they will be put to shame
who are treacherous without
excuse.

25:4 [u] Ex 33:13

[4] Show me your ways, O LORD,
teach me your paths;[u]
[5] guide me in your truth and teach
me,
for you are God my Savior,
and my hope is in you all day
long.

25:6 [v] Ps 103:17; Isa 63:7,15

[6] Remember, O LORD, your great
mercy and love,[v]
for they are from of old.

25:7 [w] Job 13:26; Jer 3:25 [x] Ps 51:1

[7] Remember not the sins of my
youth[w]
and my rebellious ways;
according to your love[x] remember
me,
for you are good, O LORD.

25:8 [y] Ps 92:15

[8] Good and upright[y] is the LORD;

[a] 4 Or *swear falsely* [b] 6 Two Hebrew manuscripts and Syriac (see also Septuagint); most Hebrew manuscripts *face, Jacob* [c] This psalm is an acrostic poem, the verses of which begin with the successive letters of the Hebrew alphabet.

THE KING IS COMING

King David was stalked by a powerful man (see 2 Samuel 19:1–2), and he himself arranged to have a man murdered after he had been involved in an affair with the man's wife (2 Samuel 11:17). As a direct result David's infant son died (2 Samuel 12:19), and later in life another of his sons turned against him (2 Samuel 15:12). Despite all of this, however, David continued to write songs of praise to God the Father. He knew that God would provide him with everything that he needed and protect him from harm. Psalms 22, 23 and 24 together form a vivid picture of God. In Psalm 22 David poured out the anguish of his soul but also acknowledged God as both provider and protector. Psalm 23, one of the best-loved passages in the entire Bible, shows us how God cares as a shepherd for his sheep, and Psalm 24 alludes to his power and glory as our great King.

David started with what he knew: pain, confusion, isolation. Even so, he was confident that God would not disappoint him. The situation may have appeared bleak, but God would take care of him (Psalm 22:5). Jesus reminded his followers (and us) of the same thing: "Look at the birds of the air; they do not sow or reap or store away in barns, and yet your heavenly Father feeds them. Are you not much more valuable than they?" (Matthew 6:26).

David may not have felt like a glorious historical figure—people mocked him and taunted his God (Psalm 22:7–8)—but he realized that God was the giver of both his life and his faith. Jesus warned us to expect much the same inglorious treatment from others but included a wonderful promise in the same breath: "All men will hate you because of me, but he who stands firm to the end will be saved" (Mark 13:13). Even though David was surrounded, frightened, emaciated and wounded, he held fast to the promise that God would both provide for him (Psalm 22:26–27) and protect him (verses 20–21).

Psalm 23 opens with a ringing testimony: "The LORD is my shepherd, I shall not be in want." As Creator of the universe, God owes us nothing—but he chooses to give us everything—rest, refreshment, restoration, guidance, fellowship, reassurance and victory. Jesus Christ is the Good Shepherd who cares for his "sheep" in the same way (John 10:14–15; 1 Peter 5:4). Our Lord himself has chosen each of us to be members of his flock (Psalm 23:5; 95:7; 100:3), and there can be no better assurance of his provision than that!

Finally, in Psalm 24, David described how God, the King of Glory, longs for a relationship with us. As our King and Creator, he could demand that we come into his presence, but instead he draws us with promises to care for us and to bless us (verse 4). He sent his Son to cleanse our hands and purify our hearts, and we now have confidence (Hebrews 10:19–22) to enter the holy presence of our King. More than anything else, God wants the people he has created to seek him and devote themselves to him in love.

Self-Discovery: *Pause a moment to think about your infinite worth in the eyes of God. How has Jesus opened the way for you to enjoy a restored relationship with God the Father?*

GO TO DISCOVERY 131 ON PAGE 703

25:8 z Ps 32:8 therefore he instructs[z] sinners in
his ways.
25:9 a Ps 23:3 b Ps 27:11 9 He guides[a] the humble in what is
right
and teaches them[b] his way.
10 All the ways of the LORD are loving
25:10 c Ps 40:11 d Ps 103:18 and faithful[c]
for those who keep the demands
of his covenant.[d]
25:11 e Ps 31:3; 79:9 11 For the sake of your name,[e] O LORD,
forgive my iniquity, though it is
great.
12 Who, then, is the man that fears
the LORD?
25:12 f Ps 37:23 He will instruct him in the way[f]
chosen for him.
25:13 g Pr 19:23 h Ps 37:11 13 He will spend his days in prosperity,[g]
and his descendants will inherit
the land.[h]
25:14 i Pr 3:32 j Jn 7:17 14 The LORD confides[i] in those who
fear him;
he makes his covenant known[j]
to them.
25:15 k Ps 141:8 15 My eyes are ever on the LORD,[k]
for only he will release my feet
from the snare.
25:16 l Ps 69:16 16 Turn to me[l] and be gracious to me,
for I am lonely and afflicted.
17 The troubles of my heart have
multiplied;
25:17 m Ps 107:6 free me from my anguish.[m]
18 Look upon my affliction and my
25:18 n 2Sa 16:12 distress[n]
and take away all my sins.
25:19 o Ps 3:1 19 See how my enemies[o] have
increased
and how fiercely they hate me!
25:20 p Ps 86:2 20 Guard my life[p] and rescue me;
let me not be put to shame,
for I take refuge in you.
25:21 q Ps 41:12 21 May integrity[q] and uprightness
protect me,
because my hope is in you.
25:22 r Ps 130:8 22 Redeem Israel,[r] O God,
from all their troubles!

PSALM 26

Of David.

1 Vindicate me, O LORD,
26:1 s Ps 7:8; Pr 20:7 t Ps 28:7 u 2Ki 20:3; Heb 10:23 for I have led a blameless life;[s]
I have trusted[t] in the LORD
without wavering.[u]
26:2 v Ps 17:3 w Ps 7:9 2 Test me,[v] O LORD, and try me,
examine my heart and my mind;[w]
3 for your love is ever before me, 26:3
and I walk continually[x] in your x 2Ki 20:3
truth.
4 I do not sit[y] with deceitful men, 26:4 y Ps 1:1
nor do I consort with hypocrites;
5 I abhor[z] the assembly of evildoers 26:5 z Ps 31:6; 139:21
and refuse to sit with the wicked.
6 I wash my hands in innocence,[a] 26:6 a Ps 73:13
and go about your altar, O LORD,
7 proclaiming aloud your praise
and telling of all your wonderful 26:7 b Ps 9:1
deeds.[b]
8 I love[c] the house where you live, 26:8 c Ps 27:4
O LORD,
the place where your glory
dwells.
9 Do not take away my soul along
with sinners, 26:9 d Ps 28:3
my life with bloodthirsty men,[d]
10 in whose hands are wicked
schemes,
whose right hands are full of 26:10 e 1Sa 8:3
bribes.[e]
11 But I lead a blameless life; 26:11 f Ps 69:18
redeem me[f] and be merciful to
me.
12 My feet stand on level ground;[g] 26:12 g Ps 27:11; 40:2
in the great assembly[h] I will h Ps 22:22
praise the LORD.

PSALM 27

Of David.

1 The LORD is my light[i] and my 27:1 i Isa 60:19
salvation[j]— j Ex 15:2
whom shall I fear? k Ps 118:6
The LORD is the stronghold of my
life—
of whom shall I be afraid?[k]
2 When evil men advance against me
to devour my flesh,[a]
when my enemies and my foes
attack me, 27:2
they will stumble and fall.[l] l Ps 9:3; 14:4
3 Though an army besiege me, 27:3
my heart will not fear;[m] m Ps 3:6
though war break out against me, n Job 4:6
even then will I be confident.[n]
4 One thing[o] I ask of the LORD,
this is what I seek:
that I may dwell in the house of the
LORD 27:4 o Ps 90:17
all the days of my life,[p] p Ps 23:6; 26:8

a 2 Or *to slander me*

to gaze upon the beauty of the
LORD
and to seek him in his temple.
5 For in the day of trouble
he will keep me safe in his
dwelling;
27:5 [q] Ps 17:8; 31:20 [r] Ps 40:2
he will hide me[q] in the shelter of
his tabernacle
and set me high upon a rock.[r]
27:6 [s] Ps 3:3 [t] Ps 107:22
6 Then my head will be exalted[s]
above the enemies who
surround me;
at his tabernacle will I sacrifice[t]
with shouts of joy;
I will sing and make music to
the LORD.

7 Hear my voice when I call, O LORD;
27:7 [u] Ps 13:3
be merciful to me and answer
me.[u]
8 My heart says of you, "Seek his[a]
face!"
Your face, LORD, I will seek.
27:9 [v] Ps 69:17
9 Do not hide your face[v] from me,

JESUS AND YOU

NO FEAR

In Psalm 27 David gave expression to his absolute confidence in God's abiding love: "The LORD is my light and my salvation—whom shall I fear . . . of whom shall I be afraid?" Much later the apostle Paul reveled in that same assurance, expressing it in these terms: "If God is for us, who can be against us? . . . Who shall separate us from the love of Christ? . . . We are more than conquerors through him who loved us" (Romans 8:31–39). Paul, like David, understood that God would never turn his back on his people. Our Lord Jesus during his time on earth had earlier reminded the people of this same truth (John 6:39; 10:28–29). Instead of worrying about our lives, we can relax and focus on the things of the Lord (Matthew 6:25,33). We all experience fears and worries. Sometimes we feel alone and in bondage to pain, and it feels as though the hurting will never stop. Sometimes we worry about our ability to meet our financial obligations for the coming month. No matter what causes anxiety in our lives, we can rest in the blessed assurance that God is greater than any problem and any force of darkness in our lives (1 John 4:4). He promises to take care of our every need—but more than that, he promises to be with us as we go through the challenges of life (Matthew 28:20; John 14:18).

do not turn your servant away in
anger;
you have been my helper.
Do not reject me or forsake me,
O God my Savior.
10 Though my father and mother
forsake me,
the LORD will receive me.
11 Teach me your way, O LORD;
27:11 [w] Ps 5:8; 25:4; 86:11
lead me in a straight path[w]
because of my oppressors.
12 Do not turn me over to the desire
of my foes,
27:12 [x] Mt 26:60; Ac 9:1
for false witnesses[x] rise up
against me,
breathing out violence.
13 I am still confident of this:
27:13 [y] Ps 31:19 [z] Jer 11:19; Eze 26:20
I will see the goodness of the
LORD[y]
in the land of the living.[z]
27:14 [a] Ps 40:1
14 Wait[a] for the LORD;
be strong and take heart
and wait for the LORD.

PSALM 28

Of David.

1 To you I call, O LORD my Rock;
28:1 [b] Ps 83:1 [c] Ps 88:4
do not turn a deaf ear to me.
For if you remain silent,[b]
I will be like those who have
gone down to the pit.[c]
28:2 [d] Ps 138:2; 140:6 [e] Ps 5:7
2 Hear my cry for mercy[d]
as I call to you for help,
as I lift up my hands
toward your Most Holy Place.[e]

3 Do not drag me away with the
wicked,
with those who do evil,
who speak cordially with their
neighbors
28:3 [f] Ps 12:2; Ps 26:9; Jer 9:8
but harbor malice in their
hearts.[f]
4 Repay them for their deeds
and for their evil work;
28:4 [g] 2Ti 4:14; Rev 22:12 [h] Rev 18:6
repay them for what their hands
have done[g]
and bring back upon them what
they deserve.[h]
5 Since they show no regard for the
works of the LORD
28:5 [i] Isa 5:12
and what his hands have done,[i]
he will tear them down

[a] 8 Or *To you, O my heart, he has said, "Seek my*

and never build them up again.

[6] Praise be to the LORD,
for he has heard my cry for mercy.

28:7 [j] Ps 18:1 [k] Ps 13:5 [l] Ps 40:3; 69:30

[7] The LORD is my strength[j] and my shield;
my heart trusts[k] in him, and I am helped.
My heart leaps for joy
and I will give thanks to him in song.[l]

28:8 [m] Ps 20:6

[8] The LORD is the strength of his people,
a fortress of salvation for his anointed one.[m]

28:9 [n] Dt 9:29; Ezr 1:4 [o] Isa 40:11 [p] Dt 1:31; 32:11

[9] Save your people and bless your inheritance;[n]
be their shepherd[o] and carry them[p] forever.

PSALM 29

A psalm of David.

29:1 [q] 1Ch 16:28 [r] Ps 96:7-9

[1] Ascribe to the LORD,[q] O mighty ones,
ascribe to the LORD glory[r] and strength.

29:2 [s] 2Ch 20:21

[2] Ascribe to the LORD the glory due his name;
worship the LORD in the splendor of his[a] holiness.[s]

29:3 [t] Job 37:5 [u] Ps 18:13

[3] The voice[t] of the LORD is over the waters;
the God of glory thunders,[u]
the LORD thunders over the mighty waters.

29:4 [v] Ps 68:33

[4] The voice of the LORD is powerful;[v]
the voice of the LORD is majestic.

29:5 [w] Jdg 9:15

[5] The voice of the LORD breaks the cedars;
the LORD breaks in pieces the cedars of Lebanon.[w]

29:6 [x] Ps 114:4 [y] Dt 3:9

[6] He makes Lebanon skip[x] like a calf,
Sirion[b][y] like a young wild ox.
[7] The voice of the LORD strikes
with flashes of lightning.

29:8 [z] Nu 13:26

[8] The voice of the LORD shakes the desert;
the LORD shakes the Desert of Kadesh.[z]

29:9 [a] Ps 26:8

[9] The voice of the LORD twists the oaks[c]
and strips the forests bare.
And in his temple all cry, "Glory!"[a]

29:10 [b] Ge 6:17 [c] Ps 10:16

[10] The LORD sits[d] enthroned over the flood;[b]
the LORD is enthroned as King forever.[c]

29:11 [d] Ps 28:8 [e] Ps 37:11

[11] The LORD gives strength to his people;[d]
the LORD blesses his people with peace.[e]

THE KNOWLEDGE OF THE EVER-PRESENT CHRIST CAN REACH DOWN INTO THE HIDDEN DEPTHS AND ASSURE LONELY MODERN MAN THAT HE IS NOT ALONE.

Stephen Neill, *Church Historian*

PSALM 30

A psalm. A song. For the dedication of the temple.[e] Of David.

30:1 [f] Ps 25:2; 28:9

[1] I will exalt you, O LORD,
for you lifted me out of the depths
and did not let my enemies gloat over me.[f]

30:2 [g] Ps 88:13 [h] Ps 6:2

[2] O LORD my God, I called to you for help[g]
and you healed me.[h]

30:3 [i] Ps 28:1; 86:13

[3] O LORD, you brought me up from the grave[f];
you spared me from going down into the pit.[i]

30:4 [j] Ps 149:1 [k] Ps 97:12

[4] Sing to the LORD, you saints[j] of his;
praise his holy name.[k]

30:5 [l] Ps 103:9 [m] 2Co 4:17

[5] For his anger[l] lasts only a moment,
but his favor lasts a lifetime;
weeping may remain for a night,
but rejoicing comes in the morning.[m]

[6] When I felt secure, I said,
"I will never be shaken."

30:7 [n] Dt 31:17; Ps 104:29

[7] O LORD, when you favored me,
you made my mountain[g] stand firm;
but when you hid your face,[n]
I was dismayed.

[8] To you, O LORD, I called;
to the Lord I cried for mercy:

[a] 2 Or *LORD with the splendor of* [b] 6 That is, Mount Hermon [c] 9 Or *LORD makes the deer give birth* [d] 10 Or *sat* [e] Title: Or *palace* [f] 3 Hebrew *Sheol* [g] 7 Or *hill country*

DISCOVERY 131

Mourning Into Dancing

Being a follower of Jesus Christ does not imply that bad times will never come. In fact, some circumstances in the lives of believers may even become more difficult. Walking with God entails marching out-of-step with the world, and the psalms are replete with prayers uttered from pits of darkness and despair.

Deep pits are very real in our lives, even when we are walking with God. One of the most common phrases used in the Old Testament to describe suffering is "the depths." This word picture can refer to sickness (Psalm 30:2) or to a state near death (verse 3). At other times the metaphor might describe God's silence (Psalm 94:17), darkness (Psalm 88:6,12), destruction (Psalm 30:9) or the experience of being "stuck" in a particular place (or rut) in life (Psalm 40:2).

We live in a world polluted by sin and are compelled daily to deal with the consequences of that sin—both our own and that of other people. We do not escape the effects of sin just because we accept Jesus and his forgiveness. But the difference should be the manner in which we approach the painful aspects of life. If we know God we can trust him in everything—even in those situations which we refer to as "the pits." We can testify, "I will exalt you, O LORD, for you lifted me out of the depths" (Psalm 30:1).

We can talk to God when we are deep in trouble or despair. When we walk through difficult valleys, God wants to see that we place our trust in him (James 1:2–8). We all tend to feel secure when things are going our way (Psalm 30:6) but often want to give up completely when we experience reversals (verse 7). It is when we are groping in a deep, dark place that we really learn to count on God to get us through. When the props we have erected to keep our balance are knocked out from beneath us and we begin to sink into the slimy mire, we come face-to-face with the fact that God himself is the only One strong enough to rescue us.

The depths are very real, but they will not last forever: "Weeping may remain for a night, but rejoicing comes in the morning" (verse 5). When God rescued David, David exalted him—God had turned his mourning into dancing (verse 11). We sometimes remember to thank God for what he has done to rescue us, but we usually neglect to celebrate with a party as David did!

At the end of his life the apostle John was exiled to the island of Patmos. Like King David and many of God's people throughout the centuries, John was "in the depths." But he also knew that God was with him, and Jesus himself came to visit and comfort the apostle (Revelation 1:12–13). And when we feel ourselves sinking into the "Slough of Despond" as Christian experienced in *Pilgrim's Progress*, we are often surprised to discover that Jesus is present with us in a very special way. It is during these times that we experience new dimensions in our relationship with him and receive fresh new assurances of his unceasing care.

Self-Discovery: *Try to recall a situation in which your relationship with Jesus has developed and deepened following a period of despondency or trial. What are some of the truths about Jesus you learned as a result of your crying out to him for help?*

GO TO DISCOVERY 132 ON PAGE 706

[9] "What gain is there in my
destruction,[a]
in my going down into the pit?
Will the dust praise you?
Will it proclaim your
faithfulness?[o]
[10] Hear, O LORD, and be merciful to me;
O LORD, be my help."

[11] You turned my wailing into dancing;
you removed my sackcloth and
clothed me with joy,[p]
[12] that my heart may sing to you and
not be silent.
O LORD my God, I will give you
thanks[q] forever.[r]

30:9 [o] Ps 6:5
30:11 [p] Ps 4:7; Jer 31:4, 13
30:12 [q] Ps 16:9 [r] Ps 44:8

PSALM 31

For the director of music. A psalm of David.

[1] In you, O LORD, I have taken refuge;
let me never be put to shame;
deliver me in your
righteousness.
[2] Turn your ear to me,
come quickly to my rescue;
be my rock of refuge,[s]
a strong fortress to save me.
[3] Since you are my rock and my
fortress,[t]
for the sake of your name[u] lead
and guide me.
[4] Free me from the trap that is set
for me,
for you are my refuge.[v]
[5] Into your hands I commit my
spirit;[w]
redeem me, O LORD, the God of
truth.

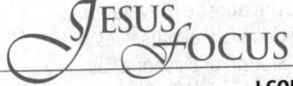

[6] I hate those who cling to worthless
idols;
I trust in the LORD.[x]
[7] I will be glad and rejoice in your
love,
for you saw my affliction[y]
and knew the anguish[z] of my
soul.
[8] You have not handed me over[a] to
the enemy
but have set my feet in a
spacious place.

[9] Be merciful to me, O LORD, for I am
in distress;
my eyes grow weak with sorrow,[b]
my soul and my body with grief.
[10] My life is consumed by anguish
and my years by groaning;[c]
my strength fails because of my
affliction,[b]
and my bones grow weak.[d]
[11] Because of all my enemies,
I am the utter contempt of my
neighbors;[e]
I am a dread to my friends—
those who see me on the street
flee from me.
[12] I am forgotten by them as though I
were dead;[f]
I have become like broken
pottery.
[13] For I hear the slander of many;
there is terror on every side;[g]
they conspire against me
and plot to take my life.[h]

[14] But I trust[i] in you, O LORD;
I say, "You are my God."
[15] My times[j] are in your hands;
deliver me from my enemies
and from those who pursue me.
[16] Let your face shine[k] on your
servant;
save me in your unfailing love.
[17] Let me not be put to shame,[l]
O LORD,

31:2 [s] Ps 18:2
31:3 [t] Ps 18:2 [u] Ps 23:3
31:4 [v] Ps 25:15
31:5 [w] Lk 23:46; Ac 7:59
31:6 [x] Jnh 2:8
31:7 [y] Ps 90:14 [z] Ps 10:14; Jn 10:27
31:8 [a] Dt 32:30
31:9 [b] Ps 6:7
31:10 [c] Ps 13:2 [d] Ps 38:3; 39:11
31:11 [e] Job 19:13; Ps 38:11; 64:8; Isa 53:4
31:12 [f] Ps 88:4
31:13 [g] Jer 20:3,10; La 2:22 [h] Mt 27:1
31:14 [i] Ps 140:6
31:15 [j] Job 24:1; Ps 143:9
31:16 [k] Nu 6:25; Ps 4:6
31:17 [l] Ps 25:2-3

[a] 9 Or *there if I am silenced* [b] 10 Or *guilt*

JESUS FOCUS

I COMMIT MY SPIRIT

Jesus' final words from the cross before he breathed his last (Luke 23:46) originally appeared in Psalm 31:5: "Father, into your hands I commit my spirit." To commit your spirit into God's hands entails relinquishing control of your life to him, trusting God with every bit of yourself and with your eternal destiny. This is the ultimate expression of our acceptance of God's will for our lives. Jesus was God the Son born as a human being. As a true human being Jesus endured every kind of temptation and every kind of suffering a person can experience (Hebrews 2:18; 4:15), especially in those final, dying moments, and he could do nothing other than commit his life to the Father. He died in our place for our sin—an act preordained by the Father himself—as a humble, ordinary man. His suffering, pain and death were all very real. He recognized, just as we must, that his "times" were secure in the hands of his loving and faithful Father (Psalm 31:15).

for I have cried out to you;
31:17 but let the wicked be put to shame
[m]Ps 115:17 and lie silent[m] in the grave.[a]
31:18 [18] Let their lying lips[n] be silenced,
[n]Ps 120:2 for with pride and contempt
[o]Ps 94:4 they speak arrogantly[o] against
the righteous.

31:19 [19] How great is your goodness,[p]
[p]Ro 11:22 which you have stored up for
[q]Isa 64:4 those who fear you,
which you bestow in the sight of
men[q]
on those who take refuge in you.
31:20 [20] In the shelter of your presence you
[r]Ps 27:5 hide[r] them
[s]Job 5:21 from the intrigues of men;[s]
in your dwelling you keep them safe
from accusing tongues.

[21] Praise be to the LORD,
31:21 for he showed his wonderful
[t]Ps 17:7 love[t] to me
[u]1Sa 23:7 when I was in a besieged city.[u]
31:22 [22] In my alarm[v] I said,
[v]Ps 116:11 "I am cut off from your sight!"
[w]La 3:54 Yet you heard my cry[w] for mercy
when I called to you for help.

31:23 [23] Love the LORD, all his saints![x]
[x]Ps 34:9 The LORD preserves the faithful,[y]
[y]Ps 145:20 but the proud he pays back[z] in
[z]Ps 94:2 full.
31:24 [24] Be strong and take heart,[a]
[a]Ps 27:14 all you who hope in the LORD.

PSALM 32

Of David. A *maskil.*[b]

[1] Blessed is he
whose transgressions are
forgiven,
32:1 whose sins are covered.[b]
[b]Ps 85:2 [2] Blessed is the man
whose sin the LORD does not
32:2 count against him[c]
[c]Ro 4:7-8*; 2Co 5:19 and in whose spirit is no deceit.[d]
[d]Jn 1:47

[3] When I kept silent,
32:3 my bones wasted away[e]
[e]Ps 31:10 through my groaning all day long.
32:4 [4] For day and night
[f]Job 33:7 your hand was heavy[f] upon me;
my strength was sapped
as in the heat of summer. *Selah*
[5] Then I acknowledged my sin to you
and did not cover up my iniquity.
I said, "I will confess[g] 32:5
my transgressions[h] to the [g]Pr 28:13
LORD"— [h]Ps 103:12
and you forgave [i]Lev 26:40
the guilt of my sin.[i] *Selah*

[6] Therefore let everyone who is godly
pray to you
while you may be found;[j] 32:6
surely when the mighty waters rise, [j]Ps 69:13; Isa 55:6
they will not reach him.[k] [k]Isa 43:2
[7] You are my hiding place;
you will protect me from trouble[l] 32:7
and surround me with songs of [l]Ps 9:9
deliverance.[m] *Selah* [m]Ex 15:1
[8] I will instruct[n] you and teach you 32:8
in the way you should go; [n]Ps 25:8
I will counsel you and watch [o]Ps 33:18
over[o] you.
[9] Do not be like the horse or the
mule,
which have no understanding
but must be controlled by bit and 32:9
bridle[p] [p]Pr 26:3
or they will not come to you.
[10] Many are the woes of the wicked,[q] 32:10
but the LORD's unfailing love [q]Ro 2:9
surrounds the man who trusts[r] [r]Pr 16:20
in him.

[11] Rejoice in the LORD[s] and be glad, 32:11
you righteous; [s]Ps 64:10
sing, all you who are upright in
heart!

[a] *17* Hebrew *Sheol* [b] Title: Probably a literary or musical term

JESUS AND YOU

PREAPPROVED CREDIT

Paul referred to Psalm 32:1–2 to declare that our status with God—forgiven and credited with righteousness—is a free gift from God himself (Romans 4:6–8). Because Jesus died in our place, God makes, so to speak, a deposit to our "righteousness account," a deposit we did not earn and could not have provided on our own. He at the same time makes a withdrawal from our sin account and declares us forgiven. We benefit both ways! God both credits us with righteousness by his grace and cancels our debt of sin (Romans 4:3,5). What he asks of us is simply that we believe what he says. Theologians call this truth (that we are credited with Jesus' righteousness) the doctrine of *imputation*, but we could also refer to it as the doctrine of God's preapproved credit.

DISCOVERY 132

IN OUR PLACE

The Bible uses a variety of words to describe the cause of our broken relationship with God. In Psalm 32 David used the terms *transgression*, *sin* and *iniquity*. The words mean essentially the same thing, but each has nuances that the others do not.

Transgression refers to rebellion against God's right to be in control. As Creator and Lord of the universe, he has determined absolute standards for right and wrong. When we go against those standards, when we step outside the guidelines God has set up, we are transgressing.

The word *sin* means, literally, missing the target, like an arrow that veers off to one side or the other. God's goal or mark for us is nothing short of perfection. When we fail to hit the bull's-eye of that target, we deviate from the straight course that God has in mind for our lives. The Bible calls this deflection *sin*.

Similarly, *iniquity* is straying from a straight path. God's path is marked by truth, but the effects of sin are all around us and within us, and there are many distractions that can cause us to become sidetracked or to follow dead-end tangents.

David's focus in Psalm 32 is not on sin; his exuberant theme is that God does not hold our sin against us. At any time we can admit to him that we have sinned and get back on the right path. A person who is right with God, who is traveling with him according to the "way" he has laid out, is "blessed" or very fortunate. Forgiveness is God's gracious work on our behalf. Through no merit of our own, God has made a way through the redeeming work of his precious Son to set us free from the grip of sin and secure for us our eternal home.

In the New Testament the apostle Paul cited verses from Psalm 32 to explain how God will "credit righteousness" to anyone who believes "in him who raised Jesus our Lord from the dead" (Romans 4:22–25). The theological word for this truth is *imputation*. It teaches that when Jesus died on the cross, he received what *we* deserved—the necessary and just punishment for sin. When we accept him, we in turn acquire what *he* deserved—a perfect relationship with God that will last through all eternity.

To catch a glimpse of the full impact of this truth, imagine yourself in heaven, in your glorified, sinless state. Did you know that from God's perspective you are just as pure and holy now as you will be then? You have been given the righteousness of Jesus Christ as an incomparable gift—through no merit or effort of your own. As Paul stated in 2 Corinthians 5:21, "God made him [Jesus] who had no sin to be sin for us, so that in him we might become the righteousness of God."

Self-Discovery: *Reflect for a moment on the incalculable price Jesus paid for your sins. Have you ever voluntarily taken someone else's punishment? Or has someone taken yours? What kinds of feelings have these experiences aroused in you?*

GO TO DISCOVERY 133 ON PAGE 709

PSALM 33

[1] Sing joyfully to the LORD, you righteous;
it is fitting[t] for the upright[u] to praise him.

33:1 [t] Ps 147:1 [u] Ps 32:11

[2] Praise the LORD with the harp;
make music to him on the ten-stringed lyre.[v]

33:2 [v] Ps 92:3

[3] Sing to him a new song;[w]
play skillfully, and shout for joy.

33:3 [w] Ps 96:1

[4] For the word of the LORD is right[x] and true;
he is faithful in all he does.

33:4 [x] Ps 19:8

[5] The LORD loves righteousness and justice;[y]
the earth is full of his unfailing love.[z]

33:5 [y] Ps 11:7 [z] Ps 119:64

[6] By the word[a] of the LORD were the heavens made,
their starry host by the breath of his mouth.

33:6 [a] Heb 11:3

[7] He gathers the waters of the sea into jars[a];
he puts the deep into storehouses.
[8] Let all the earth fear the LORD;
let all the people of the world revere him.[b]

33:8 [b] Ps 67:7; 96:9

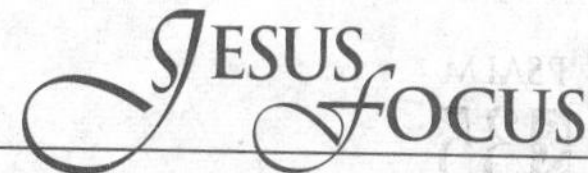

LORD OF SONG

Music has always been a vital expression of honor and thanks to God. We sing about him because he is the Lord of song. He gives us the songs (Psalm 42:8; John 35:10), and he is the one about whom we sing (Psalm 95:2; 101:1; 145:7). Psalm 33, like many other psalms, was intended to be sung with heartfelt passion and joy. Phrases such as "sing joyfully" and "shout for joy" remind God's people that true worship entails celebration. At the end of the meal we refer to as the Last Supper, Jesus and the disciples joined together in a song, most probably a psalm (Matthew 26:30). This tradition has been carried forward to this day at the close of Jewish Passover celebrations. The apostle Paul encouraged God's people to "speak to one another with psalms, hymns and spiritual songs" (Ephesians 5:19; see also Colossians 3:16). What a gloriously appropriate way to express the joy of our salvation and to thank God for the wonderful gift of Jesus!

[9] For he spoke, and it came to be;
he commanded,[c] and it stood firm.

33:9 [c] Ge 1:3; Ps 148:5

[10] The LORD foils the plans of the nations;[d]
he thwarts the purposes of the peoples.

33:10 [d] Isa 8:10

[11] But the plans of the LORD stand firm forever,
the purposes[e] of his heart through all generations.

33:11 [e] Job 23:13

[12] Blessed is the nation whose God is the LORD,[f]
the people he chose[g] for his inheritance.

33:12 [f] Ps 144:15 [g] Ex 19:5; Dt 7:6

[13] From heaven the LORD looks down
and sees all mankind;[h]

33:13 [h] Job 28:24; Ps 11:4

[14] from his dwelling place[i] he watches
all who live on earth—

33:14 [i] 1Ki 8:39

[15] he who forms[j] the hearts of all,
who considers everything they do.[k]

33:15 [j] Job 10:8 [k] Jer 32:19

[16] No king is saved by the size of his army;[l]
no warrior escapes by his great strength.

33:16 [l] Ps 44:6

[17] A horse[m] is a vain hope for deliverance;
despite all its great strength it cannot save.

33:17 [m] Ps 20:7; Pr 21:31

[18] But the eyes[n] of the LORD are on those who fear him,
on those whose hope is in his unfailing love,[o]

33:18 [n] Job 36:7; Ps 34:15 [o] Ps 147:11

[19] to deliver them from death
and keep them alive in famine.[p]

33:19 [p] Job 5:20

[20] We wait[q] in hope for the LORD;
he is our help and our shield.

33:20 [q] Ps 130:6

[21] In him our hearts rejoice,[r]
for we trust in his holy name.

33:21 [r] Zec 10:7; Jn 16:22

[22] May your unfailing love rest upon us, O LORD,
even as we put our hope in you.

PSALM 34[b]

Of David. When he pretended to be insane before Abimelech, who drove him away, and he left.

[1] I will extol the LORD at all times;[s]
his praise will always be on my lips.

34:1 [s] Ps 71:6; Eph 5:20

[a] 7 Or *sea as into a heap* [b] This psalm is an acrostic poem, the verses of which begin with the successive letters of the Hebrew alphabet.

2 My soul will boast[t] in the LORD;
let the afflicted hear and rejoice.[u]
3 Glorify the LORD with me;
let us exalt[v] his name together.

4 I sought the LORD,[w] and he
answered me;
he delivered me from all my fears.
5 Those who look to him are radiant;[x]
their faces are never covered
with shame.[y]
6 This poor man called, and the
LORD heard him;
he saved him out of all his
troubles.
7 The angel of the LORD[z] encamps
around those who fear him,
and he delivers them.

8 Taste and see that the LORD is good;[a]
blessed is the man who takes
refuge[b] in him.
9 Fear the LORD, you his saints,
for those who fear him lack
nothing.[c]
10 The lions may grow weak and
hungry,
but those who seek the LORD
lack no good thing.[d]

11 Come, my children, listen to me;
I will teach you[e] the fear of the
LORD.
12 Whoever of you loves life[f]
and desires to see many good
days,
13 keep your tongue from evil
and your lips from speaking
lies.[g]
14 Turn from evil and do good;[h]
seek peace[i] and pursue it.

15 The eyes of the LORD[j] are on the
righteous[k]
and his ears are attentive to
their cry;
16 the face of the LORD is against[l]
those who do evil,[m]
to cut off the memory[n] of them
from the earth.

17 The righteous cry out, and the
LORD hears[o] them;
he delivers them from all their
troubles.
18 The LORD is close[p] to the
brokenhearted[q]
and saves those who are crushed
in spirit.

19 A righteous man may have many
troubles,[r]
but the LORD delivers him from
them all;[s]
20 he protects all his bones,
not one of them will be broken.[t]

21 Evil will slay the wicked;[u]
the foes of the righteous will be
condemned.
22 The LORD redeems[v] his servants;
no one will be condemned who
takes refuge in him.

34:2 [t] Jer 9:24; 1Co 1:31 [u] Ps 119:74
34:3 [v] Lk 1:46
34:4 [w] Mt 7:7
34:5 [x] Ps 36:9 [y] Ps 25:3
34:7 [z] 2Ki 6:17; Da 6:22
34:8 [a] 1Pe 2:3 [b] Ps 2:12
34:9 [c] Ps 23:1
34:10 [d] Ps 84:11
34:11 [e] Ps 32:8
34:12 [f] 1Pe 3:10
34:13 [g] 1Pe 2:22
34:14 [h] Ps 37:27 [i] Heb 12:14
34:15 [j] Ps 33:18 [k] Job 36:7
34:16 [l] Lev 17:10; Jer 44:11 [m] 1Pe 3:10-12* [n] Pr 10:7
34:17 [o] Ps 145:19
34:18 [p] Ps 145:18 [q] Isa 57:15
34:19 [r] ver 17 [s] ver 4,6; Pr 24:16
34:20 [t] Jn 19:36*
34:21 [u] Ps 94:23
34:22 [v] 1Ki 1:29; Ps 71:23

NO BONES BROKEN

The apostle John quoted Psalm 34:20 as a prophecy that none of Jesus' bones would be broken at the time of his death (John 19:36). In fact, the Roman soldiers did not break Jesus' legs as he hung on the cross, although history reveals that breaking the legs of a crucified criminal was common practice. John even informs us that when the soldiers came to break his legs, our Lord was already dead (John 19:32–33). Instead, the soldiers pierced his side with a spear (John 19:34). Jesus fulfills the prophecies from the psalms, just as he does all other prophecies in the Old Testament. The psalms depict his sacrifice as well as his coronation, his suffering as well as his glory.

PSALM 35

Of David.

1 Contend, O LORD, with those who
contend with me;
fight[w] against those who fight
against me.
2 Take up shield and buckler;
arise[x] and come to my aid.
3 Brandish spear and javelin[a]
against those who pursue me.
Say to my soul,
"I am your salvation."

4 May those who seek my life
be disgraced[y] and put to shame;
may those who plot my ruin
be turned back in dismay.
5 May they be like chaff[z] before the
wind,
with the angel of the LORD
driving them away;

35:1 [w] Ps 43:1
35:2 [x] Ps 62:2
35:4 [y] Ps 70:2
35:5 [z] Job 21:18; Ps 1:4; Isa 29:5

[a] 3 Or *and block the way*

Hated Without Reason

David was forced to deal with numerous enemies, and he often wrote about these struggles in his psalms. King Saul was one of his avowed adversaries, despite the fact that David had been a trustworthy servant in the palace. David had served both as musician and warrior for the king, but Saul despised him because God had chosen David as Saul's successor. Later on during David's reign David's own son Absalom attempted to overthrow him (2 Samuel 15). And many people seemed to resent David for no obvious reason (Psalm 35:4–8,11–15).

In truth, this apparently random hatred was motivated by selfishness. David didn't do precisely what *they* wanted when *they* wanted him to. In the New Testament, on the night when Judas turned Jesus over to the authorities, Jesus recited some of David's words from verse 19: "But now they have seen these miracles, and yet they have hated both me and my Father. But this is to fulfill what is written in their Law: 'They hated me without reason' " (John 15:24–25).

Jesus too had many enemies, despite the fact that he was doing exactly what God wanted him to do. The religious leaders and teachers of the law aspired to positions of power and desired the highest level of respect from the common people. They envisioned an independent nation of Israel with themselves in the leadership role. They had some very strong opinions about precisely what God's promised Messiah would be like; in their mind he would appear as a formidable political figure—exactly what they themselves wanted to be.

The teachings and demeanor of Jesus were in direct contrast to everything these religious leaders represented and anticipated; he was a constant thorn in their side, and they determined early on that their best recourse would be to rid themselves of this nettling influence, to remove this itinerant rabble-rouser from the path of their ambitions (Matthew 12:25–37; 26:14–16).

Jesus knew, however, that his primary enemy, Satan, was the force behind all the hatred. The Lord even inflamed the religious leaders by informing them that they belonged to their father, the devil, "[who] was a murderer from the beginning, not holding to the truth, for there is no truth in him" (John 8:44). Satan himself challenged Jesus, boldly suggesting that he would grant Jesus control over the entire earth if only Jesus would honor him instead of the Father. Jesus reminded his adversary, in no uncertain terms, that only God deserves our devotion (Matthew 4:9–10). When the religious leaders and teachers turned against Jesus, they were, along with Satan, pitting themselves against God himself (John 8:47). Because God is in control of everything, even his enemies are obligated in the final analysis to conform to his plan (Psalm 103:19).

Because the world has always opposed God's people (John 15:18–25) and Satan desires to distract us from following Jesus, we should not be surprised when people seem to hate us for no apparent reason. Rather than giving in to discouragement, we can remember that Jesus experienced the same resistance—and that we will one day enjoy the reward for our faithfulness, sharing in the blessings of Jesus Christ if we stand firm to the end (Hebrews 3:15).

Self-Discovery: *Have you ever experienced being hated for no apparent reason? How did you deal with the situation? How does the example of Jesus encourage you?*

GO TO DISCOVERY 134 ON PAGE 712

[6] may their path be dark and
slippery,
with the angel of the LORD
pursuing them.
[7] Since they hid their net for me
without cause
and without cause dug a pit for
me,
[8] may ruin overtake them by
35:8 a 1Th 5:3 b Ps 9:15
surprise—[a]
may the net they hid entangle
them,
may they fall into the pit,[b] to
their ruin.
35:9 c Lk 1:47 d Isa 61:10
[9] Then my soul will rejoice[c] in the
LORD
and delight in his salvation.[d]
[10] My whole being will exclaim,
35:10 e Ex 15:11 f Ps 18:17 g Ps 37:14
"Who is like you,[e] O LORD?
You rescue the poor from those too
strong[f] for them,
the poor and needy[g] from those
who rob them."
35:11 h Ps 27:12
[11] Ruthless witnesses[h] come forward;
they question me on things I
know nothing about.
35:12 i Jn 10:32
[12] They repay me evil for good[i]
and leave my soul forlorn.
[13] Yet when they were ill, I put on
sackcloth
35:13 j Job 30:25; Ps 69:10
and humbled myself with fasting.[j]
When my prayers returned to me
unanswered,
[14] I went about mourning
as though for my friend or
brother.
I bowed my head in grief
as though weeping for my
mother.
[15] But when I stumbled, they
gathered in glee;
attackers gathered against me
when I was unaware.
35:15 k Job 30:1,8
They slandered[k] me without
ceasing.
[16] Like the ungodly they maliciously
mocked*a*;
35:16 l Job 16:9; La 2:16
they gnashed their teeth[l] at me.
[17] O Lord, how long[m] will you look on?
35:17 m Hab 1:13 n Ps 22:20
Rescue my life from their ravages,
my precious life[n] from these lions.
[18] I will give you thanks in the great
35:18 o Ps 22:25 p Ps 22:22
assembly;[o]
among throngs of people I will
praise you.[p]
[19] Let not those gloat over me
who are my enemies without
cause;
let not those who hate me without
35:19 q Ps 38:19; 69:4; Jn 15:25* r Ps 13:4; Pr 6:13
reason[q]
maliciously wink the eye.[r]
[20] They do not speak peaceably,
but devise false accusations
against those who live quietly in
the land.
35:21 s Ps 22:13 t Ps 40:15
[21] They gape[s] at me and say, "Aha!
Aha![t]
With our own eyes we have seen
it."
35:22 u Ex 3:7 v Ps 10:1; 28:1
[22] O LORD, you have seen[u] this; be not
silent.
Do not be far[v] from me, O Lord.
35:23 w Ps 44:23
[23] Awake,[w] and rise to my defense!
Contend for me, my God and
Lord.
[24] Vindicate me in your righteousness,
O LORD my God;
do not let them gloat over me.
[25] Do not let them think, "Aha, just
what we wanted!"
35:25 x La 2:16
or say, "We have swallowed him
up."[x]
35:26 y Ps 40:14; 109:29 z Ps 38:16
[26] May all who gloat over my distress
be put to shame[y] and confusion;
may all who exalt themselves over
me[z]
be clothed with shame and
disgrace.
35:27 a Ps 9:4 b Ps 32:11 c Ps 40:16; 147:11
[27] May those who delight in my
vindication[a]
shout for joy[b] and gladness;
may they always say, "The LORD be
exalted,
who delights[c] in the well-being
of his servant."
35:28 d Ps 51:14
[28] My tongue will speak of your
righteousness[d]
and of your praises all day long.

PSALM 36

For the director of music. Of David the servant of the LORD.

[1] An oracle is within my heart
concerning the sinfulness of the
wicked:*b*
36:1 e Ro 3:18*
There is no fear of God
before his eyes.[e]

a 16 Septuagint; Hebrew may mean *ungodly circle of mockers.* *b 1* Or *heart: / Sin proceeds from the wicked.*

[2] For in his own eyes he flatters
himself
too much to detect or hate his
sin.

36:3 [f] Ps 10:7 [g] Ps 94:8 [h] Jer 4:22

[3] The words of his mouth[f] are
wicked and deceitful;
he has ceased to be wise[g] and to
do good.[h]

36:4 [i] Pr 4:16; Mic 2:1 [j] Isa 65:2 [k] Ps 52:3; Ro 12:9

[4] Even on his bed he plots evil;[i]
he commits himself to a sinful
course[j]
and does not reject what is
wrong.[k]

[5] Your love, O LORD, reaches to the
heavens,
your faithfulness to the skies.
[6] Your righteousness is like the
mighty mountains,
your justice like the great deep.[l]
O LORD, you preserve both man
and beast.

36:6 [l] Job 11:8; Ps 77:19; Ro 11:33

[7] How priceless is your unfailing
love!
Both high and low among men
find[a] refuge in the shadow of
your wings.[m]

36:7 [m] Ru 2:12; Ps 17:8

[8] They feast on the abundance of
your house;[n]
you give them drink from your
river[o] of delights.

36:8 [n] Ps 65:4 [o] Job 20:17; Rev 22:1

[9] For with you is the fountain of life;[p]
in your light[q] we see light.

36:9 [p] Jer 2:13 [q] 1Pe 2:9

[10] Continue your love to those who
know you,
your righteousness to the
upright in heart.
[11] May the foot of the proud not
come against me,
nor the hand of the wicked drive
me away.
[12] See how the evildoers lie fallen—
thrown down, not able to rise![r]

36:12 [r] Ps 140:10

PSALM 37[b]

Of David.

[1] Do not fret because of evil men
or be envious[s] of those who do
wrong;[t]

37:1 [s] Pr 23:17-18 [t] Ps 73:3

[2] for like the grass they will soon
wither,
like green plants they will soon
die away.[u]

37:2 [u] Ps 90:6

[3] Trust in the LORD and do good;
dwell in the land[v] and enjoy safe
pasture.[w]

37:3 [v] Dt 30:20 [w] Isa 40:11; Jn 10:9

[4] Delight[x] yourself in the LORD
and he will give you the desires
of your heart.

37:4 [x] Isa 58:14

[5] Commit your way to the LORD;
trust in him[y] and he will do
this:

37:5 [y] Ps 4:5; Ps 55:22; Pr 16:3; 1Pe 5:7

[6] He will make your righteousness[z]
shine like the dawn,[a]
the justice of your cause like the
noonday sun.

37:6 [z] Mic 7:9 [a] Job 11:17

[7] Be still[b] before the LORD and wait
patiently[c] for him;
do not fret when men succeed in
their ways,
when they carry out their
wicked schemes.

37:7 [b] Ps 62:5; La 3:26 [c] Ps 40:1

[8] Refrain from anger[d] and turn from
wrath;
do not fret—it leads only to evil.

37:8 [d] Eph 4:31; Col 3:8

[9] For evil men will be cut off,
but those who hope in the LORD
will inherit the land.[e]

37:9 [e] Isa 57:13; 60:21

[a] 7 Or *love, O God! / Men find;* or *love! / Both heavenly beings and men / find* [b] This psalm is an acrostic poem, the stanzas of which begin with the successive letters of the Hebrew alphabet.

HEART DESIRES

Many of us wonder from time to time whether living in a relationship with God is really worthwhile. The psalmist assures us that if we place our trust in God, live our lives according to his will and take delight in getting to know our Creator, "he will give [us] the desires of [our] heart" (Psalm 37:4). Real faith focuses on the God who has made the promises. When we trust *him*, everything he has promised is ours.

Peter, the impetuous and outspoken disciple, reminded Jesus that he and the others had left everything to follow him and then in essence challenged Jesus, "So what's in it for us?" Jesus' answer was that no matter what we leave behind, living with him is infinitely better. He will bless us in the here and now, but he also gives us his promise that we will be with him forever (Matthew 19:27–29). We can't lose when we accept and live according to the promises of God. They are forever because he is forever; they are trustworthy because he is trustworthy (1 Corinthians 1:8–9).

Meekness: Power Under Control

Early in Israel's history the Lord promised his people a particular area of land, a place they would be able to call home, a haven of peace and prosperity. Hundreds of years later Jesus quoted Psalm 37:11 as part of his Sermon on the Mount. Jesus surprised his listeners by stating that the meek, not the powerful, are blessed and will inherit the entire earth (Matthew 5:5). Jesus was saying that the person who has discovered the secret of meekness has uncovered a priceless treasure. This lifestyle of seeming insignificance will be rewarded by God.

Later in his ministry Jesus used the same word, this time translated in the English as *gentle*, to describe himself: "Come to me, all you who are weary and burdened, and I will give you rest . . . for I am gentle and humble in heart, and you will find rest for your souls" (Matthew 11:28–29).

We often assume that a meek person is spineless and incompetent. Yet surely we would not use these adjectives to describe Jesus! Our Lord had all the infinite resources of God at his disposal—he had authority to calm the storm, heal the sick, raise the dead and drive out demons. True meekness may be defined as power under control, as the ability to be tender *because of* great strength. We cannot become meek simply by consciously willing ourselves to be gentle or working to become virtuous. There are, however, certain steps that will move us along the path toward that objective.

The first step is reverence for God. David challenged each of God's people to "delight [ourselves] in the LORD" (Psalm 37:4). Keeping in mind who God is and seeking him above our own often egocentric desires will help us to develop an attitude of respect. The second step is obedience. Verse 3 reminds us to "trust in the LORD and do good." When we reject our own sinful inclinations in favor of doing God's bidding, we will learn to be meek. The third step toward a life of meekness is the practice of patient endurance, no matter what our circumstances: "Be still before the LORD and wait patiently for him" (verse 7).

We will encounter many obstacles as we seek to live a life of meekness. Arrogance is the opposite of meekness; it comes to expression when we place ourselves at the center of things, thereby robbing God of the honor he alone deserves. Arrogance leads to the desire to dominate others—but God commands us to do exactly the opposite. As we learn to become sensitive to the needs and interests of other people, we will stop analyzing their faults. It is far too easy to develop the habit of seeing only what is wrong in a situation and never affirming the good. We literally become "joy robbers," squelching the spirit of trust and contentment that should reflect our relationship with God, and, by extension, with others.

The attitude of arrogance also encourages us to consider our weaknesses as diseases we can cure if we will only work hard enough. Instead, we need to accept that our weaknesses, the chinks in our armor, offer unique openings through which God can penetrate our spirits, reveal his goodness and remind us to imitate the gentle spirit of Jesus in all of our relationships.

Self-Discovery: *What are some ways you might cultivate meekness in your life? What can you learn from the life and example of Jesus that could help you develop the powerful yet tender virtue of gentleness?*

GO TO DISCOVERY 135 ON PAGE 716

10 A little while, and the wicked will
be no more;[f]
though you look for them, they
will not be found.
11 But the meek will inherit the land[g]
and enjoy great peace.

12 The wicked plot against the
righteous
and gnash their teeth[h] at them;
13 but the Lord laughs at the wicked,
for he knows their day is coming.[i]

14 The wicked draw the sword
and bend the bow[j]
to bring down the poor and needy,[k]
to slay those whose ways are
upright.
15 But their swords will pierce their
own hearts,[l]
and their bows will be broken.

16 Better the little that the righteous
have
than the wealth[m] of many
wicked;
17 for the power of the wicked will be
broken,[n]
but the LORD upholds the
righteous.

18 The days of the blameless are
known to the LORD,[o]
and their inheritance will
endure forever.
19 In times of disaster they will not
wither;
in days of famine they will enjoy
plenty.

20 But the wicked will perish:
The LORD's enemies will be like
the beauty of the fields,
they will vanish—vanish like
smoke.[p]

21 The wicked borrow and do not
repay,
but the righteous give
generously;[q]
22 those the LORD blesses will inherit
the land,
but those he curses[r] will be cut
off.

23 If the LORD delights[s] in a man's way,
he makes his steps firm;[t]
24 though he stumble, he will not
fall,[u]
for the LORD upholds[v] him with
his hand.

37:10 [f] Job 7:10; 24:24
37:11 [g] Mt 5:5
37:12 [h] Ps 35:16
37:13 [i] 1Sa 26:10; Ps 2:4
37:14 [j] Ps 11:2 [k] Ps 35:10
37:15 [l] Ps 9:16
37:16 [m] Pr 15:16
37:17 [n] Job 38:15; Ps 10:15
37:18 [o] Ps 1:6
37:20 [p] Ps 102:3
37:21 [q] Ps 112:5
37:22 [r] Job 5:3; Pr 3:33
37:23 [s] Ps 147:11 [t] 1Sa 2:9
37:24 [u] Pr 24:16 [v] Ps 145:14; 147:6

25 I was young and now I am old,
yet I have never seen the
righteous forsaken[w]
or their children begging bread.
26 They are always generous and lend
freely;
their children will be blessed.[x]

27 Turn from evil and do good;[y]
then you will dwell in the land
forever.
28 For the LORD loves the just
and will not forsake his faithful
ones.

They will be protected forever,
but the offspring of the wicked
will be cut off;[z]
29 the righteous will inherit the land[a]
and dwell in it forever.
30 The mouth of the righteous man
utters wisdom,
and his tongue speaks what is
just.
31 The law of his God is in his heart;[b]
his feet do not slip.[c]

32 The wicked lie in wait[d] for the
righteous,
seeking their very lives;
33 but the LORD will not leave them in
their power
or let them be condemned when
brought to trial.[e]

34 Wait for the LORD[f]
and keep his way.
He will exalt you to inherit the
land;
when the wicked are cut off, you
will see[g] it.

35 I have seen a wicked and ruthless
man
flourishing[h] like a green tree in
its native soil,
36 but he soon passed away and was
no more;
though I looked for him, he
could not be found.[i]

37 Consider the blameless, observe
the upright;
there is a future[*a*] for the man of
peace.[j]
38 But all sinners will be destroyed;
the future[*b*] of the wicked will be
cut off.[k]

37:25 [w] Heb 13:5
37:26 [x] Ps 147:13
37:27 [y] Ps 34:14
37:28 [z] Ps 21:10; Isa 14:20
37:29 [a] ver 9; Pr 2:21
37:31 [b] Dt 6:6; Ps 40:8; Isa 51:7 [c] ver 23
37:32 [d] Ps 10:8
37:33 [e] Ps 109:31; 2Pe 2:9
37:34 [f] Ps 27:14 [g] Ps 52:6
37:35 [h] Job 5:3
37:36 [i] Job 20:5
37:37 [j] Isa 57:1-2
37:38 [k] Ps 1:4

[*a*] *37* Or *there will be posterity* [*b*] *38* Or *posterity*

37:39 [l] Ps 3:8 [m] Ps 9:9

39 The salvation[l] of the righteous
comes from the LORD;
he is their stronghold in time of
trouble.[m]

37:40 [n] 1Ch 5:20 [o] Isa 31:5

40 The LORD helps[n] them and
delivers[o] them;
he delivers them from the
wicked and saves them,
because they take refuge in him.

PSALM 38

A psalm of David. A petition.

38:1 [p] Ps 6:1

1 O LORD, do not rebuke me in your
anger
or discipline me in your wrath.[p]

38:2 [q] Job 6:4; Ps 32:4

2 For your arrows[q] have pierced me,
and your hand has come down
upon me.

38:3 [r] Ps 6:2; Isa 1:6

3 Because of your wrath there is no
health in my body;
my bones[r] have no soundness
because of my sin.

38:4 [s] Ezr 9:6

4 My guilt has overwhelmed me
like a burden too heavy to bear.[s]

38:5 [t] Ps 69:5

5 My wounds fester and are
loathsome
because of my sinful folly.[t]

38:6 [u] Job 30:28; Ps 35:14; 42:9

6 I am bowed down and brought
very low;
all day long I go about
mourning.[u]

38:7 [v] Ps 102:3

7 My back is filled with searing pain;[v]
there is no health in my body.

38:8 [w] Ps 22:1

8 I am feeble and utterly crushed;
I groan[w] in anguish of heart.

38:9 [x] Job 3:24; Ps 6:6; 10:17

9 All my longings lie open before
you, O Lord;
my sighing[x] is not hidden from
you.

38:10 [y] Ps 31:10 [z] Ps 6:7

10 My heart pounds, my strength
fails[y] me;
even the light has gone from my
eyes.[z]

38:11 [a] Ps 31:11

11 My friends and companions avoid
me because of my wounds;[a]
my neighbors stay far away.

38:12 [b] Ps 140:5 [c] Ps 35:4; 54:3 [d] Ps 35:20

12 Those who seek my life set their
traps,[b]
those who would harm me talk
of my ruin;[c]
all day long they plot deception.[d]

13 I am like a deaf man, who cannot
hear,
like a mute, who cannot open
his mouth;

14 I have become like a man who does
not hear,
whose mouth can offer no reply.

38:15 [e] Ps 39:7 [f] Ps 17:6

15 I wait[e] for you, O LORD;
you will answer,[f] O Lord my God.

38:16 [g] Ps 35:26 [h] Ps 13:4

16 For I said, "Do not let them gloat[g]
or exalt themselves over me
when my foot slips."[h]

17 For I am about to fall,
and my pain is ever with me.

38:18 [i] Ps 32:5

18 I confess my iniquity;[i]
I am troubled by my sin.

38:19 [j] Ps 18:17 [k] Ps 35:19

19 Many are those who are my
vigorous enemies;[j]
those who hate me without
reason[k] are numerous.

38:20 [l] Ps 35:12; 1Jn 3:12

20 Those who repay my good with evil[l]
slander me when I pursue what
is good.

38:21 [m] Ps 35:22

21 O LORD, do not forsake me;
be not far[m] from me, O my God.

38:22 [n] Ps 40:13 [o] Ps 27:1

22 Come quickly to help me,[n]
O Lord my Savior.[o]

PSALM 39

For the director of music. For Jeduthun.
A psalm of David.

39:1 [p] 1Ki 2:4 [q] Job 2:10; Jas 3:2

1 I said, "I will watch my ways[p]
and keep my tongue from sin;[q]
I will put a muzzle on my mouth
as long as the wicked are in my
presence."

39:2 [r] Ps 38:13

2 But when I was silent[r] and still,
not even saying anything good,
my anguish increased.

3 My heart grew hot within me,
and as I meditated, the fire
burned;
then I spoke with my tongue:

39:4 [s] Ps 90:12 [t] Ps 103:14

4 "Show me, O LORD, my life's end
and the number of my days;[s]
let me know how fleeting is my
life.[t]

39:5 [u] Ps 89:45 [v] Ps 62:9

5 You have made my days[u] a mere
handbreadth;
the span of my years is as
nothing before you.
Each man's life is but a breath.[v]
Selah

39:6 [w] 1Pe 1:24

6 Man is a mere phantom[w] as he
goes to and fro:

39:6 [x]Ps 127:2 [y]Lk 12:20

He bustles about, but only in
vain;[x]
he heaps up wealth, not
knowing who will get it.[y]

39:7 [z]Ps 38:15

7 "But now, Lord, what do I look for?
My hope is in you.[z]

39:8 [a]Ps 51:9 [b]Ps 44:13

8 Save me[a] from all my
transgressions;[b]
do not make me the scorn of
fools.

39:9 [c]Job 2:10

9 I was silent; I would not open my
mouth,[c]
for you are the one who has
done this.
10 Remove your scourge from me;

39:10 [d]Job 9:34; Ps 32:4

I am overcome by the blow of
your hand.[d]

39:11 [e]2Pe 2:16 [f]Job 13:28

11 You rebuke[e] and discipline men for
their sin;
you consume their wealth like a
moth[f]—
each man is but a breath. *Selah*

12 "Hear my prayer, O LORD,
listen to my cry for help;
be not deaf to my weeping.

39:12 [g]1Pe 2:11 [h]Heb 11:13

For I dwell with you as an alien,[g]
a stranger,[h] as all my fathers were.

39:13 [i]Job 10:21; 14:10

13 Look away from me, that I may
rejoice again
before I depart and am no more."[i]

PSALM 40

For the director of music. Of David. A psalm.

40:1 [j]Ps 27:14 [k]Ps 34:15

1 I waited patiently[j] for the LORD;
he turned to me and heard my
cry.[k]

40:2 [l]Ps 69:14 [m]Ps 27:5

2 He lifted me out of the slimy pit,
out of the mud and mire;[l]
he set my feet on a rock[m]
and gave me a firm place to
stand.

40:3 [n]Ps 33:3

3 He put a new song[n] in my mouth,
a hymn of praise to our God.
Many will see and fear
and put their trust in the LORD.

40:4 [o]Ps 34:8 [p]Ps 84:12

4 Blessed is the man[o]
who makes the LORD his trust,[p]
who does not look to the proud,
to those who turn aside to false
gods.[a]

40:5 [q]Ps 136:4 [r]Ps 139:18; Isa 55:8

5 Many, O LORD my God,
are the wonders[q] you have done.
The things you planned for us
no one can recount[r] to you;
were I to speak and tell of them,
they would be too many to
declare.

40:6 [s]1Sa 15:22; Am 5:22 [t]Isa 1:11

6 Sacrifice and offering you did not
desire,[s]
but my ears you have pierced[b,c];
burnt offerings[t] and sin offerings
you did not require.
7 Then I said, "Here I am, I have
come—
it is written about me in the
scroll.[d]

40:8 [u]Jn 4:34 [v]Ps 37:31

8 I desire to do your will,[u] O my God;
your law is within my heart."[v]

40:9 [w]Ps 22:25 [x]Jos 22:22; Ps 119:13

9 I proclaim righteousness in the
great assembly;[w]
I do not seal my lips,
as you know,[x] O LORD.
10 I do not hide your righteousness in
my heart;

40:10 [y]Ps 89:1 [z]Ac 20:20

I speak of your faithfulness[y] and
salvation.
I do not conceal your love and your
truth
from the great assembly.[z]

40:11 [a]Pr 20:28 [b]Ps 43:3

11 Do not withhold your mercy from
me, O LORD;
may your love[a] and your truth[b]
always protect me.

40:12 [c]Ps 116:3 [d]Ps 38:4 [e]Ps 69:4 [f]Ps 73:26

12 For troubles[c] without number
surround me;
my sins have overtaken me, and
I cannot see.[d]
They are more than the hairs of my
head,[e]
and my heart fails[f] within me.

40:13 [g]Ps 70:1

13 Be pleased, O LORD, to save me;
O LORD, come quickly to help
me.[g]

40:14 [h]Ps 35:4

14 May all who seek to take my life
be put to shame and confusion;
may all who desire my ruin[h]
be turned back in disgrace.
15 May those who say to me, "Aha!
Aha!"
be appalled at their own shame.

40:16 [i]Ps 35:27

16 But may all who seek you
rejoice and be glad in you;
may those who love your salvation
always say,
"The LORD be exalted!"[i]

[a] 4 Or *to falsehood* [b] 6 Hebrew; Septuagint *but a body you have prepared for me* (see also Symmachus and Theodotion) [c] 6 Or *opened* [d] 7 Or *come / with the scroll written for me*

DISCOVERY 135

The Secret of a Joyful Life

David knew God intimately and trusted him completely for deliverance. In Psalm 40 David revealed a confident faith based on his assurance that salvation comes only from God. Despite the incredible stresses he was facing, David relinquished his frustrations to the Lord and rested in his strength. During the time of David, if a servant loved his master, he would make a lifelong covenant to remain in his service (Exodus 21:6). To signify this promise, the master would pierce the ears of the servant with a sharp awl. David used this practice as a metaphor for his love and devotion to God. He loved the Lord and had entered into a lifelong covenant of obedience to him (Psalm 40:6). He understood that the secret to a joyful life does not lie in empty sacrifice but in a lifestyle completely yielded to God's will: "I desire to do your will" (verse 8). Although David was literally running for his life, he made it a practice to talk with God about his frustrations and found delight in obedience.

Jesus is the perfect example of this kind of approach to life. Although he knew the high price he would have to pay, he loved God so much that he "became obedient to death—even death on a cross!" (Philippians 2:8). Like the bond slave in David's day, Jesus determined to be completely obedient no matter what the cost. In Hebrews 10:7 God the Son affirmed his purpose by addressing the Father with nearly identical words to those written by David: "I have come to do your will." Because he loved his Father with a perfect love, Jesus submitted to the Father's will and offered his life as the ultimate sacrifice (see also Luke 22:42; John 4:34). While he endured unspeakable personal anguish during his life on earth, and particularly during his final days, he was at the same time filled with overflowing joy because he knew he was doing what God had asked of him. The writer to the Hebrews invites us to "fix our eyes on Jesus, the author and perfecter of our faith, who for the joy set before him endured the cross, scorning its shame, and sat down at the right hand of the throne of God" (Hebrews 12:2).

A joy-filled life does not depend on outward circumstances, economic security or robust health. Joy ensues when we understand who God is and live our lives as he wants us to, with the attitude expressed by Jesus in the garden of Gethsemane: "Not my will, but yours be done" (Luke 22:42). When we obey God we enjoy the same fellowship with him that Jesus knew. When the Holy Spirit reveals an area in our life that is out-of-step with God's Word, we need to pay close attention.

Sin causes us to look elsewhere for joy (a futile endeavor), but compliance with God's will allows us to accept his best. The real difference between the lives of Christians who are growing and those who are not is *obedience.*

Self-Discovery: *Identify certain situations in your life where you are especially vulnerable to the desire to have things your own way. Ask God for the strength to give up control and to follow the lead of Jesus, who models for you a life of blessed submission to the perfect will of the Father.*

GO TO DISCOVERY 136 ON PAGE 718

40:17 [j]Ps 70:5

[17] Yet I am poor and needy;
may the Lord think of me.
You are my help and my deliverer;
O my God, do not delay.[j]

PSALM 41

For the director of music. A psalm of David.

41:1 [k]Ps 82:3-4; Pr 14:21

[1] Blessed is he who has regard for
the weak;[k]
the LORD delivers him in times of
trouble.

41:2 [l]Ps 37:22 [m]Ps 27:12

[2] The LORD will protect him and
preserve his life;
he will bless him in the land[l]
and not surrender him to the
desire of his foes.[m]
[3] The LORD will sustain him on his
sickbed
and restore him from his bed of
illness.

41:4 [n]Ps 6:2 [o]Ps 51:4

[4] I said, "O LORD, have mercy[n] on me;
heal me, for I have sinned[o]
against you."
[5] My enemies say of me in malice,
"When will he die and his name

41:5 [p]Ps 38:12

perish?[p]"

41:6 [q]Ps 12:2 [r]Pr 26:24

[6] Whenever one comes to see me,
he speaks falsely,[q] while his
heart gathers slander;[r]
then he goes out and spreads it
abroad.

41:7 [s]Ps 56:5; 71:10-11

[7] All my enemies whisper together[s]
against me;
they imagine the worst for me,
saying,
[8] "A vile disease has beset him;
he will never get up from the
place where he lies."

41:9 [t]2Sa 15:12; Ps 55:12 [u]Job 19:19; Ps 55:20; Mt 26:23; Jn 13:18*

[9] Even my close friend,[t] whom I
trusted,
he who shared my bread,
has lifted up his heel against me.[u]
[10] But you, O LORD, have mercy on
me;

41:10 [v]Ps 3:3

raise me up,[v] that I may repay
them.

41:11 [w]Ps 147:11 [x]Ps 25:2

[11] I know that you are pleased with
me,[w]
for my enemy does not triumph
over me.[x]

41:12 [y]Ps 37:17 [z]Job 36:7

[12] In my integrity you uphold me[y]
and set me in your presence
forever.[z]

41:13 [a]Ps 72:18 [b]Ps 89:52; 106:48

[13] Praise be to the LORD, the God of
Israel,[a]
from everlasting to everlasting.
Amen and Amen.[b]

BOOK II

Psalms 42–72

PSALM 42[a]

For the director of music. A *maskil*[b] of the
Sons of Korah.

42:1 [c]Ps 119:131

[1] As the deer pants for streams of
water,
so my soul pants[c] for you,
O God.

42:2 [d]Ps 63:1 [e]Jer 10:10 [f]Ps 43:4

[2] My soul thirsts[d] for God, for the
living God.[e]
When can I go[f] and meet with
God?

42:3 [g]Ps 80:5 [h]Ps 79:10

[3] My tears[g] have been my food
day and night,
while men say to me all day long,
"Where is your God?"[h]
[4] These things I remember
as I pour out my soul:
how I used to go with the
multitude,

42:4 [i]Isa 30:29 [j]Ps 100:4

leading the procession to the
house of God,[i]
with shouts of joy and
thanksgiving[j]
among the festive throng.

42:5 [k]Ps 38:6; 77:3 [l]La 3:24 [m]Ps 44:3

[5] Why are you downcast,[k] O my
soul?
Why so disturbed within me?
Put your hope in God,[l]
for I will yet praise him,
my Savior[m] and [6]my God.
My[c] soul is downcast within me;
therefore I will remember you
from the land of the Jordan,
the heights of Hermon—from
Mount Mizar.
[7] Deep calls to deep
in the roar of your waterfalls;

42:7 [n]Ps 88:7; Jnh 2:3

all your waves and breakers
have swept over me.[n]

[a] In many Hebrew manuscripts Psalms 42 and 43 constitute one psalm. [b] Title: Probably a literary or musical term [c] *5,6* A few Hebrew manuscripts, Septuagint and Syriac; most Hebrew manuscripts *praise him for his saving help.* / [6] *O my God, my*

DISCOVERY 136

Letting Go of Hatred

Hatred toward another person comes to expression in an inner voice that fumes, "I don't want you in my life anymore!" Harboring hatred toward a husband or wife can erect a dividing wall of hostility between spouses, either emotionally or through the ultimate separation of divorce. Hatred can alienate children from parents, brothers from sisters, believers from other Christians with whom they cannot see eye-to-eye.

Psalm 41 is written from the perspective of a person who finds himself hated by someone he once trusted. David knew the pain of hearing former companions express a wish for his death (verses 2,5), of having a former friend make up lies about him (verse 6), of knowing that his reputation had been tarnished to the point that most people were willing to assume the worst about him (verses 7–8), of having even his best friend turn against him (verse 9).

Even when everyone else seemed to be letting him down, however, David knew that God had not in the past, wasn't doing so in the present and would not in the future. God was on his side (verse 10), was pleased with him (verse 11) and would always be there for him (verses 12–13).

God himself knows the awful sting of being hated. It might seem incredible that someone could actively despise the God of love, but if hating someone equates to wanting that person out of one's life, there are indeed many people who *hate* God. Jesus Christ, the very Son of God himself, the Word become flesh, knew the searing pain of betrayal like no one else: One of his closest associates hated him so much that he turned him over to the authorities. The name *Judas* has become synonymous with betrayal because of his heinous deed.

And Judas didn't merely turn Jesus in—he led the authorities to the Lord as Jesus was praying. Judas *kissed* his "dear friend" on the cheek as a signal that he was the one the soldiers were looking for. Ironically, Judas sold Jesus for a paltry amount—only 30 pieces of silver—which he ended up throwing at the feet of his fellow schemers in a moment of remorse (Matthew 27:1–5). Jesus had ample reason to retaliate, but when Judas and the authorities arrived to arrest him, he looked Judas squarely in the eye and invited, "Friend, do what you came for" (Matthew 26:50). Jesus appeared almost to have given Judas permission to betray him, knowing that what God had in mind was infinitely more significant than anything he could have done to get back at Judas (Matthew 26:54).

God's Word asks us to follow the example of Jesus: "Love your enemies and pray for those who persecute you" (Matthew 5:44). Rather than thinking of ways to get back at people who have hurt us, a commitment to having the mind of Christ Jesus means seeing the difficult people in our lives in a new way. Instead of planning choice words that search and destroy or plotting revenge, we can pray for them and learn to love them. God can do amazing things through us when he teaches us a new attitude. The rewards are peace with God, peace with others and peace of mind.

Self-Discovery: *Think of moments in your life when you might have been so disappointed by God that you wondered whether he had abandoned you. In what ways did God remind you of his love and his faithfulness?*

GO TO DISCOVERY 137 ON PAGE 721

42:8 [o]Ps 57:3 [p]Job 35:10 [q]Ps 63:6; 149:5

8 By day the LORD directs his love,[o]
at night[p] his song[q] is with me—
a prayer to the God of my life.

9 I say to God my Rock,
"Why have you forgotten me?
Why must I go about mourning,[r]
oppressed by the enemy?"

42:9 [r]Ps 38:6

10 My bones suffer mortal agony
as my foes taunt me,
saying to me all day long,
"Where is your God?"

11 Why are you downcast, O my soul?
Why so disturbed within me?
Put your hope in God,
for I will yet praise him,
my Savior and my God.[s]

42:11 [s]Ps 43:5

PSALM 43[a]

1 Vindicate me, O God,
and plead my cause[t] against an
ungodly nation;
rescue me from deceitful and
wicked men.[u]

43:1 [t]1Sa 24:15; Ps 26:1; 35:1 [u]Ps 5:6

2 You are God my stronghold.
Why have you rejected[v] me?
Why must I go about mourning,
oppressed by the enemy?[w]

43:2 [v]Ps 44:9 [w]Ps 42:9

3 Send forth your light[x] and your
truth,
let them guide me;
let them bring me to your holy
mountain,[y]
to the place where you dwell.[z]

43:3 [x]Ps 36:9 [y]Ps 42:4 [z]Ps 84:1

4 Then will I go to the altar[a] of God,
to God, my joy and my delight.
I will praise you with the harp,[b]
O God, my God.

43:4 [a]Ps 26:6 [b]Ps 33:2

5 Why are you downcast, O my soul?
Why so disturbed within me?
Put your hope in God,
for I will yet praise him,
my Savior and my God.[c]

43:5 [c]Ps 42:6

PSALM 44

For the director of music. Of the Sons of Korah.
A *maskil.*[b]

1 We have heard with our ears,
O God;
our fathers have told us[d]
what you did in their days,
in days long ago.

44:1 [d]Ex 12:26; Ps 78:3

2 With your hand you drove out[e] the
nations
and planted[f] our fathers;
you crushed the peoples
and made our fathers flourish.[g]

44:2 [e]Ps 78:55 [f]Ex 15:17 [g]Ps 80:9

3 It was not by their sword[h] that they
won the land,
nor did their arm bring them
victory;
it was your right hand, your arm,[i]
and the light of your face, for
you loved[j] them.

44:3 [h]Dt 8:17; Jos 24:12 [i]Ps 77:15 [j]Dt 4:37; 7:7-8

4 You are my King[k] and my God,
who decrees[c] victories for Jacob.

44:4 [k]Ps 74:12

5 Through you we push back our
enemies;
through your name we trample[l]
our foes.

44:5 [l]Ps 108:13

6 I do not trust in my bow,[m]
my sword does not bring me
victory;

44:6 [m]Ps 33:16

7 but you give us victory[n] over our
enemies,
you put our adversaries to
shame.[o]

44:7 [n]Ps 136:24 [o]Ps 53:5

8 In God we make our boast[p] all day
long,
and we will praise your name
forever.[q] *Selah*

44:8 [p]Ps 34:2 [q]Ps 30:12

9 But now you have rejected[r] and
humbled us;
you no longer go out with our
armies.[s]

44:9 [r]Ps 74:1 [s]Ps 60:1,10

10 You made us retreat[t] before the
enemy,
and our adversaries have
plundered us.

44:10 [t]Lev 26:17; Jos 7:8; Ps 89:41

11 You gave us up to be devoured like
sheep[u]
and have scattered us among the
nations.[v]

44:11 [u]Ro 8:36 [v]Dt 4:27; 28:64; Ps 106:27

12 You sold your people for a
pittance,[w]
gaining nothing from their sale.

44:12 [w]Isa 52:3; Jer 15:13; 52:3; Jer 15:13

13 You have made us a reproach to
our neighbors,[x]
the scorn[y] and derision of those
around us.

44:13 [x]Ps 79:4; 80:6 [y]Dt 28:37

14 You have made us a byword among
the nations;
the peoples shake their heads[z]
at us.

44:14 [z]Ps 109:25; Jer 24:9

[a] In many Hebrew manuscripts Psalms 42 and 43 constitute one psalm. [b] Title: Probably a literary or musical term [c] 4 Septuagint, Aquila and Syriac; Hebrew *King, O God; / command*

15 My disgrace is before me all day
long,
and my face is covered with
shame
16 at the taunts of those who
reproach and revile[a] me,
because of the enemy, who is
bent on revenge.

44:16
[a] Ps 74:10

17 All this happened to us,
though we had not forgotten[b]
you
or been false to your covenant.

44:17
[b] Ps 78:7,57; Da 9:13

18 Our hearts had not turned[c] back;
our feet had not strayed from
your path.

44:18
[c] Job 23:11

19 But you crushed[d] us and made us a
haunt for jackals
and covered us over with deep
darkness.[e]

44:19
[d] Ps 51:8
[e] Job 3:5

20 If we had forgotten[f] the name of
our God
or spread out our hands to a
foreign god,[g]
21 would not God have discovered it,
since he knows the secrets of the
heart?[h]

44:20
[f] Ps 78:11
[g] Dt 6:14; Ps 81:9

44:21
[h] Ps 139:1-2; Jer 17:10

22 Yet for your sake we face death all
day long;
we are considered as sheep to be
slaughtered.[i]

44:22
[i] Isa 53:7; Ro 8:36*

23 Awake,[j] O Lord! Why do you sleep?[k]
Rouse yourself! Do not reject us
forever.[l]

44:23
[j] Ps 7:6
[k] Ps 78:65
[l] Ps 77:7

24 Why do you hide your face[m]
and forget our misery and
oppression?[n]

44:24
[m] Job 13:24
[n] Ps 42:9

25 We are brought down to the dust;[o]
our bodies cling to the ground.

44:25
[o] Ps 119:25

26 Rise up[p] and help us;
redeem[q] us because of your
unfailing love.

44:26
[p] Ps 35:2
[q] Ps 25:22

PSALM 45

For the director of music. To ˻the tune of˼ "Lilies." Of the Sons of Korah. A *maskil.*[a] A wedding song.

1 My heart is stirred by a noble theme
as I recite my verses for the king;
my tongue is the pen of a skillful
writer.

2 You are the most excellent of men
and your lips have been
anointed with grace,[r]
since God has blessed you forever.

45:2
[r] Lk 4:22

3 Gird your sword[s] upon your side,
O mighty one;[t]
clothe yourself with splendor
and majesty.

45:3
[s] Heb 4:12; Rev 1:16
[t] Isa 9:6

4 In your majesty ride forth
victoriously[u]
in behalf of truth, humility and
righteousness;
let your right hand display
awesome deeds.

45:4
[u] Rev 6:2

5 Let your sharp arrows pierce the
hearts of the king's enemies;
let the nations fall beneath your
feet.
6 Your throne, O God, will last for
ever and ever;[v]
a scepter of justice will be the
scepter of your kingdom.

45:6
[v] Ps 93:2; 98:9

7 You love righteousness[w] and hate
wickedness;
therefore God, your God, has set
you above your companions
by anointing[x] you with the oil of
joy.[y]

45:7
[w] Ps 33:5
[x] Isa 61:1
[y] Ps 21:6; Heb 1:8-9*

8 All your robes are fragrant[z] with
myrrh and aloes and cassia;
from palaces adorned with ivory
the music of the strings makes
you glad.

45:8
[z] SS 1:3

9 Daughters of kings[a] are among
your honored women;
at your right hand[b] is the royal
bride in gold of Ophir.

45:9
[a] SS 6:8
[b] 1Ki 2:19

10 Listen, O daughter, consider and
give ear:
Forget your people[c] and your
father's house.

45:10
[c] Dt 21:13

11 The king is enthralled by your
beauty;
honor[d] him, for he is your lord.[e]

45:11
[d] Ps 95:6
[e] Isa 54:5

12 The Daughter of Tyre will come
with a gift,[b][f]
men of wealth will seek your
favor.

45:12
[f] Ps 22:29; Isa 49:23

13 All glorious[g] is the princess within
˻her chamber˼;
her gown is interwoven with
gold.

45:13
[g] Isa 61:10

14 In embroidered garments she is led
to the king;[h]
her virgin companions follow
her
and are brought to you.

45:14
[h] SS 1:4

[a] Title: Probably a literary or musical term
[b] 12 Or *A Tyrian robe is among the gifts*

DISCOVERY 137

JESUS' HOLY BRIDE

A wedding day is usually filled with celebration and song. The day of a king's marriage is even more festive. Psalm 45 was written to commemorate just such an occasion. First we catch a glimpse of the king, and then we gaze on the lovely bride. After God's people had been taken into captivity and the nation dissolved as a separate entity, the people realized that this song also referred to God's promised Messiah, the final and ultimate King (verses 6–7).

The people pictured their king as a particular kind of person. First, the king of Israel would rank as the "most excellent of men," and God would bless his family line forever (verse 2). In the New Testament the promised Messiah was born as a human, died for our sin and rose from the dead, after which God the Father "exalted him to the highest place" (Philippians 2:7–9). Jesus is truly the "most excellent of men," and he is "[clothed with] splendor and majesty" (Psalm 45:3).

The king is also someone who works on behalf of "truth, humility and righteousness" (verse 4) for his people. Jesus fulfilled all three criteria: He is truth (John 14:6), he is the epitome of humility (Mark 10:45; Philippians 2:8) and he challenged people repeatedly to get their lives on track with God for the cause of righteousness (Matthew 5:6; 6:33).

Finally, the king of God's choosing would always defeat his enemies (Psalm 45:5), establish a throne that would last forever (verses 6–7), and reign in majesty and beauty (verses 8–9). This psalm ultimately points to Jesus, God's promised One—to Jesus, the ultimate King who will reign for all eternity (Hebrews 1:8–9).

There would be no wedding day without a bride for the groom. The king's bride as depicted in Psalm 45 was unusual because she came from a foreign country. She would have many children and be remembered through all the generations to come.

In the New Testament God's people are referred to collectively as Jesus' "bride" (Revelation 19:7; see also Ephesians 5:32). Though God's people were originally identified with the nation of Israel, it was never God's plan to exclude other nations. His desire was that Israel's national integrity would demonstrate that she belonged to the one true God so that other nations would also turn to him as their God and King (Isaiah 42:6; 49:6; 60:1–3; Romans 1:16).

Like the bride of Israel's king in the psalm, Jesus' bride has many children. The book of Romans likens God's chosen nation to a tree into which branches have been grafted. God's Good News is for anyone who will believe it and incorporate its truth into his or her life. Any such person is "grafted" into God's family tree (Romans 11:17–21).

Each of us individually has a share in Christ's church, his holy bride. Every member of the body of Christ, his church, has the opportunity to leave the legacy of a person who loved Jesus wholeheartedly and through whose witness others have been engrafted into his family. Will we be remembered that way by future generations? We are all acquainted with people who have turned their backs on God. It is God's desire that we freely share the gospel news so that more and more new brothers and sisters may be welcomed into the family circle.

***Self-Discovery:** Does your personal integrity demonstrate to others that you belong to Jesus and draw them to his side?*

GO TO DISCOVERY 138 ON PAGE 723

15 They are led in with joy and
gladness;
they enter the palace of the
king.

16 Your sons will take the place of
your fathers;
you will make them princes
throughout the land.

45:17 [i] Mal 1:11 [j] Ps 138:4
17 I will perpetuate your memory
through all generations;[i]
therefore the nations will praise
you[j] for ever and ever.

PSALM 46

For the director of music. Of the Sons of Korah. According to *alamoth*.[a] A song.

46:1 [k] Ps 9:9; 14:6 [l] Dt 4:7
1 God is our refuge[k] and strength,
an ever-present[l] help in trouble.

46:2 [m] Ps 23:4 [n] Ps 82:5 [o] Ps 18:7
2 Therefore we will not fear,[m] though
the earth give way[n]
and the mountains fall[o] into the
heart of the sea,

46:3 [p] Ps 93:3
3 though its waters roar[p] and foam
and the mountains quake with
their surging. *Selah*

46:4 [q] Ps 48:1,8; Isa 60:14
4 There is a river whose streams
make glad the city of God,[q]
the holy place where the Most
High dwells.

46:5 [r] Isa 12:6; Eze 43:7 [s] Ps 37:40
5 God is within her,[r] she will not fall;
God will help[s] her at break of
day.

46:6 [t] Ps 2:1 [u] Ps 68:32 [v] Mic 1:4
6 Nations[t] are in uproar, kingdoms[u]
fall;
he lifts his voice, the earth
melts.[v]

46:7 [w] 2Ch 13:12 [x] Ps 9:9
7 The LORD Almighty is with us;[w]
the God of Jacob is our fortress.[x]
Selah

46:8 [y] Ps 66:5 [z] Isa 61:4
8 Come and see the works of the
LORD,[y]
the desolations[z] he has brought
on the earth.

46:9 [a] Isa 2:4 [b] Ps 76:3 [c] Eze 39:9
9 He makes wars[a] cease to the ends
of the earth;
he breaks the bow[b] and shatters
the spear,
he burns the shields[b] with fire.[c]

46:10 [d] Ps 100:3 [e] Isa 2:11
10 "Be still, and know that I am
God;[d]
I will be exalted[e] among the
nations,
I will be exalted in the earth."

11 The LORD Almighty is with us;
the God of Jacob is our fortress.
Selah

PSALM 47

For the director of music. Of the Sons of Korah. A psalm.

47:1 [f] Ps 98:8; Isa 55:12 [g] Ps 106:47
1 Clap your hands,[f] all you nations;
shout to God with cries of joy.[g]

47:2 [h] Dt 7:21 [i] Mal 1:14
2 How awesome[h] is the LORD Most
High,
the great King[i] over all the earth!

47:3 [j] Ps 18:39,47
3 He subdued[j] nations under us,
peoples under our feet.

47:4 [k] 1Pe 1:4
4 He chose our inheritance[k] for us,
the pride of Jacob, whom he
loved. *Selah*

5 God has ascended amid shouts of
joy,

47:5 [l] Ps 68:33; 98:6
the LORD amid the sounding of
trumpets.[l]

47:6 [m] Ps 68:4; 89:18
6 Sing praises[m] to God, sing praises;
sing praises to our King, sing
praises.

47:7 [n] Zec 14:9 [o] Col 3:16
7 For God is the King of all the
earth;[n]
sing to him a psalm[c][o] of praise.

47:8 [p] 1Ch 16:31
8 God reigns[p] over the nations;
God is seated on his holy throne.

9 The nobles of the nations assemble
as the people of the God of
Abraham,

47:9 [q] Ps 72:11; 89:18 [r] Ps 97:9
for the kings[d] of the earth belong
to God;[q]
he is greatly exalted.[r]

PSALM 48

A song. A psalm of the Sons of Korah.

48:1 [s] Ps 96:4 [t] Ps 46:4 [u] Isa 2:2-3; Mic 4:1; Zec 8:3
1 Great is the LORD,[s] and most
worthy of praise,
in the city of our God,[t] his holy
mountain.[u]

48:2 [v] Ps 50:2; La 2:15 [w] Mt 5:35
2 It is beautiful[v] in its loftiness,
the joy of the whole earth.
Like the utmost heights of
Zaphon[e] is Mount Zion,
the[f] city of the Great King.[w]

[a] Title: Probably a musical term [b] 9 Or *chariots* [c] 7 Or *a maskil* (probably a literary or musical term) [d] 9 Or *shields* [e] 2 *Zaphon* can refer to a sacred mountain or the direction north. [f] 2 Or *earth, / Mount Zion, on the northern side / of the*

DISCOVERY 138

The City of God

Many cities in the Bible are remembered for the part they play in God's plan—whether in the past or in the future. The names Ur, Babylon, Bethlehem, Nazareth, Jerusalem and Corinth carry vivid images of people and events we associate with them. Psalm 46 is one of many psalms that refer to the "city of God." In the Old Testament "Zion," or Jerusalem, was known as God's chosen city, and while there is no specific mention of either name in the psalm, the author clearly intended to remind his audience that wherever God is present, there is abundant reason for unwavering confidence.

The psalmist wrote, "There is a river whose streams make glad the city of God" (verse 4). The city of Jerusalem *lacks* a physical river, but God's people can rest in the knowledge that he provides everything they need. God himself was to Jerusalem what a river was to other cities—and so much more! This city is the place "where the Most High dwells." And because God is in the city she will not fall; he will help Jerusalem even in, especially in, the most dangerous of times.

The city of Jerusalem demonstrates a magnificent truth about God: No one can violate, penetrate or defeat the "city" in which he has taken up residence. As long as her citizens continue to follow God's truth and walk with him, he remains in their midst. God protects the city's inhabitants to the degree that their enemies can only turn around and flee in terror. He leads his chosen ones and keeps them safe.

"One day Jesus said to his disciples, 'Let's go over to the other side of the lake.' So they got into a boat and set out. As they sailed, he fell asleep. A squall came down on the lake, so that the boat was being swamped, and they were in great danger. The disciples went and woke him, saying, 'Master, Master, we're going to drown.' He got up and rebuked the wind and the raging waters; the storm subsided and all was calm. 'Where is your faith?' he asked his disciples" (Luke 8:22–25). The disciples should have known that God was present and that he would provide a refuge from the storm. Even though the "waters roar and foam" (Psalm 46:3), there is no need to fear. God is an "ever-present help" (verse 3) and will always protect his people.

And so today, when we accept Jesus into our lives, God is present with us. Belief in Jesus is the only avenue to a right relationship with God (John 3:16; Acts 16:31; Romans 10:9). We can experience firsthand what it is to enjoy comfort, security, protection, guidance and blessing when we know Jesus as *Immanuel*, "God with us."

One day Jesus will recreate his city to be what he intended from the very beginning. He will live with his people forever—and they will bask in inconceivable joy and blessing for the rest of eternity (Revelation 21:2–4,9–27; see also 1 Corinthians 2:9).

Self-Discovery: *Picture God's provision for you as coming in the form of a river. How might this river provide not only your daily sustenance but pleasure and relaxation as well?*

GO TO DISCOVERY 139 ON PAGE 727

3 God is in her citadels;
48:3 he has shown himself to be her
x Ps 46:7 fortress.[x]

4 When the kings joined forces,
48:4 y 2Sa 10:1-19 when they advanced together,[y]
48:5 5 they saw ⌞her⌟ and were astounded;
z Ex 15:16 they fled in terror.[z]
6 Trembling seized them there,
pain like that of a woman in
labor.
7 You destroyed them like ships of
48:7 Tarshish
a Jer 18:17; shattered by an east wind.[a]
Eze 27:26
8 As we have heard,
so have we seen
in the city of the LORD Almighty,
in the city of our God:
48:8 God makes her secure forever.[b]
b Ps 87:5 *Selah*

9 Within your temple, O God,
we meditate on your unfailing
48:9 love.[c]
c Ps 26:3
48:10 10 Like your name,[d] O God,
d Dt 28:58; your praise reaches to the ends
Jos 7:9 of the earth;[e]
e Isa 41:10 your right hand is filled with
righteousness.
11 Mount Zion rejoices,
the villages of Judah are glad
48:11 because of your judgments.[f]
f Ps 97:8

12 Walk about Zion, go around her,
count her towers,
48:13 13 consider well her ramparts,
g ver 3; Ps 122:7 view her citadels,[g]
h Ps 78:6 that you may tell of them to the
next generation.[h]
14 For this God is our God for ever
and ever;
48:14 he will be our guide[i] even to the
i Ps 23:4 end.

PSALM 49

For the director of music. Of the Sons of Korah.
A psalm.

49:1 1 Hear this, all you peoples;[j]
j Ps 78:1 listen, all who live in this world,[k]
k Ps 33:8 2 both low and high,
rich and poor alike:
49:3 3 My mouth will speak words of
l Ps 37:30 wisdom;[l]
m Ps 119:130 the utterance from my heart will
give understanding.[m]
49:4 4 I will turn my ear to a proverb;[n]
n Ps 78:2 with the harp I will expound my
riddle:[o] 49:4 o Nu 12:8

5 Why should I fear[p] when evil days 49:5
come, p Ps 23:4
when wicked deceivers surround
me—
6 those who trust in their wealth[q] 49:6 q Job 31:24
and boast of their great riches?
7 No man can redeem the life of
another
or give to God a ransom for
him—
8 the ransom for a life is costly,
no payment is ever enough—[r] 49:8 r Mt 16:26
9 that he should live on[s] forever 49:9
and not see decay. s Ps 22:29; 89:48
10 For all can see that wise men die;[t] 49:10 t Ecc 2:16
the foolish and the senseless u Ecc 2:18,21
alike perish
and leave their wealth to
others.[u]
11 Their tombs will remain their
houses[a] forever,
their dwellings for endless
generations, 49:11
though they had[b] named[v] lands v Ge 4:17;
after themselves. Dt 3:14

12 But man, despite his riches, does
not endure;
he is[c] like the beasts that perish.

[a] 11 Septuagint and Syriac; Hebrew *In their thoughts their houses will remain* [b] 11 Or / *for they have* [c] 12 Hebrew; Septuagint and Syriac read verse 12 the same as verse 20.

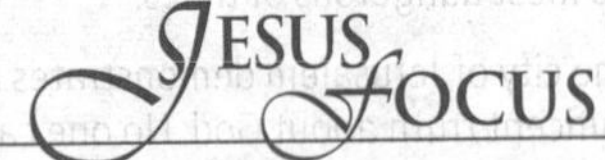

REDEEMED!

As powerful a force as money is in this life, it can guarantee nothing for the life to come. A hefty bankroll cannot ward off death, and Psalm 49 reminds us that no amount of money can ransom anyone from death. But there is hope for the person who chooses God as her security: "God will redeem my life from the grave; he will surely take me to himself" (verse 15). God promises that we will be brought back to life from death—and *that* is the hope of eternal life. Jesus came "to give his life as a ransom for many" (Matthew 20:28). Paul later expanded on this concept, stating in essence that there is only one God and one mediator between God and humankind, Jesus Christ, who gave his own life to purchase freely what money could never buy (1 Timothy 2:5–6).

49:13 [w]Lk 12:20

13 This is the fate of those who trust
in themselves,[w]
and of their followers, who
approve their sayings.
Selah

49:14 [x]Job 24:19; Ps 9:17 [y]Da 7:18; Mal 4:3; 1Co 6:2; Rev 2:26

14 Like sheep they are destined for
the grave,[a][x]
and death will feed on them.
The upright will rule[y] over them in
the morning;
their forms will decay in the
grave,[a]
far from their princely
mansions.

49:15 [z]Ps 56:13; Hos 13:14 [a]Ps 73:24

15 But God will redeem my life[b] from
the grave;[z]
he will surely take me to
himself.[a]
Selah

16 Do not be overawed when a man
grows rich,
when the splendor of his house
increases;

49:17 [b]Ps 17:14; 1Ti 6:7

17 for he will take nothing with him
when he dies,
his splendor will not descend
with him.[b]

49:18 [c]Dt 29:19; Lk 12:19

18 Though while he lived he counted
himself blessed—[c]
and men praise you when you
prosper—

49:19 [d]Ge 15:15 [e]Job 33:30

19 he will join the generation of his
fathers,[d]
who will never see the light[e]
⌊of life⌋.

49:20 [f]Ecc 3:19

20 A man who has riches without
understanding
is like the beasts that perish.[f]

PSALM 50

A psalm of Asaph.

50:1 [g]Jos 22:22 [h]Ps 113:3

1 The Mighty One, God, the LORD,[g]
speaks and summons the earth
from the rising of the sun to the
place where it sets.[h]

50:2 [i]Ps 48:2 [j]Dt 33:2; Ps 80:1

2 From Zion, perfect in beauty,[i]
God shines forth.[j]

50:3 [k]Ps 96:13 [l]Ps 97:3; Da 7:10

3 Our God comes[k] and will not be
silent;
a fire devours before him,[l]
and around him a tempest rages.

50:4 [m]Dt 4:26; Isa 1:2

4 He summons the heavens above,
and the earth,[m] that he may
judge his people:

50:5 [n]Ps 30:4 [o]Ex 24:7

5 "Gather to me my consecrated
ones,[n]
who made a covenant[o] with me
by sacrifice."

50:6 [p]Ps 89:5 [q]Ps 75:7

6 And the heavens proclaim[p] his
righteousness,
for God himself is judge.[q] *Selah*

50:7 [r]Ps 81:8 [s]Ex 20:2

7 "Hear, O my people, and I will speak,
O Israel, and I will testify[r]
against you:
I am God, your God.[s]

50:8 [t]Ps 40:6; Hos 6:6

8 I do not rebuke you for your
sacrifices
or your burnt offerings,[t] which
are ever before me.

50:9 [u]Ps 69:31

9 I have no need of a bull[u] from your
stall
or of goats from your pens,

50:10 [v]Ps 104:24

10 for every animal of the forest is
mine,
and the cattle on a thousand
hills.[v]
11 I know every bird in the mountains,
and the creatures of the field are
mine.

50:12 [w]Ex 19:5

12 If I were hungry I would not tell
you,
for the world[w] is mine, and all
that is in it.
13 Do I eat the flesh of bulls
or drink the blood of goats?

50:14 [x]Heb 13:15 [y]Dt 23:21

14 Sacrifice thank offerings[x] to God,
fulfill your vows[y] to the Most
High,

50:15 [z]Ps 81:7 [a]Ps 22:23

15 and call[z] upon me in the day of
trouble;
I will deliver you, and you will
honor[a] me."

16 But to the wicked, God says:

50:16 [b]Isa 29:13

"What right have you to recite my
laws
or take my covenant on your
lips?[b]

50:17 [c]Ne 9:26; Ro 2:21-22

17 You hate my instruction
and cast my words behind[c] you.

50:18 [d]Ro 1:32; 1Ti 5:22

18 When you see a thief, you join[d]
with him;
you throw in your lot with
adulterers.

50:19 [e]Ps 10:7; 52:2

19 You use your mouth for evil
and harness your tongue to
deceit.[e]

50:20 [f]Mt 10:21

20 You speak continually against your
brother[f]

[a] *14* Hebrew *Sheol;* also in verse 15 [b] *15* Or *soul*

and slander your own mother's
son.
21 These things you have done and I
kept silent;[g]
you thought I was altogether[a]
like you.
But I will rebuke you
and accuse[h] you to your face.

50:21 [g] Ecc 8:11; Isa 42:14 [h] Ps 90:8

22 "Consider this, you who forget
God,[i]
or I will tear you to pieces, with
none to rescue:[j]
23 He who sacrifices thank offerings
honors me,
and he prepares the way[k]
so that I may show him[b] the
salvation of God.[l]"

50:22 [i] Job 8:13; Ps 9:17 [j] Ps 7:2

50:23 [k] Ps 85:13 [l] Ps 91:16

PSALM 51

For the director of music. A psalm of David. When the prophet Nathan came to him after David had committed adultery with Bathsheba.

1 Have mercy on me, O God,
according to your unfailing love;
according to your great
compassion
blot out[m] my transgressions.[n]
2 Wash away[o] all my iniquity
and cleanse[p] me from my sin.
3 For I know my transgressions,
and my sin is always before me.[q]
4 Against you, you only, have I
sinned
and done what is evil in your
sight,[r]
so that you are proved right when
you speak
and justified when you judge.[s]
5 Surely I was sinful[t] at birth,
sinful from the time my mother
conceived me.
6 Surely you desire truth in the inner
parts[c];
you teach[d] me wisdom[u] in the
inmost place.[v]
7 Cleanse me with hyssop,[w] and I
will be clean;
wash me, and I will be whiter
than snow.[x]
8 Let me hear joy and gladness;[y]
let the bones you have crushed
rejoice.
9 Hide your face from my sins[z]
and blot out all my iniquity.
10 Create in me a pure heart,[a] O God,
and renew a steadfast spirit
within me.[b]
11 Do not cast me from your presence
or take your Holy Spirit[c] from
me.
12 Restore to me the joy of your
salvation[d]
and grant me a willing spirit, to
sustain me.
13 Then I will teach transgressors
your ways,[e]
and sinners will turn back to
you.[f]
14 Save me from bloodguilt,[g] O God,
the God who saves me,[h]
and my tongue will sing of your
righteousness.[i]
15 O Lord, open my lips,[j]
and my mouth will declare your
praise.
16 You do not delight in sacrifice,[k] or I
would bring it;
you do not take pleasure in
burnt offerings.
17 The sacrifices of God are[e] a broken
spirit;
a broken and contrite heart,[l]
O God, you will not despise.
18 In your good pleasure make Zion[m]
prosper;
build up the walls of Jerusalem.
19 Then there will be righteous
sacrifices,[n]
whole burnt offerings[o] to delight
you;
then bulls[p] will be offered on
your altar.

51:1 [m] Ac 3:19 [n] Isa 43:25; Col 2:14
51:2 [o] 1Jn 1:9 [p] Heb 9:14
51:3 [q] Isa 59:12
51:4 [r] Ge 20:6; Lk 15:21 [s] Ro 3:4*
51:5 [t] Job 14:4
51:6 [u] Pr 2:6 [v] Ps 15:2
51:7 [w] Lev 14:4; Heb 9:19 [x] Isa 1:18
51:8 [y] Isa 35:10
51:9 [z] Jer 16:17
51:10 [a] Ps 78:37; Ac 15:9 [b] Eze 18:31
51:11 [c] Eph 4:30
51:12 [d] Ps 13:5
51:13 [e] Ac 9:21-22 [f] Ps 22:27
51:14 [g] 2Sa 12:9 [h] Ps 25:5 [i] Ps 35:28
51:15 [j] Ps 9:14
51:16 [k] 1Sa 15:22; Ps 40:6
51:17 [l] Ps 34:18
51:18 [m] Ps 102:16; Isa 51:3
51:19 [n] Ps 4:5 [o] Ps 66:13 [p] Ps 66:15

PSALM 52

For the director of music. A *maskil*[f] of David. When Doeg the Edomite[q] had gone to Saul and told him: "David has gone to the house of Ahimelech."

1 Why do you boast of evil, you
mighty man?
Why do you boast[r] all day long,

52:1 [q] 1Sa 22:9 [r] Ps 94:4

[a] 21 Or *thought the 'I AM' was* [b] 23 Or *and to him who considers his way / I will show* [c] 6 The meaning of the Hebrew for this phrase is uncertain. [d] 6 Or *you desired . . .; / you taught* [e] 17 Or *My sacrifice, O God, is* [f] Title: Probably a literary or musical term

DISCOVERY 139

THE GOD OF SECOND CHANCES

David lived a life of devotion to God, but by no means did he live a perfect life. The greatest tragedy of his life was that he had an affair with a married woman and arranged to have her husband killed when she discovered that she was pregnant with David's baby. Psalm 51 allows us to listen in as David tells God, with all the emotion of a broken heart, about his sin. We also overhear David's solemn promise to turn back to his Creator and Father, the God of the second chance.

Sin is first and foremost a violation against God. To be sure, Bathsheba, Uriah and David's infant son were wronged by David's poor choices. But the relationship that suffered the greatest breach was the one between himself and God: "Against you, you only, have I sinned" (verse 4).

Sin has consequences—very serious ones. After David had turned away from God, he eventually experienced the full weight of what he'd done and felt crushed inside (verse 8). David knew that his relationship with the Father had been affected, and he had earlier seen God remove his presence from Saul after Saul had first turned his back on God (1 Samuel 16:1,14; 2 Samuel 7:15). When we sin we lose the sense of peace and joy that comes from right living. Some of the most miserable people in the world are God's people who are living with unconfessed sin. When we grieve God's Holy Spirit (Ephesians 4:30) we feel his sorrow, because he lives in us and produces his fruit in us (Galatians 5:22).

Our relationship with God, however, doesn't have to remain fractured. David found the path leading back to God, and the same path is there for us. When we admit to God that we have sinned against him and betrayed his trust, when we direct our steps back toward home, he forgives us and no longer holds our sin against us (2 Corinthians 5:17–19; 1 John 1:9). God looks for a truly "broken and contrite heart" that seeks a restored relationship (Psalm 51:1–2,17). He is the God of second chances. Not only did he forgive David, but he later used David to lead others back to himself (verse 13).

David, of course, lived long before the birth of the promised Messiah, sent by God to take upon himself the burden of sin for all who would believe (Isaiah 53:6; 2 Corinthians 5:16–21). While we certainly need to confess our sins daily and strive more and more to live a life modeled after that of our Savior, the reality is that our sins have *already* been forgiven through the blood of Jesus Christ; when God looks at us, he sees our hearts as pure and clean—as pristine as the newfallen snow (Isaiah 1:18).

John affirmed this truth in his Gospel, and John 3:16–17 are among the best-loved verses in all of Scripture: "For God so loved the world that he gave his one and only Son, that whoever believes in him shall not perish but have eternal life. For God did not send his Son into the world to condemn the world, but to save the world through him."

Self-Discovery: *Have you ever worried that your sins are unforgivable—too terrible to bring before God? If so, remember David's example. Reflect too on your righteous standing in God's sight based on the sacrifice of Jesus.*

GO TO DISCOVERY 140 ON PAGE 731

you who are a disgrace in the
eyes of God?
[2] Your tongue plots destruction;
52:2 [s] Ps 57:4 it is like a sharpened razor,[s]
[t] Ps 50:19 you who practice deceit.[t]
[3] You love evil rather than good,
52:3 [u] Jer 9:5 falsehood[u] rather than speaking
the truth. *Selah*
52:4 [v] Ps 120:2,3 [4] You love every harmful word,
O you deceitful tongue![v]
[5] Surely God will bring you down to
everlasting ruin:
52:5 [w] Isa 22:19 He will snatch you up and tear[w]
[x] Pr 2:22 you from your tent;
[y] Ps 27:13 he will uproot[x] you from the
land of the living.[y] *Selah*
52:6 [6] The righteous will see and fear;
[z] Job 22:19; Ps 37:34; 40:3 they will laugh[z] at him, saying,
[7] "Here now is the man
who did not make God his
52:7 [a] Ps 49:6 stronghold
but trusted in his great wealth[a]
and grew strong by destroying
others!"
52:8 [b] Jer 11:16
[c] Ps 13:5 [8] But I am like an olive tree[b]
flourishing in the house of God;
I trust[c] in God's unfailing love
52:9 for ever and ever.
[d] Ps 30:12 [9] I will praise you forever[d] for what
[e] Ps 54:6 you have done;
in your name I will hope, for
your name is good.[e]
I will praise you in the presence
of your saints.

PSALM 53

For the director of music. According to *mahalath.*[a] A *maskil*[b] of David.

53:1 [f] Ps 14:1-7; Ro 3:10 [g] Ps 10:4 [1] The fool[f] says in his heart,
"There is no God."[g]
They are corrupt, and their ways
are vile;
there is no one who does good.
53:2 [h] Ps 33:13 [2] God looks down from heaven[h]
[i] 2Ch 15:2 on the sons of men
to see if there are any who
understand,
any who seek God.[i]
[3] Everyone has turned away,
they have together become
corrupt;
53:3 there is no one who does good,
[j] Ro 3:10-12* not even one.[j]

[4] Will the evildoers never learn—
those who devour my people as
men eat bread
and who do not call on God?
[5] There they were, overwhelmed
with dread,
where there was nothing to 53:5
dread.[k] [k] Lev 26:17 [l] Eze 6:5
God scattered the bones[l] of those
who attacked you;
you put them to shame, for God
despised them.
[6] Oh, that salvation for Israel would
come out of Zion!
When God restores the fortunes
of his people,
let Jacob rejoice and Israel be
glad!

PSALM 54

For the director of music. With stringed instruments. A *maskil*[b] of David. When the Ziphites had gone to Saul and said, "Is not David hiding among us?"

[1] Save me, O God, by your name;[m] 54:1 [m] Ps 20:1
vindicate me by your might.[n] [n] 2Ch 20:6
[2] Hear my prayer, O God;[o] 54:2
listen to the words of my [o] Ps 5:1; 55:1
mouth.
[3] Strangers are attacking me;[p] 54:3 [p] Ps 86:14
ruthless men seek my life[q]— [q] Ps 40:14
men without regard for God.[r] [r] Ps 36:1
Selah
[4] Surely God is my help;[s] 54:4 [s] Ps 118:7
the Lord is the one who sustains [t] Ps 41:12
me.[t]
[5] Let evil recoil[u] on those who 54:5 [u] Ps 94:23
slander me; [v] Ps 89:49; 143:12
in your faithfulness[v] destroy
them.
[6] I will sacrifice a freewill offering[w] 54:6 [w] Ps 50:14
to you; [x] Ps 52:9
I will praise your name, O LORD,
for it is good.[x]
[7] For he has delivered me[y] from all 54:7 [y] Ps 34:6
my troubles, [z] Ps 59:10
and my eyes have looked in
triumph on my foes.[z]

[a] Title: Probably a musical term [b] Title: Probably a literary or musical term

PSALM 55

For the director of music. With stringed instruments. A *maskil*[a] of David.

[1] Listen to my prayer, O God,
do not ignore my plea;[a]
[2] hear me and answer me.[b]
My thoughts trouble me and I am
distraught[c]
[3] at the voice of the enemy,
at the stares of the wicked;
for they bring down suffering upon
me[d]
and revile me in their anger.[e]

[4] My heart is in anguish within me;
the terrors[f] of death assail me.
[5] Fear and trembling[g] have beset me;
horror has overwhelmed me.
[6] I said, "Oh, that I had the wings of a
dove!
I would fly away and be at rest—
[7] I would flee far away
and stay in the desert; *Selah*
[8] I would hurry to my place of shelter,
far from the tempest and
storm.[h]"

[9] Confuse the wicked, O Lord,
confound their speech,
for I see violence and strife[i] in
the city.
[10] Day and night they prowl about on
its walls;
malice and abuse are within it.
[11] Destructive forces[j] are at work in
the city;
threats and lies[k] never leave its
streets.

[12] If an enemy were insulting me,
I could endure it;
if a foe were raising himself against
me,
I could hide from him.
[13] But it is you, a man like myself,
my companion, my close friend,[l]
[14] with whom I once enjoyed sweet
fellowship
as we walked with the throng at
the house of God.[m]

[15] Let death take my enemies by
surprise;[n]
let them go down alive to the
grave,[b][o]
for evil finds lodging among
them.

[16] But I call to God,
and the LORD saves me.
[17] Evening,[p] morning[q] and noon
I cry out in distress,
and he hears my voice.
[18] He ransoms me unharmed
from the battle waged against
me,
even though many oppose me.
[19] God, who is enthroned forever,[r]
will hear[s] them and afflict
them— *Selah*
men who never change their ways
and have no fear of God.

[20] My companion attacks his friends;[t]
he violates his covenant.[u]
[21] His speech is smooth as butter,
yet war is in his heart;
his words are more soothing than
oil,[v]
yet they are drawn swords.[w]

[22] Cast your cares on the LORD
and he will sustain you;[x]
he will never let the righteous
fall.[y]
[23] But you, O God, will bring down
the wicked
into the pit[z] of corruption;
bloodthirsty and deceitful men[a]
will not live out half their days.[b]

But as for me, I trust in you.[c]

[a] Title: Probably a literary or musical term
[b] 15 Hebrew *Sheol*

55:1 [a] Ps 27:9; 61:1
55:2 [b] Ps 66:19 [c] Ps 77:3; Isa 38:14
55:3 [d] 2Sa 16:6-8; Ps 17:9 [e] Ps 71:11
55:4 [f] Ps 116:3
55:5 [g] Job 21:6; Ps 119:120
55:8 [h] Isa 4:6
55:9 [i] Jer 6:7
55:11 [j] Ps 5:9 [k] Ps 10:7
55:13 [l] 2Sa 15:12; Ps 41:9
55:14 [m] Ps 42:4
55:15 [n] Ps 64:7 [o] Nu 16:30,33
55:17 [p] Ps 141:2; Ac 3:1 [q] Ps 5:3
55:19 [r] Dt 33:27 [s] Ps 78:59
55:20 [t] Ps 7:4 [u] Ps 89:34
55:21 [v] Pr 5:3 [w] Ps 28:3; Ps 57:4; 59:7
55:22 [x] Ps 37:5; Mt 6:25-34; 1Pe 5:7 [y] Ps 37:24
55:23 [z] Ps 73:18 [a] Ps 5:6 [b] Job 15:32; Pr 10:27 [c] Ps 25:2

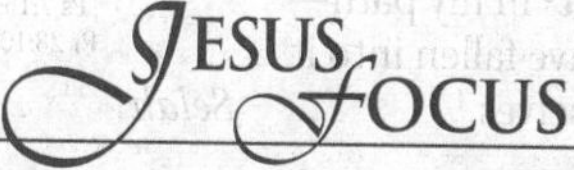

A FRIEND'S BETRAYAL

It's difficult enough to be assaulted by an enemy, but betrayal by a close friend is truly heartbreaking. David may have had his son Absalom in mind when he prayed in Psalm 55 for deliverance from his "companion" and "close friend" (verse 13). Because this psalm directs our attention to God's promised Messiah, however, we realize that David's words reach beyond his personal situation to point to Jesus' ultimate betrayer—Judas Iscariot. In the account in Matthew 26:50, when Judas arrived at Gethsemane with the men who would arrest Jesus, Jesus still addressed him as "friend." Judas responded by betraying Jesus with a kiss on the cheek—a sign of deep affection and friendship. Both David and Jesus knew the pain of being betrayed by close friends.

PSALM 56

For the director of music. To ⌊the tune of⌋ "A Dove on Distant Oaks." Of David. A *miktam*.[a] When the Philistines had seized him in Gath.

56:1 [1]Be merciful to me, O God, for men
d Ps 57:1-3 hotly pursue me;[d]
all day long they press their
attack.
56:2 [2]My slanderers pursue me all day
e Ps 57:3 long;[e]
f Ps 35:1 many are attacking me in their
pride.[f]

56:3 [3]When I am afraid,[g]
g Ps 55:4-5 I will trust in you.
[4]In God, whose word I praise,
in God I trust; I will not be
afraid.
56:4 What can mortal man do to
h Ps 118:6; Heb 13:6 me?[h]

56:5 [5]All day long they twist my
i Ps 41:7 words;[i]
they are always plotting to harm
me.
56:6 [6]They conspire,[j] they lurk,
j Ps 59:3 they watch my steps,
k Ps 71:10 eager to take my life.[k]
[7]On no account let them escape;
56:7 in your anger, O God, bring
l Ps 36:12; 55:23 down the nations.[l]
[8]Record my lament;
list my tears on your
56:8 scroll[b]—
m Mal 3:16 are they not in your record?[m]
56:9 [9]Then my enemies will turn back[n]
n Ps 9:3
o Ps 102:2 when I call for help.[o]
p Ro 8:31 By this I will know that God is
for me.[p]
[10]In God, whose word I praise,
in the LORD, whose word I
praise—
[11]in God I trust; I will not be
afraid.
What can man do to me?

56:12 [12]I am under vows[q] to you, O God;
q Ps 50:14 I will present my thank offerings
to you.
56:13 [13]For you have delivered me[c] from
r Ps 116:8
s Job 33:30 death[r]
and my feet from stumbling,
that I may walk before God
in the light of life.[d][s]

PSALM 57

For the director of music. ⌊To the tune of⌋ "Do Not Destroy." Of David. A *miktam*.[a] When he had fled from Saul into the cave.

[1]Have mercy on me, O God, have
mercy on me,
for in you my soul takes refuge.[t] 57:1
I will take refuge in the shadow of t Ps 2:12
your wings[u] u Ps 17:8
until the disaster has passed.[v] v Isa 26:20

[2]I cry out to God Most High,
to God, who fulfills ⌊his purpose⌋ 57:2
for me.[w] w Ps 138:8
[3]He sends from heaven and saves 57:3
me,[x] x Ps 18:9,16
rebuking those who hotly pursue y Ps 56:1
me;[y] *Selah* z Ps 40:11
God sends his love and his
faithfulness.[z]

[4]I am in the midst of lions;[a] 57:4
a Ps 35:17
I lie among ravenous beasts— b Ps 55:21; Pr 30:14
men whose teeth are spears and
arrows,
whose tongues are sharp
swords.[b]

[5]Be exalted, O God, above the
heavens;
let your glory be over all the 57:5
earth.[c] c Ps 108:5

[6]They spread a net for my feet— 57:6
I was bowed down[d] in distress. d Ps 145:14
They dug a pit[e] in my path— e Ps 35:7
but they have fallen into it f Ps 7:15; Pr 28:10
themselves.[f] *Selah*

[7]My heart is steadfast, O God, 57:7
my heart is steadfast;[g] g Ps 108:1
I will sing and make music.
[8]Awake, my soul! 57:8
Awake, harp and lyre![h] h Ps 16:9; 30:12; 150:3
I will awaken the dawn.

[9]I will praise you, O Lord, among
the nations;
I will sing of you among the
peoples.
[10]For great is your love, reaching to
the heavens;
your faithfulness reaches to the 57:10
skies.[i] i Ps 36:5; 103:11

[a] Title: Probably a literary or musical term
[b] 8 Or */ put my tears in your wineskin* [c] 13 Or *my soul* [d] 13 Or *the land of the living*

Jesus First

Psalm 57 declares that God is preeminent in everything: "Be exalted, O God, above the heavens; let your glory be over all the earth" (verse 11). Because God is supreme in everything, he is the only One to whom we can turn in all situations. When David was being pursued by men who wanted to kill him, he talked to God about his situation and pleaded with him for help: "Have mercy on me . . . for in you my soul takes refuge" (verse 1).

We might not encounter people who are trying to kill us, but we are surrounded by problems, responsibilities and enticements that could easily overwhelm us. People do on occasion say cruel things about us and to us. We are not immune to experiences of stress and danger. But God takes care of us: "Great is your love, reaching to the heavens; your faithfulness reaches to the skies" (verse 10).

All of creation points us to the glory of Jesus. The Bible teaches that he is first in all things. He is first in creation itself—God the Son created the entire cosmos and keeps the planets spinning (1 Corinthians 8:6; Hebrews 1:2); he is the "firstborn over all creation" (Colossians 1:15–17). Jesus is also God's "Word," and he was with God the Father in the beginning when everything was created (John 1:1–3). Jesus is the first in salvation; he conquered death—the penalty for turning away from God—by his resurrection (Romans 4:23–25; 1 Corinthians 15:26,54; 2 Timothy 2:10). Because he lives forever, we rest in the solid hope that we will enjoy eternity with him (1 Corinthians 15:20).

God the Son is first in the church; he is the "head of the body," the church; "the beginning and the firstborn" (Colossians 1:18). Because of this we as the church draw our strength and power from him (Ephesians 4:15–16). Jesus is the "chief cornerstone" of the church, having built it on the foundation of the prophets and apostles (Ephesians 2:20).

And one day Jesus will reign as our eternal King and everyone will admit that he is Lord (Philippians 2:10–11), because he is first in the kingdom that "has become the kingdom of our Lord and of his Christ" (Revelation 11:15). "Then the end will come, when he hands over the kingdom to God the Father after he has destroyed all dominion, authority and power. For he must reign until he has put all his enemies under his feet. The last enemy to be destroyed is death. When he has done this, then the Son himself will be made subject to him who put everything under him, so that God may be all in all" (1 Corinthians 15:24–26,28).

At that time the psalmist's prayers will be completely answered. God will be exalted above the heavens (Psalm 57:5), and his glory will be over all the earth (verse 11).

Although he is the Lord of lords and King of kings (Revelation 19:16), Jesus never forces himself into anyone's life. He wants a relationship with us based on love and commitment rather than on coercion. He waits to be invited (Revelation 3:20), and it is up to each of us to choose to walk with him (Romans 12:1–2).

***Self-Discovery:** In what ways have you allowed Jesus to be exalted to the number one position in your life?*

GO TO DISCOVERY 141 ON PAGE 735

57:11 [j] ver 5
[11] Be exalted, O God, above the heavens;
let your glory be over all the earth.[j]

PSALM 58

For the director of music. ⌞To the tune of⌟ "Do Not Destroy." Of David. A *miktam*.[a]

58:1 [k] Ps 82:2
[1] Do you rulers indeed speak justly?[k]
Do you judge uprightly among men?
[2] No, in your heart you devise injustice,
58:2 [l] Ps 94:20; Mal 3:15
and your hands mete out violence on the earth.[l]

RIGHTEOUS VENGEANCE

A number of psalms contain statements that strike us as harsh and abrasive, such as "break the teeth in their mouths" (Psalm 58:6) or "let them vanish" (verse 7). Sentiments such as these seem antithetical to the aspects of God's nature we prefer to emphasize—his forgiveness, love, mercy and compassion. After all, Jesus himself identified the greatest commandment of all: to love God above all else and to love other people as we love ourselves (Matthew 22:37–40). Certain people over the years have gone so far as to claim that psalms like Psalm 58, because of their vindictive language, are "less than Christian." But we might be surprised to discover that similar statements appear in the New Testament. Jesus quoted from Psalm 41:8–10 as a pronouncement of God's vengeance against Judas for his betrayal (Matthew 26:23–24). And the apostle Paul pronounced a curse on people for preaching a false gospel (Galatians 1:8–9). Revelation 18:20 calls us to rejoice when God exercises judgment in the world, because there can be no *justice* unless there is *judgment*. The necessity of judgment is part of what we mean when we confess that God is just and holy and that our sin is such an affront to his supreme majesty that it must be punished. But because God desired that we would be restored to a relationship with him, he made provision for his own Son to die an accursed death, carrying the full weight of God's just judgment for sin on his own shoulders, so that we might be set free and made right with him (Romans 5:6–21; Galatians 2:10–14; Ephesians 2:1–10).

[3] Even from birth the wicked go astray;
from the womb they are wayward and speak lies.
[4] Their venom is like the venom of a snake,[m] 58:4 [m] Ps 140:3; Ecc 10:11
like that of a cobra that has stopped its ears,
[5] that will not heed the tune of the charmer,
however skillful the enchanter may be.

[6] Break the teeth in their mouths, O God;[n] 58:6 [n] Ps 3:7 [o] Job 4:10
tear out, O LORD, the fangs of the lions![o]
[7] Let them vanish like water that flows away;[p] 58:7 [p] Jos 7:5; Ps 112:10 [q] Ps 64:3
when they draw the bow, let their arrows be blunted.[q]
[8] Like a slug melting away as it moves along,
like a stillborn child,[r] may they not see the sun. 58:8 [r] Job 3:16

[9] Before your pots can feel ⌞the heat of⌟ the thorns[s]— 58:9 [s] Ps 118:12 [t] Pr 10:25
whether they be green or dry—
the wicked will be swept away.[b][t]
[10] The righteous will be glad when they are avenged,[u] 58:10 [u] Ps 64:10; 91:8 [v] Ps 68:23
when they bathe their feet in the blood of the wicked.[v]
[11] Then men will say,
"Surely the righteous still are rewarded;
surely there is a God who judges the earth."[w] 58:11 [w] Ps 9:8; 18:20

PSALM 59

For the director of music. ⌞To the tune of⌟ "Do Not Destroy." Of David. A *miktam*.[a] When Saul had sent men to watch David's house in order to kill him.

[1] Deliver me from my enemies, O God;[x] 59:1 [x] Ps 143:9
protect me from those who rise up against me.
[2] Deliver me from evildoers
and save me from bloodthirsty men.[y] 59:2 [y] Ps 139:19

[a] Title: Probably a literary or musical term
[b] 9 The meaning of the Hebrew for this verse is uncertain.

[3] See how they lie in wait for me!
Fierce men conspire[z] against me
for no offense or sin of mine,
O LORD.
[4] I have done no wrong, yet they are
ready to attack me.[a]
Arise to help me; look on my
plight!
[5] O LORD God Almighty, the God of
Israel,
rouse yourself to punish all the
nations;
show no mercy to wicked
traitors.[b] *Selah*

[6] They return at evening,
snarling like dogs,[c]
and prowl about the city.
[7] See what they spew from their
mouths—
they spew out swords[d] from
their lips,
and they say, "Who can hear
us?"[e]
[8] But you, O LORD, laugh at them;[f]
you scoff at all those nations.[g]

[9] O my Strength, I watch for you;
you, O God, are my fortress,[h]
[10] my loving God.

God will go before me
and will let me gloat over those
who slander me.
[11] But do not kill them, O Lord our
shield,[a][i]
or my people will forget.[j]
In your might make them wander
about,
and bring them down.[k]
[12] For the sins of their mouths,[l]
for the words of their lips,[m]
let them be caught in their
pride.[n]
For the curses and lies they utter,
[13] consume them in wrath,
consume them till they are no
more.[o]
Then it will be known to the ends
of the earth
that God rules over Jacob.[p]
Selah

[14] They return at evening,
snarling like dogs,
and prowl about the city.
[15] They wander about for food[q]
and howl if not satisfied.
[16] But I will sing of your strength,[r]
in the morning[s] I will sing of
your love;[t]
for you are my fortress,
my refuge in times of trouble.[u]

[17] O my Strength, I sing praise to you;
you, O God, are my fortress, my
loving God.

59:3 [z] Ps 56:6
59:4 [a] Ps 35:19,23
59:5 [b] Jer 18:23
59:6 [c] ver 14
59:7 [d] Ps 57:4 [e] Ps 10:11
59:8 [f] Ps 37:13; Pr 1:26 [g] Ps 2:4
59:9 [h] Ps 9:9; 62:2
59:11 [i] Ps 84:9 [j] Dt 4:9 [k] Ps 106:27
59:12 [l] Ps 10:7 [m] Pr 12:13 [n] Zep 3:11
59:13 [o] Ps 104:35 [p] Ps 83:18
59:15 [q] Job 15:23
59:16 [r] Ps 21:13
59:16 [s] Ps 88:13 [t] Ps 101:1 [u] Ps 46:1

PSALM 60

For the director of music. To ⌊the tune of⌋ "The Lily of the Covenant." A *miktam*[b] of David. For teaching. When he fought Aram Naharaim[c] and Aram Zobah,[d] and when Joab returned and struck down twelve thousand Edomites in the Valley of Salt.

[1] You have rejected us,[v] O God, and
burst forth upon us;
you have been angry[w]—now
restore us![x]
[2] You have shaken the land[y] and
torn it open;
mend its fractures,[z] for it is
quaking.
[3] You have shown your people
desperate times;[a]
you have given us wine that
makes us stagger.[b]

[4] But for those who fear you, you
have raised a banner
to be unfurled against the bow.
Selah

[5] Save us and help us with your right
hand,[c]
that those you love[d] may be
delivered.
[6] God has spoken from his sanctuary:
"In triumph I will parcel out
Shechem[e]
and measure off the Valley of
Succoth.
[7] Gilead[f] is mine, and Manasseh is
mine;
Ephraim is my helmet,
Judah[g] my scepter.[h]
[8] Moab is my washbasin,
upon Edom I toss my sandal;
over Philistia I shout in
triumph.[i]"

[9] Who will bring me to the fortified
city?

60:1 [v] 2Sa 5:20; Ps 44:9 [w] Ps 79:5 [x] Ps 80:3
60:2 [y] Ps 18:7 [z] 2Ch 7:14
60:3 [a] Ps 71:20 [b] Isa 51:17; Jer 25:16
60:5 [c] Ps 17:7; 108:6 [d] Ps 127:2
60:6 [e] Ge 12:6
60:7 [f] Jos 13:31 [g] Dt 33:17 [h] Ge 49:10
60:8 [i] 2Sa 8:1

[a] *11* Or *sovereign* [b] Title: Probably a literary or musical term [c] Title: That is, Arameans of Northwest Mesopotamia [d] Title: That is, Arameans of central Syria

Who will lead me to Edom?
[10] Is it not you, O God, you who have
rejected us
and no longer go out with our
armies?[j]
[11] Give us aid against the enemy,
for the help of man is worthless.[k]
[12] With God we will gain the victory,
and he will trample down our
enemies.[l]

60:10 [j] Jos 7:12; Ps 44:9; 108:11
60:11 [k] Ps 146:3
60:12 [l] Nu 24:18; Ps 44:5

PSALM 61

For the director of music. With stringed instruments. Of David.

[1] Hear my cry, O God;[m]
listen to my prayer.[n]
[2] From the ends of the earth I call to
you,
I call as my heart grows faint;[o]
lead me to the rock[p] that is
higher than I.
[3] For you have been my refuge,[q]
a strong tower against the foe.[r]
[4] I long to dwell[s] in your tent forever
and take refuge in the shelter of
your wings.[t] *Selah*
[5] For you have heard my vows,[u]
O God;
you have given me the heritage of
those who fear your name.[v]

[6] Increase the days of the king's life,
his years for many generations.[w]
[7] May he be enthroned in God's
presence forever;[x]
appoint your love and
faithfulness to protect him.[y]

[8] Then will I ever sing praise to your
name[z]
and fulfill my vows day after day.

61:1 [m] Ps 64:1 [n] Ps 86:6
61:2 [o] Ps 77:3 [p] Ps 18:2
61:3 [q] Ps 62:7 [r] Pr 18:10
61:4 [s] Ps 23:6 [t] Ps 91:4
61:5 [u] Ps 56:12 [v] Ps 86:11
61:6 [w] Ps 21:4
61:7 [x] Ps 41:12 [y] Ps 40:11
61:8 [z] Ps 65:1; 71:22

PSALM 62

For the director of music. For Jeduthun. A psalm of David.

[1] My soul finds rest[a] in God alone;
my salvation comes from him.
[2] He alone is my rock[b] and my
salvation;
he is my fortress, I will never be
shaken.
[3] How long will you assault a man?
Would all of you throw him
down—
this leaning wall,[c] this tottering
fence?
[4] They fully intend to topple him
from his lofty place;
they take delight in lies.
With their mouths they bless,
but in their hearts they curse.[d]
Selah

[5] Find rest, O my soul, in God alone;
my hope comes from him.
[6] He alone is my rock and my
salvation;
he is my fortress, I will not be
shaken.
[7] My salvation and my honor
depend on God[a];
he is my mighty rock, my
refuge.[e]
[8] Trust in him at all times, O people;
pour out your hearts to him,[f]
for God is our refuge. *Selah*

[9] Lowborn men are but a breath,[g]
the highborn are but a lie;
if weighed on a balance,[h] they are
nothing;
together they are only a breath.
[10] Do not trust in extortion
or take pride in stolen goods;[i]
though your riches increase,
do not set your heart on them.[j]

[11] One thing God has spoken,
two things have I heard:
that you, O God, are strong,
[12] and that you, O Lord, are loving.
Surely you will reward each person
according to what he has done.[k]

62:1 [a] Ps 33:20
62:2 [b] Ps 89:26
62:3 [c] Isa 30:13
62:4 [d] Ps 28:3
62:7 [e] Ps 46:1; 85:9; Jer 3:23
62:8 [f] 1Sa 1:15; Ps 42:4; La 2:19
62:9 [g] Ps 39:5,11 [h] Isa 40:15
62:10 [i] Isa 61:8 [j] Job 31:25; 1Ti 6:6-10
62:12 [k] Job 34:11; Mt 16:27

PSALM 63

A psalm of David. When he was in the Desert of Judah.

[1] O God, you are my God,
earnestly I seek you;
my soul thirsts for you,[l]
my body longs for you,
in a dry and weary land
where there is no water.

[2] I have seen you in the sanctuary[m]
and beheld your power and your
glory.

63:1 [l] Ps 42:2; 84:2
63:2 [m] Ps 27:4

[a] 7 Or / *God Most High is my salvation and my honor*

Resting in God's Arms

Some people believe that David penned Psalm 62 after his son Absalom had tried to usurp the throne from him. Exiled from Jerusalem, hunted by his enemies and in peril for his life, David knew that he would learn to be at peace with his circumstances only by giving up his reliance on himself and learning to lean on God in every area of his life.

David began his song by asserting that his "soul [found] rest in God alone." The word *rest* has many connotations in the Bible. It can refer to national peace (Deuteronomy 12:10), death (Genesis 47:30) or the Sabbath (Leviticus 23:3). In Deuteronomy 12:9 Moses told God's people that they "[had] not yet reached the resting place" (Hebrew *menuhah*) the Lord had prepared for them across the Jordan, the place where they would come to a settled and restful position. David used the same Hebrew word in Psalm 95:11: "They shall never enter my rest." Some people refuse to turn back to God and receive what he so desperately wants to give them. His ultimate blessing for us is to be settled and safe with him.

We need rest for a number of reasons. Our bodies and spirits require respite from the hard work that is an inevitable part of this life. Because Adam and Eve turned away from God, they suffered the consequences: "By the sweat of your brow you will eat your food until you return to the ground" (Genesis 3:19). From holding down a job to caring for a family to attending to the myriad responsibilities each of us faces daily, life is exhausting. We need rest in order to possess the spiritual, mental and emotional resources to resist Satan's schemes.

We also need freedom from ourselves, relief from the limitations and struggles that are the result of our weakened sinful natures. While we are here "in this tent, we groan and are burdened, because we . . . wish to be . . . clothed with our heavenly dwelling, so that what is mortal may be swallowed up by life" (2 Corinthians 5:1–4). God created us to live with him forever; life as we know it now is temporary. There is a deep yearning in us for the more permanent, perfect body God intended us to have.

True rest is spiritual, eternal rest, a place of refuge with God where we can be released from the burdens and struggles of this physical life. Notice the many ways David describes God in this psalm. He rests because God is his salvation (verse 1), his rock, his fortress (verse 2), his hope (verse 5) and his refuge (verse 7). In this world of stress and unrest, "the promise of entering [God's] rest still stands" (Hebrews 4:1). We can experience God's peace in our lives when, by faith, we place our confidence in him and allow him to work through us, rather than trying to live by our own ability or insight. Jesus offers us the rest we so desperately crave: "Come to me, all you who are weary and burdened, and I will give you rest" (Matthew 11:28). And at the end is the fulfillment of his promise that the day is coming when our rest will be forever (Revelation 14:13).

Self-Discovery: *Are you feeling stressed or anxious right now? Imagine Jesus, with his arms outstretched, asking you to come to him and find rest. Will you come?*

GO TO DISCOVERY 142 ON PAGE 739

63:3 [n] Ps 69:16
[3] Because your love is better than
life,[n]
my lips will glorify you.
63:4 [o] Ps 104:33 [p] Ps 28:2
[4] I will praise you as long as I live,[o]
and in your name I will lift up
my hands.[p]
63:5 [q] Ps 36:8
[5] My soul will be satisfied as with the
richest of foods;[q]
with singing lips my mouth will
praise you.

[6] On my bed I remember you;
63:6 [r] Ps 42:8
I think of you through the
watches of the night.[r]
63:7 [s] Ps 27:9
[7] Because you are my help,[s]
I sing in the shadow of your
wings.
63:8 [t] Ps 18:35
[8] My soul clings to you;
your right hand upholds me.[t]
63:9 [u] Ps 40:14 [v] Ps 55:15
[9] They who seek my life will be
destroyed;[u]
they will go down to the depths
of the earth.[v]
[10] They will be given over to the sword
and become food for jackals.
[11] But the king will rejoice in God;
63:11 [w] Dt 6:13; Ps 21:1; Isa 45:23
all who swear by God's name will
praise him,[w]
while the mouths of liars will be
silenced.

PSALM 64

For the director of music. A psalm of David.

64:1 [x] Ps 55:2 [y] Ps 140:1
[1] Hear me, O God, as I voice my
complaint;[x]
protect my life from the threat of
the enemy.[y]
64:2 [z] Ps 56:6; 59:2
[2] Hide me from the conspiracy of the
wicked,[z]
from that noisy crowd of
evildoers.

[3] They sharpen their tongues like
swords
64:3 [a] Ps 58:7
and aim their words like deadly
arrows.[a]
64:4 [b] Ps 11:2 [c] Ps 55:19
[4] They shoot from ambush at the
innocent man;[b]
they shoot at him suddenly,
without fear.[c]

[5] They encourage each other in evil
plans,
they talk about hiding their
snares;

> HIDE ME, O MY SAVIOR HIDE,
> TILL THE STORM OF LIFE BE PAST;
> SAFE INTO THE HAVEN GUIDE,
> O RECEIVE MY SOUL AT LAST.
>
> Charles Wesley, *British Hymnwriter*

64:5 [d] Ps 10:11
they say, "Who will see them[a]?"[d]
[6] They plot injustice and say,
"We have devised a perfect
plan!"
Surely the mind and heart of
man are cunning.

[7] But God will shoot them with
arrows;
suddenly they will be struck
down.
64:8 [e] Ps 9:3; Pr 18:7 [f] Ps 22:7
[8] He will turn their own tongues
against them[e]
and bring them to ruin;
all who see them will shake their
heads[f] in scorn.
[9] All mankind will fear;
they will proclaim the works of
64:9 [g] Jer 51:10
God
and ponder what he has done.[g]
[10] Let the righteous rejoice in the
LORD
64:10 [h] Ps 25:20 [i] Ps 32:11
and take refuge in him;[h]
let all the upright in heart praise
him![i]

PSALM 65

For the director of music. A psalm of David.
A song.

65:1 [j] Ps 116:18
[1] Praise awaits[b] you, O God, in Zion;
to you our vows will be fulfilled.[j]
65:2 [k] Isa 66:23
[2] O you who hear prayer,
to you all men will come.[k]
65:3 [l] Ps 38:4 [m] Heb 9:14
[3] When we were overwhelmed by
sins,[l]
you forgave[c] our
transgressions.[m]
65:4 [n] Ps 4:3; 33:12 [o] Ps 36:8
[4] Blessed are those you choose[n]
and bring near to live in your
courts!
We are filled with the good things
of your house,[o]
of your holy temple.

[a] *5* Or *us* [b] *1* Or *befits*; the meaning of the Hebrew for this word is uncertain. [c] *3* Or *made atonement for*

[5] You answer us with awesome
deeds of righteousness,
O God our Savior,[p]
the hope of all the ends of the
earth
and of the farthest seas,[q]
[6] who formed the mountains by
your power,
having armed yourself with
strength,[r]
[7] who stilled the roaring of the seas,[s]
the roaring of their waves,
and the turmoil of the nations.[t]
[8] Those living far away fear your
wonders;
where morning dawns and
evening fades
you call forth songs of joy.

[9] You care for the land and water it;[u]
you enrich it abundantly.
The streams of God are filled with
water
to provide the people with
grain,[v]
for so you have ordained it.[a]
[10] You drench its furrows
and level its ridges;
you soften it with showers
and bless its crops.
[11] You crown the year with your
bounty,
and your carts overflow with
abundance.
[12] The grasslands of the desert
overflow;[w]
the hills are clothed with
gladness.
[13] The meadows are covered with
flocks[x]
and the valleys are mantled with
grain;[y]
they shout for joy and sing.[z]

65:5 [p] Ps 85:4
65:5 [q] Ps 107:23
65:6 [r] Ps 93:1
65:7 [s] Mt 8:26 [t] Isa 17:12-13
65:9 [u] Ps 68:9-10 [v] Ps 46:4; 104:14
65:12 [w] Job 28:26
65:13 [x] Ps 144:13 [y] Ps 72:16 [z] Ps 98:8; Isa 55:12

PSALM 66

For the director of music. A song. A psalm.

[1] Shout with joy to God, all the
earth![a]
[2] Sing the glory of his name;[b]
make his praise glorious!
[3] Say to God, "How awesome are
your deeds![c]
So great is your power
that your enemies cringe[d] before
you.
[4] All the earth bows down[e] to you;
they sing praise[f] to you,
they sing praise to your name."
Selah

[5] Come and see what God has done,
how awesome his works[g] in
man's behalf!
[6] He turned the sea into dry land,[h]
they passed through the waters
on foot—
come, let us rejoice in him.
[7] He rules forever[i] by his power,
his eyes watch[j] the nations—
let not the rebellious[k] rise up
against him. *Selah*

[8] Praise[l] our God, O peoples,
let the sound of his praise be
heard;
[9] he has preserved our lives
and kept our feet from
slipping.[m]
[10] For you, O God, tested us;
you refined us like silver.[n]
[11] You brought us into prison
and laid burdens[o] on our backs.
[12] You let men ride over our heads;[p]
we went through fire and water,
but you brought us to a place of
abundance.[q]

[13] I will come to your temple with
burnt offerings
and fulfill my vows[r] to you—
[14] vows my lips promised and my
mouth spoke
when I was in trouble.
[15] I will sacrifice fat animals to you
and an offering of rams;
I will offer bulls and goats.[s]
Selah

[16] Come and listen,[t] all you who fear
God;
let me tell[u] you what he has
done for me.
[17] I cried out to him with my mouth;
his praise was on my tongue.
[18] If I had cherished sin in my heart,
the Lord would not have
listened;[v]
[19] but God has surely listened
and heard my voice[w] in prayer.
[20] Praise be to God,
who has not rejected[x] my
prayer
or withheld his love from me!

66:1 [a] Ps 100:1
66:2 [b] Ps 79:9
66:3 [c] Ps 65:5 [d] Ps 18:44
66:4 [e] Ps 22:27 [f] Ps 67:3
66:5 [g] Ps 106:22
66:6 [h] Ex 14:22
66:7 [i] Ps 145:13 [j] Ps 11:4 [k] Ps 140:8
66:8 [l] Ps 98:4
66:9 [m] Ps 121:3
66:10 [n] Ps 17:3; Isa 48:10; Zec 13:9; 1Pe 1:6-7
66:11 [o] La 1:13
66:12 [p] Isa 51:23 [q] Isa 43:2
66:13 [r] Ecc 5:4
66:15 [s] Nu 6:14; Ps 51:19
66:16 [t] Ps 34:11 [u] Ps 71:15,24
66:18 [v] Job 36:21; Isa 1:15; Jas 4:3
66:19 [w] Ps 116:1-2
66:20 [x] Ps 22:24; 68:35

[a] 9 Or *for that is how you prepare the land*

PSALM 67

For the director of music. With stringed instruments. A psalm. A song.

[1]May God be gracious to us and
bless us
and make his face shine upon
us,[y] *Selah*
[2]that your ways may be known on
earth,
your salvation[z] among all
nations.[a]

[3]May the peoples praise you, O God;
may all the peoples praise you.
[4]May the nations be glad and sing
for joy,
for you rule the peoples justly[b]
and guide the nations of the
earth. *Selah*
[5]May the peoples praise you, O God;
may all the peoples praise you.

[6]Then the land will yield its harvest,[c]
and God, our God, will bless us.
[7]God will bless us,
and all the ends of the earth will
fear him.[d]

PSALM 68

For the director of music. Of David. A psalm. A song.

[1]May God arise, may his enemies be
scattered;
may his foes flee[e] before him.
[2]As smoke[f] is blown away by the
wind,
may you blow them away;
as wax melts[g] before the fire,
may the wicked perish before
God.
[3]But may the righteous be glad
and rejoice[h] before God;
may they be happy and joyful.

[4]Sing to God, sing praise to his
name,[i]
extol him who rides on the
clouds[a][j]—
his name is the LORD[k]—
and rejoice before him.
[5]A father to the fatherless,[l] a
defender of widows,[m]
is God in his holy dwelling.[n]
[6]God sets the lonely in families,[b][o]
he leads forth the prisoners[p]
with singing;
but the rebellious live in a sun-
scorched land.[q]

[7]When you went out[r] before your
people, O God,
when you marched through the
wasteland, *Selah*
[8]the earth shook,
the heavens poured down rain,[s]
before God, the One of Sinai,[t]
before God, the God of Israel.
[9]You gave abundant showers,[u]
O God;
you refreshed your weary
inheritance.
[10]Your people settled in it,
and from your bounty, O God,
you provided[v] for the poor.

[11]The Lord announced the word,
and great was the company of
those who proclaimed it:
[12]"Kings and armies flee[w] in haste;
in the camps men divide the
plunder.
[13]Even while you sleep among the
campfires,[c][x]
the wings of ⌊my⌋ dove are
sheathed with silver,
its feathers with shining gold."
[14]When the Almighty[d] scattered[y] the
kings in the land,
it was like snow fallen on Zalmon.

[15]The mountains of Bashan are
majestic mountains;
rugged are the mountains of
Bashan.
[16]Why gaze in envy, O rugged
mountains,
at the mountain where God
chooses[z] to reign,
where the LORD himself will
dwell forever?
[17]The chariots of God are tens of
thousands
and thousands of thousands;[a]
the Lord ⌊has come⌋ from Sinai
into his sanctuary.
[18]When you ascended on high,
you led captives[b] in your train;
you received gifts from men,[c]
even from[e] the rebellious—

[a] 4 Or / *prepare the way for him who rides through the deserts* [b] 6 Or *the desolate in a homeland* [c] 13 Or *saddlebags* [d] 14 Hebrew *Shaddai* [e] 18 Or *gifts for men, / even*

67:1 [y] Nu 6:24-26; Ps 4:6
67:2 [z] Isa 52:10 [a] Tit 2:11
67:4 [b] Ps 96:10-13
67:6 [c] Lev 26:4; Ps 85:12; Eze 34:27
67:7 [d] Ps 33:8
68:1 [e] Nu 10:35; Isa 33:3
68:2 [f] Hos 13:3 [g] Isa 9:18; Mic 1:4
68:3 [h] Ps 32:11
68:4 [i] Ps 66:2 [j] Dt 33:26 [k] Ex 6:3; Ps 83:18
68:5 [l] Ps 10:14 [m] Dt 10:18 [n] Dt 26:15
68:6 [o] Ps 113:9 [p] Ac 12:6 [q] Ps 107:34
68:7 [r] Ex 13:21; Jdg 4:14
68:8 [s] Jdg 5:4 [t] Ex 19:16,18
68:9 [u] Dt 11:11
68:10 [v] Ps 74:19
68:12 [w] Jos 10:16
68:13 [x] Ge 49:14
68:14 [y] Jos 10:10
68:16 [z] Dt 12:5
68:17 [a] Dt 33:2; Da 7:10
68:18 [b] Jdg 5:12 [c] Eph 4:8*

DISCOVERY 142

OUR TRIUMPHANT LORD

Place a wax candle next to a campfire and the wax loses all substance—soon the once-solid pillar is nothing but a shapeless pool. Smoke from the smaller fire rises toward the sky in a column so distinct that you can almost grasp it—until a breeze rustles through the nearby branches and it is dissolved. God's presence has the same effect on anything that is opposed to him. Nothing unholy can survive it (Psalm 68:2).

This psalm pictures God as a victorious warrior. He rides on the clouds (verse 4) and shakes the earth (verse 8). "Kings and armies flee in haste" when God comes to defend his people. He scatters the kings like flakes of snow (verse 14). He is accompanied by "tens of thousands and thousands of thousands" (verse 17). Who would be foolish enough to try to oppose the Almighty God, to dare to be his enemy?

In Romans 5:10 Paul stated that, in fact, "we were God's enemies." But in spite of our sin and animosity, "God demonstrates his own love for us in this: While we were still sinners, Christ died for us" (Romans 5:8). Those of us who have received Jesus as our Savior and Lord have become his servants (Acts 2:18). Better than that, we have been made his friends (John 15:15). Better still, he has made us his own children (1 John 3:1). Through the death of Jesus we have become righteous (Psalm 38:3), and, like David, we enjoy a relationship with God that fills us with joy (Psalm 68:3), praise (verse 19) and singing (verses 4,32).

Even though Psalm 68 was written hundreds of years before Jesus was born, it hints at the glorious culmination of his life's work—the day on which he would return victoriously to the Father's side (Psalm 68:18; John 17:1–5; Ephesians 4:8–13). Jesus provides us with a place to belong; through him we are adopted into God's family and no longer trapped by sin (Psalm 68:5–6; Titus 3:7). Jesus stated, "Everyone who sins is a slave to sin. A slave has no permanent place in the family, but a son belongs to it forever. So if the Son sets you free, you will be free indeed" (John 8:34–36).

The struggles of this life can leave us feeling as though we have much in common with the Israelites wandering in the desert. Our situation can seem barren, tedious, hopeless, lonely. But through Jesus Christ God leads us in and through the "wasteland" (Psalm 68:7). His spirit refreshes us with "living water"—water that brings with it eternal life and settles the restlessness in our souls.

Life does not have to defeat us. The God of the universe will, through his precious Son Jesus, scatter his enemies. He is the God "who daily bears our burdens" (Psalm 68:19; Matthew 11:29–30). Jesus' death on the cross banished the reign of sin forever, and through Jesus' resurrection he has destroyed the power of death and the grave; we no longer need to fear death (Psalm 68:20; 1 Corinthians 15:26). Our Lord has already overcome evil, and he has given us everything we need to live the life of victory (John 16:33; Ephesians 1:5).

***Self-Discovery:** Have you ever lived through a spiritual "wasteland" experience? In what specific ways did Jesus lead you through it back to the living water?*

GO TO DISCOVERY 143 ON PAGE 741

that you,[a] O LORD God, might
dwell there.

68:19 [d]Ps 65:5 [e]Ps 55:22
19 Praise be to the Lord, to God our
Savior,[d]
who daily bears our burdens.[e]
Selah

68:20 [f]Ps 56:13
20 Our God is a God who saves;
from the Sovereign LORD comes
escape from death.[f]

68:21 [g]Ps 110:5; Hab 3:13
21 Surely God will crush the heads[g] of
his enemies,
the hairy crowns of those who
go on in their sins.
22 The Lord says, "I will bring them
from Bashan;
68:22 [h]Nu 21:33
I will bring them from the
depths of the sea,[h]
68:23 [i]Ps 58:10 [j]1Ki 21:19
23 that you may plunge your feet in
the blood of your foes,[i]
while the tongues of your dogs[j]
have their share."

24 Your procession has come into
view, O God,
68:24 [k]Ps 63:2
the procession of my God and
King into the sanctuary.[k]
25 In front are the singers, after them
the musicians;
68:25 [l]Jdg 11:34; 1Ch 13:8
with them are the maidens
playing tambourines.[l]
26 Praise God in the great
congregation;
68:26 [m]Ps 26:12; Isa 48:1
praise the LORD in the assembly
of Israel.[m]
68:27 [n]1Sa 9:21
27 There is the little tribe[n] of
Benjamin, leading them,
there the great throng of Judah's
princes,
and there the princes of Zebulun
and of Naphtali.

28 Summon your power, O God[b];
show us your strength, O God, as
you have done before.
29 Because of your temple at
Jerusalem
68:29 [o]Ps 72:10
kings will bring you gifts.[o]
68:30 [p]Ps 22:12 [q]Ps 89:10
30 Rebuke the beast among the reeds,
the herd of bulls[p] among the
calves of the nations.
Humbled, may it bring bars of silver.
Scatter the nations[q] who delight
in war.
68:31 [r]Isa 19:19; 45:14
31 Envoys will come from Egypt;[r]
Cush[c] will submit herself to God.

32 Sing to God, O kingdoms of the
earth,
sing praise to the Lord, *Selah*
68:33 [s]Ps 18:10 [t]Ps 29:4
33 to him who rides[s] the ancient skies
above,
who thunders with mighty voice.[t]
68:34 [u]Ps 29:1
34 Proclaim the power[u] of God,
whose majesty is over Israel,
whose power is in the skies.
35 You are awesome, O God, in your
sanctuary;
68:35 [v]Ps 29:11 [w]Ps 66:20
the God of Israel gives power
and strength to his people.[v]

Praise be to God![w]

PSALM 69

For the director of music. To ⌊the tune of⌋ "Lilies."
Of David.

69:1 [x]Jnh 2:5
1 Save me, O God,
for the waters have come up to
my neck.[x]
69:2 [y]Ps 40:2
2 I sink in the miry depths,[y]
where there is no foothold.
I have come into the deep waters;
69:3 [z]Ps 6:6 [a]Ps 119:82; Isa 38:14
the floods engulf me.
3 I am worn out calling for help;[z]
my throat is parched.
My eyes fail,[a]
looking for my God.
69:4 [b]Jn 15:25* [c]Ps 35:19; 38:19
4 Those who hate me without
reason[b]
outnumber the hairs of my head;
many are my enemies without
cause,[c]
those who seek to destroy me.
I am forced to restore
what I did not steal.

69:5 [d]Ps 38:5 [e]Ps 44:21
5 You know my folly,[d] O God;
my guilt is not hidden from
you.[e]

6 May those who hope in you
not be disgraced because of me,
O Lord, the LORD Almighty;
may those who seek you
not be put to shame because of
me,
O God of Israel.
69:7 [f]Jer 15:15 [g]Ps 44:15
7 For I endure scorn for your sake,[f]
and shame covers my face.[g]
69:8 [h]Ps 31:11; Isa 53:3
8 I am a stranger to my brothers,
an alien to my own mother's
sons;[h]

[a] 18 Or *they* [b] 28 Many Hebrew manuscripts, Septuagint and Syriac; most Hebrew manuscripts *Your God has summoned power for you*
[c] 31 That is, the upper Nile region

DISCOVERY 143

Our Suffering Savior

One of the psalms quoted most frequently in the New Testament is Psalm 69, generally in connection with the ministry and suffering of Jesus. At the time of writing David was drowning in a sea of trouble and cried out for God. He implored God to save him (verse 1), answer him (verse 13), rescue him (verse 14), come near to him (verse 18) and protect him (verse 29). Even though he could envision no way out of his distress, David was confident that God would take care of him—and found the inspiration to end his song with a burst of praise.

Some of David's descriptions of his own difficulties are paralleled in the Gospel accounts of Jesus' sufferings. David's enemies hated him for no apparent reason, and Jesus—despite his miracles and perfect life of love—was despised as well (John 15:24–25). David was estranged from his own brothers (Psalm 69:8), and Jesus' brothers refused at first to believe that he was the Messiah (John 7:5). David demonstrated exemplary zeal for God no matter what the outward circumstances (Psalm 69:9), and Jesus exhibited the same passion when he drove the money changers from the temple (John 2:12–25).

David was insulted again and again; he described himself in verse 19 of Psalm 69 as "scorned, disgraced and shamed," and the apostle Paul later referred to the insults Jesus was compelled to endure (Romans 15:3). David found no sympathy anywhere—interestingly, he likened his desperate circumstances to being offered vinegar to quench his thirst (Psalm 69:21). Each of these statements in Psalm 69 is not only a lament about David's own situation but part of a detailed prophecy about what Jesus would suffer (Matthew 27:24; Mark 15:23; Luke 23:26; John 19:28–30). David pleaded with God to deal with his enemies: "May their place be deserted; let there be no one to dwell in their tents" (Psalm 69:25), and Peter would later quote David to describe what happened to Judas after he turned Jesus over to the authorities (Acts 1:20).

God never abandoned either David or his Son Jesus (see Discovery #249, page 1315), and he will never desert us. The writer to the Hebrews referred back to Deuteronomy 31:6,8 when he quoted God as saying, "Never will I leave you; never will I forsake you" (Hebrews 13:5). Whatever our circumstances, he will give us the strength to carry on, because he is the Almighty God who will never stop loving us: "The LORD appeared to us in the past, saying: 'I have loved you with an everlasting love; I have drawn you with loving-kindness' " (Jeremiah 31:3).

Because Jesus suffered insult, betrayal and unspeakable anguish of body and spirit, he knows how we feel when we grow weary and bruised from life's blows (Hebrews 4:14–16). He truly understands, and he is at our side to encourage us to "run with perseverance the race marked out for us" as we keep our eyes fixed on him, the One who has gone before to show the way (Hebrews 12:1–3).

Self-Discovery: *Picture yourself as a runner with your eye fixed firmly on the finish line. Does this image help to provide direction in your life? What Scripture verses are especially meaningful to you when you feel as though you can't take another step?*

GO TO DISCOVERY 144 ON PAGE 745

[9] for zeal for your house consumes
69:9 [i] Jn 2:17* [j] Ps 89:50-51; Ro 15:3* me,[i]
and the insults of those who
insult you fall on me.[j]
69:10 [k] Ps 35:13 [10] When I weep and fast,[k]
I must endure scorn;
69:11 [l] Ps 35:13 [11] when I put on sackcloth,[l]
people make sport of me.
[12] Those who sit at the gate mock me,
69:12 [m] Job 30:9 and I am the song of the
drunkards.[m]
69:13 [n] Isa 49:8; 2Co 6:2 [o] Ps 51:1 [13] But I pray to you, O LORD,
in the time of your favor;[n]
in your great love,[o] O God,
answer me with your sure
salvation.
[14] Rescue me from the mire,
do not let me sink;
deliver me from those who hate
69:14 [p] ver 2; Ps 144:7 me,
from the deep waters.[p]
69:15 [q] Ps 124:4-5 [r] Nu 16:33 [15] Do not let the floodwaters[q] engulf
me
or the depths swallow me up[r]
or the pit close its mouth over
me.
69:16 [s] Ps 63:3 [16] Answer me, O LORD, out of the
goodness of your love;[s]
in your great mercy turn to me.
69:17 [t] Ps 27:9 [u] Ps 66:14 [17] Do not hide your face[t] from your
servant;
answer me quickly, for I am in
trouble.[u]
69:18 [v] Ps 49:15 [18] Come near and rescue me;
redeem[v] me because of my foes.

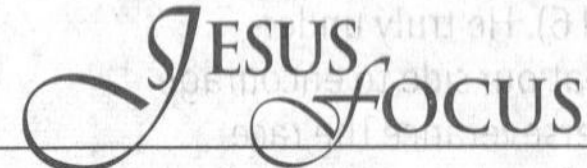

ZEAL FOR GOD

The New Testament identifies Jesus as the righteous sufferer mentioned in Psalm 69. This psalm was written by David to express his plea that God would save him from his enemies, but it also foretells what Jesus would have to endure. When John recorded the incident of Jesus expelling the money changers from the temple, he quoted verse 9 of this psalm: "Zeal for your house will consume me" (John 2:17). Jesus was angry with those who were perverting the temple, because it was intended to be a "house of prayer." Just as David's fervor demonstrated that his heart was devoted to God, so Jesus' zeal expressed his total devotion to his Father. David and Jesus both remind us that our own individual "houses of prayer and worship" must be set apart to bring honor to our Almighty God.

[19] You know how I am scorned,[w] 69:19 [w] Ps 22:6
disgraced and shamed;
all my enemies are before you.
[20] Scorn has broken my heart
and has left me helpless;
I looked for sympathy, but there
was none,
for comforters,[x] but I found 69:20 [x] Job 16:2
none.[y] [y] Isa 63:5
[21] They put gall in my food
and gave me vinegar for my 69:21 [z] Mt 27:34;
thirst.[z] Mk 15:23; Jn 19:28-30
[22] May the table set before them
become a snare;
may it become retribution and[a]
a trap.
[23] May their eyes be darkened so they
cannot see, 69:23
and their backs be bent forever.[a] [a] Isa 6:9-10; Ro 11:9-10*
[24] Pour out your wrath[b] on them;
let your fierce anger overtake 69:24 [b] Ps 79:6
them.
[25] May their place be deserted;[c] 69:25 [c] Mt 23:38
let there be no one to dwell in [d] Ac 1:20*
their tents.[d]
[26] For they persecute those you
wound
and talk about the pain of those 69:26 [e] Isa 53:4;
you hurt.[e] Zec 1:15
[27] Charge them with crime upon 69:27
crime;[f] [f] Ne 4:5
do not let them share in your [g] Ps 109:14; Isa 26:10
salvation.[g]
[28] May they be blotted out of the 69:28
book of life[h] [h] Ex 32:32-33;
and not be listed with the Lk 10:20; Php 4:3
righteous.[i] [i] Eze 13:9
[29] I am in pain and distress;
may your salvation, O God,
protect me.[j] 69:29 [j] Ps 59:1; 70:5
[30] I will praise God's name in song[k] 69:30 [k] Ps 28:7
and glorify him[l] with [l] Ps 34:3
thanksgiving.
[31] This will please the LORD more
than an ox,
more than a bull with its horns
and hoofs.[m] 69:31 [m] Ps 50:9-13
[32] The poor will see and be glad[n]— 69:32
you who seek God, may your [n] Ps 34:2
hearts live![o] [o] Ps 22:26
[33] The LORD hears the needy[p] 69:33
and does not despise his captive [p] Ps 12:5; 68:6
people.

[34] Let heaven and earth praise him,

[a] 22 Or *snare / and their fellowship become*

the seas and all that move in
them,[q]
35 for God will save Zion[r]
and rebuild the cities of Judah.[s]
Then people will settle there and
possess it;
36 the children of his servants will
inherit it,
and those who love his name
will dwell there.[t]

69:34 [q] Ps 96:11; 148:1; Isa 44:23; 49:13; 55:12
69:35 [r] Ob 1:17 [s] Ps 51:18; Isa 44:26
69:36 [t] Ps 37:29; 102:28

PSALM 70

For the director of music. Of David. A petition.

1 Hasten, O God, to save me;
O LORD, come quickly to help
me.[u]
2 May those who seek my life[v]
be put to shame and confusion;
may all who desire my ruin
be turned back in disgrace.[w]
3 May those who say to me, "Aha!
Aha!"
turn back because of their shame.
4 But may all who seek you
rejoice and be glad in you;
may those who love your salvation
always say,
"Let God be exalted!"

5 Yet I am poor and needy;[x]
come quickly to me,[y] O God.
You are my help and my deliverer;
O LORD, do not delay.

70:1 [u] Ps 40:13
70:2 [v] Ps 35:4 [w] Ps 35:26
70:5 [x] Ps 40:17 [y] Ps 141:1

PSALM 71

1 In you, O LORD, I have taken refuge;
let me never be put to shame.[z]
2 Rescue me and deliver me in your
righteousness;
turn your ear[a] to me and save me.
3 Be my rock of refuge,
to which I can always go;
give the command to save me,
for you are my rock and my
fortress.[b]
4 Deliver me, O my God, from the
hand of the wicked,[c]
from the grasp of evil and cruel
men.

5 For you have been my hope,
O Sovereign LORD,
my confidence[d] since my youth.
6 From birth[e] I have relied on you;
you brought me forth from my
mother's womb.[f]
I will ever praise[g] you.
7 I have become like a portent[h] to
many,
but you are my strong refuge.[i]
8 My mouth[j] is filled with your praise,
declaring your splendor[k] all day
long.

9 Do not cast[l] me away when I am
old;[m]
do not forsake me when my
strength is gone.
10 For my enemies speak against me;
those who wait to kill[n] me
conspire[o] together.
11 They say, "God has forsaken him;
pursue him and seize him,
for no one will rescue[p] him."
12 Be not far[q] from me, O God;
come quickly, O my God, to
help[r] me.
13 May my accusers perish in shame;
may those who want to harm me
be covered with scorn and
disgrace.[s]

14 But as for me, I will always have
hope;[t]
I will praise you more and more.
15 My mouth will tell[u] of your
righteousness,
of your salvation all day long,
though I know not its measure.
16 I will come and proclaim your
mighty acts,[v] O Sovereign
LORD;
I will proclaim your
righteousness, yours alone.
17 Since my youth, O God, you have
taught[w] me,
and to this day I declare your
marvelous deeds.[x]
18 Even when I am old and gray,[y]
do not forsake me, O God,
till I declare your power to the next
generation,
your might to all who are to
come.[z]

19 Your righteousness reaches to the
skies,[a] O God,
you who have done great things.[b]
Who, O God, is like you?[c]
20 Though you have made me see
troubles,[d] many and bitter,
you will restore[e] my life again;

71:1 [z] Ps 25:2-3; 31:1
71:2 [a] Ps 17:6
71:3 [b] Ps 18:2; 31:2-3; 44:4
71:4 [c] Ps 140:4
71:5 [d] Job 4:6; Jer 17:7
71:6 [e] Ps 22:10 [f] Ps 22:9; Isa 46:3 [g] Ps 9:1; 34:1; 52:9; 119:164; 145:2
71:7 [h] Isa 8:18; 1Co 4:9 [i] 2Sa 22:3; Ps 61:3
71:8 [j] Ps 51:15; 63:5 [k] Ps 35:28; 96:6; 104:1
71:9 [l] Ps 51:11 [m] ver 18; Ps 92:14; Isa 46:4
71:10 [n] Ps 10:8; 59:3; Pr 1:18 [o] Ps 31:13; 56:6; Mt 12:14
71:11 [p] Ps 7:2
71:12 [q] Ps 35:22; 38:21 [r] Ps 38:22; 70:1
71:13 [s] ver 24
71:14 [t] Ps 130:7
71:15 [u] Ps 35:28; 40:5
71:16 [v] Ps 106:2
71:17 [w] Dt 4:5 [x] Ps 26:7
71:18 [y] ver 9 [z] Ps 22:30,31; 78:4
71:19 [a] Ps 36:5; 57:10 [b] Ps 126:2; Lk 1:49 [c] Ps 35:10
71:20 [d] Ps 60:3 [e] Hos 6:2

from the depths of the earth
you will again bring me up.
21 You will increase my honor[f]
and comfort[g] me once again.
22 I will praise you with the harp[h]
for your faithfulness, O my God;
I will sing praise to you with the
lyre,[i]
O Holy One of Israel.[j]
23 My lips will shout for joy
when I sing praise to you—
I, whom you have redeemed.[k]
24 My tongue will tell of your
righteous acts
all day long,[l]
for those who wanted to harm me[m]
have been put to shame and
confusion.

71:21 [f] Ps 18:35 [g] Ps 23:4; 86:17; Isa 12:1; 49:13
71:22 [h] Ps 33:2 [i] Ps 92:3; 144:9 [j] 2Ki 19:22
71:23 [k] Ps 103:4
71:24 [l] Ps 35:28 [m] ver 13

PSALM 72

Of Solomon.

1 Endow the king with your justice,
O God,
the royal son with your
righteousness.
2 He will[a] judge your people in
righteousness,[n]
your afflicted ones with justice.
3 The mountains will bring
prosperity to the people,
the hills the fruit of
righteousness.
4 He will defend the afflicted among
the people
and save the children of the
needy;[o]
he will crush the oppressor.
5 He will endure[b] as long as the sun,
as long as the moon, through all
generations.
6 He will be like rain[p] falling on a
mown field,
like showers watering the earth.
7 In his days the righteous will
flourish;[q]
prosperity will abound till the
moon is no more.
8 He will rule from sea to sea
and from the River[c][r] to the ends
of the earth.[d][s]
9 The desert tribes will bow before
him
and his enemies will lick the
dust.
10 The kings of Tarshish and of
distant shores
will bring tribute to him;
the kings of Sheba[t] and Seba
will present him gifts.[u]
11 All kings will bow down to him
and all nations will serve him.
12 For he will deliver the needy who
cry out,
the afflicted who have no one to
help.
13 He will take pity on the weak and
the needy
and save the needy from death.
14 He will rescue[v] them from
oppression and violence,
for precious[w] is their blood in
his sight.
15 Long may he live!
May gold from Sheba[x] be given
him.
May people ever pray for him
and bless him all day long.
16 Let grain abound throughout the
land;
on the tops of the hills may it
sway.
Let its fruit flourish like Lebanon;[y]
let it thrive like the grass of the
field.
17 May his name endure forever;[z]
may it continue as long as the
sun.[a]

All nations will be blessed through
him,
and they will call him blessed.[b]

18 Praise be to the LORD God, the God
of Israel,[c]
who alone does marvelous
deeds.[d]
19 Praise be to his glorious name
forever;
may the whole earth be filled
with his glory.[e]
Amen and Amen.[f]

20 This concludes the prayers of
David son of Jesse.

72:2 [n] Isa 9:7; 11:4-5; 32:1
72:4 [o] Isa 11:4
72:6 [p] Dt 32:2; Hos 6:3
72:7 [q] Ps 92:12; Isa 2:4
72:8 [r] Ex 23:31 [s] Zec 9:10
72:10 [t] Ge 10:7 [u] 2Ch 9:24
72:14 [v] Ps 69:18 [w] 1Sa 26:21; Ps 116:15
72:15 [x] Isa 60:6
72:16 [y] Ps 104:16
72:17 [z] Ex 3:15 [a] Ps 89:36 [b] Ge 12:3; Lk 1:48
72:18 [c] 1Ch 29:10; Ps 41:13; 106:48 [d] Job 5:9
72:19 [e] Nu 14:21; Ne 9:5 [f] Ps 41:13

[a] 2 Or *May he*; similarly in verses 3–11 and 17
[b] 5 Septuagint; Hebrew *You will be feared*
[c] 8 That is, the Euphrates
[d] 8 Or *the end of the land*

DISCOVERY 144

God's Royal Son

Witnessing the crowning of a new king is generally a once-in-a-lifetime event. Westminster Abbey, the church in London at which coronations and other major political and royal ceremonies take place, is scrubbed from top to bottom for nearly a full year in preparation for such a momentous event. The situation in Israel was no different, either in terms of the extensive preparations or the anticipation and excitement. Psalm 72 was most likely sung as part of a coronation ceremony for the new king. In it the people describe the kind of man they want their king to be—a man committed to God's priorities.

The new king is most often the son of the previous monarch (verse 1). The people ask God to endow "the royal son" with his own righteousness. This psalm has long been considered by both Jews and Christians to be a description of God's promised Messiah. The New Testament identifies that Messiah as Jesus, referring to him as the son of David whom God promised would rule on the throne forever (Psalm 72:5; Daniel 7:14; Matthew 1:1; 2:2; Philippians 2:11; Revelation 11:15).

We can observe what this Royal Son is like by the way in which he conducts himself and how he treats his people. If a king's own life exhibited integrity, the people could be assured that their monarch was serious about doing what was right. The uprightness of Jesus' own life reflects the Father's heart (Psalm 72:1; John 17:25). As Jesus stated in John 14:9–10, "Anyone who has seen me has seen the Father . . . Don't you believe that I am in the Father, and that the Father is in me? The words I say to you are not just my own. Rather, it is the Father, living in me, who is doing the work."

Jesus is passionate about justice and compassionate toward the needy, especially those who have no one to turn to, and he expects the same of his people (Psalm 72:7; Matthew 25:31–46). He takes a special interest in children, often the most victimized members of a society (Psalm 72:4; Matthew 18:2), stating in Matthew 18:10, "See that you do not look down on one of these little ones. For I tell you that their angels in heaven always see the face of my Father in heaven."

He stands opposed to the oppressor; by his very mission statement proclaimed at the beginning of his earthly ministry he demonstrates his love for the oppressed (Psalm 72:4; Luke 4:18–19). God promised that the nation would prosper provided the king were to model this kind of concern for justice and righteousness (Psalm 72:7–8).

We also discover what the Royal Son is like because of the way his subjects live (John 13:34–35). Because he is personally committed to God's ways, righteousness will flourish in the lives of his people as well (Psalm 72:7; Galatians 5:16–25; 1 John 3:7). His enemies will become like dust, because nothing can stand in the way of God's purposes; because of his righteousness, however, his people will prosper (Luke 1:70–75), possessing everything they need—and more!

Self-Discovery: *Take some time to reflect on the life of Jesus as recorded in the Gospels. What are some specific behaviors and attitudes that Jesus modeled for which you can have a passion in your life today?*

GO TO DISCOVERY 145 ON PAGE 750

BOOK III

Psalms 73–89

PSALM 73

A psalm of Asaph.

73:1 1 Surely God is good to Israel,
[g]Mt 5:8 to those who are pure in heart.[g]

2 But as for me, my feet had almost
slipped;
73:3 I had nearly lost my foothold.
[h]Ps 37:1; 3 For I envied[h] the arrogant
Pr 23:17 when I saw the prosperity of the
[i]Job 21:7; Jer 12:1 wicked.[i]

4 They have no struggles;
their bodies are healthy and
strong.[a]
73:5 5 They are free[j] from the burdens
[j]Job 21:9 common to man;
they are not plagued by human
ills.
73:6 [k]Ge 41:42 6 Therefore pride is their necklace;[k]
[l]Ps 109:18 they clothe themselves with
violence.[l]
73:7 [m]Ps 17:10 7 From their callous hearts[m] comes
iniquity[b];
the evil conceits of their minds
know no limits.

73:8 8 They scoff, and speak with malice;
[n]Ps 17:10; in their arrogance[n] they
Jude 16 threaten oppression.
9 Their mouths lay claim to heaven,
and their tongues take
possession of the earth.
10 Therefore their people turn to them
and drink up waters in
abundance.[c]
11 They say, "How can God know?
Does the Most High have
knowledge?"

12 This is what the wicked are like—
73:12 always carefree, they increase in
[o]Ps 49:6 wealth.[o]

73:13 13 Surely in vain[p] have I kept my
[p]Job 21:15; 34:9 heart pure;
[q]Ps 26:6 in vain have I washed my hands
in innocence.[q]
14 All day long I have been plagued;
I have been punished every
morning.

15 If I had said, "I will speak thus,"
I would have betrayed your
children.

16 When I tried to understand[r] all this, 73:16
it was oppressive to me [r]Ecc 8:17
17 till I entered the sanctuary[s] of God; 73:17
then I understood their final [s]Ps 77:13 [t]Ps 37:38
destiny.[t]

18 Surely you place them on slippery 73:18
ground;[u] [u]Ps 35:6
you cast them down to ruin.
19 How suddenly[v] are they destroyed, 73:19
completely swept away by terrors! [v]Isa 47:11
20 As a dream[w] when one awakes,[x] 73:20 [w]Job 20:8
so when you arise, O Lord, [x]Ps 78:65
you will despise them as
fantasies.

21 When my heart was grieved
and my spirit embittered, 73:22
22 I was senseless[y] and ignorant; [y]Ps 49:10; 92:6
I was a brute beast[z] before you. [z]Ecc 3:18
23 Yet I am always with you;
you hold me by my right hand.
24 You guide[a] me with your counsel,[b] 73:24 [a]Ps 48:14
and afterward you will take me [b]Ps 32:8
into glory.
25 Whom have I in heaven but you?
And earth has nothing I desire 73:25
besides you.[c] [c]Php 3:8
26 My flesh and my heart[d] may fail,[e] 73:26
but God is the strength of my [d]Ps 84:2
heart [e]Ps 40:12
and my portion forever.

27 Those who are far from you will 73:27
perish;[f] [f]Ps 119:155
you destroy all who are
unfaithful to you.
28 But as for me, it is good to be near 73:28
God.[g] [g]Heb 10:22;
I have made the Sovereign Lord Jas 4:8 [h]Ps 40:5
my refuge;
I will tell of all your deeds.[h]

PSALM 74

A *maskil*[d] of Asaph.

1 Why have you rejected us forever,[i] 74:1
O God? [i]Dt 29:20;
Why does your anger smolder Ps 44:23
against the sheep of your [j]Ps 79:13; 95:7;
pasture?[j] 100:3

[a] 4 With a different word division of the Hebrew; Masoretic Text *struggles at their death; / their bodies are healthy* [b] 7 Syriac (see also Septuagint); Hebrew *Their eyes bulge with fat* [c] 10 The meaning of the Hebrew for this verse is uncertain. [d] Title: Probably a literary or musical term

[2] Remember the people you purchased[k] of old,[l]
the tribe of your inheritance, whom you redeemed[m]—
Mount Zion, where you dwelt.[n]
[3] Turn your steps toward these everlasting ruins,
all this destruction the enemy has brought on the sanctuary.

[4] Your foes roared[o] in the place where you met with us;
they set up their standards[p] as signs.
[5] They behaved like men wielding axes
to cut through a thicket of trees.[q]
[6] They smashed all the carved[r] paneling
with their axes and hatchets.
[7] They burned your sanctuary to the ground;
they defiled the dwelling place of your Name.
[8] They said in their hearts, "We will crush[s] them completely!"
They burned every place where God was worshiped in the land.

[9] We are given no miraculous signs;
no prophets[t] are left,
and none of us knows how long this will be.

[10] How long will the enemy mock you, O God?
Will the foe revile[u] your name forever?
[11] Why do you hold back your hand, your right hand?[v]
Take it from the folds of your garment and destroy them!

[12] But you, O God, are my king[w] from of old;
you bring salvation upon the earth.
[13] It was you who split open the sea[x] by your power;
you broke the heads of the monster[y] in the waters.
[14] It was you who crushed the heads of Leviathan
and gave him as food to the creatures of the desert.
[15] It was you who opened up springs[z] and streams;
you dried up[a] the ever flowing rivers.
[16] The day is yours, and yours also the night;
you established the sun and moon.[b]
[17] It was you who set all the boundaries[c] of the earth;
you made both summer and winter.[d]

[18] Remember how the enemy has mocked you, O LORD,
how foolish people[e] have reviled your name.
[19] Do not hand over the life of your dove to wild beasts;
do not forget the lives of your afflicted[f] people forever.
[20] Have regard for your covenant,[g]
because haunts of violence fill the dark places of the land.
[21] Do not let the oppressed[h] retreat in disgrace;
may the poor and needy[i] praise your name.

[22] Rise up, O God, and defend your cause;
remember how fools[j] mock you all day long.
[23] Do not ignore the clamor of your adversaries,[k]
the uproar of your enemies, which rises continually.

PSALM 75

For the director of music. ⌊To the tune of⌋ "Do Not Destroy." A psalm of Asaph. A song.

[1] We give thanks to you, O God,
we give thanks, for your Name is near;[l]
men tell of your wonderful deeds.[m]

[2] You say, "I choose the appointed time;
it is I who judge uprightly.
[3] When the earth and all its people quake,[n]
it is I who hold its pillars[o] firm. *Selah*
[4] To the arrogant I say, 'Boast no more,'
and to the wicked, 'Do not lift up your horns.[p]
[5] Do not lift your horns against heaven;

74:2 [k] Ex 15:16 [l] Dt 32:7 [m] Ex 15:13 [n] Ps 68:16
74:4 [o] La 2:7 [p] Nu 2:2
74:5 [q] Jer 46:22
74:6 [r] 1Ki 6:18
74:8 [s] Ps 83:4
74:9 [t] 1Sa 3:1
74:10 [u] Ps 44:16
74:11 [v] La 2:3
74:12 [w] Ps 44:4
74:13 [x] Ex 14:21 [y] Isa 51:9; Eze 29:3
74:15 [z] Ex 17:6; Nu 20:11 [a] Jos 2:10; 3:13
74:16 [b] Ge 1:16; Ps 136:7-9
74:17 [c] Dt 32:8; Ac 17:26 [d] Ge 8:22
74:18 [e] Dt 32:6; Ps 39:8
74:19 [f] Ps 9:18
74:20 [g] Ge 17:7; Ps 106:45
74:21 [h] Ps 103:6 [i] Ps 35:10
74:22 [j] Ps 53:1
74:23 [k] Ps 65:7
75:1 [l] Ps 145:18 [m] Ps 44:1; 71:16
75:3 [n] Isa 24:19 [o] 1Sa 2:8
75:4 [p] Zec 1:21

do not speak with outstretched
neck.' "
6 No one from the east or the west
or from the desert can exalt a
man.
7 But it is God who judges:[q]
He brings one down, he exalts
another.[r]
8 In the hand of the LORD is a cup
full of foaming wine mixed[s] with
spices;
he pours it out, and all the wicked
of the earth
drink it down to its very dregs.[t]
9 As for me, I will declare[u] this
forever;
I will sing praise to the God of
Jacob.
10 I will cut off the horns of all the
wicked,
but the horns of the righteous
will be lifted up.[v]

75:7 [q] Ps 50:6 [r] 1Sa 2:7; Ps 147:6; Da 2:21
75:8 [s] Pr 23:30 [t] Job 21:20; Jer 25:15
75:9 [u] Ps 40:10
75:10 [v] Ps 89:17; 92:10; 148:14

PSALM 76

For the director of music. With stringed instruments. A psalm of Asaph. A song.

1 In Judah God is known;
his name is great in Israel.
2 His tent is in Salem,[w]
his dwelling place in Zion.
3 There he broke the flashing arrows,
the shields and the swords, the
weapons of war.[x] *Selah*
4 You are resplendent with light,
more majestic than mountains
rich with game.
5 Valiant men lie plundered,
they sleep their last sleep;[y]
not one of the warriors
can lift his hands.
6 At your rebuke, O God of Jacob,
both horse and chariot[z] lie still.
7 You alone are to be feared.[a]
Who can stand[b] before you
when you are angry?[c]
8 From heaven you pronounced
judgment,
and the land feared[d] and was
quiet—
9 when you, O God, rose up to
judge,[e]
to save all the afflicted of the
land. *Selah*
10 Surely your wrath against men
brings you praise,[f]
and the survivors of your wrath
are restrained.[a]
11 Make vows to the LORD your God
and fulfill them;[g]
let all the neighboring lands
bring gifts[h] to the One to be
feared.
12 He breaks the spirit of rulers;
he is feared by the kings of the
earth.

76:2 [w] Ge 14:18
76:3 [x] Ps 46:9
76:5 [y] Ps 13:3
76:6 [z] Ex 15:1
76:7 [a] 1Ch 16:25 [b] Ezr 9:15; Rev 6:17 [c] Ps 2:5; Na 1:6
76:8 [d] 1Ch 16:30; 2Ch 20:29-30
76:9 [e] Ps 9:8
76:10 [f] Ex 9:16; Ro 9:17
76:11 [g] Ps 50:14; Ecc 5:4-5 [h] 2Ch 32:23; Ps 68:29

PSALM 77

For the director of music. For Jeduthun. Of Asaph. A psalm.

1 I cried out to God[i] for help;
I cried out to God to hear me.
2 When I was in distress,[j] I sought
the Lord;
at night I stretched out untiring
hands[k]
and my soul refused to be
comforted.[l]
3 I remembered you, O God, and I
groaned;
I mused, and my spirit grew
faint.[m] *Selah*
4 You kept my eyes from closing;
I was too troubled to speak.
5 I thought about the former days,[n]
the years of long ago;
6 I remembered my songs in the
night.
My heart mused and my spirit
inquired:
7 "Will the Lord reject forever?
Will he never show his favor[o]
again?
8 Has his unfailing love vanished
forever?
Has his promise[p] failed for all
time?
9 Has God forgotten to be
merciful?[q]
Has he in anger withheld his
compassion?[r]" *Selah*
10 Then I thought, "To this I will
appeal:
the years of the right hand[s] of
the Most High."

77:1 [i] Ps 3:4
77:2 [j] Ps 50:15; Isa 26:9,16 [k] Job 11:13 [l] Ge 37:35
77:3 [m] Ps 143:4
77:5 [n] Dt 32:7; Ps 44:1; 143:5; Isa 51:9
77:7 [o] Ps 85:1
77:8 [p] 2Pe 3:9
77:9 [q] Ps 25:6; 40:11; 51:1 [r] Isa 49:15
77:10 [s] Ps 31:22

[a] 10 Or *Surely the wrath of men brings you praise, / and with the remainder of wrath you arm yourself*

11 I will remember the deeds of the
LORD;
77:11 [t] Ps 143:5
yes, I will remember your
miracles[t] of long ago.
12 I will meditate on all your works
and consider all your mighty
deeds.

77:13 [u] Ex 15:11; Ps 71:19; 86:8
13 Your ways, O God, are holy.
What god is so great as our God?[u]
14 You are the God who performs
miracles;
you display your power among
the peoples.
77:15 [v] Ex 6:6; Dt 9:29
15 With your mighty arm you
redeemed your people,[v]
the descendants of Jacob and
Joseph. *Selah*
77:16 [w] Ex 14:21,28; Hab 3:8 [x] Ps 114:4; Hab 3:10
16 The waters[w] saw you, O God,
the waters saw you and
writhed;[x]
the very depths were convulsed.
77:17 [y] Jdg 5:4
17 The clouds poured down water,[y]
the skies resounded with
thunder;
your arrows flashed back and
forth.
18 Your thunder was heard in the
whirlwind,
77:18 [z] Jdg 5:4
your lightning lit up the world;
the earth trembled and quaked.[z]
77:19 [a] Hab 3:15
19 Your path led through the sea,[a]
your way through the mighty
waters,
though your footprints were not
seen.
77:20 [b] Ex 13:21 [c] Ps 78:52; Isa 63:11
20 You led your people[b] like a flock[c]
by the hand of Moses and Aaron.

PSALM 78

A *maskil*[a] of Asaph.

78:1 [d] Isa 51:4; 55:3
1 O my people, hear my teaching;[d]
listen to the words of my mouth.
78:2 [e] Ps 49:4; Mt 13:35*
2 I will open my mouth in parables,[e]
I will utter hidden things, things
from of old—
78:3 [f] Ps 44:1
3 what we have heard and known,
what our fathers have told us.[f]
78:4 [g] Dt 11:19 [h] Ps 26:7; 71:17
4 We will not hide them from their
children;[g]
we will tell the next generation
the praiseworthy deeds[h] of the LORD,
his power, and the wonders he
has done.

78:5 [i] Ps 19:7; 81:5 [j] Ps 147:19
5 He decreed statutes[i] for Jacob[j]
and established the law in Israel,
which he commanded our
forefathers
to teach their children,
6 so the next generation would know
them,
78:6 [k] Ps 22:31; 102:18
even the children yet to be born,[k]
and they in turn would tell their
children.
7 Then they would put their trust in
God
78:7 [l] Dt 6:12 [m] Dt 5:29
and would not forget[l] his deeds
but would keep his commands.[m]
78:8 [n] 2Ch 30:7 [o] Ex 32:9 [p] ver 37; Isa 30:9
8 They would not be like their
forefathers[n]—
a stubborn[o] and rebellious[p]
generation,
whose hearts were not loyal to God,
whose spirits were not faithful
to him.
78:9 [q] ver 57; 1Ch 12:2 [r] Jdg 20:39
9 The men of Ephraim, though
armed with bows,[q]
turned back on the day of battle;[r]
78:10 [s] 2Ki 17:15
10 they did not keep God's covenant[s]
and refused to live by his law.
78:11 [t] Ps 106:13
11 They forgot what he had done,[t]
the wonders he had shown them.
78:12 [u] Ps 106:22 [v] Ex 7-12 [w] Nu 13:22
12 He did miracles[u] in the sight of
their fathers
in the land of Egypt,[v] in the
region of Zoan.[w]
78:13 [x] Ex 14:21; Ps 136:13 [y] Ex 15:8
13 He divided the sea[x] and led them
through;
he made the water stand firm
like a wall.[y]
78:14 [z] Ex 13:21; Ps 105:39
14 He guided them with the cloud by
day
and with light from the fire all
night.[z]
78:15 [a] Nu 20:11; 1Co 10:4
15 He split the rocks[a] in the desert
and gave them water as
abundant as the seas;
16 he brought streams out of a rocky
crag
and made water flow down like
rivers.
78:17 [b] Dt 9:22; Isa 63:10; Heb 3:16
17 But they continued to sin[b] against
him,
rebelling in the desert against
the Most High.
78:18 [c] 1Co 10:9 [d] Ex 16:2; Nu 11:4
18 They willfully put God to the test[c]
by demanding the food they
craved.[d]
78:19 [e] Nu 21:5
19 They spoke against God,[e] saying,

[a] Title: Probably a literary or musical term

DISCOVERY 145

WORTH A THOUSAND WORDS

One of the most anticipated events of the day for many children is story time, that special moment of nestling close to Mom or Dad or crowding around a teacher as a story is either told from memory or read from a book. Curious young minds are filled with vivid pictures as the narrative unfolds, and childish imaginations run wild. Truth be told, we never outgrow our love for a good story. Some people lament, though, that our society has to a large extent lost the art of storytelling. In part because of the variety of distractions available to children and the resulting sensory overload, fewer grandchildren are interested in sitting quietly while Grandpa or Grandma recalls the events that have shaped his or her life. Sadly, these children miss out when the richness of family legacy is replaced by the lure of video game action.

God's stories need to be passed along as well. Throughout history God's faithful people have recounted the stories of the Bible, as well as memories of God's dealings in their own lives, to impressionable new generations, and these children in turn to their own. Moses warned the children of Israel: "Only be careful, and watch yourselves closely so that you do not forget the things your eyes have seen or let them slip from your heart as long as you live. Tell them to your children and to their children after them" (Deuteronomy 3:9).

Matthew quoted Psalm 78:2 to make a comment about Jesus' ministry—Jesus told stories, frequently in the form of parables, everywhere he went (Matthew 13:34–35). Whether he was teaching his disciples, preaching to the crowds or debating with the Jewish leaders, our Lord used stories to drive home his point. People related to Jesus' homespun illustrations from everyday life, regardless of their spiritual or religious background (Matthew 13:15).

Perhaps Jesus' best-known parable is that of the lost, or "prodigal," son (Luke 15:11–32). The story line is simple: A son requests his inheritance from his father, leaves home to indulge in a reckless lifestyle, realizes that he has made a horrible mistake and trudges off toward home, penitent, only to discover that his father had been watching eagerly for him the whole time. The father then hosts a gala celebration in honor of the prodigal's homecoming. The point is just as simple: No matter how far we run from God, the Father waits patiently for our return and begins to celebrate as soon as our weary, plodding figure appears on the horizon.

Our lives themselves are parables that tell others the story of Jesus—that he loves us and that a life changes when he steps into it. If we have been touched by Jesus, we will tell our world the same story with our lives as with our words.

Self-Discovery: *If you were asked to create a short story that would communicate the essence of your life, what would it say? How would Jesus appear to your audience? When the occasion presents itself, tell someone your own story, including detail both from the time before and after you met Jesus.*

GO TO DISCOVERY 146 ON PAGE 754

"Can God spread a table in the
desert?
20 When he struck the rock, water
gushed out,[f]
and streams flowed abundantly.
But can he also give us food?
Can he supply meat[g] for his
people?"
21 When the LORD heard them, he was
very angry;
his fire broke out[h] against Jacob,
and his wrath rose against Israel,
22 for they did not believe in God
or trust[i] in his deliverance.
23 Yet he gave a command to the
skies above
and opened the doors of the
heavens;[j]
24 he rained down manna[k] for the
people to eat,
he gave them the grain of
heaven.
25 Men ate the bread of angels;
he sent them all the food they
could eat.
26 He let loose the east wind[l] from the
heavens
and led forth the south wind by
his power.
27 He rained meat down on them like
dust,
flying birds like sand on the
seashore.
28 He made them come down inside
their camp,
all around their tents.
29 They ate till they had more than
enough,[m]
for he had given them what they
craved.
30 But before they turned from the
food they craved,
even while it was still in their
mouths,[n]
31 God's anger rose against them;
he put to death the sturdiest[o]
among them,
cutting down the young men of
Israel.

32 In spite of all this, they kept on
sinning;
in spite of his wonders,[p] they did
not believe.[q]
33 So he ended their days in futility[r]
and their years in terror.
34 Whenever God slew them, they
would seek[s] him;
they eagerly turned to him again.
35 They remembered that God was
their Rock,[t]
that God Most High was their
Redeemer.[u]
36 But then they would flatter him
with their mouths,[v]
lying to him with their tongues;
37 their hearts were not loyal[w] to him,
they were not faithful to his
covenant.
38 Yet he was merciful;[x]
he forgave[y] their iniquities[z]
and did not destroy them.
Time after time he restrained his
anger
and did not stir up his full wrath.
39 He remembered that they were but
flesh,[a]
a passing breeze[b] that does not
return.

40 How often they rebelled[c] against
him in the desert[d]
and grieved him[e] in the
wasteland!
41 Again and again they put God to
the test;[f]
they vexed the Holy One of
Israel.[g]
42 They did not remember his
power—
the day he redeemed them from
the oppressor,
43 the day he displayed his
miraculous signs in Egypt,
his wonders in the region of
Zoan.
44 He turned their rivers to blood;[h]
they could not drink from their
streams.
45 He sent swarms of flies[i] that
devoured them,
and frogs[j] that devastated them.
46 He gave their crops to the
grasshopper,
their produce to the locust.[k]
47 He destroyed their vines with hail[l]
and their sycamore-figs with
sleet.
48 He gave over their cattle to the hail,
their livestock[m] to bolts of
lightning.
49 He unleashed against them his hot
anger,[n]
his wrath, indignation and
hostility—
a band of destroying angels.

78:20 [f] Nu 20:11 [g] Nu 11:18
78:21 [h] Nu 11:1
78:22 [i] Dt 1:32; Heb 3:19
78:23 [j] Ge 7:11; Mal 3:10
78:24 [k] Ex 16:4; Jn 6:31*
78:26 [l] Nu 11:31
78:29 [m] Nu 11:20
78:30 [n] Nu 11:33
78:31 [o] Isa 10:16
78:32 [p] ver 11 [q] ver 22
78:33 [r] Nu 14:29,35
78:34 [s] Hos 5:15
78:35 [t] Dt 32:4 [u] Dt 9:26
78:36 [v] Eze 33:31
78:37 [w] ver 8; Ac 8:21
78:38 [x] Ex 34:6 [y] Isa 48:10 [z] Nu 14:18,20
78:39 [a] Ge 6:3; Ps 103:14 [b] Job 7:7; Jas 4:14
78:40 [c] Heb 3:16 [d] Ps 95:8; 106:14 [e] Eph 4:30
78:41 [f] Nu 14:22 [g] 2Ki 19:22; Ps 89:18
78:44 [h] Ex 7:20-21; Ps 105:29
78:45 [i] Ex 8:24; Ps 105:31 [j] Ex 8:2,6
78:46 [k] Ex 10:13
78:47 [l] Ex 9:23; Ps 105:32
78:48 [m] Ex 9:25
78:49 [n] Ex 15:7

[50]He prepared a path for his anger;
he did not spare them from death
but gave them over to the plague.
[51]He struck down all the firstborn of Egypt,[o]
the firstfruits of manhood in the tents of Ham.[p]
[52]But he brought his people out like a flock;[q]
he led them like sheep through the desert.
[53]He guided them safely, so they were unafraid;
but the sea engulfed[r] their enemies.[s]
[54]Thus he brought them to the border of his holy land,
to the hill country his right hand[t] had taken.
[55]He drove out nations[u] before them
and allotted their lands to them as an inheritance;[v]
he settled the tribes of Israel in their homes.

[56]But they put God to the test
and rebelled against the Most High;
they did not keep his statutes.
[57]Like their fathers[w] they were disloyal and faithless,
as unreliable as a faulty bow.[x]
[58]They angered him[y] with their high places;[z]
they aroused his jealousy with their idols.[a]
[59]When God heard them, he was very angry;
he rejected Israel[b] completely.
[60]He abandoned the tabernacle of Shiloh,[c]
the tent he had set up among men.
[61]He sent ⌞the ark of⌟ his might[d] into captivity,[e]
his splendor into the hands of the enemy.
[62]He gave his people over to the sword;
he was very angry with his inheritance.
[63]Fire consumed[f] their young men,
and their maidens had no wedding songs;[g]
[64]their priests were put to the sword,[h]
and their widows could not weep.

[65]Then the Lord awoke as from sleep,[i]
as a man wakes from the stupor of wine.
[66]He beat back his enemies;
he put them to everlasting shame.[j]
[67]Then he rejected the tents of Joseph,
he did not choose the tribe of Ephraim;
[68]but he chose the tribe of Judah,
Mount Zion,[k] which he loved.
[69]He built his sanctuary like the heights,
like the earth that he established forever.
[70]He chose David[l] his servant
and took him from the sheep pens;
[71]from tending the sheep he brought him
to be the shepherd[m] of his people Jacob,
of Israel his inheritance.
[72]And David shepherded them with integrity of heart;[n]
with skillful hands he led them.

PSALM 79

A psalm of Asaph.

[1]O God, the nations have invaded your inheritance;[o]
they have defiled your holy temple,
they have reduced Jerusalem to rubble.[p]
[2]They have given the dead bodies of your servants
as food to the birds of the air,
the flesh of your saints to the beasts of the earth.[q]
[3]They have poured out blood like water
all around Jerusalem,
and there is no one to bury the dead.[r]
[4]We are objects of reproach to our neighbors,
of scorn and derision to those around us.[s]

[5]How long,[t] O LORD? Will you be angry[u] forever?
How long will your jealousy burn like fire?[v]

78:51 [o]Ex 12:29; Ps 135:8 [p]Ps 105:23; 106:22
78:52 [q]Ps 77:20
78:53 [r]Ex 14:28 [s]Ps 106:10
78:54 [t]Ex 15:17; Ps 44:3
78:55 [u]Ps 44:2 [v]Jos 13:7
78:57 [w]Eze 20:27 [x]Hos 7:16
78:58 [y]Jdg 2:12 [z]Lev 26:30 [a]Ex 20:4; Dt 32:21
78:59 [b]Dt 32:19
78:60 [c]Jos 18:1
78:61 [d]Ps 132:8 [e]1Sa 4:17
78:63 [f]Nu 11:1 [g]Jer 7:34; 16:9
78:64 [h]1Sa 4:17; 22:18
78:65 [i]Ps 44:23
78:66 [j]1Sa 5:6
78:68 [k]Ps 87:2
78:70 [l]1Sa 16:1
78:71 [m]2Sa 5:2; Ps 28:9
78:72 [n]1Ki 9:4
79:1 [o]Ps 74:2 [p]2Ki 25:9
79:2 [q]Dt 28:26; Jer 7:33
79:3 [r]Jer 16:4
79:4 [s]Ps 44:13; 80:6
79:5 [t]Ps 74:10 [u]Ps 74:1; 85:5 [v]Dt 29:20; Ps 89:46; Zep 3:8

79:6 w Ps 69:24; Rev 16:1 x Jer 10:25; 2Th 1:8 y Ps 14:4

6 Pour out your wrath[w] on the nations
that do not acknowledge[x] you,
on the kingdoms
that do not call on your name;[y]
7 for they have devoured Jacob
and destroyed his homeland.

79:8 z Isa 64:9 a Ps 116:6; 142:6

8 Do not hold against us the sins of the fathers;[z]
may your mercy come quickly to meet us,
for we are in desperate need.[a]

79:9 b 2Ch 14:11 c Ps 25:11; 31:3; Jer 14:7

9 Help us,[b] O God our Savior,
for the glory of your name;
deliver us and forgive our sins
for your name's sake.[c]

79:10 d Ps 42:10 e Ps 94:1

10 Why should the nations say,
"Where is their God?"[d]
Before our eyes, make known
among the nations
that you avenge[e] the outpoured
blood of your servants.
11 May the groans of the prisoners
come before you;
by the strength of your arm
preserve those condemned to die.

79:12 f Isa 65:6; Jer 32:18 g Ge 4:15

12 Pay back into the laps[f] of our
neighbors seven times[g]
the reproach they have hurled at
you, O Lord.

79:13 h Ps 74:1; 95:7 i Ps 44:8

13 Then we your people, the sheep of
your pasture,[h]
will praise you forever;[i]
from generation to generation
we will recount your praise.

PSALM 80

For the director of music. To ⌊the tune of⌋ "The Lilies of the Covenant." Of Asaph. A psalm.

80:1 j Ps 77:20 k Ex 25:22

1 Hear us, O Shepherd of Israel,
you who lead Joseph like a flock;[j]
you who sit enthroned between the
cherubim,[k] shine forth

80:2 l Nu 2:18-24 m Ps 35:23

2 before Ephraim, Benjamin and
Manasseh.[l]
Awaken[m] your might;
come and save us.

80:3 n Ps 85:4; La 5:21 o Nu 6:25

3 Restore[n] us,[o] O God;
make your face shine upon us,
that we may be saved.

4 O LORD God Almighty,
how long will your anger smolder
against the prayers of your
people?
5 You have fed them with the bread
of tears;
you have made them drink tears
by the bowlful.[p]

80:5 p Ps 42:3; Isa 30:20

6 You have made us a source of
contention to our
neighbors,
and our enemies mock us.[q]

80:6 q Ps 79:4

7 Restore us, O God Almighty;
make your face shine upon us,
that we may be saved.

8 You brought a vine[r] out of Egypt;
you drove out[s] the nations and
planted it.

80:8 r Isa 5:1-2; Jer 2:21 s Jos 13:6; Ac 7:45

9 You cleared the ground for it,
and it took root and filled the
land.
10 The mountains were covered with
its shade,
the mighty cedars with its
branches.
11 It sent out its boughs to the Sea,[a]
its shoots as far as the River.[b][t]

80:11 t Ps 72:8

12 Why have you broken down its
walls[u]
so that all who pass by pick its
grapes?

80:12 u Ps 89:40; Isa 5:5

13 Boars from the forest ravage[v] it
and the creatures of the field
feed on it.

80:13 v Jer 5:6

14 Return to us, O God Almighty!
Look down from heaven and
see![w]

80:14 w Isa 63:15

Watch over this vine,
15 the root your right hand has
planted,
the son[c] you have raised up for
yourself.

16 Your vine is cut down, it is burned
with fire;
at your rebuke[x] your people
perish.

80:16 x Ps 39:11; 76:6

17 Let your hand rest on the man at
your right hand,
the son of man you have raised
up for yourself.
18 Then we will not turn away from
you;
revive us, and we will call on
your name.

19 Restore us, O LORD God Almighty;

[a] 11 Probably the Mediterranean [b] 11 That is, the Euphrates [c] 15 Or *branch*

AT GOD'S RIGHT HAND

In many ancient cultures the "right hand" or the host's right side was a place of prestige. If a person were invited to a party or dinner and asked to sit in this particular position, everyone present would immediately recognize that this individual was the most honored guest. While the "man at your right hand" (Psalm 80:17) refers primarily to Israel, we can also see in it the Messiah, God the Son, sitting in the place of honor at the Father's right hand. The New Testament makes it clear that Jesus is that esteemed Son (Matthew 26:64; Mark 16:19; Romans 8:34; Hebrews 12:2; 1 Peter 3:22).

There are several significant aspects to this image. First of all, Jesus is *sitting*. We all know what it's like to rest after we have finished a project into which we've poured a great deal of time and energy. When people arrive home after a day's work, they often sit and elevate their feet on a footstool or sit back in a recliner. Similarly, after Jesus' ascension "he sat down at the right hand of the Majesty in heaven" (Hebrews 1:3). He could sit because his earthly mission had been completed.

Jesus *waits* for the day God will repair the damage caused by sin, the day on which everyone everywhere will witness his glorious return (Acts 2:33–35).

And as he waits, he also *intercedes* for us. When Satan accuses us before God, Jesus contradicts him, because our Savior is living proof that the sin of humanity has been forgiven. The apostle Paul asked in Romans 8:33–34: "Who will bring any charge against those whom God has chosen? It is God who justifies. Who is he that condemns? Christ Jesus, who died—more than that, who was raised to life—is at the right hand of God and is also interceding for us."

Sometimes when we stumble, and especially when we fall, we have a hard time believing that God still accepts us—let alone defends us. But when God the Father inspects us he sees the perfection of Jesus. When we accept Jesus' payment on our behalf, God transfers our sin to him and gives us the gift of his righteousness. "God made [Jesus] who had no sin to be sin for us, so that in him we might become the righteousness of God" (2 Corinthians 5:21).

Jesus isn't always seated, however; The New Testament pictures him in one instance as standing—when Stephen, the first Christian martyr, was about to be stoned to death (Acts 7:56). Stephen gazed skyward and saw heaven opened and Jesus standing at God's right side. Many Christians believe that Jesus stood to welcome Stephen into God's kingdom. As followers of Jesus Christ, our goal is to live in such a way that our Redeemer will honor our homecoming with a standing ovation and the words we long to hear: "Well done, good and faithful servant . . . Come and share your Master's happiness . . . Come, you who are blessed by my Father, take your inheritance, the kingdom prepared for you since the creation of the world" (Matthew 25:23,34).

Self-Discovery: *The next time you pray for forgiveness of your sins, pause a moment to envision Jesus interceding with the Father on your behalf.*

GO TO DISCOVERY 147 ON PAGE 756

make your face shine upon us,
that we may be saved.

PSALM 81

For the director of music. According to *gittith.*[a] Of Asaph.

81:1 [y]Ps 66:1
[1] Sing for joy to God our strength;
shout aloud to the God of Jacob![y]
81:2 [z]Ex 15:20 [a]Ps 92:3
[2] Begin the music, strike the tambourine,[z]
play the melodious harp[a] and lyre.
[3] Sound the ram's horn at the New Moon,
and when the moon is full, on the day of our Feast;
[4] this is a decree for Israel,
an ordinance of the God of Jacob.
[5] He established it as a statute for Joseph
81:5 [b]Ex 11:4 [c]Ps 114:1
when he went out against Egypt,[b]
where we heard a language we did not understand.[b c]

81:6 [d]Isa 9:4
[6] He says, "I removed the burden from their shoulders;[d]
their hands were set free from the basket.
81:7 [e]Ex 2:23; Ps 50:15 [f]Ex 19:19 [g]Ex 17:7
[7] In your distress you called[e] and I rescued you,
I answered[f] you out of a thundercloud;
I tested you at the waters of Meribah.[g] *Selah*
81:8 [h]Ps 50:7
[8] "Hear, O my people,[h] and I will warn you—
if you would but listen to me, O Israel!
81:9 [i]Ex 20:3; Dt 32:12; Isa 43:12
[9] You shall have no foreign god[i] among you;
you shall not bow down to an alien god.
[10] I am the LORD your God,
81:10 [j]Ex 20:2 [k]Ps 107:9
who brought you up out of Egypt.[j]
Open wide your mouth and I will fill[k] it.

[11] "But my people would not listen to me;
81:11 [l]Ex 32:1-6
Israel would not submit to me.[l]
81:12 [m]Ac 7:42; Ro 1:24
[12] So I gave them over[m] to their stubborn hearts
to follow their own devices.

81:13 [n]Dt 5:29; Isa 48:18
[13] "If my people would but listen to me,[n]
if Israel would follow my ways,
81:14 [o]Ps 47:3 [p]Am 1:8
[14] how quickly would I subdue[o] their enemies
and turn my hand against[p] their foes!
[15] Those who hate the LORD would cringe before him,
and their punishment would last forever.
81:16 [q]Dt 32:14
[16] But you would be fed with the finest of wheat;[q]
with honey from the rock I would satisfy you."

PSALM 82

A psalm of Asaph.

82:1 [r]Ps 58:11; Isa 3:13
[1] God presides in the great assembly;
he gives judgment[r] among the "gods":

[2] "How long will you[c] defend the unjust
82:2 [s]Dt 1:17 [t]Ps 58:1-2; Pr 18:5
and show partiality[s] to the wicked?[t] *Selah*
82:3 [u]Dt 24:17 [v]Jer 22:16
[3] Defend the cause of the weak and fatherless;[u]
maintain the rights of the poor[v] and oppressed.
[4] Rescue the weak and needy;
deliver them from the hand of the wicked.

82:5 [w]Ps 14:4; Mic 3:1 [x]Isa 59:9 [y]Ps 11:3
[5] "They know nothing, they understand nothing.[w]
They walk about in darkness;[x]
all the foundations[y] of the earth are shaken.

82:6 [z]Jn 10:34*
[6] "I said, 'You are "gods";[z]
you are all sons of the Most High.'
82:7 [a]Ps 49:12; Eze 31:14
[7] But you will die[a] like mere men;
you will fall like every other ruler."

82:8 [b]Ps 12:5 [c]Ps 2:8; Rev 11:15
[8] Rise up,[b] O God, judge the earth,
for all the nations are your inheritance.[c]

[a] Title: Probably a musical term [b] 5 Or / *and we heard a voice we had not known* [c] 2 The Hebrew is plural.

THE SON OF GOD

The list is long; there are all kinds of "gods" that people conjure up in their own minds and then stubbornly embrace as their source of life and strength. Some people trust in their careers and social connections to see them through life. Others rely on their own creativity or determination, their friends or spouses, their burgeoning bank accounts, or politicians and their platforms. The human heart intuitively latches on to someone or something to worship, but until we know God the Father through his Son Jesus we can't be certain who God really is or what he is like.

The writer of Psalm 82 was speaking a word of judgment specifically to national leaders—the kings, judges and other authority figures in Israel. In ancient cultures such a leader was often referred to as a "god" or "son of god" because of his or her power and position. God accused these ungodly leaders of failing to rule with his priorities and heart as their guiding force. They refused to stand up for the people who couldn't stand alone and declined to rescue those who had no one else to come to their defense (verse 2–4).

Years later Jesus would appear on the scene, entering the world with the same agenda and heart of compassion as his Father. Many people would refuse to acknowledge him for who he really was, alleging that he was no different from all those other "gods" (rulers or judges), a "mere man" claiming to be God. But Jesus had an answer from the very Word of God, quoting a portion of verse 6 of Psalm 82, in which God says of the leaders of the people: "I said, 'You are "gods"; you are all sons of the Most High.' But you will die like mere men; you will fall like every other ruler." God was pointing out that those who rule or judge do so by God's appointment and thus act as his representatives, whether or not they are willing to acknowledge it. Jesus' exact words were: "Is it not written in your Law, 'I have said you are gods'? If he called them 'gods,' to whom the word of God came—and the Scripture cannot be broken—what about the one whom the Father set apart as his very own and sent into the world? Why then do you accuse me of blasphemy because I said, 'I am God's Son' "? (John 10:34–36).

While humans function like little "gods" wherever they rule or take charge over certain areas, in a far greater way Jesus, who does the works of God and demonstrates his rule over disease, death and evil, is the Lord God, the one and only Son of God. Jesus was using reason with the teachers of the law, something on which they prided themselves. But when it came right down to it, they simply didn't want to hear what he had to say or see him for who he is.

As God voluntarily taking on human flesh, Jesus did exactly what the Father had always intended human leaders to do. He was a living expression of the Father's compassion, and he pointed people to the one true God (Matthew 9:35–36) and to the kind of relationship the Father desires to have with all of his children (Matthew 11:28–30).

Self-Discovery: *What affords you the greatest sense of security in life? If you can honestly state that your relationship with Jesus Christ comes first, what takes second place?*

GO TO DISCOVERY 148 ON PAGE 761

PSALM 83

A song. A psalm of Asaph.

83:1 [d] Ps 28:1; 35:22

1 O God, do not keep silent;[d]
be not quiet, O God, be not still.

83:2 [e] Ps 2:1; Isa 17:12 [f] Jdg 8:28; Ps 81:15

2 See how your enemies are astir,[e]
how your foes rear their heads.[f]

83:3 [g] Ps 31:13

3 With cunning they conspire[g]
against your people;
they plot against those you
cherish.

83:4 [h] Est 3:6 [i] Jer 11:19

4 "Come," they say, "let us destroy[h]
them as a nation,
that the name of Israel be
remembered[i] no more."

83:5 [j] Ps 2:2

5 With one mind they plot together;[j]
they form an alliance against
you—

83:6 [k] Ps 137:7 [l] 2Ch 20:1 [m] Ge 25:16

6 the tents of Edom[k] and the
Ishmaelites,
of Moab[l] and the Hagrites,[m]

83:7 [n] Jos 13:5 [o] Eze 27:3

7 Gebal,[a n] Ammon and Amalek,
Philistia, with the people of
Tyre.[o]

83:8 [p] Dt 2:9

8 Even Assyria has joined them
to lend strength to the
descendants of Lot.[p] *Selah*

83:9 [q] Jdg 7:1-23 [r] Jdg 4:23-24

9 Do to them as you did to Midian,[q]
as you did to Sisera and Jabin at
the river Kishon,[r]

83:10 [s] Zep 1:17

10 who perished at Endor
and became like refuse[s] on the
ground.

83:11 [t] Jdg 7:25 [u] Jdg 8:12,21

11 Make their nobles like Oreb and
Zeeb,[t]
all their princes like Zebah and
Zalmunna,[u]

83:12 [v] 2Ch 20:11

12 who said, "Let us take possession[v]
of the pasturelands of God."

83:13 [w] Ps 35:5; Isa 17:13

13 Make them like tumbleweed, O my
God,
like chaff[w] before the wind.

83:14 [x] Dt 32:22; Isa 9:18

14 As fire consumes the forest
or a flame sets the mountains
ablaze,[x]

83:15 [y] Job 9:17

15 so pursue them with your tempest
and terrify them with your
storm.[y]

83:16 [z] Ps 109:29; 132:18

16 Cover their faces with shame[z]
so that men will seek your name,
O LORD.

83:17 [a] Ps 35:4

17 May they ever be ashamed and
dismayed;
may they perish in disgrace.[a]

83:18 [b] Ps 59:13

18 Let them know that you, whose
name is the LORD—
that you alone are the Most High
over all the earth.[b]

PSALM 84

For the director of music. According to *gittith*.[b]
Of the Sons of Korah. A psalm.

84:1 [c] Ps 27:4; 43:3; 132:5

1 How lovely is your dwelling place,[c]
O LORD Almighty!

84:2 [d] Ps 42:1-2

2 My soul yearns,[d] even faints,
for the courts of the LORD;
my heart and my flesh cry out
for the living God.

84:3 [e] Ps 43:4 [f] Ps 5:2

3 Even the sparrow has found a
home,
and the swallow a nest for herself,
where she may have her young—
a place near your altar,[e]
O LORD Almighty, my King and
my God.[f]

4 Blessed are those who dwell in
your house;
they are ever praising you. *Selah*

84:5 [g] Ps 81:1 [h] Jer 31:6

5 Blessed are those whose strength[g]
is in you,
who have set their hearts on
pilgrimage.[h]

84:6 [i] Joel 2:23

6 As they pass through the Valley of
Baca,
they make it a place of springs;
the autumn[i] rains also cover it
with pools.[c]

84:7 [j] Pr 4:18 [k] Dt 16:16

7 They go from strength to strength,[j]
till each appears[k] before God in
Zion.

8 Hear my prayer, O LORD God
Almighty;
listen to me, O God of Jacob.
Selah

84:9 [l] Ps 59:11 [m] 1Sa 16:6; Ps 2:2; 132:17

9 Look upon our shield,[d l] O God;
look with favor on your anointed
one.[m]

84:10 [n] 1Ch 23:5

10 Better is one day in your courts
than a thousand elsewhere;
I would rather be a doorkeeper[n] in
the house of my God
than dwell in the tents of the
wicked.

84:11 [o] Isa 60:19; Rev 21:23 [p] Ge 15:1

11 For the LORD God is a sun[o] and
shield;[p]

[a] 7 That is, Byblos [b] Title: Probably a musical term [c] 6 Or *blessings* [d] 9 Or *sovereign*

the LORD bestows favor and
honor;
84:11 [q]Ps 34:10
no good thing does he withhold[q]
from those whose walk is
blameless.

84:12 [r]Ps 2:12
12 O LORD Almighty,
blessed[r] is the man who trusts in
you.

PSALM 85

For the director of music. Of the Sons of Korah.
A psalm.

1 You showed favor to your land,
85:1 [s]Ps 14:7; Jer 30:18; Eze 39:25
O LORD;
you restored the fortunes[s] of
Jacob.
85:2 [t]Nu 14:19 [u]Ps 78:38
2 You forgave[t] the iniquity[u] of your
people
and covered all their sins. *Selah*
85:3 [v]Ps 106:23 [w]Ex 32:12; Dt 13:17; Ps 78:38; Jnh 3:9
3 You set aside all your wrath[v]
and turned from your fierce
anger.[w]

4 Restore[x] us again, O God our
85:4 [x]Ps 80:3,7
Savior,
and put away your displeasure
toward us.
85:5 [y]Ps 79:5
5 Will you be angry with us forever?[y]
Will you prolong your anger
through all generations?
85:6 [z]Ps 80:18; Hab 3:2
6 Will you not revive[z] us again,
that your people may rejoice in
you?
7 Show us your unfailing love, O LORD,
and grant us your salvation.

8 I will listen to what God the LORD
will say;
85:8 [a]Zec 9:10
he promises peace[a] to his
people, his saints—
but let them not return to folly.
85:9 [b]Isa 46:13 [c]Zec 2:5
9 Surely his salvation[b] is near those
who fear him,
that his glory[c] may dwell in our
land.

85:10 [d]Ps 89:14; Pr 3:3 [e]Ps 72:2-3; Isa 32:17
10 Love and faithfulness[d] meet
together;
righteousness[e] and peace kiss
each other.
11 Faithfulness springs forth from the
earth,
85:11 [f]Isa 45:8
and righteousness[f] looks down
from heaven.
85:12 [g]Ps 84:11; Jas 1:17
12 The LORD will indeed give what is
good,[g]
85:12 [h]Lev 26:4; Ps 67:6; Zec 8:12
and our land will yield[h] its
harvest.
13 Righteousness goes before him
and prepares the way for his
steps.

PSALM 86

A prayer of David.

86:1 [i]Ps 17:6
1 Hear, O LORD, and answer[i] me,
for I am poor and needy.
2 Guard my life, for I am devoted to
you.
You are my God; save your
servant
86:2 [j]Ps 25:2; 31:14
who trusts in you.[j]
86:3 [k]Ps 4:1; 57:1 [l]Ps 88:9
3 Have mercy[k] on me, O Lord,
for I call[l] to you all day long.
4 Bring joy to your servant,
for to you, O Lord,
86:4 [m]Ps 25:1; 143:8
I lift[m] up my soul.

5 You are forgiving and good,
86:5 [n]Ex 34:6; Ne 9:17; Ps 103:8; 145:8; Joel 2:13; Jnh 4:2
O Lord,
abounding in love[n] to all who
call to you.
6 Hear my prayer, O LORD;
listen to my cry for mercy.
86:7 [o]Ps 50:15
7 In the day of my trouble[o] I will call
to you,
for you will answer me.

HEART SURGERY

When the Bible talks about a person's "heart," it is referring to the whole person, to the core of the person's being, rather than simply to his or her emotions. In Psalm 86 David asked God for an "undivided" heart (verse 11)—it was his deepest desire to give *all* of himself to God. Having an undivided heart means that we have learned to focus in a single direction: on getting to know God better and learning to trust him more and more. Jesus expressed the same concept: "No one can serve two masters. Either he will hate the one and love the other, or he will be devoted to the one and despise the other" (Matthew 6:24). Jesus used the example of eyes (Matthew 6:22–23): Just as our eyes must focus together in order for our sight to be undistorted, so our hearts, even as we face concerns and distractions, must maintain their focus on being wholly devoted to God.

86:8 [p]Ex 15:11; Dt 3:24; Ps 89:6

[8]Among the gods there is none like
you,[p] O Lord;
no deeds can compare with yours.

86:9 [q]Ps 66:4; Rev 15:4 [r]Isa 43:7

[9]All the nations you have made
will come and worship[q] before
you, O Lord;
they will bring glory[r] to your
name.

86:10 [s]Ps 72:18 [t]Dt 6:4; Mk 12:29; 1Co 8:4

[10]For you are great and do marvelous
deeds;[s]
you alone[t] are God.

86:11 [u]Ps 25:5 [v]Jer 32:39

[11]Teach me your way,[u] O LORD,
and I will walk in your truth;
give me an undivided[v] heart,
that I may fear your name.
[12]I will praise you, O Lord my God,
with all my heart;
I will glorify your name forever.
[13]For great is your love toward me;
you have delivered me from the
depths of the grave.[a]

86:14 [w]Ps 54:3

[14]The arrogant are attacking me,
O God;
a band of ruthless men seeks my
life—
men without regard for you.[w]

86:15 [x]Ps 103:8 [y]Ex 34:6; Ne 9:17; Joel 2:13

[15]But you, O Lord, are a
compassionate and
gracious[x] God,
slow to anger, abounding in love
and faithfulness.[y]

86:16 [z]Ps 116:16

[16]Turn to me and have mercy on me;
grant your strength to your
servant
and save the son of your
maidservant.[b][z]
[17]Give me a sign of your goodness,
that my enemies may see it and
be put to shame,
for you, O LORD, have helped me
and comforted me.

PSALM 87

Of the Sons of Korah. A psalm. A song.

87:2 [a]Ps 78:68

[1]He has set his foundation on the
holy mountain;
[2] the LORD loves the gates of Zion[a]
more than all the dwellings of
Jacob.

87:3 [b]Ps 46:4; Isa 60:1

[3]Glorious things are said of you,
O city of God:[b] *Selah*

87:4 [c]Job 9:13 [d]Ps 45:12 [e]Isa 19:25

[4]"I will record Rahab[c][c] and Babylon
among those who acknowledge
me—
Philistia too, and Tyre[d], along with
Cush[d]—
and will say, 'This[e] one was born
in Zion.[e]' "
[5]Indeed, of Zion it will be said,
"This one and that one were
born in her,
and the Most High himself will
establish her."

87:6 [f]Ps 69:28; Isa 4:3; Eze 13:9

[6]The LORD will write in the register[f]
of the peoples:
"This one was born in Zion."
Selah

87:7 [g]Ps 149:3 [h]Ps 36:9

[7]As they make music[g] they will sing,
"All my fountains[h] are in you."

PSALM 88

A song. A psalm of the Sons of Korah. For the director of music. According to *mahalath leannoth*.[f] A *maskil*[g] of Heman the Ezrahite.

88:1 [i]Ps 51:14 [j]Ps 22:2; 27:9; Lk 18:7

[1]O LORD, the God who saves me,[i]
day and night I cry out[j] before
you.
[2]May my prayer come before you;
turn your ear to my cry.

88:3 [k]Ps 107:18,26

[3]For my soul is full of trouble
and my life draws near the
grave.[a][k]

88:4 [l]Ps 28:1

[4]I am counted among those who go
down to the pit;[l]
I am like a man without strength.

88:5 [m]Ps 31:22; Isa 53:8

[5]I am set apart with the dead,
like the slain who lie in the
grave,
whom you remember no more,
who are cut off[m] from your care.

88:6 [n]Ps 69:15; La 3:55

[6]You have put me in the lowest pit,
in the darkest depths.[n]

88:7 [o]Ps 42:7

[7]Your wrath lies heavily upon me;
you have overwhelmed me with
all your waves.[o] *Selah*

88:8 [p]Job 19:13; Ps 31:11 [q]Jer 32:2

[8]You have taken from me my closest
friends[p]
and have made me repulsive to
them.
I am confined[q] and cannot escape;

88:9 [r]Ps 38:10

[9] my eyes[r] are dim with grief.

[a] *13,3* Hebrew *Sheol* [b] *16* Or *save your faithful son* [c] *4* A poetic name for Egypt [d] *4* That is, the upper Nile region [e] *4* Or *"O Rahab and Babylon, / Philistia, Tyre and Cush, / I will record concerning those who acknowledge me: / 'This*
[f] Title: Possibly a tune, "The Suffering of Affliction"
[g] Title: Probably a literary or musical term

88:9 [s]Ps 86:3 [t]Job 11:13; Ps 143:6

I call[s] to you, O LORD, every day;
I spread out my hands[t] to you.
10 Do you show your wonders to the dead?
Do those who are dead rise up and praise you?[u] *Selah*

88:10 [u]Ps 6:5

11 Is your love declared in the grave,
your faithfulness[v] in Destruction[a]?

88:11 [v]Ps 30:9

12 Are your wonders known in the place of darkness,
or your righteous deeds in the land of oblivion?

13 But I cry to you for help,[w] O LORD;
in the morning[x] my prayer comes before you.[y]

88:13 [w]Ps 30:2 [x]Ps 5:3 [y]Ps 119:147

14 Why, O LORD, do you reject[z] me
and hide your face[a] from me?

88:14 [z]Ps 43:2 [a]Job 13:24; Ps 13:1

15 From my youth I have been afflicted and close to death;
I have suffered your terrors[b] and am in despair.

88:15 [b]Job 6:4

16 Your wrath has swept over me;
your terrors have destroyed me.
17 All day long they surround me like a flood;[c]
they have completely engulfed me.

88:17 [c]Ps 22:16; 124:4

18 You have taken my companions[d]
and loved ones from me;
the darkness is my closest friend.

88:18 [d]ver 8; Job 19:13; Ps 38:11

PSALM 89

A *maskil*[b] of Ethan the Ezrahite.

1 I will sing[e] of the LORD's great love forever;
with my mouth I will make your faithfulness known[f]
through all generations.
2 I will declare that your love stands firm forever,
that you established your faithfulness in heaven itself.[g]

89:1 [e]Ps 59:16; Ps 101:1 [f]Ps 36:5; 40:10

89:2 [g]Ps 36:5

3 You said, "I have made a covenant with my chosen one,
I have sworn to David my servant,
4 'I will establish your line forever
and make your throne firm through all generations.' "[h] *Selah*

89:4 [h]2Sa 7:12-16; 1Ki 8:16; Ps 132:11-12; Isa 9:7; Lk 1:33

5 The heavens[i] praise your wonders, O LORD,
your faithfulness too, in the assembly of the holy ones.

89:5 [i]Ps 19:1

6 For who in the skies above can compare with the LORD?
Who is like the LORD among the heavenly beings?[j]

89:6 [j]Ps 113:5

7 In the council of the holy ones God is greatly feared;
he is more awesome than all who surround him.[k]

89:7 [k]Ps 47:2

8 O LORD God Almighty, who is like you?[l]
You are mighty, O LORD, and your faithfulness surrounds you.

89:8 [l]Ps 71:19

9 You rule over the surging sea;
when its waves mount up, you still them.[m]

89:9 [m]Ps 65:7

10 You crushed Rahab[n] like one of the slain;
with your strong arm you scattered[o] your enemies.

89:10 [n]Ps 87:4 [o]Ps 68:1

11 The heavens are yours, and yours also the earth;[p]
you founded the world and all that is in it.[q]

89:11 [p]1Ch 29:11; Ps 24:1 [q]Ge 1:1

12 You created the north and the south;
Tabor[r] and Hermon[s] sing for joy[t] at your name.

89:12 [r]Jos 19:22 [s]Dt 3:8; Jos 12:1 [t]Ps 98:8

13 Your arm is endued with power;
your hand is strong, your right hand exalted.

14 Righteousness and justice are the foundation of your throne;[u]
love and faithfulness go before you.

89:14 [u]Ps 97:2

15 Blessed are those who have learned to acclaim you,
who walk in the light[v] of your presence, O LORD.

89:15 [v]Ps 44:3

16 They rejoice in your name[w] all day long;
they exult in your righteousness.

89:16 [w]Ps 105:3

17 For you are their glory and strength,
and by your favor you exalt our horn.[c][x]

89:17 [x]Ps 75:10; 92:10; 148:14

18 Indeed, our shield[d] belongs to the LORD,
our king[y] to the Holy One of Israel.

89:18 [y]Ps 47:9

19 Once you spoke in a vision,
to your faithful people you said:

[a] 11 Hebrew *Abaddon* [b] Title: Probably a literary or musical term [c] 17 *Horn* here symbolizes strong one. [d] 18 Or *sovereign*

How Long, God?

Psalm 89 was written at one of the darkest hours in Israel's history. The nation had been defeated, the king captured and many of the citizens exiled to a foreign country. David's dynasty had been toppled when Nebuchadnezzar, king of Babylon, attacked Jerusalem (2 Kings 24:8–17). This psalm may very well have been written shortly after the battle, when the situation appeared bleakest.

Although God's people were able to observe what they perceived of only as God's harshness and judgment, and nothing of God's protection or compassion in the aftermath of this tragedy, in this instance they still turned to him, entreating him to restore David's family line and lift their nation from the rubble. The songwriter pleaded in desperation: "How long, O LORD? Will you hide yourself forever? How long will your wrath burn like fire?" (Psalm 89:46).

Circumstances in life often seem beyond our capacity to bear. When adversity strikes, when physical or emotional anguish stays with us for so long that we feel as though our very soul has been worn down to nothing, we too implore God, "How long? When are you going to make this stop?" We all pine for an end to the pain and search our hearts to determine whether we've done something to deserve such punishment. The Bible is filled with promises from God, however, and we need to remind ourselves of what those promises are. The psalmist listed a few of them: David's line will go on forever (verse 4), God will never stop loving his people (verses 28–37) and God pledges to keep his promises (verse 34).

We also need to move forward, difficult though this may seem in those times when we could simply give in to stagnation or regression. When it feels as though God has disappeared from the scene, we are hard-pressed to look forward to anything. The bad news at the time of Israel's defeat was that the nation was in exile; it appeared that David's family line had been irrevocably severed. But the good news was that the promised Messiah would indeed emerge from this line and would do much more than simply rescue one nation from another.

God's overarching plan has always been to rescue humanity from the consequences of sin in this world. As his plan unfolded, there was a time when all seemed lost. The promised Messiah, Jesus, was hanging on a cross. His Father and his best friends had forsaken him. His enemies appeared to have won. But just when everything was darkest, Jesus triumphed over sin, Satan, death and all of his human enemies.

When we face difficulty of any kind, we cannot let ourselves judge what God is doing on the basis of our specific, fleeting circumstances. When Israel was defeated, God's chosen people assumed that God had forsaken them—but the very opposite was true. Our focal point is so very limited, but God is working from the blueprint of his master plan for all of "his-story." Be patient while his plan for you unfolds.

***Self-Discovery:** What do you notice in the last verse of this psalm? Does it surprise you? Are you able to praise the Lord—the one in control—in the midst of the trials you are presently facing?*

GO TO DISCOVERY 149 ON PAGE 764

"I have bestowed strength on a
warrior;
I have exalted a young man from
among the people.

89:20 [z] Ac 13:22 [a] Ps 78:70 [b] 1Sa 16:1,12

20 I have found David[z] my servant;[a]
with my sacred oil I have
anointed[b] him.
21 My hand will sustain him;

89:21 [c] Ps 18:35

surely my arm will strengthen
him.[c]
22 No enemy will subject him to
tribute;

89:22 [d] 2Sa 7:10

no wicked man will oppress[d] him.
23 I will crush his foes before him[e]

89:23 [e] Ps 18:40 [f] 2Sa 7:9

and strike down his adversaries.[f]
24 My faithful love will be with him,[g]

89:24 [g] 2Sa 7:15

and through my name his horn[a]
will be exalted.
25 I will set his hand over the sea,

89:25 [h] Ps 72:8

his right hand over the rivers.[h]
26 He will call out to me, 'You are my

89:26 [i] 2Sa 7:14 [j] 2Sa 22:47

Father,[i]
my God, the Rock my Savior.'[j]
27 I will also appoint him my

89:27 [k] Col 1:18 [l] Nu 24:7 [m] Rev 1:5; 19:16

firstborn,[k]
the most exalted[l] of the kings[m]
of the earth.
28 I will maintain my love to him
forever,

89:28 [n] ver 33-34; Isa 55:3

and my covenant with him will
never fail.[n]
29 I will establish his line forever,

89:29 [o] ver 4,36; Dt 11:21; Jer 33:17

his throne as long as the heavens
endure.[o]
30 "If his sons forsake my law
and do not follow my statutes,
31 if they violate my decrees
and fail to keep my commands,

89:32 [p] 2Sa 7:14

32 I will punish their sin with the rod,
their iniquity with flogging;[p]

89:33 [q] 2Sa 7:15

33 but I will not take my love from
him,[q]
nor will I ever betray my
faithfulness.
34 I will not violate my covenant

89:34 [r] Nu 23:19

or alter what my lips have
uttered.[r]
35 Once for all, I have sworn by my
holiness—
and I will not lie to David—
36 that his line will continue forever
and his throne endure before me
like the sun;
37 it will be established forever like
the moon,
the faithful witness in the sky."
Selah

38 But you have rejected,[s] you have

89:38 [s] Dt 32:19; 1Ch 28:9; Ps 44:9

spurned,
you have been very angry with
your anointed one.
39 You have renounced the covenant
with your servant
and have defiled his crown in

89:39 [t] La 5:16

the dust.[t]
40 You have broken through all his

89:40 [u] Ps 80:12 [v] La 2:2

walls[u]
and reduced his strongholds[v] to
ruins.
41 All who pass by have plundered
him;
he has become the scorn of his

89:41 [w] Ps 44:13

neighbors.[w]
42 You have exalted the right hand of
his foes;
you have made all his enemies

89:42 [x] Ps 13:2; 80:6

rejoice.[x]
43 You have turned back the edge of
his sword
and have not supported him in

89:43 [y] Ps 44:10

battle.[y]
44 You have put an end to his splendor
and cast his throne to the
ground.
45 You have cut short the days of his
youth;
you have covered him with a

89:45 [z] Ps 44:15; 109:29

mantle of shame.[z] *Selah*
46 How long, O LORD? Will you hide
yourself forever?
How long will your wrath burn

89:46 [a] Ps 79:5

like fire?[a]
47 Remember how fleeting is my life.[b]

89:47 [b] Job 7:7; Ps 39:

For what futility you have
created all men!
48 What man can live and not see
death,
or save himself from the power of

89:48 [c] Ps 22:29; 49:9

the grave[b]?[c] *Selah*
49 O Lord, where is your former great
love,
which in your faithfulness you
swore to David?
50 Remember, Lord, how your servant

89:50 [d] Ps 69:19

has[c] been mocked,[d]
how I bear in my heart the
taunts of all the nations,
51 the taunts with which your enemies
have mocked, O LORD,
with which they have mocked

89:51 [e] Ps 74:10

every step of your anointed
one.[e]

[a] 24 *Horn* here symbolizes strength.
[b] 48 Hebrew *Sheol* [c] 50 Or *your servants have*

52 Praise be to the LORD forever!
Amen and Amen.[f]

89:52 [f]Ps 41:13; 72:19

BOOK IV

Psalms 90–106

PSALM 90

A prayer of Moses the man of God.

1 Lord, you have been our dwelling
place[g]
throughout all generations.
2 Before the mountains were born[h]
or you brought forth the earth
and the world,
from everlasting to everlasting
you are God.[i]

90:1 [g]Dt 33:27; Eze 11:16
90:2 [h]Job 15:7; Pr 8:25 [i]Ps 102:24-27

3 You turn men back to dust,
saying, "Return to dust, O sons
of men."[j]
4 For a thousand years in your sight
are like a day that has just gone
by,
or like a watch in the night.[k]
5 You sweep men away[l] in the sleep
of death;
they are like the new grass of the
morning—
6 though in the morning it springs
up new,
by evening it is dry and
withered.[m]

90:3 [j]Ge 3:19; Job 34:15
90:4 [k]2Pe 3:8
90:5 [l]Ps 73:20; Isa 40:6
90:6 [m]Mt 6:30; Jas 1:10

7 We are consumed by your anger
and terrified by your
indignation.
8 You have set our iniquities before
you,
our secret sins[n] in the light of
your presence.
9 All our days pass away under your
wrath;
we finish our years with a moan.[o]
10 The length of our days is seventy
years—
or eighty, if we have the strength;
yet their span[a] is but trouble and
sorrow,
for they quickly pass, and we fly
away.[p]

90:8 [n]Ps 19:12
90:9 [o]Ps 78:33
90:10 [p]Job 20:8

11 Who knows the power of your
anger?
For your wrath is as great as the
fear that is due you.[q]

90:11 [q]Ps 76:7

12 Teach us to number our days[r]
aright,
that we may gain a heart of
wisdom.[s]

90:12 [r]Ps 39:4 [s]Dt 32:29

13 Relent, O LORD! How long[t] will it be?
Have compassion on your
servants.[u]
14 Satisfy[v] us in the morning with
your unfailing love,
that we may sing for joy[w] and be
glad all our days.[x]
15 Make us glad for as many days as
you have afflicted us,
for as many years as we have
seen trouble.
16 May your deeds be shown to your
servants,
your splendor to their children.[y]

90:13 [t]Ps 6:3 [u]Dt 32:36; Ps 135:14
90:14 [v]Ps 103:5 [w]Ps 85:6 [x]Ps 31:7
90:16 [y]Ps 44:1; Hab 3:2

17 May the favor[b] of the Lord our God
rest upon us;
establish the work of our hands
for us—
yes, establish the work of our
hands.[z]

90:17 [z]Isa 26:12

PSALM 91

1 He who dwells in the shelter[a] of the
Most High
will rest in the shadow[b] of the
Almighty.[c]
2 I will say[d] of the LORD, "He is my
refuge[c] and my fortress,
my God, in whom I trust."

91:1 [a]Ps 31:20 [b]Ps 17:8
91:2 [c]Ps 142:5

3 Surely he will save you from the
fowler's snare[d]
and from the deadly pestilence.[e]
4 He will cover you with his feathers,
and under his wings you will
find refuge;[f]
his faithfulness will be your
shield[g] and rampart.
5 You will not fear[h] the terror of
night,
nor the arrow that flies by day,
6 nor the pestilence that stalks in the
darkness,
nor the plague that destroys at
midday.
7 A thousand may fall at your side,
ten thousand at your right hand,
but it will not come near you.

91:3 [d]Ps 124:7; Pr 6:5 [e]1Ki 8:37
91:4 [f]Ps 17:8 [g]Ps 35:2
91:5 [h]Job 5:21

[a] 10 Or *yet the best of them* [b] 17 Or *beauty*
[c] 1 Hebrew *Shaddai* [d] 2 Or *He says*

ANGELS WATCHING OVER US

Artistic renditions of angels appear everywhere: on coffee mugs, in picture books, on postcards, in magazines; angels are even the focus of television shows and documentaries. We are all fascinated by the suggestion that, as we live out our lives on planet earth, we are surrounded by, watched over and perhaps even protected by lovely unseen beings of light. Some people pray to angels, some worship them and still others believe that we will become angels after our deaths.

The Bible teaches that angels are spiritual beings created by God to do his will. The word *angel* means "messenger," and it comes from a root word meaning "sent." Hebrews 1:14 asks, "Are not all angels ministering spirits sent to serve those who will inherit salvation?" God sends his angels to accomplish numerous specific tasks.

When God expelled Adam and Eve from the Garden of Eden, mighty warrior angels called *cherubim* were assigned to stand on the east side of the garden to guard the tree of life (Genesis 3:24).

God sometimes sends angels to guide his people. In Genesis 24 Abraham dispatched his servant to find a wife for his son Isaac, confident that God would send an angel to lead the servant to the young woman God intended for Abraham's son of promise.

Angels worship God. Isaiah 6 provides a fascinating glimpse into the very presence of God. Isaiah saw angels called *seraphim* and described them as having six wings: "With two wings they covered their faces, with two they covered their feet, and with two they were flying. And they were calling to one another: 'Holy, holy, holy is the LORD Almighty' " (Isaiah 6:2–3) Apparently the primary role for these angels was to worship God and testify to his presence and power.

Angels protect people. Psalm 91:11–12 assures us, "For he will command his angels concerning you to guard you in all your ways; they will lift you up in their hands, so that you will not strike your foot against a stone." The Bible nowhere states that each individual person is guarded by a particular angel, but it does tell us about times when God sent angels to guard and protect his people in certain circumstances.

God also sends angels to provide strength to his people in times of temptation. When Satan tried to lure Jesus into turning away from the will of his Father, the devil cited verse 11 of this very psalm as bait. He attempted to turn God's promise into permission for Jesus to take advantage of God. God's promises of care and protection are never an invitation to carelessness, neglect or unwise choices. There is an enormous difference between trusting God and testing him. When we deliberately place ourselves in harm's way, we miss the point of his promise of protection.

Jesus resisted the temptation, and angels came to minister to him (Matthew 4:11). In our own personal journeys God sends his angels to support us (Psalm 34:7). We seldom if ever see them, but they are present at God's command, faithfully performing his will.

Self-Discovery: *Have you, or someone else you know, ever had an "angel experience," or have you heard stories of angel encounters that have been memorable to you?*

GO TO DISCOVERY 150 ON PAGE 769

8 You will only observe with your eyes
and see the punishment of the wicked.[i]
9 If you make the Most High your dwelling—
even the LORD, who is my refuge—
10 then no harm[j] will befall you,
no disaster will come near your tent.
11 For he will command his angels[k]
concerning you
to guard you in all your ways;[l]
12 they will lift you up in their hands,
so that you will not strike your foot against a stone.[m]
13 You will tread upon the lion and the cobra;
you will trample the great lion and the serpent.[n]

14 "Because he loves me," says the LORD, "I will rescue him;
I will protect him, for he acknowledges my name.
15 He will call upon me, and I will answer him;
I will be with him in trouble,
I will deliver him and honor him.[o]
16 With long life[p] will I satisfy him
and show him my salvation.[q]"

91:8 [i] Ps 37:34; 58:10; Mal 1:5
91:10 [j] Pr 12:21
91:11 [k] Heb 1:14 [l] Ps 34:7
91:12 [m] Mt 4:6*; Lk 4:10-11*
91:13 [n] Da 6:22; Lk 10:19
91:15 [o] 1Sa 2:30; Ps 50:15; Jn 12:26
91:16 [p] Dt 6:2; Ps 21:4 [q] Ps 50:23

PSALM 92

A psalm. A song. For the Sabbath day.

1 It is good to praise the LORD
and make music to your name,[r] O Most High,[s]
2 to proclaim your love in the morning[t]
and your faithfulness at night,
3 to the music of the ten-stringed lyre
and the melody of the harp.[u]

4 For you make me glad by your deeds, O LORD;
I sing for joy at the works of your hands.[v]
5 How great are your works,[w] O LORD,
how profound your thoughts![x]
6 The senseless man[y] does not know,
fools do not understand,
7 that though the wicked spring up like grass
and all evildoers flourish,
they will be forever destroyed.

8 But you, O LORD, are exalted forever.

9 For surely your enemies, O LORD,
surely your enemies will perish;
all evildoers will be scattered.[z]
10 You have exalted my horn[a][a] like that of a wild ox;
fine oils[b] have been poured upon me.
11 My eyes have seen the defeat of my adversaries;
my ears have heard the rout of my wicked foes.[c]

12 The righteous will flourish like a palm tree,
they will grow like a cedar of Lebanon;[d]
13 planted in the house of the LORD,
they will flourish in the courts of our God.[e]
14 They will still bear fruit[f] in old age,
they will stay fresh and green,
15 proclaiming, "The LORD is upright;
he is my Rock, and there is no wickedness in him.[g]"

92:1 [r] Ps 147:1 [s] Ps 135:3
92:2 [t] Ps 89:1
92:3 [u] 1Sa 10:5; Ne 12:27; Ps 33:2
92:4 [v] Ps 8:6; 143:5
92:5 [w] Rev 15:3 [x] Ps 40:5; 139:17; Isa 28:29; Ro 11:33
92:6 [y] Ps 73:22
92:9 [z] Ps 68:1; 89:10
92:10 [a] Ps 89:17 [b] Ps 23:5
92:11 [c] Ps 54:7; 91:8
92:12 [d] Ps 1:3; 52:8; Jer 17:8; Hos 14:6
92:13 [e] Ps 100:4
92:14 [f] Jn 15:2
92:15 [g] Job 34:10

PSALM 93

1 The LORD reigns,[h] he is robed in majesty;[i]
the LORD is robed in majesty
and is armed with strength.[j]
The world is firmly established;
it cannot be moved.[k]
2 Your throne was established long ago;
you are from all eternity.[l]
3 The seas[m] have lifted up, O LORD,
the seas have lifted up their voice;
the seas have lifted up their pounding waves.
4 Mightier than the thunder[n] of the great waters,
mightier than the breakers of the sea—
the LORD on high is mighty.

5 Your statutes stand firm;
holiness[o] adorns your house
for endless days, O LORD.

93:1 [h] Ps 97:1 [i] Ps 104:1 [j] Ps 65:6 [k] Ps 96:10
93:2 [l] Ps 45:6
93:3 [m] Ps 96:11
93:4 [n] Ps 65:7
93:5 [o] Ps 29:2

[a] 10 *Horn* here symbolizes strength.

PSALM 94

[1]O LORD, the God who avenges,[p]
O God who avenges, shine
forth.[q]
[2]Rise up, O Judge[r] of the earth;
pay back[s] to the proud what
they deserve.
[3]How long will the wicked, O LORD,
how long will the wicked be
jubilant?

[4]They pour out arrogant[t] words;
all the evildoers are full of
boasting.[u]
[5]They crush your people,[v] O LORD;
they oppress your inheritance.
[6]They slay the widow and the alien;
they murder the fatherless.
[7]They say, "The LORD does not see;[w]
the God of Jacob pays no heed."

[8]Take heed, you senseless ones[x]
among the people;
you fools, when will you become
wise?
[9]Does he who implanted the ear not
hear?
Does he who formed the eye not
see?[y]
[10]Does he who disciplines nations
not punish?
Does he who teaches[z] man lack
knowledge?
[11]The LORD knows the thoughts of
man;
he knows that they are futile.[a]

[12]Blessed is the man you discipline,[b]
O LORD,
the man you teach[c] from your
law;
[13]you grant him relief from days of
trouble,
till a pit[d] is dug for the wicked.
[14]For the LORD will not reject his
people;[e]
he will never forsake his
inheritance.
[15]Judgment will again be founded on
righteousness,[f]
and all the upright in heart will
follow it.

[16]Who will rise up[g] for me against
the wicked?
Who will take a stand for me
against evildoers?[h]

94:1 p Na 1:2; Ro 12:19 q Ps 80:1
94:2 r Ge 18:25 s Ps 31:23
94:4 t Ps 31:18 u Ps 52:1
94:5 v Isa 3:15
94:7 w Job 22:14; Ps 10:11
94:8 x Ps 92:6
94:9 y Ex 4:11; Pr 20:12
94:10 z Job 35:11; Isa 28:26
94:11 a 1Co 3:20*
94:12 b Job 5:17; Heb 12:5 c Dt 8:3
94:13 d Ps 55:23
94:14 e 1Sa 12:22; Ps 37:28; Ro 11:2
94:15 f Ps 97:2
94:16 g Nu 10:35; Ps 17:13 h Ps 59:2

[17]Unless the LORD had given me help,[i]
I would soon have dwelt in the
silence of death.
[18]When I said, "My foot is slipping,[j]"
your love, O LORD, supported me.
[19]When anxiety was great within me,
your consolation brought joy to
my soul.

[20]Can a corrupt throne be allied with
you—
one that brings on misery by its
decrees?[k]
[21]They band together[l] against the
righteous
and condemn the innocent[m] to
death.
[22]But the LORD has become my
fortress,
and my God the rock in whom I
take refuge.[n]
[23]He will repay[o] them for their sins
and destroy them for their
wickedness;
the LORD our God will destroy
them.

PSALM 95

[1]Come, let us sing for joy to the
LORD;
let us shout aloud[p] to the Rock[q]
of our salvation.
[2]Let us come before him[r] with
thanksgiving
and extol him with music[s] and
song.

[3]For the LORD is the great God,[t]
the great King above all gods.[u]
[4]In his hand are the depths of the
earth,
and the mountain peaks belong
to him.
[5]The sea is his, for he made it,
and his hands formed the dry
land.[v]

[6]Come, let us bow down[w] in
worship,
let us kneel[x] before the LORD our
Maker;[y]
[7]for he is our God
and we are the people of his
pasture,[z]
the flock under his care.
Today, if you hear his voice,

94:17 i Ps 124:2
94:18 j Ps 38:16
94:20 k Ps 58:2
94:21 l Ps 56:6 m Ps 106:38; Pr 17:15,26
94:22 n Ps 18:2; 59:9
94:23 o Ps 7:16
95:1 p Ps 81:1 q 2Sa 22:47
95:2 r Mic 6:6 s Ps 81:2; Eph 5:19
95:3 t Ps 48:1; 145:3 u Ps 96:4; 97:9
95:5 v Ge 1:9; Ps 146:6
95:6 w Php 2:10 x 2Ch 6:13 y Ps 100:3; 149:2; Isa 17:7; Da 6:10-11; Hos 8:14
95:7 z Ps 74:1; 79:13

8 do not harden your hearts as you did at Meribah,[a] [a]
as you did that day at Massah[b] in the desert,
9 where your fathers tested[b] and tried me,
though they had seen what I did.
10 For forty years[c] I was angry with that generation;
I said, "They are a people whose hearts go astray,
and they have not known my ways."
11 So I declared on oath[d] in my anger,
"They shall never enter my rest."[e]

95:8 [a]Ex 17:7
95:9 [b]Nu 14:22; Ps 78:18; 1Co 10:9
95:10 [c]Ac 7:36; Heb 3:17
95:11 [d]Nu 14:23 [e]Dt 1:35; Heb 4:3*

PSALM 96

1 Sing to the LORD[f] a new song;
sing to the LORD, all the earth.
2 Sing to the LORD, praise his name;
proclaim his salvation[g] day after day.
3 Declare his glory among the nations,
his marvelous deeds among all peoples.
4 For great is the LORD and most worthy of praise;[h]
he is to be feared[i] above all gods.[j]
5 For all the gods of the nations are idols,
but the LORD made the heavens.[k]
6 Splendor and majesty are before him;
strength and glory[l] are in his sanctuary.
7 Ascribe to the LORD,[m] O families of nations,[n]
ascribe to the LORD glory and strength.
8 Ascribe to the LORD the glory due his name;
bring an offering[o] and come into his courts.
9 Worship the LORD in the splendor of his[c] holiness;[p]
tremble[q] before him, all the earth.[r]
10 Say among the nations, "The LORD reigns."[s]
The world is firmly established, it cannot be moved;[t]
he will judge the peoples with equity.[u]
11 Let the heavens rejoice, let the earth be glad;[v]
let the sea resound, and all that is in it;
12 let the fields be jubilant, and everything in them.
Then all the trees of the forest[w] will sing for joy;[x]
13 they will sing before the LORD, for he comes,
he comes to judge[y] the earth.
He will judge the world in righteousness
and the peoples in his truth.

96:1 [f]1Ch 16:23
96:2 [g]Ps 71:15
96:4 [h]Ps 18:3; 145:3 [i]Ps 89:7 [j]Ps 95:3
96:5 [k]Ps 115:15
96:6 [l]Ps 29:1
96:7 [m]Ps 29:1 [n]Ps 22:27
96:8 [o]Ps 45:12; 72:10
96:9 [p]Ps 29:2 [q]Ps 114:7 [r]Ps 33:8
96:10 [s]Ps 97:1 [t]Ps 93:1 [u]Ps 67:4
96:11 [v]Ps 97:1; 98:7; Isa 49:13
96:12 [w]Isa 44:23 [x]Ps 65:13
96:13 [y]Rev 19:11

PSALM 97

1 The LORD reigns,[z] let the earth be glad;[a]
let the distant shores rejoice.

97:1 [z]Ps 96:10 [a]Ps 96:11

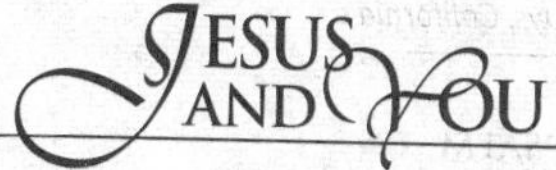

PEACE WITH GOD

When the Bible speaks of "rest," it is frequently implying a state of peaceful unity with God, a relationship in which there are no barriers between his people and himself, a relationship in which we hold nothing back but give of ourselves completely. Psalm 95 reminds us of one incident in which the Israelites refused to follow God's instructions and rebelled against Moses (Exodus 17:1–7). Because of their sin they were not permitted to settle in a place they could call home; they were unable to find the serenity for which their weary souls longed. For 40 long years they made their home in the blistering desert, moving from place to place as God directed. Psalm 95 reminded God's people of their wandering, and it also urges us to find that longed-for repose—by trusting God completely and following him persistently. We realize that we find true rest—that place to call home, that place with no barriers in our relationship with our Creator—through Jesus Christ (Ephesians 2:11–22). The author of Hebrews reminded us that we are no different from the Israelites: They failed to find rest when they refused to follow God, and we are also in danger if we harden our hearts against him (Hebrews 3:12–19). The Bible is explicit: The only way to find a place of rest (Matthew 11:28–29) is to trust in God and walk step by step with him as we love "with actions and in truth" (1 John 3:18–20).

[a] 8 *Meribah* means *quarreling.* [b] 8 *Massah* means *testing.* [c] 9 Or *LORD with the splendor of*

O FOR A THOUSAND TONGUES TO SING MY GREAT REDEEMER'S PRAISE, THE GLORIES OF MY GOD AND KING, THE TRIUMPHS OF HIS GRACE!

Charles Wesley, *British Hymnwriter*

97:2 [b] Ex 19:9; Ps 18:11 [c] Ps 89:14
97:3 [d] Da 7:10 [e] Hab 3:5 [f] Ps 18:8
97:4 [g] Ps 104:32
97:5 [h] Ps 46:2,6; Mic 1:4 [i] Jos 3:11
97:6 [j] Ps 50:6 [k] Ps 19:1
97:7 [l] Lev 26:1 [m] Jer 10:14 [n] Heb 1:6
97:8 [o] Ps 48:11

2 Clouds and thick darkness[b]
surround him;
righteousness and justice are the
foundation of his throne.[c]
3 Fire[d] goes before[e] him
and consumes[f] his foes on every
side.
4 His lightning lights up the world;
the earth sees and trembles.[g]
5 The mountains melt[h] like wax
before the LORD,
before the Lord of all the earth.[i]
6 The heavens proclaim his
righteousness,[j]
and all the peoples see his glory.[k]
7 All who worship images[l] are put to
shame,[m]
those who boast in idols—
worship him,[n] all you gods!
8 Zion hears and rejoices
and the villages of Judah are glad
because of your judgments,[o]
O LORD.

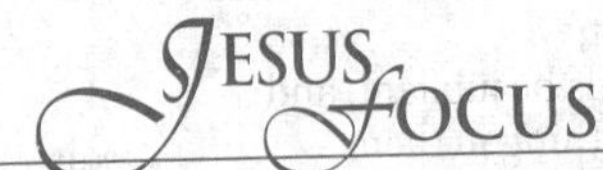

JESUS FOCUS

POWER AND GLORY

Psalm 97 paints a dramatic picture of God's reign over his creation, using large and colorful brushstrokes from nature to describe his glory: clouds and thick darkness, fire, lightning, even mountains that melt before him. The book of Revelation draws on similar images when it depicts for us what the situation will be like when Jesus comes back to free his creation from the effects of sin once and for all, to rule as our eternal King (Revelation 16:16–20). Earlier in the New Testament, when Jesus talked with his disciples about the "distress" of those final days, he employed similar language: The sun and moon will be darkened, stars will fall and the heavens will be shaken. Only then, he added, will he come to earth with amazing power and unspeakable glory (Matthew 24:29–30).

9 For you, O LORD, are the Most High
over all the earth;[p]
you are exalted[q] far above all
gods.
10 Let those who love the LORD hate
evil,[r]
for he guards the lives of his
faithful ones[s]
and delivers[t] them from the
hand of the wicked.[u]
11 Light is shed[v] upon the righteous
and joy on the upright in heart.
12 Rejoice in the LORD, you who are
righteous,
and praise his holy name.[w]

97:9 [p] Ps 83:18; 95:3 [q] Ex 18:11
97:10 [r] Ps 34:14; Am 5:15; Ro 12:9 [s] Pr 2:8 [t] Da 3:28 [u] Ps 37:40; Jer 15:21
97:11 [v] Job 22:28
97:12 [w] Ps 30:4

THE UNIQUENESS OF THE PSALMS MAKES THEM AN APPROPRIATE VEHICLE TO PRAISE THE UNIQUENESS OF CHRIST.

Jack Hayford, *Pastor, Van Nuys, California*

PSALM 98

A psalm.

1 Sing to the LORD a new song,[x]
for he has done marvelous
things;[y]
his right hand[z] and his holy arm[a]
have worked salvation for him.
2 The LORD has made his salvation
known[b]
and revealed his righteousness
to the nations.
3 He has remembered[c] his love
and his faithfulness to the house
of Israel;
all the ends of the earth have seen
the salvation of our God.

4 Shout for joy[d] to the LORD, all the
earth,
burst into jubilant song with
music;
5 make music to the LORD with the
harp,[e]
with the harp and the sound of
singing,[f]
6 with trumpets[g] and the blast of the
ram's horn—
shout for joy before the LORD,
the King.[h]

98:1 [x] Ps 96:1 [y] Ps 96:3 [z] Ex 15:6 [a] Isa 52:10
98:2 [b] Isa 52:10
98:3 [c] Lk 1:54
98:4 [d] Isa 44:23
98:5 [e] Ps 92:3 [f] Isa 51:3
98:6 [g] Nu 10:10 [h] Ps 47:7

SOMETHING NEW

Psalm 98 is a commemoration of a time when God rescued his people (verse 2), a celebration that spreads out like circles on the surface of a pond. The act of praising God for who he is begins with his own people, moves out to encompass all the people on earth and finally radiates throughout everything God has created. The only fitting song for a festivity of this magnitude is a completely *new* song describing what God has done for his people!

As God's people we are all included in an old promise of a new deal he has made through Jesus (Jeremiah 31:31–34; Luke 22:20). Sin stood as an impenetrable barrier between human beings and God, and the only just penalty was death. God himself through Jesus Christ paid that debt on our behalf, allowing each of us to participate in his offer of eternal life. When we trust in Jesus and accept his payment, that wall of sin is scaled and we enjoy a new standing before God. We have the opportunity for a brand-new start (2 Corinthians 5:17), a spiritual birth into God's family (1 Peter 1:3).

One way to describe this altered status is to say that we receive a new "self." We start afresh with a completely different lifestyle, working to rid our lives of old and unproductive habits and patterns (Colossians 3:5–14). This process continues throughout our earthly lives. The fact that the goal is so elusive can be discouraging at times, but the good news is that the Holy Spirit comes to our aid. He works from within us, helping us to *want* to live a life that pleases God and providing the inner strength and resolve to put that desire into practice (Philippians 2:12–13). Along with the new life that we enjoy, God promises each of us an attitude transplant (Ephesians 4:22–23).

In the end Jesus will repair the damage caused by sin, both throughout the world and within our souls. We can look forward to that day in which he will create "a new heaven and a new earth" in which all things will be perfect (Isaiah 43:18–19; 65:17–19; 2 Peter 3:13; Revelation 21:1–5). When we reflect on our awesome God, we can do little else but look for new ways to declare just how marvelous he is.

What has been your most meaningful worship experience? Now imagine that event beginning to spread around the world until every person on earth is shouting for joy to the Lord. Imagine that nature begins to join in, with jubilant songs of praise resounding from the sea, rivers clapping with the beat, mountains echoing with sounds of joy.

Paul depicted creation groaning because of its bondage to decay (Romans 8:19–22). Someday Jesus will come and set it free. The sons of God will be revealed, and the "the earth will be filled with the knowledge of the glory of the Lord, as the waters cover the sea" (Hebrews 2:14). Every tongue will acknowledge that Jesus is Lord and every person bow in worship (Philippians 2:9–11). What a fantastic worship experience that will be!

Self-Discovery: *Does your love for others reflect your love for Jesus in a manner that draws people to him? Do you think others sense that there is something "different"—special—about you, something that makes them wonder about your source of love and joy?*

GO TO DISCOVERY 151 ON PAGE 773

7 Let the sea resound, and
everything in it,
the world, and all who live
98:7 iPs 24:1 — in it.[i]
8 Let the rivers clap their hands,
98:8 jIsa 55:12 — let the mountains[j] sing together
for joy;
9 let them sing before the LORD,
for he comes to judge the earth.
He will judge the world in
righteousness
98:9 kPs 96:10 — and the peoples with equity.[k]

PSALM 99

99:1 lPs 97:1 mEx 25:22 — 1 The LORD reigns,[l]
let the nations tremble;
he sits enthroned between the
cherubim,[m]
let the earth shake.
99:2 nPs 48:1 oPs 97:9; 113:4 — 2 Great is the LORD[n] in Zion;
he is exalted[o] over all the
nations.
3 Let them praise your great and
99:3 pPs 76:1 — awesome name[p]—
he is holy.

99:4 qPs 11:7 rPs 98:9 — 4 The King is mighty, he loves
justice[q]—
you have established equity;[r]
in Jacob you have done
what is just and right.
99:5 sPs 132:7 — 5 Exalt[s] the LORD our God
and worship at his footstool;
he is holy.
99:6 tEx 24:6 uJer 15:1 v1Sa 7:9 — 6 Moses[t] and Aaron were among his
priests,
Samuel[u] was among those who
called on his name;
they called on the LORD
and he answered[v] them.
99:7 wEx 33:9 — 7 He spoke to them from the pillar of
cloud;[w]
they kept his statutes and the
decrees he gave them.

8 O LORD our God,
you answered them;
99:8 xNu 14:20 — you were to Israel[a] a forgiving
God,[x]
though you punished their
misdeeds.[b]
9 Exalt the LORD our God
and worship at his holy
mountain,
for the LORD our God is holy.

PSALM 100

A psalm. For giving thanks.

1 Shout for joy[y] to the LORD, all the — 100:1 yPs 98:4
earth.
2 Worship the LORD with gladness; — 100:2 zPs 95:2
come before him[z] with joyful
songs.
3 Know that the LORD is God.[a] — 100:3 aPs 46:10 bJob 10:3 cPs 74:1; Eze 34:31
It is he who made us,[b] and we
are his[c];
we are his people, the sheep of
his pasture.[c]
4 Enter his gates with thanksgiving
and his courts with praise;
give thanks to him and praise — 100:4 dPs 116:17
his name.[d]
5 For the LORD is good[e] and his love — 100:5 e1Ch 16:34; Ps 25:8 fEzr 3:11; Ps 106:1 gPs 119:90
endures forever;[f]
his faithfulness[g] continues
through all generations.

PSALM 101

Of David. A psalm.

1 I will sing of your love[h] and justice; — 101:1 hPs 51:14; 89:1; 145:7
to you, O LORD, I will sing praise.
2 I will be careful to lead a blameless
life—
when will you come to me?

I will walk in my house
with blameless heart.
3 I will set before my eyes — 101:3 iDt 15:9 jPs 40:4
no vile thing.[i]

The deeds of faithless men I hate;[j]
they will not cling to me.
4 Men of perverse heart[k] shall be far — 101:4 kPr 11:20
from me;
I will have nothing to do with
evil.

5 Whoever slanders his neighbor[l] in — 101:5 lPs 50:20 mPs 10:5; Pr 6:17
secret,
him will I put to silence;
whoever has haughty eyes[m] and a
proud heart,
him will I not endure.

6 My eyes will be on the faithful in
the land,
that they may dwell with me;

[a] 8 Hebrew *them* [b] 8 Or / *an avenger of the wrongs done to them* [c] 3 Or *and not we ourselves*

101:6 [n]Ps 119:1

he whose walk is blameless[n]
will minister to me.

7 No one who practices deceit
will dwell in my house;
no one who speaks falsely
will stand in my presence.

101:8 [o]Jer 21:12 [p]Ps 75:10 [q]Ps 118:10-12 [r]Ps 46:4

8 Every morning[o] I will put to silence
all the wicked[p] in the land;
I will cut off every evildoer[q]
from the city of the LORD.[r]

PSALM 102

A prayer of an afflicted man. When he is faint and pours out his lament before the LORD.

102:1 [s]Ex 2:23

1 Hear my prayer, O LORD;
let my cry for help[s] come to you.

102:2 [t]Ps 69:17

2 Do not hide your face[t] from me
when I am in distress.
Turn your ear to me;
when I call, answer me quickly.

102:3 [u]Jas 4:14

3 For my days vanish like smoke;[u]
my bones burn like glowing
embers.

102:4 [v]Ps 37:2

4 My heart is blighted and withered
like grass;[v]
I forget to eat my food.
5 Because of my loud groaning
I am reduced to skin and bones.

102:6 [w]Job 30:29; Isa 34:11

6 I am like a desert owl,[w]
like an owl among the ruins.

102:7 [x]Ps 77:4 [y]Ps 38:11

7 I lie awake;[x] I have become
like a bird alone[y] on a roof.
8 All day long my enemies taunt me;
those who rail against me use
my name as a curse.

102:9 [z]Ps 42:3

9 For I eat ashes as my food
and mingle my drink with tears[z]

102:10 [a]Ps 38:3

10 because of your great wrath,[a]
for you have taken me up and
thrown me aside.

102:11 [b]Job 14:2

11 My days are like the evening
shadow;[b]
I wither away like grass.

102:12 [c]Ps 9:7 [d]Ps 135:13

12 But you, O LORD, sit enthroned
forever;[c]
your renown endures[d] through
all generations.

102:13 [e]Isa 60:10

13 You will arise and have
compassion[e] on Zion,
for it is time to show favor to her;
the appointed time has come.
14 For her stones are dear to your
servants;
her very dust moves them to pity.

102:15 [f]1Ki 8:43 [g]Ps 138:4

15 The nations will fear[f] the name of
the LORD,
all the kings[g] of the earth will
revere your glory.

102:16 [h]Isa 60:1-2

16 For the LORD will rebuild Zion
and appear in his glory.[h]

102:17 [i]Ne 1:6

17 He will respond to the prayer[i] of
the destitute;
he will not despise their plea.

102:18 [j]Ro 15:4 [k]Ps 22:31

18 Let this be written[j] for a future
generation,
that a people not yet created[k]
may praise the LORD:

102:19 [l]Dt 26:15

19 "The LORD looked down[l] from his
sanctuary on high,
from heaven he viewed the earth,

102:20 [m]Ps 79:11

20 to hear the groans of the
prisoners[m]
and release those condemned to
death."

102:21 [n]Ps 22:22

21 So the name of the LORD will be
declared[n] in Zion
and his praise in Jerusalem
22 when the peoples and the
kingdoms
assemble to worship the LORD.

23 In the course of my life[a] he broke
my strength;
he cut short my days.

[a] 23 Or *By his power*

JESUS FOCUS

ALWAYS THE SAME

Psalm 102 compares us as limited, finite human beings to the unlimited, infinite and all-powerful God. We "vanish like smoke" (verse 3) but God never changes. Our physical bodies eventually deteriorate and die, but he exists "through all generations" (verse 24). These are at least two essential differences between God and ourselves: We cannot live forever of our own volition, and we inevitably vacillate and change. By contrast, the identity and nature of our Creator are firmly fixed. Over time God's people came to know that his promised Messiah would also be eternal and immutable (John 1:1; Colossians 1:15–17; Hebrews 1:12; 13:8). It's comforting to know that when we talk to Jesus in prayer, we are talking to the very same Jesus the disciples knew, the identical Jesus who is revealed to us in the Bible as the precious Son of God, our Savior and our Lord.

[24] So I said:
"Do not take me away, O my God,
in the midst of my days;
your years go on[o] through all
generations.

102:24 [o] Ps 90:2; Isa 38:10

[25] In the beginning[p] you laid the
foundations of the earth,
and the heavens are the work of
your hands.

102:25 [p] Ge 1:1; Heb 1:10-12*

[26] They will perish,[q] but you remain;
they will all wear out like a
garment.
Like clothing you will change them
and they will be discarded.

102:26 [q] Isa 34:4; Mt 24:35; 2Pe 3:7-10; Rev 20:11

[27] But you remain the same,[r]
and your years will never end.

102:27 [r] Mal 3:6; Heb 13:8; Jas 1:17

[28] The children of your servants[s] will
live in your presence;
their descendants[t] will be
established before you."

102:28 [s] Ps 69:36 [t] Ps 89:4

PSALM 103

Of David.

[1] Praise the LORD, O my soul;[u]
all my inmost being, praise his
holy name.

103:1 [u] Ps 104:1

[2] Praise the LORD, O my soul,
and forget not all his benefits—
[3] who forgives all your sins[v]
and heals[w] all your diseases,

103:3 [v] Ps 130:8 [w] Ex 15:26

[4] who redeems your life from the pit
and crowns you with love and
compassion,
[5] who satisfies your desires with
good things
so that your youth is renewed
like the eagle's.[x]

103:5 [x] Isa 40:31

[6] The LORD works righteousness
and justice for all the oppressed.

[7] He made known[y] his ways[z] to
Moses,
his deeds[a] to the people of Israel:

103:7 [y] Ps 99:7; 147:19 [z] Ex 33:13 [a] Ps 106:22

[8] The LORD is compassionate and
gracious,[b]
slow to anger, abounding in love.

103:8 [b] Ex 34:6; Ps 86:15; Jas 5:11

[9] He will not always accuse,
nor will he harbor his anger
forever;[c]

103:9 [c] Ps 30:5; Isa 57:16; Jer 3:5,12; Mic 7:18

[10] he does not treat us as our sins
deserve[d]
or repay us according to our
iniquities.

103:10 [d] Ezr 9:13

[11] For as high as the heavens are
above the earth,
so great is his love[e] for those
who fear him;

103:11 [e] Ps 57:10

[12] as far as the east is from the west,
so far has he removed our
transgressions[f] from us.

103:12 [f] 2Sa 12:13

[13] As a father has compassion[g] on his
children,
so the LORD has compassion on
those who fear him;

103:13 [g] Mal 3:17

[14] for he knows how we are formed,[h]
he remembers that we are dust.

103:14 [h] Isa 29:16

[15] As for man, his days are like grass,[i]
he flourishes like a flower[j] of the
field;

103:15 [i] Ps 90:5 [j] Job 14:2; Jas 1:10; 1Pe 1:24

[16] the wind blows[k] over it and it is
gone,
and its place[l] remembers it no
more.

103:16 [k] Isa 40:7 [l] Job 7:10

[17] But from everlasting to everlasting
the LORD's love is with those who
fear him,
and his righteousness with their
children's children—
[18] with those who keep his covenant
and remember to obey his
precepts.[m]

103:18 [m] Dt 7:9

[19] The LORD has established his
throne in heaven,
and his kingdom rules[n] over all.

103:19 [n] Ps 47:2

[20] Praise the LORD, you his angels,[o]
you mighty ones[p] who do his
bidding,
who obey his word.

103:20 [o] Ps 148:2; Heb 1:14 [p] Ps 29:1

[21] Praise the LORD, all his heavenly
hosts,[q]
you his servants who do his will.

103:21 [q] 1Ki 22:19

[22] Praise the LORD, all his works[r]
everywhere in his dominion.

103:22 [r] Ps 145:10

Praise the LORD, O my soul.

PSALM 104

[1] Praise the LORD, O my soul.[s]

104:1 [s] Ps 103:22

O LORD my God, you are very
great;
you are clothed with splendor
and majesty.
[2] He wraps[t] himself in light as with a
garment;
he stretches out the heavens[u]
like a tent

104:2 [t] Da 7:9 [u] Isa 40:22

[3] and lays the beams[v] of his upper
chambers on their waters.
He makes the clouds[w] his chariot

104:3 [v] Am 9:6 [w] Isa 19:1

As Far as East Is From West

Sometimes when we take inventory of our lives we see only the bad and find ourselves so overwhelmed that we no longer want to peer into our souls at all. When we focus only on sin and its effects, we are painfully reminded of God's justice and recoil in fear. It is at such times that we need the message of Psalm 103 to help us to direct our gaze instead upon our loving Father's mercy and compassion.

The psalmist took a long, deep look into his own soul and saw himself for who he really was. But rather than stooping in discouragement or beating himself up for his imperfection, he found himself concentrating instead on what God had done for him.

The psalmist had made a mind-boggling, life-changing discovery: God "does not treat us as our sins deserve or repay us according to our iniquities . . . for he knows how we are formed, he remembers that we are dust" (verses 10–14). God realizes that we live daily with the consequences of sin, and he hasn't left us to try to find a way out of our misery. It was his plan from the beginning of time to send Jesus, his Son, to provide for us a doorway to a renewed relationship with our Creator. It is impossible for us to begin to conceptualize the enormity of God's compassionate sacrifice. The God of the universe came down to earth and lived in a frail human body—and now he strengthens us with his Holy Spirit.

Without Jesus, the gulf separating us from God would be like the Grand Canyon—even the greatest Olympic broad jumper would fall immediately to his death should he be foolhardy enough to attempt to leap over the chasm. No matter how hard we try, there is no way for us to reach God on our own. We can go out of our way to do good deeds and search our souls for positive qualities, but there is no other way to God the Father than by asking Jesus, who died for our sins, to forgive us and to fill us with the Holy Spirit, who produces Christian character in our lives (Galatians 5:22–23).

The writer of this psalm used an interesting image to describe the absolute nature of God's forgiveness: "as far as the east is from the west" (verse 12). No matter how far you travel in an easterly direction, you will never be headed west. And no matter how far west you travel, you will never be heading east. Once God has removed our sin, there is no possibility that he will ever again hold it against us (Jeremiah 31:34; Micah 7:18–19; Romans 4:8; 2 Corinthians 5:19). The biggest problem we face in life and eternity is our sin—but the good news is that our compassionate and merciful God has seen fit to remove the problem himself through the sacrifice of our Lord Jesus Christ.

Self-Discovery: *Are you able to accept the fact that God has removed the sin problem from your life because of your faith in Jesus, or is there still an area of doubt about your personal qualifications for salvation? Simply place your confidence in the finished work of Jesus on the cross, and you can join the psalmist in expressions of praise (Psalm 103:8–12).*

GO TO DISCOVERY 152 ON PAGE 782

and rides on the wings of the
wind.[x]
4 He makes winds his messengers,[a][y]
flames of fire[z] his servants.
5 He set the earth[a] on its
foundations;
it can never be moved.
6 You covered it[b] with the deep[c] as
with a garment;
the waters stood above the
mountains.
7 But at your rebuke[d] the waters fled,
at the sound of your thunder
they took to flight;
8 they flowed over the mountains,
they went down into the valleys,
to the place you assigned[e] for
them.
9 You set a boundary they cannot
cross;
never again will they cover the
earth.
10 He makes springs[f] pour water into
the ravines;
it flows between the mountains.
11 They give water to all the beasts of
the field;
the wild donkeys quench their
thirst.
12 The birds of the air[g] nest by the
waters;
they sing among the branches.
13 He waters the mountains[h] from his
upper chambers;
the earth is satisfied by the fruit
of his work.
14 He makes grass grow[i] for the cattle,
and plants for man to cultivate—
bringing forth food[j] from the
earth:
15 wine[k] that gladdens the heart of
man,
oil[l] to make his face shine,
and bread that sustains his
heart.
16 The trees of the LORD are well
watered,
the cedars of Lebanon that he
planted.
17 There the birds[m] make their nests;
the stork has its home in the
pine trees.
18 The high mountains belong to the
wild goats;
the crags are a refuge for the
coneys.[b][n]

104:3 [x] Ps 18:10
104:4 [y] Ps 148:8; Heb 1:7* [z] 2Ki 2:11
104:5 [a] Job 26:7; Ps 24:1-2
104:6 [b] Ge 7:19 [c] Ge 1:2
104:7 [d] Ps 18:15
104:8 [e] Ps 33:7
104:10 [f] Ps 107:33; Isa 41:18
104:12 [g] Mt 8:20
104:13 [h] Ps 147:8; Jer 10:13
104:14 [i] Job 38:27; Ps 147:8 [j] Ge 1:30; Job 28:5
104:15 [k] Jdg 9:13 [l] Ps 23:5; 92:10; Lk 7:46
104:17 [m] ver 12
104:18 [n] Pr 30:26

19 The moon marks off the seasons,[o]
and the sun[p] knows when to go
down.
20 You bring darkness,[q] it becomes
night,[r]
and all the beasts of the forest[s]
prowl.
21 The lions roar for their prey
and seek their food from God.[t]
22 The sun rises, and they steal away;
they return and lie down in their
dens.[u]
23 Then man goes out to his work,[v]
to his labor until evening.
24 How many are your works,[w] O LORD!
In wisdom you made[x] them all;
the earth is full of your
creatures.
25 There is the sea,[y] vast and spacious,
teeming with creatures beyond
number—
living things both large and
small.
26 There the ships[z] go to and fro,
and the leviathan,[a] which you
formed to frolic there.

27 These all look to you
to give them their food[b] at the
proper time.
28 When you give it to them,
they gather it up;
when you open your hand,
they are satisfied[c] with good
things.
29 When you hide your face,[d]
they are terrified;
when you take away their breath,
they die and return to the dust.[e]
30 When you send your Spirit,
they are created,
and you renew the face of the
earth.

31 May the glory of the LORD endure
forever;
may the LORD rejoice in his
works[f]—
32 he who looks at the earth, and it
trembles,[g]
who touches the mountains,[h]
and they smoke.[i]

33 I will sing[j] to the LORD all my life;
I will sing praise to my God as
long as I live.

104:19 [o] Ge 1:14 [p] Ps 19:6
104:20 [q] Isa 45:7 [r] Ps 74:16 [s] Ps 50:10
104:21 [t] Job 38:39; Ps 145:15; Joel 1:20
104:22 [u] Job 37:8
104:23 [v] Ge 3:19
104:24 [w] Ps 40:5 [x] Pr 3:19
104:25 [y] Ps 69:34
104:26 [z] Ps 107:23; Eze 27:9 [a] Job 41:1
104:27 [b] Job 36:31; Ps 136:25; 145:15; 147:9
104:28 [c] Ps 145:16
104:29 [d] Dt 31:17 [e] Job 34:14; Ecc 12:7
104:31 [f] Ge 1:31
104:32 [g] Ps 97:4 [h] Ex 19:18 [i] Ps 144:5
104:33 [j] Ps 63:4

[a] 4 Or *angels* [b] 18 That is, the hyrax or rock badger

34 May my meditation be pleasing to
 him,
 as I rejoice[k] in the LORD.
35 But may sinners vanish[l] from the
 earth
 and the wicked be no more.

Praise the LORD, O my soul.

Praise the LORD.[a][m]

104:34 [k]Ps 9:2
104:35 [l]Ps 37:38 [m]Ps 105:45; 106:48

PSALM 105

1 Give thanks to the LORD,[n] call on
 his name;[o]
 make known among the nations
 what he has done.
2 Sing to him,[p] sing praise to him;
 tell of all his wonderful acts.
3 Glory in his holy name;
 let the hearts of those who seek
 the LORD rejoice.
4 Look to the LORD and his strength;
 seek his face[q] always.
5 Remember the wonders[r] he has
 done,
 his miracles, and the judgments
 he pronounced,[s]
6 O descendants of Abraham his
 servant,[t]
 O sons of Jacob, his chosen[u] ones.
7 He is the LORD our God;
 his judgments are in all the earth.
8 He remembers his covenant[v]
 forever,
 the word he commanded, for a
 thousand generations,
9 the covenant he made with
 Abraham,[w]
 the oath he swore to Isaac.
10 He confirmed it[x] to Jacob as a
 decree,
 to Israel as an everlasting
 covenant:
11 "To you I will give the land of
 Canaan[y]
 as the portion you will inherit."
12 When they were but few in
 number,[z]
 few indeed, and strangers in it,[a]
13 they wandered from nation to
 nation,
 from one kingdom to another.
14 He allowed no one to oppress[b]
 them;
 for their sake he rebuked kings:[c]

105:1 [n]1Ch 16:34 [o]Ps 99:6
105:2 [p]Ps 96:1
105:4 [q]Ps 27:8
105:5 [r]Ps 40:5 [s]Ps 77:11
105:6 [t]ver 42 [u]Ps 106:5
105:8 [v]Ps 106:45; Lk 1:72
105:9 [w]Ge 12:7; 17:2; 22:16-18; Gal 3:15-18
105:10 [x]Ge 28:13-15
105:11 [y]Ge 13:15; 15:18
105:12 [z]Ge 34:30; Dt 7:7 [a]Ge 23:4; Heb 11:9
105:14 [b]Ge 35:5 [c]Ge 12:17-20

15 "Do not touch[d] my anointed ones;
 do my prophets no harm."
16 He called down famine[e] on the land
 and destroyed all their supplies
 of food;
17 and he sent a man before them—
 Joseph, sold as a slave.[f]
18 They bruised his feet with
 shackles,[g]
 his neck was put in irons,
19 till what he foretold[h] came to pass,
 till the word of the LORD proved
 him true.
20 The king sent and released him,
 the ruler of peoples set him free.[i]
21 He made him master of his
 household,
 ruler over all he possessed,
22 to instruct his princes[j] as he
 pleased
 and teach his elders wisdom.
23 Then Israel entered Egypt;[k]
 Jacob lived as an alien in the
 land of Ham.
24 The LORD made his people very
 fruitful;
 he made them too numerous[l]
 for their foes,
25 whose hearts he turned[m] to hate
 his people,
 to conspire[n] against his
 servants.
26 He sent Moses[o] his servant,
 and Aaron, whom he had
 chosen.[p]
27 They performed[q] his miraculous
 signs among them,
 his wonders in the land of Ham.
28 He sent darkness[r] and made the
 land dark—
 for had they not rebelled against
 his words?
29 He turned their waters into blood,[s]
 causing their fish to die.[t]
30 Their land teemed with frogs,[u]
 which went up into the
 bedrooms of their rulers.
31 He spoke, and there came swarms
 of flies,[v]
 and gnats[w] throughout their
 country.
32 He turned their rain into hail,[x]
 with lightning throughout their
 land;

105:15 [d]Ge 26:11
105:16 [e]Ge 41:54; Lev 26:26; Isa 3:1; Eze 4:16
105:17 [f]Ge 37:28; 45:5; Ac 7:9
105:18 [g]Ge 40:15
105:19 [h]Ge 40:20-22
105:20 [i]Ge 41:14
105:22 [j]Ge 41:43-44
105:23 [k]Ge 46:6; Ac 13:17
105:24 [l]Ex 1:7,9
105:25 [m]Ex 4:21 [n]Ex 1:6-10; Ac 7:19
105:26 [o]Ex 3:10 [p]Nu 16:5; 17:5-8
105:27 [q]Ex 7:8-12:51
105:28 [r]Ex 10:22
105:29 [s]Ps 78:44 [t]Ex 7:21
105:30 [u]Ex 8:2,6
105:31 [v]Ex 8:21-24 [w]Ex 8:16-18
105:32 [x]Ex 9:22-25

[a] *35* Hebrew *Hallelu Yah*; in the Septuagint this line stands at the beginning of Psalm 105.

105:33 [y]Ps 78:47
33 he struck down their vines[y] and fig
trees
and shattered the trees of their
country.
105:34 [z]Ex 10:4,12-15
34 He spoke, and the locusts came,[z]
grasshoppers without number;
35 they ate up every green thing in
their land,
ate up the produce of their soil.
105:36 [a]Ex 12:29
36 Then he struck down all the
firstborn[a] in their land,
the firstfruits of all their
manhood.
105:37 [b]Ex 12:35
37 He brought out Israel, laden with
silver and gold,[b]
and from among their tribes no
one faltered.
38 Egypt was glad when they left,
105:38 [c]Ex 12:33; 15:16
because dread of Israel[c] had
fallen on them.
105:39 [d]Ex 13:21 [e]Ne 9:12; Ps 78:14
39 He spread out a cloud[d] as a
covering,
and a fire to give light at night.[e]
105:40 [f]Ps 78:18,24 [g]Ex 16:13 [h]Jn 6:31
40 They asked,[f] and he brought them
quail[g]
and satisfied them with the
bread of heaven.[h]
105:41 [i]Ex 17:6; Nu 20:11; Ps 78:15-16; 1Co 10:4
41 He opened the rock,[i] and water
gushed out;
like a river it flowed in the
desert.
105:42 [j]Ge 15:13-16
42 For he remembered his holy
promise[j]
given to his servant Abraham.
105:43 [k]Ex 15:1-18; Ps 106:12
43 He brought out his people with
rejoicing,[k]
his chosen ones with shouts of
joy;
105:44 [l]Jos 13:6-7
44 he gave them the lands of the
nations,[l]
and they fell heir to what others
had toiled for—
105:45 [m]Dt 4:40; 6:21-24
45 that they might keep his precepts
and observe his laws.[m]

Praise the LORD.[a]

PSALM 106

1 Praise the LORD.[b]

106:1 [n]Ps 100:5; 105:1
Give thanks to the LORD, for he is
good;[n]
his love endures forever.
106:2 [o]Ps 145:4,12
2 Who can proclaim the mighty
acts[o] of the LORD
or fully declare his praise?
3 Blessed are they who maintain
justice,
who constantly do what is
right.[p] 106:3 [p]Ps 15:2
4 Remember me,[q] O LORD, when you 106:4 [q]Ps 119:132
show favor to your people,
come to my aid when you save
them,
5 that I may enjoy the prosperity[r] of 106:5 [r]Ps 1:3 [s]Ps 118:15
your chosen ones,
that I may share in the joy[s] of
your nation
and join your inheritance in
giving praise.

6 We have sinned,[t] even as our 106:6 [t]Da 9:5
fathers did;
we have done wrong and acted
wickedly.
7 When our fathers were in Egypt,
they gave no thought to your
miracles;
they did not remember[u] your many 106:7 [u]Ps 78:11,42 [v]Ex 14:11-12
kindnesses,
and they rebelled by the sea,[v] the
Red Sea.[c]
8 Yet he saved them for his name's
sake,[w] 106:8 [w]Ex 9:16
to make his mighty power
known.
9 He rebuked[x] the Red Sea, and it 106:9 [x]Ps 18:15 [y]Ex 14:21; Na 1:4 [z]Isa 63:11-14
dried up;[y]
he led them through[z] the depths
as through a desert.
10 He saved them[a] from the hand of 106:10 [a]Ex 14:30 [b]Ps 107:2
the foe;
from the hand of the enemy he
redeemed them.[b]
11 The waters covered[c] their 106:11 [c]Ex 14:28; 15:5
adversaries;
not one of them survived.
12 Then they believed his promises 106:12 [d]Ex 15:1-21
and sang his praise.[d]

13 But they soon forgot[e] what he had 106:13 [e]Ex 15:24
done
and did not wait for his
counsel.
14 In the desert they gave in to their
craving;
in the wasteland they put God to 106:14 [f]1Co 10:9
the test.[f]
15 So he gave them[g] what they asked 106:15 [g]Nu 11:31
for,

[a] *45* Hebrew *Hallelu Yah* [b] *1* Hebrew *Hallelu Yah*; also in verse 48 [c] *7* Hebrew *Yam Suph*; that is, Sea of Reeds; also in verses 9 and 22

106:15 [h] Isa 10:16
but sent a wasting disease[h] upon them.

106:16 [i] Nu 16:1-3
[16] In the camp they grew envious[i] of Moses
and of Aaron, who was consecrated to the LORD.

106:17 [j] Dt 11:6
[17] The earth opened[j] up and swallowed Dathan;
it buried the company of Abiram.

106:18 [k] Nu 16:35
[18] Fire blazed[k] among their followers;
a flame consumed the wicked.

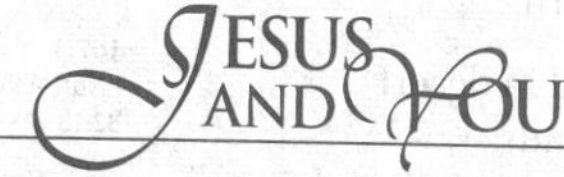

SET FREE

No one wants to live as a slave, subject to every arbitrary whim of a master, and it has never been God's plan that his people be permanently trapped in bondage of any kind. Psalm 106 reminds us of one graphic scene in which God set his people free. The mass exodus of God's people from Egypt marked the turning point in Israel's national life. After having been set free, the people were led by God through the wilderness to their promised land. The Israelites did nothing to earn their freedom; it was in every sense a free (but priceless!) gift from God. The most devastating slavery we can experience is bondage to sin, but the exodus of God's people from Egypt provides us with hope and serves as an example of the tremendous lengths to which God was willing to go to deliver his people from involuntary servitude (Romans 6:1–23; Revelation 1:4–6). When the time was right, God provided freedom for the sinful race of people through Jesus, God's promised Messiah (Galatians 4:4–5). In much the same way that the Israelites could point back to the exodus experience as a turning point in their national life, so believers today can pinpoint Jesus' death and resurrection as the pivotal moment in all of human history, the moment of final emancipation. Because Jesus loves us, he made the ultimate sacrifice to set us free both from slavery to sin and from bondage to the law—he gave his own life in our place. Believing the truth about Jesus, staking our lives on him and accepting his gift are the only actions we need to take in order to participate in that freedom. As Jesus himself said, "You will know the truth, and the truth will set you free" (John 8:32).

[19] At Horeb they made a calf[l]
and worshiped an idol cast from metal.
106:19 [l] Ex 32:4

[20] They exchanged their Glory[m]
for an image of a bull, which eats grass.
106:20 [m] Jer 2:11; Ro 1:23

[21] They forgot the God[n] who saved them,
who had done great things[o] in Egypt,
106:21 [n] Ps 78:11 [o] Dt 10:21

[22] miracles in the land of Ham[p]
and awesome deeds by the Red Sea.
106:22 [p] Ps 105:27

[23] So he said he would destroy[q] them—
had not Moses, his chosen one,
stood in the breach[r] before him
to keep his wrath from destroying them.
106:23 [q] Ex 32:10 [r] Ex 32:11-14

[24] Then they despised the pleasant land;[s]
they did not believe[t] his promise.
106:24 [s] Dt 8:7; Eze 20:6 [t] Heb 3:18-19

[25] They grumbled[u] in their tents
and did not obey the LORD.
106:25 [u] Nu 14:2

[26] So he swore[v] to them with uplifted hand
that he would make them fall in the desert,[w]
106:26 [v] Eze 20:15; Heb 3:11 [w] Nu 14:28-35

[27] make their descendants fall among the nations
and scatter[x] them throughout the lands.
106:27 [x] Lev 26:33; Ps 44:11

[28] They yoked themselves to the Baal of Peor[y]
and ate sacrifices offered to lifeless gods;
106:28 [y] Nu 25:2-3; Hos 9:10

[29] they provoked the LORD to anger by their wicked deeds,
and a plague broke out among them.

[30] But Phinehas stood up and intervened,
and the plague was checked.[z]
106:30 [z] Nu 25:8

[31] This was credited to him[a] as righteousness
for endless generations to come.
106:31 [a] Nu 25:11-13

[32] By the waters of Meribah[b] they angered the LORD,
and trouble came to Moses because of them;
106:32 [b] Nu 20:2-13; Ps 81:7

[33] for they rebelled against the Spirit of God,

and rash words came from
Moses' lips.[a][c]

106:33 [c] Nu 20:8-12

34 They did not destroy[d] the peoples
as the LORD had commanded[e]
them,

106:34 [d] Jdg 1:21 [e] Dt 7:16

35 but they mingled[f] with the nations
and adopted their customs.

106:35 [f] Jdg 3:5-6

36 They worshiped their idols,[g]
which became a snare to them.

106:36 [g] Jdg 2:12

37 They sacrificed their sons[h]
and their daughters to demons.

106:37 [h] 2Ki 16:3; 17:17

38 They shed innocent blood,
the blood of their sons[i] and
daughters,
whom they sacrificed to the idols
of Canaan,
and the land was desecrated by
their blood.

106:38 [i] Nu 35:33

39 They defiled themselves[j] by what
they did;
by their deeds they prostituted[k]
themselves.

106:39 [j] Eze 20:18 [k] Lev 17:7; Nu 15:39

40 Therefore the LORD was angry[l]
with his people
and abhorred his inheritance.[m]

106:40 [l] Jdg 2:14; Ps 78:59 [m] Dt 9:29

41 He handed them over[n] to the
nations,
and their foes ruled over them.

106:41 [n] Jdg 2:14; Ne 9:27

42 Their enemies oppressed them
and subjected them to their
power.
43 Many times he delivered them,
but they were bent on
rebellion[o]
and they wasted away in their
sin.

106:43 [o] Jdg 2:16-19

44 But he took note of their distress
when he heard their cry;[p]

106:44 [p] Jdg 3:9; 10:10

45 for their sake he remembered his
covenant[q]
and out of his great love[r] he
relented.

106:45 [q] Lev 26:42; Ps 105:8 [r] Jdg 2:18

46 He caused them to be pitied[s]
by all who held them captive.

106:46 [s] Ezr 9:9; Jer 42:12

47 Save us, O LORD our God,
and gather us[t] from the nations,
that we may give thanks to your
holy name
and glory in your praise.

106:47 [t] Ps 147:2

48 Praise be to the LORD, the God of
Israel,
from everlasting to everlasting.
Let all the people say, "Amen!"[u]

106:48 [u] Ps 41:13

Praise the LORD.

BOOK V

Psalms 107–150

PSALM 107

1 Give thanks to the LORD,[v] for he is
good;
his love endures forever.

107:1 [v] Ps 106:1

2 Let the redeemed[w] of the LORD say
this—
those he redeemed from the
hand of the foe,

107:2 [w] Ps 106:10

3 those he gathered[x] from the lands,
from east and west, from north
and south.[b]

107:3 [x] Ps 106:47; Isa 43:5-6

4 Some wandered in desert[y]
wastelands,
finding no way to a city where
they could settle.

107:4 [y] Nu 14:33; 32:13

5 They were hungry and thirsty,
and their lives ebbed away.
6 Then they cried out[z] to the LORD in
their trouble,
and he delivered them from
their distress.

107:6 [z] Ps 50:15

7 He led them by a straight way[a]
to a city where they could settle.

107:7 [a] Ezr 8:21

8 Let them give thanks to the LORD
for his unfailing love
and his wonderful deeds for men,
9 for he satisfies[b] the thirsty
and fills the hungry with good
things.[c]

107:9 [b] Ps 22:26; Lk 1:53 [c] Ps 34:10

10 Some sat in darkness[d] and the
deepest gloom,
prisoners suffering in iron
chains,[e]

107:10 [d] Lk 1:79 [e] Job 36:8

11 for they had rebelled[f] against the
words of God
and despised the counsel[g] of the
Most High.

107:11 [f] Ps 106:7; La 3:42 [g] 2Ch 36:16

12 So he subjected them to bitter
labor;
they stumbled, and there was no
one to help.[h]

107:12 [h] Ps 22:11

13 Then they cried to the LORD in
their trouble,
and he saved them from their
distress.
14 He brought them out of darkness
and the deepest gloom
and broke away their chains.[i]

107:14 [i] Ps 116:16; Lk 13:16; Ac 12:7

[a] 33 Or *against his spirit, / and rash words came from his lips* [b] 3 Hebrew *north and the sea*

[15] Let them give thanks to the LORD
for his unfailing love
and his wonderful deeds for men,
[16] for he breaks down gates of bronze
and cuts through bars of iron.

[17] Some became fools through their
rebellious ways
and suffered affliction[j] because
of their iniquities.
[18] They loathed all food[k]
and drew near the gates of
death.[l]
[19] Then they cried to the LORD in
their trouble,
and he saved them from their
distress.
[20] He sent forth his word[m] and healed
them;[n]
he rescued[o] them from the
grave.[p]
[21] Let them give thanks to the LORD
for his unfailing love
and his wonderful deeds for
men.
[22] Let them sacrifice thank offerings[q]
and tell of his works[r] with songs
of joy.
[23] Others went out on the sea in ships;
they were merchants on the
mighty waters.
[24] They saw the works of the LORD,
his wonderful deeds in the deep.
[25] For he spoke[s] and stirred up a
tempest[t]
that lifted high the waves.[u]
[26] They mounted up to the heavens
and went down to the
depths;
in their peril their courage
melted[v] away.
[27] They reeled and staggered like
drunken men;
they were at their wits' end.
[28] Then they cried out to the LORD in
their trouble,
and he brought them out of their
distress.
[29] He stilled the storm[w] to a whisper;
the waves[x] of the sea were
hushed.
[30] They were glad when it grew calm,
and he guided them to their
desired haven.
[31] Let them give thanks to the LORD
for his unfailing love
and his wonderful deeds for men.
[32] Let them exalt him in the
assembly[y] of the people
and praise him in the council of
the elders.

[33] He turned rivers into a desert,[z]
flowing springs into thirsty
ground,
[34] and fruitful land into a salt waste,[a]
because of the wickedness of
those who lived there.
[35] He turned the desert into pools of
water[b]
and the parched ground into
flowing springs;
[36] there he brought the hungry to live,
and they founded a city where
they could settle.
[37] They sowed fields and planted
vineyards[c]
that yielded a fruitful harvest;
[38] he blessed them, and their
numbers greatly
increased,[d]
and he did not let their herds
diminish.

[39] Then their numbers decreased,[e]
and they were humbled
by oppression, calamity and
sorrow;
[40] he who pours contempt on nobles[f]
made them wander in a
trackless waste.[g]
[41] But he lifted the needy[h] out of
their affliction
and increased their families like
flocks.
[42] The upright see and rejoice,[i]
but all the wicked shut their
mouths.[j]

[43] Whoever is wise,[k] let him heed
these things
and consider the great love[l] of
the LORD.

PSALM 108

A song. A psalm of David.

[1] My heart is steadfast, O God;
I will sing and make music with
all my soul.
[2] Awake, harp and lyre!
I will awaken the dawn.
[3] I will praise you, O LORD, among
the nations;

107:17 [j] Isa 65:6-7; La 3:39
107:18 [k] Job 33:20 [l] Job 33:22; Ps 9:13; 88:3
107:20 [m] Mt 8:8 [n] Ps 103:3 [o] Job 33:28 [p] Ps 30:3; 49:15
107:22 [q] Lev 7:12; [r] Ps 50:14; 116:17 [s] Ps 9:11; 73:28; 118:17
107:25 [s] Ps 105:31 [t] Jnh 1:4 [u] Ps 93:3
107:26 [v] Ps 22:14
107:29 [w] Mt 8:26 [x] Ps 89:9
107:32 [y] Ps 22:22,25; 35:18
107:33 [z] 1Ki 17:1; Ps 74:15
107:34 [a] Ge 13:10; 14:3; 19:25
107:35 [b] Ps 114:8; Isa 41:18
107:37 [c] Isa 65:21
107:38 [d] Ge 12:2; 17:16, 20; Ex 1:7
107:39 [e] 2Ki 10:32; Eze 5:12
107:40 [f] Job 12:21 [g] Job 12:24
107:41 [h] 1Sa 2:8; Ps 113:7-9
107:42 [i] Job 22:19 [j] Job 5:16; Ps 63:11; Ro 3:19
107:43 [k] Jer 9:12; Hos 14:9 [l] Ps 64:9

I will sing of you among the peoples.
4 For great is your love, higher than the heavens;
your faithfulness reaches to the skies.
5 Be exalted, O God, above the heavens,
and let your glory be over all the earth.[m]

108:5 m Ps 57:5

6 Save us and help us with your right hand,
that those you love may be delivered.
7 God has spoken from his sanctuary:
"In triumph I will parcel out Shechem
and measure off the Valley of Succoth.
8 Gilead is mine, Manasseh is mine;
Ephraim is my helmet,
Judah[n] my scepter.

108:8 n Ge 49:10

9 Moab is my washbasin,
upon Edom I toss my sandal;
over Philistia I shout in triumph."

10 Who will bring me to the fortified city?
Who will lead me to Edom?
11 Is it not you, O God, you who have rejected us
and no longer go out with our armies?[o]

108:11 o Ps 44:9

12 Give us aid against the enemy,
for the help of man is worthless.
13 With God we will gain the victory,
and he will trample down our enemies.

PSALM 109

For the director of music. Of David. A psalm.

1 O God, whom I praise,
do not remain silent,[p]

109:1 p Ps 83:1

2 for wicked and deceitful men
have opened their mouths against me;
they have spoken against me
with lying tongues.[q]

109:2 q Ps 52:4; 120:2

3 With words of hatred[r] they surround me;
they attack me without cause.[s]

109:3 r Ps 69:4 s Ps 35:7; Jn 15:25

4 In return for my friendship they accuse me,
but I am a man of prayer.[t]

109:4 t Ps 69:13

5 They repay me evil for good,[u]
and hatred for my friendship.

109:5 u Ps 35:12; 38:20

6 Appoint[a] an evil man[b] to oppose him;
let an accuser[c][v] stand at his right hand.

109:6 v Zec 3:1

7 When he is tried, let him be found guilty,
and may his prayers condemn[w] him.

109:7 w Pr 28:9

8 May his days be few;
may another take his place[x] of leadership.

109:8 x Ac 1:20*

9 May his children be fatherless
and his wife a widow.[y]

109:9 y Ex 22:24

10 May his children be wandering beggars;
may they be driven[d] from their ruined homes.
11 May a creditor seize all he has;
may strangers plunder the fruits of his labor.[z]

109:11 z Job 5:5

12 May no one extend kindness to him
or take pity[a] on his fatherless children.

109:12 a Isa 9:17

13 May his descendants be cut off,[b]
their names blotted out[c] from the next generation.

109:13 b Job 18:19; Ps 37:28 c Pr 10:7

14 May the iniquity of his fathers[d] be remembered before the LORD;
may the sin of his mother never be blotted out.

109:14 d Ex 20:5; Ne 4:5; Jer 18:23

15 May their sins always remain before the LORD,
that he may cut off the memory[e] of them from the earth.

109:15 e Job 18:17; Ps 34:16

16 For he never thought of doing a kindness,
but hounded to death the poor
and the needy[f] and the brokenhearted.[g]

109:16 f Ps 37:14,32 g Ps 34:18

17 He loved to pronounce a curse—
may it[e] come on him;[h]
he found no pleasure in blessing—
may it be[f] far from him.

109:17 h Pr 14:14; Eze 35:6

18 He wore cursing[i] as his garment;
it entered into his body like water,[j]
into his bones like oil.

109:18 i Ps 73:6 j Nu 5:22

19 May it be like a cloak wrapped about him,

a 6 Or ⌞They say:⌟ "Appoint (with quotation marks at the end of verse 19) b 6 Or *the Evil One* c 6 Or *let Satan* d 10 Septuagint; Hebrew *sought* e 17 Or *curse, / and it has* f 17 Or *blessing, / and it is*

like a belt tied forever around
him.

109:20 [k]Ps 94:23; 2Ti 4:14 [l]Ps 71:10

20 May this be the LORD's payment[k] to
my accusers,
to those who speak evil[l] of me.

21 But you, O Sovereign LORD,
deal well with me for your
name's sake;[m]
out of the goodness of your
love,[n] deliver me.

109:21 [m]Ps 79:9 [n]Ps 69:16

22 For I am poor and needy,
and my heart is wounded within
me.
23 I fade away like an evening
shadow;[o]
I am shaken off like a locust.

109:23 [o]Ps 102:11

24 My knees give[p] way from fasting;
my body is thin and gaunt.

109:24 [p]Heb 12:12

25 I am an object of scorn[q] to my
accusers;
when they see me, they shake
their heads.[r]

109:25 [q]Ps 22:6 [r]Mt 27:39; Mk 15:29

26 Help me,[s] O LORD my God;
save me in accordance with your
love.

109:26 [s]Ps 119:86

27 Let them know[t] that it is your hand,
that you, O LORD, have done it.

109:27 [t]Job 37:7

28 They may curse,[u] but you will bless;
when they attack they will be
put to shame,
but your servant will rejoice.[v]

109:28 [u]2Sa 16:12 [v]Isa 65:14

29 My accusers will be clothed with
disgrace
and wrapped in shame[w] as in a
cloak.

109:29 [w]Ps 35:26; 132:18

30 With my mouth I will greatly extol
the LORD;
in the great throng[x] I will praise
him.

109:30 [x]Ps 35:18; 111:1

31 For he stands at the right hand[y] of
the needy one,
to save his life from those who
condemn him.

109:31 [y]Ps 16:8; 73:23; 121:5

PSALM 110

Of David. A psalm.

1 The LORD says[z] to my Lord:
"Sit at my right hand
until I make your enemies
a footstool for your feet."[a]

110:1 [z]Mt 22:44*; Mk 12:36*; Lk 20:42*; Ac 2:34* [a]1Co 15:25

2 The LORD will extend your mighty
scepter[b] from Zion;
you will rule in the midst of your
enemies.

110:2 [b]Ps 45:6

3 Your troops will be willing
on your day of battle.
Arrayed in holy majesty,[c]
from the womb of the dawn
you will receive the dew of your
youth.[a]

110:3 [c]Jdg 5:2; Ps 96:9

4 The LORD has sworn
and will not change his mind:[d]
"You are a priest forever,[e]
in the order of Melchizedek."[f]

110:4 [d]Nu 23:19 [e]Heb 5:6*; 7:21* [f]Heb 7:15-17*

5 The Lord is at your right hand;[g]
he will crush kings[h] on the day
of his wrath.[i]

110:5 [g]Ps 16:8 [h]Ps 2:12 [i]Ps 2:5; Ro 2:5

6 He will judge the nations,[j] heaping
up the dead[k]
and crushing the rulers[l] of the
whole earth.

110:6 [j]Isa 2:4 [k]Isa 66:24 [l]Ps 68:21

7 He will drink from a brook beside
the way[b];
therefore he will lift up his head.[m]

110:7 [m]Ps 27:6

[a] 3 Or / *your young men will come to you like the dew* [b] 7 Or / *The One who grants succession will set him in authority*

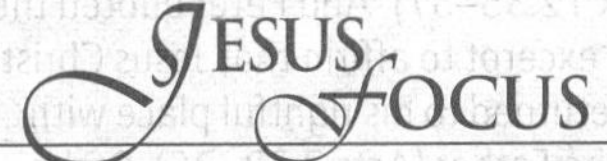

NO DEBATE

Jesus frequently referred to the Hebrew Scriptures when he spoke, and he quoted Psalm 110:1 to settle a debate with various religious leaders. The leaders had conspired to trap him with a series of questions (Matthew 22:15). The *Herodians* and the Pharisees began by quizzing him about paying taxes (Matthew 22:15–20). The *Sadducees* tried to back him into a corner on the subject of marriage in heaven (Matthew 22:23–32). And finally the *Pharisees* attempted to test him by forcing him to designate only one of God's Old Testament laws as the most significant (Matthew 22:34–40). Jesus amazed them with his answers, and then *he* asked a single question: "What do you think about the Christ? Whose son is he?" (Matthew 22:42–45). They responded without hesitation, "The son of David." The answer seemed obvious to them. At that point Jesus quoted Psalm 110 and asked: "If then David calls him 'Lord,' how can he be his son?" The religious leaders were speechless, and from that time on no one dared to ask him any more questions (Matthew 22:46). Jesus made it abundantly clear that there is no room for debate: Jesus, the Christ, the Son of God, is at the same time David's human descendant and his divine Lord.

Jesus: Our King and Priest

Many people identify Psalm 110 as one of the most significant because it is the most directly prophetic of all the psalms. It is also one of the psalms most frequently quoted in the New Testament. Its primary distinctive is that it pulls together the roles of king (verses 1–3) and priest (verses 4–7) and attributes them to a single individual, God's promised Messiah.

God had pledged to his people for generations that he would send a Savior, the One who would deliver them from their enemies and lead them as king, overcoming every obstacle and opposition. Jesus quoted this psalm to clarify the difference between David himself and the king that David was envisioning (Mark 12:35–37). And Peter quoted the same excerpt to affirm that Jesus Christ had returned to his rightful place with God the Father (Acts 2:32–36). Psalm 110 is cited to affirm that Jesus is greater than anyone or anything else in all of creation, including the angels (Hebrews 1:13).

But this Messiah would be more than a leader-king for his people. He would also function as their eternal priest. Aaron's family had served in a temporary capacity as priests, and everything they had accomplished in this role had also been temporary in its effect. Jesus, on the other hand, would come as a priest like Melchizedek: chosen by God but not of Aaron's line. Jesus is "a priest forever" (Psalm 110:4; Hebrews 7:11–28).

Under our current system of government we operate under laws that separate church and state. When Jesus returns to set up his kingdom, he will bring the two into a marvelous harmony. Government will finally be guided by righteousness and justice, and the "church" will finally have her "man in office." King Jesus will completely overthrow the power of evil on earth and usher in a reign of peace.

Those of us who have accepted Jesus as our Lord and Savior can already enjoy the rule of the King/Priest Jesus in our lives. He brings order, peace and purpose as we submit to his authority. He also functions as our high priest, continually interceding with the Father on our behalf, so that we need not be afraid of anything that comes our way (Hebrews 4:14—5:10; 7:23–25). Hebrews 7:26 assures us that "such a high priest meets our need—one who is holy, blameless, pure, set apart from sinners, exalted above the heavens."

Sin and Satan have already been defeated (2 Corinthians 2:14; Colossians 2:13–15). Because Jesus has bridged the gap, we need not fear that God is too far away to be accessible to us or that he will turn his back on us when we call: "If anyone is in Christ, he is a new creation; the old has gone, the new has come! All this is from God, who reconciled us to himself through Christ and gave us the ministry of reconciliation: that God was reconciling the world to himself in Christ, not counting men's sins against them" (2 Corinthians 5:17–19). *Nothing* can prevent us from spending eternity with God the Father.

Self-Discovery: *Are you willing to allow Jesus to be both your king and priest today? Is the kingdom of God becoming a reality in your life?*

GO TO DISCOVERY 153 ON PAGE 786

PSALM 111[a]

1 Praise the LORD.[b]

I will extol the LORD with all my heart
in the council of the upright and in the assembly.

111:2 [n]Ps 92:5; 143:5

2 Great are the works[n] of the LORD;
they are pondered by all who delight in them.
3 Glorious and majestic are his deeds,
and his righteousness endures forever.
4 He has caused his wonders to be remembered;
the LORD is gracious and compassionate.[o]

111:4 [o]Ps 103:8

111:5 [p]Mt 6:26,31-33

5 He provides food[p] for those who fear him;
he remembers his covenant forever.
6 He has shown his people the power of his works,
giving them the lands of other nations.
7 The works of his hands are faithful and just;
all his precepts are trustworthy.[q]

111:7 [q]Ps 19:7; Rev 15:3

8 They are steadfast for ever[r] and ever,
done in faithfulness and uprightness.

111:8 [r]Isa 40:8; Mt 5:18

9 He provided redemption[s] for his people;
he ordained his covenant forever—
holy and awesome[t] is his name.

111:9 [s]Lk 1:68 [t]Ps 99:3; Lk 1:49

10 The fear of the LORD is the beginning of wisdom;[u]
all who follow his precepts have good understanding.[v]
To him belongs eternal praise.[w]

111:10 [u]Pr 9:10 [v]Ecc 12:13 [w]Ps 145:2

PSALM 112[a]

1 Praise the LORD.[b]

Blessed is the man who fears the LORD,[x]
who finds great delight[y] in his commands.

112:1 [x]Ps 128:1 [y]Ps 119:14,16, 47,92

2 His children will be mighty in the land;
the generation of the upright will be blessed.
3 Wealth and riches are in his house,
and his righteousness endures forever.
4 Even in darkness light dawns[z] for the upright,
for the gracious and compassionate and righteous[a] man.[c]

112:4 [z]Job 11:17 [a]Ps 97:11

5 Good will come to him who is generous and lends freely,[b]
who conducts his affairs with justice.

112:5 [b]Ps 37:21,26

6 Surely he will never be shaken;
a righteous man will be remembered[c] forever.

112:6 [c]Pr 10:7

7 He will have no fear of bad news;
his heart is steadfast,[d] trusting in the LORD.

112:7 [d]Ps 57:7; Pr 1:33

8 His heart is secure, he will have no fear;
in the end he will look in triumph on his foes.[e]

112:8 [e]Ps 59:10

9 He has scattered abroad his gifts to the poor,[f]
his righteousness endures forever;
his horn[d] will be lifted[g] high in honor.

112:9 [f]2Co 9:9* [g]Ps 75:10

10 The wicked man will see[h] and be vexed,
he will gnash his teeth[i] and waste away;[j]
the longings of the wicked will come to nothing.[k]

112:10 [h]Ps 86:17 [i]Ps 37:12 [j]Ps 58:7-8 [k]Pr 11:7

PSALM 113

1 Praise the LORD.[e]

Praise, O servants of the LORD,[l]
praise the name of the LORD.

113:1 [l]Ps 135:1

2 Let the name of the LORD be praised,
both now and forevermore.[m]

113:2 [m]Da 2:20

3 From the rising of the sun[n] to the place where it sets,
the name of the LORD is to be praised.

113:3 [n]Isa 59:19; Mal 1:11

[a] This psalm is an acrostic poem, the lines of which begin with the successive letters of the Hebrew alphabet. [b] *1* Hebrew *Hallelu Yah* [c] *4* Or / *for* ⌞*the LORD*⌟ *is gracious and compassionate and righteous* [d] *9* *Horn* here symbolizes dignity.
[e] *1* Hebrew *Hallelu Yah*; also in verse 9

113:4 [o] Ps 99:2 [p] Ps 8:1; 97:9
[4] The LORD is exalted[o] over all the nations,
his glory above the heavens.[p]
113:5 [q] Ps 89:6 [r] Ps 103:19
[5] Who is like the LORD our God,[q]
the One who sits enthroned[r] on high,
113:6 [s] Ps 11:4; 138:6; Isa 57:15
[6] who stoops down to look[s]
on the heavens and the earth?

113:7 [t] 1Sa 2:8 [u] Ps 107:41
[7] He raises the poor[t] from the dust
and lifts the needy[u] from the ash heap;
113:8 [v] Job 36:7
[8] he seats them[v] with princes,
with the princes of their people.
113:9 [w] 1Sa 2:5; Ps 68:6; Isa 54:1
[9] He settles the barren[w] woman in her home
as a happy mother of children.

Praise the LORD.

PSALM 114

114:1 [x] Ex 13:3
[1] When Israel came out of Egypt,[x]
the house of Jacob from a people of foreign tongue,
[2] Judah became God's sanctuary,
Israel his dominion.

114:3 [y] Ex 14:21; Ps 77:16 [z] Jos 3:16
[3] The sea looked and fled,[y]
the Jordan turned back;[z]
[4] the mountains skipped like rams,
the hills like lambs.

[5] Why was it, O sea, that you fled,
O Jordan, that you turned back,
[6] you mountains, that you skipped like rams,
you hills, like lambs?

114:7 [a] Ps 96:9
[7] Tremble, O earth,[a] at the presence of the Lord,
at the presence of the God of Jacob,
114:8 [b] Ex 17:6; Nu 20:11; Ps 107:35
[8] who turned the rock into a pool,
the hard rock into springs of water.[b]

PSALM 115

115:1 [c] Ps 96:8; Isa 48:11; Eze 36:32
[1] Not to us, O LORD, not to us
but to your name be the glory,[c]
because of your love and faithfulness.

115:2 [d] Ps 42:3; 79:10
[2] Why do the nations say,
"Where is their God?"[d]
115:3 [e] Ps 103:19 [f] Ps 135:6; Da 4:35
[3] Our God is in heaven;[e]
he does whatever pleases him.[f]
115:4 [g] Dt 4:28; Jer 10:3-5
[4] But their idols are silver and gold,
made by the hands of men.[g]
115:5 [h] Jer 10:5
[5] They have mouths, but cannot speak,[h]
eyes, but they cannot see;
[6] they have ears, but cannot hear,
noses, but they cannot smell;
[7] they have hands, but cannot feel,
feet, but they cannot walk;
nor can they utter a sound with their throats.
[8] Those who make them will be like them,
and so will all who trust in them.

[9] O house of Israel, trust in the LORD—
he is their help and shield.
115:10 [i] Ps 118:3
[10] O house of Aaron,[i] trust in the LORD—
he is their help and shield.
[11] You who fear him, trust in the LORD—
he is their help and shield.

[12] The LORD remembers us and will bless us:
He will bless the house of Israel,
he will bless the house of Aaron,

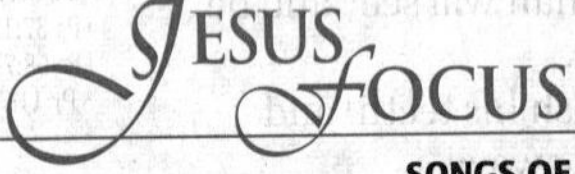

SONGS OF THE LAST MEAL

Psalms 113—118 were sung during the Passover meal every year and, in keeping with tradition, are still sung Jewish homes Psalms 113 and 114 are sung before the meal and the last four after its completion. Together this series of praise songs is referred to as the *hallel* or "praise." These psalms were likely the same songs Jesus sang during the last Passover meal with his disciples shortly before his arrest (Mark 14:26). The lyrics could not have been more appropriate for the occasion. Consider some of the phrases they include: "I will fulfill my vows to the LORD" (Psalm 116:14); "Precious in the sight of the LORD is the death of his saints" (Psalm 116:15); "The LORD is with me; I will not be afraid" (Psalm 118:6); and "I will not die but live" (Psalm 118:17). After joining together with his disciples in these hymns Jesus left for Gethsemane—fully aware that he would soon die and rise again to new life so that we could be brought back into an eternal, saving relationship with the Father (Matthew 26:30).

115:13 [j] Ps 128:1,4

13 he will bless those who fear[j] the
LORD—
small and great alike.

115:14 [k] Dt 1:11

14 May the LORD make you increase,[k]
both you and your children.

115:15 [l] Ge 1:1; 14:19; Ps 96:5

15 May you be blessed by the LORD,
the Maker of heaven[l] and earth.

115:16 [m] Ps 89:11 [n] Ps 8:6-8

16 The highest heavens belong to the
LORD,[m]
but the earth he has given[n] to
man.

115:17 [o] Ps 6:5; 88:10-12; Isa 38:18

17 It is not the dead[o] who praise the
LORD,
those who go down to silence;

115:18 [p] Ps 113:2; Da 2:20

18 it is we who extol the LORD,
both now and forevermore.[p]

Praise the LORD.[a]

PSALM 116

116:1 [q] Ps 18:1 [r] Ps 66:19

1 I love the LORD,[q] for he heard my
voice;
he heard my cry[r] for mercy.

116:2 [s] Ps 40:1

2 Because he turned his ear[s] to me,
I will call on him as long as I live.

116:3 [t] Ps 18:4-5

3 The cords of death[t] entangled me,
the anguish of the grave[b] came
upon me;
I was overcome by trouble and
sorrow.

116:4 [u] Ps 118:5 [v] Ps 22:20

4 Then I called on the name[u] of the
LORD:
"O LORD, save me![v]"

116:5 [w] Ezr 9:15; Ne 9:8; Ps 103:8; 145:17

5 The LORD is gracious and
righteous;[w]
our God is full of compassion.

116:6 [x] Ps 19:7; 79:8

6 The LORD protects the
simplehearted;
when I was in great need,[x] he
saved me.

116:7 [y] Jer 6:16; Mt 11:29 [z] Ps 13:6

7 Be at rest[y] once more, O my soul,
for the LORD has been good[z] to
you.

116:8 [a] Ps 56:13

8 For you, O LORD, have delivered my
soul[a] from death,
my eyes from tears,
my feet from stumbling,

116:9 [b] Ps 27:13

9 that I may walk before the LORD
in the land of the living.[b]

116:10 [c] 2Co 4:13*

10 I believed;[c] therefore[c] I said,
"I am greatly afflicted."

116:11 [d] Ro 3:4

11 And in my dismay I said,
"All men are liars."[d]

12 How can I repay the LORD
for all his goodness to me?

116:13 [e] Ps 16:5; 80:18

13 I will lift up the cup of salvation
and call on the name[e] of the
LORD.

116:14 [f] Ps 22:25; Jnh 2:9

14 I will fulfill my vows[f] to the LORD
in the presence of all his people.

116:15 [g] Ps 72:14

15 Precious in the sight[g] of the LORD
is the death of his saints.

116:16 [h] Ps 119:125; 143:12 [i] Ps 86:16

16 O LORD, truly I am your servant;[h]
I am your servant, the son of
your maidservant[d];[i]
you have freed me from my
chains.

116:17 [j] Lev 7:12; Ps 50:14

17 I will sacrifice a thank offering[j] to
you
and call on the name of the
LORD.

18 I will fulfill my vows to the LORD
in the presence of all his people,

116:19 [k] Ps 96:8; 135:2

19 in the courts[k] of the house of the
LORD—
in your midst, O Jerusalem.

Praise the LORD.[a]

PSALM 117

117:1 [l] Ro 15:11*

1 Praise the LORD, all you nations;[l]
extol him, all you peoples.

117:2 [m] Ps 100:5

2 For great is his love toward us,
and the faithfulness of the
LORD[m] endures forever.

Praise the LORD.[a]

PSALM 118

118:1 [n] 1Ch 16:8 [o] Ps 106:1; 136:1

1 Give thanks to the LORD,[n] for he is
good;
his love endures forever.[o]

118:2 [p] Ps 115:9

2 Let Israel say:[p]
"His love endures forever."
3 Let the house of Aaron say:
"His love endures forever."
4 Let those who fear the LORD say:
"His love endures forever."

118:5 [q] Ps 120:1 [r] Ps 18:19

5 In my anguish[q] I cried to the LORD,
and he answered[r] by setting me
free.

[a] *18,19,2* Hebrew *Hallelu Yah* [b] *3* Hebrew *Sheol* [c] *10* Or *believed even when* [d] *16* Or *servant, your faithful son*

Joy Beyond Sadness

The night before his death Jesus and his disciples celebrated the Passover together. During the meal he informed the group that one among them would turn against him. Then he broke a loaf of bread in half and poured some wine for each of them. He used the elements of the traditional feast to demonstrate for the disciples who he was and what he was about to do (Matthew 26:26–29). At the end of the meal the group sang a song and then walked together to the Mount of Olives so that Jesus could pray (Matthew 26:30) in the place called Gethsemane.

It may seem odd that the disciples were able to sing after Jesus had delivered such a solemn message. But the song was most likely the traditional psalm sung at the end of every Passover meal—Psalm 118. It is a song of suffering, describing the anguish God's promised Messiah would have to endure on behalf of those who belong to him. As Jesus and his disciples lifted their voices, however, only Jesus fully understood the significance of the words.

The first four verses of this psalm repeat four times that the Lord's "love endures forever." Since the fall of Adam and Eve, God had been promising to send a Savior who would completely atone for our sin and deliver us from Satan's power (Genesis 3:15,21). As Jesus sang this psalm he realized that his impending death was the fulfillment of all of these promises to his people, the full expression of his covenant love. Jesus had quoted Psalm 118:22–23 to warn the chief priests and the Pharisees about rejecting him as the Messiah (Matthew 2:42). Now he was allowing himself to be captured and killed by them.

In the middle of the grim psalm there bubbles up a refrain of unquenchable joy and praise: "This is the day the LORD has made; let us rejoice and be glad in it" (Psalm 118:24). Imagine for a moment the ambivalence our precious Lord must have experienced just prior to his death. He anticipated the horror he was about to face, but he also understood where these events would lead. Yes, he would suffer indescribable pain—emotional, spiritual and physical—but his gaze could penetrate the darkness of the cross because of the joy he knew would ensue (Hebrews 12:2). He realized that he would soon face indescribable agony and death, but he also knew that there was more reason to celebrate than to mourn. What he was about to accomplish would open heaven's gates and provide the means of restoration for our relationship with God.

Like Jesus we can know a joy that reaches beyond our circumstances, a certitude rooted in the reality that, despite the darkness of the moment, God always has a higher purpose. Far beyond the transient and superficial happiness for which we so often strive, we can bask in the peace and deep-seated joy of knowing that God is continually at work for our good to conform us to the likeness of his precious Son, our Savior, Jesus Christ (Romans 8:28–29; 2 Corinthians 3:18). "Give thanks to the LORD, for he is good, his love endures forever" (Psalm 118:29).

Self-Discovery: *Imagine Jesus singing this psalm just before going to the cross. What verses would have had special meaning for him? What verses have special meaning for you?*

GO TO DISCOVERY 154 ON PAGE 797

118:6 [s]Heb 13:6* [t]Ps 27:1; 56:4
6 The LORD is with me;[s] I will not be
afraid.
What can man do to me?[t]
118:7 [u]Ps 54:4 [v]Ps 59:10
7 The LORD is with me; he is my
helper.[u]
I will look in triumph on my
enemies.[v]
118:8 [w]Ps 40:4 [x]Jer 17:5
8 It is better to take refuge in the
LORD[w]
than to trust in man.[x]
9 It is better to take refuge in the
LORD
118:9 [y]Ps 146:3
than to trust in princes.[y]
10 All the nations surrounded me,
118:10 [z]Ps 18:40
but in the name of the LORD I cut
them off.[z]
118:11 [a]Ps 88:17 [b]Ps 3:6
11 They surrounded me[a] on every
side,[b]
but in the name of the LORD I cut
them off.
118:12 [c]Dt 1:44 [d]Ps 58:9
12 They swarmed around me like
bees,[c]
but they died out as quickly as
burning thorns;[d]
in the name of the LORD I cut
them off.
118:13 [e]Ps 86:17; 140:4
13 I was pushed back and about to fall,
but the LORD helped me.[e]
118:14 [f]Ex 15:2 [g]Isa 12:2
14 The LORD is my strength[f] and my
song;
he has become my salvation.[g]
118:15 [h]Ps 68:3 [i]Ps 89:13
15 Shouts of joy[h] and victory
resound in the tents of the
righteous:
"The LORD's right hand[i] has done
mighty things!
16 The LORD's right hand is lifted
high;
the LORD's right hand has done
mighty things!"
118:17 [j]Ps 6:5; Hab 1:12 [k]Ex 15:6; Ps 73:28
17 I will not die[j] but live,
and will proclaim[k] what the
LORD has done.
18 The LORD has chastened me
severely,
118:18 [l]2Co 6:9
but he has not given me over to
death.[l]
118:19 [m]Isa 26:2
19 Open for me the gates[m] of
righteousness;
I will enter and give thanks to
the LORD.
118:20 [n]Ps 24:7; Isa 35:8; Rev 22:14
20 This is the gate of the LORD
through which the righteous
may enter.[n]
21 I will give you thanks, for you
answered me;[o] 118:21 [o]Ps 116:1
you have become my salvation.
22 The stone the builders rejected 118:22 [p]Mt 21:42; Mk 12:10; Lk 20:17*; Ac 4:11*; 1Pe 2:7*
has become the capstone;[p]
23 the LORD has done this,
and it is marvelous in our eyes.
24 This is the day the LORD has made;
let us rejoice and be glad in it.
25 O LORD, save us;
O LORD, grant us success.
26 Blessed is he who comes[q] in the 118:26 [q]Mt 21:9*; Mk 11:9*; Lk 13:35*; 19:38*; Jn 12:13*
name of the LORD.
From the house of the LORD we
bless you.[a]
27 The LORD is God,
and he has made his light shine[r] 118:27 [r]1Pe 2:9
upon us.
With boughs in hand, join in the
festal procession
up[b] to the horns of the altar.
28 You are my God, and I will give you
thanks;
you are my God,[s] and I will 118:28 [s]Isa 25:1 [t]Ex 15:2
exalt[t] you.
29 Give thanks to the LORD, for he is
good;
his love endures forever.

PSALM 119[c]

א Aleph

1 Blessed are they whose ways are
blameless,
who walk[u] according to the law 119:1 [u]Ps 128:1
of the LORD.
2 Blessed are they who keep his
statutes
and seek him with all their 119:2 [v]Dt 6:5
heart.[v]
3 They do nothing wrong;[w] 119:3 [w]1Jn 3:9; 5:18
they walk in his ways.
4 You have laid down precepts
that are to be fully obeyed.
5 Oh, that my ways were steadfast
in obeying your decrees!
6 Then I would not be put to shame
when I consider all your
commands.

[a] 26 The Hebrew is plural. [b] 27 Or *Bind the festal sacrifice with ropes / and take it* [c] This psalm is an acrostic poem; the verses of each stanza begin with the same letter of the Hebrew alphabet.

[7] I will praise you with an upright
heart
as I learn your righteous laws.
[8] I will obey your decrees;
do not utterly forsake me.

ב Beth

[9] How can a young man keep his
way pure?
By living according to your word.[x]
[10] I seek you with all my heart;[y]
do not let me stray from your
commands.[z]
[11] I have hidden your word in my
heart[a]
that I might not sin against you.
[12] Praise be to you, O LORD;
teach me your decrees.[b]
[13] With my lips I recount
all the laws that come from your
mouth.[c]
[14] I rejoice in following your statutes
as one rejoices in great riches.
[15] I meditate on your precepts[d]
and consider your ways.
[16] I delight[e] in your decrees;
I will not neglect your word.

119:9 x2Ch 6:16
119:10 y2Ch 15:15 zver 21,118
119:11 aPs 37:31; Lk 2:19,51
119:12 bver 26
119:13 cPs 40:9
119:15 dPs 1:2
119:16 ePs 1:2

ג Gimel

[17] Do good to your servant,[f] and I will
live;
I will obey your word.
[18] Open my eyes that I may see
wonderful things in your law.

119:17 fPs 13:6; 116:7

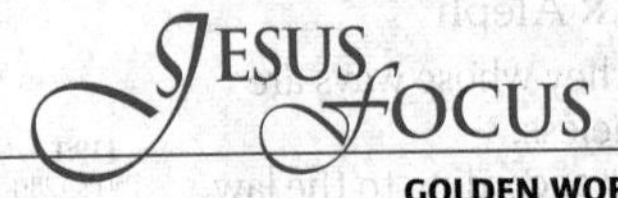

GOLDEN WORDS FROM GOD

Psalm 119 is the most lengthy of the psalms, containing 176 verses, all centered around believing God completely and walking intimately with him. The song in the original Hebrew comprises a cleverly designed *acrostic* poem, meaning that all of the verses of each stanza begin with the same letter of the Hebrew alphabet, and each succeeding section uses the next consecutive letter of the alphabet. There are many different ways to refer to God's word: laws, statutes, ways, precepts, decrees, commands. In the New Testament Jesus himself is called "the Word" (John 1:1). The Bible is the *written* expression of God's truth, and Jesus is the *personal* expression of that same truth. Our precious Savior is truth in the flesh, God's ultimate way of saying, "This is who I am if you want to get to know me" (see John 8:19; 14:7).

[19] I am a stranger on earth;[g]
do not hide your commands
from me.
[20] My soul is consumed[h] with longing
for your laws[i] at all times.
[21] You rebuke the arrogant, who are
cursed
and who stray[j] from your
commands.
[22] Remove from me scorn[k] and
contempt,
for I keep your statutes.
[23] Though rulers sit together and
slander me,
your servant will meditate on
your decrees.
[24] Your statutes are my delight;
they are my counselors.

119:19 g1Ch 29:15; Ps 39:12; 2Co 5:6; Heb 11:13
119:20 hPs 42:2; 84:2 iPs 63:1
119:21 jver 10
119:22 kPs 39:8

ד Daleth

[25] I am laid low in the dust;[l]
preserve my life[m] according to
your word.
[26] I recounted my ways and you
answered me;
teach me your decrees.[n]
[27] Let me understand the teaching of
your precepts;
then I will meditate on your
wonders.[o]
[28] My soul is weary with sorrow;[p]
strengthen me[q] according to
your word.
[29] Keep me from deceitful ways;
be gracious to me through your
law.
[30] I have chosen the way of truth;
I have set my heart on your laws.
[31] I hold fast[r] to your statutes,
O LORD;
do not let me be put to shame.
[32] I run in the path of your
commands,
for you have set my heart free.

119:25 lPs 44:25 mPs 143:11
119:26 nPs 25:4; 27:11; 86:11
119:27 oPs 145:5
119:28 pPs 107:26 qPs 20:2; 1Pe 5:10
119:31 rDt 11:22

ה He

[33] Teach me,[s] O LORD, to follow your
decrees;
then I will keep them to the end.
[34] Give me understanding, and I will
keep your law
and obey it with all my heart.
[35] Direct me in the path of your
commands,
for there I find delight.
[36] Turn my heart[t] toward your statutes
and not toward selfish gain.[u]

119:33 sver 12
119:36 t1Ki 8:58 uEze 33:31; Mk 7:21-22; Lk 12:15; Heb 13:5

[37] Turn my eyes away from worthless things;
preserve my life[v] according to your word.[a]
[38] Fulfill your promise[w] to your servant,
so that you may be feared.
[39] Take away the disgrace I dread,
for your laws are good.
[40] How I long[x] for your precepts!
Preserve my life in your righteousness.

ו Waw

[41] May your unfailing love come to me, O LORD,
your salvation according to your promise;
[42] then I will answer[y] the one who taunts me,
for I trust in your word.
[43] Do not snatch the word of truth from my mouth,
for I have put my hope in your laws.
[44] I will always obey your law,
for ever and ever.
[45] I will walk about in freedom,
for I have sought out your precepts.
[46] I will speak of your statutes before kings[z]
and will not be put to shame,
[47] for I delight in your commands
because I love them.
[48] I lift up my hands to[b] your commands, which I love,
and I meditate on your decrees.

ז Zayin

[49] Remember your word to your servant,
for you have given me hope.
[50] My comfort in my suffering is this:
Your promise preserves my life.[a]
[51] The arrogant mock me[b] without restraint,
but I do not turn[c] from your law.
[52] I remember[d] your ancient laws, O LORD,
and I find comfort in them.
[53] Indignation grips me[e] because of the wicked,
who have forsaken your law.[f]
[54] Your decrees are the theme of my song
wherever I lodge.
[55] In the night I remember[g] your name, O LORD,
and I will keep your law.
[56] This has been my practice:
I obey your precepts.

ח Heth

[57] You are my portion,[h] O LORD;
I have promised to obey your words.
[58] I have sought your face with all my heart;
be gracious to me[i] according to your promise.[j]
[59] I have considered my ways[k]
and have turned my steps to your statutes.
[60] I will hasten and not delay
to obey your commands.
[61] Though the wicked bind me with ropes,
I will not forget[l] your law.
[62] At midnight[m] I rise to give you thanks
for your righteous laws.
[63] I am a friend to all who fear you,[n]
to all who follow your precepts.
[64] The earth is filled with your love,[o] O LORD;
teach me your decrees.

ט Teth

[65] Do good to your servant
according to your word, O LORD.
[66] Teach me knowledge and good judgment,
for I believe in your commands.
[67] Before I was afflicted I went astray,[p]
but now I obey your word.
[68] You are good,[q] and what you do is good;
teach me your decrees.[r]
[69] Though the arrogant have smeared me with lies,[s]
I keep your precepts with all my heart.
[70] Their hearts are callous[t] and unfeeling,
but I delight in your law.
[71] It was good for me to be afflicted
so that I might learn your decrees.
[72] The law from your mouth is more precious to me

a 37 Two manuscripts of the Masoretic Text and Dead Sea Scrolls; most manuscripts of the Masoretic Text *life in your way* *b 48* Or *for*

119:37 v Ps 71:20; Isa 33:15
119:38 w 2Sa 7:25
119:40 x ver 20
119:42 y Pr 27:11
119:46 z Mt 10:18; Ac 26:1-2
119:50 a Ro 15:4
119:51 b Jer 20:7 c ver 157; Job 23:11; Ps 44:18
119:52 d Ps 103:18
119:53 e Ezr 9:3 f Ps 89:30
119:55 g Ps 63:6
119:57 h Ps 16:5; La 3:24
119:58 i 1Ki 13:6 j ver 41
119:59 k Lk 15:17-18
119:61 l Ps 140:5
119:62 m Ac 16:25
119:63 n Ps 101:6-7
119:64 o Ps 33:5
119:67 p Jer 31:18-19; Heb 12:11
119:68 q Ps 106:1; 107:1; Mt 19:17 r ver 12
119:69 s Job 13:4; Ps 109:2
119:70 t Ps 17:10; Isa 6:10; Ac 28:27

119:72 [u] Ps 19:10; Pr 8:10-11,19

than thousands of pieces of
silver and gold.[u]

י Yodh

119:73 [v] Job 10:8; Ps 100:3; 138:8; 139:13-16

73 Your hands made me[v] and formed
me;
give me understanding to learn
your commands.

119:74 [w] Ps 34:2

74 May those who fear you rejoice[w]
when they see me,
for I have put my hope in your
word.
75 I know, O LORD, that your laws are
righteous,

119:75 [x] Heb 12:5-11

and in faithfulness[x] you have
afflicted me.
76 May your unfailing love be my
comfort,
according to your promise to
your servant.

119:77 [y] ver 41

77 Let your compassion[y] come to me
that I may live,
for your law is my delight.

119:78 [z] Jer 50:32 [a] ver 86,161

78 May the arrogant[z] be put to shame
for wronging me without
cause;[a]
but I will meditate on your
precepts.
79 May those who fear you turn to
me,
those who understand your
statutes.
80 May my heart be blameless toward
your decrees,
that I may not be put to shame.

כ Kaph

119:81 [b] Ps 84:2

81 My soul faints[b] with longing for
your salvation,
but I have put my hope in your
word.

119:82 [c] Ps 69:3; La 2:11

82 My eyes fail,[c] looking for your
promise;
I say, "When will you comfort
me?"
83 Though I am like a wineskin in the
smoke,
I do not forget your decrees.

119:84 [d] Ps 39:4; Rev 6:10

84 How long[d] must your servant wait?
When will you punish my
persecutors?

119:85 [e] Ps 35:7; Jer 18:20,22

85 The arrogant dig pitfalls[e] for me,
contrary to your law.

119:86 [f] Ps 35:19 [g] Ps 109:26 [h] ver 78

86 All your commands are
trustworthy;[f]
help me,[g] for men persecute me
without cause.[h]
87 They almost wiped me from the
earth,

119:87 [i] Isa 58:2

but I have not forsaken[i] your
precepts.
88 Preserve my life according to your
love,
and I will obey the statutes of
your mouth.

ל Lamedh

119:89 [j] Mt 24:34-35; 1Pe 1:25

89 Your word, O LORD, is eternal;[j]
it stands firm in the heavens.

119:90 [k] Ps 36:5 [l] Ps 148:6; Ecc 1:4

90 Your faithfulness[k] continues
through all generations;
you established the earth, and it
endures.[l]

119:91 [m] Jer 33:25

91 Your laws endure[m] to this day,
for all things serve you.
92 If your law had not been my
delight,
I would have perished in my
affliction.
93 I will never forget your precepts,
for by them you have preserved
my life.
94 Save me, for I am yours;
I have sought out your
precepts.
95 The wicked are waiting to destroy
me,
but I will ponder your statutes.
96 To all perfection I see a limit;
but your commands are
boundless.

מ Mem

97 Oh, how I love your law!

119:98 [n] Ps 1:2 [o] Dt 4:6

I meditate[n] on it all day long.
98 Your commands make me wiser[o]
than my enemies,
for they are ever with me.
99 I have more insight than all my
teachers,
for I meditate on your statutes.
100 I have more understanding than
the elders,

119:100 [p] Job 32:7-9

for I obey your precepts.[p]

119:101 [q] Pr 1:15

101 I have kept my feet[q] from every
evil path
so that I might obey your word.
102 I have not departed from your
laws,
for you yourself have taught me.
103 How sweet are your words to my
taste,

119:103 [r] Ps 19:10; Pr 8:11 [s] Pr 24:13-14

sweeter than honey[r] to my
mouth![s]

[104] I gain understanding from your
precepts;
therefore I hate every wrong
path.[t]

נ Nun

[105] Your word is a lamp to my feet
and a light[u] for my path.
[106] I have taken an oath[v] and
confirmed it,
that I will follow your righteous
laws.
[107] I have suffered much;
preserve my life, O LORD,
according to your word.
[108] Accept, O LORD, the willing praise
of my mouth,[w]
and teach me your laws.
[109] Though I constantly take my life
in my hands,[x]
I will not forget your law.
[110] The wicked have set a snare[y]
for me,
but I have not strayed[z] from
your precepts.
[111] Your statutes are my heritage
forever;
they are the joy of my heart.
[112] My heart is set on keeping your
decrees
to the very end.[a]

ס Samekh

[113] I hate double-minded men,[b]
but I love your law.
[114] You are my refuge and my
shield;[c]
I have put my hope[d] in your
word.
[115] Away from me,[e] you evildoers,
that I may keep the commands
of my God!
[116] Sustain me[f] according to your
promise, and I will live;
do not let my hopes be dashed.[g]
[117] Uphold me, and I will be
delivered;
I will always have regard for your
decrees.
[118] You reject all who stray from your
decrees,
for their deceitfulness is in vain.
[119] All the wicked of the earth you
discard like dross;[h]
therefore I love your statutes.
[120] My flesh trembles[i] in fear of you;
I stand in awe of your laws.

119:104 [t] ver 128
119:105 [u] Pr 6:23
119:106 [v] Ne 10:29
119:108 [w] Hos 14:2; Heb 13:15
119:109 [x] Jdg 12:3; Job 13:14
119:110 [y] Ps 140:5; 141:9
119:111 [z] ver 10
119:112 [a] ver 33
119:113 [b] Jas 1:8
119:114 [c] Ps 32:7; 91:1 [d] ver 74
119:115 [e] Ps 6:8; 139:19; Mt 7:23
119:116 [f] Ps 54:4 [g] Ps 25:2; Ro 5:5; 9:33
119:119 [h] Eze 22:18,19
119:120 [i] Hab 3:16

ע Ayin

[121] I have done what is righteous and
just;
do not leave me to my oppressors.
[122] Ensure your servant's well-being;[j]
let not the arrogant oppress me.
[123] My eyes fail, looking for your
salvation,
looking for your righteous
promise.[k]
[124] Deal with your servant according
to your love
and teach me your decrees.[l]
[125] I am your servant;[m] give me
discernment
that I may understand your
statutes.
[126] It is time for you to act, O LORD;
your law is being broken.
[127] Because I love your commands
more than gold,[n] more than
pure gold,
[128] and because I consider all your
precepts right,
I hate every wrong path.[o]

פ Pe

[129] Your statutes are wonderful;
therefore I obey them.
[130] The unfolding of your words gives
light;[p]
it gives understanding to the
simple.[q]
[131] I open my mouth and pant,[r]
longing for your commands.[s]
[132] Turn to me and have mercy[t] on me,
as you always do to those who
love your name.
[133] Direct my footsteps according to
your word;[u]
let no sin rule[v] over me.
[134] Redeem me from the oppression
of men,[w]
that I may obey your precepts.
[135] Make your face shine[x] upon your
servant
and teach me your decrees.
[136] Streams of tears[y] flow from my
eyes,
for your law is not obeyed.[z]

צ Tsadhe

[137] Righteous are you,[a] O LORD,
and your laws are right.[b]
[138] The statutes you have laid down
are righteous;[c]
they are fully trustworthy.

119:122 [j] Job 17:3
119:123 [k] ver 82
119:124 [l] ver 12
119:125 [m] Ps 116:16
119:127 [n] Ps 19:10
119:128 [o] ver 104,163
119:130 [p] Pr 6:23 [q] Ps 19:7
119:131 [r] Ps 42:1 [s] ver 20
119:132 [t] Ps 25:16; 106:4
119:133 [u] Ps 17:5 [v] Ps 19:13; Ro 6:12
119:134 [w] Ps 142:6; Lk 1:74
119:135 [x] Nu 6:25; Ps 4:6
119:136 [y] Jer 9:1,18 [z] Eze 9:4
119:137 [a] Ezr 9:15; Jer 12:1 [b] Ne 9:13
119:138 [c] Ps 19:7

119:139 [d] Ps 69:9; Jn 2:17

139 My zeal wears me out,[d]
for my enemies ignore your words.

119:140 [e] Ps 12:6

140 Your promises have been thoroughly tested,[e]
and your servant loves them.

119:141 [f] Ps 22:6

141 Though I am lowly and despised,[f]
I do not forget your precepts.

119:142 [g] Ps 19:7

142 Your righteousness is everlasting
and your law is true.[g]
143 Trouble and distress have come upon me,
but your commands are my delight.

119:144 [h] Ps 19:9

144 Your statutes are forever right;
give me understanding[h] that I may live.

ק Qoph

145 I call with all my heart; answer me, O LORD,
and I will obey your decrees.
146 I call out to you; save me
and I will keep your statutes.

119:147 [i] Ps 5:3; 57:8; 108:2

147 I rise before dawn[i] and cry for help;
I have put my hope in your word.

119:148 [j] Ps 63:6

148 My eyes stay open through the watches of the night,[j]
that I may meditate on your promises.
149 Hear my voice in accordance with your love;
preserve my life, O LORD,
according to your laws.
150 Those who devise wicked schemes are near,
but they are far from your law.

119:151 [k] Ps 34:18; 145:18 [l] ver 142

151 Yet you are near,[k] O LORD,
and all your commands are true.[l]

119:152 [m] Lk 21:33

152 Long ago I learned from your statutes
that you established them to last forever.[m]

ר Resh

119:153 [n] La 5:1 [o] Pr 3:1

153 Look upon my suffering[n] and deliver me,
for I have not forgotten[o] your law.

119:154 [p] Mic 7:9 [q] 1Sa 24:15

154 Defend my cause[p] and redeem me;[q]
preserve my life according to your promise.

119:155 [r] Job 5:4

155 Salvation is far from the wicked,
for they do not seek out[r] your decrees.

119:156 [s] 2Sa 24:14

156 Your compassion is great, O LORD;
preserve my life[s] according to your laws.

119:157 [t] Ps 7:1

157 Many are the foes who persecute me,[t]
but I have not turned from your statutes.

119:158 [u] Ps 139:21

158 I look on the faithless with loathing,[u]
for they do not obey your word.
159 See how I love your precepts;
preserve my life, O LORD,
according to your love.
160 All your words are true;
all your righteous laws are eternal.

ש Sin and Shin

119:161 [v] 1Sa 24:11

161 Rulers persecute me[v] without cause,
but my heart trembles at your word.

119:162 [w] 1Sa 30:16

162 I rejoice in your promise
like one who finds great spoil.[w]
163 I hate and abhor falsehood
but I love your law.
164 Seven times a day I praise you
for your righteous laws.

119:165 [x] Pr 3:2; Isa 26:3,12; 32:17

165 Great peace[x] have they who love your law,
and nothing can make them stumble.

119:166 [y] Ge 49:18

166 I wait for your salvation,[y] O LORD,
and I follow your commands.
167 I obey your statutes,
for I love them greatly.

119:168 [z] Pr 5:21

168 I obey your precepts and your statutes,
for all my ways are known[z] to you.

ת Taw

119:169 [a] Ps 18:6

169 May my cry come[a] before you, O LORD;
give me understanding
according to your word.

119:170 [b] Ps 28:2 [c] Ps 31:2

170 May my supplication come[b] before you;
deliver me[c] according to your promise.

119:171 [d] Ps 51:15 [e] Ps 94:12

171 May my lips overflow with praise,[d]
for you teach me[e] your decrees.
172 May my tongue sing of your word,
for all your commands are righteous.

119:173 [f] Ps 37:24 [g] Jos 24:22

173 May your hand be ready to help[f] me,
for I have chosen[g] your precepts.

119:174 [h] ver 166
[174] I long for your salvation,[h] O LORD,
and your law is my delight.
119:175 [i] Isa 55:3
[175] Let me live[i] that I may praise you,
and may your laws sustain me.
119:176 [j] Isa 53:6
[176] I have strayed like a lost sheep.[j]
Seek your servant,
for I have not forgotten your
commands.

PSALM 120

A song of ascents.

120:1 [k] Ps 102:2; Jnh 2:2
[1] I call on the LORD in my distress,[k]
and he answers me.
120:2 [l] Pr 12:22 [m] Ps 52:4
[2] Save me, O LORD, from lying lips[l]
and from deceitful tongues.[m]

[3] What will he do to you,
and what more besides,
O deceitful tongue?
120:4 [n] Ps 45:5
[4] He will punish you with a warrior's
sharp arrows,[n]
with burning coals of the broom
tree.

120:5 [o] Ge 25:13; Jer 49:28
[5] Woe to me that I dwell in Meshech,
that I live among the tents of
Kedar![o]
[6] Too long have I lived
among those who hate peace.
[7] I am a man of peace;
but when I speak, they are for war.

PSALM 121

A song of ascents.

[1] I lift up my eyes to the hills—
where does my help come from?
121:2 [p] Ps 115:15; 124:8
[2] My help comes from the LORD,
the Maker of heaven and earth.[p]

[3] He will not let your foot slip—
he who watches over you will
not slumber;
[4] indeed, he who watches over Israel
will neither slumber nor sleep.
121:5 [q] Isa 25:4
[5] The LORD watches over[q] you—
the LORD is your shade at your
right hand;
121:6 [r] Ps 91:5; Isa 49:10; Rev 7:16
[6] the sun[r] will not harm you by day,
nor the moon by night.

121:7 [s] Ps 41:2; 91:10-12
[7] The LORD will keep you from all
harm[s]—
he will watch over your life;
[8] the LORD will watch over your
coming and going
both now and forevermore.[t]
121:8 [t] Dt 28:6

PSALM 122

A song of ascents. Of David.

[1] I rejoiced with those who said to
me,
"Let us go to the house of the
LORD."
[2] Our feet are standing
in your gates, O Jerusalem.

[3] Jerusalem is built like a city
that is closely compacted
together.
[4] That is where the tribes go up,
the tribes of the LORD,
to praise the name of the LORD
according to the statute given to
Israel.
[5] There the thrones for judgment
stand,
the thrones of the house of
David.

[6] Pray for the peace of Jerusalem:
"May those who love[u] you be
secure.
122:6 [u] Ps 51:18

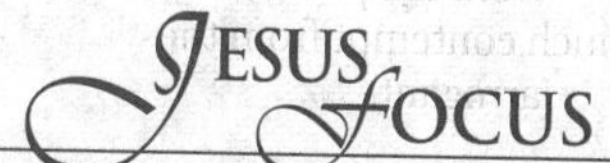

PRAY FOR JERUSALEM

Psalms 120—134 are called *songs of ascents* because they were sung by Israelites as they made annual pilgrimages to Jerusalem (Deuteronomy 16:16; Psalm 84:5–7). They literally climbed uphill from the valleys around the city, which sits 2,200 feet above sea level. These songs may also have been sung by the Levitical choirs as they ascended the steps of the temple. The psalms focus on the city of Jerusalem and the house of the Lord. In fact, Psalm 122:6 invites its readers to "pray for the peace of Jerusalem." Jesus cared very deeply for the people of this city (Matthew 23:37; Luke 19:41–44). And God desires lasting peace—not only for Jerusalem, but for all of his creation—a peace that will come to final fruition when Jesus, the Prince of Peace (Isaiah 9:6; Micah 5:2–5; Luke 2:14; Romans 5:1), takes his place as the rightful King who rules the earth when the new Jerusalem comes down out of heaven from God (Revelation 21:1–5; see also Zechariah 8:1–3; 14:8–9).

7 May there be peace within your
walls
and security within your
citadels."
8 For the sake of my brothers and
friends,
I will say, "Peace be within you."
9 For the sake of the house of the
LORD our God,
122:9 v Ne 2:10 I will seek your prosperity.[v]

PSALM 123

A song of ascents.

1 I lift up my eyes to you,
123:1 w Ps 11:4; 121:1; 141:8 to you whose throne[w] is in
heaven.
2 As the eyes of slaves look to the
hand of their master,
as the eyes of a maid look to the
hand of her mistress,
123:2 x Ps 25:15 so our eyes look to the LORD[x] our
God,
till he shows us his mercy.

3 Have mercy on us, O LORD, have
mercy on us,
for we have endured much
contempt.
4 We have endured much ridicule
from the proud,
much contempt from the
arrogant.

PSALM 124

A song of ascents. Of David.

1 If the LORD had not been on our
side—
124:1 y Ps 129:1 let Israel say[y]—
2 if the LORD had not been on our side
when men attacked us,
3 when their anger flared against us,
they would have swallowed us
alive;
4 the flood would have engulfed us,
the torrent would have swept
over us,
5 the raging waters
would have swept us away.

6 Praise be to the LORD,
who has not let us be torn by
their teeth.
7 We have escaped like a bird
out of the fowler's snare;[z] 124:7 z Ps 91:3; Pr 6:5
the snare has been broken,
and we have escaped.
8 Our help is in the name of the LORD, 124:8
the Maker of heaven[a] and earth. a Ge 1:1; Ps 121:2; 134:3

PSALM 125

A song of ascents.

1 Those who trust in the LORD are
like Mount Zion, 125:1
which cannot be shaken[b] but b Ps 46:5
endures forever.
2 As the mountains surround
Jerusalem, 125:2
so the LORD surrounds[c] his c Ps 121:8; Zec 2:4-5
people
both now and forevermore.

3 The scepter of the wicked will not 125:3
remain[d] d Ps 89:22; Pr 22:8; Isa 14:5
over the land allotted to the e 1Sa 24:10; Ps 55:20
righteous,
for then the righteous might use
their hands to do evil.[e]
4 Do good, O LORD,[f] to those who are 125:4
good, f Ps 119:68
to those who are upright in g Ps 7:10; 36:10; 94:15
heart.[g]
5 But those who turn[h] to crooked 125:5
ways[i] h Job 23:11
the LORD will banish with the i Pr 2:15; Isa 59:8
evildoers. j Ps 128:6

Peace be upon Israel.[j]

PSALM 126

A song of ascents.

1 When the LORD brought back[k] the 126:1
captives to[a] Zion, k Ps 85:1; Hos 6:11
we were like men who dreamed.[b]
2 Our mouths were filled with
laughter, 126:2
our tongues with songs of joy.[l] l Job 8:21; Ps 51:14
Then it was said among the m Ps 71:19
nations,
"The LORD has done great
things[m] for them."
3 The LORD has done great things for
us, 126:3
and we are filled with joy.[n] n Isa 25:9

[a] 1 Or *LORD restored the fortunes of* [b] 1 Or *men restored to health*

[4]Restore our fortunes,[a] O LORD,
like streams in the Negev.[o]
[5]Those who sow in tears
will reap with songs of joy.[p]
[6]He who goes out weeping,
carrying seed to sow,
will return with songs of joy,
carrying sheaves with him.

126:4 [o]Isa 35:6; 43:19
126:5 [p]Isa 35:10

PSALM 127

A song of ascents. Of Solomon.

[1]Unless the LORD builds[q] the house,
its builders labor in vain.
Unless the LORD watches[r] over the city,
the watchmen stand guard in vain.
[2]In vain you rise early
and stay up late,
toiling for food[s] to eat—
for he grants sleep[t] to[b] those he loves.
[3]Sons are a heritage from the LORD,
children a reward[u] from him.
[4]Like arrows in the hands of a warrior
are sons born in one's youth.
[5]Blessed is the man
whose quiver is full of them.
They will not be put to shame
when they contend with their enemies[v] in the gate.

127:1 [q]Ps 78:69 [r]Ps 121:4
127:2 [s]Ge 3:17 [t]Job 11:18
127:3 [u]Ge 33:5
127:5 [v]Pr 27:11

PSALM 128

A song of ascents.

[1]Blessed are all who fear the LORD,[w]
who walk in his ways.[x]
[2]You will eat the fruit of your labor;[y]
blessings and prosperity[z] will be yours.
[3]Your wife will be like a fruitful vine[a]
within your house;
your sons will be like olive shoots[b]
around your table.
[4]Thus is the man blessed
who fears the LORD.

[5]May the LORD bless you from Zion[c]
all the days of your life;
may you see the prosperity of Jerusalem,
[6]and may you live to see your
children's children.[d]

Peace be upon Israel.[e]

128:1 [w]Ps 112:1 [x]Ps 119:1-3
128:2 [y]Isa 3:10 [z]Ecc 8:12
128:3 [a]Eze 19:10 Ps 52:8; 144:12
128:5 [c]Ps 20:2; 134:3
128:6 [d]Ge 50:23; Job 42:16 [e]Ps 125:5

PSALM 129

A song of ascents.

[1]They have greatly oppressed me
from my youth[f]—
let Israel say[g]—
[2]they have greatly oppressed me
from my youth,
but they have not gained the victory[h] over me.
[3]Plowmen have plowed my back
and made their furrows long.
[4]But the LORD is righteous;[i]
he has cut me free from the cords of the wicked.

[5]May all who hate Zion[j]
be turned back in shame.[k]
[6]May they be like grass on the roof,
which withers[l] before it can grow;
[7]with it the reaper cannot fill his hands,
nor the one who gathers fill his arms.
[8]May those who pass by not say,
"The blessing of the LORD be upon you;
we bless you[m] in the name of the LORD."

129:1 [f]Ps 88:15; Hos 2:15 [g]Ps 124:1
129:2 [h]Mt 16:18
129:4 [i]Ps 119:137
129:5 [j]Mic 4:11 [k]Ps 71:13
129:6 [l]Ps 37:2
129:8 [m]Ru 2:4; Ps 118:26

PSALM 130

A song of ascents.

[1]Out of the depths[n] I cry to you,
O LORD;
[2]O Lord, hear my voice.[o]
Let your ears be attentive[p]
to my cry for mercy.
[3]If you, O LORD, kept a record of sins,
O Lord, who could stand?[q]
[4]But with you there is forgiveness;[r]
therefore you are feared.[s]

[5]I wait for the LORD,[t] my soul waits,
and in his word[u] I put my hope.
[6]My soul waits for the Lord

130:1 [n]Ps 42:7; 69:2; La 3:55
130:2 [o]Ps 28:2 [p]2Ch 6:40; Ps 64:1
130:3 [q]Ps 76:7; 143:2
130:4 [r]Ex 34:7; Isa 55:7; Jer 33:8 [s]1Ki 8:40
130:5 [t]Ps 27:14; 33:20; Isa 8:17 [u]Ps 119:81

[a] 4 Or *Bring back our captives* [b] 2 Or *eat— / for while they sleep he provides for*

130:6 more than watchmen[v] wait for
the morning,
more than watchmen wait for
the morning.[w]

v Ps 63:6 w Ps 119:147

130:7 [7] O Israel, put your hope[x] in the
LORD,
for with the LORD is unfailing
love
and with him is full redemption.

x Ps 131:3

130:8 [8] He himself will redeem[y] Israel
from all their sins.

y Lk 1:68

PSALM 131

A song of ascents. Of David.

131:1 [1] My heart is not proud,[z] O LORD,
my eyes are not haughty;
I do not concern myself with great
matters
or things too wonderful for me.
[2] But I have stilled and quieted my
soul;
like a weaned child with its
mother,
131:2 like a weaned child is my soul[a]
within me.

z Ps 101:5; Ro 12:16

a Mt 18:3; 1Co 14:20

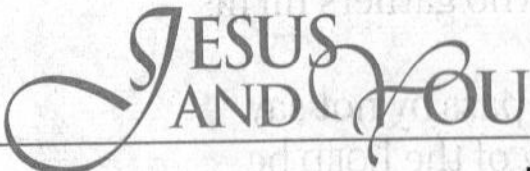

NO RECORD OF SIN

Sometimes God's people attempt to write out a list of their sins as a kind of spiritual checkup. If we are truly honest with ourselves, we are totally overwhelmed by the prevalence of sin in our lives—our deliberate cruelty, selfish ambition, apathy to the needs around us, major offenses and seemingly minor indiscretions. Because we are in fact oblivious to so many of our own sins, it would be easy to assume that God must maintain a much more comprehensive list than we could even imagine! But Psalm 130 reminds us that God does not keep a written record to use as evidence against us: "If you, O LORD, kept a record of sins . . . who could stand? But with you there is forgiveness" (verses 3–4). When we accept Jesus' death as payment for our sin, God forgives us, no longer holding that sin against us 2 Corinthians 5:18–19). Because Jesus died in our place God "canceled the written code" that had condemned us. Jesus "took it away, nailing it to the cross" (Colossians 2:14). "For God did not send his Son into the world to condemn the world, but to save the world through him" (John 3:17).

[3] O Israel, put your hope[b] in the LORD 131:3
both now and forevermore.

b Ps 130:7

PSALM 132

A song of ascents.

[1] O LORD, remember David
and all the hardships he endured.

[2] He swore an oath to the LORD
and made a vow to the Mighty 132:2
One of Jacob:[c]
[3] "I will not enter my house
or go to my bed—
[4] I will allow no sleep to my eyes,
no slumber to my eyelids,
[5] till I find a place[d] for the LORD, 132:5
a dwelling for the Mighty One of
Jacob."

c Ge 49:24

d Ac 7:46

[6] We heard it in Ephrathah,[e] 132:6
we came upon it in the fields of
Jaar:[a,b][f]
[7] "Let us go to his dwelling place;[g] 132:7
let us worship at his footstool[h]—
[8] arise, O LORD,[i] and come to your 132:8
resting place,
you and the ark of your might.
[9] May your priests be clothed with 132:9
righteousness;[j]
may your saints sing for joy."

e 1Sa 17:12 f 1Sa 7:2

g Ps 5:7 h Ps 99:5

i Nu 10:35; Ps 78:61

j Job 29:14; Isa 61:3,10

[10] For the sake of David your servant,
do not reject your anointed one.

[11] The LORD swore an oath to David,[k] 132:11
a sure oath that he will not
revoke:
"One of your own descendants[l]
I will place on your throne—
[12] if your sons keep my covenant
and the statutes I teach them,
then their sons will sit 132:12
on your throne[m] for ever and
ever."

k Ps 89:3-4,35 l 2Sa 7:12

m Lk 1:32; Ac 2:30

[13] For the LORD has chosen Zion,[n] 132:13
he has desired it for his dwelling:
[14] "This is my resting place for ever 132:14
and ever;[o]
here I will sit enthroned, for I
have desired it—
[15] I will bless her with abundant
provisions; 132:15
her poor will I satisfy with food.[p]

n Ps 48:1-2

o Ps 68:16

p Ps 107:9; 147:14

[a] 6 That is, Kiriath Jearim [b] 6 Or *heard of it in Ephrathah, / we found it in the fields of Jaar.* (And no quotes around verses 7–9)

DISCOVERY 154

Quiet in Our Souls

Psalm 131 is brief and unpretentious. David didn't provide biographical background information to clue us in as to where he was on his life's journey, but we know that he was experiencing a time during which his relationship with the Father seemed whole and intact. In essence, he expressed two thoughts in this short psalm: 1) His heart was not proud; he did not concern himself with matters "too wonderful for [him]" (verse 1), and 2) he desired that his soul be stilled and quieted like a weaned child with its mother (verse 2).

What a beautiful image of our relationship with God! We, like the infant nestled in her mother's protecting arms, can experience absolute security in fellowship with our Lord. Moses had many years earlier spoken to the Israelites just prior to his death. One of the memorable verses in his address is Deuteronomy 33:27: "The eternal God is your refuge, and underneath are the everlasting arms." And our Lord Jesus expressed a similar desire to enfold the children of Jerusalem to himself, as a hen gathers her chicks under her wings (Matthew 23:37).

And still today, amid the frenetic activity of our daily lives, we carry a deep desire within our souls to be stilled and quieted. Seldom in our busy world of television, traffic noise and even "white noise" in our offices do we experience the phenomenon of complete and utter silence, broken only by the twitter of a bird or the crack of a twig. Perhaps on a camping trip we have wondered at silence, or we may have been caught by surprise during the night by a moment so uncannily still that we consciously held our breath to listen and enjoy.

One of our deepest longings is for "the peace of God, which transcends all understanding" to "guard [our] hearts and [our] minds in Christ Jesus" (Philippians 4:7). Jesus in the same lengthy discourse twice juxtaposed the lack of peace we experience in our world with the serenity that he alone can provide. In John 14:27 he told his disciples, "Peace I leave with you; my peace I give you. I do not give to you as the world gives." And again in John 16:33: "I have told you these things, so that in me you may have peace. In this world you will have trouble. But take heart! I have overcome the world."

Jesus invites us to "come to me, all you who are weary and burdened, and I will give you rest" (Matthew 11:28). Even our prayer life can so easily deteriorate into a hurried activity, sandwiched into our busy day at the "appropriate" moments. But God invites us to commune with him during those quiet moments when we sense him reaching out to us and offering his gift of peace.

David stated in Psalm 63:6: "On my bed I remember you; I think of you through the watches of the night." We can commune with God while waiting in traffic, thanking God for our little ones as we watch them sleeping or marveling at God's provision as we pay our bills; we can experience God's peace while sitting quietly, open Bible in hand, waiting for him to reveal to us his words of grace and truth, words that will meet us at our very point of need.

Self-Discovery: *Think of being stilled and quieted like a baby with its mother. What images or adjectives come to mind to describe the feelings of the child? Are you able to rest in the arms of Jesus like a small child?*

GO TO DISCOVERY 155 ON PAGE 800

132:16 [q]2Ch 6:41

[16] I will clothe her priests[q] with
salvation,
and her saints will ever sing for
joy.

132:17 [r]Eze 29:21; Lk 1:69 [s]1Ki 11:36; 2Ch 21:7

[17] "Here I will make a horn[a] grow[r] for
David
and set up a lamp[s] for my
anointed one.

132:18 [t]Ps 35:26; 109:29

[18] I will clothe his enemies with
shame,[t]
but the crown on his head will
be resplendent."

PSALM 133

A song of ascents. Of David.

133:1 [u]Ge 13:8; Heb 13:1

[1] How good and pleasant it is
when brothers live together[u] in
unity!

133:2 [v]Ex 30:25

[2] It is like precious oil poured on the
head,[v]
running down on the beard,
running down on Aaron's beard,
down upon the collar of his
robes.

133:3 [w]Dt 4:48 [x]Lev 25:21; Dt 28:8 [y]Ps 42:8

[3] It is as if the dew of Hermon[w]
were falling on Mount Zion.
For there the LORD bestows his
blessing,[x]
even life forevermore.[y]

PSALM 134

A song of ascents.

134:1 [z]Ps 135:1-2 [a]1Ch 9:33

[1] Praise the LORD, all you servants[z] of
the LORD
who minister by night[a] in the
house of the LORD.

134:2 [b]Ps 28:2; 1Ti 2:8

[2] Lift up your hands[b] in the
sanctuary
and praise the LORD.

134:3 [c]Ps 124:8 [d]Ps 128:5

[3] May the LORD, the Maker of
heaven[c] and earth,
bless you from Zion.[d]

PSALM 135

[1] Praise the LORD.[b]

135:1 [e]Ps 113:1; 134:1

Praise the name of the LORD;
praise him, you servants[e] of the
LORD,

135:2 [f]Lk 2:37 [g]Ps 116:19

[2] you who minister in the house[f] of
the LORD,
in the courts[g] of the house of
our God.

135:3 [h]Ps 119:68 [i]Ps 147:1

[3] Praise the LORD, for the LORD is
good;[h]
sing praise to his name, for that
is pleasant.[i]

135:4 [j]Dt 10:15; 1Pe 2:9 [k]Ex 19:5; Dt 7:6

[4] For the LORD has chosen Jacob[j] to
be his own,
Israel to be his treasured
possession.[k]

135:5 [l]Ps 48:1 [m]Ps 97:9

[5] I know that the LORD is great,[l]
that our Lord is greater than all
gods.[m]

135:6 [n]Ps 115:3

[6] The LORD does whatever pleases
him,[n]
in the heavens and on the earth,
in the seas and all their depths.

135:7 [o]Jer 10:13; Zec 10:1 [p]Job 28:25 [q]Job 38:22

[7] He makes clouds rise from the
ends of the earth;
he sends lightning with the rain[o]
and brings out the wind[p] from
his storehouses.[q]

135:8 [r]Ex 12:12; Ps 78:51

[8] He struck down the firstborn[r] of
Egypt,
the firstborn of men and animals.

135:9 [s]Dt 6:22 [t]Ps 136:10-15

[9] He sent his signs[s] and wonders
into your midst, O Egypt,
against Pharaoh and all his
servants.[t]

135:10 [u]Nu 21:21-25; Ps 136:17-21

[10] He struck down many[u] nations
and killed mighty kings—

135:11 [v]Nu 21:21 [w]Jos 12:7-24

[11] Sihon[v] king of the Amorites,
Og king of Bashan
and all the kings of Canaan[w]—

135:12 [x]Ps 78:55

[12] and he gave their land as an
inheritance,[x]
an inheritance to his people
Israel.

135:13 [y]Ex 3:15 [z]Ps 102:12

[13] Your name, O LORD, endures
forever,[y]
your renown,[z] O LORD, through
all generations.

135:14 [a]Dt 32:36

[14] For the LORD will vindicate his
people
and have compassion on his
servants.[a]

[15] The idols of the nations are silver
and gold,
made by the hands of men.

[16] They have mouths, but cannot
speak,

[a] 17 *Horn* here symbolizes strong one, that is, king.
[b] 1 Hebrew *Hallelu Yah*; also in verses 3 and 21

eyes, but they cannot see;
17 they have ears, but cannot hear,
nor is there breath in their mouths.
18 Those who make them will be like them,
and so will all who trust in them.

19 O house of Israel, praise the LORD;
O house of Aaron, praise the LORD;
20 O house of Levi, praise the LORD;
you who fear him, praise the LORD.
135:21 [b] Ps 134:3
21 Praise be to the LORD from Zion,[b]
to him who dwells in Jerusalem.

Praise the LORD.

PSALM 136

136:1 [c] Ps 106:1 [d] 1Ch 16:34; 2Ch 20:21
1 Give thanks to the LORD, for he is good.[c]
His love endures forever.[d]
136:2 [e] Dt 10:17
2 Give thanks to the God of gods.[e]
His love endures forever.
3 Give thanks to the Lord of lords:
His love endures forever.

136:4 [f] Ps 72:18
4 to him who alone does great wonders,[f]
His love endures forever.
136:5 [g] Pr 3:19; Jer 51:15 [h] Ge 1:1
5 who by his understanding[g] made the heavens,[h]
His love endures forever.
136:6 [i] Ge 1:9; Jer 10:12 [j] Ps 24:2
6 who spread out the earth[i] upon the waters,[j]
His love endures forever.
136:7 [k] Ge 1:14,16
7 who made the great lights[k]—
His love endures forever.
136:8 [l] Ge 1:16
8 the sun to govern[l] the day,
His love endures forever.
9 the moon and stars to govern the night;
His love endures forever.

136:10 [m] Ex 12:29; Ps 135:8
10 to him who struck down the firstborn[m] of Egypt
His love endures forever.
136:11 [n] Ex 6:6; 12:51
11 and brought Israel out[n] from among them
His love endures forever.
136:12 [o] Dt 4:34; Ps 44:3
12 with a mighty hand and outstretched arm;[o]
His love endures forever.
136:13 [p] Ex 14:21; Ps 78:13
13 to him who divided the Red Sea[a][p] asunder
His love endures forever.
136:14 [q] Ex 14:22
14 and brought Israel through[q] the midst of it,
His love endures forever.
136:15 [r] Ex 14:27; Ps 135:9
15 but swept Pharaoh and his army into the Red Sea;[r]
His love endures forever.

136:16 [s] Ex 13:18
16 to him who led his people through the desert,[s]
His love endures forever.
136:17 [t] Ps 135:9-12
17 who struck down great kings,[t]
His love endures forever.
136:18 [u] Dt 29:7
18 and killed mighty kings[u]—
His love endures forever.
136:19 [v] Nu 21:21-25
19 Sihon king of the Amorites[v]
His love endures forever.
20 and Og king of Bashan—
His love endures forever.
136:21 [w] Jos 12:1
21 and gave their land[w] as an inheritance,
His love endures forever.
22 an inheritance to his servant Israel;
His love endures forever.

136:23 [x] Ps 113:7
23 to the One who remembered us[x] in our low estate
His love endures forever.
136:24 [y] Ps 107:2
24 and freed us from our enemies,[y]
His love endures forever.
136:25 [z] Ps 104:27; 145:15
25 and who gives food[z] to every creature.
His love endures forever.
26 Give thanks to the God of heaven.
His love endures forever.

PSALM 137

137:1 [a] Eze 1:1,3 [b] Ne 1:4
1 By the rivers of Babylon[a] we sat and wept[b]
when we remembered Zion.
2 There on the poplars
we hung our harps,
3 for there our captors asked us for songs,
137:3 [c] Ps 80:6
our tormentors demanded[c] songs of joy;
they said, "Sing us one of the songs of Zion!"
4 How can we sing the songs of the LORD
while in a foreign land?
5 If I forget you, O Jerusalem,
may my right hand forget ⌊its skill⌋.

[a] *13* Hebrew *Yam Suph;* that is, Sea of Reeds; also in verse 15

GOD'S UNFAILING LOVE

God's people have always exhibited creativity in the ways they have chosen to worship him. Just as we do today the people of Israel often sang songs with echoes or repeated refrains. A number of the people would intone a few lines, after which the rest of the group would respond with the next line or lines. Psalm 136 was sung in this manner. The first group would exclaim, "Give thanks to the LORD, for he is good," and the second would chant, "His love endures forever." This pattern would continue through the end of the song.

There are many ways to describe God's love for his people. The Hebrew word used for love in Psalm 136 focuses on God's faithfulness in keeping the covenant promise he had made to Israel. Two specific ways in which God exhibits this love to his people are reflected in this psalm. First, he demonstrates his love by his acts of creation. God designed the cosmos and everything within it as an expression of his love. Second, he demonstrates his love by freeing us from that which holds us back from being all that he intended us to be. An example for the people of Israel was their liberation from slavery in Egypt.

God's very essence is love—he can be nothing less (1 John 4:16). Much of the "love" we experience from other people is conditional: "I'll love you *as long as* . . ." The requirements each of us impose on others are different depending on our felt needs. But God never says, "I'll continue to love you *provided* . . ." He never warns us that he will love us *only* if we always obey him, finally get ourselves straightened out or express our love to him first.

In fact, God is the One who initiated the love relationship with his people. His Son Jesus Christ not only died for us "while we were still sinners" (Romans 5:8) but came back to life so that we would never again have to experience separation from God. Paul stated in Romans 6:4–6: "We were therefore buried with him through baptism into death in order that, just as Christ was raised from the dead through the glory of the Father, we too may live a new life. If we have been united with him like this in his death, we will certainly also be united with him in his resurrection. For we know that our old self was crucified with him so that the body of sin might be done away with, that we should no longer be slaves to sin."

Most of us at one time or another question God's love: "If God loves me, why would he allow this to happen? Has he forgotten about me?" But Paul reminds us with a rhetorical question that we can *know* that God is on our side: "He who did not spare his own Son, but gave him up for us all—how will he not also, along with him, graciously give us all things?" (Romans 8:32).

Self-Discovery: *Identify a time in your life in which you have been offered conditional love? What about unconditional love? How did you respond to each? How have you responded to God's unconditional love for you: "Dear friends, since God so loved us, we also ought to love one another"? (1 John 4:11).*

GO TO DISCOVERY 156 ON PAGE 805

137:6 [d]Eze 3:26

6 May my tongue cling to the roof[d]
of my mouth
if I do not remember you,
if I do not consider Jerusalem
my highest joy.

137:7 [e]Jer 49:7; La 4:21-22; Eze 25:12 [f]Ob 1:11

7 Remember, O LORD, what the
Edomites[e] did
on the day Jerusalem fell.[f]
"Tear it down," they cried,
"tear it down to its foundations!"

137:8 [g]Isa 13:1,19; Jer 25:12,26; Jer 50:15; Rev 18:6

8 O Daughter of Babylon, doomed to
destruction,[g]
happy is he who repays you
for what you have done to us—

137:9 [h]2Ki 8:12; Isa 13:16

9 he who seizes your infants
and dashes them[h] against the
rocks.

PSALM 138

Of David.

138:1 [i]Ps 95:3; 96:4

1 I will praise you, O LORD, with all
my heart;
before the "gods"[i] I will sing your
praise.

138:2 [j]1Ki 8:29; Ps 5:7; 28:2 [k]Isa 42:21

2 I will bow down toward your holy
temple[j]
and will praise your name
for your love and your
faithfulness,
for you have exalted above all things
your name and your word.[k]

138:3 [l]Ps 28:7

3 When I called, you answered me;
you made me bold and
stouthearted.[l]

138:4 [m]Ps 102:15

4 May all the kings of the earth[m]
praise you, O LORD,
when they hear the words of
your mouth.
5 May they sing of the ways of the
LORD,
for the glory of the LORD is great.

138:6 [n]Ps 113:6; Isa 57:15 [o]Pr 3:34; Jas 4:6

6 Though the LORD is on high, he
looks upon the lowly,[n]
but the proud[o] he knows from
afar.

138:7 [p]Ps 23:4 [q]Jer 51:25 [r]Ps 20:6 [s]Ps 71:20

7 Though I walk[p] in the midst of
trouble,
you preserve my life;
you stretch out your hand against
the anger of my foes,[q]
with your right hand[r] you save
me.[s]

138:8 [t]Ps 57:2; Php 1:6 [u]Job 10:3,8; 14:15

8 The LORD will fulfill ⌊his purpose⌋[t]
for me;
your love, O LORD, endures
forever—
do not abandon the works of
your hands.[u]

PSALM 139

For the director of music. Of David. A psalm.

139:1 [v]Ps 17:3 [w]Jer 12:3

1 O LORD, you have searched me[v]
and you know[w] me.

139:2 [x]2Ki 19:27 [y]Mt 9:4; Jn 2:24

2 You know when I sit and when I
rise;[x]
you perceive my thoughts[y] from
afar.

139:3 [z]Job 31:4

3 You discern my going out and my
lying down;
you are familiar with all my
ways.[z]

139:4 [a]Heb 4:13

4 Before a word is on my tongue
you know it completely,[a] O LORD.

139:5 [b]Ps 34:7

5 You hem me in[b]—behind and
before;
you have laid your hand upon
me.

139:6 [c]Job 42:3; Ro 11:33

6 Such knowledge is too wonderful
for me,
too lofty[c] for me to attain.

139:7 [d]Jer 23:24; Jnh 1:3

7 Where can I go from your Spirit?
Where can I flee[d] from your
presence?

139:8 [e]Am 9:2-3 [f]Pr 15:11

8 If I go up to the heavens,[e] you are
there;
if I make my bed[f] in the depths,[a]
you are there.
9 If I rise on the wings of the dawn,
if I settle on the far side of the
sea,

139:10 [g]Ps 23:3

10 even there your hand will guide me,[g]
your right hand will hold me fast.
11 If I say, "Surely the darkness will
hide me
and the light become night
around me,"

139:12 [h]Job 34:22; Da 2:22

12 even the darkness will not be dark[h]
to you;
the night will shine like the day,
for darkness is as light to you.

139:13 [i]Ps 119:73 [j]Job 10:11

13 For you created my inmost being;[i]
you knit me together[j] in my
mother's womb.

[a] 8 Hebrew *Sheol*

THE ETERNAL BEING . . . BECAME NOT ONLY A MAN BUT (BEFORE THAT) A BABY, AND BEFORE THAT A FETUS INSIDE A WOMAN'S BODY.

C. S. Lewis, *British Author*

[14] I praise you because I am fearfully
and wonderfully made;
your works are wonderful,[k]
I know that full well.
[15] My frame was not hidden from
you
when I was made in the secret
place.
When I was woven together[l] in the
depths of the earth,[m]
[16] your eyes saw my unformed
body.
All the days ordained for me
were written in your book
before one of them came to be.

[17] How precious to[a] me are your
thoughts, O God![n]
How vast is the sum of them!
[18] Were I to count them,
they would outnumber the
grains of sand.
When I awake,
I am still with you.

[19] If only you would slay the wicked,[o]
O God!
Away from me,[p] you
bloodthirsty men!
[20] They speak of you with evil intent;
your adversaries misuse your
name.[q]
[21] Do I not hate those[r] who hate you,
O LORD,
and abhor those who rise up
against you?
[22] I have nothing but hatred for
them;
I count them my enemies.
[23] Search me,[s] O God, and know my
heart;[t]
test me and know my anxious
thoughts.
[24] See if there is any offensive way in
me,
and lead me[u] in the way
everlasting.

139:14 [k] Ps 40:5
139:15 [l] Job 10:11 [m] Ps 63:9
139:17 [n] Ps 40:5
139:19 [o] Isa 11:4 [p] Ps 119:115
139:20 [q] Jude 15
139:21 [r] 2Ch 19:2; Ps 31:6; 119:113; Ps 119:158
139:23 [s] Job 31:6; Ps 26:2 [t] Jer 11:20
139:24 [u] Ps 5:8; 143:10; Pr 15:9

PSALM 140

For the director of music. A psalm of David.

[1] Rescue me,[v] O LORD, from evil men;
protect me from men of
violence,[w]
[2] who devise evil plans[x] in their
hearts
and stir up war every day.
[3] They make their tongues as sharp
as[y] a serpent's;
the poison of vipers[z] is on their
lips. *Selah*
[4] Keep me,[a] O LORD, from the hands
of the wicked;[b]
protect me from men of violence
who plan to trip my feet.
[5] Proud men have hidden a snare for
me;
they have spread out the cords
of their net
and have set traps[c] for me along
my path. *Selah*

140:1 [v] Ps 17:13 [w] Ps 18:48
140:2 [x] Ps 36:4; 56:6
140:3 [y] Ps 57:4 [z] Ps 58:4; Jas 3:8
140:4 [a] Ps 141:9 [b] Ps 71:4
140:5 [c] Ps 31:4; 35:7

[a] 17 Or *concerning*

JESUS FOCUS

JUSTICE FOR THE POOR

Poor people tend to be easy targets for injustice. Because they lack the power and resources to create options for themselves or to alter their circumstances and destiny, they frequently find themselves in a position of dependency, hoping that someone will take an interest in them and champion their cause. Because of the pervasive effects of sin on human nature, it often seems that few people are willing to invest the time or accept the risk implicit in becoming involved. But God himself is vitally concerned about the needy, and he "secures justice for the poor" (Psalm 140:12). What's more, he expects his people to do the same. Jesus even told two disciples of John the Baptist that one way to verify that he was indeed the Messiah, the One God had promised, was to take note that he preached the good news to the poor (Matthew 11:5; Luke 4:18; see also Isaiah 61:1). Throughout the New Testament we can see God building on the theme of his concern of justice for the underprivileged (Romans 15:26; Galatians 2:10; 1 Timothy 6:9–10; James 1:27; 2:1–5). Clearly, God's heart of compassion is big for those who have very little.

140:6 [d]Ps 16:2 [e]Ps 116:1; 143:1

[6] O LORD, I say to you, "You are my
God."[d]
Hear, O LORD, my cry for mercy.[e]

140:7 [f]Ps 28:8

[7] O Sovereign LORD,[f] my strong
deliverer,
who shields my head in the day
of battle—

140:8 [g]Ps 10:2-3

[8] do not grant the wicked[g] their
desires, O LORD;
do not let their plans succeed,
or they will become proud. *Selah*

[9] Let the heads of those who
surround me

140:9 [h]Ps 7:16

be covered with the trouble their
lips have caused.[h]

140:10 [i]Ps 11:6; 21:9

[10] Let burning coals fall upon them;
may they be thrown into the fire,[i]
into miry pits, never to rise.
[11] Let slanderers not be established
in the land;
may disaster hunt down men of

140:11 [j]Ps 34:21

violence.[j]

[12] I know that the LORD secures
justice for the poor

140:12 [k]Ps 9:4 [l]Ps 35:10

and upholds the cause[k] of the
needy.[l]

140:13 [m]Ps 97:12 [n]Ps 11:7

[13] Surely the righteous will praise
your name[m]
and the upright will live[n] before
you.

PSALM 141

A psalm of David.

141:1 [o]Ps 22:19; 70:5 [p]Ps 143:1

[1] O LORD, I call to you; come quickly[o]
to me.
Hear my voice[p] when I call to
you.

141:2 [q]Rev 5:8; 8:3 [r]1Ti 2:8 [s]Ex 29:39,41

[2] May my prayer be set before you
like incense;[q]
may the lifting up of my hands[r]
be like the evening
sacrifice.[s]

[3] Set a guard over my mouth, O LORD;
keep watch over the door of my
lips.
[4] Let not my heart be drawn to what
is evil,
to take part in wicked deeds
with men who are evildoers;

141:4 [t]Pr 23:6

let me not eat of their
delicacies.[t]

[5] Let a righteous man[a] strike me—it
is a kindness;

141:5 [u]Pr 9:8 [v]Ps 23:5

let him rebuke me[u]—it is oil on
my head.[v]
My head will not refuse it.

Yet my prayer is ever against the
deeds of evildoers;
[6] their rulers will be thrown down
from the cliffs,
and the wicked will learn that
my words were well spoken.
[7] ⌊They will say,⌋ "As one plows and
breaks up the earth,

141:7 [w]Ps 53:5

so our bones have been scattered
at the mouth[w] of the grave.[b]"

141:8 [x]Ps 25:15 [y]Ps 2:12

[8] But my eyes are fixed[x] on you,
O Sovereign LORD;
in you I take refuge[y]—do not
give me over to death.

141:9 [z]Ps 140:4 [a]Ps 38:12

[9] Keep me[z] from the snares they
have laid for me,
from the traps set[a] by evildoers.

141:10 [b]Ps 35:8

[10] Let the wicked fall[b] into their own
nets,
while I pass by in safety.

PSALM 142

A *maskil*[c] of David. When he was in the cave. A prayer.

[1] I cry aloud to the LORD;

142:1 [c]Ps 30:8

I lift up my voice to the LORD for
mercy.[c]

142:2 [d]Isa 26:16

[2] I pour out my complaint[d] before
him;
before him I tell my trouble.

142:3 [e]Ps 140:5; 143:4,7

[3] When my spirit grows faint[e] within
me,
it is you who know my way.
In the path where I walk
men have hidden a snare for me.
[4] Look to my right and see;
no one is concerned for me.
I have no refuge;

142:4 [f]Ps 31:11; Jer 30:17

no one cares[f] for my life.

142:5 [g]Ps 46:1 [h]Ps 16:5 [i]Ps 27:13

[5] I cry to you, O LORD;
I say, "You are my refuge,[g]
my portion[h] in the land of the
living."[i]

142:6 [j]Ps 17:1 [k]Ps 79:8; 116:6

[6] Listen to my cry,[j]
for I am in desperate need;[k]
rescue me from those who pursue
me,
for they are too strong for me.

[a] 5 Or *Let the Righteous One* [b] 7 Hebrew *Sheol*
[c] Title: Probably a literary or musical term

142:7 [l] Ps 146:7 [m] Ps 13:6

7 Set me free from my prison,[l]
that I may praise your name.
Then the righteous will gather
about me
because of your goodness to
me.[m]

PSALM 143

A psalm of David.

143:1 [n] Ps 140:6 [o] Ps 89:1-2 [p] Ps 71:2

1 O LORD, hear my prayer,
listen to my cry for mercy;[n]
in your faithfulness[o] and
righteousness[p]
come to my relief.

143:2 [q] Ps 14:3; Ecc 7:20; Ro 3:20

2 Do not bring your servant into
judgment,
for no one living is righteous[q]
before you.
3 The enemy pursues me,
he crushes me to the ground;
he makes me dwell in darkness
like those long dead.

143:4 [r] Ps 142:3

4 So my spirit grows faint within me;
my heart within me is dismayed.[r]

143:5 [s] Ps 77:6

5 I remember[s] the days of long ago;
I meditate on all your works
and consider what your hands
have done.

143:6 [t] Ps 63:1; 88:9

6 I spread out my hands[t] to you;
my soul thirsts for you like a
parched land. *Selah*

143:7 [u] Ps 69:17 [v] Ps 27:9; 28:1

7 Answer me quickly,[u] O LORD;
my spirit fails.
Do not hide your face[v] from me
or I will be like those who go
down to the pit.

143:8 [w] Ps 46:5; 90:14 [x] Ps 27:11 [y] Ps 25:1-2

8 Let the morning bring me word of
your unfailing love,[w]
for I have put my trust in you.
Show me the way[x] I should go,
for to you I lift up my soul.[y]

143:9 [z] Ps 31:15

9 Rescue me from my enemies,[z]
O LORD,
for I hide myself in you.
10 Teach me to do your will,
for you are my God;

143:10 [a] Ne 9:20; Ps 23:3; 25:4-5

may your good Spirit
lead[a] me on level ground.

143:11 [b] Ps 119:25 [c] Ps 31:1

11 For your name's sake, O LORD,
preserve my life;[b]
in your righteousness,[c] bring me
out of trouble.

143:12 [d] Ps 52:5; 54:5 [e] Ps 116:16

12 In your unfailing love, silence my
enemies;
destroy all my foes,[d]
for I am your servant.[e]

PSALM 144

Of David.

144:1 [f] Ps 18:2,34

1 Praise be to the LORD my Rock,[f]
who trains my hands for war,
my fingers for battle.

144:2 [g] Ps 59:9; 91:2 [h] Ps 84:9

2 He is my loving God and my
fortress,[g]
my stronghold and my deliverer,
my shield,[h] in whom I take refuge,
who subdues peoples[a] under me.

144:3 [i] Ps 8:4; Heb 2:6

3 O LORD, what is man[i] that you care
for him,
the son of man that you think of
him?

144:4 [j] Ps 39:11; 102:11

4 Man is like a breath;
his days are like a fleeting
shadow.[j]

144:5 [k] Ps 18:9; Isa 64:1 [l] Ps 104:32

5 Part your heavens,[k] O LORD, and
come down;
touch the mountains, so that
they smoke.[l]

144:6 [m] Ps 7:12-13; 18:14

6 Send forth lightning and scatter
⌊the enemies⌋;
shoot your arrows[m] and rout
them.
7 Reach down your hand from on
high;

144:7 [n] Ps 69:2 [o] Ps 18:44

deliver me and rescue me
from the mighty waters,[n]
from the hands of foreigners[o]

144:8 [p] Ps 12:2

8 whose mouths are full of lies,[p]
whose right hands are deceitful.
9 I will sing a new song to you,
O God;

144:9 [q] Ps 33:2-3

on the ten-stringed lyre[q] I will
make music to you,
10 to the One who gives victory to
kings,

144:10 [r] Ps 18:50

who delivers his servant David[r]
from the deadly sword.
11 Deliver me and rescue me

144:11 [s] Ps 12:2; Isa 44:20

from the hands of foreigners
whose mouths are full of lies,
whose right hands are deceitful.[s]

[a] 2 Many manuscripts of the Masoretic Text, Dead Sea Scrolls, Aquila, Jerome and Syriac; most manuscripts of the Masoretic Text *subdues my people*

DOES GOD REALLY CARE ABOUT ME?

Every one of us reading these words is alive today, but none of us has a guarantee about tomorrow. The Bible likens us to a vapor or to a breath that exists for only for a moment (Psalms 35:5; 39:4–6; 144:4). James said it this way: "What is your life? You are a mist that appears for a little while and then vanishes" (James 4:14). We live with that reality every day and sometimes have a hard time comprehending that God cares for each one of us *as though we were the only person on earth*.

God intended for each of our lives to be much more than transitory and insignificant. He reaches out to us with all the intensity of the love that fills his Father heart. God is not conserving that love, doling it out in miniscule portions or reserving it for a vague "someday." He offers his vigilant concern to its full extent right now, even though we have a tendency to spurn his care and go our own way.

God could have pronounced final and irrevocable judgment against sin at any time. Instead he waited to unveil his perfect plan of redemption and to welcome us back to the heart and home of the Father (Luke 15:11–24)—until the time was exactly right (Galatians 4:4–5). We were lost, but Jesus came down to earth to find us (Luke 19:9–10). God is intimately concerned with every detail of our lives—even more than we ourselves are (Matthew 10:30).

The psalmist asked: "O LORD, what is man that you care for him, the son of man that you think of him?" (Psalm 144:3). Human beings are vulnerable and of little consequence when compared with God. The author to the Hebrews quoted this verse and pointed out that the incarnation of Jesus Christ has changed everything. Someday everything in the universe will be subjected to Jesus' authority. Through Jesus, all those who place their faith in him will also be exalted with him and share his glory. The angels look on in wonder and amazement at the grace of God "(1 Peter 1:12).

Many in our world have never experienced an awareness of God's solicitous care. We make presuppositions about love and nurture from earliest childhood based on our encounters with imperfect people who have offered love only conditionally or perhaps even grudgingly. But Jesus is different: While on earth he visited, touched and encouraged people no one else would even approach. Jesus even cares about the seemingly minor details we would have expected him to dismiss as insignificant—such as what the guests would drink at a wedding (see John 2:1–11).

Jesus wants each of us to establish a relationship with him that will last forever. He cares and always will—about every nuance, every complication, every ache, every delight in our lives. This is the message of Psalm 144. David affirmed that God cares deeply for us (Psalms 8:4; 144:3). Even though life is as fleeting as a vapor, our existence is of infinite significance to our Maker. The greatest possible blessing in life is a personal relationship with God (Psalm 144:15).

Self-Discovery: *Do you ever feel as though human love has to be conserved and doled out in small portions to make certain there is enough to go around? What about the love of Jesus? How does it make you feel to hear that the awesome Creator of all things cares about you?*

GO TO DISCOVERY 157 ON PAGE 809

12 Then our sons in their youth
144:12 t Ps 128:3 will be like well-nurtured plants,[t]
and our daughters will be like
pillars
carved to adorn a palace.
13 Our barns will be filled
with every kind of provision.
Our sheep will increase by
thousands,
by tens of thousands in our
fields;
14 our oxen will draw heavy loads.[a]
There will be no breaching of walls,
no going into captivity,
no cry of distress in our streets.

144:15 u Ps 33:12 15 Blessed are the people[u] of whom
this is true;
blessed are the people whose
God is the LORD.

PSALM 145[b]

A psalm of praise. Of David.

145:1 v Ps 30:1; 34:1 w Ps 5:2 1 I will exalt you,[v] my God the King;[w]
I will praise your name for ever
and ever.
145:2 x Ps 71:6 2 Every day I will praise[x] you
and extol your name for ever
and ever.

3 Great is the LORD and most worthy
of praise;
145:3 y Job 5:9; Ps 147:5; Ro 11:33 his greatness no one can
fathom.[y]
4 One generation[z] will commend
145:4 z Isa 38:19 your works to another;
they will tell of your mighty acts.
5 They will speak of the glorious
splendor of your majesty,
145:5 a Ps 119:27 and I will meditate on your
wonderful works.[c] [a]
145:6 b Ps 66:3 c Dt 32:3 6 They will tell of the power of your
awesome works,[b]
and I will proclaim[c] your great
deeds.
145:7 d Isa 63:7 e Ps 51:14 7 They will celebrate your abundant
goodness[d]
and joyfully sing of your
righteousness.[e]

145:8 f Ps 86:15 g Ex 34:6; Nu 14:18 8 The LORD is gracious and
compassionate,[f]
slow to anger and rich in love.[g]
9 The LORD is good[h] to all;
145:9 h Ps 100:5 he has compassion on all he has
made.

10 All you have made will praise you,[i] 145:10 i Ps 19:1 j Ps 68:26
O LORD;
your saints will extol you.[j]
11 They will tell of the glory of your
kingdom
and speak of your might,
12 so that all men may know of your 145:12 k Ps 105:1
mighty acts[k]
and the glorious splendor of
your kingdom.
13 Your kingdom is an everlasting 145:13 l 1Ti 1:17; 2Pe 1:11
kingdom,[l]
and your dominion endures
through all generations.

The LORD is faithful to all his
promises
and loving toward all he has
made.[d]
14 The LORD upholds[m] all those who 145:14 m Ps 37:24 n Ps 146:8
fall
and lifts up all[n] who are bowed
down.
15 The eyes of all look to you, 145:15 o Ps 104:27; 136:25
and you give them their food[o] at
the proper time.
16 You open your hand 145:16 p Ps 104:28
and satisfy the desires[p] of every
living thing.

17 The LORD is righteous in all his ways
and loving toward all he has
made.
18 The LORD is near[q] to all who call on 145:18 q Dt 4:7 r Jn 4:24
him,[r]
to all who call on him in truth.
19 He fulfills the desires[s] of those who 145:19 s Ps 37:4 t Pr 15:29
fear him;
he hears their cry[t] and saves
them.
20 The LORD watches over all who love 145:20 u Ps 31:23; 97:10 v Ps 9:5
him,[u]
but all the wicked he will destroy.[v]
21 My mouth will speak[w] in praise of 145:21 w Ps 71:8 x Ps 65:2
the LORD.
Let every creature[x] praise his
holy name
for ever and ever.

[a] 14 Or *our chieftains will be firmly established*
[b] This psalm is an acrostic poem, the verses of which (including verse 13b) begin with the successive letters of the Hebrew alphabet.
[c] 5 Dead Sea Scrolls and Syriac (see also Septuagint); Masoretic Text *On the glorious splendor of your majesty / and on your wonderful works I will meditate*
[d] 13 One manuscript of the Masoretic Text, Dead Sea Scrolls and Syriac (see also Septuagint); most manuscripts of the Masoretic Text do not have the last two lines of verse 13.

PSALM 146

1 Praise the LORD.[a]

146:1 [y]Ps 103:1
Praise the LORD,[y] O my soul.
146:2 [z]Ps 104:33
2 I will praise the LORD all my life;[z]
I will sing praise to my God as long as I live.

146:3 [a]Ps 118:9 [b]Isa 2:22
3 Do not put your trust in princes,[a]
in mortal men,[b] who cannot save.
146:4 [c]Ps 104:29; Ecc 12:7 [d]Ps 33:10; 1Co 2:6
4 When their spirit departs, they return to the ground;[c]
on that very day their plans come to nothing.[d]
146:5 [e]Ps 144:15; Jer 17:7 [f]Ps 71:5
5 Blessed is he[e] whose help[f] is the God of Jacob,
whose hope is in the LORD his God,
146:6 [g]Ps 115:15; Ac 14:15; Rev 14:7 [h]Ps 117:2
6 the Maker of heaven[g] and earth,
the sea, and everything in them—
the LORD, who remains faithful[h] forever.
146:7 [i]Ps 103:6 [j]Ps 107:9 [k]Ps 68:6
7 He upholds the cause of the oppressed[i]
and gives food to the hungry.[j]
The LORD sets prisoners free,[k]
146:8 [l]Mt 9:30
8 the LORD gives sight to the blind,[l]
the LORD lifts up those who are bowed down,
the LORD loves the righteous.
146:9 [m]Ex 22:22; Dt 10:18; Ps 68:5
9 The LORD watches over the alien
and sustains the fatherless and the widow,[m]
but he frustrates the ways of the wicked.

146:10 [n]Ex 15:18; Ps 10:16
10 The LORD reigns[n] forever,
your God, O Zion, for all generations.

Praise the LORD.

PSALM 147

1 Praise the LORD.[b]

How good it is to sing praises to our God,
147:1 [o]Ps 135:3 [p]Ps 33:1
how pleasant[o] and fitting to praise him![p]

147:2 [q]Ps 102:16 [r]Dt 30:3
2 The LORD builds up Jerusalem;[q]
he gathers the exiles[r] of Israel.
3 He heals the brokenhearted
and binds up their wounds.
147:4 [s]Isa 40:26
4 He determines the number of the stars[s]
and calls them each by name.
147:5 [t]Ps 48:1 [u]Isa 40:28
5 Great is our Lord[t] and mighty in power;
his understanding has no limit.[u]
147:6 [v]Ps 146:8-9
6 The LORD sustains the humble[v]
but casts the wicked to the ground.

147:7 [w]Ps 33:3
7 Sing to the LORD[w] with thanksgiving;
make music to our God on the harp.
8 He covers the sky with clouds;
147:8 [x]Job 38:26
he supplies the earth with rain[x]

[a] 1 Hebrew *Hallelu Yah*; also in verse 10
[b] 1 Hebrew *Hallelu Yah*; also in verse 20

SPECIAL PRIVILEGES

Throughout Old Testament history God's people had enjoyed a position of privilege, because he had chosen them out of all the nations of the earth (Exodus 19:3–6; Deuteronomy 7:6; 14:1–2; Psalm 135:4). No matter how many times they had wandered away, God had always brought them back to himself. Psalm 147 celebrated one of those reunions. The Lord had rebuilt Jerusalem, gathered those who had been sent away and healed their wounds. We frequently visualize God as angry and judgmental, while in reality he is unbelievably patient, offering us more "fresh starts" than we can count (1 Timothy 2:4; 2 Peter 3:9). And he does that simply because he has also chosen us (1 Peter 2:9). The nation of Israel had been endowed with many advantages (Romans 3:1–2). God had trusted the Israelites with his words, laws, atonement stipulations and worship. Yet the apostle Paul came to the realization that "there is no difference [between Jews and Gentiles], for all have sinned and fall short of the glory of God" (Romans 3:22–23). We all need a Savior—no matter whether we have been born "with a silver spoon in [our] mouth" or in the dregs of poverty. Because of the work of the precious Son of God, all of humanity is offered the privilege of living in the company of God forever—we have only to place our trust in him and learn to walk in his ways (Romans 5:1–11).

147:8 [y]Ps 104:14

and makes grass grow[y] on the
hills.

147:9 [z]Ps 104:27-28; Mt 6:26 [a]Job 38:41

9 He provides food[z] for the cattle
and for the young ravens[a] when
they call.

147:10 [b]1Sa 16:7 [c]Ps 33:16-17

10 His pleasure is not in the strength[b]
of the horse,[c]
nor his delight in the legs of a
man;
11 the LORD delights in those who fear
him,
who put their hope in his
unfailing love.

12 Extol the LORD, O Jerusalem;
praise your God, O Zion,
13 for he strengthens the bars of your
gates
and blesses your people within
you.

147:14 [d]Isa 60:17-18 [e]Ps 132:15

14 He grants peace[d] to your borders
and satisfies you[e] with the finest
of wheat.

147:15 [f]Job 37:12

15 He sends his command[f] to the
earth;
his word runs swiftly.

147:16 [g]Job 37:6 [h]Job 38:29

16 He spreads the snow[g] like wool
and scatters the frost[h] like ashes.
17 He hurls down his hail like pebbles.
Who can withstand his icy blast?

147:18 [i]Ps 33:9

18 He sends his word[i] and melts them;
he stirs up his breezes, and the
waters flow.

147:19 [j]Dt 33:4; Mal 4:4

19 He has revealed his word to Jacob,
his laws and decrees[j] to Israel.

147:20 [k]Dt 4:7-8,32-34

20 He has done this for no other
nation;[k]
they do not know his laws.

Praise the LORD.

PSALM 148

1 Praise the LORD.[a]

Praise the LORD from the heavens,
praise him in the heights above.

148:2 [l]Ps 103:20

2 Praise him, all his angels,[l]
praise him, all his heavenly
hosts.
3 Praise him, sun and moon,
praise him, all you shining stars.

148:4 [m]Ge 1:7; 1Ki 8:27

4 Praise him, you highest heavens
and you waters above the skies.[m]
5 Let them praise the name of the
LORD,
for he commanded[n] and they
were created.

148:5 [n]Ge 1:1,6; Ps 33:6,9

6 He set them in place for ever and
ever;
he gave a decree[o] that will never
pass away.

148:6 [o]Job 38:33; Ps 89:37; Jer 33:25

7 Praise the LORD from the earth,
you great sea creatures[p] and all
ocean depths,

148:7 [p]Ps 74:13-14

8 lightning and hail, snow and clouds,
stormy winds that do his
bidding,[q]

148:8 [q]Ps 147:15-18

9 you mountains and all hills,[r]
fruit trees and all cedars,

148:9 [r]Isa 44:23; 49:13; 55:12

10 wild animals and all cattle,
small creatures and flying birds,
11 kings of the earth and all nations,
you princes and all rulers on
earth,
12 young men and maidens,
old men and children.

13 Let them praise the name of the
LORD,[s]
for his name alone is exalted;
his splendor is above the earth
and the heavens.[t]

148:13 [s]Isa 12:4 [t]Ps 8:1; 113:4

14 He has raised up for his people a
horn,[b][u]
the praise of all his saints,
of Israel, the people close to his
heart.

148:14 [u]Ps 75:10

Praise the LORD.

PSALM 149

1 Praise the LORD.[c][v]

149:1 [v]Ps 33:2 [w]Ps 35:18

Sing to the LORD a new song,
his praise in the assembly[w] of
the saints.

2 Let Israel rejoice in their Maker;[x]
let the people of Zion be glad in
their King.[y]

149:2 [x]Ps 95:6 [y]Ps 47:6; Zec 9:9

3 Let them praise his name with
dancing
and make music to him with
tambourine and harp.[z]

149:3 [z]Ps 81:2; 150:4

4 For the LORD takes delight[a] in his
people;
he crowns the humble with
salvation.[b]

149:4 [a]Ps 35:27 [b]Ps 132:16

[a] *1* Hebrew *Hallelu Yah*; also in verse 14
[b] *14* *Horn* here symbolizes strong one, that is, king.
[c] *1* Hebrew *Hallelu Yah*; also in verse 9

Our Finest Praise

Dancing has an unfavorable reputation in some Christian circles. And because dancing implies using one's body as a means for expressing and evoking emotion, the potential is there for this activity to deteriorate into an expression that is sensuous and displeasing to God. But dancing also affords a medium by which God's people may celebrate the God who created the marvel of the human body. The word for dancing used in the Bible refers to an activity involving jumping, turning and twisting.

There are valid reasons to praise God with our entire bodies rather than simply with our voices. God fashioned our bodies; he gifted us with flexibility, coordination, strength, rhythm, spatial orientation, poise and grace of movement, as well as with the desire to express our emotions both through motion and music. He is our King and so he is worthy of a holistic expression of thanks, one involving all of our abilities and aptitudes (Psalm 149:2). He deserves our finest expressions of praise because he has rescued us, and he defeats anyone or anything that comes against us (verse 6–9). But what may be most important of all is the simple truth that God finds delight in our adoration (verse 4). When we try to envision just how great our God really is, we might just get so excited that we can't sit still anymore! Our intense emotion will engage all of our senses, and we will rise to our feet in awe.

In chapter 6 of his Gospel, Luke included an abbreviated version of the Beatitudes (see also Matthew 5:3–12). In verse 22 Luke quoted Jesus' statement that his followers are blessed when they are hated, excluded, insulted or rejected because of their faith in the Son of Man. In light of the rather gloomy tone of this verse, verse 23 comes as a surprise: "Rejoice in that day and leap for joy, because great is your reward in heaven. For that is how their fathers treated the prophets." Jesus was telling the gathered crowd to look beyond the fleeting trials of the present day to the glory that is to come (see also 1 Peter 1:6–9; 5:10).

While we certainly enjoy many of the rich rewards of following Christ Jesus in the here and now, much of the glory we will one day enjoy will be experienced only after Jesus' second coming. But we can be joy-filled Christians despite our outward circumstances, because we possess the hope of glory which comes to its ultimate expression in Jesus (Colossians 1:27).

Paul spoke of deferred hope in Romans 5: "We rejoice in the hope of the glory of God. Not only so, but we also rejoice in our sufferings, because we know that suffering produces perseverance; perseverance, character; and character hope. And hope does not disappoint us, because God has poured out his love into our hearts by the Holy Spirit, whom he has given us" (Romans 5:2–5). We who enjoy the blessings of fellowship with Jesus Christ should of all people have reason to sing a new song and rejoice with dancing (Psalm 149:1,3).

Self-Discovery: *What expressions of love and praise come most naturally and feel most comfortable to you? Think of the wide variety of worship styles in our churches today. What kinds of feelings do your reflections on these various styles arouse in you? Are you tolerant of worship styles that are markedly different from your own?*

GO TO DISCOVERY 158 ON PAGE 813

JESUS WAS NO IVORY-TOWER THEOLOGIAN EXPOUNDING ABSTRACT AND ABSTRUSE THEORIES; HE WAS . . . ABLE TO TALK TO ORDINARY PEOPLE IN ORDINARY TERMS.

David Wenham, *Theologian, Oxford University*

149:5 [c]Ps 132:16 [d]Job 35:10
149:6 [e]Ps 66:17 [f]Heb 4:12; Rev 1:16
149:9 [g]Dt 7:1; Eze 28:26 [h]Ps 148:14

5 Let the saints rejoice[c] in this honor
and sing for joy on their beds.[d]
6 May the praise of God be in their mouths[e]
and a double-edged[f] sword in their hands,
7 to inflict vengeance on the nations
and punishment on the peoples,
8 to bind their kings with fetters,
their nobles with shackles of iron,
9 to carry out the sentence written against them.[g]
This is the glory of all his saints.[h]

Praise the LORD.

PSALM 150

1 Praise the LORD.[a]

Praise God in his sanctuary;[i]
praise him in his mighty heavens.[j]
2 Praise him for his acts of power;[k]
praise him for his surpassing greatness.[l]
3 Praise him with the sounding of the trumpet,
praise him with the harp and lyre,[m]
4 praise him with tambourine and dancing,[n]
praise him with the strings[o] and flute,
5 praise him with the clash of cymbals,[p]
praise him with resounding cymbals.

6 Let everything[q] that has breath praise the LORD.

Praise the LORD.

[a] 1 Hebrew *Hallelu Yah*; also in verse 6

150:1 [i]Ps 102:19 [j]Ps 19:1
150:2 [k]Dt 3:24 [l]Ps 145:5-6
150:3 [m]Ps 149:3
150:4 [n]Ex 15:20 [o]Isa 38:20
150:5 [p]1Ch 13:8; 15:16
150:6 [q]Ps 145:21

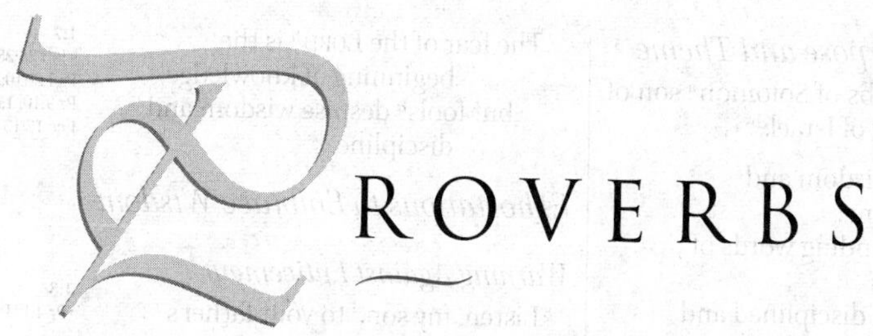

PROVERBS

Jesus in Proverbs There is a vast difference between knowing an intellectual concept and knowing a close personal friend. God has always desired that his people become acquainted with him, not in the sense of learning about him but of getting to know him as a confidant and then learning to walk step-by-step and hand in hand with him as they put that intimate knowledge into practice. That is what the Bible means when it talks about "wisdom"—God's wisdom "takes on a body" (*our* body), so to speak, as we live life the way he wants us to. The book of Proverbs begins by describing wisdom as a person with whom we can have a close personal relationship. In the Old Testament God gave his people the law to enable them to know wisdom in *principle.* In the New Testament, however, the eternal Son of God was born as the embodiment of God's wisdom, and now we know wisdom in a *person.* "It is because of [God] that you are in Christ Jesus, who has become for us wisdom from God" (1 Corinthians 1:30).

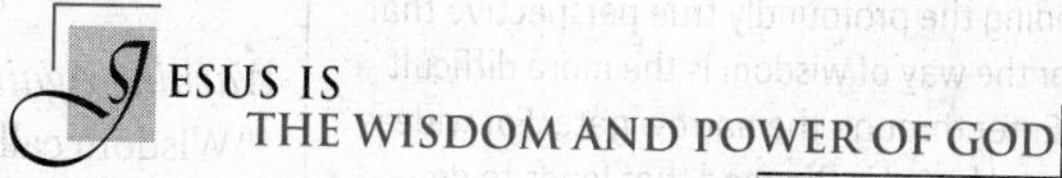

JESUS IS
THE WISDOM AND POWER OF GOD

What explanation may be offered when God-fearing people are poor or unhealthy? (Proverbs 22:4)

♦*Like other proverbs, this one makes a general observation about life—one which is usually true. Occasionally, though, as expressed by Jesus in John 9:1–3, God allows God-fearing people to suffer so that he might display his mighty work in them.*

When are rest and sleep okay? (Proverbs 24:30–34)

♦*Either laziness or workaholism can distort the concept of labor out of all proportion. Yet rest has been part of God's design from the beginning. Jesus, who had a great sense of urgency for ministry, took time off (Mark 6:30–32). In fact, busyness can distract us from cultivating an intimate relationship with Jesus (see Luke 10:38–42).*

What is the New Testament significance of the series of questions posed in Proverbs 30:4?

♦*While talking to Nicodemus, a leading Bible scholar of the day, Jesus applied this description to himself—an astounding claim of his deity (see John 3:13).*

Prologue: Purpose and Theme

1:1 [a] 1Ki 4:29-34 [b] Pr 10:1; 25:1; Ecc 1:1

1 The proverbs of Solomon[a] son of David, king of Israel:[b]

[2] for attaining wisdom and discipline;
for understanding words of insight;
[3] for acquiring a disciplined and prudent life,
doing what is right and just and fair;

1:4 [c] Pr 8:5 [d] Pr 2:10-11; 8:12

[4] for giving prudence to the simple,[c]
knowledge and discretion[d] to the young—

1:5 [e] Pr 9:9

[5] let the wise listen and add to their learning,[e]
and let the discerning get guidance—

1:6 [f] Ps 49:4; 78:2 [g] Nu 12:8

[6] for understanding proverbs and parables,[f]
the sayings and riddles[g] of the wise.

TWO CHOICES

The *proverbs* were collected and written down to help us make one of the most vital and basic choices in life—the choice between wisdom and folly, walking with God or walking on our own. In the book of Proverbs both wisdom and folly are described as people who walk through the streets of the city and call out to us, hawking their wares and beckoning us to taste a sample (Proverbs 1). Each offers specific choices, but these very different options ultimately result in the adoption of opposite lifestyles. The proverbs remind us that the direction and quality of our lives are frequently the direct result of the choices we have made along the way. Jesus said essentially the same thing, adding the profoundly true perspective that opting for the way of wisdom is the more difficult choice: "Enter through the narrow gate. For wide is the gate and broad is the road that leads to destruction, and many enter through it. But small is the gate and narrow the road that leads to life, and only a few find it" (Matthew 7:13–14). Walking with God may be demanding, and it certainly will be costly (Mark 8:34–38; Luke 9:57–62; 14:25–35), but it is the only choice that leads to freedom and joy—and in the final analysis to life itself, lived in fellowship with Jesus, who enables us to have life to the full (John 10:10).

1:7 [h] Job 28:28; Ps 111:10; Pr 9:10; 15:33; Ecc 12:13

[7] The fear of the LORD[h] is the beginning of knowledge,
but fools[a] despise wisdom and discipline.

Exhortations to Embrace Wisdom

Warning Against Enticement

1:8 [i] Pr 4:1 [j] Pr 6:20

[8] Listen, my son,[i] to your father's instruction
and do not forsake your mother's teaching.[j]

1:9 [k] Pr 4:1-9

[9] They will be a garland to grace your head
and a chain to adorn your neck.[k]

1:10 [l] Ge 39:7 [m] Dt 13:8 [n] Pr 16:29; Eph 5:11

[10] My son, if sinners entice[l] you,
do not give in[m] to them.[n]

1:11 [o] Ps 10:8

[11] If they say, "Come along with us;
let's lie in wait[o] for someone's blood,
let's waylay some harmless soul;

1:12 [p] Ps 28:1

[12] let's swallow them alive, like the grave,[b]
and whole, like those who go down to the pit;[p]
[13] we will get all sorts of valuable things
and fill our houses with plunder;
[14] throw in your lot with us,
and we will share a common purse"—

1:15 [q] Ps 119:101 [r] Ps 1:1; Pr 4:14

[15] my son, do not go along with them,
do not set foot[q] on their paths;[r]

1:16 [s] Pr 6:18; Isa 59:7

[16] for their feet rush into sin,
they are swift to shed blood.[s]
[17] How useless to spread a net
in full view of all the birds!
[18] These men lie in wait for their own blood;
they waylay only themselves!

1:19 [t] Pr 15:27

[19] Such is the end of all who go after ill-gotten gain;
it takes away the lives of those who get it.[t]

Warning Against Rejecting Wisdom

1:20 [u] Pr 8:1; 9:1-3, 13-15

[20] Wisdom calls aloud[u] in the street,
she raises her voice in the public squares;
[21] at the head of the noisy streets[c] she cries out,
in the gateways of the city she makes her speech:

[a] 7 The Hebrew words rendered *fool* in Proverbs, and often elsewhere in the Old Testament, denote one who is morally deficient. [b] 12 Hebrew *Sheol* [c] 21 Hebrew; Septuagint / *on the tops of the walls*

DISCOVERY 158

JESUS: WISDOM FROM GOD

What attitudes and actions does God look for in our lives? The practical book of Proverbs opens by listing several qualities that help to define the lifestyle God wants from his children. He desires that we live wisely and attentively, exercise self-control, develop insight and awareness based on the experiences of ourselves and others, exhibit and pass along common sense, and learn to know God intimately, recognizing his voice and understanding who he is and what he expects of us (Proverbs 1:2–4).

The entire book of Proverbs focuses on wisdom—on distinguishing between those patterns that will help us to live rightly and those that will lead to ruin. But the word *wisdom* doesn't refer to storing up in our minds an impressive amount of factual data; the person who knows a lot isn't necessarily the wise individual. Wisdom is all about putting what we do know about God and about life into practice. It has little to do with our intelligence quotient and everything to do with the quality of our relationship with God and our ability to get along well with other people. Wisdom involves active outpouring rather than passive assimilation.

Wisdom is so active, in fact, that the writer of Proverbs describes it in terms of a person rather than an idea. This "person" called Wisdom, referred to so frequently in Proverbs, is all around us, calling to us to follow her. Jesus is God's ultimate expression of his wisdom. When critics challenged his actions, Jesus responded, "Wisdom is proved right by her actions" (Matthew 11:19). We can look wise, sound wise, even possess the degrees to indicate wisdom, but ultimately the results of our actions prove whether or not we are truly wise.

From his youth people knew that Jesus' wisdom was remarkable (Luke 2:52). In him "are hidden all the treasures of wisdom and knowledge" (Colossians 2:3). When we are unsure or feeling foolish, he invites us to come to him for wisdom: "If any of you lacks wisdom, he should ask God, who gives generously to all without finding fault, and it will be given to him" (James 1:5). Jesus Christ "has become for us wisdom from God," showing us what it means to be in a right relationship with God, modeling holiness and offering us redemption (1 Corinthians 1:30).

Paul was contrasting the "wisdom" of our world with the wisdom that comes from God. The two ways of approaching life and thought are diametrically opposed to one another, and people who have never entered into a relationship with God can make no sense of his truth or his ways (Romans 8:6–7; 1 Corinthians 2:6–16; James 3:13–18). But one thing is certain: Living life according to what God deems to be wise means that we can't pride ourselves on our own insight. Our only valid reason for boasting is the fact that God's Holy Spirit is at work within us to change our hearts. Paul even referred to his own efforts to make sense of life as "rubbish." The single most important manifestation of wisdom is a relationship with Jesus Christ (Philippians 3:8–9), "in whom are hidden all the treasures of wisdom and knowledge" (Colossians 2:3).

***Self-Discovery:** How would you assess your "wisdom quotient"? Unlike your IQ, has it changed over the past several years?*

GO TO DISCOVERY 159 ON PAGE 816

1:22 [v] Pr 8:5; 9:4,16
[22] "How long will you simple ones[a][v]
love your simple ways?
How long will mockers delight
in mockery
and fools hate knowledge?
[23] If you had responded to my rebuke,
I would have poured out my
heart to you
and made my thoughts known
to you.
1:24 [w] Isa 65:12; 66:4; Jer 7:13; Zec 7:11
[24] But since you rejected me when I
called[w]
and no one gave heed when I
stretched out my hand,
[25] since you ignored all my advice
1:26 [x] Ps 2:4 [y] Pr 6:15; 10:24
and would not accept my rebuke,
[26] I in turn will laugh[x] at your disaster;
I will mock when calamity
overtakes you[y]—
[27] when calamity overtakes you like a
storm,
when disaster sweeps over you
like a whirlwind,
when distress and trouble
1:28 [z] 1Sa 8:18; Isa 1:15; Jer 11:11; Mic 3:4
overwhelm you.
[28] "Then they will call to me but I will
not answer;[z]

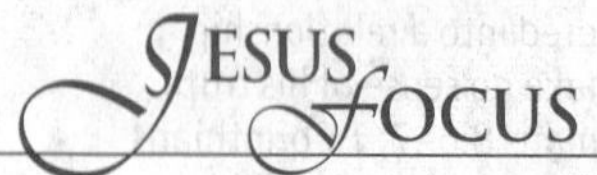

ONE YOUNG FOOL

The "fool" in Proverbs represents the individual who chooses not to walk with God and rejects the voice of his wisdom (Proverbs 1—2). Other names used in Proverbs to describe fools are "simple ones" and "mockers." While "simple ones" may not have enough sense to make an informed choice, those who mock make a conscious decision to adopt the lifestyle of folly. The tragedy is that those who reject God will eventually be rejected by him. In the New Testament Jesus frequently used examples that remind us of the pithy statements in Proverbs. Our Lord once told a parable about a rich man who built more and more barns to store his goods, planning to take life easy. In the end, however, he died in his sleep, unable to take any of his riches with him. Jesus referred to this man as a fool (Luke 12:20–21). Relinquishing control of our life to Jesus is the only response that truly makes sense in the end. For when it comes right down to it, "What good will it be for a man if he gains the whole world, yet forfeits his soul? Or what can a man give in exchange for his soul?" (Matthew 16:26).

they will look for me but will not 1:28 [a] Job 27:9; Pr 8:17; Eze 8:18; Zec 7:13
find me.[a]
[29] Since they hated knowledge
and did not choose to fear the
LORD,[b] 1:29 [b] Job 21:14
[30] since they would not accept my
advice
and spurned my rebuke,[c] 1:30 [c] ver 25; Ps 81:11
[31] they will eat the fruit of their ways
and be filled with the fruit of 1:31 [d] Job 4:8; Pr 14:14; Isa 3:11; Jer 6:19
their schemes.[d]
[32] For the waywardness of the simple
will kill them,
and the complacency of fools 1:32 [e] Jer 2:19
will destroy them;[e]
[33] but whoever listens to me will live
in safety[f] 1:33 [f] Ps 25:12; Pr 3:23 [g] Ps 112:8
and be at ease, without fear of
harm."[g]

Moral Benefits of Wisdom

2 My son, if you accept my words
and store up my commands
within you,
[2] turning your ear to wisdom
and applying your heart to 2:2 [h] Pr 22:17
understanding,[h]
[3] and if you call out for insight
and cry aloud for understanding,
[4] and if you look for it as for silver
and search for it as for hidden 2:4 [i] Job 3:21; Pr 3:14; Mt 13:44
treasure,[i]
[5] then you will understand the fear
of the LORD
and find the knowledge of God.[j] 2:5 [j] Pr 1:7
[6] For the LORD gives wisdom,[k]
and from his mouth come 2:6 [k] 1Ki 3:9,12; Jas 1:5
knowledge and
understanding.
[7] He holds victory in store for the
upright,
he is a shield[l] to those whose 2:7 [l] Pr 30:5-6 [m] Ps 84:11
walk is blameless,[m]
[8] for he guards the course of the just
and protects the way of his 2:8 [n] 1Sa 2:9; Ps 66:9
faithful ones.[n]
[9] Then you will understand what is
right and just
and fair—every good path.
[10] For wisdom will enter your heart,[o] 2:10 [o] Pr 14:33
and knowledge will be pleasant
to your soul.
[11] Discretion will protect you,

[a] *22* The Hebrew word rendered *simple* in Proverbs generally denotes one without moral direction and inclined to evil.

2:11 and understanding will guard
[p] Pr 4:6; 6:22 you.[p]

12 Wisdom will save you from the
ways of wicked men,
from men whose words are
perverse,
2:13 13 who leave the straight paths
[q] Pr 4:19; Jn 3:19 to walk in dark ways,[q]
14 who delight in doing wrong
2:14 and rejoice in the perverseness
[r] Pr 10:23; Jer 11:15 of evil,[r]
15 whose paths are crooked[s]
2:15 [s] Ps 125:5 and who are devious in their
[t] Pr 21:8 ways.[t]
2:16 [u] Pr 5:1-6; 6:20-29; 7:5-27 16 It will save you also from the
adulteress,[u]
from the wayward wife with her
seductive words,
17 who has left the partner of her
youth
and ignored the covenant she
2:17 [v] Mal 2:14 made before God.[a][v]
18 For her house leads down to death
2:18 and her paths to the spirits of
[w] Pr 7:27 the dead.[w]
2:19 19 None who go to her return
[x] Ecc 7:26 or attain the paths of life.[x]

20 Thus you will walk in the ways of
good men
and keep to the paths of the
righteous.
2:21 21 For the upright will live in the land,[y]
[y] Ps 37:29 and the blameless will remain in
it;
22 but the wicked will be cut off from
2:22 [z] Job 18:17; Ps 37:38 the land,[z]
[a] Dt 28:63; Pr 10:30 and the unfaithful will be torn
from it.[a]

Further Benefits of Wisdom

3:1 **3** My son, do not forget my
[b] Pr 4:5 teaching,[b]
but keep my commands in your
heart,
2 for they will prolong your life many
3:2 years[c]
[c] Pr 4:10 and bring you prosperity.

3 Let love and faithfulness never
leave you;
bind them around your neck,
3:3 [d] Ex 13:9; Pr 6:21; 7:3; 2Co 3:3 write them on the tablet of your
heart.[d]
3:4 4 Then you will win favor and a good
name
[e] 1Sa 2:26; Lk 2:52 in the sight of God and man.[e]

5 Trust in the LORD[f] with all your 3:5 [f] Ps 37:3,5
heart
and lean not on your own
understanding;
6 in all your ways acknowledge him, 3:6 [g] 1Ch 28:9
and he will make your paths[g] [h] Pr 16:3; Isa 45:13
straight.[b][h]

7 Do not be wise in your own eyes;[i] 3:7 [i] Ro 12:16
fear the LORD and shun evil.[j] [j] Job 1:1; Pr 16:6
8 This will bring health to your
body[k] 3:8 [k] Pr 4:22
and nourishment to your bones.[l] [l] Job 21:24

9 Honor the LORD with your wealth,
with the firstfruits[m] of all your 3:9 [m] Ex 22:29; 23:19; Dt 26:1-15
crops;
10 then your barns will be filled[n] to
overflowing, 3:10 [n] Dt 28:8
and your vats will brim over with [o] Joel 2:24
new wine.[o]

11 My son, do not despise the LORD's 3:11
discipline[p] [p] Job 5:17
and do not resent his rebuke,
12 because the LORD disciplines those 3:12 [q] Pr 13:24;
he loves,[q] Rev 3:19
as a father[c] the son he delights [r] Dt 8:5; Heb 12:5-6*
in.[r]

[a] 17 Or *covenant of her God* [b] 6 Or *will direct your paths* [c] 12 Hebrew; Septuagint */ and he punishes*

WALKING WITH HIM

It can be relatively easy to say the "right" things, but it requires authentic commitment and devotion to God to truly walk with him. Proverbs 3 urges us to know God "in all [our] ways" (verse 6). In the New Testament God refers to a person who displays this attitude and exhibits this lifestyle as his *disciple.* It is never enough to nod approval in God's direction or agree in principle with what he says while going about living our lives exactly as we please. Every aspect of our lives must be devoted to our Lord. To walk with God on the path of his choosing, as opposed to wandering or drifting along, implies selecting a destination, setting a course and staying on the path. That path is our precious Savior and Lord Jesus, who proclaimed, "I am the way and the truth and the life" (John 14:6). Jesus is the way to the Father, for he is not only the One who *shows* us the true and life-enhancing way to live, but he is himself the truth and life (John 1:1–14; 11:25).

The Essence of Trust

Proverbs 3:5–6 is a passage that is frequently committed to memory and that has afforded comfort to many believers. We sometimes use the word *trust* rather glibly, and everyone seems to have a different notion of what it means. A woman trusts her banker when she deposits her money. A man trusts his mechanic to repair his transmission. A parent trusts the doctor to correctly diagnose and treat a childhood illness. These examples have one thing in common: the giving over of responsibility for someone or something to another's care. And when the Bible encourages us to trust God, it is inviting us to relinquish all the issues of our life—finances, disappointments, relationships, recreation, career decisions, medical conditions—into God's care.

Jesus, God's Son, modeled trust for us by placing literally everything in the hands of God the Father. Time and again Jesus reminded people that the Father was in charge of his life (see John 4:34; 5:19; 6:38). The will of God the Father dominated Jesus' thinking even to the very end. In his agonizing prayer in the garden of Gethsemane shortly before his arrest, Jesus poured out his soul to the Father, including these heartrending words: "Father, if you are willing, take this cup from me; yet not my will, but yours be done" (Luke 22:42).

We are told in the next verses that "an angel from heaven appeared to [Jesus] and strengthened him. And being in anguish, he prayed more earnestly, and his sweat was like drops of blood falling to the ground" (Luke 22:43–44). God was the inspiration for everything Jesus taught and every miracle he performed; Jesus' relationship with God was the focal point of his life and the determining factor in all of his actions.

Even at the very end of his earthly life, when he hung dying on the cross, Jesus gasped, "Father, into your hands I commit my spirit" (Luke 23:46). He trusted his Father with his death and with the events that would transpire afterward. He knew and accepted that his Father's plan from all eternity had been for him to die for our sins (Galatians 4:4–5; Philippians 2:8).

Trusting God has been described as a sort of spiritual super glue: It doesn't take very much of it to make a big difference. Either you are glued to God or you aren't. Our tendency, since the Garden of Eden, has been to rely solely on our own understanding, to try to stay in control, to do things our own way. But our way will only get us into trouble. Instead, we need to get to know God in order to learn what he wants—that is what trusting God is all about.

Trust for the believer is more than an action verb; it is a noun that represents the Christian's total mind-set and lifestyle. As Paul wrote in Romans: "In the gospel a righteousness from God is revealed, a righteousness that is by faith from first to last, just as it is written: 'the righteous will live by faith' " (Romans 1:17).

***Self-Discovery:** Based on the example of spiritual super glue, above, in what ways would you say that you are you glued to God? Do you know him well enough to gain a sense of his desire for your life? How does he convey this to you? Do you trust him in any and all circumstances to do what is best for you?*

GO TO DISCOVERY 160 ON PAGE 818

13 Blessed is the man who finds
wisdom,
the man who gains
understanding,
14 for she is more profitable than silver

3:14 [s]Job 28:15; Pr 8:19; 16:16

and yields better returns than
gold.[s]
15 She is more precious than rubies;[t]

3:15 [t]Job 28:18 [u]Pr 8:11

nothing you desire can compare
with her.[u]
16 Long life is in her right hand;

3:16 [v]Pr 8:18

in her left hand are riches and
honor.[v]
17 Her ways are pleasant ways,

3:17 [w]Pr 16:7; Mt 11:28-30

and all her paths are peace.[w]
18 She is a tree of life[x] to those who

3:18 [x]Ge 2:9; Pr 11:30; Rev 2:7

embrace her;
those who lay hold of her will be
blessed.

3:19 [y]Ps 104:24 [z]Pr 8:27-29

19 By wisdom the LORD laid the earth's
foundations,[y]
by understanding he set the
heavens[z] in place;
20 by his knowledge the deeps were
divided,
and the clouds let drop the dew.

21 My son, preserve sound judgment
and discernment,

3:21 [a]Pr 4:20-22

do not let them out of your
sight;[a]

3:22 [b]Pr 1:8-9

22 they will be life for you,
an ornament to grace your neck.[b]
23 Then you will go on your way in
safety,

3:23 [c]Ps 37:24; Pr 4:12

and your foot will not stumble;[c]
24 when you lie down,[d] you will not

3:24 [d]Lev 26:6; Ps 3:5 [e]Job 11:18

be afraid;
when you lie down, your sleep[e]
will be sweet.
25 Have no fear of sudden disaster
or of the ruin that overtakes the
wicked,

3:26 [f]1Sa 2:9

26 for the LORD will be your confidence
and will keep your foot[f] from
being snared.

27 Do not withhold good from those
who deserve it,
when it is in your power to act.
28 Do not say to your neighbor,
"Come back later; I'll give it
tomorrow"—

3:28 [g]Lev 19:13; Dt 24:15

when you now have it with you.[g]
29 Do not plot harm against your
neighbor,
who lives trustfully near you.

30 Do not accuse a man for no
reason—
when he has done you no harm.

3:31 [h]Ps 37:1; Pr 24:1-2

31 Do not envy[h] a violent man
or choose any of his ways,
32 for the LORD detests a perverse

3:32 [i]Pr 11:20 [j]Job 29:4; Ps 25:14

man[i]
but takes the upright into his
confidence.[j]

3:33 [k]Dt 11:28; Mal 2:2 [l]Zec 5:4 [m]Ps 1:3

33 The LORD's curse[k] is on the house
of the wicked,[l]
but he blesses the home of the
righteous.[m]
34 He mocks proud mockers

3:34 [n]Jas 4:6*; 1Pe 5:5*

but gives grace to the humble.[n]
35 The wise inherit honor,
but fools he holds up to shame.

THE MAN OR WOMAN WHO IS COMPELLED BY JESUS' LOVE AND EMPOWERED BY HIS SPIRIT DOES THE WILL OF GOD FROM THE HEART.

F. F. Bruce, *British Scholar*

Wisdom Is Supreme

4:1 [o]Pr 1:8

4 Listen, my sons,[o] to a father's
instruction;
pay attention and gain
understanding.
2 I give you sound learning,
so do not forsake my teaching.
3 When I was a boy in my father's
house,
still tender, and an only child of
my mother,
4 he taught me and said,
"Lay hold of my words with all
your heart;

4:4 [p]Pr 7:2

keep my commands and you will
live.[p]

4:5 [q]Pr 16:16

5 Get wisdom,[q] get understanding;
do not forget my words or
swerve from them.
6 Do not forsake wisdom, and she

4:6 [r]2Th 2:10

will protect you;[r]
love her, and she will watch over
you.
7 Wisdom is supreme; therefore get
wisdom.

4:7 [s]Mt 13:44-46 [t]Pr 23:23

Though it cost all[s] you have,[a] get
understanding.[t]

[a] 7 Or *Whatever else you get*

DISCOVERY 160

THE HEART OF THE MATTER

When someone uses the phrase "above all else" (Proverbs 4:23) we are alerted to his or her top priority, the foundational principle on which this person's life philosophy is based. Proverbs 4 contains a great deal of advice and instruction that is based on action verbs, counseling us to pay attention, hold on, remember, guard, walk and even run toward a more intimate relationship with God (verses 1–2, 4–6,8,10,12–13,20–21). All of these actions are based on our response to externals; they deal with how we interact with the world around us and with our God. But the main thrust of the entire book of Proverbs has to do with our character. Our most important task is to take care of what's on the *inside*: We are to guard our hearts, because our behavior has its root in the kind of people we are.

What does the Bible mean by the "heart" of a person? God directs us to apply our hearts to understanding, to keep his commandments in our hearts, to trust him with all our hearts. Simply put, a person's heart reflects the kind of individual he or she is on the inside; it reveals to other people our true attitudes and priorities. When a person is experiencing inner peace, he enjoys a full life (Proverbs 14:30). When someone is happy, it shows on her face (Proverbs 15:13). What is inside of us inevitably finds its way out in one way or another, because it is the driving force behind our thoughts, decisions, conversations, aspirations and emotions.

It is tempting to think that we can *act* the part of a Christian by sheer force of will, never divulging to those around us the real thoughts and aspirations we harbor in our hearts. But Jesus specified that it is impossible for us to camouflage our true identities. In Matthew 6:21 our Lord reminded us that our heart will be wherever our real treasure is. If the guiding principle of our lives is service to God, our actions will reflect the heart of a servant, and others will see Jesus in us. If, on the other hand, the deepest desire of our heart is for more and more material possessions, no amount of religious activity will mask our real passion.

And the same is true of our speech. "Out of the overflow of the heart the mouth speaks," Jesus declared in Matthew 12:34. Listen to someone for a little while, and you will readily observe the truth of this statement. If a person's heart is attuned to God's Word and Spirit, her conversations will be "always full of grace, seasoned with salt" (Colossians 4:10). By contrast, if an individual's driving ambition centers around self-fulfillment in one area or another, he will continually direct every conversation toward his "pet" area of interest.

The core advice from the philosopher in Proverbs is this: "Above all else, guard your heart, for it is the wellspring of life" (Proverbs 4:23). One of the ways we can guard our heart is by memorization of Scripture. The more we take God's Word to heart, the more we internalize his truth so that it becomes a part of us, the more our hearts will be guarded by that truth.

Self-Discovery: *Finish the following sentence as honestly as you can: "I desire above all else________________."*

GO TO DISCOVERY 161 ON PAGE 824

8 Esteem her, and she will exalt you;
embrace her, and she will honor
you.[u]
9 She will set a garland of grace on
your head
and present you with a crown of
splendor.[v]"

10 Listen, my son, accept what I say,
and the years of your life will be
many.[w]
11 I guide[x] you in the way of wisdom
and lead you along straight paths.
12 When you walk, your steps will not
be hampered;
when you run, you will not
stumble.[y]
13 Hold on to instruction, do not let it
go;
guard it well, for it is your life.[z]
14 Do not set foot on the path of the
wicked
or walk in the way of evil men.[a]
15 Avoid it, do not travel on it;
turn from it and go on your way.
16 For they cannot sleep till they do
evil;[b]
they are robbed of slumber till
they make someone fall.
17 They eat the bread of wickedness
and drink the wine of violence.

18 The path of the righteous[c] is like
the first gleam of dawn,
shining ever brighter till the full
light of day.[d]
19 But the way of the wicked is like
deep darkness;[e]
they do not know what makes
them stumble.

20 My son, pay attention to what I say;
listen closely to my words.[f]
21 Do not let them out of your sight,[g]
keep them within your heart;
22 for they are life to those who find
them
and health to a man's whole
body.[h]
23 Above all else, guard your heart,
for it is the wellspring of life.[i]
24 Put away perversity from your
mouth;
keep corrupt talk far from your
lips.
25 Let your eyes look straight ahead,
fix your gaze directly before you.
26 Make level[a] paths for your feet[j]
and take only ways that are firm.

4:8 [u] 1Sa 2:30; Pr 3:18
4:9 [v] Pr 1:8-9
4:10 [w] Pr 3:2
4:11 [x] 1Sa 12:23
4:12 [y] Job 18:7; Pr 3:23
4:13 [z] Pr 3:22
4:14 [a] Ps 1:1; Pr 1:15
4:16 [b] Ps 36:4; Mic 2:1
4:18 [c] Isa 26:7 [d] 2Sa 23:4; Da 12:3; Mt 5:14; Php 2:15
4:19 [e] Job 18:5; Pr 2:13; Isa 59:9-10; Jn 12:35
4:20 [f] Pr 5:1
4:21 [g] Pr 3:21; 7:1-2
4:22 [h] Pr 3:8; 12:18
4:23 [i] Mt 12:34; Lk 6:45
4:26 [j] Heb 12:13*

27 Do not swerve to the right or the
left;[k]
keep your foot from evil.

Warning Against Adultery

5 My son, pay attention to my
wisdom,
listen well to my words[l] of
insight,
2 that you may maintain discretion
and your lips may preserve
knowledge.
3 For the lips of an adulteress drip
honey,
and her speech is smoother than
oil;[m]
4 but in the end she is bitter as gall,[n]
sharp as a double-edged sword.
5 Her feet go down to death;
her steps lead straight to the
grave.[b][o]
6 She gives no thought to the way of
life;
her paths are crooked, but she
knows it not.[p]

7 Now then, my sons, listen[q] to me;
do not turn aside from what I say.
8 Keep to a path far from her,[r]
do not go near the door of her
house,
9 lest you give your best strength to
others
and your years to one who is
cruel,
10 lest strangers feast on your wealth
and your toil enrich another
man's house.
11 At the end of your life you will
groan,
when your flesh and body are
spent.
12 You will say, "How I hated discipline!
How my heart spurned
correction![s]
13 I would not obey my teachers
or listen to my instructors.
14 I have come to the brink of utter
ruin
in the midst of the whole
assembly."

15 Drink water from your own cistern,
running water from your own
well.
16 Should your springs overflow in
the streets,

4:27 [k] Dt 5:32; 28:14
5:1 [l] Pr 4:20; 22:17
5:3 [m] Ps 55:21; Pr 2:16; 7:5
5:4 [n] Ecc 7:26
5:5 [o] Pr 7:26-27
5:6 [p] Pr 30:20
5:7 [q] Pr 7:24
5:8 [r] Pr 7:1-27
5:12 [s] Pr 1:29; 12:1

[a] 26 Or *Consider the* [b] 5 Hebrew *Sheol*

your streams of water in the
public squares?
17 Let them be yours alone,
never to be shared with strangers.

5:18 [t]SS 4:12-15 [u]Ecc 9:9; Mal 2:14

18 May your fountain[t] be blessed,
and may you rejoice in the wife
of your youth.[u]

5:19 [v]SS 2:9; 4:5

19 A loving doe, a graceful deer[v]—
may her breasts satisfy you
always,
may you ever be captivated by
her love.
20 Why be captivated, my son, by an
adulteress?
Why embrace the bosom of
another man's wife?

5:21 [w]Ps 119:168; Hos 7:2 [x]Job 14:16; Job 31:4; 34:21; Pr 15:3; Jer 16:17; 32:19; Heb 4:13

21 For a man's ways are in full view[w]
of the LORD,
and he examines all his paths.[x]
22 The evil deeds of a wicked man
ensnare him;[y]
the cords of his sin hold him
fast.[z]

5:22 [y]Ps 9:16 [z]Nu 32:23; Ps 7:15-16; Pr 1:31-32

23 He will die for lack of discipline,[a]
led astray by his own great folly.

5:23 [a]Job 4:21; 36:12

Warnings Against Folly

6:1 [b]Pr 17:18

6 My son, if you have put up
security for your neighbor,[b]
if you have struck hands in
pledge[c] for another,

6:1 [c]Pr 11:15; 22:26-27

2 if you have been trapped by what
you said,
ensnared by the words of your
mouth,
3 then do this, my son, to free yourself,
since you have fallen into your
neighbor's hands:
Go and humble yourself;
press your plea with your
neighbor!
4 Allow no sleep to your eyes,
no slumber to your eyelids.[d]

6:4 [d]Ps 132:4

5 Free yourself, like a gazelle from
the hand of the hunter,
like a bird from the snare of the
fowler.[e]

6:5 [e]Ps 91:3

6 Go to the ant, you sluggard;[f]
consider its ways and be wise!

6:6 [f]Pr 20:4

7 It has no commander,
no overseer or ruler,
8 yet it stores its provisions in
summer
and gathers its food at harvest.[g]

6:8 [g]Pr 10:4

9 How long will you lie there, you
sluggard?[h]
When will you get up from your
sleep?

6:9 [h]Pr 24:30-34

10 A little sleep, a little slumber,
a little folding of the hands to
rest[i]—

6:10 [i]Pr 24:33

11 and poverty[j] will come on you like
a bandit
and scarcity like an armed man.[a]

6:11 [j]Pr 24:30-34

12 A scoundrel and villain,
who goes about with a corrupt
mouth,
13 who winks with his eye,[k]
signals with his feet
and motions with his fingers,

6:13 [k]Ps 35:19

14 who plots evil[l] with deceit in his
heart—
he always stirs up dissension.[m]

6:14 [l]Mic 2:1 [m]ver 16-19

15 Therefore disaster will overtake
him in an instant;
he will suddenly be destroyed—
without remedy.[n]

6:15 [n]2Ch 36:16

16 There are six things the LORD hates,
seven that are detestable to him:
17 haughty eyes,
a lying tongue,[o]
hands that shed innocent
blood,[p]

6:17 [o]Ps 120:2; Pr 12:22 [p]Dt 19:10; Isa 1:15; 59:7

[a] 11 *Or like a vagrant / and scarcity like a beggar*

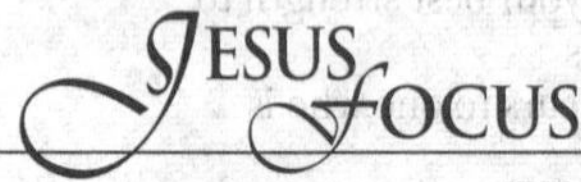

THE LURE OF MONEY

Handling money can be a tricky business, and Proverbs teaches us balance in this difficult area of life. Those who handle their financial resources wisely, says Proverbs, are on the right path toward becoming generous and prosperous. But there are implicit dangers involved in money management as well—co-signing notes, incurring excessive debt and charging exorbitant interest rates are just a few of the issues addressed in this book (see also Proverbs 11:15; 17:18; 22:26–27). The love of money and the seductive lure of the things it can buy can completely destroy a person's love for God and passion for the things of the Spirit (Mark 4:18–19; 10:21–31; Luke 12:32–34; 1 Timothy 6:6–10). Jesus put it this way: "No one can serve two masters" (Matthew 6:24). Serving God and being enslaved to our bank account are simply incompatible. Our Lord reminded his disciples to seek God before anything else and promised that God will in turn take care of the material needs of those who trust him (Matthew 6:33).

18 a heart that devises wicked schemes,
feet that are quick to rush into evil,[q]
19 a false witness[r] who pours out lies
and a man who stirs up dissension among brothers.[s]

6:18 q Ge 6:5
6:19 r Ps 27:12 s ver 12-15

Warning Against Adultery

20 My son, keep your father's commands
and do not forsake your mother's teaching.[t]
21 Bind them upon your heart forever;
fasten them around your neck.[u]
22 When you walk, they will guide you;
when you sleep, they will watch over you;
when you awake, they will speak to you.
23 For these commands are a lamp,
this teaching is a light,[v]
and the corrections of discipline
are the way to life,
24 keeping you from the immoral woman,
from the smooth tongue of the wayward wife.[w]
25 Do not lust in your heart after her beauty
or let her captivate you with her eyes,
26 for the prostitute reduces you to a loaf of bread,
and the adulteress preys upon your very life.[x]
27 Can a man scoop fire into his lap
without his clothes being burned?
28 Can a man walk on hot coals
without his feet being scorched?
29 So is he who sleeps[y] with another man's wife;[z]
no one who touches her will go unpunished.
30 Men do not despise a thief if he steals
to satisfy his hunger when he is starving.
31 Yet if he is caught, he must pay sevenfold,[a]
though it costs him all the wealth of his house.
32 But a man who commits adultery[b] lacks judgment;[c]

6:20 t Pr 1:8
6:21 u Pr 3:3; 7:1-3
6:23 v Ps 19:8; 119:105
6:24 w Pr 2:16; 7:5
6:26 x Pr 7:22-23; 29:3
6:29 y Ex 20:14 z Pr 2:16-19; 5:8
6:31 a Ex 22:1-14
6:32 b Ex 20:14 c Pr 7:7; 9:4,16

whoever does so destroys himself.
33 Blows and disgrace are his lot,
and his shame will never[d] be wiped away;
34 for jealousy[e] arouses a husband's fury,[f]
and he will show no mercy when he takes revenge.
35 He will not accept any compensation;
he will refuse the bribe, however great it is.[g]

6:33 d Pr 5:9-14
6:34 e Nu 5:14 f Ge 34:7
6:35 g Job 31:9-11; SS 8:7

Warning Against the Adulteress

7 My son,[h] keep my words
and store up my commands within you.
2 Keep my commands and you will live;[i]
guard my teachings as the apple of your eye.
3 Bind them on your fingers;
write them on the tablet of your heart.[j]
4 Say to wisdom, "You are my sister,"
and call understanding your kinsman;
5 they will keep you from the adulteress,
from the wayward wife with her seductive words.[k]
6 At the window of my house
I looked out through the lattice.
7 I saw among the simple,
I noticed among the young men,
a youth who lacked judgment.[l]
8 He was going down the street near her corner,
walking along in the direction of her house
9 at twilight,[m] as the day was fading,
as the dark of night set in.
10 Then out came a woman to meet him,
dressed like a prostitute and with crafty intent.
11 (She is loud[n] and defiant,
her feet never stay at home;
12 now in the street, now in the squares,
at every corner she lurks.)[o]
13 She took hold of him[p] and kissed him
and with a brazen face she said:[q]

7:1 h Pr 1:8; 2:1
7:2 i Pr 4:4
7:3 j Dt 6:8; Pr 3:3
7:5 k ver 21; Job 31:9; Pr 2:16; 6:24
7:7 l Pr 1:22; 6:32
7:9 m Job 24:15
7:11 n Pr 9:13; 1Ti 5:13
7:12 o Pr 8:1-36; 23:26-28
7:13 p Ge 39:12 q Pr 1:20

14 "I have fellowship offerings[a][r] at home;
today I fulfilled my vows.
15 So I came out to meet you;
I looked for you and have found you!
16 I have covered my bed
with colored linens from Egypt.
17 I have perfumed my bed[s]
with myrrh,[t] aloes and cinnamon.
18 Come, let's drink deep of love till morning;
let's enjoy ourselves with love![u]
19 My husband is not at home;
he has gone on a long journey.
20 He took his purse filled with money
and will not be home till full moon."

21 With persuasive words she led him astray;
she seduced him with her smooth talk.[v]
22 All at once he followed her
like an ox going to the slaughter,
like a deer[b] stepping into a noose[c][w]
23 till an arrow pierces[x] his liver,
like a bird darting into a snare,
little knowing it will cost him his life.[y]

24 Now then, my sons, listen[z] to me;
pay attention to what I say.
25 Do not let your heart turn to her ways
or stray into her paths.[a]
26 Many are the victims she has brought down;
her slain are a mighty throng.
27 Her house is a highway to the grave,[d]
leading down to the chambers of death.[b]

Wisdom's Call

8 Does not wisdom call out?[c]
Does not understanding raise her voice?
2 On the heights along the way,
where the paths meet, she takes her stand;
3 beside the gates leading into the city,
at the entrances, she cries aloud:[d]
4 "To you, O men, I call out;
I raise my voice to all mankind.

7:14 [r] Lev 7:11-18 **7:17** [s] Est 1:6; Isa 57:7; Eze 23:41; Am 6:4 [t] Ge 37:25 **7:18** [u] Ge 39:7 **7:21** [v] Pr 5:3 **7:22** [w] Job 18:10 **7:23** [x] Job 15:22; 16:13 [y] Pr 6:26; Ecc 7:26; 9:12 **7:24** [z] Pr 1:8-9; 5:7; 8:32 **7:25** [a] Pr 5:7-8 **7:27** [b] Pr 2:18; 5:5; 9:18; Rev 22:15 **8:1** [c] Pr 1:20; 9:3 **8:3** [d] Job 29:7

5 You who are simple,[e] gain prudence;[f]
you who are foolish, gain understanding.
6 Listen, for I have worthy things to say;
I open my lips to speak what is right.
7 My mouth speaks what is true,[g]
for my lips detest wickedness.
8 All the words of my mouth are just;
none of them is crooked or perverse.
9 To the discerning all of them are right;
they are faultless to those who have knowledge.
10 Choose my instruction instead of silver,
knowledge rather than choice gold,[h]
11 for wisdom is more precious[i] than rubies,
and nothing you desire can compare with her.[j]

12 "I, wisdom, dwell together with prudence;
I possess knowledge and discretion.[k]
13 To fear the LORD is to hate evil;[l]
I hate[m] pride and arrogance,
evil behavior and perverse speech.
14 Counsel and sound judgment are mine;
I have understanding and power.[n]
15 By me kings reign
and rulers[o] make laws that are just;
16 by me princes govern,
and all nobles who rule on earth.[e]
17 I love those who love me,[p]
and those who seek me find me.[q]
18 With me are riches and honor,[r]
enduring wealth and prosperity.[s]
19 My fruit is better than fine gold;
what I yield surpasses choice silver.[t]
20 I walk in the way of righteousness,
along the paths of justice,

8:5 [e] Pr 1:22 [f] Pr 1:4 **8:7** [g] Ps 37:30; Jn 8:14 **8:10** [h] Pr 3:14-15 **8:11** [i] Job 28:17-19 [j] Pr 3:13-15 **8:12** [k] Pr 1:4 **8:13** [l] Pr 16:6 [m] Jer 44:4 **8:14** [n] Pr 21:22; Ecc 7:19 **8:15** [o] Da 2:21; Ro 13:1 **8:17** [p] 1Sa 2:30; Ps 91:14; Jn 14:21-24 [q] Pr 1:28; Jas 1: **8:18** [r] Pr 3:16 [s] Dt 8:18; Mt 6:33 **8:19** [t] Pr 3:13-14; 10:20

[a] 14 Traditionally *peace offerings* [b] 22 Syriac (see also Septuagint); Hebrew *fool* [c] 22 The meaning of the Hebrew for this line is uncertain. [d] 27 Hebrew *Sheol* [e] 16 Many Hebrew manuscripts and Septuagint; most Hebrew manuscripts *and nobles—all righteous rulers*

[21] bestowing wealth on those who love me
and making their treasuries full.[u]

[22] "The LORD brought me forth as the first of his works,[a,b]
before his deeds of old;
[23] I was appointed[c] from eternity,
from the beginning, before the world began.
[24] When there were no oceans, I was given birth,
when there were no springs abounding with water;[v]
[25] before the mountains were settled in place,
before the hills, I was given birth,[w]
[26] before he made the earth or its fields
or any of the dust of the world.[x]
[27] I was there when he set the heavens in place,[y]
when he marked out the horizon on the face of the deep,
[28] when he established the clouds above
and fixed securely the fountains of the deep,
[29] when he gave the sea its boundary[z]
so the waters would not overstep his command,[a]
and when he marked out the foundations of the earth.[b]
[30] Then I was the craftsman at his side.[c]
I was filled with delight day after day,
rejoicing always in his presence,
[31] rejoicing in his whole world
and delighting in mankind.[d]

[32] "Now then, my sons, listen to me;
blessed are[e] those who keep my ways.[f]
[33] Listen to my instruction and be wise;
do not ignore it.
[34] Blessed is the man who listens[g] to me,
watching daily at my doors,
waiting at my doorway.
[35] For whoever finds me[h] finds life
and receives favor from the LORD.[i]
[36] But whoever fails to find me harms himself;[j]
all who hate me love death."

8:21 [u] Pr 24:4
8:24 [v] Ge 7:11
8:25 [w] Job 15:7
8:26 [x] Ps 90:2
8:27 [y] Pr 3:19
8:29 [z] Ge 1:9; Job 38:10; Ps 16:6 [a] Ps 104:9
8:29 [b] Job 38:5
8:30 [c] Jn 1:1-3
8:31 [d] Ps 16:3; 104:1-30
8:32 [e] Lk 11:28 [f] Ps 119:1-2
8:34 [g] Pr 3:13,18
8:35 [h] Pr 3:13-18 [i] Pr 12:2
8:36 [j] Pr 15:32

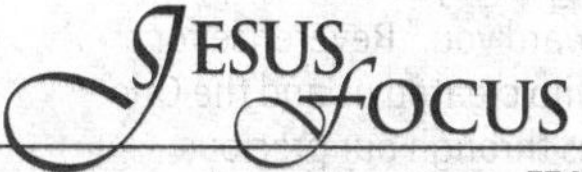

FEAR OF THE LORD

The phrase "fear of the LORD" appears repeatedly throughout the book of Proverbs (see Proverbs 9:10). "Fear" is the sense of awe we experience when we see God for who he is. Fearing God, then, doesn't mean living in terror of his wrath and his judgment. Instead it means being in a relationship with him that is based on reverence, respect and trust. Those who do not fear him in this way miss out on what he has planned for their lives because they miss *him*. Jesus' mother Mary composed and sang a beautiful song during her visit with Elizabeth prior to Jesus' birth. In it she expressed a magnificent truth: "[God's] mercy extends to those who fear him, from generation to generation" (Luke 1:50). And the apostle John in the book of Revelation included a resounding shout of triumph: "Praise our God, all you his servants, you who fear him . . . For the wedding of the Lamb [Jesus] has come, and his bride [his church] has made herself ready" (Revelation 19:5,7).

CHRIST HAS FLUNG THE DOOR OF MERCY WIDE OPEN AND STANDS IN THE DOOR CALLING AND CRYING WITH A LOUD VOICE TO POOR SINNERS.

Jonathan Edwards, *American Puritan Pastor*

Invitations of Wisdom and of Folly

9 Wisdom has built[k] her house;
she has hewn out its seven pillars.
[2] She has prepared her meat and mixed her wine;
she has also set her table.[l]
[3] She has sent out her maids, and she calls[m]
from the highest point of the city.[n]
[4] "Let all who are simple come in here!"
she says to those who lack judgment.[o]
[5] "Come, eat my food
and drink the wine I have mixed.[p]
[6] Leave your simple ways and you will live;[q]

9:1 [k] Eph 2:20-22; 1Pe 2:5
9:2 [l] Lk 14:16-23
9:3 [m] Pr 8:1-3 [n] ver 14
9:4 [o] Pr 6:32
9:5 [p] Isa 55:1
9:6 [q] Pr 8:35

[a] 22 Or *way*; or *dominion* [b] 22 Or *The LORD possessed me at the beginning of his work*; or *The LORD brought me forth at the beginning of his work* [c] 23 Or *fashioned*

A Choice for Life

Many people do not believe in a distinction between right and wrong; such people want to make their own decisions and resent the idea of absolute truth. Many have concluded that there are too many good options for a single one to be the only right way. But the Bible tells us explicitly that God gave us his Word as a guide so that we might live in a way that delights him—and that involves the ability to distinguish right from wrong.

A person can choose to follow one of two paths in life. The first is the way of wisdom—following the way God has revealed as best, making life decisions that please him. When we become acquainted with God, he gives us insight into what he wants and expects for our lives. Right living results in incredible rewards and can even lead to a longer life (Deuteronomy 30:19–20).

The second possible choice is referred to in Proverbs as *folly*. This option implies choosing *what* we want *when* we want it. Proverbs describes a foolish individual as loud, undisciplined and totally lacking in integrity. Folly is like an unprincipled woman who calls out to men to join her in a sensuous and totally unrestrained lifestyle. She has no qualms about taking what she wants and using it for her own purposes.

The Bible often contrasts these two ways of living. But whether the writer is referring to light versus darkness (Isaiah 9:2), right versus wrong (Luke 7:29), a narrow road versus a wide road (Matthew 7:13–14) or truth contrasted with lies (1 Timothy 2:7), one thing is clear: The first way is God's way (John 8:42–44). Choosing to disregard God's desires and expectations is neither a passive nor neutral decision; it is a deliberate choice to follow Satan.

Proverbs 9 spells out a reality we already know from experience: Both ways of living plead for our attention. Wisdom and folly compete for our minds, our hearts, our souls and our bodies. God wants us to give our lives to him, but only because *we* want to. The choice is a matter of life or death—literally. When we choose folly, the eventual consequence is death (verse 18).

But verses 10–12 sum up the heart of Wisdom's message, a message she has faithfully proclaimed throughout the first nine chapters of the book of Proverbs: "The fear of the LORD is the beginning of wisdom, and knowledge of the Holy One is understanding . . . If you are wise, your wisdom will reward you." Reverence for God, the One who created us and the One who redeems us through our precious Savior Jesus—this is the path of life and security. The only way we can enter into a relationship with God is by accepting Jesus' sacrifice for our sin. Jesus Christ is "the way and the truth and the life" (John 14:6–7).

***Self-Discovery:** Have you built your life on the words of Jesus? He doesn't guarantee that you won't have storms—just that you will be able to survive them.*

GO TO DISCOVERY 162 ON PAGE 826

walk in the way of
understanding.

7 "Whoever corrects a mocker
invites insult;
whoever rebukes a wicked man
incurs abuse.[r]

8 Do not rebuke a mocker[s] or he will
hate you;
rebuke a wise man and he will
love you.[t]

9 Instruct a wise man and he will be
wiser still;
teach a righteous man and he
will add to his learning.[u]

10 "The fear of the LORD[v] is the
beginning of wisdom,
and knowledge of the Holy One
is understanding.

11 For through me your days will be
many,
and years will be added to your
life.[w]

12 If you are wise, your wisdom will
reward you;
if you are a mocker, you alone
will suffer."

13 The woman Folly is loud;[x]
she is undisciplined and without
knowledge.[y]

14 She sits at the door of her house,
on a seat at the highest point of
the city,[z]

15 calling out to those who pass by,
who go straight on their way.

16 "Let all who are simple come in
here!"
she says to those who lack
judgment.

17 "Stolen water is sweet;
food eaten in secret is delicious![a]"

18 But little do they know that the
dead are there,
that her guests are in the depths
of the grave.[a][b]

9:7 [r]Pr 23:9
9:8 [s]Pr 15:12 [t]Ps 141:5
9:9 [u]Pr 1:5,7
9:10 [v]Job 28:28; Pr 1:7
9:11 [w]Pr 3:16; 10:27
9:13 [x]Pr 7:11 [y]Pr 5:6
9:14 [z]ver 3
9:17 [a]Pr 20:17
9:18 [b]Pr 2:18; 7:26-27

Proverbs of Solomon

10 The proverbs of Solomon:[c]

A wise son brings joy to his father,[d]
but a foolish son grief to his
mother.

2 Ill-gotten treasures are of no
value,[e]
but righteousness delivers from
death.[f]

10:1 [c]Pr 1:1 [d]Pr 15:20; 29:3
10:2 [e]Pr 21:6 [f]Pr 11:4,19

3 The LORD does not let the
righteous go hungry[g]
but he thwarts the craving of the
wicked.

4 Lazy hands make a man poor,[h]
but diligent hands bring wealth.[i]

5 He who gathers crops in summer is
a wise son,
but he who sleeps during
harvest is a disgraceful son.

6 Blessings crown the head of the
righteous,
but violence overwhelms the
mouth of the wicked.[b][j]

7 The memory of the righteous[k] will
be a blessing,
but the name of the wicked[l] will
rot.[m]

8 The wise in heart accept
commands,
but a chattering fool comes to
ruin.[n]

9 The man of integrity[o] walks
securely,[p]
but he who takes crooked paths
will be found out.[q]

10 He who winks maliciously[r] causes
grief,
and a chattering fool comes to
ruin.

11 The mouth of the righteous is a
fountain of life,[s]
but violence overwhelms the
mouth of the wicked.[t]

12 Hatred stirs up dissension,
but love covers over all wrongs.[u]

13 Wisdom is found on the lips of the
discerning,[v]
but a rod is for the back of him
who lacks judgment.[w]

14 Wise men store up knowledge,
but the mouth of a fool invites
ruin.[x]

15 The wealth of the rich is their
fortified city,[y]
but poverty is the ruin of the
poor.[z]

16 The wages of the righteous bring
them life,

[a] *18* Hebrew *Sheol* [b] *6* Or *but the mouth of the wicked conceals violence*; also in verse 11

10:3 [g]Mt 6:25-34
10:4 [h]Pr 19:15 [i]Pr 12:24; 13:4; 21:5
10:6 [j]ver 8,11,14
10:7 [k]Ps 112:6 [l]Ps 109:13 [m]Ps 9:6
10:8 [n]Mt 7:24-27
10:9 [o]Isa 33:15 [p]Ps 23:4 [q]Pr 28:18
10:10 [r]Ps 35:19
10:11 [s]Ps 37:30; Pr 13:12,14,19 [t]ver 6
10:12 [u]Pr 17:9; 1Co 13:4-7; 1Pe 4:8
10:13 [v]ver 31 [w]Pr 26:3
10:14 [x]Pr 18:6,7
10:15 [y]Pr 18:11 [z]Pr 19:7

LIVING GOD'S WAY

God's way is perfect—which makes sense because *he* is perfect. God never does anything or recommends that we do anything that is flawed in any way: "As for God, his way is perfect; the word of the LORD is flawless; He is a shield for all who take refuge in him" (2 Samuel 22:31). Throughout Scripture God's people have repeatedly pleaded with him for guidance. David implored in Psalm 25:4–5, "Show me your ways, O LORD, teach me your paths; guide me in your truth and teach me, for you are God my Savior, and my hope is in you all day long."

We all need help getting through life, and God's Word provides all of the direction and correction we require. God's perfect instruction offers us the hope of a long and satisfying life, while ignoring God's Word and living life on our own terms eventually result in destruction and grief (Deuteronomy 6:1–3; 1 Samuel 2:22–36).

Proverbs 10:9 tells us that "the man of integrity walks securely, but he who takes crooked paths will be found out." When we stumble or wander from his will, God as a loving Father takes our hand and gently but firmly leads us back to the right path. God's discipline is a necessary part of our learning. He will correct us; yet, though it may be painful for a time he will never harm us.

Jesus not only *showed* us the way to get to know the Father—he *is* the only way to a relationship with God: "I am the way and the truth and the life. No one comes to the Father except through me" (John 14:6). He wants us to live as he intended—abundantly and joyfully (John 15:9–11). The writer to the Hebrews referred to our access to the Father through the shed blood of Jesus Christ as "a new and living way opened for us through the curtain, that is, [Jesus'] body" (Hebrews 10:20).

In one instance, when Jesus was visiting friends in Bethany, Martha was distracted and worried about all of the extra work necessary in order to entertain her guest with the hospitality he deserved. Martha's sister Mary ignored the myriad tasks that needed to be done, and she sat, spellbound, at Jesus' feet, listening, learning and relishing his presence. Martha implored Jesus to insist that her sister help with the meal preparations, but the Lord gently rebuked her: "You are worried and upset about many things, but only one thing is needed. Mary has chosen what is better, and it will not be taken away from her" (Luke 10:41–42).

Jesus corrected Martha, and later on she professed to him that she knew him to be God's promised Messiah (John 11:27). Earlier, Jesus had set Martha straight on her priorities. Now she demonstrated to her Master that those priorities were back on track; she relinquished control of her life to Jesus, who is the resurrection and the life (John 11:25). What a marvelous declaration of faith in Jesus, the Christ, the Messiah, the One who shows us how to walk the straight path of integrity.

Self-Discovery: *Proverbs 10:9 states that someone who takes "crooked paths will be found out." How might this verse be applied to your own life experience? If you find that you've gotten off track, ask Jesus, "the way and the truth and the life," to help you get back on the right path.*

GO TO DISCOVERY 163 ON PAGE 835

but the income of the wicked
brings them punishment.[a]

17 He who heeds discipline shows the
way to life,[b]
but whoever ignores correction
leads others astray.

18 He who conceals his hatred has
lying lips,
and whoever spreads slander is a
fool.

19 When words are many, sin is not
absent,
but he who holds his tongue is
wise.[c]

20 The tongue of the righteous is
choice silver,
but the heart of the wicked is of
little value.

21 The lips of the righteous nourish
many,
but fools die for lack of
judgment.[d]

22 The blessing of the LORD brings
wealth,[e]
and he adds no trouble to it.

23 A fool finds pleasure in evil
conduct,[f]
but a man of understanding
delights in wisdom.

24 What the wicked dreads[g] will
overtake him;
what the righteous desire will be
granted.[h]

25 When the storm has swept by, the
wicked are gone,
but the righteous stand firm[i]
forever.[j]

26 As vinegar to the teeth and smoke
to the eyes,
so is a sluggard to those who
send him.[k]

27 The fear of the LORD adds length to
life,[l]
but the years of the wicked are
cut short.[m]

28 The prospect of the righteous is
joy,
but the hopes of the wicked
come to nothing.[n]

29 The way of the LORD is a refuge for
the righteous,
but it is the ruin of those who do
evil.[o]

30 The righteous will never be
uprooted,
but the wicked will not remain
in the land.[p]

31 The mouth of the righteous brings
forth wisdom,[q]
but a perverse tongue will be cut
out.

32 The lips of the righteous know
what is fitting,[r]
but the mouth of the wicked
only what is perverse.

11 The LORD abhors dishonest
scales,[s]
but accurate weights are his
delight.[t]

2 When pride comes, then comes
disgrace,[u]
but with humility comes
wisdom.[v]

3 The integrity of the upright guides
them,
but the unfaithful are destroyed
by their duplicity.[w]

4 Wealth is worthless in the day of
wrath,[x]
but righteousness delivers from
death.[y]

5 The righteousness of the blameless
makes a straight way for
them,
but the wicked are brought down
by their own wickedness.[z]

6 The righteousness of the upright
delivers them,
but the unfaithful are trapped by
evil desires.

7 When a wicked man dies, his hope
perishes;
all he expected from his power
comes to nothing.[a]

8 The righteous man is rescued from
trouble,
and it comes on the wicked
instead.[b]

9 With his mouth the godless
destroys his neighbor,
but through knowledge the
righteous escape.

10:16 [a] Pr 11:18-19
10:17 [b] Pr 6:23
10:19 [c] Pr 17:28; Ecc 5:3; Jas 1:19; 3:2-12
10:21 [d] Pr 5:22-23; Hos 4:1,6,14
10:22 [e] Ge 24:35; Ps 37:22
10:23 [f] Pr 2:14; 15:21
10:24 [g] Isa 66:4 [h] Ps 145:17-19; Mt 5:6; 1Jn 5:14-15
10:25 [i] Ps 15:5 [j] Pr 12:3,7; Mt 7:24-27
10:26 [k] Pr 26:6
10:27 [l] Pr 9:10-11 [m] Job 15:32
10:28 [n] Job 8:13; Pr 11:7
10:29 [o] Pr 21:15
10:30 [p] Ps 37:9,28-29; Pr 2:20-22
10:31 [q] Ps 37:30
10:32 [r] Ecc 10:12
11:1 [s] Lev 19:36; Dt 25:13-16; Pr 20:10,23 [t] Pr 16:11
11:2 [u] Pr 16:18 [v] Pr 18:12; 29:23
11:3 [w] Pr 13:6
11:4 [x] Eze 7:19; Zep 1:18 [y] Ge 7:1; Pr 10:2
11:5 [z] Pr 5:21-23
11:7 [a] Pr 10:28
11:8 [b] Pr 21:18

11:10 [c]Pr 28:12

10 When the righteous prosper, the
city rejoices;[c]
when the wicked perish, there
are shouts of joy.

11:11 [d]Pr 29:8

11 Through the blessing of the
upright a city is exalted,
but by the mouth of the wicked
it is destroyed.[d]

11:12 [e]Pr 14:21

12 A man who lacks judgment derides
his neighbor,[e]
but a man of understanding
holds his tongue.

11:13 [f]Lev 19:16; Pr 20:19; 1Ti 5:13

13 A gossip betrays a confidence,[f]
but a trustworthy man keeps a
secret.

11:14 [g]Pr 20:18 [h]Pr 15:22; 24:6

14 For lack of guidance a nation falls,[g]
but many advisers make victory
sure.[h]

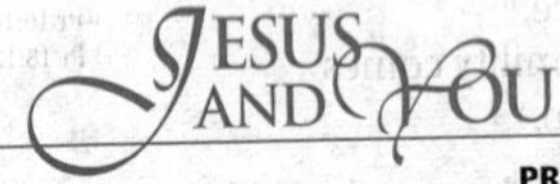

PRINCIPLES FOR LIFE

The proverbs teach truths that apply to life *in general*, but there are always exceptions to general principles. For example, the statement that "the righteous man is rescued from trouble, and it comes on the wicked instead" (Proverbs 11:8) is generally true, but there are certainly examples of godly people who have not been rescued and ungodly people who have been remarkably free from trouble. Many people suffer as a result of their faith in Jesus, and countless Christians are still martyred each year as a direct consequence of their commitment to him. Jesus used the same kind of broad generalizations in his Sermon on the Mount (Matthew 5:3–12). The poor, the meek and the merciful do certainly receive certain blessings from God in this life and will without doubt inherit eternal life in the age to come and enjoy its inexpressible benefits, but they are not thereby exempted from pain and trouble in this earthly life (John 16:33). And treating others with kindness does not in and of itself guarantee reciprocal kindness from others (Proverbs 11:16–17,24–25). Yet the Bible urges us to be kind regardless of how others respond (Ephesians 4:32; Colossians 3:12). When we read the promises of God's Word we need to understand the concept of general principles. However, we need also to embrace the reality that God's overall plan for each of us is "to prosper [us] and not to harm [us] . . . to give [us] hope and a future" (Jeremiah 29:11).

15 He who puts up security[i] for
another will surely suffer,
but whoever refuses to strike
hands in pledge is safe.

11:15 [i]Pr 6:1

16 A kindhearted woman gains
respect,[j]
but ruthless men gain only
wealth.

11:16 [j]Pr 31:31

17 A kind man benefits himself,
but a cruel man brings trouble
on himself.

18 The wicked man earns deceptive
wages,
but he who sows righteousness
reaps a sure reward.[k]

11:18 [k]Hos 10:12-13

19 The truly righteous man attains life,
but he who pursues evil goes to
his death.

20 The LORD detests men of perverse
heart
but he delights in those whose
ways are blameless.[l]

11:20 [l]1Ch 29:17; Ps 119:1; Pr 12:2,22

21 Be sure of this: The wicked will not
go unpunished,
but those who are righteous will
go free.[m]

11:21 [m]Pr 16:5

22 Like a gold ring in a pig's snout
is a beautiful woman who shows
no discretion.

23 The desire of the righteous ends
only in good,
but the hope of the wicked only
in wrath.

24 One man gives freely, yet gains
even more;
another withholds unduly, but
comes to poverty.

25 A generous man will prosper;
he who refreshes others will
himself be refreshed.[n]

11:25 [n]Mt 5:7; 2Co 9:6-9

26 People curse the man who hoards
grain,
but blessing crowns him who is
willing to sell.

27 He who seeks good finds goodwill,
but evil comes to him who
searches for it.[o]

11:27 [o]Est 7:10; Ps 7:15-16

28 Whoever trusts in his riches will
fall,[p]
but the righteous will thrive like
a green leaf.[q]

11:28 [p]Job 31:24-28; Ps 49:6; 52:7; Mk 10:25; 1Ti 6:17 [q]Ps 1:3; 92:12-14; Jer 17:8

[29] He who brings trouble on his family will inherit only wind,
11:29 [r] Pr 14:19
and the fool will be servant to the wise.[r]
11:30 [s] Jas 5:20
[30] The fruit of the righteous is a tree of life,[s]
and he who wins souls is wise.
11:31 [t] Pr 13:21; Jer 25:29; 1Pe 4:18
[31] If the righteous receive their due[t] on earth,
how much more the ungodly and the sinner!

12 Whoever loves discipline loves knowledge,
12:1 [u] Pr 9:7-9; 15:5, 10,12,32
but he who hates correction is stupid.[u]
[2] A good man obtains favor from the LORD,
but the LORD condemns a crafty man.
[3] A man cannot be established through wickedness,
12:3 [v] Pr 10:25
but the righteous cannot be uprooted.[v]
[4] A wife of noble character is her husband's crown,
12:4 [w] Pr 14:30
but a disgraceful wife is like decay in his bones.[w]
[5] The plans of the righteous are just,
but the advice of the wicked is deceitful.
[6] The words of the wicked lie in wait for blood,
12:6 [x] Pr 14:3
but the speech of the upright rescues them.[x]
12:7 [y] Ps 37:36 [z] Pr 10:25
[7] Wicked men are overthrown and are no more,[y]
but the house of the righteous stands firm.[z]
[8] A man is praised according to his wisdom,
but men with warped minds are despised.
[9] Better to be a nobody and yet have a servant
than pretend to be somebody and have no food.
[10] A righteous man cares for the needs of his animal,
but the kindest acts of the wicked are cruel.

IF YOU FIND IT HARD TO BELIEVE IN GOD, I STRONGLY ADVISE YOU TO BEGIN YOUR SEARCH NOT WITH PHILOSOPHICAL QUESTIONS . . . BUT WITH JESUS OF NAZARETH.

John Stott, *Pastor, London, England*

[11] He who works his land will have abundant food,
but he who chases fantasies lacks judgment.[a] 12:11 [a] Pr 28:19
[12] The wicked desire the plunder of evil men,
but the root of the righteous flourishes.
[13] An evil man is trapped by his sinful talk,[b] 12:13 [b] Pr 18:7 [c] Pr 21:23; 2Pe 2:9
but a righteous man escapes trouble.[c]
[14] From the fruit of his lips a man is filled with good things[d] 12:14 [d] Pr 13:2; 15:23; 18:20 [e] Isa 3:10-11
as surely as the work of his hands rewards him.[e]
[15] The way of a fool seems right to him,[f] 12:15 [f] Pr 14:12; 16:2, 25; Lk 18:11
but a wise man listens to advice.
[16] A fool shows his annoyance at once,
but a prudent man overlooks an insult.[g] 12:16 [g] Pr 29:11
[17] A truthful witness gives honest testimony,
but a false witness tells lies.[h] 12:17 [h] Pr 14:5,25
[18] Reckless words pierce like a sword,[i] 12:18 [i] Ps 57:4 [j] Pr 15:4
but the tongue of the wise brings healing.[j]
[19] Truthful lips endure forever,
but a lying tongue lasts only a moment.
[20] There is deceit in the hearts of those who plot evil,
but joy for those who promote peace.
[21] No harm befalls the righteous,[k] 12:21 [k] Ps 91:10
but the wicked have their fill of trouble.
[22] The LORD detests lying lips,[l] 12:22 [l] Pr 6:17; Rev 22:15

but he delights in men who are
truthful.[m]

12:22 [m] Pr 11:20

[23] A prudent man keeps his
knowledge to himself,[n]
but the heart of fools blurts out
folly.

12:23 [n] Pr 10:14; 13:16

[24] Diligent hands will rule,
but laziness ends in slave labor.[o]

12:24 [o] Pr 10:4

[25] An anxious heart weighs a man
down,[p]
but a kind word cheers him up.

12:25 [p] Pr 15:13; Isa 50:4

[26] A righteous man is cautious in
friendship,[a]
but the way of the wicked leads
them astray.

[27] The lazy man does not roast[b] his
game,
but the diligent man prizes his
possessions.

[28] In the way of righteousness there is
life;[q]
along that path is immortality.

12:28 [q] Dt 30:15

13

A wise son heeds his father's
instruction,
but a mocker does not listen to
rebuke.[r]

13:1 [r] Pr 10:1

[2] From the fruit of his lips a man
enjoys good things,[s]
but the unfaithful have a craving
for violence.

13:2 [s] Pr 12:14

[3] He who guards his lips[t] guards his
life,[u]
but he who speaks rashly will
come to ruin.[v]

13:3 [t] Jas 3:2 [u] Pr 21:23 [v] Pr 18:7,20-21

[4] The sluggard craves and gets
nothing,
but the desires of the diligent are
fully satisfied.

[5] The righteous hate what is false,
but the wicked bring shame and
disgrace.

[6] Righteousness guards the man of
integrity,
but wickedness overthrows the
sinner.[w]

13:6 [w] Pr 11:3,5

[7] One man pretends to be rich, yet
has nothing;
another pretends to be poor, yet
has great wealth.[x]

13:7 [x] 2Co 6:10

[8] A man's riches may ransom his life,
but a poor man hears no threat.

[9] The light of the righteous shines
brightly,
but the lamp of the wicked is
snuffed out.[y]

13:9 [y] Job 18:5; Pr 4:18-19; 24:20

[10] Pride only breeds quarrels,
but wisdom is found in those
who take advice.

[11] Dishonest money dwindles away,[z]
but he who gathers money little
by little makes it grow.

13:11 [z] Pr 10:2

[12] Hope deferred makes the heart sick,
but a longing fulfilled is a tree of
life.

[a] 26 Or *man is a guide to his neighbor* [b] 27 The meaning of the Hebrew for this word is uncertain.

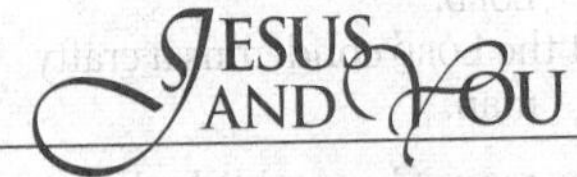

GROWING WISE

We are taught in Proverbs to evaluate every idea and possible course of action according to one standard: Is it *wise*? The book of Proverbs is not simply a collection of helpful maxims or good ideas. It contains life-changing instruction on living for God and learning to become increasingly wise. We do not come into this world already endowed with a measure of wisdom in the same way that the intelligence quotient of an individual is likely to remain fairly constant throughout life. A child can possess wisdom, and children do in fact frequently surprise us by their insightful words, but wisdom is a quality that (hopefully) increases with age and experience. Proverbs 13:1 talks about a "wise son" (note that the boy is already credited with some wisdom) but goes on to define him as a son who listens to and takes to heart his father's instruction. In other words, he is progressing along a path.

Even Jesus, the one and only Son of God, as a young man "grew in wisdom and stature, and in favor with God and men" (Luke 2:52). Because our Lord himself had to go through developmental stages and gain wisdom through experience (although, unlike ourselves, his progression did not involve trial and error), we can be assured that he empathizes with our weaknesses and struggles (Hebrews 2:18; 4:15), that he understands what it means to have not yet "arrived." But because he is God, we can be equally confident that Jesus will help us to overcome those weaknesses and gain life-empowering insight through those struggles.

13:13 [a] Nu 15:31; 2Ch 36:16

13 He who scorns instruction will pay
for it,[a]
but he who respects a command
is rewarded.

13:14 [b] Pr 10:11 [c] Pr 14:27

14 The teaching of the wise is a
fountain of life,[b]
turning a man from the snares
of death.[c]

15 Good understanding wins favor,
but the way of the unfaithful is
hard.[a]

13:16 [d] Pr 12:23

16 Every prudent man acts out of
knowledge,
but a fool exposes his folly.[d]

13:17 [e] Pr 25:13

17 A wicked messenger falls into
trouble,
but a trustworthy envoy brings
healing.[e]

13:18 [f] Pr 15:5,31-32

18 He who ignores discipline comes
to poverty and shame,
but whoever heeds correction is
honored.[f]

19 A longing fulfilled is sweet to the
soul,
but fools detest turning from evil.

13:20 [g] Pr 15:31

20 He who walks with the wise grows
wise,
but a companion of fools suffers
harm.[g]

13:21 [h] Ps 32:10

21 Misfortune pursues the sinner,
but prosperity is the reward of
the righteous.[h]

13:22 [i] Job 27:17; Ecc 2:26

22 A good man leaves an inheritance
for his children's children,
but a sinner's wealth is stored up
for the righteous.[i]

23 A poor man's field may produce
abundant food,
but injustice sweeps it away.

13:24 [j] Pr 19:18; 22:15; 23:13-14; 29:15, 17; Heb 12:7

24 He who spares the rod hates his
son,
but he who loves him is careful
to discipline him.[j]

13:25 [k] Ps 34:10; Pr 10:3

25 The righteous eat to their hearts'
content,
but the stomach of the wicked
goes hungry.[k]

14:1 [l] Pr 24:3

14 The wise woman builds her
house,[l]
but with her own hands the
foolish one tears hers down.

2 He whose walk is upright fears the
LORD,
but he whose ways are devious
despises him.

14:3 [m] Pr 12:6

3 A fool's talk brings a rod to his back,
but the lips of the wise protect
them.[m]

4 Where there are no oxen, the
manger is empty,
but from the strength of an ox
comes an abundant harvest.

14:5 [n] Pr 6:19; 12:17

5 A truthful witness does not deceive,
but a false witness pours out
lies.[n]

6 The mocker seeks wisdom and
finds none,
but knowledge comes easily to
the discerning.

7 Stay away from a foolish man,
for you will not find knowledge
on his lips.

14:8 [o] ver 24

8 The wisdom of the prudent is to
give thought to their ways,
but the folly of fools is
deception.[o]

9 Fools mock at making amends for
sin,
but goodwill is found among the
upright.

10 Each heart knows its own
bitterness,
and no one else can share its joy.

14:11 [p] Pr 3:33; 12:7

11 The house of the wicked will be
destroyed,
but the tent of the upright will
flourish.[p]

14:12 [q] Pr 12:15 [r] Pr 16:25

12 There is a way that seems right to a
man,[q]
but in the end it leads to death.[r]

14:13 [s] Ecc 2:2

13 Even in laughter[s] the heart may
ache,
and joy may end in grief.

14:14 [t] Pr 1:31 [u] Pr 12:14

14 The faithless will be fully repaid for
their ways,[t]
and the good man rewarded for
his.[u]

15 A simple man believes anything,
but a prudent man gives
thought to his steps.

[a] 15 Or *unfaithful does not endure*

16 A wise man fears the LORD and
shuns evil,[v]
but a fool is hotheaded and
reckless.

14:16 [v]Pr 22:3

17 A quick-tempered man does
foolish things,[w]
and a crafty man is hated.

14:17 [w]ver 29

18 The simple inherit folly,
but the prudent are crowned
with knowledge.

19 Evil men will bow down in the
presence of the good,
and the wicked at the gates of
the righteous.[x]

14:19 [x]Pr 11:29

20 The poor are shunned even by
their neighbors,
but the rich have many friends.[y]

14:20 [y]Pr 19:4,7

21 He who despises his neighbor sins,[z]
but blessed is he who is kind to
the needy.[a]

14:21 [z]Pr 11:12 [a]Ps 41:1; Pr 19:17

22 Do not those who plot evil go
astray?
But those who plan what is good
find[a] love and faithfulness.

23 All hard work brings a profit,
but mere talk leads only to
poverty.

24 The wealth of the wise is their
crown,
but the folly of fools yields folly.

25 A truthful witness saves lives,
but a false witness is deceitful.[b]

14:25 [b]ver 5

26 He who fears the LORD has a secure
fortress,[c]
and for his children it will be a
refuge.

14:26 [c]Pr 18:10; 19:23; Isa 33:6

27 The fear of the LORD is a fountain
of life,
turning a man from the snares
of death.[d]

14:27 [d]Pr 13:14

28 A large population is a king's glory,
but without subjects a prince is
ruined.

29 A patient man has great
understanding,
but a quick-tempered man
displays folly.[e]

14:29 [e]Ecc 7:8-9; Jas 1:19

30 A heart at peace gives life to the
body,
but envy rots the bones.[f]

14:30 [f]Pr 12:4

31 He who oppresses the poor shows
contempt for their Maker,[g]
but whoever is kind to the needy
honors God.

14:31 [g]Pr 17:5

32 When calamity comes, the wicked
are brought down,[h]
but even in death the righteous
have a refuge.[i]

14:32 [h]Pr 6:15 [i]Job 13:15; 2Ti 4:18

33 Wisdom reposes in the heart of the
discerning[j]
and even among fools she lets
herself be known.[b]

14:33 [j]Pr 2:6-10

34 Righteousness exalts a nation,[k]
but sin is a disgrace to any
people.

14:34 [k]Pr 11:11

35 A king delights in a wise servant,
but a shameful servant incurs
his wrath.[l]

14:35 [l]Mt 24:45-51; 25:14-30

15 A gentle answer turns away
wrath,[m]
but a harsh word stirs up anger.

15:1 [m]Pr 25:15

2 The tongue of the wise commends
knowledge,

[a] *22* Or *show* [b] *33* Hebrew; Septuagint and Syriac / *but in the heart of fools she is not known*

JESUS FOCUS

BLESSING FOR THE NATION

What is true on an individual level is equally true on a national level: "Righteousness exalts a nation, but sin is a disgrace to any people" (Proverbs 14:34). God promised to bless Israel corporately, as a nation, if his people chose to walk with him, but it is clear from this verse that *any* nation will be blessed when its citizens choose to follow God's ways. The early Christians wrestled with this concept. Although Proverbs had been written centuries earlier, the notion of God blessing other nations represented a radical deviation from their traditional belief system. When many Gentiles came to faith in Jesus Christ, Peter reminded the Jewish believers that "God . . . accepts men from every nation who fear him and do what is right" (Acts 10:34–35). Early Jewish Christians are to be credited for accepting Gentile believers as equal brothers and sisters in God's family (Ephesians 2:11–22; Colossians 1:25–27). It is largely because they were willing to reach out to *all* people that the early church was able to gain a foothold and the message of Jesus Christ could so quickly reach many nations.

but the mouth of the fool gushes
folly.[n]
[3] The eyes[o] of the LORD are
everywhere,[p]
keeping watch on the wicked
and the good.[q]
[4] The tongue that brings healing is a
tree of life,
but a deceitful tongue crushes
the spirit.

[5] A fool spurns his father's
discipline,
but whoever heeds correction
shows prudence.[r]
[6] The house of the righteous
contains great treasure,[s]
but the income of the wicked
brings them trouble.
[7] The lips of the wise spread
knowledge;
not so the hearts of fools.

[8] The LORD detests the sacrifice of
the wicked,[t]
but the prayer of the upright
pleases him.[u]
[9] The LORD detests the way of the
wicked
but he loves those who pursue
righteousness.[v]
[10] Stern discipline awaits him who
leaves the path;
he who hates correction will
die.[w]
[11] Death and Destruction[a] lie open
before the LORD[x]—
how much more the hearts of
men![y]
[12] A mocker resents correction;[z]
he will not consult the wise.
[13] A happy heart makes the face
cheerful,
but heartache crushes the
spirit.[a]
[14] The discerning heart seeks
knowledge,[b]
but the mouth of a fool feeds on
folly.
[15] All the days of the oppressed are
wretched,
but the cheerful heart has a
continual feast.[c]

[16] Better a little with the fear of the
LORD
than great wealth with turmoil.[d]
[17] Better a meal of vegetables where
there is love
than a fattened calf with hatred.[e]
[18] A hot-tempered man stirs up
dissension,[f]
but a patient man calms a
quarrel.[g]

[19] The way of the sluggard is blocked
with thorns,[h]
but the path of the upright is a
highway.
[20] A wise son brings joy to his father,[i]
but a foolish man despises his
mother.
[21] Folly delights a man who lacks
judgment,[j]
but a man of understanding
keeps a straight course.

[22] Plans fail for lack of counsel,
but with many advisers they
succeed.[k]
[23] A man finds joy in giving an apt
reply[l]—
and how good is a timely word![m]
[24] The path of life leads upward for
the wise
to keep him from going down to
the grave.[b]
[25] The LORD tears down the proud
man's house[n]
but he keeps the widow's
boundaries intact.[o]
[26] The LORD detests the thoughts of
the wicked,[p]
but those of the pure are
pleasing to him.
[27] A greedy man brings trouble to his
family,
but he who hates bribes will live.[q]
[28] The heart of the righteous weighs
its answers,[r]
but the mouth of the wicked
gushes evil.
[29] The LORD is far from the wicked
but he hears the prayer of the
righteous.[s]

[a] *11* Hebrew *Sheol and Abaddon* [b] *24* Hebrew *Sheol*

15:2 [n] Pr 12:23
15:3 [o] 2Ch 16:9 [p] Job 31:4; Heb 4:13 [q] Job 34:21; Jer 16:17
15:5 [r] Pr 13:1
15:6 [s] Pr 8:21
15:8 [t] Pr 21:27; Isa 1:11; Jer 6:20 [u] ver 29
15:9 [v] Pr 21:21; 1Ti 6:11
15:10 [w] Pr 1:31-32; 5:12
15:11 [x] Job 26:6; Ps 139:8 [y] 2Ch 6:30; Ps 44:21
15:12 [z] Am 5:10
15:13 [a] Pr 12:25; 17:22; 18:14
15:14 [b] Pr 18:15
15:15 [c] ver 13
15:16 [d] Ps 37:16-17; Pr 16:8; 1Ti 6:6
15:17 [e] Pr 17:1
15:18 [f] Pr 26:21 [g] Ge 13:8
15:19 [h] Pr 22:5
15:20 [i] Pr 10:1
15:21 [j] Pr 10:23
15:22 [k] Pr 11:14
15:23 [l] Pr 12:14 [m] Pr 25:11
15:25 [n] Pr 12:7 [o] Dt 19:14; Ps 68:5-6; Pr 23:10-11
15:26 [p] Pr 6:16
15:27 [q] Ex 23:8; Isa 33:15
15:28 [r] 1Pe 3:15
15:29 [s] Ps 145:18-19

[30] A cheerful look brings joy to the heart,
and good news gives health to the bones.

[31] He who listens to a life-giving rebuke
will be at home among the wise.[t]

15:31 [t]ver 5

[32] He who ignores discipline despises himself,[u]
but whoever heeds correction gains understanding.

15:32 [u]Pr 1:7

[33] The fear of the LORD[v] teaches a man wisdom,[a]
and humility comes before honor.[w]

15:33 [v]Pr 1:7 [w]Pr 18:12

16

To man belong the plans of the heart,
but from the LORD comes the reply of the tongue.[x]

16:1 [x]Pr 19:21

[2] All a man's ways seem innocent to him,
but motives are weighed by the LORD.[y]

16:2 [y]Pr 21:2

[3] Commit to the LORD whatever you do,
and your plans will succeed.[z]

16:3 [z]Ps 37:5-6; Pr 3:5-6

[4] The LORD works out everything for his own ends[a]—
even the wicked for a day of disaster.[b]

16:4 [a]Isa 43:7 [b]Ro 9:22

[5] The LORD detests all the proud of heart.[c]
Be sure of this: They will not go unpunished.[d]

16:5 [c]Pr 6:16 [d]Pr 11:20-21

[6] Through love and faithfulness sin is atoned for;
through the fear of the LORD a man avoids evil.[e]

16:6 [e]Pr 14:16

[7] When a man's ways are pleasing to the LORD,
he makes even his enemies live at peace with him.

[8] Better a little with righteousness
than much gain[f] with injustice.

16:8 [f]Ps 37:16

[9] In his heart a man plans his course,
but the LORD determines his steps.[g]

16:9 [g]Jer 10:23

[10] The lips of a king speak as an oracle,
and his mouth should not betray justice.

[11] Honest scales and balances are from the LORD;
all the weights in the bag are of his making.[h]

16:11 [h]Pr 11:1

[12] Kings detest wrongdoing,
for a throne is established through righteousness.[i]

16:12 [i]Pr 25:5

[13] Kings take pleasure in honest lips;
they value a man who speaks the truth.[j]

16:13 [j]Pr 14:35

[14] A king's wrath is a messenger of death,[k]
but a wise man will appease it.

16:14 [k]Pr 19:12

[15] When a king's face brightens, it means life;[l]
his favor is like a rain cloud in spring.

16:15 [l]Job 29:24

[16] How much better to get wisdom than gold,
to choose understanding rather than silver![m]

16:16 [m]Pr 8:10,19

[17] The highway of the upright avoids evil;
he who guards his way guards his life.

[18] Pride goes before destruction,
a haughty spirit before a fall.[n]

16:18 [n]Pr 11:2; 18:12

[19] Better to be lowly in spirit and among the oppressed
than to share plunder with the proud.

[20] Whoever gives heed to instruction prospers,
and blessed is he who trusts in the LORD.[o]

16:20 [o]Ps 2:12; 34:8; Pr 19:8; Jer 17:7

[21] The wise in heart are called discerning,
and pleasant words promote instruction.[b][p]

16:21 [p]ver 23

[22] Understanding is a fountain of life to those who have it,[q]
but folly brings punishment to fools.

16:22 [q]Pr 13:14

[23] A wise man's heart guides his mouth,
and his lips promote instruction.[c]

[24] Pleasant words are a honeycomb,

[a] 33 Or *Wisdom teaches the fear of the LORD*
[b] 21 Or *words make a man persuasive*
[c] 23 Or *mouth / and makes his lips persuasive*

No Alternate Route

We are all headed for eternity—but our eternal destinations will not all be the same, and there are two very different roads we can take. One leads us to eternal life with God (Matthew 25:34–36), while the other follows a detour away from him into an eternity separated from his love and goodness (Matthew 25:41–43). One of the greatest tragedies in this life is for a person to make an assumption of traveling on the right road only to discover that he or she is not only far from the intended destination but is in fact hopelessly lost.

The writer of Proverbs warns us that "there is a way that seems right to a man, but in the end it leads to death" (Proverbs 16:25). The people of Israel made this mistake, presupposing that because they were God's chosen people and the recipients of his law for right living, they were on the road to eternal life (Romans 9:1–8,30–33). But they forgot that the only way to live forever with God is by trusting him (Proverbs 3:5–6). An individual's family heritage or personal code of morality is not enough. Many philosophies may seem like thoroughfares directly to heaven, but there is no alternate route to the one pictured in the Bible—the way of faith in Jesus Christ, God's precious Son (John 14:6).

In his great Sermon on the Mount, where Jesus shared wonderful words of wisdom for moral living with his disciples, Jesus described two roads. The one, pictured as being entered through a wide gate, can be thought of as a smooth, six-lane turnpike with lovely landscaping and frequent rest stops; the other, pictured as being entered through a narrow gate, can be thought of as a steep, rocky two-track, overgrown with weeds, that twists and turns up a mountainside. At each of the gates a decision has to be made. The first gate boasts a set of shiny tollbooths with smiling attendants and an express lane for those fortunate enough to have exact change. The second must be entered through a simple wooden gate that must be opened by hand. One of the roads looks relaxing and inviting—it is the wide, open road of living our own way, according to our own set of rules. But this expressway will only lead us farther away from God with every mile marker. The other road appears narrow and in places barely passable, and Jesus is the only gate. That is the road, however, that winds its way into true life in the presence of God, blessed life that will never end (Matthew 7:13–14).

Jesus used a parable to warn his followers about the final destination of the easy road. A prosperous man, who ran out of space to store his wealth, said to himself, "You have plenty of good things laid up for many years. Take life easy; eat, drink and be merry" (Luke 12:19). Sound familiar? The world around us advises us to "take it easy" and "be happy." This is the way that seems right to us. "But God said to [the rich man], 'You fool! This very night your life will be demanded from you. Then who will get what you have prepared for yourself?' " (Luke12:20).

Self-Discovery: *How would you respond to someone who asserted that there are many different religions but that all lead in the end to the same God?*

GO TO DISCOVERY 164 ON PAGE 839

sweet to the soul and healing to
the bones.[r]

16:24 [r] Pr 24:13-14

[25] There is a way that seems right to a
man,[s]
but in the end it leads to death.[t]

16:25 [s] Pr 12:15 [t] Pr 14:12

[26] The laborer's appetite works for him;
his hunger drives him on.

[27] A scoundrel plots evil,
and his speech is like a
scorching fire.[u]

16:27 [u] Jas 3:6

[28] A perverse man stirs up
dissension,[v]
and a gossip separates close
friends.[w]

16:28 [v] Pr 15:18 [w] Pr 17:9

[29] A violent man entices his neighbor
and leads him down a path that
is not good.[x]

16:29 [x] Pr 1:10; 12:26

[30] He who winks with his eye is
plotting perversity;
he who purses his lips is bent on
evil.

[31] Gray hair is a crown of splendor;[y]
it is attained by a righteous life.

16:31 [y] Pr 20:29

[32] Better a patient man than a
warrior,
a man who controls his temper
than one who takes a city.

[33] The lot is cast into the lap,
but its every decision is from the
LORD.[z]

16:33 [z] Pr 18:18; 29:26

17

[1] Better a dry crust with peace
and quiet
than a house full of feasting,[*a*]
with strife.[a]

17:1 [a] Pr 15:16,17

[2] A wise servant will rule over a
disgraceful son,
and will share the inheritance as
one of the brothers.

[3] The crucible for silver and the
furnace for gold,[b]
but the LORD tests the heart.[c]

17:3 [b] Pr 27:21 [c] 1Ch 29:17; Ps 26:2; Jer 17:10

[4] A wicked man listens to evil lips;
a liar pays attention to a
malicious tongue.

[5] He who mocks the poor shows
contempt for their Maker;[d]
whoever gloats over disaster[e]
will not go unpunished.[f]

17:5 [d] Pr 14:31 [e] Job 31:29 [f] Ob 1:12

[6] Children's children[g] are a crown to
the aged,
and parents are the pride of
their children.

17:6 [g] Pr 13:22

[7] Arrogant[*b*] lips are unsuited to a
fool—
how much worse lying lips to a
ruler!

[8] A bribe is a charm to the one who
gives it;
wherever he turns, he succeeds.

[9] He who covers over an offense
promotes love,[h]
but whoever repeats the matter
separates close friends.[i]

17:9 [h] Pr 10:12 [i] Pr 16:28

[10] A rebuke impresses a man of
discernment
more than a hundred lashes a
fool.

[11] An evil man is bent only on
rebellion;
a merciless official will be sent
against him.

[12] Better to meet a bear robbed of her
cubs
than a fool in his folly.

[13] If a man pays back evil[j] for good,
evil will never leave his house.

17:13 [j] Ps 109:4-5; Jer 18:20

[14] Starting a quarrel is like breaching
a dam;
so drop the matter before a
dispute breaks out.[k]

17:14 [k] Pr 20:3

[15] Acquitting the guilty and
condemning the
innocent[l]—
the LORD detests them both.[m]

17:15 [l] Pr 18:5 [m] Ex 23:6-7; Isa 5:23

[16] Of what use is money in the hand
of a fool,
since he has no desire to get
wisdom?[n]

17:16 [n] Pr 23:23

[17] A friend loves at all times,
and a brother is born for
adversity.

[18] A man lacking in judgment strikes
hands in pledge
and puts up security for his
neighbor.[o]

17:18 [o] Pr 6:1-5; 11:15; 22:26-27

[19] He who loves a quarrel loves sin;
he who builds a high gate invites
destruction.

a *1* Hebrew *sacrifices* *b* *7* Or *Eloquent*

20 A man of perverse heart does not
prosper;
he whose tongue is deceitful
falls into trouble.

21 To have a fool for a son brings
grief;
there is no joy for the father of a
fool.[p]

17:21 [p] Pr 10:1

22 A cheerful heart is good medicine,
but a crushed spirit dries up the
bones.[q]

17:22 [q] Ps 22:15; Pr 15:13

23 A wicked man accepts a bribe[r] in
secret
to pervert the course of justice.

17:23 [r] Ex 23:8

24 A discerning man keeps wisdom in
view,
but a fool's eyes[s] wander to the
ends of the earth.

17:24 [s] Ecc 2:14

25 A foolish son brings grief to his
father
and bitterness to the one who
bore him.[t]

17:25 [t] Pr 10:1

26 It is not good to punish an
innocent man,[u]
or to flog officials for their
integrity.

17:26 [u] Pr 18:5

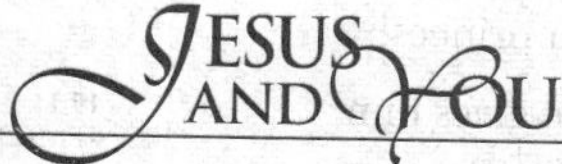

A BEST FRIEND

So called "fair-weather friends" come and go, depending on what's going on in our lives and their own, but a *true friend* is there for us through any and all circumstances (Proverbs 17:17). In fact, a good friend "sticks closer than a brother" (Proverbs 18:24). Many of the proverbs mention being a good friend or neighbor, and this concept was a deeply held value in Jewish life.

In the New Testament one expert in the law challenged Jesus: "And who is my neighbor?" (Luke 10:29). Apparently, he wanted exact parameters as to how far he was expected to extend his kindness. Jesus used a story to get his point across. In fact, he put a Samaritan—a person who represented a despised ethnic group (see John 4:9)—in the role of the man who was a true neighbor (Luke 10:29–37). As always, Jesus lived what he taught, and he was frequently criticized for being a friend of "sinners" (Matthew 11:19). But our Lord wasn't bothered by such accusations; then as now he stands ready to befriend *all* who need him.

27 A man of knowledge uses words
with restraint,
and a man of understanding is
even-tempered.[v]

17:27 [v] Pr 14:29; Jas 1:19

28 Even a fool is thought wise if he
keeps silent,
and discerning if he holds his
tongue.[w]

17:28 [w] Job 13:5

18 An unfriendly man pursues
selfish ends;
he defies all sound judgment.

2 A fool finds no pleasure in
understanding
but delights in airing his own
opinions.[x]

18:2 [x] Pr 12:23

3 When wickedness comes, so does
contempt,
and with shame comes disgrace.

4 The words of a man's mouth are
deep waters,
but the fountain of wisdom is a
bubbling brook.

5 It is not good to be partial to the
wicked[y]
or to deprive the innocent of
justice.[z]

18:5 [y] Lev 19:15; Pr 24:23-25; 28:21 [z] Ps 82:2; Pr 17:15

6 A fool's lips bring him strife,
and his mouth invites a beating.

7 A fool's mouth is his undoing,
and his lips are a snare[a] to his
soul.[b]

18:7 [a] Ps 140:9 [b] Ps 64:8; Pr 10:14; 12:13; 13:3; Ecc 10:12

8 The words of a gossip are like
choice morsels;
they go down to a man's inmost
parts.[c]

18:8 [c] Pr 26:22

9 One who is slack in his work
is brother to one who destroys.[d]

18:9 [d] Pr 28:24

10 The name of the LORD is a strong
tower;[e]
the righteous run to it and are
safe.

18:10 [e] 2Sa 22:3; Ps 61:3

11 The wealth of the rich is their
fortified city;[f]
they imagine it an unscalable
wall.

18:11 [f] Pr 10:15

12 Before his downfall a man's heart is
proud,
but humility comes before honor.[g]

18:12 [g] Pr 11:2; 15:33; 16:18

13 He who answers before listening—
that is his folly and his shame.[h]

18:13 [h] Pr 20:25; Jn 7:51

14 A man's spirit sustains him in
sickness,
but a crushed spirit who can
bear?[i]

18:14 [i] Pr 15:13; 17:22

15 The heart of the discerning
acquires knowledge;[j]
the ears of the wise seek it out.

18:15 [j] Pr 15:14

16 A gift[k] opens the way for the giver
and ushers him into the
presence of the great.

18:16 [k] Ge 32:20

17 The first to present his case seems
right,
till another comes forward and
questions him.

18 Casting the lot settles disputes[l]
and keeps strong opponents
apart.

18:18 [l] Pr 16:33

19 An offended brother is more
unyielding than a fortified
city,
and disputes are like the barred
gates of a citadel.

20 From the fruit of his mouth a man's
stomach is filled;
with the harvest from his lips he
is satisfied.[m]

18:20 [m] Pr 12:14

21 The tongue has the power of life
and death,
and those who love it will eat its
fruit.[n]

18:21 [n] Pr 13:2-3; Mt 12:37

22 He who finds a wife finds what is
good[o]
and receives favor from the
LORD.[p]

18:22 [o] Pr 12:4 [p] Pr 19:14; 31:10

23 A poor man pleads for mercy,
but a rich man answers harshly.

24 A man of many companions may
come to ruin,
but there is a friend who sticks
closer than a brother.[q]

18:24 [q] Pr 17:17; Jn 15:13-15

19

Better a poor man whose
walk is blameless
than a fool whose lips are
perverse.[r]

19:1 [r] Pr 28:6

2 It is not good to have zeal without
knowledge,
nor to be hasty and miss the
way.[s]

19:2 [s] Pr 29:20

3 A man's own folly ruins his life,
yet his heart rages against the
LORD.

4 Wealth brings many friends,
but a poor man's friend deserts
him.[t]

19:4 [t] Pr 14:20

5 A false witness[u] will not go
unpunished,
and he who pours out lies will
not go free.[v]

19:5 [u] Ex 23:1 [v] Dt 19:19; Pr 21:28

6 Many curry favor with a ruler,[w]
and everyone is the friend of a
man who gives gifts.[x]

19:6 [w] Pr 29:26 [x] Pr 17:8; 18:16

7 A poor man is shunned by all his
relatives—
how much more do his friends
avoid him!
Though he pursues them with
pleading,
they are nowhere to be found.[a][y]

19:7 [y] ver 4; Ps 38:11

8 He who gets wisdom loves his own
soul;
he who cherishes understanding
prospers.[z]

19:8 [z] Pr 16:20

9 A false witness will not go
unpunished,
and he who pours out lies will
perish.[a]

19:9 [a] ver 5

10 It is not fitting for a fool[b] to live in
luxury—
how much worse for a slave to
rule over princes![c]

19:10 [b] Pr 26:1 [c] Pr 30:21-23; Ecc 10:5-7

11 A man's wisdom gives him
patience;[d]
it is to his glory to overlook an
offense.

19:11 [d] Pr 16:32

12 A king's rage is like the roar of a
lion,
but his favor is like dew[e] on the
grass.[f]

19:12 [e] Ps 133:3 [f] Pr 16:14-15

13 A foolish son is his father's ruin,[g]
and a quarrelsome wife is like a
constant dripping.[h]

19:13 [g] Pr 10:1 [h] Pr 21:9

14 Houses and wealth are inherited
from parents,[i]
but a prudent wife is from the
LORD.[j]

19:14 [i] 2Co 12:14 [j] Pr 18:22

15 Laziness brings on deep sleep,
and the shiftless man goes
hungry.[k]

19:15 [k] Pr 6:9; 10:4

16 He who obeys instructions guards
his life,

[a] 7 The meaning of the Hebrew for this sentence is uncertain.

DISCOVERY 164

REFLECTING GOD'S FATHER HEART

There are many reasons poverty exists in our world, and there are no easy answers to why so many of the world's people have so little of the necessary resources. Whether or not we understand the complex issues involved, we realize that God's paternal heart goes out to the disadvantaged. As his people we are to reflect the same heart of compassion; each of us has a personal responsibility to reach out to the needy among us. When we care for the hurting, we are in fact giving something back to God, and he will reward us for our kindness. Jesus took the analogy one step further, reminding us that when we are kind to people in need we are in fact showing love to him: "Whatever you did for one of the least of these brothers of mine, you did for me" (Matthew 25:40).

Jesus began his talk to his disciples on the Mount of Olives (Matthew 24) with a discussion about the end of the world and the signs of his imminent return. He then reminded his hearers to live their lives in such a way that they would always be prepared for his second coming. Some people, he said in essence, can look the part of a devoted follower of Jesus Christ, but their motivation isn't coming from the heart. When our service is prompted by a heartfelt desire to alleviate the pain of others, we don't expect anything back or keep a detailed account of our service record in order to receive credit at a later time (Matthew 25:35–36).

In caring for other people we demonstrate to God that we are concerned about the same issues that he is. There are many troubled and destitute people in our world who are desperately crying out for our love. Hungry people crave food, and thirsty people need something to drink. Many lack a warm and safe place to lay their heads at night or adequate clothing to protect from the bone-chilling winds of winter. When people are sick, they need someone to care for them, and when they're in prison they yearn to know that someone cares enough to visit. Sometimes the needs are purely physical, but just as often the deep-seated cravings stem from excruciating hurts and unmet needs buried deep within the human psyche.

God doesn't expect us to fix every human problem or meet every human need. He simply wants us to reflect his concern for the one individual or family he may choose to point out to us today. When we ignore such people, we disregard what matters to Jesus and miss out on the blessings God has in store for us. Proverbs 19:17 tells us that "he who is kind to the poor lends to the LORD, and he will reward him for what he has done."

Self-Discovery: *If Jesus were to return today, would you be ready? What "unfinished business" would you want to take care of first? As you go about your day, be ready for the Lord to reveal to you that person or persons who most need your caring touch.*

GO TO DISCOVERY 165 ON PAGE 841

but he who is contemptuous of
his ways will die.[l]

[17] He who is kind to the poor lends to
the LORD,
and he will reward him for what
he has done.[m]

[18] Discipline your son, for in that
there is hope;
do not be a willing party to his
death.[n]

[19] A hot-tempered man must pay the
penalty;
if you rescue him, you will have
to do it again.

[20] Listen to advice and accept
instruction,[o]
and in the end you will be wise.[p]

[21] Many are the plans in a man's heart,
but it is the LORD's purpose that
prevails.[q]

[22] What a man desires is unfailing
love[a];
better to be poor than a liar.

[23] The fear of the LORD leads to life:
Then one rests content,
untouched by trouble.[r]

[24] The sluggard buries his hand in the
dish;
he will not even bring it back to
his mouth![s]

[25] Flog a mocker, and the simple will
learn prudence;
rebuke a discerning man, and he
will gain knowledge.[t]

[26] He who robs his father and drives
out his mother[u]
is a son who brings shame and
disgrace.

[27] Stop listening to instruction, my
son,
and you will stray from the
words of knowledge.

[28] A corrupt witness mocks at justice,
and the mouth of the wicked
gulps down evil.[v]

[29] Penalties are prepared for mockers,
and beatings for the backs of
fools.[w]

20 Wine is a mocker and beer a
brawler;
whoever is led astray by them is
not wise.[x]

[2] A king's wrath is like the roar of a
lion;[y]
he who angers him forfeits his
life.[z]

[3] It is to a man's honor to avoid
strife,
but every fool is quick to
quarrel.[a]

[4] A sluggard does not plow in
season;
so at harvest time he looks but
finds nothing.

[5] The purposes of a man's heart are
deep waters,
but a man of understanding
draws them out.

[6] Many a man claims to have
unfailing love,
but a faithful man who can find?[b]

[7] The righteous man leads a
blameless life;
blessed are his children after
him.[c]

[8] When a king sits on his throne to
judge,
he winnows out all evil with his
eyes.[d]

[9] Who can say, "I have kept my heart
pure;
I am clean and without sin"?[e]

[10] Differing weights and differing
measures—
the LORD detests them both.[f]

[11] Even a child is known by his
actions,
by whether his conduct is pure[g]
and right.

[12] Ears that hear and eyes that see—
the LORD has made them both.[h]

[13] Do not love sleep or you will grow
poor;[i]
stay awake and you will have
food to spare.

[14] "It's no good, it's no good!" says the
buyer;
then off he goes and boasts
about his purchase.

[a] 22 Or *A man's greed is his shame*

9:16 [l] Pr 16:17; Lk 10:28
19:17 [m] Mt 10:42; 2Co 9:6-8
19:18 [n] Pr 13:24; 23:13-14
19:20 [o] Pr 4:1 [p] Pr 12:15
19:21 [q] Ps 33:11; Pr 16:9; Isa 14:24,27
19:23 [r] Ps 25:13; Pr 12:21; 1Ti 4:8
19:24 [s] Pr 26:15
19:25 [t] Pr 9:9; 21:11
19:26 [u] Pr 28:24
19:28 [v] Job 15:16
19:29 [w] Pr 26:3
20:1 [x] Pr 31:4
20:2 [y] Pr 19:12 [z] Pr 8:36
20:3 [a] Pr 17:14
20:6 [b] Ps 12:1
20:7 [c] Ps 37:25-26; 112:2
20:8 [d] ver 26; Pr 25:4-5
20:9 [e] 1Ki 8:46; Ecc 7:20; 1Jn 1:8
20:10 [f] ver 23; Pr 11:1
20:11 [g] Mt 7:16
20:12 [h] Ps 94:9
20:13 [i] Pr 6:11; 19:15

Our Eternal Inheritance

The book of Proverbs, although divided into 31 separate chapters, for the most part consists of pithy and often unrelated nuggets of wisdom, many of them "one-liners" that hit their target and then retreat, to be succeeded by an entirely new thought. Proverbs 20:21 is one such verse: "An inheritance quickly gained at the beginning will not be blessed at the end." In our contemporary idiom, we might say something like "easy come, easy go." The writer does not elaborate, and there is probably no need to do so.

The verse calls to mind the class of people in our own time commonly referred to as "new money." Such people are often stereotyped as flashy, extravagant and wasteful, as well as lacking in the social graces that stem from generations of "breeding." All too frequently such people throw away, give away or gamble away their fortunes, or they mortgage their lives to the hilt to make certain they are perceived as "keeping up with the Joneses." Obviously, this description does not apply to everyone who has gained an inheritance by means of a windfall or climbed the ladder of success in a "rags to riches" story. But we all recognize the pattern.

Jesus talked about the opposite kind of inheritance in his Sermon on the Mount: "Blessed are the meek, for they will inherit the earth" (Matthew 5:5). Our Lord was referring to the humble, the unassuming, those who go through life with a servant attitude, without regard for their net worth in a financial sense. Such people have a secure inheritance, so secure that it is held in safekeeping for them. Peter expressed it this way: Praise be to the God and Father of our Lord Jesus Christ! In his great mercy he has given us new birth into a living hope through the resurrection of Jesus Christ from the dead, and into an inheritance that can never perish, spoil or fade—kept in heaven for you" (1 Peter 1:3–4).

In the "topsy-turvy" logic of our Lord, so utterly incomprehensible to many in our world, "many who are first will be last, and many who are last will be first" (Matthew 19:30). Jesus preceded these words in verse 29 of the same chapter with another statement about inheritance: "Everyone who has left houses or brothers or sisters or father or mother or children or fields for my sake will receive a hundred times as much and will inherit eternal life." Storing up treasures on earth leaves us vulnerable not only to moth, rust and thieves (Matthew 6:19), but also to stock market fluctuations, bankruptcy due to dwindling market share, or loss of position or even loss of everything through death (see Mark 10:17–23; Luke 12:13–21; Luke 16:19–31).

Once again, the concept is familiar to us, and we have an idiom to cover it: "You can't take it with you." While this saying is certainly true, we can interpret it and live it out in one of two ways. Either we can enjoy "the good life," flaunting our wealth and wasting our financial and health reserves, or we can follow Jesus' example and live the *real* good life, serving God and our neighbor, practicing good stewardship of the resources God has so graciously provided and caring for our bodies as temples of God's Holy Spirit (1 Corinthians 6:19).

Self-Discovery: *What is your definition of the good life? If you could select the lifestyle of your choice, what would it look like? What role would Jesus play? Would he sit in the place of honor in your heart?*

GO TO DISCOVERY 166 ON PAGE 847

[15]Gold there is, and rubies in
abundance,
but lips that speak knowledge
are a rare jewel.

[16]Take the garment of one who puts
up security for a stranger;
hold it in pledge[j] if he does it for
a wayward woman.[k]

20:16 [j]Ex 22:26 [k]Pr 27:13

[17]Food gained by fraud tastes sweet
to a man,[l]
but he ends up with a mouth full
of gravel.

20:17 [l]Pr 9:17

[18]Make plans by seeking advice;
if you wage war, obtain
guidance.[m]

20:18 [m]Pr 11:14; 24:6

[19]A gossip betrays a confidence;[n]
so avoid a man who talks too
much.

20:19 [n]Pr 11:13

[20]If a man curses his father or
mother,[o]
his lamp will be snuffed out in
pitch darkness.[p]

20:20 [o]Pr 30:11 [p]Ex 21:17; Job 18:5

[21]An inheritance quickly gained at
the beginning
will not be blessed at the end.

[22]Do not say, "I'll pay you back for
this wrong!"[q]
Wait for the LORD, and he will
deliver you.[r]

20:22 [q]Pr 24:29 [r]Ro 12:19

[23]The LORD detests differing weights,
and dishonest scales do not
please him.[s]

20:23 [s]ver 10

[24]A man's steps are directed by the
LORD.
How then can anyone
understand his own way?[t]

20:24 [t]Jer 10:23

[25]It is a trap for a man to dedicate
something rashly
and only later to consider his
vows.[u]

20:25 [u]Ecc 5:2,4-5

[26]A wise king winnows out the
wicked;
he drives the threshing wheel
over them.[v]

20:26 [v]ver 8

[27]The lamp of the LORD searches the
spirit of a man[a];
it searches out his inmost being.

[28]Love and faithfulness keep a king
safe;
through love his throne is made
secure.[w]

20:28 [w]Pr 29:14

[29]The glory of young men is their
strength,
gray hair the splendor of the old.[x]

20:29 [x]Pr 16:31

[30]Blows and wounds cleanse[y] away
evil,
and beatings purge the inmost
being.

20:30 [y]Pr 22:15

21

The king's heart is in the
hand of the LORD;
he directs it like a watercourse
wherever he pleases.

[2]All a man's ways seem right to him,
but the LORD weighs the heart.[z]

21:2 [z]Pr 16:2; 24:12; Lk 16:15

[3]To do what is right and just
is more acceptable to the LORD
than sacrifice.[a]

21:3 [a]1Sa 15:22; Pr 15:8; Isa 1:11; Hos 6:6; Mic 6:6-8

[4]Haughty eyes[b] and a proud heart,
the lamp of the wicked, are sin!

21:4 [b]Pr 6:17

[5]The plans of the diligent lead to
profit[c]
as surely as haste leads to poverty.

21:5 [c]Pr 10:4; 28:22

[6]A fortune made by a lying tongue
is a fleeting vapor and a deadly
snare.[b][d]

21:6 [d]2Pe 2:3

[7]The violence of the wicked will
drag them away,
for they refuse to do what is right.

[8]The way of the guilty is devious,[e]
but the conduct of the innocent
is upright.

21:8 [e]Pr 2:15

[9]Better to live on a corner of the roof
than share a house with a
quarrelsome wife.[f]

21:9 [f]Pr 25:24

[10]The wicked man craves evil;
his neighbor gets no mercy from
him.

[11]When a mocker is punished, the
simple gain wisdom;
when a wise man is instructed,
he gets knowledge.[g]

21:11 [g]Pr 19:25

[12]The Righteous One[c] takes note of
the house of the wicked
and brings the wicked to ruin.[h]

21:12 [h]Pr 14:11

[13]If a man shuts his ears to the cry of
the poor,
he too will cry out and not be
answered.[i]

21:13 [i]Mt 18:30-34; Jas 2:13

[a] 27 Or *The spirit of man is the LORD's lamp*
[b] 6 Some Hebrew manuscripts, Septuagint and Vulgate; most Hebrew manuscripts *vapor for those who seek death* [c] 12 Or *The righteous man*

14 A gift given in secret soothes anger,
and a bribe concealed in the
cloak pacifies great wrath.[j]

21:14 j Pr 18:16; 19:6

15 When justice is done, it brings joy
to the righteous
but terror to evildoers.[k]

21:15 k Pr 10:29

16 A man who strays from the path of
understanding
comes to rest in the company of
the dead.[l]

21:16 l Ps 49:14

17 He who loves pleasure will become
poor;
whoever loves wine and oil will
never be rich.[m]

21:17 m Pr 23:20-21, 29-35

18 The wicked become a ransom[n] for
the righteous,
and the unfaithful for the
upright.

21:18 n Pr 11:8; Isa 43:3

19 Better to live in a desert
than with a quarrelsome and ill-
tempered wife.[o]

21:19 o ver 9

20 In the house of the wise are stores
of choice food and oil,
but a foolish man devours all he
has.

21 He who pursues righteousness and
love
finds life, prosperity[a] and honor.[p]

21:21 p Mt 5:6

22 A wise man attacks the city of the
mighty[q]
and pulls down the stronghold
in which they trust.

21:22 q Ecc 9:15-16

23 He who guards his mouth[r] and his
tongue
keeps himself from calamity.[s]

21:23 r Jas 3:2 s Pr 12:13; 13:3

24 The proud and arrogant[t] man—
"Mocker" is his name;
he behaves with overweening
pride.

21:24 t Ps 1:1; Pr 1:22; Isa 16:6; Jer 48:29

25 The sluggard's craving will be the
death of him,[u]
because his hands refuse to
work.

21:25 u Pr 13:4

26 All day long he craves for more,
but the righteous give without
sparing.[v]

21:26 v Ps 37:26; Mt 5:42; Eph 4:28

27 The sacrifice of the wicked is
detestable[w]—
how much more so when
brought with evil intent![x]

21:27 w Isa 66:3; Jer 6:20; Am 5:22 x Pr 15:8

28 A false witness will perish,[y]
and whoever listens to him will
be destroyed forever.[b]

21:28 y Pr 19:5

29 A wicked man puts up a bold front,
but an upright man gives
thought to his ways.

30 There is no wisdom,[z] no insight, no
plan
that can succeed against the
LORD.[a]

21:30 z Jer 9:23 a Isa 8:10; Ac 5:39

31 The horse is made ready for the
day of battle,
but victory rests with the LORD.[b]

21:31 b Ps 3:8; 33:12-19; Isa 31:1

22

1 A good name is more
desirable than great riches;
to be esteemed is better than
silver or gold.[c]

22:1 c Ecc 7:1

2 Rich and poor have this in
common:
The LORD is the Maker of them
all.[d]

22:2 d Job 31:15

3 A prudent man sees danger and
takes refuge,[e]
but the simple keep going and
suffer for it.[f]

22:3 e Pr 14:16 f Pr 27:12

4 Humility and the fear of the LORD
bring wealth and honor and life.

5 In the paths of the wicked lie
thorns and snares,[g]
but he who guards his soul stays
far from them.

22:5 g Pr 15:19

6 Train[c] a child in the way he should
go,[h]
and when he is old he will not
turn from it.

22:6 h Eph 6:4

7 The rich rule over the poor,
and the borrower is servant to
the lender.

8 He who sows wickedness reaps
trouble,[i]
and the rod of his fury will be
destroyed.[j]

22:8 i Job 4:8 j Ps 125:3

9 A generous man will himself be
blessed,[k]
for he shares his food with the
poor.[l]

22:9 k 2Co 9:6 l Pr 19:17

10 Drive out the mocker, and out goes
strife;
quarrels and insults are ended.[m]

22:10 m Pr 18:6; 26:20

[a] 21 Or *righteousness* [b] 28 Or / *but the words of an obedient man will live on* [c] 6 Or *Start*

[11] He who loves a pure heart and
whose speech is gracious
will have the king for his friend.[n]
[12] The eyes of the LORD keep watch
over knowledge,
but he frustrates the words of
the unfaithful.

[13] The sluggard says, "There is a lion
outside!"[o]
or, "I will be murdered in the
streets!"

[14] The mouth of an adulteress is a
deep pit;[p]
he who is under the LORD's wrath
will fall into it.[q]

[15] Folly is bound up in the heart of a
child,
but the rod of discipline will
drive it far from him.[r]

[16] He who oppresses the poor to
increase his wealth
and he who gives gifts to the
rich—both come to poverty.

Sayings of the Wise

[17] Pay attention and listen to the
sayings of the wise;[s]
apply your heart to what I teach,
[18] for it is pleasing when you keep
them in your heart
and have all of them ready on
your lips.
[19] So that your trust may be in the
LORD,
I teach you today, even you.
[20] Have I not written thirty[a] sayings
for you,
sayings of counsel and
knowledge,
[21] teaching you true and reliable
words,[t]
so that you can give sound
answers
to him who sent you?

[22] Do not exploit the poor[u] because
they are poor
and do not crush the needy in
court,[v]
[23] for the LORD will take up their
case[w]
and will plunder those who
plunder them.[x]

[24] Do not make friends with a hot-
tempered man,
do not associate with one easily
angered,
[25] or you may learn his ways
and get yourself ensnared.[y]

[26] Do not be a man who strikes hands
in pledge[z]
or puts up security for debts;
[27] if you lack the means to pay,
your very bed will be snatched
from under you.[a]

[28] Do not move an ancient boundary
stone[b]
set up by your forefathers.

[29] Do you see a man skilled in his
work?
He will serve[c] before kings;
he will not serve before obscure
men.

23 When you sit to dine with a
ruler,
note well what[b] is before you,
[2] and put a knife to your throat
if you are given to gluttony.
[3] Do not crave his delicacies,[d]
for that food is deceptive.

[4] Do not wear yourself out to get
rich;
have the wisdom to show
restraint.
[5] Cast but a glance at riches, and
they are gone,
for they will surely sprout wings
and fly off to the sky like an
eagle.[e]

[6] Do not eat the food of a stingy man,
do not crave his delicacies;[f]
[7] for he is the kind of man
who is always thinking about
the cost.[c]
"Eat and drink," he says to you,
but his heart is not with you.
[8] You will vomit up the little you
have eaten
and will have wasted your
compliments.

[9] Do not speak to a fool,
for he will scorn the wisdom of
your words.[g]

[10] Do not move an ancient boundary
stone[h]

[a] 20 Or *not formerly written;* or *not written excellent* [b] 1 Or *who* [c] 7 Or *for as he thinks within himself, / so he is;* or *for as he puts on a feast, / so he is*

22:11 [n] Pr 16:13; Mt 5:8
22:13 [o] Pr 26:13
22:14 [p] Pr 2:16; 5:3-5; 7:5; 23:27 [q] Ecc 7:26
22:15 [r] Pr 13:24; 23:14
22:17 [s] Pr 5:1
22:21 [t] Lk 1:3-4; 1Pe 3:15
22:22 [u] Zec 7:10 [v] Ex 23:6; Mal 3:5
22:23 [w] Ps 12:5 [x] 1Sa 25:39; Pr 23:10-11
22:25 [y] 1Co 15:33
22:26 [z] Pr 11:15
22:27 [a] Pr 17:18
22:28 [b] Dt 19:14; Pr 23:10
22:29 [c] Ge 41:46
23:3 [d] ver 6-8
23:5 [e] Pr 27:24
23:6 [f] Ps 141:4
23:9 [g] Pr; 1:7; 9:7; Mt 7:6
23:10 [h] Dt 19:14; Pr 22:28

or encroach on the fields of the
fatherless,
11 for their Defender[i] is strong;
he will take up their case against
you.[j]

23:11 [i]Job 19:25 [j]Pr 22:22-23

12 Apply your heart to instruction
and your ears to words of
knowledge.

13 Do not withhold discipline from a
child;
if you punish him with the rod,
he will not die.
14 Punish him with the rod
and save his soul from death.[a]

15 My son, if your heart is wise,
then my heart will be glad;
16 my inmost being will rejoice
when your lips speak what is
right.[k]

23:16 [k]ver 24; Pr 27:11

17 Do not let your heart envy[l] sinners,
but always be zealous for the
fear of the LORD.

23:17 [l]Ps 37:1; Pr 28:14

18 There is surely a future hope for
you,
and your hope will not be cut
off.[m]

23:18 [m]Ps 9:18; Pr 24:14,19-20

19 Listen, my son, and be wise,
and keep your heart on the right
path.
20 Do not join those who drink too
much wine[n]
or gorge themselves on meat,
21 for drunkards and gluttons
become poor,[o]
and drowsiness clothes them in
rags.

23:20 [n]Isa 5:11,22; Ro 13:13; Eph 5:18

23:21 [o]Pr 21:17

22 Listen to your father, who gave you
life,
and do not despise your mother
when she is old.[p]
23 Buy the truth and do not sell it;
get wisdom, discipline and
understanding.[q]
24 The father of a righteous man has
great joy;
he who has a wise son delights
in him.[r]
25 May your father and mother be
glad;
may she who gave you birth
rejoice!

23:22 [p]Lev 19:32; Pr 1:8; 30:17; Eph 6:1-2

23:23 [q]Pr 4:7

23:24 [r]ver 15-16; Pr 10:1; 15:20

26 My son,[s] give me your heart
and let your eyes keep to my
ways,[t]
27 for a prostitute is a deep pit[u]
and a wayward wife is a narrow
well.
28 Like a bandit she lies in wait,[v]
and multiplies the unfaithful
among men.

23:26 [s]Pr 3:1; 5:1-6 [t]Ps 18:21; Pr 4:4

23:27 [u]Pr 22:14

23:28 [v]Pr 7:11-12; Ecc 7:26

29 Who has woe? Who has sorrow?
Who has strife? Who has
complaints?
Who has needless bruises? Who
has bloodshot eyes?
30 Those who linger over wine,[w]
who go to sample bowls of
mixed wine.
31 Do not gaze at wine when it is red,
when it sparkles in the cup,
when it goes down smoothly!
32 In the end it bites like a snake
and poisons like a viper.
33 Your eyes will see strange sights
and your mind imagine
confusing things.
34 You will be like one sleeping on the
high seas,
lying on top of the rigging.
35 "They hit me," you will say, "but I'm
not hurt!
They beat me, but I don't feel it!
When will I wake up
so I can find another drink?"

23:30 [w]Ps 75:8; Isa 5:11; Eph 5:18

24 Do not envy[x] wicked men,
do not desire their company;
2 for their hearts plot violence,
and their lips talk about making
trouble.[y]

24:1 [x]Ps 37:1; 73:3; Pr 3:31-32; 23:17-18

24:2 [y]Ps 10:7

3 By wisdom a house is built,[z]
and through understanding it is
established;
4 through knowledge its rooms are
filled
with rare and beautiful treasures.[a]

24:3 [z]Pr 14:1

24:4 [a]Pr 8:21

5 A wise man has great power,
and a man of knowledge
increases strength;
6 for waging war you need guidance,
and for victory many advisers.[b]

24:6 [b]Pr 11:14; 20:18; Lk 14:31

7 Wisdom is too high for a fool;
in the assembly at the gate he
has nothing to say.

8 He who plots evil
will be known as a schemer.
9 The schemes of folly are sin,
and men detest a mocker.

a 14 Hebrew *Sheol*

24:10 [c]Job 4:5; Jer 51:46; Heb 12:3

[10] If you falter in times of trouble,
how small is your strength![c]

[11] Rescue those being led away to
death;
hold back those staggering
toward slaughter.[d]

24:11 [d]Ps 82:4; Isa 58:6-7

[12] If you say, "But we knew nothing
about this,"
does not he who weighs[e] the
heart perceive it?
Does not he who guards your life
know it?
Will he not repay each person
according to what he has
done?[f]

24:12 [e]Pr 21:2 [f]Job 34:11; Ps 62:12; Ro 2:6*

[13] Eat honey, my son, for it is good;
honey from the comb is sweet to
your taste.
[14] Know also that wisdom is sweet to
your soul;
if you find it, there is a future
hope for you,
and your hope will not be cut
off.[g h]

24:14 [g]Ps 119:103; Pr 16:24 [h]Pr 23:18

[15] Do not lie in wait like an outlaw
against a righteous man's
house,
do not raid his dwelling place;
[16] for though a righteous man falls
seven times, he rises again,
but the wicked are brought
down by calamity.[i]

24:16 [i]Job 5:19; Ps 34:19; Mic 7:8

[17] Do not gloat[j] when your enemy
falls;
when he stumbles, do not let
your heart rejoice,[k]
[18] or the LORD will see and
disapprove
and turn his wrath away from
him.

24:17 [j]Ob 1:12 [k]Job 31:29

[19] Do not fret[l] because of evil men
or be envious of the wicked,
[20] for the evil man has no future
hope,
and the lamp of the wicked will
be snuffed out.[m]

24:19 [l]Ps 37:1

24:20 [m]Job 18:5; Pr 13:9; 23:17-18

[21] Fear the LORD and the king,[n] my
son,
and do not join with the
rebellious,
[22] for those two will send sudden
destruction upon them,
and who knows what calamities
they can bring?

24:21 [n]Ro 13:1-5; 1Pe 2:17

Further Sayings of the Wise

[23] These also are sayings of the wise:[o]

To show partiality[p] in judging is
not good:[q]
[24] Whoever says to the guilty, "You
are innocent"[r]—
peoples will curse him and
nations denounce him.
[25] But it will go well with those who
convict the guilty,
and rich blessing will come upon
them.

24:23 [o]Pr 1:6 [p]Lev 19:15 [q]Pr 28:21

24:24 [r]Pr 17:15

[26] An honest answer
is like a kiss on the lips.

[27] Finish your outdoor work
and get your fields ready;
after that, build your house.

[28] Do not testify against your
neighbor without cause,[s]
or use your lips to deceive.
[29] Do not say, "I'll do to him as he has
done to me;
I'll pay that man back for what
he did."[t]

24:28 [s]Ps 7:4; Pr 25:18; Eph 4:25

24:29 [t]Pr 20:22; Mt 5:38-41; Ro 12:17

[30] I went past the field of the
sluggard,[u]
past the vineyard of the man
who lacks judgment;
[31] thorns had come up everywhere,
the ground was covered with
weeds,
and the stone wall was in ruins.
[32] I applied my heart to what I
observed
and learned a lesson from what I
saw:
[33] A little sleep, a little slumber,
a little folding of the hands to
rest[v]—
[34] and poverty will come on you like a
bandit
and scarcity like an armed
man.[a w]

24:30 [u]Pr 6:6-11; 26:13-16

24:33 [v]Pr 6:10

24:34 [w]Pr 10:4; Ecc 10:18

More Proverbs of Solomon

25 These are more proverbs[x] of
Solomon, copied by the men of
Hezekiah king of Judah:[y]

25:1 [x]1Ki 4:32 [y]Pr 1:1

[2] It is the glory of God to conceal a
matter;
to search out a matter is the
glory of kings.[z]

25:2 [z]Pr 16:10-15

[a] 34 Or *like a vagrant / and scarcity like a beggar*

Dealing With Our Enemies

We as human beings tend to set lots of conditions for the ways in which we relate to other people. We buy into the world's values when it tells us that we should assert ourselves, not allow others to walk all over us, look out for Number One and stand up for our rights: "Whatever they do to you, do it back to them—an eye for an eye and a tooth for a tooth." Even though the basic injunction behind this philosophy comes directly from the Bible (Exodus 21:22–25), it was never intended as a license for revenge. God's law pointed out that there are consequences for injuring someone else, but the heart of that law has always been compassion. Just two chapters later the Israelites were instructed to return a lost article to an enemy if they were to come upon it (Exodus 23:4).

The lifestyle to which God calls us involves offering kindness to everyone—even an enemy. The writer of Proverbs tells us that when we treat our enemies with compassion or courtesy, the act is like pouring hot coals on their heads (Proverbs 25:22). This simile points out that our very act of kindness is itself a form of punishment for people who have harbored a hateful or bitter attitude toward us, because it pricks their consciences and makes them uncomfortable with themselves. That thoughtful deed might also be exactly the impetus that person needs in order to consider a new way of living. And God will reward us for acting in a manner that pleases him. While we may never observe an attitude change in that spiteful or vindictive individual, we can find comfort in the knowledge that we are pleasing our God.

Jesus realized that it is in keeping with human nature for us to love our friends and despise our enemies. He encouraged us instead to love the very people with whom we are experiencing conflict and even to dialogue with God the Father about our relationship with them: "You have heard that it was said, 'Love your neighbor and hate your enemy.' But I tell you: Love your enemies and pray for those who persecute you . . . If you love those who love you, what reward will you get? . . . And if you greet only your brothers, what are you doing more than others? Do not even pagans do that? Be perfect, therefore, as your heavenly Father is perfect" (Matthew 5:43–44,46–48).

We are surrounded by philosophical, cultural and political "enemies," whether these enemies are people or ideologies. Instead of resenting them, asserting our rights and fighting back, we need to ask God for guidance as to how he wants us to deal with them. The apostle Paul even said that the act of loving our enemies causes good to overcome evil in the world (Romans 12:19–21).

We must leave judgment to God; our role is simply to reflect his character by living the way he wants us to live, the way of Christlike tenderness and love.

Self-Discovery: *How do you respond to conflict? Do you tend to be reactive or confrontational? Do you avoid discord altogether? Do you respond with an open attitude that conveys grace and love in spite of your opinion with respect to the issue at hand? How would Jesus respond if he were in your place?*

GO TO DISCOVERY 167 ON PAGE 850

3 As the heavens are high and the
earth is deep,
so the hearts of kings are
unsearchable.

4 Remove the dross from the silver,
and out comes material for*[a]* the
silversmith;
5 remove the wicked from the king's
presence,[a]
and his throne will be
established[b] through
righteousness.[c]

25:5 [a] Pr 20:8 [b] 2Sa 7:13 [c] Pr 16:12; 29:14

6 Do not exalt yourself in the king's
presence,
and do not claim a place among
great men;
7 it is better for him to say to you,
"Come up here,"[d]
than for him to humiliate you
before a nobleman.

25:7 [d] Lk 14:7-10

What you have seen with your eyes
8 do not bring*[b]* hastily to court,
for what will you do in the end
if your neighbor puts you to
shame?[e]

25:8 [e] Mt 5:25-26

9 If you argue your case with a
neighbor,
do not betray another man's
confidence,
10 or he who hears it may shame you
and you will never lose your bad
reputation.

11 A word aptly spoken
is like apples of gold in settings
of silver.[f]

25:11 [f] ver 12; Pr 15:23

12 Like an earring of gold or an
ornament of fine gold
is a wise man's rebuke to a
listening ear.[g]

25:12 [g] ver 11; Ps 141:5; Pr 13:18; 15:31

13 Like the coolness of snow at
harvest time
is a trustworthy messenger to
those who send him;
he refreshes the spirit of his
masters.[h]

25:13 [h] Pr 10:26; 13:17

14 Like clouds and wind without rain
is a man who boasts of gifts he
does not give.

15 Through patience a ruler can be
persuaded,[i]
and a gentle tongue can break a
bone.[j]

25:15 [i] Ecc 10:4 [j] Pr 15:1

16 If you find honey, eat just enough—
too much of it, and you will
vomit.[k]

25:16 [k] ver 27

17 Seldom set foot in your neighbor's
house—
too much of you, and he will
hate you.

18 Like a club or a sword or a sharp
arrow
is the man who gives false
testimony against his
neighbor.[l]

25:18 [l] Ps 57:4; Pr 12:18

19 Like a bad tooth or a lame foot
is reliance on the unfaithful in
times of trouble.

20 Like one who takes away a
garment on a cold day,
or like vinegar poured on soda,
is one who sings songs to a
heavy heart.

21 If your enemy is hungry, give him
food to eat;
if he is thirsty, give him water to
drink.
22 In doing this, you will heap
burning coals[m] on his head,
and the LORD will reward you.[n]

25:22 [m] Ps 18:8 [n] 2Sa 16:12; 2Ch 28:15; Mt 5:44; Ro 12:20*

23 As a north wind brings rain,
so a sly tongue brings angry
looks.

24 Better to live on a corner of the roof
than share a house with a
quarrelsome wife.[o]

25:24 [o] Pr 21:9

25 Like cold water to a weary soul
is good news from a distant
land.[p]

25:25 [p] Pr 15:30

26 Like a muddied spring or a
polluted well
is a righteous man who gives
way to the wicked.

27 It is not good to eat too much
honey,[q]
nor is it honorable to seek one's
own honor.[r]

25:27 [q] ver 16 [r] Pr 27:2; Mt 23:12

28 Like a city whose walls are broken
down
is a man who lacks self-control.

26

Like snow in summer or
rain[s] in harvest,
honor is not fitting for a fool.[t]

26:1 [s] 1Sa 12:17 [t] ver 8; Pr 19:10

a 4 Or *comes a vessel from* *b* 7,8 Or *nobleman / on whom you had set your eyes. / 8Do not go*

2 Like a fluttering sparrow or a
darting swallow,
an undeserved curse does not
come to rest.[u]

26:2 [u] Nu 23:8; Dt 23:5

3 A whip for the horse, a halter for
the donkey,[v]
and a rod for the backs of fools![w]

26:3 [v] Ps 32:9 [w] Pr 10:13

4 Do not answer a fool according to
his folly,
or you will be like him yourself.[x]

26:4 [x] ver 5; Isa 36:21

5 Answer a fool according to his folly,
or he will be wise in his own
eyes.[y]

26:5 [y] ver 4; Pr 3:7

6 Like cutting off one's feet or
drinking violence
is the sending of a message by
the hand of a fool.[z]

26:6 [z] Pr 10:26

7 Like a lame man's legs that hang
limp
is a proverb in the mouth of a
fool.[a]

26:7 [a] ver 9

8 Like tying a stone in a sling
is the giving of honor to a fool.[b]

26:8 [b] ver 1

9 Like a thornbush in a drunkard's
hand
is a proverb in the mouth of a
fool.[c]

26:9 [c] ver 7

10 Like an archer who wounds at
random
is he who hires a fool or any
passer-by.

11 As a dog returns to its vomit,[d]
so a fool repeats his folly.[e]

26:11 [d] 2Pe 2:22* [e] Ex 8:15; Ps 85:8

12 Do you see a man wise in his own
eyes?[f]
There is more hope for a fool
than for him.[g]

26:12 [f] Pr 3:7 [g] Pr 29:20

13 The sluggard says,[h] "There is a lion
in the road,
a fierce lion roaming the streets!"[i]

26:13 [h] Pr 6:6-11; 24:30-34 [i] Pr 22:13

14 As a door turns on its hinges,
so a sluggard turns on his bed.[j]

26:14 [j] Pr 6:9

15 The sluggard buries his hand in the
dish;
he is too lazy to bring it back to
his mouth.[k]

26:15 [k] Pr 19:24

16 The sluggard is wiser in his own
eyes
than seven men who answer
discreetly.

17 Like one who seizes a dog by the
ears
is a passer-by who meddles in a
quarrel not his own.

18 Like a madman shooting
firebrands or deadly arrows
19 is a man who deceives his neighbor
and says, "I was only joking!"

20 Without wood a fire goes out;
without gossip a quarrel dies
down.[l]

26:20 [l] Pr 22:10

21 As charcoal to embers and as wood
to fire,
so is a quarrelsome man for
kindling strife.[m]

26:21 [m] Pr 14:17; 15:18

22 The words of a gossip are like
choice morsels;
they go down to a man's inmost
parts.[n]

26:22 [n] Pr 18:8

23 Like a coating of glaze[a] over
earthenware
are fervent lips with an evil
heart.

24 A malicious man disguises himself
with his lips,[o]
but in his heart he harbors
deceit.[p]

26:24 [o] Ps 31:18 [p] Ps 41:6; Pr 10:18; 12:20

25 Though his speech is charming,[q]
do not believe him,
for seven abominations fill his
heart.[r]

26:25 [q] Ps 28:3 [r] Jer 9:4-8

26 His malice may be concealed by
deception,
but his wickedness will be
exposed in the assembly.

27 If a man digs a pit,[s] he will fall into
it;[t]
if a man rolls a stone, it will roll
back on him.[u]

26:27 [s] Ps 7:15 [t] Est 6:13 [u] Est 2:23; 7:9; Ps 35:8; 141:10; Pr 28:10; 29:6; Isa 50:11

28 A lying tongue hates those it hurts,
and a flattering mouth[v] works
ruin.

26:28 [v] Ps 12:3; Pr 29:5

27

Do not boast[w] about
tomorrow,
for you do not know what a day
may bring forth.[x]

27:1 [w] 1Ki 20:11 [x] Mt 6:34; Lk 12:19-20; Jas 4:13-16

2 Let another praise you, and not
your own mouth;
someone else, and not your own
lips.[y]

27:2 [y] Pr 25:27

[a] 23 With a different word division of the Hebrew; Masoretic Text *of silver dross*

GLORY TO . . . ME?

Most of us have a longing deep within us to be noticed. Our world tells us that if we don't distinguish ourselves in some way, no one will pay attention to us. We believe that we will never be appreciated as we deserve unless we do something to propel ourselves into the limelight. But when we do enjoy recognition, we tend to bask in the attention at the expense of anyone else who may have helped us along the way. Part of our human need to be in control impels us to make certain we are placed on a pedestal before anyone else can climb the platform first.

Jesus faced life with a completely different approach. First of all, he didn't worry about the future and counseled his disciples not to be anxious either (see Matthew 6:25–34). Still today he wants us as his people to focus our attention on his priorities rather than our own, to relax in the knowledge that our destiny rests with him and with his perfect plan, not in our own achievements and self-aggrandizement.

It may be appropriate at one point or another for each of us to receive public recognition, but the timing is totally in the Lord's hands. When two of his disciples were bickering about which of them would be more prominent in heaven, our Lord reminded them that human pride and competition mean nothing to God. Jesus used the example of a small child to drive home his point: "He who is least among you all—he is the greatest" (Luke 9:48).

John the Baptist showed us how to handle human praise (see Discovery #187, page 939). The Jewish leaders came to ask him whether or not he was the Messiah, and he replied without equivocation, "I am not the Christ" (John 1:20). They continued to press him for his true identity. Finally "John replied in the words of Isaiah the prophet, 'I am the voice of one calling in the desert, "make straight the way for the Lord"'" (John 1:23). Then John pointed them to Jesus: "He is the one who comes after me, the thongs of whose sandals I am not worthy to untie" (John 1:27). And later John stated of Jesus, "He must become greater, I must become less" (John 3:30).

Though he literally had every reason in the universe to do so, Jesus never boasted about himself. Rather, he came to earth as a servant, a living example of God's kingdom values. Someday everyone on earth will acknowledge Jesus for who he is, and his people will proclaim to the world why he is worthy of infinite and unparalleled honor (Philippians 2:7–11).

The book of Proverbs warns us that when we place ourselves on a pedestal of pride, the fall to the ground will be a long way down and the landing brutal and destructive (Proverbs 16:18). It is much less painful to allow God to be in control of our future, including the amount of attention and appreciation we will enjoy (Proverbs 27:1–2). When we approach God with humility, offering him all the glory no matter what our station in life, he promises to lift us up (Matthew 23:12; James 4:10; 1 Peter 5:6).

Self-Discovery: *As you look in the mirror today, say to yourself, "I am not the One. Jesus is. 'He must become greater, I must become less'" (John 3:30).*

GO TO DISCOVERY 168 ON PAGE 859

27:3 [z] Job 6:3

3 Stone is heavy and sand[z] a burden,
but provocation by a fool is heavier than both.

4 Anger is cruel and fury overwhelming,
27:4 [a] Nu 5:14
but who can stand before jealousy?[a]

5 Better is open rebuke
than hidden love.

6 Wounds from a friend can be trusted,
27:6 [b] Ps 141:5; Pr 28:23
but an enemy multiplies kisses.[b]

7 He who is full loathes honey,
but to the hungry even what is bitter tastes sweet.

27:8 [c] Isa 16:2
8 Like a bird that strays from its nest[c]
is a man who strays from his home.

27:9 [d] Est 2:12; Ps 45:8
9 Perfume[d] and incense bring joy to the heart,
and the pleasantness of one's friend springs from his earnest counsel.

10 Do not forsake your friend and the friend of your father,
27:10 [e] Pr 17:17; 18:24
and do not go to your brother's house when disaster[e] strikes you—
better a neighbor nearby than a brother far away.

27:11 [f] Pr 10:1; 23:15-16 [g] Ge 24:60
11 Be wise, my son, and bring joy to my heart;[f]
then I can answer anyone who treats me with contempt.[g]

12 The prudent see danger and take refuge,
27:12 [h] Pr 22:3
but the simple keep going and suffer for it.[h]

13 Take the garment of one who puts up security for a stranger;
27:13 [i] Pr 20:16
hold it in pledge if he does it for a wayward woman.[i]

14 If a man loudly blesses his neighbor early in the morning,
it will be taken as a curse.

27:15 [j] Est 1:18; Pr 19:13
15 A quarrelsome wife is like
a constant dripping[j] on a rainy day;
16 restraining her is like restraining the wind
or grasping oil with the hand.

17 As iron sharpens iron,
so one man sharpens another.

18 He who tends a fig tree will eat its fruit,[k] 27:18 [k] 1Co 9:7 [l] Lk 19:12-27
and he who looks after his master will be honored.[l]

19 As water reflects a face,
so a man's heart reflects the man.

20 Death and Destruction[a] are never satisfied,[m] 27:20 [m] Pr 30:15-16; Hab 2:5 [n] Ecc 1:8; 6:7
and neither are the eyes of man.[n]

21 The crucible for silver and the furnace for gold,[o] 27:21 [o] Pr 17:3
but man is tested by the praise he receives.

22 Though you grind a fool in a mortar,
grinding him like grain with a pestle,
you will not remove his folly from him.

23 Be sure you know the condition of your flocks,[p] 27:23 [p] Pr 12:10
give careful attention to your herds;
24 for riches do not endure forever,[q] 27:24 [q] Pr 23:5
and a crown is not secure for all generations.
25 When the hay is removed and new growth appears
and the grass from the hills is gathered in,
26 the lambs will provide you with clothing,
and the goats with the price of a field.
27 You will have plenty of goats' milk
to feed you and your family
and to nourish your servant girls.

28

1 The wicked man flees[r] 28:1 [r] 2Ki 7:7 [s] Lev 26:17; Ps 53:5 [t] Ps 138:3
though no one pursues,[s]
but the righteous are as bold as a lion.[t]

2 When a country is rebellious, it has many rulers,
but a man of understanding and knowledge maintains order.

[a] 20 Hebrew *Sheol and Abaddon*

3 A ruler[a] who oppresses the poor
is like a driving rain that leaves
no crops.

4 Those who forsake the law praise
the wicked,
but those who keep the law
resist them.

5 Evil men do not understand
justice,
but those who seek the LORD
understand it fully.

6 Better a poor man whose walk is
blameless
than a rich man whose ways are
perverse.[u]

28:6 [u] Pr 19:1

7 He who keeps the law is a
discerning son,
but a companion of gluttons
disgraces his father.[v]

28:7 [v] Pr 23:19-21

8 He who increases his wealth by
exorbitant interest[w]
amasses it for another,[x] who will
be kind to the poor.[y]

28:8 [w] Ex 18:21 [x] Job 27:17; Pr 13:22 [y] Ps 112:9; Pr 14:31; Lk 14:12-14

9 If anyone turns a deaf ear to the
law,
even his prayers are detestable.[z]

28:9 [z] Ps 66:18; 109:7; Pr 15:8; Isa 1:13

10 He who leads the upright along an
evil path
will fall into his own trap,[a]
but the blameless will receive a
good inheritance.

28:10 [a] Pr 26:27

11 A rich man may be wise in his own
eyes,
but a poor man who has
discernment sees through
him.

12 When the righteous triumph, there
is great elation;[b]
but when the wicked rise to
power, men go into hiding.[c]

28:12 [b] 2Ki 11:20 [c] Pr 11:10; 29:2

13 He who conceals his sins[d] does not
prosper,
but whoever confesses and
renounces them finds
mercy.[e]

28:13 [d] Job 31:33 [e] Ps 32:1-5; 1Jn 1:9

14 Blessed is the man who always
fears the LORD,
but he who hardens his heart
falls into trouble.

15 Like a roaring lion or a charging
bear
is a wicked man ruling over a
helpless people.

16 A tyrannical ruler lacks judgment,
but he who hates ill-gotten gain
will enjoy a long life.

17 A man tormented by the guilt of
murder
will be a fugitive[f] till death;
let no one support him.

28:17 [f] Ge 9:6

18 He whose walk is blameless is kept
safe,
but he whose ways are perverse
will suddenly fall.[g]

28:18 [g] Pr 10:9

19 He who works his land will have
abundant food,
but the one who chases fantasies
will have his fill of poverty.[h]

28:19 [h] Pr 12:11

20 A faithful man will be richly
blessed,
but one eager to get rich will not
go unpunished.[i]

28:20 [i] ver 22; Pr 10:6; 1Ti 6:9

21 To show partiality is not good[j]—
yet a man will do wrong for a
piece of bread.[k]

28:21 [j] Pr 18:5 [k] Eze 13:19

22 A stingy man is eager to get rich
and is unaware that poverty
awaits him.[l]

28:22 [l] ver 20; Pr 23:6

23 He who rebukes a man will in the
end gain more favor
than he who has a flattering
tongue.[m]

28:23 [m] Pr 27:5-6

24 He who robs his father or mother[n]
and says, "It's not wrong"—
he is partner to him who
destroys.[o]

28:24 [n] Pr 19:26 [o] Pr 18:9

25 A greedy man stirs up dissension,
but he who trusts in the LORD[p]
will prosper.

28:25 [p] Pr 29:25

26 He who trusts in himself is a fool,[q]
but he who walks in wisdom is
kept safe.

28:26 [q] Ps 4:5; Pr 3:5

27 He who gives to the poor will lack
nothing,[r]
but he who closes his eyes to
them receives many curses.

28:27 [r] Dt 15:7; 24:19; Pr 19:17; 22:9

28 When the wicked rise to power,
people go into hiding;[s]
but when the wicked perish, the
righteous thrive.

28:28 [s] ver 12

[a] 3 Or *A poor man*

29 A man who remains stiff-necked after many rebukes
will suddenly be destroyed—
without remedy.[t]

29:1 [t] 2Ch 36:16; Pr 6:15

2 When the righteous thrive, the people rejoice;[u]
when the wicked rule, the people groan.[v]

29:2 [u] Est 8:15 [v] Pr 28:12

3 A man who loves wisdom brings joy to his father,[w]
but a companion of prostitutes squanders his wealth.[x]

29:3 [w] Pr 10:1 [x] Pr 5:8-10; Lk 15:11-32

4 By justice a king gives a country stability,[y]
but one who is greedy for bribes tears it down.

29:4 [y] Pr 8:15-16

5 Whoever flatters his neighbor
is spreading a net for his feet.

6 An evil man is snared by his own sin,[z]
but a righteous one can sing and be glad.

29:6 [z] Ecc 9:12

7 The righteous care about justice for the poor,[a]
but the wicked have no such concern.

29:7 [a] Job 29:16; Ps 41:1; Pr 31:8-9

8 Mockers stir up a city,
but wise men turn away anger.[b]

29:8 [b] Pr 11:11; 16:14

9 If a wise man goes to court with a fool,
the fool rages and scoffs, and there is no peace.

10 Bloodthirsty men hate a man of integrity
and seek to kill the upright.[c]

29:10 [c] 1Jn 3:12

11 A fool gives full vent to his anger,
but a wise man keeps himself under control.[d]

29:11 [d] Pr 12:16; 19:11

12 If a ruler listens to lies,
all his officials become wicked.

13 The poor man and the oppressor have this in common:
The LORD gives sight to the eyes of both.[e]

29:13 [e] Pr 22:2; Mt 5:45

14 If a king judges the poor with fairness,
his throne will always be secure.[f]

29:14 [f] Ps 72:1-5; Pr 16:12

15 The rod of correction imparts wisdom,
but a child left to himself
disgraces his mother.[g]

29:15 [g] Pr 10:1; 13:24; 17:21,25

16 When the wicked thrive, so does sin,
but the righteous will see their downfall.[h]

29:16 [h] Ps 37:35-36; 58:10; 91:8; 92:11

17 Discipline your son, and he will give you peace;
he will bring delight to your soul.[i]

29:17 [i] ver 15; Pr 10:1

18 Where there is no revelation, the people cast off restraint;
but blessed is he who keeps the law.[j]

29:18 [j] Ps 1:1-2; 119:1-2; Jn 13:17

19 A servant cannot be corrected by mere words;
though he understands, he will not respond.

20 Do you see a man who speaks in haste?
There is more hope for a fool than for him.[k]

29:20 [k] Pr 26:12; Jas 1:19

21 If a man pampers his servant from youth,
he will bring grief[a] in the end.

22 An angry man stirs up dissension,
and a hot-tempered one commits many sins.[l]

29:22 [l] Pr 14:17; 15:18; 26:21

23 A man's pride brings him low,
but a man of lowly spirit gains honor.[m]

29:23 [m] Pr 11:2; 15:33; 16:18; Isa 66:2; Mt 23:12

24 The accomplice of a thief is his own enemy;
he is put under oath and dare not testify.[n]

29:24 [n] Lev 5:1

25 Fear of man will prove to be a snare,
but whoever trusts in the LORD[o] is kept safe.

29:25 [o] Pr 28:25

26 Many seek an audience with a ruler,[p]
but it is from the LORD that man gets justice.

29:26 [p] Pr 19:6

27 The righteous detest the dishonest;
the wicked detest the upright.[q]

29:27 [q] ver 10

Sayings of Agur

30 The sayings of Agur son of Jakeh—an oracle[b]:

[a] *21* The meaning of the Hebrew for this word is uncertain. [b] *1* Or *Jakeh of Massa*

This man declared to Ithiel,
to Ithiel and to Ucal:[a]

2 "I am the most ignorant of men;
I do not have a man's
understanding.
3 I have not learned wisdom,
nor have I knowledge of the Holy
One.[r]
4 Who has gone up[s] to heaven and
come down?
Who has gathered up the wind
in the hollow[t] of his hands?
Who has wrapped up the waters[u]
in his cloak?[v]
Who has established all the ends
of the earth?
What is his name,[w] and the name
of his son?
Tell me if you know!

5 "Every word of God is flawless;[x]
he is a shield[y] to those who take
refuge in him.
6 Do not add[z] to his words,
or he will rebuke you and prove
you a liar.

7 "Two things I ask of you, O LORD;
do not refuse me before I die:
8 Keep falsehood and lies far from
me;
give me neither poverty nor
riches,
but give me only my daily
bread.[a]
9 Otherwise, I may have too much
and disown[b] you
and say, 'Who is the LORD?'[c]
Or I may become poor and steal,
and so dishonor the name of my
God.[d]

10 "Do not slander a servant to his
master,
or he will curse you, and you will
pay for it.

11 "There are those who curse their
fathers
and do not bless their mothers;[e]
12 those who are pure in their own
eyes[f]
and yet are not cleansed of their
filth;[g]
13 those whose eyes are ever so
haughty,[h]
whose glances are so disdainful;
14 those whose teeth[i] are swords
and whose jaws are set with
knives[j]
to devour[k] the poor[l] from the
earth,
the needy from among
mankind.[m]

15 "The leech has two daughters.
'Give! Give!' they cry.

"There are three things that are
never satisfied,[n]
four that never say, 'Enough!':
16 the grave,[b][o] the barren womb,
land, which is never satisfied
with water,
and fire, which never says,
'Enough!'

17 "The eye that mocks[p] a father,
that scorns obedience to a
mother,
will be pecked out by the ravens of
the valley,
will be eaten by the vultures.[q]

18 "There are three things that are too
amazing for me,
four that I do not understand:
19 the way of an eagle in the sky,
the way of a snake on a rock,
the way of a ship on the high seas,
and the way of a man with a
maiden.

20 "This is the way of an adulteress:
She eats and wipes her mouth
and says, 'I've done nothing
wrong.'[r]

21 "Under three things the earth
trembles,
under four it cannot bear up:
22 a servant who becomes king,[s]
a fool who is full of food,
23 an unloved woman who is married,
and a maidservant who
displaces her mistress.

24 "Four things on earth are small,
yet they are extremely wise:
25 Ants are creatures of little
strength,
yet they store up their food in
the summer;[t]
26 coneys[c][u] are creatures of little
power,

a 1 Masoretic Text; with a different word division of the Hebrew *declared, "I am weary, O God; / I am weary, O God, and faint.* *b 16* Hebrew *Sheol* *c 26* That is, the hyrax or rock badger

30:3 [r] Pr 9:10
30:4 [s] Ps 24:1-2; Jn 3:13; Eph 4:7-10 [t] Ps 104:3; Isa 40:12 [u] Job 26:8; 38:8-9 [v] Ge 1:2 [w] Rev 19:12
30:5 [x] Ps 12:6; 18:30 [y] Ge 15:1; Ps 84:11
30:6 [z] Dt 4:2; 12:32; Rev 22:18
30:8 [a] Mt 6:11
30:9 [b] Jos 24:27; Isa 1:4; 59:13 [c] Dt 6:12; 8:10-14; Hos 13:6 [d] Dt 8:12
30:11 [e] Pr 20:20
30:12 [f] Pr 16:2; Lk 18:11 [g] Jer 2:23,35
30:13 [h] 2Sa 22:28; Job 41:34; Ps 131:1; Pr 6:17
30:14 [i] Job 4:11; 29:17; Ps 3:7
30:14 [j] Ps 57:4 [k] Job 24:9; Ps 14:4 [l] Am 8:4; Mic 2:2 [m] Job 19:22
30:15 [n] Pr 27:20
30:16 [o] Pr 27:20; Isa 5:14; 14:9, 11; Hab 2:5
30:17 [p] Dt 21:18-21; Pr 23:22 [q] Job 15:23
30:20 [r] Pr 5:6
30:22 [s] Pr 19:10; 29:2
30:25 [t] Pr 6:6-8
30:26 [u] Ps 104:18

yet they make their home in the
crags;
30:27 [v]Ex 10:4 [27] locusts[v] have no king,
yet they advance together in
ranks;
[28] a lizard can be caught with the
hand,
yet it is found in kings' palaces.

[29] "There are three things that are
stately in their stride,
four that move with stately
bearing:
[30] a lion, mighty among beasts,
who retreats before nothing;
[31] a strutting rooster, a he-goat,
and a king with his army around
him.[a]

[32] "If you have played the fool and
exalted yourself,
or if you have planned evil,
30:32 [w]Job 21:5; 29:9 clap your hand over your
mouth![w]
[33] For as churning the milk produces
butter,
and as twisting the nose
produces blood,
so stirring up anger produces
strife."

Sayings of King Lemuel

31:1 [x]Pr 22:17 31 The sayings[x] of King Lemuel—
an oracle[b] his mother taught
him:

31:2 [y]Jdg 11:30; Isa 49:15 [2] "O my son, O son of my womb,
O son of my vows,[c y]
31:3 [z]Dt 17:17; 1Ki 11:3; Ne 13:26; Pr 5:1-14 [3] do not spend your strength on
women,
your vigor on those who ruin
kings.[z]

31:4 [a]Pr 20:1; Ecc 10:16-17; Isa 5:22 [4] "It is not for kings, O Lemuel—
not for kings to drink wine,[a]
not for rulers to crave beer,
31:5 [b]1Ki 16:9 [c]Pr 16:12; Hos 4:11 [5] lest they drink[b] and forget what
the law decrees,[c]
and deprive all the oppressed of
their rights.
[6] Give beer to those who are
perishing,
31:6 [d]Ge 14:18 wine[d] to those who are in
anguish;
31:7 [e]Est 1:10 [7] let them drink[e] and forget their
poverty
and remember their misery no
more.

[8] "Speak[f] up for those who cannot 31:8 [f]1Sa 19:4; Job 29:12-17
speak for themselves,
for the rights of all who are
destitute.
[9] Speak up and judge fairly; 31:9 [g]Lev 19:15; Dt 1:16; Pr 24:23; 29:7; Isa 1:17; Jer 22:16
defend the rights of the poor
and needy."[g]

Epilogue: The Wife of Noble Character

[10d] A wife of noble character[h] who can 31:10 [h]Ru 3:11; Pr 12:4; 18:22 [i]Pr 8:35; 19:14
find?[i]
She is worth far more than
rubies.
[11] Her husband[j] has full confidence 31:11 [j]Ge 2:18 [k]Pr 12:4
in her
and lacks nothing of value.[k]
[12] She brings him good, not harm,
all the days of her life.
[13] She selects wool and flax
and works with eager hands.[l] 31:13 [l]1Ti 2:9-10
[14] She is like the merchant ships,
bringing her food from afar.
[15] She gets up while it is still dark;
she provides food for her family
and portions for her servant
girls.

[a] 31 Or *king secure against revolt* [b] 1 Or *of Lemuel king of Massa, which* [c] 2 Or / *the answer to my prayers* [d] 10 Verses 10–31 are an acrostic, each verse beginning with a successive letter of the Hebrew alphabet.

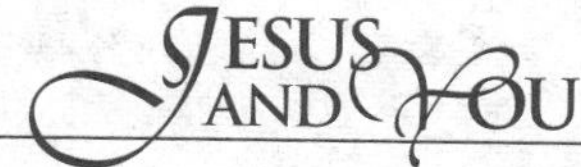

SPEAK UP!

God expects his people to reflect who he is (2 Corinthians 3:18), and so he expects us to be a voice for people who cannot speak up for themselves (Proverbs 31:8–9). Every person who walks with God has a responsibility to advocate for those who are unjustly persecuted—no matter who they are. Espousing the cause of the voiceless ones, those in our society who suffer injustice, whether in the political arena or on an individual basis, does not always help Christians to win a popularity contest. But Jesus offers a word of encouragement for his brothers and sisters who are tirelessly and often thanklessly working behind-the-scenes to bring the light of Jesus into their dark world: "Blessed are you when people insult you, persecute you and falsely say all kinds of evil against you because of me. Rejoice and be glad, because great is your reward in heaven" (Matthew 5:11–12; see also verses 13–16).

[16] She considers a field and buys it;
out of her earnings she plants a vineyard.
[17] She sets about her work vigorously;
her arms are strong for her tasks.
[18] She sees that her trading is profitable,
and her lamp does not go out at night.
[19] In her hand she holds the distaff
and grasps the spindle with her fingers.
[20] She opens her arms to the poor
and extends her hands to the needy.[m]
[21] When it snows, she has no fear for her household;
for all of them are clothed in scarlet.
[22] She makes coverings for her bed;
she is clothed in fine linen and purple.
[23] Her husband is respected at the city gate,
where he takes his seat among the elders[n] of the land.
[24] She makes linen garments and sells them,
and supplies the merchants with sashes.
[25] She is clothed with strength and dignity;
she can laugh at the days to come.
[26] She speaks with wisdom,
and faithful instruction is on her tongue.[o]
[27] She watches over the affairs of her household
and does not eat the bread of idleness.
[28] Her children arise and call her blessed;
her husband also, and he praises her:
[29] "Many women do noble things,
but you surpass them all."
[30] Charm is deceptive, and beauty is fleeting;
but a woman who fears the LORD is to be praised.
[31] Give her the reward she has earned,
and let her works bring her praise[p] at the city gate.

31:20 [m] Dt 15:11; Eph 4:28; Heb 13:16
31:23 [n] Ex 3:16; Ru 4:1,11; Pr 12:4
31:26 [o] Pr 10:31
31:31 [p] Pr 11:16

Is everything in this world meaningless? (Ecclesiastes 2:3–11)

♦ *The Teacher explored many different avenues in an attempt to find significance in life. When we read his words we must constantly keep in mind that he was speaking of things apart from God—things under the sun. As a whole the Bible teaches that meaning in life can only be found in pursuing the things of Jesus (see Philippians 3:7–11).*

Are the wise no better than fools? (Ecclesiastes 2:13–16)

♦ *The Teacher acknowledged that wisdom has its advantages over folly. But he was looking for more: life's ultimate meaning. The Teacher believed that death rendered everything in life futile. He could not foresee that Jesus would triumph over death so that we might live forever.*

Jesus in Ecclesiastes In the book of Ecclesiastes the Teacher took a long, hard look at life and recorded his findings based on his life experiences. This book of ancient wisdom focuses on the meaning and purpose of life. After passing judgment on a number of possible life directions as meaningless, dead-ended rabbit trails, the Teacher came to this conclusion: "Fear God and keep his commandments, for this is the whole duty of man" (Ecclesiastes 12:13).

The Teacher in Ecclesiastes foreshadows Jesus, who was frequently addressed as Teacher during his years on earth (see, for example, Matthew 8:19). In fact, Jesus himself *is* the meaning and purpose of our lives. While the Teacher had only the Shepherd of Israel, the one true God (Genesis 49:4; Psalms 23:1; 80:1) in mind when he wrote that the wise draw wisdom and guidance from "the Shepherd," we who live in the era after Jesus' birth know that Jesus, God's one and only Son, is "the good shepherd [who] lays down his life for the sheep" (John 10:11).

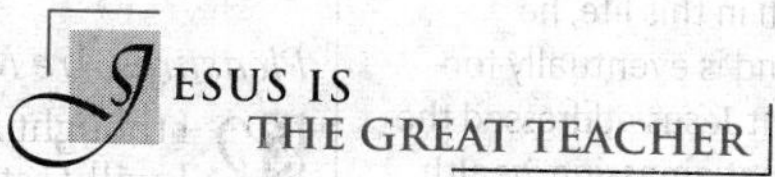
JESUS IS
THE GREAT TEACHER

Everything Is Meaningless

1:1 **1** The words of the Teacher,[a][a] son of
[a] ver 12; David, king in Jerusalem:[b]
Ecc 7:27; 12:10
[b] Pr 1:1

2 "Meaningless! Meaningless!"
says the Teacher.
1:2 "Utterly meaningless!
[c] Ps 39:5-6; 62:9; Everything is meaningless."[c]
144:4; Ecc 12:8;
Ro 8:20-21 3 What does man gain from all his
labor
1:3
[d] Ecc 2:11,22; at which he toils under the sun?[d]
3:9; 5:15-16 4 Generations come and generations
1:4 go,
[e] Ps 104:5; but the earth remains forever.[e]
119:90
5 The sun rises and the sun sets,
and hurries back to where it
1:5
[f] Ps 19:5-6 rises.[f]
6 The wind blows to the south
and turns to the north;
round and round it goes,
ever returning on its course.
7 All streams flow into the sea,
yet the sea is never full.
To the place the streams come
from,
1:7 there they return again.[g]
[g] Job 36:28 8 All things are wearisome,
more than one can say.
The eye never has enough of
1:8
[h] Pr 27:20 seeing,[h]
nor the ear its fill of hearing.
9 What has been will be again,
what has been done will be done 1:9
again;[i] [i] Ecc 2:12; 3:15
there is nothing new under the
sun.
10 Is there anything of which one can
say,
"Look! This is something new"?
It was here already, long ago;
it was here before our time.
11 There is no remembrance of men
of old,
and even those who are yet to
come
will not be remembered 1:11
by those who follow.[j] [j] Ecc 2:16

Wisdom Is Meaningless

12 I, the Teacher,[k] was king over Israel 1:12
in Jerusalem. 13 I devoted myself to study [k] ver 1
and to explore by wisdom all that is
done under heaven. What a heavy bur- 1:13
den God has laid on men![l] 14 I have seen [l] Ge 3:17;
all the things that are done under the Ecc 3:10
sun; all of them are meaningless, a chas- 1:14
ing after the wind.[m] [m] Ecc 2:11,17

15 What is twisted cannot be 1:15
straightened;[n] [n] Ecc 7:13
what is lacking cannot be
counted.

16 I thought to myself, "Look, I have
grown and increased in wisdom more
than anyone who has ruled over 1:16
Jerusalem before me;[o] I have experi- [o] 1Ki 3:12; 4:30;
enced much of wisdom and knowledge." Ecc 2:9
17 Then I applied myself to the under- 1:17
standing of wisdom,[p] and also of mad- [p] Ecc 7:23
ness and folly,[q] but I learned that this, [q] Ecc 2:3,12;
too, is a chasing after the wind. 7:25

18 For with much wisdom comes
much sorrow;
the more knowledge, the more 1:18
grief.[r] [r] Ecc 2:23; 12:12

Pleasures Are Meaningless

2 I thought in my heart, "Come now, 2:1
I will test you with pleasure[s] to [s] Ecc 7:4; 8:15;
find out what is good." But that also Lk 12:19
proved to be meaningless. 2 "Laughter,"[t] 2:2
I said, "is foolish. And what does plea- [t] Pr 14:13;
sure accomplish?" 3 I tried cheering my- Ecc 7:6
self with wine,[u] and embracing folly[v]— 2:3
my mind still guiding me with wisdom. [u] ver 24-25;
I wanted to see what was worthwhile for Ecc 3:12-13
[v] Ecc 1:17

[a] 1 Or *leader of the assembly*; also in verses 2 and 12

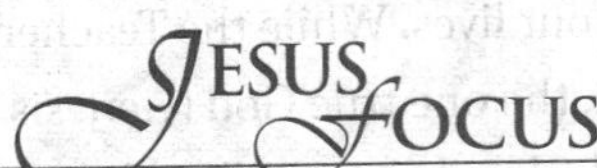

WITHOUT MEANING

"Meaningless! Meaningless!" The Teacher's opening words in Ecclesiastes come as a surprise and quickly grab our attention. The Teacher went on to explain that life without God is a pointless repetition of vicious cycles—he called it "a chasing after the wind" (Ecclesiastes 2:17). No matter what we accumulate or accomplish in this life, he lamented, it all disappears and is eventually forgotten. In the New Testament Jesus addressed the same issue. He told people that amassing wealth or storing up treasures on earth is a waste of energy, because material things are subject to decay, rust and theft. Instead, our Lord encouraged us to pursue the things that really matter—the things of God. Jesus knew that our love and loyalty will belong to whatever our heart embraces as most important. If we invest our energy in getting to know God, our primary devotion will be to him (Matthew 6:19–21).

The Quest for Fulfillment

Many people spend their entire lifetime on a quest for something to infuse them with hope and a sense of self-worth. The book of Ecclesiastes was written by just such a man, most likely King Solomon. As king over all Israel, Solomon was in a position to acquire anything his heart desired. He set out to fill his life with a myriad of pleasures and possessions—both good and bad.

Solomon did more than anyone else in history to beautify Jerusalem. He read books and applied himself to learning all he could. He accumulated money and treasures, led armies, and sought meaning in sexual intimacy and other physical pleasures. But in the book of Ecclesiastes he lamented that all of his endeavors at finding fulfillment were as futile as chasing after the wind. His conclusion was that the only thing that matters, the only reason for human existence, is to get to know God and live life in a manner that pleases him (Ecclesiastes 12:13).

Solomon referred to himself as "the Teacher," the same title people often used to address Jesus (see, for example, Matthew 8:19; Mark 4:38; Luke 10:25; John 13:13–14). Jesus' focus was on living a life that pleased the Father, and he constantly reminded others to do the same. While here on earth our Lord spent a great deal of time discussing the distinctives of a right relationship with God.

After Jesus had died and come back to life, he ascended into heaven to take up his rightful position next to God the Father. The task he left with his people was simple: teach others how to live lives pleasing to God (Matthew 28:19–20). God's people have always been instructors: from Moses to Solomon to Jesus—who left this legacy for each of us to follow. The apostle Paul passed on the task of education to Timothy: "Preach the Word . . . with great patience and careful instruction" (2 Timothy 4:2).

Solomon spent a lifetime searching for ultimate truth, and Jesus *is* the truth of God. Solomon both sought and taught wisdom, and Jesus embodies God's wisdom (1 Corinthians 1:30). Solomon recognized that walking with God constitutes the bottom line for each of us, and Jesus Christ emphasized that loving God entails loving the One he has sent—our Savior himself (John 3:16–17,31–36; 6:29,57). Just as Solomon devoted his life to gaining and teaching wisdom, so we must commit our lives to developing an intimate relationship with Jesus and allowing him to operate unimpeded in our hearts through the powerful working of the Holy Spirit.

Life without God is meaningless—like trying to capture the wind, only to find it whistling through your fingers. Jesus came as God's perfect Son to offer us eternal life and the opportunity for a personal relationship with God, and nothing on earth could have more meaning that that! He said, "I have come that [those who follow me] may have life, and have it to the full" (John 10:10).

Self-Discovery: *Have you experienced the deep, inner satisfaction that comes from a close relationship with Jesus? Read John 14:23 and Revelation 3:20 to find out how to begin.*

GO TO DISCOVERY 169 ON PAGE 861

TO BECOME CHRIST LIKE IS THE ONLY THING IN THE WHOLE WORLD WORTH CARING FOR, THE THING BEFORE WHICH EVERY AMBITION OF MAN IS FOLLY AND ALL LOWER ACHIEVEMENT VAIN.

Henry Drummond, *Scottish Evangelist*

men to do under heaven during the few
days of their lives.
[4]I undertook great projects: I built
2:4 [w]1Ki 7:1-12 [x]SS 8:11 houses for myself[w] and planted vineyards.[x] [5]I made gardens and parks and
planted all kinds of fruit trees in them. [6]I
made reservoirs to water groves of flourishing trees. [7]I bought male and female
slaves and had other slaves who were
born in my house. I also owned more
herds and flocks than anyone in Jerusalem before me. [8]I amassed silver and
2:8 [y]1Ki 9:28; 10:10,14,21 [z]2Sa 19:35 gold[y] for myself, and the treasure of
kings and provinces. I acquired men and
women singers,[z] and a harem[a] as well—
the delights of the heart of man. [9]I be-
2:9 [a]1Ch 29:25; Ecc 1:16 came greater by far than anyone in
Jerusalem before me.[a] In all this my wis-
dom stayed with me.

[10]I denied myself nothing my eyes
desired;
I refused my heart no pleasure.
My heart took delight in all my work,
and this was the reward for all
my labor.
[11]Yet when I surveyed all that my
hands had done
and what I had toiled to achieve,
everything was meaningless, a
2:11 [b]Ecc 1:14 [c]Ecc 1:3 chasing after the wind;[b]
nothing was gained under the
sun.[c]

Wisdom and Folly Are Meaningless

[12]Then I turned my thoughts to
consider wisdom,
2:12 [d]Ecc 1:17 [e]Ecc 1:9; 7:25 and also madness and folly.[d]
What more can the king's
successor do
than what has already been
done?[e]
2:13 [f]Ecc 7:19; 9:18 [g]Ecc 7:11-12 [13]I saw that wisdom[f] is better than
folly,[g]
just as light is better than
darkness.
[14]The wise man has eyes in his head,
while the fool walks in the
darkness;
but I came to realize
that the same fate overtakes 2:14 [h]Ps 49:10; Pr 17:24; Ecc 3:19; 6:6; 7:2; 9:3,11-12
them both.[h]

[15]Then I thought in my heart,

"The fate of the fool will overtake
me also.
What then do I gain by being 2:15 [i]Ecc 6:8
wise?"[i]
I said in my heart,
"This too is meaningless."
[16]For the wise man, like the fool, will
not be long remembered;
in days to come both will be 2:16 [j]Ecc 1:11; 9:5
forgotten.[j]
Like the fool, the wise man too
must die!

Toil Is Meaningless

[17]So I hated life, because the work
that is done under the sun was grievous
to me. All of it is meaningless, a chasing
after the wind.[k] [18]I hated all the things I 2:17 [k]Ecc 4:2

[a] *8* The meaning of the Hebrew for this phrase is uncertain.

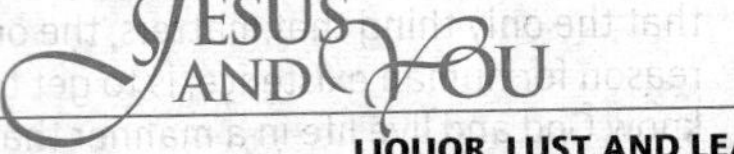

LIQUOR, LUST AND LEARNING

In his search for meaning in life, the Teacher related that he had chased after many of the same goals our own society glamorizes: Think deeper, party harder, experiment with more options, experience all you can (Ecclesiastes 1—2). But the Teacher discovered what many of us have learned: It's all a waste of time in the end, for "with much wisdom comes much sorrow" (Ecclesiastes 1:18). In other words, sometimes the more we learn from experience, the worse we feel. Ignorance can indeed be bliss! And it can take a lot of false starts for us to find out what really matters, leaving us with a deep and pervading sense of regret and futility. Life begins to make sense for us only when we learn to trust God and take his words seriously. Jesus was explicit about his purpose for us: "I have come that they may have life, and have it to the full" (John 10:10). Living for Jesus brings true fulfillment to life, and our searching souls find satisfaction only when we realize that *he* is the One we have been looking for all along, the One who alone can fill our hungry souls with all we need for true joy (John 6:35,48–51).

DISCOVERY 169

EMPTINESS: JESUS IS THE ANSWER

A businessman sat across the table from a pastor, describing his personal journey. "I thought I had it all: expensive car, elegant house, successful business. I divorced my wife because I found marriage too limiting. I started living it up, partying every night and going from one woman to another. But I kept wanting more—bigger, better, faster, prettier, more exotic. It just never lasted." Despite all of his chaotic and frantic pursuits, he was always left feeling discontented and empty.

Solomon had experienced the same frustration and disillusionment. He had tried it all, and the businessman might have been echoing Solomon's own sentiments from the book of Ecclesiastes. Solomon summarized his quest for wisdom and pleasure with words that went something like this: "I devoted myself to explore by wisdom everything under heaven. I tested pleasure to find out what was good. I stimulated myself with wine and careless living. I took on great projects—vineyards, gardens, parks, reservoirs. I bought slaves, owned livestock, amassed a great deal of money. I even kept a harem. And it all left me dissatisfied and empty" (Ecclesiastes 1:13; 2:1,3–11). We can almost envision Solomon wringing his hands as he bemoaned: "Utterly meaningless! Everything is meaningless" (Ecclesiastes 1:2). In the end, there is nothing new to be found, owned or experienced.

The apostle Paul could have related to Solomon's experience. For a long time he felt perfectly content with his education, religion, accomplishments and morality (see Philippians 3:4–6). But eventually all of these things lost their appeal. Paul realized that, ultimately, everything he'd learned or accomplished was of no more worth than a heap of garbage.

But neither Solomon nor Paul leaves us feeling hopeless. Instead, both revealed for us what *does* matter in this life. Solomon summarized his conclusion in Ecclesiastes 12:13: "Now all has been heard; here is the conclusion of the matter: Fear God and keep his commandments, for this is the whole duty of man." And Paul's statement has echoed throughout the centuries down to this very day and on to the very end of time: "I consider everything [religion, education, possessions, achievement] a loss compared to the surpassing greatness of knowing Christ Jesus my Lord" (Philippians 3:8). Now there's something that's utterly meaningful—knowing Christ Jesus as Savior and Lord, living to serve him, striving to become more like him—the answer to our emptiness.

Jesus made an offer to those who are frustrated and disillusioned with life: "If anyone is thirsty, let him come to me and drink. Whoever believes in me, as the Scripture has said, streams of living water will flow from within him" (John 7:37). Jesus not only promises to satisfy our deep inner longings, but he will also make us a source of refreshment for others.

***Self-Discovery:** What value do you place on knowing Jesus? Can you honestly say that every other goal or pleasure in your life pales by comparison? What difference for your life today does knowing Jesus make?*

GO TO DISCOVERY 170 ON PAGE 863

had toiled for under the sun, because I
2:18 must leave them to the one who comes
l Ps 39:6; 49:10 after me.[l] 19And who knows whether he
will be a wise man or a fool? Yet he will
have control over all the work into
which I have poured my effort and skill
under the sun. This too is meaningless.
20So my heart began to despair over all
my toilsome labor under the sun. 21For a
man may do his work with wisdom,
knowledge and skill, and then he must
leave all he owns to someone who has
not worked for it. This too is meaningless and a great misfortune. 22What does
a man get for all the toil and anxious
2:22 striving with which he labors under the
m Ecc 1:3; 3:9 sun?[m] 23All his days his work is pain and
2:23 grief;[n] even at night his mind does not
n Job 5:7; 14:1; Ecc 1:18 rest. This too is meaningless.
24A man can do nothing better than
2:24 to eat and drink[o] and find satisfaction in
o Ecc 8:15; 1Co 15:32 his work.[p] This too, I see, is from the
p Ecc 3:22 hand of God,[q] 25for without him, who
q Ecc 3:12-13; 5:17-19; 9:7-10 can eat or find enjoyment? 26To the man
who pleases him, God gives wisdom,
knowledge and happiness, but to the
sinner he gives the task of gathering and
2:26 storing up wealth[r] to hand it over to the
r Job 27:17 one who pleases God.[s] This too is mean-
s Pr 13:22 ingless, a chasing after the wind.

A Time for Everything

3:1 **3** There is a time[t] for everything,
t ver 11,17; Ecc 8:6 and a season for every activity
under heaven:

2 a time to be born and a time to
die,
a time to plant and a time to
uproot,
3 a time to kill and a time to heal,
a time to tear down and a time
to build,
4 a time to weep and a time to
laugh,
a time to mourn and a time to
dance,
5 a time to scatter stones and a
time to gather them,
a time to embrace and a time to
refrain,
6 a time to search and a time to
give up,
a time to keep and a time to
throw away,
3:7 7 a time to tear and a time to mend,
u Am 5:13 a time to be silent[u] and a time to
speak,
8 a time to love and a time to hate,
a time for war and a time for
peace.

9What does the worker gain from his 3:9
toil?[v] 10I have seen the burden God has v Ecc 1:3
laid on men.[w] 11He has made everything 3:10
beautiful in its time.[x] He has also set w Ecc 1:13
eternity in the hearts of men; yet they 3:11
cannot fathom[y] what God has done x ver 1
from beginning to end.[z] 12I know that y Job 11:7; Ecc 8:17
there is nothing better for men than to z Job 28:23; Ro 11:33
be happy and do good while they live.
13That everyone may eat and drink,[a] and 3:13
find satisfaction[b] in all his toil—this is a Ecc 2:3
the gift of God.[c] 14I know that every- b Ps 34:12
thing God does will endure forever; c Dt 12:7,18; Ecc 2:24; 5:19
nothing can be added to it and nothing 3:14
taken from it. God does it so that men d Job 23:15; Ecc 5:7; 7:18;
will revere him.[d] 8:12-13; Jas 1:17

15Whatever is has already been,[e] 3:15
and what will be has been e Ecc 6:10
before;[f] f Ecc 1:9
and God will call the past to
account.[a]

16And I saw something else under the
sun:

In the place of judgment—
wickedness was there,
in the place of justice—
wickedness was there.

17I thought in my heart,

"God will bring to judgment[g] 3:17
both the righteous and the g Job 19:29; Ecc 11:9;
wicked, Mt 16:27; Ro 2:6-8;
for there will be a time for every 2Th 1:6-7
activity, h ver 1
a time for every deed."[h]

18I also thought, "As for men, God tests 3:18
them so that they may see that they are i Ps 73:22
like the animals.[i] 19Man's fate[j] is like that 3:19
of the animals; the same fate awaits j Ecc 2:14
them both: As one dies, so dies the other. All have the same breath[b]; man has no
advantage over the animal. Everything is
meaningless. 20All go to the same place;
all come from dust, and to dust all re- 3:20
turn.[k] 21Who knows if the spirit of man k Ge 2:7; 3:19; Job 34:15
rises upward[l] and if the spirit of the ani- 3:21
mal[c] goes down into the earth?" l Ecc 12:7
22So I saw that there is nothing better 3:22
for a man than to enjoy his work,[m] m Ecc 2:24; 5:18

[a] 15 Or *God calls back the past* [b] 19 Or *spirit*
[c] 21 Or *Who knows the spirit of man, which rises upward, or the spirit of the animal, which*

Eternity in Our Hearts

No one has ever been to heaven and come back again to describe the experience for us, yet we are convinced that there is something beyond this temporal life. We live in a world of yesterdays, todays and tomorrows, and we think in terms of "living" in the past, the present or the future. Our concept of time has been limited by these categories, so what makes us so confident that there is something beyond tomorrow, that there is indeed a "forever"?

The answer is simply that God has implanted that knowledge within us. The book of Ecclesiastes expresses this concept by stating that he "has set eternity in the hearts of men" (Ecclesiastes 3:11). God is eternal. He doesn't continually consult a wristwatch, fretting about the possibility of running out of time or about everything he needs to accomplish tomorrow. He simply *is*—he's always been there and always will be.

Every attribute that defines who God is also lasts forever. His love for us is eternal (1 Kings 10:9), and he will always be in complete charge of the universe (Daniel 4:3). Similarly, in Ecclesiastes 3:14 Solomon asserted that "everything God does will endure forever; nothing can be added to it and nothing taken from it." God's ways and his word are changeless and eternal (Psalm 119:89; Habakkuk 3:6).

This eternal God created us to be in relationship with him, and he has fashioned each of us in his own image so that we might reflect to those around us who he is. For example, we, like God, have the ability to love and care for other people. And although we have not been alive forever, he did plant within us an expectation that we will be around for the rest of eternity—with or without him.

The only way we can hope to live with God forever is to experience a brand-new relationship with him—one without sin! Jesus, God's precious Son, was born to die in our place, completely atoning for our sin, but he came back to life to prove that death doesn't have the final word (1 Corinthians 15:54–57). Some day God's people will live with him for endless days (Revelation 21:3).

He has planted in each of us a deep longing for a "forever" with him. He offers this eternal destination to all who believe in his wonderful Son, Jesus, who gave his life so that we might be brought back into fellowship with God (John 3:16–17; Acts 16:31; Romans 10:9; 1 John 1:2–3). Jesus said, "I tell you the truth, whoever hears my word and believes him who sent me has eternal life and will not be condemned; he has crossed over from death to life" (John 5:24).

Self-Discovery: *Imagine for a moment that Jesus had not died to atone for your sins, that this life really is "all there is." Would the pleasures and achievements of life seem more or less important than they do now? Now, knowing that there is more to life, how does this reality affect the way you live today?*

GO TO DISCOVERY 171 ON PAGE 865

3:22 [n]Job 31:2 because that is his lot.[n] For who can
bring him to see what will happen after
him?

Oppression, Toil, Friendlessness

4:1 [o]Ps 12:5; Ecc 3:16 [p]La 1:16 4 Again I looked and saw all the oppression[o] that was taking place
under the sun:

I saw the tears of the oppressed—
and they have no comforter;
power was on the side of their
oppressors—
and they have no comforter.[p]
4:2 [q]Jer 20:17-18; 22:10 [r]Job 3:17; 10:18 2 And I declared that the dead,[q]
who had already died,
are happier than the living,
who are still alive.[r]
3 But better than both
4:3 [s]Job 3:16; Ecc 6:3 [t]Job 3:22 is he who has not yet been,[s]
who has not seen the evil
that is done under the sun.[t]

4 And I saw that all labor and all
achievement spring from man's envy of
his neighbor. This too is meaningless, a
4:4 [u]Ecc 1:14 chasing after the wind.[u]

4:5 [v]Pr 6:10 5 The fool folds his hands[v]
and ruins himself.
4:6 [w]Pr 15:16-17; 16:8 6 Better one handful with tranquillity
than two handfuls with toil[w]
and chasing after the wind.

7 Again I saw something meaningless
under the sun:

8 There was a man all alone;
he had neither son nor brother.
There was no end to his toil,
4:8 [x]Pr 27:20 yet his eyes were not content[x]
with his wealth.
"For whom am I toiling," he asked,
"and why am I depriving myself
of enjoyment?"
This too is meaningless—
a miserable business!

9 Two are better than one,
because they have a good return
for their work:
10 If one falls down,
his friend can help him up.
But pity the man who falls
and has no one to help him up!
11 Also, if two lie down together, they
will keep warm.
But how can one keep warm
alone?
12 Though one may be overpowered,
two can defend themselves.
A cord of three strands is not
quickly broken.

Advancement Is Meaningless

13 Better a poor but wise youth than an
old but foolish king who no longer
knows how to take warning. 14 The youth
may have come from prison to the kingship, or he may have been born in poverty within his kingdom. 15 I saw that all
who lived and walked under the sun followed the youth, the king's successor.
16 There was no end to all the people who
were before them. But those who came
later were not pleased with the successor. This too is meaningless, a chasing after the wind.

Stand in Awe of God

5 Guard your steps when you go to
the house of God. Go near to listen rather than to offer the sacrifice of
fools, who do not know that they do
wrong.

2 Do not be quick with your mouth,
do not be hasty in your heart 5:2 [y]Jdg 11:35
to utter anything before God.[y] [z]Job 6:24; Pr 10:19; 20:25
God is in heaven
and you are on earth,
so let your words be few.[z]
3 As a dream[a] comes when there are 5:3 [a]Job 20:8
many cares, [b]Ecc 10:14
so the speech of a fool when
there are many words.[b]

4 When you make a vow to God, do 5:4 [c]Dt 23:21;
not delay in fulfilling it.[c] He has no Jdg 11:35;
pleasure in fools; fulfill your vow.[d] 5 It is Ps 119:60 [d]Nu 30:2;
better not to vow than to make a vow Ps 66:13-14;
and not fulfill it.[e] 6 Do not let your 76:11
mouth lead you into sin. And do not 5:5
protest to the ⌞temple⌟ messenger, "My [e]Nu 30:2-4; Pr 20:25;
vow was a mistake." Why should God be Jnh 2:9; Ac 5:4
angry at what you say and destroy the
work of your hands? 7 Much dreaming
and many words are meaningless.
Therefore stand in awe of God.[f] 5:7 [f]Ecc 3:14; 12:13

Riches Are Meaningless

8 If you see the poor oppressed[g] in a 5:8 [g]Ps 12:5;
district, and justice and rights denied, do Ecc 4:1
not be surprised at such things; for one
official is eyed by a higher one, and over
them both are others higher still. 9 The
increase from the land is taken by all; the
king himself profits from the fields.

ENOUGH IS NEVER ENOUGH

Few of us have ever taken a vow of poverty. When we find ourselves with little or no disposable cash, it is not usually because we have *chosen* to be in this situation. Most of us instead live daily with the uneasy and somewhat paradoxical tension of possessing more than what we really need and yet at times longing for more than what we have.

Money isn't bad or good in and of itself, but it can be dangerous (see 1 Timothy 6:10) when we allow it to become "the love of our life." When we allow our financial portfolio to become our top priority, *enough* never is enough. As Solomon expressed it in Ecclesiastes 5:10, "Whoever loves money never has money enough; whoever loves wealth is never satisfied with his income."

Just like anything else we value, money can become our god—what we love, work for, rely on and allow to become the basis for our sense of self-esteem and well-being. In fact, the love of money can be so powerful a force in tearing our focus away from God that Jesus spoke more on the subject of money than he did on heaven or hell. We seem to be able to invest our primary energy in only one thing at a time. Jesus described it this way: "No one can serve two masters. Either he will hate the one and love the other, or he will be devoted to the one and despise the other. You cannot serve both God and Money" (Matthew 6:24).

How do we handle the challenge of living in a world in which the exchange of currency is critical to our existence? First of all, we can stop worrying about whether or not we will have enough to see us through or to support the lifestyle we crave (Matthew 6:25–34).

We often pursue the elusive "more" simply because we are afraid of the future. Knowing that we have a "nest egg" set aside or invested in a diverse portfolio can enhance our sense of security. But the true bottom line for all people is that each of us will eventually depart this world taking with us no more than what we brought in. Preparing for the future, even here on earth, is wise, but putting our trust in money is not. We need to trust the eternal, changeless God to take care of us.

We can also strive to keep our priorities in line with what is important to God. When we truly allow God and his Word to occupy first place in our lives, he promises to take care of everything else we need (Matthew 6:33). If we spend most of our time worrying about what will or might happen, making certain we are prepared for any circumstance that could conceivably come our way, we won't enjoy or even notice the good things God is causing to happen in our lives right now.

Self-Discovery: *As the years go by, do you devote more thought and energy to the status of your retirement portfolio or to the quality of your relationship with Jesus? What are some ways you can be a good steward of your possessions, including your most cherished "possession"—your relationship with Jesus?*

GO TO DISCOVERY 172 ON PAGE 872

10 Whoever loves money never has
money enough;
whoever loves wealth is never
satisfied with his income.
This too is meaningless.

11 As goods increase,
so do those who consume them.
And what benefit are they to the
owner
except to feast his eyes on them?

12 The sleep of a laborer is sweet,
whether he eats little or much,
but the abundance of a rich man
5:12 [h]Job 20:20
permits him no sleep.[h]

13 I have seen a grievous evil under the
5:13 [i]Ecc 6:1-2
sun:[i]

wealth hoarded to the harm of its
owner,
14 or wealth lost through some
misfortune,
so that when he has a son
there is nothing left for him.
15 Naked a man comes from his
5:15 [j]Job 1:21 [k]Ps 49:17; 1Ti 6:7 [l]Ecc 1:3
mother's womb,
and as he comes, so he departs.[j]
He takes nothing from his labor[k]
that he can carry in his hand.[l]

16 This too is a grievous evil:

As a man comes, so he departs,
5:16 [m]Pr 11:29; Ecc 1:3
and what does he gain,
since he toils for the wind?[m]
17 All his days he eats in darkness,
with great frustration, affliction
and anger.

18 Then I realized that it is good and
5:18 [n]Ecc 2:3 [o]Ecc 2:10,24
proper for a man to eat and drink,[n] and
to find satisfaction in his toilsome labor[o] under the sun during the few days
of life God has given him—for this is his
5:19 [p]1Ch 29:12; 2Ch 1:12 [q]Ecc 6:2 [r]Job 31:2 [s]Ecc 2:24; 3:13
lot. 19 Moreover, when God gives any
man wealth and possessions,[p] and enables him to enjoy them,[q] to accept his
lot[r] and be happy in his work—this is a
gift of God.[s] 20 He seldom reflects on the
5:20 [t]Dt 12:7,18
days of his life, because God keeps him
occupied with gladness of heart.[t]

6 I have seen another evil under the
sun, and it weighs heavily on men:
2 God gives a man wealth, possessions
and honor, so that he lacks nothing his
heart desires, but God does not enable
6:2 [u]Ps 17:14; Ecc 5:19 [v]Ecc 5:13
him to enjoy them,[u] and a stranger enjoys them instead. This is meaningless,
a grievous evil.[v]

3 A man may have a hundred children
and live many years; yet no matter how
long he lives, if he cannot enjoy his prosperity and does not receive proper buri-
al, I say that a stillborn[w] child is better 6:3 [w]Job 3:16; Ecc 4:3 [x]Job 3:3
off than he.[x] 4 It comes without meaning,
it departs in darkness, and in darkness
its name is shrouded. 5 Though it never
saw the sun or knew anything, it has
more rest than does that man— 6 even if
he lives a thousand years twice over but
fails to enjoy his prosperity. Do not all go
to the same place?

7 All man's efforts are for his mouth,
yet his appetite is never
satisfied.[y] 6:7 [y]Pr 16:26; 27:20
8 What advantage has a wise man
over a fool?[z] 6:8 [z]Ecc 2:15
What does a poor man gain
by knowing how to conduct
himself before others?
9 Better what the eye sees
than the roving of the appetite.
This too is meaningless,
a chasing after the wind.[a] 6:9 [a]Ecc 1:14

10 Whatever exists has already been
named,
and what man is has been
known;
no man can contend
with one who is stronger than he.
11 The more the words,
the less the meaning,
and how does that profit
anyone?

12 For who knows what is good for a
man in life, during the few and mean-
ingless days[b] he passes through like a 6:12 [b]Job 10:20
shadow?[c] Who can tell him what will [c]Job 14:2;
happen under the sun after he is gone? Ps 39:6; Jas 4:14

Wisdom

7 A good name is better than fine
perfume,[d] 7:1 [d]Pr 22:1; SS 1:3
and the day of death better than
the day of birth.
2 It is better to go to a house of
mourning
than to go to a house of feasting,
for death[e] is the destiny[f] of every 7:2 [e]Pr 11:19 [f]Ps 90:12
man;
the living should take this to
heart.
3 Sorrow is better than laughter,[g] 7:3 [g]Pr 14:13
because a sad face is good for
the heart.

[4]The heart of the wise is in the
house of mourning,
but the heart of fools is in the
house of pleasure.[h]
[5]It is better to heed a wise man's
rebuke[i]
than to listen to the song of
fools.
[6]Like the crackling of thorns[j] under
the pot,
so is the laughter[k] of fools.
This too is meaningless.

[7]Extortion turns a wise man into a
fool,
and a bribe[l] corrupts the heart.

[8]The end of a matter is better than
its beginning,
and patience[m] is better than
pride.
[9]Do not be quickly provoked[n] in
your spirit,
for anger resides in the lap of
fools.
[10]Do not say, "Why were the old days
better than these?"
For it is not wise to ask such
questions.

[11]Wisdom, like an inheritance, is a
good thing[o]
and benefits those who see the
sun.[p]
[12]Wisdom is a shelter
as money is a shelter,
but the advantage of knowledge is
this:
that wisdom preserves the life of
its possessor.

[13]Consider what God has done:[q]

Who can straighten
what he has made crooked?[r]
[14]When times are good, be happy;
but when times are bad,
consider:
God has made the one
as well as the other.
Therefore, a man cannot discover
anything about his future.

[15]In this meaningless life[s] of mine I
have seen both of these:

a righteous man perishing in his
righteousness,
and a wicked man living long in
his wickedness.[t]

[16]Do not be overrighteous,
neither be overwise—
why destroy yourself?
[17]Do not be overwicked,
and do not be a fool—
why die before your time?[u]
[18]It is good to grasp the one
and not let go of the other.
The man who fears God[v] will
avoid all ⌊extremes⌋.[a]

[19]Wisdom[w] makes one wise man
more powerful[x]
than ten rulers in a city.

[20]There is not a righteous man[y] on
earth
who does what is right and
never sins.[z]

[21]Do not pay attention to every word
people say,
or you[a] may hear your servant
cursing you—
[22]for you know in your heart
that many times you yourself
have cursed others.

7:4 [h]Ecc 2:1; Jer 16:8
7:5 [i]Ps 141:5; Pr 13:18; 15:31-32
7:6 [j]Ps 58:9; 118:12 [k]Ecc 2:2
7:7 [l]Ex 18:21; 23:8; Dt 16:19
7:8 [m]Pr 14:29; Gal 5:22; Eph 4:2
7:9 [n]Mt 5:22; Pr 14:17; Jas 1:19
7:11 [o]Pr 8:10-11; Ecc 2:13 [p]Ecc 11:7
7:13 [q]Ecc 2:24 [r]Ecc 1:15
7:15 [s]Job 7:7 [t]Ecc 8:12-14; Jer 12:1
7:17 [u]Job 15:32; Ps 55:23
7:18 [v]Ecc 3:14
7:19 [w]Ecc 2:13 [x]Ecc 9:13-18
7:20 [y]Ps 14:3 [z]1Ki 8:46; 2Ch 6:36; Pr 20:9; Ro 3:23
7:21 [a]Pr 30:10

[a] *18* Or *will follow them both*

JESUS FOCUS

A BALANCED LIFE

Ecclesiastes 7 encourages us to live a *balanced* life as we get to know God. "Avoid all extremes" (verse 18) is sound advice for wise living. Living balanced lives is also the best way to avoid both legalistic fanaticism and a "holier-than-thou" attitude toward others. The Lord Jesus himself faced criticism from religious leaders who were complacent in the certainty that they knew more details about God's laws and followed them more precisely than anyone else. These leaders were self-righteous and arrogant, believing themselves to be more godly than the average person. But Jesus applied a wonderful metaphor to these men, calling them "blind guides (who) strain out a gnat but swallow a camel" (Matthew 23:24). Our Lord also accused them of failing to practice what they were preaching, which he likened to tying a heavy load on another person's shoulders and refusing to lift a finger to help that person carry the burden (Matthew 23:3–4). The religious leaders managed to make walking with God a very difficult proposition for people, but Jesus stated that his "yoke is easy and [his] burden is light" (Matthew 11:30).

23 All this I tested by wisdom and I
said,

7:23 [b] Ecc 1:17; Ro 1:22

"I am determined to be wise"[b]—
but this was beyond me.
24 Whatever wisdom may be,
it is far off and most profound—
who can discover it?[c]

7:24 [c] Job 28:12

25 So I turned my mind to understand,
to investigate and to search out
wisdom and the scheme of
things[d]
and to understand the stupidity of
wickedness
and the madness of folly.[e]

7:25 [d] Job 28:3 [e] Ecc 1:17

26 I find more bitter than death
the woman who is a snare,[f]
whose heart is a trap
and whose hands are chains.
The man who pleases God will
escape her,
but the sinner she will ensnare.[g]

7:26 [f] Ex 10:7; Jdg 14:15 [g] Pr 2:16-19; 5:3-5; 7:23; 22:14

27 "Look," says the Teacher,[a][h] "this is
what I have discovered:

7:27 [h] Ecc 1:1

"Adding one thing to another to
discover the scheme of
things—
28 while I was still searching
but not finding—
I found one ⌊upright⌋ man among a
thousand,
but not one ⌊upright⌋ woman[i]
among them all.
29 This only have I found:
God made mankind upright,
but men have gone in search of
many schemes."

7:28 [i] 1Ki 11:3

8 Who is like the wise man?
Who knows the explanation of
things?
Wisdom brightens a man's face
and changes its hard appearance.

Obey the King

2 Obey the king's command, I say, because you took an oath before God. 3 Do
not be in a hurry to leave the king's presence.[j] Do not stand up for a bad cause,
for he will do whatever he pleases. 4 Since
a king's word is supreme, who can say to
him, "What are you doing?[k]"

8:3 [j] Ecc 10:4

8:4 [k] Job 9:12; Est 1:19; Da 4:35

5 Whoever obeys his command will
come to no harm,
and the wise heart will know the
proper time and procedure.
6 For there is a proper time and
procedure for every matter,[l]
though a man's misery weighs
heavily upon him.

8:6 [l] Ecc 3:1

7 Since no man knows the future,
who can tell him what is to
come?
8 No man has power over the wind
to contain it[b];
so no one has power over the
day of his death.
As no one is discharged in time of
war,
so wickedness will not release
those who practice it.

9 All this I saw, as I applied my mind to
everything done under the sun. There is
a time when a man lords it over others
to his own[c] hurt. 10 Then too, I saw the
wicked buried[m]—those who used to
come and go from the holy place and receive praise[d] in the city where they did
this. This too is meaningless.

8:10 [m] Ecc 1:11

11 When the sentence for a crime is
not quickly carried out, the hearts of the
people are filled with schemes to do
wrong. 12 Although a wicked man commits a hundred crimes and still lives a
long time, I know that it will go better[n]
with God-fearing men,[o] who are reverent before God.[p] 13 Yet because the
wicked do not fear God,[q] it will not go
well with them, and their days[r] will not
lengthen like a shadow.

8:12 [n] Dt 12:28; Ps 37:11,18-19; Pr 1:32-33; Isa 3:10-11 [o] Ex 1:20 [p] Ecc 3:14

8:13 [q] Ecc 3:14; Isa 3:11 [r] Dt 4:40; Job 5:26; Ps 34:12; Isa 65:20

14 There is something else meaningless that occurs on earth: righteous men
who get what the wicked deserve, and
wicked men who get what the righteous
deserve.[s] This too, I say, is meaningless.[t]
15 So I commend the enjoyment of life[u],
because nothing is better for a man under the sun than to eat and drink[v] and
be glad.[w] Then joy will accompany him
in his work all the days of the life God
has given him under the sun.

8:14 [s] Job 21:7; Ps 73:14; Mal 3:15 [t] Ecc 7:15

8:15 [u] Ps 42:8 [v] Ex 32:6; Ecc 2:3 [w] Ecc 2:24; 3:12-13; 5:18; 9:7

16 When I applied my mind to know
wisdom[x] and to observe man's labor on
earth[y]—his eyes not seeing sleep day or
night— 17 then I saw all that God has
done.[z] No one can comprehend what
goes on under the sun. Despite all his efforts to search it out, man cannot discover its meaning. Even if a wise man

8:16 [x] Ecc 1:17 [y] Ecc 1:13

8:17 [z] Job 28:3

[a] *27* Or *leader of the assembly* [b] *8* Or *over his spirit to retain it* [c] *9* Or *to their* [d] *10* Some Hebrew manuscripts and Septuagint (Aquila); most Hebrew manuscripts *and are forgotten*

8:17 [a]Job 5:9; 28:23; Ecc 3:11; Ro 11:33

claims he knows, he cannot really comprehend it.[a]

A Common Destiny for All

9:1 [b]Dt 33:3; Job 12:10; Ecc 10:14

9 So I reflected on all this and concluded that the righteous and the
wise and what they do are in God's
hands, but no man knows whether love
or hate awaits him.[b] 2All share a common destiny—the righteous and the
wicked, the good and the bad,[a] the clean
and the unclean, those who offer sacrifices and those who do not.

9:2 [c]Job 9:22; Ecc 2:14; 6:6; 7:2

As it is with the good man,
so with the sinner;
as it is with those who take oaths,
so with those who are afraid to
take them.[c]

9:3 [d]Job 9:22; Ecc 2:14 [e]Jer 11:8; 13:10; 16:12; 17:9 [f]Job 21:26

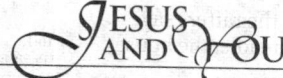

3This is the evil in everything that
happens under the sun: The same destiny overtakes all.[d] The hearts of men,
moreover, are full of evil and there is
madness in their hearts while they live,[e]
and afterward they join the dead.[f] 4Any-
one who is among the living has hope[b]—
even a live dog is better off than a dead
lion!

JESUS AND YOU

LIFE IS UNFAIR

Life seems unfair much of the time. People who live according to God's way seem to suffer as much as, and sometimes more than, those who blatantly disregard the Creator. In fact, it frequently appears as though what happens in life is in essence a matter of timing and chance. There may be periods in our lives during which we think God has forgotten justice. The Teacher reflected on many injustices in Ecclesiastes 8 and 9 and came to the conclusion that despite what others may think, it is better to walk with God in his wisdom than to appear to have it all together by the world's standards (Ecclesiastes 9:16–17). God knows what is right and fair, and the New Testament reminds us that he has chosen a day when he will bring true justice into the world through Jesus, his promised Messiah (Acts 17:31). Jesus said much the same thing to his followers: "The Father . . . has entrusted all judgment to the Son" (John 5:22). Our lives and futures are in our precious Savior's hands. He knows when we have been treated unfairly, and we can trust him to balance the scales of justice according to his good and perfect will.

5For the living know that they will
die,
but the dead know nothing;[g]
they have no further reward,
and even the memory of them[h]
is forgotten.[i]
6Their love, their hate
and their jealousy have long
since vanished;
never again will they have a part
in anything that happens under
the sun.[j]

9:5 [g]Job 14:21 [h]Ps 9:6 [i]Ecc 1:11; 2:16; Isa 26:14

9:6 [j]Job 21:21

7Go, eat your food with gladness, and
drink your wine[k] with a joyful heart,[l] for
it is now that God favors what you do.
8Always be clothed in white,[m] and always anoint your head with oil. 9Enjoy
life with your wife,[n] whom you love, all
the days of this meaningless life that
God has given you under the sun— all
your meaningless days. For this is your
lot[o] in life and in your toilsome labor under the sun. 10Whatever[p] your hand
finds to do, do it with all your might,[q] for
in the grave,[c][r] where you are going, there
is neither working nor planning nor
knowledge nor wisdom.[s]

9:7 [k]Nu 6:20 [l]Ecc 2:24; 8:15

9:8 [m]Ps 23:5; Rev 3:4

9:9 [n]Pr 5:18 [o]Job 31:2

9:10 [p]1Sa 10:7 [q]Ecc 11:6; Ro 12:11; Col 3:23 [r]Nu 16:33 [s]Ecc 2:24

11I have seen something else under
the sun:

The race is not to the swift
or the battle to the strong,[t]
nor does food come to the wise[u]
or wealth to the brilliant
or favor to the learned;
but time and chance[v] happen to
them all.[w]

9:11 [t]Am 2:14-15 [u]Job 32:13; Isa 47:10; Jer 9:23 [v]Ecc 2:14 [w]Dt 8:18

12Moreover, no man knows when his
hour will come:

As fish are caught in a cruel net,
or birds are taken in a snare,
so men are trapped by evil times[x]
that fall unexpectedly upon
them.[y]

9:12 [x]Pr 29:6 [y]Ps 73:22; Ecc 2:14; 8:7

Wisdom Better Than Folly

13I also saw under the sun this example of wisdom[z] that greatly impressed
me: 14There was once a small city with
only a few people in it. And a powerful
king came against it, surrounded it and
built huge siegeworks against it. 15Now

9:13 [z]2Sa 20:22

[a] 2 Septuagint (Aquila), Vulgate and Syriac; Hebrew does not have *and the bad.* [b] 4 Or *What then is to be chosen? With all who live, there is hope* [c] 10 Hebrew *Sheol*

there lived in that city a man poor but
wise, and he saved the city by his wisdom. But nobody remembered that
poor man.[a] 16So I said, "Wisdom is better than strength." But the poor man's
wisdom is despised, and his words are
no longer heeded.[b]

9:15 [a] Ge 40:14; Ecc 1:11; 2:16; 4:13
9:16 [b] Pr 21:22; Ecc 7:19

17 The quiet words of the wise are
more to be heeded
than the shouts of a ruler of
fools.
18 Wisdom[c] is better than weapons of
war,
but one sinner destroys much
good.

9:18 [c] ver 16

10 As dead flies give perfume a
bad smell,
so a little folly[d] outweighs
wisdom and honor.
2 The heart of the wise inclines to
the right,
but the heart of the fool to the
left.
3 Even as he walks along the road,
the fool lacks sense
and shows everyone[e] how stupid
he is.
4 If a ruler's anger rises against you,
do not leave your post;[f]
calmness can lay great errors to
rest.[g]
5 There is an evil I have seen under
the sun,
the sort of error that arises from
a ruler:
6 Fools are put in many high
positions,[h]
while the rich occupy the low
ones.
7 I have seen slaves on horseback,
while princes go on foot like
slaves.[i]
8 Whoever digs a pit may fall into it;[j]
whoever breaks through a wall
may be bitten by a snake.[k]
9 Whoever quarries stones may be
injured by them;
whoever splits logs may be
endangered by them.[l]
10 If the ax is dull
and its edge unsharpened,
more strength is needed
but skill will bring success.
11 If a snake bites before it is charmed,
there is no profit for the
charmer.[m]
12 Words from a wise man's mouth
are gracious,[n]
but a fool is consumed by his
own lips.[o]
13 At the beginning his words are
folly;
at the end they are wicked
madness—
14 and the fool multiplies words.[p]
No one knows what is coming—
who can tell him what will
happen after him?[q]
15 A fool's work wearies him;
he does not know the way to
town.
16 Woe to you, O land whose king was
a servant[a][r]
and whose princes feast in the
morning.
17 Blessed are you, O land whose king
is of noble birth
and whose princes eat at a
proper time—
for strength and not for
drunkenness.[s]
18 If a man is lazy, the rafters sag;
if his hands are idle, the house
leaks.[t]
19 A feast is made for laughter,
and wine[u] makes life merry,
but money is the answer for
everything.
20 Do not revile the king[v] even in your
thoughts,
or curse the rich in your
bedroom,
because a bird of the air may carry
your words,
and a bird on the wing may
report what you say.

10:1 [d] Pr 13:16; 18:2
10:3 [e] Pr 13:16; 18:2
10:4 [f] Ecc 8:3 [g] Pr 16:14; 25:15
10:6 [h] Pr 29:2
10:7 [i] Pr 19:10
10:8 [j] Ps 7:15; 57:6; Pr 26:27 [k] Est 2:23; Ps 9:16; Am 5:19
10:9 [l] Pr 26:27
10:11 [m] Ps 58:5; Isa 3:3
10:12 [n] Pr 10:32 [o] Pr 10:14; 14:3; 15:2; 18:7
10:14 [p] Pr 15:2; Ecc 5:3; 6:12; 8:7 [q] Ecc 9:1
10:16 [r] Isa 3:4-5,12
10:17 [s] Dt 14:26; 1Sa 25:36; Pr 31:4
10:18 [t] Pr 20:4; 24:30-34
10:19 [u] Ge 14:18; Jdg 9:13
10:20 [v] Ex 22:28

Bread Upon the Waters

11 Cast[w] your bread upon the
waters,
for after many days you will find
it again.[x]
2 Give portions to seven, yes to eight,
for you do not know what
disaster may come upon
the land.

11:1 [w] ver 6; Isa 32:20; Hos 10:12 [x] Dt 24:19; Pr 19:17; Mt 10:42

[a] 16 Or *king is a child*

3 If clouds are full of water,
they pour rain upon the earth.
Whether a tree falls to the south or
to the north,
in the place where it falls, there
will it lie.
4 Whoever watches the wind will not
plant;
whoever looks at the clouds will
not reap.
11:5 [y]Jn 3:8-10 [z]Ps 139:14-16 5 As you do not know the path of the
wind,[y]
or how the body is formed[a] in a
mother's womb,[z]
so you cannot understand the
work of God,
the Maker of all things.
11:6 [a]Ecc 9:10 6 Sow your seed in the morning,
and at evening let not your
hands be idle,[a]
for you do not know which will
succeed,
whether this or that,
or whether both will do equally
well.

Remember Your Creator While Young

7 Light is sweet,
11:7 [b]Ecc 7:11 and it pleases the eyes to see the
sun.[b]
8 However many years a man may
live,
let him enjoy them all.
11:8 [c]Ecc 12:1 But let him remember[c] the days of
darkness,
for they will be many.
Everything to come is
meaningless.
9 Be happy, young man, while you
are young,
and let your heart give you joy in
the days of your youth.
Follow the ways of your heart
11:9 [d]Job 19:29; Ecc 2:24; 3:17; 12:14; Ro 14:10 and whatever your eyes see,
but know that for all these things
God will bring you to judgment.[d]
11:10 [e]Ps 94:19 [f]Ecc 2:24 10 So then, banish anxiety[e] from your
heart
and cast off the troubles of your
body,
for youth and vigor are
meaningless.[f]

12:1 [g]Ecc 11:8 [h]2Sa 19:35 **12** Remember[g] your Creator
in the days of your youth,
before the days of trouble[h] come
and the years approach when
you will say,
"I find no pleasure in them"—
2 before the sun and the light
and the moon and the stars
grow dark,
and the clouds return after the
rain;
3 when the keepers of the house
tremble,
and the strong men stoop,
when the grinders cease because
they are few,
and those looking through the
windows grow dim;
4 when the doors to the street are
closed
and the sound of grinding fades;
when men rise up at the sound of
birds, 12:4 [i]Jer 25:10
but all their songs grow faint;[i]
5 when men are afraid of heights
and of dangers in the streets;
when the almond tree blossoms
and the grasshopper drags
himself along
and desire no longer is stirred.
Then man goes to his eternal home[j] 12:5 [j]Job 17:13; 10:21 [k]Jer 9:17; Am 5:16
and mourners[k] go about the
streets.

6 Remember him—before the silver
cord is severed,
or the golden bowl is broken;
before the pitcher is shattered at
the spring,
or the wheel broken at the well,

[a] 5 Or *know how life* (or *the spirit*) / *enters the body being formed*

THE ADVANTAGE OF YOUTH

In the end, after pursuing all kinds of pleasures and accomplishments in a futile effort to find fulfillment, the Teacher concluded that walking with God is the best possible lifestyle option—and that the best way to acquire this mind-set is to make it a practice early in life (Ecclesiastes 12:1). A young person who commits his or her life to God can devote an entire lifetime to learning to follow God's will and ways. Jesus expressed the same focus, encouraging very young children to come to him and urging his adult hearers to model their spiritual walk after that of these ingenuous and trusting little ones (Luke 18:16).

God's Gentle Goad

The *goad* has gotten a bad reputation. When we refer to someone as having been "goaded into" something, we're usually talking about a person who has been incited to aggressive action. In ancient times a goad was simply a long stick used by farmers to keep their animals moving in the right direction. When Solomon observed that the words of a wise man are like a goad, he wasn't implying that God's people are to offer their opinions in a rude or hurtful manner. Instead, we should encourage the people around us to pattern their lifestyle according to the teachings of God's Word (Ecclesiastes 12:11).

Ecclesiastes also says that the words of wise men are like nails driven deep into wood (verse 11). Again, the emphasis isn't on the sharp points of the nails but on how long they will stay put, on how securely they will support the structure. God's wisdom isn't frivolous; it is instead a guiding force that stimulates people to live in a way that pleases him, even during the most difficult of times.

The writer to the Hebrews likened the word of God to a sword. Like the analogy of the nails above, the issue is not the potential of the blade to hurt or kill. Instead, this author pointed to the ability of God's words to penetrate, to cut to the heart of the matter: "For the word of God is living and active. Sharper than any double-edged sword, it penetrates even to dividing soul and spirit, joints and marrow; it judges the thoughts and attitudes of the heart" (Hebrews 4:12).

The writer followed up this rather ominous image with a proclamation of Good News: "Therefore, since we have a great high priest who has gone through the heavens, Jesus the Son of God, let us hold firmly to the faith we profess. For we do not have a high priest who is unable to sympathize with our weaknesses, but we have one who has been tempted in every way, just as we are—yet was without sin" (Hebrews 4:14–15). In other words, even though the Word of God may be likened to a goad, to nails or to a sword, our Savior knows that we need more than the words to prod us. Because of our innate weaknesses and inability to keep God's commands, we need Jesus, our great high priest, and the Holy Spirit to intercede for us with the Father (Romans 8:26; Hebrews 7:25).

When the risen Jesus confronted the apostle Paul (then Saul) on the road to Damascus, our Lord observed, "It is hard for you to kick against the goads" (Acts 26:14). It was common knowledge that an ox that resisted the farmer's goad would accomplish nothing except inviting repeated pokes. Paul had assumed that he was doing the right thing by arresting and persecuting Christians. But he was actually headed in the wrong direction, and the Lord needed to prod him back onto the right path.

God the Holy Spirit lives within his people to gently but firmly goad us back in the right direction when we have gotten off track. A life committed to walking with God will produce a conscience sensitive to his will.

***Self-Discovery:** Can you recall a time when God's Word was like a sharp sword or a gentle goad for you, when you felt absolutely convicted by a particular verse or passage? Did you follow through with the needed change in your life?*

GO TO DISCOVERY 173 ON PAGE 876

12:7 [l] Ge 3:19; Job 34:15; Ps 146:4 [m] Ecc 3:21 [n] Job 20:8; Zec 12:1

7 and the dust returns[l] to the ground
it came from,
and the spirit returns to God[m]
who gave it.[n]

12:8 [o] Ecc 1:2

8 "Meaningless! Meaningless!" says
the Teacher.[a]
"Everything is meaningless![o]"

The Conclusion of the Matter

9 Not only was the Teacher wise, but
also he imparted knowledge to the people. He pondered and searched out and
12:9 [p] 1Ki 4:32 set in order many proverbs.[p] 10 The
Teacher searched to find just the right
12:10 [q] Pr 22:20-21 words, and what he wrote was upright
and true.[q]

11 The words of the wise are like goads,
12:11 [r] Ezr 9:8 their collected sayings like firmly em-
bedded nails[r]—given by one Shepherd.
12 Be warned, my son, of anything in addition to them.

12:12 [s] Ecc 1:18 Of making many books there is no
end, and much study wearies the body.[s]

I BELIEVE THAT [JESUS] IS THE ANSWER TO EVERY INDIVIDUAL'S SEARCH FOR MEANING.

Billy Graham, *American Evangelist*

13 Now all has been heard;
here is the conclusion of the
matter:
Fear God and keep his
commandments,[t] 12:13 [t] Dt 4:2; 10:12 [u] Mic 6:8
for this is the whole ⌊duty⌋ of
man.[u]

14 For God will bring every deed into
judgment,[v] 12:14 [v] Ecc 3:17 [w] Mt 10:26; 1Co 4:5
including every hidden
thing,[w]
whether it is good or evil.

[a] 8 Or *the leader of the assembly*; also in verses 9 and 10

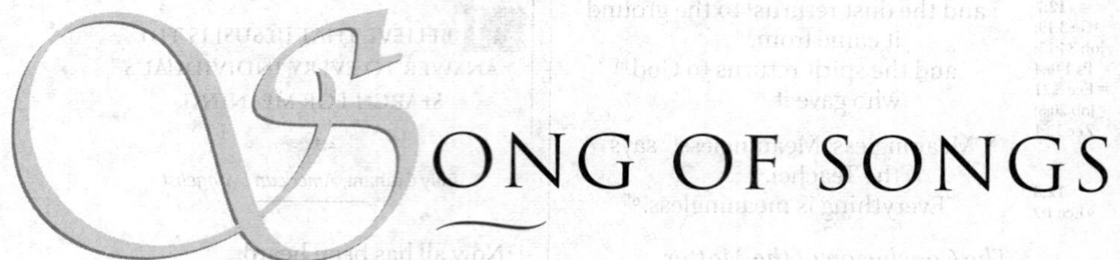

SONG OF SONGS

What is the significance of this unusual book?

♦ *The most likely explanation is that this book belongs to Biblical wisdom literature and that it is wisdom's description of an amorous relationship. The Bible speaks of both wisdom and love as gifts of God, to be received with gratitude and celebration. This understanding of Song of Songs contrasts with the view that it presents an intentional allegory of the love relationship between God and Israel, or between Jesus and the church, or between Jesus and the soul.*

Is there significance to the reference to myrrh? (Song of Songs 1:13)

♦ *Myrrh was an aromatic gum exuding from the bark of a balsam tree. It was used as an alluring fragrance (Esther 2:2, Proverbs 7:17) to perfume royal nuptual robes (Psalm 45:8). The Magi brought myrrh to young Jesus as a gift fit for a king (Matthew 2:2,11).*

Jesus in Song of Songs Song of Songs paints an enchanting poetic portrait. It depicts the love and untiring pursuit of a man for a woman. The young lover is believed by many to be King Solomon, disguised as a shepherd. He falls in love with a young Shulammite woman, whom he seeks out and woos, seemingly without rest. The energetic advances of the young man remind us of God's tireless, loving quest for a relationship with each of us through his Son Jesus Christ, the ultimate lover of our souls, although this is very likely not intentional symbolism. Like Solomon, Jesus is our shepherd (John 10:11–16), and he promises to return to take us to a "wedding banquet" at his Father's house (Matthew 25:1–13; Revelation 19:7–9). When he does return, he will come as the King of kings, and we will live in the joy of his glorious presence forever (Revelation 5:10; 19:16).

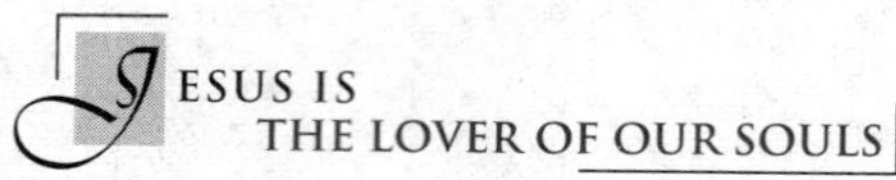

JESUS IS THE LOVER OF OUR SOULS

1:1 [a] 1Ki 4:32

1 Solomon's Song of Songs.[a]

Beloved[a]

[2] Let him kiss me with the kisses of his mouth—
for your love[b] is more delightful than wine.

1:2 [b] SS 4:10

[3] Pleasing is the fragrance of your perfumes;[c]
your name[d] is like perfume poured out.
No wonder the maidens[e] love you!

1:3 [c] SS 4:10 [d] Ecc 7:1 [e] Ps 45:14

[4] Take me away with you—let us hurry!
Let the king bring me into his chambers.[f]

1:4 [f] Ps 45:15

Friends

We rejoice and delight in you[b];
we will praise your love more than wine.

Beloved

How right they are to adore you!

[5] Dark am I, yet lovely,[g]
O daughters of Jerusalem,[h]
dark like the tents of Kedar,
like the tent curtains of Solomon.[c]

1:5 [g] SS 2:14; 4:3 [h] SS 2:7; 5:8; 5:16

[6] Do not stare at me because I am dark,
because I am darkened by the sun.
My mother's sons were angry with me
and made me take care of the vineyards;[i]
my own vineyard I have neglected.

1:6 [i] Ps 69:8; SS 8:12

[7] Tell me, you whom I love, where you graze your flock
and where you rest your sheep[j] at midday.
Why should I be like a veiled woman
beside the flocks of your friends?

1:7 [j] SS 3:1-4; Isa 13:20

Friends

[8] If you do not know, most beautiful of women,[k]
follow the tracks of the sheep
and graze your young goats
by the tents of the shepherds.

1:8 [k] SS 5:9; 6:1

> **MAN IS SOON CHANGED AND LIGHTLY FALLETH AWAY, BUT CHRIST ABIDETH FOREVER AND STANDETH STRONGLY WITH HIS LOVER UNTO THE END.**
>
> Thomas á Kempis, *German Mystic*

Lover

[9] I liken you, my darling, to a mare
harnessed to one of the chariots[l] of Pharaoh.

1:9 [l] 2Ch 1:17

[10] Your cheeks[m] are beautiful with earrings,
your neck with strings of jewels.[n]

1:10 [m] SS 5:13 [n] Isa 61:10

[11] We will make you earrings of gold,
studded with silver.

Beloved

[12] While the king was at his table,
my perfume spread its fragrance.[o]

1:12 [o] SS 4:11-14

[13] My lover is to me a sachet of myrrh
resting between my breasts.
[14] My lover is to me a cluster of henna[p] blossoms
from the vineyards of En Gedi.[q]

1:14 [p] SS 4:13 [q] 1Sa 23:29

Lover

[15] How beautiful[r] you are, my darling!
Oh, how beautiful!
Your eyes are doves.[s]

1:15 [r] SS 4:7 [s] SS 2:14; 4:1; 5:2,12; 6:9

Beloved

[16] How handsome you are, my lover!
Oh, how charming!
And our bed is verdant.

Lover

[17] The beams of our house are cedars;[t]
our rafters are firs.

1:17 [t] 1Ki 6:9

Beloved[d]

2 I am a rose[e][u] of Sharon,[v]
a lily[w] of the valleys.

2:1 [u] Isa 35:1 [v] S 1Ch 27:29 [w] SS 5:13; Hos 14:5

[a] Primarily on the basis of the gender of the Hebrew pronouns used, male and female speakers are indicated in the margins by the captions *Lover* and *Beloved* respectively. The words of others are marked *Friends.* In some instances the divisions and their captions are debatable. [b] *4* The Hebrew is masculine singular. [c] *5* Or *Salma* [d] *1* Or *Lover* [e] *1* Possibly a member of the crocus family

Divine Love Song

The Song of Songs is a lengthy love poem that allows us to listen in on a series of intimate exchanges between a man and woman who are very much in love. The two describe each other with some of the most beautiful (and to our modern ears some of the most overblown!) word pictures found anywhere in literature. The young woman is identified simply as a Shulammite (Song of Songs 6:13), and the young man is assumed by many to be King Solomon, disguising himself as a shepherd (Song of Songs 1:7–8). The lovers are totally attuned to one another. Nothing in the world can separate them or extinguish the fire of their passion.

The groom eloquently describes the unparalleled beauty he perceives in his beloved, and she also portrays him in glowing terms: "My lover is radiant and ruddy, outstanding among ten thousand" (Song of Songs 5:10). He had pursued her when she had nothing but herself to offer, and now she cannot even conceive of a relationship with any other man.

The couple shares much more than mutual attraction and romantic passion, however. A warm affection has developed to the point that she can refer to him as a "friend" who is "altogether lovely" (Song of Songs 5:16). And he demonstrates his love and respect for her by honoring her at parties and other social gatherings (Song of Songs 2:4).

There are at least five distinct songs in this book, forming an exquisite collage of poetry committed to the beauty of love and friendship. The Bible tells us that all God-centered marriages should reflect this kind of devotion, even when challenged by the hard work of mutual submission (Ephesians 5:21) and times of struggle (1 Corinthians 7:1–5; Hebrews 13:4).

The Song of Songs can also be interpreted as a picture of God's love for the nation of Israel. The prophet Hosea frequently used this image of a bride and groom to describe God's intimacy with his chosen nation (Hosea 1:7; 11:4; 14:1–9). The same metaphor appears in the New Testament to describe the relationship between Jesus and the church (Ephesians 5:21–33), although no human love relationship could begin to compare with the devotion of Jesus for his bride. Jesus willingly carried out the ultimate demonstration of love: He died for our sin (Ephesians 5:25). His love doesn't ebb and flow based on fleeting circumstances or fickle feelings (Hebrews 13:5), and there are no strings attached (1 Corinthians 13:4–8).

Jesus is the perfect Lover for our souls, and every description of love in the Song of Songs applies to him as to no other. Our Redeemer is truly outstanding among ten thousand (Song of Songs 5:10), the Rose of Sharon, the Lily of the Valley (Song of Songs 2:1). He is altogether lovely and loving and wants us to be committed to him as he is to us (1 John 5:1–3).

Self-Discovery: Jesus wants to hear your expressions of love for him. He also wants you to know the feelings of love he has toward you. When have you last told him that you love him? When have you most recently heard him express his love for you?

GO TO DISCOVERY 174 ON PAGE 881

Lover

[2]Like a lily among thorns
is my darling among the maidens.

Beloved

[3]Like an apple tree among the trees
of the forest
is my lover[x] among the young
men.
I delight[y] to sit in his shade,
and his fruit is sweet to my
taste.[z]

2:3 [x]SS 1:14 [y]SS 1:4 [z]SS 4:16

[4]He has taken me to the banquet
hall,[a]
and his banner[b] over me is love.

2:4 [a]Est 1:11 [b]Nu 1:52

[5]Strengthen me with raisins,
refresh me with apples,[c]
for I am faint with love.[d]

2:5 [c]SS 7:8 [d]SS 5:8

[6]His left arm is under my head,
and his right arm embraces me.[e]

2:6 [e]SS 8:3

[7]Daughters of Jerusalem, I charge
you[f]
by the gazelles and by the does
of the field:
Do not arouse or awaken love
until it so desires.[g]

2:7 [f]SS 5:8 [g]SS 3:5; 8:4

[8]Listen! My lover!
Look! Here he comes,
leaping across the mountains,
bounding over the hills.[h]

2:8 [h]ver 17; SS 8:14

[9]My lover is like a gazelle[i] or a
young stag.[j]
Look! There he stands behind
our wall,
gazing through the windows,
peering through the lattice.

2:9 [i]2Sa 2:18 [j]ver 17; SS 8:14

[10]My lover spoke and said to me,
"Arise, my darling,
my beautiful one, and come with
me.
[11]See! The winter is past;
the rains are over and gone.
[12]Flowers appear on the earth;
the season of singing has come,
the cooing of doves
is heard in our land.
[13]The fig tree forms its early fruit;[k]
the blossoming[l] vines spread
their fragrance.
Arise, come, my darling;
my beautiful one, come with me."

2:13 [k]Isa 28:4; Jer 24:2; Hos 9:10; Mic 7:1; Na 3:12 [l]SS 7:12

Lover

[14]My dove[m] in the clefts of the rock,
in the hiding places on the
mountainside,
show me your face,
let me hear your voice;
for your voice is sweet,
and your face is lovely.[n]

2:14 [m]Ge 8:8; SS 1:15 [n]SS 1:5; 8:13

[15]Catch for us the foxes,[o]
the little foxes
that ruin the vineyards,[p]
our vineyards that are in bloom.[q]

2:15 [o]Jdg 15:4 [p]SS 1:6 [q]SS 7:12

Beloved

[16]My lover is mine and I am his;[r]
he browses among the lilies.[s]
[17]Until the day breaks
and the shadows flee,[t]
turn, my lover,[u]
and be like a gazelle
or like a young stag[v]
on the rugged hills.[a][w]

2:16 [r]SS 7:10 [s]SS 4:5; 6:3

2:17 [t]SS 4:6 [u]SS 1:14 [v]ver 9 [w]ver 8

3 All night long on my bed
I looked[x] for the one my heart
loves;
I looked for him but did not find
him.
[2]I will get up now and go about the
city,
through its streets and squares;
I will search for the one my heart
loves.
So I looked for him but did not
find him.
[3]The watchmen found me

3:1 [x]SS 5:6; Isa 26:9

[a] 17 Or *the hills of Bether*

A BANNER OVER ME

A "banner" (Song of Songs 2:4) was a military flag that held together a fighting unit during battle. Soldiers vowed unconditional allegiance to their banner and would risk their lives for all who fought under it. The mutual devotion of the lovers in Song of Songs was so apparent that it could not have been made more obvious if a huge banner had been waving over their heads. Just as a new bride can bask in the security of her husband's love, so we too can rest with complete confidence in Jesus. He loves us with obvious passion, so much so that he gave up his own life so that we could be with him (Galatians 1:4; Ephesians 5:25–27). We love him because he pursued and courted us in love (1 John 4:19). When he died on the cross and came back again to life, Jesus raised a "banner" of love over us as a promise to come back and take us to be with him (John 14:3).

3:3 [y] SS 5:7

as they made their rounds in the
city.[y]
"Have you seen the one my heart
loves?"
[4] Scarcely had I passed them
when I found the one my heart
loves.
I held him and would not let him go
till I had brought him to my

3:4 [z] SS 8:2 [a] SS 6:9

mother's house,[z]
to the room of the one who
conceived me.[a]

3:5 [b] SS 2:7 [c] SS 8:4

[5] Daughters of Jerusalem, I charge
you[b]
by the gazelles and by the does
of the field:
Do not arouse or awaken love
until it so desires.[c]

3:6 [d] SS 8:5 [e] SS 1:13; 4:6,14 [f] Ex 30:34

[6] Who is this coming up from the
desert[d]
like a column of smoke,
perfumed with myrrh[e] and incense
made from all the spices[f] of the
merchant?

3:7 [g] 1Sa 8:11

[7] Look! It is Solomon's carriage,
escorted by sixty warriors,[g]
the noblest of Israel,
[8] all of them wearing the sword,
all experienced in battle,
each with his sword at his side,

3:8 [h] Job 15:22; Ps 91:5

prepared for the terrors of the
night.[h]
[9] King Solomon made for himself
the carriage;
he made it of wood from
Lebanon.
[10] Its posts he made of silver,
its base of gold.
Its seat was upholstered with
purple,
its interior lovingly inlaid
by*[a]* the daughters of Jerusalem.

3:11 [i] Isa 4:4 [j] Isa 62:5

[11] Come out, you daughters of Zion,[i]
and look at King Solomon
wearing the crown,
the crown with which his
mother crowned him
on the day of his wedding,
the day his heart rejoiced.[j]

Lover

4 How beautiful you are, my darling!
Oh, how beautiful!
Your eyes behind your veil are
doves.[k]

4:1 [k] SS 1:15; 5:12 [l] SS 6:5; Mic 7:14

Your hair is like a flock of goats
descending from Mount Gilead.[l]
[2] Your teeth are like a flock of sheep
just shorn,
coming up from the washing.
Each has its twin;
not one of them is alone.[m]

4:2 [m] SS 6:6

[3] Your lips are like a scarlet ribbon;
your mouth[n] is lovely.
Your temples behind your veil
are like the halves of a
pomegranate.[o]

4:3 [n] SS 5:16 [o] SS 6:7

[4] Your neck is like the tower[p] of
David,
built with elegance*[b]*;
on it hang a thousand shields,[q]
all of them shields of warriors.

4:4 [p] SS 7:4 [q] Eze 27:10

[5] Your two breasts[r] are like two
fawns,
like twin fawns of a gazelle[s]
that browse among the lilies.[t]

4:5 [r] SS 7:3 [s] Pr 5:19 [t] SS 2:16; 6:2-3

[6] Until the day breaks
and the shadows flee,[u]
I will go to the mountain of myrrh[v]
and to the hill of incense.

4:6 [u] SS 2:17 [v] ver 14

[7] All beautiful[w] you are, my darling;
there is no flaw in you.

4:7 [w] SS 1:15

[8] Come with me from Lebanon, my
bride,[x]
come with me from Lebanon.
Descend from the crest of Amana,
from the top of Senir,[y] the
summit of Hermon,[z]
from the lions' dens
and the mountain haunts of the
leopards.

4:8 [x] SS 5:1 [y] Dt 3:9 [z] 1Ch 5:23

[9] You have stolen my heart, my sister,
my bride;
you have stolen my heart
with one glance of your eyes,
with one jewel of your necklace.[a]

4:9 [a] Ge 41:42

[10] How delightful[b] is your love[c], my
sister, my bride!
How much more pleasing is your
love than wine,
and the fragrance of your
perfume than any spice!

4:10 [b] SS 7:6 [c] SS 1:2

[11] Your lips drop sweetness as the
honeycomb, my bride;
milk and honey are under your
tongue.[d]
The fragrance of your garments
is like that of Lebanon.[e]

4:11 [d] Ps 19:10; SS 5:1 [e] Hos 14:6

[12] You are a garden locked up, my
sister, my bride;

a 10 Or *its inlaid interior a gift of love / from*
b 4 The meaning of the Hebrew for this word is uncertain.

you are a spring enclosed, a
sealed fountain.[f]

4:12
[f] Pr 5:15-18

13 Your plants are an orchard of
pomegranates[g]
with choice fruits,
with henna[h] and nard,

4:13
[g] SS 6:11; 7:12
[h] SS 1:14

14 nard and saffron,
calamus and cinnamon,[i]
with every kind of incense tree,
with myrrh[j] and aloes
and all the finest spices.[k]

4:14
[i] Ex 30:23
[j] SS 3:6 [k] SS 1:12

15 You are[a] a garden fountain,
a well of flowing water
streaming down from Lebanon.

Beloved

16 Awake, north wind,
and come, south wind!
Blow on my garden,
that its fragrance may spread
abroad.
Let my lover come into his garden
and taste its choice fruits.[l]

4:16
[l] SS 2:3; 5:1

Lover

5 I have come into my garden, my
sister, my bride;[m]
I have gathered my myrrh with
my spice.
I have eaten my honeycomb and
my honey;
I have drunk my wine and my
milk.[n]

5:1
[m] SS 4:8
[n] SS 4:11; Isa 55:1

Friends

Eat, O friends, and drink;
drink your fill, O lovers.

Beloved

2 I slept but my heart was awake.
Listen! My lover is knocking:
"Open to me, my sister, my darling,
my dove, my flawless[o] one.[p]
My head is drenched with dew,
my hair with the dampness of
the night."

5:2
[o] SS 4:7 [p] SS 6:9

3 I have taken off my robe—
must I put it on again?
I have washed my feet—
must I soil them again?
4 My lover thrust his hand through
the latch-opening;
my heart began to pound for him.
5 I arose to open for my lover,
and my hands dripped with
myrrh,[q]
my fingers with flowing myrrh,
on the handles of the lock.

5:5
[q] ver 13

6 I opened for my lover,[r]
but my lover had left; he was
gone.[s]
My heart sank at his departure.[b]
I looked[t] for him but did not find
him.
I called him but he did not
answer.

5:6
[r] SS 6:1 [s] SS 6:2
[t] SS 3:1

7 The watchmen found me
as they made their rounds in the
city.[u]
They beat me, they bruised me;
they took away my cloak,
those watchmen of the walls!

5:7
[u] SS 3:3

8 O daughters of Jerusalem, I charge
you[v]—
if you find my lover,
what will you tell him?
Tell him I am faint with love.[w]

5:8
[v] SS 2:7; 3:5
[w] SS 2:5

Friends

9 How is your beloved better than
others,
most beautiful of women?[x]
How is your beloved better than
others,
that you charge us so?

5:9
[x] SS 1:8; 6:1

Beloved

10 My lover is radiant and ruddy,
outstanding among ten
thousand.[y]

5:10
[y] Ps 45:2

11 His head is purest gold;
his hair is wavy
and black as a raven.
12 His eyes are like doves[z]
by the water streams,
washed in milk,[a]
mounted like jewels.

5:12
[z] SS 1:15; 4:1
[a] Ge 49:12

13 His cheeks[b] are like beds of spice[c]
yielding perfume.
His lips are like lilies[d]
dripping with myrrh.

5:13
[b] SS 1:10 [c] SS 6:2
[d] SS 2:1

14 His arms are rods of gold
set with chrysolite.
His body is like polished ivory
decorated with sapphires.[c][e]

5:14
[e] Job 28:6

15 His legs are pillars of marble
set on bases of pure gold.
His appearance is like Lebanon,[f]
choice as its cedars.

5:15
[f] 1Ki 4:33; SS 7:4

16 His mouth[g] is sweetness itself;
he is altogether lovely.

5:16
[g] SS 4:3

[a] 15 Or *I am* (spoken by the *Beloved*) [b] 6 Or *heart had gone out to him when he spoke* [c] 14 Or *lapis lazuli*

5:16 [h] SS 7:9 [i] SS 1:5 This is my lover,[h] this my friend,
O daughters of Jerusalem.[i]

Friends

6:1 [j] SS 5:6 [k] SS 1:8 **6** Where has your lover[j] gone,
most beautiful of women?[k]
Which way did your lover turn,
that we may look for him with
you?

Beloved

6:2 [l] SS 5:6 [m] SS 4:12 [n] SS 5:13 [2] My lover has gone[l] down to his
garden,[m]
to the beds of spices,[n]
to browse in the gardens
and to gather lilies.
[3] I am my lover's and my lover is
6:3 [o] SS 7:10 [p] SS 2:16 mine;[o]
he browses among the lilies.[p]

Lover

[4] You are beautiful, my darling, as
6:4 [q] Jos 12:24 [r] Ps 48:2; 50:2 [s] ver 10 Tirzah,[q]
lovely as Jerusalem,[r]
majestic as troops with
banners.[s]
[5] Turn your eyes from me;
they overwhelm me.
6:5 [t] SS 4:1 Your hair is like a flock of goats
descending from Gilead.[t]
[6] Your teeth are like a flock of sheep
coming up from the washing.
6:6 [u] SS 4:2 Each has its twin,
not one of them is alone.[u]

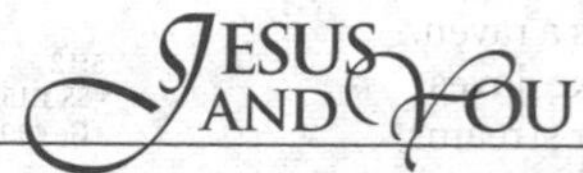

MY LOVER, MY FRIEND

It has often been observed that a good *friendship* is the basis for a good *romance*. In any godly relationship between a husband and wife there is a healthy balance of romance and friendship. In Song of Songs the young woman referred to the young man as "my lover, my friend" (Song of Songs 5:16). Their love was ignited by physical attraction, but the relationship held together because of their maturing friendship. The New Testament shows us that Jesus is both our lover and our friend (see John 15:9–15). His love for us is so complete and so passionate that nothing can ever separate us from it (Romans 8:39). And John 15:13 tells us that Jesus expressed his love in the fullest way possible—by giving up his life so that we might be saved: "Greater love has no one than this, that he lay down his life for his friends."

[7] Your temples behind your veil[v] 6:7 [v] Ge 24:65 [w] SS 4:3
are like the halves of a
pomegranate.[w]
[8] Sixty queens[x] there may be, 6:8 [x] Ps 45:9 [y] Ge 22:24
and eighty concubines,[y]
and virgins beyond number;
[9] but my dove,[z] my perfect one,[a] is 6:9 [z] SS 1:15 [a] SS 5:2 [b] SS 3:4
unique,
the only daughter of her mother,
the favorite of the one who bore
her.[b]
The maidens saw her and called
her blessed;
the queens and concubines
praised her.

Friends

[10] Who is this that appears like the
dawn,
fair as the moon, bright as the
sun,
majestic as the stars in
procession?

Lover

[11] I went down to the grove of nut
trees
to look at the new growth in the
valley,
to see if the vines had budded
or the pomegranates were in 6:11 [c] SS 7:12
bloom.[c]
[12] Before I realized it,
my desire set me among the royal
chariots of my people.[a]

Friends

[13] Come back, come back,
O Shulammite;
come back, come back, that we
may gaze on you!

Lover

Why would you gaze on the
Shulammite
as on the dance[d] of Mahanaim? 6:13 [d] Ex 15:20

7 How beautiful your sandaled
feet, 7:1 [e] Ps 45:13
O prince's[e] daughter!
Your graceful legs are like jewels,
the work of a craftsman's hands.
[2] Your navel is a rounded goblet
that never lacks blended wine.
Your waist is a mound of wheat
encircled by lilies.

[a] 12 Or *among the chariots of Amminadab*; or *among the chariots of the people of the prince*

DISCOVERY 174

THE ULTIMATE TEST OF LOVE

Love is one of the most beautiful words in any language—and one of the most difficult to define. At least in the English-speaking world we use the word in a variety of ways, many of which trivialize its true implications. We speak of loving a husband or wife, our children, a pet, a sport, a favorite food. The Song of Songs celebrates the physical and sexual aspects of romantic love, and for many people these elements are all there is to the "love" between a man and a woman.

But sprinkled throughout the declarations of attraction in the Song of Songs is another theme, one that God views as critical to any love relationship: Love is a commitment. Real love is much more than just a feeling, more than merely a physical, sexual, or even mental or intellectual attraction to another person. The young woman does not hesitate to verbalize the couple's mutual devotion: "I am my lover's and my lover is mine" (Song of Songs 6:3).

Even the first love story ever recorded—that of Adam and Eve—is one that speaks of loving commitment (see Genesis 2:24). The apostle Paul reminded the church in Ephesus that God's ideal for marriage is that it be founded on the total dedication of the partners to one another (Ephesians 5:21). Love in a godly marriage is not a fifty–fifty negotiated partnership; it is the one hundred percent commitment of each party toward the other.

Our very ability to love each other derives from God's love for us. He committed himself to us to a degree beyond what anyone else ever has or ever will. God loved the world with such passion, such ardor, that he sent his only Son to walk the dusty roads in our shoes and ultimately to die in our stead. Jesus' sacrifice frees us to experience the overwhelming and unconditional love of our Creator.

When we trust the One who loves us so fervently and commit our very lives to him, he offers us his abiding presence: "God has said, 'Never will I leave you; never will I forsake you.' So we say with confidence, 'The Lord is my helper; I will not be afraid. What can man do to me?' " (Hebrews 13:5–6). Our God, who is the God of commitment, gives us the strength we need to live for him today (2 Peter 1:3) and the bright hope that guarantees our safety, both now (Hebrews 6:17–20) and for the life to come (1 Peter 1:3–5).

"Grace and peace . . . from Jesus Christ, who is the faithful witness, the firstborn from the dead, and the ruler of the kings of the earth. To him who loved us and has freed us from our sins by his blood, and has made us to be a kingdom and priests to serve his God and Father—to him be glory and power forever and ever! Amen" (Revelation 1:4–6).

Self-Discovery: *Take a moment to express to Jesus how much you love him and how thankful you are for his incomparable gift to you. How does it make you feel to know that his love for you is based on an eternal, unwavering commitment?*

GO TO DISCOVERY 175 ON PAGE 883

7:3 [f]SS 4:5 [3]Your breasts[f] are like two fawns,
twins of a gazelle.
7:4 [g]Ps 144:12; SS 4:4 [4]Your neck is like an ivory tower.[g]
Your eyes are the pools of
[h]Nu 21:26 Heshbon[h]
[i]SS 5:15 by the gate of Bath Rabbim.
Your nose is like the tower of
Lebanon[i]
looking toward Damascus.
[5]Your head crowns you like Mount
7:5 [j]Isa 35:2 Carmel.[j]
Your hair is like royal tapestry;
the king is held captive by its
tresses.
7:6 [k]SS 1:15 [6]How beautiful[k] you are and how
[l]SS 4:10 pleasing,
O love, with your delights![l]
[7]Your stature is like that of the
palm,
7:7 [m]SS 4:5 and your breasts[m] like clusters
of fruit.
[8]I said, "I will climb the palm tree;
I will take hold of its fruit."
May your breasts be like the
clusters of the vine,
7:8 the fragrance of your breath like
[n]SS 2:5 apples,[n]
[9]and your mouth like the best
wine.

Beloved

May the wine go straight to my
7:9 [o]SS 5:16 lover,[o]
flowing gently over lips and
teeth.[*a*]
[10]I belong to my lover,
7:10 [p]Ps 45:11 and his desire[p] is for me.[q]
[q]SS 2:16; 6:3 [11]Come, my lover, let us go to the
countryside,
let us spend the night in the
villages.[*b*]
7:12 [r]SS 1:6 [s]SS 2:15 [12]Let us go early to the vineyards[r]
[t]SS 2:13 to see if the vines have budded,[s]
[u]SS 4:13 if their blossoms[t] have opened,
[v]SS 6:11 and if the pomegranates[u] are in
bloom[v]—
there I will give you my love.
7:13 [w]Ge 30:14 [13]The mandrakes[w] send out their
[x]SS 4:16 fragrance,
and at our door is every delicacy,
both new and old,
that I have stored up for you, my
lover.[x]

8 If only you were to me like a
brother,
who was nursed at my mother's
breasts!
Then, if I found you outside,
I would kiss you,
and no one would despise me.
[2]I would lead you
and bring you to my mother's 8:2 [y]SS 3:4
house[y]—
she who has taught me.
I would give you spiced wine to
drink,
the nectar of my pomegranates.
[3]His left arm is under my head 8:3
and his right arm embraces me.[z] [z]SS 2:6
[4]Daughters of Jerusalem, I charge
you:
Do not arouse or awaken love 8:4
until it so desires.[a] [a]SS 2:7; 3:5

Friends

8:5 [5]Who is this coming up from the [b]SS 3:6 [c]SS 3:4
desert[b]
leaning on her lover?

Beloved

Under the apple tree I roused you;
there your mother conceived[c]
you,
there she who was in labor gave
you birth.
[6]Place me like a seal over your
heart,
like a seal on your arm; 8:6
for love[d] is as strong as death, [d]SS 1:2 [e]Nu 5:14
its jealousy[*c*][e] unyielding as the
grave.[*d*]
It burns like blazing fire,
like a mighty flame.[*e*]
[7]Many waters cannot quench love;
rivers cannot wash it away.
If one were to give
all the wealth of his house for
love, 8:7
it[*f*] would be utterly scorned.[f] [f]Pr 6:35

Friends

[8]We have a young sister,
and her breasts are not yet grown.
What shall we do for our sister
for the day she is spoken for?
[9]If she is a wall,
we will build towers of silver on
her.
If she is a door,
we will enclose her with panels
of cedar.

[*a*] 9 Septuagint, Aquila, Vulgate and Syriac; Hebrew *lips of sleepers* [*b*] 11 Or *henna bushes* [*c*] 6 Or *ardor* [*d*] 6 Hebrew *Sheol* [*e*] 6 Or / *like the very flame of the* LORD [*f*] 7 Or *he*

The Incredible Power of Love

The Song of Songs concludes with a description of love's power. The writer declares that love is as strong as death (Song of Songs 8:6), the most feared and inescapable passage of a human life. Even with our modern technology and advanced medical techniques, no one is immune from death. It is stronger than any other force in our lives—except love, which, as the apostle Paul observed, is the "most excellent way" to exercise all spiritual gifts (1 Corinthians 13).

Love is consuming, like a blazing fire that licks up everything in its path (Song of Songs 8:6). It is a passion that burns, driving people on some occasions to perform the noblest acts. People sacrifice their very lives for love of freedom, their time and energy for love of family, and their individual desires and aspirations for love of husband or wife. While love drives a person once the fire has been ignited, it also warms others when it touches them. Love is invincible. It overcomes the raging storms of life. Difficulties, disappointments and failures cannot destroy a godly love; in fact, these tragedies only intensify the bond. And love is a gift that cannot be purchased (verse 7).

Hundreds of years after this Song of Songs had been composed, Jesus was born to be the Singer of God's love song to us. His love is so intense that nothing can separate us from it (Romans 8:38–39). That love consumed our Lord to the extent that he died on our behalf. Jesus' commitment overcomes all obstacles and enemies—including death. It is a most gracious gift. There is nothing we can do to cause him to care for us any less (1 John 3:16). We are forever secure in the grip of his boundless love.

The apostle Paul expressed the incredible richness of Jesus' love in a resounding declaration: "I pray that you, being rooted and established in love, may have power, together with all the saints, to grasp how wide and long and high and deep is the love of Christ, and to know this love that surpasses knowledge—that you may be filled to the measure of all the fullness of God" (Ephesians 3:17–19).

Jesus' love is not only immense, but it is also eternally secure. Paul asked, "Who shall separate us from the love of Christ? Shall trouble or hardship or famine or nakedness or danger or sword? . . . No, in all these things we are more than conquerors through him who loved us. For I am convinced that neither death nor life, neither angels nor demons, neither the present nor the future, nor any powers, neither height nor depth, nor anything else in all creation, will be able to separate us from the love of God that is in Christ Jesus our Lord" (Romans 8:35,37–39).

Self-Discovery: *Pause to reflect on the magnitude of Jesus' love for you. Think of that love in terms of infinite width, length, height and depth. Concede that you are unable in your own power to grasp the concept of such love. Then bask for a moment in its warmth, and let it seep into your spirit to strengthen you for your service.*

GO TO DISCOVERY 176 ON PAGE 887

Beloved

10 I am a wall,
and my breasts are like towers.
Thus I have become in his eyes

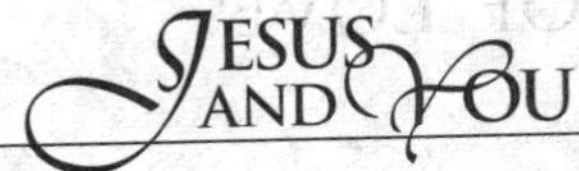

COME AWAY

Song of Songs ends with an appeal: "Come away, my lover" (Song of Songs 8:14). When the young man returned, he took his loved one with him because he longed to be in her company. In the New Testament Jesus promised to return for his "bride," the church, and, like the suitor in Song of Songs, he longs for that day. Although he had informed his disciples that he was going away to get things ready, he promised to come back for his own (John 14:2–4). Jesus loves us so much that he wants to spend eternity with us. He also wants us to become more intimate with him every day as we live our lives now—because he is the lover of our souls (1 Thessalonians 4:16–17). No one will ever love us like he does. We can trust him with all our hearts, because his love is eternally changeless and faithful (Psalm 136).

like one bringing contentment.
11 Solomon had a vineyard[g] in Baal
Hamon;
he let out his vineyard to
tenants.
Each was to bring for its fruit
a thousand shekels[a][h] of silver.
12 But my own vineyard[i] is mine to
give;
the thousand shekels are for you,
O Solomon,
and two hundred[b] are for those
who tend its fruit.

Lover

13 You who dwell in the gardens
with friends in attendance,
let me hear your voice!

Beloved

14 Come away, my lover,
and be like a gazelle[j]
or like a young stag[k]
on the spice-laden mountains.[l]

[a] *11* That is, about 25 pounds (about 11.5 kilograms); also in verse 12 [b] *12* That is, about 5 pounds (about 2.3 kilograms)

8:11 [g] Ecc 2:4 [h] Isa 7:23
8:12 [i] SS 1:6
8:14 [j] Pr 5:19 [k] SS 2:9 [l] SS 2:8,17

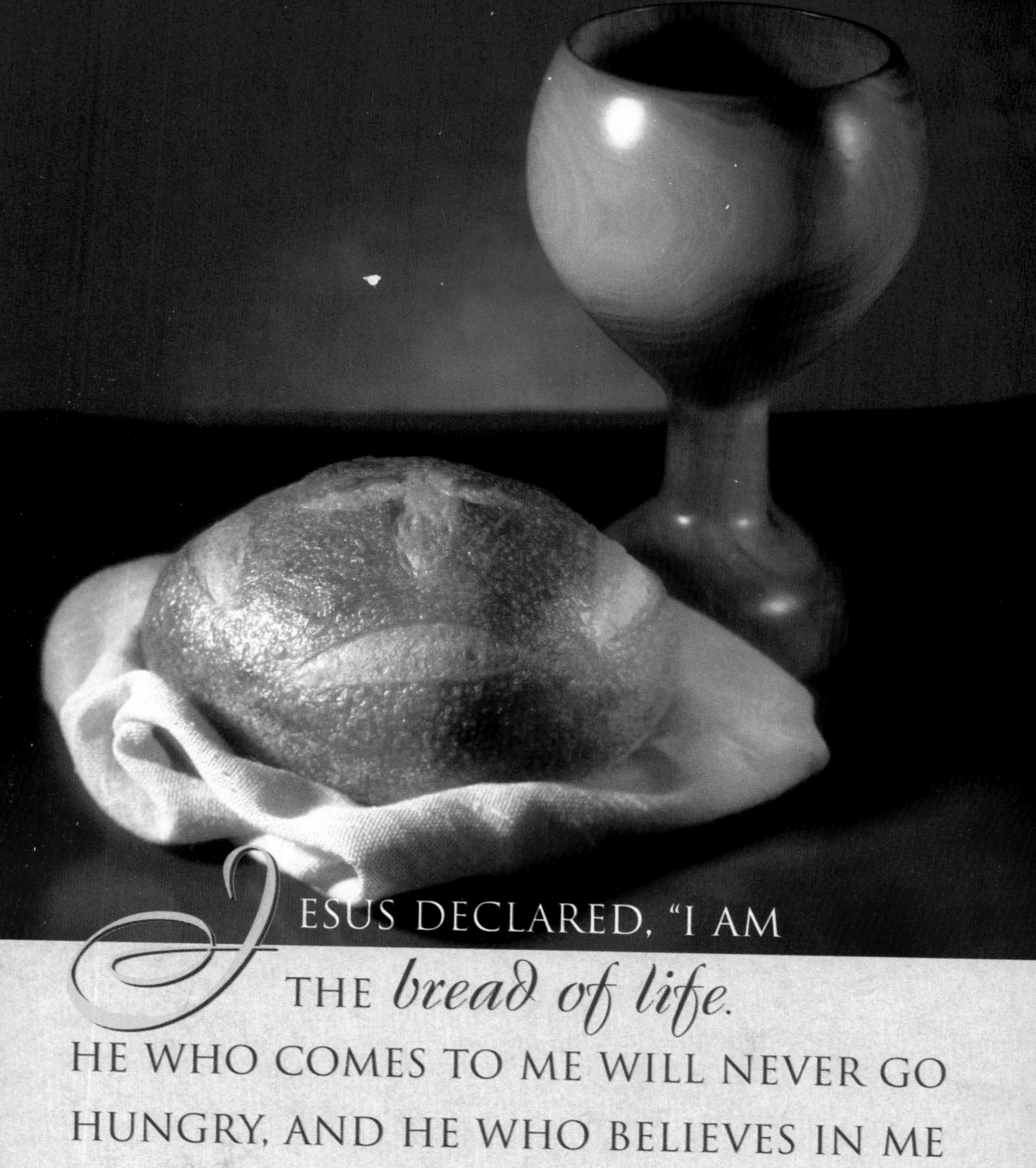

JESUS DECLARED, "I AM THE *bread of life.* HE WHO COMES TO ME WILL NEVER GO HUNGRY, AND HE WHO BELIEVES IN ME WILL NEVER BE THIRSTY."

—JOHN 6:35—

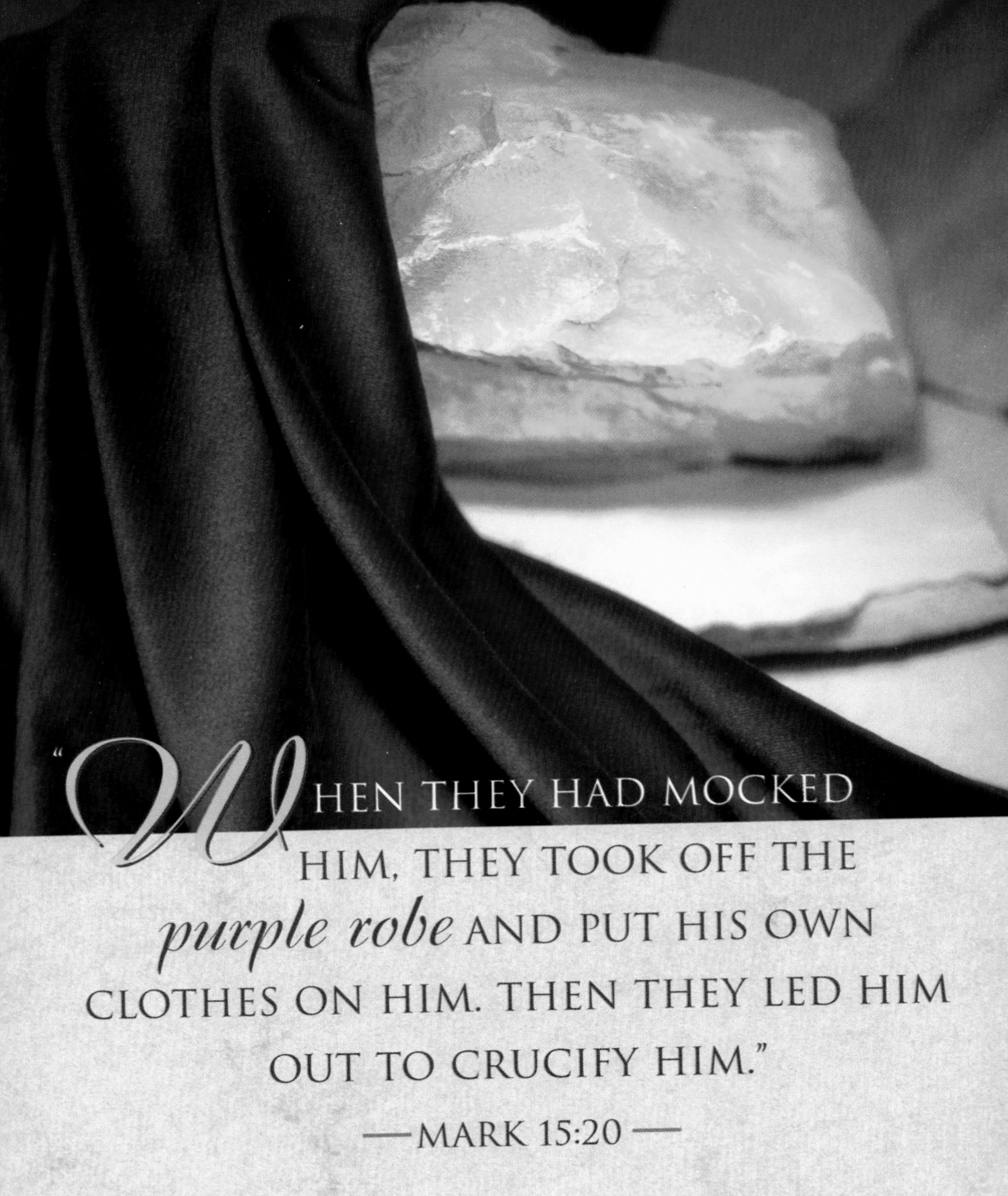

"WHEN THEY HAD MOCKED HIM, THEY TOOK OFF THE *purple robe* AND PUT HIS OWN CLOTHES ON HIM. THEN THEY LED HIM OUT TO CRUCIFY HIM."

—MARK 15:20—

Why call Jesse's descendant a branch? (Isaiah 11:1)

♦ *Isaiah played on the picture of a family tree. From the stump of Jesse a new branch would sprout, a future Messiah whom we now know as Jesus Christ (Matthew 16:16; Romans 1:2–4). Because the Messiah would be a branch of Jesse's family tree, the word* branch *became a Messianic title.*

In what way would the servant be a light for the Gentiles? (Isaiah 42:6)

♦ *The Messiah would welcome Gentiles as well as Jews into the family of God through his sacrificial atonement. Jesus fulfilled God's purpose of reaching out to the whole world both through his chosen people and through his promised Messiah (Isaiah 60:1–14).*

How are we healed by wounds given to someone else? (Isaiah 53:5)

♦ *A modern analogy might be a heart transplant; one person lives because another dies. That physical analogy pictures the spiritual healing God makes available to us through the atoning death of his Son, Jesus Christ.*

Jesus in Isaiah The book of Isaiah is filled with prophecies about God's promised Messiah. Isaiah foresaw the coming Savior as the "anointed" one (Isaiah 61:1), the virgin's son (Isaiah 7:14) who was destined to rule on David's throne (Isaiah 9:6–7), suffer for our sins (Isaiah 53:3–11) and triumph over evil (Isaiah 66:15–24). Isaiah called the Messiah by several different names: Immanuel, meaning "God with us" (Isaiah 7:14); the Branch (Isaiah 11:1); Wonderful Counselor, Mighty God, Prince of Peace (Isaiah 9:6); the servant of the Lord (Isaiah 42:1); the Redeemer (Isaiah 44:6; 48:17); the Holy One and your King (Isaiah 43:15). The New Testament makes it clear that Jesus is that promised Messiah because "all the prophets testify about him" (Acts 10:43). Jesus himself referred in the Gospels to prophecies of Isaiah (Matthew 13:14–15; 15:7–9; Mark 7:6–7), and the Gospel writers speak in several other instances about the fulfillment of Isaiah's prophecies (Matthew 1:21–23; 4:13–16; 12:17–21; Luke 4:17–19; 22:37; John 12:38).

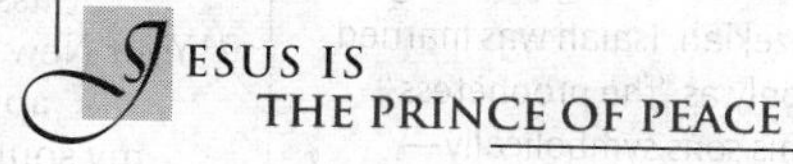

1:1
[a] Nu 12:6
[b] Isa 40:9
[c] Isa 2:1
[d] 2Ch 26:22
[e] 2Ki 16:1

1 The vision[a] concerning Judah and Jerusalem[b] that Isaiah son of Amoz saw[c] during the reigns of Uzziah,[d] Jotham, Ahaz[e] and Hezekiah, kings of Judah.

A Rebellious Nation

1:2
[f] Mic 1:2
[g] Isa 30:1,9; 65:2

2 Hear, O heavens! Listen, O earth!
For the LORD has spoken:[f]
"I reared children and brought them up,
but they have rebelled[g] against me.
3 The ox knows his master,
the donkey his owner's manger,
but Israel does not know,[h]
my people do not understand."

1:3
[h] Jer 8:7; 9:3,6

4 Ah, sinful nation,
a people loaded with guilt,
a brood of evildoers,[i]
children given to corruption!
They have forsaken the LORD;
they have spurned the Holy One[j] of Israel
and turned their backs on him.

1:4
[i] Isa 14:20
[j] Isa 5:19,24

5 Why should you be beaten anymore?
Why do you persist in rebellion?[k]
Your whole head is injured,
your whole heart afflicted.[l]

1:5
[k] Isa 31:6
[l] Isa 33:6,24

6 From the sole of your foot to the top of your head
there is no soundness[m]—
only wounds and welts
and open sores,
not cleansed or bandaged[n]
or soothed with oil.[o]

1:6
[m] Ps 38:3

1:6
[n] Isa 30:26; Jer 8:22
[o] Lk 10:34

7 Your country is desolate,[p]
your cities burned with fire;
your fields are being stripped by foreigners
right before you,
laid waste as when overthrown by strangers.

1:7
[p] Lev 26:34

8 The Daughter of Zion is left
like a shelter in a vineyard,
like a hut[q] in a field of melons,
like a city under siege.

1:8
[q] Job 27:18

9 Unless the LORD Almighty
had left us some survivors,[r]
we would have become like Sodom,
we would have been like Gomorrah.[s]

1:9
[r] Isa 10:20-22; 37:4,31-32
[s] Ge 19:24; Ro 9:29*

10 Hear the word of the LORD,[t]
you rulers of Sodom;[u]
listen to the law[v] of our God,
you people of Gomorrah!

1:10
[t] Isa 28:14
[u] Isa 3:9; Eze 16:49; Ro 9:29; Rev 11:8
[v] Isa 8:20

11 "The multitude of your sacrifices—
what are they to me?" says the LORD.
"I have more than enough of burnt offerings,
of rams and the fat of fattened animals;[w]
I have no pleasure
in the blood of bulls[x] and lambs and goats.[y]

1:11
[w] Ps 50:8
[x] Jer 6:20
[y] 1Sa 15:22; Mal 1:10

12 When you come to appear before me,
who has asked this of you,[z]
this trampling of my courts?

1:12
[z] Ex 23:17

13 Stop bringing meaningless offerings![a]
Your incense[b] is detestable to me.
New Moons, Sabbaths and convocations[c]—
I cannot bear your evil assemblies.

1:13
[a] Isa 66:3
[b] Jer 7:9
[c] 1Ch 23:31

14 Your New Moon festivals and your appointed feasts[d]
my soul hates.
They have become a burden to me;
I am weary[e] of bearing them.

1:14
[d] Lev 23:1-44; Nu 28:11-29:39; Isa 29:1
[e] Isa 7:13; 43:22, 24

15 When you spread out your hands in prayer,
I will hide[f] my eyes from you;
even if you offer many prayers,
I will not listen.
Your hands are full of blood;[g]
16 wash and make yourselves clean.

1:15
[f] Isa 8:17; 59:2; Mic 3:4
[g] Isa 59:3

ISAIAH

PRINCE OF PROPHETS

Isaiah, whose name means "the LORD saves," was the son of a prominent citizen in Jerusalem named Amoz (Isaiah 1:1). Isaiah's ministry began after the death of King Uzziah, around 740 B.C., and extended through the reigns of Jotham, Ahaz and Hezekiah. Isaiah was married but referred to his wife only as "the prophetess" (Isaiah 8:3). He named his sons symbolically—Shear-Jashub means "a remnant will return" (Isaiah 7:3) while Maher-Shalal-Hash-Baz means "quick to the plunder, swift to the spoil" (Isaiah 8:3). Isaiah's prophecies spell out that God's promised Messiah would be born to rule the people of Israel. God also used this noteworthy prophet in several situations that were crucial to the survival of the Messiah's family line (Isaiah 7:1–16; 37:1–4).

God Gets the Red Out

Anyone who has ever observed a child wearing a white tee shirt slurp a cherry popsicle on a hot summer day knows about red dye. Red dye creates stains—and on a white shirt they are usually permanent. Even if some of the dye does wash out, a faint discoloration stays behind. Sin is like red dye on our souls. It may be insidious, but it is never invisible. There is always a stain, and the blot is often humiliating. Sin is not superficial; it penetrates into every thread of the fabric of our lives. But God's Good News is that it doesn't have to stay that way.

God's plan from the beginning has been to remove the ugly smudge sin has left in the world (Isaiah 1:18). He warned us when humankind first decided to turn away from him that sin results in death (Genesis 2:17; 3:19). Rather than wiping people off the face of the earth, however, God set up a sacrificial system to keep the sin of each generation "covered" with blood (Leviticus 16:15–19; 17:11). Later, when the time was right, Jesus came to die that he might make atonement for our sins (Hebrews 2:17; 9:11–28; 1 John 2:2; 4:10). His blood removes the stain of sin *forever*, and God "remembers [our] sins no more" (Isaiah 43:25).

God wants us to simply accept Jesus' death in exchange for our own. He will forgive us unconditionally (Psalm 103:11–12) as he draws us to himself through Jesus (John 12:32). We become a new person in him and are granted a fresh, clean start (2 Corinthians 5:17).

The first snow of winter is pristine, sparkling and clean. It covers over the decaying leaves and the dying grass and makes the world appear breathtakingly new. Jesus' blood does much more, however, than merely *covering* our sin like snow hiding dead autumn leaves—it removes the stain completely (1 John 1:7–9). He allows us to enter into a new relationship with God—not tarnished in any way because it is based on the righteousness of the sinless Son, the One whom God made "to be sin for us so that in him we might become the righteousness of God" (2 Corinthians 5:21; see also Hebrews 10:19–24).

The writer of Hebrews invites us to "draw near to God with a sincere heart in full assurance of faith, having our hearts sprinkled to cleanse us from a guilty conscience and having our bodies washed with pure water" (Hebrews 10:22). And John refers in Revelation 7:14 to those who "have washed their robes and made them white in the blood of the Lamb." Truly, no detergent can rival the cleansing, wonder-working power of Jesus' blood!

Self-Discovery: *Think of the ugliest sin smudge in your life, past or present. Do you truly believe that Jesus has removed that spot and now presents you before the Father as completely pure and sinless? Are you able to let go of the guilt and allow thankfulness to take its place?*

GO TO DISCOVERY 177 ON PAGE 889

Take your evil deeds
out of my sight![h]
Stop doing wrong,[i]
17 learn to do right!
Seek justice,[j]
encourage the oppressed.[a]
Defend the cause of the fatherless,[k]
plead the case of the widow.

18 "Come now, let us reason together,"[l]
says the LORD.
"Though your sins are like scarlet,
they shall be as white as snow;[m]
though they are red as crimson,
they shall be like wool.
19 If you are willing and obedient,
you will eat the best from the
land;[n]
20 but if you resist and rebel,
you will be devoured by the
sword."[o]
For the mouth of the LORD
has spoken.[p]
21 See how the faithful city
has become a harlot![q]
She once was full of justice;
righteousness used to dwell in
her—
but now murderers!
22 Your silver has become dross,
your choice wine is diluted with
water.
23 Your rulers are rebels,
companions of thieves;
they all love bribes[r]
and chase after gifts.
They do not defend the cause of
the fatherless;
the widow's case does not come
before them.[s]
24 Therefore the Lord, the LORD
Almighty,
the Mighty One of Israel, declares:
"Ah, I will get relief from my foes
and avenge[t] myself on my
enemies.
25 I will turn my hand against you;
I will thoroughly purge away
your dross
and remove all your impurities.[u]
26 I will restore your judges as in days
of old,[v]
your counselors as at the
beginning.
Afterward you will be called
the City of Righteousness,[w]
the Faithful City.[x]"

27 Zion will be redeemed with justice,
her penitent ones with
righteousness.[y]
28 But rebels and sinners will both be
broken,
and those who forsake the LORD
will perish.[z]

29 "You will be ashamed because of
the sacred oaks[a]
in which you have delighted;
you will be disgraced because of
the gardens[b]
that you have chosen.
30 You will be like an oak with fading
leaves,
like a garden without water.
31 The mighty man will become
tinder
and his work a spark;
both will burn together,
with no one to quench the fire.[c]"

The Mountain of the LORD

2 This is what Isaiah son of Amoz
saw concerning Judah and Jerusalem:[d]

2 In the last days
the mountain[e] of the LORD's temple
will be established
as chief among the mountains;
it will be raised above the hills,
and all nations will stream to it.

3 Many peoples will come and say,
"Come, let us go up to the
mountain of the LORD,
to the house of the God of Jacob.
He will teach us his ways,
so that we may walk in his
paths."
The law[f] will go out from Zion,
the word of the LORD from
Jerusalem.[g]
4 He will judge between the nations
and will settle disputes for many
peoples.
They will beat their swords into
plowshares
and their spears into pruning
hooks.[h]
Nation will not take up sword
against nation,[i]
nor will they train for war
anymore.

a 17 Or / *rebuke the oppressor*

1:16 [h] Isa 52:11 [i] Isa 55:7; Jer 25:5
1:17 [j] Zep 2:3 [k] Ps 82:3
1:18 [l] Isa 41:1; 43:9, 26 [m] Ps 51:7; Rev 7:14
1:19 [n] Dt 30:15-16; Isa 55:2
1:20 [o] Isa 3:25; 65:12 [p] Isa 34:16; 40:5; 58:14; Mic 4:4
1:21 [q] Isa 57:3-9; Jer 2:20
1:23 [r] Ex 23:8 [s] Isa 10:2; Jer 5:28; Eze 22:6-7; Zec 7:10
1:24 [t] Isa 35:4; 59:17; 61:2; 63:4
1:25 [u] Eze 22:22; Mal 3:3
1:26 [v] Jer 33:7,11 [w] Isa 33:5; 62:1; Zec 8:3 [x] Isa 60:14; 62:2
1:27 [y] Isa 35:10; 62:12; 63:4
1:28 [z] Ps 9:5; Isa 24:20; 66:24; 2Th 1:8-9
1:29 [a] Isa 57:5 [b] Isa 65:3; 66:17
1:31 [c] Isa 5:24; 9:18-19; 26:11; 33:14; 66:15-16,24
2:1 [d] Isa 1:1
2:2 [e] Isa 27:13; 56:7; 66:20; Mic 4:7
2:3 [f] Isa 51:4,7 [g] Lk 24:47
2:4 [h] Joel 3:10 [i] Ps 46:9; Isa 9:5; 11:6-9; 32:18; Hos 2:18; Zec 9:10
2:5 [j] Isa 58:1

God's Invitation

We as human beings are fascinated with predictions and speculations about what lies ahead. From the beginning of time God has promised his people a future that will contain everything he intended for his world and his people in the first place. We cannot pinpoint exactly when that time will come, but we do know that God wants us to be prepared. No matter what might be happening in the world around us, one truth remains constant: God asks us to walk with him (Isaiah 2:5).

Throughout the Bible there are many descriptions of earth's final days. Life will not be pleasant for anyone living at that time. Even as Christians we are tempted to take pride in what we can accomplish without God, and our world is full of evil enticements that do not come from his Fatherly hand. Many people would prefer to trust superstitions, Eastern philosophies, horoscopes, chance, even themselves—anything or anyone except God (verses 6–8).

Ultimately all of these distractions and "idols" lead us away from the one true God. God promises to humble humankind, to put us in our place, so to speak (verse 9). His plan has always been for people to live together in harmony with him and in obedience to his way. He desires personal fellowship with each of us, a relationship in which he himself will be our guide and mentor (verse 3). He wants to be the sole focus of our devotion, the only One to whom we can turn for justice and wisdom.

This desire to be close to us is one of the reasons that the Father sent Jesus, his one and only Son. Not only was Jesus born into the human race to show us firsthand what God is like, but he also died for our sins so that we might be made right with God (2 Corinthians 5:16–21). Jesus is the One whom God had promised for generations to send, the One who will be worshiped forever (Philippians 2:9–11).

Until that day, what does God expect from us? "Let us walk in the light of the LORD," invited the prophet in Isaiah 2:5. Jesus himself elaborated in John 8:12: "I am the light of the world. Whoever follows me will never walk in darkness, but will have the light of life." As we live to please our Savior, we promote his way in the world around us. We show people by the light that shines in our hearts and lives what it means to truly worship God: "God, who said, 'Let light shine out of darkness,' made his light shine in our hearts to give us the light of the knowledge of the glory of God in the face of Christ" (2 Corinthians 4:6).

And we can in turn offer his peace and his promise of hope to a broken world. In the words of the apostle Paul, "Let your gentleness be evident to all. The Lord is near. Do not be anxious about anything, but in everything, by prayer and petition, with thanksgiving, present your requests to God. And the peace of God, which transcends all understanding, will guard your hearts and your minds in Christ Jesus" (Philippians 5:5–8).

Self-Discovery: *List some descriptive words for darkness and others for light. If you prefer to walk in the light, identify some reasons. Then reflect on the concept of walking daily in the sunshine with Jesus, the light of the world.*

GO TO DISCOVERY 178 ON PAGE 895

5 Come, O house of Jacob,[j]
let us walk in the light[k] of the
LORD.

The Day of the LORD

6 You have abandoned[l] your people,
the house of Jacob.
They are full of superstitions from
the East;
they practice divination like the
Philistines[m]
and clasp hands[n] with pagans.[o]
7 Their land is full of silver and gold;
there is no end to their treasures.
Their land is full of horses;[p]
there is no end to their chariots.[q]
8 Their land is full of idols;[r]
they bow down to the work of
their hands,
to what their fingers[s] have made.
9 So man will be brought low[t]
and mankind humbled[u]—
do not forgive them.[a][v]

10 Go into the rocks,
hide in the ground
from dread of the LORD
and the splendor of his majesty![w]
11 The eyes of the arrogant man will
be humbled
and the pride[x] of men brought
low;
the LORD alone will be exalted in
that day.

12 The LORD Almighty has a day in
store
for all the proud and lofty,
for all that is exalted[y]
(and they will be humbled),[z]
13 for all the cedars of Lebanon, tall
and lofty,
and all the oaks of Bashan,[a]
14 for all the towering mountains
and all the high hills,[b]
15 for every lofty tower
and every fortified wall,[c]
16 for every trading ship[b][d]
and every stately vessel.
17 The arrogance of man will be
brought low
and the pride of men humbled;
the LORD alone will be exalted in
that day,[e]
18 and the idols will totally
disappear.[f]

19 Men will flee to caves in the rocks
and to holes in the ground
from dread of the LORD
and the splendor of his majesty,
when he rises to shake the earth.[g]
20 In that day men will throw away
to the rodents and bats[h]
their idols of silver and idols of gold,
which they made to worship.
21 They will flee to caverns in the rocks
and to the overhanging crags
from dread of the LORD
and the splendor of his majesty,
when he rises to shake the earth.[i]

22 Stop trusting in man,[j]
who has but a breath in his
nostrils.
Of what account is he?[k]

Judgment on Jerusalem and Judah

3 See now, the Lord,
the LORD Almighty,
is about to take from Jerusalem
and Judah
both supply and support:
all supplies of food[l] and all
supplies of water,[m]
2 the hero and warrior,[n]
the judge and prophet,
the soothsayer and elder,[o]
3 the captain of fifty and man of rank,
the counselor, skilled craftsman
and clever enchanter.

4 I will make boys their officials;
mere children will govern them.[p]
5 People will oppress each other—
man against man, neighbor
against neighbor.[q]
The young will rise up against the
old,
the base against the honorable.

6 A man will seize one of his brothers
at his father's home, and say,
"You have a cloak, you be our leader;
take charge of this heap of ruins!"
7 But in that day he will cry out,
"I have no remedy.[r]
I have no food or clothing in my
house;
do not make me the leader of
the people."

8 Jerusalem staggers,
Judah is falling;[s]
their words[t] and deeds are against
the LORD,

a 9 Or *not raise them up* *b* 16 Hebrew *every ship of Tarshish*

2:5 k Isa 60:1,19-20; 1Jn 1:5,7
2:6 l Dt 31:17 m 2Ki 1:2 n Pr 6:1 o 2Ki 16:7
2:7 p Dt 17:16 q Isa 31:1; Mic 5:10
2:8 r Isa 10:9-11 s Isa 17:8
2:9 t Ps 62:9 u Isa 5:15 v Ne 4:5
2:10 w 2Th 1:9; Rev 6:15-16
2:11 x Isa 5:15; 37:23
2:12 y Isa 24:4,21; Mal 4:1 z Job 40:11
2:13 a Zec 11:2
2:14 b Isa 30:25; 40:4
2:15 c Isa 25:2,12
2:16 d 1Ki 10:22
2:17 e ver 11
2:18 f Isa 21:9
2:19 g Heb 12:26
2:20 h Lev 11:19
2:21 i ver 19
2:22 j Ps 146:3; Jer 17:5 k Ps 8:4; 144:3; Isa 40:15; Jas 4:14
3:1 l Lev 26:26 m Isa 5:13; Eze 4:16
3:2 n Eze 17:13 o 2Ki 24:14; Isa 9:14-15
3:4 p Ecc 10:16 *fn*
3:5 q Isa 9:19; Jer 9:8; Mic 7:2,6
3:7 r Eze 34:4; Hos 5:13
3:8 s Isa 1:7 t Isa 9:15,17

3:8 u Ps 73:9,11
defying[u] his glorious presence.
9 The look on their faces testifies
against them;
3:9 v Ge 13:13 w Pr 8:36; Ro 6:23
they parade their sin like Sodom;[v]
they do not hide it.
Woe to them!
They have brought disaster[w]
upon themselves.

3:10 x Dt 28:1-14 y Ps 128:2
10 Tell the righteous it will be well[x]
with them,
for they will enjoy the fruit of
their deeds.[y]
3:11 z Dt 28:15-68
11 Woe to the wicked! Disaster[z] is
upon them!
They will be paid back for what
their hands have done.

3:12 a ver 4 b Isa 9:16
12 Youths[a] oppress my people,
women rule over them.
O my people, your guides lead you
astray;[b]
they turn you from the path.

13 The LORD takes his place in court;
3:13 c Mic 6:2
he rises to judge[c] the people.
3:14 d Job 22:4 e Job 24:9; Jas 2:6
14 The LORD enters into judgment[d]
against the elders and leaders of
his people:
"It is you who have ruined my
vineyard;
the plunder[e] from the poor is in
your houses.
3:15 f Ps 94:5
15 What do you mean by crushing my
people[f]
and grinding the faces of the
poor?"
declares the Lord,
the LORD Almighty.

3:16 g SS 3:11
16 The LORD says,
"The women of Zion[g] are
haughty,
walking along with outstretched
necks,
flirting with their eyes,
tripping along with mincing steps,
with ornaments jingling on their
ankles.
17 Therefore the Lord will bring sores
on the heads of the women
of Zion;
the LORD will make their scalps
bald."

18 In that day the Lord will snatch
3:18 h Jdg 8:21
away their finery: the bangles and headbands and crescent necklaces,[h] 19 the
3:20 i Ex 39:28
earrings and bracelets and veils, 20 the
headdresses[i] and ankle chains and
sashes, the perfume bottles and charms,
21 the signet rings and nose rings, 22 the
fine robes and the capes and cloaks, the
purses 23 and mirrors, and the linen garments and tiaras and shawls.

24 Instead of fragrance[j] there will be a 3:24 j Est 2:12 k Pr 31:24 l Isa 22:12 m La 2:10; Eze 27:30-31 n 1Pe 3:3
stench;
instead of a sash,[k] a rope;
instead of well-dressed hair,
baldness;[l]
instead of fine clothing,
sackcloth;[m]
instead of beauty,[n] branding.
25 Your men will fall by the sword,[o] 3:25 o Isa 1:20
your warriors in battle.
26 The gates of Zion will lament and
mourn;[p] 3:26 p Jer 14:2 q La 2:10
destitute, she will sit on the
ground.[q]

4 In that day seven women 4:1 r Isa 13:12 s 2Th 3:12 t Ge 30:23
will take hold of one man[r]
and say, "We will eat our own food[s]
and provide our own clothes;
only let us be called by your name.
Take away our disgrace!"[t]

The Branch of the LORD

2 In that day the Branch of the LORD[u] 4:2 u Isa 11:1-5; 53:2; Jer 23:5-6; Zec 3:8; 6:12 v Ps 72:16
will be beautiful and glorious, and the
fruit[v] of the land will be the pride and
glory of the survivors in Israel. 3 Those

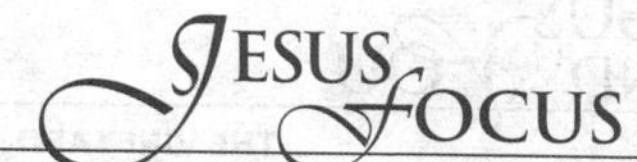

THE BRANCH

Isaiah referred to God's promised Messiah as "the Branch of the LORD" (Isaiah 4:2) and described him as issuing from the family line of King David (Isaiah 11:1). Here, God promised that there would come a day in which David's family line would sprout and blossom in a new way. The Messiah's appearance would bring God's glory back to his chosen people. Sometimes we fail to see beyond Isaiah's severe warnings, but these prophecies also offer tremendous hope for the future.

The Messiah is referred to as the "Branch" in several other places in the Bible (see Jeremiah 23:5; 33:15 and Zechariah 3:8; 6:12). Although David's family line had been cut down like a tree, the roots remained alive. When the time was right (Galatians 4:4–5), God himself fulfilled the promise he had made toDavid (2 Samuel 7:11–16)—sending Jesus to be our eternal King and precious Savior.

4:3 wRo 11:5 xIsa 52:1; 60:21 yLk 10:20

who are left in Zion, who remain[w] in
Jerusalem, will be called holy,[x] all who
are recorded[y] among the living in Jerusalem. 4 The Lord will wash away the

4:4 zIsa 3:24 aIsa 1:15 bIsa 28:6 cIsa 1:31; Mt 3:11

filth[z] of the women of Zion; he will
cleanse the bloodstains[a] from Jerusalem
by a spirit[a] of judgment[b] and a spirit[a] of
fire.[c] 5 Then the LORD will create over all
of Mount Zion and over those who assemble there a cloud of smoke by day

4:5 dEx 13:21 eIsa 60:1

and a glow of flaming fire by night;[d] over
all the glory[e] will be a canopy. 6 It will be

4:6 fPs 27:5 gIsa 25:4

a shelter[f] and shade from the heat of the
day, and a refuge[g] and hiding place from
the storm and rain.

The Song of the Vineyard

5:1 hPs 80:8-9

5 I will sing for the one I love
a song about his vineyard:[h]
My loved one had a vineyard
on a fertile hillside.
2 He dug it up and cleared it of
stones

5:2 iJer 2:21 jMt 21:19; Mk 11:13; Lk 13:6

and planted it with the choicest
vines.[i]
He built a watchtower in it
and cut out a winepress as well.
Then he looked for a crop of good
grapes,
but it yielded only bad fruit.[j]

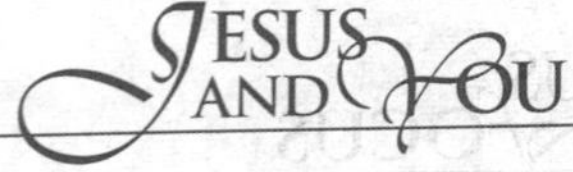

THE VINEYARD

The "Song of the Vineyard" creatively communicates God's message to his people. Israel was God's "vineyard," and he had carefully and lovingly tended his people, only to watch them produce "bad fruit" (Isaiah 5:2). God wants his people to reflect the quality of their relationship with him in who they are and how they act, but his people are all too frequently more concerned with living their own way. In the New Testament Jesus also more than once used the image of a vineyard in his parables. He talked about vineyard workers (Matthew 20:1–16), vineyard tenants (Mark 12:1–12) and a fig tree growing in a vineyard (Luke 13:6–9). Each parable teaches that "good fruit" in a person's life is the evidence of a changed heart and a life committed to walking with God. Jesus called himself "the true vine" (John 15:1) and those who choose to walk with him are the branches: "If a man remains in me and I in him, he will bear much fruit" (John 15:5).

3 "Now you dwellers in Jerusalem
and men of Judah,
judge between me and my
vineyard.[k]

5:3 kMt 21:40

4 What more could have been done
for my vineyard
than I have done for it?[l]

5:4 l2Ch 36:15; Jer 2:5-7; Mic 6:3-4; Mt 23:37

When I looked for good grapes,
why did it yield only bad?
5 Now I will tell you
what I am going to do to my
vineyard:
I will take away its hedge,
and it will be destroyed;

5:5 mPs 80:12 nIsa 28:3,18; La 1:15; Lk 21:24

I will break down its wall,[m]
and it will be trampled.[n]
6 I will make it a wasteland,
neither pruned nor cultivated,

5:6 oIsa 7:23,24; Heb 6:8

and briers and thorns[o] will grow
there.
I will command the clouds
not to rain on it."

5:7 pPs 80:8 qIsa 59:15

7 The vineyard[p] of the LORD Almighty
is the house of Israel,
and the men of Judah
are the garden of his delight.
And he looked for justice,[q] but saw
bloodshed;
for righteousness, but heard
cries of distress.

Woes and Judgments

5:8 rJer 22:13 sMic 2:2; Hab 2:9-12

8 Woe[r] to you who add house to
house
and join field to field[s]
till no space is left
and you live alone in the land.

5:9 tIsa 22:14 uIsa 6:11-12; Mt 23:38

9 The LORD Almighty has declared in
my hearing:[t]

"Surely the great houses will
become desolate,[u]
the fine mansions left without
occupants.
10 A ten-acre[b] vineyard will produce
only a bath[c] of wine,

5:10 vLev 26:26

a homer[d] of seed only an ephah[e]
of grain."[v]

11 Woe to those who rise early in the
morning
to run after their drinks,

[a] 4 Or *the Spirit* [b] 10 Hebrew *ten-yoke,* that is, the land plowed by 10 yoke of oxen in one day [c] 10 That is, probably about 6 gallons (about 22 liters) [d] 10 That is, probably about 6 bushels (about 220 liters) [e] 10 That is, probably about 3/5 bushel (about 22 liters)

who stay up late at night
till they are inflamed with wine.[w]
12 They have harps and lyres at their
banquets,
tambourines and flutes and
wine,
but they have no regard[x] for the
deeds of the LORD,
no respect for the work of his
hands.[y]
13 Therefore my people will go into
exile[z]
for lack of understanding;[a]
their men of rank will die of hunger
and their masses will be parched
with thirst.
14 Therefore the grave[a][b] enlarges its
appetite
and opens its mouth[c] without
limit;
into it will descend their nobles
and masses
with all their brawlers and
revelers.
15 So man will be brought low[d]
and mankind humbled,[e]
the eyes of the arrogant[f]
humbled.
16 But the LORD Almighty will be
exalted by his justice,[g]
and the holy God will show
himself holy[h] by his
righteousness.
17 Then sheep will graze as in their
own pasture;[i]
lambs will feed[b] among the
ruins of the rich.

18 Woe to those who draw sin along
with cords of deceit,
and wickedness[j] as with cart
ropes,
19 to those who say, "Let God hurry,
let him hasten his work
so we may see it.
Let it approach,
let the plan of the Holy One of
Israel come,
so we may know it."[k]

20 Woe to those who call evil good
and good evil,
who put darkness for light
and light for darkness,[l]
who put bitter for sweet
and sweet for bitter.[m]

21 Woe to those who are wise in their
own eyes[n]

5:11 [w]Pr 23:29-30
5:12 [x]Job 34:27 [y]Ps 28:5; Am 6:5-6
5:13 [z]Hos 4:6 [a]Isa 1:3; Hos 4:6
5:14 [b]Pr 30:16 [c]Nu 16:30
5:15 [d]Isa 10:33 [e]Isa 2:9 [f]Isa 2:11
5:16 [g]Isa 28:17; 30:18; 33:5; 61:8 [h]Isa 29:23
5:17 [i]Isa 7:25; Zep 2:6,14
5:18 [j]Isa 59:4-8; Jer 23:14
5:19 [k]Jer 17:15; Eze 12:22; 2Pe 3:4
5:20 [l]Mt 6:22-23; Lk 11:34-35 [m]Am 5:7
5:21 [n]Pr 3:7; Ro 12:16; 1Co 3:18-20

and clever in their own sight.

22 Woe to those who are heroes at
drinking wine[o]
and champions at mixing drinks,
23 who acquit the guilty for a bribe,[p]
but deny justice[q] to the
innocent.[r]
24 Therefore, as tongues of fire lick up
straw
and as dry grass sinks down in
the flames,
so their roots will decay[s]
and their flowers blow away like
dust;
for they have rejected the law of
the LORD Almighty
and spurned the word[t] of the
Holy One of Israel.
25 Therefore the LORD's anger[u] burns
against his people;
his hand is raised and he strikes
them down.
The mountains shake,
and the dead bodies are like
refuse[v] in the streets.

Yet for all this, his anger is not
turned away,[w]
his hand is still upraised.[x]

26 He lifts up a banner for the distant
nations,
he whistles[y] for those at the
ends of the earth.[z]
Here they come,
swiftly and speedily!
27 Not one of them grows tired or
stumbles,
not one slumbers or sleeps;
not a belt is loosened at the waist,[a]
not a sandal thong is broken.[b]
28 Their arrows are sharp,[c]
all their bows[d] are strung;
their horses' hoofs seem like flint,
their chariot wheels like a
whirlwind.
29 Their roar is like that of the lion,[e]
they roar like young lions;
they growl as they seize[f] their prey
and carry it off with no one to
rescue.[g]
30 In that day they will roar over it
like the roaring of the sea.[h]
And if one looks at the land,
he will see darkness and
distress;[i]

5:22 [o]Pr 23:20
5:23 [p]Ex 23:8 [q]Isa 10:2 [r]Ps 94:21; Jas 5:6
5:24 [s]Job 18:16 [t]Isa 8:6; 30:9,12
5:25 [u]2Ki 22:13 [v]2Ki 9:37 [w]Jer 4:8; Da 9:16 [x]Isa 9:12,17,21; 10:4
5:26 [y]Isa 7:18; Zec 10:8 [z]Dt 28:49; Isa 13:5; 18:3
5:27 [a]Job 12:18 [b]Joel 2:7-8
5:28 [c]Ps 45:5 [d]Ps 7:12
5:29 [e]Jer 51:38; Zep 3:3; Zec 11:3 [f]Isa 10:6; 49:24-25 [g]Isa 42:22; Mic 5:8
5:30 [h]Lk 21:25 [i]Isa 8:22; Jer 4:23-28

[a] *14* Hebrew *Sheol* [b] *17* Septuagint; Hebrew / *strangers will eat*

5:30 [j]Joel 2:10

even the light will be darkened[j]
by the clouds.

Isaiah's Commission

6:1 [k]2Ch 26:22,23 [l]2Ki 15:7 [m]Jn 12:41 [n]Rev 4:2

6 In the year that King Uzziah[k]
died,[l] I saw the Lord[m] seated on a
throne,[n] high and exalted, and the train
of his robe filled the temple. 2Above him

6:2 [o]Rev 4:8 [p]Eze 1:11

were seraphs,[o] each with six wings: With
two wings they covered their faces, with
two they covered their feet,[p] and with
two they were flying. 3And they were
calling to one another:

"Holy, holy, holy is the LORD
Almighty;
the whole earth is full of his
glory."[q]

6:3 [q]Ps 72:19; Rev 4:8

4At the sound of their voices the doorposts and thresholds shook and the
temple was filled with smoke.
5"Woe to me!" I cried. "I am ruined!

6:5 [r]Jer 9:3-8 [s]Jer 51:57

For I am a man of unclean lips, and I live
among a people of unclean lips,[r] and my
eyes have seen the King,[s] the LORD Almighty."
6Then one of the seraphs flew to me
with a live coal in his hand, which he had
taken with tongs from the altar. 7With it

6:7 [t]Jer 1:9 [u]1Jn 1:7

he touched my mouth and said, "See,
this has touched your lips;[t] your guilt is
taken away and your sin atoned for.[u]"

6:8 [v]Ac 9:4

8Then I heard the voice[v] of the Lord
saying, "Whom shall I send? And who
will go for us?"
And I said, "Here am I. Send me!"

6:9 [w]Eze 3:11 [x]Mt 13:15*; Lk 8:10*

9He said, "Go[w] and tell this people:

" 'Be ever hearing, but never
understanding;
be ever seeing, but never
perceiving.'[x]

6:10 [y]Dt 32:15; Ps 119:70 [z]Jer 5:21 [a]Mt 13:13-15; Mk 4:12*; Ac 28:26-27*

10Make the heart of this people
calloused;[y]
make their ears dull
and close their eyes.[a]
Otherwise they might see with
their eyes,
hear with their ears,[z]
understand with their hearts,
and turn and be healed."[a]

6:11 [b]Ps 79:5 [c]Lev 26:31

11Then I said, "For how long, O Lord?"[b]
And he answered:

"Until the cities lie ruined[c]
and without inhabitant,
until the houses are left deserted
and the fields ruined and
ravaged,

6:12 [d]Dt 28:64 [e]Jer 4:29

12until the LORD has sent everyone
far away[d]
and the land is utterly forsaken.[e]

6:13 [f]Isa 1:9 [g]Job 14:7

13And though a tenth remains[f] in
the land,
it will again be laid waste.
But as the terebinth and oak
leave stumps when they are cut
down,
so the holy seed will be the
stump in the land."[g]

The Sign of Immanuel

7:1 [h]2Ki 15:37 [i]2Ch 28:5 [j]2Ki 15:25

7 When Ahaz son of Jotham, the
son of Uzziah, was king of Judah,
King Rezin[h] of Aram[i] and Pekah[j] son of
Remaliah king of Israel marched up to
fight against Jerusalem, but they could
not overpower it.

7:2 [k]ver 13; Isa 22:22 [l]Isa 9:9

2Now the house of David[k] was told,
"Aram has allied itself with[b] Ephraim[l]";
so the hearts of Ahaz and his people

[a] 9,10 Hebrew; Septuagint *'You will be ever hearing, but never understanding; / you will be ever seeing, but never perceiving.' / 10This people's heart has become calloused; / they hardly hear with their ears, / and they have closed their eyes* [b] 2 Or *has set up camp in*

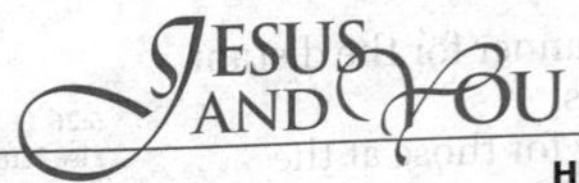

HEAVEN'S THRONE

Isaiah's portrayal of heaven's throne room is similar to John's depiction in Revelation 4. In both accounts, God the Father sits enthroned in the heavenly temple. Both describe winged angelic creatures ("seraphs"), ablaze with God's glory and crying out for all to hear that the Lord Almighty is "holy, holy, holy" (Isaiah 6:2–3; Revelation 4:6–8). Both Isaiah and John were overwhelmed by God's glory and presence. Isaiah cried out, "Woe to me!" (Isaiah 6:5), while John simply "wept and wept" (Revelation 5:4). Both men knew the awesome privilege of standing in God's presence. John testified that God alone is worthy of ultimate praise and worship: "You are worthy, our Lord and God, to receive glory and honor and power" (Revelation 4:11). Isaiah described the Lord as "high and exalted" (Isaiah 6:1). This phrase applies both to God the Father (Isaiah 57:15) and to God the Son, the suffering servant (Isaiah 52:13), confirming that God the Father and God the Son are one, sharing the same attributes and being worthy of our highest honor and praise (Acts 2:33; 3:13; Ephesians 1:20–23; Philippians 2:9–11).

DISCOVERY 178

A Model of Forgiveness

There are many different notions in our world about the meaning of the word *forgiveness*: "Forgive but never forget." "To err is human; to forgive divine." "Forgive? Not on your life! He'll never live this one down." God has a very different idea, however.

Isaiah 6 describes what we all know to be the human condition. We envy other people to the point of bitterness. We murder others, either literally or with gossip that just as surely maligns the reputation. We lie, cheat and grasp for ourselves what belongs to others. Even Isaiah, one of God's great prophets, knew that he had no hope of standing in the presence of a holy God: "I am ruined! For I am a man of unclean lips, and I live among a people of unclean lips" (verse 5).

Both God's Word and our own experience cry out that each of us is a sinner. Yet our downfall is not as thoroughgoing and final as it first appears. God recognized our desperate situation and has provided a way to repair the ravages caused by sin. The process begins when the Holy Spirit convicts us to admit that our sin keeps us apart from the holy God who created us (John 16:8). When we perceive God as he really is—in all his beauty, majesty and perfection—we start realizing just how far we have wandered from his presence. We begin to develop an acute awareness of our failures, of the sins that mark and mar our lives, such as arrogance, selfishness, jealousy, lust, rage and inappropriately expressed anger.

When we admit our shortcomings and turn to God, he forgives us: "Your guilt is taken away and your sin atoned for" (Isaiah 6:7). Isaiah didn't *do* anything to induce God to forgive him; God offered forgiveness to him as a free gift. We can indeed have an intimate relationship with the holy God. We don't have to be trapped by passions, addictions or past choices that would otherwise lead us down a destructive path. When we are willing to believe God, accept his forgiveness and learn to live according to his will, we have the opportunity for a brand-new start (2 Corinthians 5:17).

Jesus Christ is the One who made it possible for God to forgive us. From the beginning, the cost of turning away from God has been the reality of a jagged and gaping abyss separating us eternally from him. But because of Jesus' atoning sacrifice, God no longer holds our sin against us (Romans 4:7–8; 2 Corinthians 5:16–21), and we, like the prophet Isaiah experienced when the angel touched his lips with a coal, are made completely clean. In the same way Jesus touches and transforms the life of every person who turns to him.

Self-Discovery: *Are you willing, using the model of Jesus, to offer your forgiveness to others as a free gift? Are you selective, or can you offer this gift to anyone who has wronged you? How is your life different as a result of having received God's forgiveness?*

GO TO DISCOVERY 179 ON PAGE 897

were shaken, as the trees of the forest
are shaken by the wind.
3 Then the LORD said to Isaiah, "Go
out, you and your son Shear-Jashub,[a] to
meet Ahaz at the end of the aqueduct of
7:3 the Upper Pool, on the road to the
m 2Ki 18:17; Isa 36:2 Washerman's Field.[m] 4 Say to him, 'Be
careful, keep calm[n] and don't be afraid.[o]
7:4 Do not lose heart[p] because of these two
n Isa 30:15 o Isa 35:4 smoldering stubs[q] of firewood—be-
p Dt 20:3 cause of the fierce anger[r] of Rezin and
q Zec 3:2 r Isa 10:24 Aram and of the son of Remaliah.
5 Aram, Ephraim and Remaliah's son
have plotted your ruin, saying, 6 "Let us
invade Judah; let us tear it apart and divide it among ourselves, and make the
son of Tabeel king over it." 7 Yet this is
what the Sovereign LORD says:
7:7 " 'It will not take place,
s Isa 8:10; Ac 4:25 it will not happen,[s]
8 for the head of Aram is Damascus,[t]
7:8 t Ge 14:15 and the head of Damascus is
only Rezin.
Within sixty-five years
Ephraim will be too shattered[u] 7:8 u Isa 17:1-3
to be a people.
9 The head of Ephraim is Samaria,
and the head of Samaria is only
Remaliah's son.
If you do not stand firm in your 7:9
faith,[v] v 2Ch 20:20
you will not stand at all.' "[w] w Isa 8:6-8; 30:12-14

10 Again the LORD spoke to Ahaz,
11 "Ask the LORD your God for a sign,
whether in the deepest depths or in the
highest heights."
12 But Ahaz said, "I will not ask; I will
not put the LORD to the test."

> **NOWHERE IS GOD SO NEAR TO MAN AS IN JESUS CHRIST.**
>
> Richard Baxter, *Puritan Pastor*

13 Then Isaiah said, "Hear now, you
house of David! Is it not enough to try
the patience of men? Will you try the
patience of my God[x] also? 14 Therefore 7:13 x Isa 25:1
the Lord himself will give you[b] a sign:
The virgin will be with child and will 7:14
give birth to a son,[y] and[c] will call him y Lk 1:31
Immanuel.[d z] 15 He will eat curds and z Isa 8:8,10; Mt 1:23*
honey[a] when he knows enough to reject 7:15
the wrong and choose the right. 16 But a ver 22
before the boy knows[b] enough to reject
the wrong and choose the right, the land 7:16
of the two kings you dread will be laid b Isa 8:4
waste.[c] 17 The LORD will bring on you and c Isa 17:3; Hos 5:9,13; Am 1:3-5
on your people and on the house of your
father a time unlike any since Ephraim
broke away[d] from Judah—he will bring 7:17 d 1Ki 12:16
the king of Assyria.[e]" e 2Ch 28:20
18 In that day the LORD will whistle[f] for 7:18
flies from the distant streams of Egypt f Isa 5:26
and for bees from the land of Assyria.[g] g Isa 13:5
19 They will all come and settle in the
steep ravines and in the crevices[h] in the 7:19 h Isa 2:19
rocks, on all the thornbushes and at all
the water holes. 20 In that day the Lord will 7:20
use[i] a razor hired from beyond the Riv- i Isa 10:15
er[e]—the king of Assyria[j]—to shave your j Isa 8:7; 10:5
head and the hair of your legs, and to take
off your beards also. 21 In that day, a man
will keep alive a young cow and two
goats. 22 And because of the abundance of

[a] 3 *Shear-Jashub* means *a remnant will return.*
[b] 14 The Hebrew is plural.
[c] 14 Masoretic Text; Dead Sea Scrolls *and he* or *and they*
[d] 14 *Immanuel* means *God with us.*
[e] 20 That is, the Euphrates

GOD WITH US

When other kings went to war against him, King Ahaz repeatedly found that he was in danger of losing the throne (Isaiah 7). So God sent Isaiah to instruct Ahaz to ask for a sign of God's promise that the throne would be safe. King Ahaz refused to specify a sign, so God selected his own: A boy would be born to a virgin as a sign to Ahaz that the sovereign and all-knowing God had the situation under control. Some Bible scholars believe that the word *virgin* simply refers to a "young woman." However, the Hebrew word used (*almah*) applies specifically to an unmarried woman who has never had sexual relations. This prophecy was intended for the house of David and not simply for Ahaz. In the fullness of time, the Messiah would be born of that house in the most unusual manner imaginable—without the intervention of a human father. He was to be the means of salvation, not simply from physical foes but ultimately from sin (Matthew 1:21). In the New Testament, Matthew referred back to Isaiah 7:14 to demonstrate that Jesus was indeed the One God had promised, the One who is, in fullness of meaning, God with us (Matthew 1:23). Jesus, as the Messiah, was born with two natures: He is the human child of Mary, and he is the divine Son of God.

Born of a Virgin

The words of Isaiah in verse 14 of chapter 7 foreshadow the birth of the promised Messiah to a virgin nearly 700 years after the time of Isaiah. A virgin? How could that be possible?

Over the years people have debated about what the Bible means by this phrase. Some contend that the word *virgin* should be translated "young woman." The New Testament makes it clear, however, that God ultimately had in mind an unmarried woman who had never experienced sexual intercourse (Matthew 1:18–23). Jesus was conceived within Mary without the intervention of a human father. This was a miracle by anyone's definition—and the doctrine of the virgin birth of Jesus is one of the basic beliefs of Christianity.

Jesus' earthly conception and birth did not constitute his beginning, however. God the Son has always existed (Galatians 4:4). Jesus himself testified that he had come from heaven (John 6:38), and Paul later attested that Jesus had willingly relinquished his position of honor in heaven for a time in order to become a servant here on earth (Philippians 2:6–11). God prepared his people for this birth repeatedly many centuries before it occurred. In fact, the first mention of this blessed event appears within the context of Adam and Eve's original act of sin. God promised already then that one of Eve's descendants would be the one to remedy the problem of sin forever (see Genesis 3:15). Isaiah took the prediction one step further by specifying that this Promised One would be born of a virgin and that the child would be referred to as *Immanuel*, the Hebrew word for "God with us."

It was imperative that God's Son be born of a virgin. A child conceived by sinful parents is born in sin just as they were. Even if a man born with a sinful nature could die to atone for his own sin, he could not do so on behalf of anyone else. Jesus was born as Mary's son with the assistance of the Holy Spirit of God, allowing him to enter the world as God's *holy* Son (Luke 1:34–35). Jesus was completely pure and untainted by sin, and so he could offer himself to God the Father as a substitute for fallen humanity (Hebrews 9:14).

The eternal Son of God, who is and remains true and eternal God, took upon himself a truly human nature—in all things like us except for sin (Hebrews 4:15; 7:26–27). He was given to us to set us completely free and to make us right with God (1 Corinthians 1:30). He was born with two natures, the nature of God and the nature of a man—with the exception that he was without sin (Hebrews 4:15). Jesus is not simply a perfectly good and moral religious leader we can learn from. He is "the only-begotten Son of God, begotten of the Father before all worlds; God of God; Light of Light; very God of very God; begotten, not made, being of one substance with the Father, by whom all things were made" (Nicene Creed).

Self-Discovery: *Personalize the beautiful name* Immanuel *by repeating the sentence, "Jesus means God with me!" Take a moment to think about the implications of what you have just stated. What difference will this truth make in your life today?*

GO TO DISCOVERY 180 ON PAGE 900

the milk they give, he will have curds to
eat. All who remain in the land will eat
curds and honey. 23 In that day, in every
place where there were a thousand vines
7:23 worth a thousand silver shekels,[a] there
k Isa 5:6 will be only briers and thorns.[k] 24 Men will
go there with bow and arrow, for the land
will be covered with briers and thorns.
25 As for all the hills once cultivated by the
hoe, you will no longer go there for fear of
the briers and thorns; they will become
7:25 places where cattle are turned loose and
l Isa 5:17 where sheep run.[l]

Assyria, the LORD's Instrument

8:1 8 The LORD said to me, "Take a large
m Isa 30:8; Hab 2:2 n ver 3; scroll[m] and write on it with an or-
Hab 2:2 dinary pen: Maher-Shalal-Hash-Baz.[b n]
8:2 2 And I will call in Uriah[o] the priest and
o 2Ki 16:10 Zechariah son of Jeberekiah as reliable
witnesses for me."

3 Then I went to the prophetess, and
she conceived and gave birth to a son.
And the LORD said to me, "Name him
8:4 Maher-Shalal-Hash-Baz. 4 Before the boy
p Isa 7:16 knows[p] how to say 'My father' or 'My
q Isa 7:8 mother,' the wealth of Damascus and the
plunder of Samaria will be carried off by
the king of Assyria."[q]

5 The LORD spoke to me again:

8:6 r Isa 5:24 s Jn 9:7 6 "Because this people has rejected[r]
t Isa 7:1 the gently flowing waters of
Shiloah[s]
and rejoices over Rezin
and the son of Remaliah,[t]
7 therefore the Lord is about to bring
against them
8:7 the mighty floodwaters[u] of the
u Isa 17:12-13 River[c]—
v Isa 7:20 the king of Assyria[v] with all his
pomp.
It will overflow all its channels,
run over all its banks
8 and sweep on into Judah, swirling
over it,
passing through it and reaching
up to the neck.
Its outspread wings will cover the
breadth of your land,
8:8 w Isa 7:14 O Immanuel[d]!"[w]

8:9 9 Raise the war cry,[e x] you nations,
x Isa 17:12-13 y Joel 3:9 and be shattered!
Listen, all you distant lands.
Prepare[y] for battle, and be shattered!
Prepare for battle, and be
shattered!

> **IT IS ALL TOO EASY TO BELIEVE IN A JESUS WHO IS LARGELY A CONSTRUCTION OF OUR OWN IMAGINATION — AN INOFFENSIVE PERSON WHOM NO ONE WOULD REALLY TROUBLE TO CRUCIFY.**
>
> F. F. Bruce, *British Scholar*

8:10 z Job 5:12 10 Devise your strategy, but it will be
a Isa 7:7 thwarted;[z]
b Isa 7:14; Ro 8:31 propose your plan, but it will not
stand,[a]
for God is with us.[f b]

Fear God

8:11 11 The LORD spoke to me with his
c Eze 3:14 strong hand upon me,[c] warning me not
d Eze 2:8 to follow[d] the way of this people. He
said:

8:12 e Isa 7:2; 30:1 f 1Pe 3:14* 12 "Do not call conspiracy[e]
everything that these people call
conspiracy[g];
do not fear what they fear,
8:13 and do not dread it.[f]
g Nu 20:12 13 The LORD Almighty is the one you
h Isa 29:23 are to regard as holy,[g]
he is the one you are to fear,
8:14 he is the one you are to dread,[h]
i Isa 4:6; Eze 11:16 14 and he will be a sanctuary;[i]
j Lk 2:34; Ro 9:33*; but for both houses of Israel he
1Pe 2:8* will be
k Isa 24:17-18 a stone that causes men to stumble
and a rock that makes them fall.[j]
And for the people of Jerusalem he
will be
8:15 a trap and a snare.[k]
l Isa 28:13; 59:10; Lk 20:18; 15 Many of them will stumble;[l]
Ro 9:32 they will fall and be broken,
they will be snared and captured."

8:16 16 Bind up the testimony
m Isa 29:11-12 and seal[m] up the law among my
8:17 disciples.
n Hab 2:3 17 I will wait[n] for the LORD,
o Dt 31:17; who is hiding[o] his face from the
Isa 54:8 house of Jacob.
I will put my trust in him.

[a] 23 That is, about 25 pounds (about 11.5 kilograms) [b] 1 *Maher-Shalal-Hash-Baz* means *quick to the plunder, swift to the spoil*; also in verse 3. [c] 7 That is, the Euphrates [d] 8 *Immanuel* means *God with us.* [e] 9 Or *Do your worst* [f] 10 Hebrew *Immanuel* [g] 12 Or *Do not call for a treaty / every time these people call for a treaty*

OUR TROUBLE IS WE WANT THE PEACE WITHOUT THE PRINCE.

Addison H. Leitch, *American Theologian*

8:18 [p]Heb 2:13* [q]Lk 2:34 [r]Ps 9:11
18Here am I, and the children the
LORD has given me.[p] We are signs[q] and
symbols in Israel from the LORD Almighty, who dwells on Mount Zion.[r]
8:19 [s]1Sa 28:8 [t]Isa 29:4
19When men tell you to consult[s] mediums and spiritists, who whisper and
mutter,[t] should not a people inquire of
8:20 [u]Isa 1:10; Lk 16:29 [v]Mic 3:6
their God? Why consult the dead on behalf of the living? 20To the law[u] and to the
testimony! If they do not speak according to this word, they have no light[v] of
dawn. 21Distressed and hungry, they will
8:21 [w]Rev 16:11
roam through the land; when they are
famished, they will become enraged and,
looking upward, will curse[w] their king
and their God. 22Then they will look to-
8:22 [x]ver 20; Isa 5:30
ward the earth and see only distress and
darkness and fearful gloom, and they
will be thrust into utter darkness.[x]

To Us a Child Is Born

9:1 [y]2Ki 15:29
9 Nevertheless, there will be no
more gloom for those who were in
distress. In the past he humbled the land
of Zebulun and the land of Naphtali,[y]
but in the future he will honor Galilee of
the Gentiles, by the way of the sea, along
the Jordan—

9:2 [z]Eph 5:8 [a]Lk 1:79 [b]Mt 4:15-16*
2The people walking in darkness
have seen a great light;[z]
on those living in the land of the
shadow of death[a] [a]
a light has dawned.[b]
3You have enlarged the nation
and increased their joy;
they rejoice before you
as people rejoice at the harvest,
as men rejoice
9:4 [c]Jdg 7:25 [d]Isa 14:25 [e]Isa 10:27 [f]Isa 14:4; 49:26; 51:13; 54:14
when dividing the plunder.
4For as in the day of Midian's defeat,[c]
you have shattered
the yoke[d] that burdens them,
the bar across their shoulders,[e]
the rod of their oppressor.[f]
5Every warrior's boot used in battle
and every garment rolled in blood
9:5 [g]Isa 2:4
will be destined for burning,[g]
will be fuel for the fire.
9:6 [h]Isa 53:2; Lk 2:11 [i]Jn 3:16
6For to us a child is born,[h]
to us a son is given,[i]
9:6 [j]Mt 28:18 [k]Isa 28:29 [l]Isa 10:21; 11:2 [m]Isa 26:3,12; 66:12
and the government[j] will be on
his shoulders.
And he will be called
Wonderful Counselor,[b] [k] Mighty
God,[l]
Everlasting Father, Prince of
Peace.[m]
7Of the increase of his government
and peace
9:7 [n]Da 2:44; Lk 1:33 [o]Isa 11:4; 16:5; 32:1,16 [p]Isa 37:32; 59:17
there will be no end.[n]
He will reign on David's throne
and over his kingdom,
establishing and upholding it
with justice[o] and righteousness
from that time on and forever.
The zeal[p] of the LORD Almighty
will accomplish this.

The LORD's Anger Against Israel

8The Lord has sent a message
against Jacob;
it will fall on Israel.
9All the people will know it—
9:9 [q]Isa 7:9
Ephraim and the inhabitants of
Samaria[q]—
who say with pride

[a] 2 Or *land of darkness* [b] 6 Or *Wonderful, Counselor*

A CHILD IS BORN

One of the most descriptive Messianic sections in the Old Testament is found in Isaiah 7—12. Isaiah's prophecy of a birth as a sign to his contemporaries foreshadowed the virgin birth of Jesus, the promised One (Isaiah 7:14), who fulfills this prophecy in fullest measure. We also learn that the Messiah would have distinctive titles—Wonderful Counselor, Mighty God, Everlasting Father and Prince of Peace (Isaiah 9:6)—and that he would come from Galilee (verses 1–2).

God's people had understood for a long time that the Messiah's kingdom would be glorious, his throne eternal and his reign peaceful. But Isaiah shocked his hearers with an almost unimaginable revelation: The Messiah would be God himself coming to live with his people! (Isaiah 7:14; Matthew 1:23; John 1:1–14). Matthew confirmed in his Gospel that Isaiah 9:1–2 refers to Jesus—God the Son, born as a human being to die in our place in order that he could live with his people forever. Is it any wonder that when Jesus was born, the angel announced, "He will be great and will be called the Son of the Most High"? (Luke 1:32).

DISCOVERY 180

Isaiah's Prophetic Vision

Some of the Bible's references to and descriptions of God's promised Messiah are somewhat indistinct. In Isaiah 9, however, God provides us with the most detailed portrayal in the Old Testament. Isaiah specified that the Messiah would "honor Galilee of the Gentiles, by the way of the sea, along the Jordan" (Isaiah 9:1). That is the region from which Jesus' family came.

Immediately following this explicit statement Isaiah penned the following memorable words: "The people walking in darkness have seen a great light; on those living in the land of the shadow of death a light has dawned" (verse 2). God's Son arrived on the scene at the optimal moment in history (Galatians 4:4–5). People were groping in darkness with no clear idea of how to relate to God. Jesus referred to himself as the light of the world (John 8:12), asserting that whoever walks with him will never again walk in darkness.

God's people already understood that the Promised One would be born to a human mother like any other child—but that he would be *unlike* any other infant in that God would be his Father—literally! Jesus, God the Son, did later come to earth and fulfill every prophecy ever made about the Messiah—even the somber prediction that his own people would reject him (Isaiah 53:3; John 1:11).

Many of the prophetic visions will still be fulfilled in the future. For example, God's people expected the Messiah to function as a government leader or ruler because Isaiah had explicitly stated that "the government will be on his shoulders" (Isaiah 9:6). When Jesus entered Jerusalem astride a borrowed donkey prior to his arrest and crucifixion, the people chanted, "Blessed is he who comes in the name of the Lord" (Matthew 21:1–9). They fully expected Jesus to become their triumphant king at that very moment. Jesus did issue from David's royal family line (Luke 1:32), and one day the entire world *will* recognize him as Lord and King—but that will happen when he comes back for his people (Romans 14:9; Philippians 2:9–11).

It is sometimes difficult to comprehend prophecies, because God gave the prophets many pieces of a puzzle, not all of which would be fulfilled simultaneously. The prophets often recorded what God had told them without separating the prophecies, so Jesus' birth isn't always depicted as a separate event from his second coming. Isaiah almost certainly didn't realize that there would be a gap in history—the gap in which we are now living. God's primary message is not concerned with the sequence of events. He simply wants us to know that he has a plan for the universe—and that Jesus is at the center of that plan. Christ Jesus *will* return to reign as King forever, just as surely as every last one of the prophecies concerning his birth, life, death and resurrection have come to fulfillment (Revelation 11:15).

Self-Discovery: *Visualize our solar system, with the stationary sun at its center and the planets orbiting gracefully around it. Then use the same model, picturing Jesus, God the Son, as the stabilizing center of all human life. What other associations come to mind? Light? Warmth? Life itself?*

GO TO DISCOVERY 181 ON PAGE 904

9:9 [r] Isa 46:12

and arrogance[r] of heart,
[10] "The bricks have fallen down,
but we will rebuild with dressed stone;
the fig trees have been felled,
but we will replace them with cedars."

9:11 [s] Isa 7:8

[11] But the LORD has strengthened
Rezin's[s] foes against them
and has spurred their enemies on.

9:12 [t] 2Ki 16:6 [u] 2Ch 28:18 [v] Ps 79:7 [w] Isa 5:25

[12] Arameans[t] from the east and
Philistines[u] from the west
have devoured[v] Israel with open mouth.

Yet for all this, his anger is not turned away,
his hand is still upraised.[w]

9:13 [x] Jer 5:3 [y] Isa 31:1; Hos 7:7,10

[13] But the people have not returned
to him who struck[x] them,
nor have they sought[y] the LORD Almighty.
[14] So the LORD will cut off from Israel
both head and tail,

9:14 [z] Isa 19:15 [a] Rev 18:8

both palm branch and reed[z] in a single day;[a]

9:15 [b] Isa 3:2-3

[15] the elders[b] and prominent men are the head,
the prophets who teach lies are the tail.

9:16 [c] Mt 15:14; 23:16,24 [d] Isa 3:12

[16] Those who guide[c] this people mislead them,
and those who are guided are led astray.[d]

9:17 [e] Jer 18:21 [f] Isa 27:11 [g] Isa 10:6 [h] Isa 1:4 [i] Mt 12:34 [j] Isa 5:25

[17] Therefore the Lord will take no
pleasure in the young men,[e]
nor will he pity[f] the fatherless and widows,
for everyone is ungodly[g] and wicked,[h]
every mouth speaks vileness.[i]
Yet for all this, his anger is not turned away,
his hand is still upraised.[j]

9:18 [k] Mal 4:1 [l] Ps 83:14

[18] Surely wickedness burns like a fire;[k]
it consumes briers and thorns,
it sets the forest thickets ablaze,[l]
so that it rolls upward in a column of smoke.

9:19 [m] Isa 13:9,13 [n] Isa 1:31 [o] Mic 7:2,6

[19] By the wrath[m] of the LORD Almighty
the land will be scorched
and the people will be fuel for the fire;[n]
no one will spare his brother.[o]

9:20 [p] Lev 26:26 [q] Isa 49:26

[20] On the right they will devour,
but still be hungry;[p]
on the left they will eat,[q]
but not be satisfied.
Each will feed on the flesh of his own offspring[a]:

9:21 [r] 2Ch 28:6 [s] Isa 5:25

[21] Manasseh will feed on Ephraim,
and Ephraim on Manasseh;
together they will turn against Judah.[r]

Yet for all this, his anger is not turned away,
his hand is still upraised.[s]

10:1 [t] Ps 58:2

10 Woe to those who make unjust laws,
to those who issue oppressive decrees,[t]

10:2 [u] Isa 3:14 [v] Isa 5:23

[2] to deprive[u] the poor of their rights
and withhold justice from the oppressed of my people,[v]
making widows their prey
and robbing the fatherless.

10:3 [w] Job 31:14; Hos 9:7 [x] Lk 19:44 [y] Isa 20:6

[3] What will you do on the day of reckoning,[w]
when disaster[x] comes from afar?
To whom will you run for help?[y]
Where will you leave your riches?

10:4 [z] Isa 24:22 [a] Isa 22:2; 34:3; 66:16 [b] Isa 5:25

[4] Nothing will remain but to cringe
among the captives[z]
or fall among the slain.[a]
Yet for all this, his anger is not turned away,[b]
his hand is still upraised.

God's Judgment on Assyria

10:5 [c] Isa 14:25; Zep 2:13 [d] Jer 51:20 [e] Isa 13:3,5,13; 30:30; 66:14

[5] "Woe to the Assyrian,[c] the rod of my anger,
in whose hand is the club[d] of my wrath![e]

10:6 [f] Isa 9:17 [g] Isa 9:19 [h] Isa 5:29

[6] I send him against a godless[f] nation,
I dispatch him against a people who anger me,[g]
to seize loot and snatch plunder,[h]
and to trample them down like mud in the streets.

10:7 [i] Ge 50:20; Ac 4:23-28

[7] But this is not what he intends,[i]
this is not what he has in mind;
his purpose is to destroy,
to put an end to many nations.

10:8 [j] 2Ki 18:24

[8] 'Are not my commanders[j] all kings?' he says.

10:9 [k] Ge 10:10 [l] 2Ch 35:20

[9] 'Has not Calno[k] fared like Carchemish?[l]

[a] 20 Or *arm*

10:9 [m]2Ki 17:6 [n]2Ki 16:9
10:10 [o]2Ki 19:18

Is not Hamath like Arpad,
and Samaria[m] like Damascus?[n]
[10] As my hand seized the kingdoms
of the idols,[o]
kingdoms whose images excelled
those of Jerusalem and
Samaria—
[11] shall I not deal with Jerusalem and
her images
as I dealt with Samaria and her
idols?' "

10:12 [p]Isa 28:21-22; 65:7 [q]2Ki 19:31 [r]Jer 50:18

[12] When the Lord has finished all his
work[p] against Mount Zion[q] and Jerusalem, he will say, "I will punish the
king of Assyria[r] for the willful pride of
his heart and the haughty look in his
eyes. [13] For he says:

10:13 [s]Isa 37:24; Da 4:30 [t]Eze 28:4

" 'By the strength of my hand I have
done this,[s]
and by my wisdom, because I
have understanding.
I removed the boundaries of
nations,
I plundered their treasures;[t]
like a mighty one I subdued[a]
their kings.

10:14 [u]Jer 49:16; Ob 1:4 [v]Job 31:25

[14] As one reaches into a nest,[u]
so my hand reached for the
wealth[v] of the nations;
as men gather abandoned eggs,
so I gathered all the countries;
not one flapped a wing,
or opened its mouth to chirp.' "

10:15 [w]Isa 45:9; Ro 9:20-21 [x]ver 5

[15] Does the ax raise itself above him
who swings it,
or the saw boast against him
who uses it?[w]
As if a rod were to wield him who
lifts it up,
or a club[x] brandish him who is
not wood!

10:16 [y]ver 18; Isa 17:4 [z]Isa 8:7

[16] Therefore, the Lord, the LORD
Almighty,
will send a wasting disease[y]
upon his sturdy warriors;
under his pomp[z] a fire will be
kindled
like a blazing flame.

10:17 [a]Isa 31:9 [b]Isa 37:23 [c]Nu 11:1-3 [d]Isa 9:18

[17] The Light of Israel will become a
fire,[a]
their Holy One[b] a flame;
in a single day it will burn and
consume
his thorns[c] and his briers.[d]

10:18 [e]2Ki 19:23

[18] The splendor of his forests[e] and
fertile fields
it will completely destroy,
as when a sick man wastes away.

10:19 [f]Isa 21:17

[19] And the remaining trees of his
forests will be so few[f]
that a child could write them
down.

The Remnant of Israel

10:20 [g]Isa 11:10,11 [h]2Ki 16:7 [i]2Ch 28:20 [j]Isa 17:7

[20] In that day[g] the remnant of Israel,
the survivors of the house of
Jacob,
will no longer rely[h] on him
who struck them down[i]
but will truly rely[j] on the LORD,
the Holy One of Israel.

10:21 [k]Isa 6:13 [l]Isa 9:6

[21] A remnant[k] will return,[b] a remnant
of Jacob
will return to the Mighty God.[l]

10:22 [m]Ro 9:27-28 [n]Isa 28:22; Da 9:27

[22] Though your people, O Israel, be
like the sand by the sea,
only a remnant will return.[m]
Destruction has been decreed,[n]
overwhelming and righteous.

10:23 [o]Isa 28:22; Ro 9:27-28*

[23] The Lord, the LORD Almighty, will
carry out
the destruction decreed upon
the whole land.[o]

10:24 [p]Ps 87:5-6 [q]Ex 5:14

[24] Therefore, this is what the Lord, the
LORD Almighty, says:

"O my people who live in Zion,[p]
do not be afraid of the Assyrians,
who beat[q] you with a rod
and lift up a club against you, as
Egypt did.

10:25 [r]Isa 17:14 [s]ver 5; Da 11:36

[25] Very soon[r] my anger against you
will end
and my wrath[s] will be directed
to their destruction."

10:26 [t]Isa 37:36-38 [u]Isa 9:4 [v]Ex 14:16

[26] The LORD Almighty will lash[t] them
with a whip,
as when he struck down Midian[u]
at the rock of Oreb;
and he will raise his staff over the
waters,[v]
as he did in Egypt.

10:27 [w]Isa 9:4 [x]Isa 14:25

[27] In that day their burden will be
lifted from your shoulders,
their yoke[w] from your neck;[x]
the yoke will be broken
because you have grown so fat.[c]

10:28 [y]1Sa 14:2

[28] They enter Aiath;
they pass through Migron;[y]

[a] 13 Or / *I subdued the mighty,* [b] 21 Hebrew *shear-jashub*; also in verse 22 [c] 27 Hebrew; Septuagint *broken / from your shoulders*

10:28 [z] 1Sa 13:2 they store supplies at Micmash.[z]
29 They go over the pass, and say,
"We will camp overnight at Geba."
10:29 [a] Jos 18:25 Ramah[a] trembles;
Gibeah of Saul flees.
10:30 [b] 1Sa 25:44 [c] Ne 11:32 30 Cry out, O Daughter of Gallim![b]
Listen, O Laishah!
Poor Anathoth![c]
31 Madmenah is in flight;
10:32 [d] 1Sa 21:1 [e] Jer 6:23 the people of Gebim take cover.
32 This day they will halt at Nob;[d]
they will shake their fist
at the mount of the Daughter of
Zion,[e]
at the hill of Jerusalem.
33 See, the Lord, the LORD Almighty,
will lop off the boughs with great
power.
The lofty trees will be felled,
10:33 [f] Am 2:9 the tall[f] ones will be brought low.
34 He will cut down the forest
thickets with an ax;
Lebanon will fall before the
Mighty One.

The Branch From Jesse

11:1 [g] ver 10; Isa 9:7; Rev 5:5 [h] Isa 4:2 11 A shoot will come up from
the stump of Jesse;[g]
from his roots a Branch[h] will
bear fruit.

THE NEW SHOOT

God promised to send the Messiah through David's family line, so if God removed any king who came after David, the Messiah's own reign would be at risk. Yet that is exactly what Isaiah predicted: While David's line was still on the throne, the house of Jesse would be cut down like a tree. Yet God never leaves his people without hope. He promised that a "shoot" would grow from the stump that remained (Isaiah 11:1)—a single and unexpected shoot that would become the Lord's own Branch. Not only would this Branch bear fruit, but God's Spirit would rest on this chosen and protected family member. Jesus, God's one and only Son, is that Branch (Hebrews 7:14). When Jesus was born, the angel Gabriel made clear to Mary exactly who had come to earth: "The Lord God will give him the throne of his father David and he will reign . . . forever" (Luke 1:32–33). This baby was the divine Son of God, the long-expected Messiah, now appearing in human flesh.

2 The Spirit[i] of the LORD will rest on
him— 11:2 [i] Isa 42:1; 48:16; 61:1; Mt 3:16; Jn 1:32-33 [j] Eph 1:17 [k] 2Ti 1:7
the Spirit of wisdom[j] and of
understanding,
the Spirit of counsel and of
power,[k]
the Spirit of knowledge and of
the fear of the LORD—
3 and he will delight in the fear of the
LORD.

He will not judge by what he sees
with his eyes,[l] 11:3 [l] Jn 7:24 [m] Jn 2:25
or decide by what he hears with
his ears;[m]
4 but with righteousness[n] he will 11:4 [n] Ps 72:2 [o] Isa 9:7 [p] Isa 3:14 [q] Mal 4:6 [r] Job 4:9; 2Th 2:8
judge the needy,
with justice[o] he will give decisions
for the poor[p] of the earth.
He will strike[q] the earth with the
rod of his mouth;
with the breath[r] of his lips he
will slay the wicked.
5 Righteousness will be his belt
and faithfulness[s] the sash 11:5 [s] Isa 25:1 [t] Eph 6:14
around his waist.[t]
6 The wolf will live with the lamb,[u] 11:6 [u] Isa 65:25
the leopard will lie down with
the goat,
the calf and the lion and the
yearling[a] together;
and a little child will lead them.
7 The cow will feed with the bear,
their young will lie down
together,
and the lion will eat straw like
the ox.
8 The infant will play near the hole
of the cobra,
and the young child put his
hand into the viper's nest.
9 They will neither harm nor destroy[v] 11:9 [v] Job 5:23 [w] Ps 98:2-3; Isa 52:10 [x] Isa 45:6,14; Hab 2:14
on all my holy mountain,
for the earth[w] will be full of the
knowledge[x] of the LORD
as the waters cover the sea.

10 In that day the Root of Jesse will 11:10 [y] Jn 12:32 [z] Isa 49:23; Lk 2:32 [a] Ro 15:12* [b] Isa 14:3; 28:12; 32:17-18
stand as a banner[y] for the peoples; the
nations[z] will rally to him,[a] and his place
of rest[b] will be glorious. 11 In that day[c] the
Lord will reach out his hand a second 11:11 [c] Isa 10:20 [d] Isa 19:24; Hos 11:11; Mic 7:12; Zec 10:10
time to reclaim the remnant that is left
of his people from Assyria,[d] from Lower
Egypt, from Upper Egypt,[b] from Cush,[c]

[a] 6 Hebrew; Septuagint *lion will feed*
[b] 11 Hebrew *from Pathros* [c] 11 That is, the upper Nile region

Cut Off—But Not Destroyed

When the Babylonians conquered Jerusalem in 586 B.C., the tragic event marked the end of David's family rule. Even though the people eventually returned from exile to rebuild Jerusalem and the temple, the monarchy was not restored. From that day until the present, no descendant of David's family has ever again reigned over Israel. The family tree was cut down by the Babylonians, left as nothing more than a stump (Isaiah 11:1).

But that was not the end of the story. God promised that a new shoot, a future member of David's royal family, would emerge from the stump. This "Branch" would bear fruit like none God's people had ever before seen. For one thing God's Spirit would be on this new King. In the New Testament, when John baptized Jesus, the Holy Spirit descended from heaven and alighted on Jesus (Matthew 3:16–17). Later, while he was teaching in the synagogue in Nazareth, Jesus himself affirmed that the Spirit of the Lord was on him (Luke 4:18).

This new "Branch," Isaiah predicted, would judge the wicked, and God the Father did in fact later give that role to Jesus (John 5:22). God's promised Savior would not be a judge who would *condemn* the people, however (John 3:17). Instead, his role would be to *remove the sin* that stood between God and humanity (Romans 5:1—6:14; 8:1–17). This promised branch of David's family tree did in fact reverse all of the effects of sin, so that peace is now possible—peace with God, with nature and with one another.

The day on which Jerusalem and the temple were ransacked and destroyed by the Babylonians was most assuredly a dark and desolate one in the history of the Jews. Their anchor of hope, everything they had expected for their future as God's people, seemed to crumble along with the city walls. But this tragedy did not mark the end. God promised to do something greater than they could have imagined in their wildest dreams: He pledged that he would send the ultimate Branch who would never be cut off—Jesus, the Christ, the precious Son of God.

We all face times during which we feel cut off, as though all of our hope has evaporated and everything meaningful in our lives has dissipated into thin air. An unexpected turn of events can make our lives feel as though they've been reduced to a mere stump of what they once were. At those times in particular we must remember the promises in Isaiah. All is not lost, and God has a fabulous future planned for each one of us. Despite the despair that rules the moment, God promises restoration beyond our ability to imagine (1 Corinthians 2:9). If we are willing to focus on him instead of on the seeming futility of the current situation, our eyes will be opened, and we will see Jesus in a new and vital way as the One who brings us back to the heart and the home of the Father.

Self-Discovery: *Think of specific ways to celebrate today Jesus' promise of faithfulness that comes from an intimate union and fellowship with him, the "true vine" (John 15:1).*

GO TO DISCOVERY 182 ON PAGE 908

11:11 [e] Ge 10:22 [f] Isa 42:4,10,12; 66:19

from Elam,[e] from Babylonia,[a] from Hamath and from the islands[f] of the sea.

[12] He will raise a banner for the nations
and gather the exiles of Israel;
he will assemble the scattered people[g] of Judah
from the four quarters of the earth.

11:12 [g] Zep 3:10

[13] Ephraim's jealousy will vanish,
and Judah's enemies[b] will be cut off;
Ephraim will not be jealous of Judah,
nor Judah hostile toward Ephraim.[h]

11:13 [h] Jer 3:18; Eze 37:16-17, 22; Hos 1:11

[14] They will swoop down on the slopes of Philistia to the west;
together they will plunder the people to the east.
They will lay hands on Edom[i] and Moab,[j]
and the Ammonites will be subject to them.

11:14 [i] Da 11:41; Joel 3:19 [j] Isa 16:14; 25:10

[15] The LORD will dry up
the gulf of the Egyptian sea;
with a scorching wind he will sweep his hand[k]
over the Euphrates River.[c][l]
He will break it up into seven streams

11:15 [k] Isa 19:16 [l] Isa 7:20

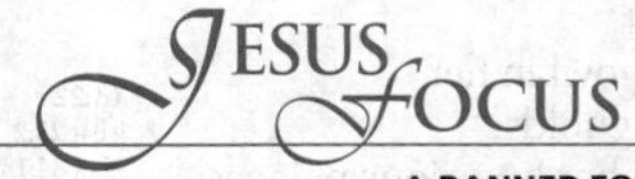

A BANNER FOR THE NATIONS

Isaiah referred to God's Messiah as the "Root of Jesse" and specified that this promised One would be a "banner for the peoples" and that "the nations [would] rally to him" (Isaiah 11:10). A banner was used for assembling troops or groups of people. And Isaiah foretold that God would gather "the remnant" of Israel—those whose hearts were still devoted to him—back into a relationship with himself (verse 11). God allowed Isaiah to see beyond the time when the people would return from captivity in Babylon to yet another "return." Someday God's chosen people will gather under the banner of Jesus the Messiah. The precious Lord over the whole earth will be recognized as the One who has rescued them from their sin, and the whole world will know that "the Holy One of Israel [is] among [us]" (Isaiah 12:6). Immanuel, "God with us," will reign over the nations, and his banner of love and grace will be unfurled and soar in triumph forever (Matthew 1:23).

so that men can cross over in sandals.
[16] There will be a highway[m] for the remnant of his people
that is left from Assyria,
as there was for Israel
when they came up from Egypt.[n]

11:16 [m] Isa 19:23; 62:10 [n] Ex 14:26-31

Songs of Praise

12 In that day you will say:

"I will praise[o] you, O LORD.
Although you were angry with me,
your anger has turned away
and you have comforted me.

12:1 [o] Isa 25:1

[2] Surely God is my salvation;
I will trust[p] and not be afraid.
The LORD, the LORD, is my strength and my song;
he has become my salvation.[q]"

12:2 [p] Isa 26:3 [q] Ex 15:2; Ps 118:14

[3] With joy you will draw water[r]
from the wells of salvation.

12:3 [r] Jn 4:10,14

[4] In that day you will say:

"Give thanks to the LORD, call on his name;[s]
make known among the nations what he has done,
and proclaim that his name is exalted.

12:4 [s] Ps 105:1; Isa 24:15

[5] Sing[t] to the LORD, for he has done glorious things;[u]
let this be known to all the world.

12:5 [t] Ex 15:1 [u] Ps 98:1

[6] Shout aloud and sing for joy, people of Zion,
for great is the Holy One of Israel[v] among you.[w]"

12:6 [v] Isa 49:26 [w] Zep 3:14-17

A Prophecy Against Babylon

13 An oracle concerning Babylon that Isaiah son of Amoz saw:

[2] Raise a banner[x] on a bare hilltop,
shout to them;
beckon to them
to enter the gates of the nobles.

13:2 [x] Jer 50:2; 51:27

[3] I have commanded my holy ones;
I have summoned my warriors[y]
to carry out my wrath—
those who rejoice[z] in my triumph.

13:3 [y] Joel 3:11 [z] Ps 149:2

[4] Listen, a noise on the mountains,
like that of a great multitude![a]

13:4 [a] Joel 3:14

[a] 11 Hebrew *Shinar* [b] 13 Or *hostility*
[c] 15 Hebrew *the River*

Listen, an uproar among the
kingdoms,
like nations massing together!
The LORD Almighty is mustering
an army for war.
5 They come from faraway lands,
from the ends of the heavens[b]—
the LORD and the weapons of his
wrath—
to destroy[c] the whole country.

6 Wail,[d] for the day[e] of the LORD is
near;
it will come like destruction
from the Almighty.[a]
7 Because of this, all hands will go
limp,
every man's heart will melt.[f]
8 Terror[g] will seize them,
pain and anguish will grip them;
they will writhe like a woman in
labor.
They will look aghast at each other,
their faces aflame.[h]

9 See, the day of the LORD is coming
—a cruel day, with wrath and
fierce anger—
to make the land desolate
and destroy the sinners within
it.
10 The stars of heaven and their
constellations
will not show their light.
The rising sun[i] will be darkened[j]
and the moon will not give its
light.[k]
11 I will punish[l] the world for its evil,
the wicked for their sins.
I will put an end to the arrogance
of the haughty
and will humble the pride of the
ruthless.
12 I will make man[m] scarcer than
pure gold,
more rare than the gold of Ophir.
13 Therefore I will make the heavens
tremble;[n]
and the earth will shake from its
place
at the wrath of the LORD Almighty,
in the day of his burning anger.

14 Like a hunted gazelle,
like sheep without a shepherd,[o]
each will return to his own people,
each will flee to his native land.[p]
15 Whoever is captured will be thrust
through;
all who are caught will fall[q] by
the sword.[r]
16 Their infants[s] will be dashed to
pieces before their eyes;
their houses will be looted and
their wives ravished.

17 See, I will stir up[t] against them the
Medes,
who do not care for silver
and have no delight in gold.[u]
18 Their bows will strike down the
young men;
they will have no mercy on
infants
nor will they look with
compassion on children.
19 Babylon, the jewel of kingdoms,
the glory[v] of the Babylonians'[b]
pride,
will be overthrown[w] by God
like Sodom and Gomorrah.[x]
20 She will never be inhabited[y]
or lived in through all
generations;
no Arab[z] will pitch his tent there,
no shepherd will rest his flocks
there.
21 But desert creatures[a] will lie there,
jackals will fill her houses;
there the owls will dwell,
and there the wild goats will leap
about.
22 Hyenas will howl in her
strongholds,[b]
jackals[c] in her luxurious palaces.
Her time is at hand,[d]
and her days will not be
prolonged.

14 The LORD will have
compassion[e] on Jacob;
once again he will choose[f] Israel
and will settle them in their own
land.
Aliens[g] will join them
and unite with the house of
Jacob.
2 Nations will take them
and bring[h] them to their own
place.
And the house of Israel will possess
the nations[i]
as menservants and
maidservants in the LORD's
land.

13:5 [b] Isa 5:26 [c] Isa 24:1
13:6 [d] Eze 30:2 [e] Isa 2:12; Joel 1:15
13:7 [f] Eze 21:7
13:8 [g] Isa 21:4 [h] Na 2:10
13:10 [i] Isa 24:23 [j] Isa 5:30; Rev 8:12 [k] Eze 32:7; Mt 24:29*; Mk 13:24*
13:11 [l] Isa 3:11; 11:4; 26:21
13:12 [m] Isa 4:1
13:13 [n] Isa 34:4; 51:6; Hag 2:6
13:14 [o] 1Ki 22:17 [p] Jer 50:16
13:15 [q] Jer 51:4 [r] Isa 14:19; Jer 50:25
13:16 [s] Ps 137:9
13:17 [t] Jer 51:1 [u] Pr 6:34-35
13:19 [v] Da 4:30 [w] Rev 14:8 [x] Ge 19:24
13:20 [y] Isa 14:23; 34:10-15 [z] 2Ch 17:11
13:21 [a] Rev 18:2
13:22 [b] Isa 25:2 [c] Isa 34:13 [d] Jer 51:33
14:1 [e] Ps 102:13; Isa 49:10,13; 54:7-8,10 [f] Isa 41:8; 44:1; 49:7; Zec 1:17; 2:12 [g] Eph 2:12-19
14:2 [h] Isa 60:9 [i] Isa 49:7,23

[a] 6 Hebrew *Shaddai* [b] 19 Or *Chaldeans'*

They will make captives of their
captors
14:2 [j]Isa 60:14; 61:5
and rule over their oppressors.[j]
14:3 [k]Isa 11:10
3 On the day the LORD gives you relief[k]
from suffering and turmoil and cruel
14:4 [l]Hab 2:6 [m]Isa 9:4
bondage, 4 you will take up this taunt[l]
against the king of Babylon:

How the oppressor[m] has come to
an end!
How his fury[a] has ended!
14:5 [n]Ps 125:3
5 The LORD has broken the rod of the
wicked,[n]
the scepter of the rulers,
6 which in anger struck down
14:6 [o]Isa 10:14 [p]Isa 47:6
peoples[o]
with unceasing blows,
and in fury subdued nations
with relentless aggression.[p]
7 All the lands are at rest and at
14:7 [q]Ps 98:1; 126:1-3
peace;
they break into singing.[q]
14:8 [r]Eze 31:16
8 Even the pine trees[r] and the cedars
of Lebanon
exult over you and say,
"Now that you have been laid low,
no woodsman comes to cut us
down."
14:9 [s]Eze 32:21
9 The grave[b][s] below is all astir
to meet you at your coming;
it rouses the spirits of the departed
to greet you—
all those who were leaders in the
world;
it makes them rise from their
thrones—
all those who were kings over
the nations.
10 They will all respond,
they will say to you,
"You also have become weak, as we
are;
you have become like us."[t] 14:10 [t]Eze 32:21
11 All your pomp has been brought
down to the grave,
along with the noise of your
harps;
maggots are spread out beneath
you
and worms[u] cover you. 14:11 [u]Isa 51:8
12 How you have fallen[v] from heaven, 14:12 [v]Isa 34:4; Lk 10:18 [w]2Pe 1:19; Rev 2:28; 8:10; 9:1
O morning star,[w] son of the
dawn!
You have been cast down to the
earth,
you who once laid low the
nations!
13 You said in your heart,
"I will ascend[x] to heaven; 14:13 [x]Da 5:23; 8:10; Mt 11:23 [y]Eze 28:2; 2Th 2:4
I will raise my throne[y]
above the stars of God;
I will sit enthroned on the mount
of assembly,
on the utmost heights of the
sacred mountain.[c]
14 I will ascend above the tops of the
clouds;
I will make myself like the Most
High."[z] 14:14 [z]Isa 47:8; 2Th 2:4
15 But you are brought down to the
grave, 14:15 [a]Mt 11:23; Lk 10:15
to the depths[a] of the pit.
16 Those who see you stare at you, 14:16 [b]Jer 50:23
they ponder your fate:[b]
"Is this the man who shook the
earth
and made kingdoms tremble,
17 the man who made the world a 14:17 [c]Joel 2:3
desert,[c]
who overthrew its cities
and would not let his captives go
home?"

[a] 4 Dead Sea Scrolls, Septuagint and Syriac; the meaning of the word in the Masoretic Text is uncertain. [b] 9 Hebrew *Sheol*; also in verses 11 and 15 [c] 13 Or *the north*; Hebrew *Zaphon*

JESUS FOCUS

SATAN'S FALL

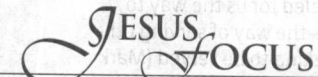

Although Isaiah's message is directed against the king of Babylon, some believe the images can apply to the fall of Satan as well. The evil one may have control of things on earth for the time being, but God's precious and glorious Son ultimately outshines Satan and all his forces—just as the brightest morning star fades in the light of the rising sun. Revelation 12:7–12 expands on Isaiah's vision, describing the ultimate ruin of Satan and all his "stars." Jesus himself gave us victory over the enemy when he resisted Satan's temptation (Matthew 4:1–11) and again when he conquered the devastating penalty and power of sin by coming back to life (Romans 4:25). To this day Satan stands defeated because Jesus died in our place for our sin (Colossians 1:13–14; 2:13–15)—and then defeated death itself through the power of his resurrection (Ephesians 1:18–23; Philippians 3:10), gaining for us eternal life (see Romans 8:32,37–39; 1 Corinthians 15:51–57).

DISCOVERY 182

The Cure for Pride

Satan is alive and doing quite well on Planet Earth. The Bible describes him as a roaring lion that wanders the earth looking for people to devour (1 Peter 5:8). He is God's avowed adversary and the enemy of all of humanity (Genesis 3:14–15). But we might be surprised by the fact that Satan was not *always* God's enemy. He was once, in fact, an angel. While Isaiah specifically had the king of Babylon in view here in these verses (Isaiah 14:3–23), the passage indirectly points to Satan, whose own proud aspirations for equal status with God proved disastrous. Isaiah referred to him as "morning star" and "son of the dawn" (verse 12). Satan wasn't content to be subservient to God, though, and "fell" from his position.

Satan wanted to *be* God. His attitude is reflected in the boasts attributed to the king of Babylon in verses 13–14: "I will ascend to heaven; I will raise my throne; I will sit enthroned; I will ascend; I will make myself like the Most High." The most telling aspect of these words is the repetition of the phrase *I will*—the essence of pride. And that conceit is what ultimately caused Satan's fall from God's presence and his grace. God plunged him from his high position to the depths of the pit (Isaiah 14:15).

Satan wanted more, just as we do. Adam and Eve each succumbed to the temptation to possess the power to make decisions only God has the wisdom to make. They desired the one thing God had held back from them: autonomy. Satan, in the form of a serpent, convinced them that doing what God had expressly forbidden—eating fruit from the one tree to which he'd denied them access—would make them like God (Genesis 3:5). Out of arrogance and with total disregard for God's command, they ate the fruit. Because of their disobedience they were expelled from the idyllic environment of the garden—just as Satan had been evicted from his residence in heaven. The first couple learned a lesson we all eventually confront: Pride will result in a fall of some kind (Proverbs 16:18), because an insolent, arrogant attitude separates us from God.

Later on Satan again appealed to human pride when he tempted Jesus. The devil essentially taunted, "If you are really God, *prove* it" (Matthew 4:3). But Jesus resisted that temptation. Unlike Satan, who wanted to become more than what he really was, Jesus already was God, but even so he refused to demand his rights as God while he lived as a man. Instead, he acted as a humble servant (Philippians 2:7–11). Satan, Adam and Eve all tried to *ascend* to greatness. By contrast, Jesus *descended*. He became one of us, and by so doing he modeled for us the way to overcome pride—the way of serving others instead of seeking to be served (Mark 10:45; Philippians 2:1–4).

It may come wrapped in as many different packages as there are people, but every one of us struggles with conceit. *Acting* humble is not a cure-all for a heart filled with pride. Only as we allow the Holy Spirit to change our hearts (Galatians 5:22–23) will we learn to follow Jesus' example (Matthew 11:29).

Self-Discovery: If the words I will *are associated with arrogance, identify some phrases that might be associated with humility. Then put these phrases into the context of some sentences that convey a humble spirit before God.*

GO TO DISCOVERY 183 ON PAGE 915

18 All the kings of the nations lie in state,
each in his own tomb.

14:19 [d] Isa 22:16-18 [e] Jer 41:7-9

19 But you are cast out[d] of your tomb
like a rejected branch;
you are covered with the slain,
with those pierced by the sword,
those who descend to the stones of the pit.[e]
Like a corpse trampled underfoot,
20 you will not join them in burial,
for you have destroyed your land
and killed your people.

14:20 [f] Job 18:19 [g] Isa 1:4 [h] Ps 21:10

The offspring[f] of the wicked[g]
will never be mentioned[h] again.
21 Prepare a place to slaughter his sons

14:21 [i] Ex 20:5; Lev 26:39

for the sins of their forefathers;[i]
they are not to rise to inherit the land
and cover the earth with their cities.
22 "I will rise up against them,"
declares the LORD Almighty.
"I will cut off from Babylon her name and survivors,

14:22 [j] 1Ki 14:10; Job 18:19

her offspring and descendants,[j]"
declares the LORD.

14:23 [k] Isa 34:11-15; Zep 2:14

23 "I will turn her into a place for owls[k]
and into swampland;
I will sweep her with the broom of destruction,"
declares the LORD Almighty.

A Prophecy Against Assyria

14:24 [l] Isa 45:23 [m] Ac 4:28

24 The LORD Almighty has sworn,[l]
"Surely, as I have planned, so it will be,
and as I have purposed, so it will stand.[m]

14:25 [n] Isa 10:5,12 [o] Isa 9:4 [p] Isa 10:27

25 I will crush the Assyrian[n] in my land;
on my mountains I will trample him down.
His yoke[o] will be taken from my people,
and his burden removed from their shoulders.[p]"

14:26 [q] Isa 23:9 [r] Ex 15:12

26 This is the plan[q] determined for the whole world;
this is the hand[r] stretched out over all nations.
27 For the LORD Almighty has purposed, and who can thwart him?

14:27 [s] 2Ch 20:6; Isa 43:13; Da 4:35

His hand is stretched out, and who can turn it back?[s]

A Prophecy Against the Philistines

14:28 [t] Isa 13:1 [u] 2Ki 16:20

28 This oracle[t] came in the year King
Ahaz[u] died:

14:29 [v] 2Ch 26:6 [w] Isa 11:8

29 Do not rejoice, all you Philistines,[v]
that the rod that struck you is broken;
from the root of that snake will spring up a viper,[w]
its fruit will be a darting, venomous serpent.

14:30 [x] Isa 3:15 [y] Isa 7:21-22 [z] Isa 8:21; 9:20; 51:19 [a] Jer 25:16

30 The poorest of the poor will find pasture,
and the needy[x] will lie down in safety.[y]
But your root I will destroy by famine;[z]
it will slay[a] your survivors.

14:31 [b] Isa 3:26 [c] Jer 1:14

31 Wail, O gate![b] Howl, O city!
Melt away, all you Philistines!
A cloud of smoke comes from the north,[c]
and there is not a straggler in its ranks.

14:32 [d] Isa 37:9 [e] Ps 87:2,5; Isa 44:28; 54:11 [f] Isa 4:6; Jas 2:5

32 What answer shall be given
to the envoys[d] of that nation?
"The LORD has established Zion,[e]
and in her his afflicted people will find refuge.[f]"

A Prophecy Against Moab

15:1 [g] Isa 11:14 [h] Jer 48:24,41

15 An oracle concerning Moab:[g]
Ar in Moab is ruined,[h]
destroyed in a night!
Kir in Moab is ruined,
destroyed in a night!

15:2 [i] Jer 48:35 [j] Lev 21:5

2 Dibon goes up to its temple,
to its high places[i] to weep;
Moab wails over Nebo and Medeba.
Every head is shaved[j]
and every beard cut off.

15:3 [k] Jer 48:38 [l] Isa 22:4

3 In the streets they wear sackcloth;
on the roofs and in the public squares[k]
they all wail,
prostrate with weeping.[l]

15:4 [m] Nu 32:3

4 Heshbon and Elealeh[m] cry out,
their voices are heard all the way to Jahaz.
Therefore the armed men of Moab cry out,
and their hearts are faint.

15:5 [n] Jer 48:31 [o] Jer 48:3,34 [p] Jer 4:20; 48:5

5 My heart cries out over Moab;[n]
her fugitives flee as far as Zoar,
as far as Eglath Shelishiyah.
They go up the way to Luhith,
weeping as they go;
on the road to Horonaim[o]
they lament their destruction.[p]

15:6 [q] Isa 19:5-7; Jer 48:34 [r] Joel 1:12

6 The waters of Nimrim are dried up[q]
and the grass is withered;[r]
the vegetation is gone
and nothing green is left.

15:7 [s] Isa 30:6; Jer 48:36

7 So the wealth they have acquired[s]
and stored up
they carry away over the Ravine
of the Poplars.
8 Their outcry echoes along the
border of Moab;
their wailing reaches as far as
Eglaim,
their lamentation as far as Beer
Elim.
9 Dimon's[a] waters are full of blood,
but I will bring still more upon
Dimon[a]—

15:9 [t] 2Ki 17:25

a lion[t] upon the fugitives of Moab
and upon those who remain in
the land.

16:1 [u] 2Ki 3:4 [v] 2Ki 14:7 [w] Isa 10:32

16 Send lambs[u] as tribute
to the ruler of the land,
from Sela,[v] across the desert,
to the mount of the Daughter of
Zion.[w]

16:2 [x] Pr 27:8 [y] Nu 21:13-14; Jer 48:20

2 Like fluttering birds
pushed from the nest,[x]
so are the women of Moab
at the fords of the Arnon.[y]
3 "Give us counsel,
render a decision.
Make your shadow like night—
at high noon.

16:3 [z] 1Ki 18:4

Hide the fugitives,[z]
do not betray the refugees.
4 Let the Moabite fugitives stay with
you;
be their shelter from the
destroyer."

16:4 [a] Isa 9:4

The oppressor[a] will come to an end,
and destruction will cease;
the aggressor will vanish from
the land.

16:5 [b] Da 7:14; Mic 4:7 [c] Lk 1:32 [d] Isa 9:7

5 In love a throne[b] will be established;
in faithfulness a man will sit on
it—
one from the house[b] of David[c]—
one who in judging seeks justice[d]
and speeds the cause of
righteousness.

16:6 [e] Am 2:1; Zep 2:8 [f] Ob 1: Zep 2:10

6 We have heard of Moab's[e] pride[f]—
her overweening pride and
conceit,
her pride and her insolence—
but her boasts are empty.

16:7 [g] Jer 48:20 [h] 1Ch 16:3 [i] 2Ki 3:25

7 Therefore the Moabites wail,[g]
they wail together for Moab.
Lament and grieve
for the men[c][h] of Kir Hareseth.[i]
8 The fields of Heshbon wither,
the vines of Sibmah also.
The rulers of the nations
have trampled down the
choicest vines,
which once reached Jazer
and spread toward the desert.
Their shoots spread out
and went as far as the sea.

16:9 [j] Isa 15:3 [k] Jer 40:12

9 So I weep,[j] as Jazer weeps,
for the vines of Sibmah.
O Heshbon, O Elealeh,
I drench you with tears!
The shouts of joy over your ripened
fruit
and over your harvests[k] have
been stilled.

16:10 [l] Isa 24:7-8 [m] Jdg 9:27 [n] Job 24:11

10 Joy and gladness are taken away
from the orchards;[l]
no one sings or shouts in the
vineyards;
no one treads[m] out wine at the
presses,[n]
for I have put an end to the
shouting.

16:11 [o] Isa 15:5 [p] Isa 63:15; Hos 11:8; Php 2:1

11 My heart laments for Moab[o] like a
harp,
my inmost being[p] for Kir
Hareseth.

16:12 [q] Isa 15:2 [r] 1Ki 18:29

12 When Moab appears at her high
place,
she only wears herself out;
when she goes to her shrine[q] to
pray,
it is to no avail.[r]

16:14 [s] Isa 25:10; Jer 48:42 [t] Isa 21:17

13 This is the word the LORD has already spoken concerning Moab. 14 But
now the LORD says: "Within three years,
as a servant bound by contract would
count them, Moab's splendor and all her
many people will be despised,[s] and her
survivors will be very few and feeble."[t]

[a] 9 Masoretic Text; Dead Sea Scrolls, some Septuagint manuscripts and Vulgate *Dibon*
[b] 5 Hebrew *tent*
[c] 7 Or "*raisin cakes*," a wordplay

An Oracle Against Damascus

17:1 [u]Ge 14:15; Jer 49:23; Ac 9:2 [v]Isa 25:2; Am 1:3; Zec 9:1

17 An oracle concerning Damascus:[u]

"See, Damascus will no longer be a city
but will become a heap of ruins.[v]

17:2 [w]Isa 7:21; Eze 25:5 [x]Jer 7:33; Mic 4:4

2 The cities of Aroer will be deserted
and left to flocks,[w] which will lie down,
with no one to make them afraid.[x]
3 The fortified city will disappear from Ephraim,
and royal power from Damascus;

17:3 [y]ver 4; Hos 9:11 [z]Isa 7:8,16; 8:4

the remnant of Aram will be
like the glory[y] of the Israelites,"[z]
declares the LORD Almighty.

17:4 [a]Isa 10:16

4 "In that day the glory of Jacob will fade;
the fat of his body will waste[a] away.

17:5 [b]ver 11; Jer 51:33; Joel 3:13; Mt 13:30

5 It will be as when a reaper gathers the standing grain
and harvests[b] the grain with his arm—
as when a man gleans heads of grain
in the Valley of Rephaim.

17:6 [c]Dt 4:27; Isa 24:13 [d]Isa 27:12

6 Yet some gleanings will remain,[c]
as when an olive tree is beaten,[d]
leaving two or three olives on the topmost branches,
four or five on the fruitful boughs,"
declares the LORD, the God of Israel.

17:7 [e]Isa 10:20 [f]Mic 7:7

7 In that day men will look[e] to their Maker
and turn their eyes to the Holy One[f] of Israel.

17:8 [g]Isa 2:18,20; 30:22

8 They will not look to the altars,
the work of their hands,[g]
and they will have no regard for the Asherah poles[a]
and the incense altars their fingers have made.

9 In that day their strong cities, which
they left because of the Israelites, will be
like places abandoned to thickets and
undergrowth. And all will be desolation.

17:10 [h]Isa 51:13 [i]Ps 68:19; Isa 12:2

10 You have forgotten[h] God your Savior;[i]
you have not remembered the Rock, your fortress.
Therefore, though you set out the finest plants
and plant imported vines,

17:11 [j]Ps 90:6 [k]Hos 8:7 [l]Job 4:8

11 though on the day you set them out, you make them grow,
and on the morning[j] when you plant them, you bring them to bud,
yet the harvest will be as nothing[k]
in the day of disease and incurable pain.[l]

17:12 [m]Ps 18:4; Jer 6:23; Lk 21:25

12 Oh, the raging of many nations—
they rage like the raging sea![m]
Oh, the uproar of the peoples—
they roar like the roaring of great waters!

17:13 [n]Ps 9:5 [o]Isa 13:14 [p]Isa 41:2,15-16 [q]Job 21:18

13 Although the peoples roar like the roar of surging waters,
when he rebukes[n] them they flee[o] far away,
driven before the wind like chaff[p] on the hills,
like tumbleweed before a gale.[q]

17:14 [r]2Ki 19:35

14 In the evening, sudden terror!
Before the morning, they are gone![r]
This is the portion of those who loot us,
the lot of those who plunder us.

A Prophecy Against Cush

18:1 [s]Isa 20:3-5; Eze 30:4-5,9; Zep 2:12; 3:10

18 Woe to the land of whirring wings[b]
along the rivers of Cush,[c][s]

18:2 [t]Ex 2:3 [u]Ge 10:8-9; 2Ch 12:3 [v]ver 7

2 which sends envoys by sea
in papyrus[t] boats over the water.

Go, swift messengers,
to a people tall and smooth-skinned,
to a people feared far and wide,
an aggressive[u] nation of strange speech,
whose land is divided by rivers.[v]

18:3 [w]Isa 5:26

3 All you people of the world,
you who live on the earth,
when a banner[w] is raised on the mountains,
you will see it,
and when a trumpet sounds,
you will hear it.
4 This is what the LORD says to me:

[a] *8* That is, symbols of the goddess Asherah
[b] *1* Or *of locusts* [c] *1* That is, the upper Nile region

“I will remain quiet and will look
on from my dwelling place,[x]
like shimmering heat in the
sunshine,
like a cloud of dew[y] in the heat
of harvest.”
[5] For, before the harvest, when the
blossom is gone
and the flower becomes a
ripening grape,
he will cut off the shoots with
pruning knives,
and cut down and take away the
spreading branches.[z]
[6] They will all be left to the
mountain birds of prey
and to the wild animals;[a]
the birds will feed on them all
summer,
the wild animals all winter.

[7] At that time gifts will be brought to
the LORD Almighty

from a people tall and
smooth-skinned,
from a people feared far and
wide,
an aggressive nation of strange
speech,
whose land is divided by rivers—

the gifts will be brought to Mount Zion, the place of the Name of the LORD Almighty.[b]

18:4 [x] Isa 26:21; Hos 5:15 [y] Isa 26:19; Hos 14:5
18:5 [z] Isa 17:10-11; Eze 17:6
18:6 [a] Isa 56:9; Jer 7:33; Eze 32:4; 39:17
18:7 [b] Ps 68:31

A Prophecy About Egypt

19 An oracle[c] concerning Egypt:[d e]

See, the LORD rides on a swift
cloud[f]
and is coming to Egypt.
The idols of Egypt tremble before
him,
and the hearts of the Egyptians
melt[g] within them.

[2] “I will stir up Egyptian against
Egyptian—
brother will fight against
brother,[h]
neighbor against neighbor,
city against city,
kingdom against kingdom.[i]
[3] The Egyptians will lose heart,
and I will bring their plans to
nothing;
they will consult the idols and the
spirits of the dead,
the mediums and the spiritists.[j]
[4] I will hand the Egyptians over
to the power of a cruel master,
and a fierce king[k] will rule over
them,”
declares the Lord, the LORD
Almighty.

[5] The waters of the river will dry up,[l]
and the riverbed will be parched
and dry.
[6] The canals will stink;[m]
the streams of Egypt will
dwindle and dry up.[n]
The reeds and rushes will wither,[o]
[7] also the plants along the Nile,
at the mouth of the river.
Every sown field[p] along the Nile
will become parched, will blow
away and be no more.
[8] The fishermen[q] will groan and
lament,
all who cast hooks[r] into the Nile;
those who throw nets on the water
will pine away.
[9] Those who work with combed flax
will despair,
the weavers of fine linen[s] will
lose hope.
[10] The workers in cloth will be
dejected,
and all the wage earners will be
sick at heart.

[11] The officials of Zoan[t] are nothing
but fools;
the wise counselors of Pharaoh
give senseless advice.
How can you say to Pharaoh,
“I am one of the wise men,[u]
a disciple of the ancient kings”?
[12] Where are your wise men[v] now?
Let them show you and make
known
what the LORD Almighty
has planned[w] against Egypt.
[13] The officials of Zoan have become
fools,
the leaders of Memphis[a x] are
deceived;
the cornerstones of her peoples
have led Egypt astray.
[14] The LORD has poured into them
a spirit of dizziness;[y]
they make Egypt stagger in all that
she does,

[a] *13* Hebrew *Noph*

19:1 [c] Isa 13:1; Jer 43:12 [d] Joel 3:19 [e] Ex 12:12 [f] Ps 18:10; 104:3; Rev 1:7 [g] Jos 2:11
19:2 [h] Jdg 7:22; Mt 10:21,36 [i] 2Ch 20:23
19:3 [j] Isa 8:19; 47:13; Da 2:2,10
19:4 [k] Isa 20:4; Jer 46:26; Eze 29:19
19:5 [l] Jer 51:36
19:6 [m] Ex 7:18 [n] Isa 37:25; Eze 30:12 [o] Isa 15:6
19:7 [p] Isa 23:3
19:8 [q] Eze 47:10 [r] Hab 1:15
19:9 [s] Pr 7:16; Eze 27:7
19:11 [t] Nu 13:22 [u] 1Ki 4:30; Ac 7:22
19:12 [v] 1Co 1:20 [w] Isa 14:24; Ro 9:17
19:13 [x] Jer 2:16; Eze 30:13,16
19:14 [y] Mt 17:17

as a drunkard staggers around
in his vomit.
15 There is nothing Egypt can do—
head or tail, palm branch or
reed.[z]

16 In that day the Egyptians will be like
women.[a] They will shudder with fear[b] at
the uplifted hand[c] that the LORD
Almighty raises against them. 17 And the
land of Judah will bring terror to the
Egyptians; everyone to whom Judah is
mentioned will be terrified, because of
what the LORD Almighty is planning[d]
against them.

18 In that day five cities in Egypt will
speak the language of Canaan and swear
allegiance[e] to the LORD Almighty. One of
them will be called the City of Destruction.[a]

19 In that day there will be an altar[f] to
the LORD in the heart of Egypt, and a
monument[g] to the LORD at its border.
20 It will be a sign and witness to the
LORD Almighty in the land of Egypt.
When they cry out to the LORD because
of their oppressors, he will send them a
savior and defender, and he will rescue[h]
them. 21 So the LORD will make himself
known to the Egyptians, and in that day
they will acknowledge[i] the LORD. They
will worship[j] with sacrifices and grain
offerings; they will make vows to the
LORD and keep them. 22 The LORD will
strike[k] Egypt with a plague; he will
strike them and heal them. They
will turn[l] to the LORD, and he will respond to their pleas and heal[m] them.

23 In that day there will be a highway[n]
from Egypt to Assyria. The Assyrians
will go to Egypt and the Egyptians to
Assyria. The Egyptians and Assyrians
will worship[o] together. 24 In that day Israel will be the third, along with Egypt
and Assyria, a blessing on the earth.
25 The LORD Almighty will bless them,
saying, "Blessed be Egypt my people,[p]
Assyria my handiwork,[q] and Israel my
inheritance.[r]"

19:15 [z] Isa 9:14
19:16 [a] 50:37; 51:30; Na 3:13 [b] Heb 10:31 [c] Isa 11:15
19:17 [d] Isa 14:24
19:18 [e] Zep 3:9
19:19 [f] Jos 22:10 [g] Ge 28:18
19:20 [h] Isa 49:24-26
19:21 [i] Isa 11:9 [j] Isa 56:7; Mal 1:11
19:22 [k] Heb 12:11 [l] Isa 45:14; Hos 14:1 [m] Dt 32:39
19:23 [n] Isa 11:16 [o] Isa 27:13
19:25 [p] Ps 100:3 [q] Isa 29:23; 45:11; 60:21; 64:8; Eph 2:10 [r] Hos 2:23

A Prophecy Against Egypt and Cush

20 In the year that the supreme
commander,[s] sent by Sargon
king of Assyria, came to Ashdod and attacked and captured it— 2 at that time
the LORD spoke through Isaiah son of
Amoz.[t] He said to him, "Take off the
sackcloth[u] from your body and the sandals[v] from your feet." And he did so, going around stripped[w] and barefoot.[x]

3 Then the LORD said, "Just as my servant Isaiah has gone stripped and barefoot for three years, as a sign[y] and portent against Egypt and Cush,[b][z] 4 so the
king[a] of Assyria will lead away stripped
and barefoot the Egyptian captives and
Cushite exiles, young and old, with buttocks bared—to Egypt's shame.[b] 5 Those
who trusted in Cush and boasted in
Egypt[c] will be afraid and put to shame.
6 In that day the people who live on this
coast will say, 'See what has happened to
those we relied on, those we fled to for
help[d] and deliverance from the king of
Assyria! How then can we escape?[e]' "

20:1 [s] 2Ki 18:17
20:2 [t] Isa 13:1 [u] Zec 13:4; Mt 3:4
20:2 [v] Eze 24:17,23 [w] 1Sa 19:24 [x] Mic 1:8
20:3 [y] Isa 8:18 [z] Isa 37:9; 43:3
20:4 [a] Isa 19:4 [b] Isa 47:3; Jer 13:22,26
20:5 [c] 2Ki 18:21; Isa 30:5
20:6 [d] Isa 10:3 [e] Jer 30:15-17; Mt 23:33; 1Th 5:3; Heb 2:3

A Prophecy Against Babylon

21 An oracle concerning the
Desert[f] by the Sea:

Like whirlwinds sweeping through
the southland,[g]
an invader comes from the
desert,
from a land of terror.

2 A dire[h] vision has been shown to
me:
The traitor betrays,[i] the looter
takes loot.
Elam,[j] attack! Media, lay siege!
I will bring to an end all the
groaning she caused.

3 At this my body is racked with pain,
pangs seize me, like those of a
woman in labor;[k]
I am staggered by what I hear,
I am bewildered by what I see.
4 My heart falters,
fear makes me tremble;
the twilight I longed for
has become a horror to me.

5 They set the tables,
they spread the rugs,
they eat, they drink![l]
Get up, you officers,
oil the shields!

6 This is what the Lord says to me:

"Go, post a lookout
and have him report what he sees.

21:1 [f] Isa 13:21; Jer 51:43 [g] Zec 9:14
21:2 [h] Ps 60:3 [i] Isa 33:1 [j] Isa 22:6; Jer 49:34
21:3 [k] Ps 48:6; Isa 26:17
21:5 [l] Jer 51:39,57; Da 5:2

[a] 18 Most manuscripts of the Masoretic Text; some manuscripts of the Masoretic Text, Dead Sea Scrolls and Vulgate *City of the Sun* (that is, Heliopolis) [b] 3 That is, the upper Nile region; also in verse 5

21:7 m ver 9

[7]When he sees chariots[m]
with teams of horses,
riders on donkeys
or riders on camels,
let him be alert,
fully alert."

21:8 n Hab 2:1

[8]And the lookout[a n] shouted,

"Day after day, my lord, I stand on
the watchtower;
every night I stay at my post.
[9]Look, here comes a man in a chariot
with a team of horses.
And he gives back the answer:
'Babylon[o] has fallen,[p] has fallen!
All the images of its gods[q]
lie shattered on the ground!'"

21:9 o Rev 14:8 p Jer 51:8; Rev 18:2 q Isa 46:1; Jer 50:2; 51:44

[10]O my people, crushed on the
threshing floor,[r]
I tell you what I have heard
from the LORD Almighty,
from the God of Israel.

21:10 r Jer 51:33

A Prophecy Against Edom

[11]An oracle concerning Dumah[b]:[s]

Someone calls to me from Seir,[t]
"Watchman, what is left of the
night?
Watchman, what is left of the
night?"
[12]The watchman replies,
"Morning is coming, but also the
night.
If you would ask, then ask;
and come back yet again."

21:11 s Ge 25:14 t Ge 32:3

A Prophecy Against Arabia

[13]An oracle[u] concerning Arabia:

21:13 u Isa 13:1

You caravans of Dedanites,
who camp in the thickets of
Arabia,
[14] bring water for the thirsty;
you who live in Tema,[v]
bring food for the fugitives.
[15]They flee[w] from the sword,
from the drawn sword,
from the bent bow
and from the heat of battle.

21:14 v Ge 25:15

21:15 w Isa 13:14

[16]This is what the Lord says to me:
"Within one year, as a servant bound by
contract[x] would count it, all the pomp[y]
of Kedar[z] will come to an end. [17]The survivors of the bowmen, the warriors of
Kedar, will be few.[a]" The LORD, the God
of Israel, has spoken.

21:16 x Isa 16:14 y Isa 17:3 z Ps 120:5; Isa 60:7

21:17 a Isa 10:19

A Prophecy About Jerusalem

22 An oracle[b] concerning the Valley[c] of Vision:

22:1 b Isa 13:1 c Ps 125:2; Jer 21:13; Joel 3:2,12,14

What troubles you now,
that you have all gone up on the
roofs,
[2]O town full of commotion,
O city of tumult and revelry?[d]
Your slain were not killed by the
sword,
nor did they die in battle.
[3]All your leaders have fled together;
they have been captured without
using the bow.
All you who were caught were
taken prisoner together,
having fled while the enemy was
still far away.
[4]Therefore I said, "Turn away from
me;
let me weep[e] bitterly.
Do not try to console me
over the destruction of my
people."[f]

22:2 d Isa 32:13

22:4 e Isa 15:3; Lk 19:41 f Jer 9:1

[5]The Lord, the LORD Almighty, has a
day
of tumult and trampling and
terror[g]
in the Valley of Vision,
a day of battering down walls
and of crying out to the
mountains.
[6]Elam[h] takes up the quiver,[i]
with her charioteers and horses;
Kir[j] uncovers the shield.
[7]Your choicest valleys are full of
chariots,
and horsemen are posted at the
city gates;[k]
[8] the defenses of Judah are
stripped away.

22:5 g La 1:5

22:6 h Isa 21:2 i Jer 49:35 j 2Ki 16:9

22:7 k 2Ch 32:1-2

And you looked in that day
to the weapons[l] in the Palace of
the Forest;[m]
[9]you saw that the City of David
had many breaches in its
defenses;
you stored up water
in the Lower Pool.[n]
[10]You counted the buildings in
Jerusalem
and tore down houses to
strengthen the wall.

22:8 l 2Ch 32:5 m 1Ki 7:2

22:9 n 2Ch 32:4

[a] *8* Dead Sea Scrolls and Syriac; Masoretic Text *A lion* [b] *11* *Dumah* means *silence* or *stillness,* a wordplay on *Edom.*

THE KEY OF DAVID

In the Bible an open door symbolizes several things. First, the open door (or gate) is an illustration for a means of entry into God's family. Jesus declared that he himself was the door of the sheepfold (John 10:7–10). The open door also represents the opportunities God gives us to serve him (Revelation 3:8). Finally, the open door symbolizes fellowship with Jesus, who stands patiently waiting at the entrance to our hearts, desiring to enter our lives (Revelation 3:20).

God promised Hilkiah that he would replace Shebna as the palace administrator. In that role Hilkiah would receive the key to the house of David (Isaiah 22:15–24). This Old Testament promise aptly describes the character of Jesus. The second and third chapters of Revelation contain seven messages from Jesus to seven churches in Asia. Each of the messages begins with a description of Jesus Christ. The message to the church in Philadelphia reads in part as follows: "These are the words of him who is holy and true, who holds the key of David. What he opens no one can shut, and what he shuts no one can open" (Revelation 3:7).

The "key of David" probably refers to access to the kingdom of God and the blessings associated with it. Jesus not only *holds* the key to the spiritual kingdom, but he in fact *is* that key (John 14:6). And Jesus is more than simply the key to eternal life and the blessings of the kingdom; he also opens doors of opportunity for us to minister to others. The letter from Jesus to the church at Philadelphia goes on to recognize all the work this congregation had done for Jesus: "See, I have placed before you an open door that no one can shut" (Revelation 3:8).

Paul was very conscious of the doors of opportunity that had been opened for him. He went to Troas to preach the gospel and "found that the Lord had opened a door for me" (2 Corinthians 2:12). What are God's "open doors" like? For one thing, we find them in the ordinary activities of life. Paul did not wait for word that there was a door opening in Troas. He simply went where he knew God wanted him to go and discovered what God had in mind for him as he went about his daily activities.

Just because a door opens for us does not mean that we will encounter no opposition. In fact, Paul discovered that opposition often goes hand-in-hand with an open door. Ephesus represented a place of conflict for Paul: "A great door for effective work has opened to me, and there are many who oppose me" (1 Corinthians 16:9). But because it is God who opens any and all doors he chooses to open, we can be encouraged by the knowledge that we are partnering with him. He opens, and we walk through.

There are opportunities all around us—to tell other people about Jesus, to give of our financial resources to support others, to pray, love, encourage . . . the list is endless. As we ask God to make us aware of the doors he is opening, he will equip us with the grace and courage to walk through them—no matter what opposition we might face.

***Self-Discovery:** Identify some doors that have been opened (or closed) in your life. Looking back, can you begin to trace how God's plan for your life was unfolding?*

GO TO DISCOVERY 184 ON PAGE 920

22:11 [o]2Ki 25:4; Jer 39:4 [p]2Ch 32:4

11 You built a reservoir between the
two walls[o]
for the water of the Old Pool,[p]
but you did not look to the One
who made it,
or have regard for the One who
planned it long ago.

22:12 [q]Joel 2:17 [r]Mic 1:16 [s]Joel 1:13

12 The Lord, the LORD Almighty,
called you on that day
to weep[q] and to wail,
to tear out your hair[r] and put on
sackcloth.[s]
13 But see, there is joy and revelry,
slaughtering of cattle and killing
of sheep,
eating of meat and drinking of
wine![t]

22:13 [t]Isa 5:22; 28:7-8; 56:12; Lk 17:26-29 [u]1Co 15:32*

"Let us eat and drink," you say,
"for tomorrow we die!"[u]

22:14 [v]Isa 5:9 [w]Isa 13:11; 26:21; 30:13-14; Eze 24:13

14 The LORD Almighty has revealed
this in my hearing:[v] "Till your dying day
this sin will not be atoned[w] for," says the
Lord, the LORD Almighty.

15 This is what the Lord, the LORD
Almighty, says:

22:15 [x]2Ki 18:18; Isa 36:3

"Go, say to this steward,
to Shebna,[x] who is in charge of
the palace:
16 What are you doing here and who
gave you permission

22:16 [y]Mt 27:60

to cut out a grave[y] for yourself
here,

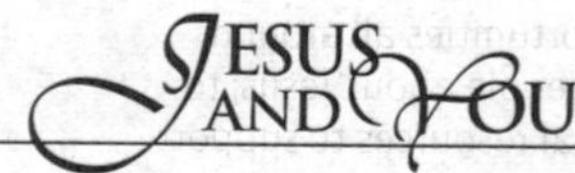

TWICE DESTROYED

The Israelites complacently believed that God would never allow Jerusalem to fall into enemy hands, yet in order to prepare for war they reinforced the city walls and reservoirs. The prophet Isaiah warned the people to turn away from their sins and back to God before it was too late (Isaiah 22:12–13), but the nation failed to listen, and in 605 B.C. the city of Jerusalem fell to the Babylonians. Some 20 years later, in 586 B.C., this magnificent city was reduced to a pile of smoldering ashes. Centuries later Jesus predicted that Jerusalem would again be destroyed, and this event did occur 40 years afterward, when the Romans ransacked and burned the city in A.D. 70. Twice Jerusalem suffered the same fate, because in each instance the people had refused to change their ways (Matthew 24:1–2,15–20).

hewing your grave on the height
and chiseling your resting place
in the rock?

17 "Beware, the LORD is about to take
firm hold of you
and hurl you away, O you mighty
man.
18 He will roll you up tightly like a ball
and throw[z] you into a large
country.
There you will die
and there your splendid chariots
will remain—
you disgrace to your master's
house!

22:18 [z]Isa 17:13

19 I will depose you from your office,
and you will be ousted from your
position.

20 "In that day I will summon my servant, Eliakim[a] son of Hilkiah. 21 I will
clothe him with your robe and fasten
your sash around him and hand your
authority over to him. He will be a father
to those who live in Jerusalem and to the
house of Judah. 22 I will place on his
shoulder the key[b] to the house of David;[c]
what he opens no one can shut, and
what he shuts no one can open.[d] 23 I will
drive him like a peg[e] into a firm place;[f]
he will be a seat[a] of honor[g] for the house
of his father. 24 All the glory of his family
will hang on him: its offspring and off-
shoots—all its lesser vessels, from the
bowls to all the jars.

22:20 [a]2Ki 18:18; Isa 36:3

22:22 [b]Rev 3:7 [c]Isa 7:2 [d]Job 12:14

22:23 [e]Zec 10:4 [f]Ezr 9:8 [g]1Sa 2:7-8; Job 36:7

25 "In that day," declares the LORD
Almighty, "the peg[h] driven into the firm
place will give way; it will be sheared off
and will fall, and the load hanging on it
will be cut down." The LORD has spoken.[i]

22:25 [h]ver 23 [i]Isa 46:11; Mic 4:4

A Prophecy About Tyre

23 An oracle concerning Tyre:[j]

Wail, O ships[k] of Tarshish![l]
For Tyre is destroyed
and left without house or harbor.
From the land of Cyprus[b]
word has come to them.

23:1 [j]Jos 19:29; 1Ki 5:1; Jer 47:4; Eze 26,27,28; Joel 3:4-8; Am 1:9-10; Zec 9:2-4 [k]1Ki 10:22 [l]Ge 10:4; Isa 2:16 *fn*

2 Be silent, you people of the island
and you merchants of Sidon,
whom the seafarers have
enriched.
3 On the great waters
came the grain of the Shihor;

[a] 23 Or *throne* [b] 1 Hebrew *Kittim*

23:3 [m]Isa 19:7 [n]Eze 27:3

the harvest of the Nile[a][m] was the
revenue of Tyre,[n]
and she became the marketplace
of the nations.

23:4 [o]Ge 10:15,19

4 Be ashamed, O Sidon,[o] and you,
O fortress of the sea,
for the sea has spoken:
"I have neither been in labor nor
given birth;
I have neither reared sons nor
brought up daughters."
5 When word comes to Egypt,
they will be in anguish at the
report from Tyre.

6 Cross over to Tarshish;
wail, you people of the island.

23:7 [p]Isa 22:2; 32:13

7 Is this your city of revelry,[p]
the old, old city,
whose feet have taken her
to settle in far-off lands?
8 Who planned this against Tyre,
the bestower of crowns,
whose merchants are princes,
whose traders are renowned in
the earth?

23:9 [q]Job 40:11 [r]Isa 13:11 [s]Isa 5:13; 9:15

9 The LORD Almighty planned it,
to bring low[q] the pride of all
glory
and to humble[r] all who are
renowned[s] on the earth.

10 Till[b] your land as along the Nile,
O Daughter of Tarshish,
for you no longer have a harbor.

23:11 [t]Ex 14:21 [u]Isa 25:2; Zec 9:3-4

11 The LORD has stretched out his
hand[t] over the sea
and made its kingdoms tremble.
He has given an order concerning
Phoenicia[c]
that her fortresses be destroyed.[u]

23:12 [v]Rev 18:22 [w]Isa 47:1

12 He said, "No more of your reveling,[v]
O Virgin Daughter[w] of Sidon,
now crushed!

"Up, cross over to Cyprus[d];
even there you will find no rest."
13 Look at the land of the
Babylonians,[e]
this people that is now of no
account!

23:13 [x]Isa 10:5 [y]Isa 10:7

The Assyrians[x] have made it
a place for desert creatures;
they raised up their siege towers,
they stripped its fortresses bare
and turned it into a ruin.[y]

23:14 [z]Isa 2:16 *fn*

14 Wail, you ships of Tarshish;[z]
your fortress is destroyed!

23:15 [a]Jer 25:22

15 At that time Tyre[a] will be forgotten
for seventy years, the span of a king's life.
But at the end of these seventy years, it
will happen to Tyre as in the song of the
prostitute:

16 "Take up a harp, walk through the
city,
O prostitute forgotten;
play the harp well, sing many a
song,
so that you will be remembered."

23:17 [b]Eze 16:26; Na 3:4; Rev 17:1

23:18 [c]Ex 28:36; Ps 72:10 [d]Isa 60:5-9; Mic 4:13

17 At the end of seventy years, the LORD
will deal with Tyre. She will return to her
hire as a prostitute[b] and will ply her
trade with all the kingdoms on the face
of the earth. 18 Yet her profit and her
earnings will be set apart for the LORD;[c]
they will not be stored up or hoarded.
Her profits will go to those who live before the LORD,[d] for abundant food and
fine clothes.

The LORD's Devastation of the Earth

24:1 [e]ver 20; Isa 2:19-21; 33:9

24 See, the LORD is going to lay
waste the earth[e]
and devastate it;
he will ruin its face
and scatter its inhabitants—

24:2 [f]Hos 4:9 [g]Eze 7:12 [h]Lev 25:35-37; Dt 23:19-20

2 it will be the same
for priest as for people,[f]
for master as for servant,
for mistress as for maid,
for seller as for buyer,[g]
for borrower as for lender,
for debtor as for creditor.[h]

24:3 [i]Isa 6:11-12

3 The earth will be completely laid
waste
and totally plundered.[i]
The LORD has spoken
this word.

24:4 [j]Isa 2:12

4 The earth dries up and withers,
the world languishes and
withers,
the exalted[j] of the earth
languish.

24:5 [k]Ge 3:17; Nu 35:33 [l]Isa 10:6; 59:12

5 The earth is defiled[k] by its people;
they have disobeyed[l] the laws,
violated the statutes
and broken the everlasting
covenant.

[a] *2,3* Masoretic Text; one Dead Sea Scroll *Sidon, / who cross over the sea; / your envoys ³are on the great waters. / The grain of the Shihor, / the harvest of the Nile,* [b] *10* Dead Sea Scrolls and some Septuagint manuscripts; Masoretic Text *Go through* [c] *11* Hebrew *Canaan* [d] *12* Hebrew *Kittim* [e] *13* Or *Chaldeans*

6 Therefore a curse consumes the earth;
its people must bear their guilt.
Therefore earth's inhabitants are burned up,[m]
and very few are left.
7 The new wine dries up and the vine withers;[n]
all the merrymakers groan.[o]
8 The gaiety of the tambourines[p] is stilled,
the noise[q] of the revelers has stopped,
the joyful harp[r] is silent.[s]
9 No longer do they drink wine[t] with a song;
the beer is bitter[u] to its drinkers.
10 The ruined city lies desolate;
the entrance to every house is barred.
11 In the streets they cry out for wine;
all joy turns to gloom,[v]
all gaiety is banished from the earth.
12 The city is left in ruins,
its gate is battered to pieces.
13 So will it be on the earth
and among the nations,
as when an olive tree is beaten,[w]
or as when gleanings are left after the grape harvest.

14 They raise their voices, they shout for joy;[x]
from the west they acclaim the LORD's majesty.
15 Therefore in the east give glory[y] to the LORD;
exalt[z] the name of the LORD, the God of Israel,
in the islands of the sea.
16 From the ends of the earth we hear singing:
"Glory[a] to the Righteous One."

But I said, "I waste away, I waste away!
Woe to me!
The treacherous betray!
With treachery the treacherous betray![b]"
17 Terror and pit and snare[c] await you,
O people of the earth.
18 Whoever flees at the sound of terror
will fall into a pit;
whoever climbs out of the pit
will be caught in a snare.

24:6 [m] Isa 1:31
24:7 [n] Joel 1:10-12 [o] Isa 16:8-10
24:8 [p] Isa 5:12 [q] Jer 7:34; 16:9; 25:10; Hos 2:11 [r] Rev 18:22 [s] Eze 26:13
24:9 [t] Isa 5:11,22 [u] Isa 5:20
24:11 [v] Isa 16:10; 32:13; Jer 14:3
24:13 [w] Isa 17:6
24:14 [x] Isa 12:6
24:15 [y] Isa 66:19 [z] Isa 25:3; Mal 1:11
24:16 [a] Isa 28:5 [b] Isa 21:2; Jer 5:11
24:17 [c] Jer 48:43

The floodgates of the heavens[d] are opened,
the foundations of the earth shake.[e]
19 The earth is broken up,
the earth is split asunder,[f]
the earth is thoroughly shaken.
20 The earth reels like a drunkard,[g]
it sways like a hut in the wind;
so heavy upon it is the guilt of its rebellion[h]
that it falls—never to rise again.

21 In that day the LORD will punish[i]
the powers in the heavens above
and the kings on the earth below.
22 They will be herded together
like prisoners[j] bound in a dungeon;[k]
they will be shut up in prison
and be punished[a] after many days.[l]
23 The moon will be abashed, the sun[m] ashamed;
for the LORD Almighty will reign[n]
on Mount Zion[o] and in Jerusalem,
and before its elders, gloriously.[p]

24:18 [d] Ge 7:11 [e] Ps 18:7
24:19 [f] Dt 11:6
24:20 [g] Isa 19:14 [h] Isa 1:2,28; 43:27
24:21 [i] Isa 10:12
24:22 [j] Isa 10:4 [k] Isa 42:7,22 [l] Eze 38:8
24:23 [m] Isa 13:10 [n] Rev 22:5 [o] Heb 12:22 [p] Isa 60:19

Praise to the LORD

25 O LORD, you are my God;
I will exalt you and praise your name,
for in perfect faithfulness
you have done marvelous things,[q]
things planned[r] long ago.
2 You have made the city a heap of rubble,[s]
the fortified[t] town a ruin,
the foreigners' stronghold[u] a city no more;
it will never be rebuilt.
3 Therefore strong peoples will honor you;
cities of ruthless[v] nations will revere you.
4 You have been a refuge[w] for the poor,
a refuge for the needy in his distress,
a shelter from the storm
and a shade from the heat.
For the breath of the ruthless[x]
is like a storm driving against a wall
5 and like the heat of the desert.

25:1 [q] Ps 98:1 [r] Nu 23:19
25:2 [s] Isa 17:1 [t] Isa 17:3 [u] Isa 13:22
25:3 [v] Isa 13:11
25:4 [w] Isa 4:6; 17:10; 27:5; 33:16 [x] Isa 29:5; 49:25

[a] 22 Or *released*

25:5 [y]Jer 51:55

You silence[y] the uproar of
foreigners;
as heat is reduced by the shadow
of a cloud,
so the song of the ruthless is
stilled.

25:6 [z]Isa 2:2 [a]Isa 1:19; Mt 8:11; 22:4 [b]Pr 9:2

6 On this mountain[z] the LORD
Almighty will prepare
a feast[a] of rich food for all
peoples,
a banquet of aged wine—
the best of meats and the finest
of wines.[b]

25:7 [c]2Co 3:15-16; Eph 4:18

7 On this mountain he will destroy
the shroud[c] that enfolds all
peoples,
the sheet that covers all nations;

25:8 [d]Hos 13:14; 1Co 15:54-55* [e]Isa 30:19; 35:10; 51:11; 65:19; Rev 7:17; 21:4 [f]Mt 5:11; 1Pe 4:14

8 he will swallow up death[d] forever.
The Sovereign LORD will wipe away
the tears[e]
from all faces;
he will remove the disgrace[f] of his
people
from all the earth.
The LORD has spoken.

25:9 [g]Isa 40:9 [h]Ps 20:5; Isa 33:22; 35:4; 49:25-26; 60:16

9 In that day they will say,

"Surely this is our God;[g]
we trusted in him, and he saved[h]
us.

JESUS AND YOU

PROMISES TO COUNT ON

Isaiah foresaw the future kingdom of God as a time of unrestrained celebration and rejoicing (Isaiah 25:6–8). God's victorious Messiah will "swallow up death forever" (verse 8), and eternal life will be offered to all who have put their trust in God (verse 9). The whole earth will be judged, but this event need not instill fear in God's people, and it will be followed by the incomparable experience of a glorious future. Death and pain will be abolished, tears will be wiped away and Jesus will reign in perfect peace and perfect justice. The apostle John described the same future experience, referring to the new heaven and the new earth that God will bring about (Revelation 21:1–27). God has an incredible future planned for his family—for all who are willing to take him at his word and surrender control of their lives to him, trusting in his precious son Jesus for forgiveness of sins and the gracious gift of eternal life (John 3:36).

This is the LORD, we trusted in him;
let us rejoice[i] and be glad in his
salvation."

25:9 [i]Isa 35:2,10

10 The hand of the LORD will rest on
this mountain;
but Moab[j] will be trampled
under him
as straw is trampled down in the
manure.

25:10 [j]Am 2:1-3

11 They will spread out their hands in
it,
as a swimmer spreads out his
hands to swim.
God will bring down[k] their pride[l]
despite the cleverness[a] of their
hands.

25:11 [k]Isa 5:25; 14:26; 16:14 [l]Job 40:12

12 He will bring down your high
fortified walls
and lay them low;[m]
he will bring them down to the
ground,
to the very dust.

25:12 [m]Isa 15:1

A Song of Praise

26 In that day this song will be sung in the land of Judah:

We have a strong city;[n]
God makes salvation
its walls[o] and ramparts.

26:1 [n]Isa 14:32 [o]Isa 60:18

2 Open the gates
that the righteous[p] nation may
enter,
the nation that keeps faith.

26:2 [p]Isa 54:14; 58:8; 62:2

3 You will keep in perfect peace
him whose mind is steadfast,
because he trusts in you.

4 Trust[q] in the LORD forever,
for the LORD, the LORD, is the
Rock eternal.

26:4 [q]Isa 12:2; 50:10

5 He humbles those who dwell on
high,
he lays the lofty city low;
he levels it to the ground[r]
and casts it down to the dust.

26:5 [r]Isa 25:12

6 Feet trample it down—
the feet of the oppressed,
the footsteps of the poor.[s]

26:6 [s]Isa 3:15

7 The path of the righteous is level;
O upright One, you make the way
of the righteous smooth.[t]

26:7 [t]Isa 42:16

8 Yes, LORD, walking in the way of
your laws,[b][u]
we wait for you;
your name[v] and renown

26:8 [u]Isa 56:1 [v]Isa 12:4

[a] *11* The meaning of the Hebrew for this word is uncertain. [b] *8* Or *judgments*

Perfect Peace

Turmoil is unavoidable in our world. "In this world you will have trouble," stated our precious Lord Jesus in John 16:33. But in Isaiah 26:3 the prophet voiced a wonderful promise worth remembering every day—especially in the middle of life's storms: "You will keep in perfect peace him whose mind is steadfast, because he trusts in you." God is the source of our peace, the One who holds us steady when everything around us is faltering and the foundations are shaking.

There are two kinds of peace mentioned in the Bible. First, there is peace *with* God. This kind of peace comes only when we believe that Jesus died for our sin (Romans 5:1). Before God opened the way back into a relationship with himself through his Son, we were God's enemies (Colossians 1:21)—alienated from God, hostile toward him, in spiritual turmoil, at war with our Creator.

Second, there is the peace *of* God. When we enjoy a relationship with him, we can lay all of our anxieties and confusion before him in prayer, learning to trust him with everything, and he will give us an inner tranquility that cannot be explained or understood: "Do not be anxious about anything, but in everything, by prayer and petition, with thanksgiving, present your requests to God. And the peace of God, which transcends all understanding, will guard your hearts and your minds in Christ Jesus" (Philippians 4:6–7). No matter what the tragedy—the death of a child, the loss of a job, the diagnosis of a terminal disease—the lives of God's people are undergirded by the steady assurance that he is continually at work behind the scenes to fulfill his perfect purposes for his creation.

God's peace is perfect, complete, all we need in any given situation. As we learn to trust God, he blesses us with his peace (Psalm 29:11). Relying on God and his wisdom is the only choice that will never disappoint us, the only option that teaches us godly wisdom. Only when we turn to Jesus can we enjoy the certainty that our salvation is real ("Since we have been justified through faith, we have peace with God through our Lord Jesus Christ, through whom we have gained access by faith into this grace in which we now stand" [Romans 5:1–2]) and gain the repose that comes from answered prayer (Philippians 4:6–7).

Peace is so intrinsic to the nature of God that the Bible uses it as his name. The Father is the "God of peace" (Philippians 4:9), and Jesus the Messiah is the "Prince of Peace" (Isaiah 9:6). Finally, God the Holy Spirit is the One who produces peace in our lives (Romans 8:6; Galatians 5:22). Jesus said, "Peace I leave with you; my peace I give you. I do not give to you as the world gives. Do not let your heart be troubled and do not be afraid" (John 14:27).

Self-Discovery: *Look up the word* peace *in the concordance at the back of this Bible. Take a moment to look up some of the passages. What is your response after reading several of them?*

GO TO DISCOVERY 185 ON PAGE 923

are the desire of our hearts.
9 My soul yearns for you in the night;
in the morning my spirit longs[w]
for you.
When your judgments come upon
the earth,
the people of the world learn
righteousness.[x]
10 Though grace is shown to the
wicked,
they do not learn righteousness;
even in a land of uprightness they
go on doing evil[y]
and regard[z] not the majesty of
the LORD.
11 O LORD, your hand is lifted high,
but they do not see[a] it.
Let them see your zeal for your
people and be put to shame;
let the fire[b] reserved for your
enemies consume them.

12 LORD, you establish peace for us;
all that we have accomplished
you have done for us.
13 O LORD, our God, other lords[c]
besides you have ruled over
us,
but your name alone do we
honor.[d]
14 They are now dead,[e] they live no
more;
those departed spirits do not rise.
You punished them and brought
them to ruin;[f]
you wiped out all memory of
them.
15 You have enlarged the nation,
O LORD;
you have enlarged the nation.
You have gained glory for yourself;
you have extended all the
borders[g] of the land.

16 LORD, they came to you in their
distress;[h]
when you disciplined them,
they could barely whisper a
prayer.[a]
17 As a woman with child and about
to give birth[i]
writhes and cries out in her
pain,
so were we in your presence,
O LORD.
18 We were with child, we writhed in
pain,
but we gave birth[j] to wind.

26:9 [w] Ps 63:1; 78:34; Isa 55:6 [x] Mt 6:33
26:10 [y] Isa 32:6 [z] Isa 22:12-13; Hos 11:7; Jn 5:37-38; Ro 2:4
26:11 [a] Isa 44:9,18 [b] Heb 10:27
26:13 [c] Isa 2:8; 10:5,11 [d] Isa 63:7
26:14 [e] Dt 4:28 [f] Isa 10:3
26:15 [g] Isa 33:17
26:16 [h] Hos 5:15
26:17 [i] Jn 16:21
26:18 [j] Isa 33:11; 59:4

We have not brought salvation[k] to
the earth;
we have not given birth to
people of the world.
19 But your dead[l] will live;
their bodies will rise.
You who dwell in the dust,
wake up and shout for joy.
Your dew is like the dew of the
morning;
the earth will give birth to her
dead.[m]

20 Go, my people, enter your rooms
and shut the doors[n] behind you;
hide[o] yourselves for a little while
until his wrath has passed by.[p]
21 See, the LORD is coming[q] out of his
dwelling[r]
to punish[s] the people of the
earth for their sins.
The earth will disclose the blood[t]
shed upon her;
she will conceal her slain no
longer.

Deliverance of Israel

27 In that day,
the LORD will punish with his
sword,[u]
his fierce, great and powerful
sword,
Leviathan[v] the gliding serpent,
Leviathan the coiling serpent;
he will slay the monster[w] of the
sea.

2 In that day—

"Sing about a fruitful vineyard:[x]
3 I, the LORD, watch over it;
I water[y] it continually.
I guard it day and night
so that no one may harm it.
4 I am not angry.
If only there were briers and thorns
confronting me!
I would march against them in
battle;
I would set them all on fire.[z]
5 Or else let them come to me for
refuge;[a]
let them make peace[b] with me,
yes, let them make peace with
me."

[a] 16 The meaning of the Hebrew for this clause is uncertain.

26:18 [k] Ps 17:14
26:19 [l] Isa 25:8; Eph 5:14 [m] Eze 37:1-14; Da 12:2
26:20 [n] Ex 12:23 [o] Ps 91:1,4 [p] Ps 30:5; Isa 54:7-8
26:21 [q] Jude 1:14 [r] Mic 1:3 [s] Isa 13:9,11; 30:12-14 [t] Job 16:18; Lk 11:50-51
27:1 [u] Isa 34:6; 66:16 [v] Job 3:8 [w] Ps 74:13
27:2 [x] Jer 2:21
27:3 [y] Isa 58:11
27:4 [z] Isa 10:17; Mt 3:12; Heb 6:8
27:5 [a] Isa 25:4 [b] Job 22:21; Ro 5:1; 2Co 5:20

27:6 [c]Hos 14:5-6 [d]Isa 37:31

6 In days to come Jacob will take root,
Israel will bud and blossom[c]
and fill all the world with fruit.[d]

27:7 [e]Isa 37:36-38

7 Has ⌞the LORD⌟ struck her
as he struck[e] down those who
struck her?
Has she been killed
as those were killed who killed
her?

27:8 [f]Isa 50:1; 54:7

8 By warfare[a] and exile[f] you contend
with her—
with his fierce blast he drives her
out,
as on a day the east wind blows.

27:9 [g]Ro 11:27* [h]Ex 34:13

9 By this, then, will Jacob's guilt be
atoned for,
and this will be the full fruitage
of the removal of his sin:[g]
When he makes all the altar stones
to be like chalk stones crushed
to pieces,
no Asherah poles[b][h] or incense
altars
will be left standing.

27:10 [i]Isa 32:14; Jer 26:6 [j]Isa 17:2

10 The fortified city stands desolate,[i]
an abandoned settlement,
forsaken like the desert;
there the calves graze,
there they lie down;[j]
they strip its branches bare.
11 When its twigs are dry, they are
broken off
and women come and make
fires with them.

27:11 [k]Dt 32:28; Isa 1:3; Jer 8:7 [l]Dt 32:18; Isa 43:1,7,15; 44:1-2,21,24 [m]Isa 9:17

For this is a people without
understanding;[k]
so their Maker has no
compassion on them,
and their Creator[l] shows them
no favor.[m]

27:12 [n]Ge 15:18 [o]Dt 30:4; Isa 11:12; 17:6
27:13 [p]Lev 25:9; Mt 24:31 [q]Isa 19:21,25

12 In that day the LORD will thresh
from the flowing Euphrates[c] to the Wadi
of Egypt,[n] and you, O Israelites, will be
gathered[o] up one by one. 13 And in that
day a great trumpet[p] will sound. Those
who were perishing in Assyria and those
who were exiled in Egypt[q] will come and
worship the LORD on the holy mountain
in Jerusalem.

Woe to Ephraim

28:1 [r]ver 3; Isa 9:9 [s]ver 4 [t]Hos 7:5

28 Woe to that wreath, the pride
of Ephraim's[r] drunkards,
to the fading flower, his glorious
beauty,
set on the head of a fertile valley[s]—
to that city, the pride of those
laid low by wine![t]

28:2 [u]Isa 40:10 [v]Isa 30:30; Eze 13:11 [w]Isa 29:6 [x]Isa 8:7

2 See, the Lord has one who is
powerful[u] and strong.
Like a hailstorm[v] and a
destructive wind,[w]
like a driving rain and a flooding[x]
downpour,
he will throw it forcefully to the
ground.

28:3 [y]ver 1

3 That wreath, the pride of
Ephraim's[y] drunkards,
will be trampled underfoot.

28:4 [z]ver 1 [a]Hos 9:10; Na 3:12

4 That fading flower, his glorious
beauty,
set on the head of a fertile valley,[z]
will be like a fig[a] ripe before
harvest—
as soon as someone sees it and
takes it in his hand,
he swallows it.

28:5 [b]Isa 62:3

5 In that day the LORD Almighty
will be a glorious crown,[b]
a beautiful wreath
for the remnant of his people.

28:6 [c]Isa 11:2-4; 32:1,16 [d]Jn 5:30 [e]2Ch 32:8

6 He will be a spirit of justice[c]
to him who sits in judgment,[d]
a source of strength
to those who turn back the
battle[e] at the gate.

28:7 [f]Isa 22:13 [g]Isa 56:10-12 [h]Isa 24:2 [i]Isa 9:15 [j]Isa 29:11; Hos 4:11

7 And these also stagger from wine[f]
and reel[g] from beer:
Priests[h] and prophets[i] stagger
from beer
and are befuddled with wine;
they reel from beer,
they stagger when seeing
visions,[j]
they stumble when rendering
decisions.

28:8 [k]Jer 48:26

8 All the tables are covered with
vomit[k]
and there is not a spot without
filth.

28:9 [l]ver 26; Isa 30:20; 48:17; 50:4; 54:13 [m]Ps 131:2 [n]Heb 5:12-13

9 "Who is it he is trying to teach?[l]
To whom is he explaining his
message?
To children weaned[m] from their
milk,[n]
to those just taken from the
breast?
10 For it is:
Do and do, do and do,

[a] *8* See Septuagint; the meaning of the Hebrew for this word is uncertain. [b] *9* That is, symbols of the goddess Asherah [c] *12* Hebrew *River*

Resting on a Rock

Very few people can relax on a boat during a raging thunderstorm with swelling waves and pummeling rain, or in an airplane surging through turbulent winds, or in the midst of an earthquake. Maybe you've experienced being aboard a small boat surrounded by buffeting waves. Maybe you know what it's like to grope for a secure place to stand. When we are in situations like this, we find ourselves stumbling, grasping for anything to hold us steady—and praying for a firm foothold on steady ground. But there *is* a sure foundation on which to stand, Someone who will keep us safe and guide us by the hand through the most intense turmoil imaginable, Someone who will allow us to find rest when all around us is tumultuous and threatening.

God's message to the northern kingdom was that the people could find their rest in God. It hadn't taken long for the Israelites to become rigid and ritualistic in their observance of God's law. Rather than getting to know God, they had turned his words into a rule book. Their basis for facing life's issues had become adherence to an inflexible list of do's and don'ts. Rules in and of themselves, however, are insecure and ultimately unsatisfying. Isaiah captured the essence of the philosophy of the Israelites of his day by referring to it as a complex system of "Do and do, do and do, rule on rule, rule on rule; a little here, a little there—so that they will go and fall backward, be injured and snared and captured" (Isaiah 28:13).

The children of God were so preoccupied with obeying all the rules that they had begun stumbling all over one another. Surprisingly God's counsel to his people was to slow down and be still—to rest. We can almost hear God's gentle appeal, whispering on the winds of the storm: "Quit trying so hard. There is nothing you need to do except *enjoy me.* I have provided everything for you, so step out of the storm you have created and relax."

Isaiah reminded the people that there was a "stone" on which they could rest without ever experiencing dismay. This stone is one hundred percent safe and secure, a place of reprieve from the endless round of *doing* and rule-keeping. That stone is Jesus, God's Son, the "sure foundation" (verse 16) for all of life (see also Psalm 118:22; 1 Corinthians 3:11).

Peter quoted Isaiah's words and encouraged believers to become people of integrity who are not blown away by the storms of life. As we live holy lives we become strong and immovable (see 1 Peter 2:4–12). So relax, settle down, trust him—and find joy in your journey of faith (Matthew 11:28).

Self-Discovery: *Imagine yourself stretching out atop a huge rock after a grueling mountain hike. Gaze upward at the blueness of the sky. Look around you at the breathtaking scenery. Now picture that rock as Jesus. What associations come to mind?*

GO TO DISCOVERY 186 ON PAGE 933

rule on rule, rule on rule[a];
a little here, a little there."

28:11 [o] Isa 33:19 [p] 1Co 14:21*

11 Very well then, with foreign lips
and strange tongues[o]
God will speak to this people,[p]
12 to whom he said,

28:12 [q] Isa 11:10; Mt 11:28-29

"This is the resting place, let the
weary rest";[q]
and, "This is the place of repose"—
but they would not listen.
13 So then, the word of the LORD to
them will become:
Do and do, do and do,
rule on rule, rule on rule;
a little here, a little there—
so that they will go and fall
backward,

28:13 [r] Mt 21:44 [s] Isa 8:15

be injured[r] and snared and
captured.[s]

28:14 [t] Isa 1:10

14 Therefore hear the word of the
LORD,[t] you scoffers
who rule this people in Jerusalem.
15 You boast, "We have entered into a
covenant with death,
with the grave[b] we have made an
agreement.

28:15 [u] ver 2,18; Isa 8:7-8; 30:28; Da 11:22 [v] Isa 9:15 [w] Isa 29:15

When an overwhelming scourge
sweeps by,[u]
it cannot touch us,
for we have made a lie[v] our refuge
and falsehood[c] our hiding
place.[w]"

16 So this is what the Sovereign LORD
says:

28:16 [x] Ps 118:22; Isa 8:14-15; Mt 21:42; Ac 4:11; Eph 2:20 [y] Ro 9:33*; 10:11*; 1Pe 2:6*

"See, I lay a stone in Zion,
a tested stone,[x]
a precious cornerstone for a sure
foundation;
the one who trusts will never be
dismayed.[y]

28:17 [z] Isa 5:16 [a] 2Ki 21:13

17 I will make justice[z] the measuring
line
and righteousness the plumb
line;[a]
hail will sweep away your refuge,
the lie,
and water will overflow your
hiding place.
18 Your covenant with death will be
annulled;

28:18 [b] Isa 7:7 [c] ver 15 [d] Da 8:13

your agreement with the grave
will not stand.[b]
When the overwhelming scourge
sweeps by,[c]
you will be beaten down[d] by it.

28:19 [e] 2Ki 24:2 [f] Job 18:11

19 As often as it comes it will carry
you away;[e]
morning after morning, by day
and by night,
it will sweep through."

The understanding of this message
will bring sheer terror.[f]
20 The bed is too short to stretch out
on,

28:20 [g] Isa 59:6

the blanket too narrow to wrap
around you.[g]

28:21 [h] 1Ch 14:11 [i] Jos 10:10,12; 1Ch 14:16 [j] Isa 10:12; Lk 19:41-44

21 The LORD will rise up as he did at
Mount Perazim,[h]
he will rouse himself as in the
Valley of Gibeon[i]—
to do his work,[j] his strange work,
and perform his task, his alien
task.
22 Now stop your mocking,
or your chains will become
heavier;
the Lord, the LORD Almighty, has
told me

28:22 [k] Isa 10:22 [l] Isa 10:23

of the destruction decreed[k]
against the whole land.[l]

23 Listen and hear my voice;
pay attention and hear what I say.
24 When a farmer plows for planting,
does he plow continually?
Does he keep on breaking up
and harrowing the soil?
25 When he has leveled the surface,
does he not sow caraway and
scatter cummin?[m]

28:25 [m] Mt 23:23 [n] Ex 9:32

Does he not plant wheat in its
place,[d]
barley in its plot,[d]
and spelt[n] in its field?
26 His God instructs him
and teaches him the right way.

27 Caraway is not threshed with a
sledge,
nor is a cartwheel rolled over
cummin;
caraway is beaten out with a rod,
and cummin with a stick.
28 Grain must be ground to make
bread;
so one does not go on threshing
it forever.

[a] *10* Hebrew / *sav lasav sav lasav / kav lakav kav lakav* (possibly meaningless sounds; perhaps a mimicking of the prophet's words); also in verse 13
[b] *15* Hebrew *Sheol*; also in verse 18 [c] *15* Or *false gods* [d] *25* The meaning of the Hebrew for this word is uncertain.

Though he drives the wheels of his
threshing cart over it,
his horses do not grind it.
29 All this also comes from the LORD
Almighty,
28:29 [o]Isa 9:6 [p]Ro 11:33 wonderful in counsel[o] and
magnificent in wisdom.[p]

Woe to David's City

29:1 [q]Isa 22:12-13 [r]2Sa 5:9 [s]Isa 1:14 **29** Woe[q] to you, Ariel, Ariel,[r]
the city where David settled!
Add year to year
and let your cycle of festivals[s] go
on.
29:2 [t]Isa 3:26; La 2:5 2 Yet I will besiege Ariel;
she will mourn and lament,[t]
she will be to me like an altar
hearth.[a]
3 I will encamp against you all
around;
29:3 [u]Lk 19:43-44 I will encircle[u] you with towers
and set up my siege works
against you.
4 Brought low, you will speak from
the ground;
29:4 [v]Isa 8:19 your speech will mumble[v] out of
the dust.
Your voice will come ghostlike
from the earth;
out of the dust your speech will
whisper.
5 But your many enemies will
become like fine dust,
the ruthless hordes like blown 29:5 [w]Isa 17:13 [x]Isa 17:14; 1Th 5:3
chaff.[w]
Suddenly,[x] in an instant,
6 the LORD Almighty will come
with thunder and earthquake[y] and 29:6 [y]Mt 24:7; Mk 13:8; Lk 21:11; Rev 11:19
great noise,
with windstorm and tempest and
flames of a devouring fire.
7 Then the hordes of all the nations[z] 29:7 [z]Mic 4:11-12; Zec 12:9 [a]Job 20:8
that fight against Ariel,
that attack her and her fortress
and besiege her,
will be as it is with a dream,[a]
with a vision in the night—
8 as when a hungry man dreams that
he is eating,
but he awakens,[b] and his hunger 29:8 [b]Ps 73:20
remains;
as when a thirsty man dreams that
he is drinking,
but he awakens faint, with his
thirst unquenched.
So will it be with the hordes of all
the nations
that fight against Mount Zion.

9 Be stunned and amazed,
blind yourselves and be sightless; 29:9 [c]Isa 51:17 [d]Isa 51:21-22
be drunk,[c] but not from wine,[d]
stagger, but not from beer.
10 The LORD has brought over you a
deep sleep:
He has sealed your eyes[e] (the 29:10 [e]Ps 69:23; Isa 6:9-10; Ro 11:8* [f]Mic 3:6 [g]1Sa 9:9
prophets);[f]
he has covered your heads (the
seers).[g]

11 For you this whole vision is nothing 29:11 [h]Isa 8:16; Mt 13:11; Rev 5:1-2
but words sealed[h] in a scroll. And if you
give the scroll to someone who can read,
and say to him, "Read this, please," he
will answer, "I can't; it is sealed." 12 Or if
you give the scroll to someone who cannot read, and say, "Read this, please," he
will answer, "I don't know how to read."
13 The Lord says:

"These people come near to me
with their mouth
and honor me with their lips, 29:13 [i]Eze 33:31
but their hearts are far from me.[i]
Their worship of me

[a] 2 The Hebrew for *altar hearth* sounds like the Hebrew for *Ariel.*

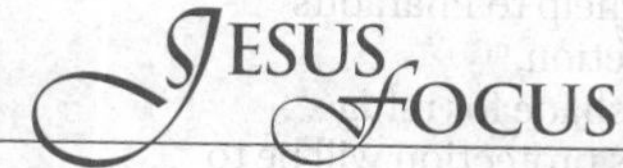

RELIGIOUS PRETENDERS

Ariel, meaning "altar hearth" in Hebrew, is another name for Jerusalem (Isaiah 29:1). Jerusalem was more than just the capital of Judah; it was the focal point for Israel's worship. However, over the years Israel's religion had degenerated into meaningless ritual, and God was warning the people that if they did not turn back to him, he would turn the entire city into an altar hearth of sacrificial fires. Isaiah's prophecies remind us of Jesus' warnings about empty religion and God's coming judgment on those who appeared clean on the outside but were dirty on the inside (Matthew 23:1—24:51). God did punish the Israelites when they were taken captive and their city destroyed by the Babylonians in 586 B.C. He dealt so severely with his own nation because the Israelites, of *all* people, knew better! They talked about God and went through the motions of worship, but their hearts were not devoted to him (Isaiah 29:13). Jesus quoted this verse, applying it to the people of his own day (Mark 7:6–7).

> **WHOEVER SEES CHRIST AS A MIRROR OF THE FATHER'S HEART, ACTUALLY WALKS THROUGH THE WORLD WITH NEW EYES.**
>
> Martin Luther, *German Reformer*

29:13 [j]Mt 15:8-9*; Mk 7:6-7*; Col 2:22

is made up only of rules taught
by men.[a][j]

29:14 [k]Hab 1:5 [l]Jer 8:9; 49:7 [m]Isa 6:9-10; 1Co 1:19*

14 Therefore once more I will astound
these people
with wonder upon wonder;[k]
the wisdom of the wise[l] will perish,
the intelligence of the intelligent
will vanish.[m]"
15 Woe to those who go to great
depths
to hide their plans from the LORD,
who do their work in darkness and
think,

29:15 [n]Ps 10:11-13; 94:7; Isa 57:12 [o]Job 22:13

"Who sees us?[n] Who will
know?"[o]
16 You turn things upside down,
as if the potter were thought to
be like the clay!
Shall what is formed say to him
who formed it,

29:16 [p]Isa 45:9; 64:8; Ro 9:20-21*

"He did not make me"?
Can the pot say of the potter,[p]
"He knows nothing"?
17 In a very short time, will not
Lebanon be turned into a
fertile field[q]
and the fertile field seem like a
forest?[r]

29:17 [q]Ps 84:6 [r]Isa 32:15

29:18 [s]Mk 7:37 [t]Isa 32:3; 35:5; Mt 11:5

18 In that day the deaf[s] will hear the
words of the scroll,
and out of gloom and darkness
the eyes of the blind will see.[t]

29:19 [u]Isa 61:1; Mt 5:5; 11:29 [v]Isa 14:30; Mt 11:5; Jas 1:9; 2:5

19 Once more the humble[u] will rejoice
in the LORD;
the needy[v] will rejoice in the
Holy One of Israel.

29:20 [w]Isa 28:22 [x]Isa 59:4; Mic 2:1

20 The ruthless will vanish,
the mockers[w] will disappear,
and all who have an eye for evil[x]
will be cut down—
21 those who with a word make a
man out to be guilty,

29:21 [y]Am 5:10,15 [z]Isa 2:7

who ensnare the defender in
court[y]
and with false testimony deprive
the innocent of justice.[z]
22 Therefore this is what the LORD, who
redeemed Abraham,[a] says to the house
of Jacob:

29:22 [a]Isa 41:8; 63:16 [b]Isa 49:23

"No longer will Jacob be ashamed;[b]
no longer will their faces grow
pale.
23 When they see among them their
children,[c]

29:23 [c]Isa 49:20-26 [d]Isa 19:25

the work of my hands,[d]
they will keep my name holy;
they will acknowledge the
holiness of the Holy One of
Jacob,
and will stand in awe of the God
of Israel.
24 Those who are wayward[e] in spirit
will gain understanding;[f]
those who complain will accept
instruction."[g]

29:24 [e]Isa 28:7; Heb 5:2 [f]Isa 41:20; 60:16 [g]Isa 30:21

Woe to the Obstinate Nation

30 "Woe[h] to the obstinate
children,"[i]
declares the LORD,
"to those who carry out plans that
are not mine,
forming an alliance,[j] but not by
my Spirit,
heaping sin upon sin;

30:1 [h]Isa 29:15 [i]Isa 1:2 [j]Isa 8:12

2 who go down to Egypt[k]
without consulting[l] me;
who look for help to Pharaoh's
protection,[m]
to Egypt's shade for refuge.

30:2 [k]Isa 31:1 [l]Nu 27:21 [m]Isa 36:9

3 But Pharaoh's protection will be to
your shame,
Egypt's shade will bring you
disgrace.[n]

30:3 [n]Isa 20:4-5; 36:6

4 Though they have officials in Zoan[o]
and their envoys have arrived in
Hanes,

30:4 [o]Isa 19:11

5 everyone will be put to shame
because of a people[p] useless to
them,
who bring neither help nor
advantage,
but only shame and disgrace."

30:5 [p]ver 7

6 An oracle concerning the animals of
the Negev:

Through a land of hardship and
distress,[q]
of lions and lionesses,
of adders and darting snakes,[r]
the envoys carry their riches on
donkeys' backs,

30:6 [q]Ex 5:10,21; Isa 8:22; Jer 11:4 [r]Dt 8:15

[a] 13 Hebrew; Septuagint *They worship me in vain; / their teachings are but rules taught by men*

30:6 [s]Isa 15:7 their treasures[s] on the humps of
camels,
to that unprofitable nation,
7 to Egypt, whose help is utterly
useless.
Therefore I call her
Rahab the Do-Nothing.
8 Go now, write it on a tablet for
them,
30:8 [t]Isa 8:1; Hab 2:2 inscribe it on a scroll,[t]
that for the days to come
it may be an everlasting witness.
9 These are rebellious people,
30:9 [u]Isa 28:15; 59:3-4 [v]Isa 1:10 deceitful[u] children,
children unwilling to listen to
the LORD's instruction.[v]
10 They say to the seers,
30:10 [w]Jer 11:21; Am 7:13 [x]1Ki 22:8 [y]Eze 13:7; Ro 16:18 "See no more visions[w]!"
and to the prophets,
"Give us no more visions of what
is right!
Tell us pleasant things,[x]
prophesy illusions.[y]
11 Leave this way,
get off this path,
30:11 [z]Job 21:14 and stop confronting[z] us
with the Holy One of Israel!"

12 Therefore, this is what the Holy One
of Israel says:

30:12 [a]Isa 5:24 [b]Isa 5:7 "Because you have rejected this
message,[a]
relied on oppression[b]
and depended on deceit,
13 this sin will become for you
30:13 [c]Ps 62:3 [d]1Ki 20:30 [e]Isa 29:5 like a high wall,[c] cracked and
bulging,
that collapses[d] suddenly,[e] in an
instant.
30:14 [f]Ps 2:9; Jer 19:10-11 14 It will break in pieces like pottery,[f]
shattered so mercilessly
that among its pieces not a
fragment will be found
for taking coals from a hearth
or scooping water out of a
cistern."

15 This is what the Sovereign LORD, the
Holy One of Israel, says:

"In repentance and rest is your
salvation,
30:15 [g]Isa 32:17 in quietness and trust[g] is your
strength,
but you would have none of it.
30:16 [h]Isa 31:1,3 16 You said, 'No, we will flee on
horses.'[h]
Therefore you will flee!
You said, 'We will ride off on swift
horses.'
Therefore your pursuers will be
swift!
17 A thousand will flee
at the threat of one;
at the threat of five[i] 30:17 [i]Lev 26:8; Jos 23:10
you will all flee[j] away, [j]Lev 26:36; Dt 28:25
till you are left
like a flagstaff on a mountaintop,
like a banner on a hill."
18 Yet the LORD longs[k] to be gracious 30:18 [k]Isa 42:14; 2Pe 3:9,15
to you;
he rises to show you compassion. [l]Isa 5:16
For the LORD is a God of justice.[l] [m]Isa 25:9
Blessed are all who wait for him![m]

19 O people of Zion, who live in Jeru- 30:19 [n]Isa 60:20; 61:3
salem, you will weep no more.[n] How gra- [o]Ps 50:15;
cious he will be when you cry for help! Isa 58:9; 65:24;
As soon as he hears, he will answer[o] you. Mt 7:7-11
20 Although the Lord gives you the 30:20
bread[p] of adversity and the water of af- [p]1Ki 22:27
fliction, your teachers will be hidden[q] no [q]Ps 74:9;
more; with your own eyes you will see Am 8:11
them. 21 Whether you turn to the right or
to the left, your ears will hear a voice[r] be- 30:21 [r]Isa 29:24
hind you, saying, "This is the way; walk
in it." 22 Then you will defile your idols[s] 30:22 [s]Ex 32:4
overlaid with silver and your images
covered with gold; you will throw them
away like a menstrual cloth and say to
them, "Away with you!"

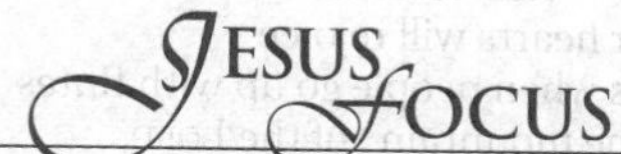

THIS IS THE WAY!

After announcing that God was preparing to judge his people, Isaiah offered words of consolation (Isaiah 30:18–21). Their troubles—"bread of adversity" and "water of affliction" (verse 20)—would become their teachers to bring them back to God. In their time of uncertainty and struggle they would hear a voice saying, "This is the way; walk in it" (verse 21).

Jesus would later remind his disciples of the same gracious offer of guidance during their hour of greatest need: "Do not let your hearts be troubled. Trust in God; trust also in me" (John 14:1). He went on to inform them that he would soon be leaving to prepare a place for them, and Thomas inquired in bewilderment, "How can we know the way?" (John 14:5). "I am the way and the truth and the life," was Jesus' response (John 14:6), and this precious truth still holds true for us today.

23 He will also send you rain[t] for the
seed you sow in the ground, and the
food that comes from the land will be
rich and plentiful. In that day your cattle will graze in broad meadows.[u] 24 The
oxen and donkeys that work the soil will
eat fodder and mash, spread out with
fork[v] and shovel. 25 In the day of great
slaughter, when the towers[w] fall, streams
of water will flow[x] on every high mountain and every lofty hill. 26 The moon will
shine like the sun,[y] and the sunlight will
be seven times brighter, like the light of
seven full days, when the LORD binds up
the bruises of his people and heals[z] the
wounds he inflicted.

27 See, the Name[a] of the LORD comes
from afar,
with burning anger[b] and dense
clouds of smoke;
his lips are full of wrath,[c]
and his tongue is a consuming
fire.
28 His breath[d] is like a rushing
torrent,
rising up to the neck.[e]
He shakes the nations in the sieve[f]
of destruction;
he places in the jaws of the
peoples
a bit[g] that leads them astray.
29 And you will sing
as on the night you celebrate a
holy festival;
your hearts will rejoice
as when people go up with flutes
to the mountain[h] of the LORD,
to the Rock of Israel.
30 The LORD will cause men to hear
his majestic voice
and will make them see his arm
coming down
with raging anger and consuming
fire,
with cloudburst, thunderstorm
and hail.
31 The voice of the LORD will shatter
Assyria;[i]
with his scepter he will strike[j]
them down.
32 Every stroke the LORD lays on them
with his punishing rod
will be to the music of
tambourines and harps,
as he fights them in battle with
the blows of his arm.[k]
33 Topheth[l] has long been prepared;
it has been made ready for the
king.
Its fire pit has been made deep and
wide,
with an abundance of fire and
wood;
the breath of the LORD,
like a stream of burning sulfur,[m]
sets it ablaze.

30:23 [t] Isa 65:21-22 [u] Ps 65:13
30:24 [v] Mt 3:12; Lk 3:17
30:25 [w] Isa 2:15 [x] Isa 41:18
30:26 [y] Isa 24:23; 60:19-20; Rev 21:23; 22:5 [z] Dt 32:39; Isa 1:5
30:27 [a] Isa 59:19 [b] Isa 66:14 [c] Isa 10:5
30:28 [d] Isa 11:4 [e] Isa 8:8 [f] Am 9:9 [g] 2Ki 19:28; Isa 37:29
30:29 [h] Ps 42:4
30:31 [i] Isa 10:5,12 [j] Isa 11:4
30:32 [k] Isa 11:15; Eze 32:10
30:33 [l] 2Ki 23:10 [m] Ge 19:24

Woe to Those Who Rely on Egypt

31 Woe to those who go down
to Egypt[n] for help,
who rely on horses,
who trust in the multitude of their
chariots[o]
and in the great strength of their
horsemen,
but do not look to the Holy One of
Israel,
or seek help from the LORD.[p]
2 Yet he too is wise[q] and can bring
disaster;[r]
he does not take back his words.[s]
He will rise up against the house of
the wicked,[t]
against those who help evildoers.
3 But the Egyptians[u] are men and
not God;[v]
their horses are flesh and not
spirit.
When the LORD stretches out his
hand,[w]
he who helps will stumble,
he who is helped[x] will fall;
both will perish together.
4 This is what the LORD says to me:
"As a lion[y] growls,
a great lion over his prey—
and though a whole band of
shepherds
is called together against him,
he is not frightened by their shouts
or disturbed by their clamor—
so the LORD Almighty will come
down[z]
to do battle on Mount Zion and
on its heights.
5 Like birds hovering overhead,
the LORD Almighty will shield[a]
Jerusalem;
he will shield it and deliver[b] it,
he will 'pass over' it and will
rescue it."

6 Return to him you have so greatly revolted against, O Israelites. 7 For in that

31:1 [n] Dt 17:16; Isa 30:2,5 [o] Isa 2:7 [p] Ps 20:7; Da 9:13
31:2 [q] Ro 16:27 [r] Isa 45:7 [s] Nu 23:19 [t] Isa 32:6
31:3 [u] Isa 36:9 [v] Eze 28:9; 2Th 2:4 [w] Isa 9:17,21 [x] Isa 30:5-7
31:4 [y] Nu 24:9; Hos 11:10; Am 3:8 [z] Isa 42:13
31:5 [a] Ps 91:4 [b] Isa 37:35; 38:6

31:7 day every one of you will reject the idols
[c]Isa 2:20; 30:22 of silver and gold[c] your sinful hands
have made.

31:8 [d]Isa 10:12 [e]Isa 14:25; 37:7 [f]Ge 49:15
8 "Assyria[d] will fall by a sword that is
not of man;
a sword, not of mortals, will
devour[e] them.
They will flee before the sword
and their young men will be put
to forced labor.[f]

31:9 [g]Dt 32:31,37 [h]Isa 10:17
9 Their stronghold[g] will fall because
of terror;
at sight of the battle standard
their commanders will
panic,"
declares the LORD,
whose fire[h] is in Zion,
whose furnace is in Jerusalem.

The Kingdom of Righteousness

32:1 [i]Eze 37:24 [j]Ps 72:1-4; Isa 9:7
32 See, a king[i] will reign in
righteousness
and rulers will rule with justice.[j]

32:2 [k]Isa 4:6
2 Each man will be like a shelter[k]
from the wind
and a refuge from the storm,
like streams of water in the desert
and the shadow of a great rock
in a thirsty land.

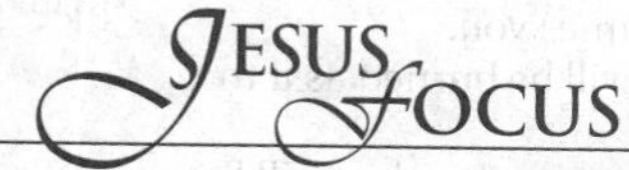

KINGDOM BLESSINGS

Isaiah did more than envision a future kingdom in a golden age of righteousness (Isaiah 32); he projected himself into it. Even though many of the events he recounted are yet to be fulfilled, he wrote as though he were seeing them himself. Isaiah predicted the second coming of God's promised Messiah to rule in righteousness (verse 1) and included powerful imagery to describe that time. God will bring streams of water in the desert and the shadow of a great rock in a thirsty land (verse 2). Isaiah also foretold that God's "Spirit [would be] poured upon us from on high" (verse 15). The apostle Peter quoted a similar passage from another book, that of the prophet Joel. Jesus had already returned to his Father (Acts 1:9–11), and his followers were gathering together. In Acts 2:16–17 Peter included a description from Joel 2:28–32, containing a promise that God's Spirit would be given to his followers. On the Day of Pentecost the Spirit of God filled Jesus' followers (Acts 2:1–4)—and the Christian church was born.

3 Then the eyes of those who see will
no longer be closed,[l] 32:3 [l]Isa 29:18
and the ears of those who hear
will listen.
4 The mind of the rash will know
and understand,[m] 32:4 [m]Isa 29:24
and the stammering tongue will
be fluent and clear.
5 No longer will the fool[n] be called 32:5 [n]1Sa 25:25
noble
nor the scoundrel be highly
respected.
6 For the fool speaks folly,[o] 32:6 [o]Pr 19:3
his mind is busy with evil: [p]Isa 9:17
He practices ungodliness[p] [q]Isa 9:16
and spreads error[q] concerning [r]Isa 3:15
the LORD;
the hungry he leaves empty[r]
and from the thirsty he
withholds water.
7 The scoundrel's methods are
wicked,[s] 32:7 [s]Jer 5:26-28
he makes up evil schemes[t] [t]Mic 7:3
to destroy the poor with lies, [u]Isa 61:1
even when the plea of the needy[u]
is just.
8 But the noble man makes noble
plans, 32:8
and by noble deeds[v] he stands. [v]Pr 11:25

The Women of Jerusalem

9 You women who are so complacent, 32:9
rise up and listen[w] to me; [w]Isa 28:23
you daughters who feel secure,[x] [x]Isa 47:8;
hear what I have to say! Am 6:1; Zep 2:15
10 In little more than a year
you who feel secure will tremble;
the grape harvest will fail,[y] 32:10 [y]Isa 5:5-6; 24:7
and the harvest of fruit will not
come.
11 Tremble, you complacent women;
shudder, you daughters who feel
secure!
Strip off your clothes,[z] 32:11 [z]Isa 47:2
put sackcloth around your
waists.
12 Beat your breasts[a] for the pleasant 32:12 [a]Na 2:7
fields,
for the fruitful vines
13 and for the land of my people,
a land overgrown with thorns 32:13
and briers[b]— [b]Isa 5:6
yes, mourn for all houses of [c]Isa 22:2
merriment
and for this city of revelry.[c]
14 The fortress[d] will be abandoned, 32:14
the noisy city deserted;[e] [d]Isa 13:22 [e]Isa 6:11; 27:10

32:14 [f] Isa 34:13 [g] Ps 104:11

citadel and watchtower[f] will
become a wasteland forever,
the delight of donkeys,[g] a
pasture for flocks,

32:15 [h] Isa 11:2; Joel 2:28 [i] Ps 107:35; Isa 35:1-2 [j] Isa 29:17

15 till the Spirit[h] is poured upon us
from on high,
and the desert becomes a fertile
field,[i]
and the fertile field seems like a
forest.[j]
16 Justice will dwell in the desert
and righteousness live in the
fertile field.

32:17 [k] Ps 119:165; Ro 14:17; Jas 3:18 [l] Isa 30:15

17 The fruit of righteousness will be
peace;[k]
the effect of righteousness will
be quietness and
confidence[l] forever.
18 My people will live in peaceful
dwelling places,

32:18 [m] Hos 2:18-23

in secure homes,
in undisturbed places of rest.[m]

32:19 [n] Isa 28:17; 30:30 [o] Isa 10:19; Zec 11:2 [p] Isa 24:10; 27:10

19 Though hail[n] flattens the forest[o]
and the city is leveled[p]
completely,
20 how blessed you will be,
sowing[q] your seed by every
stream,

32:20 [q] Ecc 11:1 [r] Isa 30:24

and letting your cattle and
donkeys range free.[r]

Distress and Help

33:1 [s] Hab 2:8; Mt 7:2 [t] Isa 21:2

33 Woe to you, O destroyer,
you who have not been
destroyed!
Woe to you, O traitor,
you who have not been betrayed!
When you stop destroying,
you will be destroyed;[s]
when you stop betraying,
you will be betrayed.[t]

33:2 [u] Isa 40:10; 51:9; 59:16 [v] Isa 25:9

2 O LORD, be gracious to us;
we long for you.
Be our strength[u] every morning,
our salvation[v] in time of distress.

33:3 [w] Isa 59:16-18

3 At the thunder of your voice, the
peoples flee;
when you rise up,[w] the nations
scatter.
4 Your plunder, O nations, is
harvested as by young
locusts;
like a swarm of locusts men
pounce on it.

33:5 [x] Ps 97:9 [y] Isa 28:6 [z] Isa 1:26

5 The LORD is exalted,[x] for he dwells
on high;
he will fill Zion with justice[y] and
righteousness.[z]
6 He will be the sure foundation for
your times,

33:6 [a] Isa 51:6 [b] Isa 11:2-3; Mt 6:33

a rich store of salvation[a] and
wisdom and knowledge;
the fear[b] of the LORD is the key
to this treasure.[a]
7 Look, their brave men cry aloud in
the streets;

33:7 [c] 2Ki 18:37

the envoys[c] of peace weep
bitterly.
8 The highways are deserted,
no travelers are on the roads.[d]

33:8 [d] Jdg 5:6; Isa 35:8

The treaty is broken,
its witnesses[b] are despised,
no one is respected.
9 The land mourns[c][e] and wastes
away,

33:9 [e] Isa 3:26 [f] Isa 2:13; 35:2 [g] Isa 24:4

Lebanon[f] is ashamed and
withers;[g]
Sharon is like the Arabah,
and Bashan and Carmel drop
their leaves.

33:10 [h] Ps 12:5; Isa 2:21

10 "Now will I arise,[h]" says the LORD.
"Now will I be exalted;
now will I be lifted up.

33:11 [i] Ps 7:14; Isa 59:4; Jas 1:15 [j] Isa 26:18 [k] Isa 1:31

11 You conceive[i] chaff,
you give birth[j] to straw;
your breath is a fire[k] that
consumes you.
12 The peoples will be burned as if to
lime;

33:12 [l] Isa 10:17

like cut thornbushes they will be
set ablaze.[l]"

33:13 [m] Ps 48:10; 49:1 [n] Isa 49:1

13 You who are far away,[m] hear[n] what
I have done;
you who are near, acknowledge
my power!
14 The sinners in Zion are terrified;

33:14 [o] Isa 32:11 [p] Isa 30:30; Heb 12:29

trembling[o] grips the godless:
"Who of us can dwell with the
consuming fire?[p]
Who of us can dwell with
everlasting burning?"

33:15 [q] Isa 58:8 [r] Ps 15:2; 24:4 [s] Ps 119:37

15 He who walks righteously[q]
and speaks what is right,[r]
who rejects gain from extortion
and keeps his hand from
accepting bribes,
who stops his ears against plots of
murder
and shuts his eyes[s] against
contemplating evil—

[a] 6 Or *is a treasure from him* [b] 8 Dead Sea Scrolls; Masoretic Text / *the cities* [c] 9 Or *dries up*

[16] this is the man who will dwell on
the heights,
whose refuge[t] will be the
mountain fortress.[u]
His bread will be supplied,
and water will not fail[v] him.

33:16 [t] Isa 25:4 [u] Isa 26:1 [v] Isa 49:10

[17] Your eyes will see the king[w] in his
beauty
and view a land that stretches
afar.[x]

33:17 [w] Isa 6:5 [x] Isa 26:15

[18] In your thoughts you will ponder
the former terror:[y]
"Where is that chief officer?
Where is the one who took the
revenue?
Where is the officer in charge of
the towers?"

33:18 [y] Isa 17:14

[19] You will see those arrogant people
no more,
those people of an obscure
speech,
with their strange,
incomprehensible tongue.[z]

33:19 [z] Isa 28:11; Jer 5:15

[20] Look upon Zion, the city of our
festivals;
your eyes will see Jerusalem,
a peaceful abode,[a] a tent that
will not be moved;[b]
its stakes will never be pulled up,
nor any of its ropes broken.

33:20 [a] Isa 32:18 [b] Ps 46:5; 125:1-2

[21] There the LORD will be our Mighty
One.
It will be like a place of broad
rivers and streams.[c]
No galley with oars will ride them,
no mighty ship will sail them.

33:21 [c] Isa 41:18; 48:18; 66:12

[22] For the LORD is our judge,[d]
the LORD is our lawgiver,[e]
the LORD is our king;[f]
it is he who will save[g] us.

33:22 [d] Isa 11:4 [e] Isa 2:3; Jas 4:12 [f] Ps 89:18 [g] Isa 25:9

[23] Your rigging hangs loose:
The mast is not held secure,
the sail is not spread.
Then an abundance of spoils will
be divided
and even the lame[h] will carry off
plunder.[i]

33:23 [h] 2Ki 7:8 [i] 2Ki 7:16

[24] No one living in Zion will say, "I am
ill";[j]
and the sins of those who dwell
there will be forgiven.[k]

33:24 [j] Isa 30:26 [k] Jer 50:20; 1Jn 1:7-9

Judgment Against the Nations

34 Come near, you nations, and
listen;[l]
pay attention, you peoples!
Let the earth[m] hear, and all that is
in it,
the world, and all that comes out
of it![n]

34:1 [l] Isa 41:1; 43:9 [m] Ps 49:1 [n] Dt 32:1

[2] The LORD is angry with all nations;
his wrath is upon all their armies.
He will totally destroy[a][o] them,
he will give them over to
slaughter.[p]

34:2 [o] Isa 13:5 [p] Isa 30:25

[3] Their slain will be thrown out,
their dead bodies will send up a
stench;[q]
the mountains will be soaked
with their blood.[r]

34:3 [q] Joel 2:20; Am 4:10 [r] ver 7; Eze 14:19; 35:6; 38:22

[4] All the stars of the heavens will be
dissolved[s]
and the sky rolled up[t] like a
scroll;
all the starry host will fall[u]
like withered leaves from the
vine,
like shriveled figs from the fig
tree.

34:4 [s] Isa 13:13; 2Pe 3:10 [t] Eze 32:7-8 [u] Joel 2:31; Mt 24:29*; Rev 6:13

[5] My sword[v] has drunk its fill in the
heavens;
see, it descends in judgment on
Edom,[w]
the people I have totally
destroyed.[x]

34:5 [v] Dt 32:41-42; Jer 46:10; Eze 21:5 [w] Am 1:11-12 [x] Isa 24:6; Mal 1:4

[6] The sword of the LORD is bathed in
blood,
it is covered with fat—
the blood of lambs and goats,
fat from the kidneys of rams.

[a] 2 The Hebrew term refers to the irrevocable giving over of things or persons to the LORD, often by totally destroying them; also in verse 5.

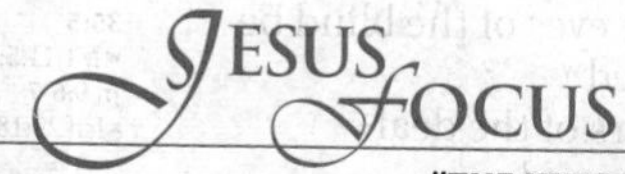

"THE KING IN HIS BEAUTY"

Isaiah foretold that God's promised Messiah would rule over the entire world (Isaiah 33:13–17) and referred to him as the "king in his beauty" (verse 17), who would appear in Israel. This prophetic passage does not apply to all the kings of Judah. Instead, Isaiah described a king who would rule in splendor over the whole world—One who would be majestic and victorious beyond any of the historic kings of Israel and Judah. Isaiah described the glory and magnitude of this king's reign much as John depicted the glory of the new Jerusalem in Revelation 21:16–17. Jesus himself will be our Judge, Lawgiver, King and Savior (Isaiah 33:22).

For the LORD has a sacrifice in Bozrah
and a great slaughter in Edom.
7 And the wild oxen will fall with them,
the bull calves and the great bulls.[y]
Their land will be drenched with blood,
and the dust will be soaked with fat.

34:7 [y] Ps 68:30

8 For the LORD has a day of vengeance,[z]
a year of retribution, to uphold Zion's cause.
9 Edom's streams will be turned into pitch,
her dust into burning sulfur;
her land will become blazing pitch!
10 It will not be quenched night and day;
its smoke will rise forever.[a]
From generation to generation it will lie desolate;[b]
no one will ever pass through it again.

34:8 [z] Isa 63:4
34:10 [a] Rev 14:10-11; 19:3 [b] Isa 13:20; 24:1; Eze 29:12; Mal 1:3

11 The desert owl[a][c] and screech owl[a] will possess it;
the great owl[a] and the raven will nest there.
God will stretch out over Edom
the measuring line of chaos
and the plumb line[d] of desolation.
12 Her nobles will have nothing there to be called a kingdom,
all her princes[e] will vanish[f] away.
13 Thorns will overrun her citadels,
nettles and brambles her strongholds.[g]
She will become a haunt for jackals,[h]
a home for owls.
14 Desert creatures will meet with hyenas,[i]
and wild goats will bleat to each other;
there the night creatures will also repose
and find for themselves places of rest.
15 The owl will nest there and lay eggs,
she will hatch them, and care for her young under the shadow of her wings;
there also the falcons[j] will gather,
each with its mate.

34:11 [c] Zep 2:14; Rev 18:2 [d] 2Ki 21:13; La 2:8
34:12 [e] Jer 27:20; 39:6 [f] Isa 41:11-12
34:13 [g] Isa 13:22; 32:13 [h] Ps 44:19; Jer 9:11; 10:22
34:14 [i] Isa 13:22
34:15 [j] Dt 14:13

16 Look in the scroll[k] of the LORD and read:

None of these will be missing,
not one will lack her mate.
For it is his mouth[l] that has given the order,
and his Spirit will gather them together.
17 He allots their portions;[m]
his hand distributes them by measure.
They will possess it forever
and dwell there from generation to generation.[n]

34:16 [k] Isa 30:8 [l] Isa 1:20; 58:14
34:17 [m] Isa 17:14; Jer 13:25 [n] ver 10

Joy of the Redeemed

35 The desert[o] and the parched land will be glad;
the wilderness will rejoice and blossom.[p]
Like the crocus, 2 it will burst into bloom;
it will rejoice greatly and shout for joy.[q]
The glory of Lebanon[r] will be given to it,
the splendor of Carmel[s] and Sharon;
they will see the glory of the LORD,
the splendor of our God.[t]

35:1 [o] Isa 27:10; 41:18-19 [p] Isa 51:3
35:2 [q] Isa 25:9; 55:12 [r] Isa 32:15 [s] SS 7:5 [t] Isa 25:9

3 Strengthen the feeble hands,
steady the knees[u] that give way;
4 say to those with fearful hearts,
"Be strong, do not fear;
your God will come,
he will come with vengeance;[v]
with divine retribution
he will come to save you."

35:3 [u] Job 4:4; Heb 12:12
35:4 [v] Isa 1:24; 34:8

5 Then will the eyes of the blind be opened[w]
and the ears of the deaf[x] unstopped.
6 Then will the lame[y] leap like a deer,
and the mute tongue[z] shout for joy.
Water will gush forth in the wilderness
and streams[a] in the desert.
7 The burning sand will become a pool,
the thirsty ground bubbling springs.[b]
In the haunts where jackals[c] once lay,

35:5 [w] Mt 11:5; Jn 9:6-7 [x] Isa 29:18; 50:4
35:6 [y] Mt 15:30; Jn 5:8-9; Ac 3:8 [z] Isa 32:4; Mt 9:32-33; 12:22; Lk 11:14 [a] Isa 41:18; Jn 7:38
35:7 [b] Isa 49:10 [c] Isa 13:22

[a] *11* The precise identification of these birds is uncertain.

DISCOVERY 186

Caught Up in Praise

One of Isaiah's prevailing themes was that God would bless his people when the Messiah appeared. The thirty-fifth chapter of his book is devoted to this topic. It identifies the kind of world that would exist (verses 1–7) and the kind of people who would inhabit it (verse 8–10). God wanted to remind his people of their future hope, because the nation was in the throes of despair at the time.

The prophet identified three major changes that would occur. First, the desert would be infused with new life: Flowers would bloom in the wilderness, and the parched and thirsty ground would gurgle with fresh springs (verses 1–2,7). When the Messiah arrived, he would strengthen feeble hands, knees and hearts (verses 3–4). Finally, the sick and broken, the blind, deaf, lame and mute would all be healed (verses 5–6).

These promises are fulfilled both physically and spiritually in Jesus Christ. When John the Baptist entertained second thoughts about whether or not Jesus was really the promised One, he sent some of his followers to ask the Lord point-blank (Matthew 11:3). Jesus directed them to go tell John what they had seen: "The blind receive sight, the lame walk, those who have leprosy are cured, the deaf hear, the dead are raised, and the good news is preached to the poor" (Matthew 11:4–5). He was in effect pointing to the evidence and affirming, "I am the one Isaiah wrote about."

The wilderness Isaiah described may be viewed as symbolic of the human condition without Jesus—a mere subsistence in an arid desert with no water for life. Jesus came to offer abundant life lived in fellowship with him, both now and in the age to come, and to quench the spiritual thirst of our souls (John 4:13–14).

Isaiah said that those who live as members of the Messiah's kingdom will be distinct, a "clean" people who will walk in the "Way of Holiness" (Isaiah 35:8), a redeemed people (verse 9). This is a marvelous description of our salvation in Jesus. We are declared holy and righteous because we trust in him (Romans 3:21–26; 5:1–2). His blood "bought" us because he died in our place (Ephesians 1:7; 1 Timothy 2:5–6; 1 Peter 1:18–19).

The blessings of the Messiah's kingdom will profoundly influence those who receive them. Their lives will overflow with joy, and they will be awestruck at God's presence. Those lonely times of sorrow during which they can do nothing but sigh will vanish in God's presence as they lift up their song of praise (Isaiah 35:10).

Many of us know what it is to be crushed by fear, sadness and even the strain of over-commitment. But what about joy? As we learn what God has done and what he yet intends to do for us, we will experience instead what it means to be caught up in praise and honor for God.

Self-Discovery: *In what ways is your life abundant because of the presence of Jesus? Spend time in prayer, thanking God specifically for each way he has brought joy and purpose into your life.*

GO TO DISCOVERY 187 ON PAGE 939

grass and reeds and papyrus will
grow.

35:8 [d] Isa 11:16; 33:8; Mt 7:13-14 [e] Isa 4:3; 1Pe 1:15 [f] Isa 52:1

[8] And a highway[d] will be there;
it will be called the Way of
Holiness.[e]
The unclean[f] will not journey on it;
it will be for those who walk in
that Way;
wicked fools will not go about
on it.[a]

35:9 [g] Isa 30:6 [h] Isa 34:14 [i] Isa 51:11; 62:12; 63:4

[9] No lion[g] will be there,
nor will any ferocious beast[h] get
up on it;
they will not be found there.
But only the redeemed[i] will walk
there,
[10] and the ransomed of the LORD
will return.

35:10 [j] Isa 25:9 [k] Isa 30:19; 51:11; Rev 7:17; 21:4

They will enter Zion with singing;
everlasting joy[j] will crown their
heads.
Gladness and joy will overtake
them,
and sorrow and sighing will flee
away.[k]

Sennacherib Threatens Jerusalem

36:1 [l] 2Ch 32:1

36 In the fourteenth year of King
Hezekiah's reign, Sennacherib[l]
king of Assyria attacked all the fortified
cities of Judah and captured them.
[2] Then the king of Assyria sent his field
commander with a large army from Lachish to King Hezekiah at Jerusalem.
When the commander stopped at the

36:2 [m] Isa 7:3

aqueduct of the Upper Pool, on the road
to the Washerman's Field,[m] [3] Eliakim[n]

36:3 [n] Isa 22:20-21 [o] 2Ki 18:18

son of Hilkiah the palace administrator,
Shebna[o] the secretary, and Joah son of
Asaph the recorder went out to him.
[4] The field commander said to them,
"Tell Hezekiah,

" 'This is what the great king, the
king of Assyria, says: On what are
you basing this confidence of
yours? [5] You say you have strategy
and military strength—but you
speak only empty words. On whom

36:5 [p] 2Ki 18:7

are you depending, that you rebel[p]
against me? [6] Look now, you are de-

36:6 [q] Isa 30:2,5 [r] Eze 29:6-7

pending on Egypt,[q] that splintered
reed[r] of a staff, which pierces a
man's hand and wounds him if he
leans on it! Such is Pharaoh king of
Egypt to all who depend on him.
[7] And if you say to me, "We are depending on the LORD our God"—
isn't he the one whose high places

36:7 [s] 2Ki 18:4 [t] Dt 12:2-5

and altars Hezekiah removed,[s] saying to Judah and Jerusalem, "You
must worship before this altar"?[t]
[8] " 'Come now, make a bargain
with my master, the king of Assyria: I will give you two thousand
horses—if you can put riders on
them! [9] How then can you repulse
one officer of the least of my mas-

36:9 [u] Isa 31:3 [v] Isa 30:2-5

ter's officials, even though you are
depending on Egypt[u] for chariots
and horsemen?[v] [10] Furthermore,
have I come to attack and destroy

36:10 [w] 1Ki 13:18

this land without the LORD?
The LORD himself told[w] me to
march against this country and
destroy it.' "

[11] Then Eliakim, Shebna and Joah said

36:11 [x] Ezr 4:7

to the field commander, "Please speak to
your servants in Aramaic,[x] since we understand it. Don't speak to us in Hebrew
in the hearing of the people on the wall."
[12] But the commander replied, "Was it
only to your master and you that my
master sent me to say these things, and
not to the men sitting on the wall—who,
like you, will have to eat their own filth
and drink their own urine?"
[13] Then the commander stood and

36:13 [y] 2Ch 32:18

called out in Hebrew,[y] "Hear the words
of the great king, the king of Assyria!
[14] This is what the king says: Do not let
Hezekiah deceive you. He cannot deliver you! [15] Do not let Hezekiah persuade
you to trust in the LORD when he says,
'The LORD will surely deliver us; this city
will not be given into the hand of the

36:15 [z] Isa 37:10

king of Assyria.'[z]
[16] "Do not listen to Hezekiah. This is
what the king of Assyria says: Make
peace with me and come out to me.

36:16 [a] 1Ki 4:25; Zec 3:10 [b] Pr 5:15

Then every one of you will eat from his
own vine and fig tree[a] and drink water
from his own cistern,[b] [17] until I come
and take you to a land like your own—a
land of grain and new wine, a land of
bread and vineyards.
[18] "Do not let Hezekiah mislead you
when he says, 'The LORD will deliver us.'
Has the god of any nation ever delivered
his land from the hand of the king of Assyria? [19] Where are the gods of Hamath
and Arpad? Where are the gods of

[a] 8 Or / *the simple will not stray from it*

36:20 Sepharvaim? Have they rescued Samaria
c 1Ki 20:23 from my hand? 20Who of all the gods[c] of
these countries has been able to save his
land from me? How then can the LORD
deliver Jerusalem from my hand?"
21But the people remained silent and
36:21 said nothing in reply, because the king
d Pr 9:7-8; 26:4 had commanded, "Do not answer him."[d]
22Then Eliakim son of Hilkiah the
palace administrator, Shebna the secretary, and Joah son of Asaph the recorder
went to Hezekiah, with their clothes
torn, and told him what the field commander had said.

Jerusalem's Deliverance Foretold

37 When King Hezekiah heard
this, he tore his clothes and put
on sackcloth and went into the temple
of the LORD. 2He sent Eliakim the palace
administrator, Shebna the secretary, and
the leading priests, all wearing sack-
37:2 cloth, to the prophet Isaiah son of
e Isa 1:1 Amoz.[e] 3They told him, "This is what
Hezekiah says: This day is a day of dis-
37:3 tress and rebuke and disgrace, as when
f Isa 26:18; 66:9; children come to the point of birth[f] and
Hos 13:13 there is no strength to deliver them. 4It
may be that the LORD your God will hear
the words of the field commander,
whom his master, the king of Assyria,
has sent to ridicule the living God, and
37:4 that he will rebuke him for the words the
g Isa 36:13,18- LORD your God has heard.[g] Therefore
20 h Isa 1:9 pray for the remnant[h] that still survives."
5When King Hezekiah's officials came
to Isaiah, 6Isaiah said to them, "Tell your
master, 'This is what the LORD says: Do
37:6 not be afraid[i] of what you have heard—
i Isa 7:4 those words with which the underlings
of the king of Assyria have blasphemed
me. 7Listen! I am going to put a spirit in
him so that when he hears a certain re-
37:7 port,[j] he will return to his own country,
j ver 9 and there I will have him cut down with
the sword.' "
8When the field commander heard
that the king of Assyria had left Lachish,
he withdrew and found the king fighting
37:8 k Nu 33:20 against Libnah.[k]
37:9 9Now Sennacherib received a report[l]
l ver 7 that Tirhakah, the Cushite[a] king ⌞of
Egypt⌟, was marching out to fight
against him. When he heard it, he sent
messengers to Hezekiah with this word:
10"Say to Hezekiah king of Judah: Do not
let the god you depend on deceive you
when he says, 'Jerusalem will not be
handed over to the king of Assyria.'[m] 37:10
11Surely you have heard what the kings m Isa 36:15
of Assyria have done to all the countries,
destroying them completely. And will 37:11
you be delivered?[n] 12Did the gods of the n Isa 36:18-20
nations that were destroyed by my fore-
fathers[o] deliver them—the gods of Go- 37:12 o 2Ki 18:11
zan, Haran,[p] Rezeph and the people of p Ge 11:31;
Eden who were in Tel Assar? 13Where is 12:1-4; Ac 7:2
the king of Hamath, the king of Arpad,
the king of the city of Sepharvaim, or of
Hena or Ivvah?"

Hezekiah's Prayer

14Hezekiah received the letter from
the messengers and read it. Then he
went up to the temple of the LORD and
spread it out before the LORD. 15And
Hezekiah prayed to the LORD: 16"O LORD
Almighty, God of Israel, enthroned be-
tween the cherubim, you alone are God[q] 37:16 q Dt 10:17;
over all the kingdoms of the earth. You Ps 86:10;
have made heaven and earth. 17Give ear, 136:2-3
O LORD, and hear;[r] open your eyes, 37:17 r 2Ch 6:40
O LORD, and see;[s] listen to all the words s Da 9:18
Sennacherib has sent to insult the living
God.
18"It is true, O LORD, that the Assyrian
kings have laid waste all these peoples 37:18
and their lands.[t] 19They have thrown t 2Ki 15:29;
their gods into the fire and destroyed Na 2:11-12
them,[u] for they were not gods[v] but only 37:19
wood and stone, fashioned by human u Isa 26:14
hands. 20Now, O LORD our God, deliver v Isa 41:24,29
us from his hand, so that all kingdoms
on earth may know that you alone, 37:20
O LORD, are God.[b][w]" w Ps 46:10

Sennacherib's Fall

21Then Isaiah son of Amoz[x] sent a 37:21 x ver 2
message to Hezekiah: "This is what the
LORD, the God of Israel, says: Because
you have prayed to me concerning Sennacherib king of Assyria, 22this is the
word the LORD has spoken against him:

"The Virgin Daughter of Zion
despises and mocks you.
The Daughter of Jerusalem 37:22
tosses her head[y] as you flee. y Job 16:4
23 Who is it you have insulted and
blasphemed?[z] 37:23 z ver 4
Against whom have you raised
your voice

[a] 9 That is, from the upper Nile region
[b] 20 Dead Sea Scrolls (see also 2 Kings 19:19); Masoretic Text *alone are the LORD*

37:23 [a]Isa 2:11

and lifted your eyes in pride?[a]
Against the Holy One of Israel!
[24] By your messengers
you have heaped insults on the Lord.
And you have said,
'With my many chariots
I have ascended the heights of the mountains,
the utmost heights of Lebanon.[b]
I have cut down its tallest cedars,
the choicest of its pines.
I have reached its remotest heights,
the finest of its forests.
[25] I have dug wells in foreign lands[a]
and drunk the water there.
With the soles of my feet
I have dried up all the streams of Egypt.[c]'

37:24 [b]Isa 14:8
37:25 [c]Dt 11:10

[26] "Have you not heard?
Long ago I ordained[d] it.
In days of old I planned[e] it;
now I have brought it to pass,
that you have turned fortified cities
into piles of stone.[f]
[27] Their people, drained of power,
are dismayed and put to shame.
They are like plants in the field,
like tender green shoots,
like grass sprouting on the roof,[g]
scorched[b] before it grows up.

37:26 [d]Ac 2:23; 4:27-28; 1Pe 2:8 [e]Isa 10:6; 25:1 [f]Isa 25:2
37:27 [g]Ps 129:6

[28] "But I know where you stay
and when you come and go[h]
and how you rage[i] against me.
[29] Because you rage against me
and because your insolence[j] has
reached my ears,
I will put my hook in your nose[k]
and my bit in your mouth,
and I will make you return
by the way you came.[l]

37:28 [h]Ps 139:1-3 [i]Ps 2:1
37:29 [j]Isa 10:12 [k]Isa 30:28; Eze 38:4 [l]ver 34

[30] "This will be the sign for you, O Hezekiah:

"This year you will eat what grows by itself,
and the second year what springs from that.
But in the third year sow and reap,
plant vineyards and eat their fruit.
[31] Once more a remnant of the house of Judah
will take root below and bear fruit[m] above.
[32] For out of Jerusalem will come a remnant,
and out of Mount Zion a band of survivors.
The zeal[n] of the LORD Almighty
will accomplish this.

37:31 [m]Isa 27:6
37:32 [n]Isa 9:7

[33] "Therefore this is what the LORD says concerning the king of Assyria:

"He will not enter this city
or shoot an arrow here.
He will not come before it with shield
or build a siege ramp against it.
[34] By the way that he came he will return;[o]
he will not enter this city,"
declares the LORD.
[35] "I will defend[p] this city and save it,
for my sake[q] and for the sake of David[r] my servant!"

37:34 [o]ver 29
37:35 [p]Isa 31:5; 38:6 [q]Isa 43:25; 48:9, 11 [r]2Ki 20:6

[36] Then the angel of the LORD went out
and put to death a hundred and eighty-
five thousand men in the Assyrian[s]
camp. When the people got up the next
morning—there were all the dead bodies! [37] So Sennacherib king of Assyria
broke camp and withdrew. He returned
to Nineveh[t] and stayed there.
[38] One day, while he was worshiping in
the temple of his god Nisroch, his sons
Adrammelech and Sharezer cut him
down with the sword, and they escaped
to the land of Ararat.[u] And Esarhaddon
his son succeeded him as king.

37:36 [s]Isa 10:12
37:37 [t]Ge 10:11
37:38 [u]Ge 8:4; Jer 51:27

Hezekiah's Illness

38 In those days Hezekiah became
ill and was at the point of
death. The prophet Isaiah son of Amoz[v]
went to him and said, "This is what the
LORD says: Put your house in order,[w] because you are going to die; you will not
recover."
[2] Hezekiah turned his face to the wall
and prayed to the LORD, [3] "Remember,
O LORD, how I have walked[x] before you
faithfully and with wholehearted devotion[y] and have done what is good in your
eyes.[z]" And Hezekiah wept[a] bitterly.
[4] Then the word of the LORD came to
Isaiah: [5] "Go and tell Hezekiah, 'This is

38:1 [v]Isa 37:2 [w]2Sa 17:23
38:3 [x]Ne 13:14; Ps 26:3 [y]1Ch 29:19 [z]Dt 6:18 [a]Ps 6:8

a 25 Dead Sea Scrolls (see also 2 Kings 19:24); Masoretic Text does not have *in foreign lands.*
b 27 Some manuscripts of the Masoretic Text, Dead Sea Scrolls and some Septuagint manuscripts (see also 2 Kings 19:26); most manuscripts of the Masoretic Text *roof / and terraced fields*

what the LORD, the God of your father
38:5 David, says: I have heard your prayer and
[b] 2Ki 18:2 seen your tears; I will add fifteen years[b]
to your life. [6]And I will deliver you and
38:6 this city from the hand of the king of As-
[c] Isa 31:5; 37:35 syria. I will defend[c] this city.
38:7 [7]" 'This is the LORD's sign[d] to you that
[d] Isa 7:11,14 the LORD will do what he has promised:
[8]I will make the shadow cast by the sun
go back the ten steps it has gone down
on the stairway of Ahaz.' " So the sun-
38:8 light went back the ten steps it had gone
[e] Jos 10:13 down.[e]

[9]A writing of Hezekiah king of Judah
after his illness and recovery:

38:10 [10]I said, "In the prime of my life[f]
[f] Ps 102:24 must I go through the gates of
[g] Ps 107:18; 2Co 1:9 death[a][g]
[h] Job 17:11 and be robbed of the rest of my
years?[h]"
[11]I said, "I will not again see the LORD,
38:11 the LORD, in the land of the living;[i]
[i] Ps 27:13; 116:9 no longer will I look on mankind,
or be with those who now dwell
38:12 in this world.[b]
[j] 2Co 5:1,4; 2Pe 1:13-14 [12]Like a shepherd's tent[j] my house
[k] Job 4:21 has been pulled down[k] and
[l] Heb 1:12 taken from me.
[m] Job 7:6 Like a weaver I have rolled[l] up my
[n] Ps 73:14 life,
and he has cut me off from the
loom;[m]
day and night[n] you made an end
of me.
38:13 [13]I waited patiently till dawn,
[o] Ps 51:8 but like a lion he broke[o] all my
[p] Job 10:16; Da 6:24 bones;[p]
day and night you made an end
of me.
38:14 [14]I cried like a swift or thrush,
[q] Isa 59:11 I moaned like a mourning dove.[q]
[r] Job 17:3 My eyes grew weak as I looked to
the heavens.
I am troubled; O Lord, come to
my aid!"[r]

[15]But what can I say?
38:15 He has spoken to me, and he
[s] Ps 39:9 himself has done this.[s]
[t] 1Ki 21:27 I will walk humbly[t] all my years
[u] Job 7:11 because of this anguish of my
soul.[u]
[16]Lord, by such things men live;
and my spirit finds life in them
too.
38:16 You restored me to health
[v] Ps 119:25 and let me live.[v]
[17]Surely it was for my benefit
that I suffered such anguish.
In your love you kept me
from the pit[w] of destruction; 38:17
you have put all my sins[x] [w] Ps 30:3
behind your back.[y] [x] Jer 31:34
[18]For the grave[a][z] cannot praise you, [y] Isa 43:25; Mic 7:19
death cannot sing your praise;[a] 38:18 [z] Ecc 9:10
those who go down to the pit[b] [a] Ps 6:5; 88:10-11; 115:17
cannot hope for your [b] Ps 30:9
faithfulness.
[19]The living, the living—they praise[c] 38:19
you, [c] Dt 6:7; Ps 118:17; 119:175
as I am doing today;
fathers tell their children[d] [d] Dt 11:19
about your faithfulness.

[20]The LORD will save me,
and we will sing[e] with stringed 38:20 [e] Ps 68:25
instruments[f] [f] Ps 33:2
all the days of our lives[g] [g] Ps 116:2
in the temple[h] of the LORD. [h] Ps 116:17-19

[21]Isaiah had said, "Prepare a poultice
of figs and apply it to the boil, and he
will recover."
[22]Hezekiah had asked, "What will be
the sign that I will go up to the temple of
the LORD?"

Envoys From Babylon

39 At that time Merodach-Baladan son of Baladan king of Bab- 39:1
ylon[i] sent Hezekiah letters and a gift, [i] 2Ch 32:31
because he had heard of his illness and
recovery. [2]Hezekiah received the envoys[j] 39:2
gladly and showed them what was in his [j] 2Ch 32:31 [k] 2Ki 18:15
storehouses—the silver, the gold,[k] the
spices, the fine oil, his entire armory and
everything found among his treasures.
There was nothing in his palace or in all
his kingdom that Hezekiah did not
show them.
[3]Then Isaiah the prophet went to
King Hezekiah and asked, "What did
those men say, and where did they come
from?"
"From a distant land,[l]" Hezekiah 39:3
replied. "They came to me from Babylon." [l] Dt 28:49
[4]The prophet asked, "What did they
see in your palace?"
"They saw everything in my palace,"
Hezekiah said. "There is nothing among
my treasures that I did not show them."
[5]Then Isaiah said to Hezekiah, "Hear

[a] 10,18 Hebrew *Sheol* [b] 11 A few Hebrew manuscripts; most Hebrew manuscripts *in the place of cessation*

the word of the LORD Almighty: 6The
time will surely come when everything
in your palace, and all that your fathers
have stored up until this day, will be carried off to Babylon.[m] Nothing will be left,
says the LORD. 7And some of your descendants, your own flesh and blood
who will be born to you, will be taken
away, and they will become eunuchs in
the palace of the king of Babylon.[n]"
8"The word of the LORD you have spoken is good," Hezekiah replied. For he
thought, "There will be peace and security in my lifetime.[o]"

39:6 [m] 2Ki 24:13; Jer 20:5
39:7 [n] 2Ki 24:15; Da 1:1-7
39:8 [o] 2Ch 32:26

Comfort for God's People

40 Comfort, comfort[p] my
people,
says your God.
2 Speak tenderly[q] to Jerusalem,
and proclaim to her
that her hard service has been
completed,[r]
that her sin has been paid for,
that she has received from the
LORD's hand
double[s] for all her sins.

3 A voice of one calling:
"In the desert prepare
the way[t] for the LORD[a];
make straight in the wilderness
a highway for our God.[b][u]
4 Every valley shall be raised up,
every mountain and hill made
low;
the rough ground shall become
level,[v]
the rugged places a plain.
5 And the glory of the LORD will be
revealed,
and all mankind together will
see it.[w]
For the mouth of the LORD
has spoken."[x]

6 A voice says, "Cry out."
And I said, "What shall I cry?"
"All men are like grass,[y]
and all their glory is like the
flowers of the field.
7 The grass withers and the flowers
fall,
because the breath[z] of the LORD
blows on them.
Surely the people are grass.
8 The grass withers and the flowers
fall,
but the word[a] of our God stands
forever.[b]"
9 You who bring good tidings[c] to
Zion,
go up on a high mountain.
You who bring good tidings to
Jerusalem,[c]
lift up your voice with a shout,
lift it up, do not be afraid;
say to the towns of Judah,
"Here is your God!"[d]
10 See, the Sovereign LORD comes[e]
with power,
and his arm[f] rules[g] for him.
See, his reward[h] is with him,
and his recompense
accompanies him.
11 He tends his flock like a shepherd:[i]
He gathers the lambs in his arms
and carries them close to his heart;
he gently leads those that have
young.
12 Who has measured the waters[j] in
the hollow of his hand,[k]
or with the breadth of his hand
marked off the heavens?[l]
Who has held the dust of the earth
in a basket,
or weighed the mountains on
the scales

40:1 [p] Isa 12:1; 49:13; 51:3,12; 52:9; 61:2; 66:13; Jer 31:13; Zep 3:14-17; 2Co 1:3
40:2 [q] Isa 35:4 [r] Isa 41:11-13; 49:25 [s] Isa 61:7; Jer 16:18; Zec 9:12; Rev 18:6
40:3 [t] Mal 3:1 [u] Mt 3:3*; Mk 1:3*; Jn 1:23*
40:4 [v] Isa 45:2,13
40:5 [w] Isa 52:10; Lk 3:4-6* [x] Isa 1:20; 58:14
40:6 [y] Job 14:2
40:7 [z] Job 41:21
40:8 [a] Isa 55:11; 59:21 [b] Mt 5:18; 1Pe 1:24-25*
40:9 [c] Isa 52:7-10; 61:1; Ro 10:15 [d] Isa 25:9
40:10 [e] Rev 22:7 [f] Isa 59:16 [g] Isa 9:6-7 [h] Isa 62:11; Rev 22:12
40:11 [i] Eze 34:23; Mic 5:4; Jn 10:11
40:12 [j] Job 38:10 [k] Pr 30:4 [l] Heb 1:10-12

[a] 3 Or *A voice of one calling in the desert: / "Prepare the way for the LORD* [b] 3 Hebrew; Septuagint *make straight the paths of our God* [c] 9 Or *O Zion, bringer of good tidings, / go up on a high mountain. / O Jerusalem, bringer of good tidings*

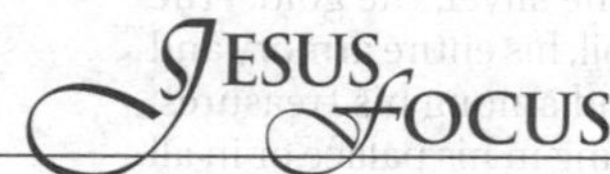

"HERE IS YOUR GOD"

In Chapter 40 Isaiah shifted his focus from judgment to hope. God's prophet knew that the promised Messiah would appear—that God himself was coming to earth: "Here is your God!" he proclaimed (verse 9). The Messiah would be both fully divine and fully human. In the New Testament, John the Baptist, another great prophet and the forerunner of Jesus, referred to himself as the "voice . . . in the desert" (John 1:23), enjoining the people of Israel to repent and prepare for the Messiah. And when he saw Jesus, John exclaimed, "Look, the Lamb of God, who takes away the sin of the world! This is the one I meant when I said, 'A man who comes after me has surpassed me because he was before me'" (John 1:29–30).

DISCOVERY 187

Pointing to Jesus

God's ways are often surprising, yet he often graciously prepares us in one way or another to understand them. Through Isaiah God declared that he would provide "a voice" before the appearance of the Messiah to alert the people that the day was approaching (Isaiah 40:3). The "voice" Isaiah was referring to was John the Baptist, who was sent by God to prepare the way for Jesus (Matthew 3:3; Mark 1:3, Luke 3:4; John 1:23). Isaiah included many details that would help to identify this messenger.

Bear in mind that John was not *the* voice; he was only *a* voice. His purpose was simply to point to *the* voice—Jesus Christ. When the priests and Levites questioned John as to whether or not he was the Christ or Elijah or "the Prophet," he emphatically stated that he was not, specifying that his role was to be a voice (John 1:19–23). At long last John was able to make the announcement: "Look, the Lamb of God, who takes away the sin of the world" (John 1:29).

John's voice implored people to turn from their sins and follow God (Matthew 3:1). This forerunner of Jesus realized that the people needed to be willing to listen to God in order to recognize God's Son for who he was.

John was no ordinary prophet. He made his home in the desert, wearing rude clothing made of rough camel hair and eating locusts and wild honey (Mark 1:6). John did not travel to meet the crowds; instead, the people came to him.

It would have been an easy task for John to establish his own following and give birth to his own movement, but he resisted this temptation, recognizing that his life's calling was simply to prepare people to open their lives and hearts to Jesus. Even when John's disciples argued with Jesus' disciples about which of the two was the greater, John allowed no room for doubt, stating that "He must become greater; I must become less" (John 3:30). Once Jesus appeared on the scene, John's task was complete, and he was content to fade into the background.

God wants each of us to be a voice for him as well. Our purpose is to point people to Jesus rather than to demonstrate how good or how committed we are. And the message we call out is the same as John's—that God wants people to turn from their sin and give control of their lives to Jesus. We are called to be faithful to God wherever he places us—in the city, in the desert, in the midst of crowds, in obscurity.

But we are called to be more than Jesus' voice—he asks us to be his hands and feet as well. In the Master's name we are to feed the hungry, offer a cup of cold water to the thirsty, show hospitality to the stranger, clothe the needy, look after the needs of the sick and visit those in prison (Matthew 26:34–46). The writer to the Hebrews urged us to "keep on loving each other as brothers. Do not forget to entertain strangers, for by so doing some people have entertained angels without knowing it" (Hebrews 13:1–2).

***Self-Discovery:** In what concrete ways can you be Jesus' voice, hands and feet to someone near you?*

GO TO DISCOVERY 188 ON PAGE 943

YOU SHOULD POINT TO THE WHOLE MAN JESUS AND SAY, "THAT IS GOD."

Martin Luther, *German Reformer*

and the hills in a balance?
13 Who has understood the mind[a] of the LORD,
or instructed him as his counselor?[m]
14 Whom did the LORD consult to enlighten him,
and who taught him the right way?
Who was it that taught him knowledge[n]
or showed him the path of understanding?
15 Surely the nations are like a drop in a bucket;
they are regarded as dust on the scales;
he weighs the islands as though they were fine dust.
16 Lebanon is not sufficient for altar fires,
nor its animals[o] enough for burnt offerings.
17 Before him all the nations[p] are as nothing;[q]
they are regarded by him as worthless
and less than nothing.[r]
18 To whom, then, will you compare God?[s]
What image[t] will you compare him to?
19 As for an idol,[u] a craftsman casts it,
and a goldsmith[v] overlays it with gold[w]
and fashions silver chains for it.
20 A man too poor to present such an offering
selects wood that will not rot.
He looks for a skilled craftsman
to set up an idol that will not topple.[x]

21 Do you not know?
Have you not heard?
Has it not been told[y] you from the beginning?
Have you not understood[z] since the earth was founded?[a]
22 He sits enthroned above the circle of the earth,
and its people are like grasshoppers.[b]
He stretches out the heavens like a canopy,[c]
and spreads them out like a tent[d] to live in.
23 He brings princes[e] to naught
and reduces the rulers of this world to nothing.[f]
24 No sooner are they planted,
no sooner are they sown,
no sooner do they take root in the ground,
than he blows[g] on them and they wither,
and a whirlwind sweeps them away like chaff.

25 "To whom will you compare me?[h]
Or who is my equal?" says the Holy One.
26 Lift your eyes and look to the heavens:[i]
Who created[j] all these?
He who brings out the starry host[k] one by one,
and calls them each by name.
Because of his great power and mighty strength,
not one of them is missing.[l]

27 Why do you say, O Jacob,
and complain, O Israel,
"My way is hidden from the LORD;
my cause is disregarded by my God"?[m]
28 Do you not know?
Have you not heard?[n]
The LORD is the everlasting[o] God,
the Creator of the ends of the earth.
He will not grow tired or weary,
and his understanding no one can fathom.[p]
29 He gives strength to the weary[q]
and increases the power of the weak.
30 Even youths grow tired and weary,
and young men[r] stumble and fall;
31 but those who hope[s] in the LORD
will renew their strength.[t]
They will soar on wings like eagles;[u]
they will run and not grow weary,
they will walk and not be faint.[v]

a 13 Or *Spirit*; or *spirit*

40:13 [m] Ro 11:34*; 1Co 2:16*
40:14 [n] Job 21:22; Col 2:3
40:16 [o] Ps 50:9-11; Mic 6:7; Heb 10:5-9
40:17 [p] Isa 30:28 [q] Isa 29:7 [r] Da 4:35
40:18 [s] Ex 8:10; 1Sa 2:2; Isa 46:5 [t] Ac 17:29
40:19 [u] Ps 115:4 [v] Isa 41:7; Jer 10:3 [w] Isa 2:20
40:20 [x] 1Sa 5:3
40:21 [y] Ps 19:1; 50:6; Ac 14:17 [z] Ro 1:19 [a] Isa 48:13; 51:13
40:22 [b] Nu 13:33; Ps 104:2; Isa 42:5 [c] Job 22:14 [d] Job 36:29
40:23 [e] Isa 34:12 [f] Job 12:21; Ps 107:40
40:24 [g] Isa 41:16
40:25 [h] ver 18
40:26 [i] Isa 51:6 [j] Ps 89:11-13; Isa 42:5 [k] Ps 147:4 [l] Isa 34:16
40:27 [m] Job 27:2; Lk 18:7-8
40:28 [n] ver 21 [o] Ps 90:2 [p] Ps 147:5; Ro 11:33
40:29 [q] Isa 50:4; Jer 31:25
40:30 [r] Isa 9:17; Jer 6:11; 9:21
40:31 [s] Lk 18:1 [t] 2Co 4:16 [u] Ex 19:4; Ps 103:5 [v] 2Co 4:1; Heb 12:1-3

The Helper of Israel

41:1 [w]Hab 2:20; Zec 2:13 [x]Isa 11:11 [y]Isa 48:16 [z]Isa 1:18; 34:1; 50:8

41 "Be silent[w] before me, you
islands![x]
Let the nations renew their
strength!
Let them come forward[y] and speak;
let us meet together[z] at the
place of judgment.

41:2 [a]Ezr 1:2 [b]ver 25; Isa 45:1,13 [c]2Sa 22:43 [d]Isa 40:24

2 "Who has stirred[a] up one from the
east,[b]
calling him in righteousness to
his service[a]?
He hands nations over to him
and subdues kings before him.
He turns them to dust[c] with his
sword,
to windblown chaff[d] with his
bow.
3 He pursues them and moves on
unscathed,
by a path his feet have not
traveled before.
4 Who has done this and carried it
through,
calling forth the generations
from the beginning?[e]
I, the LORD—with the first of them
and with the last[f]—I am he."

41:4 [e]ver 26; Isa 46:10 [f]Isa 44:6; 48:12; Rev 1:8,17; 22:13

41:5 [g]Eze 26:17-18

5 The islands[g] have seen it and fear;
the ends of the earth tremble.
They approach and come forward;
6 each helps the other
and says to his brother, "Be
strong!"
7 The craftsman encourages the
goldsmith,[h]
and he who smooths with the
hammer
spurs on him who strikes the
anvil.
He says of the welding, "It is good."
He nails down the idol so it will
not topple.

41:7 [h]Isa 40:19

8 "But you, O Israel, my servant,
Jacob, whom I have chosen,
you descendants of Abraham[i]
my friend,[j]
9 I took you from the ends of the
earth,[k]
from its farthest corners I called
you.
I said, 'You are my servant';
I have chosen[l] you and have not
rejected you.
10 So do not fear, for I am with you;[m]
do not be dismayed, for I am
your God.
I will strengthen you and help[n] you;
I will uphold you with my
righteous right hand.

41:8 [i]Isa 29:22; 51:2; 63:16 [j]2Ch 20:7; Jas 2:23

41:9 [k]Isa 11:12 [l]Dt 7:6

41:10 [m]Jos 1:9; Isa 43:2,5; Ro 8:31 [n]ver 13-14; Isa 44:2; 49:8

11 "All who rage[o] against you
will surely be ashamed and
disgraced;[p]
those who oppose[q] you
will be as nothing and perish.[r]
12 Though you search for your
enemies,
you will not find them.[s]
Those who wage war against you
will be as nothing[t] at all.
13 For I am the LORD, your God,
who takes hold of your right
hand[u]
and says to you, Do not fear;
I will help[v] you.
14 Do not be afraid, O worm Jacob,
O little Israel,
for I myself will help you," declares
the LORD,
your Redeemer, the Holy One of
Israel.
15 "See, I will make you into a
threshing sledge,[w]
new and sharp, with many teeth.
You will thresh the mountains and
crush them,

41:11 [o]Isa 17:12 [p]Isa 45:24 [q]Ex 23:22 [r]Isa 29:8

41:12 [s]Ps 37:35-36 [t]Isa 17:14

41:13 [u]Isa 42:6; 45:1 [v]ver 10

41:15 [w]Mic 4:13

[a] 2 Or / *whom victory meets at every step*

OUR REDEEMER

The Messiah would be the "Redeemer, the Holy One of Israel" (Isaiah 41:14). Isaiah employed majestic language in chapters 40 through 46 to portray God as Master of the universe. People and nations might think highly of themselves and of their own power, but from God's omniscient and omnipotent perspective people are like "grasshoppers" (Isaiah 40:22), nations like a "drop in a bucket" (Isaiah 40:15), Jacob a feeble and despised "worm" and Israel strikingly "little" (Isaiah 41:14). But God persisted in his love for his people and promised to send a Redeemer who would bring them back to him. The New Testament reveals Jesus to be that Redeemer and describes what he did on our behalf to make possible a restored and intimate relationship with God (Mark 10:45; Romans 3:24; Galatians 3:13–14; Titus 2:14; Hebrews 9:12–15; 1 Peter 1:18–21).

and reduce the hills to chaff.

41:16 [x] Jer 51:2 [y] Isa 45:25

16 You will winnow[x] them, the wind
will pick them up,
and a gale will blow them away.
But you will rejoice in the LORD
and glory[y] in the Holy One of
Israel.

41:17 [z] Isa 43:20 [a] Isa 30:19

17 "The poor and needy search for
water,[z]
but there is none;
their tongues are parched with
thirst.
But I the LORD will answer[a] them;
I, the God of Israel, will not
forsake them.

41:18 [b] Isa 30:25 [c] Isa 43:19 [d] Isa 35:7

18 I will make rivers flow[b] on barren
heights,
and springs within the valleys.
I will turn the desert[c] into pools of
water,
and the parched ground into
springs.[d]
19 I will put in the desert
the cedar and the acacia, the
myrtle and the olive.

41:19 [e] Isa 60:13

I will set pines in the wasteland,
the fir and the cypress together,[e]
20 so that people may see and know,
may consider and understand,
that the hand of the LORD has done
this,

41:20 [f] Job 12:9

that the Holy One of Israel has
created[f] it.

21 "Present your case," says the LORD.
"Set forth your arguments," says

41:21 [g] Isa 43:15

Jacob's King.[g]

41:22 [h] Isa 43:9; 45:21 [i] Isa 46:10

22 "Bring in ⌞your idols⌟ to tell us
what is going to happen.[h]
Tell us what the former things were,
so that we may consider them
and know their final outcome.
Or declare to us the things to come,[i]
23 tell us what the future holds,

41:23 [j] Isa 42:9; 44:7-8; 45:3 [k] Jer 10:5

so we may know[j] that you are
gods.
Do something, whether good or
bad,[k]
so that we will be dismayed and
filled with fear.

41:24 [l] Isa 37:19; 44:9; 1Co 8:4 [m] Ps 115:8

24 But you are less than nothing[l]
and your works are utterly
worthless;
he who chooses you is
detestable.[m]

41:25 [n] ver 2

25 "I have stirred up one from the
north,[n] and he comes—
one from the rising sun who
calls on my name.

41:25 [o] 2Sa 22:43

He treads[o] on rulers as if they were
mortar,
as if he were a potter treading
the clay.
26 Who told of this from the
beginning, so we could
know,
or beforehand, so we could say,
'He was right'?
No one told of this,
no one foretold it,

41:26 [p] Hab 2:18-19

no one heard any words[p] from
you.

41:27 [q] Isa 48:3,16 [r] Isa 40:9

27 I was the first to tell[q] Zion, 'Look,
here they are!'
I gave to Jerusalem a messenger
of good tidings.[r]

41:28 [s] Isa 50:2; 59:16; 63:5 [t] Isa 40:13-14

28 I look but there is no one[s]—
no one among them to give
counsel,[t]
no one to give answer when I ask
them.
29 See, they are all false!

41:29 [u] ver 24 [v] Jer 5:13

Their deeds amount to
nothing;[u]
their images are but wind[v] and
confusion.

The Servant of the LORD

42:1 [w] Isa 43:10; Lk 9:35; 1Pe 2:4,6 [x] Isa 11:2; Mt 3:16-17; Jn 3:34

42 "Here is my servant, whom I
uphold,
my chosen one[w] in whom I
delight;
I will put my Spirit[x] on him
and he will bring justice to the
nations.
2 He will not shout or cry out,
or raise his voice in the streets.
3 A bruised reed he will not break,
and a smoldering wick he will
not snuff out.

42:3 [y] Ps 72:2

In faithfulness he will bring forth
justice;[y]
4 he will not falter or be
discouraged
till he establishes justice on earth.

42:4 [z] Ge 49:10; Mt 12:18-21*

In his law the islands will put
their hope."[z]

5 This is what God the LORD says—
he who created the heavens and
stretched them out,

42:5 [a] Ps 24:2 [b] Ac 17:25

who spread out the earth and all
that comes out of it,[a]
who gives breath[b] to its people,
and life to those who walk on it:

Called to Service

There are several sections of Isaiah's prophecy that are referred to as the "Servant passages," because they describe how we can live in a way that positively influences other people (see chapters 42, 49, 50, 52 and 53). These chapters also point ahead to God's ultimate Servant, Jesus Christ.

Though Isaiah's prophecies were recorded hundreds of years before Jesus' birth, the attitudes and behavior Isaiah described delineate Jesus in detail. The first thing Isaiah wrote in these "servant songs" is that the Lord's Servant would manifest a spirit of sensitivity and restraint. The Gospels never refer to Jesus as brash or boisterous. Instead, his power was always demonstrated in a gentle and humble manner. Isaiah 42:2 states that the servant "[would] not shout or cry out, or raise his voice in the streets." His sensitivity would also be apparent by his compassion: "A bruised reed he will not break, and a smoldering wick he will not snuff out" (verse 3). Jesus constantly aligned himself with fairness, righteousness, integrity, honesty and an absolute adherence to truth. He spent himself on those who were oppressed, misjudged, misunderstood, victimized. This often startled and angered his opponents, who failed to comprehend the true meaning of service.

One morning, while Jesus was teaching in the temple, the Jewish leaders brought to him a woman who had been caught in the act of adultery (see Discovery #277, page 1425). The woman was like a bruised reed, caught in a sinful attempt to meet the deep longings of her soul. Jesus lovingly protected her from the violence of the self-righteous mob. He did not condone her sin, but neither did he condemn her. By his grace, he allowed a bruised reed to stand tall again (John 8:3–11).

But acting as God's servant is not a role reserved for Jesus alone. As his followers, we take on the same attitude and accountability. The Bible tells us that "[our] attitude should be the same as that of Christ Jesus" (Philippians 2:5). Just as God's Son made himself nothing, taking on the nature and demeanor of a servant, so we must devote ourselves to humble and faithful service to others (Ephesians 4:2). And again, Paul stated in Galatians 5:13, "You . . . were called to be free. But do not use your freedom to indulge the sinful nature; rather, serve one another in love."

Following this mandate is difficult, even impossible, when we try to do it on our own. But we can depend on the Holy Spirit who lives within us. When we are weak, he infuses us with his strength. When we are foolish, he proves himself wise. We carry with us the indelible impression of God everywhere we go (2 Corinthians 2:14—3:18). If the world is to see God's character, people must observe Jesus' characteristics in his servants. Mark 10:44–45 inspires us with these words: "And whoever wants to be first must be slave of all. For even the Son of Man did not come to be served, but to serve, and to give his life as a ransom for many."

Self-Discovery: *Have you ever felt like a bruised reed or a smoldering wick? Can you recall Jesus' tender touch during this vulnerable period of your life? What were some of the ways he comforted and restored you, keeping you from snapping or burning out?*

GO TO DISCOVERY 189 ON PAGE 954

42:6 [c] Isa 43:1 [d] Jer 23:6 [e] Isa 26:3 [f] Isa 49:8 [g] Lk 2:32; Ac 13:47

6 "I, the LORD, have called[c] you in
righteousness;[d]
I will take hold of your hand.
I will keep[e] you and will make you
to be a covenant[f] for the people
and a light for the Gentiles,[g]

42:7 [h] Isa 35:5 [i] Isa 49:9; 61:1 [j] Lk 4:19; 2Ti 2:26; Heb 2:14-15

7 to open eyes that are blind,[h]
to free[i] captives from prison[j]
and to release from the dungeon
those who sit in darkness.

42:8 [k] Ex 3:15 [l] Isa 48:11

8 "I am the LORD; that is my name![k]
I will not give my glory to
another[l]
or my praise to idols.
9 See, the former things have taken
place,
and new things I declare;
before they spring into being
I announce them to you."

Song of Praise to the LORD

42:10 [m] Ps 33:3; 40:3; 98:1 [n] Isa 49:6 [o] 1Ch 16:32; Ps 96:11

10 Sing to the LORD a new song,[m]
his praise from the ends of the
earth,[n]
you who go down to the sea, and
all that is in it,[o]
you islands, and all who live in
them.

42:11 [p] Isa 32:16 [q] Isa 60:7 [r] Isa 52:7; Na 1:15

11 Let the desert[p] and its towns raise
their voices;
let the settlements where Kedar[q]
lives rejoice.
Let the people of Sela sing for joy;
let them shout from the
mountaintops.[r]

42:12 [s] Isa 24:15

12 Let them give glory[s] to the LORD
and proclaim his praise in the
islands.

42:13 [t] Isa 9:6 [u] Isa 26:11 [v] Hos 11:10 [w] Isa 66:14

13 The LORD will march out like a
mighty[t] man,
like a warrior he will stir up his
zeal;[u]
with a shout[v] he will raise the
battle cry
and will triumph over his
enemies.[w]

14 "For a long time I have kept silent,
I have been quiet and held
myself back.
But now, like a woman in childbirth,
I cry out, I gasp and pant.

42:15 [x] Eze 38:20 [y] Isa 50:2; Na 1:4-6

15 I will lay waste[x] the mountains and
hills
and dry up all their vegetation;
I will turn rivers into islands
and dry up[y] the pools.

42:16 [z] Lk 1:78-79 [a] Isa 32:3 [b] Lk 3:5 [c] Heb 13:5

16 I will lead[z] the blind[a] by ways they
have not known,
along unfamiliar paths I will
guide them;
I will turn the darkness into light
before them
and make the rough places
smooth.[b]
These are the things I will do;
I will not forsake[c] them.

42:17 [d] Ps 97:7; Isa 1:29; 44:11; 45:16

17 But those who trust in idols,
who say to images, 'You are our
gods,'
will be turned back in utter
shame.[d]

Israel Blind and Deaf

42:18 [e] Isa 35:5

18 "Hear, you deaf;[e]
look, you blind, and see!

42:19 [f] Isa 43:8; Eze 12:2 [g] Isa 41:8-9 [h] Isa 44:26 [i] Isa 26:3

19 Who is blind[f] but my servant,[g]
and deaf like the messenger[h] I
send?
Who is blind like the one
committed[i] to me,
blind like the servant of the
LORD?

42:20 [j] Jer 6:10

20 You have seen many things, but
have paid no attention;
your ears are open, but you hear
nothing."[j]

42:21 [k] ver 4

21 It pleased the LORD
for the sake of his righteousness
to make his law[k] great and
glorious.

42:22 [l] Isa 24:18 [m] Isa 24:22

22 But this is a people plundered and
looted,
all of them trapped in pits[l]
or hidden away in prisons.[m]
They have become plunder,
with no one to rescue them;
they have been made loot,
with no one to say, "Send them
back."

42:23 [n] Isa 48:18

23 Which of you will listen to this
or pay close attention[n] in time
to come?
24 Who handed Jacob over to become
loot,
and Israel to the plunderers?
Was it not the LORD,
against whom we have sinned?

42:24 [o] Isa 30:15

For they would not follow[o] his
ways;
they did not obey his law.
25 So he poured out on them his
burning anger,
the violence of war.

It enveloped them in flames,[p] yet
they did not understand;
it consumed them, but they did
not take it to heart.[q]

Israel's Only Savior

43 But now, this is what the LORD says—
he who created you, O Jacob,
he who formed[r] you, O Israel:[s]
"Fear not, for I have redeemed[t]
you;
I have summoned you by name;[u]
you are mine.
2 When you pass through the
waters,[v]
I will be with you;[w]
and when you pass through the
rivers,
they will not sweep over you.
When you walk through the fire,[x]
you will not be burned;
the flames will not set you
ablaze.[y]
3 For I am the LORD, your God,[z]
the Holy One of Israel, your
Savior;
I give Egypt for your ransom,
Cush[a][a] and Seba in your stead.[b]
4 Since you are precious and
honored in my sight,
and because I love[c] you,
I will give men in exchange for you,
and people in exchange for your
life.
5 Do not be afraid,[d] for I am with
you;[e]
I will bring your children[f] from
the east
and gather you from the west.
6 I will say to the north, 'Give them
up!'
and to the south,[g] 'Do not hold
them back.'
Bring my sons from afar
and my daughters[h] from the
ends of the earth—
7 everyone who is called by my
name,[i]
whom I created for my glory,
whom I formed and made.[j]"
8 Lead out those who have eyes but
are blind,[k]
who have ears but are deaf,[l]
9 All the nations gather together[m]
and the peoples assemble.
Which of them foretold[n] this
and proclaimed to us the former
things?
Let them bring in their witnesses
to prove they were right,
so that others may hear and say,
"It is true."
10 "You are my witnesses," declares
the LORD,
"and my servant[o] whom I have
chosen,
so that you may know and believe
me
and understand that I am he.
Before me no god[p] was formed,
nor will there be one after me.
11 I, even I, am the LORD,
and apart from me there is no
savior.[q]
12 I have revealed and saved and
proclaimed—
I, and not some foreign god[r]
among you.
You are my witnesses,[s]" declares
the LORD, "that I am God.
13 Yes, and from ancient days[t] I am
he.
No one can deliver out of my hand.
When I act, who can reverse
it?"[u]

[a] 3 That is, the upper Nile region

42:25 p 2Ki 25:9 q Isa 29:13; 47:7; 57:1,11; Hos 7:9
43:1 r ver 7 s Ge 32:28; Isa 44:21 t Isa 44:2,6 u Isa 42:6; 45:3-4
43:2 v Isa 8:7 w Dt 31:6,8 x Isa 29:6; 30:27 y Ps 66:12; Da 3:25-27
43:3 z Ex 20:2 a Isa 20:3 b Pr 21:18
43:4 c Isa 63:9
43:5 d Isa 44:2 e Jer 30:10-11 f Isa 41:8
43:6 g Ps 107:3 h 2Co 6:18
43:7 i Isa 56:5; 63:19; Jas 2:7 j ver 1, 21; Ps 100:3; Eph 2:10; Eph 2:10
43:8 k Isa 6:9-10 l Isa 42:20; Eze 12:2
43:9 m Isa 41:1 n Isa 41:26
43:10 o Isa 41:8-9 p Isa 44:6,8
43:11 q Isa 45:21
43:12 r Dt 32:12; Ps 81:9 s Isa 44:8
43:13 t Ps 90:2 u Job 9:12; Isa 14:27

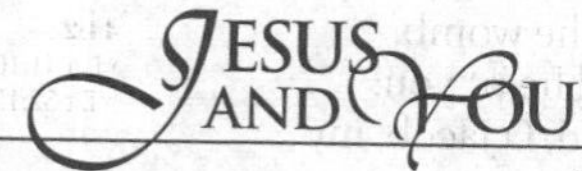

WITNESS FOR GOD

God's people have always enjoyed a special relationship with him, and in Isaiah 43:1 he once again pledged his tender and undying love for his people: "I have redeemed you . . . you are mine." Whatever difficulties may intrude into our lives, he reminds us that he is our God, our Savior and our King (verses 3,15). God chose Israel to be his covenant people, but the nation was too frequently unfaithful in response to him. In the New Testament, when Jesus gave his final commission to the disciples just before his ascension, he made certain that they understood their assignment: "You will receive power when the Holy Spirit comes on you; and you will be my witnesses in Jerusalem, and in all Judea and Samaria, and to the ends of the earth" (Acts 1:8). The disciples' mission is still ours today. God wants us as his faithful people to communicate in word and in deed to those around us the Good News of who he is and what he has done for us.

God's Mercy and Israel's Unfaithfulness

14 This is what the LORD says—
your Redeemer, the Holy One of Israel:
"For your sake I will send to Babylon
and bring down as fugitives[v] all the Babylonians,[a][w]
in the ships in which they took pride.
15 I am the LORD, your Holy One,
Israel's Creator, your King."

16 This is what the LORD says—
he who made a way through the sea,
a path through the mighty waters,[x]
17 who drew out[y] the chariots and horses,
the army and reinforcements together,[z]
and they lay there, never to rise again,
extinguished, snuffed out like a wick:
18 "Forget the former things;
do not dwell on the past.
19 See, I am doing a new thing![a]
Now it springs up; do you not perceive it?
I am making a way in the desert[b]
and streams in the wasteland.
20 The wild animals honor me,
the jackals[c] and the owls,
because I provide water[d] in the desert
and streams in the wasteland,
to give drink to my people, my chosen,
21 the people I formed for myself
that they may proclaim my praise.[e]

22 "Yet you have not called upon me, O Jacob,
you have not wearied yourselves for me, O Israel.[f]
23 You have not brought me sheep for burnt offerings,
nor honored[g] me with your sacrifices.[h]
I have not burdened you with grain offerings
nor wearied you with demands[i] for incense.[j]
24 You have not bought any fragrant calamus[k] for me,
or lavished on me the fat of your sacrifices.
But you have burdened me with your sins
and wearied[l] me with your offenses.[m]

25 "I, even I, am he who blots out
your transgressions,[n] for my own sake,[o]
and remembers your sins no more.[p]
26 Review the past for me,
let us argue the matter together;[q]
state the case[r] for your innocence.
27 Your first father sinned;
your spokesmen[s] rebelled against me.
28 So I will disgrace the dignitaries of your temple,
and I will consign Jacob to destruction[b]
and Israel to scorn.[t]

Israel the Chosen

44 "But now listen, O Jacob, my servant,[u]
Israel, whom I have chosen.
2 This is what the LORD says—
he who made you, who formed you in the womb,
and who will help[v] you:
Do not be afraid, O Jacob, my servant,
Jeshurun,[w] whom I have chosen.
3 For I will pour water[x] on the thirsty land,
and streams on the dry ground;
I will pour out my Spirit[y] on your offspring,
and my blessing on your descendants.[z]
4 They will spring up like grass in a meadow,
like poplar trees[a] by flowing streams.[b]
5 One will say, 'I belong to the LORD';
another will call himself by the name of Jacob;
still another will write on his hand,[c] 'The LORD's,'[d]
and will take the name Israel.

[a] 14 Or *Chaldeans* [b] 28 The Hebrew term refers to the irrevocable giving over of things or persons to the LORD, often by totally destroying them.

43:14 [v] Isa 13:14-15 [w] Isa 23:13
43:16 [x] Ps 77:19; Isa 11:15; 51:10
43:17 [y] Ps 118:12; Isa 1:31 [z] Ex 14:9
43:19 [a] 2Co 5:17; Rev 21:5 [b] Ex 17:6; Nu 20:11
43:20 [c] Isa 13:22 [d] Isa 48:21
43:21 [e] Ps 102:18; 1Pe 2:9
43:22 [f] Isa 30:11
43:23 [g] Zec 7:5-6; Mal 1:6-8 [h] Am 5:25 [i] Jer 7:22 [j] Ex 30:35; Lev 2:1
43:24 [k] Ex 30:23 [l] Isa 1:14; 7:13 [m] Mal 2:17
43:25 [n] Ac 3:19 [o] Isa 37:35; Eze 36:22 [p] Isa 38:17; Jer 31:34
43:26 [q] Isa 1:18 [r] Isa 41:1; 50:8
43:27 [s] Isa 9:15; 28:7; Jer 5:31
43:28 [t] Jer 24:9; Eze 5:15
44:1 [u] ver 21; Jer 30:10; 46:27-28
44:2 [v] Isa 41:10 [w] Dt 32:15
44:3 [x] Joel 3:18 [y] Joel 2:28; Ac 2:17 [z] Isa 61:9; 65:23
44:4 [a] Lev 23:40 [b] Job 40:22
44:5 [c] Ex 13:9 [d] Zec 8:20-22

The LORD, Not Idols

[6] "This is what the LORD says—
Israel's King[e] and Redeemer,[f] the LORD Almighty:
I am the first and I am the last;[g]
apart from me there is no God.
[7] Who then is like me? Let him proclaim it.
Let him declare and lay out before me
what has happened since I established my ancient people,
and what is yet to come—
yes, let him foretell[h] what will come.
[8] Do not tremble, do not be afraid.
Did I not proclaim this and foretell it long ago?
You are my witnesses. Is there any God[i] besides me?
No, there is no other Rock;[j] I know not one."
[9] All who make idols are nothing,
and the things they treasure are worthless.[k]
Those who would speak up for them are blind;
they are ignorant, to their own shame.
[10] Who shapes a god and casts an idol,
which can profit him nothing?[l]
[11] He and his kind will be put to shame;[m]
craftsmen are nothing but men.
Let them all come together and take their stand;
they will be brought down to terror and infamy.[n]
[12] The blacksmith[o] takes a tool
and works with it in the coals;
he shapes an idol with hammers,
he forges it with the might of his arm.[p]
He gets hungry and loses his strength;
he drinks no water and grows faint.
[13] The carpenter[q] measures with a line
and makes an outline with a marker;
he roughs it out with chisels
and marks it with compasses.
He shapes it in the form of man,[r]
of man in all his glory,
that it may dwell in a shrine.[s]
[14] He cut down cedars,
or perhaps took a cypress or oak.
He let it grow among the trees of the forest,
or planted a pine, and the rain made it grow.
[15] It is man's fuel[t] for burning;
some of it he takes and warms himself,
he kindles a fire and bakes bread.
But he also fashions a god and worships it;
he makes an idol and bows[u] down to it.
[16] Half of the wood he burns in the fire;
over it he prepares his meal,
he roasts his meat and eats his fill.
He also warms himself and says,
"Ah! I am warm; I see the fire."
[17] From the rest he makes a god, his idol;
he bows down to it and worships.
He prays[v] to it and says,
"Save[w] me; you are my god."
[18] They know nothing, they understand[x] nothing;
their eyes[y] are plastered over so they cannot see,
and their minds closed so they cannot understand.
[19] No one stops to think,
no one has the knowledge or understanding[z] to say,

44:6 [e] Isa 41:21 [f] Isa 43:1 [g] Isa 41:4; Rev 1:8,17; 22:13
44:7 [h] Isa 41:22,26
44:8 [i] Isa 43:10 [j] Dt 4:35; 1Sa 2:2
44:9 [k] Isa 41:24
44:10 [l] Isa 41:29; Jer 10:5; Ac 19:26
44:11 [m] Isa 1:29 [n] Isa 42:17
44:12 [o] Isa 40:19; 41:6-7 [p] Jer 10:3-5; Ac 17:29
44:13 [q] Isa 41:7 [r] Ps 115:4-7 [s] Jdg 17:4-5
44:15 [t] ver 19 [u] 2Ch 25:14
44:17 [v] 1Ki 18:26 [w] Isa 45:20
44:18 [x] Isa 1:3 [y] Isa 6:9-10
44:19 [z] Isa 5:13; 27:11; 45:20

ISRAEL'S TRUE KING

The Old Testament stresses throughout its pages that there is only one God and that his name is *Yahweh* ("the LORD"). "I am the first and I am the last; apart from me there is no God," he declared (Isaiah 44:6). In the same verse God referred to himself as "Israel's King and Redeemer." Similarly in the New Testament, Jesus officially presented himself as both the King of Israel and the promised Messiah when he entered Jerusalem for the final time (Matthew 21:1–5). And he is our Redeemer who died for our sins and rose again to new life in order to open the door for our resurrection and glorification in the age to come (Romans 6:1–14; 1 Corinthians 15:12–28; Philippians 3:20–21; Hebrews 9:11–15).

"Half of it I used for fuel;
I even baked bread over its coals,
I roasted meat and I ate.
Shall I make a detestable[a] thing
from what is left?
Shall I bow down to a block of wood?"
20 He feeds on ashes,[b] a deluded[c] heart misleads him;
he cannot save himself, or say,
"Is not this thing in my right hand a lie?[d]"

21 "Remember[e] these things, O Jacob,
for you are my servant, O Israel.
I have made you, you are my servant;[f]
O Israel, I will not forget you.[g]
22 I have swept away[h] your offenses like a cloud,
your sins like the morning mist.
Return[i] to me,
for I have redeemed[j] you."

23 Sing for joy,[k] O heavens, for the LORD has done this;
shout aloud, O earth[l] beneath.
Burst into song, you mountains,[m]
you forests and all your trees,
for the LORD has redeemed Jacob,
he displays his glory[n] in Israel.

Jerusalem to Be Inhabited

24 "This is what the LORD says—
your Redeemer,[o] who formed you in the womb:

I am the LORD,
who has made all things,
who alone stretched out the heavens,[p]
who spread out the earth by myself,
25 who foils[q] the signs of false prophets
and makes fools of diviners,[r]
who overthrows the learning of the wise[s]
and turns it into nonsense,[t]
26 who carries out the words[u] of his servants
and fulfills[v] the predictions of his messengers,

who says of Jerusalem, 'It shall be inhabited,'
of the towns of Judah, 'They shall be built,'
and of their ruins, 'I will restore them,'[w]
27 who says to the watery deep, 'Be dry,
and I will dry up your streams,'
28 who says of Cyrus,[x] 'He is my shepherd
and will accomplish all that I please;
he will say of Jerusalem,[y] "Let it be rebuilt,"
and of the temple,[z] "Let its foundations be laid." '

44:19 [a] Dt 27:15
44:20 [b] Ps 102:9 [c] Job 15:31; Ro 1:21-23,28; 2Th 2:11; 2Ti 3:13 [d] Isa 59:3,4,13; Ro 1:25
44:21 [e] Isa 46:8; Zec 10:9 [f] ver 1-2 [g] Isa 49:15
44:22 [h] Isa 43:25; Ac 3:19 [i] Isa 55:7 [j] 1Co 6:20
44:23 [k] Isa 42:10 [l] Ps 148:7 [m] Ps 98:8 [n] Isa 61:3
44:24 [o] Isa 43:14 [p] Isa 42:5
44:25 [q] Ps 33:10 [r] Isa 47:13 [s] 1Co 1:27 [t] 2Sa 15:31; 1Co 1:19-20
44:26 [u] Zec 1:6 [v] Isa 55:11; Mt 5:18 [w] Isa 49:8-21
44:28 [x] 2Ch 36:22 [y] Isa 14:32 [z] Ezr 1:2-4

45 "This is what the LORD says to his anointed,
to Cyrus, whose right hand I take hold[a] of
to subdue nations[b] before him
and to strip kings of their armor,
to open doors before him
so that gates will not be shut:
2 I will go before you
and will level[c] the mountains[a];
I will break down gates of bronze
and cut through bars of iron.[d]
3 I will give you the treasures[e] of darkness,
riches stored in secret places,[f]
so that you may know[g] that I am the LORD,
the God of Israel, who summons you by name.[h]
4 For the sake of Jacob my servant,[i]
of Israel my chosen,
I summon you by name
and bestow on you a title of honor,
though you do not acknowledge[j] me.
5 I am the LORD, and there is no other;[k]
apart from me there is no God.[l]
I will strengthen you,[m]
though you have not acknowledged me,
6 so that from the rising of the sun
to the place of its setting[n]
men may know there is none besides me.[o]
I am the LORD, and there is no other.
7 I form the light and create darkness,
I bring prosperity and create disaster;[p]
I, the LORD, do all these things.

45:1 [a] Ps 73:23; Isa 41:13; 42:6 [b] Jer 50:35
45:2 [c] Isa 40:4 [d] Ps 107:16; Jer 51:30
45:3 [e] Jer 50:37 [f] Jer 41:8 [g] Isa 41:23 [h] Ex 33:12; Isa 43:1
45:4 [i] Isa 41:8-9 [j] Ac 17:23
45:5 [k] Isa 44:8 [l] Ps 18:31 [m] Ps 18:39
45:6 [n] Isa 43:5; Mal 1:11 [o] ver 5, 18
45:7 [p] Isa 31:2; Am 3:6

a 2 Dead Sea Scrolls and Septuagint; the meaning of the word in the Masoretic Text is uncertain.

8 “You heavens above, rain[q] down
righteousness;[r]
let the clouds shower it down.
Let the earth open wide,
let salvation[s] spring up,
let righteousness grow with it;
I, the LORD, have created it.

9 “Woe to him who quarrels[t] with
his Maker,
to him who is but a potsherd
among the potsherds on
the ground.
Does the clay say to the potter,[u]
‘What are you making?’
Does your work say,
‘He has no hands’?
10 Woe to him who says to his father,
‘What have you begotten?’
or to his mother,
‘What have you brought to
birth?’

11 “This is what the LORD says—
the Holy One of Israel, and its
Maker:
Concerning things to come,
do you question me about my
children,
or give me orders about the
work of my hands?[v]
12 It is I who made the earth
and created mankind upon it.
My own hands stretched out the
heavens;[w]
I marshaled their starry hosts.[x]
13 I will raise up Cyrus[a][y] in my
righteousness:
I will make all his ways straight.
He will rebuild my city
and set my exiles free,
but not for a price or reward,[z]
says the LORD Almighty.”

14 This is what the LORD says:
“The products of Egypt and the
merchandise of Cush,[b]
and those tall Sabeans—
they will come over to you
and will be yours;
they will trudge behind you,
coming over to you in chains.[a]
They will bow down before you
and plead[b] with you, saying,
‘Surely God is with you,[c] and there
is no other;
there is no other god.’ ”

45:8 [q] Ps 72:6; Joel 3:18 [r] Ps 85:11; Isa 60:21; 61:10, 11; Hos 10:12 [s] Isa 12:3
45:9 [t] Job 15:25 [u] Isa 29:16; Ro 9:20-21*
45:11 [v] Isa 19:25
45:12 [w] Ge 2:1; Isa 42:5 [x] Ne 9:6
45:13 [y] 2Ch 36:22; Isa 41:2 [z] Isa 52:3
45:14 [a] Isa 14:1-2 [b] Jer 16:19; Zec 8:20-23 [c] 1Co 14:25

15 Truly you are a God who hides[d]
himself,
O God and Savior of Israel.
16 All the makers of idols will be put
to shame and disgraced;[e]
they will go off into disgrace
together.
17 But Israel will be saved[f] by the LORD
with an everlasting salvation;[g]
you will never be put to shame or
disgraced,
to ages everlasting.

18 For this is what the LORD says—
he who created the heavens,
he is God;
he who fashioned and made the
earth,
he founded it;
he did not create it to be empty,[h]
but formed it to be inhabited[i]—
he says:
“I am the LORD,
and there is no other.[j]
19 I have not spoken in secret,[k]
from somewhere in a land of
darkness;
I have not said to Jacob’s
descendants,[l]
‘Seek me in vain.’
I, the LORD, speak the truth;
I declare what is right.[m]

20 “Gather together[n] and come;
assemble, you fugitives from the
nations.
Ignorant[o] are those who carry[p]
about idols of wood,
who pray to gods that cannot
save.[q]
21 Declare what is to be, present it—
let them take counsel together.
Who foretold[r] this long ago,
who declared it from the distant
past?
Was it not I, the LORD?
And there is no God apart from
me,[s]
a righteous God and a Savior;
there is none but me.

22 “Turn[t] to me and be saved,[u]
all you ends of the earth;[v]
for I am God, and there is no
other.
23 By myself I have sworn,[w]

a 13 Hebrew *him* *b* 14 That is, the upper Nile region

45:15 [d] Ps 44:24
45:16 [e] Isa 44:9,11
45:17 [f] Ro 11:26 [g] Isa 26:4
45:18 [h] Ge 1:2 [i] Ge 1:26; Isa 42:5 [j] ver 5
45:19 [k] Isa 48:16 [l] Isa 41:8 [m] Dt 30:11
45:20 [n] Isa 43:9 [o] Isa 44:19 [p] Isa 46:1; Jer 10:5 [q] Isa 44:17; 46:6-7
45:21 [r] Isa 41:22 [s] ver 5
45:22 [t] Zec 12:10 [u] Nu 21:8-9; 2Ch 20:12 [v] Isa 49:6,12
45:23 [w] Ge 22:16

my mouth has uttered in all
integrity[x]
a word that will not be revoked:[y]
Before me every knee will bow;
by me every tongue will swear.[z]
24 They will say of me, 'In the LORD
alone
are righteousness[a] and
strength.' "
All who have raged against him
will come to him and be put to
shame.[b]
25 But in the LORD all the descendants
of Israel
will be found righteous and will
exult.[c]

Gods of Babylon

46 Bel[d] bows down, Nebo
stoops low;
their idols are borne by beasts of
burden.[a]
The images that are carried[e] about
are burdensome,
a burden for the weary.
2 They stoop and bow down
together;
unable to rescue the burden,
they themselves go off into
captivity.[f]
3 "Listen[g] to me, O house of Jacob,
all you who remain of the house
of Israel,
you whom I have upheld since you
were conceived,
and have carried since your birth.
4 Even to your old age and gray hairs[h]
I am he,[i] I am he who will
sustain you.
I have made you and I will carry
you;
I will sustain you and I will
rescue you.

5 "To whom will you compare me or
count me equal?
To whom will you liken me that
we may be compared?[j]
6 Some pour out gold from their bags
and weigh out silver on the
scales;
they hire a goldsmith[k] to make it
into a god,
and they bow down and worship
it.[l]
7 They lift it to their shoulders and
carry[m] it;
they set it up in its place, and
there it stands.
From that spot it cannot move.
Though one cries out to it, it does
not answer;
it cannot save[n] him from his
troubles.

8 "Remember[o] this, fix it in mind,
take it to heart, you rebels.
9 Remember the former things,
those of long ago;[p]
I am God, and there is no other;
I am God, and there is none like
me.[q]
10 I make known the end from the
beginning,
from ancient times,[r] what is still
to come.
I say: My purpose will stand,[s]
and I will do all that I please.
11 From the east I summon a bird of
prey;
from a far-off land, a man to
fulfill my purpose.
What I have said, that will I bring
about;
what I have planned, that will I
do.
12 Listen[t] to me, you stubborn-
hearted,
you who are far from
righteousness.[u]
13 I am bringing my righteousness
near,
it is not far away;
and my salvation will not be
delayed.
I will grant salvation to Zion,
my splendor[v] to Israel.

The Fall of Babylon

47 "Go down, sit in the dust,
Virgin Daughter[w] of Babylon;
sit on the ground without a throne,
Daughter of the Babylonians.[b][x]
No more will you be called
tender or delicate.[y]
2 Take millstones[z] and grind[a] flour;
take off your veil.[b]
Lift up your skirts,[c] bare your legs,
and wade through the streams.
3 Your nakedness[d] will be exposed
and your shame[e] uncovered.
I will take vengeance;[f]
I will spare no one."

[a] *1* Or *are but beasts and cattle* [b] *1* Or *Chaldeans*; also in verse 5

45:23 [x] Heb 6:13 [y] Isa 55:11 [z] Ps 63:11; Isa 19:18; Ro 14:11*; Php 2:10-11
45:24 [a] Jer 33:16 [b] Isa 41:11
45:25 [c] Isa 41:16
46:1 [d] Isa 21:9; Jer 50:2; 51:44 [e] Isa 45:20
46:2 [f] Jdg 18:17-18; 2Sa 5:21
46:3 [g] ver 12
46:4 [h] Ps 71:18 [i] Isa 43:13
46:5 [j] Isa 40:18,25
46:6 [k] Isa 40:19 [l] Isa 44:17
46:7 [m] ver 1 [n] Isa 44:17; Isa 45:20
46:8 [o] Isa 44:21
46:9 [p] Dt 32:7 [q] Isa 45:5,21
46:10 [r] Isa 45:21 [s] Pr 19:21; Ac 5:39
46:12 [t] ver 3 [u] Ps 119:150; Isa 48:1; Jer 2:5
46:13 [v] Isa 44:23
47:1 [w] Isa 23:12 [x] Ps 137:8; Jer 50:42; 51:33; Zec 2:7 [y] Dt 28:56
47:2 [z] Ex 11:5; Mt 24:41 [a] Jdg 16:21 [b] Ge 24:65 [c] Isa 32:11
47:3 [d] Eze 16:37; Na 3:5 [e] Isa 20:4 [f] Isa 34:8

4 Our Redeemer—the LORD
Almighty is his name[g]—
is the Holy One of Israel.

47:4 [g] Jer 50:34

5 "Sit in silence, go into darkness,[h]
Daughter of the Babylonians;
no more will you be called
queen of kingdoms.[i]

47:5 [h] Isa 13:10 [i] Isa 13:19

6 I was angry[j] with my people
and desecrated my inheritance;
I gave them into your hand,[k]
and you showed them no mercy.
Even on the aged
you laid a very heavy yoke.

47:6 [j] 2Ch 28:9 [k] Isa 10:13

7 You said, 'I will continue forever—
the eternal queen!'[l]
But you did not consider these
things
or reflect[m] on what might
happen.[n]

47:7 [l] ver 5; Rev 18:7 [m] Isa 42:23,25 [n] Dt 32:29

8 "Now then, listen, you wanton
creature,
lounging in your security[o]
and saying to yourself,
'I am, and there is none besides
me.[p]
I will never be a widow[q]
or suffer the loss of children.'

47:8 [o] Isa 32:9 [p] Isa 45:6; Zep 2:15 [q] Rev 18:7

9 Both of these will overtake you
in a moment,[r] on a single day:
loss of children[s] and
widowhood.
They will come upon you in full
measure,
in spite of your many sorceries[t]
and all your potent spells.[u]

47:9 [r] Ps 73:19; 1Th 5:3; Rev 18:8-10 [s] Isa 13:18 [t] Na 3:4 [u] Rev 18:23

10 You have trusted[v] in your
wickedness
and have said, 'No one sees me.'[w]
Your wisdom[x] and knowledge
mislead[y] you
when you say to yourself,
'I am, and there is none besides
me.'

47:10 [v] Ps 52:7; 62:10 [w] Isa 29:15 [x] Isa 5:21 [y] Isa 44:20

11 Disaster will come upon you,
and you will not know how to
conjure it away.
A calamity will fall upon you
that you cannot ward off with a
ransom;
a catastrophe you cannot foresee
will suddenly[z] come upon you.

47:11 [z] 1Th 5:3

12 "Keep on, then, with your magic
spells
and with your many sorceries,[a]
which you have labored at since
childhood.
Perhaps you will succeed,
perhaps you will cause terror.

47:12 [a] ver 9

13 All the counsel you have received
has only worn you out![b]
Let your astrologers[c] come
forward,
those stargazers who make
predictions month by
month,
let them save[d] you from what is
coming upon you.

47:13 [b] Isa 57:10; Jer 51:58 [c] Isa 44:25 [d] ver 15

14 Surely they are like stubble;[e]
the fire will burn them up.
They cannot even save themselves
from the power of the flame.[f]
Here are no coals to warm anyone;
here is no fire to sit by.

47:14 [e] Isa 5:24; Na 1:10 [f] Isa 10:17; Jer 51:30,32,58

15 That is all they can do for you—
these you have labored with
and trafficked[g] with since
childhood.
Each of them goes on in his error;
there is not one that can save
you.

47:15 [g] Rev 18:11

Stubborn Israel

48 "Listen to this, O house of
Jacob,
you who are called by the name
of Israel
and come from the line of Judah,
you who take oaths in the name of
the LORD
and invoke[h] the God of Israel—
but not in truth[i] or
righteousness—

48:1 [h] Isa 58:2 [i] Jer 4:2

2 you who call yourselves citizens of
the holy city[j]
and rely[k] on the God of Israel—
the LORD Almighty is his name:

48:2 [j] Isa 52:1 [k] Isa 10:20; Mic 3:11; Ro 2:17

3 I foretold the former things[l] long
ago,
my mouth announced[m] them
and I made them known;
then suddenly I acted, and they
came to pass.

48:3 [l] Isa 41:22 [m] Isa 45:21

4 For I knew how stubborn[n] you
were;
the sinews of your neck[o] were
iron,
your forehead[p] was bronze.

48:4 [n] Dt 31:27 [o] Ex 32:9; Ac 7:51 [p] Eze 3:9

5 Therefore I told you these things
long ago;
before they happened I
announced them to you
so that you could not say,
'My idols did them;[q]

48:5 [q] Jer 44:15-18

my wooden image and metal
god ordained them.'
6 You have heard these things; look
at them all.
Will you not admit them?
"From now on I will tell you of new
things,
of hidden things unknown to
you.
7 They are created now, and not long
ago;
you have not heard of them
before today.
So you cannot say,
'Yes, I knew of them.'
8 You have neither heard nor
understood;
from of old your ear has not
been open.
Well do I know how treacherous
you are;
you were called a rebel[r] from
birth.
9 For my own name's sake I delay my
wrath;[s]
for the sake of my praise I hold it
back from you,
so as not to cut you off.[t]
10 See, I have refined you, though not
as silver;
I have tested you in the furnace[u]
of affliction.
11 For my own sake,[v] for my own
sake, I do this.
How can I let myself be
defamed?[w]
I will not yield my glory to
another.[x]

Israel Freed

12 "Listen[y] to me, O Jacob,
Israel, whom I have called:
I am he;
I am the first and I am the last.[z]
13 My own hand laid the foundations
of the earth,[a]
and my right hand spread out
the heavens;[b]
when I summon them,
they all stand up together.[c]
14 "Come together,[d] all of you, and
listen:
Which of ⌞the idols⌟ has foretold
these things?
The LORD's chosen ally
will carry out his purpose[e]
against Babylon;
his arm will be against the
Babylonians.[a]
15 I, even I, have spoken;
yes, I have called[f] him.
I will bring him,
and he will succeed in his
mission.
16 "Come near[g] me and listen to this:
"From the first announcement I
have not spoken in secret;[h]
at the time it happens, I am
there."
And now the Sovereign LORD has
sent[i] me,
with his Spirit.
17 This is what the LORD says—
your Redeemer,[j] the Holy One[k]
of Israel:
"I am the LORD your God,
who teaches you what is best for
you,
who directs[l] you in the way[m]
you should go.
18 If only you had paid attention[n] to
my commands,
your peace[o] would have been
like a river,
your righteousness[p] like the
waves of the sea.
19 Your descendants would have been
like the sand,
your children like its numberless
grains;[q]
their name would never be cut off[r]
nor destroyed from before me."
20 Leave Babylon,
flee[s] from the Babylonians!
Announce this with shouts of joy[t]
and proclaim it.
Send it out to the ends of the
earth;
say, "The LORD has redeemed[u]
his servant Jacob."
21 They did not thirst[v] when he led
them through the deserts;
he made water flow[w] for them
from the rock;
he split the rock
and water gushed out.[x]
22 "There is no peace," says the LORD,
"for the wicked."[y]

[a] *14* Or *Chaldeans*; also in verse 20

48:8 r Dt 9:7,24; Ps 58:3
48:9 s Ps 78:38; Isa 30:18 t Ne 9:31
48:10 u 1Ki 8:51
48:11 v 1Sa 12:22; Isa 37:35 w Dt 32:27; Jer 14:7,21; Eze 20:9,14,22, 44 x Isa 42:8
48:12 y Isa 46:3 z Isa 41:4; Rev 1:17; 22:13
48:13 a Heb 1:10-12 b Ex 20:11 c Isa 40:26
48:14 d Isa 43:9
48:14 e Isa 46:10-11
48:15 f Isa 45:1
48:16 g Isa 41:1 h Isa 45:19 i Zec 2:9,11
48:17 j Isa 49:7 k Isa 43:14 l Isa 49:10 m Ps 32:8
48:18 n Dt 32:29 o Ps 119:165; Isa 66:12 p Isa 45:8
48:19 q Ge 22:17 r Isa 56:5; 66:22
48:20 s Jer 50:8; 51:6, 45; Zec 2:6-7; Rev 18:4 t Isa 49:13 u Isa 52:9; 63:9
48:21 v Isa 41:17 w Isa 30:25 x Ex 17:6; Nu 20:11; Ps 105:41; Isa 35:6
48:22 y Isa 57:21

The Servant of the LORD

49:1 [z] Isa 44:24; 46:3; Mt 1:20 [a] Isa 7:14; 9:6; 44:2; Jer 1:5; Gal 1:15

49 Listen to me, you islands;
hear this, you distant nations:
Before I was born[z] the LORD called[a]
me;
from my birth he has made
mention of my name.

49:2 [b] Isa 11:4; Rev 1:16

2 He made my mouth like a
sharpened sword,[b]
in the shadow of his hand he hid
me;
he made me into a polished
arrow
and concealed me in his quiver.

49:3 [c] Zec 3:8 [d] Isa 44:23

3 He said to me, "You are my
servant,[c]
Israel, in whom I will display my
splendor.[d]"

49:4 [e] Isa 65:23 [f] Isa 35:4

4 But I said, "I have labored to no
purpose;
I have spent my strength in vain[e]
and for nothing.
Yet what is due me is in the LORD's
hand,
and my reward[f] is with my God."

49:5 [g] Isa 11:12 [h] Isa 43:4

5 And now the LORD says—
he who formed me in the womb
to be his servant
to bring Jacob back to him
and gather Israel[g] to himself,
for I am honored[h] in the eyes of the
LORD
and my God has been my
strength—
6 he says:
"It is too small a thing for you to be
my servant
to restore the tribes of Jacob
and bring back those of Israel I
have kept.

49:6 [i] Lk 2:32 [j] Ac 13:47*

I will also make you a light for the
Gentiles,[i]
that you may bring my salvation
to the ends of the earth."[j]

49:7 [k] Isa 48:17 [l] Ps 22:6; 69:7-9 [m] Isa 52:15

7 This is what the LORD says—
the Redeemer and Holy One of
Israel[k]—
to him who was despised[l] and
abhorred by the nation,
to the servant of rulers:
"Kings[m] will see you and rise up,
princes will see and bow down,
because of the LORD, who is
faithful,
the Holy One of Israel, who has
chosen you."

CHRIST WAS SHOWN TO HOLY MEN OF OLD, THAT THEY MIGHT BE SAVED BY FAITH IN HIS PASSION TO COME, JUST AS WE ARE SAVED BY FAITH IN HIS PASSION ALREADY PAST.

Augustine, *Catholic Theologian*

Restoration of Israel

49:8 [n] Ps 69:13 [o] 2Co 6:2* [p] Isa 26:3 [q] Isa 42:6 [r] Isa 44:26

8 This is what the LORD says:
"In the time of my favor[n] I will
answer you,
and in the day of salvation I will
help you;[o]
I will keep[p] you and will make you
to be a covenant for the people,[q]
to restore the land[r]
and to reassign its desolate
inheritances,

49:9 [s] Isa 42:7; 61:1; Lk 4:19 [t] Isa 41:18

9 to say to the captives,[s] 'Come out,'
and to those in darkness, 'Be
free!'
"They will feed beside the roads
and find pasture on every barren
hill.[t]

49:10 [u] Isa 33:16 [v] Ps 121:6; Rev 7:16 [w] Isa 14:1 [x] Isa 35:7

10 They will neither hunger nor thirst,[u]
nor will the desert heat or the
sun beat upon them.[v]
He who has compassion[w] on them
will guide them
and lead them beside springs[x] of
water.
11 I will turn all my mountains into
roads,

49:11 [y] Isa 11:16 [z] Isa 40:4

and my highways[y] will be raised
up.[z]

49:12 [a] Isa 43:5-6

12 See, they will come from afar[a]—
some from the north, some from
the west,
some from the region of
Aswan.[a]"
13 Shout for joy, O heavens;
rejoice, O earth;

49:13 [b] Isa 44:23 [c] Isa 40:1

burst into song, O mountains![b]
For the LORD comforts[c] his people
and will have compassion on his
afflicted ones.

14 But Zion said, "The LORD has
forsaken me,
the Lord has forgotten me."

[a] *12* Dead Sea Scrolls; Masoretic Text *Sinim*

A Light to the Gentiles

The Old Testament contains hundreds of predictions about the Messiah. There are so many details provided that some Jews who believe in Jesus refer to the New Testament as the "Renewed" Testament. Isaiah 49 is one of the passages in which the predictions are crystal clear.

Jesus was with the Father from the beginning (verse 1). Before God had created anything, he and Jesus already existed as two of the three persons who make up the triune God. Not only was Jesus *with* God, but he *is* God (John 1:1–2). Another inferred reference to Jesus being present with God in creation is Genesis 1:26, where God said, "Let *us* make man in *our* image." Paul in Colossians 1:16 stated that "by [Jesus] all things were created . . . All things were created by him and for him."

Jesus is God's servant (Isaiah 49:3), and his role is to bring glory to God rather than to himself (John 14:13; 17:4), to make God known to us (John 17:26). Just prior to one of our Lord's most impressive miracles—raising Lazarus from the dead—Jesus lifted his face toward heaven and told his Father that he would be performing the miracle so that those who would observe it might believe that God had sent him (John 11:41–42).

But Isaiah also prophesied that the Messiah would be rejected by his own people (Isaiah 53:3). And that is exactly what Jesus faced: He "came to that which was his own, but his own did not receive him" (John 1:11). The day Jesus rode into Jerusalem on a donkey at the end of his public ministry on earth he wept over the people who had turned away from his free offer of salvation (Luke 19:41–42). Instead of recognizing him as the promised Messiah, the crowds would soon chant "Crucify him!" (Luke 23:21).

Jesus has a message of salvation that is for all people everywhere (Isaiah 49:6). He *started* with Israel, offering to restore the chosen nation to God. But that was "too small a thing." The good news of Jesus is for everybody; he wants us to carry the message to the ends of the earth. God's purpose in redeeming humanity extends to every family lineage, every ethnic or tribal group, every nationality, because of the unifying and reconciling work of Jesus Christ, God's precious Son (1 Corinthians 12:13; Ephesians 3:6), who has destroyed "the dividing wall of hostility" (Ephesians 2:14) and has brought believers together "from every tribe and language and people and nation" (Revelation 5:9) and "made them to be a kingdom and priests to serve our God" (Revelation 5:10).

***Self-Discovery:** What is the extent of the influence God has allowed you to have on others? Is it possible that Jesus may have larger plans for your life? Is there something you can do that will help expand his kingdom beyond your city, beyond your state, beyond your country to the ends of the earth?*

GO TO DISCOVERY 190 ON PAGE 960

15 "Can a mother forget the baby at her breast
and have no compassion on the child she has borne?
Though she may forget,
I will not forget you![d]
16 See, I have engraved[e] you on the palms of my hands;
your walls[f] are ever before me.
17 Your sons hasten back,
and those who laid you waste[g] depart from you.
18 Lift up your eyes and look around;
all your sons gather[h] and come to you.
As surely as I live,[i]" declares the LORD,
"you will wear[j] them all as ornaments;
you will put them on, like a bride.

19 "Though you were ruined and made desolate[k]
and your land laid waste,[l]
now you will be too small for your people,[m]
and those who devoured you will be far away.
20 The children born during your bereavement
will yet say in your hearing,
'This place is too small for us;
give us more space to live in.'[n]
21 Then you will say in your heart,
'Who bore me these?
I was bereaved and barren;
I was exiled and rejected.[o]
Who brought these up?
I was left[p] all alone,
but these—where have they come from?' "

22 This is what the Sovereign LORD says:

"See, I will beckon to the Gentiles,
I will lift up my banner[q] to the peoples;
they will bring your sons in their arms
and carry your daughters on their shoulders.[r]
23 Kings[s] will be your foster fathers,
and their queens your nursing mothers.[t]
They will bow down before you with their faces to the ground;
they will lick the dust[u] at your feet.
Then you will know that I am the LORD;[v]
those who hope in me will not be disappointed."

24 Can plunder be taken from warriors,[w]
or captives rescued from the fierce[a]?

25 But this is what the LORD says:

"Yes, captives[x] will be taken from warriors,[y]
and plunder retrieved from the fierce;
I will contend with those who contend with you,
and your children I will save.[z]
26 I will make your oppressors[a] eat[b] their own flesh;
they will be drunk on their own blood,[c] as with wine.
Then all mankind will know[d]
that I, the LORD, am your Savior,
your Redeemer, the Mighty One of Jacob."

Israel's Sin and the Servant's Obedience

50 This is what the LORD says:

"Where is your mother's certificate of divorce[e]
with which I sent her away?
Or to which of my creditors
did I sell[f] you?
Because of your sins you were sold;[g]
because of your transgressions your mother was sent away.
2 When I came, why was there no one?
When I called, why was there no one to answer?[h]
Was my arm too short[i] to ransom you?
Do I lack the strength[j] to rescue you?
By a mere rebuke I dry up the sea,[k]
I turn rivers into a desert;
their fish rot for lack of water
and die of thirst.
3 I clothe the sky with darkness

[a] 24 Dead Sea Scrolls, Vulgate and Syriac (see also Septuagint and verse 25); Masoretic Text *righteous*

49:15 [d] Isa 44:21
49:16 [e] SS 8:6 [f] Ps 48:12-13; Isa 62:6
49:17 [g] Isa 10:6
49:18 [h] Isa 43:5; 54:7; Isa 60:4 [i] Isa 45:23 [j] Isa 52:1
49:19 [k] Isa 54:1,3 [l] Isa 5:6 [m] Zec 10:10
49:20 [n] Isa 54:1-3
49:21 [o] Isa 5:13 [p] Isa 1:8
49:22 [q] Isa 11:10 [r] Isa 60:4
49:23 [s] Isa 60:3,10-11 [t] Isa 60:16
49:23 [u] Ps 72:9 [v] Mic 7:17
49:24 [w] Mt 12:29; Lk 11:21
49:25 [x] Isa 14:2 [y] Jer 50:33-34 [z] Isa 25:9; 35:4
49:26 [a] Isa 9:4 [b] Isa 9:20 [c] Rev 16:6 [d] Eze 39:7
50:1 [e] Dt 24:1; Jer 3:8; Hos 2:2 [f] Ne 5:5; Mt 18:25 [g] Dt 32:30; Isa 52:3
50:2 [h] Isa 41:28 [i] Nu 11:23; Isa 59:1 [j] Ge 18:14 [k] Ex 14:22; Jos 3:16

and make sackcloth[l] its covering."

4 The Sovereign LORD has given me
an instructed tongue,[m]
to know the word that sustains the weary.[n]
He wakens me morning by morning,[o]
wakens my ear to listen like one being taught.
5 The Sovereign LORD has opened my ears,[p]
and I have not been rebellious;[q]
I have not drawn back.
6 I offered my back to those who beat[r] me,
my cheeks to those who pulled out my beard;
I did not hide my face
from mocking and spitting.[s]
7 Because the Sovereign LORD helps[t] me,
I will not be disgraced.
Therefore have I set my face like flint,[u]
and I know I will not be put to shame.
8 He who vindicates me is near.
Who then will bring charges against me?[v]
Let us face each other![w]
Who is my accuser?
Let him confront me!
9 It is the Sovereign LORD who helps[x] me.
Who is he that will condemn me?

50:3 [l] Rev 6:12
50:4 [m] Ex 4:12 [n] Mt 11:28 [o] Ps 5:3; 119:147; 143:8
50:5 [p] Isa 35:5 [q] Mt 26:39; Jn 8:29; 14:31; 15:10; Ac 26:19; Heb 5:8
50:6 [r] Isa 53:5; Mt 27:30; Mk 14:65; 15:19; Lk 22:63 [s] La 3:30; Mt 26:67
50:7 [t] Isa 42:1 [u] Eze 3:8-9
50:8 [v] Isa 43:26; Ro 8:32-34 [w] Isa 41:1
50:9 [x] Isa 41:10

JESUS FOCUS

THE SUFFERING SERVANT

In chapter 50 Isaiah pictures the Messiah as the Lord's Suffering Servant, as One who will be beaten and spit on by his accusers: "I offered my back to those who beat me, my cheeks to those who pulled out my beard. I did not hide my face from mocking and spitting" (verse 6). In the New Testament, Jesus' trial and execution are described in similar terms (Matthew 26:67; 27:26–31; Mark 15:15–20; Luke 23:16; John 19:1–3). Peter wrote that Jesus was wounded on our behalf (1 Peter 2:24; see also Isaiah 53:5), and Hebrews 2:10 describes Jesus' suffering and death for our sins as the ultimate statement of his love for us (see also John 3:16–17; 15:13).

They will all wear out like a garment;
the moths[y] will eat them up.
10 Who among you fears the LORD
and obeys the word of his servant?[z]
Let him who walks in the dark,
who has no light,
trust[a] in the name of the LORD
and rely on his God.
11 But now, all you who light fires
and provide yourselves with flaming torches,[b]
go, walk in the light of your fires[c]
and of the torches you have set ablaze.
This is what you shall receive from my hand:
You will lie down in torment.[d]

Everlasting Salvation for Zion

51 "Listen[e] to me, you who pursue righteousness[f]
and who seek the LORD:
Look to the rock from which you were cut
and to the quarry from which you were hewn;
2 look to Abraham,[g] your father,
and to Sarah, who gave you birth.
When I called him he was but one,
and I blessed him and made him many.[h]
3 The LORD will surely comfort[i] Zion
and will look with compassion on all her ruins;[j]
he will make her deserts like Eden,[k]
her wastelands like the garden of the LORD.
Joy and gladness[l] will be found in her,
thanksgiving and the sound of singing.

4 "Listen to me, my people;[m]
hear me, my nation:
The law will go out from me;
my justice[n] will become a light to the nations.[o]
5 My righteousness draws near speedily,
my salvation is on the way,[p]
and my arm[q] will bring justice to the nations.
The islands will look to me
and wait in hope for my arm.

50:9 [y] Job 13:28; Isa 51:8
50:10 [z] Isa 49:3 [a] Isa 26:4
50:11 [b] Pr 26:18 [c] Jas 3:6 [d] Isa 65:13-15
51:1 [e] Isa 46:3 [f] ver 7; Ps 94:15; Ro 9:30-31
51:2 [g] Isa 29:22; Ro 4:16; Heb 11:11 [h] Ge 12:2
51:3 [i] Isa 40:1 [j] Isa 52:9 [k] Ge 2:8 [l] Isa 25:9; 66:10
51:4 [m] Ps 50:7 [n] Isa 2:4 [o] Isa 42:4,6
51:5 [p] Isa 46:13 [q] Isa 40:10; 63:1,5

6 Lift up your eyes to the heavens,
look at the earth beneath;
the heavens will vanish like smoke,[r]
the earth will wear out like a garment[s]
and its inhabitants die like flies.
But my salvation will last forever,
my righteousness will never fail.

7 "Hear me, you who know what is right,[t]
you people who have my law in your hearts:[u]
Do not fear the reproach of men
or be terrified by their insults.[v]
8 For the moth will eat them up like a garment;[w]
the worm will devour them like wool.
But my righteousness will last forever,[x]
my salvation through all generations."

9 Awake, awake! Clothe yourself with strength,[y]
O arm of the LORD;
awake, as in days gone by,
as in generations of old.[z]
Was it not you who cut Rahab to pieces,
who pierced that monster[a] through?
10 Was it not you who dried up the sea,[b]
the waters of the great deep,
who made a road in the depths of the sea
so that the redeemed might cross over?
11 The ransomed[c] of the LORD will return.
They will enter Zion with singing;
everlasting joy will crown their heads.
Gladness and joy[d] will overtake them,
and sorrow and sighing will flee away.[e]

12 "I, even I, am he who comforts[f] you.
Who are you that you fear mortal men,[g]
the sons of men, who are but grass,[h]
13 that you forget[i] the LORD your Maker,[j]
who stretched out the heavens[k]
and laid the foundations of the earth,
that you live in constant terror[l] every day
because of the wrath of the oppressor,
who is bent on destruction?
For where is the wrath of the oppressor?
14 The cowering prisoners will soon be set free;
they will not die in their dungeon,
nor will they lack bread.[m]
15 For I am the LORD your God,
who churns up the sea[n] so that its waves roar—
the LORD Almighty is his name.
16 I have put my words in your mouth[o]
and covered you with the shadow of my hand[p]—
I who set the heavens in place,
who laid the foundations of the earth,
and who say to Zion, 'You are my people.' "

The Cup of the LORD's Wrath

17 Awake, awake![q]
Rise up, O Jerusalem,
you who have drunk from the hand of the LORD
the cup of his wrath,[r]
you who have drained to its dregs
the goblet that makes men stagger.[s]
18 Of all the sons[t] she bore
there was none to guide her;[u]
of all the sons she reared
there was none to take her by the hand.
19 These double calamities[v] have come upon you—
who can comfort you?—
ruin and destruction, famine[w] and sword—
who can[a] console you?
20 Your sons have fainted;
they lie at the head of every street,[x]
like antelope caught in a net.
They are filled with the wrath of the LORD
and the rebuke of your God.

21 Therefore hear this, you afflicted one,

a 19 Dead Sea Scrolls, Septuagint, Vulgate and Syriac; Masoretic Text / *how can I*

51:6 [r] Mt 24:35; 2Pe 3:10 [s] Ps 102:25-26
51:7 [t] ver 1 [u] Ps 37:31 [v] Mt 5:11; Ac 5:41
51:8 [w] Isa 50:9 [x] ver 6
51:9 [y] Isa 52:1 [z] Dt 4:34 [a] Ps 74:13
51:10 [b] Ex 14:22
51:11 [c] Isa 35:9 [d] Jer 33:11 [e] Rev 7:17
51:12 [f] 2Co 1:4 [g] Ps 118:6; Isa 2:22 [h] Isa 40:6-7; 1Pe 1:24
51:13 [i] Isa 17:10 [j] Isa 45:11 [k] Ps 104:2; Isa 48:13 [l] Isa 7:4
51:14 [m] Isa 49:10
51:15 [n] Jer 31:35
51:16 [o] Dt 18:18; Isa 59:21 [p] Ex 33:22
51:17 [q] Isa 52:1 [r] Job 21:20; Rev 14:10; 16:19 [s] Ps 60:3
51:18 [t] Ps 88:18 [u] Isa 49:21
51:19 [v] Isa 47:9 [w] Isa 14:30
51:20 [x] Isa 5:25; Jer 14:16

51:21 [y]ver 17; Isa 29:9

made drunk,[y] but not with wine.
22 This is what your Sovereign LORD says,

51:22 [z]Isa 49:25 [a]ver 17

your God, who defends[z] his people:
"See, I have taken out of your hand
the cup[a] that made you stagger;
from that cup, the goblet of my wrath,
you will never drink again.

51:23 [b]Isa 49:26; Jer 25:15-17,26, 28; 49:12 [c]Zec 12:2 [d]Jos 10:24

23 I will put it into the hands of your tormentors,[b]
who said to you,
'Fall prostrate[c] that we may walk[d] over you.'
And you made your back like the ground,
like a street to be walked over."

52:1 [e]Isa 51:17 [f]Isa 51:9 [g]Ex 28:2,40; Ps 110:3; Zec 3:4 [h]Ne 11:1; Mt 4:5; Rev 21:2 [i]Na 1:15; Rev 21:27

52 Awake, awake,[e] O Zion,
clothe yourself with strength.[f]
Put on your garments of splendor,[g]
O Jerusalem, the holy city.[h]
The uncircumcised and defiled
will not enter you again.[i]

52:2 [j]Isa 29:4

2 Shake off your dust;[j]
rise up, sit enthroned,
O Jerusalem.
Free yourself from the chains on your neck,
O captive Daughter of Zion.

52:3 [k]Ps 44:12 [l]Isa 45:13

3 For this is what the LORD says:

"You were sold for nothing,[k]
and without money[l] you will be redeemed."

4 For this is what the Sovereign LORD says:

52:4 [m]Ge 46:6

"At first my people went down to Egypt[m] to live;
lately, Assyria has oppressed them.

5 "And now what do I have here?" declares the LORD.

"For my people have been taken away for nothing,
and those who rule them mock,[a]"
declares the LORD.
"And all day long
my name is constantly blasphemed.[n]

52:5 [n]Eze 36:20; Ro 2:24*

52:6 [o]Isa 49:23

6 Therefore my people will know[o] my name;
therefore in that day they will know
that it is I who foretold it.
Yes, it is I."

7 How beautiful on the mountains
are the feet of those who bring good news,[p]
who proclaim peace,[q]
who bring good tidings,
who proclaim salvation,
who say to Zion,
"Your God reigns!"[r]

52:7 [p]Isa 40:9; Ro 10:15* [q]Na 1:15; Eph 6:15 [r]Ps 93:1

52:8 [s]Isa 62:6

8 Listen! Your watchmen[s] lift up their voices;
together they shout for joy.
When the LORD returns to Zion,
they will see it with their own eyes.

52:9 [t]Ps 98:4 [u]Isa 51:3 [v]Isa 48:20

9 Burst into songs of joy[t] together,
you ruins[u] of Jerusalem,
for the LORD has comforted his people,
he has redeemed Jerusalem.[v]

52:10 [w]Isa 66:18 [x]Ps 98:2-3; Lk 3:6

10 The LORD will lay bare his holy arm
in the sight of all the nations,[w]
and all the ends of the earth will see
the salvation[x] of our God.

52:11 [y]Isa 48:20 [z]Isa 1:16; 2Co 6:17* [a]2Ti 2:19

11 Depart,[y] depart, go out from there!
Touch no unclean thing![z]
Come out from it and be pure,[a]
you who carry the vessels of the LORD.

52:12 [b]Ex 12:11 [c]Mic 2:13

12 But you will not leave in haste[b]
or go in flight;
for the LORD will go before you,[c]

[a] 5 Dead Sea Scrolls and Vulgate; Masoretic Text *wail*

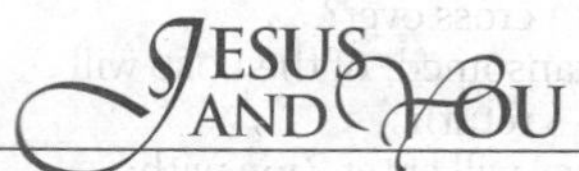

BEAUTIFUL FEET

There is great satisfaction and joy in carrying good news to people who desperately need it. Even the travel-worn, dirt-encrusted feet of the courier are "beautiful" to those anxiously awaiting his message of hope (Isaiah 52:7). The New Testament word for "good news" is *evangelion*, or gospel. Paul quoted this passage to describe people who carry the Good News about Jesus to others (Romans 10:15). Elsewhere, the apostle summarized the Good News of the gospel, the news that is still "of first importance" to us today: "that Christ died for our sins . . . that he was buried, that he was raised on the third day according to the Scriptures" (1 Corinthians 15:3–4).

52:12 the God of Israel will be your
dEx 14:19 rear guard.[d]

The Suffering and Glory of the Servant

52:13 [13] See, my servant[e] will act wisely[a];
eIsa 42:1 he will be raised and lifted up
fIsa 57:15; Php 2:9 and highly exalted.[f]
[14] Just as there were many who were
appalled at him[b]—
his appearance was so disfigured
beyond that of any man
and his form marred beyond
human likeness—
[15] so will he sprinkle many nations,[c]
and kings will shut their mouths
because of him.
For what they were not told, they
will see,
52:15 and what they have not heard,
gRo 15:21*; Eph 3:4-5 they will understand.[g]

53:1 **53** Who has believed our
hRo 10:16* message[h]
iJn 12:38* and to whom has the arm of the
LORD been revealed?[i]
[2] He grew up before him like a
tender shoot,
and like a root out of dry
ground.
He had no beauty or majesty to
53:2 attract us to him,
jIsa 52:14 nothing in his appearance[j] that
we should desire him.
[3] He was despised and rejected by
men,
a man of sorrows, and familiar
53:3 with suffering.[k]
kver 4,10; Lk 18:31-33 Like one from whom men hide
lPs 22:6; Jn 1:10-11 their faces
he was despised,[l] and we
esteemed him not.

53:4 [4] Surely he took up our infirmities
mMt 8:17* and carried our sorrows,[m]
nJn 19:7 yet we considered him stricken by
God,[n]
smitten by him, and afflicted.
53:5 [5] But he was pierced for our
oRo 4:25; 1Co 15:3; Heb 9:28 transgressions,[o]
pIPe 2:24-25 he was crushed for our
iniquities;
the punishment that brought us
peace was upon him,
and by his wounds we are
healed.[p]
[6] We all, like sheep, have gone astray,
each of us has turned to his own
way;

HIS HUMILIATION EXPIATES OUR PRIDE; HIS PERFECT LOVE ATONES FOR OUR INGRATITUDE; HIS EXQUISITE TENDERNESS PLEADS FOR OUR INSENSIBILITY.

John Newton, *British Pastor*

and the LORD has laid on him
the iniquity of us all.
[7] He was oppressed and afflicted,
yet he did not open his mouth;[q] 53:7
he was led like a lamb to the qMk 14:61
slaughter,
and as a sheep before her
shearers is silent,
so he did not open his mouth.
[8] By oppression[d] and judgment he
was taken away.
And who can speak of his
descendants?
For he was cut off from the land of 53:8
the living;[r] rDa 9:26; Ac 8:32-33*
for the transgression[s] of my sver 12
people he was stricken.[e]
[9] He was assigned a grave with the
wicked, 53:9
and with the rich[t] in his death, tMt 27:57-60
though he had done no violence,[u] uIsa 42:1-3
nor was any deceit in his mouth.[v] v1Pe 2:22*
[10] Yet it was the LORD's will[w] to crush[x] 53:10
him and cause him to wIsa 46:10
suffer,[y] xver 5 yver 3
and though the LORD makes[f] his zPs 22:30
life a guilt offering,
he will see his offspring[z] and
prolong his days,
and the will of the LORD will
prosper in his hand.
[11] After the suffering[a] of his soul, 53:11
he will see the light ⌞of life⌟[g] and aJn 10:14-18
be satisfied[h]; bRo 5:18-19
by his knowledge[i] my righteous
servant will justify[b] many,

[a] 13 Or *will prosper* [b] 14 Hebrew *you* [c] 15 Hebrew; Septuagint *so will many nations marvel at him* [d] 8 Or *From arrest* [e] 8 Or *away. / Yet who of his generation considered / that he was cut off from the land of the living / for the transgression of my people, / to whom the blow was due?* [f] 10 Hebrew *though you make* [g] 11 Dead Sea Scrolls (see also Septuagint); Masoretic Text does not have *the light ⌞of life⌟.* [h] 11 Or (with Masoretic Text) [11] *He will see the result of the suffering of his soul / and be satisfied* [i] 11 Or *by knowledge of him*

THE OBEDIENT SERVANT SUFFERS

Isaiah 53 is the most detailed prophecy in the Old Testament dealing with the Messiah's suffering. Each phrase and every word demands thoughtful attention. The passage was written in poetic form and is so replete with meaning that every time we read it we notice more than before. There are five sections to the poem. The first describes the *program* of God's Servant (Isaiah 52:13–15), followed by a discussion of his *person* (Isaiah 53:1–3), his *passion* (verses 4–6), his *patience* (verses 7–9) and finally his *provision* (verses 10–12).

The heart of the prophecy is in the third section, which describes the Servant's "passion" or suffering. Isaiah told us (using the past tense) that the Suffering Servant "took up our infirmities and carried our sorrows" (verse 4). The Hebrew word for "took up" connotes lifting something and carrying it away. Jesus *took up* our sin, and the necessary punishment, and carried them away (1 Peter 2:24). Recognizing our Savior's death for what it was means viewing his act of love as taking God's righteous judgment on *himself* for our sake (Romans 5:6–11). Isaiah referred to the Messiah as "stricken" by God for our sin (Isaiah 53:4).

In another graphic image Isaiah stated that God's Son was "pierced for our transgressions" (verse 5). The word here means "to pierce through," carrying the connotation of violent and excruciating torture. We can also recognize the reference to crucifixion—Jesus' hands and feet were literally "pierced through" with nails as he hung on the cross (John 20:25; Acts 2:23; see also John 19:34).

Isaiah also used an agricultural term, stating that Jesus was (or would be) "crushed" for our iniquities, like harvested grapes trampled in a vat until they have burst and the juice is released. In the "winepress" of God's wrath (Revelation 14:19), Jesus was crushed until his spirit was broken (Psalm 34:18) and his blood gushed forth in atonement for our sin (Romans 3:25; 1 John 2:2).

Jesus assumed God's punishment for our sin so that we could have peace with the Father (Romans 5:1; Ephesians 2:14–17; Colossians 1:19–20). Punishment and peace strike us as a strange combination. But it is only because Jesus was punished for our sin that we are restored to fellowship with the holy God and granted *shalom*—the peace for which God's people had waited for centuries.

Finally, we are *healed* because Jesus was *wounded*. This beautiful passage in Isaiah 53 includes a reminder of the desperate human condition that required Jesus to undergo such suffering: We are like sheep, lost and in rebellion against God. Verse 6 both begins and ends with a collective reference to all people. "We all" were lost—but God has laid on Jesus' shoulders the weight of the sin of "us all." But Jesus' suffering would not be the end of his story. Isaiah pointed, this time in future tense, beyond the anguish of the cross: "After the suffering of his soul, [Jesus] will see the light of life and be satisfied; by his knowledge my righteous servant will justify many, and he will bear their iniquities" (verse 11).

Self-Discovery: *Picture Jesus easing the burden of sin from your shoulders and carrying it away. Notice the feeling of lightness and the ease of movement, and consciously appreciate your freedom in Jesus.*

GO TO DISCOVERY 191 ON PAGE 963

> HE WHO MADE MAN, WAS MADE MAN . . . HE CRIED LIKE A BABE IN THE MANGER IN SPEECHLESS INFANCY—THIS WORD WITHOUT WHICH HUMAN ELOQUENCE IS SPEECHLESS.
>
> Augustine, *Catholic Theologian*

and he will bear their iniquities.
[12] Therefore I will give him a portion
among the great,[a][c]
and he will divide the spoils with
the strong,[b]
because he poured out his life unto
death,[d]
and was numbered with the
transgressors.[e]
For he bore the sin of many,
and made intercession for the
transgressors.

53:12 [c] Php 2:9 [d] Mt 26:28,38,39,42 [e] Mk 15:27*; Lk 22:37*; 23:32

The Future Glory of Zion

54 "Sing, O barren woman,
you who never bore a child;
burst into song, shout for joy,
you who were never in labor;
because more are the children[f] of
the desolate woman
than of her who has a husband,[g]"
says the LORD.
[2] "Enlarge the place of your tent,[h]
stretch your tent curtains wide,
do not hold back;
lengthen your cords,
strengthen your stakes.[i]
[3] For you will spread out to the right
and to the left;
your descendants will dispossess
nations
and settle in their desolate[j] cities.
[4] "Do not be afraid; you will not
suffer shame.
Do not fear disgrace; you will
not be humiliated.
You will forget the shame of your
youth
and remember no more the
reproach[k] of your
widowhood.
[5] For your Maker is your husband[l]—
the LORD Almighty is his name—
the Holy One of Israel is your
Redeemer;[m]
he is called the God of all the
earth.[n]
[6] The LORD will call you back[o]
as if you were a wife deserted[p]
and distressed in spirit—
a wife who married young,
only to be rejected," says your
God.
[7] "For a brief moment[q] I abandoned
you,
but with deep compassion I will
bring you back.[r]
[8] In a surge of anger[s]
I hid my face from you for a
moment,
but with everlasting kindness[t]
I will have compassion on you,"
says the LORD your Redeemer.
[9] "To me this is like the days of Noah,
when I swore that the waters of
Noah would never again
cover the earth.[u]
So now I have sworn not to be
angry[v] with you,
never to rebuke you again.
[10] Though the mountains be shaken[w]
and the hills be removed,
yet my unfailing love for you will
not be shaken[x]
nor my covenant[y] of peace be
removed,"

54:1 [f] Isa 49:20 [g] 1Sa 2:5; Gal 4:27*
54:2 [h] Isa 49:19-20 [i] Ex 35:18; 39:40
54:3 [j] Isa 49:19
54:4 [k] Isa 51:7
54:5 [l] Jer 3:14 [m] Isa 48:17
54:5 [n] Isa 6:3
54:6 [o] Isa 49:14-21 [p] Isa 50:1-2; 62:4,12
54:7 [q] Isa 26:20 [r] Isa 49:18
54:8 [s] Isa 60:10 [t] ver 10
54:9 [u] Ge 8:21 [v] Isa 12:1
54:10 [w] Ps 46:2 [x] Isa 51:6 [y] Ps 89:34

[a] 12 Or *many* [b] 12 Or *numerous*

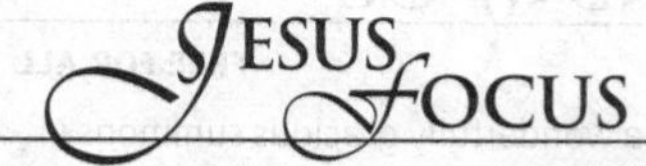

A NEW JERUSALEM

Isaiah adamantly declared that God would not reject Israel permanently. There would come a time, he predicted, when the ruined city of Jerusalem would be rebuilt and achieve a greatness far beyond anything it had previously enjoyed (Isaiah 54:11–12). And the day is coming when Jesus, God's promised Messiah, will return on the clouds with power and great glory (Matthew 24:30; 26:64; Revelation 1:7) to reign over his eternal kingdom. John's vision of the new Jerusalem in Revelation 21 echoes Isaiah's description. Both Isaiah and John foresaw a time when there will be no more sin and suffering, when God's people will live in peace with God and with one another. The new Jerusalem will be "the bride, the wife of the Lamb" (Revelation 21:9), a beautiful picture of the glorified community of God's people living in eternal unity with their precious Savior and Lord.

THE BLOOD OF CHRIST STANDS . . . NOT SIMPLY FOR GOD'S SORROW OVER SIN BUT FOR GOD'S WRATH ON SIN.

P. T. Forsyth, *British Theologian*

says the LORD, who has
compassion[z] on you.

11 "O afflicted[a] city, lashed by storms[b]
and not comforted,[c]
I will build you with stones of
turquoise,[a][d]
your foundations[e] with
sapphires.[b]
12 I will make your battlements of
rubies,
your gates of sparkling jewels,
and all your walls of precious
stones.
13 All your sons will be taught by the
LORD,[f]
and great will be your children's
peace.[g]
14 In righteousness you will be
established:
Tyranny[h] will be far from you;
you will have nothing to fear.
Terror will be far removed;
it will not come near you.
15 If anyone does attack you, it will
not be my doing;
whoever attacks you will
surrender[i] to you.
16 "See, it is I who created the
blacksmith
who fans the coals into flame
and forges a weapon fit for its
work.
And it is I who have created the
destroyer to work havoc;
17 no weapon forged against you
will prevail,[j]
and you will refute[k] every
tongue that accuses you.
This is the heritage of the servants
of the LORD,
and this is their vindication
from me,"
declares the LORD.

Invitation to the Thirsty

55 "Come, all you who are
thirsty,[l]
come to the waters;
and you who have no money,
come, buy[m] and eat!
Come, buy wine and milk[n]
without money and without
cost.[o]
2 Why spend money on what is not
bread,
and your labor on what does not
satisfy?[p]
Listen, listen to me, and eat what is
good,[q]
and your soul will delight in the
richest of fare.
3 Give ear and come to me;
hear me, that your soul may live.[r]
I will make an everlasting
covenant[s] with you,
my faithful love[t] promised to
David.[u]
4 See, I have made him a witness to
the peoples,
a leader and commander[v] of the
peoples.
5 Surely you will summon nations[w]
you know not,
and nations that do not know
you will hasten to you,
because of the LORD your God,

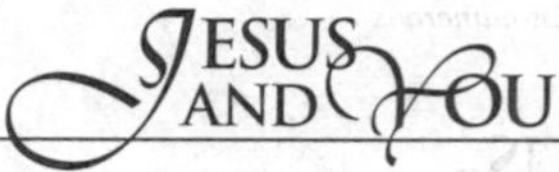

FREE FOR ALL

Isaiah offered a wonderfully gracious summons in chapter 55 to all who are hungry and thirsty: Come and eat and drink freely. He urged the people to seek God while he can be found (verse 6). The entire chapter is an invitation from God himself to his people to find spiritual refreshment for our souls. The Holy Spirit voiced a similar call in Revelation 22:17, where he urged all people to respond to the invitation to join the kingdom of God.

Isaiah also prophesied that from David's family line would come "a witness . . . leader and commander" for Jews and Gentiles alike (Isaiah 55:4–5)—fulfilled ultimately in our Lord Jesus Christ! Paul in Acts 13:34 quoted Isaiah 55:3, pointing out that the faithful love (or "the holy and sure blessings") God had promised to David have indeed been fulfilled in Jesus. God still offers the same enduring love and unconditional acceptance to all who believe in his Son Jesus (Romans 10:9–13).

54:10 [z] ver 8
54:11 [a] Isa 14:32 [b] Isa 28:2; 29:6 [c] Isa 51:19 [d] 1Ch 29:2; Rev 21:18 [e] Isa 28:16; Rev 21:19-20
54:13 [f] Jn 6:45* [g] Isa 48:18
54:14 [h] Isa 9:4
54:15 [i] Isa 41:11-16
54:17 [j] Isa 29:8 [k] Isa 45:24-25
55:1 [l] Jn 4:14; 7:37 [m] La 5:4; Mt 13:44; Rev 3:18 [n] SS 5:1 [o] Hos 14:4; Mt 10:8; Rev 21:6
55:2 [p] Ps 22:26; Ecc 6:2; Hos 8:7 [q] Isa 1:19
55:3 [r] Lev 18:5; Ro 10:5 [s] Isa 61:8 [t] Isa 54:8 [u] Ac 13:34*
55:4 [v] Jer 30:9; Eze 34:23-24
55:5 [w] Isa 49:6

[a] 11 The meaning of the Hebrew for this word is uncertain. [b] 11 Or *lapis lazuli*

COME!

Water and food are essential to life. But just as we need to eat and drink in order to sustain our physical bodies, so we require spiritual "bread" and "water" for vital spiritual lives. Jesus often used these elements to illustrate our spiritual hunger and thirst for God.

On one occasion he met a woman at the well in Sychar (John 4:1–26), a town in Samaria. The Lord, parched after his long journey, requested a drink of water. The woman was puzzled. She was a Samaritan, and this stranger was obviously a Jew—the two of them represented two groups of people who habitually despised and went out of their way to avoid one another! Why would this man even deign to speak to her, let alone stoop to ask her for something so mundane as a drink of water?

Jesus used the woman's questions to turn the conversation in an unusual direction. He advised her that he was able to supply her with water that would quench her thirst to the degree that she would never have to drink again—clearly using the metaphor of water to refer to eternal life with God (John 4:9–14).

In another instance Jesus proclaimed that he is the "bread of life" (John 6:35). He had just satisfied more than 5,000 famished people with only five barley loaves and two small fish (John 6:1–14). But Jesus wanted the crowd to focus on a reality beyond the obvious—that bread made from barley or any other grain will eventually spoil and that it cannot keep a person alive forever. Only Jesus Christ can do that: "He who comes to me will never go hungry, and he who believes in me will never be thirsty" (John 6:35).

Every one of us is born with a spiritual craving that will not be satisfied until we eat and drink the spiritual bread and water of life—Jesus himself. Through the prophet Isaiah God offered his people a gentle and simple invitation: "Come." (Isaiah 55:1).

Isaiah further advised the people how they could receive the blessings of spiritual refreshment from God. First, we have to be willing to *come* to the Father on his terms (verse 1). As long as we feed our souls with the junk food the world offers, we cannot experience wholesome nourishment from God. Second, we have to *listen* (verse 2) to God's promises as he reveals himself in the Bible. Third, we must *seek* him (verse 6)—now! God isn't waiting for a more agreeable day to show us his love, nor does he want us to delay beginning a relationship with him until after it is too late to respond to the invitation (Matthew 25:1–13; 2 Corinthians 6:1–2). Finally, we need to *call* on the Lord (verse 6), to invoke his help and wisdom in every decision and situation we face.

Jesus stands ready to satisfy our spiritual hunger and thirst as we open our lives to him. The book of Revelation tells us that he stands at the door to our lives, knocking and waiting for us to invite him in (Revelation 3:20). When we answer his knock, he will enter and share a meal with us that will be more satisfying than any earthly feast we could ever imagine!

Self-Discovery: *Recall a time when you were so thirsty that a glass of ice cold water was the only thing on your mind. Remember the satisfaction when you finally took your first swallow. Then imagine how it would feel for you never to be thirsty again. In what specific ways does Jesus satisfy your thirst?*

GO TO DISCOVERY 192 ON PAGE 965

the Holy One of Israel,
for he has endowed you with
splendor."[x]

55:5 [x]Isa 60:9

6 Seek the LORD while he may be
found;[y]
call[z] on him while he is near.
7 Let the wicked forsake his way
and the evil man his thoughts.[a]
Let him turn[b] to the LORD, and he
will have mercy[c] on him,
and to our God, for he will freely
pardon.[d]

55:6 [y]Ps 32:6; Isa 49:8; 2Co 6:1-2 [z]Isa 65:24
55:7 [a]Isa 32:7; 59:7 [b]Isa 44:22 [c]Isa 54:10 [d]Isa 1:18; 40:2

8 "For my thoughts are not your
thoughts,
neither are your ways my ways,"[e]
declares the LORD.
9 "As the heavens are higher than the
earth,[f]
so are my ways higher than your
ways
and my thoughts than your
thoughts.
10 As the rain[g] and the snow
come down from heaven,
and do not return to it
without watering the earth
and making it bud and flourish,
so that it yields seed for the
sower and bread for the
eater,[h]
11 so is my word that goes out from
my mouth:
It will not return to me empty,[i]
but will accomplish what I desire
and achieve the purpose[j] for
which I sent it.
12 You will go out in joy
and be led forth in peace;[k]
the mountains and hills
will burst into song before you,
and all the trees[l] of the field
will clap their hands.[m]
13 Instead of the thornbush will grow
the pine tree,
and instead of briers[n] the
myrtle[o] will grow.
This will be for the LORD's renown,[p]
for an everlasting sign,
which will not be destroyed."

55:8 [e]Isa 53:6
55:9 [f]Ps 103:11
55:10 [g]Isa 30:23 [h]2Co 9:10
55:11 [i]Isa 45:23 [j]Isa 44:26
55:12 [k]Isa 54:10,13 [l]1Ch 16:33 [m]Ps 98:8
55:13 [n]Isa 5:6 [o]Isa 41:19 [p]Isa 63:12

Salvation for Others

56 This is what the LORD says:

"Maintain justice[q]
and do what is right,
for my salvation[r] is close at hand
and my righteousness will soon
be revealed.
2 Blessed[s] is the man who does this,
the man who holds it fast,
who keeps the Sabbath[t] without
desecrating it,
and keeps his hand from doing
any evil."

56:1 [q]Isa 1:17 [r]Ps 85:9
56:2 [s]Ps 119:2 [t]Ex 20:8,10; Isa 58:13

3 Let no foreigner who has bound
himself to the LORD say,
"The LORD will surely exclude
me from his people."
And let not any eunuch[u] complain,
"I am only a dry tree."
4 For this is what the LORD says:

"To the eunuchs who keep my
Sabbaths,
who choose what pleases me
and hold fast to my covenant—
5 to them I will give within my
temple and its walls[v]
a memorial and a name
better than sons and daughters;
I will give them an everlasting name
that will not be cut off.[w]
6 And foreigners who bind
themselves to the LORD
to serve[x] him,
to love the name of the LORD,
and to worship him,
all who keep the Sabbath[y] without
desecrating it
and who hold fast to my
covenant—

56:3 [u]Jer 38:7 *fn*; Ac 8:27
56:5 [v]Isa 26:1; 60:18 [w]Isa 48:19; 55:13
56:6 [x]Isa 60:7,10; 61:5 [y]ver 2,4

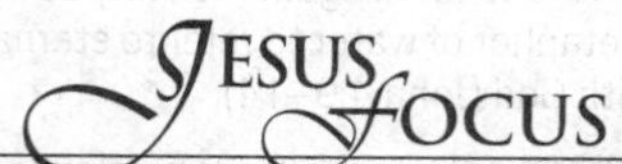

HOUSE OF PRAYER

Early on in the history of Israel foreigners were not permitted to participate in the formal worship of God (Exodus 12:43; Deuteronomy 23:1–8). Isaiah, however, described a time when God would open the temple as a house of prayer to anyone and everyone who desired to come and worship him (Isaiah 56:7). In the New Testament, Jesus was outraged that merchants had turned the temple into a "den of robbers" rather than honoring it as a "house of prayer for all nations" (Mark 11:17). New Testament Christians, following Jesus' example, welcomed both Jews and Gentiles into their fellowship, but they needed periodic reminders of the true nature and purpose of the church (Acts 10:34–36; 1 Corinthians 11:17–34; Ephesians 2:11–22; Revelation 2—3).

God's Word Will Accomplish Its Purpose

God reveals himself to us in both the natural and the spiritual realms. He is in complete control of the world, and whatever he determines happens just as he says. Rain from heaven falls down to earth, enabling the ground to produce food for the present, seeds for the future, and beauty in foliage and flowers. The same is true in the spiritual realm. God's actions always have a purpose, and that purpose is always "fruitful." God's Word produces "soul food" now, leaves seeds for a future spiritual harvest and creates inner beauty in the process: "As the rain and the snow come down from heaven, and do not return to it without watering the earth and making it bud and flourish, so that it yields seed for the sower and bread for the eater, so is my word that goes out from my mouth: It will not return to me empty, but will accomplish what I desire and achieve the purpose for which I sent it" (Isaiah 55:10–11).

God spoke the world into existence, and we see people, animals and the earth itself as evidence (Exodus 9:29; Psalm 24:1–2; 104). God speaks in the spiritual world as well. Both Old and New Testaments record incidents in which God spoke directly to human beings—to Adam and Eve in the Garden of Eden (Genesis 2:16), to Moses from the burning bush (Exodus 3:4), and to Isaiah and Peter in visions (Isaiah 1:1–2; Acts 10:9–16). And the Bible is God's means of speaking directly to us throughout the ages, of revealing his nature and of training us in right living (Psalm 119:9–11). The apostle Paul stated that "all Scripture is God-breathed and is useful for teaching rebuking, correcting and training in righteousness, so that the man of God may be thoroughly equipped in every good work" (2 Timothy 3:16).

God desired to relate to us even more personally, however, and so he sent his Son, Jesus, to connect with people and to reveal in the most intimate manner who our God really is (John 1:1–18; Hebrews 1:1–3). The apostle Paul declared that Jesus "is the image of the invisible God, the firstborn over all creation . . . He is before all things, and in him all things hold together" (Colossians 1:15,17).

Jesus, the embodiment of God's Word, also has a purpose. Like rain that falls on the earth, Jesus Christ brings eternal life (John 3:16–17) and bears much fruit for the Father (John 6:35–40; 10:27–30; 17:1–5), the fruit of lives brought into a saving relationship with the Lord. In the world around us, water doesn't evaporate until it has accomplished what God sent it to do—nourish the plant life so that fruit may sprout. In the same way Jesus, the Word *par excellence*, came down from heaven, "watered" his people spiritually and then returned to the Father with his mission accomplished. At the end of his life Jesus prayed to the Father, "I have brought you glory on earth by completing the work you gave me to do" (John 17:4).

Self-Discovery: *Picture the refreshment of a cooling afternoon shower on a sweltering summer day. Imagine lifting your arms and allowing your whole face and body to be soaked with the revitalizing water. Then think of those raindrops as spiritual blessings from Jesus.*

GO TO DISCOVERY 193 ON PAGE 969

56:7
[z] Isa 2:2
[a] Ro 12:1; Heb 13:15
[b] Mt 21:13*; Lk 19:46*
[c] Mk 11:17*

7 these I will bring to my holy
mountain[z]
and give them joy in my house of
prayer.
Their burnt offerings and sacrifices[a]
will be accepted on my altar;
for my house will be called
a house of prayer for all
nations.[b]"[c]
8 The Sovereign LORD declares—
he who gathers the exiles of
Israel:

56:8
[d] Isa 11:12; 60:3-11; Jn 10:16

"I will gather[d] still others to them
besides those already gathered."

God's Accusation Against the Wicked

56:9
[e] Isa 18:6; Jer 12:9

9 Come, all you beasts of the field,[e]
come and devour, all you beasts
of the forest!

56:10
[f] Eze 3:17
[g] Na 3:18

10 Israel's watchmen[f] are blind,
they all lack knowledge;
they are all mute dogs,
they cannot bark;
they lie around and dream,
they love to sleep.[g]
11 They are dogs with mighty
appetites;
they never have enough.

56:11
[h] Eze 34:2
[i] Isa 1:3
[j] Isa 57:17; Eze 13:19; Mic 3:11

They are shepherds[h] who lack
understanding;[i]
they all turn to their own way,
each seeks his own gain.[j]
12 "Come," each one cries, "let me get
wine!
Let us drink our fill of beer!

56:12
[k] Ps 10:6; Lk 12:18-19

And tomorrow will be like today,
or even far better."[k]

57:1
[l] Ps 12:1
[m] Isa 42:25
[n] 2Ki 22:20

57 The righteous perish,[l]
and no one ponders it in his
heart;[m]
devout men are taken away,
and no one understands
that the righteous are taken away
to be spared from evil.[n]

57:2
[o] Isa 26:7

2 Those who walk uprightly[o]
enter into peace;
they find rest as they lie in death.
3 "But you—come here, you sons of
a sorceress,

57:3
[p] Mt 16:4
[q] Isa 1:21

you offspring of adulterers[p] and
prostitutes![q]
4 Whom are you mocking?
At whom do you sneer
and stick out your tongue?
Are you not a brood of rebels,
the offspring of liars?

57:5
[r] 2Ki 16:4
[s] Lev 18:21; Ps 106:37-38; Eze 16:20

5 You burn with lust among the oaks
and under every spreading tree;[r]
you sacrifice your children[s] in the
ravines
and under the overhanging crags.

57:6
[t] Jer 3:9
[u] Jer 7:18
[v] Jer 5:9,29; 9:9

6 ⌊The idols⌋[t] among the smooth
stones of the ravines are
your portion;
they, they are your lot.
Yes, to them you have poured out
drink offerings[u]
and offered grain offerings.
In the light of these things,
should I relent?[v]

57:7
[w] Jer 3:6; Eze 16:16

7 You have made your bed on a high
and lofty hill;[w]
there you went up to offer your
sacrifices.
8 Behind your doors and your
doorposts
you have put your pagan
symbols.
Forsaking me, you uncovered your
bed,
you climbed into it and opened
it wide;

57:8
[x] Eze 16:26; 23:7
[y] Eze 23:18

you made a pact with those whose
beds you love,[x]
and you looked on their
nakedness.[y]
9 You went to Molech[a] with olive oil
and increased your perfumes.

57:9
[z] Eze 23:16,40

You sent your ambassadors[b][z] far
away;
you descended to the grave[c]
itself!
10 You were wearied by all your ways,

57:10
[a] Jer 2:25; 18:12

but you would not say, 'It is
hopeless.'[a]
You found renewal of your
strength,
and so you did not faint.

57:11
[b] Pr 29:25
[c] Jer 2:32; 3:21
[d] Ps 50:21

11 "Whom have you so dreaded and
feared[b]
that you have been false to me,
and have neither remembered[c] me
nor pondered this in your
hearts?
Is it not because I have long been
silent[d]
that you do not fear me?

57:12
[e] Isa 29:15; Mic 3:2-4,8

12 I will expose your righteousness
and your works,[e]
and they will not benefit you.

57:13
[f] Jer 22:20; 30:15

13 When you cry out[f] for help,

[a] 9 Or *to the king* [b] 9 Or *idols* [c] 9 Hebrew *Sheol*

let your collection ⌊of idols⌋ save
you!
The wind will carry all of them off,
a mere breath will blow them
away.
But the man who makes me his
refuge
will inherit the land[g]
and possess my holy
mountain."[h]

Comfort for the Contrite

14 And it will be said:

"Build up, build up, prepare the
road!
Remove the obstacles out of the
way of my people."[i]
15 For this is what the high and lofty[j]
One says—
he who lives forever,[k] whose
name is holy:
"I live in a high and holy place,
but also with him who is
contrite[l] and lowly in
spirit,[m]
to revive the spirit of the lowly
and to revive the heart of the
contrite.[n]
16 I will not accuse forever,
nor will I always be angry,[o]
for then the spirit of man would
grow faint before me—
the breath of man that I have
created.
17 I was enraged by his sinful
greed;[p]
I punished him, and hid my face
in anger,
yet he kept on in his willful
ways.[q]
18 I have seen his ways, but I will heal[r]
him;
I will guide him and restore
comfort[s] to him,
19 creating praise on the lips[t] of the
mourners in Israel.
Peace, peace,[u] to those far and
near,"[v]
says the LORD. "And I will heal
them."
20 But the wicked[w] are like the
tossing sea,
which cannot rest,
whose waves cast up mire and
mud.
21 "There is no peace,"[x] says my God,
"for the wicked."[y]

57:13 [g] Ps 37:9 [h] Isa 65:9-11
57:14 [i] Isa 62:10; Jer 18:15
57:15 [j] Isa 52:13 [k] Dt 33:27 [l] Ps 147:3 [m] Ps 34:18; 51:17; Isa 66:2 [n] Isa 61:1
57:16 [o] Ps 85:5; 103:9; Mic 7:18
57:17 [p] Isa 56:11 [q] Isa 1:4
57:18 [r] Isa 30:26 [s] Isa 61:1-3
57:19 [t] Isa 6:7; Heb 13:15 [u] Eph 2:17 [v] Ac 2:39
57:20 [w] Job 18:5-21
57:21 [x] Isa 59:8 [y] Isa 48:22

True Fasting

58 "Shout it aloud,[z] do not hold
back.
Raise your voice like a trumpet.
Declare to my people their
rebellion[a]
and to the house of Jacob their
sins.
2 For day after day they seek[b] me
out;
they seem eager to know my
ways,
as if they were a nation that does
what is right
and has not forsaken the
commands of its God.
They ask me for just decisions
and seem eager for God to come
near[c] them.
3 'Why have we fasted,'[d] they say,
'and you have not seen it?
Why have we humbled ourselves,
and you have not noticed?'[e]

"Yet on the day of your fasting, you
do as you please[f]
and exploit all your workers.
4 Your fasting ends in quarreling and
strife,[g]
and in striking each other with
wicked fists.
You cannot fast as you do today
and expect your voice to be
heard[h] on high.
5 Is this the kind of fast[i] I have
chosen,
only a day for a man to humble[j]
himself?
Is it only for bowing one's head like
a reed
and for lying on sackcloth and
ashes?[k]
Is that what you call a fast,
a day acceptable to the LORD?

6 "Is not this the kind of fasting I
have chosen:
to loose the chains of injustice[l]
and untie the cords of the yoke,
to set the oppressed[m] free
and break every yoke?
7 Is it not to share your food with the
hungry[n]
and to provide the poor
wanderer with shelter[o]—
when you see the naked, to clothe[p]
him,

58:1 [z] Isa 40:6 [a] Isa 48:8
58:2 [b] Isa 48:1; Tit 1:16; Jas 4:8 [c] Isa 29:13
58:3 [d] Lev 16:29 [e] Mal 3:14 [f] Isa 22:13; Zec 7:5-6
58:4 [g] 1Ki 21:9-13; Isa 59:6 [h] Isa 59:2
58:5 [i] Zec 7:5 [j] 1Ki 21:27 [k] Job 2:8
58:6 [l] Ne 5:10-11 [m] Jer 34:9
58:7 [n] Eze 18:16; Lk 3:11 [o] Isa 16:4; Heb 13:2 [p] Job 31:19-20; Mt 25:36

58:7 [q]Ge 29:14; Lk 10:31-32

and not to turn away from your
own flesh and blood?[q]
8 Then your light will break forth
like the dawn,[r]
and your healing[s] will quickly
appear;
then your righteousness[a] will go
before you,
and the glory of the LORD will be
your rear guard.[t]

58:8 [r]Job 11:17 [s]Isa 30:26 [t]Ex 14:19

9 Then you will call,[u] and the LORD
will answer;
you will cry for help, and he will
say: Here am I.

"If you do away with the yoke of
oppression,
with the pointing finger[v] and
malicious talk,[w]
10 and if you spend yourselves in
behalf of the hungry
and satisfy the needs of the
oppressed,[x]
then your light[y] will rise in the
darkness,
and your night will become like
the noonday.[z]

58:9 [u]Ps 50:15 [v]Pr 6:13 [w]Ps 12:2; Isa 59:13

58:10 [x]Dt 15:7-8 [y]Isa 42:16 [z]Job 11:17

11 The LORD will guide you always;
he will satisfy your needs[a] in a
sun-scorched land
and will strengthen your frame.
You will be like a well-watered
garden,[b]
like a spring[c] whose waters
never fail.

58:11 [a]Ps 107:9 [b]SS 4:15 [c]Jn 4:14

12 Your people will rebuild the
ancient ruins[d]
and will raise up the age-old
foundations;[e]
you will be called Repairer of
Broken Walls,
Restorer of Streets with
Dwellings.

58:12 [d]Isa 49:8 [e]Isa 44:28

13 "If you keep your feet from
breaking the Sabbath[f]
and from doing as you please on
my holy day,
if you call the Sabbath a delight[g]
and the LORD's holy day
honorable,
and if you honor it by not going
your own way
and not doing as you please or
speaking idle words,
14 then you will find your joy[h] in the
LORD,
and I will cause you to ride on
the heights[i] of the land
and to feast on the inheritance
of your father Jacob."
The mouth of the LORD
has spoken.[j]

58:13 [f]Isa 56:2 [g]Ps 84:2,10

58:14 [h]Job 22:26

58:14 [i]Dt 32:13 [j]Isa 1:20

Sin, Confession and Redemption

59 Surely the arm of the LORD is
not too short[k] to save,
nor his ear too dull to hear.[l]
2 But your iniquities have separated
you from your God;
your sins have hidden his face from
you,
so that he will not hear.[m]
3 For your hands are stained with
blood,[n]
your fingers with guilt.
Your lips have spoken lies,
and your tongue mutters wicked
things.
4 No one calls for justice;
no one pleads his case with
integrity.
They rely on empty arguments and
speak lies;
they conceive trouble and give
birth to evil.[o]
5 They hatch the eggs of vipers
and spin a spider's web.[p]
Whoever eats their eggs will die,
and when one is broken, an
adder is hatched.
6 Their cobwebs are useless for
clothing;
they cannot cover themselves
with what they make.[q]
Their deeds are evil deeds,
and acts of violence[r] are in their
hands.
7 Their feet rush into sin;
they are swift to shed innocent
blood.[s]
Their thoughts are evil thoughts;[t]
ruin and destruction mark their
ways.[u]
8 The way of peace they do not
know;
there is no justice in their paths.
They have turned them into
crooked roads;
no one who walks in them will
know peace.[v]

9 So justice is far from us,

59:1 [k]Nu 11:23; Isa 50:2 [l]Isa 58:9; 65:24

59:2 [m]Isa 1:15; 58:4

59:3 [n]Isa 1:15

59:4 [o]Job 15:35; Ps 7:14

59:5 [p]Job 8:14

59:6 [q]Isa 28:20 [r]Isa 58:4

59:7 [s]Pr 6:17 [t]Mk 7:21-22 [u]Ro 3:15-17*

59:8 [v]Isa 57:21; Lk 1:79

[a] 8 Or *your righteous One*

When God Seems Not to Answer

When it comes to our prayers, God generally answers in one of three ways: *yes, no* or *wait*. There is one situation in particular in which God could grant our request but often chooses to decline: when there is repeated, and unconfessed, sin in our life. "Surely the arm of the LORD is not too short to save, nor his ear too dull," Isaiah pointed out to the errant Israelites. "But your iniquities have separated you from your God; your sins have hidden his face from you, so that he will not hear. For your hands are stained with blood, your fingers with guilt. Your lips have spoken lies, and your tongue mutters wicked things" (Isaiah 59:1–3). While sin separates us from God, it does not separate God from us. Isaiah told us that *we* are the ones who have distanced ourselves.

There are always serious consequences when we are complacent about our wrongdoing, and one of these is the negative impact on our prayer life. Sin robs us of the joy we could claim if we would only realize that Jesus gave his life to atone for the corrupt attitudes and actions to which we so tenaciously cling. "Restore to me the joy of your salvation and grant me a willing spirit, to sustain me" implored David (Psalm 51:12). While sin may feel good for a time, in the end it leaves us entangled in misery. It can also lead to physical sickness and even premature death (1 Corinthians 11:27–30). And it can mean losing the things that mean the most to us (1 Corinthians 9:26–27).

More than anything else, however, sin is a gross insult to God. It is so offensive that no sinner can enter God's holy presence. The unrepentant will be tormented forever in hell (Matthew 8:12; 13:37–43; Galatians 5:19–21; Revelation 26:8–11). God himself paid an enormous price when his Son Jesus died for us, and because God hates evil so vehemently, so should we! It is not enough to admit that there are offenses in our lives; we need to turn away from wickedness and focus on right living. Sin must be confessed. In the words of Isaiah, "Our offenses are many in your sight, and our sins testify against us. Our offenses are ever with us, and we acknowledge our iniquities" (Isaiah 59:12).

We all struggle with sin. The difference in the case of a believer is the assurance that God has forgiven us and that our intimate relationship with him has been fully restored. If we confess our trespasses to him, he pledges that he *will* forgive and purify us (1 John 1:9).

Because our prayers are hindered by our sin, it makes sense that we devote part of our prayer time to analyzing our lives and identifying particular misdeeds that we have not confessed—wrong things that we have done as well as right things that we have left undone. As we look to Jesus, the One who was "tempted in every way, just as we are—yet was without sin," we may find the courage to approach God's throne of grace humbly and confidently, knowing that there we will "receive mercy and find grace to help us in our time of need" (Hebrews 7:15–16).

Self-Discovery: *Is there an unconfessed sin that might be hindering your prayer life? Why not take a moment to talk to the Lord about it?*

GO TO DISCOVERY 194 ON PAGE 973

and righteousness does not
reach us.

59:9 [w] Isa 5:30; 8:20

We look for light, but all is
darkness;[w]
for brightness, but we walk in
deep shadows.

59:10 [x] Dt 28:29 [y] Isa 8:15 [z] La 3:6

10 Like the blind[x] we grope along the
wall,
feeling our way like men without
eyes.
At midday we stumble[y] as if it were
twilight;
among the strong, we are like
the dead.[z]

59:11 [a] Isa 38:14; Eze 7:16

11 We all growl like bears;
we moan mournfully like doves.[a]
We look for justice, but find none;
for deliverance, but it is far away.

59:12 [b] Ezr 9:6 [c] Isa 3:9

12 For our offenses[b] are many in your
sight,
and our sins testify[c] against us.
Our offenses are ever with us,
and we acknowledge our
iniquities:

59:13 [d] Pr 30:9; Mt 10:33; Tit 1:16 [e] Isa 5:7 [f] Mk 7:21-22

13 rebellion and treachery against the
LORD,
turning our backs[d] on our God,
fomenting oppression[e] and revolt,
uttering lies[f] our hearts have
conceived.

59:14 [g] Isa 1:21 [h] Isa 48:1

14 So justice is driven back,
and righteousness[g] stands at a
distance;
truth[h] has stumbled in the streets,
honesty cannot enter.
15 Truth is nowhere to be found,
and whoever shuns evil becomes
a prey.
The LORD looked and was
displeased
that there was no justice.

59:16 [i] Isa 41:28 [j] Ps 98:1; Isa 63:5

16 He saw that there was no one,[i]
he was appalled that there was
no one to intervene;
so his own arm worked salvation[j]
for him,
and his own righteousness
sustained him.

59:17 [k] Eph 6:14 [l] Eph 6:17; 1Th 5:8 [m] Isa 63:3 [n] Isa 9:7

17 He put on righteousness as his
breastplate,[k]
and the helmet[l] of salvation on
his head;
he put on the garments[m] of
vengeance
and wrapped himself in zeal[n] as
in a cloak.

18 According to what they have done,
so will he repay
wrath to his enemies
and retribution to his foes;
he will repay the islands their
due.

59:19 [o] Isa 49:12 [p] Ps 113:3

19 From the west,[o] men will fear the
name of the LORD,
and from the rising of the sun,[p]
they will revere his glory.
For he will come like a pent-up
flood
that the breath of the LORD
drives along.[a]

59:20 [q] Ac 2:38-39; Ro 11:26-27*

20 "The Redeemer will come to Zion,
to those in Jacob who repent of
their sins,"[q]
declares the LORD.

59:21 [r] Isa 11:2; 44:3

21 "As for me, this is my covenant with
them," says the LORD. "My Spirit,[r] who is
on you, and my words that I have put in
your mouth will not depart from your
mouth, or from the mouths of your children, or from the mouths of their descendants from this time on and forever," says the LORD.

The Glory of Zion

60:1 [s] Isa 52:2 [t] Eph 5:14

60 "Arise,[s] shine, for your light[t]
has come,
and the glory of the LORD rises
upon you.

60:2 [u] Jer 13:16; Col 1:13

2 See, darkness covers the earth
and thick darkness[u] is over the
peoples,
but the LORD rises upon you
and his glory appears over you.

60:3 [v] Isa 45:14; Rev 21:24 [w] Isa 49:23

3 Nations[v] will come to your light,
and kings[w] to the brightness of
your dawn.

60:4 [x] Isa 11:12 [y] Isa 43:6 [z] Isa 49:20-22

4 "Lift up your eyes and look about
you:
All assemble[x] and come to you;
your sons come from afar,
and your daughters[y] are carried
on the arm.[z]
5 Then you will look and be radiant,
your heart will throb and swell
with joy;
the wealth on the seas will be
brought to you,
to you the riches of the nations
will come.

[a] 19 Or *When the enemy comes in like a flood, / the Spirit of the LORD will put him to flight*

60:6 [a] Ge 25:2 [b] Ge 25:4 [c] Ps 72:10 [d] Isa 43:23; Mt 2:11 [e] Isa 42:10
60:7 [f] Ge 25:13 [g] ver 13; Hag 2:3,7,9

6 Herds of camels will cover your land,
young camels of Midian[a] and Ephah.[b]
And all from Sheba[c] will come,
bearing gold and incense[d]
and proclaiming the praise[e] of the LORD.
7 All Kedar's[f] flocks will be gathered to you,
the rams of Nebaioth will serve you;
they will be accepted as offerings on my altar,
and I will adorn my glorious temple.[g]

60:8 [h] Isa 49:21
60:9 [i] Isa 11:11 [j] Isa 2:16 *fn* [k] Isa 14:2; 43:6 [l] Isa 55:5

8 "Who are these[h] that fly along like clouds,
like doves to their nests?
9 Surely the islands[i] look to me;
in the lead are the ships of Tarshish,[a][j]
bringing[k] your sons from afar,
with their silver and gold,
to the honor of the LORD your God,
the Holy One of Israel,
for he has endowed you with splendor.[l]

60:10 [m] Isa 14:1-2 [n] Isa 49:23; Rev 21:24 [o] Isa 54:8
60:11 [p] ver 18; Isa 62:10; Rev 21:25 [q] ver 5; Rev 21:26 [r] Ps 149:8
60:12 [s] Isa 14:2
60:13 [t] Isa 35:2 [u] Isa 41:19 [v] 1Ch 28:2; Ps 132:7
60:14 [w] Isa 14:2 [x] Isa 49:23; Rev 3:9

10 "Foreigners[m] will rebuild your walls,
and their kings[n] will serve you.
Though in anger I struck you,
in favor I will show you compassion.[o]
11 Your gates[p] will always stand open,
they will never be shut, day or night,
so that men may bring you the wealth of the nations[q]—
their kings[r] led in triumphal procession.
12 For the nation or kingdom that will not serve[s] you will perish;
it will be utterly ruined.
13 "The glory of Lebanon[t] will come to you,
the pine, the fir and the cypress together,[u]
to adorn the place of my sanctuary;
and I will glorify the place of my feet.[v]
14 The sons of your oppressors[w] will come bowing before you;
all who despise you will bow down[x] at your feet
and will call you the City of the LORD,
Zion[y] of the Holy One of Israel.

60:14 [y] Heb 12:22
60:15 [z] Isa 1:7-9; 6:12 [a] Isa 33:8 [b] Isa 4:2 [c] Isa 65:18
60:16 [d] Isa 49:23; 66:11,12 [e] Isa 59:20

15 "Although you have been forsaken[z] and hated,
with no one traveling[a] through,
I will make you the everlasting pride[b]
and the joy[c] of all generations.
16 You will drink the milk of nations
and be nursed[d] at royal breasts.
Then you will know that I, the LORD, am your Savior,
your Redeemer,[e] the Mighty One of Jacob.
17 Instead of bronze I will bring you gold,
and silver in place of iron.
Instead of wood I will bring you bronze,
and iron in place of stones.
I will make peace your governor
and righteousness your ruler.
18 No longer will violence be heard in your land,
nor ruin or destruction within your borders,
but you will call your walls Salvation[f]
and your gates Praise.

60:18 [f] Isa 26:1
60:19 [g] Rev 22:5 [h] Zec 2:5; Rev 21:23
60:20 [i] Isa 30:26 [j] Isa 35:10
60:21 [k] Rev 21:27 [l] Ps 37:11,22; Isa 57:13; 61:7 [m] Mt 15:13 [n] Isa 19:25; 29:23; Eph 2:10 [o] Isa 52:1

19 The sun will no more be your light by day,
nor will the brightness of the moon shine on you,
for the LORD will be your everlasting light,[g]
and your God will be your glory.[h]
20 Your sun[i] will never set again,
and your moon will wane no more;
the LORD will be your everlasting light,
and your days of sorrow[j] will end.
21 Then will all your people be righteous[k]
and they will possess[l] the land forever.
They are the shoot I have planted,[m]
the work of my hands,[n]
for the display of my splendor.[o]
22 The least of you will become a thousand,
the smallest a mighty nation.
I am the LORD;
in its time I will do this swiftly."

[a] 9 Or *the trading ships*

The Year of the LORD's Favor

61:1 [p] Isa 11:2 [q] Ps 45:7 [r] Mt 11:5; Lk 7:22 [s] Isa 57:15 [t] Isa 42:7; 49:9

61 The Spirit[p] of the Sovereign
LORD is on me,
because the LORD has anointed[q]
me
to preach good news to the
poor.[r]
He has sent me to bind up[s] the
brokenhearted,
to proclaim freedom for the
captives[t]
and release from darkness for
the prisoners,[a]

61:2 [u] Isa 49:8; Lk 4:18-19* [v] Isa 34:8 [w] Isa 57:18; Mt 5:4

2 to proclaim the year of the LORD's
favor[u]
and the day of vengeance[v] of our
God,
to comfort[w] all who mourn,
3 and provide for those who grieve
in Zion—
to bestow on them a crown of
beauty
instead of ashes,
the oil of gladness
instead of mourning,
and a garment of praise
instead of a spirit of despair.
They will be called oaks of
righteousness,
a planting of the LORD
for the display of his splendor.[x]

61:3 [x] Isa 60:20-21

61:4 [y] Isa 49:8; Eze 36:33; Am 9:14

4 They will rebuild the ancient ruins[y]
and restore the places long
devastated;
they will renew the ruined cities
that have been devastated for
generations.

61:5 [z] Isa 14:1-2

5 Aliens[z] will shepherd your flocks;
foreigners will work your fields
and vineyards.

61:6 [a] Ex 19:6; 1Pe 2:5 [b] Isa 60:11

6 And you will be called priests[a] of
the LORD,
you will be named ministers of
our God.
You will feed on the wealth[b] of
nations,
and in their riches you will
boast.

61:7 [c] Isa 40:2; Zec 9:12

7 Instead of their shame
my people will receive a double[c]
portion,
and instead of disgrace
they will rejoice in their
inheritance;
and so they will inherit a double
portion in their land,
and everlasting joy will be theirs.

61:8 [d] Ps 11:7; Isa 5:16 [e] Isa 55:3

8 "For I, the LORD, love justice;[d]
I hate robbery and iniquity.
In my faithfulness I will reward
them
and make an everlasting
covenant[e] with them.
9 Their descendants will be known
among the nations
and their offspring among the
peoples.
All who see them will acknowledge
that they are a people the LORD
has blessed."

61:10 [f] Isa 25:9; Hab 3:18 [g] Ps 132:9; Isa 52:1 [h] Isa 49:18; Rev 21:2

10 I delight greatly in the LORD;
my soul rejoices[f] in my God.
For he has clothed me with
garments of salvation
and arrayed me in a robe of
righteousness,[g]
as a bridegroom adorns his head
like a priest,
and as a bride[h] adorns herself
with her jewels.

61:11 [i] Ps 85:1

11 For as the soil makes the sprout
come up
and a garden causes seeds to
grow,
so the Sovereign LORD will make
righteousness[i] and praise
spring up before all nations.

[a] 1 Hebrew; Septuagint *the blind*

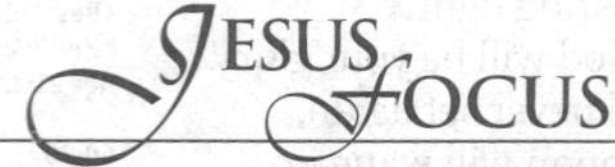

A GOOD PLACE TO START

When Jesus began his public ministry he quoted a dramatic passage from Isaiah (Isaiah 61:1–2; Luke 4:18–21). Immediately afterward he announced to the assembled worshipers in the synagogue that, without a doubt, "*today* this scripture is fulfilled in your hearing" (Luke 4:21, italics added). Later, when John the Baptist sought reassurance of Jesus' identity and divinity, our Lord again used the language of Isaiah, alluding both to Psalm 35:5–6 and to Isaiah 61:1: "The blind receive sight, the lame walk . . . the deaf hear, the dead are raised, and the good news is preached to the poor" (Matthew 11:5). How interesting that Jesus did not cite the "vengeance" portions of Isaiah 35 (verse 4) and 61 (verse 2). That day of vengeance will come when Jesus returns.

DISCOVERY 194

GOOD NEWS TO THE POOR

It was the Sabbath day in the town of Nazareth. Jesus was in town, and he attended the service at the synagogue. He stood up and read from the scroll, selecting Isaiah 61:1–2, a passage pointing ahead to God's coming Messiah. Following the reading he made a shocking (in the ears of the hearers even an audacious) announcement: "Today this scripture is fulfilled in your hearing" (Luke 4:21).

Isaiah's prophecies were meticulously detailed. He had written that the Messiah would be unlike any other prophet before him in what he *said* and in what he *did*. First, the Messiah would be anointed by God to preach good news to the poor (Isaiah 61:1). The word *anointed* comes from the same root as the title *Messiah*. God anointed individuals during Old Testament times as heralds of his Good News to his beloved people. Jesus came to do just that, but with one very distinctive difference: He came to tell the spiritually poor that God had chosen to adopt even them to become his own children (Matthew 5:3).

Second, the prophet had predicted that the Messiah would heal those with broken hearts and liberate captives and prisoners. God's chosen One would announce that God's favor had become available to humanity in and through the precious Son of God (Ephesians 2:8–9). Jesus came to minister to the needy, focusing on those who were hurting and shattered inside. Jesus recognized that his purpose was to seek out lost sinners—not those already complacent in their own perceived "righteousness"—and bring them back to the Father (Luke 15:1–32; 19:1–10).

Jesus referred again to Isaiah 61:1 shortly after reading the passage in the synagogue, this time to substantiate his claim to being the Messiah. John the Baptist, languishing in a prison cell, had apparently begun to doubt the authenticity of Jesus' Messianic role, having expected faster and more dramatic results from the Lord's ministry. Seeking reassurance, he sent two of his disciples to Jesus, asking, "Are you the one who was to come, or should we expect someone else?" (Luke 7:18–19). Jesus merely pointed to the evidence, instructing them to "go back and report to John what you have seen and heard: The blind receive sight, the lame walk, those who have leprosy are cured, the deaf hear, the dead are raised, and the good news is preached to the poor" (Luke 7:22).

Like John's disciples, we too have only to look at the evidence to see Jesus Christ at work in the world. At times he works directly, healing the sick by miraculous means. More often he ministers indirectly, through the selfless benevolence of us, his servants. Just as John's disciples were instructed to go back and report to him, so the love of Christ Jesus will be recounted around the world when God's people are faithful in their task. Paul addressed the church in Rome: "I thank my God through Jesus Christ for all of you, because your faith is being reported all over the world" (Romans 1:8). We as members of Christ's church are called to be his witnesses (Acts 1:8), both in word and in deed.

Self-Discovery: *Recall a time when Jesus has worked through you to alleviate someone else's pain. Then remember a time when you have felt his healing touch through the selfless love of a fellow believer.*

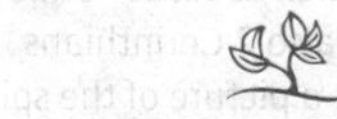

GO TO DISCOVERY 195 ON PAGE 977

Zion's New Name

62 For Zion's sake I will not
keep silent,
for Jerusalem's sake I will not
remain quiet,
till her righteousness[j] shines out
like the dawn,
her salvation like a blazing
torch.
2 The nations[k] will see your
righteousness,
and all kings your glory;
you will be called by a new name[l]
that the mouth of the LORD will
bestow.
3 You will be a crown[m] of splendor in
the LORD's hand,
a royal diadem in the hand of
your God.
4 No longer will they call you
Deserted,[n]
or name your land Desolate.
But you will be called Hephzibah,[a]
and your land Beulah[b];
for the LORD will take delight[o] in
you,
and your land will be married.[p]
5 As a young man marries a maiden,
so will your sons[c] marry you;
as a bridegroom rejoices over his
bride,
so will your God rejoice[q] over
you.
6 I have posted watchmen[r] on your
walls, O Jerusalem;
they will never be silent day or
night.
You who call on the LORD,
give yourselves no rest,
7 and give him no rest[s] till he
establishes Jerusalem
and makes her the praise of the
earth.

8 The LORD has sworn by his right
hand
and by his mighty arm:
"Never again will I give your grain[t]
as food for your enemies,
and never again will foreigners
drink the new wine
for which you have toiled;
9 but those who harvest it will eat it
and praise the LORD,
and those who gather the grapes
will drink it
in the courts of my sanctuary."
10 Pass through, pass through the
gates![u]
Prepare the way for the people.
Build up, build up the highway![v][w]
Remove the stones.
Raise a banner[x] for the nations.

11 The LORD has made proclamation
to the ends of the earth:
"Say to the Daughter of Zion,[y]
'See, your Savior comes![z]
See, his reward is with him,
and his recompense
accompanies him.' "[a]
12 They will be called[b] the Holy
People,[c]
the Redeemed[d] of the LORD;
and you will be called Sought After,
the City No Longer Deserted.[e]

God's Day of Vengeance and Redemption

63 Who is this coming from
Edom,
from Bozrah,[f] with his garments
stained crimson?
Who is this, robed in splendor,
striding forward in the greatness
of his strength?

"It is I, speaking in righteousness,
mighty to save."[g]

2 Why are your garments red,

a 4 *Hephzibah* means *my delight is in her.*
b 4 *Beulah* means *married.* *c* 5 Or *Builder*

62:1 j Isa 1:26
62:2 k Isa 52:10; 60:3 l ver 4,12
62:3 m Isa 28:5; Zec 9:16; 1Th 2:19
62:4 n Isa 54:6 o Jer 32:41; Zep 3:17 p Jer 3:14; Hos 2:19
62:5 q Isa 65:19
62:6 r Isa 52:8; Eze 3:17
62:7 s Mt 15:21-28; Lk 18:1-8
62:8 t Dt 28:30-33; Isa 1:7; Jer 5:17
62:10 u Isa 60:11 v Isa 57:14 w Isa 11:16 x Isa 11:10
62:11 y Zec 9:9; Mt 21:5 z Rev 22:12 a Isa 40:10
62:12 b ver 4 c 1Pe 2:9 d Isa 35:9 e Isa 42:16
63:1 f Am 1:12 g Zep 3:17

JESUS AND YOU

GOD'S "BEULAH" LAND

Isaiah described Israel as being married to God (Isaiah 62:4; Isaiah 54:5–8; see also Hosea 2:16–20). No longer would the nation be forsaken or desolate. Instead, Israel would be called *Hephzibah*, which means "my delight is in her," and her land *Beulah*, meaning "married." The name *Beulah* symbolizes the future prosperity of God's people, and it refers to temporal as well as eternal blessings. In the New Testament Jesus is referred to as the "bridegroom" (Matthew 9:15; 25:1–13; John 3:29), and the Christian church as Jesus' "bride" (Revelation 19:7; 21:2; see also 2 Corinthians 11:2). God uses marriage as a picture of the spiritual union between Christians and Jesus (Romans 7:1–4; Ephesians 5:25–33).

like those of one treading the
winepress?

63:3 [h] Rev 14:20; 19:15 [i] Isa 22:5 [j] Rev 19:13

3 "I have trodden the winepress[h]
alone;
from the nations no one was
with me.
I trampled them in my anger
and trod them down in my
wrath;[i]
their blood spattered my garments,[j]
and I stained all my clothing.
4 For the day of vengeance was in my
heart,
and the year of my redemption
has come.

63:5 [k] Isa 41:28 [l] Ps 44:3; 98:1 [m] Isa 59:16

5 I looked, but there was no one[k] to
help,
I was appalled that no one gave
support;
so my own arm[l] worked salvation
for me,
and my own wrath sustained
me.[m]

63:6 [n] Isa 29:9 [o] Isa 34:3

6 I trampled the nations in my anger;
in my wrath I made them drunk[n]
and poured their blood[o] on the
ground."

Praise and Prayer

63:7 [p] Isa 54:8

7 I will tell of the kindnesses[p] of the
LORD,
the deeds for which he is to be
praised,
according to all the LORD has
done for us—
yes, the many good things he has
done
for the house of Israel,
according to his compassion[q]
and many kindnesses.

63:7 [q] Ps 51:1; Eph 2:4

63:8 [r] Isa 51:4

8 He said, "Surely they are my
people,[r]
sons who will not be false to me";
and so he became their Savior.
9 In all their distress he too was
distressed,
and the angel of his presence[s]
saved them.
In his love and mercy he redeemed[t]
them;
he lifted them up and carried[u]
them
all the days of old.

63:9 [s] Ex 33:14 [t] Dt 7:7-8 [u] Dt 1:31

63:10 [v] Ps 78:40 [w] Ps 51:11; Ac 7:51; Eph 4:30 [x] Ps 106:40

10 Yet they rebelled[v]
and grieved his Holy Spirit.[w]
So he turned and became their
enemy[x]
and he himself fought against
them.

11 Then his people recalled[a] the days
of old,
the days of Moses and his
people—
where is he who brought them
through the sea,[y]
with the shepherd of his flock?
Where is he who set
his Holy Spirit[z] among them,

63:11 [y] Ex 14:22,30 [z] Nu 11:17

12 who sent his glorious arm of power
to be at Moses' right hand,
who divided the waters[a] before
them,
to gain for himself everlasting
renown,

63:12 [a] Ex 14:21-22; Isa 11:15

13 who led[b] them through the depths?
Like a horse in open country,
they did not stumble;[c]

63:13 [b] Dt 32:12 [c] Jer 31:9

14 like cattle that go down to the plain,
they were given rest by the Spirit
of the LORD.
This is how you guided your people
to make for yourself a glorious
name.

15 Look down from heaven[d] and see
from your lofty throne,[e] holy and
glorious.
Where are your zeal[f] and your
might?
Your tenderness and
compassion[g] are withheld
from us.
16 But you are our Father,

63:15 [d] Dt 26:15; Ps 80:14 [e] Ps 123:1 [f] Isa 9:7; 26:11 [g] Jer 31:20; Hos 11:8

[a] 11 Or *But may he recall*

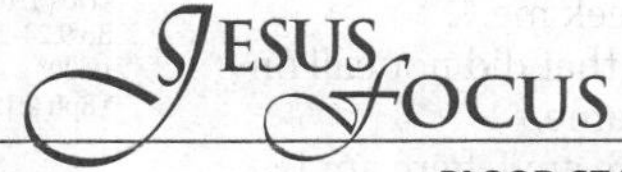

BLOOD-STAINED CLOTHES

When Jesus returns in glory he will triumph over his enemies (Isaiah 63:3–6). God's "day of vengeance" (Isaiah 61:2) will be fulfilled when the bloodstained Savior treads the "winepress" of God (Isaiah 63:3). The image recorded in Isaiah is identical to John's vision in Revelation 19:13–16: "He is dressed in a robe dipped in blood, and his name is the Word of God . . . He treads the winepress of the fury of the wrath of God Almighty . . . He has this name written: KING OF KINGS AND LORD OF LORDS." Both Isaiah and John knew that God's promised Messiah would redeem both his own people and all of creation from the consequences of sin (Romans 8:18–25).

though Abraham does not know
us
or Israel acknowledge[h] us;
you, O LORD, are our Father,
our Redeemer[i] from of old is
your name.

63:16 [h] Job 14:21 [i] Isa 41:14; 44:6

[17] Why, O LORD, do you make us
wander from your ways
and harden our hearts so we do
not revere[j] you?
Return[k] for the sake of your
servants,
the tribes that are your
inheritance.

63:17 [j] Isa 29:13 [k] Nu 10:36

[18] For a little while your people
possessed your holy place,
but now our enemies have
trampled down your
sanctuary.[l]

63:18 [l] Ps 74:3-8

[19] We are yours from of old;
but you have not ruled over them,
they have not been called by
your name.[a]

64 Oh, that you would rend the
heavens[m] and come down,[n]
that the mountains[o] would
tremble before you!

64:1 [m] Ps 18:9; 144:5 [n] Mic 1:3 [o] Ex 19:18

[2] As when fire sets twigs ablaze
and causes water to boil,
come down to make your name
known to your enemies
and cause the nations to quake[p]
before you!

64:2 [p] Ps 99:1; Jer 5:22; 33:9

[3] For when you did awesome[q] things
that we did not expect,
you came down, and the
mountains trembled before
you.

64:3 [q] Ps 65:5

[4] Since ancient times no one has
heard,
no ear has perceived,
no eye has seen any God besides
you,
who acts on behalf of those who
wait for him.[r]

64:4 [r] Isa 30:18; 1Co 2:9*

[5] You come to the help of those who
gladly do right,[s]
who remember your ways.
But when we continued to sin
against them,
you were angry.
How then can we be saved?

64:5 [s] Isa 26:8

[6] All of us have become like one who
is unclean,
and all our righteous[t] acts are
like filthy rags;
we all shrivel up like a leaf,[u]
and like the wind our sins sweep
us away.

64:6 [t] Isa 46:12; 48:1 [u] Ps 90:5-6

[7] No one[v] calls on your name
or strives to lay hold of you;
for you have hidden[w] your face
from us
and made us waste away[x]
because of our sins.

64:7 [v] Isa 59:4 [w] Dt 31:18; Isa 1:15; 54:8 [x] Isa 9:18

[8] Yet, O LORD, you are our Father.[y]
We are the clay, you are the
potter;[z]
we are all the work of your hand.

64:8 [y] Isa 63:16 [z] Isa 29:16

[9] Do not be angry[a] beyond measure,
O LORD;
do not remember our sins[b]
forever.
Oh, look upon us, we pray,
for we are all your people.

64:9 [a] Isa 57:17; 60:10 [b] Isa 43:25

[10] Your sacred cities have become a
desert;
even Zion is a desert, Jerusalem
a desolation.
[11] Our holy and glorious temple,[c]
where our fathers praised
you,
has been burned with fire,
and all that we treasured[d] lies in
ruins.

64:11 [c] Ps 74:3-7 [d] La 1:7,10

[12] After all this, O LORD, will you hold
yourself back?[e]
Will you keep silent[f] and punish
us beyond measure?

64:12 [e] Ps 74:10-11; Isa 42:14 [f] Ps 83:1

Judgment and Salvation

65 "I revealed myself to those
who did not ask for me;
I was found by those who did
not seek me.[g]
To a nation[h] that did not call on
my name,
I said, 'Here am I, here am I.'

65:1 [g] Hos 1:10; Ro 9:24-26; 10:20* [h] Eph 2:12

[2] All day long I have held out my
hands
to an obstinate people,[i]
who walk in ways not good,
pursuing their own
imaginations[j]—

65:2 [i] Isa 1:2,23; Ro 10:21* [j] Ps 81:11-12; Isa 66:18

[3] a people who continually provoke
me
to my very face,[k]
offering sacrifices in gardens[l]
and burning incense on altars of
brick;

65:3 [k] Job 1:11 [l] Isa 1:29

[4] who sit among the graves

[a] 19 Or *We are like those you have never ruled, / like those never called by your name*

DISCOVERY 195

GOD'S INITIATIVE

It is obvious from Scripture that God is the One who initiates a relationship with us rather than the other way around. God is the first to speak, the first to listen, the first to act and the first to love. The apostle John stated it this way: "This is love: not that we loved God, but that he loved us" (1 John 4:10). From the beginning of creation to the end of humanity's temporal existence, when he will fulfill his promise to create a new heaven and a new earth (Genesis 1:1; Revelation 21:2), God takes the first step.

Isaiah was explicit on this subject: Humankind does not ask for God's help or presence or seek him out. Isaiah opened chapter 65 with these poignant words of God: "I revealed myself to those who did not ask for me; I was found by those who did not seek me. To a nation that did not call on my name, I said, 'Here am I, here am I' " (verse 1).

Paul later wrote to the church in Rome: "There is no one righteous, not even one; there is no one who understands, no one who seeks God. All have turned away, they have together become worthless; there is no one who does good, not even one" (Romans 3:10–12). Paul used some pretty strong language to make the point that we can do nothing to impress God. When we try, we are really only seeking our own gratification. The inescapable reality is that God had to come looking for us, like a shepherd who had lost a sheep (Luke 15:1–7) or a woman who had lost a silver coin (Luke 15:8–10).

Jesus also took the initiative to meet with people. Once he told a man named Zacchaeus that "the Son of Man came to seek and to save what was lost" (Luke 19:10). Jesus took the first step by reaching out to Zacchaeus, and Zacchaeus responded with joy and obedience. Sadly, however, not everyone took Jesus seriously: "He was in the world, and though the world was made through him, the world did not recognize him. He came to that which was his own, but his own did not receive him" (John 1:10–11).

Jesus' greatest desire is for us to respond as Zacchaeus did—to love him wholeheartedly and put into practice what he teaches. It is just that simple: God initiates, and all we need to do is respond in grateful obedience and humble service. "Yet to all who received him," the apostle John continued in the beautiful first chapter of his Gospel, "to those who believed in his name, he gave the right to become children of God—children born not of natural descent, nor of human decision or a husband's will, but born of God" (John 1:12–13).

***Self-Discovery:** Does the thought of God pursuing you as the divine Seeker fill you with fear, or with relief? Picture in your mind's eye the all-knowing, all-loving Lord meeting you face-to-face. What would he say to you? What would you say to him?*

GO TO DISCOVERY 196 ON PAGE 984

and spend their nights keeping
secret vigil;
65:4 [m] Lev 11:7
who eat the flesh of pigs,[m]
and whose pots hold broth of
unclean meat;
5 who say, 'Keep away; don't come
near me,
65:5 [n] Mt 9:11; Lk 7:39; 18:9-12
for I am too sacred[n] for you!'
Such people are smoke in my
nostrils,
a fire that keeps burning all day.
65:6 [o] Ps 50:3 [p] Jer 16:18 [q] Ps 79:12
6 "See, it stands written before me:
I will not keep silent[o] but will
pay back[p] in full;
I will pay it back into their
laps[q]—
65:7 [r] Isa 22:14 [s] Ex 20:5 [t] Isa 57:7
7 both your sins[r] and the sins of your
fathers,"[s]
says the LORD.
"Because they burned sacrifices on
the mountains
and defied me on the hills,[t]
I will measure into their laps
the full payment for their former
deeds."

8 This is what the LORD says:

"As when juice is still found in a
cluster of grapes
and men say, 'Don't destroy it,
there is yet some good in it,'
so will I do in behalf of my
servants;
I will not destroy them all.
65:9 [u] Isa 45:19 [v] Am 9:11-15 [w] Isa 32:18
9 I will bring forth descendants[u]
from Jacob,
and from Judah those who will
possess[v] my mountains;
my chosen people will inherit them,
and there will my servants live.[w]
65:10 [x] Isa 35:2 [y] Jos 7:26 [z] Isa 51:1
10 Sharon[x] will become a pasture for
flocks,
and the Valley of Achor[y] a
resting place for herds,
for my people who seek[z] me.

65:11 [a] Dt 29:24-25; Isa 1:28
11 "But as for you who forsake[a] the
LORD
and forget my holy mountain,
who spread a table for Fortune
and fill bowls of mixed wine for
Destiny,
65:12 [b] Isa 27:1 [c] Pr 1:24-25; Isa 41:28; 66:4 [d] 2Ch 36:15-16; Jer 7:13
12 I will destine you for the sword,[b]
and you will all bend down for
the slaughter;
for I called but you did not answer,[c]
I spoke but you did not listen.[d]
You did evil in my sight
and chose what displeases me."

13 Therefore this is what the Sovereign
LORD says:

65:13 [e] Isa 1:19 [f] Isa 41:17 [g] Isa 44:9
"My servants will eat,[e]
but you will go hungry;
my servants will drink,
but you will go thirsty;[f]
my servants will rejoice,
but you will be put to shame.[g]
14 My servants will sing
out of the joy of their hearts,
65:14 [h] Mt 8:12; Lk 13:28
but you will cry out[h]
from anguish of heart
and wail in brokenness of spirit.
15 You will leave your name
65:15 [i] Zec 8:13
to my chosen ones as a curse;[i]
the Sovereign LORD will put you to
death,
but to his servants he will give
another name.
16 Whoever invokes a blessing in the
land
65:16 [j] Ps 31:5 [k] Isa 19:18
will do so by the God of truth;[j]
he who takes an oath in the land
will swear[k] by the God of truth.
For the past troubles will be
forgotten
and hidden from my eyes.

New Heavens and a New Earth

17 "Behold, I will create
65:17 [l] Isa 66:22; 2Pe 3:13 [m] Isa 43:18; Jer 3:16
new heavens and a new earth.[l]
The former things will not be
remembered,[m]
nor will they come to mind.
65:18 [n] Ps 98:1-9; Isa 25:9
18 But be glad and rejoice[n] forever
in what I will create,
for I will create Jerusalem to be a
delight
and its people a joy.
65:19 [o] Isa 35:10; 62:5 [p] Isa 25:8; Rev 7:17
19 I will rejoice[o] over Jerusalem
and take delight in my people;
the sound of weeping and of
crying[p]
will be heard in it no more.

20 "Never again will there be in it
an infant who lives but a few
days,
65:20 [q] Ecc 8:13
or an old man who does not live
out his years;[q]
he who dies at a hundred
will be thought a mere youth;
he who fails to reach[a] a hundred

[a] 20 Or / *the sinner who reaches*

will be considered accursed.

65:21 [r] Isa 32:18 [s] Isa 37:30; Am 9:14

21 They will build houses[r] and dwell
in them;
they will plant vineyards and eat
their fruit.[s]
22 No longer will they build houses
and others live in them,
or plant and others eat.

65:22 [t] Ps 92:12-14 [u] Ps 21:4; 91:16

For as the days of a tree,[t]
so will be the days[u] of my people;
my chosen ones will long enjoy
the works of their hands.
23 They will not toil in vain
or bear children doomed to
misfortune;

65:23 [v] Dt 28:3-12; Isa 61:9 [w] Ac 2:39

for they will be a people blessed[v] by
the LORD,
they and their descendants[w]
with them.

65:24 [x] Isa 55:6 [y] Da 9:20-23; 10:12

24 Before they call[x] I will answer;
while they are still speaking[y] I
will hear.

65:25 [z] Isa 11:6 [a] Ge 3:14; Mic 7:17

25 The wolf and the lamb[z] will feed
together,
and the lion will eat straw like
the ox,
but dust will be the serpent's[a]
food.
They will neither harm nor destroy
on all my holy mountain,"
says the LORD.

Judgment and Hope

66:1 [b] Mt 23:22 [c] 1Ki 8:27; Mt 5:34-35 [d] 2Sa 7:7; Jn 4:20-21; Ac 7:49*; 17:24

66 This is what the LORD says:
"Heaven is my throne,[b]
and the earth is my footstool.[c]
Where is the house[d] you will build
for me?
Where will my resting place be?

66:2 [e] Isa 40:26; Ac 7:50* [f] Isa 57:15; Mt 5:3-4; Lk 18:13-14 [g] Ezr 9:4

2 Has not my hand made all these
things,[e]
and so they came into being?"
declares the LORD.
"This is the one I esteem:
he who is humble and contrite
in spirit,[f]
and trembles at my word.[g]

66:3 [h] Isa 1:11 [i] Lev 2:2

3 But whoever sacrifices a bull[h]
is like one who kills a man,
and whoever offers a lamb,
like one who breaks a dog's neck;
whoever makes a grain offering
is like one who presents pig's
blood,
and whoever burns memorial
incense,[i]
like one who worships an idol.

66:3 [j] Isa 57:17

They have chosen their own ways,[j]
and their souls delight in their
abominations;
4 so I also will choose harsh
treatment for them

66:4 [k] Pr 10:24 [l] Pr 1:24; Jer 7:13 [m] 2Ki 21:2,4,6 [n] Isa 65:12

and will bring upon them what
they dread.[k]
For when I called, no one
answered,[l]
when I spoke, no one listened.
They did evil[m] in my sight
and chose what displeases me."[n]
5 Hear the word of the LORD,

66:5 [o] Ps 38:20; Isa 60:15 [p] Lk 13:17

you who tremble at his word:
"Your brothers who hate[o] you,
and exclude you because of my
name, have said,
'Let the LORD be glorified,
that we may see your joy!'
Yet they will be put to shame.[p]
6 Hear that uproar from the city,
hear that noise from the temple!
It is the sound of the LORD

66:6 [q] Isa 65:6; Joel 3:7

repaying[q] his enemies all they
deserve.

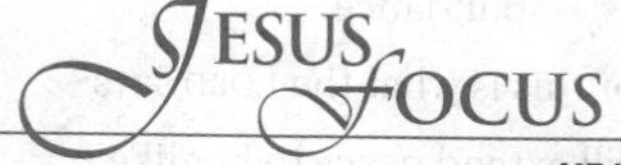

HEAVEN AND HELL

Isaiah 66, the final chapter in this lengthy prophecy, is one of the more unusual chapters in the Bible. It begins with heaven but ends with hell. God first speaks from heaven and promises to hear the prayers of sinners who turn back to him for forgiveness (verse 1–2). He will restore Jerusalem with mind-boggling speed (verse 8). He promises that peace will flow through the nations like a river and that he will care for this new nation like a nursing mother cares for her infant (verses 12–13). But without warning the tone becomes ominous. The Lord will come "with fire and with his sword" and "many will be . . . slain" (verses 16). Similar judgments are described in Revelation 14—19 and 2 Thessalonians 1:7–10, where Jesus, who came to earth to suffer and die on our behalf, will return as judge. Those who have refused to follow in God's ways will be cast into hell, where the "worm will not die, nor . . . [the] fire be quenched" (Isaiah 66:24). This final chapter in Isaiah reminds us that at the very gate of heaven there is also a wide and alluring gate into hell—and that each of us must make a choice between the two (Matthew 7:13–14).

66:7 [r] Isa 54:1 [s] Rev 12:5

7 "Before she goes into labor,[r]
she gives birth;
before the pains come upon her,
she delivers a son.[s]
8 Who has ever heard of such a
thing?

66:8 [t] Isa 64:4

Who has ever seen[t] such things?
Can a country be born in a day
or a nation be brought forth in a
moment?
Yet no sooner is Zion in labor
than she gives birth to her
children.

66:9 [u] Isa 37:3

9 Do I bring to the moment of birth[u]
and not give delivery?" says the
LORD.
"Do I close up the womb
when I bring to delivery?" says
your God.

66:10 [v] Dt 32:43; Ro 15:10 [w] Ps 26:8

10 "Rejoice[v] with Jerusalem and be
glad for her,
all you who love[w] her;
rejoice greatly with her,
all you who mourn over her.

66:11 [x] Isa 60:16

11 For you will nurse[x] and be satisfied
at her comforting breasts;
you will drink deeply
and delight in her overflowing
abundance."

12 For this is what the LORD says:

66:12 [y] Isa 48:18 [z] Ps 72:3; Isa 60:5; 61:6 [a] Isa 60:4

"I will extend peace to her like a
river,[y]
and the wealth[z] of nations like a
flooding stream;
you will nurse and be carried[a] on
her arm
and dandled on her knees.

66:13 [b] Isa 40:1; 2Co 1:4

13 As a mother comforts her child,
so will I comfort[b] you;
and you will be comforted over
Jerusalem."
14 When you see this, your heart will
rejoice
and you will flourish like grass;
the hand of the LORD will be made
known to his servants,

66:14 [c] Isa 10:5

but his fury[c] will be shown to his
foes.

66:15 [d] Ps 68:17

15 See, the LORD is coming with fire,
and his chariots[d] are like a
whirlwind;
he will bring down his anger with
fury,

66:15 [e] Ps 9:5

and his rebuke[e] with flames of
fire.

66:16 [f] Isa 30:30 [g] Isa 27:1

16 For with fire[f] and with his sword[g]
the LORD will execute judgment
upon all men,
and many will be those slain by
the LORD.

66:17 [h] Isa 1:29 [i] Lev 11:7 [j] Ps 37:20; Isa 1:28

17 "Those who consecrate and purify
themselves to go into the gardens,[h] following the one in the midst of[a] those
who eat the flesh of pigs[i] and rats and
other abominable things—they will
meet their end[j] together," declares the
LORD.
18 "And I, because of their actions and
their imaginations, am about to come[b]
and gather all nations and tongues, and
they will come and see my glory.

66:19 [k] Isa 11:10; 49:22 [l] Isa 2:16 [m] Eze 27:10 [n] Ge 10:2 [o] Isa 11:11 [p] 1Ch 16:24; Isa 24:15

19 "I will set a sign[k] among them, and
I will send some of those who survive to
the nations—to Tarshish,[l] to the Libyans[c] and Lydians[m] (famous as archers),
to Tubal[n] and Greece, and to the distant
islands[o] that have not heard of my fame
or seen my glory.[p] They will proclaim my
glory among the nations. 20 And they will
bring all your brothers, from all the nations, to my holy mountain in Jerusalem
as an offering to the LORD—on horses, in
chariots and wagons, and on mules and
camels," says the LORD. "They will bring

66:20 [q] Isa 52:11

them, as the Israelites bring their grain
offerings, to the temple of the LORD in
ceremonially clean vessels.[q] 21 And I will

66:21 [r] Ex 19:6; Isa 61:6; 1Pe 2:5,9

select some of them also to be priests[r]
and Levites," says the LORD.

66:22 [s] Isa 65:17; Heb 12:26-27; 2Pe 3:13; Rev 21:1 [t] Jn 10:27-29; 1Pe 1:4-5

22 "As the new heavens and the new
earth[s] that I make will endure before
me," declares the LORD, "so will your
name and descendants endure.[t] 23 From
one New Moon to another and from one
Sabbath[u] to another, all mankind will

66:23 [u] Eze 46:1-3 [v] Isa 19:21

come and bow down[v] before me," says
the LORD. 24 "And they will go out and

66:24 [w] Isa 14:11 [x] Isa 1:31; Mk 9:48*

look upon the dead bodies of those who
rebelled against me; their worm[w] will
not die, nor will their fire be quenched,[x]
and they will be loathsome to all
mankind."

[a] *17* Or *gardens behind one of your temples, and*
[b] *18* The meaning of the Hebrew for this clause is uncertain.
[c] *19* Some Septuagint manuscripts *Put* (Libyans); Hebrew *Pul*

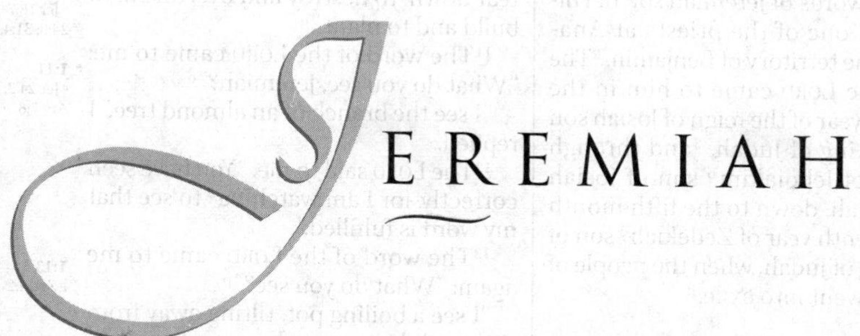

JEREMIAH

How is the Messiah linked to Israel's return from captivity? (Jeremiah 23:5–8)

♦*We must be careful to distinguish between the first coming of Jesus and his second, between the captivity of Babylon and the captivity of sin. The complete promise of restoration will be fulfilled only when Jesus establishes his kingdom on earth at the end of the age.*

How much prophecy did Jeremiah understand? (Jeremiah 23:5–6)

♦*Jeremiah was pointing to a future day, to a coming king similar to David who would fulfill all of God's covenant promises. It is quite possible that his view was limited, allowing him primarily to foresee a physical renewal of Israel (Jeremiah 30:3). Jeremiah did know that the name of the righteous Branch would be "The LORD Our Righteousness" (verse 6).*

What kind of safety was offered for the city of Jerusalem? (Jeremiah 33:16)

♦*God's promise came with conditions: It was offered to those who would allow the righteous Branch (verse 15) to rule over them. This was a prophecy of a future Messiah whose kingdom would not be of this world.*

Jesus in Jeremiah In the book of Jeremiah God promised that the Messiah's family line would survive—the family tree was still alive, and "a righteous Branch" would sprout when the time was right (Jeremiah 23:5). Unlike the kings that Israel had always known, this One would rule wisely and be called "The LORD Our Righteousness" (verse 6). Although God did curse the family lines of Jehoiachin (Jeremiah 22:30) and Jehoiakim (Jeremiah 36:30–31) because they had turned away from him, he also promised that David's family line would never fail (Jeremiah 33:17). This promise was fulfilled when the Messiah, God the Son himself, was born into David's family and given the name Jesus, "because he will save his people from their sins" (Matthew 1:21; Luke 1:31–33). Watch for Jeremiah's encouraging tone about Judah's future redemption. Beyond release from exile, Jeremiah heralded the advent of Jesus—a new day in which God's covenantal promises would be fulfilled in a manner that transcended all of his mercies of the past.

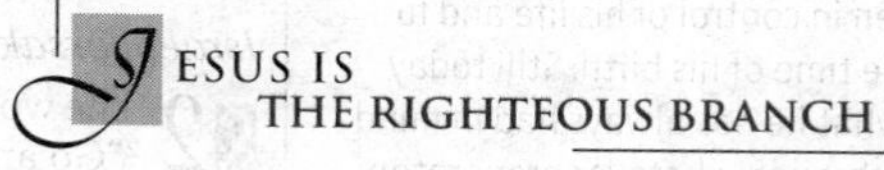

JESUS IS THE RIGHTEOUS BRANCH

1:1 [a]Jos 21:18; 1Ch 6:60; Jer 32:7-9

1:3 [b]2Ki 23:34 [c]2Ki 24:17; Jer 39:2 [d]Jer 52:15

1 The words of Jeremiah son of Hilkiah, one of the priests at Anathoth[a] in the territory of Benjamin. 2The
word of the LORD came to him in the
thirteenth year of the reign of Josiah son
of Amon king of Judah, 3and through
the reign of Jehoiakim[b] son of Josiah
king of Judah, down to the fifth month
of the eleventh year of Zedekiah[c] son of
Josiah king of Judah, when the people of
Jerusalem went into exile.[d]

The Call of Jeremiah

4The word of the LORD came to me,
saying,

1:5 [e]Ps 139:16 [f]Isa 49:1 [g]ver 10; Jer 25:15-26

5"Before I formed you in the womb I
knew[a][e] you,
before you were born[f] I set you
apart;
I appointed you as a prophet to
the nations.[g]"

1:6 [h]Ex 4:10; 6:12 [i]1Ki 3:7

6"Ah, Sovereign LORD," I said, "I do not
know how to speak;[h] I am only a child."[i]
7But the LORD said to me, "Do not say,
'I am only a child.' You must go to everyone I send you to and say whatever I
command you. 8Do not be afraid[j] of
them, for I am with you[k] and will rescue
you," declares the LORD.

1:8 [j]Eze 2:6 [k]Jos 1:5; Jer 15:20

9Then the LORD reached out his hand
and touched[l] my mouth and said to me,
"Now, I have put my words in your
mouth.[m] 10See, today I appoint you over
nations and kingdoms to uproot and
tear down, to destroy and overthrow, to
build and to plant."[n]

1:9 [l]Isa 6:7 [m]Ex 4:12

1:10 [n]Jer 18:7-10; 24:6; 31:4,28

11The word of the LORD came to me:
"What do you see, Jeremiah?"[o]
"I see the branch of an almond tree," I
replied.

1:11 [o]Jer 24:3; Am 7:8

12The LORD said to me, "You have seen
correctly, for I am watching[b] to see that
my word is fulfilled."
13The word of the LORD came to me
again: "What do you see?"[p]
"I see a boiling pot, tilting away from
the north," I answered.

1:13 [p]Zec 4:2

14The LORD said to me, "From the
north disaster will be poured out on all
who live in the land. 15I am about to
summon all the peoples of the northern
kingdoms," declares the LORD.

"Their kings will come and set up
their thrones
in the entrance of the gates of
Jerusalem;
they will come against all her
surrounding walls
and against all the towns of
Judah.[q]

1:15 [q]Jer 4:16; 9:11

16I will pronounce my judgments on
my people
because of their wickedness[r] in
forsaking me,[s]
in burning incense to other gods[t]
and in worshiping what their
hands have made.

1:16 [r]Dt 28:20 [s]Jer 17:13 [t]Jer 7:9; 19:4

17"Get yourself ready! Stand up and say
to them whatever I command you. Do
not be terrified[u] by them, or I will terrify
you before them. 18Today I have made
you[v] a fortified city, an iron pillar and a
bronze wall to stand against the whole
land—against the kings of Judah, its officials, its priests and the people of the
land. 19They will fight against you but will
not overcome you, for I am with you[w]
and will rescue[x] you," declares the LORD.

1:17 [u]Eze 2:6

1:18 [v]Isa 50:7

1:19 [w]Jer 20:11 [x]ver 8

Israel Forsakes God

2 The word of the LORD came to me:
2"Go and proclaim in the hearing
of Jerusalem:

" 'I remember the devotion of your
youth,[y]
how as a bride you loved me
and followed me through the
desert,[z]

2:2 [y]Eze 16:8-14, 60; Hos 2:15 [z]Dt 2:7

[a]5 Or *chose* [b]12 The Hebrew for *watching* sounds like the Hebrew for *almond tree.*

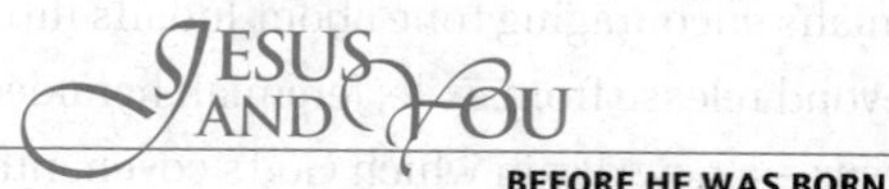

BEFORE HE WAS BORN

God's calling of Jeremiah as a prophet was dramatic: "Before you were born I set you apart," he declared (Jeremiah 1:5). Jeremiah argued that he was too young to speak for God, but God reminded him of who had been in control of his life and future even before the time of his birth. Still today God calls us to do what he has always had in mind for us and takes us through whatever preparatory training is needed. God's call to us is always supported by his grace, enabling us to walk with him along whatever paths he has chosen for us to experience. The prophecies about the Messiah's birth contain similar principles: God had chosen from time immemorial where and how his promised Messiah would be born (Matthew 1:18–23; Galatians 4:4–5).

through a land not sown.
[3] Israel was holy[a] to the LORD,[b]
the firstfruits[c] of his harvest;
all who devoured[d] her were held
guilty,[e]
and disaster overtook them,' "
declares the LORD.

2:3 [a] Dt 7:6 [b] Ex 19:6 [c] Jas 1:18; Rev 14:4 [d] Isa 41:11; Jer 30:16 [e] Jer 50:7

[4] Hear the word of the LORD, O house
of Jacob,
all you clans of the house of Israel.

[5] This is what the LORD says:

"What fault did your fathers find in
me,
that they strayed so far from me?
They followed worthless idols
and became worthless[f]
themselves.
[6] They did not ask, 'Where is the
LORD,
who brought us up out of Egypt[g]
and led us through the barren
wilderness,
through a land of deserts[h] and
rifts,[i]
a land of drought and darkness,[a]
a land where no one travels and
no one lives?'
[7] I brought you into a fertile land
to eat its fruit and rich produce.[j]
But you came and defiled my land
and made my inheritance
detestable.[k]
[8] The priests did not ask,
'Where is the LORD?'
Those who deal with the law did
not know me;[l]
the leaders rebelled against me.
The prophets prophesied by Baal,[m]
following worthless idols.[n]

2:5 [f] 2Ki 17:15
2:6 [g] Hos 13:4 [h] Dt 8:15 [i] Dt 32:10
2:7 [j] Nu 13:27; Dt 8:7-9; 11:10-12 [k] Ps 106:34-39; Jer 16:18
2:8 [l] Jer 4:22 [m] Jer 23:13 [n] Jer 16:19

[9] "Therefore I bring charges[o] against
you again,"
declares the LORD.
"And I will bring charges against
your children's children.
[10] Cross over to the coasts of Kittim[b]
and look,
send to Kedar[c] and observe
closely;
see if there has ever been
anything like this:
[11] Has a nation ever changed its gods?
(Yet they are not gods[p] at all.)
But my people have exchanged
their[d] Glory[q]
for worthless idols.

2:9 [o] Eze 20:35-36; Mic 6:2
2:11 [p] Isa 37:19; Jer 16:20 [q] Ps 106:20; Ro 1:23

[12] Be appalled at this, O heavens,
and shudder with great horror,"
declares the LORD.
[13] "My people have committed two
sins:
They have forsaken me,
the spring of living water,[r]
and have dug their own cisterns,
broken cisterns that cannot hold
water.
[14] Is Israel a servant, a slave[s] by birth?
Why then has he become
plunder?
[15] Lions[t] have roared;
they have growled at him.
They have laid waste[u] his land;
his towns are burned and
deserted.
[16] Also, the men of Memphis[e][v] and
Tahpanhes[w]
have shaved the crown of your
head.[f]
[17] Have you not brought this on
yourselves[x]
by forsaking the LORD your God
when he led you in the way?
[18] Now why go to Egypt[y]
to drink water from the Shihor[g]?[z]
And why go to Assyria
to drink water from the River[h]?
[19] Your wickedness will punish you;
your backsliding[a] will rebuke[b]
you.
Consider then and realize
how evil and bitter[c] it is for you
when you forsake the LORD your
God
and have no awe[d] of me,"
declares the Lord,
the LORD Almighty.

2:13 [r] Ps 36:9; Jn 4:14
2:14 [s] Ex 4:22
2:15 [t] Jer 4:7; 50:17 [u] Isa 1:7
2:16 [v] Isa 19:13 [w] Jer 43:7-9
2:17 [x] Jer 4:18
2:18 [y] Isa 30:2 [z] Jos 13:3
2:19 [a] Jer 3:11,22 [b] Isa 3:9; Hos 5:5 [c] Job 20:14; Am 8:10 [d] Ps 36:1

[20] "Long ago you broke off your yoke[e]
and tore off your bonds;
you said, 'I will not serve you!'
Indeed, on every high hill[f]
and under every spreading tree[g]
you lay down as a prostitute.
[21] I had planted[h] you like a choice
vine[i]
of sound and reliable stock.
How then did you turn against me
into a corrupt,[j] wild vine?

2:20 [e] Lev 26:13 [f] Isa 57:7; Jer 17:2 [g] Dt 12:2
2:21 [h] Ex 15:17 [i] Ps 80:8 [j] Isa 5:4

[a] *6* Or *and the shadow of death* [b] *10* That is, Cyprus and western coastlands [c] *10* The home of Bedouin tribes in the Syro-Arabian desert [d] *11* Masoretic Text; an ancient Hebrew scribal tradition *my* [e] *16* Hebrew *Noph* [f] *16* Or *have cracked your skull* [g] *18* That is, a branch of the Nile [h] *18* That is, the Euphrates

Springs of Living Water

Thirst. We can all identify with that human condition! The tongue seems to stick to the roof of the mouth, we have barely enough saliva to swallow . . . and we fantasize that a tall, icy glass of water would satisfy our needs forever! When hiking, thirst can become a very demanding craving, and it seems that the higher we climb the more frequently we have to stop to take a drink.

The prophet Jeremiah confronted God's people about the length of time they had been straying from God. Though God had been faithful to them and the nation had prospered, the people he had chosen to bless had in response deserted him. Their sin, God told them through Jeremiah, was that they had "forsaken [him], the spring of living water" (Jeremiah 2:13). They had ignored the only One who could rejuvenate and refresh them in their moments of spiritual "cottonmouth."

But water is more than a welcome relief when we're thirsty; it is a basic necessity for living. And in the same way, without the "water of life" we die spiritually. That is the lesson Jesus wanted to teach the woman from Samaria whom he met at the town well (John 4; see also Discovery #191, page 963, and #275, page 1415). Jesus told her, "If you knew the gift of God and who it is that asks you for a drink, you would have asked him and he would have given you living water" (John 4:10).

The water Jesus was referring to is the same refreshment he offers us when we are spiritually parched. Without the living water, the Lord Jesus, there is no real life at all.

Jesus gives us a satisfaction that is permanent. Even frequent sips of cool water when we are struggling up a mountain path provide only temporary relief from thirst. There are numerous things in life that we try to "drink," and many of these can alleviate our thirst momentarily—possessions, position, pleasure, prominence. But only Jesus can provide peace, joy, contentment, hope, strength and wisdom—in a cup that will forever overflow: "Jesus answered, 'Everyone who drinks this water will be thirsty again, but whoever drinks the water I give him will never thirst. Indeed, the water I give him will become in him a spring of water welling up to eternal life'" (John 4:13–14).

Jesus desires that we live an *abundant* life here on earth. As we allow him to delight us with his bottomless cup of blessing (John 1:16), we understand what that abundant joy is all about (John 10:10). Rather than "[digging] . . . broken cisterns that cannot hold water" by chasing elusive things that seem so important, we can go to Jesus, the true, the utterly satisfying "spring of living water" (Jeremiah 2:13).

Self-Discovery: *Have you ever thought about Jesus' blessings as coming from a bottomless cup? Spend a few moments listing, and giving thanks for, the many blessings, large and small, that you receive from "the fullness of his grace" (John 1:16).*

GO TO DISCOVERY 197 ON PAGE 996

22 Although you wash yourself with soda
and use an abundance of soap,
the stain of your guilt is still before me,"
declares the Sovereign LORD.

2:23 [k]Pr 30:12 [l]Jer 9:14 [m]Jer 7:31 [n]ver 33; Jer 31:22

23 "How can you say, 'I am not defiled;[k]
I have not run after the Baals'?[l]
See how you behaved in the valley;[m]
consider what you have done.
You are a swift she-camel
running[n] here and there,

2:24 [o]Jer 14:6

24 a wild donkey[o] accustomed to the desert,
sniffing the wind in her craving—
in her heat who can restrain her?
Any males that pursue her need not tire themselves;
at mating time they will find her.
25 Do not run until your feet are bare
and your throat is dry.
But you said, 'It's no use!
I love foreign gods,[p]
and I must go after them.'

2:25 [p]Dt 32:16; Jer 3:13; 14:10

2:26 [q]Jer 48:27

26 "As a thief is disgraced[q] when he is caught,
so the house of Israel is disgraced—
they, their kings and their officials,
their priests and their prophets.
27 They say to wood, 'You are my father,'
and to stone,[r] 'You gave me birth.'
They have turned their backs to me
and not their faces;[s]
yet when they are in trouble,[t] they say,
'Come and save us!'

2:27 [r]Jer 3:9 [s]Jer 18:17; 32:33 [t]Jdg 10:10; Isa 26:16

2:28 [u]Isa 45:20 [v]Dt 32:37 [w]2Ki 17:29; Jer 11:13

28 Where then are the gods[u] you made for yourselves?
Let them come if they can save you
when you are in trouble![v]
For you have as many gods
as you have towns,[w] O Judah.

29 "Why do you bring charges against me?
You have all[x] rebelled against me,"
declares the LORD.

2:29 [x]Jer 5:1; 6:13; Da 9:11

30 "In vain I punished your people;
they did not respond to correction.
Your sword has devoured your prophets[y]
like a ravening lion.

2:30 [y]Ne 9:26; Ac 7:52; 1Th 2:15

31 "You of this generation, consider the word of the LORD:

"Have I been a desert to Israel
or a land of great darkness?[z]
Why do my people say, 'We are free to roam;
we will come to you no more'?

2:31 [z]Isa 45:19

32 Does a maiden forget her jewelry,
a bride her wedding ornaments?
Yet my people have forgotten me,
days without number.
33 How skilled you are at pursuing love!
Even the worst of women can learn from your ways.
34 On your clothes men find
the lifeblood[a] of the innocent poor,
though you did not catch them breaking in.[b]
Yet in spite of all this
35 you say, 'I am innocent;
he is not angry with me.'
But I will pass judgment[c] on you
because you say, 'I have not sinned.'[d]

2:34 [a]2Ki 21:16 [b]Ex 22:2

2:35 [c]Jer 25:31 [d]1Jn 1:8,10

36 Why do you go about so much,
changing[e] your ways?
You will be disappointed by Egypt[f]
as you were by Assyria.

2:36 [e]Jer 31:22 [f]Isa 30:2,3,7

37 You will also leave that place
with your hands on your head,[g]
for the LORD has rejected those you trust;
you will not be helped[h] by them.

2:37 [g]2Sa 13:19 [h]Jer 37:7

3 "If a man divorces[i] his wife
and she leaves him and marries another man,
should he return to her again?
Would not the land be completely defiled?
But you have lived as a prostitute
with many lovers[j]—
would you now return to me?"
declares the LORD.

3:1 [i]Dt 24:1-4 [j]Jer 2:20,25; Eze 16:26,29

2 "Look up to the barren heights and see.
Is there any place where you have not been ravished?
By the roadside[k] you sat waiting for lovers,
sat like a nomad[a] in the desert.
You have defiled the land[l]
with your prostitution and wickedness.

3:2 [k]Ge 38:14; Eze 16:25 [l]Jer 2:7

[a] 2 Or *an Arab*

3:3 [m] Lev 26:19 [n] Jer 14:4 [o] Jer 6:15; 8:12; Zep 3:5

3 Therefore the showers have been
withheld,[m]
and no spring rains[n] have fallen.
Yet you have the brazen look of a
prostitute;
you refuse to blush with shame.[o]

3:4 [p] ver 19 [q] Jer 2:2

4 Have you not just called to me:
'My Father,[p] my friend from my
youth,[q]

3:5 [r] Ps 103:9; Isa 57:16

5 will you always be angry?[r]
Will your wrath continue
forever?'
This is how you talk,
but you do all the evil you can."

Unfaithful Israel

3:6 [s] Jer 17:2 [t] Jer 2:20

6 During the reign of King Josiah, the LORD said to me, "Have you seen what faithless Israel has done? She has gone up on every high hill and under every spreading tree[s] and has committed adultery[t] there. 7 I thought that after she had done all this she would return to me but she did not, and her unfaithful sister[u] Judah saw it. 8 I gave faithless Israel her certificate of divorce and sent her away because of all her adulteries. Yet I saw that her unfaithful sister Judah had no fear;[v] she also went out and committed adultery. 9 Because Israel's immorality mattered so little to her, she defiled the land[w] and committed adultery with stone[x] and wood.[y] 10 In spite of all this, her unfaithful sister Judah did not return to me with all her heart, but only in pretense,[z]" declares the LORD.

3:7 [u] Eze 16:46

3:8 [v] Eze 16:47; 23:11

3:9 [w] ver 2 [x] Isa 57: [y] Jer 2:27

3:10 [z] Jer 12:2

11 The LORD said to me, "Faithless Israel is more righteous[a] than unfaithful[b] Judah. 12 Go, proclaim this message toward the north:[c]

3:11 [a] Eze 16:52; 23:11 [b] ver 7

3:12 [c] 2Ki 17:3-6 [d] ver 14; Jer 31:21,22; Eze 33:11 [e] Ps 86:15

" 'Return,[d] faithless Israel,' declares
the LORD,
'I will frown on you no longer,
for I am merciful,' declares the LORD,
'I will not be angry[e] forever.
13 Only acknowledge[f] your guilt—
you have rebelled against the
LORD your God,
you have scattered your favors to
foreign gods[g]
under every spreading tree,[h]
and have not obeyed[i] me,' "
declares the LORD.

3:13 [f] Dt 30:1-3; Jer 14:20; 1Jn 1:9 [g] Jer 2:25 [h] Dt 12:2 [i] ver 25

14 "Return,[j] faithless people," declares the LORD, "for I am your husband. I will choose you—one from a town and two from a clan—and bring you to Zion. 15 Then I will give you shepherds[k] after my own heart, who will lead you with knowledge and understanding. 16 In those days, when your numbers have increased greatly in the land," declares the LORD, "men will no longer say, 'The ark of the covenant of the LORD.' It will never enter their minds or be remembered;[l] it will not be missed, nor will another one be made. 17 At that time they will call Jerusalem The Throne[m] of the LORD, and all nations will gather in Jerusalem to honor[n] the name of the LORD. No longer will they follow the stubbornness of their evil hearts.[o] 18 In those days the house of Judah will join the house of Israel,[p] and together[q] they will come from a northern[r] land to the land[s] I gave your forefathers as an inheritance.

3:14 [j] Hos 2:19

3:15 [k] Ac 20:28

3:16 [l] Isa 65:17

3:17 [m] Jer 17:12; Eze 43:7 [n] Isa 60:9 [o] Jer 11:8

3:18 [p] Hos 1:11 [q] Isa 11:13; Jer 50:4 [r] Jer 16:15; 31:8 [s] Am 9:15

19 "I myself said,

" 'How gladly would I treat you like
sons
and give you a desirable land,

JESUS FOCUS

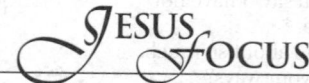

REAL FORGIVENESS

God often used the image of marriage to describe his relationship with his people (Isaiah 54:5–7; 62:4; Hosea 2:16–20; 2 Corinthians 11:2). Jeremiah 3 begins by citing the laws of divorce and remarriage that God had established in Deuteronomy 24:1–4. These laws would not allow a husband and wife, once divorced, to remarry one another. Sin separates God from his people much as a divorce separates a husband from a wife, and without the intervention of the sacrificial death and resurrection of his Son Jesus Christ the consequences would be irrevocable.

But God used those same laws to describe his limitless love for his people. God was not excusing their sin—in fact, he was about to judge them severely for it. But he was at the same time pledging his faithfulness to his covenant despite the people's unfaithfulness. Jeremiah defined the worship of other gods as spiritual prostitution (Jeremiah 3:1), but God would show his undying love for his people by sending a Messiah to save them. In the New Testament that Messiah, Jesus, reminded people of the message Jeremiah had preached so long before—that our total devotion should be to God the Father and that our failure to surrender our lives completely to God constitutes spiritual adultery (Matthew 12:39; 16:4; Mark 8:38).

the most beautiful inheritance
of any nation.'
3:19 I thought you would call me
t ver 4; Isa 63:16 'Father'[t]
and not turn away from
following me.
[20] But like a woman unfaithful to her
husband,
so you have been unfaithful to
me, O house of Israel,"
declares the LORD.

3:21 [21] A cry is heard on the barren
u ver 2 heights,[u]
the weeping and pleading of the
people of Israel,
because they have perverted their
ways
and have forgotten the LORD
their God.

3:22 [22] "Return,[v] faithless people;
v Hos 14:4 I will cure[w] you of backsliding."
w Jer 33:6;
Hos 6:1

"Yes, we will come to you,
for you are the LORD our God.
[23] Surely the ⌊idolatrous⌋ commotion
on the hills
and mountains is a deception;
3:23 surely in the LORD our God
x Ps 3:8; is the salvation[x] of Israel.
Jer 17:14
3:24 [24] From our youth shameful[y] gods
y Hos 9:10 have consumed
the fruits of our fathers' labor—
their flocks and herds,
their sons and daughters.
3:25 [25] Let us lie down in our shame,[z]
z Ezr 9:6 and let our disgrace cover us.
a Jer 22:21 We have sinned against the LORD
our God,
both we and our fathers;
from our youth[a] till this day
we have not obeyed the LORD our
God."

4:1 **4** "If you will return[b], O Israel,
b Jer 3:1,22; return to me,"
Joel 2:12
c Jer 35:15 declares the LORD.
"If you put your detestable idols[c]
out of my sight
and no longer go astray,
[2] and if in a truthful, just and
righteous way
4:2 you swear,[d] 'As surely as the
d Dt 10:20; LORD lives,'[e]
Isa 65:16
e Jer 12:16 then the nations will be blessed[f] by
f Ge 22:18; him
Gal 3:8
and in him they will glory."

[3] This is what the LORD says to the
men of Judah and to Jerusalem:

"Break up your unplowed ground[g] 4:3
and do not sow among thorns.[h] g Hos 10:12
h Mk 4:18
[4] Circumcise yourselves to the LORD,
circumcise your hearts,[i] 4:4
you men of Judah and people of i Dt 10:16;
Jerusalem, Jer 9:26;
or my wrath[j] will break out and Ro 2:28-29
burn like fire j Zep 2:2
because of the evil you have k Am 5:6
done—
burn with no one to quench[k] it.

Disaster From the North

[5] "Announce in Judah and proclaim
in Jerusalem and say:
'Sound the trumpet throughout
the land!'
Cry aloud and say:
'Gather together!
Let us flee to the fortified cities!'[l] 4:5
[6] Raise the signal to go to Zion! l Jos 10:20;
Flee for safety without delay! Jer 8:14
For I am bringing disaster from the
north,[m] 4:6
even terrible destruction." m Jer 1:13-15;
50:3

JESUS FOCUS

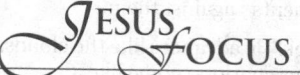

MORE THAN A RITUAL

Every male Jewish baby had to be circumcised as a physical sign of the covenant between God and his people, marking this nation as different from those around it—as dedicated to God. However, the rite of circumcision frequently degenerated into an empty ritual. Jeremiah reminded God's chosen nation of the underlying meaning of the symbol. "Circumcise your hearts," he directed the people in Jeremiah 4:4. God is more interested in devotion to himself from the motivation of genuine love than he is in meaningless tradition callously and carelessly carried out. The prophet compared spiritual circumcision to the plowing of ground in preparation for planting seeds (verse 3). In the New Testament Jesus used similar word pictures, reminding the people of the importance of a soft and yielding heart, a heart ready to hear and respond to God's call and desires (Matthew 13:3–8,18–23). Later the apostle Paul pointed out that it is only through a relationship with Jesus that our hearts are softened so that we might respond to God as we receive his astounding gift of new life and the victory over our sinful nature and the forces of darkness (Jeremiah 4:13–15; Colossians 2:11).

[7] A lion[n] has come out of his lair;
a destroyer of nations has set out.
He has left his place
to lay waste[o] your land.
Your towns will lie in ruins[p]
without inhabitant.
[8] So put on sackcloth,[q]
lament and wail,
for the fierce anger[r] of the LORD
has not turned away from us.

[9] "In that day," declares the LORD,
"the king and the officials will
lose heart,
the priests will be horrified,
and the prophets will be
appalled."[s]

[10] Then I said, "Ah, Sovereign LORD,
how completely you have deceived[t] this
people and Jerusalem by saying, 'You
will have peace,'[u] when the sword is at
our throats."

[11] At that time this people and Jerusalem will be told, "A scorching wind[v] from
the barren heights in the desert blows
toward my people, but not to winnow or
cleanse; [12] a wind too strong for that
comes from me.[a] Now I pronounce my
judgments[w] against them."

[13] Look! He advances like the clouds,[x]
his chariots[y] come like a
whirlwind,[z]
his horses are swifter than eagles.[a]
Woe to us! We are ruined!
[14] O Jerusalem, wash[b] the evil from
your heart and be saved.
How long will you harbor wicked
thoughts?
[15] A voice is announcing from Dan,[c]
proclaiming disaster from the
hills of Ephraim.
[16] "Tell this to the nations,
proclaim it to Jerusalem:
'A besieging army is coming from a
distant land,
raising a war cry[d] against the
cities of Judah.
[17] They surround[e] her like men
guarding a field,
because she has rebelled[f]
against me,'"
declares the LORD.
[18] "Your own conduct and actions[g]
have brought this upon you.[h]
This is your punishment.
How bitter[i] it is!
How it pierces to the heart!"

4:7 [n] 2Ki 24:1; Jer 2:15 [o] Isa 1:7 [p] Jer 25:9
4:8 [q] Isa 22:12; Jer 6:26 [r] Jer 30:24
4:9 [s] Isa 29:9
4:10 [t] 2Th 2:11 [u] Jer 14:13
4:11 [v] Eze 17:10; Hos 13:15
4:12 [w] Jer 1:16
4:13 [x] Isa 19:1 [y] Isa 66:15 [z] Isa 5:28 [a] Dt 28:49; Hab 1:8
4:14 [b] Jas 4:8
4:15 [c] Jer 8:16
4:16 [d] Eze 21:22
4:17 [e] 2Ki 25:1,4 [f] Jer 5:23
4:18 [g] Ps 107:17; Isa 50:1 [h] Jer 2:17 [i] Jer 2:19

[19] Oh, my anguish, my anguish![j]
I writhe in pain.
Oh, the agony of my heart!
My heart pounds within me,
I cannot keep silent.[k]
For I have heard the sound of the
trumpet;
I have heard the battle cry.[l]
[20] Disaster follows disaster;[m]
the whole land lies in ruins.
In an instant my tents[n] are
destroyed,
my shelter in a moment.
[21] How long must I see the battle
standard
and hear the sound of the
trumpet?

[22] "My people are fools;[o]
they do not know me.[p]
They are senseless children;
they have no understanding.
They are skilled in doing evil;[q]
they know not how to do good."[r]

[23] I looked at the earth,
and it was formless and empty;[s]
and at the heavens,
and their light was gone.
[24] I looked at the mountains,
and they were quaking;[t]
all the hills were swaying.
[25] I looked, and there were no people;
every bird in the sky had flown
away.[u]
[26] I looked, and the fruitful land was
a desert;
all its towns lay in ruins
before the LORD, before his fierce
anger.

[27] This is what the LORD says:

"The whole land will be ruined,
though I will not destroy[v] it
completely.
[28] Therefore the earth will mourn[w]
and the heavens above grow
dark,[x]
because I have spoken and will not
relent,[y]
I have decided and will not turn
back."[z]

[29] At the sound of horsemen and
archers[a]
every town takes to flight.[b]
Some go into the thickets;

4:19 [j] Isa 16:11; 22:4; Jer 9:10 [k] Jer 20:9 [l] Nu 10:9
4:20 [m] Ps 42:7; Eze 7:26 [n] Jer 10:20
4:22 [o] Jer 10:8 [p] Jer 2:8 [q] Jer 13:23; 1Co 14:20 [r] Ro 16:19
4:23 [s] Ge 1:2
4:24 [t] Isa 5:25; Eze 38:20
4:25 [u] Jer 9:10; 12:4; Zep 1:3
4:27 [v] Jer 5:10,18; 12:12; 30:11; 46:28
4:28 [w] Jer 12:4,11; 14:2; Hos 4:3 [x] Isa 5:30; 50:3 [y] Nu 23:19 [z] Jer 23:20; 30:24
4:29 [a] Jer 6:23 [b] 2Ki 25:4

[a] 12 Or *comes at my command*

4:29 [c] ver 7

some climb up among the rocks.
All the towns are deserted;[c]
no one lives in them.

4:30 [d] Isa 10:3-4 [e] Eze 23:40 [f] 2Ki 9:30 [g] La 1:2; Eze 23:9,22

30 What are you doing,[d] O devastated one?
Why dress yourself in scarlet
and put on jewels[e] of gold?
Why shade your eyes with paint?[f]
You adorn yourself in vain.
Your lovers[g] despise you;
they seek your life.

4:31 [h] Jer 13:21 [i] Isa 42:14 [j] Isa 1:15; La 1:17

31 I hear a cry as of a woman in labor,[h]
a groan as of one bearing her first child—
the cry of the Daughter of Zion
gasping for breath,[i]
stretching out her hands[j] and saying,
"Alas! I am fainting;
my life is given over to murderers."

Not One Is Upright

5:1 [k] 2Ch 16:9; Eze 22:30 [l] Ge 18:32 [m] Ge 18:24

5 "Go up and down[k] the streets of Jerusalem,
look around and consider,
search through her squares.
If you can find but one person[l]
who deals honestly and seeks the truth,
I will forgive[m] this city.

5:2 [n] Jer 4:2

2 Although they say, 'As surely as the LORD lives,'[n]
still they are swearing falsely."

5:3 [o] 2Ch 16:9 [p] Isa 9:13 [q] Jer 2:30; Zep 3:2 [r] Jer 7:26; 19:15; Eze 3:8-9

3 O LORD, do not your eyes[o] look for truth?
You struck[p] them, but they felt no pain;
you crushed them, but they refused correction.[q]
They made their faces harder than stone[r]
and refused to repent.

5:4 [s] Jer 8:7

4 I thought, "These are only the poor;
they are foolish,
for they do not know[s] the way of the LORD,
the requirements of their God.

5:5 [t] Mic 3:1,9 [u] Ps 2:3; Jer 2:20

5 So I will go to the leaders[t]
and speak to them;
surely they know the way of the LORD,
the requirements of their God."
But with one accord they too had
broken off the yoke
and torn off the bonds.[u]

5:6 [v] Hos 13:7 [w] Jer 30:14

6 Therefore a lion from the forest
will attack them,
a wolf from the desert will ravage them,
a leopard[v] will lie in wait near their towns
to tear to pieces any who venture out,
for their rebellion is great
and their backslidings many.[w]

5:7 [x] Jos 23:7; Zep 1:5 [y] Dt 32:21; Jer 2:11; Gal 4:8 [z] Nu 25:1

7 "Why should I forgive you?
Your children have forsaken me
and sworn[x] by gods that are not gods.[y]
I supplied all their needs,
yet they committed adultery[z]
and thronged to the houses of prostitutes.

5:8 [a] Jer 29:23; Eze 22:11

8 They are well-fed, lusty stallions,
each neighing for another man's wife.[a]

5:9 [b] ver 29; Jer 9:9

9 Should I not punish them for this?"[b]
declares the LORD.
"Should I not avenge myself
on such a nation as this?

5:10 [c] Jer 4:27

10 "Go through her vineyards and ravage them,
but do not destroy them completely.[c]
Strip off her branches,
for these people do not belong to the LORD.

5:11 [d] Jer 3:20

11 The house of Israel and the house of Judah
have been utterly unfaithful[d] to me,"
declares the LORD.

5:12 [e] Jer 23:17 [f] 2Ch 36:16; Jer 14:13

12 They have lied about the LORD;
they said, "He will do nothing!
No harm will come to us;[e]
we will never see sword or famine.[f]

5:13 [g] Jer 14:15

13 The prophets[g] are but wind
and the word is not in them;
so let what they say be done to them."

5:14 [h] Jer 1:9; Hos 6:5 [i] Jer 23:29

14 Therefore this is what the LORD God Almighty says:

"Because the people have spoken these words,
I will make my words in your mouth[h] a fire[i]
and these people the wood it consumes.
15 O house of Israel," declares the LORD,

5:15 [j] Dt 28:49; Isa 5:26; Jer 4:16 [k] Isa 28:11

"I am bringing a distant nation[j] against you—
an ancient and enduring nation,
a people whose language[k] you do not know,
whose speech you do not understand.
16 Their quivers are like an open grave;
all of them are mighty warriors.

5:17 [l] Jer 8:16 [m] Lev 26:16 [n] Jer 50:7,17 [o] Dt 28:32 [p] Dt 28:31 [q] Dt 28:33

17 They will devour[l m] your harvests and food,
devour[n o] your sons and daughters;
they will devour[p] your flocks and herds,
devour your vines and fig trees.
With the sword they will destroy
the fortified cities in which you trust.[q]

5:18 [r] Jer 4:27
5:19 [s] Dt 29:24-26; 1Ki 9:9 [t] Jer 16:13 [u] Dt 28:48

18 "Yet even in those days," declares the
LORD, "I will not destroy[r] you completely. 19 And when the people ask,[s] 'Why has
the LORD our God done all this to us?'
you will tell them, 'As you have forsaken
me and served foreign gods[t] in your own
land, so now you will serve foreigners[u]
in a land not your own.'

20 "Announce this to the house of Jacob
and proclaim it in Judah:
21 Hear this, you foolish and senseless people,
who have eyes[v] but do not see,
who have ears but do not hear:[w]

5:21 [v] Isa 6:10; Eze 12:2 [w] Mt 13:15; Mk 8:18
5:22 [x] Dt 28:58

22 Should you not fear[x] me?" declares the LORD.
"Should you not tremble in my presence?
I made the sand a boundary for the sea,
an everlasting barrier it cannot cross.
The waves may roll, but they cannot prevail;
they may roar, but they cannot cross it.

5:23 [y] Dt 21:18

23 But these people have stubborn and rebellious[y] hearts;
they have turned aside and gone away.
24 They do not say to themselves,
'Let us fear the LORD our God,
who gives autumn and spring rains[z] in season,
who assures us of the regular weeks of harvest.'[a]

5:24 [z] Ps 147:8; Joel 2:23 [a] Ge 8:22; Ac 14:17

25 Your wrongdoings have kept these away;
your sins have deprived you of good.

5:26 [b] Ps 10:8; Pr 1:11

26 "Among my people are wicked men
who lie in wait[b] like men who snare birds
and like those who set traps to catch men.

5:27 [c] Jer 9:6 [d] Jer 12:1

27 Like cages full of birds,
their houses are full of deceit;[c]
they have become rich[d] and powerful
28 and have grown fat[e] and sleek.
Their evil deeds have no limit;
they do not plead the case of the fatherless[f] to win it,
they do not defend the rights of the poor.[g]

5:28 [e] Dt 32:15 [f] Zec 7:10 [g] Isa 1:23; Jer 7:6

29 Should I not punish them for this?"
declares the LORD.
"Should I not avenge myself
on such a nation as this?

5:30 [h] Jer 23:14; Hos 6:10
5:31 [i] Eze 13:6; Mic 2:11

30 "A horrible[h] and shocking thing
has happened in the land:
31 The prophets prophesy lies,[i]
the priests rule by their own authority,
and my people love it this way.
But what will you do in the end?

Jerusalem Under Siege

6 "Flee for safety, people of Benjamin!
Flee from Jerusalem!
Sound the trumpet in Tekoa![j]
Raise the signal over Beth Hakkerem![k]
For disaster looms out of the north,[l]
even terrible destruction.
2 I will destroy the Daughter of Zion,
so beautiful and delicate.

6:1 [j] 2Ch 11:6 [k] Ne 3:14 [l] Jer 4:6
6:3 [m] Jer 12:10 [n] 2Ki 25:4; Lk 19:43

3 Shepherds[m] with their flocks will come against her;
they will pitch their tents around[n] her,
each tending his own portion."

6:4 [o] Jer 15:8

4 "Prepare for battle against her!
Arise, let us attack at noon![o]
But, alas, the daylight is fading,
and the shadows of evening grow long.
5 So arise, let us attack at night
and destroy her fortresses!"

[6]This is what the LORD Almighty says:

6:6 [p]Dt 20:19-20 [q]Jer 32:24

"Cut down the trees[p]
and build siege ramps[q] against
Jerusalem.
This city must be punished;
it is filled with oppression.
[7] As a well pours out its water,

6:7 [r]Ps 55:9; Eze 7:11,23 [s]Jer 20:8

so she pours out her wickedness.
Violence[r] and destruction[s]
resound in her;
her sickness and wounds are
ever before me.
[8] Take warning, O Jerusalem,

6:8 [t]Eze 23:18; Hos 9:12

or I will turn away[t] from you
and make your land desolate
so no one can live in it."

[9]This is what the LORD Almighty says:

"Let them glean the remnant of
Israel
as thoroughly as a vine;
pass your hand over the branches
again,
like one gathering grapes."
[10] To whom can I speak and give
warning?
Who will listen to me?

6:10 [u]Ac 7:51 [v]Jer 20:8

Their ears are closed[a][u]
so they cannot hear.
The word[v] of the LORD is offensive
to them;
they find no pleasure in it.

6:11 [w]Jer 7:20 [x]Job 32:20; Jer 20:9 [y]Jer 9:21

[11] But I am full of the wrath[w] of the
LORD,
and I cannot hold it in.[x]

"Pour it out on the children in the
street
and on the young men[y] gathered
together;
both husband and wife will be
caught in it,
and the old, those weighed down
with years.

6:12 [z]Dt 28:30 [a]Jer 8:10; 38:22 [b]Isa 5:25

[12] Their houses will be turned over to
others,[z]
together with their fields and
their wives,[a]
when I stretch out my hand[b]
against those who live in the
land,"
declares the LORD.

6:13 [c]Isa 56:11 [d]Jer 8:10

[13] "From the least to the greatest,
all are greedy for gain;[c]
prophets and priests alike,
all practice deceit.[d]
[14] They dress the wound of my people
as though it were not serious.

6:14 [e]Jer 4:10; 8:11; Eze 13:10

'Peace, peace,' they say,
when there is no peace.[e]
[15] Are they ashamed of their
loathsome conduct?
No, they have no shame at all;

6:15 [f]Jer 3:3; 8:10-12

they do not even know how to
blush.[f]
So they will fall among the fallen;
they will be brought down when
I punish them,"
says the LORD.

[16]This is what the LORD says:

6:16 [g]Jer 18:15 [h]Ps 119:3 [i]Mt 11:29

"Stand at the crossroads and look;
ask for the ancient paths,[g]
ask where the good way[h] is, and
walk in it,
and you will find rest[i] for your
souls.
But you said, 'We will not walk
in it.'

6:17 [j]Eze 3:17 [k]Jer 11:7-8; 25:4

[17] I appointed watchmen[j] over you
and said,
'Listen to the sound of the
trumpet!'
But you said, 'We will not listen.'[k]
[18] Therefore hear, O nations;
observe, O witnesses,
what will happen to them.

6:19 [l]Isa 1:2; Jer 22:29 [m]Pr 1:31 [n]Jer 8:9

[19] Hear, O earth:[l]
I am bringing disaster on this
people,
the fruit of their schemes,[m]
because they have not listened to
my words
and have rejected my law.[n]
[20] What do I care about incense from
Sheba

6:20 [o]Ex 30:23 [p]Am 5:22 [q]Ps 50:8-10; Jer 7:21; Mic 6:7-8 [r]Isa 1:11

or sweet calamus[o] from a
distant land?
Your burnt offerings are not
acceptable;[p]
your sacrifices[q] do not please
me."[r]

[21]Therefore this is what the LORD says:

"I will put obstacles before this
people.

6:21 [s]Isa 8:14

Fathers and sons alike will
stumble[s] over them;
neighbors and friends will perish."

[22]This is what the LORD says:

6:22 [t]Jer 1:15; 10:22

"Look, an army is coming
from the land of the north;[t]

[a] 10 Hebrew *uncircumcised*

a great nation is being stirred up
from the ends of the earth.
23 They are armed with bow and
spear;
6:23 [u]Isa 13:18 [v]Jer 4:29 they are cruel and show no
mercy.[u]
They sound like the roaring sea
as they ride on their horses;[v]
they come like men in battle
formation
to attack you, O Daughter of
Zion."

24 We have heard reports about them,
and our hands hang limp.
6:24 [w]Jer 4:19 [x]Jer 4:31; 50:41-43 Anguish[w] has gripped us,
pain like that of a woman in
labor.[x]
25 Do not go out to the fields
or walk on the roads,
6:25 [y]Jer 49:29 for the enemy has a sword,
and there is terror on every side.[y]
6:26 [z]Jer 4:8 [a]Jer 25:34; Mic 1:10 [b]Zec 12:10 26 O my people, put on sackcloth[z]
and roll in ashes;[a]
mourn with bitter wailing
as for an only son,[b]
for suddenly the destroyer
will come upon us.

6:27 [c]Jer 9:7 27 "I have made you a tester[c] of metals
and my people the ore,
that you may observe
and test their ways.
6:28 [d]Jer 5:23 [e]Jer 9:4 [f]Eze 22:18 28 They are all hardened rebels,[d]
going about to slander.[e]
They are bronze and iron;[f]
they all act corruptly.
29 The bellows blow fiercely
to burn away the lead with fire,
but the refining goes on in vain;
the wicked are not purged out.
6:30 [g]Ps 119:119; Jer 7:29; Hos 9:17 30 They are called rejected silver,
because the LORD has rejected
them."[g]

False Religion Worthless

7 This is the word that came to Jer-
7:2 [h]Jer 17:19 emiah from the LORD: 2 "Stand[h] at
the gate of the LORD's house and there
proclaim this message:
" 'Hear the word of the LORD, all you
people of Judah who come through
these gates to worship the LORD. 3 This is
7:3 [i]Jer 18:11; 26:13 what the LORD Almighty, the God of Israel, says: Reform your ways[i] and your
actions, and I will let you live in this
7:4 [j]Mic 3:11 place. 4 Do not trust in deceptive[j] words
and say, "This is the temple of the LORD,
the temple of the LORD, the temple of the
LORD!" 5 If you really change your ways
and your actions and deal with each 7:5 [k]Jer 22:3
other justly,[k] 6 if you do not oppress the
alien, the fatherless or the widow and do
not shed innocent blood[l] in this place, 7:6 [l]Jer 2:34; 19:4
and if you do not follow other gods[m] to [m]Dt 8:19
your own harm, 7 then I will let you live
in this place, in the land[n] I gave your 7:7 [n]Dt 4:40
forefathers for ever and ever. 8 But look,
you are trusting in deceptive words that
are worthless.
9 " 'Will you steal and murder, commit 7:9
adultery and perjury,[a] burn incense to [o]Jer 11:13,17
Baal[o] and follow other gods[p] you have [p]Ex 20:3
not known, 10 and then come and stand 7:10
before me in this house,[q] which bears [q]Jer 32:34; Eze 23:38-39
my Name, and say, "We are safe"—safe
to do all these detestable things? 11 Has 7:11 [r]Isa 56:7
this house,[r] which bears my Name, be- [s]Mt 21:13*; Mk 11:17*;
come a den of robbers[s] to you? But I Lk 19:46*
have been watching![t] declares the LORD. [t]Jer 29:23
12 " 'Go now to the place in Shiloh[u] 7:12
where I first made a dwelling for my [u]Jos 18:1
Name, and see what I did[v] to it because [v]1Sa 4:10-11, 22; Ps 78:60-64

[a] 9 Or *and swear by false gods*

JESUS FOCUS

A DEN OF ROBBERS

The Jewish people relied on the temple as a sort of "security blanket," assuming that no harm would come to Jerusalem as long as the temple was standing. They presumed that they were secure because they were God's chosen people, and the temple in their midst served as what they considered to be irrefutable proof of their invulnerability. But when they turned away from God, their sins followed them even into the temple. Jeremiah referred to the temple as a "den of robbers" (see also Matthew 21:13; Mark 11:17; Luke 19:46) because, like thieves who hide in caves and think themselves to be safe, the people surmised that the temple itself afforded them protection (Jeremiah 7:11).

In the New Testament Jesus said much the same thing to the people of his day. Jesus quoted Jeremiah when he drove out the people who were using the temple courtyard in a way God had never intended (Mark 11:17). God will remove any obstacle from our lives that stands in the way of our devotion to him—and over the course of time he has permitted the destruction of the tabernacle (1 Samuel 4:1—6:21) and two temples to prove this point! (2 Kings 25:9; Matthew 24:1–2).

of the wickedness of my people Israel. 13While you were doing all these things, declares the LORD, I spoke to you again and again,[w] but you did not listen;[x] I called you, but you did not answer.[y] 14Therefore, what I did to Shiloh I will now do to the house that bears my Name,[z] the temple you trust in, the place I gave to you and your fathers. 15I will thrust you from my presence, just as I did all your brothers, the people of Ephraim.'[a]

16"So do not pray for this people nor offer any plea[b] or petition for them; do not plead with me, for I will not listen to you. 17Do you not see what they are doing in the towns of Judah and in the streets of Jerusalem? 18The children gather wood, the fathers light the fire, and the women knead the dough and make cakes of bread for the Queen of Heaven.[c] They pour out drink offerings[d] to other gods to provoke[e] me to anger. 19But am I the one they are provoking? declares the LORD. Are they not rather harming themselves, to their own shame?[f]

20" 'Therefore this is what the Sovereign LORD says: My anger[g] and my wrath will be poured out on this place, on man and beast, on the trees of the field and on the fruit of the ground, and it will burn and not be quenched.

21" 'This is what the LORD Almighty, the God of Israel, says: Go ahead, add your burnt offerings to your other sacrifices[h] and eat[i] the meat yourselves! 22For when I brought your forefathers out of Egypt and spoke to them, I did not just give them commands about burnt offerings and sacrifices,[j] 23but I gave them this command: Obey[k] me, and I will be your God and you will be my people.[l] Walk in all the ways I command you, that it may go well[m] with you. 24But they did not listen or pay attention;[n] instead, they followed the stubborn inclinations of their evil hearts. They went backward and not forward. 25From the time your forefathers left Egypt until now, day after day, again and again I sent you my servants the prophets.[o] 26But they did not listen to me or pay attention. They were stiff-necked and did more evil than their forefathers.'[p]

27"When you tell[q] them all this, they will not listen[r] to you; when you call to them, they will not answer. 28Therefore say to them, 'This is the nation that has not obeyed the LORD its God or responded to correction. Truth has perished; it has vanished from their lips. 29Cut off[s] your hair and throw it away; take up a lament on the barren heights, for the LORD has rejected and abandoned[t] this generation that is under his wrath.

7:13 [w] 2Ch 36:15 [x] Isa 65:12 [y] Jer 35:17
7:14 [z] 1Ki 9:7
7:15 [a] Ps 78:67
7:16 [b] Ex 32:10; Dt 9:14; Jer 15:1
7:18 [c] Jer 44:17-19 [d] Jer 19:13 [e] 1Ki 14:9
7:19 [f] Jer 9:19
7:20 [g] Jer 42:18; La 2:3-5
7:21 [h] Isa 1:11; Am 5:21-22 [i] Hos 8:13
7:22 [j] 1Sa 15:22; Ps 51:16; Hos 6:6
7:23 [k] Ex 19:5 [l] Lev 26:12 [m] Ex 15:26
7:24 [n] Ps 81:11-12; Jer 11:8
7:25 [o] Jer 25:4
7:26 [p] Jer 16:12
7:27 [q] Eze 2:7 [r] Eze 3:7
7:29 [s] Job 1:20; Isa 15:2; Mic 1:16 [t] Jer 6:30

The Valley of Slaughter

30" 'The people of Judah have done evil in my eyes, declares the LORD. They have set up their detestable idols[u] in the house that bears my Name and have defiled[v] it. 31They have built the high places of Topheth[w] in the Valley of Ben Hinnom to burn their sons and daughters[x] in the fire—something I did not command, nor did it enter my mind.[y] 32So beware, the days are coming, declares the LORD, when people will no longer call it Topheth or the Valley of Ben Hinnom, but the Valley of Slaughter,[z] for they will bury[a] the dead in Topheth until there is no more room. 33Then the carcasses of this people will become food[b] for the birds of the air and the beasts of the earth, and there will be no one to frighten them away. 34I will bring an end to the sounds[c] of joy and gladness and to the voices of bride and bridegroom[d] in the towns of Judah and the streets of Jerusalem, for the land will become desolate.[e]

8 " 'At that time, declares the LORD, the bones of the kings and officials of Judah, the bones of the priests and prophets, and the bones of the people of Jerusalem will be removed from their graves. 2They will be exposed to the sun and the moon and all the stars of the heavens, which they have loved and served[f] and which they have followed and consulted and worshiped. They will not be gathered up or buried, but will be like refuse lying on the ground. 3Wherever I banish them, all the survivors of this evil nation will prefer death to life,[g] declares the LORD Almighty.'

Sin and Punishment

4"Say to them, 'This is what the LORD says:

" 'When men fall down, do they not
get up?[h]
When a man turns away, does he
not return?

7:30 [u] Eze 7:20-22 [v] Jer 32:34
7:31 [w] 2Ki 23:10 [x] Ps 106:38 [y] Jer 19:5
7:32 [z] Jer 19:6 [a] Jer 19:11
7:33 [b] Dt 28:26
7:34 [c] Isa 24:8; Eze 26:13 [d] Rev 18:23 [e] Lev 26:34
8:2 [f] 2Ki 23:5; Ac 7:42
8:3 [g] Job 3:22; Rev 9:6
8:4 [h] Pr 24:16

8:5 [i] Jer 5:27 [j] Jer 7:24; 9:6
8:6 [k] Rev 9:20 [l] Ps 14:1-3
8:7 [m] Isa 1:3; Jer 5:4-5
8:8 [n] Ro 2:17
8:9 [o] Jer 6:15 [p] Jer 6:19
8:10 [q] Jer 6:12 [r] Isa 56:11
8:11 [s] Jer 6:14
8:12 [t] Jer 3:3 [u] Ps 52:5-7; Isa 3:9 [v] Jer 6:15
8:13 [w] Joel 1:7

5 Why then have these people
turned away?
Why does Jerusalem always turn
away?
They cling to deceit;[i]
they refuse to return.[j]
6 I have listened attentively,
but they do not say what is right.
No one repents[k] of his wickedness,
saying, "What have I done?"
Each pursues his own course[l]
like a horse charging into battle.
7 Even the stork in the sky
knows her appointed seasons,
and the dove, the swift and the
thrush
observe the time of their
migration.
But my people do not know[m]
the requirements of the LORD.
8 " 'How can you say, "We are wise,
for we have the law[n] of the LORD,"
when actually the lying pen of the
scribes
has handled it falsely?
9 The wise[o] will be put to shame;
they will be dismayed and
trapped.
Since they have rejected the word[p]
of the LORD,
what kind of wisdom do they
have?
10 Therefore I will give their wives to
other men
and their fields to new owners.[q]
From the least to the greatest,
all are greedy for gain;[r]
prophets and priests alike,
all practice deceit.
11 They dress the wound of my people
as though it were not serious.
"Peace, peace," they say,
when there is no peace.[s]
12 Are they ashamed of their
loathsome conduct?
No, they have no shame[t] at all;
they do not even know how to
blush.
So they will fall among the fallen;
they will be brought down when
they are punished,[u]
says the LORD.[v]

13 " 'I will take away their harvest,
declares the LORD.
There will be no grapes on the
vine.[w]
There will be no figs[x] on the tree,
and their leaves will wither.[y]
What I have given them
will be taken[z] from them.[a]' "

14 "Why are we sitting here?
Gather together!
Let us flee to the fortified cities[a]
and perish there!
For the LORD our God has doomed
us to perish
and given us poisoned water[b] to
drink,
because we have sinned[c] against
him.
15 We hoped for peace[d]
but no good has come,
for a time of healing
but there was only terror.[e]
16 The snorting of the enemy's horses
is heard from Dan;[f]
at the neighing of their stallions
the whole land trembles.
They have come to devour
the land and everything in it,
the city and all who live there."

17 "See, I will send venomous snakes[g]
among you,
vipers that cannot be charmed,[h]
and they will bite you,"
declares the LORD.

18 O my Comforter[b] in sorrow,
my heart is faint[i] within me.
19 Listen to the cry of my people
from a land far away:[j]
"Is the LORD not in Zion?
Is her King no longer there?"
"Why have they provoked me to
anger with their images,
with their worthless foreign
idols?"[k]

20 "The harvest is past,
the summer has ended,
and we are not saved."

21 Since my people are crushed, I am
crushed;
I mourn,[l] and horror grips me.
22 Is there no balm in Gilead?[m]
Is there no physician there?
Why then is there no healing[n]
for the wound of my people?

8:13 [x] Lk 13:6 [y] Mt 21:19 [z] Jer 5:17
8:14 [a] Jer 4:5; Jer 35:11 [b] Dt 29:18; Jer 9:15; 23:15 [c] Jer 14:7,20
8:15 [d] ver 11 [e] Jer 14:19
8:16 [f] Jer 4:15
8:17 [g] Nu 21:6; Dt 32:24 [h] Ps 58:5
8:18 [i] La 5:17
8:19 [j] Jer 9:16 [k] Dt 32:21
8:21 [l] Jer 14:17
8:22 [m] Ge 37:25 [n] Jer 30:12

[a] *13* The meaning of the Hebrew for this sentence is uncertain. [b] *18* The meaning of the Hebrew for this word is uncertain.

9 1 Oh, that my head were a
spring of water
and my eyes a fountain of tears!
I would weep[o] day and night
for the slain of my people.[p]
2 Oh, that I had in the desert
a lodging place for travelers,
so that I might leave my people
and go away from them;
for they are all adulterers,[q]
a crowd of unfaithful people.

3 "They make ready their tongue
like a bow, to shoot lies;[r]
it is not by truth
that they triumph[a] in the land.
They go from one sin to another;
they do not acknowledge me,"
declares the LORD.

4 "Beware of your friends;
do not trust your brothers.[s]
For every brother is a deceiver,[b][t]
and every friend a slanderer.
5 Friend deceives friend,
and no one speaks the truth.
They have taught their tongues to
lie;
they weary themselves with
sinning.
6 You[c] live in the midst of
deception;[u]
in their deceit they refuse to
acknowledge me,"
declares the LORD.

7 Therefore this is what the LORD Almighty says:

"See, I will refine[v] and test[w] them,
for what else can I do
because of the sin of my people?
8 Their tongue[x] is a deadly arrow;
it speaks with deceit.
With his mouth each speaks
cordially to his neighbor,
but in his heart he sets a trap[y]
for him.
9 Should I not punish them for this?"
declares the LORD.
"Should I not avenge[z] myself
on such a nation as this?"

10 I will weep and wail for the
mountains
and take up a lament concerning
the desert pastures.
They are desolate and untraveled,
and the lowing of cattle is not
heard.
The birds of the air[a] have fled
and the animals are gone.

11 "I will make Jerusalem a heap of
ruins,
a haunt of jackals;[b]
and I will lay waste the towns of
Judah
so no one can live there."[c]

12 What man is wise[d] enough to understand this? Who has been instructed
by the LORD and can explain it? Why has
the land been ruined and laid waste like
a desert that no one can cross?
13 The LORD said, "It is because they
have forsaken my law, which I set before
them; they have not obeyed me or followed my law.[e] 14 Instead, they have followed[f] the stubbornness of their hearts;[g]
they have followed the Baals, as their fathers taught them." 15 Therefore, this is
what the LORD Almighty, the God of Israel, says: "See, I will make this people eat
bitter food[h] and drink poisoned water.[i]
16 I will scatter them among nations[j] that
neither they nor their fathers have
known,[k] and I will pursue them with the
sword[l] until I have destroyed them."[m]

17 This is what the LORD Almighty says:

"Consider now! Call for the wailing
women[n] to come;
send for the most skillful of them.
18 Let them come quickly
and wail over us
till our eyes overflow with tears
and water streams from our
eyelids.[o]
19 The sound of wailing is heard from
Zion:
'How ruined[p] we are!
How great is our shame!
We must leave our land
because our houses are in ruins.'"
20 Now, O women, hear the word of
the LORD;
open your ears to the words of
his mouth.
Teach your daughters how to wail;
teach one another a lament.[q]
21 Death has climbed in through our
windows
and has entered our fortresses;

[a] 3 Or *lies; / they are not valiant for truth* [b] 4 Or *a deceiving Jacob* [c] 6 That is, Jeremiah (the Hebrew is singular)

9:1 [o] Jer 13:17; La 2:11,18 [p] Isa 22:4
9:2 [q] Jer 5:7-8; 23:10; Hos 4:2
9:3 [r] Ps 64:3
9:4 [s] Mic 7:5-6 [t] Ge 27:35
9:6 [u] Jer 5:27
9:7 [v] Isa 1:25 [w] Jer 6:27
9:8 [x] ver 3 [y] Jer 5:26
9:9 [z] Jer 5:9,29
9:10 [a] Jer 4:25; 12:4; Hos 4:3
9:11 [b] Isa 34:13 [c] Isa 25:2; Jer 26:9
9:12 [d] Ps 107:43; Hos 14:9
9:13 [e] 2Ch 7:19; Ps 89:30-32
9:14 [f] Jer 2:8,23 [g] Jer 7:24
9:15 [h] La 3:15 [i] Jer 8:14
9:16 [j] Lev 26:33 [k] Dt 28:64 [l] Eze 5:2 [m] Jer 44:27; Eze 5:12
9:17 [n] 2Ch 35:25; Ecc 12:5; Am 5:16
9:18 [o] Jer 14:17
9:19 [p] Jer 4:13
9:20 [q] Isa 32:9-13

THE WEEPING PROPHET

Boys in Western or European cultures frequently grow up with the admonition that "big boys don't cry." They often train for a lifetime to repress their emotions, perceiving tears as a sign of weakness. But the prophet Jeremiah was not afraid to cry. In fact, he is known as the "weeping prophet." In addition to the book that bears his name, Jeremiah wrote the book of Lamentations—a book of unabashed and unrestrained *crying* and *mourning*.

What moved God's prophet so? Well, Jeremiah was given the task of pronouncing God's judgment against Judah's sins. He boldly declared that divine judgment and refused to water down the message, preaching with fire and passion (Jeremiah 5:14; 20:9; 23:29). Jeremiah was also heartbroken because God had revealed to him what was going to happen: "Oh, that my head were a spring of water and my eyes a fountain of tears! I would weep day and night for the slain of my people . . . See, I will refine and test them, for what else can I do because of the sin of my people?" (Jeremiah 9:1,7).

The prophet's message of judgment was preached through tears that flowed from a wellspring of deep compassion. God's truth, even when that truth demands that evildoers must be judged, is never void of love. The experience of encountering sin should affect us in much the same way. We are often very good at condemning other people and asking God to judge them for their sin—but do we *cry* for the people who are enslaved to sin? Jeremiah did!

Our Lord Jesus expressed similar emotion in his lengthy discourse recorded in Matthew 23. The message is a pronouncement of "woe" (calamity or affliction) on the teachers of the law and the Pharisees, whom Jesus was accusing in large part of misleading the population and blinding the people to the truth. In a moment of genuine pathos, Jesus cried, "O Jerusalem, Jerusalem, you who kill the prophets and stone those sent to you, how often I have longed to gather your children together, as a hen gathers her chicks under her wings, but you were not willing" (Matthew 23:37).

The apostle Paul addressed the believers in Corinth in a similar vein: "I am afraid that when I come again my God will humble me before you, and I will be grieved over many who have sinned earlier and have not repented of the impurity, sexual sin and debauchery in which they have indulged" (2 Corinthians 12:21).

We are people created in the image of God in every sense (including the emotional realm). Heartache over sin—our own and that of others—is both appropriate and necessary if we are truly to place our trust in Jesus as the sacrificial Lamb who gave his life to atone for the sin of the world (Mark 1:14–15; John 1:29). Our God expects from us "a broken and contrite heart," and he will never respond to our sorrow over sin with contempt or apathy or rejection (Psalm 51:17).

Self-Discovery: *Have you ever experienced a broken heart because of your sin? Did it occur to you that you were offering God the best kind of sacrifice—one that he has promised not to reject? Did you realize that your broken heart provided an open door through which Jesus could enter?*

GO TO DISCOVERY 198 ON PAGE 1006

it has cut off the children from the
streets
and the young men[r] from the
public squares.

[22]Say, "This is what the LORD declares:

" 'The dead bodies of men will lie
like refuse[s] on the open field,
like cut grain behind the reaper,
with no one to gather them.' "

[23]This is what the LORD says:

"Let not the wise man boast of his
wisdom[t]
or the strong man boast of his
strength[u]
or the rich man boast of his
riches,[v]
[24]but let him who boasts boast[w]
about this:
that he understands and knows
me,
that I am the LORD,[x] who exercises
kindness,[y]
justice and righteousness[z] on
earth,
for in these I delight,"
declares the LORD.

[25]"The days are coming," declares the
LORD, "when I will punish all who are circumcised only in the flesh[a]— [26]Egypt,
Judah, Edom, Ammon, Moab and all
who live in the desert in distant
places.[a][b] For all these nations are really
uncircumcised, and even the whole
house of Israel is uncircumcised in
heart.[c]"

9:21 [r]2Ch 36:17
9:22 [s]Jer 8:2
9:23 [t]Ecc 9:11 [u]1Ki 20:11 [v]Eze 28:4-5
9:24 [w]1Co 1:31*; Gal 6:14 [x]2Co 10:17* [y]Ps 51:1; Mic 7:18 [z]Ps 36:6
9:25 [a]Ro 2:8-9
9:26 [b]Jer 25:23
9:26 [c]Lev 26:41; Ac 7:51; Ro 2:28

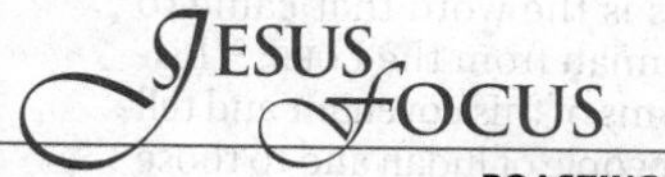

BOASTING ABOUT GOD

Bragging about our financial stability, our popularity or our service to God is a waste of time. In fact, when we stop to think about it, most of the goals we spend our lives pursuing are ultimately of very little value. Jesus devoted much of his time to interacting with the outcasts and throwaways of society, reaching out indiscriminately to fishermen, farmers, common people, tax collectors and prostitutes. The apostle Paul quoted Jeremiah 9:23–24 when he reminded the Corinthians that God chooses the despised, weak and destitute people of this world to serve his purposes and that the only legitimate boasting is boasting in the Lord (1 Corinthians 1:31; see also Matthew 25:31–46 for a remarkable story of Jesus' love for those the world considered to be "least").

God and Idols

10 Hear what the LORD says to you, O house of Israel. [2]This is what the LORD says:

"Do not learn the ways of the
nations[d]
or be terrified by signs in the sky,
though the nations are terrified
by them.
[3]For the customs of the peoples are
worthless;
they cut a tree out of the forest,
and a craftsman[e] shapes it with
his chisel.
[4]They adorn it with silver and gold;
they fasten it with hammer and
nails
so it will not totter.[f]
[5]Like a scarecrow in a melon patch,
their idols cannot speak;[g]
they must be carried
because they cannot walk.[h]
Do not fear them;
they can do no harm
nor can they do any good."[i]

[6]No one is like you, O LORD;
you are great,[j]
and your name is mighty in
power.
[7]Who should not revere you,
O King of the nations?[k]
This is your due.
Among all the wise men of the
nations
and in all their kingdoms,
there is no one like you.
[8]They are all senseless and foolish;[l]
they are taught by worthless
wooden idols.
[9]Hammered silver is brought from
Tarshish
and gold from Uphaz.
What the craftsman and goldsmith
have made[m]
is then dressed in blue and
purple—
all made by skilled workers.
[10]But the LORD is the true God;
he is the living God, the eternal
King.

[a]26 Or *desert and who clip the hair by their foreheads*

10:2 [d]Lev 20:23
10:3 [e]Isa 40:19
10:4 [f]Isa 41:7
10:5 [g]1Co 12:2 [h]Ps 115:5,7 [i]Isa 41:24; 46:7
10:6 [j]Ps 48:1
10:7 [k]Ps 22:28; Rev 15:4
10:8 [l]Isa 40:19; Jer 4:22
10:9 [m]Ps 115:4; Isa 40:19

When he is angry, the earth
trembles;
the nations cannot endure his
wrath.[n]

10:10 [n]Ps 76:7

11 "Tell them this: 'These gods, who
did not make the heavens and the earth,
will perish[o] from the earth and from under the heavens.' "[a]

10:11 [o]Ps 96:5; Isa 2:18

12 But God made the earth by his
power;
he founded the world by his
wisdom
and stretched out the heavens[p]
by his understanding.
13 When he thunders,[q] the waters in
the heavens roar;
he makes clouds rise from the
ends of the earth.
He sends lightning with the rain[r]
and brings out the wind from his
storehouses.

10:12 [p]Ge 1:1,8; Job 9:8; Isa 40:22
10:13 [q]Job 36:29 [r]Ps 135:7

14 Everyone is senseless and without
knowledge;
every goldsmith is shamed by
his idols.
His images are a fraud;
they have no breath in them.
15 They are worthless,[s] the objects of
mockery;
when their judgment comes,
they will perish.
16 He who is the Portion[t] of Jacob is
not like these,
for he is the Maker of all things,[u]
including Israel, the tribe of his
inheritance[v]—
the LORD Almighty is his name.[w]

10:15 [s]Isa 41:24; Jer 14:22
10:16 [t]Dt 32:9; Ps 119:57 [u]ver 12 [v]Ps 74:2 [w]Jer 31:35; 32:18

Coming Destruction

17 Gather up your belongings[x] to
leave the land,
you who live under siege.
18 For this is what the LORD says:
"At this time I will hurl[y] out
those who live in this land;
I will bring distress on them
so that they may be captured."

10:17 [x]Eze 12:3-12
10:18 [y]1Sa 25:29

19 Woe to me because of my injury!
My wound[z] is incurable!
Yet I said to myself,
"This is my sickness, and I must
endure[a] it."
20 My tent[b] is destroyed;
all its ropes are snapped.
My sons are gone from me and are
no more;[c]
no one is left now to pitch my
tent
or to set up my shelter.
21 The shepherds are senseless
and do not inquire of the LORD;
so they do not prosper
and all their flock is scattered.[d]
22 Listen! The report is coming—
a great commotion from the
land of the north!
It will make the towns of Judah
desolate,
a haunt of jackals.[e]

10:19 [z]Jer 14:17 [a]Mic 7:9
10:20 [b]Jer 4:20
10:20 [c]Jer 31:15; La 1:5
10:21 [d]Jer 23:2
10:22 [e]Jer 9:11

Jeremiah's Prayer

23 I know, O LORD, that a man's life is
not his own;
it is not for man to direct his
steps.[f]
24 Correct me, LORD, but only with
justice—
not in your anger,[g]
lest you reduce me to nothing.[h]
25 Pour out your wrath on the
nations[i]
that do not acknowledge you,
on the peoples who do not call
on your name.[j]
For they have devoured[k] Jacob;
they have devoured him
completely
and destroyed his homeland.[l]

10:23 [f]Pr 20:24
10:24 [g]Ps 6:1; 38:1 [h]Jer 30:11
10:25 [i]Zep 3:8 [j]Job 18:21; Ps 14:4 [k]Ps 79:7; Jer 8:16 [l]Ps 79:6-7

The Covenant Is Broken

11 This is the word that came to
Jeremiah from the LORD: 2"Lis-
ten to the terms of this covenant and tell
them to the people of Judah and to those
who live in Jerusalem. 3Tell them that
this is what the LORD, the God of Israel,
says: 'Cursed[m] is the man who does not
obey the terms of this covenant— 4the
terms I commanded your forefathers
when I brought them out of Egypt, out of
the iron-smelting furnace.[n]' I said,
'Obey[o] me and do everything I command you, and you will be my people,[p]
and I will be your God. 5Then I will fulfill
the oath I swore[q] to your forefathers, to
give them a land flowing with milk and
honey'—the land you possess today."
I answered, "Amen, LORD."
6The LORD said to me, "Proclaim all
these words in the towns of Judah and in

11:3 [m]Dt 27:26; Gal 3:10
11:4 [n]Dt 4:20; 1Ki 8:51 [o]Ex 24:8 [p]Jer 7:23; 31:33
11:5 [q]Ex 13:5; Dt 7:12; Ps 105:8-11

[a] 11 The text of this verse is in Aramaic.

11:6 the streets of Jerusalem: 'Listen to the
[r] Dt 15:5; terms of this covenant and follow[r] them.
Ro 2:13; Jas 1:22 [7]From the time I brought your forefa-
11:7 thers up from Egypt until today, I
[s] 2Ch 36:15 warned them again and again,[s] saying,
11:8 "Obey me." [8]But they did not listen or
[t] Jer 7:26 pay attention;[t] instead, they followed
[u] Lev 26:14-43 the stubbornness of their evil hearts. So
I brought on them all the curses[u] of the
covenant I had commanded them to follow but that they did not keep.'"
11:9 [9]Then the LORD said to me, "There is
[v] Eze 22:25 a conspiracy[v] among the people of Judah and those who live in Jerusalem.
11:10 [10]They have returned to the sins of their
[w] Dt 9:7 forefathers,[w] who refused to listen to my
[x] Jdg 2:12-13 words. They have followed other gods[x]
to serve them. Both the house of Israel
and the house of Judah have broken the
covenant I made with their forefathers.
11:11 [11]Therefore this is what the LORD says: 'I
[y] 2Ki 22:16; [z] Jer 14:12; will bring on them a disaster[y] they can-
Eze 8:18 not escape. Although they cry[z] out to
[a] ver 14; Pr 1:28; Isa 1:15; me, I will not listen[a] to them. [12]The
Zec 7:13 towns of Judah and the people of Jerusa-
lem will go and cry out to the gods to
11:12 [b] Jer 44:17 whom they burn incense,[b] but they will
[c] Dt 32:37 not help them at all when disaster[c]
strikes. [13]You have as many gods as you
11:13 have towns, O Judah; and the altars you
[d] Jer 7:9 have set up to burn incense[d] to that

JESUS AND YOU

COMING TO TERMS

God chose the nation of Israel simply because he wanted them, not because there was anything special about this group of people (Exodus 19:4–6; Deuteronomy 7:6–9). He promised to be with them and to give them a land to call their own (Genesis 12:1–3; 15:1–21; 17:1–8). This type of commitment is called an "unconditional" covenant. Even though the promise was God's alone, however, he still expected the people to live his way. In this sense the covenant was "conditional" as well (Deuteronomy 27:1—28:68). The blessings and curses of the covenant demonstrated the results of either adhering to or ignoring its provisions, and Jeremiah repeated those terms in Jeremiah 11. Blessings were evident when the people were walking with God and curses when they were not. The New Testament actually represents a new covenant established by Jesus when he died on the cross for our sins (Matthew 26:28), a new covenant predicted by Jeremiah (Jeremiah 31:31).

shameful[e] god Baal are as many as the 11:13
streets of Jerusalem.' [e] Jer 3:24
[14]"Do not pray[f] for this people nor of- 11:14
fer any plea or petition for them, be- [f] Ex 32:10
cause I will not listen[g] when they call to [g] ver 11
me in the time of their distress.

[15]"What is my beloved doing in my
temple
as she works out her evil
schemes with many?
Can consecrated meat avert
⌞your punishment⌟?
When you engage in your
wickedness,
then you rejoice.[a]"
[16]The LORD called you a thriving
olive tree
with fruit beautiful in form.
But with the roar of a mighty storm 11:16
he will set it on fire,[h] [h] Jer 21:14
and its branches will be broken.[i] [i] Isa 27:11; Ro 11:17-24

[17]The LORD Almighty, who planted[j] you, 11:17
has decreed disaster for you, because [j] Isa 5:2; Jer 12:2
the house of Israel and the house of Ju- [k] Jer 7:9
dah have done evil and provoked me to
anger by burning incense to Baal.[k]

Plot Against Jeremiah

[18]Because the LORD revealed their plot
to me, I knew it, for at that time he
showed me what they were doing. [19]I
had been like a gentle lamb led to the
slaughter; I did not realize that they had 11:19
plotted[l] against me, saying, [l] Jer 18:18; 20:10

"Let us destroy the tree and its fruit; [m] Job 28:13; Isa 53:8
let us cut him off from the land [n] Ps 83:4
of the living,[m]
that his name be remembered[n]
no more."
[20]But, O LORD Almighty, you who
judge righteously
and test the heart and mind,[o] 11:20
let me see your vengeance upon [o] Ps 7:9
them,
for to you I have committed my
cause.

[21]"Therefore this is what the LORD
says about the men of Anathoth who are
seeking your life[p] and saying, 'Do not 11:21
prophesy in the name of the LORD or you [p] Jer 12:6
will die[q] by our hands'— [22]therefore this [q] Jer 26:8,11; 38:4
is what the LORD Almighty says: 'I will
punish them. Their young men[r] will die 11:22 [r] Jer 18:21

[a] 15 Or *Could consecrated meat avert your punishment? / Then you would rejoice*

11:23 [s]Jer 6:9 [t]Jer 23:12

by the sword, their sons and daughters
by famine. 23 Not even a remnant[s] will be
left to them, because I will bring disaster on the men of Anathoth in the year
of their punishment.[t]"

Jeremiah's Complaint

12:1 [u]Ezr 9:15 [v]Jer 5:27-28

12 You are always righteous,[u] O LORD,
when I bring a case before you.
Yet I would speak with you about your justice:
Why does the way of the wicked prosper?[v]
Why do all the faithless live at ease?

12:2 [w]Jer 11:17 [x]Isa 29:13; Jer 3:10; Mt 15:8; Tit 1:16

2 You have planted[w] them, and they have taken root;
they grow and bear fruit.
You are always on their lips
but far from their hearts.[x]

12:3 [y]Ps 7:9; 11:5; 139:1-4; Jer 11:20 [z]Jer 17:18

3 Yet you know me, O LORD;
you see me and test[y] my thoughts about you.
Drag them off like sheep to be butchered!
Set them apart for the day of slaughter![z]

12:4 [a]Jer 4:28 [b]Joel 1:10-12 [c]Jer 4:25; 9:10

4 How long will the land lie parched[a][a]
and the grass in every field be withered?[b]
Because those who live in it are wicked,
the animals and birds have perished.[c]
Moreover, the people are saying,
"He will not see what happens to us."

God's Answer

12:5 [d]Jer 49:19; 50:44

5 "If you have raced with men on foot
and they have worn you out,
how can you compete with horses?
If you stumble in safe country,[b]
how will you manage in the thickets[d] by[c] the Jordan?

12:6 [e]Pr 26:24-25; Jer 9:4 [f]Ps 12:2

6 Your brothers, your own family—
even they have betrayed you;
they have raised a loud cry against you.[e]
Do not trust them,
though they speak well of you.[f]

12:7 [g]Jer 7:29

7 "I will forsake my house,
abandon[g] my inheritance;
I will give the one I love
into the hands of her enemies.

12:8 [h]Hos 9:15; Am 6:8

8 My inheritance has become to me
like a lion in the forest.
She roars at me;
therefore I hate her.[h]

12:9 [i]Isa 56:9; Jer 15:3; Eze 23:25

9 Has not my inheritance become to me
like a speckled bird of prey
that other birds of prey surround and attack?
Go and gather all the wild beasts;
bring them to devour.[i]

12:10 [j]Jer 23:1 [k]Isa 5:1-7

10 Many shepherds[j] will ruin my vineyard
and trample down my field;
they will turn my pleasant field
into a desolate wasteland.[k]

12:11 [l]ver 4; Isa 42:25; Jer 23:10

11 It will be made a wasteland,
parched and desolate before me;[l]
the whole land will be laid waste
because there is no one who cares.

12:12 [m]Jer 47:6

12 Over all the barren heights in the desert
destroyers will swarm,
for the sword of the LORD[m] will devour

[a] 4 Or *land mourn* [b] 5 Or *If you put your trust in a land of safety* [c] 5 Or *the flooding of*

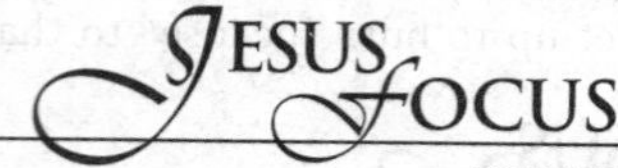

HOPE FOR THE GENTILES

God desired that the people of Israel would demonstrate to the other nations that they enjoyed a relationship with the one true God (Isaiah 42:6; 49:6; 60:3). He never intended Israel to be the only people to whom he related and desired that the Israelites extend an invitation to the nations around them to join them in worshiping God. When God first divulged to Abraham his plan to make him the forefather of a great nation, he included all peoples and nations in the blessing (Genesis 12:2–3). Jesus Christ, God's one and only Son, would be born of Jewish descent, but he would be the Savior for all people everywhere (John 3:16). Even though Jeremiah pronounced judgment on Israel's Gentile neighbors because they had not put their trust in God, he also declared to them that God would have compassion on them (Jeremiah 12:15–16). When Jesus the Messiah was born, the hope that *all* people could have a relationship with God was clearly extended to people from every tribe and language and people and nation (Luke 2:32; Revelation 5:9).

from one end of the land to the
other;[n]
no one will be safe.
13 They will sow wheat but reap
thorns;
they will wear themselves out
but gain nothing.[o]
So bear the shame of your harvest
because of the LORD's fierce
anger."[p]

14 This is what the LORD says: "As for all my wicked neighbors who seize the inheritance I gave my people Israel, I will uproot[q] them from their lands and I will uproot the house of Judah from among them. 15 But after I uproot them, I will again have compassion and will bring[r] each of them back to his own inheritance and his own country. 16 And if they learn well the ways of my people and swear by my name, saying, 'As surely as the LORD lives'[s]—even as they once taught my people to swear by Baal[t]—then they will be established among my people.[u] 17 But if any nation does not listen, I will completely uproot and destroy[v] it," declares the LORD.

A Linen Belt

13 This is what the LORD said to me: "Go and buy a linen belt and put it around your waist, but do not let it touch water." 2 So I bought a belt, as the LORD directed, and put it around my waist.

3 Then the word of the LORD came to me a second time: 4 "Take the belt you bought and are wearing around your waist, and go now to Perath[a] and hide it there in a crevice in the rocks." 5 So I went and hid it at Perath, as the LORD told me.[w]

6 Many days later the LORD said to me, "Go now to Perath and get the belt I told you to hide there." 7 So I went to Perath and dug up the belt and took it from the place where I had hidden it, but now it was ruined and completely useless.

8 Then the word of the LORD came to me: 9 "This is what the LORD says: 'In the same way I will ruin the pride of Judah and the great pride[x] of Jerusalem. 10 These wicked people, who refuse to listen to my words, who follow the stubbornness of their hearts[y] and go after other gods[z] to serve and worship them, will be like this belt—completely useless! 11 For as a belt is bound around a man's waist, so I bound the whole house of Israel and the whole house of Judah to me,' declares the LORD, 'to be my people for my renown[a] and praise and honor.[b] But they have not listened.'[c]

12:12 [n] Jer 3:2
12:13 [o] Lev 26:20; Dt 28:38; Mic 6:15; Hag 1:6 [p] Jer 4:26
12:14 [q] Zec 2:7-9
12:15 [r] Am 9:14-15
12:16 [s] Jer 4:2 [t] Jos 23:7 [u] Isa 49:6; Jer 3:17
12:17 [v] Isa 60:12
13:5 [w] Ex 40:16
13:9 [x] Lev 26:19
13:10 [y] Jer 11:8; 16:12 [z] Jer 9:14

Wineskins

12 "Say to them: 'This is what the LORD, the God of Israel, says: Every wineskin should be filled with wine.' And if they say to you, 'Don't we know that every wineskin should be filled with wine?' 13 then tell them, 'This is what the LORD says: I am going to fill with drunkenness[d] all who live in this land, including the kings who sit on David's throne, the priests, the prophets and all those living in Jerusalem. 14 I will smash them one against the other, fathers and sons alike, declares the LORD. I will allow no pity or mercy or compassion[e] to keep me from destroying[f] them.' "

Threat of Captivity

15 Hear and pay attention,
do not be arrogant,
for the LORD has spoken.
16 Give glory[g] to the LORD your God
before he brings the darkness,
before your feet stumble[h]
on the darkening hills.
You hope for light,
but he will turn it to thick
darkness
and change it to deep gloom.[i]
17 But if you do not listen,
I will weep in secret
because of your pride;
my eyes will weep bitterly,
overflowing with tears,[k]
because the LORD's flock[l] will be
taken captive.[m]
18 Say to the king and to the queen
mother,
"Come down from your thrones,
for your glorious crowns
will fall from your heads."
19 The cities in the Negev will be shut
up,
and there will be no one to open
them.
All Judah[n] will be carried into exile,
carried completely away.
20 Lift up your eyes and see

[a] 4 Or possibly *the Euphrates*; also in verses 5-7

13:11 [a] Jer 32:20; 33:9 [b] Ex 19:5-6 [c] Jer 7:26
13:13 [d] Ps 60:3; 75:8; Isa 51:17; 63:6; Jer 51:57
13:14 [e] Jer 16:5 [f] Dt 29:20; Eze 5:10
13:16 [g] Jos 7:19 [h] Jer 23:12 [i] Isa 59:9
13:17 [j] Mal 2:2 [k] Jer 9:1 [l] Ps 80:1; Jer 23:1 [m] Jer 14:18
13:19 [n] Jer 20:4; 52:30

those who are coming from the north.[o]
Where is the flock[p] that was entrusted to you,
the sheep of which you boasted?
21 What will you say when ⌞the LORD⌟ sets over you
those you cultivated as your special allies?[q]
Will not pain grip you
like that of a woman in labor?[r]
22 And if you ask yourself,
"Why has this happened to me?"—
it is because of your many sins[s]
that your skirts have been torn off
and your body mistreated.[t]
23 Can the Ethiopian[a] change his skin
or the leopard its spots?
Neither can you do good
who are accustomed to doing evil.

24 "I will scatter you like chaff[u]
driven by the desert wind.[v]
25 This is your lot,
the portion[w] I have decreed for you,"
declares the LORD,
"because you have forgotten me
and trusted in false gods.
26 I will pull up your skirts over your face
that your shame may be seen[x]—
27 your adulteries and lustful neighings,
your shameless prostitution![y]
I have seen your detestable acts
on the hills and in the fields.[z]
Woe to you, O Jerusalem!
How long will you be unclean?"[a]

Drought, Famine, Sword

14 This is the word of the LORD to Jeremiah concerning the drought:

2 "Judah mourns,[b]
her cities languish;
they wail for the land,
and a cry goes up from Jerusalem.
3 The nobles send their servants for water;
they go to the cisterns
but find no water.[c]
They return with their jars unfilled;
dismayed and despairing,
they cover their heads.[d]

13:20 [o] Jer 6:22; Hab 1:6 [p] Jer 23:2
13:21 [q] Jer 38:22 [r] Jer 4:31
13:22 [s] Jer 9:2-6; 16:10-12 [t] Eze 16:37; Na 3:5-6
13:24 [u] Ps 1:4 [v] Lev 26:33
13:25 [w] Job 20:29; Mt 24:51
13:26 [x] La 1:8; Eze 16:37; Hos 2:10
13:27 [y] Jer 2:20 [z] Eze 6:13 [a] Hos 8:5
14:2 [b] Isa 3:26; Jer 8:21
14:3 [c] 2Ki 18:31; Job 6:19-20 [d] 2Sa 15:30

4 The ground is cracked
because there is no rain in the land;[e]
the farmers are dismayed
and cover their heads.
5 Even the doe in the field
deserts her newborn fawn
because there is no grass.[f]
6 Wild donkeys stand on the barren heights[g]
and pant like jackals;
their eyesight fails
for lack of pasture."
7 Although our sins testify[h] against us,
O LORD, do something for the sake of your name.
For our backsliding[i] is great;
we have sinned[j] against you.
8 O Hope[k] of Israel,
its Savior in times of distress,
why are you like a stranger in the land,
like a traveler who stays only a night?
9 Why are you like a man taken by surprise,
like a warrior powerless to save?[l]
You are among[m] us, O LORD,
and we bear your name;[n]
do not forsake us!

10 This is what the LORD says about this people:

"They greatly love to wander;
they do not restrain their feet.[o]
So the LORD does not accept[p] them;
he will now remember[q] their wickedness
and punish them for their sins."[r]

11 Then the LORD said to me, "Do not
pray[s] for the well-being of this people.
12 Although they fast, I will not listen to
their cry;[t] though they offer burnt offerings[u] and grain offerings, I will not accept[v] them. Instead, I will destroy them
with the sword, famine and plague."
13 But I said, "Ah, Sovereign LORD, the
prophets keep telling them, 'You will not
see the sword or suffer famine.[w] Indeed, I
will give you lasting peace in this place.'"
14 Then the LORD said to me, "The
prophets are prophesying lies[x] in my
name. I have not sent[y] them or appoint-

[a] 23 Hebrew *Cushite* (probably a person from the upper Nile region)

14:4 [e] Jer 3:3
14:5 [f] Isa 15:6
14:6 [g] Job 39:5-6; Jer 2:24
14:7 [h] Hos 5:5 [i] Jer 5:6 [j] Jer 8:14
14:8 [k] Jer 17:13
14:9 [l] Isa 50:2 [m] Jer 8:19 [n] Isa 63:19; Jer 15:16
14:10 [o] Ps 119:101; Jer 2:25 [p] Jer 6:20; Am 5:22 [q] Hos 9:9 [r] Jer 44:21-23; Hos 8:13
14:11 [s] Ex 32:10
14:12 [t] Isa 1:15; Jer 11:11 [u] Jer 7:21 [v] Jer 6:20
14:13 [w] Jer 5:12
14:14 [x] Jer 27:14 [y] Jer 23:21,32

ed them or spoken to them. They are prophesying to you false visions,[z] divinations,[a] idolatries[a] and the delusions of their own minds. 15 Therefore, this is what the LORD says about the prophets who are prophesying in my name: I did not send them, yet they are saying, 'No sword or famine will touch this land.' Those same prophets will perish[b] by sword and famine.[c] 16 And the people they are prophesying to will be thrown out into the streets of Jerusalem because of the famine and sword. There will be no one to bury[d] them or their wives, their sons or their daughters.[e] I will pour out on them the calamity they deserve.[f]

14:14 [z]Jer 23:16 [a]Eze 12:24
14:15 [b]Eze 14:9 [c]Jer 5:12-13
14:16 [d]Ps 79:3 [e]Jer 7:33 [f]Pr 1:31

17 "Speak this word to them:

" 'Let my eyes overflow with tears[g]
night and day without ceasing;
for my virgin daughter—my people—
has suffered a grievous wound,
a crushing blow.[h]
18 If I go into the country,
I see those slain by the sword;
if I go into the city,
I see the ravages of famine.[i]
Both prophet and priest
have gone to a land they know not.' "

14:17 [g]Jer 9:1 [h]Jer 8:21
14:18 [i]Eze 7:15

19 Have you rejected Judah completely?[j]
Do you despise Zion?
Why have you afflicted us
so that we cannot be healed?[k]
We hoped for peace
but no good has come,
for a time of healing
but there is only terror.[l]
20 O LORD, we acknowledge our wickedness
and the guilt of our fathers;
we have indeed sinned[m] against you.
21 For the sake of your name[n] do not despise us;
do not dishonor your glorious throne.[o]
Remember your covenant with us
and do not break it.
22 Do any of the worthless idols of the nations bring rain?[p]
Do the skies themselves send down showers?
No, it is you, O LORD our God.
Therefore our hope is in you,
for you are the one who does all this.

14:19 [j]Jer 7:29 [k]Jer 30:12-13 [l]Jer 8:15
14:20 [m]Da 9:7-8
14:21 [n]ver 7 [o]Jer 3:17
14:22 [p]Ps 135:7

15 Then the LORD said to me: "Even if Moses[q] and Samuel[r] were to stand before me, my heart would not go out to this people.[s] Send them away from my presence![t] Let them go! 2 And if they ask you, 'Where shall we go?' tell them, 'This is what the LORD says:

" 'Those destined for death, to death;
those for the sword, to the sword;[u]
those for starvation, to starvation;[v]
those for captivity, to captivity.'[w]

3 "I will send four kinds of destroyers[x] against them," declares the LORD, "the sword to kill and the dogs to drag away and the birds[y] of the air and the beasts of the earth to devour and destroy.[z] 4 I will make them abhorrent[a] to all the kingdoms of the earth[b] because of what Manasseh[c] son of Hezekiah king of Judah did in Jerusalem.

15:1 [q]Ex 32:11; Nu 14:13-20 [r]1Sa 7:9 [s]Jer 7:16; Eze 14:14,20 [t]2Ki 17:20
15:2 [u]Jer 43:11 [v]Jer 14:12 [w]Rev 13:10
15:3 [x]Lev 26:16 [y]Dt 28:26 [z]Lev 26:22; Eze 14:21
15:4 [a]Jer 24:9; 29:18 [b]Dt 28:25 [c]2Ki 21:2; 23:26-27

5 "Who will have pity[d] on you, O Jerusalem?
Who will mourn for you?
Who will stop to ask how you are?
6 You have rejected[e] me," declares the LORD.
"You keep on backsliding.
So I will lay hands[f] on you and destroy you;
I can no longer show compassion.
7 I will winnow them with a winnowing fork
at the city gates of the land.
I will bring bereavement and destruction on my people,[g]
for they have not changed their ways.
8 I will make their widows more numerous
than the sand of the sea.
At midday I will bring a destroyer[h]
against the mothers of their young men;
suddenly I will bring down on them
anguish and terror.
9 The mother of seven will grow faint[i]
and breathe her last.
Her sun will set while it is still day;

15:5 [d]Isa 51:19; Jer 13:14; 21:7; Na 3:7
15:6 [e]Jer 6:19; 7:24 [f]Zep 1:4
15:7 [g]Jer 18:21
15:8 [h]Jer 6:4
15:9 [i]1Sa 2:5

[a] 14 Or *visions, worthless divinations*

she will be disgraced and
humiliated.
15:9 [j]Jer 21:7
I will put the survivors to the sword[j]
before their enemies,"
declares the LORD.

15:10 [k]Job 3:1 [l]Jer 1:19 [m]Lev 25:36
10 Alas, my mother, that you gave me
birth,[k]
a man with whom the whole
land strives and contends![l]
I have neither lent[m] nor borrowed,
yet everyone curses me.

11 The LORD said,
15:11 [n]Jer 40:4 [o]Jer 21:1-2; 37:3; 42:1-3
"Surely I will deliver you[n] for a
good purpose;
surely I will make your enemies
plead[o] with you
in times of disaster and times of
distress.

15:12 [p]Jer 28:14
12 "Can a man break iron—
iron from the north[p]—or bronze?
15:13 [q]Ps 44:12 [r]Jer 17:3
13 Your wealth and your treasures
I will give as plunder, without
charge,[q]
because of all your sins
throughout your country.[r]
15:14 [s]Dt 28:36; Jer 16:13 [t]Dt 32:22; Ps 21:9
14 I will enslave you to your enemies
in[a] a land you do not know,[s]
for my anger will kindle a fire[t]
that will burn against you."

15 You understand, O LORD;
15:15 [u]Jer 12:3 [v]Ps 69:7-9
remember me and care for me.
Avenge me on my persecutors.[u]
You are long-suffering—do not
take me away;
think of how I suffer reproach
for your sake.[v]
15:16 [w]Eze 3:3; Rev 10:10 [x]Ps 119:72,103 [y]Jer 14:9
16 When your words came, I ate[w]
them;
they were my joy and my heart's
delight,[x]
for I bear your name,[y]
O LORD God Almighty.
15:17 [z]Ps 1:1; 26:4-5; Jer 16:8
17 I never sat[z] in the company of
revelers,
never made merry with them;
I sat alone because your hand was
on me
and you had filled me with
indignation.
18 Why is my pain unending
15:18 [a]Jer 30:15; Mic 1:9 [b]Job 6:15
and my wound grievous and
incurable?[a]
Will you be to me like a deceptive
brook,
like a spring that fails?[b]

19 Therefore this is what the LORD says:
15:19 [c]Zec 3:7
"If you repent, I will restore you
that you may serve[c] me;
if you utter worthy, not worthless,
words,
you will be my spokesman.
Let this people turn to you,
but you must not turn to them.
20 I will make you a wall to this
people,
a fortified wall of bronze;
they will fight against you
but will not overcome you,
15:20 [d]Jer 20:11; Eze 3:8
for I am with you
to rescue and save you,"[d]
declares the LORD.
21 "I will save you from the hands of
the wicked
15:21 [e]Jer 50:34 [f]Ge 48:16
and redeem[e] you from the grasp
of the cruel."[f]

Day of Disaster

16 Then the word of the LORD
came to me: 2 "You must not
16:2 [g]1Co 7:26-27
marry[g] and have sons or daughters in
this place." 3 For this is what the LORD
says about the sons and daughters born
in this land and about the women who
are their mothers and the men who are
16:3 [h]Jer 6:21
their fathers:[h] 4 "They will die of deadly
diseases. They will not be mourned or
16:4 [i]Jer 25:33 [j]Ps 83:10; Jer 9:22 [k]Ps 79:1-3; Jer 15:3; 34:20
buried[i] but will be like refuse lying on
the ground.[j] They will perish by sword
and famine, and their dead bodies will
become food for the birds of the air and
the beasts of the earth."[k]
5 For this is what the LORD says: "Do
not enter a house where there is a funeral meal; do not go to mourn or show
sympathy, because I have withdrawn my
blessing, my love and my pity from this
people," declares the LORD. 6 "Both high
16:6 [l]Eze 9:5-6 [m]Lev 19:28 [n]Jer 41:5; 47:5
and low will die in this land.[l] They will
not be buried or mourned, and no one
will cut[m] himself or shave[n] his head for
them. 7 No one will offer food to comfort
16:7 [o]Eze 24:17; Hos 9:4
those who mourn[o] for the dead—not
even for a father or a mother—nor will
anyone give them a drink to console
them.
16:8 [p]Ecc 7:2-4; Jer 15:17
8 "And do not enter a house where
there is feasting and sit down to eat and
drink.[p] 9 For this is what the LORD Al-

[a] *14* Some Hebrew manuscripts, Septuagint and Syriac (see also Jer. 17:4); most Hebrew manuscripts *I will cause your enemies to bring you / into*

mighty, the God of Israel, says: Before
your eyes and in your days I will bring an
end to the sounds[q] of joy and gladness
and to the voices of bride and bridegroom in this place.[r]
10 "When you tell these people all this
and they ask you, 'Why has the LORD decreed such a great disaster against us?
What wrong have we done? What sin
have we committed against the LORD
our God?'[s] 11 then say to them, 'It is because your fathers forsook me,' declares
the LORD, 'and followed other gods and
served and worshiped them. They forsook me and did not keep my law.[t] 12 But
you have behaved more wickedly than
your fathers.[u] See how each of you is following the stubbornness of his evil
heart[v] instead of obeying me. 13 So I will
throw you out of this land into a land
neither you nor your fathers have
known,[w] and there you will serve other
gods[x] day and night, for I will show you
no favor.'[y]
14 "However, the days are coming," declares the LORD, "when men will no
longer say, 'As surely as the LORD lives,
who brought the Israelites up out of
Egypt,'[z] 15 but they will say, 'As surely as
the LORD lives, who brought the Israelites up out of the land of the north and
out of all the countries where he had
banished them.'[a] For I will restore[b] them
to the land I gave their forefathers.
16 "But now I will send for many fishermen," declares the LORD, "and they will
catch them.[c] After that I will send for
many hunters, and they will hunt[d] them
down on every mountain and hill and
from the crevices of the rocks.[e] 17 My
eyes are on all their ways; they are not
hidden[f] from me, nor is their sin concealed from my eyes.[g] 18 I will repay them
double[h] for their wickedness and their
sin, because they have defiled my land[i]
with the lifeless forms of their vile images and have filled my inheritance with
their detestable idols."

19 O LORD, my strength and my
fortress,
my refuge in time of distress,
to you the nations will come[j]
from the ends of the earth and
say,
"Our fathers possessed nothing but
false gods,[k]

16:9 [q] Isa 24:8; Eze 26:13; Hos 2:11 [r] Rev 18:23
16:10 [s] Dt 29:24; Jer 5:19
16:11 [t] Dt 29:25-26; 1Ki 9:9; Ps 106:35-43; Jer 22:9
16:12 [u] Jer 7:26 [v] Ecc 9:3; Jer 13:10
16:13 [w] Dt 28:36; Jer 5:19 [x] Dt 4:28 [y] Jer 15:5
16:14 [z] Dt 15:15; Jer 23:7-8
16:15 [a] Isa 11:11; Jer 23:8 [b] Jer 24:6
16:16 [c] Am 4:2; Hab 1:14-15 [d] Am 9:3; Mic 7:2 [e] 1Sa 26:20
16:17 [f] 1Co 4:5; Heb 4:13 [g] Pr 15:3
16:18 [h] Isa 40:2; Rev 18:6 [i] Nu 35:34; Jer 2:7
16:19 [j] Isa 2:2; Jer 3:17 [k] Ps 4:2

worthless idols that did them no
good.
20 Do men make their own gods?
Yes, but they are not gods!"[l]

21 "Therefore I will teach them—
this time I will teach them
my power and might.
Then they will know
that my name is the LORD.

17 "Judah's sin is engraved with
an iron tool,[m]
inscribed with a flint point,
on the tablets of their hearts[n]
and on the horns of their altars.
2 Even their children remember
their altars and Asherah poles[a][o]
beside the spreading trees
and on the high hills.[p]
3 My mountain in the land
and your[b] wealth and all your
treasures
I will give away as plunder,[q]
together with your high places,[r]
because of sin throughout your
country.[s]
4 Through your own fault you will
lose
the inheritance[t] I gave you.
I will enslave you to your enemies[u]
in a land[v] you do not know,
for you have kindled my anger,
and it will burn[w] forever."

5 This is what the LORD says:

"Cursed is the one who trusts in
man,[x]
who depends on flesh for his
strength
and whose heart turns away
from the LORD.
6 He will be like a bush in the
wastelands;
he will not see prosperity when
it comes.
He will dwell in the parched places
of the desert,
in a salt[y] land where no one
lives.

7 "But blessed is the man who
trusts[z] in the LORD,
whose confidence is in him.
8 He will be like a tree planted by the
water

16:20 [l] Ps 115:4-7; Isa 37:19; Jer 2:11
17:1 [m] Job 19:24 [n] Pr 3:3; 2Co 3:3
17:2 [o] 2Ch 24:18 [p] Jer 2:20
17:3 [q] 2Ki 24:13 [r] Jer 26:18; Mic 3:12 [s] Jer 15:13
17:4 [t] La 5:2 [u] Dt 28:48; Jer 12:7 [v] Jer 16:13 [w] Jer 7:20; 15:14
17:5 [x] Isa 2:22; 30:1-3
17:6 [y] Dt 29:23; Job 39:6
17:7 [z] Ps 34:8; 40:4; Pr 16:20

[a] *2* That is, symbols of the goddess Asherah
[b] *2,3* Or *hills* / [3]*and the mountains of the land.* / *Your*

A Heart Transplant

Throughout Scripture God is quite clear about what he expects of his people. Over and over he reiterates that he desires obedience, service, worship, loyalty and love. If God is so explicit, why do we have such difficulty getting it right? Jeremiah spelled out the answer: "The heart is deceitful above all things and beyond cure" (Jeremiah 17:9).

In the ancient world the heart was thought to be the "command post" of a person's life, and actions and behaviors were said to flow directly from it. God's Word frequently describes the "condition" of the hearts of particular individuals. While God's people were slaves in Egypt, Pharaoh's heart is described as "hard," with the result that "he would not listen to [Moses and Aaron]" (Exodus 7:13). Although King Solomon started strong, "as [he] grew old, his wives turned his heart after other gods, and his heart was not fully devoted to the LORD his God" (1 Kings 11:4). Psalm 10:3 observes that a wicked man "boasts of the cravings of his heart." The heart of King Nebuchadnezzar of Babylon is said to have become "arrogant and hardened with pride" (Daniel 5:20). And Ananias and Sapphira lied to the Holy Spirit because Satan had filled their hearts (Acts 5:3).

Hard hearts, *wandering* hearts, *boastful* hearts, *arrogant* hearts, *lying* hearts—there seems to be no end to the corruption of which the human heart is capable. Our hearts are so insidious because of someone else who has a heart problem—Satan himself. The Bible records that God's enemy boasted to himself, "I will ascend to heaven; I will raise my throne above the stars of God" (Isaiah 14:13). Satan presumed that he could raise himself to the same plane as God and then set out to convince human beings that they too could achieve this godlike status (Genesis 3:5–5). His schemes in the Garden of Eden achieved his dastardly purpose, and ever since that time he has constantly been tempting others to buy into the same lie (John 8:44; 1 Peter 5:8).

The only cure for a deceitful heart is Jesus. When we accept his Holy Spirit into our lives he comes with a housewarming gift: a new, *pure* heart, In Paul's words to Titus: "At one time we too were foolish, disobedient, deceived and enslaved by all kinds of passions and pleasures. We lived in malice and envy, being hated and hating one another. But when the kindness and love of God our Savior appeared, he saved us, not because of righteous things we had done, but because of his mercy. He saved us through the washing of rebirth and renewal by the Holy Spirit, whom he poured out on us generously through Jesus Christ our Savior, so that, having been justified by his grace, we might become heirs, having the hope of eternal life" (Titus 3:3–7).

And this new heart transforms us from the inside out (Ezekiel 11:19; 36:26–27). Jesus Christ wants us to know that he is waiting and that we have only to invite him in: "Here I am! I stand at the door and knock. If anyone hears my voice and opens the door, I will come in" (Revelation 3:20).

***Self-Discovery:** If Jesus were to knock on your door, would you invite him into your home? What difference would his presence make? If you have not consciously done so, invite him into your heart today.*

GO TO DISCOVERY 199 ON PAGE 1009

that sends out its roots by the
stream.
It does not fear when heat comes;
its leaves are always green.
It has no worries in a year of
drought[a]
and never fails to bear fruit."[b]

17:8 [a]Jer 14:1-6 [b]Ps 1:3; 92:12-14

9 The heart[c] is deceitful above all
things
and beyond cure.
Who can understand it?

17:9 [c]Ecc 9:3; Mt 13:15; Mk 7:21-22

10 "I the LORD search the heart[d]
and examine the mind,[e]
to reward[f] a man according to his
conduct,
according to what his deeds
deserve."[g]

17:10 [d]1Sa 16:7; Rev 2:23 [e]Ps 17:3; 139:23; Jer 11:20; 20:12; Ro 8:27 [f]Ps 62:12; Jer 32:19 [g]Ro 2:6

11 Like a partridge that hatches eggs
it did not lay
is the man who gains riches by
unjust means.
When his life is half gone, they will
desert him,
and in the end he will prove to
be a fool.[h]

17:11 [h]Lk 12:20

12 A glorious throne,[i] exalted from
the beginning,
is the place of our sanctuary.

17:12 [i]Jer 3:17

13 O LORD, the hope[j] of Israel,
all who forsake[k] you will be put
to shame.
Those who turn away from you will
be written in the dust
because they have forsaken the
LORD,
the spring of living water.

17:13 [j]Jer 14:8 [k]Isa 1:28; Jer 2:17

14 Heal me, O LORD, and I will be
healed;
save me and I will be saved,
for you are the one I praise.[l]

17:14 [l]Ps 109:1

15 They keep saying to me,
"Where is the word of the LORD?
Let it now be fulfilled!"[m]

17:15 [m]Isa 5:19; 2Pe 3:4

16 I have not run away from being
your shepherd;
you know I have not desired the
day of despair.
What passes my lips is open
before you.

17 Do not be a terror[n] to me;
you are my refuge[o] in the day of
disaster.

17:17 [n]Ps 88:15-16 [o]Jer 16:19; Na 1:7

18 Let my persecutors be put to
shame,
but keep me from shame;
let them be terrified,
but keep me from terror.
Bring on them the day of disaster;
destroy them with double
destruction.[p]

17:18 [p]Ps 35:1-8

Keeping the Sabbath Holy

19 This is what the LORD said to me:
"Go and stand at the gate of the people,
through which the kings of Judah go in
and out; stand also at all the other gates
of Jerusalem.[q] 20 Say to them, 'Hear the
word of the LORD, O kings of Judah and
all people of Judah and everyone living in
Jerusalem[r] who come through these
gates.[s] 21 This is what the LORD says: Be
careful not to carry a load on the Sabbath[t] day or bring it through the gates of
Jerusalem. 22 Do not bring a load out of
your houses or do any work on the Sabbath, but keep the Sabbath day holy, as I
commanded your forefathers.[u] 23 Yet they
did not listen or pay attention;[v] they
were stiff-necked[w] and would not listen
or respond to discipline.[x] 24 But if you are
careful to obey me, declares the LORD,
and bring no load through the gates of
this city on the Sabbath, but keep the
Sabbath day holy by not doing any work
on it, 25 then kings who sit on David's
throne[y] will come through the gates of
this city with their officials. They and
their officials will come riding in chariots and on horses, accompanied by the
men of Judah and those living in Jerusalem, and this city will be inhabited forever. 26 People will come from the towns of
Judah and the villages around Jerusalem,
from the territory of Benjamin and the
western foothills, from the hill country
and the Negev,[z] bringing burnt offerings
and sacrifices, grain offerings, incense
and thank offerings to the house of the
LORD. 27 But if you do not obey[a] me to
keep the Sabbath day holy by not carrying any load as you come through the
gates of Jerusalem on the Sabbath day,
then I will kindle an unquenchable fire[b]
in the gates of Jerusalem that will consume her fortresses.' "[c]

17:19 [q]Jer 7:2; 26:2
17:20 [r]Jer 19:3 [s]Jer 22:2
17:21 [t]Nu 15:32-36; Ne 13:15-21; Jn 5:10
17:22 [u]Ex 20:8; 31:13; Isa 56:2-6; Eze 20:12
17:23 [v]Jer 7:26 [w]Jer 19:15 [x]Jer 7:28
17:25 [y]2Sa 7:13; Isa 9:7; Jer 22:2, 4; Lk 1:32
17:26 [z]Jer 32:44; 33:13; Zec 7:7
17:27 [a]Jer 22:5 [b]Jer 7:20 [c]2Ki 25:9; Am 2:5

At the Potter's House

18 This is the word that came to
Jeremiah from the LORD: 2 "Go
down to the potter's house, and there I
will give you my message." 3 So I went
down to the potter's house, and I saw

him working at the wheel. 4But the pot
he was shaping from the clay was
marred in his hands; so the potter
formed it into another pot, shaping it as
seemed best to him.
5Then the word of the LORD came to
me: 6"O house of Israel, can I not do with
18:6 [d] Isa 45:9; Ro 9:20-21 you as this potter does?" declares the
LORD. "Like clay[d] in the hand of the pot-
ter, so are you in my hand, O house of Israel. 7If at any time I announce that a na-
18:7 [e] Jer 1:10 tion or kingdom is to be uprooted,[e] torn
down and destroyed, 8and if that nation
18:8 [f] Jer 26:13; Jnh 3:8-10 [g] Eze 18:21; Hos 11:8-9 I warned repents of its evil, then I will relent[f] and not inflict on it the disaster[g] I
had planned. 9And if at another time I
announce that a nation or kingdom is to
18:9 [h] Jer 1:10; 31:28 be built[h] up and planted, 10and if it does
evil[i] in my sight and does not obey me,
then I will reconsider[j] the good I had in-
18:10 [i] Eze 33:18 [j] 1Sa 2:29-30 tended to do for it.
11"Now therefore say to the people of
Judah and those living in Jerusalem,
18:11 [k] Jer 4:6 [l] 2Ki 17:13; Isa 1:16-19 [m] Jer 7:3 'This is what the LORD says: Look! I am
preparing a disaster[k] for you and devis-
ing a plan against you. So turn[l] from
your evil ways,[m] each one of you, and re-
18:12 [n] Isa 57:10; Jer 2:25 form your ways and your actions.' 12But
they will reply, 'It's no use.[n] We will con-
tinue with our own plans; each of us will
follow the stubbornness of his evil
heart.' "

13Therefore this is what the LORD says:

"Inquire among the nations:
18:13 [o] Isa 66:8; Jer 2:10 [p] Jer 5:30 Who has ever heard anything
like this?[o]
A most horrible[p] thing has been
done
by Virgin Israel.
14 Does the snow of Lebanon
ever vanish from its rocky slopes?
Do its cool waters from distant
sources
ever cease to flow?[a]
15 Yet my people have forgotten me;
18:15 [q] Jer 10:15 [r] Jer 6:16 [s] Isa 57:14; 62:10 they burn incense to worthless
idols,[q]
which made them stumble in their
ways
and in the ancient paths.[r]
They made them walk in bypaths
and on roads not built up.[s]
18:16 [t] Jer 25:9 [u] Jer 19:8 [v] Ps 22:7 16 Their land will be laid waste,[t]
an object of lasting scorn;[u]
all who pass by will be appalled
and will shake their heads.[v]

17 Like a wind[w] from the east, 18:17 [w] Jer 13:24 [x] Jer 2:27
I will scatter them before their
enemies;
I will show them my back and not
my face[x]
in the day of their disaster."

18They said, "Come, let's make plans[y] 18:18 [y] Jer 11:19 [z] Mal 2:7 [a] Jer 5:13 [b] Ps 52:2
against Jeremiah; for the teaching of the
law by the priest[z] will not be lost, nor
will counsel from the wise, nor the word
from the prophets.[a] So come, let's attack
him with our tongues[b] and pay no attention to anything he says."

19 Listen to me, O LORD;
hear what my accusers are saying!
20 Should good be repaid with evil?
Yet they have dug a pit[c] for me. 18:20 [c] Ps 35:7; 57:6 [d] Ps 106:23
Remember that I stood before you
and spoke in their behalf[d]
to turn your wrath away from
them.
21 So give their children over to
famine;[e] 18:21 [e] Jer 11:22 [f] Ps 109:9
hand them over to the power of
the sword.
Let their wives be made childless
and widows;[f]
let their men be put to death,
their young men slain by the
sword in battle.
22 Let a cry[g] be heard from their 18:22 [g] Jer 6:26 [h] Ps 140:5
houses
when you suddenly bring
invaders against them,
for they have dug a pit to capture
me
and have hidden snares[h] for my
feet.
23 But you know, O LORD,
all their plots to kill[i] me. 18:23 [i] Jer 11:21 [j] Ps 109:14
Do not forgive[j] their crimes
or blot out their sins from your
sight.
Let them be overthrown before you;
deal with them in the time of
your anger.

19 This is what the LORD says: "Go
and buy a clay jar from a pot- 19:1 [k] Jer 18:2 [l] Nu 11:17
ter.[k] Take along some of the elders[l] of
the people and of the priests 2and go out 19:2 [m] Jos 15:8
to the Valley of Ben Hinnom,[m] near the
entrance of the Potsherd Gate. There
proclaim the words I tell you, 3and say,

[a] 14 The meaning of the Hebrew for this sentence is uncertain.

DISCOVERY 199

GOD IS THE POTTER

Oftentimes a visual aid has a more powerful impact on us than a verbal message. In one instance an artist demonstrated the truth of Jeremiah 18 to the members of a church he was visiting. As he sat down at the pottery wheel, he explained the properties of the clay, the use of the instruments and the process. As he deftly fashioned an exquisite piece of pottery, he made several significant connections between Biblical truth and the process of molding clay. His nimble fingers formed and finessed his pot, and then—right in the middle of a sentence, while the pot was spinning—he smashed it with his fist until it was again just a lump of clay.

"I have the right to do that," he informed the congregation with a smile. "After all, I made the pot! Now, if *you* had smashed it, I would have been angry because *you* did not make it!"

This is precisely the lesson God wanted to teach his people through the ministry of Jeremiah. God sent the prophet to a potter's house. The potter sculpted a vessel that turned out to be flawed, so he pounded it back down to a gob of clay and started over. The message is not that we should cower in fear of our Creator God lest he smash us. His message is simply that he can do what he likes with us because he has fashioned us: "Like clay in the hand of the potter, so are you in my hand, O house of Israel" (verse 6). Because he was trying to guide and mold his people, he did not want them to continue in their arrogant and stubborn resistance.

The apostle Paul addressed the same issue in Romans 9: "One of you will say to me: 'Then why does God still blame us? For who resists his will?' . . . Shall what is formed say to him who formed it, 'Why did you make me like this?' Does not the potter have the right to make out of the same lump of clay some pottery for noble purposes and some for common use?" (Romans 9:19–21).

Sometimes God's ways appear harsh to us. We want to gasp in shock or raise an objection just like the audience when the potter destroyed the clay pot. But clay does not argue with the artist! God may rearrange our life or alter our prospects in a manner that seems unfair, but we must remember that his hand is both sovereign and loving. It is only when we resist that his touch seems harsh.

Jesus modeled perfectly the ideal of cooperating with God. On the night he was to be arrested he prayed that there might be some way for him to avoid the imminent anguish and desolation. At the same time, he realized that his Father had a perfect plan in mind, so he surrendered control and submitted himself to the Father's loving hand: "Not as I will, but as you will" (Matthew 26:39).

Self-Discovery: *Think about the qualities of a lump of clay. Would any of these adjectives describe you in terms of your relationship with Jesus?*

GO TO DISCOVERY 200 ON PAGE 1015

19:3 [n]Jer 17:20 'Hear the word of the LORD, O kings[n] of
[o]Jer 6:19 Judah and people of Jerusalem. This is
[p]1Sa 3:11 what the LORD Almighty, the God of Israel, says: Listen! I am going to bring a
disaster[o] on this place that will make
19:4 the ears of everyone who hears of it tin-
[q]Dt 28:20; gle.[p] 4For they have forsaken[q] me and
Isa 65:11 made this a place of foreign gods; they
[r]Lev 18:21 have burned sacrifices[r] in it to gods that
[s]2Ki 21:16; neither they nor their fathers nor the
Jer 2:34 kings of Judah ever knew, and they have
filled this place with the blood of the in-
19:5 nocent.[s] 5They have built the high places
[t]Lev 18:21; of Baal to burn their sons[t] in the fire as
Ps 106:37-38 offerings to Baal—something I did not
[u]Jer 7:31; 32:35 command or mention, nor did it enter
my mind.[u] 6So beware, the days are
coming, declares the LORD, when people
19:6 will no longer call this place Topheth or
[v]Jos 15:8 the Valley of Ben Hinnom,[v] but the Val-
[w]Jer 7:32 ley of Slaughter.[w]
7" 'In this place I will ruin[a] the plans
of Judah and Jerusalem. I will make
them fall by the sword before their ene-
19:7 mies,[x] at the hands of those who seek
[x]Lev 26:17; Dt 28:25 their lives, and I will give their carcass-
[y]Jer 16:4; 34:20 es[y] as food[z] to the birds of the air and
[z]Ps 79:2 the beasts of the earth. 8I will devastate
19:8 [a]Jer 18:16 this city and make it an object of scorn;[a]
all who pass by will be appalled and will
19:9 scoff because of all its wounds. 9I will
[b]Lev 26:29; make them eat[b] the flesh of their sons
Dt 28:49-57; and daughters, and they will eat one an-
La 4:10 other's flesh during the stress of the
[c]Isa 9:20 siege imposed on them by the enemies[c]
who seek their lives.'
19:10 10"Then break the jar[d] while those
[d]ver 1 who go with you are watching, 11and say
19:11 [e]Ps 2:9; to them, 'This is what the LORD Al-
Isa 30:14 mighty says: I will smash[e] this nation
[f]Jer 7:32 and this city just as this potter's jar is
smashed and cannot be repaired. They
will bury[f] the dead in Topheth until
there is no more room. 12This is what I
will do to this place and to those who
19:13 live here, declares the LORD. I will make
[g]Jer 32:29; this city like Topheth. 13The houses[g] in
52:13 [h]Dt 4:19; Jerusalem and those of the kings of Ju-
Ac 7:42 dah will be defiled like this place, To-
[i]Jer 7:18; pheth—all the houses where they
Eze 20:28 burned incense on the roofs to all the
starry hosts[h] and poured out drink offerings[i] to other gods.' "
14Jeremiah then returned from To-
19:14 pheth, where the LORD had sent him to
[j]2Ch 20:5; prophesy, and stood in the court[j] of the
Jer 26:2 LORD's temple and said to all the people,
15"This is what the LORD Almighty, the
God of Israel, says: 'Listen! I am going to
bring on this city and the villages
around it every disaster I pronounced
against them, because they were stiff- 19:15
necked[k] and would not listen to my [k]Ne 9:16;
words.' " Jer 7:26; 17:23

Jeremiah and Pashhur

20 When the priest Pashhur son of 20:1
Immer,[l] the chief officer[m] in the [l]1Ch 24:14
temple of the LORD, heard Jeremiah [m]2Ki 25:18
prophesying these things, 2he had Jere- 20:2
miah the prophet beaten[n] and put in the [n]Jer 1:19 [o]Job 13:27
stocks[o] at the Upper Gate of Benjamin[p] [p]Jer 37:13; 38:7;
at the LORD's temple. 3The next day, Zec 14:10
when Pashhur released him from the
stocks, Jeremiah said to him, "The LORD's
name for you is not Pashhur, but Magor- 20:3
Missabib.[b][q] 4For this is what the LORD [q]ver 10
says: 'I will make you a terror to yourself
and to all your friends; with your own 20:4
eyes[r] you will see them fall by the sword [r]Jer 29:21
of their enemies. I will hand[s] all Judah [s]Jer 21:10 [t]Jer 52:27
over to the king of Babylon, who will car-
ry[t] them away to Babylon or put them to
the sword. 5I will hand over to their ene- 20:5
mies all the wealth[u] of this city—all its [u]Jer 17:3
products, all its valuables and all the [v]2Ki 20:17
treasures of the kings of Judah. They will
take it away[v] as plunder and carry it off
to Babylon. 6And you, Pashhur, and all
who live in your house will go into exile
to Babylon. There you will die and be 20:6
buried, you and all your friends to whom [w]Jer 14:15;
you have prophesied[w] lies.' " La 2:14

Jeremiah's Complaint

7O LORD, you deceived[c] me, and I
was deceived[c];
you overpowered me and
prevailed.
I am ridiculed all day long;
everyone mocks me.
8Whenever I speak, I cry out
proclaiming violence and 20:8
destruction.[x] [x]Jer 6:7
So the word of the LORD has [y]2Ch 36:16;
brought me Jer 6:10
insult and reproach[y] all day long.
9But if I say, "I will not mention him
or speak any more in his name," 20:9
his word is in my heart like a fire,[z] [z]Ps 39:3
a fire shut up in my bones.

[a] 7 The Hebrew for *ruin* sounds like the Hebrew for *jar* (see verses 1 and 10). [b] 3 *Magor-Missabib* means *terror on every side.* [c] 7 Or *persuaded*

20:9 [a]Job 32:18-20; Ac 4:20

I am weary of holding it in;[a]
indeed, I cannot.

20:10 [b]Ps 31:13; Jer 6:25 [c]Isa 29:21 [d]Ps 41:9 [e]Lk 11:53-54 [f]1Ki 19:2

10 I hear many whispering,
"Terror[b] on every side!
Report[c] him! Let's report him!"
All my friends[d]
are waiting for me to slip,[e]
saying,
"Perhaps he will be deceived;
then we will prevail[f] over him
and take our revenge on him."

20:11 [g]Jer 1:8; Ro 8:31 [h]Jer 17:18 [i]Jer 15:20 [j]Jer 23:40

11 But the LORD[g] is with me like a
mighty warrior;
so my persecutors[h] will stumble
and not prevail.[i]
They will fail and be thoroughly
disgraced;[j]
their dishonor will never be
forgotten.

20:12 [k]Jer 17:10 [l]Ps 54:7; 59:10 [m]Ps 62:8; Jer 11:20

12 O LORD Almighty, you who
examine the righteous
and probe the heart and mind,[k]
let me see your vengeance[l] upon
them,
for to you I have committed[m] my
cause.

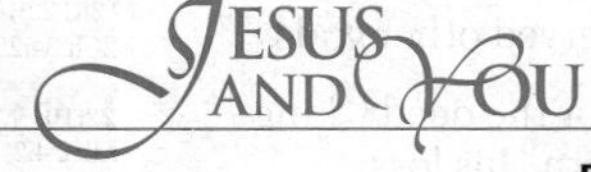

FIRE IN HIS BONES

Jeremiah didn't possess a ticket to the easy life just because God had tapped him to serve as a prophet. In fact, Jeremiah complained to God that life as a prophet was much too difficult (Jeremiah 20:7–18). Despite constant threats on his life, he still felt compelled to tell the people what God wanted them to know, because God's words were like a raging fire within him (verse 9). Eventually, however, God made his word known in another way—he sent the Messiah, his one and only Son, literally as his Word in the flesh (John 1:14). When John the Baptist saw Jesus approaching, he, like Jeremiah, found himself unable to keep quiet and cried out, "Look, the Lamb of God, who takes away the sin of the world!" (John 1:29). When the apostle Paul met the Lord for the first time, the entire direction of his life changed, and he too knew that he could not keep the amazing news to himself (Acts 26:19–20). God's people throughout the centuries have experienced the same passionate desire. As we walk with God, he transforms us in such a way that we find ourselves ready and eager to tell other people about our Savior (1 Peter 3:15–16).

20:13 [n]Ps 35:10

13 Sing to the LORD!
Give praise to the LORD!
He rescues[n] the life of the needy
from the hands of the wicked.

20:14 [o]Job 3:3; Jer 15:10

14 Cursed be the day I was born![o]
May the day my mother bore me
not be blessed!
15 Cursed be the man who brought
my father the news,
who made him very glad, saying,
"A child is born to you—a son!"

20:16 [p]Ge 19:25

16 May that man be like the towns[p]
the LORD overthrew without pity.
May he hear wailing in the
morning,
a battle cry at noon.

20:17 [q]Job 10:18-19

17 For he did not kill me in the womb,[q]
with my mother as my grave,
her womb enlarged forever.
18 Why did I ever come out of the
womb
to see trouble and sorrow
and to end my days in shame?[r]

20:18 [r]Ps 90:9

God Rejects Zedekiah's Request

21:1 [s]2Ki 24:18; Jer 52:1 [t]Jer 38:1 [u]2Ki 25:18; Jer 29:25; 37:3
21:2 [v]Jer 37:3,7 [w]2Ki 25:1 [x]Ps 44:1-4; Jer 32:17

21 The word came to Jeremiah from the LORD when King Zedekiah[s] sent to him Pashhur[t] son of Malkijah and the priest Zephaniah[u] son of
Maaseiah. They said: 2"Inquire[v] now of
the LORD for us because Nebuchadnezzar[a][w] king of Babylon is attacking us.
Perhaps the LORD will perform wonders[x]
for us as in times past so that he will
withdraw from us."

3But Jeremiah answered them, "Tell
Zedekiah, 4'This is what the LORD, the
God of Israel, says: I am about to turn[y]
against you the weapons of war that are
in your hands, which you are using to
fight the king of Babylon and the Babylonians[b] who are outside the wall besieging[z] you. And I will gather them inside this city. 5I myself will fight against
you with an outstretched hand[a] and a
mighty arm in anger and fury and great
wrath. 6I will strike down those who live
in this city—both men and animals—
and they will die of a terrible plague.[b]
7After that, declares the LORD, I will
hand over Zedekiah[c] king of Judah, his
officials and the people in this city who
survive the plague, sword and famine, to

21:4 [y]Jer 32:5 [z]Jer 37:8-10
21:5 [a]Jer 6:12
21:6 [b]Jer 14:12
21:7 [c]2Ki 25:7; Jer 52:9

[a] 2 Hebrew *Nebuchadrezzar,* of which *Nebuchadnezzar* is a variant; here and often in Jeremiah and Ezekiel [b] 4 Or *Chaldeans*; also in verse 9

21:7 [d]Jer 37:17; 39:5 [e]2Ch 36:17; Eze 7:9; Hab 1:6

Nebuchadnezzar king of Babylon[d] and
to their enemies who seek their lives. He
will put them to the sword; he will show
them no mercy or pity or compassion.'[e]
8"Furthermore, tell the people, 'This is
what the LORD says: See, I am setting before you the way of life and the way of
death. 9Whoever stays in this city will
die by the sword, famine or plague.[f] But
whoever goes out and surrenders to the
Babylonians who are besieging you will
live; he will escape with his life.[g] 10I have
determined to do this city harm[h] and
not good, declares the LORD. It will be
given into the hands[i] of the king of Babylon, and he will destroy it with fire.'[j]
11"Moreover, say to the royal house[k] of
Judah, 'Hear the word of the LORD;
12O house of David, this is what the LORD
says:

21:9 [f]Jer 14:12 [g]Jer 38:2,17; 39:18; 45:5
21:10 [h]Jer 44:11,27; Am 9:4 [i]Jer 32:28; 38:2-3 [j]Jer 52:13
21:11 [k]Jer 13:18
21:12 [l]Jer 22:3 [m]Isa 1:31

" 'Administer justice[l] every
morning;
rescue from the hand of his
oppressor
the one who has been robbed,
or my wrath will break out and
burn like fire
because of the evil you have
done—
burn with no one to quench[m] it.
13I am against[n] you, ⌊Jerusalem,⌋
you who live above this valley[o]
on the rocky plateau,
declares the LORD—
you who say, "Who can come
against us?
Who can enter our refuge?"[p]
14I will punish you as your deeds[q]
deserve,
declares the LORD.
I will kindle a fire[r] in your forests[s]
that will consume everything
around you.' "

21:13 [n]Eze 13:8 [o]Ps 125:2 [p]Jer 49:4; Ob 1:3-4
21:14 [q]Isa 3:10-11 [r]2Ch 36:19; Jer 52:13 [s]Eze 20:47

Judgment Against Evil Kings

22 This is what the LORD says: "Go
down to the palace of the king
of Judah and proclaim this message
there: 2'Hear the word of the LORD, O
king of Judah, you who sit on David's
throne[t]—you, your officials and your
people who come through these gates.[u]
3This is what the LORD says: Do what is
just[v] and right. Rescue from the hand of
his oppressor[w] the one who has been
robbed. Do no wrong or violence to the
alien, the fatherless or the widow,[x] and
do not shed innocent blood in this
place. 4For if you are careful to carry out
these commands, then kings[y] who sit on
David's throne will come through the
gates of this palace, riding in chariots
and on horses, accompanied by their officials and their people. 5But if you do
not obey[z] these commands, declares the
LORD, I swear[a] by myself that this palace
will become a ruin.' "

22:2 [t]Jer 17:25; Lk 1:32 [u]Jer 17:20
22:3 [v]Mic 6:8; Zec 7:9 [w]Ps 72:4; Jer 21:12 [x]Ex 22:22
22:4 [y]Jer 17:25
22:5 [z]Jer 17:27 [a]Heb 6:13

6For this is what the LORD says about
the palace of the king of Judah:

"Though you are like Gilead to me,
like the summit of Lebanon,
I will surely make you like a desert,[b]
like towns not inhabited.
7I will send destroyers[c] against you,
each man with his weapons,
and they will cut[d] up your fine
cedar beams
and throw them into the fire.

22:6 [b]Mic 3:12
22:7 [c]Jer 4:7 [d]Isa 10:34

8"People from many nations will pass
by this city and will ask one another,
'Why has the LORD done such a thing to
this great city?'[e] 9And the answer will be:
'Because they have forsaken the covenant of the LORD their God and have
worshiped and served other gods.'[f] "

22:8 [e]Dt 29:25-26; 1Ki 9:8-9; Jer 16:10-11
22:9 [f]2Ki 22:17; 2Ch 34:25

10Do not weep for the dead[g] ⌊king⌋
or mourn[h] his loss;
rather, weep bitterly for him who
is exiled,
because he will never return
nor see his native land again.

22:10 [g]Ecc 4:2 [h]ver 18

11For this is what the LORD says about
Shallum[a][i] son of Josiah, who succeeded
his father as king of Judah but has gone
from this place: "He will never return.
12He will die[j] in the place where they
have led him captive; he will not see this
land again."

22:11 [i]2Ki 23:31
22:12 [j]2Ki 23:34

13"Woe to him who builds[k] his
palace by unrighteousness,
his upper rooms by injustice,
making his countrymen work for
nothing,
not paying[l] them for their labor.
14He says, 'I will build myself a great
palace[m]
with spacious upper rooms.'
So he makes large windows in it,
panels it with cedar[n]
and decorates it in red.

22:13 [k]Mic 3:10; Hab 2:9 [l]Lev 19:13; Jas 5:4
22:14 [m]Isa 5:8-9 [n]2Sa 7:2

[a] 11 Also called *Jehoahaz*

15 "Does it make y[...]ou a king
to have mo[...]e and more cedar?
Did not y[...]ther have food and
[...]
[...]was right and just,[o]
[...]ell[p] with him.
[...]e cause of the poor
[...]dy,[q]
[...]nt well.
[...] it means to know
[...]ORD.
[...]nd your heart
[...]n dishonest gain,
[...]ocent blood[r]
[...]ssion and
[...]n."
[...]s what the LORD says
[...]n son of Josiah king of Ju-
[...]
[...]ey will not mourn for him:
'Alas, my brother! Alas, my sister!'
They will not mourn for him:
'Alas, my master! Alas, his
splendor!'
19 He will have the burial of a
donkey—
dragged away and thrown[s]
outside the gates of Jerusalem."

20 "Go up to Lebanon and cry out,
let your voice be heard in
Bashan,
cry out from Abarim,[t]
for all your allies are crushed.
21 I warned you when you felt secure,
but you said, 'I will not listen!'
This has been your way from your
youth;[u]
you have not obeyed[v] me.
22 The wind will drive all your
shepherds away,
and your allies will go into exile.
Then you will be ashamed and
disgraced
because of all your wickedness.
23 You who live in 'Lebanon,[a]'
who are nestled in cedar
buildings,
how you will groan when pangs
come upon you,
pain[w] like that of a woman in
labor!

24 "As surely as I live," declares the
LORD, "even if you, Jehoiachin[b][x] son of Jehoiakim king of Judah, were a signet
ring on my right hand, I would still pull
you off. 25 I will hand you over[y] to those
who seek your life, those you fear—to
Nebuchadnezzar king of Babylon and to
the Babylonians.[c] 26 I will hurl[z] you and
the mother who gave you birth into another country, where neither of you was
born, and there you both will die. 27 You
will never come back to the land you
long to return to."

28 Is this man Jehoiachin a despised,
broken pot,[a]
an object no one wants?
Why will he and his children be
hurled[b] out,
cast into a land[c] they do not
know?
29 O land,[d] land, land,
hear the word of the LORD!
30 This is what the LORD says:
"Record this man as if childless,[e]
a man who will not prosper[f] in
his lifetime,
for none of his offspring will
prosper,
none will sit on the throne[g] of
David
or rule anymore in Judah."

The Righteous Branch

23 "Woe to the shepherds[h] who
are destroying and scattering[i]
the sheep of my pasture!"[j] declares the
LORD. 2 Therefore this is what the LORD,
the God of Israel, says to the shepherds
who tend my people: "Because you have
scattered my flock and driven them
away and have not bestowed care on
them, I will bestow punishment on you
for the evil[k] you have done," declares the
LORD. 3 "I myself will gather the remnant[l]
of my flock out of all the countries
where I have driven them and will bring
them back to their pasture, where they
will be fruitful and increase in number.
4 I will place shepherds[m] over them who
will tend them, and they will no longer
be afraid[n] or terrified, nor will any be
missing,[o]" declares the LORD.

5 "The days are coming," declares the
LORD,
"when I will raise up to David[d] a
righteous Branch,[p]

22:15 [o] 2Ki 23:25 [p] Ps 128:2; Isa 3:10
22:16 [q] Ps 72:[...]
22:19 [s] Jer 36:30
22:20 [t] Nu 27:12
22:21 [u] Jer 3:25; 32:30 [v] Jer 7:23-28
22:23 [w] Jer 4:31
22:24 [x] 2Ki 24:6,8; Jer 37:1
22:25 [y] 2Ki 24:16; Jer 34:20
22:26 [z] 2Ki 24:8; 2Ch 36:10
22:28 [a] Ps 31:12; Jer 48:38; Hos 8:8 [b] Jer 15:1 [c] Jer 17:4
22:29 [d] Jer 6:19; Mic 1:2
22:30 [e] 1Ch 3:18; Mt 1:12 [f] Jer 10:21 [g] Ps 94:20
23:1 [h] Jer 10:21; Eze 34:1-10; Zec 11:15-17 [i] Isa 56:11 [j] Eze 34:31
23:2 [k] Jer 21:12
23:3 [l] Isa 11:10-12; Jer 32:37; Eze 34:11-16
23:4 [m] Jer 3:15; 31:10; Eze 34:23 [n] Jer 30:10; 46:27-28 [o] Jn 6:39
23:5 [p] Isa 4:2

[a] 23 That is, the palace in Jerusalem (see 1 Kings 7:2) [b] 24 Hebrew *Coniah*, a variant of *Jehoiachin*; also in verse 28 [c] 25 Or *Chaldeans* [d] 5 Or *up from David's line*

23:5 [q] Isa 9:7 [r] Isa 11:1; Zec 6:12
23:6 [s] Jer 33:16; Mt 1:21-23 [t] Ro 3:21-22; 1Co 1:30
23:7 [u] Jer 16:14
23:8 [v] Isa 43:5-6; Am 9:14-15

a King who will reign[q] wisely
and do what is just and right[r] in
the land.
6 In his days Judah will be saved
and Israel will live in safety.
This is the name[s] by which he will
be called:
The LORD Our Righteousness.[t]

7 "So then, the days are coming," declares
the LORD, "when people will no longer
say, 'As surely as the LORD lives, who
brought the Israelites up out of Egypt,'[u]
8 but they will say, 'As surely as the LORD
lives, who brought the descendants of
Israel up out of the land of the north and
out of all the countries where he had
banished them.' Then they will live in
their own land."[v]

Lying Prophets

23:9 [w] Jer 20:8-9
23:10 [x] Jer 9:2 [y] Ps 107:34; Jer 9:10 [z] Hos 4:2-3
23:11 [a] Jer 6:13; 8:10; Zep 3:4 [b] Jer 7:10
23:12 [c] Ps 35:6; Jer 13:16 [d] Jer 11:23
23:13 [e] Jer 2:8
23:14 [f] Jer 5:30 [g] Jer 29:23

9 Concerning the prophets:
My heart is broken within me;
all my bones tremble.
I am like a drunken man,
like a man overcome by wine,
because of the LORD
and his holy words.[w]
10 The land is full of adulterers;[x]
because of the curse[a] the land
lies parched[b]
and the pastures[y] in the desert
are withered.[z]
The ⌊prophets⌋ follow an evil course
and use their power unjustly.

11 "Both prophet and priest are
godless;[a]
even in my temple[b] I find their
wickedness,"
declares the LORD.
12 "Therefore their path will become
slippery;[c]
they will be banished to darkness
and there they will fall.
I will bring disaster on them
in the year they are punished,[d]"
declares the LORD.

13 "Among the prophets of Samaria
I saw this repulsive thing:
They prophesied by Baal[e]
and led my people Israel astray.
14 And among the prophets of
Jerusalem
I have seen something horrible:[f]
They commit adultery and live a
lie.[g]
They strengthen th[e] hands of
evildoers,[h]
so that no one turn[s from his]
wickedness.
They are all like Sodom[i]
the people of Jerusalem
Gomorrah."[j]

23:14 [h] Eze 13:22 [i] Ge 18:20

15 Therefore, this is what th[e LORD]
Almighty says concerning the pro[phets]:

"I will make them eat bitter food
and drink poisoned water,[k]
because from the prophets of
Jerusalem
ungodliness has spread
throughout the land."

23:1[6] [l] Jer 2[3:…]; Mt 7:1[5] [m] Jer 14[:14] [n] Jer 9:20
23:17 [o] Jer 8:11 [p] Jer 13:10 [q] Jer 5:12; Am 9:10; Mic 3:11
23:19 [r] Jer 25:32; 30:23
23:20 [s] 2Ki 23:26 [t] Jer 30:24
23:21 [u] Jer 14:14; 27:15

16 This is what the LORD Almighty says:

"Do not listen[l] to what the
prophets are prophesying
to you;
they fill you with false hopes.
They speak visions[m] from their
own minds,
not from the mouth[n] of the LORD.
17 They keep saying to those who
despise me,
'The LORD says: You will have
peace.'[o]
And to all who follow the
stubbornness[p] of their
hearts
they say, 'No harm[q] will come to
you.'
18 But which of them has stood in the
council of the LORD
to see or to hear his word?
Who has listened and heard his
word?
19 See, the storm[r] of the LORD
will burst out in wrath,
a whirlwind swirling down
on the heads of the wicked.
20 The anger[s] of the LORD will not
turn back[t]
until he fully accomplishes
the purposes of his heart.
In days to come
you will understand it clearly.
21 I did not send[u] these prophets,
yet they have run with their
message;
I did not speak to them,
yet they have prophesied.
22 But if they had stood in my council,

[a] 10 Or *because of these things* [b] 10 Or *land mourns*

Righteous Branch

…kings who descended …ne were spiritually …lly corrupt. The proph- …med that Judah's king …not prosper and that …ould rule over the na- …30). But God had prom- …descendants would be …ael's throne *forever*!

…tinued on in the very …his prophecy to use one …hrases to introduce a mes- … for the future: *The days are* …eremiah 23:5). One day, he …ed, God would raise up a "righ- …s Branch." That King would descend …om David's family line and would reign forever in a kingdom of perfect harmony.

God didn't promise a towering shade tree or even a branch emerging from the main stump. Instead this promised King would be an offshoot, a "sprout" that would emerge from the root after the tree had been cut down (Isaiah 6:13; 11:1). This branch would be *righteous*, acting in full accord with God's own characteristics, as well as being free from guilt and sin (Isaiah 9:7; Hebrews 7:26).

Paul pointed out to the Corinthian believers that Jesus Christ "has become for us wisdom from God—that is, our righteousness, holiness and redemption" (1 Corinthians 1:30). And Peter had these words to say about Jesus: " 'He committed no sin, and no deceit was found in his mouth.' When they hurled their insults at him, he did not retaliate; when he suffered, he made no threats. Instead, he entrusted himself to him who judges justly. He himself bore our sins in his body on the tree, so that we might die to sins and live for righteousness; by his wounds you have been healed" (1 Peter 2:22–24).

The Old Testament writers repeatedly used the word *Branch* to describe the Messiah (Isaiah 4:2-4; Jeremiah 33:15; Zechariah 3:8). This coming King, the hope of the entire world, would spring from the *fallen* dynasty of David. He would execute justice and righteousness as his ancestor David had done (2 Samuel 8:15). The nation of Israel would be reunited, and the Messiah would save his people (Ezekiel 37:19). The world would at long last experience the peace and security for which it had been yearning (see Isaiah 40).

We all need Jesus in our lives, because he offers us a chance for new life to sprout from the putrid decay of our sin and selfishness. Like plants straining toward the sunshine, our souls long to grow closer to the light and peace he alone offers (John 16:33; Philippians 4:7). "Peace I leave with you," Jesus assured his disciples near the end of his life on earth. "My peace I give you. I do not give to you as the world gives. Do not let your hearts be troubled and do not be afraid" (John 14:27).

Self-Discovery: *Visualize a pot of flowers in a windowsill with all of the buds and blossoms facing the outside, straining toward the light. Picture yourself and your family, friends or neighbors as these flowers. Stretch as close to Jesus as you can, enjoying the light and warmth. Allow your spirit to open up to him as a full-blown flower, reflecting his glory in your brilliant colors.*

GO TO DISCOVERY 201 ON PAGE 1023

they would have proclaimed my
23:22 [v] Jer 25:5; Zec 1:4 words to my people
and would have turned[v] them from
their evil ways
and from their evil deeds.

23:23 [w] Ps 139:1-10 23 "Am I only a God nearby,[w]"
declares the LORD,
"and not a God far away?
23:24 [x] Job 22:12-14 [y] 1Ki 8:27 24 Can anyone hide[x] in secret places
so that I cannot see him?"
declares the LORD.
"Do not I fill heaven and earth?"[y]
declares the LORD.

25 "I have heard what the prophets say
23:25 [z] Jer 14:14 [a] ver 28,32; Jer 29:8 who prophesy lies[z] in my name. They
say, 'I had a dream![a] I had a dream!'
26 How long will this continue in the
23:26 [b] 1Ti 4:1-2 hearts of these lying prophets, who
prophesy the delusions[b] of their own
minds? 27 They think the dreams they
tell one another will make my people
23:27 [c] Dt 13:1-3; Jer 29:8 [d] Jdg 3:7; 8:33-34 forget[c] my name, just as their fathers
forgot[d] my name through Baal worship.
28 Let the prophet who has a dream tell
his dream, but let the one who has my
word speak it faithfully. For what has
straw to do with grain?" declares the
23:29 [e] Jer 5:14 LORD. 29 "Is not my word like fire,"[e] declares the LORD, "and like a hammer that
23:30 [f] Ps 34:16 [g] Dt 18:20; Jer 14:15 breaks a rock in pieces?
30 "Therefore," declares the LORD, "I am
against[f] the prophets[g] who steal from
one another words su
31 Yes," declares the LO
the prophets who wag t
and yet declare, 'The L
32 Indeed, I am against th
esy false dreams,[i]" decla
"They tell them and lead 23:31 [h] ver 17
astray with their reckless li
not send or appoint them. Th 23:32 [i] Jer 7:8;
benefit[j] these people in the l
clares the LORD.

False Oracles and False Prophe

33 "When these people, or a proph
a priest, ask you, 'What is the oracle
the LORD?' say to them, 'What oracle
will forsake[l] you, declares the LORD.' 34 I
prophet or a priest or anyone else claims
'This is the oracle[m] of the LORD,' I wil
punish[n] that man and his household.
35 This is what each of you keeps on saying to his friend or relative: 'What is the 23 [o] Je
LORD's answer?'[o] or 'What has the LORD
spoken?' 36 But you must not mention
'the oracle of the LORD' again, because
every man's own word becomes his ora- 23:36
cle and so you distort[p] the words of the [p] Gal 1:7-
living God, the LORD Almighty, our God. 2Pe 3:16
37 This is what you keep saying to a
prophet: 'What is the LORD's answer to
you?' or 'What has the LORD spoken?'
38 Although you claim, 'This is the oracle
of the LORD,' this is what the LORD says:
You used the words, 'This is the oracle of
the LORD,' even though I told you that
you must not claim, 'This is the oracle of
the LORD.' 39 Therefore, I will surely forget 23:39
you and cast[q] you out of my presence [q] Jer 7:15
along with the city I gave to you and your
fathers. 40 I will bring upon you everlast- 23:40
ing disgrace[r]—everlasting shame that [r] Jer 20:11; Eze 5:14-15
will not be forgotten."

Two Baskets of Figs

24 After Jehoiachin[c][s] son of Je- 24:1 [s] 2Ki 24:16;
hoiakim king of Judah and the 2Ch 36:9; Jer 29:2 [t] Am 8:1-2
officials, the craftsmen and the artisans
of Judah were carried into exile from Jerusalem to Babylon by Nebuchadnezzar
king of Babylon, the LORD showed me
two baskets of figs[t] placed in front of the
temple of the LORD. 2 One basket had
very good figs, like those that ripen ear-

TELLING THE TRUTH

Compared to the messages of the optimistic, yet false, prophets of his day, Jeremiah's warnings stood out like a sour note from a fifth grade band student. The false prophets claimed that their dreams and visions were from God, but their prophecies were in fact the very opposite of what God had to say about the way the people were living and what they could expect as a result. God objected that they "prophesy lies in my name" (Jeremiah 23:25). The situation didn't change much from Jeremiah's day to Jesus' time. Jesus warned his own generation about people who wrongly claim to speak God's words: "Watch out that no one deceives you . . . many false prophets will appear and deceive many people" (Matthew 24:4,11). Jesus, like Jeremiah, was especially critical of counterfeit religious leaders, referring to them as "hypocrites" and "blind guides" (Matthew 23:23–24).

[a] 33 Or *burden* (see Septuagint and Vulgate)
[b] 33 Hebrew; Septuagint and Vulgate *'You are the burden.* (The Hebrew for *oracle* and *burden* is the same.)
[c] 1 Hebrew *Jeconiah,* a variant of *Jehoiachin*

d very poor[u] figs,
24:2 [u]Isa 5:4 ly; the other be eaten.
so bad they ked me, "What do
24:3 [v]Jer 1:11; Am 8:2 3Then The good ones are
you se oor ones are so bad
"
f the LORD came to
he LORD, the God of
se good figs, I regard
from Judah, whom I
s place to the land of
6My eyes will watch
good, and I will bring
is land. I will build[x]
tear them down; I will
ot uproot them. 7I will
to know me, that I am
ill be my people,[y] and I
, for they will return[z] to
ir heart.[a]
e the poor[b] figs, which are so
cannot be eaten,' says the LORD,
I deal with Zedekiah king of Ju-
h, his officials[c] and the survivors[d]
from Jerusalem, whether they remain in
24:9 this land or live in Egypt.[e] 9I will make
, 34:17 them abhorrent[f] and an offense to all
Dt 28:25; 1Ki 9:7 the kingdoms of the earth, a reproach
[h]Jer 29:18 and a byword,[g] an object of ridicule and
[i]Dt 28:37 cursing,[h] wherever I banish[i] them. 10I
24:10 will send the sword,[j] famine and plague[k]
[j]Isa 51:19 against them until they are destroyed
[k]Jer 27:8 from the land I gave to them and their
fathers.' "

Seventy Years of Captivity

25 The word came to Jeremiah
concerning all the people of Ju-
25:1 dah in the fourth year of Jehoiakim[l] son
[l]2Ki 24:2; Jer 36:1 of Josiah king of Judah, which was the
[m]2Ki 24:1 first year of Nebuchadnezzar[m] king of
Babylon. 2So Jeremiah the prophet said
25:2 to all the people of Judah[n] and to all
[n]Jer 18:11 those living in Jerusalem: 3For twenty-
25:3 three years—from the thirteenth year of
[o]Jer 1:2 Josiah[o] son of Amon king of Judah until
[p]Jer 11:7; 26:5 this very day—the word of the LORD has
[q]Jer 7:26 come to me and I have spoken to you
again and again,[p] but you have not listened.[q]
25:4 4And though the LORD has sent all his
[r]Jer 7:25 servants the prophets[r] to you again and
again, you have not listened or paid any
attention. 5They said, "Turn now, each
of you, from your evil ways and your evil
practices, and you can stay in the land

the LORD gave to you and your fathers
for ever and ever. 6Do not follow other 25:6
gods[s] to serve and worship them; do not [s]Dt 8:19
provoke me to anger with what your
hands have made. Then I will not harm
you."
7"But you did not listen to me," declares the LORD, "and you have provoked 25:7
me with what your hands have made,[t] [t]Dt 32:21
and you have brought harm[u] to your- [u]2Ki 21:15
selves."
8Therefore the LORD Almighty says
this: "Because you have not listened to 25:9
my words, 9I will summon[v] all the peo- [v]Isa 13:3-5
ples of the north[w] and my servant[x] Neb- [w]Jer 1:15
uchadnezzar king of Babylon," declares [x]Jer 27:6
the LORD, "and I will bring them against [y]Jer 18:16
this land and its inhabitants and against
all the surrounding nations. I will completely destroy[b] them and make them
an object of horror and scorn,[y] and an
everlasting ruin. 10I will banish from 25:10
them the sounds[z] of joy and gladness, [z]Isa 24:8; Eze 26:13
the voices of bride and bridegroom,[a] the [a]Jer 7:34
sound of millstones[b] and the light of the [b]Ecc 12:3-4
lamp.[c] 11This whole country will be- [c]Rev 18:22-23
come a desolate wasteland,[d] and these 25:11
nations will serve the king of Babylon [d]Jer 4:26-27; 12:11-12
seventy years.[e] [e]2Ch 36:21
12"But when the seventy years[f] are ful- 25:12
filled, I will punish the king of Babylon [f]Jer 29:10

[a]5 Or *Chaldeans* [b]9 The Hebrew term refers to the irrevocable giving over of things or persons to the LORD, often by totally destroying them.

EXACTLY TIMED

Jeremiah predicted that the exact duration of the Babylonian captivity would be 70 years (Jeremiah 25:11) and that Babylon itself would fall at the end of that time (verse 12). The fact that Israel would be exiled for a relatively short period of time must have instilled in God's people hope for the future. In the meantime Daniel, another prophet who lived during Jeremiah's lifetime, was deeply moved by reading Jeremiah's prediction (Daniel 9:2). After prayer and fasting, Daniel received a vision from God that the promised Messiah would come to the people (Daniel 9:25). God used both Jeremiah and Daniel to remind his people that he had neither abandoned them during their exile nor forgotten his promise of a Messiah who would carry out God's perfect plan of redemption (Ephesians 1:3–10; Colossians 1:13–14).

and his nation, the land of the Babyloni-
25:12 ans,[a] for their guilt," declares the LORD,
g Isa 13:19-22; "and will make it desolate[g] forever. [13]I
14:22-23 will bring upon that land all the things I
have spoken against it, all that are written in this book and prophesied by Jeremiah against all the nations. [14]They
25:14 h Jer 27:7 themselves will be enslaved[h] by many
i Jer 50:9; 51:27- nations[i] and great kings; I will repay[j]
28 j Jer 51:6 them according to their deeds and the
work of their hands."

The Cup of God's Wrath

[15]This is what the LORD, the God of Is-
25:15 rael, said to me: "Take from my hand
k Isa 51:17; this cup[k] filled with the wine of my
Ps 75:8; Rev 14:10 wrath and make all the nations to whom
I send you drink it. [16]When they drink it,
25:16 l Na 3:11 they will stagger[l] and go mad[m] because
m Jer 51:7 of the sword I will send among them."
[17]So I took the cup from the LORD's
hand and made all the nations to whom
25:17 n Jer 1:10 he sent[n] me drink it: [18]Jerusalem and the
towns of Judah, its kings and officials, to
make them a ruin and an object of hor-
25:18 o Jer 24:9 ror and scorn and cursing,[o] as they are
p Jer 44:22 today;[p] [19]Pharaoh king of Egypt, his attendants, his officials and all his people,
[20]and all the foreign people there; all the
25:20 q Job 1:1 kings of Uz;[q] all the kings of the Philis-
r Jer 47:5 tines (those of Ashkelon,[r] Gaza, Ekron,
25:21 and the people left at Ashdod); [21]Edom,
s Jer 49:1 Moab and Ammon;[s] [22]all the kings of
25:22 Tyre and Sidon;[t] the kings of the coast-
t Jer 47:4 lands[u] across the sea; [23]Dedan, Tema,
u Jer 31:10 Buz and all who are in distant places[b];[v]
25:23 [24]all the kings of Arabia[w] and all the
v Jer 9:26; 49:32 kings of the foreign people who live in
25:24 the desert; [25]all the kings of Zimri,
w 2Ch 9:14 Elam[x] and Media; [26]and all the kings of
25:25 the north,[y] near and far, one after the
x Ge 10:22 other—all the kingdoms on the face of
25:26 the earth. And after all of them, the king
y Jer 50:3,9 z Jer 51:41 of Sheshach[c][z] will drink it too.
[27]"Then tell them, 'This is what the
25:27 LORD Almighty, the God of Israel, says:
a ver 16,28; Drink, get drunk[a] and vomit, and fall to
Hab 2:16 b Eze 21:4 rise no more because of the sword[b] I will
send among you.' [28]But if they refuse to
take the cup from your hand and drink,
tell them, 'This is what the LORD
25:29 Almighty says: You must drink it! [29]See, I
c Jer 13:12-14 am beginning to bring disaster[c] on the
d 1Pe 4:17 city that bears my Name,[d] and will you
e Pr 11:31 indeed go unpunished?[e] You will not go
unpunished, for I am calling down a

sword upon all[f] who
declares the LORD Alm
[30]"Now prophesy a
against them and say to ... rth,
25:29 f ver 30-31

" 'The LORD will roar[g] fro
he will thunder[h] from h
dwelling
and roar mightily against
land.
He will shout like those who t
the grapes,
shout against all who live on t
earth.
[31]The tumult will resound to the
ends of the earth,
for the LORD will bring charges[i]
against the nations;
he will bring judgment on all
mankind
and put the wicked to the
sword,' "

declares the LORD.

[32]This is what the LORD Almighty says:

"Look! Disaster is spreading 25:32
from nation to nation;[j] j Isa 34:2
a mighty storm[k] is rising k Jer 23:19
from the ends of the earth."

[33]At that time those slain[l] by the LORD 25:33 l Isa 66:16;
will be everywhere—from one end of the Eze 39:17-20
earth to the other. They will not be m Jer 16:4
mourned or gathered[m] up or buried,[n] but n Ps 79:3
will be like refuse lying on the ground.

[34]Weep and wail, you shepherds; 25:34
roll[o] in the dust, you leaders of o Jer 6:26
the flock. p Isa 34:6; Jer 50:27
For your time to be slaughtered[p]
has come;
you will fall and be shattered like
fine pottery.
[35]The shepherds will have nowhere
to flee,
the leaders of the flock no place 25:35
to escape.[q] q Job 11:20
[36]Hear the cry of the shepherds,
the wailing of the leaders of the
flock,
for the LORD is destroying their
pasture.
[37]The peaceful meadows will be laid
waste
because of the fierce anger of the
LORD.

[a] 12 Or *Chaldeans* [b] 23 Or *who clip the hair by their foreheads* [c] 26 *Sheshach* is a cryptogram for Babylon.

25:38 38Like a lion[r] he will leave his lair,
r Jer 4:7 and their land will become
desolate
because of the sword[a] of the
oppressor
and because of the LORD's fierce
anger.

Jeremiah Threatened With Death

26:1 s 2Ki 23:36 26 Early in the reign of Jehoiakim[s]
son of Josiah king of Judah, this
word came from the LORD: 2“This is
26:2 what the LORD says: Stand in the court-
t Jer 19:14 yard[t] of the LORD's house and speak to
u Jer 1:17; all the people of the towns of Judah who
Mt 28:20; Ac 20:27 come to worship in the house of the
v Dt 4:2 LORD. Tell[u] them everything I command
26:3 you; do not omit[v] a word. 3Perhaps they
w Jer 36:7 will listen and each will turn[w] from his
x Jer 18:8 evil way. Then I will relent[x] and not
bring on them the disaster I was planning because of the evil they have done.
26:4 4Say to them, 'This is what the LORD
y Lev 26:14 says: If you do not listen[y] to me and fol-
z 1Ki 9:6 low my law,[z] which I have set before you,
5and if you do not listen to the words of
my servants the prophets, whom I have
26:5 sent to you again and again (though you
a Jer 25:4 have not listened[a]), 6then I will make
26:6 b Jos 18:1 this house like Shiloh[b] and this city an
c 2Ki 22:19 object of cursing[c] among all the nations
of the earth.' ”

7The priests, the prophets and all the
people heard Jeremiah speak these
words in the house of the LORD. 8But as
soon as Jeremiah finished telling all the
people everything the LORD had commanded him to say, the priests, the
prophets and all the people seized him
and said, “You must die! 9Why do you
prophesy in the LORD's name that this
26:9 house will be like Shiloh and this city
d Jer 9:11 will be desolate and deserted?”[d] And all
the people crowded around Jeremiah in
the house of the LORD.

10When the officials of Judah heard
about these things, they went up from
the royal palace to the house of the LORD
and took their places at the entrance of
the New Gate of the LORD's house.
11Then the priests and the prophets said
26:11 to the officials and all the people, “This
e Dt 18:20; man should be sentenced to death[e] be-
Jer 18:23; 38:4; Mt 26:66; cause he has prophesied against this
Ac 6:11 city. You have heard it with your own
ears!”

12Then Jeremiah said to all the officials[f] and all the people: “The LORD sent 26:12
me to prophesy[g] against this house and f Jer 1:18
this city all the things you have heard.[h] g Am 7:15; Ac 4:18-20; 5:29
13Now reform[i] your ways and your ac- h ver 2,15
tions and obey the LORD your God. Then 26:13
the LORD will relent and not bring the di- i Jer 7:5;
saster he has pronounced against you. Joel 2:12-14
14As for me, I am in your hands;[j] do with 26:14
me whatever you think is good and j Jer 38:5
right. 15Be assured, however, that if you
put me to death, you will bring the guilt
of innocent blood on yourselves and on
this city and on those who live in it, for
in truth the LORD has sent me to you to
speak all these words in your hearing.”

16Then the officials[k] and all the peo- 26:16
ple said to the priests and the prophets, k Ac 23:9 l Ac 5:34-39;
“This man should not be sentenced to 23:29
death![l] He has spoken to us in the name
of the LORD our God.”

17Some of the elders of the land
stepped forward and said to the entire
assembly of people, 18“Micah[m] of Mo- 26:18
resheth prophesied in the days of Heze- m Mic 1:1
kiah king of Judah. He told all the peo- n Isa 2:3 o Ne 4:2; Jer 9:11
ple of Judah, 'This is what the LORD p Mic 4:1; Zec 8:3
Almighty says: q Jer 17:3

“ 'Zion[n] will be plowed like a field,
Jerusalem will become a heap of
rubble,[o]
the temple hill[p] a mound
overgrown with thickets.'[b][q]

19“Did Hezekiah king of Judah or anyone
else in Judah put him to death? Did not 26:19
Hezekiah[r] fear the LORD and seek his fa- r 2Ch 32:24-26;
vor? And did not the LORD relent,[s] so that Isa 37:14-20 s Ex 32:14;
he did not bring the disaster[t] he pro- 2Sa 24:16
nounced against them? We are about to t Jer 44:7 u Hab 2:10
bring a terrible disaster[u] on ourselves!”

20(Now Uriah son of Shemaiah from
Kiriath Jearim[v] was another man who 26:20 v Jos 9:17
prophesied in the name of the LORD; he
prophesied the same things against this
city and this land as Jeremiah did.
21When King Jehoiakim[w] and all his of- 26:21 w 1Ki 19:2
ficers and officials heard his words, the x Mt 10:23
king sought to put him to death. But
Uriah heard of it and fled[x] in fear to
Egypt. 22King Jehoiakim, however, sent 26:22
Elnathan[y] son of Acbor to Egypt, along y Jer 36:12,25
with some other men. 23They brought
Uriah out of Egypt and took him to King
Jehoiakim, who had him struck down

a 38 Some Hebrew manuscripts and Septuagint (see also Jer. 46:16 and 50:16); most Hebrew manuscripts *anger* b 18 Micah 3:12

with a sword and his body thrown into
the burial place of the common people.)
26:24 24Furthermore, Ahikam[z] son of Sha-
z 2Ki 22:12 phan supported Jeremiah, and so he was
not handed over to the people to be put
to death.

Judah to Serve Nebuchadnezzar

27:1 27 Early in the reign of Zedekiah[a a]
a 2Ch 36:11 son of Josiah king of Judah, this
word came to Jeremiah from the LORD:
2This is what the LORD said to me: "Make
27:2 b Jer 28:10,13 a yoke[b] out of straps and crossbars and
put it on your neck. 3Then send word to
27:3 c Jer 25:21 the kings of Edom, Moab, Ammon,[c]
Tyre and Sidon through the envoys who
have come to Jerusalem to Zedekiah
king of Judah. 4Give them a message for
their masters and say, 'This is what the
LORD Almighty, the God of Israel, says:
"Tell this to your masters: 5With my
27:5 d Dt 9:29 great power and outstretched arm[d] I
e Ps 115:16 made the earth and its people and the
animals that are on it, and I give[e] it to
27:6 anyone I please. 6Now I will hand all
f Jer 25:9 your countries over to my servant[f] Neb-
g Jer 21:7; Eze 29:18-20 uchadnezzar[g] king of Babylon; I will
h Jer 28:14; Da 2:37-38 make even the wild animals subject to
him.[h] 7All nations will serve[i] him and
27:7 i 2Ch 36:20 his son and his grandson until the time[j]
j Jer 25:12 for his land comes; then many nations
k Jer 25:14; Da 5:28 and great kings will subjugate[k] him.
8" ' "If, however, any nation or king-
dom will not serve Nebuchadnezzar
king of Babylon or bow its neck under
his yoke, I will punish that nation with
the sword, famine and plague, declares
the LORD, until I destroy it by his hand.
9So do not listen to your prophets, your
27:9 diviners, your interpreters of dreams,
l Dt 18:11 your mediums[l] or your sorcerers who
27:10 tell you, 'You will not serve the king of
m Jer 23:25 Babylon.' 10They prophesy lies[m] to you
that will only serve to remove you far
from your lands; I will banish you and
27:11 you will perish. 11But if any nation will
n Jer 21:9 bow its neck under the yoke[n] of the king
of Babylon and serve him, I will let that
nation remain in its own land to till it
and to live there, declares the LORD." ' "
12I gave the same message to Zedekiah king of Judah. I said, "Bow your neck
under the yoke of the king of Babylon;
serve him and his people, and you will
27:13 o Eze 18:31 live. 13Why will you and your people die[o]
by the sword, famine and plague with
which the LORD has threatened any nation that will not serve the king of Babylon? 14Do not listen to the words of the
prophets who say to you, 'You will not
serve the king of Babylon,' for they are 27:14
prophesying lies[p] to you. 15'I have not p Jer 14:14
sent[q] them,' declares the LORD. 'They are 27:15
prophesying lies in my name.[r] There- q Jer 23:21
fore, I will banish you and you will per- r Jer 29:9 s Jer 6:15
ish,[s] both you and the prophets who
prophesy to you.' "
16Then I said to the priests and all
these people, "This is what the LORD
says: Do not listen to the prophets who 27:16
say, 'Very soon now the articles[t] from t 2Ki 24:13; 2Ch 36:7,10;
the LORD's house will be brought back Jer 28:3; Da 1:2
from Babylon.' They are prophesying lies
to you. 17Do not listen to them. Serve the
king of Babylon, and you will live. Why
should this city become a ruin? 18If they
are prophets and have the word of the 27:18
LORD, let them plead[u] with the LORD u 1Sa 7:8
Almighty that the furnishings remaining in the house of the LORD and in the
palace of the king of Judah and in Jerusalem not be taken to Babylon. 19For this
is what the LORD Almighty says about

a 1 A few Hebrew manuscripts and Syriac (see also Jer. 27:3, 12 and 28:1); most Hebrew manuscripts *Jehoiakim* (Most Septuagint manuscripts do not have this verse.)

JESUS FOCUS

PREVAILING JUDGMENTS

God sent judgment to his people Israel in order to turn them away from sin and draw them back into a right relationship with himself. While it wasn't always clear to the people what God was doing, the details of the judgment were always under his control. God moved Nebuchadnezzar of Babylon to destroy Jerusalem but to preserve the vessels of worship from the temple (Jeremiah 27:21–22). Later on God employed Cyrus of Persia to defeat the Babylonians and send both the people and the worship vessels back to the land (Ezra 1:3,7). In both cases God's true prophets had foretold with exact precision who the conquerors would be (Isaiah 45:1–3). In the New Testament, when Jesus predicted that Jerusalem would again be destroyed, he was equally as accurate (Matthew 24:2–28), stating that "not one stone here will be left on another; every one will be thrown down" (Matthew 24:2), a prediction that was literally fulfilled in A.D. 70 when the Romans completely destroyed Jerusalem and the temple buildings.

the movable stands
things[w] that are left
h Nebuchadnezzar
not take away when
chin[a y] son of Je-
ah into exile from Je-
ı, along with all the
d Jerusalem— 21yes,
D Almighty, the God
t the things that are
the LORD and in the
f Judah and in Jeru-
e taken[z] to Babylon
remain until the day[a]
declares the LORD.
them back and re-
place.' "

Hananiah

month of that same
ourth year, early in the
h[c] king of Judah, the
niah son of Azzur, who
beon,[d] said to me in the
e LORD in the presence of the
d all the people: 2"This is what
RD Almighty, the God of Israel,
I will break the yoke[e] of the king of
bylon. 3Within two years I will bring
back to this place all the articles[f] of the
LORD's house that Nebuchadnezzar king
of Babylon removed from here and took
to Babylon. 4I will also bring back to this
28:4 22:24-27 place Jehoiachin[a g] son of Jehoiakim king
of Judah and all the other exiles from Ju-
dah who went to Babylon,' declares the
LORD, 'for I will break the yoke of the
king of Babylon.' "
5Then the prophet Jeremiah replied to
the prophet Hananiah before the priests
and all the people who were standing in
the house of the LORD. 6He said, "Amen!
May the LORD do so! May the LORD fulfill
the words you have prophesied by bringing the articles of the LORD's house and
all the exiles back to this place from
Babylon. 7Nevertheless, listen to what I
have to say in your hearing and in the
hearing of all the people: 8From early
times the prophets who preceded you
28:8 and me have prophesied war, disaster
h Lev 26:14-17; Isa 5:5-7 and plague[h] against many countries and
great kingdoms. 9But the prophet who
prophesies peace will be recognized as
28:9 one truly sent by the LORD only if his
i Dt 18:22 prediction comes true.[i]"
10Then the prophet Hananiah took
the yoke[j] off the neck of the prophet Jer- 28:10 j Jer 27:2
emiah and broke it, 11and he said[k] before
all the people, "This is what the LORD 28:11 k Jer 14:14; 27:10
says: 'In the same way will I break the
yoke of Nebuchadnezzar king of Babylon off the neck of all the nations within two years.' " At this, the prophet Jeremiah went on his way.
12Shortly after the prophet Hananiah
had broken the yoke off the neck of the
prophet Jeremiah, the word of the LORD
came to Jeremiah: 13"Go and tell Hananiah, 'This is what the LORD says: You have
broken a wooden yoke, but in its place
you will get a yoke of iron. 14This is what
the LORD Almighty, the God of Israel, 28:14
says: I will put an iron yoke[l] on the necks l Dt 28:48
of all these nations to make them serve[m] m Jer 25:11
Nebuchadnezzar king of Babylon, and n Jer 27:6
they will serve him. I will even give him
control over the wild animals.[n]' "
15Then the prophet Jeremiah said to
Hananiah the prophet, "Listen, Hanani- 28:15
ah! The LORD has not sent[o] you, yet you o Jer 29:31
have persuaded this nation to trust in p Jer 20:6; 29:21; La 2:14;
lies.[p] 16Therefore, this is what the LORD Eze 13:6
says: 'I am about to remove you from the 28:16
face of the earth.[q] This very year you are q Ge 7:4
going to die, because you have preached r Dt 13:5; Jer 29:32
rebellion[r] against the LORD.' "
17In the seventh month of that same
year, Hananiah the prophet died.

A Letter to the Exiles

29 This is the text of the letter that
the prophet Jeremiah sent from
Jerusalem to the surviving elders among
the exiles and to the priests, the prophets and all the other people Nebuchadnezzar had carried into exile from Jeru- 29:1
salem to Babylon.[s] 2(This was after King s 2Ch 36:10
Jehoiachin[a t] and the queen mother, the 29:2
court officials and the leaders of Judah t 2Ki 24:12; Jer 22:24-28
and Jerusalem, the craftsmen and the
artisans had gone into exile from Jerusalem.) 3He entrusted the letter to Elasah
son of Shaphan and to Gemariah son of
Hilkiah, whom Zedekiah king of Judah
sent to King Nebuchadnezzar in Babylon. It said:

4This is what the LORD Almighty,
the God of Israel, says to all those I
carried[u] into exile from Jerusalem 29:4 u Jer 24:5
to Babylon: 5"Build[v] houses and 29:5
settle down; plant gardens and eat v ver 28

[a] 20,4,2 Hebrew *Jeconiah,* a variant of *Jehoiachin*

what they produce. [6]Marry and
have sons and daughters; find
wives for your sons and give your
daughters in marriage, so that they
too may have sons and daughters.
Increase in number there; do not
decrease. [7]Also, seek the peace and
29:7
prosperity of the city to which I
[w]Ezr 6:10; 1Ti 2:1-2
have carried you into exile. Pray[w]
to the LORD for it, because if it prospers, you too will prosper." [8]Yes, this
is what the LORD Almighty, the God
of Israel, says: "Do not let the
prophets and diviners among you
29:8
[x]Jer 37:9
deceive[x] you. Do not listen to the
[y]Jer 23:27
dreams you encourage them to
29:9
have.[y] [9]They are prophesying lies[z]
[z]Jer 14:14; 27:15
to you in my name. I have not sent
them," declares the LORD.
29:10
[10]This is what the LORD says:
[a]2Ch 36:21; Jer 25:12; Da 9:2
"When seventy years[a] are complet-
[b]Jer 21:22
ed for Babylon, I will come to you
and fulfill my gracious promise to
bring you back[b] to this place. [11]For
29:11
[c]Ps 40:5
I know the plans[c] I have for you,"
declares the LORD, "plans to prosper you and not to harm you, plans
to give you hope and a future.
[12]Then you will call upon me and
29:12
come and pray to me, and I will lis-
[d]Ps 145:19
ten[d] to you. [13]You will seek[e] me and
29:13
find me when you seek me with all
[e]Mt 7:7
your heart.[f] [14]I will be found by
[f]Dt 4:29; Jer 24:7
you," declares the LORD, "and will
bring you back[g] from captivity.[a] I
29:14
will gather you from all the nations
[g]Dt 30:3; Jer 30:3
and places where I have banished
[h]Jer 23:3-4
you," declares the LORD, "and will
bring you back to the place from
which I carried you into exile."[h]
[15]You may say, "The LORD has
raised up prophets for us in Babylon," [16]but this is what the LORD
says about the king who sits on David's throne and all the people who
remain in this city, your countrymen who did not go with you into
exile— [17]yes, this is what the LORD
29:17
Almighty says: "I will send the
[i]Jer 27:8
sword, famine and plague[i] against
[j]Jer 24:8-10
them and I will make them like
poor figs[j] that are so bad they cannot be eaten. [18]I will pursue them
with the sword, famine and plague
29:18
and will make them abhorrent[k] to
[k]Jer 15:4
all the kingdoms of the earth and
[l]Dt 28:25; Jer 42:18
an object of cursing and horror,[l] of

scorn and reproach, a
nations where I drive
they have not listen
words,"[m] declares the LO
that I sent to them again
by my servants the prophe
you exiles have not listened
declares the LORD.
[20]Therefore, hear the word
LORD, all you exiles whom I
sent[o] away from Jerusalem to
ylon. [21]This is what the L
Almighty, the God of Israel, sa
about Ahab son of Kolaiah an
Zedekiah son of Maaseiah, who ar
prophesying lies[p] to you in my
name: "I will hand them over to
Nebuchadnezzar king of Babylon,
and he will put them to death before your very eyes. [22]Because of
them, all the exiles from Judah who
are in Babylon will use this curse:
'The LORD treat you like Zedekiah
and Ahab, whom the king of Bab- 29:2
ylon burned[q] in the fire.' [23]For they [q]Da
have done outrageous things in Is-
rael; they have committed adul- 29:23
tery[r] with their neighbors' wives [r]Jer 23:14
and in my name have spoken lies, [s]Heb 4:13
which I did not tell them to do. I
know[s] it and am a witness to it,"
declares the LORD.

Message to Shemaiah

[24]Tell Shemaiah the Nehelamite,
[25]"This is what the LORD Almighty, the
God of Israel, says: You sent letters in
your own name to all the people in Jeru- 29:25
salem, to Zephaniah[t] son of Maaseiah [t]2Ki 25:18; Jer 21:1
the priest, and to all the other priests.
You said to Zephaniah, [26]'The LORD has
appointed you priest in place of Jehoiada to be in charge of the house of the 29:26
LORD; you should put any madman[u] who [u]2Ki 9:11; Hos 9:7;
acts like a prophet into the stocks[v] and Jn 10:20
neck-irons. [27]So why have you not repri- [v]Jer 20:2
manded Jeremiah from Anathoth, who
poses as a prophet among you? [28]He has
sent this message[w] to us in Babylon: It 29:28
will be a long time.[x] Therefore build[y] [w]ver 1 [x]ver 10
houses and settle down; plant gardens [y]ver 5
and eat what they produce.' "
[29]Zephaniah the priest, however, read
the letter to Jeremiah the prophet.
[30]Then the word of the LORD came to Jeremiah: [31]"Send this message to all the

[a] 14 Or *will restore your fortunes*

DISCOVERY 201

God's Eternal Plan

Jeremiah 29:11 is a favorite verse for many people, a beautiful nugget hidden within a rather gloomy passage like a pearl tucked away within an oyster, just waiting to be discovered. Despite the fact that God through Jeremiah was predicting a 70-year exile, this particular verse is one of the most hopeful in Scripture: " 'I know the plans I have for you,' declares the LORD, 'plans to prosper you and not to harm you, plans to give you hope and a future.' " Jeremiah went on to repeat God's words that he, the loving Father, would listen to his people, provided they would seek him wholeheartedly (verse 13), that he would be found by them and bring them back from captivity, gathering them from all the nations and places to which he had banished them (verse 14).

True, this prediction was speaking of the future, and 70 years would be a long time for Israel to have to wait (not to mention that deliverance would come outside of the life span of most of the individuals hearing Jeremiah's words). It would be easy for us in our contemporary "insta-culture" to scoff at such a long-range promise, to cancel out its significance because of the seemingly interminable time span. But God was speaking not only to and about Israel in the sense of the corporate "you"; he was directing his promise to the current generation, and ultimately to each of us individually.

Liberation from Babylonian exile might not be accomplished within the lives of most of Jeremiah's audience, but God's plans for hope and a future were for them as well. God's plan of well-being and prosperity rather than harm, of listening to his people and being available to them, would certainly find partial fulfillment during the period of exile—and ultimate fulfillment not only in the deliverance from exile but in the deliverance from sin that would be brought about through the sacrificial death of Jesus, God's one and only Son. God's desire and intention for his people (in fact, for all people he has created) is always for the good. He loves his entire creation and longs for all people everywhere to come to him and enter into a love relationship with him (Ezekiel 18:23,32; 33:11; John 3:16–17; 1 Timothy 2:4; 4:10; Titus 2:11; 2 Peter 3:9).

The apostle Paul expressed a similar sentiment in yet another verse that is a "pearl" for many believers: "We know that in all things God works for the good of those who love him, who have been called according to his purpose" (Romans 8:28). *All things?* We want to ask. *Are you certain, Paul? "Trouble or hardship or persecution or famine or nakedness or danger or sword"?* (Romans 8:35; italics added). Paul's response is emphatic and resounding: "In all these things we are more than conquerors through him who loved us. For I am convinced that . . . [nothing] in all creation, will be able to separate us from the love of God that is in Christ Jesus our Lord" (Romans 8:37–39).

***Self-Discovery:** What does it mean to you that God plans to give you hope and a future? How will this promise help you to withstand the daily ups and downs of life?*

GO TO DISCOVERY 202 ON PAGE 1027

29:31 [z] ver 24 [a] Jer 14:14; 28:15
29:32 [b] 1Sa 2:30-33 [c] ver 10 [d] Jer 28:16

exiles: 'This is what the LORD says about
Shemaiah[z] the Nehelamite: Because
Shemaiah has prophesied to you, even
though I did not send[a] him, and has led
you to believe a lie, 32 this is what the
LORD says: I will surely punish Shemaiah
the Nehelamite and his descendants.[b]
He will have no one left among this people, nor will he see the good[c] things I will
do for my people, declares the LORD, because he has preached rebellion[d]
against me.' "

Restoration of Israel

30:2 [e] Isa 30:8
30:3 [f] Jer 29:14 [g] Jer 16:15

30 This is the word that came to
Jeremiah from the LORD: 2 "This
is what the LORD, the God of Israel, says:
'Write[e] in a book all the words I have
spoken to you. 3 The days are coming,'
declares the LORD, 'when I will bring[f] my
people Israel and Judah back from captivity[a] and restore[g] them to the land I
gave their forefathers to possess,' says
the LORD."

4 These are the words the LORD spoke
concerning Israel and Judah: 5 "This is
what the LORD says:

30:5 [h] Jer 6:25
30:6 [i] Jer 4:31
30:7 [j] Isa 2:12; Joel 2:11 [k] Zep 1:15 [l] ver 10

" 'Cries of fear[h] are heard—
terror, not peace.
6 Ask and see:
Can a man bear children?
Then why do I see every strong
man
with his hands on his stomach
like a woman in labor,[i]
every face turned deathly pale?
7 How awful that day[j] will be!
None will be like it.
It will be a time of trouble[k] for
Jacob,
but he will be saved[l] out of it.

30:8 [m] Isa 9:4 [n] Eze 34:27

8 " 'In that day,' declares the LORD
Almighty,
'I will break the yoke[m] off their
necks
and will tear off their bonds;
no longer will foreigners enslave
them.[n]

30:9 [o] Isa 55:3-4; Lk 1:69; Ac 2:30; 13:23 [p] Eze 34:23-24; 37:24; Hos 3:5

9 Instead, they will serve the LORD
their God
and David[o] their king,[p]
whom I will raise up for them.

30:10 [q] Isa 43:5; Jer 46:27-28 [r] Isa 44:2

10 " 'So do not fear,[q] O Jacob my
servant;[r]
do not be dismayed, O Israel,'
declares the LORD.

30:10 [s] Jer 29:14 [t] Isa 35:9

'I will surely save[s] you out of a
distant place,
your descendants from the land
of their exile.
Jacob will again have peace and
security,[t]
and no one will make him afraid.

30:11 [u] Jer 4:27; 46:28 [v] Jer 10:24 [w] Am 9:8

11 I am with you and will save you,'
declares the LORD.
'Though I completely destroy all
the nations
among which I scatter you,
I will not completely destroy[u]
you.
I will discipline[v] you but only with
justice;
I will not let you go entirely
unpunished.'[w]

12 "This is what the LORD says:

30:12 [x] Jer 15:18
30:13 [y] Jer 8:22; 14:19; 46:11
30:14 [z] Jer 22:20; La 1:2 [a] Job 13:24 [b] Job 30:21 [c] Jer 5:6

" 'Your wound is incurable,
your injury beyond healing.[x]
13 There is no one to plead your cause,
no remedy for your sore,
no healing[y] for you.
14 All your allies[z] have forgotten you;
they care nothing for you.
I have struck you as an enemy[a]
would
and punished you as would the
cruel,[b]
because your guilt is so great
and your sins[c] so many.
15 Why do you cry out over your
wound,
your pain that has no cure?
Because of your great guilt and
many sins
I have done these things to you.

30:16 [d] Isa 33:1; Jer 2:3; 10:25 [e] Isa 14:2; Joel 3:4-8 [f] Jer 50:10
30:17 [g] Jer 33:24

16 " 'But all who devour[d] you will be
devoured;
all your enemies will go into
exile.[e]
Those who plunder[f] you will be
plundered;
all who make spoil of you I will
despoil.
17 But I will restore you to health
and heal your wounds,'
declares the LORD,
'because you are called an outcast,[g]
Zion for whom no one cares.'

18 "This is what the LORD says:

[a] 3 Or *will restore the fortunes of my people Israel and Judah*

30:18 [h]ver 3; Jer 31:23 [i]Ps 102:13 [j]Jer 31:4,24,38

" 'I will restore the fortunes[h] of
Jacob's tents
and have compassion[i] on his
dwellings;
the city will be rebuilt[j] on her ruins,
and the palace will stand in its
proper place.

30:19 [k]Isa 35:10; 51:11 [l]Isa 51:3 [m]Ps 126:1-2; Jer 31:4 [n]Jer 33:22 [o]Isa 60:9

19 From them will come songs[k] of
thanksgiving[l]
and the sound of rejoicing.[m]
I will add to their numbers,[n]
and they will not be decreased;
I will bring them honor,[o]
and they will not be disdained.

30:20 [p]Isa 54:13; Jer 31:17 [q]Isa 54:14

20 Their children[p] will be as in days of
old,
and their community will be
established[q] before me;
I will punish all who oppress
them.

30:21 [r]ver 9 [s]Nu 16:5

21 Their leader[r] will be one of their
own;
their ruler will arise from among
them.
I will bring him near[s] and he will
come close to me,
for who is he who will devote
himself
to be close to me?'
declares the LORD.
22 " 'So you will be my people,
and I will be your God.' "

30:23 [t]Jer 23:19

23 See, the storm[t] of the LORD
will burst out in wrath,
a driving wind swirling down
on the heads of the wicked.

30:24 [u]Jer 4:8 [v]Jer 4:28 [w]Jer 23:19-20

24 The fierce anger[u] of the LORD will
not turn back[v]
until he fully accomplishes
the purposes of his heart.
In days to come
you will understand[w] this.

31:1 [x]Jer 30:22

31 "At that time," declares the
LORD, "I will be the God[x] of all
the clans of Israel, and they will be my
people."
2 This is what the LORD says:

31:2 [y]Nu 14:20 [z]Ex 33:14

"The people who survive the sword
will find favor[y] in the desert;
I will come to give rest[z] to Israel."
3 The LORD appeared to us in the past,[a]
saying:

31:3 [a]Dt 4:37 [b]Hos 11:4

"I have loved[a] you with an
everlasting love;
I have drawn[b] you with
loving-kindness.

31:4 [c]Jer 30:19

4 I will build you up again
and you will be rebuilt, O Virgin
Israel.
Again you will take up your
tambourines
and go out to dance with the
joyful.[c]

31:5 [d]Jer 50:19 [e]Isa 65:21; Am 9:14

5 Again you will plant vineyards
on the hills of Samaria;[d]
the farmers will plant them
and enjoy their fruit.[e]

31:6 [f]Isa 2:3; Jer 50:4-5; Mic 4:2

6 There will be a day when
watchmen cry out
on the hills of Ephraim,
'Come, let us go up to Zion,
to the LORD our God.' "[f]
7 This is what the LORD says:

31:7 [g]Dt 28:13; Isa 61:9 [h]Ps 14:7; 28:9 [i]Isa 37:31

"Sing with joy for Jacob;
shout for the foremost[g] of the
nations.
Make your praises heard, and say,
'O LORD, save[h] your people,
the remnant[i] of Israel.'

31:8 [j]Jer 3:18; 23:8 [k]Dt 30:4; Eze 34:12-14 [l]Isa 42:16 [m]Eze 34:16; Mic 4:6

8 See, I will bring them from the land
of the north[j]
and gather[k] them from the ends
of the earth.
Among them will be the blind[l] and
the lame,[m]
expectant mothers and women
in labor;
a great throng will return.

31:9 [n]Ps 126:5 [o]Isa 63:13 [p]Isa 49:11 [q]Ex 4:22; Jer 3:4

9 They will come with weeping;[n]
they will pray as I bring them
back.
I will lead[o] them beside streams of
water
on a level[p] path where they will
not stumble,
because I am Israel's father,[q]
and Ephraim is my firstborn son.

31:10 [r]Isa 66:19; Jer 25:22 [s]Jer 50:19 [t]Isa 40:11; Eze 34:12

10 "Hear the word of the LORD,
O nations;
proclaim it in distant
coastlands:[r]
'He who scattered Israel will
gather[s] them
and will watch over his flock like
a shepherd.'[t]

31:11 [u]Isa 44:23; 48:20 [v]Ps 142:6

11 For the LORD will ransom Jacob
and redeem[u] them from the hand
of those stronger[v] than they.

[a] 3 Or *LORD has appeared to us from afar*

31:12 [w] Eze 17:23; Mic 4:1 [x] Joel 3:18 [y] Hos 2:21-22 [z] Isa 58:11 [a] Isa 65:19; Jn 16:22; Rev 7:17

12 They will come and shout for joy
on the heights[w] of Zion;
they will rejoice in the bounty[x]
of the LORD—
the grain, the new wine and the oil,[y]
the young of the flocks and herds.
They will be like a well-watered
garden,[z]
and they will sorrow[a] no more.
13 Then maidens will dance and be
glad,
young men and old as well.
I will turn their mourning[b] into
gladness;
I will give them comfort and joy[c]
instead of sorrow.
14 I will satisfy[d] the priests with
abundance,
and my people will be filled with
my bounty,"
declares the LORD.

31:13 [b] Isa 61:3 [c] Ps 30:11; Isa 51:11

31:14 [d] ver 25

15 This is what the LORD says:

"A voice is heard in Ramah,[e]
mourning and great weeping,
Rachel weeping for her children
and refusing to be comforted,[f]
because her children are no
more."[g]

31:15 [e] Jos 18:25 [f] Ge 37:35 [g] Jer 10:20; Mt 2:17-18*

16 This is what the LORD says:

"Restrain your voice from weeping
and your eyes from tears,[h]
for your work will be rewarded,[i]"
declares the LORD.

31:16 [h] Isa 25:8; 30:19 [i] Ru 2:12

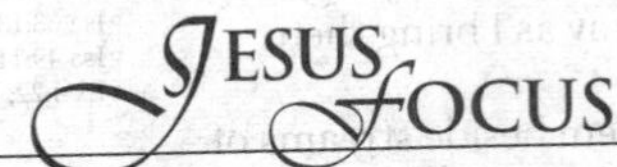

RACHEL WEEPS

The Babylonians gathered the Israelites in Ramah and deported them from there to Babylon (Jeremiah 40:1). Jeremiah 31:15 refers to "Rachel weeping for her children" in Ramah, which is a way of saying that there was such great agony over the exile of the people that even their ancestors were crying. In the New Testament, Matthew 2:18 likens another tragic event to this one. King Herod slaughtered every baby boy in the vicinity of Bethlehem in a futile attempt to eliminate the Messiah. Both tragedies refer back to Jacob's wife, Rachel, who died at Bethlehem while giving birth to Benjamin (Genesis 35:16–20). And in both cases God has promised to overrule the nation's sorrow for her ultimate joy (Jeremiah 31:16–17,20; Luke 1:31–33; 2:10–11).

"They will return[j] from the land
of the enemy.
17 So there is hope for your future,"
declares the LORD.
"Your children will return to
their own land.

31:16 [j] Jer 30:3; Eze 11:17

18 "I have surely heard Ephraim's
moaning:
'You disciplined[k] me like an
unruly calf,[l]
and I have been disciplined.
Restore[m] me, and I will return,
because you are the LORD my
God.
19 After I strayed,[n]
I repented;
after I came to understand,
I beat[o] my breast.
I was ashamed and humiliated
because I bore the disgrace of
my youth.'
20 Is not Ephraim my dear son,
the child in whom I delight?
Though I often speak against him,
I still remember[p] him.
Therefore my heart yearns for him;
I have great compassion[q] for
him,"
declares the LORD.

31:18 [k] Job 5:17 [l] Hos 4:16 [m] Ps 80:3

31:19 [n] Eze 36:31 [o] Eze 21:12; Lk 18:13

31:20 [p] Hos 4:4; 11:8 [q] Isa 55:7; 63:15; Mic 7:18

21 "Set up road signs;
put up guideposts.
Take note of the highway,[r]
the road that you take.
Return,[s] O Virgin[t] Israel,
return to your towns.
22 How long will you wander,[u]
O unfaithful[v] daughter?
The LORD will create a new thing
on earth—
a woman will surround[a] a man."

31:21 [r] Jer 50:5 [s] Isa 52:11 [t] ver 4

31:22 [u] Jer 2:23 [v] Jer 3:6

23 This is what the LORD Almighty, the
God of Israel, says: "When I bring them
back from captivity,[b][w] the people in the
land of Judah and in its towns will once
again use these words: 'The LORD bless
you, O righteous dwelling,[x] O sacred
mountain.'[y] 24 People will live[z] together
in Judah and all its towns—farmers and
those who move about with their flocks.
25 I will refresh the weary and satisfy the
faint."[a]
26 At this I awoke[b] and looked around.
My sleep had been pleasant to me.
27 "The days are coming," declares the

31:23 [w] Jer 30:18 [x] Isa 1:26 [y] Ps 48:1; Zec 8:3

31:24 [z] Zec 8:4-8

31:25 [a] Jn 4:14

31:26 [b] Zec 4:1

[a] 22 Or *will go about ⌞seeking⌟;* or *will protect*
[b] 23 Or *I restore their fortunes*

HE NEW COVENANT

omise under the "old
humanity was that he
new covenant" with his
ah 31:31). This prophecy
nt that it comprises the
Testament quote from the
ent; it is quoted in its entirety
8:8–12 and again in
: "This is the covenant I will
h them after that time, says the
will put my laws in their hearts,
and I will write them on their minds . . . Their sins and lawless acts I will remember no more." This is also the only Old Testament passage in which the phrase *new covenant* appears.

Jeremiah wanted God's people to begin to grasp the contrast between the two covenants. Although they were in some ways similar and were both pledges made by Almighty God, one was complete and the other was not.

The old covenant referred to the promises God had made to Israel when he had delivered his people from slavery in Egypt. God made the promise through Moses on Mount Sinai that he would bless the nation if the people would only keep his law (Exodus 19:5; 2 Corinthians 3:14). Part of that law included the necessity of worshiping God—first at the tabernacle and later at the temple.

Both the tabernacle and the temple provided the people with a focal point from which to direct their attention to God, as well as a designated location to offer sacrifices for sin. The animal sacrifices, however, offered only a temporary provision from God to "cover" sin until the arrival of the final Sacrifice who would remove sin forever.

The new covenant centers around that one final Sacrifice—Jesus Christ—and it is a covenant of forgiveness (Jeremiah 31:34). The New Testament writers tell us that Jesus is "superior" to the animal sacrifices because his shed blood eradicated our sin forever (Hebrews 8:6; 9:11–28). The new covenant between God and us is not only superior to the old one, but it replaces the first covenant with something far better (Hebrews 8:13).

Jesus' sacrifice was the only one that offered reconciliation with God *one* time for *all* time; the sacrifice made only once covers the sin of all humanity for eternity (Hebrews 10:11–12). When we truly repent and ask God for forgiveness, he deliberately blots our sin from his memory and no longer holds it against us (Hebrews 8:17).

Self-Discovery: *When someone has wronged you, are you able not only to forgive but also to "forget"? What do you think forgetting really means in this context?*

GO TO DISCOVERY 203 ON PAGE 1031

WE ARE NEVER NEARER CHRIST THAN WHEN WE FIND OURSELVES LOST IN A HOLY AMAZEMENT AT HIS UNSPEAKABLE LOVE.

John Owen, *Puritan Pastor*

31:27 [c] Eze 36:9-11; Hos 2:23
LORD, "when I will plant[c] the house of Israel and the house of Judah with the offspring of men and of animals. 28Just as I
watched over them to uproot and tear
31:28 [d] Jer 18:8; 44:27 [e] Jer 1:10
down, and to overthrow, destroy and
bring disaster,[d] so I will watch over them
to build and to plant,"[e] declares the
LORD. 29"In those days people will no
longer say,

31:29 [f] La 5:7 [g] Eze 18:2
'The fathers[f] have eaten sour
grapes,
and the children's teeth are set
on edge.'[g]

31:30 [h] Isa 3:11; Gal 6:7
30Instead, everyone will die for his own
sin;[h] whoever eats sour grapes—his own
teeth will be set on edge.

31"The time is coming," declares the
LORD,
31:31 [i] Jer 32:40; Eze 37:26; Lk 22:20; Heb 8:8-12*; 10:16-17
"when I will make a new
covenant[i]
with the house of Israel
and with the house of Judah.
31:32 [j] Ex 24:8 [k] Dt 5:3
32It will not be like the covenant[j]
I made with their forefathers[k]
when I took them by the hand
to lead them out of Egypt,
because they broke my covenant,
though I was a husband to[a]
them,[b]"
declares the LORD.
33"This is the covenant I will make
with the house of Israel
after that time," declares the
LORD.
31:33 [l] 2Co 3:3 [m] Jer 24:7; Heb 10:16
"I will put my law in their minds
and write it on their hearts.[l]
I will be their God,
and they will be my people.[m]
31:34 [n] 1Jn 2:27 [o] Jn 6:45
34No longer will a man teach[n] his
neighbor,
or a man his brother, saying,
'Know the LORD,'
because they will all know[o] me,
from the least of them to the
greatest,"
declares the LORD.
"For I will forgive
and will rememb
more."

35This is what the LORD

he who appoints[r] the sun
to shine by day,
who decrees the moon and s
to shine by night,[s]
who stirs up the sea
so that its waves roar—
the LORD Almighty is his name:[t]

31:34 [p] Isa 54:13; Jer 33:8; 50:20 [q] Ro 11:27; ... 7:19; ... 17*

36"Only if these decrees[u] vanish from
my sight,"
declares the LORD,
"will the descendants[v] of Israel
ever cease
to be a nation before me."

37This is what the LORD says:
"Only if the heavens above can be
measured[w]
and the foundations of the earth
below be searched out
will I reject[x] all the descendants of
Israel
because of all they have done,"
declares the LORD.

31:37 [w] Jer 33:22 [x] Jer 33:24-26; Ro 11:1-5

38"The days are coming," declares the
LORD, "when this city will be rebuilt[y] for
me from the Tower of Hananel[z] to the
Corner Gate.[a] 39The measuring line will
stretch from there straight to the hill of
Gareb and then turn to Goah. 40The
whole valley[b] where dead bodies[c] and
ashes are thrown, and all the terraces
out to the Kidron Valley[d] on the east as
far as the corner of the Horse Gate,[e] will
be holy[f] to the LORD. The city will never
again be uprooted or demolished."

31:38 [y] Jer 30:18 [z] Ne 3:1 [a] 2Ki 14:13; Zec 14:10
31:40 [b] Jer 7:31-32 [c] Jer 8:2 [d] 2Sa 15:23; Jn 18:1 [e] 2Ki 11:16 [f] Joel 3:17; Zec 14:21

Jeremiah Buys a Field

32 This is the word that came to
Jeremiah from the LORD in the
tenth[g] year of Zedekiah king of Judah,
which was the eighteenth[h] year of Nebuchadnezzar. 2The army of the king of
Babylon was then besieging Jerusalem,
and Jeremiah the prophet was confined
in the courtyard of the guard[i] in the royal palace of Judah.
3Now Zedekiah king of Judah had imprisoned him there, saying, "Why do you
prophesy[j] as you do? You say, 'This is
what the LORD says: I am about to hand

32:1 [g] 2Ki 25:1 [h] Jer 25:1; 39:1
32:2 [i] Ne 3:25; Jer 37:21
32:3 [j] Jer 26:8-9

[a] 32 Hebrew; Septuagint and Syriac / *and I turned away from* [b] 32 Or *was their master*

32:3 this city over to the king of Babylon, and
[k]ver 28; Jer 34:2-3 he will capture[k] it. [4]Zedekiah king of Judah will not escape[l] out of the hands of
32:4 [l]Jer 38:18,23; 39:5-7; 52:9 the Babylonians[a] but will certainly be
handed over to the king of Babylon, and
32:5 will speak with him face to face and see
[m]Jer 39:7; Eze 12:13 him with his own eyes. [5]He will take[m]
[n]Jer 21:4 Zedekiah to Babylon, where he will remain until I deal with him, declares the
LORD. If you fight against the Babylonians, you will not succeed.'"[n]

[6]Jeremiah said, "The word of the LORD
came to me: [7]Hanamel son of Shallum
your uncle is going to come to you and
say, 'Buy my field at Anathoth, because
32:7 as nearest relative it is your right and
[o]Lev 25:24-25; Ru 4:3-4; Mt 27:10* duty[o] to buy it.'

[8]"Then, just as the LORD had said, my
cousin Hanamel came to me in the
courtyard of the guard and said, 'Buy my
field at Anathoth in the territory of Benjamin. Since it is your right to redeem it
and possess it, buy it for yourself.'

"I knew that this was the word of the
LORD; [9]so I bought the field at Anathoth
from my cousin Hanamel and weighed
32:9 [p]Ge 23:16 out for him seventeen shekels[b] of silver.[p]
[10]I signed and sealed the deed, had it
32:10 [q]Ru 4:9 witnessed,[q] and weighed out the silver
on the scales. [11]I took the deed of purchase—the sealed copy containing the
terms and conditions, as well as the unsealed copy— [12]and I gave this deed to

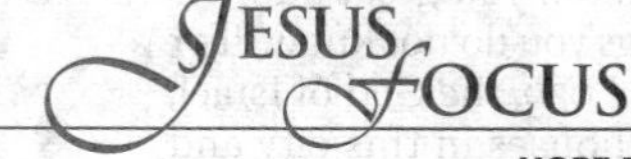

HOPE FOR THE FUTURE

Jeremiah bought some property while Jerusalem was under siege and about to fall to the Babylonians (Jeremiah 32:8–9). The plot was virtually worthless under the circumstances, but eventually the property would be passed down to Jeremiah's heirs following their return from exile. Jeremiah literally put his money where his mouth was. He demonstrated his conviction that God would keep his promise to bring the people back to the land. The prophet knew that there would be a "new" covenant (Jeremiah 31:31), one that would both fulfill the first and complete it forever (Jeremiah 32:40). In the New Testament Paul emphasized that the "new" promise God made to his people was through Jesus, the ultimate hope for the future (2 Corinthians 2:12—3:18). And Jesus himself affirmed that the new covenant was sealed in his blood (Matthew 26:28; Luke 22:20).

Baruch[r] son of Neriah,[s] the son of Mah- 32:12
seiah, in the presence of my cousin Han- [r]ver 16; Jer 36:4; 43:3,6; 45:1
amel and of the witnesses who had [s]Jer 51:59
signed the deed and of all the Jews sitting in the courtyard of the guard.

[13]"In their presence I gave Baruch
these instructions: [14]'This is what the
LORD Almighty, the God of Israel, says:
Take these documents, both the sealed
and unsealed copies of the deed of purchase, and put them in a clay jar so they
will last a long time. [15]For this is what
the LORD Almighty, the God of Israel,
says: Houses, fields and vineyards will 32:15
again be bought in this land.'[t] [t]ver 43-44; Jer 30:18; Am 9:14-15

[16]"After I had given the deed of purchase to Baruch son of Neriah, I prayed
to the LORD:

[17]"Ah, Sovereign LORD,[u] you have 32:17
made the heavens and the earth by [u]Jer 1:6
your great power and outstretched [v]2Ki 19:15; Ps 102:25
arm.[v] Nothing is too hard[w] for you. [w]Mt 19:26
[18]You show love[x] to thousands but 32:18
bring the punishment for the fa- [x]Dt 5:10
thers' sins into the laps of their [y]Ex 20:5
children[y] after them. O great and [z]Jer 10:16
powerful God, whose name is the
LORD Almighty,[z] [19]great are your
purposes and mighty are your 32:19
deeds.[a] Your eyes are open to all the [a]Isa 28:29
ways of men;[b] you reward everyone [b]Pr 5:21; Jer 16:17
according to his conduct and as his [c]Jer 17:10; Mt 16:27
deeds deserve.[c] [20]You performed
miraculous signs and wonders in
Egypt[d] and have continued them 32:20 [d]Ex 9:16
to this day, both in Israel and
among all mankind, and have
gained the renown that is still
yours. [21]You brought your people 32:21
Israel out of Egypt with signs and [e]Ex 6:6; 1Ch 17:21; Da 9:15
wonders, by a mighty hand[e] and an [f]Dt 26:8
outstretched arm and with great
terror.[f] [22]You gave them this land
you had sworn to give their forefathers, a land flowing with milk and 32:22
honey.[g] [23]They came in and took [g]Ex 3:8; Jer 11:5
possession[h] of it, but they did not 32:23
obey you or follow your law;[i] they [h]Ps 44:2; 78:54-55 [i]Ne 9:26; Jer 11:8
did not do what you commanded
them to do. So you brought all this [j]Da 9:14
disaster[j] upon them.

[24]"See how the siege ramps are
built up to take the city. Because of 32:24
the sword, famine and plague,[k] the [k]Jer 14:12
city will be handed over to the

[a]4 Or *Chaldeans*; also in verses 5, 24, 25, 28, 29 and 43 [b]9 That is, about 7 ounces (about 200 grams)

32:24 Babylonians who are attacking it.
[l]Dt 4:25-26; What you said[l] has happened, as
Jos 23:15-16 you now see. 25And though the city
will be handed over to the Babylonians, you, O Sovereign LORD, say to
me, 'Buy the field with silver and
have the transaction witnessed.' "

26Then the word of the LORD came to
32:27 Jeremiah: 27"I am the LORD, the God of all
[m]Nu 16:22 mankind.[m] Is anything too hard for me?
28Therefore, this is what the LORD says: I
am about to hand this city over to the
32:28 Babylonians and to Nebuchadnezzar[n]
[n]2Ch 36:17 [o]ver 3 king of Babylon, who will capture it.[o]
29The Babylonians who are attacking
32:29 this city will come in and set it on fire;
[p]2Ch 36:19; they will burn it down,[p] along with the
Jer 21:10; 37:8, 10; 52:13 houses[q] where the people provoked me
[q]Jer 19:13 to anger by burning incense on the roofs
[r]Jer 44:18 to Baal and by pouring out drink offerings[r] to other gods.

30"The people of Israel and Judah have
done nothing but evil in my sight from
32:30 their youth;[s] indeed, the people of Israel
[s]Jer 22:21 [t]Jer 8:19 have done nothing but provoke[t] me
[u]Jer 25:7 with what their hands have made,[u] declares the LORD. 31From the day it was
built until now, this city has so aroused
32:31 my anger and wrath that I must remove[v]
[v]2Ki 23:27; 24:3 it from my sight. 32The people of Israel
and Judah have provoked me by all the
32:32 evil[w] they have done—they, their kings
[w]Isa 1:4-6; Da 9:8 and officials, their priests and prophets,
the men of Judah and the people of Jeru-
32:33 salem. 33They turned their backs[x] to me
[x]Jer 2:27; Eze 8:16 and not their faces; though I taught[y]
[y]Jer 7:13 them again and again, they would not
listen or respond to discipline. 34They
set up their abominable idols in the
32:34 house that bears my Name and defiled[z]
[z]Jer 7:30 it. 35They built high places for Baal in the
Valley of Ben Hinnom to sacrifice their
32:35 sons and daughters[a] to Molech,[a] though
[a]Lev 18:21 I never commanded, nor did it enter my
[b]Jer 7:31; 19:5 mind,[b] that they should do such a detestable thing and so make Judah sin.

32:36 36"You are saying about this city, 'By
[c]ver 24 the sword, famine and plague[c] it will be
handed over to the king of Babylon'; but
32:37 this is what the LORD, the God of Israel,
[d]Jer 23:3,6 says: 37I will surely gather[d] them from all
[e]Dt 30:3; Eze 34:28 the lands where I banish them in my furious anger and great wrath; I will bring
32:38 them back to this place and let them live
[f]Jer 24:7; 2Co 6:16* in safety.[e] 38They will be my people,[f] and
I will be their God. 39I will give them sin-
32:39 [g]Eze 11:19 gleness[g] of heart and action, so that they

will always fear me for their own good
and the good of their children after
them. 40I will make an everlasting cov- 32:40
enant[h] with them: I will never stop doing [h]Isa 55:3
good to them, and I will inspire them to [i]Jer 24:7
fear me, so that they will never turn away
from me.[i] 41I will rejoice in doing them 32:41
good[j] and will assuredly plant[k] them in [j]Dt 30:9 [k]Jer 24:6; 31:28;
this land with all my heart and soul. Am 9:15

42"This is what the LORD says: As I
have brought all this great calamity on
this people, so I will give them all the
prosperity I have promised[l] them. 32:42 [l]Jer 31:28
43Once more fields will be bought[m] in 32:43
this land of which you say, 'It is a deso- [m]ver 15
late waste, without men or animals, for
it has been handed over to the Babylonians.' 44Fields will be bought for silver, 32:44
and deeds[n] will be signed, sealed and [n]ver 10
witnessed in the territory of Benjamin, [o]Jer 17:26 [p]Jer 33:7,11,26
in the villages around Jerusalem, in the
towns of Judah and in the towns of the
hill country, of the western foothills and
of the Negev,[o] because I will restore[p]
their fortunes,[b] declares the LORD."

Promise of Restoration

33 While Jeremiah was still con- 33:1
fined in the courtyard[q] of the [q]Jer 32:2-3;
guard, the word of the LORD came to him 37:21; 38:28
a second time: 2"This is what the LORD 33:2
says, he who made the earth,[r] the LORD [r]Jer 10:16
who formed it and established it—the [s]Ex 3:15; 15:3
LORD is his name:[s] 3'Call[t] to me and I will 33:3
answer you and tell you great and un- [t]Isa 55:6;
searchable things you do not know.' 4For Jer 29:12
this is what the LORD, the God of Israel,
says about the houses in this city and
the royal palaces of Judah that have been 33:4
torn down to be used against the siege[u] [u]Eze 4:2
ramps[v] and the sword 5in the fight with [v]Jer 32:24; Hab 1:10
the Babylonians[c]: 'They will be filled
with the dead bodies of the men I will 33:5
slay in my anger and wrath.[w] I will hide [w]Jer 21:4-7
my face[x] from this city because of all its [x]Isa 8:17
wickedness.

6" 'Nevertheless, I will bring health 33:7
and healing to it; I will heal my peo- [y]Jer 32:44
ple and will let them enjoy abundant [z]Jer 30:3; Am 9:14
peace and security. 7I will bring Judah[y] [a]Isa 1:26
and Israel back from captivity[d] [z] and will 33:8
rebuild them as they were before.[a] 8I will [b]Heb 9:13-14
cleanse[b] them from all the sin they have [c]Jer 31:34; Mic 7:18;
committed against me and will forgive[c] Zec 13:1

[a] 35 Or *to make their sons and daughters pass through the fire,* [b] 44 Or *will bring them back from captivity* [c] 5 Or *Chaldeans* [d] 7 Or *will restore the fortunes of Judah and Israel*

DISCOVERY 203

A Glimmer of Light

The situation in Jerusalem was desperate—and rapidly deteriorating. The houses had been torn down and the stones used to fortify the walls of Jerusalem against the final assault of the Babylonians (Jeremiah 33:4–5). Judah was defeated in the ensuing battle, and the city was left a "desolate waste, without men or animals" (verse 10). This moment did in many ways appear to be the death rattle in Jewish history. But Jeremiah realized that God would ultimately bring about healing out of the suffering (verse 6). In this black hour the prophet reminded the beleaguered people who God is and what he had promised.

Jeremiah pointed out to the disconsolate Israelites that the Lord is the Creator of the universe. Yes, Jerusalem had been destroyed; undeniably, the kingdom had been lost; sadly, their prophet was in prison. But God was still God, and he remained in control of the universe. This Almighty Creator was not in despair over Israel's plight. He was yet at work!

God held out an invitation to his people: "Call to me and I will answer you and tell you great and unsearchable things you do not know" (verse 3). God doesn't always *do* something to extricate us from our current plight, because that is not his primary purpose. Instead, he wants to *reveal* himself to his children.

Even though there had been repeated warnings that God would judge their sin and allow his people to be exiled to a foreign land, the Father held out the promise of a coming Messiah who would reign forever (verses 15–16). The "Branch" is one of many symbols used to describe the Messiah (see Isaiah 11:1), and Jeremiah here identified this branch as "The LORD Our Righteousness" (Jeremiah 33:16).

Jesus is the "wisdom from God . . . our righteousness, holiness and redemption" (1 Corinthians 1:30). Because the righteous Son of God took our sin upon himself and died in our place, when we place our trust in him God credits us with *his* righteousness (Romans 4:5,11,22–25; 2 Corinthians 5:21).

Even during those times when we strain our eyes into the murky distance but catch no glimmer of hope, we need to remember that God has always promised better days to come. His people who lived before Jesus' birth took comfort from the promise that a Savior would one day rescue them. Today we look forward to the new heaven and the new earth that Jesus Christ will establish when he returns in splendor as our eternal King (2 Peter 3:13; Revelation 21:1–5).

Self-Discovery: *Consider the implications of being credited with Jesus' righteousness. What does it mean to you that this credit to your spiritual account wipes out your sin debt—not only from the past but any that you might incur in the future? Pause for a moment to thank your benefactor!*

GO TO DISCOVERY 204 ON PAGE 1039

all their sins of rebellion against me.
33:9 9Then this city will bring me renown, joy,
[d] Jer 13:11 praise[d] and honor[e] before all nations on
[e] Isa 62:7; earth that hear of all the good things I
Jer 3:17 do for it; and they will be in awe and will
tremble at the abundant prosperity and
peace I provide for it.'
10"This is what the LORD says: 'You say
about this place, "It is a desolate waste,
33:10 without men or animals."[f] Yet in the
[f] Jer 32:43 towns of Judah and the streets of Jerusalem that are deserted, inhabited by nei-
ther men nor animals, there will be
33:11 heard once more 11the sounds of joy and
[g] Isa 51:3 gladness,[g] the voices of bride and bride-
[h] Lev 7:12 groom, and the voices of those who
[i] 1Ch 16:8; Ps 136:1 bring thank offerings[h] to the house of
[j] 1Ch 16:34; 2Ch 5:13; Ps 100:4-5 the LORD, saying,

"Give thanks to the LORD Almighty,
for the LORD is good;[i]
his love endures forever."[j]

For I will restore the fortunes of the land
as they were before,' says the LORD.
33:12 12"This is what the LORD Almighty
[k] Jer 32:43 says: 'In this place, desolate[k] and with-
[l] Isa 65:10; out men or animals—in all its towns
Eze 34:11-15 there will again be pastures for shepherds to rest their flocks.[l] 13In the towns
33:13 of the hill country, of the western
[m] Jer 17:26 foothills and of the Negev,[m] in the terri-
[n] Lev 27:32 tory of Benjamin, in the villages around
Jerusalem and in the towns of Judah,
flocks will again pass under the hand[n] of
the one who counts them,' says the LORD.
14" 'The days are coming,' declares the
33:14 LORD, 'when I will fulfill the gracious
[o] Jer 29:10 promise[o] I made to the house of Israel
and to the house of Judah.

33:15 15" 'In those days and at that time
[p] Ps 72:2 I will make a righteous[p] Branch[q]
[q] Isa 4:2; 11:1; sprout from David's line;
Jer 23:5 he will do what is just and right
in the land.
33:16 16In those days Judah will be saved[r]
[r] Isa 45:17 and Jerusalem will live in safety.
[s] 1Co 1:30 This is the name by which it[a] will
be called:
The LORD Our Righteousness.'[s]

33:17 17For this is what the LORD says: 'David
[t] 2Sa 7:13; will never fail[t] to have a man to sit on the
1Ki 2:4; Ps 89:29-37; throne of the house of Israel, 18nor will
Lk 1:33 the priests, who are Levites,[u] ever fail to
33:18 have a man to stand before me continu-
[u] Dt 18:1 ally to offer burnt offerings, to burn grain
[v] Heb 13:15 offerings and to present sacrifices.[v]' "

19The word of the LORD came to Jeremiah: 20"This is what the LORD says: 'If
you can break my covenant with the 33:20
day[w] and my covenant with the night, so [w] Ps 89:36
that day and night no longer come at
their appointed time, 21then my cov- 33:21
enant[x] with David my servant—and my [x] Ps 89:34
covenant with the Levites who are [y] 2Ch 7:18
priests ministering before me—can be
broken and David will no longer have a
descendant to reign on his throne.[y] 22I
will make the descendants of David my
servant and the Levites who minister
before me as countless[z] as the stars of 33:22
the sky and as measureless as the sand [z] Ge 15:5
on the seashore.' "
23The word of the LORD came to Jeremiah: 24"Have you not noticed that these
people are saying, 'The LORD has reject- 33:24
ed the two kingdoms[b][a] he chose'? So [a] Eze 37:22
they despise[b] my people and no longer [b] Ne 4:4
regard them as a nation.[c] 25This is what [c] Jer 30:17
the LORD says: 'If I have not established 33:25
my covenant with day and night[d] and [d] Jer 31:35-36
the fixed laws of heaven and earth,[e] [e] Ps 74:16-17
26then I will reject[f] the descendants of 33:26
Jacob[g] and David my servant and will [f] Jer 31:37
not choose one of his sons to rule over [g] Isa 14:1 [h] ver 7
the descendants of Abraham, Isaac and
Jacob. For I will restore their fortunes[c][h]
and have compassion on them.' "

Warning to Zedekiah

34 While Nebuchadnezzar king of
Babylon and all his army and all 34:1
the kingdoms and peoples[i] in the em- [i] Jer 27:7
pire he ruled were fighting against Jeru- [j] 2Ki 25:1;
salem[j] and all its surrounding towns, Jer 39:1
this word came to Jeremiah from the
LORD: 2"This is what the LORD, the God 34:2
of Israel, says: Go to Zedekiah[k] king of [k] 2Ch 36:11
Judah and tell him, 'This is what the [l] ver 22;
LORD says: I am about to hand this city Jer 32:29; 37:8
over to the king of Babylon, and he will
burn it down.[l] 3You will not escape from
his grasp but will surely be captured and 34:3
handed over[m] to him. You will see the [m] 2Ki 25:7;
king of Babylon with your own eyes, and Jer 21:7; 32:4
he will speak with you face to face. And
you will go to Babylon.
4" 'Yet hear the promise of the LORD,
O Zedekiah king of Judah. This is what
the LORD says concerning you: You will
not die by the sword; 5you will die peace- 34:5
fully. As people made a funeral fire[n] in [n] 2Ch 16:14; 21:19

[a] 16 Or *he* [b] 24 Or *families* [c] 26 Or *will bring them back from captivity*

honor of your fathers, the former kings who preceded you, so they will make a fire in your honor and lament, "Alas,[o] O master!" I myself make this promise, declares the LORD.' "

6 Then Jeremiah the prophet told all this to Zedekiah king of Judah, in Jerusalem, 7 while the army of the king of Babylon was fighting against Jerusalem and the other cities of Judah that were still holding out—Lachish[p] and Azekah.[q] These were the only fortified cities left in Judah.

Freedom for Slaves

8 The word came to Jeremiah from the LORD after King Zedekiah had made a covenant with all the people[r] in Jerusalem to proclaim freedom[s] for the slaves. 9 Everyone was to free his Hebrew slaves, both male and female; no one was to hold a fellow Jew in bondage.[t] 10 So all the officials and people who entered into this covenant agreed that they would free their male and female slaves and no longer hold them in bondage. They agreed, and set them free. 11 But afterward they changed their minds and took back the slaves they had freed and enslaved them again.

12 Then the word of the LORD came to Jeremiah: 13 "This is what the LORD, the God of Israel, says: I made a covenant with your forefathers[u] when I brought them out of Egypt, out of the land of slavery. I said, 14 'Every seventh year each of you must free any fellow Hebrew who has sold himself to you. After he has served you six years, you must let him go free.'[a][v] Your fathers, however, did not listen to me or pay attention[w] to me. 15 Recently you repented and did what is right in my sight: Each of you proclaimed freedom to his countrymen.[x] You even made a covenant before me in the house that bears my Name.[y] 16 But now you have turned around[z] and profaned[a] my name; each of you has taken back the male and female slaves you had set free to go where they wished. You have forced them to become your slaves again.

17 "Therefore, this is what the LORD says: You have not obeyed me; you have not proclaimed freedom for your fellow countrymen. So I now proclaim 'freedom' for you,[b] declares the LORD—'freedom' to fall by the sword, plague and famine. I will make you abhorrent to all the kingdoms of the earth.[c] 18 The men who have violated my covenant and have not fulfilled the terms of the covenant they made before me, I will treat like the calf they cut in two and then walked between its pieces.[d] 19 The leaders of Judah and Jerusalem, the court officials,[e] the priests and all the people of the land who walked between the pieces of the calf, 20 I will hand over[f] to their enemies who seek their lives.[g] Their dead bodies will become food for the birds of the air and the beasts of the earth.[h]

21 "I will hand Zedekiah[i] king of Judah and his officials[j] over to their enemies who seek their lives, to the army of the king of Babylon, which has withdrawn[k] from you. 22 I am going to give the order, declares the LORD, and I will bring them back to this city. They will fight against it, take[l] it and burn[m] it down. And I will lay waste the towns of Judah so no one can live there."

The Recabites

35 This is the word that came to Jeremiah from the LORD during the reign of Jehoiakim[n] son of Josiah king of Judah: 2 "Go to the Recabite[o] family and invite them to come to one of the side rooms[p] of the house of the LORD and give them wine to drink."

3 So I went to get Jaazaniah son of Jeremiah, the son of Habazziniah, and his brothers and all his sons—the whole family of the Recabites. 4 I brought them into the house of the LORD, into the room of the sons of Hanan son of Igdaliah the man of God.[q] It was next to the room of the officials, which was over that of Maaseiah son of Shallum[r] the doorkeeper.[s] 5 Then I set bowls full of wine and some cups before the men of the Recabite family and said to them, "Drink some wine."

6 But they replied, "We do not drink wine, because our forefather Jonadab[t] son of Recab gave us this command: 'Neither you nor your descendants must ever drink wine.[u] 7 Also you must never build houses, sow seed or plant vineyards; you must never have any of these things, but must always live in tents.[v] Then you will live a long time in the

34:5 [o] Jer 22:18
34:7 [p] Jos 10:3 [q] Jos 10:10; 2Ch 11:9
34:8 [r] 2Ki 11:17 [s] Ex 21:2; Lev 25:10,39-41; Ne 5:5-8
34:9 [t] Lev 25:39-46
34:13 [u] Ex 24:8
34:14 [v] Ex 21:2 [w] Dt 15:12; 2Ki 17:14
34:15 [x] ver 8 [y] Jer 7:10-11; 32:34
34:16 [z] Eze 3:20; 18:24 [a] Ex 20:7; Lev 19:12
34:17 [b] Mt 7:2; Gal 6:7
34:17 [c] Dt 28:25,64; Jer 29:18
34:18 [d] Ge 15:10
34:19 [e] Zep 3:3-4
34:20 [f] Jer 21:7 [g] Jer 11:21 [h] Dt 28:26; Jer 7:33; 19:7
34:21 [i] Jer 32:4 [j] Jer 39:6; 52:24-27 [k] Jer 37:5
34:22 [l] Jer 39:1-2 [m] Jer 39:8
35:1 [n] 2Ch 36:5
35:2 [o] 2Ki 10:15; 1Ch 2:55 [p] 1Ki 6:5
35:4 [q] Dt 33:1 [r] 1Ch 9:19 [s] 2Ki 12:9
35:6 [t] 2Ki 10:15 [u] Lev 10:9; Nu 6:2-4; Lk 1:15
35:7 [v] Heb 11:9

[a] 14 Deut. 15:12

land[w] where you are nomads.' 8We have obeyed everything our forefather[x] Jonadab son of Recab commanded us. Neither we nor our wives nor our sons and daughters have ever drunk wine 9or built houses to live in or had vineyards, fields or crops.[y] 10We have lived in tents and have fully obeyed everything our forefather Jonadab commanded us. 11But when Nebuchadnezzar king of Babylon invaded[z] this land, we said, 'Come, we must go to Jerusalem[a] to escape the Babylonian[a] and Aramean armies.' So we have remained in Jerusalem."

12Then the word of the LORD came to Jeremiah, saying: 13"This is what the LORD Almighty, the God of Israel, says: Go and tell the men of Judah and the people of Jerusalem, 'Will you not learn a lesson[b] and obey my words?' declares the LORD. 14'Jonadab son of Recab ordered his sons not to drink wine and this command has been kept. To this day they do not drink wine, because they obey their forefather's command. But I have spoken to you again and again,[c] yet you have not obeyed[d] me. 15Again and again I sent all my servants the prophets[e] to you. They said, "Each of you must turn[f] from your wicked ways and reform[g] your actions; do not follow other gods to serve them. Then you will live in the land[h] I have given to you and your fathers." But you have not paid attention or listened[i] to me. 16The descendants of Jonadab son of Recab have carried out the command their forefather[j] gave them, but these people have not obeyed me.'

17"Therefore, this is what the LORD God Almighty, the God of Israel, says: 'Listen! I am going to bring on Judah and on everyone living in Jerusalem every disaster[k] I pronounced against them. I spoke to them, but they did not listen;[l] I called to them, but they did not answer.' "[m]

18Then Jeremiah said to the family of the Recabites, "This is what the LORD Almighty, the God of Israel, says: 'You have obeyed the command of your forefather Jonadab and have followed all his instructions and have done everything he ordered.' 19Therefore, this is what the LORD Almighty, the God of Israel, says: 'Jonadab son of Recab will never fail[n] to have a man to serve[o] me.' "

35:7 w Ex 20:12; Eph 6:2-3
35:8 x Pr 1:8; Col 3:20
35:9 y 1Ti 6:6
35:11 z 2Ki 24:1 a Jer 8:14
35:13 b Jer 6:10; 32:33
35:14 c Jer 7:13; 25:3 d Isa 30:9
35:15 e Jer 7:25 f Jer 26:3 g Isa 1:16-17; Jer 4:1; 18:11; Eze 18:30 h Jer 25:5 i Jer 7:26
35:16 j Mal 1:6
35:17 k Jos 23:15; Jer 21:4-7 l Pr 1:24; Ro 10:21 m Isa 65:12; 66:4; Jer 7:13
35:19 n Jer 33:17 o Jer 15:19

Jehoiakim Burns Jeremiah's Scroll

36 In the fourth year of Jehoiakim[p] son of Josiah king of Judah, this word came to Jeremiah from the LORD: 2"Take a scroll[q] and write on it all the words I have spoken to you concerning Israel, Judah and all the other nations from the time I began speaking to you in the reign of Josiah[r] till now. 3Perhaps[s] when the people of Judah hear[t] about every disaster I plan to inflict on them, each of them will turn[u] from his wicked way; then I will forgive[v] their wickedness and their sin."

4So Jeremiah called Baruch[w] son of Neriah, and while Jeremiah dictated[x] all the words the LORD had spoken to him, Baruch wrote them on the scroll.[y] 5Then Jeremiah told Baruch, "I am restricted; I cannot go to the LORD's temple. 6So you go to the house of the LORD on a day of fasting[z] and read to the people from the scroll the words of the LORD that you wrote as I dictated. Read them to all the people of Judah who come in from their towns. 7Perhaps they will bring their petition before the LORD, and each will turn[a] from his wicked ways, for the anger[b] and wrath pronounced against this people by the LORD are great."

8Baruch son of Neriah did everything Jeremiah the prophet told him to do; at the LORD's temple he read the words of the LORD from the scroll. 9In the ninth month[c] of the fifth year of Jehoiakim son of Josiah king of Judah, a time of fasting[d] before the LORD was proclaimed for all the people in Jerusalem and those who had come from the towns of Judah. 10From the room of Gemariah son of Shaphan the secretary,[e] which was in the upper courtyard at the entrance of the New Gate[f] of the temple, Baruch read to all the people at the LORD's temple the words of Jeremiah from the scroll.

11When Micaiah son of Gemariah, the son of Shaphan, heard all the words of the LORD from the scroll, 12he went down to the secretary's room in the royal palace, where all the officials were sitting: Elishama the secretary, Delaiah son of Shemaiah, Elnathan[g] son of Acbor, Gemariah son of Shaphan, Zedekiah son of Hananiah, and all the other officials. 13After Micaiah told them everything he

36:1 p 2Ch 36:5
36:2 q Ex 17:14; Jer 30:2; Hab 2:2 r Jer 1:2; 25:3
36:3 s ver 7; Eze 12:3 t Mk 4:12 u Jer 26:3; Jnh 3:8; Ac 3:19 v Jer 18:8
36:4 w Jer 32:12 x ver 18 y Eze 2:9
36:6 z ver 9
36:7 a Jer 26:3 b Dt 31:17
36:9 c ver 22 d 2Ch 20:3
36:10 e Jer 52:25 f Jer 26:10
36:12 g Jer 26:22

[a] *11* Or *Chaldean*

had heard Baruch read to the people
36:14 from the scroll, 14 all the officials sent Je-
h ver 21 hudi[h] son of Nethaniah, the son of
Shelemiah, the son of Cushi, to say to
Baruch, "Bring the scroll from which
you have read to the people and come."
So Baruch son of Neriah went to them
with the scroll in his hand. 15 They said
to him, "Sit down, please, and read it
to us."

So Baruch read it to them. 16 When
they heard all these words, they looked
at each other in fear and said to Baruch,
"We must report all these words to the
king." 17 Then they asked Baruch, "Tell
us, how did you come to write all this?
Did Jeremiah dictate it?"

36:18 18 "Yes," Baruch replied, "he dictated[i]
i ver 4 all these words to me, and I wrote them
in ink on the scroll."

36:19 19 Then the officials said to Baruch,
j 1Ki 17:3 "You and Jeremiah, go and hide.[j] Don't
let anyone know where you are."

20 After they put the scroll in the room
of Elishama the secretary, they went to
the king in the courtyard and reported
everything to him. 21 The king sent Jehu-
36:21 di[k] to get the scroll, and Jehudi brought
k ver 14 it from the room of Elishama the secre-
l 2Ki 22:10 tary and read it to the king[l] and all the
officials standing beside him. 22 It was
36:22 the ninth month and the king was sit-
m Am 3:15 ting in the winter apartment,[m] with a
fire burning in the firepot in front of
him. 23 Whenever Jehudi had read three
or four columns of the scroll, the king
cut them off with a scribe's knife and
36:23 threw them into the firepot, until the
n 1Ki 22:8 entire scroll was burned in the fire.[n]
36:24 24 The king and all his attendants who
o Ps 36:1 heard all these words showed no fear,[o]
p Ge 37:29; 2Ki 22:11; Isa 37:1 nor did they tear their clothes.[p] 25 Even
though Elnathan, Delaiah and Gemari-
ah urged the king not to burn the scroll,
he would not listen to them. 26 Instead,
the king commanded Jerahmeel, a son
of the king, Seraiah son of Azriel and
36:26 Shelemiah son of Abdeel to arrest[q] Bar-
q Mt 23:34 uch the scribe and Jeremiah the proph-
r Jer 15:21 et. But the LORD had hidden[r] them.

27 After the king burned the scroll
containing the words that Baruch had
36:27 written at Jeremiah's dictation,[s] the
s ver 4 word of the LORD came to Jeremiah:
28 "Take another scroll and write on it all
the words that were on the first scroll,
which Jehoiakim king of Judah burned
up. 29 Also tell Jehoiakim king of Judah,
'This is what the LORD says: You burned
that scroll and said, "Why did you write
on it that the king of Babylon would certainly come and destroy this land and 36:29
cut off both men and animals from it?"[t] t Isa 30:10
30 Therefore, this is what the LORD says
about Jehoiakim king of Judah: He will
have no one to sit on the throne of Da- 36:30
vid; his body will be thrown out[u] and ex- u Jer 22:19
posed to the heat by day and the frost by
night. 31 I will punish him and his children and his attendants for their
wickedness; I will bring on them and
those living in Jerusalem and the people 36:31
of Judah every disaster[v] I pronounced v Pr 29:1
against them, because they have not listened.' "

32 So Jeremiah took another scroll and
gave it to the scribe Baruch son of Neri- 36:32
ah, and as Jeremiah dictated,[w] Baruch w ver 4 x Ex 34:1 y ver 23
wrote[x] on it all the words of the scroll
that Jehoiakim king of Judah had
burned[y] in the fire. And many similar
words were added to them.

JESUS FOCUS

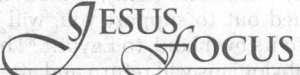

JEHOIAKIM'S CURSE

Jehoiakim (also called Eliakim) reigned in Judah from 609–598 B.C. (2 Kings 23:34–37; 2 Chronicles 36:4–8). He ruled as a vassal to the kings of Babylon, which means that he entered into a covenant with them for protection. Jeremiah predicted that Jehoiakim would die because he had turned to other nations rather than to God for protection and that there would be no one left to rule in Israel (Jeremiah 36:30–31). Jehoiakim was briefly replaced, however, by his son Jehoiachin, who usurped the throne and "ruled" for three months in defiance of the Babylonians. Because his succession was not valid, Jehoiachin's brief reign did not contradict Jeremiah's prophecy. Jehoiachin was immediately besieged by Nebuchadnezzar of Babylon, and he surrendered and was sent into exile. Jehoiachin's uncle, Zedekiah, did became Judah's last king. Although Jehoiachin tried to wrest control of the throne for himself despite what God had stated through Jeremiah, the prophet's prediction still came true. And the promise still stands today: The only descendant in David's family line who will sit on the throne is the Messiah himself—Jesus Christ (Matthew 1:11; Luke 1:31–32), the King of kings and Lord of lords (Revelation 17:14; 19:16).

Jeremiah in Prison

37:1 z2Ki 24:17 aEze 17:13 b2Ki 24:8,12; 2Ch 36:10; Jer 22:24 37 Zedekiah[z] son of Josiah was
made king[a] of Judah by Nebu-
chadnezzar king of Babylon; he reigned
in place of Jehoiachin[a][b] son of Jehoiakim. 2Neither he nor his attendants nor
37:2 c2Ki 24:19; 2Ch 36:12,14 the people of the land paid any attention[c] to the words the LORD had spoken
through Jeremiah the prophet.
3King Zedekiah, however, sent Jehucal
son of Shelemiah with the priest Zepha-
37:3 dJer 29:25; 52:24 e1Ki 13:6; Jer 21:1-2; 42:2 niah[d] son of Maaseiah to Jeremiah the
prophet with this message: "Please pray[e]
to the LORD our God for us."
4Now Jeremiah was free to come and
37:4 fver 15; Jer 32:2 go among the people, for he had not yet
been put in prison.[f] 5Pharaoh's army had
37:5 gEze 17:15 hJer 34:21 i2Ki 24:7 marched out of Egypt,[g] and when the
Babylonians[b] who were besieging Jeru-
salem heard the report about them, they
withdrew[h] from Jerusalem.[i]
6Then the word of the LORD came to
Jeremiah the prophet: 7"This is what the
37:7 j2Ki 22:18 kJer 2:36; La 4:17 LORD, the God of Israel, says: Tell the
king of Judah, who sent you to inquire[j]
of me, 'Pharaoh's army, which has
marched out to support you, will go
back to its own land, to Egypt.[k] 8Then
37:8 lJer 34:22; 39:8 the Babylonians will return and attack
this city; they will capture it and burn[l] it
down.'
9"This is what the LORD says: Do not
37:9 mJer 29:8 deceive[m] yourselves, thinking, 'The
Babylonians will surely leave us.' They
will not! 10Even if you were to defeat the
entire Babylonian[c] army that is attacking you and only wounded men were left
in their tents, they would come out and
burn this city down."
37:11 nver 5 11After the Babylonian army had
withdrawn[n] from Jerusalem because of
Pharaoh's army, 12Jeremiah started to
leave the city to go to the territory of
37:12 oJer 32:9 Benjamin to get his share of the property[o] among the people there. 13But when
he reached the Benjamin Gate, the captain of the guard, whose name was Irijah
son of Shelemiah, the son of Hananiah,
arrested him and said, "You are deserting to the Babylonians!"
14"That's not true!" Jeremiah said. "I
am not deserting to the Babylonians."
37:14 pJer 40:4 But Irijah would not listen to him; instead, he arrested[p] Jeremiah and
brought him to the officials. 15They were
37:15 qJer 20:2 rJer 38:26 angry with Jeremiah and had him beat-
en[q] and imprisoned in the house[r] of
Jonathan the secretary, which they had
made into a prison.
16Jeremiah was put into a vaulted cell
in a dungeon, where he remained a long
time. 17Then King Zedekiah sent for him
and had him brought to the palace,
where he asked[s] him privately,[t] "Is there 37:17 sJer 15:11 tJer 38:16 uJer 21:7
any word from the LORD?"
"Yes," Jeremiah replied, "you will be
handed over[u] to the king of Babylon."
18Then Jeremiah said to King Zedeki- 37:18 v1Sa 26:18; Jn 10:32; Ac 25:8
ah, "What crime[v] have I committed
against you or your officials or this people, that you have put me in prison?
19Where are your prophets who prophesied to you, 'The king of Babylon will not
attack you or this land'? 20But now, my
lord the king, please listen. Let me bring
my petition before you: Do not send me
back to the house of Jonathan the secretary, or I will die there."
21King Zedekiah then gave orders for
Jeremiah to be placed in the courtyard of 37:21 wIsa 33:16; Jer 38:9 x2Ki 25:3; Jer 52:6 yJer 32:2; 38:6, 13,28
the guard and given bread from the
street of the bakers each day until all the
bread[w] in the city was gone.[x] So Jeremiah remained in the courtyard of the
guard.[y]

Jeremiah Thrown Into a Cistern

38 Shephatiah son of Mattan, Ged-
aliah son of Pashhur, Jehucal[d][z] 38:1 zJer 37:3
son of Shelemiah, and Pashhur son of
Malkijah heard what Jeremiah was
telling all the people when he said, 2"This
is what the LORD says: 'Whoever stays in
this city will die by the sword, famine or 38:2 aJer 34:17 bJer 21:9; 39:18; 45:5
plague,[a] but whoever goes over to the
Babylonians[e] will live. He will escape
with his life; he will live.'[b] 3And this is
what the LORD says: 'This city will cer-
tainly be handed over to the army of the 38:3 cJer 21:4,10; 32:3
king of Babylon, who will capture it.' "[c]
4Then the officials[d] said to the king, 38:4 dJer 36:12 eJer 26:11
"This man should be put to death.[e] He is
discouraging the soldiers who are left in
this city, as well as all the people, by the
things he is saying to them. This man is
not seeking the good of these people but
their ruin."
5"He is in your hands," King Zedekiah
answered. "The king can do nothing to
oppose you."

[a] *1* Hebrew *Coniah*, a variant of *Jehoiachin*
[b] *5* Or *Chaldeans*; also in verses 8, 9, 13 and 14
[c] *10* Or *Chaldean*; also in verse 11
[d] *1* Hebrew *Jucal*, a variant of *Jehucal*
[e] *2* Or *Chaldeans*; also in verses 18, 19 and 23

[6]So they took Jeremiah and put him
into the cistern of Malkijah, the king's
38:6 son, which was in the courtyard of the
[f]Jer 37:21 guard.[f] They lowered Jeremiah by ropes
into the cistern; it had no water in it,
only mud, and Jeremiah sank down into
the mud.
38:7 [7]But Ebed-Melech,[g] a Cushite,[a] an of-
[g]Jer 39:16 [h]Ac 8:27 ficial[b][h] in the royal palace, heard that
[i]Job 29:7 they had put Jeremiah into the cistern.
While the king was sitting in the Benjamin Gate,[i] [8]Ebed-Melech went out of the
palace and said to him, [9]"My lord the
king, these men have acted wickedly in
all they have done to Jeremiah the prophet. They have thrown him into a cistern,
38:9 where he will starve to death when there
[j]Jer 37:21 is no longer any bread[j] in the city."
[10]Then the king commanded Ebed-
Melech the Cushite, "Take thirty men
from here with you and lift Jeremiah the
prophet out of the cistern before he
dies."
[11]So Ebed-Melech took the men with
him and went to a room under the
treasury in the palace. He took some old
rags and worn-out clothes from there
and let them down with ropes to Jeremiah in the cistern. [12]Ebed-Melech the
Cushite said to Jeremiah, "Put these old
rags and worn-out clothes under your
arms to pad the ropes." Jeremiah did so,
[13]and they pulled him up with the ropes
and lifted him out of the cistern. And
Jeremiah remained in the courtyard of 38:13
the guard.[k] [k]Jer 37:21

Zedekiah Questions Jeremiah Again

[14]Then King Zedekiah sent for Jeremiah the prophet and had him brought
to the third entrance to the temple of
the LORD. "I am going to ask you something," the king said to Jeremiah. "Do 38:14
not hide[l] anything from me." [l]1Sa 3:17
[15]Jeremiah said to Zedekiah, "If I give
you an answer, will you not kill me? Even
if I did give you counsel, you would not
listen to me."
[16]But King Zedekiah swore this oath 38:16
secretly[m] to Jeremiah: "As surely as the [m]Jer 37:17
LORD lives, who has given us breath,[n] I [n]Isa 42:5; 57:16 [o]ver 4
will neither kill you nor hand you over to
those who are seeking your life."[o]
[17]Then Jeremiah said to Zedekiah,
"This is what the LORD God Almighty, the
God of Israel, says: 'If you surrender to the
officers of the king of Babylon, your life
will be spared and this city will not be
burned down; you and your family will 38:17 [p]2Ki 24:12;
live.[p] [18]But if you will not surrender to the Jer 21:9
officers of the king of Babylon, this city
will be handed over[q] to the Babylonians 38:18 [q]ver 3; Jer 34:3
and they will burn[r] it down; you yourself [r]Jer 37:8
will not escape[s] from their hands.'" [s]Jer 24:8; 32:4
[19]King Zedekiah said to Jeremiah, "I 38:19
am afraid[t] of the Jews who have gone [t]Isa 51:12;
over[u] to the Babylonians, for the Bab- Jn 12:42 [u]Jer 39:9
ylonians may hand me over to them and
they will mistreat me."
[20]"They will not hand you over," Jere- 38:20
miah replied. "Obey[v] the LORD by doing [v]Jer 11:4
what I tell you. Then it will go well with [w]Isa 55:3
you, and your life[w] will be spared. [21]But
if you refuse to surrender, this is what
the LORD has revealed to me: [22]All the 38:22
women[x] left in the palace of the king of [x]Jer 6:12
Judah will be brought out to the officials
of the king of Babylon. Those women
will say to you:

"'They misled you and overcame
you—
those trusted friends of yours.

[a]7 Probably from the upper Nile region [b]7 Or *a eunuch*

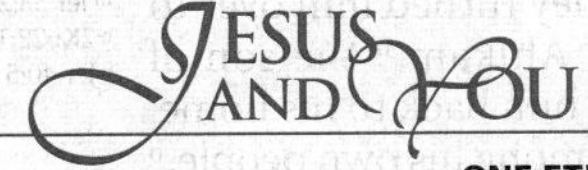

ONE ETHIOPIAN EUNUCH

Ebed-Melech was a eunuch from Cush (Ethiopia) and an official serving King Zedekiah. Jeremiah 38:7–13 recounts the manner in which Ebed-Melech stepped in to save Jeremiah's life. The prophet had been imprisoned at the bottom of an empty cistern during the final siege of Jerusalem (verse 6), and the only person willing to come to his aid was this foreigner. Because Ebed-Melech was willing to help, God gave him a special promise of personal deliverance (Jeremiah 39:15–18). In the New Testament another Ethiopian eunuch put his faith in God and was blessed (Acts 8:26–39). In both cases, God spoke to Gentiles through his Jewish messengers. Peter was taught the truth of the gospel in a most striking way: "I now realize how true it is that God does not show favoritism but accepts men from every nation who fear him and do what is right" (Acts 10:34; see also Romans 2:11). God's grace is available to all people—regardless of their racial, ethnic, social, economic or denominational background. Paul assured us in Galatians 3:28 that, on the basis of the finished work of Jesus Christ, we are all one in the Lord (see also Romans 10:12; 1 Corinthians 12:13; Ephesians 2:15–16).

Your feet are sunk in the mud;
your friends have deserted you.'

38:23 [y] 2Ki 25:6 [z] Jer 41:10

23 "All your wives and children[y] will be brought out to the Babylonians. You yourself will not escape from their hands but will be captured[z] by the king of Babylon; and this city will[a] be burned down."

24 Then Zedekiah said to Jeremiah, "Do not let anyone know about this conversation, or you may die. 25 If the officials hear that I talked with you, and they come to you and say, 'Tell us what you said to the king and what the king said to you; do not hide it from us or we will kill you,' 26 then tell them, 'I was pleading with the king not to send me back to Jonathan's house[a] to die there.' "

38:26 [a] Jer 37:15

27 All the officials did come to Jeremiah and question him, and he told them everything the king had ordered him to say. So they said no more to him, for no one had heard his conversation with the king.

28 And Jeremiah remained in the courtyard of the guard[b] until the day Jerusalem was captured.

38:28 [b] Jer 37:21; 39:14

The Fall of Jerusalem

39 This is how Jerusalem was taken: 1 In the ninth year of Zedekiah king of Judah, in the tenth month, Nebuchadnezzar king of Babylon marched against Jerusalem with his whole army and laid siege[c] to it. 2 And on the ninth day of the fourth month of Zedekiah's eleventh year, the city wall was broken through. 3 Then all the officials[d] of the king of Babylon came and took seats in the Middle Gate: Nergal-Sharezer of Samgar, Nebo-Sarsekim[b] a chief officer, Nergal-Sharezer a high official and all the other officials of the king of Babylon. 4 When Zedekiah king of Judah and all the soldiers saw them, they fled; they left the city at night by way of the king's garden, through the gate between the two walls, and headed toward the Arabah.[c]

39:1 [c] 2Ki 25:1; Jer 52:4; Eze 24:2

39:3 [d] Jer 21:4

5 But the Babylonian[d] army pursued them and overtook Zedekiah[e] in the plains of Jericho. They captured him and took him to Nebuchadnezzar king of Babylon at Riblah[f] in the land of Hamath, where he pronounced sentence on him. 6 There at Riblah the king of Babylon slaughtered the sons of Zedekiah before his eyes and also killed all the nobles of Judah. 7 Then he put out Zedekiah's eyes[g] and bound him with bronze shackles to take him to Babylon.[h]

39:5 [e] Jer 32:4 [f] 2Ki 23:33

39:7 [g] Eze 12:13 [h] Jer 32:5

8 The Babylonians[e] set fire[i] to the royal palace and the houses of the people and broke down the walls[j] of Jerusalem. 9 Nebuzaradan commander of the imperial guard carried into exile to Babylon the people who remained in the city, along with those who had gone over to him, and the rest of the people.[k] 10 But Nebuzaradan the commander of the guard left behind in the land of Judah some of the poor people, who owned nothing; and at that time he gave them vineyards and fields.

39:8 [i] Jer 38:18 [j] Ne 1:3

39:9 [k] Jer 40:1

11 Now Nebuchadnezzar king of Babylon had given these orders about Jeremiah through Nebuzaradan commander of the imperial guard: 12 "Take him and look after him; don't harm[l] him but do for him whatever he asks." 13 So Nebuzaradan the commander of the guard, Nebushazban a chief officer, Nergal-Sharezer a high official and all the other officers of the king of Babylon 14 sent and had Jeremiah taken out of the courtyard of the guard.[m] They turned him over to Gedaliah son of Ahikam,[n] the son of Shaphan, to take him back to his home. So he remained among his own people.[o]

39:12 [l] Pr 16:7; 1Pe 3:13

39:14 [m] Jer 38:28 [n] 2Ki 22:12 [o] Jer 40:5

15 While Jeremiah had been confined in the courtyard of the guard, the word of the LORD came to him: 16 "Go and tell Ebed-Melech[p] the Cushite, 'This is what the LORD Almighty, the God of Israel, says: I am about to fulfill my words against this city through disaster,[q] not prosperity. At that time they will be fulfilled before your eyes. 17 But I will rescue[r] you on that day, declares the LORD; you will not be handed over to those you fear. 18 I will save you; you will not fall by the sword[s] but will escape with your life,[t] because you trust[u] in me, declares the LORD.' "

39:16 [p] Jer 38:7 [q] Jer 21:10; Da 9:12

39:17 [r] Ps 41:1-2

39:18 [s] Jer 45:5 [t] Jer 21:9; 38:2 [u] Jer 17:7

Jeremiah Freed

40 The word came to Jeremiah from the LORD after Nebuzaradan commander of the imperial guard had released him at Ramah. He had found Jeremiah bound in chains among

[a] 23 Or *and you will cause this city to* [b] 3 Or *Nergal-Sharezer, Samgar-Nebo, Sarsekim* [c] 4 Or *the Jordan Valley* [d] 5 Or *Chaldean* [e] 8 Or *Chaldeans*

God's Wake-Up Call

Sometimes when disaster enters the lives of believers we are immediately tempted to blame the devil. Some tragedies really are the work of Satan (consider Job's suffering, for example). But God can also use adversity as a wake-up call when we have failed to take him seriously. Even when Satan really is the direct cause of our troubles, he can only work within the parameters of God's permission (Job 1:12; 2:6). When Jerusalem finally fell to the Babylonians, as Jeremiah had been predicting for years, God sent the disturbing message that *he* was bringing disaster rather than prosperity on Jerusalem (Jeremiah 39:15–16).

God allowed Israel to make her own choices as a nation, but he also warned his people about the inevitable consequences of bad decisions: "See, I am setting before you today a blessing and a curse—the blessing if you obey the commands of the LORD your God that I am giving you today; the curse if you disobey the commands of the LORD your God" (Deuteronomy 11:26–28). Part of the curse for disobedience would be utter defeat at the hands of their enemies (Deuteronomy 28:25). God still works with us the same way. When we obey him we bask in his blessings; when we disobey we suffer the consequences (Galatians 6:7–8).

God warned Israel *repeatedly* that he was about to call down disaster. His people simply could not claim to have forgotten these signals. God had first provided his clear-cut law but then reinforced the message by sending prophets to remind the people. Jeremiah reiterated the warning again and again, hoping his countrymen and women would turn back to God. And God was patient; only after years and years did he finally allow the catastrophe to materialize. It was his *mercy*, not his justice, that God really yearned for his people to know (2 Peter 3:9).

During Noah's lifetime God had observed the wickedness of humanity, and his heart had been broken. He had waited for more than 100 years for the people to turn back to him, but they had refused (Genesis 6). And God finally did send disaster on the whole earth in the form of a cataclysmic flood.

Although there can be no doubt that our own bad choices can lead to disaster in this life (and, if the pattern remains unbroken, will result in calamity in the life to come), the mercy of our Lord is indeed remarkable. The apostle Paul marveled at the seemingly limitless patience of Jesus (Romans 2:4). Despite the fact that Paul had zealously devoted his considerable energies to persecuting Christians, the resurrected Jesus met him along the road to Damascus and turned his life around. Paul wrote to Timothy: "Christ Jesus came into the world to save sinners—of whom I am the worst. But for that very reason I was shown mercy so that in me, the worst of sinners, Christ Jesus might display his unlimited patience as an example for those who would believe on him and receive eternal life" (1 Timothy 1:15–16).

Self-Discovery: *In what specific ways has Jesus displayed his unlimited patience in your life?*

GO TO DISCOVERY 205 ON PAGE 1051

all the captives from Jerusalem and Judah who were being carried into exile to
Babylon. 2When the commander of the
guard found Jeremiah, he said to him,
"The LORD your God decreed this disaster for this place.[v] 3And now the LORD
has brought it about; he has done just as
he said he would. All this happened because you people sinned[w] against the
LORD and did not obey[x] him. 4But today
I am freeing you from the chains on your
wrists. Come with me to Babylon, if you
like, and I will look after you; but if you
do not want to, then don't come. Look,
the whole country lies before you; go
wherever you please."[y] 5However, before
Jeremiah turned to go,[a] Nebuzaradan
added, "Go back to Gedaliah[z] son of
Ahikam, the son of Shaphan, whom the
king of Babylon has appointed over the
towns of Judah, and live with him
among the people, or go anywhere else
you please."[a]

Then the commander gave him provisions and a present and let him go. 6So
Jeremiah went to Gedaliah son of Ahikam at Mizpah[b] and stayed with him
among the people who were left behind
in the land.

Gedaliah Assassinated

7When all the army officers and their
men who were still in the open country
heard that the king of Babylon had appointed Gedaliah son of Ahikam as governor over the land and had put him in
charge of the men, women and children
who were the poorest[c] in the land and
who had not been carried into exile to
Babylon, 8they came to Gedaliah at Mizpah[d]—Ishmael[e] son of Nethaniah, Johanan and Jonathan the sons of Kareah,
Seraiah son of Tanhumeth, the sons of
Ephai the Netophathite,[f] and Jaazaniah[b]
the son of the Maacathite,[g] and their
men. 9Gedaliah son of Ahikam, the son
of Shaphan, took an oath to reassure
them and their men. "Do not be afraid
to serve[h] the Babylonians,[c]" he said.
"Settle down in the land and serve the
king of Babylon, and it will go well with
you.[i] 10I myself will stay at Mizpah[j] to
represent you before the Babylonians
who come to us, but you are to harvest
the wine, summer fruit and oil, and put
them in your storage jars, and live in the
towns you have taken over."[k]

40:2 [v]Jer 50:7
40:3 [w]Da 9:11 [x]Dt 29:24-28; Ro 2:5-9
40:4 [y]Ge 13:9; Jer 39:11-12
40:5 [z]2Ki 25:22 [a]Jer 39:14
40:6 [b]Jdg 20:1; 1Sa 7:5-17
40:7 [c]Jer 39:10
40:8 [d]ver 13 [e]ver 14; Jer 41:1,2 [f]2Sa 23:28 [g]Dt 3:14
40:9 [h]Jer 27:11 [i]Jer 38:20
40:10 [j]ver 6 [k]Dt 1:39

11When all the Jews in Moab,[l] Ammon, Edom and all the other countries
heard that the king of Babylon had left a
remnant in Judah and had appointed
Gedaliah son of Ahikam, the son of Shaphan, as governor over them, 12they all
came back to the land of Judah, to Gedaliah at Mizpah, from all the countries
where they had been scattered.[m] And
they harvested an abundance of wine
and summer fruit.

13Johanan son of Kareah and all the
army officers still in the open country
came to Gedaliah at Mizpah[n] 14and said
to him, "Don't you know that Baalis king
of the Ammonites[o] has sent Ishmael son
of Nethaniah to take your life?" But Gedaliah son of Ahikam did not believe
them.

15Then Johanan son of Kareah said
privately to Gedaliah in Mizpah, "Let me
go and kill Ishmael son of Nethaniah,
and no one will know it. Why should he
take your life and cause all the Jews who
are gathered around you to be scattered
and the remnant of Judah to perish?"

16But Gedaliah son of Ahikam said to
Johanan son of Kareah, "Don't do such a
thing! What you are saying about Ishmael is not true."

41 In the seventh month Ishmael[p]
son of Nethaniah, the son of
Elishama, who was of royal blood and
had been one of the king's officers, came
with ten men to Gedaliah son of Ahikam at Mizpah. While they were eating
together there, 2Ishmael[q] son of Nethaniah and the ten men who were with
him got up and struck down Gedaliah
son of Ahikam, the son of Shaphan, with
the sword, killing the one whom the
king of Babylon had appointed[r] as governor over the land.[s] 3Ishmael also killed
all the Jews who were with Gedaliah at
Mizpah, as well as the Babylonian[d] soldiers who were there.

4The day after Gedaliah's assassina-
tion, before anyone knew about it,
5eighty men who had shaved off their
beards,[t] torn their clothes and cut themselves came from Shechem,[u] Shiloh[v] and
Samaria,[w] bringing grain offerings and
incense with them to the house of the
LORD.[x] 6Ishmael son of Nethaniah went

40:11 [l]Nu 25:1
40:12 [m]Jer 43:5
40:13 [n]ver 8
40:14 [o]2Sa 10:1-19; Jer 25:21; 41:10
41:1 [p]Jer 40:8
41:2 [q]Ps 41:9; 109:5 [r]Jer 40:5 [s]2Sa 3:27; 20:9-10
41:5 [t]Lev 19:27 [u]Ge 33:18; Jdg 9:1-57; 1Ki 12:1 [v]Jos 18:1 [w]1Ki 16:24 [x]2Ki 25:9

[a]5 Or *Jeremiah answered* [b]8 Hebrew *Jezaniah,* a variant of *Jaazaniah* [c]9 Or *Chaldeans*; also in verse 10 [d]3 Or *Chaldean*

out from Mizpah to meet them, weeping[y] as he went. When he met them, he
said, "Come to Gedaliah son of Ahikam."
7When they went into the city, Ishmael
son of Nethaniah and the men who were
with him slaughtered them and threw
them into a cistern. 8But ten of them
said to Ishmael, "Don't kill us! We have
wheat and barley, oil and honey, hidden
in a field."[z] So he let them alone and did
not kill them with the others. 9Now the
cistern where he threw all the bodies of
the men he had killed along with Gedaliah was the one King Asa[a] had made as
part of his defense[b] against Baasha[c]
king of Israel. Ishmael son of Nethaniah
filled it with the dead.
10Ishmael made captives of all the rest
of the people[d] who were in Mizpah—the
king's daughters along with all the others who were left there, over whom Nebuzaradan commander of the imperial
guard had appointed Gedaliah son of
Ahikam. Ishmael son of Nethaniah took
them captive and set out to cross over to
the Ammonites.[e]
11When Johanan[f] son of Kareah and
all the army officers who were with him
heard about all the crimes Ishmael son
of Nethaniah had committed, 12they
took all their men and went to fight Ishmael son of Nethaniah. They caught up
with him near the great pool[g] in Gibeon.
13When all the people[h] Ishmael had with
him saw Johanan son of Kareah and the
army officers who were with him, they
were glad. 14All the people Ishmael had
taken captive at Mizpah turned and
went over to Johanan son of Kareah.
15But Ishmael son of Nethaniah and
eight of his men escaped[i] from Johanan
and fled to the Ammonites.

Flight to Egypt

16Then Johanan son of Kareah and all
the army officers who were with him led
away all the survivors[j] from Mizpah
whom he had recovered from Ishmael
son of Nethaniah after he had assassinated Gedaliah son of Ahikam: the soldiers, women, children and court officials he had brought from Gibeon. 17And
they went on, stopping at Geruth Kimham[k] near Bethlehem on their way to
Egypt[l] 18to escape the Babylonians.[a]
They were afraid[m] of them because Ishmael son of Nethaniah had killed Gedaliah[n] son of Ahikam, whom the king of
Babylon had appointed as governor over
the land.

42 Then all the army officers, including Johanan[o] son of Kareah
and Jezaniah[b] son of Hoshaiah, and all
the people from the least to the greatest[p] approached 2Jeremiah the prophet
and said to him, "Please hear our petition and pray[q] to the LORD your God for
this entire remnant.[r] For as you now see,
though we were once many, now only a
few[s] are left. 3Pray that the LORD your
God will tell us where we should go and
what we should do."[t]
4"I have heard you," replied Jeremiah
the prophet. "I will certainly pray[u] to the
LORD your God as you have requested; I
will tell you everything the LORD says
and will keep nothing back from you."[v]
5Then they said to Jeremiah, "May the
LORD be a true and faithful witness[w]
against us if we do not act in accordance
with everything the LORD your God
sends you to tell us. 6Whether it is favorable or unfavorable, we will obey the
LORD our God, to whom we are sending
you, so that it will go well[x] with us, for
we will obey[y] the LORD our God."
7Ten days later the word of the LORD
came to Jeremiah. 8So he called together Johanan son of Kareah and all the
army officers[z] who were with him and
all the people from the least to the
greatest. 9He said to them, "This is what
the LORD, the God of Israel, to whom you
sent me to present your petition, says:[a]
10'If you stay in this land, I will build[b]
you up and not tear you down; I will
plant[c] you and not uproot you,[d] for I am
grieved over the disaster I have inflicted
on you.[e] 11Do not be afraid of the king of
Babylon,[f] whom you now fear.[g] Do not
be afraid of him, declares the LORD, for I
am with you and will save[h] you and deliver you from his hands.[i] 12I will show
you compassion so that he will have
compassion on you and restore you to
your land.'[j]
13"However, if you say, 'We will not
stay in this land,' and so disobey[k] the
LORD your God, 14and if you say, 'No, we
will go and live in Egypt,[l] where we will
not see war or hear the trumpet or be
hungry for bread,' 15then hear the word

a 18 Or *Chaldeans* *b* 1 Hebrew; Septuagint (see also 43:2) *Azariah*

41:6 y2Sa 3:16
41:8 zIsa 45:3
41:9 a1Ki 15:22; 2Ch 16:6 bJdg 6:2 c2Ch 16:1
41:10 dJer 40:7,12 eJer 40:14
41:11 fJer 40:8
41:12 g2Sa 2:13
41:13 hver 10
41:15 iJob 21:30; Pr 28:17
41:16 jJer 43:4
41:17 k2Sa 19:37 lJer 42:14
41:18 mIsa 51:12; Jer 42:16; Lk 12:4-5 nJer 40:5
42:1 oJer 40:13; 41:11 pJer 6:13; 44:12
42:2 qJer 36:7; Ac 8:24; Jas 5:16 rIsa 1:9 sLev 26:22; La 1:1
42:3 tPs 86:11; Pr 3:6
42:4 uEx 8:29; 1Sa 12:23 v1Ki 22:14; 1Sa 3:17
42:5 wGe 31:50
42:6 xDt 5:29; 6:3; Jer 7:23 yEx 24:7; Jos 24:24
42:8 zver 1
42:9 a2Ki 22:15
42:10 bJer 24:6 cJer 31:28 dEze 36:36 eJer 18:8
42:11 fJer 27:11 gNu 14:9 hIsa 43:5 iJer 1:8; Ro 8:31
42:12 jPs 106:44-46
42:13 kJer 44:16
42:14 lNu 11:4-5

of the LORD, O remnant of Judah. This is what the LORD Almighty, the God of Israel, says: 'If you are determined to go to Egypt and you do go to settle there, 16then the sword[m] you fear will overtake you there, and the famine you dread will follow you into Egypt, and there you will die. 17Indeed, all who are determined to go to Egypt to settle there will die by the sword, famine and plague;[n] not one of them will survive or escape the disaster I will bring on them.' 18This is what the LORD Almighty, the God of Israel, says: 'As my anger and wrath[o] have been poured out on those who lived in Jerusalem,[p] so will my wrath be poured out on you when you go to Egypt. You will be an object of cursing and horror,[q] of condemnation and reproach; you will never see this place again.'[r]

19"O remnant of Judah, the LORD has told you, 'Do not go to Egypt.'[s] Be sure of this: I warn you today 20that you made a fatal mistake[a] when you sent me to the LORD your God and said, 'Pray to the LORD our God for us; tell us everything he says and we will do it.'[t] 21I have told you today, but you still have not obeyed the LORD your God in all he sent me to tell you.[u] 22So now, be sure of this: You will die by the sword, famine and plague[v] in the place where you want to go to settle."[w]

43 When Jeremiah finished telling the people all the words of the LORD their God—everything the LORD had sent him to tell them[x]— 2Azariah son of Hoshaiah and Johanan[y] son of Kareah and all the arrogant men said to Jeremiah, "You are lying! The LORD our God has not sent you to say, 'You must not go to Egypt to settle there.' 3But Baruch son of Neriah is inciting you against us to hand us over to the Babylonians,[b] so they may kill us or carry us into exile to Babylon."[z]

4So Johanan son of Kareah and all the army officers and all the people disobeyed the LORD's command[a] to stay in the land of Judah.[b] 5Instead, Johanan son of Kareah and all the army officers led away all the remnant of Judah who had come back to live in the land of Judah from all the nations where they had been scattered.[c] 6They also led away all the men, women and children and the king's daughters whom Nebuzaradan commander of the imperial guard had left with Gedaliah son of Ahikam, the son of Shaphan, and Jeremiah the prophet and Baruch son of Neriah. 7So they entered Egypt in disobedience to the LORD and went as far as Tahpanhes.[d]

8In Tahpanhes[e] the word of the LORD came to Jeremiah: 9"While the Jews are watching, take some large stones with you and bury them in clay in the brick pavement at the entrance to Pharaoh's palace in Tahpanhes. 10Then say to them, 'This is what the LORD Almighty, the God of Israel, says: I will send for my servant[f] Nebuchadnezzar king of Babylon, and I will set his throne over these stones I have buried here; he will spread his royal canopy above them. 11He will come and attack Egypt,[g] bringing death to those destined for death, captivity to those destined for captivity, and the sword to those destined for the sword.[h] 12He[c] will set fire to the temples of the gods[i] of Egypt; he will burn their temples and take their gods captive. As a shepherd wraps[j] his garment around him, so will he wrap Egypt around himself and depart from there unscathed. 13There in the temple of the sun[d] in Egypt he will demolish the sacred pillars and will burn down the temples of the gods of Egypt.' "

Disaster Because of Idolatry

44 This word came to Jeremiah concerning all the Jews living in Lower Egypt—in Migdol,[k] Tahpanhes[l] and Memphis[e][m]—and in Upper Egypt[f]:[n] 2"This is what the LORD Almighty, the God of Israel, says: You saw the great disaster I brought on Jerusalem and on all the towns of Judah. Today they lie deserted and in ruins[o] 3because of the evil they have done. They provoked me to anger by burning incense and by worshiping other gods[p] that neither they nor you nor your fathers[q] ever knew. 4Again and again[r] I sent my servants the prophets,[s] who said, 'Do not do this detestable thing that I hate!' 5But they did not listen or pay attention; they did not turn from their wickedness or stop burning incense to other gods.[t] 6Therefore, my fierce anger was poured out; it

42:16 [m] Eze 11:8
42:17 [n] ver 22; Jer 44:13
42:18 [o] Dt 29:18-20; Jer 7:20 [p] 2Ch 36:19; Jer 39:1-9 [q] Jer 29:18 [r] Jer 22:10
42:19 [s] Dt 17:16; Isa 30:7
42:20 [t] ver 2
42:21 [u] Eze 2:7; Zec 7:11-12
42:22 [v] ver 17; Eze 6:11 [w] Hos 9:6
43:1 [x] Jer 26:8; 42:9-22
43:2 [y] Jer 42:1
43:3 [z] Jer 38:4
43:4 [a] Jer 42:5-6 [b] Jer 42:10
43:5 [c] Jer 40:12
43:7 [d] Jer 2:16; 44:1
43:8 [e] Jer 2:16
43:10 [f] Isa 44:28; Jer 25:9; 27:6
43:11 [g] Jer 46:13-26; Eze 29:19-20 [h] Jer 15:2; 44:13; Zec 11:9
43:12 [i] Jer 46:25; Eze 30:13 [j] Ps 104:2; 109:18-19
44:1 [k] Ex 14:2 [l] Jer 43:7,8 [m] Isa 19:13 [n] Isa 11:11; Jer 46:14
44:2 [o] Isa 6:11; Jer 9:11; 34:22
44:3 [p] ver 8; Dt 13:6-11; 29:26 [q] Dt 32:17; Jer 19:4
44:4 [r] Jer 7:13 [s] Jer 7:25; 25:4; 26:5
44:5 [t] Jer 11:8-10

[a] 20 Or *you erred in your hearts* [b] 3 Or *Chaldeans* [c] 12 Or *I* [d] 13 Or *in Heliopolis* [e] 1 Hebrew *Noph* [f] 1 Hebrew *in Pathros*

raged against the towns of Judah and the streets of Jerusalem and made them the desolate ruins they are today.

7“Now this is what the LORD God Almighty, the God of Israel, says: Why bring such great disaster[u] on yourselves by cutting off from Judah the men and women,[v] the children and infants, and so leave yourselves without a remnant? 8Why provoke me to anger with what your hands have made,[w] burning incense to other gods in Egypt, where you have come to live?[x] You will destroy yourselves and make yourselves an object of cursing and reproach[y] among all the nations on earth. 9Have you forgotten the wickedness committed by your fathers and by the kings and queens of Judah and the wickedness committed by you and your wives in the land of Judah and the streets of Jerusalem?[z] 10To this day they have not humbled themselves or shown reverence, nor have they followed my law[a] and the decrees I set before you and your fathers.[b]

11“Therefore, this is what the LORD Almighty, the God of Israel, says: I am determined to bring disaster[c] on you and to destroy all Judah. 12I will take away the remnant[d] of Judah who were determined to go to Egypt to settle there. They will all perish in Egypt; they will fall by the sword or die from famine. From the least to the greatest, they will die by sword or famine.[e] They will become an object of cursing and horror, of condemnation and reproach.[f] 13I will punish those who live in Egypt with the sword, famine and plague,[g] as I punished Jerusalem. 14None of the remnant of Judah who have gone to live in Egypt will escape or survive to return to the land of Judah, to which they long to return and live; none will return except a few fugitives.”[h]

15Then all the men who knew that their wives were burning incense to other gods, along with all the women who were present—a large assembly—and all the people living in Lower and Upper Egypt,[a] said to Jeremiah, 16“We will not listen[i] to the message you have spoken to us in the name of the LORD! 17We will certainly do everything we said we would:[j] We will burn incense to the Queen of Heaven[k] and will pour out drink offerings to her just as we and our fathers, our kings and our officials did in the towns of Judah and in the streets of Jerusalem. At that time we had plenty of food and were well off and suffered no harm.[l] 18But ever since we stopped burning incense to the Queen of Heaven and pouring out drink offerings to her, we have had nothing and have been perishing by sword and famine.[m]”

19The women added, “When we burned incense to the Queen of Heaven[n] and poured out drink offerings to her, did not our husbands know that we were making cakes like her image and pouring out drink offerings to her?”

20Then Jeremiah said to all the people, both men and women, who were answering him, 21“Did not the LORD remember[o] and think about the incense[p] burned in the towns of Judah and the streets of Jerusalem[q] by you and your fathers,[r] your kings and your officials and the people of the land? 22When the LORD could no longer endure your wicked actions and the detestable things you did, your land became an object of cursing[s] and a desolate waste without inhabitants, as it is today.[t] 23Because you have burned incense and have sinned against the LORD and have not obeyed him or followed his law or his decrees or his stipulations, this disaster[u] has come upon you, as you now see.”[v]

24Then Jeremiah said to all the people, including the women,[w] “Hear the word of the LORD, all you people of Judah in Egypt.[x] 25This is what the LORD Almighty, the God of Israel, says: You and your wives have shown by your actions what you promised when you said, ‘We will certainly carry out the vows we made to burn incense and pour out drink offerings to the Queen of Heaven.’[y]

“Go ahead then, do what you promised! Keep your vows![z] 26But hear the word of the LORD, all Jews living in Egypt: ‘I swear[a] by my great name,’ says the LORD, ‘that no one from Judah living anywhere in Egypt will ever again invoke my name or swear, “As surely as the Sovereign LORD lives.”[b] 27For I am watching over them for harm,[c] not for good; the Jews in Egypt will perish by sword and famine until they are all destroyed. 28Those who escape the sword and return to the land of Judah from Egypt will

44:7 [u] Jer 26:19 [v] Jer 51:22
44:8 [w] Jer 25:6-7 [x] 1Co 10:22 [y] Jer 42:18
44:9 [z] ver 17,21
44:10 [a] Jos 1:7 [b] 1Ki 9:6-9
44:11 [c] Jer 21:10; Am 9:4
44:12 [d] ver 7 [e] Isa 1:28 [f] Jer 29:18; 42:15-18
44:13 [g] Jer 42:17
44:14 [h] ver 28; Jer 22:24-27; Ro 9:27
44:16 [i] Jer 11:8-10
44:17 [j] Dt 23:23 [k] ver 25; Jer 7:18
44:17 [l] Hos 2:5-13
44:18 [m] Mal 3:13-15
44:19 [n] Jer 7:18
44:21 [o] Isa 64:9; Jer 14:10 [p] Jer 11:13 [q] ver 9 [r] Ps 79:8
44:22 [s] Jer 25:18 [t] Ge 19:13; Ps 107:33-34
44:23 [u] Jer 40:2 [v] 1Ki 9:9; Jer 7:13-15; Da 9:11-12
44:24 [w] ver 15 [x] Jer 43:7
44:25 [y] ver 17 [z] Eze 20:39
44:26 [a] Ge 22:16; Isa 48:1; Heb 6:13-17 [b] Dt 32:40; Ps 50:16
44:27 [c] Jer 31:28

[a] 15 Hebrew *in Egypt and Pathros*

be very few.[d] Then the whole remnant of Judah who came to live in Egypt will know whose word will stand—mine or theirs.[e]

29 " 'This will be the sign to you that I will punish you in this place,' declares the LORD, 'so that you will know that my threats of harm against you will surely stand.'[f] 30 This is what the LORD says: 'I am going to hand Pharaoh[g] Hophra king of Egypt over to his enemies who seek his life, just as I handed Zedekiah[h] king of Judah over to Nebuchadnezzar king of Babylon, the enemy who was seeking his life.' "[i]

A Message to Baruch

45 This is what Jeremiah the prophet told Baruch[j] son of Neriah in the fourth year of Jehoiakim[k] son of Josiah king of Judah, after Baruch had written on a scroll the words Jeremiah was then dictating: 2 "This is what the LORD, the God of Israel, says to you, Baruch: 3 You said, 'Woe to me! The LORD has added sorrow to my pain; I am worn out with groaning[l] and find no rest.' "

4 ⌊The LORD said,⌋ "Say this to him: 'This is what the LORD says: I will overthrow what I have built and uproot what I have planted,[m] throughout the land.[n] 5 Should you then seek great things for yourself? Seek them not.[o] For I will bring disaster on all people, declares the LORD, but wherever you go I will let you escape with your life.' "[p]

A Message About Egypt

46 This is the word of the LORD that came to Jeremiah the prophet concerning the nations:[q]

2 Concerning Egypt:

This is the message against the army of Pharaoh Neco[r] king of Egypt, which was defeated at Carchemish[s] on the Euphrates River by Nebuchadnezzar king of Babylon in the fourth year of Jehoiakim[t] son of Josiah king of Judah:

3 "Prepare your shields,[u] both large
and small,
and march out for battle!
4 Harness the horses,
mount the steeds!
Take your positions
with helmets on!
Polish[v] your spears,
put on your armor![w]
5 What do I see?
They are terrified,
they are retreating,
their warriors are defeated.
They flee[x] in haste
without looking back,
and there is terror[y] on every side,"
declares the LORD.
6 "The swift cannot flee[z]
nor the strong escape.
In the north by the River Euphrates
they stumble and fall.[a]

7 "Who is this that rises like the Nile,
like rivers of surging waters?[b]
8 Egypt rises like the Nile,
like rivers of surging waters.
She says, 'I will rise and cover the
earth;
I will destroy cities and their
people.'
9 Charge, O horses!
Drive furiously, O charioteers![c]
March on, O warriors—
men of Cush[a] and Put who carry
shields,
men of Lydia[d] who draw the bow.
10 But that day[e] belongs to the Lord,
the LORD Almighty—
a day of vengeance, for
vengeance on his foes.
The sword will devour[f] till it is
satisfied,
till it has quenched its thirst
with blood.
For the Lord, the LORD Almighty,
will offer sacrifice[g]
in the land of the north by the
River Euphrates.

11 "Go up to Gilead and get balm,[h]
O Virgin[i] Daughter of Egypt.
But you multiply remedies in vain;
there is no healing[j] for you.
12 The nations will hear of your
shame;
your cries will fill the earth.
One warrior will stumble over
another;
both will fall[k] down together."

13 This is the message the LORD spoke to Jeremiah the prophet about the coming of Nebuchadnezzar king of Babylon to attack Egypt:[l]

[a] 9 That is, the upper Nile region

44:28 [d] ver 13-14; Isa 10:19 [e] ver 17,25-26
44:29 [f] Pr 19:21
44:30 [g] Jer 46:26; Eze 30:21 [h] 2Ki 25:1-7 [i] Jer 39:5
45:1 [j] Jer 32:12; 36:4, 18,32 [k] 2Ch 36:5
45:3 [l] Ps 69:3
45:4 [m] Jer 11:17 [n] Isa 5:5-7; Jer 18:7-10
45:5 [o] Mt 6:25-27,33 [p] Jer 21:9; 38:2; 39:18
46:1 [q] Jer 1:10; 25:15-38
46:2 [r] 2Ki 23:29 [s] 2Ch 35:20 [t] Jer 45:1
46:3 [u] Isa 21:5; Jer 51:11-12
46:4 [v] Eze 21:9-11 [w] 1Sa 17:5,38; 2Ch 26:14; Ne 4:16
46:5 [x] ver 21 [y] Jer 49:29
46:6 [z] Isa 30:16 [a] ver 12,16; Da 11:19
46:7 [b] Jer 47:2
46:9 [c] Jer 47:3 [d] Isa 66:19
46:10 [e] Joel 1:15 [f] Dt 32:42 [g] Zep 1:7
46:11 [h] Jer 8:22 [i] Isa 47:1 [j] Jer 30:13; Mic 1:9
46:12 [k] Isa 19:4; Na 3:8-10
46:13 [l] Isa 19:1

14 "Announce this in Egypt, and
proclaim it in Migdol;
proclaim it also in Memphis[a]
and Tahpanhes:[m]
'Take your positions and get ready,
for the sword devours those
around you.'

46:14 [m] Jer 43:8

15 Why will your warriors be laid low?
They cannot stand, for the LORD
will push them down.[n]

46:15 [n] Isa 66:15-16

16 They will stumble[o] repeatedly;
they will fall[p] over each other.
They will say, 'Get up, let us go back
to our own people and our
native lands,
away from the sword of the
oppressor.'

46:16 [o] Lev 26:37 [p] ver 6

17 There they will exclaim,
'Pharaoh king of Egypt is only a
loud noise;
he has missed his opportunity.[q]'

46:17 [q] Isa 19:11-16

18 "As surely as I live," declares the
King,[r]
whose name is the LORD
Almighty,
"one will come who is like Tabor[s]
among the mountains,
like Carmel[t] by the sea.

46:18 [r] Jer 48:15 [s] Jos 19:22 [t] 1Ki 18:42

19 Pack your belongings for exile,[u]
you who live in Egypt,
for Memphis will be laid waste
and lie in ruins without
inhabitant.

46:19 [u] Isa 20:4

20 "Egypt is a beautiful heifer,
but a gadfly is coming
against her from the north.[v]

46:20 [v] ver 24; Jer 47:2

21 The mercenaries[w] in her ranks
are like fattened calves.
They too will turn and flee[x]
together,
they will not stand their ground,
for the day[y] of disaster is coming
upon them,
the time for them to be
punished.

46:21 [w] 2Ki 7:6 [x] ver 5 [y] Ps 37:13

22 Egypt will hiss like a fleeing serpent
as the enemy advances in force;
they will come against her with
axes,
like men who cut down trees.
23 They will chop down her forest,"
declares the LORD,
"dense though it be.
They are more numerous than
locusts,[z]
they cannot be counted.

46:23 [z] Jdg 7:12

24 The Daughter of Egypt will be put
to shame,
handed over to the people of the
north.[a]"

46:24 [a] Jer 1:15

25 The LORD Almighty, the God of Israel, says: "I am about to bring punishment on Amon god of Thebes,[b][b] on
Pharaoh, on Egypt and her gods[c] and
her kings, and on those who rely[d] on
Pharaoh. 26 I will hand them over[e] to
those who seek their lives, to Nebuchadnezzar king[f] of Babylon and his officers.
Later, however, Egypt will be inhabited[g]
as in times past," declares the LORD.

46:25 [b] Eze 30:14; Na 3:8 [c] Jer 43:12 [d] Isa 20:6
46:26 [e] Jer 44:30 [f] Eze 32:11 [g] Eze 29:11-16

27 "Do not fear,[h] O Jacob my servant;
do not be dismayed, O Israel.
I will surely save you out of a
distant place,
your descendants from the land
of their exile.[i]
Jacob will again have peace and
security,
and no one will make him afraid.

46:27 [h] Isa 41:13; 43:5 [i] Isa 11:11; Jer 50:19

28 Do not fear, O Jacob my servant,
for I am with you,"[j] declares the
LORD.
"Though I completely destroy[k] all
the nations
among which I scatter you,
I will not completely destroy you.
I will discipline you but only with
justice;
I will not let you go entirely
unpunished."

46:28 [j] Isa 8:9-10 [k] Jer 4:27

A Message About the Philistines

47 This is the word of the LORD
that came to Jeremiah the
prophet concerning the Philistines before Pharaoh attacked Gaza:[l]

47:1 [l] Ge 10:19; Am 1:6; Zec 9:5-7

2 This is what the LORD says:

"See how the waters are rising in
the north;[m]
they will become an overflowing
torrent.
They will overflow the land and
everything in it,
the towns and those who live in
them.
The people will cry out;
all who dwell in the land will wail
3 at the sound of the hoofs of
galloping steeds,

47:2 [m] Isa 8:7; 14:31

[a] 14 Hebrew *Noph*; also in verse 19
[b] 25 Hebrew *No*

at the noise of enemy chariots
and the rumble of their wheels.
Fathers will not turn to help their
children;
their hands will hang limp.
4 For the day has come
to destroy all the Philistines
and to cut off all survivors

47:4 [n] Am 1:9-10; Zec 9:2-4 [o] Jer 25:22 [p] Ge 10:14; Joel 3:4 [q] Dt 2:23

who could help Tyre[n] and Sidon.[o]
The LORD is about to destroy the
Philistines,[p]
the remnant from the coasts of
Caphtor.[a][q]

47:5 [r] Jer 41:5; Mic 1:16 [s] Jer 25:20

5 Gaza will shave[r] her head in
mourning;
Ashkelon[s] will be silenced.
O remnant on the plain,
how long will you cut
yourselves?

47:6 [t] Jer 12:12

6 " 'Ah, sword[t] of the LORD,' ⌊you cry,⌋
'how long till you rest?
Return to your scabbard;
cease and be still.'
7 But how can it rest
when the LORD has commanded
it,
when he has ordered it
to attack Ashkelon and the
coast?"

A Message About Moab

48 Concerning Moab:

This is what the LORD Almighty, the God of Israel, says:

48:1 [u] Nu 32:38 [v] Nu 32:37

"Woe to Nebo,[u] for it will be ruined.
Kiriathaim[v] will be disgraced
and captured;
the stronghold[b] will be
disgraced and shattered.

48:2 [w] Isa 16:14 [x] Nu 21:25

2 Moab will be praised[w] no more;
in Heshbon[c][x] men will plot her
downfall:
'Come, let us put an end to that
nation.'
You too, O Madmen,[d] will be
silenced;
the sword will pursue you.

48:3 [y] Isa 15:5

3 Listen to the cries from Horonaim,[y]
cries of great havoc and
destruction.
4 Moab will be broken;
her little ones will cry out.[e]

48:5 [z] Isa 15:5

5 They go up the way to Luhith,[z]
weeping bitterly as they go;
on the road down to Horonaim
anguished cries over the
destruction are heard.

48:6 [a] Jer 17:6

6 Flee! Run for your lives;
become like a bush[f] in the
desert.[a]

48:7 [b] Nu 21:29 [c] Isa 46:1-2; Jer 49:3

7 Since you trust in your deeds and
riches,
you too will be taken captive,
and Chemosh[b] will go into exile,[c]
together with his priests and
officials.
8 The destroyer will come against
every town,
and not a town will escape.
The valley will be ruined
and the plateau destroyed,
because the LORD has spoken.
9 Put salt on Moab,
for she will be laid waste[g];
her towns will become desolate,
with no one to live in them.

48:10 [d] Jer 47:6 [e] 1Ki 20:42; 2Ki 13:15-19

10 "A curse on him who is lax in doing
the LORD's work!
A curse on him who keeps his
sword[d] from bloodshed![e]

48:11 [f] Zec 1:15 [g] Zep 1:12

11 "Moab has been at rest[f] from youth,
like wine left on its dregs,[g]
not poured from one jar to
another—
she has not gone into exile.
So she tastes as she did,
and her aroma is unchanged.
12 But days are coming,"
declares the LORD,
"when I will send men who pour
from jars,
and they will pour her out;
they will empty her jars
and smash her jugs.

48:13 [h] Hos 10:6

13 Then Moab will be ashamed[h] of
Chemosh,
as the house of Israel was
ashamed
when they trusted in Bethel.

48:14 [i] Ps 33:16

14 "How can you say, 'We are warriors,[i]
men valiant in battle'?
15 Moab will be destroyed and her
towns invaded;

48:15 [j] Jer 50:27

her finest young men will go
down in the slaughter,[j]"

[a] *4* That is, Crete [b] *1* Or */ Misgab* [c] *2* The Hebrew for *Heshbon* sounds like the Hebrew for *plot.* [d] *2* The name of the Moabite town Madmen sounds like the Hebrew for *be silenced.* [e] *4* Hebrew; Septuagint */ proclaim it to Zoar* [f] *6* Or *like Aroer* [g] *9* Or *Give wings to Moab, / for she will fly away*

48:15 [k]Jer 46:18 [l]Jer 51:57

declares the King,[k] whose name
is the LORD Almighty.[l]

48:16 [m]Isa 13:22

16 "The fall of Moab is at hand;[m]
her calamity will come quickly.
17 Mourn for her, all who live around
her,
all who know her fame;
say, 'How broken is the mighty
scepter,
how broken the glorious staff!'

48:18 [n]Isa 47:1 [o]Nu 21:30; Jos 13:9 [p]ver 8

18 "Come down from your glory
and sit on the parched ground,[n]
O inhabitants of the Daughter of
Dibon,[o]
for he who destroys Moab
will come up against you
and ruin your fortified cities.[p]

48:19 [q]Dt 2:36

19 Stand by the road and watch,
you who live in Aroer.[q]
Ask the man fleeing and the
woman escaping,
ask them, 'What has happened?'

48:20 [r]Isa 16:7 [s]Nu 21:13

20 Moab is disgraced, for she is
shattered.
Wail[r] and cry out!
Announce by the Arnon[s]
that Moab is destroyed.

48:21 [t]Nu 21:23; Isa 15:4 [u]Jos 13:18

21 Judgment has come to the
plateau—
to Holon, Jahzah[t] and
Mephaath,[u]

48:22 [v]Jos 13:9,17

22 to Dibon,[v] Nebo and Beth
Diblathaim,

48:23 [w]Jos 13:17

23 to Kiriathaim, Beth Gamul and
Beth Meon,[w]

48:24 [x]Am 2:2

24 to Kerioth[x] and Bozrah—
to all the towns of Moab, far and
near.

48:25 [y]Ps 75:10 [z]Ps 10:15; Eze 30:21

25 Moab's horn[a][y] is cut off;
her arm[z] is broken,"
declares the LORD.

48:26 [a]Jer 25:16,27

26 "Make her drunk,[a]
for she has defied the LORD.
Let Moab wallow in her vomit;
let her be an object of ridicule.

48:27 [b]Jer 2:26 [c]Job 16:4; Jer 18:16 [d]Mic 7:8-10

27 Was not Israel the object of your
ridicule?[b]
Was she caught among thieves,
that you shake your head[c] in
scorn[d]
whenever you speak of her?
28 Abandon your towns and dwell
among the rocks,
you who live in Moab.

48:28 [e]Ps 55:6-7 [f]Jdg 6:2

Be like a dove[e] that makes its nest
at the mouth of a cave.[f]

48:29 [g]Job 40:12; Isa 16:6

29 "We have heard of Moab's pride[g]—
her overweening pride and
conceit,
her pride and arrogance
and the haughtiness of her heart.
30 I know her insolence but it is futile,"
declares the LORD,
"and her boasts accomplish
nothing.

48:31 [h]Isa 15:5-8 [i]2Ki 3:25

31 Therefore I wail[h] over Moab,
for all Moab I cry out,
I moan for the men of Kir
Hareseth.[i]

48:32 [j]Isa 16:8-9

32 I weep for you, as Jazer weeps,
O vines of Sibmah.[j]
Your branches spread as far as the
sea;
they reached as far as the sea of
Jazer.
The destroyer has fallen
on your ripened fruit and grapes.
33 Joy and gladness are gone
from the orchards and fields of
Moab.

48:33 [k]Isa 16:10 [l]Joel 1:12

I have stopped the flow of wine[k]
from the presses;
no one treads them with shouts
of joy.[l]
Although there are shouts,
they are not shouts of joy.

48:34 [m]Nu 32:3 [n]Isa 15:4 [o]Ge 13:10 [p]Isa 15:5 [q]Isa 15:6

34 "The sound of their cry rises
from Heshbon to Elealeh[m] and
Jahaz,[n]
from Zoar[o] as far as Horonaim[p]
and Eglath Shelishiyah,
for even the waters of Nimrim
are dried up.[q]

48:35 [r]Isa 15:2; 16:12 [s]Jer 11:13

35 In Moab I will put an end
to those who make offerings on
the high places[r]
and burn incense[s] to their gods,"
declares the LORD.

48:36 [t]Isa 16:11 [u]Isa 15:7

36 "So my heart laments[t] for Moab
like a flute;
it laments like a flute for the
men of Kir Hareseth.
The wealth they acquired[u] is
gone.

48:37 [v]Isa 15:2; Jer 41:5 [w]Ge 37:34

37 Every head is shaved[v]
and every beard cut off;
every hand is slashed
and every waist is covered with
sackcloth.[w]
38 On all the roofs in Moab
and in the public squares

[a] 25 *Horn* here symbolizes strength.

there is nothing but mourning,
for I have broken Moab
like a jar[x] that no one wants,”
declares the LORD.

39 “How shattered she is! How they wail!
How Moab turns her back in shame!
Moab has become an object of ridicule,
an object of horror to all those around her.”

40 This is what the LORD says:

“Look! An eagle is swooping[y] down,
spreading its wings[z] over Moab.
41 Kerioth[a] will be captured
and the strongholds taken.
In that day the hearts of Moab’s warriors
will be like the heart of a woman in labor.[a]
42 Moab will be destroyed[b] as a nation[c]
because she defied[d] the LORD.
43 Terror and pit and snare[e] await you,
O people of Moab,”
declares the LORD.
44 “Whoever flees[f] from the terror
will fall into a pit,
whoever climbs out of the pit
will be caught in a snare;
for I will bring upon Moab
the year[g] of her punishment,”
declares the LORD.

45 “In the shadow of Heshbon
the fugitives stand helpless,
for a fire has gone out from Heshbon,
a blaze from the midst of Sihon;[h]
it burns the foreheads of Moab,
the skulls[i] of the noisy boasters.
46 Woe to you, O Moab![j]
The people of Chemosh are destroyed;
your sons are taken into exile
and your daughters into captivity.

47 “Yet I will restore[k] the fortunes of Moab
in days to come,”
declares the LORD.

Here ends the judgment on Moab.

48:38 [x] Jer 22:28
48:40 [y] Dt 28:49; Hab 1:8 [z] Isa 8:8
48:41 [a] Isa 21:3
48:42 [b] Ps 83:4; Isa 16:14 [c] ver 2 [d] ver 26
48:43 [e] Isa 24:17
48:44 [f] 1Ki 19:17; Isa 24:18 [g] Jer 11:23
48:45 [h] Nu 21:21,26-28 [i] Nu 24:17
48:46 [j] Nu 21:29
48:47 [k] Jer 12:15; 49:6, 39

A Message About Ammon

49 Concerning the Ammonites:[l]

This is what the LORD says:
“Has Israel no sons?
Has she no heirs?
Why then has Molech[b] taken possession of Gad?
Why do his people live in its towns?
2 But the days are coming,”
declares the LORD,
“when I will sound the battle cry[m]
against Rabbah[n] of the Ammonites;
it will become a mound of ruins,
and its surrounding villages will be set on fire.
Then Israel will drive out
those who drove her out,[o]”
says the LORD.
3 “Wail, O Heshbon, for Ai[p] is destroyed!
Cry out, O inhabitants of Rabbah!
Put on sackcloth and mourn;
rush here and there inside the walls,
for Molech will go into exile,[q]
together with his priests and officials.
4 Why do you boast of your valleys,
boast of your valleys so fruitful?
O unfaithful daughter,
you trust in your riches[r] and say,
‘Who will attack me?’[s]
5 I will bring terror on you
from all those around you,”
declares the Lord,
the LORD Almighty.
“Every one of you will be driven away,
and no one will gather the fugitives.

6 “Yet afterward, I will restore[t] the fortunes of the Ammonites,”
declares the LORD.

A Message About Edom

7 Concerning Edom:[u]

This is what the LORD Almighty says:

“Is there no longer wisdom in Teman?[v]

[a] 41 Or *The cities* [b] 1 Or *their king*; Hebrew *malcam*; also in verse 3

49:1 [l] Am 1:13; Zep 2:8-9
49:2 [m] Jer 4:19 [n] Dt 3:11 [o] Isa 14:2; Eze 21:28-32; 25:2-11
49:3 [p] Jos 8:28 [q] Jer 48:7
49:4 [r] Jer 9:23; 1Ti 6:17 [s] Jer 21:13
49:6 [t] ver 39; Jer 48:47
49:7 [u] Ge 25:30; Eze 25:12 [v] Ge 36:11,15,34

Has counsel perished from the prudent?
Has their wisdom decayed?
8 Turn and flee, hide in deep caves,
you who live in Dedan,[w]
for I will bring disaster on Esau
at the time I punish him.
9 If grape pickers came to you,
would they not leave a few grapes?
If thieves came during the night,
would they not steal only as much as they wanted?
10 But I will strip Esau bare;
I will uncover his hiding places,
so that he cannot conceal himself.
His children, relatives and neighbors will perish,
and he will be no more.[x]
11 Leave your orphans;[y] I will protect their lives.
Your widows too can trust in me."

12 This is what the LORD says: "If those
who do not deserve to drink the cup[z]
must drink it, why should you go unpunished?[a] You will not go unpunished,
but must drink it. 13 I swear[b] by myself,"
declares the LORD, "that Bozrah[c] will become a ruin and an object of horror, of
reproach and of cursing; and all its
towns will be in ruins forever."

14 I have heard a message from the LORD:
An envoy was sent to the nations to say,
"Assemble yourselves to attack it!
Rise up for battle!"

15 "Now I will make you small among the nations,
despised among men.
16 The terror you inspire
and the pride of your heart have deceived you,
you who live in the clefts of the rocks,
who occupy the heights of the hill.
Though you build your nest[d] as high as the eagle's,
from there I will bring you down,"
declares the LORD.
17 "Edom will become an object of horror;[e]
all who pass by will be appalled and will scoff
because of all its wounds.[f]

49:8 [w] Jer 25:23
49:10 [x] Mal 1:2-5
49:11 [y] Hos 14:3
49:12 [z] Jer 25:15 [a] Jer 25:28-29
49:13 [b] Ge 22:16 [c] Ge 36:33; Isa 34:6
49:16 [d] Job 39:27; Am 9:2
49:17 [e] ver 13 [f] Jer 50:13; Eze 35:7

18 As Sodom and Gomorrah[g] were overthrown,
along with their neighboring towns,"
says the LORD,
"so no one will live there;
no man will dwell[h] in it.

19 "Like a lion coming up from Jordan's thickets[i]
to a rich pastureland,
I will chase Edom from its land in an instant.
Who is the chosen one I will appoint for this?
Who is like me and who can challenge me?[j]
And what shepherd can stand against me?"
20 Therefore, hear what the LORD has planned against Edom,
what he has purposed[k] against those who live in Teman:
The young of the flock[l] will be dragged away;
he will completely destroy[m] their pasture because of them.
21 At the sound of their fall the earth will tremble;[n]
their cry[o] will resound to the Red Sea.[a]
22 Look! An eagle will soar and swoop[p] down,
spreading its wings over Bozrah.
In that day the hearts of Edom's warriors
will be like the heart of a woman in labor.[q]

A Message About Damascus

23 Concerning Damascus:[r]

"Hamath[s] and Arpad[t] are dismayed,
for they have heard bad news.
They are disheartened,
troubled like[b] the restless sea.[u]
24 Damascus has become feeble,
she has turned to flee
and panic has gripped her;
anguish and pain have seized her,
pain like that of a woman in labor.
25 Why has the city of renown not been abandoned,

[a] 21 Hebrew *Yam Suph*; that is, Sea of Reeds
[b] 23 Hebrew *on* or *by*

49:18 [g] Ge 19:24; Dt 29:23 [h] ver 33
49:19 [i] Jer 12:5 [j] Jer 50:44
49:20 [k] Isa 14:27 [l] Jer 50:45 [m] Mal 1:3-4
49:21 [n] Eze 26:15 [o] Jer 50:46; Eze 26:18
49:22 [p] Hos 8:1 [q] Isa 13:8; Jer 48:40-41
49:23 [r] Ge 14:15; 2Ch 16:2; Ac 9:2 [s] Isa 10:9; Am 6:2; Zec 9:2 [t] 2Ki 18:34 [u] Ge 49:4; Isa 57:20

the town in which I delight?
26 Surely, her young men will fall in
the streets;
49:26 [v]Jer 50:30 all her soldiers will be silenced[v]
in that day,"
declares the LORD Almighty.
49:27 [w]Jer 43:12; Am 1:4 [x]1Ki 15:18 27 "I will set fire[w] to the walls of
Damascus;
it will consume the fortresses of
Ben-Hadad.[x]"

A Message About Kedar and Hazor

49:28 [y]Ge 25:13 [z]Jdg 6:3 28 Concerning Kedar[y] and the kingdoms of Hazor, which Nebuchadnezzar
king of Babylon attacked:

This is what the LORD says:

"Arise, and attack Kedar
and destroy the people of the
East.[z]
29 Their tents and their flocks will be
taken;
their shelters will be carried off
with all their goods and camels.
Men will shout to them,
49:29 [a]Jer 6:25; 46:5 'Terror[a] on every side!'
30 "Flee quickly away!
Stay in deep caves, you who live
in Hazor,"
declares the LORD.
"Nebuchadnezzar king of Babylon
has plotted against you;
he has devised a plan against you.
31 "Arise and attack a nation at ease,
which lives in confidence,"
declares the LORD,
"a nation that has neither gates nor
49:31 [b]Eze 38:11 bars;[b]
its people live alone.
32 Their camels will become plunder,
and their large herds will be
booty.
49:32 [c]Jer 9:26 I will scatter to the winds those
who are in distant places[a][c]
and will bring disaster on them
from every side,"
declares the LORD.
33 "Hazor will become a haunt of
jackals,
49:33 [d]Jer 10:22 [e]ver 18; Jer 51:37 a desolate[d] place forever.
No one will live there;
no man will dwell[e] in it."

A Message About Elam

34 This is the word of the LORD that
came to Jeremiah the prophet concern-
ing Elam,[f] early in the reign of Zedeki- 49:34 [f]Ge 10:22 [g]2Ki 24:18
ah[g] king of Judah:

35 This is what the LORD Almighty says:
"See, I will break the bow[h] of Elam, 49:35 [h]Isa 22:6
the mainstay of their might.
36 I will bring against Elam the four 49:36 [i]ver 32
winds[i]
from the four quarters of the
heavens;
I will scatter them to the four winds,
and there will not be a nation
where Elam's exiles do not go.
37 I will shatter Elam before their foes,
before those who seek their lives;
I will bring disaster upon them,
even my fierce anger,"[j] 49:37 [j]Jer 30:24 [k]Jer 9:16
declares the LORD.
"I will pursue them with the sword[k]
until I have made an end of
them.
38 I will set my throne in Elam
and destroy her king and
officials,"
declares the LORD.
39 "Yet I will restore[l] the fortunes of 49:39 [l]Jer 48:47
Elam
in days to come,"
declares the LORD.

A Message About Babylon

50 This is the word the LORD spoke
through Jeremiah the prophet 50:1 [m]Ge 10:10; Isa 13:1
concerning Babylon[m] and the land of
the Babylonians[b]:

2 "Announce and proclaim[n] among 50:2 [n]Jer 4:16 [o]Jer 51:31 [p]Isa 46:1 [q]Jer 51:47
the nations,
lift up a banner and proclaim it;
keep nothing back, but say,
'Babylon will be captured;[o]
Bel[p] will be put to shame,
Marduk[q] filled with terror.
Her images will be put to shame
and her idols filled with terror.'
3 A nation from the north will attack
her
and lay waste her land. 50:3 [r]ver 13; Isa 14:22-23 [s]Zep 1:3
No one will live[r] in it;
both men and animals[s] will flee
away.
4 "In those days, at that time,"
declares the LORD,
"the people of Israel and the people 50:4 [t]Jer 3:18; Hos 1:11
of Judah together[t]

[a] 32 Or *who clip the hair by their foreheads*
[b] 1 Or *Chaldeans*; also in verses 8, 25, 35 and 45

Lost and Alone

To even conceive of the possibility that God's people might be lost in sin is a horrific notion. But to hear that their leaders have deliberately guided them in the wrong direction—that's almost unthinkable. But it happens all the time, even today. False shepherds and teachers continue to lead God's people astray, but in the final analysis we are each responsible for our own actions. The Bible places the burden of accountability squarely on the individual: "We all, like sheep, have gone astray, each of us has turned to his own way" (Isaiah 53:6). Notice that Isaiah did not say that we have been led astray, nor that we have followed a pied piper who lured us like unsuspecting children away from our home.

When we stray from God's path we can never point the finger at him. Sometimes we fail to stop to ask God for directions, hurtling along at a frenzied pace with little thought to where the detour might be leading. We are too proud to ask him for his counsel, because we smugly assume that we can figure things out by ourselves.

People who are lost with respect to God suffer two consequences. First, they forget their own resting place (Jeremiah 50:6); second, they are vulnerable to being devoured by others (verse 7). The runaway teenager, the wayward father, the homeless alcoholic, the bewildered cult member, the frightened fugitive on the lam—all are examples of individuals who may at one time have known a resting place but who have voluntarily given up their home, even forgotten it, because of whatever compulsion has driven them away. It can astound us to read of adolescents who have for one reason or another fled seemingly comfortable living situations to choose the desolate and desperate life on the streets. Lost and vulnerable, they live in constant fear for their very lives and are at risk at any time of being devoured by the thieves, thugs, pimps and opportunists all around them.

But our Lord Jesus Christ is a kind shepherd who seeks out lost men, women, boys and girls and carries them home, home to the heart of the loving Father. Our Good Shepherd knows all of his sheep by name (John 10:2–3), and they follow him (John 10:4). He cares about them to the degree of being willing to give up his own life in order to protect them (John 10:11,28). And he never stops looking for other sheep who are still missing (John 10:16). Even if 99 of 100 are safe in the fold, he will go searching for the one that is alone and defenseless (see Luke 15:1–7).

All around us are people who have lost their way—family members, neighbors, friends, working associates, casual acquaintances. Jesus wants to love them through us; he asks us to be his undershepherds for seeking the alienated, the battered, the bruised, the weary, and bringing them home to the One who offers the only true rest for the soul (Matthew 11:28–30).

Self-Discovery: *Have you ever voluntarily given up a settled resting place, either physically or spiritually? What motivated you to come back? How were you received when you returned?*

GO TO DISCOVERY 206 ON PAGE 1062

50:4 [u] Ezr 3:12; Jer 31:9 [v] Hos 3:5

will go in tears[u] to seek[v] the
LORD their God.
5 They will ask the way to Zion
and turn their faces toward it.

50:5 [w] Jer 33:7 [x] Isa 55:3; Jer 32:40; Heb 8:6-10

They will come[w] and bind
themselves to the LORD
in an everlasting covenant[x]
that will not be forgotten.

50:6 [y] Isa 53:6; Mt 9:36; 10:6 [z] Jer 3:6; Eze 34:6 [a] ver 19

6 "My people have been lost sheep;[y]
their shepherds have led them
astray
and caused them to roam on the
mountains.
They wandered over mountain and
hill[z]
and forgot their own resting
place.[a]
7 Whoever found them devoured
them;

50:7 [b] Jer 2:3 [c] Jer 14:8

their enemies said, 'We are not
guilty,[b]
for they sinned against the LORD,
their true pasture,
the LORD, the hope[c] of their
fathers.'

50:8 [d] Isa 48:20; Jer 51:6; Rev 18:4

8 "Flee[d] out of Babylon;
leave the land of the Babylonians,
and be like the goats that lead
the flock.
9 For I will stir up and bring against
Babylon
an alliance of great nations from
the land of the north.
They will take up their positions
against her,
and from the north she will be
captured.
Their arrows will be like skilled
warriors
who do not return
empty-handed.
10 So Babylonia[a] will be plundered;
all who plunder her will have
their fill,"
declares the LORD.

50:11 [e] Isa 47:6

11 "Because you rejoice and are glad,
you who pillage my inheritance,[e]
because you frolic like a heifer
threshing grain
and neigh like stallions,
12 your mother will be greatly
ashamed;
she who gave you birth will be
disgraced.
She will be the least of the
nations—
a wilderness, a dry land, a desert.
13 Because of the LORD's anger she
will not be inhabited
but will be completely desolate.

50:13 [f] Jer 18:16 [g] Jer 49:17

All who pass Babylon will be
horrified and scoff[f]
because of all her wounds.[g]

50:14 [h] ver 29,42

14 "Take up your positions around
Babylon,
all you who draw the bow.[h]
Shoot at her! Spare no arrows,
for she has sinned against the
LORD.

50:15 [i] Jer 51:14 [j] Jer 51:44,58 [k] Jer 51:6 [l] Ps 137:8; Rev 18:6

15 Shout[i] against her on every side!
She surrenders, her towers fall,
her walls[j] are torn down.
Since this is the vengeance[k] of the
LORD,
take vengeance on her;
do to her[l] as she has done to
others.

50:16 [m] Jer 25:38

16 Cut off from Babylon the sower,
and the reaper with his sickle at
harvest.
Because of the sword[m] of the
oppressor

[a] 10 Or *Chaldea*

BABYLON'S FALL

Jeremiah warned God's people not to rebel against Babylon (Jeremiah 42:9–22). God was going to discipline his people by allowing the Babylonians to conquer them, but ultimately Babylon herself would be defeated by Persia (Jeremiah 42:11–12; 50:1–3). God's message is always consistent: Sin must be judged. Even though God used the sinful Babylonians as agents to administer his discipline, he would later judge Babylon for refusing to follow him. The fall of Babylon is such a significant event in the Old Testament that it is referred to in the New Testament to describe the manner in which all of God's enemies will eventually be conquered (Revelation 17—18). Jeremiah promised that the people would return from captivity after Babylon had fallen. They would come back to the land God had promised them, once again grazing their flocks peacefully in their "own pasture"—at rest in their return to the one true God (Jeremiah 50:5,19,34). This homecoming was necessary so that the promised Messiah could be born in the land and fulfill the prophecies made about him (Micah 5:2; Matthew 2:1–6).

50:16 [n]Isa 13:14 [o]Jer 51:9

let everyone return to his own
people,[n]
let everyone flee to his own land.[o]

50:17 [p]Jer 2:15 [q]2Ki 17:6 [r]2Ki 24:10,14 [s]2Ki 25:7

17 "Israel is a scattered flock
that lions[p] have chased away.
The first to devour him
was the king[q] of Assyria;
the last to crush his bones
was Nebuchadnezzar[r] king[s] of
Babylon."

18 Therefore this is what the LORD
Almighty, the God of Israel, says:

50:18 [t]Isa 10:12 [u]Eze 31:3

"I will punish the king of Babylon
and his land
as I punished the king[t] of
Assyria.[u]

50:19 [v]Jer 31:10; Eze 34:13 [w]Jer 31:5; 33:12

19 But I will bring[v] Israel back to his
own pasture
and he will graze on Carmel and
Bashan;
his appetite will be satisfied
on the hills[w] of Ephraim and
Gilead.
20 In those days, at that time,"
declares the LORD,
"search will be made for Israel's
guilt,
but there will be none,
and for the sins[x] of Judah,
but none will be found,
for I will forgive[y] the remnant[z] I
spare.

50:20 [x]Mic 7:18,19 [y]Jer 31:34 [z]Isa 1:9

50:21 [a]Eze 23:23

21 "Attack the land of Merathaim
and those who live in Pekod.[a]
Pursue, kill and completely
destroy[a] them,"
declares the LORD.
"Do everything I have
commanded you.

50:22 [b]Jer 4:19-21; 51:54

22 The noise[b] of battle is in the land,
the noise of great destruction!
23 How broken and shattered
is the hammer of the whole earth!

50:23 [c]Isa 14:16

How desolate[c] is Babylon
among the nations!

50:24 [d]Da 5:30-31 [e]Jer 51:31 [f]Job 9:4

24 I set a trap[d] for you, O Babylon,
and you were caught before you
knew it;
you were found and captured[e]
because you opposed[f] the LORD.

50:25 [g]Isa 13:5

25 The LORD has opened his arsenal
and brought out the weapons[g] of
his wrath,
for the Sovereign LORD Almighty
has work to do
in the land of the Babylonians.[h]

50:25 [h]Jer 51:25,55

26 Come against her from afar.
Break open her granaries;
pile her up like heaps of grain.

50:26 [i]Isa 14:22-23

Completely destroy[i] her
and leave her no remnant.
27 Kill all her young bulls;
let them go down to the
slaughter!
Woe to them! For their day has
come,
the time for them to be punished.
28 Listen to the fugitives and refugees
from Babylon
declaring in Zion[j]
how the LORD our God has taken
vengeance,[k]
vengeance for his temple.

50:28 [j]Isa 48:20; Jer 51:10 [k]ver 15

29 "Summon archers against Babylon,
all those who draw the bow.[l]
Encamp all around her;
let no one escape.
Repay[m] her for her deeds;[n]
do to her as she has done.
For she has defied[o] the LORD,
the Holy One of Israel.

50:29 [l]ver 14 [m]Rev 18:6 [n]Jer 51:56 [o]Isa 47:10

50:30 [p]Isa 13:18; Jer 49:26

30 Therefore, her young men[p] will fall
in the streets;
all her soldiers will be silenced in
that day,"
declares the LORD.

50:31 [q]Jer 21:13

31 "See, I am against[q] you, O arrogant
one,"
declares the Lord, the LORD
Almighty,
"for your day has come,
the time for you to be punished.
32 The arrogant one will stumble and
fall
and no one will help her up;

50:32 [r]Jer 21:14; 49:27

I will kindle a fire[r] in her towns
that will consume all who are
around her."

33 This is what the LORD Almighty says:

50:33 [s]Isa 58:6 [t]Isa 14:17

"The people of Israel are
oppressed,[s]
and the people of Judah as well.
All their captors hold them fast,
refusing to let them go.[t]
34 Yet their Redeemer is strong;
the LORD Almighty[u] is his name.
He will vigorously defend their
cause[v]

50:34 [u]Jer 51:19 [v]Jer 15:21; 51:36

[a] *21* The Hebrew term refers to the irrevocable giving over of things or persons to the LORD, often by totally destroying them; also in verse 26.

50:34 [w]Isa 14:7

so that he may bring rest[w] to
their land,
but unrest to those who live in
Babylon.

50:35 [x]Jer 47:6 [y]Da 5:7

35 "A sword[x] against the Babylonians!"
declares the LORD—
"against those who live in Babylon
and against her officials and
wise[y] men!
36 A sword against her false prophets!
They will become fools.

50:36 [z]Jer 49:22

A sword against her warriors![z]
They will be filled with terror.
37 A sword against her horses and
chariots[a]

50:37 [a]Jer 51:21 [b]Jer 51:30; Na 3:13

and all the foreigners in her ranks!
They will become women.[b]
A sword against her treasures!
They will be plundered.
38 A drought on[a] her waters!

50:38 [c]Jer 51:36 [d]ver 2

They will dry[c] up.
For it is a land of idols,[d]
idols that will go mad with terror.

39 "So desert creatures and hyenas
will live there,
and there the owl will dwell.

50:39 [e]Isa 13:19-22; 34:13-15; Jer 51:37; Rev 18:2

It will never again be inhabited
or lived in from generation to
generation.[e]
40 As God overthrew Sodom and
Gomorrah[f]

50:40 [f]Ge 19:24

along with their neighboring
towns,"
declares the LORD,
"so no one will live there;
no man will dwell in it.
41 "Look! An army is coming from the
north;[g]

50:41 [g]Jer 6:22 [h]Isa 13:4; Jer 51:22-28

a great nation and many kings
are being stirred up from the
ends of the earth.[h]

50:42 [i]ver 14 [j]Isa 13:18 [k]Isa 5:30 [l]Jer 6:23

42 They are armed with bows[i] and
spears;
they are cruel and without
mercy.[j]
They sound like the roaring sea[k]
as they ride on their horses;
they come like men in battle
formation
to attack you, O Daughter of
Babylon.[l]
43 The king of Babylon has heard
reports about them,
and his hands hang limp.
Anguish has gripped him,
pain like that of a woman in labor.
44 Like a lion coming up from Jordan's
thickets
to a rich pastureland,
I will chase Babylon from its land
in an instant.

50:44 [m]Nu 16:5 [n]Job 41:10; Isa 46:9; Jer 49:19

Who is the chosen[m] one I will
appoint for this?
Who is like me and who can
challenge me?[n]
And what shepherd can stand
against me?"
45 Therefore, hear what the LORD has
planned against Babylon,

50:45 [o]Ps 33:11; Isa 14:24; Jer 51:11

what he has purposed[o] against
the land of the Babylonians:
The young of the flock will be
dragged away;
he will completely destroy their
pasture because of them.
46 At the sound of Babylon's capture
the earth will tremble;

50:46 [p]Rev 18:9-10

its cry[p] will resound among the
nations.

51

This is what the LORD says:

"See, I will stir up the spirit of a
destroyer
against Babylon and the people
of Leb Kamai.[b]
2 I will send foreigners to Babylon

51:2 [q]Isa 41:16; Jer 15:7; Mt 3:12

to winnow[q] her and to devastate
her land;
they will oppose her on every side
in the day of her disaster.

51:3 [r]Jer 50:29 [s]Jer 46:4

3 Let not the archer string his bow,[r]
nor let him put on his armor.[s]
Do not spare her young men;
completely destroy[c] her army.

51:4 [t]Isa 13:15 [u]Jer 49:26; 50:30

4 They will fall[t] down slain in
Babylon,[d]
fatally wounded in her streets.[u]

51:5 [v]Isa 54:6-8 [w]Hos 4:1

5 For Israel and Judah have not been
forsaken[v]
by their God, the LORD Almighty,
though their land[e] is full of guilt[w]
before the Holy One of Israel.

51:6 [x]Jer 50:8 [y]Nu 16:26; Rev 18:4 [z]Jer 50:15

6 "Flee[x] from Babylon!
Run for your lives!
Do not be destroyed because of
her sins.[y]
It is time for the LORD's vengeance;[z]

[a] 38 Or *A sword against* [b] 1 *Leb Kamai* is a cryptogram for Chaldea, that is, Babylonia. [c] 3 The Hebrew term refers to the irrevocable giving over of things or persons to the LORD, often by totally destroying them. [d] 4 Or *Chaldea* [e] 5 Or / *and the land* ⌊*of the Babylonians*⌋

51:6 [a]Jer 25:14 he will pay[a] her what she
deserves.
51:7 [b]Jer 25:15-16; Rev 14:8-10; 17:4 [7]Babylon was a gold cup[b] in the
LORD's hand;
she made the whole earth drunk.
The nations drank her wine;
therefore they have now gone
mad.
51:8 [c]Isa 21:9; Rev 14:8 [d]Jer 46:11 [8]Babylon will suddenly fall[c] and be
broken.
Wail over her!
Get balm[d] for her pain;
perhaps she can be healed.

[9]" 'We would have healed Babylon,
but she cannot be healed;
51:9 [e]Isa 13:14; Jer 50:16 [f]Rev 18:4-5 let us leave[e] her and each go to his
own land,
for her judgment[f] reaches to the
skies,
it rises as high as the clouds.'

51:10 [g]Mic 7:9 [h]Jer 50:28 [10]" 'The LORD has vindicated[g] us;
come, let us tell in Zion
what the LORD our God has
done.'[h]

51:11 [i]Jer 50:9 [j]Jer 46:4 [k]ver 28 [l]Jer 50:45 [m]Jer 50:28 [11]"Sharpen the arrows,[i]
take up the shields![j]
The LORD has stirred up the kings
of the Medes,[k]
because his purpose[l] is to
destroy Babylon.
The LORD will take vengeance,
vengeance for his temple.[m]
[12]Lift up a banner against the walls
of Babylon!
Reinforce the guard,
station the watchmen,
prepare an ambush!
The LORD will carry out his purpose,
his decree against the people of
Babylon.
51:13 [n]Rev 17:1,15 [o]Isa 45:3; Hab 2:9 [13]You who live by many waters[n]
and are rich in treasures,[o]
your end has come,
the time for you to be cut off.
51:14 [p]Am 6:8 [q]ver 27; Na 3:15 [r]Jer 50:15 [14]The LORD Almighty has sworn by
himself:[p]
I will surely fill you with men, as
with a swarm of locusts,[q]
and they will shout[r] in triumph
over you.

[15]"He made the earth by his power;
he founded the world by his
51:15 [s]Ge 1:1; Job 9:8; Ps 104:2 wisdom
and stretched[s] out the heavens
by his understanding.

51:16 [t]Ps 18:11-13 [u]Ps 135:7; Jnh 1:4 [16]When he thunders,[t] the waters in
the heavens roar;
he makes clouds rise from the
ends of the earth.
He sends lightning with the rain
and brings out the wind from his
storehouses.[u]

[17]"Every man is senseless and
without knowledge;
every goldsmith is shamed by
his idols.
51:17 [v]Isa 44:20; Hab 2:18-19 His images are a fraud;[v]
they have no breath in them.
51:18 [w]Jer 18:15 [18]They are worthless,[w] the objects of
mockery;
when their judgment comes,
they will perish.
[19]He who is the Portion of Jacob is
not like these,
for he is the Maker of all things,
including the tribe of his
inheritance—
the LORD Almighty is his name.
51:20 [x]Isa 10:5 [y]Mic 4:13 [20]"You are my war club,[x]
my weapon for battle—
with you I shatter[y] nations,
with you I destroy kingdoms,
51:21 [z]Ex 15:1 [21]with you I shatter horse and rider,[z]
with you I shatter chariot and
driver,
[22]with you I shatter man and woman,
with you I shatter old man and
youth,
51:22 [a]2Ch 36:17; Isa 13:17-18 with you I shatter young man
and maiden,[a]
[23]with you I shatter shepherd and
flock,
with you I shatter farmer and
oxen,
51:23 [b]ver 57 with you I shatter governors and
officials.[b]

51:24 [c]Jer 50:15 [24]"Before your eyes I will repay[c] Babylon and all who live in Babylonia[a] for all
the wrong they have done in Zion," declares the LORD.

[25]"I am against you, O destroying
mountain,
you who destroy the whole earth,"
declares the LORD.
"I will stretch out my hand against
you,
roll you off the cliffs,
51:25 [d]Zec 4:7 and make you a burned-out
mountain.[d]

[a] *24* Or *Chaldea*; also in verse 35

26 No rock will be taken from you for
a cornerstone,
nor any stone for a foundation,
for you will be desolate[e] forever,"
declares the LORD.

27 "Lift up a banner[f] in the land!
Blow the trumpet among the
nations!
Prepare the nations for battle
against her;
summon against her these
kingdoms:[g]
Ararat,[h] Minni and Ashkenaz.[i]
Appoint a commander against her;
send up horses like a swarm of
locusts.
28 Prepare the nations for battle
against her—
the kings of the Medes,[j]
their governors and all their
officials,
and all the countries they rule.
29 The land trembles and writhes,
for the LORD's purposes against
Babylon stand—
to lay waste the land of Babylon
so that no one will live there.[k]
30 Babylon's warriors[l] have stopped
fighting;
they remain in their strongholds.
Their strength is exhausted;
they have become like women.[m]
Her dwellings are set on fire;
the bars[n] of her gates are broken.
31 One courier[o] follows another
and messenger follows
messenger
to announce to the king of Babylon
that his entire city is captured,
32 the river crossings seized,
the marshes set on fire,
and the soldiers terrified.[p]"

33 This is what the LORD Almighty, the
God of Israel, says:

"The Daughter of Babylon is like a
threshing floor[q]
at the time it is trampled;
the time to harvest[r] her will
soon come."

34 "Nebuchadnezzar[s] king of Babylon
has devoured us,
he has thrown us into confusion,
he has made us an empty jar.
Like a serpent he has swallowed us
and filled his stomach with our
delicacies,
and then has spewed us out.
35 May the violence done to our flesh[a]
be upon Babylon,"
say the inhabitants of Zion.
"May our blood be on those who
live in Babylonia,"
says Jerusalem.[t]

36 Therefore, this is what the LORD
says:

"See, I will defend your cause[u]
and avenge[v] you;
I will dry up[w] her sea
and make her springs dry.
37 Babylon will be a heap of ruins,
a haunt[x] of jackals,
an object of horror and scorn,
a place where no one lives.[y]
38 Her people all roar like young lions,
they growl like lion cubs.
39 But while they are aroused,
I will set out a feast for them
and make them drunk,
so that they shout with laughter—
then sleep forever and not
awake,"
declares the LORD.[z]

40 "I will bring them down
like lambs to the slaughter,
like rams and goats.

41 "How Sheshach[b][a] will be
captured,[b]
the boast of the whole earth
seized!
What a horror Babylon will be
among the nations!
42 The sea will rise over Babylon;
its roaring waves[c] will cover her.
43 Her towns will be desolate,
a dry and desert land,
a land where no one lives,
through which no man travels.[d]
44 I will punish Bel[e] in Babylon
and make him spew out[f] what
he has swallowed.
The nations will no longer stream
to him.
And the wall[g] of Babylon will
fall.
45 "Come out[h] of her, my people!
Run[i] for your lives!

51:26 [e] ver 29; Isa 13:19-22; Jer 50:12
51:27 [f] Isa 13:2; Jer 50:2 [g] Jer 25:14 [h] Ge 8:4 [i] Ge 10:3
51:28 [j] ver 11
51:29 [k] ver 43; Isa 13:20
51:30 [l] Jer 50:36 [m] Isa 19:16 [n] Isa 45:2; La 2:9; Na 3:13
51:31 [o] 2Sa 18:19-31
51:32 [p] Jer 50:36
51:33 [q] Isa 21:10 [r] Isa 17:5; Hos 6:11
51:34 [s] Jer 50:17
51:35 [t] ver 24; Ps 137:8
51:36 [u] Ps 140:12; Jer 50:34; La 3:58 [v] ver 6; Ro 12:19 [w] Jer 50:38
51:37 [x] Isa 13:22; Rev 18:2 [y] Jer 50:13,39
51:39 [z] ver 57
51:41 [a] Jer 25:26 [b] Isa 13:19
51:42 [c] Isa 8:7
51:43 [d] ver 29,62; Isa 13:20; Jer 2:6
51:44 [e] Isa 46:1 [f] ver 34 [g] ver 58; Jer 50:15
51:45 [h] Rev 18:4 [i] ver 6; Isa 48:20; Jer 50:8

[a] 35 Or *done to us and to our children*
[b] 41 *Sheshach* is a cryptogram for Babylon.

Run from the fierce anger of the
51:46 LORD.
[j]Jer 46:27 46 Do not lose heart or be afraid[j]
[k]2Ki 19:7 when rumors[k] are heard in the
land;
one rumor comes this year,
another the next,
rumors of violence in the land
and of ruler against ruler.
51:47 47 For the time will surely come
[l]ver 52; when I will punish the idols[l] of
Isa 46:1-2; Jer 50:2 Babylon;
[m]Jer 50:12 her whole land will be disgraced[m]
and her slain will all lie fallen
within her.
48 Then heaven and earth and all that
51:48 is in them
[n]Isa 44:23; will shout[n] for joy over Babylon,
Rev 18:20 [o]ver 11 for out of the north[o]
destroyers will attack her,"
declares the LORD.
49 "Babylon must fall because of
Israel's slain,
51:49 just as the slain in all the earth
[p]Ps 137:8; Jer 50:29 have fallen because of Babylon.[p]
50 You who have escaped the sword,
51:50 [q]ver 45 leave[q] and do not linger!
[r]Ps 137:6 Remember[r] the LORD in a distant
land,
and think on Jerusalem."
51:51 [s]Ps 44:13-16; 79:4 [t]La 1:10 51 "We are disgraced,[s]
for we have been insulted
and shame covers our faces,
because foreigners have entered
the holy places of the LORD's
house."[t]
52 "But days are coming," declares the
LORD,
51:52 [u]ver 47 "when I will punish her idols,[u]
and throughout her land
the wounded will groan.
51:53 [v]Ge 11:4; Isa 14:13-14 53 Even if Babylon reaches the sky[v]
[w]Jer 49:16 and fortifies her lofty
stronghold,
I will send destroyers[w] against
her,"
declares the LORD.
54 "The sound of a cry comes from
Babylon,
51:54 [x]Jer 50:22 the sound of great destruction[x]
from the land of the
Babylonians.[a]
55 The LORD will destroy Babylon;
he will silence her noisy din.
Waves[y] of enemies will rage like 51:55 [y]Ps 18:4
great waters;
the roar of their voices will
resound.
56 A destroyer[z] will come against 51:56 [z]ver 48 [a]Ps 46:9
Babylon; [b]ver 6; Ps 94:1-2;
her warriors will be captured, Hab 2:8
and their bows will be broken.[a]
For the LORD is a God of
retribution;
he will repay[b] in full.
57 I will make her officials and wise
men drunk,
her governors, officers and
warriors as well;
they will sleep[c] forever and not 51:57 [c]Ps 76:5;
awake," Jer 25:27
declares the King,[d] whose name [d]Jer 46:18;
is the LORD Almighty. 48:15

58 This is what the LORD Almighty says:
"Babylon's thick wall[e] will be 51:58 [e]ver 44 [f]ver 64
leveled [g]Hab 2:13
and her high gates set on fire;
the peoples[f] exhaust themselves
for nothing,
the nations' labor is only fuel for
the flames."[g]

59 This is the message Jeremiah gave to
the staff officer Seraiah son of Neriah,[h] 51:59 [h]Jer 36:4
the son of Mahseiah, when he went to [i]Jer 52:1
Babylon with Zedekiah[i] king of Judah in [j]Jer 28:1
the fourth[j] year of his reign. 60 Jeremiah
had written on a scroll[k] about all the di- 51:60 [k]Jer 30:2; 36:2
sasters that would come upon Bab-
ylon—all that had been recorded con-
cerning Babylon. 61 He said to Seraiah, 51:62 [l]Isa 13:20;
"When you get to Babylon, see that you Jer 50:13,39
read all these words aloud. 62 Then say,
'O LORD, you have said you will destroy
this place, so that neither man nor animal will live in it; it will be desolate[l] forever.' 63 When you finish reading this
scroll, tie a stone to it and throw it into
the Euphrates. 64 Then say, 'So will Babylon sink to rise no more because of the
disaster I will bring upon her. And her 51:64 [m]ver 58
people[m] will fall.'" [n]Job 31:40

The words of Jeremiah end[n] here.

The Fall of Jerusalem

52 Zedekiah[o] was twenty-one 52:1 [o]2Ki 24:17
years old when he became king,
and he reigned in Jerusalem eleven years.
His mother's name was Hamutal daugh-

[a] 54 Or *Chaldeans*

ter of Jeremiah; she was from Libnah.[p]
2 He did evil in the eyes of the LORD, just
as Jehoiakim[q] had done. 3 It was because
of the LORD's anger that all this happened
to Jerusalem and Judah,[r] and in the end
he thrust them from his presence.

Now Zedekiah rebelled[s] against the
king of Babylon.

4 So in the ninth year of Zedekiah's
reign, on the tenth[t] day of the tenth
month, Nebuchadnezzar king of Babylon marched against Jerusalem[u] with
his whole army. They camped outside
the city and built siege works all around
it.[v] 5 The city was kept under siege until
the eleventh year of King Zedekiah.

6 By the ninth day of the fourth month
the famine in the city had become so severe that there was no food for the people to eat.[w] 7 Then the city wall was broken through, and the whole army fled.
They left the city at night through the
gate between the two walls near the
king's garden, though the Babylonians[a]
were surrounding the city. They fled toward the Arabah,[b] 8 but the Babylonian[c]
army pursued King Zedekiah and overtook him in the plains of Jericho. All his
soldiers were separated from him and
scattered, 9 and he was captured.[x]

He was taken to the king of Babylon
at Riblah[y] in the land of Hamath,[z] where
he pronounced sentence on him.
10 There at Riblah the king of Babylon
slaughtered the sons[a] of Zedekiah before his eyes; he also killed all the officials of Judah. 11 Then he put out Zedekiah's eyes, bound him with bronze
shackles and took him to Babylon,
where he put him in prison till the day of
his death.[b]

12 On the tenth day of the fifth[c]
month, in the nineteenth year of Nebuchadnezzar king of Babylon, Nebuzaradan[d] commander of the imperial
guard, who served the king of Babylon,
came to Jerusalem. 13 He set fire[e] to the
temple[f] of the LORD, the royal palace and
all the houses of Jerusalem. Every important building he burned down. 14 The
whole Babylonian army under the commander of the imperial guard broke
down all the walls[g] around Jerusalem.
15 Nebuzaradan the commander of the
guard carried into exile some of the
poorest people and those who remained
in the city, along with the rest of the
craftsmen[d] and those who had gone
over to the king of Babylon. 16 But Nebuzaradan left behind[h] the rest of the
poorest people of the land to work the
vineyards and fields.

17 The Babylonians broke up the
bronze pillars,[i] the movable stands[j] and
the bronze Sea[k] that were at the temple
of the LORD and they carried all the
bronze to Babylon.[l] 18 They also took
away the pots, shovels, wick trimmers,
sprinkling bowls, dishes and all the
bronze articles used in the temple service.[m] 19 The commander of the imperial guard took away the basins, censers,[n]
sprinkling bowls, pots, lampstands,
dishes and bowls used for drink offerings—all that were made of pure gold or
silver.

20 The bronze from the two pillars, the
Sea and the twelve bronze bulls under it,
and the movable stands, which King Solomon had made for the temple of the
LORD, was more than could be weighed.[o]
21 Each of the pillars was eighteen cubits
high and twelve cubits in circumference[e]; each was four fingers thick, and
hollow.[p] 22 The bronze capital[q] on top of
the one pillar was five cubits[f] high and
was decorated with a network and
pomegranates of bronze all around. The
other pillar, with its pomegranates, was
similar. 23 There were ninety-six pomegranates on the sides; the total number
of pomegranates[r] above the surrounding network was a hundred.

24 The commander of the guard took
as prisoners Seraiah[s] the chief priest,
Zephaniah[t] the priest next in rank and
the three doorkeepers. 25 Of those still in
the city, he took the officer in charge of
the fighting men, and seven royal advisers. He also took the secretary who was
chief officer in charge of conscripting
the people of the land and sixty of his
men who were found in the city. 26 Nebuzaradan[u] the commander took them
all and brought them to the king of Babylon at Riblah. 27 There at Riblah, in the
land of Hamath, the king had them executed.

So Judah went into captivity, away[v]

52:1 [p] Jos 10:29; 2Ki 8:22
52:2 [q] Jer 36:30
52:3 [r] Isa 3:1 [s] Eze 17:12-16
52:4 [t] Zec 8:19 [u] 2Ki 25:1-7; Jer 39:1 [v] Eze 24:1-2
52:6 [w] Isa 3:1
52:9 [x] Jer 32:4 [y] Nu 34:11 [z] Nu 13:21
52:10 [a] Jer 22:30
52:11 [b] Eze 12:13
52:12 [c] Zec 7:5; 8:19 [d] Jer 39:9
52:13 [e] 2Ch 36:19; Ps 74:8; La 2:6 [f] Ps 79:1; Mic 3:12
52:14 [g] Ne 1:3
52:16 [h] Jer 40:6
52:17 [i] 1Ki 7:15 [j] 1Ki 7:27-37 [k] 1Ki 7:23 [l] Jer 27:19-22
52:18 [m] Ex 27:3; 1Ki 7:45
52:19 [n] 1Ki 7:50
52:20 [o] 1Ki 7:47
52:21 [p] 1Ki 7:15
52:22 [q] 1Ki 7:16
52:23 [r] 1Ki 7:20
52:24 [s] 2Ki 25:18 [t] Jer 21:1; 37:3
52:26 [u] ver 12
52:27 [v] Jer 20:4

[a] *7* Or *Chaldeans*; also in verse 17 [b] *7* Or *the Jordan Valley* [c] *8* Or *Chaldean*; also in verse 14 [d] *15* Or *populace* [e] *21* That is, about 27 feet (about 8.1 meters) high and 18 feet (about 5.4 meters) in circumference [f] *22* That is, about 7 1/2 feet (about 2.3 meters)

from her land. 28This is the number of
52:28 the people Nebuchadnezzar carried into
w 2Ki 24:14-16; 2Ch 36:20 exile:[w]

in the seventh year, 3,023 Jews;
29in Nebuchadnezzar's eighteenth year,
832 people from Jerusalem;
30in his twenty-third year,
745 Jews taken into exile by Nebuzaradan the commander of the imperial guard.
There were 4,600 people in all.

Jehoiachin Released

31In the thirty-seventh year of the exile of Jehoiachin king of Judah, in the
year Evil-Merodach[a] became king of
Babylon, he released Jehoiachin king of
Judah and freed him from prison on the
twenty-fifth day of the twelfth month.
32He spoke kindly to him and gave him
a seat of honor higher than those of the
other kings who were with him in Babylon. 33So Jehoiachin put aside his
52:33 prison clothes and for the rest of his life
x 2Sa 9:7 ate regularly at the king's table.[x] 34Day
by day the king of Babylon gave Je-
hoiachin a regular allowance[y] as long as 52:34
he lived, till the day of his death. y 2Sa 9:10

[a] *31* Also called *Amel-Marduk*

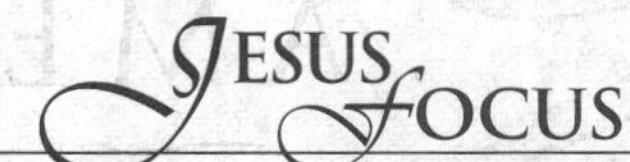

A RAY OF HOPE

Jeremiah's ministry was very unpopular because his prophecies were often bleak. However, he ended his book with a ray of hope for the future—Jehoiachin had been released from prison. Despite the curse on Jehoiachin's immediate successors to the throne of David, the old kings represented the only link to the future Messiah. Jehoiachin's survival guaranteed the eventual perpetuity of the Messianic line (see Matthew 1:11). This final "footnote" assured Jeremiah's readers that there was still hope for the future. When Jesus' birth was announced to Mary, the angel Gabriel said: "He will be . . . called the Son of the Most High. The Lord God will give him the throne of his father David . . . his kingdom will never end: (Luke 1:32–33). This could only be said about God's promised Messiah—Jesus Christ (Luke 1:32–33).

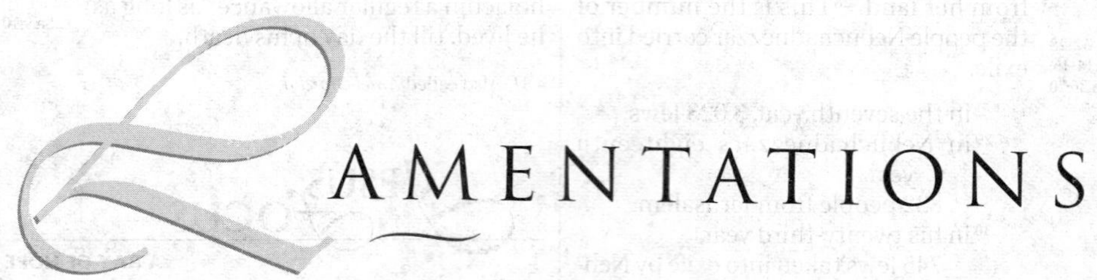

LAMENTATIONS

How do the quotations from Jesus in Matthew 23:37–39 and Luke 13:34–35 remind the reader of the laments found in this book?

- *In a manner reminiscent of the cries of the writer of Lamentations, Jesus lamented over Jerusalem. His words express the ironic coupling of the kindness and severity of God that is central to the gospel message (see Romans 11:22–23).*

Should we ask for revenge? (Lamentations 3:64)

- *Even in the Old Testament, vengeance was solely God's prerogative (Deuteronomy 32:35). Modern believers should expect, work toward and pray for justice on earth (Matthew 16:27; 2 Timothy 4:14). But Jesus also commanded his followers to love their enemies (Luke 23:34). God will ultimately right every wrong.*

Is there a point of no return? (Lamentations 5:22)

- *In an emotional finish, Jeremiah wavered in his confidence: What if God didn't give Judah another chance? But God specializes in second chances. Only if we reject God and Jesus Christ, his provision for our sins, will we be beyond the point of return (Romans 8:35–39).*

Jesus in Lamentations Jeremiah is traditionally thought to be the author of Lamentations—a beautiful yet bleak book that deals with the pain of loss. Jeremiah's primary purpose in this emotional book was to express grief over Jerusalem's slide from orderliness to a state of chaos.

There are notable similarities between Jeremiah, the Weeping Prophet, and Jesus. Jesus, like Jeremiah, wept for God's holy city as he predicted Jerusalem's destruction (Matthew 23:37—24:2; Luke 19:41–44). Both were rejected by the citizens of Jerusalem, but each continued to call the people back to God. At the time Jeremiah wrote, Jerusalem had been razed and the temple burned. Yet God heard the plea of his people to draw them back to himself (Lamentations 5:21). Despite the darkness of the moment, Jeremiah wanted the people to hold on to this certain truth: God is the Lord of hope (Lamentations 3:21,34–25), of love (verse 22), of faithfulness (verse 23) and of salvation (verse 26), and he was still at work to bring about redemption through his Son Jesus (Galatians 4:4–5).

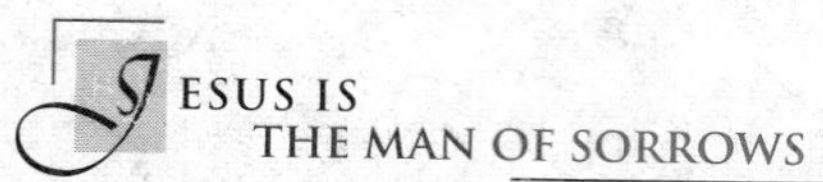

JESUS IS THE MAN OF SORROWS

1 [a] How deserted lies the city,
once so full of people!
How like a widow[a] is she,
who once was great[b] among the
nations!
She who was queen among the
provinces
has now become a slave.[c]

1:1
[a] Isa 47:8
[b] 1Ki 4:21
[c] Isa 3:26;
Jer 40:9

2 Bitterly she weeps[d] at night,
tears are upon her cheeks.
Among all her lovers[e]
there is none to comfort her.
All her friends have betrayed[f] her;
they have become her enemies.[g]

1:2
[d] Ps 6:6 [e] Jer 3:1
[f] Jer 4:30;
Mic 7:5 [g] ver 16

3 After affliction and harsh labor,
Judah has gone into exile.[h]
She dwells among the nations;
she finds no resting place.[i]
All who pursue her have overtaken
her
in the midst of her distress.

1:3
[h] Jer 13:19
[i] Dt 28:65

4 The roads to Zion mourn,
for no one comes to her
appointed feasts.
All her gateways are desolate,[j]
her priests groan,
her maidens grieve,
and she is in bitter anguish.[k]

1:4
[j] Jer 9:11
[k] Joel 1:8-13

5 Her foes have become her masters;
her enemies are at ease.
The LORD has brought her grief[l]
because of her many sins.
Her children have gone into exile,[m]
captive before the foe.

1:5
[l] Jer 30:15
[m] Jer 39:9;
52:28-30

6 All the splendor has departed
from the Daughter of Zion.[n]
Her princes are like deer
that find no pasture;
in weakness they have fled
before the pursuer.

1:6
[n] Jer 13:18

7 In the days of her affliction and
wandering
Jerusalem remembers all the
treasures
that were hers in days of old.
When her people fell into enemy
hands,
there was no one to help her.[o]
Her enemies looked at her
and laughed at her destruction.

1:7
[o] Jer 37:7;
La 4:17

8 Jerusalem has sinned[p] greatly
and so has become unclean.
All who honored her despise her,
for they have seen her
nakedness;[q]
she herself groans[r]
and turns away.

1:8
[p] ver 20;
Isa 59:2-13
[q] Jer 13:22,26
[r] ver 21,22

9 Her filthiness clung to her skirts;
she did not consider her future.[s]
Her fall[t] was astounding;
there was none to comfort[u] her.
"Look, O LORD, on my affliction,[v]
for the enemy has triumphed."

1:9
[s] Dt 32:28-29;
Isa 47:7;
Eze 24:13
[t] Jer 13:18
[u] Ecc 4:1;
Jer 16:7
[v] Ps 25:18

10 The enemy laid hands
on all her treasures;[w]
she saw pagan nations
enter her sanctuary[x]—
those you had forbidden[y]
to enter your assembly.

1:10
[w] Isa 64:11
[x] Ps 74:7-8;
Jer 51:51
[y] Dt 23:3

11 All her people groan[z]
as they search for bread;[a]
they barter their treasures for food
to keep themselves alive.
"Look, O LORD, and consider,
for I am despised."

1:11
[z] Ps 38:8
[a] Jer 52:6

12 "Is it nothing to you, all you who
pass by?[b]
Look around and see.
Is any suffering like my suffering[c]

1:12
[b] Jer 18:16
[c] ver 18

a This chapter is an acrostic poem, the verses of which begin with the successive letters of the Hebrew alphabet.

JESUS AND YOU

THE TEMPLE DESTROYED

When the Babylonians conquered Jerusalem, they burned and plundered Solomon's temple (Lamentations 1:10; see also 2 Kings 25:9,13–17). People who had been devoted to worshiping there were deeply shaken, feeling as though God had deserted them. Even today orthodox Jews recognize the anniversary of the temple's destruction by reading the book of Lamentations aloud and by reciting Jeremiah's prayers. In the New Testament Jesus echoed Jeremiah's sorrow when he predicted that both the city and the rebuilt temple would again be destroyed (Matthew 24:1–28). Jesus was so passionate about God's holy city that he cried out as he stood in the temple: "O Jerusalem, Jerusalem . . . how often I have longed to gather your children together, as a hen gathers her chicks under her wings, but you were not willing" (Matthew 23:37). It has always been God's deepest desire that we turn to him, knowing him as intimately as baby chicks know their own mother.

DISCOVERY 206

HOPE IN DESPAIR

Despair is a nearly intolerable emotion. When storms slam into our lives, people often surrender to despair and simply give up hope. The author of Lamentations voiced such hopelessness in the first chapter of his book of lament, in which he mourned the fall of Jerusalem. In verse 12 he cried out, "Is it nothing to you, all you who pass by? Look around and see. Is any suffering like my suffering that was inflicted on me, that the LORD brought on me in the day of his fierce anger?"

But God is always there to meet us at our point of need. Just two chapters later the writer of Lamentations made this beautiful confession: "Because of the LORD's great love we are not consumed, for his compassions never fail. They are new every morning; great is [his] faithfulness" (Lamentations 3:22–23).

No matter what dilemma we face, there is cause for optimism for the future. Many people around the world suffer under oppressive governments. When access to God's Word is denied, people live in hopelessness. Political oppression, economic instability and social limitations work together to sap public and private morale. People seldom smile; storefronts lack color; even clothing is drab. *Everything* can appear gray and bleak when people feel that they are without possibilities. But when the Good News of Jesus Christ is presented to such people, both young and old discover truth that brings a gleam to the eye and a spring to the step—in spite of otherwise unchanged circumstances.

In the New Testament we learn more about the Messiah through whom God promised he would bring lasting hope to his people (Ephesians 2:12–13). When we trust Jesus, we know that he will care for all of our needs—food to eat, clothes to wear, breath in our lungs (Matthew 6:25–34). And beyond our physical needs he imbues us with strength to face hardships: "No temptation has seized you except what is common to man. And God is faithful; he will not let you be tempted beyond what you can bear. But when you are tempted, he will also provide a way out so that you can stand up under it" (1 Corinthians 10:13).

What an unspeakable consolation for us as believers to rest in the certainty that there is absolutely no situation too difficult for God (Matthew 19:26; Luke 1:37; Romans 4:21). He is forever faithful, and when we trust him his peace will dominate our lives (Philippians 4:6). No matter how trying the problems we face, we can rejoice in the certain knowledge that "[we] can do everything through [Jesus Christ] who gives [us] strength (Philippians 4:13).

No, our Lord is not promising that we can become "supermen" and "superwomen," able to leap over the troubles of life in a powerful single bound, but he is offering his absolute pledge that he will see us through any situation, no matter how demanding, all the way through the dark tunnel until we emerge at the other end and our faces once again bask in the brilliant light of the new day of joy that comes from Jesus (Psalm 30:5; Isaiah 35:10; John 16:20–24; 17:13).

***Self-Discovery:** Name some specific ways in which God's "compassions" or blessings are new every morning.*

GO TO DISCOVERY 207 ON PAGE 1072

that was inflicted on me,
that the LORD brought on me
in the day of his fierce anger?[d]

13 "From on high he sent fire,
sent it down into my bones.[e]
He spread a net for my feet
and turned me back.
He made me desolate,[f]
faint[g] all the day long.

14 "My sins have been bound into a
yoke[a];[h]
by his hands they were woven
together.
They have come upon my neck
and the Lord has sapped my
strength.
He has handed me over[i]
to those I cannot withstand.

15 "The Lord has rejected
all the warriors in my midst;[j]
he has summoned an army[k]
against me
to[b] crush my young men.[l]
In his winepress the Lord has
trampled
the Virgin Daughter of Judah.

16 "This is why I weep
and my eyes overflow with
tears.[m]
No one is near to comfort[n] me,
no one to restore my spirit.
My children are destitute
because the enemy has
prevailed."[o]

17 Zion stretches out her hands,[p]
but there is no one to comfort her.
The LORD has decreed for Jacob
that his neighbors become his
foes;
Jerusalem has become
an unclean thing among them.

18 "The LORD is righteous,
yet I rebelled[q] against his
command.
Listen, all you peoples;
look upon my suffering.[r]
My young men and maidens
have gone into exile.[s]

19 "I called to my allies
but they betrayed me.
My priests and my elders
perished[t] in the city
while they searched for food
to keep themselves alive.

1:12 [d] Isa 13:13; Jer 30:24
1:13 [e] Job 30:30 [f] Jer 44:6 [g] Hab 3:16
1:14 [h] Dt 28:48; Isa 47:6 [i] Jer 32:5
1:15 [j] Jer 37:10 [k] Isa 41:2 [l] Isa 28:18; Jer 18:21
1:16 [m] La 2:11,18; 3:48-49 [n] Ps 69:20; Ecc 4:1 [o] ver 2; Jer 13:17; 14:17
1:17 [p] Jer 4:31
1:18 [q] 1Sa 12:14 [r] ver 12 [s] Dt 28:32,41
1:19 [t] Jer 14:15; La 2:20

20 "See, O LORD, how distressed[u] I am!
I am in torment[v] within,
and in my heart I am disturbed,
for I have been most rebellious.
Outside, the sword bereaves;
inside, there is only death.[w]

21 "People have heard my groaning,[x]
but there is no one to comfort
me.[y]
All my enemies have heard of my
distress;
they rejoice[z] at what you have
done.
May you bring the day[a] you have
announced
so they may become like me.

22 "Let all their wickedness come
before you;
deal with them
as you have dealt with me
because of all my sins.[b]
My groans are many
and my heart is faint."

2

[c] How the Lord has covered the
Daughter of Zion
with the cloud of his anger[d]![c]
He has hurled down the splendor
of Israel
from heaven to earth;
he has not remembered his
footstool[d]
in the day of his anger.

2 Without pity[e] the Lord has
swallowed[f] up
all the dwellings of Jacob;
in his wrath he has torn down
the strongholds[g] of the
Daughter of Judah.
He has brought her kingdom and
its princes
down to the ground[h] in dishonor.

3 In fierce anger he has cut off
every horn[e][i] of Israel.
He has withdrawn his right hand[j]
at the approach of the enemy.
He has burned in Jacob like a
flaming fire

1:20 [u] Jer 4:19 [v] La 2:11 [w] Dt 32:25; Eze 7:15
1:21 [x] ver 8 [y] ver 4 [z] La 2:15 [a] Isa 47:11; Jer 30:16
1:22 [b] Ne 4:5
2:1 [c] La 3:44 [d] Ps 99:5; 132:7
2:2 [e] La 3:43 [f] Ps 21:9 [g] Ps 89:39-40; Mic 5:11 [h] Isa 25:12
2:3 [i] Ps 75:5,10 [j] Ps 74:11

[a] *14* Most Hebrew manuscripts; Septuagint *He kept watch over my sins* [b] *15* Or *has set a time for me / when he will* [c] This chapter is an acrostic poem, the verses of which begin with the successive letters of the Hebrew alphabet. [d] *1* Or *How the Lord in his anger / has treated the Daughter of Zion with contempt* [e] *3* Or */ all the strength*; or *every king*; *horn* here symbolizes strength.

that consumes everything
around it.[k]

4 Like an enemy he has strung his
bow;[l]
his right hand is ready.
Like a foe he has slain
all who were pleasing to the eye;[m]
he has poured out his wrath like
fire[n]
on the tent of the Daughter of
Zion.

5 The Lord is like an enemy;[o]
he has swallowed up Israel.
He has swallowed up all her palaces
and destroyed her strongholds.[p]
He has multiplied mourning and
lamentation
for the Daughter of Judah.[q]

6 He has laid waste his dwelling like
a garden;
he has destroyed his place of
meeting.[r]
The LORD has made Zion forget
her appointed feasts and her
Sabbaths;[s]
in his fierce anger he has spurned
both king and priest.[t]

7 The Lord has rejected his altar
and abandoned his sanctuary.
He has handed over to the enemy
the walls of her palaces;[u]
they have raised a shout in the
house of the LORD
as on the day of an appointed
feast.

8 The LORD determined to tear down
the wall around the Daughter of
Zion.
He stretched out a measuring line[v]
and did not withhold his hand
from destroying.
He made ramparts and walls
lament;
together they wasted away.[w]

9 Her gates[x] have sunk into the
ground;
their bars he has broken and
destroyed.
Her king and her princes are
exiled[y] among the nations,
the law[z] is no more,
and her prophets no longer find
visions[a] from the LORD.

10 The elders of the Daughter of Zion
sit on the ground in silence;
they have sprinkled dust on their
heads[b]
and put on sackcloth.[c]
The young women of Jerusalem
have bowed their heads to the
ground.[d]

11 My eyes fail from weeping,[e]
I am in torment within,[f]
my heart is poured out[g] on the
ground
because my people are destroyed,
because children and infants faint[h]
in the streets of the city.

12 They say to their mothers,
"Where is bread and wine?"
as they faint like wounded men
in the streets of the city,
as their lives ebb away
in their mothers' arms.[i]

13 What can I say for you?
With what can I compare you,
O Daughter of Jerusalem?
To what can I liken you,
that I may comfort you,
O Virgin Daughter of Zion?[j]
Your wound is as deep as the sea.[k]
Who can heal you?

14 The visions of your prophets
were false and worthless;
they did not expose your sin
to ward off your captivity.[l]
The oracles they gave you
were false and misleading.[m]

15 All who pass your way
clap their hands at you;[n]
they scoff[o] and shake their heads
at the Daughter of Jerusalem:
"Is this the city that was called
the perfection of beauty,[p]
the joy of the whole earth?"[q]

16 All your enemies open their mouths
wide against you;[r]
they scoff and gash their teeth[s]
and say, "We have swallowed her
up.[t]
This is the day we have waited for;
we have lived to see it."

17 The LORD has done what he
planned;
he has fulfilled his word,
which he decreed long ago.[u]
He has overthrown you without
pity,[v]

2:3 [k] Isa 42:25; Jer 21:4-5,14
2:4 [l] Job 16:13; La 3:12-13 [m] Eze 24:16,25 [n] Isa 42:25; Jer 7:20
2:5 [o] Jer 30:14 [p] ver 2 [q] Jer 9:17-20
2:6 [r] Jer 52:13 [s] La 1:4; Zep 3:18 [t] La 4:16
2:7 [u] Ps 74:7-8; Isa 64:11; Jer 33:4-5
2:8 [v] 2Ki 21:13; Isa 34:11 [w] Isa 3:26
2:9 [x] Ne 1:3 [y] Dt 28:36; 2Ki 24:15 [z] 2Ch 15:3 [a] Jer 14:14
2:10 [b] Job 2:12 [c] Isa 15:3 [d] Job 2:13; Isa 3:26
2:11 [e] La 1:16; 3:48-51 [f] La 1:20 [g] ver 19; Ps 22:14 [h] La 4:4
2:12 [i] La 4:4
2:13 [j] Isa 37:22 [k] Jer 14:17; La 1:12
2:14 [l] Isa 58:1 [m] Jer 2:8; 23:25-32,33-40; 29:9; Eze 13:3; 22:28
2:15 [n] Eze 25:6 [o] Jer 19:8 [p] Ps 50:2 [q] Ps 48:2
2:16 [r] Ps 56:2; La 3:46 [s] Job 16:9 [t] Ps 35:25
2:17 [u] Dt 28:15-45 [v] ver 2; Eze 5:11

he has let the enemy gloat over
you,
he has exalted the horn[a] of your
foes.[w]

2:17 [w]Ps 89:42

18 The hearts of the people
cry out to the Lord.[x]
O wall of the Daughter of Zion,
let your tears[y] flow like a river
day and night;[z]
give yourself no relief,
your eyes no rest.[a]

2:18 [x]Ps 119:145 [y]La 1:16 [z]Jer 9:1 [a]La 3:49

19 Arise, cry out in the night,
as the watches of the night begin;
pour out your heart[b] like water
in the presence of the Lord.[c]
Lift up your hands to him
for the lives of your children,
who faint[d] from hunger
at the head of every street.

2:19 [b]1Sa 1:15; Ps 62:8 [c]Isa 26:9 [d]Isa 51:20

20 "Look, O LORD, and consider:
Whom have you ever treated like
this?
Should women eat their offspring,[e]
the children they have cared for?[f]
Should priest and prophet be
killed[g]
in the sanctuary of the Lord?

2:20 [e]Dt 28:53; Jer 19:9 [f]La 4:10 [g]Ps 78:64; Jer 14:15

21 "Young and old lie together
in the dust of the streets;
my young men and maidens
have fallen by the sword.[h]
You have slain them in the day of
your anger;
you have slaughtered them
without pity.[i]

2:21 [h]2Ch 36:17; Ps 78:62-63; Jer 6:11 [i]Jer 13:14; La 3:43; Zec 11:6

22 "As you summon to a feast day,
so you summoned against me
terrors[j] on every side.
In the day of the LORD's anger
no one escaped or survived;
those I cared for and reared,[k]
my enemy has destroyed."

2:22 [j]Ps 31:13; Jer 6:25 [k]Hos 9:13

3[b] I am the man who has seen
affliction
by the rod of his wrath.[l]
2 He has driven me away and made
me walk
in darkness[m] rather than light;
3 indeed, he has turned his hand
against me[n]
again and again, all day long.
4 He has made my skin and my flesh
grow old
and has broken my bones.[o]

3:1 [l]Job 19:21; Ps 88:7
3:2 [m]Jer 4:23
3:3 [n]Isa 5:25
3:4 [o]Ps 51:8; Isa 38:13; Jer 50:17

5 He has besieged me and
surrounded me
with bitterness[p] and hardship.[q]
6 He has made me dwell in darkness
like those long dead.[r]

3:5 [p]ver 19 [q]Jer 23:15
3:6 [r]Ps 88:5-6

7 He has walled me in so I cannot
escape;[s]
he has weighed me down with
chains.[t]
8 Even when I call out or cry for help,
he shuts out my prayer.[u]
9 He has barred my way with blocks
of stone;
he has made my paths crooked.[v]

3:7 [s]Job 3:23 [t]Jer 40:4
3:8 [u]Job 30:20; Ps 22:2
3:9 [v]Isa 63:17; Hos 2:6

10 Like a bear lying in wait,
like a lion in hiding,
11 he dragged me from the path and
mangled[w] me
and left me without help.
12 He drew his bow[x]
and made me the target[y] for his
arrows.[z]

3:11 [w]Hos 6:1
3:12 [x]La 2:4 [y]Job 7:20 [z]Ps 7:12-13; 38:2

13 He pierced my heart
with arrows from his quiver.[a]
14 I became the laughingstock[b] of all
my people;
they mock me in song[c] all day
long.
15 He has filled me with bitter herbs
and sated me with gall.[d]

3:13 [a]Job 6:4
3:14 [b]Jer 20:7 [c]Job 30:9
3:15 [d]Jer 9:15

16 He has broken my teeth with
gravel;[e]
he has trampled me in the dust.
17 I have been deprived of peace;
I have forgotten what prosperity
is.
18 So I say, "My splendor is gone
and all that I had hoped from
the LORD."[f]

3:16 [e]Pr 20:17
3:18 [f]Job 17:15

19 I remember my affliction and my
wandering,
the bitterness and the gall.
20 I well remember them,
and my soul is downcast[g] within
me.[h]
21 Yet this I call to mind
and therefore I have hope:

3:20 [g]Ps 42:5 [h]Ps 42:11

22 Because of the LORD's great love we
are not consumed,
for his compassions never fail.[i]

3:22 [i]Ps 78:38; Mal 3:6

[a] *17 Horn* here symbolizes strength. [b] This chapter is an acrostic poem; the verses of each stanza begin with the successive letters of the Hebrew alphabet, and the verses within each stanza begin with the same letter.

23 They are new every morning;
3:23 [j]Zep 3:5 great is your faithfulness.[j]
24 I say to myself, "The LORD is my
3:24 [k]Ps 16:5 portion;[k]
therefore I will wait for him."

25 The LORD is good to those whose
hope is in him,
3:25 [l]Isa 25:9; 30:18 to the one who seeks him;[l]
26 it is good to wait quietly
3:26 [m]Ps 37:7; 40:1 for the salvation of the LORD.[m]
27 It is good for a man to bear the yoke
while he is young.

3:28 [n]Jer 15:17 28 Let him sit alone in silence,[n]
for the LORD has laid it on him.
3:29 [o]Jer 31:17 29 Let him bury his face in the dust—
there may yet be hope.[o]
3:30 [p]Job 16:10; Isa 50:6 30 Let him offer his cheek to one who
would strike him,[p]
and let him be filled with
disgrace.

31 For men are not cast off
3:31 [q]Ps 94:14; Isa 54:7 by the Lord forever.[q]
32 Though he brings grief, he will
show compassion,
3:32 [r]Ps 78:38; Hos 11:8 so great is his unfailing love.[r]
33 For he does not willingly bring
3:33 [s]Eze 33:11 affliction
or grief to the children of men.[s]

34 To crush underfoot
all prisoners in the land,
35 to deny a man his rights
before the Most High,
36 to deprive a man of justice—
3:36 [t]Jer 22:3; Hab 1:13 would not the Lord see such
things?[t]

3:37 [u]Ps 33:9-11 37 Who can speak and have it happen
if the Lord has not decreed it?[u]
38 Is it not from the mouth of the
3:38 [v]Job 2:10; Isa 45:7; Jer 32:42 Most High
that both calamities and good
things come?[v]
39 Why should any living man
3:39 [w]Jer 30:15; Mic 7:9 complain
when punished for his sins?[w]

3:40 [x]2Co 13:5 [y]Ps 119:59; 139:23-24 40 Let us examine our ways and test
them,[x]
and let us return to the LORD.[y]
41 Let us lift up our hearts and our
3:41 [z]Ps 25:1; 28:2 hands
to God in heaven,[z] and say:
3:42 [a]Da 9:5 [b]Jer 5:7-9 42 "We have sinned and rebelled[a]
and you have not forgiven.[b]

43 "You have covered yourself with
anger and pursued us;
you have slain without pity.[c] 3:43 [c]La 2:2,17,21
44 You have covered yourself with a
cloud[d] 3:44 [d]Ps 97:2 [e]ver 8
so that no prayer[e] can get
through.
45 You have made us scum[f] and refuse 3:45 [f]1Co 4:13
among the nations.

46 "All our enemies have opened their
mouths 3:46 [g]La 2:16
wide against us.[g]
47 We have suffered terror and 3:47 [h]Jer 48:43 [i]Isa 24:17-18; 51:19
pitfalls,[h]
ruin and destruction."[i]
48 Streams of tears flow from my eyes[j] 3:48 [j]La 1:16 [k]La 2:11
because my people are
destroyed.[k]

49 My eyes will flow unceasingly, 3:49 [l]Jer 14:17
without relief,[l]
50 until the LORD looks down 3:50 [m]Isa 63:15
from heaven and sees.[m]
51 What I see brings grief to my soul
because of all the women of my
city.

52 Those who were my enemies
without cause 3:52 [n]Ps 35:7
hunted me like a bird.[n]
53 They tried to end my life in a pit[o] 3:53 [o]Jer 37:16
and threw stones at me;
54 the waters closed over my head,[p] 3:54 [p]Ps 69:2; Jnh 2:3-5
and I thought I was about to be
cut off.

55 I called on your name, O LORD, 3:55 [q]Ps 130:1; Jnh 2:2
from the depths of the pit.[q]
56 You heard my plea:[r] "Do not close 3:56 [r]Ps 55:1
your ears
to my cry for relief."
57 You came near when I called you, 3:57 [s]Isa 41:10
and you said, "Do not fear."[s]

58 O Lord, you took up my case;[t] 3:58 [t]Jer 51:36 [u]Ps 34:22; Jer 50:34
you redeemed my life.[u]
59 You have seen, O LORD, the wrong
done to me.[v] 3:59 [v]Jer 18:19-20
Uphold my cause!
60 You have seen the depth of their 3:60 [w]Jer 11:20; 18:18
vengeance,
all their plots against me.[w]

61 O LORD, you have heard their
insults,
all their plots against me—
62 what my enemies whisper and
mutter 3:62 [x]Eze 36:3
against me all day long.[x]
63 Look at them! Sitting or standing,
they mock me in their songs.

64 Pay them back what they deserve,
O LORD,
3:64 [y] Ps 28:4
for what their hands have done.[y]
65 Put a veil over their hearts,[z]
3:65 [z] Isa 6:10
and may your curse be on them!
66 Pursue them in anger and destroy
them
from under the heavens of the
LORD.

4[a] How the gold has lost its
luster,
the fine gold become dull!
4:1 [a] Eze 7:19
The sacred gems are scattered
at the head of every street.[a]

2 How the precious sons of Zion,
once worth their weight in gold,
are now considered as pots of clay,
the work of a potter's hands!

3 Even jackals offer their breasts
to nurse their young,
but my people have become
heartless
4:3 [b] Job 39:16
like ostriches in the desert.[b]

4:4 [c] Ps 22:15 [d] La 2:11,12
4 Because of thirst the infant's tongue
sticks to the roof of its mouth;[c]
the children beg for bread,
but no one gives it to them.[d]

5 Those who once ate delicacies
4:5 [e] Jer 6:2 [f] Am 6:3-7
are destitute in the streets.
Those nurtured in purple[e]
now lie on ash heaps.[f]

4:6 [g] Ge 19:25
6 The punishment of my people
is greater than that of Sodom,[g]
which was overthrown in a
moment
without a hand turned to help
her.

7 Their princes were brighter than
snow
and whiter than milk,
their bodies more ruddy than
rubies,
their appearance like sapphires.[b]

4:8 [h] Job 30:28 [i] Ps 102:3-5
8 But now they are blacker[h] than
soot;
they are not recognized in the
streets.
Their skin has shriveled on their
bones;[i]
it has become as dry as a stick.

9 Those killed by the sword are
better off
than those who die of famine;
racked with hunger, they waste
away
4:9 [j] Jer 15:2; 16:4
for lack of food from the field.[j]

10 With their own hands
4:10 [k] Lev 26:29; Dt 28:53-57; Jer 19:9; La 2:20; Eze 5:10
compassionate women
have cooked their own
children,[k]
who became their food
when my people were destroyed.

11 The LORD has given full vent to his
wrath;
he has poured out his fierce
anger.
4:11 [l] Jer 17:27 [m] Dt 32:22; Jer 7:20; Eze 22:31
He kindled a fire[l] in Zion
that consumed her
foundations.[m]

12 The kings of the earth did not
believe,
nor did any of the world's
people,
4:12 [n] 1Ki 9:9; Jer 21:13
that enemies and foes could enter
the gates of Jerusalem.[n]

13 But it happened because of the
4:13 [o] Jer 5:31; 6:13; Eze 22:28; Mic 3:11
sins of her prophets
and the iniquities of her priests,[o]
who shed within her
the blood of the righteous.

14 Now they grope through the
streets
4:14 [p] Isa 59:10 [q] Jer 2:34; 19:4
like men who are blind.[p]
They are so defiled with blood[q]
that no one dares to touch their
garments.

15 "Go away! You are unclean!" men
cry to them.
"Away! Away! Don't touch us!"
When they flee and wander about,
people among the nations say,
4:15 [r] Lev 13:46
"They can stay here no longer."[r]

16 The LORD himself has scattered
them;
he no longer watches over
4:16 [s] Isa 9:14-16 [t] La 5:12
them.[s]
The priests are shown no honor,
the elders[t] no favor.

17 Moreover, our eyes failed,
4:17 [u] Isa 20:5; Eze 29:16 [v] La 1:7 [w] Jer 37:7
looking in vain[u] for help;[v]
from our towers we watched
for a nation[w] that could not save
us.

[a] This chapter is an acrostic poem, the verses of which begin with the successive letters of the Hebrew alphabet. [b] 7 Or *lapis lazuli*

18 Men stalked us at every step,
so we could not walk in our
streets.
Our end was near, our days were
numbered,
for our end had come.[x]

4:18 [x]Eze 7:2-12; Am 8:2

19 Our pursuers were swifter
than eagles[y] in the sky;
they chased us[z] over the mountains
and lay in wait for us in the
desert.

4:19 [y]Dt 28:49 [z]Isa 5:26-28

20 The LORD's anointed,[a] our very life
breath,
was caught in their traps.[b]
We thought that under his shadow
we would live among the
nations.

4:20 [a]2Sa 19:21 [b]Jer 39:5; Eze 12:12-13; 19:4,8

21 Rejoice and be glad, O Daughter of
Edom,
you who live in the land of Uz.
But to you also the cup[c] will be
passed;
you will be drunk and stripped
naked.[d]

4:21 [c]Jer 25:15 [d]Isa 34:6-10; Am 1:11-12; Ob 1:16

22 O Daughter of Zion, your
punishment will end;[e]
he will not prolong your exile.
But, O Daughter of Edom, he will
punish your sin
and expose your wickedness.[f]

4:22 [e]Isa 40:2; Jer 33:8 [f]Ps 137:7; Mal 1:4

5 Remember, O LORD, what has
happened to us;
look, and see our disgrace.[g]
2 Our inheritance[h] has been turned
over to aliens,
our homes[i] to foreigners.
3 We have become orphans and
fatherless,
our mothers like widows.[j]
4 We must buy the water we drink;
our wood can be had only at a
price.[k]
5 Those who pursue us are at our
heels;
we are weary[l] and find no rest.
6 We submitted to Egypt and
Assyria[m]
to get enough bread.
7 Our fathers sinned and are no
more,
and we bear their punishment.[n]
8 Slaves[o] rule over us,
and there is none to free us from
their hands.[p]

5:1 [g]Ps 44:13-16; 89:50
5:2 [h]Ps 79:1 [i]Zep 1:13
5:3 [j]Jer 15:8; 18:21
5:4 [k]Isa 3:1
5:5 [l]Ne 9:37
5:6 [m]Hos 9:3
5:7 [n]Jer 14:20; 16:12
5:8 [o]Ne 5:15 [p]Zec 11:6

9 We get our bread at the risk of our
lives
because of the sword in the
desert.
10 Our skin is hot as an oven,
feverish from hunger.[q]
11 Women have been ravished[r] in
Zion,
and virgins in the towns of
Judah.

5:10 [q]La 4:8-9
5:11 [r]Zec 14:2

JESUS FOCUS

WHERE IS OUR HOPE?

The average citizen of Israel was devastated when the people were taken into captivity by the Babylonians. Women were raped, princes hung and the general populace enslaved. All joy seemed to vanish, so much so that "dancing [had] turned to mourning" (Lamentations 5:15). In spite of this appalling situation, Jeremiah ended his book with an expression of his realization of the people's need for God to move them to contrition and repentance: "Restore us to yourself, O LORD, that we may return; renew our days as of old" (verse 21).

But this hopeful sentence is continued on a very different note in verse 22 without so much as a comma intervening: ". . . unless you have utterly rejected us and are angry with us beyond measure." At first blush this sentence sounds like a horrible afterthought that hangs suspended in the air. We are accustomed to a book ending with all of the loose ends neatly tucked in. But Jeremiah's thought seems to trail off into oblivion, as though the prophet were second-guessing himself in a moment of profound doubt. Yet the words of Psalm 51, written by David as a cry for mercy, build to a crescendo of triumph with his declaration in verse 17: "The sacrifices of God are a broken spirit; a broken and a contrite heart, O God, you will not despise."

We have the blessing today of the New Testament when we face times of spiritual emptiness or doubt. What better passage than the words of Paul in Romans 8 to bolster us in our down times? The apostle expressed his confidence in these resounding terms: "Who shall separate us from the love of Christ? Shall trouble or hardship or persecution or famine or nakedness or danger or sword? . . . No, in all these thing we are more than conquerors through him who loved us. For I am convinced that . . . [nothing] in all creation, will be able to separate us from the love of God that is in Christ Jesus our Lord" (Romans 8:35,37–39).

[12] Princes have been hung up by their
hands;
5:12 [s] La 4:16 elders are shown no respect.[s]
[13] Young men toil at the millstones;
boys stagger under loads of wood.
[14] The elders are gone from the city
gate;
5:14 [t] Isa 24:8; Jer 7:34 the young men have stopped
their music.[t]
5:15 [u] Jer 25:10 [15] Joy is gone from our hearts;
our dancing has turned to
mourning.[u]
5:16 [v] Ps 89:39 [w] Isa 3:11 [16] The crown[v] has fallen from our
head.
Woe to us, for we have sinned![w]
5:17 [x] Isa 1:5 [17] Because of this our hearts[x] are
faint,
because of these things our eyes[y] 5:17 [y] Ps 6:7
grow dim
[18] for Mount Zion, which lies 5:18 [z] Mic 3:12
desolate,[z]
with jackals prowling over it.

[19] You, O LORD, reign forever; 5:19 [a] Ps 45:6; 102:12,24-27
your throne endures[a] from
generation to generation.
[20] Why do you always forget us?[b] 5:20 [b] Ps 13:1; 44:24
Why do you forsake us so long?
[21] Restore[c] us to yourself, O LORD, 5:21 [c] Ps 80:3
that we may return;
renew our days as of old
[22] unless you have utterly rejected us
and are angry with us beyond 5:22 [d] Isa 64:9
measure.[d]

Ezekiel

How was the Lord a sanctuary? (Ezekiel 11:16)

♦ *Before the exile God's people associated Jerusalem and the temple with God's presence among them. Now God showed his people that he himself could be their sanctuary. God was with them in their exile. Later, Jesus came to replace the temple (John 2:19–21).*

What is the significance of the phrase "when I make atonement for you"? (Ezekiel 16:63)

♦ *God assured Jerusalem that he would make adequate provision for her sins, allowing him to reestablish his relationship with his people. In the progress of revelation and history, we discover that God views Jesus' death as the sacrifice that enables him to make peace with sinners and restore them to his favor (Romans 5:1–2).*

How could David, long dead, lead Israel again? (Ezekiel 34:23–24)

♦ *It was clear that the vision was of a coming Messiah—a descendant of David. David's name in the prophecy not only indicated his descendant, but it also indicated someone who would be like David—a man after God's own heart (see 1 Samuel 13:14).*

Jesus in Ezekiel The unusual title "son of man" is used of Ezekiel more than 90 times in this book—as a way for God to emphasize the limitations of being human. Only one other Old Testament prophet, Daniel, was called "son of man" (Daniel 8:17). There is one other person, however, whose humanity was so incomparably significant that he could be called the "Son of Man," namely Jesus. In fact, Jesus identified himself more frequently by that name than by any other, thereby letting people know that he was genuinely and completely human, as well as fully divine. We also see in the book of Ezekiel the vivid depiction of the departure of the divine glory from the temple (Ezekiel 8—11) and its ultimate and final return at the end of the age (Ezekiel 43). In Jesus the glory of God is present once again with his people (John 1:14; 8:54; 13:31–32; 17:1,5,10,22), and the day is coming when he will return "with power and great glory" (Matthew 24:30) to usher in his eternal kingdom (Revelation 11:15–17).

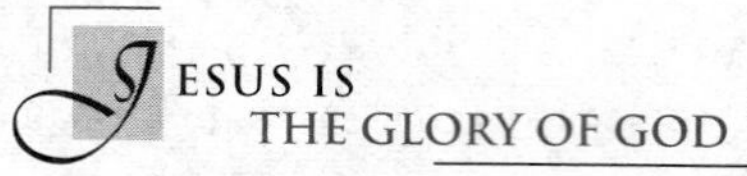
JESUS IS
THE GLORY OF GOD

The Living Creatures and the Glory of the Lord

1 In the[a] thirtieth year, in the fourth month on the fifth day, while I was among the exiles[a] by the Kebar River, the heavens were opened[b] and I saw visions[c] of God.

2 On the fifth of the month—it was the fifth year of the exile of King Jehoiachin[d]— 3 the word of the Lord came to Ezekiel the priest, the son of Buzi,[b] by the Kebar River in the land of the Babylonians.[c] There the hand of the Lord was upon him.[e]

4 I looked, and I saw a windstorm coming out of the north[f]—an immense cloud with flashing lightning and surrounded by brilliant light. The center of the fire looked like glowing metal,[g] 5 and in the fire was what looked like four living creatures.[h] In appearance their form was that of a man,[i] 6 but each of them had four faces[j] and four wings. 7 Their legs were straight; their feet were like those of a calf and gleamed like burnished bronze.[k] 8 Under their wings on their four sides they had the hands of a man.[l] All four of them had faces and wings, 9 and their wings touched one another. Each one went straight ahead; they did not turn as they moved.[m]

10 Their faces looked like this: Each of the four had the face of a man, and on the right side each had the face of a lion, and on the left the face of an ox; each also had the face of an eagle.[n] 11 Such were their faces. Their wings[o] were spread out upward; each had two wings, one touching the wing of another creature on either side, and two wings covering its body. 12 Each one went straight ahead. Wherever the spirit would go, they would go, without turning as they went. 13 The appearance of the living creatures was like burning coals of fire or like torches. Fire moved back and forth among the creatures; it was bright, and lightning[p] flashed out of it. 14 The creatures sped back and forth like flashes of lightning.[q]

15 As I looked at the living creatures, I saw a wheel on the ground beside each creature with its four faces. 16 This was the appearance and structure of the wheels: They sparkled like chrysolite,[r] and all four looked alike. Each appeared to be made like a wheel intersecting a wheel. 17 As they moved, they would go in any one of the four directions the creatures faced; the wheels did not turn[s] about[d] as the creatures went. 18 Their rims were high and awesome, and all four rims were full of eyes[t] all around.

19 When the living creatures moved, the wheels beside them moved; and when the living creatures rose from the ground, the wheels also rose. 20 Wherever the spirit would go, they would go,[u] and the wheels would rise along with them, because the spirit of the living creatures was in the wheels. 21 When the creatures moved, they also moved; when the creatures stood still, they also stood still; and when the creatures rose from the ground, the wheels rose along with them, because the spirit of the living creatures was in the wheels.[v]

22 Spread out above the heads of the living creatures was what looked like an expanse,[w] sparkling like ice, and awesome. 23 Under the expanse their wings were stretched out one toward the other, and each had two wings covering its body. 24 When the creatures moved, I heard the sound of their wings, like the roar of rushing waters, like the voice[x] of the Almighty,[e] like the tumult of an army.[y] When they stood still, they lowered their wings.

1:1 [a] Eze 11:24-25 [b] Mt 3:16; Ac 7:56 [c] Ex 24:10
1:2 [d] 2Ki 24:15
1:3 [e] 2Ki 3:15; Eze 3:14,22
1:4 [f] Jer 1:14 [g] Eze 8:2
1:5 [h] Rev 4:6 [i] ver 26
1:6 [j] Eze 10:14
1:7 [k] Da 10:6; Rev 1:15
1:8 [l] Eze 10:8
1:9 [m] Eze 10:22
1:10 [n] Eze 10:14; Rev 4:7
1:11 [o] Isa 6:2
1:13 [p] Rev 4:5
1:14 [q] Ps 29:7
1:16 [r] Eze 10:9-11; Da 10:6
1:17 [s] ver 9
1:18 [t] Eze 10:12; Rev 4:6
1:20 [u] ver 12
1:21 [v] Eze 10:17
1:22 [w] Eze 10:1
1:24 [x] Eze 10:5; 43:2; Da 10:6; Rev 1:15; 19:6 [y] 2Ki 7:6

[a] *1* Or ⌊*my*⌋ [b] *3* Or *Ezekiel son of Buzi the priest* [c] *3* Or *Chaldeans* [d] *17* Or *aside* [e] *24* Hebrew *Shaddai*

Jesus Focus

SEEING THE GLORY

This book of prophecy opens in chapter 1 with a spectacular burst of God's glory. There are striking similarities between Ezekiel's vision here and John's vision in Revelation. Both Ezekiel and John witnessed the brilliance of heaven flashing in front of them (Ezekiel 1:4; Revelation 4:2–6). Ezekiel's description of the living creatures (Ezekiel 1:5–14) is similar to John's in Revelation 4:7, including the symbols of a man, a lion, an ox and an eagle. Both men also observed what looked like a rainbow around God's throne (Ezekiel 1:28; Revelation 4:3), and both saw the eternal, majestic Son of God. John perceived Jesus both as being "like a son of man" (Revelation 1:13) and as the Lamb (Revelation 5). Ezekiel mentioned "a figure like that of a man" (Ezekiel 1:26) who embodied the radiant glory of the Lord.

DISCOVERY 207

SON OF MAN

The title *son of man* is used 93 times in the book of Ezekiel to refer to the prophet through whom Almighty God was speaking. The phrase highlights the fact that the spokesman was mortal and could not compare to God in his glory. The term places the prophet at a distance from God (Psalm 8:4). In fact, when Ezekiel was instructed to stand up, he let his readers know that he was able to do so only with the help of the God's Holy Spirit (Ezekiel 2:2).

In the New Testament Jesus described himself as the Son of Man more frequently than he used any other title. This phrase appears 78 times in the Gospel accounts. While in Ezekiel's case the title emphasized his *distance from God*, in Jesus' situation it emphasizes his *nearness to us*. He is a "son of man" (see Daniel 7:13) and so one of us. But because he is also a distinct member of the Trinity, the one, true, eternal God, he is not separated from the Father like the prophets before him.

There are many things Jesus came to show us, as the Word became flesh (John 1:14; Romans 8:3; Philippians 2:8; Hebrews 2:17). He wanted us to know that he loves us beyond all else. Though he is God, he relinquished the privileges of heaven to be born as a human so that he could seek and save the lost (Luke 19:10). He walked the earth as an itinerant preacher and healer, moving from place to place as he reached out to all kinds of people with his love (Matthew 8:20).

Jesus Christ served humbly and ultimately died to atone for our sins (Mark 10:45; John 3:14). Jesus came to complete God's law, and he is Lord over it (Matthew 12:8). One day he will return as reigning royalty, and all the nations will mourn their judgment (Matthew 24:30). Until that day, he is with his church, guiding and nurturing his people (Matthew 28:20).

Jesus asks us to follow him. We are invited to cast off the life of sin in order to enjoy the full life he intended for us (John 10:10; Romans 6:2–13; Colossians 3:5–14). As we receive Christ Jesus as Lord and continue to live in him (Colossians 2:6), we can let others know about the Son of Man who has set us free from darkness and brought us into his glorious kingdom of light and life (Mark 8:38; Colossians 1:13–14).

Self-Discovery: *Because sin so permeates every area of our lives, it may be difficult for you to picture Jesus as a human being who did not sin. Identify some other aspects of the human condition that Jesus did experience. How might your reflections on Jesus' humanity help you to feel that he understands your needs?*

GO TO DISCOVERY 208 ON PAGE 1080

25Then there came a voice from above
the expanse over their heads as they
stood with lowered wings. 26Above the
1:26 expanse over their heads was what
[z] Ex 24:10; looked like a throne of sapphire,[a][z] and
Eze 10:1 high above on the throne was a figure
[a] Rev 1:13 like that of a man.[a] 27I saw that from
what appeared to be his waist up he
looked like glowing metal, as if full of
fire, and that from there down he looked
1:27 like fire; and brilliant light surrounded
[b] Eze 8:2 him.[b] 28Like the appearance of a rain-
1:28 bow[c] in the clouds on a rainy day, so was
[c] Ge 9:13; Rev 10:1 the radiance around him.[d]
[d] Rev 4:2 This was the appearance of the like-
[e] Eze 8:4 ness of the glory[e] of the LORD. When I
[f] Eze 3:23; Da 8:17; saw it, I fell facedown,[f] and I heard the
Rev 1:17 voice of one speaking.

Ezekiel's Call

2:1 **2** He said to me, "Son of man,
[g] Da 10:11 stand[g] up on your feet and I will
2:2 speak to you." 2As he spoke, the Spirit
[h] Eze 3:24; came into me and raised me[h] to my feet,
Da 8:18 and I heard him speaking to me.
3He said: "Son of man, I am sending
you to the Israelites, to a rebellious nation that has rebelled against me; they
2:3 and their fathers have been in revolt
[i] Jer 3:25; against me to this very day.[i] 4The people
Eze 20:8-24 to whom I am sending you are obstinate
2:4 and stubborn.[j] Say to them, 'This is
[j] Eze 3:7 what the Sovereign LORD says.' 5And
2:5 whether they listen or fail to listen[k]—for
[k] Eze 3:11 they are a rebellious house[l]—they will
[l] Eze 3:27 [m] Eze 33:33 know that a prophet has been among
2:6 them.[m] 6And you, son of man, do not be
[n] Jer 1:8,17 afraid[n] of them or their words. Do not be
[o] Isa 9:18; afraid, though briers and thorns[o] are all
Mic 7:4 around you and you live among scorpi-
[p] Eze 3:9 ons. Do not be afraid of what they say or
terrified by them, though they are a rebellious house.[p] 7You must speak my
2:7 words to them, whether they listen or
[q] Jer 1:7; fail to listen, for they are rebellious.[q]
Eze 3:10-11 8But you, son of man, listen to what I say
2:8 to you. Do not rebel like that rebellious
[r] Isa 50:5 house;[r] open your mouth and eat[s] what
[s] Jer 15:16; Rev 10:9 I give you."
9Then I looked, and I saw a hand[t]
2:9 [t] Eze 8:3 stretched out to me. In it was a scroll,
10which he unrolled before me. On both
2:10 sides of it were written words of lament
[u] Rev 8:13 and mourning and woe.[u]

3 And he said to me, "Son of man,
eat what is before you, eat this
scroll; then go and speak to the house of
Israel." 2So I opened my mouth, and he
gave me the scroll to eat.
3Then he said to me, "Son of man, eat
this scroll I am giving you and fill your 3:3
stomach with it." So I ate[v] it, and it tast- [v] Jer 15:16
ed as sweet as honey[w] in my mouth. [w] Ps 19:10; Ps 119:103;
4He then said to me: "Son of man, go Rev 10:9-10
now to the house of Israel and speak my
words to them. 5You are not being sent
to a people of obscure speech and diffi-
cult language,[x] but to the house of Isra- 3:5 [x] Isa 28:11;
el— 6not to many peoples of obscure Jnh 1:2
speech and difficult language, whose
words you cannot understand. Surely if I
had sent you to them, they would have 3:6
listened to you.[y] 7But the house of Israel [y] Mt 11:21-23
is not willing to listen to you because
they are not willing to listen to me, for 3:7 [z] Eze 2:4;
the whole house of Israel is hardened Jn 15:20-23
and obstinate.[z] 8But I will make you as 3:8
unyielding and hardened as they are.[a] [a] Jer 1:18

[a] 26 Or *lapis lazuli*

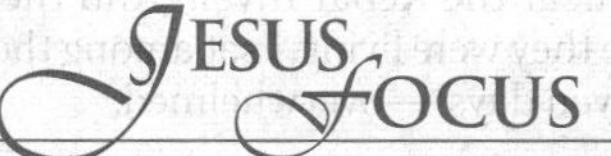

A SCROLL TO EAT

Life as a prophet of God was often a bittersweet experience, and in fact generally more painful than pleasant. In Ezekiel 3 God asked Ezekiel to eat a scroll, an act that symbolized Ezekiel's internalization of God's message. The scroll didn't look particularly edible, but Ezekiel soon discovered that it tasted as sweet as honey (verses 1–3). The message it contained was another matter: It was full of lament and woe (Ezekiel 2:9–10). In the New Testament God instructed the apostle John to do the same thing. The scroll John ate was also sweet to the taste, but it turned his stomach sour (Revelation 10:9–11). God's truth can cut both ways. It is a sweet experience to be empowered to speak God's truth, but it is also bitter in the sense that the message may be one of condemnation for our sin. God is always consistent, and God the Son spoke the same message as the Father. While he was on earth Jesus told people the Good News about God's love and forgiveness, but he balanced that truth with the "bitter" message that because of our sins we are sick and in need of healing (Mark 2:17), lost and in need of being found (Luke 15:1–32), over our heads in debt and in need of forgiveness and deliverance (Matthew 18:21–35). Thank God that the answer to our misery comes in and through our precious Jesus, who saves us by his grace (Ephesians 2:1–10).

9 I will make your forehead like the hardest stone, harder than flint. Do not be afraid of them or terrified by them, though they are a rebellious house.[b]"

10 And he said to me, "Son of man, listen carefully and take to heart all the words I speak to you. 11 Go now to your countrymen in exile and speak to them. Say to them, 'This is what the Sovereign LORD says,' whether they listen or fail to listen.[c]"

12 Then the Spirit lifted me up,[d] and I heard behind me a loud rumbling sound—May the glory of the LORD be praised in his dwelling place!— 13 the sound of the wings of the living creatures brushing against each other and the sound of the wheels beside them, a loud rumbling sound.[e] 14 The Spirit then lifted me up and took me away, and I went in bitterness and in the anger of my spirit, with the strong hand of the LORD upon me. 15 I came to the exiles who lived at Tel Abib near the Kebar River.[f] And there, where they were living, I sat among them for seven days[g]—overwhelmed.

Warning to Israel

16 At the end of seven days the word of the LORD came to me:[h] 17 "Son of man, I have made you a watchman[i] for the house of Israel; so hear the word I speak and give them warning from me. 18 When I say to a wicked man, 'You will surely die,' and you do not warn him or speak out to dissuade him from his evil ways in order to save his life, that wicked man will die for[a] his sin, and I will hold you accountable for his blood.[j] 19 But if you do warn the wicked man and he does not turn from his wickedness or from his evil ways, he will die for his sin; but you will have saved yourself.[k]

20 "Again, when a righteous man turns from his righteousness and does evil, and I put a stumbling block before him, he will die. Since you did not warn him, he will die for his sin. The righteous things he did will not be remembered, and I will hold you accountable for his blood.[l] 21 But if you do warn the righteous man not to sin and he does not sin, he will surely live because he took warning, and you will have saved yourself.[m]"

22 The hand of the LORD[n] was upon me there, and he said to me, "Get up and go[o] out to the plain,[p] and there I will speak to you." 23 So I got up and went out to the plain. And the glory of the LORD was standing there, like the glory I had seen by the Kebar River,[q] and I fell facedown.[r]

24 Then the Spirit came into me and raised me[s] to my feet. He spoke to me and said: "Go, shut yourself inside your house. 25 And you, son of man, they will tie with ropes; you will be bound so that you cannot go out among the people.[t] 26 I will make your tongue stick to the roof of your mouth so that you will be silent and unable to rebuke them, though they are a rebellious house.[u] 27 But when I speak to you, I will open your mouth and you shall say to them, 'This is what the Sovereign LORD says.'[v] Whoever will listen let him listen, and whoever will refuse let him refuse; for they are a rebellious house.[w]

Siege of Jerusalem Symbolized

4 "Now, son of man, take a clay tablet, put it in front of you and draw the city of Jerusalem on it. 2 Then lay siege to it: Erect siege works against it, build a ramp[x] up to it, set up camps against it and put battering rams around it.[y] 3 Then take an iron pan, place it as an iron wall between you and the city and turn your face toward it. It will be under siege, and you shall besiege it. This will be a sign[z] to the house of Israel.[a]

4 "Then lie on your left side and put the sin of the house of Israel upon yourself.[b] You are to bear their sin for the number of days you lie on your side. 5 I have assigned you the same number of days as the years of their sin. So for 390 days you will bear the sin of the house of Israel.

6 "After you have finished this, lie down again, this time on your right side, and bear the sin of the house of Judah. I have assigned you 40 days, a day for each year.[b] 7 Turn your face toward the siege of Jerusalem and with bared arm prophesy against her. 8 I will tie you up with ropes so that you cannot turn from one side to the other until you have finished the days of your siege.[c]

9 "Take wheat and barley, beans and lentils, millet and spelt;[d] put them in a storage jar and use them to make bread for yourself. You are to eat it during the

a 18 Or *in*; also in verses 19 and 20 *b* 4 Or *your side*

3:9 [b] Isa 50:7; Eze 2:6; Mic 3:8
3:11 [c] Eze 2:4-5,7
3:12 [d] Eze 8:3; Ac 8:39
3:13 [e] Eze 1:24; 10:5, 16-17
3:15 [f] Ps 137:1 [g] Job 2:13
3:16 [h] Jer 42:7
3:17 [i] Isa 52:8; Jer 6:17; Eze 33:7-9
3:18 [j] ver 20; Eze 33:6
3:19 [k] 2Ki 17:13; Eze 14:14,20; Ac 18:6; 20:26; 1Ti 4:14-16
3:20 [l] Ps 125:5; Eze 18:24; 33:12,18
3:21 [m] Ac 20:31
3:22 [n] Eze 1:3 [o] Ac 9:6 [p] Eze 8:4
3:23 [q] Eze 1:1 [r] Eze 1:28
3:24 [s] Eze 2:2
3:25 [t] Eze 4:8
3:26 [u] Eze 2:5; 24:27; 33:22
3:27 [v] ver 11 [w] Eze 12:3; 24:27; 33:22
4:2 [x] Jer 6:6 [y] Eze 21:22
4:3 [z] Isa 8:18; 20:3; Eze 12:3-6; 24:24,27 [a] Jer 39:1
4:6 [b] Nu 14:34; Da 9:24-26; 12:11-12
4:8 [c] Eze 3:25
4:9 [d] Isa 28:25

390 days you lie on your side. 10Weigh out twenty shekels[a] of food to eat each day and eat it at set times. 11Also measure out a sixth of a hin[b] of water and drink it at set times. 12Eat the food as you would a barley cake; bake it in the sight of the people, using human excrement[e] for fuel.” 13The LORD said, “In this way the people of Israel will eat defiled food among the nations where I will drive them.”[f]

14Then I said, “Not so, Sovereign LORD![g] I have never defiled myself. From my youth until now I have never eaten anything found dead[h] or torn by wild animals. No unclean meat has ever entered my mouth.[i]”

15“Very well,” he said, “I will let you bake your bread over cow manure instead of human excrement.”

16He then said to me: “Son of man, I will cut off[j] the supply of food in Jerusalem. The people will eat rationed food in anxiety and drink rationed water in despair,[k] 17for food and water will be scarce. They will be appalled at the sight of each other and will waste away because of[c] their sin.[l]

5 “Now, son of man, take a sharp sword and use it as a barber's razor[m] to shave[n] your head and your beard.[o] Then take a set of scales and divide up the hair. 2When the days of your siege come to an end, burn a third of the hair with fire inside the city. Take a third and strike it with the sword all around the city. And scatter a third to the wind. For I will pursue them with drawn sword.[p] 3But take a few strands of hair and tuck them away in the folds of your garment.[q] 4Again, take a few of these and throw them into the fire and burn them up. A fire will spread from there to the whole house of Israel.

5“This is what the Sovereign LORD says: This is Jerusalem, which I have set in the center of the nations, with countries all around her. 6Yet in her wickedness she has rebelled against my laws and decrees more than the nations and countries around her. She has rejected my laws and has not followed my decrees.[r]

7“Therefore this is what the Sovereign LORD says: You have been more unruly than the nations around you and have not followed my decrees or kept my laws. You have not even[d] conformed to the standards of the nations around you.[s]

8“Therefore this is what the Sovereign LORD says: I myself am against you, Jerusalem, and I will inflict punishment on you in the sight of the nations.[t] 9Because of all your detestable idols, I will do to you what I have never done before and will never do again.[u] 10Therefore in your midst fathers will eat their children, and children will eat their fathers.[v] I will inflict punishment on you and will scatter all your survivors to the winds.[w] 11Therefore as surely as I live, declares the Sovereign LORD, because you have defiled my sanctuary with all your vile images[x] and detestable practices,[y] I myself will withdraw my favor; I will not look on you with pity or spare you.[z] 12A third of your people will die of the plague or perish by famine inside you; a third will fall by the sword outside your walls; and a third I will scatter to the winds and pursue with drawn sword.[a]

13“Then my anger will cease and my wrath[b] against them will subside, and I will be avenged.[c] And when I have spent my wrath upon them, they will know that I the LORD have spoken in my zeal.

14“I will make you a ruin and a reproach among the nations around you, in the sight of all who pass by.[d] 15You will be a reproach and a taunt, a warning and an object of horror to the nations around you when I inflict punishment on you in anger and in wrath and with stinging rebuke.[e] I the LORD have spoken.[f] 16When I shoot at you with my deadly and destructive arrows of famine, I will shoot to destroy you. I will bring more and more famine upon you and cut off your supply of food.[g] 17I will send famine and wild beasts against you, and they will leave you childless. Plague and bloodshed[h] will sweep through you, and I will bring the sword against you. I the LORD have spoken.[i]”

A Prophecy Against the Mountains of Israel

6 The word of the LORD came to me: 2“Son of man, set your face against the mountains[j] of Israel; proph-

4:12 [e] Isa 36:12
4:13 [f] Hos 9:3
4:14 [g] Jer 1:6; Eze 9:8; 20:49 [h] Lev 11:39 [i] Ex 22:31; Dt 14:3; Ac 10:14
4:16 [j] Ps 105:16; Eze 5:16 [k] ver 10-11; Lev 26:26; Isa 3:1; Eze 12:19
4:17 [l] Lev 26:39; Eze 24:23; 33:10
5:1 [m] Isa 7:20 [n] Eze 44:20 [o] Lev 21:5
5:2 [p] ver 12; Lev 26:33
5:3 [q] Jer 39:10
5:6 [r] Jer 11:10; Eze 16:47-51; Zec 7:11
5:7 [s] 2Ch 33:9; Jer 2:10-11; Eze 16:47
5:8 [t] Eze 15:7
5:9 [u] Da 9:12; Mt 24:21
5:10 [v] Lev 26:29; La 2:20 [w] Lev 26:33; Ps 44:11; Eze 12:14; Zec 2:6
5:11 [x] Eze 7:20 [y] 2Ch 36:14; Eze 8:6 [z] Eze 7:4,9
5:12 [a] ver 2,17; Jer 15:2; 21:9; Eze 6:11-12; 12:14
5:13 [b] Eze 21:17; 36:6 [c] Isa 1:24
5:14 [d] Lev 26:32; Ne 2:17; Ps 74:3-10; 79:1-4
5:15 [e] 1Ki 9:7; Jer 22:8-9; 24:9 [f] Eze 25:17
5:16 [g] Dt 32:24
5:17 [h] Eze 38:22 [i] Eze 14:21
6:2 [j] Eze 36:1

[a] *10* That is, about 8 ounces (about 0.2 kilogram)
[b] *11* That is, about 2/3 quart (about 0.6 liter)
[c] *17* Or *away in*
[d] *7* Most Hebrew manuscripts; some Hebrew manuscripts and Syriac *You have*

esy against them ³and say: 'O mountains
of Israel, hear the word of the Sovereign
LORD. This is what the Sovereign LORD
6:3 says to the mountains and hills, to the
k Eze 36:4 ravines and valleys:[k] I am about to bring
l Lev 26:30 a sword against you, and I will destroy
your high places.[l] ⁴Your altars will be de-
6:4 m 2Ch 14:5 molished and your incense altars[m] will
be smashed; and I will slay your people
in front of your idols. ⁵I will lay the dead
bodies of the Israelites in front of their
6:5 n Jer 8:1-2 idols, and I will scatter your bones[n]
around your altars. ⁶Wherever you live,
the towns will be laid waste and the high
places demolished, so that your altars
6:6 will be laid waste and devastated, your
o Mic 1:7; idols[o] smashed and ruined, your incense
Zec 13:2 p Lev 26:30 altars[p] broken down, and what you have
q Isa 6:11; made wiped out.[q] ⁷Your people will fall
Eze 5:14 slain among you, and you will know that
I am the LORD.

⁸" 'But I will spare some, for some of
6:8 r Jer 44:28 you will escape[r] the sword when you are
s Isa 6:13; scattered among the lands and nations.[s]
Jer 44:14; Eze 12:16; 14:22 ⁹Then in the nations where they have
been carried captive, those who escape
will remember me—how I have been
6:9 t Ps 78:40; grieved[t] by their adulterous hearts, which
Isa 7:13 have turned away from me, and by their
u Eze 20:7,24 eyes, which have lusted after their idols.[u]
v Eze 20:43; 36:31 They will loathe themselves for the evil
they have done and for all their de-
testable practices.[v] ¹⁰And they will know
that I am the LORD; I did not threaten in
vain to bring this calamity on them.

¹¹" 'This is what the Sovereign LORD
says: Strike your hands together and
stamp your feet and cry out "Alas!" because of all the wicked and detestable
practices of the house of Israel, for they
will fall by the sword, famine and
6:11 w Eze 5:12; 21:14,17; 25:6 plague.[w] ¹²He that is far away will die of
the plague, and he that is near will fall by
the sword, and he that survives and is
spared will die of famine. So will I spend
6:12 x Eze 5:12 my wrath upon them.[x] ¹³And they will
know that I am the LORD, when their
people lie slain among their idols around
their altars, on every high hill and on all
6:13 y Isa 57:5 the mountaintops, under every spread-
z 1Ki 14:23; Jer 2:20; ing tree and every leafy oak[y]—places
Eze 20:28; where they offered fragrant incense to all
Hos 4:13 their idols.[z] ¹⁴And I will stretch out my
6:14 a Isa 5:25 hand[a] against them and make the land a
b Eze 14:13 desolate waste from the desert to Dib-
lah[a]—wherever they live. Then they will
know that I am the LORD.[b]' "

The End Has Come

7 The word of the LORD came to me:
²"Son of man, this is what the Sovereign LORD says to the land of Israel:
The end![c] The end has come upon the 7:2 c Am 8:2,10
four corners[d] of the land. ³The end is d Rev 7:1; 20:8
now upon you and I will unleash my
anger against you. I will judge you according to your conduct and repay you
for all your detestable practices. ⁴I will
not look on you with pity[e] or spare you; 7:4 e Eze 5:11
I will surely repay you for your conduct
and the detestable practices among you.
Then you will know that I am the LORD.

⁵"This is what the Sovereign LORD 7:5
says: Disaster![f] An unheard-of[b] disaster f 2Ki 21:12
is coming. ⁶The end has come! The end
has come! It has roused itself against
you. It has come! ⁷Doom has come upon
you—you who dwell in the land. The
time has come, the day is near;[g] there is 7:7 g Eze 12:23;
panic, not joy, upon the mountains. ⁸I Zep 1:14

[a] *14* Most Hebrew manuscripts; a few Hebrew manuscripts *Riblah* [b] *5* Most Hebrew manuscripts; some Hebrew manuscripts and Syriac *Disaster after*

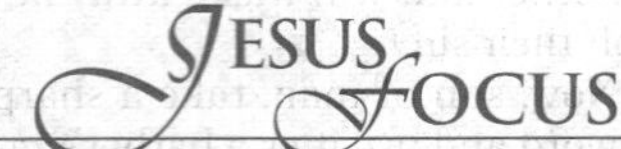

"THE END HAS COME!"

Predictions about the end of the world typically cause us to perk up our ears and pay attention. Our natural human curiosity longs to know how close the end is. In the book of Ezekiel God made a clear announcement through his prophet: "The end has come!" (Ezekiel 7:6). It was too late to turn back the hand of judgment, too late to even prepare for the devastation; Jerusalem would be destroyed and fall to the enemy. Centuries later, in the New Testament, Jesus' followers asked him how they could know that the end of the age was near. Jesus informed them that there would be wars, famines and earthquakes—but these events weren't particularly out of the ordinary (Matthew 24:6–7). And then Jesus went on to declare that "this gospel of the kingdom will be preached in the whole world as a testimony to all nations, and then the end will come" (Matthew 24:14). God is not so much concerned that we try to identify the precise endpoint of history and begin preparing only when we see it approaching as he is that we live *every moment* as his faithful and obedient people. That way, when Jesus returns to earth as our eternal King, we will already be prepared for his coming (Matthew 24:44).

He will be called
Wonderful Counselor,
Mighty God, Everlasting Father,
Prince of Peace.

—Isaiah 9:6—

AS JESUS WAS COMING UP
OUT OF THE WATER, HE SAW HEAVEN
BEING TORN OPEN AND THE SPIRIT
DESCENDING ON HIM LIKE A *dove*.
AND A VOICE CAME FROM HEAVEN:
"YOU ARE *my Son*, WHOM I LOVE;
WITH YOU I AM WELL PLEASED."

—MARK 1:10-11—

7:8 h Isa 42:25; Eze 9:8; 14:19; Na 1:6 i Eze 20:8,21; 36:19 am about to pour out my wrath[h] on you
and spend my anger against you; I will
judge you according to your conduct
and repay you for all your detestable
practices.[i] 9 I will not look on you with
pity or spare you; I will repay you in accordance with your conduct and the detestable practices among you. Then you
will know that it is I the LORD who
strikes the blow.

7:10 j Ps 89:32; Isa 10:5 10 "The day is here! It has come! Doom
has burst forth, the rod[j] has budded, ar-
rogance has blossomed! 11 Violence has
grown into[a] a rod to punish wickedness;
none of the people will be left, none of
that crowd—no wealth, nothing of val-
7:11 k Jer 16:6; Zep 1:18 ue.[k] 12 The time has come, the day has
arrived. Let not the buyer rejoice nor the
7:12 l ver 7; Isa 5:13-14; Eze 30:3 seller grieve, for wrath is upon the whole
crowd.[l] 13 The seller will not recover the
land he has sold as long as both of them
live, for the vision concerning the whole
crowd will not be reversed. Because of
their sins, not one of them will preserve
7:13 m Lev 25:24-28 his life.[m] 14 Though they blow the trumpet and get everything ready, no one will
go into battle, for my wrath is upon the
whole crowd.

15 "Outside is the sword, inside are
plague and famine; those in the country
7:15 n Dt 32:25; Jer 14:18; La 1:20; Eze 5:12 will die by the sword, and those in the
city will be devoured by famine and
plague.[n] 16 All who survive and escape
will be in the mountains, moaning like
7:16 o Isa 59:11 p Ezr 9:15; Eze 6:8 doves[o] of the valleys, each because of his
sins.[p] 17 Every hand will go limp,[q] and
every knee will become as weak as water.
18 They will put on sackcloth and be
7:17 q Isa 13:7; Eze 21:7; 22:14 clothed with terror.[r] Their faces will be
covered with shame and their heads will
be shaved.[s] 19 They will throw their silver
7:18 r Ps 55:5 s Isa 15:2-3; Eze 27:31; Am 8:10 into the streets, and their gold will be an
unclean thing. Their silver and gold will
not be able to save them in the day of the
LORD's wrath.[t] They will not satisfy their
7:19 t Eze 13:5; Zep 1:7,18 u Eze 14:3 v Pr 11:4 hunger or fill their stomachs with it, for
it has made them stumble[u] into sin.[v]
20 They were proud of their beautiful jewelry and used it to make their detestable
7:20 w Jer 7:30 idols and vile images.[w] Therefore I will
turn these into an unclean thing for
them. 21 I will hand it all over as plunder
to foreigners and as loot to the wicked of
7:21 x 2Ki 24:13 the earth, and they will defile it.[x] 22 I will
turn my face[y] away from them, and they
7:22 y Eze 39:23-24 will desecrate my treasured place; robbers will enter it and desecrate it.

23 "Prepare chains, because the land is
full of bloodshed[z] and the city is full of 7:23 z 2Ki 21:16
violence. 24 I will bring the most wicked
of the nations to take possession of their
houses; I will put an end to the pride of 7:24 a Eze 24:21 b 2Ch 7:20; Eze 28:7
the mighty, and their sanctuaries[a] will
be desecrated.[b] 25 When terror comes,
they will seek peace, but there will be
none.[c] 26 Calamity upon calamity[d] will 7:25 c Eze 13:10,16
come, and rumor upon rumor. They will
try to get a vision from the prophet; the 7:26 d Jer 4:20 e Isa 47:11; Eze 20:1-3; Mic 3:6
teaching of the law by the priest will be
lost, as will the counsel of the elders.[e]
27 The king will mourn, the prince will be
clothed with despair,[f] and the hands of 7:27 f Ps 109:19; Eze 26:16 g Eze 18:20 h ver 4
the people of the land will tremble. I will
deal with them according to their conduct,[g] and by their own standards I will
judge them. Then they will know that I
am the LORD.[h]"

Idolatry in the Temple

8 In the sixth year, in the sixth
month on the fifth day, while I
was sitting in my house and the elders[i] 8:1 i Eze 14:1 j Eze 33:31 k Eze 1:1-3
of Judah were sitting before[j] me, the
hand of the Sovereign LORD came upon
me there.[k] 2 I looked, and I saw a figure
like that of a man.[b] From what appeared
to be his waist down he was like fire, and
from there up his appearance was as
bright as glowing metal.[l] 3 He stretched 8:2 l Eze 1:4,26-27
out what looked like a hand and took
me by the hair of my head. The Spirit 8:3 m Eze 3:12; 11:1 n Ex 20:5; Dt 32:16
lifted me up[m] between earth and heav-
en and in visions of God he took me to
Jerusalem, to the entrance to the north
gate of the inner court, where the idol
that provokes to jealousy[n] stood. 4 And
there before me was the glory[o] of the 8:4 o Eze 1:28 p Eze 3:22
God of Israel, as in the vision I had seen
in the plain.[p]

5 Then he said to me, "Son of man,
look toward the north." So I looked, and
in the entrance north of the gate of the 8:5 q Ps 78:58; Jer 32:34
altar I saw this idol[q] of jealousy.

6 And he said to me, "Son of man, do
you see what they are doing—the utter-
ly detestable[r] things the house of Israel 8:6 r Eze 5:11
is doing here, things that will drive me
far from my sanctuary? But you will see
things that are even more detestable."

7 Then he brought me to the entrance
to the court. I looked, and I saw a hole in
the wall. 8 He said to me, "Son of man,

[a] 11 Or *The violent one has become* [b] 2 Or *saw a fiery figure*

now dig into the wall." So I dug into the wall and saw a doorway there.

9 And he said to me, "Go in and see the wicked and detestable things they are doing here." 10 So I went in and looked, and I saw portrayed all over the walls all kinds of crawling things and detestable animals and all the idols of the house of Israel.[s] 11 In front of them stood seventy elders of the house of Israel, and Jaazaniah son of Shaphan was standing among them. Each had a censer[t] in his hand, and a fragrant cloud of incense[u] was rising.

12 He said to me, "Son of man, have you seen what the elders of the house of Israel are doing in the darkness, each at the shrine of his own idol? They say, 'The LORD does not see[v] us; the LORD has forsaken the land.' " 13 Again, he said, "You will see them doing things that are even more detestable."

14 Then he brought me to the entrance to the north gate of the house of the LORD, and I saw women sitting there, mourning for Tammuz. 15 He said to me, "Do you see this, son of man? You will see things that are even more detestable than this."

16 He then brought me into the inner court of the house of the LORD, and there at the entrance to the temple, between the portico and the altar,[w] were about twenty-five men. With their backs toward the temple of the LORD and their faces toward the east, they were bowing down to the sun in the east.[x]

17 He said to me, "Have you seen this, son of man? Is it a trivial matter for the house of Judah to do the detestable things they are doing here? Must they also fill the land with violence[y] and continually provoke me to anger?[z] Look at them putting the branch to their nose! 18 Therefore I will deal with them in anger; I will not look on them with pity[a] or spare them. Although they shout in my ears, I will not listen[b] to them."

8:10 [s] Ex 20:4
8:11 [t] Nu 16:17 [u] Nu 16:35
8:12 [v] Ps 10:11; Isa 29:15; Eze 9:9
8:16 [w] Joel 2:17 [x] Dt 4:19; 17:3; Job 31:28; Jer 2:27; Eze 11:1,12
8:17 [y] Eze 9:9 [z] Eze 16:26
8:18 [a] Eze 9:10; 24:14 [b] Isa 1:15; Jer 11:11; Mic 3:4; Zec 7:13

Idolaters Killed

9 Then I heard him call out in a loud voice, "Bring the guards of the city here, each with a weapon in his hand." 2 And I saw six men coming from the direction of the upper gate, which faces north, each with a deadly weapon in his hand. With them was a man clothed in linen[c] who had a writing kit at his side. They came in and stood beside the bronze altar.

3 Now the glory[d] of the God of Israel went up from above the cherubim,[e] where it had been, and moved to the threshold of the temple. Then the LORD called to the man clothed in linen who had the writing kit at his side 4 and said to him, "Go throughout the city of Jerusalem and put a mark[f] on the foreheads of those who grieve and lament[g] over all the detestable things that are done in it.[h]"

5 As I listened, he said to the others, "Follow him through the city and kill, without showing pity[i] or compassion. 6 Slaughter old men, young men and maidens, women and children, but do not touch anyone who has the mark. Begin at my sanctuary." So they began with the elders[j] who were in front of the temple.[k]

7 Then he said to them, "Defile the temple and fill the courts with the slain. Go!" So they went out and began killing throughout the city. 8 While they were killing and I was left alone, I fell facedown,[l] crying out, "Ah, Sovereign LORD! Are you going to destroy the entire remnant of Israel in this outpouring of your wrath on Jerusalem?[m]"

9 He answered me, "The sin of the house of Israel and Judah is exceedingly great; the land is full of bloodshed and the city is full of injustice.[n] They say, 'The LORD has forsaken the land; the LORD does not see.'[o] 10 So I will not look on them with pity[p] or spare them, but I will bring down on their own heads what they have done.[q]"

11 Then the man in linen with the writing kit at his side brought back word, saying, "I have done as you commanded."

The Glory Departs From the Temple

10 I looked, and I saw the likeness of a throne[r] of sapphire[a][s] above the expanse[t] that was over the heads of the cherubim. 2 The LORD said to the man clothed in linen,[u] "Go in among the wheels[v] beneath the cherubim. Fill[w] your hands with burning coals from among the cherubim and scatter them over the city." And as I watched, he went in.

[a] 1 Or *lapis lazuli*

9:2 [c] Lev 16:4; Eze 10:2; Rev 15:6
9:3 [d] Eze 10:4 [e] Eze 11:22
9:4 [f] Ex 12:7; 2Co 1:22; Rev 7:3; 9:4 [g] Ps 119:136; Jer 13:17; Eze 21:6 [h] Ps 119:53
9:5 [i] Eze 5:11
9:6 [j] Eze 8:11-13,16 [k] 2Ch 36:17; Jer 25:29; 1Pe 4:17
9:8 [l] Jos 7:6 [m] Eze 11:13; Am 7:1-6
9:9 [n] Eze 22:29 [o] Job 22:13; Eze 8:12
9:10 [p] Eze 7:4; 8:18 [q] Isa 65:6; Eze 11:21
10:1 [r] Rev 4:2 [s] Ex 24:10 [t] Eze 1:22
10:2 [u] Eze 9:2 [v] Eze 1:15 [w] Rev 8:5

3 Now the cherubim were standing on
the south side of the temple when the
man went in, and a cloud filled the inner
(10:4 x Eze 1:28; 9:3) court. 4 Then the glory of the LORD[x] rose
from above the cherubim and moved to
the threshold of the temple. The cloud
filled the temple, and the court was full
of the radiance of the glory of the LORD.
5 The sound of the wings of the cherubim
(10:5) could be heard as far away as the outer
(y Job 40:9; Eze 1:24) court, like the voice[y] of God Almighty[a]
when he speaks.
6 When the LORD commanded the
man in linen, "Take fire from among the
wheels, from among the cherubim," the
man went in and stood beside a wheel.
7 Then one of the cherubim reached out
his hand to the fire that was among
them. He took up some of it and put it
into the hands of the man in linen, who
took it and went out. 8 (Under the wings
of the cherubim could be seen what
(10:8 z Eze 1:8) looked like the hands of a man.)[z]
9 I looked, and I saw beside the cheru-
bim four wheels, one beside each of the
(10:9) cherubim; the wheels sparkled like
(a Eze 1:15-16; Rev 21:20) chrysolite.[a] 10 As for their appearance,
the four of them looked alike; each was
like a wheel intersecting a wheel. 11 As
they moved, they would go in any one of
the four directions the cherubim faced;
the wheels did not turn about[b] as the
cherubim went. The cherubim went in
whatever direction the head faced, without turning as they went. 12 Their entire
bodies, including their backs, their
hands and their wings, were completely
(10:12 b Rev 4:6-8) full of eyes,[b] as were their four wheels.[c]
(c Eze 1:15-21) 13 I heard the wheels being called "the
(10:14) whirling wheels." 14 Each of the cheru-
(d 1Ki 7:36) bim[d] had four faces:[e] One face was that
(e Eze 1:6 f Eze 1:10;) of a cherub, the second the face of a
(Rev 4:7) man, the third the face of a lion, and the
fourth the face of an eagle.[f]
15 Then the cherubim rose upward.
(10:15 g Eze 1:3,5) These were the living creatures[g] I had
seen by the Kebar River. 16 When the cher-
ubim moved, the wheels beside them
moved; and when the cherubim spread
their wings to rise from the ground, the
wheels did not leave their side. 17 When
the cherubim stood still, they also stood
still; and when the cherubim rose, they
rose with them, because the spirit of the
(10:17 h Eze 1:20-21) living creatures was in them.[h]
18 Then the glory of the LORD departed
from over the threshold of the temple
and stopped above the cherubim.[i] (10:18 i Ps 18:10)
19 While I watched, the cherubim spread
their wings and rose from the ground,
and as they went, the wheels went with (10:19)
them.[j] They stopped at the entrance to (j Eze 11:1,22)
the east gate of the LORD's house, and the
glory of the God of Israel was above them.
20 These were the living creatures I had
seen beneath the God of Israel by the (10:20)
Kebar River,[k] and I realized that they (k Eze 1:1)
were cherubim. 21 Each had four faces[l] (10:21)
and four wings,[m] and under their wings (l Eze 41:18 m Eze 1:6)
was what looked like the hands of a
man. 22 Their faces had the same appearance as those I had seen by the Kebar River. Each one went straight ahead.

Judgment on Israel's Leaders

11 Then the Spirit lifted me up
and brought me to the gate of
the house of the LORD that faces east.
There at the entrance to the gate were
twenty-five men, and I saw among them
Jaazaniah son of Azzur and Pelatiah son (11:1)
of Benaiah, leaders of the people.[n] 2 The (n Eze 8:16;)
LORD said to me, "Son of man, these are (10:19; 43:4-5)
the men who are plotting evil and giving
wicked advice in this city. 3 They say,
'Will it not soon be time to build (11:3)
houses?[c] This city is a cooking pot,[o] and (o Jer 1:13;)
we are the meat.'[p] 4 Therefore prophesy[q] (Eze 24:3 p ver 7,)
against them; prophesy, son of man." (11)
5 Then the Spirit of the LORD came (11:4)
upon me, and he told me to say: "This is (q Eze 3:4,17)
what the LORD says: That is what you are
saying, O house of Israel, but I know (11:5)
what is going through your mind.[r] 6 You (r Jer 17:10)
have killed many people in this city and (11:6)
filled its streets with the dead.[s] (s Eze 7:23; 22:6)
7 "Therefore this is what the Sovereign
LORD says: The bodies you have thrown
there are the meat and this city is the (11:7)
pot, but I will drive you out of it.[t] 8 You (t Eze 24:3-13;)
fear the sword, and the sword is what I (Mic 3:2-3)
will bring against you, declares the Sov- (11:8)
ereign LORD.[u] 9 I will drive you out of the (u Pr 10:24)
city and hand you over[v] to foreigners (11:9)
and inflict punishment on you.[w] 10 You (v Ps 106:41 w Dt 28:36;)
will fall by the sword, and I will execute (Eze 5:8)
judgment on you at the borders of Isra- (11:10)
el.[x] Then you will know that I am the (x 2Ki 14:25)
LORD. 11 This city will not be a pot[y] for (11:11)
you, nor will you be the meat in it; I will (y ver 3)
execute judgment on you at the borders
of Israel. 12 And you will know that I am

[a] 5 Hebrew *El-Shaddai* [b] 11 Or *aside* [c] 3 Or *This is not the time to build houses.*

DISCOVERY 208

Representing God's Glory

Throughout the Old Testament God's "glory" served as confirmation to his people that he was with them, as a visible demonstration of his beauty and majesty. The glory of God settled on first the tabernacle and later the temple, and when Moses entered the tabernacle, God's glory filled it like a cloud (Exodus 40:34–35). Later, when Solomon built the temple, God's glory filled it in the form of fire (2 Chronicles 7:1–2). It was during Ezekiel's ministry among the exiles in Babylon that God removed his glory, his presence, from the temple in Jerusalem (Ezekiel 10:18–19; 11:22–23).

God did so because the people who remained in Jerusalem were blatantly sinning. Their sin had even permeated their worship to the point that they were paying homage to pagan idols in the temple courts (Ezekiel 8:3,14–16) and had painted likenesses of pagan gods on the walls of the temple (Ezekiel 8:9–11).

It is interesting to note that God removed his glory gradually—almost as though he were reluctant to do so. Ezekiel wrote that God's glory first rose above the cherubim (Ezekiel 9:3), then moved to the threshold of the temple (Ezekiel 10:4), then hovered above the temple itself (Ezekiel 10:19) and finally went up from the city and stopped above the Mount of Olives (Ezekiel 11:23). Not long after this departure the original temple was destroyed by the Babylonians (2 Chronicles 36:19). And nowhere in the Bible do we read that God's glory ever returned to the rebuilt temple begun by Zerubbabel in 536 B.C. and completed in 516 B.C. (Ezra 6:13–15).

But God's glory did return to us—in the person of his precious Son Jesus: "The Word became flesh and made his dwelling among us. We have seen his glory, the glory of the One and Only" (John 1:14). Jesus embodies the glory of God. Thirty-three years after his birth Jesus Christ returned to heaven—from the Mount of Olives (Acts 1:8–11), the same point from which God's glory had finally departed in the Ezekiel account.

But that doesn't mean that God's glory is no longer with us. When Jesus left this earth he promised that the Holy Spirit would be with his people forever (John 14:16), and now *we* reflect the Lord's glory and are being changed into Jesus' likeness "with ever-increasing glory" (2 Corinthians 3:18). Today we represent God's presence in our families, communities and churches.

***Self-Discovery:** What does it mean to you that you are in the process of being changed into Jesus' likeness with ever-increasing glory? What implications does this have for how you live your life?*

GO TO DISCOVERY 209 ON PAGE 1089

the LORD, for you have not followed my decrees[z] or kept my laws but have conformed to the standards of the nations around you.[a]"

13 Now as I was prophesying, Pelatiah[b] son of Benaiah died. Then I fell facedown and cried out in a loud voice, "Ah, Sovereign LORD! Will you completely destroy the remnant of Israel?[c]"

14 The word of the LORD came to me: 15 "Son of man, your brothers—your brothers who are your blood relatives[a] and the whole house of Israel—are those of whom the people of Jerusalem have said, 'They are[b] far away from the LORD; this land was given to us as our possession.'[d]

Promised Return of Israel

16 "Therefore say: 'This is what the Sovereign LORD says: Although I sent them far away among the nations and scattered them among the countries, yet for a little while I have been a sanctuary[e] for them in the countries where they have gone.'

17 "Therefore say: 'This is what the Sovereign LORD says: I will gather you from the nations and bring you back from the countries where you have been scattered, and I will give you back the land of Israel again.'[f]

18 "They will return to it and remove all its vile images[g] and detestable idols.[h] 19 I will give them an undivided heart[i] and put a new spirit in them; I will remove from them their heart of stone[j] and give them a heart of flesh.[k] 20 Then they will follow my decrees and be careful to keep my laws.[l] They will be my people, and I will be their God.[m] 21 But as for those whose hearts are devoted to their vile images and detestable idols, I will bring down on their own heads what they have done, declares the Sovereign LORD.[n]"

22 Then the cherubim, with the wheels beside them, spread their wings, and the glory of the God of Israel was above them.[o] 23 The glory[p] of the LORD went up from within the city and stopped above the mountain[q] east of it. 24 The Spirit[r] lifted me up and brought me to the exiles in Babylonia[c] in the vision[s] given by the Spirit of God.

Then the vision I had seen went up from me, 25 and I told the exiles everything the LORD had shown me.[t]

11:12 [z] Lev 18:4; Eze 18:9 [a] Eze 8:10
11:13 [b] ver 1 [c] Eze 9:8
11:15 [d] Eze 33:24
11:16 [e] Ps 90:1; 91:9; Isa 8:14
11:17 [f] Jer 3:18; 24:5-6; Eze 28:25; 34:13
11:18 [g] Eze 5:11 [h] Eze 37:23
11:19 [i] Jer 32:39 [j] Zec 7:12 [k] Eze 18:31; 36:26; 2Co 3:3
11:20 [l] Ps 105:45 [m] Eze 14:11; 36:26-28
11:21 [n] Eze 9:10; 16:43
11:22 [o] Eze 10:19
11:23 [p] Eze 8:4; 10:4 [q] Zec 14:4
11:24 [r] Eze 8:3 [s] 2Co 12:2-4
11:25 [t] Eze 3:4,11

The Exile Symbolized

12 The word of the LORD came to me: 2 "Son of man, you are living among a rebellious people. They have eyes to see but do not see and ears to hear but do not hear, for they are a rebellious people.[u]

3 "Therefore, son of man, pack your belongings for exile and in the daytime, as they watch, set out and go from where you are to another place. Perhaps[v] they will understand,[w] though they are a rebellious house.[x] 4 During the daytime, while they watch, bring out your belongings packed for exile. Then in the evening, while they are watching, go out like those who go into exile.[y] 5 While they watch, dig through the wall and take your belongings out through it. 6 Put them on your shoulder as they are watching and carry them out at dusk. Cover your face so that you cannot see the land, for I have made you a sign[z] to the house of Israel."

7 So I did as I was commanded.[a] During the day I brought out my things packed for exile. Then in the evening I dug through the wall with my hands. I took my belongings out at dusk, carrying them on my shoulders while they watched.

8 In the morning the word of the LORD came to me: 9 "Son of man, did not that rebellious house of Israel ask you, 'What are you doing?'[b]

10 "Say to them, 'This is what the Sovereign LORD says: This oracle concerns the prince in Jerusalem and the whole house of Israel who are there.' 11 Say to them, 'I am a sign to you.'

"As I have done, so it will be done to them. They will go into exile as captives.[c]

12 "The prince among them will put his things on his shoulder at dusk[d] and leave, and a hole will be dug in the wall for him to go through. He will cover his face so that he cannot see the land.[e] 13 I will spread my net[f] for him, and he will be caught in my snare;[g] I will bring him to Babylonia, the land of the Chaldeans, but he will not see[h] it, and there he will die.[i] 14 I will scatter to the winds all those around him—his staff and all his

a 15 Or *are in exile with you* (see Septuagint and Syriac) *b* 15 Or *those to whom the people of Jerusalem have said, 'Stay* *c* 24 Or *Chaldea*

12:2 [u] Isa 6:10; Eze 2:6-8; Mt 13:15
12:3 [v] Jer 36:3 [w] Jer 26:3 [x] 2Ti 2:25-26
12:4 [y] ver 12; Jer 39:4
12:6 [z] ver 12; Isa 8:18; 20:3; Eze 4:3; 24:24
12:7 [a] Eze 24:18; 37:10
12:9 [b] Eze 17:12; 20:49; 24:19
12:11 [c] 2Ki 25:7; Jer 15:2; 52:15
12:12 [d] Jer 39:4 [e] Jer 52:7
12:13 [f] Eze 17:20; 19:8; Hos 7:12 [g] Isa 24:17-18 [h] Jer 39:7 [i] Jer 52:11; Eze 17:16

troops—and I will pursue them with drawn sword.[j]

15 "They will know that I am the LORD, when I disperse them among the nations and scatter them through the countries. 16 But I will spare a few of them from the sword, famine and plague, so that in the nations where they go they may acknowledge all their detestable practices. Then they will know that I am the LORD.[k]"

17 The word of the LORD came to me: 18 "Son of man, tremble as you eat your food,[l] and shudder in fear as you drink your water. 19 Say to the people of the land: 'This is what the Sovereign LORD says about those living in Jerusalem and in the land of Israel: They will eat their food in anxiety and drink their water in despair, for their land will be stripped of everything[m] in it because of the violence of all who live there.[n] 20 The inhabited towns will be laid waste and the land will be desolate. Then you will know that I am the LORD.[o]' "

21 The word of the LORD came to me: 22 "Son of man, what is this proverb you have in the land of Israel: 'The days go by and every vision comes to nothing'?[p] 23 Say to them, 'This is what the Sovereign LORD says: I am going to put an end to this proverb, and they will no longer quote it in Israel.' Say to them, 'The days are near when every vision will be fulfilled.[q] 24 For there will be no more false visions or flattering divinations[r] among the people of Israel. 25 But I the LORD will speak what I will, and it shall be fulfilled without delay. For in your days, you rebellious house, I will fulfill whatever I say, declares the Sovereign LORD.[s]' "

26 The word of the LORD came to me: 27 "Son of man, the house of Israel is saying, 'The vision he sees is for many years from now, and he prophesies about the distant future.'[t]

28 "Therefore say to them, 'This is what the Sovereign LORD says: None of my words will be delayed any longer; whatever I say will be fulfilled, declares the Sovereign LORD.' "

12:14 [j] 2Ki 25:5; Eze 5:10,12
12:16 [k] Jer 22:8-9; Eze 6:8-10; 14:22
12:18 [l] La 5:9; Eze 4:16
12:19 [m] Eze 6:6-14; Mic 7:13; Zec 7:14 [n] Eze 4:16; 23:33
12:20 [o] Isa 7:23-24; Jer 4:7
12:22 [p] Eze 11:3; Am 6:3; 2Pe 3:4
12:23 [q] Ps 37:13; Joel 2:1; Zep 1:14
12:24 [r] Jer 14:14; Eze 13:23; Zec 13:2-4
12:25 [s] Isa 14:24; Hab 1:5
12:27 [t] Da 10:14

False Prophets Condemned

13 The word of the LORD came to me: 2 "Son of man, prophesy against the prophets of Israel who are now prophesying. Say to those who prophesy out of their own imagination: 'Hear the word of the LORD![u] 3 This is what the Sovereign LORD says: Woe to the foolish[a] prophets[v] who follow their own spirit and have seen nothing![w] 4 Your prophets, O Israel, are like jackals among ruins. 5 You have not gone up to the breaks in the wall to repair[x] it for the house of Israel so that it will stand firm in the battle on the day of the LORD.[y] 6 Their visions are false and their divinations a lie. They say, "The LORD declares," when the LORD has not sent them; yet they expect their words to be fulfilled.[z] 7 Have you not seen false visions and uttered lying divinations when you say, "The LORD declares," though I have not spoken?

8 " 'Therefore this is what the Sovereign LORD says: Because of your false words and lying visions, I am against you, declares the Sovereign LORD. 9 My hand will be against the prophets who see false visions and utter lying divinations. They will not belong to the council of my people or be listed in the records[a] of the house of Israel, nor will they enter the land of Israel. Then you will know that I am the Sovereign LORD.[b]

10 " 'Because they lead my people astray,[c] saying, "Peace," when there is no peace, and because, when a flimsy wall is built, they cover it with whitewash,[d] 11 therefore tell those who cover it with whitewash that it is going to fall. Rain will come in torrents, and I will send hailstones hurtling down, and violent winds will burst forth.[e] 12 When the wall collapses, will people not ask you, "Where is the whitewash you covered it with?"

13 " 'Therefore this is what the Sovereign LORD says: In my wrath I will unleash a violent wind, and in my anger hailstones[f] and torrents of rain will fall with destructive fury.[g] 14 I will tear down the wall you have covered with whitewash and will level it to the ground so that its foundation[h] will be laid bare. When it[b] falls,[i] you will be destroyed in it; and you will know that I am the LORD. 15 So I will spend my wrath against the wall and against those who covered it with whitewash. I will say to you, "The wall is gone and so are those who whitewashed it, 16 those prophets of Israel who

13:2 [u] ver 17; Jer 23:16; 37:19
13:3 [v] La 2:14 [w] Jer 23:25-32
13:5 [x] Isa 58:12; Eze 22:30 [y] Eze 7:19
13:6 [z] Jer 28:15; Eze 22:28
13:9 [a] Jer 17:13 [b] Eze 20:38
13:10 [c] Jer 50:6 [d] Eze 7:25; 22:28
13:11 [e] Eze 38:22
13:13 [f] Rev 11:19; 16:21 [g] Ex 9:25; Isa 30:30
13:14 [h] Mic 1:6 [i] Jer 6:15

[a] 3 Or *wicked* [b] 14 Or *the city*

prophesied to Jerusalem and saw visions
13:16 of peace for her when there was no
j Isa 57:21; Jer 6:14 peace, declares the Sovereign LORD.[j]" '
17"Now, son of man, set your face
13:17 against the daughters[k] of your people
k Rev 2:20 l ver 2 who prophesy out of their own imagination. Prophesy against them[l] 18and say,
'This is what the Sovereign LORD says:
Woe to the women who sew magic
charms on all their wrists and make veils
of various lengths for their heads in order to ensnare people. Will you ensnare
the lives of my people but preserve your
13:19 own? 19You have profaned[m] me among
m Eze 20:39; 22:26 n Pr 28:21 my people for a few handfuls of barley
and scraps of bread. By lying to my peo-
ple, who listen to lies, you have killed
those who should not have died and have
spared those who should not live.[n]
20" 'Therefore this is what the Sovereign LORD says: I am against your magic
charms with which you ensnare people
like birds and I will tear them from your
arms; I will set free the people that you
ensnare like birds. 21I will tear off your
veils and save my people from your

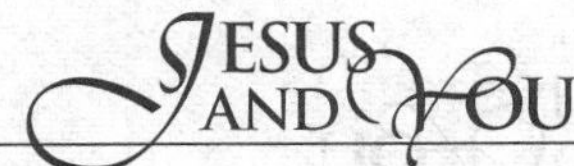

WHITEWASHED LIES

The Hebrew word translated "whitewashed" (Ezekiel 13:15) literally means "to plaster over," conveying the idea of filling in a crack in a wall with plaster and then painting over it to conceal the repair (Ezekiel 13:10–11). Ezekiel as one of God's true prophets reminded the people that false prophets merely whitewashed the problem of sin. Sin is undeniably real, like an enormous and unsightly crack in the plaster of our spiritual lives. We might be able to make the wall look good by covering it over, but underneath the paint it is about to crumble. Jesus used the same image, comparing the religious leaders to "whitewashed tombs" (Matthew 23:27–28). A tomb may look presentable on the outside, but inside it is full of decaying flesh and the bones of the dead. Although our lives might appear intact to other people, unless the crumbling fracture of sin has been attacked and addressed at the very core, any superficial cosmetic attempts we make to cover over our miserable condition are destined to fail. Only Jesus Christ can repair the damage from the inside out, enabling us to stand erect and strong and to enjoy a right and pure relationship with God (Romans 6:1–14; 2 Corinthians 5:17).

hands, and they will no longer fall prey
to your power. Then you will know that 13:21
I am the LORD.[o] 22Because you disheart- o Ps 91:3
ened the righteous with your lies, when
I had brought them no grief, and because you encouraged the wicked not to
turn from their evil ways and so save 13:22
their lives,[p] 23therefore you will no p Jer 23:14; Eze 33:14-16
longer see false visions or practice div-
ination.[q] I will save my people from your 13:23
hands. And then you will know that I am q ver 6; Eze 12:24
the LORD.[r]' " r Mic 3:6

Idolaters Condemned

14 Some of the elders of Israel
came to me and sat down in 14:1
front of me.[s] 2Then the word of the LORD s Eze 8:1; 20:1
came to me: 3"Son of man, these men
have set up idols in their hearts and put 14:3
wicked stumbling blocks[t] before their t ver 7; Eze 7:19
faces. Should I let them inquire of me at u Isa 1:15; Eze 20:31
all?[u] 4Therefore speak to them and tell
them, 'This is what the Sovereign LORD
says: When any Israelite sets up idols in
his heart and puts a wicked stumbling
block before his face and then goes to a
prophet, I the LORD will answer him myself in keeping with his great idolatry. 5I
will do this to recapture the hearts of the
people of Israel, who have all deserted[v] 14:5
me for their idols.'[w] v Zec 11:8 w Jer 2:11
6"Therefore say to the house of Israel,
'This is what the Sovereign LORD says:
Repent! Turn from your idols and re- 14:6
nounce all your detestable practices![x] x Isa 2:20; 30:22
7" 'When any Israelite or any alien[y] liv- 14:7
ing in Israel separates himself from me y Ex 12:48; 20:10
and sets up idols in his heart and puts a
wicked stumbling block before his face
and then goes to a prophet to inquire of
me, I the LORD will answer him myself. 8I
will set my face against[z] that man and 14:8
make him an example and a byword.[a] I z Eze 15:7 a Eze 5:15
will cut him off from my people. Then
you will know that I am the LORD.
9" 'And if the prophet[b] is enticed[c] to 14:9
utter a prophecy, I the LORD have enticed b Jer 14:15 c Jer 4:10
that prophet, and I will stretch out my d 1Ki 22:23
hand against him and destroy him from
among my people Israel.[d] 10They will
bear their guilt—the prophet will be as
guilty as the one who consults him.
11Then the people of Israel will no longer 14:11
stray[e] from me, nor will they defile them- e Eze 48:11
selves anymore with all their sins. They f Eze 11:19-20; 37:23
will be my people, and I will be their God,
declares the Sovereign LORD.[f]' "

Judgment Inescapable

12 The word of the LORD came to me:
13 "Son of man, if a country sins against
me by being unfaithful and I stretch out
14:13 my hand against it to cut off its food
g Lev 26:26 supply[g] and send famine upon it and kill
h Eze 5:16; 6:14; its men and their animals,[h] 14 even if
15:8 these three men—Noah,[i] Daniel[a][j] and
14:14 Job[k]—were in it, they could save only
i Ge 6:8 j ver 20; Eze 28:3; themselves by their righteousness,[l] de-
Da 1:6; 6:13 k Job 1:1 clares the Sovereign LORD.
l Job 42:9; 15 "Or if I send wild beasts[m] through
Jer 15:1; Eze 18:20 that country and they leave it childless
and it becomes desolate so that no one
14:15 can pass through it because of the
m Eze 5:17 n Lev 26:22 beasts,[n] 16 as surely as I live, declares the
Sovereign LORD, even if these three men
were in it, they could not save their own
14:16 sons or daughters. They alone would be
o Eze 18:20 saved, but the land would be desolate.[o]
14:17 17 "Or if I bring a sword[p] against that
p Lev 26:25; country and say, 'Let the sword pass
Eze 5:12; 21:3-4 throughout the land,' and I kill its men
q Eze 25:13; Zep 1:3 and their animals,[q] 18 as surely as I live,
declares the Sovereign LORD, even if
these three men were in it, they could
not save their own sons or daughters.
They alone would be saved.
14:19 19 "Or if I send a plague into that land
r Eze 7:8 and pour out my wrath[r] upon it through
s Eze 38:22 bloodshed, killing its men and their animals,[s] 20 as surely as I live, declares the
Sovereign LORD, even if Noah, Daniel
and Job were in it, they could save nei-
14:20 ther son nor daughter. They would save
t ver 14 only themselves by their righteousness.[t]
21 "For this is what the Sovereign LORD
says: How much worse will it be when I
send against Jerusalem my four dreadful
judgments—sword and famine and wild
14:21 beasts and plague—to kill its men and
u Jer 15:3; Eze 5:17; 33:27; their animals![u] 22 Yet there will be some
Am 4:6-10; Rev 6:8 survivors—sons and daughters who will
be brought out of it.[v] They will come to
14:22 you, and when you see their conduct[w]
v Eze 12:16 w Eze 20:43 and their actions, you will be consoled
regarding the disaster I have brought
upon Jerusalem—every disaster I have
brought upon it. 23 You will be consoled
when you see their conduct and their
actions, for you will know that I have
14:23 done nothing in it without cause, de-
x Jer 22:8-9 clares the Sovereign LORD.[x]"

Jerusalem, A Useless Vine

15 The word of the LORD came to
me: 2 "Son of man, how is the
15:2 y Isa 5:1-7; wood of a vine[y] better than that of a
Jer 2:21; branch on any of the trees in the forest?
Hos 10:1 3 Is wood ever taken from it to make anything useful? Do they make pegs from it
to hang things on? 4 And after it is
thrown on the fire as fuel and the fire
15:4 burns both ends and chars the middle,
z Eze 19:14; Jn 15:6 is it then useful for anything?[z] 5 If it was
not useful for anything when it was
whole, how much less can it be made
into something useful when the fire has
burned it and it is charred?
6 "Therefore this is what the Sovereign
LORD says: As I have given the wood of
the vine among the trees of the forest as
fuel for the fire, so will I treat the people
15:7 living in Jerusalem. 7 I will set my face
a Ps 34:16; Eze 14:8 against[a] them. Although they have
b Isa 24:18; come out of the fire, the fire will yet con-
Am 9:1-4 sume them. And when I set my face
against them, you will know that I am
the LORD.[b] 8 I will make the land deso-
15:8 c Eze 14:13 late[c] because they have been unfaith-
d Eze 17:20 ful,[d] declares the Sovereign LORD."

[a] 14 Or *Danel*; the Hebrew spelling may suggest a person other than the prophet Daniel; also in verse 20.

JESUS AND YOU

USELESS VINES

The symbol of a grapevine, or vineyard, is frequently used in the Bible to represent Israel (Genesis 49:22; Psalm 80:8; Isaiah 3:14; 5:1; 27:2; Jeremiah 2:21; Hosea 10:1). Ezekiel added a surprising twist to the image, however, referring to the vine as useless firewood (Ezekiel 15:4). God was declaring through Ezekiel that he would treat the people of Jerusalem like a grapevine that was producing no grapes (verse 6) and that the city would be destroyed. Jesus later compared the people of Jerusalem to a fig tree that failed to produce fruit (Mark 11:12–14). "May no one ever eat fruit from you again," he cursed the tree, and the blighted tree immediately withered. When we are graciously and lovingly drawn close to the Father's heart, our lives will reflect our gratitude by what we say and by what we do. Only God the Son is the true, living vine, and God the Father is the gardener. Jesus stated that every branch that does not bear fruit will be cut off, thrown into the fire and burned (John 15:1–6). The evidence of real growth in the life of an individual is the quality of the fruit produced in that person's life (Galatians 5:22–23; Ephesians 5:9; Philippians 1:11).

An Allegory of Unfaithful Jerusalem

16 The word of the LORD came to
me: 2"Son of man, confront Jerusalem with her detestable practices[e]
3and say, 'This is what the Sovereign
LORD says to Jerusalem: Your ancestry[f]
and birth were in the land of the
Canaanites; your father was an Amorite
and your mother a Hittite.[g] 4On the day
you were born[h] your cord was not cut,
nor were you washed with water to
make you clean, nor were you rubbed
with salt or wrapped in cloths. 5No one
looked on you with pity or had compassion enough to do any of these things for
you. Rather, you were thrown out into
the open field, for on the day you were
born you were despised.

6" 'Then I passed by and saw you kicking about in your blood, and as you lay
there in your blood I said to you,
"Live!"[a][i] 7I made you grow[j] like a plant of
the field. You grew up and developed
and became the most beautiful of jewels.[b] Your breasts were formed and your
hair grew, you who were naked and
bare.[k]

8" 'Later I passed by, and when I
looked at you and saw that you were old
enough for love, I spread the corner of
my garment[l] over you and covered your
nakedness. I gave you my solemn oath
and entered into a covenant with you,
declares the Sovereign LORD, and you became mine.[m]

9" 'I bathed[c] you with water and
washed[n] the blood from you and put
ointments on you. 10I clothed you with
an embroidered[o] dress and put leather
sandals on you. I dressed you in fine
linen[p] and covered you with costly garments.[q] 11I adorned you with jewelry:[r] I
put bracelets[s] on your arms and a necklace[t] around your neck, 12and I put a
ring on your nose,[u] earrings on your ears
and a beautiful crown[v] on your head.
13So you were adorned with gold and silver; your clothes were of fine linen and
costly fabric and embroidered cloth.
Your food was fine flour, honey and olive
oil.[w] You became very beautiful and rose
to be a queen.[x] 14And your fame[y] spread
among the nations on account of your
beauty,[z] because the splendor I had giv-
en you made your beauty perfect, declares the Sovereign LORD.

15" 'But you trusted in your beauty and
used your fame to become a prostitute.
You lavished your favors on anyone who
passed by[a] and your beauty became
his.[d][b] 16You took some of your garments
to make gaudy high places, where you
carried on your prostitution.[c] Such
things should not happen, nor should
they ever occur. 17You also took the fine
jewelry I gave you, the jewelry made of
my gold and silver, and you made for
yourself male idols and engaged in prostitution with them.[d] 18And you took your
embroidered clothes to put on them, and
you offered my oil and incense before
them. 19Also the food I provided for
you—the fine flour, olive oil and honey I
gave you to eat—you offered as fragrant
incense before them. That is what happened, declares the Sovereign LORD.[e]

16:2 [e] Eze 20:4; 22:2
16:3 [f] Eze 21:30 [g] ver 45
16:4 [h] Hos 2:3
16:6 [i] Ex 19:4
16:7 [j] Dt 1:10
16:7 [k] Ex 1:7
16:8 [l] Ru 3:9 [m] Jer 2:2; Hos 2:7,19-20
16:9 [n] Ru 3:3
16:10 [o] Ex 26:36 [p] Eze 27:16 [q] ver 18
16:11 [r] Eze 23:40 [s] Isa 3:19; Eze 23:42 [t] Ge 41:42
16:12 [u] Isa 3:21 [v] Isa 28:5; Jer 13:18
16:13 [w] 1Sa 10:1 [x] Dt 32:13-14; 1Ki 4:21
16:14 [y] 1Ki 10:24 [z] La 2:15
16:15 [a] ver 25 [b] Isa 57:8; Jer 2:20; Eze 23:3; 27:3
16:16 [c] 2Ki 23:7
16:17 [d] Eze 7:20
16:19 [e] Hos 2:8

JESUS FOCUS

AN ABANDONED BABY

In Ezekiel 16:1–5 God described Jerusalem as an abandoned baby, and he went so far as to taunt the people in a seemingly derisive tone: "Your father was an Amorite and your mother a Hittite" (verse 3). These two nations represented the people who had originally lived in Jerusalem before God had chosen it as his holy city and given it to the Israelites (Joshua 11:3; 15:63; Judges 3:5–6; 2 Samuel 5:6–9). The people had forgotten where they had been before God had found them, and in goading them like this God was reminding his arrogant people that he alone was the One who had provided both for themselves and for their city. In a later century Jesus repeatedly confronted the citizens of Jerusalem with the fact that they were taking their position of favor with God for granted. Jesus also frequently spoke harsh words in order to get his point across. In one instance he informed the people that their father wasn't God at all but the murdering and lying Satan (John 8:44), adding tersely that "the reason you do not hear is that you do not belong to God" (John 8:47). Because of their sins, the people had once again become like a helpless infant abandoned and at the mercy of the elements.

[a] 6 A few Hebrew manuscripts, Septuagint and Syriac; most Hebrew manuscripts *"Live!" And as you lay there in your blood I said to you, "Live!"*
[b] 7 Or *became mature*
[c] 9 Or *I had bathed*
[d] 15 Most Hebrew manuscripts; one Hebrew manuscript (see some Septuagint manuscripts) *by. Such a thing should not happen*

16:20 20 “ ‘And you took your sons and
f Jer 7:31 daughters[f] whom you bore to me[g] and
g Ex 13:2 sacrificed them as food to the idols. Was
h Ps 106:37-38; your prostitution not enough?[h] 21 You
Isa 57:5; slaughtered my children and sacrificed
Eze 23:37 16:21 them[a] to the idols.[i] 22 In all your de-
i 2Ki 17:17; testable practices and your prostitution
Jer 19:5 you did not remember the days of your
16:22 youth,[j] when you were naked and bare,
j Jer 2:2; Hos 11:1 k ver 6 kicking about in your blood.[k]
23 “ ‘Woe! Woe to you, declares the
Sovereign LORD. In addition to all your
16:24 other wickedness, 24 you built a mound
l ver 31; Isa 57:7 for yourself and made a lofty shrine[l] in
m Ps 78:58; every public square.[m] 25 At the head of
Jer 2:20; 3:2; every street you built your lofty shrines
Eze 20:28 and degraded your beauty, offering your
16:25 body with increasing promiscuity to
n ver 15; Pr 9:14 anyone who passed by.[n] 26 You engaged
16:26 in prostitution with the Egyptians, your
o Eze 8:17 lustful neighbors, and provoked[o] me to
p Eze 20:8; anger with your increasing promiscu-
23:19-21 ity.[p] 27 So I stretched out my hand[q]
16:27 against you and reduced your territory;
q Eze 20:33 I gave you over to the greed of your ene-
r 2Ch 28:18 mies, the daughters of the Philistines,[r]
who were shocked by your lewd con-
duct. 28 You engaged in prostitution with
16:28 the Assyrians[s] too, because you were in-
s 2Ki 16:7 satiable; and even after that, you still
were not satisfied. 29 Then you increased
16:29 your promiscuity to include Babylonia,[b][t]
t Eze 23:14-17 a land of merchants, but even with this
you were not satisfied.
30 “ ‘How weak-willed you are, declares
the Sovereign LORD, when you do all
these things, acting like a brazen prosti-
16:30 tute![u] 31 When you built your mounds at
u Jer 3:3 the head of every street and made your
16:31 lofty shrines[v] in every public square, you
v ver 24 were unlike a prostitute, because you
scorned payment.
32 “ ‘You adulterous wife! You prefer
strangers to your own husband! 33 Every
prostitute receives a fee, but you give
16:33 gifts[w] to all your lovers, bribing them to
w Isa 30:6; 57:9 come to you from everywhere for your
x Hos 8:9-10 illicit favors.[x] 34 So in your prostitution
you are the opposite of others; no one
runs after you for your favors. You are
the very opposite, for you give payment
and none is given to you.
35 “ ‘Therefore, you prostitute, hear the
word of the LORD! 36 This is what the Sovereign LORD says: Because you poured
out your wealth[c] and exposed your
nakedness in your promiscuity with
your lovers, and because of all your detestable idols, and because you gave 16:36
them your children's blood,[y] 37 therefore y Jer 19:5;
I am going to gather all your lovers, with Eze 23:10
whom you found pleasure, those you
loved as well as those you hated. I will
gather them against you from all around
and will strip you in front of them, and 16:37
they will see all your nakedness.[z] 38 I will z Jer 13:22
sentence you to the punishment of
women who commit adultery and who 16:38
shed blood;[a] I will bring upon you the a Eze 23:45
blood vengeance of my wrath and jeal- b Lev 20:10;
ous anger.[b] 39 Then I will hand you over Eze 23:25
to your lovers, and they will tear down
your mounds and destroy your lofty
shrines. They will strip you of your
clothes and take your fine jewelry and 16:39
leave you naked and bare.[c] 40 They will c Eze 23:26;
bring a mob against you, who will stone[d] Hos 2:3
you and hack you to pieces with their 16:40
swords. 41 They will burn down[e] your d Jn 8:5,7
houses and inflict punishment on you in 16:41
the sight of many women.[f] I will put a e Dt 13:16
stop[g] to your prostitution, and you will f Eze 23:10
no longer pay your lovers. 42 Then my g Eze 23:27,48
wrath against you will subside and my
jealous anger will turn away from you; I 16:42
will be calm and no longer angry.[h] h Isa 54:9;
43 “ ‘Because you did not remember[i] Eze 5:13; 39:29
the days of your youth but enraged me 16:43
with all these things, I will surely bring i Ps 78:42
down[j] on your head what you have j Eze 22:31
done, declares the Sovereign LORD. Did k ver 22;
you not add lewdness to all your other Eze 11:21
detestable practices?[k]
44 “ ‘Everyone who quotes proverbs
will quote this proverb about you: “Like
mother, like daughter.” 45 You are a true
daughter of your mother, who despised
her husband and her children; and you
are a true sister of your sisters, who despised their husbands and their children. Your mother was a Hittite and 16:45
your father an Amorite.[l] 46 Your older sis- l Eze 23:2
ter was Samaria, who lived to the north
of you with her daughters; and your
younger sister, who lived to the south of 16:46
you with her daughters, was Sodom.[m] m Ge 13:10-13;
47 You not only walked in their ways and Eze 23:4
copied their detestable practices, but in
all your ways you soon became more de- 16:47
praved than they.[n] 48 As surely as I live, n 2Ki 21:9;
declares the Sovereign LORD, your sister Eze 5:7
Sodom and her daughters never did

[a] 21 Or *and made them pass through ⌞the fire⌟*
[b] 29 Or *Chaldea* [c] 36 Or *lust*

16:48 [o] Mt 10:15; 11:23-24 what you and your daughters have
done.[o]
49“ ‘Now this was the sin of your sister
16:49 [p] Ge 13:13 [q] Ps 138:6 [r] Eze 18:7,12,16; Lk 12:16-20 Sodom:[p] She and her daughters were arrogant,[q] overfed and unconcerned; they
did not help the poor and needy.[r] 50They
were haughty and did detestable things
before me. Therefore I did away with
16:50 [s] Ge 18:20-21; 19:5 them as you have seen.[s] 51Samaria did
not commit half the sins you did. You
have done more detestable things than
they, and have made your sisters seem
righteous by all these things you have
16:51 [t] Jer 3:8-11 done.[t] 52Bear your disgrace, for you have
furnished some justification for your sis-
ters. Because your sins were more vile
than theirs, they appear more righteous
than you. So then, be ashamed and bear
your disgrace, for you have made your
sisters appear righteous.
16:53 [u] Isa 19:24-25 53“ ‘However, I will restore[u] the fortunes of Sodom and her daughters and
of Samaria and her daughters, and your
fortunes along with them, 54so that you
16:54 [v] Jer 2:26; Eze 14:22 may bear your disgrace[v] and be
ashamed of all you have done in giving
them comfort. 55And your sisters, Sodom with her daughters and Samaria
with her daughters, will return to what
they were before; and you and your
daughters will return to what you were
16:55 [w] Mal 3:4 before.[w] 56You would not even mention
your sister Sodom in the day of your
pride, 57before your wickedness was uncovered. Even so, you are now scorned
16:57 [x] 2Ki 16:6 by the daughters of Edom[a x] and all her
neighbors and the daughters of the Phi-
listines—all those around you who despise you. 58You will bear the consequences of your lewdness and your
16:58 [y] Eze 23:49 detestable practices, declares the LORD.[y]
59“ ‘This is what the Sovereign LORD
says: I will deal with you as you deserve,
because you have despised my oath by
16:59 [z] Eze 17:19 breaking the covenant.[z] 60Yet I will remember the covenant I made with you
in the days of your youth, and I will es-
16:60 [a] Jer 32:40; Eze 37:26 tablish an everlasting covenant[a] with
you. 61Then you will remember your
16:61 [b] Eze 20:43 ways and be ashamed[b] when you receive
your sisters, both those who are older
than you and those who are younger. I
will give them to you as daughters, but
not on the basis of my covenant with
16:62 [c] Jer 24:7; Eze 20:37,43-44; Hos 2:19-20 you. 62So I will establish my covenant
with you, and you will know that I am
the LORD.[c] 63Then, when I make atone-
ment[d] for you for all you have done, you 16:63 [d] Ps 65:3; 79:9 [e] Ro 3:19 [f] Ps 39:9; Da 9:7-8
will remember and be ashamed and
never again open your mouth[e] because
of your humiliation, declares the Sovereign LORD.[f]”

Two Eagles and a Vine

17 The word of the LORD came to
me: 2“Son of man, set forth an
allegory and tell the house of Israel a 17:2 [g] Eze 20:49
parable.[g] 3Say to them, ‘This is what the
Sovereign LORD says: A great eagle[h] with 17:3 [h] Hos 8:1 [i] Jer 22:23
powerful wings, long feathers and full
plumage of varied colors came to Lebanon.[i] Taking hold of the top of a cedar,
4he broke off its topmost shoot and carried it away to a land of merchants,
where he planted it in a city of traders.
5“ ‘He took some of the seed of your
land and put it in fertile soil. He planted 17:5 [j] Dt 8:7-9; Isa 44:4
it like a willow by abundant water,[j] 6and
it sprouted and became a low, spreading
vine. Its branches turned toward him,
but its roots remained under it. So it became a vine and produced branches and
put out leafy boughs.
7“ ‘But there was another great eagle
with powerful wings and full plumage.
The vine now sent out its roots toward
him from the plot where it was planted
and stretched out its branches to him 17:7 [k] Eze 31:4
for water.[k] 8It had been planted in good
soil by abundant water so that it would
produce branches, bear fruit and become a splendid vine.’
9“Say to them, ‘This is what the Sovereign LORD says: Will it thrive? Will it
not be uprooted and stripped of its fruit
so that it withers? All its new growth
will wither. It will not take a strong arm
or many people to pull it up by the roots.
10Even if it[l] is transplanted, will it thrive? 17:10 [l] Hos 13:15
Will it not wither completely when the
east wind strikes it—wither away in the
plot where it grew?’ ”
11Then the word of the LORD came to
me: 12“Say to this rebellious house, ‘Do
you not know what these things 17:12 [m] Eze 12:9 [n] 2Ki 24:15 [o] Eze 24:19
mean?[m]’ Say to them: ‘The king of Bab-
ylon went to Jerusalem and carried off
her king and her nobles,[n] bringing them
back with him to Babylon.[o] 13Then he
took a member of the royal family and
made a treaty with him, putting him un-

[a] 57 Many Hebrew manuscripts and Syriac; most Hebrew manuscripts, Septuagint and Vulgate *Aram*

der oath.[p] He also carried away the leading men of the land, 14so that the kingdom would be brought low,[q] unable to
rise again, surviving only by keeping his
treaty. 15But the king rebelled[r] against
him by sending his envoys to Egypt to
get horses and a large army.[s] Will he succeed? Will he who does such things escape? Will he break the treaty and yet
escape?[t]

16" 'As surely as I live, declares the Sovereign LORD, he shall die[u] in Babylon, in
the land of the king who put him on the
throne, whose oath he despised and
whose treaty he broke.[v] 17Pharaoh[w] with
his mighty army and great horde will be
of no help to him in war, when ramps[x]
are built and siege works erected to destroy many lives.[y] 18He despised the oath
by breaking the covenant. Because he
had given his hand in pledge[z] and yet
did all these things, he shall not escape.

19" 'Therefore this is what the Sovereign LORD says: As surely as I live, I will
bring down on his head my oath that he
despised and my covenant that he broke.[a]
20I will spread my net[b] for him, and he will
be caught in my snare. I will bring him to
Babylon and execute judgment[c] upon
him there because he was unfaithful to
me. 21All his fleeing troops will fall by the
sword,[d] and the survivors[e] will be scattered to the winds.[f] Then you will know
that I the LORD have spoken.

22" 'This is what the Sovereign LORD
says: I myself will take a shoot from the
very top of a cedar and plant it; I will
break off a tender sprig from its topmost
shoots and plant it on a high and lofty
mountain.[g] 23On the mountain heights
of Israel I will plant it; it will produce
branches and bear fruit and become a
splendid cedar. Birds of every kind will
nest in it; they will find shelter in the
shade of its branches.[h] 24All the trees of
the field[i] will know that I the LORD bring
down the tall tree and make the low tree
grow tall. I dry up the green tree and
make the dry tree flourish.

" 'I the LORD have spoken, and I will
do it.[j] "

17:13 p 2Ch 36:13
17:14 q Eze 29:14
17:15 r Jer 52:3 s Dt 17:16 t Jer 34:3; 38:18
17:16 u Jer 52:11; Eze 12:13 v 2Ki 24:17
17:17 w Jer 37:7 x Eze 4:2 y Isa 36:6; Jer 37:5; Eze 29:6-7
17:18 z 1Ch 29:24
17:19 a Eze 16:59
17:20 b Eze 12:13; 32:3 c Jer 2:35; Eze 20:36
17:21 d Eze 12:14 e 2Ki 25:11 f 2Ki 25:5
17:22 g Jer 23:5; Eze 20:40; 36:1, 36; 37:22
17:23 h Ps 92:12; Isa 2:2; Eze 31:6; Da 4:12; Hos 14:5-7; Mt 13:32
17:24 i Ps 96:12 j Eze 19:12; 21:26; 22:14; Am 9:11

The Soul Who Sins Will Die

18 The word of the LORD came to
me: 2"What do you people
mean by quoting this proverb about the
land of Israel:

" 'The fathers eat sour grapes,
and the children's teeth are set
on edge'?[k]

3"As surely as I live, declares the Sovereign LORD, you will no longer quote
this proverb in Israel. 4For every living
soul belongs to me, the father as well as
the son—both alike belong to me. The
soul who sins is the one who will die.[l]

5"Suppose there is a righteous man
who does what is just and right.
6He does not eat at the mountain[m]
shrines
or look to the idols[n] of the house
of Israel.
He does not defile his neighbor's wife
or lie with a woman during her
period.
7He does not oppress[o] anyone,
but returns what he took in
pledge[p] for a loan.
He does not commit robbery
but gives his food to the hungry
and provides clothing for the
naked.[q]
8He does not lend at usury
or take excessive interest.[a][r]
He withholds his hand from doing
wrong
and judges fairly[s] between man
and man.
9He follows my decrees
and faithfully keeps my laws.
That man is righteous;[t]
he will surely live,[u]
declares the Sovereign
LORD.

10"Suppose he has a violent son, who
sheds blood[v] or does any of these other
things[b] 11(though the father has done
none of them):

"He eats at the mountain shrines.
He defiles his neighbor's wife.
12He oppresses the poor[w] and needy.
He commits robbery.
He does not return what he took in
pledge.
He looks to the idols.
He does detestable things.[x]
13He lends at usury and takes
excessive interest.[y]

Will such a man live? He will not! Because he has done all these detestable

18:2 k Isa 3:15; Jer 31:29; La 5:7
18:4 l ver 20; Isa 42:5; Ro 6:23
18:6 m Eze 22:9 n Dt 4:19; Eze 6:13; 20:24
18:7 o Ex 22:21 p Ex 22:26; Dt 24:12 q Dt 15:11; Mt 25:36
18:8 r Ex 22:25; Lev 25:35-37; Dt 23:19-20 s Zec 8:16
18:9 t Hab 2:4 u Lev 18:5; Eze 20:11; Am 5:4
18:10 v Ex 21:12
18:12 w Am 4:1 x 2Ki 21:11; Isa 59:6-7; Jer 22:17; Eze 8:6,17
18:13 y Ex 22:25

[a] 8 Or *take interest*; similarly in verses 13 and 17
[b] 10 Or *things to a brother*

THE BLAME GAME

A popular maxim during Ezekiel's day went like this: "The fathers eat sour grapes, and the children's teeth are set on edge" (Ezekiel 18:2). The prophet Jeremiah had cited this proverb as well, predicting that the days of this saying were numbered in the land (Jeremiah 31:29). Now Ezekiel was declaring that the day had come; by divine decree this proverb was no longer to be quoted in Israel (Ezekiel 18:3) but was to be replaced with a new thesis: "The soul that sins is the one who will die" (verses 4,20).

Rightly applied, the "sour grapes" proverb isn't necessarily a bad one. The Bible does teach that people's sins can and often do have a negative effect on their descendants (Exodus 20:5; 34:6–7; Numbers 14:18). Certainly much of the suffering experienced during the exile could be traced back to the persistent rebellion, idolatry and covenant unfaithfulness of previous generations of Israelites (Ezekiel 16:1–59). The exile was, in effect, the appropriate consequence for these accumulating acts of disobedience.

The problem for the people in the time of Jeremiah and Ezekiel was that they had seized on this idea as an ideal way to disavow personal responsibility and remove themselves from blame. In essence, they were positioning themselves as innocent victims of an unfair God, snared in the trap of divine retribution meted out indiscriminately.

But Ezekiel, serving as an instrument to declare God's truth, would refuse to endorse the "blame game." Ezekiel eloquently made the case that everyone was equally accountable before God for the stewardship of life. The only appropriate response to the "bad news" of personal accountability is the Good News of God's offer of forgiveness to all who turn to him in repentance and faith.

The Old Testament prophet sounds strikingly similar to the New Testament prophet John the Baptist: "Repent and live!" (Ezekiel 18:32; see also Matthew 3:2; Mark 1:15). The great Good News of the gospel is this: God removes our guilt, erasing it forever from our record (Psalms 51:1,9; 103:11–12; Micah 7:18–19; Acts 3:19; Hebrews 8:12) because of the redemptive work of our precious Savior, Jesus Christ, God's one and only Son (Romans 5:6–11; Ephesians 2:1–8; Colossians 1:19–22).

The wonderful promise of salvation through the blood of Jesus and the gift of the empowering Holy Spirit are for us and for our children (Acts 2:39), to be accepted anew by each individual member of each succeeding generation. God's desire for each of us, a desire he has gone to great lengths to communicate to us, is life—full, abundant, overflowing life (Ezekiel 16:6; 18:23,32; 1 Timothy 2:4; 2 Peter 3:9). This life he has given us in Jesus Christ, his Son, the One whose very purpose in coming to this earth was "that [we] may have life, and have it to the full" (John 10:10).

Self-Discovery: *Can you think of some examples from your own life when you shifted blame from yourself to someone or something else? You may want to spend some time in personal confession, acknowledging your responsibility and receiving the Lord's refreshing and grace-filled offer of forgiveness and a fresh start.*

GO TO DISCOVERY 210 ON PAGE 1099

things, he will surely be put to death and
his blood will be on his own head.[z]
14"But suppose this son has a son who
sees all the sins his father commits, and
though he sees them, he does not do
such things:[a]

15"He does not eat at the mountain
shrines
or look to the idols of the house
of Israel.
He does not defile his neighbor's
wife.
16He does not oppress anyone
or require a pledge for a loan.
He does not commit robbery
but gives his food to the hungry
and provides clothing for the
naked.[b]
17He withholds his hand from sin[a]
and takes no usury or excessive
interest.
He keeps my laws and follows my
decrees.

He will not die for his father's sin; he will
surely live. 18But his father will die for his
own sin, because he practiced extortion,
robbed his brother and did what was
wrong among his people.
19"Yet you ask, 'Why does the son not
share the guilt of his father?' Since the
son has done what is just and right and
has been careful to keep all my decrees,
he will surely live.[c] 20The soul who sins is
the one who will die. The son will not
share the guilt of the father, nor will the
father share the guilt of the son. The righteousness of the righteous man will be
credited to him, and the wickedness of
the wicked will be charged against him.[d]
21"But if a wicked man turns away
from all the sins he has committed and
keeps all my decrees and does what is
just and right, he will surely live; he will
not die.[e] 22None of the offenses he has
committed will be remembered against
him. Because of the righteous things he
has done, he will live.[f] 23Do I take any
pleasure in the death of the wicked? declares the Sovereign LORD. Rather, am I
not pleased[g] when they turn from their
ways and live?[h]
24"But if a righteous man turns from
his righteousness and commits sin and
does the same detestable things the
wicked man does, will he live? None of
the righteous things he has done will be

18:13 [z] Eze 33:4-5
18:14 [a] 2Ch 34:21; Pr 23:24
18:16 [b] Ps 41:1; Isa 58:10
18:19 [c] Ex 20:5; Dt 5:9; Jer 15:4; Zec 1:3-6
18:20 [d] Dt 24:16; 1Ki 8:32; 2Ki 14:6; Isa 3:11; Mt 16:27; Ro 2:9
18:21 [e] Eze 33:12,19
18:22 [f] Ps 18:20-24; Isa 43:25; Mic 7:19
18:23 [g] Ps 147:11 [h] Eze 33:11; 1Ti 2:4

remembered. Because of the unfaithfulness he is guilty of and because of the
sins he has committed, he will die.[i]
25"Yet you say, 'The way of the Lord is
not just.' Hear, O house of Israel: Is my
way unjust?[j] Is it not your ways that are
unjust? 26If a righteous man turns from
his righteousness and commits sin, he
will die for it; because of the sin he has
committed he will die. 27But if a wicked
man turns away from the wickedness he
has committed and does what is just and
right, he will save his life.[k] 28Because he
considers all the offenses he has committed and turns away from them, he will
surely live; he will not die. 29Yet the house
of Israel says, 'The way of the Lord is not
just.' Are my ways unjust, O house of Israel? Is it not your ways that are unjust?
30"Therefore, O house of Israel, I will
judge you, each one according to his
ways, declares the Sovereign LORD. Repent![l] Turn away from all your offenses;
then sin will not be your downfall.[m]
31Rid yourselves of all the offenses you
have committed, and get a new heart[n]
and a new spirit. Why will you die,
O house of Israel?[o] 32For I take no pleasure in the death of anyone, declares the
Sovereign LORD. Repent and live![p]

A Lament for Israel's Princes

19 "Take up a lament[q] concerning
the princes[r] of Israel 2and say:

"'What a lioness was your mother
among the lions!
She lay down among the young
lions
and reared her cubs.
3She brought up one of her cubs,
and he became a strong lion.
He learned to tear the prey
and he devoured men.
4The nations heard about him,
and he was trapped in their pit.
They led him with hooks
to the land of Egypt.[s]

5"'When she saw her hope
unfulfilled,
her expectation gone,
she took another of her cubs
and made him a strong lion.[t]
6He prowled among the lions,
for he was now a strong lion.

[a] *17* Septuagint (see also verse 8); Hebrew *from the poor*

18:24 [i] 1Sa 15:11; 2Ch 24:17-20; Eze 3:20; 20:27; 2Pe 2:20-22
18:25 [j] Ge 18:25; Jer 12:1; Eze 33:17; Zep 3:5; Mal 2:17; 3:13-15
18:27 [k] Isa 1:18
18:30 [l] Mt 3:2 [m] Eze 7:3; 33:20; Hos 12:6
18:31 [n] Ps 51:10 [o] Isa 1:16-17; Eze 11:19; 36:26
18:32 [p] Eze 33:11
19:1 [q] Eze 26:17; 27:2,32 [r] 2Ki 24:6
19:4 [s] 2Ki 23:33-34; 2Ch 36:4
19:5 [t] 2Ki 23:34

He learned to tear the prey
and he devoured men.[u]
7 He broke down[a] their strongholds
and devastated[v] their towns.
The land and all who were in it
were terrified by his roaring.
8 Then the nations[w] came against him,
those from regions round about.
They spread their net for him,
and he was trapped in their pit.[x]
9 With hooks they pulled him into a cage
and brought him to the king of Babylon.[y]
They put him in prison,
so his roar was heard no longer
on the mountains of Israel.[z]

10 " 'Your mother was like a vine in your vineyard[b]
planted by the water;
it was fruitful and full of branches
because of abundant water.[a]
11 Its branches were strong,
fit for a ruler's scepter.
It towered high
above the thick foliage,
conspicuous for its height
and for its many branches.[b]
12 But it was uprooted[c] in fury
and thrown to the ground.
The east wind made it shrivel,
it was stripped of its fruit;
its strong branches withered

19:6 [u] 2Ki 24:9; 2Ch 36:9
19:7 [v] Eze 30:12
19:8 [w] 2Ki 24:2 [x] 2Ki 24:11
19:9 [y] 2Ch 36:6 [z] 2Ki 24:15
19:10 [a] Ps 80:8-11
19:11 [b] Eze 31:3; Da 4:11
19:12 [c] Eze 17:10

JESUS FOCUS

THE LION'S ROAR

The lion, renowned for its agility and strength as well as for its spine-tingling roar, was the symbol of the tribe of Judah (Genesis 49:9). In Ezekiel 19:1–9 the prophet used the image of a lion in an unusual way in order to provide the people with yet another clear illustration of how they were behaving—like docile lion cubs captured one after another by hunters, the first being transported to Egypt and the second to Babylon. When the kings from David's royal family had been expelled from power, Judah's roar was silenced. But we read in the New Testament that "the Lion of the tribe of Judah, the Root of David, has triumphed" (Revelation 5:5). With the death and resurrection of Jesus, God's conquering Son, the Lion of Judah sprang back to life and its mighty roar shattered the silence once again.

and fire consumed them.[d]
13 Now it is planted in the desert,[e]
in a dry and thirsty land.[f]
14 Fire spread from one of its main[c] branches
and consumed[g] its fruit.
No strong branch is left on it
fit for a ruler's scepter.'[h]

This is a lament and is to be used as a lament."

Rebellious Israel

20 In the seventh year, in the fifth month on the tenth day, some of the elders of Israel came to inquire of the LORD, and they sat down in front of me.[i]

2 Then the word of the LORD came to me: 3 "Son of man, speak to the elders of Israel and say to them, 'This is what the Sovereign LORD says: Have you come to inquire[j] of me? As surely as I live, I will not let you inquire of me, declares the Sovereign LORD.[k]'

4 "Will you judge them? Will you judge them, son of man? Then confront them with the detestable practices of their fathers[l] 5 and say to them: 'This is what the Sovereign LORD says: On the day I chose[m] Israel, I swore with uplifted hand to the descendants of the house of Jacob and revealed myself to them in Egypt. With uplifted hand I said to them, "I am the LORD your God.[n]" 6 On that day I swore to them that I would bring them out of Egypt into a land I had searched out for them, a land flowing with milk and honey,[o] the most beautiful of all lands.[p] 7 And I said to them, "Each of you, get rid of the vile images[q] you have set your eyes on, and do not defile yourselves with the idols of Egypt. I am the LORD your God.[r]"

8 " 'But they rebelled against me and would not listen to me; they did not get rid of the vile images they had set their eyes on, nor did they forsake the idols of Egypt.[s] So I said I would pour out my wrath on them and spend my anger against them in Egypt.[t] 9 But for the sake of my name I did what would keep it from being profaned in the eyes of the nations they lived among and in whose sight I had revealed myself to the Israel-

[a] 7 Targum (see Septuagint); Hebrew *He knew*
[b] 10 Two Hebrew manuscripts; most Hebrew manuscripts *your blood*
[c] 14 Or *from under its*

19:12 [d] Isa 27:11; Eze 28:17; Hos 13:15
19:13 [e] Eze 20:35 [f] Hos 2:3
19:14 [g] Eze 20:47 [h] Eze 15:4
20:1 [i] Eze 8:1
20:3 [j] Eze 14:3 [k] Mic 3:7
20:4 [l] Eze 16:2; 22:2; Mt 23:32
20:5 [m] Dt 7:6 [n] Ex 6:7
20:6 [o] Ex 3:8; Jer 32:22 [p] Dt 8:7; Ps 48:2; Da 8:9
20:7 [q] Ex 20:4 [r] Ex 20:2; Lev 18:3; Dt 29:18
20:8 [s] Eze 7:8 [t] Isa 63:10

ites by bringing them out of Egypt.[u] 10 Therefore I led them out of Egypt and brought them into the desert.[v] 11 I gave them my decrees and made known to them my laws, for the man who obeys them will live by them.[w] 12 Also I gave them my Sabbaths as a sign[x] between us, so they would know that I the LORD made them holy.

13 " 'Yet the people of Israel rebelled[y] against me in the desert. They did not follow my decrees but rejected my laws—although the man who obeys them will live by them—and they utterly desecrated my Sabbaths. So I said I would pour out my wrath[z] on them and destroy them in the desert.[a] 14 But for the sake of my name I did what would keep it from being profaned in the eyes of the nations in whose sight I had brought them out.[b] 15 Also with uplifted hand I swore to them in the desert that I would not bring them into the land I had given them—a land flowing with milk and honey, most beautiful of all lands[c]— 16 because they rejected my laws and did not follow my decrees and desecrated my Sabbaths. For their hearts[d] were devoted to their idols.[e] 17 Yet I looked on them with pity and did not destroy them or put an end to them in the desert. 18 I said to their children in the desert, "Do not follow the statutes of your fathers[f] or keep their laws or defile yourselves with their idols. 19 I am the LORD your God;[g] follow my decrees and be careful to keep my laws.[h] 20 Keep my Sabbaths holy, that they may be a sign between us. Then you will know that I am the LORD your God.[i]"

21 " 'But the children rebelled against me: They did not follow my decrees, they were not careful to keep my laws—although the man who obeys them will live by them—and they desecrated my Sabbaths. So I said I would pour out my wrath on them and spend my anger against them in the desert. 22 But I withheld[j] my hand, and for the sake of my name I did what would keep it from being profaned in the eyes of the nations in whose sight I had brought them out. 23 Also with uplifted hand I swore to them in the desert that I would disperse them among the nations and scatter[k] them through the countries, 24 because they had not obeyed my laws but had rejected my decrees and desecrated my Sabbaths,[l] and their eyes ⌊lusted⌋ after[m] their fathers' idols.[n] 25 I also gave them over[o] to statutes that were not good and laws they could not live by;[p] 26 I let them become defiled through their gifts—the sacrifice of every firstborn[a]—that I might fill them with horror so they would know that I am the LORD.[q]'

27 "Therefore, son of man, speak to the people of Israel and say to them, 'This is what the Sovereign LORD says: In this also your fathers blasphemed[r] me by forsaking me:[s] 28 When I brought them into the land[t] I had sworn to give them and they saw any high hill or any leafy tree, there they offered their sacrifices, made offerings that provoked me to anger, presented their fragrant incense and poured out their drink offerings.[u] 29 Then I said to them: What is this high place you go to?' " (It is called Bamah[b] to this day.)

Judgment and Restoration

30 "Therefore say to the house of Israel: 'This is what the Sovereign LORD says: Will you defile yourselves[v] the way your fathers did and lust after their vile images?[w] 31 When you offer your gifts—the sacrifice of your sons[x] in[c] the fire—you continue to defile yourselves with all your idols to this day. Am I to let you inquire of me, O house of Israel? As surely as I live, declares the Sovereign LORD, I will not let you inquire of me.[y]

32 " 'You say, "We want to be like the nations, like the peoples of the world, who serve wood and stone." But what you have in mind will never happen. 33 As surely as I live, declares the Sovereign LORD, I will rule over you with a mighty hand and an outstretched arm and with outpoured wrath.[z] 34 I will bring you from the nations[a] and gather you from the countries where you have been scattered—with a mighty hand and an outstretched arm and with outpoured wrath.[b] 35 I will bring you into the desert of the nations and there, face to face, I will execute judgment[c] upon you. 36 As I judged your fathers in the desert of the land of Egypt, so I will judge you, declares the Sovereign LORD.[d] 37 I will take note of you as you pass under my

[a] 26 Or *—making every firstborn pass through ⌊the fire⌋* [b] 29 *Bamah* means *high place.* [c] 31 Or *—making your sons pass through*

20:9 [u] Eze 36:22; 39:7
20:10 [v] Ex 13:18
20:11 [w] Lev 18:5; Dt 4:7-8; Ro 10:5
20:12 [x] Ex 31:13
20:13 [y] Ps 78:40 [z] Dt 9:8 [a] Nu 14:29; Ps 95:8-10; Isa 56:6
20:14 [b] Eze 36:23
20:15 [c] Ps 95:11; 106:26
20:16 [d] Nu 15:39 [e] Am 5:26
20:18 [f] Zec 1:4
20:19 [g] Ex 20:2 [h] Dt 5:32-33; 6:1-2; 8:1; 11:1; 12:1
20:20 [i] Jer 17:22
20:22 [j] Ps 78:38
20:23 [k] Lev 26:33; Dt 28:64
20:24 [l] ver 13 [m] Eze 6:9 [n] ver 16
20:25 [o] Ps 81:12 [p] 2Th 2:11
20:26 [q] 2Ki 17:17
20:27 [r] Ro 2:24 [s] Eze 18:24
20:28 [t] Ps 78:55,58 [u] Eze 6:13
20:30 [v] ver 43 [w] Jer 16:12
20:31 [x] Eze 16:20 [y] Ps 106:37-39; Jer 7:31
20:33 [z] Jer 21:5
20:34 [a] 2Co 6:17* [b] Isa 27:12-13; Jer 44:6; La 2:4
20:35 [c] Jer 2:35
20:36 [d] Nu 11:1-35; 1Co 10:5-10

20:37 e Lev 27:32; rod,[e] and I will bring you into the bond
Jer 33:13 of the covenant.[f] 38 I will purge[g] you of
f Eze 16:62 those who revolt and rebel against me.
20:38 Although I will bring them out of the
g Eze 34:17-22; land where they are living, yet they will
Am 9:9-10 not enter the land of Israel. Then you
h Ps 95:11; will know that I am the LORD.[h]
Jer 44:14; 39 " 'As for you, O house of Israel, this is
Eze 13:9; Mal 3:3; Heb 4:3 what the Sovereign LORD says: Go and
20:39 i Jer 44:25 serve your idols,[i] every one of you! But
j Isa 1:13; afterward you will surely listen to me
Eze 43:7; and no longer profane my holy name
Am 4:4 with your gifts and idols.[j] 40 For on my
holy mountain, the high mountain of Israel, declares the Sovereign LORD, there
in the land the entire house of Israel will
20:40 serve me, and there I will accept them.
k Isa 60:7 There I will require your offerings[k] and
l Isa 56:7; your choice gifts,[a] along with all your
Mal 3:4 holy sacrifices.[l] 41 I will accept you as fragrant incense when I bring you out from
the nations and gather you from the
20:41 countries where you have been scat-
m Eze 28:25; tered, and I will show myself holy[m]
36:23 among you in the sight of the nations.[n]
n Eze 11:17 42 Then you will know that I am the
20:42 o Eze 38:23 LORD,[o] when I bring you into the land of
p Eze 34:13; Israel,[p] the land I had sworn with uplift-
36:24 ed hand to give to your fathers. 43 There
you will remember your conduct and all
the actions by which you have defiled
20:43 yourselves, and you will loathe your-
q Eze 6:9; 16:61; selves for all the evil you have done.[q]
Hos 5:15 44 You will know that I am the LORD,
20:44 r Eze 36:22 when I deal with you for my name's sake[r]
s Eze 24:24 and not according to your evil ways and
your corrupt practices, O house of Israel, declares the Sovereign LORD.[s]' "

Prophecy Against the South

45 The word of the LORD came to me:
46 "Son of man, set your face toward the
20:46 south; preach against the south and
t Eze 21:2; Am 7:16 prophesy against[t] the forest of the
u Isa 30:6; southland.[u] 47 Say to the southern forest:
Jer 13:19 'Hear the word of the LORD. This is what
the Sovereign LORD says: I am about to
set fire to you, and it will consume all
your trees, both green and dry. The blazing flame will not be quenched, and
20:47 every face from south to north will be
v Isa 9:18-19; scorched by it.[v] 48 Everyone will see that
13:8; Jer 21:14 I the LORD have kindled it; it will not be
20:48 w Jer 7:20 quenched.[w]' "
49 Then I said, "Ah, Sovereign LORD!
20:49 They are saying of me, 'Isn't he just
x Mt 13:13; Jn 16:25 telling parables?[x]' "

Babylon, God's Sword of Judgment

21 The word of the LORD came to
me: 2 "Son of man, set your face
against Jerusalem and preach against 21:2
the sanctuary. Prophesy against[y] the y Eze 20:46
land of Israel 3 and say to her: 'This is 21:3
what the LORD says: I am against you.[z] I z Jer 21:13 a ver 9-11;
will draw my sword from its scabbard Job 9:22
and cut off from you both the righteous
and the wicked.[a] 4 Because I am going to
cut off the righteous and the wicked, my
sword will be unsheathed against every- 21:4
one from south to north.[b] 5 Then all peo- b Eze 20:47
ple will know that I the LORD have drawn
my sword from its scabbard; it will not 21:5
return[c] again.'[d] c ver 30 d Na 1:9
6 "Therefore groan, son of man! Groan
before them with broken heart and bit- 21:6
ter grief.[e] 7 And when they ask you, 'Why e Isa 22:4
are you groaning?' you shall say, 'Be-
cause of the news that is coming. Every 21:7
heart will melt and every hand go limp;[f] f Eze 22:14; 7:17
every spirit will become faint and every
knee become as weak as water.' It is
coming! It will surely take place, declares
the Sovereign LORD."

[a] 40 Or *and the gifts of your firstfruits*

UNPOPULAR PREACHING

The Lord instructed his prophet Ezekiel to "preach against the sanctuary" (Ezekiel 21). The people of Israel did not want to hear disparaging words about what was going on in their place of worship or to acknowledge that God's intentions toward themselves and their temple might be less than favorable. When Ezekiel informed the Israelites that God's glory had departed from the temple (Ezekiel 10), he might just as well have stated that the lights had gone out in the house of God. The Most Holy Place was dark and ominously empty now that God's glory—his very presence and majesty—no longer filled its area. Jesus Christ would later protest the empty rituals of the temple of his day (Matthew 23) and predict its destruction as well (Matthew 24:1–2). In fact, after he had been arrested and put on trial, Jesus himself was accused of threatening to destroy the temple (Matthew 26:61). But neither Ezekiel nor Jesus harbored negative feelings against the temple itself. Instead, both protested the way in which God's people had desecrated the place intended for the worship of the one true God.

8 The word of the LORD came to me:
9 "Son of man, prophesy and say, 'This is
what the Lord says:

" 'A sword, a sword,
sharpened and polished—

21:10 [g] Ps 110:5-6; Isa 34:5-6

10 sharpened for the slaughter,[g]
polished to flash like lightning!

" 'Shall we rejoice in the scepter of my
son ⌊Judah⌋? The sword despises every
such stick.

21:11 [h] Jer 46:4

11 " 'The sword is appointed to be
polished,[h]
to be grasped with the hand;
it is sharpened and polished,
made ready for the hand of the
slayer.
12 Cry out and wail, son of man,
for it is against my people;
it is against all the princes of
Israel.
They are thrown to the sword
along with my people.

21:12 [i] Jer 31:19

Therefore beat your breast.[i]

13 " 'Testing will surely come. And
what if the scepter ⌊of Judah⌋, which the
sword despises, does not continue? declares the Sovereign LORD.'

21:14 [j] Nu 24:10 [k] Eze 6:11; 30:24

14 "So then, son of man, prophesy
and strike your hands[j] together.
Let the sword strike twice,
even three times.
It is a sword for slaughter—
a sword for great slaughter,
closing in on them from every
side.[k]

21:15 [l] 2Sa 17:10 [m] Ps 22:14

15 So that hearts may melt[l]
and the fallen be many,
I have stationed the sword for
slaughter[a]
at all their gates.
Oh! It is made to flash like lightning,
it is grasped for slaughter.[m]
16 O sword, slash to the right,
then to the left,

21:17 [n] ver 14; Eze 22:13 [o] Eze 5:13

wherever your blade is turned.
17 I too will strike my hands[n] together,
and my wrath[o] will subside.
I the LORD have spoken."

18 The word of the LORD came to me:
19 "Son of man, mark out two roads for
the sword of the king of Babylon to take,
both starting from the same country.
Make a signpost where the road
branches off to the city. 20 Mark out one
road for the sword to come against Rabbah of the Ammonites[p] and another
against Judah and fortified Jerusalem.
21 For the king of Babylon will stop at the
fork in the road, at the junction of the
two roads, to seek an omen: He will cast
lots[q] with arrows, he will consult his
idols, he will examine the liver.[r] 22 Into
his right hand will come the lot for Jerusalem, where he is to set up battering
rams, to give the command to slaughter,
to sound the battle cry, to set battering
rams against the gates, to build a ramp
and to erect siege works.[s] 23 It will seem
like a false omen to those who have
sworn allegiance to him, but he will remind[t] them of their guilt and take them
captive.

21:20 [p] Dt 3:11; Jer 49:2; Am 1:14

21:21 [q] Pr 16:33 [r] Nu 22:7; 23:23

21:22 [s] Eze 4:2; 26:9

21:23 [t] Nu 5:15

24 "Therefore this is what the Sovereign LORD says: 'Because you people
have brought to mind your guilt by your
open rebellion, revealing your sins in all
that you do—because you have done
this, you will be taken captive.

25 " 'O profane and wicked prince of Israel, whose day has come, whose time of
punishment has reached its climax,[u]
26 this is what the Sovereign LORD says:
Take off the turban, remove the crown.[v]
It will not be as it was: The lowly will be
exalted and the exalted will be brought
low.[w] 27 A ruin! A ruin! I will make it a
ruin! It will not be restored until he
comes to whom it rightfully belongs; to
him I will give it.'[x]

21:25 [u] Eze 35:5

21:26 [v] Jer 13:18 [w] Ps 75:7; Eze 17:24

21:27 [x] Ps 2:6; Jer 23:5-6; Eze 37:24; Hag 2:21-22

28 "And you, son of man, prophesy and
say, 'This is what the Sovereign LORD
says about the Ammonites[y] and their
insults:

21:28 [y] Zep 2:8 [z] Jer 12:12

" 'A sword,[z] a sword,
drawn for the slaughter,
polished to consume
and to flash like lightning!
29 Despite false visions concerning
you
and lying divinations about you,
it will be laid on the necks
of the wicked who are to be slain,
whose day has come,
whose time of punishment has
reached its climax.[a]

21:29 [a] ver 25; Eze 22:28; 35:5

30 Return the sword to its scabbard.[b]
In the place where you were
created,
in the land of your ancestry,[c]

21:30 [b] Jer 47:6 [c] Eze 16:3

a 15 Septuagint; the meaning of the Hebrew for this word is uncertain.

I will judge you.'
31 I will pour out my wrath upon you
and breathe out my fiery anger[d]
against you;
I will hand you over to brutal men,
men skilled in destruction.[e]
32 You will be fuel for the fire,[f]
your blood will be shed in your
land,
you will be remembered[g] no more;
for I the LORD have spoken.' "

21:31 [d] Eze 22:20-21 [e] Jer 51:20-23
21:32 [f] Mal 4:1 [g] Eze 25:10

Jerusalem's Sins

22 The word of the LORD came to
me: 2 "Son of man, will you
judge her? Will you judge this city of
bloodshed?[h] Then confront her with all
her detestable practices[i] 3 and say: 'This
is what the Sovereign LORD says: O city
that brings on herself doom by shedding
blood[j] in her midst and defiles herself by
making idols, 4 you have become guilty
because of the blood you have shed[k] and
have become defiled by the idols you
have made. You have brought your days
to a close, and the end of your years has
come.[l] Therefore I will make you an object of scorn to the nations and a laughingstock to all the countries.[m] 5 Those
who are near and those who are far away
will mock you, O infamous city, full of
turmoil.
6 " 'See how each of the princes of Israel who are in you uses his power to shed
blood.[n] 7 In you they have treated father
and mother with contempt;[o] in you they
have oppressed the alien and mistreated
the fatherless and the widow.[p] 8 You have
despised my holy things and desecrated
my Sabbaths.[q] 9 In you are slanderous
men[r] bent on shedding blood; in you are
those who eat at the mountain shrines[s]
and commit lewd acts.[t] 10 In you are
those who dishonor their fathers' bed; in
you are those who violate women during
their period, when they are ceremonially unclean.[u] 11 In you one man commits
a detestable offense with his neighbor's
wife, another shamefully defiles his
daughter-in-law,[v] and another violates
his sister,[w] his own father's daughter. 12 In
you men accept bribes[x] to shed blood;
you take usury and excessive interest[a]
and make unjust gain from your neighbors[y] by extortion. And you have forgotten me, declares the Sovereign LORD.
13 " 'I will surely strike my hands[z] together at the unjust gain[a] you have
made and at the blood[b] you have shed in
your midst. 14 Will your courage endure
or your hands be strong in the day I deal
with you? I the LORD have spoken,[c] and
I will do it.[d] 15 I will disperse you among
the nations and scatter[e] you through the
countries; and I will put an end to your
uncleanness.[f] 16 When you have been defiled[b] in the eyes of the nations, you will
know that I am the LORD.' "
17 Then the word of the LORD came to
me: 18 "Son of man, the house of Israel
has become dross[g] to me; all of them are
the copper, tin, iron and lead left inside
a furnace. They are but the dross of silver.[h] 19 Therefore this is what the Sovereign LORD says: 'Because you have all become dross, I will gather you into
Jerusalem. 20 As men gather silver, copper, iron, lead and tin into a furnace to
melt it with a fiery blast, so will I gather
you in my anger and my wrath and put
you inside the city and melt you.[i] 21 I will
gather you and I will blow on you with
my fiery wrath, and you will be melted
inside her. 22 As silver is melted[j] in a furnace, so you will be melted inside her,
and you will know that I the LORD have
poured out my wrath upon you.' "[k]
23 Again the word of the LORD came to
me: 24 "Son of man, say to the land, 'You
are a land that has had no rain or showers[c] in the day of wrath.'[l] 25 There is a
conspiracy[m] of her princes[d] within her
like a roaring lion tearing its prey; they
devour people,[n] take treasures and precious things and make many widows[o]
within her. 26 Her priests do violence to
my law[p] and profane my holy things;
they do not distinguish between the
holy and the common;[q] they teach that
there is no difference between the unclean and the clean;[r] and they shut their
eyes to the keeping of my Sabbaths, so
that I am profaned among them.[s] 27 Her
officials within her are like wolves tearing their prey; they shed blood and kill
people to make unjust gain.[t] 28 Her
prophets whitewash[u] these deeds for
them by false visions and lying divinations. They say, 'This is what the Sovereign LORD says'—when the LORD has not
spoken.[v] 29 The people of the land prac-

22:2 [h] Eze 24:6,9; Na 3:1 [i] Eze 16:2
22:3 [j] ver 6,13,27; Eze 23:37,45
22:4 [k] 2Ki 21:16 [l] Eze 21:25 [m] Eze 5:14
22:6 [n] Isa 1:23
22:7 [o] Dt 5:16; 27:16 [p] Ex 22:21-22
22:8 [q] Eze 23:38-39
22:9 [r] Lev 19:16 [s] Eze 18:11 [t] Hos 4:10,14
22:10 [u] Lev 18:8,19
22:11 [v] Lev 18:15 [w] Lev 18:9; 2Sa 13:14
22:12 [x] Dt 27:25; Mic 7:3 [y] Lev 19:13
22:13 [z] Eze 21:17
22:13 [a] Isa 33:15 [b] ver 3
22:14 [c] Eze 24:14 [d] Eze 17:24; 21:7
22:15 [e] Dt 4:27; Zec 7:14 [f] Eze 23:27
22:18 [g] Ps 119:119; Isa 1:22 [h] Jer 6:28-30
22:20 [i] Mal 3:2
22:22 [j] Isa 1:25 [k] Eze 20:8,33
22:24 [l] Eze 24:13
22:25 [m] Jer 11:9 [n] Hos 6:9 [o] Jer 15:8
22:26 [p] Mal 2:7-8 [q] Eze 44:23 [r] Lev 10:10 [s] 1Sa 2:12-17; Jer 2:8,26; Hag 2:11-14
22:27 [t] Isa 1:23
22:28 [u] Eze 13:10 [v] Eze 13:2,6-7

[a] 12 Or *usury and interest* [b] 16 Or *When I have allotted you your inheritance* [c] 24 Septuagint; Hebrew *has not been cleansed or rained on* [d] 25 Septuagint; Hebrew *prophets*

22:29 [w] Ex 22:21; 23:9 [x] Isa 5:7
22:30 [y] Eze 13:5 [z] Ps 106:23; Jer 5:1
22:31 [a] Eze 16:43 [b] Eze 7:8-9; 9:10; Ro 2:8

tice extortion and commit robbery; they
oppress the poor and needy and mistreat the alien,[w] denying them justice.[x]
30 "I looked for a man among them
who would build up the wall[y] and stand
before me in the gap on behalf of the
land so I would not have to destroy it,
but I found none.[z] 31 So I will pour out
my wrath on them and consume them
with my fiery anger, bringing down[a] on
their own heads all they have done, declares the Sovereign LORD.[b]"

Two Adulterous Sisters

23:2 [c] Jer 3:7; Eze 16:45
23:3 [d] Jos 24:14 [e] Lev 17:7

23 The word of the LORD came to
me: 2 "Son of man, there were
two women, daughters of the same
mother.[c] 3 They became prostitutes in
Egypt,[d] engaging in prostitution[e] from
their youth. In that land their breasts
were fondled and their virgin bosoms
caressed. 4 The older was named Oholah,
and her sister was Oholibah. They were

JESUS AND YOU

STANDING IN THE GAP

God always follows through with both his warnings and his promises to his people. He had warned the Israelites for generations that he would destroy the nation because of her sin, and in Ezekiel 22:30 he issued one final ultimatum, stating in essence: "If there is one person who is willing to 'stand before me in the gap,' I will not judge the sin of the people." God was asking through his messenger, the prophet, for a single individual to intercede with God on behalf of the nation and to call the people to repentance. For whatever reason God appears to have singled out Ezekiel as the one to *communicate* his message to the princes, the prophets, the priests and the people, and Ezekiel seems to have been exempted from this search for the one person who would stand in the gap. Not a single individual could be found to fill this role, however, and consequently God's judgment fell on the entire city. We can never underestimate the potential influence of only one individual who is willing to take God at his word. You yourself might conceivably be the only one standing between God's blessing and his judgment! Ultimately, we know that Jesus is standing before the Father on our behalf, as we receive through faith his forgiveness and the payment he has offered for our sin—his own death (Romans 8:34; 1 Timothy 2:5; 1 John 2:1).

mine and gave birth to sons and daughters. Oholah is Samaria, and Oholibah is
Jerusalem.
5 "Oholah engaged in prostitution
while she was still mine; and she lusted
after her lovers, the Assyrians[f]—warriors[g] 6 clothed in blue, governors and
commanders, all of them handsome
young men, and mounted horsemen.
7 She gave herself as a prostitute to all the
elite of the Assyrians and defiled herself
with all the idols of everyone she lusted
after.[h] 8 She did not give up the prostitution she began in Egypt,[i] when during
her youth men slept with her, caressed
her virgin bosom and poured out their
lust upon her.[j]
9 "Therefore I handed her over[k] to her
lovers, the Assyrians, for whom she lusted.[l] 10 They stripped[m] her naked, took
away her sons and daughters and killed
her with the sword. She became a byword among women,[n] and punishment
was inflicted on her.[o]
11 "Her sister Oholibah saw this, yet in
her lust and prostitution she was more
depraved than her sister.[p] 12 She too lusted after the Assyrians—governors and
commanders, warriors in full dress,
mounted horsemen, all handsome
young men.[q] 13 I saw that she too defiled
herself; both of them went the same way.
14 "But she carried her prostitution
still further. She saw men portrayed on a
wall,[r] figures of Chaldeans[a] portrayed in
red,[s] 15 with belts around their waists
and flowing turbans on their heads; all
of them looked like Babylonian chariot
officers, natives of Chaldea.[b] 16 As soon
as she saw them, she lusted after them
and sent messengers to them in Chaldea. 17 Then the Babylonians came to
her, to the bed of love, and in their lust
they defiled her. After she had been defiled by them, she turned away from
them in disgust. 18 When she carried on
her prostitution openly and exposed her
nakedness, I turned away[t] from her in
disgust, just as I had turned away from
her sister.[u] 19 Yet she became more and
more promiscuous as she recalled the
days of her youth, when she was a prostitute in Egypt. 20 There she lusted after
her lovers, whose genitals were like
those of donkeys and whose emission

23:5 [f] 2Ki 16:7; Hos 5:13 [g] Hos 8:9
23:7 [h] Hos 5:3; 6:10
23:8 [i] Ex 32:4 [j] Eze 16:15
23:9 [k] 2Ki 18:11 [l] Hos 11:5
23:10 [m] Hos 2:10 [n] Eze 16:41 [o] Eze 16:36
23:11 [p] Jer 3:8-11; Eze 16:51
23:12 [q] 2Ki 16:7-15; 2Ch 28:16
23:14 [r] Eze 8:10 [s] Jer 22:14
23:18 [t] Ps 78:59; 106:40; Jer 6:8 [u] Jer 12:8; Am 5:21

[a] 14 Or *Babylonians* [b] 15 Or *Babylonia*; also in verse 16

was like that of horses. 21 So you longed
for the lewdness of your youth, when in
23:21 Egypt your bosom was caressed and
v Eze 16:26 your young breasts fondled.[a][v]
22 "Therefore, Oholibah, this is what
the Sovereign LORD says: I will stir up
your lovers against you, those you
turned away from in disgust, and I will
23:22 bring them against you from every
w Eze 16:37 side[w]— 23 the Babylonians[x] and all the
23:23 Chaldeans, the men of Pekod[y] and Shoa
x 2Ki 20:14-18 y Jer 50:21 and Koa, and all the Assyrians with
z 2Ki 24:2 them, handsome young men, all of them
governors and commanders, chariot officers and men of high rank, all mounted on horses.[z] 24 They will come against
23:24 you with weapons,[b] chariots and wag-
a Jer 47:3; Eze 26:7,10; ons[a] and with a throng of people; they
Na 2:4 will take up positions against you on
b Jer 39:5-6 every side with large and small shields
and with helmets. I will turn you over to
them for punishment,[b] and they will
punish you according to their standards.
25 I will direct my jealous anger against
you, and they will deal with you in fury.
They will cut off your noses and your
ears, and those of you who are left will
fall by the sword. They will take away
23:25 c ver 47 your sons and daughters,[c] and those of
d Eze 20:47-48 you who are left will be consumed by
23:26 fire.[d] 26 They will also strip[e] you of your
e Jer 13:22 f Isa 3:18-23; clothes and take your fine jewelry.[f] 27 So
Eze 16:39 I will put a stop[g] to the lewdness and
23:27 prostitution you began in Egypt. You
g Eze 16:41 will not look on these things with longing or remember Egypt anymore.

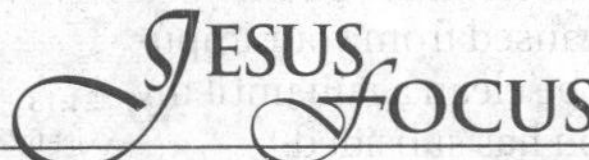

TWO SINFUL SISTERS

In Ezekiel 23 Samaria and Jerusalem are described as two sisters who have had many lovers. Samaria was the capital of Israel's northern kingdom and Jerusalem the capital of Judah, the southern kingdom. Samaria was the first to turn away from God to worship idols, but Jerusalem soon followed suit—and God referred to their spiritual unfaithfulness as adultery and prostitution (verses 1–4). Jesus used similar words to describe his contemporaries—"a wicked and adulterous generation" (Matthew 12:39). Ironically, Jesus received a warmer reception from the people of Samaria, who had first turned away from God, than from those in Jerusalem (see Matthew 23:37–39; John 4:39–42).

28 "For this is what the Sovereign LORD 23:28
says: I am about to hand you over[h] to h Jer 34:20
those you hate, to those you turned
away from in disgust. 29 They will deal
with you in hatred and take away everything you have worked for. They will
leave you naked and bare, and the
shame of your prostitution will be ex- 23:29
posed. Your lewdness and promiscuity[i] i Dt 28:48
30 have brought this upon you, because
you lusted after the nations and defiled 23:30
yourself with their idols.[j] 31 You have j Eze 6:9
gone the way of your sister; so I will put 23:31
her cup[k] into your hand.[l] k Jer 25:15 l 2Ki 21:13
32 "This is what the Sovereign LORD
says:

"You will drink your sister's cup,
a cup large and deep;
it will bring scorn and derision, 23:32
for it holds so much.[m] m Ps 60:3; Isa 51:17;
33 You will be filled with drunkenness Jer 25:15
and sorrow,
the cup of ruin and desolation, 23:33
the cup of your sister Samaria.[n] n Jer 25:15-16
34 You will drink it[o] and drain it dry; 23:34
you will dash it to pieces o Ps 75:8;
and tear your breasts. Isa 51:17

I have spoken, declares the Sovereign
LORD.

35 "Therefore this is what the Sovereign LORD says: Since you have forgot- 23:35
ten[p] me and thrust me behind your p Isa 17:10; Jer 3:21
back,[q] you must bear the consequences q 1Ki 14:9
of your lewdness and prostitution."
36 The LORD said to me: "Son of man,
will you judge Oholah and Oholibah?
Then confront[r] them with their de- 23:36 r Eze 16:2
testable practices,[s] 37 for they have com- s Isa 58:1; Eze 22:2;
mitted adultery and blood is on their Mic 3:8
hands. They committed adultery with
their idols; they even sacrificed their
children, whom they bore to me,[c] as 23:37
food for them.[t] 38 They have also done t Eze 16:36
this to me: At that same time they defiled my sanctuary and desecrated my
Sabbaths. 39 On the very day they sacrificed their children to their idols, they 23:39
entered my sanctuary and desecrated[u] u 2Ki 21:4
it. That is what they did in my house.[v] v Jer 7:10
40 "They even sent messengers for 23:40
men who came from far away,[w] and w Isa 57:9

[a] 21 Syriac (see also verse 3); Hebrew *caressed because of your young breasts* [b] 24 The meaning of the Hebrew for this word is uncertain. [c] 37 Or *even made the children they bore to me pass through ⌊the fire⌋*

when they arrived you bathed yourself
for them, painted your eyes[x] and put on
your jewelry.[y] 41 You sat on an elegant
couch,[z] with a table[a] spread before it on
which you had placed the incense and
oil that belonged to me.
42 "The noise of a carefree crowd was
around her; Sabeans[a] were brought from
the desert along with men from the rabble, and they put bracelets[b] on the arms
of the woman and her sister and beautiful crowns on their heads.[c] 43 Then I said
about the one worn out by adultery,
'Now let them use her as a prostitute,[d]
for that is all she is.' 44 And they slept with
her. As men sleep with a prostitute, so
they slept with those lewd women, Oholah and Oholibah. 45 But righteous men
will sentence them to the punishment of
women who commit adultery and shed
blood, because they are adulterous and
blood is on their hands.[e]
46 "This is what the Sovereign LORD
says: Bring a mob[f] against them and give
them over to terror and plunder. 47 The
mob will stone them and cut them
down with their swords; they will kill
their sons and daughters and burn[g]
down their houses.[h]
48 "So I will put an end to lewdness in
the land, that all women may take warning and not imitate you.[i] 49 You will suffer the penalty for your lewdness and
bear the consequences of your sins of
idolatry. Then you will know that I am
the Sovereign LORD."

23:40 [x] 2Ki 9:30 [y] Jer 4:30; Eze 16:13-19
23:41 [z] Est 1:6; Pr 7:17; Am 6:4 [a] Isa 65:11; Eze 44:16
23:42 [b] Ge 24:30 [c] Eze 16:11-12
23:43 [d] ver 3
23:45 [e] Lev 20:10; Eze 16:38; Hos 6:5
23:46 [f] Eze 16:40
23:47 [g] 2Ch 36:19 [h] 2Ch 36:17; Eze 16:40-41
23:48 [i] 2Pe 2:6
23:49 [j] Eze 7:4; 9:10; 20:38

The Cooking Pot

24 In the ninth year, in the tenth
month on the tenth day, the
word of the LORD came to me:[k] 2 "Son of
man, record this date, this very date, because the king of Babylon has laid siege
to Jerusalem this very day.[l] 3 Tell this rebellious house[m] a parable[n] and say to
them: 'This is what the Sovereign LORD
says:

" 'Put on the cooking pot;[o] put it on
and pour water into it.
4 Put into it the pieces of meat,
all the choice pieces—the leg
and the shoulder.
Fill it with the best of these bones;
5 take the pick of the flock.[p]
Pile wood beneath it for the bones;
bring it to a boil
and cook the bones in it.[q]

24:1 [k] Eze 8:1
24:2 [l] 2Ki 25:1; Jer 39:1; 52:4
24:3 [m] Isa 1:2; Eze 2:3,6 [n] Eze 17:2; 20:49 [o] Jer 1:13; Eze 11:3
24:5 [p] Jer 52:10 [q] Jer 52:24-27

6 " 'For this is what the Sovereign LORD
says:

" 'Woe to the city of bloodshed,[r]
to the pot now encrusted,
whose deposit will not go away!
Empty it piece by piece
without casting lots[s] for them.

7 " 'For the blood she shed is in her
midst:
She poured it on the bare rock;
she did not pour it on the ground,
where the dust would cover it.[t]
8 To stir up wrath and take revenge
I put her blood on the bare rock,
so that it would not be covered.

9 " 'Therefore this is what the Sovereign
LORD says:

" 'Woe to the city of bloodshed!
I, too, will pile the wood high.
10 So heap on the wood
and kindle the fire.
Cook the meat well,
mixing in the spices;
and let the bones be charred.
11 Then set the empty pot on the coals
till it becomes hot and its
copper glows
so its impurities may be melted
and its deposit burned away.[u]
12 It has frustrated all efforts;
its heavy deposit has not been
removed,
not even by fire.

13 " 'Now your impurity is lewdness.
Because I tried to cleanse you but you
would not be cleansed from your impurity, you will not be clean again until my
wrath against you has subsided.[v]

14 " 'I the LORD have spoken. The time
has come for me to act. I will not hold
back; I will not have pity, nor will I relent.
You will be judged according to your
conduct and your actions,[w] declares the
Sovereign LORD.[x]' "

Ezekiel's Wife Dies

15 The word of the LORD came to me:
16 "Son of man, with one blow I am about
to take away from you the delight of your
eyes. Yet do not lament or weep or shed
any tears.[y] 17 Groan quietly; do not mourn
for the dead. Keep your turban fastened
and your sandals on your feet; do not

24:6 [r] Eze 22:2 [s] Ob 1:11; Na 3:10
24:7 [t] Lev 17:13
24:11 [u] Jer 21:10; Eze 22:15
24:13 [v] Jer 6:28-30; Eze 16:42; 22:24
24:14 [w] Eze 36:19 [x] Eze 18:30
24:16 [y] Jer 13:17; 16:5; 22:10

[a] 42 Or *drunkards*

DISCOVERY 210

A God of Love?

The death of Ezekiel's beloved wife, the "delight" of his eyes, was predicted by God in what might easily strike us as cold and callous terms. Ezekiel recorded this tragedy in straightforward and sparse language, adding no emotional commentary (Ezekiel 24:15–17). Our initial reaction might well be to reread the passage. Perhaps we have inadvertently misread the verses. Perhaps there is some clue that we have missed to help us to somehow relate to this seemingly heartless passage.

Reading ahead, we soon discover that God was about to predict (and administer!) a calamity far greater than that of this individual death. Jerusalem would fall, the temple (the "delight" of the people's eyes) would be desecrated, the people taken into exile and their sons and daughters murdered (verses 20–22). But none of this sounds like the God whom we have come to know and trust. Assuming that we have not all along been incorrect in our understanding of his divine nature, how are we to interpret these seemingly paradoxical predictions?

While this passage does not itself directly address our burning questions, we recognize that God through Ezekiel was making a commentary on suffering. Elsewhere in his Word we are told that while God does not remove suffering from our human experience, he does promise to sustain us through our difficult times (Psalm 23:4). We learn in fact that suffering may serve a purpose in our lives: to test our faith (1 Peter 1:7; 4:12–13) or strengthen it (Matthew 15:27; Acts 6:5; Romans 4:19–20), to discipline, teach (Hebrews 12:7) or humble us (Deuteronomy 8:2–3; 1 Corinthians 1:3–7), or to demonstrate God's power at work through our weakness (2 Corinthians 12:9).

While Ezekiel 24 nowhere states that the death of Ezekiel's wife was an object lesson, the death of this seemingly innocent individual does foreshadow that of the only truly innocent person who has ever lived: our Lord Jesus Christ. The apostle Paul referred to God's love and the death of Jesus Christ in a single breath: "But God demonstrates his own love for us in this: While we were still sinners, Christ died for us" (Romans 5:8). In other words, God the Father allowed his innocent Son to die as a manifestation of the intensity both of his judgment and of his love.

It is only in this context that the death of Ezekiel's wife can begin to make sense to us. Just as Israel as a nation needed to "die" in order to be purified, restored and resurrected, so we as Christians need to "die" to our old sinful natures in order to be raised to new life: "We were therefore buried with [Jesus] through baptism into death in order that, just as Christ was raised from the dead through the glory of the Father, we too may live a new life" (Romans 6:4).

We may never make the assumption that God is either heartless or apathetic when it comes to human pain. Although we may not always understand his ways (Isaiah 55:9), we can rest in the assurance that his plan is perfect (Jeremiah 29:11) and that he works in *all things* for the good of those who love him (Romans 8:28).

***Self-Discovery:** Reflect on a period of suffering in your life. Looking back, can you identify a purpose? How has Jesus made his love real to you?*

GO TO DISCOVERY 211 ON PAGE 1111

cover the lower part of your face or eat
the customary food ⌊of mourners⌋.[z]"
18So I spoke to the people in the
morning, and in the evening my wife
died. The next morning I did as I had
been commanded.
19Then the people asked me, "Won't
you tell us what these things have to do
with us?[a]"
20So I said to them, "The word of the
LORD came to me: 21Say to the house of
Israel, 'This is what the Sovereign LORD
says: I am about to desecrate my sanctuary—the stronghold in which you
take pride, the delight of your eyes,[b] the
object of your affection. The sons and
daughters[c] you left behind will fall by
the sword.[d] 22And you will do as I have
done. You will not cover the lower part
of your face or eat the customary food
⌊of mourners⌋.[e] 23You will keep your turbans on your heads and your sandals on
your feet. You will not mourn[f] or weep
but will waste away because of[a] your
sins and groan among yourselves.[g]
24Ezekiel will be a sign[h] to you; you will
do just as he has done. When this happens, you will know that I am the Sovereign LORD.'
25"And you, son of man, on the day I
take away their stronghold, their joy and
glory, the delight of their eyes, their
heart's desire, and their sons and daughters[i] as well— 26on that day a fugitive
will come to tell you[j] the news. 27At that
time your mouth will be opened; you
will speak with him and will no longer
be silent. So you will be a sign to them,
and they will know that I am the LORD.[k]"

24:17 [z]Jer 16:7
24:19 [a]Eze 12:9; 37:18
24:21 [b]Ps 27:4 [c]Eze 23:25 [d]Jer 7:14,15; Eze 23:47
24:22 [e]Jer 16:7
24:23 [f]Job 27:15 [g]Ps 78:64
24:24 [h]Isa 20:3; Eze 4:3; 12:11
24:25 [i]Jer 11:22
24:26 [j]1Sa 4:12; Job 1:15-19
24:27 [k]Eze 3:26; 33:22

A Prophecy Against Ammon

25 The word of the LORD came to
me: 2"Son of man, set your face
against the Ammonites[l] and prophesy
against them.[m] 3Say to them, 'Hear the
word of the Sovereign LORD. This is what
the Sovereign LORD says: Because you
said "Aha![n]" over my sanctuary when it
was desecrated and over the land of Israel when it was laid waste and over the
people of Judah when they went into exile,[o] 4therefore I am going to give you to
the people of the East[p] as a possession.
They will set up their camps and pitch
their tents among you; they will eat your
fruit and drink your milk.[q] 5I will turn
Rabbah[r] into a pasture for camels and
Ammon into a resting place for sheep.[s]
Then you will know that I am the LORD.
6For this is what the Sovereign LORD
says: Because you have clapped your
hands and stamped your feet, rejoicing
with all the malice of your heart against
the land of Israel,[t] 7therefore I will
stretch out my hand[u] against you and
give you as plunder to the nations. I will
cut you off from the nations and exterminate you from the countries. I will destroy[v] you, and you will know that I am
the LORD.[w]'"

25:2 [l]Eze 21:28; Zep 2:8-9 [m]Jer 49:1-6
25:3 [n]Eze 26:2; 36:2 [o]Pr 17:5
25:4 [p]Jdg 6:3 [q]Dt 28:33,51; Jdg 6:33
25:5 [r]Dt 3:11; Eze 21:20
25:5 [s]Isa 17:2
25:6 [t]Ob 1:12; Zep 2:8
25:7 [u]Zep 1:4 [v]Eze 21:31 [w]Am 1:14-15

A Prophecy Against Moab

8"This is what the Sovereign LORD
says: 'Because Moab[x] and Seir said,
"Look, the house of Judah has become
like all the other nations," 9therefore I
will expose the flank of Moab, beginning
at its frontier towns—Beth Jeshimoth[y],
Baal Meon[z] and Kiriathaim[a]—the glory
of that land. 10I will give Moab along
with the Ammonites to the people of the
East as a possession, so that the Ammonites will not be remembered[b]
among the nations; 11and I will inflict
punishment on Moab. Then they will
know that I am the LORD.'"

25:8 [x]Jer 48:1; Am 2:1
25:9 [y]Nu 33:49 [z]Nu 32:3; Jos 13:17 [a]Nu 32:37; Jos 13:19
25:10 [b]Eze 21:32

A Prophecy Against Edom

12"This is what the Sovereign LORD
says: 'Because Edom[c] took revenge on
the house of Judah and became very
guilty by doing so, 13therefore this is
what the Sovereign LORD says: I will
stretch out my hand against Edom and
kill its men and their animals.[d] I will lay
it waste, and from Teman to Dedan[e]
they will fall by the sword. 14I will take
vengeance on Edom by the hand of my
people Israel, and they will deal with
Edom in accordance with my anger[f] and
my wrath; they will know my vengeance,
declares the Sovereign LORD.'"

25:12 [c]2Ch 28:17
25:13 [d]Eze 29:8 [e]Jer 25:23
25:14 [f]Eze 35:11

A Prophecy Against Philistia

15"This is what the Sovereign LORD
says: 'Because the Philistines[g] acted in
vengeance and took revenge with malice
in their hearts, and with ancient hostility sought to destroy Judah, 16therefore
this is what the Sovereign LORD says: I
am about to stretch out my hand
against the Philistines,[h] and I will cut off
the Kerethites[i] and destroy those re-

25:15 [g]2Ch 28:18
25:16 [h]Jer 47:1-7 [i]1Sa 30:14; Zep 2:4-5

[a] 23 Or *away in*

maining along the coast. 17 I will carry out great vengeance on them and punish them in my wrath. Then they will know that I am the LORD, when I take vengeance on them.' "

A Prophecy Against Tyre

26 In the eleventh year, on the first day of the month, the word of the LORD came to me: 2 "Son of man, because Tyre[j] has said of Jerusalem, 'Aha![k] The gate to the nations is broken, and its doors have swung open to me; now that she lies in ruins I will prosper,' 3 therefore this is what the Sovereign LORD says: I am against you, O Tyre, and I will bring many nations against you, like the sea[l] casting up its waves. 4 They will destroy[m] the walls of Tyre[n] and pull down her towers; I will scrape away her rubble and make her a bare rock. 5 Out in the sea[o] she will become a place to spread fishnets, for I have spoken, declares the Sovereign LORD. She will become plunder[p] for the nations, 6 and her settlements on the mainland will be ravaged by the sword. Then they will know that I am the LORD.

7 "For this is what the Sovereign LORD says: From the north I am going to bring against Tyre Nebuchadnezzar[a][q] king of Babylon, king of kings,[r] with horses and chariots,[s] with horsemen and a great army. 8 He will ravage your settlements on the mainland with the sword; he will set up siege works[t] against you, build a ramp[u] up to your walls and raise his shields against you. 9 He will direct the blows of his battering rams against your walls and demolish your towers with his weapons. 10 His horses will be so many that they will cover you with dust. Your walls will tremble at the noise of the war horses, wagons and chariots[v] when he enters your gates as men enter a city whose walls have been broken through. 11 The hoofs[w] of his horses will trample all your streets; he will kill your people with the sword, and your strong pillars[x] will fall to the ground.[y] 12 They will plunder your wealth and loot your merchandise; they will break down your walls and demolish your fine houses and throw your stones, timber and rubble into the sea.[z] 13 I will put an end[a] to your noisy songs, and the music of your harps[b] will be heard no more.[c] 14 I will make you a bare rock, and you will become a place to spread fishnets. You will never be rebuilt,[d] for I the LORD have spoken, declares the Sovereign LORD.

15 "This is what the Sovereign LORD says to Tyre: Will not the coastlands[e] tremble[f] at the sound of your fall, when the wounded groan and the slaughter takes place in you? 16 Then all the princes of the coast will step down from their thrones and lay aside their robes and take off their embroidered garments. Clothed[g] with terror, they will sit on the ground, trembling[h] every moment, appalled[i] at you. 17 Then they will take up a lament[j] concerning you and say to you:

" 'How you are destroyed, O city of
renown,
peopled by men of the sea!
You were a power on the seas,
you and your citizens;
you put your terror
on all who lived there.[k]
18 Now the coastlands tremble
on the day of your fall;

26:2 [j] 2Sa 5:11; Isa 23 [k] Eze 25:3
26:3 [l] Isa 5:30; Jer 50:42; 51:42
26:4 [m] Isa 23:1,11 [n] Am 1:10
26:5 [o] Eze 27:32 [p] Eze 29:19
26:7 [q] Jer 27:6 [r] Ezr 7:12; Da 2:37 [s] Eze 23:24; Na 2:3-4
26:8 [t] Jer 6:6 [u] Eze 21:22
26:10 [v] Jer 4:13
26:11 [w] Isa 5:28 [x] Jer 43:13 [y] Isa 26:5
26:12 [z] Isa 23:8; Eze 27:3-27; 28:8
26:13 [a] Jer 7:34 [b] Isa 14:11 [c] Jer 25:10; Rev 18:22
26:14 [d] Job 12:14; Mal 1:4
26:15 [e] Eze 27:35 [f] Jer 49:21
26:16 [g] Job 8:22 [h] Hos 11:10 [i] Eze 32:10
26:17 [j] Eze 19:1; 27:32 [k] Isa 14:12

[a] 7 Hebrew *Nebuchadrezzar,* of which *Nebuchadnezzar* is a variant; here and often in Ezekiel and Jeremiah

JESUS FOCUS

TYRE DESTROYED FOREVER

Tyre was a Phoenician city off the coast of Lebanon, north of Israel. Known for its shipping and commerce, it exercised great influence in the ancient Mediterranean world. The larger portion of the city had been built on a man-made island off the mainland. Hiram, at one time the king of Tyre, had been a personal friend of both David and Solomon (2 Samuel 5:11; 1 Kings 5:1–12) and had assisted them in the construction of the temple. In Ezekiel's day, however, Tyre was a pagan commercial center that had completely forgotten the one true God, and the prophet predicted that it would be completely destroyed (Ezekiel 26:2–6). In 571 B.C., after a 15-year siege that began shortly after the fall of Jerusalem, Nebuchadnezzar of Babylon demolished the mainland part of the city. The island city offshore surrendered to Alexander the Great in 332 B.C. Interestingly, Jesus' only ministry outside of Israel was in the "vicinity of Tyre" where he healed the demon-possessed daughter of a Greek woman from Syrian Phoenicia (Mark 7:24–30).

the islands in the sea
are terrified at your collapse.'[l]

19"This is what the Sovereign LORD
says: When I make you a desolate city,
like cities no longer inhabited, and when
I bring the ocean depths over you and its
vast waters cover you,[m] 20then I will
bring you down with those who go down
to the pit,[n] to the people of long ago. I
will make you dwell in the earth below,
as in ancient ruins, with those who go
down to the pit, and you will not return
or take your place[a] in the land of the living.[o] 21I will bring you to a horrible end
and you will be no more. You will be
sought, but you will never again be
found, declares the Sovereign LORD."[p]

A Lament for Tyre

27 The word of the LORD came to
me: 2"Son of man, take up a
lament concerning Tyre. 3Say to Tyre,
situated at the gateway to the sea,[q] merchant of peoples on many coasts, 'This
is what the Sovereign LORD says:

" 'You say, O Tyre,
"I am perfect in beauty.[r]"
4Your domain was on the high seas;
your builders brought your
beauty to perfection.
5They made all your timbers
of pine trees from Senir[b];[s]
they took a cedar from Lebanon
to make a mast for you.
6Of oaks[t] from Bashan
they made your oars;
of cypress wood[c] from the coasts of
Cyprus[d][u]
they made your deck, inlaid with
ivory.
7Fine embroidered linen from Egypt
was your sail
and served as your banner;
your awnings were of blue and
purple[v]
from the coasts of Elishah.
8Men of Sidon and Arvad[w] were
your oarsmen;
your skilled men, O Tyre, were
aboard as your seamen.[x]
9Veteran craftsmen of Gebal[e][y] were
on board
as shipwrights to caulk your
seams.
All the ships of the sea and their
sailors

26:18 [l] Isa 23:5; 41:5; Eze 27:35
26:19 [m] Isa 8:7-8
26:20 [n] Eze 32:18; Am 9:2; Jnh 2:2, 6 [o] Eze 32:24,30
26:21 [p] Eze 27:36; 28:19; Rev 18:21
27:3 [q] ver 33 [r] Eze 28:2
27:5 [s] Dt 3:9
27:6 [t] Nu 21:33; Jer 22:20; Zec 11:2 [u] Ge 10:4; Isa 23:12
27:7 [v] Ex 25:4; Jer 10:9
27:8 [w] Ge 10:18 [x] 1Ki 9:27
27:9 [y] Jos 13:5; 1Ki 5:18

came alongside to trade for your
wares.
10" 'Men of Persia,[z] Lydia and Put[a]
served as soldiers in your army.
They hung their shields and
helmets on your walls,
bringing you splendor.
11Men of Arvad and Helech
manned your walls on every side;
men of Gammad
were in your towers.
They hung their shields around
your walls;
they brought your beauty to
perfection.

12" 'Tarshish[b] did business with you
because of your great wealth of goods;[c]
they exchanged silver, iron, tin and lead
for your merchandise.
13" 'Greece, Tubal and Meshech[d] traded with you; they exchanged slaves[e] and
articles of bronze for your wares.
14" 'Men of Beth Togarmah[f] exchanged work horses, war horses and
mules for your merchandise.
15" 'The men of Rhodes[f][g] traded with
you, and many coastlands[h] were your
customers; they paid you with ivory[i]
tusks and ebony.
16" 'Aram[g][j] did business with you because of your many products; they exchanged turquoise,[k] purple fabric, embroidered work, fine linen, coral and
rubies for your merchandise.
17" 'Judah and Israel traded with you;
they exchanged wheat from Minnith[l]
and confections,[h] honey, oil and balm
for your wares.
18" 'Damascus,[m] because of your
many products and great wealth of
goods, did business with you in wine
from Helbon and wool from Zahar.
19" 'Danites and Greeks from Uzal
bought your merchandise; they exchanged wrought iron, cassia and calamus for your wares.
20" 'Dedan traded in saddle blankets
with you.
21" 'Arabia and all the princes of Kedar[n] were your customers; they did

27:10 [z] Eze 38:5 [a] Eze 30:5
27:12 [b] Ge 10:4 [c] ver 18,33
27:13 [d] Ge 10:2; Isa 66:19; Eze 38:2 [e] Rev 18:13
27:14 [f] Ge 10:3; Eze 38:6
27:15 [g] Ge 10:7 [h] Jer 25:22 [i] 1Ki 10:22; Rev 18:12
27:16 [j] Jdg 10:6; Isa 7:1-8 [k] Eze 28:13
27:17 [l] Jdg 11:33
27:18 [m] Ge 14:15; Eze 47:16-18
27:21 [n] Ge 25:13; Isa 60:7

[a] 20 Septuagint; Hebrew *return, and I will give glory* [b] 5 That is, Hermon [c] 6 Targum; the Masoretic Text has a different division of the consonants. [d] 6 Hebrew *Kittim* [e] 9 That is, Byblos [f] 15 Septuagint; Hebrew *Dedan* [g] 16 Most Hebrew manuscripts; some Hebrew manuscripts and Syriac *Edom* [h] 17 The meaning of the Hebrew for this word is uncertain.

business with you in lambs, rams and
goats.

27:22 [o]Ge 10:7,28; 1Ki 10:1-2; Isa 60:6 [p]Ge 43:11

22“ ‘The merchants of Sheba[o] and Raamah traded with you; for your merchandise they exchanged the finest of all
kinds of spices[p] and precious stones,
and gold.

27:23 [q]2Ki 19:12 [r]Isa 37:12

23“ ‘Haran,[q] Canneh and Eden[r] and
merchants of Sheba, Asshur and Kilmad
traded with you. 24In your marketplace
they traded with you beautiful garments, blue fabric, embroidered work
and multicolored rugs with cords twisted and tightly knotted.

27:25 [s]Isa 2:16 *fn*

25“ ‘The ships of Tarshish[s] serve
as carriers for your wares.
You are filled with heavy cargo
in the heart of the sea.
26Your oarsmen take you
out to the high seas.

27:26 [t]Ps 48:7; Jer 18:17

But the east wind[t] will break you to
pieces
in the heart of the sea.

27:27 [u]Pr 11:4

27Your wealth,[u] merchandise and
wares,
your mariners, seamen and
shipwrights,
your merchants and all your
soldiers,
and everyone else on board
will sink into the heart of the sea
on the day of your shipwreck.

27:28 [v]Eze 26:15

28The shorelands will quake[v]
when your seamen cry out.
29All who handle the oars
will abandon their ships;
the mariners and all the seamen
will stand on the shore.
30They will raise their voice
and cry bitterly over you;

27:30 [w]2Sa 1:2 [x]Jer 6:26 [y]Rev 18:18-19

they will sprinkle dust[w] on their
heads
and roll[x] in ashes.[y]
31They will shave their heads
because of you
and will put on sackcloth.

27:31 [z]Isa 16:9 [a]Isa 22:12; Eze 7:18

They will weep[z] over you with
anguish of soul
and with bitter mourning.[a]

27:32 [b]Eze 26:17

32As they wail and mourn over you,
they will take up a lament[b]
concerning you:
“Who was ever silenced like Tyre,
surrounded by the sea?”
33When your merchandise went out
on the seas,
you satisfied many nations;

27:33 [c]ver 12; Eze 28:4-5

with your great wealth[c] and your
wares
you enriched the kings of the
earth.
34Now you are shattered by the sea
in the depths of the waters;

27:34 [d]Zec 9:4

your wares and all your company
have gone down with you.[d]

27:35 [e]Eze 26:15

35All who live in the coastlands[e]
are appalled at you;
their kings shudder with horror
and their faces are distorted
with fear.

27:36 [f]Jer 18:16; 19:8; 49:17; 50:13; Zep 2:15 [g]Ps 37:10,36; Eze 26:21

36The merchants among the nations
hiss at you;[f]
you have come to a horrible end
and will be no more.[g]’ ”

A Prophecy Against the King of Tyre

28 The word of the LORD came to
me: 2“Son of man, say to the
ruler of Tyre, ‘This is what the Sovereign
LORD says:

“ ‘In the pride of your heart
you say, “I am a god;

28:2 [h]Isa 14:13 [i]Ps 9:20; 82:6-7; Isa 31:3; 2Th 2:4

I sit on the throne[h] of a god
in the heart of the seas.”
But you are a man and not a god,
though you think you are as wise
as a god.[i]

28:3 [j]Da 1:20; 5:11-12

3Are you wiser than Daniel[a]?[j]
Is no secret hidden from you?
4By your wisdom and understanding
you have gained wealth for
yourself

28:4 [k]Zec 9:3

and amassed gold and silver
in your treasuries.[k]
5By your great skill in trading
you have increased your wealth,

28:5 [l]Job 31:25; Ps 52:7; 62:10; Hos 12:8; 13:6

and because of your wealth
your heart has grown proud.[l]

6“ ‘Therefore this is what the Sovereign LORD says:

“ ‘Because you think you are wise,
as wise as a god,
7I am going to bring foreigners
against you,

28:7 [m]Eze 30:11; 31:12; 32:12; Hab 1:6

the most ruthless of nations;[m]
they will draw their swords against
your beauty and wisdom
and pierce your shining
splendor.

28:8 [n]Eze 32:30

8They will bring you down to the
pit,[n]

[a] 3 Or *Danel*; the Hebrew spelling may suggest a person other than the prophet Daniel.

and you will die a violent death
28:8 [o] Eze 27:27
in the heart of the seas.[o]
[9] Will you then say, "I am a god,"
in the presence of those who kill
you?
You will be but a man, not a god,
in the hands of those who slay
you.
28:10 [p] Eze 31:18; 32:19,24
[10] You will die the death of the
uncircumcised[p]
at the hands of foreigners.

I have spoken, declares the Sovereign
LORD.' "

[11] The word of the LORD came to me:
28:12 [q] Eze 19:1 [r] Eze 27:2-4
[12] "Son of man, take up a lament[q] concerning the king of Tyre and say to him:
'This is what the Sovereign LORD says:

" 'You were the model of
perfection,
full of wisdom and perfect in
beauty.[r]
28:13 [s] Ge 2:8 [t] Eze 31:8-9 [u] Eze 27:16
[13] You were in Eden,[s]
the garden of God;[t]
every precious stone adorned you:
ruby, topaz and emerald,
chrysolite, onyx and jasper,
sapphire,[a] turquoise[u] and beryl.[b]
Your settings and mountings[c] were
made of gold;
on the day you were created they
were prepared.
28:14 [v] Ex 30:26; 40:9 [w] Ex 25:17-20
[14] You were anointed[v] as a guardian
cherub,[w]
for so I ordained you.
You were on the holy mount of
God;
you walked among the fiery
stones.
[15] You were blameless in your ways
from the day you were created
till wickedness was found in you.
[16] Through your widespread trade
28:16 [x] Hab 2:17 [y] Ge 3:24
you were filled with violence,[x]
and you sinned.
So I drove you in disgrace from the
mount of God,
and I expelled you, O guardian
cherub,[y]
from among the fiery stones.
28:17 [z] Eze 31:10
[17] Your heart became proud[z]
on account of your beauty,
and you corrupted your wisdom
because of your splendor.
So I threw you to the earth;
I made a spectacle of you before
kings.
[18] By your many sins and dishonest
trade
you have desecrated your
sanctuaries.
So I made a fire come out from
you,
and it consumed you,
28:18 [a] Mal 4:3
and I reduced you to ashes[a] on the
ground
in the sight of all who were
watching.
[19] All the nations who knew you
are appalled at you;
you have come to a horrible end
28:19 [b] Jer 51:64; Eze 26:21; 27:36
and will be no more.[b]' "

A Prophecy Against Sidon

28:21 [c] Eze 6:2 [d] Ge 10:15; Jer 25:22
[20] The word of the LORD came to me:
[21] "Son of man, set your face against[c] Sidon;[d] prophesy against her [22] and say:
'This is what the Sovereign LORD says:

28:22 [e] Eze 39:13 [f] Eze 30:19
" 'I am against you, O Sidon,
and I will gain glory[e] within you.
They will know that I am the LORD,
when I inflict punishment[f] on
her
and show myself holy within her.
[23] I will send a plague upon her
and make blood flow in her
streets.
The slain will fall within her,
with the sword against her on
every side.
28:23 [g] Eze 38:22
Then they will know that I am the
LORD.[g]

[24] " 'No longer will the people of Israel
28:24 [h] Nu 33:55; Jos 23:13; Eze 2:6
have malicious neighbors who are
painful briers and sharp thorns.[h] Then
they will know that I am the Sovereign
LORD.
28:25 [i] Ps 106:47; Jer 32:37 [j] Isa 11:12 [k] Eze 20:41 [l] Jer 23:8; Eze 11:17; 34:27; 37:25
[25] " 'This is what the Sovereign LORD
says: When I gather[i] the people of Israel
from the nations where they have been
scattered,[j] I will show myself holy[k]
among them in the sight of the nations.
Then they will live in their own land,
28:26 [m] Jer 23:6 [n] Isa 65:21; Jer 32:15; Eze 38:8; Am 9:14-15
which I gave to my servant Jacob.[l]
[26] They will live there in safety[m] and will
build houses and plant vineyards; they
will live in safety when I inflict punishment on all their neighbors who maligned them. Then they will know that I
am the LORD their God.[n]' "

[a] *13* Or *lapis lazuli* [b] *13* The precise identification of some of these precious stones is uncertain. [c] *13* The meaning of the Hebrew for this phrase is uncertain.

A Prophecy Against Egypt

29 In the tenth year, in the tenth month on the twelfth day, the word of the LORD came to me:[o] 2"Son of man, set your face against Pharaoh king of Egypt[p] and prophesy against him and against all Egypt.[q] 3Speak to him and say: 'This is what the Sovereign LORD says:

" 'I am against you, Pharaoh[r] king
of Egypt,
you great monster[s] lying among
your streams.
You say, "The Nile is mine;
I made it for myself."
4But I will put hooks[t] in your jaws
and make the fish of your
streams stick to your scales.
I will pull you out from among
your streams,
with all the fish sticking to your
scales.[u]
5I will leave you in the desert,
you and all the fish of your
streams.
You will fall on the open field
and not be gathered or picked up.
I will give you as food
to the beasts of the earth and
the birds of the air.[v]

6Then all who live in Egypt will know that I am the LORD.

" 'You have been a staff of reed[w] for the house of Israel. 7When they grasped you with their hands, you splintered[x] and you tore open their shoulders; when they leaned on you, you broke and their backs were wrenched.[a][y]

8" 'Therefore this is what the Sovereign LORD says: I will bring a sword against you and kill your men and their animals.[z] 9Egypt will become a desolate wasteland. Then they will know that I am the LORD.

" 'Because you said, "The Nile is mine; I made it,[a]" 10therefore I am against you and against your streams, and I will make the land of Egypt a ruin and a desolate waste from Migdol to Aswan,[b] as far as the border of Cush.[b] 11No foot of man or animal will pass through it; no one will live there for forty years.[c] 12I will make the land of Egypt desolate among devastated lands, and her cities will lie desolate forty years among ruined cities. And I will disperse the Egyptians among the nations and scatter them through the countries.[d]

13" 'Yet this is what the Sovereign LORD says: At the end of forty years I will gather the Egyptians from the nations where they were scattered. 14I will bring them back from captivity and return them to Upper Egypt,[c][e] the land of their ancestry. There they will be a lowly[f] kingdom. 15It will be the lowliest of kingdoms and will never again exalt itself above the other nations.[g] I will make it so weak that it will never again rule over the nations. 16Egypt will no longer be a source of confidence[h] for the people of Israel but will be a reminder of their sin in turning to her for help. Then they will know that I am the Sovereign LORD.[i]' "

17In the twenty-seventh year, in the first month on the first day, the word of the LORD came to me:[j] 18"Son of man, Nebuchadnezzar[k] king of Babylon drove his army in a hard campaign against Tyre; every head was rubbed bare[l] and every shoulder made raw. Yet he and his army got no reward from the campaign he led against Tyre. 19Therefore this is what the Sovereign LORD says: I am going to give Egypt to Nebuchadnezzar king of Babylon, and he will carry off its wealth. He will loot and plunder the land as pay for his army.[m] 20I have given him Egypt as a reward for his efforts because he and his army did it for me, declares the Sovereign LORD.[n]

21"On that day I will make a horn[d][o] grow for the house of Israel, and I will open your mouth[p] among them. Then they will know that I am the LORD.[q]"

A Lament for Egypt

30 The word of the LORD came to me: 2"Son of man, prophesy and say: 'This is what the Sovereign LORD says:

" 'Wail[r] and say,
"Alas for that day!"
3For the day is near,[s]
the day of the LORD[t] is near—
a day of clouds,
a time of doom for the nations.
4A sword will come against Egypt,

[a] *7* Syriac (see also Septuagint and Vulgate); Hebrew *and you caused their backs to stand*
[b] *10* That is, the upper Nile region
[c] *14* Hebrew *to Pathros*
[d] *21* *Horn* here symbolizes strength.

29:1 [o] ver 17; Eze 26:1
29:2 [p] Jer 25:19 [q] Isa 19:1-17; Jer 46:2; Eze 30:1-26; 31:1-18; 32:1-32
29:3 [r] Jer 44:30 [s] Ps 74:13; Isa 27:1; Eze 32:2
29:4 [t] 2Ki 19:28 [u] Eze 38:4
29:5 [v] Jer 7:33; 34:20; Eze 32:4-6; 39:4
29:6 [w] 2Ki 18:21; Isa 36:6
29:7 [x] Isa 36:6 [y] Eze 17:15-17
29:8 [z] Eze 14:17; 32:11-13
29:9 [a] Eze 30:7-8,13-19
29:10 [b] Eze 30:6
29:11 [c] Eze 32:13
29:12 [d] Jer 46:19; Eze 30:7,23,26
29:14 [e] Eze 30:14 [f] Eze 17:14
29:15 [g] Zec 10:11
29:16 [h] Isa 36:4,6 [i] Isa 30:2; Hos 8:13
29:17 [j] Eze 24:1
29:18 [k] Jer 27:6; Eze 26:7-8 [l] Jer 48:37
29:19 [m] Jer 43:10-13; Eze 30:4,10,24-25
29:20 [n] Isa 10:6-7; 45:1; Jer 25:9
29:21 [o] Ps 132:17 [p] Eze 33:22 [q] Eze 24:27
30:2 [r] Isa 13:6
30:3 [s] Eze 7:7; Joel 2:1,11; Ob 1:15 [t] ver 18; Eze 7:12,19

and anguish will come upon
Cush.[a]
When the slain fall in Egypt,
30:4 her wealth will be carried away
u Eze 29:19 and her foundations torn down.[u]
30:5 5 Cush and Put.[v] Lydia and all Arabia,
v Eze 27:10 w Jer 25:20 Libya[b] and the people[w] of the covenant
land will fall by the sword along with
Egypt.
6 " 'This is what the LORD says:
" 'The allies of Egypt will fall
and her proud strength will fail.
30:6 From Migdol to Aswan[x]
x Eze 29:10 they will fall by the sword within
her,
declares the Sovereign
LORD.
7 " 'They will be desolate
among desolate lands,
and their cities will lie
30:7 y Eze 29:12 among ruined cities.[y]
8 Then they will know that I am the
LORD,
when I set fire to Egypt
and all her helpers are crushed.

30:9 9 " 'On that day messengers will go out
z Isa 18:1-2 from me in ships to frighten Cush[z] out
a Isa 23:5 of her complacency. Anguish[a] will take
b Eze 32:9-10 hold of them on the day of Egypt's
doom, for it is sure to come.[b]

10 " 'This is what the Sovereign LORD
says:
" 'I will put an end to the hordes of
Egypt
by the hand of Nebuchadnezzar
30:10 c Eze 29:19 king of Babylon.[c]
11 He and his army—the most
30:11 d Eze 28:7 ruthless of nations[d]—
will be brought in to destroy the
land.
They will draw their swords
against Egypt
and fill the land with the slain.
30:12 12 I will dry up[e] the streams of the
e Isa 19:6 f Eze 29:9 Nile[f]
and sell the land to evil men;
by the hand of foreigners
I will lay waste the land and
everything in it.

I the LORD have spoken.

13 " 'This is what the Sovereign LORD
says:
30:13 g Jer 43:12 " 'I will destroy the idols[g]
and put an end to the images in
Memphis.[c][h] 30:13 h Isa 19:13
No longer will there be a prince in i Zec 10:11
Egypt,[i]
and I will spread fear throughout
the land.
14 I will lay[j] waste Upper Egypt,[d] 30:14 j Eze 29:14
set fire to Zoan[k] k Ps 78:12,43
and inflict punishment on l Jer 46:25
Thebes.[e][l]
15 I will pour out my wrath on
Pelusium,[f]
the stronghold of Egypt,
and cut off the hordes of Thebes.
16 I will set fire to Egypt;
Pelusium will writhe in agony.
Thebes will be taken by storm;
Memphis will be in constant
distress.
17 The young men of Heliopolis[g][m] 30:17 m Ge 41:45
and Bubastis[h]
will fall by the sword,
and the cities themselves will go
into captivity.
18 Dark will be the day at Tahpanhes
when I break the yoke of Egypt;[n] 30:18 n Lev 26:13
there her proud strength will o ver 3
come to an end.
She will be covered with clouds,
and her villages will go into
captivity.[o]
19 So I will inflict punishment on
Egypt,
and they will know that I am the
LORD.' "

20 In the eleventh year, in the first
month on the seventh day, the word of 30:20 p Eze 26:1;
the LORD came to me:[p] 21 "Son of man, I 29:17; 31:1
have broken the arm[q] of Pharaoh king of 30:21
Egypt. It has not been bound up for q Jer 48:25
healing[r] or put in a splint so as to be- r Jer 30:13; 46:11
come strong enough to hold a sword.
22 Therefore this is what the Sovereign
LORD says: I am against Pharaoh king of 30:22
Egypt.[s] I will break both his arms, the s Jer 46:25 t Ps 37:17
good arm as well as the broken one, and
make the sword fall from his hand.[t] 23 I
will disperse the Egyptians among the 30:23 u Eze 29:12
nations and scatter them through the
countries.[u] 24 I will strengthen[v] the arms 30:24 v Zec 10:6,12
of the king of Babylon and put my w Eze 21:14;
sword[w] in his hand, but I will break the Zep 2:12

[a] 4 That is, the upper Nile region; also in verses 5 and 9 [b] 5 Hebrew *Cub* [c] 13 Hebrew *Noph*; also in verse 16 [d] 14 Hebrew *waste Pathros* [e] 14 Hebrew *No*; also in verses 15 and 16 [f] 15 Hebrew *Sin*; also in verse 16 [g] 17 Hebrew *Awen* (or *On*) [h] 17 Hebrew *Pi Beseth*

arms of Pharaoh, and he will groan before him like a mortally wounded man.
25I will strengthen the arms of the king
of Babylon, but the arms of Pharaoh will
fall limp. Then they will know that I am
the LORD, when I put my sword into the
hand of the king of Babylon and he
brandishes it against Egypt. 26I will disperse the Egyptians among the nations
and scatter them through the countries.
30:26 [x] Eze 29:12 Then they will know that I am the
LORD.[x]"

A Cedar in Lebanon

31:1 [y] Jer 52:5 [z] Eze 30:20 31 In the eleventh year,[y] in the
third month on the first day,
the word of the LORD came to me:[z] 2"Son
of man, say to Pharaoh king of Egypt
and to his hordes:

" 'Who can be compared with you
in majesty?
3Consider Assyria, once a cedar in
Lebanon,
with beautiful branches
overshadowing the forest;
31:3 [a] Isa 10:34 it towered on high,
its top above the thick foliage.[a]
4The waters nourished it,
deep springs made it grow tall;
their streams flowed
all around its base
and sent their channels
to all the trees of the field.
5So it towered higher
than all the trees of the field;
its boughs increased
and its branches grew long,
31:5 [b] Eze 17:5 spreading because of abundant
waters.[b]
6All the birds of the air
nested in its boughs,
all the beasts of the field
gave birth under its branches;
31:6 [c] Eze 17:23; Mt 13:32 all the great nations
lived in its shade.[c]
7It was majestic in beauty,
with its spreading boughs,
for its roots went down
to abundant waters.
31:8 [d] Ps 80:10 [e] Ge 2:8-9 8The cedars[d] in the garden of God
could not rival it,
nor could the pine trees
equal its boughs,
nor could the plane trees
compare with its branches—
no tree in the garden of God
could match its beauty.[e]
9I made it beautiful
with abundant branches, 31:9 [f] Ge 2:8 [g] Ge 13:10; Eze 28:13
the envy of all the trees of Eden[f]
in the garden of God.[g]

10" 'Therefore this is what the Sovereign LORD says: Because it towered on
high, lifting its top above the thick fo- 31:10 [h] Isa 14:13-14; Eze 28:17
liage, and because it was proud[h] of its
height, 11I handed it over to the ruler of
the nations, for him to deal with accord- 31:11 [i] Da 5:20
ing to its wickedness. I cast it aside,[i]
12and the most ruthless of foreign na- 31:12 [j] Eze 28:7 [k] Eze 32:5; 35:8 [l] Eze 32:11-12; Da 4:14
tions[j] cut it down and left it. Its boughs
fell on the mountains and in all the valleys;[k] its branches lay broken in all the
ravines of the land. All the nations of the
earth came out from under its shade
and left it.[l] 13All the birds of the air set-
tled on the fallen tree, and all the beasts 31:13 [m] Isa 18:6; Eze 29:5; 32:4
of the field were among its branches.[m]
14Therefore no other trees by the waters
are ever to tower proudly on high, lifting
their tops above the thick foliage. No
other trees so well-watered are ever to
reach such a height; they are all destined 31:14 [n] Ps 82:7 [o] Ps 63:9; Eze 26:20; 32:24
for death,[n] for the earth below, among
mortal men, with those who go down to
the pit.[o]
15" 'This is what the Sovereign LORD
says: On the day it was brought down to
the grave[a] I covered the deep springs
with mourning for it; I held back its
streams, and its abundant waters were
restrained. Because of it I clothed Lebanon with gloom, and all the trees of the
field withered away. 16I made the nations 31:16 [p] Eze 26:15 [q] Isa 14:8 [r] Eze 14:22; 32:31 [s] Isa 14:15; Eze 32:18
tremble[p] at the sound of its fall when I
brought it down to the grave with those
who go down to the pit. Then all the
trees[q] of Eden, the choicest and best of
Lebanon, all the trees that were well-watered, were consoled[r] in the earth below.[s] 17Those who lived in its shade, its
allies among the nations, had also gone
down to the grave with it, joining those 31:17 [t] Ps 9:17
killed by the sword.[t]
18" 'Which of the trees of Eden can be
compared with you in splendor and
majesty? Yet you, too, will be brought
down with the trees of Eden to the
earth below; you will lie among the un- 31:18 [u] Jer 9:26; Eze 32:19,21
circumcised,[u] with those killed by the
sword.
" 'This is Pharaoh and all his hordes,
declares the Sovereign LORD.' "

[a] 15 Hebrew *Sheol*; also in verses 16 and 17

A Lament for Pharaoh

32 In the twelfth year, in the twelfth month on the first day, the word of the LORD came to me:[v] 2"Son of man, take up a lament[w] concerning Pharaoh king of Egypt and say to him:

" 'You are like a lion[x] among the nations;
you are like a monster in the seas
thrashing about in your streams,
churning the water with your feet
and muddying the streams.[y]

3" 'This is what the Sovereign LORD says:

" 'With a great throng of people
I will cast my net over you,
and they will haul you up in my net.[z]
4I will throw you on the land
and hurl you on the open field.
I will let all the birds of the air
settle on you
and all the beasts of the earth
gorge themselves on you.[a]
5I will spread your flesh on the mountains
and fill the valleys[b] with your remains.
6I will drench the land with your flowing blood[c]
all the way to the mountains,
and the ravines will be filled with your flesh.
7When I snuff you out, I will cover the heavens
and darken their stars;
I will cover the sun with a cloud,
and the moon will not give its light.[d]
8All the shining lights in the heavens
I will darken over you;
I will bring darkness over your land,
declares the Sovereign LORD.
9I will trouble the hearts of many peoples
when I bring about your destruction among the nations,
among[a] lands you have not known.
10I will cause many peoples to be appalled at you,
and their kings will shudder
with horror because of you
when I brandish my sword
before them.
On the day[e] of your downfall
each of them will tremble
every moment for his life.[f]

11" 'For this is what the Sovereign LORD says:

" 'The sword of the king of Babylon[g]
will come against you.
12I will cause your hordes to fall
by the swords of mighty men—
the most ruthless of all nations.[h]
They will shatter the pride of Egypt,
and all her hordes will be overthrown.[i]
13I will destroy all her cattle
from beside abundant waters
no longer to be stirred by the foot of man
or muddied by the hoofs of cattle.[j]
14Then I will let her waters settle
and make her streams flow like oil,
declares the Sovereign LORD.
15When I make Egypt desolate
and strip the land of everything in it,
when I strike down all who live there,
then they will know that I am the LORD.[k]

16"This is the lament[l] they will chant
for her. The daughters of the nations will
chant it; for Egypt and all her hordes they
will chant it, declares the Sovereign LORD."

17In the twelfth year, on the fifteenth
day of the month, the word of the LORD
came to me:[m] 18"Son of man, wail for the
hordes of Egypt and consign[n] to the
earth below both her and the daughters
of mighty nations, with those who go
down to the pit.[o] 19Say to them, 'Are you
more favored than others? Go down and
be laid among the uncircumcised.'[p]
20They will fall among those killed by the
sword. The sword is drawn; let her be
dragged[q] off with all her hordes. 21From
within the grave[b][r] the mighty leaders will

32:1 [v] Eze 31:1; 33:21
32:2 [w] Eze 19:1; 27:2 [x] Eze 19:3,6; Na 2:11-13 [y] Eze 29:3; 34:18
32:3 [z] Eze 12:13
32:4 [a] Isa 18:6; Eze 31:12-13
32:5 [b] Eze 31:12
32:6 [c] Isa 34:3
32:7 [d] Isa 13:10; 34:4; Eze 30:3; Joel 2:2,31; 3:15; Mt 24:29; Rev 8:12
32:10 [e] Jer 46:10 [f] Eze 26:16; 27:35
32:11 [g] Jer 46:26
32:12 [h] Eze 28:7 [i] Eze 31:11-12
32:13 [j] Eze 29:8,11
32:15 [k] Ex 7:5; 14:4,18; Ps 107:33-34; Eze 6:7
32:16 [l] 2Sa 1:17; 2Ch 35:25; Eze 26:17
32:17 [m] ver 1
32:18 [n] Jer 1:10 [o] Eze 31:14,16; Mic 1:8
32:19 [p] ver 29-30; Eze 28:10; 31:18
32:20 [q] Ps 28:3
32:21 [r] Isa 14:9

[a] 9 Hebrew; Septuagint *bring you into captivity among the nations, / to* [b] 21 Hebrew *Sheol*; also in verse 27

say of Egypt and her allies, 'They have come down and they lie with the uncircumcised, with those killed by the sword.'

22"Assyria is there with her whole army; she is surrounded by the graves of all her slain, all who have fallen by the sword. 23Their graves are in the depths of the pit[s] and her army lies around her grave. All who had spread terror in the land of the living are slain, fallen by the sword.

24"Elam[t] is there, with all her hordes around her grave. All of them are slain, fallen by the sword.[u] All who had spread terror in the land of the living[v] went down uncircumcised to the earth below. They bear their shame with those who go down to the pit.[w] 25A bed is made for her among the slain, with all her hordes around her grave. All of them are uncircumcised, killed by the sword. Because their terror had spread in the land of the living, they bear their shame with those who go down to the pit; they are laid among the slain.

26"Meshech and Tubal[x] are there, with all their hordes around their graves. All of them are uncircumcised, killed by the sword because they spread their terror in the land of the living. 27Do they not lie with the other uncircumcised warriors who have fallen, who went down to the grave with their weapons of war, whose swords were placed under their heads? The punishment for their sins rested on their bones, though the terror of these warriors had stalked through the land of the living.

28"You too, O Pharaoh, will be broken and will lie among the uncircumcised, with those killed by the sword.

29"Edom[y] is there, her kings and all her princes; despite their power, they are laid with those killed by the sword. They lie with the uncircumcised, with those who go down to the pit.[z]

30"All the princes of the north[a] and all the Sidonians[b] are there; they went down with the slain in disgrace despite the terror caused by their power. They lie uncircumcised with those killed by the sword and bear their shame with those who go down to the pit.

31"Pharaoh—he and all his army—will see them and he will be consoled[c] for all his hordes that were killed by the sword, declares the Sovereign LORD. 32Although I had him spread terror in the land of the living, Pharaoh and all his hordes will be laid among the uncircumcised, with those killed by the sword, declares the Sovereign LORD."

32:23 [s] Isa 14:15
32:24 [t] Ge 10:22 [u] Jer 49:37 [v] Job 28:13 [w] Eze 26:20
32:26 [x] Ge 10:2; Eze 27:13
32:29 [y] Isa 34:5-15; Jer 49:7; Eze 35:15; Ob 1:1 [z] Eze 25:12-14
32:30 [a] Jer 25:26; Eze 38:6; 39:2 [b] Jer 25:22; Eze 28:21
32:31 [c] Eze 14:22; 31:16

Ezekiel a Watchman

33 The word of the LORD came to me: 2"Son of man, speak to your countrymen and say to them: 'When I bring the sword[d] against a land, and the people of the land choose one of their men and make him their watchman,[e] 3and he sees the sword coming against the land and blows the trumpet[f] to warn the people, 4then if anyone hears the trumpet but does not take warning[g] and the sword comes and takes his life, his blood will be on his own head.[h] 5Since he heard the sound of the trumpet but did not take warning, his blood will be on his own head. If he had taken warning, he would have saved himself. 6But if the watchman sees the sword coming and does not blow the trumpet to warn the people and the sword comes and takes the life of one of them, that man will be taken away because of his sin, but I will hold the watchman accountable for his blood.'[i]

7"Son of man, I have made you a watchman for the house of Israel; so hear the word I speak and give them warning from me.[j] 8When I say to the wicked, 'O wicked man, you will surely die,[k]' and you do not speak out to dissuade him from his ways, that wicked man will die for[a] his sin, and I will hold you accountable for his blood.[l] 9But if you do warn the wicked man to turn from his ways and he does not do so, he will die for his sin, but you will have saved yourself.[m]

10"Son of man, say to the house of Israel, 'This is what you are saying: "Our offenses and sins weigh us down, and we are wasting away[n] because of[b] them. How then can we live?[o]" ' 11Say to them, 'As surely as I live, declares the Sovereign LORD, I take no pleasure in the death of the wicked, but rather that they turn from their ways and live.[p] Turn! Turn from your evil ways! Why will you die, O house of Israel?'[q]

12"Therefore, son of man, say to your countrymen, 'The righteousness of the righteous man will not save him when

[a] 8 Or *in*; also in verse 9 [b] 10 Or *away in*

33:2 [d] Jer 12:12 [e] Eze 3:11
33:3 [f] Hos 8:1
33:4 [g] 2Ch 25:16 [h] Jer 6:17; Eze 18:13; Zec 1:4; Ac 18:6
33:6 [i] Eze 3:18
33:7 [j] Jer 26:2; Eze 3:17
33:8 [k] ver 14 [l] Eze 18:4
33:9 [m] Eze 3:17-19
33:10 [n] Eze 24:23 [o] Lev 26:39; Eze 4:17
33:11 [p] Eze 18:32; 2Pe 3:9 [q] Eze 18:23

he disobeys, and the wickedness of the
wicked man will not cause him to fall
when he turns from it. The righteous
man, if he sins, will not be allowed to live
because of his former righteousness.'[r]
13 If I tell the righteous man that he will
surely live, but then he trusts in his righteousness and does evil, none of the
righteous things he has done will be remembered; he will die for the evil he has
done.[s] 14 And if I say to the wicked man,
'You will surely die,' but he then turns
away from his sin and does what is just[t]
and right— 15 if he gives back what he
took in pledge for a loan, returns what
he has stolen,[u] follows the decrees that
give life, and does no evil, he will surely
live; he will not die.[v] 16 None of the sins
he has committed will be remembered
against him. He has done what is just
and right; he will surely live.[w]
17 "Yet your countrymen say, 'The way
of the Lord is not just.' But it is their way
that is not just. 18 If a righteous man
turns from his righteousness and does
evil, he will die for it.[x] 19 And if a wicked
man turns away from his wickedness
and does what is just and right, he will
live by doing so. 20 Yet, O house of Israel,
you say, 'The way of the Lord is not just.'
But I will judge each of you according to
his own ways."

Jerusalem's Fall Explained

21 In the twelfth year of our exile, in
the tenth month on the fifth day, a man
who had escaped[y] from Jerusalem came
to me and said, "The city has fallen![z]"
22 Now the evening before the man arrived, the hand of the LORD was upon
me,[a] and he opened my mouth[b] before
the man came to me in the morning. So
my mouth was opened and I was no
longer silent.[c]
23 Then the word of the LORD came to
me: 24 "Son of man, the people living in
those ruins[d] in the land of Israel are saying, 'Abraham was only one man, yet he
possessed the land. But we are many;
surely the land has been given to us as
our possession.'[e] 25 Therefore say to
them, 'This is what the Sovereign LORD
says: Since you eat meat with the blood[f]
still in it and look to your idols and shed
blood, should you then possess the
land?[g] 26 You rely on your sword, you do
detestable things, and each of you defiles his neighbor's wife.[h] Should you
then possess the land?'
27 "Say this to them: 'This is what the
Sovereign LORD says: As surely as I live,
those who are left in the ruins will fall by
the sword, those out in the country I will
give to the wild animals to be devoured,
and those in strongholds and caves will
die of a plague.[i] 28 I will make the land a
desolate waste, and her proud strength
will come to an end, and the mountains
of Israel will become desolate so that no
one will cross them. 29 Then they will
know that I am the LORD, when I have
made the land a desolate waste because
of all the detestable things they have
done.'
30 "As for you, son of man, your countrymen are talking together about you
by the walls and at the doors of the
houses, saying to each other, 'Come and
hear the message that has come from
the LORD.' 31 My people come to you, as
they usually do, and sit before[j] you to listen to your words, but they do not put
them into practice. With their mouths
they express devotion, but their hearts
are greedy for unjust gain.[k] 32 Indeed, to
them you are nothing more than one
who sings love songs with a beautiful
voice and plays an instrument well, for
they hear your words but do not put
them into practice.[l]
33 "When all this comes true—and it
surely will—then they will know that a
prophet has been among them.[m]"

Shepherds and Sheep

34 The word of the LORD came to
me: 2 "Son of man, prophesy
against the shepherds of Israel; prophesy and say to them: 'This is what the
Sovereign LORD says: Woe to the shepherds of Israel who only take care of
themselves! Should not shepherds take
care of the flock?[n] 3 You eat the curds,
clothe yourselves with the wool and
slaughter the choice animals, but you do
not take care of the flock.[o] 4 You have not
strengthened the weak or healed the
sick or bound up the injured. You have
not brought back the strays or searched
for the lost. You have ruled them harshly and brutally.[p] 5 So they were scattered
because there was no shepherd,[q] and
when they were scattered they became
food for all the wild animals.[r] 6 My sheep

33:12 r 2Ch 7:14; Eze 3:20
33:13 s Eze 18:24; Heb 10:38; 2Pe 2:20-21
33:14 t Eze 18:27
33:15 u Ex 22:1-4; Lev 6:2-5 v Eze 20:11; Lk 19:8
33:16 w Isa 43:25; Eze 18:22
33:18 x Eze 3:20; Eze 18:26
33:21 y Eze 24:26 z 2Ki 25:4,10; Jer 39:1-2; Eze 32:1
33:22 a Eze 1:3 b Lk 1:64 c Eze 3:26-27; 24:27
33:24 d Eze 36:4 e Isa 51:2; Jer 40:7; Eze 11:15; Ac 7:5
33:25 f Ge 9:4; Dt 12:16 g Jer 7:9-10; Eze 22:6,27
33:26 h Eze 22:11
33:27 i 1Sa 13:6; Isa 2:19; Jer 42:22; Eze 39:4
33:31 j Eze 8:1 k Ps 78:36-37; Isa 29:13; Eze 22:27; Mt 13:22; 1Jn 3:18
33:32 l Mk 6:20
33:33 m 1Sa 3:20; Jer 28:9; Eze 2:5
34:2 n Ps 78:70-72; Isa 40:11; Jer 3:15; 23:1; Mic 3:11; Jn 10:11; 21:15-17
34:3 o Isa 56:11; Eze 22:27; Zec 11:16
34:4 p Zec 11:15-17
34:5 q Nu 27:17 r ver 28; Isa 56:9

The Lord Our Shepherd

God described his tender concern for his people as that of a shepherd for his flock. This illustration encompasses both the manner in which he cares for us and the way he wants spiritual leaders to attend to the needs of those for whom they are responsible. Through his prophet Ezekiel God condemned the priests of Israel, promising that one day he would himself lead his people (Ezekiel 34:11–16).

There are many promises God has made to us, his "sheep." He will search for us when we are lost and rescue us in times of trouble (verses 11–12). He will point the way to pastures where we can feast on the choicest grass (verses 13–14). He will tend to our needs (verse 15), bind up our wounds and invigorate us when we are weak (verse 16).

In the New Testament the role of pastors and other church leaders is described in much the same way. As shepherds of God's flock, they are to follow the guidelines for compassion established by God himself (1 Peter 5:2). Jesus, God's Son, has always been the role model for his undershepherds. He referred to himself as the "good shepherd" (John 10:11), and in this role he still calls us each by name, leads us (John 10:3–4) and protects us to the point of having offered up his own life to rescue us from danger (John 10:11–13). Jesus' sacrificial death in fact entitles him to be called the "great Shepherd" (Hebrews 13:20).

The apostle Paul did not mince words when he addressed the elders in Ephesus shortly before his departure to continue on to Jerusalem: "Keep watch over yourselves and all the flock of which the Holy Spirit has made you overseers. Be shepherds of the church of God, which he bought with his own blood. I know that after I leave, savage wolves will come in among you and will not spare the flock" (Acts 20:28–29).

While we are quick to hold up a high standard for church officers and members of the clergy (as well we should!), there is a very real sense in which we as Christians are all Christ's undershepherds. Our Great Shepherd calls each of his children to reflect his tender love in our concern for other people—children, parents, neighbors, friends, working associates, acquaintances, strangers with whom we come into contact. It may well be that through the faithful service of willing Christians many lost sheep will be brought safely home to the fold.

Self-Discovery: *Think about the fact that Jesus, your Great Shepherd, has called you to be his undershepherd. Identify the people in your life who make up your flock. How can you lead them compassionately and sacrificially?*

GO TO DISCOVERY 212 ON PAGE 1115

wandered over all the mountains and on
every high hill. They were scattered over
34:6 [s]Ps 142:4; 1Pe 2:25 the whole earth, and no one searched or
looked for them.[s]
7“ ‘Therefore, you shepherds, hear the
word of the LORD: 8As surely as I live, declares the Sovereign LORD, because my
flock lacks a shepherd and so has been
plundered and has become food for all
the wild animals, and because my shepherds did not search for my flock but
cared for themselves rather than for my
flock, 9therefore, O shepherds, hear the
34:10 [t]Jer 21:13 [u]Ps 72:14 [v]1Sa 2:29-30; Zec 10:3 word of the LORD: 10This is what the Sovereign LORD says: I am against[t] the shep-
herds and will hold them accountable
for my flock. I will remove them from
tending the flock so that the shepherds
can no longer feed themselves. I will rescue[u] my flock from their mouths, and it
will no longer be food for them.[v]
11“ ‘For this is what the Sovereign
LORD says: I myself will search for my
34:12 [w]Isa 40:11; Jer 31:10; Lk 19:10 [x]Eze 30:3 sheep and look after them. 12As a shepherd[w] looks after his scattered flock
when he is with them, so will I look after
my sheep. I will rescue them from all the
places where they were scattered on a
day of clouds and darkness.[x] 13I will
bring them out from the nations and
gather them from the countries, and I
will bring them into their own land. I will
34:13 [y]Jer 23:3 pasture them on the mountains of Israel, in the ravines and in all the settlements in the land.[y] 14I will tend them in
34:14 [z]Eze 20:40 [a]Ps 23:2 [b]Eze 36:29-30 a good pasture, and the mountain
heights of Israel[z] will be their grazing
land. There they will lie down in good
grazing land, and there they will feed in
a rich pasture[a] on the mountains of Israel.[b] 15I myself will tend my sheep and
34:15 [c]Ps 23:1-2 have them lie down, declares the Sovereign LORD.[c] 16I will search for the lost and
34:16 [d]Mic 4:6 [e]Isa 10:16; Lk 5:32 bring back the strays. I will bind up the
injured and strengthen the weak,[d] but
the sleek and the strong I will destroy. I
will shepherd the flock with justice.[e]
17“ ‘As for you, my flock, this is what
the Sovereign LORD says: I will judge be-
34:17 [f]Mt 25:32-33 tween one sheep and another, and between rams and goats.[f] 18Is it not
enough for you to feed on the good pasture? Must you also trample the rest of
your pasture with your feet? Is it not
enough for you to drink clear water?
Must you also muddy the rest with your
feet? 19Must my flock feed on what you
have trampled and drink what you have
muddied with your feet?
20“ ‘Therefore this is what the Sovereign LORD says to them: See, I myself will
judge between the fat sheep and the lean
sheep. 21Because you shove with flank
and shoulder, butting all the weak sheep
with your horns[g] until you have driven 34:21 [g]Dt 33:17
them away, 22I will save my flock, and
they will no longer be plundered. I will 34:22 [h]Ps 72:12-14; Jer 23:2-3
judge between one sheep and another.[h]
23I will place over them one shepherd,
my servant David, and he will tend[i] 34:23 [i]Isa 40:11
them; he will tend them and be their 34:24 [j]Eze 36:28 [k]Jer 30:9
shepherd. 24I the LORD will be their God,[j]
and my servant David will be prince
among them. I the LORD have spoken.[k]
25“ ‘I will make a covenant of peace
with them and rid the land of wild 34:25 [l]Lev 26:6 [m]Isa 11:6-9; Hos 2:18
beasts[l] so that they may live in the
desert and sleep in the forests in safety.[m]
26I will bless[n] them and the places sur-
rounding my hill.[a] I will send down 34:26 [n]Ge 12:2 [o]Ps 68:9 [p]Dt 11:13-15; Isa 44:3
showers in season;[o] there will be show-
ers of blessing.[p] 27The trees of the field
will yield their fruit and the ground will
yield its crops; the people will be secure
in their land. They will know that I am
the LORD, when I break the bars of their 34:27 [q]Lev 26:13 [r]Jer 30:8
yoke[q] and rescue them from the hands
of those who enslaved them.[r] 28They will
no longer be plundered by the nations,
nor will wild animals devour them. They 34:28 [s]Jer 30:10; Eze 39:26
will live in safety, and no one will make
them afraid.[s] 29I will provide for them a
land renowned[t] for its crops, and they 34:29 [t]Isa 4:2 [u]Eze 36:29 [v]Eze 36:6 [w]Eze 36:15
will no longer be victims of famine[u] in
the land or bear the scorn[v] of the nations.[w] 30Then they will know that I, the
LORD their God, am with them and that
they, the house of Israel, are my people, 34:30 [x]Eze 14:11; 37:27
declares the Sovereign LORD.[x] 31You my
sheep, the sheep of my pasture,[y] are peo-
ple, and I am your God, declares the 34:31 [y]Ps 100:3; Jer 23:1
Sovereign LORD.’ ”

A Prophecy Against Edom

35 The word of the LORD came to
me: 2“Son of man, set your face
against Mount Seir; prophesy against it
3and say: ‘This is what the Sovereign
LORD says: I am against you, Mount Seir,
and I will stretch out my hand[z] against 35:3 [z]Jer 6:12 [a]Eze 25:12-14
you and make you a desolate waste.[a] 4I
will turn your towns into ruins and you

[a] 26 Or *I will make them and the places surrounding my hill a blessing*

will be desolate. Then you will know that
I am the LORD.[b]
5" 'Because you harbored an ancient
hostility and delivered the Israelites over
to the sword at the time of their calamity, the time their punishment reached
its climax,[c] 6therefore as surely as I live,
declares the Sovereign LORD, I will give
you over to bloodshed and it will pursue
you.[d] Since you did not hate bloodshed,
bloodshed will pursue you. 7I will make
Mount Seir a desolate waste and cut off
from it all who come and go. 8I will fill
your mountains with the slain; those
killed by the sword will fall on your hills
and in your valleys and in all your ravines.[e] 9I will make you desolate forever;
your towns will not be inhabited. Then
you will know that I am the LORD.[f]
10" 'Because you have said, "These two
nations and countries will be ours and
we will take possession[g] of them," even
though I the LORD was there, 11therefore

35:4 [b]ver 9
35:5 [c]Ps 137:7; Eze 21:29
35:6 [d]Isa 63:2-6
35:8 [e]Eze 31:12
35:9 [f]Jer 49:13
35:10 [g]Ps 83:12; Eze 36:2,5

EDOM IS CONDEMNED

In Ezekiel 35:3 God through his prophet addressed some harsh words to the nation of Edom: "I am against you . . and I will stretch out my hand against you and make you a desolate waste." Israel (Jacob's descendants) and Edom (descendants of his brother Esau) were long-time enemies (Genesis 27:41). Esau's family had despised the nation of Israel for years, to the point of celebrating when Israel suffered reversals or losses (Ezekiel 35:12–15; see also the book of Obadiah). When the Babylonians burned Jerusalem, the Edomites looted the city (Obadiah 12–14). But their attitude went beyond contempt for the people of the city; the Edomites were actually belittling God and his work among his chosen people. Because of Edom's continuing hatred of Israel, God gave the Edomites over to devastation and spiritual barrenness. Still today Petra and Teman, the great ancient cities of Edom, lie in total ruin. Ezekiel's prophecy has a similar tone to Jesus' message in Matthew 25:31–46, in which our Lord informed the people that he would separate the nations who would one day gather before him as "a shepherd separates the sheep from the goats" (Matthew 25:32). When Jesus comes back for his people, some nations will be blessed but others severely condemned for their callous attitude toward God and his people.

as surely as I live, declares the Sovereign
LORD, I will treat you in accordance with
the anger[h] and jealousy you showed in
your hatred of them and I will make myself known among them when I judge
you.[i] 12Then you will know that I the
LORD have heard all the contemptible
things you have said against the mountains of Israel. You said, "They have been
laid waste and have been given over to
us to devour.[j]" 13You boasted against me
and spoke against me without restraint,
and I heard it.[k] 14This is what the Sovereign LORD says: While the whole earth
rejoices, I will make you desolate.[l] 15Be-
cause you rejoiced[m] when the inheritance of the house of Israel became desolate, that is how I will treat you. You will
be desolate, O Mount Seir,[n] you and all
of Edom.[o] Then they will know that I am
the LORD.' "

A Prophecy to the Mountains of Israel

36 "Son of man, prophesy to the
mountains of Israel and say,
'O mountains of Israel, hear the word of
the LORD. 2This is what the Sovereign
LORD says: The enemy said of you, "Aha![p]
The ancient heights[q] have become our
possession.[r]" ' 3Therefore prophesy and
say, 'This is what the Sovereign LORD
says: Because they ravaged and hounded you from every side so that you became the possession of the rest of the
nations and the object of people's malicious talk and slander,[s] 4therefore,
O mountains of Israel, hear the word of
the Sovereign LORD: This is what the
Sovereign LORD says to the mountains
and hills, to the ravines and valleys,[t] to
the desolate ruins and the deserted
towns that have been plundered and
ridiculed by the rest of the nations
around you[u]— 5this is what the Sovereign LORD says: In my burning zeal I
have spoken against the rest of the nations, and against all Edom, for with glee
and with malice in their hearts they
made my land their own possession so
that they might plunder its pastureland.'[v] 6Therefore prophesy concerning
the land of Israel and say to the mountains and hills, to the ravines and valleys:
'This is what the Sovereign LORD says: I
speak in my jealous wrath because you
have suffered the scorn of the nations.[w]
7Therefore this is what the Sovereign

35:11 [h]Eze 25:14 [i]Ps 9:16; Mt 7:2
35:12 [j]Jer 50:7
35:13 [k]Da 11:36
35:14 [l]Jer 51:48
35:15 [m]Ob 1:12 [n]ver 3 [o]Isa 34:5-6,11; Jer 50:11-13; La 4:21
36:2 [p]Eze 25:3 [q]Dt 32:13 [r]Eze 35:10
36:3 [s]Ps 44:13-14
36:4 [t]Eze 6:3 [u]Dt 11:11; Ps 79:4; Eze 34:28
36:5 [v]Jer 50:11; Eze 25:12-14; 35:10,15
36:6 [w]Ps 123:3-4; Eze 34:29

LORD says: I swear with uplifted hand
that the nations around you will also
suffer scorn.
36:8 8" 'But you, O mountains of Israel, will
x Isa 27:6 produce branches and fruit[x] for my people Israel, for they will soon come home.
9I am concerned for you and will look on
you with favor; you will be plowed and
sown, 10and I will multiply the number of
people upon you, even the whole house
36:10 of Israel. The towns will be inhabited and
y ver 33; the ruins rebuilt.[y] 11I will increase the
Isa 49:17-23 number of men and animals upon you,
and they will be fruitful and become numerous. I will settle people on you as in
36:11 z Mic 7:14 the past[z] and will make you prosper
a Jer 31:28; more than before.[a] Then you will know
Eze 16:55 that I am the LORD. 12I will cause people,
my people Israel, to walk upon you. They
36:12 will possess you, and you will be their in-
b Eze 47:14,22 heritance;[b] you will never again deprive
them of their children.
13" 'This is what the Sovereign LORD
36:13 says: Because people say to you, "You de-
c Nu 13:32 vour men[c] and deprive your nation of its
children," 14therefore you will no longer
devour men or make your nation childless, declares the Sovereign LORD. 15No
longer will I make you hear the taunts of
the nations, and no longer will you suffer the scorn of the peoples or cause
36:15 your nation to fall, declares the Sover-
d Ps 89:50-51; Eze 34:29 eign LORD.[d] "
16Again the word of the LORD came to
me: 17"Son of man, when the people of
Israel were living in their own land, they
defiled it by their conduct and their ac-
36:17 tions. Their conduct was like a woman's
e Jer 2:7 monthly uncleanness in my sight.[e] 18So
36:18 I poured out[f] my wrath on them be-
f 2Ch 34:21 cause they had shed blood in the land
and because they had defiled it with
36:19 their idols. 19I dispersed them among
g Dt 28:64 the nations, and they were scattered[g]
h Eze 39:24 through the countries; I judged them according to their conduct and their ac-
36:20 tions.[h] 20And wherever they went
i Ro 2:24 among the nations they profaned[i] my
j Isa 52:5; holy name, for it was said of them,
Jer 33:24; 'These are the LORD's people, and yet
Eze 12:16 they had to leave his land.'[j] 21I had concern for my holy name, which the house
36:21 k Ps 74:18; of Israel profaned among the nations
Isa 48:9 where they had gone.[k]
22"Therefore say to the house of Israel, 'This is what the Sovereign LORD says:
It is not for your sake, O house of Israel,

that I am going to do these things, but
for the sake of my holy name, which you 36:22
have profaned[l] among the nations l Ro 2:24*
where you have gone.[m] 23I will show the m Ps 106:8
holiness of my great name, which has
been profaned among the nations, the
name you have profaned among them.
Then the nations will know that I am
the LORD, declares the Sovereign LORD, 36:23
when I show myself holy[n] through you n Eze 20:41
before their eyes.[o] o Ps 126:2; Isa 5:16
24" 'For I will take you out of the nations; I will gather you from all the coun- 36:24
tries and bring you back into your own p Eze 34:13; 37:21
land.[p] 25I will sprinkle[q] clean water on
you, and you will be clean; I will cleanse[r] 36:25
you from all your impurities and from all q Heb 9:13; 10:22 r Ps 51:2,7
your idols.[s] 26I will give you a new heart[t] s Zec 13:2
and put a new spirit in you; I will remove 36:26
from you your heart of stone and give t Jer 24:7 u Ps 51:10;
you a heart of flesh.[u] 27And I will put my Eze 11:19
Spirit[v] in you and move you to follow my
decrees and be careful to keep my laws. 36:27
28You will live in the land I gave your fore- v Eze 37:14
fathers; you will be my people,[w] and I will 36:28 w Jer 30:22
be your God.[x] 29I will save you from all x Eze 14:11; 37:14,27
your uncleanness. I will call for the grain
and make it plentiful and will not bring 36:29
famine[y] upon you. 30I will increase the y Eze 34:29
fruit of the trees and the crops of the
field, so that you will no longer suffer dis- 36:30
grace among the nations because of z Lev 26:4-5;
famine.[z] 31Then you will remember your Eze 34:27;
evil ways and wicked deeds, and you will Hos 2:21-22
loathe yourselves for your sins and de-
testable practices.[a] 32I want you to know 36:31 a Eze 6:9; 20:43
that I am not doing this for your sake,
declares the Sovereign LORD. Be ashamed
and disgraced for your conduct, O house 36:32
of Israel![b] b Dt 9:5
33" 'This is what the Sovereign LORD
says: On the day I cleanse you from all
your sins, I will resettle your towns, and
the ruins will be rebuilt. 34The desolate
land will be cultivated instead of lying
desolate in the sight of all who pass
through it. 35They will say, "This land
that was laid waste has become like the 36:35
garden of Eden;[c] the cities that were ly- c Joel 2:3
ing in ruins, desolate and destroyed, are d Isa 51:3
now fortified and inhabited.[d]" 36Then
the nations around you that remain will
know that I the LORD have rebuilt what
was destroyed and have replanted what 36:36
was desolate. I the LORD have spoken, e Eze 17:22;
and I will do it.'[e] 22:14; 37:14;
37"This is what the Sovereign LORD 39:27-28

DISCOVERY 212

Radical Transformation

One of the pitfalls we face in following Jesus is the temptation to focus on how our lives look to others rather than on how God is changing us from the inside out—one day at a time. Matters of the heart are God's chief concern. We can be quick to judge the Old Testament Israelites for losing their focus on God in the context of what looks to us like the clutter of endless rituals, but aren't we tempted also to take our eyes off the Lord and concentrate on our outward appearance of spirituality, on how we present ourselves both to others and to God?

God promised Ezekiel that he would provide the nation of Israel with a new heart and a new spirit. The people would experience a fundamental transformation from the inside out, and this radical change of heart and spirit would inevitably lead to a life of obedience (Ezekiel 36:26–27).

First, God promised a new heart. Sin rejoices in prompting us to deny the truth, but God is explicit in his analysis: "The heart is deceitful above all things and beyond cure" (Jeremiah 17:9). Our entire self has been permeated and corrupted by sin, and we are powerless to change that fact.

But God is a heart surgeon of incomparable skill—in fact, he administers a total heart transplant! He removes the old heart of stone (Ezekiel 36:26) that has resisted his will and replaces it with a new, softer version—one that is vital and responsive. A new heart offers new life, new direction, new desires and new possibilities.

Second, God promised that along with their new heart would come the very Spirit of God (verse 27). In the Old Testament the Spirit of God *came on* people but did not *live in* people. God's promise of his indwelling Spirit must have sounded strange to the ears of Old Testament believers. Much later Jesus promised that the Holy Spirit would be present after his ascension to guide the disciples into all truth (John 16:5–15). The outpouring of the Spirit occurred in a dramatic way on the day of Pentecost (Acts 2:1-4). It is that same Spirit within our own hearts who infuses in us the power to resist sin and to obey the Lord (Galatians 5:16–26).

Jesus made it abundantly clear that we are incapable of camouflaging that which lies deepest within our hearts. In his Sermon on the Mount our Lord made the profound statement that "where [our] treasure is, there [our] heart will be also" (Matthew 6:21). Later on he told a group of Pharisees that "out of the overflow of the heart the mouth speaks" (Matthew 12:34).

Finally, Jesus summarized the intent behind the law, the seemingly exacting Ten Commandments, indicating that the spirit of the law is in essence a matter of the heart: "Love the Lord your God with all your heart and with all your soul and with all your mind and with all your strength" (Mark 12:30). With heart, soul, mind and strength—in other words, with everything we are—we are called to love our God. And out of this love will inevitably flow an outpouring of heartfelt and selfless service, service that the world will see and recognize as the genuine article.

Self-Discovery: *What images or implications come to mind when you think of the Holy Spirit living in your heart?*

GO TO DISCOVERY 213 ON PAGE 1117

says: Once again I will yield to the plea of
the house of Israel and do this for them:
I will make their people as numerous as
36:38 [f]1Ki 8:63; 2Ch 35:7-9 sheep, 38 as numerous as the flocks for
offerings[f] at Jerusalem during her ap-
pointed feasts. So will the ruined cities
be filled with flocks of people. Then they
will know that I am the LORD."

The Valley of Dry Bones

37:1 [g]Eze 1:3; 8:3 [h]Eze 11:24; Lk 4:1; Ac 8:39 [i]Jer 7:32 [j]Jer 8:2; Eze 40:1 37 The hand of the LORD was upon
me,[g] and he brought me out by
the Spirit[h] of the LORD and set me in the
middle of a valley;[i] it was full of bones.[j]
2 He led me back and forth among them,
and I saw a great many bones on the
floor of the valley, bones that were very
dry. 3 He asked me, "Son of man, can
37:3 [k]Dt 32:39; 1Sa 2:6; Isa 26:19 these bones live?"

I said, "O Sovereign LORD, you alone
know.[k]"

4 Then he said to me, "Prophesy to
37:4 [l]Jer 22:29 these bones and say to them, 'Dry bones,
hear the word of the LORD![l] 5 This is what
the Sovereign LORD says to these bones:
37:5 [m]Ge 2:7; Ps 104:29-30 I will make breath[a] enter you, and you
will come to life.[m] 6 I will attach tendons
to you and make flesh come upon you
and cover you with skin; I will put breath
37:6 [n]Eze 38:23; Joel 2:27; 3:17 in you, and you will come to life. Then
you will know that I am the LORD.[n]' "

7 So I prophesied as I was commanded. And as I was prophesying, there was
a noise, a rattling sound, and the bones
came together, bone to bone. 8 I looked,
and tendons and flesh appeared on
them and skin covered them, but there
was no breath in them.

9 Then he said to me, "Prophesy to the
37:9 [o]Ps 104:30 breath;[o] prophesy, son of man, and say
to it, 'This is what the Sovereign LORD
says: Come from the four winds,
O breath, and breathe into these slain,
that they may live.' " 10 So I prophesied as
he commanded me, and breath entered
37:10 [p]Rev 11:11 them; they came to life and stood up on
their feet—a vast army.[p]

11 Then he said to me: "Son of man,
these bones are the whole house of Isra-
37:11 [q]La 3:54 el. They say, 'Our bones are dried up and
our hope is gone; we are cut off.'[q]
12 Therefore prophesy and say to them:
37:12 [r]Dt 32:39; 1Sa 2:6; Isa 26:19; Hos 13:14; Am 9:14-15 'This is what the Sovereign LORD says:
O my people, I am going to open your
graves and bring you up from them; I
will bring you back to the land of Israel.[r]
13 Then you, my people, will know that I
am the LORD, when I open your graves
and bring you up from them. 14 I will put 37:14 [s]Joel 2:28-29 [t]Eze 36:27-28, 36
my Spirit[s] in you and you will live, and I
will settle you in your own land. Then
you will know that I the LORD have spoken, and I have done it, declares the
LORD.[t]' "

One Nation Under One King

15 The word of the LORD came to me:
16 "Son of man, take a stick of wood and
write on it, 'Belonging to Judah and the
Israelites[u] associated with him.'[v] Then 37:16 [u]1Ki 12:20; 2Ch 10:17-19 [v]Nu 17:2-3; 2Ch 15:9
take another stick of wood, and write on
it, 'Ephraim's stick, belonging to Joseph
and all the house of Israel associated
with him.' 17 Join them together into one 37:17 [w]ver 24; Isa 11:13; Jer 50:4; Hos 1:11
stick so that they will become one in
your hand.[w]

18 "When your countrymen ask you,
'Won't you tell us what you mean by
this?'[x] 19 say to them, 'This is what the 37:18 [x]Eze 24:19
Sovereign LORD says: I am going to take
the stick of Joseph—which is in Ephraim's hand—and of the Israelite tribes associated with him, and join it to Judah's
stick, making them a single stick of
wood, and they will become one in my
hand.'[y] 20 Hold before their eyes the 37:19 [y]Zec 10:6
sticks you have written on 21 and say to
them, 'This is what the Sovereign LORD
says: I will take the Israelites out of the
nations where they have gone. I will
gather them from all around and bring 37:21 [z]Isa 43:5-6; Eze 36:24; 39:27
them back into their own land.[z] 22 I will
make them one nation in the land, on
the mountains of Israel. There will be
one king over all of them and they will
never again be two nations or be divid- 37:22 [a]Isa 11:13; Jer 3:18; Hos 1:11
ed into two kingdoms.[a] 23 They will no
longer defile[b] themselves with their
idols and vile images or with any of their 37:23 [b]Eze 36:25; 43:7 [c]Eze 11:18; 36:28
offenses, for I will save them from all
their sinful backsliding,[b] and I will
cleanse them. They will be my people,
and I will be their God.[c]

24 " 'My servant David[d] will be king 37:24 [d]Hos 3:5 [e]Isa 40:11; Eze 34:23 [f]Ps 78:70-71
over them, and they will all have one
shepherd.[e] They will follow my laws and
be careful to keep my decrees.[f] 25 They
will live in the land I gave to my servant
Jacob, the land where your fathers lived.[g] 37:25 [g]Eze 28:25
They and their children and their chil-

[a] 5 The Hebrew for this word can also mean *wind* or *spirit* (see verses 6–14). [b] 23 Many Hebrew manuscripts (see also Septuagint); most Hebrew manuscripts *all their dwelling places where they sinned*

DISCOVERY 213

Revitalizing Dry Bones

God accompanied his servant Ezekiel on an incredible trip—a spiritual journey to a land of dry bones. In this vision the Lord asked Ezekiel whether the piles of bones could come back to life. Simple question with an obvious answer—or so Ezekiel assumed. And yet he refused to give a definite response one way or the other. If he were to have reminded God that bones can't live, he would have been expressing doubt concerning God's power. On the other hand, accepting the premise that the bones could indeed come back to life would have implied endorsing a human impossibility. The prophet responded with what seemed the only plausible answer, "O Sovereign Lord, you alone know" (Ezekiel 37:3).

Ezekiel did not formulate his own plan of action but instead placed his trust in God's ability to act. After Ezekiel had responded in faith, God gave him what seemed a ludicrous directive: "Prophesy to these bones and say to them . . . 'You will come to life' " (verses 4–5).

It is one thing to believe that God can accomplish the impossible but quite another to become personally involved in the process. Ezekiel, however, did exactly as God had requested. Incredibly, those bones did take on flesh and become animate. Before long, an entire army stood at attention. On that day God performed a phenomenal miracle for Ezekiel's benefit in order to remind his people that he is indeed the Lord (verse 13) and that his promises are powerful and true.

When God's Word is faithfully taught, that which is dead in our souls is revitalized through the working of God's Holy Spirit. Paul enthused, "I can do everything through [Jesus] who gives me strength" (Philippians 4:13). And Jesus told his disciples that "apart from [him they could] do nothing" (John 15:5). The same Jesus who raised Lazarus from the dead, healed the sick and fed more than 5,000 people with a few fish and loaves of bread can do the seemingly impossible for us. He can transform our listless spirits and make of us a powerful army of servants. God can breathe life into the most desperate of situations.

Oftentimes our strength becomes depleted to the point of discouragement or even despair. At such times we can trust the truth of God's Word to instill new vitality into our monotonous routine. *Nothing* is impossible for our God!

Self-Discovery: What do you think Paul meant when he claimed that Jesus provided him with the ability to do all things? What are the implications of these words for your life?

GO TO DISCOVERY 214 ON PAGE 1133

dren's children will live there forever,[h] and David my servant will be their prince forever.[i] 26 I will make a covenant of peace[j] with them; it will be an everlasting covenant. I will establish them and increase their numbers,[k] and I will put my sanctuary among them forever.[l] 27 My dwelling place[m] will be with them; I will be their God, and they will be my people.[n] 28 Then the nations will know that I the LORD make Israel holy,[o] when my sanctuary is among them forever.' "

A Prophecy Against Gog

38 The word of the LORD came to me: 2 "Son of man, set your face against Gog, of the land of Magog,[p] the chief prince of[a] Meshech and Tubal;[q] prophesy against him 3 and say: 'This is what the Sovereign LORD says: I am against you, O Gog, chief prince of[b] Meshech and Tubal.[r] 4 I will turn you around, put hooks[s] in your jaws and bring you out with your whole army—your horses, your horsemen fully armed, and a great horde with large and small shields, all of them brandishing their swords.[t] 5 Persia, Cush[c][u] and Put[v] will be with them, all with shields and helmets, 6 also Gomer[w] with all its troops, and Beth Togarmah[x] from the far north with all its troops—the many nations with you.

7 " 'Get ready; be prepared,[y] you and all the hordes gathered about you, and take command of them. 8 After many days[z] you will be called to arms. In future years you will invade a land that has recovered from war, whose people were gathered from many nations[a] to the mountains of Israel, which had long been desolate. They had been brought out from the nations, and now all of them live in safety.[b] 9 You and all your troops and the many nations with you will go up, advancing like a storm;[c] you will be like a cloud[d] covering the land.

10 " 'This is what the Sovereign LORD says: On that day thoughts will come into your mind and you will devise an evil scheme.[e] 11 You will say, "I will invade a land of unwalled villages; I will attack a peaceful and unsuspecting people—all of them living without walls and without gates and bars.[f] 12 I will plunder and loot and turn my hand against the resettled ruins and the people gathered from the nations, rich in livestock and goods, living at the center of the land." 13 Sheba[g] and Dedan and the merchants of Tarshish and all her villages[d] will say to you, "Have you come to plunder? Have you gathered your hordes to loot, to carry off silver and gold, to take away livestock and goods and to seize much plunder?[h]" '

14 "Therefore, son of man, prophesy and say to Gog: 'This is what the Sovereign LORD says: In that day, when my people Israel are living in safety,[i] will you not take notice of it? 15 You will come from your place in the far north, you and many nations with you, all of them riding on horses, a great horde, a mighty army.[j] 16 You will advance against my people Israel like a cloud[k] that covers the land. In days to come, O Gog, I will bring you against my land, so that the nations may know me when I show myself holy through you before their eyes.[l]

17 " 'This is what the Sovereign LORD says: Are you not the one I spoke of in former days by my servants the prophets of Israel? At that time they prophesied for years that I would bring you against them. 18 This is what will happen in that day: When Gog attacks the land of Israel, my hot anger will be aroused, declares the Sovereign LORD. 19 In my zeal and fiery wrath I declare that at that time there shall be a great earthquake in the land of Israel.[m] 20 The fish of the sea, the birds of the air, the beasts of the field, every creature that moves along the ground, and all the people on the face of the earth will tremble at my presence. The mountains will be overturned, the cliffs will crumble and every wall will fall to the ground.[n] 21 I will summon a sword[o] against Gog on all my mountains, declares the Sovereign LORD. Every man's sword will be against his brother.[p] 22 I will execute judgment[q] upon him with plague and bloodshed; I will pour down torrents of rain, hailstones[r] and burning sulfur on him and on his troops and on the many nations with him. 23 And so I will show my greatness and my holiness, and I will make myself known in the sight of many nations. Then they will know that I am the LORD.[s]'

[a] 2 Or *the prince of Rosh,* [b] 3 Or *Gog, prince of Rosh,* [c] 5 That is, the upper Nile region [d] 13 Or *her strong lions*

37:25 h Am 9:15 i Isa 11:1
37:26 j Isa 55:3 k Jer 30:19 l Eze 16:62
37:27 m Lev 26:11; Jn 1:14 n 2Co 6:16*
37:28 o Ex 31:13; Eze 20:12
38:2 p Ge 10:2 q Rev 20:8
38:3 r Eze 39:1
38:4 s 2Ki 19:28 t Eze 29:4; Da 11:40
38:5 u Ge 10:6 v Eze 27:10
38:6 w Ge 10:2 x Eze 27:14
38:7 y Isa 8:9
38:8 z Isa 24:22 a Isa 11:11 b Jer 23:6
38:9 c Isa 28:2 d Jer 4:13; Joel 2:2
38:10 e Ps 36:4; Mic 2:1
38:11 f Jer 49:31; Zec 2:4
38:13 g Eze 27:22 h Isa 10:6; Jer 15:13
38:14 i ver 8; Zec 2:5
38:15 j Eze 39:2
38:16 k ver 9 l Isa 29:23; Eze 39:21
38:19 m Ps 18:7; Eze 5:13; Hag 2:6,21
38:20 n Hos 4:3; Na 1:5
38:21 o Eze 14:17 p 1Sa 14:20; 2Ch 20:23; Hag 2:22
38:22 q Isa 66:16; Jer 25:31 r Ps 18:12; Rev 16:21
38:23 s Eze 36:23

39 "Son of man, prophesy against Gog and say: 'This is what the Sovereign LORD says: I am against you, O Gog, chief prince of[a] Meshech and Tubal.[t] 2I will turn you around and drag you along. I will bring you from the far north and send you against the mountains of Israel. 3Then I will strike your bow[u] from your left hand and make your arrows[v] drop from your right hand. 4On the mountains of Israel you will fall, you and all your troops and the nations with you. I will give you as food to all kinds of carrion birds and to the wild animals.[w] 5You will fall in the open field, for I have spoken, declares the Sovereign LORD. 6I will send fire[x] on Magog and on those who live in safety in the coastlands,[y] and they will know that I am the LORD.

7" 'I will make known my holy name among my people Israel. I will no longer let my holy name be profaned,[z] and the nations will know that I the LORD am the Holy One in Israel.[a] 8It is coming! It will surely take place, declares the Sovereign LORD. This is the day I have spoken of.

9" 'Then those who live in the towns of Israel will go out and use the weapons for fuel and burn them up—the small and large shields, the bows and arrows, the war clubs and spears. For seven years they will use them for fuel.[b] 10They will not need to gather wood from the fields or cut it from the forests, because they will use the weapons for fuel. And they will plunder those who plundered them and loot those who looted them, declares the Sovereign LORD.[c]

11" 'On that day I will give Gog a burial place in Israel, in the valley of those who travel east toward[b] the Sea.[c] It will block the way of travelers, because Gog and all his hordes will be buried there. So it will be called the Valley of Hamon Gog.[d][d]

12" 'For seven months the house of Israel will be burying them in order to cleanse the land.[e] 13All the people of the land will bury them, and the day I am glorified[f] will be a memorable day for them, declares the Sovereign LORD.

14" 'Men will be regularly employed to cleanse the land. Some will go throughout the land and, in addition to them, others will bury those that remain on the ground. At the end of the seven months they will begin their search. 15As they go through the land and one of them sees a human bone, he will set up a marker beside it until the gravediggers have buried it in the Valley of Hamon Gog. 16(Also a town called Hamonah[e] will be there.) And so they will cleanse the land.'

17"Son of man, this is what the Sovereign LORD says: Call out to every kind of bird[g] and all the wild animals: 'Assemble and come together from all around to the sacrifice I am preparing for you, the great sacrifice on the mountains of Israel. There you will eat flesh and drink blood. 18You will eat the flesh of mighty men and drink the blood of the princes of the earth as if they were rams and lambs, goats and bulls—all of them fattened animals from Bashan.[h] 19At the sacrifice I am preparing for you, you will eat fat till you are glutted and drink blood till you are drunk. 20At my table you will eat your fill of horses and riders, mighty men and soldiers of every kind,' declares the Sovereign LORD.[i]

21"I will display my glory among the nations, and all the nations will see the punishment I inflict and the hand I lay upon them.[j] 22From that day forward the house of Israel will know that I am the LORD their God. 23And the nations will know that the people of Israel went into exile for their sin, because they were unfaithful to me. So I hid my face from them and handed them over to their enemies, and they all fell by the sword.[k] 24I dealt with them according to their uncleanness and their offenses, and I hid my face from them.[l]

25"Therefore this is what the Sovereign LORD says: I will now bring Jacob back from captivity[f][m] and will have compassion[n] on all the people of Israel, and I will be zealous for my holy name.[o] 26They will forget their shame and all the unfaithfulness they showed toward me when they lived in safety[p] in their land with no one to make them afraid.[q] 27When I have brought them back from the nations and have gathered them from the countries of their enemies, I will show myself holy through them in the sight of many nations.[r] 28Then they

a 1 Or *Gog, prince of Rosh,* *b 11* Or *of* *c 11* That is, the Dead Sea *d 11* *Hamon Gog* means *hordes of Gog.* *e 16* *Hamonah* means *horde.* *f 25* Or *now restore the fortunes of Jacob*

39:1 t Eze 38:2,3
39:3 u Hos 1:5 v Ps 76:3
39:4 w ver 17-20; Eze 29:5; 33:27
39:6 x Eze 30:8; Am 1:4 y Jer 25:22
39:7 z Ex 20:7 a Isa 12:6; Eze 36:16,23
39:9 b Ps 46:9
39:10 c Isa 14:2; 33:1; Hab 2:8
39:11 d Eze 38:2
39:12 e Dt 21:23
39:13 f Eze 28:22
39:17 g Rev 19:17
39:18 h Ps 22:12; Jer 51:40
39:20 i Rev 19:17-18
39:21 j Ex 9:16; Isa 37:20; Eze 38:16
39:23 k Isa 1:15; 59:2; Jer 22:8-9; 44:23
39:24 l Jer 2:17,19; 4:18; Eze 36:19
39:25 m Jer 33:7; Eze 34:13 n Jer 30:18 o Isa 27:12-13
39:26 p 1Ki 4:25 q Isa 17:2; Eze 34:28; Mic 4:4
39:27 r Eze 36:23-24; 37:21; 38:16

will know that I am the LORD their God, for though I sent them into exile among the nations, I will gather them to their own land, not leaving any behind. 29 I will no longer hide my face from them, for I will pour out my Spirit[s] on the house of Israel, declares the Sovereign LORD."

The New Temple Area

40 In the twenty-fifth year of our exile, at the beginning of the year, on the tenth of the month, in the fourteenth year after the fall of the city[t]—on that very day the hand of the LORD was upon me[u] and he took me there. 2 In visions[v] of God he took me to the land of Israel and set me on a very high mountain,[w] on whose south side were some buildings that looked like a city. 3 He took me there, and I saw a man whose appearance was like bronze;[x] he was standing in the gateway with a linen cord and a measuring rod[y] in his hand. 4 The man said to me, "Son of man, look with your eyes and hear with your ears and pay attention to everything I am going to show you, for that is why you have been brought here. Tell[z] the house of Israel everything you see.[a]"

The East Gate to the Outer Court

5 I saw a wall completely surrounding the temple area. The length of the measuring rod in the man's hand was six long cubits, each of which was a cubit[a] and a handbreadth.[b] He measured[b] the wall; it was one measuring rod thick and one rod high.

6 Then he went to the gate facing east.[c] He climbed its steps and measured the threshold of the gate; it was one rod deep.[c] 7 The alcoves[d] for the guards were one rod long and one rod wide, and the projecting walls between the alcoves were five cubits thick. And the threshold of the gate next to the portico facing the temple was one rod deep.

8 Then he measured the portico of the gateway; 9 it[d] was eight cubits deep and its jambs were two cubits thick. The portico of the gateway faced the temple.

10 Inside the east gate were three alcoves on each side; the three had the same measurements, and the faces of the projecting walls on each side had the same measurements. 11 Then he measured the width of the entrance to the gateway; it was ten cubits and its length was thirteen cubits. 12 In front of each alcove was a wall one cubit high, and the alcoves were six cubits square. 13 Then he measured the gateway from the top of the rear wall of one alcove to the top of the opposite one; the distance was twenty-five cubits from one parapet opening to the opposite one. 14 He measured along the faces of the projecting walls all around the inside of the gateway—sixty cubits. The measurement was up to the portico[e] facing the courtyard.[f][e] 15 The distance from the entrance of the gateway to the far end of its portico was fifty cubits. 16 The alcoves and the projecting walls inside the gateway were surmounted by narrow parapet openings all around, as was the portico; the openings all around faced inward. The faces of the projecting walls were decorated with palm trees.[f]

The Outer Court

17 Then he brought me into the outer court.[g] There I saw some rooms and a pavement that had been constructed all around the court; there were thirty rooms[h] along the pavement.[i] 18 It abutted the sides of the gateways and was as wide as they were long; this was the lower pavement. 19 Then he measured the distance from the inside of the lower gateway to the outside of the inner court;[j] it was a hundred cubits[k] on the east side as well as on the north.

The North Gate

20 Then he measured the length and width of the gate facing north, leading into the outer court. 21 Its alcoves[l]—three on each side—its projecting walls and its portico had the same measurements as those of the first gateway. It was fifty cubits long and twenty-five cubits wide. 22 Its openings, its portico[m] and its palm tree decorations had the same measurements as those of the gate facing east. Seven steps led up to it, with

39:29 [s] Joel 2:28; Ac 2:17
40:1 [t] 2Ki 25:7; Jer 39:1-10; 52:4-11; Eze 33:21 [u] Eze 1:3
40:2 [v] Da 7:1,7 [w] Eze 17:22; Rev 21:10
40:3 [x] Eze 1:7; Da 10:6; Rev 1:15 [y] Eze 47:3; Zec 2:1-2; Rev 11:1; 21:15
40:4 [z] Jer 26:2 [a] Eze 44:5
40:5 [b] Eze 42:20
40:6 [c] Eze 8:16
40:7 [d] ver 36
40:14 [e] Ex 27:9
40:16 [f] ver 21-22; 2Ch 3:5; Eze 41:26
40:17 [g] Rev 11:2 [h] Eze 41:6 [i] Eze 42:1
40:19 [j] Eze 46:1 [k] ver 23,27
40:21 [l] ver 7
40:22 [m] ver 49

[a] 5 The common cubit was about 1 1/2 feet (about 0.5 meter). [b] 5 That is, about 3 inches (about 8 centimeters) [c] 6 Septuagint; Hebrew *deep, the first threshold, one rod deep* [d] 8,9 Many Hebrew manuscripts, Septuagint, Vulgate and Syriac; most Hebrew manuscripts *gateway facing the temple; it was one rod deep. 9 Then he measured the portico of the gateway; it* [e] 14 Septuagint; Hebrew *projecting wall* [f] 14 The meaning of the Hebrew for this verse is uncertain.

its portico opposite them. 23There was a
gate to the inner court facing the north
gate, just as there was on the east. He
40:23 measured from one gate to the opposite
n ver 19 one; it was a hundred cubits.[n]

The South Gate

24Then he led me to the south side
and I saw a gate facing south. He measured its jambs and its portico, and they
had the same measurements as the others. 25The gateway and its portico had
narrow openings all around, like the
openings of the others. It was fifty cubits
40:25 long and twenty-five cubits wide.[o] 26Sev-
o ver 33 en steps led up to it, with its portico opposite them; it had palm tree decora-
tions on the faces of the projecting walls
40:26 on each side.[p] 27The inner court[q] also
p ver 22 had a gate facing south, and he mea-
40:27 sured from this gate to the outer gate on
q ver 32 the south side; it was a hundred cubits.

Gates to the Inner Court

28Then he brought me into the inner
court through the south gate, and he
40:28 measured the south gate; it had the
r ver 35 same measurements[r] as the others. 29Its
alcoves, its projecting walls and its portico had the same measurements as the
others. The gateway and its portico had
openings all around. It was fifty cubits
long and twenty-five cubits wide. 30(The
40:30 porticoes[s] of the gateways around the
s ver 21 inner court were twenty-five cubits wide
40:31 and five cubits deep.) 31Its portico[t] faced
t ver 22 the outer court; palm trees decorated its
jambs, and eight steps led up to it.

32Then he brought me to the inner
court on the east side, and he measured
the gateway; it had the same measurements as the others. 33Its alcoves, its
projecting walls and its portico had the
same measurements as the others. The
gateway and its portico had openings all
around. It was fifty cubits long and
40:34 twenty-five cubits wide. 34Its portico[u]
u ver 22 faced the outer court; palm trees decorated the jambs on either side, and eight
steps led up to it.

35Then he brought me to the north
40:35 gate[v] and measured it. It had the same
v Eze 44:4; 47:2 measurements as the others, 36as did its
40:36 alcoves,[w] its projecting walls and its por-
w ver 7 tico, and it had openings all around. It
was fifty cubits long and twenty-five cubits wide. 37Its portico[a] faced the outer
court; palm trees decorated the jambs
on either side, and eight steps led up
to it.

The Rooms for Preparing Sacrifices

38A room with a doorway was by the
portico in each of the inner gateways,
where the burnt offerings[x] were washed. 40:38 x 2Ch 4:6;
39In the portico of the gateway were two Eze 42:13
tables on each side, on which the burnt 40:39
offerings,[y] sin offerings[z] and guilt offer- y Eze 46:2
ings[a] were slaughtered. 40By the outside z Lev 4:3,28
wall of the portico of the gateway, near a Lev 7:1
the steps at the entrance to the north
gateway were two tables, and on the
other side of the steps were two tables.
41So there were four tables on one side of
the gateway and four on the other—
eight tables in all—on which the sacrifices were slaughtered. 42There were also
four tables of dressed stone[b] for the 40:42 b Ex 20:25
burnt offerings, each a cubit and a half c ver 39
long, a cubit and a half wide and a cubit
high. On them were placed the utensils
for slaughtering the burnt offerings and
the other sacrifices.[c] 43And double-
pronged hooks, each a handbreadth
long, were attached to the wall all
around. The tables were for the flesh of
the offerings.

Rooms for the Priests

44Outside the inner gate, within the
inner court, were two rooms, one[b] at the
side of the north gate and facing south,
and another at the side of the south[c]
gate and facing north. 45He said to me,
"The room facing south is for the priests
who have charge of the temple,[d] 46and 40:45 d 1Ch 9:23
the room facing north[e] is for the priests 40:46
who have charge of the altar.[f] These are e Eze 42:13
the sons of Zadok,[g] who are the only Le- f Nu 18:5
vites who may draw near to the LORD to g 1Ki 2:35
minister before him.[h]" h Nu 16:5;
Eze 43:19;
44:15; 45:4;
48:11

47Then he measured the court: It was
square—a hundred cubits long and a
hundred cubits wide. And the altar was
in front of the temple.

The Temple

48He brought me to the portico of the
temple[i] and measured the jambs of the 40:48 i 1Ki 6:2
portico; they were five cubits wide on either side. The width of the entrance was

[a] 37 Septuagint (see also verses 31 and 34); Hebrew *jambs* [b] 44 Septuagint; Hebrew *were rooms for singers, which were* [c] 44 Septuagint; Hebrew *east*

fourteen cubits and its projecting walls
40:49 were[a] three cubits wide on either side.
j ver 22; 1Ki 6:3 49The portico[j] was twenty cubits wide,
k 1Ki 7:15 and twelve[b] cubits from front to back. It
was reached by a flight of stairs,[c] and
there were pillars[k] on each side of the
jambs.

41:1 **41** Then the man brought me to
l ver 23 the outer sanctuary[l] and measured the jambs; the width of the jambs
was six cubits[d] on each side.[e] 2The entrance was ten cubits wide, and the projecting walls on each side of it were five
cubits wide. He also measured the outer
sanctuary; it was forty cubits long and
41:2 m 2Ch 3:3 twenty cubits wide.[m]
3Then he went into the inner sanctuary and measured the jambs of the entrance; each was two cubits wide. The
entrance was six cubits wide, and the
projecting walls on each side of it were
seven cubits wide. 4And he measured
the length of the inner sanctuary; it was
twenty cubits, and its width was twenty
41:4 cubits across the end of the outer sanc-
n 1Ki 6:20 tuary.[n] He said to me, "This is the Most
o Ex 26:33; Heb 9:3-8 Holy Place.[o]"
5Then he measured the wall of the
temple; it was six cubits thick, and each
side room around the temple was four
41:6 cubits wide. 6The side rooms were on
p Eze 40:17 three levels, one above another, thirty[p]
q 1Ki 6:5 on each level. There were ledges all
around the wall of the temple to serve as
supports for the side rooms, so that the
supports were not inserted into the wall
of the temple.[q] 7The side rooms all
around the temple were wider at each
successive level. The structure surrounding the temple was built in ascending stages, so that the rooms
widened as one went upward. A stair-
41:7 way[r] went up from the lowest floor to
r 1Ki 6:8 the top floor through the middle floor.
8I saw that the temple had a raised
base all around it, forming the foundation of the side rooms. It was the length
of the rod, six long cubits. 9The outer
wall of the side rooms was five cubits
thick. The open area between the side
rooms of the temple 10and the ⌊priests'⌋
rooms was twenty cubits wide all around
the temple. 11There were entrances to
the side rooms from the open area, one
on the north and another on the south;
and the base adjoining the open area
was five cubits wide all around.

12The building facing the temple
courtyard on the west side was seventy
cubits wide. The wall of the building was
five cubits thick all around, and its
length was ninety cubits.
13Then he measured the temple; it
was a hundred cubits long, and the temple courtyard and the building with its
walls were also a hundred cubits long.
14The width of the temple courtyard on
the east, including the front of the tem- 41:14
ple, was a hundred cubits.[s] s Eze 40:47
15Then he measured the length of the
building facing the courtyard at the rear 41:15
of the temple, including its galleries[t] on t Eze 42:3
each side; it was a hundred cubits.
The outer sanctuary, the inner sanctuary and the portico facing the court,
16as well as the thresholds and the nar- 41:16
row windows[u] and galleries around the u 1Ki 6:4
three of them—everything beyond and v ver 25-26;
including the threshold was covered 1Ki 6:15;
with wood. The floor, the wall up to the Eze 42:3
windows, and the windows were cov-
ered.[v] 17In the space above the outside of
the entrance to the inner sanctuary and
on the walls at regular intervals all
around the inner and outer sanctuary
18were carved[w] cherubim[x] and palm 41:18
trees.[y] Palm trees alternated with cheru- w 1Ki 6:18 x Ex 37:7;
bim. Each cherub had two faces:[z] 19the 2Ch 3:7
face of a man toward the palm tree on y 1Ki 6:29; 7:36
one side and the face of a lion toward the z Eze 10:21
palm tree on the other. They were carved 41:19
all around the whole temple.[a] 20From the a Eze 10:14
floor to the area above the entrance,
cherubim and palm trees were carved on
the wall of the outer sanctuary.
21The outer sanctuary[b] had a rectan- 41:21
gular doorframe, and the one at the b ver 1
front of the Most Holy Place was similar. 41:22
22There was a wooden altar[c] three cubits c Ex 30:1
high and two cubits square[f]; its corners, d Ex 25:23;
its base[g] and its sides were of wood. The Eze 23:41;
man said to me, "This is the table[d] that 44:16; Mal 1:7,
is before the LORD." 23Both the outer 12
sanctuary[e] and the Most Holy Place had 41:23
double doors.[f] 24Each door had two e ver 1 f 1Ki 6:32
leaves—two hinged leaves[g] for each 41:24
door. 25And on the doors of the outer g 1Ki 6:34
sanctuary were carved cherubim and

[a] *48* Septuagint; Hebrew *entrance was*
[b] *49* Septuagint; Hebrew *eleven* [c] *49* Hebrew; Septuagint *Ten steps led up to it* [d] *1* The common cubit was about 1 1/2 feet (about 0.5 meter). [e] *1* One Hebrew manuscript and Septuagint; most Hebrew manuscripts *side, the width of the tent* [f] *22* Septuagint; Hebrew *long*
[g] *22* Septuagint; Hebrew *length*

palm trees like those carved on the
walls, and there was a wooden overhang
on the front of the portico. [26]On the
sidewalls of the portico were narrow
41:26 windows with palm trees carved on
[h]ver 15-16; each side. The side rooms of the temple
Eze 40:16 also had overhangs.[h]

Rooms for the Priests

42 Then the man led me north-
ward into the outer court and
42:1 [i]ver 13 brought me to the rooms[i] opposite the
[j]Eze 41:12-14 temple courtyard[j] and opposite the out-
[k]Eze 40:17 er wall on the north side.[k] [2]The building
whose door faced north was a hundred
cubits[a] long and fifty cubits wide. [3]Both
in the section twenty cubits from the inner court and in the section opposite
42:3 [l]Eze 41:15 the pavement of the outer court, gallery[l]
[m]Eze 41:16 faced gallery at the three levels.[m] [4]In
front of the rooms was an inner pas-
sageway ten cubits wide and a hundred
42:4 cubits[b] long. Their doors were on the
[n]Eze 46:19 north.[n] [5]Now the upper rooms were nar-
rower, for the galleries took more space
from them than from the rooms on the
lower and middle floors of the building.
[6]The rooms on the third floor had no
pillars, as the courts had; so they were
smaller in floor space than those on the
lower and middle floors. [7]There was an
outer wall parallel to the rooms and the
outer court; it extended in front of the
rooms for fifty cubits. [8]While the row of
rooms on the side next to the outer
court was fifty cubits long, the row on
the side nearest the sanctuary was a
hundred cubits long. [9]The lower rooms
42:9 had an entrance[o] on the east side as one
[o]Eze 44:5; 46:19 enters them from the outer court.
[10]On the south side[c] along the length
of the wall of the outer court, adjoining
the temple courtyard and opposite the
42:10 outer wall, were rooms[p] [11]with a pas-
[p]ver 1 sageway in front of them. These were
like the rooms on the north; they had
the same length and width, with similar
exits and dimensions. Similar to the
doorways on the north [12]were the doorways of the rooms on the south. There
was a doorway at the beginning of the
passageway that was parallel to the corresponding wall extending eastward, by
which one enters the rooms.
42:13 [13]Then he said to me, "The north[q]
[q]Eze 40:46 and south rooms facing the temple
courtyard are the priests' rooms, where
the priests who approach the LORD will
eat the most holy offerings. There they
will put the most holy offerings—the
grain offerings, the sin offerings[r] and the 42:13 [r]Lev 10:17; 6:25
guilt offerings[s]—for the place is holy.[t] [s]Lev 14:13
[14]Once the priests enter the holy [t]Ex 29:31;
precincts, they are not to go into the Lev 6:29; 7:6; 10:12-13;
outer court until they leave behind the Nu 18:9-10
garments[u] in which they minister, for 42:14 [u]Eze 44:19
these are holy. They are to put on other [v]Ex 29:9;
clothes before they go near the places Lev 8:7-9
that are for the people.[v]"
[15]When he had finished measuring
what was inside the temple area, he led
me out by the east gate[w] and measured 42:15 [w]Eze 43:1
the area all around: [16]He measured the
east side with the measuring rod; it was
five hundred cubits.[d] [17]He measured the
north side; it was five hundred cubits[e]
by the measuring rod. [18]He measured
the south side; it was five hundred cubits by the measuring rod. [19]Then he
turned to the west side and measured; it
was five hundred cubits by the measur-
ing rod. [20]So he measured[x] the area on 42:20 [x]Eze 40:5
all four sides. It had a wall around it,[y] [y]Zec 2:5
five hundred cubits long and five hun- [z]Eze 45:2;
dred cubits wide,[z] to separate the holy Rev 21:16 [a]Eze 22:26
from the common.[a]

The Glory Returns to the Temple

43 Then the man brought me to
the gate facing east,[b] [2]and I saw 43:1 [b]Eze 10:19; 42:15; 44:1; 46:1
the glory of the God of Israel coming
from the east. His voice was like the roar 43:2
of rushing waters,[c] and the land was ra- [c]Rev 1:15
diant with his glory.[d] [3]The vision I saw [d]Isa 6:3; Eze 11:23;
was like the vision I had seen when he[f] Rev 18:1
came to destroy the city and like the visions I had seen by the Kebar River, and
I fell facedown. [4]The glory[e] of the LORD 43:4 [e]Eze 1:28
entered the temple through the gate fac- [f]Eze 10:19
ing east.[f] [5]Then the Spirit[g] lifted me up[h] 43:5
and brought me into the inner court, and [g]Eze 11:24
the glory of the LORD filled the temple. [h]Eze 3:12; 8:3
[6]While the man was standing beside
me, I heard someone speaking to me
from inside the temple. [7]He said: "Son of
man, this is the place of my throne and
the place for the soles of my feet. This is
where I will live among the Israelites for-

[a] *2* The common cubit was about 1 1/2 feet (about 0.5 meter). [b] *4* Septuagint and Syriac; Hebrew *and one cubit* [c] *10* Septuagint; Hebrew *Eastward* [d] *16* See Septuagint of verse 17; Hebrew *rods*; also in verses 18 and 19. [e] *17* Septuagint; Hebrew *rods* [f] *3* Some Hebrew manuscripts and Vulgate; most Hebrew manuscripts *I*

ever. The house of Israel will never again
defile my holy name—neither they nor
their kings—by their prostitution[a] and
43:7 [i]Lev 26:30 the lifeless idols[b] of their kings at their
high places.[i] 8When they placed their
threshold next to my threshold and
their doorposts beside my doorposts,
with only a wall between me and them,
they defiled my holy name by their detestable practices. So I destroyed them
in my anger. 9Now let them put away
from me their prostitution and the lifeless idols of their kings, and I will live
43:9 [j]Eze 37:26-28 among them forever.[j]
10"Son of man, describe the temple to
43:10 [k]Eze 16:61 the people of Israel, that they may be
ashamed[k] of their sins. Let them con-
sider the plan, 11and if they are ashamed
of all they have done, make known to
them the design of the temple—its
arrangement, its exits and entrances—
its whole design and all its regulations[c]
and laws. Write these down before them
so that they may be faithful to its design
43:11 [l]Eze 44:5 and follow all its regulations.[l]
12"This is the law of the temple: All
43:12 [m]Eze 40:2 the surrounding area[m] on top of the
mountain will be most holy. Such is the
law of the temple.

The Altar

13"These are the measurements of the
43:13 [n]2Ch 4:1 altar[n] in long cubits, that cubit being a
cubit[d] and a handbreadth[e]: Its gutter is
a cubit deep and a cubit wide, with a rim
of one span[f] around the edge. And this
is the height of the altar: 14From the gutter on the ground up to the lower ledge
it is two cubits high and a cubit wide,
and from the smaller ledge up to the
larger ledge it is four cubits high and a
cubit wide. 15The altar hearth is four cu-
43:15 [o]Ex 27:2 bits high, and four horns[o] project upward from the hearth. 16The altar hearth
is square, twelve cubits long and twelve
cubits wide. 17The upper ledge also is
square, fourteen cubits long and fourteen cubits wide, with a rim of half a cu-
43:17 [p]Ex 20:26 bit and a gutter of a cubit all around.
The steps[p] of the altar face east."
18Then he said to me, "Son of man,
43:18 [q]Ex 40:29 [r]Lev 1:5,11; Heb 9:21-22 this is what the Sovereign LORD says:
These will be the regulations for sacri-
ficing burnt offerings[q] and sprinkling
blood[r] upon the altar when it is built:
43:19 [s]Lev 4:3; Eze 45:18-19 19You are to give a young bull[s] as a sin offering to the priests, who are Levites, of
the family of Zadok,[t] who come near[u] to 43:19 [t]Eze 44:15 [u]Nu 16:40; Eze 40:46
minister before me, declares the Sover-
eign LORD. 20You are to take some of its
blood and put it on the four horns of the
altar and on the four corners of the up-
per ledge[v] and all around the rim, and so 43:20 [v]ver 17 [w]Lev 16:19
purify the altar[w] and make atonement
for it. 21You are to take the bull for the
sin offering and burn it in the designat-
ed part of the temple area outside the 43:21 [x]Ex 29:14; Heb 13:11
sanctuary.[x]
22"On the second day you are to offer
a male goat without defect for a sin offering, and the altar is to be purified as it
was purified with the bull. 23When you
have finished purifying it, you are to offer a young bull and a ram from the flock,
both without defect.[y] 24You are to offer 43:23 [y]Ex 29:1
them before the LORD, and the priests are 43:24 [z]Lev 2:13; Mk 9:49-50
to sprinkle salt[z] on them and sacrifice
them as a burnt offering to the LORD.
25"For seven days[a] you are to provide 43:25 [a]Lev 8:33 [b]Ex 29:37
a male goat daily for a sin offering; you
are also to provide a young bull and a
ram from the flock, both without defect.[b] 26For seven days they are to make
atonement for the altar and cleanse it;
thus they will dedicate it. 27At the end of 43:27 [c]Lev 9:1 [d]Lev 17:5
these days, from the eighth day[c] on, the
priests are to present your burnt offerings and fellowship offerings[g][d] on the altar. Then I will accept you, declares the
Sovereign LORD."

The Prince, the Levites, the Priests

44 Then the man brought me back
to the outer gate of the sanctu-
ary, the one facing east,[e] and it was shut. 44:1 [e]Eze 43:1
2The LORD said to me, "This gate is to re-
main shut. It must not be opened; no 44:2 [f]Eze 43:4-5
one may enter through it.[f] It is to remain
shut because the LORD, the God of Israel, has entered through it. 3The prince
himself is the only one who may sit inside the gateway to eat in the presence[g]
of the LORD. He is to enter by way of the 44:3 [g]Ex 24:9-11 [h]Eze 46:2,8
portico of the gateway and go out the
same way.[h]"
4Then the man brought me by way of
the north gate to the front of the temple.

[a] 7 Or *their spiritual adultery*; also in verse 9 [b] 7 Or *the corpses*; also in verse 9 [c] 11 Some Hebrew manuscripts and Septuagint; most Hebrew manuscripts *regulations and its whole design* [d] 13 The common cubit was about 1 1/2 feet (about 0.5 meter). [e] 13 That is, about 3 inches (about 8 centimeters) [f] 13 That is, about 9 inches (about 22 centimeters) [g] 27 Traditionally *peace offerings*

I looked and saw the glory of the LORD
filling the temple[i] of the LORD, and I fell
facedown.[j]
5 The LORD said to me, "Son of man,
look carefully, listen closely and give attention to everything I tell you concerning all the regulations regarding the
temple of the LORD. Give attention to the
entrance of the temple and all the exits
of the sanctuary.[k] 6 Say to the rebellious
house[l] of Israel, 'This is what the Sovereign LORD says: Enough of your detestable practices, O house of Israel! 7 In
addition to all your other detestable
practices, you brought foreigners uncircumcised in heart[m] and flesh into my
sanctuary, desecrating my temple while
you offered me food, fat and blood, and
you broke my covenant.[n] 8 Instead of
carrying out your duty in regard to my
holy things, you put others in charge of
my sanctuary.[o] 9 This is what the Sovereign LORD says: No foreigner uncircumcised in heart and flesh is to enter my
sanctuary, not even the foreigners who
live among the Israelites.[p]
10 " 'The Levites who went far from me
when Israel went astray[q] and who wandered from me after their idols must
bear the consequences of their sin.[r]
11 They may serve in my sanctuary, having charge of the gates of the temple and
serving in it; they may slaughter the
burnt offerings[s] and sacrifices for the
people and stand before the people and
serve them.[t] 12 But because they served
them in the presence of their idols and
made the house of Israel fall into sin,
therefore I have sworn with uplifted
hand[u] that they must bear the consequences of their sin, declares the Sovereign LORD.[v] 13 They are not to come near
to serve me as priests or come near any
of my holy things or my most holy offerings; they must bear the shame[w] of their
detestable practices.[x] 14 Yet I will put
them in charge of the duties of the temple and all the work that is to be done
in it.[y]
15 " 'But the priests, who are Levites
and descendants of Zadok and who
faithfully carried out the duties of my
sanctuary when the Israelites went
astray from me, are to come near to minister before me; they are to stand before
me to offer sacrifices of fat and blood, declares the Sovereign LORD.[z] 16 They alone

44:4 [i]Isa 6:4; Rev 15:8 [j]Eze 1:28; 3:23
44:5 [k]Eze 40:4; 43:10-11
44:6 [l]Eze 3:9
44:7 [m]Lev 26:41 [n]Ge 17:14; Ex 12:48; Lev 22:25
44:8 [o]Lev 22:2; Nu 18:7
44:9 [p]Joel 3:17; Zec 14:21
44:10 [q]2Ki 23:8 [r]Nu 18:23
44:11 [s]2Ch 29:34 [t]Nu 3:5-37; 16:9; 1Ch 26:12-19
44:12 [u]Ps 106:26 [v]2Ki 16:10-16
44:13 [w]Eze 16:61 [x]Nu 18:3
44:14 [y]Nu 18:4; 1Ch 23:28-32
44:15 [z]Jer 33:18; Eze 40:46; Zec 3:7

are to enter my sanctuary; they alone are
to come near my table[a] to minister before me and perform my service.[b]
17 " 'When they enter the gates of the
inner court, they are to wear linen
clothes;[c] they must not wear any woolen
garment while ministering at the gates
of the inner court or inside the temple.
18 They are to wear linen turbans[d] on
their heads and linen undergarments[e]
around their waists. They must not wear
anything that makes them perspire.[f]
19 When they go out into the outer court
where the people are, they are to take off
the clothes they have been ministering
in and are to leave them in the sacred
rooms, and put on other clothes, so that
they do not consecrate[g] the people by
means of their garments.[h]
20 " 'They must not shave their heads
or let their hair grow long, but they are
to keep the hair of their heads trimmed.[i]
21 No priest is to drink wine when he enters the inner court.[j] 22 They must not
marry widows or divorced women; they
may marry only virgins of Israelite descent or widows of priests.[k] 23 They are
to teach my people the difference between the holy and the common[l] and
show them how to distinguish between
the unclean and the clean.[m]
24 " 'In any dispute, the priests are to
serve as judges[n] and decide it according
to my ordinances. They are to keep my
laws and my decrees for all my appointed feasts, and they are to keep my Sabbaths holy.[o]
25 " 'A priest must not defile himself by
going near a dead person; however, if the
dead person was his father or mother,
son or daughter, brother or unmarried
sister, then he may defile himself.[p] 26 After he is cleansed, he must wait seven
days.[q] 27 On the day he goes into the inner court of the sanctuary to minister in
the sanctuary, he is to offer a sin offering
for himself, declares the Sovereign LORD.
28 " 'I am to be the only inheritance[r]
the priests have. You are to give them no
possession in Israel; I will be their possession. 29 They will eat the grain offerings, the sin offerings and the guilt offerings; and everything in Israel
devoted[a] to the LORD[s] will belong to
them.[t] 30 The best of all the firstfruits[u]

a 29 The Hebrew term refers to the irrevocable giving over of things or persons to the LORD.

44:16 [a]Eze 41:22 [b]Nu 18:5
44:17 [c]Ex 39:27-28; Rev 19:8
44:18 [d]Ex 28:39; Isa 3:20 [e]Ex 28:42 [f]Lev 16:4
44:19 [g]Lev 6:27; Eze 46:20 [h]Lev 6:10-11; Eze 42:14
44:20 [i]Lev 21:5; Nu 6:5
44:21 [j]Lev 10:9
44:22 [k]Lev 21:7
44:23 [l]Eze 22:26 [m]Mal 2:7
44:24 [n]Dt 17:8-9; 1Ch 23:4 [o]2Ch 19:8
44:25 [p]Lev 21:1-4
44:26 [q]Nu 19:14
44:28 [r]Nu 18:20; Dt 10:9; 18:1-2; Jos 13:33
44:29 [s]Lev 27:21 [t]Nu 18:9,14
44:30 [u]Nu 18:12-13

and of all your special gifts will belong to
the priests. You are to give them the first
portion of your ground meal[v] so that a
blessing[w] may rest on your household.[x]
31 The priests must not eat anything,
bird or animal, found dead or torn by
wild animals.[y]

44:30 [v] Nu 15:18-21 [w] Mal 3:10 [x] Ne 10:35-37
44:31 [y] Ex 22:31; Lev 22:8

Division of the Land

45 "'When you allot the land as an
inheritance,[z] you are to present
to the LORD a portion of the land as a sacred district, 25,000 cubits long and
20,000[a] cubits wide; the entire area will
be holy.[a] 2 Of this, a section 500 cubits
square[b] is to be for the sanctuary, with
50 cubits around it for open land. 3 In the
sacred district, measure off a section
25,000 cubits[b] long and 10,000 cubits[c]
wide. In it will be the sanctuary, the
Most Holy Place. 4 It will be the sacred
portion of the land for the priests,[c] who
minister in the sanctuary and who draw
near to minister before the LORD. It will
be a place for their houses as well as a
holy place for the sanctuary.[d] 5 An area
25,000 cubits long and 10,000 cubits
wide will belong to the Levites, who
serve in the temple, as their possession
for towns to live in.[d][e]

6 "'You are to give the city as its property an area 5,000 cubits wide and
25,000 cubits long, adjoining the sacred
portion; it will belong to the whole
house of Israel.[f]

7 "'The prince will have the land bordering each side of the area formed by
the sacred district and the property of
the city. It will extend westward from the
west side and eastward from the east
side, running lengthwise from the western to the eastern border parallel to one
of the tribal portions.[g] 8 This land will be
his possession in Israel. And my princes
will no longer oppress my people but
will allow the house of Israel to possess
the land according to their tribes.[h]

9 "'This is what the Sovereign LORD
says: You have gone far enough, O
princes of Israel! Give up your violence
and oppression and do what is just and
right.[i] Stop dispossessing my people, declares the Sovereign LORD. 10 You are to
use accurate scales,[j] an accurate
ephah[e][k] and an accurate bath.[f] 11 The
ephah[l] and the bath are to be the same
size, the bath containing a tenth of a

45:1 [z] Eze 47:21-22 [a] Eze 48:8-9,29
45:2 [b] Eze 42:20
45:4 [c] Eze 40:46 [d] Eze 48:10-11
45:5 [e] Eze 48:13
45:6 [f] Eze 48:15-18
45:7 [g] Eze 48:21
45:8 [h] Nu 26:53; Eze 46:18
45:9 [i] Jer 22:3; Zec 7:9-10; 8:16
45:10 [j] Dt 25:15; Pr 11:1; Am 8:4-6; Mic 6:10-11 [k] Lev 19:36
45:11 [l] Isa 5:10

homer[g] and the ephah a tenth of a homer; the homer is to be the standard
measure for both. 12 The shekel[h] is to
consist of twenty gerahs.[m] Twenty
shekels plus twenty-five shekels plus fifteen shekels equal one mina.[i]

Offerings and Holy Days

13 "'This is the special gift you are to
offer: a sixth of an ephah from each homer of wheat and a sixth of an ephah
from each homer of barley. 14 The prescribed portion of oil, measured by the
bath, is a tenth of a bath from each cor
(which consists of ten baths or one homer, for ten baths are equivalent to a homer). 15 Also one sheep is to be taken
from every flock of two hundred from
the well-watered pastures of Israel.
These will be used for the grain offerings, burnt offerings[n] and fellowship offerings[j] to make atonement[o] for the
people, declares the Sovereign LORD.
16 All the people of the land will participate in this special gift for the use of the
prince in Israel. 17 It will be the duty of
the prince to provide the burnt offerings, grain offerings and drink offerings
at the festivals, the New Moons and the
Sabbaths[p]—at all the appointed feasts
of the house of Israel. He will provide the
sin offerings, grain offerings, burnt offerings and fellowship offerings to make
atonement for the house of Israel.[q]

18 "'This is what the Sovereign LORD
says: In the first month[r] on the first day
you are to take a young bull without defect[s] and purify the sanctuary.[t] 19 The
priest is to take some of the blood of the
sin offering and put it on the doorposts
of the temple, on the four corners of the
upper ledge[u] of the altar[v] and on the
gateposts of the inner court. 20 You are to
do the same on the seventh day of the
month for anyone who sins unintentionally[w] or through ignorance; so you
are to make atonement for the temple.

21 "'In the first month on the four-

45:12 [m] Ex 30:13; Lev 27:25; Nu 3:47
45:15 [n] Lev 1:4 [o] Lev 6:30
45:17 [p] Lev 23:38; Isa 66:23 [q] 1Ki 8:62; 2Ch 31:3; Eze 46:4-12
45:18 [r] Ex 12:2 [s] Lev 22:20; Heb 9:14 [t] Lev 16:16,33
45:19 [u] Eze 43:17 [v] Lev 16:18-19; Eze 43:20
45:20 [w] Lev 4:27

[a] 1 Septuagint (see also verses 3 and 5 and 48:9); Hebrew *10,000* [b] 3 That is, about 7 miles (about 12 kilometers) [c] 3 That is, about 3 miles (about 5 kilometers) [d] 5 Septuagint; Hebrew *temple; they will have as their possession 20 rooms*
[e] 10 An ephah was a dry measure. [f] 10 A bath was a liquid measure. [g] 11 A homer was a dry measure. [h] 12 A shekel weighed about 2/5 ounce (about 11.5 grams). [i] 12 That is, 60 shekels; the common mina was 50 shekels.
[j] 15 Traditionally *peace offerings;* also in verse 17

45:21 teenth day you are to observe the Pass-
[x] Ex 12:11; over,[x] a feast lasting seven days, during
Lev 23:5-6 which you shall eat bread made without
yeast. 22On that day the prince is to provide a bull as a sin offering for himself
45:22 [y] Lev 4:14 and for all the people of the land.[y]
23Every day during the seven days of the
45:23 Feast he is to provide seven bulls and
[z] Job 42:8 seven rams[z] without defect as a burnt
[a] Nu 28:16-25 offering to the LORD, and a male goat for
a sin offering.[a] 24He is to provide as a
45:24 [b] Nu 28:12-13 grain offering[b] an ephah for each bull
[c] Eze 46:5-7 and an ephah for each ram, along with a
hin[*a*] of oil for each ephah.[c]
25"'During the seven days of the
45:25 [d] Dt 16:13 Feast,[d] which begins in the seventh
[e] Lev 23:34-43; month on the fifteenth day, he is to make
Nu 29:12-38 the same provision for sin offerings,
burnt offerings, grain offerings and oil.[e]

46 "'This is what the Sovereign
LORD says: The gate of the inner
46:1 [f] Eze 40:19 court[f] facing east[g] is to be shut on the
[g] 1Ch 9:18 six working days, but on the Sabbath
[h] ver 6; Isa 66:23 day and on the day of the New Moon[h] it
is to be opened. 2The prince is to enter
46:2 [i] ver 8 [j] ver 12; from the outside through the portico[i] of
Eze 44:3 the gateway and stand by the gatepost.
The priests are to sacrifice his burnt offering and his fellowship offerings.[*b*] He
is to worship at the threshold of the
gateway and then go out, but the gate
will not be shut until evening.[j] 3On the
Sabbaths and New Moons the people of
the land are to worship in the presence
of the LORD at the entrance to that gate-
46:3 [k] Lk 1:10 way.[k] 4The burnt offering the prince
brings to the LORD on the Sabbath day is
to be six male lambs and a ram, all without defect. 5The grain offering given
with the ram is to be an ephah,[*c*] and the
grain offering with the lambs is to be as
46:5 [l] ver 11; much as he pleases, along with a hin[*a*] of
Eze 45:24 oil for each ephah.[l] 6On the day of the
46:6 New Moon[m] he is to offer a young bull,
[m] ver 1; six lambs and a ram, all without defect.
Nu 10:10 7He is to provide as a grain offering one
ephah with the bull, one ephah with the
ram, and with the lambs as much as he
wants to give, along with a hin of oil
46:7 [n] Eze 45:24 with each ephah.[n] 8When the prince en-
46:8 ters, he is to go in through the portico[o]
[o] ver 2 of the gateway, and he is to come out the
[p] Eze 44:3 same way.[p]
9"'When the people of the land come
46:9 [q] Ex 23:14; before the LORD at the appointed feasts,[q]
34:20 whoever enters by the north gate to
worship is to go out the south gate; and

whoever enters by the south gate is to go
out the north gate. No one is to return
through the gate by which he entered,
but each is to go out the opposite gate.
10The prince is to be among them, going
in when they go in and going out when 46:10 [r] 2Sa 6:14-15;
they go out.[r] Ps 42:4
11"'At the festivals and the appointed
feasts, the grain offering is to be an
ephah with a bull, an ephah with a ram,
and with the lambs as much as one
pleases, along with a hin of oil for each 46:11 [s] ver 5
ephah.[s] 12When the prince provides[t] a
freewill offering[u] to the LORD—whether 46:12 [t] Eze 45:17
a burnt offering or fellowship offer- [u] Lev 7:16
ings—the gate facing east is to be [v] ver 2
opened for him. He shall offer his burnt
offering or his fellowship offerings as he
does on the Sabbath day. Then he shall
go out, and after he has gone out, the
gate will be shut.[v]
13"'Every day you are to provide a
year-old lamb without defect for a burnt
offering to the LORD; morning by morn- 46:13
ing you shall provide it.[w] 14You are also [w] Ex 29:38;
to provide with it morning by morning a Nu 28:3
grain offering, consisting of a sixth of an
ephah with a third of a hin of oil to
moisten the flour. The presenting of this
grain offering to the LORD is a lasting or- 46:14
dinance.[x] 15So the lamb and the grain of- [x] Da 8:11
fering and the oil shall be provided 46:15 [y] Ex 29:42
morning by morning for a regular[y] [z] Ex 29:38;
burnt offering.[z] Nu 28:5-6
16"'This is what the Sovereign LORD
says: If the prince makes a gift from his
inheritance to one of his sons, it will also
belong to his descendants; it is to be
their property by inheritance.[a] 17If, how- 46:16 [a] 2Ch 21:3
ever, he makes a gift from his inheri-
tance to one of his servants, the servant 46:17
may keep it until the year of freedom;[b] [b] Lev 25:10
then it will revert to the prince. His inheritance belongs to his sons only; it is
theirs. 18The prince must not take any of 46:18
the inheritance[c] of the people, driving [c] Lev 25:23;
them off their property. He is to give his Eze 45:8;
sons their inheritance out of his own Mic 2:1-2
property, so that none of my people will
be separated from his property.'"
19Then the man brought me through
the entrance[d] at the side of the gate to 46:19 [d] Eze 42:9
the sacred rooms facing north, which
belonged to the priests, and showed me

[*a*] *24,5* That is, probably about 4 quarts (about 4 liters) [*b*] *2* Traditionally *peace offerings*; also in verse 12 [*c*] *5* That is, probably about 3/5 bushel (about 22 liters)

a place at the western end. 20 He said to me, "This is the place where the priests will cook the guilt offering and the sin offering and bake the grain offering, to avoid bringing them into the outer court and consecrating[e] the people."[f]

46:20 e Lev 6:27 f Zec 14:20

21 He then brought me to the outer court and led me around to its four corners, and I saw in each corner another court. 22 In the four corners of the outer court were enclosed[a] courts, forty cubits long and thirty cubits wide; each of the courts in the four corners was the same size. 23 Around the inside of each of the four courts was a ledge of stone, with places for fire built all around under the ledge. 24 He said to me, "These are the kitchens where those who minister at the temple will cook the sacrifices of the people."

The River From the Temple

47 The man brought me back to the entrance of the temple, and I saw water[g] coming out from under the threshold of the temple toward the east (for the temple faced east). The water was coming down from under the south side of the temple, south of the altar.[h] 2 He then brought me out through the north gate and led me around the outside to the outer gate facing east, and the water was flowing from the south side.

47:1 g Isa 55:1 h Ps 46:4; Joel 3:18; Rev 22:1

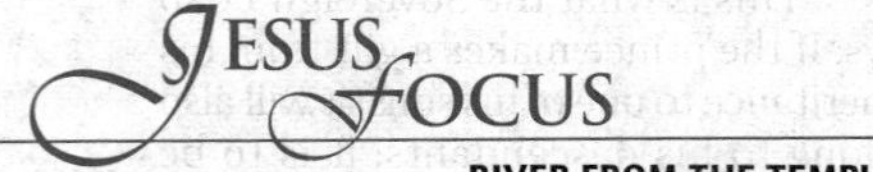

RIVER FROM THE TEMPLE

Ezekiel 47:1–12 describes the image of a river that flows from the temple into the Jordan Valley and on through the land of Israel to the Dead Sea in the south. The miraculous powers of this river reverse the saltiness of the Dead Sea, and trees begin to grow on its banks (verse 7). Much later the apostle John used a similar image to describe the new Jerusalem that he had seen in his own vision. John had observed a river of life flowing from God's throne, with the tree of life, whose leaves were for the "healing of the nations" (Revelation 22:2), growing on its bank. Both visions peer ahead into a glorious future in which God's presence and provision are clearly and unmistakably central. Jesus likened himself to the river of life when he declared, "Whoever drinks the water I give him will never thirst . . . [It] will become in him a spring of water welling up to eternal life" (John 4:13–14).

3 As the man went eastward with a measuring line[i] in his hand, he measured off a thousand cubits[b] and then led me through water that was ankle-deep. 4 He measured off another thousand cubits and led me through water that was knee-deep. He measured off another thousand and led me through water that was up to the waist. 5 He measured off another thousand, but now it was a river that I could not cross, because the water had risen and was deep enough to swim in—a river that no one could cross.[j] 6 He asked me, "Son of man, do you see this?"

47:3 i Eze 40:3

47:5 j Isa 11:9; Hab 2:14

Then he led me back to the bank of the river. 7 When I arrived there, I saw a great number of trees on each side of the river.[k] 8 He said to me, "This water flows toward the eastern region and goes down into the Arabah,[c][l] where it enters the Sea.[d] When it empties into the Sea,[d] the water there becomes fresh.[m] 9 Swarms of living creatures will live wherever the river flows. There will be large numbers of fish, because this water flows there and makes the salt water fresh; so where the river flows everything will live.[n] 10 Fishermen[o] will stand along the shore; from En Gedi[p] to En Eglaim there will be places for spreading nets.[q] The fish will be of many kinds[r]—like the fish of the Great Sea.[e][s] 11 But the swamps and marshes will not become fresh; they will be left for salt.[t] 12 Fruit trees of all kinds will grow on both banks of the river.[u] Their leaves will not wither, nor will their fruit[v] fail. Every month they will bear, because the water from the sanctuary flows to them. Their fruit will serve for food and their leaves for healing.[w]"

47:7 k ver 12; Rev 22:2

47:8 l Dt 3:17; Jos 3:16 m Isa 41:18

47:9 n Isa 12:3; 55:1; Jn 4:14; 7:37-38

47:10 o Mt 4:19 p Jos 15:62 q Eze 26:5 r Ps 104:25; Mt 13:47 s Nu 34:6

47:11 t Dt 29:23

47:12 u ver 7; Rev 22:2 v Ps 1:3 w Ge 2:9; Jer 17:8

The Boundaries of the Land

13 This is what the Sovereign LORD says: "These are the boundaries[x] by which you are to divide the land for an inheritance among the twelve tribes of Israel, with two portions for Joseph.[y] 14 You are to divide it equally among them. Because I swore with uplifted hand to give it to your forefathers, this land will become your inheritance.[z]

47:13 x Nu 34:2-12 y Ge 48:5

47:14 z Ge 12:7; Dt 1:8; Eze 20:5-6

[a] *22* The meaning of the Hebrew for this word is uncertain. [b] *3* That is, about 1,500 feet (about 450 meters) [c] *8* Or *the Jordan Valley* [d] *8* That is, the Dead Sea [e] *10* That is, the Mediterranean; also in verses 15, 19 and 20

15 "This is to be the boundary of the land:

"On the north side it will run from the Great Sea by the Hethlon road[a] past Lebo[a] Hamath to Zedad, 16 Berothah[b b] and Sibraim (which lies on the border between Damascus and Hamath),[c] as far as Hazer Hatticon, which is on the border of Hauran. 17 The boundary will extend from the sea to Hazar Enan,[c] along the northern border of Damascus, with the border of Hamath to the north. This will be the north boundary.[d]

18 "On the east side the boundary will run between Hauran and Damascus, along the Jordan between Gilead and the land of Israel, to the eastern sea and as far as Tamar.[d] This will be the east boundary.

19 "On the south side it will run from Tamar as far as the waters of Meribah Kadesh,[e] then along the Wadi ⌊of Egypt⌋[f] to the Great Sea.[g] This will be the south boundary.

20 "On the west side, the Great Sea will be the boundary to a point opposite Lebo[e] Hamath.[h] This will be the west boundary.[i]

21 "You are to distribute this land among yourselves according to the tribes of Israel. 22 You are to allot it as an inheritance for yourselves and for the aliens[j] who have settled among you and who have children. You are to consider them as native-born Israelites; along with you they are to be allotted an inheritance among the tribes of Israel.[k] 23 In whatever tribe the alien settles, there you are to give him his inheritance," declares the Sovereign LORD.

The Division of the Land

48 "These are the tribes, listed by name: At the northern frontier, Dan[l] will have one portion; it will follow the Hethlon road[m] to Lebo[f] Hamath;[n] Hazar Enan and the northern border of Damascus next to Hamath will be part of its border from the east side to the west side.

2 "Asher[o] will have one portion; it will border the territory of Dan from east to west.

3 "Naphtali[p] will have one portion; it will border the territory of Asher from east to west.

4 "Manasseh[q] will have one portion; it will border the territory of Naphtali from east to west.

5 "Ephraim[r] will have one portion; it will border the territory of Manasseh[s] from east to west.[t]

6 "Reuben[u] will have one portion; it will border the territory of Ephraim from east to west.

7 "Judah[v] will have one portion; it will border the territory of Reuben from east to west.

8 "Bordering the territory of Judah from east to west will be the portion you are to present as a special gift. It will be 25,000 cubits[g] wide, and its length from east to west will equal one of the tribal portions; the sanctuary will be in the center of it.[w]

9 "The special portion you are to offer to the LORD will be 25,000 cubits long and 10,000 cubits[h] wide.[x] 10 This will be the sacred portion for the priests. It will be 25,000 cubits long on the north side, 10,000 cubits wide on the west side, 10,000 cubits wide on the east side and 25,000 cubits long on the south side. In the center of it will be the sanctuary of the LORD.[y] 11 This will be for the consecrated priests, the Zadokites,[z] who were faithful in serving me[a] and did not go astray as the Levites did when the Israelites went astray.[b] 12 It will be a special gift to them from the sacred portion of the land, a most holy portion, bordering the territory of the Levites.

13 "Alongside the territory of the priests, the Levites will have an allotment 25,000 cubits long and 10,000 cubits wide. Its total length will be 25,000 cubits and its width 10,000 cubits.[c] 14 They must not sell or exchange any of it. This is the best of the land and must not pass into other hands, because it is holy to the LORD.[d]

15 "The remaining area, 5,000 cubits wide and 25,000 cubits long, will be for the common use of the city, for houses

47:15 [a] Eze 48:1
47:16 [b] 2Sa 8:8 [c] Nu 13:21; Eze 48:1
47:17 [d] Eze 48:1
47:19 [e] Dt 32:51 [f] Isa 27:12 [g] Eze 48:28
47:20 [h] Eze 48:1 [i] Nu 34:6
47:22 [j] Isa 14:1 [k] Nu 26:55-56; Isa 56:6-7; Ro 10:12; Eph 2:12-16; 3:6; Col 3:11
48:1 [l] Ge 30:6 [m] Eze 47:15-17 [n] Eze 47:20
48:2 [o] Jos 19:24-31
48:3 [p] Jos 19:32-39
48:4 [q] Jos 17:1-11
48:5 [r] Jos 16:5-9 [s] Jos 17:7-10 [t] Jos 17:17
48:6 [u] Jos 13:15-21
48:7 [v] Jos 15:1-63
48:8 [w] ver 21
48:9 [x] Eze 45:1
48:10 [y] ver 21; Eze 45:3-4
48:11 [z] 2Sa 8:17 [a] Lev 8:35 [b] Eze 14:11; 44:15
48:13 [c] Eze 45:5
48:14 [d] Lev 25:34; 27:10,28

[a] 15 Or *past the entrance to* [b] 15,16 See Septuagint and Ezekiel 48:1; Hebrew *road to go into Zedad, 16 Hamath, Berothah* [c] 17 Hebrew *Enon,* a variant of *Enan* [d] 18 Septuagint and Syriac; Hebrew *Israel. You will measure to the eastern sea* [e] 20 Or *opposite the entrance to* [f] 1 Or *to the entrance to* [g] 8 That is, about 7 miles (about 12 kilometers) [h] 9 That is, about 3 miles (about 5 kilometers)

and for pastureland. The city will be in
the center of it 16and will have these
measurements: the north side 4,500 cubits, the south side 4,500 cubits, the east
48:16 side 4,500 cubits, and the west side 4,500
[e]Rev 21:16 cubits.[e] 17The pastureland for the city
will be 250 cubits on the north, 250 cu-
bits on the south, 250 cubits on the east,
and 250 cubits on the west. 18What remains of the area, bordering on the sacred portion and running the length of
it, will be 10,000 cubits on the east side
and 10,000 cubits on the west side. Its
48:18 produce will supply food for the workers
[f]Eze 45:6 of the city.[f] 19The workers from the city
who farm it will come from all the tribes
of Israel. 20The entire portion will be a
square, 25,000 cubits on each side. As a
special gift you will set aside the sacred
portion, along with the property of the
city.

21"What remains on both sides of the
area formed by the sacred portion and
the city property will belong to the
prince. It will extend eastward from the
25,000 cubits of the sacred portion to
the eastern border, and westward from
the 25,000 cubits to the western border.
Both these areas running the length of
the tribal portions will belong to the
prince, and the sacred portion with the
temple sanctuary will be in the center of

THE GATES OF THE CITY

In the final vision in the book of Ezekiel, the prophet saw 12 gates, each named after one of the 12 tribes of Israel (Ezekiel 48:30–35). The apostle John later viewed the same gates in his own vision of the new Jerusalem (Revelation 21:12). Both visions focused on God's presence in his eternal city. Ezekiel 48:35 specifies that the very name of the city will be "THE LORD IS THERE," and Revelation 21:3 expresses the same idea: "Now the dwelling of God is with men, and he will live with them." From the very beginning of time God's plan has been to have a pure and permanent relationship with his people. Jesus Christ made that relationship possible, first by dying on the cross to remove the sin barrier between God the Father and humankind and then by coming back to life so that we might live with him forever in the new Jerusalem (Ephesians 2:4–9,13,17; 1 Peter 3:18; Revelation 22:3–5).

them.[g] 22So the property of the Levites 48:21 [g]ver 8,10;
and the property of the city will lie in the Eze 45:7
center of the area that belongs to the
prince. The area belonging to the prince
will lie between the border of Judah and
the border of Benjamin.

23"As for the rest of the tribes: Benjamin[h] will have one portion; it will ex- 48:23
tend from the east side to the west side. [h]Jos 18:11-28

24"Simeon[i] will have one portion; it 48:24 [i]Ge 29:33;
will border the territory of Benjamin Jos 19:1-9
from east to west.

25"Issachar[j] will have one portion; it 48:25
will border the territory of Simeon from [j]Jos 19:17-23
east to west.

26"Zebulun[k] will have one portion; it 48:26
will border the territory of Issachar from [k]Jos 19:10-16
east to west.

27"Gad[l] will have one portion; it will 48:27
border the territory of Zebulun from [l]Jos 13:24-28
east to west.

28"The southern boundary of Gad will
run south from Tamar[m] to the waters of 48:28 [m]Ge 14:7
Meribah Kadesh, then along the Wadi [n]Eze 47:19
⌞of Egypt⌟ to the Great Sea.[a][n]

29"This is the land you are to allot as
an inheritance to the tribes of Israel, and
these will be their portions," declares the
Sovereign LORD.

The Gates of the City

30"These will be the exits of the city:
Beginning on the north side, which is
4,500 cubits long, 31the gates of the city
will be named after the tribes of Israel.
The three gates on the north side will be
the gate of Reuben, the gate of Judah
and the gate of Levi.

32"On the east side, which is 4,500 cubits long, will be three gates: the gate of
Joseph, the gate of Benjamin and the
gate of Dan.

33"On the south side, which measures
4,500 cubits, will be three gates: the gate
of Simeon, the gate of Issachar and the
gate of Zebulun.

34"On the west side, which is 4,500 cu-
bits long, will be three gates: the gate of
Gad, the gate of Asher and the gate of
Naphtali.

35"The distance all around will be
18,000 cubits. 48:35 [o]Isa 12:6; 24:23;

"And the name of the city from that Jer 3:17; 14:9;
time on will be: Jer 33:16; Joel 3:21;

THE LORD IS THERE.[o]" Zec 2:10; Rev 21:3

[a]28 That is, the Mediterranean

Who was the fourth man in the furnace? (Daniel 3:25)

♦*Nebuchadnezzar realized that he was seeing a supernatural being and described the man as an angel (Daniel 3:28). Some believe the figure was an angel; others feel he was literally the Son of God making an appearance more than five centuries before his earthly birth.*

Is there significance to the term son of man? (Daniel 7:13)

♦*This expression usually referred in the Old Testament to a human being. But many believe that in this context it refers to Jesus, stressing his humanity as well as the authority and power given him (Matthew 28:18). Jesus frequently applied this title to himself (Mark 8:31; John 1:51). Because Jesus is not yet worshiped by every people and nation (Daniel 7:14), the events pictured in this passage are apparently still to come.*

Jesus in Daniel The most significant appearance of Jesus in the book of Daniel is Daniel's a vision of the "son of man" coming on the clouds to bring judgment and salvation (Daniel 7:13–14). Daniel used the term to refer to a future ruler of God's kingdom and presented this being as a person distinct from God the Father who will receive an eternal kingdom. The clouds of heaven likely represent clouds of glory (Exodus 40:34,38; Acts 1:9,11; 1 Thessalonians 4:17; Revelation 1:7), indicating that the son of man is indeed the divine Son (Matthew 26:64), our Lord Jesus Christ (Luke 21:27; John 1:51).

Daniel also described the Messiah as a rock that would crush earthly kingdoms (Daniel 2:34–25) and as "the Anointed One, the ruler," who would come and then be cut off (Daniel 9:25–26), referring to Jesus' earthly ministry and crucifixion. Finally, some Bible students believe that both the fourth man in the fiery furnace (Daniel 3:25) and the man in the vision of Daniel 10:5–9 may have been the preincarnate Jesus.

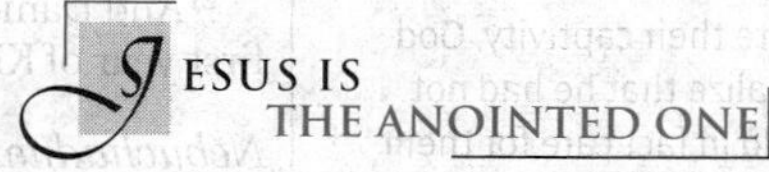
JESUS IS
THE ANOINTED ONE

Daniel's Training in Babylon

1 In the third year of the reign of Jehoiakim king of Judah, Nebuchadnezzar[a] king of Babylon came to Jerusalem and besieged it.[b] 2 And the Lord delivered Jehoiakim king of Judah into his hand, along with some of the articles from the temple of God. These he carried off to the temple of his god in Babylonia*[a]* and put in the treasure house of his god.[c]

3 Then the king ordered Ashpenaz, chief of his court officials, to bring in some of the Israelites from the royal family and the nobility[d]— 4 young men without any physical defect, handsome, showing aptitude for every kind of learning, well informed, quick to understand, and qualified to serve in the king's palace. He was to teach them the language and literature of the Babylonians.*[b]* 5 The king assigned them a daily amount of food and wine[e] from the king's table. They were to be trained for three years, and after that they were to enter the king's service.[f]

6 Among these were some from Judah: Daniel,[g] Hananiah, Mishael and Azariah. 7 The chief official gave them new names: to Daniel, the name Belteshazzar;[h] to Hananiah, Shadrach; to Mishael, Meshach; and to Azariah, Abednego.[i]

8 But Daniel resolved not to defile[j] himself with the royal food and wine, and he asked the chief official for permission not to defile himself this way. 9 Now God had caused the official to show favor[k] and sympathy[l] to Daniel, 10 but the official told Daniel, "I am afraid of my lord the king, who has assigned your*[c]* food and drink. Why should he see you looking worse than the other young men your age? The king would then have my head because of you."

11 Daniel then said to the guard whom the chief official had appointed over Daniel, Hananiah, Mishael and Azariah, 12 "Please test your servants for ten days: Give us nothing but vegetables to eat and water to drink. 13 Then compare our appearance with that of the young men who eat the royal food, and treat your servants in accordance with what you see." 14 So he agreed to this and tested them for ten days.

15 At the end of the ten days they looked healthier and better nourished than any of the young men who ate the royal food.[m] 16 So the guard took away their choice food and the wine they were to drink and gave them vegetables instead.[n]

17 To these four young men God gave knowledge and understanding[o] of all kinds of literature and learning.[p] And Daniel could understand visions and dreams of all kinds.[q]

18 At the end of the time[r] set by the king to bring them in, the chief official presented them to Nebuchadnezzar. 19 The king talked with them, and he found none equal to Daniel, Hananiah, Mishael and Azariah; so they entered the king's service.[s] 20 In every matter of wisdom and understanding about which the king questioned them, he found them ten times better than all the magicians and enchanters in his whole kingdom.[t]

21 And Daniel remained there until the first year of King Cyrus.[u]

Nebuchadnezzar's Dream

2 In the second year of his reign, Nebuchadnezzar had dreams;[v] his mind was troubled[w] and he could not sleep.[x] 2 So the king summoned the

1:1 [a] 2Ki 24:1 [b] 2Ch 36:6
1:2 [c] 2Ch 36:7; Jer 27:19-20; Zec 5:5-11
1:3 [d] 2Ki 20:18; 24:15; Isa 39:7
1:5 [e] ver 8,10 [f] ver 19
1:6 [g] Eze 14:14
1:7 [h] Da 4:8; 5:12 [i] Da 2:49; 3:12
1:8 [j] Eze 4:13-14
1:9 [k] Ge 39:21; Pr 16:7 [l] 1Ki 8:50; Ps 106:46
1:15 [m] Ex 23:25
1:16 [n] ver 12-13
1:17 [o] 1Ki 3:12 [p] Da 2:23; Jas 1:5 [q] Da 2:19,30; 7:1; 8:1
1:18 [r] ver 5
1:19 [s] Ge 41:46
1:20 [t] 1Ki 4:30; Da 2:13,28
1:21 [u] Da 6:28; 10:1
2:1 [v] Job 33:15,18; Da 4:5 [w] Ge 41:8 [x] Est 6:1; Da 6:18

a 2 Hebrew *Shinar* *b* 4 Or *Chaldeans*
c 10 The Hebrew for *your* and *you* in this verse is plural.

JESUS FOCUS

REMINDING OTHERS OF THE PROMISES

Daniel was still a teenager when taken captive (Daniel 1), and his life spanned the entire period of captivity; he served under both the Babylonians and the Persians. By the time he was thrown into the den of lions (Daniel 6:16), Daniel must have been somewhere in his eighties. His long life and futuristic visions provided the people with an important link to God's promise that he would one day send a Messiah. Despite their captivity, God wanted the Israelites to realize that he had not abandoned them. He would in fact care for them and protect them, despite their circumstances, until the coming of his Anointed One (Daniel 9:25). In the continual ebb and flow of human history, many nations would rise and fall between the time of the captivity and the birth of Jesus, but God would remain firmly in control of the situation at all times.

DISCOVERY 214

The Unshakable Rock

Have you ever faced apparently insurmountable obstacles? Of all the men to ever walk this earth, surely this man for whom this Bible book is named did. The powerful King Nebuchadnezzar had experienced a troubling dream. He demanded that his astrologers, sorcerers and wise men interpret the dream for him, but in order to verify their honesty he demanded that they first recount the dream and then explain its significance! Their failure to do so enraged the king to the point that he decreed the execution of every wise man in the land.

Daniel was at this time one of the wisest of those wise men (Daniel 1:20), and soldiers were dispatched to carry out the king's decree. Unlike the others, however, Daniel did not despair, because he was intimately acquainted with the God who "reveals deep and hidden things" (Daniel 2:22). When we face "impossible" circumstances, it is not how stacked the odds seem to be against us but our view of God that matters. Daniel knew that God was bigger than the death threats of an arrogant king.

After having received a revelation from God in a dream, Daniel appeared before King Nebuchadnezzar and described the full content of his dream as well as its explanation. The dream had to do with a large and dazzling statue with a head of gold, chest and arms of silver, belly and thighs of bronze, legs of iron and feet of iron and clay. The statue represented a series of world empires.

In the middle of the dream a rock, pried from the ground by unseen hands, smashed the statue's feet. The statue was broken to pieces and blown away like chaff, so that not a trace remained. The rock then became a "huge mountain [that] filled the whole earth" (verse 35). This rock is a clear reference to Jesus, who will eventually crush all earthly kingdoms and establish his own kingdom of righteousness.

In Psalm 118 we read that the very "stone the builders rejected has become the capstone (Psalm 118:22). In the New Testament Jesus quoted this psalm with reference to his rejection by his own people (Luke 20:17). Later, when Peter stood before the Sanhedrin, he also referred back to Psalm 118 to prove that Jesus had indeed risen from the dead (Acts 4:10–11).

Jesus is our Rock. He reigns supreme over all the kingdoms of this world, and no power on earth can stand against him (Daniel 2:34). Jesus Christ was rejected—and still is by many people—but he remains the capstone (Psalm 118:22–23), the chief cornerstone (Ephesians 2:20; 1 Peter 2:4–7), the only hope we have for rescue (Isaiah 28:16). When we face circumstances that rob us of hope, we can keep our eyes focused on Jesus, the Rock who can never be shaken.

Self-Discovery: *Can you think of some other illustrations from life that remind you of Jesus being a capstone or cornerstone? What does this image mean to you?*

GO TO DISCOVERY 215 ON PAGE 1137

magicians,[y] enchanters, sorcerers[z] and astrologers[a a] to tell him what he had dreamed.[b] When they came in and stood before the king, [3]he said to them, "I have had a dream that troubles[c] me and I want to know what it means.[b]"

[4]Then the astrologers answered the king in Aramaic,[c d] "O king, live forever![e] Tell your servants the dream, and we will interpret it."

[5]The king replied to the astrologers, "This is what I have firmly decided: If you do not tell me what my dream was and interpret it, I will have you cut into pieces[f] and your houses turned into piles of rubble.[g] [6]But if you tell me the dream and explain it, you will receive from me gifts and rewards and great honor.[h] So tell me the dream and interpret it for me."

[7]Once more they replied, "Let the king tell his servants the dream, and we will interpret it."

[8]Then the king answered, "I am certain that you are trying to gain time, because you realize that this is what I have firmly decided: [9]If you do not tell me the dream, there is just one penalty[i] for you. You have conspired to tell me misleading and wicked things, hoping the situation will change. So then, tell me the dream, and I will know that you can interpret it for me."[j]

[10]The astrologers answered the king, "There is not a man on earth who can do what the king asks! No king, however great and mighty, has ever asked such a thing of any magician or enchanter or astrologer.[k] [11]What the king asks is too difficult. No one can reveal it to the king except the gods,[l] and they do not live among men."

[12]This made the king so angry and furious[m] that he ordered the execution[n] of all the wise men of Babylon. [13]So the decree was issued to put the wise men to death, and men were sent to look for Daniel and his friends to put them to death.[o]

[14]When Arioch, the commander of the king's guard, had gone out to put to death the wise men of Babylon, Daniel spoke to him with wisdom and tact. [15]He asked the king's officer, "Why did the king issue such a harsh decree?" Arioch then explained the matter to Daniel. [16]At this, Daniel went in to the king and asked for time, so that he might interpret the dream for him.

[17]Then Daniel returned to his house and explained the matter to his friends Hananiah, Mishael and Azariah.[p] [18]He urged them to plead for mercy[q] from the God of heaven concerning this mystery,[r] so that he and his friends might not be executed with the rest of the wise men of Babylon. [19]During the night the mystery[s] was revealed to Daniel in a vision.[t] Then Daniel praised the God of heaven [20]and said:

"Praise be to the name of God for
 ever and ever;[u]
 wisdom and power[v] are his.
[21]He changes times and seasons;[w]
 he sets up kings and deposes[x]
 them.
He gives wisdom[y] to the wise
 and knowledge to the discerning.
[22]He reveals deep and hidden things;[z]
 he knows what lies in darkness,[a]
 and light[b] dwells with him.
[23]I thank and praise you, O God of
 my fathers:[c]
You have given me wisdom[d] and
 power,
you have made known to me what
 we asked of you,
 you have made known to us the
 dream of the king."

Daniel Interprets the Dream

[24]Then Daniel went to Arioch,[e] whom the king had appointed to execute the wise men of Babylon, and said to him, "Do not execute the wise men of Babylon. Take me to the king, and I will interpret his dream for him."

[25]Arioch took Daniel to the king at once and said, "I have found a man among the exiles from Judah[f] who can tell the king what his dream means."

[26]The king asked Daniel (also called Belteshazzar),[g] "Are you able to tell me what I saw in my dream and interpret it?"

[27]Daniel replied, "No wise man, enchanter, magician or diviner can explain to the king the mystery he has asked about,[h] [28]but there is a God in heaven who reveals mysteries.[i] He has shown King Nebuchadnezzar what will happen in days to come.[j] Your dream and the vi-

2:2 [y]Ge 41:8 [z]Ex 7:11 [a]ver 10; Da 5:7 [b]Da 4:6
2:3 [c]Da 4:5
2:4 [d]Ezr 4:7 [e]Da 3:9; 5:10
2:5 [f]ver 12 [g]Ezr 6:11; Da 3:29
2:6 [h]ver 48; Da 5:7, 16
2:9 [i]Est 4:11 [j]Isa 41:22-24
2:10 [k]ver 27
2:11 [l]Da 5:11
2:12 [m]Da 3:13,19 [n]ver 5
2:13 [o]Da 1:20
2:17 [p]Da 1:6
2:18 [q]Isa 37:4 [r]Jer 33:3
2:19 [s]ver 28 [t]Job 33:15; Da 1:17
2:20 [u]Ps 113:2; 145:1-2 [v]Jer 32:19
2:21 [w]Da 7:25 [x]Job 12:19; Ps 75:6-7 [y]Jas 1:5
2:22 [z]Job 12:22; Ps 25:14; Da 5:11 [a]Ps 139:11-12; Jer 23:24; Heb 4:13 [b]Isa 45:7; Jas 1:17
2:23 [c]Ex 3:15 [d]Da 1:17
2:24 [e]ver 14
2:25 [f]Da 1:6; 5:13; 6:13
2:26 [g]Da 1:7
2:27 [h]ver 10
2:28 [i]Ge 40:8; Am 4:13 [j]Ge 49:1; Da 10:14

[a] 2 Or *Chaldeans*; also in verses 4, 5 and 10
[b] 3 Or *was*
[c] 4 The text from here through chapter 7 is in Aramaic.

2:28 [k]Da 4:5 sions that passed through your mind[k] as
you lay on your bed are these:
[29]"As you were lying there, O king,
your mind turned to things to come,
and the revealer of mysteries showed
2:30 [l]Isa 45:3; Da 1:17; Am 4:13 you what is going to happen. [30]As for
me, this mystery has been revealed[l] to
me, not because I have greater wisdom
than other living men, but so that you,
O king, may know the interpretation
and that you may understand what
went through your mind.
[31]"You looked, O king, and there be-
2:31 [m]Hab 1:7 fore you stood a large statue—an enormous, dazzling statue,[m] awesome in appearance. [32]The head of the statue was
made of pure gold, its chest and arms of
silver, its belly and thighs of bronze, [33]its
legs of iron, its feet partly of iron and
partly of baked clay. [34]While you were
watching, a rock was cut out, but not by
2:34 [n]Zec 4:6 [o]ver 44-45; Ps 2:9; Isa 60:12; Da 8:25 human hands.[n] It struck the statue on its
feet of iron and clay and smashed them.[o]
[35]Then the iron, the clay, the bronze, the
silver and the gold were broken to pieces
at the same time and became like chaff
2:35 [p]Ps 1:4; 37:10; Isa 17:13 [q]Isa 2:3; Mic 4:1 on a threshing floor in the summer. The
wind swept them away[p] without leaving
a trace. But the rock that struck the statue became a huge mountain[q] and filled
the whole earth.
[36]"This was the dream, and now we
2:37 [r]Eze 26:7 [s]Jer 27:7 will interpret it to the king. [37]You, O king,
are the king of kings.[r] The God of heav-
en has given you dominion[s] and power
and might and glory; [38]in your hands he
has placed mankind and the beasts of
2:38 [t]Jer 27:6; Da 4:21-22 the field and the birds of the air. Wherever they live, he has made you ruler over
them all.[t] You are that head of gold.
[39]"After you, another kingdom will
rise, inferior to yours. Next, a third kingdom, one of bronze, will rule over the
whole earth. [40]Finally, there will be a
fourth kingdom, strong as iron—for
iron breaks and smashes everything—
and as iron breaks things to pieces, so it
2:40 [u]Da 7:7,23 will crush and break all the others.[u]
[41]Just as you saw that the feet and toes
were partly of baked clay and partly of
iron, so this will be a divided kingdom;
yet it will have some of the strength of
iron in it, even as you saw iron mixed
with clay. [42]As the toes were partly iron
and partly clay, so this kingdom will be
partly strong and partly brittle. [43]And
just as you saw the iron mixed with
baked clay, so the people will be a mixture and will not remain united, any
more than iron mixes with clay.
[44]"In the time of those kings, the God
of heaven will set up a kingdom that will
never be destroyed, nor will it be left to 2:44 [v]Ps 2:9; 1Co 15:24 [w]Isa 60:12 [x]Ps 145:13; Isa 9:7; Da 4:34; 6:26; 7:14,27; Mic 4:7,13; Lk 1:33
another people. It will crush[v] all those
kingdoms[w] and bring them to an end,
but it will itself endure forever.[x] [45]This is
the meaning of the vision of the rock[y]
cut out of a mountain, but not by human hands[z]—a rock that broke the iron,
the bronze, the clay, the silver and the 2:45 [y]Isa 28:16 [z]Da 8:25
gold to pieces.
"The great God has shown the king
what will take place in the future. The
dream is true and the interpretation is
trustworthy."
[46]Then King Nebuchadnezzar fell
prostrate[a] before Daniel and paid him 2:46 [a]Da 8:17; Ac 10:25 [b]Ac 14:13
honor and ordered that an offering[b] and
incense be presented to him. [47]The king
said to Daniel, "Surely your God is the 2:47 [c]Da 11:36 [d]Da 4:25 [e]ver 22,28
God of gods[c] and the Lord of kings[d] and
a revealer of mysteries,[e] for you were
able to reveal this mystery."
[48]Then the king placed Daniel in a
high position and lavished many gifts on
him. He made him ruler over the entire
province of Babylon and placed him in 2:48 [f]ver 6; Da 4:9; 5:11
charge of all its wise men.[f] [49]Moreover, at
Daniel's request the king appointed Shadrach, Meshach and Abednego admin-
istrators over the province of Babylon,[g] 2:49 [g]Da 1:7
while Daniel himself remained at the
royal court.

The Image of Gold and the Fiery Furnace

3 King Nebuchadnezzar made an
image[h] of gold, ninety feet high 3:1 [h]Isa 46:6; Jer 16:20; Hab 2:19
and nine feet[a] wide, and set it up on the
plain of Dura in the province of Babylon.
[2]He then summoned the satraps, prefects, governors, advisers, treasurers,
judges, magistrates and all the other
provincial officials[i] to come to the dedi- 3:2 [i]ver 27; Da 6:7
cation of the image he had set up. [3]So
the satraps, prefects, governors, advisers, treasurers, judges, magistrates and
all the other provincial officials assembled for the dedication of the image that
King Nebuchadnezzar had set up, and
they stood before it.
[4]Then the herald loudly proclaimed,

[a] *1* Aramaic *sixty cubits high and six cubits wide* (about 27 meters high and 2.7 meters wide)

"This is what you are commanded to do,
O peoples, nations and men of every
3:4 language:[j] 5As soon as you hear the
[j]Da 4:1; 6:25 sound of the horn, flute, zither, lyre,
harp, pipes and all kinds of music, you
3:5 [k]ver 10,15 must fall down and worship the image
of gold that King Nebuchadnezzar has
3:6 [l]ver 11,15,21; set up.[k] 6Whoever does not fall down
Jer 29:22; and worship will immediately be thrown
Da 6:7; Mt 13:42,50; into a blazing furnace."[l]
Rev 13:15 7Therefore, as soon as they heard the
sound of the horn, flute, zither, lyre, harp
and all kinds of music, all the peoples,
nations and men of every language fell
3:7 down and worshiped the image of gold
[m]ver 5 that King Nebuchadnezzar had set up.[m]
3:8 8At this time some astrologers[a] [n] came
[n]Da 2:10 forward and denounced the Jews. 9They
3:9 said to King Nebuchadnezzar, "O king,
[o]Ne 2:3; live forever![o] 10You have issued a decree,[p]
Da 5:10; 6:6 O king, that everyone who hears the
3:10 [p]Da 6:12 sound of the horn, flute, zither, lyre, harp,
[q]ver 4-6 pipes and all kinds of music must fall
down and worship the image of gold,[q]
11and that whoever does not fall down
and worship will be thrown into a blazing furnace. 12But there are some Jews
whom you have set over the affairs of the
3:12 province of Babylon—Shadrach, Me-
[r]Da 2:49 shach and Abednego[r]—who pay no at-
[s]Da 6:13 [t]Est 3:3 tention[s] to you, O king. They neither
serve your gods nor worship the image of
3:13 gold you have set up."[t]
[u]Da 2:12 13Furious[u] with rage, Nebuchadnezzar summoned Shadrach, Meshach and
Abednego. So these men were brought
before the king, 14and Nebuchadnezzar
said to them, "Is it true, Shadrach, Me-
3:14 shach and Abednego, that you do not
[v]Isa 46:1; serve my gods[v] or worship the image[w] of
Jer 50:2 [w]ver 1 gold I have set up? 15Now when you hear
the sound of the horn, flute, zither, lyre,
harp, pipes and all kinds of music, if you
are ready to fall down and worship the
image I made, very good. But if you do
not worship it, you will be thrown im-
3:15 mediately into a blazing furnace. Then
[x]Isa 36:18-20 [y]Ex 5:2; what god[x] will be able to rescue[y] you
2Ch 32:15 from my hand?"
3:16 16Shadrach, Meshach and Abednego[z]
[z]Da 1:7 replied to the king, "O Nebuchadnezzar,
we do not need to defend ourselves before you in this matter. 17If we are
3:17 thrown into the blazing furnace, the
[a]Ps 27:1-2 God we serve is able to save[a] us from it,
[b]Job 5:19; and he will rescue[b] us from your hand,
Jer 1:8 O king. 18But even if he does not, we

want you to know, O king, that we will
not serve your gods or worship the im- 3:18 [c]ver 28;
age of gold you have set up.[c]" Jos 24:15
19Then Nebuchadnezzar was furious
with Shadrach, Meshach and Abednego,
and his attitude toward them changed. 3:19
He ordered the furnace heated seven[d] [d]Lev 26:18-28
times hotter than usual 20and com-
manded some of the strongest soldiers
in his army to tie up Shadrach, Meshach
and Abednego and throw them into the
blazing furnace. 21So these men, wearing
their robes, trousers, turbans and other
clothes, were bound and thrown into the
blazing furnace. 22The king's command
was so urgent and the furnace so hot
that the flames of the fire killed the soldiers who took up Shadrach, Meshach 3:22
and Abednego,[e] 23and these three men, [e]Da 1:7
firmly tied, fell into the blazing furnace.
24Then King Nebuchadnezzar leaped
to his feet in amazement and asked his
advisers, "Weren't there three men that
we tied up and threw into the fire?"
They replied, "Certainly, O king."
25He said, "Look! I see four men walking around in the fire, unbound and unharmed, and the fourth looks like a son
of the gods."
26Nebuchadnezzar then approached
the opening of the blazing furnace and
shouted, "Shadrach, Meshach and
Abednego, servants of the Most High 3:26
God,[f] come out! Come here!" [f]Da 4:2,34
So Shadrach, Meshach and Abednego
came out of the fire, 27and the satraps, 3:27
prefects, governors and royal advisers[g] [g]ver 2
crowded around them.[h] They saw that [h]Isa 43:2; Heb 11:32-34
the fire[i] had not harmed their bodies, [i]Da 6:23
nor was a hair of their heads singed;
their robes were not scorched, and there
was no smell of fire on them.
28Then Nebuchadnezzar said, "Praise
be to the God of Shadrach, Meshach and
Abednego, who has sent his angel[j] and 3:28 [j]Ps 34:7;
rescued his servants! They trusted[k] in Da 6:22; Ac 5:19
him and defied the king's command and [k]Job 13:15; Ps 26:1; 84:12;
were willing to give up their lives rather Jer 17:7 [l]ver 18
than serve or worship any god except 3:29
their own God.[l] 29Therefore I decree[m] [m]Da 6:26
that the people of any nation or lan- [n]Ezr 6:11 [o]Da 6:27
guage who say anything against the God
of Shadrach, Meshach and Abednego be
cut into pieces and their houses be
turned into piles of rubble,[n] for no other god can save[o] in this way."

[a] 8 Or *Chaldeans*

DISCOVERY 215

THE ANGEL OF THE LORD

As a young man Daniel had demonstrated wisdom and maturity beyond his years. His friends, Shadrach, Meshach and Abednego, were undoubtedly inspired by Daniel's example. So when the king decreed that all of his subjects were to fall on their faces and worship a golden image, the three young men paid no heed. As a result they were bound and thrown into a blazing furnace—but not before they had informed the king that they would have no need to defend themselves against the wrath-induced actions of Nebuchadnezzar (Daniel 3:16–18).

As he stood surveying the roaring bonfire, the king was baffled. He was quite certain that three men had been thrown into the fire, but as he peered into the licking flames he clearly saw *four*, all of them unshackled and unharmed. And the mysterious fourth man looked "like a son of the gods" (Daniel 3:25).

Some might interpret this image as a mirage, a figment of the king's imagination, wishful thinking or even a hallucination. But it was none of those. Nebuchadnezzar believed in the existence of many gods, so he concluded that the fourth figure was an angel sent by a god. Although the king was confused, he was actually quite close to the truth. The fourth man in the fire was indeed a messenger from God—some believe him to have been the "angel of the LORD," possibly the preincarnate Jesus himself.

In Isaiah 63:9 we read about another instance in which the angel of the Lord intervened, rescuing Israel from her oppressive and abusive enemies. In his love and grace Jesus redeemed Israel, just as today he reclaims us from the grip of sin: "The angel of the LORD encamps around those who fear him, and he delivers them" (Psalm 34:7). Jesus Christ did that for Shadrach, Meshach and Abednego. The three young men experienced the presence of the true *Immanuel*, or "God with us."

Life invariably brings fiery trials. But during these crisis moments we can cling to the promise that Jesus is walking with us. There is no circumstance, no trial, no pending decision in which he is not present as our refuge, our strong tower in whom we rest secure (Psalm 31:1–5; 61:3). He wants to help us, because he has both God's glory and our best interest at heart. In Jesus we truly find our "wisdom . . . righteousness, holiness and redemption" (1 Corinthians 1:30).

Self-Discovery: *Recall a time when Jesus walked with you through a fiery trial. In what way was his presence apparent to you?*

GO TO DISCOVERY 216 ON PAGE 1143

30 Then the king promoted Shadrach,
3:30 Meshach and Abednego in the province
p Da 2:49 of Babylon.[p]

Nebuchadnezzar's Dream of a Tree

4 King Nebuchadnezzar,

To the peoples, nations and men
4:1 q Da 3:4 of every language,[q] who live in all
r Da 6:25 the world:

May you prosper greatly![r]

2 It is my pleasure to tell you
4:2 about the miraculous signs[s] and
s Ps 74:9 wonders that the Most High God[t]
t Da 3:26 has performed for me.

3 How great are his signs,
how mighty his wonders![u]
4:3 u Ps 105:27; His kingdom is an eternal
Da 6:27 kingdom;
v Da 2:44 his dominion endures[v] from
generation to generation.

4 I, Nebuchadnezzar, was at
4:4 home in my palace, contented[w]
w Ps 30:6 and prosperous. 5 I had a dream[x]
4:5 x Da 2:1 that made me afraid. As I was lying
y Da 2:28 in my bed, the images and visions
that passed through my mind[y] terrified me. 6 So I commanded that all
4:6 the wise men of Babylon be
z Da 2:2 brought before me to interpret[z] the
4:7 dream for me. 7 When the magi-
a Ge 41:8 cians,[a] enchanters, astrologers[a]
b Isa 44:25; and diviners[b] came, I told them the
Da 2:2 c Da 2:10 dream, but they could not interpret
it for me.[c] 8 Finally, Daniel came
into my presence and I told him the
4:8 dream. (He is called Belteshazzar,[d]
d Da 1:7 after the name of my god, and the
e Da 5:11,14 spirit of the holy gods[e] is in him.)
4:9 9 I said, "Belteshazzar, chief[f] of
f Da 2:48 the magicians, I know that the spir-
g Da 5:11-12 it of the holy gods[g] is in you, and no
mystery is too difficult for you.
Here is my dream; interpret it for
me. 10 These are the visions I saw
4:10 h ver 5 while lying in my bed:[h] I looked,
i Eze 31:3-4 and there before me stood a tree in
the middle of the land. Its height
was enormous.[i] 11 The tree grew
large and strong and its top
touched the sky; it was visible to
the ends of the earth. 12 Its leaves
were beautiful, its fruit abundant,
and on it was food for all. Under it
the beasts of the field found shelter,
and the birds of the air lived in its
branches;[j] from it every creature 4:12 j Eze 17:23;
was fed. Mt 13:32
13 "In the visions I saw while lying
in my bed,[k] I looked, and there be- 4:13 k Da 7:1 l ver 23;
fore me was a messenger,[b] a holy Dt 33:2; Da 8:13
one,[l] coming down from heaven.
14 He called in a loud voice: 'Cut
down the tree and trim off its
branches; strip off its leaves and
scatter its fruit. Let the animals flee
from under it and the birds from its
branches.[m] 15 But let the stump and 4:14 m Eze 31:12;
its roots, bound with iron and Mt 3:10
bronze, remain in the ground, in
the grass of the field.
" 'Let him be drenched with the
dew of heaven, and let him live with
the animals among the plants of
the earth. 16 Let his mind be
changed from that of a man and let
him be given the mind of an animal,
till seven times[c] pass by for him.[n] 4:16 n ver 23,32
17 " 'The decision is announced
by messengers, the holy ones declare the verdict, so that the living
may know that the Most High[o] is 4:17 o ver 2,25;
sovereign[p] over the kingdoms of Ps 83:18
men and gives them to anyone he p Jer 27:5-7;
wishes and sets over them the Da 2:21; 5:18-21
lowliest[q] of men.' q Da 11:21
18 "This is the dream that I, King
Nebuchadnezzar, had. Now, Belteshazzar, tell me what it means, for
none of the wise men in my king-
dom can interpret it for me.[r] But 4:18 r Ge 41:8;
you can,[s] because the spirit of the Da 5:8,15
holy gods is in you."[t] s Ge 41:15 t ver 7-9

Daniel Interprets the Dream

19 Then Daniel (also called Belteshazzar) was greatly perplexed for
a time, and his thoughts terrified[u] 4:19 u Da 7:15,28;
him. So the king said, "Beltesha- 8:27; 10:16-17
zar, do not let the dream or its
meaning alarm you."

Belteshazzar answered, "My
lord, if only the dream applied to
your enemies and its meaning to
your adversaries! 20 The tree you
saw, which grew large and strong,
with its top touching the sky, visible to the whole earth, 21 with beautiful leaves and abundant fruit, pro-

[a] 7 Or *Chaldeans* [b] 13 Or *watchman*; also in verses 17 and 23 [c] 16 Or *years*; also in verses 23, 25 and 32

viding food for all, giving shelter to
the beasts of the field, and having
nesting places in its branches for
the birds of the air— 22you, O king,
4:22 [v] 2Sa 12:7 [w] Jer 27:7; Da 2:37-38; 5:18-19
are that tree![v] You have become
great and strong; your greatness
has grown until it reaches the sky,
and your dominion extends to distant parts of the earth.[w]
4:23 [x] ver 13 [y] Da 5:21
23"You, O king, saw a messenger,
a holy one,[x] coming down from
heaven and saying, 'Cut down the
tree and destroy it, but leave the
stump, bound with iron and
bronze, in the grass of the field,
while its roots remain in the
ground. Let him be drenched with
the dew of heaven; let him live like
the wild animals, until seven times
pass by for him.'[y]
24"This is the interpretation,
4:24 [z] Job 40:12; Ps 107:40
O king, and this is the decree[z] the
Most High has issued against my
lord the king: 25You will be driven
away from people and will live with
the wild animals; you will eat grass
like cattle and be drenched with
the dew of heaven. Seven times will
4:25 [a] ver 17; Ps 83:18 [b] Jer 27:5; Da 5:21
pass by for you until you acknowl-
edge that the Most High[a] is sovereign over the kingdoms of men and
gives them to anyone he wishes.[b]
4:26 [c] ver 15 [d] Da 2:37
26The command to leave the stump
of the tree with its roots[c] means
that your kingdom will be restored
to you when you acknowledge that
Heaven rules.[d] 27Therefore, O king,
be pleased to accept my advice: Renounce your sins by doing what is
4:27 [e] Isa 55:6-7 [f] 1Ki 21:29; Ps 41:3; Eze 18:22
right, and your wickedness by be-
ing kind to the oppressed.[e] It may
be that then your prosperity will
continue."[f]

The Dream Is Fulfilled

4:28 [g] Nu 23:19
28All this happened[g] to King
Nebuchadnezzar. 29Twelve months
later, as the king was walking on
the roof of the royal palace of Babylon, 30he said, "Is not this the great
Babylon I have built as the royal
4:30 [h] Isa 37:24-25; Da 5:20; Hab 2:4
residence, by my mighty power and
for the glory of my majesty?"[h]
31The words were still on his lips
when a voice came from heaven,
"This is what is decreed for you,
King Nebuchadnezzar: Your royal
authority has been taken from you.
32You will be driven away from people and will live with the wild animals; you will eat grass like cattle.
Seven times will pass by for you until you acknowledge that the Most
High is sovereign over the kingdoms of men and gives them to
anyone he wishes."
33Immediately what had been
said about Nebuchadnezzar was
fulfilled. He was driven away from
people and ate grass like cattle. His
body was drenched with the dew of
heaven until his hair grew like the
feathers of an eagle and his nails
like the claws of a bird.[i] 4:33 [i] Da 5:20-21

34At the end of that time, I, Nebuchadnezzar, raised my eyes toward heaven, and my sanity was restored. Then I praised the Most
High; I honored and glorified him 4:34 [j] Da 12:7; Rev 4:10 [k] Ps 145:13; Da 2:44; 5:21; 6:26; Lk 1:33
who lives forever.[j]

His dominion is an eternal
dominion;
his kingdom endures from
generation to generation.[k]
35All the peoples of the earth
are regarded as nothing.[l] 4:35 [l] Isa 40:17 [m] Ps 115:3; 135:6 [n] Isa 45:9; Ro 9:20
He does as he pleases[m]
with the powers of heaven
and the peoples of the earth.
No one can hold back his hand
or say to him: "What have you
done?"[n]

36At the same time that my sanity was restored, my honor and
splendor were returned to me for
the glory of my kingdom.[o] My ad- 4:36 [o] Pr 22:4
visers and nobles sought me out,
and I was restored to my throne
and became even greater than before. 37Now I, Nebuchadnezzar,
praise and exalt and glorify the 4:37 [p] Dt 32:4; Ps 33:4-5 [q] Ex 18:11; Job 40:11-12; Da 5:20,23
King of heaven, because everything
he does is right and all his ways are
just.[p] And those who walk in pride
he is able to humble.[q]

The Writing on the Wall

5 King Belshazzar gave a great ban- 5:1 [r] Est 1:3
quet[r] for a thousand of his nobles
and drank wine with them. 2While
Belshazzar was drinking his wine, he
gave orders to bring in the gold and sil- 5:2 [s] 2Ki 24:13; Jer 52:19
ver goblets[s] that Nebuchadnezzar his

father[a] had taken from the temple in Jerusalem, so that the king and his nobles, his wives and his concubines might drink from them.[t] 3 So they brought in the gold goblets that had been taken from the temple of God in Jerusalem, and the king and his nobles, his wives and his concubines drank from them. 4 As they drank the wine, they praised the gods of gold and silver, of bronze, iron, wood and stone.[u]

5 Suddenly the fingers of a human hand appeared and wrote on the plaster of the wall, near the lampstand in the royal palace. The king watched the hand as it wrote. 6 His face turned pale and he was so frightened[v] that his knees knocked together and his legs gave way.[w]

7 The king called out for the enchanters, astrologers[b] and diviners[x] to be brought and said to these wise[y] men of Babylon, "Whoever reads this writing and tells me what it means will be clothed in purple and have a gold chain placed around his neck,[z] and he will be made the third highest ruler in the kingdom."[a]

8 Then all the king's wise men came in, but they could not read the writing or tell the king what it meant.[b] 9 So King Belshazzar became even more terrified[c] and his face grew more pale. His nobles were baffled.

10 The queen,[c] hearing the voices of the king and his nobles, came into the banquet hall. "O king, live forever!"[d] she said. "Don't be alarmed! Don't look so pale! 11 There is a man in your kingdom who has the spirit of the holy gods[e] in him. In the time of your father he was found to have insight and intelligence and wisdom[f] like that of the gods. King Nebuchadnezzar your father—your father the king, I say—appointed him chief of the magicians, enchanters, astrologers and diviners.[g] 12 This man Daniel, whom the king called Belteshazzar,[h] was found to have a keen mind and knowledge and understanding, and also the ability to interpret dreams, explain riddles and solve difficult problems.[i] Call for Daniel, and he will tell you what the writing means."

13 So Daniel was brought before the king, and the king said to him, "Are you Daniel, one of the exiles my father the king brought from Judah?[j] 14 I have heard that the spirit of the gods is in you and that you have insight, intelligence and outstanding wisdom. 15 The wise men and enchanters were brought before me to read this writing and tell me what it means, but they could not explain it. 16 Now I have heard that you are able to give interpretations and to solve difficult problems. If you can read this writing and tell me what it means, you will be clothed in purple and have a gold chain placed around your neck, and you will be made the third highest ruler in the kingdom."

17 Then Daniel answered the king, "You may keep your gifts for yourself and give your rewards to someone else.[k] Nevertheless, I will read the writing for the king and tell him what it means.

18 "O king, the Most High God gave your father Nebuchadnezzar sovereignty and greatness and glory and splendor.[l] 19 Because of the high position he gave him, all the peoples and nations and men of every language dreaded and feared him. Those the king wanted to put to death, he put to death;[m] those he wanted to spare, he spared; those he wanted to promote, he promoted; and those he wanted to humble, he humbled. 20 But when his heart became arrogant and hardened with pride,[n] he was deposed from his royal throne and stripped[o] of his glory.[p] 21 He was driven away from people and given the mind of an animal; he lived with the wild donkeys and ate grass like cattle; and his body was drenched with the dew of heaven, until he acknowledged that the Most High God is sovereign[q] over the kingdoms of men and sets over them anyone he wishes.[r]

22 "But you his son,[d] O Belshazzar, have not humbled[s] yourself, though you knew all this. 23 Instead, you have set yourself up against[t] the Lord of heaven. You had the goblets from his temple brought to you, and you and your nobles, your wives and your concubines drank wine from them. You praised the gods of silver and gold, of bronze, iron, wood and stone, which cannot see or hear or understand.[u] But you did not honor the God who holds in his hand your life[v] and all

5:2 [t] Est 1:7; Da 1:2
5:4 [u] Ps 135:15-18; Hab 2:19; Rev 9:20
5:6 [v] Da 4:5 [w] Eze 7:17
5:7 [x] Isa 44:25 [y] Da 4:6-7 [z] Ge 41:42 [a] Da 2:5-6,48; 6:2-3
5:8 [b] Da 2:10,27
5:9 [c] Isa 21:4
5:10 [d] Da 3:9
5:11 [e] Da 4:8-9,19 [f] ver 14; Da 1:17 [g] Da 2:47-48
5:12 [h] Da 1:7 [i] ver 14-16; Da 6:3
5:13 [j] Da 6:13
5:17 [k] 2Ki 5:16
5:18 [l] Jer 27:7; Da 2:37-38
5:19 [m] Da 2:12-13; 3:6
5:20 [n] Da 4:30 [o] Jer 13:18 [p] Job 40:12; Isa 14:13-15
5:21 [q] Eze 17:24 [r] Da 4:16-17,35
5:22 [s] Ex 10:3; 2Ch 33:23
5:23 [t] Jer 50:29 [u] Ps 115:4-8; Hab 2:19 [v] Job 12:10

[a] 2 Or *ancestor*; or *predecessor*; also in verses 11, 13 and 18 [b] 7 Or *Chaldeans*; also in verse 11
[c] 10 Or *queen mother* [d] 22 Or *descendant*; or *successor*

5:23 [w] Job 31:4; your ways.[w] 24Therefore he sent the hand
Jer 10:23 that wrote the inscription.
25"This is the inscription that was
written:

MENE, MENE, TEKEL, PARSIN[a]

26"This is what these words mean:
Mene[b]: God has numbered the
5:26 [x] Jer 27:7 days[x] of your reign and
[y] Isa 13:6 brought it to an end.[y]
27 *Tekel*[c]: You have been weighed
on the scales and found
5:27 [z] Ps 62:9 wanting.[z]
5:28 28 *Peres*[d]: Your kingdom is divided
[a] Isa 13:17 and given to the Medes[a]
[b] Da 6:28 and Persians."[b]

29Then at Belshazzar's command,
Daniel was clothed in purple, a gold
chain was placed around his neck, and
he was proclaimed the third highest
5:30 ruler in the kingdom.
[c] ver 1 [d] Isa 21:9; 30That very night Belshazzar,[c] king of
Jer 51:31 the Babylonians,[e] was slain,[d] 31and Da-
5:31 rius[e] the Mede took over the kingdom,
[e] Da 6:1; 9:1 at the age of sixty-two.

Daniel in the Den of Lions

6:1 **6** It pleased Darius[f] to appoint 120
[f] Da 5:31 [g] Est 1:1 satraps[g] to rule throughout the
kingdom, 2with three administrators
6:2 over them, one of whom was Daniel.[h]
[h] Da 2:48-49 [i] Ezr 4:22 The satraps were made accountable[i] to
them so that the king might not suffer
loss. 3Now Daniel so distinguished himself among the administrators and the
satraps by his exceptional qualities that
the king planned to set him over the
6:3 whole kingdom.[j] 4At this, the adminis-
[j] Ge 41:41; trators and the satraps tried to find
Est 10:3; Da 5:12-14 grounds for charges against Daniel in
his conduct of government affairs, but
they were unable to do so. They could
find no corruption in him, because he
was trustworthy and neither corrupt
nor negligent. 5Finally these men said,
"We will never find any basis for charges
against this man Daniel unless it has
something to do with the law of his
6:5 [k] Ac 24:13-16 God."[k]
6So the administrators and the sa-
6:6 traps went as a group to the king and
[l] Ne 2:3; Da 2:4 said: "O King Darius, live forever![l] 7The
6:7 royal administrators, prefects, satraps,
[m] Da 3:2 advisers and governors[m] have all agreed
that the king should issue an edict and
enforce the decree that anyone who
prays to any god or man during the next
thirty days, except to you, O king, shall 6:7
be thrown into the lions' den.[n] 8Now, [n] Ps 59:3; 64:2-6;
O king, issue the decree and put it in Da 3:6
writing so that it cannot be altered—in
accordance with the laws of the Medes
and Persians, which cannot be repealed."[o] 9So King Darius put the decree 6:8
in writing. [o] Est 1:19
10Now when Daniel learned that the
decree had been published, he went
home to his upstairs room where the
windows opened toward[p] Jerusalem. 6:10 [p] 1Ki 8:48-49
Three times a day he got down on his

[a] 25 Aramaic *UPARSIN* (that is, *AND PARSIN*)
[b] 26 *Mene* can mean *numbered* or *mina* (a unit of money). [c] 27 *Tekel* can mean *weighed* or *shekel.*
[d] 28 *Peres* (the singular of *Parsin*) can mean *divided* or *Persia* or *a half mina* or *a half shekel.*
[e] 30 Or *Chaldeans*

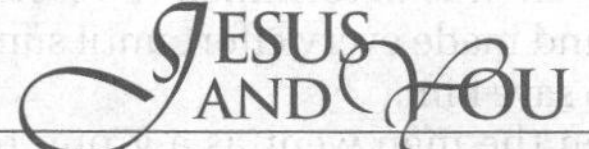

IN THE LIONS' DEN

At various times throughout history rulers have used lions to torture and kill those who have opposed them. Particularly during periods of persecution during the first centuries following Jesus' death, members of the fledgling church were repeatedly thrown to the lions because their decision to walk with God and stake their lives on faith in his Son ran counter to the official government stance. While Darius was ruler of Babylon, Daniel was accused of treason and thrown into a den full of restless, ravenous lions (Daniel 6:16–21). God protected his servant, however, by providing an angel to prevent the lions from attacking (verse 22).

The very fact of choosing to walk with God involves a second implicit choice, a choice to walk out of step with this world (Romans 12:2; 1 John 2:15), and Satan makes certain that believers will feel the consequences of this decision (Job 1:7; 1 Peter 5:8). Jesus warned his followers that they would be "handed over . . . and put to death, and [that they would be] . . . hated by all nations because of their [faith in him]" (Matthew 24:9). Jesus had also addressed this issue when he began his Sermon on the Mount with the recitation of the much-loved Beatitudes, stating that: "Blessed are you when people insult you, persecute you and falsely say all kinds of evil against you because of me. Rejoice and be glad, because great is your reward in heaven, for in the same way they persecuted the prophets who were before you" (Matthew 5:11–12).

6:10 knees[q] and prayed, giving thanks to his
[q]Ps 95:6 [r]Ac 5:29 God, just as he had done before.[r] 11 Then
these men went as a group and found
Daniel praying and asking God for help.
12 So they went to the king and spoke to
him about his royal decree: "Did you not
publish a decree that during the next
thirty days anyone who prays to any god
or man except to you, O king, would be
thrown into the lions' den?"

The king answered, "The decree
stands—in accordance with the laws of
6:12 [s]Est 1:19; the Medes and Persians, which cannot
Da 3:8-12 be repealed."[s]

13 Then they said to the king, "Daniel,
6:13 who is one of the exiles from Judah,[t]
[t]Da 2:25; 5:13 [u]Est 3:8; pays no attention[u] to you, O king, or to
Da 3:12 the decree you put in writing. He still
prays three times a day." 14 When the
king heard this, he was greatly dis-
6:14 [v]Mk 6:26 tressed;[v] he was determined to rescue
Daniel and made every effort until sun-
down to save him.

15 Then the men went as a group to
the king and said to him, "Remember,
O king, that according to the law of the
6:15 Medes and Persians no decree or edict
[w]Est 8:8 that the king issues can be changed."[w]

16 So the king gave the order, and they
brought Daniel and threw him into the
6:16 [x]ver 7 lions' den.[x] The king said to Daniel,
[y]Job 5:19; "May your God, whom you serve contin-
Ps 37:39-40 ually, rescue[y] you!"

17 A stone was brought and placed
over the mouth of the den, and the king
6:17 sealed[z] it with his own signet ring and
[z]Mt 27:66 with the rings of his nobles, so that Daniel's situation might not be changed.
18 Then the king returned to his palace
6:18 [a]2Sa 12:17 and spent the night without eating[a] and
[b]Est 6:1; Da 2:1 without any entertainment being
brought to him. And he could not sleep.[b]

19 At the first light of dawn, the king
got up and hurried to the lions' den.
20 When he came near the den, he called
to Daniel in an anguished voice, "Daniel,
servant of the living God, has your God,
6:20 whom you serve continually, been able
[c]Da 3:17 to rescue you from the lions?"[c]

6:21 21 Daniel answered, "O king, live forev-
[d]Da 2:4 er![d] 22 My God sent his angel,[e] and he
6:22 shut the mouths of the lions.[f] They have
[e]Da 3:28 not hurt me, because I was found inno-
[f]Ps 91:11-13; Heb 11:33 cent in his sight.[g] Nor have I ever done
[g]Ac 12:11; 2Ti 4:17 any wrong before you, O king."

23 The king was overjoyed and gave orders to lift Daniel out of the den. And
when Daniel was lifted from the den, no
wound[h] was found on him, because he 6:23 [h]Da 3:27
had trusted[i] in his God. [i]1Ch 5:20

24 At the king's command, the men
who had falsely accused Daniel were
brought in and thrown into the lions' 6:24
den,[j] along with their wives and chil- [j]Dt 19:18-19; Est 7:9-10; Ps 54:5
dren.[k] And before they reached the floor
of the den, the lions overpowered them [k]Dt 24:16; 2Ki 14:6
and crushed all their bones.[l] [l]Isa 38:13

25 Then King Darius wrote to all the
peoples, nations and men of every language throughout the land:

"May you prosper greatly![m] 6:25 [m]Da 4:1

26 "I issue a decree that in every
part of my kingdom people must
fear and reverence the God of Dan- 6:26 [n]Ps 99:1-3;
iel.[n] Da 3:29 [o]Da 2:44; 4:34

"For he is the living God
and he endures forever;
his kingdom will not be destroyed,
his dominion will never end.[o]
27 He rescues and he saves; 6:27
he performs signs and wonders[p] [p]Da 4:3 [q]ver 22
in the heavens and on the earth.
He has rescued Daniel
from the power of the lions."[q]

28 So Daniel prospered during the 6:28
reign of Darius and the reign of Cyrus[a] [r] [r]2Ch 36:22;
the Persian. Da 1:21

Daniel's Dream of Four Beasts

7 In the first year of Belshazzar[s] king 7:1
of Babylon, Daniel had a dream, [s]Da 5:1 [t]Da 1:17
and visions passed through his mind[t] as [u]Jer 36:4
he was lying on his bed. He wrote[u] down
the substance of his dream.

2 Daniel said: "In my vision at night I
looked, and there before me were the four 7:2
winds of heaven[v] churning up the great [v]Rev 7:1
sea. 3 Four great beasts,[w] each different 7:3
from the others, came up out of the sea. [w]Rev 13:1

4 "The first was like a lion,[x] and it had 7:4
the wings of an eagle.[y] I watched until [x]Jer 4:7 [y]Eze 17:3
its wings were torn off and it was lifted
from the ground so that it stood on two
feet like a man, and the heart of a man
was given to it.

5 "And there before me was a second
beast, which looked like a bear. It was
raised up on one of its sides, and it had
three ribs in its mouth between its teeth.
It was told, 'Get up and eat your fill of
flesh!'[z] 7:5 [z]Da 2:39

[a] 28 Or *Darius, that is, the reign of Cyrus*

God in the Midst of Chaos

The world situation is always plagued by instability, and the problems and conflicts all around can seem overwhelming. We can't help but ask the question, "Is God really in control?" We know intellectually that he is, but that knowledge is often at odds with our experience.

Daniel understood what it was like to live in a hostile and pagan environment. He had been taken captive and now found himself serving in a position of authority within the Babylonian royal court. Yet God reminded Daniel that the Lord Almighty, the Ancient of Days (Daniel 7:9) was still sovereign and proceeded to give the young man several visions to drive home his point.

One of these visions was of wind, the sea and four beasts (Daniel 7:1–3). The wind represented the all-powerful movement of God (Genesis 8:1; Exodus 10:13), the sea was a picture of humanity (Isaiah 17:12–13) and the four beasts represented four separate empires (Babylonia, Medo-Persia, Greece and Rome) that would in turn rise and fall (Daniel 7:15–17). The message of the vision was that God choreographs the whirling, dizzying dance of history. Powers and dominions ebb and flow according to his will, but two truths still afford us confidence and hope in an ever-changing environment.

The first is that God is in control (verses 9–10). Far from sitting aloof as an absentee landlord, he is intimately involved in the affairs of human history. Second, according to his perfect plan in his perfect timing God would send his Son, the Messiah, to secure our deliverance from the penalty and the power of sin (Galatians 4:4–5).

This passage in Daniel (Daniel 7:13) marks the first time in Scripture in which the title "son of man" was used with reference to the Messiah, although in the New Testament Jesus would frequently refer to himself in this way (Matthew 9:6; Mark 10:45; Luke 22:69; John 3:13–14; 12:23). Daniel 7:14, part of a powerful prophecy that will come to its final culmination when Jesus comes again to be enthroned as ruler over the whole earth, exults: "He was given authority, glory and sovereign power; all peoples, nations and men of every language worshiped him. His dominion is an everlasting dominion that will not pass away, and his kingdom is one that will never be destroyed."

Self-Discovery: *The media bombards us daily with bad news from around the planet. Do you sometimes wonder whether or not God is really in control or why he doesn't intervene? Have the circumstances of life ever caused you to doubt God's goodness? If so, how did you resolve the issue in your own mind?*

GO TO DISCOVERY 217 ON PAGE 1147

6“After that, I looked, and there before
me was another beast, one that looked
7:6 like a leopard.[a] And on its back it had
a Rev 13:2 four wings like those of a bird. This beast
had four heads, and it was given author-
ity to rule.
7“After that, in my vision at night I
looked, and there before me was a
fourth beast—terrifying and frightening
7:7 b Da 2:40 and very powerful. It had large iron[b]
c Rev 12:3 teeth; it crushed and devoured its victims and trampled underfoot whatever
was left. It was different from all the former beasts, and it had ten horns.[c]
8“While I was thinking about the
horns, there before me was another
7:8 horn, a little[d] one, which came up
d Da 8:9 e Rev 9:7 among them; and three of the first horns
f Ps 12:3; were uprooted before it. This horn had
Rev 13:5-6 eyes like the eyes of a man[e] and a mouth
that spoke boastfully.[f]
9“As I looked,

“thrones were set in place,
and the Ancient of Days took his
seat.
His clothing was as white as snow;
the hair of his head was white
7:9 like wool.[g]
g Rev 1:14 h Eze 1:15; 10:6 His throne was flaming with fire,
and its wheels[h] were all ablaze.
7:10 i Ps 50:3; 97:3; 10 A river of fire[i] was flowing,
Isa 30:27 coming out from before him.[j]
j Dt 33:2; Thousands upon thousands
Ps 68:17; attended him;
Rev 5:11 k Rev 20:11-15 ten thousand times ten
thousand stood before him.
The court was seated,
and the books[k] were opened.

11“Then I continued to watch because
of the boastful words the horn was
speaking. I kept looking until the beast
7:11 was slain and its body destroyed and
l Rev 19:20 thrown into the blazing fire.[l] 12(The other beasts had been stripped of their authority, but were allowed to live for a period of time.)
13“In my vision at night I looked, and
7:13 there before me was one like a son of
m Mt 8:20*; Rev 1:13* man,[m] coming with the clouds of heav-
n Mt 24:30; Rev 1:7 en.[n] He approached the Ancient of Days
and was led into his presence. 14He was
7:14 o Mt 28:18 given authority,[o] glory and sovereign
p Ps 72:11; power; all peoples, nations and men of
102:22; 1Co 15:27; every language worshiped him.[p] His do-
Eph 1:22 minion is an everlasting dominion that

will not pass away, and his kingdom is 7:14
one that will never be destroyed.[q] q Da 2:44; Heb 12:28; Rev 11:15

The Interpretation of the Dream

15“I, Daniel, was troubled in spirit, and
the visions that passed through my 7:15
mind disturbed me.[r] 16I approached one r Da 4:19
of those standing there and asked him
the true meaning of all this.
“So he told me and gave me the inter- 7:16
pretation[s] of these things: 17‘The four s Da 8:16; 9:22;
great beasts are four kingdoms that will Zec 1:9
rise from the earth. 18But the saints of
the Most High will receive the kingdom 7:18
and will possess it forever—yes, for ever t Isa 60:12-14;
and ever.’[t] Rev 2:26; 20:4
19“Then I wanted to know the true
meaning of the fourth beast, which was
different from all the others and most
terrifying, with its iron teeth and bronze
claws—the beast that crushed and devoured its victims and trampled underfoot whatever was left. 20I also wanted to
know about the ten horns on its head
and about the other horn that came up,
before which three of them fell—the
horn that looked more imposing than
the others and that had eyes and a
mouth that spoke boastfully. 21As I
watched, this horn was waging war 7:21
against the saints and defeating them,[u] u Rev 13:7
22until the Ancient of Days came and
pronounced judgment in favor of the
saints of the Most High, and the time
came when they possessed the kingdom.
23“He gave me this explanation: ‘The
fourth beast is a fourth kingdom that
will appear on earth. It will be different
from all the other kingdoms and will devour the whole earth, trampling it down 7:23
and crushing it.[v] 24The ten horns[w] are v Da 2:40
ten kings who will come from this king- 7:24
dom. After them another king will arise, w Rev 17:12
different from the earlier ones; he will
subdue three kings. 25He will speak 7:25
against the Most High[x] and oppress his x Isa 37:23; Da 11:36
saints and try to change the set times[y] y Da 2:21
and the laws. The saints will be handed z Da 8:24; 12:7;
over to him for a time, times and half a Rev 12:14
time.[a][z]
26“ ‘But the court will sit, and his power will be taken away and completely destroyed forever. 27Then the sovereignty,
power and greatness of the kingdoms
under the whole heaven will be handed
over to the saints, the people of the Most

a 25 Or *for a year, two years and half a year*

High. His kingdom will be an everlasting[a] kingdom, and all rulers will worship[b] and obey him.'
28"This is the end of the matter. I,
Daniel, was deeply troubled[c] by my
thoughts, and my face turned pale, but I
kept the matter to myself."

Daniel's Vision of a Ram and a Goat

8 In the third year of King Belshazzar's reign, I, Daniel, had a vision,
after the one that had already appeared
to me. 2In my vision I saw myself in the
citadel of Susa[d] in the province of Elam;[e]
in the vision I was beside the Ulai Canal.
3I looked up,[f] and there before me was a
ram with two horns, standing beside the
canal, and the horns were long. One of
the horns was longer than the other but
grew up later. 4I watched the ram as he
charged toward the west and the north
and the south. No animal could stand
against him, and none could rescue
from his power. He did as he pleased[g]
and became great.
5As I was thinking about this, suddenly a goat with a prominent horn between his eyes came from the west,
crossing the whole earth without touching the ground. 6He came toward the
two-horned ram I had seen standing beside the canal and charged at him in
great rage. 7I saw him attack the ram furiously, striking the ram and shattering
his two horns. The ram was powerless to
stand against him; the goat knocked
him to the ground and trampled on
him,[h] and none could rescue the ram
from his power. 8The goat became very
great, but at the height of his power his
large horn was broken off,[i] and in its
place four prominent horns grew up toward the four winds of heaven.[j]
9Out of one of them came another
horn, which started small but grew in
power to the south and to the east and
toward the Beautiful Land.[k] 10It grew
until it reached[l] the host of the heavens,
and it threw some of the starry host
down to the earth[m] and trampled[n] on
them. 11It set itself up to be as great as
the Prince of the host;[o] it took away the
daily sacrifice[p] from him, and the place
of his sanctuary was brought low.[q] 12Be-
cause of rebellion, the host ⌞of the
saints⌟[a] and the daily sacrifice were giv-
en over to it. It prospered in everything
it did, and truth was thrown to the
ground.
13Then I heard a holy one[r] speaking,
and another holy one said to him, "How
long will it take for the vision to be fulfilled[s]—the vision concerning the daily
sacrifice, the rebellion that causes desolation, and the surrender of the sanctuary and of the host that will be trampled[t] underfoot?"
14He said to me, "It will take 2,300
evenings and mornings; then the sanctuary will be reconsecrated."[u]

The Interpretation of the Vision

15While I, Daniel, was watching the
vision[v] and trying to understand it,
there before me stood one who looked
like a man.[w] 16And I heard a man's voice
from the Ulai calling, "Gabriel,[x] tell this
man the meaning of the vision."
17As he came near the place where I
was standing, I was terrified and fell
prostrate.[y] "Son of man," he said to me,
"understand that the vision concerns
the time of the end."[z]
18While he was speaking to me, I was
in a deep sleep, with my face to the
ground.[a] Then he touched me and
raised me to my feet.[b]

7:27 [a]Da 2:44; 4:34; Lk 1:33; Rev 11:15; 22:5 [b]Ps 22:27; 72:11; 86:9
7:28 [c]Da 4:19
8:2 [d]Est 1:2 [e]Ge 10:22
8:3 [f]Da 10:5
8:4 [g]Da 11:3,16
8:7 [h]Da 7:7
8:8 [i]2Ch 26:16-21; Da 5:20 [j]Da 7:2; Rev 7:1
8:9 [k]Da 11:16
8:10 [l]Isa 14:13 [m]Rev 12:4 [n]Da 7:7
8:11 [o]Da 11:36-37 [p]Eze 46:13-14 [q]Da 11:31; 12:11
8:13 [r]Da 4:23 [s]Da 12:6 [t]Lk 21:24; Rev 11:2
8:14 [u]Da 12:11-12
8:15 [v]ver 1 [w]Da 10:16-18
8:16 [x]Da 9:21; Lk 1:19
8:17 [y]Eze 1:28; Da 2:46; Rev 1:17 [z]Hab 2:3
8:18 [a]Da 10:9 [b]Eze 2:2; Da 10:16-18

a 12 Or *rebellion, the armies*

JESUS FOCUS

THE END OF TIME

The angel Gabriel informed Daniel that his vision pertained to the "time of the end" (Daniel 8:17). Daniel was directed to "seal up the vision" (verse 26), implying that because it concerned events in the distant future it wasn't yet time for the people to fully grasp its implications. Centuries later, when God gave the apostle John a vision about the end times, the angel instructed him, "Do not seal up the words of the prophecy of this book, because the time is near" (Revelation 22:10). Both the book of Daniel and the book of Revelation focus on events that will occur in the final days of human history. Both allude to a climactic battle between God and Satan, a confrontation in which God will triumph (Daniel 11:40–45; Revelation 16:13–16). Both Daniel and John assure us that God will keep his promises to Israel when Jesus, his Anointed One, reigns as King over God's eternal kingdom here on earth (Daniel 9:26; Revelation 19:11–16).

19He said: "I am going to tell you what will happen later in the time of wrath, because the vision concerns the appointed time of the end.[a][c] 20The two-horned ram that you saw represents the kings of Media and Persia. 21The shaggy goat is the king of Greece,[d] and the large horn between his eyes is the first king.[e] 22The four horns that replaced the one that was broken off represent four kingdoms that will emerge from his nation but will not have the same power.

23"In the latter part of their reign, when rebels have become completely wicked, a stern-faced king, a master of intrigue, will arise. 24He will become very strong, but not by his own power. He will cause astounding devastation and will succeed in whatever he does. He will destroy the mighty men and the holy people.[f] 25He will cause deceit to prosper, and he will consider himself superior. When they feel secure, he will destroy many and take his stand against the Prince of princes.[g] Yet he will be destroyed, but not by human power.[h]

26"The vision of the evenings and mornings that has been given you is true,[i] but seal[j] up the vision, for it concerns the distant future."[k]

27I, Daniel, was exhausted and lay ill for several days. Then I got up and went about the king's business.[l] I was appalled[m] by the vision; it was beyond understanding.

8:19 c Hab 2:3
8:21 d Da 10:20 e Da 11:3
8:24 f Da 7:25; 11:36
8:25 g Da 11:36 h Da 2:34; 11:21
8:26 i Da 10:1 j Rev 22:10 k Da 10:14
8:27 l Da 2:48 m Da 7:28

Daniel's Prayer

9 In the first year of Darius[n] son of Xerxes[b] (a Mede by descent), who was made ruler over the Babylonian[c] kingdom— 2in the first year of his reign, I, Daniel, understood from the Scriptures, according to the word of the LORD given to Jeremiah the prophet, that the desolation of Jerusalem would last seventy[o] years. 3So I turned to the Lord God and pleaded with him in prayer and petition, in fasting, and in sackcloth and ashes.[p]

4I prayed to the LORD my God and confessed:

"O Lord, the great and awesome God,[q] who keeps his covenant of love[r] with all who love him and obey his commands, 5we have sinned and done wrong.[s] We have been wicked and have rebelled; we have turned away[t] from your commands and laws.[u] 6We have not listened to your servants the prophets,[v] who spoke in your name to our kings, our princes and our fathers, and to all the people of the land.

7"Lord, you are righteous, but this day we are covered with shame[w]—the men of Judah and people of Jerusalem and all Israel, both near and far, in all the countries where you have scattered[x] us because of our unfaithfulness to you.[y] 8O LORD, we and our kings, our princes and our fathers are covered with shame because we have sinned against you. 9The Lord our God is merciful and forgiving,[z] even though we have rebelled against him;[a] 10we have not obeyed the LORD our God or kept the laws he gave us through his servants the prophets.[b] 11All Israel has transgressed your law and turned away, refusing to obey you.

"Therefore the curses and sworn judgments written in the Law of Moses, the servant of God, have been poured out on us, because we have sinned[c] against you. 12You have fulfilled[d] the words spoken against us and against our rulers by bringing upon us great disaster. Under the whole heaven nothing has ever been done like what has been done to Jerusalem.[e] 13Just as it is written in the Law of Moses, all this disaster has come upon us, yet we have not sought the favor of the LORD our God by turning from our sins and giving attention to your truth.[f] 14The LORD did not hesitate to bring the disaster[g] upon us, for the LORD our God is righteous in everything he does; yet we have not obeyed him.[h]

15"Now, O Lord our God, who brought your people out of Egypt with a mighty hand[i] and who made for yourself a name[j] that endures to this day, we have sinned, we have done wrong. 16O Lord, in keeping with all your righteous acts,[k] turn away your anger and your wrath from Jerusalem,[l] your city, your

9:1 n Da 5:31
9:2 o 2Ch 36:21; Jer 29:10; Zec 7:5
9:3 p Ne 1:4; Jer 29:12
9:4 q Dt 7:21 r Dt 7:9
9:5 s Ps 106:6
9:5 t Isa 53:6 u ver 11; La 1:20
9:6 v 2Ch 36:16; Jer 44:5
9:7 w Ps 44:15 x Dt 4:27; Am 9:9 y Jer 3:25
9:9 z Ps 130:4 a Ne 9:17; Jer 14:7
9:10 b 2Ki 17:13-15; 18:12
9:11 c Isa 1:4-6; Jer 8:5-10
9:12 d Isa 44:26; Zec 1:6 e Jer 44:2-6; Eze 5:9
9:13 f Isa 9:13; Jer 2:30
9:14 g Jer 44:27 h Ne 9:33
9:15 i Jer 32:21 j Ne 9:10
9:16 k Ps 31:1 l Jer 32:32

[a] 19 Or *because the end will be at the appointed time* [b] 1 Hebrew *Ahasuerus* [c] 1 Or *Chaldean*

Waiting for Deliverance

To those who cared, it seemed as though God had broken all of his promises. His people had been exiled from the land he had given them, the temple had been destroyed and David's family was no longer occupying the throne. Some of the Israelites may have started to believe that the gods of the Babylonians were more powerful than the God of their fathers! Then God sent a prophet named Daniel to remind them that the God of Israel was anything but a weakling. It wasn't God who had changed his mind. The people had turned away from him and had missed out on what he had planned for them—but only for a time. No matter where they were or what they faced, the word of God remained true. And he wanted their complete devotion.

Daniel's greatest anguish was not over the sin of unbelievers; it was prompted by the iniquity of God's own people. Even though our heavenly Father disciplines us for disobeying him, we are still prone to faithlessness. Yet instead of terrorizing us, God lovingly preserves us and guides us in his ways. Even in the midst of an evil world he promises that we will be restored. In the middle of Daniel's prophecy about God's wrath toward sin, God promised that there would come a time of complete atonement for all sin (Daniel 9:24).

It would be another 490 years before the Messiah would be born (Matthew 1:1). As he had promised, God the Father would send Jesus to die in our place so that the chasm caused by sin might be bridged forever (Romans 5:6–8; Hebrews 9:26–28). Jesus promised to come back to take his people to be with him in heaven (John 14:2–3), and our anticipation of that day has stretched to two millennia. Because that elusive event seems so far removed from our daily struggle, many people fail to make personal holiness a priority. But this fact remains: God promises a better future for us when we are willing to walk with him. In the New Testament the apostle Paul stated it this way: "Let us not become weary in doing good, for at the proper time we will reap a harvest if we do not give up" (Galatians 6:9).

The world and its evil will run their course, but our task is to be witnesses to God's call and to the redemption that is ours in Jesus Christ (Philippians 2:14–16). The book of Daniel doesn't diminish the pain and despair generated by living so long in a sinful world, but neither does Daniel allow us to give up on following our faithful God. As the evil of the world stretches into the future, we can rest assured that it will be overcome by the power of our sovereign God (Daniel 5:21). Daniel's visions always show God as triumphant (Daniel 7:11,26–27; 8:25; 9:27; 11:45; 12:13). With Daniel we look forward to the climax of God's sovereignty as described in the book of Revelation: "The kingdom of the world has become the kingdom of our Lord and of his Christ, and he will reign forever and ever" (Revelation 11:15; see also Daniel 2:44; 7:27).

Self-Discovery: *If you are familiar with Georg Friederich Handel's masterful oratorio,* The Messiah, *recall the music and lyrics to the climactic section based on Revelation 11:15. Allow your spirit to worship the Lord by offering up to him the memory of this inspiring music.*

GO TO DISCOVERY 218 ON PAGE 1155

9:16 holy hill.[m] Our sins and the iniqui-
m Zec 8:3 ties of our fathers have made Jeru-
n Eze 5:14 salem and your people an object of
scorn[n] to all those around us.
17"Now, our God, hear the prayers
and petitions of your servant. For
9:17 your sake, O Lord, look with favor[o]
o Nu 6:24-26; Ps 80:19 on your desolate sanctuary. 18Give
ear, O God, and hear; open your eyes
9:18 and see[p] the desolation of the city
p Ps 80:14 that bears your Name.[q] We do not
q Isa 37:17; Jer 7:10-12; 25:29 make requests of you because we
are righteous, but because of your
9:19 great mercy. 19O Lord, listen! O Lord,
r Ps 44:23 forgive![r] O Lord, hear and act! For
your sake, O my God, do not delay,
because your city and your people
bear your Name."

The Seventy "Sevens"

20While I was speaking and praying,
confessing my sin and the sin of my people Israel and making my request to the
9:20 LORD my God for his holy hill[s]— 21while
s ver 3; Ps 145:18; I was still in prayer, Gabriel,[t] the man I
Isa 58:9 had seen in the earlier vision, came to
9:21 me in swift flight about the time of the
t Da 8:16; Lk 1:19 evening sacrifice.[u] 22He instructed me
u Ex 29:39 and said to me, "Daniel, I have now
come to give you insight and understanding. 23As soon as you began to
9:23 pray, an answer was given, which I have
v Da 10:19; Lk 1:28 come to tell you, for you are highly es-
w Da 10:11-12; teemed.[v] Therefore, consider the mes-
Mt 24:15 sage and understand the vision:[w]

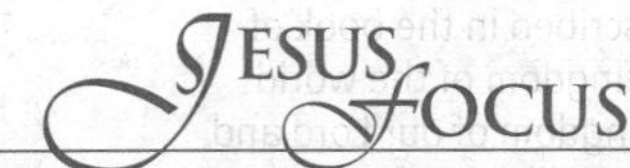

CUT OFF AND MADE NOTHING

Daniel's prophecy includes a description of the Messiah as "the Anointed One, the ruler" (Daniel 9:25), who would come and then be "cut off" (verse 26). Jesus, the precious Son of God, came as a tiny baby (Luke 2:1–14) and was handed over to be crucified (Matthew 27:15–26; Acts 3:13–15) so that we might be set free from the penalty and power of sin (Romans 6:1–23; Galatians 3:13). The One who is in very nature God "made himself nothing" (Philippians 2:7) to do his Father's will. Many years before Jesus came to earth Daniel received from the angel Gabriel this prophecy that the Messiah would suffer and die the most degrading of deaths—death on a cross—"cut off" and literally "made . . . nothing" so that we could find all we need for life eternal in and through him.

24"Seventy 'sevens'[a] are decreed for
your people and your holy city to finish[b]
transgression, to put an end to sin, to 9:24
atone[x] for wickedness, to bring in ever- x Isa 53:10
lasting righteousness,[y] to seal up vision y Isa 56:1
and prophecy and to anoint the most
holy.[c]
25"Know and understand this: From
the issuing of the decree[d] to restore and
rebuild[z] Jerusalem until the Anointed 9:25 z Ezr 4:24
One,[e][a] the ruler, comes, there will be sev- a Jn 4:25
en 'sevens,' and sixty-two 'sevens.' It will
be rebuilt with streets and a trench, but
in times of trouble. 26After the sixty-two
'sevens,' the Anointed One will be cut
off[b] and will have nothing.[f] The people 9:26 b Isa 53:8
of the ruler who will come will destroy c Na 1:8
the city and the sanctuary. The end will
come like a flood:[c] War will continue
until the end, and desolations have been
decreed. 27He will confirm a covenant
with many for one 'seven.'[g] In the middle
of the 'seven'[g] he will put an end to sacrifice and offering. And on a wing ⌊of the
temple⌋ he will set up an abomination
that causes desolation, until the end 9:27
that is decreed[d] is poured out on him.[h]"[i] d Isa 10:22

Daniel's Vision of a Man

10 In the third year of Cyrus[e] king 10:1 e Da 1:21
of Persia, a revelation was given f Da 1:7
to Daniel (who was called Belteshaz- g Da 8:26
zar).[f] Its message was true[g] and it concerned a great war.[j] The understanding
of the message came to him in a vision. 10:2
2At that time I, Daniel, mourned[h] for h Ezr 9:4
three weeks. 3I ate no choice food; no
meat or wine touched my lips; and I
used no lotions at all until the three
weeks were over.
4On the twenty-fourth day of the first 10:4
month, as I was standing on the bank of i Ge 2:14
the great river, the Tigris,[i] 5I looked up 10:5
and there before me was a man dressed j Eze 9:2;
in linen,[j] with a belt of the finest gold[k] Rev 15:6
around his waist. 6His body was like k Jer 10:9
chrysolite, his face like lightning,[l] his 10:6 l Mt 17:2
eyes like flaming torches,[m] his arms and m Rev 19:12
legs like the gleam of burnished bronze,[n] n Rev 1:15

[a] 24 Or *'weeks'*; also in verses 25 and 26 [b] 24 Or *restrain* [c] 24 Or *Most Holy Place*; or *most holy One* [d] 25 Or *word* [e] 25 Or *an anointed one*; also in verse 26 [f] 26 Or *off and will have no one*; or *off, but not for himself* [g] 27 Or *'week'* [h] 27 Or *it* [i] 27 Or *And one who causes desolation will come upon the pinnacle of the abominable ⌊temple⌋, until the end that is decreed is poured out on the desolated ⌊city⌋* [j] 1 Or *true and burdensome*

and his voice like the sound of a multitude.
7 I, Daniel, was the only one who saw
10:7 the vision; the men with me did not see
[o] 2Ki 6:17-20; Ac 9:7 it,[o] but such terror overwhelmed them
that they fled and hid themselves. 8 So I
10:8 was left alone,[p] gazing at this great vi-
[p] Ge 32:24 [q] Da 8:27 sion; I had no strength left,[q] my face
[r] Hab 3:16 turned deathly pale and I was helpless.[r]
9 Then I heard him speaking, and as I lis-
10:9 tened to him, I fell into a deep sleep, my
[s] Da 8:18 face to the ground.[s]
10:10 10 A hand touched me[t] and set me
[t] Jer 1:9 [u] Rev 1:17 trembling on my hands and knees.[u] 11 He
said, "Daniel, you who are highly es-
10:11 teemed,[v] consider carefully the words I
[v] Da 9:23 [w] Eze 2:1 am about to speak to you, and stand
up,[w] for I have now been sent to you."
And when he said this to me, I stood up
trembling.
12 Then he continued, "Do not be
afraid, Daniel. Since the first day that
you set your mind to gain understand- 10:12
ing and to humble[x] yourself before your [x] Da 9:3
God, your words were heard, and I have [y] Da 9:20
come in response to them.[y] 13 But the
prince of the Persian kingdom resisted 10:13
me twenty-one days. Then Michael,[z] one [z] ver 21;
of the chief princes, came to help me, Da 12:1; Jude 1:9
because I was detained there with the
king of Persia. 14 Now I have come to ex- 10:14
plain[a] to you what will happen to your [a] Da 9:22
people in the future, for the vision con- [b] Da 2:28; 8:26;
cerns a time yet to come.[b]" Hab 2:3
15 While he was saying this to me, I
bowed with my face toward the ground 10:15
and was speechless.[c] 16 Then one who [c] Eze 24:27;
looked like a man[a] touched my lips, and Lk 1:20
I opened my mouth and began to
speak.[d] I said to the one standing before 10:16
me, "I am overcome with anguish[e] be- [d] Isa 6:7; Jer 1:9;
cause of the vision, my lord, and I am Da 8:15-18 [e] Isa 21:3
helpless. 17 How can I, your servant, talk
with you, my lord? My strength is gone
and I can hardly breathe."[f] 10:17 [f] Da 4:19
18 Again the one who looked like a
man touched[g] me and gave me strength. 10:18 [g] ver 16
19 "Do not be afraid, O man highly es-
teemed," he said. "Peace![h] Be strong 10:19
now; be strong."[i] [h] Jdg 6:23; Isa 35:4 [i] Jos 1:9 [j] Isa 6:1-8
When he spoke to me, I was strength-
ened and said, "Speak, my lord, since
you have given me strength."[j]
20 So he said, "Do you know why I have
come to you? Soon I will return to fight
against the prince of Persia, and when I 10:20
go, the prince of Greece[k] will come; [k] Da 8:21; 11:2
21 but first I will tell you what is written 10:21
in the Book of Truth.[l] (No one supports [l] Da 11:2
me against them except Michael,[m] your [m] ver 13; Jude 1:9

11 prince. 1 And in the first year of 11:1
Darius[n] the Mede, I took my [n] Da 5:31
stand to support and protect him.)

The Kings of the South and the North

2 "Now then, I tell you the truth:[o] 11:2
Three more kings will appear in Persia, [o] Da 10:21 [p] Da 10:20
and then a fourth, who will be far richer
than all the others. When he has gained
power by his wealth, he will stir up
everyone against the kingdom of
Greece.[p] 3 Then a mighty king will appear, who will rule with great power and
do as he pleases.[q] 4 After he has ap- 11:3
peared, his empire will be broken up and [q] Da 8:4,21

a 16 Most manuscripts of the Masoretic Text; one manuscript of the Masoretic Text, Dead Sea Scrolls and Septuagint *Then something that looked like a man's hand*

JESUS AND YOU

SPIRITUAL BATTLES

The angel allowed Daniel to glimpse what transpires in the spiritual world when God's people are struggling. He informed Daniel that he had come to strengthen him, because Daniel was physically depleted and mentally exhausted both from his personal experiences and from the intense emotions involved in receiving God's revelations (Daniel 10:18–19). But the angel was compelled to leave again to "fight against the prince of Persia" (verse 20). That which we can observe around us with our physical eyes is never a complete picture of our situation. When it appears as though God is taking too long to act, when we fear that we're simply too exhausted to go on, it might well be that a conflict is raging behind the scenes in the spiritual realm. The apostle Paul would later address this same reality in a very direct manner: "Our struggle is not against flesh and blood, but . . . against the powers of this dark world and against the spiritual forces of evil in the heavenly realms" (Ephesians 6:12). From Daniel's struggle we see evidence of what we know to be true in our own lives: God is continually at work counteracting the schemes of Satan and his forces. Jesus has already defeated Satan by dying for our sins and rising again in triumph (Luke 10:18; Romans 16:20; Colossians 2:13–15). Far from fighting a losing battle, we can be assured that we are on the winning side in the aftermath of a conflict whose outcome has long ago been decided.

11:4 parceled out toward the four winds of
r Da 7:2; 8:22 heaven.[r] It will not go to his descendants, nor will it have the power he exercised, because his empire will be uprooted and given to others.
5 "The king of the South will become
strong, but one of his commanders will
become even stronger than he and will
rule his own kingdom with great power.
6 After some years, they will become allies. The daughter of the king of the
South will go to the king of the North to
make an alliance, but she will not retain
her power, and he and his power[a] will
not last. In those days she will be handed over, together with her royal escort
and her father[b] and the one who supported her.
7 "One from her family line will arise to
take her place. He will attack the forces
11:7 s ver 6 of the king of the North[s] and enter his
fortress; he will fight against them and
be victorious. 8 He will also seize their
11:8 gods,[t] their metal images and their valu-
t Isa 37:19; 46:1-2 able articles of silver and gold and carry
u Jer 43:12 them off to Egypt.[u] For some years he
will leave the king of the North alone.
9 Then the king of the North will invade
the realm of the king of the South but
will retreat to his own country. 10 His
sons will prepare for war and assemble a
great army, which will sweep on like an
irresistible flood[v] and carry the battle as 11:10 v Isa 8:8;
far as his fortress. Jer 46:8; Da 9:26
11 "Then the king of the South will
march out in a rage and fight against the
king of the North, who will raise a large 11:11
army, but it will be defeated.[w] 12 When w Da 8:7-8
the army is carried off, the king of the
South will be filled with pride and will
slaughter many thousands, yet he will
not remain triumphant. 13 For the king
of the North will muster another army,
larger than the first; and after several
years, he will advance with a huge army
fully equipped.
14 "In those times many will rise
against the king of the South. The violent men among your own people will
rebel in fulfillment of the vision, but
without success. 15 Then the king of the
North will come and build up siege 11:15
ramps[x] and will capture a fortified city. x Eze 4:2
The forces of the South will be powerless
to resist; even their best troops will not
have the strength to stand. 16 The invad- 11:16
er will do as he pleases;[y] no one will be y Da 8:4
able to stand against him.[z] He will es- z Jos 1:5; Da 8:7
tablish himself in the Beautiful Land a Da 8:9
and will have the power to destroy it.[a]
17 He will determine to come with the
might of his entire kingdom and will
make an alliance with the king of the
South. And he will give him a daughter
in marriage in order to overthrow the
kingdom, but his plans[c] will not suc-
ceed[b] or help him. 18 Then he will turn 11:17 b Ps 20:4
his attention to the coastlands[c] and will 11:18
take many of them, but a commander c Isa 66:19;
will put an end to his insolence and will Jer 25:22
turn his insolence back upon him.[d] 19 Af- d Hos 12:14
ter this, he will turn back toward the
fortresses of his own country but will 11:19
stumble and fall,[e] to be seen no more.[f] e Ps 27:2 f Ps 37:36;
20 "His successor will send out a tax Eze 26:21
collector to maintain the royal splendor.[g] In a few years, however, he will be 11:20
destroyed, yet not in anger or in battle. g Isa 60:17
21 "He will be succeeded by a con- 11:21
temptible[h] person who has not been h Da 4:17
given the honor of royalty.[i] He will in- i Da 8:25
vade the kingdom when its people feel

[a] 6 Or *offspring* [b] 6 Or *child* (see Vulgate and Syriac) [c] 17 Or *but she*

JESUS FOCUS

THE ANTICHRIST

Antiochus IV was a tyrant who presumed to take on himself the arrogant name of *Epiphanes*, meaning "God made manifest." Daniel's words in chapter 11 focus on this pagan king who apparently believed that he himself was plainly and unmistakably God in the flesh. Some people suggest that part of Daniel's prophecy goes beyond Antiochus and alludes to God's final enemy, the "antichrist" (1 John 2:18), who will also make outrageous claims about his own irresistible authority and extraordinary prowess. The apostle Paul would refer to the antichrist as "the man doomed to destruction," who will make the same audacious claim to divinity and will set himself up to be worshiped (2 Thessalonians 2:3–4). In the book of Revelation John referred to the antichrist as the "beast" and predicted that all who have sided with the worldly kingdom will in fact bow down before him (Revelation 13:8). In the end, however, the glorious, all-powerful Son of God will triumph over this false god (Revelation 19:19–20) and will begin his glorious reign over all creation, an eternal kingship characterized by perfection, love and righteousness.

secure, and he will seize it through intrigue. 22 Then an overwhelming army will be swept away before him; both it and a prince of the covenant will be destroyed.[j] 23 After coming to an agreement with him, he will act deceitfully,[k] and with only a few people he will rise to power. 24 When the richest provinces feel secure, he will invade them and will achieve what neither his fathers nor his forefathers did. He will distribute plunder, loot and wealth among his followers.[l] He will plot the overthrow of fortresses—but only for a time.

25 "With a large army he will stir up his strength and courage against the king of the South. The king of the South will wage war with a large and very powerful army, but he will not be able to stand because of the plots devised against him. 26 Those who eat from the king's provisions will try to destroy him; his army will be swept away, and many will fall in battle. 27 The two kings, with their hearts bent on evil,[m] will sit at the same table and lie[n] to each other, but to no avail, because an end will still come at the appointed time.[o] 28 The king of the North will return to his own country with great wealth, but his heart will be set against the holy covenant. He will take action against it and then return to his own country.

29 "At the appointed time he will invade the South again, but this time the outcome will be different from what it was before. 30 Ships of the western coastlands[a][p] will oppose him, and he will lose heart. Then he will turn back and vent his fury against the holy covenant. He will return and show favor to those who forsake the holy covenant.

31 "His armed forces will rise up to desecrate the temple fortress and will abolish the daily sacrifice. Then they will set up the abomination that causes desolation.[q] 32 With flattery he will corrupt those who have violated the covenant, but the people who know their God will firmly resist[r] him.

33 "Those who are wise will instruct[s] many, though for a time they will fall by the sword or be burned or captured or plundered.[t] 34 When they fall, they will receive a little help, and many who are not sincere[u] will join them. 35 Some of the wise will stumble, so that they may be refined,[v] purified and made spotless until the time of the end, for it will still come at the appointed time.

The King Who Exalts Himself

36 "The king will do as he pleases. He will exalt and magnify himself above every god and will say unheard-of things[w] against the God of gods.[x] He will be successful until the time of wrath[y] is completed, for what has been determined must take place. 37 He will show no regard for the gods of his fathers or for the one desired by women, nor will he regard any god, but will exalt himself above them all. 38 Instead of them, he will honor a god of fortresses; a god unknown to his fathers he will honor with gold and silver, with precious stones and costly gifts. 39 He will attack the mightiest fortresses with the help of a foreign god and will greatly honor those who acknowledge him. He will make them rulers over many people and will distribute the land at a price.[b]

40 "At the time of the end the king of the South[z] will engage him in battle, and the king of the North will storm[a] out against him with chariots and cavalry and a great fleet of ships. He will invade many countries and sweep through them like a flood.[b] 41 He will also invade the Beautiful Land. Many countries will fall, but Edom,[c] Moab[d] and the leaders of Ammon will be delivered from his hand. 42 He will extend his power over many countries; Egypt will not escape. 43 He will gain control of the treasures of gold and silver and all the riches of Egypt,[e] with the Libyans[f] and Nubians in submission. 44 But reports from the east and the north will alarm him, and he will set out in a great rage to destroy and annihilate many. 45 He will pitch his royal tents between the seas at[c] the beautiful holy mountain. Yet he will come to his end, and no one will help him.

The End Times

12 "At that time Michael,[g] the great prince who protects your people, will arise. There will be a time of distress[h] such as has not happened from the beginning of nations until then. But

11:22 [j] Da 8:10-11
11:23 [k] Da 8:25
11:24 [l] Ne 9:25
11:27 [m] Ps 64:6 [n] Ps 12:2; Jer 9:5 [o] Hab 2:3
11:30 [p] Ge 10:4
11:31 [q] Da 8:11-13; 9:27; Mt 24:15*; Mk 13:14*
11:32 [r] Mic 5:7-9
11:33 [s] Mal 2:7 [t] Mt 24:9; Jn 16:2; Heb 11:32-38
11:34 [u] Mt 7:15; Ro 16:18
11:35 [v] Ps 78:38; Da 12:10; Zec 13:9; Jn 15:2
11:36 [w] Rev 13:5-6 [x] Dt 10:17; Isa 14:13-14; Da 7:25; 8:11-12,25; 2Th 2:4 [y] Isa 10:25; 26:20
11:40 [z] Isa 21:1 [a] Isa 5:28 [b] Eze 38:4
11:41 [c] Isa 11:14 [d] Jer 48:47
11:43 [e] Eze 30:4 [f] 2Ch 12:3; Na 3:9
12:1 [g] Da 10:13 [h] Da 9:12; Mt 24:21; Mk 13:19; Rev 16:18

[a] 30 Hebrew *of Kittim* [b] 39 Or *land for a reward* [c] 45 Or *the sea and*

12:1 [i]Ex 32:32; at that time your people—everyone
Ps 56:8 [j]Jer 30:7 whose name is found written in the
book[i]—will be delivered.[j] 2 Multitudes
12:2 [k]Isa 26:19; who sleep in the dust of the earth will
Mt 25:46; awake: some to everlasting life, others to
Jn 5:28-29 shame and everlasting contempt.[k]
12:3 3 Those who are wise[a][l] will shine[m] like
[l]Da 11:33 the brightness of the heavens, and those
[m]Mt 13:43; Jn 5:35 who lead many to righteousness, like the

SHINING LIKE STARS

The phrase *everlasting life* appears only once in the Old Testament, here in the book of Daniel (Daniel 12:2) There are other passages in which God's promise of life eternal is implied (see, for example, Job 19:25–26; Psalm 16:10; 49:15; Isaiah 25:8; 45:17; Ezekiel 37:1–14), but this is the first instance in which God makes it clear that there will be distinct eternal destinations for all people. Daniel stated explicitly that "multitudes . . . will awake: some to everlasting life, others to . . . everlasting contempt." The righteous ones—those who have put their faith in God and his Son Jesus—are described as "stars" that will shine forever. Our Lord Jesus would later make a similar statement, alerting people that there will come a time when "all who are in their graves" will hear God's voice and come out. "Those who have done good will rise to live, and those who have done evil will rise to be condemned" (John 5:28–29). Daniel instilled hope in the people based on the assurance that God had not turned away from them and that they would spend eternity with him if they were to draw near to him in wisdom and faith (1 Corinthians 2:6–7; Hebrews10:22; James 4:8). And Jesus, the precious Son of God, is the One who makes that hope a reality for each of us today (John 14:6; Colossians 1:27; 1 Timothy 1:1; Titus 2:11–14; Hebrews 6:18–19; 1 Peter 1:3–13).

stars for ever and ever.[n] 4 But you, Daniel, 12:3 [n]1Co 15:42
close up and seal[o] the words of the scroll
until the time of the end.[p] Many will go 12:4 [o]Isa 8:16
here and there to increase knowledge." [p]ver 9,13; Rev 22:10

5 Then I, Daniel, looked, and there before me stood two others, one on this
bank of the river and one on the oppo-
site bank.[q] 6 One of them said to the man 12:5 [q]Da 10:4
clothed in linen,[r] who was above the wa-
ters of the river, "How long will it be be- 12:6 [r]Eze 9:2
fore these astonishing things are ful- [s]Da 8:13
filled?"[s]
7 The man clothed in linen, who was 12:7 [t]Rev 10:5-6
above the waters of the river, lifted his [u]Da 7:25
right hand and his left hand toward [v]Da 8:24
heaven, and I heard him swear by him [w]Lk 21:24;
who lives forever,[t] saying, "It will be for a Rev 10:7
time, times and half a time.[b][u] When the
power of the holy people[v] has been finally broken, all these things will be
completed.[w]"
8 I heard, but I did not understand. So
I asked, "My lord, what will the outcome
of all this be?"
9 He replied, "Go your way, Daniel, because the words are closed up and 12:9
sealed until the time of the end.[x] 10 Many [x]ver 4
will be purified, made spotless and re-
fined,[y] but the wicked will continue to 12:10 [y]Da 11:35
be wicked.[z] None of the wicked will un- [z]Isa 32:7;
derstand, but those who are wise will Rev 22:11
understand.[a] [a]Hos 14:9
11 "From the time that the daily sacri- 12:11
fice is abolished and the abomination [b]Da 8:11; 9:27;
that causes desolation[b] is set up, there Mt 24:15*;
will be 1,290 days. 12 Blessed is the one Mk 13:14*
who waits[c] for and reaches the end of 12:12 [c]Isa 30:18
the 1,335 days.[d] [d]Da 8:14
13 "As for you, go your way till the end. 12:13
You will rest,[e] and then at the end of the [e]Isa 57:2
days you will rise to receive your allotted [f]Ps 16:5;
inheritance.[f]" Rev 14:13

[a] 3 Or *who impart wisdom* [b] 7 Or *a year, two years and half a year*

HOSEA

What is the New Testament significance of the references to ransom and redemption from death? (Hosea 13:14)

- *Hosea's reference was to the death of the nation (verse 1). The apostle Paul would later apply this passage from Hosea to the resurrection victory accomplished in Jesus Christ (1 Corinthians 15:55).*

Have God's promises to Israel been fulfilled? (Hosea 14:5–7)

- *While some Bible scholars point to certain aspects of these promises that have been fulfilled at various stages of Israel's history, the ultimate fulfillment is yet to come, at the second coming of Jesus.*

Jesus in Hosea In his prophetic book Hosea pictured God as a faithful and forgiving husband whose relationship to Israel was one of love (Hosea 2:16–19; 10:12). Through the graphic illustration of Hosea's dealings with his adulterous wife, whom God had instructed him to marry, God revealed to his people that he will do whatever is necessary to bring us back to himself after we have wandered off. God's message through Hosea is that he has set his heart on us and will not give us up.

Although Hosea made no explicit reference to Jesus, the pattern of God's dealings with his people as expressed in this prophetic book undeniably looks ahead to that of his future gracious dealings with all of humanity in the sending of Jesus as Redeemer (Ephesians 1:1–8). Hosea did make an oblique reference to the flight of the holy family into Egypt (and their subsequent return) in Hosea 11:1–2 (see also Matthew 2:14–15), although this symbolic passage refers more openly to God calling his son, Israel, out of Egypt at the time of the exodus.

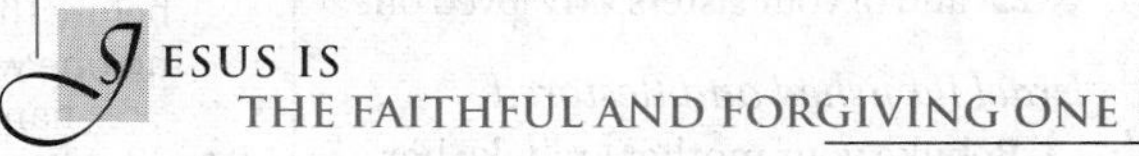

JESUS IS THE FAITHFUL AND FORGIVING ONE

1 The word of the LORD that came to Hosea son of Beeri during the reigns of Uzziah, Jotham, Ahaz and Hezekiah, kings of Judah,[a] and during the reign of Jeroboam[b] son of Jehoash[a] king of Israel:[c]

Hosea's Wife and Children

2 When the LORD began to speak through Hosea, the LORD said to him, "Go, take to yourself an adulterous[d] wife and children of unfaithfulness, because the land is guilty of the vilest adultery[e] in departing from the LORD." 3 So he married Gomer daughter of Diblaim, and she conceived and bore him a son.

4 Then the LORD said to Hosea, "Call him Jezreel,[f] because I will soon punish the house of Jehu for the massacre at Jezreel, and I will put an end to the kingdom of Israel. 5 In that day I will break Israel's bow in the Valley of Jezreel.[g]"

6 Gomer[h] conceived again and gave birth to a daughter. Then the LORD said to Hosea, "Call her Lo-Ruhamah,[b] for I will no longer show love to the house of Israel,[i] that I should at all forgive them. 7 Yet I will show love to the house of Judah; and I will save them—not by bow,[j] sword or battle, or by horses and horsemen, but by the LORD their God.[k]"

8 After she had weaned Lo-Ruhamah, Gomer had another son. 9 Then the LORD said, "Call him Lo-Ammi,[c] for you are not my people, and I am not your God.

10 "Yet the Israelites will be like the sand on the seashore, which cannot be measured or counted.[l] In the place where it was said to them, 'You are not my people,' they will be called 'sons of the living God.'[m] 11 The people of Judah and the people of Israel will be reunited,[n] and they will appoint one leader[o] and will come up out of the land,[p] for great will be the day of Jezreel.

2 "Say of your brothers, 'My people,' and of your sisters, 'My loved one.'[q]

Israel Punished and Restored

2 "Rebuke your mother,[r] rebuke her,
for she is not my wife,
and I am not her husband.
Let her remove the adulterous[s]
look from her face
and the unfaithfulness from
between her breasts.
3 Otherwise I will strip her naked
and make her as bare as on the
day she was born;[t]
I will make her like a desert,[u]
turn her into a parched land,
and slay her with thirst.
4 I will not show my love to her
children,[v]
because they are the children of
adultery.
5 Their mother has been unfaithful
and has conceived them in
disgrace.
She said, 'I will go after my lovers,[w]
who give me my food and my
water,
my wool and my linen, my oil
and my drink.'[x]
6 Therefore I will block her path with
thornbushes;
I will wall her in so that she
cannot find her way.[y]
7 She will chase after her lovers but
not catch them;
she will look for them but not
find them.[z]
Then she will say,
'I will go back to my husband as
at first,[a]
for then I was better off[b] than
now.'
8 She has not acknowledged[c] that I
was the one
who gave her the grain, the new
wine and oil,
who lavished on her the silver and
gold—
which they used for Baal.[d]
9 "Therefore I will take away my
grain[e] when it ripens,
and my new wine[f] when it is
ready.
I will take back my wool and my
linen,
intended to cover her
nakedness.
10 So now I will expose her lewdness
before the eyes of her lovers;
no one will take her out of my
hands.[g]
11 I will stop[h] all her celebrations:
her yearly festivals, her New
Moons,
her Sabbath days—all her
appointed feasts.[i]

1:1 [a] Isa 1:1; Mic 1:1 [b] 2Ki 13:13 [c] Am 1:1
1:2 [d] Jer 3:1; Hos 2:2,5; 3:1 [e] Dt 31:16; Jer 3:14; Eze 23:3-21; Hos 5:3
1:4 [f] 2Ki 10:1-14; Hos 2:22
1:5 [g] 2Ki 15:29
1:6 [h] ver 3 [i] Hos 2:4
1:7 [j] Ps 44:6 [k] Zec 4:6
1:10 [l] Ge 22:17; Jer 33:22 [m] ver 9; Ro 9:26*
1:11 [n] Isa 11:12,13 [o] Jer 23:5-8 [p] Eze 37:15-28
2:1 [q] ver 23
2:2 [r] ver 5; Isa 50:1; Hos 1:2 [s] Eze 23:45
2:3 [t] Eze 16:4,22 [u] Isa 32:13-14
2:4 [v] Eze 8:18
2:5 [w] Jer 3:6 [x] Jer 44:17-18
2:6 [y] Job 3:23; 19:8; La 3:9
2:7 [z] Hos 5:13 [a] Jer 2:2; 3:1 [b] Eze 16:8
2:8 [c] Isa 1:3 [d] Eze 16:15-19; Hos 8:4
2:9 [e] Hos 8:7 [f] Hos 9:2
2:10 [g] Eze 16:37
2:11 [h] Jer 7:34 [i] Isa 1:14; Jer 16:9; Hos 3:4; Am 8:10

[a] *1* Hebrew *Joash,* a variant of *Jehoash* [b] *6* *Lo-Ruhamah* means *not loved.* [c] *9* *Lo-Ammi* means *not my people.*

Redeemed and Restored

Many people relish a good love story, and one of the most incredible such stories in the Bible is that of Hosea and Gomer. Hosea ministered faithfully as a full-time prophet, but then God directed him to marry a prostitute named Gomer—certainly not the typical pastor's wife!

Gomer bore three children—two sons and a daughter—but Hosea was painfully aware that he was not the father (Hosea 1:2). Imagine how the prophet must have felt. But the story gets worse. Gomer left Hosea, the couple was divorced (Hosea 2:2) and she continued to drift from one liaison to the next. To Gomer this was the good life: No need to answer to anyone, no long-term commitments, no end to excitement and variety (verse 5). But at the culmination of every superficial relationship Gomer went away empty. Finally, Hosea found her groveling in poverty and provided her anonymously with grain, wine, oil and money. Gomer proceeded to squander these gifts in the worship of Baal (verse 8).

Hosea must have felt like a sucker to end all suckers. He had married a woman of questionable character who had been, not surprisingly, unfaithful to him. Finally she had left him, participated in trysts with a string of lovers and ended up with nothing at all to show for it. And then this apparently gullible ex-husband had passed her food and money in secret!

At last Gomer hit rock bottom. She found herself stripped naked and compelled to stand in front of a jeering, catcalling crowd to be auctioned off as a slave. Hosea stood among the gawking spectators that day. But Hosea had come with a single agenda, with the express purpose of buying Gomer back—not as a slave but as his *wife*! God had instructed him to love this adulterous wife, just as God continued to love Israel regardless of how many times the nation had rejected him and violated his trust.

Each of us is like Gomer. No, perhaps we do not lead lives of flagrant sin, flaunting our bodies in complete abandonment. But we do rebel and run from God in pursuit of whatever we fancy will provide us pleasure. We flee, but God doggedly pursues us—down whatever dark alleys we may choose to hide (Psalm 139:7–10; Luke 19:10). When we, like Gomer, were helpless to save ourselves, God sent the most valuable gift of all: his own Son (Romans 5:6–11). On the cross Jesus Christ purchased us from the "slave market" of sin and redeemed us from the fate we deserved (Romans 6:1–23). And, like Hosea, our Savior has restored us to the position of his beloved (Ephesians 5:2).

Self-Discovery: *What emotion does the reality of God's love arouse in you? Think of ways you can respond today in gratitude for the undeserved love shown you in Jesus.*

GO TO DISCOVERY 219 ON PAGE 1171

2:12 [j]Isa 7:23; Jer 8:13 [k]Isa 5:6 [l]Hos 13:8

12 I will ruin her vines[j] and her fig trees,
which she said were her pay from her lovers;
I will make them a thicket,[k]
and wild animals will devour them.[l]

2:13 [m]Hos 11:2 [n]Eze 16:17 [o]Hos 4:13 [p]Hos 4:6; 8:14; 13:6

13 I will punish her for the days
she burned incense to the Baals;[m]
she decked herself with rings and jewelry,[n]
and went after her lovers,[o]
but me she forgot,[p]"
declares the LORD.

14 "Therefore I am now going to allure her;
I will lead her into the desert
and speak tenderly to her.

2:15 [q]Jos 7:24,26 [r]Ex 15:1-18 [s]Jer 2:2 [t]Hos 12:9

15 There I will give her back her vineyards,
and will make the Valley of Achor[a][q] a door of hope.
There she will sing[b][r] as in the days of her youth,[s]
as in the day she came up out of Egypt.[t]

16 "In that day," declares the LORD,
"you will call me 'my husband';
you will no longer call me 'my master.[c]'

2:17 [u]Ex 23:13; Ps 16:4 [v]Jos 23:7

17 I will remove the names of the Baals from her lips;[u]
no longer will their names be invoked.[v]

2:18 [w]Job 5:22 [x]Isa 2:4 [y]Jer 23:6; Eze 34:25

18 In that day I will make a covenant for them
with the beasts of the field and the birds of the air
and the creatures that move along the ground.[w]
Bow and sword and battle
I will abolish[x] from the land,
so that all may lie down in safety.[y]

2:19 [z]Isa 62:4 [a]Isa 1:27

19 I will betroth[z] you to me forever;
I will betroth you in[d] righteousness and justice,[a]
in[e] love and compassion.

2:20 [b]Jer 31:34; Hos 6:6; 13:4

20 I will betroth you in faithfulness,
and you will acknowledge[b] the LORD.

2:21 [c]Isa 55:10; Zec 8:12

21 "In that day I will respond,"
declares the LORD—
"I will respond[c] to the skies,
and they will respond to the earth;

2:22 [d]Jer 31:12; Joel 2:19

22 and the earth will respond to the grain,
the new wine and oil,[d]
and they will respond to Jezreel.[f]

2:23 [e]Jer 31:27 [f]Hos 1:6 [g]Hos 1:10 [h]Ro 9:25*; 1Pe 2:10

23 I will plant[e] her for myself in the land;
I will show my love to the one I called 'Not my loved one.[g][f]'
I will say to those called 'Not my people,[h]' 'You are my people';[g]
and they will say, 'You are my God.[h]' "

Hosea's Reconciliation With His Wife

3 The LORD said to me, "Go, show your love to your wife again, though she is loved by another and is an

[a] 15 *Achor* means *trouble.* [b] 15 Or *respond* [c] 16 Hebrew *baal* [d] 19 Or *with*; also in verse 20 [e] 19 Or *with* [f] 22 *Jezreel* means *God plants.* [g] 23 Hebrew *Lo-Ruhamah* [h] 23 Hebrew *Lo-Ammi*

JESUS AND YOU

RETURNING TO THE LORD

Most people have good intentions when they state their wedding vows. Eventually, however, the pressures and disappointments of life leave us vulnerable to various temptations—and sometimes the temptation is adultery. In the book of Hosea God directed the prophet to marry an adulterous woman who would ultimately leave him for liaisons with other men (Hosea 1:2). We are not privy to Hosea's reaction to this seemingly bizarre instruction; we know only that he obeyed. God used Gomer's behavior to illustrate to the people of Israel their habitual unfaithfulness to him. But although the Israelites had repeatedly betrayed God, he announced that he would never forget his promises to them. He assured them, in fact, that "afterward the Israelites will return and seek the LORD their God and David their king. They will come trembling to the LORD and to his blessings in the last days" (Hosea 3:5). Although Jesus was a descendant of David and was in fact the true Son of God and the long-awaited Messiah, many people in his day still refused to accept him for who he was or to honor him as their King. But in a manner reminiscent of God's promise in Hosea 3:5 the Father again pledged through the apostle Paul that someday "every knee [shall] bow . . . and every tongue confess that Jesus Christ is Lord" (Philippians 2:10–11).

3:1 [i] Hos 1:2 [j] 2Sa 6:19

adulteress.[i] Love her as the LORD loves
the Israelites, though they turn to other
gods and love the sacred raisin cakes.[j]"
2 So I bought her for fifteen shekels[a] of
silver and about a homer and a lethek[b]
of barley. 3 Then I told her, "You are to
live with[c] me many days; you must not
be a prostitute or be intimate with any
man, and I will live with[c] you."
4 For the Israelites will live many days
without king or prince,[k] without sacrifice[l] or sacred stones, without ephod or
idol.[m] 5 Afterward the Israelites will return and seek the LORD their God and
David their king.[n] They will come trembling to the LORD and to his blessings in
the last days.[o]

3:4 [k] Hos 13:11 [l] Da 11:31; Hos 2:11 [m] Jdg 17:5-6; Zec 10:2

3:5 [n] Eze 34:23-24 [o] Jer 50:4-5

The Charge Against Israel

4 Hear the word of the LORD, you Israelites,
because the LORD has a charge to bring
against you who live in the land:
"There is no faithfulness, no love,
no acknowledgment[p] of God in the land.
2 There is only cursing,[d] lying[q] and murder,[r]
stealing[s] and adultery;
they break all bounds,
and bloodshed follows bloodshed.
3 Because of this the land mourns,[e][t]
and all who live in it waste away;[u]
the beasts of the field and the birds of the air
and the fish of the sea are dying.[v]

4 "But let no man bring a charge,
let no man accuse another,
for your people are like those
who bring charges against a priest.[w]
5 You stumble[x] day and night,
and the prophets stumble with you.
So I will destroy your mother[y]—
6 my people are destroyed from lack of knowledge.[z]

"Because you have rejected knowledge,
I also reject you as my priests;
because you have ignored the law[a] of your God,
I also will ignore your children.
7 The more the priests increased,
the more they sinned against me;
they exchanged[f] their[g] Glory[b]
for something disgraceful.[c]
8 They feed on the sins of my people
and relish their wickedness.[d]
9 And it will be: Like people, like priests.[e]
I will punish both of them for their ways
and repay them for their deeds.[f]

10 "They will eat but not have enough;[g]
they will engage in prostitution
but not increase,
because they have deserted[h] the LORD
to give themselves 11 to prostitution,[i]
to old wine and new,
which take away the understanding[j] 12 of my people.
They consult a wooden idol[k]
and are answered by a stick of wood.[l]
A spirit of prostitution leads them astray;[m]
they are unfaithful to their God.
13 They sacrifice on the mountaintops
and burn offerings on the hills,
under oak,[n] poplar and terebinth,
where the shade is pleasant.[o]
Therefore your daughters turn to prostitution[p]
and your daughters-in-law to adultery.[q]

14 "I will not punish your daughters
when they turn to prostitution,
nor your daughters-in-law
when they commit adultery,
because the men themselves
consort with harlots[r]
and sacrifice with shrine prostitutes—
a people without understanding
will come to ruin!

15 "Though you commit adultery, O Israel,
let not Judah become guilty.

4:1 [p] Jer 7:28

4:2 [q] Hos 7:3; 10:4 [r] Hos 6:9 [s] Hos 7:1

4:3 [t] Jer 4:28 [u] Isa 33:9 [v] Jer 4:25; Zep 1:3

4:4 [w] Dt 17:12; Eze 3:26

4:5 [x] Eze 14:7 [y] Hos 2:2

4:6 [z] Hos 2:13; Mal 2:7-8 [a] Hos 8:1,12

4:7 [b] Hab 2:16 [c] Hos 10:1,6; 13:6

4:8 [d] Isa 56:11; Mic 3:11

4:9 [e] Isa 24:2 [f] Jer 5:31; Hos 8:13; 9:9,15

4:10 [g] Lev 26:26; Mic 6:14 [h] Hos 7:14; 9:17

4:11 [i] Hos 5:4 [j] Pr 20:1

4:12 [k] Jer 2:27 [l] Hab 2:19 [m] Isa 44:20

4:13 [n] Isa 1:29 [o] Jer 3:6; Hos 11:2 [p] Jer 2:20; Am 7:17 [q] Hos 2:13

4:14 [r] ver 11

[a] 2 That is, about 6 ounces (about 170 grams)
[b] 2 That is, probably about 10 bushels (about 330 liters)
[c] 3 Or *wait for*
[d] 2 That is, to pronounce a curse upon
[e] 3 Or *dries up*
[f] 7 Syriac and an ancient Hebrew scribal tradition; Masoretic Text *I will exchange*
[g] 7 Masoretic Text; an ancient Hebrew scribal tradition *my*

"Do not go to Gilgal;[s]
do not go up to Beth Aven.[a]
And do not swear, 'As surely as
the LORD lives!'
16 The Israelites are stubborn,
like a stubborn heifer.
How then can the LORD pasture
them
like lambs[t] in a meadow?
17 Ephraim is joined to idols;
leave him alone!
18 Even when their drinks are gone,
they continue their prostitution;
their rulers dearly love shameful
ways.
19 A whirlwind[u] will sweep them away,
and their sacrifices will bring
them shame.[v]

Judgment Against Israel

5 "Hear this, you priests!
Pay attention, you Israelites!
Listen, O royal house!
This judgment is against you:
You have been a snare[w] at Mizpah,
a net spread out on Tabor.
2 The rebels are deep in slaughter.[x]
I will discipline all of them.[y]
3 I know all about Ephraim;
Israel is not hidden from me.
Ephraim, you have now turned to
prostitution;
Israel is corrupt.[z]
4 "Their deeds do not permit them
to return to their God.
A spirit of prostitution[a] is in their
heart;
they do not acknowledge[b] the
LORD.
5 Israel's arrogance testifies[c] against
them;
the Israelites, even Ephraim,
stumble in their sin;
Judah also stumbles with them.
6 When they go with their flocks and
herds
to seek the LORD,[d]
they will not find him;
he has withdrawn[e] himself from
them.
7 They are unfaithful[f] to the LORD;
they give birth to illegitimate[g]
children.
Now their New Moon festivals
will devour[h] them and their fields.
8 "Sound the trumpet in Gibeah,[i]
the horn in Ramah.[j]
Raise the battle cry in Beth Aven[a];[k]
lead on, O Benjamin.
9 Ephraim will be laid waste
on the day of reckoning.[l]
Among the tribes of Israel
I proclaim what is certain.[m]
10 Judah's leaders are like those
who move boundary stones.[n]
I will pour out my wrath[o] on them
like a flood of water.
11 Ephraim is oppressed,
trampled in judgment,
intent on pursuing idols.[b][p]
12 I am like a moth[q] to Ephraim,
like rot to the people of Judah.

13 "When Ephraim saw his sickness,
and Judah his sores,
then Ephraim turned to Assyria,[r]
and sent to the great king for
help.[s]
But he is not able to cure[t] you,
not able to heal your sores.[u]
14 For I will be like a lion[v] to Ephraim,
like a great lion to Judah.
I will tear them to pieces and go
away;
I will carry them off, with no one
to rescue them.[w]
15 Then I will go back to my place
until they admit their guilt.
And they will seek my face;[x]
in their misery[y] they will
earnestly seek me.[z]"

Israel Unrepentant

6 "Come, let us return to the LORD.
He has torn us to pieces[a]
but he will heal us;
he has injured us
but he will bind up our wounds.[b]
2 After two days he will revive us;[c]
on the third day he will restore us,
that we may live in his presence.
3 Let us acknowledge the LORD;
let us press on to acknowledge
him.
As surely as the sun rises,
he will appear;
he will come to us like the winter
rains,[d]
like the spring rains that water
the earth.[e]"

[a] 15,8 *Beth Aven* means *house of wickedness* (a name for Bethel, which means *house of God*).
[b] 11 The meaning of the Hebrew for this word is uncertain.

4:15 s Hos 9:15; 12:11; Am 4:4
4:16 t Isa 5:17; 7:25
4:19 u Hos 12:1; 13:15 v Isa 1:29
5:1 w Hos 6:9; 9:8
5:2 x Hos 4:2 y Hos 9:15
5:3 z Hos 6:10
5:4 a Hos 4:11 b Hos 4:6
5:5 c Hos 7:10
5:6 d Mic 6:6-7 e Pr 1:28; Isa 1:15; Eze 8:6
5:7 f Hos 6:7 g Hos 2:4 h Hos 2:11-12
5:8 i Hos 9:9; 10:9
5:8 j Isa 10:29 k Hos 4:15
5:9 l Isa 37:3; Hos 9:11-17 m Isa 46:10; Zec 1:6
5:10 n Dt 19:14 o Eze 7:8
5:11 p Hos 9:16; Mic 6:16
5:12 q Isa 51:8
5:13 r Hos 7:11; 8:9 s Hos 10:6 t Hos 14:3 u Jer 30:12
5:14 v Am 3:4 w Mic 5:8
5:15 x Hos 3:5 y Jer 2:27 z Isa 64:9
6:1 a Hos 5:14 b Dt 32:39; Jer 30:17; Hos 14:4
6:2 c Ps 30:5
6:3 d Joel 2:23 e Ps 72:6

6:4 [f]Hos 11:8 [g]Hos 7:1; 13:3

4 "What can I do with you, Ephraim?[f]
What can I do with you, Judah?
Your love is like the morning mist,
like the early dew that
disappears.[g]
5 Therefore I cut you in pieces with
my prophets,
I killed you with the words of my
mouth;[h]

6:5 [h]Jer 1:9-10; 23:29 [i]Heb 4:12

my judgments flashed like
lightning upon you.[i]

6:6 [j]Isa 1:11; Mt 9:13*; 12:7* [k]Hos 2:20

6 For I desire mercy, not sacrifice,[j]
and acknowledgment[k] of God
rather than burnt offerings.

6:7 [l]Hos 8:1 [m]Hos 5:7

7 Like Adam,[a] they have broken the
covenant[l]—
they were unfaithful[m] to me
there.
8 Gilead is a city of wicked men,
stained with footprints of blood.
9 As marauders lie in ambush for a
man,
so do bands of priests;
they murder on the road to
Shechem,
committing shameful crimes.[n]

6:9 [n]Jer 7:9-10; Eze 22:9; Hos 7:1

10 I have seen a horrible[o] thing
in the house of Israel.
There Ephraim is given to
prostitution
and Israel is defiled.[p]

6:10 [o]Jer 5:30 [p]Hos 5:3

11 "Also for you, Judah,
a harvest[q] is appointed.

6:11 [q]Jer 51:33; Joel 3:13

"Whenever I would restore the
fortunes of my people,

7

1 whenever I would heal Israel,
the sins of Ephraim are exposed
and the crimes of Samaria
revealed.[r]
They practice deceit,[s]
thieves break into houses,[t]
bandits rob in the streets;

7:1 [r]Hos 6:4 [s]ver 13 [t]Hos 4:2

2 but they do not realize
that I remember[u] all their evil
deeds.
Their sins engulf them;[v]
they are always before me.

7:2 [u]Jer 14:10; Hos 8:13 [v]Jer 2:19

3 "They delight the king with their
wickedness,
the princes with their lies.[w]

7:3 [w]Hos 4:2; Mic 7:3

4 They are all adulterers,[x]
burning like an oven
whose fire the baker need not stir
from the kneading of the dough
till it rises.

7:4 [x]Jer 9:2

5 On the day of the festival of our king
the princes become inflamed
with wine,[y]
and he joins hands with the
mockers.

7:5 [y]Isa 28:1,7

6 Their hearts are like an oven;[z]
they approach him with
intrigue.
Their passion smolders all night;
in the morning it blazes like a
flaming fire.

7:6 [z]Ps 21:9

7 All of them are hot as an oven;
they devour their rulers.
All their kings fall,
and none of them calls[a] on me.

7:7 [a]ver 16

8 "Ephraim mixes[b] with the nations;
Ephraim is a flat cake not
turned over.

7:8 [b]ver 11; Ps 106:35; Hos 5:13

9 Foreigners sap his strength,[c]
but he does not realize it.
His hair is sprinkled with gray,
but he does not notice.

7:9 [c]Isa 1:7; Hos 8:7

[a] 7 Or *As at Adam*; or *Like men*

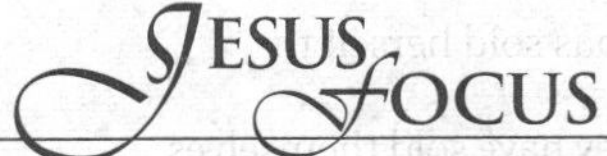

THE SPIRIT OF THE LAW

On two separate occasions Jesus quoted the words of his Father recorded in Hosea 6:6: "I desire mercy, not sacrifice." In the first scenario Jesus was being criticized by the Pharisees for his association with tax collectors and "sinners" (Matthew 9:11), and he instructed them to "go and learn what this means: 'I desire mercy, not sacrifice'" (Matthew 9:13). In the second instance our Lord was again responding to a reproach from the Pharisees, this time over the issue of "unlawful" Sabbath activities—in this case picking and eating grain from a field (Matthew 12:1–2). Jesus reminded the Pharisees of two Old Testament instances of Sabbath "desecration," one involving King David and the other priests in the temple (Matthew 12:3–5). His final words were intended to be convicting: "If you had known what these words mean, 'I desire mercy, not sacrifice,' you would not have condemned the innocent. For the Son of Man is Lord of the Sabbath" (Matthew 12:7–8). But the Pharisees failed to get the message and, miffed at Jesus' reply, almost immediately challenged him about the permissibility of healing on the Sabbath. Jesus responded with a question for them and concluded that it is lawful to "do good" on the Sabbath (Matthew 12:11–12). Sacrifice and ritual constituted the "letter" of the law; mercy and goodness were, and remain, its proper spirit and its righteous objective.

7:10 [d] Hos 5:5 [e] Isa 9:13

[10] Israel's arrogance testifies against
him,[d]
but despite all this
he does not return to the LORD his
God
or search[e] for him.

7:11 [f] Hos 11:11 [g] Hos 5:13; 12:1

[11] "Ephraim is like a dove,[f]
easily deceived and senseless—
now calling to Egypt,
now turning to Assyria.[g]

7:12 [h] Eze 12:13

[12] When they go, I will throw my net[h]
over them;
I will pull them down like birds
of the air.
When I hear them flocking together,
I will catch them.

7:13 [i] Hos 9:12 [j] Jer 14:10; Eze 34:4-6; Hos 9:17 [k] ver 1; Mt 23:37

[13] Woe[i] to them,
because they have strayed[j] from
me!
Destruction to them,
because they have rebelled
against me!
I long to redeem them
but they speak lies against me.[k]

7:14 [l] Jer 3:10 [m] Am 2:8 [n] Hos 13:16

[14] They do not cry out to me from
their hearts[l]
but wail upon their beds.
They gather together[a] for grain
and new wine[m]
but turn away from me.[n]
[15] I trained them and strengthened
them,

7:15 [o] Na 1:9,11

but they plot evil[o] against me.

7:16 [p] Ps 78:9,57 [q] Eze 23:32 [r] Hos 9:3

[16] They do not turn to the Most High;
they are like a faulty bow.[p]
Their leaders will fall by the sword
because of their insolent words.
For this they will be ridiculed[q]
in the land of Egypt.[r]

Israel to Reap the Whirlwind

8:1 [s] Dt 28:49; Jer 4:13 [t] Hos 4:6; 6:7

8 "Put the trumpet to your lips!
An eagle[s] is over the house of the
LORD
because the people have broken
my covenant
and rebelled against my law.[t]
[2] Israel cries out to me,
'O our God, we acknowledge you!'
[3] But Israel has rejected what is good;
an enemy will pursue him.
[4] They set up kings without my
consent;

8:4 [u] Hos 13:10 [v] Hos 2:8

they choose princes without my
approval.[u]
With their silver and gold
they make idols[v] for themselves
to their own destruction.

8:5 [w] Hos 10:5 [x] Jer 13:27

[5] Throw out your calf-idol,
O Samaria![w]
My anger burns against them.
How long will they be incapable of
purity?[x]
[6] They are from Israel!
This calf—a craftsman has made it;
it is not God.
It will be broken in pieces,
that calf of Samaria.

8:7 [y] Pr 22:8; Isa 66:15; Hos 10:12-13; Na 1:3 [z] Hos 2:9

[7] "They sow the wind
and reap the whirlwind.[y]
The stalk has no head;
it will produce no flour.
Were it to yield grain,
foreigners would swallow it up.[z]

8:8 [a] Jer 51:34 [b] Jer 22:28

[8] Israel is swallowed up;[a]
now she is among the nations
like a worthless[b] thing.
[9] For they have gone up to Assyria
like a wild donkey wandering
alone.
Ephraim has sold herself to
lovers.

8:10 [c] Eze 16:37; 22:20 [d] Jer 42:2

[10] Although they have sold themselves
among the nations,
I will now gather them together.[c]
They will begin to waste away[d]
under the oppression of the
mighty king.

8:11 [e] Hos 10:1; 12:11

[11] "Though Ephraim built many
altars for sin offerings,
these have become altars for
sinning.[e]
[12] I wrote for them the many things
of my law,
but they regarded them as
something alien.

8:13 [f] Jer 7:21 [g] Hos 7:2 [h] Hos 4:9 [i] Hos 9:3,6

[13] They offer sacrifices given to me
and they eat[f] the meat,
but the LORD is not pleased with
them.
Now he will remember[g] their
wickedness
and punish their sins:[h]
They will return to Egypt.[i]

8:14 [j] Dt 32:18; Hos 2:13 [k] Jer 17:27

[14] Israel has forgotten[j] his Maker
and built palaces;
Judah has fortified many towns.
But I will send fire upon their cities
that will consume their
fortresses."[k]

a 14 Most Hebrew manuscripts; some Hebrew manuscripts and Septuagint *They slash themselves*

Punishment for Israel

9 Do not rejoice, O Israel;
do not be jubilant[l] like the other
nations.
For you have been unfaithful[m] to
your God;
you love the wages of a prostitute
at every threshing floor.
2 Threshing floors and winepresses
will not feed the people;
the new wine[n] will fail them.
3 They will not remain[o] in the LORD's
land;
Ephraim will return to Egypt[p]
and eat unclean[a] food in Assyria.[q]
4 They will not pour out wine
offerings to the LORD,
nor will their sacrifices please[r]
him.
Such sacrifices will be to them like
the bread of mourners;
all who eat them will be unclean.[s]
This food will be for themselves;
it will not come into the temple
of the LORD.

5 What will you do[t] on the day of
your appointed feasts,[u]
on the festival days of the LORD?
6 Even if they escape from
destruction,
Egypt will gather them,
and Memphis[v] will bury them.
Their treasures of silver will be
taken over by briers,
and thorns[w] will overrun their
tents.
7 The days of punishment[x] are
coming,
the days of reckoning are at hand.
Let Israel know this.
Because your sins[y] are so many
and your hostility so great,
the prophet is considered a fool,[z]
the inspired man a maniac.
8 The prophet, along with my God,
is the watchman over Ephraim,[b]
yet snares[a] await him on all his
paths,
and hostility in the house of his
God.
9 They have sunk deep into
corruption,
as in the days of Gibeah.[b]
God will remember[c] their
wickedness
and punish them for their sins.

9:1 [l] Isa 22:12-13 [m] Hos 10:5
9:2 [n] Hos 2:9
9:3 [o] Lev 25:23 [p] Hos 8:13 [q] Eze 4:13; Hos 7:11
9:4 [r] Jer 6:20; Hos 8:13 [s] Hag 2:13-14
9:5 [t] Isa 10:3; Jer 5:31 [u] Hos 2:11
9:6 [v] Isa 19:13 [w] Isa 5:6; Hos 10:8
9:7 [x] Isa 34:8; Jer 10:15; Mic 7:4 [y] Jer 16:18 [z] Isa 44:25; La 2:14; Eze 14:9-10
9:8 [a] Hos 5:1
9:9 [b] Jdg 19:16-30; Hos 5:8; 10:9 [c] Hos 8:13

10 "When I found Israel,
it was like finding grapes in the
desert;
when I saw your fathers,
it was like seeing the early fruit
on the fig tree.
But when they came to Baal Peor,[d]
they consecrated themselves to
that shameful idol[e]
and became as vile as the thing
they loved.
11 Ephraim's glory will fly away like a
bird[f]—
no birth, no pregnancy, no
conception.[g]
12 Even if they rear children,
I will bereave them of every one.
Woe[h] to them
when I turn away from them![i]
13 I have seen Ephraim, like Tyre,
planted in a pleasant place.[j]
But Ephraim will bring out
their children to the slayer."

14 Give them, O LORD—
what will you give them?
Give them wombs that miscarry
and breasts that are dry.[k]

15 "Because of all their wickedness in
Gilgal,[l]
I hated them there.
Because of their sinful deeds,[m]
I will drive them out of my house.
I will no longer love them;
all their leaders are rebellious.[n]
16 Ephraim[o] is blighted,
their root is withered,
they yield no fruit.[p]
Even if they bear children,
I will slay[q] their cherished
offspring."

17 My God will reject them
because they have not obeyed[r]
him;
they will be wanderers among
the nations.[s]

10 Israel was a spreading vine;[t]
he brought forth fruit for
himself.
As his fruit increased,
he built more altars;[u]
as his land prospered,
he adorned his sacred stones.[v]

9:10 [d] Nu 25:1-5; Ps 106:28-29 [e] Jer 11:13; Hos 4:14
9:11 [f] Hos 4:7; 10:5 [g] ver 14
9:12 [h] Hos 7:13 [i] Dt 31:17
9:13 [j] Eze 27:3
9:14 [k] ver 11; Lk 23:29
9:15 [l] Hos 4:15 [m] Hos 7:2 [n] Isa 1:23; Hos 4:9; 5:2
9:16 [o] Hos 5:11 [p] Hos 8:7 [q] ver 12
9:17 [r] Hos 4:10 [s] Dt 28:65; Hos 7:13
10:1 [t] Eze 15:2 [u] 1Ki 14:23 [v] Hos 8:11; 12:11

[a] 3 That is, ceremonially unclean [b] 8 Or *The prophet is the watchman over Ephraim, / the people of my God*

10:2
w 1Ki 18:21
x Hos 13:16
y ver 8
z Mic 5:13

[2] Their heart is deceitful,[w]
and now they must bear their guilt.[x]
The LORD will demolish their altars[y]
and destroy their sacred stones.[z]
[3] Then they will say, "We have no king
because we did not revere the LORD.
But even if we had a king,
what could he do for us?"
[4] They make many promises,
take false oaths[a]
and make agreements;[b]
therefore lawsuits spring up
like poisonous weeds in a plowed field.
[5] The people who live in Samaria fear
for the calf-idol of Beth Aven.[a c]
Its people will mourn over it,
and so will its idolatrous priests,[d]
those who had rejoiced over its splendor,
because it is taken from them into exile.[e]
[6] It will be carried to Assyria[f]
as tribute for the great king.[g]
Ephraim will be disgraced;[h]
Israel will be ashamed of its wooden idols.[b]
[7] Samaria and its king will float away[i]
like a twig on the surface of the waters.
[8] The high places of wickedness[c j]
will be destroyed—
it is the sin of Israel.
Thorns[k] and thistles will grow up
and cover their altars.[l]
Then they will say to the mountains, "Cover us!"
and to the hills, "Fall on us!"[m]

[9] "Since the days of Gibeah,[n] you have sinned, O Israel,
and there you have remained.[d]
Did not war overtake
the evildoers in Gibeah?
[10] When I please, I will punish[o] them;
nations will be gathered against them
to put them in bonds for their double sin.
[11] Ephraim is a trained heifer
that loves to thresh;
so I will put a yoke
on her fair neck.
I will drive Ephraim,
Judah must plow,
and Jacob must break up the ground.
[12] Sow for yourselves righteousness,[p]
reap the fruit of unfailing love,
and break up your unplowed ground;[q]
for it is time to seek[r] the LORD,
until he comes
and showers righteousness[s] on you.
[13] But you have planted wickedness,
you have reaped evil,[t]
you have eaten the fruit of deception.

10:4
a Hos 4:2
b Eze 17:19; Am 5:7

10:5
c Hos 5:8
d 2Ki 23:5
e Hos 8:5; 9:1,3, 11

10:6
f Hos 11:5
g Hos 5:13
h Isa 30:3; Hos 4:7

10:7
i Hos 13:11

10:8
j 1Ki 12:28-30; Hos 4:13
k Hos 9:6 l ver 2; Isa 32:13
m Lk 23:30*; Rev 6:16

10:9
n Hos 5:8

10:10
o Eze 5:13; Hos 4:9

10:12
p Pr 11:18
q Jer 4:3
r Hos 12:6
s Isa 45:8

10:13
t Job 4:8; Hos 7:3; 11:12; Gal 6:7-8

[a] 5 *Beth Aven* means *house of wickedness* (a name for Bethel, which means *house of God*). [b] 6 Or *its counsel* [c] 8 Hebrew *aven,* a reference to Beth Aven (a derogatory name for Bethel) [d] 9 Or *there a stand was taken*

JESUS FOCUS

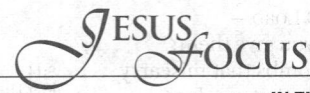

IN THE RIGHT SPIRIT

In order to drive home his point about the corruptness and deceitfulness of God's people, Hosea sarcastically referred to *Bethel*, which means "house of God," as *Beth Aven*, or "house of wickedness" (Hosea 10:5). When Jeroboam was king of the northern kingdom, he disobeyed God by establishing Bethel in Samaria, in place of Jerusalem, as his primary religious sanctuary, thereby leading the people away from true worship of God (1 Kings 12:28–33). Years later, when Hosea was a prophet, God's people were still intermingling religions and diluting the truth. In fact, in the New Testament Jesus spoke with a woman from Samaria, who raised the question of the definition of true worship: "Our fathers worshiped on this mountain," she challenged, "but you Jews claim that the place where we must worship is in Jerusalem" (John 4:20). Jesus initially informed her that "salvation is from the Jews" (John 4:22), meaning that God's Anointed One, the Messiah, the One who would redeem his people, would be a Jew, but he went on to say that God has always wanted his people to worship him "in spirit and in truth" (John 4:24). He desires a relationship with each of us that calls us to go beyond merely observing religious rituals to offering our very lives, in heart, mind and will, as living sacrifices (Romans 12:1)and worshiping him through our obedient service.

Because you have depended on
your own strength

10:13 [u]Ps 33:16

and on your many warriors,[u]
14 the roar of battle will rise against
your people,
so that all your fortresses will be

10:14 [v]Isa 17:3 [w]Hos 13:16

devastated[v]—
as Shalman devastated Beth Arbel
on the day of battle,
when mothers were dashed to
the ground with their
children.[w]
15 Thus will it happen to you,
O Bethel,
because your wickedness is great.
When that day dawns,
the king of Israel will be

10:15 [x]ver 7

completely destroyed.[x]

God's Love for Israel

11:1 [y]Ex 4:22; Hos 12:9,13; 13:4; Mt 2:15*

11 "When Israel was a child, I
loved him,
and out of Egypt I called my son.[y]

11:2 [z]Hos 2:13 [a]2Ki 17:15; Isa 65:7; Jer 18:15

2 But the more I[a] called Israel,
the further they went from me.[b]
They sacrificed to the Baals[z]
and they burned incense to
images.[a]

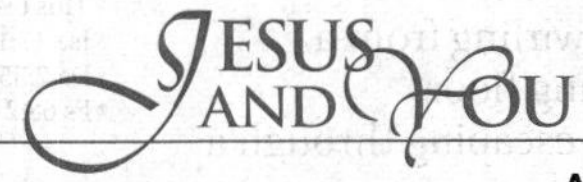

A REBELLIOUS SON

God had already memorably illustrated for his eighth-century people his love for them through Hosea's experience with Gomer, his promiscuous and unfaithful wife. In Hosea 11 God introduced another word picture—that of a rebellious son. According to Deuteronomy 21:18–21, a son who rebelled against his parents could be stoned to death. But because God loved his people and realized that they were unable of their own accord to repair the rift in their relationship with himself, he held off on executing the sentence (Hosea 11:8–9), offering them still another chance. God's heart of compassion never changes, and Jesus confirmed this truth when he told his listeners the parable of the son who left his father's house for the temporarily satisfying thrills of a decadent lifestyle (Luke 15:11–32). Yet when the boy returned home—broken and bankrupt both financially and in spirit—the father welcomed him back with celebration and open arms. God is waiting in the wings to welcome all of his wandering children in the same way; we have only to turn from our sinful ways and accept Jesus with our whole heart.

3 It was I who taught Ephraim to
walk,

11:3 [b]Dt 1:31; Hos 7:15 [c]Jer 30:17

taking them by the arms;[b]
but they did not realize
it was I who healed[c] them.
4 I led them with cords of human
kindness,

11:4 [d]Jer 31:2-3 [e]Lev 26:13 [f]Ex 16:32; Ps 78:25

with ties of love;[d]
I lifted the yoke[e] from their neck
and bent down to feed[f] them.

11:5 [g]Hos 7:16 [h]Hos 10:6

5 "Will they not return to Egypt[g]
and will not Assyria[h] rule over
them
because they refuse to repent?

11:6 [i]Hos 13:16

6 Swords[i] will flash in their cities,
will destroy the bars of their gates
and put an end to their plans.

11:7 [j]Jer 3:6-7; 8:5

7 My people are determined to turn
from me.[j]
Even if they call to the Most
High,
he will by no means exalt them.

11:8 [k]Hos 6:4 [l]Ge 14:8

8 "How can I give you up, Ephraim?[k]
How can I hand you over, Israel?
How can I treat you like Admah?
How can I make you like
Zeboiim?[l]
My heart is changed within me;
all my compassion is aroused.

11:9 [m]Dt 13:17; Jer 30:11 [n]Mal 3:6 [o]Nu 23:19

9 I will not carry out my fierce anger,[m]
nor will I turn and devastate[n]
Ephraim.
For I am God, and not man[o]—
the Holy One among you.
I will not come in wrath.[c]
10 They will follow the LORD;
he will roar like a lion.
When he roars,
his children will come trembling

11:10 [p]Hos 6:1-3

from the west.[p]
11 They will come trembling
like birds from Egypt,

11:11 [q]Isa 11:11 [r]Eze 28:26

like doves from Assyria.[q]
I will settle them in their homes,"[r]
declares the LORD.

Israel's Sin

11:12 [s]Hos 4:2

12 Ephraim has surrounded me with
lies,[s]
the house of Israel with deceit.
And Judah is unruly against God,
even against the faithful Holy
One.

[a] 2 Some Septuagint manuscripts; Hebrew *they*
[b] 2 Septuagint; Hebrew *them*
[c] 9 Or *come against any city*

12:1 [t] Eze 17:10 [u] 2Ki 17:4

12 [1] Ephraim feeds on the wind;[t]
he pursues the east wind all day
and multiplies lies and violence.
He makes a treaty with Assyria
and sends olive oil to Egypt.[u]

12:2 [v] Mic 6:2 [w] Hos 4:9

[2] The LORD has a charge[v] to bring
against Judah;
he will punish Jacob[a] according
to his ways
and repay him according to his
deeds.[w]

12:3 [x] Ge 25:26 [y] Ge 32:24-29

[3] In the womb he grasped his
brother's heel;[x]
as a man he struggled[y] with
God.
[4] He struggled with the angel and
overcame him;
he wept and begged for his favor.

12:4 [z] Ge 28:12-15; 35:15

He found him at Bethel[z]
and talked with him there—
[5] the LORD God Almighty,

12:5 [a] Ex 3:15

the LORD is his name[a] of renown!

12:6 [b] Mic 6:8 [c] Hos 6:1-3; 10:12; Mic 7:7

[6] But you must return to your God;
maintain love and justice,[b]
and wait for your God always.[c]

12:7 [d] Am 8:5

[7] The merchant uses dishonest
scales;[d]
he loves to defraud.
[8] Ephraim boasts,

12:8 [e] Ps 62:10; Rev 3:17

"I am very rich; I have become
wealthy.[e]
With all my wealth they will not
find in me
any iniquity or sin."

[9] "I am the LORD your God,
⌞who brought you⌟ out of[b]

12:9 [f] Lev 23:43; Hos 11:1 [g] Ne 8:17

Egypt;[f]
I will make you live in tents[g] again,
as in the days of your appointed
feasts.
[10] I spoke to the prophets,
gave them many visions

12:10 [h] Eze 20:49 [i] 2Ki 17:13; Jer 7:25

and told parables[h] through
them."[i]

12:11 [j] Hos 6:8 [k] Hos 4:15 [l] Hos 8:11

[11] Is Gilead wicked?[j]
Its people are worthless!
Do they sacrifice bulls in Gilgal?[k]
Their altars will be like piles of
stones
on a plowed field.[l]
[12] Jacob fled to the country of

12:12 [m] Ge 28:5 [n] Ge 29:18

Aram[c];[m]
Israel served to get a wife,
and to pay for her he tended
sheep.[n]

[13] The LORD used a prophet to bring
Israel up from Egypt,

12:13 [o] Ex 13:3; Isa 63:11-14

by a prophet he cared for him.[o]
[14] But Ephraim has bitterly provoked
him to anger;

12:14 [p] Eze 18:13 [q] Da 11:18

his Lord will leave upon him the
guilt of his bloodshed[p]
and will repay him for his
contempt.[q]

The LORD's Anger Against Israel

13:1 [r] Jdg 12:1 [s] Jdg 8:1 [t] Hos 11:2

13 When Ephraim spoke, men
trembled;[r]
he was exalted[s] in Israel.
But he became guilty of Baal
worship[t] and died.
[2] Now they sin more and more;

13:2 [u] Isa 46:6; Jer 10:4 [v] Isa 44:17-20

they make idols for themselves
from their silver,[u]
cleverly fashioned images,
all of them the work of
craftsmen.
It is said of these people,
"They offer human sacrifice
and kiss[d] the calf-idols.[v]"
[3] Therefore they will be like the
morning mist,
like the early dew that

13:3 [w] Hos 6:4 [x] Isa 17:13 [y] Da 2:35 [z] Ps 68:2

disappears,[w]
like chaff[x] swirling from a
threshing floor,[y]
like smoke[z] escaping through a
window.

[4] "But I am the LORD your God,
⌞who brought you⌟ out of[b]

13:4 [a] Hos 12:9 [b] Ex 20:3 [c] Isa 43:11; 45:21-22

Egypt.[a]
You shall acknowledge no God but
me,[b]
no Savior[c] except me.
[5] I cared for you in the desert,
in the land of burning heat.
[6] When I fed them, they were
satisfied;
when they were satisfied, they

13:6 [d] Dt 32:12-15; Hos 2:13

became proud;
then they forgot me.[d]
[7] So I will come upon them like a
lion,
like a leopard I will lurk by the

13:8 [e] 2Sa 17:8

path.
[8] Like a bear robbed of her cubs,[e]
I will attack them and rip them
open.

[a] 2 *Jacob* means *he grasps the heel* (figuratively, *he deceives*). [b] 9,4 Or *God / ever since you were in* [c] 12 That is, Northwest Mesopotamia [d] 2 Or *"Men who sacrifice / kiss*

Like a lion I will devour them;
a wild animal will tear them
apart.[f]
9 "You are destroyed, O Israel,
because you are against me,[g]
against your helper.[h]
10 Where is your king,[i] that he may
save you?
Where are your rulers in all your
towns,
of whom you said,
'Give me a king and princes'?[j]
11 So in my anger I gave you a king,
and in my wrath I took him
away.[k]
12 The guilt of Ephraim is stored up,
his sins are kept on record.[l]
13 Pains as of a woman in childbirth[m]
come to him,
but he is a child without
wisdom;
when the time arrives,
he does not come to the opening
of the womb.[n]

14 "I will ransom them from the
power of the grave[a];[o]
I will redeem them from death.
Where, O death, are your plagues?
Where, O grave,[a] is your
destruction?[p]

"I will have no compassion,
15 even though he thrives[q] among
his brothers.
An east wind[r] from the LORD will
come,
blowing in from the desert;
his spring will fail
and his well dry up.[s]
His storehouse will be plundered[t]
of all its treasures.
16 The people of Samaria must bear
their guilt,[u]
because they have rebelled[v]
against their God.
They will fall by the sword;[w]
their little ones will be dashed[x]
to the ground,
their pregnant women[y] ripped
open."

13:8 [f] Ps 50:22
13:9 [g] Jer 2:17-19 [h] Dt 33:29
13:10 [i] 2Ki 17:4 [j] 1Sa 8:6; Hos 8:4
13:11 [k] 1Ki 14:10; Hos 10:7
13:12 [l] Dt 32:34
13:13 [m] Isa 13:8; Mic 4:9-10 [n] Isa 66:9
13:14 [o] Ps 49:15; Eze 37:12-13 [p] 1Co 15:55*
13:15 [q] Hos 10:1 [r] Eze 19:12 [s] Jer 51:36 [t] Jer 20:5
13:16 [u] Hos 10:2 [v] Hos 7:14 [w] Hos 11:6 [x] 2Ki 8:12; Hos 10:14 [y] 2Ki 15:16; Isa 13:16

Repentance to Bring Blessing

14 Return, O Israel, to the LORD
your God.
Your sins have been your
downfall![z]
2 Take words with you

14:1 [z] Hos 5:5

THE VERY BRIGHTNESS OF JESUS' LIFE SHOWS UP THE DARK CORNERS OF OUR OWN. WE DO NOT WANT TO GET TOO CLOSE TO HIM BECAUSE WE HAVE A NASTY SUSPICION THAT HE WOULD EXPECT SOME MAJOR CHANGES IN OUR LIFESTYLE.

Michael Green, *British Scholar*

and return to the LORD.
Say to him:
"Forgive all our sins
and receive us graciously,[a]
that we may offer the fruit of our
lips.[b][b]
3 Assyria cannot save us;
we will not mount war-horses.[c]
We will never again say 'Our gods'[d]
to what our own hands have
made,
for in you the fatherless[e] find
compassion."

4 "I will heal[f] their waywardness
and love them freely,[g]
for my anger has turned away
from them.
5 I will be like the dew to Israel;
he will blossom like a lily.[h]
Like a cedar of Lebanon[i]
he will send down his roots;[j]
6 his young shoots will grow.

14:2 [a] Mic 7:18-19 [b] Heb 13:15
14:3 [c] Ps 33:17; Isa 31:1 [d] Hos 8:6 [e] Ps 10:14; 68:5
14:4 [f] Hos 6:1 [g] Zep 3:17
14:5 [h] SS 2:1 [i] Isa 35:2 [j] Job 29:19

[a] 14 Hebrew *Sheol* [b] 2 Or *offer our lips as sacrifices of bulls*

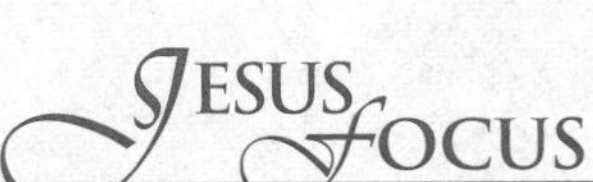

NEW HOPE

Most of Hosea's messages to the people spoke of their unfaithfulness to God, but he ended his book with words of hope for a different and better future. Hosea employed vivid imagery of trees laden with luscious fruit and of abundant crops (Hosea 14:5–8). This was God's description of the time when the Messiah, God's precious Son, will rule the nations (see also Isaiah 27:6). In Revelation 22, the final chapter of the Bible, the apostle John used similar nature imagery. When Jesus returns as the triumphant King of creation, his people will enjoy unspeakable blessings and abundant fruitfulness for all eternity (Revelation 22:1–6).

14:6 [k] Ps 52:8; Jer 11:16 [l] SS 4:11

His splendor will be like an olive
tree,[k]
his fragrance like a cedar of
Lebanon.[l]

14:7 [m] Ps 91:1-4 [n] Hos 2:22 [o] Eze 17:23

7 Men will dwell again in his shade.[m]
He will flourish like the grain.
He will blossom like a vine,
and his fame will be like the
wine[n] from Lebanon.[o]

14:8 [p] ver 3

8 O Ephraim, what more have I[a] to
do with idols?[p]
I will answer him and care for
him.
I am like a green pine tree;
your fruitfulness comes from
me."

14:9 [q] Ps 107:43 [r] Pr 10:29; Isa 1:28 [s] Ps 111:7-8; Zep 3:5; Ac 13:10 [t] Isa 26:7

9 Who is wise?[q] He will realize these
things.
Who is discerning? He will
understand them.[r]
The ways of the LORD are right;[s]
the righteous walk[t] in them,
but the rebellious stumble in
them.

[a] 8 Or *What more has Ephraim*

Jesus in Joel The book of Joel divides easily into two sections. The opening section (Joel 1:1—2:17) tells of an invasion of locusts and records the response of the Israelites to this catastrophe. The remaining section (Joel 2:18—3:21) takes us to the distant future and describes the coming "day of the LORD."

Watch closely throughout the book for God's plan for his people, a plan that comes to ultimate fulfillment in the redemption accomplished in Jesus Christ, God's precious Son. Look for the connections between the natural disaster of the locust invasion and Joel's words about the future. God will one day take charge of this world, but Joel indicates that God's judgment would also be carried out in his own day through natural catastrophes.

Joel's words in Joel 2:28–32 point to the new age in Jesus, the One in whom salvation is found (Acts 4:12; 10:43; Romans 10:8–13), and to the outpouring of the Holy Spirit at Pentecost (Acts 2:1–4,16–21). But his message is clear that restoration must be preceded by repentance.

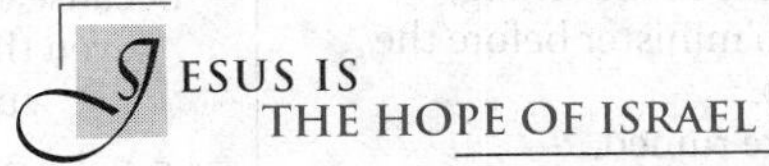

JESUS IS
THE HOPE OF ISRAEL

When will the moon turn to blood? (Joel 2:30–32)

♦*This will occur at the final judgment when Jesus returns. The "last days" officially began with the coming of the Holy Spirit on all believers at Pentecost (Acts 2:14–21). At the end of the last days, God will judge the earth. The moon will appear blood red, signaling the end of human rule on earth and the subsequent reign of Jesus (Matthew 24:29–30; Revelation 6:12–14).*

When will Jerusalem finally be holy and safe? (Joel 3:17)

♦*Some say that Jerusalem's security will occur as soon as Jesus returns to rout Satan and his enemies (Matthew 24:30–31). Others, believing in a literal thousand-year peaceful reign of Jesus on earth (Revelation 20:4), conclude that Jerusalem will be secure in the end.*

1:1 [a]Jer 1:2 [b]Ac 2:16

1 The word of the LORD that came[a] to Joel[b] son of Pethuel.

An Invasion of Locusts

1:2 [c]Hos 5:1 [d]Hos 4:1 [e]Joel 2:2

2 Hear this,[c] you elders;
listen, all who live in the land.[d]
Has anything like this ever
happened in your days
or in the days of your
forefathers?[e]

1:3 [f]Ex 10:2; Ps 78:4

3 Tell it to your children,[f]
and let your children tell it to
their children,
and their children to the next
generation.

1:4 [g]Dt 28:39; Na 3:15

4 What the locust swarm has left
the great locusts have eaten;
what the great locusts have left
the young locusts have eaten;
what the young locusts have left
other locusts[a] have eaten.[g]

1:5 [h]Joel 3:3

5 Wake up, you drunkards, and
weep!
Wail, all you drinkers of wine;[h]
wail because of the new wine,
for it has been snatched from
your lips.

1:6 [i]Joel 2:2,11,25 [j]Rev 9:8

6 A nation has invaded my land,
powerful and without number;[i]
it has the teeth[j] of a lion,
the fangs of a lioness.

1:7 [k]Isa 5:6 [l]Am 4:9

7 It has laid waste[k] my vines
and ruined my fig trees.[l]
It has stripped off their bark
and thrown it away,
leaving their branches white.

1:8 [m]ver 13; Isa 22:12; Am 8:10

8 Mourn like a virgin[b] in sackcloth[m]
grieving for the husband[c] of her
youth.

1:9 [n]Hos 9:4; Joel 2:14,17

9 Grain offerings and drink
offerings[n]
are cut off from the house of the
LORD.
The priests are in mourning,
those who minister before the
LORD.

1:10 [o]Isa 24:4 [p]Hos 9:2

10 The fields are ruined,
the ground is dried up[d];[o]
the grain is destroyed,
the new wine[p] is dried up,
the oil fails.

1:11 [q]Jer 14:3-4; Am 5:16 [r]Isa 17:11

11 Despair, you farmers,[q]
wail, you vine growers;
grieve for the wheat and the barley,
because the harvest of the field
is destroyed.[r]

1:12 [s]Hag 2:19

12 The vine is dried up
and the fig tree is withered;
the pomegranate, the palm and the
apple tree—
all the trees of the field—are
dried up.[s]
Surely the joy of mankind
is withered away.

A Call to Repentance

1:13 [t]Jer 4:8 [u]Joel 2:17 [v]ver 9

13 Put on sackcloth,[t] O priests, and
mourn;
wail, you who minister[u] before
the altar.
Come, spend the night in sackcloth,
you who minister before my
God;
for the grain offerings and drink
offerings[v]
are withheld from the house of
your God.

1:14 [w]2Ch 20:3 [x]Jnh 3:8

14 Declare a holy fast;[w]
call a sacred assembly.
Summon the elders
and all who live in the land
to the house of the LORD your God,
and cry out[x] to the LORD.

1:15 [y]Jer 30:7 [z]Isa 13:6,9; Joel 2:1,11,31

15 Alas for that[y] day!
For the day of the LORD[z] is near;
it will come like destruction
from the Almighty.[e]

1:16 [a]Isa 3:7 [b]Dt 12:7

16 Has not the food been cut off[a]
before our very eyes—
joy and gladness
from the house of our God?[b]

1:17 [c]Isa 17:10-11

17 The seeds are shriveled
beneath the clods.[f][c]
The storehouses are in ruins,
the granaries have been broken
down,
for the grain has dried up.

18 How the cattle moan!
The herds mill about
because they have no pasture;
even the flocks of sheep are
suffering.

1:19 [d]Ps 50:15 [e]Am 7:4 [f]Jer 9:10

19 To you, O LORD, I call,[d]
for fire[e] has devoured the open
pastures[f]
and flames have burned up all
the trees of the field.

a 4 The precise meaning of the four Hebrew words used here for locusts is uncertain. *b* 8 Or *young woman* *c* 8 Or *betrothed* *d* 10 Or *ground mourns* *e* 15 Hebrew *Shaddai* *f* 17 The meaning of the Hebrew for this word is uncertain.

[20] Even the wild animals pant for
you;[g]
the streams of water have dried
up[h]
and fire has devoured the open
pastures.

An Army of Locusts

2 Blow the trumpet[i] in Zion;[j]
sound the alarm on my holy
hill.
Let all who live in the land tremble,
for the day of the LORD[k] is
coming.
It is close at hand[l]—
[2] a day of darkness[m] and gloom,[n]
a day of clouds and blackness.
Like dawn spreading across the
mountains
a large and mighty army[o] comes,
such as never was of old[p]
nor ever will be in ages to come.
[3] Before them fire devours,
behind them a flame blazes.
Before them the land is like the
garden of Eden,[q]
behind them, a desert waste[r]—
nothing escapes them.
[4] They have the appearance of
horses;[s]
they gallop along like cavalry.
[5] With a noise like that of chariots[t]
they leap over the
mountaintops,
like a crackling fire[u] consuming
stubble,
like a mighty army drawn up for
battle.
[6] At the sight of them, nations are in
anguish;[v]
every face turns pale.[w]
[7] They charge like warriors;
they scale walls like soldiers.
They all march in line,
not swerving[x] from their course.
[8] They do not jostle each other;
each marches straight ahead.
They plunge through defenses
without breaking ranks.
[9] They rush upon the city;
they run along the wall.
They climb into the houses;
like thieves they enter through
the windows.[y]
[10] Before them the earth shakes,[z]
the sky trembles,
the sun and moon are
darkened,[a]
and the stars no longer shine.[b]
[11] The LORD[c] thunders
at the head of his army;
his forces are beyond number,
and mighty are those who obey
his command.
The day of the LORD is great;[d]
it is dreadful.
Who can endure it?[e]

Rend Your Heart

[12] "Even now," declares the LORD,
"return[f] to me with all your
heart,
with fasting and weeping and
mourning."
[13] Rend your heart[g]
and not your garments.[h]
Return to the LORD your God,
for he is gracious and
compassionate,
slow to anger and abounding in
love,[i]
and he relents from sending
calamity.[j]
[14] Who knows? He may turn[k] and
have pity
and leave behind a blessing[l]—
grain offerings and drink
offerings[m]
for the LORD your God.
[15] Blow the trumpet[n] in Zion,
declare a holy fast,[o]
call a sacred assembly.[p]
[16] Gather the people,
consecrate[q] the assembly;
bring together the elders,
gather the children,
those nursing at the breast.
Let the bridegroom[r] leave his
room
and the bride her chamber.
[17] Let the priests, who minister
before the LORD,
weep between the temple porch
and the altar.[s]
Let them say, "Spare your people,
O LORD.
Do not make your inheritance
an object of scorn,[t]
a byword among the nations.
Why should they say among the
peoples,
'Where is their God?[u]' "

1:20 [g] Ps 104:21 [h] 1Ki 17:7
2:1 [i] Jer 4:5 [j] ver 15 [k] Joel 1:15; Zep 1:14-16 [l] Ob 1:15
2:2 [m] Am 5:18 [n] Da 9:12 [o] Joel 1:6 [p] Joel 1:2
2:3 [q] Ge 2:8 [r] Ps 105:34-35
2:4 [s] Rev 9:7
2:5 [t] Rev 9:9 [u] Isa 5:24; 30:30
2:6 [v] Isa 13:8 [w] Na 2:10
2:7 [x] Isa 5:27
2:9 [y] Jer 9:21
2:10 [z] Ps 18:7
2:10 [a] Mt 24:29 [b] Isa 13:10; Eze 32:8
2:11 [c] Joel 1:15 [d] Zep 1:14; Rev 18:8 [e] Eze 22:14
2:12 [f] Jer 4:1; Hos 12:6
2:13 [g] Ps 34:18; Isa 57:15 [h] Job 1:20 [i] Ex 34:6 [j] Jer 18:8
2:14 [k] Jer 26:3 [l] Hag 2:19 [m] Joel 1:13
2:15 [n] Nu 10:2 [o] Jer 36:9 [p] Joel 1:14
2:16 [q] Ex 19:10,22 [r] Ps 19:5
2:17 [s] Eze 8:16; Mt 23:35 [t] Dt 9:26-29; Ps 44:13 [u] Ps 42:3

The LORD's Answer

2:18 [v]Zec 1:14

18 Then the LORD will be jealous[v] for
his land
and take pity on his people.
19 The LORD will reply[a] to them:

2:19 [w]Jer 31:12 [x]Eze 34:29

"I am sending you grain, new wine
and oil,[w]
enough to satisfy you fully;
never again will I make you
an object of scorn[x] to the
nations.

2:20 [y]Jer 1:14-15 [z]Zec 14:8 [a]Isa 34:3

20 "I will drive the northern army[y] far
from you,
pushing it into a parched and
barren land,
with its front columns going into
the eastern[z] sea[b]
and those in the rear into the
western sea.[c]
And its stench[a] will go up;
its smell will rise."

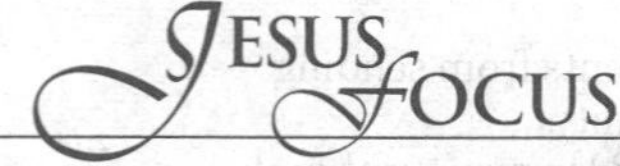

CALLING ON JESUS' NAME

After the miraculous outpouring of the Holy Spirit on the day of Pentecost, Peter addressed the crowd and delivered a rousing sermon, part of which included a recitation, with some slight variations, of Joel 2:28–32 (see Acts 2:16–21). Peter went on to remind his listeners that Jesus had been "accredited by God to [them] by miracles, wonders and signs" and "handed over to [them] by God's set purpose and foreknowledge" to be put to death on the cross (Acts 2:22–23). "But God," the apostle continued joyfully, "raised him from the dead, freeing him from the agony of death, because it was impossible for death to keep its hold on him . . . Exalted to the right hand of God, he has received from the Father the promised Holy Spirit and has poured out what you now see and hear" (Acts 2:24,33). Peter concluded his sermon with words that "cut" the audience "to the heart" (Acts 2:37): "Therefore let all Israel be assured of this: God has made this Jesus, whom you crucified, both Lord and Christ" (Acts 2:36). This Jesus, who is the hope of Israel, is our only hope as well. This is the truth of the good news about Jesus: "That if you confess with your mouth, 'Jesus is Lord,' and believe in your heart that God raised him from the dead, you will be saved . . . Everyone who calls on the name of the Lord will be saved" (Romans 10:9,13).

Surely he has done great things.[d]

2:21 [b]Isa 54:4; Zep 3:16-17 [c]Ps 126:3

21 Be not afraid,[b] O land;
be glad and rejoice.
Surely the LORD has done great
things.[c]

2:22 [d]Ps 65:12 [e]Joel 1:18-20

22 Be not afraid, O wild animals,
for the open pastures are
becoming green.[d]
The trees are bearing their fruit;
the fig tree and the vine yield
their riches.[e]

2:23 [f]Ps 149:2; Isa 12:6; 41:16; Hab 3:18; Zec 10:7 [g]Lev 26:4

23 Be glad, O people of Zion,
rejoice[f] in the LORD your God,
for he has given you
the autumn rains in
righteousness.[e]
He sends you abundant showers,
both autumn and spring rains,[g]
as before.

2:24 [h]Lev 26:10; Mal 3:10 [i]Am 9:13

24 The threshing floors will be filled
with grain;
the vats will overflow[h] with new
wine[i] and oil.
25 "I will repay you for the years the
locusts have eaten—
the great locust and the young
locust,
the other locusts and the locust
swarm[f]—
my great army that I sent among
you.

2:26 [j]Lev 26:5 [k]Isa 62:9 [l]Ps 126:3; Isa 25:1

26 You will have plenty to eat, until
you are full,[j]
and you will praise[k] the name of
the LORD your God,
who has worked wonders[l] for
you;
never again will my people be
shamed.

2:27 [m]Joel 3:17

27 Then you will know that I am in
Israel,
that I am the LORD[m] your God,
and that there is no other;
never again will my people be
shamed.

The Day of the LORD

2:28 [n]Eze 39:29

28 "And afterward,
I will pour out my Spirit[n] on all
people.

[a] 18,19 Or *LORD was jealous . . . / and took pity . . . / 19The LORD replied* [b] 20 That is, the Dead Sea [c] 20 That is, the Mediterranean [d] 20 Or *rise. / Surely it has done great things."* [e] 23 Or / *the teacher for righteousness:* [f] 25 The precise meaning of the four Hebrew words used here for locusts is uncertain.

THE OUTPOURING OF THE SPIRIT

The outpouring of the Holy Spirit on the day of Pentecost was a remarkable event (Acts 2:1–13). Luke, who authored the book of Acts, wrote that the coming of the Spirit sounded like the blowing of a "violent wind" and that those assembled observed what appeared to be "tongues of fire" resting on everyone present. All were filled with the Holy Spirit and miraculously started proclaiming the Good News about Jesus in every known language. A crowd was quickly attracted to this phenomenon, and people hailing from a wide variety of homelands were astonished that each could understand the message (Acts 2:1–4).

Not everyone was impressed, however. Some mocked the disciples and accused them of drunkenness. Then Peter spoke up, reminding the crowd of the prophecy in Joel 2:28–32. This was the very event God's people had so long been awaiting! Peter called to their attention some important truths:

1. *God's Holy Spirit came to be with his people.* This incident opened a new chapter in the saga of God's relationship with human beings. His Spirit had come to indwell his people. No longer would God's presence be confined to a tent or the temple. Instead, the holy God would take up residence within the heart of each individual believer!

2. *It included everyone.* God the Holy Spirit showed no discrimination, resting on men and women, young and old. The possibility exists already at this early date that Gentiles were included as well. Certainly the message was intended for Gentile ears.

3. *People would be saved by calling on God.* The prophet Joel was foretelling the availability of salvation to anyone who would accept the redemption Jesus Christ would offer through his death. Joel 2:32 states: "Everyone who calls on the name of the LORD will be saved; for on Mount Zion and in Jerusalem there will be deliverance."

But Joel was not the only one who had predicted the coming of the Holy Spirit. Before Jesus went out to the Jordan River to be baptized by John the Baptist, John had announced that Jesus himself would "baptize [the crowds] with the Holy Spirit and with fire" (Matthew 3:11). Later, Jesus stood up at a feast and invited, "If anyone is thirsty, let him come to me and drink" (John 7:37). He was referring to the life-giving "streams" of the Holy Spirit (John 7:38–39), who lives in us and transforms us into the people God intended us to be.

There are two important facts to remember about Pentecost. First of all, this was not a spontaneous event. God's prophet Joel had predicted this outpouring hundreds of years earlier, and the actual occurrence clearly fulfilled every detail. Second, the arrival of the Spirit happened exactly as Jesus had promised. God's Word is continuous from start to finish: Jesus came both to fulfill Old Testament prophecy and to provide additional insight into that prophecy. And now that Jesus has returned to heaven, the Holy Spirit continues to guide us (John 16:12–13).

Self-Discovery: *In what way does the Holy Spirit provide life-giving streams that flow from within you?*

GO TO DISCOVERY 220 ON PAGE 1178

Your sons and daughters will
prophesy,
your old men will dream dreams,
your young men will see visions.
2:29 [o]1Co 12:13; 29 Even on my servants,[o] both men
Gal 3:28 and women,
I will pour out my Spirit in those
days.
30 I will show wonders in the
2:30 heavens[p]
[p]Lk 21:11 and on the earth,[q]
[q]Mk 13:24-25 blood and fire and billows of
smoke.
31 The sun will be turned to
2:31 darkness[r]
[r]Mt 24:29 and the moon to blood
[s]Isa 13:9-10; before the coming of the great
Mal 4:1,5 and dreadful day of the
LORD.[s]
32 And everyone who calls
2:32 on the name of the LORD will be
[t]Ac 2:17-21*; saved;[t]
Ro 10:13* for on Mount Zion[u] and in
[u]Isa 46:13 Jerusalem
[v]Ob 1:17 there will be deliverance,[v]
[w]Isa 11:11; as the LORD has said,
Mic 4:7; Ro 9:27 among the survivors[w]
whom the LORD calls.

The Nations Judged

3:1 **3** "In those days and at that time,
[x]Jer 16:15 when I restore the fortunes[x] of
Judah and Jerusalem,
2 I will gather all nations
and bring them down to the
Valley of Jehoshaphat.[a]
3:2 [y]Eze 36:5 There I will enter into judgment[y]
against them
concerning my inheritance, my
people Israel,
for they scattered my people
among the nations
and divided up my land.
3 They cast lots for my people
and traded boys for prostitutes;
3:3 they sold girls for wine[z]
[z]Am 2:6 that they might drink.

3:4 4 "Now what have you against me,
[a]Mt 11:21 O Tyre and Sidon[a] and all you regions of
[b]Isa 34:8 Philistia? Are you repaying me for something I have done? If you are paying me
back, I will swiftly and speedily return
on your own heads what you have
done.[b] 5 For you took my silver and my
gold and carried off my finest treasures
3:5 to your temples.[c] 6 You sold the people of
[c]2Ch 21:16-17 Judah and Jerusalem to the Greeks, that
you might send them far from their
homeland.

7 "See, I am going to rouse them out of 3:7
the places to which you sold them,[d] and [d]Isa 43:5-6;
I will return on your own heads what Jer 23:8
you have done. 8 I will sell your sons[e] and 3:8
daughters to the people of Judah,[f] and [e]Isa 60:14
they will sell them to the Sabeans, a na- [f]Isa 14:2
tion far away." The LORD has spoken.

9 Proclaim this among the nations: 3:9
Prepare for war![g] [g]Isa 8:9
Rouse the warriors![h] [h]Jer 46:4
Let all the fighting men draw
near and attack.
10 Beat your plowshares into swords 3:10
and your pruning hooks[i] into [i]Isa 2:4; Mic 4:3
spears. [j]Zec 12:8
Let the weakling[j] say,
"I am strong!"
11 Come quickly, all you nations from
every side, 3:11
and assemble[k] there. [k]Eze 38:15-16;
Bring down your warriors,[l] Zep 3:8
O LORD! [l]Isa 13:3

12 "Let the nations be roused;
let them advance into the Valley
of Jehoshaphat,
for there I will sit
to judge[m] all the nations on 3:12 [m]Isa 2:4
every side.
13 Swing the sickle, 3:13
for the harvest[n] is ripe. [n]Hos 6:11;
Come, trample the grapes, Mt 13:39;
for the winepress[o] is full Rev 14:15-19
and the vats overflow— [o]Rev 14:20
so great is their wickedness!"

14 Multitudes, multitudes
in the valley of decision!
For the day of the LORD[p] is near 3:14 [p]Isa 34:2-8;
in the valley of decision. Joel 1:15
15 The sun and moon will be
darkened,
and the stars no longer shine.
16 The LORD will roar from Zion 3:16
and thunder from Jerusalem;[q] [q]Am 1:2
the earth and the sky will [r]Eze 38:19
tremble.[r] [s]Jer 16:19
But the LORD will be a refuge for his
people,
a stronghold[s] for the people of
Israel.

[a] 2 *Jehoshaphat* means *the LORD judges*; also in verse 12.

Blessings for God's People

3:17 [t] Joel 2:27 [u] Isa 4:3
17 "Then you will know that I, the LORD your God,[t]
dwell in Zion,[u] my holy hill.
Jerusalem will be holy;
never again will foreigners invade her.

3:18 [v] Ex 3:8 [w] Isa 30:25; 35:6 [x] Rev 22:1-2 [y] Eze 47:1; Am 9:13
18 "In that day the mountains will drip new wine,
and the hills will flow with milk;[v]
all the ravines of Judah will run with water.[w]
A fountain will flow out of the LORD's house[x]
and will water the valley of acacias.[a][y]
19 But Egypt will be desolate,
Edom a desert waste,
because of violence[z] done to the people of Judah,
in whose land they shed innocent blood.
20 Judah will be inhabited forever[a]
and Jerusalem through all generations.
21 Their bloodguilt, which I have not pardoned,
I will pardon.[b]"

The LORD dwells in Zion!

3:19 [z] Ob 1:10

3:20 [a] Am 9:15

3:21 [b] Eze 36:25

[a] 18 Or *Valley of Shittim*

Jesus in Amos Despite the inevitability of judgment on the northern kingdom of Israel, Amos related God's promise to restore his relationship with his people. The Messiah God had promised from David's "fallen tent" (Amos 9:11) would rule as King forever. Jesus would fulfill God's promise to David's family that they would never again be "uprooted" (Amos 9:15; Luke 1:32–33).

While Amos's contemporary Hosea emphasized the need for a personal relationship between God and his people, Amos was more concerned with calling the people back to an outward lifestyle that reflects justice and righteousness (Amos 5:24). Despite his overall focus on judgment, however, Amos concluded his prophecy with a beautiful word picture of eventual restoration, a time when there would be an outpouring of future blessings reserved by God for his people and a glorious hope beyond the coming judgment (Amos 9:11–15). The house of David would again rule over Israel (in the person of Jesus), this rule would extend to many nations (Amos 9:12), and Israel would once again be secure, feasting on wine and fruit (Amos 9:14–15).

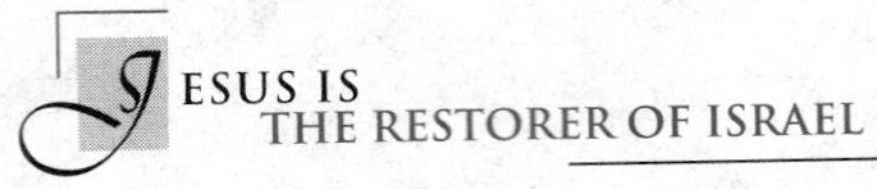

How did Amos relate the unique history of deliverance the Israelites had already experienced to the coming penalties for their current rebellion? (Amos 2:6–16)

- *Although salvation through Jesus was not yet a reality, God had already blessed Israel with many redemption experiences, from the time of the exodus through that of the prophets. Amos asserted that by means of their corrupt lifestyles, the Israelites of his day were denying their history and increasing the severity of the inevitable consequences of their rebellious behavior.*

What other nations will "bear [God's] name"? (Amos 9:12)

- *The reference is to every nation whose people turn to faith in Jesus. This prophecy began to be fulfilled shortly after Jesus' death, and the fulfillment continues today. Through Jesus' atoning sacrifice people from every tribe and language and people and nation (Revelation 5:9) are all invited into a relationship with God, and all those who follow Jesus bear God's name.*

1 The words of Amos, one of the shepherds of Tekoa[a]—what he saw concerning Israel two years before the earthquake,[b] when Uzziah[c] was king of Judah and Jeroboam[d] son of Jehoash[a] was king of Israel.[e]

2 He said:

"The LORD roars[f] from Zion
and thunders from Jerusalem;[g]
the pastures of the shepherds dry up,[b]
and the top of Carmel[h] withers."[i]

Judgment on Israel's Neighbors

3 This is what the LORD says:

"For three sins of Damascus,[j]
even for four, I will not turn back ⌞my wrath⌟.[k]
Because she threshed Gilead
with sledges having iron teeth,
4 I will send fire[l] upon the house of Hazael
that will consume the fortresses[m] of Ben-Hadad.[n]
5 I will break down the gate[o] of Damascus;
I will destroy the king who is in[c] the Valley of Aven[d]
and the one who holds the scepter in Beth Eden.
The people of Aram will go into exile to Kir,[p]"
says the LORD.

6 This is what the LORD says:

"For three sins of Gaza,[q]
even for four, I will not turn back ⌞my wrath⌟.
Because she took captive whole communities
and sold them to Edom,[r]
7 I will send fire upon the walls of Gaza
that will consume her fortresses.
8 I will destroy the king[e] of Ashdod[s]
and the one who holds the scepter in Ashkelon.
I will turn my hand[t] against Ekron,
till the last of the Philistines[u] is dead,"
says the Sovereign LORD.[v]

9 This is what the LORD says:

"For three sins of Tyre,[w]
even for four, I will not turn back ⌞my wrath⌟.

1:1 [a] 2Sa 14:2 [b] Zec 14:5 [c] 2Ch 26:23 [d] 2Ki 14:23 [e] Hos 1:1
1:2 [f] Isa 42:13 [g] Joel 3:16 [h] Am 9:3 [i] Jer 12:4
1:3 [j] Isa 8:4; 17:1-3 [k] Am 2:6
1:4 [l] Jer 49:27 [m] Jer 17:27 [n] 1Ki 20:1; 2Ki 6:24
1:5 [o] Jer 51:30 [p] 2Ki 16:9
1:6 [q] 1Sa 6:17; Zep 2:4 [r] Ob 1:11
1:8 [s] 2Ch 26:6 [t] Ps 81:14 [u] Eze 25:16 [v] Isa 14:28-32; Zep 2:4-7
1:9 [w] 1Ki 5:1; 9:11-14; Isa 23:1-18; Jer 25:22; Joel 3:4; Mt 11:21

Because she sold whole communities of captives to Edom,
disregarding a treaty of brotherhood,
10 I will send fire upon the walls of Tyre
that will consume her fortresses.[x]"

11 This is what the LORD says:

"For three sins of Edom,[y]
even for four, I will not turn back ⌞my wrath⌟.
Because he pursued his brother with a sword,
stifling all compassion,[f]
because his anger raged continually
and his fury flamed unchecked,[z]
12 I will send fire upon Teman[a]
that will consume the fortresses of Bozrah."

13 This is what the LORD says:

"For three sins of Ammon,[b]
even for four, I will not turn back ⌞my wrath⌟.
Because he ripped open the pregnant women[c] of Gilead
in order to extend his borders,
14 I will set fire to the walls of Rabbah[d]
that will consume her fortresses
amid war cries[e] on the day of battle,
amid violent winds on a stormy day.
15 Her king[g] will go into exile,
he and his officials together,"
says the LORD.

2 This is what the LORD says:

"For three sins of Moab,
even for four, I will not turn back ⌞my wrath⌟.
Because he burned, as if to lime,
the bones of Edom's king,
2 I will send fire upon Moab
that will consume the fortresses of Kerioth.[h]
Moab will go down in great tumult
amid war cries and the blast of the trumpet.

1:10 [x] Zec 9:1-4
1:11 [y] Nu 20:14-21; 2Ch 28:17; Jer 49:7-22 [z] Eze 25:12-14
1:12 [a] Ob 1:9-10
1:13 [b] Jer 49:1-6; Eze 21:28; 25:2-7 [c] Hos 13:16
1:14 [d] Dt 3:11 [e] Am 2:2

a 1 Hebrew *Joash,* a variant of *Jehoash* *b* 2 Or *shepherds mourn* *c* 5 Or *the inhabitants of* *d* 5 *Aven* means *wickedness.* *e* 8 Or *inhabitants* *f* 11 Or *sword / and destroyed his allies* *g* 15 Or / *Molech;* Hebrew *malcam* *h* 2 Or *of her cities*

[3] I will destroy her ruler[f]
and kill all her officials with
him,"[g]
says the LORD.

[4] This is what the LORD says:

"For three sins of Judah,[h]
even for four, I will not turn back
⌊my wrath⌋.
Because they have rejected the law[i]
of the LORD
and have not kept his decrees,[j]
because they have been led astray[k]
by false gods,[a][l]
the gods[b] their ancestors
followed,[m]
[5] I will send fire upon Judah
that will consume the fortresses
of Jerusalem.[n]"

Judgment on Israel

[6] This is what the LORD says:

"For three sins of Israel,
even for four, I will not turn back
⌊my wrath⌋.
They sell the righteous for silver,
and the needy for a pair of
sandals.[o]
[7] They trample on the heads of the
poor
as upon the dust of the ground
and deny justice to the
oppressed.
Father and son use the same girl
and so profane my holy name.[p]
[8] They lie down beside every altar
on garments taken in pledge.[q]
In the house of their god
they drink wine[r] taken as fines.

[9] "I destroyed the Amorite[s] before
them,
though he was tall as the cedars
and strong as the oaks.
I destroyed his fruit above
and his roots[t] below.

[10] "I brought you up out of Egypt,[u]
and I led you forty years in the
desert[v]
to give you the land of the
Amorites.[w]
[11] I also raised up prophets[x] from
among your sons
and Nazirites[y] from among your
young men.
Is this not true, people of Israel?"
declares the LORD.

2:3 [f]Ps 2:10 [g]Isa 40:23
2:4 [h]2Ki 17:19; Hos 12:2 [i]Jer 6:19 [j]Eze 20:24 [k]Isa 9:16 [l]Isa 28:15 [m]2Ki 22:13; Jer 16:12
2:5 [n]Jer 17:27; Hos 8:14
2:6 [o]Joel 3:3; Am 8:6
2:7 [p]Am 5:11-12; 8:4
2:8 [q]Ex 22:26 [r]Am 4:1; 6:6
2:9 [s]Nu 21:23-26; Jos 10:12 [t]Eze 17:9; Mal 4:1
2:10 [u]Ex 20:2; Am 3:1 [v]Dt 2:7 [w]Ex 3:8; Am 9:7
2:11 [x]Dt 18:18; Jer 7:25 [y]Nu 6:2-3; Jdg 13:5

[12] "But you made the Nazirites drink
wine
and commanded the prophets
not to prophesy.[z]

[13] "Now then, I will crush you
as a cart crushes when loaded
with grain.
[14] The swift will not escape,
the strong[a] will not muster their
strength,
and the warrior will not save his
life.[b]
[15] The archer[c] will not stand his
ground,
the fleet-footed soldier will not
get away,
and the horseman will not save
his life.
[16] Even the bravest warriors[d]
will flee naked on that day,"
declares the LORD.

Witnesses Summoned Against Israel

3 Hear this word the LORD has spoken against you, O people of Israel—against the whole family I brought
up out of Egypt:[e]

[2] "You only have I chosen[f]
of all the families of the earth;
therefore I will punish you
for all your sins.[g]"

[3] Do two walk together
unless they have agreed to do so?
[4] Does a lion roar in the thicket
when he has no prey?[h]
Does he growl in his den
when he has caught nothing?
[5] Does a bird fall into a trap on the
ground
where no snare has been set?
Does a trap spring up from the
earth
when there is nothing to catch?
[6] When a trumpet sounds in a city,
do not the people tremble?
When disaster comes to a city,
has not the LORD caused it?[i]
[7] Surely the Sovereign LORD does
nothing
without revealing his plan[j]
to his servants the prophets.[k]

[8] The lion has roared—
who will not fear?

2:12 [z]Isa 30:10; Jer 11:21; Am 7:12-13; Mic 2:6
2:14 [a]Jer 9:23 [b]Ps 33:16; Isa 30:16-17
2:15 [c]Eze 39:3
2:16 [d]Jer 48:41
3:1 [e]Am 2:10
3:2 [f]Dt 7:6; Lk 12:47 [g]Jer 14:10
3:4 [h]Ps 104:21; Hos 5:14
3:6 [i]Isa 14:24-27; 45:7
3:7 [j]Ge 18:17; Da 9:22; Jn 15:15; Rev 10:7 [k]Jer 23:22

[a] 4 Or *by lies* [b] 4 Or *lies*

3:8 [l]Jer 20:9; Jnh 1:1-3; 3:1-3; Ac 4:20

The Sovereign LORD has spoken—
who can but prophesy?[l]

[9] Proclaim to the fortresses of
Ashdod
and to the fortresses of Egypt:
"Assemble yourselves on the
mountains of Samaria;[m]

3:9 [m]Am 4:1; 6:1

see the great unrest within her
and the oppression among her
people."

3:10 [n]Jer 4:22; Am 5:7; 6:12 [o]Hab 2:8 [p]Zep 1:9

[10] "They do not know how to do
right,[n]" declares the LORD,
"who hoard plunder[o] and loot in
their fortresses."[p]

[11] Therefore this is what the Sovereign
LORD says:

"An enemy will overrun the land;
he will pull down your
strongholds
and plunder your fortresses.[q]"

3:11 [q]Am 2:5; 6:14

[12] This is what the LORD says:

"As a shepherd saves from the
lion's[r] mouth
only two leg bones or a piece of
an ear,
so will the Israelites be saved,
those who sit in Samaria
on the edge of their beds
and in Damascus on their
couches.[a][s]"

3:12 [r]1Sa 17:34 [s]Am 6:4

[13] "Hear this and testify[t] against the
house of Jacob," declares the Lord, the
LORD God Almighty.

3:13 [t]Eze 2:7

[14] "On the day I punish Israel for her
sins,
I will destroy the altars of
Bethel;[u]
the horns of the altar will be cut off
and fall to the ground.

3:14 [u]Am 5:5-6

[15] I will tear down the winter house[v]
along with the summer house;[w]
the houses adorned with ivory[x] will
be destroyed
and the mansions will be
demolished,"
declares the LORD.

3:15 [v]Jer 36:22 [w]Jdg 3:20 [x]1Ki 22:39

Israel Has Not Returned to God

4 Hear this word, you cows of
Bashan[y] on Mount
Samaria,[z]
you women who oppress the
poor and crush the needy
and say to your husbands, "Bring
us some drinks![a]"

4:1 [y]Ps 22:12; Eze 39:18 [z]Am 3:9 [a]Am 2:8; 5:11; 8:6

[2] The Sovereign LORD has sworn by
his holiness:
"The time will surely come
when you will be taken away[b] with
hooks,
the last of you with fishhooks.

4:2 [b]Am 6:8

[3] You will each go straight out
through breaks in the wall,[c]
and you will be cast out toward
Harmon,[b]"
declares the LORD.

4:3 [c]Eze 12:5

[4] "Go to Bethel and sin;
go to Gilgal[d] and sin yet more.
Bring your sacrifices every
morning,[e]
your tithes[f] every three years.[c][g]

4:4 [d]Hos 4:15 [e]Nu 28:3 [f]Dt 14:28 [g]Eze 20:39; Am 5:21-22

[5] Burn leavened bread[h] as a thank
offering
and brag about your freewill
offerings[i]—
boast about them, you Israelites,
for this is what you love to do,"
declares the Sovereign
LORD.

4:5 [h]Lev 7:13 [i]Lev 22:18-21

[6] "I gave you empty stomachs[d] in
every city
and lack of bread in every town,
yet you have not returned to me,"
declares the LORD.[j]

4:6 [j]Isa 3:1; Jer 5:3; Hag 2:17

[7] "I also withheld rain from you
when the harvest was still three
months away.
I sent rain on one town,
but withheld it from another.[k]
One field had rain;
another had none and dried up.

4:7 [k]Ex 9:4,26; Dt 11:17; 2Ch 7:13

[8] People staggered from town to
town for water[l]
but did not get enough to drink,
yet you have not returned[m] to
me,"
declares the LORD.[n]

4:8 [l]Eze 4:16-17 [m]Jer 3:7 [n]Jer 14:4

[9] "Many times I struck your gardens
and vineyards,
I struck them with blight and
mildew.[o]
Locusts devoured your fig and
olive trees,[p]
yet you have not returned[q] to me,"
declares the LORD.

4:9 [o]Dt 28:22 [p]Joel 1:7 [q]Jer 3:10; Hag 2:17

[a] *12* The meaning of the Hebrew for this line is uncertain. [b] *3* Masoretic Text; with a different word division of the Hebrew (see Septuagint) *out, O mountain of oppression* [c] *4* Or *tithes on the third day* [d] *6* Hebrew *you cleanness of teeth*

ARE YOU READY?

Most of us have observed on at least one occasion a person walking down a sidewalk wearing a sign that bears a message for the world. "Sandwich boards," sometimes called "billboards," might announce a local event, menu prices, or Bible verses or truths from God's Word. If the prophet Amos were to have worn such a sign, it would undoubtedly have announced: "Prepare to meet your God" (Amos 4:12). Many people would have rushed right past him, oblivious to his message, just as they do today on our busy sidewalks, but there is no reminder we need more than that one!

How do we go about preparing to meet the incomparable God of the universe?

1. *Approach him on his terms.* We need to confess that our sin separates us from God and accept the reality that Jesus died in our place. He is the only One who can forgive our sin and bring us back to God (Ephesians 1:7; Colossians 1:21–22). Meeting the Almighty God need no longer be a frightening prospect, because this reunion means communing with our faithful and loving Father face-to-face. Death is merely the process of leaving this earthly life to join our heavenly family. It is with God that we find our true home (2 Corinthians 5:1–5; Philippians 3:20).

2. *Live every day to please him.* God wants us to construct our lives on the foundation of belief in his Son Jesus. That is the only basis on which the Father will accept us as holy (1 Corinthians 3:10–15). Jesus reminded his followers of the only approach to life acceptable to God: "Store up for yourselves treasures in heaven, where moth and rust do not destroy, and where thieves do not break in and steal. For where your treasure is, there your heart will be also" (Matthew 6:19–21). We prepare to meet our Lord by learning to have an eternal perspective.

Everything we possess or accomplish here on earth is ultimately worthless—except for the character God builds in us and the investment we make in other people's lives. That is how we build up treasure in heaven. The Holy Spirit works within us to transform us into the people God intended us to be—and we take that transformation with us into eternity.

Self-Discovery: *What character changes can you detect in your own life as you continue to become more like Jesus? Is there a particular habit or unconfessed sin that is standing in the way of your character development?*

GO TO DISCOVERY 221 ON PAGE 1187

10 "I sent plagues[r] among you
as I did to Egypt.
I killed your young men with the
sword,
along with your captured horses.
I filled your nostrils with the
stench of your camps,
yet you have not returned to me,"
declares the LORD.[s]

11 "I overthrew some of you
as I[a] overthrew Sodom and
Gomorrah.[t]
You were like a burning stick
snatched from the fire,
yet you have not returned to me,"
declares the LORD.

12 "Therefore this is what I will do to
you, Israel,
and because I will do this to you,
prepare to meet your God,
O Israel."

13 He who forms the mountains,[u]
creates the wind,
and reveals his thoughts[v] to
man,
he who turns dawn to darkness,
and treads the high places of the
earth[w]—
the LORD God Almighty is his
name.[x]

A Lament and Call to Repentance

5 Hear this word, O house of Israel,
this lament[y] I take up concerning
you:

2 "Fallen is Virgin[z] Israel,
never to rise again,
deserted in her own land,
with no one to lift her up.[a]"

3 This is what the Sovereign LORD says:
"The city that marches out a
thousand strong for Israel
will have only a hundred left;
the town that marches out a
hundred strong
will have only ten left.[b]"

4 This is what the LORD says to the
house of Israel:

"Seek me and live;[c]
5 do not seek Bethel,
do not go to Gilgal,[d]
do not journey to Beersheba.[e]
For Gilgal will surely go into exile,

4:10 r Ex 9:3; Dt 28:27 s Isa 9:13
4:11 t Ge 19:24; Jer 23:14
4:13 u Ps 65:6 v Da 2:28 w Mic 1:3 x Isa 47:4; Am 5:8,27; 9:6
5:1 y Eze 19:1
5:2 z Jer 14:17 a Jer 50:32; Am 8:14
5:3 b Isa 6:13; Am 6:9
5:4 c Isa 55:3; Jer 29:13
5:5 d 1Sa 11:14; Am 4:4 e Am 8:14

and Bethel will be reduced to
nothing.[b][f]"
6 Seek[g] the LORD and live,[h]
or he will sweep through the
house of Joseph like a fire;[i]
it will devour,
and Bethel[j] will have no one to
quench it.

7 You who turn justice into
bitterness[k]
and cast righteousness to the
ground
8 (he who made the Pleiades and
Orion,[l]
who turns blackness into dawn[m]
and darkens day into night,[n]
who calls for the waters of the sea
and pours them out over the
face of the land—
the LORD is his name[o]—
9 he flashes destruction on the
stronghold
and brings the fortified city to
ruin),[p]
10 you hate the one who reproves in
court[q]
and despise him who tells the
truth.[r]

11 You trample on the poor[s]
and force him to give you grain.
Therefore, though you have built
stone mansions,[t]
you will not live in them;
though you have planted lush
vineyards,
you will not drink their wine.[u]
12 For I know how many are your
offenses
and how great your sins.

You oppress the righteous and take
bribes
and you deprive the poor of
justice in the courts.[v]
13 Therefore the prudent man keeps
quiet in such times,
for the times are evil.

14 Seek good, not evil,
that you may live.
Then the LORD God Almighty will
be with you,
just as you say he is.
15 Hate evil,[w] love good;

a 11 Hebrew *God* b 5 Or *grief;* or *wickedness;* Hebrew *aven,* a reference to Beth Aven (a derogatory name for Bethel)

5:5 f 1Sa 7:16
5:6 g Isa 55:6 h ver 14 i Dt 4:24 j Am 3:14
5:7 k Am 6:12
5:8 l Job 9:9 m Isa 42:16 n Ps 104:20; Am 8:9 o Ps 104:6-9; Am 4:13
5:9 p Mic 5:11
5:10 q Isa 29:21 r 1Ki 22:8
5:11 s Am 8:6 t Am 3:15 u Mic 6:15
5:12 v Isa 5:23; Am 2:6-7
5:15 w Ps 97:10; Ro 12:9

maintain justice in the courts.
Perhaps the LORD God Almighty
will have mercy[x]
on the remnant[y] of Joseph.

5:15 [x] Joel 2:14 [y] Mic 5:7,8

[16]Therefore this is what the Lord, the
LORD God Almighty, says:

5:16 [z] Jer 9:17 [a] Joel 1:11

"There will be wailing[z] in all the
streets
and cries of anguish in every
public square.
The farmers[a] will be summoned to
weep
and the mourners to wail.
[17] There will be wailing in all the
vineyards,
for I will pass through[b] your
midst,"
says the LORD.[c]

5:17 [b] Ex 12:12 [c] Isa 16:10; Jer 48:33

The Day of the LORD

[18] Woe to you who long
for the day of the LORD![d]
Why do you long for the day of the
LORD?
That day will be darkness,[e] not
light.[f]
[19] It will be as though a man fled
from a lion
only to meet a bear,
as though he entered his house
and rested his hand on the wall
only to have a snake bite him.[g]
[20] Will not the day of the LORD be
darkness, not light—
pitch-dark, without a ray of
brightness?[h]

5:18 [d] Joel 1:15 [e] Joel 2:2 [f] Isa 5:19,30; Jer 30:7
5:19 [g] Job 20:24; Isa 24:17-18; Jer 15:2-3; 48:44
5:20 [h] Isa 13:10; Zep 1:15

[21] "I hate, I despise your religious
feasts;[i]
I cannot stand your assemblies.[j]
[22] Even though you bring me burnt
offerings and grain
offerings,
I will not accept them.
Though you bring choice
fellowship offerings,[a]
I will have no regard for them.[k l]
[23] Away with the noise of your songs!
I will not listen to the music of
your harps.[m]
[24] But let justice[n] roll on like a river,
righteousness like a never-
failing stream![o]
[25] "Did you bring me sacrifices[p] and
offerings
forty years[q] in the desert,
O house of Israel?
[26] You have lifted up the shrine of
your king,
the pedestal of your idols,
the star of your god[b]—
which you made for yourselves.
[27] Therefore I will send you into exile
beyond Damascus,"
says the LORD, whose name is
God Almighty.[r]

5:21 [i] Lev 26:31 [j] Isa 1:11-16
5:22 [k] Am 4:4; Mic 6:6-7 [l] Isa 66:3
5:23 [m] Am 6:5
5:24 [n] Jer 22:3 [o] Mic 6:8
5:25 [p] Isa 43:23 [q] Dt 32:17
5:27 [r] Am 4:13; Ac 7:42-43*

Woe to the Complacent

6 Woe to you[s] who are
complacent in Zion,
and to you who feel secure on
Mount Samaria,
you notable men of the foremost
nation,
to whom the people of Israel
come![t]
[2] Go to Calneh[u] and look at it;
go from there to great Hamath,[v]
and then go down to Gath[w] in
Philistia.
Are they better off than[x] your two
kingdoms?
Is their land larger than yours?
[3] You put off the evil day
and bring near a reign of terror.[y]
[4] You lie on beds inlaid with ivory
and lounge on your couches.
You dine on choice lambs
and fattened calves.[z]
[5] You strum away on your harps[a]
like David
and improvise on musical
instruments.[b]
[6] You drink wine[c] by the bowlful
and use the finest lotions,
but you do not grieve[d] over the
ruin of Joseph.
[7] Therefore you will be among the
first to go into exile;
your feasting and lounging will
end.

6:1 [s] Lk 6:24 [t] Isa 32:9-11
6:2 [u] Ge 10:10 [v] 2Ki 18:34 [w] 2Ch 26:6 [x] Na 3:8
6:3 [y] Isa 56:12; Am 9:10
6:4 [z] Eze 34:2-3; Am 3:12
6:5 [a] Isa 5:12; Am 5:23 [b] 1Ch 15:16
6:6 [c] Am 2:8 [d] Eze 9:4

The LORD Abhors the Pride of Israel

[8]The Sovereign LORD has sworn by
himself[e]—the LORD God Almighty declares:

"I abhor[f] the pride of Jacob[g]

6:8 [e] Ge 22:16; Heb 6:13 [f] Lev 26:30 [g] Ps 47:4

[a] 22 Traditionally *peace offerings* [b] 26 Or *lifted up Sakkuth your king / and Kaiwan your idols, / your star-gods;* Septuagint *lifted up the shrine of Molech / and the star of your god Rephan, / their idols*

and detest his fortresses;
I will deliver up[h] the city
and everything in it.[i]"

9If ten[j] men are left in one house, they
too will die. 10And if a relative who is to
burn the bodies[k] comes to carry them
out of the house and asks anyone still
hiding there, "Is anyone with you?" and
he says, "No," then he will say, "Hush![l]
We must not mention the name of the
LORD."

11For the LORD has given the
command,
and he will smash the great
house[m] into pieces
and the small house into bits.[n]

12Do horses run on the rocky crags?
Does one plow there with oxen?
But you have turned justice into
poison[o]
and the fruit of righteousness
into bitterness[p]—
13you who rejoice in the conquest of
Lo Debar[a]
and say, "Did we not take
Karnaim[b] by our own
strength?[q]"

14For the LORD God Almighty
declares,
"I will stir up a nation[r] against
you, O house of Israel,
that will oppress you all the way
from Lebo[c] Hamath[s] to the
valley of the Arabah.[t]"

Locusts, Fire and a Plumb Line

7 This is what the Sovereign LORD
showed me:[u] He was preparing
swarms of locusts[v] after the king's share
had been harvested and just as the second crop was coming up. 2When they
had stripped the land clean,[w] I cried out,
"Sovereign LORD, forgive! How can Jacob
survive?[x] He is so small![y]"
3So the LORD relented.[z]
"This will not happen," the LORD said.[a]
4This is what the Sovereign LORD
showed me: The Sovereign LORD was
calling for judgment by fire;[b] it dried up
the great deep and devoured[c] the land.
5Then I cried out, "Sovereign LORD, I beg
you, stop! How can Jacob survive? He is
so small![d]"
6So the LORD relented.[e]

6:8 [h] Am 4:2 [i] Dt 32:19
6:9 [j] Am 5:3
6:10 [k] 1Sa 31:12 [l] Am 8:3
6:11 [m] Am 3:15 [n] Isa 55:11
6:12 [o] Hos 10:4 [p] Am 5:7
6:13 [q] Job 8:15; Isa 28:14-15
6:14 [r] Jer 5:15 [s] 1Ki 8:65 [t] Am 3:11
7:1 [u] Am 8:1 [v] Joel 1:4
7:2 [w] Ex 10:15 [x] Isa 37:4 [y] Eze 11:13
7:3 [z] Dt 32:36; Jer 26:19; Jnh 3:10 [a] Hos 11:8
7:4 [b] Isa 66:16 [c] Dt 32:22
7:5 [d] ver 1-2; Joel 2:17
7:6 [e] Jnh 3:10

"This will not happen either," the Sovereign LORD said.

7This is what he showed me: The Lord
was standing by a wall that had been
built true to plumb, with a plumb line in
his hand. 8And the LORD asked me,
"What do you see,[f] Amos?[g]"
"A plumb line,[h]" I replied.
Then the Lord said, "Look, I am setting a plumb line among my people Israel; I will spare them no longer.[i]

9"The high places of Isaac will be
destroyed
and the sanctuaries[j] of Israel will
be ruined;
with my sword I will rise against
the house of Jeroboam.[k]"

Amos and Amaziah

10Then Amaziah the priest of Bethel[l]
sent a message to Jeroboam[m] king of Israel: "Amos is raising a conspiracy[n]
against you in the very heart of Israel.
The land cannot bear all his words.[o]
11For this is what Amos is saying:

" 'Jeroboam will die by the sword,
and Israel will surely go into
exile,
away from their native land.' "

12Then Amaziah said to Amos, "Get
out, you seer! Go back to the land of Judah. Earn your bread there and do your
prophesying there.[p] 13Don't prophesy
anymore at Bethel, because this is the
king's sanctuary and the temple of the
kingdom.[q]"
14Amos answered Amaziah, "I was
neither a prophet[r] nor a prophet's son,
but I was a shepherd, and I also took
care of sycamore-fig trees. 15But the
LORD took me from tending the flock[s]
and said to me, 'Go, prophesy to my people Israel.'[t] 16Now then, hear the word of
the LORD. You say,

" 'Do not prophesy against[u] Israel,
and stop preaching against the
house of Isaac.'

17"Therefore this is what the LORD
says:

" 'Your wife will become a
prostitute[v] in the city,

[a] 13 *Lo Debar* means *nothing.* [b] 13 *Karnaim* means *horns*; *horn* here symbolizes strength.
[c] 14 Or *from the entrance to*

7:8 [f] Jer 1:11,13 [g] Isa 28:17; La 2:8; Am 8:2 [h] 2Ki 21:13 [i] Jer 15:6; Eze 7:2-9
7:9 [j] Lev 26:31 [k] 2Ki 15:9; Isa 63:18; Hos 10:8
7:10 [l] 1Ki 12:32 [m] 2Ki 14:23 [n] Jer 38:4 [o] Jer 26:8-11
7:12 [p] Mt 8:34
7:13 [q] Am 2:12; Ac 4:18
7:14 [r] 2Ki 2:5; 4:38
7:15 [s] 2Sa 7:8 [t] Jer 7:1-2; Eze 2:3-4
7:16 [u] Eze 20:46; Mic 2:6
7:17 [v] Hos 4:13

and your sons and daughters
will fall by the sword.
Your land will be measured and
divided up,
and you yourself will die in a
pagan[a] country.
7:17 [w] 2Ki 17:6; Eze 4:13; Hos 9:3 And Israel will certainly go into
exile,
away from their native land.[w]' "

A Basket of Ripe Fruit

8 This is what the Sovereign LORD
showed me: a basket of ripe fruit.
8:2 [x] Jer 24:3 [y] Am 7:8 [z] Eze 7:2-9 2"What do you see,[x] Amos?[y]" he asked.
"A basket of ripe fruit," I answered.
Then the LORD said to me, "The time
is ripe for my people Israel; I will spare
them no longer.[z]
3"In that day," declares the Sovereign
LORD, "the songs in the temple will turn
8:3 [a] Am 5:16 [b] Am 5:23; 6:10 to wailing.[b][a] Many, many bodies—flung
everywhere! Silence![b]"

4 Hear this, you who trample the
needy
8:4 [c] Pr 30:14 [d] Ps 14:4; Am 2:7 and do away with the poor[c] of
the land,[d]

5 saying,

"When will the New Moon be over
that we may sell grain,
and the Sabbath be ended
that we may market wheat?"—
skimping the measure,
boosting the price
8:5 [e] 2Ki 4:23; Ne 13:15-16; Hos 12:7; Mic 6:10-11 and cheating with dishonest
scales,[e]
6 buying the poor with silver
and the needy for a pair of
sandals,
selling even the sweepings with
8:6 [f] Am 2:6 the wheat.[f]

8:7 [g] Am 6:8 [h] Hos 8:13 7 The LORD has sworn by the Pride of
Jacob:[g] "I will never forget[h] anything
they have done.

8:8 [i] Hos 4:3 [j] Ps 18:7; Jer 46:8; Am 9:5 8"Will not the land tremble[i] for this,
and all who live in it mourn?
The whole land will rise like the
Nile;
it will be stirred up and then
sink
like the river of Egypt.[j]

9"In that day," declares the Sovereign
LORD,

"I will make the sun go down at
noon
and darken the earth in broad 8:9 [k] Job 5:14; Isa 59:9-10; Jer 15:9; Am 5:8; Mic 3:6
daylight.[k]
10 I will turn your religious feasts into
mourning
and all your singing into
weeping.
I will make all of you wear
sackcloth[l] 8:10 [l] Jer 48:37 [m] Jer 6:26; Zec 12:10 [n] Eze 7:18
and shave your heads.
I will make that time like
mourning for an only son[m]
and the end of it like a bitter
day.[n]

11 "The days are coming," declares the
Sovereign LORD,
"when I will send a famine
through the land—
not a famine of food or a thirst for
water,
but a famine of hearing the
words of the LORD.[o] 8:11 [o] 1Sa 3:1; 2Ch 15:3; Eze 7:26
12 Men will stagger from sea to sea
and wander from north to east,
searching for the word of the LORD, 8:12 [p] Eze 20:3,31
but they will not find it.[p]

13"In that day

"the lovely young women and
strong young men 8:13 [q] Isa 41:17; Hos 2:3
will faint because of thirst.[q]
14 They who swear by the shame[c] of
Samaria,

[a] 17 Hebrew *an unclean* [b] 3 Or *"the temple singers will wail* [c] 14 Or *by Ashima*; or *by the idol*

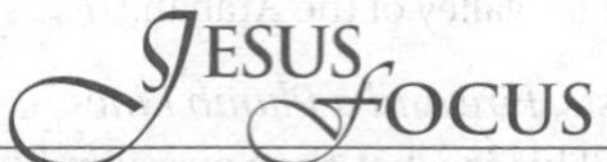

GOD'S SILENCE

Amos 8 describes how God's people would be devastated if they did not turn back to him. The prophet predicted that the most unbearable judgment of all would be God's silence, a famine of words (Amos 8:11). Amos predicted that there would be no message from God through his prophets through the upcoming judgment and ultimately through an agonizing period of four hundred "silent years"—the period of time we now call the "intertestamental period." After Malachi, the final Old Testament prophet, God did not send another messenger for four centuries. His silence was finally broken when John the Baptist announced that God's promised Messiah—Jesus—had come as the "Lamb of God, who takes away the sin of the world!" (John 1:29).

8:14 [r]1Ki 12:29 [s]Am 5:5 [t]Am 5:2

or say, 'As surely as your god
lives, O Dan,'[r]
or, 'As surely as the god[a] of
Beersheba[s] lives'—
they will fall,
never to rise again.[t]"

Israel to Be Destroyed

9 I saw the Lord standing by the altar, and he said:

"Strike the tops of the pillars
so that the thresholds shake.
9:1 [u]Ps 68:21
Bring them down on the heads[u] of
all the people;
those who are left I will kill with
the sword.
Not one will get away,
none will escape.
9:2 [v]Ps 139:8 [w]Jer 51:53 [x]Ob 1:4
2 Though they dig down to the
depths of the grave,[b][v]
from there my hand will take
them.
Though they climb up to the
heavens,[w]
from there I will bring them
down.[x]
9:3 [y]Am 1:2 [z]Ps 139:8-10 [a]Jer 16:16-17
3 Though they hide themselves on
the top of Carmel,[y]
there I will hunt them down and
seize them.[z]
Though they hide from me at the
bottom of the sea,
there I will command the
serpent to bite them.[a]
4 Though they are driven into exile
by their enemies,
9:4 [b]Lev 26:33; Eze 5:12 [c]Jer 21:10 [d]Jer 39:16 [e]Jer 44:11
there I will command the sword[b]
to slay them.
I will fix my eyes upon them
for evil[c] and not for good.[d]"[e]

5 The Lord, the LORD Almighty,
he who touches the earth and it
melts,[f]
9:5 [f]Ps 46:2; Mic 1:4 [g]Am 8:8
and all who live in it mourn—
the whole land rises like the Nile,
then sinks like the river of
Egypt[g]—
6 he who builds his lofty palace[c] in
the heavens
and sets its foundation[d] on the
earth,
who calls for the waters of the sea
and pours them out over the
face of the land—
9:6 [h]Ps 104:1-3,5-6, 13; Am 5:8
the LORD is his name.[h]

7 "Are not you Israelites
the same to me as the
Cushites[e]?"[i]
declares the LORD.
9:7 [i]Isa 20:4; 43:3 [j]Dt 2:23; Jer 47:4 [k]2Ki 16:9; Isa 22:6; Am 1:5; 2:10
"Did I not bring Israel up from
Egypt,
the Philistines from Caphtor[f][j]
and the Arameans from Kir?[k]

8 "Surely the eyes of the Sovereign
LORD
are on the sinful kingdom.
I will destroy it
from the face of the earth—
yet I will not totally destroy
the house of Jacob,"
declares the LORD.[l]
9:8 [l]Jer 44:27
9 "For I will give the command,
and I will shake the house of
Israel
among all the nations
9:9 [m]Lk 22:31 [n]Isa 30:28
as grain[m] is shaken in a sieve,[n]
and not a pebble will reach the
ground.
10 All the sinners among my people
will die by the sword,
all those who say,

[a] 14 Or *power* [b] 2 Hebrew *to Sheol* [c] 6 The meaning of the Hebrew for this phrase is uncertain. [d] 6 The meaning of the Hebrew for this word is uncertain. [e] 7 That is, people from the upper Nile region [f] 7 That is, Crete

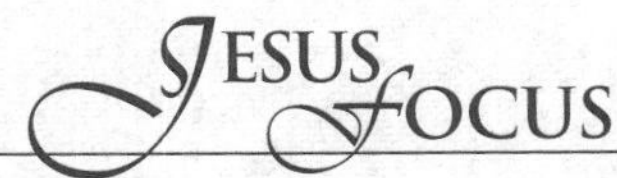

DAVID'S TENT

Most of what the prophet Amos had to say pertained to the destruction of the northern kingdom of Israel. But his closing verses assured the people that their relationship with God would be repaired, "never again to be uprooted" (Amos 9:11–15). Amos looked forward to the time when God would restore "David's fallen tent," the family line, to the position God had promised. At the time of Amos's prophecy, the northern half of the nation had already broken away from the rule of David's family in Jerusalem, and it would eventually fall to the Assyrians. Not long afterward the southern kingdom would be laid waste by the Babylonians. David's "tent" had most certainly collapsed! Centuries later, however, an angel came to speak with a young woman named Mary. He informed her that she would have a baby "who will be called the Son of the Most High" and that "the Lord God will give him the throne of his father David, and he will reign over the house of Jacob forever" (Luke 1:32–33).

'Disaster will not overtake or
meet us.'[o]

9:10 [o] Am 6:3

Israel's Restoration

11 "In that day I will restore
David's fallen tent.
I will repair its broken places,
restore its ruins,
and build it as it used to be,[p]
12 so that they may possess the
remnant of Edom[q]
and all the nations that bear my
name,[a][r]"
declares the LORD,
who will do these things.[s]

9:11 [p] Ps 80:12
9:12 [q] Nu 24:18 [r] Isa 43:7 [s] Ac 15:16-17*

13 "The days are coming," declares the
LORD,

"when the reaper will be overtaken
by the plowman[t]
and the planter by the one
treading grapes.
New wine will drip from the
mountains
and flow from all the hills.[u]
14 I will bring back my exiled[b] people
Israel;
they will rebuild the ruined
cities[v] and live in them.
They will plant vineyards and
drink their wine;
they will make gardens and eat
their fruit.[w]
15 I will plant[x] Israel in their own
land,
never again to be uprooted
from the land I have given
them,"

says the LORD your God.[y]

9:13 [t] Lev 26:5 [u] Joel 3:18
9:14 [v] Isa 61:4 [w] Jer 30:18; 31:28; Eze 28:25-26
9:15 [x] Isa 60:21 [y] Jer 24:6; Eze 34:25-28; 37:12,25

[a] *12* Hebrew; Septuagint *so that the remnant of men / and all the nations that bear my name may seek* ⌊*the Lord*⌋ [b] *14* Or *will restore the fortunes of my*

OBADIAH

What message does this short book have for beleaguered Christians today?

♦ *The book of Obadiah stresses the justice of God, his ongoing concern for his persecuted people and his behind-the-scenes working on our behalf. Obadiah's promises regarding the coming kingdom of God have passed into our possession today and come to fullest expression in Jesus Christ, God's precious Son, the faithful Deliverer of his people.*

What is the significance of the clause, "Deliverers will go up on Mount Zion"? (Obadiah 21)

♦ *This refers to future leaders who would restore God's people as a nation. Edom would vanish and Judah would rise from the ashes, demonstrating God's faithfulness to his people. Many think this alludes in the end to the Messiah who one day will deliver his people.*

Jesus in Obadiah Obadiah directed his words against the cruel nation of Edom, distant relatives of the Israelites who had periodically helped other nations to attack Israel. Obadiah's words promised God's ultimate judgment on Edom for taking advantage of Israel.

Jesus is pictured in Obadiah as the ultimate Judge of the nations and the Defender of Israel (Obadiah 15–20), as well as the Deliverer who will go up to Mount Zion (verse 21). This may well be an allusion to Jesus, who is the Deliverer *par excellence* (see second sidebar question and answer). See Revelation 11:15 for a ringing affirmation of this prophecy about the final outcome of history: "The kingdom of the world has become the kingdom of our Lord and of his Christ, and he will reign for ever and ever." Jesus' arrival, however, will also be associated with fire (verse 18). 2 Thessalonians 1:7–9 reinforces this prediction, stating that Jesus will be "revealed from heaven in blazing fire . . . He will punish those who do not know God . . . with everlasting destruction."

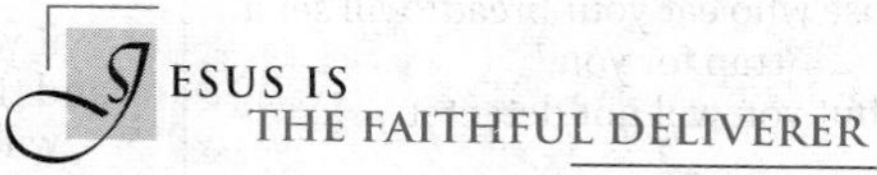

JESUS IS THE FAITHFUL DELIVERER

1 The vision of Obadiah.

This is what the Sovereign LORD says about Edom[a]—

We have heard a message from the
  LORD:
An envoy[b] was sent to the
  nations to say,
"Rise, and let us go against her for
  battle"[c]—

2 "See, I will make you small among
  the nations;
you will be utterly despised.
3 The pride[d] of your heart has
  deceived you,
you who live in the clefts of the
  rocks[a]
and make your home on the
  heights,
you who say to yourself,
'Who can bring me down to the
  ground?'[e]
4 Though you soar like the eagle
and make your nest[f] among the
  stars,
from there I will bring you
  down,"[g]
    declares the LORD.[h]
5 "If thieves came to you,
if robbers in the night—
Oh, what a disaster awaits you—
would they not steal only as
  much as they wanted?
If grape pickers came to you,
would they not leave a few
  grapes?[i]
6 But how Esau will be ransacked,
his hidden treasures pillaged!
7 All your allies[j] will force you to the
  border;
your friends will deceive and
  overpower you;
those who eat your bread[k] will set a
  trap for you,[b]
but you will not detect it.

8 "In that day," declares the LORD,
"will I not destroy[l] the wise men
  of Edom,
men of understanding in the
  mountains of Esau?
9 Your warriors, O Teman,[m] will be
  terrified,
and everyone in Esau's
  mountains
will be cut down in the slaughter.
10 Because of the violence[n] against
  your brother Jacob,[o]
you will be covered with shame;
you will be destroyed forever.[p]
11 On the day you stood aloof
while strangers carried off his
  wealth
and foreigners entered his gates
and cast lots[q] for Jerusalem,
you were like one of them.
12 You should not look down on your
  brother
in the day of his misfortune,
nor rejoice[r] over the people of
  Judah
in the day of their destruction,[s]
nor boast so much
in the day of their trouble.[t]
13 You should not march through the
  gates of my people
in the day of their disaster,
nor look down on them in their
  calamity[u]
in the day of their disaster,
nor seize their wealth
in the day of their disaster.
14 You should not wait at the
  crossroads
to cut down their fugitives,
nor hand over their survivors
in the day of their trouble.

15 "The day of the LORD is near[v]
for all nations.
As you have done, it will be done to
  you;
your deeds[w] will return upon
  your own head.
16 Just as you drank on my holy hill,
so all the nations will drink[x]
  continually;
they will drink and drink
and be as if they had never been.
17 But on Mount Zion will be
  deliverance;[y]
it will be holy,[z]
and the house of Jacob
will possess its inheritance.
18 The house of Jacob will be a fire
and the house of Joseph a flame;
the house of Esau will be stubble,
and they will set it on fire and
  consume[a] it.
There will be no survivors
from the house of Esau."
    The LORD has spoken.

[a] 3 Or *of Sela*   [b] 7 The meaning of the Hebrew for this clause is uncertain.

1:1 [a] Isa 63:1-6; Jer 49:7-22; Eze 25:12-14; Am 1:11-12 [b] Isa 18:2 [c] Jer 6:4-5
1:3 [d] Isa 16:6 [e] Isa 14:13-15; Rev 18:7
1:4 [f] Hab 2:9 [g] Isa 14:13 [h] Job 20:6
1:5 [i] Dt 24:21
1:7 [j] Jer 30:14 [k] Ps 41:9
1:8 [l] Job 5:12; Isa 29:14
1:9 [m] Ge 36:11,34
1:10 [n] Joel 3:19 [o] Ps 137:7; Am 1:11-12 [p] Eze 35:9
1:11 [q] Na 3:10
1:12 [r] Eze 35:15 [s] Pr 17:5 [t] Mic 4:11
1:13 [u] Eze 35:5
1:15 [v] Eze 30:3 [w] Jer 50:29; Hab 2:8
1:16 [x] Jer 25:15; 49:12
1:17 [y] Am 9:11-15 [z] Isa 4:3
1:18 [a] Zec 12:6

DISCOVERY 222

The Sign of Jonah

People of all ages enjoy fishing. And the myths they like to perpetuate are many: the one that got away, the creative manner in which one was caught, the size of the fish he or she landed . . . and the list goes on.

The "fish tale" related by Jonah is a classic. It is a difficult story to "swallow," like many of the scenarios related after a long day of "wetting a line," but Jonah's narrative is truthful in every detail.

Perhaps the most incredible claim in the story is the statement that "the LORD provided a great fish to swallow Jonah, and Jonah was inside the fish three days and three nights" (Jonah 1:17). A fish large enough to swallow a man whole? A man who survived to tell about it? Jonah engaging in an intimate and intense conversation with God from within the body of this improbable "rescuer"? And finally God instructing the fish to vomit Jonah alive onto dry ground? The whole narrative sounds like an elaborate fable designed to teach a lesson. But Jonah himself would testify to the reality of the experience with impassioned conviction!

God used the implausible story of Jonah's fish experience to present a vivid picture of the events that would surround the death and resurrection of Jesus. The connection became clear as the events recounted in the Gospels continued to unfold. After Jesus' death his body was laid in a tomb, and there it remained for three days (Matthew 27:62–66; Luke 24:7). But on the third day, by the command of God the Father and the power of his Holy Spirit, that body took on new life (Mark 16:1–8). Matthew explained that Jonah's close encounter with the great fish was a sign that Jesus would come to life again—not only in a spiritual sense but physically as well (Matthew 12:40).

Jonah's extraordinary adventure really happened, and so did Jesus' resurrection. Jesus is infinitely more than simply an historical figure or a fictitious model of good behavior from whom we can learn some good moral lessons. Our faith in Jesus Christ is not lifeless or futile, not based on some ingenious fable. That faith has substance because the One in whom we place our trust is indeed alive and well! And we have assurance that when we relinquish control of our lives to him, we will one day live in his presence forever—because his resurrection guarantees our own (1 Corinthians 15:20–28).

We can believe both Jonah's tale and Jesus' story because we understand the extent of God's power: There is *nothing* he cannot do (Matthew 19:26; Luke 1:37). The power of sin and death has caused unspeakable devastation, but the vitality available to us through faith in Jesus Christ is infinitely greater! Death may appear ominous, but it has already been conquered by life (1 Corinthians 15:54–57).

Self-Discovery: *To what evidence would you point if you found yourself in the position of explaining Jesus' resurrection to a skeptic?*

GO TO DISCOVERY 223 ON PAGE 1199

10And the LORD commanded the fish,
and it vomited Jonah onto dry land.

Jonah Goes to Nineveh

3 Then the word of the LORD came
3:1 [f]Jnh 1:1 to Jonah[f] a second time: 2"Go to
the great city of Nineveh and proclaim
to it the message I give you."
3Jonah obeyed the word of the LORD
and went to Nineveh. Now Nineveh was
a very important city—a visit required
three days. 4On the first day, Jonah started into the city. He proclaimed: "Forty
more days and Nineveh will be overturned." 5The Ninevites believed God.
They declared a fast, and all of them,
3:5 [g]Da 9:3; from the greatest to the least, put on
Lk 11:32 sackcloth.[g]
6When the news reached the king of
Nineveh, he rose from his throne, took
3:6 off his royal robes, covered himself with
[h]Job 2:8,13; sackcloth and sat down in the dust.[h]
Eze 27:30-31 7Then he issued a proclamation in Nineveh:

"By the decree of the king and his nobles:

Do not let any man or beast,
herd or flock, taste anything; do
3:7 [i]2Ch 20:3 not let them eat or drink.[i] 8But let
man and beast be covered with
3:8 sackcloth. Let everyone call[j] ur-
[j]Ps 130:1; Jnh 1:6 gently on God. Let them give up
their evil ways and their violence.
3:9 9Who knows?[k] God may yet relent
[k]2Sa 12:22 [l]Joel 2:14 and with compassion turn[l] from
his fierce anger so that we will not
perish."

10When God saw what they did and
how they turned from their evil ways, he
3:10 had compassion[m] and did not bring
[m]Am 7:6 [n]Jer 18:8 upon them the destruction[n] he had
[o]Ex 32:14 threatened.[o]

Jonah's Anger at the LORD's Compassion

4 But Jonah was greatly displeased
4:1 [p]ver 4; Lk 15:28 and became angry.[p] 2He prayed to
the LORD, "O LORD, is this not what I said
when I was still at home? That is why I
4:2 was so quick to flee to Tarshish. I knew[q]
[q]Jer 20:7-8 [r]Ex 34:6; that you are a gracious and compas-
Ps 86:5,15 sionate God, slow to anger and abound-
[s]Joel 2:13 ing in love,[r] a God who relents from
sending calamity.[s] 3Now, O LORD, take
4:3 [t]1Ki 19:4 away my life,[t] for it is better for me to
[u]Job 7:15 die[u] than to live."

4But the LORD replied, "Have you any
right to be angry?"[v] 4:4 [v]Mt 20:11-15
5Jonah went out and sat down at a
place east of the city. There he made
himself a shelter, sat in its shade and
waited to see what would happen to the
city. 6Then the LORD God provided a vine
and made it grow up over Jonah to give
shade for his head to ease his discomfort, and Jonah was very happy about
the vine. 7But at dawn the next day God
provided a worm, which chewed the
vine so that it withered.[w] 8When the sun 4:7 [w]Joel 1:12
rose, God provided a scorching east
wind, and the sun blazed on Jonah's
head so that he grew faint. He wanted to
die, and said, "It would be better for me
to die than to live."
9But God said to Jonah, "Do you have
a right to be angry about the vine?"

JESUS FOCUS

A COMMISSION AND A RESPONSE

Jonah was not the first individual to run away from what God wanted him to do—and he will not be the last. God has always desired that his people share with others the Good News that they can have a relationship with him, but we all too often come up with a long list of other things we'd rather do. God instructed Jonah to travel northeast to Nineveh, which was in Assyria, but the obstinate prophet instead boarded a boat and deliberately headed west into the Mediterranean Sea. We are not told precisely why Jonah refused to follow God's command. We do know that the Assyrians were Israel's enemies and that later when the people of Nineveh did turn back to God, Jonah was angry with God for showing compassion to his enemies (Jonah 4:1–3). Interestingly, this sullen attitude was manifested *after* Jonah's amazing three-day encounter with the great fish, which of all possible experiences should have been an eye-opener! And God had a strong challenge for the prophet: "Have you any right to be angry?" (verse 4). God went on to explain how he views all of humanity—with a heart of compassion, tenderness and forgiveness. During his earthly ministry Jesus commissioned his followers to do the same thing God had asked Jonah to do: to "make disciples of all nations" (Matthew 28:19), to go everywhere and tell everyone who he is and what he came to do (Mark 16:15).

"I do," he said. "I am angry enough to die."

10 But the LORD said, "You have been concerned about this vine, though you did not tend it or make it grow. It sprang up overnight and died overnight.

11 But Nineveh[x] has more than a hundred and twenty thousand people who cannot tell their right hand from their left, and many cattle as well. Should I not be concerned[y] about that great city?"

4:11
[x] Jnh 1:2; 3:2
[y] Jnh 3:10

MICAH

What is the significance of Micah 5:2?

♦ *Centuries later the religious leaders would use this verse to tell King Herod where the Messiah would be born (Matthew 2:6).*

Did Micah realize that he was prophesying about the Messiah? (Micah 5:2–4)

♦ *Yes, although he may not have recognized that his vision wouldn't be fulfilled for centuries. He described the coming ideal ruler in terms meaningful to the people of his day.*

Will Assyria again be a power in the last days? (Micah 5:5)

♦ *Assyria will probably be a power only in a figurative sense. Assyria serves as a model to represent God's enemies. When God rules through his Messianic King, his people will no longer need to fear cruel, would-be oppressors like the Assyrians, for the Messiah will protect God's people.*

Jesus in Micah Micah covered a lot of ground in this prophetic book, painting a panoramic portrait of history that exploded with proclamations about events that would span many centuries. Try reading Micah as a series of short sermons. Determine who is speaking—God, Micah or the people—and then reflect on the meaning. Note that these short sermons divide easily into three distinct sections: God's judgment for the sins of Israel and Judah, prophecies about the coming Messiah and the marvelous future God is planning, and the fate of the guilty nations.

Micah predicted exactly where God's promised Messiah would be born—in Bethlehem (Micah 5:2). Of all the kings of Judah, only David himself was born in Bethlehem, which makes Micah's prophecy all the more specific and unique. David's greater Son would come from Bethlehem to "shepherd his flock" (Micah 5:4). Micah linked God's promised Messiah with the shepherd image so familiar in the area around Bethlehem. Centuries later, shepherds would welcome the Savior when he was born there (Luke 2:8–16).

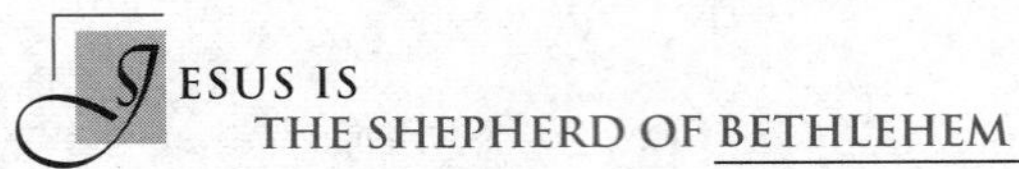

JESUS IS THE SHEPHERD OF BETHLEHEM

1 The word of the LORD that came to Micah of Moresheth[a] during the reigns of Jotham,[b] Ahaz[c] and Hezekiah, kings of Judah[d]—the vision[e] he saw concerning Samaria and Jerusalem.

2 Hear, O peoples, all of you,[f]
listen, O earth[g] and all who are in it,
that the Sovereign LORD may witness[h] against you,
the Lord from his holy temple.[i]

Judgment Against Samaria and Jerusalem

3 Look! The LORD is coming from his dwelling[j] place;
he comes down and treads the high places of the earth.[k]
4 The mountains melt[l] beneath him
and the valleys split apart,[m]
like wax before the fire,
like water rushing down a slope.
5 All this is because of Jacob's transgression,
because of the sins of the house of Israel.
What is Jacob's transgression?
Is it not Samaria?[n]
What is Judah's high place?
Is it not Jerusalem?

6 "Therefore I will make Samaria a heap of rubble,
a place for planting vineyards.
I will pour her stones[o] into the valley
and lay bare her foundations.[p]
7 All her idols[q] will be broken to pieces;
all her temple gifts will be burned with fire;
I will destroy all her images.[r]
Since she gathered her gifts from the wages of prostitutes,[s]
as the wages of prostitutes they will again be used."

Weeping and Mourning

8 Because of this I will weep[t] and wail;
I will go about barefoot and naked.
I will howl like a jackal
and moan like an owl.
9 For her wound[u] is incurable;
it has come to Judah.[v]
It[a] has reached the very gate[w] of my people,
even to Jerusalem itself.
10 Tell it not in Gath[b];
weep not at all.[c]
In Beth Ophrah[d]
roll in the dust.
11 Pass on in nakedness[x] and shame,
you who live in Shaphir.[e]
Those who live in Zaanan[f]
will not come out.
Beth Ezel is in mourning;
its protection is taken from you.
12 Those who live in Maroth[g] writhe in pain,
waiting for relief,[y]
because disaster has come from the LORD,
even to the gate of Jerusalem.
13 You who live in Lachish,[h][z]
harness the team to the chariot.
You were the beginning of sin
to the Daughter of Zion,
for the transgressions of Israel
were found in you.
14 Therefore you will give parting gifts[a]
to Moresheth Gath.
The town of Aczib[i][b] will prove deceptive[c]
to the kings of Israel.
15 I will bring a conqueror against you
who live in Mareshah.[j][d]
He who is the glory of Israel
will come to Adullam.[e]
16 Shave[f] your heads in mourning
for the children in whom you delight;
make yourselves as bald as the vulture,
for they will go from you into exile.

Man's Plans and God's

2 Woe to those who plan iniquity,
to those who plot evil on their beds![g]
At morning's light they carry it out
because it is in their power to do it.
2 They covet fields[h] and seize them,

1:1 [a] Jer 26:18 [b] 1Ch 3:12 [c] 1Ch 3:13 [d] Hos 1:1 [e] Isa 1:1
1:2 [f] Ps 50:7 [g] Jer 6:19 [h] Ge 31:50; Dt 4:26; Isa 1:2 [i] Ps 11:4
1:3 [j] Isa 18:4 [k] Am 4:13
1:4 [l] Ps 46:2,6 [m] Nu 16:31; Na 1:5
1:5 [n] Am 8:14
1:6 [o] Am 5:11 [p] Eze 13:14
1:7 [q] Eze 6:6 [r] Dt 9:21 [s] Dt 23:17-18
1:8 [t] Isa 15:3
1:9 [u] Jer 46:11 [v] 2Ki 18:13 [w] Isa 3:26
1:11 [x] Eze 23:29
1:12 [y] Jer 14:19
1:13 [z] Jos 10:3
1:14 [a] 2Ki 16:8 [b] Jos 15:44 [c] Jer 15:18
1:15 [d] Jos 15:44 [e] Jos 12:15
1:16 [f] Job 1:20
2:1 [g] Ps 36:4
2:2 [h] Isa 5:8

[a] 9 Or *He* [b] 10 *Gath* sounds like the Hebrew for *tell.* [c] 10 Hebrew; Septuagint may suggest *not in Acco.* The Hebrew for *in Acco* sounds like the Hebrew for *weep.* [d] 10 *Beth Ophrah* means *house of dust.* [e] 11 *Shaphir* means *pleasant.* [f] 11 *Zaanan* sounds like the Hebrew for *come out.* [g] 12 *Maroth* sounds like the Hebrew for *bitter.* [h] 13 *Lachish* sounds like the Hebrew for *team.* [i] 14 *Aczib* means *deception.* [j] 15 *Mareshah* sounds like the Hebrew for *conqueror.*

and houses, and take them.
2:2 [i] Jer 22:17 They defraud[i] a man of his home,
a fellowman of his inheritance.

3 Therefore, the LORD says:

2:3 [j] Jer 18:11; Am 3:1-2 [k] Isa 2:12 "I am planning disaster[j] against
this people,
from which you cannot save
yourselves.
You will no longer walk proudly,[k]
for it will be a time of calamity.
4 In that day men will ridicule you;
they will taunt you with this
mournful song:
2:4 [l] Jer 4:13 'We are utterly ruined;[l]
my people's possession is divided
up.
He takes it from me!
He assigns our fields to traitors.' "
5 Therefore you will have no one in
the assembly of the LORD
2:5 [m] Jos 18:4 to divide the land[m] by lot.

False Prophets

6 "Do not prophesy," their prophets
say.
"Do not prophesy about these
things;
2:6 [n] Mic 6:16 [o] Am 2:12 disgrace[n] will not overtake us.[o]"
7 Should it be said, O house of Jacob:
"Is the Spirit of the LORD angry?
Does he do such things?"

2:7 [p] Ps 119:65 [q] Ps 15:2; 84:11 "Do not my words do good[p]
to him whose ways are upright?[q]
8 Lately my people have risen up
like an enemy.
You strip off the rich robe
from those who pass by without
a care,
like men returning from battle.

JESUS FOCUS

A SHEPHERD-KING

Micah 2 describes the restorer of Israel as a Shepherd-King who would "bring [Israel] together like . . . a flock in its pasture" (verse 12)—and who would be the Lord himself! Micah gazed ahead in time and saw that the Messiah would lead his people into blessing just as a shepherd leads his sheep to food, water and safety (Micah 5:4–5). Jesus later fulfilled this prophecy: "I am the good shepherd. The good shepherd lays down his life for the sheep" (John 10:11).

9 You drive the women of my people
from their pleasant homes.[r] 2:9 [r] Jer 10:20
You take away my blessing
from their children forever.
10 Get up, go away!
For this is not your resting place,[s] 2:10 [s] Dt 12:9
because it is defiled,[t] [t] Lev 18:25-29;
it is ruined, beyond all remedy. Ps 106:38-39
11 If a liar and deceiver[u] comes and 2:11 [u] Jer 5:31
says, [v] Isa 30:10
'I will prophesy for you plenty of
wine and beer,'
he would be just the prophet for
this people![v]

Deliverance Promised

12 "I will surely gather all of you,
O Jacob;
I will surely bring together the 2:12
remnant[w] of Israel. [w] Mic 4:7; 5:7; 7:18
I will bring them together like
sheep in a pen,
like a flock in its pasture;
the place will throng with people.
13 One who breaks open the way will
go up before[x] them; 2:13 [x] Isa 52:12
they will break through the gate
and go out.
Their king will pass through before
them,
the LORD at their head."

Leaders and Prophets Rebuked

3 Then I said,

"Listen, you leaders[y] of Jacob, 3:1 [y] Jer 5:5
you rulers of the house of Israel.
Should you not know justice,
2 you who hate good and love evil;
who tear the skin from my people 3:2
and the flesh from their bones;[z] [z] Ps 53:4; Eze 22:27
3 who eat my people's flesh,[a]
strip off their skin 3:3 [a] Ps 14:4
and break their bones in pieces;[b] [b] Zep 3:3
who chop them up like meat for [c] Eze 11:7
the pan,
like flesh for the pot?[c]"
4 Then they will cry out to the LORD, 3:4
but he will not answer them.[d] [d] Ps 18:41; Isa 1:15
At that time he will hide his face[e] [e] Dt 31:17
from them
because of the evil they have
done.

5 This is what the LORD says:

"As for the prophets
who lead my people astray,[f] 3:5 [f] Isa 3:12; 9:16

if one feeds them,
they proclaim 'peace';
if he does not,
they prepare to wage war
against him.
[6] Therefore night will come over you,
without visions,
and darkness, without
divination.[g]
The sun will set for the prophets,[h]
and the day will go dark for them.
[7] The seers will be ashamed[i]
and the diviners disgraced.[j]
They will all cover their faces
because there is no answer from
God."
[8] But as for me, I am filled with
power,
with the Spirit of the LORD,
and with justice and might,
to declare to Jacob his
transgression,
to Israel his sin.[k]
[9] Hear this, you leaders of the house
of Jacob,
you rulers of the house of Israel,
who despise justice
and distort all that is right;[l]
[10] who build[m] Zion with bloodshed,[n]
and Jerusalem with wickedness.[o]
[11] Her leaders judge for a bribe,
her priests teach for a price,
and her prophets tell fortunes
for money.[p]
Yet they lean upon the LORD and
say,
"Is not the LORD among us?
No disaster will come upon us."[q]
[12] Therefore because of you,
Zion will be plowed like a field,
Jerusalem will become a heap of
rubble,[r]
the temple hill a mound
overgrown with thickets.

The Mountain of the LORD

4 In the last days
the mountain[s] of the LORD's temple
will be established
as chief among the mountains;
it will be raised above the hills,[t]
and peoples will stream to it.[u]
[2] Many nations will come and say,
"Come, let us go up to the
mountain of the LORD,[v]
to the house of the God of
Jacob.[w]
He will teach us his ways,[x]
so that we may walk in his paths."
The law will go out from Zion,
the word of the LORD from
Jerusalem.
[3] He will judge between many
peoples
and will settle disputes for strong
nations far and wide.[y]
They will beat their swords into
plowshares
and their spears into pruning
hooks.[z]
Nation will not take up sword
against nation,
nor will they train for war
anymore.[a]
[4] Every man will sit under his own
vine
and under his own fig tree,[b]
and no one will make them afraid,[c]

3:6 [g] Isa 8:19-22 [h] Isa 29:10
3:7 [i] Mic 7:16 [j] Isa 44:25
3:8 [k] Isa 58:1
3:9 [l] Ps 58:1-2; Isa 1:23
3:10 [m] Jer 22:13 [n] Hab 2:12 [o] Eze 22:27
3:11 [p] Isa 1:23; Jer 6:13; Hos 4:8,18 [q] Jer 7:4
3:12 [r] Jer 26:18
4:1 [s] Zec 8:3 [t] Eze 17:22 [u] Ps 22:27; 86:9; Jer 3:17
4:2 [v] Jer 31:6 [w] Zec 2:11; 14:16 [x] Ps 25:8-9; Isa 54:13
4:3 [y] Isa 11:4 [z] Joel 3:10 [a] Isa 2:4
4:4 [b] 1Ki 4:25 [c] Lev 26:6

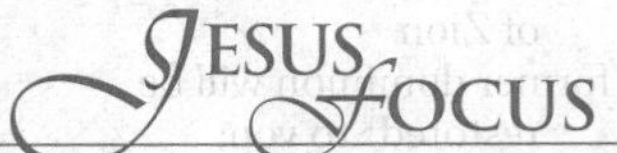

THE GOLDEN AGE

Micah lived during the same time period as the prophet Isaiah. In fact, Micah 4:1–3 is similar to Isaiah 2:2–4. Both of these prophets were aware that there would come a future time in which God's promised Messiah would rule the nations, a kind of "golden age" when God would bless the nation of Israel as never before. God revealed to Micah that the time during which his chosen Messiah would reign as King would be a period of blessing, peace and prosperity. Regardless of when this golden age will occur, the wonderful promises of God were initially fulfilled in the coming of the Messiah to usher in the firstfruits of the blessings. They continue to be fulfilled in the present as people from all nations turn to Jesus as Savior and Lord and experience the power of God's Spirit to bring healing for hurts and freedom from bondage, and they will finally and fully be consummated when Jesus comes again.

Micah offered words of tremendous encouragement and consolation in Micah 4:6–8, where he proclaimed that God was not overlooking the present distress of his people but was at work through his power to mend and make new. The passage pulsates with a spirit of compassion—the same spirit so obvious in Jesus, the Messiah, who knows the sorry state of his people and enters into their distress (Matthew 9:36).

4:4 [d] Isa 1:20; Zec 3:10
4:5 [e] 2Ki 17:29 [f] Jos 24:14-15; Isa 26:8; Zec 10:12
4:6 [g] Ps 147:2 [h] Eze 34:13,16; 37:21; Zep 3:19
4:7 [i] Mic 2:12 [j] Da 7:14; Lk 1:33; Rev 11:15
4:8 [k] Isa 1:26
4:9 [l] Jer 8:19 [m] Jer 30:6
4:10 [n] 2Ki 20:18; Isa 43:14 [o] Isa 48:20
4:11 [p] La 2:16; Ob 1:12
4:12 [q] Isa 55:8; Ro 11:33-34

for the LORD Almighty has
spoken.[d]
5 All the nations may walk
in the name of their gods;[e]
we will walk in the name of the
LORD
our God for ever and ever.[f]

The LORD's Plan

6 "In that day," declares the LORD,

"I will gather the lame;
I will assemble the exiles[g]
and those I have brought to
grief.[h]
7 I will make the lame a remnant,[i]
those driven away a strong
nation.
The LORD will rule over them in
Mount Zion
from that day and forever.[j]
8 As for you, O watchtower of the
flock,
O stronghold[a] of the Daughter
of Zion,
the former dominion will be
restored[k] to you;
kingship will come to the
Daughter of Jerusalem."
9 Why do you now cry aloud—
have you no king?[l]
Has your counselor perished,
that pain seizes you like that of a
woman in labor?[m]
10 Writhe in agony, O Daughter of
Zion,
like a woman in labor,
for now you must leave the city
to camp in the open field.
You will go to Babylon;[n]
there you will be rescued.
There the LORD will redeem[o] you
out of the hand of your enemies.
11 But now many nations
are gathered against you.
They say, "Let her be defiled,
let our eyes gloat[p] over Zion!"
12 But they do not know
the thoughts of the LORD;
they do not understand his plan,[q]
he who gathers them like sheaves
to the threshing floor.
13 "Rise and thresh, O Daughter of
Zion,
for I will give you horns of iron;
I will give you hoofs of bronze

THE MOST FOUNDATIONAL CHRISTIAN BELIEF ABOUT JESUS HAS BEEN THAT HE WAS THE MESSIAH PROMISED IN THE HEBREW SCRIPTURES.

Markus Bockmuehl,
Lecturer, Cambridge University

and you will break to pieces
many nations."[r] 4:13 [r] Da 2:44
You will devote their ill-gotten
gains to the LORD,
their wealth to the Lord of all
the earth.

A Promised Ruler From Bethlehem

5 Marshal your troops, O city of
troops,[b]
for a siege is laid against us.
They will strike Israel's ruler
on the cheek[s] with a rod. 5:1 [s] La 3:30

2 "But you, Bethlehem[t] Ephrathah,[u]
though you are small among the
clans[c] of Judah,
out of you will come for me
one who will be ruler over Israel,
whose origins[d] are from of old,[v]
from ancient times.[e]"[w]
3 Therefore Israel will be abandoned
until the time when she who is
in labor gives birth
and the rest of his brothers return
to join the Israelites.
4 He will stand and shepherd his
flock[x]
in the strength of the LORD,
in the majesty of the name of the
LORD his God.
And they will live securely, for then
his greatness[y]
will reach to the ends of the
earth.
5 And he will be their peace.[z]

5:2 [t] Jn 7:42 [u] Ge 48:7 [v] Ps 102:25 [w] Mt 2:6*
5:4 [x] Isa 40:11; 49:9; Eze 34:11-15, 23; Mic 7:14 [y] Isa 52:13; Lk 1:32
5:5 [z] Isa 9:6; Lk 2:14; Col 1:19-20 [a] Isa 8:7

Deliverance and Destruction

When the Assyrian invades[a] our
land
and marches through our
fortresses,

[a] 8 Or *hill* [b] 1 Or *Strengthen your walls, O walled city* [c] 2 Or *rulers* [d] 2 Hebrew *goings out* [e] 2 Or *from days of eternity*

Bethlehem

Many of us were born in out-of-the-way, obscure towns unfamiliar to most people. Maybe your hometown was Drain, Oregon or Dunamoney, Ireland.

Or maybe Bethlehem Ephrathah. The prophet Micah foretold that the birth of God's promised Messiah would take place in Bethlehem (Micah 5:2), a name meaning "house of bread." In ancient times the availability of bread was essential to life. And Jesus, who entered the world in a lowly stable in this insignificant town, later referred to himself as the "bread of life." Jesus Christ promised that he would satisfy the spiritual hunger of everyone who would come to him for bread (John 6:35). His is the loaf that does more than satisfy us until our next meal—its nourishment lasts forever (John 6:50–51).

Bethlehem sits a few miles south of Jerusalem. It is the setting for much of the book of Ruth. Ruth, a young woman from Moab, immigrated there with her Jewish mother-in-law Naomi after both of their husbands had died. The two arrived destitute and with little hope for more than a meager subsistence. Boaz, a wealthy landowner, took an interest in Ruth and allowed her to gather leftover grain from his field. Once he discovered that he was in a position to redeem Naomi's ancestral land, Boaz married Ruth, and she became King David's great-grandmother. The book of Ruth, like several other Old Testament stories, gives us a foreshadowing of Jesus Christ, God's one and only Son, who would later come to redeem us from sin and accept us as his "bride."

God's people were aware for many generations that the Messiah would be born in Bethlehem, because the prophet Micah had predicted the event (Micah 5:2). In fact, when the Magi from the east arrived in Jerusalem and asked the religious leaders where the "one who had been born king of the Jews" could be found, they answered immediately and accurately by pointing to the prophecy of Micah (Matthew 2:1–6).

Why did God the Father choose Bethlehem as the birthplace of his beloved Son? Perhaps the answer will become apparent to us someday in glory. In the meantime, we can marvel at the fact that God did select this unpretentious village to become one of the most significant sites in all of human history!

Self-Discovery: *Does your life sometimes seem insignificant? ordinary? mundane? Regardless of whatever limitations you may face, remember that God has a specific plan for you and that your life is of eternal significance to him.*

GO TO DISCOVERY 224 ON PAGE 1205

we will raise against him seven
shepherds,
even eight leaders of men.[b]
[6] They will rule[a] the land of Assyria
with the sword,
the land of Nimrod[c] with drawn
sword.[b][d]
He will deliver us from the
Assyrian
when he invades our land
and marches into our borders.[e]
[7] The remnant[f] of Jacob will be
in the midst of many peoples
like dew from the LORD,
like showers on the grass,[g]
which do not wait for man
or linger for mankind.
[8] The remnant of Jacob will be
among the nations,
in the midst of many peoples,
like a lion among the beasts of the
forest,[h]
like a young lion among flocks
of sheep,
which mauls and mangles[i] as it
goes,
and no one can rescue.[j]
[9] Your hand will be lifted up[k] in
triumph over your enemies,
and all your foes will be
destroyed.

[10] "In that day," declares the LORD,

"I will destroy your horses from
among you
and demolish your chariots.[l]
[11] I will destroy the cities[m] of your
land
and tear down all your
strongholds.[n]
[12] I will destroy your witchcraft
and you will no longer cast
spells.[o]
[13] I will destroy your carved images
and your sacred stones from
among you;
you will no longer bow down
to the work of your hands.[p]
[14] I will uproot from among you your
Asherah poles[c][q]
and demolish your cities.
[15] I will take vengeance[r] in anger and
wrath
upon the nations that have not
obeyed me."

5:5 [b] Isa 10:24-27
5:6 [c] Ge 10:8 [d] Zep 2:13 [e] Na 2:11-13
5:7 [f] Mic 2:12 [g] Isa 44:4
5:8 [h] Ge 49:9 [i] Mic 4:13; Zec 10:5 [j] Ps 50:22; Hos 5:14
5:9 [k] Ps 10:12
5:10 [l] Hos 14:3; Zec 9:10
5:11 [m] Isa 6:11 [n] Hos 10:14; Am 5:9
5:12 [o] Dt 18:10-12; Isa 2:6; 8:19
5:13 [p] Eze 6:9; Zec 13:2
5:14 [q] Ex 34:13
5:15 [r] Isa 65:12

JESUS IS THE GOD WHOM WE CAN APPROACH WITHOUT PRIDE AND BEFORE WHOM WE CAN HUMBLE OURSELVES WITHOUT DESPAIR.

Blaise Pascal, *French Philosopher*

The LORD's Case Against Israel

6 Listen to what the LORD says:

"Stand up, plead your case before
the mountains;[s]
let the hills hear what you have
to say.
[2] Hear,[t] O mountains, the LORD's
accusation;[u]
listen, you everlasting
foundations of the earth.
For the LORD has a case against his
people;
he is lodging a charge[v] against
Israel.
[3] "My people, what have I done to
you?
How have I burdened[w] you?
Answer me.
[4] I brought you up out of Egypt
and redeemed you from the land
of slavery.[x]
I sent Moses[y] to lead you,
also Aaron[z] and Miriam.[a]
[5] My people, remember
what Balak[b] king of Moab
counseled
and what Balaam son of Beor
answered.
Remember ⌊your journey⌋ from
Shittim[c] to Gilgal,[d]
that you may know the righteous
acts[e] of the LORD."
[6] With what shall I come before the
LORD
and bow down before the
exalted God?
Shall I come before him with burnt
offerings,
with calves a year old?[f]
[7] Will the LORD be pleased with
thousands of rams,[g]
with ten thousand rivers of oil?[h]
Shall I offer my firstborn[i] for my
transgression,

6:1 [s] Ps 50:1; Eze 6:2
6:2 [t] Dt 32:1 [u] Hos 12:2 [v] Ps 50:7
6:3 [w] Jer 2:5
6:4 [x] Dt 7:8 [y] Ex 4:16 [z] Ps 77:20 [a] Ex 15:20
6:5 [b] Nu 22:5-6 [c] Nu 25:1 [d] Jos 5:9-10 [e] Jdg 5:11; 1Sa 12:7
6:6 [f] Ps 40:6-8; 51:16-17
6:7 [g] Isa 40:16 [h] Ps 50:8-10 [i] Lev 18:21

[a] *6* Or *crush* [b] *6* Or *Nimrod in its gates*
[c] *14* That is, symbols of the goddess Asherah

6:7 [j]2Ki 16:3

the fruit of my body for the sin
of my soul?[j]
[8] He has showed you, O man, what is
good.
And what does the LORD require
of you?
To act justly[k] and to love mercy
and to walk humbly[l] with your
God.[m]

6:8 [k]Isa 1:17; Jer 22:3 [l]Isa 57:15 [m]Dt 10:12-13; 1Sa 15:22; Hos 6:6

Israel's Guilt and Punishment

[9] Listen! The LORD is calling to the
city—
and to fear your name is
wisdom—
"Heed the rod and the One who
appointed it.[a]
[10] Am I still to forget, O wicked
house,
your ill-gotten treasures
and the short ephah,[b] which is
accursed?[n]
[11] Shall I acquit a man with dishonest
scales,[o]
with a bag of false weights?
[12] Her rich men are violent;[p]
her people are liars[q]
and their tongues speak
deceitfully.[r]

6:10 [n]Eze 45:9-10; Am 3:10; 8:4-6

6:11 [o]Lev 19:36; Hos 12:7

6:12 [p]Isa 1:23 [q]Isa 3:8 [r]Jer 9:3

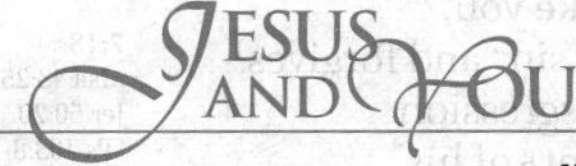

WHAT GOD WANTS

From Micah we have a clear statement of what God expects from his people: "to act justly and to love mercy and to walk humbly with your God" (Micah 6:8). These are the qualities that really matter to God, and the expectation will never change—because such qualities reflect God's heart. While Jesus was here on earth he informed the Pharisees that he was not impressed in the least with religious hypocrisy. Just as the people of Israel during the time of Micah, the Pharisees of Jesus' day had the outward details of religiosity down to an exact science (see Micah 6:6–7), even making certain that they offered a tenth of their spices to God. But they neglected "the more important matters of the law—justice, mercy and faithfulness" (Matthew 23:23–24). Using another word picture, Jesus pointed out to them that they were so busy straining out a gnat that they were swallowing a whole camel! God's "requirements" are not tedious. He wants us to learn to walk humbly with him as we increasingly become the kind of people he desires—people with hearts like his.

[13] Therefore, I have begun to destroy[s]
you,
to ruin you because of your sins.
[14] You will eat but not be satisfied;[t]
your stomach will still be
empty.[c]
You will store up but save nothing,[u]
because what you save I will give
to the sword.
[15] You will plant but not harvest;[v]
you will press olives but not use
the oil on yourselves,
you will crush grapes but not
drink the wine.[w]
[16] You have observed the statutes of
Omri[x]
and all the practices of Ahab's[y]
house,
and you have followed their
traditions.[z]
Therefore I will give you over to
ruin[a]
and your people to derision;
you will bear the scorn[b] of the
nations.[d]"

6:13 [s]Isa 1:7; 6:11

6:14 [t]Isa 9:20 [u]Isa 30:6

6:15 [v]Dt 28:38; Jer 12:13 [w]Am 5:11; Zep 1:13

6:16 [x]1Ki 16:25 [y]1Ki 16:29-33 [z]Jer 7:24 [a]Jer 25:9 [b]Jer 51:51

Israel's Misery

7 What misery is mine!
I am like one who gathers
summer fruit
at the gleaning of the vineyard;
there is no cluster of grapes to eat,
none of the early figs that I
crave.
[2] The godly have been swept from
the land;[c]
not one upright man remains.
All men lie in wait to shed blood;[d]
each hunts his brother with a
net.[e]
[3] Both hands are skilled in doing
evil;[f]
the ruler demands gifts,
the judge accepts bribes,
the powerful dictate what they
desire—
they all conspire together.
[4] The best of them is like a brier,[g]
the most upright worse than a
thorn hedge.
The day of your watchmen has
come,
the day God visits you.

7:2 [c]Ps 12:1 [d]Mic 3:10 [e]Jer 5:26

7:3 [f]Pr 4:16

7:4 [g]Eze 2:6

[a] *9* The meaning of the Hebrew for this line is uncertain. [b] *10* An ephah was a dry measure. [c] *14* The meaning of the Hebrew for this word is uncertain. [d] *16* Septuagint; Hebrew *scorn due my people*

7:4 [h] Isa 22:5; Hos 9:7

Now is the time of their
confusion.[h]
[5] Do not trust a neighbor;

7:5 [i] Jer 9:4

put no confidence in a friend.[i]
Even with her who lies in your
embrace
be careful of your words.
[6] For a son dishonors his father,
a daughter rises up against her
mother,[j]

7:6 [j] Eze 22:7 [k] Mt 10:35-36*

a daughter-in-law against her
mother-in-law—
a man's enemies are the members
of his own household.[k]

7:7 [l] Ps 130:5; Isa 25:9 [m] Ps 4:3

[7] But as for me, I watch in hope[l] for
the LORD,
I wait for God my Savior;
my God will hear[m] me.

Israel Will Rise

7:8 [n] Pr 24:17 [o] Ps 37:24; Am 9:11 [p] Isa 9:2

[8] Do not gloat over me,[n] my enemy!
Though I have fallen, I will rise.[o]
Though I sit in darkness,
the LORD will be my light.[p]
[9] Because I have sinned against him,

7:9 [q] La 3:39-40 [r] Isa 46:13

I will bear the LORD's wrath,[q]
until he pleads my case
and establishes my right.
He will bring me out into the light;
I will see his righteousness.[r]
[10] Then my enemy will see it

7:10 [s] Ps 35:26 [t] Isa 51:23 [u] Zec 10:5

and will be covered with shame,[s]
she who said to me,
"Where is the LORD your God?"
My eyes will see her downfall;[t]
even now she will be trampled[u]
underfoot
like mire in the streets.

7:11 [v] Isa 54:11

[11] The day for building your walls[v]
will come,
the day for extending your
boundaries.
[12] In that day people will come to you
from Assyria and the cities of
Egypt,
even from Egypt to the Euphrates
and from sea to sea
and from mountain to

7:12 [w] Isa 19:23-25

mountain.[w]

[13] The earth will become desolate
because of its inhabitants,

7:13 [x] Isa 3:10-11

as the result of their deeds.[x]

Prayer and Praise

7:14 [y] Mic 5:4 [z] Ps 23:4 [a] Jer 50:19

[14] Shepherd[y] your people with your
staff,[z]
the flock of your inheritance,
which lives by itself in a forest,
in fertile pasturelands.[a]
Let them feed in Bashan and
Gilead[a]
as in days long ago.

[15] "As in the days when you came out
of Egypt,

7:15 [b] Ex 3:20; Ps 78:12

I will show them my wonders.[b]"
[16] Nations will see and be ashamed,[c]

7:16 [c] Isa 26:11

deprived of all their power.
They will lay their hands on their
mouths
and their ears will become deaf.
[17] They will lick dust like a snake,
like creatures that crawl on the
ground.
They will come trembling out of
their dens;

7:17 [d] Isa 25:3; 49:23; 59:19

they will turn in fear[d] to the
LORD our God
and will be afraid of you.
[18] Who is a God like you,

7:18 [e] Isa 43:25; Jer 50:20 [f] Ps 103:8-13 [g] Mic 2:12 [h] Ex 34:9 [i] Ps 103:9 [j] Jer 32:41

who pardons sin[e] and forgives[f]
the transgression
of the remnant[g] of his
inheritance?[h]
You do not stay angry[i] forever
but delight to show mercy.[j]
[19] You will again have compassion on
us;
you will tread our sins underfoot

7:19 [k] Isa 43:25 [l] Jer 31:34

and hurl all our iniquities[k] into
the depths of the sea.[l]
[20] You will be true to Jacob,
and show mercy to Abraham,
as you pledged on oath to our

7:20 [m] Dt 7:8; Lk 1:72

fathers[m]
in days long ago.

a 14 Or *in the middle of Carmel*

NAHUM

In what way is God's justice as portrayed in Nahum redemptive?

♦ *God destroys the forces of evil to create a new world of freedom (Nahum 1:13) and peace. His acts of retribution play a part in his ultimate plan of fulfilling his covenant promises for his people. Nahum's prophecy underlines the necessity of Jesus' sacrifice on the cross as a means of satisfying God's righteous demand for justice.*

When will the peace promised in this verse come? (Nahum 1:15)

♦ *The people of Judah heard great news: Nineveh had been utterly destroyed (612 B.C.) and, soon afterward, Assyrian forces had suffered their final defeat (609 B.C.). The second promise of peace tells the good news of the Messiah: He breaks the power of evil and will achieve final victory at his second coming.*

Jesus in Nahum Nahum, whose name means "comfort," predicted the fall of Nineveh, Assyria's capital, and spoke a word of consolation to the beleaguered Israelites (Nahum 2:2). This comfort, however, stems not so much from the prediction of the downfall of Nineveh as from the promise that God would uphold justice and establish true peace. Without explicitly saying so, Nahum directed us to Jesus, who will later establish the kingdom of peace (Micah 5:4–5; Romans 5:1; Ephesians 2:14).

Nahum's prophecy depicts God as a "jealous and avenging God" (Nahum 1:2) whose way is often "in the whirlwind and the storm" (verse 3). But God also "cares for those who trust in him" (verse 7). God's justice and mercy come together in Jesus, to whom the Father has entrusted all judgment (John 4:22; 9:39). When the time comes for God to judge sin, Jesus will separate those who have aligned themselves with his heart of righteousness from those who have lived life without regard for him. Those who trust in Jesus' atoning sacrifice will live with him eternally (Matthew 25:31–46).

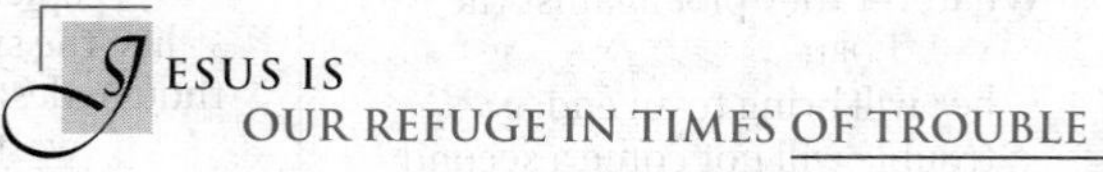

JESUS IS OUR REFUGE IN TIMES OF TROUBLE

1:1 [a] Isa 13:1; 19:1; Jer 23:33-34 [b] Jnh 1:2; Na 2:8; Zep 2:13

1 An oracle[a] concerning Nineveh.[b] The book of the vision of Nahum the Elkoshite.

The LORD's Anger Against Nineveh

1:2 [c] Ex 20:5 [d] Dt 32:41; Ps 94:1

2 The LORD is a jealous[c] and
avenging God;
the LORD takes vengeance[d] and
is filled with wrath.
The LORD takes vengeance on his
foes
and maintains his wrath against
his enemies.

1:3 [e] Ne 9:17 [f] Ex 34:7 [g] Ps 104:3

3 The LORD is slow to anger[e] and
great in power;
the LORD will not leave the guilty
unpunished.[f]
His way is in the whirlwind and the
storm,
and clouds[g] are the dust of his
feet.
4 He rebukes the sea and dries it up;
he makes all the rivers run dry.

1:4 [h] Isa 33:9

Bashan and Carmel[h] wither
and the blossoms of Lebanon
fade.

1:5 [i] Ex 19:18 [j] Mic 1:4

5 The mountains quake[i] before him
and the hills melt away.[j]
The earth trembles at his presence,
the world and all who live in it.
6 Who can withstand his
indignation?

1:6 [k] Mal 3:2 [l] Jer 10:10 [m] 1Ki 19:11

Who can endure[k] his fierce
anger?
His wrath is poured out like fire;[l]
the rocks are shattered[m] before
him.

1:7 [n] Jer 33:11 [o] Ps 1:6

7 The LORD is good,[n]
a refuge in times of trouble.
He cares for[o] those who trust in
him,
8 but with an overwhelming flood
he will make an end of ⌞Nineveh⌟;
he will pursue his foes into
darkness.

9 Whatever they plot against the
LORD
he[a] will bring to an end;
trouble will not come a second
time.

1:10 [p] 2Sa 23:6 [q] Isa 5:24; Mal 4:1

10 They will be entangled among
thorns[p]
and drunk from their wine;
they will be consumed like dry
stubble.[b][q]

11 From you, ⌞O Nineveh,⌟ has one
come forth
who plots evil against the LORD
and counsels wickedness.

12 This is what the LORD says:

1:12 [r] Isa 10:34 [s] Isa 54:6-8; La 3:31-32

"Although they have allies and are
numerous,
they will be cut off[r] and pass
away.
Although I have afflicted you,
⌞O Judah,⌟
I will afflict you no more.[s]

1:13 [t] Isa 9:4

13 Now I will break their yoke[t] from
your neck
and tear your shackles away."

14 The LORD has given a command
concerning you, ⌞Nineveh⌟:

1:14 [u] Isa 14:22 [v] Mic 5:13 [w] Eze 32:22-23

"You will have no descendants to
bear your name.[u]
I will destroy the carved images[v]
and cast idols
that are in the temple of your
gods.
I will prepare your grave,[w]
for you are vile."

15 Look, there on the mountains,

1:15 [x] Isa 40:9; Ro 10:15 [y] Isa 52:7 [z] Lev 23:2-4 [a] Isa 52:1

the feet of one who brings good
news,[x]
who proclaims peace![y]
Celebrate your festivals,[z] O Judah,
and fulfill your vows.
No more will the wicked invade
you;[a]
they will be completely
destroyed.

Nineveh to Fall

2:1 [b] Jer 51:20

2 An attacker[b] advances against
you, ⌞Nineveh⌟.
Guard the fortress,
watch the road,
brace yourselves,
marshal all your strength!

2:2 [c] Eze 37:23 [d] Isa 60:15

2 The LORD will restore[c] the
splendor[d] of Jacob
like the splendor of Israel,
though destroyers have laid them
waste
and have ruined their vines.

2:3 [e] Eze 23:14-15

3 The shields of his soldiers are red;
the warriors are clad in scarlet.[e]

[a] 9 Or *What do you foes plot against the LORD? / He*
[b] 10 The meaning of the Hebrew for this verse is uncertain.

DISCOVERY 224

HOPE THROUGH HARD TIMES

There are many situations in life that cause indescribable pain. During those seasons it is easy to cry out in bewilderment, "If God is so good, then why is this happening to me?" The message of the prophet Nahum is that God is good—all of the time—no matter what life hurls our way at any given moment.

Nahum referred to God as "a refuge in times of trouble" who "cares for those who trust in him" (Nahum 1:7). Although God's goodness doesn't guarantee a trouble-free life, it does sustain us through troubled times. Even when our world seems to be spinning out of control and the walls appear to be crashing in all around us, we know that God's loving arms offer a safe retreat. In fact, he is the only safe place to which we can run and hide (Psalm 31:1–5; 71:1–3).

When we are plodding along through times of loss and grief, mornings can be the most difficult time. Sometimes it requires more energy than we can muster simply to crawl out of bed and face another day. But if we're willing to start the day focusing our attention on our loving Father, we will find that God will imbue us with the inner strength to meet the demands of each hour.

Jesus empathizes with our pain, because he personally endured untold agony and grief on account of our sin. The writer to the Hebrews offers words of hope in the midst of our darkness: "Since we have a great high priest who has gone through the heavens, Jesus the Son of God, let us hold firmly to the faith we profess. For we do not have a high priest who is unable to sympathize with our weaknesses, but we have one who has been tempted in every way, just as we are—yet was without sin. Let us then approach the throne of grace with confidence, so that we may receive mercy and find grace to help us in our time of need" (Hebrews 4:14–16).

Like the Canaanite woman whose daughter was suffering terribly from demon-possession, we can approach Jesus with a simple but impassioned request: "Lord, help me!" (Matthew 15:25), and he will respond with love and grace to our deep need. When our resources are spent, he will surround us with people who will reach out with his love. When we cannot bring ourselves to utter even a one-sentence prayer, when the load of grief is so heavy that we feel as though we cannot endure another hour, our Lord will move his people to encourage us, reach out to us, pray for us and cry with us.

Self-Discovery: *Do you feel the need to explain your situation to God in detail? Are you anxious about using the "proper" format or just the right words in prayer? When have you last cried out, "Lord, help me!" Did he hear you? How do you know?*

GO TO DISCOVERY 225 ON PAGE 1210

The metal on the chariots flashes
on the day they are made ready;
the spears of pine are
brandished.[a]

2:4 [f]Jer 4:13
[4] The chariots[f] storm through the
streets,
rushing back and forth through
the squares.
They look like flaming torches;
they dart about like lightning.

[5] He summons his picked troops,
2:5 [g]Jer 46:12
yet they stumble[g] on their way.
They dash to the city wall;
the protective shield is put in
place.
2:6 [h]Na 3:13
[6] The river gates[h] are thrown open
and the palace collapses.
[7] It is decreed[b] that ⌊the city⌋
be exiled and carried away.
2:7 [i]Isa 59:11 [j]Isa 32:12
Its slave girls moan[i] like doves
and beat upon their breasts.[j]
[8] Nineveh is like a pool,
and its water is draining away.
"Stop! Stop!" they cry,
but no one turns back.
[9] Plunder the silver!
Plunder the gold!
The supply is endless,
the wealth from all its treasures!
[10] She is pillaged, plundered,
stripped!
Hearts melt, knees give way,
bodies tremble, every face grows
2:10 [k]Isa 29:22
pale.[k]
2:11 [l]Isa 5:29
[11] Where now is the lions' den,[l]
the place where they fed their
young,
where the lion and lioness went,
and the cubs, with nothing to
fear?
2:12 [m]Jer 51:34
[12] The lion killed[m] enough for his
cubs
and strangled the prey for his
mate,
filling his lairs with the kill
and his dens with the prey.

2:13 [n]Jer 21:13; Na 3:5 [o]Ps 46:9
[13] "I am against[n] you,"
declares the LORD Almighty.
"I will burn up your chariots in
smoke,[o]
and the sword will devour your
young lions.
I will leave you no prey on the
earth.
The voices of your messengers
will no longer be heard."

Woe to Nineveh

3:1 [p]Eze 22:2; Mic 3:10
3 Woe to the city of blood,[p]
full of lies,
full of plunder,
never without victims!
[2] The crack of whips,
the clatter of wheels,
galloping horses
and jolting chariots!
[3] Charging cavalry,
flashing swords
and glittering spears!
Many casualties,
piles of dead,
bodies without number,
3:3 [q]2Ki 19:35; Isa 34:3
people stumbling over the
corpses[q]—
[4] all because of the wanton lust of a
harlot,
alluring, the mistress of
3:4 [r]Isa 47:9 [s]Isa 23:17; Eze 16:25-29
sorceries,[r]
who enslaved nations by her
prostitution[s]
and peoples by her witchcraft.

3:5 [t]Na 2:13 [u]Jer 13:22 [v]Isa 47:3
[5] "I am against[t] you," declares the
LORD Almighty.
"I will lift your skirts[u] over your
face.
I will show the nations your
nakedness[v]
and the kingdoms your shame.
3:6 [w]Job 9:31 [x]1Sa 2:30; Jer 51:37 [y]Isa 14:16
[6] I will pelt you with filth,[w]
I will treat you with contempt[x]
and make you a spectacle.[y]
[7] All who see you will flee from you
and say,
3:7 [z]Na 1:1 [a]Jer 15:5 [b]Isa 51:19
'Nineveh[z] is in ruins—who will
mourn for her?'[a]
Where can I find anyone to
comfort[b] you?"

3:8 [c]Am 6:2 [d]Jer 46:25 [e]Isa 19:6-9
[8] Are you better than[c] Thebes,[c] [d]
situated on the Nile,[e]
with water around her?
The river was her defense,
the waters her wall.
3:9 [f]2Ch 12:3 [g]Eze 27:10 [h]Eze 30:5
[9] Cush[d] [f] and Egypt were her
boundless strength;
Put[g] and Libya[h] were among her
allies.
3:10 [i]Isa 20:4 [j]Isa 13:16; Hos 13:16
[10] Yet she was taken captive[i]
and went into exile.
Her infants were dashed[j] to pieces

[a] 3 Hebrew; Septuagint and Syriac / *the horsemen rush to and fro* [b] 7 The meaning of the Hebrew for this word is uncertain. [c] 8 Hebrew *No Amon* [d] 9 That is, the upper Nile region

at the head of every street.
Lots were cast for her nobles,
and all her great men were put
in chains.
3:11 k Isa 49:26 11 You too will become drunk;[k]
l Isa 2:10 you will go into hiding[l]
and seek refuge from the enemy.

12 All your fortresses are like fig trees
with their first ripe fruit;
when they are shaken,
3:12 m Isa 28:4 the figs[m] fall into the mouth of
the eater.
3:13 13 Look at your troops—
n Isa 19:16; they are all women![n]
Jer 50:37 The gates[o] of your land
o Na 2:6 are wide open to your enemies;
p Isa 45:2 fire has consumed their bars.[p]
3:14 14 Draw water for the siege,[q]
q 2Ch 32:4 r Na 2:1 strengthen your defenses![r]
Work the clay,
tread the mortar,
repair the brickwork!
15 There the fire will devour you;
the sword will cut you down
and, like grasshoppers, consume
you.
3:15 Multiply like grasshoppers,
s Joel 1:4 multiply like locusts![s]

16 You have increased the number of
your merchants
till they are more than the stars
of the sky,
but like locusts they strip the land
and then fly away.
17 Your guards are like locusts,[t] 3:17 t Jer 51:27
your officials like swarms of
locusts
that settle in the walls on a cold
day—
but when the sun appears they fly
away,
and no one knows where.

18 O king of Assyria, your shepherds[a] 3:18
slumber;[u] u Ps 76:5-6
your nobles lie down to rest.[v] v Isa 56:10
Your people are scattered[w] on the w 1Ki 22:17
mountains
with no one to gather them. 3:19
19 Nothing can heal your wound;[x] x Jer 30:13;
your injury is fatal. Mic 1:9
Everyone who hears the news y Job 27:23;
about you La 2:15;
claps his hands[y] at your fall, Zep 2:15
for who has not felt
your endless cruelty?

[a] 18 Or *rulers*

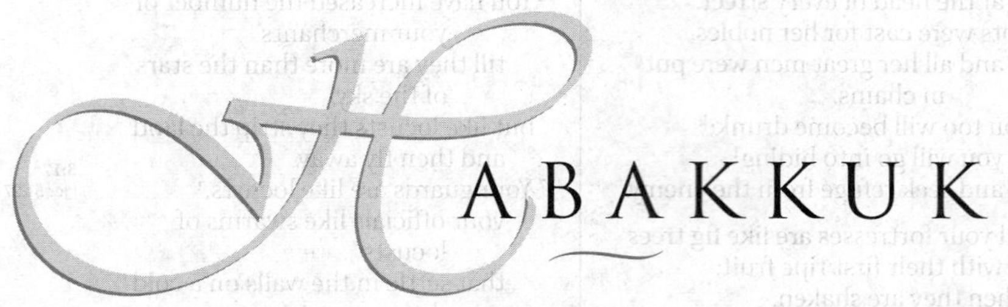
HABAKKUK

What is the significance of the expression, "be utterly amazed"? (Habakkuk 1:5)

- *Centuries after Habakkuk wrote his short book, the apostle Paul quoted him to support the point that God will judge those who reject Jesus (Acts 13:41).*

What answer did Habakkuk receive from God regarding his painful questions about injustice? (Habakkuk 2:1–4)

- *Habakkuk learned that, despite the devastating circumstances of a given moment in time, God's promises are unfailing and his purposes consistent. This understanding instilled hope and confidence in the prophet. God's perfect plan for humanity reached its zenith in the atoning death and resurrection of his Son.*

Jesus in Habakkuk Most Old Testament prophets spoke for God, but Habakkuk addressed God on behalf of the people. His first two chapters consist of two questions or complaints and two unexpected and unwelcome answers from God. Habakkuk foresaw a devastating invasion by a more powerful nation. While God's power is infinitely greater than anything on earth, he seemed to be silent while Babylon grew increasingly powerful. Examine Habakkuk's feelings as he questioned God. Then notice the change in the prophet's perspective in chapter 3. Read especially Habakkuk 3:17–18 for a beautiful confession that, because God is his Savior, Habakkuk and all God's people, past, present and future, could rejoice regardless of external circumstances.

In Habakkuk we see Jesus both as the One who reveals the future (Habakkuk 2:2–3; see Hebrews 1:1–2) and as the object of our faith (Habakkuk 2:4). Habakkuk used the clause "the righteous will live by his faith," which is quoted several times in the New Testament (see Romans 1:17; Galatians 3:11; Hebrews 10:38). Our faith in God's promises powers up our confidence in Jesus, his promised One.

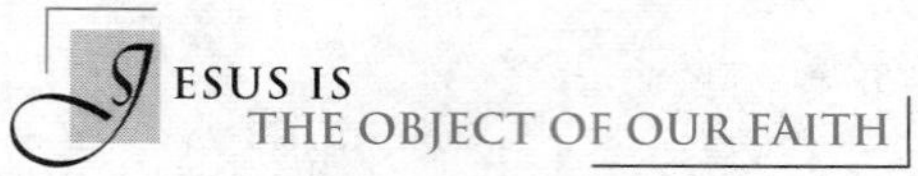
JESUS IS
THE OBJECT OF OUR FAITH

1:1 [a]Na 1:1 **1** The oracle[a] that Habakkuk the prophet received.

Habakkuk's Complaint

[2]How long, O LORD, must I call for
help,
1:2 [b]Ps 13:1-2; 22:1-2 [c]Jer 14:9 but you do not listen?[b]
Or cry out to you, "Violence!"
but you do not save?[c]
[3]Why do you make me look at
injustice?
1:3 [d]ver 13 [e]Jer 20:8 [f]Ps 55:9 Why do you tolerate[d] wrong?
Destruction and violence[e] are
before me;
there is strife,[f] and conflict
abounds.
1:4 [g]Ps 119:126 [h]Job 19:7; Isa 1:23; 5:20; Eze 9:9 [4]Therefore the law[g] is paralyzed,
and justice never prevails.
The wicked hem in the righteous,
so that justice is perverted.[h]

The LORD's Answer

[5]"Look at the nations and watch—
1:5 [i]Isa 29:9 [j]Ac 13:41* and be utterly amazed.[i]
For I am going to do something in
your days
that you would not believe,
even if you were told.[j]
1:6 [k]2Ki 24:2 [6]I am raising up the Babylonians,[a][k]
that ruthless and impetuous
people,
who sweep across the whole earth
to seize dwelling places not their
own.[l] 1:6 [l]Jer 13:20
[7]They are a feared and dreaded
people;[m] 1:7 [m]Isa 18:7; Jer 39:5-9
they are a law to themselves
and promote their own honor.
[8]Their horses are swifter[n] than
leopards, 1:8 [n]Jer 4:13
fiercer than wolves at dusk.
Their cavalry gallops headlong;
their horsemen come from afar.
They fly like a vulture swooping to
devour;
[9] they all come bent on violence.
Their hordes[b] advance like a desert
wind
and gather prisoners[o] like sand. 1:9 [o]Hab 2:5
[10]They deride kings
and scoff at rulers.[p] 1:10 [p]2Ch 36:6
They laugh at all fortified cities;
they build earthen ramps and
capture them.
[11]Then they sweep past like the
wind[q] and go on— 1:11 [q]Jer 4:11-12 [r]Da 4:30
guilty men, whose own strength
is their god."[r]

Habakkuk's Second Complaint

[12]O LORD, are you not from
everlasting?
My God, my Holy One,[s] we will
not die. 1:12 [s]Isa 31:1 [t]Isa 10:6
O LORD, you have appointed[t] them
to execute judgment;
O Rock, you have ordained them
to punish.
[13]Your eyes are too pure to look on
evil;
you cannot tolerate wrong.[u] 1:13 [u]La 3:34-36
Why then do you tolerate the
treacherous?
Why are you silent while the
wicked
swallow up those more
righteous than themselves?
[14]You have made men like fish in the
sea,
like sea creatures that have no
ruler.
[15]The wicked foe pulls all of them up
with hooks,[v] 1:15 [v]Isa 19:8 [w]Jer 16:16
he catches them in his net,[w]

NO AUTOMATIC ENTITLEMENT

How could a loving God abandon his chosen people to the cruel and pagan Babylonians? Such a notion might have seemed unthinkable, but the walls can suddenly come crashing down when people begin to assume that they are automatically entitled to God's blessings. God is more concerned with our spiritual walk than with our degree of physical or emotional comfort.

Generations after the prophet Habakkuk had proclaimed God's message to the people of Israel, Paul quoted Habakkuk 1:5 while speaking to a congregation in a Jewish synagogue. He encouraged his hearers not to allow complacency to prevent them from accepting Jesus as God's Messiah (Acts 13:40–41). Just as God had instructed Habakkuk and his people that he was at work to punish evil and establish righteousness, to bring about an amazing redemption of his people in the end, so Paul reminded his hearers of how foolish it would be to fail to see God at work in and through his precious Son, Jesus Christ, the Promised One.

[a]6 Or *Chaldeans* [b]9 The meaning of the Hebrew for this word is uncertain.

Yet I Will Rejoice

Sometimes the prophets in the Old Testament strike us as a bit intimidating. They appear to be spiritual superheroes as they speak God's truth in the face of nearly insufferable persecution and sometimes surprising directives from God. Many of us can relate immediately to Habakkuk, however. He began his book by complaining! Then, despite his numerous questions and doubts, he discovered amazing truths about his God.

Habakkuk's initial complaint seems quite valid (Habakkuk 1:1–4). He observed the moral decay all around him and wondered where God was. How could the Lord just sit back and allow these terrible injustices to go unchecked?

God's response was interesting (verses 5–11). He wasn't preoccupied with other things. He was watching and keeping an account of wrongs. And he was about to do something about sin and evil. The only problem for the prophet was that God's solution was the *last* thing the prophet had expected. Certainly God intended to judge the wicked—but he was planning to carry out that justice by sending the Babylonians to conquer the nation of Israel!

Now we're as confused as Habakkuk (verses 12–17). How can God punish evil with *more* evil? Doesn't that go against his nature? If God is holy and unable to tolerate impurity, how can he *use* it for his own purposes?

God then responded in Habakkuk 2:2–20 to the prophet's second complaint to God: "Why are you silent while the wicked swallow up those more righteous than themselves?" (Habakkuk 1:13). In this passage the Lord directed his people as to how he wanted them to live—despite the evil all around them: "The righteous will live by his faith" (Habakkuk 2:4). This statement first implies that *God's people accept God's methods and his timing*, even when they don't understand. Habakkuk needed to come to terms with the fact that the despised nation of Babylon fit into God's plan—whether or not the Babylonians realized it.

Living by faith means that *God's people accept God's words*. It means believing that even if every shred of evidence points in the opposite direction, God is in the right, and we can bank on God's word as our only reliable investment. There may be times when we doubt God's purpose because of our inability to see a situation from his perspective, but as we get to know him better, we can declare along with the prophet: "Yet I will rejoice in the LORD, I will be joyful in God my Savior" (Habakkuk 3:18).

Our Lord Jesus struggled with the same issue of trusting God's plan as he poured out his soul to his Father in Gethsemane just prior to his arrest. "My Father," he pleaded, "if it is possible, may this cup be taken from me. Yet not as I will, but as you will" (Matthew 26:36). Could good really result from such unspeakable evil? Could God's plan truly be to offer ultimate hope to humanity through the sacrifice of his own Son in one of the most bitter scenes in all of human history? Notice that Jesus, like Habakkuk, used the word *yet*. "Yet I will rejoice in the LORD," asserted Habakkuk. "Yet not as I will, but as you will," declared Jesus Christ in his exemplary prayer of submission to his Father's perfect plan.

Self-Discovery: *Finish the following sentence in a way that is meaningful to you in terms of your Christian walk: "Even though____________________, yet I will__________________________."*

GO TO DISCOVERY 226 ON PAGE 1218

he gathers them up in his dragnet;
and so he rejoices and is glad.
16 Therefore he sacrifices to his net
and burns incense[x] to his dragnet,
for by his net he lives in luxury
and enjoys the choicest food.
17 Is he to keep on emptying his net,
destroying nations without mercy?[y]

1:16 [x] Jer 44:8
1:17 [y] Isa 14:6; 19:8

2

1 I will stand at my watch[z]
and station myself on the ramparts;[a]
I will look to see what he will say[b] to me,
and what answer I am to give to this complaint.[a][c]

2:1 [z] Isa 21:8 [a] Ps 48:13 [b] Ps 85:8 [c] Ps 5:3

The LORD's Answer

2 Then the LORD replied:

"Write[d] down the revelation
and make it plain on tablets
so that a herald[b] may run with it.
3 For the revelation awaits an appointed time;
it speaks of the end[e]
and will not prove false.
Though it linger, wait[f] for it;
it[c] will certainly come and will not delay.[g]

2:2 [d] Rev 1:19
2:3 [e] Da 8:17; 10:14 [f] Ps 27:14 [g] Eze 12:25; Heb 10:37-38

4 "See, he is puffed up;
his desires are not upright—
but the righteous will live by his faith[d][h]—

2:4 [h] Ro 1:17*; Gal 3:11*; Heb 10:37-38*

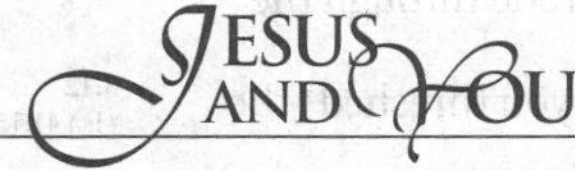

A CLEAR MESSAGE

God instructed Habakkuk to "write down the revelation and make it plain on tablets so that a herald may run with it" (Habakkuk 2:2). He wanted the people to understand, without any room for misinterpretation or doubt, what he was saying, and he wanted to make certain that each and every individual received the word. The message was about the future of God's people, the "time . . . of the end" (verse 3). In the New Testament God gave the apostle John a more exact vision of the end times, referring to the message as "the revelation of Jesus Christ" (Revelation 1:1). Jesus is the One who reveals the future, as well as the only One we can trust to take us through whatever comes our way in the days ahead.

5 indeed, wine[i] betrays him;
he is arrogant and never at rest.
Because he is as greedy as the grave[e]
and like death is never satisfied,[j]
he gathers to himself all the nations
and takes captive all the peoples.

2:5 [i] Pr 20:1 [j] Pr 27:20; 30:15-16

6 "Will not all of them taunt[k] him with ridicule and scorn, saying,

" 'Woe to him who piles up stolen goods
and makes himself wealthy by extortion![l]
How long must this go on?'
7 Will not your debtors[f] suddenly arise?
Will they not wake up and make you tremble?
Then you will become their victim.[m]
8 Because you have plundered many nations,
the peoples who are left will plunder you.[n]
For you have shed man's blood;[o]
you have destroyed lands and cities and everyone in them.

2:6 [k] Isa 14:4 [l] Am 2:8
2:7 [m] Pr 29:1
2:8 [n] Isa 33:1; Zec 2:8-9 [o] ver 17

9 "Woe to him who builds[p] his realm by unjust gain
to set his nest on high,
to escape the clutches of ruin!
10 You have plotted the ruin[q] of many peoples,
shaming[r] your own house and forfeiting your life.
11 The stones[s] of the wall will cry out,
and the beams of the woodwork will echo it.

2:9 [p] Jer 22:13
2:10 [q] Jer 26:19 [r] ver 16
2:11 [s] Jos 24:27; Lk 19:40

12 "Woe to him who builds a city with bloodshed[t]
and establishes a town by crime!
13 Has not the LORD Almighty determined
that the people's labor is only fuel for the fire,[u]
that the nations exhaust themselves for nothing?[v]
14 For the earth will be filled with the knowledge of the glory[w] of the LORD,
as the waters cover the sea.[x]

2:12 [t] Mic 3:10
2:13 [u] Isa 50:11 [v] Isa 47:13
2:14 [w] Nu 14:21 [x] Isa 11:9

[a] 1 Or *and what to answer when I am rebuked*
[b] 2 Or *so that whoever reads it*
[c] 3 Or *Though he linger, wait for him; / he*
[d] 4 Or *faithfulness*
[e] 5 Hebrew *Sheol*
[f] 7 Or *creditors*

15 "Woe to him who gives drink to his
neighbors,
pouring it from the wineskin till
they are drunk,
so that he can gaze on their
naked bodies.

2:16 [y] ver 10 [z] La 4:21 [a] Isa 51:22

16 You will be filled with shame[y]
instead of glory.
Now it is your turn! Drink and
be exposed[a]![z]
The cup[a] from the LORD's right
hand is coming around to
you,
and disgrace will cover your
glory.

2:17 [b] Jer 51:35 [c] Jer 50:15 [d] ver 8

17 The violence[b] you have done to
Lebanon will overwhelm
you,
and your destruction of animals
will terrify you.[c]
For you have shed man's blood;[d]
you have destroyed lands and
cities and everyone in
them.

2:18 [e] Jer 5:21 [f] Ps 115:4-5; Jer 10:14

18 "Of what value is an idol,[e] since a
man has carved it?
Or an image that teaches lies?
For he who makes it trusts in his
own creation;
he makes idols that cannot
speak.[f]
19 Woe to him who says to wood,
'Come to life!'

2:19 [g] 1Ki 18:27 [h] Jer 10:4

Or to lifeless stone, 'Wake up!'[g]
Can it give guidance?
It is covered with gold and
silver;[h]
there is no breath in it.

2:20 [i] Ps 11:4 [j] Isa 41:1

20 But the LORD is in his holy temple;[i]
let all the earth be silent[j] before
him."

Habakkuk's Prayer

3 A prayer of Habakkuk the prophet. On *shigionoth*.[b]

3:2 [k] Ps 44:1 [l] Ps 119:120 [m] Ps 85:6 [n] Isa 54:8

2 LORD, I have heard[k] of your fame;
I stand in awe[l] of your deeds,
O LORD.
Renew[m] them in our day,
in our time make them known;
in wrath remember mercy.[n]

3 God came from Teman,
the Holy One from Mount Paran.
Selah[c]

3:3 [o] Ps 48:10

His glory covered the heavens
and his praise filled the earth.[o]
4 His splendor was like the sunrise;
rays flashed from his hand,
where his power was hidden.
5 Plague went before him;
pestilence followed his steps.
6 He stood, and shook the earth;
he looked, and made the nations
tremble.

3:6 [p] Ps 114:1-6

The ancient mountains crumbled
and the age-old hills collapsed.[p]
His ways are eternal.

3:7 [q] Jdg 7:24-25 [r] Ex 15:14

7 I saw the tents of Cushan in
distress,
the dwellings of Midian[q] in
anguish.[r]

3:8 [s] Ex 7:20 [t] Ps 68:17

8 Were you angry with the rivers,[s]
O LORD?
Was your wrath against the
streams?
Did you rage against the sea
when you rode with your horses
and your victorious chariots?[t]

3:9 [u] Ps 7:12-13

9 You uncovered your bow,
you called for many arrows.[u]
Selah
You split the earth with rivers;
10 the mountains saw you and
writhed.

3:10 [v] Ps 98:7 [w] Ps 93:3

Torrents of water swept by;
the deep roared[v]
and lifted its waves[w] on high.

3:11 [x] Jos 10:13 [y] Ps 18:14

11 Sun and moon stood still[x] in the
heavens
at the glint of your flying arrows,[y]
at the lightning of your flashing
spear.

3:12 [z] Isa 41:15

12 In wrath you strode through the
earth
and in anger you threshed[z] the
nations.

3:13 [a] Ps 20:6; 28:8 [b] Ps 68:21; 110:6

13 You came out to deliver[a] your
people,
to save your anointed one.
You crushed[b] the leader of the land
of wickedness,
you stripped him from head to
foot. *Selah*
14 With his own spear you pierced his
head

3:14 [c] Jdg 7:22

when his warriors stormed out
to scatter us,[c]
gloating as though about to devour

[a] *16* Masoretic Text; Dead Sea Scrolls, Aquila, Vulgate and Syriac (see also Septuagint) *and stagger* [b] *1* Probably a literary or musical term [c] *3* A word of uncertain meaning; possibly a musical term; also in verses 9 and 13

3:14
[d] Ps 64:2-5

the wretched[d] who were in
hiding.
15 You trampled the sea with your
horses,
churning the great waters.[e]

3:15
[e] Ex 15:8;
Ps 77:19

16 I heard and my heart pounded,
my lips quivered at the sound;
decay crept into my bones,
and my legs trembled.
Yet I will wait patiently for the day
of calamity
to come on the nation invading
us.
17 Though the fig tree does not bud
and there are no grapes on the
vines,
though the olive crop fails
and the fields produce no food,[f]
though there are no sheep in the
pen
and no cattle in the stalls,[g]

3:17
[f] Joel 1:10-12,18
[g] Jer 5:17

18 yet I will rejoice in the LORD,[h]
I will be joyful in God my Savior.

3:18
[h] Isa 61:10;
Php 4:4

19 The Sovereign LORD is my
strength;[i]
he makes my feet like the feet of
a deer,
he enables me to go on the
heights.[j]

3:19
[i] Dt 33:29;
Ps 46:1-5
[j] Dt 32:13;
2Sa 22:34;
Ps 18:33

For the director of music. On my
stringed instruments.

ZEPHANIAH

In what way does the tone of Zephaniah change from beginning to end?

♦ *Zephaniah begins with a warning of judgment (Zephaniah 1:2–3) and ends with a ringing affirmation of coming salvation for both the nations (Zephaniah 3:9) and the remnant of Israel (Zephaniah 3:19–20). Note the change in tone from the warnings to the hope expressed in chapter 3:14–17. The message of salvation is clear and is expressed with exuberance.*

Why would God reward Judah? (Zephaniah 2:7)

♦ *Judah had broken her covenant with God and deserved nothing but punishment. But after the judgment God would fulfill his promise to make his people into a great nation and give them all of the promised land as an eternal possession. It is certainly significant that the long-awaited Messiah would proceed from Judah.*

Jesus in Zephaniah The book of Zephaniah is set in the time of King Josiah (640–609 B.C.) and underscores the decadent conditions that led to Josiah's attempts at reform. Look for the prophet's vivid, emotionally charged language, and notice the balance Zephaniah painted between God's anger and his compassion.

Zephaniah follows a logical progression from its brief introduction through its discussion of the coming judgment of Judah and Jerusalem. The last portion deals with God's judgment of the nations surrounding Judah and the promise of the restoration of Jerusalem.

Although there is no overt mention of the Messiah, it is certainly possible to see Jesus in Zephaniah's description of the all-powerful King of Israel (Zephaniah 3:15) and of the One who defends the meek, the humble and the poor (Zephaniah 2:2; 3:12; Matthew 5:3,5; Luke 1:52–53). He is coming on the "day of the LORD" (Zephaniah 1:14) to judge those who have turned against him and to destroy wicked civilizations, while restoring all of creation to the way he intended it to be (Matthew 13:40–42; 24:29–31; Revelation 6:7; 21:1–5).

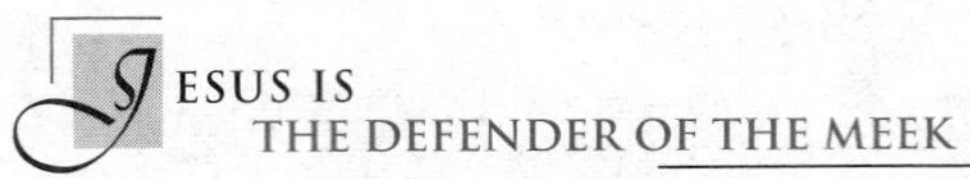

JESUS IS THE DEFENDER OF THE MEEK

1 The word of the LORD that came to Zephaniah son of Cushi, the son of Gedaliah, the son of Amariah, the son of Hezekiah, during the reign of Josiah[a] son of Amon king of Judah:

Warning of Coming Destruction

2 "I will sweep away everything
from the face of the earth,"[b]
declares the LORD.
3 "I will sweep away both men and animals;
I will sweep away the birds of the air[c]
and the fish of the sea.
The wicked will have only heaps of rubble[*a*]
when I cut off man from the face of the earth,"[d]
declares the LORD.

Against Judah

4 "I will stretch out my hand[e] against Judah
and against all who live in Jerusalem.
I will cut off from this place every remnant of Baal,[f]
the names of the pagan and the idolatrous priests[g]—
5 those who bow down on the roofs
to worship the starry host,
those who bow down and swear by the LORD
and who also swear by Molech,[*b*][h]
6 those who turn back from following[i] the LORD
and neither seek[j] the LORD nor inquire[k] of him.
7 Be silent[l] before the Sovereign LORD,
for the day of the LORD[m] is near.
The LORD has prepared a sacrifice;[n]
he has consecrated those he has invited.
8 On the day of the LORD's sacrifice
I will punish[o] the princes
and the king's sons[p]
and all those clad
in foreign clothes.
9 On that day I will punish
all who avoid stepping on the threshold,[*c*]
who fill the temple of their gods
with violence and deceit.[q]
10 "On that day," declares the LORD,
"a cry will go up from the Fish Gate,[r]

1:1 [a] 2Ki 22:1; 2Ch 34:1-35:25
1:2 [b] Ge 6:7
1:3 [c] Jer 4:25 [d] Hos 4:3
1:4 [e] Jer 6:12 [f] Mic 5:13 [g] Hos 10:5
1:5 [h] Jer 5:7
1:6 [i] Isa 1:4; Jer 2:13 [j] Isa 9:13 [k] Hos 7:7
1:7 [l] Hab 2:20; Zec 2:13 [m] ver 14; Isa 13:6 [n] Isa 34:6; Jer 46:10
1:8 [o] Isa 24:21 [p] Jer 39:6
1:9 [q] Am 3:10
1:10 [r] 2Ch 33:14

wailing from the New Quarter,
and a loud crash from the hills.
11 Wail,[s] you who live in the market district[*d*];
all your merchants will be wiped out,
all who trade with[*e*] silver will be ruined.[t]
12 At that time I will search Jerusalem with lamps
and punish those who are complacent,[u]
who are like wine left on its dregs,[v]
who think, 'The LORD will do nothing,[w]
either good or bad.'
13 Their wealth will be plundered,[x]
their houses demolished.
They will build houses
but not live in them;
they will plant vineyards
but not drink the wine.[y]

The Great Day of the LORD

14 "The great day of the LORD[z] is near[a]—
near and coming quickly.
Listen! The cry on the day of the LORD will be bitter,
the shouting of the warrior there.
15 That day will be a day of wrath,
a day of distress and anguish,
a day of trouble and ruin,
a day of darkness and gloom,
a day of clouds and blackness,[b]
16 a day of trumpet and battle cry[c]
against the fortified cities
and against the corner towers.[d]
17 I will bring distress on the people
and they will walk like blind[e] men,
because they have sinned
against the LORD.
Their blood will be poured out[f] like dust
and their entrails like filth.[g]
18 Neither their silver nor their gold
will be able to save them
on the day of the LORD's wrath.[h]
In the fire of his jealousy
the whole world will be consumed,[i]

1:11 [s] Jas 5:1 [t] Hos 9:6
1:12 [u] Am 6:1 [v] Jer 48:11 [w] Eze 8:12
1:13 [x] Jer 15:13 [y] Dt 28:30,39; Am 5:11; Mic 6:15
1:14 [z] ver 7; Joel 1:15 [a] Eze 7:7
1:15 [b] Isa 22:5; Joel 2:2
1:16 [c] Jer 4:19 [d] Isa 2:15
1:17 [e] Isa 59:10 [f] Ps 79:3 [g] Jer 9:22
1:18 [h] Eze 7:19 [i] ver 2-3; Zep 3:8

a 3 The meaning of the Hebrew for this line is uncertain. *b 5* Hebrew *Malcam,* that is, Milcom *c 9* See 1 Samuel 5:5. *d 11* Or *the Mortar* *e 11* Or *in*

for he will make a sudden end
of all who live in the earth.[j]"

1:18 j Ge 6:7

2 Gather together,[k] gather together,
O shameful[l] nation,
2 before the appointed time arrives
and that day sweeps on like
chaff,[m]
before the fierce anger[n] of the LORD
comes upon you,
before the day of the LORD's
wrath comes upon you.
3 Seek[o] the LORD, all you humble of
the land,
you who do what he commands.
Seek righteousness, seek humility;[p]
perhaps you will be sheltered[q]
on the day of the LORD's anger.

2:1 k 2Ch 20:4; Joel 1:14 l Jer 3:3; 6:15
2:2 m Isa 17:13; Hos 13:3 n La 4:11
2:3 o Am 5:6 p Ps 45:4; Am 5:14-15 q Ps 57:1

Against Philistia

4 Gaza[r] will be abandoned
and Ashkelon left in ruins.
At midday Ashdod will be emptied
and Ekron uprooted.
5 Woe to you who live by the sea,
O Kerethite[s] people;
the word of the LORD is against you,[t]
O Canaan, land of the Philistines.

"I will destroy you,
and none will be left."[u]

6 The land by the sea, where the
Kerethites[a] dwell,
will be a place for shepherds and
sheep pens.[v]
7 It will belong to the remnant of the
house of Judah;
there they will find pasture.
In the evening they will lie down
in the houses of Ashkelon.
The LORD their God will care for
them;
he will restore their fortunes.[b] [w]

2:4 r Am 1:6,7-8; Zec 9:5-7
2:5 s Eze 25:16 t Am 3:1 u Isa 14:30
2:6 v Isa 5:17
2:7 w Ps 126:4; Jer 32:44

Against Moab and Ammon

8 "I have heard the insults[x] of Moab
and the taunts of the
Ammonites,
who insulted[y] my people
and made threats against their
land.
9 Therefore, as surely as I live,"
declares the LORD Almighty, the
God of Israel,
"surely Moab[z] will become like
Sodom,[a]
the Ammonites[b] like
Gomorrah—
a place of weeds and salt pits,
a wasteland forever.
The remnant of my people will
plunder[c] them;
the survivors of my nation will
inherit their land.[d]"

10 This is what they will get in return
for their pride,[e]
for insulting[f] and mocking the
people of the LORD
Almighty.
11 The LORD will be awesome[g] to them
when he destroys all the gods[h] of
the land.
The nations on every shore will
worship him,[i]
every one in its own land.

2:8 x Jer 48:27 y Eze 25:3
2:9 z Isa 15:1-16:14; Jer 48:1-47 a Dt 29:23 b Jer 49:1-6; Eze 25:1-7
2:9 c Isa 11:14 d Am 2:1-3
2:10 e Isa 16:6 f Jer 48:27
2:11 g Joel 2:11 h Zep 1:4 i Zep 3:9

Against Cush

12 "You too, O Cushites,[c] [j]
will be slain by my sword.[k]"

2:12 j Isa 18:1; 20:4 k Jer 46:10

Against Assyria

13 He will stretch out his hand
against the north
and destroy Assyria,
leaving Nineveh[l] utterly desolate
and dry as the desert.[m]
14 Flocks and herds will lie down
there,
creatures of every kind.
The desert owl[n] and the screech
owl
will roost on her columns.
Their calls will echo through the
windows,
rubble will be in the doorways,
the beams of cedar will be
exposed.
15 This is the carefree[o] city
that lived in safety.[p]
She said to herself,
"I am, and there is none besides
me."[q]
What a ruin she has become,
a lair for wild beasts!
All who pass by her scoff[r]
and shake their fists.

2:13 l Na 1:1 m Mic 5:6
2:14 n Isa 14:23
2:15 o Isa 32:9 p Isa 47:8 q Eze 28:2 r Na 3:19

The Future of Jerusalem

3 Woe to the city of oppressors,[s]
rebellious and defiled![t]
2 She obeys[u] no one,
she accepts no correction.[v]

3:1 s Jer 6:6 t Eze 23:30
3:2 u Jer 22:21 v Jer 7:28

[a] 6 The meaning of the Hebrew for this word is uncertain. [b] 7 Or *will bring back their captives*
[c] 12 That is, people from the upper Nile region

She does not trust in the LORD,
she does not draw near[w] to her God.
3 Her officials are roaring lions,
her rulers are evening wolves,[x]
who leave nothing for the morning.
4 Her prophets are arrogant;
they are treacherous[y] men.
Her priests profane the sanctuary
and do violence to the law.[z]
5 The LORD within her is righteous;
he does no wrong.[a]
Morning by morning he dispenses his justice,
and every new day he does not fail,
yet the unrighteous know no shame.
6 "I have cut off nations;
their strongholds are demolished.
I have left their streets deserted,
with no one passing through.
Their cities are destroyed;[b]
no one will be left—no one at all.
7 I said to the city,
'Surely you will fear me
and accept correction!'
Then her dwelling would not be cut off,
nor all my punishments come upon her.
But they were still eager
to act corruptly[c] in all they did.
8 Therefore wait[d] for me," declares the LORD,
"for the day I will stand up to testify.[a]
I have decided to assemble the nations,[e]
to gather the kingdoms
and to pour out my wrath on them—
all my fierce anger.
The whole world will be consumed[f]
by the fire of my jealous anger.

9 "Then will I purify the lips of the peoples,
that all of them may call[g] on the name of the LORD
and serve[h] him shoulder to shoulder.
10 From beyond the rivers of Cush[b][i]
my worshipers, my scattered people,
will bring me offerings.[j]
11 On that day you will not be put to shame[k]
for all the wrongs you have done to me,
because I will remove from this city
those who rejoice in their pride.
Never again will you be haughty
on my holy hill.
12 But I will leave within you
the meek[l] and humble,
who trust[m] in the name of the LORD.
13 The remnant[n] of Israel will do no wrong;[o]
they will speak no lies,[p]
nor will deceit be found in their mouths.
They will eat and lie down[q]
and no one will make them afraid.[r]"

14 Sing, O Daughter of Zion;[s]
shout aloud,[t] O Israel!
Be glad and rejoice with all your heart,
O Daughter of Jerusalem!

[a] 8 Septuagint and Syriac; Hebrew *will rise up to plunder* [b] 10 That is, the upper Nile region

3:2 [w] Ps 73:28; Jer 5:3
3:3 [x] Eze 22:27
3:4 [y] Jer 9:4 [z] Eze 22:26
3:5 [a] Dt 32:4
3:6 [b] Lev 26:31
3:7 [c] Hos 9:9
3:8 [d] Ps 27:14 [e] Joel 3:2 [f] Zep 1:18
3:9 [g] Zep 2:11 [h] Isa 19:18
3:10 [i] Ps 68:31
3:10 [j] Isa 60:7
3:11 [k] Joel 2:26-27
3:12 [l] Isa 14:32 [m] Na 1:7
3:13 [n] Isa 10:21; Mic 4:7 [o] Ps 119:3 [p] Rev 14:5 [q] Eze 34:15; Zep 2:7 [r] Eze 34:25-28
3:14 [s] Zec 2:10 [t] Isa 12:6

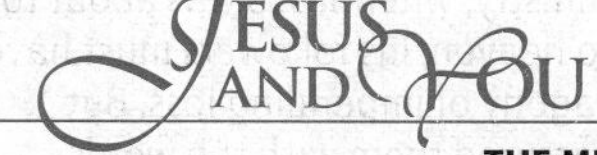

THE MEEK WILL INHERIT

Jesus' teaching in Matthew 5:1–12 reflects God's heart—a heart that desires to bless his people and to enjoy an intimate love relationship with them. The prophets in the Old Testament informed the people both about God's love and about his hatred of evil, and Jesus gave the same message to his generation. Zephaniah asserted that the meek—those who are gentle and peaceful—will inherit the earth (Zephaniah 2:3; 3:12), and Jesus made the same statement in Matthew 5:5. Jesus wasn't implying that we are to be passive or apathetic. Rather, our Lord intended to convey that humility and sincerity should motivate all our actions. The prophet Zephaniah stated that the "day of the LORD" (Zephaniah 1:14) will sweep away the effects of sin on civilization and that those who have turned away from God will be separated from him forever. Only those who walk humbly with God will enjoy eternity with him (Isaiah 57:15; see also Micah 6:8; James 4:6–10).

Something to Shout About

There are times when, as followers of Jesus, we celebrate with unparalleled joy. Zephaniah described that kind of celebration. He invited the people to sing, shout aloud, be glad, rejoice with all their heart. Zephaniah 3:14 marks a turning point in Zephaniah's prophecy. The beginning of the book concentrates on God's judgment, but then the mood lightens and the prophet focuses on the Lord's future promises for his people: promises of restoration, healing and blessing. When the Messiah would come to establish his kingdom, Zephaniah predicted, there would be a celebration to exceed all others.

Many of the promises in Zephaniah deal with Jesus' second coming, but there are others for which we experience daily fulfillment. Consider what God does. First of all, *God is with us* (verse 17), and he always has been. Many years after Zephaniah's ministry, when Jesus was about to return to heaven, his followers must have felt the agony of impending loss. But Jesus reassured them with the words, "Surely I am with you always, to the very end of the age" (Matthew 28:20). His presence comes in different forms at different times, but he is never far from us (Acts 17:27).

God also saves us. In the New Testament Peter and John were brought before the Sanhedrin, a Jewish council, for questioning. Peter reminded those assembled that the only way to be delivered from sin is through Jesus, God's Son. "Salvation is found in no one else," he stated emphatically, "for there is no other name under heaven given to men by which we must be saved" (Acts 4:12).

Sometimes the reality is difficult to comprehend, but *God delights in us* (Zephaniah 3:17). He is vitally interested in our lives. His love for us is so great that he sent his one and only Son to die for our sin so that we might have the opportunity to experience the rekindling of the fire of our relationship with him.

God "quiets" us with his love (Zephaniah 3:17). We are restless creatures, worrying that God might not actually be "out there" or that he might not really care about us. His love is not demonstrated by reproach; it is soothing and completely fulfilling. How much more could he love us than to die for us? (John 15:13).

Finally, *God rejoices over us* (Zephaniah 3:17). The Bible has much to say about singing and rejoicing in God's honor, but Zephaniah made the amazing announcement that God sings and rejoices over *us*! What profound encouragement we can take from this declaration!

We all have something to shout about, no matter how trying and painful our particular circumstances might be. The God of the universe has saved us from our sin. He is right by our side, wherever we go. God loves us, delights in us, rejoices over us. Is it any wonder that all of heaven honors Jesus by shouting aloud? (Revelation 5:12). And we are invited to join in the chorus.

***Self-Discovery:** Identify some specific ways in which you feel the presence of Jesus in your life. Take a few moments to ponder the wonder of the all-powerful, sovereign Lord of the universe singing and rejoicing over you.*

GO TO DISCOVERY 227 ON PAGE 1222

[15] The LORD has taken away your
punishment,
he has turned back your enemy.
The LORD, the King of Israel, is with
you;[u]
never again will you fear[v] any
harm.
[16] On that day they will say to
Jerusalem,
"Do not fear, O Zion;
do not let your hands hang
limp.[w]
[17] The LORD your God is with you,
he is mighty to save.[x]
He will take great delight[y] in you,
he will quiet you with his love,
he will rejoice over you with
singing."
[18] "The sorrows for the appointed
feasts
I will remove from you;
they are a burden and a reproach
to you.[a]
[19] At that time I will deal
with all who oppressed you;
I will rescue the lame
and gather those who have been
scattered.[z]
I will give them praise[a] and honor
in every land where they were
put to shame.
[20] At that time I will gather you;
at that time I will bring[b] you
home.
I will give you honor[c] and praise
among all the peoples of the
earth
when I restore your fortunes[b][d]
before your very eyes,"
says the LORD.

3:15 [u] Eze 37:26-28 [v] Isa 54:14
3:16 [w] Job 4:3; Isa 35:3-4; Heb 12:12
3:17 [x] Isa 63:1 [y] Isa 62:4
3:19 [z] Eze 34:16; Mic 4:6 [a] Isa 60:18
3:20 [b] Jer 29:14; Eze 37:12 [c] Isa 56:5; 66:22 [d] Joel 3:1

[a] 18 Or *"I will gather you who mourn for the appointed feasts; / your reproach is a burden to you*
[b] 20 Or *I bring back your captives*

HAGGAI

HAGGAI

How would God "shake the heavens and the earth"? (Haggai 2:6–7)

♦ *This is a picture of judgment, probably describing some form of political and military turmoil that would alter the structure of the world order. Some suggest that Alexander's conquests almost 200 years later were an initial fulfillment of this prophecy. Haggai told of a final judgment before a Messianic kingdom would be established (verses 20–23).*

Why has "a little while" taken so long? (Haggai 2:6)

♦ *Some explain this puzzling phrase by remembering that God's perspective on time is quite different from ours. Others say it refers to the period of time about five centuries prior to the Messianic age. Still others think the phrase was an expression that simply referred to the future in general.*

What is the significance of the expression "desired of all nations"? (Haggai 2:7)

♦ *Many believe this phrase refers to Jesus. Others think it speaks of desirable things, such as wealth, to be sent by the nations as tribute to the Lord when he reigns in Jerusalem. See Isaiah 60:5–9 and Zechariah 14:14.*

Jesus in Haggai If you've ever felt discouraged or complacent about your spiritual life, Haggai has some encouraging, as well as convicting, words for you. While his prophecy was aimed at correcting a particular problem in the life of God's people (they were giving a higher priority to building their own homes than to rebuilding the Lord's house), the lessons remain relevant for today. Note the close connection Haggai established between obedience and blessing.

Chapter 2 ultimately points to the appearance of Jesus, the "desired of all nations" (verse 7), whose coming would fill the rebuilt temple with glory (verse 9). God's promise to send a Messiah was remembered by the Israelites, but while they languished in captivity they began to wonder whether it would ever be fulfilled. But the people dared to hope again after Zerubbabel had returned to Jerusalem to rebuild Solomon's temple (Haggai 1:18). Zerubbabel was Jesus' ancestor (Matthew 1:12; Luke 3:27) and part of the royal line (1 Chronicles 3:19). God would make Zerubbabel, then governor of Judah, his "signet ring" (Haggai 2:23), a guarantee to all Israel that the promised Messiah would someday come.

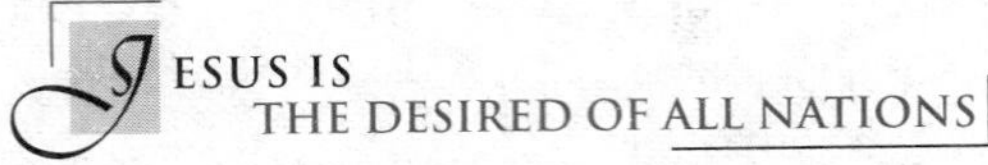
JESUS IS
THE DESIRED OF ALL NATIONS

A Call to Build the House of the LORD

1 In the second year of King Darius,[a] on the first day of the sixth month, the word of the LORD came through the prophet Haggai[b] to Zerubbabel[c] son of Shealtiel, governor[d] of Judah, and to Joshua[a][e] son of Jehozadak,[f] the high priest:

2 This is what the LORD Almighty says: "These people say, 'The time has not yet come for the LORD's house to be built.' "

3 Then the word of the LORD came through the prophet Haggai:[g] 4 "Is it a time for you yourselves to be living in your paneled houses,[h] while this house remains a ruin?[i]"

5 Now this is what the LORD Almighty says: "Give careful thought[j] to your ways. 6 You have planted much, but have harvested little.[k] You eat, but never have enough. You drink, but never have your fill. You put on clothes, but are not warm. You earn wages,[l] only to put them in a purse with holes in it."

7 This is what the LORD Almighty says: "Give careful thought to your ways. 8 Go up into the mountains and bring down timber and build the house, so that I may take pleasure[m] in it and be honored," says the LORD. 9 "You expected much, but see, it turned out to be little. What you brought home, I blew away. Why?" declares the LORD Almighty. "Because of my house, which remains a ruin,[n] while each of you is busy with his own house. 10 Therefore, because of you the heavens have withheld their dew and the earth its crops.[o] 11 I called for a drought[p] on the fields and the mountains, on the grain, the new wine, the oil and whatever the ground produces, on men and cattle, and on the labor of your hands.[q]"

12 Then Zerubbabel[r] son of Shealtiel, Joshua son of Jehozadak, the high priest, and the whole remnant[s] of the people obeyed[t] the voice of the LORD their God and the message of the prophet Haggai, because the LORD their God had sent him. And the people feared[u] the LORD.

13 Then Haggai, the LORD's messenger, gave this message of the LORD to the people: "I am with[v] you," declares the LORD. 14 So the LORD stirred up the spirit of Zerubbabel[w] son of Shealtiel, governor of Judah, and the spirit of Joshua son of Jehozadak, the high priest, and the spirit of the whole remnant[x] of the people. They came and began to work on the house of the LORD Almighty, their God, 15 on the twenty-fourth day of the sixth month[y] in the second year of King Darius.

The Promised Glory of the New House

2 On the twenty-first day of the seventh month, the word of the LORD came through the prophet Haggai: 2 "Speak to Zerubbabel son of Shealtiel, governor of Judah, to Joshua son of Jehozadak, the high priest, and to the remnant of the people. Ask them, 3 'Who of you is left who saw this house[z] in its former glory? How does it look to you now? Does it not seem to you like nothing?[a] 4 But now be strong, O Zerubbabel,' declares the LORD. 'Be strong,[b] O Joshua son of Jehozadak, the high priest. Be strong, all you people of the land,' declares the LORD, 'and work. For I am with[c] you,' declares the LORD Almighty. 5 'This is what I covenanted with you when you came out of Egypt.[d] And my Spirit[e] remains among you. Do not fear.'

6 "This is what the LORD Almighty says: 'In a little while[f] I will once more shake the heavens and the earth,[g] the sea and the dry land. 7 I will shake all nations, and the desired of all nations will come, and I will fill this house[h] with glory,' says the LORD Almighty. 8 'The silver is mine and the gold is mine,' declares the LORD Almighty. 9 'The glory[i] of this present house will be greater than the glory of the former house,' says the LORD Almighty. 'And in this place I will grant peace,' declares the LORD Almighty."

Blessings for a Defiled People

10 On the twenty-fourth day of the ninth month,[j] in the second year of Darius, the word of the LORD came to the prophet Haggai: 11 "This is what the LORD Almighty says: 'Ask the priests[k] what the law says: 12 If a person carries consecrated meat in the fold of his garment, and that fold touches some bread or stew, some wine, oil or other food, does it become consecrated?[l] ' "

The priests answered, "No."

[a] *1* A variant of *Jeshua*; here and elsewhere in Haggai

1:1 [a] Ezr 4:24 [b] Ezr 5:1 [c] Mt 1:12-13 [d] Ezr 5:3 [e] Ezr 2:2 [f] 1Ch 6:15; Ezr 3:2
1:3 [g] Ezr 5:1
1:4 [h] 2Sa 7:2 [i] ver 9; Jer 33:12
1:5 [j] La 3:40
1:6 [k] Dt 28:38 [l] Hag 2:16; Zec 8:10
1:8 [m] Ps 132:13-14
1:9 [n] ver 4
1:10 [o] Lev 26:19; Dt 28:23
1:11 [p] Dt 28:22; 1Ki 17:1 [q] Hag 2:17
1:12 [r] ver 1 [s] ver 14; Isa 1:9; Hag 2:2 [t] Isa 50:10 [u] Dt 31:12
1:13 [v] Mt 28:20; Ro 8:31
1:14 [w] Ezr 5:2 [x] ver 12
1:15 [y] ver 1
2:3 [z] Ezr 3:12 [a] Zec 4:10
2:4 [b] 1Ch 28:20; Zec 8:9; Eph 6:10 [c] 2Sa 5:10; Ac 7:9
2:5 [d] Ex 29:46 [e] Ne 9:20; Isa 63:11
2:6 [f] Isa 10:25 [g] Heb 12:26*
2:7 [h] Isa 60:7
2:9 [i] Ps 85:9
2:10 [j] ver 1
2:11 [k] Lev 10:10-11; Dt 17:8-11; Mal 2:7
2:12 [l] Lev 6:27; Mt 23:19

Our Lord's Model for Service

After 70 years of exile in Babylon a band of Jewish men and their families, under Zerubbabel's leadership, returned to Jerusalem to rebuild God's holy temple (Ezra 1:2–3). Although this return had long been awaited, the work would evoke ambivalent feelings in the hearts of the people, and God's messages to Haggai would be needed to infuse them with the will to continue.

As the workers began the demanding task of rebuilding, they became discouraged and downhearted. The rebuilt temple would lack the silver, the gold and the grandeur of Solomon's temple. The negative comparison weakened their resolve, and the builders were tempted to give up on the project. But God reminded them that he was the One who had asked them to leave Babylon (Ezra 1:5) in order to build the temple (Haggai 1:14), and he encouraged them to press on with the task because he would continue to be present with them (Haggai 2:4).

The prophet Haggai reminded the builders that they were working for God's purposes (verses 6–9). All of the silver and gold in the world already belonged to God (1 Chronicles 29:14,16; Haggai 2:8), and the Lord did not need a sacrifice, because every animal was already his as well (Psalm 50:9–10). Haggai knew that God could have provided whatever would have been necessary to refurbish the temple to its original splendor, but God chose to work in a different way. All he asked was that his people remain faithful.

God has never been impressed by the scope of human achievement or by the beneficence of the individual who gives in order to receive glory from other human beings (Matthew 6:4). In one particular instance Jesus observed a widow offering two very small copper coins for the temple treasury. To the astonishment of the onlookers, our Lord declared that "this poor widow has put in more than all the others. All these people gave their gifts out of their wealth; but she out of her poverty put in all she had to live on" (Luke 21:3).

The apostle Paul wrote to the believers in Corinth about the generosity of the Macedonian churches, who despite extreme poverty had expressed their overflowing joy in the blessings of the gospel by giving "beyond their ability" (2 Corinthians 8:1–3). Paul went on to encourage the Corinthian believers as well to demonstrate a similar spirit of eager giving: "Now finish the work, so that your eager willingness to do it may be matched by your completion of it, according to your means. For if the willingness is there, the gift is acceptable according to what one has" (2 Corinthians 8:11–12).

The incentive Paul offered for giving? "For you know the grace of our Lord Jesus Christ, that though he was rich, yet for your sakes he became poor, so that you through his poverty might become rich" (2 Corinthians 8:9). In other words, said Paul, we are called to give of our talents and resources as we are able, with thankfulness in our hearts and in accordance with the model of our Lord and Savior Jesus Christ.

Self-Discovery: What are some specific kinds of service that you can render in the name of Jesus? Identify some impromptu gifts that you can give today, even if they seem to you to be quite small and insignificant (words of encouragement, a prayer for one who is hurting, a postcard?).

GO TO DISCOVERY 228 ON PAGE 1228

13Then Haggai said, “If a person defiled by contact with a dead body
touches one of these things, does it become defiled?”
“Yes,” the priests replied, “it becomes
2:13 [m]Lev 22:4-6 defiled.[m]”
14Then Haggai said, “ ‘So it is with this
people and this nation in my sight,’ de-
2:14 clares the LORD. ‘Whatever they do and
[n]Isa 1:13 whatever they offer[n] there is defiled.
2:15 15“ ‘Now give careful thought[o] to this
[o]Hag 1:5 from this day on[a]—consider how things
[p]Ezr 3:10 were before one stone was laid[p] on an-
[q]Ezr 4:24 other in the LORD's temple.[q] 16When
anyone came to a heap of twenty measures, there were only ten. When anyone
went to a wine vat to draw fifty mea-
sures, there were only twenty.[r] 17I struck 2:16 [r]Hag 1:6
all the work of your hands[s] with blight,[t]
mildew and hail, yet you did not turn to 2:17 [s]Hag 1:11
me,' declares the LORD.[u] 18'From this day [t]Dt 28:22;
on, from this twenty-fourth day of the 1Ki 8:37; Am 4:9
ninth month, give careful thought to the [u]Am 4:6
day when the foundation[v] of the LORD's
temple was laid. Give careful thought: 2:18 [v]Zec 8:9
19Is there yet any seed left in the barn?
Until now, the vine and the fig tree, the
pomegranate and the olive tree have not
borne fruit.
“ ‘From this day on I will bless you.’ ”

Zerubbabel the LORD's Signet Ring

20The word of the LORD came to Haggai a second time on the twenty-fourth
day of the month: 21“Tell Zerubbabel[w] 2:21 [w]Ezr 5:2
governor of Judah that I will shake the
heavens and the earth. 22I will overturn
royal thrones and shatter the power of
the foreign kingdoms.[x] I will overthrow 2:22
chariots[y] and their drivers; horses and [x]Da 2:44 [y]Mic 5:10
their riders will fall, each by the sword of [z]Jdg 7:22
his brother.[z]
23“ ‘On that day,’ declares the LORD
Almighty, ‘I will take you, my servant[a] 2:23 [a]Isa 43:10
Zerubbabel son of Shealtiel,’ declares the
LORD, ‘and I will make you like my signet
ring, for I have chosen you,’ declares the
LORD Almighty.”

[a] 15 Or *to the days past*

JESUS FOCUS

FAMILY TIES

A full 78 years before Haggai's prophecy, God had rejected King Jehoiachin: "Even if you . . . were a signet ring on my right hand, I would still pull you off" (Jeremiah 22:24). But Jehoiachin's grandson Zerubbabel returned to Jerusalem to rebuild the temple, and God referred to him as "my signet ring" (Haggai 2:23). God punished Jehoiachin for turning away from him, but that punishment was not permanent. Although none of Jehoiachin's immediate descendants became kings in Israel, the Messiah's family line was preserved through Zerubbabel, an ancestor of both of Jesus' earthly parents (Matthew 1:13; Luke 3:27). God proved once again that he always keeps his promises, even when it looks as though all hope is lost .

ZECHARIAH

ZECHARIAH

Could a priest also be a king in Israel? (Zechariah 6:13)

♦ *Priests had to belong to the tribe of Levi, while kings were to come from the line of David (from the tribe of Judah). A priest, therefore, could not also be a king. This was apparently a symbolic statement that pointed ahead to the Messiah, the One in whom the two offices and functions would be united (Psalm 110; Hebrews 7).*

What is the New Testament significance to the term* cornerstone? *(Zechariah 10:4)

♦ *This is a name for the Messiah that suggests his key role in the construction of God's plan of salvation (1 Peter 2:6). Jesus is also the nail, the One on whom God's glory hangs, as well as the battle bow through whom God will ultimately triumph.*

Why give names to pieces of wood? (Zechariah 11:7)

♦ *These were tools used by the shepherd to lead the flock. The shepherd would lead the people with favor and unity—gently, with grace, to bring them together with God. This is most likely a picture of the ministry of the coming Messiah, the good shepherd (John 10:11).*

Jesus in Zechariah Zechariah contains numerous images foreshadowing the Messiah. These fascinating and complex chapters helped the New Testament believers to understand Jesus' suffering, death and resurrection and provided a backdrop for John's words in Revelation concerning the last days. Jesus is pictured as the "Branch" of David's family line that God had promised to preserve (Zechariah 3:8; 6:12). In another description, the Messianic Servant-Messenger (likely the preincarnate Jesus) stands alongside two olive trees, one of which represents Zerubbabel and the royal ministry, and the other Joshua and the priestly ministry, symbolizing our Lord's role as both King and Priest (Zechariah 4:11–14). The prophet also received messages from the Lord that the Messiah would one day ride into Jerusalem astride a donkey (Zechariah 9:9; Matthew 21:5), be betrayed for 30 pieces of silver (Zechariah 11:12–13; Matthew 26:14–15) and be killed by his own people (Zechariah 12:10; 13:6; Matthew 27:20). In the end, however, Jesus will triumph over all of God's enemies and reign over Jerusalem as "the King, the LORD Almighty" (Zechariah 14:17).

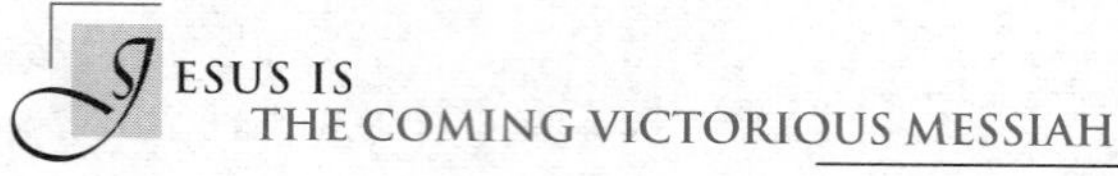
JESUS IS
THE COMING VICTORIOUS MESSIAH

A Call to Return to the LORD

1 In the eighth month of the second
1:1 [a] Ezr 4:24; 6:15 year of Darius,[a] the word of the
[b] Ezr 5:1 LORD came to the prophet Zechariah[b]
[c] Mt 23:35; Lk 11:51 [d] ver 7; son of Berekiah,[c] the son of Iddo:[d]
Ne 12:4 2"The LORD was very angry[e] with your
1:2 forefathers. 3Therefore tell the people:
[e] 2Ch 36:16 This is what the LORD Almighty says:
'Return to me,' declares the LORD Al-
1:3 [f] Mal 3:7; Jas 4:8 mighty, 'and I will return to you,'[f] says
the LORD Almighty. 4Do not be like your
1:4 [g] 2Ch 36:15 forefathers,[g] to whom the earlier proph-
[h] Ps 106:6 ets proclaimed: This is what the LORD
[i] 2Ch 24:19; Ps 78:8; Jer 6:17 Almighty says: 'Turn from your evil
ways[h] and your evil practices.' But they
would not listen or pay attention to me,[i]
declares the LORD. 5Where are your forefathers now? And the prophets, do they
live forever? 6But did not my words and
my decrees, which I commanded my
servants the prophets, overtake your
forefathers?
"Then they repented and said, 'The
1:6 LORD Almighty has done to us what our
[j] Jer 12:14-17; ways and practices deserve,[j] just as he
La 2:17 determined to do.' "

The Man Among the Myrtle Trees

7On the twenty-fourth day of the
eleventh month, the month of Shebat, in
the second year of Darius, the word of
the LORD came to the prophet Zechariah son of Berekiah, the son of Iddo.
8During the night I had a vision—and
1:8 [k] Rev 6:4 there before me was a man riding a red[k]
horse! He was standing among the myr-
tle trees in a ravine. Behind him were
red, brown and white horses.[l] 1:8 [l] Zec 6:2-7
9I asked, "What are these, my lord?"
The angel[m] who was talking with me 1:9 [m] Zec 4:1,4-5
answered, "I will show you what they
are."
10Then the man standing among the
myrtle trees explained, "They are the
ones the LORD has sent to go throughout
the earth."[n] 1:10 [n] Zec 6:5-8
11And they reported to the angel of
the LORD, who was standing among the
myrtle trees, "We have gone throughout
the earth and found the whole world at
rest and in peace."[o] 1:11 [o] Isa 14:7
12Then the angel of the LORD said,
"LORD Almighty, how long will you withhold mercy from Jerusalem and from
the towns of Judah, which you have been
angry with these seventy[p] years?" 13So 1:12 [p] Da 9:2
the LORD spoke kind and comforting
words to the angel who talked with me.[q] 1:13 [q] Zec 4:1
14Then the angel who was speaking to
me said, "Proclaim this word: This is
what the LORD Almighty says: 'I am very
jealous[r] for Jerusalem and Zion, 15but I 1:14 [r] Joel 2:18;
am very angry with the nations that feel Zec 8:2
secure.[s] I was only a little angry, but they 1:15
added to the calamity.'[t] [s] Jer 48:11 [t] Ps 123:3-4;
16"Therefore, this is what the LORD Am 1:11
says: 'I will return[u] to Jerusalem with 1:16
mercy, and there my house will be re- [u] Zec 8:3
built. And the measuring line[v] will be [v] Zec 2:1-2
stretched out over Jerusalem,' declares
the LORD Almighty.
17"Proclaim further: This is what the
LORD Almighty says: 'My towns will
again overflow with prosperity, and the 1:17
LORD will again comfort[w] Zion and [w] Isa 51:3 [x] Isa 14:1
choose[x] Jerusalem.' "[y] [y] Zec 2:12

Four Horns and Four Craftsmen

18Then I looked up—and there before
me were four horns! 19I asked the angel
who was speaking to me, "What are
these?"
He answered me, "These are the
horns[z] that scattered Judah, Israel and 1:19 [z] Am 6:13
Jerusalem."
20Then the LORD showed me four
craftsmen. 21I asked, "What are these
coming to do?"
He answered, "These are the horns
that scattered Judah so that no one
could raise his head, but the craftsmen
have come to terrify them and throw
down these horns of the nations who

JESUS FOCUS

THE FOUR HORSEMEN

Zechariah first saw the "angel of the LORD" (thought by many to be the preincarnate Jesus himself) standing among the myrtle trees in the valley. Men on red, brown and white horses came to report that the whole earth was at peace (Zechariah 1:8–11). This vision is very similar to that of the apostle John centuries later. In John's vision Jesus opened the seals of the scroll of judgment (Revelation 6:1–8). The first four seals were associated with four horsemen who also rode on colorful horses—white, red, black and pale. These horsemen are associated with God's judgment of the earth at the end of time. In Zechariah 6:1–8 they are called the "four spirits of heaven," indicating that they were sent by God.

lifted up their horns[a] against the land of Judah to scatter its people."[b]

A Man With a Measuring Line

2 Then I looked up—and there before me was a man with a measuring line in his hand! 2 I asked, "Where are you going?"

He answered me, "To measure Jerusalem, to find out how wide and how long it is."[c]

3 Then the angel who was speaking to me left, and another angel came to meet him 4 and said to him: "Run, tell that young man, 'Jerusalem will be a city without walls[d] because of the great number[e] of men and livestock in it. 5 And I myself will be a wall[f] of fire around it,' declares the LORD, 'and I will be its glory[g] within.'

6 "Come! Come! Flee from the land of the north," declares the LORD, "for I have scattered you to the four winds of heaven,"[h] declares the LORD.

7 "Come, O Zion! Escape, you who live in the Daughter of Babylon!"[i] 8 For this is what the LORD Almighty says: "After he has honored me and has sent me against the nations that have plundered you—for whoever touches you touches the apple of his eye[j]— 9 I will surely raise my hand against them so that their slaves will plunder them.[a][k] Then you will know that the LORD Almighty has sent me.[l]

10 "Shout and be glad, O Daughter of Zion.[m] For I am coming,[n] and I will live among you,"[o] declares the LORD. 11 "Many nations will be joined with the LORD in that day and will become my people. I will live among you and you will know that the LORD Almighty has sent me to you. 12 The LORD will inherit[p] Judah as his portion in the holy land and will again choose[q] Jerusalem. 13 Be still[r] before the LORD, all mankind, because he has roused himself from his holy dwelling."

Clean Garments for the High Priest

3 Then he showed me Joshua[b][s] the high priest standing before the angel of the LORD, and Satan[c][t] standing at his right side to accuse him. 2 The LORD said to Satan, "The LORD rebuke you,[u] Satan! The LORD, who has chosen[v] Jerusalem, rebuke you! Is not this man a burning stick snatched from the fire?"[w]

3 Now Joshua was dressed in filthy clothes as he stood before the angel. 4 The angel said to those who were standing before him, "Take off his filthy clothes."

Then he said to Joshua, "See, I have taken away your sin,[x] and I will put rich garments[y] on you."

5 Then I said, "Put a clean turban[z] on his head." So they put a clean turban on

1:21 [a] Ps 75:4 [b] Ps 75:10
2:2 [c] Eze 40:3; Rev 21:15
2:4 [d] Eze 38:11 [e] Isa 49:20; Jer 30:19; 33:22
2:5 [f] Isa 26:1 [g] Rev 21:23
2:6 [h] Eze 17:21
2:7 [i] Isa 48:20
2:8 [j] Dt 32:10
2:9 [k] Isa 14:2 [l] Zec 4:9
2:10 [m] Zep 3:14 [n] Zec 9:9 [o] Lev 26:12; Zec 8:3
2:12 [p] Dt 32:9; Ps 33:12; Jer 10:16 [q] Zec 1:17
2:13 [r] Hab 2:20
3:1 [s] Hag 1:1; Zec 6:11 [t] Ps 109:6
3:2 [u] Jude 1:9 [v] Isa 14:1 [w] Am 4:11; Jude 1:23
3:4 [x] Eze 36:25; Mic 7:18 [y] Isa 52:1; Rev 19:8
3:5 [z] Ex 29:6

[a] *8,9* Or *says after . . . eye: 9 "I . . . plunder them."*
[b] *1* A variant of *Joshua;* here and elsewhere in Zechariah
[c] *1* *Satan* means *accuser.*

JESUS FOCUS

MEASURING THE CITY

In his vision the prophet Zechariah saw a man going out to measure Jerusalem—"a city without walls" (Zechariah 2:4). The vision reminded God's people that he would at some point in the future restore the city in terms of size, population, wealth and security. The same imagery was used in the visions of Ezekiel and John (Ezekiel 40:2–3; Revelation 11:1–3; 21:15–21), both of whom also saw someone measuring the temple and God's holy city. The one who holds the measuring line in Ezekiel is an angelic guide (see Ezekiel 40:3,5), who may have been God the Son. The Lord takes care of his people, and he will one day rebuild Jerusalem as God's eternal city (Hebrews 11:10; Revelation 21:2–4,9–27).

CONDEMNING SATAN, OUR ACCUSER

Zechariah was allowed to witness a very unusual sight: Satan stood next to Joshua, God's high priest, and accused him of spiritual inadequacy (Zechariah 3:1–2). But God let Satan know that Joshua was one of God's own and that God himself had made him acceptable. Zechariah is not the only Biblical character to have observed Satan accusing one of God's people. John also saw Satan as the "accuser of our brothers, who accuses them before our God" (Revelation 12:10). But we have no need to fear accusations from Satan, because we have a defender standing with us before God: "We have One who speaks to the Father in our defense—Jesus Christ, the Righteous One" (1 John 2:1). In Zechariah 3 "the angel of the LORD" stood by Joshua's side (verse 5). Zechariah observed the angel speaking to Joshua and offering forgiveness and fresh, clean robes in which he could serve God.

his head and clothed him, while the angel of the LORD stood by.
6The angel of the LORD gave this
charge to Joshua: 7"This is what the
LORD Almighty says: 'If you will walk in
3:7 my ways and keep my requirements,
a Dt 17:8-11; then you will govern my house[a] and
Eze 44:15-16 have charge of my courts, and I will give
you a place among these standing here.
8" 'Listen, O high priest Joshua and
your associates seated before you, who
3:8 are men symbolic[b] of things to come: I
b Eze 12:11 am going to bring my servant, the
c Isa 4:2 Branch.[c] 9See, the stone I have set in
front of Joshua! There are seven eyes[a] on
3:9 that one stone,[d] and I will engrave an in-
d Isa 28:16 scription on it,' says the LORD Almighty,
e Jer 50:20 'and I will remove the sin[e] of this land in
a single day.
10" 'In that day each of you will invite
3:10 his neighbor to sit under his vine and fig
f 1Ki 4:25; tree,[f]' declares the LORD Almighty.' "
Mic 4:4

The Gold Lampstand and the Two
4:1 *Olive Trees*
g Da 8:18 **4** Then the angel who talked with
h Jer 31:26 me returned and wakened[g] me, as
4:2 a man is wakened from his sleep.[h] 2He
i Jer 1:13 asked me, "What do you see?"[i]
j Ex 25:31; I answered, "I see a solid gold lamp-
Rev 1:12 stand[j] with a bowl at the top and seven
k Rev 4:5 lights[k] on it, with seven channels to the
4:3 lights. 3Also there are two olive trees[l] by
l ver 11;
Rev 11:4

it, one on the right of the bowl and the
other on its left."
4I asked the angel who talked with
me, "What are these, my lord?"
5He answered, "Do you not know
what these are?" 4:5
"No, my lord," I replied.[m] m Zec 1:9
6So he said to me, "This is the word of 4:6
the LORD to Zerubbabel:[n] 'Not by might n Ezr 5:2
nor by power, but by my Spirit,'[o] says the o Isa 11:2-4;
LORD Almighty. Hos 1:7
7"What[b] are you, O mighty mountain? Before Zerubbabel you will be- 4:7
come level ground.[p] Then he will bring p Jer 51:25
out the capstone[q] to shouts of 'God q Ps 118:22
bless it! God bless it!' "
8Then the word of the LORD came to
me: 9"The hands of Zerubbabel have laid
the foundation[r] of this temple; his 4:9
hands will also complete it.[s] Then you r Ezr 3:11
will know that the LORD Almighty has s Ezr 3:8; 6:15;
sent me[t] to you. Zec 6:12
10"Who despises the day of small t Zec 2:9
things?[u] Men will rejoice when they see 4:10
the plumb line in the hand of Zerubba- u Hag 2:3
bel. v Zec 3:9;
"(These seven are the eyes[v] of the Rev 5:6
LORD, which range throughout the
earth.)"
11Then I asked the angel, "What are 4:11
these two olive trees[w] on the right and w ver 3; Rev 11:4
the left of the lampstand?"
12Again I asked him, "What are these
two olive branches beside the two gold
pipes that pour out golden oil?"
13He replied, "Do you not know what
these are?"
"No, my lord," I said.
14So he said, "These are the two who 4:14
are anointed[x] to[c] serve the Lord of all x Ex 29:7; 40:15;
the earth." Da 9:24-26;
Zec 3:1-7

The Flying Scroll
5 I looked again—and there before
me was a flying scroll![y] 5:1
2He asked me, "What do you see?" y Eze 2:9;
I answered, "I see a flying scroll, thir- Rev 5:1
ty feet long and fifteen feet wide.[d]" 5:3
3And he said to me, "This is the curse[z] z Isa 24:6; 43:28;
that is going out over the whole land; for Mal 3:9; 4:6
according to what it says on one side, a Ex 20:15;
every thief[a] will be banished, and ac- Mal 3:8
cording to what it says on the other, b Isa 48:1
everyone who swears falsely[b] will be

[a] 9 Or *facets* [b] 7 Or *Who* [c] 14 Or *two who bring oil and* [d] 2 Hebrew *twenty cubits long and ten cubits wide* (about 9 meters long and 4.5 meters wide)

JESUS FOCUS

TWO VISIONS

The governor Zerubbabel (Ezra 2:2) and Joshua, the high priest (Ezra 3:2), were seen by Zechariah in his vision as two olive trees (Zechariah 4:11–14), both chosen to serve the Lord. Together they reflect Jesus' role as both our King and our High Priest (Hebrews 7:1–28; 10:9–25). Zechariah also saw a golden lampstand surrounded by seven lights. Centuries later the apostle John would view a similar vision of Jesus, the risen Savior of God's people, moving among seven golden lampstands (Revelation 1:12–20). The lampstand, or candlestick, was made of pure gold and symbolizes Jesus as our Light (John 8:12) and as the eternal Son of God (Revelation 1:5). The "anointed" One is the Messiah, whom God sent as the branch from David's family tree to be both Ruler and Priest (Zechariah 3:8; 4:14).

God of Small Successes

"Who despises the day of small things?" the Lord asked the prophet Zechariah (Zechariah 4:10). The truth is that most of us do. Much of the time things don't happen as quickly as we would like them to. It takes longer to break a destructive habit than we feel it should. Telephone lines are busy, or we are forced to leave a message. There are two persons ahead of us at the ATM machine. We complain that our computer response time is woeful. Service at a restaurant is too slow. God doesn't act quickly enough in response to our requests, even when our ideas seem ironclad and we can present him with solutions for every contingency. Human beings have always been impatient.

Zechariah prophesied during the time God's people were rebuilding the temple and the city walls following the Babylonian exile (see Ezra 7—10; Nehemiah 11—12). The people had become discouraged because the progress could be measured only in small increments. There was a great deal of work to be done to repair the devastation wrought by the Babylonians, and the people already living in the area mocked the builders and did everything they could think of to hinder their progress. The easiest "solution" would have been to give up, conceding that the task was simply too difficult.

We also tend to forget that big projects are frequently accomplished one tentative step at a time, but God is committed to any worthwhile project undertaken in his name. His words to Zechariah could just as well apply to our own situation: "This is the word of the LORD to Zerubbabel [the governor]: 'Not by might nor by power, but by my Spirit,' says the LORD Almighty. What are you, O mighty mountain? Before Zerubbabel you will become level ground. Then he will bring out the capstone to shouts of 'God bless it!' " (Zechariah 4:6–7).

The manner God chose to deliver us from our sins sounds preposterous to some, but the incontrovertible fact remains that Jesus Christ, the eternal Son of God, was born to die in our place. God delights to work through circumstances that might seem insurmountable or impossible; he does this in order to showcase his own great power (2 Corinthians 4:7).

When God lays the foundation, there is no mistaking who is involved (Isaiah 28:16), especially when so many obstacles join forces against us. And when Jesus was raised from the dead there was no mistaking that this miracle was the work of the heavenly Father (1 Peter 1:20–21). God promises to continue to work in our lives until he has finished what he has begun (Philippians 1:6).

Self-Discovery: What special work has Jesus begun in your life? Is there a particular area in which you can see yourself blossoming and developing? Has the development been slow and steady, or has it progressed rapidly?

GO TO DISCOVERY 229 ON PAGE 1232

banished. 4The LORD Almighty declares,
'I will send it out, and it will enter the
house of the thief and the house of him
5:4 who swears falsely by my name. It will
[c] Lev 14:34-45; remain in his house and destroy it, both
Hab 2:9-11; Mal 3:5 its timbers and its stones.[c]' "

The Woman in a Basket

5Then the angel who was speaking to
me came forward and said to me, "Look
up and see what this is that is appearing."
6I asked, "What is it?"
He replied, "It is a measuring basket.[a]" And he added, "This is the iniquity[b] of the people throughout the land."
7Then the cover of lead was raised,
and there in the basket sat a woman! 8He
said, "This is wickedness," and he pushed
her back into the basket and pushed the
5:8 [d] Mic 6:11 lead cover down over its mouth.[d]
9Then I looked up—and there before
me were two women, with the wind in
their wings! They had wings like those of
5:9 a stork,[e] and they lifted up the basket
[e] Lev 11:19 between heaven and earth.
10"Where are they taking the basket?"
I asked the angel who was speaking
to me.
11He replied, "To the country of Bab-
5:11 [f] Ge 10:10 ylonia[c][f] to build a house[g] for it. When it
[g] Jer 29:5,28 is ready, the basket will be set there in its
[h] Da 1:2 place."[h]

Four Chariots

6:1 **6** I looked up again—and there be-
[i] ver 5 fore me were four chariots[i] coming out from between two mountains—
mountains of bronze! 2The first chariot
6:2 had red horses, the second black,[j] 3the
[j] Rev 6:5 third white,[k] and the fourth dappled—
6:3 all of them powerful. 4I asked the angel
[k] Rev 6:2 who was speaking to me, "What are
these, my lord?"
5The angel answered me, "These are
6:5 [l] Eze 37:9; the four spirits[d][l] of heaven, going out
Mt 24:31; from standing in the presence of the
Rev 7:1 Lord of the whole world. 6The one with
the black horses is going toward the
north country, the one with the white
horses toward the west,[e] and the one
with the dappled horses toward the
south."
7When the powerful horses went out,
they were straining to go throughout the
6:7 [m] Zec 1:10 earth.[m] And he said, "Go throughout
the earth!" So they went throughout the
earth.

8Then he called to me, "Look, those
going toward the north country have 6:8
given my Spirit[f] rest[n] in the land of the [n] Eze 5:13; 24:13
north."

A Crown for Joshua

9The word of the LORD came to me:
10"Take ⌊silver and gold⌋ from the exiles
Heldai, Tobijah and Jedaiah, who have
arrived from Babylon.[o] Go the same day 6:10 [o] Ezr 7:14-16;
to the house of Josiah son of Zephaniah. Jer 28:6
11Take the silver and gold and make a
crown,[p] and set it on the head of the 6:11 [p] Ps 21:3
high priest, Joshua[q] son of Jehozadak.[r] [q] Zec 3:1
12Tell him this is what the LORD Al- [r] Ezr 3:2
mighty says: 'Here is the man whose
name is the Branch,[s] and he will branch 6:12 [s] Isa 4:2; Zec 3:8
out from his place and build the temple [t] Ezr 3:8-10;
of the LORD.[t] 13It is he who will build the Zec 4:6-9
temple of the LORD, and he will be
clothed with majesty and will sit and
rule on his throne. And he will be a
priest[u] on his throne. And there will be 6:13 [u] Ps 110:4
harmony between the two.' 14The crown
will be given to Heldai,[g] Tobijah, Jedaiah
and Hen[h] son of Zephaniah as a memorial in the temple of the LORD. 15Those
who are far away will come and help to

[a] 6 Hebrew *an ephah;* also in verses 7–11 [b] 6 Or *appearance* [c] 11 Hebrew *Shinar* [d] 5 Or *winds* [e] 6 Or *horses after them* [f] 8 Or *spirit* [g] 14 Syriac; Hebrew *Helem* [h] 14 Or *and the gracious one, the*

JESUS FOCUS

GLORIOUS KING AND PRIEST

One day Jesus the Messiah will be anointed as our eternal King and Priest. In his vision Zechariah was able to witness the spectacular installation of Joshua as a royal high priest in Jerusalem (Zechariah 6:9–15). At the same time the prophet caught a glimpse of a still greater day—when the Messiah himself will be crowned as the central figure in God's future kingdom. The images that Zechariah described are very similar to those depicted by other prophets. Both Isaiah and Jeremiah referred to the "tender shoot" who would spring up as the "righteous Branch" from David's family line (Isaiah 53:2; Jeremiah 33:15). And the psalmist predicted that a son of David would be installed by God as a King and Priest in the future (Psalm 110:4–7). The book of Hebrews identifies Jesus as the Messiah, God the Son, as well as our eternal King and heavenly High Priest (Hebrews 4:14–16; 7:14–28; 9:11–15).

6:15 build the temple of the LORD,[v] and you
[v] Isa 60:10 will know that the LORD Almighty has
[w] Zec 2:9-11 sent me to you.[w] This will happen if you
[x] Isa 58:12; Jer 7:23; Zec 3:7 diligently obey[x] the LORD your God."

Justice and Mercy, Not Fasting

7 In the fourth year of King Darius,
the word of the LORD came to
7:1 Zechariah on the fourth day of the ninth
[y] Ne 1:1 month, the month of Kislev.[y] 2The people of Bethel had sent Sharezer and Re-
gem-Melech, together with their men, to
7:2 entreat[z] the LORD 3by asking the priests
[z] Jer 26:19; Zec 8:21 of the house of the LORD Almighty and
7:3 the prophets, "Should I mourn[a] and fast
[a] Zec 12:12-14; [b] Jer 52:12-14; Zec 8:19 in the fifth[b] month, as I have done for so
many years?"
4Then the word of the LORD Almighty
7:5 came to me: 5"Ask all the people of the
[c] Isa 58:5 land and the priests, 'When you fasted[c]
and mourned in the fifth and seventh
months for the past seventy years, was it
really for me that you fasted? 6And when
you were eating and drinking, were you
not just feasting for yourselves? 7Are
these not the words the LORD pro-
7:7 claimed through the earlier prophets[d]
[d] Zec 1:4 when Jerusalem and its surrounding
[e] Jer 22:21 towns were at rest[e] and prosperous, and
[f] Jer 17:26 the Negev and the western foothills[f]
were settled?' "
8And the word of the LORD came
again to Zechariah: 9"This is what the
LORD Almighty says: 'Administer true
7:9 justice;[g] show mercy and compassion to
[g] Zec 8:16 one another. 10Do not oppress the wid-
7:10 ow or the fatherless, the alien[h] or the
[h] Ex 22:21 [i] Ex 22:22; Isa 1:17 poor. In your hearts do not think evil of
each other.'[i]
11"But they refused to pay attention;
stubbornly they turned their backs and
7:11 stopped up their ears.[j] 12They made
[j] Jer 8:5; 11:10; 17:23 their hearts as hard as flint[k] and would
7:12 not listen to the law or to the words that
[k] Jer 17:1; Eze 11:19 the LORD Almighty had sent by his Spir-
[l] Ne 9:29 it through the earlier prophets.[l] So the
[m] Da 9:12 LORD Almighty was very angry.[m]
13" 'When I called, they did not lis-
7:13 ten;[n] so when they called, I would not
[n] Pr 1:24 [o] Isa 1:15; Jer 11:11; 14:12; Mic 3:4 listen,'[o] says the LORD Almighty.[p] 14'I
scattered[q] them with a whirlwind[r]
[p] Pr 1:28 among all the nations, where they were
7:14 strangers. The land was left so desolate
[q] Dt 4:27; 28:64-67 behind them that no one could come or
[r] Jer 23:19 go. This is how they made the pleasant
[s] Jer 44:6 land desolate.[s]' "

The LORD Promises to Bless Jerusalem

8 Again the word of the LORD Almighty came to me. 2This is what
the LORD Almighty says: "I am very jealous for Zion; I am burning with jealousy
for her."
3This is what the LORD says: "I will re- 8:3
turn[t] to Zion and dwell in Jerusalem.[u] [t] Zec 1:16
Then Jerusalem will be called the City of [u] Zec 2:10
Truth, and the mountain of the LORD
Almighty will be called the Holy Mountain."
4This is what the LORD Almighty says:
"Once again men and women of ripe old 8:4
age will sit in the streets of Jerusalem,[v] [v] Isa 65:20
each with cane in hand because of his
age. 5The city streets will be filled with 8:5
boys and girls playing there.[w]" [w] Jer 30:20; 31:13
6This is what the LORD Almighty says:
"It may seem marvelous to the remnant 8:6
of this people at that time,[x] but will it [x] Ps 118:23; 126:1-3
seem marvelous to me?[y]" declares the [y] Jer 32:17,27
LORD Almighty.
7This is what the LORD Almighty says:
"I will save my people from the countries
of the east and the west.[z] 8I will bring 8:7
them back[a] to live in Jerusalem; they will [z] Ps 107:3; Isa 11:11; 43:5
be my people,[b] and I will be faithful and 8:8
righteous to them as their God." [a] Zec 10:10
9This is what the LORD Almighty says: [b] Eze 11:19-20; 36:28; Zec 2:11
"You who now hear these words spoken
by the prophets[c] who were there when 8:9
the foundation was laid for the house of [c] Ezr 5:1
the LORD Almighty, let your hands be [d] Hag 2:4
strong[d] so that the temple may be built. 8:10
10Before that time there were no wages[e] [e] Hag 1:6
for man or beast. No one could go about
his business safely because of his enemy,
for I had turned every man against his
neighbor. 11But now I will not deal with
the remnant of this people as I did in the
past,"[f] declares the LORD Almighty. 8:11 [f] Isa 12:1
12"The seed will grow well, the vine 8:12
will yield its fruit,[g] the ground will pro- [g] Joel 2:22
duce its crops,[h] and the heavens will [h] Ps 67:6
drop their dew.[i] I will give all these [i] Ge 27:28
things as an inheritance[j] to the remnant [j] Ob 1:17
of this people. 13As you have been an ob-
ject of cursing[k] among the nations, O Ju- 8:13 [k] Jer 42:18
dah and Israel, so will I save you, and you [l] Ge 12:2
will be a blessing.[l] Do not be afraid, but
let your hands be strong."
14This is what the LORD Almighty says:
"Just as I had determined to bring disas- 8:14
ter[m] upon you and showed no pity when [m] Jer 31:28;
your fathers angered me," says the LORD Eze 24:14
Almighty, 15"so now I have determined

8:15 [n] ver 13; Jer 29:11; Mic 7:18-20 to do good[n] again to Jerusalem and Judah. Do not be afraid. 16 These are the
things you are to do: Speak the truth[o] to
8:16 [o] Ps 15:2; Eph 4:25 [p] Zec 7:9 each other, and render true and sound
judgment in your courts;[p] 17 do not plot
evil[q] against your neighbor, and do not
love to swear falsely.[r] I hate all this," de-
8:17 [q] Pr 3:29 [r] Pr 6:16-19 clares the LORD.

18 Again the word of the LORD Almighty came to me. 19 This is what the
8:19 [s] Jer 39:2 [t] Jer 52:12 [u] 2Ki 25:25 [v] Jer 52:4 [w] Ps 30:11 [x] ver 16 LORD Almighty says: "The fasts of the
fourth,[s] fifth,[t] seventh[u] and tenth[v]
months will become joyful[w] and glad
occasions and happy festivals for Judah.
Therefore love truth[x] and peace."

20 This is what the LORD Almighty says:
"Many peoples and the inhabitants of
many cities will yet come, 21 and the inhabitants of one city will go to another
8:21 [y] Zec 7:2 and say, 'Let us go at once to entreat[y] the
LORD and seek the LORD Almighty. I my-
self am going.' 22 And many peoples and
powerful nations will come to Jerusalem
8:22 [z] Ps 117:1; Isa 60:3; Zec 2:11 to seek the LORD Almighty and to entreat him."[z]

23 This is what the LORD Almighty says:
"In those days ten men from all languages and nations will take firm hold
of one Jew by the hem of his robe and
8:23 [a] Isa 45:14; 1Co 14:25 say, 'Let us go with you, because we have
heard that God is with you.' "[a]

Judgment on Israel's Enemies

An Oracle

9 The word of the LORD is against
the land of Hadrach
9:1 [b] Isa 17:1 and will rest upon Damascus[b]—
for the eyes of men and all the
tribes of Israel
9:2 [c] Jer 49:23 [d] Eze 28:1-19 are on the LORD—[a]
2 and upon Hamath[c] too, which
borders on it,
and upon Tyre[d] and Sidon,
though they are very skillful.
3 Tyre has built herself a stronghold;
she has heaped up silver like
dust,
9:3 [e] Job 27:16; Eze 28:4 and gold like the dirt of the
streets.[e]
4 But the Lord will take away her
possessions
9:4 [f] Isa 23:1; Eze 26:3-5; 28:18 and destroy her power on the sea,
and she will be consumed by fire.[f]
5 Ashkelon will see it and fear;
Gaza will writhe in agony,
and Ekron too, for her hope will
wither.
Gaza will lose her king
and Ashkelon will be deserted.
6 Foreigners will occupy Ashdod,
and I will cut off the pride of the
Philistines.
7 I will take the blood from their
mouths,
the forbidden food from
between their teeth.
Those who are left will belong to
our God
and become leaders in Judah,
and Ekron will be like the
Jebusites.
8 But I will defend my house
against marauding forces.
Never again will an oppressor
overrun my people,
for now I am keeping watch.[g] 9:8 [g] Isa 52:1; 54:14

The Coming of Zion's King

9 Rejoice greatly, O Daughter of Zion!
Shout, Daughter of Jerusalem!
See, your king[b] comes to you,
righteous and having salvation,[h] 9:9 [h] Isa 9:6-7; 43:3-11; Jer 23:5-6; Zep 3:14-15; Zec 2:10 [i] Mt 21:5*; Jn 12:15*
gentle and riding on a donkey,
on a colt, the foal of a donkey.[i]
10 I will take away the chariots from
Ephraim
and the war-horses from
Jerusalem,
and the battle bow will be 9:10 [j] Hos 1:7; 2:18; Mic 4:3; 5:10; Zec 10:4 [k] Ps 72:8
broken.[j]
He will proclaim peace to the
nations.
His rule will extend from sea to
sea
and from the River[c] to the ends
of the earth.[d][k]
11 As for you, because of the blood of 9:11 [l] Ex 24:8 [m] Isa 42:7
my covenant[l] with you,
I will free your prisoners[m] from
the waterless pit.
12 Return to your fortress,[n] 9:12 [n] Joel 3:16
O prisoners of hope;
even now I announce that I will
restore twice as much to
you.
13 I will bend Judah as I bend my bow 9:13 [o] Isa 49:2 [p] Joel 3:6 [q] Jer 51:20
and fill it with Ephraim.[o]
I will rouse your sons, O Zion,
against your sons, O Greece,[p]
and make you like a warrior's
sword.[q]

[a] 1 Or *Damascus. / For the eye of the LORD is on all mankind, / as well as on the tribes of Israel,*
[b] 9 Or *King* [c] 10 That is, the Euphrates
[d] 10 Or *the end of the land*

DISCOVERY 229

Why a Donkey?

Donkeys are not known for their speed and grace. Nor are they generally associated with nobility and pride. God's promised Messiah would make his grand entrance into Jerusalem astride a donkey, however—Zechariah was clear about that (Zechariah 9:9). The Bible tells us that Jesus later did this very thing in order to fulfill Zechariah's prophecy (Matthew 21:1–11). But *why* did God want his Son to ride that donkey?

Donkeys were service animals, and as such they were used for many purposes: trampling grain, pulling plows, transporting heavy loads for long distances, turning millstones to grind grain. In spite of their diminutive size these animals were capable of tremendous amounts of work, and they served people well. And Jesus chose a donkey to remind us that he had come to earth to serve.

Just before Jesus' triumphal entry into Jerusalem, the mother of James and John had entreated the Lord to allow her sons to sit on either side of him in heaven. Jesus had informed her that priorities in his heavenly kingdom would be different from the ones with which we are familiar here on earth. Anyone who desired to be first would instead have to become a slave to others. Jesus "did not come to be served, but to serve, and to give his life as a ransom for many" (Matthew 20:28). Immediately after Jesus had said this, he dispatched two disciples to procure the donkey for him.

Donkeys were also associated with peace. A warrior would not dream of riding a donkey into battle (Zechariah 9:10). Jesus wanted to convey that he had not come to earth to overthrow the Roman government, even though that was the one accomplishment most of the people expected of the Messiah. His purpose was instead to bring peace with God through his own suffering and death (Romans 5:1–2; Ephesians 2:14–18). One day he will return, this time riding a horse and prepared for battle. He will at that time eliminate sin from the world forever and establish his eternal kingdom (Revelation 19:11–16).

Donkeys are gentle animals, not as high-strung as horses and more predictable. The Messiah himself would not be an avenger in the way the people were expecting. Instead, he came to us "gentle and riding on a donkey" (Zechariah 9:9; Matthew 21:5).

Today donkeys are not generally considered to be desirable animals. But it was a donkey that God used to accomplish his purpose. We may not think of our own lives as significant, either, but still today God has use for the unlikely and the different. He frequently accomplishes his purposes through people or ideas that we would view as foolish or weak (1 Corinthians 1:27–30; 2 Corinthians 4:7).

***Self-Discovery:** Take a moment to reflect on how God chooses to use you. As you identify your personal characteristics, offer each to God to use as he sees fit.*

GO TO DISCOVERY 230 ON PAGE 1235

The LORD Will Appear

[14] Then the LORD will appear over
them;[r]
his arrow will flash like
lightning.[s]
The Sovereign LORD will sound the
trumpet;
he will march in the storms[t] of
the south,
[15] and the LORD Almighty will
shield[u] them.
They will destroy
and overcome with slingstones.
They will drink and roar as with
wine;
they will be full like a bowl
used for sprinkling[a] the corners[v]
of the altar.
[16] The LORD their God will save them
on that day
as the flock of his people.
They will sparkle in his land
like jewels in a crown.[w]
[17] How attractive and beautiful they
will be!
Grain will make the young men
thrive,
and new wine the young women.

9:14 [r] Isa 31:5 [s] Ps 18:14; Hab 3:11 [t] Isa 21:1; 66:15
9:15 [u] Isa 37:35; Zec 12:8 [v] Ex 27:2
9:16 [w] Isa 62:3; Jer 31:11

The LORD Will Care for Judah

10 Ask the LORD for rain in the
springtime;
it is the LORD who makes the
storm clouds.
He gives showers of rain to men,
and plants of the field to
everyone.
[2] The idols[x] speak deceit,
diviners see visions that lie;
they tell dreams that are false,
they give comfort in vain.
Therefore the people wander like
sheep
oppressed for lack of a shepherd.[y]

[3] "My anger burns against the
shepherds,
and I will punish the leaders;[z]
for the LORD Almighty will care
for his flock, the house of Judah,
and make them like a proud
horse in battle.
[4] From Judah will come the
cornerstone,
from him the tent peg,[a]
from him the battle bow,[b]
from him every ruler.
[5] Together they[b] will be like mighty
men
trampling the muddy streets in
battle.[c]
Because the LORD is with them,
they will fight and overthrow the
horsemen.[d]

[6] "I will strengthen the house of
Judah
and save the house of Joseph.
I will restore them
because I have compassion on
them.[e]
They will be as though
I had not rejected them,
for I am the LORD their God
and I will answer[f] them.
[7] The Ephraimites will become like
mighty men,
and their hearts will be glad as
with wine.[g]
Their children will see it and be
joyful;
their hearts will rejoice in the
LORD.
[8] I will signal[h] for them
and gather them in.
Surely I will redeem them;
they will be as numerous[i] as
before.
[9] Though I scatter them among the
peoples,
yet in distant lands they will
remember me.[j]
They and their children will
survive,
and they will return.
[10] I will bring them back from Egypt
and gather them from Assyria.[k]
I will bring them to Gilead[l] and
Lebanon,
and there will not be room[m]
enough for them.
[11] They will pass through the sea of
trouble;
the surging sea will be subdued
and all the depths of the Nile will
dry up.[n]
Assyria's pride[o] will be brought
down
and Egypt's scepter[p] will pass
away.
[12] I will strengthen them in the LORD
and in his name they will walk,"[q]
declares the LORD.

10:2 [x] Eze 21:21 [y] Eze 34:5; Hos 3:4; Mt 9:36
10:3 [z] Jer 25:34
10:4 [a] Isa 22:23 [b] Zec 9:10
10:5 [c] 2Sa 22:43 [d] Am 2:15; Hag 2:22
10:6 [e] Zec 8:7-8 [f] Zec 13:9
10:7 [g] Zec 9:15
10:8 [h] Isa 5:26 [i] Jer 33:22; Eze 36:11
10:9 [j] Eze 6:9
10:10 [k] Isa 11:11 [l] Jer 50:19 [m] Isa 49:19
10:11 [n] Isa 19:5-7; 51:10 [o] Zep 2:13 [p] Eze 30:13
10:12 [q] Mic 4:5

[a] 15 Or *bowl, / like* [b] 4,5 Or *ruler, all of them together. / [5]They*

11:1 [r] Eze 31:3 **11** Open your doors,
O Lebanon,[r]
so that fire may devour your
cedars!
2 Wail, O pine tree, for the cedar has
fallen;
the stately trees are ruined!
11:2 Wail, oaks of Bashan;
[s] Isa 32:19 the dense forest[s] has been cut
down!
3 Listen to the wail of the shepherds;
their rich pastures are destroyed!
Listen to the roar of the lions;
11:3 the lush thicket of the Jordan is
[t] Jer 2:15; 50:44 ruined![t]

Two Shepherds

4 This is what the LORD my God says:
"Pasture the flock marked for slaughter.
5 Their buyers slaughter them and go unpunished. Those who sell them say,
'Praise the LORD, I am rich!' Their own
11:5 [u] Jer 50:7; shepherds do not spare them.[u] 6 For I will
Eze 34:2-3 no longer have pity on the people of the
land," declares the LORD. "I will hand
everyone over to his neighbor[v] and his 11:6 [v] Zec 14:13
king. They will oppress the land, and I [w] Isa 9:19-21;
will not rescue them from their hands."[w] Jer 13:14;
7 So I pastured the flock marked for Mic 5:8; 7:2-6
slaughter, particularly the oppressed of
the flock. Then I took two staffs and
called one Favor and the other Union,
and I pastured the flock. 8 In one month
I got rid of the three shepherds.
The flock detested me, and I grew
weary of them 9 and said, "I will not be
your shepherd. Let the dying die, and 11:9
the perishing perish.[x] Let those who are [x] Jer 15:2; 43:11
left eat one another's flesh."
10 Then I took my staff called Favor[y] 11:10 [y] ver 7
and broke it, revoking[z] the covenant I [z] Ps 89:39;
had made with all the nations. 11 It was Jer 14:21
revoked on that day, and so the afflicted
of the flock who were watching me
knew it was the word of the LORD.
12 I told them, "If you think it best, give
me my pay; but if not, keep it." So they 11:12
paid me thirty pieces of silver.[a] [a] Ex 21:32;
13 And the LORD said to me, "Throw it Mt 26:15
to the potter"—the handsome price at
which they priced me! So I took the thirty pieces of silver and threw them into 11:13
the house of the LORD to the potter.[b] [b] Mt 27:9-10*;
14 Then I broke my second staff called Ac 1:18-19
Union, breaking the brotherhood be-
tween Judah and Israel.
15 Then the LORD said to me, "Take
again the equipment of a foolish shepherd. 16 For I am going to raise up a shepherd over the land who will not care for
the lost, or seek the young, or heal the
injured, or feed the healthy, but will eat
the meat of the choice sheep, tearing off
their hoofs.

17 "Woe to the worthless shepherd,[c] 11:17
who deserts the flock! [c] Jer 23:1
May the sword strike his arm[d] and [d] Eze 30:21-22
his right eye! [e] Jer 23:1
May his arm be completely
withered,
his right eye totally blinded!"[e]

Jerusalem's Enemies to Be Destroyed

An Oracle

12 This is the word of the LORD concerning Israel. The LORD, who 12:1 [f] Isa 42:5;
stretches out the heavens,[f] who lays the Jer 51:15
foundation of the earth,[g] and who forms [g] Ps 102:25;
the spirit of man[h] within him, declares: Heb 1:10 [h] Isa 57:16
2 "I am going to make Jerusalem a cup[i] 12:2
that sends all the surrounding peoples [i] Ps 75:8

JESUS FOCUS

REJECTING THE SHEPHERD

God frequently described himself as a shepherd who leads his people (Genesis 48:15; Psalm 23:1; 80:1; Isaiah 40:11), and he employed the same image to describe individuals who lead God's people in his ways (2 Samuel 5:2; Psalm 78:70–72; Jeremiah 3:15; 23:1–4; Ezekiel 34:1–2). God's intention was, of course, that the leaders guide the people in the same way God does—in compassion, truth and mercy—but we are aware from our reading of Scripture that it didn't always happen. God informed Zechariah that he was angry with the leaders of Judah, and he promised to shepherd the nation himself (Zechariah 10:3). Zechariah possessed two shepherd's staffs, one symbolizing God's blessing and the other national unity. God broke both staffs because the people had turned away from him (Zechariah 11:4–17). Centuries later God's people would reject the Good Shepherd (Jesus Christ) once again (John 10:1–18; see Matthew 21:42; Mark 8:31). The prophet Zechariah predicted that the leaders of the people would pay 30 pieces of silver in exchange for Jesus' life, and Matthew recorded that Judas was paid precisely that amount to turn Jesus over to the authorities (Zechariah 11:12–13; Matthew 27:9–10).

DISCOVERY 230

Death by Crucifixion

Human beings have throughout the centuries developed many methods for torturing and killing one another, but crucifixion remains one of the cruelest. The Romans used this style of execution on a regular basis. The person hung on a cross was either tied by his or her hands and feet or nailed to the wood. This position prevented blood from circulating to the vital organs. The agony was compounded by the fact that the only way to breathe was to raise up the body. That necessity entailed excruciating pain as the dying individual pulled with the hands and pushed with the feet. Eventually exhaustion would take over, and the victim would die. Part of what makes this form of execution so horrific is the fact that the person could hang in this way for up to several days before succumbing to death. The Jewish people hated this form of execution and viewed anyone who was crucified as being cursed by God (Deuteronomy 21:23).

It was shocking to God's people first to even conceive of his promised Messiah as having to die. And even if the Jews were to accept this as a possibility, that he would die in such a cursed way was unthinkable. And yet the prophet Zechariah predicted just that, going so far as to specify that the Savior would be "pierced" (Zechariah 12:10). Zechariah was not the only Old Testament writer to make such a prediction. Psalm 22:16 says the same thing, as does Isaiah 53:5: "He was pierced for our transgressions." Just as Jesus' birth was predicted in great detail, many of the details about Jesus death were foretold in the Old Testament.

It is the very fact that Jesus died, as well as the manner of his death, that has prevented many Jewish people throughout the centuries from accepting him as the Messiah. Everything about our Lord's crucifixion constitutes an affront to their understanding of God's teachings. By contrast, Jesus' followers have always viewed the crucifixion as a source for celebration. The apostle Paul stated, "May I never boast except in the cross of our Lord Jesus Christ, through which the world has been crucified to me, and I to the world" (Galatians 6:14).

The cross represents our only hope for salvation, because it is at the foot of that cross that we find forgiveness and become "crucified" to our sinful selves so that the living God can become preeminent in our lives (Romans 6:6; Galatians 2:19–21). We can become all that God intended us to be only after he has forgiven our sins and begun working in our lives to make us more like his Son (2 Corinthians 3:18; Philippians 2:1–13; 1 John 3:2).

One day there will be no more doubt. The entire human race will understand that Jesus was "pierced" for our sin: "Look, he is coming with the clouds, and every eye will see him, even those who pierced him" (Revelation 1:7).

Self-Discovery: *As you ponder the anguish Jesus suffered on the cross, pause to express your response in a time of prayer.*

GO TO DISCOVERY 231 ON PAGE 1241

12:2 reeling.[j] Judah[k] will be besieged as well as
jIsa 51:23 Jerusalem. 3On that day, when all the na-
kZec 14:14 tions[l] of the earth are gathered against
12:3 lZec 14:2 her, I will make Jerusalem an immovable
mDa 2:34-35 rock[m] for all the nations. All who try to
nMt 21:44 move it will injure[n] themselves. 4On that
day I will strike every horse with panic
and its rider with madness," declares the
LORD. "I will keep a watchful eye over the
12:4 house of Judah, but I will blind all the
oPs 76:6 horses of the nations.[o] 5Then the leaders
of Judah will say in their hearts, 'The people of Jerusalem are strong, because the
LORD Almighty is their God.'
6"On that day I will make the leaders
12:6 pIsa 10:17-18; of Judah like a firepot[p] in a woodpile,
Zec 11:1 like a flaming torch among sheaves.
qOb 1:18 They will consume[q] right and left all the
surrounding peoples, but Jerusalem will
remain intact in her place.
7"The LORD will save the dwellings of
Judah first, so that the honor of the house
of David and of Jerusalem's inhabitants
12:7 rJer 30:18; may not be greater than that of Judah.[r]
Am 9:11 8On that day the LORD will shield[s] those
who live in Jerusalem, so that the feeblest
12:8 sJoel 3:16; among them will be like David, and the
Zec 9:15 house of David will be like God,[t] like the
tPs 82:6 uMic 7:8 Angel of the LORD going before[u] them.
9On that day I will set out to destroy all
12:9 vZec 14:2-3 the nations that attack Jerusalem.[v]

Mourning for the One They Pierced

10"And I will pour out on the house of
David and the inhabitants of Jerusalem
12:10 wIsa 44:3; a spirit[a] of grace and supplication.[w]
Eze 39:29; They will look on[b] me, the one they have
Joel 2:28-29 xJn 19:34,37*; pierced,[x] and they will mourn for him as
Rev 1:7 one mourns for an only child, and grieve
bitterly for him as one grieves for a firstborn son. 11On that day the weeping in
Jerusalem will be great, like the weeping
of Hadad Rimmon in the plain of Me-
12:11 y2Ki 23:29 giddo.[y] 12The land will mourn,[z] each
clan by itself, with their wives by them-
12:12 zMt 24:30; selves: the clan of the house of David
Rev 1:7 and their wives, the clan of the house of
Nathan and their wives, 13the clan of the
house of Levi and their wives, the clan of
Shimei and their wives, 14and all the rest
of the clans and their wives.

Cleansing From Sin

13:1 aJer 17:13 13 "On that day a fountain[a] will be
bPs 51:2; opened to the house of David
Heb 9:14 and the inhabitants of Jerusalem, to
cleanse[b] them from sin and impurity.

2"On that day, I will banish the names
of the idols[c] from the land, and they will 13:2 cEx 23:13;
be remembered no more," declares the Eze 36:25;
LORD Almighty. "I will remove both the Hos 2:17 d1Ki 22:22;
prophets[d] and the spirit of impurity Jer 23:14-15
from the land. 3And if anyone still
prophesies, his father and mother, to
whom he was born, will say to him, 'You
must die, because you have told lies in
the LORD's name.' When he prophesies, 13:3
his own parents will stab him.[e] eDt 13:6-11;
4"On that day every prophet will be 18:20; Jer 23:34;
ashamed[f] of his prophetic vision. He will Eze 14:9
not put on a prophet's garment[g] of hair[h] 13:4
in order to deceive. 5He will say, 'I am not fJer 6:15;
a prophet. I am a farmer; the land has Mic 3:6-7 gMt 3:4
been my livelihood since my youth.[c][i] 6If h2Ki 1:8; Isa 20:2
someone asks him, 'What are these 13:5
wounds on your body[d]?' he will answer, iAm 7:14
'The wounds I was given at the house of
my friends.'

The Shepherd Struck, the Sheep Scattered

7"Awake, O sword,[j] against my 13:7 jJer 47:6
shepherd,[k] kIsa 40:11; 53:4; Eze 37:24
against the man who is close to lMt 26:31*;
me!" Mk 14:27*
declares the LORD Almighty.
"Strike the shepherd,
and the sheep will be scattered,[l]
and I will turn my hand against
the little ones.
8In the whole land," declares the
LORD,
"two-thirds will be struck down
and perish;
yet one-third will be left in it.[m] 13:8 mEze 5:2-4,12
9This third I will bring into the fire;[n] 13:9
I will refine them like silver[o] nMal 3:2
and test them like gold. oIsa 48:10; 1Pe 1:6-7
They will call[p] on my name pPs 50:15
and I will answer[q] them; qZec 10:6 rJer 30:22
I will say, 'They are my people,'[r] sJer 29:12
and they will say, 'The LORD is
our God.'[s]

The LORD Comes and Reigns

14 A day of the LORD[t] is coming 14:1
when your plunder will be di- tIsa 13:9;
vided among you. Mal 4:1
2I will gather all the nations to Jerusalem to fight against it; the city will be
captured, the houses ransacked, and the

[a] 10 Or *the Spirit* [b] 10 Or *to* [c] 5 Or *farmer; a man sold me in my youth* [d] 6 Or *wounds between your hands*

women raped. Half of the city will go
14:2 [u]Isa 13:6; Zec 13:8 into exile, but the rest of the people will
not be taken from the city.[u]
3Then the LORD will go out and fight[v]
14:3 [v]Zec 9:14-15 against those nations, as he fights in the
day of battle. 4On that day his feet will
14:4 [w]Eze 11:23 stand on the Mount of Olives,[w] east of
Jerusalem, and the Mount of Olives will
14:5 [x]Am 1:1 [y]Isa 29:6; 66:15-16 [z]Mt 16:27; 25:31 be split in two from east to west, forming a great valley, with half of the moun-
tain moving north and half moving
south. 5You will flee by my mountain
valley, for it will extend to Azel. You will
flee as you fled from the earthquake[a][x] in
the days of Uzziah king of Judah. Then
the LORD my God will come,[y] and all the
holy ones with him.[z]
14:6 [a]Isa 13:10; Jer 4:23 6On that day there will be no light,[a] no
cold or frost. 7It will be a unique[b] day,
without daytime or nighttime[c]—a day
14:7 [b]Jer 30:7 [c]Rev 21:23-25; 22:5 [d]Isa 30:26 known to the LORD. When evening
comes, there will be light.[d]
8On that day living water[e] will flow
14:8 [e]Eze 47:1-12; Jn 7:38; Rev 22:1-2 [f]Joel 2:20 out from Jerusalem, half to the eastern[f]
sea[b] and half to the western sea,[c] in
summer and in winter.
9The LORD will be king over the whole
14:9 [g]Dt 6:4; Isa 45:24; Rev 11:15 [h]Eph 4:5-6 earth.[g] On that day there will be one
LORD, and his name the only name.[h]
10The whole land, from Geba[i] to Rimmon, south of Jerusalem, will become
14:10 [i]1Ki 15:22 [j]Jer 30:18; Am 9:11 [k]Zec 12:6 like the Arabah. But Jerusalem will be
raised up[j] and remain in its place,[k] from
the Benjamin Gate to the site of the First
Gate, to the Corner Gate, and from the
Tower of Hananel to the royal winepresses. 11It will be inhabited; never
again will it be destroyed. Jerusalem will
14:11 [l]Eze 34:25-28 be secure.[l]
12This is the plague with which the
LORD will strike all the nations that
fought against Jerusalem: Their flesh
will rot while they are still standing on
their feet, their eyes will rot in their
sockets, and their tongues will rot in
14:12 [m]Lev 26:16; Dt 28:22 their mouths.[m] 13On that day men will
be stricken by the LORD with great pan-
ic. Each man will seize the hand of an-
14:13 [n]Zec 11:6 other, and they will attack each other.[n]
14:14 [o]Zec 12:2 [p]Isa 23:18 14Judah[o] too will fight at Jerusalem. The
wealth of all the surrounding nations
will be collected[p]—great quantities of
gold and silver and clothing. 15A similar
14:15 [q]ver 12 plague[q] will strike the horses and mules,
the camels and donkeys, and all the an-
imals in those camps.
16Then the survivors from all the nations that have attacked Jerusalem will
go up year after year to worship the
King, the LORD Almighty, and to cele-
brate the Feast of Tabernacles.[r] 17If any 14:16 [r]Isa 60:6-9
of the peoples of the earth do not go up
to Jerusalem to worship the King, the 14:17 [s]Jer 14:4; Am 4:7
LORD Almighty, they will have no rain.[s]
18If the Egyptian people do not go up
and take part, they will have no rain. The
LORD[d] will bring on them the plague he
inflicts on the nations that do not go up
to celebrate the Feast of Tabernacles.[t] 14:18 [t]ver 12
19This will be the punishment of Egypt
and the punishment of all the nations
that do not go up to celebrate the Feast
of Tabernacles.
20On that day HOLY TO THE LORD will be
inscribed on the bells of the horses, and
the cooking pots[u] in the LORD's house 14:20 [u]Eze 46:20 [v]Zec 9:15
will be like the sacred bowls[v] in front of
the altar. 21Every pot in Jerusalem and
Judah will be holy[w] to the LORD Al- 14:21 [w]Ro 14:6-7; 1Co 10:31 [x]Ne 8:10 [y]Zec 9:8 [z]Eze 44:9
mighty, and all who come to sacrifice
will take some of the pots and cook in
them. And on that day[x] there will no
longer be a Canaanite[e][y] in the house of
the LORD Almighty.[z]

[a] 5 Or *5My mountain valley will be blocked and will extend to Azel. It will be blocked as it was blocked because of the earthquake* [b] 8 That is, the Dead Sea [c] 8 That is, the Mediterranean [d] 18 Or *part, then the LORD* [e] 21 Or *merchant*

JESUS FOCUS

HOLY TO THE LORD

Old Testament law stipulated that there was a difference between the sacred and the secular. The words "HOLY TO THE LORD" were to be inscribed on a plate attached to the front of the priests' turbans as a sign that the priests had been set apart for God's service (Exodus 28:36), and Zechariah predicted that there would come a time when such words would adorn houses and when even ordinary cooking pots would be set apart as sacred (Zechariah 14:21). Generations later God revealed the same picture to another man. The apostle John witnessed a vision of the "new" Jerusalem (Revelation 21—22), a glorious and flawless place where God's name will be written on our foreheads (Revelation 22:4). Only those who have entered into a restored relationship with God through the atoning sacrifice of God the Son, "those whose names are written in the Lamb's book of life" (Revelation 21:27), will be allowed to enter the holy and eternal city of God.

What is the significance of the reference to "the sun of righteousness"? (Malachi 4:2)

◆ *After the firestorm sweeps through, a new day will dawn. The sunrise Malachi had in mind was the coming of God's Son, Jesus Christ.*

How do wings heal? (Malachi 4:2)

◆ *Just as the sun rises and spreads its rays (wings) in every direction, bringing light and warmth, so Jesus, when he appears in human lives, brings light and warmth that are totally healing.*

How would Elijah return? (Malachi 4:5–6)

◆ *Jesus said that John the Baptist fulfilled that great expectation, preparing the way for Jesus Christ himself (Matthew 11:7–14)*

Jesus in Malachi Malachi records a debate between a loving father and his sinful children. God urges his children to change their wicked ways, but they refuse, responding instead with fretful complaints and stinging accusations. This debate provides a glimpse into God's passionate love for his people. Many topics are covered, but all stem from God's desire for his children to reciprocate his love by exhibiting integrity, purity, faithfulness and justice in their daily lives.

Chapters 3 and 4 point toward the coming of Jesus, the messenger of God's covenant (Malachi 3:1) and the "sun of righteousness [who] will rise with healing in [his] wings" (Malachi 4:2). These descriptions set the backdrop for the Gospel narratives immediately to follow.

God's final words through Malachi reverberate with hope: "I will send you the prophet Elijah" (Malachi 4:5). When Jesus began his work, he identified John the Baptist as that promised prophet (Matthew 11:14), the one who would minister "in the spirit and power of Elijah" (Luke 1:17) and prepare the way for Jesus, "the Lamb of God, who takes away the sin of the world" (John 1:29).

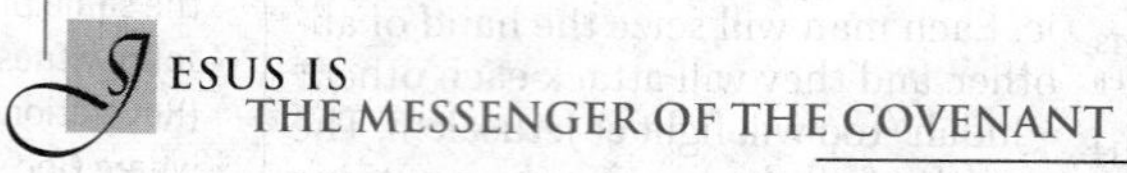
JESUS IS
THE MESSENGER OF THE COVENANT

1:1 [a]Na 1:1 **1** An oracle:[a] The word[b] of the LORD
[b]1Pe 4:11 to Israel through Malachi.[a]

Jacob Loved, Esau Hated

1:2 2"I have loved[c] you," says the LORD.
[c]Dt 4:37 "But you ask, 'How have you
[d]Ro 9:13* loved us?'
"Was not Esau Jacob's brother?" the
LORD says. "Yet I have loved Jacob,[d] 3but
Esau I have hated, and I have turned his
1:3 [e]Isa 34:10 mountains into a wasteland[e] and left his
[f]Eze 35:3-9 inheritance to the desert jackals.[f]"
1:4 4Edom may say, "Though we have
[g]Isa 9:10 been crushed, we will rebuild[g] the ruins."
[h]Eze 25:12-14 But this is what the LORD Almighty
says: "They may build, but I will demolish. They will be called the Wicked Land,
a people always under the wrath of the
1:5 LORD.[h] 5You will see it with your own
[i]Ps 35:27; Mic 5:4 eyes and say, 'Great[i] is the LORD—even
[j]Am 1:11-12 beyond the borders of Israel!'[j]

Blemished Sacrifices

6"A son honors his father, and a servant his master. If I am a father, where is
the honor due me? If I am a master,
1:6 where is the respect[k] due me?" says the
[k]Isa 1:2 LORD Almighty.[l] "It is you, O priests, who
[l]Job 5:17 show contempt for my name.
"But you ask, 'How have we shown
contempt for your name?'
1:7 7"You place defiled food[m] on my altar.
[m]ver 12; Lev 21:6 "But you ask, 'How have we defiled
you?'
"By saying that the LORD's table is
contemptible. 8When you bring blind
animals for sacrifice, is that not wrong?
When you sacrifice crippled or diseased
1:8 animals,[n] is that not wrong? Try offering
[n]Lev 22:22; Dt 15:21 them to your governor! Would he be
[o]Isa 43:23 pleased with you? Would he accept
you?" says the LORD Almighty.[o]
9"Now implore God to be gracious to
1:9 [p]Lev 23:33-44 us. With such offerings[p] from your
hands, will he accept you?"—says the
LORD Almighty.
10"Oh, that one of you would shut the
temple doors, so that you would not
1:10 light useless fires on my altar! I am not
[q]Hos 5:6 pleased[q] with you," says the LORD
[r]Isa 1:11-14; Jer 14:12 Almighty, "and I will accept no offering[r]
from your hands. 11My name will be
great among the nations, from the rising
to the setting of the sun. In every place
1:11 incense[s] and pure offerings will be
[s]Isa 60:6-7; Rev 8:3 brought to my name, because my name
will be great among the nations," says
the LORD Almighty.
12"But you profane it by saying of the
Lord's table, 'It is defiled,' and of its 1:12
food,[t] 'It is contemptible.' 13And you say, [t]ver 7
'What a burden!'[u] and you sniff at it con- 1:13
temptuously," says the LORD Almighty. [u]Isa 43:22-24
"When you bring injured, crippled or
diseased animals and offer them as sacrifices, should I accept them from your
hands?" says the LORD. 14"Cursed is the
cheat who has an acceptable male in his
flock and vows to give it, but then sacri- 1:14
fices a blemished animal[v] to the Lord. [v]Lev 22:18-21
For I am a great king,[w]" says the LORD [w]1Ti 6:15
Almighty, "and my name is to be feared
among the nations.

Admonition for the Priests

2 "And now this admonition is for
you, O priests.[x] 2If you do not lis- 2:1 [x]ver 7
ten, and if you do not set your heart to
honor my name," says the LORD Al- 2:2
mighty, "I will send a curse[y] upon you, [y]Dt 28:20
and I will curse your blessings. Yes, I
have already cursed them, because you
have not set your heart to honor me.
3"Because of you I will rebuke[b] your
descendants[c]; I will spread on your faces 2:3
the offal[z] from your festival sacrifices, [z]Ex 29:14
and you will be carried off with it.[a] 4And [a]1Ki 14:10
you will know that I have sent you this
admonition so that my covenant with 2:4
Levi[b] may continue," says the LORD [b]Nu 3:12
Almighty. 5"My covenant was with him,
a covenant[c] of life and peace,[d] and I gave 2:5 [c]Dt 33:9
them to him; this called for reverence [d]Nu 25:12
and he revered me and stood in awe of
my name. 6True instruction[e] was in his 2:6
mouth and nothing false was found on [e]Dt 33:10
his lips. He walked with me in peace and [f]Jer 23:22; Jas 5:19-20
uprightness, and turned many from sin.[f]
7"For the lips of a priest[g] ought to pre- 2:7
serve knowledge, and from his mouth [g]Jer 18:18 [h]Lev 10:11
men should seek instruction[h]—because [i]Nu 27:21
he is the messenger[i] of the LORD Almighty. 8But you have turned from the
way and by your teaching have caused 2:8
many to stumble;[j] you have violated the [j]Jer 18:15
covenant with Levi," says the LORD
Almighty. 9"So I have caused you to be 2:9
despised[k] and humiliated before all the [k]1Sa 2:30
people, because you have not followed
my ways but have shown partiality in
matters of the law."

[a] 1 *Malachi* means *my messenger.* [b] 3 Or *cut off* (see Septuagint) [c] 3 Or *will blight your grain*

Judah Unfaithful

2:10 [l]1Co 8:6 [m]Ex 19:5 10Have we not all one Father[a]?[l] Did
not one God create us? Why do we pro-
fane the covenant[m] of our fathers by
breaking faith with one another?
11Judah has broken faith. A detestable
thing has been committed in Israel and
in Jerusalem: Judah has desecrated the
2:11 [n]Ne 13:23 sanctuary the LORD loves, by marrying[n]
[o]Ezr 9:1; Jer 3:7-9 the daughter of a foreign god.[o] 12As for
the man who does this, whoever he may
2:12 [p]Eze 24:21 be, may the LORD cut him off[p] from the
[q]Mal 1:10 tents of Jacob[b]—even though he brings
offerings[q] to the LORD Almighty.
13Another thing you do: You flood the
LORD's altar with tears. You weep and
wail because he no longer pays atten-
2:13 [r]Jer 14:12 tion[r] to your offerings or accepts them
with pleasure from your hands. 14You
ask, "Why?" It is because the LORD is acting as the witness between you and the
2:14 [s]Pr 5:18 wife of your youth,[s] because you have
broken faith with her, though she is your
partner, the wife of your marriage covenant.
2:15 [t]Ge 2:24; Mt 19:4-6 15Has not ⌊the LORD⌋ made them one?[t]
In flesh and spirit they are his. And why
[u]1Co 7:14 one? Because he was seeking godly offspring.[c][u] So guard yourself in your spirit, and do not break faith with the wife of
your youth.
2:16 [v]Dt 24:1; 16"I hate divorce,"[v] says the LORD God
Mt 5:31-32; of Israel, "and I hate a man's covering
19:4-9 himself[d] with violence as well as with his
garment," says the LORD Almighty.
So guard yourself in your spirit, and
do not break faith.

The Day of Judgment

2:17 [w]Isa 43:24 17You have wearied[w] the LORD with
your words.
"How have we wearied him?" you ask.
By saying, "All who do evil are good in
the eyes of the LORD, and he is pleased
with them" or "Where is the God of justice?"
3 "See, I will send my messenger,
who will prepare the way before
3:1 [x]Isa 40:3; me.[x] Then suddenly the Lord you are
Mt 11:10*; seeking will come to his temple; the
Mk 1:2*; messenger of the covenant, whom you
Lk 7:27* desire, will come," says the LORD Almighty.
3:2 [y]Eze 22:14; 2But who can endure[y] the day of his
Rev 6:17 coming? Who can stand when he ap-
[z]Zec 13:9; pears? For he will be like a refiner's fire[z]
Mt 3:10-12 or a launderer's soap. 3He will sit as a refiner and purifier of silver;[a] he will puri- 3:3 [a]Da 12:10
fy[b] the Levites and refine them like gold [b]Isa 1:25
and silver. Then the LORD will have men
who will bring offerings in righteous-
ness, 4and the offerings[c] of Judah and Je- 3:4 [c]2Ch 7:12;
rusalem will be acceptable to the LORD, Ps 51:19; Mal 1:11
as in days gone by, as in former years.[d] [d]2Ch 7:3
5"So I will come near to you for judg-
ment. I will be quick to testify against
sorcerers, adulterers and perjurers,[e] 3:5 [e]Jer 7:9
against those who defraud laborers of [f]Lev 19:13;
their wages,[f] who oppress the widows[g] Jas 5:4 [g]Ex 22:22
and the fatherless, and deprive aliens of
justice, but do not fear me," says the
LORD Almighty.

Robbing God

6"I the LORD do not change.[h] So you, 3:6 [h]Nu 23:19;
O descendants of Jacob, are not de- Jas 1:17
stroyed. 7Ever since the time of your
forefathers you have turned away[i] from 3:7 [i]Jer 7:26;
my decrees and have not kept them. Re- Ac 7:51 [j]Zec 1:3
turn to me, and I will return to you,"[j]
says the LORD Almighty.
"But you ask, 'How are we to return?'
8"Will a man rob God? Yet you
rob me.
"But you ask, 'How do we rob you?'
"In tithes[k] and offerings. 9You are 3:8 [k]Ne 13:10-12

[a] 10 Or *father* [b] 12 Or *12May the LORD cut off from the tents of Jacob anyone who gives testimony in behalf of the man who does this* [c] 15 Or *15But the one ⌊who is our father⌋ did not do this, not as long as life remained in him. And what was he seeking? An offspring from God* [d] 16 Or *his wife*

JESUS FOCUS

PREPARING THE WAY

The Old Testament closes with both a promise and a warning. The promise was that a "messenger" or prophet would come to prepare the hearts of the people for the coming Messiah, whom Malachi referred to as the "messenger of the covenant" (Malachi 3:1–3). The New Testament identifies the first messenger as John the Baptist (Matthew 11:14; John 1:19–27) and the second as Jesus Christ himself (Matthew 3:11–17; John 1:29–34; see also Isaiah 4:6; Jeremiah 31:31–34; Hebrews 8:6–13; 9:15). The warning was that God would curse the land if the people opted to reject the messages of the forerunner and the Messiah (Malachi 4:6). The Old Testament ends with the people still looking for God's promised Messiah, and the New Testament heralds that he has come and identifies him as Jesus (Luke 2:11,29–32).

DISCOVERY 231

When God Is Silent

There are stagnant periods in the lives of many believers during which God seems almost strangely silent. Perhaps that has never been more true than during the four centuries between the end of the Old Testament and the beginning of the New. Malachi was the last of the Old Testament prophets, and after his death God did not send a successor until the birth of John the Baptist.

It isn't too difficult to visualize dour Old Testament prophets whose primary role it was to pronounce doom and gloom on God's unfaithful people. But Malachi closed his prophecy with words that should have infused all future generations with hope: "Surely the day [was] coming" when people would see God's righteousness, and there would be healing for God's people when "Elijah" appeared (Malachi 4:1–6). The "Elijah" to whom Malachi pointed would be John the Baptist, and his purpose would be to prepare the people for the ministry of the One who would set them free from slavery to sin.

What must it have been like to be alive during the intertestamental period? No prophets, no message from God—only a seemingly endless void. Some people very likely assumed that God had forgotten them. Others may have concluded that he no longer cared. We all live through times during which it seems we are unable to make contact with our Lord, and we inevitably experience the same fears and doubts. Living during these times of apparent one-way communication requires faith.

But even though there had been no prophet since Malachi, the people had already received God's promises; they already had access to the word of the Lord. The faith of some no doubt matured during that communication vacuum as they continued to turn to God in faith and cling to his promises.

In the final analysis God is never really silent (see Hebrews 1:1–3). He might not furnish new revelation, but we always have his eternal and completely reliable Word to inspire hope in our hearts. After all, we serve the infinite and all-powerful God who pledges that he will ever be "faithful to all his promises and loving toward all he has made" (Psalm 145:13), and nowhere has this promise been more beautifully expressed than in the gift of his precious Son, our Lord and Savior Jesus Christ.

Self-Discovery: *Have you gone through a period during which God seemed silent and your faith in Jesus stagnant? What are some of the things you learned from this experience?*

GO TO DISCOVERY 232 ON PAGE 1259

under a curse—the whole nation of
3:10 you—because you are robbing me.
[l]Ne 13:12 [10]Bring the whole tithe into the store-
[m]2Ki 7:2 house,[l] that there may be food in my
house. Test me in this," says the LORD
Almighty, "and see if I will not throw
open the floodgates[m] of heaven and
pour out so much blessing that you will
not have room enough for it. [11]I will prevent pests from devouring your crops,
and the vines in your fields will not cast
their fruit," says the LORD Almighty.
3:12 [n]Isa 61:9 [12]"Then all the nations will call you
[o]Isa 62:4 blessed,[n] for yours will be a delightful
land,"[o] says the LORD Almighty.
3:13 [p]Mal 2:17 [13]"You have said harsh things[p] against
me," says the LORD.
"Yet you ask, 'What have we said
3:14 against you?'
[q]Ps 73:13 [14]"You have said, 'It is futile[q] to serve
[r]Isa 58:3 God. What did we gain by carrying out
his requirements and going about like
mourners[r] before the LORD Almighty?
[15]But now we call the arrogant blessed.
3:15 [s]Jer 7:10 Certainly the evildoers[s] prosper, and
even those who challenge God escape.'"
[16]Then those who feared the LORD
3:16 talked with each other, and the LORD lis-
[t]Ps 34:15 tened and heard.[t] A scroll[u] of remem-
[u]Ps 56:8 brance was written in his presence concerning those who feared the LORD and
honored his name.
[17]"They will be mine," says the LORD
3:17 Almighty, "in the day when I make up
[v]Dt 7:6 my treasured possession.[a][v] I will spare[w]
[w]Ps 103:13; Isa 26:20 them, just as in compassion a man
spares his son who serves him. [18]And
3:18 you will again see the distinction be-
[x]Ge 18:25 tween the righteous[x] and the wicked,

FOR WHAT IS GRACE BUT THE BEAMS OF CHRIST, THE SUN OF RIGHTEOUSNESS?

Richard Sibbes, *Puritan Pastor*

between those who serve God and those
who do not.

The Day of the LORD

4:1 [y]Joel 2:31 4 "Surely the day is coming;[y] it will
[z]Isa 5:24; Ob 1:18 burn like a furnace. All the arrogant and every evildoer will be stubble,[z]
and that day that is coming will set
them on fire," says the LORD Almighty.
"Not a root or a branch will be left to
them. [2]But for you who revere my name,
4:2 [a]Lk 1:78; Eph 5:14 the sun of righteousness[a] will rise with
healing[b] in its wings. And you will go out
[b]Isa 30:26 and leap[c] like calves released from the
[c]Isa 35:6 stall. [3]Then you will trample[d] down the
4:3 wicked; they will be ashes[e] under the
[d]Job 40:12 soles of your feet on the day when I do
[e]Eze 28:18 these things," says the LORD Almighty.
4:4 [4]"Remember the law[f] of my servant
[f]Ps 147:19 Moses, the decrees and laws I gave him
at Horeb for all Israel.
4:5 [5]"See, I will send you the prophet Eli-
[g]Mt 11:14; Lk 1:17 jah[g] before that great and dreadful day
[h]Joel 2:31 of the LORD comes.[h] [6]He will turn the
4:6 hearts of the fathers to their children,[i]
[i]Lk 1:17 and the hearts of the children to their fa-
[j]Isa 11:4; Rev 19:15 thers; or else I will come and strike[j] the
[k]Zec 5:3 land with a curse."[k]

[a] 17 Or *Almighty, "my treasured possession, in the day when I act*

FROM MALACHI TO JESUS

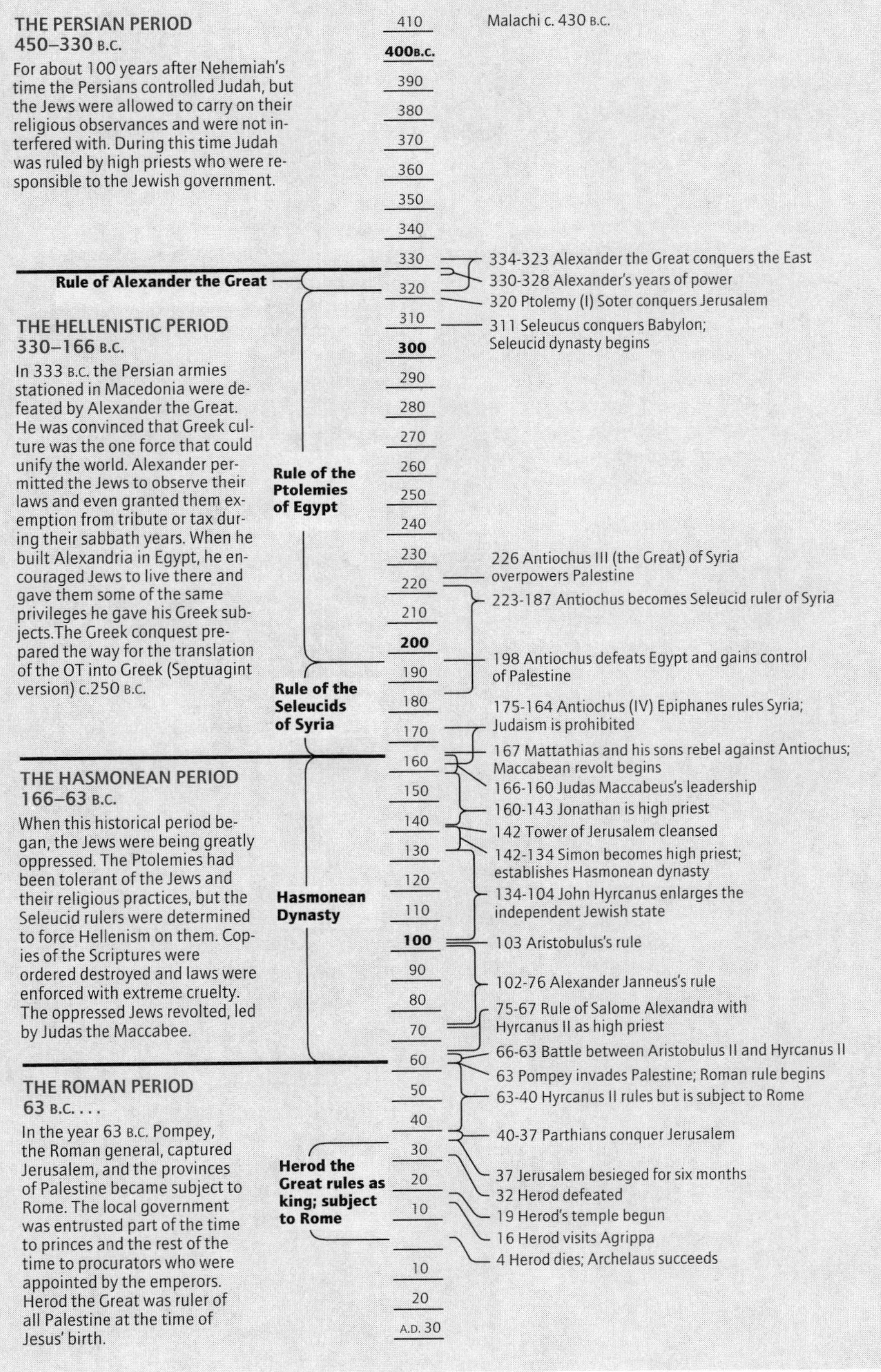

THE PERSIAN PERIOD
450–330 B.C.
For about 100 years after Nehemiah's time the Persians controlled Judah, but the Jews were allowed to carry on their religious observances and were not interfered with. During this time Judah was ruled by high priests who were responsible to the Jewish government.
410
400B.C.
390
380
370
360
350
340
330
320
310
300
290
280
270
260
250
240
230
220
210
200
190
180
170
160
150
140
130
120
110
100
90
80
70
60
50
40
30
20
10
10
20
A.D. 30
Malachi c. 430 B.C.
Rule of Alexander the Great
334-323 Alexander the Great conquers the East
330-328 Alexander's years of power
320 Ptolemy (I) Soter conquers Jerusalem
311 Seleucus conquers Babylon; Seleucid dynasty begins
THE HELLENISTIC PERIOD
330–166 B.C.
In 333 B.C. the Persian armies stationed in Macedonia were defeated by Alexander the Great. He was convinced that Greek culture was the one force that could unify the world. Alexander permitted the Jews to observe their laws and even granted them exemption from tribute or tax during their sabbath years. When he built Alexandria in Egypt, he encouraged Jews to live there and gave them some of the same privileges he gave his Greek subjects.The Greek conquest prepared the way for the translation of the OT into Greek (Septuagint version) c.250 B.C.
Rule of the Ptolemies of Egypt
226 Antiochus III (the Great) of Syria overpowers Palestine
223-187 Antiochus becomes Seleucid ruler of Syria
198 Antiochus defeats Egypt and gains control of Palestine
Rule of the Seleucids of Syria
175-164 Antiochus (IV) Epiphanes rules Syria; Judaism is prohibited
167 Mattathias and his sons rebel against Antiochus; Maccabean revolt begins
166-160 Judas Maccabeus's leadership
160-143 Jonathan is high priest
142 Tower of Jerusalem cleansed
142-134 Simon becomes high priest; establishes Hasmonean dynasty
134-104 John Hyrcanus enlarges the independent Jewish state
103 Aristobulus's rule
102-76 Alexander Janneus's rule
75-67 Rule of Salome Alexandra with Hyrcanus II as high priest
66-63 Battle between Aristobulus II and Hyrcanus II
THE HASMONEAN PERIOD
166–63 B.C.
When this historical period began, the Jews were being greatly oppressed. The Ptolemies had been tolerant of the Jews and their religious practices, but the Seleucid rulers were determined to force Hellenism on them. Copies of the Scriptures were ordered destroyed and laws were enforced with extreme cruelty. The oppressed Jews revolted, led by Judas the Maccabee.
Hasmonean Dynasty
63 Pompey invades Palestine; Roman rule begins
63-40 Hyrcanus II rules but is subject to Rome
40-37 Parthians conquer Jerusalem
37 Jerusalem besieged for six months
32 Herod defeated
19 Herod's temple begun
16 Herod visits Agrippa
4 Herod dies; Archelaus succeeds
THE ROMAN PERIOD
63 B.C. . . .
In the year 63 B.C. Pompey, the Roman general, captured Jerusalem, and the provinces of Palestine became subject to Rome. The local government was entrusted part of the time to princes and the rest of the time to procurators who were appointed by the emperors. Herod the Great was ruler of all Palestine at the time of Jesus' birth.
Herod the Great rules as king; subject to Rome

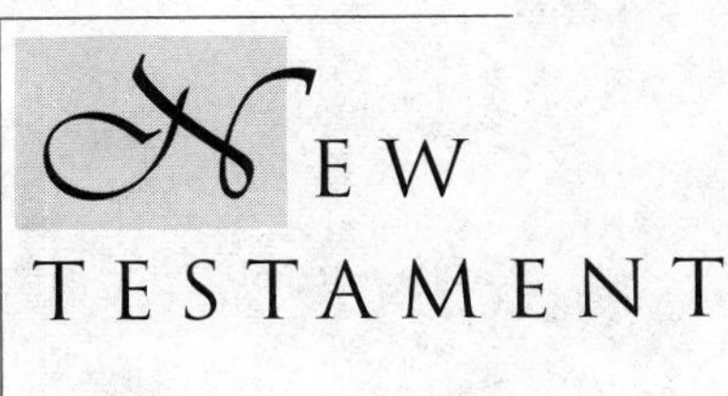
NEW
TESTAMENT

The Time Between the Testaments

The time between the Testaments was one of ferment and change—a time of the realignment of traditional power blocs and the passing of a Near Eastern cultural tradition that had been dominant for almost 3,000 years.

In Biblical history, the approximately 400 years that separate the time of Nehemiah from the birth of Christ are known as the intertestamental period (c. 432—5 B.C.). Sometimes called the "silent" years, they were anything but silent. The events, literature and social forces of these years would shape the world of the New Testament.

History

With the Babylonian captivity, Israel ceased to be an independent nation and became a minor territory in a succession of larger empires. Very little is known about the latter years of Persian domination because the Jewish historian Josephus, our primary source for the intertestamental period, all but ignores them.

With Alexander the Great's acquisition of Palestine (332 B.C.), a new and more insidious threat to Israel emerged. Alexander was committed to the creation of a world united by Greek language and culture, a policy followed by his successors. This policy, called Hellenization, had a dramatic impact on the Jews. At Alexander's death (323 B.C.) the empire he had won was divided among his generals. Two of them founded dynasties—the Ptolemies of Egypt and the Seleucids in Syria and Mesopotamia—that would contend for control of Palestine for over a century.

The rule of the Ptolemies was considerate of Jewish religious sensitivities, but in 198 B.C. the Seleucids took control and paved the way for one of the most heroic periods in Jewish history.

The early Seleucid years were largely a continuation of the tolerant rule of the Ptolemies, but Antiochus IV Epiphanes (whose title means "God made manifest" and who ruled 175—164 B.C.) changed that when he attempted to consolidate his fading empire through a policy of radical Hellenization. While a segment of the Jewish aristocracy had already adopted Greek ways, the majority of Jews were outraged.

Antiochus's atrocities were aimed at the eradication of Jewish religion. He prohibited some of the central elements of Jewish practice, attempted to destroy all copies of the Torah (the Pentateuch) and required offerings to the Greek god Zeus. His crowning outrage was the erection of a statue of Zeus and the sacrificing of a pig in the Jerusalem temple itself.

Opposition to Antiochus was led by Mattathias, an elderly villager from a priestly family, and his five sons: Judas (Maccabeus), Jonathan, Simon, John and Eleazar. Mattathias destroyed a Greek altar established in his village, Modein, and killed Antiochus's emissary. This triggered the Maccabean revolt, a 24-year war (166—142 B.C.) that resulted in the independence of Judah until the Romans took control in 63 B.C.

The victory of Mattathias's family was hollow, however. With the death of his last son, Simon, the Hasmonean dynasty that they founded soon evolved into an aristocratic, Hellenistic regime sometimes hard to distinguish from that of the Seleucids. During the reign of Simon's son, John Hyrcanus, the orthodox Jews who had supported the Maccabees fell out of favor. With only a few exceptions, the rest of the Hasmoneans supported the Jewish Hellenizers. The Pharisees were actually persecuted by Alexander Janneus (103—76 B.C.).

The Hasmonean dynasty ended when, in 63 B.C., an expanding Roman empire intervened in a dynastic clash between the two sons of Janneus, Aristobulus II and Hyrcanus II. Pompey, the general who subdued the East for Rome, took Jerusalem after a three-month siege of the temple area, massacring priests in the performance of their duties and entering the Most Holy Place. This sacrilege began Roman rule in a way that Jews could neither forgive nor forget.

Literature

During these unhappy years of oppression and internal strife, the Jewish people produced a sizable body of literature that both recorded and addressed their era. Three of the more significant works are the Septuagint, the Apocrypha and the Dead Sea Scrolls.

Septuagint. Jewish legend says that 72 scholars, under the sponsorship of Ptolemy Philadelphus (c. 250 B.C.), were brought together on the island of Pharos, near Alexandria, where they produced a Greek translation of the Old Testament in 72 days. From this tradition the Latin word for 70, "Septuagint," became the name attached to the translation. The Roman numeral for 70, LXX, is used as an abbreviation for it.

Behind the legend lies the probability that at least the Torah (the five books of Moses) was translated into Greek c. 250 B.C. for the use of the Greek-speaking Jews of Alexandria. The rest of the Old Testament and some noncanonical books were also included in the LXX before the dawning of the Christian era, though it is difficult to be certain when.

The Septuagint quickly became the Bible of the Jews outside Palestine who, like the Alexandrians, no longer spoke Hebrew. It would be difficult to overestimate its influence. It made the Scriptures available both to the Jews who no longer spoke their ancestral language and to the entire Greek-speaking world. It later became the Bible of the early church. Also, its widespread popularity and use contributed to the retention of the Apocrypha by some branches of Christendom.

Apocrypha. Derived from a Greek word that means "hidden," Apocrypha has acquired the meaning "false," but in a technical sense it describes a specific body of writings. This collection consists of a variety of books and additions to canonical books that, with the exception of 2 Esdras (c. A.D. 90), were written during the intertestamental period. Their recognition as authoritative in Roman and Eastern Christianity is the result of a complex historical process.

The canon of the Old Testament accepted by Protestants today was very likely established by the dawn of the second century A.D., though after the fall of Jerusalem and the destruction of the temple in 70. The precise scope of the Old Testament was discussed among the Jews until the Council of Jamnia (c. 90). This Hebrew canon was not accepted by the early church, which used the Septuagint. In spite of disagreements among some of the church fathers as to which books were canonical and which were not, the Apocryphal books continued in common use by most Christians until the Reformation. During this period most Protestants decided to follow the original Hebrew canon while Rome, at the Council of Trent (1546) and more recently at the First Vatican Council (1869—70), affirmed the larger "Alexandrian" canon that includes the Apocrypha.

The Apocryphal books have retained their place primarily through the weight of ecclesiastical authority, without which they would not commend themselves as canonical literature. There is no clear evidence that Jesus or the apostles ever quoted any Apocryphal works as Scripture (but see note on Jude 14). The Jewish community that produced them repudiated them, and the historical surveys in the apostolic sermons recorded in Acts completely ignore the period they cover. Even the sober, historical account of 1 Maccabees is tarnished by numerous errors and anachronisms.

There is nothing of theological value in the Apocryphal books that cannot be duplicated in canonical Scripture, and they contain much that runs counter to its teachings. Nonetheless, this body of literature does provide a valuable source of information for the study of the intertestamental period.

Dead Sea Scrolls. In the spring of 1947 an Arab shepherd chanced upon a cave in the hills overlooking the southwestern shore of the Dead Sea that contained what has been called "the greatest manuscript discovery of modern times." The documents and fragments of documents found in those caves, dubbed the "Dead Sea Scrolls," included Old Testament books, a few books of the Apocrypha, apocalyptic works, pseudepigrapha (books that purport to be the work of ancient heroes of the faith), and a number of books peculiar to the sect that produced them.

Approximately a third of the documents are Biblical, with Psalms, Deuteronomy and Isaiah—the books quoted most often in the New Testament—occurring most frequently. One of the most remarkable finds was a complete 24-foot-long scroll of Isaiah.

The Scrolls have made a significant contribution to the quest for a form of the Old Testament texts most accurately reflecting the original manuscripts; they provide copies 1,000 years closer to the originals than were previously known. The understanding of Biblical Hebrew and Aramaic and knowledge of the development of Judaism between the Testaments have been increased significantly. Of great importance to readers of the Bible is the demonstration of the care with which Old Testament texts were copied, thus providing objective evidence for the general reliability of those texts.

Social developments

The Judaism of Jesus' day is, to a large extent, the result of changes that came about in response to the pressures of the intertestamental period.

Diaspora. The Diaspora (dispersion) of Israel begun in the exile accelerated during these years until a writer of the day could say that Jews filled "every land and sea."

Jews outside Palestine, cut off from the temple, concentrated their religious life in the study of the Torah and the life of the synagogue (see below). The missionaries of the early church began their Gentile ministries among the Diaspora, using their Greek translation of the Old Testament.

Sadducees. In Palestine, the Greek world made its greatest impact through the party of the Sadducees. Made up of aristocrats, it became the temple party. Because of their position, the Sadducees had a vested interest in the status quo.

Relatively few in number, they wielded disproportionate political power and controlled the high priesthood. They rejected all religious writings except the Torah, as well as any doctrine (such as the resurrection) not found in those five books.

Synagogue. During the exile, Israel was cut off from the temple, divested of nationhood and surrounded by pagan religious practices. Her faith was threatened with extinction. Under these circumstances, the exiles turned their religious focus from what they had lost to what they retained—the Torah and the belief that they were God's people. They concentrated on the law rather than nationhood, on personal piety rather than sacramental rectitude, and on prayer as an acceptable replacement for the sacrifices denied to them.

When they returned from the exile, they brought with them this new form of religious expression, as well as the synagogue (its center), and Judaism became a faith that could be practiced wherever the Torah could be carried. The emphases on personal piety and a relationship with God, which characterized synagogue worship, not only helped preserve Judaism but also prepared the way for the Christian gospel.

Pharisees. As the party of the synagogue, the Pharisees strove to reinterpret the law. They built a "hedge" around it to enable Jews to live righteously before God in a world that had changed drastically since the days of Moses. Although they were comparatively few in number, the Pharisees enjoyed the support of the people and influenced popular opinion if not national policy. They were the only party to survive the destruction of the temple in A.D. 70 and were the spiritual progenitors of modern Judaism.

Essenes. An almost forgotten Jewish sect until the discovery of the Dead Sea Scrolls, the Essenes were a small, separatist group that grew out of the conflicts of the Maccabean age. Like the Pharisees, they stressed strict legal observance, but they considered the temple priesthood corrupt and rejected much of the temple ritual and sacrificial system. Mentioned by several ancient writers, the precise nature of the Essenes is still not certain, though it is generally agreed that the Qumran community that produced the Dead Sea Scrolls was an Essene group.

Because they were convinced that they were the true remnant, these Qumran Essenes had separated themselves from Judaism at large and devoted themselves to personal purity and preparation for the final war between the "Sons of Light and the Sons of Darkness." They practiced an apocalyptic faith, looking back to the contributions of their "Teacher of Righteousness" and forward to the coming of two, and possibly three, Messiahs. The destruction of the temple in A.D. 70, however, seems to have delivered a death blow to their apocalyptic expectations.

Attempts have been made to equate aspects of the beliefs of the Qumran community with the origins of Christianity. Some have seen a prototype of Jesus in their "Teacher of Righteousness," and both John the Baptist and Jesus have been assigned membership in the sect. There is, however, only a superficial, speculative base for these conjectures.

Social Developments

The Judaism of Jesus' day is, to a large extent, the result of changes that came about in response to the pressures of the intertestamental period.

Diaspora. The Diaspora (dispersion) of Israel beginning in the exile accelerated during these years until a writer of the day could say that Jews filled "every land and sea."

Jews outside Palestine, cut off from the temple, concentrated their religious life in the study of the Torah and the life of the synagogue (see below). The missionaries of the early church began their Gentile ministries among the Diaspora, using their Greek translation of the Old Testament.

Sadducees. In Palestine, the Greek world made its greatest impact through the party of the Sadducees. Made up of aristocrats, it became the temple party. Because of their position, the Sadducees had a vested interest in the status quo.

Relatively few in number, they wielded disproportionate political power and controlled the high priesthood. They rejected all religious writings except the Torah, as well as any doctrine (such as the resurrection) not found in these five books.

Synagogue. During the exile, Israel was cut off from the temple, divested of nationhood and surrounded by pagan religious practices. Her faith was threatened with extinction. Under these circumstances, the exiles turned their religious focus from what they had lost to what they retained—the Torah and the belief that they were God's people. They concentrated on the law rather than nationhood, on personal piety rather than sacramental rectitude, and on prayer as an acceptable replacement for the sacrifices denied to them.

When they returned from the exile, they brought with them this new form of religious expression, as well as the synagogue (its center), and Judaism became a faith that could be practiced wherever the Torah could be carried. The emphases on personal piety and a relationship with God, which characterized synagogue worship, not only helped preserve Judaism but also prepared the way for the Christian gospel.

Pharisees. As the party of the synagogue, the Pharisees strove to reinterpret the law. They built a "hedge" around it to enable Jews to live righteously before God in a world that had changed drastically since the days of Moses. Although they were comparatively few in number, the Pharisees enjoyed the support of the people and influenced popular opinion if not national policy. They were the only party to survive the destruction of the temple in A.D. 70 and were the spiritual progenitors of modern Judaism.

Essenes. An almost forgotten Jewish sect until the discovery of the Dead Sea Scrolls, the Essenes were a small, separatist group that grew out of the conflicts of the Maccabean age. Like the Pharisees, they stressed strict legal observance, but they considered the temple priesthood corrupt and rejected much of the temple ritual and sacrificial system. Mentioned by several ancient writers, the precise nature of the Essenes is still not certain, though it is generally agreed that the Qumran community that produced the Dead Sea Scrolls was an Essene group.

Because they were convinced that they were the true remnant, these Qumran Essenes had separated themselves from Judaism at large and devoted themselves to personal purity and preparation for the final war between the "Sons of Light and the Sons of Darkness." They practiced an apocalyptic faith, looking back to the contributions of their "Teacher of Righteousness" and forward to the coming of two, and possibly three, Messiahs. The destruction of the temple in A.D. 70, however, seems to have delivered a death blow to their apocalyptic expectations.

Attempts have been made to equate aspects of the beliefs of the Qumran community with the origins of Christianity. Some have seen a prototype of Jesus in their "Teacher of Righteousness," and both John the Baptist and Jesus have been assigned membership in the sect. There is, however, only a superficial, speculative base for these conjectures.

The Life of Jesus

CHILDHOOD

Birth of Jesus, BETHLEHEM, C. 6/5 B.C., Mt 1:18–25; Lk 2:1–7

Visit by shepherds, BETHLEHEM, Lk 2:8–20

Presentation in the temple, JERUSALEM, Lk 2:21–40

Visit by the Magi, BETHLEHEM, Mt 2:1–12

Escape to Egypt, NILE DELTA, Mt 2:13–18

Return to Nazareth, LOWER GALILEE, Mt 2:19–23

Visit to temple as a boy, JERUSALEM, C A.D. 7/8, Lk 2:41–52

YEAR OF INAUGURATION

YEAR OF POPULARITY

YEAR OF OPPOSITION

Begin less than full year of ministry

10 5 B.C. | A.D. 5 10 15 20 25 30 35

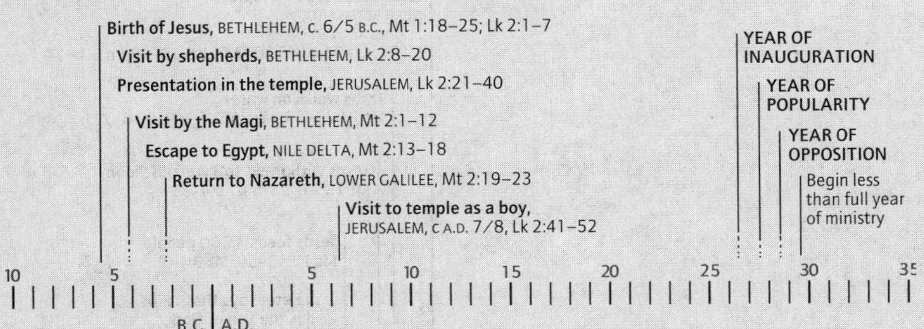

Jesus baptized
JORDAN RIVER
C. A.D. 26
Mt 3:13–17; Mk 1:9–11; Lk 3:21–23; Jn 1:29–39

Jesus tempted by Satan
DESERT
Mt 4:1–11; Mk 1:12–13; Lk 4:1–13

Jesus' first miracle
CANA
Jn 2:1–11

4 fishermen become Jesus' followers
SEA OF GALILEE AT CAPERNAUM
A.D. 27
Mt 4:18–22; Mk 1:16–20; Lk 5:1–11

Jesus heals Peter's mother-in-law
CAPERNAUM
Mt 8:14–17; Mk 1:29–34; Lk 4:38–41

YEAR OF INAUGURATION — **YEAR OF POPULARITY**

A.D. 27: FALL, WINTER, SPRING, SUMMER, FALL; 28: WINTER

Jesus' cleansing of the temple
A.D. 27
Jn 2:14–22

Jesus and Nicodemus
JERUSALEM
A.D. 27
Jn 3:1–21

Jesus talks to the Samaritan woman
SAMARIA
Jn 4:5–42

Jesus heals an official's son
CANA
Jn 4:46–54

The people of Jesus' hometown try to kill him
NAZARETH
Lk 4:16–31

Jesus begins his first preaching trip through Galilee
Mt 4:23–25; Mk 1:35–39; Lk 4:42–44

Matthew decides to follow Jesus
CAPERNAUM
Mt 9:9–13; Mk 2:13–17; Lk 5:27–32

Jesus chooses the 12 disciples
A.D. 28
Mk 3:13–19; Lk 6:12–15

Jesus preaches the "Sermon on the Mount"
Mt 5:1–7:29; Lk 6:20–49

THE LIFE OF JESUS

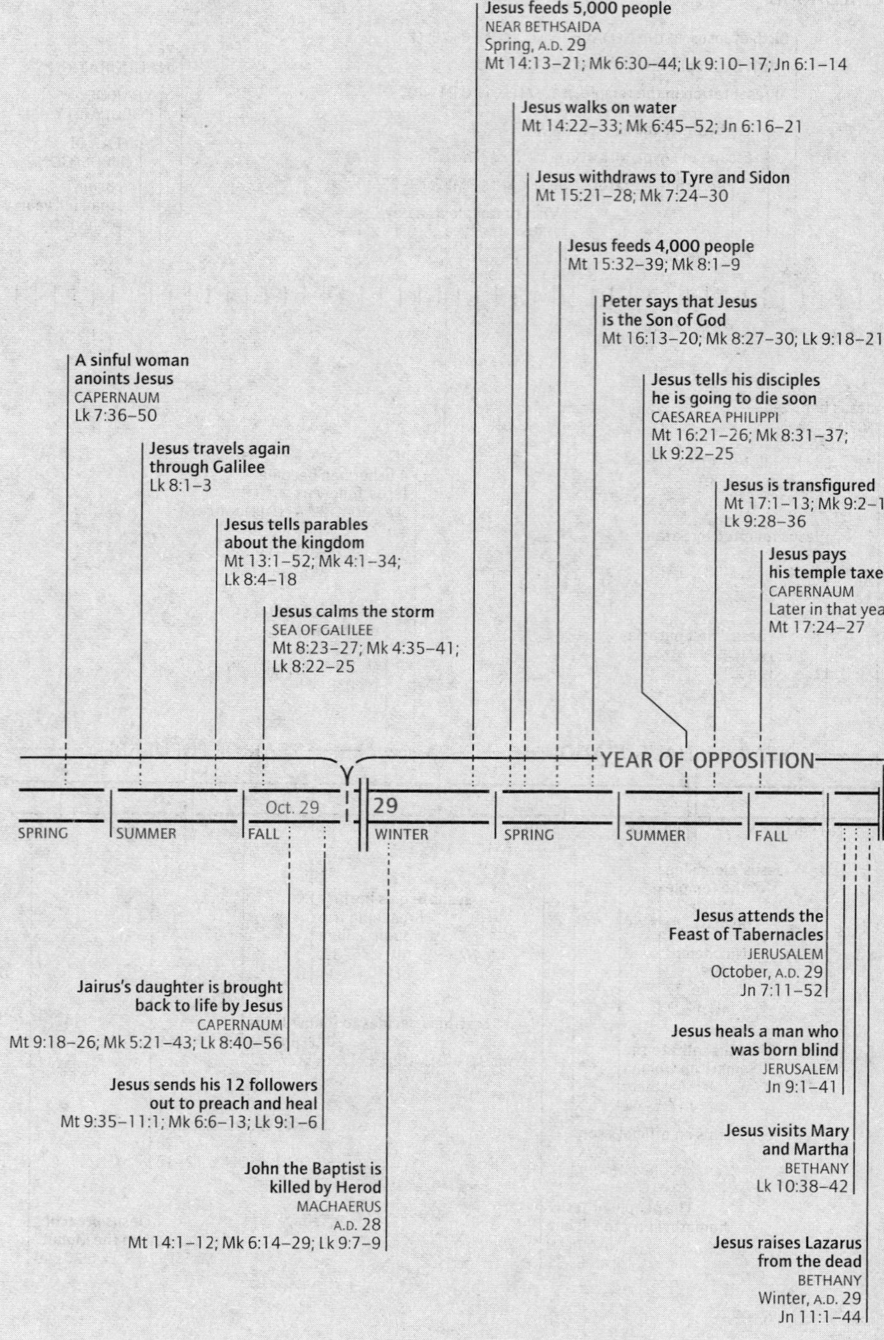

Jesus feeds 5,000 people
NEAR BETHSAIDA
Spring, A.D. 29
Mt 14:13–21; Mk 6:30–44; Lk 9:10–17; Jn 6:1–14
Jesus walks on water
Mt 14:22–33; Mk 6:45–52; Jn 6:16–21
Jesus withdraws to Tyre and Sidon
Mt 15:21–28; Mk 7:24–30
Jesus feeds 4,000 people
Mt 15:32–39; Mk 8:1–9
Peter says that Jesus is the Son of God
Mt 16:13–20; Mk 8:27–30; Lk 9:18–21
A sinful woman anoints Jesus
CAPERNAUM
Lk 7:36–50
Jesus tells his disciples he is going to die soon
CAESAREA PHILIPPI
Mt 16:21–26; Mk 8:31–37; Lk 9:22–25
Jesus travels again through Galilee
Lk 8:1–3
Jesus is transfigured
Mt 17:1–13; Mk 9:2–13; Lk 9:28–36
Jesus tells parables about the kingdom
Mt 13:1–52; Mk 4:1–34; Lk 8:4–18
Jesus pays his temple taxes
CAPERNAUM
Later in that year
Mt 17:24–27
Jesus calms the storm
SEA OF GALILEE
Mt 8:23–27; Mk 4:35–41; Lk 8:22–25
YEAR OF OPPOSITION
Oct. 29
29
SPRING
SUMMER
FALL
WINTER
SPRING
SUMMER
FALL
Jesus attends the Feast of Tabernacles
JERUSALEM
October, A.D. 29
Jn 7:11–52
Jairus's daughter is brought back to life by Jesus
CAPERNAUM
Mt 9:18–26; Mk 5:21–43; Lk 8:40–56
Jesus heals a man who was born blind
JERUSALEM
Jn 9:1–41
Jesus sends his 12 followers out to preach and heal
Mt 9:35–11:1; Mk 6:6–13; Lk 9:1–6
Jesus visits Mary and Martha
BETHANY
Lk 10:38–42
John the Baptist is killed by Herod
MACHAERUS
A.D. 28
Mt 14:1–12; Mk 6:14–29; Lk 9:7–9
Jesus raises Lazarus from the dead
BETHANY
Winter, A.D. 29
Jn 11:1–44

THE LIFE OF JESUS

Jesus begins his last trip to Jerusalem
A.D. 30
Lk 17:11

Jesus blesses the little children
ACROSS THE JORDAN
Mt 19:13–15; Mk 10:13–16; Lk 18:15–17

Jesus talks to the rich young man
ACROSS THE JORDAN
Mt 19:16–30; Mk 10:17–31; Lk 18:18–30

Jesus again tells about his death and resurrection
NEAR THE JORDAN
Mt 20:17–19; Mk 10:32–34; Lk 18:31–34

Jesus heals blind Bartimaeus
JERICHO
Mt 20:29–34; Mk 10:46–52; Lk 18:35–43

Jesus talks to Zacchaeus
JERICHO
Lk 19:1–10

Jesus returns to Bethany to visit Mary and Martha
BETHANY
Jn 11:55—12:1

THE LAST WEEK

The Triumphal Entry, JERUSALEM, Sunday
Mt 21:1–11; Mk 11:1–10; Lk 19:29–44; Jn 12:12–19

Jesus curses the fig tree, Monday
Mt 21:18–19; Mk 11:12–14

Jesus cleanses the temple, Monday
Mt 21:12–13; Mk 11:15–18

The authority of Jesus questioned, Tuesday
Mt 21:23–27; Mk 11:27–33; Lk 20:1–8

Jesus teaches in the temple, Tuesday
Mt 21:28—23:39; Mk 12:1–44; Lk 20:9—21:4

Jesus anointed, BETHANY, Tuesday
Mt 26:6–13; Mk 14:3–9; Jn 12:2–11

The plot against Jesus, Wednesday
Mt 26:14–16; Mk 14:10–11; Lk 22:3–6

The Last Supper, Thursday
Mt 26:17–29; Mk 14:12–25; Lk 22:7–20; Jn 13:1–38

Jesus comforts the disciples, Thursday
Jn 14:1–16:33

Gethsemane, Thursday
Mt 26:36–46; Mk 14:32–42; Lk 22:40–46

Jesus' arrest and trial, Thursday night and Friday
Mt 26:47—27:26; Mk 14:43—15:15; Lk 22:47—23:25; Jn 18:2—19:16

Jesus' crucifixion and death, GOLGOTHA, Friday
Mt 27:27–56; Mk 15:16–41; Lk 23:26–49; Jn 19:17–30

The burial of Jesus, JOSEPH'S TOMB, Friday
Mt 27:57–66; Mk 15:42–47; Lk 23:50–56; Jn 19:31–42

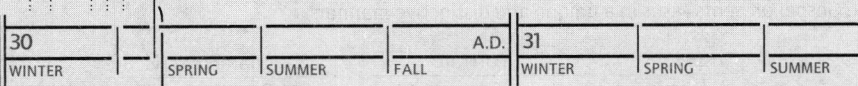

30 WINTER | SPRING | SUMMER | FALL | A.D. 31 WINTER | SPRING | SUMMER

AFTER THE RESURRECTION

The empty tomb, JERUSALEM, Sunday
Mt 28:1–10; Mk 16:1–8; Lk 24:1–12; Jn 20:1–10

Mary Magdalene sees Jesus in the garden
JERUSALEM, Sunday
Mt 16:9–11; Jn 20:11–18

Jesus appears to the two going to Emmaus
Sunday
Mk 16:12–13; Lk 24:13–35

Jesus appears to 10 disciples
JERUSALEM, Sunday
Mk 16:14; Lk 24:36–43; Jn 20:19–25

Jesus appears to the 11 disciples
JERUSALEM, One week later
Jn 20:26–31

Jesus talks with some of his disciples
SEA OF GALILEE, One week later
Jn 21:1–25

Jesus ascends to his Father in heaven
MOUNT OF OLIVES, 40 days later
Mt 28:16–20; Mk 16:19–20; Lk 24:44–53

Dotted lines leading to the timeline are meant to define sequence of events only. Exact dates, even year dates, are generally unknown.

Jesus in the New Testament

BY EDWARD HINDSON, D. PHIL.

Jesus is the primary figure in the New Testament. From the very beginning Jesus is pictured as the One who fulfills the prophecies of the Messiah. His arrival on the scene of humanity changed the course of history. His ministry was characterized by the announcement that a new covenant with God was being inaugurated, not as a repudiation of the old covenant but as its final fulfillment.

The German scholar E. W. Hengstenberg observed that God had prepared the Jewish people to look for the One the prophets had promised in the Hebrew Scriptures. For the rest of the world, he suggested that God had sent the Redeemer only after centuries of allowing "diseased humanity to seek in vain to heal itself, in the absence of the divine physician."[1] God was preparing Jews and Gentiles alike to receive the "Good News" of his grace in Jesus Christ.

The unity of the Testaments points to the same God, the same theology and the same divine promises. The Christian faith is the expression of confidence in those promises, the belief that Jesus of Nazareth is indeed the Son of God—the promised Messiah, the Savior and Redeemer of humankind, the One of whom "all the prophets testify" (Acts 10:43).

The Gospel Portraits

The four Gospels are like four separate portraits of the same person. Each focuses on a different aspect of that individual, and the various poses, angles of lighting and facial expressions each have their own story to tell. Therefore, the theme and structure of each Gospel is unique. The men who wrote these accounts were convinced that they were true. Therefore, the Gospels overflow with the confidence that the subject of all four of the portraits was indeed the Savior—God's promised One.

Each Gospel presents Jesus in a unique and distinctive manner:

Gospel	Portrait	Characteristic
Matthew	King	Royalty
Mark	Servant	Ministry
Luke	Son of Man	Humanity
John	Son of God	Deity

A New Testament Overview

The New Testament completes the picture of Jesus Christ that was introduced in the prophecies, foreshadowings and images of the Old Testament. Biblical terms like *Messiah, redeemer, shepherd, son of man* and *son of David* originate in the Old Testament and find their ultimate significance in the New Testament. The story begun in the Hebrew Bible is completed in the Greek New Testament. The Biblical picture of Jesus unfolds in each section of the New Testament.

Gospels	Manifestation of Jesus
Acts	Propagation of the Good News of Jesus
Epistles	Explanation of Jesus
Revelation	Consummation in Jesus

Person of Jesus Christ

One cannot read the New Testament without being confronted by Jesus Christ. His person is overwhelming. His character is irresistibly attractive. His teachings are life-changing. British scholar Michael Green wrote: "The claims of Jesus are so startling that they stop us in our tracks and challenge us to make up our minds about this most remarkable person. Was He just a great teacher? Or was He much more?"[2]

The more closely you examine the person, character and claims of Jesus the more you will be compelled to see that he was more than just a man. Oxford scholar C. S. Lewis observed: "A man who was merely a man and said the sort of things Jesus said would not be a great moral teacher. He would either be a lunatic—on the level with a man who says he is a poached egg—or else he would be the Devil of Hell. Either this man was, and is, the Son of God, or else a madman or something worse."[3]

Jesus was born in obscurity, raised in poverty and crucified in ignominy. Yet he transformed the ancient world and continues to transform lives today. Those who put their faith in him find him to be more than sufficient to meet their deepest needs. New Testament scholar Robert Stein noted: "There is a certain wholeness about the Jesus who preached the arrival of the kingdom of God, who ate with tax collectors and sinners, who healed the sick and raised the dead, who died sacrificially on the cross and rose triumphantly from the dead . . . Attempts to strip the supernatural from Jesus' life can only produce a Jesus so radically different that he is unrecognizable and his impact on history unexplainable."[4]

Charles H. Spurgeon said it best over a century ago when the great British pastor wrote: "You may study, look, and meditate, but Jesus is a greater Savior than you think Him to be, even when your thoughts are at their highest."[5]

[1] E. W. Hengstenberg, *Christology of the Old Testament* (Grand Rapids: Kregel, 1970), p. 1.
[2] Michael Green, *Who Is This Jesus?* (Nashville: Thomas Nelson, 1992), p. 6.
[3] C. S. Lewis, *Mere Christianity* (New York: Macmillan, 1960), p. 56.
[4] Robert Stein, *Jesus the Messiah* (Downers Grove, IL: Intervarsity Press, 1996), p. 24.
[5] Charles Spurgeon, quoted in *No Greater Savior* (Eugene, OR: Harvest House, 1995), p. 11.

"Surely he was the Son of God" (Matthew 27:54).

MATTHEW

Why was it necessary that Jesus' birth be a virgin birth? (Matthew 1:23)

♦ *Some think it was because Adam's original sin has been passed down to humanity through sinful parents. They say that Jesus, to be free of sin, needed to circumvent the natural method and be conceived in a supernatural way. Jesus' birth, a miraculous birth to a sexually pure young woman, most emphatically served to underscore his divinity.*

In what sense was the kingdom of heaven already near? (Matthew 4:17)

♦ *The kingdom of heaven was near because the King was near. Jesus was introducing God's plan of salvation, of which he was the central figure. When men and women repent, they leave the kingdom of the world and enter the kingdom of heaven. Not until Jesus returns, though, will God's rule be fully realized on earth.*

Jesus in Matthew Reading a sequel to a novel without having read the original story can be frustrating unless a transitional story line is provided. The Gospel of Matthew provides such a transition, connecting the stories of the Old and New Testaments.

Because he was a former tax collector, Matthew recorded the life of Jesus in an accountant's style, with facts grouped topically instead of chronologically. Matthew pulled together Jesus' teachings into five major groupings: the Sermon on the Mount in chapters 5—7; Jesus' words to his disciples in chapter 10; parables about the kingdom of God in chapter 13; teachings about the church in chapter 18; and Jesus' observations about religious rituals and his words about the future in chapters 23—25. Woven throughout these passages are snapshots of Jesus' life and ministry.

Matthew quoted at least 40 Old Testament passages, emphasizing the fulfillment of prophecies from the Hebrew Scripture and focusing on the significance of the law (Matthew 5:17–18) and Jesus' identity as the Shepherd-King who had come to reclaim the "lost sheep of Israel" (Matthew 10:6).

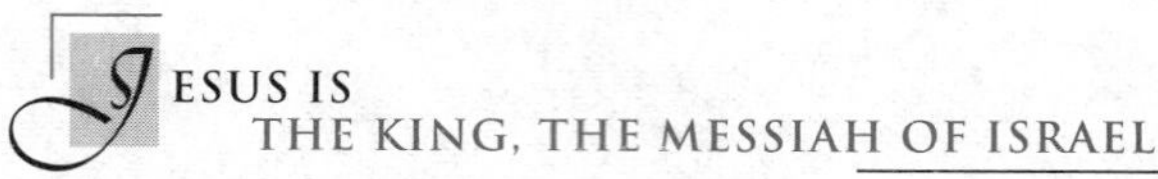

JESUS IS THE KING, THE MESSIAH OF ISRAEL

THE MOST BASIC CHRISTIAN BELIEF ABOUT JESUS IS THAT HE WAS THE MESSIAH.

Marcus Bockmeuhl, *Cambridge University*

The Genealogy of Jesus

1:1 [a]2Sa 7:12-16; Isa 9:6,7; 11:1; Jer 23:5,6; Mt 9:27; Lk 1:32,69; Ro 1:3; Rev 22:16 [b]Ge 22:18; Gal 3:16

1 A record of the genealogy of Jesus Christ the son of David,[a] the son of Abraham:[b]

1:2 [c]Ge 21:3,12 [d]Ge 25:26 [e]Ge 29:35

2 Abraham was the father of Isaac,[c]
Isaac the father of Jacob,[d]
Jacob the father of Judah and his brothers,[e]

1:3 [f]Ge 38:27-30

3 Judah the father of Perez and Zerah, whose mother was Tamar,[f]
Perez the father of Hezron,
Hezron the father of Ram,
4 Ram the father of Amminadab,
Amminadab the father of Nahshon,
Nahshon the father of Salmon,
5 Salmon the father of Boaz, whose mother was Rahab,
Boaz the father of Obed, whose mother was Ruth,
Obed the father of Jesse,

1:6 [g]1Sa 16:1; 17:12 [h]2Sa 12:24

6 and Jesse the father of King David.[g]

David was the father of Solomon, whose mother had been Uriah's wife,[h]
7 Solomon the father of Rehoboam,
Rehoboam the father of Abijah,
Abijah the father of Asa,
8 Asa the father of Jehoshaphat,
Jehoshaphat the father of Jehoram,
Jehoram the father of Uzziah,
9 Uzziah the father of Jotham,
Jotham the father of Ahaz,
Ahaz the father of Hezekiah,

1:10 [i]2Ki 20:21

10 Hezekiah the father of Manasseh,[i]
Manasseh the father of Amon,
Amon the father of Josiah,

1:11 [j]2Ki 24:14-16; Jer 27:20; Da 1:2

11 and Josiah the father of Jeconiah[a] and his brothers at the time of the exile to Babylon.[j]

1:12 [k]1Ch 3:17 [l]1Ch 3:19; Ezr 3:2

12 After the exile to Babylon:
Jeconiah was the father of Shealtiel,[k]
Shealtiel the father of Zerubbabel,[l]
13 Zerubbabel the father of Abiud,
Abiud the father of Eliakim,
Eliakim the father of Azor,
14 Azor the father of Zadok,
Zadok the father of Akim,
Akim the father of Eliud,
15 Eliud the father of Eleazar,
Eleazar the father of Matthan,
Matthan the father of Jacob,

1:16 [m]Lk 1:27 [n]Mt 27:17

16 and Jacob the father of Joseph, the husband of Mary,[m] of whom was born Jesus, who is called Christ.[n]

17 Thus there were fourteen generations in all from Abraham to David, fourteen from David to the exile to Babylon, and fourteen from the exile to the Christ.[b]

The Birth of Jesus Christ

18 This is how the birth of Jesus Christ came about: His mother Mary was pledged to be married to Joseph, but be-

[a] *11* That is, Jehoiachin; also in verse 12 [b] *17* Or *Messiah.* "The Christ" (Greek) and "the Messiah" (Hebrew) both mean "the Anointed One."

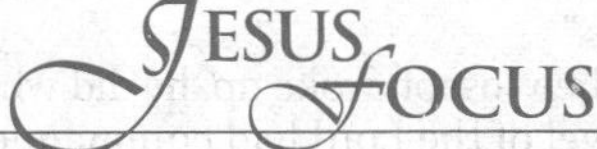

A SURPRISING LIST

Matthew began his Gospel by delineating Jesus' family line (Matthew 1:1–16). What may surprise us is the appearance of several individuals who were not of Jewish descent. For example, three women—*Tamar* (Genesis 38), *Rahab* (Joshua 2:1–6) and *Ruth* (Ruth 1—4)—none of whom was an Israelite by birth, all appear in the genealogy of Jesus. Already throughout Old Testament history God the Father was setting the stage for the inclusion of Gentiles, not only into the earthly lineage of his Son Jesus but also into his eternal family. While a Biblical genealogy may at first strike us as about as inspiring as an expired page of newspaper classified ads, a little study can reveal some interesting themes. Notice also that there were "questionable" people in Jesus' background (Ahaz, Manasseh and Jeconiah [or Jehoiachin], for example; see Matthew 1:9–11), just as there are in every family tree. It should not surprise us, however, given the nature of our God, that he works in and through woefully sinful people to carry out his gracious plans.

> INCREASINGLY THE GOSPELS ARE SEEN AS BIOGRAPHY . . . FOUR PICTURES, ALL DIFFERENT . . . YET ALL ARE OF ONE AND THE SAME MAN.
>
> Richard A. Burridge, *King's College, London*

fore they came together, she was found
to be with child through the Holy Spir-
1:18 [o]Lk 1:35 it.[o] 19Because Joseph her husband was a
righteous man and did not want to ex-
1:19 [p]Dt 24:1 pose her to public disgrace, he had in
mind to divorce[p] her quietly.
20But after he had considered this, an
angel of the Lord appeared to him in a
dream and said, "Joseph son of David, do
not be afraid to take Mary home as your
wife, because what is conceived in her is
from the Holy Spirit. 21She will give birth
1:21 to a son, and you are to give him the
[q]Lk 1:31 name Jesus,[a][q] because he will save his
[r]Lk 2:11; people from their sins."[r]
Ac 5:31; 13:23, 28 22All this took place to fulfill what the
Lord had said through the prophet:
23"The virgin will be with child and will
give birth to a son, and they will call
1:23 him Immanuel"[b][s]—which means, "God
[s]Isa 7:14; 8:8,10 with us."
24When Joseph woke up, he did what
the angel of the Lord had commanded
him and took Mary home as his wife.
25But he had no union with her until she
gave birth to a son. And he gave him the 1:25
name Jesus.[t] [t]ver 21

The Visit of the Magi

2 After Jesus was born in Bethle- 2:1
hem in Judea,[u] during the time of [u]Lk 2:4-7 [v]Lk 1:5
King Herod,[v] Magi[c] from the east came
to Jerusalem 2and asked, "Where is the
one who has been born king of the 2:2
Jews?[w] We saw his star[x] in the east[d] and [w]Jer 23:5;
have come to worship him." Mt 27:11;
3When King Herod heard this he was Mk 15:2;
disturbed, and all Jerusalem with him. Jn 1:49; 18:33-
4When he had called together all the 37 [x]Nu 24:17
people's chief priests and teachers of the
law, he asked them where the Christ[e] 2:5
was to be born. 5"In Bethlehem[y] in Ju- [y]Jn 7:42
dea," they replied, "for this is what the
prophet has written:

6" 'But you, Bethlehem, in the land
of Judah,
are by no means least among the
rulers of Judah;
for out of you will come a ruler
who will be the shepherd of my 2:6
people Israel.'[f]"[z] [z]Mic 5:2; 2Sa 5:2

7Then Herod called the Magi secretly

[a] 21 *Jesus* is the Greek form of *Joshua,* which means *the LORD saves.* [b] 23 Isaiah 7:14
[c] 1 Traditionally *Wise Men* [d] 2 Or *star when it rose* [e] 4 Or *Messiah* [f] 6 Micah 5:2

JESUS FOCUS

A VIRGIN'S BABY

Isaiah had predicted that the Messiah would be born of a virgin (Isaiah 7:14), and this miraculous conception is one of the foundational truths of Christianity. Had Jesus' biological mother been Mary and his biological father Joseph, he would have been just another man. But Isaiah's message about the virgin birth had been explicit. Matthew quoted Isaiah when he described Jesus' birth, leaving no doubt that Jesus himself fulfilled Isaiah's prophecy (Matthew 1:23). Jesus is more than simply a special and unique man sent from God. The Messiah is God himself in human flesh—he is *Immanuel*, "God with us." When Jesus was born, God had arrived on the human scene to live and interact directly with his people (John 1:14; Philippians 2:6–8).

JOSEPH

STEPFATHER FOR GOD'S SON

Joseph, Mary's husband, was Jesus' stepfather. Matthew made it unmistakably clear that Joseph was not Jesus' biological father (Matthew 1:16,18). On three separate occasions an angel appeared to give Joseph a special message about his unique role (Matthew 1:20; 2:13,22). Each time Joseph acted exactly as God had directed him. Jesus grew up watching Joseph's unquestioning compliance with God's instruction. In Joseph the young Jesus observed a role model of character, faith and virtue. Joseph was a carpenter, possibly a stonecutter (the same Greek word applies to both trades), by trade. He lived out most of his life in Nazareth, with the exceptions of a brief stay in Bethlehem and a slightly longer residence in Egypt. The last time Joseph is mentioned is when Jesus was twelve years old (Luke 2:41–52). Because his name does not come up again, some surmise that he may have died, leaving Mary a widow.

DISCOVERY 232

WHO EXACTLY IS JESUS?

Many of us cannot remember the time we first heard about Jesus. We may have been reared in a home in which he was loved and honored. Others receive the Good News about him during their school years or in their adult life. Some come to a point in life at which they commit themselves to him, while others make a conscious decision to reject his call. Sadly, millions speak his name only in the context of a swear word.

But who exactly is Jesus? Because his sayings and teachings were so extraordinarily wise, many view him as a great teacher. Because he championed the cause of the oppressed and offered them freedom, and because he confounded the religious and social establishments of his day, some perceive him as a social revolutionary. Because he touched those who suffered from leprosy, healed the sick and raised the dead, many remember him as a great healer. Because his life serves as a model for leadership development, others envision him as the ultimate corporate leader, the perfect CEO.

But who is Jesus really? As we try to introduce our Lord to others within a modern context we may be in danger of missing the purpose of his life. Certainly, he was a teacher and a social revolutionary, a healer and a leader—but he was so much more. An angel directed Joseph to name Mary's infant son Jesus, meaning "the LORD saves," because "he [would] save his people from their sins" (Matthew 1:21).

To understand why our Savior came, we first have to have a realistic understanding of the human condition. Each one of us is separated from the holy God, because each has turned away from him. The Bible refers to that act of turning from God as sin (Romans 3:23). The inescapable punishment for sin is death, or eternal separation from the one true and loving God (Romans 6:23). Paul used several different word pictures to describe the human dilemma: Without Jesus Christ we are lost, held in slavery, groping in darkness and living without hope! Our culture continually attempts to redefine sin, to water down the problem with euphemisms and excuses, to shift the blame to others—but the sinful heart of each individual is a totally personal issue.

Happily, in sharp contrast to the terrible news of the darkness and hopelessness of our condition is the great good news of peace and joy and restoration (Luke 2:10)—in the person of Jesus, who came to set us free from the bondage and penalty of our sin by dying on the cross in our place. Infinitely more than a teacher, counselor, revolutionary leader, healer, friend or brother, Jesus—God in human flesh (John 1:14), Immanuel, "God with us" (Matthew 1:23)—is the Savior of the world. If we will only accept his sacrifice, he will gladly and graciously forgive our sins, liberate us from Satan's kingdom of darkness and usher us into his glorious kingdom of light (1 Peter 2:9).

Self-Discovery: *Can you recall the precise moment at which you gave your life to Jesus? Or have you loved Jesus since early childhood? Either way, take a moment to offer a prayer of thanksgiving to God.*

GO TO DISCOVERY 233 ON PAGE 1261

> IT IS A MARVEL THAT TO HIM, THE BABE, THEY OF HIS OWN HOUSE HASTED WITH THEIR SWORDS, AND THEY THAT WERE STRANGERS WITH THEIR OFFERINGS.
>
> Ephraim the Syrian, *Early Church Father*

and found out from them the exact time
the star had appeared. 8He sent them to
Bethlehem and said, "Go and make a
careful search for the child. As soon as
you find him, report to me, so that I too
may go and worship him."
9After they had heard the king, they
went on their way, and the star they had
seen in the east[a] went ahead of them
until it stopped over the place where the
child was. 10When they saw the star,
they were overjoyed. 11On coming to the
2:11 house, they saw the child with his moth-
a Isa 60:3 er Mary, and they bowed down and wor-
b Ps 72:10 shiped him.[a] Then they opened their
2:12 treasures and presented him with gifts[b]
c Heb 11:7 d ver 13,19,22; of gold and of incense and of myrrh.
Mt 27:19 12And having been warned[c] in a dream[d]

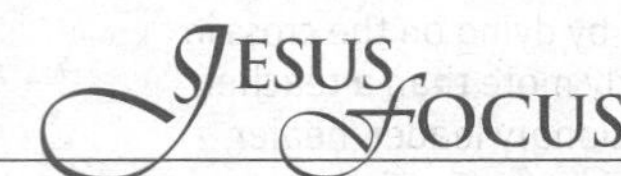

KING OF THE JEWS

The great King Herod was distracted and apprehensive (Matthew 2:3). Before him stood dignitaries from a distant country, matter-of-factly asking the whereabouts of the newborn king of Israel (verse 2). They had of course approached Herod first, because he governed the area—and, as far as Herod himself was concerned, functioned as the king of the Jews! Herod was from the region of Idumea (Edom). He had been appointed as a local Roman governor, sometimes referred to as a "king," to rule Judea and Galilee under Caesar Augustus. The Roman empire was at the time in a state of continual political upheaval, and Herod's position was shaky. King Herod was in power from 37 B.C. until 4 B.C., and his paranoia about his position is well documented in history. In fact, this tragic and insecure figure ruthlessly executed many people—including every Bethlehemite baby boy under the age of two years, after he had received word of Jesus' birth (verse 16)—in a frenetic attempt to cling to his tenuous station.

not to go back to Herod, they returned
to their country by another route.

The Escape to Egypt

13When they had gone, an angel[e] of 2:13 e Ac 5:19
the Lord appeared to Joseph in a dream.[f] f ver 12,19,22
"Get up," he said, "take the child and his
mother and escape to Egypt. Stay there
until I tell you, for Herod is going to
search for the child to kill him."
14So he got up, took the child and his
mother during the night and left for
Egypt, 15where he stayed until the death
of Herod. And so was fulfilled what the
Lord had said through the prophet: "Out 2:15 g Hos 11:1;
of Egypt I called my son."[b][g] Ex 4:22,23
16When Herod realized that he had
been outwitted by the Magi, he was furious, and he gave orders to kill all the boys
in Bethlehem and its vicinity who were
two years old and under, in accordance
with the time he had learned from the

[a] 9 Or *seen when it rose* [b] 15 Hosea 11:1

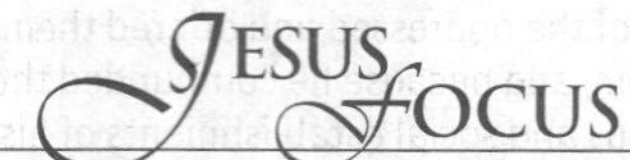

EXILE IN EGYPT

When Herod ordered the execution of every Jewish baby boy in Bethlehem and its vicinity who was under the age of two years, Jesus' family fled from Bethlehem to Egypt (Matthew 2:13). God's people had frequently sought refuge in Egypt over the centuries (see Jeremiah 43—44), and a fairly large Jewish community had been established there. God's prophet Hosea had long ago predicted that God would call his "son" out of Egypt (Hosea 11:1). When Hosea penned these words, he was no doubt referring to the manner in which God had freed his people from slavery in Egypt. However, we recognize in retrospect that this was also a prophecy about God's promised Messiah. Matthew in fact quoted this Old Testament prophecy in verse 15 of chapter 2, applying it to Jesus.

It may strike us as ironic that Joseph and Mary fled with their infant to the very country from which the Israelite nation had earlier taken flight, and we cannot help but recall Pharaoh's edict that every Israelite baby boy be murdered (Exodus 1:22). God's Old Testament servant Moses had escaped execution at that time because of his adoption by Pharaoh's daughter (Exodus 2:10). A further similarity is that God brought about deliverance for his people first through Moses and ultimately through Jesus.

DISCOVERY 233

HOW WILL YOU RESPOND?

Matthew included in his Gospel the captivating story of the Magi, pictured by many as exotic foreigners traveling on the backs of camels, who undertook a long and arduous journey in search of the young Jesus. We do know that these men were from the East, probably Persia or Southern Arabia. By New Testament times the term *Magi* had come to cover a wide variety of men interested in dreams, astrology, magic, books thought to contain mysterious references to the future, and the like.

Although the Magi arrived in Bethlehem spurred on by astrological calculations, they had probably built up their expectation of a kingly figure by working through assorted Jewish books. It is possible that they were familiar with the oracle, spoken by Balaam, who had come "from the eastern mountains" (see Numbers 23:7) that "a star will come out of Jacob; a scepter will rise out of Israel" (Numbers 24:17). Apparently they were genuinely seeking God, and consequently he met them in the language they understood, that of the stars.

The Magi informed King Herod that they had come to *worship* the One born king of the Jews (Matthew 2:2). While the term *worship* can simply mean "do homage," Matthew painted a picture that suggests that the Magi worshiped Jesus better than they themselves realized! Verse 10 indicates that the Magi were "overjoyed" when the star finally stopped over the place where the child was, and verse 11 portrays them bowing down and worshiping the young Jesus, opening their treasures and presenting him with costly and extravagant gifts. It is certainly apparent that these travel-weary foreigners had gone to great lengths to locate and worship a small child born as "king" over a powerless group of people living under Roman rule.

The news of Jesus' birth did indeed cause many diverse reactions. The Magi traveled for months, single-mindedly bent on finding the baby Jesus, and they were not disconcerted when they located him in a humble house rather than in the fine palace in Jerusalem. Herod felt so threatened that he ordered the murder of all boys in the vicinity of Bethlehem under the age of two years (Matthew 2:16). Mary sat quietly in awe of the implications of her infant's birth. But the religious leaders in Jerusalem simply could not be bothered. Despite their wealth of knowledge of the Hebrew Scriptures, despite their intimate acquaintance with Old Testament Messianic prophecy, when the crowning event of all of human history arrived they lacked the curiosity to make the short trip from Jerusalem to Bethlehem to check out the rumors for themselves.

Formal knowledge of Scripture, Matthew was apparently implying, does not in itself lead to knowing who Jesus is. The apostle John made a poignant statement in the first chapter of his Gospel: "[Jesus] was in the world, and though the world was made through him, the world did not recognize him. He came to that which was his own, but his own did not receive him. Yet to all who received him . . . he gave the right to become children of God" (John 1:10–12).

Self-Discovery: It is easy for Christians to become so familiar with the Christmas story that the marvel ceases to move us. Take a moment to ponder, along with Mary, the wonder of the incarnation, and then bow down in your spirit along with the Magi in adoration of Jesus Christ, your Lord and Savior.

GO TO DISCOVERY 234 ON PAGE 1264

Magi. 17Then what was said through the
prophet Jeremiah was fulfilled:

> 18"A voice is heard in Ramah,
> weeping and great mourning,
> Rachel weeping for her children
> and refusing to be comforted,
> 2:18 [h]Jer 31:15 — because they are no more."[a][h]

The Return to Nazareth

19After Herod died, an angel of the
2:19 [i]ver 12,13,22 — Lord appeared in a dream[i] to Joseph in
Egypt 20and said, "Get up, take the child
and his mother and go to the land of Israel, for those who were trying to take
the child's life are dead."

21So he got up, took the child and his
mother and went to the land of Israel.
22But when he heard that Archelaus was
reigning in Judea in place of his father
2:22 [j]ver 12,13,19; Mt 27:19 [k]Lk 2:39 — Herod, he was afraid to go there. Having
been warned in a dream,[j] he withdrew to
the district of Galilee,[k] 23and he went
and lived in a town called Nazareth.[l] So
2:23 [l]Lk 1:26; Jn 1:45,46 [m]Mt 1:22 [n]Mk 1:24 — was fulfilled[m] what was said through the
prophets: "He will be called a Nazarene."[n]

John the Baptist Prepares the Way

3:1 [o]Lk 1:13,57-66; 3:2-19 — 3 In those days John the Baptist[o]
came, preaching in the Desert of
Judea 2and saying, "Repent, for the king- — 3:2 [p]Da 2:44; Mt 4:17; 6:10; Lk 11:20; 21:31; Jn 3:3,5; Ac 1:3, 6
dom of heaven[p] is near." 3This is he who
was spoken of through the prophet Isaiah:

> "A voice of one calling in the desert,
> 'Prepare the way for the Lord, — 3:3 [q]Isa 40:3; Mal 3:1; Lk 1:76; Jn 1:23
> make straight paths for him.' "[b][q]

4John's clothes were made of camel's
hair, and he had a leather belt around his
waist.[r] His food was locusts[s] and wild — 3:4 [r]2Ki 1:8 [s]Lev 11:22
honey. 5People went out to him from Jerusalem and all Judea and the whole region of the Jordan. 6Confessing their
sins, they were baptized by him in the
Jordan River.

7But when he saw many of the Pharisees and Sadducees coming to where he
was baptizing, he said to them: "You
brood of vipers![t] Who warned you to flee — 3:7 [t]Mt 12:34; 23:33 [u]Ro 1:18; 1Th 1:10
from the coming wrath?[u] 8Produce fruit
in keeping with repentance.[v] 9And do
not think you can say to yourselves, 'We — 3:8 [v]Ac 26:20
have Abraham as our father.' I tell you
that out of these stones God can raise up
children for Abraham. 10The ax is already
at the root of the trees, and every tree
that does not produce good fruit will be — 3:10 [w]Mt 7:19; Lk 13:6-9; Jn 15:2,6
cut down and thrown into the fire.[w]

11"I baptize you with[c] water for repentance. But after me will come one
who is more powerful than I, whose sandals I am not fit to carry. He will baptize — 3:11 [x]Mk 1:8 [y]Isa 4:4; Ac 2:3,4
you with the Holy Spirit[x] and with fire.[y]
12His winnowing fork is in his hand, and
he will clear his threshing floor, gathering his wheat into the barn and burning — 3:12 [z]Mt 13:30
up the chaff with unquenchable fire."[z]

JOHN THE BAPTIST
THE MESSIAH'S FORERUNNER

John the Baptist is sometimes referred to as the forerunner of Jesus, because God had sent him ahead of Jesus as a herald to let the people know that the Messiah had arrived and to call them to prepare their hearts for accepting his message. John was the son of Zechariah, a priest, and his wife Elizabeth, and was a relative of Jesus (Luke 1:36), and Jesus stated that John had come in the spirit of Elijah to fulfill Malachi 4:5 (Matthew 11:14). John began his ministry in the 15th year of the reign of Tiberias Caesar, approximately A.D. 25 or 26 (Luke 3:1). John urged Israel to turn back to God because the Messiah had at long last arrived, bringing the kingdom of God with him (Matthew 3:2; John 1:6–8,19–22). John the Baptist was the first person to identify Jesus as the "Lamb of God" (John 1:29), and many of John's disciples later became followers of Jesus, because John had made clear to them that his job was simply to prepare the way for God's Messiah. John was eventually arrested and executed by Herod Antipas (Matthew 14:1–12).

> THE LORD JESUS HIMSELF HAS NOT ONLY, AS GOD, GIVEN THE HOLY SPIRIT, BUT ALSO, AS MAN, HE HAS RECEIVED HIM.
>
> Augustine, *Catholic Theologian*

The Baptism of Jesus

13Then Jesus came from Galilee to the — 3:13 [a]Mk 1:4
Jordan to be baptized by John.[a] 14But John
tried to deter him, saying, "I need to be
baptized by you, and do you come to me?"

15Jesus replied, "Let it be so now; it is
proper for us to do this to fulfill all righteousness." Then John consented.

[a] *18* Jer. 31:15 [b] *3* Isaiah 40:3 [c] *11* Or *in*

3:16 [b]Isa 11:2; 42:1 16 As soon as Jesus was baptized, he
went up out of the water. At that mo-
3:17 [c]Mt 17:5; Jn 12:28 ment heaven was opened, and he saw
the Spirit of God[b] descending like a dove
[d]Ps 2:7; 2Pe 1:17,18 and lighting on him. 17 And a voice from
[e]Isa 42:1; Mt 12:18; 17:5; Mk 1:11; 9:7; Lk 9:35 heaven[c] said, "This is my Son,[d] whom I
love; with him I am well pleased."[e]

CHRIST'S TEMPTATIONS WERE UTTER NONSENSE IF HE WERE ONLY A MAN. WHAT MAN WOULD EVER BE CHALLENGED TO CHANGE A ROCK INTO A LOAF OF BREAD?

Anonymous

The Temptation of Jesus

4 Then Jesus was led by the Spirit
into the desert to be tempted by
4:2 [f]Ex 34:28; 1Ki 19:8 the devil. 2 After fasting forty days and
forty nights,[f] he was hungry. 3 The
4:3 [g]1Th 3:5 [h]Mt 3:17; Jn 5:25; Ac 9:20 tempter[g] came to him and said, "If you
are the Son of God,[h] tell these stones to
become bread."
4 Jesus answered, "It is written: 'Man
does not live on bread alone, but on
4:4 [i]Dt 8:3 every word that comes from the mouth
of God.'[a]"[i]

IMMEDIATELY UPON COMMENCING HIS PUBLIC MINISTRY, JESUS BEGAN TO TEACH AND DEMONSTRATE THAT HE WAS MORE THAN HUMAN, THAT IN FACT HE WAS GOD COME IN THE FLESH.

Tim LaHaye,
Christian Author and Speaker

5 Then the devil took him to the holy 4:5 [j]Ne 11:1; Da 9:24; Mt 27:53
city[j] and had him stand on the highest
point of the temple. 6 "If you are the Son
of God," he said, "throw yourself down.
For it is written:

" 'He will command his angels
concerning you,
and they will lift you up in their
hands,
so that you will not strike your foot
against a stone.'[b]"[k] 4:6 [k]Ps 91:11,12

7 Jesus answered him, "It is also writ-
ten: 'Do not put the Lord your God to 4:7 [l]Dt 6:16
the test.'[c]"[l]
8 Again, the devil took him to a very

[a] 4 Deut. 8:3 [b] 6 Psalm 91:11,12 [c] 7 Deut. 6:16

JESUS' BAPTISM AND TEMPTATION

Events surrounding Jesus' baptism reveal the intense religious excitement and social ferment of the early days of John the Baptist's ministry. Herod had been rapacious and extravagant; Roman military occupation was harsh. Some agitation centered around the change of procurators from Gratus to Pilate in A.D. 26. Most of the people hoped for a religious solution to their low political fortunes, and when they heard of a new prophet, they flocked out into the desert to hear him. The religious sect (Essenes) from Qumran professed similar doctrines of repentance and baptism. Jesus was baptized at Bethany on the other side of the Jordan (see Jn 1:28). John also baptized at "Aenon near Salim" (Jn 3:23).

The temptation took place in (1) the desert region of the lower Jordan Valley, (2) a high mountain (possibly one of the abrupt cliffs near Jericho that present an unsurpassed panorama) and (3) the pinnacle of the temple, from which the priests sounded the trumpet to call the city's attention to important events.

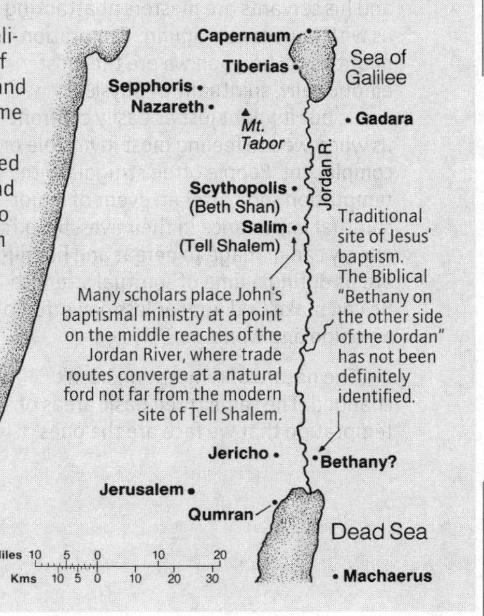

OVERCOMING TEMPTATION

Temptation is a universal human struggle. But for Jesus' followers the fight often seems doubly difficult, because we squirm under our acute awareness of God's holy standard and because the devil targets us for specific and sustained attack. Jesus himself was personally tempted by Satan, but he stood firm and unwavering in his commitment to the Father. His victory imbues us with encouragement, because we know that he empathizes with our struggle. The difference between Jesus and us is that Jesus knew the lure of temptation but refrained from sinning (Hebrews 4:15). We can learn a great deal about dealing with temptation from observing Jesus' response to Satan's enticements.

Jesus was tempted immediately after having spent 40 days fasting in the desert in the presence of the Spirit (Matthew 4:1–11). Although God the Son was undoubtedly on a spiritual high, he was physically depleted and vulnerable. Satan and his servants are masters at attacking us with impeccable timing. Temptation might assail us when we are the most emotionally, spiritually or physically weak, but it might just as easily confront us when we are feeling most invincible or complacent. People often struggle with temptation soon after an event of major spiritual importance in their lives. If God's enemy can manage to defeat and humiliate us during a time of spiritual strength, he can make God appear less powerful to an onlooking world.

The nature of temptation hasn't changed. The same three basic areas of temptation that we face are the ones that lured Eve and Adam to disobey God. They are "the cravings of sinful man, the lust of his eyes and the boasting of what he has and does" (1 John 2:16). Compare this description with the narrative in Genesis 3:6: "When the woman saw that the fruit of the tree was good for food and pleasing to the eye, and also desirable for gaining wisdom, she took some and ate it."

Jesus' reaction to the first temptation reveals that he refused to use his power for his own convenience, his response to the second that he declined to act recklessly and then expect God to deliver him, and his reply to the third that he would under no circumstances compromise with Satan.

There is one fail-safe method available to each of us for resisting temptation, and Jesus modeled it for us. Like Jesus Christ, we have to fight back with God's truth. Each time Jesus was tempted his response began with the same phrase: *It is written*. The more intimately we know God through his Word, the more resolute and successful we can be in the face of evil. We can do no better than to do as the psalmist did: "I have hidden your word in my heart that I might not sin against you" (Psalm 119:11).

Self-Discovery: Can you recall facing a particularly strong temptation during or shortly after a spiritual "high"? Were you able to resist the temptation? Why or why not?

GO TO DISCOVERY 235 ON PAGE 1267

high mountain and showed him all the
kingdoms of the world and their splendor. 9 "All this I will give you," he said, "if
you will bow down and worship me."
10 Jesus said to him, "Away from me,
Satan![m] For it is written: 'Worship the
Lord your God, and serve him only.'[a]"[n]
11 Then the devil left him, and angels
came and attended him.[o]

Jesus Begins to Preach

12 When Jesus heard that John had
been put in prison,[p] he returned to Galilee.[q] 13 Leaving Nazareth, he went and
lived in Capernaum,[r] which was by the
lake in the area of Zebulun and Naphtali— 14 to fulfill what was said through the
prophet Isaiah:

15 "Land of Zebulun and land of
Naphtali,
the way to the sea, along the
Jordan,
Galilee of the Gentiles—
16 the people living in darkness
have seen a great light;
on those living in the land of the
shadow of death
a light has dawned."[b][s]

17 From that time on Jesus began to
preach, "Repent, for the kingdom of
heaven[t] is near."

4:10 [m] 1Ch 21:1 [n] Dt 6:13
4:11 [o] Mt 26:53; Lk 22:43; Heb 1:14
4:12 [p] Mt 14:3 [q] Mk 1:14
4:13 [r] Mk 1:21; Lk 4:23,31; Jn 2:12; 4:46,47
4:16 [s] Isa 9:1,2; Lk 2:32
4:17 [t] Mt 3:2

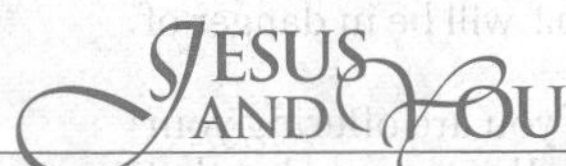

FISHING FOR PEOPLE

When Jesus began his public ministry, he repeatedly asked people to turn to God because the "kingdom of heaven [was] near" (Matthew 4:17). He also began gathering his disciples, a band of 12 full-time followers, several of whom were fishermen. Jesus promised Peter and Andrew that if they were to cast their lot with him, he would teach them how to "catch" people rather than fish (verse 19)! James and John also spontaneously dropped their fishing nets to follow Jesus and learn from him. Discipleship is never easy—Jesus asked this small group of men to renounce everything from their pasts, to leave all without so much as a farewell glance, and to follow him without question or foreknowledge of their destinations or destinies. And still today when God asks us to join his team, he demands that we lay aside all of our own ideals and ideas in order to follow him in faithful obedience wherever he may lead.

The Calling of the First Disciples

18 As Jesus was walking beside the Sea
of Galilee,[u] he saw two brothers, Simon
called Peter[v] and his brother Andrew.
They were casting a net into the lake, for
they were fishermen. 19 "Come, follow
me,"[w] Jesus said, "and I will make you
fishers of men." 20 At once they left their
nets and followed him.
21 Going on from there, he saw two
other brothers, James son of Zebedee
and his brother John.[x] They were in a
boat with their father Zebedee, preparing their nets. Jesus called them, 22 and
immediately they left the boat and their
father and followed him.

Jesus Heals the Sick

23 Jesus went throughout Galilee,[y]
teaching in their synagogues,[z] preaching
the good news[a] of the kingdom,[b] and
healing every disease and sickness
among the people.[c] 24 News about him
spread all over Syria,[d] and people
brought to him all who were ill with various diseases, those suffering severe pain,
the demon-possessed,[e] those having seizures,[f] and the paralyzed,[g] and he healed
them. 25 Large crowds from Galilee, the
Decapolis,[c] Jerusalem, Judea and the region across the Jordan followed him.[h]

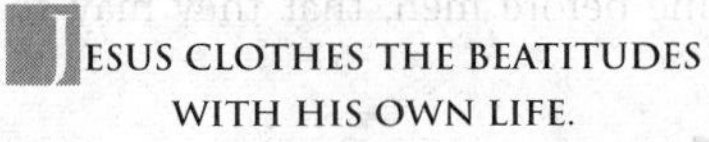

JESUS CLOTHES THE BEATITUDES WITH HIS OWN LIFE.

Carl F. H. Henry, *American Theologian*

The Beatitudes

5 Now when he saw the crowds, he
went up on a mountainside and
sat down. His disciples came to him,
2 and he began to teach them, saying:

3 "Blessed are the poor in spirit,
for theirs is the kingdom of
heaven.[i]
4 Blessed are those who mourn,
for they will be comforted.[j]
5 Blessed are the meek,
for they will inherit the earth.[k]
6 Blessed are those who hunger and
thirst for righteousness,
for they will be filled.[l]
7 Blessed are the merciful,

4:18 [u] Mt 15:29; Mk 7:31; Jn 6:1 [v] Mt 16:17,18
4:19 [w] Mk 10:21,28, 52
4:21 [x] Mt 20:20
4:23 [y] Mk 1:39; Lk 4:15,44 [z] Mt 9:35; 13:54; Mk 1:21; Lk 4:15; Jn 6:59 [a] Mk 1:14 [b] Mt 3:2; Ac 20:25 [c] Mt 8:16; 15:30; Ac 10:38
4:24 [d] Lk 2:2 [e] Mt 8:16,28; 9:32; 15:22; Mk 1:32; 5:15, 16,18 [f] Mt 17:15 [g] Mt 8:6; 9:2; Mk 2:3
4:25 [h] Mk 3:7,8; Lk 6:17
5:3 [i] ver 10,19; Mt 25:34
5:4 [j] Isa 61:2,3; Rev 7:17
5:5 [k] Ps 37:11; Ro 4:13
5:6 [l] Isa 55:1,2

[a] *10* Deut. 6:13 [b] *16* Isaiah 9:1,2 [c] *25* That is, the Ten Cities

5:8 for they will be shown mercy.
[m] Ps 24:3,4 8 Blessed are the pure in heart,[m]
[n] Heb 12:14; Rev 22:4 for they will see God.[n]
9 Blessed are the peacemakers,
5:9 for they will be called sons of
[o] ver 44,45; Ro 8:14 God.[o]
10 Blessed are those who are
persecuted because of
5:10 [p] 1Pe 3:14 righteousness,[p]
for theirs is the kingdom of
heaven.

5:11 11 "Blessed are you when people insult
[q] 1Pe 4:14 you,[q] persecute you and falsely say all
5:12 kinds of evil against you because of me.
[r] Ac 5:41; 1Pe 4:13,16 12 Rejoice and be glad,[r] because great is
[s] Mt 23:31,37; your reward in heaven, for in the same
Ac 7:52; way they persecuted the prophets who
1Th 2:15 were before you.[s]

Salt and Light

13 "You are the salt of the earth. But if
the salt loses its saltiness, how can it be
made salty again? It is no longer good
5:13 [t] Mk 9:50; for anything, except to be thrown out
Lk 14:34,35 and trampled by men.[t]
14 "You are the light of the world.[u] A
5:14 [u] Jn 8:12 city on a hill cannot be hidden. 15 Neither
do people light a lamp and put it under
a bowl. Instead they put it on its stand,
and it gives light to everyone in the
5:15 [v] Mk 4:21; house.[v] 16 In the same way, let your light
Lk 8:16 shine before men, that they may see
your good deeds and praise[w] your Fa- 5:16 [w] Mt 9:8
ther in heaven.

The Fulfillment of the Law

17 "Do not think that I have come to
abolish the Law or the Prophets; I have
not come to abolish them but to fulfill 5:17
them.[x] 18 I tell you the truth, until heav- [x] Ro 3:31
en and earth disappear, not the smallest
letter, not the least stroke of a pen, will
by any means disappear from the Law 5:18
until everything is accomplished.[y] [y] Lk 16:17
19 Anyone who breaks one of the least of 5:19
these commandments[z] and teaches [z] Jas 2:10
others to do the same will be called least
in the kingdom of heaven, but whoever
practices and teaches these commands
will be called great in the kingdom of
heaven. 20 For I tell you that unless your
righteousness surpasses that of the
Pharisees and the teachers of the law,
you will certainly not enter the kingdom
of heaven.

Murder

21 "You have heard that it was said to 5:21
the people long ago, 'Do not murder,[a a] [a] Ex 20:13;
and anyone who murders will be subject Dt 5:17
to judgment.' 22 But I tell you that anyone
who is angry with his brother[b] will be 5:22
subject to judgment.[b] Again, anyone [b] 1Jn 3:15
who says to his brother, 'Raca,[c]' is an- [c] Mt 26:59
swerable to the Sanhedrin.[c] But anyone [d] Jas 3:6
who says, 'You fool!' will be in danger of
the fire of hell.[d]
23 "Therefore, if you are offering your
gift at the altar and there remember that
your brother has something against you,
24 leave your gift there in front of the altar. First go and be reconciled to your
brother; then come and offer your gift.
25 "Settle matters quickly with your adversary who is taking you to court. Do it
while you are still with him on the way, or
he may hand you over to the judge, and
the judge may hand you over to the officer, and you may be thrown into prison.
26 I tell you the truth, you will not get out
until you have paid the last penny.[d]

Adultery

27 "You have heard that it was said, 5:27
'Do not commit adultery.'[e e] 28 But I tell [e] Ex 20:14;
you that anyone who looks at a woman Dt 5:18

[a] 21 Exodus 20:13 [b] 22 Some manuscripts *brother without cause* [c] 22 An Aramaic term of contempt [d] 26 Greek *kodrantes* [e] 27 Exodus 20:14

JESUS FOCUS

JESUS AND THE LAW

Jesus was accused by some of trying to thrust aside or overturn God's law, but that was never his intention. By contrast, Jesus actually came to fulfill the law, demonstrating that God considered his law an essential component of Jewish life (Matthew 5:17). Throughout the centuries the religious leaders had written voluminous interpretations and applications of the law, but many of these explications missed the very spirit of how God intended his people to live. Jesus challenged not the law itself but its rigid interpretations, stating repeatedly words to this effect: "You have heard this, but I tell you there's more to it!" (see Matthew 5:21—7:29). Jesus Christ wanted people to understand who God is, and in order to grow in their understanding they needed the ability to see beyond the legal restrictions to the essential character of the One who had made the laws.

Empty But Open Hands

Jesus taught many principles that run counter to the normal responses of our human nature, and the pithy statements in the Beatitudes sum up his unique value system. To a world that places a high premium on wealth, success, power, self-satisfaction, independence, relativism, aggressiveness and popularity, Jesus' astonishing pronouncements come as a shock. He tells us that the ones who are blessed (joyful at the core of their being and beautiful in God's sight) are those who are poor in spirit, who mourn for their sins, who are meek, who hunger and thirst for righteousness, who demonstrate mercy, who are pure in heart, who are peacemakers, who endure persecution in the name of Jesus Christ (Matthew 5:3–10).

Jesus' initial statement is fundamental to all of the rest: "Blessed are the poor in spirit." There are two different Greek words in the New Testament to describe the poor. The first one, *penes*, refers to someone who barely ekes out a living through working hard with his or her hands (Luke 21:2). The second, *ptochos*, connotes a beggar, an individual who is totally devoid of resources and completely dependent on the generosity of others. In Luke 16:19–21 Jesus portrayed just such a man to illustrate devotion to God and the ensuing rewards. The beggar Lazarus was so destitute that he hungered for the few meager crumbs that might fall from the rich man's table.

According to the world's value system, it would have been logical for Jesus to have used the first Greek word for "poor"—something like: "Blessed are *those who work hard with their hands*, for they will be blessed by God." The implication would have been that if a person attends church services, spends time in the Word, prays, donates money and time and helps other people, God will reward him or her. But Jesus did not use the first Greek word, in effect stating instead: "Blessed are *the beggars*, those who have nothing to offer to God, those who are totally dependent on God as their source of life and strength, those who have learned to trust in God rather than in themselves."

This principle is foundational to living the way God wants us to live. We are saved because we trust that Jesus died for our sins, not because we could ever begin to be good enough to win God's approval. The apostle Paul stated this truth in unforgettable terms in Galatians 2:20: "I have been crucified with Christ and I no longer live, but Christ lives in me. The life I live in the body, I live by faith in the Son of God, who loved me and gave himself for me." And in Ephesians 2:8–9 Paul reiterated the message: "It is by grace you have been saved, through faith—not of works, so that no one can boast."

When it comes to pleasing God, we approach him as beggars with an empty but open hand. True joy and comfort are found in relying on God every day, acknowledging that he is our source of protection, strength and sustenance. We cannot have it any other way.

Self-Discovery: *Visualize yourself approaching Jesus as a beggar, with your upturned palms outstretched to him. What expression do you see on his face? How does he respond? In what ways does this image of Jesus influence your relationship with him right now?*

GO TO DISCOVERY 236 ON PAGE 1274

lustfully has already committed adul-
5:28 [f]Pr 6:25 tery with her in his heart.[f] [29]If your right
5:29 eye causes you to sin,[g] gouge it out and
[g]Mt 18:6,8,9; throw it away. It is better for you to lose
Mk 9:42-47 one part of your body than for your
whole body to be thrown into hell.
[30]And if your right hand causes you to
sin, cut it off and throw it away. It is better for you to lose one part of your body
than for your whole body to go into hell.

Divorce

[31]"It has been said, 'Anyone who divorces his wife must give her a certifi-
5:31 [h]Dt 24:1-4 cate of divorce.'[a][h] [32]But I tell you that
anyone who divorces his wife, except for
marital unfaithfulness, causes her to become an adulteress, and anyone who
5:32 marries the divorced woman commits
[i]Lk 16:18 adultery.[i]

Oaths

[33]"Again, you have heard that it was
5:33 said to the people long ago, 'Do not
[j]Lev 19:12 break your oath,[j] but keep the oaths you
[k]Nu 30:2; have made to the Lord.'[k] [34]But I tell you,
Dt 23:21; Do not swear at all:[l] either by heaven, for
Mt 23:16-22 it is God's throne;[m] [35]or by the earth, for
5:34 [l]Jas 5:12 it is his footstool; or by Jerusalem, for it
[m]Isa 66:1; is the city of the Great King.[n] [36]And do
Mt 23:22 not swear by your head, for you cannot
5:35 make even one hair white or black.
[n]Ps 48:2 [37]Simply let your 'Yes' be 'Yes,' and your
5:37 [o]Jas 5:12 'No,' 'No';[o] anything beyond this comes
[p]Mt 6:13; 13:19, from the evil one.[p]
38; Jn 17:15;
2Th 3:3;

An Eye for an Eye

1Jn 2:13,14;
3:12; 5:18,19 [38]"You have heard that it was said,
5:38 'Eye for eye, and tooth for tooth.'[b][q] [39]But
[q]Ex 21:24; I tell you, Do not resist an evil person. If
Lev 24:20; someone strikes you on the right cheek,
Dt 19:21 turn to him the other also.[r] [40]And if
5:39 someone wants to sue you and take
[r]Lk 6:29; your tunic, let him have your cloak as
Ro 12:17,19; well. [41]If someone forces you to go one
1Co 6:7; 1Pe 3:9 mile, go with him two miles. [42]Give to
5:42 [s]Dt 15:8; the one who asks you, and do not turn
Lk 6:30 away from the one who wants to borrow
5:43 from you.[s]
[t]Lev 19:18
[u]Dt 23:6

Love for Enemies

5:44 [43]"You have heard that it was said,
[v]Lk 6:27,28; 'Love your neighbor[c][t] and hate your en-
23:34; Ac 7:60; emy.'[u] [44]But I tell you: Love your ene-
Ro 12:14; 1Co 4:12; mies[d] and pray for those who persecute
1Pe 2:23 you,[v] [45]that you may be sons[w] of your
5:45 [w]ver 9 Father in heaven. He causes his sun to
rise on the evil and the good, and sends
rain on the righteous and the unrigh- 5:45
teous.[x] [46]If you love those who love you, [x]Job 25:3
what reward will you get?[y] Are not even 5:46
the tax collectors doing that? [47]And if [y]Lk 6:32
you greet only your brothers, what are 5:48
you doing more than others? Do not [z]Lev 19:2;
even pagans do that? [48]Be perfect, there- 1Pe 1:16
fore, as your heavenly Father is perfect.[z]

Giving to the Needy

6 "Be careful not to do your 'acts of
righteousness' before men, to be 6:1
seen by them.[a] If you do, you will have [a]Mt 23:5
no reward from your Father in heaven.
[2]"So when you give to the needy, do
not announce it with trumpets, as the
hypocrites do in the synagogues and on
the streets, to be honored by men. I tell
you the truth, they have received their
reward in full. [3]But when you give to the
needy, do not let your left hand know
what your right hand is doing, [4]so that
your giving may be in secret. Then your
Father, who sees what is done in secret, 6:4 [b]ver 6,18;
will reward you.[b] Col 3:23,24

Prayer

[5]"And when you pray, do not be like
the hypocrites, for they love to pray 6:5
standing[c] in the synagogues and on the [c]Mk 11:25;
street corners to be seen by men. I tell Lk 18:10-14
you the truth, they have received their
reward in full. [6]But when you pray, go
into your room, close the door and pray 6:6
to your Father,[d] who is unseen. Then [d]2Ki 4:33
your Father, who sees what is done in secret, will reward you. [7]And when you 6:7
pray, do not keep on babbling[e] like pa- [e]Ecc 5:2
gans, for they think they will be heard [f]1Ki 18:26-29
because of their many words.[f] [8]Do not
be like them, for your Father knows 6:8
what you need[g] before you ask him. [g]ver 32
[9]"This, then, is how you should pray:

"'Our Father in heaven,
hallowed be your name,
[10]your kingdom[h] come, 6:10 [h]Mt 3:2
your will be done[i] [i]Mt 26:39
on earth as it is in heaven. 6:11
[11]Give us today our daily bread.[j] [j]Pr 30:8
[12]Forgive us our debts,
as we also have forgiven our 6:12
debtors.[k] [k]Mt 18:21-35

[a] *31* Deut. 24:1 [b] *38* Exodus 21:24; Lev. 24:20; Deut. 19:21 [c] *43* Lev. 19:18 [d] *44* Some late manuscripts *enemies, bless those who curse you, do good to those who hate you*

"YOUR THRONE . . . WILL LAST
FOR EVER AND EVER . . .
YOU HAVE LOVED RIGHTEOUSNESS AND
HATED WICKEDNESS; THEREFORE GOD . . .
HAS SET YOU ABOVE YOUR COMPANIONS
BY ANOINTING YOU WITH
THE *oil of joy.*"
—HEBREWS 1:8-9—

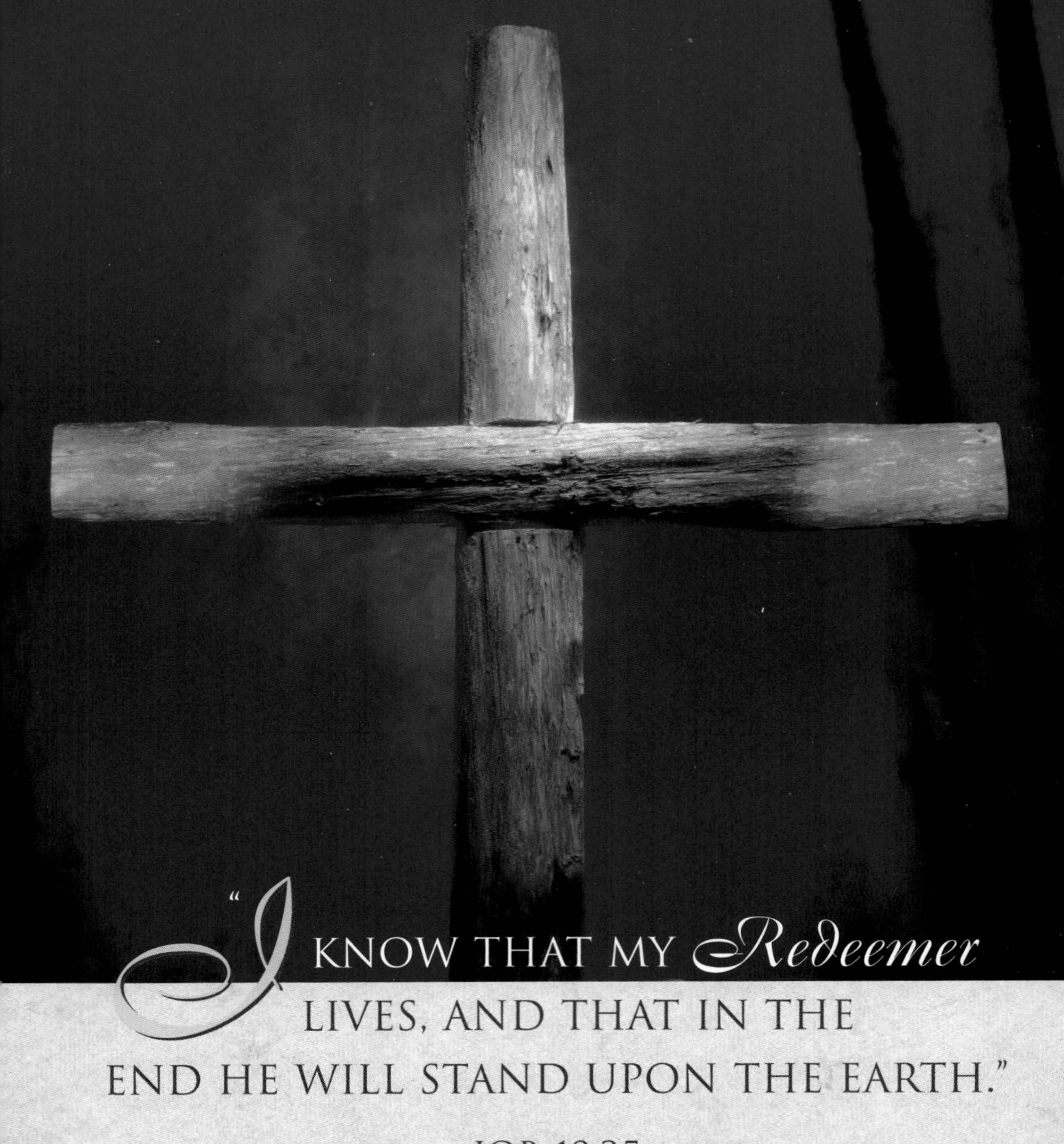

"I KNOW THAT MY *Redeemer* LIVES, AND THAT IN THE END HE WILL STAND UPON THE EARTH."

— JOB 19:25 —

6:13 [13] And lead us not into temptation,[l]
[l]Jas 1:13 [m]Mt 5:37 but deliver us from the evil one.[a] [m]
6:14 [n]Mt 18:21-35; [14]For if you forgive men when they sin
Mk 11:25,26; against you, your heavenly Father will
Eph 4:32; also forgive you.[n] [15]But if you do not for-
Col 3:13 give men their sins, your Father will not
6:15 [o]Mt 18:35 forgive your sins.[o]

Fasting

6:16 [p]Isa 58:5 [16]"When you fast, do not look
somber[p] as the hypocrites do, for they
disfigure their faces to show men they
are fasting. I tell you the truth, they have
received their reward in full. [17]But when
you fast, put oil on your head and wash
your face, [18]so that it will not be obvious
to men that you are fasting, but only to
your Father, who is unseen; and your Father, who sees what is done in secret, will
6:18 [q]ver 4,6 reward you.[q]

Treasures in Heaven

6:19 [r]Pr 23:4; [19]"Do not store up for yourselves trea-
Heb 13:5 sures on earth,[r] where moth and rust
[s]Jas 5:2,3 destroy,[s] and where thieves break in and
6:20 steal. [20]But store up for yourselves trea-
[t]Mt 19:21; sures in heaven,[t] where moth and rust
Lk 12:33; 18:22; do not destroy, and where thieves do not
1Ti 6:19 [u]Lk 12:33 break in and steal.[u] [21]For where your
treasure is, there your heart will be also.[v]
6:21 [v]Lk 12:34 [22]"The eye is the lamp of the body. If
your eyes are good, your whole body will
be full of light. [23]But if your eyes are bad,
your whole body will be full of darkness.
If then the light within you is darkness,
how great is that darkness!

[24]"No one can serve two masters. Either he will hate the one and love the
other, or he will be devoted to the one
6:24 and despise the other. You cannot serve
[w]Lk 16:13 both God and Money.[w]

Do Not Worry

6:25 [x]ver 27,28,31, [25]"Therefore I tell you, do not worry[x]
34; Lk 10:41; about your life, what you will eat or
12:11,22; Php 4:6; 1Pe 5:7 drink; or about your body, what you will
wear. Is not life more important than
food, and the body more important than
clothes? [26]Look at the birds of the air;
they do not sow or reap or store away in
6:26 barns, and yet your heavenly Father feeds
[y]Job 38:41; them.[y] Are you not much more valuable
Ps 147:9 [z]Mt 10:29-31 than they?[z] [27]Who of you by worrying
6:27 can add a single hour to his life[b]?[a]
[a]Ps 39:5 [28]"And why do you worry about
clothes? See how the lilies of the field
grow. They do not labor or spin. [29]Yet I

> **OF ALL THE SYSTEMS OF MORALITY, ANCIENT OR MODERN, WHICH HAVE COME UNDER MY OBSERVATION, NONE APPEARS TO ME SO PURE AS THAT OF JESUS.**
>
> 
>
> Thomas Jefferson, *American President*

tell you that not even Solomon in all his 6:29
splendor[b] was dressed like one of these. [b]1Ki 10:4-7
[30]If that is how God clothes the grass of
the field, which is here today and tomorrow is thrown into the fire, will he not
much more clothe you, O you of little 6:30
faith?[c] [31]So do not worry, saying, 'What [c]Mt 8:26; 14:31;
shall we eat?' or 'What shall we drink?' or 16:8
'What shall we wear?' [32]For the pagans
run after all these things, and your heav- 6:32
enly Father knows that you need them.[d] [d]ver 8
[33]But seek first his kingdom and his righteousness, and all these things will be 6:33
given to you as well.[e] [34]Therefore do not [e]Mt 19:29;
worry about tomorrow, for tomorrow Mk 10:29-30
will worry about itself. Each day has
enough trouble of its own.

Judging Others

7 "Do not judge, or you too will be 7:1
judged.[f] [2]For in the same way you [f]Lk 6:37; Ro 14:4,10,13;
judge others, you will be judged, and 1Co 4:5;
with the measure you use, it will be Jas 4:11,12
measured to you.[g] 7:2 [g]Mk 4:24;
[3]"Why do you look at the speck of Lk 6:38
sawdust in your brother's eye and pay no
attention to the plank in your own eye?
[4]How can you say to your brother, 'Let
me take the speck out of your eye,' when
all the time there is a plank in your own
eye? [5]You hypocrite, first take the plank
out of your own eye, and then you will
see clearly to remove the speck from
your brother's eye.

[6]"Do not give dogs what is sacred; do
not throw your pearls to pigs. If you do, 7:7
they may trample them under their feet, [h]Mt 21:22;
and then turn and tear you to pieces. Mk 11:24; Jn 14:13,14;
15:7,16; 16:23,

Ask, Seek, Knock 24; Jas 1:5-8; 4:2,3; 1Jn 3:22;

[7]"Ask and it will be given to you;[h] seek 5:14,15
and you will find; knock and the door 7:8
will be opened to you. [8]For everyone [i]Pr 8:17; Jer 29:12,13
who asks receives; he who seeks finds;[i]

[a] 13 Or *from evil*; some late manuscripts *one, / for yours is the kingdom and the power and the glory forever. Amen.* [b] 27 Or *single cubit to his height*

and to him who knocks, the door will be
opened.
9“Which of you, if his son asks for
bread, will give him a stone? 10Or if he
asks for a fish, will give him a snake? 11If
you, then, though you are evil, know
how to give good gifts to your children,
how much more will your Father in
heaven give good gifts to those who ask
7:12 him! 12So in everything, do to others
j Lk 6:31 what you would have them do to you,[j]
k Ro 13:8-10; for this sums up the Law and the
Gal 5:14 Prophets.[k]

The Narrow and Wide Gates

7:13 13“Enter through the narrow gate.[l] For
l Lk 13:24 wide is the gate and broad is the road
that leads to destruction, and many enter through it. 14But small is the gate and
narrow the road that leads to life, and
only a few find it.

A Tree and Its Fruit

7:15 15“Watch out for false prophets.[m]
m Jer 23:16; They come to you in sheep's clothing,
Mt 24:24; Mk 13:22; but inwardly they are ferocious wolves.[n]
Lk 6:26; 2Pe 2:1; 16By their fruit you will recognize them.[o]
1Jn 4:1; Rev 16:13 Do people pick grapes from thorn-
n Ac 20:29 bushes, or figs from thistles?[p] 17Likewise
7:16 every good tree bears good fruit, but a
o Mt 12:33; bad tree bears bad fruit. 18A good tree
Lk 6:44 p Jas 3:12 cannot bear bad fruit, and a bad tree
cannot bear good fruit. 19Every tree that
does not bear good fruit is cut down and 7:19
thrown into the fire.[q] 20Thus, by their q Mt 3:10
fruit you will recognize them.
21“Not everyone who says to me, 7:21
‘Lord, Lord,’[r] will enter the kingdom of r Hos 8:2; Mt 25:11
heaven, but only he who does the will of s Ro 2:13;
my Father who is in heaven.[s] 22Many will Jas 1:22
say to me on that day,[t] ‘Lord, Lord, did 7:22
we not prophesy in your name, and in t Mt 10:15
your name drive out demons and per- u 1Co 13:1-3
form many miracles?’[u] 23Then I will tell
them plainly, ‘I never knew you. Away 7:23
from me, you evildoers!’[v] v Ps 6:8; Mt 25:12,41; Lk 13:25-27

The Wise and Foolish Builders

24“Therefore everyone who hears
these words of mine and puts them into 7:24
practice[w] is like a wise man who built w Jas 1:22-25
his house on the rock. 25The rain came
down, the streams rose, and the winds
blew and beat against that house; yet it
did not fall, because it had its foundation on the rock. 26But everyone who
hears these words of mine and does not
put them into practice is like a foolish
man who built his house on sand. 27The
rain came down, the streams rose, and
the winds blew and beat against that
house, and it fell with a great crash.”
28When Jesus had finished saying 7:28
these things,[x] the crowds were amazed x Mt 11:1; 13:53; 19:1; 26:1
at his teaching,[y] 29because he taught as y Mt 13:54;
one who had authority, and not as their Mk 1:22; 6:2;
teachers of the law. Lk 4:32; Jn 7:46

The Man With Leprosy

8 When he came down from the
mountainside, large crowds fol- 8:2
lowed him. 2A man with leprosy[a][z] came z Lk 5:12
and knelt before him[a] and said, “Lord, if a Mt 9:18; 15:25;
you are willing, you can make me clean.” 18:26; 20:20
3Jesus reached out his hand and
touched the man. “I am willing,” he said.
“Be clean!” Immediately he was cured[b]
of his leprosy. 4Then Jesus said to him, 8:4
“See that you don't tell anyone.[b] But go, b Mt 9:30;
show yourself to the priest and offer the Mk 5:43; 7:36;
gift Moses commanded,[c] as a testimony 8:30 c Lev 14:2-32
to them.”

The Faith of the Centurion

5When Jesus had entered Capernaum,
a centurion came to him, asking for

[a] 2 The Greek word was used for various diseases affecting the skin—not necessarily leprosy.
[b] 3 Greek *made clean*

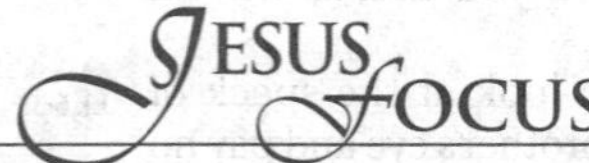

THE GOLDEN RULE

Many of us have been taught from early childhood that “the golden rule” is to do to (or for) others what we would like them to do to (or for) us. While Jesus didn't call it “the golden rule,” the statement itself summarizes the essence of the ethical behavior he urges his followers to demonstrate. Jesus' words encourage us to live out our obedience to God's law by treating others the way we ourselves would want to be treated. Jesus did not teach that we can be made right with God or “earn” salvation because we have been kind to others. The very next verses in fact tell us that we can come into God's kingdom only by the narrow way—through a relationship with Jesus, the Son of God (John 14:6). But merely saying that we believe in Jesus isn't sufficient for those who are kingdom citizens. A natural outgrowth of that faith entails putting it into action by living life in a way that pleases God (Matthew 7:21; Galatians 5:6; James 2:14–26).

help. 6"Lord," he said, "my servant lies at
home paralyzed and in terrible suffering."
7Jesus said to him, "I will go and heal
him."
8The centurion replied, "Lord, I do
not deserve to have you come under my
roof. But just say the word, and my ser-
8:8 vant will be healed.[d] 9For I myself am a
[d]Ps 107:20 man under authority, with soldiers under me. I tell this one, 'Go,' and he goes;
and that one, 'Come,' and he comes. I say
to my servant, 'Do this,' and he does it."
10When Jesus heard this, he was as-
8:10 tonished and said to those following
[e]Mt 15:28 him, "I tell you the truth, I have not
8:11 found anyone in Israel with such great
[f]Ps 107:3; Isa 49:12; 59:19; Mal 1:11 faith.[e] 11I say to you that many will come
from the east and the west,[f] and will
take their places at the feast with Abraham, Isaac and Jacob in the kingdom of 8:11
heaven.[g] 12But the subjects of the king- [g]Lk 13:29
dom[h] will be thrown outside, into the 8:12
darkness, where there will be weeping [h]Mt 13:38
and gnashing of teeth."[i] [i]Mt 13:42,50; 22:13; 24:51; 25:30; Lk 13:28
13Then Jesus said to the centurion,
"Go! It will be done just as you believed 8:13
it would."[j] And his servant was healed at [j]Mt 9:22
that very hour.

Jesus Heals Many

14When Jesus came into Peter's house,
he saw Peter's mother-in-law lying in
bed with a fever. 15He touched her hand
and the fever left her, and she got up and
began to wait on him.
16When evening came, many who
were demon-possessed were brought to
him, and he drove out the spirits with a 8:16
word and healed all the sick.[k] 17This was [k]Mt 4:23,24
to fulfill[l] what was spoken through the 8:17
prophet Isaiah: [l]Mt 1:22 [m]Isa 53:4

> "He took up our infirmities
> and carried our diseases."[a][m]

The Cost of Following Jesus

18When Jesus saw the crowd around
him, he gave orders to cross to the other 8:18
side of the lake.[n] 19Then a teacher of the [n]Mk 4:35
law came to him and said, "Teacher, I
will follow you wherever you go."
20Jesus replied, "Foxes have holes and 8:20
birds of the air have nests, but the Son of [o]Da 7:13;
Man[o] has no place to lay his head." Mt 12:8,32,40; 16:13,27,28;
21Another disciple said to him, "Lord, 17:9; 19:28;
first let me go and bury my father." Mk 2:10; 8:31
22But Jesus told him, "Follow me,[p] and 8:22
let the dead bury their own dead." [p]Mt 4:19

Jesus Calms the Storm

23Then he got into the boat and his
disciples followed him. 24Without warning, a furious storm came up on the lake,
so that the waves swept over the boat.
But Jesus was sleeping. 25The disciples
went and woke him, saying, "Lord, save
us! We're going to drown!" 8:26
26He replied, "You of little faith,[q] why [q]Mt 6:30
are you so afraid?" Then he got up and [r]Ps 65:7; 89:9; 107:29
rebuked the winds and the waves, and it
was completely calm.[r]
27The men were amazed and asked,
"What kind of man is this? Even the
winds and the waves obey him!"

[a] *17* Isaiah 53:4

JESUS AND YOU

A NON-EXCLUSIVE SAVIOR

When the servant of the Roman centurion became deathly ill, the centurion sought out Jesus, who offered to go to the man's house to heal the servant despite the fact that this action would have constituted a violation of Jewish protocol (according to Jewish law, a Jew ceremonially defiled himself by entering a Gentile's house; see Acts 10:28). The centurion had something else in mind, however. Surprisingly, this Roman official first asserted that he did not deserve to have Jesus come under his roof and then urged the Master to "just say the word, and my servant will be healed" (Matthew 8:8). The centurion reminded Jesus that he himself was in a position of authority and that he could command his servants to perform specific tasks and then expect that they would comply. Without explicitly saying so, he was acknowledging that Jesus too possessed the authority to speak a word and expect obedience, that Jesus could perform a miracle without being physically present at the scene. Neither Jesus himself nor the skeptical crowd would have expected such profound faith from a Roman soldier, and we wonder how the centurion had come to this point of belief. Jesus commended the man for his faith, stating emphatically: "I tell you the truth, I have not found anyone in Israel with such great faith. I say to you that many will come from the east and from the west, and will take their places at the feast with Abraham, Isaac and Jacob in the kingdom of heaven" (verses 10–11).

Miracles of Jesus

Healing Miracles	Matthew	Mark	Luke	John
Man with leprosy	8:2–4	1:40–42	5:12–13	
Roman centurion's servant	8:5–13		7:1–10	
Peter's mother-in-law	8:14–15	1:30–31	4:38–35	
Two men from Gadara	8:28–34	5:1–15	8:27–35	
Paralyzed man	9:2–7	2:3–12	5:18–25	
Woman with bleeding	9:20–22	5:25–29	8:43–48	
Two blind men	9:27–31			
Mute, demon-possessed man	9:32–33			
Man with a shriveled hand	12:10–13	3:1–5	6:6–10	
Blind, mute, demon-possessed man	12:22		11:14	
Canaanite woman's daughter	15:21–28	7:24–30		
Boy with a demon	17:14–18	9:17–29	9:38–43	
Two blind men (including Bartimaeus)	20:29–34	10:46–52	18:35–43	
Deaf mute		7:31–37		
Possessed man in synagogue		1:23–26	4:33–35	
Blind man at Bethsaida		8:22–26		
Crippled woman			13:11–13	
Man with dropsy			14:1–4	
Ten men with leprosy			17:11–19	
The high priest's servant			22:50–51	
Official's son at Capernaum				4:46–54
Sick man at pool of Bethesda				5:1–9
Man born blind				9:1–7
Miracles showing power over nature				
Calming the storm	8:23–27	4:37–41	8:22–25	
Walking on water	14:25	6:48–51		6:19–21
Feeding of the 5,000	14:15–21	6:35–44	9:12–17	6:6–13
Feeding of the 4,000	15:32–38	8:1–9		
Coin in fish	17:24–27			
Fig tree withered	21:18–22	11:12–14,20–25		
Large catch of fish			5:4–11	
Water turned into wine				2:1–11
Another large catch of fish				21:1–11
Miracles of raising the dead				
Jairus's daughter	9:18–19,23–25	5:22–24,38–42	8:41–42,49–56	
Widow's son at Nain			7:11–15	
Lazarus				11:1–44

The Healing of Two Demon-possessed Men

28When he arrived at the other side in
the region of the Gadarenes,[a] two de-
8:28 s Mt 4:24 mon-possessed[s] men coming from the
tombs met him. They were so violent
8:29 t Jdg 11:12; that no one could pass that way. 29"What
2Sa 16:10; do you want with us,[t] Son of God?" they
1Ki 17:18; shouted. "Have you come here to torture
Mk 1:24; Lk 4:34; Jn 2:4 us before the appointed time?"[u]
u 2Pe 2:4 30Some distance from them a large
herd of pigs was feeding. 31The demons
begged Jesus, "If you drive us out, send
us into the herd of pigs."
32He said to them, "Go!" So they came
out and went into the pigs, and the
whole herd rushed down the steep bank
into the lake and died in the water.
33Those tending the pigs ran off, went
into the town and reported all this, including what had happened to the demon-possessed men. 34Then the whole
town went out to meet Jesus. And when
they saw him, they pleaded with him to
8:34 v Lk 5:8; Ac 16:39 leave their region.[v]

Jesus Heals a Paralytic

9:1 w Mt 4:13 **9** Jesus stepped into a boat, crossed
over and came to his own town.[w]
9:2 x Mt 4:24 2Some men brought to him a paralytic,[x]
y ver 22 lying on a mat. When Jesus saw their
z Jn 16:33 faith,[y] he said to the paralytic, "Take
a Lk 7:48 heart,[z] son; your sins are forgiven."[a]
3At this, some of the teachers of the
9:3 b Mt 26:65; law said to themselves, "This fellow is
Jn 10:33 blaspheming!"[b]
4Knowing their thoughts,[c] Jesus said,
9:4 c Ps 94:11; "Why do you entertain evil thoughts in
Mt 12:25; Lk 6:8; 9:47; your hearts? 5Which is easier: to say,
11:17 'Your sins are forgiven,' or to say, 'Get up
and walk'? 6But so that you may know
9:6 d Mt 8:20 that the Son of Man[d] has authority on
earth to forgive sins . . ." Then he said to
the paralytic, "Get up, take your mat and
go home." 7And the man got up and
9:8 went home. 8When the crowd saw this,
e Mt 5:16; 15:31; they were filled with awe; and they
Lk 7:16; 13:13; 17:15; 23:47; praised God,[e] who had given such au-
Jn 15:8; Ac 4:21; 11:18; 21:20 thority to men.

The Calling of Matthew

9As Jesus went on from there, he saw
a man named Matthew sitting at the tax
collector's booth. "Follow me," he told
him, and Matthew got up and followed
him.
10While Jesus was having dinner at

JESUS EQUIPPED UNQUALIFIED, UNLIKELY AND UNFIT MEN FOR KINGDOM SERVICE.

Mose Pleasure, Jr., *Director, Hope III Housing Program, Memphis, Tennessee*

Matthew's house, many tax collectors
and "sinners" came and ate with him
and his disciples. 11When the Pharisees
saw this, they asked his disciples, "Why
does your teacher eat with tax collectors
and 'sinners'?"[f] 9:11 f Mt 11:19;
12On hearing this, Jesus said, "It is not Lk 5:30; 15:2;
the healthy who need a doctor, but the Gal 2:15
sick. 13But go and learn what this means: 9:13
'I desire mercy, not sacrifice.'[b][g] For I have g Hos 6:6;
not come to call the righteous, but sin- Mic 6:6-8; Mt 12:7
ners."[h] h 1Ti 1:15

Jesus Questioned About Fasting

14Then John's disciples came and
asked him, "How is it that we and the 9:14
Pharisees fast,[i] but your disciples do not i Lk 18:12
fast?"
15Jesus answered, "How can the
guests of the bridegroom mourn while 9:15
he is with them?[j] The time will come j Jn 3:29
when the bridegroom will be taken from k Ac 13:2,3; 14:23
them; then they will fast.[k]
16"No one sews a patch of unshrunk
cloth on an old garment, for the patch
will pull away from the garment, making
the tear worse. 17Neither do men pour
new wine into old wineskins. If they do,
the skins will burst, the wine will run out
and the wineskins will be ruined. No,
they pour new wine into new wineskins,
and both are preserved."

A Dead Girl and a Sick Woman

18While he was saying this, a ruler 9:18
came and knelt before him[l] and said, l Mt 8:2
"My daughter has just died. But come m Mk 5:23
and put your hand on her,[m] and she will
live." 19Jesus got up and went with him,
and so did his disciples.
20Just then a woman who had been
subject to bleeding for twelve years
came up behind him and touched the 9:20
edge of his cloak.[n] 21She said to herself, n Mt 14:36;
"If I only touch his cloak, I will be Mk 3:10
healed."

a 28 Some manuscripts *Gergesenes*; others *Gerasenes* *b* 13 Hosea 6:6

A Friend of Sinners

Jesus associated with all kinds of people, and his relationships could not be compartmentalized into neat categories. He was a friend to the rich and greedy as well as to the poor and needy. And there were few people in Jesus' day known to be more avaricious and corrupt than the tax collectors. These men were Jews who had forged an alliance with the Roman government and who made their livelihood collecting taxes for the Romans. No respectable Jew would ever socialize with a tax collector.

Except Jesus. Not only did he associate with this class of individual, but he even asked Matthew, a tax collector by trade, to be his disciple and then proceeded to enjoy a party with Matthew's friends. Mystified, the Jewish leaders questioned Jesus' disciples as to why he was acting in such a shameful manner (Matthew 9:11). It didn't take long for Jesus to gain an undeserved reputation for being "a glutton and a drunkard, a friend of tax collectors and 'sinners' " (Matthew 11:19). Jesus' response to the complaint of the religious leaders was simple but profound: "It is not the healthy who need a doctor, but the sick . . . I have not come to call the righteous, but sinners" (Matthew 9:12–13).

Sadly, God's people have throughout the generations earned a reputation, sometimes deserved, for isolating themselves from "sinners." Still today many insulate themselves by narrowing their circle of friends and associates to a group that shares their own Christian principles and lifestyle. The argument may be made that there is Biblical precedent for an isolationist mind-set. The apostle Paul directed the Corinthian believers to: "'come out from them [unbelievers] and be separate, says the Lord. Touch no unclean thing, and I will receive you' " (2 Corinthians 6:17). But we need to remember the context of Paul's cautionary words. He was speaking about being "yoked together with unbelievers" in the context of a marital relationship (2 Corinthians 6:14). Similarly, God through his Old Testament spokesmen regularly chided the Israelites for intermingling with the nations around them, but the focus was once again on intermarriage (Deuteronomy 7:3; Joshua 23:12; 1 Kings 11:2; Ezra 9:14), as well as idolatry (Deuteronomy 7:5; 12:3; 29:17; Ezekiel 20:7; 23:30). "Depart, depart," stated Isaiah. "Touch no unclean thing! Come out . . . and be pure" (Isaiah 52:11).

Jesus' mandate in the Great Commission (Matthew 28:18–20) and elsewhere is precisely the opposite of separatism. While it is indisputably true that we must avoid temptations that would draw us into a lifestyle that might compromise our Christian beliefs and practices, Jesus mandated us as his followers to infiltrate the world with the Good News of the gospel.

The apostle Paul not only identified with sinners but identified himself as the "worst" of the lot: "Christ Jesus came into the world to save sinners . . . For that very reason I was shown mercy so that in me, the worst of sinners, Christ Jesus might display his unlimited patience as an example for those who would believe on him and receive eternal life" (1 Timothy 1:15–16).

Self-Discovery: *In what way could you reach out like Jesus today to share the message of salvation with someone else who could eternally benefit from the Good News you have to offer?*

GO TO DISCOVERY 237 ON PAGE 1276

> I HAVE READ THE STORIES OF JESUS MANY TIMES, BUT I HAVE NEVER LOST THAT SENSE OF NEW DISCOVERY AND EXCITEMENT. JESUS REMAINS AS COMPELLING AS EVER.
>
> John Drane, *British Scholar*

22Jesus turned and saw her. "Take
9:22 heart, daughter," he said, "your faith has
o Mk 10:52; healed you."[o] And the woman was
Lk 7:50; 17:19; 18:42 p Mt 15:28 healed from that moment.[p]
23When Jesus entered the ruler's house
9:23 and saw the flute players and the noisy
q 2Ch 35:25; crowd,[q] 24he said, "Go away. The girl is
Jer 9:17,18 not dead[r] but asleep."[s] But they laughed
9:24 at him. 25After the crowd had been put
r Ac 20:10 outside, he went in and took the girl by
s Jn 11:11-14 the hand, and she got up. 26News of this
9:26 t Mt 4:24 spread through all that region.[t]

Jesus Heals the Blind and Mute

27As Jesus went on from there, two
9:27 blind men followed him, calling out,
u Mt 15:22; Mk 10:47; "Have mercy on us, Son of David!"[u]
Lk 18:38-39 28When he had gone indoors, the
blind men came to him, and he asked
them, "Do you believe that I am able to
do this?"
"Yes, Lord," they replied.
29Then he touched their eyes and
9:29 said, "According to your faith will it be
v ver 22 done to you";[v] 30and their sight was re-
9:30 stored. Jesus warned them sternly, "See
w Mt 8:4 that no one knows about this."[w] 31But
9:31 they went out and spread the news
x ver 26; Mk 7:36 about him all over that region.[x]
32While they were going out, a man
9:32 who was demon-possessed[y] and could
y Mt 4:24 z Mt 12:22-24 not talk[z] was brought to Jesus. 33And
when the demon was driven out, the
man who had been mute spoke. The
9:33 crowd was amazed and said, "Nothing
a Mk 2:12 like this has ever been seen in Israel."[a]
34But the Pharisees said, "It is by the
9:34 b Mt 12:24; prince of demons that he drives out
Lk 11:15 demons."[b]

The Workers Are Few

35Jesus went through all the towns
and villages, teaching in their synagogues, preaching the good news of the
9:35 kingdom and healing every disease and
c Mt 4:23 sickness.[c] 36When he saw the crowds, he
had compassion on them,[d] because they 9:36
were harassed and helpless, like sheep d Mt 14:14
without a shepherd.[e] 37Then he said to e Nu 27:17; Eze 34:5,6;
his disciples, "The harvest[f] is plentiful Zec 10:2;
but the workers are few.[g] 38Ask the Lord Mk 6:34
of the harvest, therefore, to send out 9:37
workers into his harvest field." f Jn 4:35 g Lk 10:2

Jesus Sends Out the Twelve

10 He called his twelve disciples to
him and gave them authority to 10:1
drive out evil[a] spirits[h] and to heal every h Mk 3:13-15;
disease and sickness. Lk 9:1
2These are the names of the twelve
apostles: first, Simon (who is called Peter) and his brother Andrew; James son
of Zebedee, and his brother John; 3Phil-
ip and Bartholomew; Thomas and Matthew the tax collector; James son of Alphaeus, and Thaddaeus; 4Simon the 10:4
Zealot and Judas Iscariot, who betrayed i Mt 26:14-16,
him.[i] 25,47; Jn 13:2, 26,27
5These twelve Jesus sent out with the
following instructions: "Do not go 10:5
among the Gentiles or enter any town of j 2Ki 17:24;
the Samaritans.[j] 6Go rather to the lost Lk 9:52; Jn 4:4-
sheep of Israel.[k] 7As you go, preach this 26,39,40; Ac 8:5,25
message: 'The kingdom of heaven[l] is
near.' 8Heal the sick, raise the dead, 10:6
cleanse those who have leprosy,[b] drive k Jer 50:6; Mt 15:24
out demons. Freely you have received,
freely give. 9Do not take along any gold 10:7 l Mt 3:2
or silver or copper in your belts;[m] 10take
no bag for the journey, or extra tunic, or 10:9 m Lk 22:35
sandals or a staff; for the worker is worth 10:10
his keep.[n] n 1Ti 5:18
11"Whatever town or village you enter,
search for some worthy person there and
stay at his house until you leave. 12As you
enter the home, give it your greeting.[o] 13If 10:12 o 1Sa 25:6
the home is deserving, let your peace rest
on it; if it is not, let your peace return to 10:14 p Ne 5:13;
you. 14If anyone will not welcome you or Lk 10:11;
listen to your words, shake the dust off Ac 13:51
your feet[p] when you leave that home or 10:15
town. 15I tell you the truth, it will be more q 2Pe 2:6 r Mt 12:36;
bearable for Sodom and Gomorrah[q] on 2Pe 2:9; 1Jn 4:17
the day of judgment[r] than for that town.[s] s Mt 11:22,24
16I am sending you out like sheep among 10:16
wolves.[t] Therefore be as shrewd as t Lk 10:3 u Ro 16:19
snakes and as innocent as doves.[u]
17"Be on your guard against men; they 10:17
will hand you over to the local councils[v] v Mt 5:22 w Mt 23:34;
and flog you in their synagogues.[w] 18On Mk 13:9; Ac 5:40; 26:11

[a] *1* Greek *unclean* [b] *8* The Greek word was used for various diseases affecting the skin—not necessarily leprosy.

DISCOVERY 237

Disciple, Apostle, Christian

Jesus chose 12 followers (Matthew 10:2–4) who, with the exception of Judas, would eventually comprise the core group of the early leadership of his church. In the New Testament there are at least three names used to identify this group: *disciples*, *apostles* and *Christians*. Each of these names in its own way reminds us of what it means to follow our Master.

A *disciple* is one who learns from another. In ancient cultures teachers would gather a group of students or disciples who would live with and learn from them on a full-time basis. This education involved both listening to the teacher's words and observing and imitating his lifestyle. And so today, being one of Jesus' disciples implies that we are students of both his teaching and his manner of living. We continually learn from him and incorporate what we are learning into our own lives.

Jesus offered the same invitation to everyone: "Learn from me" (Matthew 11:29). When Paul approached the end of his life, having already written a number of letters that would eventually become part of the New Testament, he still desired to discover more about his Savior. In fact, just prior to his execution this remarkable church father asked for his scrolls and parchments of God's Word (2 Timothy 4:13). To the end, Paul was a true disciple.

An *apostle* is a "sent one," one who is on a mission for another. Following Jesus means not only that we learn from him but also that we do what he asks and go where he instructs. Just before Jesus ascended into heaven he reminded his apostles of their mission: "Go and make disciples" (Matthew 28:19). We are disciples, but we are also sent to invite others to join our ranks, to learn from Jesus by giving their lives to him and then bearing witness to him themselves as they meet others with whom they can share the Good News..

The name *Christian* is the one most often used today. Literally, it means one who is like Christ or one who belongs to him and identifies with him. Jesus' followers were first called Christians in Antioch, after Jesus had returned to heaven (Acts 11:26). We usually talk first about "becoming a Christian" and then about "being discipled." What we have in mind is making a decision to follow Jesus and then learning from a teacher how to live as a Christian. The process the Bible describes, however, is exactly the opposite: First a person is a disciple, learning about Jesus, and *then*, with the help of God's Holy Spirit, he or she becomes a "Christian" or Christlike person who possesses the very attitude of Jesus, an attitude of self-sacrificing humility and love for others (Philippians 2:1–11).

Self-Discovery: *Bearing the name* Christian *carries enormous responsibility. In what ways do you think your friends and neighbors or working associates view you as a "Christlike" person? Identify some specific areas in which you might better reflect the heart and spirit of Jesus.*

GO TO DISCOVERY 238 ON PAGE 1279

10:18 my account you will be brought before
x Ac 25:24-26 governors and kings[x] as witnesses to
them and to the Gentiles. 19But when
10:19 they arrest you, do not worry about
y Ex 4:12 what to say or how to say it.[y] At that
time you will be given what to say, 20for
10:20 it will not be you speaking, but the Spir-
z Ac 4:8 it of your Father[z] speaking through you.
21"Brother will betray brother to
10:21 death, and a father his child; children
a ver 35,36; will rebel against their parents[a] and
Mic 7:6 have them put to death. 22All men will
10:22 hate you because of me, but he who
b Mt 24:13; stands firm to the end will be saved.[b]
Mk 13:13 23When you are persecuted in one place,
flee to another. I tell you the truth, you
will not finish going through the cities of
Israel before the Son of Man comes.
10:24 24"A student is not above his teacher,
c Lk 6:40; nor a servant above his master.[c] 25It is
Jn 13:16; 15:20 enough for the student to be like his
teacher, and the servant like his master.
10:25 If the head of the house has been called
d Mk 3:22 Beelzebub,[a][d] how much more the members of his household!
26"So do not be afraid of them. There
is nothing concealed that will not be dis-
10:26 closed, or hidden that will not be made
e Mk 4:22; known.[e] 27What I tell you in the dark,
Lk 8:17 speak in the daylight; what is whispered
in your ear, proclaim from the roofs.
28Do not be afraid of those who kill the
10:28 body but cannot kill the soul. Rather, be
f Isa 8:12,13; afraid of the One[f] who can destroy both
Heb 10:31 soul and body in hell. 29Are not two
sparrows sold for a penny[b]? Yet not one
of them will fall to the ground apart
10:30 from the will of your Father. 30And even
g 1Sa 14:45; the very hairs of your head are all num-
2Sa 14:11; Lk 21:18; bered.[g] 31So don't be afraid; you are
Ac 27:34 worth more than many sparrows.[h]
10:31 32"Whoever acknowledges me before
h Mt 12:12 men,[i] I will also acknowledge him before
10:32 my Father in heaven. 33But whoever dis-
i Ro 10:9 owns me before men, I will disown him
before my Father in heaven.[j]
10:33 34"Do not suppose that I have come to
j Mk 8:38; 2Ti 2:12 bring peace to the earth. I did not come
to bring peace, but a sword. 35For I have
come to turn

"'a man against his father,
a daughter against her mother,
10:35 a daughter-in-law against her
k ver 21 mother-in-law[k]—
36 'a man's enemies will be the
members of his own
10:36 l Mic 7:6 household.'[c][l]

37"Anyone who loves his father or
mother more than me is not worthy of
me; anyone who loves his son or daugh-
ter more than me is not worthy of me;[m] 10:37 m Lk 14:26
38and anyone who does not take his
cross and follow me is not worthy of 10:38
me.[n] 39Whoever finds his life will lose it, n Mt 16:24;
and whoever loses his life for my sake Lk 14:27
will find it.[o] 10:39
40"He who receives you receives me,[p] o Lk 17:33; Jn 12:25
and he who receives me receives the one 10:40
who sent me.[q] 41Anyone who receives a p Mt 18:5;
prophet because he is a prophet will re- Gal 4:14; q Lk 9:48;
ceive a prophet's reward, and anyone Jn 12:44; 13:20
who receives a righteous man because
he is a righteous man will receive a righteous man's reward. 42And if anyone
gives even a cup of cold water to one of
these little ones because he is my disci- 10:42
ple, I tell you the truth, he will certainly r Mt 25:40;
not lose his reward."[r] Mk 9:41; Heb 6:10

Jesus and John the Baptist

11 After Jesus had finished in- 11:1
structing his twelve disciples,[s] s Mt 7:28
he went on from there to teach and
preach in the towns of Galilee.[d] 11:2
2When John heard in prison[t] what t Mt 14:3
Christ was doing, he sent his disciples
3to ask him, "Are you the one who was to 11:3
come,[u] or should we expect someone u Ps 118:26;
else?" Jn 11:27; Heb 10:37
4Jesus replied, "Go back and report to
John what you hear and see: 5The blind
receive sight, the lame walk, those who
have leprosy[e] are cured, the deaf hear,
the dead are raised, and the good news 11:5
is preached to the poor.[v] 6Blessed is the v Isa 35:4-6;
man who does not fall away on account 61:1; Lk 4:18,19
of me."[w] 11:6
7As John's[x] disciples were leaving, w Mt 13:21
Jesus began to speak to the crowd about 11:7
John: "What did you go out into the x Mt 3:1
desert to see? A reed swayed by the
wind? 8If not, what did you go out to
see? A man dressed in fine clothes? No,
those who wear fine clothes are in kings'
palaces. 9Then what did you go out to 11:9
see? A prophet?[y] Yes, I tell you, and y Mt 21:26;
more than a prophet. 10This is the one Lk 1:76
about whom it is written:

a 25 Greek *Beezeboul* or *Beelzeboul* *b* 29 Greek *an assarion* *c* 36 Micah 7:6 *d* 1 Greek *in their towns* *e* 5 The Greek word was used for various diseases affecting the skin—not necessarily leprosy.

> **JESUS OFTEN FOUND HIMSELF SURROUNDED BY A LARGE CROWD OF IRRELIGIOUS PEOPLE . . . UNDESIRABLES. THE UNCONVINCED. THE SPIRITUALLY CONFUSED. THE MORALLY BANKRUPT. PEOPLE GOD WOULDN'T POSSIBLY HAVE ANY USE FOR!**
>
> Bill Hybels, *Pastor, Chicago, Illinois*

"'I will send my messenger ahead
of you,
who will prepare your way
before you.'[a][z]
11I tell you the truth: Among those born
of women there has not risen anyone
greater than John the Baptist; yet he
who is least in the kingdom of heaven is
greater than he. 12From the days of John
the Baptist until now, the kingdom of
heaven has been forcefully advancing,
and forceful men lay hold of it. 13For all
the Prophets and the Law prophesied
until John. 14And if you are willing to accept it, he is the Elijah who was to
come.[a] 15He who has ears, let him hear.[b]
16"To what can I compare this generation? They are like children sitting in the
marketplaces and calling out to others:
17"'We played the flute for you,
and you did not dance;
we sang a dirge,
and you did not mourn.'
18For John came neither eating[c] nor
drinking,[d] and they say, 'He has a demon.' 19The Son of Man came eating and
drinking, and they say, 'Here is a glutton
and a drunkard, a friend of tax collectors and "sinners."'[e] But wisdom is
proved right by her actions."

Woe on Unrepentant Cities

20Then Jesus began to denounce the
cities in which most of his miracles had
been performed, because they did not
repent. 21"Woe to you, Korazin! Woe to
you, Bethsaida![f] If the miracles that were
performed in you had been performed
in Tyre and Sidon,[g] they would have repented long ago in sackcloth and ashes.[h]
22But I tell you, it will be more bearable

11:10 [z] Mal 3:1; Mk 1:2
11:14 [a] Mal 4:5; Mt 17:10-13; Mk 9:11-13; Lk 1:17; Jn 1:21
11:15 [b] Mt 13:9,43; Mk 4:23; Lk 14:35; Rev 2:7
11:18 [c] Mt 3:4 [d] Lk 1:15
11:19 [e] Mt 9:11
11:21 [f] Mk 6:45; Lk 9:10; Jn 12:21 [g] Mt 15:21; Lk 6:17; Ac 12:20 [h] Jnh 3:5-9

for Tyre and Sidon on the day of judgment than for you.[i] 23And you, Capernaum,[j] will you be lifted up to the skies?
No, you will go down to the depths.[b][k] If
the miracles that were performed in you
had been performed in Sodom, it would
have remained to this day. 24But I tell
you that it will be more bearable for Sodom on the day of judgment than for
you."[l]

Rest for the Weary

25At that time Jesus said, "I praise you,
Father,[m] Lord of heaven and earth, because you have hidden these things
from the wise and learned, and revealed
them to little children.[n] 26Yes, Father, for
this was your good pleasure.
27"All things have been committed to
me[o] by my Father.[p] No one knows the
Son except the Father, and no one
knows the Father except the Son and
those to whom the Son chooses to reveal
him.[q]
28"Come to me,[r] all you who are weary
and burdened, and I will give you rest.
29Take my yoke upon you and learn from
me,[s] for I am gentle and humble in
heart, and you will find rest for your
souls.[t] 30For my yoke is easy and my burden is light."[u]

[a] 10 Mal. 3:1 [b] 23 Greek *Hades*

11:22 [i] ver 24; Mt 10:15
11:23 [j] Mt 4:13 [k] Isa 14:13-15
11:24 [l] Mt 10:15
11:25 [m] Lk 22:42; Jn 11:41 [n] 1Co 1:26-29
11:27 [o] Mt 28:18 [p] Jn 3:35; 13:3; 17:2 [q] Jn 10:15
11:28 [r] Jn 7:37
11:29 [s] Jn 13:15; Php 2:5; 1Pe 2:21; 1Jn 2:6 [t] Jer 6:16
11:30 [u] 1Jn 5:3

JESUS FOCUS

MIRACLES AREN'T ENOUGH

Jesus' miracles attracted great attention, but they did not always result in people turning to God in faith. In Matthew 11:20–24 Jesus condemned the towns of Koran, Bethsaida and Capernaum because they had seen with their own eyes who he was and what he had done and yet had failed to believe. Witnessing miracles does not always lead people to want to get to know God. Only God's grace can bring about a change in our hearts. These miracles may have constituted irrefutable evidence that Jesus was indeed the Messiah, but miracles cannot in and of themselves soften and change unyielding hearts of stone. Jesus desires our commitment, not our applause, our worship rather than merely our wonder, our repentance rather than simply our respect. The greatest miracle anyone can experience is having his or her heart transformed by the touch of God's love and grace (Matthew 13:11–17; Ephesians 2:4–10).

DISCOVERY 238

"YOKED" WITH JESUS

"Come to me, all you who are weary and burdened, and I will give you rest . . . for my yoke is easy and my burden is light" (Matthew 11:28,30). These are some of the most comforting words in all of Scripture. They are a gracious invitation to anyone who is weary and overburdened—and that includes each of us at one time or another.

Then why is the average daily experience of many Christians exactly the opposite of the rest-filled existence we crave and Jesus promises to provide? We live in a world of nerve-jangling noise, ever-accelerating pace, frenetic activity and endless demands. Yet we yearn for repose. The paradox is that in order for us to be *un*burdened, we first have to be *burdened* by Jesus' guidance and expectations. Yes, our Lord makes demands on us, but he tells us that what he asks of us is "easy" and that the load he asks us to shoulder is "light."

The burden of which Jesus speaks is his expectation that we be gentle and humble in heart. It is the quality of remaining serene and tranquil in the midst of the raging deluge of challenges life hurls at us. Jesus' rest entails an inner peace that is not dependent on circumstances. Even if we have never personally experienced this rest, we can see it modeled in the life of Jesus.

While the disciples grew panicky in a storm on the Sea of Galilee, Jesus slept soundly in the bottom of the lurching boat (Matthew 8:24). Our Lord was never in a hurry, never frantic. Busy? Always—but not weary or burdened by the staggering weight of responsibility. Paul reminds us that we too can experience that kind of inner quietness, because God's peace guards our hearts and minds (Philippians 4:4–7).

Many people today have no frame of reference for understanding the word *yoke*, but the people listening to Jesus knew exactly what he was referring to. A yoke fit around the neck of an ox, and reins and a plow were attached to it. When the ox strained against the yoke he at the same time pulled the plow. The yoke represented backbreaking work—for both ox and farmer.

Jesus told us that his yoke is easy, but that seems contradictory—until we consider how young oxen were trained to plow. An inexperienced ox was yoked with a well-trained animal. Everywhere the more experienced and stronger ox went, the younger plodded along as well. It learned to plow, but without exerting much effort. The trained ox did all the real pulling.

When we give our lives to Jesus, we are "yoked" together with him. He does the pulling, and we follow and learn, thereby finding real joy and purpose and rest. It is only when we choose to tug in an opposite direction from him that the yoke becomes an irritant, and we chafe at the instruction that the Lord intends to use as a means to draw us closer to himself.

Self-Discovery: *Do you view the responsibilities of your Christian life as burdensome, or do you feel that Jesus' burden for you is light? If you do feel overburdened, think of some ways in which you can readjust your priorities. Try to see yourself today as a disciple of Jesus, walking with him and imitating his every move, his every attitude and action.*

GO TO DISCOVERY 239 ON PAGE 1286

Lord of the Sabbath

12 At that time Jesus went through
the grainfields on the Sabbath.
His disciples were hungry and began to
12:1 [v] Dt 23:25 pick some heads of grain[v] and eat them.
2 When the Pharisees saw this, they said
12:2 [w] ver 10; Lk 13:14; 14:3; Jn 5:10; 7:23; 9:16 to him, "Look! Your disciples are doing
what is unlawful on the Sabbath."[w]
3 He answered, "Haven't you read what
David did when he and his companions
12:3 [x] 1Sa 21:6 were hungry?[x] 4 He entered the house of
God, and he and his companions ate the
consecrated bread—which was not law-
12:4 [y] Lev 24:5,9 ful for them to do, but only for the
priests.[y] 5 Or haven't you read in the Law
12:5 [z] Nu 28:9,10; Jn 7:22,23 that on the Sabbath the priests in the
temple desecrate the day[z] and yet are in-
nocent? 6 I tell you that one[a] greater than
12:6 [a] ver 41,42 the temple is here.[a] 7 If you had known
what these words mean, 'I desire mercy,
12:7 [b] Hos 6:6; Mic 6:6-8; Mt 9:13 not sacrifice,'[b][b] you would not have condemned the innocent. 8 For the Son of
Man[c] is Lord of the Sabbath."
12:8 [c] Mt 8:20 9 Going on from that place, he went
into their synagogue, 10 and a man with
a shriveled hand was there. Looking for
12:10 [d] ver 2; Lk 13:14; 14:3; Jn 9:16 a reason to accuse Jesus, they asked him,
"Is it lawful to heal on the Sabbath?"[d]
11 He said to them, "If any of you has a
sheep and it falls into a pit on the Sab-
12:11 [e] Lk 14:5 bath, will you not take hold of it and lift
it out?[e] 12 How much more valuable is a
12:12 [f] Mt 10:31 man than a sheep![f] Therefore it is lawful
to do good on the Sabbath."
13 Then he said to the man, "Stretch
out your hand." So he stretched it out
and it was completely restored, just as
sound as the other. 14 But the Pharisees
went out and plotted how they might 12:14 [g] Mt 26:4; 27:1; Mk 3:6; Lk 6:11; Jn 5:18; 11:53
kill Jesus.[g]

God's Chosen Servant

15 Aware of this, Jesus withdrew from
that place. Many followed him, and he 12:15 [h] Mt 4:23
healed all their sick,[h] 16 warning them
not to tell who he was.[i] 17 This was to ful- 12:16 [i] Mt 8:4
fill what was spoken through the proph-
et Isaiah:

18 "Here is my servant whom I have
chosen,
the one I love, in whom I delight;[j] 12:18 [j] Mt 3:17
I will put my Spirit on him,
and he will proclaim justice to
the nations.
19 He will not quarrel or cry out;
no one will hear his voice in the
streets.
20 A bruised reed he will not break,
and a smoldering wick he will
not snuff out,
till he leads justice to victory.
21 In his name the nations will put
their hope."[c][k] 12:21 [k] Isa 42:1-4

Jesus and Beelzebub

22 Then they brought him a demon-
possessed man who was blind and
mute, and Jesus healed him, so that he 12:22 [l] Mt 4:24; 9:32-33
could both talk and see.[l] 23 All the people
were astonished and said, "Could this be
the Son of David?"[m] 12:23 [m] Mt 9:27
24 But when the Pharisees heard this,
they said, "It is only by Beelzebub,[d][n] the 12:24 [n] Mk 3:22
prince of demons, that this fellow drives [o] Mt 9:34
out demons."[o]
25 Jesus knew their thoughts[p] and said 12:25 [p] Mt 9:4
to them, "Every kingdom divided
against itself will be ruined, and every
city or household divided against itself
will not stand. 26 If Satan[q] drives out Sa- 12:26 [q] Mt 4:10
tan, he is divided against himself. How
then can his kingdom stand? 27 And if I
drive out demons by Beelzebub, by
whom do your people[r] drive them out? 12:27 [r] Ac 19:13
So then, they will be your judges. 28 But if
I drive out demons by the Spirit of God,
then the kingdom of God has come
upon you.

[a] 6 Or *something*; also in verses 41 and 42
[b] 7 Hosea 6:6 [c] 21 Isaiah 42:1-4 [d] 24 Greek *Beezeboul* or *Beelzeboul*; also in verse 27

LORD OF THE SABBATH

One of the major themes of Matthew's Gospel is that Jesus is Lord. When the Pharisees were offended because Jesus' disciples had seemingly ignored a Sabbath prohibition, Jesus reminded them of an incident in which the temple priests had been in violation of one of their rules (Matthew 12:1–14). God cares a great deal about our character, and he gave his people the law as a guideline for learning his will. At this time Jesus made two radical statements. First, he informed the scandalized Pharisees that "one greater than the temple is here" (verse 6), thereby claiming that God's presence was now with the people in human form. Jesus further stated that "the Son of Man is Lord of the Sabbath" (verse 8). And Jesus immediately proceeded to authenticate each statement by healing a man's shriveled hand—on the Sabbath.

29“Or again, how can anyone enter a
strong man’s house and carry off his
possessions unless he first ties up the
strong man? Then he can rob his house.
30“He who is not with me is against
12:30 s Mk 9:40; Lk 11:23 me, and he who does not gather with me
scatters.[s] 31And so I tell you, every sin
and blasphemy will be forgiven men, but
12:31 t Mk 3:28,29; Lk 12:10 the blasphemy against the Spirit will not
be forgiven.[t] 32Anyone who speaks a
word against the Son of Man will be forgiven, but anyone who speaks against
12:32 u Tit 2:12 v Mk 10:30; Lk 20:34,35; Eph 1:21; Heb 6:5 the Holy Spirit will not be forgiven, either in this age[u] or in the age to come.[v]
33“Make a tree good and its fruit will
be good, or make a tree bad and its fruit
will be bad, for a tree is recognized by its
12:33 w Mt 7:16,17; Lk 6:43,44 fruit.[w] 34You brood of vipers,[x] how can
you who are evil say anything good? For
out of the overflow of the heart the
12:34 x Mt 3:7; 23:33 y Mt 15:18; Lk 6:45 mouth speaks.[y] 35The good man brings
good things out of the good stored up in
him, and the evil man brings evil things
out of the evil stored up in him. 36But I
tell you that men will have to give account on the day of judgment for every
careless word they have spoken. 37For by
your words you will be acquitted, and by
your words you will be condemned.”

The Sign of Jonah

38Then some of the Pharisees and
teachers of the law said to him, “Teacher,
12:38 z Mt 16:1; Mk 8:11,12; Lk 11:16; Jn 2:18; 6:30; 1Co 1:22 we want to see a miraculous sign from
you.”[z]
39He answered, “A wicked and adulterous generation asks for a miraculous
12:39 a Mt 16:4; Lk 11:29 sign! But none will be given it except the
sign of the prophet Jonah.[a] 40For as Jo-
nah was three days and three nights in
12:40 b Jnh 1:17 c Mt 8:20 d Mt 16:21 the belly of a huge fish,[b] so the Son of
Man[c] will be three days and three nights
in the heart of the earth.[d] 41The men of
12:41 e Jnh 1:2 f Jnh 3:5 Nineveh[e] will stand up at the judgment
with this generation and condemn it; for
they repented at the preaching of Jonah,[f]
and now one[a] greater than Jonah is here.
42The Queen of the South will rise at the
judgment with this generation and con-
12:42 g 1Ki 10:1; 2Ch 9:1 demn it; for she came[g] from the ends of
the earth to listen to Solomon’s wisdom,
and now one greater than Solomon is
here.
43“When an evil[b] spirit comes out of a
man, it goes through arid places seeking
rest and does not find it. 44Then it says,
‘I will return to the house I left.’ When it
arrives, it finds the house unoccupied,
swept clean and put in order. 45Then it
goes and takes with it seven other spirits more wicked than itself, and they go
in and live there. And the final condition
of that man is worse than the first.[h] That 12:45 h 2Pe 2:20
is how it will be with this wicked gener-
ation.”

Jesus’ Mother and Brothers

46While Jesus was still talking to the 12:46 i Mt 1:18; 2:11, 13,14,20; Lk 1:43; 2:33, 34,48,51; Jn 2:1, 5; 19:25,26 j Mt 13:55; Jn 2:12; 7:3,5; Ac 1:14; 1Co 9:5; Gal 1:19
crowd, his mother[i] and brothers[j] stood
outside, wanting to speak to him.
47Someone told him, “Your mother and
brothers are standing outside, wanting
to speak to you.”[c]
48He replied to him, “Who is my
mother, and who are my brothers?”
49Pointing to his disciples, he said, “Here
are my mother and my brothers. 50For
whoever does the will of my Father in 12:50 k Jn 15:14
heaven[k] is my brother and sister and
mother.”

JESUS PLANTED THE SEED
OF HIMSELF IN THE SOIL OF
HISTORY [AND] IN EVERY
HEART THAT WOULD LISTEN.

Lloyd John Oglivie, *Chaplain, U.S. Senate*

The Parable of the Sower

13 That same day Jesus went out of
the house[l] and sat by the lake. 13:1 l ver 36; Mt 9:28
2Such large crowds gathered around him 13:2 m Lk 5:3
that he got into a boat[m] and sat in it,
while all the people stood on the shore.
3Then he told them many things in parables, saying: “A farmer went out to sow
his seed. 4As he was scattering the seed,
some fell along the path, and the birds
came and ate it up. 5Some fell on rocky
places, where it did not have much soil. It
sprang up quickly, because the soil was
shallow. 6But when the sun came up, the
plants were scorched, and they withered
because they had no root. 7Other seed fell
among thorns, which grew up and
choked the plants. 8Still other seed fell on
good soil, where it produced a crop—a 13:8 n Ge 26:12
hundred,[n] sixty or thirty times what was
sown. 9He who has ears, let him hear.”[o] 13:9 o Mt 11:15

[a] 41 Or *something*; also in verse 42 [b] 43 Greek *unclean* [c] 47 Some manuscripts do not have verse 47.

Parables of Jesus

Parable	Matthew	Mark	Luke
Lamp under a bowl	5:14–15	4:21–22	8:16; 11:33
Wise and foolish builders	7:24–27		6:47–49
New cloth on an old coat	9:16	2:21	5:36
New wine in old wineskins	9:17	2:22	5:37–38
Sower and the soils	13:3–8,18–23	4:3–8,14–20	8:5–8,11–15
Weeds	13:24–30,36–43		
Mustard seed	13:31–32	4:30–32	13:18–19
Yeast	13:33		13:20–21
Hidden treasure	13:44		
Valuable pearl	13:45–46		
Net	13:47–50		
Owner of a house	13:52		
Lost sheep	18:12–14		15:4–7
Unmerciful servant	18:23–34		
Workers in the vineyard	20:1–16		
Two sons	21:28–32		
Tenants	21:33–44	12:1–11	20:9–18
Wedding banquet	22:2–14		
Fig tree	24:32–35	13:28–29	21:29–31
Faithful and wise servant	24:45–51		12:42–48
Ten virgins	25:1–13		
Talents (minas)	25:14–30		19:12–27
Sheep and goats	25:31–46		
Growing seed		4:26–29	
Watchful servants		13:35–37	12:35–40
Moneylender			7:41–43
Good Samaritan			10:30–37
Friend in need			11:5–8
Rich fool			12:16–21
Unfruitful fig tree			13:6–9
Lowest seat at the feast			14:7–14
Great banquet			14:16–24
Cost of discipleship			14:28–33
Lost coin			15:8–10
Lost (prodigal) son			15:11–32
Shrewd manager			16:1–8
Rich man and Lazarus			16:19–31
Master and his servant			17:7–10
Persistent widow			18:2–8
Pharisee and tax collector			18:10–14

10 The disciples came to him and asked, "Why do you speak to the people in parables?"

11 He replied, "The knowledge of the secrets of the kingdom of heaven has been given to you,[p] but not to them. 12 Whoever has will be given more, and he will have an abundance. Whoever does not have, even what he has will be taken from him.[q] 13 This is why I speak to them in parables:

"Though seeing, they do not see;
 though hearing, they do not hear
  or understand.[r]

14 In them is fulfilled the prophecy of Isaiah:

" 'You will be ever hearing but
  never understanding;
 you will be ever seeing but never
  perceiving.
15 For this people's heart has become
  calloused;
 they hardly hear with their ears,
 and they have closed their eyes.
Otherwise they might see with
  their eyes,
 hear with their ears,
 understand with their hearts
and turn, and I would heal them.'[a][s]

16 But blessed are your eyes because they see, and your ears because they hear.[t] 17 For I tell you the truth, many prophets and righteous men longed to see what you see[u] but did not see it, and to hear what you hear but did not hear it.

18 "Listen then to what the parable of the sower means: 19 When anyone hears the message about the kingdom[v] and does not understand it, the evil one[w] comes and snatches away what was sown in his heart. This is the seed sown along the path. 20 The one who received the seed that fell on rocky places is the man who hears the word and at once receives it with joy. 21 But since he has no root, he lasts only a short time. When trouble or persecution comes because of the word, he quickly falls away.[x] 22 The one who received the seed that fell among the thorns is the man who hears the word, but the worries of this life and the deceitfulness of wealth[y] choke it, making it unfruitful. 23 But the one who received the seed that fell on good soil is the man who hears the word and understands it. He produces a crop, yielding a hundred, sixty or thirty times what was sown."[z]

13:11 p Mt 11:25; 16:17; 19:11; Jn 6:65; 1Co 2:10,14; Col 1:27; 1Jn 2:20,27
13:12 q Mt 25:29; Lk 19:26
13:13 r Dt 29:4; Jer 5:21; Eze 12:2
13:15 s Isa 6:9,10; Jn 12:40; Ac 28:26,27; Ro 11:8
13:16 t Mt 16:17
13:17 u Jn 8:56; Heb 11:13; 1Pe 1:10-12
13:19 v Mt 4:23 w Mt 5:37
13:21 x Mt 11:6
13:22 y Mt 19:23; 1Ti 6:9,10,17

The Parable of the Weeds

24 Jesus told them another parable: "The kingdom of heaven is like[a] a man who sowed good seed in his field. 25 But while everyone was sleeping, his enemy came and sowed weeds among the wheat, and went away. 26 When the wheat sprouted and formed heads, then the weeds also appeared.

27 "The owner's servants came to him and said, 'Sir, didn't you sow good seed in your field? Where then did the weeds come from?'

28 " 'An enemy did this,' he replied.

"The servants asked him, 'Do you want us to go and pull them up?'

29 " 'No,' he answered, 'because while you are pulling the weeds, you may root up the wheat with them. 30 Let both grow together until the harvest. At that time I will tell the harvesters: First collect the weeds and tie them in bundles to be burned; then gather the wheat and bring it into my barn.' "[b]

The Parables of the Mustard Seed and the Yeast

31 He told them another parable: "The kingdom of heaven is like[c] a mustard seed,[d] which a man took and planted in his field. 32 Though it is the smallest of all your seeds, yet when it grows, it is the largest of garden plants and becomes a tree, so that the birds of the air come and perch in its branches."[e]

33 He told them still another parable: "The kingdom of heaven is like[f] yeast that a woman took and mixed into a large amount[b] of flour[g] until it worked all through the dough."[h]

34 Jesus spoke all these things to the crowd in parables; he did not say anything to them without using a parable.[i] 35 So was fulfilled what was spoken through the prophet:

"I will open my mouth in parables,
 I will utter things hidden since
  the creation of the world."[c][j]

a 15 Isaiah 6:9,10 *b 33* Greek *three satas* (probably about 1/2 bushel or 22 liters)
c 35 Psalm 78:2

13:23 z ver 8
13:24 a ver 31,33,45, 47; Mt 18:23; 20:1; 22:2; 25:1; Mk 4:26,30
13:30 b Mt 3:12
13:31 c ver 24 d Mt 17:20; Lk 17:6
13:32 e Ps 104:12; Eze 17:23; 31:6; Da 4:12
13:33 f ver 24 g Ge 18:6 h Gal 5:9
13:34 i Mk 4:33; Jn 16:25
13:35 j Ps 78:2; Ro 16:25,26; 1Co 2:7; Eph 3:9; Col 1:26

The Parable of the Weeds Explained

36Then he left the crowd and went
into the house. His disciples came to
13:36 him and said, "Explain to us the para-
k Mt 15:15 ble[k] of the weeds in the field."

37He answered, "The one who sowed
13:37 the good seed is the Son of Man.[l] 38The
l Mt 8:20 field is the world, and the good seed
stands for the sons of the kingdom. The
13:38 weeds are the sons of the evil one,[m]
m Jn 8:44,45; 1Jn 3:10 39and the enemy who sows them is the
13:39 devil. The harvest[n] is the end of the age,[o]
n Joel 3:13 and the harvesters are angels.[p]
o Mt 24:3; 28:20

p Rev 14:15 40"As the weeds are pulled up and
burned in the fire, so it will be at the end
13:41 of the age. 41The Son of Man[q] will send
q Mt 8:20 out his angels,[r] and they will weed out of
r Mt 24:31 his kingdom everything that causes sin
and all who do evil. 42They will throw
13:42 them into the fiery furnace, where there
s ver 50; Mt 8:12 will be weeping and gnashing of teeth.[s]
43Then the righteous will shine like the
13:43 sun[t] in the kingdom of their Father. He
t Da 12:3 who has ears, let him hear.[u]
u Mt 11:15

The Parables of the Hidden Treasure and the Pearl

13:44 44"The kingdom of heaven is like[v]
v ver 24 treasure hidden in a field. When a man
w Isa 55:1; Php 3:7,8 found it, he hid it again, and then in his
joy went and sold all he had and bought
that field.[w]

13:45 45"Again, the kingdom of heaven is
x ver 24 like[x] a merchant looking for fine pearls.
46When he found one of great value, he
went away and sold everything he had
and bought it.

The Parable of the Net

13:47 47"Once again, the kingdom of heaven
y ver 24 is like[y] a net that was let down into the
z Mt 22:10 lake and caught all kinds[z] of fish.
48When it was full, the fishermen pulled
it up on the shore. Then they sat down
and collected the good fish in baskets,
but threw the bad away. 49This is how it
will be at the end of the age. The angels
13:49 will come and separate the wicked from
a Mt 25:32 the righteous[a] 50and throw them into
13:50 the fiery furnace, where there will be
b Mt 8:12 weeping and gnashing of teeth.[b]

51"Have you understood all these
things?" Jesus asked.

"Yes," they replied.

52He said to them, "Therefore every
teacher of the law who has been instructed about the kingdom of heaven is
like the owner of a house who brings out
of his storeroom new treasures as well as
old."

A Prophet Without Honor

53When Jesus had finished these par- 13:53
ables,[c] he moved on from there. 54Com- c Mt 7:28
ing to his hometown, he began teaching 13:54
the people in their synagogue,[d] and they d Mt 4:23
were amazed.[e] "Where did this man get e Mt 7:28
this wisdom and these miraculous pow-
ers?" they asked. 55"Isn't this the carpen- 13:55
ter's son?[f] Isn't his mother's[g] name Mary, f Lk 3:23; Jn 6:42
and aren't his brothers James, Joseph, Si- g Mt 12:46
mon and Judas? 56Aren't all his sisters
with us? Where then did this man get all 13:57
these things?" 57And they took offense[h] h Jn 6:61
at him. i Lk 4:24; Jn 4:44

But Jesus said to them, "Only in his
hometown and in his own house is a
prophet without honor."[i]

58And he did not do many miracles
there because of their lack of faith.

John the Baptist Beheaded

14 At that time Herod[j] the te- 14:1 j Mk 8:15;
trarch heard the reports about Lk 3:1,19; 13:31; 23:7,8;
Jesus,[k] 2and he said to his attendants, Ac 4:27; 12:1 k Lk 9:7-9
"This is John the Baptist;[l] he has risen
from the dead! That is why miraculous 14:2
powers are at work in him." l Mt 3:1

3Now Herod had arrested John and

JESUS AND YOU

A HOMETOWN BOY

Jesus began his public teaching in his hometown synagogue—nearly inciting a riot in Nazareth (Luke 4:16–30). Later, when he returned, he aroused great curiosity but very little response of faith. The local people just couldn't believe that the carpenter's son they'd watched grow up was now teaching like a rabbi and performing amazing miracles (Matthew 13:55). Jesus understood the situation, commenting that "only in his hometown and in his own house is a prophet without honor" (verse 57). Because his own townspeople refused to accept him, Jesus chose not to perform many miracles in the vicinity of Nazareth. The people who should have known the most about him understood him the least, tragically missing the joy of developing a personal relationship with the long-awaited Savior God had sent. Like so many today, these people were so close to the truth that they were unable to see it.

bound him and put him in prison[m] because of Herodias, his brother Philip's wife,[n] 4for John had been saying to him: "It is not lawful for you to have her."[o] 5Herod wanted to kill John, but he was afraid of the people, because they considered him a prophet.[p]

6On Herod's birthday the daughter of Herodias danced for them and pleased Herod so much 7that he promised with an oath to give her whatever she asked. 8Prompted by her mother, she said, "Give me here on a platter the head of John the Baptist." 9The king was distressed, but because of his oaths and his dinner guests, he ordered that her request be granted 10and had John beheaded[q] in the prison. 11His head was brought in on a platter and given to the girl, who carried it to her mother. 12John's disciples came and took his body and buried it.[r] Then they went and told Jesus.

14:3 [m] Mt 4:12; 11:2 [n] Lk 3:19,20
14:4 [o] Lev 18:16; 20:21
14:5 [p] Mt 11:9
14:10 [q] Mt 17:12
14:12 [r] Ac 8:2

Jesus Feeds the Five Thousand

13When Jesus heard what had happened, he withdrew by boat privately to a solitary place. Hearing of this, the crowds followed him on foot from the towns. 14When Jesus landed and saw a large crowd, he had compassion on them[s] and healed their sick.[t]

15As evening approached, the disciples came to him and said, "This is a remote place, and it's already getting late. Send the crowds away, so they can go to the villages and buy themselves some food."

16Jesus replied, "They do not need to go away. You give them something to eat."

17"We have here only five loaves[u] of bread and two fish," they answered.

18"Bring them here to me," he said. 19And he directed the people to sit down on the grass. Taking the five loaves and the two fish and looking up to heaven, he gave thanks and broke the loaves.[v] Then he gave them to the disciples, and the disciples gave them to the people. 20They all ate and were satisfied, and the disciples picked up twelve basketfuls of broken pieces that were left over. 21The number of those who ate was about five thousand men, besides women and children.

14:14 [s] Mt 9:36 [t] Mt 4:23
14:17 [u] Mt 16:9
14:19 [v] 1Sa 9:13; Mt 26:26; Mk 8:6; Lk 24:30; Ac 2:42; 27:35; 1Ti 4:4

Jesus Walks on the Water

22Immediately Jesus made the disciples get into the boat and go on ahead of him to the other side, while he dismissed the crowd. 23After he had dismissed them, he went up on a mountainside by himself to pray.[w] When evening came, he was there alone, 24but the boat was already a considerable distance[a] from land, buffeted by the waves because the wind was against it.

25During the fourth watch of the night Jesus went out to them, walking on the lake. 26When the disciples saw him walking on the lake, they were terrified. "It's a ghost,"[x] they said, and cried out in fear.

27But Jesus immediately said to them: "Take courage![y] It is I. Don't be afraid."[z]

28"Lord, if it's you," Peter replied, "tell me to come to you on the water."

29"Come," he said.

Then Peter got down out of the boat, walked on the water and came toward Jesus. 30But when he saw the wind, he was afraid and, beginning to sink, cried out, "Lord, save me!"

31Immediately Jesus reached out his hand and caught him. "You of little faith,"[a] he said, "why did you doubt?"

32And when they climbed into the boat, the wind died down. 33Then those who were in the boat worshiped him, saying, "Truly you are the Son of God."[b]

34When they had crossed over, they landed at Gennesaret. 35And when the men of that place recognized Jesus, they sent word to all the surrounding country. People brought all their sick to him 36and begged him to let the sick just touch the edge of his cloak,[c] and all who touched him were healed.

14:23 [w] Lk 3:21
14:26 [x] Lk 24:37
14:27 [y] Mt 9:2; Ac 23:11 [z] Da 10:12; Mt 17:7; 28:10; Lk 1:13,30; 2:10; Ac 18:9; 23:11; Rev 1:17
14:31 [a] Mt 6:30
14:33 [b] Ps 2:7; Mt 4:3
14:36 [c] Mt 9:20

Clean and Unclean

15 Then some Pharisees and teachers of the law came to Jesus from Jerusalem and asked, 2"Why do your disciples break the tradition of the elders? They don't wash their hands before they eat!"[d]

3Jesus replied, "And why do you break the command of God for the sake of your tradition? 4For God said, 'Honor your father and mother'[b][e] and 'Anyone who curses his father or mother must be put to death.'[c][f] 5But you say that if a man says to his father or mother, 'Whatever help you might otherwise have received from me is a gift devoted to God,' 6he is

15:2 [d] Lk 11:38
15:4 [e] Ex 20:12; Dt 5:16; Eph 6:2 [f] Ex 21:17; Lev 20:9

[a] 24 Greek *many stadia* [b] 4 Exodus 20:12; Deut. 5:16 [c] 4 Exodus 21:17; Lev. 20:9

DISCOVERY 239

A Walk on the Water

The incident of Jesus walking on the water took place immediately after the feeding of the five thousand (see Discovery #276, page 1421). Jesus instructed the disciples to go ahead of him by boat while he dismissed the crowd, after which he went up on the mountainside by himself to pray (Matthew 14:22–23).

Looking back to the beginning of chapter 14, we read about the tragic beheading of John the Baptist (verses 1–12). Verse 13 informs us that, "when Jesus heard what had happened, he withdrew by boat privately to a solitary place" only to be followed by the insistent crowds. Despite his personal anguish over John's death and probable physical exhaustion, Jesus was driven by compassion for the people to stretch himself to minister to them (verse 14).

After the last of the crowd had drifted off into the darkness, Jesus communed with God for several hours (from the onset of the evening until the fourth watch of the night, somewhere between 3 A.M. and 6 A.M.). By that point, our Lord evidently felt sufficiently revitalized in spirit to desire to join his struggling disciples, who had all night been battling contrary waves. John's narrative is sparse on details, telling us simply that Jesus went out to the disciples, walking on the water (verse 25).

It is little wonder that the beleaguered disciples were alarmed to the point of terror, jumping to the conclusion that a ghost was approaching their tiny vessel. Jesus' response, "Take courage! It is I. Don't be afraid" (verse 27), would most likely have put them at ease during ordinary circumstances, but their overall exhaustion and the eerie conditions no doubt clouded their perception. The ever-impetuous Peter responded immediately with a test: "Lord, if it's you, . . . tell me to come to you on the water" (verse 28). As is the case with Jesus' one-word revelation of himself to Mary Magdalene at the scene of the empty tomb ("Mary") (John 20:16), his brief response to Peter ("Come") (Matthew 14:29) strikes us as full of pathos and love.

Peter's impetuous gesture of climbing out of the boat to meet his Lord on the water demonstrates a significant level of faith, but his relapse into doubt and panic, resulting in his beginning to sink (verse 30), reveals his human side. The disciples had been battling the waves for eight or more hours, following a taxing day. The beauty of the situation is that Jesus understood perfectly the limitations under which Peter was functioning; he immediately reached out his hand and caught Peter.

The reality of Jesus' humanity affords us a degree of comfort we could not have experienced had he spent his 33 years on earth simply as deity. Jesus understands our limited reserves, our discouragement, doubt and fatigue. The writer to the Hebrews expressed this truth in memorable terms: "We do not have a high priest who is unable to sympathize with our weaknesses, but we have one who has been tempted in every way, just as we are—yet without sin. Let us then approach the throne of grace with confidence, so that we may receive mercy and find grace to help us in our time of need" (Hebrews 4:15–16).

Self-Discovery: *In what ways do you find comfort in the ability of Jesus to empathize with your human weaknesses?*

GO TO DISCOVERY 240 ON PAGE 1289

not to 'honor his father[a]' with it. Thus
you nullify the word of God for the sake
of your tradition. 7 You hypocrites! Isaiah
was right when he prophesied about
you:

8 " 'These people honor me with
their lips,
but their hearts are far from me.
15:9 [g] Col 2:20-22 9 They worship me in vain;
[h] Isa 29:13; their teachings are but rules
Mal 2:2 taught by men.[g] [b] [h]' "

10 Jesus called the crowd to him and
said, "Listen and understand. 11 What
goes into a man's mouth does not make
15:11 him 'unclean,'[i] but what comes out of
[i] Ac 10:14,15 his mouth, that is what makes him 'un-
[j] ver 18 clean.' "[j]

12 Then the disciples came to him and
asked, "Do you know that the Pharisees
were offended when they heard this?"

15:13 13 He replied, "Every plant that my
[k] Isa 60:21; 61:3; heavenly Father has not planted[k] will be
Jn 15:2 pulled up by the roots. 14 Leave them; they
15:14 are blind guides.[c] [l] If a blind man leads a
[l] Mt 23:16,24; blind man, both will fall into a pit."[m]
Ro 2:19
[m] Lk 6:39 15 Peter said, "Explain the parable
to us."[n]

15:15 16 "Are you still so dull?"[o] Jesus asked
[n] Mt 13:36 them. 17 "Don't you see that whatever en-
15:16 ters the mouth goes into the stomach
[o] Mt 16:9 and then out of the body? 18 But the
15:18 things that come out of the mouth come
[p] Mt 12:34; from the heart,[p] and these make a man
Lk 6:45; Jas 3:6 'unclean.' 19 For out of the heart come
evil thoughts, murder, adultery, sexual
immorality, theft, false testimony, slan-
15:19 der.[q] 20 These are what make a man 'un-
[q] Gal 5:19-21 clean';[r] but eating with unwashed hands
15:20 [r] Ro 14:14 does not make him 'unclean.' "

The Faith of the Canaanite Woman

21 Leaving that place, Jesus withdrew
15:21 [s] Mt 11:21 to the region of Tyre and Sidon.[s] 22 A
Canaanite woman from that vicinity
15:22 came to him, crying out, "Lord, Son of
[t] Mt 9:27 David,[t] have mercy on me! My daughter
[u] Mt 4:24 is suffering terribly from demon-possession."[u]

23 Jesus did not answer a word. So his
disciples came to him and urged him,
"Send her away, for she keeps crying out
after us."

15:24 24 He answered, "I was sent only to the
[v] Mt 10:6,23; Ro 15:8 lost sheep of Israel."[v]

25 The woman came and knelt before
15:25 [w] Mt 8:2 him.[w] "Lord, help me!" she said.

26 He replied, "It is not right to take the
children's bread and toss it to their dogs."

27 "Yes, Lord," she said, "but even the
dogs eat the crumbs that fall from their
masters' table."

28 Then Jesus answered, "Woman, you
have great faith![x] Your request is grant- 15:28 [x] Mt 9:22
ed." And her daughter was healed from
that very hour.

Jesus Feeds the Four Thousand

29 Jesus left there and went along the
Sea of Galilee. Then he went up on a
mountainside and sat down. 30 Great
crowds came to him, bringing the lame,
the blind, the crippled, the mute and
many others, and laid them at his feet; 15:30
and he healed them.[y] 31 The people were [y] Mt 4:23
amazed when they saw the mute speak-
ing, the crippled made well, the lame
walking and the blind seeing. And they 15:31
praised the God of Israel.[z] [z] Mt 9:8

32 Jesus called his disciples to him and
said, "I have compassion for these peo- 15:32
ple;[a] they have already been with me [a] Mt 9:36
three days and have nothing to eat. I do
not want to send them away hungry, or
they may collapse on the way."

33 His disciples answered, "Where
could we get enough bread in this remote place to feed such a crowd?"

34 "How many loaves do you have?"
Jesus asked.

"Seven," they replied, "and a few small
fish."

35 He told the crowd to sit down on the
ground. 36 Then he took the seven loaves
and the fish, and when he had given 15:36
thanks, he broke them[b] and gave them [b] Mt 14:19
to the disciples, and they in turn to the
people. 37 They all ate and were satisfied.
Afterward the disciples picked up seven
basketfuls of broken pieces that were 15:37
left over.[c] 38 The number of those who [c] Mt 16:10
ate was four thousand, besides women
and children. 39 After Jesus had sent the
crowd away, he got into the boat and
went to the vicinity of Magadan.

The Demand for a Sign

16 The Pharisees and Sadducees[d] 16:1 [d] Ac 4:1
came to Jesus and tested him [e] Mt 12:38
by asking him to show them a sign from
heaven.[e]

[a] 6 Some manuscripts *father or his mother*
[b] 9 Isaiah 29:13 [c] 14 Some manuscripts *guides of the blind*

> **ABOVE ALL THE GRACE AND THE GIFTS THAT CHRIST GIVES TO HIS BELOVED IS THAT OF OVERCOMING SELF.**
>
> St. Francis of Assisi, *Catholic Theologian*

2He replied,[a] "When evening comes,
you say, 'It will be fair weather, for the
sky is red,' 3and in the morning, 'Today it
will be stormy, for the sky is red and
overcast.' You know how to interpret the
16:3 appearance of the sky, but you cannot
f Lk 12:54-56 interpret the signs of the times.[f] 4A
wicked and adulterous generation looks
for a miraculous sign, but none will be
16:4 given it except the sign of Jonah."[g] Jesus
g Mt 12:39 then left them and went away.

The Yeast of the Pharisees and Sadducees

5When they went across the lake, the
disciples forgot to take bread. 6"Be careful," Jesus said to them. "Be on your
16:6 guard against the yeast of the Pharisees
h Lk 12:1 and Sadducees."[h]
7They discussed this among themselves and said, "It is because we didn't
bring any bread."
16:8 8Aware of their discussion, Jesus
i Mt 6:30 asked, "You of little faith,[i] why are you
talking among yourselves about having
no bread? 9Do you still not understand?
Don't you remember the five loaves for
16:9 the five thousand, and how many bas-
j Mt 14:17-21 ketfuls you gathered?[j] 10Or the seven
16:10 loaves for the four thousand, and how
k Mt 15:34-38 many basketfuls you gathered?[k] 11How
is it you don't understand that I was not
talking to you about bread? But be on
your guard against the yeast of the Pharisees and Sadducees." 12Then they understood that he was not telling them to
guard against the yeast used in bread,
16:12 but against the teaching of the Pharisees
l Ac 4:1 and Sadducees.[l]

Peter's Confession of Christ

13When Jesus came to the region of
Caesarea Philippi, he asked his disciples,
"Who do people say the Son of Man is?"
16:14 14They replied, "Some say John the
m Mt 3:1; 14:2 Baptist;[m] others say Elijah; and still oth-
n Mk 6:15; Jn 1:21 ers, Jeremiah or one of the prophets."[n]
15"But what about you?" he asked.
"Who do you say I am?" 16:16
16Simon Peter answered, "You are the o Mt 4:3;
Christ,[b] the Son of the living God."[o] Ps 42:2; Jn 11:27;
17Jesus replied, "Blessed are you, Si- Ac 14:15;
mon son of Jonah, for this was not re- 2Co 6:16; 1Th 1:9;
vealed to you by man,[p] but by my Father 1Ti 3:15;
in heaven. 18And I tell you that you are Heb 10:31;
Peter,[c][q] and on this rock I will build my 12:22
church,[r] and the gates of Hades[d] will not 16:17
overcome it.[e] 19I will give you the keys[s] p 1Co 15:50; Gal 1:16;
of the kingdom of heaven; whatever you Eph 6:12;
bind on earth will be[f] bound in heaven, Heb 2:14
and whatever you loose on earth will be[f] 16:18
loosed in heaven."[t] 20Then he warned his q Jn 1:42 r Eph 2:20
disciples not to tell anyone[u] that he was 16:19
the Christ. s Isa 22:22;
Rev 3:7
t Mt 18:18;
Jn 20:23
16:20
u Mk 8:30

> **HAD HE NOT EXISTED, I DOUBT WE WOULD HAVE HAD THE GUTS TO IMAGINE HIM.**
>
> Bill Oberst, Jr., *American Actor*

Jesus Predicts His Death

21From that time on Jesus began to
explain to his disciples that he must go 16:21
to Jerusalem and suffer many things[v] at v Mk 10:34;
the hands of the elders, chief priests and Lk 17:25 w Jn 2:19
teachers of the law, and that he must be x Mt 17:22,23;
killed and on the third day[w] be raised to 27:63; Mk 9:31; Lk 9:22; 18:31-
life.[x] 33; 24:6,7
22Peter took him aside and began to
rebuke him. "Never, Lord!" he said. "This
shall never happen to you!"
23Jesus turned and said to Peter, "Get
behind me, Satan![y] You are a stumbling 16:23
block to me; you do not have in mind the y Mt 4:10
things of God, but the things of men."
24Then Jesus said to his disciples, "If
anyone would come after me, he must
deny himself and take up his cross and 16:24
follow me.[z] 25For whoever wants to save z Mt 10:38; Lk 14:27
his life[g] will lose it, but whoever loses his 16:25
life for me will find it.[a] 26What good will a Jn 12:25
it be for a man if he gains the whole
world, yet forfeits his soul? Or what can
a man give in exchange for his soul? 16:27
27For the Son of Man[b] is going to come[c] b Mt 8:20
in his Father's glory with his angels, and c Ac 1:11

[a] 2 Some early manuscripts do not have the rest of verse 2 and all of verse 3. [b] 16 Or *Messiah*; also in verse 20 [c] 18 *Peter* means *rock.* [d] 18 Or *hell* [e] 18 Or *not prove stronger than it* [f] 19 Or *have been* [g] 25 The Greek word means either *life* or *soul*; also in verse 26.

DISCOVERY 240

"Who Do You Say I Am?"

During Jesus' earthly ministry there was much discussion about who he really was. Some people surmised that he was John the Baptist come back to life. Others conjectured that he was Elijah, Jeremiah or one of the other prophets (Matthew 16:14). But Jesus was primarily concerned about what his own disciples thought. Peter's confession was immediate and emphatic: "You are the Christ, the Son of the living God" (verse 16).

Peter actually professed two separate truths about Jesus' identity. First, he is the Christ, God's promised Messiah, the anointed One sent by God to be our prophet, priest and king. But Peter further declared that Jesus is the Son of God.

Peter was characterized by his impetuous actions and outbursts and frequently spoke what was on his mind without sufficient forethought. In this instance, however, he is to be applauded for his insightful statement of faith. But before we cheer too loudly, we must look ahead at the ensuing event.

Shortly after this conversation Jesus began preparing his disciples for his coming death (verse 21). These words did not sit well with Peter, and he spoke out in rebuke: "Never, Lord! . . . This shall never happen to you!" (verse 22). Peter understood who Jesus was but failed utterly to grasp the nature of his mission, assuming that, because Jesus was the Messiah, he had come to establish an earthly kingdom and to overthrow the Roman government. Peter was right about who Jesus was but wrong about why he had come.

And the issue was critical—critical enough for Jesus to respond to Peter with uncharacteristic harshness. If Jesus were not to die in accordance with his Father's plan, then Satan would win the victory in the battle for the human soul and destiny, and Peter was in effect voicing Satan's opinion!

Peter had structured his conception of Jesus to fit within the parameters of his own expectations. The consummate man of action wanted a king and a kingdom—not death and apparent defeat. We often do the same thing. We are quick to confess that Jesus is the Son of God, but then we proceed to try to force him into the misshapen opening that represents our own image, perspectives and needs.

Our human nature wants to make Jesus Christ palatable to our modern culture rather than allowing him to shine forth before the world as a crucified and risen Savior. But when we redefine Jesus, we do the work of Satan. At that point we, like Peter, understand neither our leader nor our enemy.

Self-Discovery: *If you were asked to explain in a sentence or two who Jesus is, what would be the most important characteristics or truths you would want to include? After you have identified these, formulate your brief statement: Jesus is____.*

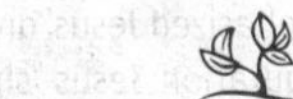

GO TO DISCOVERY 241 ON PAGE 1291

DISCOVERY 241

Cultivating Our Faith

While Jesus was up on the mountain with Peter, James and John, the rest of the disciples continued their ministry in the valley. One distraught father brought his demon-possessed son to them, but they were unable to drive out the demon. Ironically, the disciples had been given authority by Jesus to correct just this kind of problem (Mark 3:15–16), and they had done it so many times before (Matthew 10:1).

After Jesus had returned from the mountain, the agonized father approached and knelt before him. " 'Lord, have mercy on my son,' he said. 'He has seizures and is suffering greatly. He often falls into the fire or into the water. I brought him to your disciples, but they could not heal him' " (Matthew 17:15–16). Jesus had merely to rebuke the demon, and it immediately relinquished its hold on the boy.

Afterward, in private, the mystified disciples questioned Jesus as to why they had failed. Jesus' reply was straightforward: "Because you have so little faith. I tell you the truth, if you have faith as small as a mustard seed, you can say to this mountain, 'Move from here to there' and it will move. Nothing will be impossible for you" (verses 20–21). Faith as infinitesimal as the tiniest of seeds can work miracles, Jesus told them—but apparently they had lacked even that degree of trust when they had attempted to liberate the boy on their own.

Faith can be cultivated in one way: through prayer (Mark 9:29), but the disciples had forgotten that fundamental discipline. Without prayer we are as helpless as the disciples in the face of satanic opposition. It is not enough to be *called* to ministry, to be *gifted* for ministry, to have *experience* in ministry or to have achieved some *success* in ministry. We must continually practice the discipline of real prayer as we do what Jesus asks of us.

Neglecting to pray robs us of our power and may reduce our faith to a level of usefulness in God's kingdom far smaller than what God desires to exercise in us. As we draw closer to our precious Lord Jesus we will echo the words of the apostle Paul, who found the secret to his contentment and the source of his strength in Jesus alone: "I can do everything through him who gives me strength" (Philippians 4:13).

Self-Discovery: *What do you think Jesus meant by his statement to the disciples in Matthew 17:20–21? How do you reconcile these words with the reality that you do not receive everything you ask for in prayer? Do you attribute the "problem" with respect to "unanswered prayer" to your own lack of faith? What other possible explanations might there be?*

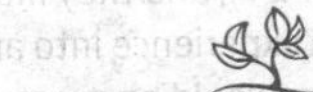

GO TO DISCOVERY 242 ON PAGE 1293

> I PROPOSE THAT JESUS WAS A JOYFUL SPIRIT WHEN HE WALKED ON THIS EARTH — A MAN OF GREAT WIT, WHO USED HUMOR IN HIS HEALING MINISTRY. A GLOOMY MESSIAH WOULD NOT HAVE ATTRACTED CHILDREN, THE DEPRESSED, THE SICK TO HIM BY THE THOUSANDS.
>
> Cal Samra, *Author*

17:25 [x]Mt 22:17-21; Ro 13:7 whom do the kings of the earth collect
duty and taxes[x]—from their own sons
or from others?"
26"From others," Peter answered.
"Then the sons are exempt," Jesus said
17:27 [y]Jn 6:61 to him. 27"But so that we may not offend[y] them, go to the lake and throw out
your line. Take the first fish you catch;
open its mouth and you will find a four-
drachma coin. Take it and give it to
them for my tax and yours."

The Greatest in the Kingdom of Heaven

18 At that time the disciples came
to Jesus and asked, "Who is the
greatest in the kingdom of heaven?"
2He called a little child and had him
stand among them. 3And he said: "I tell

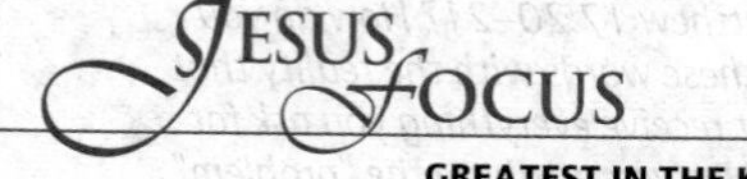

GREATEST IN THE KINGDOM

The disciples learned a great many life-changing lessons during the time they spent with Jesus, but they made mistakes along the way. One time, they failed to exorcise a demon who was torturing a young boy (Matthew 17:14–21), and they moved directly from that humbling experience into an argument about which of them would be greatest in God's kingdom. Jesus used their argument as an opportunity to teach them a lesson in humility. He called a small child to his side and addressed the disciples: "Whoever humbles himself like this child is the greatest in the kingdom of heaven" (Matthew 18:4). In Jesus' day, children were on the lowest rung of the social ladder. By using a child as an example for grown men, Jesus presented two implicit messages: Children are fully as significant as adults in God's kingdom, and God values the virtue of humility.

you the truth, unless you change and be-
come like little children,[z] you will never 18:3 [z]Mt 19:14; 1Pe 2:2 [a]Mt 3:2
enter the kingdom of heaven.[a] 4There-
fore, whoever humbles himself like this
child is the greatest in the kingdom of 18:4 [b]Mk 9:35
heaven.[b]
5"And whoever welcomes a little child 18:5 [c]Mt 10:40
like this in my name welcomes me.[c]
6But if anyone causes one of these little 18:6 [d]Mt 5:29 [e]Mk 9:42; Lk 17:2
ones who believe in me to sin,[d] it would
be better for him to have a large millstone hung around his neck and to be
drowned in the depths of the sea.[e]
7"Woe to the world because of the
things that cause people to sin! Such
things must come, but woe to the man 18:7 [f]Lk 17:1
through whom they come![f] 8If your
hand or your foot causes you to sin,[g] cut 18:8 [g]Mt 5:29; Mk 9:43,45
it off and throw it away. It is better for
you to enter life maimed or crippled
than to have two hands or two feet and
be thrown into eternal fire. 9And if your 18:9 [h]Mt 5:29 [i]Mt 5:22
eye causes you to sin,[h] gouge it out and
throw it away. It is better for you to enter life with one eye than to have two
eyes and be thrown into the fire of hell.[i]

The Parable of the Lost Sheep

10"See that you do not look down on
one of these little ones. For I tell you that 18:10 [j]Ge 48:16; Ps 34:7; Ac 12:11,15; Heb 1:14
their angels[j] in heaven always see the
face of my Father in heaven.[a]
12"What do you think? If a man owns
a hundred sheep, and one of them wanders away, will he not leave the ninety-
nine on the hills and go to look for the
one that wandered off? 13And if he finds
it, I tell you the truth, he is happier
about that one sheep than about the
ninety-nine that did not wander off. 14In
the same way your Father in heaven is
not willing that any of these little ones
should be lost.

A Brother Who Sins Against You

18:15 [k]Lev 19:17; Lk 17:3; Gal 6:1; Jas 5:19,20
15"If your brother sins against you,[b] go
and show him his fault,[k] just between
the two of you. If he listens to you, you 18:16 [l]Nu 35:30; Dt 17:6; 19:15; Jn 8:17; 2Co 13:1; 1Ti 5:19; Heb 10:28
have won your brother over. 16But if he
will not listen, take one or two others
along, so that 'every matter may be established by the testimony of two or
three witnesses.'[c][l] 17If he refuses to listen
to them, tell it to the church;[m] and if he 18:17 [m]1Co 6:1-6

[a] 10 Some manuscripts *heaven.* 11*The Son of Man came to save what was lost.* [b] 15 Some manuscripts do not have *against you.* [c] 16 Deut. 19:15

DISCOVERY 242

UNLIMITED FORGIVENESS

When someone else has wronged us, we expect a certain chain of events to be set in motion. We have already been *hurt*, and we sense that the responsible person *owes* us something—be it some form of restitution or at the very least a remorseful apology. Finally, we feel vindicated and are willing to "forgive" the debt because it has been paid in some way.

But godly forgiveness overlooks the second step; it implies a voluntary decision to release the other person from the debt he or she would otherwise have owed for the injury. The process of forgiveness always begins with the person who has been wronged, not with the person who did the hurting. In Matthew 18 Jesus taught that when we feel as though we've been treated unjustly, we should as a first step approach the offending brother or sister and attempt to resolve the issue. The initiative must come from our side, because the person who wounded us may not even realize the extent of the harm he or she has inflicted. Jesus instructs us that in the event the person refuses to listen, we are to approach the individual a second time, taking one or two witnesses along with us. If the person still declines to cooperate, the matter may be dealt with by the church.

Even if we do initially follow the course of action Jesus has mapped out for us, as human beings we tend to want to know how far we are obliged to carry the principle. "What if that same person hurts me over and over again?" we ask. "Do I have to keep forgiving her?" Peter vocalized the same question, although it was most likely on the minds of all of the disciples. Peter immediately went on to suggest an answer to his own question, and the proposal at first blush sounded rather generous: "Up to seven times?" But Jesus' answer took everyone aback: "I tell you, not seven times, but seventy-seven times" (verse 22). His point was that there is no limit to forgiveness. We are called on to forgive—even the same individual, for the same offense—to infinity! And Jesus went on in verse 35 to stipulate that we go beyond simply forgiving someone who has wronged us to forgiving "from your heart."

"Bear with each other," urged the apostle Paul, "and forgive whatever grievances you may have against one another. Forgive as the Lord forgave you. And over all [other] virtues put on love, which binds them all together in perfect unity" (Colossians 3:13–14). And again in Ephesians 4:32: "Be kind and compassionate to one another, forgiving each other, just as in Christ God forgave you."

Forgiveness can occur only in the context of genuine love. The emotional debts that we as sinful people would otherwise owe to one another have been canceled through the shed blood of Jesus Christ our Savior. Our only outstanding debt, said Paul, should be "the continuing debt to love one another, for he who loves his fellowman has fulfilled the law" (Romans 13:8). Paul entreated Philemon to accept back his runaway slave Onesimus "no longer as a slave, but better than a slave, as a dear brother" (Philemon 16). What an uplifting model of love and forgiveness for us as Christians!

Self-Discovery: *Bow your head and ask the Lord Jesus to grant you the power to initiate forgiveness, no matter what injustice may be rankling you today.*

GO TO DISCOVERY 243 ON PAGE 1297

refuses to listen even to the church, treat
18:17 [n] Ro 16:17; 2Th 3:6,14 him as you would a pagan or a tax collector.[n]
18“I tell you the truth, whatever you
bind on earth will be[a] bound in heaven,
18:18 [o] Mt 16:19; Jn 20:23 and whatever you loose on earth will be[a]
loosed in heaven.[o]
19“Again, I tell you that if two of you
18:19 [p] Mt 7:7 on earth agree about anything you ask
for, it will be done for you[p] by my Father
in heaven. 20For where two or three
come together in my name, there am I
with them.”

The Parable of the Unmerciful Servant

21Then Peter came to Jesus and asked,
18:21 [q] Mt 6:14 [r] Lk 17:4 “Lord, how many times shall I forgive
my brother when he sins against me?[q]
Up to seven times?”[r]
18:22 [s] Ge 4:24 22Jesus answered, “I tell you, not sev-
en times, but seventy-seven times.[b][s]
18:23 [t] Mt 13:24 [u] Mt 25:19 23“Therefore, the kingdom of heaven
is like[t] a king who wanted to settle ac-
counts[u] with his servants. 24As he began
the settlement, a man who owed him
18:25 [v] Lk 7:42 [w] Lev 25:39; 2Ki 4:1; Ne 5:5,8 ten thousand talents[c] was brought to
him. 25Since he was not able to pay,[v] the
master ordered that he and his wife and
his children and all that he had be sold[w]
to repay the debt.
18:26 [x] Mt 8:2 26“The servant fell on his knees before
him.[x] ‘Be patient with me,’ he begged,
‘and I will pay back everything.’ 27The
servant’s master took pity on him, canceled the debt and let him go.

MATTHEW AND MONEY

As a former tax collector Matthew focused a good deal of his attention on money. For instance, Matthew was the only Gospel writer to record the stories of the unmerciful servant (Matthew 18:23–35), the vineyard workers (Matthew 20:1–16) and the servants who were entrusted with sums of money by their master (Matthew 25:14–30). Matthew, who turned his back on a life of extortion and greed to follow Jesus, recorded Jesus’ strongest words about the use and misuse of money, as well as about the appropriate treatment of the poor. Matthew’s choice to follow Jesus affected every aspect of his life—including his system of ethics. When God gets hold of our hearts, he changes our values and teaches us to hone in on what is really important in life.

28“But when that servant went out, he
found one of his fellow servants who
owed him a hundred denarii.[d] He
grabbed him and began to choke him.
‘Pay back what you owe me!’ he demanded.
29“His fellow servant fell to his knees
and begged him, ‘Be patient with me,
and I will pay you back.’
30“But he refused. Instead, he went off
and had the man thrown into prison until he could pay the debt. 31When the
other servants saw what had happened,
they were greatly distressed and went
and told their master everything that
had happened.
32“Then the master called the servant
in. ‘You wicked servant,’ he said, ‘I canceled all that debt of yours because you
begged me to. 33Shouldn’t you have had
mercy on your fellow servant just as I
had on you?’ 34In anger his master
turned him over to the jailers to be tortured, until he should pay back all he
owed.
35“This is how my heavenly Father will
treat each of you unless you forgive your 18:35 [y] Mt 6:14; Jas 2:13
brother from your heart.”[y]

Divorce

19 When Jesus had finished saying
these things,[z] he left Galilee and 19:1 [z] Mt 7:28
went into the region of Judea to the oth-
er side of the Jordan. 2Large crowds fol- 19:2 [a] Mt 4:23
lowed him, and he healed them[a] there.
3Some Pharisees came to him to test
him. They asked, “Is it lawful for a man
to divorce his wife[b] for any and every 19:3 [b] Mt 5:31
reason?”
4“Haven’t you read,” he replied, “that
at the beginning the Creator ‘made
them male and female,’[e][c] 5and said, ‘For 19:4 [c] Ge 1:27; 5:2
this reason a man will leave his father
and mother and be united to his wife,
and the two will become one flesh’[f]?[d] 19:5 [d] Ge 2:24; 1Co 6:16; Eph 5:31
6So they are no longer two, but one.
Therefore what God has joined together,
let man not separate.”
7“Why then,” they asked, “did Moses
command that a man give his wife a cer- 19:7 [e] Dt 24:1-4; Mt 5:31
tificate of divorce and send her away?”[e]
8Jesus replied, “Moses permitted you
to divorce your wives because your
hearts were hard. But it was not this way

[a] *18* Or *have been* [b] *22* Or *seventy times seven* [c] *24* That is, millions of dollars [d] *28* That is, a few dollars [e] *4* Gen. 1:27 [f] *5* Gen. 2:24

from the beginning. 9 I tell you that anyone who divorces his wife, except for
19:9 [f]Mt 5:32; Lk 16:18 marital unfaithfulness, and marries another woman commits adultery."[f]
10 The disciples said to him, "If this is
the situation between a husband and
wife, it is better not to marry."
11 Jesus replied, "Not everyone can ac-
19:11 [g]Mt 13:11; 1Co 7:7-9,17 cept this word, but only those to whom
it has been given.[g] 12 For some are eu-
nuchs because they were born that way;
others were made that way by men; and
others have renounced marriage[a] because of the kingdom of heaven. The
one who can accept this should accept it."

The Little Children and Jesus

13 Then little children were brought to
19:13 [h]Mk 5:23 Jesus for him to place his hands on
them[h] and pray for them. But the disciples rebuked those who brought them.
14 Jesus said, "Let the little children
19:14 [i]Mt 25:34 [j]Mt 18:3; 1Pe 2:2 come to me, and do not hinder them, for
the kingdom of heaven belongs[i] to such
as these."[j] 15 When he had placed his
hands on them, he went on from there.

The Rich Young Man

16 Now a man came up to Jesus and
19:16 [k]Mt 25:46 [l]Lk 10:25 asked, "Teacher, what good thing must I
do to get eternal life[k]?"[l]
17 "Why do you ask me about what is
good?" Jesus replied. "There is only One

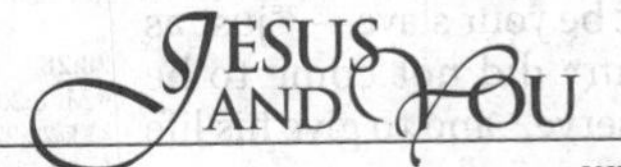

WHAT'S MISSING?

A wealthy and influential young man alleged to Jesus that he had kept God's commandments all of his life. Even so, he felt as though he was missing something: "What do I still lack?" he queried (Matthew 19:20). Jesus wanted the young man to see that there is more to God's law than adherence to a stringent set of rules. The spirit of the law comes from God's heart and should penetrate to the depths of our own hearts. So Jesus instructed his visitor to sell everything he possessed, donate all of the money to charity and follow Jesus (verse 21). The young man went away disheartened and disillusioned, choosing to walk away from what God really wanted, saying in essence, "I love myself—not God or my neighbor." God asks that we learn to walk in a way that pleases him—loving him and other people from the heart.

who is good. If you want to enter life, 19:17 [m]Lev 18:5
obey the commandments."[m]
18 "Which ones?" the man inquired.
Jesus replied, " 'Do not murder, do not 19:18 [n]Jas 2:11
commit adultery,[n] do not steal, do not
give false testimony, 19 honor your father 19:19 [o]Ex 20:12-16; Dt 5:16-20 [p]Lev 19:18; Mt 5:43
and mother,'[b][o] and 'love your neighbor
as yourself.'[c]"[p]
20 "All these I have kept," the young
man said. "What do I still lack?"
21 Jesus answered, "If you want to be 19:21 [q]Mt 5:48 [r]Lk 12:33; Ac 2:45; 4:34-35 [s]Mt 6:20
perfect,[q] go, sell your possessions and
give to the poor,[r] and you will have treasure in heaven.[s] Then come, follow me."
22 When the young man heard this, he
went away sad, because he had great
wealth.
23 Then Jesus said to his disciples, "I
tell you the truth, it is hard for a rich 19:23 [t]Mt 13:22; 1Ti 6:9,10
man[t] to enter the kingdom of heaven.
24 Again I tell you, it is easier for a camel
to go through the eye of a needle than for
a rich man to enter the kingdom of God."
25 When the disciples heard this, they
were greatly astonished and asked,
"Who then can be saved?"
26 Jesus looked at them and said, 19:26 [u]Ge 18:14; Job 42:2; Jer 32:17; Zec 8:6; Lk 1:37; 18:27; Ro 4:21
"With man this is impossible, but with
God all things are possible."[u]
27 Peter answered him, "We have left
everything to follow you![v] What then
will there be for us?"
28 Jesus said to them, "I tell you the 19:27 [v]Mt 4:19
truth, at the renewal of all things, when
the Son of Man sits on his glorious 19:28 [w]Mt 20:21; 25:31 [x]Lk 22:28-30; Rev 3:21; 4:4; 20:4
throne,[w] you who have followed me will
also sit on twelve thrones, judging the
twelve tribes of Israel.[x] 29 And everyone
who has left houses or brothers or sisters or father or mother[d] or children or
fields for my sake will receive a hundred
times as much and will inherit eternal 19:29 [y]Mt 6:33; 25:46
life.[y] 30 But many who are first will be
last, and many who are last will be first.[z] 19:30 [z]Mt 20:16; Mk 10:31; Lk 13:30

The Parable of the Workers in the Vineyard

20 "For the kingdom of heaven is 20:1 [a]Mt 13:24 [b]Mt 21:28,33
like[a] a landowner who went out
early in the morning to hire men to work
in his vineyard.[b] 2 He agreed to pay them
a denarius for the day and sent them
into his vineyard.

[a] 12 Or *have made themselves eunuchs*
[b] 19 Exodus 20:12-16; Deut. 5:16-20
[c] 19 Lev. 19:18 [d] 29 Some manuscripts *mother or wife*

> **CHRIST'S MIRACLES WERE PARABLES IN DEEDS, AND HIS PARABLES WERE MIRACLES IN WORDS.**
>
> W. Graham Scroggie, *Scottish Theologian*

3“About the third hour he went out
and saw others standing in the marketplace doing nothing. 4He told them, ‘You
also go and work in my vineyard, and I
will pay you whatever is right.’ 5So they
went.
“He went out again about the sixth
hour and the ninth hour and did the
same thing. 6About the eleventh hour he
went out and found still others standing
around. He asked them, ‘Why have you
been standing here all day long doing
nothing?’
7“ ‘Because no one has hired us,’ they
answered.
“He said to them, ‘You also go and
work in my vineyard.’
20:8 [c]Lev 19:13; Dt 24:15
8“When evening came,[c] the owner of
the vineyard said to his foreman, ‘Call
the workers and pay them their wages,
beginning with the last ones hired and
going on to the first.’
9“The workers who were hired about
the eleventh hour came and each received a denarius. 10So when those came
who were hired first, they expected to receive more. But each one of them also re-
20:11 [d]Jnh 4:1
ceived a denarius. 11When they received
it, they began to grumble[d] against the
landowner. 12‘These men who were hired
last worked only one hour,’ they said, ‘and
you have made them equal to us who
20:12 [e]Jnh 4:8; Lk 12:55; Jas 1:11
have borne the burden of the work and
the heat[e] of the day.’
13“But he answered one of them,
20:13 [f]Mt 22:12; 26:50
‘Friend,[f] I am not being unfair to you.
Didn't you agree to work for a denarius?
14Take your pay and go. I want to give
the man who was hired last the same as
I gave you. 15Don't I have the right to do
20:15 [g]Dt 15:9; Mk 7:22
what I want with my own money? Or are
you envious because I am generous?’[g]
16“So the last will be first, and the first
20:16 [h]Mt 19:30
will be last.”[h]

Jesus Again Predicts His Death

17Now as Jesus was going up to Jerusalem, he took the twelve disciples aside
and said to them, 18“We are going up to
20:18 [i]Lk 9:51 [j]Mt 8:20 [k]Mt 16:21; 27:1,2
Jerusalem,[i] and the Son of Man[j] will be
betrayed to the chief priests and the
teachers of the law.[k] They will condemn
him to death 19and will turn him over to
20:19 [l]Mt 16:21 [m]Ac 2:23 [n]Mt 16:21 [o]Mt 16:21
the Gentiles to be mocked and flogged[l]
and crucified.[m] On the third day[n] he will
be raised to life!”[o]

A Mother's Request

20:20 [p]Mt 4:21 [q]Mt 8:2
20Then the mother of Zebedee's sons[p]
came to Jesus with her sons and, kneeling down,[q] asked a favor of him.
21“What is it you want?” he asked.
She said, “Grant that one of these two
sons of mine may sit at your right and
20:21 [r]Mt 19:28
the other at your left in your kingdom.”[r]
22“You don't know what you are ask-
20:22 [s]Isa 51:17,22; Jer 49:12; Mt 26:39,42; Mk 14:36; Lk 22:42; Jn 18:11
ing,” Jesus said to them. “Can you drink
the cup[s] I am going to drink?”
“We can,” they answered.
23Jesus said to them, “You will indeed
drink from my cup,[t] but to sit at my
20:23 [t]Ac 12:2; Rev 1:9
right or left is not for me to grant. These
places belong to those for whom they
have been prepared by my Father.”
20:24 [u]Lk 22:24,25
24When the ten heard about this, they
were indignant[u] with the two brothers.
25Jesus called them together and said,
“You know that the rulers of the Gentiles lord it over them, and their high officials exercise authority over them.
26Not so with you. Instead, whoever
20:26 [v]Mt 23:11; Mk 9:35
wants to become great among you must
be your servant,[v] 27and whoever wants
to be first must be your slave— 28just as
20:28 [w]Mt 8:20 [x]Lk 22:27; Jn 13:13-16; 2Co 8:9; Php 2:7 [y]Isa 53:10; Mt 26:28; 1Ti 2:6; Tit 2:14; Heb 9:28; 1Pe 1:18,19
the Son of Man[w] did not come to be
served, but to serve,[x] and to give his life
as a ransom[y] for many.”

Two Blind Men Receive Sight

29As Jesus and his disciples were leaving Jericho, a large crowd followed him.
30Two blind men were sitting by the
roadside, and when they heard that
20:30 [z]Mt 9:27
Jesus was going by, they shouted, “Lord,
Son of David,[z] have mercy on us!”
31The crowd rebuked them and told
them to be quiet, but they shouted all
the louder, “Lord, Son of David, have
mercy on us!”
32Jesus stopped and called them.
“What do you want me to do for you?”
he asked.
33“Lord,” they answered, “we want our
sight.”
34Jesus had compassion on them and

DISCOVERY 243

Is God Unfair?

We expect our heavenly Father to exercise "fairness," but he doesn't always meet our criteria in this regard. In order to illustrate God's seemingly paradoxical system of justice, Jesus told a parable about workers in a vineyard. Some toiled all day with bent backs under a beating sun. At five different times during the course of the day the owner hired additional workers, and the final group to be hired picked for only one hour. When all of the men were paid at the end of the day, each received exactly the same amount! Those who had labored from sunup to sundown were understandably miffed. But the owner of the vineyard pointed out that he had followed exactly all the conditions of his agreement with each of the workers. God's sense of justice does not always match ours, because his value system differs from that of the world.

To begin with, God looks for *faithfulness*, not for length of service. In his eyes all of his children are equal—and all of them are loved unconditionally. The sainted individual who has faithfully served God for 50 years is no more valuable in his sight than the three-minute Christian bursting with the wonder and joy of her newfound peace.

Second, God is *generous* with his rewards. None of the workers was disgruntled about being paid one denarius for one day's work. That was the standard wage, and they all considered it equitable—at least at time of hire. The problem came as they began to compare themselves to others who hadn't worked as hard or as long as they had. What they didn't understand is that paying a full denarius to those who had worked for only one hour was not unfair—it was a marvelous expression of generosity. God the Father doesn't give us as little as possible; he always blesses us with far more than we deserve.

Heaven's value system is the exact opposite of the one the world teaches us. Under God's standard those who are looked on as "last" by the world, be they underdogs and social misfits or humble servants, may very well enter the kingdom first, while the ones the world would perceive as "top dogs" may be last through heaven's door. The important truth for us to remember is that God is always fair—according to his own standards.

In the final analysis, of course, none of us deserves God's blessings. "Every good and perfect gift is from above, coming down from the Father of the heavenly lights, who does not change like shifting shadows" (James 1:17). *Everything* we enjoy, including the very air we breathe, is a gift from God, who "gives all men life and breath and everything else" (Acts 17:25).

The ultimate gift is available to all people for the asking: "For the wages of sin is death, but the gift of God is eternal life in Christ Jesus our Lord" (Romans 6:23). The real beauty of the gospel message lies precisely in the truth that "while we were still sinners, Christ died for us" (Romans 5:8).

Self-Discovery: *What is your personal reaction to the parable about the vineyard? Does a part of you feel that the owner's behavior was unfair? How can you reconcile Jesus' explanation of fairness with that which is generally accepted in our culture?*

GO TO DISCOVERY 244 ON PAGE 1299

touched their eyes. Immediately they received their sight and followed him.

The Triumphal Entry

21:1 [a] Mt 24:3; 26:30; Mk 14:26; Lk 19:37; 21:37; 22:39; Jn 8:1; Ac 1:12

21 As they approached Jerusalem and came to Bethphage on the Mount of Olives,[a] Jesus sent two disciples, 2saying to them, "Go to the village ahead of you, and at once you will find a donkey tied there, with her colt by her. Untie them and bring them to me. 3If anyone says anything to you, tell him that the Lord needs them, and he will send them right away."

4This took place to fulfill what was spoken through the prophet:

5"Say to the Daughter of Zion,
'See, your king comes to you,
gentle and riding on a donkey,
on a colt, the foal of a donkey.' "[a][b]

21:5 [b] Zec 9:9; Isa 62:11

6The disciples went and did as Jesus had instructed them. 7They brought the donkey and the colt, placed their cloaks on them, and Jesus sat on them. 8A very large crowd spread their cloaks[c] on the road, while others cut branches from the trees and spread them on the road. 9The crowds that went ahead of him and those that followed shouted,

21:8 [c] 2Ki 9:13

"Hosanna[b] to the Son of David!"[d]

"Blessed is he who comes in the
name of the Lord!"[c][e]

"Hosanna[b] in the highest!"[f]

21:9 [d] ver 15; Mt 9:27 [e] Ps 118:26; Mt 23:39 [f] Lk 2:14

10When Jesus entered Jerusalem, the whole city was stirred and asked, "Who is this?"

11The crowds answered, "This is Jesus, the prophet[g] from Nazareth in Galilee."

21:11 [g] Lk 7:16,39; 24:19; Jn 1:21,25; 6:14; 7:40

Jesus at the Temple

12Jesus entered the temple area and drove out all who were buying[h] and selling there. He overturned the tables of the money changers[i] and the benches of those selling doves.[j] 13"It is written," he said to them, " 'My house will be called a house of prayer,'[d][k] but you are making it a 'den of robbers.'[e]"[l]

21:12 [h] Dt 14:26 [i] Ex 30:13 [j] Lev 1:14

21:13 [k] Isa 56:7 [l] Jer 7:11

14The blind and the lame came to him at the temple, and he healed them.[m] 15But when the chief priests and the teachers of the law saw the wonderful things he did and the children shouting in the temple area, "Hosanna to the Son of David,"[n] they were indignant.[o]

21:14 [m] Mt 4:23

21:15 [n] ver 9; Mt 9:27 [o] Lk 19:39

16"Do you hear what these children are saying?" they asked him.

"Yes," replied Jesus, "have you never read,

" 'From the lips of children and
infants
you have ordained praise'[f]?"[p]

21:16 [p] Ps 8:2

17And he left them and went out of the city to Bethany,[q] where he spent the night.

21:17 [q] Mt 26:6; Mk 11:1; Lk 24:50; Jn 11:1,18; 12:1

The Fig Tree Withers

18Early in the morning, as he was on his way back to the city, he was hungry. 19Seeing a fig tree by the road, he went up to it but found nothing on it except leaves. Then he said to it, "May you never bear fruit again!" Immediately the tree withered.[r]

21:19 [r] Isa 34:4; Jer 8:13

20When the disciples saw this, they were amazed. "How did the fig tree wither so quickly?" they asked.

21Jesus replied, "I tell you the truth, if you have faith and do not doubt,[s] not only can you do what was done to the fig tree, but also you can say to this mountain, 'Go, throw yourself into the sea,' and it will be done. 22If you believe, you will receive whatever you ask for[t] in prayer."

21:21 [s] Mt 17:20; Lk 17:6; 1Co 13:2; Jas 1:6

21:22 [t] Mt 7:7

The Authority of Jesus Questioned

23Jesus entered the temple courts, and, while he was teaching, the chief priests and the elders of the people came to him. "By what authority[u] are you doing these things?" they asked. "And who gave you this authority?"

21:23 [u] Ac 4:7; 7:27

24Jesus replied, "I will also ask you one question. If you answer me, I will tell you by what authority I am doing these things. 25John's baptism—where did it come from? Was it from heaven, or from men?"

They discussed it among themselves and said, "If we say, 'From heaven,' he will ask, 'Then why didn't you believe him?' 26But if we say, 'From men'—we are afraid of the people, for they all hold that John was a prophet."[v]

21:26 [v] Mt 11:9; Mk 6:20

27So they answered Jesus, "We don't know."

[a] *5* Zech. 9:9 [b] *9* A Hebrew expression meaning "Save!" which became an exclamation of praise; also in verse 15 [c] *9* Psalm 118:26 [d] *13* Isaiah 56:7 [e] *13* Jer. 7:11 [f] *16* Psalm 8:2

WHO IS JESUS?

The final week of Jesus' life began with a parade in his honor and culminated in his execution. How did things change so quickly?

Jesus' "triumphal entry" into Jerusalem touched off a mass celebration, enlisting the applause and support of the crowds. Jesus rode into Jerusalem on a donkey to fulfill an Old Testament prophecy (Zechariah 9:9; Matthew 21:1–3). A donkey is a docile animal—not the sort of "steed" on whose back a skilled warrior would make his charge to bring about his victory. If Jesus had come to earth with the ultimate goal of overthrowing the Roman government, he probably would have entered Jerusalem in full battle regalia astride a spirited stallion. One day he will do just that, declaring war against Satan and his armies (Revelation 19:11–16), but for the time being he was making his slow and plodding advance while riding an animal associated with peace (Isaiah 9:6). The masses, sadly, still missed the point, still envisioning that Jesus had come to conquer.

Crowds lined the streets as Jesus was conveyed into the city. Some people threw their outer garments and tree branches along the road, recalling the response of the masses years before when Jehu had become the king of Israel (2 Kings 9:13). The people, fickle as they would soon turn out to be, were at this particular moment proclaiming Jesus as their king. In so doing the crowd chanted three phrases:

"Hosanna to the Son of David." Hosanna means "Save!" They were asking Jesus to deliver them from political domination and to become their earthly king, "the Son of David."

"Blessed is he who comes in the name of the Lord." This quotation came straight from the Hebrew Scripture, Psalm 118:26. The people to their credit realized that Jesus was no ordinary person—that he possessed the authority and power of God himself.

"Hosanna in the highest." The throng recognized that Jesus had come from the "highest" place—the dwelling place of God (Psalm 148:1–2; Luke 2:14).

Jesus captured the attention of the entire city, and people began to ask in wonder, "Who is this?" (Matthew 21:10). Each of us today needs to answer for ourselves the same question, and our conclusion will have eternal significance. If we deduce that Jesus was just another prophet or gifted public speaker, then we may respect his teaching—but not much more than that. But if we accept that he is indeed the Messiah, our Savior, we can do nothing less than fall at his feet in awe and worship, echoing the words of the throngs around the throne in heaven: "Worthy is the Lamb, who was slain, to receive power and wealth and wisdom and strength and honor and glory and blessing!" (Revelation 5:12).

Self-Discovery: *Try to recall the last time you were overcome with your awe and love for Jesus? What inspired these feelings (a sunset? a hymn? a passage of Scripture that touched you in a special way? an unexpected blessing just when you needed it?)? How did you respond?*

GO TO DISCOVERY 245 ON PAGE 1303

Then he said, "Neither will I tell you
by what authority I am doing these
things.

The Parable of the Two Sons

28"What do you think? There was a
man who had two sons. He went to the
21:28 [w] ver 33; Mt 20:1 — first and said, 'Son, go and work today in
the vineyard.'[w]
29" 'I will not,' he answered, but later
he changed his mind and went.
30"Then the father went to the other
son and said the same thing. He answered, 'I will, sir,' but he did not go.
31"Which of the two did what his father wanted?"

"The first," they answered.

Jesus said to them, "I tell you the
21:31 [x] Lk 7:29 [y] Lk 7:50 — truth, the tax collectors[x] and the prostitutes[y] are entering the kingdom of God
21:32 [z] Mt 3:1-12 [a] Lk 3:12,13; 7:29 [b] Lk 7:36-50 [c] Lk 7:30 — ahead of you. 32For John came to you to
show you the way of righteousness,[z] and
you did not believe him, but the tax collectors[a] and the prostitutes[b] did. And
even after you saw this, you did not repent[c] and believe him.

The Parable of the Tenants

21:33 [d] Ps 80:8 [e] Isa 5:1-7 [f] Mt 25:14,15 — 33"Listen to another parable: There
was a landowner who planted[d] a vine-
yard. He put a wall around it, dug a
winepress in it and built a watchtower.[e]
Then he rented the vineyard to some
farmers and went away on a journey.[f]
21:34 [g] Mt 22:3 — 34When the harvest time approached, he
sent his servants[g] to the tenants to col-
lect his fruit.
35"The tenants seized his servants;
21:35 [h] 2Ch 24:21; Mt 23:34,37; Heb 11:36,37 — they beat one, killed another, and stoned
a third.[h] 36Then he sent other servants[i]
to them, more than the first time, and
21:36 [i] Mt 22:4 — the tenants treated them the same way.
37Last of all, he sent his son to them.
'They will respect my son,' he said.
38"But when the tenants saw the son,
21:38 [j] Heb 1:2 [k] Mt 12:14 [l] Ps 2:8 — they said to each other, 'This is the heir.[j]
Come, let's kill him[k] and take his inher-
itance.'[l] 39So they took him and threw
him out of the vineyard and killed him.
40"Therefore, when the owner of the
vineyard comes, what will he do to those
tenants?"
41"He will bring those wretches to a
21:41 [m] Mt 8:11,12 [n] Ac 13:46; 18:6; 28:28 — wretched end,"[m] they replied, "and he
will rent the vineyard to other tenants,[n]
who will give him his share of the crop at
harvest time."

42Jesus said to them, "Have you never
read in the Scriptures:

" 'The stone the builders rejected
has become the capstone[a];
the Lord has done this,
and it is marvelous in our eyes'[b]?[o] 21:42 [o] Ps 118:22,23; Ac 4:11; 1Pe 2:7

43"Therefore I tell you that the king-
dom of God will be taken away from 21:43 [p] Mt 8:12
you[p] and given to a people who will produce its fruit. 44He who falls on this
stone will be broken to pieces, but he on 21:44 [q] Lk 2:34
whom it falls will be crushed."[c][q]
45When the chief priests and the
Pharisees heard Jesus' parables, they
knew he was talking about them. 46They
looked for a way to arrest him, but they
were afraid of the crowd because the 21:46 [r] ver 11,26
people held that he was a prophet.[r]

The Parable of the Wedding Banquet

22 Jesus spoke to them again in
parables, saying: 2"The king-
dom of heaven is like[s] a king who pre- 22:2 [s] Mt 13:24
pared a wedding banquet for his son.
3He sent his servants[t] to those who had 22:3 [t] Mt 21:34
been invited to the banquet to tell them
to come, but they refused to come.

[a] 42 Or *cornerstone* [b] 42 Psalm 118:22,23
[c] 44 Some manuscripts do not have verse 44.

JESUS FOCUS

PROPERLY DRESSED

The parable of the wedding clothes illustrates two important truths (Matthew 22:1–14). First, because God's chosen people had rejected him, he had broadened his focus to include those outside of Abraham's family. Second, we need God's grace in order to enter into a relationship with him. Jesus' parable began with the sending out of invitations to a wedding banquet. The people invited first—the Jews—declined the invitations, so the father invited others—the Gentiles. However, only those who were dressed in appropriate wedding attire were actually allowed to enjoy the festivities, even if they had arrived with an invitation in hand. God invites everyone to enjoy a relationship with him, but in order to take him up on that offer we need to accept the "clothes" of God's righteousness. Our only avenue to a relationship with God the Father is through acceptance of Jesus as his Son who died for our sins and rose again to new life so that we might never again experience separation from God (John 10:28).

22:4 4“Then he sent some more servants[u]
u Mt 21:36 and said, ‘Tell those who have been invited that I have prepared my dinner: My
oxen and fattened cattle have been
butchered, and everything is ready.
Come to the wedding banquet.’
5“But they paid no attention and went
off—one to his field, another to his business. 6The rest seized his servants, mistreated them and killed them. 7The king
was enraged. He sent his army and de-
22:7 stroyed those murderers[v] and burned
v Lk 19:27 their city.
8“Then he said to his servants, ‘The
wedding banquet is ready, but those I invited did not deserve to come. 9Go to
22:9 the street corners[w] and invite to the
w Eze 21:21 banquet anyone you find.’ 10So the servants went out into the streets and gathered all the people they could find, both
22:10 good and bad,[x] and the wedding hall
x Mt 13:47,48 was filled with guests.
11“But when the king came in to see
the guests, he noticed a man there who
22:12 was not wearing wedding clothes.
y Mt 20:13; 26:50 12‘Friend,’[y] he asked, ‘how did you get in
here without wedding clothes?’ The
man was speechless.
13“Then the king told the attendants,
‘Tie him hand and foot, and throw him
22:13 outside, into the darkness, where there
z Mt 8:12 will be weeping and gnashing of teeth.’[z]
22:14 14“For many are invited, but few are
a Rev 17:14 chosen.”[a]

Paying Taxes to Caesar

15Then the Pharisees went out and
laid plans to trap him in his words.
22:16 16They sent their disciples to him along
b Mk 3:6 with the Herodians.[b] “Teacher,” they
said, “we know you are a man of integrity and that you teach the way of God in
accordance with the truth. You aren’t
swayed by men, because you pay no at-
22:17 tention to who they are. 17Tell us then,
c Mt 17:25 what is your opinion? Is it right to pay
taxes[c] to Caesar or not?”
18But Jesus, knowing their evil intent,
said, “You hypocrites, why are you trying to trap me? 19Show me the coin
used for paying the tax.” They brought
him a denarius, 20and he asked them,
“Whose portrait is this? And whose inscription?”
21“Caesar’s,” they replied.
Then he said to them, “Give to Caesar

THE CLAIMS OF JESUS ARE SO STARTLING THAT THEY . . . CHALLENGE US TO MAKE UP OUR MINDS ABOUT THIS MOST REMARKABLE PERSON. WAS HE JUST A GREAT TEACHER OR WAS HE MUCH MORE?

Michael Green,
British Theologian

what is Caesar’s,[d] and to God what is 22:21
God’s.” d Ro 13:7
22When they heard this, they were
amazed. So they left him and went 22:22
away.[e] e Mk 12:12

Marriage at the Resurrection

23That same day the Sadducees,[f] who 22:23
say there is no resurrection,[g] came to f Ac 4:1
him with a question. 24“Teacher,” they g Ac 23:8; 1Co 15:12
said, “Moses told us that if a man dies
without having children, his brother
must marry the widow and have children for him.[h] 25Now there were seven 22:24
brothers among us. The first one mar- h Dt 25:5,6
ried and died, and since he had no children, he left his wife to his brother. 26The
same thing happened to the second and
third brother, right on down to the seventh. 27Finally, the woman died. 28Now
then, at the resurrection, whose wife will
she be of the seven, since all of them
were married to her?”
29Jesus replied, “You are in error be- 22:29
cause you do not know the Scriptures[i] i Jn 20:9
or the power of God. 30At the resurrection people will neither marry nor be 22:30
given in marriage;[j] they will be like the j Mt 24:38
angels in heaven. 31But about the resurrection of the dead—have you not read
what God said to you, 32‘I am the God of
Abraham, the God of Isaac, and the God 22:32
of Jacob’[a]?[k] He is not the God of the k Ex 3:6; Ac 7:32
dead but of the living.”
33When the crowds heard this, they 22:33
were astonished at his teaching.[l] l Mt 7:28

The Greatest Commandment

34Hearing that Jesus had silenced the 22:34
Sadducees,[m] the Pharisees got together. m Ac 4:1
35One of them, an expert in the law,[n] test- 22:35
ed him with this question: 36“Teacher, n Lk 7:30; 10:25; 11:45; 14:3

a 32 Exodus 3:6

> NO CRITIC OF JESUS HAS EVER BEEN TAKEN SERIOUSLY. HIS LIFE WAS THE EPITOME OF VIRTUE.
>
> 
>
> Richard Halverson, *Chaplain, U.S. Senate*

which is the greatest commandment in
the Law?"
37 Jesus replied: " 'Love the Lord your
22:37 God with all your heart and with all your
[o] Dt 6:5 soul and with all your mind.'[a o] 38 This is
the first and greatest commandment.
22:39 39 And the second is like it: 'Love your
[p] Lev 19:18; neighbor as yourself.'[b p] 40 All the Law
Mt 5:43; 19:19; and the Prophets hang on these two
Gal 5:14 commandments."[q]
22:40 [q] Mt 7:12

Whose Son Is the Christ?

41 While the Pharisees were gathered
22:42 together, Jesus asked them, 42 "What do
[r] Mt 9:27 you think about the Christ[c]? Whose son
is he?"
"The son of David,"[r] they replied.
43 He said to them, "How is it then that
David, speaking by the Spirit, calls him
'Lord'? For he says,

44 " 'The Lord said to my Lord:
"Sit at my right hand
22:44 [s] Ps 110:1; Ac 2:34,35; until I put your enemies
1Co 15:25; Heb 1:13; 10:13 under your feet." '[d s]

45 If then David calls him 'Lord,' how can
he be his son?" 46 No one could say a word
22:46 [t] Mk 12:34; in reply, and from that day on no one
Lk 20:40 dared to ask him any more questions.[t]

Seven Woes

23 Then Jesus said to the crowds
and to his disciples: 2 "The
23:2 [u] Ezr 7:6,25; teachers of the law[u] and the Pharisees
Ne 8:4 sit in Moses' seat. 3 So you must obey
them and do everything they tell you.
23:4 [v] Lk 11:46; But do not do what they do, for they do
Ac 15:10; not practice what they preach. 4 They tie
Gal 6:13 up heavy loads and put them on men's
23:5 shoulders, but they themselves are not
[w] Mt 6:1,2,5,16 willing to lift a finger to move them.[v]
[x] Ex 13:9; Dt 6:8 5 "Everything they do is done for men
[y] Nu 15:38; Dt 22:12 to see:[w] They make their phylacteries[e x]
23:6 wide and the tassels on their garments[y]
[z] Lk 11:43; 14:7; long; 6 they love the place of honor at
20:46 banquets and the most important seats
23:7 in the synagogues;[z] 7 they love to be
[a] ver 8; Mk 9:5; greeted in the marketplaces and to have
10:51; Jn 1:38, 49 men call them 'Rabbi.'[a]

8 "But you are not to be called 'Rabbi,'
for you have only one Master and you are
all brothers. 9 And do not call anyone on
earth 'father,' for you have one Father,[b] 23:9 [b] Mal 1:6;
and he is in heaven. 10 Nor are you to be Mt 7:11
called 'teacher,' for you have one Teacher,
the Christ.[c] 11 The greatest among you 23:11 [c] Mt 20:26;
will be your servant.[c] 12 For whoever ex- Mk 9:35
alts himself will be humbled, and who- 23:12 [d] Lk 14:11
ever humbles himself will be exalted.[d]
13 "Woe to you, teachers of the law and 23:13 [e] ver 15,23,25,
Pharisees, you hypocrites![e] You shut the 27,29 [f] Lk 11:52
kingdom of heaven in men's faces. You
yourselves do not enter, nor will you let
those enter who are trying to.[f f]
15 "Woe to you, teachers of the law and
Pharisees, you hypocrites! You travel
over land and sea to win a single con- 23:15
vert,[g] and when he becomes one, you [g] Ac 2:11; 6:5;
make him twice as much a son of hell[h] 13:43 [h] Mt 5:22
as you are.
16 "Woe to you, blind guides![i] You say, 23:16 [i] ver 24;
'If anyone swears by the temple, it Mt 15:14
means nothing; but if anyone swears by [j] Mt 5:33-35
the gold of the temple, he is bound by
his oath.'[j] 17 You blind fools! Which is
greater: the gold, or the temple that 23:17
makes the gold sacred?[k] 18 You also say, [k] Ex 30:29
'If anyone swears by the altar, it means
nothing; but if anyone swears by the gift
on it, he is bound by his oath.' 19 You
blind men! Which is greater: the gift, or 23:19
the altar that makes the gift sacred?[l] [l] Ex 29:37
20 Therefore, he who swears by the altar
swears by it and by everything on it.
21 And he who swears by the temple
swears by it and by the one who dwells[m] 23:21 [m] 1Ki 8:13;
in it. 22 And he who swears by heaven Ps 26:8
swears by God's throne and by the one 23:22
who sits on it.[n] [n] Ps 11:4; Mt 5:34
23 "Woe to you, teachers of the law and
Pharisees, you hypocrites! You give a 23:23
tenth[o] of your spices—mint, dill and [o] Lev 27:30
cummin. But you have neglected the [p] Mic 6:8; Lk 11:42
more important matters of the law—
justice, mercy and faithfulness.[p] You
should have practiced the latter, without
neglecting the former. 24 You blind 23:24
guides![q] You strain out a gnat but swal- [q] ver 16
low a camel.
25 "Woe to you, teachers of the law and

[a] *37* Deut. 6:5 [b] *39* Lev. 19:18 [c] *42,10* Or *Messiah* [d] *44* Psalm 110:1 [e] *5* That is, boxes containing Scripture verses, worn on forehead and arm [f] *13* Some manuscripts *to.* [14] *Woe to you, teachers of the law and Pharisees, you hypocrites! You devour widows' houses and for a show make lengthy prayers. Therefore you will be punished more severely.*

Walking the Talk

"The church is full of hypocrites!" We can't be a part of God's family for long before we hear those words from someone. In fact, this may be the most frequently used rationalization for dismissing the truth about Jesus and choosing not to follow him. That is why it is critical that our relationship with him be based on more than mere lip service.

In fact, Jesus' harshest criticism was directed at people who confessed one set of beliefs but lived according to an entirely different system. The religious leaders in Israel had over the centuries dissected and elaborated on God's law until Jewish daily life had come to be based on hundreds of regulations associated with every aspect of living.

Jesus spoke to and about these religious leaders on many occasions and at one point directed an entire sermon toward them (see Matthew 23:1–39). Over and over again he proclaimed, "Woe to you, teachers of the law and Pharisees." The word *woe* signifies the threat of dire calamity. In this case, Jesus was abundantly clear that religious hypocrites are under the judgment of the very God they claim to be serving through adherence to all of their own rules and regulations.

We are all guilty at one time or another of saying one thing and doing another. One of the problems with hypocrisy is that it is easier to identify the trait in someone else than to admit to it in oneself! So Jesus was explicit. There are certain characteristics that point to a hypocritical lifestyle:

Do we talk more spiritually than we live? Jesus criticized the Pharisees because they did not practice what they preached (verse 3). They were full of impressive spiritual talk but woefully deficient in their walk, making demands on other people that they themselves were unwilling to fulfill. Expressed in contemporary language, their motto might have been, "Do as I say, not as I do."

Do we serve God so that other people will be impressed? The Pharisees were undeniably devout, but they often engaged in religious activities and performed good deeds for the sole purpose of impressing others. Jesus nailed the problem head on when he noted that "everything they do is done for men to see" (verse 5).

Are we more interested in how things look on the outside than in the condition of our hearts? The Pharisees paid careful attention to living a circumspect life—with regard to the externals—making certain that everything they did aligned with what God's law called "clean" while avoiding everything "unclean." But Jesus revealed that their hearts were corrupt, permeated by greed and self-indulgence (verse 25).

Religious hypocrisy is especially deceitful and dangerous because it drives us away from the God we profess to love at the same time we think we are moving closer to him (verses 37–39). In Jesus' day hypocrisy caused many scrupulously religious people to reject him as the promised Messiah—and the same holds true today. God's desire will always be that we remain devoted to him in heartfelt love.

Self-Discovery: *Take a moment to examine your own heart for evidences of hypocrisy. Confess it to the Lord and develop a specific action plan to bring you closer to a life of integrity.*

GO TO DISCOVERY 246 ON PAGE 1306

23:25 Pharisees, you hypocrites! You clean the
r Mk 7:4 outside of the cup and dish,[r] but inside
s Lk 11:39 they are full of greed and self-indulgence.[s] 26 Blind Pharisee! First clean the
inside of the cup and dish, and then the
outside also will be clean.

27 "Woe to you, teachers of the law and
23:27 Pharisees, you hypocrites! You are like
t Lk 11:44; Ac 23:3 whitewashed tombs,[t] which look beautiful on the outside but on the inside are
full of dead men's bones and everything
unclean. 28 In the same way, on the outside you appear to people as righteous
but on the inside you are full of hypocrisy and wickedness.

29 "Woe to you, teachers of the law and
23:29 Pharisees, you hypocrites! You build
u Lk 11:47,48 tombs for the prophets[u] and decorate
the graves of the righteous. 30 And you
say, 'If we had lived in the days of our
forefathers, we would not have taken
part with them in shedding the blood of
the prophets.' 31 So you testify against
23:31 yourselves that you are the descendants
v Ac 7:51-52 of those who murdered the prophets.[v]
23:32 32 Fill up, then, the measure[w] of the sin of
w 1Th 2:16 your forefathers!

23:33 33 "You snakes! You brood of vipers![x]
x Mt 3:7; 12:34 How will you escape being condemned
y Mt 5:22 to hell?[y] 34 Therefore I am sending you
prophets and wise men and teachers.
Some of them you will kill and crucify;[z] 23:34
others you will flog in your synagogues[a] z 2Ch 36:15,16; Lk 11:49
and pursue from town to town.[b] 35 And a Mt 10:17
so upon you will come all the righteous b Mt 10:23
blood that has been shed on earth, from
the blood of righteous Abel[c] to the 23:35
blood of Zechariah son of Berekiah,[d] c Ge 4:8; Heb 11:4
whom you murdered between the tem- d Zec 1:1
ple and the altar.[e] 36 I tell you the truth, e 2Ch 24:21
all this will come upon this generation.[f] 23:36 f Mt 10:23; 24:34

37 "O Jerusalem, Jerusalem, you who
kill the prophets and stone those sent to 23:37
you,[g] how often I have longed to gather g 2Ch 24:21; Mt 5:12
your children together, as a hen gathers
her chicks under her wings, but you
were not willing. 38 Look, your house is 23:38
left to you desolate.[h] 39 For I tell you, you h 1Ki 9:7,8; Jer 22:5
will not see me again until you say,
'Blessed is he who comes in the name of 23:39
the Lord.'[a]"[i] i Ps 118:26; Mt 21:9

Signs of the End of the Age

24 Jesus left the temple and was
walking away when his disci-
ples came up to him to call his attention
to its buildings. 2 "Do you see all these
things?" he asked. "I tell you the truth,
not one stone here will be left on anoth- 24:2
er;[j] every one will be thrown down." j Lk 19:44

3 As Jesus was sitting on the Mount of 24:3
Olives,[k] the disciples came to him pri- k Mt 21:1
vately. "Tell us," they said, "when will this
happen, and what will be the sign of
your coming and of the end of the age?"

4 Jesus answered: "Watch out that no
one deceives you. 5 For many will come
in my name, claiming, 'I am the Christ,[b]' 24:5
and will deceive many.[l] 6 You will hear of l ver 11,23,24; 1Jn 2:18
wars and rumors of wars, but see to it
that you are not alarmed. Such things
must happen, but the end is still to
come. 7 Nation will rise against nation, 24:7
and kingdom against kingdom.[m] There m Isa 19:2
will be famines[n] and earthquakes in var- n Ac 11:28
ious places. 8 All these are the beginning
of birth pains.

9 "Then you will be handed over to be 24:9
persecuted[o] and put to death,[p] and you o Mt 10:17
will be hated by all nations because of p Jn 16:2
me. 10 At that time many will turn away
from the faith and will betray and hate
each other, 11 and many false prophets[q] 24:11
will appear and deceive many people. q Mt 7:15
12 Because of the increase of wickedness,
the love of most will grow cold, 13 but he

[a] 39 Psalm 118:26 [b] 5 Or *Messiah*; also in verse 23

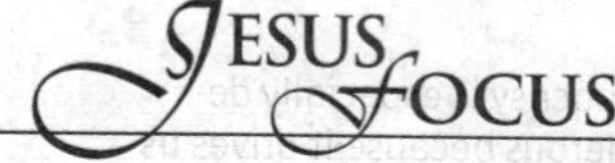

O JERUSALEM!

Although he had confronted the religious leaders (Matthew 21 and 22) and exposed their hypocrisy (Matthew 23), Jesus' heart was broken because of their refusal to recognize the fulfillment of God's promise—despite the fact that he was standing right in front of them. Our Lord mourned for the city that he had chosen as his own: "O Jerusalem . . . how often I have longed to gather your children together, as a hen gathers her chicks under her wings, but you were not willing" (verse 37). Because the people would not embrace God's Messiah, Jesus warned that Jerusalem would once again be subject to attack and that both the city and the temple would be destroyed (Matthew 24:2). But Jesus took no delight in this prediction, weeping instead over the city that was too proud to admit that the Messiah had come. The blessings that could have been theirs for the taking would of necessity be withheld until a future day (see Acts 1:6–7).

who stands firm to the end will be
24:13 r Mt 10:22 saved.[r] 14 And this gospel of the kingdom[s] will be preached in the whole
24:14 s Mt 4:23 world[t] as a testimony to all nations, and
t Ro 10:18; then the end will come.
Col 1:6,23; 15 "So when you see standing in the
Lk 2:1; 4:5; Ac 11:28; 17:6; holy place[u] 'the abomination that causes
Rev 3:10; 16:14 desolation,'[a v] spoken of through the
24:15 prophet Daniel—let the reader under-
u Ac 6:13 v Da 9:27; 11:31; stand— 16 then let those who are in Judea
12:11 flee to the mountains. 17 Let no one on
24:17 the roof of his house[w] go down to take
w 1Sa 9:25; Mt 10:27; anything out of the house. 18 Let no one
Lk 12:3; Ac 10:9 in the field go back to get his cloak.
19 How dreadful it will be in those days for
24:19 x Lk 23:29 pregnant women and nursing mothers![x]
20 Pray that your flight will not take place
in winter or on the Sabbath. 21 For then
there will be great distress, unequaled
from the beginning of the world until
24:21 y Da 12:1; now—and never to be equaled again.[y]
Joel 2:2 22 If those days had not been cut short, no
24:22 one would survive, but for the sake of the
z ver 24,31 elect[z] those days will be shortened. 23 At
that time if anyone says to you, 'Look,
24:23 here is the Christ!' or, 'There he is!' do not
a Lk 17:23; 1:8 believe it.[a] 24 For false Christs and false
prophets will appear and perform great
24:24 signs and miracles[b] to deceive even the
b 2Th 2:9-11; Rev 13:13 elect—if that were possible. 25 See, I have
told you ahead of time.
26 "So if anyone tells you, 'There he is,
out in the desert,' do not go out; or, 'Here
24:27 he is, in the inner rooms,' do not believe
c Lk 17:24 d Mt 8:20 it. 27 For as lightning[c] that comes from
the east is visible even in the west, so will
be the coming of the Son of Man.[d]
24:28 28 Wherever there is a carcass, there the
e Lk 17:37 vultures will gather.[e]
29 "Immediately after the distress of
those days

" 'the sun will be darkened,
and the moon will not give its
24:29 light;
f Isa 13:10; 34:4; Eze 32:7; the stars will fall from the sky,
Joel 2:10,31; Zep 1:15; and the heavenly bodies will be
Rev 6:12,13; 8:12 shaken.'[b f]

30 "At that time the sign of the Son of
24:30 Man will appear in the sky, and all the
g Da 7:13; Rev 1:7 nations of the earth will mourn. They
will see the Son of Man coming on the
24:31 clouds of the sky,[g] with power and great
h Mt 13:41 i Isa 27:13; glory. 31 And he will send his angels[h] with
Zec 9:14; 1Co 15:52; a loud trumpet call,[i] and they will gath-
1Th 4:16; Rev 8:2; 10:7; er his elect from the four winds, from
11:15 one end of the heavens to the other.

WE SHOULD LIVE OUR LIVES AS THOUGH CHRIST WAS COMING THIS AFTERNOON.

Jimmy Carter,
American President

32 "Now learn this lesson from the fig
tree: As soon as its twigs get tender and
its leaves come out, you know that summer is near. 33 Even so, when you see all
these things, you know that it[c] is near, 24:33
right at the door.[j] 34 I tell you the truth, j Jas 5:9
this generation[d] will certainly not pass
away until all these things have hap- 24:34
pened.[k] 35 Heaven and earth will pass k Mt 16:28; 23:36
away, but my words will never pass away.[l]

The Day and Hour Unknown 24:35 l Mt 5:18

36 "No one knows about that day or 24:36
hour, not even the angels in heaven, nor m Ac 1:7
the Son,[e] but only the Father.[m] 37 As it
was in the days of Noah,[n] so it will be at 24:37 n Ge 6:5; 7:6-23
the coming of the Son of Man. 38 For in
the days before the flood, people were
eating and drinking, marrying and giv-
ing in marriage,[o] up to the day Noah en- 24:38 o Mt 22:30
tered the ark; 39 and they knew nothing
about what would happen until the flood
came and took them all away. That is
how it will be at the coming of the Son of
Man. 40 Two men will be in the field; one 24:40
will be taken and the other left.[p] 41 Two p Lk 17:34
women will be grinding with a hand mill; 24:41
one will be taken and the other left.[q] q Lk 17:35
42 "Therefore keep watch, because you
do not know on what day your Lord will 24:42
come.[r] 43 But understand this: If the r Mt 25:13; Lk 12:40
owner of the house had known at what
time of night the thief was coming,[s] he 24:43 s Lk 12:39
would have kept watch and would not
have let his house be broken into. 44 So 24:44
you also must be ready,[t] because the Son t 1Th 5:6
of Man will come at an hour when you
do not expect him.
45 "Who then is the faithful and wise 24:45
servant,[u] whom the master has put in u Mt 25:21,23
charge of the servants in his household
to give them their food at the proper
time? 46 It will be good for that servant
whose master finds him doing so when 24:46
he returns.[v] 47 I tell you the truth, he will v Rev 16:15

a 15 Daniel 9:27; 11:31; 12:11 *b 29* Isaiah 13:10; 34:4 *c 33* Or *he* *d 34* Or *race* *e 36* Some manuscripts do not have *nor the Son.*

DISCOVERY 246

KEEPING WATCH

Jesus was very clear about one fact regarding his return: The date itself is not important. What matters is the manner in which we live our lives while we wait. As people who love God, we want to live our lives to please him, and when Jesus comes back we want to be ready for him (1 Corinthians 1:4–9; Ephesians 5:8,10; Philippians 1:9–11; 1 Thessalonians 3:13; 5:23–24). In Matthew 24:32–51 Jesus used several illustrations to define the outlook he wants us to cultivate.

The first image is that of a fig tree (verses 32–35), a tree that generally produces two crops each year. The winter figs ripen in June, while the summer figs ripen in the early autumn. One of the distinctives of a fig tree is that the fruit buds appear before the leaves. A person can be certain that the figs are ripe only after the tree has leafed out. The disciples understood that Jesus was telling them to be on the lookout for the indicators that would point to his imminent return.

The second illustration is found in verses 36–39. As we consider all that God has told us in the Bible about his return, we would expect that people would be keenly alert to what is going on in the world around them. But life goes on as usual, just as it did during the many years when Noah was constructing his ark. Suddenly, however, God will carry out precisely what he has told us all along, and even his own people will be caught by surprise. When Jesus comes back, most of the world will be living in heedless ignorance of the signs that the time is approaching. Two people, Jesus told us, will be busily engaged in some daily activity, and seemingly without warning one will be snatched away into judgment, because the time of God's wrath will have arrived (verses 40–41).

In verses 43–44 Jesus pointed out that, if a homeowner were to have received advance warning that a thief would be arriving at a precise moment, he would be on guard, armed with a plan both to protect his property and to apprehend the criminal. Jesus wants his people to look for him with the same diligence as one who waits in the darkness in anticipation of a break-in.

In the final parable in this chapter, Jesus depicted a servant who was left in charge of a household during his master's extended absence (verses 45–51). As the master's return was delayed for a longer and longer period of time, the servant became careless and surly, beating his fellow servants and feasting on the household's fine food and drink. The master did finally return without advance notification, and the wicked servant received his just punishment.

Jesus' urgent advice in this chapter is that we should "keep watch" and "be ready" (verses 42–44). As we wait for our Lord to return, we are called to demonstrate to others what it means to belong to him, to be people who reflect his character both in attitude and in action. A wise servant does what his Master asks him to do, however trivial or simple the request might seem. Whether the task is something as mundane as building a birdhouse or as grandiose as building a monument, doing God's bidding as we wait for him is never a waste of our time!

***Self-Discovery:** In what specific ways are you preparing yourself for the second coming of Jesus? Is this an issue you discuss as a family?*

GO TO DISCOVERY 247 ON PAGE 1308

24:47 w Mt 25:21,23 put him in charge of all his possessions.[w]
48But suppose that servant is wicked
and says to himself, 'My master is staying away a long time,' 49and he then begins to beat his fellow servants and to
24:49 x Lk 21:34 eat and drink with drunkards.[x] 50The
master of that servant will come on a
day when he does not expect him and at
an hour he is not aware of. 51He will cut
him to pieces and assign him a place
24:51 y Mt 8:12 with the hypocrites, where there will be
weeping and gnashing of teeth.[y]

The Parable of the Ten Virgins

25:1 z Mt 13:24 a Lk 12:35-38; Ac 20:8; Rev 4:5 b Rev 19:7; 21:2 25 "At that time the kingdom of
heaven will be like[z] ten virgins
who took their lamps[a] and went out to
meet the bridegroom.[b] 2Five of them
25:2 c Mt 24:45 were foolish and five were wise.[c] 3The
foolish ones took their lamps but did
not take any oil with them. 4The wise,
however, took oil in jars along with their
lamps. 5The bridegroom was a long time
in coming, and they all became drowsy
25:5 d 1Th 5:6 and fell asleep.[d]
6"At midnight the cry rang out: 'Here's
the bridegroom! Come out to meet him!'
7"Then all the virgins woke up and
trimmed their lamps. 8The foolish ones
25:8 e Lk 12:35 said to the wise, 'Give us some of your
oil; our lamps are going out.'[e]
9" 'No,' they replied, 'there may not be
enough for both us and you. Instead, go
to those who sell oil and buy some for
yourselves.'
10"But while they were on their way to
buy the oil, the bridegroom arrived. The
25:10 f Rev 19:9 virgins who were ready went in with him
to the wedding banquet.[f] And the door
was shut.
11"Later the others also came. 'Sir! Sir!'
they said. 'Open the door for us!'
12"But he replied, 'I tell you the truth,
I don't know you.'
25:13 g Mt 24:42,44; Mk 13:35; Lk 12:40 13"Therefore keep watch, because you
do not know the day or the hour.[g]

The Parable of the Talents

25:14 h Mt 21:33; Lk 19:12 14"Again, it will be like a man going on
a journey,[h] who called his servants and
entrusted his property to them. 15To one
he gave five talents[a] of money, to anoth-
25:15 i Mt 18:24,25 er two talents, and to another one talent, each according to his ability.[i] Then
he went on his journey. 16The man who
had received the five talents went at
once and put his money to work and
gained five more. 17So also, the one with
the two talents gained two more. 18But
the man who had received the one talent went off, dug a hole in the ground
and hid his master's money.
19"After a long time the master of
those servants returned and settled ac- 25:19 j Mt 18:23
counts with them.[j] 20The man who had
received the five talents brought the
other five. 'Master,' he said, 'you entrusted me with five talents. See, I have
gained five more.'
21"His master replied, 'Well done,
good and faithful servant! You have been
faithful with a few things; I will put you 25:21 k ver 23; Mt 24:45,47; Lk 16:10
in charge of many things.[k] Come and
share your master's happiness!'
22"The man with the two talents also
came. 'Master,' he said, 'you entrusted
me with two talents; see, I have gained
two more.'
23"His master replied, 'Well done,
good and faithful servant! You have been
faithful with a few things; I will put you 25:23 l ver 21
in charge of many things.[l] Come and
share your master's happiness!'
24"Then the man who had received
the one talent came. 'Master,' he said, 'I
knew that you are a hard man, harvesting where you have not sown and gathering where you have not scattered seed.
25So I was afraid and went out and hid
your talent in the ground. See, here is
what belongs to you.'
26"His master replied, 'You wicked,
lazy servant! So you knew that I harvest
where I have not sown and gather where
I have not scattered seed? 27Well then,
you should have put my money on deposit with the bankers, so that when I
returned I would have received it back
with interest.
28" 'Take the talent from him and give
it to the one who has the ten talents.
29For everyone who has will be given
more, and he will have an abundance.
Whoever does not have, even what he 25:29 m Mt 13:12; Mk 4:25; Lk 8:18; 19:26
has will be taken from him.[m] 30And
throw that worthless servant outside,
into the darkness, where there will be 25:30 n Mt 8:12
weeping and gnashing of teeth.'[n]

The Sheep and the Goats

31"When the Son of Man comes[o] in 25:31 o Mt 16:27; Lk 17:30
his glory, and all the angels with him, he

[a] *15* A talent was worth more than a thousand dollars.

DISCOVERY 247

Preparing for Jesus' Return

When Jesus ascended into heaven, two angels appeared to the sorrowing disciples and assured them that their Lord would come back to them in the same way he had gone (Acts 1:10–11)—and Christians have been awaiting that day for nearly two thousand years. Before his crucifixion Jesus revealed to his disciples some details about the final days just prior to his return. Most of his instruction focused on how he wants his followers to live.

The first thing Jesus stressed is that we must *be prepared*. To drive home this point Jesus related a parable about five wise and five foolish virgins (Matthew 25:1–13). All ten young women were to be involved in a wedding celebration, and they were waiting for the bridegroom to arrive. The five who were prepared had brought extra oil for their lamps in case he should be delayed (verse 4). The foolish women, on the other hand, had come with only enough oil for the amount of time they had expected to wait. When the groom failed to arrive within the anticipated time frame, those virgins were compelled to leave in order to purchase more oil. But while they were on their errand the bridegroom arrived, and they missed the entire celebration. Jesus summarized the teaching of this parable in this way: "Therefore keep watch, because you do not know the day or the hour" (verse 13).

Jesus also wants us to *be involved*, and he told a second parable to illustrate how we can invest in his kingdom (verses 14–30). A rich man who went away on a journey entrusted three servants with varying amounts of money. Upon his return he discovered that two had invested well but that the third had done nothing with the amount he had been given. This servant was punished for his lack of initiative. God blesses us with all kinds of resources—money, possessions, abilities, intellect, relationships, time—and good stewardship of any of these can result in dividends for his kingdom cause. As we serve him with all that we are and all that we have, we long for the day when we will hear those wonderful words of commendation spoken by our precious Lord: "Well done, good and faithful servant! . . . Come and share your master's happiness" (verse 21).

The third point Jesus made is that he wants us to be *compassionate*. As we wait for Jesus' glorious return, we are called to help meet the needs of those around us so that they can perceive God's love expressed in very practical ways. We must seek out people who are hungry, thirsty, homeless, naked, sick or in prison (verses 34–36), those whom the world considers "least." And when we expend ourselves for someone in need, we reach out to Jesus himself (verse 40), who invites us who have served him with no thought of reward, "Come, you who are blessed by my Father; take your inheritance, the kingdom prepared for you since the creation of the world" (verse 34).

Self-Discovery: *Envision yourself standing before Jesus and hearing the words spoken to your personally: "Well done, good and faithful servant! . . . Come and share your master's happiness." What emotions does this scene call forth in you? Pause a moment to thank the Lord for such incomparable mercy.*

GO TO DISCOVERY 248 ON PAGE 1311

25:31 will sit on his throne[p] in heavenly glory.
[p] Mt 19:28 32All the nations will be gathered before
25:32 him, and he will separate[q] the people
[q] Mal 3:18 [r] Eze 34:17,20 one from another as a shepherd separates the sheep from the goats.[r] 33He will
put the sheep on his right and the goats
on his left.

34"Then the King will say to those on
25:34 his right, 'Come, you who are blessed by
[s] Mt 3:2; 5:3,10, 19; 19:14; my Father; take your inheritance, the
Ac 20:32; kingdom[s] prepared for you since the
1Co 15:50; creation of the world.[t] 35For I was hun-
Gal 5:21; Jas 2:5 [t] Heb 4:3; 9:26; gry and you gave me something to eat, I
Rev 13:8; 17:8 was thirsty and you gave me something
25:35 to drink, I was a stranger and you invit-
[u] Job 31:32; ed me in,[u] 36I needed clothes and you
Isa 58:7; Eze 18:7; clothed me,[v] I was sick and you looked
Heb 13:2 after me,[w] I was in prison and you came
25:36 to visit me.'[x]

[v] Isa 58:7; 37"Then the righteous will answer
Eze 18:7; him, 'Lord, when did we see you hungry
Jas 2:15,16 [w] Jas 1:27 and feed you, or thirsty and give you
[x] 2Ti 1:16 something to drink? 38When did we see
you a stranger and invite you in, or
needing clothes and clothe you? 39When
did we see you sick or in prison and go
to visit you?'

40"The King will reply, 'I tell you the
truth, whatever you did for one of the
25:40 least of these brothers of mine, you did
[y] Pr 19:17; Mt 10:40,42; for me.'[y]
Heb 6:10; 13:2 41"Then he will say to those on his left,
25:41 'Depart from me,[z] you who are cursed,
[z] Mt 7:23 into the eternal fire[a] prepared for the
[a] Isa 66:24; Mt 3:12;; 5:22; devil and his angels.[b] 42For I was hungry
Mk 9:43,48; Lk 3:17; Jude 7 and you gave me nothing to eat, I was
[b] 2Pe 2:4 thirsty and you gave me nothing to
drink, 43I was a stranger and you did not
invite me in, I needed clothes and you
did not clothe me, I was sick and in
prison and you did not look after me.'

44"They also will answer, 'Lord, when
did we see you hungry or thirsty or a
25:45 stranger or needing clothes or sick or in
[c] Pr 14:31; 17:5 prison, and did not help you?'
25:46 45"He will reply, 'I tell you the truth,
[d] Mt 19:29; whatever you did not do for one of the
Jn 3:15,16,36; 17:2,3; Ro 2:7; least of these, you did not do for me.'[c]
Gal 6:8; 5:11,13, 46"Then they will go away to eternal
20 [e] Da 12:2; Jn 5:29; punishment, but the righteous to eter-
Ac 24:15; Ro 2:7,8; nal life."[d][e]
Gal 6:8

The Plot Against Jesus

26:1 **26** When Jesus had finished saying
[f] Mt 7:28 all these things,[f] he said to his
26:2 [g] Jn 11:55; 13:1 disciples, 2"As you know, the Passover[g] is

FOLLOW HIM THROUGH ALL THE SCENES OF INSULT AND OUTRAGE ON THAT NIGHT AND MORNING OF HIS ARREST AND TRIAL . . . HOW HIS INHERENT GREATNESS COMES OUT. NOT ONCE DID HE LOSE HIS NOBLE BEARING OR HIS ROYAL DIGNITY.

C. I. Scofield, *American Theologian*

two days away—and the Son of Man will
be handed over to be crucified."

3Then the chief priests and the elders 26:3
of the people assembled[h] in the palace [h] Ps 2:2 [i] ver 57;
of the high priest, whose name was Ca- Jn 11:47-53;
iaphas,[i] 4and they plotted to arrest Jesus 18:13,14,24,28
in some sly way and kill him.[j] 5"But not 26:4 [j] Mt 12:14
during the Feast," they said, "or there 26:5
may be a riot[k] among the people." [k] Mt 27:24

Jesus Anointed at Bethany

6While Jesus was in Bethany[l] in the 26:6 [l] Mt 21:17
home of a man known as Simon the
Leper, 7a woman came to him with an
alabaster jar of very expensive perfume,
which she poured on his head as he was
reclining at the table.

8When the disciples saw this, they
were indignant. "Why this waste?" they
asked. 9"This perfume could have been
sold at a high price and the money giv-
en to the poor."

10Aware of this, Jesus said to them,
"Why are you bothering this woman?
She has done a beautiful thing to me.
11The poor you will always have with 26:11 [m] Dt 15:11
you,[m] but you will not always have me.
12When she poured this perfume on my 26:12
body, she did it to prepare me for burial.[n] [n] Jn 19:40
13I tell you the truth, wherever this
gospel is preached throughout the
world, what she has done will also be
told, in memory of her."

Judas Agrees to Betray Jesus

14Then one of the Twelve—the one 26:14
called Judas Iscariot[o]—went to the chief [o] ver 25,47;
priests 15and asked, "What are you will- Mt 10:4
ing to give me if I hand him over to you?" 26:15
So they counted out for him thirty silver [p] Ex 21:32;
coins.[p] 16From then on Judas watched Zec 11:12
for an opportunity to hand him over.

THERE IS NO DEATH OF SIN WITHOUT THE DEATH OF CHRIST.

John Owen, *Puritan Pastor*

The Lord's Supper

17 On the first day of the Feast of Un-
26:17 [q]Ex 12:18-20 leavened Bread,[q] the disciples came to
Jesus and asked, "Where do you want us
to make preparations for you to eat the
Passover?"

18 He replied, "Go into the city to a cer-
26:18 [r]Jn 7:6,8,30; 12:23; 13:1; 17:1 tain man and tell him, 'The Teacher
says: My appointed time[r] is near. I am
going to celebrate the Passover with my
disciples at your house.' " 19 So the disciples did as Jesus had directed them and
prepared the Passover.

20 When evening came, Jesus was reclining at the table with the Twelve. 21 And
26:21 [s]Lk 22:21-23; Jn 13:21 while they were eating, he said, "I tell you
the truth, one of you will betray me."[s]

22 They were very sad and began to say
to him one after the other, "Surely not I,
Lord?"

23 Jesus replied, "The one who has
dipped his hand into the bowl with me
will betray me.[t] 24 The Son of Man will go 26:23 [t]Ps 41:9; Jn 13:18
just as it is written about him.[u] But woe
to that man who betrays the Son of 26:24 [u]Isa 53; Da 9:26; Mk 9:12; Lk 24:25-27,46; Ac 17:2,3; 26:22,23
Man! It would be better for him if he had
not been born."

25 Then Judas, the one who would betray him, said, "Surely not I, Rabbi?"[v]

Jesus answered, "Yes, it is you."[a]

26 While they were eating, Jesus took 26:25 [v]Mt 23:7
bread, gave thanks and broke it,[w] and
gave it to his disciples, saying, "Take and 26:26 [w]Mt 14:19; 1Co 10:16
eat; this is my body."

27 Then he took the cup, gave thanks
and offered it to them, saying, "Drink
from it, all of you. 28 This is my blood of
the[b] covenant,[x] which is poured out for 26:28 [x]Ex 24:6-8; Heb 9:20 [y]Mt 20:28; Mk 1:4
many for the forgiveness of sins.[y] 29 I tell
you, I will not drink of this fruit of the
vine from now on until that day when I
drink it anew with you[z] in my Father's 26:29 [z]Ac 10:41
kingdom."

30 When they had sung a hymn, they 26:30 [a]Mt 21:1; Mk 14:26
went out to the Mount of Olives.[a]

Jesus Predicts Peter's Denial

31 Then Jesus told them, "This very
night you will all fall away on account of 26:31 [b]Mt 11:6 [c]Zec 13:7; Jn 16:32
me,[b] for it is written:

" 'I will strike the shepherd,
and the sheep of the flock will be
scattered.'[c][c]

32 But after I have risen, I will go ahead of 26:32 [d]Mt 28:7,10,16
you into Galilee."[d]

33 Peter replied, "Even if all fall away
on account of you, I never will."

34 "I tell you the truth," Jesus answered,
"this very night, before the rooster 26:34 [e]ver 75; Jn 13:38
crows, you will disown me three times."[e]

35 But Peter declared, "Even if I have to
die with you,[f] I will never disown you." 26:35 [f]Jn 13:37
And all the other disciples said the
same.

Gethsemane

36 Then Jesus went with his disciples
to a place called Gethsemane, and he
said to them, "Sit here while I go over
there and pray." 37 He took Peter and the 26:37 [g]Mt 4:21
two sons of Zebedee[g] along with him,
and he began to be sorrowful and troubled. 38 Then he said to them, "My soul is
overwhelmed with sorrow[h] to the point 26:38 [h]Jn 12:27 [i]ver 40,41
of death. Stay here and keep watch
with me."[i]

[a] 25 Or *"You yourself have said it"* [b] 28 Some manuscripts *the new* [c] 31 Zech. 13:7

ONE LAST MEAL

Jesus ate a final Passover meal with his disciples on the night prior to his crucifixion. This Passover celebration, like all others before it, included all of the required elements: bread, wine, roasted lamb and bitter herbs. Jesus employed two Passover symbols to explain the meaning of his own imminent death. The bread symbolized his body and the cup of wine his blood. By making this association, Jesus ordained a new celebration: the sacrament of the Lord's Supper (Matthew 26:17–29). Jesus himself would be the "lamb" who would be sacrificed for our sins, and the shedding of his blood would do more than any prior sacrifice could ever have accomplished (John 1:29; Ephesians 1:7; 1 Peter 1:18–19; Revelation 5:9). Rather than glossing over our sin, Jesus' death on our behalf eradicated that sin entirely. Jesus was the Passover lamb who removed once and for all the bitter herbs of sin (Isaiah 53:7; 1 Corinthians 5:7). But he left behind the bread and the wine as a memorial of what he was about to do for his people (1 Corinthians 11:23–26).

DISCOVERY 248

Not as I Will

Gethsemane—the name has come to signify a place of intense suffering and courageous submission. After Jesus had celebrated the Passover with his disciples, the group went together to the garden of Gethsemane. Jesus asked his friends to keep watch while he prayed alone a short distance away. That prayer was so full of anguish that "his sweat was like drops of blood falling to the ground" (Luke 22:44).

Prayer is one of the disciplines of a godly life believers frequently find difficult to completely understand. To an outsider who is unfamiliar with the language many Christians use in prayer, the whole concept may seem intimidating or even baffling. But God never intended that talking with him should be threatening. His desire is that prayer be more like an intimate conversation than a profound theological discourse. Jesus began his own prayer with "my Father," and he had instructed his disciples to address God in the same manner when they approached him in prayer (see Luke 11:2).

True prayer requires honesty—both with ourselves and with God. That night in the garden Jesus knew full well that he was about to be arrested, and with every ounce of human emotion he dreaded and resisted the prospect of death on a cross. "If it is possible," he pleaded with his Father, "may this cup be taken from me" (Matthew 26:39). Jesus of course knew that his request ran contrary to God's eternal design, but he expressed his emotions honestly. "If it [were] possible" he would have preferred to avoid the anguish ahead of him. This entreaty was not a sign of weakness, however; it was an expression of candor and authenticity. In the same way, when we face seemingly unbearable suffering, it is perfectly legitimate for us to plead with our heavenly Father to deliver us from the pain.

But when we approach God in a prayer like this, we have to be willing in advance to submit to whatever he decides is best. Jesus didn't look forward to the pain, but he had the wisdom and the courage to add, "Yet not as I will, but as you will," an acknowledgement that his Father's will had to take priority over his own personal preference. When we come into God's presence in this spirit of humble submission, of willingness to surrender control, to let go into the loving arms of the Father, we know in advance that while he may not change our circumstances he will most definitely change *us* through the experience.

Self-Discovery: *Think back to a particular situation in which you found it difficult to surrender control and submit to God's will. In what way did he reveal to you that your particular request or desire was not in line with his will? How did the Holy Spirit help you to resolve the issue?*

GO TO DISCOVERY 249 ON PAGE 1315

39Going a little farther, he fell with his
26:39 [j] Mt 20:22; [k] ver 42; Ps 40:6-8; Isa 50:5; Jn 5:30; 6:38 face to the ground and prayed, "My Father, if it is possible, may this cup[j] be
taken from me. Yet not as I will, but as
you will."[k]
40Then he returned to his disciples
and found them sleeping. "Could you
26:40 [l] ver 38 men not keep watch with me[l] for one
hour?" he asked Peter. 41"Watch and
26:41 [m] Mt 6:13 pray so that you will not fall into temptation.[m] The spirit is willing, but the
body is weak."
42He went away a second time and
prayed, "My Father, if it is not possible
for this cup to be taken away unless I
drink it, may your will be done."
43When he came back, he again found
them sleeping, because their eyes were
heavy. 44So he left them and went away
once more and prayed the third time,
saying the same thing.
45Then he returned to the disciples
26:45 [n] ver 18 and said to them, "Are you still sleeping
and resting? Look, the hour[n] is near, and
the Son of Man is betrayed into the
hands of sinners. 46Rise, let us go! Here
comes my betrayer!"

Jesus Arrested

47While he was still speaking, Judas,
one of the Twelve, arrived. With him was
a large crowd armed with swords and
clubs, sent from the chief priests and the
elders of the people. 48Now the betrayer
had arranged a signal with them: "The
one I kiss is the man; arrest him." 49Go-
ing at once to Jesus, Judas said, "Greet-
26:49 [o] ver 25 ings, Rabbi!"[o] and kissed him.
50Jesus replied, "Friend,[p] do what you
26:50 [p] Mt 20:13; 22:12 came for."[a]
Then the men stepped forward,
seized Jesus and arrested him. 51With
that, one of Jesus' companions reached
26:51 [q] Lk 22:36,38 [r] Jn 18:10 for his sword,[q] drew it out and struck
the servant of the high priest, cutting off
his ear.[r]
52"Put your sword back in its place,"
26:52 [s] Ge 9:6; Rev 13:10 Jesus said to him, "for all who draw the
sword will die by the sword.[s] 53Do you
think I cannot call on my Father, and he
26:53 [t] 2Ki 6:17; Da 7:10; Mt 4:11 will at once put at my disposal more
than twelve legions of angels?[t] 54But how
then would the Scriptures be fulfilled[u]
26:54 [u] ver 24 that say it must happen in this way?"
55At that time Jesus said to the crowd,
"Am I leading a rebellion, that you have
come out with swords and clubs to cap-

> THE ROMANS SAW HIM AS A TROUBLEMAKER . . . BUT I DON'T THINK THEY FELT HE WAS A DANGEROUS REVOLUTIONARY. IN THAT CASE, THEY WOULD HAVE KILLED THE WHOLE BAND.
>
> 
>
> Karen Armstrong, *American Author*

ture me? Every day I sat in the temple 26:55 [v] Mk 12:35; Lk 21:37; Jn 7:14,28; 18:20
courts teaching,[v] and you did not arrest
me. 56But this has all taken place that
the writings of the prophets might be
fulfilled."[w] Then all the disciples desert- 26:56 [w] ver 24
ed him and fled.

Before the Sanhedrin

57Those who had arrested Jesus took 26:57 [x] ver 3
him to Caiaphas,[x] the high priest, where
the teachers of the law and the elders
had assembled. 58But Peter followed him
at a distance, right up to the courtyard
of the high priest.[y] He entered and sat 26:58 [y] Jn 18:15 [z] Jn 7:32,45,46
down with the guards[z] to see the out-
come.
59The chief priests and the whole San-
hedrin[a] were looking for false evidence 26:59 [a] Mt 5:22
against Jesus so that they could put him
to death. 60But they did not find any,
though many false witnesses[b] came for- 26:60 [b] Ps 27:12; 35:11; Ac 6:13 [c] Dt 19:15
ward.
Finally two[c] came forward 61and declared, "This fellow said, 'I am able to destroy the temple of God and rebuild it in 26:61 [d] Jn 2:19
three days.' "[d]
62Then the high priest stood up and
said to Jesus, "Are you not going to answer? What is this testimony that these
men are bringing against you?" 63But
Jesus remained silent.[e] 26:63 [e] Mt 27:12,14 [f] Lev 5:1 [g] Mt 16:16
The high priest said to him, "I charge
you under oath[f] by the living God:[g] Tell
us if you are the Christ,[b] the Son of God."
64"Yes, it is as you say," Jesus replied.
"But I say to all of you: In the future you
will see the Son of Man sitting at the
right hand of the Mighty One[h] and com- 26:64 [h] Ps 110:1 [i] Da 7:13; Rev 1:7
ing on the clouds of heaven."[i]
65Then the high priest tore his
clothes[j] and said, "He has spoken blas- 26:65 [j] Mk 14:63
phemy! Why do we need any more wit-
nesses? Look, now you have heard the
blasphemy. 66What do you think?"

[a] 50 Or *"Friend, why have you come?"* [b] 63 Or *Messiah*; also in verse 68

26:66 [k]Lev 24:16; Jn 19:7 "He is worthy of death,"[k] they answered.
26:67 [l]Mt 16:21; 27:30 67Then they spit in his face and struck
him with their fists.[l] Others slapped him
26:68 [m]Lk 22:63-65 68and said, "Prophesy to us, Christ. Who
hit you?"[m]

Peter Disowns Jesus

69Now Peter was sitting out in the
courtyard, and a servant girl came to
him. "You also were with Jesus of Galilee," she said.
70But he denied it before them all. "I
don't know what you're talking about,"
he said.
71Then he went out to the gateway,
where another girl saw him and said to
the people there, "This fellow was with
Jesus of Nazareth."
72He denied it again, with an oath: "I
don't know the man!"
73After a little while, those standing
there went up to Peter and said, "Surely
you are one of them, for your accent
gives you away."
74Then he began to call down curses
on himself and he swore to them, "I
don't know the man!"
Immediately a rooster crowed. 75Then
Peter remembered the word Jesus had
spoken: "Before the rooster crows, you
will disown me three times."[n] And he 26:75 [n]ver 34; Jn 13:38
went outside and wept bitterly.

Judas Hangs Himself

27 Early in the morning, all the
chief priests and the elders of
the people came to the decision to put 27:1 [o]Mt 12:14; Mk 15:1; Lk 22:66
Jesus to death.[o] 2They bound him, led
him away and handed him over[p] to Pi-
late, the governor.[q] 27:2 [p]Mt 20:19 [q]Mk 15:1; Lk 13:1; Ac 3:13; 1Ti 6:13
3When Judas, who had betrayed him,[r]
saw that Jesus was condemned, he was
seized with remorse and returned the
thirty silver coins[s] to the chief priests
and the elders. 4"I have sinned," he said, 27:3 [r]Mt 10:4 [s]Mt 26:14,15
"for I have betrayed innocent blood."
"What is that to us?" they replied.
"That's your responsibility."[t] 27:4 [t]ver 24
5So Judas threw the money into the
temple[u] and left. Then he went away 27:5 [u]Lk 1:9,21 [v]Ac 1:18
and hanged himself.[v]
6The chief priests picked up the coins
and said, "It is against the law to put this
into the treasury, since it is blood money." 7So they decided to use the money to
buy the potter's field as a burial place for
foreigners. 8That is why it has been 27:8 [w]Ac 1:19
called the Field of Blood[w] to this day.
9Then what was spoken by Jeremiah the 27:9 [x]Mt 1:22
prophet was fulfilled:[x] "They took the
thirty silver coins, the price set on him
by the people of Israel, 10and they used
them to buy the potter's field, as the 27:10 [y]Zec 11:12,13; Jer 32:6-9
Lord commanded me."[a][y]

Jesus Before Pilate

11Meanwhile Jesus stood before the
governor, and the governor asked him, 27:11 [z]Mt 2:2
"Are you the king of the Jews?"[z]
"Yes, it is as you say," Jesus replied.
12When he was accused by the chief
priests and the elders, he gave no an- 27:12 [a]Mt 26:63; Mk 14:61; Jn 19:9
swer.[a] 13Then Pilate asked him, "Don't
you hear the testimony they are bring-
ing against you?"[b] 14But Jesus made no 27:13 [b]Mt 26:62
reply,[c] not even to a single charge—to
the great amazement of the governor. 27:14 [c]Mk 14:61
15Now it was the governor's custom at
the Feast to release a prisoner[d] chosen 27:15 [d]Jn 18:39
by the crowd. 16At that time they had a
notorious prisoner, called Barabbas. 17So

[a] 10 See Zech. 11:12,13; Jer. 19:1–13; 32:6–9.

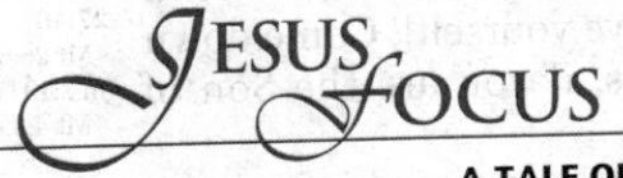

A TALE OF TWO CHOICES

Judas and Peter were two men with radically different characters and destinies. Judas was the only Judean among the disciples, and he held a position of honor as their treasurer. But in the end he fell victim to the lure of the very money he had so closely guarded when, as the prophet Zechariah had predicted, he turned Jesus over to the authorities for 30 pieces of silver (Zechariah 11:12). Peter also was a trusted leader and spokesman for the group. He swore that he would never fall away (Matthew 26:31–35), but sadly, when Jesus was on trial, Peter three times denied that he even knew the Master (verses 69–75). Each of these disciples failed miserably, but we remember the two with drastically different emotions. After turning away from Jesus, Judas continued running and ended up taking his own life in despair. But Peter stopped short, turned back and mourned that he had ever allowed his fear to dictate his actions. Peter, like Judas, could have missed the opportunity for reconciliation, but he didn't. The breaking of Peter's pride set the scene for the making of his character, and he was restored to his place of service (see John 21:15–19).

when the crowd had gathered, Pilate
asked them, "Which one do you want
27:17 me to release to you: Barabbas, or Jesus
[e] ver 22; Mt 1:16 who is called Christ?"[e] 18For he knew it
was out of envy that they had handed
Jesus over to him.
27:19 19While Pilate was sitting on the
[f] Jn 19:13 [g] ver 24 judge's seat,[f] his wife sent him this mes-
[h] Ge 20:6; Nu 12:6; sage: "Don't have anything to do with
1Ki 3:5; that innocent[g] man, for I have suffered a
Job 33:14-16; great deal today in a dream[h] because of
Mt 1:20; 2:12, 13,19,22 him."
20But the chief priests and the elders
27:20 persuaded the crowd to ask for Barab-
[i] Ac 3:14 bas and to have Jesus executed.[i]
21"Which of the two do you want me
to release to you?" asked the governor.
"Barabbas," they answered.
27:22 22"What shall I do, then, with Jesus
[j] Mt 1:16 who is called Christ?"[j] Pilate asked.
They all answered, "Crucify him!"
23"Why? What crime has he committed?" asked Pilate.
But they shouted all the louder, "Crucify him!"
24When Pilate saw that he was getting
27:24 [k] Mt 26:5 nowhere, but that instead an uproar[k]
[l] Ps 26:6 was starting, he took water and washed
[m] Dt 21:6-8 [n] ver 4 his hands[l] in front of the crowd. "I am
innocent of this man's blood,"[m] he said.
"It is your responsibility!"[n]
27:25 25All the people answered, "Let his
[o] Jos 2:19; Ac 5:28 blood be on us and on our children!"[o]
27:26 26Then he released Barabbas to them.
[p] Isa 53:5; But he had Jesus flogged,[p] and handed
Jn 19:1 him over to be crucified.

The Soldiers Mock Jesus

27:27 27Then the governor's soldiers took
[q] Jn 18:28,33; Jesus into the Praetorium[q] and gathered
19:9 the whole company of soldiers around
27:28 him. 28They stripped him and put a
[r] Jn 19:2 scarlet robe on him,[r] 29and then twisted
together a crown of thorns and set it on
his head. They put a staff in his right
hand and knelt in front of him and
27:29 mocked him. "Hail, king of the Jews!"
[s] Isa 53:3; Jn 19:2,3 they said.[s] 30They spit on him, and took
27:30 the staff and struck him on the head
[t] Mt 16:21; again and again.[t] 31After they had
26:67 mocked him, they took off the robe and
27:31 put his own clothes on him. Then they
[u] Isa 53:7 led him away to crucify him.[u]

27:32 *The Crucifixion*

[v] Heb 13:12 [w] Ac 2:10; 6:9; 32As they were going out,[v] they met a
11:20; 13:1 man from Cyrene,[w] named Simon, and

THE CROSS OF CHRIST MUST BE EITHER THE DARKEST SPOT OF ALL IN THE MYSTERY OF EXISTENCE OR A SEARCHLIGHT BY THE AID OF WHICH WE MAY PENETRATE THE SURROUNDING GLOOM.

Burnett H. Streeter, *Oxford Professor*

they forced him to carry the cross.[x] 27:32 [x] Mk 15:21;
33They came to a place called Golgotha Lk 23:26
(which means The Place of the Skull).[y] 27:33
34There they offered Jesus wine to drink, [y] Jn 19:17
mixed with gall;[z] but after tasting it, he
refused to drink it. 35When they had 27:34
crucified him, they divided up his [z] ver 48; Ps 69:21
clothes by casting lots.[a a] 36And sitting 27:35
down, they kept watch[b] over him there. [a] Ps 22:18
37Above his head they placed the written 27:36
charge against him: THIS IS JESUS, THE KING [b] ver 54
OF THE JEWS. 38Two robbers were cruci- 27:38
fied with him,[c] one on his right and one [c] Isa 53:12
on his left. 39Those who passed by
hurled insults at him, shaking their 27:39
heads[d] 40and saying, "You who are going [d] Ps 22:7;
to destroy the temple and build it in 109:25; La 2:15
three days,[e] save yourself![f] Come down 27:40
from the cross, if you are the Son of [e] Mt 26:61;
God!"[g] Jn 2:19 [f] ver 42 [g] Mt 4:3,6
41In the same way the chief priests,
the teachers of the law and the elders
mocked him. 42"He saved others," they
said, "but he can't save himself! He's the
King of Israel![h] Let him come down now 27:42 [h] Jn 1:49; 12:13
from the cross, and we will believe[i] in [i] Jn 3:15
him. 43He trusts in God. Let God rescue 27:43
him[j] now if he wants him, for he said, 'I [j] Ps 22:8
am the Son of God.'" 44In the same way
the robbers who were crucified with him
also heaped insults on him.

The Death of Jesus

45From the sixth hour until the ninth 27:45
hour darkness[k] came over all the land. [k] Am 8:9
46About the ninth hour Jesus cried out
in a loud voice, *"Eloi, Eloi,*[b] *lama
sabachthani?"*—which means, "My God, 27:46
my God, why have you forsaken me?"[c l] [l] Ps 22:1
47When some of those standing there
heard this, they said, "He's calling Elijah."
48Immediately one of them ran and

[a] 35 A few late manuscripts *lots that the word spoken by the prophet might be fulfilled: "They divided my garments among themselves and cast lots for my clothing"* (Psalm 22:18) [b] 46 Some manuscripts *Eli, Eli* [c] 46 Psalm 22:1

DISCOVERY 249

Forsaken But Not Abandoned

As Jesus hung dying on the cross, an eerie and impenetrable darkness enveloped the land from noon until three o'clock. In the Bible darkness is often used as a metaphor for God's judgment: When Jesus comes back again and God judges the world for having refused his offer of life through his Son, "the sun will be darkened, and the moon will not give its light" (Matthew 24:29). Darkness is also used to describe the appalling terrors of hell (Matthew 8:12; 2 Peter 2:17). Jesus hung on the cross enshrouded in darkness, enduring both the Father's judgment and the anguish of hell on our behalf.

When the three hours of darkness had come to an end, Jesus cried out to his Father in torment: "My God, my God, why have you forsaken me?" (Matthew 27:46). Did God actually abandon his own Son? If so, we wonder how he could have done something so horrendous—this would, after all, have implied God abandoning God! Being abandoned, however, is not the same as being forsaken. Jesus knew in advance precisely what his suffering and death would entail, and yet he had declared to his disciples that, even though *they* would abandon him, his Father in heaven would never do so (John 16:32).

To abandon someone means to turn away from that individual and to leave him or her utterly alone. The word *forsake* has a different meaning: to leave someone temporarily alone to bear the consequences of his present circumstances, to decline to intervene on her behalf (Acts 2:27,31). Jesus was not implying that his Father had abandoned him, never to return. Rather, he was crying out: "Why are you leaving me on the cross? Why have you not delivered me?" (see Psalm 22). As God, Jesus had known from the beginning of time the why of his crucifixion, but as man he still cried out for deliverance. At the same time Jesus was fully aware that if God were to have intervened there would have been no possibility of atonement for our sins, and we would have been left without hope, ourselves abandoned to the despair of eternal darkness and separation from God (Ephesians 2:11–13).

God is always at our side, but he does not always intervene to ease or remove our sufferings (1 Peter 1:6). In the same way that God the Father allowed his own Son to die on the cross so that he could accomplish the greatest act of all time, our eternal salvation from sin, so God sometimes allows us to walk "alone" through a dark valley in order that he might accomplish a greater purpose in our life (Hebrews 12:1–3; 1 Peter 5:10).

Self-Discovery: *Can you recall a time when you felt forsaken or alone? Try to recall the feelings associated with this difficult time. Then try to imagine how Jesus must have felt during the time he was forsaken by his Father.*

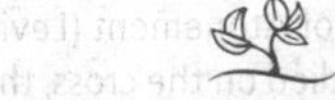

GO TO DISCOVERY 250 ON PAGE 1317

27:48 got a sponge. He filled it with wine vine-
[m] ver 34; gar,[m] put it on a stick, and offered it to
Ps 69:21 Jesus to drink. 49 The rest said, "Now
leave him alone. Let's see if Elijah comes
to save him."
27:50 50 And when Jesus had cried out again
[n] Jn 19:30 in a loud voice, he gave up his spirit.[n]
27:51 51 At that moment the curtain of the
[o] Ex 26:31-33; temple[o] was torn in two from top to bot-
Heb 9:3,8 tom. The earth shook and the rocks
[p] ver 54 split.[p] 52 The tombs broke open and the
bodies of many holy people who had
died were raised to life. 53 They came out
27:53 of the tombs, and after Jesus' resurrec-
[q] Mt 4:5 tion they went into the holy city[q] and
appeared to many people.
54 When the centurion and those with
27:54 him who were guarding[r] Jesus saw the
[r] ver 36 [s] Mt 4:3; 17:5 earthquake and all that had happened,
they were terrified, and exclaimed,
"Surely he was the Son[a] of God!"[s]
55 Many women were there, watching
from a distance. They had followed Jesus
27:55 from Galilee to care for his needs.[t]
[t] Lk 8:2,3 56 Among them were Mary Magdalene,
27:56 Mary the mother of James and Joses,
[u] Mk 15:47; Lk 24:10; Jn 19:25 and the mother of Zebedee's sons.[u]

The Burial of Jesus

57 As evening approached, there came
a rich man from Arimathea, named Joseph, who had himself become a disciple of Jesus. 58 Going to Pilate, he asked
for Jesus' body, and Pilate ordered that it
be given to him. 59 Joseph took the body,
wrapped it in a clean linen cloth, 60 and
placed it in his own new tomb[v] that he 27:60 [v] Mt 27:66; 28:2;
had cut out of the rock. He rolled a big Mk 16:4
stone in front of the entrance to the
tomb and went away. 61 Mary Magdalene
and the other Mary were sitting there
opposite the tomb.

The Guard at the Tomb

62 The next day, the one after Preparation Day, the chief priests and the Pharisees went to Pilate. 63 "Sir," they said, "we
remember that while he was still alive
that deceiver said, 'After three days I will
rise again.'[w] 64 So give the order for the 27:63 [w] Mt 16:21
tomb to be made secure until the third
day. Otherwise, his disciples may come
and steal the body and tell the people
that he has been raised from the dead.
This last deception will be worse than
the first."
65 "Take a guard,"[x] Pilate answered. 27:65 [x] ver 66;
"Go, make the tomb as secure as you Mt 28:11
know how." 66 So they went and made the
tomb secure by putting a seal[y] on the 27:66 [y] Da 6:17
stone[z] and posting the guard.[a] [z] ver 60; Mt 28:2 [a] Mt 28:11

> THE DAY OF THE CRUCIFIXION IS OF HISTORICAL INTEREST, BUT WHAT IS OF ETERNAL IMPORTANCE . . . IS NOT WHEN CHRIST DIED BUT THAT HE DIED.
>
> W. Graham Scroggie, *British Theologian*

The Resurrection

28 After the Sabbath, at dawn on
the first day of the week, Mary
Magdalene and the other Mary[b] went to 28:1 [b] Mt 27:56
look at the tomb.
2 There was a violent earthquake,[c] for 28:2 [c] Mt 27:51
an angel[d] of the Lord came down from [d] Jn 20:12
heaven and, going to the tomb, rolled
back the stone and sat on it. 3 His appearance was like lightning, and his 28:3
clothes were white as snow.[e] 4 The [e] Da 10:6; Mk 9:3; Jn 20:12
guards were so afraid of him that they
shook and became like dead men.
5 The angel said to the women, "Do 28:5
not be afraid,[f] for I know that you are [f] ver 10; Mt 14:27
looking for Jesus, who was crucified. 6 He
is not here; he has risen, just as he said.[g] 28:6 [g] Mt 16:21
Come and see the place where he lay.

[a] 54 Or *a son*

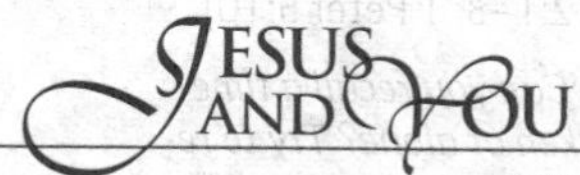

THE CURTAIN IS TORN

A massive curtain hung in Jerusalem's temple, separating the Most Holy Place from the rest of the temple (Exodus 26:31–33). Only the high priest was allowed to go behind the curtain into God's presence—and he was permitted to do so only once each year on the Day of Atonement (Leviticus 16:1–17). When Jesus died on the cross, that massive curtain was miraculously torn from top to bottom (Matthew 27:51) as a sign to God's people that they no longer had to be separated from him (see Hebrews 9:1–14; 10:19–22). Today we too can approach God the Father unhindered (Ephesians 2:18; 3:12; Hebrews 4:14–16), because the shed blood of Jesus has eradicated our sins and given us the incredible opportunity of free and direct access to God.

The Great Commission

The last recorded words of Jesus in Matthew's Gospel are: "All authority in heaven and on earth has been given to me. Therefore go and make disciples of all nations, baptizing them in the name of the Father and of the Son and of the Holy Spirit, and teaching them to obey everything I have commanded you. And surely I am with you always, to the very end of the age" (Matthew 28:18–20). We call these words the "Great Commission." For centuries Jesus' directive has served as the "marching orders" for his church, reminding us of his purpose, a purpose he has passed on to his followers.

Our mission has one priority: "Make disciples." Jesus didn't ask us to construct imposing edifices in his name or to administer well-organized and well-funded programs. He directed us only to help other people to get to know him, to encourage and teach them what it means to follow him.

Jesus even instructed us as to how to go about fulfilling this mission. First, we are to talk to other people about him. Next we should encourage them to be baptized as a way of identifying with Jesus and his people. Finally, we are to teach them the things of God and help to build them up in their faith. As they get to know God they will naturally begin to talk to others about him, and the cycle of discipleship will continue.

Finally, our Savior's words have left us with two promises. God had endowed Jesus with the authority to do whatever was necessary, and before the Son's ascension Jesus passed that same awesome authority on to each of us. Even more important, Jesus pledged that he would always go with us—we will never walk alone in our ministry of shining the light of Jesus wherever we go.

Of what greater honor could we begin to conceive than that of being called to be witnesses for our Lord Jesus Christ? Luke tells us that, just prior to Jesus' ascension, he empowered his disciples with these stirring words: "You will receive power when the Holy Spirit comes on you; and you will be my witnesses in Jerusalem, and in all Judea and Samaria, and to the ends of the earth" (Acts 1:7–8).

Already in the Old Testament the prophet Isaiah used an image that, while referring immediately to the messengers who ran from the scene of a battle to bring news of the outcome to a waiting king and people, prefigured the faithful witnesses who would bring to the world the Good News of salvation: "How beautiful on the mountains are the feet of those who bring good news, who proclaim peace, who bring good tidings, who proclaim salvation" (Isaiah 52:7).

May we take our commission seriously, whether we are called to share the gospel message in our own corner of the world (to our spouses, children, grandchildren, parents, brothers, sisters, next-door neighbors, colleagues, mothers in our children's play group, or "chance" associates) or in far-flung places. Pray for the Spirit's empowerment, and rejoice that you have been given the privilege of sharing the "reason for the hope that you have" (1 Peter 3:15).

Self-Discovery: *When was the last time you presented the gospel message to someone? When was the last time you could have done so but didn't make the effort. What prevented you?*

GO TO DISCOVERY 251 ON PAGE 1323

7 Then go quickly and tell his disciples:
28:7 [h] ver 10,16; Mt 26:32 'He has risen from the dead and is going
ahead of you into Galilee.[h] There you
will see him.' Now I have told you."
8 So the women hurried away from the
tomb, afraid yet filled with joy, and ran
28:9 [i] Jn 20:14-18 to tell his disciples. 9 Suddenly Jesus met
them.[i] "Greetings," he said. They came
to him, clasped his feet and worshiped
28:10 [j] Jn 20:17; Ro 8:29; Heb 2:11-13,17 him. 10 Then Jesus said to them, "Do not
be afraid. Go and tell my brothers[j] to go
to Galilee; there they will see me."

The Guards' Report

11 While the women were on their way,
28:11 [k] Mt 27:65,66 some of the guards[k] went into the city
and reported to the chief priests every-
thing that had happened. 12 When the
chief priests had met with the elders and
devised a plan, they gave the soldiers a
large sum of money, 13 telling them, "You
are to say, 'His disciples came during the
night and stole him away while we were
asleep.' 14 If this report gets to the gover-
28:14 [l] Mt 27:2 nor,[l] we will satisfy him and keep you
out of trouble." 15 So the soldiers took the
money and did as they were instructed.
And this story has been widely circulat-
28:16 [m] ver 7,10; Mt 26:32 ed among the Jews to this very day.

The Great Commission

28:18 [n] Da 7:13,14; Lk 10:22; Jn 3:35; 17:2; 1Co 15:27; Eph 1:20-22; Php 2:9,10 16 Then the eleven disciples went to
Galilee, to the mountain where Jesus
had told them to go.[m] 17 When they saw
him, they worshiped him; but some
doubted. 18 Then Jesus came to them
28:19 [o] Mk 16:15,16; Lk 24:47; Ac 1:8; 14:21 [p] Ac 2:38; 8:16; Ro 6:3,4 and said, "All authority in heaven and on
earth has been given to me.[n] 19 Therefore
go and make disciples of all nations,[o]
baptizing them in[a] the name of the Father and of the Son and of the Holy Spir-
28:20 [q] Ac 2:42 [r] Mt 18:20; Ac 18:10 [s] Mt 13:39 it,[p] 20 and teaching[q] them to obey everything I have commanded you. And
surely I am with you[r] always, to the very
end of the age."[s]

[a] *19* Or *into*; see Acts 8:16; 19:5; Romans 6:3; 1 Cor. 1:13; 10:2 and Gal. 3:27.

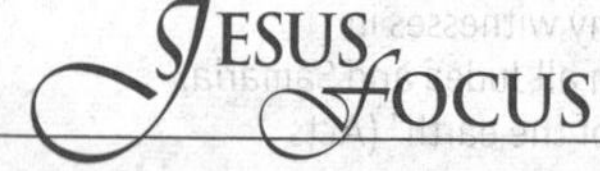

ALIVE AGAIN

Jesus was more than just a great teacher. He proved that he is God's cherished Son by coming back to life from the grave, and it is this truth that separates him from every other religious leader in history. In fact, it is our Lord's own resurrection that establishes his power to grant us eternal life (1 Corinthians 15:20–23; Ephesians 1:18–21). There were too many eyewitnesses for us to doubt the reality of the resurrection—hundreds of them, in fact (1 Corinthians 15:6). Not only that, but his followers were so committed to this truth that they preached it at the risk of death at every possible opportunity.

The Bible explicitly states that the gravestone had been moved and that our Savior's body was missing (Matthew 28). An angel of the Lord had in fact rolled back the stone that sealed the grave—not to let Jesus *out,* because he was already gone—but to let us *in* to see for ourselves the evidence of the empty tomb. That amazing truth still resonates in our souls today: "He is not here; he has risen" (verse 6).

CHRIST COMMISSIONED HIS DISCIPLES . . . THROUGHOUT THE CENTURIES TO CONTINUE HIS MINISTRY OF SEEKING AND SAVING THE LOST.

Bill Bright, *founder,*
Campus Crusade for Christ International

Why is self-denial a prerequisite to being a Christian? (Mark 8:34)

- *The kingdom of heaven belongs to those who are "poor in spirit" (Matthew 5:3)—those who recognize their spiritual poverty and acknowledge their need for God's help. Without asking us to deny our self-worth, Jesus asks us to deny our self-centeredness so that his priorities might become ours.*

Was Jesus advocating slavery in Mark 10:43–45?

- *Jesus wasn't endorsing the institution of slavery, but he used it as an object lesson in humility. His own willingness to submit to the Father's will, even to the point of death, is an example of servanthood lived out to its fullest.*

Why didn't Jesus know when he would come back on the clouds? (Mark 13:32)

- *When Jesus became human, he gave up the right to use his divine abilities for his own purposes (Philippians 2:6–8). Because Jesus submitted to the Father in everything, he left the matter of the timing of his return to the Father too.*

Jesus in Mark Mark's Gospel reads like a newspaper, written in simple sentences with action-packed scenes. Mark's fast-paced approach introduces Jesus Christ as the Servant of the Lord. Because of Mark's simple style, this Gospel is the best place to start for someone who doesn't know much about Jesus.

Mark's simple, uncomplicated style is primarily chronological as it follows Jesus' life and presents an overview of Jesus' ministry as he experiences both great popularity and deadly opposition. Mark's Gospel was directed to a non-Jewish audience, so references to the Old Testament are infrequent in his account. The majority of Mark's information also appears in the other three Gospel narratives, but pay careful attention to the emotional impact of this action-packed Gospel. More than forty percent of Mark focuses on the suffering and sacrifice of Jesus. As you read this book, look at the facts Mark recorded and pause to think about why Mark would have included them. Why were they important to the people in Jesus' day? Why are they important to you today?

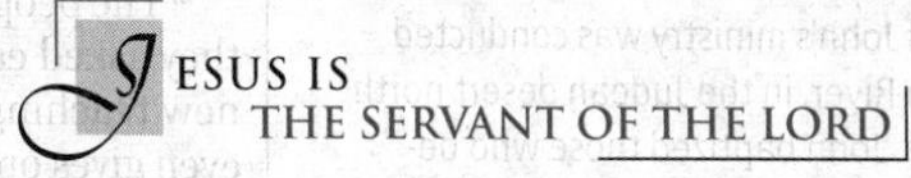

John the Baptist Prepares the Way

1 The beginning of the gospel about
1:1 a Mt 4:3 Jesus Christ, the Son of God.[a][a]

[2]It is written in Isaiah the prophet:

“I will send my messenger ahead of
1:2 b Mal 3:1; Mt 11:10; Lk 7:27 you,
who will prepare your way”[b][b]—
[3]“a voice of one calling in the desert,
1:3 ‘Prepare the way for the Lord,
c Isa 40:3; Jn 1:23 make straight paths for him.’ ”[c][c]

[4]And so John[d] came, baptizing in the
1:4 d Mt 3:1 desert region and preaching a baptism
e Ac 13:24 of repentance[e] for the forgiveness of
f Lk 1:77 sins.[f] [5]The whole Judean countryside
and all the people of Jerusalem went out
to him. Confessing their sins, they were
baptized by him in the Jordan River.
[6]John wore clothing made of camel's
hair, with a leather belt around his waist,
1:6 g Lev 11:22 and he ate locusts[g] and wild honey.
[7]And this was his message: “After me
will come one more powerful than I, the
thongs of whose sandals I am not wor-
1:7 h Ac 13:25 thy to stoop down and untie.[h] [8]I baptize
you with[d] water, but he will baptize you
1:8 i Isa 44:3; Joel 2:28; Ac 1:5; 2:4; 11:16; 19:4-6 with the Holy Spirit.”[i]

The Baptism and Temptation of Jesus

[9]At that time Jesus came from Naza-
1:9 j Mt 2:23 reth[j] in Galilee and was baptized by
John in the Jordan. [10]As Jesus was coming up out of the water, he saw heaven
being torn open and the Spirit descend-

JESUS FOCUS

A VOICE IN THE DESERT

John the Baptist appeared on the scene as a lone prophet, pleading with the nation of Israel to turn back to God because the Messiah was coming. In Mark 1:2–3 Mark quoted both Malachi 3:1 and Isaiah 40:3 as prophecies pointing to John the Baptist, the messenger who was to come before the Messiah as “a voice of one calling in the desert.” Most of John's ministry was conducted near the Jordan River, in the Judean desert north of the Dead Sea. John baptized those who believed his message to demonstrate that they had turned from their sins to prepare for the coming Messiah (Mark 1:4), but later on many of John's followers were baptized again after professing their belief that Jesus was truly the Son of God, the promised Messiah (Acts 19:1–7).

ing on him like a dove.[k] [11]And a voice 1:10 k Jn 1:32
came from heaven: “You are my Son,[l]
whom I love; with you I am well pleased.” 1:11 l Mt 3:17
[12]At once the Spirit sent him out into
the desert, [13]and he was in the desert
forty days, being tempted by Satan.[m] He 1:13 m Mt 4:10
was with the wild animals, and angels
attended him.

The Calling of the First Disciples

[14]After John was put in prison, Jesus 1:14 n Mt 4:12
went into Galilee,[n] proclaiming the good o Mt 4:23
news of God.[o] [15]“The time has come,”[p]
he said. “The kingdom of God is near. 1:15 p Gal 4:4;
Repent and believe the good news!”[q] Eph 1:10
[16]As Jesus walked beside the Sea of q Ac 20:21
Galilee, he saw Simon and his brother
Andrew casting a net into the lake, for
they were fishermen. [17]“Come, follow
me,” Jesus said, “and I will make you fishers of men.” [18]At once they left their nets
and followed him.
[19]When he had gone a little farther, he
saw James son of Zebedee and his
brother John in a boat, preparing their
nets. [20]Without delay he called them,
and they left their father Zebedee in the
boat with the hired men and followed
him.

Jesus Drives Out an Evil Spirit

[21]They went to Capernaum, and when
the Sabbath came, Jesus went into the 1:21
synagogue and began to teach.[r] [22]The r Mt 4:23;
people were amazed at his teaching, be- Mk 10:1
cause he taught them as one who had 1:22
authority, not as the teachers of the law.[s] s Mt 7:28,29
[23]Just then a man in their synagogue
who was possessed by an evil[e] spirit
cried out, [24]“What do you want with us,[t] 1:24 t Mt 8:29
Jesus of Nazareth?[u] Have you come to u Mt 2:23; Lk 24:19;
destroy us? I know who you are—the Ac 24:5
Holy One of God!”[v] v Lk 1:35; Jn 6:69; Ac 3:14
[25]“Be quiet!” said Jesus sternly. “Come
out of him!”[w] [26]The evil spirit shook the 1:25 w ver 34
man violently and came out of him with
a shriek.[x] 1:26 x Mk 9:20
[27]The people were all so amazed[y] that
they asked each other, “What is this? A 1:27 y Mk 10:24,32
new teaching—and with authority! He
even gives orders to evil spirits and they
obey him.” [28]News about him spread 1:28
quickly over the whole region[z] of Gali- z Mt 9:26
lee.

[a] *1* Some manuscripts do not have *the Son of God.*
[b] *2* Mal. 3:1 [c] *3* Isaiah 40:3 [d] *8* Or *in*
[e] *23* Greek *unclean;* also in verses 26 and 27

Jesus Heals Many

1:29 29As soon as they left the synagogue,[a]
a ver 21,23 they went with James and John to the
home of Simon and Andrew. 30Simon's
mother-in-law was in bed with a fever,
and they told Jesus about her. 31So he
1:31 went to her, took her hand and helped
b Lk 7:14 her up.[b] The fever left her and she began
to wait on them.
32That evening after sunset the people brought to Jesus all the sick and de-
1:32 c Mt 4:24 mon-possessed.[c] 33The whole town
1:34 gathered at the door, 34and Jesus healed
d Mt 4:23 many who had various diseases.[d] He
e Mk 3:12; also drove out many demons, but he
Ac 16:17,18 would not let the demons speak because
they knew who he was.[e]

Jesus Prays in a Solitary Place

35Very early in the morning, while it
was still dark, Jesus got up, left the house
1:35 and went off to a solitary place, where he
f Lk 3:21 prayed.[f] 36Simon and his companions
went to look for him, 37and when they
found him, they exclaimed: "Everyone is
looking for you!"
38Jesus replied, "Let us go somewhere
else—to the nearby villages—so I can
1:38 preach there also. That is why I have
g Isa 61:1 come."[g] 39So he traveled throughout Gal-
1:39 ilee, preaching in their synagogues[h] and
h Mt 4:23 driving out demons.[i]
i Mt 4:24

A Man With Leprosy

1:40 40A man with leprosy[a] came to him
j Mk 10:17 and begged him on his knees,[j] "If you
are willing, you can make me clean."
41Filled with compassion, Jesus
reached out his hand and touched the
man. "I am willing," he said. "Be clean!"
42Immediately the leprosy left him and
he was cured.
43Jesus sent him away at once with a
1:44 strong warning: 44"See that you don't tell
k Mt 8:4 this to anyone.[k] But go, show yourself to
l Lev 13:49 m Lev 14:1-32 the priest[l] and offer the sacrifices that
Moses commanded for your cleansing,[m]
as a testimony to them." 45Instead he
went out and began to talk freely, spreading the news. As a result, Jesus could no
1:45 longer enter a town openly but stayed
n Lk 5:15,16 outside in lonely places.[n] Yet the people
o Mk 2:13; Lk 5:17; Jn 6:2 still came to him from everywhere.[o]

Jesus Heals a Paralytic

2 A few days later, when Jesus again
entered Capernaum, the people

> **WHAT WOULD HAPPEN IF CHRIST WALKED INTO A CHURCH AND HAD (LONG HAIR) AND SMELLED LIKE A HOMELESS PERSON AND SAID, "LISTEN EVERYBODY, I WANT YOU ALL TO QUIT YOUR JOBS, RENOUNCE YOUR WORLDLY GOODS AND GIVE AWAY EVERYTHING YOU HAVE, AND COME WALK AROUND WITH ME"? I DON'T THINK HE'D GET VERY FAR. PEOPLE WOULD LOOK AT HIM AND SAY, "THIS IS NOT THE FORM OF GOD WE'RE USED TO!"**

Moby, *Secular Recording Artist*

heard that he had come home. 2So 2:2
many[p] gathered that there was no room p ver 13;
left, not even outside the door, and he Mk 1:45
preached the word to them. 3Some men 2:3
came, bringing to him a paralytic,[q] car- q Mt 4:24
ried by four of them. 4Since they could
not get him to Jesus because of the
crowd, they made an opening in the roof
above Jesus and, after digging through
it, lowered the mat the paralyzed man
was lying on. 5When Jesus saw their
faith, he said to the paralytic, "Son, your 2:5
sins are forgiven."[r] r Lk 7:48
6Now some teachers of the law were
sitting there, thinking to themselves,
7"Why does this fellow talk like that?
He's blaspheming! Who can forgive sins 2:7
but God alone?"[s] s Isa 43:25
8Immediately Jesus knew in his spirit
that this was what they were thinking in
their hearts, and he said to them, "Why
are you thinking these things? 9Which is
easier: to say to the paralytic, 'Your sins
are forgiven,' or to say, 'Get up, take your
mat and walk'? 10But that you may know
that the Son of Man[t] has authority on 2:10 t Mt 8:20
earth to forgive sins . . ." He said to the
paralytic, 11"I tell you, get up, take your
mat and go home." 12He got up, took his
mat and walked out in full view of them
all. This amazed everyone and they 2:12
praised God,[u] saying, "We have never u Mt 9:8
seen anything like this!"[v] v Mt 9:33

a 40 The Greek word was used for various diseases affecting the skin—not necessarily leprosy.

The Calling of Levi

2:13 13 Once again Jesus went out beside
w Mk 1:45; the lake. A large crowd came to him,[w]
Lk 5:15; Jn 6:2 and he began to teach them. 14 As he
walked along, he saw Levi son of Al-
phaeus sitting at the tax collector's
2:14 booth. "Follow me,"[x] Jesus told him, and
x Mt 4:19 Levi got up and followed him.
15 While Jesus was having dinner at
Levi's house, many tax collectors and
"sinners" were eating with him and his
disciples, for there were many who followed him. 16 When the teachers of the
2:16 y Ac 23:9 law who were Pharisees[y] saw him eating
z Mt 9:11 with the "sinners" and tax collectors,
they asked his disciples: "Why does he
eat with tax collectors and 'sinners'?"[z]
17 On hearing this, Jesus said to them,
"It is not the healthy who need a doctor,
2:17 but the sick. I have not come to call the
a Lk 19:10; 1Ti 1:15 righteous, but sinners."[a]

Jesus Questioned About Fasting

18 Now John's disciples and the Phar-
2:18 b Mt 6:16-18; isees were fasting.[b] Some people came
Ac 13:2 and asked Jesus, "How is it that John's
disciples and the disciples of the Pharisees are fasting, but yours are not?"
19 Jesus answered, "How can the guests
of the bridegroom fast while he is with
them? They cannot, so long as they have
him with them. 20 But the time will come
2:20 when the bridegroom will be taken from
c Lk 17:22 them,[c] and on that day they will fast.
21 "No one sews a patch of unshrunk
cloth on an old garment. If he does, the
new piece will pull away from the old,
making the tear worse. 22 And no one
pours new wine into old wineskins. If he
does, the wine will burst the skins, and
both the wine and the wineskins will be
ruined. No, he pours new wine into new
wineskins."

Lord of the Sabbath

23 One Sabbath Jesus was going
through the grainfields, and as his disci-
2:23 ples walked along, they began to pick
d Dt 23:25 some heads of grain.[d] 24 The Pharisees
2:24 said to him, "Look, why are they doing
e Mt 12:2 what is unlawful on the Sabbath?"[e]
25 He answered, "Have you never read
what David did when he and his com-
2:26 panions were hungry and in need? 26 In
f 1Ch 24:6; the days of Abiathar the high priest,[f] he
2Sa 8:17 entered the house of God and ate the
consecrated bread, which is lawful only

> I WANT TO KNOW ONE THING—THE WAY TO HEAVEN. GOD HIMSELF HAS SHOWN THE WAY. FOR THIS PURPOSE JESUS CAME FROM HEAVEN.
>
> 
>
> John Wesley,
> *Methodist Evangelist*

for priests to eat.[g] And he also gave 2:26 g Lev 24:5-9
some to his companions."[h] h 1Sa 21:1-6
27 Then he said to them, "The Sabbath 2:27
was made for man,[i] not man for the i Ex 23:12;
Sabbath.[j] 28 So the Son of Man[k] is Lord Dt 5:14
even of the Sabbath." j Col 2:16

3 Another time he went into the 2:28
synagogue,[l] and a man with a k Mt 8:20
shriveled hand was there. 2 Some of them 3:1
were looking for a reason to accuse Jesus, l Mt 4:23;
so they watched him closely[m] to see if he Mk 1:21
would heal him on the Sabbath.[n] 3 Jesus 3:2 m Mt 12:10
said to the man with the shriveled hand, n Lk 14:1
"Stand up in front of everyone."
4 Then Jesus asked them, "Which is
lawful on the Sabbath: to do good or to
do evil, to save life or to kill?" But they
remained silent.
5 He looked around at them in anger
and, deeply distressed at their stubborn
hearts, said to the man, "Stretch out
your hand." He stretched it out, and his
hand was completely restored. 6 Then
the Pharisees went out and began to 3:6 o Mt 22:16;
plot with the Herodians[o] how they Mk 12:13
might kill Jesus.[p] p Mt 12:14

Crowds Follow Jesus

7 Jesus withdrew with his disciples to
the lake, and a large crowd from Galilee 3:7
followed.[q] 8 When they heard all he was q Mt 4:25
doing, many people came to him from
Judea, Jerusalem, Idumea, and the regions across the Jordan and around Tyre 3:8
and Sidon.[r] 9 Because of the crowd he r Mt 11:21
told his disciples to have a small boat
ready for him, to keep the people from 3:10 s Mt 4:23
crowding him. 10 For he had healed t Mt 9:20
many,[s] so that those with diseases were
pushing forward to touch him.[t] 11 When- 3:11 u Mt 4:3;
ever the evil[a] spirits saw him, they fell Mk 1:23,24
down before him and cried out, "You are 3:12 v Mt 8:4;
the Son of God."[u] 12 But he gave them Mk 1:24,25,34;
strict orders not to tell who he was.[v] Ac 16:17,18

[a] 11 Greek *unclean*; also in verse 30

Being With Jesus

Innumerable articles have been written over the years on the subject of discipleship. Seminars, training courses and workshops are conducted on a regular basis. While there are myriad applications for different situations, however, the essence of discipleship as Jesus taught it is captured by three words: *be*, *do* and *have*.

"[Jesus] appointed twelve—designating them apostles—that they might *be* with him" (Mark 3:14, italics added). At first they worked alongside him, but he eventually began dispatching them to heal and teach on their own (Matthew 10:1–42). They responded by *doing* what Jesus had asked of them. He also enabled them with authority over demons. In this context they possessed (or *had*) the resources they needed to exercise this authority. Most of what has been written about discipleship focuses on *doing* and *having*, but relatively little has been written about *being*. And it is really this aspect of discipleship that is foundational (Mark 3:14).

We can spend time with Jesus in different ways: the first spiritually, by reading and meditating on his Word. Like Mary, we can sit engrossed at our Savior's feet, hanging on to his every word (Luke 10:39). If we want to know the mind of Christ, we have to become intimately familiar with the words he spoke. If we want to know his heart, we can pay special attention to the values that were important to him and to the way he treated people. If we want to know what our Lord expects from us, we'll want to read and reread his directives as recorded in Scripture. We can spend time in prayer with Jesus, pouring out our souls to him and listening for his answers. As expressed by the apostle Paul, we are called to "devote [ourselves] to prayer, being watchful and thankful" (Colossians 4:2). Finally, if we want to develop Christlike characteristics, we will benefit by spending time with seasoned believers who reflect the mind and heart of the Savior.

When we spend time with Jesus, our knowledge of him will go infinitely beyond knowing about him. We will know him on an entirely personal level, in the same intimate manner that we know our spouse, our child, our most trusted friend. Jesus referred to himself as the good shepherd and went on the state: "I know my sheep and my sheep know me—just as the Father knows me and I know the Father—and I lay down my life for the sheep . . . My sheep listen to my voice; I know them, and they follow me. I give them eternal life, and they shall never perish; no one can snatch them out of my hand. My Father, who has given them to me, is greater than all; no one can snatch them out of my Father's hand. I and the Father are one" (John 10:14–15,27–29). We are indeed *with* Jesus Christ, so intimately connected with him that we are forever in the grip of his hand.

Self-Discovery: *Jesus longs for intimacy with you (Revelation 3:20). Will you open the door of your life today so that you can be with him?*

GO TO DISCOVERY 252 ON PAGE 1326

THE CHARACTER OF JESUS IS IMMENSELY ATTRACTIVE. IT EMBODIES ALL THAT WE OURSELVES WOULD, IN OUR BEST MOMENTS, LIKE TO BE.

Michael Green, *British Scholar*

The Appointing of the Twelve Apostles

[13]Jesus went up on a mountainside
3:13 and called to him those he wanted, and
w Mt 5:1 they came to him.[w] [14]He appointed
3:14 twelve—designating them apostles[a x]—
x Mk 6:30 that they might be with him and that he
3:15 might send them out to preach [15]and to
y Mt 10:1 have authority to drive out demons.[y]
3:16 [16]These are the twelve he appointed: Si-
z Jn 1:42 mon (to whom he gave the name Peter);[z]
[17]James son of Zebedee and his brother
John (to them he gave the name Boaner-
ges, which means Sons of Thunder);
[18]Andrew, Philip, Bartholomew, Matthew, Thomas, James son of Alphaeus,
Thaddaeus, Simon the Zealot [19]and Judas Iscariot, who betrayed him.

Jesus and Beelzebub

3:20 [20]Then Jesus entered a house, and
a ver 7 b Mk 6:31 again a crowd gathered,[a] so that he and
his disciples were not even able to eat.[b]
[21]When his family heard about this, they
3:21 went to take charge of him, for they said,
c Jn 10:20; Ac 26:24 "He is out of his mind."[c]
[22]And the teachers of the law who
3:22 came down from Jerusalem[d] said, "He is
d Mt 15:1 possessed by Beelzebub[b]![e] By the prince
e Mt 10:25; 11:18; 12:24; Jn 7:20; 8:48,52; 10:20 of demons he is driving out demons."[f]
f Mt 9:34 [23]So Jesus called them and spoke to
them in parables:[g] "How can Satan[h]
3:23 drive out Satan? [24]If a kingdom is divid-
g Mk 4:2 h Mt 4:10 ed against itself, that kingdom cannot
stand. [25]If a house is divided against itself, that house cannot stand. [26]And if
Satan opposes himself and is divided, he
cannot stand; his end has come. [27]In
fact, no one can enter a strong man's
house and carry off his possessions un-
3:27 less he first ties up the strong man. Then
i Isa 49:24,25 he can rob his house.[i] [28]I tell you the
truth, all the sins and blasphemies of
men will be forgiven them. [29]But whoever blasphemes against the Holy Spirit
3:29 will never be forgiven; he is guilty of an
j Mt 12:31,32; Lk 12:10 eternal sin."[j]

[30]He said this because they were saying, "He has an evil spirit."

Jesus' Mother and Brothers

[31]Then Jesus' mother and brothers ar- 3:31
rived.[k] Standing outside, they sent k ver 21
someone in to call him. [32]A crowd was
sitting around him, and they told him,
"Your mother and brothers are outside
looking for you."
[33]"Who are my mother and my brothers?" he asked.
[34]Then he looked at those seated in a
circle around him and said, "Here are
my mother and my brothers! [35]Whoever
does God's will is my brother and sister
and mother."

The Parable of the Sower

4 Again Jesus began to teach by the 4:1
lake.[l] The crowd that gathered l Mk 2:13; 3:7
around him was so large that he got into
a boat and sat in it out on the lake, while
all the people were along the shore at the 4:2
water's edge. [2]He taught them many m ver 11;
things by parables,[m] and in his teaching Mk 3:23
said: [3]"Listen! A farmer went out to sow 4:3
his seed.[n] [4]As he was scattering the seed, n ver 26

[a] *14* Some manuscripts do not have *designating them apostles.* [b] *22* Greek *Beezeboul* or *Beelzeboul*

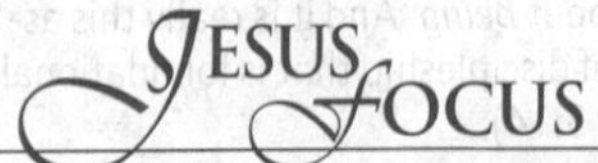

THE ABRIDGED EDITION

Mark's record of Jesus' life is the "abridged edition," ideal for readers-on-the-run. Mark recorded almost as many parables as the other Gospel writers, but he devoted much less space to each of them, focusing instead on Jesus' miracles. Mark 4:26–29 relates one parable, however, that is unique to Mark's Gospel—the parable of the growing seed—and this is immediately followed by the parable of the mustard seed (verses 30–32). Both focus on how God's kingdom grows from an insignificant beginning. Although the symbolism in the parables was straightforward, many people failed to grasp the implications, especially those who wanted to avoid facing the stark truth about their own shortcomings (verses 12–13). But Jesus "explained everything" to his followers (verse 34). Jesus' parables were brief stories or illustrations that reflected God's truth, but they were intelligible only through the working of God's grace to those who were willing to listen.

some fell along the path, and the birds
came and ate it up. 5Some fell on rocky
places, where it did not have much soil.
It sprang up quickly, because the soil
was shallow. 6But when the sun came
up, the plants were scorched, and they
withered because they had no root.
7Other seed fell among thorns, which
grew up and choked the plants, so that
they did not bear grain. 8Still other seed
fell on good soil. It came up, grew and
4:8 produced a crop, multiplying thirty, six-
o Jn 15:5; Col 1:6 ty, or even a hundred times."[o]
4:9 9Then Jesus said, "He who has ears to
p ver 23; hear, let him hear."[p]
Mt 11:15 10When he was alone, the Twelve and
the others around him asked him about
4:11 the parables. 11He told them, "The secret
q Mt 3:2 of the kingdom of God[q] has been given
r 1Co 5:12,13; to you. But to those on the outside[r]
Col 4:5; 1Th 4:12; everything is said in parables 12so that,
1Ti 3:7

" 'they may be ever seeing but
never perceiving,
and ever hearing but never
understanding;
4:12 s Isa 6:9,10; otherwise they might turn and be
Mt 13:13-15 forgiven!'[a]"[s]

13Then Jesus said to them, "Don't you
understand this parable? How then will
4:14 you understand any parable? 14The
t Mk 16:20; farmer sows the word.[t] 15Some people
Lk 1:2; Ac 4:31; 8:4; 16:6; 17:11; are like seed along the path, where the
Php 1:14 word is sown. As soon as they hear it, Sa-
4:15 u Mt 4:10 tan[u] comes and takes away the word
that was sown in them. 16Others, like
seed sown on rocky places, hear the word
and at once receive it with joy. 17But
since they have no root, they last only a
short time. When trouble or persecution
comes because of the word, they quickly
fall away. 18Still others, like seed sown
among thorns, hear the word; 19but the
4:19 worries of this life, the deceitfulness of
v Mt 19:23; wealth[v] and the desires for other things
1Ti 6:9,10,17; 1Jn 2:15-17 come in and choke the word, making it
unfruitful. 20Others, like seed sown on
good soil, hear the word, accept it, and
produce a crop—thirty, sixty or even a
hundred times what was sown."

A Lamp on a Stand

21He said to them, "Do you bring in a
4:21 lamp to put it under a bowl or a bed? In-
w Mt 5:15 stead, don't you put it on its stand?[w]
22For whatever is hidden is meant to be
disclosed, and whatever is concealed is
meant to be brought out into the open.[x] 4:22 x Jer 16:17;
23If anyone has ears to hear, let him Mt 10:26;
hear."[y] Lk 8:17; 12:2

24"Consider carefully what you hear," 4:23
he continued. "With the measure you y ver 9; Mt 11:15
use, it will be measured to you—and 4:24
even more.[z] 25Whoever has will be given z Mt 7:2; Lk 6:38
more; whoever does not have, even what 4:25
he has will be taken from him."[a] a Mt 13:12; 25:29

The Parable of the Growing Seed

26He also said, "This is what the king- 4:26
dom of God is like.[b] A man scatters seed b Mt 13:24
on the ground. 27Night and day, whether
he sleeps or gets up, the seed sprouts and
grows, though he does not know how.
28All by itself the soil produces grain—
first the stalk, then the head, then the full
kernel in the head. 29As soon as the grain
is ripe, he puts the sickle to it, because 4:29
the harvest has come."[c] c Rev 14:15

The Parable of the Mustard Seed

30Again he said, "What shall we say 4:30
the kingdom of God is like,[d] or what d Mt 13:24
parable shall we use to describe it? 31It is
like a mustard seed, which is the smallest seed you plant in the ground. 32Yet
when planted, it grows and becomes the
largest of all garden plants, with such big
branches that the birds of the air can
perch in its shade."

33With many similar parables Jesus
spoke the word to them, as much as 4:33
they could understand.[e] 34He did not say e Jn 16:12
anything to them without using a para- 4:34
ble.[f] But when he was alone with his f Jn 16:25
own disciples, he explained everything.

Jesus Calms the Storm

35That day when evening came, he
said to his disciples, "Let us go over to
the other side." 36Leaving the crowd behind, they took him along, just as he 4:36
was, in the boat.[g] There were also other g ver 1; Mk 3:9;
boats with him. 37A furious squall came 5:2,21; 6:32,45
up, and the waves broke over the boat,
so that it was nearly swamped. 38Jesus
was in the stern, sleeping on a cushion.
The disciples woke him and said to him,
"Teacher, don't you care if we drown?"
39He got up, rebuked the wind and
said to the waves, "Quiet! Be still!" Then
the wind died down and it was completely calm.
40He said to his disciples, "Why are

[a] *12* Isaiah 6:9,10

DISCOVERY 252

What Kind of Man Is This?

The Sea of Galilee is not a "sea" in the sense that we would expect. Compared with the oceans and other great bodies of water on the planet, it is a relatively small lake. But it is a significant body of water in Israel, which is primarily a desert environment. It is also known to be unpredictable, and any change in wind direction or velocity can spawn an instant storm. One can start across the lake by boat with the sun shining and the lake surface as smooth as glass, but in a matter of minutes the wind can pick up and the waves become turgid.

In one particular instance, after Jesus had boarded a fishing boat with his disciples to cross over to the other side of the sea, a "furious squall" arose, with waves high enough to swamp the small vessel. Jesus, no doubt exhausted from the labors of the day, slept soundly on a cushion while the disciples grew more and more panicky. Finally, they shook him awake in desperation and asked, possibly with a note of cynicism, whether or not he cared about their lives (Mark 4:38). Jesus responded by standing and addressing the storm: "Quiet! Be still!" (verse 39). Immediately, the storm winds sighed their last and the waves subsided; once again the boat glided through placid waters. Reflecting back on this story, including the conversation between Jesus and his disciples after the calming of the storm, we note that three significant questions were asked.

The first came from the disciples: "Teacher, don't you care if we drown?" (verse 38). It appeared to the disciples as though Jesus was either oblivious or aloof to their plight. How could the Master be sound asleep during such a crisis, as though he hadn't a care in the world? The group had evidently already forgotten what Jesus had told them before they had boarded the boat: that they were going *to the other side* (verse 35).

Next it was Jesus' turn to ask a question. Immediately after he had rebuked the storm, Jesus addressed his disciples: "Why are you so afraid? Do you still have no faith?" (verse 40). Because we are human beings who experience human emotions, fear and faith can never be mutually exclusive. However, our fear can become progressively lessened as we grow in our faith. As we come to have a stronger faith it begins to exert a greater control over our fear.

The final question was asked by the disciples: "Who is this?" What kind of man has authority over the wind and the waves? In view of what Jesus had just done, the only answer to this question was: He is the very Son of God! God's presence, as well as his power, was demonstrated (see Psalm 65:7; 107:25–30; Proverbs 30:4). Mark indicated his answer to this question in the opening line of his Gospel: "The beginning of the gospel about Jesus Christ, the Son of God" (Mark 1:1). What kind of man has authority over the wind and waves? Only the One who created the elements in the first place!

***Self-Discovery:** Identify an area in your life in which your faith has helped you to overcome a particular fear. Reflect back to your childhood if necessary. Were you afraid of the dark? of a thunderstorm? of your neighbor's dog? How were you able to relate your growing faith to this situation?*

GO TO DISCOVERY 253 ON PAGE 1329

CHRIST'S LIFE OUTWARDLY
WAS ONE OF THE MOST TROUBLED
LIVES THAT WAS EVER LIVED . . .
BUT THE INNER LIFE WAS A SEA OF
GLASS. THE GREAT CALM WAS
ALWAYS THERE.

Henry Drummond, *Scottish Evangelist*

4:40 you so afraid? Do you still have no
h Mt 14:31; faith?"[h]
Mk 16:14 41They were terrified and asked each
other, "Who is this? Even the wind and
the waves obey him!"

The Healing of a Demon-possessed Man

5 They went across the lake to the
5:2 region of the Gerasenes.[a] 2When
i Mk 4:1 Jesus got out of the boat,[i] a man with an
j Mk 1:23 evil[b] spirit[j] came from the tombs to
meet him. 3This man lived in the tombs,
and no one could bind him any more,
not even with a chain. 4For he had often
been chained hand and foot, but he tore
the chains apart and broke the irons on
his feet. No one was strong enough to
subdue him. 5Night and day among the
tombs and in the hills he would cry out
and cut himself with stones.

6When he saw Jesus from a distance,
he ran and fell on his knees in front of
5:7 him. 7He shouted at the top of his voice,
k Mt 8:29 "What do you want with me,[k] Jesus, Son
l Mt 4:3; Lk 1:32; 6:35; of the Most High God?[l] Swear to God
Ac 16:17; that you won't torture me!" 8For Jesus
Heb 7:1 had said to him, "Come out of this man,
you evil spirit!"

9Then Jesus asked him, "What is your
5:9 name?"
m ver 15 "My name is Legion,"[m] he replied, "for
we are many." 10And he begged Jesus
again and again not to send them out of
the area.

11A large herd of pigs was feeding on
the nearby hillside. 12The demons
begged Jesus, "Send us among the pigs;
allow us to go into them." 13He gave
them permission, and the evil spirits
came out and went into the pigs. The
herd, about two thousand in number,
rushed down the steep bank into the
lake and were drowned.

14Those tending the pigs ran off and
reported this in the town and countryside, and the people went out to see
what had happened. 15When they came
to Jesus, they saw the man who had been 5:15
possessed by the legion[n] of demons,[o] n ver 9 o ver 16,
sitting there, dressed and in his right 18; Mt 4:24
mind; and they were afraid. 16Those who
had seen it told the people what had
happened to the demon-possessed
man—and told about the pigs as well.
17Then the people began to plead with
Jesus to leave their region.

18As Jesus was getting into the boat,
the man who had been demon-possessed begged to go with him. 19Jesus
did not let him, but said, "Go home to 5:19
your family and tell them[p] how much p Mt 8:4
the Lord has done for you, and how he
has had mercy on you." 20So the man
went away and began to tell in the De- 5:20
capolis[c][q] how much Jesus had done for q Mt 4:25;
him. And all the people were amazed. Mk 7:31

A Dead Girl and a Sick Woman

21When Jesus had again crossed over
by boat to the other side of the lake,[r] a 5:21 r Mt 9:1 s Mk 4:1
large crowd gathered around him while
he was by the lake.[s] 22Then one of the 5:22
synagogue rulers,[t] named Jairus, came t ver 35,36,38;
there. Seeing Jesus, he fell at his feet Lk 13:14;
23and pleaded earnestly with him, "My Ac 13:15; 18:8, 17
little daughter is dying. Please come and 5:23
put your hands on[u] her so that she will u Mt 19:13;
be healed and live." 24So Jesus went with Mk 6:5; 7:32; 8:23; 16:18;
him. Lk 4:40; 13:13;
A large crowd followed and pressed Ac 6:6
around him. 25And a woman was there 5:25
who had been subject to bleeding[v] for v Lev 15:25-30
twelve years. 26She had suffered a great
deal under the care of many doctors and
had spent all she had, yet instead of getting better she grew worse. 27When she
heard about Jesus, she came up behind
him in the crowd and touched his cloak,
28because she thought, "If I just touch 5:28
his clothes,[w] I will be healed." 29Immedi- w Mt 9:20
ately her bleeding stopped and she felt 5:29
in her body that she was freed from her x ver 34
suffering.[x]

30At once Jesus realized that power[y] 5:30 y Lk 5:17; 6:19
had gone out from him. He turned
around in the crowd and asked, "Who
touched my clothes?"

31"You see the people crowding

[a] *1* Some manuscripts *Gadarenes*; other manuscripts *Gergesenes* [b] *2* Greek *unclean*; also in verses 8 and 13 [c] *20* That is, the Ten Cities

> THE MIRACLES OF JESUS WERE THE ORDINARY WORKS OF HIS FATHER, WROUGHT SMALL AND SWIFT THAT WE MIGHT TAKE THEM IN.
>
> 
>
> George MacDonald, *Scottish Theologian*

against you," his disciples answered, "and
yet you can ask, 'Who touched me?' "
32But Jesus kept looking around to see
who had done it. 33Then the woman,
knowing what had happened to her,
came and fell at his feet and, trembling
with fear, told him the whole truth. 34He
5:34 said to her, "Daughter, your faith has
z Mt 9:22 healed you.[z] Go in peace[a] and be freed
a Ac 15:33 from your suffering."
35While Jesus was still speaking, some
5:35 men came from the house of Jairus, the
b ver 22 synagogue ruler.[b] "Your daughter is
dead," they said. "Why bother the
teacher any more?"
36Ignoring what they said, Jesus told
the synagogue ruler, "Don't be afraid;
just believe."
37He did not let anyone follow him ex-
5:37 cept Peter, James and John the brother of
c Mt 4:21 James.[c] 38When they came to the home
5:38 of the synagogue ruler,[d] Jesus saw a
d ver 22 commotion, with people crying and
wailing loudly. 39He went in and said to
them, "Why all this commotion and
5:39 wailing? The child is not dead but
e Mt 9:24 asleep."[e] 40But they laughed at him.
After he put them all out, he took the
child's father and mother and the disciples who were with him, and went in
5:41 where the child was. 41He took her by the
f Mk 1:31 hand[f] and said to her, *"Talitha koum!"*
g Lk 7:14; (which means, "Little girl, I say to you,
Ac 9:40 get up!").[g] 42Immediately the girl stood
up and walked around (she was twelve
years old). At this they were completely
5:43 astonished. 43He gave strict orders not to
h Mt 8:4 let anyone know about this,[h] and told
them to give her something to eat.

A Prophet Without Honor

6:1 6 Jesus left there and went to his
i Mt 2:23 hometown,[i] accompanied by his
6:2 disciples. 2When the Sabbath came,[j] he
j Mk 1:21 began to teach in the synagogue,[k] and
k Mt 4:23
l Mt 7:28 many who heard him were amazed.[l]
"Where did this man get these
things?" they asked. "What's this wisdom that has been given him, that he
even does miracles! 3Isn't this the carpenter? Isn't this Mary's son and the
brother of James, Joseph,[a] Judas and Si- 6:3
mon?[m] Aren't his sisters here with us?" m Mt 12:46
And they took offense at him.[n] n Mt 11:6;
4Jesus said to them, "Only in his Jn 6:61
hometown, among his relatives and in
his own house is a prophet without 6:4
honor."[o] 5He could not do any miracles o Lk 4:24;
there, except lay his hands on[p] a few sick Jn 4:44
people and heal them. 6And he was 6:5
amazed at their lack of faith. p Mk 5:23

Jesus Sends Out the Twelve

Then Jesus went around teaching 6:6 q Mt 9:35;
from village to village.[q] 7Calling the Mk 1:39;
Twelve to him,[r] he sent them out two by Lk 13:22
two[s] and gave them authority over evil[b] 6:7
spirits.[t] r Mk 3:13
8These were his instructions: "Take s Dt 17:6; Lk 10:1
nothing for the journey except a staff— t Mt 10:1
no bread, no bag, no money in your belts.
9Wear sandals but not an extra tunic.
10Whenever you enter a house, stay there
until you leave that town. 11And if any
place will not welcome you or listen to
you, shake the dust off your feet[u] when 6:11 u Mt 10:14
you leave, as a testimony against them."

[a] 3 Greek *Joses*, a variant of *Joseph* [b] 7 Greek *unclean*

JESUS FOCUS

FINDING TIME TO REST

Wherever Jesus went people followed him, pressing around him and pleading with him to come and heal their sick loved ones. The pressure must have been physically, emotionally and spiritually draining. Mark recorded five separate instances when Jesus took his disciples to "a quiet place" to get away from the crowds (see Mark 3:7–9; 6:31,45; 7:24; 9:30). These efforts were not always successful, however. Once, when Jesus and his disciples were trying to revitalize themselves through a brief period of rest and relaxation, they ended up organizing an impromptu dinner for 5,000 men, along with their families (Mark 6:31–44). Although Jesus' human body craved rest, his divine compassion could not resist helping the hurting. Like each of us, Jesus faced the challenge of balancing the meeting of fundamental human needs with the urgency of his sense of calling from God.

DISCOVERY 253

A Prophet Without Honor

No matter what we do with our lives after we become adults, how far we travel or how much we learn, returning to our hometown, especially after a prolonged absence, is always an emotional experience! Most people will at one time or another speak nostalgically about their childhood remembrances. To some degree people make sense of their daily experiences through the filter of the patterns and recollections of their youth. In subtle ways each of us will be forever affected by something of what we were as a small child.

Jesus understood these feelings about childhood experiences. When he returned to Nazareth and taught in the synagogue, the people were amazed by his wisdom and miracles but found themselves unable to reconcile what they were seeing and hearing with the fact that Jesus was a local carpenter's son (Mark 6:2–3). Within the close-knit circle of small-town life, they had watched him grow up, and their response to his teaching was skewed by their recollections of what had been in many ways an ordinary childhood.

Within this context Jesus' words of rebuke ring true: "Only in his hometown, among his relatives and in his own house is a prophet without honor" (verse 4). And not much has changed. For example, in the contemporary world of business, corporations regularly bring in outside consultants to help with problem-solving, while there are probably knowledgeable and capable persons on staff who could accomplish the same result with a less effort.

The citizens of Nazareth lacked faith, but Jesus refused to simply walk away and give up on them. He did not perform a great many miracles in Nazareth, but he did perform some (verses 5–6).

The reaction that stung the most, however, had to be that of his own family. Mark related in an earlier chapter that Jesus' own family had questioned his sanity: "Jesus entered a house, and again a crowd gathered, so that he and his disciples were not even able to eat. When his family heard about this, they went to take charge of him, for they said, 'He is out of his mind' " (Mark 3:20–21). And the apostle John stated simply in John 7:5 that "even his own brothers did not believe in him."

Similarly in our own lives, it can sometimes be most difficult to discuss the reality of Jesus' love and salvation with those who know us best. They may listen to what we say and even acknowledge that they can observe a change in our demeanor since we first met the Savior, but they will almost invariably judge us through the family lens. They are most skeptical because they remember too much.

But even when our parents, brothers or sisters reject our words or are embarrassed by our devotion to Jesus, we cannot simply resign ourselves to their entrenched attitudes. Eventually, Jesus' own family did come to the point of belief (Acts 1:14). That which will speak the loudest is not the idea that we are perfect but the observation that we are consistent. The example of an altered lifestyle will make a difference over time.

Self-Discovery: *Thinking about your faith in Jesus and your Christian walk, in what ways are you the same person you were when you were five years old? 12 years old? 18? In what ways are you different?*

GO TO DISCOVERY 254 ON PAGE 1334

> **HOW THE GOSPELS EXPLAIN THAT JESUS HAPPENED TO BE IN GALILEE IN GENERAL, AND NAZARETH IN PARTICULAR, RINGS WITH HISTORIC AUTHENTICITY.**
>
> Bishop John Spong, *Anglican Theologian*

12 They went out and preached that
6:12 v Lk 9:6 people should repent.[v] 13 They drove out
many demons and anointed many sick
6:13 w Jas 5:14 people with oil[w] and healed them.

John the Baptist Beheaded

14 King Herod heard about this, for
6:14 Jesus' name had become well known.
x Mt 3:1 Some were saying,[a] "John the Baptist[x]
has been raised from the dead, and that
is why miraculous powers are at work in
him."
6:15 y Mal 4:5 15 Others said, "He is Elijah."[y]
z Mt 21:11 And still others claimed, "He is a
a Mt 16:14; Mk 8:28 prophet,[z] like one of the prophets of
long ago."[a]
16 But when Herod heard this, he said,
"John, the man I beheaded, has been
raised from the dead!"
17 For Herod himself had given orders
6:17 to have John arrested, and he had him
b Mt 4:12; 11:2; bound and put in prison.[b] He did this
Lk 3:19,20 because of Herodias, his brother Philip's
wife, whom he had married. 18 For John
6:18 had been saying to Herod, "It is not law-
c Lev 18:16; 20:21 ful for you to have your brother's wife."[c]
19 So Herodias nursed a grudge against
John and wanted to kill him. But she
was not able to, 20 because Herod feared
6:20 John and protected him, knowing him
d Mt 11:9; 21:26 to be a righteous and holy man.[d] When
Herod heard John, he was greatly puz-
zled[b]; yet he liked to listen to him.
6:21 21 Finally the opportune time came.
e Est 1:3; 2:18 On his birthday Herod gave a banquet[e]
f Lk 3:1 for his high officials and military commanders and the leading men of Gali-
lee.[f] 22 When the daughter of Herodias
came in and danced, she pleased Herod
and his dinner guests.
The king said to the girl, "Ask me for
anything you want, and I'll give it to
you." 23 And he promised her with an
6:23 oath, "Whatever you ask I will give you,
g Est 5:3,6; 7:2 up to half my kingdom."[g]
24 She went out and said to her mother, "What shall I ask for?"

"The head of John the Baptist," she
answered.
25 At once the girl hurried in to the
king with the request: "I want you to
give me right now the head of John the
Baptist on a platter."
26 The king was greatly distressed, but
because of his oaths and his dinner
guests, he did not want to refuse her.
27 So he immediately sent an execution-
er with orders to bring John's head. The
man went, beheaded John in the prison,
28 and brought back his head on a platter.
He presented it to the girl, and she gave
it to her mother. 29 On hearing of this,
John's disciples came and took his body
and laid it in a tomb.

Jesus Feeds the Five Thousand 6:30

30 The apostles[h] gathered around Jesus h Mt 10:2; Lk 9:10; 17:5;
and reported to him all they had done 22:14; 24:10;
and taught.[i] 31 Then, because so many Ac 1:2,26 i Lk 9:10
people were coming and going that they
did not even have a chance to eat,[j] he 6:31 j Mk 3:20
said to them, "Come with me by your-
selves to a quiet place and get some rest."
32 So they went away by themselves in 6:32
a boat[k] to a solitary place. 33 But many k ver 45; Mk 4:36
who saw them leaving recognized them
and ran on foot from all the towns and
got there ahead of them. 34 When Jesus
landed and saw a large crowd, he had
compassion on them, because they were 6:34
like sheep without a shepherd.[l] So he be- l Mt 9:36
gan teaching them many things.
35 By this time it was late in the day, so
his disciples came to him. "This is a remote place," they said, "and it's already
very late. 36 Send the people away so they
can go to the surrounding countryside
and villages and buy themselves something to eat."
37 But he answered, "You give them 6:37
something to eat."[m] m 2Ki 4:42-44
They said to him, "That would take
eight months of a man's wages[c]! Are we
to go and spend that much on bread and
give it to them to eat?"
38 "How many loaves do you have?" he
asked. "Go and see."
When they found out, they said, 6:38 n Mt 15:34;
"Five—and two fish."[n] Mk 8:5
39 Then Jesus directed them to have all
the people sit down in groups on the

[a] 14 Some early manuscripts *He was saying*
[b] 20 Some early manuscripts *he did many things*
[c] 37 Greek *take two hundred denarii*

green grass. 40So they sat down in
groups of hundreds and fifties. 41Taking
the five loaves and the two fish and looking up to heaven, he gave thanks and
6:41 broke the loaves.[o] Then he gave them to
o Mt 14:19 his disciples to set before the people. He
also divided the two fish among them
all. 42They all ate and were satisfied,
43and the disciples picked up twelve basketfuls of broken pieces of bread and
fish. 44The number of the men who had
eaten was five thousand.

Jesus Walks on the Water

6:45 45Immediately Jesus made his disci-
p ver 32 ples get into the boat[p] and go on ahead
q Mt 11:21 of him to Bethsaida,[q] while he dismissed
6:46 the crowd. 46After leaving them, he went
r Lk 3:21 up on a mountainside to pray.[r]
47When evening came, the boat was
in the middle of the lake, and he was
alone on land. 48He saw the disciples
straining at the oars, because the wind
was against them. About the fourth
watch of the night he went out to them,
walking on the lake. He was about to
pass by them, 49but when they saw him
walking on the lake, they thought he
was a ghost.[s] They cried out, 50because 6:49
they all saw him and were terrified. s Lk 24:37
Immediately he spoke to them and
said, "Take courage! It is I. Don't be 6:50
afraid."[t] 51Then he climbed into the t Mt 14:27
boat[u] with them, and the wind died 6:51 u ver 32
down.[v] They were completely amazed, v Mk 4:39
52for they had not understood about the 6:52
loaves; their hearts were hardened.[w] w Mk 8:17-21
53When they had crossed over, they
landed at Gennesaret and anchored 6:53
there.[x] 54As soon as they got out of the x Jn 6:24,25
boat, people recognized Jesus. 55They
ran throughout that whole region and
carried the sick on mats to wherever
they heard he was. 56And wherever he
went—into villages, towns or countryside—they placed the sick in the marketplaces. They begged him to let them
touch even the edge of his cloak,[y] and all 6:56
who touched him were healed. y Mt 9:20

Clean and Unclean

7 The Pharisees and some of the
teachers of the law who had come
from Jerusalem gathered around Jesus
and 2saw some of his disciples eating 7:2
food with hands that were "unclean,"[z] z Ac 10:14,28;
that is, unwashed. 3(The Pharisees and 11:8; Ro 14:14
all the Jews do not eat unless they give
their hands a ceremonial washing, hold- 7:3
ing to the tradition of the elders.[a] 4When a ver 5,8,9,13;
they come from the marketplace they do Lk 11:38
not eat unless they wash. And they observe many other traditions, such as the 7:4
washing of cups, pitchers and kettles.[a])[b] b Mt 23:25;
5So the Pharisees and teachers of the Lk 11:39
law asked Jesus, "Why don't your disciples live according to the tradition of the 7:5
elders[c] instead of eating their food with c ver 3; Gal 1:14;
'unclean' hands?" Col 2:8
6He replied, "Isaiah was right when he
prophesied about you hypocrites; as it is
written:

"'These people honor me with
their lips,
but their hearts are far from me.
7They worship me in vain;
their teachings are but rules 7:7
taught by men.'[b][d] d Isa 29:13

8You have let go of the commands of
God and are holding on to the traditions 7:8
of men."[e] e ver 3
9And he said to them: "You have a fine

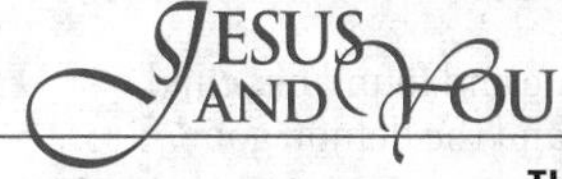

THEY DIDN'T GET IT

After Jesus had miraculously satisfied the hunger of the people, he sent his disciples across the lake by boat. Later that evening the Master crossed the lake himself, walking on top of the water to meet the disciples in the boat. The terrified band assumed that a ghost was drifting toward them, but Jesus allayed their fears with three simple words: "Don't be afraid" (Mark 6:50). When he climbed into the boat, the disciples were "completely amazed," probably sitting in shocked silence. Verse 52 tells us that "they had not understood about the loaves." In other words, the disciples just didn't get it. They had just witnessed Jesus feeding more than 5,000 people with a handful of food, and they were still astonished that he could walk on water. Only through experience did they finally begin to see that Jesus can do anything—and it is the same with each of us. Only as we get to know Jesus on an intimate level do we learn that he can do anything in and through our lives. The more we observe him carrying out his plans for our lives, the less astounded we'll be when he performs what seems unimaginable to us.

a 4 Some early manuscripts *pitchers, kettles and dining couches* b 6,7 Isaiah 29:13

way of setting aside the commands of
7:9 God in order to observe[a] your own tradi-
f ver 3 tions![f] 10For Moses said, 'Honor your fa-
7:10 ther and your mother,'[b][g] and, 'Anyone
g Ex 20:12; who curses his father or mother must be
Dt 5:16 h Ex 21:17; put to death.'[c][h] 11But you say[i] that if a
Lev 20:9 man says to his father or mother: 'What-
7:11 ever help you might otherwise have re-
i Mt 23:16,18 ceived from me is Corban' (that is, a gift
devoted to God), 12then you no longer let
him do anything for his father or mother.
7:13 13Thus you nullify the word of God[j] by
j Heb 4:12 k ver 3 your tradition[k] that you have handed
down. And you do many things like that."
14Again Jesus called the crowd to him
and said, "Listen to me, everyone, and
understand this. 15Nothing outside a
man can make him 'unclean' by going
into him. Rather, it is what comes out of
a man that makes him 'unclean.'[d]"
7:17 17After he had left the crowd and en-
l Mk 9:28 tered the house, his disciples asked him[l]
about this parable. 18"Are you so dull?"
he asked. "Don't you see that nothing
that enters a man from the outside can
make him 'unclean'? 19For it doesn't go
7:19 into his heart but into his stomach, and
m Ro 14:1-12; then out of his body." (In saying this,
Col 2:16; 1Ti 4:3-5 Jesus declared all foods[m] "clean.")[n]
n Ac 10:15 20He went on: "What comes out of a
man is what makes him 'unclean.' 21For
from within, out of men's hearts, come
evil thoughts, sexual immorality, theft,
murder, adultery, 22greed,[o] malice, de- 7:22 o Mt 20:15
ceit, lewdness, envy, slander, arrogance
and folly. 23All these evils come from inside and make a man 'unclean.'"

The Faith of a Syrophoenician Woman

24Jesus left that place and went to the 7:24
vicinity of Tyre.[e][p] He entered a house p Mt 11:21
and did not want anyone to know it; yet
he could not keep his presence secret.
25In fact, as soon as she heard about
him, a woman whose little daughter was
possessed by an evil[f] spirit[q] came and 7:25 q Mt 4:24
fell at his feet. 26The woman was a
Greek, born in Syrian Phoenicia. She
begged Jesus to drive the demon out of
her daughter.
27"First let the children eat all they
want," he told her, "for it is not right to
take the children's bread and toss it to
their dogs."
28"Yes, Lord," she replied, "but even
the dogs under the table eat the children's crumbs."
29Then he told her, "For such a reply,
you may go; the demon has left your
daughter."
30She went home and found her child
lying on the bed, and the demon gone.

The Healing of a Deaf and Mute Man

31Then Jesus left the vicinity of Tyre[r] 7:31 r ver 24; Mt 11:21
and went through Sidon, down to the s Mt 4:18
Sea of Galilee[s] and into the region of t Mt 4:25; Mk 5:20
the Decapolis.[g][t] 32There some people
brought to him a man who was deaf and 7:32
could hardly talk,[u] and they begged him u Mt 9:32; Lk 11:14
to place his hand on[v] the man. v Mk 5:23
33After he took him aside, away from
the crowd, Jesus put his fingers into the
man's ears. Then he spit[w] and touched 7:33 w Mk 8:23
the man's tongue. 34He looked up to
heaven[x] and with a deep sigh[y] said to 7:34 x Mk 6:41;
him, "*Ephphatha!*" (which means, "Be Jn 11:41
opened!"). 35At this, the man's ears were y Mk 8:12
opened, his tongue was loosened and he 7:35
began to speak plainly.[z] z Isa 35:5,6
36Jesus commanded them not to tell 7:36
anyone.[a] But the more he did so, the a Mt 8:4

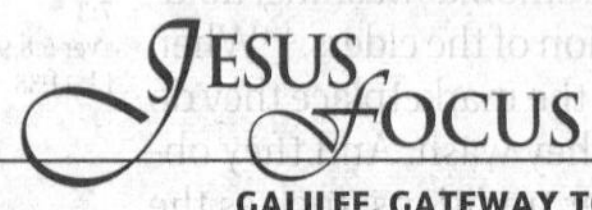

GALILEE, GATEWAY TO THE GENTILES

The region of Galilee lies in the extreme northern part of Israel and surrounds the Sea of Galilee, a freshwater lake fed by the Jordan River. Isaiah referred to the region as "Galilee of the Gentiles" (Isaiah 9:1), because much Gentile traffic passed through the area as a result of its location (see Mark 7:31). A large percentage of Jesus' ministry took place in Galilee. It was here that he preached the Sermon on the Mount (Matthew 5—7) and fed 5,000 men and their families (John 6:1–15), and it was here that Peter confessed that Jesus is "the Christ, the Son of the living God" (Matthew 16:16). It was also in this region that Jesus commissioned his disciples to go into the entire world to tell people about him (Matthew 28:16–20). Jesus' ministry in Galilee fulfilled what God had predicted through his prophet Isaiah hundreds of years earlier: A "great light" would shine in Galilee after the arrival of the Messiah (Isaiah 9:1–2) and would touch Jew and Gentile alike (Isaiah 49:6; Acts 26:23; see also Luke 2:29–32; John 8:12).

a 9 Some manuscripts *set up* *b 10* Exodus 20:12; Deut. 5:16 *c 10* Exodus 21:17; Lev. 20:9
d 15 Some early manuscripts *'unclean.' 16If anyone has ears to hear, let him hear.* *e 24* Many early manuscripts *Tyre and Sidon* *f 25* Greek *unclean*
g 31 That is, the Ten Cities

more they kept talking about it. 37People
were overwhelmed with amazement.
"He has done everything well," they said.
"He even makes the deaf hear and the
mute speak."

Jesus Feeds the Four Thousand

8 During those days another large
crowd gathered. Since they had
nothing to eat, Jesus called his disciples
to him and said, 2"I have compassion for
8:2 these people;[b] they have already been
b Mt 9:36 with me three days and have nothing to
eat. 3If I send them home hungry, they
will collapse on the way, because some
of them have come a long distance."
4His disciples answered, "But where
in this remote place can anyone get
enough bread to feed them?"
5"How many loaves do you have?"
Jesus asked.
"Seven," they replied.
6He told the crowd to sit down on the
ground. When he had taken the seven
loaves and given thanks, he broke them
and gave them to his disciples to set before the people, and they did so. 7They
had a few small fish as well; he gave
8:7 thanks for them also and told the disci-
c Mt 14:19 ples to distribute them.[c] 8The people ate
and were satisfied. Afterward the disci-
8:8 ples picked up seven basketfuls of bro-
d ver 20 ken pieces that were left over.[d] 9About
four thousand men were present. And
having sent them away, 10he got into the
boat with his disciples and went to the
region of Dalmanutha.
11The Pharisees came and began to
question Jesus. To test him, they asked
8:11 him for a sign from heaven.[e] 12He sighed
e Mt 12:38 deeply[f] and said, "Why does this gener-
8:12 ation ask for a miraculous sign? I tell
f Mk 7:34 you the truth, no sign will be given to it."
13Then he left them, got back into the
boat and crossed to the other side.

The Yeast of the Pharisees and Herod

14The disciples had forgotten to bring
bread, except for one loaf they had with
them in the boat. 15"Be careful," Jesus
8:15 warned them. "Watch out for the yeast[g]
g 1Co 5:6-8 h Lk 12:1 of the Pharisees[h] and that of Herod."[i]
i Mt 14:1; Mk 12:13 16They discussed this with one another and said, "It is because we have no
bread."
17Aware of their discussion, Jesus
asked them: "Why are you talking about

I HAVE LOVED TO HEAR MY
LORD SPOKEN OF, AND WHEREVER
I HAVE SEEN THE PRINT OF HIS
SHOE IN THE EARTH, THERE I HAVE
COVETED TO PUT MINE ALSO.

John Bunyan, *Puritan Pastor*

having no bread? Do you still not see or
understand? Are your hearts hardened?[j] 8:17 j Isa 6:9,10; Mk 6:52
18Do you have eyes but fail to see, and
ears but fail to hear? And don't you remember? 19When I broke the five loaves
for the five thousand, how many basketfuls of pieces did you pick up?" 8:19
"Twelve,"[k] they replied. k Mt 14:20;
20"And when I broke the seven loaves Mk 6:41-44; Lk 9:17; Jn 6:13
for the four thousand, how many bas-
ketfuls of pieces did you pick up?" 8:20
They answered, "Seven."[l] l ver 6-9; Mt 15:37
21He said to them, "Do you still not 8:21
understand?"[m] m Mk 6:52

The Healing of a Blind Man at Bethsaida

22They came to Bethsaida,[n] and some 8:22 n Mt 11:21
people brought a blind man[o] and o Mk 10:46;
begged Jesus to touch him. 23He took the Jn 9:1
blind man by the hand and led him out-
side the village. When he had spit[p] on 8:23 p Mk 7:33
the man's eyes and put his hands on[q] q Mk 5:23
him, Jesus asked, "Do you see anything?"
24He looked up and said, "I see people;
they look like trees walking around."
25Once more Jesus put his hands on
the man's eyes. Then his eyes were
opened, his sight was restored, and he
saw everything clearly. 26Jesus sent him
home, saying, "Don't go into the village.[a]"

Peter's Confession of Christ

27Jesus and his disciples went on to
the villages around Caesarea Philippi.
On the way he asked them, "Who do
people say I am?"
28They replied, "Some say John the 8:28 r Mt 3:1
Baptist;[r] others say Elijah;[s] and still oth- s Mal 4:5
ers, one of the prophets."
29"But what about you?" he asked.
"Who do you say I am?" 8:29
Peter answered, "You are the Christ.[b]"[t] t Jn 6:69; 11:27

[a] 26 Some manuscripts *Don't go and tell anyone in the village* [b] 29 Or *Messiah*. "The Christ" (Greek) and "the Messiah" (Hebrew) both mean "the Anointed One."

The Sacrifice of Following Jesus

When people consider the claims and conditions of Christianity, their first question is often, "What will I have to give up?" They want to know whether they will be required to relinquish dancing, smoking, drugs, alcohol or sexual promiscuity. The list goes on and changes over time. But Jesus made the issue crystal clear: His demands are infinitely more encompassing; he wants us to give up *ourselves*.

The first action we must take is to *deny ourselves*, and the first step toward achieving this goal is to admit that we are by nature self-centered and captive to sin (Genesis 8:21; Psalm 51:5; Romans 3:23; 5:12; Ephesians 2:3). Jesus stressed that we must say no to that egotistical self, much as we might firmly enforce a rule prohibiting sweets before dinnertime with our three-year-old child.

Selfishness was at the core of Eve and Adam's first sin (Genesis 3:6). They chose to disregard God's implicit mandate in order to satisfy their own curiosity and desire. But Jesus' followers have to learn to say no to whatever contradicts God's demands. Once we have begun to practice this principle, our lives will become more and more centered on God and on other people rather than on ourselves (Mark 8:34).

Another aspect of giving up everything for Jesus is the act of *taking up our cross* (verse 34). This entails surrendering our "right" to the future we have been expecting. The cross in this context is not a symbol of the difficulties we will inevitably endure in this life. It represents the place of death, and "taking up our cross" signifies our declaration that our future belongs exclusively to God. We "die" to living life our own way and begin a new life lived according to God's way (Romans 6:1–23; 8:1–17).

To *lose our life* has a different connotation (Mark 8:35). Losing this life implies renouncing our pursuit of material possessions. If we attempt to protect our lives by accumulating all the wealth we can, we will still lose everything in the end. But if we give our lives away for God we will in the final analysis gain everything. We trade the temporary and material for the permanent and spiritual.

We also need to *let go of our pride* and our concern about following the ways of the world (verse 38). If we are ashamed of Jesus and of living his way, he will be ashamed of us one day when we stand before God.

What then do we have to give up to follow Jesus? The answer is simple: Everything!

But what do we gain from doing so? The answer is breathtakingly wonderful—beyond our wildest dreams: *Everything*!

Self-Discovery: *In what ways have you denied yourself in order to follow Jesus? Or is it difficult to identify activities, associations or possessions that you have done without? Is there a need in your life for change in this area?*

GO TO DISCOVERY 255 ON PAGE 1336

8:30 [u]Mt 8:4; 16:20; 17:9; Mk 9:9; Lk 9:21 30Jesus warned them not to tell anyone about him.[u]

Jesus Predicts His Death

8:31 [v]Mt 8:20 [w]Mt 16:21 [x]Mt 27:1,2 [y]Ac 2:23; 3:13 [z]Mt 16:21 [a]Mt 16:21 31He then began to teach them that
the Son of Man[v] must suffer many
things[w] and be rejected by the elders,
chief priests and teachers of the law,[x]
and that he must be killed[y] and after
8:32 three days[z] rise again.[a] 32He spoke plain-
[b]Jn 18:20 ly[b] about this, and Peter took him aside
and began to rebuke him.
33But when Jesus turned and looked
at his disciples, he rebuked Peter. "Get
8:33 [c]Mt 4:10 behind me, Satan!"[c] he said. "You do not
have in mind the things of God, but the
things of men."
34Then he called the crowd to him
along with his disciples and said: "If anyone would come after me, he must deny
himself and take up his cross and follow
8:34 [d]Mt 10:38; Lk 14:27 me.[d] 35For whoever wants to save his
life[a] will lose it, but whoever loses his life
8:35 [e]Jn 12:25 for me and for the gospel will save it.[e]
36What good is it for a man to gain the
whole world, yet forfeit his soul? 37Or
what can a man give in exchange for his
soul? 38If anyone is ashamed of me and
my words in this adulterous and sinful
8:38 [f]Mt 8:20 [g]Mt 10:33; Lk 12:9 [h]1Th 2:19 generation, the Son of Man[f] will be
ashamed of him[g] when he comes[h] in his
Father's glory with the holy angels."
9 And he said to them, "I tell you
the truth, some who are standing
9:1 [i]Mk 13:30; Lk 22:18 [j]Mt 24:30; 25:31 here will not taste death before they see
the kingdom of God come[i] with power."[j]

The Transfiguration

2After six days Jesus took Peter, James
9:2 [k]Mt 4:21 and John[k] with him and led them up a
high mountain, where they were all
alone. There he was transfigured before
them. 3His clothes became dazzling
9:3 [l]Mt 28:3 white,[l] whiter than anyone in the world
could bleach them. 4And there appeared
before them Elijah and Moses, who were
talking with Jesus.
9:5 [m]Mt 23:7 5Peter said to Jesus, "Rabbi,[m] it is good
for us to be here. Let us put up three
shelters—one for you, one for Moses and
one for Elijah." 6(He did not know what
to say, they were so frightened.)
7Then a cloud appeared and enveloped them, and a voice came from
9:7 [n]Ex 24:16 [o]Mt 3:17 the cloud:[n] "This is my Son, whom I
love. Listen to him!"[o]
8Suddenly, when they looked around,
they no longer saw anyone with them
except Jesus.
9As they were coming down the
mountain, Jesus gave them orders not to 9:9 [p]Mk 8:30 [q]Mt 8:20
tell anyone[p] what they had seen until
the Son of Man[q] had risen from the
dead. 10They kept the matter to themselves, discussing what "rising from the
dead" meant.
11And they asked him, "Why do the
teachers of the law say that Elijah must
come first?"
12Jesus replied, "To be sure, Elijah does
come first, and restores all things. Why
then is it written that the Son of Man[r] 9:12 [r]Mt 8:20 [s]Mt 16:21 [t]Lk 23:11
must suffer much[s] and be rejected?[t]
13But I tell you, Elijah has come,[u] and
they have done to him everything they 9:13 [u]Mt 11:14
wished, just as it is written about him."

The Healing of a Boy With an Evil Spirit

14When they came to the other disciples, they saw a large crowd around
them and the teachers of the law arguing with them. 15As soon as all the people saw Jesus, they were overwhelmed
with wonder and ran to greet him.
16"What are you arguing with them
about?" he asked.
17A man in the crowd answered,
"Teacher, I brought you my son, who is
possessed by a spirit that has robbed
him of speech. 18Whenever it seizes him,
it throws him to the ground. He foams at
the mouth, gnashes his teeth and becomes rigid. I asked your disciples to
drive out the spirit, but they could not."
19"O unbelieving generation," Jesus
replied, "how long shall I stay with you?
How long shall I put up with you? Bring
the boy to me."
20So they brought him. When the
spirit saw Jesus, it immediately threw
the boy into a convulsion. He fell to the
ground and rolled around, foaming at 9:20 [v]Mk 1:26
the mouth.[v]
21Jesus asked the boy's father, "How
long has he been like this?"
"From childhood," he answered. 22"It
has often thrown him into fire or water
to kill him. But if you can do anything,
take pity on us and help us." 9:23 [w]Mt 21:21; Mk 11:23; Jn 11:40
23"'If you can'?" said Jesus. "Every-
thing is possible for him who believes."[w]

a 35 The Greek word means either *life* or *soul*; also in verse 36.

The First Shall Be Last

Most of us have an aversion to wasting our precious minutes by waiting in a long and slow-moving line. But our irritation is exacerbated when someone cuts in line ahead of us. The degree of hostility that can be generated by such a simple act is amazing. Why do we object to people cutting us off? Because we feel that it is unfair for them to push others aside and reach the goal before we do, when we have, after all, been following the rules and patiently waiting. But this very attitude, minor as the incident may seem, lies at the heart of selfishness and represents exactly the opposite of the manner in which Jesus wants his people to live.

Throughout Jesus' earthly ministry his disciples eagerly anticipated his overthrowing the hated Roman government and establishing his own godly kingdom. Beyond this, they repeatedly argued about which of them would be the greatest, about who would make his way to the front of the line first. Imagine their dismay when Jesus informed them that the only way to be first in his kingdom . . . was to be last (Mark 9:35). What is our Lord really telling us?

First, he wants us to put the interests of other people *ahead* of our own. Jesus exemplified this attitude throughout his earthly ministry. Even though he created and controls the world, he did not *demand* that fallen humanity serve him. Instead he *invited* us to serve him by modeling this lifestyle for us; he spent himself in the act of serving us (Mark 10:45; John 13:17; Philippians 2:3–5).

Second, Jesus wants us to guard against an inflated sense of our own importance. The apostle Paul cautioned the believers in Rome: "For by the grace given me I say to every one of you: Do not think of yourself more highly than you ought, but rather think of yourself with sober judgment, in accordance with the measure of faith God has given you" (Romans 12:3). And again in 1 Corinthians 4:7: "Who makes you different from anyone else? What do you have that you did not receive? And if you did receive it, why do you boast as though you did not?"

Paul was asking us to assess our own situation in light of the fact that everything we have and everything we are is a gift from God. And, in Jesus' own words, "From everyone who has been given much, much will be demanded; and from the one who has been entrusted with much, much more will be asked" (Luke 12:48).

We are to live our lives with the servant attitude exemplified by Jesus Christ himself when he stooped to wash the disciples' dusty feet (John 13:14–15). We are to spend ourselves in Jesus' service to the degree to which we have been gifted by him to do so. We are to place ourselves last, not from a mistaken lack of self-esteem but from a sincere love for people and a compelling desire to share the incomparable gifts with which our Lord has showered us.

Self-Discovery: *Imagine that Jesus is kneeling in front of you now, washing your feet. How does this make you feel? Did you know that each act of loving service done for others is accepted by Jesus as an act done for him? (Matthew 25:31–40). In what way can you wash the feet of Jesus today?*

GO TO DISCOVERY 256 ON PAGE 1339

[24]Immediately the boy's father exclaimed, "I do believe; help me overcome
my unbelief!"
9:25 [25]When Jesus saw that a crowd was
x ver 15 running to the scene,[x] he rebuked the
evil[a] spirit. "You deaf and mute spirit,"
he said, "I command you, come out of
him and never enter him again."
[26]The spirit shrieked, convulsed him
violently and came out. The boy looked
so much like a corpse that many said,
"He's dead." [27]But Jesus took him by the
hand and lifted him to his feet, and he
stood up.
9:28 [28]After Jesus had gone indoors, his
y Mk 7:17 disciples asked him privately,[y] "Why
couldn't we drive it out?"
[29]He replied, "This kind can come out
only by prayer.[b]"
[30]They left that place and passed
through Galilee. Jesus did not want anyone to know where they were, [31]because
9:31 he was teaching his disciples. He said to
z Mt 8:20 them, "The Son of Man[z] is going to be
a ver 12; Ac 2:23; 3:13 betrayed into the hands of men. They
b Mt 16:21 will kill him,[a] and after three days[b] he
c Mt 16:21 will rise."[c] [32]But they did not understand
9:32 what he meant[d] and were afraid to ask
d Lk 2:50; 9:45; 18:34; Jn 12:16 him about it.

Who Is the Greatest?

9:33 e Mt 4:13 [33]They came to Capernaum.[e] When
f Mk 1:29 he was in the house,[f] he asked them,
"What were you arguing about on the
road?" [34]But they kept quiet because on
9:34 the way they had argued about who was
g Lk 22:24 the greatest.[g]
[35]Sitting down, Jesus called the
Twelve and said, "If anyone wants to be
9:35 h Mt 18:4; 20:26; first, he must be the very last, and the
Mk 10:43; Lk 22:26 servant of all."[h]
[36]He took a little child and had him
stand among them. Taking him in his
9:36 i Mk 10:16 arms,[i] he said to them, [37]"Whoever welcomes one of these little children in my
name welcomes me; and whoever wel-
9:37 comes me does not welcome me but the
j Mt 10:40 one who sent me."[j]

Whoever Is Not Against Us Is for Us

[38]"Teacher," said John, "we saw a man
driving out demons in your name and
9:38 we told him to stop, because he was not
k Nu 11:27-29 one of us."[k]
[39]"Do not stop him," Jesus said. "No
one who does a miracle in my name can
in the next moment say anything bad
about me, [40]for whoever is not against 9:40
us is for us.[l] [41]I tell you the truth, anyone l Mt 12:30; Lk 11:23
who gives you a cup of water in my
name because you belong to Christ will 9:41
certainly not lose his reward.[m] m Mt 10:42

Causing to Sin

[42]"And if anyone causes one of these 9:42
little ones who believe in me to sin,[n] it n Mt 5:29
would be better for him to be thrown o Mt 18:6; Lk 17:2
into the sea with a large millstone tied
around his neck.[o] [43]If your hand causes
you to sin,[p] cut it off. It is better for you 9:43 p Mt 5:29
to enter life maimed than with two q Mt 5:30; 18:8
hands to go into hell,[q] where the fire r Mt 25:41
never goes out.[c r] [45]And if your foot 9:45
causes you to sin,[s] cut it off. It is better s Mt 5:29
for you to enter life crippled than to t Mt 18:8
have two feet and be thrown into hell.[d t] 9:47
[47]And if your eye causes you to sin,[u] u Mt 5:29
pluck it out. It is better for you to enter v Mt 5:29; 18:9
the kingdom of God with one eye than
to have two eyes and be thrown into
hell,[v] [48]where

" 'their worm does not die, 9:48 w Isa 66:24; Mt 25:41
and the fire is not quenched.'[e w]

[49]Everyone will be salted[x] with fire. 9:49 x Lev 2:13
[50]"Salt is good, but if it loses its salti-
ness, how can you make it salty again?[y] 9:50 y Mt 5:13; Lk 14:34,35
Have salt in yourselves,[z] and be at peace z Col 4:6
with each other."[a] a Ro 12:18; 2Co 13:11; 1Th 5:13

Divorce

10 Jesus then left that place and
went into the region of Judea 10:1
and across the Jordan.[b] Again crowds of b Mk 1:5; Jn 10:40; 11:7
people came to him, and as was his cus- c Mt 4:23; Mk 2:13; 4:2; 6:6,34
tom, he taught them.[c]
[2]Some Pharisees[d] came and tested
him by asking, "Is it lawful for a man to 10:2
divorce his wife?" d Mk 2:16
[3]"What did Moses command you?"
he replied.
[4]They said, "Moses permitted a man
to write a certificate of divorce and send 10:4
her away."[e] e Dt 24:1-4; Mt 5:31
[5]"It was because your hearts were
hard[f] that Moses wrote you this law," 10:5 f Ps 95:8; Heb 3:15
Jesus replied. [6]"But at the beginning of
creation God 'made them male and fe- 10:6
male.'[f g] [7]"For this reason a man will leave g Ge 1:27; 5:2

[a] *25* Greek *unclean* [b] *29* Some manuscripts *prayer and fasting* [c] *43* Some manuscripts *out, [44]where / " 'their worm does not die, / and the fire is not quenched.'* [d] *45* Some manuscripts *hell, [46]where / " 'their worm does not die, / and the fire is not quenched.'* [e] *48* Isaiah 66:24 [f] *6* Gen. 1:27

his father and mother and be united to
10:8 h Ge 2:24; 1Co 6:16 his wife,[a] 8and the two will become one
flesh.'[b][h] So they are no longer two, but
one. 9Therefore what God has joined together, let man not separate."
10When they were in the house again,
the disciples asked Jesus about this. 11He
answered, "Anyone who divorces his
10:11 i Mt 5:32; Lk 16:18 wife and marries another woman commits adultery against her.[i] 12And if she
divorces her husband and marries an-
10:12 j Ro 7:3; 1Co 7:10,11 other man, she commits adultery."[j]

The Little Children and Jesus

13People were bringing little children
to Jesus to have him touch them, but the
disciples rebuked them. 14When Jesus
saw this, he was indignant. He said to
them, "Let the little children come to
me, and do not hinder them, for the
10:14 k Mt 25:34 kingdom of God belongs to such as
these.[k] 15I tell you the truth, anyone who
10:15 l Mt 18:3 will not receive the kingdom of God like
a little child will never enter it."[l] 16And
10:16 m Mk 9:36 he took the children in his arms,[m] put
his hands on them and blessed them.

The Rich Young Man

10:17 n Mk 1:40; o Lk 10:25; Ac 20:32 17As Jesus started on his way, a man
ran up to him and fell on his knees[n] be-
fore him. "Good teacher," he asked,
"what must I do to inherit eternal life?"[o]
18"Why do you call me good?" Jesus
answered. "No one is good—except God
alone. 19You know the commandments:
'Do not murder, do not commit adultery,
do not steal, do not give false testimony,
10:19 p Ex 20:12-16; Dt 5:16-20 do not defraud, honor your father and
mother.'[c][p]
20"Teacher," he declared, "all these I
have kept since I was a boy."
21Jesus looked at him and loved him.
"One thing you lack," he said. "Go, sell
10:21 q Ac 2:45; r Mt 6:20; Lk 12:33; s Mt 4:19 everything you have and give to the
poor,[q] and you will have treasure in
heaven.[r] Then come, follow me."[s]
22At this the man's face fell. He went
away sad, because he had great wealth.
10:23 t Ps 52:7; 62:10; 1Ti 6:9,10,17 23Jesus looked around and said to his
disciples, "How hard it is for the rich[t] to
enter the kingdom of God!"
24The disciples were amazed at his
words. But Jesus said again, "Children,
10:24 u Mt 7:13,14 how hard it is[d] to enter the kingdom of
God![u] 25It is easier for a camel to go
10:25 v Lk 12:16-20 through the eye of a needle than for a
rich man to enter the kingdom of God."[v]

26The disciples were even more
amazed, and said to each other, "Who
then can be saved?"
27Jesus looked at them and said, "With
man this is impossible, but not with 10:27 w Mt 19:26
God; all things are possible with God."[w]
28Peter said to him, "We have left 10:28 x Mt 4:19
everything to follow you!"[x]
29"I tell you the truth," Jesus replied,
"no one who has left home or brothers
or sisters or mother or father or children
or fields for me and the gospel 30will fail
to receive a hundred times as much[y] in 10:30 y Mt 6:33; z Mt 12:32; a Mt 25:46
this present age (homes, brothers, sis-
ters, mothers, children and fields—and
with them, persecutions) and in the age
to come,[z] eternal life.[a] 31But many who 10:31 b Mt 19:30
are first will be last, and the last first."[b]

Jesus Again Predicts His Death

32They were on their way up to Jerusalem, with Jesus leading the way, and the
disciples were astonished, while those
who followed were afraid. Again he took 10:32 c Mk 3:16-19
the Twelve[c] aside and told them what
was going to happen to him. 33"We are 10:33 d Lk 9:51; e Mt 8:20; f Mt 27:1,2
going up to Jerusalem,"[d] he said, "and
the Son of Man[e] will be betrayed to the
chief priests and teachers of the law.[f]
They will condemn him to death and
will hand him over to the Gentiles,
34who will mock him and spit on him, 10:34 g Mt 16:21; h Ac 2:23; 3:13; i Mt 16:21; j Mt 16:21
flog him[g] and kill him.[h] Three days lat-
er[i] he will rise."[j]

The Request of James and John

35Then James and John, the sons of
Zebedee, came to him. "Teacher," they
said, "we want you to do for us whatever we ask."
36"What do you want me to do for
you?" he asked.
37They replied, "Let one of us sit at
your right and the other at your left in 10:37 k Mt 19:28
your glory."[k]
38"You don't know what you are ask- 10:38 l Job 38:2; m Mt 20:22; n Lk 12:50
ing,"[l] Jesus said. "Can you drink the
cup[m] I drink or be baptized with the
baptism I am baptized with?"[n]
39"We can," they answered.
Jesus said to them, "You will drink the
cup I drink and be baptized with the 10:39 o Ac 12:2; Rev 1:9
baptism I am baptized with,[o] 40but to sit
at my right or left is not for me to grant.

[a] *7* Some early manuscripts do not have *and be united to his wife.* [b] *8* Gen. 2:24 [c] *19* Exodus 20:12–16; Deut. 5:16–20 [d] *24* Some manuscripts *is for those who trust in riches*

DISCOVERY 256

WHAT DO YOU WANT?

"What do you want me to do for you?" If Jesus were to appear before you this very moment and ask that straightforward question, how would you respond? For a man named Bartimaeus there could be no hesitation at all: You see, he had been blind from birth (Mark 10:51). "Rabbi," he pleaded, "I want to see." And Jesus immediately healed him.

In order to experience all that Jesus has for us, it is imperative that we first of all *realize that we lack something*. Bartimaeus not only knew that he lacked sight, but he just as surely recognized that he could do nothing to correct the situation himself and, more significantly, that Jesus alone had the power to heal him. A miracle of transformation can occur only after we have admitted our own limitations and acknowledged that Jesus alone can meet the need. In our spiritual blindness we are tempted to falsely assume that we can work things out for ourselves if we will only exercise initiative and creativity.

In order to open the door for a miracle in our lives, we must also seek Jesus and *ignore public opinion*. When Bartimaeus called out to Jesus, the people in the crowd implored him to be quiet (verse 48). Perhaps they assumed that this sorry specimen of a man would bother the busy Jesus or that their own needs were far more important than those of a useless beggar, or maybe they even felt embarrassed by the unwanted interruption. In our lives as well, the "crowd" will often discourage us from getting to know God and taking Jesus seriously. But God is in the business of performing miracles in spite of public cynicism or outcry.

To set the groundwork for miraculous intervention in our lives, we must also, like Bartimaeus, *be persistent*. This blind beggar understood that only Jesus was in a position to heal him, and he was determined to do whatever was necessary to reach him and catch his attention. Had Bartimaeus simply given up when the crowd had rebuffed him, he would have remained blind.

And so it is with us. If we experience doubt as to whether God has heard us the first time (which is never really in question, although he sometimes forces us to wait as a test of our faith), we have to call out again.

It is also critical that we *approach God in faith* when it comes to asking for a miracle. When Bartimaeus asked for sight, Jesus' directive was simple: "Go, your faith has healed you" (verse 52). The power of God healed the blind man, but the healing came about because of the man's faith. It was not the *size* of his faith that mattered but the fact that he was placing his trust in the right person. Even when our faith is weak or wavering, if it is focused on God it can move mountains (Matthew 17:20; 21:21–22).

Self-Discovery: *When you are facing a crisis or a serious need, are you persistent in prayer? How well do you handle having to wait for an answer? How do you respond to those situations in which you perceive a lack of response to a specific prayer?*

GO TO DISCOVERY 257 ON PAGE 1343

WHAT IS SO DIFFICULT ABOUT ACCEPTING THAT THE CLAIM OF JESUS MIGHT BE TRUE? AYE, THERE'S THE RUB: TO DO THIS WILL COST NOT LESS THAN EVERYTHING.

N. T. Wright, *Chaplain, Oxford University*

These places belong to those for whom
they have been prepared."
41When the ten heard about this, they
became indignant with James and John.
42Jesus called them together and said,
"You know that those who are regarded
as rulers of the Gentiles lord it over
them, and their high officials exercise
authority over them. 43Not so with you.
10:43 Instead, whoever wants to become great
p Mk 9:35 among you must be your servant,[p] 44and
whoever wants to be first must be slave
10:45 of all. 45For even the Son of Man did not
q Mt 20:28 come to be served, but to serve,[q] and to
r Mt 20:28 give his life as a ransom for many."[r]

Blind Bartimaeus Receives His Sight

46Then they came to Jericho. As Jesus
and his disciples, together with a large
crowd, were leaving the city, a blind
man, Bartimaeus (that is, the Son of Ti-
maeus), was sitting by the roadside beg-
10:47 ging. 47When he heard that it was Jesus
s Mk 1:24 of Nazareth,[s] he began to shout, "Jesus,
t Mt 9:27 Son of David,[t] have mercy on me!"
48Many rebuked him and told him to
be quiet, but he shouted all the more,
"Son of David, have mercy on me!"
49Jesus stopped and said, "Call him."
So they called to the blind man,
"Cheer up! On your feet! He's calling
you." 50Throwing his cloak aside, he
jumped to his feet and came to Jesus.
51"What do you want me to do for
10:51 you?" Jesus asked him.
u Mt 23:7 The blind man said, "Rabbi,[u] I want to
see."
10:52 52"Go," said Jesus, "your faith has
v Mt 9:22 healed you."[v] Immediately he received his
w Mt 4:19 sight and followed[w] Jesus along the road.

The Triumphal Entry

11 As they approached Jerusalem
11:1 and came to Bethphage and
x Mt 21:17 Bethany[x] at the Mount of Olives,[y] Jesus
y Mt 21:1 sent two of his disciples, 2saying to
them, "Go to the village ahead of you,
and just as you enter it, you will find a
colt tied there, which no one has ever 11:2
ridden.[z] Untie it and bring it here. 3If z Nu 19:2;
anyone asks you, 'Why are you doing Dt 21:3; 1Sa 6:7
this?' tell him, 'The Lord needs it and
will send it back here shortly.' "
4They went and found a colt outside 11:4
in the street, tied at a doorway.[a] As they a Mk 14:16
untied it, 5some people standing there
asked, "What are you doing, untying that
colt?" 6They answered as Jesus had told
them to, and the people let them go.
7When they brought the colt to Jesus and
threw their cloaks over it, he sat on it.
8Many people spread their cloaks on the
road, while others spread branches they
had cut in the fields. 9Those who went
ahead and those who followed shouted,

"Hosanna![a]"

"Blessed is he who comes in the 11:9
name of the Lord!"[b] [b] b Ps 118:25,26;
Mt 23:39
10"Blessed is the coming kingdom of
our father David!"

"Hosanna in the highest!"[c] 11:10
c Lk 2:14

11Jesus entered Jerusalem and went to
the temple. He looked around at everything, but since it was already late, he 11:11
went out to Bethany with the Twelve.[d] d Mt 21:12,17

Jesus Clears the Temple

12The next day as they were leaving
Bethany, Jesus was hungry. 13Seeing in
the distance a fig tree in leaf, he went to
find out if it had any fruit. When he
reached it, he found nothing but leaves, 11:13
because it was not the season for figs.[e] e Lk 13:6-9
14Then he said to the tree, "May no one
ever eat fruit from you again." And his
disciples heard him say it.
15On reaching Jerusalem, Jesus entered the temple area and began driving
out those who were buying and selling
there. He overturned the tables of the
money changers and the benches of
those selling doves, 16and would not allow anyone to carry merchandise
through the temple courts. 17And as he
taught them, he said, "Is it not written:

" 'My house will be called 11:17
a house of prayer for all f Isa 56:7
nations'[c]?[f]

[a] 9 A Hebrew expression meaning "Save!" which became an exclamation of praise; also in verse 10
[b] 9 Psalm 118:25,26 [c] 17 Isaiah 56:7

11:17 But you have made it 'a den of rob-
gJer 7:11 bers.'[a]"[g]
18 The chief priests and the teachers of
11:18 hMt 21:46; the law heard this and began looking for
Mk 12:12; a way to kill him, for they feared him,[h]
Lk 20:19 iMt 7:28 because the whole crowd was amazed at
his teaching.[i]
11:19 19 When evening came, they[b] went out
jLk 21:37 of the city.[j]

The Withered Fig Tree

20 In the morning, as they went along,
they saw the fig tree withered from the
roots. 21 Peter remembered and said to
11:21 kMt 23:7 Jesus, "Rabbi,[k] look! The fig tree you
cursed has withered!"
22 "Have[c] faith in God," Jesus answered.
23 "I tell you the truth, if anyone says to
this mountain, 'Go, throw yourself into
the sea,' and does not doubt in his heart
11:23 but believes that what he says will hap-
lMt 21:21 pen, it will be done for him.[l] 24 Therefore
I tell you, whatever you ask for in prayer,
believe that you have received it, and it
11:24 mMt 7:7 will be yours.[m] 25 And when you stand
praying, if you hold anything against
11:25 anyone, forgive him, so that your Father
nMt 6:14 in heaven may forgive you your sins."[d][n]

The Authority of Jesus Questioned

27 They arrived again in Jerusalem,
and while Jesus was walking in the temple courts, the chief priests, the teachers
of the law and the elders came to him.
28 "By what authority are you doing these
things?" they asked. "And who gave you
authority to do this?"
29 Jesus replied, "I will ask you one
question. Answer me, and I will tell you
by what authority I am doing these
things. 30 John's baptism—was it from
heaven, or from men? Tell me!"
31 They discussed it among themselves and said, "If we say, 'From heaven,'
he will ask, 'Then why didn't you believe
him?' 32 But if we say, 'From men' . . ."
11:32 (They feared the people, for everyone
oMt 11:9 held that John really was a prophet.)[o]
33 So they answered Jesus, "We don't
know."
Jesus said, "Neither will I tell you by
what authority I am doing these things."

The Parable of the Tenants

12 He then began to speak to them
in parables: "A man planted a
12:1 pIsa 5:1-7 vineyard.[p] He put a wall around it, dug a
pit for the winepress and built a watch-
tower. Then he rented the vineyard to
some farmers and went away on a journey. 2 At harvest time he sent a servant to
the tenants to collect from them some of
the fruit of the vineyard. 3 But they seized
him, beat him and sent him away empty-
handed. 4 Then he sent another servant
to them; they struck this man on the
head and treated him shamefully. 5 He
sent still another, and that one they
killed. He sent many others; some of
them they beat, others they killed.
6 "He had one left to send, a son, 12:6
whom he loved. He sent him last of all,[q] qHeb 1:1-3
saying, 'They will respect my son.'
7 "But the tenants said to one another,
'This is the heir. Come, let's kill him, and
the inheritance will be ours.' 8 So they
took him and killed him, and threw him
out of the vineyard.
9 "What then will the owner of the
vineyard do? He will come and kill those
tenants and give the vineyard to others.
10 Haven't you read this scripture:

" 'The stone the builders rejected 12:10
has become the capstone[e];[r] rAc 4:11
11 the Lord has done this,
and it is marvelous in our 12:11
eyes'[f]?"[s] sPs 118:22,23

12 Then they looked for a way to arrest
him because they knew he had spoken
the parable against them. But they were 12:12
afraid of the crowd;[t] so they left him and tMk 11:18
went away.[u] uMt 22:22

Paying Taxes to Caesar

13 Later they sent some of the Phar- 12:13
isees and Herodians[v] to Jesus to catch vMt 22:16;
him[w] in his words. 14 They came to him Mk 3:6
and said, "Teacher, we know you are a wMt 12:10
man of integrity. You aren't swayed by
men, because you pay no attention to
who they are; but you teach the way of
God in accordance with the truth. Is it
right to pay taxes to Caesar or not?
15 Should we pay or shouldn't we?"
But Jesus knew their hypocrisy. "Why
are you trying to trap me?" he asked.
"Bring me a denarius and let me look at
it." 16 They brought the coin, and he

[a] 17 Jer. 7:11 [b] 19 Some early manuscripts *he*
[c] 22 Some early manuscripts *If you have*
[d] 25 Some manuscripts *sins. 26But if you do not forgive, neither will your Father who is in heaven forgive your sins.*
[e] 10 Or *cornerstone*
[f] 11 Psalm 118:22,23

asked them, "Whose portrait is this?
And whose inscription?"
"Caesar's," they replied.
17Then Jesus said to them, "Give to
12:17 Caesar what is Caesar's and to God what
[x] Ro 13:7 is God's."[x]
And they were amazed at him.

Marriage at the Resurrection

12:18 [y] Ac 4:1 18Then the Sadducees,[y] who say there
[z] Ac 23:8; is no resurrection,[z] came to him with a
1Co 15:12 question. 19"Teacher," they said, "Moses
wrote for us that if a man's brother dies
and leaves a wife but no children, the
12:19 man must marry the widow and have
[a] Dt 25:5 children for his brother.[a] 20Now there
were seven brothers. The first one married and died without leaving any children. 21The second one married the widow, but he also died, leaving no child. It
was the same with the third. 22In fact,
none of the seven left any children. Last
of all, the woman died too. 23At the resurrection[a] whose wife will she be, since
the seven were married to her?"
12:24 24Jesus replied, "Are you not in error
[b] 2Ti 3:15-17 because you do not know the Scriptures[b]
or the power of God? 25When the dead
rise, they will neither marry nor be given
12:25 in marriage; they will be like the angels in
[c] 1Co 15:42,49, heaven.[c] 26Now about the dead rising—
52 have you not read in the book of Moses,
in the account of the bush, how God said
12:26 to him, 'I am the God of Abraham, the
[d] Ex 3:6 God of Isaac, and the God of Jacob'[b]?[d]
27He is not the God of the dead, but of the
living. You are badly mistaken!"

The Greatest Commandment

12:28 [e] Lk 10:25-28; 28One of the teachers of the law[e] came
20:39 and heard them debating. Noticing that
Jesus had given them a good answer, he
asked him, "Of all the commandments,
which is the most important?"
29"The most important one," answered Jesus, "is this: 'Hear, O Israel, the
Lord our God, the Lord is one.[c] 30Love
the Lord your God with all your heart
12:30 and with all your soul and with all your
[f] Dt 6:4,5 mind and with all your strength.'[d][f] 31The
12:31 second is this: 'Love your neighbor as
[g] Lev 19:18; yourself.'[e][g] There is no commandment
Mt 5:43 greater than these."
12:32 32"Well said, teacher," the man replied.
[h] Dt 4:35,39; "You are right in saying that God is one
Isa 45:6,14; 46:9 and there is no other but him.[h] 33To love
him with all your heart, with all your understanding and with all your strength,
and to love your neighbor as yourself is
more important than all burnt offerings 12:33
and sacrifices."[i] [i] 1Sa 15:22;
34When Jesus saw that he had an- Hos 6:6; Mic 6:6-8;
swered wisely, he said to him, "You are Heb 10:8
not far from the kingdom of God."[j] And 12:34
from then on no one dared ask him any [j] Mt 3:2 [k] Mt 22:46;
more questions.[k] Lk 20:40

Whose Son Is the Christ?

35While Jesus was teaching in the 12:35
temple courts,[l] he asked, "How is it that [l] Mt 26:55
the teachers of the law say that the [m] Mt 9:27
Christ[f] is the son of David?[m] 36David
himself, speaking by the Holy Spirit,[n] 12:36
declared: [n] 2Sa 23:2 [o] Ps 110:1;

" 'The Lord said to my Lord: Mt 22:44
"Sit at my right hand
until I put your enemies
under your feet." '[g][o]

37David himself calls him 'Lord.' How
then can he be his son?" 12:37
The large crowd[p] listened to him with [p] Jn 12:9
delight.
38As he taught, Jesus said, "Watch out
for the teachers of the law. They like to
walk around in flowing robes and be
greeted in the marketplaces, 39and have
the most important seats in the synagogues and the places of honor at ban- 12:39
quets.[q] 40They devour widows' houses [q] Lk 11:43
and for a show make lengthy prayers.
Such men will be punished most severely."

The Widow's Offering

41Jesus sat down opposite the place 12:41
where the offerings were put[r] and [r] 2Ki 12:9;
watched the crowd putting their money Jn 8:20
into the temple treasury. Many rich people threw in large amounts. 42But a poor
widow came and put in two very small
copper coins,[h] worth only a fraction of a
penny.[i]
43Calling his disciples to him, Jesus
said, "I tell you the truth, this poor widow has put more into the treasury than
all the others. 44They all gave out of their
wealth; but she, out of her poverty, put in 12:44
everything—all she had to live on."[s] [s] 2Co 8:12

[a] *23* Some manuscripts *resurrection, when men rise from the dead,* [b] *26* Exodus 3:6 [c] *29* Or *the Lord our God is one Lord* [d] *30* Deut. 6:4,5 [e] *31* Lev. 19:18 [f] *35* Or *Messiah* [g] *36* Psalm 110:1 [h] *42* Greek *two lepta* [i] *42* Greek *kodrantes*

The Secret of Giving

How we spend our money is a clear indication of where our priorities lie. Jesus held very strong opinions about money. In fact, he talked about this subject more than about heaven or hell. One of the ways in which we can demonstrate our commitment to him is through the willing donation of our financial resources for the Lord and his work. In the Bible we read about three different kinds of giving:

First, there is *systematic giving*. God asks us to contribute a set percentage of our income on a regular basis. This consistent pattern of giving reminds us that Jesus is Lord of our finances (1 Corinthians 16:2).

Second, there is *spontaneous giving*. When we meet people with specific needs we should be prepared to offer our own resources on an impromptu basis. James encouraged us to give to others freely whenever the need arises (James 2:16).

Finally, the Bible urges believers to participate in *sacrificial giving*—offering gifts above and beyond what we think we can afford. This kind of giving alters our personal lifestyle and costs us in a significant way (2 Corinthians 8:2–3). Jesus' own life is an example of this highest form of giving: "Though he was rich, yet for your sakes he became poor, so that you through his poverty might become rich" (2 Corinthians 8:9).

One day, as people were making their offerings at the temple, Jesus singled out one woman, a destitute widow, as one who served as an example of a generous heart. Many rich people were donating large quantities of gold and silver, but the widow contributed only two small copper coins. But Jesus made a startling observation: She had actually sacrificed *more* than all of the others put together—because she had given everything she had! (Mark 12:43–44).

God's perspective on giving has little to do with an impressive balance in our checkbook. God's promise in Scripture will be true for you as well: "Now he who supplies seed to the sower and bread for food will also supply and increase your store of seed and will enlarge the harvest of your righteousness. You will be made rich in every way so that you can be generous on every occasion, and through us your generosity will result in thanksgiving to God" (2 Corinthians 9:10–11). What God is looking for is a generous heart and an attitude that puts others first. A person who gives sacrificially does so because she trusts that God will provide whatever she needs.

Self-Discovery: *Grade yourself in the areas of systematic and spontaneous giving? Which comes more easily to you, and why?*

GO TO DISCOVERY 258 ON PAGE 1347

Signs of the End of the Age

13 As he was leaving the temple,
one of his disciples said to him,
"Look, Teacher! What massive stones!
What magnificent buildings!"
2"Do you see all these great buildings?" replied Jesus. "Not one stone here
13:2 will be left on another; every one will be
t Lk 19:44 thrown down."[t]
3As Jesus was sitting on the Mount of
13:3 Olives[u] opposite the temple, Peter,
u Mt 21:1 v Mt 4:21 James, John[v] and Andrew asked him privately, 4"Tell us, when will these things
happen? And what will be the sign that
they are all about to be fulfilled?"
13:5 5Jesus said to them: "Watch out that
w ver 22; no one deceives you.[w] 6Many will come
Jer 29:8; Eph 5:6; in my name, claiming, 'I am he,' and will
2Th 2:3,10-12; deceive many. 7When you hear of wars
1Ti 4:1; 2Ti 3:13; 1Jn 4:6 and rumors of wars, do not be alarmed.
Such things must happen, but the end is
still to come. 8Nation will rise against
nation, and kingdom against kingdom.
There will be earthquakes in various
places, and famines. These are the beginning of birth pains.
9"You must be on your guard. You will
be handed over to the local councils and
13:9 x Mt 10:17 flogged in the synagogues.[x] On account
of me you will stand before governors
and kings as witnesses to them. 10And
the gospel must first be preached to all
nations. 11Whenever you are arrested
and brought to trial, do not worry beforehand about what to say. Just say
13:11 whatever is given you at the time, for it
y Mt 10:19,20; Lk 12:11,12 is not you speaking, but the Holy Spirit.[y]
12"Brother will betray brother to
death, and a father his child. Children
13:12 will rebel against their parents and have
z Mic 7:6; Mt 10:21; them put to death.[z] 13All men will hate
Lk 12:51-53 you because of me,[a] but he who stands
firm to the end will be saved.[b]
13:13 a Jn 15:21 14"When you see 'the abomination
b Mt 10:22 that causes desolation'[a][c] standing where
13:14 it[b] does not belong—let the reader un-
c Da 9:27; 11:31; 12:11 derstand—then let those who are in Judea flee to the mountains. 15Let no one
on the roof of his house go down or enter the house to take anything out. 16Let
no one in the field go back to get his
cloak. 17How dreadful it will be in those
days for pregnant women and nursing
13:17 d Lk 23:29 mothers![d] 18Pray that this will not take
place in winter, 19because those will be
days of distress unequaled from the be-
13:19 e Mk 10:6 ginning, when God created the world,[e]
until now—and never to be equaled
again.[f] 20If the Lord had not cut short 13:19
those days, no one would survive. But f Da 9:26; 12:1; Joel 2:2
for the sake of the elect, whom he has
chosen, he has shortened them. 21At
that time if anyone says to you, 'Look,
here is the Christ[c]!' or, 'Look, there he is!' 13:21
do not believe it.[g] 22For false Christs and g Lk 17:23; 21:8
false prophets[h] will appear and perform 13:22
signs and miracles[i] to deceive the h Mt 7:15 i Jn 4:48;
elect—if that were possible. 23So be on 2Th 2:9,10
your guard;[j] I have told you everything 13:23
ahead of time. j 2Pe 3:17
24"But in those days, following that
distress,

" 'the sun will be darkened,
and the moon will not give its
light;
25the stars will fall from the sky,
and the heavenly bodies will be 13:25 k Isa 13:10; 34:4;
shaken.'[d][k] Mt 24:29

26"At that time men will see the Son of 13:26
Man coming in clouds[l] with great pow- l Da 7:13;
er and glory. 27And he will send his an- Mt 16:27; Rev 1:7
gels and gather his elect from the four
winds, from the ends of the earth to the
ends of the heavens.[m] 13:27 m Zec 2:6
28"Now learn this lesson from the fig
tree: As soon as its twigs get tender and
its leaves come out, you know that summer is near. 29Even so, when you see
these things happening, you know that
it is near, right at the door. 30I tell you the 13:30
truth, this generation[e][n] will certainly n Lk 17:25
not pass away until all these things have o Mk 9:1
happened.[o] 31Heaven and earth will pass
away, but my words will never pass 13:31
away.[p] p Mt 5:18

The Day and Hour Unknown

32"No one knows about that day or
hour, not even the angels in heaven, nor
the Son, but only the Father.[q] 33Be on 13:32 q Ac 1:7;
guard! Be alert[f]![r] You do not know when 1Th 5:1,2
that time will come. 34It's like a man go- 13:33
ing away: He leaves his house and puts r 1Th 5:6
his servants[s] in charge, each with his as- 13:34
signed task, and tells the one at the door s Mt 25:14
to keep watch.
35"Therefore keep watch because you
do not know when the owner of the
house will come back—whether in
the evening, or at midnight, or when the

[a] *14* Daniel 9:27; 11:31; 12:11 [b] *14* Or *he*; also in verse 29 [c] *21* Or *Messiah* [d] *25* Isaiah 13:10; 34:4 [e] *30* Or *race* [f] *33* Some manuscripts *alert and pray*

> CALL ON THE COMING JUDGE
> TO BE YOUR PRESENT SAVIOR.
> AS JUDGE, HE IS THE LAW,
> BUT AS SAVIOR, HE IS THE GOSPEL.
>
> 
>
> J. I. Packer,
> *British Theologian*

rooster crows, or at dawn. 36If he comes
suddenly, do not let him find you sleeping. 37What I say to you, I say to every-
13:37 [t]Lk 12:35-40 one: 'Watch!' "[t]

Jesus Anointed at Bethany

14:1 [u]Jn 11:55; 13:1 14 Now the Passover[u] and the
[v]Mt 12:14 Feast of Unleavened Bread were
only two days away, and the chief priests
and the teachers of the law were looking
for some sly way to arrest Jesus and kill
him.[v] 2"But not during the Feast," they
said, "or the people may riot."
14:3 [w]Mt 21:17 3While he was in Bethany,[w] reclining
[x]Lk 7:37-39 at the table in the home of a man known
as Simon the Leper, a woman came with
an alabaster jar of very expensive perfume, made of pure nard. She broke the
jar and poured the perfume on his head.[x]
4Some of those present were saying
indignantly to one another, "Why this
waste of perfume? 5It could have been
sold for more than a year's wages[a] and
the money given to the poor." And they
rebuked her harshly.
6"Leave her alone," said Jesus. "Why
are you bothering her? She has done a
beautiful thing to me. 7The poor you will
always have with you, and you can help
14:7 [y]Dt 15:11 them any time you want.[y] But you will
not always have me. 8She did what she
14:8 [z]Jn 19:40 could. She poured perfume on my body
beforehand to prepare for my burial.[z] 9I
14:9 [a]Mt 24:14; tell you the truth, wherever the gospel is
Mk 16:15 preached throughout the world,[a] what
she has done will also be told, in memory of her."
14:10 [b]Mk 3:16-19 10Then Judas Iscariot, one of the
[c]Mt 10:4 Twelve,[b] went to the chief priests to betray Jesus to them.[c] 11They were delighted to hear this and promised to give him
money. So he watched for an opportunity to hand him over.

The Lord's Supper

12On the first day of the Feast of Unleavened Bread, when it was customary
to sacrifice the Passover lamb,[d] Jesus' 14:12 [d]Ex 12:1-11;
disciples asked him, "Where do you Dt 16:1-4;
want us to go and make preparations for 1Co 5:7
you to eat the Passover?"
13So he sent two of his disciples, telling
them, "Go into the city, and a man carrying a jar of water will meet you. Follow
him. 14Say to the owner of the house he
enters, 'The Teacher asks: Where is my
guest room, where I may eat the Passover
with my disciples?' 15He will show you a 14:15
large upper room,[e] furnished and ready. [e]Ac 1:13
Make preparations for us there."
16The disciples left, went into the city
and found things just as Jesus had told
them. So they prepared the Passover.
17When evening came, Jesus arrived
with the Twelve. 18While they were reclining at the table eating, he said, "I tell
you the truth, one of you will betray
me—one who is eating with me."
19They were saddened, and one by
one they said to him, "Surely not I?"
20"It is one of the Twelve," he replied,
"one who dips bread into the bowl with 14:20
me.[f] 21The Son of Man[g] will go just as it [f]Jn 13:18-27
is written about him. But woe to that 14:21
man who betrays the Son of Man! It [g]Mt 8:20
would be better for him if he had not
been born."
22While they were eating, Jesus took 14:22
bread, gave thanks and broke it,[h] and [h]Mt 14:19
gave it to his disciples, saying, "Take it;
this is my body."
23Then he took the cup, gave thanks
and offered it to them, and they all 14:23
drank from it.[i] [i]1Co 10:16
24"This is my blood of the[b] covenant,[j] 14:24
which is poured out for many," he said to [j]Mt 26:28
them. 25"I tell you the truth, I will not
drink again of the fruit of the vine until
that day when I drink it anew in the 14:25
kingdom of God."[k] [k]Mt 3:2
26When they had sung a hymn, they 14:26
went out to the Mount of Olives.[l] [l]Mt 21:1

Jesus Predicts Peter's Denial

27"You will all fall away," Jesus told
them, "for it is written:

" 'I will strike the shepherd,
and the sheep will be 14:27
scattered.'[c][m] [m]Zec 13:7

28But after I have risen, I will go ahead of 14:28
you into Galilee."[n] [n]Mk 16:7

[a]5 Greek *than three hundred denarii* [b]24 Some manuscripts *the new* [c]27 Zech. 13:7

29 Peter declared, "Even if all fall away,
I will not."
30 "I tell you the truth," Jesus answered,
"today—yes, tonight—before the roost-
14:30 er crows twice[a] you yourself will disown
[o] ver 66-72; Lk 22:34; me three times."[o]
Jn 13:38 31 But Peter insisted emphatically,
14:31 "Even if I have to die with you,[p] I will
[p] Lk 22:33; never disown you." And all the others
Jn 13:37 said the same.

Gethsemane

32 They went to a place called Gethsemane, and Jesus said to his disciples,
"Sit here while I pray." 33 He took Peter,
14:33 [q] Mt 4:21 James and John[q] along with him, and he
began to be deeply distressed and trou-
14:34 bled. 34 "My soul is overwhelmed with
[r] Jn 12:27 sorrow to the point of death,"[r] he said to
them. "Stay here and keep watch."
35 Going a little farther, he fell to the
14:35 ground and prayed that if possible the
[s] ver 41; hour[s] might pass from him. 36 *"Abba,*[b] Fa-
Mt 26:18 ther,"[t] he said, "everything is possible for
14:36 you. Take this cup[u] from me. Yet not
[t] Ro 8:15; what I will, but what you will."[v]
Gal 4:6
[u] Mt 20:22 37 Then he returned to his disciples
[v] Mt 26:39 and found them sleeping. "Simon," he
said to Peter, "are you asleep? Could you
not keep watch for one hour? 38 Watch
14:38 and pray so that you will not fall into
[w] Mt 6:13 temptation.[w] The spirit is willing, but
[x] Ro 7:22,23 the body is weak."[x]

JESUS FOCUS

A PLACE OF TRIUMPH

Gethsemane is an olive garden east of Jerusalem on the slope of a mountain called the Mount of Olives. It sits directly across from the temple and the eastern gate, overlooking Jerusalem across the Kidron Valley. Jesus apparently loved this secluded retreat and frequently went there to pray (Luke 22:39; John 18:1–2).

On the night before his death Jesus entered this wooded sanctuary to address the Father in privacy (Mark 14:32). It was here that Judas and others in the arresting group located him and from here that Jesus was taken back to the city for questioning by the high priest. While we often identify Gethsemane as a place of suffering because of Jesus' anguished prayer there, it was ultimately a place of triumph—it was in his beloved Gethsemane that Jesus finally and completely accepted the Father's will that he die for our sins.

39 Once more he went away and
prayed the same thing. 40 When he came
back, he again found them sleeping, because their eyes were heavy. They did
not know what to say to him.
41 Returning the third time, he said to
them, "Are you still sleeping and resting? 14:41
Enough! The hour[y] has come. Look, the [y] ver 35; Mt 26:18
Son of Man is betrayed into the hands of
sinners. 42 Rise! Let us go! Here comes my
betrayer!"

Jesus Arrested

43 Just as he was speaking, Judas,[z] one 14:43 [z] Mt 10:4
of the Twelve, appeared. With him was a
crowd armed with swords and clubs,
sent from the chief priests, the teachers
of the law, and the elders.
44 Now the betrayer had arranged a
signal with them: "The one I kiss is the
man; arrest him and lead him away under guard." 45 Going at once to Jesus, Ju- 14:45
das said, "Rabbi!"[a] and kissed him. 46 The [a] Mt 23:7
men seized Jesus and arrested him.
47 Then one of those standing near drew
his sword and struck the servant of the
high priest, cutting off his ear.
48 "Am I leading a rebellion," said Jesus,
"that you have come out with swords
and clubs to capture me? 49 Every day I
was with you, teaching in the temple 14:49
courts,[b] and you did not arrest me. But [b] Mt 26:55
the Scriptures must be fulfilled."[c] 50 Then [c] Isa 53:7-12;
everyone deserted him and fled.[d] Mt 1:22
51 A young man, wearing nothing but 14:50
a linen garment, was following Jesus. [d] ver 27
When they seized him, 52 he fled naked,
leaving his garment behind.

Before the Sanhedrin

53 They took Jesus to the high priest,
and all the chief priests, elders and
teachers of the law came together. 54 Peter followed him at a distance, right into 14:54
the courtyard of the high priest.[e] There [e] Mt 26:3
he sat with the guards and warmed him- [f] Jn 18:18
self at the fire.[f]
55 The chief priests and the whole San- 14:55
hedrin[g] were looking for evidence [g] Mt 5:22
against Jesus so that they could put him
to death, but they did not find any.
56 Many testified falsely against him, but
their statements did not agree.
57 Then some stood up and gave this
false testimony against him: 58 "We

[a] 30 Some early manuscripts do not have *twice.*
[b] 36 Aramaic for *Father*

DISCOVERY 258

JUDAS, THE TRAITOR

Not many of us would name our son Judas, and few have done so since the day that name became synonymous with being a traitor. The name of the "disciple" who betrayed Jesus has come to represent evil, darkness, sin, betrayal—and Satan himself. But who was Judas before he became the most infamous traitor of all time?

First of all, Judas was a man singled out by Jesus himself to follow him and learn from him (Mark 3:13–19). Like the other disciples Judas spent three years in the presence of God the Son. He witnessed the same miracles as the other 11 disciples, listened to the same parables, heard the same teaching, ate the same food and slept in the same places. He even went out with the others to preach, heal the sick and drive out demons (Mark 3:14–15).

Judas was also responsible for the group's finances, and, as treasurer-turned-thief, he was inordinately concerned about "proper" use of funds. Once, when Jesus' friend Mary poured expensive perfume on Jesus' feet and wiped it off with her hair, Judas objected vehemently to her extravagant gesture: "Why wasn't this perfume sold and the money given to the poor?" But John 12:4 states clearly that Judas didn't really care about the poor; he was concerned only with lining his own pocketbook. His final act of lascivious greed, predicted by Jesus in Mark 14:18–21 and carried out in verses 43–46, was the natural outgrowth of a long-time pattern of behavior. And underlining Judas' total lack of scruples was the tragic reality that he betrayed his "Lord" with a kiss!

God had foretold in the Old Testament that the Messiah would be betrayed, but Judas was still responsible for his actions (Psalm 41:9). James asked the question in James 4:4: "Don't you know that friendship with the world is hatred toward God?" If Jesus Christ does not have mastery over our lives, another master will move in quickly to fill the void. "Don't you know," asked the apostle Paul, "that when you offer yourselves to someone to obey him as slaves, you are slaves to the one whom you obey—whether you are slaves to sin, which leads to death, or to obedience, which leads to righteousness" (Romans 6:16). Yes, Judas most certainly had a choice, and his tragedy is compounded by the fact that he of all people had been given the opportunity to sit at the Master's feet for three years.

No one's Christian character is caught by osmosis, nor does the Christian faith "rub off" on a child from a godly parent. Both Scripture and our own lives are replete with examples of people who, despite every spiritual advantage, have opted to throw away the gift that has been placed in their lap from early childhood. By the same token, each of us can point to examples of believers who have overcome seemingly insurmountable obstacles to follow Jesus. It is imperative that we as Christian parents and friends model our faith and nurture those who come behind us. But we must also impress on them the need for an individual decision for Christ Jesus.

Self-Discovery: *Can you identify anything in your life or in the lives of those you love that could grow, like spiritual cancer, and gradually replace loyalty to Jesus? The apostle James gave an effective prescription in James 4:6–10.*

GO TO DISCOVERY 259 ON PAGE 1350

MAN OF SORROWS! WHAT A NAME
FOR THE SON OF GOD, WHO CAME
RUINED SINNERS TO RECLAIM.
HALLELUJAH! WHAT A SAVIOR!

Philip Bliss, *American Hymn Writer*

heard him say, 'I will destroy this man-
made temple and in three days will build
14:58 h Mk 15:29; another,[h] not made by man.' " 59 Yet even
Jn 2:19 then their testimony did not agree.
60 Then the high priest stood up before
them and asked Jesus, "Are you not going to answer? What is this testimony
that these men are bringing against
14:61 you?" 61 But Jesus remained silent and
i Isa 53:7; Mt 27:12,14; gave no answer.[i]
Mk 15:5; Lk 23:9; Jn 19:9 Again the high priest asked him, "Are
j Mt 16:16; Jn 4:25,26 you the Christ,[a] the Son of the Blessed
One?"[j]
62 "I am," said Jesus. "And you will see
the Son of Man sitting at the right hand
14:62 of the Mighty One and coming on the
k Rev 1:7 clouds of heaven."[k]
14:63 63 The high priest tore his clothes.[l]
l Lev 10:6; 21:10; "Why do we need any more witnesses?"
Nu 14:6; Ac 14:14 he asked. 64 "You have heard the blasphemy. What do you think?"
14:64 They all condemned him as worthy of
m Lev 24:16 death.[m] 65 Then some began to spit at
him; they blindfolded him, struck him
14:65 with their fists, and said, "Prophesy!"
n Mt 16:21 And the guards took him and beat him.[n]

Peter Disowns Jesus

14:66 66 While Peter was below in the court-
o ver 54 yard,[o] one of the servant girls of the high
14:67 priest came by. 67 When she saw Peter
p ver 54 q Mk 1:24 warming himself,[p] she looked closely at
him.
"You also were with that Nazarene,
Jesus,"[q] she said.
14:68 68 But he denied it. "I don't know or un-
r ver 30,72 derstand what you're talking about,"[r] he
said, and went out into the entryway.[b]
69 When the servant girl saw him
there, she said again to those standing
14:70 around, "This fellow is one of them."
s ver 30,68,72 t Ac 2:7 70 Again he denied it.[s]
After a little while, those standing
near said to Peter, "Surely you are one of
them, for you are a Galilean."[t]
71 He began to call down curses on
14:71 himself, and he swore to them, "I don't
u ver 30,72 know this man you're talking about."[u]
72 Immediately the rooster crowed the
second time.[c] Then Peter remembered
the word Jesus had spoken to him: "Before the rooster crows twice[d] you will 14:72
disown me three times."[v] And he broke v ver 30,68
down and wept.

Jesus Before Pilate

15 Very early in the morning, the
chief priests, with the elders, 15:1
the teachers of the law[w] and the whole w Mt 27:1;
Sanhedrin,[x] reached a decision. They Lk 22:66 x Mt 5:22
bound Jesus, led him away and handed y Mt 27:2
him over to Pilate.[y]
2 "Are you the king of the Jews?"[z] 15:2 z ver 9,12,18,26;
asked Pilate. Mt 2:2
"Yes, it is as you say," Jesus replied.
3 The chief priests accused him of
many things. 4 So again Pilate asked him,
"Aren't you going to answer? See how
many things they are accusing you of." 15:5
5 But Jesus still made no reply,[a] and Pi- a Mk 14:61
late was amazed.
6 Now it was the custom at the Feast
to release a prisoner whom the people
requested. 7 A man called Barabbas was
in prison with the insurrectionists who
had committed murder in the uprising.
8 The crowd came up and asked Pilate to
do for them what he usually did.
9 "Do you want me to release to you 15:9
the king of the Jews?"[b] asked Pilate, b ver 2
10 knowing it was out of envy that the
chief priests had handed Jesus over to
him. 11 But the chief priests stirred up
the crowd to have Pilate release Barab- 15:11
bas[c] instead. c Ac 3:14
12 "What shall I do, then, with the one
you call the king of the Jews?" Pilate
asked them.
13 "Crucify him!" they shouted.
14 "Why? What crime has he committed?" asked Pilate.
But they shouted all the louder, "Crucify him!"
15 Wanting to satisfy the crowd, Pilate
released Barabbas to them. He had Jesus 15:15
flogged,[d] and handed him over to be d Isa 53:6
crucified.

The Soldiers Mock Jesus

16 The soldiers led Jesus away into the 15:16
palace[e] (that is, the Praetorium) and e Jn 18:28,33;
called together the whole company of 19:9

[a] 61 Or *Messiah* [b] 68 Some early manuscripts *entryway and the rooster crowed* [c] 72 Some early manuscripts do not have *the second time.* [d] 72 Some early manuscripts do not have *twice.*

soldiers. 17They put a purple robe on
him, then twisted together a crown of
thorns and set it on him. 18And they be-
15:18 gan to call out to him, "Hail, king of the
[f] ver 2 Jews!"[f] 19Again and again they struck
him on the head with a staff and spit on
him. Falling on their knees, they paid
homage to him. 20And when they had
mocked him, they took off the purple
15:20 robe and put his own clothes on him.
[g] Heb 13:12 Then they led him out[g] to crucify him.

The Crucifixion

15:21 [h] Mt 27:32 21A certain man from Cyrene,[h] Si-
[i] Ro 16:13 mon, the father of Alexander and Ru-
[j] Mt 27:32; fus,[i] was passing by on his way in from
Lk 23:26 the country, and they forced him to carry the cross.[j] 22They brought Jesus to the
place called Golgotha (which means The
15:23 Place of the Skull). 23Then they offered
[k] ver 36; Ps 69:21; him wine mixed with myrrh,[k] but he did
Pr 31:6 not take it. 24And they crucified him. Di-
15:24 viding up his clothes, they cast lots[l] to
[l] Ps 22:18 see what each would get.
25It was the third hour when they crucified him. 26The written notice of the
15:26 charge against him read: THE KING OF THE
[m] ver 2 JEWS.[m] 27They crucified two robbers with
him, one on his right and one on his
left.[a] 29Those who passed by hurled in-
15:29 sults at him, shaking their heads[n] and
[n] Ps 22:7; 109:25 [o] Mk 14:58; saying, "So! You who are going to destroy
Jn 2:19 the temple and build it in three days,[o]
30come down from the cross and save
yourself!"
31In the same way the chief priests
and the teachers of the law mocked
15:31 him[p] among themselves. "He saved oth-
[p] Ps 22:7 ers," they said, "but he can't save him-
15:32 [q] Mk 14:61 self! 32Let this Christ,[b][q] this King of Is-
[r] ver 2 rael,[r] come down now from the cross,
that we may see and believe." Those crucified with him also heaped insults on
him.

The Death of Jesus

33At the sixth hour darkness came
15:33 over the whole land until the ninth
[s] Am 8:9 hour.[s] 34And at the ninth hour Jesus
cried out in a loud voice, *"Eloi, Eloi, lama*
sabachthani?"—which means, "My God,
15:34 my God, why have you forsaken me?"[c][t]
[t] Ps 22:1 35When some of those standing near
heard this, they said, "Listen, he's calling
Elijah."
15:36 [u] ver 23; 36One man ran, filled a sponge with
Ps 69:21 wine vinegar,[u] put it on a stick, and offered it to Jesus to drink. "Now leave him
alone. Let's see if Elijah comes to take
him down," he said.
37With a loud cry, Jesus breathed his 15:37
last.[v] [v] Jn 19:30
38The curtain of the temple was torn 15:38
in two from top to bottom.[w] 39And when [w] Heb 10:19,20
the centurion,[x] who stood there in front 15:39
of Jesus, heard his cry and[d] saw how he [x] ver 45
died, he said, "Surely this man was the [y] Mk 1:1,11; 9:7;
Son[e] of God!"[y] Mt 4:3
40Some women were watching from a 15:40
distance.[z] Among them were Mary [z] Ps 38:11
Magdalene, Mary the mother of James [a] Mk 16:1;
the younger and of Joses, and Salome.[a] Lk 24:10; Jn 19:25
41In Galilee these women had followed
him and cared for his needs. Many other women who had come up with him to 15:41
Jerusalem were also there.[b] [b] Mt 27:55,56; Lk 8:2,3

YOU HAVE TRUSTED CHRIST AS YOUR DYING SAVIOR; NOW TRUST HIM AS YOUR LIVING SAVIOR. JUST AS MUCH AS HE CAME TO DELIVER YOU FROM FUTURE PUNISHMENT, DID HE ALSO COME TO DELIVER YOU FROM PRESENT BONDAGE.

Hannah Whitall Smith, *Christian Author*

The Burial of Jesus

42It was Preparation Day (that is, the 15:42
day before the Sabbath).[c] So as evening [c] Mt 27:62; Jn 19:31
approached, 43Joseph of Arimathea, a
prominent member of the Council,[d] 15:43
who was himself waiting for the king- [d] Mt 5:22 [e] Mt 3:2;
dom of God,[e] went boldly to Pilate and Lk 2:25,38
asked for Jesus' body. 44Pilate was surprised to hear that he was already dead.
Summoning the centurion, he asked
him if Jesus had already died. 45When he
learned from the centurion[f] that it was 15:45 [f] ver 39
so, he gave the body to Joseph. 46So Jo-
seph bought some linen cloth, took
down the body, wrapped it in the linen,
and placed it in a tomb cut out of rock.
Then he rolled a stone against the en- 15:46
trance of the tomb.[g] 47Mary Magdalene [g] Mk 16:3
and Mary the mother of Joses[h] saw 15:47
where he was laid. [h] ver 40

[a] 27 Some manuscripts *left, 28and the scripture was fulfilled which says, "He was counted with the lawless ones"* (Isaiah 53:12) [b] 32 Or *Messiah* [c] 34 Psalm 22:1 [d] 39 Some manuscripts do not have *heard his cry and* [e] 39 Or *a son*

He Is Risen!

Among all of the religious leaders who have ever lived, Jesus Christ is unique. He is the only One of whom his followers can claim with remarkable confidence that he died and three days later came back to life. The Christian faith stands or falls on the validity of this seemingly outrageous claim. If Jesus did not rise from the dead, our faith is empty, nothing but pious sentiment based on a myth (1 Corinthians 15:17). On the other hand, if Jesus *did* walk out of the tomb, then he is exactly who he claimed to be—the very Son of God.

The story that Jesus would (or did) return from the dead did not begin to be told after the fact. Jesus had stated all along that he would die and rise again (Matthew 20:17–19), going so far as to point out that his resurrection would be the only sure sign that he really was the promised Messiah (Matthew 12:38–40). In fact, prior to Jesus' burial there was already so much talk about this claim that the authorities did all they could to secure the body. The religious leaders asked Pilate to guard Jesus' tomb in order to prevent the disciples from stealing the body and then spreading the news that their Lord had been raised from the dead (Matthew 27:62–66).

But there is no way for skeptics, either at that time or today, to explain away the fact that the tomb was indeed empty following Jesus' resurrection. When the women came to anoint Jesus' body on the third day, concerned as to who might be available to roll away the heavy stone, an angel informed them that their beloved Master was gone (Mark 16:6). We know that Jesus' body had been placed in a tomb and that the tomb had been sealed. And we know that three days later that tomb lay open and empty. Many people have tried to explain away this phenomenon—but there is no plausible explanation other than the fact that Jesus arose just as he had said he would (Matthew 28:6).

The evidence is clear: Jesus did arise from the grave—not just in a spiritual sense but physically as well. The authorities did everything they could to prevent this miracle, but the risen Christ burst forth from his tomb, rejuvenated and glorious, and appeared to hundreds of people over the next several weeks (John 20:10–31; 1 Corinthians 15:3–8). Among all the religious leaders who have lived in bygone centuries, Jesus is unique—he is the only One who still lives!

Self-Discovery: *Have you ever seriously doubted an aspect of Christianity? In what way did Jesus lead you through this period of questioning?*

GO TO DISCOVERY 260 ON PAGE 1355

The Resurrection

16 When the Sabbath was over,
Mary Magdalene, Mary the
16:1 mother of James, and Salome bought
[i]Lk 23:56; spices[i] so that they might go to anoint
Jn 19:39,40 Jesus' body. [2]Very early on the first day of
the week, just after sunrise, they were on
their way to the tomb [3]and they asked
16:3 each other, "Who will roll the stone away
[j]Mk 15:46 from the entrance of the tomb?"[j]

[4]But when they looked up, they saw
that the stone, which was very large, had
been rolled away. [5]As they entered the
16:5 tomb, they saw a young man dressed in
[k]Jn 20:12 a white robe[k] sitting on the right side,
and they were alarmed.

[6]"Don't be alarmed," he said. "You are
16:6 looking for Jesus the Nazarene,[l] who was
[l]Mk 1:24 crucified. He has risen! He is not here.
See the place where they laid him. [7]But
go, tell his disciples and Peter, 'He is go-
16:7 ing ahead of you into Galilee. There you
[m]Jn 21:1-23 [n]Mk 14:28 will see him,[m] just as he told you.' "[n]

[8]Trembling and bewildered, the
women went out and fled from the
tomb. They said nothing to anyone, because they were afraid.

[The earliest manuscripts and some other ancient witnesses do not have Mark 16:9–20.]

[9]When Jesus rose early on the first
day of the week, he appeared first to
16:9 Mary Magdalene,[o] out of whom he had
[o]Jn 20:11-18 driven seven demons. [10]She went and
told those who had been with him and
who were mourning and weeping.
[11]When they heard that Jesus was alive

> IF CHRIST DID NOT RISE FROM THE DEAD, HE WOULD BE NO DIFFERENT FROM ANY OTHER RELIGIOUS LEADER.
>
> 
>
> Charles Stanley, *Pastor, Atlanta, Georgia*

and that she had seen him, they did not 16:11
believe it.[p] [p]ver 13,14; Lk 24:11

[12]Afterward Jesus appeared in a different form to two of them while they
were walking in the country.[q] [13]These 16:12 [q]Lk 24:13-32
returned and reported it to the rest; but
they did not believe them either.

[14]Later Jesus appeared to the Eleven
as they were eating; he rebuked them for
their lack of faith and their stubborn refusal to believe those who had seen him 16:14
after he had risen.[r] [r]Lk 24:36-43

[15]He said to them, "Go into all the 16:15
world and preach the good news to all [s]Mt 28:18-20; Lk 24:47,48
creation.[s] [16]Whoever believes and is
baptized will be saved, but whoever does 16:16
not believe will be condemned.[t] [17]And [t]Jn 3:16,18,36; Ac 16:31
these signs will accompany those who
believe: In my name they will drive out 16:17 [u]Mk 9:38;
demons;[u] they will speak in new Lk 10:17; Ac 5:16; 8:7;
tongues;[v] [18]they will pick up snakes[w] 16:18; 19:13-16
with their hands; and when they drink [v]Ac 2:4; 10:46;
deadly poison, it will not hurt them at 19:6; 1Co 12:10, 28,30
all; they will place their hands on[x] sick
people, and they will get well." 16:18 [w]Lk 10:19; Ac 28:3-5

[19]After the Lord Jesus had spoken to [x]Ac 6:6
them, he was taken up into heaven[y] and
he sat at the right hand of God.[z] [20]Then 16:19
the disciples went out and preached [y]Lk 24:50,51; Jn 6:62; Ac 1:9-11; 1Ti 3:16
everywhere, and the Lord worked with [z]Ps 110:1;
them and confirmed his word by the Ro 8:34; Col 3:1;
signs that accompanied it. Heb 1:3; 12:2

LUKE

How much did Mary know about Jesus? (Luke 1:46–55)

♦ *Mary recognized that Jesus was a promised gift of God, the Messiah (Luke 1:31–35). But the incident recorded in Luke 2:41–52 indicates that she didn't realize that Jesus was God in human flesh.*

Was there any risk that Jesus might yield to Satan's temptations? (Luke 4:3–13)

♦ *Some say that the Spirit could never have put Jesus at risk since our Lord's divine nature would never have succumbed to temptation. Others say that because Jesus was human his temptations were legitimate. Had this been merely a mock spiritual battle, they say, our salvation could not be legitimate (see Hebrews 2:14–18; 4:15).*

Why did Jesus pray for his captors' forgiveness? (Luke 23:34)

♦ *Jesus desired forgiveness not only for those who crucified him, but for everyone. God's forgiveness is extended to everyone, but no one is forgiven against his or her own will. Each must respond to God's call to repent and turn to him in order to be forgiven.*

Jesus in Luke Luke, a doctor, was a trusted friend and traveling companion of the apostle Paul (Colossians 4:14; 2 Timothy 4:11). As a new believer in the early church, Luke sensed the need for a clear and accurate account of the life of Jesus. Although he probably did not know Jesus personally, Luke interviewed eyewitnesses and reviewed existing records in order to write his book. His narrative begins before the birth of Jesus and ends with Jesus' ascension into heaven.

Watch for ways that Luke elaborated on the accounts of Matthew and Mark. You'll find familiar stories such as the Good Samaritan, the Lost Son and Luke's detailed account of Jesus' birth. As you read Luke, notice the importance to Jesus of people and relationships and especially his association with women. Note Luke's detailed character descriptions, as well as his personal perspective as he recorded events that demonstrate Jesus' interest in the non-Jewish world and the poor. Pay careful attention also to the two large sections of material that are unique to Luke in chapters 1—2 and chapters 10—19.

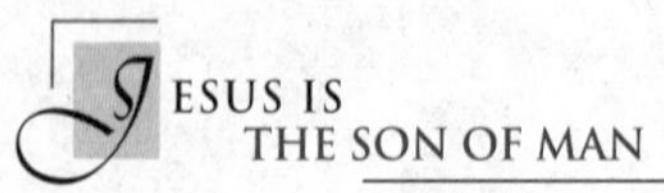

JESUS IS THE SON OF MAN

Introduction

1 Many have undertaken to draw
up an account of the things that
have been fulfilled[a] among us, 2just as
they were handed down to us by those
who from the first[a] were eyewitnesses[b]
and servants of the word.[c] 3Therefore,
since I myself have carefully investigated everything from the beginning, it
seemed good also to me to write an orderly account[d] for you, most excellent[e]
Theophilus,[f] 4so that you may know the
certainty of the things you have been
taught.[g]

1:2 [a]Mk 1:1; Jn 15:27; Ac 1:21,22 [b]Heb 2:3; 1Pe 5:1; 2Pe 1:16; 1Jn 1:1 [c]Mk 4:14
1:3 [d]Ac 11:4 [e]Ac 24:3; 26:25 [f]Ac 1:1
1:4 [g]Jn 20:31

The Birth of John the Baptist Foretold

5In the time of Herod king of Judea[h]
there was a priest named Zechariah,
who belonged to the priestly division of
Abijah;[i] his wife Elizabeth was also a descendant of Aaron. 6Both of them were
upright in the sight of God, observing all
the Lord's commandments and regulations blamelessly.[j] 7But they had no children, because Elizabeth was barren; and
they were both well along in years.
8Once when Zechariah's division was
on duty and he was serving as priest before God,[k] 9he was chosen by lot, according to the custom of the priesthood, to
go into the temple of the Lord and burn
incense.[l] 10And when the time for the
burning of incense came, all the assembled worshipers were praying outside.[m]
11Then an angel[n] of the Lord appeared to him, standing at the right side
of the altar of incense.[o] 12When Zechariah saw him, he was startled and was
gripped with fear.[p] 13But the angel said
to him: "Do not be afraid,[q] Zechariah;
your prayer has been heard. Your wife
Elizabeth will bear you a son, and you
are to give him the name John.[r] 14He will
be a joy and delight to you, and many
will rejoice because of his birth,[s] 15for he
will be great in the sight of the Lord. He
is never to take wine or other fermented
drink,[t] and he will be filled with the Holy
Spirit even from birth.[b][u] 16Many of the
people of Israel will he bring back to the
Lord their God. 17And he will go on before the Lord,[v] in the spirit and power of
Elijah,[w] to turn the hearts of the fathers
to their children[x] and the disobedient to
the wisdom of the righteous—to make
ready a people prepared for the Lord."
18Zechariah asked the angel, "How

1:5 [h]Mt 2:1 [i]1Ch 24:10
1:6 [j]Ge 7:1; 1Ki 9:4
1:8 [k]1Ch 24:19; 2Ch 8:14
1:9 [l]Ex 30:7,8; 1Ch 23:13; 2Ch 29:11
1:10 [m]Lev 16:17
1:11 [n]Ac 5:19 [o]Ex 30:1-10
1:12 [p]Jdg 6:22,23; 13:22
1:13 [q]ver 30; Mt 14:27 [r]ver 60,63
1:14 [s]ver 58
1:15 [t]Nu 6:3; Jdg 13:4; Lk 7:33 [u]Jer 1:5; Gal 1:15
1:17 [v]ver 76 [w]Mt 11:14 [x]Mal 4:5,6

can I be sure of this? I am an old man
and my wife is well along in years."[y]
19The angel answered, "I am Gabriel.[z]
I stand in the presence of God, and I
have been sent to speak to you and to
tell you this good news. 20And now you
will be silent and not able to speak[a] until the day this happens, because you did
not believe my words, which will come
true at their proper time."
21Meanwhile, the people were waiting
for Zechariah and wondering why he
stayed so long in the temple. 22When he
came out, he could not speak to them.
They realized he had seen a vision in the
temple, for he kept making signs[b] to
them but remained unable to speak.
23When his time of service was completed, he returned home. 24After this
his wife Elizabeth became pregnant and
for five months remained in seclusion.
25"The Lord has done this for me," she
said. "In these days he has shown his favor and taken away my disgrace[c] among
the people."

1:18 [y]ver 34; Ge 17:17
1:19 [z]ver 26; Mt 18:10; Da 8:16; 9:21
1:20 [a]Eze 3:26
1:22 [b]ver 62
1:25 [c]Ge 30:23; Isa 4:1

The Birth of Jesus Foretold

26In the sixth month, God sent the angel Gabriel[d] to Nazareth,[e] a town in Galilee, 27to a virgin pledged to be married
to a man named Joseph,[f] a descendant
of David. The virgin's name was Mary.
28The angel went to her and said, "Greetings, you who are highly favored! The
Lord is with you."
29Mary was greatly troubled at his
words and wondered what kind of greeting this might be. 30But the angel said to
her, "Do not be afraid,[g] Mary, you have
found favor with God. 31You will be with
child and give birth to a son, and you are
to give him the name Jesus.[h] 32He will be
great and will be called the Son of the
Most High.[i] The Lord God will give him
the throne of his father David, 33and he
will reign over the house of Jacob forever; his kingdom[j] will never end."[k]
34"How will this be," Mary asked the
angel, "since I am a virgin?"
35The angel answered, "The Holy
Spirit will come upon you,[l] and the power of the Most High[m] will overshadow
you. So the holy one[n] to be born will be
called[c] the Son of God.[o] 36Even Eliza-

1:26 [d]ver 19 [e]Mt 2:23
1:27 [f]Mt 1:16,18,20; Lk 2:4
1:30 [g]ver 13; Mt 14:27
1:31 [h]Isa 7:14; Mt 1:21,25; Lk 2:21
1:32 [i]ver 35,76; Mk 5:7
1:33 [j]Mt 28:18 [k]Da 2:44; 7:14, 27; Mic 4:7; Heb 1:8
1:35 [l]Mt 1:18 [m]ver 32,76 [n]Mk 1:24 [o]Mt 4:3

a 1 Or *been surely believed* *b 15* Or *from his mother's womb* *c 35* Or *So the child to be born will be called holy,*

JESUS—THERE'S JUST SOMETHING ABOUT THAT NAME! MASTER, SAVIOR, JESUS . . . LET ALL HEAVEN AND EARTH PROCLAIM; KINGS AND KINGDOMS WILL ALL PASS AWAY, BUT THERE'S SOMETHING ABOUT THAT NAME!

Bill and Gloria Gaither, *American Hymn Writers*

beth your relative is going to have a child
in her old age, and she who was said to
1:37 be barren is in her sixth month. 37For
p Mt 19:26 nothing is impossible with God."[p]
38"I am the Lord's servant," Mary answered. "May it be to me as you have
said." Then the angel left her.

Mary Visits Elizabeth

39At that time Mary got ready and
1:39 hurried to a town in the hill country of
q ver 65 Judea,[q] 40where she entered Zechariah's
home and greeted Elizabeth. 41When
Elizabeth heard Mary's greeting, the
baby leaped in her womb, and Elizabeth
was filled with the Holy Spirit. 42In a loud
1:42 voice she exclaimed: "Blessed are you
r Jdg 5:24 among women,[r] and blessed is the child
you will bear! 43But why am I so favored,
that the mother of my Lord should come
to me? 44As soon as the sound of your
greeting reached my ears, the baby in my
womb leaped for joy. 45Blessed is she who
has believed that what the Lord has said
to her will be accomplished!"

Mary's Song

46And Mary said:

1:46 s Ps 34:2,3 "My soul glorifies the Lord[s]
47 and my spirit rejoices in God my
1:47 t 1Ti 1:1; 2:3 Savior,[t]
48 for he has been mindful
1:48 u Ps 138:6 of the humble state of his
v Lk 11:27 servant.[u]
From now on all generations will
call me blessed,[v]
1:49 49 for the Mighty One has done
w Ps 71:19 great things[w] for me—
x Ps 111:9 holy is his name.[x]
1:50 50 His mercy extends to those who
y Ex 20:6; Ps 103:17 fear him,
from generation to generation.[y]
1:51 51 He has performed mighty deeds
z Ps 98:1; Isa 40:10 with his arm;[z]
he has scattered those who are
proud in their inmost
thoughts.
52 He has brought down rulers from
their thrones
but has lifted up the humble.
53 He has filled the hungry with good
things[a] 1:53 a Ps 107:9
but has sent the rich away empty.
54 He has helped his servant Israel, 1:54
remembering to be merciful[b] b Ps 98:3
55 to Abraham and his descendants[c]
forever, 1:55 c Ge 17:19;
even as he said to our fathers." Ps 132:11; Gal 3:16

56Mary stayed with Elizabeth for about
three months and then returned home.

The Birth of John the Baptist

57When it was time for Elizabeth to
have her baby, she gave birth to a son.
58Her neighbors and relatives heard that
the Lord had shown her great mercy,
and they shared her joy.
59On the eighth day they came to circumcise[d] the child, and they were going 1:59
to name him after his father Zechariah, d Ge 17:12; Lev 12:3;
60but his mother spoke up and said, "No! Lk 2:21; Php 3:5
He is to be called John."[e] 1:60
61They said to her, "There is no one e ver 13,63
among your relatives who has that
name."
62Then they made signs[f] to his father, 1:62 f ver 22
to find out what he would like to name
the child. 63He asked for a writing tablet,
and to everyone's astonishment he
wrote, "His name is John."[g] 64Immedi- 1:63
ately his mouth was opened and his g ver 13,60
tongue was loosed, and he began to
speak,[h] praising God. 65The neighbors 1:64 h ver 20
were all filled with awe, and throughout
the hill country of Judea[i] people were 1:65 i ver 39
talking about all these things. 66Every-
one who heard this wondered about it,
asking, "What then is this child going to 1:66
be?" For the Lord's hand was with him.[j] j Ge 39:2; Ac 11:21

Zechariah's Song

67His father Zechariah was filled with 1:67 k Joel 2:28
the Holy Spirit and prophesied:[k]

68 "Praise be to the Lord, the God of 1:68 l Ps 72:18
Israel,[l] m Ps 111:9; Lk 7:16
because he has come and has
redeemed his people.[m] 1:69
69 He has raised up a horn[a][n] of n 1Sa 2:1,10; Ps 18:2; 89:17;
salvation for us 132:17; Eze 29:21

[a] 69 *Horn* here symbolizes strength.

DISCOVERY 260

The Song of Mary

Songs often accompany special events, and there are many examples of this throughout Scripture. Moses and the Israelites sang together after they had crossed the Red Sea (Exodus 15:1–21), Hannah after she had brought Samuel to the house of the Lord (1 Samuel 2:1–10), Deborah and Barak after they had defeated the Canaanites (Judges 5:1–31). The entire book of Psalms comprises a hymnal of praise; in fact, most, if not all, of the psalms have been set to music and are still sung in "Psalters." Finally, the expectant Mary burst into song after she had visited Elizabeth, the mother-to-be of John the Baptist. Both women carried miracle babies: Elizabeth was expecting in her old age, and Mary was pregnant without the intervention of a human father.

Mary's song was a shining example of both praise and submission to God. There are four parts to it. First, she confessed her understanding of who God is and of who she was in comparison to him (Luke 1:46–48). Next, she described what God is like (verses 49–50) and then marveled at his intimate concern for the details of her life (verses 51–53). Finally, she reflected back on God's covenant with Abraham (verses 54–55).

God had chosen Mary from among all of the women who have ever lived to bear his son. She was blessed with a one-of-a-kind privilege. No other woman has been offered so great an honor either before or since! Elizabeth was correct when she exclaimed, "Blessed are you among women, and blessed is the child you will bear" (verse 42). But Mary was also caught in a social trap. She found herself in the awkward position of being pregnant and unmarried, and in her culture this represented utter disgrace. Even so, her response to God was remarkable: "My soul glorifies the Lord and my spirit rejoices in God my Savior" (verse 46–47).

The word *glorify* means "to make large, to increase or to grow." More than anything else, Mary wanted to honor God more and more in her life. She also *rejoiced* in God her Savior. Even though she was vulnerable to ridicule and denunciation, her joy was firmly planted in God—not in the opinions of others or in her own troubling circumstances. Circumstances change daily, and there is always the possibility that people will misunderstand us, but our desire that God's influence grow larger in our souls should never wane.

One of the most remarkable aspects about Mary's song is her impressive knowledge of Jewish history and Hebrew Scripture. She referred to 12 different Old Testament prayers in her song. She had very probably woven the lyrics together with tender care and then memorized them. Mary truly *knew* him of whom she sang!

Because Mary trusted and loved her God, she was not devastated by the thought of the heartless barbs of others. Though still a teenager, she had read and memorized God's Word, and she could take comfort in the familiar truths she had discovered there. In the same way, when we face difficulties in life, it is our knowledge of God and of his ways that ultimately sustains us. The better we get to know him through the pages of his Word, the more natural it becomes to recall his promises and to give control of our lives over to him.

Self-Discovery: *Think about the last time you were unjustly criticized. Did you find it necessary or important to explain yourself, or were you willing to let the matter go, knowing that you were innocent of the accusation? What was the outcome of the situation?*

GO TO DISCOVERY 261 ON PAGE 1359

1:69 [o]Mt 1:1 in the house of his servant David[o]
[70](as he said through his holy
1:70 [p]Jer 23:5 prophets of long ago),[p]
[71]salvation from our enemies
and from the hand of all who
hate us—
1:72 [q]Mic 7:20 [72]to show mercy to our fathers[q]
[r]Ps 105:8,9; and to remember his holy
106:45; covenant,[r]
Eze 16:60 [73]the oath he swore to our father
1:73 Abraham:[s]
[s]Ge 22:16-18 [74]to rescue us from the hand of our
enemies,
1:74 and to enable us to serve him[t]
[t]Heb 9:14 without fear
1:75 [75]in holiness and righteousness[u]
[u]Eph 4:24 before him all our days.

[76]And you, my child, will be called a
1:76 prophet[v] of the Most High;[w]
[v]Mt 11:9
[w]ver 32,35 for you will go on before the Lord
[x]ver 17; Mal 3:1 to prepare the way for him,[x]
[77]to give his people the knowledge of
salvation
through the forgiveness of their
1:77 sins,[y]
[y]Jer 31:34; Mk 1:4 [78]because of the tender mercy of our
God,
1:78 [z]Mal 4:2 by which the rising sun[z] will
come to us from heaven
[79]to shine on those living in darkness
1:79 and in the shadow of death,[a]
[a]Isa 9:2; 59:9; Mt 4:16; to guide our feet into the path of
Ac 26:18 peace."

[80]And the child grew and became
1:80 [b]Lk 2:40,52 strong in spirit;[b] and he lived in the
desert until he appeared publicly to Is-
rael.

The Birth of Jesus

2:1 [c]Lk 3:1; **2** In those days Caesar Augustus[c]
Mt 22:17 issued a decree that a census
[d]Mt 24:14 should be taken of the entire Roman
world.[d] [2](This was the first census that

> THE MOST SIGNIFICANT EVENT
> OF THE CENTURIES TOOK PLACE
> IN . . . A STABLE. . . . YES, MARY
> HAD A LITTLE LAMB THAT NIGHT.
> AND HER PRECIOUS LITTLE LAMB
> WAS DESTINED . . .
> FOR GOLGOTHA'S ALTAR.
>
> 
>
> Charles R. Swindoll,
> *President, Dallas Theological Seminary*

took place while Quirinius was governor
of Syria.)[e] [3]And everyone went to his 2:2 [e]Mt 4:24
own town to register.
[4]So Joseph also went up from the
town of Nazareth in Galilee to Judea, to
Bethlehem[f] the town of David, because 2:4 [f]Jn 7:42
he belonged to the house and line of Da-
vid. [5]He went there to register with
Mary, who was pledged to be married to
him and was expecting a child. [6]While
they were there, the time came for the
baby to be born, [7]and she gave birth to
her firstborn, a son. She wrapped him in
cloths and placed him in a manger, because there was no room for them in the
inn.

The Shepherds and the Angels

[8]And there were shepherds living out
in the fields nearby, keeping watch over
their flocks at night. [9]An angel[g] of the 2:9 [g]Lk 1:11;
Lord appeared to them, and the glory of Ac 5:19
the Lord shone around them, and they
were terrified. [10]But the angel said to
them, "Do not be afraid.[h] I bring you 2:10 [h]Mt 14:27
good news of great joy that will be for all
the people. [11]Today in the town of David
a Savior[i] has been born to you; he is 2:11 [i]Mt 1:21;
Christ[a][j] the Lord. [12]This will be a sign[k] Jn 4:42; Ac 5:31
to you: You will find a baby wrapped in [j]Mt 1:16; 16:16,
cloths and lying in a manger." 20; Jn 11:27; Ac 2:36
[13]Suddenly a great company of the
heavenly host appeared with the angel, 2:12 [k]1Sa 2:34;
praising God and saying, 2Ki 19:29; Isa 7:14

[14]"Glory to God in the highest,
and on earth peace[l] to men on 2:14 [l]Lk 1:79; Ro 5:1;
whom his favor rests." Eph 2:14,17

[15]When the angels had left them and
gone into heaven, the shepherds said to
one another, "Let's go to Bethlehem and
see this thing that has happened, which
the Lord has told us about."
[16]So they hurried off and found Mary
and Joseph, and the baby, who was lying
in the manger. [17]When they had seen
him, they spread the word concerning
what had been told them about this
child, [18]and all who heard it were
amazed at what the shepherds said to
them. [19]But Mary treasured up all these
things and pondered them in her 2:19 [m]ver 51
heart.[m] [20]The shepherds returned, glori- 2:20
fying and praising God[n] for all the [n]Mt 9:8

[a] *11* Or *Messiah.* "The Christ" (Greek) and "the Messiah" (Hebrew) both mean "the Anointed One"; also in verse 26.

things they had heard and seen, which
were just as they had been told.

Jesus Presented in the Temple

2:21 21On the eighth day, when it was time
o Lk 1:59 to circumcise him,[o] he was named Jesus,
p Lk 1:31 the name the angel had given him before he had been conceived.[p]
2:22 22When the time of their purification
q Lev 12:2-8 according to the Law of Moses[q] had
been completed, Joseph and Mary took
him to Jerusalem to present him to the
Lord 23(as it is written in the Law of the
2:23 Lord, "Every firstborn male is to be con-
r Ex 13:2,12,15; secrated to the Lord"[a]),[r] 24and to offer a
Nu 3:13 sacrifice in keeping with what is said in
the Law of the Lord: "a pair of doves or
2:24 two young pigeons."[b][s]
s Lev 12:8 25Now there was a man in Jerusalem
called Simeon, who was righteous and
2:25 t Lk 1:6 u ver 38; devout.[t] He was waiting for the consola-
Isa 52:9; tion of Israel,[u] and the Holy Spirit was
Lk 23:51 upon him. 26It had been revealed to him
by the Holy Spirit that he would not die
before he had seen the Lord's Christ.
27Moved by the Spirit, he went into the
temple courts. When the parents
brought in the child Jesus to do for him
2:27 v ver 22 what the custom of the Law required,[v]
28Simeon took him in his arms and
praised God, saying:

> 29"Sovereign Lord, as you have
> 2:29 promised,[w]
> w ver 26
> x Ac 2:24 you now dismiss[c] your servant
> in peace.[x]
> 30For my eyes have seen your
> 2:30 y Isa 52:10; salvation,[y]
> Lk 3:6 31 which you have prepared in the
> sight of all people,
> 32a light for revelation to the Gentiles
> 2:32 and for glory to your people
> z Isa 42:6; 49:6; Israel."[z]
> Ac 13:47; 26:23

33The child's father and mother marveled at what was said about him. 34Then
Simeon blessed them and said to Mary,
2:34 his mother:[a] "This child is destined to
a Mt 12:46 b Isa 8:14; cause the falling[b] and rising of many in
Mt 21:44; Israel, and to be a sign that will be spo-
1Co 1:23; ken against, 35so that the thoughts of
2Co 2:16; many hearts will be revealed. And a
1Pe 2:7,8
2:36 sword will pierce your own soul too."
c Ac 21:9 36There was also a prophetess,[c] Anna,
the daughter of Phanuel, of the tribe of
Asher. She was very old; she had lived
with her husband seven years after her
marriage, 37and then was a widow until

> THEY ALL WERE LOOKING FOR A KING TO SLAY THEIR FOES AND LIFT THEM HIGH. THOU CAM'ST, A LITTLE BABY THING THAT MADE A WOMAN CRY.
>
> 
>
> George MacDonald, *Scottish Pastor*

she was eighty-four.[d][d] She never left the 2:37
temple but worshiped night and day, d 1Ti 5:9
fasting and praying.[e] 38Coming up to e Ac 13:3; 14:23;
them at that very moment, she gave 1Ti 5:5
thanks to God and spoke about the
child to all who were looking forward to 2:38
the redemption of Jerusalem.[f] f ver 25;
39When Joseph and Mary had done Isa 40:2;
everything required by the Law of the Lk 1:68; 24:21
Lord, they returned to Galilee to their 2:39
own town of Nazareth.[g] 40And the child g ver 51; Mt 2:23
grew and became strong; he was filled
with wisdom, and the grace of God was 2:40
upon him.[h] h ver 52; Lk 1:80

The Boy Jesus at the Temple

41Every year his parents went to Jeru- 2:41
salem for the Feast of the Passover.[i] i Ex 23:15;
42When he was twelve years old, they Dt 16:1-8
went up to the Feast, according to the
custom. 43After the Feast was over, while
his parents were returning home, the
boy Jesus stayed behind in Jerusalem,
but they were unaware of it. 44Thinking
he was in their company, they traveled
on for a day. Then they began looking for
him among their relatives and friends.
45When they did not find him, they went
back to Jerusalem to look for him. 46Af-
ter three days they found him in the
temple courts, sitting among the teachers, listening to them and asking them
questions. 47Everyone who heard him 2:47
was amazed[j] at his understanding and j Mt 7:28
his answers. 48When his parents saw 2:48
him, they were astonished. His mother[k] k Mt 12:46
said to him, "Son, why have you treated l Lk 3:23; 4:22
us like this? Your father[l] and I have been
anxiously searching for you."
49"Why were you searching for me?"
he asked. "Didn't you know I had to be 2:49
in my Father's house?"[m] 50But they did m Jn 2:16
not understand what he was saying to 2:50
them.[n] n Mk 9:32

[a] 23 Exodus 13:2,12 [b] 24 Lev. 12:8 [c] 29 Or *promised, / now dismiss* [d] 37 Or *widow for eighty-four years*

> JESUS WAS A MAN WHO WAS CONCERNED FOR THE WHOLE PERSON . . . HE HAD A TRIANGULAR CONCERN OF MIND, BODY AND SPIRIT.
>
> 
>
> Calvin D. Butts, *African American Pastor*

51Then he went down to Nazareth
with them[o] and was obedient to them.
But his mother treasured all these
things in her heart.[p] 52And Jesus grew in
wisdom and stature, and in favor with
God and men.[q]

John the Baptist Prepares the Way

3 In the fifteenth year of the reign of
Tiberius Caesar—when Pontius
Pilate[r] was governor of Judea, Herod[s] tetrarch of Galilee, his brother Philip tetrarch of Iturea and Traconitis, and Ly-
sanias tetrarch of Abilene— 2during the
high priesthood of Annas and Caiaphas,[t] the word of God came to John[u]
son of Zechariah[v] in the desert. 3He
went into all the country around the Jordan, preaching a baptism of repentance
for the forgiveness of sins.[w] 4As is written in the book of the words of Isaiah
the prophet:

"A voice of one calling in the desert,
'Prepare the way for the Lord,
make straight paths for him.
5Every valley shall be filled in,
every mountain and hill made
low.
The crooked roads shall become
straight,
the rough ways smooth.
6And all mankind will see God's
salvation.' "[a][x]

7John said to the crowds coming out
to be baptized by him, "You brood of
vipers![y] Who warned you to flee from
the coming wrath?[z] 8Produce fruit in
keeping with repentance. And do not
begin to say to yourselves, 'We have
Abraham as our father.'[a] For I tell you
that out of these stones God can raise up
children for Abraham. 9The ax is already
at the root of the trees, and every tree
that does not produce good fruit will be
cut down and thrown into the fire."[b]

10"What should we do then?"[c] the
crowd asked.
11John answered, "The man with two
tunics should share with him who has
none, and the one who has food should
do the same."[d]
12Tax collectors also came to be baptized.[e] "Teacher," they asked, "what
should we do?"
13"Don't collect any more than you are
required to,"[f] he told them.
14Then some soldiers asked him, "And
what should we do?"
He replied, "Don't extort money and
don't accuse people falsely[g]—be content
with your pay."
15The people were waiting expectantly and were all wondering in their hearts
if John[h] might possibly be the Christ.[b][i]
16John answered them all, "I baptize you
with[c] water.[j] But one more powerful
than I will come, the thongs of whose
sandals I am not worthy to untie. He will
baptize you with the Holy Spirit and
with fire.[k] 17His winnowing fork[l] is in his
hand to clear his threshing floor and to
gather the wheat into his barn, but he
will burn up the chaff with unquenchable fire."[m] 18And with many other
words John exhorted the people and
preached the good news to them.
19But when John rebuked Herod[n] the
tetrarch because of Herodias, his brother's wife, and all the other evil things he
had done, 20Herod added this to them
all: He locked John up in prison.[o]

The Baptism and Genealogy of Jesus

21When all the people were being
baptized, Jesus was baptized too. And
as he was praying,[p] heaven was opened
22and the Holy Spirit descended on
him[q] in bodily form like a dove. And a
voice came from heaven: "You are my
Son,[r] whom I love; with you I am well
pleased."[s]
23Now Jesus himself was about thirty
years old when he began his ministry.[t]
He was the son, so it was thought, of
Joseph,[u]

the son of Heli, 24the son of Matthat,
the son of Levi, the son of Melki,
the son of Jannai, the son of Joseph,
25the son of Mattathias, the son of
Amos,

[a] 6 Isaiah 40:3-5 [b] 15 Or *Messiah* [c] 16 Or *in*

2:51 [o] ver 39; Mt 2:23 [p] ver 19
2:52 [q] ver 40; 1Sa 2:26; Lk 1:80
3:1 [r] Mt 27:2 [s] Mt 14:1
3:2 [t] Mt 26:3; Jn 18:13; Ac 4:6 [u] Mt 3:1 [v] Lk 1:13
3:3 [w] ver 16; Mk 1:4
3:6 [x] Isa 40:3-5; Ps 98:2; Isa 42:16; 52:10; Lk 2:30
3:7 [y] Mt 12:34; 23:33 [z] Ro 1:18
3:8 [a] Isa 51:2; Lk 19:9; Jn 8:33, 39; Ac 13:26; Ro 4:1,11,12,16, 17; Gal 3:7
3:9 [b] Mt 3:10
3:10 [c] ver 12,14; Ac 2:37; 16:30
3:11 [d] Isa 58:7
3:12 [e] Lk 7:29
3:13 [f] Lk 19:8
3:14 [g] Ex 23:1; Lev 19:11
3:15 [h] Mt 3:1 [i] Jn 1:19,20; Ac 13:25
3:16 [j] ver 3; Mk 1:4 [k] Jn 1:26,33; Ac 1:5; 11:16; 19:4
3:17 [l] Isa 30:24 [m] Mt 13:30; 25:41
3:19 [n] ver 1
3:20 [o] Mt 14:3,4; Mk 6:17-18
3:21 [p] Mt 14:23; Mk 1:35; 6:46; Lk 5:16; 6:12; 9:18,28; 11:1
3:22 [q] Isa 42:1; Jn 1:32,33; Ac 10:38 [r] Mt 3:17 [s] Mt 3:17
3:23 [t] Mt 4:17; Ac 1:1 [u] Lk 1:27

You Are My Son, Whom I Love

John the Baptist baptized people as a sign and symbol that those individuals had turned away from sin. Baptism symbolizes cleansing, a washing away of our sins through the blood of Jesus, a drowning to the old sinful nature and a rising with a new Christlike nature. But Jesus had never sinned, so it strikes us as odd that he would even go to John for baptism. Jesus had several good reasons for doing so, however. First, this act represented for Jesus a way of identifying with human beings and their sin.

Another reason for Jesus' baptism was that this occasion would mark the official beginning of his public ministry. For 30 years he had lived in relative obscurity as the son of a carpenter. Now he would begin to do God's work in a very public way. And everyone present recognized God's approval when the Holy Spirit came down from heaven and the voice of God the Father informed the gathered crowd that Jesus was indeed his beloved Son to whom they should listen.

Jesus' participation in the sacrament of baptism symbolized not only that he identified with us in our sinful condition but also that he had come to cleanse us from that sin, to shoulder our burden for us and to suffer the penalty on our behalf (Isaiah 53:5–6,8,10,12). After Jesus had been baptized, John introduced him by saying, "Look, the Lamb of God, who takes away the sin of the world" (John 1:29).

Jesus was baptized in order to remove any doubt that he was indeed God's promised Messiah. God had earlier informed John that he would be able to identify the Messiah after the Holy Spirit had descended from heaven on a particular person and then remained with that individual (verses 33–34).

But there was yet another reason that Jesus' baptism was significant: It is one of the few instances in the Bible in which all three members of the Trinity are present and clearly identified. God the Holy Spirit descended on Jesus (God the Son) in the form of a dove—a gentle bird valued as a symbol of purity (Psalm 68:13). The main reason for the visible presence of the Holy Spirit was to graphically demonstrate that he was empowering Jesus for what the Father had called him to do. Finally, God the Father spoke from heaven and declared his love for his Son (Luke 3:22).

God made it clear that he was pleased with Jesus. Up to that point his Son had lived in relative anonymity. He had not performed a single miracle, preached a single sermon or even begun his public ministry. But God was still delighted with Jesus.

It is not necessary for us, either, to be engaged in full-time ministry in order to please God. Jesus pleased his Father by interacting with the villagers of Nazareth and attending to the family business. God asks only that we love him with all our hearts and that we are willing to serve wherever he might choose to place us: "Whatever you do, work at it with all your heart, as working for the Lord, not for men" (Colossians 3:23).

Self-Discovery: *Picture yourself as one who is tenderly and passionately loved by the Lord. How might you live differently knowing that he is pleased with you and calls you his son or his daughter?*

GO TO DISCOVERY 262 ON PAGE 1363

the son of Nahum, the son of Esli,
the son of Naggai, 26 the son of Ma-
ath,
the son of Mattathias, the son of
Semein,
the son of Josech, the son of Joda,
27 the son of Joanan, the son of Rhesa,
3:27 v Mt 1:12 the son of Zerubbabel,[v] the son of
Shealtiel,
the son of Neri, 28 the son of Melki,
the son of Addi, the son of Cosam,
the son of Elmadam, the son of Er,
29 the son of Joshua, the son of Eliezer,
the son of Jorim, the son of Matthat,
the son of Levi, 30 the son of Simeon,
the son of Judah, the son of Joseph,
the son of Jonam, the son of Eliakim,
31 the son of Melea, the son of Menna,
3:31 w 2Sa 5:14; 1Ch 3:5 the son of Mattatha, the son of Nathan,[w]
the son of David, 32 the son of Jesse,
the son of Obed, the son of Boaz,
the son of Salmon,[a] the son of Nahshon,
33 the son of Amminadab, the son of
Ram,[b]
3:33 x Ru 4:18-22; 1Ch 2:10-12 the son of Hezron, the son of Perez,[x]
the son of Judah, 34 the son of Jacob,
3:34 y Ge 11:24,26 the son of Isaac, the son of Abraham,
the son of Terah, the son of Nahor,[y]
35 the son of Serug, the son of Reu,
the son of Peleg, the son of Eber,
the son of Shelah, 36 the son of Cainan,
the son of Arphaxad,[z] the son of 3:36 z Ge 11:12
Shem, a Ge 5:28-32
the son of Noah, the son of Lamech,[a]
37 the son of Methuselah, the son of
Enoch,
the son of Jared, the son of Mahalalel,
the son of Kenan, 38 the son of Enosh,
the son of Seth, the son of Adam,
the son of God.[b] 3:38 b Ge 5:1,2,6-9

The Temptation of Jesus

4 Jesus, full of the Holy Spirit,[c] re- 4:1 c ver 14,18
turned from the Jordan[d] and was d Lk 3:3,21
led by the Spirit[e] in the desert, 2 where e Lk 2:27
for forty days[f] he was tempted by the 4:2 f Ex 34:28; 1Ki 19:8
devil. He ate nothing during those days,
and at the end of them he was hungry.
3 The devil said to him, "If you are the
Son of God, tell this stone to become
bread."
4 Jesus answered, "It is written: 'Man 4:4
does not live on bread alone.'[c]"[g] g Dt 8:3
5 The devil led him up to a high place
and showed him in an instant all the
kingdoms of the world.[h] 6 And he said to 4:5 h Mt 24:14
him, "I will give you all their authority
and splendor, for it has been given to
me,[i] and I can give it to anyone I want to. 4:6 i Jn 12:31; 14:30; 1Jn 5:19
7 So if you worship me, it will all be yours."
8 Jesus answered, "It is written: 'Worship the Lord your God and serve him
only.'[d]"[j] 4:8 j Dt 6:13
9 The devil led him to Jerusalem and
had him stand on the highest point of
the temple. "If you are the Son of God,"
he said, "throw yourself down from here.
10 For it is written:

" 'He will command his angels
concerning you
to guard you carefully;
11 they will lift you up in their hands,
so that you will not strike your
foot against a stone.'[e]"[k] 4:11 k Ps 91:11,12

12 Jesus answered, "It says: 'Do not put 4:12
the Lord your God to the test.'[f]"[l] l Dt 6:16
13 When the devil had finished all this 4:13
tempting,[m] he left him[n] until an oppor- m Heb 4:15
tune time. n Jn 14:30

Jesus Rejected at Nazareth

14 Jesus returned to Galilee[o] in the 4:14
power of the Spirit, and news about him o Mt 4:12

a 32 Some early manuscripts *Sala* *b* 33 Some manuscripts *Amminadab, the son of Admin, the son of Arni*; other manuscripts vary widely.
c 4 Deut. 8:3 *d* 8 Deut. 6:13 *e* 11 Psalm 91:11,12 *f* 12 Deut. 6:16

JESUS FOCUS

GOOD NEWS FOR ALL PEOPLE

Luke, as the only Gentile writer in the New Testament, did not emphasize the fact that Jesus was of Jewish descent. While Matthew, whose reading audience was Jewish, traced Jesus' lineage back to Abraham, the father of the Hebrew race, Luke took his genealogy all the way back to Adam, the father of the entire human race. In so doing Luke made an implicit statement that all peoples—Jews and Gentiles alike—are invited into a relationship with God through Jesus. Luke's point was not that all of humanity will be saved but that salvation is equally offered to all of humanity. By placing this all-inclusive genealogy at the beginning of Jesus' ministry, Luke indicated that the benefits of Jesus' ministry would be available to all (Luke 24:46–47; Acts 1:8; 13:46–48; 26:23; 28:28).

> **N**AZARETH AS A TOWN TURNED ITS BACK ON THE ONE WHO WOULD GIVE THEM THEIR ONLY PLACE IN WORLD HISTORY.
>
> 
>
> John Pollock, *British Author*

4:14 [p]Mt 9:26 spread through the whole countryside.[p]
4:15 15 He taught in their synagogues,[q] and
[q]Mt 4:23 everyone praised him.
4:16 16 He went to Nazareth,[r] where he had
[r]Mt 2:23 been brought up, and on the Sabbath
[s]Mt 13:54 day he went into the synagogue,[s] as was
his custom. And he stood up to read.
17 The scroll of the prophet Isaiah was
handed to him. Unrolling it, he found
the place where it is written:

4:18 [t]Jn 3:34 18 "The Spirit of the Lord is on me,[t]
because he has anointed me
to preach good news to the poor.
He has sent me to proclaim
freedom for the prisoners
and recovery of sight for the
blind,
to release the oppressed,
19 to proclaim the year of the
4:19 [u]Isa 61:1,2; Lev 25:10 Lord's favor."[a][u]

20 Then he rolled up the scroll, gave it
4:20 [v]ver 17; Mt 26:55 back to the attendant and sat down.[v]
The eyes of everyone in the synagogue
were fastened on him, 21 and he began by
saying to them, "Today this scripture is
fulfilled in your hearing."
22 All spoke well of him and were
amazed at the gracious words that came
from his lips. "Isn't this Joseph's son?"
4:22 [w]Mt 13:54,55; Jn 6:42; 7:15 they asked.[w]
23 Jesus said to them, "Surely you will
quote this proverb to me: 'Physician,
heal yourself! Do here in your home-
4:23 [x]ver 16 town[x] what we have heard that you did
[y]Mk 1:21-28; 2:1-12 in Capernaum.'"[y]
24 "I tell you the truth," he continued,
"no prophet is accepted in his home-
4:24 [z]Mt 13:57; Jn 4:44 town.[z] 25 I assure you that there were
many widows in Israel in Elijah's time,
when the sky was shut for three and a
half years and there was a severe famine
4:25 [a]1Ki 17:1; 18:1; Jas 5:17,18 throughout the land.[a] 26 Yet Elijah was
not sent to any of them, but to a widow
4:26 [b]1Ki 17:8-16; Mt 11:21 in Zarephath in the region of Sidon.[b]
27 And there were many in Israel with
leprosy[b] in the time of Elisha the prophet, yet not one of them was cleansed— 4:27
only Naaman the Syrian."[c] [c]2Ki 5:1-14
28 All the people in the synagogue
were furious when they heard this.
29 They got up, drove him out of the
town,[d] and took him to the brow of the 4:29 [d]Nu 15:35;
hill on which the town was built, in or- Ac 7:58;
der to throw him down the cliff. 30 But he Heb 13:12
walked right through the crowd and 4:30
went on his way.[e] [e]Jn 8:59; 10:39

Jesus Drives Out an Evil Spirit

31 Then he went down to Capernaum,[f] 4:31 [f]ver 23; Mt 4:13
a town in Galilee, and on the Sabbath
began to teach the people. 32 They were
amazed at his teaching,[g] because his 4:32 [g]Mt 7:28
message had authority.[h] [h]ver 36; Mt 7:29
33 In the synagogue there was a man
possessed by a demon, an evil[c] spirit. He
cried out at the top of his voice, 34 "Ha!
What do you want with us,[i] Jesus of 4:34 [i]Mt 8:29
Nazareth?[j] Have you come to destroy [j]Mk 1:24
us? I know who you are[k]—the Holy One [k]Jas 2:19
of God!"[l] [l]ver 41; Mk 1:24
35 "Be quiet!" Jesus said sternly.[m] 4:35 [m]ver 39,41;
"Come out of him!" Then the demon Mt 8:26; Lk 8:24

a *19* Isaiah 61:1,2 *b* *27* The Greek word was used for various diseases affecting the skin—not necessarily leprosy. *c* *33* Greek *unclean*; also in verse 36

JESUS FOCUS

JESUS AND WOMEN

Luke showed a great interest in women and included in his Gospel numerous stories about women, many of them unique to his account of the life and ministry of Jesus (he also included more specific names of women than did the other Gospel writers). He continued this interest throughout Acts, the sequel to Luke (see Acts 1:14). Luke related stories about healing (Luke 4:38–39; 8:1–3,40–56; 13:11–17; 17:11–17) and faith (Luke 4:26; 7:36–50; 8:48; 18:1–8; 21:1–4) of women and emphasized stories of women involved in discipleship (Luke 8:19–21; 11:27–28), particularly in the detailed account of Jesus' dialogue with Mary and Martha (Luke 10:38–42) and in the reports of the female disciples who traveled with Jesus (Luke 8:1–3). Women are prominent in the stories of the births of both Jesus and John the Baptist (Mary, Elizabeth and Anna; Luke 1—2) and are described in both the passion and resurrection narratives (Luke 23:49; 23:55—28:12).

threw the man down before them all
and came out without injuring him.
4:36 [n] Mt 7:28; [o] ver 32; Mt 7:29; Mt 10:1 — 36 All the people were amazed[n] and
said to each other, "What is this teach-
ing? With authority[o] and power he gives
orders to evil spirits and they come out!"
37 And the news about him spread
4:37 [p] ver 14; Mt 9:26 — throughout the surrounding area.[p]

Jesus Heals Many

38 Jesus left the synagogue and went to
the home of Simon. Now Simon's mother-in-law was suffering from a high
fever, and they asked Jesus to help her.
4:39 [q] ver 35,41 — 39 So he bent over her and rebuked[q] the
fever, and it left her. She got up at once
and began to wait on them.
40 When the sun was setting, the people brought to Jesus all who had various
kinds of sickness, and laying his hands
4:40 [r] Mk 5:23 [s] Mt 4:23 — on each one,[r] he healed them.[s] 41 Moreover, demons came out of many people,
shouting, "You are the Son of God!"[t] But
4:41 [t] Mt 4:3 [u] ver 35 [v] Mt 8:4 — he rebuked[u] them and would not allow
them to speak,[v] because they knew he
was the Christ.[a]
42 At daybreak Jesus went out to a solitary place. The people were looking for
him and when they came to where he
was, they tried to keep him from leaving
them. 43 But he said, "I must preach the
4:43 [w] Mt 3:2 — good news of the kingdom of God[w] to
the other towns also, because that is
why I was sent." 44 And he kept on
4:44 [x] Mt 4:23 — preaching in the synagogues of Judea.[b][x]

The Calling of the First Disciples

5 One day as Jesus was standing by
the Lake of Gennesaret,[c] with the
people crowding around him and listen-
5:1 [y] Mk 4:14; Heb 4:12 — ing to the word of God,[y] 2 he saw at the
water's edge two boats, left there by the
fishermen, who were washing their nets.
3 He got into one of the boats, the one belonging to Simon, and asked him to put
out a little from shore. Then he sat down
5:3 [z] Mt 13:2 — and taught the people from the boat.[z]
4 When he had finished speaking, he
said to Simon, "Put out into deep water,
5:4 [a] Jn 21:6 — and let down[d] the nets for a catch."[a]
5 Simon answered, "Master,[b] we've
5:5 [b] Lk 8:24,45; 9:33,49; 17:13 [c] Jn 21:3 — worked hard all night and haven't
caught anything.[c] But because you say
so, I will let down the nets."
6 When they had done so, they caught
such a large number of fish that their
5:6 [d] Jn 21:11 — nets began to break.[d] 7 So they signaled
their partners in the other boat to come
and help them, and they came and filled
both boats so full that they began to
sink.
8 When Simon Peter saw this, he fell at
Jesus' knees and said, "Go away from me, — **5:8**
Lord; I am a sinful man!"[e] 9 For he and all — [e] Ge 18:27;
his companions were astonished at the — Job 42:6; Isa 6:5
catch of fish they had taken, 10 and so
were James and John, the sons of Zebedee, Simon's partners.
Then Jesus said to Simon, "Don't be
afraid;[f] from now on you will catch — **5:10** [f] Mt 14:27
men." 11 So they pulled their boats up on
shore, left everything and followed him.[g] — **5:11** [g] ver 28; Mt 4:19

The Man With Leprosy

12 While Jesus was in one of the towns,
a man came along who was covered
with leprosy.[e][h] When he saw Jesus, he — **5:12** [h] Mt 8:2
fell with his face to the ground and
begged him, "Lord, if you are willing, you
can make me clean."
13 Jesus reached out his hand and
touched the man. "I am willing," he said.
"Be clean!" And immediately the leprosy
left him.
14 Then Jesus ordered him, "Don't tell
anyone,[i] but go, show yourself to the — **5:14** [i] Mt 8:4
priest and offer the sacrifices that Moses — [j] Lev 14:2-32
commanded[j] for your cleansing, as a
testimony to them."
15 Yet the news about him spread all
the more,[k] so that crowds of people — **5:15** [k] Mt 9:26
came to hear him and to be healed of
their sicknesses. 16 But Jesus often with- — **5:16** [l] Mt 14:23;
drew to lonely places and prayed.[l] — Lk 3:21

Jesus Heals a Paralytic

17 One day as he was teaching, Phar-
isees and teachers of the law,[m] who had — **5:17** [m] Mt 15:1;
come from every village of Galilee and — Lk 2:46
from Judea and Jerusalem, were sitting — [n] Mk 5:30; Lk 6:19
there. And the power of the Lord was
present for him to heal the sick.[n] 18 Some
men came carrying a paralytic on a mat
and tried to take him into the house to
lay him before Jesus. 19 When they could
not find a way to do this because of the
crowd, they went up on the roof and
lowered him on his mat through the
tiles into the middle of the crowd, right
in front of Jesus.

[a] *41* Or *Messiah* [b] *44* Or *the land of the Jews*; some manuscripts *Galilee* [c] *1* That is, Sea of Galilee [d] *4* The Greek verb is plural. [e] *12* The Greek word was used for various diseases affecting the skin—not necessarily leprosy.

Following Jesus

A fisherman named Peter was washing his nets after an unproductive night on the lake, and Jesus stood nearby teaching. As the crowd pressed around him, Jesus climbed into Peter's beached boat and asked him to push it a short distance from shore. From this "pulpit" our Lord sat down and finished his sermon. Afterward Jesus instructed Peter to row back into the deep water and to throw his nets once again into the lake for a catch. Peter objected mildly, indicating that he and his fellow fishermen had fished all night unsuccessfully. "But," he conceded, "because you say so, I will let down the nets" (Luke 5:5). The result was an astonishing catch of fish, so many that the nets began to tear. Peter signaled his partners on shore for assistance, and both boats were filled to such capacity that they began to sink.

Peter recognized immediately that Jesus was special, as did the other fishermen, James and John. In his characteristic impetuous fashion, Peter confessed his sins, and all three pulled their boats onto the shore and left everything behind to become Jesus' disciples. At first glance this action may strike us as impulsive, but these three very ordinary fishermen had just witnessed a most extraordinary miracle. The decision to align ourselves with Jesus can be made on the spot or evolve from early childhood, but that first step along the Savior's path must never be taken lightly. There are important implications to consider before we make this momentous life decision.

First, following Jesus involves listening to his words. This story began with a crowd spellbound by Jesus' teaching, and no doubt Jesus' words held Peter's attention as well. Following Jesus involves more than merely passive listening, however; it also entails taking Jesus' words seriously. Sometimes God asks us to do something that seems outside the bounds of everyday common sense, but when we are devoted to him we will trust him and follow without equivocation.

A third characteristic of following Jesus is that of keeping him as our central focus. Peter witnessed the miracle of the great catch of fish and immediately fell to his knees, crying, "Go away from me, Lord; I am a sinful man!" (verse 8). Peter was overcome by his own sinfulness and unworthiness in the face of the incomparably worthy Son of God.

We also have to understand Jesus' mission. Jesus informed Peter that "from now on [he would] catch men" (verse 10). Peter would continue "fishing," but he would devote the remainder of his life to "catching" people for the Savior (Matthew 4:19; Mark 1:17).

In the final analysis following Jesus implies total abandonment to him. True disciples turn their backs on all of the encumbrances and earthly baggage that might pull them back or slow them down (Luke 5:11). Peter, James and John relinquished their careers, their boats (apparently still laden with fish!), their families, *everything* to follow in the footsteps of their newfound Master. It may seem as though we are called on to give up a great deal to follow our Lord, but the blessings we will receive from such a commitment will go beyond what we could ever have imagined (Luke 18:28–30; 1 Corinthians 2:9).

Self-Discovery: *Offer a brief, one-sentence prayer to Jesus in the following format: "Dear Lord, because you say so, I will____."*

GO TO DISCOVERY 263 ON PAGE 1367

5:20 20When Jesus saw their faith, he said,
o Lk 7:48,49 "Friend, your sins are forgiven."[o]
21The Pharisees and the teachers of
the law began thinking to themselves,
"Who is this fellow who speaks blasphe-
5:21 my? Who can forgive sins but God
p Isa 43:25 alone?"[p]
22Jesus knew what they were thinking
and asked, "Why are you thinking these
things in your hearts? 23Which is easier:
to say, 'Your sins are forgiven,' or to say,
5:24 'Get up and walk'? 24But that you may
q Mt 8:20 know that the Son of Man[q] has authority on earth to forgive sins . . ." He said to
the paralyzed man, "I tell you, get up,
take your mat and go home." 25Immedi-
ately he stood up in front of them, took
what he had been lying on and went
home praising God. 26Everyone was
5:26 amazed and gave praise to God.[r] They
r Mt 9:8 were filled with awe and said, "We have
seen remarkable things today."

The Calling of Levi

27After this, Jesus went out and saw a
tax collector by the name of Levi sitting
5:27 at his tax booth. "Follow me,"[s] Jesus said
s Mt 4:19 to him, 28and Levi got up, left everything
5:28 and followed him.[t]
t ver 11; Mt 4:19 29Then Levi held a great banquet for
5:29 Jesus at his house, and a large crowd of
u Lk 15:1 tax collectors[u] and others were eating
with them. 30But the Pharisees and the
teachers of the law who belonged to
5:30 their sect[v] complained to his disciples,
v Ac 23:9 w Mt 9:11 "Why do you eat and drink with tax collectors and 'sinners'?"[w]
31Jesus answered them, "It is not the
healthy who need a doctor, but the sick.
32I have not come to call the righteous,
5:32 but sinners to repentance."[x]
x Jn 3:17

Jesus Questioned About Fasting

5:33 33They said to him, "John's disciples[y]
y Lk 7:18; Jn 1:35; 3:25,26 often fast and pray, and so do the disciples of the Pharisees, but yours go on
eating and drinking."
5:34 34Jesus answered, "Can you make the
z Jn 3:29 guests of the bridegroom[z] fast while he
is with them? 35But the time will come
when the bridegroom will be taken from
5:35 them;[a] in those days they will fast."
a Lk 9:22; 17:22; Jn 16:5-7 36He told them this parable: "No one
tears a patch from a new garment and
sews it on an old one. If he does, he will
have torn the new garment, and the
patch from the new will not match the
old. 37And no one pours new wine into
old wineskins. If he does, the new wine
will burst the skins, the wine will run out
and the wineskins will be ruined. 38No,
new wine must be poured into new
wineskins. 39And no one after drinking
old wine wants the new, for he says, 'The
old is better.' "

Lord of the Sabbath

6 One Sabbath Jesus was going
through the grainfields, and his
disciples began to pick some heads of
grain, rub them in their hands and eat 6:1
the kernels.[b] 2Some of the Pharisees b Dt 23:25
asked, "Why are you doing what is un- 6:2
lawful on the Sabbath?"[c] c Mt 12:2
3Jesus answered them, "Have you never read what David did when he and his
companions were hungry?[d] 4He entered 6:3
the house of God, and taking the conse- d 1Sa 21:6
crated bread, he ate what is lawful only
for priests to eat.[e] And he also gave 6:4 e Lev 24:5,9
some to his companions." 5Then Jesus
said to them, "The Son of Man[f] is Lord 6:5 f Mt 8:20
of the Sabbath."
6On another Sabbath[g] he went into 6:6 g ver 1
the synagogue and was teaching, and a
man was there whose right hand was
shriveled. 7The Pharisees and the teachers of the law were looking for a reason
to accuse Jesus, so they watched him
closely[h] to see if he would heal on the 6:7 h Mt 12:10
Sabbath.[i] 8But Jesus knew what they i Mt 12:2
were thinking[j] and said to the man with 6:8
the shriveled hand, "Get up and stand in j Mt 9:4
front of everyone." So he got up and
stood there.
9Then Jesus said to them, "I ask you,
which is lawful on the Sabbath: to do
good or to do evil, to save life or to destroy it?"
10He looked around at them all, and
then said to the man, "Stretch out your
hand." He did so, and his hand was com-
pletely restored. 11But they were furious[k] 6:11 k Jn 5:18
and began to discuss with one another
what they might do to Jesus.

The Twelve Apostles

12One of those days Jesus went out to
a mountainside to pray, and spent the 6:12
night praying to God.[l] 13When morning l Lk 3:21
came, he called his disciples to him and
chose twelve of them, whom he also designated apostles:[m] 14Simon (whom he 6:13 m Mk 6:30
named Peter), his brother Andrew,

As to Jesus of Nazareth . . . I think his system of morals and his religion, as he left them to us, is the best the world ever saw, or is likely to see.

Benjamin Franklin, *American Statesman*

James, John, Philip, Bartholomew,
6:15 n Mt 9:9 15 Matthew,[n] Thomas, James son of Alphaeus, Simon who was called the Zeal-
ot, 16 Judas son of James, and Judas Iscariot, who became a traitor.

Blessings and Woes

17 He went down with them and stood
on a level place. A large crowd of his disciples was there and a great number of
people from all over Judea, from Jerusalem, and from the coast of Tyre and Si-
6:17 o Mt 4:25; Mt 11:21; Mk 3:7,8 don,[o] 18 who had come to hear him and
to be healed of their diseases. Those
troubled by evil[a] spirits were cured,
6:19 p Mt 9:20 q Mt 14:36; Mk 5:30; Lk 5:17 19 and the people all tried to touch him,[p]
because power was coming from him
and healing them all.[q]
20 Looking at his disciples, he said:

"Blessed are you who are poor,
6:20 r Mt 25:34 for yours is the kingdom of God.[r]
6:21 s Isa 55:1,2; Mt 5:6 t Isa 61:2, 3; Mt 5:4; Rev 7:17 21 Blessed are you who hunger now,
for you will be satisfied.[s]
Blessed are you who weep now,
for you will laugh.[t]
22 Blessed are you when men hate
you,
6:22 u Jn 9:22; 16:2 v Isa 51:7 w Jn 15:21 when they exclude you[u] and
insult you[v]
and reject your name as evil,
because of the Son of Man.[w]

6:23 x Mt 5:12 y Mt 5:12 23 "Rejoice in that day and leap for joy,[x]
because great is your reward in heaven.
For that is how their fathers treated the
prophets.[y]

6:24 z Jas 5:1 a Lk 16:25 24 "But woe to you who are rich,[z]
for you have already received
your comfort.[a]
6:25 b Isa 65:13 c Pr 14:13 25 Woe to you who are well fed now,
for you will go hungry.[b]
Woe to you who laugh now,
for you will mourn and weep.[c]
26 Woe to you when all men speak
well of you,
for that is how their fathers
treated the false prophets.[d] 6:26 d Mt 7:15

Love for Enemies

27 "But I tell you who hear me: Love
your enemies, do good to those who 6:27 e ver 35; Mt 5:44; Ro 12:20
hate you,[e] 28 bless those who curse you,
pray for those who mistreat you.[f] 29 If
someone strikes you on one cheek, turn
to him the other also. If someone takes 6:28 f Mt 5:44
your cloak, do not stop him from taking
your tunic. 30 Give to everyone who asks
you, and if anyone takes what belongs to
you, do not demand it back.[g] 31 Do to 6:30 g Dt 15:7,8,10; Pr 21:26
others as you would have them do to
you.[h]
32 "If you love those who love you, 6:31 h Mt 7:12
what credit is that to you?[i] Even 'sin-
ners' love those who love them. 33 And if 6:32 i Mt 5:46
you do good to those who are good to
you, what credit is that to you? Even
'sinners' do that. 34 And if you lend to
those from whom you expect repay- 6:34 j Mt 5:42
ment, what credit is that to you?[j] Even
'sinners' lend to 'sinners,' expecting to be

[a] *18* Greek *unclean*

GOD'S GOLDEN RULE

Over the course of the years one of Jesus' statements has become known as the *Golden Rule*: "Do to others as you would have them do to you" (Luke 6:31). God created us to be in fellowship with him, and he wants our relationships with others to reflect that closeness. What Jesus taught was revolutionary at the time—and would be considered fully as radical if it had first been announced in our own day and culture. The generally accepted political tactic throughout all ages, as well as our natural human instinct, is to hate our enemies and look for ways to belittle, deride or injure them—physically, financially, in terms of reputation—in any way we can. Jesus instead promoted the unthinkable, urging people to love their enemies and choose not to fight back after having been cheated or hurt. His teaching goes against the grain of our common sense, because common sense is based on our faulty, unregenerate human nature, untouched by the grace and power of Jesus. The truth is that we are more like Jesus when we are suffering than at any other time (Romans 8:17; 2 Corinthians 1:5; 4:10; Philippians 3:10; Colossians 1:24; 1 Peter 4:13).

repaid in full. 35 But love your enemies,
6:35 [k]ver 27 [l]Ro 8:14 [m]Mk 5:7 do good to them,[k] and lend to them
without expecting to get anything back.
6:36 [n]Jas 2:13 [o]Mt 5:48; 6:1; Lk 11:2; 12:32; Ro 8:15; Eph 4:6; 1Pe 1:17; 1Jn 1:3; 3:1 Then your reward will be great, and you
will be sons[l] of the Most High,[m] because
he is kind to the ungrateful and wicked.
36 Be merciful,[n] just as your Father[o] is
merciful.

Judging Others

37 "Do not judge, and you will not be
6:37 [p]Mt 7:1 [q]Mt 6:14 judged.[p] Do not condemn, and you will
not be condemned. Forgive, and you will
be forgiven.[q] 38 Give, and it will be given
to you. A good measure, pressed down,
6:38 [r]Ps 79:12; Isa 65:6,7 [s]Mt 7:2; Mk 4:24 shaken together and running over, will
be poured into your lap.[r] For with the
measure you use, it will be measured to
you."[s]
39 He also told them this parable: "Can
a blind man lead a blind man? Will they
6:39 [t]Mt 15:14 not both fall into a pit?[t] 40 A student is
6:40 [u]Mt 10:24; Jn 13:16 not above his teacher, but everyone who
is fully trained will be like his teacher.[u]
41 "Why do you look at the speck of
sawdust in your brother's eye and pay no
attention to the plank in your own eye?
42 How can you say to your brother,
'Brother, let me take the speck out of
your eye,' when you yourself fail to see
the plank in your own eye? You hypocrite, first take the plank out of your eye,
and then you will see clearly to remove
the speck from your brother's eye.

A Tree and Its Fruit

43 "No good tree bears bad fruit, nor
does a bad tree bear good fruit. 44 Each
6:44 [v]Mt 12:33 tree is recognized by its own fruit.[v] People do not pick figs from thornbushes, or
grapes from briers. 45 The good man
brings good things out of the good
stored up in his heart, and the evil man
6:45 [w]Pr 4:23; Mt 12:34,35; Mk 7:20 brings evil things out of the evil stored
up in his heart. For out of the overflow
of his heart his mouth speaks.[w]

The Wise and Foolish Builders

6:46 [x]Jn 13:13 [y]Mal 1:6; Mt 7:21 46 "Why do you call me, 'Lord, Lord,'[x]
and do not do what I say?[y] 47 I will show
you what he is like who comes to me
6:47 [z]Lk 8:21; 11:28; Jas 1:22-25 and hears my words and puts them into
practice.[z] 48 He is like a man building a
house, who dug down deep and laid the
foundation on rock. When a flood came,
the torrent struck that house but could
not shake it, because it was well built.
49 But the one who hears my words and
does not put them into practice is like a
man who built a house on the ground
without a foundation. The moment the
torrent struck that house, it collapsed
and its destruction was complete."

The Faith of the Centurion

7 When Jesus had finished saying
all this[a] in the hearing of the peo- 7:1 [a]Mt 7:28
ple, he entered Capernaum. 2 There a
centurion's servant, whom his master
valued highly, was sick and about to die.
3 The centurion heard of Jesus and sent
some elders of the Jews to him, asking
him to come and heal his servant.
4 When they came to Jesus, they pleaded
earnestly with him, "This man deserves
to have you do this, 5 because he loves
our nation and has built our synagogue."
6 So Jesus went with them.
He was not far from the house when
the centurion sent friends to say to him:
"Lord, don't trouble yourself, for I do not
deserve to have you come under my
roof. 7 That is why I did not even consider myself worthy to come to you. But say
the word, and my servant will be
healed.[b] 8 For I myself am a man under 7:7 [b]Ps 107:20
authority, with soldiers under me. I tell
this one, 'Go,' and he goes; and that one,
'Come,' and he comes. I say to my servant, 'Do this,' and he does it."
9 When Jesus heard this, he was
amazed at him, and turning to the
crowd following him, he said, "I tell you,
I have not found such great faith even in
Israel." 10 Then the men who had been
sent returned to the house and found
the servant well.

Jesus Raises a Widow's Son

11 Soon afterward, Jesus went to a
town called Nain, and his disciples and a
large crowd went along with him. 12 As he
approached the town gate, a dead person
was being carried out—the only son of
his mother, and she was a widow. And a
large crowd from the town was with her.
13 When the Lord[c] saw her, his heart went 7:13 [c]ver 19; Lk 10:1; 13:15; 17:5; 22:61; 24:34; Jn 11:2
out to her and he said, "Don't cry."
14 Then he went up and touched the
coffin, and those carrying it stood still.
He said, "Young man, I say to you, get 7:14 [d]Mt 9:25; Mk 1:31; Lk 8:54; Jn 11:43; Ac 9:40
up!"[d] 15 The dead man sat up and began
to talk, and Jesus gave him back to his
mother.

DISCOVERY 263

DEALING WITH DOUBT

John the Baptist had been given an exclusive assignment by God the Father: to be the forerunner for the Messiah (Luke 1:17). He had prepared the hearts of people so that they would be receptive to Jesus when he began his public ministry (Matthew 3:1–12; Mark 1:1–8). But John eventually found himself thrown into prison by Herod. Before long this stalwart preacher began experiencing doubts about whether Jesus really was the Messiah after all.

He dispatched two of his disciples to ask Jesus outright, "Are you the one who was to come, or should we expect someone else?" (Luke 7:19). What a remarkable question coming from the chosen forerunner, the very one who had baptized Jesus (Luke 3:21–22), introduced him as the Lamb of God (John 1:29) and known in advance that the Holy Spirit would descend from heaven to rest on him (John 1:33–34).

John the Baptist's birth, life and ministry were integral to God's salvation plan from the beginning. Yet when the circumstances of his life became thorny, John found himself plagued by insecurity. The Bible does not tell us what precipitated his doubts. Perhaps he felt abandoned. If Jesus were truly the Messiah, why did he not free John from prison? Our doubts are often rooted in the same emotion. When we find ourselves imprisoned in one way or another—seemingly forgotten and alone—we begin to question the reality of Jesus' love and power: "If Jesus is God and if he really loves me, then why doesn't he help me *right now*?"

John's disciples approached Jesus expecting a yes or no answer to John's question. John 7:21 tells us that "at that very time Jesus cured many who had diseases, sicknesses and evil spirits, and gave sight to many who were blind." Jesus reminded John's disciples of what had already been prophesied in the Old Testament: "Go back and report to John what you have seen and heard: The blind receive sight, the lame walk, those who have leprosy are cured, the deaf hear, the dead are raised, and the good news is preached to the poor" (Luke 7:22; see also Isaiah 29:18–21; 35:5–6; 61:1–2). No elaboration was needed. Because Jesus was doing what God had clearly stated only the Messiah would do, then he must indeed be the Promised One.

God doesn't chastise us for doubting. He desires to prove himself, and he will point us back to his Word every time. Circumstances in life can easily become catalysts for doubt—or they can become agents for helping us to grow closer to the Savior and more deeply rooted in his Word. There is only one way that our faith in God can flourish: "Faith comes from hearing the message, and the message is heard through the word of Christ" (Romans 10:17).

Self-Discovery: *Reflect back to the last time a difficult experience strengthened your faith and deepened your relationship with Jesus. Were you able to hold on to this spiritual "gain," or did you find yourself losing ground after the problem had been resolved.*

GO TO DISCOVERY 264 ON PAGE 1373

7:16 e Lk 1:65 16They were all filled with awe[e] and
f Mt 9:8 g ver 39; praised God.[f] "A great prophet[g] has ap-
Mt 21:11 peared among us," they said. "God has
h Lk 1:68 come to help his people."[h] 17This news
7:17 about Jesus spread throughout Judea[a]
i Mt 9:26 and the surrounding country.[i]

Jesus and John the Baptist

7:18 j Mt 3:1 18John's[j] disciples[k] told him about all
k Lk 5:33 these things. Calling two of them, 19he
sent them to the Lord to ask, "Are you
the one who was to come, or should we
expect someone else?"

20When the men came to Jesus, they
said, "John the Baptist sent us to you to
ask, 'Are you the one who was to come,
or should we expect someone else?' "

7:21 21At that very time Jesus cured many
l Mt 4:23 who had diseases, sicknesses[l] and evil
spirits, and gave sight to many who were
blind. 22So he replied to the messengers,
"Go back and report to John what you
have seen and heard: The blind receive
sight, the lame walk, those who have
leprosy[b] are cured, the deaf hear, the
dead are raised, and the good news is
7:22 m Isa 29:18,19; preached to the poor.[m] 23Blessed is the
35:5,6; 61:1,2; man who does not fall away on account
Lk 4:18 of me."

24After John's messengers left, Jesus
began to speak to the crowd about John:
"What did you go out into the desert to
see? A reed swayed by the wind? 25If not,
what did you go out to see? A man
dressed in fine clothes? No, those who
wear expensive clothes and indulge in
7:26 luxury are in palaces. 26But what did you
n Mt 11:9 go out to see? A prophet?[n] Yes, I tell you,
and more than a prophet. 27This is the
one about whom it is written:

" 'I will send my messenger ahead
of you,
7:27 o Mal 3:1; who will prepare your way
Mt 11:10; before you.'[c][o]
Mk 1:2

28I tell you, among those born of women
7:28 there is no one greater than John; yet the
p Mt 3:2 one who is least in the kingdom of God[p]
is greater than he."

29(All the people, even the tax collectors, when they heard Jesus' words, acknowledged that God's way was right,
because they had been baptized by
7:29 q Mt 21:32; John.[q] 30But the Pharisees and experts in
Mk 1:5; Lk 3:12 the law[r] rejected God's purpose for
7:30 themselves, because they had not been
r Mt 22:35 baptized by John.)

31"To what, then, can I compare the
people of this generation? What are they
like? 32They are like children sitting in
the marketplace and calling out to each
other:

" 'We played the flute for you,
and you did not dance;
we sang a dirge,
and you did not cry.'

33For John the Baptist came neither eating bread nor drinking wine,[s] and you 7:33
say, 'He has a demon.' 34The Son of Man s Lk 1:15
came eating and drinking, and you say,
'Here is a glutton and a drunkard, a 7:34
friend of tax collectors and "sinners." '[t] t Lk 5:29,30;
35But wisdom is proved right by all her 15:1,2
children."

> NO ONE ELSE HOLDS OR HAS HELD THE PLACE IN THE HEART OF THE WORLD WHICH JESUS HOLDS. OTHER GODS HAVE BEEN AS DEVOUTLY WORSHIPPED; NO OTHER MAN HAS BEEN SO DEVOUTLY LOVED.
>
> John Knox, *Scottish Reformer*

Jesus Anointed by a Sinful Woman

36Now one of the Pharisees invited
Jesus to have dinner with him, so he
went to the Pharisee's house and reclined at the table. 37When a woman
who had lived a sinful life in that town
learned that Jesus was eating at the
Pharisee's house, she brought an alabaster jar of perfume, 38and as she
stood behind him at his feet weeping,
she began to wet his feet with her tears.
Then she wiped them with her hair,
kissed them and poured perfume on
them.

39When the Pharisee who had invited
him saw this, he said to himself, "If this
man were a prophet,[u] he would know 7:39
who is touching him and what kind of u ver 16;
woman she is—that she is a sinner." Mt 21:11

40Jesus answered him, "Simon, I have
something to tell you."

"Tell me, teacher," he said.

41"Two men owed money to a certain

[a] 17 Or *the land of the Jews* [b] 22 The Greek word was used for various diseases affecting the skin—not necessarily leprosy. [c] 27 Mal. 3:1

moneylender. One owed him five hundred denarii,[a] and the other fifty. 42Nei-
ther of them had the money to pay him
back, so he canceled the debts of both.
Now which of them will love him more?"
43Simon replied, "I suppose the one
who had the bigger debt canceled."
"You have judged correctly," Jesus
said.
44Then he turned toward the woman
and said to Simon, "Do you see this
7:44 woman? I came into your house. You did
v Ge 18:4; 19:2; not give me any water for my feet,[v] but
43:24; Jdg 19:21; she wet my feet with her tears and wiped
Jn 13:4-14; 1Ti 5:10 them with her hair. 45You did not give
7:45 me a kiss,[w] but this woman, from the
w Lk 22:47,48; time I entered, has not stopped kissing
Ro 16:16 my feet. 46You did not put oil on my
7:46 head,[x] but she has poured perfume on
x Ps 23:5; Ecc 9:8 my feet. 47Therefore, I tell you, her many
sins have been forgiven—for she loved
much. But he who has been forgiven little loves little."
48Then Jesus said to her, "Your sins are
7:48 y Mt 9:2 forgiven."[y]
49The other guests began to say
among themselves, "Who is this who
7:50 z Mt 9:22; even forgives sins?"
Mk 5:34; Lk 8:48 50Jesus said to the woman, "Your faith
a Ac 15:33 has saved you;[z] go in peace."[a]

The Parable of the Sower

8 After this, Jesus traveled about
from one town and village to another, proclaiming the good news of the
8:1 b Mt 4:23 kingdom of God.[b] The Twelve were with
him, 2and also some women who had
been cured of evil spirits and diseases:
8:2 c Mt 27:55,56 Mary (called Magdalene)[c] from whom
seven demons had come out; 3Joanna
8:3 the wife of Cuza, the manager of Her-
d Mt 14:1 od's[d] household; Susanna; and many
others. These women were helping to
support them out of their own means.
4While a large crowd was gathering
and people were coming to Jesus from
town after town, he told this parable: 5"A
farmer went out to sow his seed. As he
was scattering the seed, some fell along
the path; it was trampled on, and the
birds of the air ate it up. 6Some fell on
rock, and when it came up, the plants
withered because they had no moisture.
7Other seed fell among thorns, which
grew up with it and choked the plants.
8Still other seed fell on good soil. It came
up and yielded a crop, a hundred times
more than was sown."
When he said this, he called out, "He
who has ears to hear, let him hear."[e] 8:8 e Mt 11:15
9His disciples asked him what this
parable meant. 10He said, "The knowledge of the secrets of the kingdom of
God has been given to you,[f] but to oth- 8:10 f Mt 13:11
ers I speak in parables, so that, g Isa 6:9; Mt 13:13,14

> " 'though seeing, they may not see;
> though hearing, they may not
> understand.'[b][g]

11"This is the meaning of the parable:
The seed is the word of God.[h] 12Those 8:11 h Heb 4:12
along the path are the ones who hear,
and then the devil comes and takes away
the word from their hearts, so that they
may not believe and be saved. 13Those on
the rock are the ones who receive the
word with joy when they hear it, but they
have no root. They believe for a while,
but in the time of testing they fall away.[i] 8:13 i Mt 11:6
14The seed that fell among thorns stands
for those who hear, but as they go on
their way they are choked by life's wor- 8:14 j Mt 19:23; 1Ti 6:9,10,17
ries, riches[j] and pleasures, and they do

[a] 41 A denarius was a coin worth about a day's wages. [b] 10 Isaiah 6:9

MARY MAGDALENE

DEVOTED DISCIPLE

Mary was a common Jewish name. In fact, there were four different women with this name who were closely associated with Jesus: his mother; James's mother, sometimes referred to as "the other Mary"; Mary of Bethany, sister to Martha and Lazarus; and Mary "Magdalene." Mary "Magdalene" came from a tiny village called Magdala, which lay between Tiberias and Capernaum on the western shore of the Sea of Galilee. She had first made Jesus' acquaintance when he had driven out from her seven evil spirits, or demons, and she had been one of the faithful women who had helped care for and support Jesus and his disciples throughout the remainder of his ministry (Matthew 27:55–56; Luke 8:2). She stayed with our Lord during his crucifixion and was present at his burial (Matthew 27:61). Mary Magdalene was one of the women who went to the tomb on Sunday morning—only to find it empty (Luke 24:1–12), and she holds the honor of having been the one to divulge to the stunned disciples that Jesus had come back to life (Luke 24:10; John 20:18).

> GANDHI SAID THAT WHAT HE FOUND MOST ATTRACTIVE ABOUT JESUS WAS THAT HE WASN'T JUST SOMEONE WHO TAUGHT IT, AS MANY OF THE ASIAN SAGES DID. HE DID IT, HE ACTUALLY LIVED IT. HE LOVED HIS NEIGHBORS, HIS ENEMIES. HE STAYED AMONG THE POOR. HE WAS AN EXEMPLAR OF HIS OWN TEACHING.
>
> Harvey Cox, *Harvard Theologian*

not mature. 15But the seed on good soil
stands for those with a noble and good
heart, who hear the word, retain it, and
by persevering produce a crop.

A Lamp on a Stand

16"No one lights a lamp and hides it in
a jar or puts it under a bed. Instead, he
8:16 puts it on a stand, so that those who
k Mt 5:15; come in can see the light.[k] 17For there is
Mk 4:21; nothing hidden that will not be dis-
Lk 11:33 closed, and nothing concealed that will
8:17 not be known or brought out into the
l Mt 10:26; open.[l] 18Therefore consider carefully
Mk 4:22; how you listen. Whoever has will be giv-
Lk 12:2
8:18 en more; whoever does not have, even
m Mt 13:12; what he thinks he has will be taken from
25:29; Lk 19:26 him."[m]

Jesus' Mother and Brothers

19Now Jesus' mother and brothers
came to see him, but they were not able
to get near him because of the crowd.
20Someone told him, "Your mother and
8:20 n Jn 7:5 brothers[n] are standing outside, wanting
to see you."
8:21 21He replied, "My mother and broth-
o Lk 6:47; 11:28; ers are those who hear God's word and
Jn 14:21 put it into practice."[o]

Jesus Calms the Storm

22One day Jesus said to his disciples,
"Let's go over to the other side of the
lake." So they got into a boat and set out.
23As they sailed, he fell asleep. A squall
came down on the lake, so that the boat
was being swamped, and they were in
great danger.
24The disciples went and woke him,
8:24 saying, "Master, Master,[p] we're going to
p Lk 5:5 drown!"

He got up and rebuked[q] the wind and 8:24 q Lk 4:35,39,41
the raging waters; the storm subsided, r Ps 107:29;
and all was calm.[r] 25"Where is your Jnh 1:15
faith?" he asked his disciples.
In fear and amazement they asked
one another, "Who is this? He commands even the winds and the water,
and they obey him."

The Healing of a Demon-possessed Man

26They sailed to the region of the Gerasenes,[a] which is across the lake from
Galilee. 27When Jesus stepped ashore, he
was met by a demon-possessed man
from the town. For a long time this man
had not worn clothes or lived in a house,
but had lived in the tombs. 28When he
saw Jesus, he cried out and fell at his
feet, shouting at the top of his voice, 8:28
"What do you want with me,[s] Jesus, Son s Mt 8:29
of the Most High God?[t] I beg you, don't t Mk 5:7
torture me!" 29For Jesus had command-
ed the evil[b] spirit to come out of the
man. Many times it had seized him, and
though he was chained hand and foot
and kept under guard, he had broken his
chains and had been driven by the demon into solitary places.
30Jesus asked him, "What is your
name?"
"Legion," he replied, because many
demons had gone into him. 31And they
begged him repeatedly not to order 8:31
them to go into the Abyss.[u] u Rev 9:1,2,11;
32A large herd of pigs was feeding 11:7; 17:8;
there on the hillside. The demons 20:1,3
begged Jesus to let them go into them,
and he gave them permission. 33When
the demons came out of the man, they
went into the pigs, and the herd rushed 8:33
down the steep bank into the lake[v] and v ver 22,23
was drowned.
34When those tending the pigs saw
what had happened, they ran off and reported this in the town and countryside,
35and the people went out to see what
had happened. When they came to
Jesus, they found the man from whom
the demons had gone out, sitting at
Jesus' feet,[w] dressed and in his right 8:35
mind; and they were afraid. 36Those who w Lk 10:39
had seen it told the people how the de- 8:36
mon-possessed[x] man had been cured. x Mt 4:24

[a] 26 Some manuscripts *Gadarenes*; other manuscripts *Gergesenes*; also in verse 37
[b] 29 Greek *unclean*

8:37 37 Then all the people of the region of the
y Ac 16:39 Gerasenes asked Jesus to leave them,[y]
because they were overcome with fear.
So he got into the boat and left.
38 The man from whom the demons
had gone out begged to go with him, but
Jesus sent him away, saying, 39 "Return
home and tell how much God has done
for you." So the man went away and told
all over town how much Jesus had done
for him.

A Dead Girl and a Sick Woman

40 Now when Jesus returned, a crowd
welcomed him, for they were all expect-
8:41 ing him. 41 Then a man named Jairus, a
z ver 49; ruler of the synagogue,[z] came and fell at
Mk 5:22 Jesus' feet, pleading with him to come to
his house 42 because his only daughter, a
girl of about twelve, was dying.

As Jesus was on his way, the crowds
almost crushed him. 43 And a woman
was there who had been subject to
8:43 bleeding[a] for twelve years,[*a*] but no one
a Lev 15:25-30 could heal her. 44 She came up behind
8:44 him and touched the edge of his cloak,[b]
b Mt 9:20 and immediately her bleeding stopped.
45 "Who touched me?" Jesus asked.

When they all denied it, Peter said,
8:45 "Master,[c] the people are crowding and
c Lk 5:5 pressing against you."

46 But Jesus said, "Someone touched
8:46 me;[d] I know that power has gone out
d Mt 14:36; Mk 3:10 from me."[e]
e Lk 5:17; 6:19 47 Then the woman, seeing that she
could not go unnoticed, came trembling
and fell at his feet. In the presence of all
the people, she told why she had
touched him and how she had been instantly healed. 48 Then he said to her,
8:48 "Daughter, your faith has healed you.[f]
f Mt 9:22 g Ac 15:33 Go in peace."[g]

49 While Jesus was still speaking,
someone came from the house of Jairus,
8:49 the synagogue ruler.[h] "Your daughter is
h ver 41 dead," he said. "Don't bother the teacher
any more."

50 Hearing this, Jesus said to Jairus,
"Don't be afraid; just believe, and she
will be healed."

51 When he arrived at the house of Jairus, he did not let anyone go in with
8:51 him except Peter, John and James,[i] and
i Mt 4:21 the child's father and mother. 52 Mean-
8:52 while, all the people were wailing and
j Lk 23:27 k Mt 9:24; mourning[j] for her. "Stop wailing," Jesus
Jn 11:11,13 said. "She is not dead but asleep."[k]

53 They laughed at him, knowing that
she was dead. 54 But he took her by the 8:54
hand and said, "My child, get up!"[l] 55 Her l Lk 7:14
spirit returned, and at once she stood
up. Then Jesus told them to give her
something to eat. 56 Her parents were astonished, but he ordered them not to tell 8:56
anyone what had happened.[m] m Mt 8:4

CHRIST IS THE CENTER OF CHRISTIANITY. TO PRETEND ANYTHING ELSE IS NOT CHRISTIANITY, WHATEVER ELSE IT MAY BE.

Catherine Marshall, *Christian Author*

Jesus Sends Out the Twelve

9 When Jesus had called the Twelve
together, he gave them power and
authority to drive out all demons[n] and 9:1 n Mt 10:1
to cure diseases,[o] 2 and he sent them out o Mt 4:23;
to preach the kingdom of God[p] and to Lk 5:17
heal the sick. 3 He told them: "Take noth- 9:2
ing for the journey—no staff, no bag, no p Mt 3:2
bread, no money, no extra tunic.[q] 9:3
4 Whatever house you enter, stay there q Lk 10:4; 22:35
until you leave that town. 5 If people do
not welcome you, shake the dust off
your feet when you leave their town, as
a testimony against them."[r] 6 So they set 9:5
out and went from village to village, r Mt 10:14
preaching the gospel and healing people
everywhere.

7 Now Herod[s] the tetrarch heard 9:7 s Mt 14:1
about all that was going on. And he was t Mt 3:1 u ver 19
perplexed, because some were saying
that John[t] had been raised from the
dead,[u] 8 others that Elijah had ap-
peared,[v] and still others that one of the 9:8 v Mt 11:14
prophets of long ago had come back to w ver 19; Jn 1:21
life.[w] 9 But Herod said, "I beheaded John.
Who, then, is this I hear such things
about?" And he tried to see him.[x] 9:9 x Lk 23:8

Jesus Feeds the Five Thousand

10 When the apostles[y] returned, they 9:10
reported to Jesus what they had done. y Mk 6:30 z Mt 11:21
Then he took them with him and they
withdrew by themselves to a town called
Bethsaida,[z] 11 but the crowds learned
about it and followed him. He welcomed
them and spoke to them about the king-

a 43 Many manuscripts *years, and she had spent all she had on doctors*

9:11 a ver 2; Mt 3:2 dom of God,[a] and healed those who
needed healing.
12Late in the afternoon the Twelve
came to him and said, "Send the crowd
away so they can go to the surrounding
villages and countryside and find food
and lodging, because we are in a remote
place here."
13He replied, "You give them something to eat."
They answered, "We have only five
loaves of bread and two fish—unless we
go and buy food for all this crowd."
14(About five thousand men were there.)
But he said to his disciples, "Have
them sit down in groups of about fifty
each." 15The disciples did so, and everybody sat down. 16Taking the five loaves
and the two fish and looking up to heav-
9:16 b Mt 14:19 en, he gave thanks and broke them.[b]
Then he gave them to the disciples to set
before the people. 17They all ate and
were satisfied, and the disciples picked
up twelve basketfuls of broken pieces
that were left over.

AT THAT TIME LIVED JESUS, A HOLY MAN, IF MAN HE MAY BE CALLED, FOR HE PERFORMED WONDERFUL WORKS, AND TAUGHT MEN, AND JOYFULLY RECEIVED THE TRUTH. HE WAS MESSIAH.

Flavius Josephus, *Jewish Historian*

Peter's Confession of Christ

9:18 c Lk 3:21 18Once when Jesus was praying[c] in
private and his disciples were with him,
he asked them, "Who do the crowds say
I am?"
9:19 d Mt 3:1 19They replied, "Some say John the
e ver 7,8 Baptist;[d] others say Elijah; and still others, that one of the prophets of long ago
has come back to life."[e]
20"But what about you?" he asked.
9:20 f Jn 1:49; 6:66-69; 11:27 "Who do you say I am?"
Peter answered, "The Christ[a] of God."[f]
9:21 g Mt 16:20; Mk 8:30 21Jesus strictly warned them not to
tell this to anyone.[g] 22And he said, "The
Son of Man[h] must suffer many things[i]
9:22 h Mt 8:20 i Mt 16:21 and be rejected by the elders, chief
j Mt 27:1,2 priests and teachers of the law,[j] and he
k Ac 2:23; 3:13 must be killed[k] and on the third day[l] be
l Mt 16:21 raised to life."[m]
m Mt 16:21 23Then he said to them all: "If anyone
would come after me, he must deny
himself and take up his cross daily and 9:23
follow me.[n] 24For whoever wants to save n Mt 10:38; Lk 14:27
his life will lose it, but whoever loses his
life for me will save it.[o] 25What good is it 9:24
for a man to gain the whole world, and o Jn 12:25
yet lose or forfeit his very self? 26If anyone is ashamed of me and my words, the 9:26
Son of Man will be ashamed of him[p] p Mt 10:33;
when he comes in his glory and in the Lk 12:9; 2Ti 2:12
glory of the Father and of the holy an- q Mt 16:27
gels.[q] 27I tell you the truth, some who are
standing here will not taste death before
they see the kingdom of God."

The Transfiguration

28About eight days after Jesus said
this, he took Peter, John and James[r] with 9:28 r Mt 4:21
him and went up onto a mountain to s Lk 3:21
pray.[s] 29As he was praying, the appearance of his face changed, and his clothes
became as bright as a flash of lightning.
30Two men, Moses and Elijah, 31appeared in glorious splendor, talking with 9:31
Jesus. They spoke about his departure,[t] t 2Pe 1:15
which he was about to bring to fulfillment at Jerusalem. 32Peter and his companions were very sleepy,[u] but when they 9:32 u Mt 26:43
became fully awake, they saw his glory
and the two men standing with him. 33As
the men were leaving Jesus, Peter said to 9:33
him, "Master,[v] it is good for us to be here. v Lk 5:5
Let us put up three shelters—one for
you, one for Moses and one for Elijah."
(He did not know what he was saying.)
34While he was speaking, a cloud appeared and enveloped them, and they
were afraid as they entered the cloud. 35A
voice came from the cloud, saying, "This
is my Son, whom I have chosen;[w] listen 9:35 w Isa 42:1
to him."[x] 36When the voice had spoken, x Mt 3:17
they found that Jesus was alone. The disciples kept this to themselves, and told 9:36
no one at that time what they had seen.[y] y Mt 17:9

The Healing of a Boy With an Evil Spirit

37The next day, when they came down
from the mountain, a large crowd met
him. 38A man in the crowd called out,
"Teacher, I beg you to look at my son, for
he is my only child. 39A spirit seizes him
and he suddenly screams; it throws him
into convulsions so that he foams at the
mouth. It scarcely ever leaves him and is

[a] 20 Or *Messiah*

DISCOVERY 264

SELF-DENIAL FOR THE NAME

In Luke 9:18–27 Jesus asked his disciples two significant questions (see also Discovery #240, page 1289). The first was purely academic in nature: "Who do the crowds say I am?" (verse 18). The disciples responded with what the Teacher already knew. Many people were observing that Jesus was a great prophet, perhaps John the Baptist or Elijah or another Old Testament prophet come back to life (verse 19). This reply might at first blush have appeared flattering, but in fact Jesus was *not* just another prophet—he is the very Son of God.

The second question sounded deceptively simple, but it must have caused the disciples to squirm. Jesus was asking them to jump off the fence, to align themselves with him openly: "Who do you say I am?" (verse 20). Peter's reply was immediate and emphatic: "The Christ of God" (Luke 9:20; see also Matthew 16:16; Mark 8:29). Peter recognized who Jesus is and was willing to state his conviction.

After he had asked these two questions, Jesus made two surprising pronouncements. The first was an explicit prediction: "The Son of Man must suffer many things" (Luke 9:22). This must have been a shocking revelation for the disciples. They had just heard Peter's confession about Jesus being the Messiah, and they shared the popular expectation that Jesus would deliver the nation of Israel from Roman occupation and establish and rule over God's kingdom forever. But Jesus was stating exactly the opposite: that he was going to suffer and die and then come back from the dead. The course of events that would lead to the cross and the tomb was *necessary* for the salvation of humanity, and it was important to Jesus that the disciples were not operating under a false assumption (Romans 5:12–21).

Before the 12 could even begin to assimilate this astonishing news, Jesus continued with the second declaration: "If anyone would come after me, he must deny himself and take up his cross daily and follow me" (Luke 9:23). The disciples had been anticipating positions of authority and prominence in Jesus' new kingdom (Mark 9:33–37; 10:35–45) and periodically argued about which of them was destined to become the greatest leader. And now, suddenly, following Jesus didn't sound so glamorous. In lieu of prominence and political power Jesus was predicting self-denial and death. In fact, Jesus informed them that if they were to try to protect their lives, they would ultimately lose them—and that only in losing their lives would they truly find abundant life (Luke 9:24).

Jesus' revelation to his disciples still applies to us today. He expects our complete allegiance and asks us to sacrifice everything in order to live for him and to proclaim his Good News (Mark 8:35). The apostle Paul echoed Jesus' words, stating that everything he did was for the sake of the gospel (1 Corinthians 9:19–27).

***Self-Discovery:** In what ways, if any, do you feel that you are taking up your cross daily? Do you ever feel that there is something missing in your life if you are not feeling deprived in some way because of your faith? Try to put into words what you feel the Christian's attitude toward life should be.*

GO TO DISCOVERY 265 ON PAGE 1377

destroying him. 40 I begged your disciples
to drive it out, but they could not."
41 "O unbelieving and perverse gener-
9:41 [z] Dt 32:5 ation,"[z] Jesus replied, "how long shall I
stay with you and put up with you?
Bring your son here."
42 Even while the boy was coming, the
demon threw him to the ground in a
convulsion. But Jesus rebuked the evil[a]
spirit, healed the boy and gave him back
to his father. 43 And they were all amazed
at the greatness of God.
While everyone was marveling at all
that Jesus did, he said to his disciples,
44 "Listen carefully to what I am about to
9:44 tell you: The Son of Man is going to be
[a] ver 22 betrayed into the hands of men."[a] 45 But
they did not understand what this
meant. It was hidden from them, so that
9:45 [b] Mk 9:32 they did not grasp it,[b] and they were
afraid to ask him about it.

Who Will Be the Greatest?

46 An argument started among the
9:46 disciples as to which of them would be
[c] Lk 22:24 the greatest.[c] 47 Jesus, knowing their
9:47 thoughts,[d] took a little child and had
[d] Mt 9:4 him stand beside him. 48 Then he said to
them, "Whoever welcomes this little
child in my name welcomes me; and
9:48 whoever welcomes me welcomes the
[e] Mt 10:40 one who sent me.[e] For he who is least
[f] Mk 9:35 among you all—he is the greatest."[f]
9:49 49 "Master,"[g] said John, "we saw a man
[g] Lk 5:5 driving out demons in your name and
we tried to stop him, because he is not
one of us."
9:50 50 "Do not stop him," Jesus said, "for
[h] Mt 12:30; Lk 11:23 whoever is not against you is for you."[h]

Samaritan Opposition

9:51 51 As the time approached for him to
[i] Mk 16:19 [j] Lk 13:22; be taken up to heaven,[i] Jesus resolutely
17:11; 18:31; set out for Jerusalem.[j] 52 And he sent
19:28 messengers on ahead, who went into a
9:52 Samaritan[k] village to get things ready
[k] Mt 10:5 for him; 53 but the people there did not
welcome him, because he was heading
9:54 for Jerusalem. 54 When the disciples
[l] Mt 4:21 James and John[l] saw this, they asked,
[m] 2Ki 1:10,12 "Lord, do you want us to call fire down
from heaven to destroy them[b]?"[m] 55 But
Jesus turned and rebuked them, 56 and[c]
they went to another village.

The Cost of Following Jesus

57 As they were walking along the
road,[n] a man said to him, "I will follow 9:57
you wherever you go." [n] ver 51
58 Jesus replied, "Foxes have holes and
birds of the air have nests, but the Son of 9:58
Man[o] has no place to lay his head." [o] Mt 8:20
59 He said to another man, "Fol- 9:59
low me."[p] [p] Mt 4:19
But the man replied, "Lord, first let
me go and bury my father."
60 Jesus said to him, "Let the dead bury
their own dead, but you go and proclaim 9:60
the kingdom of God."[q] [q] Mt 3:2
61 Still another said, "I will follow you,
Lord; but first let me go back and say
good-by to my family."[r] 9:61 [r] 1Ki 19:20
62 Jesus replied, "No one who puts his
hand to the plow and looks back is fit for
service in the kingdom of God."

Jesus Sends Out the Seventy-two

10 After this the Lord[s] appointed 10:1 [s] Lk 7:13
seventy-two[d] others[t] and sent [t] Lk 9:1,2,51,52
them two by two[u] ahead of him to every [u] Mk 6:7
town and place where he was about to [v] Mt 10:1
go.[v] 2 He told them, "The harvest is plentiful, but the workers are few. Ask the
Lord of the harvest, therefore, to send 10:2
out workers into his harvest field.[w] 3 Go! [w] Mt 9:37,38;
I am sending you out like lambs among Jn 4:35
wolves.[x] 4 Do not take a purse or bag or 10:3
sandals; and do not greet anyone on the [x] Mt 10:16
road.
5 "When you enter a house, first say,
'Peace to this house.' 6 If a man of peace
is there, your peace will rest on him; if
not, it will return to you. 7 Stay in that
house, eating and drinking whatever
they give you, for the worker deserves
his wages.[y] Do not move around from 10:7 [y] Mt 10:10;
house to house. 1Co 9:14;
8 "When you enter a town and are wel- 1Ti 5:18
comed, eat what is set before you.[z] 9 Heal 10:8 [z] 1Co 10:27
the sick who are there and tell them,
'The kingdom of God[a] is near you.' 10 But 10:9
when you enter a town and are not wel- [a] Mt 3:2; 10:7
comed, go into its streets and say,
11 'Even the dust of your town that sticks
to our feet we wipe off against you.[b] Yet 10:11 [b] Mt 10:14;
be sure of this: The kingdom of God is Mk 6:11 [c] ver 9
near.'[c] 12 I tell you, it will be more bear-

[a] *42* Greek *unclean* [b] *54* Some manuscripts *them, even as Elijah did* [c] *55,56* Some manuscripts *them. And he said, "You do not know what kind of spirit you are of, for the Son of Man did not come to destroy men's lives, but to save them."* *56 And* [d] *1* Some manuscripts *seventy*; also in verse 17

10:12 [d]Mt 10:15 able on that day for Sodom[d] than for
[e]Mt 11:24 that town.[e]
13"Woe to you,[f] Korazin! Woe to you,
10:13 [f]Lk 6:24-26 Bethsaida! For if the miracles that were
[g]Rev 11:3 performed in you had been performed
in Tyre and Sidon, they would have repented long ago, sitting in sackcloth[g]
and ashes. 14But it will be more bearable
for Tyre and Sidon at the judgment than
10:15 for you. 15And you, Capernaum,[h] will
[h]Mt 4:13 you be lifted up to the skies? No, you will
go down to the depths.[a]
16"He who listens to you listens to me;
he who rejects you rejects me; but he
10:16 [i]Mt 10:40; who rejects me rejects him who
Jn 13:20 sent me."[i]
17The seventy-two[j] returned with joy
10:17 [j]ver 1 and said, "Lord, even the demons sub-
[k]Mk 16:17 mit to us in your name."[k]
18He replied, "I saw Satan[l] fall like
10:18 [l]Mt 4:10 lightning from heaven.[m] 19I have given
[m]Isa 14:12; you authority to trample on snakes[n] and
Rev 9:1; 12:8,9 scorpions and to overcome all the pow-
10:19 [n]Mk 16:18; er of the enemy; nothing will harm you.
Ac 28:3-5 20However, do not rejoice that the spirits
submit to you, but rejoice that your
10:20 [o]Ex 32:32; names are written in heaven."[o]
Ps 69:28; 21At that time Jesus, full of joy
Da 12:1; through the Holy Spirit, said, "I praise
Php 4:3; Heb 12:23; you, Father, Lord of heaven and earth,
Rev 13:8; 20:12; because you have hidden these things
21:27 from the wise and learned, and revealed
10:21 [p]1Co 1:26-29 them to little children.[p] Yes, Father, for
this was your good pleasure.
22"All things have been committed to
10:22 [q]Mt 28:18 me by my Father.[q] No one knows who
[r]Jn 1:18 the Son is except the Father, and no one
knows who the Father is except the Son
and those to whom the Son chooses to
reveal him."[r]
23Then he turned to his disciples and
said privately, "Blessed are the eyes that
see what you see. 24For I tell you that
many prophets and kings wanted to see
what you see but did not see it, and to
10:24 [s]1Pe 1:10-12 hear what you hear but did not hear it."[s]

The Parable of the Good Samaritan

25On one occasion an expert in the
law stood up to test Jesus. "Teacher," he
asked, "what must I do to inherit eternal
10:25 [t]Mt 19:16; life?"[t]
Lk 18:18 26"What is written in the Law?" he
replied. "How do you read it?"
27He answered: " 'Love the Lord your
God with all your heart and with all your
soul and with all your strength and with
all your mind'[b];[u] and, 'Love your neigh- 10:27 [u]Dt 6:5
bor as yourself.'[c]"[v] [v]Lev 19:18; Mt 5:43
28"You have answered correctly," Jesus
replied. "Do this and you will live."[w] 10:28
29But he wanted to justify himself,[x] so [w]Lev 18:5; Ro 7:10
he asked Jesus, "And who is my neigh-
bor?" 10:29 [x]Lk 16:15
30In reply Jesus said: "A man was going
down from Jerusalem to Jericho, when
he fell into the hands of robbers. They
stripped him of his clothes, beat him
and went away, leaving him half dead.

[a] 15 Greek *Hades* [b] 27 Deut. 6:5 [c] 27 Lev. 19:18

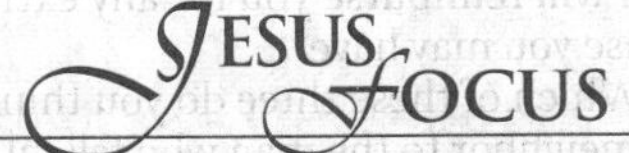

A TRUE NEIGHBOR?

The parable of the Good Samaritan is one of the most familiar stories in the Bible (Luke 10:25–37). Sometimes referred to as a "juridical parable" (one pertaining to the administration of justice), it lays out a set of circumstances and then implicitly asks the listener or reader to make a moral assessment. The story is set along the treacherous route from Jerusalem to Jericho, which ran a distance of 17 miles with a sharp descent from about 2,500 feet above sea level to about 800 below sea level. The road wound through precarious, rocky desert terrain, providing ideal vantage points from which robbers could waylay defenseless travelers. In Jesus' fabled account both a priest (a religious leader) and a Levite (a lay associate) observed a fellow Jew who had been savagely beaten and left for dead, but each decided that it would be inexpedient to get involved. After all, touching a dead body would have made them "unclean" (Leviticus 21:1–4), a situation that would have been inconvenient to say the least! But a traveler from Samaria, despised by the Jewish people because of his race, stopped without concern for his own safety to care for the man, going so far as to make financial arrangements at an inn to ensure his full recovery. The word *neighbor* as used in this story has connotations far beyond that individual similar to us in social status and lifestyle who resides in our "neighborhood"; Jesus was referring instead to that person who is willing—regardless of whether the action might be convenient, prudent or even safe—to reach out unconditionally to a fellow human being in need. Our willingness to "be bothered" has a great deal to say about the depth of our love for Jesus and the integrity of our Christian walk.

[31]A priest happened to be going down
the same road, and when he saw the
10:31 man, he passed by on the other side.[y]
y Lev 21:1-3 [32]So too, a Levite, when he came to the
place and saw him, passed by on the
10:33 z Mt 10:5 other side. [33]But a Samaritan,[z] as he
traveled, came where the man was; and
when he saw him, he took pity on him.
[34]He went to him and bandaged his
wounds, pouring on oil and wine. Then
he put the man on his own donkey, took
him to an inn and took care of him.
[35]The next day he took out two silver
coins[a] and gave them to the innkeeper.
'Look after him,' he said, 'and when I return, I will reimburse you for any extra
expense you may have.'

[36]"Which of these three do you think
was a neighbor to the man who fell into
the hands of robbers?"

[37]The expert in the law replied, "The
one who had mercy on him."

Jesus told him, "Go and do likewise."

At the Home of Martha and Mary

[38]As Jesus and his disciples were on
their way, he came to a village where a
10:38 a Jn 11:1; 12:2 woman named Martha[a] opened her
home to him. [39]She had a sister called
10:39 b Jn 11:1; 12:3 Mary,[b] who sat at the Lord's feet[c] listen-
c Lk 8:35 ing to what he said. [40]But Martha was
distracted by all the preparations that
had to be made. She came to him and
10:40 d Mk 4:38 asked, "Lord, don't you care[d] that my
sister has left me to do the work by my-
self? Tell her to help me!"

[41]"Martha, Martha," the Lord an-
10:41 e Mt 6:25-34; swered, "you are worried[e] and upset
Lk 12:11,22 about many things, [42]but only one thing
10:42 is needed.[b f] Mary has chosen what is
f Ps 27:4 better, and it will not be taken away
from her."

Jesus' Teaching on Prayer

11:1 **11** One day Jesus was praying[g] in a
g Lk 3:21 h Jn 13:13 certain place. When he finished, one of his disciples said to him,
"Lord,[h] teach us to pray, just as John
taught his disciples."

I HAVE SEEN JESUS DO MORE IN PEOPLE'S LIVES DURING TEN MINUTES OF REAL PRAYER THAN IN TEN OF MY SERMONS.

Jim Cymbala, *Pastor, Brooklyn, New York*

[2]He said to them, "When you pray,
say:

" 'Father,[c]
hallowed be your name, 11:2
your kingdom[i] come.[d] i Mt 3:2
[3]Give us each day our daily bread.
[4]Forgive us our sins,
for we also forgive everyone who
sins against us.[e j] 11:4 j Mt 18:35;
And lead us not into Mk 11:25
temptation.[f] ' "[k] k Mt 26:41; Jas 1:13

[5]Then he said to them, "Suppose one
of you has a friend, and he goes to him
at midnight and says, 'Friend, lend me
three loaves of bread, [6]because a friend
of mine on a journey has come to me,
and I have nothing to set before him.'

[7]"Then the one inside answers, 'Don't
bother me. The door is already locked,
and my children are with me in bed. I
can't get up and give you anything.' [8]I tell
you, though he will not get up and give
him the bread because he is his friend,
yet because of the man's boldness[g] he
will get up and give him as much as he
needs.[l] 11:8 l Lk 18:1-6

[9]"So I say to you: Ask and it will be
given to you;[m] seek and you will find; 11:9 m Mt 7:7
knock and the door will be opened to
you. [10]For everyone who asks receives;
he who seeks finds; and to him who
knocks, the door will be opened.

[11]"Which of you fathers, if your son
asks for[h] a fish, will give him a snake instead? [12]Or if he asks for an egg, will give
him a scorpion? [13]If you then, though
you are evil, know how to give good gifts
to your children, how much more will
your Father in heaven give the Holy Spirit to those who ask him!"

Jesus and Beelzebub

[14]Jesus was driving out a demon that
was mute. When the demon left, the
man who had been mute spoke, and the 11:14 n Mt 9:32,33
crowd was amazed.[n] [15]But some of them
said, "By Beelzebub,[i o] the prince of 11:15 o Mk 3:22
demons, he is driving out demons."[p] p Mt 9:34

[a] 35 Greek *two denarii* [b] 42 Some manuscripts *but few things are needed—or only one* [c] 2 Some manuscripts *Our Father in heaven* [d] 2 Some manuscripts *come. May your will be done on earth as it is in heaven.* [e] 4 Greek *everyone who is indebted to us* [f] 4 Some manuscripts *temptation but deliver us from the evil one* [g] 8 Or *persistence* [h] 11 Some manuscripts *for bread, will give him a stone; or if he asks for* [i] 15 Greek *Beezeboul* or *Beelzeboul;* also in verses 18 and 19

THE LORD'S PRAYER

Luke has recorded in chapter 11 of his Gospel a prayer traditionally titled "the Lord's Prayer." It might be more appropriate, however, to refer to it as "the Disciple's Prayer," because Jesus offered it to the disciples as a model to follow when they prayed. The prayer in Luke 11 is actually a slightly condensed version of the one found in Matthew 6:9–13. Some of the important elements are as follows:

Father. Once we have established a relationship with our heavenly Father through his Son Jesus, we can approach him with the same confidence as a child with her daddy (John 14:6). Our heavenly Father has promised to meet all of our needs (Matthew 7:7–12; Philippians 4:19).

Hallowed be your name. The impetus for true prayer begins with the desire to honor God (Psalm 34:3), not with the motive of calling our needs to his attention. "Hallowing" God's name means setting God's name aside as sacred from all other names, of placing the honor of that name above our own personal needs or desires.

Your kingdom come. A kingdom by its very nature requires two basic components, a king and subjects. When we ask for God's kingdom to come, we are expressing our heartfelt desire that God will reign in the hearts and lives of human beings everywhere. This includes praying for people who do not yet know God as well as pleading with him to help those who are already citizens of his kingdom to be yielded to his will.

Give us each day our daily bread. The first personal request in Jesus' model prayer addresses the issue of our daily needs. We may be tempted to ask God to meet our needs for the week, the month or even the year. While this kind of petition is not inherently wrong, we need to develop the confidence to depend on God *daily*. If God were to supply our needs in bulk quantities, we might too easily forget the source of our bounty or become greedy and lust for more than what we really need.

Forgive us our sins. God's forgiveness of our sins is directly dependent on our willingness to forgive others who have wronged us. Because God paid the staggering debts accumulated as a result of our sin through the redeeming work of Jesus, it should be incomprehensible that any of us would refuse to absolve another person. Jesus spoke frequently about the importance of forgiveness (Matthew 18:21–35; Mark 11:20–25).

Lead us not into temptation. God himself does not tempt us to sin (James 1:13). At the same time his daily guidance does not mean that we will no longer encounter temptation. Even Jesus was tested in the desert by Satan (Luke 4:1–2). When we ask God not to lead us into temptation, we are really praying that he will guide us step-by-step through the struggle, that he will uphold us and make us strong so that we might resist our enemies (Romans 5:3–5; 1 Corinthians 10:13).

Prayer always begins with praising God. From the mind-set of praise we can then bring up our own needs, because we will be doing so from a godly focus. But we'll likely be surprised at how the amount of time spent talking about ourselves decreases as we become seasoned in prayer.

Self-Discovery: *Pray the Lord's Prayer, pausing after each clause to personalize the prayer by adding a sentence or two of your own.*

GO TO DISCOVERY 266 ON PAGE 1383

11:16 16Others tested him by asking for a sign
q Mt 12:38 from heaven.[q]
17Jesus knew their thoughts[r] and said
11:17 r Mt 9:4 to them: "Any kingdom divided against
11:18 itself will be ruined, and a house divided
s Mt 4:10 against itself will fall. 18If Satan[s] is divided against himself, how can his king-
dom stand? I say this because you claim
that I drive out demons by Beelzebub.
19Now if I drive out demons by Beelzebub, by whom do your followers drive
them out? So then, they will be your
judges. 20But if I drive out demons by the
11:20 t Ex 8:19 finger of God,[t] then the kingdom of
u Mt 3:2 God[u] has come to you.
21"When a strong man, fully armed,
guards his own house, his possessions
are safe. 22But when someone stronger
attacks and overpowers him, he takes
away the armor in which the man trusted and divides up the spoils.
23"He who is not with me is against
11:23 me, and he who does not gather with
v Mt 12:30; Mk 9:40; Lk 9:50 me, scatters.[v]
24"When an evil[a] spirit comes out of a
man, it goes through arid places seeking
rest and does not find it. Then it says, 'I
will return to the house I left.' 25When it
arrives, it finds the house swept clean
and put in order. 26Then it goes and
takes seven other spirits more wicked
than itself, and they go in and live there.
11:26 And the final condition of that man is
w 2Pe 2:20 worse than the first."[w]
27As Jesus was saying these things, a
woman in the crowd called out, "Blessed
11:27 is the mother who gave you birth and
x Lk 23:29 nursed you."[x]
11:28 28He replied, "Blessed rather are those
y Heb 4:12 who hear the word of God[y] and obey it."[z]
z Pr 8:32; Lk 6:47; 8:21; Jn 14:21

The Sign of Jonah

29As the crowds increased, Jesus said,
"This is a wicked generation. It asks for
11:29 a miraculous sign,[a] but none will be giv-
a ver 16; Mt 12:38 en it except the sign of Jonah.[b] 30For as
b Jnh 1:17; Mt 16:4 Jonah was a sign to the Ninevites, so also
will the Son of Man be to this genera-
tion. 31The Queen of the South will rise
at the judgment with the men of this
generation and condemn them; for she
11:31 came from the ends of the earth to listen
c 1Ki 10:1; 2Ch 9:1 to Solomon's wisdom,[c] and now one[b]
greater than Solomon is here. 32The men
of Nineveh will stand up at the judgment with this generation and condemn
it; for they repented at the preaching of
Jonah,[d] and now one greater than Jonah 11:32 d Jnh 3:5
is here.

The Lamp of the Body

33"No one lights a lamp and puts it in
a place where it will be hidden, or under
a bowl. Instead he puts it on its stand, so
that those who come in may see the 11:33
light.[e] 34Your eye is the lamp of your e Mt 5:15;
body. When your eyes are good, your Mk 4:21; Lk 8:16
whole body also is full of light. But when
they are bad, your body also is full of
darkness. 35See to it, then, that the light
within you is not darkness. 36Therefore,
if your whole body is full of light, and no
part of it dark, it will be completely
lighted, as when the light of a lamp
shines on you."

Six Woes

37When Jesus had finished speaking,
a Pharisee invited him to eat with him;
so he went in and reclined at the table.[f] 11:37 f Lk 7:36; 14:1
38But the Pharisee, noticing that Jesus
did not first wash before the meal,[g] was 11:38 g Mk 7:3,4
surprised.
39Then the Lord[h] said to him, "Now 11:39 h Lk 7:13
then, you Pharisees clean the outside of i Mt 23:25,26;
the cup and dish, but inside you are full Mk 7:20-23
of greed and wickedness.[i] 40You foolish
people![j] Did not the one who made the 11:40 j Lk 12:20;
outside make the inside also? 41But give 1Co 15:36
what is inside ⌞the dish⌟[c] to the poor,[k] 11:41
and everything will be clean for you.[l] k Lk 12:33
42"Woe to you Pharisees, because you l Ac 10:15
give God a tenth[m] of your mint, rue and 11:42
all other kinds of garden herbs, but you m Lk 18:12
neglect justice and the love of God.[n] You n Dt 6:5; Mic 6:8
should have practiced the latter without o Mt 23:23
leaving the former undone.[o]
43"Woe to you Pharisees, because you
love the most important seats in the
synagogues and greetings in the marketplaces.[p] 11:43 p Mt 23:6,7;
44"Woe to you, because you are like Mk 12:38-39;
unmarked graves,[q] which men walk over Lk 14:7; 20:46
without knowing it." 11:44
45One of the experts in the law[r] an- q Mt 23:27
swered him, "Teacher, when you say 11:45
these things, you insult us also." r Mt 22:35
46Jesus replied, "And you experts in
the law, woe to you, because you load
people down with burdens they can
hardly carry, and you yourselves will not 11:46
lift one finger to help them.[s] s Mt 23:4

[a] 24 Greek *unclean* [b] 31 Or *something*; also in verse 32 [c] 41 Or *what you have*

47“Woe to you, because you build
tombs for the prophets, and it was your
forefathers who killed them. 48So you
testify that you approve of what your
11:48 [t]Mt 23:29-32; Ac 7:51-53
forefathers did; they killed the prophets,
and you build their tombs.[t] 49Because of
this, God in his wisdom[u] said, ‘I will
11:49 [u]1Co 1:24,30; Col 2:3 [v]Mt 23:34
send them prophets and apostles, some
of whom they will kill and others they
will persecute.’[v] 50Therefore this generation will be held responsible for the
blood of all the prophets that has been
shed since the beginning of the world,
11:51 [w]Ge 4:8 [x]2Ch 24:20,21 [y]Mt 23:35,36
51from the blood of Abel[w] to the blood of
Zechariah,[x] who was killed between the
altar and the sanctuary. Yes, I tell you,
this generation will be held responsible
for it all.[y]
52“Woe to you experts in the law, because you have taken away the key to
knowledge. You yourselves have not en-
11:52 [z]Mt 23:13
tered, and you have hindered those who
were entering.”[z]
53When Jesus left there, the Pharisees
and the teachers of the law began to op-
11:54 [a]Mt 12:10; Mk 12:13
pose him fiercely and to besiege him
with questions, 54waiting to catch him
in something he might say.[a]

Warnings and Encouragements

12 Meanwhile, when a crowd of
many thousands had gathered,
so that they were trampling on one another, Jesus began to speak first to his
disciples, saying: “Be on your guard
against the yeast of the Pharisees, which
12:1 [b]Mt 16:6,11,12; Mk 8:15
is hypocrisy.[b] 2There is nothing concealed that will not be disclosed, or hid-
12:2 [c]Mk 4:22; Lk 8:17
den that will not be made known.[c]
3What you have said in the dark will be
heard in the daylight, and what you have
whispered in the ear in the inner rooms
will be proclaimed from the roofs.
12:4 [d]Jn 15:14,15
4“I tell you, my friends,[d] do not be
afraid of those who kill the body and after that can do no more. 5But I will show
you whom you should fear: Fear him
who, after the killing of the body, has
power to throw you into hell. Yes, I tell
12:5 [e]Heb 10:31
you, fear him.[e] 6Are not five sparrows
sold for two pennies[a]? Yet not one of
them is forgotten by God. 7Indeed, the
very hairs of your head are all num-
12:7 [f]Mt 10:30 [g]Mt 12:12
bered.[f] Don’t be afraid; you are worth
more than many sparrows.[g]
8“I tell you, whoever acknowledges
me before men, the Son of Man will also
acknowledge him before the angels of
12:8 [h]Lk 15:10
God.[h] 9But he who disowns me before
men will be disowned[i] before the angels
12:9 [i]Mk 8:38; 2Ti 2:12
of God. 10And everyone who speaks a
word against the Son of Man[j] will be
forgiven, but anyone who blasphemes
12:10 [j]Mt 8:20 [k]Mt 12:31,32; Mk 3:28-29; 1Jn 5:16
against the Holy Spirit will not be forgiven.[k]
11“When you are brought before synagogues, rulers and authorities, do not
12:11 [l]Mt 10:17,19; Mk 13:11; Lk 21:12,14
worry about how you will defend yourselves or what you will say,[l] 12for the
Holy Spirit will teach you at that time
what you should say.”[m]
12:12 [m]Ex 4:12; Mt 10:20; Mk 13:11; Lk 21:15

The Parable of the Rich Fool

13Someone in the crowd said to him,
“Teacher, tell my brother to divide the
inheritance with me.”
14Jesus replied, “Man, who appointed
me a judge or an arbiter between you?”
15Then he said to them, “Watch out! Be
on your guard against all kinds of greed;
a man’s life does not consist in the abun-
12:15 [n]Job 20:20; 31:24; Ps 62:10
dance of his possessions.”[n]
16And he told them this parable: “The
ground of a certain rich man produced
a good crop. 17He thought to himself,
‘What shall I do? I have no place to store
my crops.’
18“Then he said, ‘This is what I’ll do. I
will tear down my barns and build bigger ones, and there I will store all my
grain and my goods. 19And I’ll say to myself, “You have plenty of good things laid
up for many years. Take life easy; eat,
drink and be merry.” ’
20“But God said to him, ‘You fool![o]
12:20 [o]Jer 17:11; Lk 11:40 [p]Job 27:8 [q]Ps 39:6; 49:10
This very night your life will be de-
manded from you.[p] Then who will get
what you have prepared for yourself?’[q]
21“This is how it will be with anyone
who stores up things for himself but is
12:21 [r]ver 33
not rich toward God.”[r]

Do Not Worry

22Then Jesus said to his disciples:
“Therefore I tell you, do not worry about
your life, what you will eat; or about your
body, what you will wear. 23Life is more
than food, and the body more than
clothes. 24Consider the ravens: They do
not sow or reap, they have no storeroom
12:24 [s]Job 38:41; Ps 147:9
or barn; yet God feeds them.[s] And how
much more valuable you are than birds!
25Who of you by worrying can add a sin-

[a] 6 Greek *two assaria*

gle hour to his life[a]? 26Since you cannot
do this very little thing, why do you worry about the rest?
27"Consider how the lilies grow. They
12:27 do not labor or spin. Yet I tell you, not
t 1Ki 10:4-7 even Solomon in all his splendor[t] was
dressed like one of these. 28If that is how
God clothes the grass of the field, which
is here today, and tomorrow is thrown
12:28 into the fire, how much more will he
u Mt 6:30 clothe you, O you of little faith![u] 29And do
not set your heart on what you will eat or
drink; do not worry about it. 30For the
12:30 v Lk 6:36 pagan world runs after all such things,
w Mt 6:8 and your Father[v] knows that you need
12:31 them.[w] 31But seek his kingdom,[x] and
x Mt 3:2 these things will be given to you as well.[y]
y Mt 19:29 32"Do not be afraid,[z] little flock, for
12:32 your Father has been pleased to give you
z Mt 14:27 a Mt 25:34 the kingdom.[a] 33Sell your possessions
and give to the poor.[b] Provide purses for
12:33 b Mt 19:21; yourselves that will not wear out, a
Ac 2:45 treasure in heaven[c] that will not be ex-
c Mt 6:20 hausted, where no thief comes near and
d Jas 5:2 no moth destroys.[d] 34For where your
12:34 e Mt 6:21 treasure is, there your heart will be also.[e]

Watchfulness

35"Be dressed ready for service and
keep your lamps burning, 36like men
waiting for their master to return from
a wedding banquet, so that when he
comes and knocks they can immediately open the door for him. 37It will be
12:37 good for those servants whose master
f Mt 24:42,46; finds them watching when he comes.[f] I
25:13 g Mt 20:28 tell you the truth, he will dress himself to
serve, will have them recline at the table
and will come and wait on them.[g] 38It
will be good for those servants whose
master finds them ready, even if he
comes in the second or third watch of
the night. 39But understand this: If the
12:39 owner of the house had known at what
h Mt 6:19; hour the thief[h] was coming, he would
1Th 5:2; 2Pe 3:10; not have let his house be broken into.
Rev 3:3; 16:15 40You also must be ready,[i] because the
12:40 Son of Man will come at an hour when
i Mk 13:33; you do not expect him."
Lk 21:36 41Peter asked, "Lord, are you telling
12:42 this parable to us, or to everyone?"
j Lk 7:13 42The Lord[j] answered, "Who then is
the faithful and wise manager, whom
the master puts in charge of his servants
to give them their food allowance at the
proper time? 43It will be good for that
servant whom the master finds doing so
when he returns. 44I tell you the truth, he
will put him in charge of all his possessions. 45But suppose the servant says to
himself, 'My master is taking a long time
in coming,' and he then begins to beat
the menservants and maidservants and
to eat and drink and get drunk. 46The
master of that servant will come on a
day when he does not expect him and at
an hour he is not aware of.[k] He will cut 12:46 k ver 40
him to pieces and assign him a place
with the unbelievers.
47"That servant who knows his master's will and does not get ready or does
not do what his master wants will be
beaten with many blows.[l] 48But the one 12:47 l Dt 25:2
who does not know and does things de-
serving punishment will be beaten with
few blows.[m] From everyone who has 12:48 m Lev 5:17;
been given much, much will be de- Nu 15:27-30
manded; and from the one who has
been entrusted with much, much more
will be asked.

> CHRIST HAS A HABIT OF INSERTING A CORKSCREW INTO ONE'S HEART AND THEN PULLING BACK AND FORTH.
>
> A. W. Tozer, *American Theologian*

Not Peace but Division

49"I have come to bring fire on the
earth, and how I wish it were already
kindled! 50But I have a baptism[n] to un- 12:50 n Mk 10:38
dergo, and how distressed I am until it is o Jn 19:30
completed![o] 51Do you think I came to
bring peace on earth? No, I tell you, but
division. 52From now on there will be
five in one family divided against each
other, three against two and two against
three. 53They will be divided, father
against son and son against father,
mother against daughter and daughter
against mother, mother-in-law against
daughter-in-law and daughter-in-law 12:53
against mother-in-law."[p] p Mic 7:6; Mt 10:21

Interpreting the Times

54He said to the crowd: "When you
see a cloud rising in the west, immediately you say, 'It's going to rain,' and it
does.[q] 55And when the south wind 12:54
blows, you say, 'It's going to be hot,' and q Mt 16:2

a 25 Or *single cubit to his height*

it is. 56Hypocrites! You know how to interpret the appearance of the earth and
12:56 the sky. How is it that you don't know
r Mt 16:3 how to interpret this present time?[r]
57"Why don't you judge for yourselves
what is right? 58As you are going with
your adversary to the magistrate, try
hard to be reconciled to him on the way,
or he may drag you off to the judge, and
12:58 s Mt 5:25 the judge turn you over to the officer,
and the officer throw you into prison.[s]
12:59 t Mt 5:26; 59I tell you, you will not get out until you
Mk 12:42 have paid the last penny.[a]"[t]

Repent or Perish

13 Now there were some present
at that time who told Jesus
13:1 u Mt 27:2 about the Galileans whose blood Pilate[u]
had mixed with their sacrifices. 2Jesus
answered, "Do you think that these Galileans were worse sinners than all the
other Galileans because they suffered
13:2 v Jn 9:2,3 this way?[v] 3I tell you, no! But unless you
repent, you too will all perish. 4Or those
13:4 eighteen who died when the tower in Si-
w Jn 9:7,11 loam[w] fell on them—do you think they
were more guilty than all the others living in Jerusalem? 5I tell you, no! But un- 13:5
less you repent,[x] you too will all perish." x Mt 3:2; Ac 2:38
6Then he told this parable: "A man
had a fig tree, planted in his vineyard,
and he went to look for fruit on it, but
did not find any.[y] 7So he said to the man 13:6 y Isa 5:2;
who took care of the vineyard, 'For three Jer 8:13;
years now I've been coming to look for Mt 21:19
fruit on this fig tree and haven't found
any. Cut it down![z] Why should it use up 13:7 z Mt 3:10
the soil?'
8" 'Sir,' the man replied, 'leave it alone
for one more year, and I'll dig around it
and fertilize it. 9If it bears fruit next year,
fine! If not, then cut it down.' "

A Crippled Woman Healed on the Sabbath

10On a Sabbath Jesus was teaching in 13:10
one of the synagogues,[a] 11and a woman a Mt 4:23
was there who had been crippled by a 13:11
spirit for eighteen years.[b] She was bent b ver 16
over and could not straighten up at all.
12When Jesus saw her, he called her forward and said to her, "Woman, you are
set free from your infirmity." 13Then he
put his hands on her,[c] and immediately 13:13 c Mk 5:23
she straightened up and praised God.
14Indignant because Jesus had healed
on the Sabbath,[d] the synagogue ruler[e] 13:14 d Mt 12:2;
said to the people, "There are six days Lk 14:3 e Mk 5:22
for work.[f] So come and be healed on f Ex 20:9
those days, not on the Sabbath."
15The Lord answered him, "You hypocrites! Doesn't each of you on the Sabbath untie his ox or donkey from the stall
and lead it out to give it water?[g] 16Then 13:15 g Lk 14:5
should not this woman, a daughter of 13:16
Abraham,[h] whom Satan[i] has kept bound h Lk 3:8; 19:9
for eighteen long years, be set free on the i Mt 4:10
Sabbath day from what bound her?"
17When he said this, all his opponents 13:17
were humiliated,[j] but the people were j Isa 66:5
delighted with all the wonderful things
he was doing.

The Parables of the Mustard Seed and the Yeast

18Then Jesus asked, "What is the king-
dom of God[k] like?[l] What shall I compare 13:18 k Mt 3:2
it to? 19It is like a mustard seed, which a l Mt 13:24
man took and planted in his garden. It 13:19
grew and became a tree,[m] and the birds m Lk 17:6
of the air perched in its branches."[n] n Mt 13:32
20Again he asked, "What shall I com-
pare the kingdom of God to? 21It is like

JESUS FOCUS

REPENTANCE

Many of us would enjoy being entertained at a Christian concert, inspired at a Bible seminar or challenged at a leadership conference. But being called on to repent? A bit old-fashioned, wouldn't you think—and certainly not a likely approach for drawing an enthusiastic crowd. But most of Jesus' sermons urged people to repent—to turn away from sin and turn back to God (Matthew 4:17; Luke 13:3). Jesus was not ashamed to remind people that they had wandered away from God—and that the Father was waiting in the wings to forgive them and to draw them back them into a relationship with him. Following his resurrection Jesus made clear to his followers that he wanted them to continue to relay that same message to people everywhere (Luke 24:47). For anyone who sincerely desires to walk with God, the concept of repentance is not an embarrassing religious concept for which we need to apologize any time we mention the word. The reality of our need for repentance is vitally relevant for us today. Paul's statement is as true as we enter the third millennium as it was in the first century A.D.: "God . . . commands all people everywhere to repent" (Acts 17:30).

[a] 59 Greek *lepton*

yeast that a woman took and mixed into
13:21 a large amount[a] of flour until it worked
[o] 1Co 5:6 all through the dough."[o]

The Narrow Door

[22]Then Jesus went through the towns
and villages, teaching as he made his
13:22 way to Jerusalem.[p] [23]Someone asked
[p] Lk 9:51 him, "Lord, are only a few people going
to be saved?"

He said to them, [24]"Make every effort
13:24 to enter through the narrow door,[q] be-
[q] Mt 7:13 cause many, I tell you, will try to enter
and will not be able to. [25]Once the owner of the house gets up and closes the
door, you will stand outside knocking
and pleading, 'Sir, open the door for us.'

"But he will answer, 'I don't know you
13:25 [r] Mt 7:23; 25:10-12 or where you come from.'[r]

[26]"Then you will say, 'We ate and
drank with you, and you taught in our
streets.'

[27]"But he will reply, 'I don't know you
or where you come from. Away from me,
13:27 [s] Mt 7:23; 25:41 all you evildoers!'[s]

[28]"There will be weeping there, and
13:28 [t] Mt 8:12 gnashing of teeth,[t] when you see Abraham, Isaac and Jacob and all the proph-
ets in the kingdom of God, but you yourselves thrown out. [29]People will come
13:29 [u] Mt 8:11 from east and west[u] and north and
south, and will take their places at the
feast in the kingdom of God. [30]Indeed
there are those who are last who will be
13:30 [v] Mt 19:30 first, and first who will be last."[v]

Jesus' Sorrow for Jerusalem

[31]At that time some Pharisees came
13:31 to Jesus and said to him, "Leave this
[w] Mt 14:1 place and go somewhere else. Herod[w]
wants to kill you."

[32]He replied, "Go tell that fox, 'I will
drive out demons and heal people today
13:32 and tomorrow, and on the third day I
[x] Heb 2:10 will reach my goal.'[x] [33]In any case, I must
13:33 keep going today and tomorrow and the
[y] Mt 21:11 next day—for surely no prophet[y] can die
outside Jerusalem!

[34]"O Jerusalem, Jerusalem, you who kill
the prophets and stone those sent to you,
how often I have longed to gather your
13:34 children together, as a hen gathers her
[z] Mt 23:37 chicks under her wings,[z] but you were
13:35 not willing! [35]Look, your house is left to
[a] Jer 12:17; 22:5 you desolate.[a] I tell you, you will not see
[b] Ps 118:26; Mt 21:9; Lk 19:38 me again until you say, 'Blessed is he who
comes in the name of the Lord.'[b]"[b]

Jesus at a Pharisee's House

14 One Sabbath, when Jesus went
to eat in the house of a promi- 14:1
nent Pharisee,[c] he was being carefully [c] Lk 7:36; 11:37
watched.[d] [2]There in front of him was a [d] Mt 12:10
man suffering from dropsy. [3]Jesus asked
the Pharisees and experts in the law,[e] "Is 14:3 [e] Mt 22:35
it lawful to heal on the Sabbath or not?"[f] [f] Mt 12:2
[4]But they remained silent. So taking
hold of the man, he healed him and sent
him away.

[5]Then he asked them, "If one of you
has a son[c] or an ox that falls into a well
on the Sabbath day, will you not imme-
diately pull him out?"[g] [6]And they had 14:5 [g] Lk 13:15
nothing to say.

[7]When he noticed how the guests
picked the places of honor at the table,[h] 14:7 [h] Lk 11:43
he told them this parable: [8]"When
someone invites you to a wedding feast,
do not take the place of honor, for a person more distinguished than you may
have been invited. [9]If so, the host who
invited both of you will come and say to
you, 'Give this man your seat.' Then, humiliated, you will have to take the least
important place. [10]But when you are invited, take the lowest place, so that
when your host comes, he will say to
you, 'Friend, move up to a better place.'
Then you will be honored in the presence of all your fellow guests. [11]For
everyone who exalts himself will be
humbled, and he who humbles himself 14:11 [i] Mt 23:12;
will be exalted."[i] Lk 18:14

[12]Then Jesus said to his host, "When
you give a luncheon or dinner, do not invite your friends, your brothers or relatives, or your rich neighbors; if you do,
they may invite you back and so you will
be repaid. [13]But when you give a banquet, invite the poor, the crippled, the
lame, the blind,[j] [14]and you will be 14:13 [j] ver 21
blessed. Although they cannot repay
you, you will be repaid at the resurrection of the righteous."[k] 14:14 [k] Ac 24:15

The Parable of the Great Banquet

[15]When one of those at the table with
him heard this, he said to Jesus, "Blessed 14:15
is the man who will eat at the feast[l] in [l] Isa 25:6; Mt 26:29;
the kingdom of God."[m] Lk 13:29; Rev 19:9

[16]Jesus replied: "A certain man was [m] Mt 3:2
preparing a great banquet and invited

[a] 21 Greek *three satas* (probably about 1/2 bushel or 22 liters) [b] 35 Psalm 118:26 [c] 5 Some manuscripts *donkey*

DISCOVERY 266

The Banquet Is Ready

Jesus told a parable about a grand banquet as an illustration of his offer of salvation. In the story the servant of the house went out to advise the invited guests that the banquet was ready—and one by one the invitees began to fabricate excuses for their "inability" to attend.

The first individual on the guest list declined on the basis that he had just purchased a field (Luke 14:18) which he wanted to go out and inspect. The second man excused himself based on his desire to try out the five yoke of oxen he'd just purchased (verse 19). The third had recently married and didn't want to be bothered with anything outside of his own family interests (verses 20). God does of course want us to be diligent in our business dealings and to be devoted to our loved ones, but he still expects that our first priority will be communion with him, that the need for our souls to be fed will take precedence over material or physical obligations or pleasures.

The host of the banquet in the parable, exasperated that his intended guests were declining his gracious invitation, directed his servant to seek out instead "the poor, the crippled, the blind and the lame" (verse 21). The destitute and disabled were more than willing to attend such a banquet! But there was still room in the banquet hall, so the master instructed the servant to "go out to the roads and country lanes and make them come in, so that my house will be full" (verse 23). God's great love is like that—it is absolutely inclusive, and his banquet table is set for any and all who will choose to accept his invitation.

In Jesus' parable it was the self-sufficient and the elite who missed out on the delicacies, the people who were too busy with demands of fields and oxen and families to take the time to participate in the extravagant feast. The underprivileged no doubt thoroughly appreciated the event; it is likely that many remembered this unexpected pleasure as a high point in their lives.

The bottom line is that *no one* deserved to attend the banquet. Each guest was welcomed only after having accepted an official invitation. Nothing in our busy agendas can possibly be more important than accepting that offer. In fact, Jesus invites us to enjoy an intimate dinner (communion) in our own homes (hearts) with him alone: "Here I am! I stand at the door and knock. If anyone hears my voice and opens the door, I will come in and eat with him, and he with me" (Revelation 3:20).

Self-Discovery: *Reflect on what it means to you to receive an invitation to a gala event like a banquet. Are you inclined to drop everything you have going on in your busy life in order to attend? What will you say to your precious Savior Jesus when you enter the banquet hall at which he is the host?*

GO TO DISCOVERY 267 ON PAGE 1385

many guests. 17At the time of the banquet he sent his servant to tell those
who had been invited, 'Come, for everything is now ready.'
18"But they all alike began to make excuses. The first said, 'I have just bought
a field, and I must go and see it. Please
excuse me.'
19"Another said, 'I have just bought
five yoke of oxen, and I'm on my way to
try them out. Please excuse me.'
20"Still another said, 'I just got married, so I can't come.'
21"The servant came back and reported this to his master. Then the owner of
the house became angry and ordered his
servant, 'Go out quickly into the streets
and alleys of the town and bring in the
14:21 poor, the crippled, the blind and the
[n] ver 13 lame.'[n]
22" 'Sir,' the servant said, 'what you ordered has been done, but there is still
room.'
23"Then the master told his servant,
'Go out to the roads and country lanes
and make them come in, so that my
house will be full. 24I tell you, not one of
14:24 those men who were invited will get a
[o] Mt 21:43; Ac 13:46 taste of my banquet.' "[o]

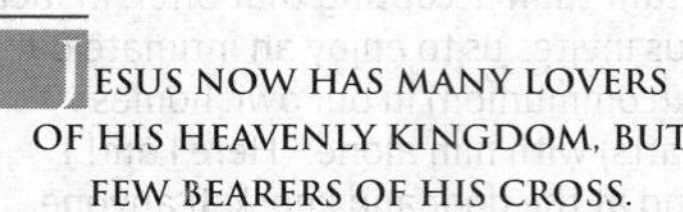
JESUS NOW HAS MANY LOVERS OF HIS HEAVENLY KINGDOM, BUT FEW BEARERS OF HIS CROSS.

Thomas á Kempis, *German Mystic*

The Cost of Being a Disciple

25Large crowds were traveling with
Jesus, and turning to them he said: 26"If
anyone comes to me and does not hate
his father and mother, his wife and children, his brothers and sisters—yes, even
14:26 his own life—he cannot be my disciple.[p]
[p] Mt 10:37; Jn 12:25 27And anyone who does not carry his
14:27 cross and follow me cannot be my disci-
[q] Mt 10:38; Lk 9:23 ple.[q]
28"Suppose one of you wants to build
a tower. Will he not first sit down and es-
timate the cost to see if he has enough
money to complete it? 29For if he lays
the foundation and is not able to finish
it, everyone who sees it will ridicule him,
30saying, 'This fellow began to build and
was not able to finish.'
31"Or suppose a king is about to go to
war against another king. Will he not
first sit down and consider whether he is
able with ten thousand men to oppose
the one coming against him with twenty thousand? 32If he is not able, he will
send a delegation while the other is still
a long way off and will ask for terms of
peace. 33In the same way, any of you who
does not give up everything he has can- 14:33
not be my disciple.[r] [r] Php 3:7,8
34"Salt is good, but if it loses its salti- 14:34
ness, how can it be made salty again?[s] [s] Mk 9:50
35It is fit neither for the soil nor for the 14:35
manure pile; it is thrown out.[t] [t] Mt 5:13
"He who has ears to hear, let him [u] Mt 11:15
hear."[u]

The Parable of the Lost Sheep

15 Now the tax collectors[v] and 15:1
"sinners" were all gathering [v] Lk 5:29
around to hear him. 2But the Pharisees
and the teachers of the law muttered,
"This man welcomes sinners and eats 15:2
with them."[w] [w] Mt 9:11
3Then Jesus told them this parable:[x] 15:3
4"Suppose one of you has a hundred [x] Mt 13:3
sheep and loses one of them. Does he
not leave the ninety-nine in the open
country and go after the lost sheep until 15:4
he finds it?[y] 5And when he finds it, he [y] Ps 23; 119:176;
joyfully puts it on his shoulders 6and Jer 31:10;
goes home. Then he calls his friends and Eze 34:11-16;
neighbors together and says, 'Rejoice Lk 5:32; 19:10

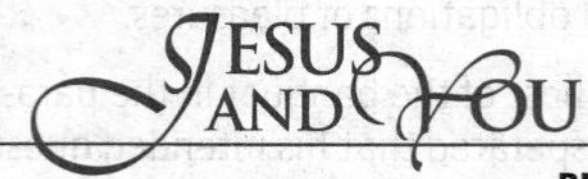

BEING HIS DISCIPLE

The cost of following Jesus and committing to live life the way he asks us to is more than many people are willing to pay. In fact, discipleship is never an easy decision. In Luke 14:25–33 Jesus challenged each of us to count the cost before making the commitment to follow him. Our Lord minced no words and allowed no room for equivocation or misinterpretation. A person *cannot* be our Lord's disciple unless following Jesus is more important to him or her than anything else in the whole world. An impossible order for us as human beings, right? Actually, the incredible truth is that as we become more intimately acquainted with the God who created us, our attachment to him *will* become more precious to us than our personal relationships (verse 26), our personal rights (verse 27) or our personal riches (verse 33). Are you ready to accept the challenge?

DISCOVERY 267

Selfishness: the Root of Sin

We've all heard that we can tell a lot about a person by the company she keeps. That's very true—so long as we know *why* she has chosen such friends. The accusation that Jesus was a "friend of sinners" was indeed valid, but his choice of companions wasn't based on mutual enjoyment of an immoral lifestyle. Jesus' parables in Luke 15 (the lost coin, the lost sheep, the lost son) explain the rationale behind his choice of friends, each illustrating our Lord's compassion for the lost.

Sin has its root in selfishness. In the final and most lengthy parable of chapter 15 the younger son demanded his share of his father's inheritance. His request began with the all-too-familiar words *give me* (verse 12), reminding us of the "gimme" culture in which we are enmeshed from early childhood on. Life with his father had been good, but the alluring pleasures of the outside world proved too strong an enticement. A similar egocentrism had lured Eve in the Garden of Eden to do what God the Father had expressly forbidden—thereby unwittingly plunging the whole human race into the devastation brought about by disobedience and sin (Genesis 3:1–7).

After the younger son had sauntered off to seek the "good life," he squandered his newfound wealth in unbridled debauchery (Luke 15:13). Inevitably the money slipped through his fingers, and he was reduced to feeding pigs on a stranger's farm. Pigs were considered unclean animals according to Jewish law, so this was a particularly abhorrent task. The Jewish people at the time referred to Gentiles as "pigs," so here was a Jewish man not only feeding pigs that belonged to a "pig" but even sneaking helpings of the slop fed to the grunting animals to try to satisfy his relentless hunger. Finally, the young son resolved to return to his father in humiliation—to offer his services as a hired hand.

To his astonishment as he trudged around the last bend in the road, he spied his father peering off into the distance, yearning for a glimpse of the prodigal. Upon the son's return the ecstatic father not only embraced and forgave him but even hosted a gala celebration in his honor. The father's compassion was reflected in his jubilant words: "This son of mine was dead and is alive again; he was lost and is found" (verse 24).

The younger son was not the only egotistical member of the family, however. His older brother, the "good son," was disgruntled because of the welcome-home party. The reality is that the brothers were not so very different from one another. One allowed selfishness to ruin his life in a very obvious way; the sullen jealousy of the other soured his outlook on life. Whether or not there is obvious sin in our lives, God is fully aware of our inner motivations, and the only way back into a right relationship with our heavenly Father is by confessing our sin and deliberately turning away from self-centered attitudes (Romans 2:7–8; 1 John 1:9).

Self-Discovery: *Would you consider yourself a "friend of sinners"? In what ways have you reached out beyond your family, church family or community to truly befriend someone in need? If you have not done so, what do you feel has been holding you back?*

GO TO DISCOVERY 268 ON PAGE 1388

15:6 [z] ver 9 with me; I have found my lost sheep.'[z] 7I
tell you that in the same way there will
be more rejoicing in heaven over one
sinner who repents than over ninety-
15:7 nine righteous persons who do not need
[a] ver 10 to repent.[a]

The Parable of the Lost Coin

8"Or suppose a woman has ten silver
coins[a] and loses one. Does she not light
a lamp, sweep the house and search
carefully until she finds it? 9And when
she finds it, she calls her friends and
neighbors together and says, 'Rejoice
15:9 [b] ver 6 with me; I have found my lost coin.'[b] 10In
the same way, I tell you, there is rejoicing
in the presence of the angels of God over
15:10 [c] ver 7 one sinner who repents."[c]

The Parable of the Lost Son

11Jesus continued: "There was a man
15:11 [d] Mt 21:28 who had two sons.[d] 12The younger one
said to his father, 'Father, give me my
15:12 [e] Dt 21:17 share of the estate.'[e] So he divided his
[f] ver 30 property[f] between them.
13"Not long after that, the younger
son got together all he had, set off for a
distant country and there squandered
15:13 [g] ver 30; Lk 16:1 his wealth[g] in wild living. 14After he had
spent everything, there was a severe
famine in that whole country, and he began to be in need. 15So he went and hired
himself out to a citizen of that country,
15:15 [h] Lev 11:7 who sent him to his fields to feed pigs.[h]
16He longed to fill his stomach with the
pods that the pigs were eating, but no
one gave him anything.
17"When he came to his senses, he
said, 'How many of my father's hired
men have food to spare, and here I am
starving to death! 18I will set out and go
back to my father and say to him: Father,
15:18 [i] Lev 26:40; Mt 3:2 I have sinned[i] against heaven and
against you. 19I am no longer worthy to
be called your son; make me like one of
your hired men.' 20So he got up and went
to his father.
"But while he was still a long way off,
his father saw him and was filled with
compassion for him; he ran to his son,
15:20 [j] Ge 45:14,15; 46:29; Ac 20:37 threw his arms around him and kissed
him.[j]
21"The son said to him, 'Father, I have
15:21 [k] Ps 51:4 sinned against heaven and against you.[k]
I am no longer worthy to be called your
son.[b]'
22"But the father said to his servants,
'Quick! Bring the best robe[l] and put it on 15:22 [l] Zec 3:4; Rev 6:11
him. Put a ring on his finger[m] and san- [m] Ge 41:42
dals on his feet. 23Bring the fattened calf
and kill it. Let's have a feast and celebrate. 24For this son of mine was dead 15:24
and is alive again;[n] he was lost and is [n] Eph 2:1,5; 5:14; 1Ti 5:6
found.' So they began to celebrate.[o] [o] ver 32
25"Meanwhile, the older son was in
the field. When he came near the house,
he heard music and dancing. 26So he
called one of the servants and asked him
what was going on. 27'Your brother has
come,' he replied, 'and your father has
killed the fattened calf because he
has him back safe and sound.'
28"The older brother became angry[p] 15:28 [p] Jnh 4:1
and refused to go in. So his father went
out and pleaded with him. 29But he answered his father, 'Look! All these years
I've been slaving for you and never disobeyed your orders. Yet you never gave
me even a young goat so I could celebrate with my friends. 30But when this
son of yours who has squandered your
property[q] with prostitutes[r] comes 15:30 [q] ver 12,13
home, you kill the fattened calf for him!' [r] Pr 29:3
31" 'My son,' the father said, 'you are
always with me, and everything I have is
yours. 32But we had to celebrate and be
glad, because this brother of yours was 15:32
dead and is alive again; he was lost and [s] ver 24; Mal 3:17
is found.' "[s]

The Parable of the Shrewd Manager

16 Jesus told his disciples: "There
was a rich man whose manager 16:1
was accused of wasting his possessions.[t] [t] Lk 15:13,30
2So he called him in and asked him,
'What is this I hear about you? Give an
account of your management, because
you cannot be manager any longer.'
3"The manager said to himself, 'What
shall I do now? My master is taking
away my job. I'm not strong enough to
dig, and I'm ashamed to beg— 4I know
what I'll do so that, when I lose my job
here, people will welcome me into their
houses.'
5"So he called in each one of his master's debtors. He asked the first, 'How
much do you owe my master?'
6" 'Eight hundred gallons[c] of olive oil,'
he replied.
"The manager told him, 'Take your

[a] *8* Greek *ten drachmas,* each worth about a day's wages [b] *21* Some early manuscripts *son. Make me like one of your hired men.* [c] *6* Greek *one hundred batous* (probably about 3 kiloliters)

bill, sit down quickly, and make it four hundred.'

7"Then he asked the second, 'And how much do you owe?'

" 'A thousand bushels[a] of wheat,' he replied.

"He told him, 'Take your bill and make it eight hundred.'

8"The master commended the dishonest manager because he had acted shrewdly. For the people of this world[u] are more shrewd[v] in dealing with their own kind than are the people of the light.[w] 9I tell you, use worldly wealth[x] to gain friends for yourselves, so that when it is gone, you will be welcomed into eternal dwellings.[y]

10"Whoever can be trusted with very little can also be trusted with much,[z] and whoever is dishonest with very little will also be dishonest with much. 11So if you have not been trustworthy in handling worldly wealth,[a] who will trust you with true riches? 12And if you have not been trustworthy with someone else's property, who will give you property of your own?

13"No servant can serve two masters. Either he will hate the one and love the other, or he will be devoted to the one and despise the other. You cannot serve both God and Money."[b]

14The Pharisees, who loved money,[c] heard all this and were sneering at Jesus.[d] 15He said to them, "You are the ones who justify yourselves[e] in the eyes of men, but God knows your hearts.[f] What is highly valued among men is detestable in God's sight.

Additional Teachings

16"The Law and the Prophets were proclaimed until John.[g] Since that time, the good news of the kingdom of God is being preached,[h] and everyone is forcing his way into it. 17It is easier for heaven and earth to disappear than for the least stroke of a pen to drop out of the Law.[i]

18"Anyone who divorces his wife and marries another woman commits adultery, and the man who marries a divorced woman commits adultery.[j]

The Rich Man and Lazarus

19"There was a rich man who was dressed in purple and fine linen and lived in luxury every day.[k] 20At his gate was laid a beggar[l] named Lazarus, covered with sores 21and longing to eat what fell from the rich man's table.[m] Even the dogs came and licked his sores.

22"The time came when the beggar died and the angels carried him to Abraham's side. The rich man also died and was buried. 23In hell,[b] where he was in torment, he looked up and saw Abraham far away, with Lazarus by his side. 24So he called to him, 'Father Abraham,[n] have pity on me and send Lazarus to dip the tip of his finger in water and cool my tongue, because I am in agony in this fire.'[o]

25"But Abraham replied, 'Son, remember that in your lifetime you received your good things, while Lazarus received bad things,[p] but now he is comforted here and you are in agony.[q] 26And besides all this, between us and you a great chasm has been fixed, so that those who want to go from here to you cannot, nor can anyone cross over from there to us.'

27"He answered, 'Then I beg you, father, send Lazarus to my father's house, 28for I have five brothers. Let him warn them,[r] so that they will not also come to this place of torment.'

29"Abraham replied, 'They have Moses[s] and the Prophets;[t] let them listen to them.'

30" 'No, father Abraham,'[u] he said, 'but if someone from the dead goes to them, they will repent.'

31"He said to him, 'If they do not listen to Moses and the Prophets, they will not be convinced even if someone rises from the dead.' "

Sin, Faith, Duty

17 Jesus said to his disciples: "Things that cause people to sin[v] are bound to come, but woe to that person through whom they come.[w] 2It would be better for him to be thrown into the sea with a millstone tied around his neck than for him to cause one of these little ones[x] to sin.[y] 3So watch yourselves.

"If your brother sins, rebuke him,[z] and if he repents, forgive him.[a] 4If he sins against you seven times in a day, and

16:8 [u] Ps 17:14 [v] Ps 18:26 [w] Jn 12:36; Eph 5:8; 1Th 5:5
16:9 [x] ver 11,13 [y] Mt 19:21; Lk 12:33
16:10 [z] Mt 25:21,23; Lk 19:17
16:11 [a] ver 9,13
16:13 [b] ver 9,11; Mt 6:24
16:14 [c] 1Ti 3:3 [d] Lk 23:35
16:15 [e] Lk 10:29 [f] 1Sa 16:7; Rev 2:23
16:16 [g] Mt 11:12,13 [h] Mt 4:23
16:17 [i] Mt 5:18
16:18 [j] Mt 5:31,32; 19:9; Mk 10:11; Ro 7:2,3; 1Co 7:10,11
16:19 [k] Eze 16:49
16:20 [l] Ac 3:2
16:21 [m] Mt 15:27
16:24 [n] ver 30; Lk 3:8 [o] Mt 5:22
16:25 [p] Ps 17:14 [q] Lk 6:21,24,25
16:28 [r] Ac 2:40; 20:23; 1Th 4:6
16:29 [s] Lk 24:27,44; Jn 5:45-47; Ac 15:21 [t] Lk 4:17; Jn 1:45
16:30 [u] ver 24; Lk 3:8
17:1 [v] Mt 5:29 [w] Mt 18:7
17:2 [x] Mk 10:24; Lk 10:21 [y] Mt 5:29
17:3 [z] Mt 18:15 [a] Eph 4:32; Col 3:13

[a] 7 Greek *one hundred korous* (probably about 35 kiloliters) [b] 23 Greek *Hades*

DISCOVERY 268

THE REALITY OF HELL

Hell is not on the top ten list of favorite topics for most people. Even pastors shy away from sermons on the subject. But Jesus spoke about hell more often than he talked about heaven. One of the most vivid Biblical descriptions of hell is found in Jesus' parable of a rich man and a beggar named Lazarus (Luke 16:19–31). There are two parts to the narrative:

The rich man and Lazarus in this life. The two men lived strikingly different lives. The rich man reveled in the lap of luxury every day, wearing the finest clothes and eating the most delectable foods. In our contemporary jargon, we might have referred to him as "filthy rich." Lazarus, on the other hand, sat at the rich man's gate and could aptly have been described as "filthy poor," so destitute that dogs would come and lick the festering sores covering his emaciated body, and he would have been satisfied with just a few crumbs from the rich man's table. But apparently those crumbs were never allowed to fall. These two men lived in close proximity to one another but existed at opposite ends of the social and economic spectrum.

The rich man and Lazarus in the life to come. The contrast between the circumstances of the two men in this life is startling, but not nearly as stark as what was to come afterward. Lazarus' ultimate destination was heaven, while the rich man found himself tormented in hell.

Hell is a very real place, and anyone who refuses God's love will end up there. The rich man found himself writhing in such agony that he pleaded with Father Abraham to ask Lazarus just to "dip the tip of his finger in water" and cool his tongue (verse 24). While the wealthy landholder would never have dreamed of touching Lazarus during the beggar's earthly life, he now begged for a drop of water from the same hand only the dogs would earlier have deigned to lick.

There is an unbridgeable chasm between heaven and hell; no one can travel from one to the other, because the decision that destines a person for hell is made prior to death. The good news is that an eternity spent in hell is not inevitable. The rich man pleaded to go back and warn his family before it was too late for them, but hell has no exit. Abraham retorted: "[Your family members] have Moses and the Prophets; let them listen to them" (verse 29).

From start to finish, God's Word declares the story of Jesus' love for us. It is not God's desire that any of the people he has so lovingly created spend eternity in hell (Ezekiel 18:23,32; 33:11; 1 Timothy 2:4; 2 Peter 3:9). Through the shed blood of his Son Jesus he offers eternal life to all of humanity (Hebrews 9:11–15). But the decision is ours—we need to reach out for the gift, unwrap it and savor it.

Self-Discovery: *Are you so familiar with the gospel story that it has ceased to grip your heart? Pause for a few moments and reflect deeply on the implications of Jesus' sacrificial death on your behalf. Try to envision that you've heard the amazing news for the very first time today. Then thank Jesus with as much conviction as you can.*

GO TO DISCOVERY 269 ON PAGE 1392

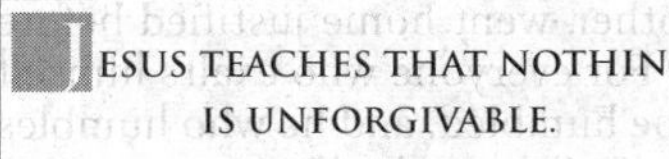

JESUS TEACHES THAT NOTHING IS UNFORGIVABLE.

John Foster Dulles, *American Statesman*

seven times comes back to you and says,
17:4 [b]Mt 18:21,22 'I repent,' forgive him."[b]
5The apostles[c] said to the Lord,[d] "In-
17:5 [c]Mk 6:30 [d]Lk 7:13 crease our faith!"
6He replied, "If you have faith as small
17:6 [e]Mt 13:31; 17:20; Lk 13:19 [f]Mt 21:21; Mk 9:23 as a mustard seed,[e] you can say to this
mulberry tree, 'Be uprooted and planted
in the sea,' and it will obey you.[f]
7"Suppose one of you had a servant
plowing or looking after the sheep.
Would he say to the servant when he
comes in from the field, 'Come along
now and sit down to eat'? 8Would he not
rather say, 'Prepare my supper, get your-
17:8 [g]Lk 12:37 self ready and wait on me[g] while I eat
and drink; after that you may eat and
drink'? 9Would he thank the servant because he did what he was told to do?
10So you also, when you have done
everything you were told to do, should
say, 'We are unworthy servants; we have
17:10 [h]1Co 9:16 only done our duty.' "[h]

Ten Healed of Leprosy

17:11 [i]Lk 9:51 [j]Lk 9:51,52; Jn 4:3,4 11Now on his way to Jerusalem,[i] Jesus
traveled along the border between
Samaria and Galilee.[j] 12As he was going
17:12 [k]Mt 8:2 [l]Lev 13:45,46 into a village, ten men who had leprosy[a][k] met him. They stood at a dis-
tance[l] 13and called out in a loud voice,
17:13 [m]Lk 5:5 "Jesus, Master,[m] have pity on us!"
14When he saw them, he said, "Go,
17:14 [n]Lev 14:2; Mt 8:4 show yourselves to the priests."[n] And as
they went, they were cleansed.
15One of them, when he saw he was
17:15 [o]Mt 9:8 healed, came back, praising God[o] in a
loud voice. 16He threw himself at Jesus'
feet and thanked him—and he was a
17:16 [p]Mt 10:5 Samaritan.[p]
17Jesus asked, "Were not all ten
cleansed? Where are the other nine?
18Was no one found to return and give
praise to God except this foreigner?"
19Then he said to him, "Rise and go; your
17:19 [q]Mt 9:22 faith has made you well."[q]

The Coming of the Kingdom of God

20Once, having been asked by the
Pharisees when the kingdom of God
17:20 [r]Mt 3:2 would come,[r] Jesus replied, "The kingdom of God does not come with your
careful observation, 21nor will people
say, 'Here it is,' or 'There it is,'[s] because 17:21 [s]ver 23
the kingdom of God is within[b] you."
22Then he said to his disciples, "The
time is coming when you will long to see
one of the days of the Son of Man,[t] but 17:22 [t]Mt 8:20 [u]Mt 9:15; Lk 5:35
you will not see it.[u] 23Men will tell you,
'There he is!' or 'Here he is!' Do not go
running off after them.[v] 24For the Son of 17:23 [v]Mt 24:23; Mk 13:21; Lk 21:8
Man in his day[c] will be like the light-
ning,[w] which flashes and lights up the
sky from one end to the other. 25But first 17:24 [w]Mt 24:27
he must suffer many things[x] and be re-
jected[y] by this generation.[z] 17:25 [x]Mt 16:21 [y]Lk 9:22; 18:32 [z]Mk 13:30; Lk 21:32
26"Just as it was in the days of Noah,[a]
so also will it be in the days of the Son of
Man. 27People were eating, drinking,
marrying and being given in marriage up
to the day Noah entered the ark. Then 17:26 [a]Ge 7:6-24
the flood came and destroyed them all.
28"It was the same in the days of Lot.[b] 17:28 [b]Ge 19:1-28
People were eating and drinking, buying
and selling, planting and building. 29But
the day Lot left Sodom, fire and sulfur
rained down from heaven and destroyed
them all.
30"It will be just like this on the day the 17:30 [c]Mt 10:23; 16:27; 24:3,27, 37,39; 25:31; 1Co 1:7; 1Th 2:19; 2Th 1:7; 2:8; 2Pe 3:4; Rev 1:7
Son of Man is revealed.[c] 31On that day no
one who is on the roof of his house, with
his goods inside, should go down to get
them. Likewise, no one in the field
should go back for anything.[d] 32Remem- 17:31 [d]Mt 24:17,18; Mk 13:15-16
ber Lot's wife![e] 33Whoever tries to keep
his life will lose it, and whoever loses his
life will preserve it.[f] 34I tell you, on that 17:32 [e]Ge 19:26
night two people will be in one bed; one
will be taken and the other left. 35Two 17:33 [f]Jn 12:25

[a] *12* The Greek word was used for various diseases affecting the skin—not necessarily leprosy.
[b] *21* Or *among* [c] *24* Some manuscripts do not have *in his day.*

WITH MATCHLESS AUTHORITY, JESUS MADE HIMSELF THE PIVOTAL POINT OF HISTORY. THE OLD TESTAMENT POINTS TOWARD HIM, AND NOW . . . HE INTRODUCES THE KINGDOM AND SHOWS HOW THE OLD TESTAMENT FINDS ITS ULTIMATE VALIDITY IN HIMSELF AND HIS TEACHING.

Donald A. Carson, *Professor, Trinity Evangelical Divinity School, Deerfield, Illinois*

women will be grinding grain together;
17:35 g Mt 24:41 one will be taken and the other left.[a]"[g]
37"Where, Lord?" they asked.
17:37 He replied, "Where there is a dead
h Mt 24:28 body, there the vultures will gather."[h]

The Parable of the Persistent Widow

18 Then Jesus told his disciples a
parable to show that they
18:1 should always pray and not give up.[i] 2He
i Isa 40:31; Lk 11:5-8; said: "In a certain town there was a
Ac 1:14; judge who neither feared God nor cared
Ro 12:12; about men. 3And there was a widow in
Eph 6:18; Col 4:2; that town who kept coming to him with
1Th 5:17 the plea, 'Grant me justice[j] against my
18:3 j Isa 1:17 adversary.'
4"For some time he refused. But finally he said to himself, 'Even though I
don't fear God or care about men, 5yet
because this widow keeps bothering me,
I will see that she gets justice, so that she
18:5 won't eventually wear me out with her
k Lk 11:8 coming!'"[k]
18:6 6And the Lord[l] said, "Listen to what
l Lk 7:13 the unjust judge says. 7And will not God
18:7 bring about justice for his chosen ones,
m Ex 22:23; who cry out[m] to him day and night? Will
Ps 88:1; he keep putting them off? 8I tell you, he
Rev 6:10 will see that they get justice, and quick-
18:8 n Mt 8:20 ly. However, when the Son of Man[n]
o Mt 16:27 comes,[o] will he find faith on the earth?"

> TILL MEN HAVE FAITH IN CHRIST, THEIR BEST SERVICES ARE BUT GLORIOUS SINS.
>
> Thomas Brooks, *Puritan Pastor*

The Parable of the Pharisee and the Tax Collector

18:9 9To some who were confident of their
p Lk 16:15 own righteousness[p] and looked down
q Isa 65:5 on everybody else,[q] Jesus told this para-
18:10 ble: 10"Two men went up to the temple
r Ac 3:1 to pray,[r] one a Pharisee and the other a
18:11 tax collector. 11The Pharisee stood up[s]
s Mt 6:5; Mk 11:25 and prayed about[b] himself: 'God, I thank
you that I am not like other men—rob-
18:12 bers, evildoers, adulterers—or even like
t Isa 58:3; Mt 9:14 this tax collector. 12I fast[t] twice a week
u Mal 3:8; Lk 11:42 and give a tenth[u] of all I get.'
18:13 13"But the tax collector stood at a dis-
v Isa 66:2; tance. He would not even look up to
Jer 31:19; heaven, but beat his breast[v] and said,
Lk 23:48 'God, have mercy on me, a sinner.'[w]
w Lk 5:32; 1Ti 1:15 14"I tell you that this man, rather than
the other, went home justified before
God. For everyone who exalts himself
will be humbled, and he who humbles 18:14
himself will be exalted."[x] x Mt 23:12; Lk 14:11

The Little Children and Jesus

15People were also bringing babies to
Jesus to have him touch them. When the
disciples saw this, they rebuked them.
16But Jesus called the children to him
and said, "Let the little children come to
me, and do not hinder them, for the
kingdom of God belongs to such as
these. 17I tell you the truth, anyone who
will not receive the kingdom of God like 18:17
a little child[y] will never enter it." y Mt 11:25; 18:3

The Rich Ruler

18A certain ruler asked him, "Good
teacher, what must I do to inherit eter- 18:18
nal life?"[z] z Lk 10:25
19"Why do you call me good?" Jesus
answered. "No one is good—except God
alone. 20You know the commandments:
'Do not commit adultery, do not murder,
do not steal, do not give false testimony, 18:20
honor your father and mother.'[c]"[a] a Ex 20:12-16;
21"All these I have kept since I was a Dt 5:16-20; Ro 13:9
boy," he said.
22When Jesus heard this, he said to
him, "You still lack one thing. Sell everything you have and give to the poor,[b] 18:22 b Ac 2:45
and you will have treasure in heaven.[c] c Mt 6:20
Then come, follow me."

[a] 35 Some manuscripts *left.* 36*Two men will be in the field; one will be taken and the other left.*
[b] 11 Or *to* [c] 20 Exodus 20:12–16; Deut. 5:16–20

LITTLE PEOPLE

Jesus cared about the little people in life, and that concern is showcased in Luke 18:9–14, a parable in which our Lord juxtaposed an arrogant individual with a humble man. The real heroes in the eyes of Jesus as portrayed in many of his parables are the underdogs—the "have-nots" who have no standing in the eyes of their more fortunate counterparts. The villains, on the other hand, are people who are heartless and unfair, pompous and condescending in their self-righteousness. Jesus wanted people to know that God's love for them has nothing to do with what they are like. Our inadequacies—or our adequacies!—don't matter to him. He simply wants our hearts.

23When he heard this, he became very
sad, because he was a man of great
wealth. 24Jesus looked at him and said,
"How hard it is for the rich to enter the
18:24 kingdom of God![d] 25Indeed, it is easier
d Pr 11:28 for a camel to go through the eye of a
needle than for a rich man to enter the
kingdom of God."
26Those who heard this asked, "Who
then can be saved?"
27Jesus replied, "What is impossible
18:27 e Mt 19:26 with men is possible with God."[e]
28Peter said to him, "We have left all
18:28 f Mt 4:19 we had to follow you!"[f]
29"I tell you the truth," Jesus said to
them, "no one who has left home or wife
or brothers or parents or children for the
sake of the kingdom of God 30will fail to
18:30 receive many times as much in this age
g Mt 12:32 h Mt 25:46 and, in the age to come,[g] eternal life."[h]

Jesus Again Predicts His Death

18:31 31Jesus took the Twelve aside and told
i Lk 9:51 j Ps 22; them, "We are going up to Jerusalem,[i]
Isa 53 k Mt 8:20 and everything that is written by the
prophets[j] about the Son of Man[k] will be
18:32 fulfilled. 32He will be handed over to the
l Lk 23:1 Gentiles.[l] They will mock him, insult
m Mt 16:21 him, spit on him, flog him[m] and kill
n Ac 2:23 him.[n] 33On the third day[o] he will rise
18:33 o Mt 16:21 again."[p]
p Mt 16:21 34The disciples did not understand
any of this. Its meaning was hidden from
18:34 them, and they did not know what he
q Mk 9:32; Lk 9:45 was talking about.[q]

A Blind Beggar Receives His Sight

18:35 35As Jesus approached Jericho,[r] a
r Lk 19:1 blind man was sitting by the roadside
begging. 36When he heard the crowd going by, he asked what was happening.
37They told him, "Jesus of Nazareth is
18:37 s Lk 19:4 passing by."[s]
38He called out, "Jesus, Son of David,[t]
18:38 t ver 39; Mt 9:27 have mercy[u] on me!"
u Mt 17:15; 39Those who led the way rebuked him
Lk 18:13 and told him to be quiet, but he shouted
18:39 all the more, "Son of David, have mercy
v ver 38 on me!"[v]
40Jesus stopped and ordered the man
to be brought to him. When he came
near, Jesus asked him, 41"What do you
want me to do for you?"
"Lord, I want to see," he replied.
42Jesus said to him, "Receive your
18:42 w Mt 9:22 sight; your faith has healed you."[w] 43Im-
mediately he received his sight and fol-
lowed Jesus, praising God. When all the 18:43
people saw it, they also praised God.[x] x Mt 9:8; Lk 13:17

Zacchaeus the Tax Collector

19 Jesus entered Jericho[y] and was 19:1
passing through. 2A man was y Lk 18:35
there by the name of Zacchaeus; he was
a chief tax collector and was wealthy.
3He wanted to see who Jesus was, but
being a short man he could not, because
of the crowd. 4So he ran ahead and
climbed a sycamore-fig[z] tree to see him, 19:4 z 1Ki 10:27;
since Jesus was coming that way.[a] 1Ch 27:28;
5When Jesus reached the spot, he Isa 9:10
looked up and said to him, "Zacchaeus, a Lk 18:37
come down immediately. I must stay at
your house today." 6So he came down at
once and welcomed him gladly.
7All the people saw this and began to
mutter, "He has gone to be the guest of a
'sinner.'"[b] 19:7 b Mt 9:11
8But Zacchaeus stood up and said to
the Lord,[c] "Look, Lord! Here and now I 19:8 c Lk 7:13
give half of my possessions to the poor, d Lk 3:12,13
and if I have cheated anybody out of e Ex 22:1; Lev 6:4,5;
anything,[d] I will pay back four times the Nu 5:7; 2Sa 12:6
amount."[e]
9Jesus said to him, "Today salvation
has come to this house, because this
man, too, is a son of Abraham.[f] 10For the 19:9 f Lk 3:8; 13:16;
Son of Man came to seek and to save Ro 4:16; Gal 3:7
what was lost."[g] 19:10

The Parable of the Ten Minas g Eze 34:12,16; Jn 3:17

11While they were listening to this, he
went on to tell them a parable, because
he was near Jerusalem and the people
thought that the kingdom of God[h] was 19:11 h Mt 3:2
going to appear at once.[i] 12He said: "A i Lk 17:20;
man of noble birth went to a distant Ac 1:6
country to have himself appointed king
and then to return. 13So he called ten of 19:13
his servants[j] and gave them ten minas.[a] j Mk 13:34
'Put this money to work,' he said, 'until I
come back.'
14"But his subjects hated him and
sent a delegation after him to say, 'We
don't want this man to be our king.'
15"He was made king, however, and
returned home. Then he sent for the servants to whom he had given the money,
in order to find out what they had
gained with it.
16"The first one came and said, 'Sir,
your mina has earned ten more.' 19:17
17" 'Well done, my good servant!'[k] his k Pr 27:18

a 13 A mina was about three months' wages.

A True Son of Abraham

Jesus was always transparent and unambiguous about his purpose: "The Son of Man came to seek and to save what was lost" (Luke 19:10). Because of physical constraints and eager crowds, it was not always convenient for people to get close to Jesus, however, and persistence and ingenuity were sometimes required. Zacchaeus was a good example of someone who wanted to see Jesus, but the odds were stacked against him. He was a chief tax collector, hated by the Jewish people because he was working against his own race as one of a group of legal extortionists for the Roman government.

To add fuel to the fire of prejudice against him, Zacchaeus was "vertically challenged"—so short, in fact, that when Jesus walked through town Zacchaeus was unable to catch a glimpse of him over the heads in the pressing crowd. Undaunted, he ran ahead and climbed a sycamore-fig tree. Sycamore-fig branches grow low to the ground, so it would have been easy for a short man to have scaled such a tree.

As Jesus approached the tree, from within whose sheltering branches Zacchaeus must certainly have hoped to gaze undetected, our Lord stopped deliberately, looked up and addressed the tax collector by name: "Zacchaeus, come down immediately. I must stay at your house today" (verse 5). Zacchaeus must have been stunned, but he was also ecstatic. The wiry little man scrambled down from the tree and confirmed the invitation for his newfound friend to enjoy an evening at his home. If Zacchaeus was surprised, those in the crowd of onlookers must have been utterly shocked. Zacchaeus was a man whom they had loved to hate, and Jesus, the man they had come to see, was taking the initiative to befriend him.

While the people stood around muttering and protesting, Zacchaeus publicly confessed his sin, offering to donate half of all he possessed to the poor. But then he went one step further, promising to repay anyone whom he had cheated—four times the amount he had extorted from each (verse 8).

We know little about Zacchaeus's spiritual journey—only that he was desperate to see Jesus and that he repented and offered reparation following his surprise encounter with the Master. Jesus' final comment to Zacchaeus probably astonished the bystanders even further: "Today salvation has come to this house, because this man, too, is a son of Abraham" (verse 9). Zacchaeus was not saved because he was promising to do good things or on the merits of his Jewish background and heritage. Instead, his actions proved that he was taking Jesus' words of invitation seriously. This man was identified as a true son of Abraham because of his faith. Paul stated in Galatians 3:29 that, "if you belong to Christ, then you are Abraham's seed, and heirs according to the promise." The apostle clarified further in Ephesians 3:6: "This mystery is that through the gospel the Gentiles are heirs together with Israel, members together of one body, and sharers together in the promise in Christ Jesus." As we reflect on the "surpassing grace" God has given to each one of us, may we echo Paul's words from 2 Corinthians 9:15: "Thanks be to God for his indescribable gift!"

Self-Discovery: *Have you ever felt surprised that Jesus chose you? If you have feelings of inadequacy in some areas (and who of us does not!), reflect on your infinite value in Jesus' eyes.*

GO TO DISCOVERY 270 ON PAGE 1396

master replied. ‘Because you have been
trustworthy in a very small matter, take
19:17 charge of ten cities.’[l]
[l]Lk 16:10 18“The second came and said, ‘Sir,
your mina has earned five more.’
19“His master answered, ‘You take
charge of five cities.’
20“Then another servant came and
said, ‘Sir, here is your mina; I have kept it
laid away in a piece of cloth. 21I was
afraid of you, because you are a hard
19:21 man. You take out what you did not put
[m]Mt 25:24 in and reap what you did not sow.’[m]
22“His master replied, ‘I will judge you
19:22 by your own words,[n] you wicked ser-
[n]2Sa 1:16; Job 15:6 vant! You knew, did you, that I am a hard
[o]Mt 25:26 man, taking out what I did not put in,
and reaping what I did not sow?[o] 23Why
then didn’t you put my money on deposit, so that when I came back, I could
have collected it with interest?’
24“Then he said to those standing by,
‘Take his mina away from him and give
it to the one who has ten minas.’
25“ ‘Sir,’ they said, ‘he already has ten!’
26“He replied, ‘I tell you that to everyone who has, more will be given, but as
for the one who has nothing, even what
19:26 he has will be taken away.[p] 27But those
[p]Mt 13:12; 25:29; Lk 8:18 enemies of mine who did not want me
to be king over them—bring them here
and kill them in front of me.’ ”

The Triumphal Entry

28After Jesus had said this, he went on
19:28 ahead, going up to Jerusalem,[q] 29As he
[q]Mk 10:32; Lk 9:51 approached Bethphage and Bethany[r] at
19:29 the hill called the Mount of Olives,[s] he
[r]Mt 21:17 sent two of his disciples, saying to them,
[s]Mt 21:1 30“Go to the village ahead of you, and as
you enter it, you will find a colt tied
there, which no one has ever ridden. Untie it and bring it here. 31If anyone asks
you, ‘Why are you untying it?’ tell him,
‘The Lord needs it.’ ”
32Those who were sent ahead went
19:32 and found it just as he had told them.[t]
[t]Lk 22:13 33As they were untying the colt, its owners asked them, “Why are you untying
the colt?”
34They replied, “The Lord needs it.”
35They brought it to Jesus, threw their
cloaks on the colt and put Jesus on it.
19:36 36As he went along, people spread their
[u]2Ki 9:13 cloaks[u] on the road.
37When he came near the place where
the road goes down the Mount of Ol-
ives,[v] the whole crowd of disciples began 19:37 [v]Mt 21:1
joyfully to praise God in loud voices for
all the miracles they had seen:

38“Blessed is the king who comes in 19:38 [w]Ps 118:26; Lk 13:35
the name of the Lord!”[a][w] [x]Lk 2:14

“Peace in heaven and glory in the
highest!”[x]

39Some of the Pharisees in the crowd
said to Jesus, “Teacher, rebuke your disciples!”[y] 19:39 [y]Mt 21:15,16
40“I tell you,” he replied, “if they keep
quiet, the stones will cry out.”[z] 19:40 [z]Hab 2:11
41As he approached Jerusalem and
saw the city, he wept over it[a] 42and said, 19:41 [a]Isa 22:4; Lk 13:34,35
“If you, even you, had only known on
this day what would bring you peace—
but now it is hidden from your eyes.
43The days will come upon you when
your enemies will build an embankment 19:43
against you and encircle you and hem [b]Isa 29:3;
you in on every side.[b] 44They will dash Jer 6:6; Eze 4:2; 26:8; Lk 21:20
you to the ground, you and the children
within your walls.[c] They will not leave 19:44 [c]Ps 137:9
one stone on another,[d] because you did [d]Mt 24:2;
not recognize the time of God’s coming[e] Mk 13:2; Lk 21:6
to you.” [e]1Pe 2:12

Jesus at the Temple

45Then he entered the temple area
and began driving out those who were
selling. 46“It is written,” he said to them,
“ ‘My house will be a house of prayer’[b],[f] 19:46 [f]Isa 56:7
but you have made it ‘a den of rob- [g]Jer 7:11
bers.’[c]”[g]

47Every day he was teaching at the
temple.[h] But the chief priests, the teach- 19:47 [h]Mt 26:55
ers of the law and the leaders among the [i]Mt 12:14;
people were trying to kill him.[i] 48Yet Mk 11:18
they could not find any way to do it, because all the people hung on his words.

The Authority of Jesus Questioned

20 One day as he was teaching the 20:1
people in the temple courts[j] [j]Mt 26:55
and preaching the gospel,[k] the chief [k]Lk 8:1
priests and the teachers of the law, together with the elders, came up to him.
2“Tell us by what authority you are doing
these things,” they said. “Who gave you 20:2
this authority?”[l] [l]Jn 2:18; Ac 4:7; 7:27
3He replied, “I will also ask you a
question. Tell me, 4John’s baptism[m]— 20:4
was it from heaven, or from men?” [m]Mk 1:4
5They discussed it among themselves

[a] 38 Psalm 118:26 [b] 46 Isaiah 56:7
[c] 46 Jer. 7:11

and said, "If we say, 'From heaven,' he
will ask, 'Why didn't you believe him?'
20:6 6But if we say, 'From men,' all the peo-
[n]Lk 7:29 ple[n] will stone us, because they are per-
[o]Mt 11:9 suaded that John was a prophet."[o]
7So they answered, "We don't know
where it was from."
8Jesus said, "Neither will I tell you by
what authority I am doing these things."

The Parable of the Tenants

9He went on to tell the people this
20:9 [p]Isa 5:1-7 parable: "A man planted a vineyard,[p]
[q]Mt 25:14 rented it to some farmers and went
away for a long time.[q] 10At harvest time
he sent a servant to the tenants so they
would give him some of the fruit of the
vineyard. But the tenants beat him and
sent him away empty-handed. 11He sent
another servant, but that one also they
beat and treated shamefully and sent
away empty-handed. 12He sent still a
third, and they wounded him and threw
him out.
13"Then the owner of the vineyard
said, 'What shall I do? I will send my son,
20:13 [r]Mt 3:17 whom I love;[r] perhaps they will respect
him.'
14"But when the tenants saw him,
they talked the matter over. 'This is the
heir,' they said. 'Let's kill him, and the inheritance will be ours.' 15So they threw
him out of the vineyard and killed him.

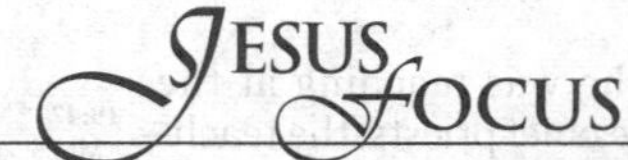

THE ULTIMATE TEACHER

Jesus is known the world over as a master teacher. Many people in fact believe that he was the greatest teacher the world has ever known. His lessons were captivating, and people "hung on his words" (Luke 19:48), recognizing that he was telling them exactly what they longed (and needed) to hear. Even the Lord's enemies were impressed by who he was and what he had to say (Luke 20:26,39). Whenever they questioned his authority, he managed to silence them by responding with his own questions—questions that they could not answer without incriminating themselves (verses 5,15,17,44). In fact, Luke stated in verse 40 that in this particular instance Jesus' questions and answers were so amazing that no one dared to confront him again. When the ultimate authority spoke, even the people on the other side of the fence stopped to listen.

"What then will the owner of the
vineyard do to them? 16He will come and
kill those tenants[s] and give the vineyard 20:16
to others." [s]Lk 19:27
When the people heard this, they
said, "May this never be!"
17Jesus looked directly at them and
asked, "Then what is the meaning of
that which is written:

" 'The stone the builders rejected 20:17
has become the capstone[a]'[b]?[t] [t]Ps 118:22; Ac 4:11

18Everyone who falls on that stone will
be broken to pieces, but he on whom it
falls will be crushed."[u] 20:18 [u]Isa 8:14,15
19The teachers of the law and the chief 20:19
priests looked for a way to arrest him[v] [v]Lk 19:47
immediately, because they knew he had [w]Mk 11:18
spoken this parable against them. But
they were afraid of the people.[w]

Paying Taxes to Caesar

20Keeping a close watch on him, they
sent spies, who pretended to be honest.
They hoped to catch Jesus in something 20:20
he said[x] so that they might hand him [x]Mt 12:10
over to the power and authority of the [y]Mt 27:2
governor.[y] 21So the spies questioned
him: "Teacher, we know that you speak
and teach what is right, and that you do
not show partiality but teach the way of 20:21
God in accordance with the truth.[z] 22Is [z]Jn 3:2
it right for us to pay taxes to Caesar or
not?"
23He saw through their duplicity and
said to them, 24"Show me a denarius.
Whose portrait and inscription are
on it?"
25"Caesar's," they replied.
He said to them, "Then give to Caesar 20:25
what is Caesar's,[a] and to God what is [a]Lk 23:2;
God's." Ro 13:7
26They were unable to trap him in
what he had said there in public. And astonished by his answer, they became
silent.

The Resurrection and Marriage

27Some of the Sadducees,[b] who say 20:27 [b]Ac 4:1
there is no resurrection,[c] came to Jesus [c]Ac 23:8;
with a question. 28"Teacher," they said, 1Co 15:12
"Moses wrote for us that if a man's
brother dies and leaves a wife but no
children, the man must marry the wid- 20:28
ow and have children for his brother.[d] [d]Dt 25:5
29Now there were seven brothers. The

[a] 17 *Or cornerstone* [b] 17 Psalm 118:22

first one married a woman and died
childless. 30The second 31and then the
third married her, and in the same way
the seven died, leaving no children. 32Fi-
nally, the woman died too. 33Now then,
at the resurrection whose wife will she
be, since the seven were married to her?"
34Jesus replied, "The people of this age
marry and are given in marriage. 35But
20:35 those who are considered worthy of tak-
[e] Mt 12:32 ing part in that age[e] and in the resurrection from the dead will neither marry
nor be given in marriage, 36and they can
20:36 no longer die; for they are like the angels.
[f] Jn 1:12; They are God's children,[f] since they are
1Jn 3:1-2 children of the resurrection. 37But in the
account of the bush, even Moses showed
that the dead rise, for he calls the Lord
'the God of Abraham, and the God of
20:37 Isaac, and the God of Jacob.'[a][g] 38He is
[g] Ex 3:6 not the God of the dead, but of the living, for to him all are alive."
39Some of the teachers of the law responded, "Well said, teacher!" 40And no
20:40 one dared to ask him any more ques-
[h] Mt 22:46; tions.[h]
Mk 12:34

Whose Son Is the Christ?

41Then Jesus said to them, "How is it
that they say the Christ[b] is the Son of
20:41 David?[i] 42David himself declares in the
[i] Mt 1:1 Book of Psalms:

" 'The Lord said to my Lord:
"Sit at my right hand
43 until I make your enemies
20:43 a footstool for your feet." '[c][j]
[j] Ps 110:1;
Mt 22:44 44David calls him 'Lord.' How then can
he be his son?"
45While all the people were listening,
Jesus said to his disciples, 46"Beware of
the teachers of the law. They like to walk
around in flowing robes and love to be
greeted in the marketplaces and have
the most important seats in the synagogues and the places of honor at ban-
20:46 quets.[k] 47They devour widows' houses
[k] Lk 11:43 and for a show make lengthy prayers.
Such men will be punished most severe-
ly."

The Widow's Offering

21 As he looked up, Jesus saw the
rich putting their gifts into the
21:1 temple treasury.[l] 2He also saw a poor
[l] Mt 27:6; widow put in two very small copper
Jn 8:20 coins.[d] 3"I tell you the truth," he said,

CHRIST HATH TOLD US HE
WILL COME, BUT NOT WHEN,
THAT WE MIGHT NEVER
PUT OFF OUR CLOTHES, OR PUT
OUT THE CANDLE.

William Gurnall, *Puritan Pastor*

"this poor widow has put in more than
all the others. 4All these people gave
their gifts out of their wealth; but she
out of her poverty put in all she had to 21:4
live on."[m] [m] 2Co 8:12

Signs of the End of the Age

5Some of his disciples were remarking
about how the temple was adorned with
beautiful stones and with gifts dedicated to God. But Jesus said, 6"As for what
you see here, the time will come when
not one stone will be left on another;[n] 21:6
every one of them will be thrown down." [n] Lk 19:44
7"Teacher," they asked, "when will
these things happen? And what will be
the sign that they are about to take
place?"
8He replied: "Watch out that you are
not deceived. For many will come in my
name, claiming, 'I am he,' and, 'The time 21:8
is near.' Do not follow them.[o] 9When you [o] Lk 17:23
hear of wars and revolutions, do not be
frightened. These things must happen
first, but the end will not come right
away."
10Then he said to them: "Nation will
rise against nation, and kingdom 21:10
against kingdom.[p] 11There will be great [p] 2Ch 15:6;
earthquakes, famines and pestilences in Isa 19:2
various places, and fearful events and 21:11
great signs from heaven.[q] [q] Isa 29:6;
Joel 2:30
12"But before all this, they will lay
hands on you and persecute you. They
will deliver you to synagogues and prisons, and you will be brought before
kings and governors, and all on account
of my name. 13This will result in your be- 21:13
ing witnesses to them.[r] 14But make up [r] Php 1:12
your mind not to worry beforehand how 21:14
you will defend yourselves.[s] 15For I will [s] Lk 12:11
give you[t] words and wisdom that none 21:15
of your adversaries will be able to resist [t] Lk 12:12
or contradict. 16You will be betrayed
even by parents, brothers, relatives and

[a] 37 Exodus 3:6 [b] 41 Or *Messiah* [c] 43 Psalm 110:1 [d] 2 Greek *two lepta*

DISCOVERY 270

SIGNS OF HIS COMING

The temple in Jerusalem was magnificent (Luke 21:5). Jesus' disciples were impressed with its beautiful stones, and God's people believed that this edifice would stand tall and glorious forever. But Jesus knew differently, announcing that "not one stone will be left on another; every one of them will be thrown down" (verse 6). The disciples were skeptical about this seemingly implausible prediction and demanded to know when this demolition would take place. Matthew stated in his Gospel that they at the same time asked for a description of the signs of Jesus' coming (Matthew 24:3). The disciples associated Jerusalem's destruction—and especially that of the temple—with the end of the world.

Jesus replied that there would be many signs of the end times: false messiahs (Luke 21:8), wars and revolutions (verse 10), natural disasters (verse 11), persecution of believers (verses 12–19), conflict in the Middle East (verses 20–24) and cosmic upheaval (verses 25–27). When they perceived those signs, Jesus directed, they were to stand up and lift up their heads, because their redemption would be drawing near (verse 28). These warnings, however, represent occurrences common enough to every era so as to leave people constantly wondering whether their generation will be the last. Jesus' purpose was not to elaborate on these harbingers themselves but to remind us to live responsibly—because we know for certain that Jesus will one day return.

If our focus is truly on our Savior, our lives will reflect that emphasis. Jesus was very clear about what God expects:

Don't waste your life on pleasure. Living lives of indulgence and self-gratification will cause us to waste our energy on matters and possessions that have no lasting value (verse 34). Instead, as the apostle Paul declared to the Colossian Christians, "Set your mind on things above, not on earthly things. For you died, and your life is now hidden with Christ in God. When Christ, who is your life, appears, then you also will appear with him in glory" (Colossians 3:2–4).

The day of Jesus' return will come unexpectedly, and, while we wait, we are called to watch and pray (Luke 21:36). The apostle Peter gave us instructions on how to live as we wait for the Lord's return: "The end of all things is near. Therefore be clear-minded and self-controlled so that you can pray. Above all, love each other deeply, because love covers over a multitude of sins" (1 Peter 4:7–8).

Finally, we can be ready for Jesus' return at any time by living a life that consistently honors Jesus. Then and only then will we be able to stand secure on that final glorious day when we will be summoned before our Lord's judgment seat (Luke 21:36), not because of anything we've done to earn his favor, but because of his great mercy (Titus 3:15).

Self-Discovery: *What kinds of pleasures do you as a Christian enjoy? What difference is there between legitimate pleasure and self-indulgence? Do you feel Jesus wants you to be happy in life? Why or why not?*

GO TO DISCOVERY 271 ON PAGE 1401

friends,[u] and they will put some of you to death. 17 All men will hate you because of me.[v] 18 But not a hair of your head will perish.[w] 19 By standing firm you will gain life.[x]

20 "When you see Jerusalem being surrounded by armies,[y] you will know that its desolation is near. 21 Then let those who are in Judea flee to the mountains, let those in the city get out, and let those in the country not enter the city.[z] 22 For this is the time of punishment[a] in fulfillment[b] of all that has been written. 23 How dreadful it will be in those days for pregnant women and nursing mothers! There will be great distress in the land and wrath against this people. 24 They will fall by the sword and will be taken as prisoners to all the nations. Jerusalem will be trampled[c] on by the Gentiles until the times of the Gentiles are fulfilled.

25 "There will be signs in the sun, moon and stars. On the earth, nations will be in anguish and perplexity at the roaring and tossing of the sea.[d] 26 Men will faint from terror, apprehensive of what is coming on the world, for the heavenly bodies will be shaken.[e] 27 At that time they will see the Son of Man[f] coming in a cloud[g] with power and great glory. 28 When these things begin to take place, stand up and lift up your heads, because your redemption is drawing near."[h]

29 He told them this parable: "Look at the fig tree and all the trees. 30 When they sprout leaves, you can see for yourselves and know that summer is near. 31 Even so, when you see these things happening, you know that the kingdom of God[i] is near.

32 "I tell you the truth, this generation[a][j] will certainly not pass away until all these things have happened. 33 Heaven and earth will pass away, but my words will never pass away.[k]

34 "Be careful, or your hearts will be weighed down with dissipation, drunkenness and the anxieties of life,[l] and that day will close on you unexpectedly[m] like a trap. 35 For it will come upon all those who live on the face of the whole earth. 36 Be always on the watch, and pray[n] that you may be able to escape all that is about to happen, and that you may be able to stand before the Son of Man."

21:16 [u] Lk 12:52,53
21:17 [v] Jn 15:21
21:18 [w] Mt 10:30
21:19 [x] Mt 10:22
21:20 [y] Lk 19:43
21:21 [z] Lk 17:31
21:22 [a] Isa 63:4; Da 9:24-27; Hos 9:7 [b] Mt 1:22
21:24 [c] Isa 5:5; 63:18; Da 8:13; Rev 11:2
21:25 [d] 2Pe 3:10,12
21:26 [e] Mt 24:29
21:27 [f] Mt 8:20 [g] Rev 1:7
21:28 [h] Lk 18:7
21:31 [i] Mt 3:2
21:32 [j] Lk 11:50; 17:25
21:33 [k] Mt 5:18
21:34 [l] Mk 4:19 [m] Lk 12:40,46; 1Th 5:2-7
21:36 [n] Mt 26:41

37 Each day Jesus was teaching at the temple,[o] and each evening he went out[p] to spend the night on the hill called the Mount of Olives,[q] 38 and all the people came early in the morning to hear him at the temple.[r]

Judas Agrees to Betray Jesus

22

Now the Feast of Unleavened Bread, called the Passover, was approaching,[s] 2 and the chief priests and the teachers of the law were looking for some way to get rid of Jesus,[t] for they were afraid of the people. 3 Then Satan[u] entered Judas, called Iscariot,[v] one of the Twelve. 4 And Judas went to the chief priests and the officers of the temple guard[w] and discussed with them how he might betray Jesus. 5 They were delighted and agreed to give him money.[x] 6 He consented, and watched for an opportunity to hand Jesus over to them when no crowd was present.

The Last Supper

7 Then came the day of Unleavened Bread on which the Passover lamb had to be sacrificed.[y] 8 Jesus sent Peter and John,[z] saying, "Go and make preparations for us to eat the Passover."

9 "Where do you want us to prepare for it?" they asked.

10 He replied, "As you enter the city, a man carrying a jar of water will meet you. Follow him to the house that he enters, 11 and say to the owner of the house, 'The Teacher asks: Where is the guest room, where I may eat the Passover with my disciples?' 12 He will show you a large upper room, all furnished. Make preparations there."

13 They left and found things just as Jesus had told them.[a] So they prepared the Passover.

14 When the hour came, Jesus and his apostles[b] reclined at the table.[c] 15 And he said to them, "I have eagerly desired to eat this Passover with you before I suffer.[d] 16 For I tell you, I will not eat it again until it finds fulfillment in the kingdom of God."[e]

17 After taking the cup, he gave thanks and said, "Take this and divide it among you. 18 For I tell you I will not drink again of the fruit of the vine until the kingdom of God comes."

[a] 32 Or *race*

21:37 [o] Mt 26:55 [p] Mk 11:19 [q] Mt 21:1
21:38 [r] Jn 8:2
22:1 [s] Jn 11:55
22:2 [t] Mt 12:14
22:3 [u] Mt 4:10; Jn 13:2 [v] Mt 10:4
22:4 [w] ver 52; Ac 4:1; 5:24
22:5 [x] Zec 11:12
22:7 [y] Ex 12:18-20; Dt 16:5-8; Mk 14:12
22:8 [z] Ac 3:1,11; 4:13,19; 8:14
22:13 [a] Lk 19:32
22:14 [b] Mk 6:30 [c] Mt 26:20; Mk 14:17,18
22:15 [d] Mt 16:21
22:16 [e] Lk 14:15; Rev 19:9

19 And he took bread, gave thanks and
22:19 f Mt 14:19 broke it,[f] and gave it to them, saying,
"This is my body given for you; do this in
remembrance of me."
20 In the same way, after the supper he
22:20 took the cup, saying, "This cup is the
g Ex 24:8; new covenant[g] in my blood, which is
Isa 42:6; poured out for you. 21 But the hand of
Jer 31:31-34; him who is going to betray me is with
Zec 9:11; 2Co 3:6; mine on the table.[h] 22 The Son of Man[i]
Heb 8:6; 9:15 will go as it has been decreed,[j] but woe
22:21 to that man who betrays him." 23 They
h Ps 41:9 began to question among themselves
22:22 i Mt 8:20 which of them it might be who would do
j Ac 2:23; 4:28 this.
24 Also a dispute arose among them as
to which of them was considered to be
22:24 greatest.[k] 25 Jesus said to them, "The
k Mk 9:34; kings of the Gentiles lord it over them;
Lk 9:46 and those who exercise authority over
them call themselves Benefactors. 26 But
you are not to be like that. Instead, the
greatest among you should be like the
22:26 youngest,[l] and the one who rules like
l 1Pe 5:5; m Mk 9:35; the one who serves.[m] 27 For who is
Lk 9:48 greater, the one who is at the table or the
one who serves? Is it not the one who is
at the table? But I am among you as one
22:27 n Mt 20:28; who serves.[n] 28 You are those who have
Lk 12:37 stood by me in my trials. 29 And I confer
22:29 on you a kingdom,[o] just as my Father
o Mt 25:34; 2Ti 2:12 conferred one on me, 30 so that you may
eat and drink at my table in my king-
22:30 dom[p] and sit on thrones, judging the
p Lk 14:15; q Mt 19:28 twelve tribes of Israel.[q]
22:31 31 "Simon, Simon, Satan has asked[r] to
r Job 1:6-12; s Am 9:9 sift you[a] as wheat.[s] 32 But I have prayed
for you,[t] Simon, that your faith may not
22:32 fail. And when you have turned back,
t Jn 17:9,15; strengthen your brothers."[u]
Ro 8:34; 33 But he replied, "Lord, I am ready to
u Jn 21:15-17 go with you to prison and to death."[v]
22:33 v Jn 11:16 34 Jesus answered, "I tell you, Peter, before the rooster crows today, you will
deny three times that you know me."
22:35 35 Then Jesus asked them, "When I
w Mt 10:9,10; Lk 9:3; 10:4 sent you without purse, bag or sandals,[w]
did you lack anything?"
"Nothing," they answered.
36 He said to them, "But now if you
have a purse, take it, and also a bag; and
if you don't have a sword, sell your cloak
and buy one. 37 It is written: 'And he was
22:37 x Isa 53:12 numbered with the transgressors'[b];[x] and
I tell you that this must be fulfilled in
me. Yes, what is written about me is
reaching its fulfillment."

38 The disciples said, "See, Lord, here
are two swords."
"That is enough," he replied.

Jesus Prays on the Mount of Olives

39 Jesus went out as usual[y] to the 22:39 y Lk 21:37
Mount of Olives,[z] and his disciples fol- z Mt 21:1
lowed him. 40 On reaching the place, he
said to them, "Pray that you will not fall
into temptation."[a] 41 He withdrew about 22:40 a Mt 6:13
a stone's throw beyond them, knelt
down[b] and prayed, 42 "Father, if you are 22:41 b Lk 18:11
willing, take this cup[c] from me; yet not
my will, but yours be done."[d] 43 An angel 22:42 c Mt 20:22
from heaven appeared to him and d Mt 26:39
strengthened him.[e] 44 And being in an- 22:43
guish, he prayed more earnestly, and his e Mt 4:11; Mk 1:13
sweat was like drops of blood falling to
the ground.[c]
45 When he rose from prayer and went
back to the disciples, he found them
asleep, exhausted from sorrow. 46 "Why
are you sleeping?" he asked them. "Get
up and pray so that you will not fall into 22:46
temptation."[f] f ver 40

Jesus Arrested

47 While he was still speaking a crowd
came up, and the man who was called
Judas, one of the Twelve, was leading
them. He approached Jesus to kiss him,
48 but Jesus asked him, "Judas, are you
betraying the Son of Man with a kiss?"
49 When Jesus' followers saw what was
going to happen, they said, "Lord, 22:49
should we strike with our swords?"[g] g ver 38
50 And one of them struck the servant of
the high priest, cutting off his right ear.
51 But Jesus answered, "No more of
this!" And he touched the man's ear and
healed him.
52 Then Jesus said to the chief priests,
the officers of the temple guard,[h] and 22:52 h ver 4
the elders, who had come for him, "Am I
leading a rebellion, that you have come
with swords and clubs? 53 Every day I
was with you in the temple courts,[i] and 22:53
you did not lay a hand on me. But this is i Mt 26:55 j Jn 12:27
your hour[j]—when darkness reigns."[k] k Mt 8:12; Jn 1:5; 3:20

Peter Disowns Jesus 22:54

54 Then seizing him, they led him away l Mt 26:57; Mk 14:53
and took him into the house of the high m Mt 26:58; Mk 14:54;
priest.[l] Peter followed at a distance.[m] Jn 18:15

[a] *31* The Greek is plural. [b] *37* Isaiah 53:12
[c] *44* Some early manuscripts do not have verses 43 and 44.

55But when they had kindled a fire in the middle of the courtyard and had sat down together, Peter sat down with them. 56A servant girl saw him seated there in the firelight. She looked closely at him and said, "This man was with him."

57But he denied it. "Woman, I don't know him," he said.

58A little later someone else saw him and said, "You also are one of them."

"Man, I am not!" Peter replied.

59About an hour later another asserted, "Certainly this fellow was with him, for he is a Galilean."[n]

60Peter replied, "Man, I don't know what you're talking about!" Just as he was speaking, the rooster crowed. 61The Lord[o] turned and looked straight at Peter. Then Peter remembered the word the Lord had spoken to him: "Before the rooster crows today, you will disown me three times."[p] 62And he went outside and wept bitterly.

The Guards Mock Jesus

63The men who were guarding Jesus began mocking and beating him. 64They blindfolded him and demanded, "Prophesy! Who hit you?" 65And they said many other insulting things to him.[q]

Jesus Before Pilate and Herod

66At daybreak the council[r] of the elders of the people, both the chief priests and teachers of the law, met together,[s] and Jesus was led before them. 67"If you are the Christ,[a]" they said, "tell us."

Jesus answered, "If I tell you, you will not believe me, 68and if I asked you, you would not answer.[t] 69But from now on, the Son of Man will be seated at the right hand of the mighty God."[u]

70They all asked, "Are you then the Son of God?"[v]

He replied, "You are right in saying I am."[w]

71Then they said, "Why do we need any more testimony? We have heard it from his own lips."

23 Then the whole assembly rose and led him off to Pilate.[x] 2And they began to accuse him, saying, "We have found this man subverting our nation.[y] He opposes payment of taxes to Caesar[z] and claims to be Christ,[b] a king."[a]

3So Pilate asked Jesus, "Are you the king of the Jews?"

"Yes, it is as you say," Jesus replied.

4Then Pilate announced to the chief priests and the crowd, "I find no basis for a charge against this man."[b]

5But they insisted, "He stirs up the people all over Judea[c] by his teaching. He started in Galilee[c] and has come all the way here."

6On hearing this, Pilate asked if the man was a Galilean.[d] 7When he learned that Jesus was under Herod's jurisdiction, he sent him to Herod,[e] who was also in Jerusalem at that time.

8When Herod saw Jesus, he was greatly pleased, because for a long time he had been wanting to see him.[f] From what he had heard about him, he hoped to see him perform some miracle. 9He plied him with many questions, but Jesus gave him no answer.[g] 10The chief priests and the teachers of the law were standing there, vehemently accusing him. 11Then Herod and his soldiers ridiculed and mocked him. Dressing him in an elegant robe,[h] they sent him back to Pilate. 12That day Herod and Pilate became friends[i]—before this they had been enemies.

13Pilate called together the chief priests, the rulers and the people, 14and said to them, "You brought me this man as one who was inciting the people to rebellion. I have examined him in your presence and have found no basis for your charges against him.[j] 15Neither has Herod, for he sent him back to us; as you can see, he has done nothing to deserve death. 16Therefore, I will punish him[k] and then release him.[d]"

18With one voice they cried out, "Away with this man! Release Barabbas to us!"[l] 19(Barabbas had been thrown into prison for an insurrection in the city, and for murder.)

20Wanting to release Jesus, Pilate appealed to them again. 21But they kept shouting, "Crucify him! Crucify him!"

22For the third time he spoke to them: "Why? What crime has this man committed? I have found in him no grounds for the death penalty. Therefore I will

[a] 67 Or *Messiah* [b] 2 Or *Messiah*; also in verses 35 and 39 [c] 5 Or *over the land of the Jews*
[d] 16 Some manuscripts *him."* *17Now he was obliged to release one man to them at the Feast.*

22:59 [n] Lk 23:6
22:61 [o] Lk 7:13 [p] ver 34
22:65 [q] Mt 16:21
22:66 [r] Mt 5:22 [s] Mt 27:1; Mk 15:1
22:68 [t] Lk 20:3-8
22:69 [u] Mk 16:19
22:70 [v] Mt 4:3 [w] Mt 27:11; Lk 23:3
23:1 [x] Mt 27:2; Mk 15:1; Jn 18:28
23:2 [y] ver 14 [z] Lk 20:22 [a] Jn 19:12
23:4 [b] ver 14,22,41; Mt 27:23; Jn 18:38; 1Ti 6:13; 2Co 5:21
23:5 [c] Mk 1:14
23:6 [d] Lk 22:59
23:7 [e] Mt 14:1; Lk 3:1
23:8 [f] Lk 9:9
23:9 [g] Mk 14:61
23:11 [h] Mk 15:17-19; Jn 19:2,3
23:12 [i] Ac 4:27
23:14 [j] ver 4
23:16 [k] ver 22; Mt 27:26; Jn 19:1; Ac 16:37; 2Co 11:23,24
23:18 [l] Ac 3:13,14

> **HOW JESUS, WITH A BODY WRACKED WITH PAIN . . . COULD SPEAK ON BEHALF OF SOME HEARTLESS THUGS IS BEYOND MY COMPREHENSION. NEVER, NEVER HAVE I SEEN SUCH LOVE.**
>
> Max Lucado, *Christian Author, Texas*

have him punished and then release
23:22 [m]ver 16 him."[m]
23 But with loud shouts they insistent-
ly demanded that he be crucified, and
their shouts prevailed. 24 So Pilate decided to grant their demand. 25 He released
the man who had been thrown into
prison for insurrection and murder, the
one they asked for, and surrendered
Jesus to their will.

The Crucifixion

26 As they led him away, they seized Si-
23:26 [n]Mt 27:32 mon from Cyrene,[n] who was on his way
[o]Mk 15:21; in from the country, and put the cross
Jn 19:17 on him and made him carry it behind
Jesus.[o] 27 A large number of people followed him, including women who
23:27 [p]Lk 8:52 mourned and wailed[p] for him. 28 Jesus
turned and said to them, "Daughters of
23:28 Jerusalem, do not weep for me; weep for
[q]Lk 19:41-44; yourselves and for your children.[q] 29 For
21:23,24 the time will come when you will say,
'Blessed are the barren women, the
wombs that never bore and the breasts
23:29 [r]Mt 24:19 that never nursed!'[r] 30 Then

"'they will say to the mountains,
"Fall on us!"
23:30 [s]Hos 10:8; Isa 2:19; and to the hills, "Cover us!"'[a][s]

Rev 6:16 31 For if men do these things when the
23:31 tree is green, what will happen when it is
[t]Eze 20:47 dry?"[t]
32 Two other men, both criminals, were
23:32 [u]Isa 53:12; also led out with him to be executed.[u]
Mt 27:38; 33 When they came to the place called the
Mk 15:27; Jn 19:18 Skull, there they crucified him, along
with the criminals—one on his right, the
23:34 other on his left. 34 Jesus said, "Father,[v]
[v]Mt 11:25 [w]Mt 5:44 forgive them, for they do not know what
[x]Ps 22:18 they are doing."[b][w] And they divided up
his clothes by casting lots.[x]
23:35 35 The people stood watching, and the
[y]Ps 22:17 rulers even sneered at him.[y] They said,
[z]Isa 42:1 "He saved others; let him save himself if
he is the Christ of God, the Chosen One."[z]

36 The soldiers also came up and 23:36 [a]Ps 22:7
mocked him.[a] They offered him wine [b]Ps 69:21;
vinegar[b] 37 and said, "If you are the king Mt 27:48
of the Jews,[c] save yourself."
38 There was a written notice above 23:37 [c]Lk 4:3,9
him, which read: THIS IS THE KING OF THE
JEWS.[d] 23:38 [d]Mt 2:2
39 One of the criminals who hung
there hurled insults at him: "Aren't you
the Christ? Save yourself and us!"[e] 23:39 [e]ver 35,37
40 But the other criminal rebuked him.
"Don't you fear God," he said, "since you
are under the same sentence? 41 We are
punished justly, for we are getting what
our deeds deserve. But this man has
done nothing wrong."[f] 23:41 [f]ver 4
42 Then he said, "Jesus, remember me
when you come into your kingdom.[c]"[g] 23:42 [g]Mt 16:27
43 Jesus answered him, "I tell you the
truth, today you will be with me in par- 23:43 [h]2Co 12:3,4;
adise."[h] Rev 2:7

> **JESUS DIED TO SAVE SUCH AS YOU. HE IS FULL OF COMPASSION.**
>
> George Whitefield, *British Evangelist*

Jesus' Death

44 It was now about the sixth hour, and
darkness came over the whole land un- 23:44
til the ninth hour,[i] 45 for the sun stopped [i]Am 8:9
shining. And the curtain of the temple[j] 23:45
was torn in two.[k] 46 Jesus called out with [j]Ex 26:31-33;
a loud voice,[l] "Father, into your hands I Heb 9:3,8 [k]Heb 10:19,20
commit my spirit."[m] When he had said
this, he breathed his last.[n] 23:46 [l]Mt 27:50
47 The centurion, seeing what had [m]Ps 31:5;
happened, praised God[o] and said, "Sure- 1Pe 2:23 [n]Jn 19:30
ly this was a righteous man." 48 When all
the people who had gathered to witness 23:47 [o]Mt 9:8
this sight saw what took place, they beat
their breasts[p] and went away. 49 But all 23:48 [p]Lk 18:13
those who knew him, including the
women who had followed him from Gal- 23:49
ilee,[q] stood at a distance,[r] watching [q]Lk 8:2
these things. [r]Ps 38:11

Jesus' Burial

50 Now there was a man named
Joseph, a member of the Council, a
good and upright man, 51 who had not
consented to their decision and action.
He came from the Judean town of

[a] 30 Hosea 10:8 [b] 34 Some early manuscripts do not have this sentence. [c] 42 Some manuscripts *come with your kingly power*

DISCOVERY 271

JESUS, REMEMBER ME

The sinless Son of God was executed on a cross, hanging helpless between two hardened criminals. At first, as the irate crowd jeered, "the robbers who were crucified with him also heaped insults on him" (Matthew 27:44). But then one of the thieves experienced a radical change of heart.

His first action was to confront the other criminal, reminding him that they as partners in crime fully deserved execution but pointing out that "this man has done nothing wrong" (Luke 23:41). The dying man didn't stop there, however, but went on to entreat Jesus for help. His request was terse and to the point, but it contains within its nine short words one of the most beautiful unsolicited confessions in the Bible: "Jesus, remember me when you come into your kingdom" (verse 42). Through some flash of revelation this man with the sordid past recognized Jesus as the Messiah and the King and realized that faith in him would provide his only access into God's eternal kingdom.

The Savior's response is equally memorable: "I tell you the truth, today you will be with me in paradise" (verse 43). This guilt-ridden criminal received a great deal more than he had bargained for. He asked only to be *remembered*, but Jesus promised to be with him. This was more than the promise of a distant future in a far-off kingdom. *Today* he would experience the glory of paradise with the God who was now dying to save him.

Jesus regularly does more than we dare to ask. The apostle Paul pointed out, in fact, that he "is able to do immeasurably more than all we ask or imagine" because his power is working in us (Ephesians 3:20–21). Here was a man who had lived only to please himself, literally almost until his last breath. And simply by placing his destiny in the hands of Jesus he experienced "immeasurably more" than he was requesting or could ever have fantasized would happen to him. Immediately following his last rasping breath, he would find himself in the place of blessedness, where he would be "at home with the Lord" (2 Corinthians 5:8; see also Philippians 1:23).

We are sometimes confused about what God expects from us. We begin to believe that our salvation is dependent on our compliance with the expectations of our Christian social circles, our families, our churches. But the thief on the cross had never been baptized. He didn't attend regular church services, didn't deposit money in the offering plate every week and undoubtedly performed many more bad deeds than good deeds. The only thing he did do was to admit his sin, acknowledge who Jesus is and ask the Savior for help.

***Self-Discovery:** Reflect on the truth that Jesus is able to do immeasurably more than all you could ask or imagine. What is the most wonderful gift you can imagine? Marvel at the reality that you can expect much more than that from him!*

GO TO DISCOVERY 272 ON PAGE 1403

Arimathea and he was waiting for the
23:51 kingdom of God.[s] [52]Going to Pilate, he
s Lk 2:25,38 asked for Jesus' body. [53]Then he took it
down, wrapped it in linen cloth and
placed it in a tomb cut in the rock, one
23:54 in which no one had yet been laid. [54]It
t Mt 27:62 was Preparation Day,[t] and the Sabbath
was about to begin.
[55]The women who had come with
23:55 u ver 49 Jesus from Galilee[u] followed Joseph and
saw the tomb and how his body was laid
in it. [56]Then they went home and pre-
23:56 v Mk 16:1; pared spices and perfumes.[v] But they
Lk 24:1 w Ex 12:16; rested on the Sabbath in obedience to
20:10 the commandment.[w]

The Resurrection

24 On the first day of the week,
very early in the morning, the
women took the spices they had pre-
24:1 x Lk 23:56 pared[x] and went to the tomb. [2]They
found the stone rolled away from the
tomb, [3]but when they entered, they did
24:3 y ver 23,24 not find the body of the Lord Jesus.[y]
[4]While they were wondering about this,
suddenly two men in clothes that
24:4 z Jn 20:12 gleamed like lightning[z] stood beside
them. [5]In their fright the women bowed
down with their faces to the ground, but
the men said to them, "Why do you look
for the living among the dead? [6]He is not
here; he has risen! Remember how he
told you, while he was still with you in
24:6 a Mt 17:22,23; Galilee:[a] [7]'The Son of Man[b] must be de-
Mk 9:30-31; livered into the hands of sinful men, be
Lk 9:22; 24:44 crucified and on the third day be raised
24:7 b Mt 8:20 again.' "[c] [8]Then they remembered his
c Mt 16:21 words.[d]
[9]When they came back from the
24:8 d Jn 2:22 tomb, they told all these things to the
Eleven and to all the others. [10]It was
Mary Magdalene, Joanna, Mary the
mother of James, and the others with
24:10 e Lk 8:1-3 them[e] who told this to the apostles.[f]
f Mk 6:30 [11]But they did not believe[g] the women,
24:11 because their words seemed to them
g Mk 16:11 like nonsense. [12]Peter, however, got up
and ran to the tomb. Bending over, he
saw the strips of linen lying by them-
24:12 h Jn 20:3-7 selves,[h] and he went away,[i] wondering to
i Jn 20:10 himself what had happened.

On the Road to Emmaus

[13]Now that same day two of them
were going to a village called Emmaus,
24:13 j Mk 16:12 about seven miles[a] from Jerusalem.[j]
[14]They were talking with each other
about everything that had happened.
[15]As they talked and discussed these
things with each other, Jesus himself
came up and walked along with them;[k] 24:15 k ver 36
[16]but they were kept from recognizing
him.[l] 24:16 l Jn 20:14; 21:4
[17]He asked them, "What are you discussing together as you walk along?"
They stood still, their faces downcast.
[18]One of them, named Cleopas,[m] asked 24:18 m Jn 19:25
him, "Are you only a visitor to Jerusalem
and do not know the things that have
happened there in these days?"
[19]"What things?" he asked.
"About Jesus of Nazareth,"[n] they re- 24:19 n Mk 1:24
plied. "He was a prophet,[o] powerful in o Mt 21:11
word and deed before God and all the
people. [20]The chief priests and our
rulers[p] handed him over to be sentenced 24:20 p Lk 23:13
to death, and they crucified him; [21]but
we had hoped that he was the one who
was going to redeem Israel.[q] And what is 24:21 q Lk 1:68; 2:38;
more, it is the third day[r] since all this 21:28 r Mt 16:21
took place. [22]In addition, some of our
women amazed us.[s] They went to the 24:22 s ver 1-10
tomb early this morning [23]but didn't
find his body. They came and told us
that they had seen a vision of angels,
who said he was alive. [24]Then some of
our companions went to the tomb and
found it just as the women had said, but
him they did not see."[t] 24:24 t ver 12
[25]He said to them, "How foolish you
are, and how slow of heart to believe all
that the prophets have spoken! [26]Did not
the Christ[b] have to suffer these things
and then enter his glory?"[u] [27]And begin- 24:26 u Heb 2:10;
ning with Moses[v] and all the Prophets,[w] 1Pe 1:11
he explained to them what was said in
all the Scriptures concerning himself.[x] 24:27 v Ge 3:15;
[28]As they approached the village to Nu 21:9;
which they were going, Jesus acted as if Dt 18:15
he were going farther. [29]But they urged w Isa 7:14; 9:6; 40:10,11; 53;
him strongly, "Stay with us, for it is near- Eze 34:23;
ly evening; the day is almost over." So he Da 9:24; Mic 7:20;
went in to stay with them. Mal 3:1 x Jn 1:45
[30]When he was at the table with
them, he took bread, gave thanks, broke
it[y] and began to give it to them. [31]Then 24:30 y Mt 14:19
their eyes were opened and they recog-
nized him,[z] and he disappeared from 24:31 z ver 16
their sight. [32]They asked each other,
"Were not our hearts burning within us[a] 24:32 a Ps 39:3
while he talked with us on the road and b ver 27,45
opened the Scriptures[b] to us?"

[a] 13 Greek *sixty stadia* (about 11 kilometers)
[b] 26 Or *Messiah*; also in verse 46

The Mystery of the Empty Tomb

It was late afternoon on the day of Jesus' resurrection, and Cleopas and a friend were making their way on foot from Jerusalem to Emmaus. The distance was about seven miles—easily walked within a couple of hours. Their conversation was, not surprisingly, centered around the events surrounding Jesus' death and burial. Even though angels had purportedly announced that Jesus was no longer dead (Luke 24:22–23), their faces were "downcast" (verse 17), because they apparently did not yet believe that God had really raised their Lord from the tomb.

As they trudged along immersed in conversation, Jesus himself appeared and joined them, although neither recognized him. The Lord joined the conversation by inquiring as to what they were talking about. The two looked at him incredulously: How could someone in such close proximity to Jerusalem not have heard the reports of what had been happening?

The two began to describe the events of the last few days and to explain who Jesus was. First, they noted that he was a prophet, "powerful in word and deed" (verse 19). While this was certainly true, their explanation did not go far enough—God's promised Messiah was in reality the last and greatest prophet.

The two wayfarers also confessed that Jesus was Israel's redeemer. It had been their avid desire that Jesus would free Israel from the Roman occupation, but he had failed to meet that expectation (verse 21). All of their dreams of a secure earthly kingdom and a victorious political Messiah had been cruelly crushed when Jesus hung dying on the cross of shame.

The problem occupying nearly everyone's thoughts at the moment was the fact that Jesus' body was missing. Some of the women had gone early in the morning to anoint his body with spices—and had found only an empty tomb. But the women had further reported something so illogical as to sound ludicrous—angels had appeared to them and declared that Jesus was alive!

At this juncture Jesus led the two on a guided tour of the Scriptures, reminding them of one prophecy after another that pointed to himself as the Messiah. Although God's people hadn't expected their deliverer to die, the prophets had explicitly declared that he would have to suffer before he could fulfill God's intention for him (Isaiah 53:1-7; Luke 24:26–27).

We have no hope of understanding the Bible without looking at Jesus. Many passages in the Old Testament point toward his coming, and the New Testament reveals how he fulfilled the Old Testament predictions. One way to describe how the two Testaments work together is to state that the New Testament is *concealed* within the Old Testament and that the Old is *revealed* in the New. And central to both is Jesus Christ.

Nearly 2,000 years later, we are blessed with two advantages that the disciples on the road to Emmaus did not have. First, we have access to the New Testament, which describes Jesus' life, teachings, death, resurrection, ascension and promised return. Second, we have his indwelling Holy Spirit who guides us into God's truth (John 16:12–13). When we've given our lives to Jesus, it is inconceivable that we will fail to grow spiritually.

Self-Discovery: *Think for a moment about the gift of the New Testament and what it means for you. Then reflect on the gift of the Holy Spirit. Pause to thank God for these incomparable blessings!*

GO TO DISCOVERY 273 ON PAGE 1409

33They got up and returned at once to
Jerusalem. There they found the Eleven
and those with them, assembled together 34and saying, "It is true! The Lord has
24:34 c1Co 15:5 risen and has appeared to Simon."[c]
35Then the two told what had happened
on the way, and how Jesus was recog-
24:35 dver 30,31 nized by them when he broke the bread.[d]

Jesus Appears to the Disciples

36While they were still talking about
24:36 eJn 20:19,21,26; 14:27 this, Jesus himself stood among them
and said to them, "Peace be with you."[e]
37They were startled and frightened,
thinking they saw a ghost.[f] 38He said to 24:37 fMk 6:49
them, "Why are you troubled, and why
do doubts rise in your minds? 39Look at
my hands and my feet. It is I myself!
Touch me and see;[g] a ghost does not 24:39 gJn 20:27; 1Jn 1:1
have flesh and bones, as you see I have."
40When he had said this, he showed
them his hands and feet. 41And while
they still did not believe it because of
joy and amazement, he asked them,
"Do you have anything here to eat?"
42They gave him a piece of broiled fish,

Resurrection Appearances

Event	Place	Day of the Week	Matthew	Mark	Luke	John	Acts	1 Cor
The empty tomb	Jerusalem	Resurrection Sunday	28:1–10	16:1–8	24:1–12	20:1–9		
To Mary Magdalene in the garden	Jerusalem	Resurrection Sunday		16:9–11		20:11–18		
To other women	Jerusalem	Resurrection Sunday	28:9–10					
To two people going to Emmaus	Road to Emmaus	Resurrection Sunday		16:12–13	24:13–32			
To Peter	Jerusalem	Resurrection Sunday			24:34			15:5
To the ten disciples in the upper room	Jerusalem	Resurrection Sunday			24:36–43	20:19–25		
To the eleven disciples in the upper room	Jerusalem	Following Sunday		16:14		20:26–31		15:5
To seven disciples fishing	Sea of Galilee	Some time later				21:1–23		
To the eleven disciples on a mountain	Galilee	Some time later	28:16–20	16:15–18				
To more than five hundred	Unknown	Some time later						15:6
To James	Unknown	Some time later						15:7
To his disciples at his ascension	Mount of Olives	Forty days after Jesus' resurrection			24:44–49		1:3–8	
To Paul	Damascus	Several years later					9:1–19 22:3–16 26:9–18	9:1

THERE ARE MANY PEOPLE TODAY WHO MEET JESUS, NOT IN GALILEE AND JUDEA, BUT IN THE GOSPEL RECORD.

F. F. Bruce, *British Scholar*

24:43 [h] Ac 10:41 43 and he took it and ate it in their presence.[h]
24:44 [i] Lk 9:45; 18:34 44 He said to them, "This is what I told
[j] Mt 16:21; you while I was still with you:[i] Every-
Lk 9:22,44; thing must be fulfilled[j] that is written
18:31-33; 22:37 about me in the Law of Moses,[k] the
[k] ver 27 [l] Ps 2; 16; 22; 69; 72; 110; 118 Prophets and the Psalms."[l]
45 Then he opened their minds so they
could understand the Scriptures. 46 He
told them, "This is what is written: The
Christ will suffer and rise from the dead
on the third day, 47 and repentance and 24:47 [m] Ac 5:31;
forgiveness of sins will be preached in 10:43; 13:38
his name[m] to all nations,[n] beginning at [n] Mt 28:19
Jerusalem. 48 You are witnesses[o] of these 24:48
things. 49 I am going to send you what my [o] Ac 1:8; 2:32; 5:32; 13:31;
Father has promised;[p] but stay in the 1Pe 5:1
city until you have been clothed with 24:49
power from on high." [p] Jn 14:16; Ac 1:4

The Ascension

50 When he had led them out to the 24:50
vicinity of Bethany,[q] he lifted up his [q] Mt 21:17
hands and blessed them. 51 While he was
blessing them, he left them and was tak-
en up into heaven.[r] 52 Then they wor- 24:51 [r] 2Ki 2:11
shiped him and returned to Jerusalem
with great joy. 53 And they stayed contin- 24:53
ually at the temple,[s] praising God. [s] Ac 2:46

John

Jesus in John Our world offers a variety of gods to worship. Yet only one religion worships a person known primarily for his sacrificial love. The Gospel of John provides a compelling profile of that God who is so marvelously revealed in the person of Jesus Christ.

John is a wonderful book for new believers. Clearly defining the basics of Christianity, John presents Jesus as God's Son, describes the problems of a sinful world and candidly outlines the plan of salvation. Note how many times Jesus reveals aspects of his character in the "I am" sayings.

John referred to images of light and life to describe God's activity in the world. Note also that he arranged various groupings of events or statements in his account in groups of seven, which was a sacred number to God's people. In this Gospel there are seven of Jesus' discourses, seven of his miracles and seven "I am" statements. The seven miracles recorded by John climax in Jesus' own resurrection, which served for John as irrefutable proof that Jesus is God's Son.

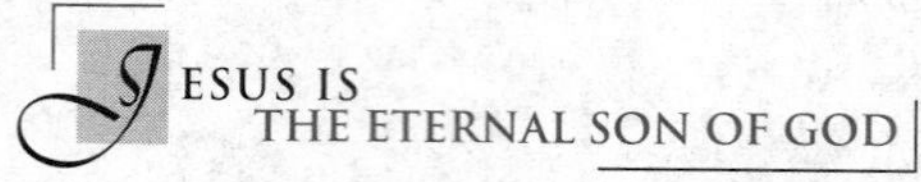

Why did Jesus hide his true identity? (John 2:24)

- *The people expected the Messiah to be a political and military figure who would lead Israel to independence from Rome. Jesus' purpose was to establish an invisible kingdom, a spiritual movement. He didn't want people thinking of him as a political activist.*

Why was Jesus reluctant to perform "signs and wonders"? (John 4:48)

- *The signs and wonders were intended only to validate Jesus' claims, not to draw attention or gather a following. Our Lord was disturbed that people were more interested in sensationalism than they were in a relationship with God. He chose to perform miracles in the hope that they would inspire faith, not simply please crowds.*

Who are the Jesus' other sheep? (John 10:16)

- *The sheep pen represents Israel, the Jewish people. By saying that he had sheep other than the Jews, Jesus was referring to the Gentiles. This verse constitutes one of Jesus' earliest and clearest references that Gentiles will be included in his kingdom.*

1:1 [a] Rev 19:13 *The Word Became Flesh*
[b] Jn 17:5; 1Jn 1:2 **1** In the beginning was the Word,[a]
[c] Php 2:6 and the Word was with God,[b] and
1:2 the Word was God.[c] 2He was with God
[d] Ge 1:1 in the beginning.[d]
1:3 3Through him all things were made;
[e] 1Co 8:6; without him nothing was made that has
Col 1:16; been made.[e] 4In him was life,[f] and that
Heb 1:2 life was the light[g] of men. 5The light
1:4 [f] Jn 5:26; 11:25; shines in the darkness, but the darkness
14:6 [g] Jn 8:12 has not understood[a] it.[h]
1:5 6There came a man who was sent
[h] Jn 3:19 from God; his name was John.[i] 7He came
1:6 as a witness to testify[j] concerning that
[i] Mt 3:1 light, so that through him all men might
1:7 believe.[k] 8He himself was not the light;
[j] ver 15,19,32 he came only as a witness to the light.
[k] ver 12 9The true light[l] that gives light to every
1:9 man[m] was coming into the world.[b]
[l] 1Jn 2:8 [m] Isa 49:6 10He was in the world, and though the

ATTRIBUTE THE HUMBLE WORDS TO THE MAN BORN OF MARY, BUT THE MORE SUBLIME AND DIVINELY SUITABLE, TO THE WORD WHO EXISTED IN THE BEGINNING.

Amphilochius of Iconium, *Early Church Father*

world was made through him,[n] the 1:10
world did not recognize him. 11He came [n] Heb 1:2
to that which was his own, but his own
did not receive him. 12Yet to all who re-
ceived him, to those who believed[o] in his 1:12 [o] ver 7 [p] 1Jn 3:23
name,[p] he gave the right to become chil- [q] Gal 3:26
dren of God[q]— 13children born not of

[a] 5 Or *darkness, and the darkness has not overcome*
[b] 9 Or *This was the true light that gives light to every man who comes into the world*

Sevens in John

John's focus was on showing that Jesus is the Son of God. John described Jesus as the eternal Word who was with God from the beginning and who, in fact, is God (John 1:1). John was also careful to write down some of the many times Jesus referred to himself by the divine name "I am." Jesus identified himself as the Bread of Life (6:35–51), the Light of the World (8:12—9:5), the Gate for the Father's Sheep (10:7–9), the Good Shepherd (10:11–14), the Resurrection and Life (11:35), the Way and the Truth (14:6), and the True Vine of God (15:1–5). John also arranged many things in his account in groups of seven, which was a sacred number to God's people. In this Gospel there are seven of Jesus' discourses, seven of his miracles and seven "I am" statements.

Seven Discourses	Seven Miracles	Seven "I am" Statements
1. New Birth (3:1–36)	1. Water Into Wine (2:1–11)	1. Bread of Life (6:35–51)
2. Water of Life (4:1–42)	2. Healing the Official's Son (4:43–54)	2. Light of the World (8:12—9:5)
3. Son of Man (5:19–47)	3. Healing the Lame Man (5:1–16)	3. Gate for the Sheep (10:7–9)
4. Bread of Life (6:22–66)	4. Feeding the 5,000 (6:1–14)	4. Good Shepherd (10:11–14)
5. Rivers of Living Water (7:1–52)	5. Walking on Water (6:16–21)	5. Resurrection and Life (11:35)
6. Light of the World (8:12–59)	6. Healing the Blind Man (9:1–12)	6. Way, Truth and Life (14:6)
7. Good Shepherd (10:1–42)	7. Raising Lazarus From the Dead (11:1–46)	7. True Vine (15:1–5)

1:13 r Jn 3:6; Jas 1:18; natural descent,[a] nor of human decision
1Pe 1:23; 1Jn 3:9 or a husband's will, but born of God.[r]
14 The Word became flesh[s] and made
1:14 s Gal 4:4; his dwelling among us. We have seen his
Php 2:7,8; glory, the glory of the One and Only,[b]
1Ti 3:16; Heb 2:14 who came from the Father, full of grace
t Jn 14:6 and truth.[t]
15 John testifies[u] concerning him. He
1:15 u ver 7 v ver 30; cries out, saying, "This was he of whom
Mt 3:11 I said, 'He who comes after me has sur-
1:16 passed me because he was before me.' "[v]
w Eph 1:23; 16 From the fullness[w] of his grace we have
Col 1:19 all received one blessing after another.
1:17 17 For the law was given through Moses;[x]
x Jn 7:19 y ver 14 grace and truth came through Jesus
1:18 Christ.[y] 18 No one has ever seen God,[z]
z Ex 33:20; Jn 6:46; but God the One and Only,[b,c][a] who is at
Col 1:15; 1Ti 6:16 the Father's side, has made him known.

a Jn 3:16,18; 1Jn 4:9

John the Baptist Denies Being the Christ

19 Now this was John's testimony when
1:19 b Jn 2:18; 5:10, the Jews[b] of Jerusalem sent priests and
16; 6:41,52 Levites to ask him who he was. 20 He did
1:20 not fail to confess, but confessed freely,
c Jn 3:28; "I am not the Christ.[d]"[c]
Lk 3:15,16 21 They asked him, "Then who are
1:21 you? Are you Elijah?"[d]
d Mt 11:14 He said, "I am not."
e Dt 18:15 "Are you the Prophet?"[e]
He answered, "No."

JOHN
THE APOSTLE

John was a son of Zebedee and a brother of James (Matthew 10:2). His family ran a thriving fishing business in Galilee (Mark 1:20), and together John and his brother were known as "Sons of Thunder" (Mark 3:17). John, James and Peter formed a kind of "inner circle" among the disciples, frequently spending time alone with Jesus (Matthew 17:1; Mark 14:33). John included in his Gospel certain specific details about his personal involvement with Jesus: that he sat beside him at the Last Supper (John 13:23), stood with Jesus' mother Mary while Jesus hung dying on the cross (John 19:26–27) and later outran Peter on the way to verify that Jesus' tomb was indeed empty (John 20:1–10). John was active in the early church (Acts 3:1–10; 4:1–22; 8:14–25), and historical tradition says that he moved to Ephesus in A.D. 66 to serve as bishop of the church. In all likelihood he did all of his writing there—his Gospel, 1, 2 and 3 John, and the book of Revelation.

22 Finally they said, "Who are you? Give
us an answer to take back to those who
sent us. What do you say about yourself?"
23 John replied in the words of Isaiah
the prophet, "I am the voice of one call-
ing in the desert,[f] 'Make straight the way 1:23 f Mt 3:1
for the Lord.' "[e][g] g Isa 40:3
24 Now some Pharisees who had been
sent 25 questioned him, "Why then do
you baptize if you are not the Christ, nor
Elijah, nor the Prophet?"
26 "I baptize with[f] water," John replied,
"but among you stands one you do not
know. 27 He is the one who comes after 1:27
me,[h] the thongs of whose sandals I am h ver 15,30
not worthy to untie."
28 This all happened at Bethany on the
other side of the Jordan,[i] where John was 1:28
baptizing. i Jn 3:26; 10:40

Jesus the Lamb of God

29 The next day John saw Jesus coming
toward him and said, "Look, the Lamb 1:29
of God,[j] who takes away the sin of the j ver 36; Isa 53:7;
world! 30 This is the one I meant when I 1Pe 1:19;
said, 'A man who comes after me has Rev 5:6
surpassed me because he was before 1:30
me.'[k] 31 I myself did not know him, but k ver 15,27
the reason I came baptizing with water
was that he might be revealed to Israel."
32 Then John gave this testimony: "I
saw the Spirit come down from heaven
as a dove and remain on him.[l] 33 I would 1:32 l Mt 3:16;
not have known him, except that the Mk 1:10
one who sent me to baptize with water[m] 1:33
told me, 'The man on whom you see the m Mk 1:4
Spirit come down and remain is he who n Mt 3:11;
will baptize with the Holy Spirit.'[n] 34 I Mk 1:8
have seen and I testify that this is the 1:34
Son of God."[o] o ver 49; Mt 4:3

Jesus' First Disciples

35 The next day John[p] was there again 1:35
with two of his disciples. 36 When he saw p Mt 3:1
Jesus passing by, he said, "Look, the
Lamb of God!"[q] 1:36 q ver 29
37 When the two disciples heard him
say this, they followed Jesus. 38 Turning
around, Jesus saw them following and
asked, "What do you want?" 1:38
They said, "Rabbi"[r] (which means r ver 49; Mt 23:7
Teacher), "where are you staying?"

[a] *13* Greek *of bloods* [b] *14,18* Or *the Only Begotten* [c] *18* Some manuscripts *but the only* (or *only begotten) Son* [d] *20* Or *Messiah.* "The Christ" (Greek) and "the Messiah" (Hebrew) both mean "the Anointed One"; also in verse 25. [e] *23* Isaiah 40:3 [f] *26* Or *in*; also in verses 31 and 33

DISCOVERY 273

THE LIVING WORD OF GOD

Words express our inner thoughts and help us to communicate those thoughts to others. In this way, words reveal what cannot be seen. Similarly, Jesus is "the Word," revealing One whom we cannot see—namely, God! Both the Jews and the Gentiles valued the concept of "word." To the Jewish people "the Word" connoted the creative, life-changing power of God. His Word was "alive," because it was active (Psalm 33:6; 147:15), a hammer and a fire that accomplished wondrous things (Isaiah 55:10–11; Jeremiah 23:29).

The Greek view was related but slightly different. The word *logos*, often translated "word" or "message," implied that there was order in the world, because the world was controlled by the reason or mind of God. The Greeks believed that this *logos* was the rational principle that governed all things and prevented total chaos. The Gospel of John begins with a declaration that Jesus is the *logos*, the Word. While Jewish people would read this and think immediately of the life-changing power of God, Greek readers would reflect on the mind of God who created and controls the universe. Both interpretations shed valuable light on the subject.

The first time John mentioned "the Word" was in relation to creation (John 1:1–3). These three compact verses carry a great deal of truth about God the Son. John declared that Jesus existed before creation, so that he is the *eternal* Word of God. And he was more than simply present when God created the universe; he was active in the process. Jesus is also *distinct* from God the Father because he was *with* God—and yet he himself *is* God because John clarified that "the Word was God."

But there's more: God's Word became flesh (verse 14). We call that remarkable occurrence the *incarnation*. Jesus did not stop being God the Son when he was born into the human race. Rather, he became the "God-man." While still possessing the nature of God, he at the same time assumed the nature of man. Jesus was made like us and was tempted to sin just as we are (Hebrews 2:17–28; 4:15). The difference, though, is that he did not yield to temptation.

Jesus is "the Word of life" (1 John 1:1), our only avenue of access into eternity with the God who loves us. On this point the Bible leaves no room for misunderstanding: "He who has the Son has life; he who does not have the Son of God does not have life" (1 John 5:12). And one day Jesus will come back as God in all glory and power. Because he died for our sins, "he is dressed in a robe dipped in blood, and his name is the Word of God" (Revelation 19:13).

Self-Discovery: *Envision yourself in a position of being asked to explain to a nonbeliever the significance of Jesus' incarnation for you. What would your response be?*

GO TO DISCOVERY 274 ON PAGE 1412

39"Come," he replied, "and you will see."
So they went and saw where he was
staying, and spent that day with him. It
was about the tenth hour.
40Andrew, Simon Peter's brother, was
one of the two who heard what John had
said and who had followed Jesus. 41The
first thing Andrew did was to find his
1:41 brother Simon and tell him, "We have
s Jn 4:25 found the Messiah" (that is, the Christ).[s]
42And he brought him to Jesus.
Jesus looked at him and said, "You are
1:42 t Ge 17:5,15 Simon son of John. You will be called[t]
u Mt 16:18 Cephas" (which, when translated, is
Peter[a]).[u]

Jesus Calls Philip and Nathanael

1:43 43The next day Jesus decided to leave
v Mt 10:3; Jn 6:5-7; 12:21, for Galilee. Finding Philip,[v] he said to
22; 14:8,9 him, "Follow me."[w]
w Mt 4:19 44Philip, like Andrew and Peter, was
1:44 from the town of Bethsaida.[x] 45Philip
x Mt 11:21; found Nathanael[y] and told him, "We
Jn 12:21 have found the one Moses wrote about
1:45 y Jn 21:2 in the Law,[z] and about whom the proph-
z Lk 24:27 a Lk 24:27 ets also wrote[a]—Jesus of Nazareth,[b] the
b Mt 2:23; son of Joseph."[c]
Mk 1:24 46"Nazareth! Can anything good come
c Lk 3:23 from there?"[d] Nathanael asked.
1:46 "Come and see," said Philip.
d Jn 7:41,42,52 47When Jesus saw Nathanael ap-
1:47 proaching, he said of him, "Here is a true
e Ro 9:4,6 Israelite,[e] in whom there is nothing
f Ps 32:2 false."[f]
48"How do you know me?" Nathanael
asked.
Jesus answered, "I saw you while you
were still under the fig tree before Philip
1:49 called you."
g ver 38; Mt 23:7 49Then Nathanael declared, "Rabbi,[g]
h ver 34; Mt 4:3 i Mt 2:2; 27:42; you are the Son of God;[h] you are the
Jn 12:13 King of Israel."[i]
50Jesus said, "You believe[b] because I
told you I saw you under the fig tree. You
shall see greater things than that." 51He
then added, "I tell you[c] the truth, you[c]
1:51 j Mt 3:16 shall see heaven open,[j] and the angels of
k Ge 28:12 God ascending and descending[k] on the
l Mt 8:20 Son of Man."[l]

Jesus Changes Water to Wine

2 On the third day a wedding took
2:1 m Jn 4:46; 21:2 place at Cana in Galilee.[m] Jesus'
n Mt 12:46 mother[n] was there, 2and Jesus and his
disciples had also been invited to the
wedding. 3When the wine was gone,
Jesus' mother said to him, "They have no
more wine."
4"Dear woman,[o] why do you involve 2:4
me?"[p] Jesus replied. "My time[q] has not o Jn 19:26 p Mt 8:29
yet come." q Mt 26:18; Jn 7:6
5His mother said to the servants, "Do
whatever he tells you."[r] 2:5
6Nearby stood six stone water jars, the r Ge 41:55
kind used by the Jews for ceremonial 2:6
washing,[s] each holding from twenty to s Mk 7:3,4; Jn 3:25
thirty gallons.[d]
7Jesus said to the servants, "Fill the
jars with water"; so they filled them to
the brim.
8Then he told them, "Now draw some
out and take it to the master of the banquet."
They did so, 9and the master of the
banquet tasted the water that had been 2:9
turned into wine.[t] He did not realize t Jn 4:46
where it had come from, though the servants who had drawn the water knew.
Then he called the bridegroom aside
10and said, "Everyone brings out the
choice wine first and then the cheaper
wine after the guests have had too much
to drink; but you have saved the best till
now."
11This, the first of his miraculous 2:11
signs,[u] Jesus performed at Cana in Gali- u ver 23; Jn 3:2;
lee. He thus revealed his glory,[v] and his 4:48; 6:2,14,26,
disciples put their faith in him.[w] 30; 12:37; 20:30 v Jn 1:14 w Ex 14:31

Jesus Clears the Temple

12After this he went down to Capernaum[x] with his mother and brothers[y] 2:12
and his disciples. There they stayed for a x Mt 4:13 y Mt 12:46
few days.
13When it was almost time for the Jewish Passover,[z] Jesus went up to Jerusa- 2:13
lem.[a] 14In the temple courts he found z Jn 11:55 a Dt 16:1-6;
men selling cattle, sheep and doves, and Lk 2:41
others sitting at tables exchanging money. 15So he made a whip out of cords, and
drove all from the temple area, both
sheep and cattle; he scattered the coins
of the money changers and overturned
their tables. 16To those who sold doves he
said, "Get these out of here! How dare you
turn my Father's house[b] into a market!" 2:16
17His disciples remembered that it is b Lk 2:49
written: "Zeal for your house will con- 2:17
sume me."[e c] c Ps 69:9

[a] 42 Both *Cephas* (Aramaic) and *Peter* (Greek) mean *rock.* [b] 50 Or *Do you believe . . . ?* [c] 51 The Greek is plural. [d] 6 Greek *two to three metretes* (probably about 75 to 115 liters) [e] 17 Psalm 69:9

18 Then the Jews demanded of him,
2:18 "What miraculous sign can you show us
d Mt 12:38 to prove your authority to do all this?"[d]
2:19 19 Jesus answered them, "Destroy this
e Mt 26:61; temple, and I will raise it again in three
27:40; Mk 14:58; 15:29 days."[e]
20 The Jews replied, "It has taken forty-
six years to build this temple, and you
are going to raise it in three days?" 21 But
the temple he had spoken of was his
2:21 f 1Co 6:19 body.[f] 22 After he was raised from the
dead, his disciples recalled what he had
2:22 g Lk 24:5-8; said.[g] Then they believed the Scripture
Jn 12:16; 14:26 and the words that Jesus had spoken.
2:23 23 Now while he was in Jerusalem at
h ver 13 the Passover Feast,[h] many people saw
the miraculous signs he was doing and
believed in his name.[a] 24 But Jesus would
not entrust himself to them, for he knew
all men. 25 He did not need man's testi-
2:25 i Mt 9:4; Jn 6:61, mony about man, for he knew what was
64; 13:11 in a man.[i]

Jesus Teaches Nicodemus

3:1 3 Now there was a man of the Phar-
j Jn 7:50; 19:39 isees named Nicodemus,[j] a mem-
k Lk 23:13 ber of the Jewish ruling council.[k] 2 He
came to Jesus at night and said, "Rabbi,
we know you are a teacher who has
come from God. For no one could per-
3:2 l Jn 9:16,33 form the miraculous signs[l] you are do-
m Ac 2:22; 10:38 ing if God were not with him."[m]
3 In reply Jesus declared, "I tell you the
truth, no one can see the kingdom of 3:3
God unless he is born again.[b]"[n] n Jn 1:13;
4 "How can a man be born when he is 1Pe 1:23
old?" Nicodemus asked. "Surely he cannot enter a second time into his mother's womb to be born!"
5 Jesus answered, "I tell you the truth,
no one can enter the kingdom of God
unless he is born of water and the Spirit.[o] 6 Flesh gives birth to flesh, but the 3:5
Spirit[c] gives birth to spirit.[p] 7 You should o Tit 3:5
not be surprised at my saying, 'You[d] 3:6
must be born again.' 8 The wind blows p Jn 1:13; 1Co 15:50
wherever it pleases. You hear its sound,
but you cannot tell where it comes from
or where it is going. So it is with everyone born of the Spirit."
9 "How can this be?"[q] Nicodemus 3:9
asked. q Jn 6:52,60

> THE ONLY PERMISSIBLE WAY [TO KNOW CHRIST] IS TO BELIEVE.
>
> Soren Kierkegaard, *Danish Philosopher*

10 "You are Israel's teacher,"[r] said Jesus, 3:10
"and do you not understand these r Lk 2:46
things? 11 I tell you the truth, we speak of 3:11
what we know,[s] and we testify to what s Jn 1:18; 7:16,17
we have seen, but still you people do not t ver 32
accept our testimony.[t] 12 I have spoken 3:13
to you of earthly things and you do not u Pr 30:4;
believe; how then will you believe if I Ac 2:34;
speak of heavenly things? 13 No one has Eph 4:8-10 v Jn 6:38,42
ever gone into heaven[u] except the one 3:14
who came from heaven[v]—the Son of w Nu 21:8,9
Man.[e] 14 Just as Moses lifted up the snake x Jn 8:28; 12:32
in the desert,[w] so the Son of Man must 3:15
be lifted up,[x] 15 that everyone who be- y ver 16,36
lieves[y] in him may have eternal life.[f] 3:16
16 "For God so loved[z] the world that z Ro 5:8;
he gave his one and only Son,[g] that Eph 2:4; 1Jn 4:9,
whoever believes in him shall not perish 10 a ver 36;
but have eternal life.[a] 17 For God did not Jn 6:29,40; 11:25,26
send his Son into the world[b] to con- 3:17
demn the world, but to save the world b Jn 6:29,57;
through him.[c] 18 Whoever believes in 10:36; 11:42; 17:8,21; 20:21
him is not condemned,[d] but whoever c Jn 12:47; 1Jn 4:14
does not believe stands condemned al- 3:18
ready because he has not believed in the d Jn 5:24
name of God's one and only Son.[h][e] e 1Jn 4:9

a 23 Or *and believed in him* *b* 3 Or *born from above*; also in verse 7 *c* 6 Or *but spirit* *d* 7 The Greek is plural. *e* 13 Some manuscripts *Man, who is in heaven* *f* 15 Or *believes may have eternal life in him* *g* 16 Or *his only begotten Son* *h* 18 Or *God's only begotten Son*

NICODEMUS

SEEKING GOD

Nicodemus, which means "conqueror of the people," needed to face and conquer his own fears in order to become a follower of Jesus (John 3:1–21). He was an orthodox Pharisee, a member of the Sanhedrin council, and a respected teacher and religious leader in the Jewish community, and he may have gone to see Jesus under cover of night for fear of criticism. Later, when the Sanhedrin discussed arresting of Jesus, Nicodemus defended his cause (John 7:50–52). And after Jesus' death it was Nicodemus who helped Joseph of Arimathea take his body from the cross so that it could be prepared for burial (John 19:38–42). The fact that John seemed so familiar with the details of Nicodemus's life suggests that Nicodemus, certainly an unlikely follower of Jesus, may have become well-known among his followers.

Born Again

Nicodemus, a wealthy religious leader (John 3:1; 19:39), came to visit Jesus furtively under cover of night in order to express his appreciation for Jesus' ministry. The interesting fact is that our Lord ignored his praise and cut right to the heart of Nicodemus's need: "No one can see the kingdom of God unless he is born again" (John 3:3). Nicodemus was undoubtedly familiar with the concept of spiritual rebirth. When a Gentile converted to Judaism, he was said to be "reborn." However, Nicodemus still confused Jesus' words with physical rebirth.

The words *born again* in this context might mean one of three things. They might imply *a radical change* of some kind. They might also mean being born *a second time*, or they could connote being born *from above*. We might easily say that Jesus was incorporating all three of these definitions: Spiritual rebirth entails being radically born a second time from above (John 1:13; James 1:18; 1 Peter 1:23; 1 John 3:9; 5:1,4). And that, according to Jesus, is the only way to heaven.

Jesus went on to elaborate on the nature of this new birth, stating that *it is a water and Spirit birth*: "No one can enter the kingdom of God unless he is born of water and the Spirit" (John 3:5). Some people believe that the phrase "water and the Spirit" incorporates both physical and spiritual birth, *water* referring to physical birth which begins after a woman's water has broken and *the Spirit* representing the new life God offers us. Others perceive water as a symbol of being cleansed from sin (Psalm 51:7; Zechariah 13:1; Titus 3:5–7). According to this interpretation *water* represents a cleansing agent that transforms us as we listen to God's Word (1 Peter 1:23), while *the Spirit* speaks of God's Holy Spirit who works the rebirth within us (Titus 3:5).

Jesus further informed his guest that this rebirth is *like the wind* (John 3:8). The wind is independent; we cannot control its velocity or direction. New birth from God is similar in that it is the work of God alone (John 1:13). While we cannot see the wind itself, we can certainly discern its presence as it moves through an area. The same is true of new birth. Although we cannot completely explain or understand it, we can witness its effects in the life of a believer (James 2:14–17).

The Bible teaches us that God offers us a brand-new start when we give over our lives to him. The apostle Paul wrote, "Therefore, if anyone is in Christ, he is a new creation; the old has gone, the new has come" (2 Corinthians 5:17). We are unable to be so diligent in following his commands that we can win his approval; the only determining factor in our being made right with our Maker is the rebirth which he offers us through Jesus Christ, a transformation so revolutionary, so radical, that it can only be termed a "new creation" (Galatians 6:15).

***Self-Discovery:** Take a moment to think about the analogy of your spiritual rebirth as being like the wind. What other associations can you think of?*

GO TO DISCOVERY 275 ON PAGE 1415

3:19 [f]Jn 1:4; 8:12 19This is the verdict: Light[f] has come
into the world, but men loved darkness
instead of light because their deeds were
evil. 20Everyone who does evil hates the
light, and will not come into the light for
3:20 [g]Eph 5:11,13 fear that his deeds will be exposed.[g]
21But whoever lives by the truth comes
into the light, so that it may be seen
plainly that what he has done has been
done through God."[a]

John the Baptist's Testimony About Jesus

22After this, Jesus and his disciples
went out into the Judean countryside,
where he spent some time with them,
3:22 [h]Jn 4:2 and baptized.[h] 23Now John also was baptizing at Aenon near Salim, because
there was plenty of water, and people
were constantly coming to be baptized.
24(This was before John was put in
3:24 [i]Mt 4:12; 14:3 prison.)[i] 25An argument developed between some of John's disciples and a cer-
tain Jew[b] over the matter of ceremonial
3:25 [j]Jn 2:6 washing.[j] 26They came to John and said
to him, "Rabbi,[k] that man who was with
3:26 [k]Mt 23:7 [l]Jn 1:7 you on the other side of the Jordan—the
one you testified[l] about—well, he is bap-
tizing, and everyone is going to him."
27To this John replied, "A man can receive only what is given him from heav-
en. 28You yourselves can testify that I
said, 'I am not the Christ[c] but am sent
3:28 [m]Jn 1:20,23 ahead of him.'[m] 29The bride belongs to
3:29 the bridegroom.[n] The friend who at-
[n]Mt 9:15 tends the bridegroom waits and listens
[o]Jn 16:24; for him, and is full of joy when he hears
17:13; Php 2:2; the bridegroom's voice. That joy is mine,
1Jn 1:4; 2Jn 12 and it is now complete.[o] 30He must become greater; I must become less.

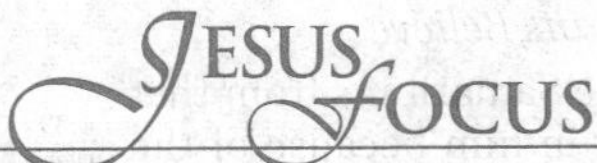

STEPPING ASIDE

It couldn't have been easy being John the Baptist. From the very beginning John understood that his ministry was only temporary and that his sole purpose was to direct people to someone else. And he was very clear about his role: "He [Jesus] must become greater; I must become less" (John 3:30). John the Baptist was the last in a long line of prophets that God had sent to his people, and his ministry marked a transition between the old covenant and the new. He willingly stepped aside when the time was right for Jesus to take center stage.

31"The one who comes from above[p] is 3:31 [p]ver 13
above all; the one who is from the earth [q]Jn 8:23; 1Jn 4:5
belongs to the earth, and speaks as one
from the earth.[q] The one who comes
from heaven is above all. 32He testifies to
what he has seen and heard,[r] but no one 3:32 [r]Jn 8:26; 15:15
accepts his testimony.[s] 33The man who [s]ver 11
has accepted it has certified that God is 3:34
truthful. 34For the one whom God has [t]ver 17
sent[t] speaks the words of God, for God[d] [u]Mt 12:18;
gives the Spirit[u] without limit. 35The Fa- Lk 4:18; Ac 10:38
ther loves the Son and has placed every- 3:35
thing in his hands.[v] 36Whoever believes [v]Mt 28:18;
in the Son has eternal life,[w] but whoev- Jn 5:20,22; 17:2
er rejects the Son will not see life, for 3:36 [w]ver 15; Jn 5:24;
God's wrath remains on him."[e] 6:47

Jesus Talks With a Samaritan Woman

4 The Pharisees heard that Jesus
was gaining and baptizing more
disciples than John,[x] 2although in fact it 4:1 [x]Jn 3:22,26
was not Jesus who baptized, but his dis-
ciples. 3When the Lord learned of this, 4:3
he left Judea[y] and went back once more [y]Jn 3:22
to Galilee.
4Now he had to go through Samaria.
5So he came to a town in Samaria called
Sychar, near the plot of ground Jacob
had given to his son Joseph.[z] 6Jacob's 4:5
well was there, and Jesus, tired as he was [z]Ge 33:19; 48:22; Jos 24:32
from the journey, sat down by the well.
It was about the sixth hour.
7When a Samaritan woman came to
draw water, Jesus said to her, "Will you
give me a drink?" 8(His disciples had 4:8
gone into the town[a] to buy food.) [a]ver 5,39
9The Samaritan woman said to him,
"You are a Jew and I am a Samaritan[b] 4:9 [b]Mt 10:5;
woman. How can you ask me for a Lk 9:52,53
drink?" (For Jews do not associate with
Samaritans.[f])
10Jesus answered her, "If you knew the
gift of God and who it is that asks you for
a drink, you would have asked him and 4:10
he would have given you living water."[c] [c]Isa 44:3;
11"Sir," the woman said, "you have Jer 2:13;
nothing to draw with and the well is Zec 14:8;
deep. Where can you get this living wa- Jn 7:37,38;
ter? 12Are you greater than our father Ja- Rev 21:6; 22:1, 17
cob, who gave us the well[d] and drank 4:12 [d]ver 6
from it himself, as did also his sons and
his flocks and herds?"

[a] *21* Some interpreters end the quotation after verse 15. [b] *25* Some manuscripts *and certain Jews* [c] *28* Or *Messiah* [d] *34* Greek *he* [e] *36* Some interpreters end the quotation after verse 30. [f] *9* Or *do not use dishes Samaritans have used*

> WHAT A DYNAMIC CONFRONTATION! THIS MAN WHO ASKED HER FOR A SIMPLE CUP OF WATER WAS NOW STANDING THERE, CLAIMING TO BE THE TRUE MESSIAH, . . . AND PROMISING TO FORGIVE HER SIN AND TRANSFORM HER.
>
> John F. MacArthur, Jr., *Pastor, Sun Valley, California*

13 Jesus answered, "Everyone who
drinks this water will be thirsty again,
4:14 14 but whoever drinks the water I give
[e] Jn 6:35 him will never thirst.[e] Indeed, the water
[f] Jn 7:38 [g] Mt 25:46 I give him will become in him a spring of
water[f] welling up to eternal life."[g]
4:15 15 The woman said to him, "Sir, give
[h] Jn 6:34 me this water so that I won't get thirsty[h]
and have to keep coming here to draw
water."
16 He told her, "Go, call your husband
and come back."
17 "I have no husband," she replied.
Jesus said to her, "You are right when
you say you have no husband. 18 The fact
is, you have had five husbands, and the
man you now have is not your husband.
What you have just said is quite true."
4:19 19 "Sir," the woman said, "I can see that
[i] Mt 21:11 you are a prophet.[i] 20 Our fathers wor-
4:20 shiped on this mountain,[j] but you Jews
[j] Dt 11:29; claim that the place where we must wor-
Jos 8:33 [k] Lk 9:53 ship is in Jerusalem."[k]
21 Jesus declared, "Believe me, woman,
4:21 [l] Jn 5:28; 16:2 a time is coming[l] when you will worship
[m] Mal 1:11; the Father neither on this mountain nor
1Ti 2:8 in Jerusalem.[m] 22 You Samaritans wor-
4:22 ship what you do not know;[n] we wor-
[n] 2Ki 17:28-41 ship what we do know, for salvation is
[o] Isa 2:3; Ro 3:1, 2; 9:4,5 from the Jews.[o] 23 Yet a time is coming
4:23 and has now come[p] when the true wor-
[p] Jn 5:25; 16:32 shipers will worship the Father in spirit[q]
[q] Php 3:3 and truth, for they are the kind of wor-
4:24 shipers the Father seeks. 24 God is spirit,[r]
[r] Php 3:3 and his worshipers must worship in
spirit and in truth."
4:25 25 The woman said, "I know that Mes-
[s] Mt 1:16 siah" (called Christ)[s] "is coming. When
he comes, he will explain everything
to us."
4:26 26 Then Jesus declared, "I who speak to
[t] Jn 8:24; 9:35-37 you am he."[t]

The Disciples Rejoin Jesus

27 Just then his disciples returned[u] and 4:27
were surprised to find him talking with [u] ver 8
a woman. But no one asked, "What do
you want?" or "Why are you talking with
her?"
28 Then, leaving her water jar, the
woman went back to the town and said
to the people, 29 "Come, see a man who
told me everything I ever did.[v] Could this 4:29 [v] ver 17,18
be the Christ[a]?"[w] 30 They came out of the [w] Mt 12:23;
town and made their way toward him. Jn 7:26,31
31 Meanwhile his disciples urged him,
"Rabbi,[x] eat something." 4:31 [x] Mt 23:7
32 But he said to them, "I have food to 4:32
eat[y] that you know nothing about." [y] Job 23:12;
33 Then his disciples said to each oth- Mt 4:4; Jn 6:27
er, "Could someone have brought him
food?"
34 "My food," said Jesus, "is to do the 4:34
will[z] of him who sent me and to finish his [z] Mt 26:39;
work.[a] 35 Do you not say, 'Four months Jn 6:38; 17:4;
more and then the harvest'? I tell you, 19:30 [a] Jn 19:30
open your eyes and look at the fields!
They are ripe for harvest.[b] 36 Even now 4:35 [b] Mt 9:37;
the reaper draws his wages, even now he Lk 10:2
harvests[c] the crop for eternal life,[d] so that 4:36
the sower and the reaper may be glad to- [c] Ro 1:13
gether. 37 Thus the saying 'One sows and [d] Mt 25:46
another reaps'[e] is true. 38 I sent you to 4:37
reap what you have not worked for. Oth- [e] Job 31:8;
ers have done the hard work, and you Mic 6:15
have reaped the benefits of their labor."

> ONE OF JESUS' SPECIALTIES IS TO MAKE SOMEBODIES OUT OF NOBODIES.
>
> Henrietta Mears, *American Bible Teacher*

Many Samaritans Believe

39 Many of the Samaritans from that
town[f] believed in him because of the 4:39 [f] ver 5 [g] ver 29
woman's testimony, "He told me every-
thing I ever did."[g] 40 So when the Samaritans came to him, they urged him to
stay with them, and he stayed two days.
41 And because of his words many more
became believers.
42 They said to the woman, "We no
longer believe just because of what you
said; now we have heard for ourselves,
and we know that this man really is the 4:42 [h] Lk 2:11;
Savior of the world."[h] 1Jn 4:14

[a] 29 Or *Messiah*

Overcoming Barriers

On the surface Nicodemus (John 3:1–21) had nothing in common with the Samaritan woman in John 4. Nicodemus sought Jesus out, while the Samaritan woman was sought out by Jesus. Nicodemus was a favored Jew and a religious leader, but the woman was a despised Samaritan and an outcast from "decent" society.

But these two disparate individuals shared a common need: to know God the Father through Jesus, his Son. Jesus looked beyond their surface differences and saw these two people for who they were on the inside. In order to even converse with the Samaritan woman, Jesus was compelled to overcome three major cultural barriers:

1. *The gender barrier*. Jewish religious law did not condone a rabbi speaking with a woman in public. Many rabbis would not even talk to their own wives or daughters outside the privacy of their homes, and some were so exacting in this standard that they would close their eyes when they saw a woman on the street.

2. *The racial barrier*. The Jewish people hated the Samaritans, and Samaritans in turn despised Jews. Centuries earlier, when the northern kingdom had been led away captive by Assyria, most of the Jewish population had been taken to Media. Foreigners were then moved to the town of Samaria, and the Jews who had been left behind intermarried with them. The Jews who had been taken to Media also intermarried, with the result that the ten northern tribes were absorbed into the surrounding pagan cultures. When men from the southern kingdom returned from captivity in Babylon, the people of Samaria offered to help them to rebuild Jerusalem. When this generous offer was refused, the Samaritans responded by opposing the building project. By the time of Jesus' earthly ministry, centuries of hatred had transpired between the two peoples.

3. *The social barrier.* Jesus was addressed by some as "rabbi," or "teacher," which indicated that, despite his lowly lifestyle, he was viewed with respect by those who heard his sermons and saw his miracles. The woman, on the other hand, had been divorced five times and was now living with a man who was not her husband (verses 17–18). The stigma of her past may explain why she had come to draw water during the hottest part of the day rather than in the company of the rest of the women in the cool of the morning. She was obviously an outcast, and merely acknowledging her could have left Jesus open to charges that he was breaking the unspoken rules of social etiquette.

Sometimes it is easier for us to reach out to people like Nicodemus—people who to some degree look like us, talk like us and are at least as well-respected as we are. Our challenge as we strive to follow Jesus' example is to step out of our comfort zones to interact with people who are radically different from ourselves. That is certainly one way in which we can follow in the footsteps of the Savior, and, when we are truly devoted to sharing the Good News with others, the Holy Spirit will help us to overcome any barriers.

Self-Discovery: *Think about a time when you stepped out of your social or cultural comfort zone to assist or encourage someone else or to share the gospel message. How did you feel about the interaction afterward? What is preventing you from making this kind of cross-cultural connection a way of life?*

GO TO DISCOVERY 276 ON PAGE 1421

Jesus in Judea and Samaria

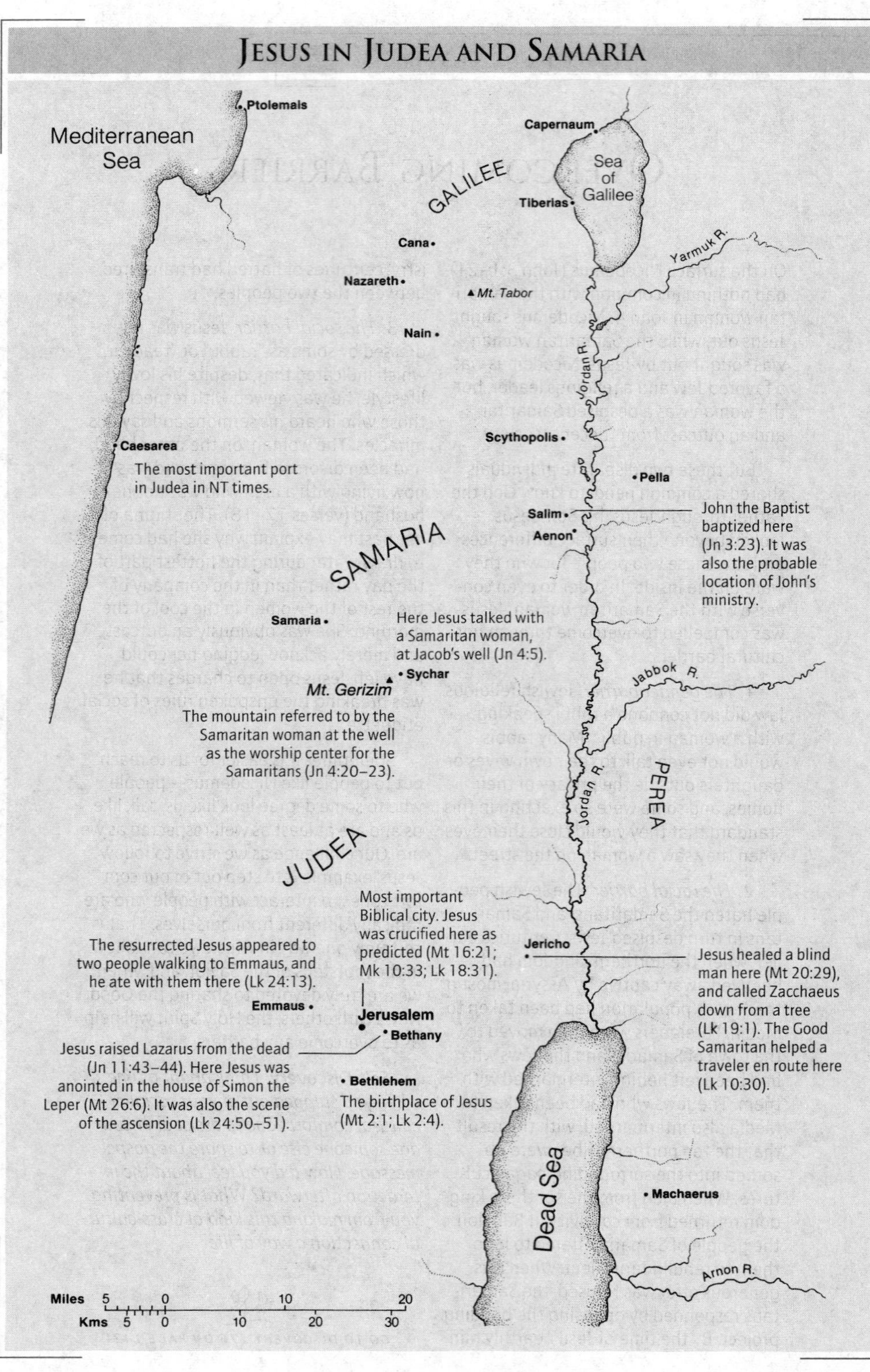

Ptolemais
Mediterranean Sea
Capernaum
Sea of Galilee
GALILEE
Tiberias
Cana
Yarmuk R.
Nazareth
Mt. Tabor
Nain
Jordan R.
Scythopolis
Caesarea
The most important port in Judea in NT times.
Pella
Salim
Aenon
John the Baptist baptized here (Jn 3:23). It was also the probable location of John's ministry.
SAMARIA
Samaria
Here Jesus talked with a Samaritan woman, at Jacob's well (Jn 4:5).
Sychar
Mt. Gerizim
Jabbok R.
The mountain referred to by the Samaritan woman at the well as the worship center for the Samaritans (Jn 4:20–23).
Jordan R.
PEREA
JUDEA
Most important Biblical city. Jesus was crucified here as predicted (Mt 16:21; Mk 10:33; Lk 18:31).
The resurrected Jesus appeared to two people walking to Emmaus, and he ate with them there (Lk 24:13).
Jericho
Jesus healed a blind man here (Mt 20:29), and called Zacchaeus down from a tree (Lk 19:1). The Good Samaritan helped a traveler en route here (Lk 10:30).
Emmaus
Jerusalem
Bethany
Jesus raised Lazarus from the dead (Jn 11:43–44). Here Jesus was anointed in the house of Simon the Leper (Mt 26:6). It was also the scene of the ascension (Lk 24:50–51).
Bethlehem
The birthplace of Jesus (Mt 2:1; Lk 2:4).
Dead Sea
Machaerus
Arnon R.
Miles 5 0 10 20
Kms 5 0 10 20 30

Jesus Heals the Official's Son

4:43 43After the two days[i] he left for Gali-
[i] ver 40 lee. 44(Now Jesus himself had pointed
out that a prophet has no honor in his
4:44 own country.)[j] 45When he arrived in
[j] Mt 13:57; Lk 4:24 Galilee, the Galileans welcomed him.
They had seen all that he had done in Je-
4:45 [k] Jn 2:23 rusalem at the Passover Feast,[k] for they
also had been there.
46Once more he visited Cana in Galilee, where he had turned the water into
4:46 [l] Jn 2:1-11 wine.[l] And there was a certain royal official whose son lay sick at Capernaum.
47When this man heard that Jesus had
4:47 arrived in Galilee from Judea,[m] he went
[m] ver 3,54 to him and begged him to come and
heal his son, who was close to death.
48"Unless you people see miraculous
4:48 [n] Da 4:2,3; signs and wonders,"[n] Jesus told him,
Jn 2:11; Ac 2:43; "you will never believe."
14:3; Ro 15:19; 2Co 12:12; 49The royal official said, "Sir, come
Heb 2:4 down before my child dies."
50Jesus replied, "You may go. Your son
will live."
The man took Jesus at his word and
departed. 51While he was still on the
way, his servants met him with the news
that his boy was living. 52When he inquired as to the time when his son got
better, they said to him, "The fever left
him yesterday at the seventh hour."
53Then the father realized that this
was the exact time at which Jesus had
said to him, "Your son will live." So he
4:53 [o] Ac 11:14 and all his household[o] believed.
54This was the second miraculous
4:54 [p] ver 48; Jn 2:11 sign[p] that Jesus performed, having come
from Judea to Galilee.

JESUS FOCUS

LONG DISTANCE MIRACLES

Although Rome had conquered Israel and was not a welcome presence in the land, Jesus never excluded the Romans from his healing touch. In John 4:43–54 John recounted the story of Jesus' second miracle, the healing of the dying son of a Roman official. There are many similarities between this healing and that of the servant of a Roman centurion (Matthew 8:5–13; Luke 7:2–10). Both were "long-distance" miracles in that at the time of the healings Jesus was nowhere near the people who so desperately needed his help. Jesus' miracles are never limited by time or distance.

The Healing at the Pool

5 Some time later, Jesus went up to
Jerusalem for a feast of the Jews.
2Now there is in Jerusalem near the
Sheep Gate[q] a pool, which in Aramaic[r] 5:2 [q] Ne 3:1; 12:39
is called Bethesda[a] and which is sur- [r] Jn 19:13,17,20;
rounded by five covered colonnades. 20:16; Ac 21:40;
3Here a great number of disabled people 22:2; 26:14
used to lie—the blind, the lame, the paralyzed.[b] 5One who was there had been
an invalid for thirty-eight years. 6When
Jesus saw him lying there and learned
that he had been in this condition for a
long time, he asked him, "Do you want
to get well?"
7"Sir," the invalid replied, "I have no
one to help me into the pool when the
water is stirred. While I am trying to get
in, someone else goes down ahead
of me."
8Then Jesus said to him, "Get up! Pick 5:8
up your mat and walk."[s] 9At once the [s] Mt 9:5,6;
man was cured; he picked up his mat Mk 2:11;
and walked. Lk 5:24
The day on which this took place was 5:9
a Sabbath,[t] 10and so the Jews[u] said to the [t] Jn 9:14
man who had been healed, "It is the Sab- 5:10
bath; the law forbids you to carry your [u] ver 16 [v] Ne 13:15-22;
mat."[v] Jer 17:21;
11But he replied, "The man who made Mt 12:2
me well said to me, 'Pick up your mat
and walk.'"
12So they asked him, "Who is this fellow who told you to pick it up and walk?"
13The man who was healed had no
idea who it was, for Jesus had slipped
away into the crowd that was there.
14Later Jesus found him at the temple
and said to him, "See, you are well again.
Stop sinning[w] or something worse may 5:14 [w] Mk 2:5;
happen to you." 15The man went away Jn 8:11
and told the Jews[x] that it was Jesus who 5:15
had made him well. [x] Jn 1:19

Life Through the Son

16So, because Jesus was doing these
things on the Sabbath, the Jews persecuted him. 17Jesus said to them, "My Fa- 5:17
ther is always at his work[y] to this very [y] Jn 9:4; 14:10
day, and I, too, am working." 18For this

[a] 2 Some manuscripts *Bethzatha*; other manuscripts *Bethsaida* [b] 3 Some less important manuscripts *paralyzed—and they waited for the moving of the waters. 4From time to time an angel of the Lord would come down and stir up the waters. The first one into the pool after each such disturbance would be cured of whatever disease he had.*

> **JESUS' OUTLANDISH CLAIM TO BEING THE ONLY WAY TO GOD PUTS CHRISTIANITY IN A CLASS BY ITSELF.**
>
> Lee Strobel, *American Journalist*

reason the Jews tried all the harder to
5:18 [z]Jn 7:1 [a]Jn 10:30,33; 19:7 kill him;[z] not only was he breaking the
Sabbath, but he was even calling God his
own Father, making himself equal with
God.[a]
19Jesus gave them this answer: "I tell
5:19 [b]ver 30; Jn 8:28 you the truth, the Son can do nothing by
himself;[b] he can do only what he sees his
Father doing, because whatever the Father does the Son also does. 20For the Fa-
5:20 [c]Jn 3:35 [d]Jn 14:12 ther loves the Son[c] and shows him all he
does. Yes, to your amazement he will
show him even greater things than
these.[d] 21For just as the Father raises the
5:21 [e]Ro 4:17; 8:11 [f]Jn 11:25 dead and gives them life,[e] even so the
Son gives life[f] to whom he is pleased to
give it. 22Moreover, the Father judges no
5:22 [g]ver 27; Jn 9:39; Ac 10:42; 17:31 one, but has entrusted all judgment to
the Son,[g] 23that all may honor the Son
just as they honor the Father. He who
does not honor the Son does not honor
5:23 [h]Lk 10:16; 1Jn 2:23 the Father, who sent him.[h]
24"I tell you the truth, whoever hears
my word and believes him who sent me
has eternal life and will not be con-
5:24 [i]Jn 3:18 [j]1Jn 3:14 demned;[i] he has crossed over from
death to life.[j] 25I tell you the truth, a time
is coming and has now come[k] when the
5:25 [k]Jn 4:23 [l]Jn 8:43,47 dead will hear[l] the voice of the Son of
God and those who hear will live. 26For
as the Father has life in himself, so he
has granted the Son to have life in him-
5:27 [m]ver 22; Ac 10:42; 17:31 self. 27And he has given him authority to
judge[m] because he is the Son of Man.

> **JESUS COMBINED . . . TENDER LOVE TO THE SINNER WITH UNCOMPROMISING SEVERITY AGAINST SIN, COMMANDING DIGNITY WITH WINNING HUMILITY, FEARLESS COURAGE WITH WISE CAUTION, UNYIELDING FIRMNESS WITH SWEET GENTLENESS!**
>
> 
>
> Philip Schaff, *Church Historian*

28"Do not be amazed at this, for a 5:28
time is coming[n] when all who are in [n]Jn 4:21
their graves will hear his voice 29and
come out—those who have done good
will rise to live, and those who have
done evil will rise to be condemned.[o] 5:29 [o]Da 12:2; Mt 25:46
30By myself I can do nothing;[p] I judge
only as I hear, and my judgment is just,[q] 5:30 [p]ver 19 [q]Jn 8:16 [r]Mt 26:39; Jn 4:34; 6:38
for I seek not to please myself but him
who sent me.[r]

Testimonies About Jesus

31"If I testify about myself, my testi-
mony is not valid.[s] 32There is another 5:31 [s]Jn 8:14
who testifies in my favor,[t] and I know
that his testimony about me is valid. 5:32 [t]ver 37; Jn 8:18
33"You have sent to John and he has 5:33
testified[u] to the truth. 34Not that I ac- [u]Jn 1:7
cept human testimony;[v] but I mention
it that you may be saved. 35John was a 5:34 [v]1Jn 5:9
lamp that burned and gave light,[w] and
you chose for a time to enjoy his light. 5:35 [w]2Pe 1:19
36"I have testimony weightier than
that of John.[x] For the very work that the 5:36 [x]1Jn 5:9
Father has given me to finish, and [y]Jn 14:11; 15:24
which I am doing,[y] testifies that the Fa- [z]Jn 3:17; 10:25
ther has sent me.[z] 37And the Father who
sent me has himself testified concern-
ing me.[a] You have never heard his voice 5:37 [a]Jn 8:18
nor seen his form,[b] 38nor does his word [b]Dt 4:12;
dwell in you,[c] for you do not believe the 1Ti 1:17; Jn 1:18
one he sent.[d] 39You diligently study[a] the 5:38
Scriptures[e] because you think that by [c]1Jn 2:14
them you possess eternal life. These are [d]Jn 3:17
the Scriptures that testify about me,[f] 5:39 [e]Ro 2:17,18
40yet you refuse to come to me to have [f]Lk 24:27,44;
life. Ac 13:27
41"I do not accept praise from men,[g] 5:41
42but I know you. I know that you do not [g]ver 44
have the love of God in your hearts. 43I
have come in my Father's name, and you
do not accept me; but if someone else
comes in his own name, you will accept
him. 44How can you believe if you accept
praise from one another, yet make no effort to obtain the praise that comes 5:44 [h]Ro 2:29
from the only God[b]?[h]
45"But do not think I will accuse you 5:45 [i]Jn 9:28
before the Father. Your accuser is Mo- [j]Ro 2:17
ses,[i] on whom your hopes are set.[j] 46If 5:46
you believed Moses, you would believe [k]Ge 3:15;
me, for he wrote about me.[k] 47But since Lk 24:27,44;
you do not believe what he wrote, how Ac 26:22
are you going to believe what I say?"[l] 5:47 [l]Lk 16:29,31

[a] 39 Or *Study diligently* (the imperative)
[b] 44 Some early manuscripts *the Only One*

Jesus Feeds the Five Thousand

6 Some time after this, Jesus
crossed to the far shore of the Sea
of Galilee (that is, the Sea of Tiberias),
2and a great crowd of people followed
6:2 him because they saw the miraculous
[m]Jn 2:11 signs[m] he had performed on the sick.
3Then Jesus went up on a mountain-
6:3 side[n] and sat down with his disciples.
[n]ver 15 4The Jewish Passover Feast[o] was near.
6:4 5When Jesus looked up and saw a
[o]Jn 2:13; 11:55 great crowd coming toward him, he said
6:5 to Philip,[p] "Where shall we buy bread for
[p]Jn 1:43 these people to eat?" 6He asked this only
to test him, for he already had in mind
what he was going to do.
7Philip answered him, "Eight months'
wages[a] would not buy enough bread for
each one to have a bite!"
6:8 8Another of his disciples, Andrew, Si-
[q]Jn 1:40 mon Peter's brother,[q] spoke up, 9"Here is
a boy with five small barley loaves and
two small fish, but how far will they go 6:9
among so many?"[r] [r]2Ki 4:43
10Jesus said, "Have the people sit
down." There was plenty of grass in that
place, and the men sat down, about five
thousand of them. 11Jesus then took the
loaves, gave thanks,[s] and distributed to 6:11
those who were seated as much as they [s]ver 23; Mt 14:19
wanted. He did the same with the fish.
12When they had all had enough to
eat, he said to his disciples, "Gather the
pieces that are left over. Let nothing be
wasted." 13So they gathered them and
filled twelve baskets with the pieces of
the five barley loaves left over by those
who had eaten.
14After the people saw the miraculous
sign[t] that Jesus did, they began to say, 6:14
"Surely this is the Prophet who is to [t]Jn 2:11

[a] 7 Greek *two hundred denarii*

Jesus in Galilee

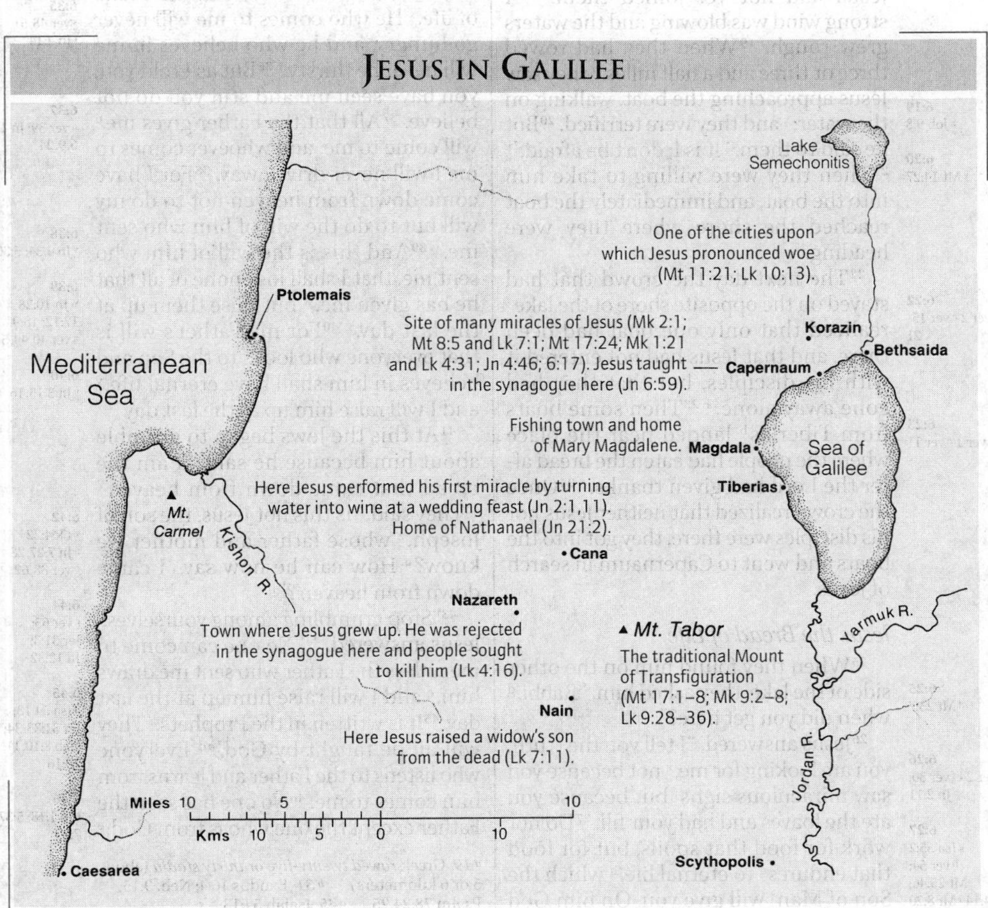

Lake Semechonitis
One of the cities upon which Jesus pronounced woe (Mt 11:21; Lk 10:13).
Ptolemais
Site of many miracles of Jesus (Mk 2:1; Mt 8:5 and Lk 7:1; Mt 17:24; Mk 1:21 and Lk 4:31; Jn 4:46; 6:17). Jesus taught in the synagogue here (Jn 6:59).
Korazin
Bethsaida
Capernaum
Mediterranean Sea
Fishing town and home of Mary Magdalene.
Magdala
Sea of Galilee
Tiberias
Here Jesus performed his first miracle by turning water into wine at a wedding feast (Jn 2:1,11). Home of Nathanael (Jn 21:2).
Mt. Carmel
Kishon R.
Cana
Nazareth
Town where Jesus grew up. He was rejected in the synagogue here and people sought to kill him (Lk 4:16).
Mt. Tabor
The traditional Mount of Transfiguration (Mt 17:1–8; Mk 9:2–8; Lk 9:28–36).
Yarmuk R.
Nain
Here Jesus raised a widow's son from the dead (Lk 7:11).
Jordan R.
Miles 10 5 0 10
Kms 10 5 0 10
Scythopolis
Caesarea

> **THE CHRIST WAS TWOFOLD: MAN IS WHAT WAS SEEN, BUT GOD IS WHAT WAS NOT SEEN. AS MAN, HE TRULY ATE AS WE DO . . . AS GOD, HE FED THE FIVE THOUSAND WITH FIVE LOAVES.**
>
> Cyril of Jerusalem, *Early Church Father*

come into the world."[u] 15 Jesus, knowing that they intended to come and make him king[v] by force, withdrew again to a mountain by himself.[w]

Jesus Walks on the Water

16 When evening came, his disciples went down to the lake, 17 where they got into a boat and set off across the lake for Capernaum. By now it was dark, and Jesus had not yet joined them. 18 A strong wind was blowing and the waters grew rough. 19 When they had rowed three or three and a half miles,[a] they saw Jesus approaching the boat, walking on the water;[x] and they were terrified. 20 But he said to them, "It is I; don't be afraid."[y] 21 Then they were willing to take him into the boat, and immediately the boat reached the shore where they were heading.

22 The next day the crowd that had stayed on the opposite shore of the lake[z] realized that only one boat had been there, and that Jesus had not entered it with his disciples, but that they had gone away alone.[a] 23 Then some boats from Tiberias[b] landed near the place where the people had eaten the bread after the Lord had given thanks.[c] 24 Once the crowd realized that neither Jesus nor his disciples were there, they got into the boats and went to Capernaum in search of Jesus.

Jesus the Bread of Life

25 When they found him on the other side of the lake, they asked him, "Rabbi,[d] when did you get here?"

26 Jesus answered, "I tell you the truth, you are looking for me,[e] not because you saw miraculous signs[f] but because you ate the loaves and had your fill. 27 Do not work for food that spoils, but for food that endures[g] to eternal life,[h] which the Son of Man[i] will give you. On him God the Father has placed his seal[j] of approval."

28 Then they asked him, "What must we do to do the works God requires?"

29 Jesus answered, "The work of God is this: to believe[k] in the one he has sent."[l]

30 So they asked him, "What miraculous sign[m] then will you give that we may see it and believe you?[n] What will you do? 31 Our forefathers ate the manna[o] in the desert; as it is written: 'He gave them bread from heaven to eat.'[b]"[p]

32 Jesus said to them, "I tell you the truth, it is not Moses who has given you the bread from heaven, but it is my Father who gives you the true bread from heaven. 33 For the bread of God is he who comes down from heaven[q] and gives life to the world."

34 "Sir," they said, "from now on give us this bread."[r]

35 Then Jesus declared, "I am the bread of life.[s] He who comes to me will never go hungry, and he who believes in me will never be thirsty.[t] 36 But as I told you, you have seen me and still you do not believe. 37 All that the Father gives me[u] will come to me, and whoever comes to me I will never drive away. 38 For I have come down from heaven not to do my will but to do the will of him who sent me.[v] 39 And this is the will of him who sent me, that I shall lose none of all that he has given me,[w] but raise them up at the last day.[x] 40 For my Father's will is that everyone who looks to the Son and believes in him shall have eternal life,[y] and I will raise him up at the last day."

41 At this the Jews began to grumble about him because he said, "I am the bread that came down from heaven." 42 They said, "Is this not Jesus, the son of Joseph,[z] whose father and mother we know?[a] How can he now say, 'I came down from heaven'?"[b]

43 "Stop grumbling among yourselves," Jesus answered. 44 "No one can come to me unless the Father who sent me draws him,[c] and I will raise him up at the last day. 45 It is written in the Prophets: 'They will all be taught by God.'[c][d] Everyone who listens to the Father and learns from him comes to me. 46 No one has seen the Father except the one who is from God;[e]

6:14 [u] Dt 18:15,18; Mt 11:3; 21:11
6:15 [v] Jn 18:36 [w] Mt 14:23; Mk 6:46
6:19 [x] Job 9:8
6:20 [y] Mt 14:27
6:22 [z] ver 2 [a] ver 15-21
6:23 [b] ver 1 [c] ver 11
6:25 [d] Mt 23:7
6:26 [e] ver 24 [f] ver 30; Jn 2:11
6:27 [g] Isa 55:2 [h] ver 54; Mt 25:46; Jn 4:14 [i] Mt 8:20 [j] Ro 4:11; 1Co 9:2; 2Co 1:22; Eph 1:13; 4:30; 2Ti 2:19; Rev 7:3
6:29 [k] 1Jn 3:23 [l] Jn 3:17
6:30 [m] Jn 2:11 [n] Mt 12:38
6:31 [o] Nu 11:7-9 [p] Ex 16:4,15; Ne 9:15; Ps 78:24; 105:40
6:33 [q] ver 50
6:34 [r] Jn 4:15
6:35 [s] ver 48,51 [t] Jn 4:14
6:37 [u] ver 39; Jn 17:2, 6,9,24
6:38 [v] Jn 4:34; 5:30
6:39 [w] Jn 10:28; 17:12; 18:9 [x] ver 40,44,54
6:40 [y] Jn 3:15,16
6:42 [z] Lk 4:22 [a] Jn 7:27,28 [b] ver 38,62
6:44 [c] ver 65; Jer 31:3; Jn 12:32
6:45 [d] Isa 54:13; Jer 31:33,34; Heb 8:10,11; 10:16
6:46 [e] Jn 1:18; 5:37; 7:29

[a] *19* Greek *rowed twenty-five or thirty stadia* (about 5 or 6 kilometers) [b] *31* Exodus 16:4; Neh. 9:15; Psalm 78:24,25 [c] *45* Isaiah 54:13

DISCOVERY 276

GOD'S LIMITLESS RESOURCES

The miracles of Jesus generated a frenzy of excitement, and crowds followed him everywhere. At one point our Lord stepped into a boat to cross the Sea of Galilee, while the unrelenting crowd walked around the lake to meet him on the other side. Jesus sat with his disciples on a mountainside and watched the approaching throng.

While they were waiting Jesus turned to Philip, asking, "Where shall we buy bread for these people to eat?" (John 6:5). But Philip had no answer. It was Andrew who offered a seemingly far-fetched solution. He had located a boy with five small barley loaves and two small fish (verse 9). Barley loaves were the cheapest available kind of bread, and the fish were most likely pickled and no larger than sardines. The fish were eaten along with the barley loaves to help in swallowing the coarse bread. It was ridiculous to presume that this meager snack could have any impact upon the dilemma of how to appease the appetites of five thousand hungry men, not to mention women and children.

But Jesus had formulated a plan. He instructed the disciples to direct the people to sit down in groups. Then he thanked his Father for the meal and began to separate and distribute the loaves and fish. To the astonishment of everyone, the supply never ran out! Every appetite was sated, and there were 12 basketfuls of leftovers.

The disciples learned some important lessons that day. For one thing, spiritual *responsibility* is never limited by human *ability*. The responsibility which Jesus had passed along to his disciples far outweighed their available resources. Similarly in our own lives, what Jesus asks of us is *always* beyond our wherewithal—After all, our every breath is a gift from God. Accepting our God-given responsibilities without concern about our limited resources and reserves teaches us to depend totally upon him.

In this situation, although there was but little food, God was there. Jesus accepted the boy's generous gift and proceeded to multiply it more than five-thousand-fold. And so today, as we put all that we possess at the Lord's disposal, he will make of it what he desires—and our little (be it time, talents, possessions or prayers) will go further than we would ever have thought possible.

The miracle Jesus performed on the hillside that afternoon formed the backdrop for his subsequent sermon (verses 25–59). After the people had eaten their fill, he reminded them of the necessity of food to sustain physical life. From that point his comparison was clear: "I am the bread of life. He who comes to me will never go hungry, and he who believes in me will never be thirsty" (verse 35). Only Jesus can fill us to the brim with the "soul food" we so desperately crave.

***Self-Discovery:** If you had been Andrew, would you even have bothered to mention the meager lunch that was available, or would you have been embarrassed to bring up one seemingly infinitesimal positive in the face of a problem so overwhelming? Elaborate on your answer.*

GO TO DISCOVERY 277 ON PAGE 1425

only he has seen the Father. 47 I tell you
the truth, he who believes has everlast-
6:48 ing life. 48 I am the bread of life.[f] 49 Your
[f] ver 35,51 forefathers ate the manna in the desert,
6:49 yet they died.[g] 50 But here is the bread
[g] ver 31,58 that comes down from heaven,[h] which a
6:50 man may eat and not die. 51 I am the liv-
[h] ver 33 ing bread that came down from heaven.
If anyone eats of this bread, he will live
6:51 forever. This bread is my flesh, which I
[i] Heb 10:10 will give for the life of the world."[i]
6:52 52 Then the Jews began to argue
[j] Jn 7:43; 9:16; sharply among themselves,[j] "How can
10:19 this man give us his flesh to eat?"
53 Jesus said to them, "I tell you the
6:53 truth, unless you eat the flesh of the Son
[k] Mt 8:20 of Man[k] and drink his blood, you have
no life in you. 54 Whoever eats my flesh
and drinks my blood has eternal life,
6:54 and I will raise him up at the last day.[l]
[l] ver 39 55 For my flesh is real food and my blood
is real drink. 56 Whoever eats my flesh
6:56 [m] Jn 15:4-7; and drinks my blood remains in me, and
1Jn 3:24; 4:15 I in him.[m] 57 Just as the living Father sent

USER-FRIENDLY CHRISTIANITY

"User-friendly" is a much-used phrase today, and it typically refers to instructions, procedures or processes that are uncomplicated and easy to follow. And many people believe that the best way to entice others to attend church services is to adapt the "user-friendly" model to this context, removing any barriers that might cause people to feel uncomfortable, either with the setting or with the message. Jesus never worried about his approach to attracting crowds, however—and sometimes he purposely drove them away! In John 6:60–71 we are told that the people who were following him and listening to his teaching complained that what he was saying was too difficult for them to accept, with the result that they turned away and refused to follow him (verse 66). The people asked for manna, but Jesus had a clear message for them. While they wanted more miracles, he desired to be their Master. People follow Jesus for a variety of different reasons—to ensure an eternal destiny in heaven, for the excitement of espousing a cause, to please family or friends or to obtain blessings, to name only a few. But Jesus asks us to follow him solely because we love him and want to know him more and more intimately. Jesus wants to be Lord of our lives, not simply our champion, our benefactor or our benefits coordinator.

me[n] and I live because of the Father, so 6:57 [n] Jn 3:17
the one who feeds on me will live be-
cause of me. 58 This is the bread that
came down from heaven. Your forefathers ate manna and died, but he who
feeds on this bread will live forever."[o] 6:58 [o] ver 49-51;
59 He said this while teaching in the syn- Jn 3:36
agogue in Capernaum.

Many Disciples Desert Jesus

60 On hearing it, many of his disciples[p] 6:60 [p] ver 66
said, "This is a hard teaching. Who can
accept it?"
61 Aware that his disciples were grumbling about this, Jesus said to them, 6:61
"Does this offend you?[q] 62 What if you [q] Mt 11:6
see the Son of Man ascend to where he 6:62
was before![r] 63 The Spirit gives life;[s] the [r] Mk 16:19;
flesh counts for nothing. The words I Jn 3:13; 17:5
have spoken to you are spirit[a] and they 6:63
are life. 64 Yet there are some of you who [s] 2Co 3:6
do not believe." For Jesus had known[t] 6:64
from the beginning which of them did [t] Jn 2:25
not believe and who would betray him.
65 He went on to say, "This is why I told
you that no one can come to me unless 6:65
the Father has enabled him."[u] [u] ver 37,44
66 From this time many of his disciples[v] turned back and no longer fol- 6:66
lowed him. [v] ver 60
67 "You do not want to leave too, do
you?" Jesus asked the Twelve.[w] 6:67 [w] Mt 10:2
68 Simon Peter answered him,[x] "Lord,
to whom shall we go? You have the 6:68 [x] Mt 16:16
words of eternal life. 69 We believe and
know that you are the Holy One of God."[y] 6:69 [y] Mk 8:29;
70 Then Jesus replied, "Have I not cho- Lk 9:20
sen you,[z] the Twelve? Yet one of you is a 6:70
devil!"[a] 71 (He meant Judas, the son of Si- [z] Jn 15:16,19
mon Iscariot, who, though one of the [a] Jn 13:27
Twelve, was later to betray him.)

Jesus Goes to the Feast of Tabernacles

7 After this, Jesus went around in
Galilee, purposely staying away 7:1
from Judea because the Jews[b] there were [b] Jn 1:19
waiting to take his life.[c] 2 But when the [c] Jn 5:18
Jewish Feast of Tabernacles[d] was near, 7:2
3 Jesus' brothers[e] said to him, "You ought [d] Lev 23:34; Dt 16:16
to leave here and go to Judea, so that
your disciples may see the miracles you 7:3
do. 4 No one who wants to become a [e] Mt 12:46
public figure acts in secret. Since you are
doing these things, show yourself to the
world." 5 For even his own brothers did 7:5
not believe in him.[f] [f] Mk 3:21

[a] *63* Or *Spirit*

7:6 6Therefore Jesus told them, "The right
g Mt 26:18 time[g] for me has not yet come; for you
any time is right. 7The world cannot
7:7 h Jn 15:18,19 hate you, but it hates me[h] because I tes-
i Jn 3:19,20 tify that what it does is evil.[i] 8You go to
7:8 the Feast. I am not yet[a] going up to this
j ver 6 Feast, because for me the right time[j] has
not yet come." 9Having said this, he
stayed in Galilee.
10However, after his brothers had left
for the Feast, he went also, not publicly,
7:11 but in secret. 11Now at the Feast the Jews
k Jn 11:56 were watching for him[k] and asking,
"Where is that man?"
12Among the crowds there was widespread whispering about him. Some
said, "He is a good man."
7:12 Others replied, "No, he deceives the
l ver 40,43 people."[l] 13But no one would say any-
7:13 m Jn 9:22; 12:42; thing publicly about him for fear of the
19:38 Jews.[m]

Jesus Teaches at the Feast

7:14 14Not until halfway through the Feast
n ver 28; Mt 26:55 did Jesus go up to the temple courts and
begin to teach.[n] 15The Jews[o] were
7:15 o Jn 1:19 amazed and asked, "How did this man
p Ac 26:24 get such learning[p] without having stud-
q Mt 13:54 ied?"[q]
7:16 16Jesus answered, "My teaching is not
r Jn 3:11; 14:24 my own. It comes from him who sent
7:17 s Ps 25:14; me.[r] 17If anyone chooses to do God's will,
Jn 8:43 he will find out[s] whether my teaching

JESUS AND YOU

PUBLIC OPINION

Jesus' brothers urged him to go to Jerusalem, Israel's political and religious center. "Show yourself to the world," they insisted (John 7:4). Jesus knew the public's mode of thought, however, and he understood the fickleness of the human heart. The crowds that came to Jerusalem were curious, but many were also skeptical. Some believed that Jesus was the Messiah, while others concluded that he was demon-possessed. Even our Lord's own brothers at that stage refused to believe that he was the Son of God (verse 5), assuming that their brother was attempting to launch a career as a public figure. Although Jesus' brothers were close to him, they failed utterly at this point in time to comprehend the purpose of his life. Happily, at least some of Jesus' brothers did later believe in him and are mentioned as members of the early church (Acts 1:14; see also Matthew 13:55; Jude 1).

comes from God or whether I speak on
my own. 18He who speaks on his own 7:18
does so to gain honor for himself,[t] but he t Jn 5:41; 8:50,54
who works for the honor of the one who
sent him is a man of truth; there is nothing false about him. 19Has not Moses giv- 7:19
en you the law?[u] Yet not one of you keeps u Jn 1:17 v ver 1;
the law. Why are you trying to kill me?"[v] Mt 12:14
20"You are demon-possessed,"[w] the 7:20
crowd answered. "Who is trying to kill w Jn 8:48; 10:20
you?"
21Jesus said to them, "I did one miracle, and you are all astonished. 22Yet, because Moses gave you circumcision[x] 7:22 x Lev 12:3
(though actually it did not come from y Ge 17:10-14
Moses, but from the patriarchs),[y] you
circumcise a child on the Sabbath.
23Now if a child can be circumcised on
the Sabbath so that the law of Moses
may not be broken, why are you angry
with me for healing the whole man on 7:24
the Sabbath? 24Stop judging by mere ap- z Isa 11:3,4;
pearances, and make a right judgment."[z] Jn 8:15

THE REAL ISSUE ... IS THIS: IS JESUS TO BE WORSHIPPED OR ONLY ADMIRED?

John Stott, *Pastor, London, England*

Is Jesus the Christ?

25At that point some of the people of
Jerusalem began to ask, "Isn't this the
man they are trying to kill? 26Here he is,
speaking publicly, and they are not say-
ing a word to him. Have the authorities[a] 7:26 a ver 48
really concluded that he is the Christ[b]? 7:27
27But we know where this man is from;[b] b Mt 13:55;
when the Christ comes, no one will Lk 4:22
know where he is from."
28Then Jesus, still teaching in the temple courts,[c] cried out, "Yes, you know 7:28
me, and you know where I am from.[d] I c ver 14 d Jn 8:14
am not here on my own, but he who sent e Jn 8:26,42
me is true.[e] You do not know him, 29but
I know him[f] because I am from him and 7:29 f Mt 11:27
he sent me."
30At this they tried to seize him, but
no one laid a hand on him,[g] because his 7:30 g ver 32,44;
time had not yet come. 31Still, many in Jn 10:39
the crowd put their faith in him.[h] They 7:31
said, "When the Christ comes, will he do h Jn 8:30
more miraculous signs[i] than this man?" i Jn 2:11

a 8 Some early manuscripts do not have *yet*.
b 26 Or *Messiah*; also in verses 27, 31, 41 and 42

32The Pharisees heard the crowd
whispering such things about him. Then
the chief priests and the Pharisees sent
temple guards to arrest him.
33Jesus said, "I am with you for only a
7:33 [j]Jn 13:33; 16:16 short time,[j] and then I go to the one who
[k]Jn 16:5,10,17, 28 sent me.[k] 34You will look for me, but you
will not find me; and where I am, you
7:34 [l]Jn 8:21; 13:33 cannot come."[l]
35The Jews said to one another,
"Where does this man intend to go that
we cannot find him? Will he go where
7:35 [m]Jas 1:1 our people live scattered[m] among the
[n]Jn 12:20; 1Pe 1:1 Greeks,[n] and teach the Greeks? 36What
did he mean when he said, 'You will look
for me, but you will not find me,' and
'Where I am, you cannot come'?"
7:37 [o]Lev 23:36 37On the last and greatest day of the
[p]Isa 55:1; Feast,[o] Jesus stood and said in a loud
Rev 22:17 voice, "If anyone is thirsty, let him come
7:38 to me and drink.[p] 38Whoever believes in
[q]Isa 58:11 me, as[a] the Scripture has said,[q] streams
[r]Jn 4:10 [s]Jn 4:14 of living water[r] will flow from within
him."[s] 39By this he meant the Spirit,[t]
7:39 [t]Joel 2:28; whom those who believed in him were
Ac 2:17,33 [u]Jn 20:22 later to receive.[u] Up to that time the
[v]Jn 12:23; 13:31, Spirit had not been given, since Jesus
32 had not yet been glorified.[v]
7:40 40On hearing his words, some of the
[w]Mt 21:11; Jn 1:21 people said, "Surely this man is the
Prophet."[w]
7:41 41Others said, "He is the Christ."
[x]ver 52; Jn 1:46 Still others asked, "How can the
7:42 Christ come from Galilee?[x] 42Does not
[y]Mt 1:1 [z]Mic 5:2; the Scripture say that the Christ will
Mt 2:5,6; Lk 2:4 come from David's family[b][y] and from
Bethlehem,[z] the town where David
7:43 [a]Jn 9:16; 10:19 lived?" 43Thus the people were divided[a]
because of Jesus. 44Some wanted to seize
7:44 [b]ver 30 him, but no one laid a hand on him.[b]

Unbelief of the Jewish Leaders

45Finally the temple guards went back
to the chief priests and Pharisees, who
asked them, "Why didn't you bring
him in?"
46"No one ever spoke the way this
7:46 [c]Mt 7:28 man does,"[c] the guards declared.
7:47 47"You mean he has deceived you
[d]ver 12 also?"[d] the Pharisees retorted. 48"Has
any of the rulers or of the Pharisees be-
7:48 [e]Jn 12:42 lieved in him?[e] 49No! But this mob that
knows nothing of the law—there is a
curse on them."
7:50 50Nicodemus,[f] who had gone to Jesus
[f]Jn 3:1; 19:39 earlier and who was one of their own
number, asked, 51"Does our law con-
demn anyone without first hearing him
to find out what he is doing?"
52They replied, "Are you from Galilee,
too? Look into it, and you will find that a 7:52
prophet[c] does not come out of Galilee."[g] [g]ver 41

[The earliest manuscripts and many other ancient witnesses do not have John 7:53–8:11.]

53Then each went to his own home.
8 But Jesus went to the Mount of
Olives.[h] 2At dawn he appeared 8:1 [h]Mt 21:1
again in the temple courts, where all the
people gathered around him, and he sat 8:2
down to teach them.[i] 3The teachers of [i]ver 20;
the law and the Pharisees brought in a Mt 26:55
woman caught in adultery. They made
her stand before the group 4and said to
Jesus, "Teacher, this woman was caught
in the act of adultery. 5In the Law Moses 8:5
commanded us to stone such women.[j] [j]Lev 20:10;
Now what do you say?" 6They were using Dt 22:22
this question as a trap,[k] in order to have 8:6
a basis for accusing him.[l] [k]Mt 22:15,18 [l]Mt 12:10
But Jesus bent down and started to
write on the ground with his finger.
7When they kept on questioning him, he
straightened up and said to them, "If
any one of you is without sin, let him be 8:7
the first to throw a stone[m] at her."[n] [m]Dt 17:7
8Again he stooped down and wrote on [n]Ro 2:1,22
the ground.
9At this, those who heard began to go
away one at a time, the older ones first,
until only Jesus was left, with the
woman still standing there. 10Jesus
straightened up and asked her, "Woman, where are they? Has no one condemned you?"
11"No one, sir," she said. 8:11
"Then neither do I condemn you,"[o] [o]Jn 3:17
Jesus declared. "Go now and leave your [p]Jn 5:14
life of sin."[p]

The Validity of Jesus' Testimony

12When Jesus spoke again to the peo- 8:12
ple, he said, "I am[q] the light of the [q]Jn 6:35 [r]Jn 1:4;
world.[r] Whoever follows me will never 12:35 [s]Pr 4:18;
walk in darkness, but will have the light Mt 5:14
of life."[s]

[a] 37,38 Or / *If anyone is thirsty, let him come to me. / And let him drink,* 38*who believes in me. / As*
[b] 42 Greek *seed* [c] 52 Two early manuscripts *the Prophet*

DISCOVERY 277

STONES AND GLASS HOUSES

In John 8 we find words of Jesus frequently quoted today by those who advocate for civility in private and public discourse: "If any one of you is without sin, let him be the first to throw a stone" (verse 7). A contemporary saying is similar: "People in glass houses shouldn't throw stones." We are all guilty of sinning, and yet we're all too often hasty to judge others—often for the same misdeeds of which we ourselves are guilty! One day as Jesus was teaching in the temple courts, the religious leaders dragged in front of him a woman who had been caught in adultery. There she stood—hair disheveled, eyes glazed with terror—a scorned object in the midst of a group of highly scrupulous but condescending men.

The Pharisees were indignant and confronted Jesus with a recitation of God's law about adultery: "Moses commanded us to stone such women. Now what do *you* say?" (verse 5, italics added). The problem was that they were only quoting part of God's law; the full provision required that *both* the man and the woman be put to death (Deuteronomy 22:22). These smug hypocrites were not really interested in the woman, in what she had done or even in the law of God. But they were very intent on challenging Jesus and trying to back him up against a wall (John 8:6). If he were to agree that the woman should be stoned, he would be in violation of Roman law, because only the Romans had the authority to carry out the death penalty. If, on the other hand, Jesus were to counsel them to look the other way and allow the woman to go free, he would be in direct violation of God's law. These teachers of the law and Pharisees had tried many times in the past to discredit Jesus, but this time they thought they had him in a noose from which there could be no escape.

But Jesus ignored their question. In fact, he simply crouched down and wrote some words in the dirt. None of the Gospel writers has recorded precisely what our Lord wrote. Whatever it was, however, the Pharisees did not comprehend his point and continued pressing Jesus for an answer to their trick question. Finally, Jesus spoke the well-remembered words recorded for us in verse 7 (above). Our Lord both upheld God's law and forced the Pharisees to confront their own sin, rather than pointing a finger of condemnation at the woman.

One by one, the accusers slipped away. They had nothing more to say, and no one wanted to be the first to pick up a rock and throw it.

When we have more in common with the Pharisees than we do with Jesus, we become prone to begin focusing on another's faults while ignoring our own. But as we allow Jesus to work in and through our lives, we become gripped by his love so tenderly offered to us and to others. And it becomes our ardent desire to introduce people to the Savior who has forgiven *all* of our sins.

Self-Discovery: *Recall a time when you were caught in a "Catch 22" situation—a dilemma of your own making from which you could see no way of escaping a winner. What were Jesus' words to you in your sin snare?*

GO TO DISCOVERY 278 ON PAGE 1429

13 The Pharisees challenged him,
8:13 “Here you are, appearing as your own
[t]Jn 5:31 witness; your testimony is not valid.”[t]
14 Jesus answered, “Even if I testify on
my own behalf, my testimony is valid,
8:14 for I know where I came from and where
[u]Jn 13:3; 16:28 [v]Jn 7:28; 9:29 I am going.[u] But you have no idea where
I come from[v] or where I am going. 15 You
8:15 judge by human standards;[w] I pass judg-
[w]Jn 7:24 [x]Jn 3:17 ment on no one.[x] 16 But if I do judge, my
decisions are right, because I am not
8:16 alone. I stand with the Father, who sent
[y]Jn 5:30 me.[y] 17 In your own Law it is written that
the testimony of two men is valid.[z] 18 I
8:17 [z]Dt 17:6; am one who testifies for myself; my oth-
Mt 18:16 er witness is the Father, who sent me.”[a]
8:18 19 Then they asked him, “Where is
[a]Jn 5:37 your father?”
8:19 “You do not know me or my Father,”[b]
[b]Jn 16:3 Jesus replied. “If you knew me, you
[c]Jn 14:7; 1Jn 2:23 would know my Father also.”[c] 20 He
spoke these words while teaching[d] in
8:20 [d]Mt 26:55 the temple area near the place where the
[e]Mk 12:41 [f]Mt 26:18; offerings were put.[e] Yet no one seized
Jn 7:30 him, because his time had not yet
come.[f]
21 Once more Jesus said to them, “I am
going away, and you will look for me,
8:21 [g]Eze 3:18 and you will die[g] in your sin. Where I go,
[h]Jn 7:34; 13:33 you cannot come.”[h]
22 This made the Jews ask, “Will he kill
himself? Is that why he says, ‘Where I go,
you cannot come’?”
23 But he continued, “You are from be-
8:23 low; I am from above. You are of this
[i]Jn 3:31; 17:14 world; I am not of this world.[i] 24 I told
you that you would die in your sins; if
8:24 you do not believe that I am ⌞the one I
[j]Jn 4:26; 13:19 claim to be⌟,[a][j] you will indeed die in your
sins.”
25 “Who are you?” they asked.
“Just what I have been claiming all
along,” Jesus replied. 26 “I have much to
say in judgment of you. But he who sent
8:26 [k]Jn 7:28 me is reliable,[k] and what I have heard
[l]Jn 3:32; 15:15 from him I tell the world.”[l]
27 They did not understand that he
was telling them about his Father. 28 So
Jesus said, “When you have lifted up the
8:28 [m]Jn 3:14; 5:19; Son of Man,[m] then you will know that I
12:32 am ⌞the one I claim to be⌟ and that I do
8:29 nothing on my own but speak just what
[n]ver 16; the Father has taught me. 29 The one who
Jn 16:32 [o]Jn 4:34; 5:30; sent me is with me; he has not left me
6:38 alone,[n] for I always do what pleases
8:30 him.”[o] 30 Even as he spoke, many put
[p]Jn 7:31 their faith in him.[p]

The Children of Abraham

31 To the Jews who had believed him,
Jesus said, “If you hold to my teaching,[q] 8:31
you are really my disciples. 32 Then you [q]Jn 15:7; 2Jn 9
will know the truth, and the truth will
set you free.”[r] 8:32 [r]Ro 8:2; Jas 2:12
33 They answered him, “We are Abra- 8:33
ham's descendants[b][s] and have never [s]ver 37,39;
been slaves of anyone. How can you say Mt 3:9
that we shall be set free?”
34 Jesus replied, “I tell you the truth,
everyone who sins is a slave to sin.[t] 8:34 [t]Ro 6:16;
35 Now a slave has no permanent place in 2Pe 2:19
the family, but a son belongs to it forev- 8:35
er.[u] 36 So if the Son sets you free, you will [u]Gal 4:30
be free indeed. 37 I know you are Abra-
ham's descendants. Yet you are ready to
kill me,[v] because you have no room for 8:37 [v]ver 39,40
my word. 38 I am telling you what I have
seen in the Father's presence,[w] and you 8:38 [w]Jn 5:19,30;
do what you have heard from your fa- 14:10,24
ther.[c]”
39 “Abraham is our father,” they answered.
“If you were Abraham's children,”[x] 8:39 [x]ver 37; Ro 9:7;
said Jesus, “then you would[d] do the Gal 3:7
things Abraham did. 40 As it is, you are
determined to kill me, a man who has
told you the truth that I heard from 8:40
God.[y] Abraham did not do such things. [y]ver 26
41 You are doing the things your own fa- 8:41
ther does.”[z] [z]ver 38,44
“We are not illegitimate children,” [a]Isa 63:16; 64:8
they protested. “The only Father we
have is God himself.”[a]

The Children of the Devil

42 Jesus said to them, “If God were 8:42
your Father, you would love me,[b] for I [b]1Jn 5:1
came from God[c] and now am here. I [c]Jn 16:27; 17:8 [d]Jn 7:28
have not come on my own;[d] but he sent [e]Jn 3:17
me.[e] 43 Why is my language not clear to
you? Because you are unable to hear
what I say. 44 You belong to your father,
the devil,[f] and you want to carry out 8:44 [f]1Jn 3:8 [g]ver 38,
your father's desire.[g] He was a murderer 41 [h]Ge 3:4
from the beginning, not holding to the
truth, for there is no truth in him. When
he lies, he speaks his native language, for
he is a liar and the father of lies.[h] 45 Yet 8:45
because I tell the truth,[i] you do not be- [i]Jn 18:37
lieve me! 46 Can any of you prove me
guilty of sin? If I am telling the truth,

[a] *24* Or *I am he*; also in verse 28 [b] *33* Greek *seed*; also in verse 37 [c] *38* Or *presence. Therefore do what you have heard from the Father.* [d] *39* Some early manuscripts *“If you are Abraham's children,” said Jesus, “then*

> **CRITICS MUST RECKON . . . WITH THE WELL-NIGH IRRESISTIBLE IMPRESSION THAT THE ETERNAL GOD IS BEST SEEN IN [JESUS'] PERSONALITY AND LIFE.**
>
> 
>
> Carl F. H. Henry, *American Theologian*

why don't you believe me? 47He who be-
8:47 jJn 18:37; longs to God hears what God says.[j] The
1Jn 4:6 reason you do not hear is that you do
not belong to God."

The Claims of Jesus About Himself

48The Jews answered him, "Aren't we
8:48 kMt 10:5 right in saying that you are a Samaritan[k]
lver 52; Jn 7:20 and demon-possessed?"[l]
49"I am not possessed by a demon,"
said Jesus, "but I honor my Father and
8:50 you dishonor me. 50I am not seeking glo-
mver 54; Jn 5:41 ry for myself;[m] but there is one who
seeks it, and he is the judge. 51I tell you
8:51 the truth, if anyone keeps my word, he
nJn 11:26 will never see death."[n]
52At this the Jews exclaimed, "Now we
know that you are demon-possessed!
Abraham died and so did the prophets,
yet you say that if anyone keeps your
word, he will never taste death. 53Are
8:53 you greater than our father Abraham?[o]
oJn 4:12 He died, and so did the prophets. Who
do you think you are?"
8:54 54Jesus replied, "If I glorify myself,[p] my
pver 50 qJn 16:14; glory means nothing. My Father, whom
17:1,5 you claim as your God, is the one who
glorifies me.[q] 55Though you do not
8:55 know him,[r] I know him.[s] If I said I did
rver 19 sJn 7:28, not, I would be a liar like you, but I do
29 tJn 15:10 know him and keep his word.[t] 56Your fa-
8:56 uver 37,39 ther Abraham[u] rejoiced at the thought
vMt 13:17; of seeing my day; he saw it[v] and was
Heb 11:13 glad."
57"You are not yet fifty years old," the
Jews said to him, "and you have seen
Abraham!"
8:58 58"I tell you the truth," Jesus answered,
wJn 1:2; 17:5,24 xEx 3:14 "before Abraham was born,[w] I am!"[x]
8:59 59At this, they picked up stones to stone
yLev 24:16; him,[y] but Jesus hid himself,[z] slipping
Jn 10:31; 11:8 zJn 12:36 away from the temple grounds.

Jesus Heals a Man Born Blind

9:2 **9** As he went along, he saw a man
aMt 23:7 bver 34; blind from birth. 2His disciples
Lk 13:2; Ac 28:4 asked him, "Rabbi,[a] who sinned,[b] this
man[c] or his parents,[d] that he was born 9:2 cEze 18:20
blind?" dEx 20:5;
3"Neither this man nor his parents Job 21:19
sinned," said Jesus, "but this happened
so that the work of God might be dis-
played in his life.[e] 4As long as it is day,[f] 9:3 eJn 11:4
we must do the work of him who sent
me. Night is coming, when no one can 9:4
work. 5While I am in the world, I am the fJn 11:9; 12:35
light of the world."[g] 9:5 gJn 1:4; 8:12;
6Having said this, he spit[h] on the 12:46
ground, made some mud with the saliva,
and put it on the man's eyes. 7"Go," he 9:6 hMk 7:33; 8:23
told him, "wash in the Pool of Siloam"[i]
(this word means Sent). So the man went 9:7 iver 11;
and washed, and came home seeing.[j] 2Ki 5:10; Lk 13:4
8His neighbors and those who had jIsa 35:5;
formerly seen him begging asked, "Isn't Jn 11:37
this the same man who used to sit and 9:8
beg?"[k] 9Some claimed that he was. kAc 3:2,10
Others said, "No, he only looks like
him."
But he himself insisted, "I am the
man."
10"How then were your eyes opened?"
they demanded.
11He replied, "The man they call Jesus
made some mud and put it on my eyes.
He told me to go to Siloam and wash. So 9:11
I went and washed, and then I could see."[l] lver 7
12"Where is this man?" they asked
him.
"I don't know," he said.

The Pharisees Investigate the Healing

13They brought to the Pharisees the
man who had been blind. 14Now the day
on which Jesus had made the mud and
opened the man's eyes was a Sabbath.[m] 9:14
15Therefore the Pharisees also asked mJn 5:9
him how he had received his sight.[n] "He 9:15
put mud on my eyes," the man replied, nver 10
"and I washed, and now I see."
16Some of the Pharisees said, "This
man is not from God, for he does not
keep the Sabbath."[o] 9:16
But others asked, "How can a sinner oMt 12:2
do such miraculous signs?" So they were pJn 6:52; 7:43; 10:19
divided.[p]
17Finally they turned again to the
blind man, "What have you to say about
him? It was your eyes he opened."
The man replied, "He is a prophet."[q] 9:17 qMt 21:11
18The Jews[r] still did not believe that
he had been blind and had received his 9:18 rJn 1:19
sight until they sent for the man's parents. 19"Is this your son?" they asked. "Is

> **A STUDY OF THE LIFE OF JESUS THAT EXCLUDES THE MIRACULOUS IS DESTINED FROM THE START TO PRODUCE A JESUS WHO IS AN ABERRATION.**
>
> Robert Stein, *American Scholar*

this the one you say was born blind?
How is it that now he can see?"
20"We know he is our son," the parents
answered, "and we know he was born
blind. 21But how he can see now, or who
opened his eyes, we don't know. Ask
him. He is of age; he will speak for him-
9:22 self." 22His parents said this because they
[s]Jn 7:13 [t]ver 34; were afraid of the Jews,[s] for already the
Lk 6:22 Jews had decided that anyone who ac-
[u]Jn 12:42; 16:2 knowledged that Jesus was the Christ[a]
would be put out[t] of the synagogue.[u]
23That was why his parents said, "He is
9:23 [v]ver 21 of age; ask him."[v]
24A second time they summoned the
man who had been blind. "Give glory to
9:24 [w]Jos 7:19 God,[b]"[w] they said. "We know this man is
[x]ver 16 a sinner."[x]
25He replied, "Whether he is a sinner
or not, I don't know. One thing I do
know. I was blind but now I see!"
26Then they asked him, "What did he
do to you? How did he open your eyes?"
27He answered, "I have told you al-
9:27 [y]ver 15 ready[y] and you did not listen. Why do
you want to hear it again? Do you want
to become his disciples, too?"
28Then they hurled insults at him and
said, "You are this fellow's disciple! We
9:28 [z]Jn 5:45 are disciples of Moses![z] 29We know that
God spoke to Moses, but as for this fel-
low, we don't even know where he comes
9:29 [a]Jn 8:14 from."[a]
30The man answered, "Now that is remarkable! You don't know where he
9:31 [b]Ge 18:23-32; comes from, yet he opened my eyes.
Ps 34:15,16; 31We know that God does not listen to
66:18; 145:19, 20; Pr 15:29; sinners. He listens to the godly man who
Isa 1:15; 59:1,2; Jn 15:7; does his will.[b] 32Nobody has ever heard
Jas 5:16-18; 1Jn 5:14,15 of opening the eyes of a man born blind.
33If this man were not from God,[c] he
9:33 [c]ver 16; Jn 3:2 could do nothing."
34To this they replied, "You were
9:34 [d]ver 2 [e]ver 22, steeped in sin at birth;[d] how dare you
35; Isa 66:5 lecture us!" And they threw him out.[e]

Spiritual Blindness

35Jesus heard that they had thrown
him out, and when he found him, he
said, "Do you believe in the Son of Man?"
36"Who is he, sir?" the man asked.
"Tell me so that I may believe in him."[f] 9:36 [f]Ro 10:14
37Jesus said, "You have now seen him;
in fact, he is the one speaking with you."[g] 9:37 [g]Jn 4:26
38Then the man said, "Lord, I believe,"
and he worshiped him.[h] 9:38 [h]Mt 28:9
39Jesus said, "For judgment[i] I have
come into this world,[j] so that the blind 9:39 [i]Jn 5:22 [j]Jn 3:19
will see[k] and those who see will become [k]Lk 4:18
blind."[l] [l]Mt 13:13
40Some Pharisees who were with him
heard him say this and asked, "What?
Are we blind too?"[m] 9:40 [m]Ro 2:19
41Jesus said, "If you were blind, you
would not be guilty of sin; but now that
you claim you can see, your guilt remains.[n] 9:41 [n]Jn 15:22,24

The Shepherd and His Flock

10 "I tell you the truth, the man
who does not enter the sheep
pen by the gate, but climbs in by some
other way, is a thief and a robber. 2The
man who enters by the gate is the shep-
herd of his sheep.[o] 3The watchman 10:2 [o]ver 11,14
opens the gate for him, and the sheep
listen to his voice.[p] He calls his own 10:3 [p]ver 4,5,14,16,
sheep by name and leads them out. 27
4When he has brought out all his own,
he goes on ahead of them, and his sheep
follow him because they know his voice.
5But they will never follow a stranger; in
fact, they will run away from him because they do not recognize a stranger's
voice." 6Jesus used this figure of speech,[q] 10:6
but they did not understand what he [q]Jn 16:25
was telling them.
7Therefore Jesus said again, "I tell you
the truth, I am the gate for the sheep. 10:8
8All who ever came before me[r] were [r]Jer 23:1,2
thieves and robbers, but the sheep did
not listen to them. 9I am the gate; whoever enters through me will be saved.[c]
He will come in and go out, and find
pasture. 10The thief comes only to steal
and kill and destroy; I have come that 10:11
they may have life, and have it to the full. [s]ver 14;
11"I am the good shepherd.[s] The good Isa 40:11;
shepherd lays down his life for the Eze 34:11-16,
23; Heb 13:20;
1Pe 5:4;
sheep.[t] 12The hired hand is not the shep- Rev 7:17 [t]Jn 15:13;
herd who owns the sheep. So when he 1Jn 3:16

[a] 22 Or *Messiah* [b] 24 A solemn charge to tell the truth (see Joshua 7:19) [c] 9 Or *kept safe*

Our Good Shepherd

A shepherd is solely responsible for the well-being of the flock. When David was a young shepherd, he fought both a lion and a bear in order to protect the sheep entrusted to his care (1 Samuel 17:34–36). If a sheep were killed, the shepherd was required to produce evidence that the incident had not been his fault (Exodus 22:13). Any conscientious shepherd would willingly risk danger for the sake of the defenseless animals (Genesis 3:39; 1 Samuel 17:34–37). In an even greater way, Jesus is our Good Shepherd who was willing to make the ultimate sacrifice and put his own life on the line for us (John 10:11). There are at least three points to consider about our Lord's sacrifice:

1. Jesus' sacrifice was *voluntary*. Jesus was not a hapless victim of the whims of circumstances, and he stated unequivocally: "No one takes [my life] from me, but I lay it down of my own accord" (verse 18). If we look at our Lord's death from a straightforward and purely historical perspective, Jesus died because Judas had betrayed him, because Pilate was a coward, because the religious leaders hated him. If we consider the crucifixion from a theological standpoint, the Son of God died for the sin of the whole world (Isaiah 53:5–6; John 1:29). But if we attempt to ponder this event vicariously from Jesus' human perspective, we cannot get around the reality that his was the supreme act of love, because he voluntarily gave up his own life for ours (Galatians 2:20; Ephesians 5:2,25).

2. Jesus' sacrifice was *total*. Our Savior set aside his glory as God the Son to enter our world as a vulnerable baby (Philippians 2:1–11). He experienced being forsaken by God the Father before he succumbed to death (Matthew 27:46). He died physically, but he also died spiritually, bearing the Father's wrath and accepting his ultimate punishment for our sin—separation from God the Father (Romans 5:6–11).

3. His sacrifice was *beneficial*. Jesus Christ died in our stead, and theologians refer to this as *substitution* (1 Peter 3:18). But he also died *for our benefit*, for which scholars use the term *vicarious atonement*. Jesus died for our sins, and God blesses us by assigning to us the results of that sacrifice (2 Corinthians 5:21; 1 Peter 2:22).

When we face difficulties in this life, we need to remember that Jesus is our loving Shepherd. He empathizes with what we are going through, because he has walked in our shoes. He knows how we feel. And he demonstrated beyond doubt that he cares, because he voluntarily laid down his own life to save us from eternal death.

Self-Discovery: *Jesus is your Good Shepherd. Name the feelings that are stirred up in you as you focus on this image.*

GO TO DISCOVERY 279 ON PAGE 1432

10:12 sees the wolf coming, he abandons the
u Zec 11:16,17 sheep and runs away.[u] Then the wolf attacks the flock and scatters it. 13 The
man runs away because he is a hired
hand and cares nothing for the sheep.
10:14 v ver 11 w ver 27 14 "I am the good shepherd;[v] I know
my sheep[w] and my sheep know me—
10:15 15 just as the Father knows me and I
x Mt 11:27 know the Father[x]—and I lay down my
10:16 life for the sheep. 16 I have other sheep[y]
y Isa 56:8 that are not of this sheep pen. I must
z Jn 11:52; Eph 2:11-19 bring them also. They too will listen to
a Eze 37:24; my voice, and there shall be one flock[z]
1Pe 2:25 and one shepherd.[a] 17 The reason my Fa-
10:17 ther loves me is that I lay down my
b ver 11,15,18 life[b]—only to take it up again. 18 No one
10:18 takes it from me, but I lay it down of my
c Mt 26:53 own accord.[c] I have authority to lay it
d Jn 15:10; down and authority to take it up again.
Php 2:8; Heb 5:8 This command I received from my Father."[d]
10:19 19 At these words the Jews were again
e Jn 7:43; 9:16 divided.[e] 20 Many of them said, "He is de-
10:20 mon-possessed[f] and raving mad.[g] Why
f Jn 7:20 g Mk 3:21 listen to him?"
10:21 21 But others said, "These are not the
h Mt 4:24 sayings of a man possessed by a de-
i Ex 4:11; mon.[h] Can a demon open the eyes of the
Jn 9:32,33 blind?"[i]

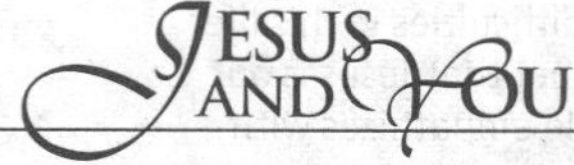

WHO ARE YOU?

People regularly confronted Jesus with one rather blunt and straightforward question: "Who are you?" The question permeates the Gospels and in one form or another still dominates many discussions about Jesus today. Was he a prophet? A radical rabble-rouser? A failed revolutionary? A wise spiritual leader? Or was he actually the Son of God? At one point the people insisted that Jesus tell them plainly whether or not he claimed to be the Messiah (John 10:24). Jesus replied that the miracles he did in the name of God the Father spoke for him because "I and the Father are one" (verse 30). The response was immediate—the crowd wanted to stone him for blasphemy because of his seemingly audacious claim (verse 31). But sooner or later each of us needs to ask the same question: Who is this man named Jesus? We can look at his life, listen to his words and examine his claims. The ultimate conclusion for each of us is a matter of the heart, but the Bible clearly teaches that Jesus is love in action, wisdom personified—the Son of God, our Savior.

The Unbelief of the Jews

22 Then came the Feast of Dedication[a]
at Jerusalem. It was winter, 23 and Jesus 10:23
was in the temple area walking in Solo- j Ac 3:11; 5:12
mon's Colonnade.[j] 24 The Jews[k] gathered
around him, saying, "How long will you 10:24 k Jn 1:19
keep us in suspense? If you are the l Jn 16:25,29
Christ,[b] tell us plainly."[l]
25 Jesus answered, "I did tell you,[m] but 10:25 m Jn 8:58
you do not believe. The miracles I do in n Jn 5:36
my Father's name speak for me,[n] 26 but 10:26
you do not believe because you are not o Jn 8:47
my sheep.[o] 27 My sheep listen to my voice; 10:27
I know them,[p] and they follow me.[q] 28 I p ver 14 q ver 4
give them eternal life, and they shall nev- 10:28
er perish; no one can snatch them out of r Jn 6:39
my hand.[r] 29 My Father, who has given 10:29
them to me,[s] is greater than all[c];[t] no one s Jn 17:2,6,24 t Jn 14:28
can snatch them out of my Father's hand.
30 I and the Father are one."[u] 10:30 u Jn 17:21-23

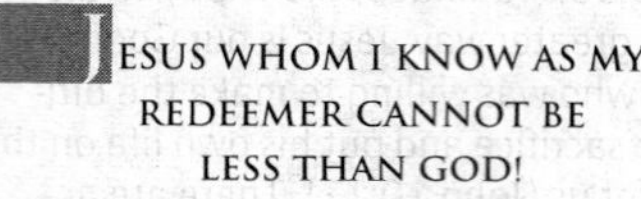

JESUS WHOM I KNOW AS MY REDEEMER CANNOT BE LESS THAN GOD!

Athanasius, *Early Church Father*

31 Again the Jews picked up stones to
stone him,[v] 32 but Jesus said to them, "I 10:31 v Jn 8:59
have shown you many great miracles
from the Father. For which of these do
you stone me?"
33 "We are not stoning you for any of
these," replied the Jews, "but for blasphemy, because you, a mere man, claim 10:33
to be God."[w] w Lev 24:16; Jn 5:18
34 Jesus answered them, "Is it not writ-
ten in your Law,[x] 'I have said you are 10:34 x Jn 8:17;
gods'[d]?[y] 35 If he called them 'gods,' to Ro 3:19 y Ps 82:6
whom the word of God came—and the
Scripture cannot be broken— 36 what
about the one whom the Father set 10:36
apart[z] as his very own[a] and sent into the z Jer 1:5 a Jn 6:69
world?[b] Why then do you accuse me of b Jn 3:17
blasphemy because I said, 'I am God's c Jn 5:17,18
Son'?[c] 37 Do not believe me unless I do 10:37 d ver 25;
what my Father does.[d] 38 But if I do it, Jn 15:24
even though you do not believe me, be-
lieve the miracles, that you may know 10:38 e Jn 14:10,11,20;
and understand that the Father is in me, 17:21
and I in the Father."[e] 39 Again they tried to 10:39
seize him,[f] but he escaped their grasp.[g] f Jn 7:30
40 Then Jesus went back across the Jor- g Lk 4:30; Jn 8:59

[a] 22 That is, Hanukkah [b] 24 Or *Messiah*
[c] 29 Many early manuscripts *What my Father has given me is greater than all* [d] 34 Psalm 82:6

10:40 h Jn 1:28 dan[h] to the place where John had been
baptizing in the early days. Here he
10:41 i Jn 2:11; 3:30 j Jn 1:26,27,30,34 stayed 41and many people came to him.
They said, "Though John never per-
formed a miraculous sign,[i] all that John
10:42 k Jn 7:31 said about this man was true."[j] 42And in
that place many believed in Jesus.[k]

The Death of Lazarus

11:1 l Mt 21:17 m Lk 10:38 11 Now a man named Lazarus
was sick. He was from Bethany,[l]
the village of Mary and her sister Martha.[m] 2This Mary, whose brother Lazarus now lay sick, was the same one who
poured perfume on the Lord and wiped
11:2 n Mk 14:3; Lk 7:38; Jn 12:3 his feet with her hair.[n] 3So the sisters
sent word to Jesus, "Lord, the one you
11:3 o ver 5,36 love[o] is sick."
4When he heard this, Jesus said, "This
11:4 p ver 40; Jn 9:3 sickness will not end in death. No, it is
for God's glory[p] so that God's Son may
be glorified through it." 5Jesus loved
Martha and her sister and Lazarus. 6Yet
when he heard that Lazarus was sick, he
stayed where he was two more days.
11:7 q Jn 10:40 7Then he said to his disciples, "Let us
go back to Judea."[q]
8"But Rabbi,"[r] they said, "a short while
11:8 r Mt 23:7 s Jn 8:59; 10:31 ago the Jews tried to stone you,[s] and yet
you are going back there?"
9Jesus answered, "Are there not twelve
hours of daylight? A man who walks by
day will not stumble, for he sees by this
11:9 t Jn 9:4; 12:35 world's light.[t] 10It is when he walks by
night that he stumbles, for he has no
light."
11After he had said this, he went on to
11:11 u ver 3 v Ac 7:60 tell them, "Our friend[u] Lazarus has fall-
en asleep;[v] but I am going there to wake
him up."
12His disciples replied, "Lord, if he
sleeps, he will get better." 13Jesus had
been speaking of his death, but his dis-
11:13 w Mt 9:24 ciples thought he meant natural sleep.[w]
14So then he told them plainly, "Laza-
rus is dead, 15and for your sake I am glad
I was not there, so that you may believe.
But let us go to him."
11:16 x Mt 10:3; Jn 14:5; 20:24-28; 21:2; Ac 1:13 16Then Thomas[x] (called Didymus)
said to the rest of the disciples, "Let us
also go, that we may die with him."

Jesus Comforts the Sisters

17On his arrival, Jesus found that Laz-
11:17 y ver 6,39 arus had already been in the tomb for
11:18 z ver 1 four days.[y] 18Bethany[z] was less than two
miles[a] from Jerusalem, 19and many Jews
had come to Martha and Mary to com-
fort them in the loss of their brother.[a] 11:19 a ver 31; Job 2:11
20When Martha heard that Jesus was
coming, she went out to meet him, but 11:20 b Lk 10:38-42
Mary stayed at home.[b]
21"Lord," Martha said to Jesus, "if you
had been here, my brother would not
have died.[c] 22But I know that even now 11:21 c ver 32,37
God will give you whatever you ask."[d]
23Jesus said to her, "Your brother will 11:22 d ver 41,42; Jn 9:31
rise again."
24Martha answered, "I know he will
rise again in the resurrection[e] at the last 11:24 e Da 12:2; Jn 5:28,29; Ac 24:15
day."
25Jesus said to her, "I am the resurrec- 11:25 f Jn 1:4
tion and the life.[f] He who believes in me
will live, even though he dies; 26and whoever lives and believes in me will never
die. Do you believe this?"
27"Yes, Lord," she told him, "I believe
that you are the Christ,[b][g] the Son of 11:27 g Lk 2:11 h Mt 16:16 i Jn 6:14
God,[h] who was to come into the world."[i]
28And after she had said this, she went
back and called her sister Mary aside.
"The Teacher[j] is here," she said, "and is 11:28 j Mt 26:18; Jn 13:13
asking for you." 29When Mary heard this,
she got up quickly and went to him.
30Now Jesus had not yet entered the village, but was still at the place where 11:30 k ver 20
Martha had met him.[k] 31When the Jews
who had been with Mary in the house, 11:31 l ver 19
comforting her,[l] noticed how quickly
she got up and went out, they followed
her, supposing she was going to the
tomb to mourn there.
32When Mary reached the place
where Jesus was and saw him, she fell at
his feet and said, "Lord, if you had been
here, my brother would not have died."[m] 11:32 m ver 21
33When Jesus saw her weeping, and
the Jews who had come along with her
also weeping, he was deeply moved[n] in 11:33 n ver 38 o Jn 12:27
spirit and troubled.[o] 34"Where have you
laid him?" he asked.
"Come and see, Lord," they replied.
35Jesus wept.[p] 11:35 p Lk 19:41
36Then the Jews said, "See how he
loved him!"[q] 11:36 q ver 3
37But some of them said, "Could not
he who opened the eyes of the blind 11:37 r Jn 9:6,7 s ver 21,32
man[r] have kept this man from dying?"[s]

Jesus Raises Lazarus From the Dead

38Jesus, once more deeply moved,[t] 11:38 t ver 33
came to the tomb. It was a cave with a

a 18 Greek *fifteen stadia* (about 3 kilometers)
b 27 Or *Messiah*

Where Were You?

Funerals are often heartrending experiences. Yet, as the apostle Paul reminded us, we who know Jesus Christ do not need "to grieve like the rest of men, who have no hope" (1 Thessalonians 4:13). When we ourselves and our departed loved one have both accepted the gift of God's forgiveness through Jesus' sacrifice, even though we miss our loved one tremendously, we can still experience the thrill of the incomparable hope of eternal life. Many pastors incorporate Jesus' words from John 11:25 into their funeral message: "I am the resurrection and the life. He who believes in me will live, even though he dies; and whoever lives and believes in me will never die."

This is the comfort Jesus held out to Martha after the death of her brother Lazarus. Jesus arrived on the scene a full four days after Lazarus had been buried, even though the frantic sisters had sent word days earlier while Lazarus had still been alive. And Martha's first words to the Master were filled with a certain pathos: "If you had been here, my brother would not have died" (verse 21).

Martha's pointed statement veiled a poignant question that cried out in effect, "Where were you when we needed you?" And this cry of reproach sounds familiar to our ears. But God is here right by our side, holding us in the midst of our grief and our pain. Our feelings of pain and loss don't nullify that reality (verses 4–5). Jesus did not rebuke Martha because of an error in her theology. Rather, he offered her an extraordinary promise: "I am the resurrection and the life" (verse 25).

Martha understood that one day God would raise all of his people from their graves but assumed incorrectly that Jesus was merely pointing ahead to that final day. Yet, in reality, he was about to enact the miracle for which she so desperately yearned. When Jesus inquired as to whether or not Martha believed what he was saying, she skirted the question and responded indirectly: "Yes, Lord, I believe that you are the Christ, the Son of God, who was to come into the world" (verse 27).

Martha could not really comprehend Jesus' specific promise until later, after he had brought Lazarus back to life. But even in her grief she was certain of one fact: Jesus was the Son of God and the promised Messiah. We are tempted to malign Martha for her apparent lack of faith. But in reality she was reaching beyond the promise itself to the Source of that promise.

We may not fully understand why things happen, and we may not always discern the full extent of God's promises. But if our faith is in the *Person*, our theology will fall into line, and we will learn that Jesus' promises will always come to pass, according to his perfect plan and in his perfect timing. How much we know is immaterial. What counts in the end is *who* we trust.

Self-Discovery: *What difference does it make to you to know that Jesus is "the resurrection and the life"?*

GO TO DISCOVERY 280 ON PAGE 1434

11:38 u Mt 27:60; Lk 24:2; Jn 20:1 stone laid across the entrance.[u] 39"Take
away the stone," he said.
"But, Lord," said Martha, the sister of
11:39 v ver 17 the dead man, "by this time there is a bad
odor, for he has been there four days."[v]
40Then Jesus said, "Did I not tell you
11:40 w ver 23-25 x ver 4 that if you believed,[w] you would see the
glory of God?"[x]
41So they took away the stone. Then
11:41 y Jn 17:1 z Mt 11:25 Jesus looked up[y] and said, "Father,[z] I
thank you that you have heard me. 42I
knew that you always hear me, but I said
this for the benefit of the people stand-
11:42 a Jn 12:30 b Jn 3:17 ing here,[a] that they may believe that you
sent me."[b]
43When he had said this, Jesus called
11:43 c Lk 7:14 in a loud voice, "Lazarus, come out!"[c]
44The dead man came out, his hands
11:44 d Jn 19:40 e Jn 20:7 and feet wrapped with strips of linen,[d]
and a cloth around his face.[e]
Jesus said to them, "Take off the grave
clothes and let him go."

The Plot to Kill Jesus

45Therefore many of the Jews who had
11:45 f ver 19 g Jn 2:23 h Ex 14:31; Jn 7:31 come to visit Mary,[f] and had seen what
Jesus did,[g] put their faith in him.[h] 46But
some of them went to the Pharisees and
11:47 i ver 57 j Mt 26:3 k Mt 5:22 l Jn 2:11 told them what Jesus had done. 47Then
the chief priests and the Pharisees[i]
called a meeting[j] of the Sanhedrin.[k]
"What are we accomplishing?" they
asked. "Here is this man performing
many miraculous signs.[l] 48If we let him
go on like this, everyone will believe in
him, and then the Romans will come
and take away both our place[a] and our
nation."
49Then one of them, named Caia-
11:49 m Mt 26:3 n ver 51; Jn 18:13,14 phas,[m] who was high priest that year,[n]
spoke up, "You know nothing at all!
50You do not realize that it is better for
you that one man die for the people
11:50 o Jn 18:14 than that the whole nation perish."[o]
51He did not say this on his own, but
as high priest that year he prophesied
that Jesus would die for the Jewish nation, 52and not only for that nation but
also for the scattered children of God, to
11:52 p Isa 49:6; Jn 10:16 bring them together and make them
one.[p] 53So from that day on they plotted
to take his life.[q]
11:53 q Mt 12:14 54Therefore Jesus no longer moved
about publicly among the Jews.[r] Instead
11:54 r Jn 7:1 he withdrew to a region near the desert,
to a village called Ephraim, where he
stayed with his disciples.

55When it was almost time for the 11:55 s Ex 12:13,23, 27; Mt 26:1,2; Mk 14:1; Jn 13:1 t 2Ch 30:17,18
Jewish Passover,[s] many went up from
the country to Jerusalem for their ceremonial cleansing[t] before the Passover.
56They kept looking for Jesus,[u] and as 11:56 u Jn 7:11
they stood in the temple area they asked
one another, "What do you think? Isn't
he coming to the Feast at all?" 57But the
chief priests and Pharisees had given orders that if anyone found out where
Jesus was, he should report it so that
they might arrest him.

Jesus Anointed at Bethany

12 Six days before the Passover,[v] 12:1 v Jn 11:55 w Mt 21:17
Jesus arrived at Bethany,[w]
where Lazarus lived, whom Jesus had
raised from the dead. 2Here a dinner was 12:2 x Lk 10:38-42
given in Jesus' honor. Martha served,[x]
while Lazarus was among those reclining at the table with him. 3Then Mary
took about a pint[b] of pure nard, an ex-
pensive perfume;[y] she poured it on 12:3 y Mk 14:3 z Jn 11:2
Jesus' feet and wiped his feet with her
hair.[z] And the house was filled with the
fragrance of the perfume.
4But one of his disciples, Judas Iscari- 12:4 a Mt 10:4
ot, who was later to betray him,[a] objected, 5"Why wasn't this perfume sold and
the money given to the poor? It was
worth a year's wages.[c]" 6He did not say
this because he cared about the poor
but because he was a thief; as keeper of 12:6 b Jn 13:29
the money bag,[b] he used to help himself
to what was put into it.
7"Leave her alone," Jesus replied. "⌊It
was intended⌋ that she should save this
perfume for the day of my burial.[c] 8You 12:7 c Jn 19:40
will always have the poor among you,[d]
but you will not always have me." 12:8 d Dt 15:11
9Meanwhile a large crowd of Jews
found out that Jesus was there and
came, not only because of him but also
to see Lazarus, whom he had raised
from the dead.[e] 10So the chief priests 12:9 e Jn 11:43,44
made plans to kill Lazarus as well, 11for
on account of him[f] many of the Jews 12:11 f ver 17,18; Jn 11:45 g Jn 7:31
were going over to Jesus and putting
their faith in him.[g]

The Triumphal Entry

12The next day the great crowd that
had come for the Feast heard that Jesus
was on his way to Jerusalem. 13They

[a] *48* Or *temple* [b] *3* Greek *a litra* (probably about 0.5 liter) [c] *5* Greek *three hundred denarii*

DISCOVERY 280

A Radical Act of Love

The beautiful narrative of Mary anointing Jesus in Bethany is one of the most memorable stories in the Gospels. Impelled by her overpowering emotion and oblivious to the censure of those around her, Mary performed an act of radical love. There are several aspects of this story that are worth our attention:

The setting. A man called "Simon the leper" hosted a dinner to honor Jesus, most likely to celebrate Simon's own healing from leprosy and Lazarus's resurrection from the dead (Matthew 26:6; John 12:1–2). Mary, Martha, Lazarus and the disciples were all in attendance.

The anointing (John 12:3). During the course of the festivities Mary entered the room carrying a jar of nard, an expensive perfume. She proceeded to pour it onto Jesus' feet and then wipe it off with her hair. Though this may strike us as somewhat bizarre, it was her way of showing reverence and devotion. It was customary to anoint the honored guest at a banquet, so the people did not question the gesture itself. What was extraordinary, however, was the cost of the perfume. Nard was an herb grown in the Himalayas, and this perfume was an expensive imported oil—so costly, in fact, that the bottle was worth the equivalent of a full year's wages (verse 5). The act of wiping off the oil with her hair was unusual for any respectable woman, because for a woman to untie her hair in public was considered disgraceful, something only a prostitute would do.

Mary was not acting impulsively, however. This was a premeditated gesture. Jesus even observed that Mary's anointing was an act of preparation for his death and burial (verse 7). The disciples may have ignored Jesus when he had predicted his own death, but Mary had not. She had sat at his feet and listened with rapt attention to his every word (Luke 10:39). She knew her Lord was destined to die and wanted to express the extent of her love while he was still alive.

The response. Judas protested that the money the jar of perfume represented could have been used for a more practical purpose, such as a donation for the poor (Matthew 26:8). He was actually annoyed because this extravagant demonstration did not benefit him in any way. As treasurer for the group he had become accustomed to embezzling a portion of the money that he controlled (John 12:6). But Mary had her priorities in the right order. She was honoring her Savior, unconcerned about the cost to herself.

Jesus' own response secures Mary's permanent position in human history: "Wherever this gospel is preached throughout the world, what she has done will also be told, in memory of her" (Matthew 26:13). Mary was, of course, by no means a perfect human being, but she was inspiringly devoted to the One who would die to set her free from the penalty of sin. She is remembered more than anything else for this one noble act of love. And as we learn to devote our lives more and more to the cause of Jesus Christ, we too will want to honor him and to express our devotion to him. Will we like Mary be remembered for the "expensive perfume" we have poured on the Savior's feet?

Self-Discovery: *What "expensive perfume" have you poured at Jesus' feet? What extravagant gesture have you made, not just to show the world the level of your commitment to Jesus, but to demonstrate to Jesus himself how much you love him?*

GO TO DISCOVERY 281 ON PAGE 1437

took palm branches and went out to
meet him, shouting,

“Hosanna![a]”

“Blessed is he who comes in the
12:13 [h]Ps 118:25,26
name of the Lord!”[b][h]
[i]Jn 1:49
“Blessed is the King of Israel!”[i]

14 Jesus found a young donkey and sat
upon it, as it is written,

15 “Do not be afraid, O Daughter of
Zion;
see, your king is coming,
12:15 [j]Zec 9:9
seated on a donkey’s colt.”[c][j]

16 At first his disciples did not under-
12:16 [k]Mk 9:32 [l]Jn 2:22; 7:39; 14:26
stand all this.[k] Only after Jesus was glorified[l] did they realize that these things
had been written about him and that
they had done these things to him.
12:17 [m]Jn 11:42
17 Now the crowd that was with him[m]
when he called Lazarus from the tomb
and raised him from the dead continued
to spread the word. 18 Many people, because they had heard that he had given
12:18 [n]ver 11
this miraculous sign,[n] went out to meet
him. 19 So the Pharisees said to one another, “See, this is getting us nowhere.
Look how the whole world has gone af-
12:19 [o]Jn 11:47,48
ter him!”[o]

Jesus Predicts His Death

12:20 [p]Jn 7:35; Ac 11:20
20 Now there were some Greeks[p]
among those who went up to worship at
the Feast. 21 They came to Philip, who
12:21 [q]Mt 11:21; Jn 1:44
was from Bethsaida[q] in Galilee, with a
request. “Sir,” they said, “we would like to
see Jesus.” 22 Philip went to tell Andrew;
Andrew and Philip in turn told Jesus.
23 Jesus replied, “The hour has come
12:23 [r]Jn 13:32; 17:1
for the Son of Man to be glorified.[r] 24 I
tell you the truth, unless a kernel of
12:24 [s]1Co 15:36
wheat falls to the ground and dies,[s] it remains only a single seed. But if it dies, it
12:25 [t]Mt 10:39; Mk 8:35; Lk 14:26
produces many seeds. 25 The man who
loves his life will lose it, while the man
who hates his life in this world will keep
it[t] for eternal life. 26 Whoever serves me
12:26 [u]Jn 14:3; 17:24; 2Co 5:8; 1Th 4:17
must follow me; and where I am, my servant also will be.[u] My Father will honor
the one who serves me.
12:27 [v]Mt 26:38,39; Jn 11:33,38; 13:21 [w]Mt 11:25 [x]ver 23
27 “Now my heart is troubled,[v] and
what shall I say? ‘Father,[w] save me from
this hour’?[x] No, it was for this very reason I came to this hour. 28 Father, glorify
your name!”
12:28 [y]Mt 3:17
Then a voice came from heaven,[y] “I
have glorified it, and will glorify it again.”
29 The crowd that was there and heard it
said it had thundered; others said an angel had spoken to him.
30 Jesus said, “This voice was for your
benefit,[z] not mine. 31 Now is the time for
12:30 [z]Jn 11:42
judgment on this world;[a] now the prince
of this world[b] will be driven out. 32 But I,
12:31 [a]Jn 16:11 [b]Jn 14:30; 16:11; 2Co 4:4; Eph 2:2; 1Jn 4:4
when I am lifted up from the earth,[c] will
draw all men to myself.”[d] 33 He said this
to show the kind of death he was going
to die.[e]
12:32 [c]ver 34; Jn 3:14; 8:28 [d]Jn 6:44
34 The crowd spoke up, “We have
heard from the Law that the Christ[d] will
remain forever,[f] so how can you say, ‘The
12:33 [e]Jn 18:32
Son of Man[g] must be lifted up’?[h] Who is
this ‘Son of Man’?”
12:34 [f]Ps 110:4; Isa 9:7; Eze 37:25; Da 7:14 [g]Mt 8:20 [h]Jn 3:14
35 Then Jesus told them, “You are go-
ing to have the light[i] just a little while
longer. Walk while you have the light,[j]
before darkness overtakes you.[k] The
man who walks in the dark does not
12:35 [i]ver 46 [j]Eph 5:8 [k]1Jn 2:11
know where he is going. 36 Put your trust
in the light while you have it, so that you
may become sons of light.”[l] When he
had finished speaking, Jesus left and hid
12:36 [l]Lk 16:8 [m]Jn 8:59
himself from them.[m]

The Jews Continue in Their Unbelief

37 Even after Jesus had done all these
12:37 [n]Jn 2:11
miraculous signs[n] in their presence,
they still would not believe in him.
38 This was to fulfill the word of Isaiah
the prophet:

“Lord, who has believed our
message
and to whom has the arm of the
12:38 [o]Isa 53:1; Ro 10:16
Lord been revealed?”[e][o]

39 For this reason they could not believe, because, as Isaiah says elsewhere:

40 “He has blinded their eyes
and deadened their hearts,
so they can neither see with their
eyes,
nor understand with their hearts,
nor turn—and I would heal
12:40 [p]Isa 6:10; Mt 13:13,15
them.”[f][p]

41 Isaiah said this because he saw Jesus’
12:41 [q]Isa 6:1-4 [r]Lk 24:27
glory[q] and spoke about him.[r]
42 Yet at the same time many even
among the leaders believed in him.[s] But
12:42 [s]ver 11; Jn 7:48 [t]Jn 7:13
because of the Pharisees[t] they would

a 13 A Hebrew expression meaning “Save!” which became an exclamation of praise *b 13* Psalm 118:25,26 *c 15* Zech. 9:9 *d 34* Or *Messiah*
e 38 Isaiah 53:1 *f 40* Isaiah 6:10

not confess their faith for fear they
12:42 [u]Jn 9:22 would be put out of the synagogue;[u]
[43]for they loved praise from men more
12:43 [v]Jn 5:44 than praise from God.[v]
[44]Then Jesus cried out, "When a man
12:44 believes in me, he does not believe in me
[w]Mt 10:40; only, but in the one who sent me.[w]
Jn 5:24 [45]When he looks at me, he sees the one
12:45 who sent me.[x] [46]I have come into the
[x]Jn 14:9 world as a light,[y] so that no one who be-
12:46 lieves in me should stay in darkness.
[y]Jn 1:4; 3:19; [47]"As for the person who hears my
8:12; 9:5 words but does not keep them, I do not
12:47 judge him. For I did not come to judge
[z]Jn 3:17 the world, but to save it.[z] [48]There is a
judge for the one who rejects me and
does not accept my words; that very
12:48 word which I spoke will condemn him[a]
[a]Jn 5:45 at the last day. [49]For I did not speak of
my own accord, but the Father who sent
12:49 [b]Jn 14:31 me commanded me[b] what to say and
how to say it. [50]I know that his command leads to eternal life. So whatever I
say is just what the Father has told me to
say."

Jesus Washes His Disciples' Feet

13 It was just before the Passover
13:1 [c]Jn 11:55 Feast.[c] Jesus knew that the time
[d]Jn 12:23 had come[d] for him to leave this world
[e]Jn 16:28 and go to the Father.[e] Having loved his
own who were in the world, he now
showed them the full extent of his love.[a]
[2]The evening meal was being served,
and the devil had already prompted Judas Iscariot, son of Simon, to betray
13:3 Jesus. [3]Jesus knew that the Father had
[f]Mt 28:18 put all things under his power,[f] and that
[g]Jn 8:42; 16:27, he had come from God[g] and was re-
28,30 turning to God; [4]so he got up from the
meal, took off his outer clothing, and
wrapped a towel around his waist. [5]Af-
13:5 ter that, he poured water into a basin
[h]Lk 7:44 and began to wash his disciples' feet,[h]
drying them with the towel that was
wrapped around him.
[6]He came to Simon Peter, who said to
him, "Lord, are you going to wash my
feet?"
[7]Jesus replied, "You do not realize
now what I am doing, but later you will
13:7 [i]ver 12 understand."[i]
[8]"No," said Peter, "you shall never
wash my feet."
Jesus answered, "Unless I wash you,
you have no part with me."
[9]"Then, Lord," Simon Peter replied,

> **WAS NOT JESUS AN EXTREMIST FOR LOVE? . . . SO THE QUESTION IS NOT WHETHER WE WILL BE EXTREMISTS, BUT WHAT KIND OF EXTREMISTS WE WILL BE.**
>
> Martin Luther King, Jr., *Civil Rights Leader*

"not just my feet but my hands and my
head as well!"
[10]Jesus answered, "A person who has
had a bath needs only to wash his feet;
his whole body is clean. And you are
clean,[j] though not every one of you." 13:10 [j]Jn 15:3
[11]For he knew who was going to betray
him, and that was why he said not every
one was clean.
[12]When he had finished washing their
feet, he put on his clothes and returned
to his place. "Do you understand what I 13:13
have done for you?" he asked them. [k]Jn 11:28
[13]"You call me 'Teacher'[k] and 'Lord,'[l] and [l]Lk 6:46;
rightly so, for that is what I am. [14]Now 1Co 12:3; Php 2:11
that I, your Lord and Teacher, have 13:14
washed your feet, you also should wash [m]1Pe 5:5
one another's feet.[m] [15]I have set you an 13:15
example that you should do as I have [n]Mt 11:29
done for you.[n] [16]I tell you the truth, no 13:16
servant is greater than his master,[o] nor [o]Mt 10:24;
is a messenger greater than the one who Lk 6:40;
sent him. [17]Now that you know these Jn 15:20
things, you will be blessed if you do 13:17
them.[p] [p]Mt 7:24,25; Lk 11:28; Jas 1:25

Jesus Predicts His Betrayal

[18]"I am not referring to all of you;[q] I 13:18 [q]ver 10
know those I have chosen.[r] But this is to [r]Jn 15:16,19
fulfill the scripture: 'He who shares my [s]Mt 26:23
bread[s] has lifted up his heel[t] against [t]Jn 6:70
me.'[b][u] [u]Ps 41:9
[19]"I am telling you now before it happens, so that when it does happen you
will believe[v] that I am He.[w] [20]I tell you 13:19 [v]Jn 14:29; 16:4
the truth, whoever accepts anyone I [w]Jn 8:24
send accepts me; and whoever accepts
me accepts the one who sent me."[x] 13:20
[21]After he had said this, Jesus was [x]Mt 10:40;
troubled in spirit[y] and testified, "I tell Lk 10:16
you the truth, one of you is going to be- 13:21
tray me."[z] [y]Jn 12:27 [z]Mt 26:21
[22]His disciples stared at one another,
at a loss to know which of them he
meant. [23]One of them, the disciple whom

[a] 1 Or *he loved them to the last* [b] 18 Psalm 41:9

DISCOVERY 281

A Servant Mind-set

It must have been a confusing as well as convicting moment for the disciples when Jesus removed his outer cloak and began washing their feet (John 13:4–5). They had gathered to celebrate the Passover, and, only moments after rebuking the disciples for arguing about who among them would be the greatest (Luke 22:24–27), Jesus quietly stood up, removed his outer garment, wrapped a towel around his waist, filled a basin with water and began, one by one, to wash their feet.

This gesture shocked the disciples, because foot washing, though it was essential in their dusty environment, represented the most menial task a person could do. In fact, this distasteful duty was generally assigned to the lowliest servant in the household. Yet in this situation the most esteemed person in the room voluntarily took on himself the most despised of household jobs. As he proceeded, Jesus preached what he was practicing: "Now that I, your Lord and Teacher, have washed your feet, you also should wash one another's feet. I have set you an example . . . No servant is greater than his master, nor is a messenger greater than the one who sent him. Now that you know these things, you will be blessed if you do them" (John 13:14–16).

Taking on a servant role will quickly squelch a competitive spirit. This was not the first incident in which the disciples had attempted to tout their own importance. Jesus had repeatedly pointed out that "many who are first will be last, and the last first" (Mark 10:31). But even on the night of the Passover celebration, the disciples were busy jockeying for position (Luke 22:24). Perhaps that explains why none of the 12 had volunteered to wash the feet of the others—which should have been done as a common courtesy shortly after the group's arrival.

Putting ourselves in the position of a servant brings us forward in our goal of becoming more Christlike. Jesus certainly had every right to be served by all of creation, yet he chose to be a servant throughout his earthly life and ultimately to die for our sin. And he asks each of us to follow this servant model (Mark 10:44–45). A slave has no choice as to who or when he will serve. A slave serves because he is a slave, and he is in the service of anyone and everyone. That is precisely what Jesus asks us to do.

A servant mind-set compels us to involve ourselves in the mundane and disagreeable tasks of everyday life. We often like to set our sights on the big and impressive tasks we desire to undertake in the service of our Lord. But living as Jesus lived means serving others in the seemingly insignificant areas too. It may mean stopping along the roadside to help someone change a tire, purchasing a cup of lemonade from a child's sidewalk stand, allowing the busy mother with an armful of grocery items to move ahead of us in the line, and countless other acts of kindness. Jesus advised his disciples that deferring to the needs of others in such seemingly trivial ways demonstrates respect for God and will be rewarded (Mark 9:41). Our Lord's gracious rewards are given to those who serve him as they offer themselves to others in simple, yet profound, ways (Matthew 25:35–40).

Self-Discovery: *What menial task have you performed in the service of Jesus? What was your true motivation?*

GO TO DISCOVERY 282 ON PAGE 1439

13:23 Jesus loved,[a] was reclining next to him.
a Jn 19:26; 20:2; 24Simon Peter motioned to this disciple
21:7,20 and said, "Ask him which one he means."
25Leaning back against Jesus, he
13:25 asked him, "Lord, who is it?"[b]
b Jn 21:20 26Jesus answered, "It is the one to
whom I will give this piece of bread
when I have dipped it in the dish." Then,
dipping the piece of bread, he gave it to
Judas Iscariot, son of Simon. 27As soon
as Judas took the bread, Satan entered
13:27 c Lk 22:3 into him.[c]
"What you are about to do, do quickly," Jesus told him, 28but no one at the
meal understood why Jesus said this to
13:29 him. 29Since Judas had charge of the
d Jn 12:6 money,[d] some thought Jesus was telling
him to buy what was needed for the
Feast, or to give something to the poor.
13:30 30As soon as Judas had taken the bread,
e Lk 22:53 he went out. And it was night.[e]

Jesus Predicts Peter's Denial

31When he was gone, Jesus said, "Now
13:31 f Jn 7:39 is the Son of Man glorified[f] and God is
g Jn 14:13; 17:4; glorified in him.[g] 32If God is glorified in
1Pe 4:11 him,[a] God will glorify the Son in him-
13:32 h Jn 17:1 self,[h] and will glorify him at once.
33"My children, I will be with you only
a little longer. You will look for me, and
13:33 just as I told the Jews, so I tell you now:
i Jn 7:33,34 Where I am going, you cannot come.[i]
13:34 34"A new command[j] I give you: Love
j 1Jn 2:7-11; 3:11 k Lev 19:18; one another.[k] As I have loved you, so you
1Th 4:9; must love one another.[l] 35By this all men
1Pe 1:22 will know that you are my disciples, if
l Jn 15:12; Eph 5:2; you love one another."[m]
1Jn 4:10,11 36Simon Peter asked him, "Lord,
13:35 where are you going?"
m 1Jn 3:14; 4:20 Jesus replied, "Where I am going, you
13:36 cannot follow now,[n] but you will follow
n ver 33; Jn 14:2 later."[o]
o Jn 21:18,19; 37Peter asked, "Lord, why can't I fol-
2Pe 1:14 low you now? I will lay down my life for
you."
38Then Jesus answered, "Will you
really lay down your life for me? I tell you
13:38 the truth, before the rooster crows, you
p Jn 18:27 will disown me three times![p]

Jesus Comforts His Disciples

14:1 q ver 27 14 "Do not let your hearts be troubled.[q] Trust in God[b]; trust also
in me. 2In my Father's house are many
rooms; if it were not so, I would have
14:2 r Jn 13:33,36 told you. I am going there[r] to prepare a
place for you. 3And if I go and prepare a

> **WHAT GOD'S SON HAS TOLD ME, TAKE FOR TRUE I DO; TRUTH HIMSELF SPEAKS TRULY OR THERE'S NOTHING TRUE.**
>
> 
>
> St. Thomas Aquinas, *Catholic Theologian*

place for you, I will come back and take
you to be with me that you also may be
where I am.[s] 4You know the way to the 14:3 s Jn 12:26
place where I am going."

Jesus the Way to the Father

5Thomas[t] said to him, "Lord, we don't 14:5 t Jn 11:16
know where you are going, so how can
we know the way?"
6Jesus answered, "I am the way[u] and 14:6 u Jn 10:9
the truth and the life.[v] No one comes to v Jn 11:25
the Father except through me. 7If you
really knew me, you would know[c] my 14:7
Father as well.[w] From now on, you do w Jn 8:19
know him and have seen him."
8Philip said, "Lord, show us the Father
and that will be enough for us."
9Jesus answered: "Don't you know me,
Philip, even after I have been among you
such a long time? Anyone who has seen
me has seen the Father.[x] How can you 14:9 x Jn 12:45;
say, 'Show us the Father'? 10Don't you be- Col 1:15;
lieve that I am in the Father, and that the Heb 1:3
Father is in me?[y] The words I say to you 14:10 y Jn 10:38
are not just my own.[z] Rather, it is the Fa- z Jn 5:19
ther, living in me, who is doing his work.
11Believe me when I say that I am in the
Father and the Father is in me; or at least
believe on the evidence of the miracles 14:11
themselves.[a] 12I tell you the truth, any- a Jn 5:36; 10:38
one who has faith[b] in me will do what I 14:12
have been doing.[c] He will do even b Mt 21:21
greater things than these, because I am c Lk 10:17
going to the Father. 13And I will do whatever you ask[d] in my name, so that the 14:13
Son may bring glory to the Father. 14You d Mt 7:7
may ask me for anything in my name,
and I will do it.

Jesus Promises the Holy Spirit

15"If you love me, you will obey what I 14:15
command.[e] 16And I will ask the Father, e ver 21,23; Jn 15:10; 1Jn 5:3
and he will give you another Counselor[f]
to be with you forever— 17the Spirit of 14:16 f Jn 15:26; 16:7

a 32 Many early manuscripts do not have *If God is glorified in him.* b 1 Or *You trust in God*
c 7 Some early manuscripts *If you really have known me, you will know*

DISCOVERY 282

Comfort in Trouble

Feeling alone and isolated during a difficult time might just be the worst of all of the emotions we experience in our lifetime. Jesus knew what was coming in his own life—his arrest, trial, execution and resurrection. But before he left his disciples to carry out God's plan to reconcile his people to himself, he wanted them to understand that they would never find themselves in the position of abandonment. He promised that his Holy Spirit would live within them as the embodiment of God's presence (John 14:16; 15:26–27; 16:7–15).

Circumstances would not always be smooth for the small group of men who had put their lives at stake to follow Jesus (Mark 10:17–31; John 15:18–27). Jesus urged his disciples, however, to allow others to see the love of God reflected in their lives instead of lashing out in hostility at the opposition marshaled against them. When we respond to others in love, we stand in sharp contrast to the value system of the world and have an opportunity to reveal to those around us the Father's heart (Philippians 2:15–16).

Jesus offered his disciples the wonderful gift of his comfort and help to take with them through their trials. His blessings are founded on his promises. Our Lord has pledged to come back for his people (John 14:3) and to answer when we call on him (verses 13–14). The Counselor, the Helper Jesus promised, has long since come and taken up residence in our hearts, continually teaching us what God wants and bringing peace to our souls (verses 26–27).

We face many difficulties, both because of the sin in our own lives and the rampant evil in the world around us. John, like other Biblical writers, continually reminded believers that God is just as real and close to us today as Jesus was to the disciples almost 2,000 years ago—even when we find ourselves unable to perceive that he is at work. Our faith can all too easily be smothered by the very real problems around us, but Paul reminds us of the confidence we can have in Jesus Christ: "Who shall separate us from the love of Christ? Shall trouble or hardship or persecution or famine or nakedness of danger or sword? . . . No, in all these things we are more than conquerors through him who loved us. For I am convinced that neither death nor life . . . nor anything else in all creation will be able to separate us from the love of God, that is in Christ Jesus our Lord" (Romans 8:35,37–40).

We have the Spirit's presence in our hearts now, and we will one day bask in Jesus' glorious presence for all eternity (John 14:3). Without Jesus everyday problems and challenges would appear random and senseless, and we would feel ourselves to be at the mercy of a cruel and inexplicable universe. When we give our lives to the Savior, however, we receive the kind of hope that gives us strength for today as we are empowered to put our daily struggles into perspective. Our steps need not be tentative when we know that the Almighty God of the universe is walking with us, stride for stride, throughout our life's journey.

Self-Discovery: *Under what circumstances have you felt hopeless, abandoned, in despair? What role did your faith in Jesus have in lifting you out of your depression?*

GO TO DISCOVERY 283 ON PAGE 1442

NO ONE CAN HAVE FAITH IN CHRIST WITHOUT ALSO HAVING FAITH IN GOD THE FATHER AND IN THE HOLY SPIRIT.

J. Greshem Machen, *Presbyterian Theologian*

14:17 truth.[g] The world cannot accept him,[h]
[g]Jn 15:26; 16:13; 1Jn 4:6 because it neither sees him nor knows
[h]1Co 2:14 him. But you know him, for he lives with
you and will be[a] in you. 18I will not leave
14:18 [i]ver 3,28 you as orphans; I will come to you.[i] 19Be-
14:19 fore long, the world will not see me any-
[j]Jn 7:33,34; more, but you will see me.[j] Because I
16:16 [k]Jn 6:57 live, you also will live.[k] 20On that day you
14:20 will realize that I am in my Father,[l] and
[l]Jn 10:38 you are in me, and I am in you. 21Who-
14:21 ever has my commands and obeys them,
[m]1Jn 5:3 he is the one who loves me.[m] He who
[n]1Jn 2:5 loves me will be loved by my Father,[n]
and I too will love him and show myself
14:22 to him."
[o]Lk 6:16; 22Then Judas[o] (not Judas Iscariot)
Ac 1:13 said, "But, Lord, why do you intend to
[p]Ac 10:41 show yourself to us and not to the
world?"[p]
23Jesus replied, "If anyone loves me, he
14:23 [q]ver 15 will obey my teaching.[q] My Father will
love him, and we will come to him and
make our home with him.[r] 24He who 14:23 [r]1Jn 2:24;
does not love me will not obey my teach- Rev 3:20
ing. These words you hear are not my
own; they belong to the Father who 14:24
sent me.[s] [s]Jn 7:16
25"All this I have spoken while still 14:26
with you. 26But the Counselor,[t] the Holy [t]Jn 15:26; 16:7
Spirit, whom the Father will send in my [u]Ac 2:33 [v]Jn 16:13;
name,[u] will teach you all things[v] and will 1Jn 2:20,27
remind you of everything I have said to [w]Jn 2:22
you.[w] 27Peace I leave with you; my peace
I give you.[x] I do not give to you as the 14:27 [x]Jn 16:33;
world gives. Do not let your hearts be Php 4:7;
troubled and do not be afraid. Col 3:15
28"You heard me say, 'I am going away
and I am coming back to you.'[y] If you 14:28 [y]ver 2-4,18
loved me, you would be glad that I am [z]Jn 5:18
going to the Father,[z] for the Father is [a]Jn 10:29; Php 2:6
greater than I.[a] 29I have told you now be-
fore it happens, so that when it does hap- 14:29
pen you will believe.[b] 30I will not speak [b]Jn 13:19; 16:4
with you much longer, for the prince of
this world[c] is coming. He has no hold on 14:30
me, 31but the world must learn that I love [c]Jn 12:31
the Father and that I do exactly what my
Father has commanded me.[d] 14:31
[d]Jn 10:18; 12:49
"Come now; let us leave.

SO MANY QUESTIONS

The disciples' heads must have been spinning. As the Passover meal progressed, their Master's words amazed them again and again (John 13—14). Jesus was predicting events that were soon to happen, but the disciples were bewildered, wondering: *Where is he going? When? Why? How?* Jesus had warned them that "the end" was coming, but none of them had expected the dire predictions they now heard him making. *Going back to heaven to the Father's house? He's leaving us?* John recorded some of their reactions: "Where are you going?" (John 13:36); "Why can't I follow you now?" (verse 37); "How can we know the way?" (John 14:5). All of Jesus' answers were direct and simple, but they were profound. On that last evening together in the upper room, the Lord answered their questions, allayed their fears and comforted them—even as he prepared them for the shock they were to receive before the night was over.

IF JESUS IS LORD THEN THE ONLY RIGHT RESPONSE TO HIM IS SURRENDER AND OBEDIENCE.

Rebecca Pippert, *Christian Author and Speaker*

The Vine and the Branches

15 "I am the true vine,[e] and my Fa- 15:1 [e]Isa 5:1-7
ther is the gardener. 2He cuts
off every branch in me that bears no
fruit, while every branch that does bear
fruit he prunes[b] so that it will be even
more fruitful. 3You are already clean because of the word I have spoken to you.[f] 15:3
4Remain in me, and I will remain in [f]Jn 13:10; 17:17; Eph 5:26
you.[g] No branch can bear fruit by itself; 15:4
it must remain in the vine. Neither can [g]Jn 6:56; 1Jn 2:6
you bear fruit unless you remain in me.
5"I am the vine; you are the branches.
If a man remains in me and I in him, he 15:5
will bear much fruit;[h] apart from me you [h]ver 16
can do nothing. 6If anyone does not remain in me, he is like a branch that is
thrown away and withers; such
branches are picked up, thrown into the

[a] 17 Some early manuscripts *and is*   [b] 2 The Greek for *prunes* also means *cleans.*

15:6 fire and burned.[i] 7If you remain in me
i ver 2 and my words remain in you, ask what-
15:7 ever you wish, and it will be given you.[j]
j Mt 7:7 8This is to my Father's glory,[k] that you
15:8 bear much fruit, showing yourselves to
k Mt 5:16 l Jn 8:31 be my disciples.[l]
15:9 9"As the Father has loved me,[m] so have
m Jn 17:23,24,26 I loved you. Now remain in my love. 10If
you obey my commands,[n] you will re-
15:10 main in my love, just as I have obeyed
n Jn 14:15 my Father's commands and remain in
his love. 11I have told you this so that my
joy may be in you and that your joy may
15:11 be complete.[o] 12My command is this:
o Jn 17:13 Love each other as I have loved you.[p]
15:12 13Greater love has no one than this, that
p Jn 13:34 he lay down his life for his friends.[q]
15:13 14You are my friends[r] if you do what I
q Jn 10:11; Ro 5:7,8 command.[s] 15I no longer call you servants, because a servant does not know
15:14 his master's business. Instead, I have
r Lk 12:4 s Mt 12:50 called you friends, for everything that I
15:15 learned from my Father I have made
t Jn 8:26 known to you.[t] 16You did not choose me,
15:16 but I chose you and appointed you[u] to
u Jn 6:70; 13:18 go and bear fruit—fruit that will last.
Then the Father will give you whatever
15:17 you ask in my name. 17This is my com-
v ver 12 mand: Love each other.[v]

The World Hates the Disciples

15:18 18"If the world hates you,[w] keep in
w 1Jn 3:13 mind that it hated me first. 19If you belonged to the world, it would love you as
15:19 its own. As it is, you do not belong to the
x ver 16 world, but I have chosen you[x] out of the
y Jn 17:14 world. That is why the world hates you.[y]
20Remember the words I spoke to you:
15:20 'No servant is greater than his master.'[a][z]
z Jn 13:16 If they persecuted me, they will perse-
a 2Ti 3:12 cute you also.[a] If they obeyed my teaching, they will obey yours also. 21They will
15:21 treat you this way because of my name,[b]
b Mt 10:22 for they do not know the One who sent
c Jn 16:3 me.[c] 22If I had not come and spoken to
them, they would not be guilty of sin.
Now, however, they have no excuse for
15:22 their sin.[d] 23He who hates me hates my
d Jn 9:41; Ro 1:20 Father as well. 24If I had not done among
15:24 them what no one else did,[e] they would
e Jn 5:36 not be guilty of sin. But now they have
seen these miracles, and yet they have
hated both me and my Father. 25But this
15:25 is to fulfill what is written in their Law:
f Ps 35:19; 69:4 'They hated me without reason.'[b][f]
15:26 26"When the Counselor[g] comes,
g Jn 14:16 whom I will send to you from the Fa-

> FOR THE SAKE OF EACH OF US HE LAID DOWN HIS LIFE — WORTH NO LESS THAN THE UNIVERSE. HE DEMANDS OF US IN RETURN OUR LIVES FOR THE SAKE OF EACH OTHER.
>
> 
>
> Clement of Alexandria, *Early Church Father*

ther,[h] the Spirit of truth[i] who goes out 15:26 h Jn 14:26
from the Father, he will testify about i Jn 14:17
me.[j] 27And you also must testify,[k] for you j 1Jn 5:7
have been with me from the beginning.[l] 15:27 k Lk 24:48;
16 "All this[m] I have told you so that 1Jn 1:2; 4:14
you will not go astray.[n] 2They l Lk 1:2
will put you out of the synagogue;[o] in 16:1
fact, a time is coming when anyone who m Jn 15:18-27
kills you will think he is offering a ser- n Mt 11:6
vice to God.[p] 3They will do such things 16:2 o Jn 9:22
because they have not known the Father p Isa 66:5;
or me.[q] 4I have told you this, so that Ac 26:9,10;
when the time comes you will remem- Rev 6:9
ber[r] that I warned you. I did not tell you 16:3 q Jn 15:21;
this at first because I was with you. 17:25; 1Jn 3:1

The Work of the Holy Spirit

16:4 r Jn 13:19
5"Now I am going to him who sent
me,[s] yet none of you asks me, 'Where 16:5 s Jn 7:33
are you going?'[t] 6Because I have said t Jn 13:36; 14:5
these things, you are filled with grief.
7But I tell you the truth: It is for your
good that I am going away. Unless I go
away, the Counselor[u] will not come to 16:7 u Jn 14:16,26;
you; but if I go, I will send him to you.[v] 15:26 v Jn 7:39
8When he comes, he will convict the
world of guilt[c] in regard to sin and righteousness and judgment: 9in regard to
sin,[w] because men do not believe in me; 16:9 w Jn 15:22
10in regard to righteousness,[x] because I 16:10
am going to the Father, where you can x Ac 3:14; 7:52;
see me no longer; 11and in regard to 1Pe 3:18
judgment, because the prince of this
world[y] now stands condemned. 16:11 y Jn 12:31
12"I have much more to say to you,
more than you can now bear.[z] 13But 16:12 z Mk 4:33
when he, the Spirit of truth,[a] comes, he
will guide you into all truth.[b] He will not 16:13 a Jn 14:17
speak on his own; he will speak only b Jn 14:26
what he hears, and he will tell you what
is yet to come. 14He will bring glory to
me by taking from what is mine and
making it known to you. 15All that be- 16:15
longs to the Father is mine.[c] That is why c Jn 17:10

a 20 John 13:16 *b 25* Psalms 35:19; 69:4 *c 8* Or *will expose the guilt of the world*

DISCOVERY 283

Never Abandoned

On the night before Jesus died he spoke with his disciples about the challenges they would face after he had returned to heaven. He forewarned them they would be banned from the synagogues and even killed because of their belief in him (John 16:2–3).

But Jesus also reminded them that even though he would be leaving this earth, they would never be abandoned. He promised that his Holy Spirit would come to stay with them forever and to help them endure through every difficulty (John 16:7; see also John 14:16–17).

The disciples were in desperate need of a counselor, because Jesus would no longer be available to mentor them in person. The word *counselor* refers to an individual who is called alongside another in order to help. Jesus himself would never forget his beloved disciples as he interceded for them at God's right hand (Romans 8:34; Hebrews 7:25), but this promised Counselor would in no way be an inferior substitute for his physical presence! God the Holy Spirit is equal in power, wisdom, love and ability to God the Father and God the Son. The Holy Spirit infuses us with the strength we need to live lives that are fully committed to Jesus (Ephesians 5:18–20) and that bear the fruit of Christian character (Galatians 5:22–23).

The Holy Spirit, Jesus promised, would also guide them (John 16:13). He is the Spirit of truth, and as such he reveals to us God's truth as we live for him. During the three years the disciples had been with Jesus, they had asked question upon question, learning all they could about their Master and his way of life. If they had failed to comprehend something Jesus had done or said, they had simply requested that he explain more fully.

How unsettling it must have been to realize that Jesus would be leaving them and that they would no longer be able to converse with him in person. Jesus wanted them to know that he would continue to answer their questions and explain his words but that from now on this help would come through his Holy Spirit—no longer face-to-face, but certainly heart-to-heart. Jesus promised that the Spirit would live within them, guide them in his truth and bring honor to Jesus himself (John 16:13–14).

But there was more: The Holy Spirit would also work in the lives of those who would oppose God's people. Part of the Spirit's role is to "convict the world of guilt in regard to sin and righteousness and judgment" (verse 8). We learn as we face adversity, just as the disciples did, that God the Holy Spirit will never leave us to face the foe in our own strength.

The Holy Spirit lives inside every person who has staked his or her life on Jesus. He is always there, prompting us, prodding us, encouraging us, guiding us, changing us, maturing us through all the twists and turns of life. And when other people challenge us in our faith, we can ask the Holy Spirit to move in the same way in their lives so that they too may respond gratefully to his love and may humbly accept his forgiveness.

Self-Discovery: *In what ways are you aware of the presence of the Holy Spirit in your heart and life? In what ways do you experience his comfort and benefit from his counsel? Bearing in mind that God can use a variety of means to accomplish his purposes, be as specific as you can.*

GO TO DISCOVERY 284 ON PAGE 1444

I said the Spirit will take from what is
mine and make it known to you.
16:16 16“In a little while[d] you will see me no
[d]Jn 7:33 more, and then after a little while you
[e]Jn 14:18-24 will see me.”[e]

The Disciples' Grief Will Turn to Joy

17Some of his disciples said to one another, “What does he mean by saying, ‘In
a little while you will see me no more,
and then after a little while you will see
16:17 me,’[f] and ‘Because I am going to the Fa-
[f]ver 16 [g]ver 5 ther’?”[g] 18They kept asking, “What does
he mean by ‘a little while’? We don't understand what he is saying.”
19Jesus saw that they wanted to ask
him about this, so he said to them, “Are
you asking one another what I meant
when I said, ‘In a little while you will see
me no more, and then after a little while
you will see me’? 20I tell you the truth,
16:20 you will weep and mourn[h] while the
[h]Lk 23:27 world rejoices. You will grieve, but your
[i]Jn 20:20 grief will turn to joy.[i] 21A woman giving
16:21 birth to a child has pain[j] because her
[j]Isa 26:17; 1Th 5:3 time has come; but when her baby is
born she forgets the anguish because of
her joy that a child is born into the
world. 22So with you: Now is your time of
16:22 grief,[k] but I will see you again[l] and you
[k]ver 6 [l]ver 16 will rejoice, and no one will take away
your joy. 23In that day you will no longer
ask me anything. I tell you the truth, my
Father will give you whatever you ask in
16:23 my name.[m] 24Until now you have not
[m]Mt 7:7; Jn 15:16 asked for anything in my name. Ask and
you will receive, and your joy will be
16:24 complete.[n]
[n]Jn 3:29; 15:11
25“Though I have been speaking figu-
16:25 ratively,[o] a time is coming[p] when I will
[o]Mt 13:34; Jn 10:6 [p]ver 2 no longer use this kind of language but
will tell you plainly about my Father. 26In
16:26 that day you will ask in my name.[q] I am
[q]ver 23,24 not saying that I will ask the Father on
your behalf. 27No, the Father himself
16:27 loves you because you have loved me[r]
[r]Jn 14:21,23 and have believed that I came from God.
28I came from the Father and entered
the world; now I am leaving the world
16:28 and going back to the Father.”[s]
[s]Jn 13:3
29Then Jesus' disciples said, “Now you
are speaking clearly and without figures
16:29 of speech.[t] 30Now we can see that you
[t]ver 25 know all things and that you do not
even need to have anyone ask you questions. This makes us believe that you
came from God.”

31“You believe at last!”[a] Jesus an-
swered. 32“But a time is coming,[u] and 16:32 [u]ver 2,25
has come, when you will be scattered,[v] [v]Mt 26:31
each to his own home. You will leave me [w]Jn 8:16,29
all alone. Yet I am not alone, for my Father is with me.[w]
33“I have told you these things, so that 16:33
in me you may have peace.[x] In this [x]Jn 14:27
world you will have trouble.[y] But take [y]Jn 15:18-21
heart! I have overcome[z] the world.” [z]Ro 8:37; 1Jn 4:4

Jesus Prays for Himself

17 After Jesus said this, he looked 17:1
toward heaven[a] and prayed: [a]Jn 11:41 [b]Jn 12:23; 13:31,32

“Father, the time has come. Glorify your Son, that your Son may
glorify you.[b] 2For you granted him
authority over all people that he 17:2
might give eternal life to all those [c]ver 6,9,24; Da 7:14; Jn 6:37, 39
you have given him.[c] 3Now this is
eternal life: that they may know 17:3
you, the only true God, and Jesus [d]ver 8,18,21,23, 25; Jn 3:17
Christ, whom you have sent.[d] 4I
have brought you glory[e] on earth 17:4
by completing the work you gave [e]Jn 13:31

[a] 31 Or *“Do you now believe?”*

SOMEONE IS PRAYING

There are times when we yearn to know that someone really cares about us, and especially that someone is praying for us. And John 17 assures us that Jesus does precisely that. On his way to the Garden of Gethsemane to pray on the eve of the final day of his earthly life, our Lord took the time to pray for the disciples who would so soon be bereft of his comfort and company, as well as for the well-being of everyone who would one day believe in him. During the course of his intimate conversation with God the Father, he passed the mantle of his earthly mission over to his disciples, fully aware that he was about to be arrested and crucified in our place. Although thoughts of the impending ordeal must have been agonizing for our Savior, Jesus was able to look beyond the pain and fear and view the coming torment as the ultimate expression of God's love for his people. What kept him steadfast and resolute that night was the thought of the people he loves so dearly—you and me. When he must have had so many other pressing concerns about which to address the Father, our Savior characteristically honed in on the needs of those he loves.

THE HIGH PRIESTLY PRAYER

The intimate conversation between Jesus and his Father recorded in John 17 is commonly referred to as "the high priestly prayer," because it depicts for us how Jesus intercedes on our behalf just as a high priest would have done in the temple (Isaiah 53:12; Romans 8:34; Hebrews 7:25; 1 John 2:1). Our Savior's words allow us a personal glimpse into his heart and his passion. Jesus prayed for himself (John 17:1–5) and for the disciples (verses 6–19)—and then he even prayed for each of us who has come to believe in Jesus (verse 20–26):

Prayer for himself. Before he was arrested and sentenced to die, Jesus communed with the Father during the "hour" of his suffering. He understood what he was about to face, but still his overriding desire was for the Father to "glorify your Son, that your Son may glorify you" (verse 1). Jesus never denied that the agony of the cross loomed ahead of him. However, he was able to direct his mind's "eye" beyond that obstacle to the glory that would follow (Hebrews 12:1–3). Jesus did not plead for his own honor based on some egocentric need; he wanted God to honor him in order that the Father would also be glorified after Jesus had returned to heaven.

Prayer for his disciples. Next Jesus prayed for those who had listened to his words and believed in the Father, those "whom [the Father] gave [the Son] out of the world" (John 17:6–8). He interceded for their protection, because he recognized that he would no longer be physically present with them (verses 11–12) and because he foresaw that they would be under direct attack from the evil one (verse 15). Finally, he prayed that they would be holy, a process that is vitally connected to knowledge of God's truth (verse 17). God has provided us with his Word as the means for our sanctification.

Prayer for us. The most remarkable aspect of Jesus' prayer is that he also focused on *us*, interceding for all who would eventually believe in him (verse 20). He pleaded with the Father for our unity in the faith, because oneness is a visible demonstration to a watching world that Jesus is indeed real, that he was sent by God, and that he still lives and continues to transform lives. When the people who are called by Jesus' name demonstrate solidarity of passion and purpose, others witness the reality of Jesus and his love. But when that bond is threatened or destroyed, our attempts to proclaim truth too often prove futile. Finally, Jesus prayed that those whom the Father had given him would someday be with him in glory (verse 24).

In the meantime, our Lord left us with a single task: to demonstrate our devotion to him through a bond of unity with one another, in order that others will be drawn to the love of Jesus Christ that is manifested in our lives: "May they be brought to complete unity to let the world know that you sent me and have loved them even as you have loved me: (verse 23).

Self-Discovery: *What priority do you place on oneness with other believers, despite differences in worship styles, doctrine or emphases? What specific steps have you taken to show that you embrace all of God's children as brothers and sisters in Christ?*

GO TO DISCOVERY 285 ON PAGE 1449

WE COULD NEVER RECOGNIZE THE FATHER'S GRACE AND MERCY EXCEPT FOR OUR LORD JESUS CHRIST, WHO IS A MIRROR OF HIS FATHER'S HEART.

Martin Luther, *German Reformer*

17:4 [f]Jn 4:34 me to do.[f] 5And now, Father, glorify me in your presence with the
17:5 [g]Php 2:6 glory I had with you[g] before the
[h]Jn 1:2 world began.[h]

Jesus Prays for His Disciples

17:6 6"I have revealed you[a][i] to those
[i]ver 26 [j]ver 2; whom you gave me[j] out of the
Jn 6:37,39 world. They were yours; you gave
them to me and they have obeyed
your word. 7Now they know that
everything you have given me
comes from you. 8For I gave them
17:8 [k]ver 14,26 the words you gave me[k] and they
[l]Jn 16:27 accepted them. They knew with
[m]ver 3,18,21, certainty that I came from you,[l]
23,25; Jn 3:17 and they believed that you sent
17:9 [n]Lk 22:32 me.[m] 9I pray for them.[n] I am not
praying for the world, but for those
you have given me, for they are
yours. 10All I have is yours, and all
17:10 [o]Jn 16:15 you have is mine.[o] And glory has
come to me through them. 11I will
remain in the world no longer, but
17:11 [p]Jn 13:1 they are still in the world,[p] and I am
[q]Jn 7:33 coming to you.[q] Holy Father, pro-
[r]ver 21-23 tect them by the power of your
[s]Jn 10:30 name—the name you gave me—so
that they may be one[r] as we are
one.[s] 12While I was with them, I
protected them and kept them safe
by that name you gave me. None
17:12 [t]Jn 6:39 has been lost[t] except the one
[u]Jn 6:70 doomed to destruction[u] so that
Scripture would be fulfilled.
13"I am coming to you now, but I
say these things while I am still in
the world, so that they may have
17:13 [v]Jn 3:29 the full measure of my joy[v] within
them. 14I have given them your
word and the world has hated
17:14 [w]Jn 15:19 them,[w] for they are not of the world
[x]Jn 8:23 any more than I am of the world.[x]
15My prayer is not that you take
them out of the world but that you
17:15 [y]Mt 5:37 protect them from the evil one.[y]
16They are not of the world, even as
I am not of it.[z] 17Sanctify[b] them by 17:16 [z]ver 14
the truth; your word is truth.[a] 18As
you sent me into the world,[b] I have 17:17 [a]Jn 15:3
sent them into the world.[c] 19For
them I sanctify myself, that they 17:18 [b]ver 3,8,21,23,
too may be truly sanctified. 25 [c]Jn 20:21

Jesus Prays for All Believers

20"My prayer is not for them
alone. I pray also for those who will
believe in me through their message, 21that all of them may be one,
Father, just as you are in me and I
am in you.[d] May they also be in us 17:21 [d]Jn 10:38
so that the world may believe that [e]ver 3,8,18,23,
you have sent me.[e] 22I have given 25; Jn 3:17
them the glory that you gave me,
that they may be one as we are
one:[f] 23I in them and you in me. 17:22 [f]Jn 14:20
May they be brought to complete
unity to let the world know that 17:23
you sent me[g] and have loved them[h] [g]Jn 3:17 [h]Jn 16:27
even as you have loved me.
24"Father, I want those you have
given me to be with me where I
am,[i] and to see my glory,[j] the glory 17:24 [i]Jn 12:26
you have given me because you [j]Jn 1:14 [k]ver 5;
loved me before the creation of the Mt 25:34
world.[k]
25"Righteous Father, though the
world does not know you,[l] I know 17:25 [l]Jn 15:21; 16:3
you, and they know that you have [m]ver 3,8,18,21,
sent me.[m] 26I have made you known 23; Jn 3:17; 7:29;
to them,[n] and will continue to make 16:27
you known in order that the love 17:26 [n]ver 6 [o]Jn 15:9
you have for me may be in them[o]
and that I myself may be in them."

Jesus Arrested

18 When he had finished praying,
Jesus left with his disciples and
crossed the Kidron Valley.[p] On the oth- 18:1 [p]2Sa 15:23
er side there was an olive grove,[q] and he [q]ver 26 [r]Mt 26:36
and his disciples went into it.[r]
2Now Judas, who betrayed him, knew
the place, because Jesus had often met
there with his disciples.[s] 3So Judas came 18:2 [s]Lk 21:37; 22:39
to the grove, guiding[t] a detachment of
soldiers and some officials from the 18:3 [t]Ac 1:16
chief priests and Pharisees.[u] They were [u]ver 12
carrying torches, lanterns and weapons.
4Jesus, knowing all that was going to
happen to him,[v] went out and asked 18:4 [v]Jn 6:64; 13:1,
them, "Who is it you want?"[w] 11 [w]ver 7

[a]6 Greek *your name*; also in verse 26 [b]17 Greek *hagiazo (set apart for sacred use* or *make holy)*; also in verse 19

5"Jesus of Nazareth," they replied.
"I am he," Jesus said. (And Judas the
traitor was standing there with them.)
6When Jesus said, "I am he," they drew
back and fell to the ground.
18:7 7Again he asked them, "Who is it you
[x] ver 4 want?"[x]
And they said, "Jesus of Nazareth."
8"I told you that I am he," Jesus answered. "If you are looking for me, then
let these men go." 9This happened so
that the words he had spoken would be
fulfilled: "I have not lost one of those you
18:9 [y] Jn 17:12 gave me."[a][y]
10Then Simon Peter, who had a sword,
drew it and struck the high priest's servant, cutting off his right ear. (The servant's name was Malchus.)
11Jesus commanded Peter, "Put your
18:11 [z] Mt 20:22 sword away! Shall I not drink the cup[z]
the Father has given me?"

Jesus Taken to Annas

12Then the detachment of soldiers
with its commander and the Jewish offi-
18:12 [a] ver 3 cials[a] arrested Jesus. They bound him
13and brought him first to Annas, who
18:13 [b] ver 24; Mt 26:3 was the father-in-law of Caiaphas,[b] the
high priest that year. 14Caiaphas was the
one who had advised the Jews that it
would be good if one man died for the **18:14**
people.[c] [c] Jn 11:49-51

Peter's First Denial

15Simon Peter and another disciple
were following Jesus. Because this disci-
ple was known to the high priest,[d] he **18:15** [d] Mt 26:3
went with Jesus into the high priest's [e] Mt 26:58;
courtyard,[e] 16but Peter had to wait out- Mk 14:54;
side at the door. The other disciple, who Lk 22:54
was known to the high priest, came
back, spoke to the girl on duty there and
brought Peter in.
17"You are not one of his disciples, are
you?" the girl at the door asked Peter.
He replied, "I am not."[f] **18:17** [f] ver 25
18It was cold, and the servants and of-
ficials stood around a fire[g] they had **18:18** [g] Jn 21:9
made to keep warm. Peter also was [h] Mk 14:54,67
standing with them, warming himself.[h]

The High Priest Questions Jesus

19Meanwhile, the high priest questioned Jesus about his disciples and his
teaching.

a 9 John 6:39

JESUS FOCUS

IF OLIVE TREES COULD WEEP

Olive trees have flourished in Gethsemane for centuries. Even in Jesus' time there were trees there that were hundreds of years old. The setting was serene and beautiful, an ideal haven for Jesus to revitalize his flagging spirit and commune with his Father in peace. The garden sits on the lower slopes of the Mount of Olives and commands a spectacular view of the Kidron Valley, the city of Jerusalem and the land beyond. The disciples met there frequently and probably sat reflecting about God's kingdom and wondering what they might be able to expect. If the olive trees had been able to listen, they would undoubtedly have overheard a multitude of hopes and dreams. But on the night of Jesus' betrayal, the tranquility of the garden was shattered by the intrusion of soldiers. Jesus was arrested there at the hand of one of his own (John 18:1–11). If olive trees could weep, they would most certainly have wept on that most dreadful of nights—not only for Jesus, but also for those who had come so close to him and yet missed him altogether!

JESUS FOCUS

CLOSE TO THE FIRE

Peter and John followed Jesus and the soldiers at a safe distance to the high priest's palace, undoubtedly desperate to see what would happen next (John 18:15–18). Before the night was over, Peter had been asked three times whether he was a follower of Jesus, but in his traumatized state he three times adamantly denied any association (John 18:15–18; see also Matthew 26:69–75; Mark 14:66–72; Luke 22:55–62). That night the people ignored Peter once he had convinced them that he was merely an interested onlooker. Jesus didn't ignore him, however. When the rooster crowed in the early morning, Jesus turned away from the men who were accusing him and looked out into the courtyard—his eyes meeting Peter's agonized glance in a tacit communication that must have spoken volumes and that no doubt haunted Peter for the rest of his life (Luke 22:61). After meeting his Lord's piercing gaze, a look that gave evidence of overflowing love and sorrow, Peter's heart broke, and he ran outside and sobbed his heart out in true repentance (Luke 22:62).

> MEN MAY LOVE HIM OR HATE HIM, BUT THEY DO IT INTENSELY.
>
> 
>
> T. R. Glover, *British Scholar*

20“I have spoken openly to the world,” Jesus replied. “I always taught in synagogues[i] or at the temple,[j] where all the Jews come together. I said nothing in secret.[k] 21Why question me? Ask those who heard me. Surely they know what I said.”

18:20 [i]Mt 4:23 [j]Mt 26:55 [k]Jn 7:26

22When Jesus said this, one of the officials[l] nearby struck him in the face.[m] “Is this the way you answer the high priest?” he demanded.

18:22 [l]ver 3 [m]Mt 16:21; Jn 19:3

23“If I said something wrong,” Jesus replied, “testify as to what is wrong. But if I spoke the truth, why did you strike me?”[n] 24Then Annas sent him, still bound, to Caiaphas[o] the high priest.[a]

18:23 [n]Mt 5:39; Ac 23:2-5
18:24 [o]ver 13; Mt 26:3

Peter’s Second and Third Denials

25As Simon Peter stood warming himself,[p] he was asked, “You are not one of his disciples, are you?”

He denied it, saying, “I am not.”[q]

26One of the high priest’s servants, a relative of the man whose ear Peter had cut off,[r] challenged him, “Didn’t I see you with him in the olive grove?”[s] 27Again Peter denied it, and at that moment a rooster began to crow.[t]

18:25 [p]ver 18 [q]ver 17
18:26 [r]ver 10 [s]ver 1
18:27 [t]Jn 13:38

Jesus Before Pilate

28Then the Jews led Jesus from Caiaphas to the palace of the Roman governor.[u] By now it was early morning, and to avoid ceremonial uncleanness the Jews did not enter the palace;[v] they wanted to be able to eat the Passover.[w] 29So Pilate came out to them and asked, “What charges are you bringing against this man?”

18:28 [u]Mt 27:2; Mk 15:1; Lk 23:1 [v]ver 33; Jn 19:9 [w]Jn 11:55

30“If he were not a criminal,” they replied, “we would not have handed him over to you.”

31Pilate said, “Take him yourselves and judge him by your own law.”

“But we have no right to execute anyone,” the Jews objected. 32This happened so that the words Jesus had spoken indicating the kind of death he was going to die[x] would be fulfilled.

18:32 [x]Mt 20:19; 26:2; Jn 3:14; 8:28; 12:32,33

33Pilate then went back inside the palace,[y] summoned Jesus and asked him, “Are you the king of the Jews?”[z]

18:33 [y]ver 28,29; Jn 19:9 [z]Lk 23:3; Mt 2:2

34“Is that your own idea,” Jesus asked, “or did others talk to you about me?”

35“Am I a Jew?” Pilate replied. “It was your people and your chief priests who handed you over to me. What is it you have done?”

36Jesus said, “My kingdom[a] is not of this world. If it were, my servants would fight to prevent my arrest by the Jews.[b] But now my kingdom is from another place.”[c]

18:36 [a]Mt 3:2 [b]Mt 26:53 [c]Lk 17:21; Jn 6:15

37“You are a king, then!” said Pilate.

Jesus answered, “You are right in saying I am a king. In fact, for this reason I was born, and for this I came into the world, to testify to the truth.[d] Everyone on the side of truth listens to me.”[e]

18:37 [d]Jn 3:32 [e]Jn 8:47; 1Jn 4:6

38“What is truth?” Pilate asked. With this he went out again to the Jews and said, “I find no basis for a charge against him.[f] 39But it is your custom for me to release to you one prisoner at the time of the Passover. Do you want me to release ‘the king of the Jews’?”

18:38 [f]Lk 23:4; Jn 19:4,6

40They shouted back, “No, not him! Give us Barabbas!” Now Barabbas had taken part in a rebellion.[g]

18:40 [g]Ac 3:14

Jesus Sentenced to Be Crucified

19 Then Pilate took Jesus and had him flogged.[h] 2The soldiers twisted together a crown of thorns and put it on his head. They clothed him in a purple robe 3and went up to him again and again, saying, “Hail, king of the Jews!”[i] And they struck him in the face.[j]

19:1 [h]Dt 25:3; Isa 50:6; 53:5; Mt 27:26
19:3 [i]Mt 27:29 [j]Jn 18:22

4Once more Pilate came out and said to the Jews, “Look, I am bringing him out[k] to you to let you know that I find no basis for a charge against him.”[l] 5When Jesus came out wearing the crown of thorns and the purple robe,[m] Pilate said to them, “Here is the man!”

19:4 [k]Jn 18:38 [l]ver 6; Lk 23:4
19:5 [m]ver 2

6As soon as the chief priests and their officials saw him, they shouted, “Crucify! Crucify!”

But Pilate answered, “You take him and crucify him.[n] As for me, I find no basis for a charge against him.”[o]

19:6 [n]Ac 3:13 [o]ver 4; Lk 23:4

7The Jews insisted, “We have a law, and according to that law he must die,[p] because he claimed to be the Son of God.”[q]

19:7 [p]Lev 24:16 [q]Mt 26:63-66; Jn 5:18; 10:33

[a] 24 Or *(Now Annas had sent him, still bound, to Caiaphas the high priest.)*

8When Pilate heard this, he was even
more afraid, 9and he went back inside
19:9 the palace.[r] "Where do you come from?"
r Jn 18:33 s Mk 14:61 he asked Jesus, but Jesus gave him no answer.[s] 10"Do you refuse to speak to me?"
Pilate said. "Don't you realize I have power either to free you or to crucify you?"
11Jesus answered, "You would have no
power over me if it were not given to you
19:11 t Ro 13:1 from above.[t] Therefore the one who
u Jn 18:28-30; Ac 3:13 handed me over to you[u] is guilty of a
greater sin."
12From then on, Pilate tried to set
Jesus free, but the Jews kept shouting, "If
19:12 you let this man go, you are no friend of
v Lk 23:2 Caesar. Anyone who claims to be a king[v]
opposes Caesar."
13When Pilate heard this, he brought
19:13 Jesus out and sat down on the judge's
w Mt 27:19 seat[w] at a place known as the Stone
x Jn 5:2 Pavement (which in Aramaic[x] is Gabba-
tha). 14It was the day of Preparation[y] of 19:14 y Mt 27:62
Passover Week, about the sixth hour.[z] z Mk 15:25
"Here is your king,"[a] Pilate said to the a ver 19,21
Jews.
15But they shouted, "Take him away!
Take him away! Crucify him!"
"Shall I crucify your king?" Pilate
asked.
"We have no king but Caesar," the
chief priests answered.
16Finally Pilate handed him over to 19:16 b Mt 27:26; Mk 15:15; Lk 23:25
them to be crucified.[b]

JESUS FOCUS

"FATHER, FORGIVE THEM"

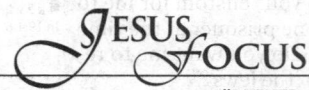

Death by crucifixion was associated in the Jewish mind with a curse from God (see Deuteronomy 21:22–23; Galatians 3:13) and represented for God's people the ultimate humiliation—a spectacle of blood, sweat, tears and shame. The victim was stripped of his clothing, beaten and in many instances nailed to the cross (John 19:1,18,23). It was dirty business, and the Romans were experts at it—known for lining the roads that led into a conquered city with people dying on crosses. The steady crack of their hammers could be heard above the screams of the victims. Each blow not only resulted in nearly intolerable agony but also reminded the victim that there was no hope left. But even in the middle of so horrific an ordeal, Jesus demonstrated his character. Unlike many others, he was no writhing, screaming, pleading victim, nor was he an angry, cursing man. Instead, as the hammers rang out, one voice could be heard to call out above the clamor, "Father, forgive them!" (Luke 23:34). The apostle Peter gave expression to this remarkable attitude on the part of our Savior: "When they hurled their insults at him, he did not retaliate; when he suffered, he made no threats. Instead, he entrusted himself to him who judges justly. He himself bore our sins in his body on the tree, so that we might die to sins and live for righteousness; by his wounds you have been healed (1 Peter 2:23–24).

JESUS WAS CRUCIFIED NOT IN A CATHEDRAL BETWEEN TWO CANDLES, BUT ON A CROSS BETWEEN TWO THIEVES.

George F. MacLeod, *Scottish Minister*

The Crucifixion

So the soldiers took charge of Jesus.
17Carrying his own cross,[c] he went out to 19:17 c Ge 22:6;
the place of the Skull[d] (which in Arama- Lk 14:27; 23:26
ic[e] is called Golgotha). 18Here they cruci- d Lk 23:33
fied him, and with him two others[f]—one e Jn 5:2
on each side and Jesus in the middle. 19:18 f Lk 23:32
19Pilate had a notice prepared and fas-
tened to the cross. It read: JESUS OF NAZA-
RETH,[g] THE KING OF THE JEWS.[h] 20Many of 19:19 g Mk 1:24
the Jews read this sign, for the place h ver 14,21
where Jesus was crucified was near the 19:20
city,[i] and the sign was written in Arama- i Heb 13:12
ic, Latin and Greek. 21The chief priests of
the Jews protested to Pilate, "Do not
write 'The King of the Jews,' but that this
man claimed to be king of the Jews."[j] 19:21 j ver 14
22Pilate answered, "What I have writ-
ten, I have written."
23When the soldiers crucified Jesus,
they took his clothes, dividing them into
four shares, one for each of them, with
the undergarment remaining. This garment was seamless, woven in one piece
from top to bottom.
24"Let's not tear it," they said to one
another. "Let's decide by lot who will
get it."
This happened that the scripture
might be fulfilled[k] which said, 19:24 k ver 28,36,37;

"They divided my garments among Mt 1:22
them l Ps 22:18
and cast lots for my clothing."[a][l]

[a] 24 Psalm 22:18

DISCOVERY 285

IT IS FINISHED

Two issues were indeed "finished" after Jesus had breathed his last. His death consummated a process which God had begun from the beginning of time: All of the Old Testament prophecies concerning the Messiah's sufferings had been fulfilled (John 19:28), and every provision necessary for our salvation from sin was now in place (verse 30).

The concept of finishing something can have several meanings. It can signal the realization of a goal or successful completion of an assignment, as when Jesus amazed the crowds by the power of his teaching (Matthew 7:28). It can also mean fulfillment of a religious, legal or social obligation or accountability. The same Greek word (*teleo*) is used with regard to Mary and Joseph having done what was required in God's law by dedicating Jesus to the Father (Luke 2:39).

One can also complete something in the same sense in which we finish a race; whether or not we come in first, we struggle to cross the finish line (2 Timothy 4:7). To finish might also signal the full repayment of a debt. After Jesus and his disciples had arrived in Capernaum, the collectors of the two-drachma tax approached Peter and asked whether or not Jesus had paid the *teleo*, the temple tax (Matthew 17:24). When Jesus mouthed the three short words, "It is finished," from the cross, he was in effect declaring that he had fulfilled all meanings: He had completed his assigned task, kept God's law, finished the race and fully paid the debt for our sin.

There are still other implications of our Savior's understated proclamation. The word he used has the connotation that something already accomplished will have an ongoing effect. Jesus' earthly task had been completed, but his death and eventual resurrection would most certainly have an ongoing impact (John 3:16) In fact, this one act of supreme sacrifice would change the outlook and history of the world for all time to come.

The task Jesus had come to accomplish was indeed finished, but Jesus himself was not. The devastated disciples concluded that the mission into which they had poured their life energy had ended with Jesus' final breath (Matthew 26:56). The soldiers who had pierced Jesus' side with a spear assumed that the social upheaval caused by the activities of this rabble-rouser were "finished" and that they wouldn't have to deal any longer with this thorn in their side (John 19:33–34). The edgy religious leaders hoped that the influence of our Lord was "finished" but asked Pilate to seal Jesus' tomb to ensure that the disciples wouldn't steal his body (Matthew 27:62–66). Satan gleefully presumed that the threat from this sworn enemy had come to an end, and he gloated in the realization that Jesus was dead and buried (Colossians 2:15).

But all of them were wrong. Three days later the Redeemer rose triumphant from the dead! (Matthew 28:1–10). His supreme act of sacrifice had been completed, but his glorious future as the exalted and triumphant Son of God was only beginning! (Philippians 2:9–11).

Self-Discovery: *Think about some specific commitments that you have made to the Lord. Which have been "finished," in terms of your having accomplished what you had pledged to do, and which are ongoing in nature, a part of your lifelong, daily walk with Jesus Christ?*

GO TO DISCOVERY 286 ON PAGE 1453

So this is what the soldiers did.
19:25 [m]Mt 27:55,56; 25Near the cross[m] of Jesus stood his
Mk 15:40,41; mother,[n] his mother's sister, Mary the
Lk 23:49 [n]Mt 12:46 wife of Clopas, and Mary Magdalene.[o]
[o]Lk 24:18 26When Jesus saw his mother[p] there,
19:26 and the disciple whom he loved[q] stand-
[p]Mt 12:46 ing nearby, he said to his mother, "Dear
[q]Jn 13:23 woman, here is your son," 27and to the
disciple, "Here is your mother." From
that time on, this disciple took her into
his home.

The Death of Jesus

19:28 28Later, knowing that all was now
[r]ver 30; Jn 13:1 completed,[r] and so that the Scripture
[s]ver 24,36,37 would be fulfilled,[s] Jesus said, "I am
19:29 thirsty." 29A jar of wine vinegar[t] was
[t]Ps 69:21 there, so they soaked a sponge in it, put
the sponge on a stalk of the hyssop
plant, and lifted it to Jesus' lips. 30When
he had received the drink, Jesus said, "It
19:30 [u]Lk 12:50; is finished."[u] With that, he bowed his
Jn 17:4 head and gave up his spirit.
19:31 31Now it was the day of Preparation,[v]
[v]ver 14,42 and the next day was to be a special Sab-
[w]Dt 21:23; bath. Because the Jews did not want the
Jos 8:29; 10:26, 27 bodies left on the crosses[w] during the
Sabbath, they asked Pilate to have the
legs broken and the bodies taken down.
32The soldiers therefore came and broke
the legs of the first man who had been

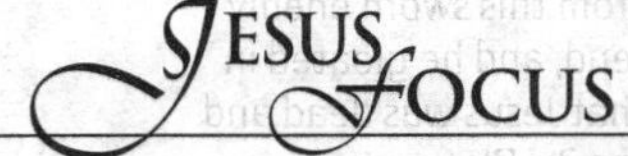

A TORTUOUS DEATH

Crucifixion was designed to be a brutal form of execution. In fact, the victim was literally tortured to death. On rare occasions some hung for several days before death overtook them, and the hideous ordeal stretched out in unspeakable agony. The average survival period, however, was about 24 hours. In order to speed the process of dying, Roman soldiers regularly broke their victims' legs as they hung on the crosses. The excruciating pain prevented the sufferers from being able to push themselves up in order to breathe, and they soon suffocated. Jesus died in only a few hours, however, and was already dead when the soldiers came to break his legs, so they did not follow through (John 19:33). Just as God had predicted centuries earlier, the Messiah's bones were not broken (Exodus 12:46; Numbers 9:12; Psalm 34:20). Instead, the soldiers drove a spear into his side (John 19:33–34), fulfilling another prediction (Zechariah 12:10).

crucified with Jesus, and then those of 19:32
the other.[x] 33But when they came to [x]ver 18
Jesus and found that he was already
dead, they did not break his legs. 34In- 19:34
stead, one of the soldiers pierced[y] Jesus' [y]Zec 12:10
side with a spear, bringing a sudden flow [z]1Jn 5:6,8
of blood and water.[z] 35The man who saw
it[a] has given testimony, and his testimo- 19:35 [a]Lk 24:48
ny is true.[b] He knows that he tells the [b]Jn 15:27; 21:24
truth, and he testifies so that you also
may believe. 36These things happened so 19:36
that the scripture would be fulfilled:[c] [c]ver 24,28,37;
"Not one of his bones will be broken,"[a][d] Mt 1:22 [d]Ex 12:46;
37and, as another scripture says, "They Nu 9:12;
will look on the one they have pierced."[b][e] Ps 34:20

19:37 [e]Zec 12:10;

The Burial of Jesus Rev 1:7

38Later, Joseph of Arimathea asked Pilate for the body of Jesus. Now Joseph
was a disciple of Jesus, but secretly because he feared the Jews. With Pilate's
permission, he came and took the body
away. 39He was accompanied by Nicode-
mus,[f] the man who earlier had visited 19:39 [f]Jn 3:1; 7:50
Jesus at night. Nicodemus brought a
mixture of myrrh and aloes, about seventy-five pounds.[c] 40Taking Jesus' body,
the two of them wrapped it, with the
spices, in strips of linen.[g] This was in ac- 19:40 [g]Lk 24:12;
cordance with Jewish burial customs.[h] Jn 11:44; 20:5,7 [h]Mt 26:12
41At the place where Jesus was crucified,
there was a garden, and in the garden a
new tomb, in which no one had ever
been laid. 42Because it was the Jewish
day of Preparation[i] and since the tomb 19:42 [i]ver 14,31
was nearby,[j] they laid Jesus there. [j]ver 20,41

The Empty Tomb

20 Early on the first day of the
week, while it was still dark,
Mary Magdalene[k] went to the tomb and 20:1
saw that the stone had been removed [k]ver 18; Jn 19:25
from the entrance.[l] 2So she came run- [l]Mt 27:60,66
ning to Simon Peter and the other disci-
ple, the one Jesus loved,[m] and said, 20:2 [m]Jn 13:23
"They have taken the Lord out of the [n]ver 13
tomb, and we don't know where they
have put him!"[n]

3So Peter and the other disciple start-
ed for the tomb.[o] 4Both were running, 20:3 [o]Lk 24:12
but the other disciple outran Peter and
reached the tomb first. 5He bent over 20:5
and looked in[p] at the strips of linen[q] ly- [p]ver 11
ing there but did not go in. 6Then Simon [q]Jn 19:40

[a] *36* Exodus 12:46; Num. 9:12; Psalm 34:20
[b] *37* Zech. 12:10 [c] *39* Greek *a hundred litrai* (about 34 kilograms)

> **THE RESURRECTION IS THE SIMPLEST, MOST PROBABLE EXPLANATION OF THE EMPTY TOMB.**
>
> William Lane Craig, *American Scholar*

Peter, who was behind him, arrived and
went into the tomb. He saw the strips of
linen lying there, 7as well as the burial
20:7 cloth that had been around Jesus' head.[r]
r Jn 11:44 The cloth was folded up by itself, separate from the linen. 8Finally the other
20:8 disciple, who had reached the tomb
s ver 4 first,[s] also went inside. He saw and be-
20:9 lieved. 9(They still did not understand
t Mt 22:29; from Scripture[t] that Jesus had to rise
Jn 2:22 u Lk 24:26,46 from the dead.)[u]

Jesus Appears to Mary Magdalene

10Then the disciples went back to
their homes, 11but Mary stood outside
the tomb crying. As she wept, she bent
20:11 over to look into the tomb[v] 12and saw
v ver 5 two angels in white,[w] seated where Jesus'
20:12 body had been, one at the head and the
w Mt 28:2,3; Mk 16:5; other at the foot.
Lk 24:4; Ac 5:19 13They asked her, "Woman, why are
20:13 you crying?"[x]
x ver 15 y ver 2 "They have taken my Lord away," she
said, "and I don't know where they have
put him."[y] 14At this, she turned around
20:14 and saw Jesus standing there,[z] but she
z Mt 28:9; Mk 16:9 did not realize that it was Jesus.[a]
a Lk 24:16; Jn 21:4 15"Woman," he said, "why are you cry-
20:15 ing?[b] Who is it you are looking for?"
b ver 13 Thinking he was the gardener, she
said, "Sir, if you have carried him away,
tell me where you have put him, and I
will get him."
16Jesus said to her, "Mary."
She turned toward him and cried out
20:16 in Aramaic,[c] "Rabboni!"[d] (which means
c Jn 5:2 d Mt 23:7 Teacher).
17Jesus said, "Do not hold on to me,
for I have not yet returned to the Father.
20:17 Go instead to my brothers[e] and tell
e Mt 28:10 f Jn 7:33 them, 'I am returning to my Father[f] and
your Father, to my God and your God.' "
20:18 18Mary Magdalene[g] went to the disci-
g ver 1 h Lk 24:10,22,23 ples[h] with the news: "I have seen the
Lord!" And she told them that he had
said these things to her.

Jesus Appears to His Disciples

19On the evening of that first day of
the week, when the disciples were together, with the doors locked for fear of 20:19
the Jews,[i] Jesus came and stood among i Jn 7:13 j Jn 14:27
them and said, "Peace[j] be with you!"[k] k ver 21,26;
20After he said this, he showed them his Lk 24:36-39
hands and side.[l] The disciples were over- 20:20 l Lk 24:39,40;
joyed[m] when they saw the Lord. Jn 19:34
21Again Jesus said, "Peace be with m Jn 16:20,22
you![n] As the Father has sent me,[o] I am 20:21
sending you."[p] 22And with that he n ver 19 o Jn 3:17
breathed on them and said, "Receive the p Mt 28:19;
Holy Spirit.[q] 23If you forgive anyone his Jn 17:18
sins, they are forgiven; if you do not for- 20:22 q Jn 7:39;
give them, they are not forgiven."[r] Ac 2:38; 8:15-17; 19:2; Gal 3:2

Jesus Appears to Thomas

24Now Thomas[s] (called Didymus), 20:23 r Mt 16:19; 18:18
one of the Twelve, was not with the dis-
ciples when Jesus came. 25So the other 20:24 s Jn 11:16
disciples told him, "We have seen the
Lord!"

TOUCH ME!

Thomas may have been skeptical by nature, although in reality none of the other disciples believed that Jesus had come back to life until after they had seen him with their own eyes. In fact, Thomas wasn't even present when Jesus first appeared to the others (John 20:24). The incredulous Thomas refused to believe (or possibly couldn't even bring himself to dare to believe) the astonishing news that the others reported to him until Jesus paid the group another visit and insisted that Thomas touch his very real wounds, still fresh from the crucifixion. For all of the disciples, seeing was believing, and Jesus took the opportunity to convey to them that those who believe without having seen him will be even more blessed by his presence (verse 29). Since Jesus ascended into heaven (Luke 24:51) God's people have not had the opportunity to see their Savior face-to-face but have faithfully trusted in Jesus based on the truth of his written Word and the internal testimony of the Holy Spirit. What happened so long ago convinced not only Thomas but also countless generations of believers who have accepted the disciples' eyewitness reports as truth and who have welcomed the Savior into their hearts and lives, confidently proclaiming with Thomas, "My Lord and my God!" (John 20:28).

JESUS NEVER GAINED DISCIPLES UNDER FALSE PRETENSES. HE NEVER HID HIS SCARS, BUT RATHER DECLARED "BEHOLD MY HANDS AND FEET."

George Sweeting, *Chancellor, Moody Bible Institute, Chicago, Illinois*

But he said to them, "Unless I see the
nail marks in his hands and put my fin-
20:25 [t] ver 20 ger where the nails were, and put my
[u] Mk 16:11 hand into his side,[t] I will not believe it."[u]
26 A week later his disciples were in
the house again, and Thomas was with
them. Though the doors were locked,
Jesus came and stood among them and
20:26 [v] Jn 14:27 said, "Peace[v] be with you!"[w] 27 Then he
[w] ver 21 said to Thomas, "Put your finger here;
see my hands. Reach out your hand and
20:27 put it into my side. Stop doubting and
[x] ver 25; Lk 24:40 believe."[x]
28 Thomas said to him, "My Lord and
my God!"
20:29 29 Then Jesus told him, "Because you
[y] Jn 3:15 have seen me, you have believed;[y]
[z] 1Pe 1:8 blessed are those who have not seen and
yet have believed."[z]
20:30 30 Jesus did many other miraculous
[a] Jn 2:11 signs[a] in the presence of his disciples,
[b] Jn 21:25 which are not recorded in this book.[b]
31 But these are written that you may[a]
20:31 [c] Jn 3:15; 19:35 believe[c] that Jesus is the Christ, the Son
[d] Mt 4:3 of God,[d] and that by believing you may
[e] Mt 25:46 have life in his name.[e]

Jesus and the Miraculous Catch of Fish

21 Afterward Jesus appeared again
21:1 [f] Jn 20:19,26 to his disciples,[f] by the Sea of
[g] Jn 6:1 Tiberias.[b][g] It happened this way: 2 Simon
21:2 Peter, Thomas[h] (called Didymus),
[h] Jn 11:16 Nathanael[i] from Cana in Galilee,[j] the
[i] Jn 1:45 [j] Jn 2:1 sons of Zebedee,[k] and two other disci-
[k] Mt 4:21 ples were together. 3 "I'm going out to
fish," Simon Peter told them, and they
said, "We'll go with you." So they went
out and got into the boat, but that night
21:3 [l] Lk 5:5 they caught nothing.[l]
4 Early in the morning, Jesus stood on
21:4 the shore, but the disciples did not real-
[m] Lk 24:16; Jn 20:14 ize that it was Jesus.[m]
5 He called out to them, "Friends,
haven't you any fish?"
"No," they answered.
6 He said, "Throw your net on the
right side of the boat and you will find
some." When they did, they were unable
to haul the net in because of the large
number of fish.[n] 21:6 [n] Lk 5:4-7
7 Then the disciple whom Jesus loved[o] 21:7
said to Peter, "It is the Lord!" As soon as [o] Jn 13:23
Simon Peter heard him say, "It is the
Lord," he wrapped his outer garment
around him (for he had taken it off) and
jumped into the water. 8 The other disciples followed in the boat, towing the net
full of fish, for they were not far from
shore, about a hundred yards.[c] 9 When
they landed, they saw a fire[p] of burning 21:9 [p] Jn 18:18
coals there with fish on it,[q] and some [q] ver 10,13
bread.
10 Jesus said to them, "Bring some of
the fish you have just caught."
11 Simon Peter climbed aboard and
dragged the net ashore. It was full of
large fish, 153, but even with so many
the net was not torn. 12 Jesus said to
them, "Come and have breakfast." None
of the disciples dared ask him, "Who are
you?" They knew it was the Lord. 13 Jesus
came, took the bread and gave it to
them, and did the same with the fish.[r] 21:13 [r] ver 9
14 This was now the third time Jesus ap-
peared to his disciples[s] after he was 21:14 [s] Jn 20:19,26
raised from the dead.

Jesus Reinstates Peter

15 When they had finished eating, Jesus
said to Simon Peter, "Simon son of John,
do you truly love me more than these?"
"Yes, Lord," he said, "you know that I
love you."[t] 21:15 [t] Mt 26:33,35;
Jesus said, "Feed my lambs."[u] Jn 13:37
16 Again Jesus said, "Simon son of [u] Lk 12:32
John, do you truly love me?"
He answered, "Yes, Lord, you know
that I love you."
Jesus said, "Take care of my sheep."[v] 21:16 [v] Mt 2:6;
17 The third time he said to him, "Si- Ac 20:28;
mon son of John, do you love me?" 1Pe 5:2,3
Peter was hurt because Jesus asked
him the third time, "Do you love me?"[w] 21:17 [w] Jn 13:38
He said, "Lord, you know all things;[x] you [x] Jn 16:30
know that I love you." [y] ver 16
Jesus said, "Feed my sheep.[y] 18 I tell
you the truth, when you were younger
you dressed yourself and went where you
wanted; but when you are old you will
stretch out your hands, and someone

[a] 31 Some manuscripts *may continue to*
[b] 1 That is, Sea of Galilee [c] 8 Greek *about two hundred cubits* (about 90 meters)

DISCOVERY 286

Do You Love Me?

Peter and several of the other disciples had spent an unsuccessful night fishing (John 21:3). As they were rowing wearily toward shore in the morning mist they observed a man standing on the beach. They failed to recognize him as the risen Jesus, but when he instructed them to try throwing their nets over the other side of the boat, they did as he said—with the amazing result that they caught 153 fish! When they reached the shore they realized that the mysterious stranger was indeed the Lord. Jesus already had a fire going and cooked some of the fish for them (verses 12–13).

After breakfast Jesus turned his attention to Peter. During their conversation Jesus interrogated Peter three times as to whether or not Peter loved him, the three questions standing in direct contrast to Peter's three denials that he knew Jesus (Mark 14:66–72).

There is an interesting play on words in the Greek, with Jesus and Peter using two different words for "love." In his first two questions Jesus spoke of *agapao*, which refers to the highest and noblest degree of love, the kind which God has for his people, a sacrificial and unconditional love (John 3:16). Peter responded with *phileo*, a term describing human love—a feeling of appreciation and affection for others. Back and forth the two volleyed, with Jesus asking the first two times whether or not Peter truly loved him with the deepest and most unselfish devotion and Peter assuring the Lord that he did indeed hold a deep affection and appreciation for him. The third time Jesus asked Peter whether he did indeed love his Master with affection or fondness (*phileo*), to which Peter replied, "Lord, you know all things; you know that I love [*phileo*] you" (John 21:17).

There was more to this exchange, however. In his first question Jesus asked Peter to make a comparison: "Do you truly love me more than these?" (verse 15). Our Lord may have been asking whether Peter loved Jesus more than he loved the other disciples or whether Peter loved Jesus more than the other disciples loved Jesus. He might even have been asking whether Peter loved Jesus more than he loved fishing, life by the sea or a combination of all of the above. Whatever he was referring to, the crux of Jesus' question was obvious: Did Peter put Jesus first and foremost, above everyone and everything else?

This degree of love requires confirmation and completion through action. "Feed my lambs," Jesus directed Peter (verse 15). Loving the Lord entails loving the people and the things he loves and doing what he asks without question or protest. For Peter this kind of obedience entailed helping to take care of God's people. And so it is with us: As we learn to love Jesus, his priorities become ours, and what matters to him becomes more and more important in our lives. We begin to demonstrate our adoration of Jesus by the way we live, not just by the words we speak (John 14:23–24; 1 John 3:18).

***Self-Discovery:** In what specific ways have you confirmed and "completed" your love for Jesus through concrete actions?*

GO TO DISCOVERY 287 ON PAGE 1457

else will dress you and lead you where
you do not want to go." 19Jesus said this
21:19 to indicate the kind of death[z] by which
[z]Jn 12:33; 18:32 Peter would glorify God.[a] Then he said to
[a]2Pe 1:14 him, "Follow me!"
20Peter turned and saw that the disci-
21:20 [b]ver 7; Jn 13:23 ple whom Jesus loved[b] was following
[c]Jn 13:25 them. (This was the one who had leaned
back against Jesus at the supper and had
said, "Lord, who is going to betray
you?")[c] 21When Peter saw him, he asked,
"Lord, what about him?"
22Jesus answered, "If I want him to re-
21:22 main alive until I return,[d] what is that to
[d]Mt 16:27; 1Co 4:5; you? You must follow me."[e] 23Because of
Rev 2:25 this, the rumor spread among the broth-
[e]ver 19 ers[f] that this disciple would not die. But
21:23 Jesus did not say that he would not die;
[f]Ac 1:16 he only said, "If I want him to remain
alive until I return, what is that to you?"
24This is the disciple who testifies to
21:24 [g]Jn 15:27 these things[g] and who wrote them down.
[h]Jn 19:35 We know that his testimony is true.[h]
21:25 25Jesus did many other things as well.[i]
[i]Jn 20:30 If every one of them were written down,
I suppose that even the whole world
would not have room for the books that
would be written.

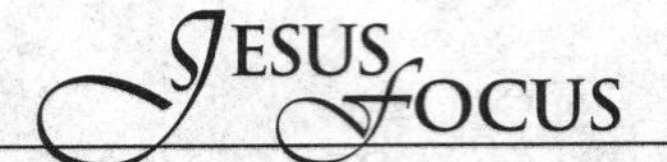

THE LAST BREAKFAST

After he had come back to life, Jesus treated seven of his disciples, including John, to an unusual breakfast. The disciples were back in Galilee, fishing and waiting to hear what Jesus wanted them to do next. After fishing all night, they were exhausted and discouraged because they had caught nothing. Then a man called to them from the shore, suggesting that they cast their nets on the other side of the boat. They took his advice, and the nets were instantly filled. They had seen this happen before (Luke 5). "It is the Lord!" John exclaimed. Peter jumped overboard in his excitement and swam to shore, leaving the others to drag in the nets. John, being a fisherman, counted the catch, and there were 153 fish in the net. When they came ashore, Jesus had breakfast waiting for them. This was the last miracle they would see Jesus perform. But the most memorable event of that day was the expression of Jesus' grace in restoring Peter to his service.

Why was Jesus' ascension such a dramatic exit? (Acts 1:9)

- *Jesus had prepared his disciples for his eventual departure. But they still had not grasped the significance of all he had taught them (verse 6). His ascension may have been a final vivid object lesson that he was leaving the physical world and returning to spiritual realms. His extraordinary departure helped the disciples to see Jesus of Nazareth as the Christ of heaven.*

Why did the risen Jesus appear only to those already convinced? (Acts 10:41)

- *The masses would not have been able to comprehend what they were seeing, nor would they have been able to respond with believing hearts. Jesus appeared especially to these individuals so that they might be made witnesses.*

Jesus in Acts In the book of Acts we read about Jesus' ascension into heaven after he had commissioned his disciples to tell people everywhere who he is and what he had come to do (Acts 1:1–11). From heaven he continued to guide the apostles through his Holy Spirit, poured out on the day of Pentecost (Acts 2:1–13). Acts demonstrates that revival and the growth of the church brought about not by human effort but only through the Spirit's power.

Filled with dramatic events from the lives of Peter and Paul, Acts provides fascinating details about the beginnings of the church. When the risen Jesus intervened in Paul's life, he spoke from heaven and left no doubt as to who he was (Acts 9:5). As you read Acts, you will be inspired as you follow the story of Paul's dramatic conversion, his acceptance by other believers and his ministry as a Christian missionary.

The apostles' teaching focused on Jesus himself because "there is no other name under heaven given to men by which we must be saved" (Acts 4:12).

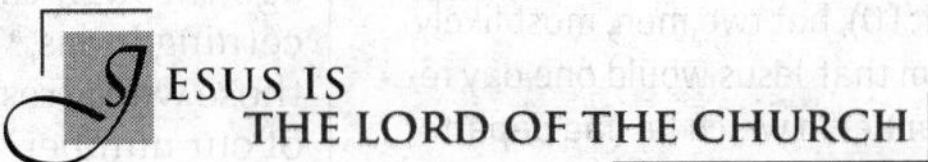
JESUS IS
THE LORD OF THE CHURCH

WE SHOULD NOT BE SURPRISED THAT A CHRIST WHO WAS RAISED FROM THE DEAD HAS ALSO ASCENDED INTO HEAVEN.

Erwin Lutzer, *Pastor, Chicago, Illinois*

Jesus Taken Up Into Heaven

1:1 [a] Lk 1:1-4 **1** In my former book,[a] Theophilus, I
[b] Lk 3:23 wrote about all that Jesus began
1:2 to do and to teach[b] 2until the day he was
[c] ver 9,11; taken up to heaven,[c] after giving in-
Mk 16:19 [d] Mt 28:19,20 structions[d] through the Holy Spirit to
[e] Mk 6:30 the apostles[e] he had chosen.[f] 3After his
[f] Jn 13:18 suffering, he showed himself to these
men and gave many convincing proofs
1:3 [g] Mt 28:17; that he was alive. He appeared to them[g]
Lk 24:34,36; over a period of forty days and spoke
Jn 20:19,26; 21:1,14; about the kingdom of God. 4On one oc-
1Co 15:5-7 casion, while he was eating with them,
he gave them this command: "Do not
1:4 [h] Lk 24:49; leave Jerusalem, but wait for the gift my
Jn 14:16; Father promised, which you have heard
Ac 2:33 me speak about.[h] 5For John baptized
with[a] water, but in a few days you will be
baptized with the Holy Spirit."
6So when they met together, they
asked him, "Lord, are you at this time 1:6
going to restore[i] the kingdom to Israel?" [i] Mt 17:11
7He said to them: "It is not for you to
know the times or dates the Father has
set by his own authority.[j] 8But you will 1:7 [j] Mt 24:36
receive power when the Holy Spirit
comes on you;[k] and you will be my wit- 1:8 [k] Ac 2:1-4
nesses[l] in Jerusalem, and in all Judea [l] Lk 24:48
and Samaria,[m] and to the ends of the [m] Ac 8:1-25 [n] Mt 28:19
earth."[n]
9After he said this, he was taken up[o] 1:9 [o] ver 2
before their very eyes, and a cloud hid
him from their sight.
10They were looking intently up into
the sky as he was going, when suddenly
two men dressed in white[p] stood beside 1:10 [p] Lk 24:4;
them. 11"Men of Galilee,"[q] they said, Jn 20:12
"why do you stand here looking into the 1:11
sky? This same Jesus, who has been tak- [q] Ac 2:7
en from you into heaven, will come [r] Mt 16:27
back[r] in the same way you have seen
him go into heaven."

Matthias Chosen to Replace Judas

12Then they returned to Jerusalem[s] 1:12
from the hill called the Mount of Olives,[t] [s] Lk 24:52 [t] Mt 21:1
a Sabbath day's walk[b] from the city.
13When they arrived, they went upstairs 1:13
to the room[u] where they were staying. [u] Ac 9:37; 20:8
Those present were Peter, John, James [v] Mt 10:2-4;
and Andrew; Philip and Thomas, Mk 3:16-19; Lk 6:14-16
Bartholomew and Matthew; James son
of Alphaeus and Simon the Zealot, and
Judas son of James.[v] 14They all joined to-
gether constantly in prayer,[w] along with 1:14 [w] Ac 2:42; 6:4
the women[x] and Mary the mother of [x] Lk 23:49,55
Jesus, and with his brothers.[y] [y] Mt 12:46
15In those days Peter stood up among
the believers[c] (a group numbering about
a hundred and twenty) 16and said,
"Brothers, the Scripture had to be ful- 1:16
filled[z] which the Holy Spirit spoke long [z] ver 20
ago through the mouth of David con- [a] Jn 13:18
cerning Judas,[a] who served as guide for
those who arrested Jesus— 17he was one
of our number[b] and shared in this min- 1:17 [b] Jn 6:70,71
istry."[c] [c] ver 25
18(With the reward[d] he got for his 1:18
wickedness, Judas bought a field;[e] there [d] Mt 26:14,15
he fell headlong, his body burst open [e] Mt 27:3-10
and all his intestines spilled out. 19Every-
one in Jerusalem heard about this, so

[a] *5* Or *in* [b] *12* That is, about 3/4 mile (about 1,100 meters) [c] *15* Greek *brothers*

JESUS GOES BACK TO HEAVEN

Following his resurrection Jesus appeared to his disciples on several occasions with "many convincing proofs" (Acts 1:3). After he had dispatched them to go into the world to tell people the Good News, our Savior returned to take his rightful place at the right hand of God the Father in heaven. There the Father glorified him and exalted him as the glorious Son of God (John 17:4–5; Philippians 2:6–11). That return to the Father's side marked his triumphal entry into heaven to fill his role as our great high priest (Romans 8:34; Hebrews 4:14—5:10; 6:19—7:28).

The disciples stood staring at the sky as Jesus disappeared (Acts 1:10), but two men, most likely angels, assured them that Jesus would one day return in the same manner in which he had departed—in the same resurrection body and in clouds and "great glory" (Matthew 24:30). Many Bible students believe that this promise of Jesus' return also reveals that Jesus will come back to the Mount of Olives, thus fulfilling the prophecy of Zechariah 14:4 which predicts that the mountain will split in two to provide a way of escape for God's people from the final onslaught of opposition.

Famous Last Words

A person's last words are often remembered long after her death as the most significant she has ever spoken. When we are granted an opportunity to offer final words, we want to make certain that they express what we most want those left behind to hold dear and never forget. One man who was about to undergo a risky heart surgery squeezed his wife's hand and whispered, "If I don't make it, I want you to know I love you." He did not survive the surgery, but those last words are firmly etched into his widow's memory.

In Acts 1 we read Jesus' last words to his disciples before his return to the Father's side: "You will receive power when the Holy Spirit comes on you; and you will be my witnesses in Jerusalem, and in all Judea and Samaria, and to the ends of the earth" (verse 8). The disciples had lived with Jesus for three years, witnessed his miracles, listened to his teaching, experienced his death and celebrated his resurrection. All along they had expected Jesus the Messiah to deliver the Jewish people from Roman rule and to set up God's eternal kingdom right there on the very soil they trod. Jesus had patiently explained to them again and again that his purpose was different, that he would establish his kingdom at a later time (John 18:36).

At the very end of his earthly life, though, they were still asking the same obtuse question: "Lord, are you at this time going to restore the kingdom to Israel?" (Acts 1:6). The 11 disciples apparently continued to entertain visions of positions of prominence and leadership in this new kingdom. But Jesus turned their attention to more immediate concerns and a more pressing mission.

"You will be my witnesses," Jesus informed the disciples (verse 8). Notice that he did not say, "You will *witness*." Jesus was more concerned about the kind of people his disciples were to become than he was about what they would say to people as they talked about him. Unfortunately, we too often find it convenient to switch the direction from "being something" to "doing something."

There was unprecedented power in the mission Jesus conferred on his disciples. This mandate was unlike any commission ever before given, and it was not something they could accomplish by their own strength. Jesus instructed them to wait until they had received the power of his Holy Spirit (verse 8). When the Spirit did come on them Peter delivered a powerful sermon to the gathered crowd (Acts 2:14–39). Three thousand people responded to the message (Acts 2:41)—a message preached only a few short weeks after the terrified Peter had opened his mouth to curse and deny any association with Jesus (Mark 14:66–72). The power of the Holy Spirit had transformed a coward into a courageous spokesman for God.

The complexion and prospects of our world have been irreversibly changed because Jesus' disciples continued (and still continue today) to be his witnesses (Acts 1:8). Witnessing for Jesus begins where we live and work, but, as we continue to carry out the Lord's commission, his Holy Spirit will empower our lives so that our testimony may have an ever-widening circle of influence.

Self-Discovery: *In what way does it make a difference in your own life to think about being a witness rather than simply witnessing?*

GO TO DISCOVERY 288 ON PAGE 1459

they called that field in their language
Akeldama, that is, Field of Blood.)
20"For," said Peter, "it is written in the
book of Psalms,

" 'May his place be deserted;
1:20 let there be no one to dwell in
[f]Ps 69:25 it,'[a f]
[g]Ps 109:8

and,

" 'May another take his place of
leadership.'[b g]

21Therefore it is necessary to choose one
of the men who have been with us the
whole time the Lord Jesus went in and
1:22 out among us, 22beginning from John's
[h]Mk 1:4 [i]ver 8 baptism[h] to the time when Jesus was
taken up from us. For one of these must
become a witness[i] with us of his resurrection."
23So they proposed two men: Joseph
called Barsabbas (also known as Justus)
1:24
[j]Ac 6:6; 14:23 and Matthias. 24Then they prayed,[j]
[k]1Sa 16:7; "Lord, you know everyone's heart.[k] Show
Jer 17:10; Ac 15:8; us which of these two you have chosen
Rev 2:23 25to take over this apostolic ministry,
which Judas left to go where he belongs."
26Then they cast lots, and the lot fell to
Matthias; so he was added to the eleven
1:26 apostles.[l]
[l]Ac 2:14

The Holy Spirit Comes at Pentecost

2:1
[m]Lev 23:15,16; **2** When the day of Pentecost[m]
Ac 20:16 came, they were all together[n] in
[n]Ac 1:14 one place. 2Suddenly a sound like the
blowing of a violent wind came from
heaven and filled the whole house where 2:2
they were sitting.[o] 3They saw what [o]Ac 4:31
seemed to be tongues of fire that separated and came to rest on each of them.
4All of them were filled with the Holy
Spirit and began to speak in other 2:4
tongues[c p] as the Spirit enabled them. [p]Mk 16:17; 1Co 12:10
5Now there were staying in Jerusalem
God-fearing[q] Jews from every nation 2:5
under heaven. 6When they heard this [q]Ac 8:2
sound, a crowd came together in bewilderment, because each one heard them
speaking in his own language. 7Utterly
amazed,[r] they asked: "Are not all these 2:7 [r]ver 12 [s]Ac 1:11
men who are speaking Galileans?[s]
8Then how is it that each of us hears
them in his own native language?
9Parthians, Medes and Elamites; residents of Mesopotamia, Judea and Cap- 2:9
padocia,[t] Pontus[u] and Asia,[v] 10Phrygia[w] [t]1Pe 1:1 [u]Ac 18:2
and Pamphylia,[x] Egypt and the parts of [v]Ac 16:6;
Libya near Cyrene;[y] visitors from Rome Ro 16:5;
11(both Jews and converts to Judaism); 1Co 16:19; 2Co 1:8
Cretans and Arabs—we hear them de-
claring the wonders of God in our own 2:10
tongues!" 12Amazed and perplexed, they [w]Ac 16:6; 18:23 [x]Ac 13:13;
asked one another, "What does this 15:38 [y]Mt 27:32
mean?"
13Some, however, made fun of them
and said, "They have had too much 2:13
wine.[d]"[z] [z]1Co 14:23

Peter Addresses the Crowd

14Then Peter stood up with the
Eleven, raised his voice and addressed
the crowd: "Fellow Jews and all of you
who live in Jerusalem, let me explain this
to you; listen carefully to what I say.
15These men are not drunk, as you sup- 2:15
pose. It's only nine in the morning![a] [a]1Th 5:7
16No, this is what was spoken by the
prophet Joel:

17" 'In the last days, God says,
I will pour out my Spirit on all
people.[b] 2:17 [b]Isa 44:3;
Your sons and daughters will Jn 7:37-39;
prophesy,[c] Ac 10:45 [c]Ac 21:9
your young men will see visions,
your old men will dream dreams.
18Even on my servants, both men
and women,
I will pour out my Spirit in those
days, 2:18
and they will prophesy.[d] [d]Ac 21:9-12

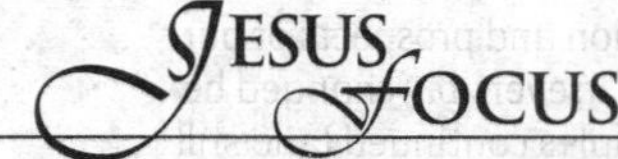

THE GUIDANCE OF THE SPIRIT

Jesus' disciples were known as the Twelve, and that number was reduced to 11 after the death of Judas. The disciples chose Matthias by lot as a substitute for Judas (Acts 1:23–26). This is the last Biblical incident in which the casting of lots is mentioned as a means for determining the Father's will, although in the Old Testament the priests cast lots frequently (see, for example, Exodus 28:30; 1 Chronicles 24:5,31; Nehemiah 10:34). However, after Jesus returned to heaven following his death and resurrection, he sent the Holy Spirit to live within us, and we have had him ever since to reveal the will of the Father and to guide us personally (John 16:5–15). The better we get to know God, the better we understand what he wants for us.

[a] *20* Psalm 69:25 [b] *20* Psalm 109:8 [c] *4* Or *languages*; also in verse 11 [d] *13* Or *sweet wine*

Peter's Pentecost Sermon

Peter made at least two significant statements in his sermon on the day of Pentecost. The first has, tragically, often been used to fuel hatred and violence against those of Jewish descent. Peter answered the implied question of *Who crucified Jesus?* by implicating the Jewish people (Acts 2:23,36), and over the centuries certain misguided individuals have argued that the relentless persecution which the Jews have endured is their just desert for putting to death the Son of God.

Yes, the Jewish masses did clamor for Jesus' death; interestingly, they also willingly acknowledged that the repercussions would be upon themselves and their children (Matthew 27:25). But others were involved in the process. First, Pontius Pilate was responsible, having ignored the warnings of his wife (Matthew 27:19) and turned Jesus over to be executed. The Jewish religious leaders were certainly accountable. They had tried to have Jesus arrested long before, and, after much plotting and scheming, had bribed Judas to betray him.

All of these individuals were only instruments in the process, however. Ultimately, *each of us* is responsible for the heinous crime of killing our Savior, because Jesus died according to the Father's perfect plan, instituted from before the beginning of time, to fully atone for the sins of all of humanity. The truth is that the crucifixion wouldn't have happened had we as a human race not turned our backs on God.

Peter's next statement answered the question of *Who exalted Jesus?* Peter informed his audience that God had made Jesus to be both Lord and Christ (Acts 2:36). When we talk about Jesus' life we sometimes divide it into two broad stages: his *humiliation* and his *exaltation*. "Humiliation" implies that Jesus Christ voluntarily renounced the glories of heaven to be born into the human race in order to suffer, die and be buried for our sin.

But then came his exaltation. He rose victorious from the dead, returned to heaven and now sits in the place of honor at the right hand of God the Father. The apostle Paul later described Jesus' exaltation as well: "Therefore God exalted him to the highest place and gave him the name that is above every name, that at the name of Jesus every knee should bow, in heaven and on earth and under the earth, and every tongue confess that Jesus Christ is Lord, to the glory of God the Father" (Philippians 2:9–11).

What does this mean for us? Sometimes we hear speakers, teachers or pastors say that we need to "make Jesus Lord." But it is not our prerogative to place him in that position: Jesus is *already* Lord of all. What he wants is for us to accept his lordship in our lives. One day, every person who has ever lived will readily admit the truth of who Jesus is, but for many it will be too late. The choice to surrender to him must be made during this earthly life.

Self-Discovery: *Have you accepted Jesus as the Lord of your life? If so, "just as you received Christ Jesus as Lord, continue to live in him" (Colossians 2:65). How can you demonstrate your submission to him today?*

GO TO DISCOVERY 289 ON PAGE 1463

[19] I will show wonders in the heaven
above
and signs on the earth below,
blood and fire and billows of
smoke.
[20] The sun will be turned to darkness
and the moon to blood[e]
before the coming of the great
and glorious day of the
Lord.
[21] And everyone who calls
on the name of the Lord will be
saved.'[a][f]

2:20 [e] Mt 24:29
2:21 [f] Ro 10:13

> THE CROSS OF CHRIST DECLARES TWO THINGS: FIRST, GOD'S INFINITE LOVE OF THE WORLD; SECOND, GOD'S INFINITE HATRED OF SIN.
>
> R. A. Torrey, *American Evangelist*

[22]"Men of Israel, listen to this: Jesus of Nazareth was a man accredited by God to you by miracles, wonders and signs,[g] which God did among you through him,[h] as you yourselves know. [23]This man was handed over to you by God's set purpose and foreknowledge;[i] and you, with the help of wicked men,[b] put him to death by nailing him to the cross.[j] [24]But God raised him from the dead,[k] freeing him from the agony of death, because it was impossible for death to keep its hold on him.[l] [25]David said about him:

2:22 [g] Jn 4:48; Ac 10:38 [h] Jn 3:2
2:23 [i] Lk 22:22; Ac 3:18; 4:28 [j] Lk 24:20; Ac 3:13
2:24 [k] ver 32; 1Co 6:14; 2Co 4:14; Eph 1:20; Col 2:12; Heb 13:20; 1Pe 1:21 [l] Jn 20:9

"'I saw the Lord always before me.
Because he is at my right hand,
I will not be shaken.
[26] Therefore my heart is glad and my
tongue rejoices;
my body also will live in hope,
[27] because you will not abandon me
to the grave,
nor will you let your Holy One
see decay.[m]
[28] You have made known to me the
paths of life;
you will fill me with joy in your
presence.'[c]

2:27 [m] ver 31; Ac 13:35

[29]"Brothers, I can tell you confidently that the patriarch[n] David died and was buried,[o] and his tomb is here[p] to this day. [30]But he was a prophet and knew that God had promised him on oath that he would place one of his descendants on his throne.[q] [31]Seeing what was ahead, he spoke of the resurrection of the Christ,[d] that he was not abandoned to the grave, nor did his body see decay.[r] [32]God has raised this Jesus to life,[s] and we are all witnesses[t] of the fact. [33]Exalted[u] to the right hand of God,[v] he has received from the Father[w] the promised Holy Spirit[x] and has poured out[y] what you now see and hear. [34]For David did not ascend to heaven, and yet he said,

2:29 [n] Ac 7:8,9 [o] Ac 13:36; 1Ki 2:10 [p] Ne 3:16
2:30 [q] 2Sa 7:12; Ps 132:11
2:31 [r] Ps 16:10
2:32 [s] ver 24 [t] Ac 1:8
2:33 [u] Php 2:9 [v] Mk 16:19 [w] Ac 1:4 [x] Jn 7:39; 14:26 [y] Ac 10:45

"'The Lord said to my Lord:
"Sit at my right hand
[35] until I make your enemies
a footstool for your feet."'[e][z]

2:35 [z] Ps 110:1; Mt 22:44

[36]"Therefore let all Israel be assured of this: God has made this Jesus, whom you crucified, both Lord and Christ."[a]

2:36 [a] Lk 2:11

[37]When the people heard this, they were cut to the heart and said to Peter and the other apostles, "Brothers, what shall we do?"[b]

2:37 [b] Lk 3:10,12,14

[38]Peter replied, "Repent and be baptized,[c] every one of you, in the name of Jesus Christ for the forgiveness of your sins.[d] And you will receive the gift of the Holy Spirit. [39]The promise is for you and your children[e] and for all who are far off[f]—for all whom the Lord our God will call."

2:38 [c] Ac 8:12,16,36,38; 22:16 [d] Lk 24:47; Ac 3:19
2:39 [e] Isa 44:3 [f] Ac 10:45; Eph 2:13

[40]With many other words he warned them; and he pleaded with them, "Save yourselves from this corrupt generation."[g] [41]Those who accepted his message were baptized, and about three thousand were added to their number that day.

2:40 [g] Dt 32:5

The Fellowship of the Believers

[42]They devoted themselves to the apostles' teaching and to the fellowship, to the breaking of bread and to prayer.[h] [43]Everyone was filled with awe, and many wonders and miraculous signs were done by the apostles.[i] [44]All the believers were together and had everything in common.[j] [45]Selling their possessions and goods, they gave to anyone as he had need.[k] [46]Every day they continued to meet together in the temple courts.[l] They broke bread[m] in their

2:42 [h] Ac 1:14
2:43 [i] Ac 5:12
2:44 [j] Ac 4:32
2:45 [k] Mt 19:21
2:46 [l] Lk 24:53; Ac 5:21,42 [m] Ac 20:7

[a] 21 Joel 2:28–32 [b] 23 Or *of those not having the law* (that is, Gentiles) [c] 28 Psalm 16:8–11
[d] 31 Or *Messiah.* "The Christ" (Greek) and "the Messiah" (Hebrew) both mean "the Anointed One"; also in verse 36. [e] 35 Psalm 110:1

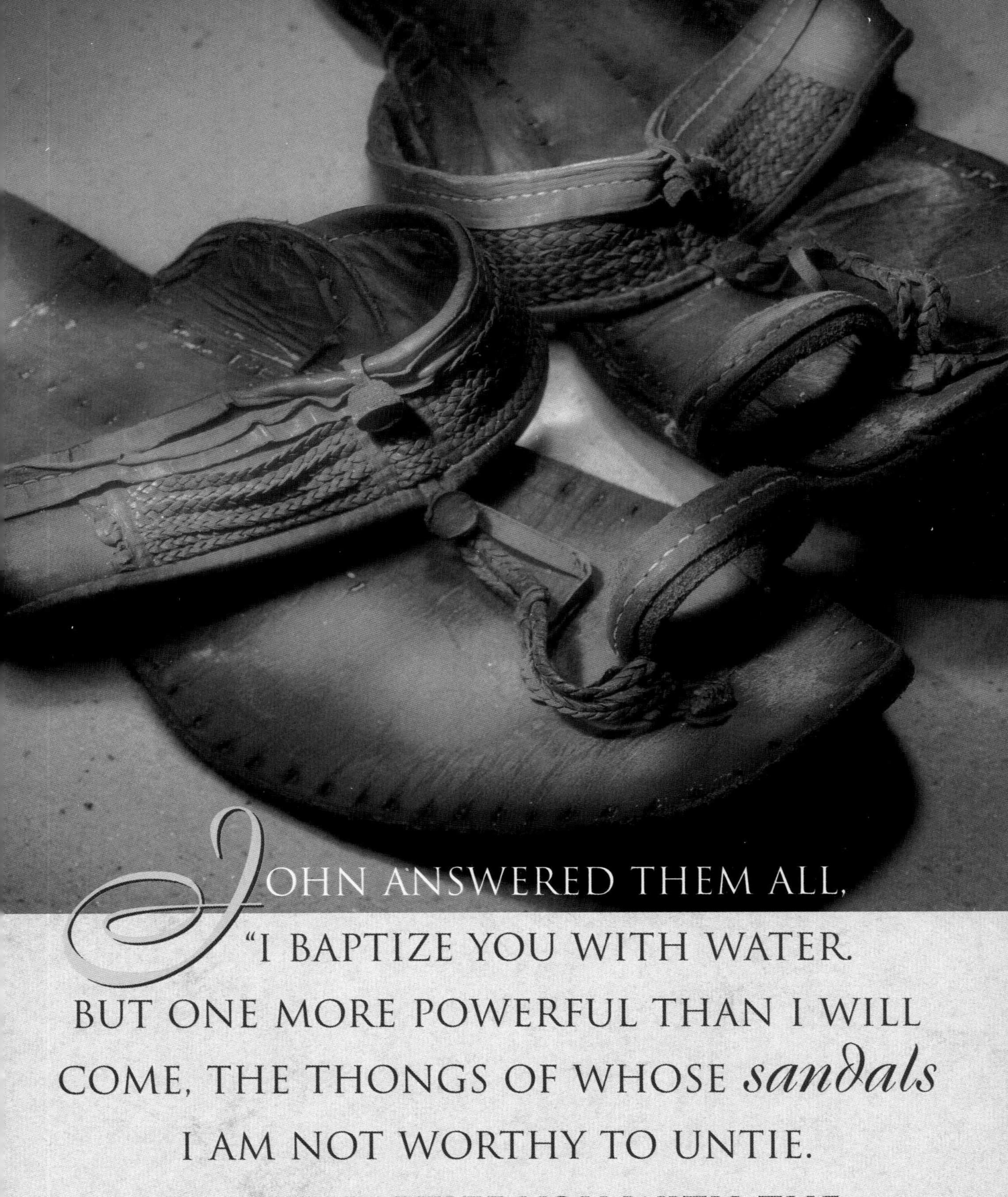

JOHN ANSWERED THEM ALL,
"I BAPTIZE YOU WITH WATER.
BUT ONE MORE POWERFUL THAN I WILL
COME, THE THONGS OF WHOSE *sandals*
I AM NOT WORTHY TO UNTIE.
HE WILL BAPTIZE YOU WITH THE
HOLY SPIRIT AND WITH FIRE."

—LUKE 3:16—

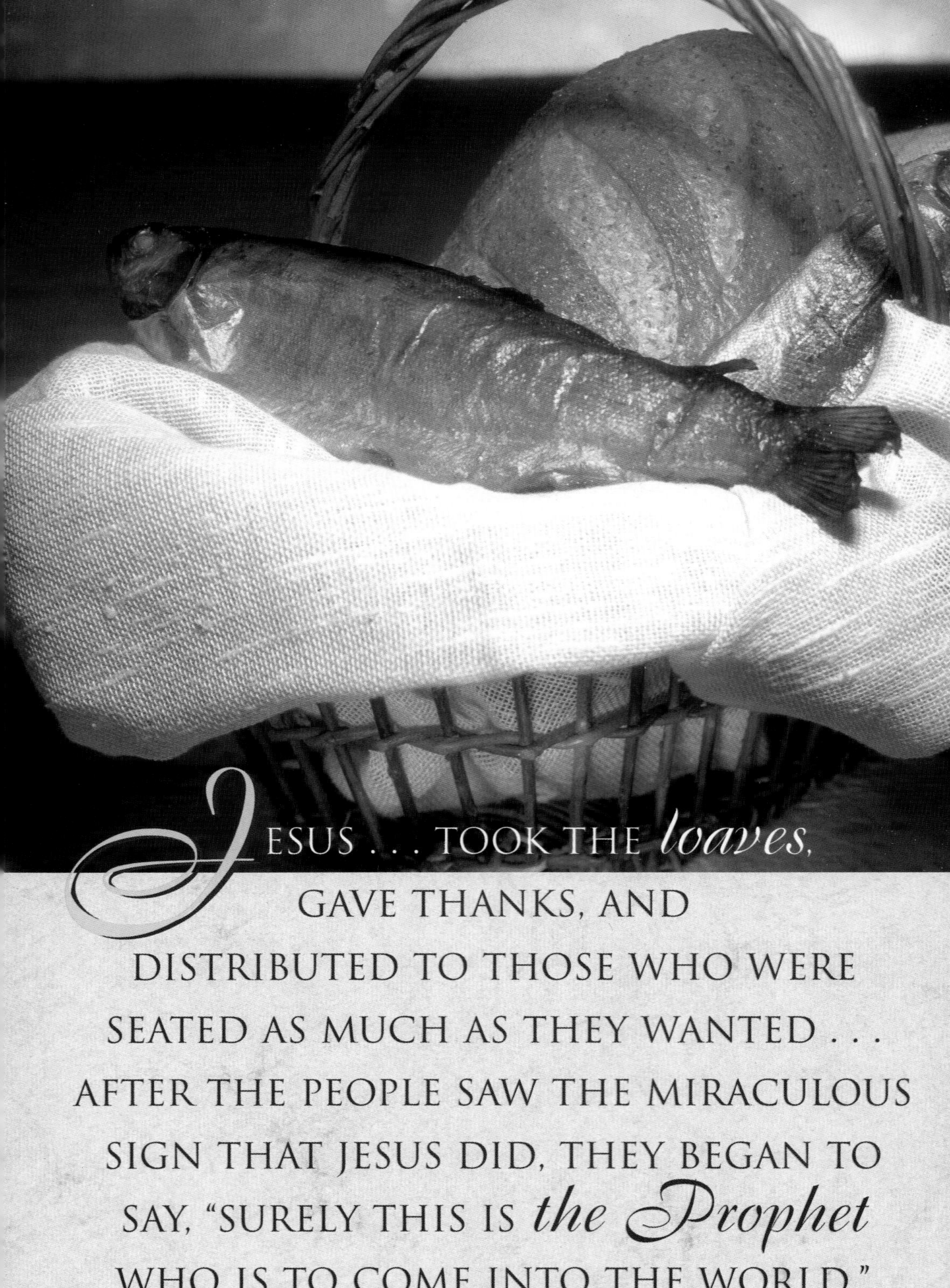

JESUS . . . TOOK THE *loaves*, GAVE THANKS, AND DISTRIBUTED TO THOSE WHO WERE SEATED AS MUCH AS THEY WANTED . . . AFTER THE PEOPLE SAW THE MIRACULOUS SIGN THAT JESUS DID, THEY BEGAN TO SAY, "SURELY THIS IS *the Prophet* WHO IS TO COME INTO THE WORLD."

— JOHN 6:11,14 —

homes and ate together with glad and
sincere hearts, 47praising God and en-
2:47 joying the favor of all the people.[n] And — n Ro 14:18
the Lord added to their number[o] daily — o ver 41; Ac 5:14
those who were being saved.

Peter Heals the Crippled Beggar

3:1 **3** One day Peter and John[p] were go- — p Lk 22:8
ing up to the temple[q] at the time — q Ac 2:46
of prayer—at three in the afternoon.[r] — r Ps 55:17
3:2 2Now a man crippled from birth[s] was — s Ac 14:8
being carried to the temple gate[t] called — t Lk 16:20
Beautiful, where he was put every day to — u Jn 9:8
beg[u] from those going into the temple
courts. 3When he saw Peter and John
about to enter, he asked them for money. 4Peter looked straight at him, as did
John. Then Peter said, "Look at us!" 5So
the man gave them his attention, expecting to get something from them.
6Then Peter said, "Silver or gold I do
not have, but what I have I give you. In
3:6 the name of Jesus Christ of Nazareth,[v] — v ver 16; Ac 4:10
walk." 7Taking him by the right hand, he
helped him up, and instantly the man's
feet and ankles became strong. 8He
jumped to his feet and began to walk.
Then he went with them into the temple
courts, walking and jumping,[w] and 3:8 w Ac 14:10
praising God. 9When all the people[x] saw
him walking and praising God, 10they 3:9 x Ac 4:16,21
recognized him as the same man who
used to sit begging at the temple gate
called Beautiful,[y] and they were filled 3:10 y ver 2
with wonder and amazement at what
had happened to him.

> **I DON'T THINK THERE ARE MANY JEWS — FANATICS AND ILL-INFORMED EXCEPTED — WHO ARE NOT FASCINATED BY THE PERSON AND TEACHING OF JESUS.**
>
> 
>
> David Flusser, *Jewish Scholar*

Peter Speaks to the Onlookers

11While the beggar held on to Peter
and John,[z] all the people were aston- 3:11 z Lk 22:8
ished and came running to them in the a Jn 10:23;
place called Solomon's Colonnade.[a] Ac 5:12
12When Peter saw this, he said to them:
"Men of Israel, why does this surprise
you? Why do you stare at us as if by our
own power or godliness we had made
this man walk? 13The God of Abraham,
Isaac and Jacob, the God of our fathers,[b] 3:13 b Ac 5:30
has glorified his servant Jesus. You c Mt 27:2
handed him over to be killed, and you d Lk 23:4
disowned him before Pilate,[c] though he
had decided to let him go.[d] 14You disowned the Holy[e] and Righteous One[f] 3:14 e Mk 1:24;
and asked that a murderer be released Ac 4:27 f Ac 7:52
to you.[g] 15You killed the author of life, g Mk 15:11; Lk 23:18-25
but God raised him from the dead.[h] We
are witnesses of this. 16By faith in the 3:15 h Ac 2:24
name of Jesus, this man whom you see
and know was made strong. It is Jesus'
name and the faith that comes through
him that has given this complete healing to him, as you can all see.
17"Now, brothers, I know that you act-
ed in ignorance,[i] as did your leaders.[j] 3:17 i Lk 23:34
18But this is how God fulfilled what he j Ac 13:27
had foretold[k] through all the prophets,[l] 3:18 k Ac 2:23
saying that his Christ[a] would suffer.[m] l Lk 24:27
19Repent, then, and turn to God, so that m Ac 17:2,3; 26:22,23
your sins may be wiped out,[n] that times
of refreshing may come from the Lord, 3:19 n Ac 2:38
20and that he may send the Christ, who
has been appointed for you—even Jesus.
21He must remain in heaven[o] until the 3:21 o Ac 1:11
time comes for God to restore every-

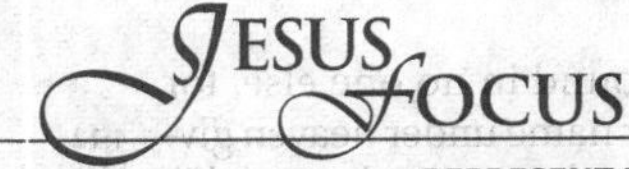

REPRESENTATIVES OF JESUS

One of the most convincing proofs that Jesus had in fact risen victorious from the dead was the radical change in his followers (Acts 3). A group of ordinary individuals—who had been so profoundly shaken on the night of Jesus' arrest that they had abandoned their Master and gone into hiding—found through the power of the Holy Spirit such unflinching courage that they set in motion a worldwide movement that has literally reshaped civilization. God, working through his people, sparked a spiritual revolution through simple but dedicated followers who had witnessed a miracle unlike any other and who were convinced beyond any doubt that Jesus had come back to life—and that he had possessed the power to do so because he was the very Son of God. Because of their unshakable convictions, the apostles spoke to people with unprecedented boldness, doing everything in Jesus' name and as his representatives. Whenever they performed a healing miracle, the apostles were careful to make clear to the person that he or she had been healed "in the name of Jesus" (see, for example, verses 6,16).

a 18 Or *Messiah*; also in verse 20

3:21 [p]Mt 17:11 thing,[p] as he promised long ago through
[q]Lk 1:70 his holy prophets.[q] 22For Moses said,
'The Lord your God will raise up for you
a prophet like me from among your own
people; you must listen to everything he
3:22 [r]Dt 18:15,18; tells you.[r] 23Anyone who does not listen
Ac 7:37 to him will be completely cut off from
3:23 among his people.'[a][s]
[s]Dt 18:19 24"Indeed, all the prophets[t] from
3:24 Samuel on, as many as have spoken,
[t]Lk 24:27 have foretold these days. 25And you are
3:25 heirs[u] of the prophets and of the cov-
[u]Ac 2:39 [v]Ro 9:4,5 enant[v] God made with your fathers. He
[w]Ge 12:3; 22:18; said to Abraham, 'Through your off-
26:4; 28:14 spring all peoples on earth will be
3:26 blessed.'[b][w] 26When God raised up[x] his
[x]ver 22; Ac 2:24 [y]Ac 13:46; servant, he sent him first[y] to you to bless
Ro 1:16 you by turning each of you from your
wicked ways."

Peter and John Before the Sanhedrin

4 The priests and the captain of the
4:1 [z]Lk 22:4 temple guard[z] and the Sad-
[a]Mt 3:7 ducees[a] came up to Peter and John while
they were speaking to the people. 2They
were greatly disturbed because the
apostles were teaching the people and
4:2 proclaiming in Jesus the resurrection of
[b]Ac 17:18 the dead.[b] 3They seized Peter and John,
4:3 and because it was evening, they put
[c]Ac 5:18 them in jail[c] until the next day. 4But
4:4 many who heard the message believed,
[d]Ac 2:41 and the number of men grew[d] to about
4:5 five thousand.
[e]Lk 23:13 5The next day the rulers,[e] elders and
teachers of the law met in Jerusalem.

JESUS FOCUS

GOOD NEWS FOR ALL

The story of Jesus' resurrection greatly alarmed the Sadducees because they did not believe in the reality of an afterlife (see also Matthew 22:23; Acts 23:6–8). At the time of Jesus' resurrection a rumor had circulated that someone had stolen Jesus' body to make it appear as though he had come back to life, but no one had been able to produce the dead body. The inability to produce a body rendered the objections of these Jewish leaders essentially ineffectual, and they must have been frustrated. What were disturbing reports to the Sadducees, however, constituted Good News for all of humanity. Many people believed the testimony of the apostles, and the number of people professing faith in Jesus Christ continued to grow (Acts 4:4).

6Annas the high priest was there, and so
were Caiaphas,[f] John, Alexander and the 4:6 [f]Mt 26:3; Lk 3:2
other men of the high priest's family.
7They had Peter and John brought before them and began to question them:
"By what power or what name did you
do this?"
8Then Peter, filled with the Holy Spirit, said to them: "Rulers and elders of the
people![g] 9If we are being called to ac- 4:8 [g]ver 5; Lk 23:13
count today for an act of kindness
shown to a cripple[h] and are asked how 4:9 [h]Ac 3:6
he was healed, 10then know this, you and
all the people of Israel: It is by the name
of Jesus Christ of Nazareth, whom you
crucified but whom God raised from the 4:10
dead,[i] that this man stands before you [i]Ac 2:24
healed. 11He is

"'the stone you builders rejected, 4:11
which has become the [j]Ps 118:22;
capstone.'[c][d][j] Isa 28:16; Mt 21:42

> CHRIST IS NOT SAID TO HAVE RECEIVED SALVATION, BUT TO BE SALVATION ITSELF.
>
> John Calvin, *Swiss Reformer*

12Salvation is found in no one else, for
there is no other name under heaven giv- 4:12 [k]Mt 1:21;
en to men by which we must be saved."[k] Ac 10:43;
13When they saw the courage of Peter 1Ti 2:5
and John[l] and realized that they were
unschooled, ordinary men,[m] they were 4:13 [l]Lk 22:8
astonished and they took note that [m]Mt 11:25
these men had been with Jesus. 14But
since they could see the man who had
been healed standing there with them,
there was nothing they could say. 15So
they ordered them to withdraw from the 4:15
Sanhedrin[n] and then conferred togeth- [n]Mt 5:22
er. 16"What are we going to do with these 4:16
men?"[o] they asked. "Everybody living in [o]Jn 11:47
Jerusalem knows they have done an out- [p]Ac 3:6-10
standing miracle,[p] and we cannot deny
it. 17But to stop this thing from spreading any further among the people, we
must warn these men to speak no longer
to anyone in this name."
18Then they called them in again and
commanded them not to speak or teach
at all in the name of Jesus.[q] 19But Peter 4:18 [q]Ac 5:40
and John replied, "Judge for yourselves

[a] *23* Deut. 18:15,18,19 [b] *25* Gen. 22:18; 26:4
[c] *11* Or *cornerstone* [d] *11* Psalm 118:22

DISCOVERY 289

ONLY ONE WAY

Many facts about Jesus are attractive to the secular mind. He exhibited a gentle spirit (Matthew 11:29) and showed great compassion for the poor and the hurting (Mark 6:34). He continually called for justice to be balanced with mercy (Matthew 9:13; Luke 6:36). His radical teachings were completely opposite of the counsel of others: Rather than advocating revenge (Matthew 5:38–48), Jesus taught people to love their neighbors in the same way in which they loved themselves (Mark 12:31–33; Luke 10:27).

But there is one claim about Jesus that is highly offensive to our pluralistic society: the truth that faith in him is the *only* way to heaven (John 14:6). Peter confronted the religious leaders of his day with that incontrovertible fact (Acts 4:12), and they were no more receptive than people are today! (verse 21).

Our post-modern mind-set is still quick to accuse Christianity of being narrow-minded. Narrow-minded? Perhaps. The truth? Without question! Jesus had been explicit all long: "I am the way and the truth and the life. No one comes to the Father except through me" (John 14:6). Jesus is not one of many options; he is the only way, the only truth and the only life. The apostle Paul reminded his young student Timothy of the same reality: "There is one God and one mediator between God and men, the man Christ Jesus" (1 Timothy 2:5).

It would be so much more "acceptable," so much "neater" if each of us were free to choose our own path to heaven, and many people still try. In fact, most other world religions promote the concept that there are different routes all leading ultimately to the same God. God certainly does allow us to make our own choices, but the direction we select will either lead us toward God or away from him. Everything ever written in Scripture "[testifies] about him that everyone who believes in him receives forgiveness of sins through his name" (Acts 10:43).

Some of us might feel as though we're doing just fine on our own, but the Bible is crystal clear: Human beings live in one of two spiritual conditions. Either they are *saved* or they are *lost* (Romans 3:9–31; 6:1–23). We are all born in a lost condition (Ephesians 2:1–3), "without hope and without God in the world" (Ephesians 2:12), and our only prospect of liberation is found in Jesus.

The fact that God's plan of salvation is so exclusive shapes how we as his children are called to set our priorities. We cannot ignore the plight of family and friends who do not know Jesus. There may well be people in our neighborhoods who have virtually no interest in Jesus, and we may even opt to travel to a foreign country to share the Good News with people who have never heard his name or the way to find life in him. Each day, as we rub shoulders with those around us, we can get into the habit of asking ourselves one question: "What can I do right now to get the message to this person who needs to see Jesus?"

***Self-Discovery:** Do you feel a sense of compulsion or urgency for spreading the Good News about Jesus Christ, either to your own family on a day-by-day basis or with neighbors, co-workers or even chance acquaintances? Try to assess and evaluate the reasons behind your answer.*

GO TO DISCOVERY 290 ON PAGE 1468

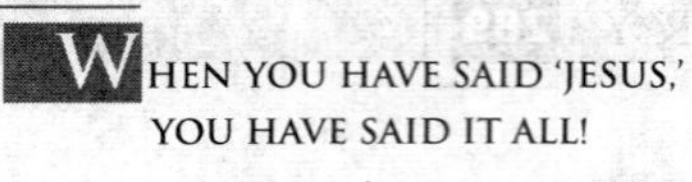

WHEN YOU HAVE SAID 'JESUS,'
YOU HAVE SAID IT ALL!

Adrian Rogers, *Pastor, Memphis, Tennessee*

4:19 whether it is right in God's sight to obey
r Ac 5:29 you rather than God.[r] 20For we cannot
help speaking about what we have seen
and heard."
21After further threats they let them
go. They could not decide how to punish
4:21 s Ac 5:26 them, because all the people[s] were prais-
t Mt 9:8 ing God[t] for what had happened. 22For
the man who was miraculously healed
was over forty years old.

The Believers' Prayer

23On their release, Peter and John
went back to their own people and reported all that the chief priests and elders had said to them. 24When they
heard this, they raised their voices together in prayer to God. "Sovereign
Lord," they said, "you made the heaven
and the earth and the sea, and everything in them. 25You spoke by the Holy
Spirit through the mouth of your ser-
4:25 u Ac 1:16 vant, our father David:[u]

" 'Why do the nations rage
and the peoples plot in vain?
26The kings of the earth take their
stand
4:26 and the rulers gather together
v Ps 2:1,2; Da 9:25; against the Lord
Lk 4:18; and against his Anointed
Ac 10:38; Heb 1:9 One.[a]'[b][v]

4:27 27Indeed Herod[w] and Pontius Pilate[x]
w Mt 14:1 met together with the Gentiles and the
x Mt 27:2; Lk 23:12 people[c] of Israel in this city to conspire
y ver 30 against your holy servant Jesus,[y] whom
you anointed. 28They did what your
4:28 power and will had decided beforehand
z Ac 2:23 should happen.[z] 29Now, Lord, consider
4:29 their threats and enable your servants to
a ver 13,31; speak your word with great boldness.[a]
Ac 9:27; 14:3; Php 1:14 30Stretch out your hand to heal and perform miraculous signs and wonders[b]
4:30 b Jn 4:48 c ver 27 through the name of your holy servant
Jesus."[c]
31After they prayed, the place where
4:31 d Ac 2:2 e ver 29 they were meeting was shaken.[d] And
they were all filled with the Holy Spirit
and spoke the word of God boldly.[e]

The Believers Share Their Possessions

32All the believers were one in heart
and mind. No one claimed that any of
his possessions was his own, but they
shared everything they had.[f] 33With 4:32 f Ac 2:44
great power the apostles continued to
testify[g] to the resurrection[h] of the Lord 4:33 g Lk 24:48
Jesus, and much grace was upon them h Ac 1:22
all. 34There were no needy persons
among them. For from time to time
those who owned lands or houses sold 4:34
them,[i] brought the money from the i Mt 19:21; Ac 2:45
sales 35and put it at the apostles' feet,[j]
and it was distributed to anyone as he 4:35 j ver 37; Ac 5:2
had need.[k] k Ac 2:45; 6:1
36Joseph, a Levite from Cyprus, whom
the apostles called Barnabas[l] (which 4:36 l Ac 9:27; 1Co 9:6
means Son of Encouragement), 37sold a
field he owned and brought the money 4:37
and put it at the apostles' feet.[m] m ver 35; Ac 5:2

Ananias and Sapphira

5 Now a man named Ananias, together with his wife Sapphira, also
sold a piece of property. 2With his wife's
full knowledge he kept back part of the
money for himself, but brought the rest 5:2
and put it at the apostles' feet.[n] n Ac 4:35,37
3Then Peter said, "Ananias, how is it 5:3
that Satan[o] has so filled your heart[p] that o Mt 4:10
you have lied to the Holy Spirit[q] and p Jn 13:2,27 q ver 9
have kept for yourself some of the mon-
ey you received for the land? 4Didn't it
belong to you before it was sold? And after it was sold, wasn't the money at your
disposal? What made you think of doing
such a thing? You have not lied to men
but to God."
5When Ananias heard this, he fell
down and died.[r] And great fear[s] seized 5:5 r ver 10 s ver 11
all who heard what had happened.
6Then the young men came forward,
wrapped up his body,[t] and carried him 5:6 t Jn 19:40
out and buried him.
7About three hours later his wife
came in, not knowing what had happened. 8Peter asked her, "Tell me, is this
the price you and Ananias got for the
land?"
"Yes," she said, "that is the price."[u] 5:8 u ver 2
9Peter said to her, "How could you
agree to test the Spirit of the Lord?[v] 5:9 v ver 3
Look! The feet of the men who buried
your husband are at the door, and they
will carry you out also."

[a] *26* That is, Christ or Messiah [b] *26* Psalm 2:1,2
[c] *27* The Greek is plural.

> I AM AMAZED BY THE SAYINGS OF CHRIST. THEY SEEM TRUER THAN ANYTHING I HAVE EVER READ AND THEY CERTAINLY TURNED THE WORLD UPSIDE DOWN.
>
> Katharine Butler Hathaway, *American Author*

10At that moment she fell down at his
5:10 [w]ver 5 feet and died.[w] Then the young men
came in and, finding her dead, carried her
out and buried her beside her husband.
5:11 [x]ver 5; Ac 19:17 11Great fear[x] seized the whole church and
all who heard about these events.

The Apostles Heal Many

12The apostles performed many
5:12 [y]Ac 2:43 miraculous signs and wonders[y] among
[z]Ac 4:32 the people. And all the believers used to
[a]Ac 3:11 meet together[z] in Solomon's Colonnade.[a] 13No one else dared join them,
5:13 even though they were highly regarded
[b]Ac 2:47; 4:21 by the people.[b] 14Nevertheless, more and
more men and women believed in the
Lord and were added to their number.
15As a result, people brought the sick
into the streets and laid them on beds
and mats so that at least Peter's shadow
might fall on some of them as he passed
5:15 by.[c] 16Crowds gathered also from the
[c]Ac 19:12 towns around Jerusalem, bringing their
sick and those tormented by evil[a] spir-
5:16 [d]Mk 16:17 its, and all of them were healed.[d]

The Apostles Persecuted

17Then the high priest and all his associates, who were members of the par-
5:17 [e]Ac 15:5 [f]Ac 4:1 ty[e] of the Sadducees,[f] were filled with
jealousy. 18They arrested the apostles
5:18 [g]Ac 4:3 and put them in the public jail.[g] 19But
during the night an angel[h] of the Lord
5:19 [h]Mt 1:20; Lk 1:11; Ac 8:26; 27:23 opened the doors of the jail[i] and
brought them out. 20"Go, stand in the
[i]Ac 16:26 temple courts," he said, "and tell the people the full message of this new life."[j]
5:20 21At daybreak they entered the tem-
[j]Jn 6:63,68 ple courts, as they had been told, and
began to teach the people.
When the high priest and his associ-
5:21 [k]Ac 4:5,6 ates[k] arrived, they called together the
[l]ver 27,34,41; Mt 5:22 Sanhedrin[l]—the full assembly of the
elders of Israel—and sent to the jail for
the apostles. 22But on arriving at the jail,
the officers did not find them there. So
they went back and reported, 23"We
found the jail securely locked, with the
guards standing at the doors; but when
we opened them, we found no one inside." 24On hearing this report, the captain of the temple guard and the chief
priests[m] were puzzled, wondering what 5:24 [m]Ac 4:1
would come of this.
25Then someone came and said,
"Look! The men you put in jail are
standing in the temple courts teaching
the people." 26At that, the captain went
with his officers and brought the apostles. They did not use force, because they 5:26
feared that the people[n] would stone [n]Ac 4:21
them. 5:27
27Having brought the apostles, they [o]Mt 5:22
made them appear before the San-
hedrin[o] to be questioned by the high 5:28 [p]Ac 4:18
priest. 28"We gave you strict orders not [q]Mt 23:35; 27:25; Ac 2:23,
to teach in this name,"[p] he said. "Yet you 36; 3:14,15; 7:52
have filled Jerusalem with your teaching
and are determined to make us guilty of 5:29 [r]Ac 4:19
this man's blood."[q]
29Peter and the other apostles replied: 5:30 [s]Ac 3:13
"We must obey God rather than men![r] [t]Ac 2:24
30The God of our fathers[s] raised Jesus [u]Ac 10:39;
from the dead[t]—whom you had killed 13:29; Gal 3:13;
by hanging him on a tree.[u] 31God exalt- 1Pe 2:24
ed him to his own right hand[v] as Prince 5:31 [v]Ac 2:33

[a] 16 Greek *unclean*

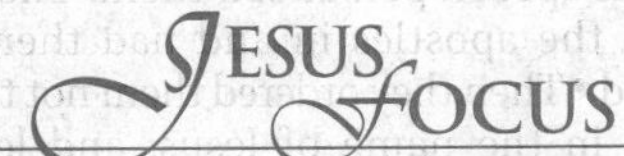

THE NAMES OF JESUS

When Peter addressed the Sanhedrin he referred to Jesus as "Prince and Savior" (Acts 5:31). The disciples used many different names to describe Jesus, including "Lord and Christ" (Acts 2:36), "Christ" (Acts 9:22), "Holy and Righteous One" (Acts 3:14), "author of life" (Acts 3:15), "Anointed One" (Acts 4:26), "Righteous One" (Acts 7:52), "Son of Man" (Acts 7:56), "the Lord Jesus" (Acts 9:17), "Savior" (Acts 13:23) and "Son of God" (Acts 9:20). These men and women of God recognized beyond any doubt that Jesus was God's promised Messiah. In fact, they were so convinced that he was the deliverer promised so many centuries earlier that they were willing to risk their very lives for him. These early apostles surrendered convenience and sacrificed personal agendas to devote their energies to a bold and relentless campaign to publicize the truth about who Jesus is and what he had done. Their faith in Jesus and the incomparable power of God's Holy Spirit fueled the churches with vitality and purpose.

5:31 [w] Lk 2:11 [x] Mt 1:21; Lk 24:47; Ac 2:38 and Savior[w] that he might give repentance and forgiveness of sins to Israel.[x]
32 We are witnesses of these things,[y] and
so is the Holy Spirit,[z] whom God has giv-
5:32 [y] Lk 24:48 [z] Jn 15:26 en to those who obey him."
33 When they heard this, they were fu-
rious[a] and wanted to put them to death.
5:33 [a] Ac 2:37; 7:54 34 But a Pharisee named Gamaliel,[b] a
teacher of the law,[c] who was honored by
5:34 [b] Ac 22:3 [c] Lk 2:46 all the people, stood up in the Sanhedrin
and ordered that the men be put outside
for a little while. 35 Then he addressed
them: "Men of Israel, consider carefully
what you intend to do to these men.
36 Some time ago Theudas appeared,
claiming to be somebody, and about
four hundred men rallied to him. He was
killed, all his followers were dispersed,
and it all came to nothing. 37 After him,
Judas the Galilean appeared in the days
5:37 [d] Lk 2:1,2 of the census[d] and led a band of people
in revolt. He too was killed, and all his
followers were scattered. 38 Therefore, in
the present case I advise you: Leave
these men alone! Let them go! For if
their purpose or activity is of human ori-
5:38 [e] Mt 15:13 gin, it will fail.[e] 39 But if it is from God,
you will not be able to stop these men;
you will only find yourselves fighting
5:39 [f] Pr 21:30; Ac 7:51; 11:17 against God."[f]
40 His speech persuaded them. They
called the apostles in and had them
5:40 [g] Mt 10:17 flogged.[g] Then they ordered them not to
speak in the name of Jesus, and let
them go.
41 The apostles left the Sanhedrin, re-
5:41 [h] Mt 5:12 [i] Jn 15:21 joicing[h] because they had been counted
worthy of suffering disgrace for the
Name.[i] 42 Day after day, in the temple
5:42 [j] Ac 2:46 courts[j] and from house to house, they
never stopped teaching and proclaiming
the good news that Jesus is the Christ.[a]

The Choosing of the Seven

6 In those days when the number of
6:1 [k] Ac 2:41 [l] Ac 9:29 [m] Ac 9:39,41 [n] Ac 4:35 disciples was increasing,[k] the Grecian Jews[l] among them complained
against the Hebraic Jews because their
widows[m] were being overlooked in the
daily distribution of food.[n] 2 So the
Twelve gathered all the disciples together and said, "It would not be right for us
to neglect the ministry of the word of
God in order to wait on tables. 3 Broth-
6:3 [o] Ac 1:16 ers,[o] choose seven men from among you
who are known to be full of the Spirit
and wisdom. We will turn this responsibility over to them 4 and will give our at-
6:4 [p] Ac 1:14 tention to prayer[p] and the ministry of
the word."
5 This proposal pleased the whole
6:5 [q] ver 8; Ac 11:19 [r] Ac 11:24 [s] Ac 8:5-40; 21:8 group. They chose Stephen,[q] a man full
of faith and of the Holy Spirit;[r] also Phil-
ip,[s] Procorus, Nicanor, Timon, Parme-
nas, and Nicolas from Antioch, a convert to Judaism. 6 They presented these
6:6 [t] Ac 1:24; 8:17; 13:3; 2Ti 1:6 [u] Nu 8:10; Ac 9:17; 1Ti 4:14 men to the apostles, who prayed[t] and
laid their hands on them.[u]
7 So the word of God spread.[v] The
number of disciples in Jerusalem increased rapidly, and a large number of
6:7 [v] Ac 12:24; 19:20 priests became obedient to the faith.

Stephen Seized

8 Now Stephen, a man full of God's
grace and power, did great wonders and
6:8 [w] Jn 4:48 miraculous signs[w] among the people.
9 Opposition arose, however, from mem-
bers of the Synagogue of the Freedmen
6:9 [x] Mt 27:32 [y] Ac 15:23,41; 22:3; 23:34 [z] Ac 2:9 (as it was called)—Jews of Cyrene[x] and
Alexandria as well as the provinces of
Cilicia[y] and Asia.[z] These men began to

[a] 42 Or *Messiah*

STEPHEN
MARTYRED FOR JESUS

Stephen was one of seven deacons the disciples chose to care for the needs of the Greek Christians in Jerusalem (Acts 6:1–5). This devoted follower of Jesus taught people faithfully about the truth of Jesus and frequently debated with groups of Jewish leaders in various synagogues (verses 8–10). Stephen was arrested and tried for heresy by the Sanhedrin council. Specifically, he was accused of blasphemy, and he was later stoned to death as a result of his teaching (Acts 7:54–60). Stephen's willingness to die for what he knew to be the truth stood as a powerful example for other Christians to follow as persecution based on allegiance to the name and cause of Jesus became more and more widespread. It is very likely that Paul first heard the truth about Jesus at Stephen's trial (Acts 7:57—8:1), although Paul was still at that time an avid persecutor of the church. Stephen's unforgettable testimony was sealed by his death. The Greek word *martyria* is most often translated "testimony" in our English Bibles, and the term *martyr* has since come to signify an individual who has been put to death as a result of his or her unwavering commitment to belief in Jesus.

argue with Stephen, 10but they could not
stand up against his wisdom or the Spirit by whom he spoke.[a]
11Then they secretly[b] persuaded some
men to say, "We have heard Stephen
speak words of blasphemy against Moses and against God."[c]
12So they stirred up the people and the
elders and the teachers of the law. They
seized Stephen and brought him before
the Sanhedrin.[d] 13They produced false
witnesses, who testified, "This fellow
never stops speaking against this holy
place[e] and against the law. 14For we have
heard him say that this Jesus of Nazareth
will destroy this place and change the
customs Moses handed down to us."[f]
15All who were sitting in the Sanhedrin[g] looked intently at Stephen, and
they saw that his face was like the face
of an angel.

Stephen's Speech to the Sanhedrin

7 Then the high priest asked him,
"Are these charges true?"
2To this he replied: "Brothers and fathers,[h] listen to me! The God of glory[i]
appeared to our father Abraham while
he was still in Mesopotamia, before he
lived in Haran.[j] 3'Leave your country
and your people,' God said, 'and go to the
land I will show you.'[a][k]
4"So he left the land of the Chaldeans
and settled in Haran. After the death of
his father, God sent him to this land
where you are now living.[l] 5He gave him
no inheritance here, not even a foot of
ground. But God promised him that he
and his descendants after him would
possess the land,[m] even though at that
time Abraham had no child. 6God spoke
to him in this way: 'Your descendants
will be strangers in a country not their
own, and they will be enslaved and mistreated four hundred years.[n] 7But I will
punish the nation they serve as slaves,'
God said, 'and afterward they will come
out of that country and worship me in
this place.'[b][o] 8Then he gave Abraham the
covenant of circumcision.[p] And Abraham became the father of Isaac and circumcised him eight days after his birth.[q]
Later Isaac became the father of Jacob,[r]
and Jacob became the father of the
twelve patriarchs.[s]
9"Because the patriarchs were jealous
of Joseph,[t] they sold him as a slave into
Egypt.[u] But God was with him[v] 10and
rescued him from all his troubles. He
gave Joseph wisdom and enabled him to
gain the goodwill of Pharaoh king of
Egypt; so he made him ruler over Egypt
and all his palace.[w]
11"Then a famine struck all Egypt and
Canaan, bringing great suffering, and
our fathers could not find food.[x] 12When
Jacob heard that there was grain in
Egypt, he sent our fathers on their first
visit.[y] 13On their second visit, Joseph told
his brothers who he was,[z] and Pharaoh
learned about Joseph's family. 14After
this, Joseph sent for his father Jacob and
his whole family,[a] seventy-five in all.[b]
15Then Jacob went down to Egypt,
where he and our fathers died.[c] 16Their
bodies were brought back to Shechem
and placed in the tomb that Abraham
had bought from the sons of Hamor at
Shechem for a certain sum of money.[d]
17"As the time drew near for God to
fulfill his promise to Abraham, the number of our people in Egypt greatly increased.[e] 18Then another king, who
knew nothing about Joseph, became
ruler of Egypt.[f] 19He dealt treacherously
with our people and oppressed our forefathers by forcing them to throw out
their newborn babies so that they would
die.[g]
20"At that time Moses was born, and
he was no ordinary child.[c] For three
months he was cared for in his father's
house.[h] 21When he was placed outside,
Pharaoh's daughter took him and
brought him up as her own son.[i] 22Mo-
ses was educated in all the wisdom of
the Egyptians[j] and was powerful in
speech and action.
23"When Moses was forty years old, he
decided to visit his fellow Israelites. 24He
saw one of them being mistreated by an
Egyptian, so he went to his defense and
avenged him by killing the Egyptian.
25Moses thought that his own people
would realize that God was using him to
rescue them, but they did not. 26The next
day Moses came upon two Israelites who
were fighting. He tried to reconcile them
by saying, 'Men, you are brothers; why do
you want to hurt each other?'
27"But the man who was mistreating
the other pushed Moses aside and said,

6:10 [a]Lk 21:15
6:11 [b]1Ki 21:10 [c]Mt 26:59-61
6:12 [d]Mt 5:22
6:13 [e]Ac 21:28
6:14 [f]Ac 15:1; 21:21; 26:3; 28:17
6:15 [g]Mt 5:22
7:2 [h]Ac 22:1 [i]Ps 29:3 [j]Ge 11:31; 15:7
7:3 [k]Ge 12:1
7:4 [l]Ge 12:5
7:5 [m]Ge 12:7; 17:8; 26:3
7:6 [n]Ex 12:40
7:7 [o]Ex 3:12
7:8 [p]Ge 17:9-14 [q]Ge 21:2-4 [r]Ge 25:26 [s]Ge 29:31-35; 30:5-13,17-24; 35:16-18,22-26
7:9 [t]Ge 37:4,11
7:9 [u]Ge 37:28; Ps 105:17 [v]Ge 39:2,21,23
7:10 [w]Ge 41:37-43
7:11 [x]Ge 41:54
7:12 [y]Ge 42:1,2
7:13 [z]Ge 45:1-4
7:14 [a]Ge 45:9,10 [b]Ge 46:26,27; Ex 1:5; Dt 10:22
7:15 [c]Ge 46:5-7; 49:33; Ex 1:6
7:16 [d]Ge 23:16-20; 33:18,19; 50:13; Jos 24:32
7:17 [e]Ex 1:7; Ps 105:24
7:18 [f]Ex 1:8
7:19 [g]Ex 1:10-22
7:20 [h]Ex 2:2; Heb 11:23
7:21 [i]Ex 2:3-10
7:22 [j]1Ki 4:30; Isa 19:11

[a] 3 Gen. 12:1 [b] 7 Gen. 15:13,14 [c] 20 Or *was fair in the sight of God*

LIVING FOR GOD

Throughout the ages every person has faced the same choice: to walk with God or to live life apart from him. Our sinful nature (Romans 8:7) incites us to choose our own way, the way that seems best or feels right to us. Despite technological advances and personal accomplishments, humanity hasn't really changed. We read the truth in Ecclesiastes that "what has been will be again, what has been done will be done again; there is nothing new under the sun" (Ecclesiastes 1:9–10).

Stephen is remembered as the first martyr for the Christian faith, stoned to death for speaking God's truth (Acts 7:54–60). What we sometimes miss in the lesson of his death is the fact that Stephen not only *died* for God but first *lived* for him; he was "a man full of God's grace and power" (Acts 6:8). Humankind has always tended to reject God's truth, and the reaction of the masses to Stephen was no different from the response of their ancestors to every prophet God had ever sent (Acts 7:51–52).

The people listened as Stephen related the history of the Old Testament; that was a subject of great interest to them. It wasn't until he began to challenge the stubborn arrogance of his own generation, making the connection between the intractable Israelites of old and his contemporaries, that the people became angry and quickly turned against him (verse 54). Stephen pointed out that the Jews of his own day were resisting God's Spirit instead of walking with him. They knew the Word of God, yet chose to ignore it. Jesus, God the Son, had even come down from heaven to live among them and teach them God's truth, but the result had been Jesus' execution (verse 52). What they failed to understand was that acceptance of Jesus' death as the atoning sacrifice for their sin would eliminate that very sin in a way that the temple sacrifices never could (Romans 3:25; 1 John 2:2; 4:10).

It has always been God's intention that we walk with him (Ezekiel 33:11; Hosea 11:3–4). Even when sin changed the dynamics of humanity's perfect relationship with God, God refused to give up. Instead, he himself repaired the breach by doing what we could not (Romans 5:6–8). Jesus, God's "Righteous One" (Acts 7:52), paid the price for sin (Ephesians 2:8–9). Now we can choose to walk in the Spirit (Galatians 5:25) and allow ourselves to be pliable enough for him to change us into the people God intends us to be.

Paul summed it up this way: "We have an obligation—but it is not to the sinful nature, to live according to it. For if you live according to the sinful nature, you will die; but if by the Spirit you put to death the misdeeds of the body, you will live, because those who are led by the Spirit of God are sons of God" (Romans 8:12–14).

***Self-Discovery:** Do you feel that the writer of Ecclesiastes was correct in stating that there is nothing new under the sun? Make a listing of things you feel are legitimately new. How many, if any, relate to human nature and our basic human cravings, incentives, and the like?*

GO TO DISCOVERY 291 ON PAGE 1471

'Who made you ruler and judge over us?
28Do you want to kill me as you killed the
Egyptian yesterday?'[a] 29When Moses
7:29 heard this, he fled to Midian, where he
[k]Ex 2:11-15 settled as a foreigner and had two sons.[k]
30"After forty years had passed, an an-
gel appeared to Moses in the flames of a
burning bush in the desert near Mount
Sinai. 31When he saw this, he was
amazed at the sight. As he went over to
look more closely, he heard the Lord's
7:31 voice:[l] 32'I am the God of your fathers,
[l]Ex 3:1-4 the God of Abraham, Isaac and Jacob.'[b]
7:32 Moses trembled with fear and did not
[m]Ex 3:6 dare to look.[m]
33"Then the Lord said to him, 'Take
off your sandals; the place where you are
7:33 standing is holy ground.[n] 34I have indeed
[n]Ex 3:5; seen the oppression of my people in
Jos 5:15 Egypt. I have heard their groaning and
7:34 have come down to set them free. Now
[o]Ex 3:7-10 come, I will send you back to Egypt.'[c o]
35"This is the same Moses whom they
had rejected with the words, 'Who made
7:35 you ruler and judge?'[p] He was sent to be
[p]ver 27 their ruler and deliverer by God himself,
7:36 through the angel who appeared to him
[q]Ex 12:41; 33:1 in the bush. 36He led them out of Egypt[q]
[r]Ex 14:21 and did wonders and miraculous signs
in Egypt, at the Red Sea[d r] and for forty
years in the desert.
37"This is that Moses who told the Israelites, 'God will send you a prophet
7:37 like me from your own people.'[e s] 38He
[s]Dt 18:15,18; Ac 3:22 was in the assembly in the desert, with
7:38 the angel[t] who spoke to him on Mount
[t]ver 53 Sinai, and with our fathers;[u] and he re-
[u]Ex 19:17 ceived living words[v] to pass on to us.[w]
[v]Dt 32:45-47; Heb 4:12 39"But our fathers refused to obey
[w]Ro 3:2 him. Instead, they rejected him and in
7:39 their hearts turned back to Egypt.[x]
[x]Nu 14:3,4 40They told Aaron, 'Make us gods who
will go before us. As for this fellow Mo-
7:40 ses who led us out of Egypt—we don't
[y]Ex 32:1,23 know what has happened to him!'[f y]
41That was the time they made an idol in
the form of a calf. They brought sacri-
7:41 fices to it and held a celebration in hon-
[z]Ex 32:4-6; Ps 106:19,20; or of what their hands had made.[z] 42But
Rev 9:20 God turned away[a] and gave them over
7:42 to the worship of the heavenly bodies.[b]
[a]Jos 24:20; This agrees with what is written in the
Isa 63:10 [b]Jer 19:13 book of the prophets:

"'Did you bring me sacrifices and
offerings
forty years in the desert, O house
of Israel?

> **FORGOTTEN IN TODAY'S "GOSPEL REVISIONISM" IS THE MESSAGE THAT SENT CHRIST TO THE CROSS AND THE DISCIPLES TO MARTYRDOM . . . JESUS CALLS US TO TAKE UP THE CROSS AND FOLLOW HIM.**
>
> Bailey Smith, *American Evangelist*

43You have lifted up the shrine of
Molech
and the star of your god Rephan,
the idols you made to worship.
Therefore I will send you into
exile'[g c] beyond Babylon. 7:43 [c]Am 5:25-27

44"Our forefathers had the tabernacle 7:44
of the Testimony[d] with them in the [d]Ex 38:21
desert. It had been made as God directed [e]Ex 25:8,9,40
Moses, according to the pattern he had
seen.[e] 45Having received the tabernacle,
our fathers under Joshua brought it with
them when they took the land from the
nations God drove out before them.[f] It re- 7:45
mained in the land until the time of Da- [f]Jos 3:14-17;
vid, 46who enjoyed God's favor and asked 18:1; 23:9; 24:18; Ps 44:2
that he might provide a dwelling place for 7:46
the God of Jacob.[h g] 47But it was Solomon [g]2Sa 7:8-16;
who built the house for him. Ps 132:1-5
48"However, the Most High does not
live in houses made by men.[h] As the 7:48 [h]1Ki 8:27;
prophet says: 2Ch 2:6

49"'Heaven is my throne,
and the earth is my footstool.[i] 7:49 [i]Mt 5:34,35
What kind of house will you build
for me?
says the Lord.
Or where will my resting place be?
50Has not my hand made all these
things?'[i j] 7:50 [j]Isa 66:1,2

51"You stiff-necked people,[k] with un- 7:51
circumcised hearts[l] and ears! You are [k]Ex 32:9; 33:3,5
just like your fathers: You always resist [l]Lev 26:41; Dt 10:16;
the Holy Spirit! 52Was there ever a Jer 4:4; 9:26
prophet your fathers did not perse- 7:52
cute?[m] They even killed those who pre- [m]2Ch 36:16; Mt 5:12
dicted the coming of the Righteous One. [n]Ac 3:14;
And now you have betrayed and mur- 1Th 2:15
dered him[n]— 53you who have received

a 28 Exodus 2:14 *b 32* Exodus 3:6
c 34 Exodus 3:5,7,8,10 *d 36* That is, Sea of Reeds
e 37 Deut. 18:15 *f 40* Exodus 32:1 *g 43* Amos 5:25-27 *h 46* Some early manuscripts *the house of Jacob* *i 50* Isaiah 66:1,2

7:53 [o]ver 38; the law that was put into effect through
Gal 3:19; angels[o] but have not obeyed it."
Heb 2:2

The Stoning of Stephen

7:54 [54]When they heard this, they were fu-
[p]Ac 5:33 rious[p] and gnashed their teeth at him.
[55]But Stephen, full of the Holy Spirit,
looked up to heaven and saw the glory of
God, and Jesus standing at the right
7:55 hand of God.[q] [56]"Look," he said, "I see
[q]Mk 16:19 heaven open[r] and the Son of Man[s]
7:56 [r]Mt 3:16 standing at the right hand of God."
[s]Mt 8:20 [57]At this they covered their ears and,
yelling at the top of their voices, they all
7:58 rushed at him, [58]dragged him out of the
[t]Lk 4:29 city[t] and began to stone him.[u] Mean-
[u]Lev 24:14,16; Dt 13:9 while, the witnesses laid their clothes[v] at
[v]Ac 22:20 [w]Ac 8:1 the feet of a young man named Saul.[w]
[59]While they were stoning him, Ste-
7:59 phen prayed, "Lord Jesus, receive my
[x]Ps 31:5; Lk 23:46 spirit."[x] [60]Then he fell on his knees[y] and
cried out, "Lord, do not hold this sin
7:60 against them."[z] When he had said this,
[y]Ac 9:40 [z]Mt 5:44 he fell asleep.
8:1 [a]Ac 7:58 **8** And Saul[a] was there, giving approval to his death.

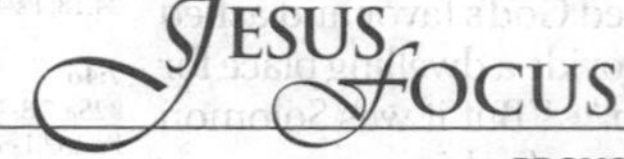

PROVOCATIVE WORDS

When Stephen began his speech to the Jewish religious leaders, they listened intently to what he had to say. He began by summarizing Jewish history and highlighting the lives of Abraham, Joseph, Moses and David. But when he went on to suggest that God's people had rejected Jesus just as their forefathers had rejected God's prophets, the crowd turned against him. The prophets, Stephen pointed out, had been sent by God to tell the people about the "Righteous One," God's promised Messiah. "And now," he informed them directly and boldly, "you have betrayed and murdered him" (Acts 7:52). Filled with rage at the accusations, the now-hostile religious leaders lost no time in dragging Stephen out of the city and stoning him to death (verse 58). But without realizing it they were actually helping to spread the Good News about Jesus. Stephen's death began a relentless wave of persecution for Christians in Jerusalem and prompted many Christian families to leave the area, taking their commitment to God's truth with them and proclaiming that truth (Acts 8:1)—which is exactly what Jesus had asked his followers to do (Acts 1:8).

The Church Persecuted and Scattered

On that day a great persecution broke
out against the church at Jerusalem, and 8:1
all except the apostles were scattered[b] [b]Ac 11:19
throughout Judea and Samaria.[c] [2]Godly [c]Ac 9:31
men buried Stephen and mourned 8:3
deeply for him. [3]But Saul[d] began to de- [d]Ac 7:58
stroy the church.[e] Going from house to [e]Ac 22:4,19; 26:10,11;
house, he dragged off men and women 1Co 15:9; Gal 1:13,23;
and put them in prison. Php 3:6; 1Ti 1:13

Philip in Samaria

[4]Those who had been scattered[f] 8:4
preached the word wherever they went.[g] [f]ver 1 [g]Ac 15:35
[5]Philip[h] went down to a city in Samaria 8:5
and proclaimed the Christ[a] there. [6]When [h]Ac 6:5
the crowds heard Philip and saw the
miraculous signs he did, they all paid
close attention to what he said. [7]With 8:7
shrieks, evil[b] spirits came out of many,[i] [i]Mk 16:17
and many paralytics and cripples were [j]Mt 4:24
healed.[j] [8]So there was great joy in that city.

Simon the Sorcerer

[9]Now for some time a man named Si- 8:9
mon had practiced sorcery[k] in the city [k]Ac 13:6
and amazed all the people of Samaria. [l]Ac 5:36
He boasted that he was someone great,[l]
[10]and all the people, both high and low,
gave him their attention and exclaimed,
"This man is the divine power known as 8:10
the Great Power."[m] [11]They followed him [m]Ac 14:11; 28:6
because he had amazed them for a long
time with his magic. [12]But when they
believed Philip as he preached the good 8:12
news of the kingdom of God[n] and the [n]Ac 1:3
name of Jesus Christ, they were bap- [o]Ac 2:38
tized,[o] both men and women. [13]Simon
himself believed and was baptized. And
he followed Philip everywhere, aston- 8:13
ished by the great signs and miracles[p] he [p]ver 6; Ac 19:11
saw.
[14]When the apostles in Jerusalem
heard that Samaria[q] had accepted the 8:14
word of God, they sent Peter and John[r] [q]ver 1 [r]Lk 22:8
to them. [15]When they arrived, they
prayed for them that they might receive 8:15
the Holy Spirit,[s] [16]because the Holy Spir- [s]Ac 2:38
it had not yet come upon any of them;[t] 8:16
they had simply been baptized into[c] the [t]Ac 19:2
name of the Lord Jesus.[u] [17]Then Peter [u]Mt 28:19; Ac 2:38
and John placed their hands on them,[v] 8:17
and they received the Holy Spirit. [v]Ac 6:6
[18]When Simon saw that the Spirit was
given at the laying on of the apostles'
hands, he offered them money [19]and

[a]5 Or *Messiah* [b]7 Greek *unclean* [c]16 Or *in*

DISCOVERY 291

TELLING THE GOOD NEWS

Philip was an evangelist whom God used in a powerful way to bring the Good News of Jesus Christ to the inhabitants of Samaria (Acts 8:5–8). At the height of Philip's successful ministry there God called him away from the crowds to speak with one individual on a lonely desert road between Jerusalem and Gaza (verses 26–27).

The man was religious; he was in fact on his way home from worshiping in Jerusalem. He was also a high public official in his home country, in charge of the treasury of Ethiopia. The two men came from disparate racial, ethnic and cultural backgrounds, but this fact was inconsequential. Jesus, speaking through an angel, asked Philip to explain God's plan of salvation to this seeker, and Philip did just that (verse 35).

The Holy Spirit prompts us to talk with others about Jesus. Philip observed that the man was sitting in his chariot reading aloud from the Old Testament prophecy of Isaiah, but it was God's Spirit who instructed Philip to run alongside the chariot and address the Ethiopian (verse 29).

Speaking to someone about our faith does not have to be complicated. Philip opened the conversation by asking a basic question: "Do you understand what you are reading?" (verse 30). And immediately the Ethiopian invited the evangelist to join him in the chariot and began asking his own questions:

"How can I unless someone explains it to me?" (verse 31)

"Tell me, please, who is the prophet talking about, himself or someone else?" (verse 34)

"Why shouldn't I be baptized?" (verse 37)

One of the most effective ways to testify about what God has done in our lives is through questions—our own and those of others. A nonthreatening but open-ended question in particular invites participation. Philip and his traveling companion started with the Old Testament, and Philip went on to explain how Jesus was the fulfillment of everything written there (see Luke 24:27; Acts 8:35; 1 Corinthians 15:1–4).

Philip was willing to cross racial, ethnic and cultural barriers in order to discourse with another man about Jesus Christ (see Discovery #275, page 1415, in which Jesus modeled this behavior in addressing the needs of the Samaritan woman). Our God is never one-sided or unjust. He created all people and loves each one of us in the same way and to the same degree (Acts 10:34).

In the end, we all belong to one race—the human race—and if we have placed our faith in Christ Jesus, we have all become brothers and sisters in God's eternal family. God has in mind one church, a church that encompasses and embraces "every nation, tribe, people and language" (Revelation 7:9).

Self-Discovery: *Are you comfortable sharing your faith with others, or do you experience a certain hesitancy or even panic when you hear the word* evangelism*? What approaches have you used in talking with nonbelievers about your relationship with the Lord, and how effective have they been?*

GO TO DISCOVERY 292 ON PAGE 1474

said, "Give me also this ability so that
everyone on whom I lay my hands may
receive the Holy Spirit."
20 Peter answered: "May your money
perish with you, because you thought
8:20 [w] 2Ki 5:16; Da 5:17; Mt 10:8; Ac 2:38 — you could buy the gift of God with money![w] 21 You have no part or share in this
ministry, because your heart is not right[x]
before God. 22 Repent of this wickedness
8:21 [x] Ps 78:37 — and pray to the Lord. Perhaps he will forgive you for having such a thought in
your heart. 23 For I see that you are full of
bitterness and captive to sin."
24 Then Simon answered, "Pray to the
8:24 [y] Ex 8:8; Nu 21:7; 1Ki 13:6 — Lord for me[y] so that nothing you have
said may happen to me."
25 When they had testified and proclaimed the word of the Lord, Peter and
John returned to Jerusalem, preaching
8:25 [z] ver 40 — the gospel in many Samaritan villages.[z]

Philip and the Ethiopian

8:26 [a] Ac 5:19 — 26 Now an angel[a] of the Lord said to
Philip, "Go south to the road—the
desert road—that goes down from Jerusalem to Gaza." 27 So he started out, and
8:27 [b] Ps 68:31; 87:4; Zep 3:10 [c] Isa 56:3-5 [d] 1Ki 8:41-43; Jn 12:20 — on his way he met an Ethiopian[a][b] eunuch,[c] an important official in charge of
all the treasury of Candace, queen of the
Ethiopians. This man had gone to Jerusalem to worship,[d] 28 and on his way
home was sitting in his chariot reading
the book of Isaiah the prophet. 29 The
8:29 [e] Ac 10:19; 11:12; 13:2; 20:23; 21:11 — Spirit told[e] Philip, "Go to that chariot
and stay near it."
30 Then Philip ran up to the chariot
and heard the man reading Isaiah the
prophet. "Do you understand what you
are reading?" Philip asked.
31 "How can I," he said, "unless someone explains it to me?" So he invited
Philip to come up and sit with him.
32 The eunuch was reading this passage of Scripture:

"He was led like a sheep to the
slaughter,
and as a lamb before the shearer
is silent,
so he did not open his mouth.
33 In his humiliation he was deprived
of justice.
Who can speak of his
descendants?
For his life was taken from the
earth."[b][f] — 8:33 [f] Isa 53:7,8

34 The eunuch asked Philip, "Tell me,
please, who is the prophet talking about,
himself or someone else?" 35 Then Philip
began[g] with that very passage of Scrip- — 8:35 [g] Mt 5:2 [h] Lk 24:27; Ac 17:2; 18:28; 28:23
ture[h] and told him the good news about
Jesus.

> YOU'RE NEVER REALLY PREACHING UNTIL YOU'RE PREACHING ABOUT JESUS.
>
> Jerry Vines, *Pastor, Jacksonville, Florida*

36 As they traveled along the road, they
came to some water and the eunuch
said, "Look, here is water. Why shouldn't
I be baptized?"[c][i] 38 And he gave orders to — 8:36 [i] Ac 10:47
stop the chariot. Then both Philip and
the eunuch went down into the water
and Philip baptized him. 39 When they — 8:39 [j] 1Ki 18:12; 2Ki 2:16; Eze 3:12,14; 8:3; 11:1,24; 43:5; 2Co 12:2
came up out of the water, the Spirit of
the Lord suddenly took Philip away,[j] and
the eunuch did not see him again, but
went on his way rejoicing. 40 Philip, how- — 8:40 [k] ver 25 [l] Ac 10:1,24; 12:19; 21:8,16; 23:23,33; 25:1,4, 6,13
ever, appeared at Azotus and traveled
about, preaching the gospel in all the
towns[k] until he reached Caesarea.[l]

Saul's Conversion

9 Meanwhile, Saul was still breath-
ing out murderous threats against — 9:1 [m] Ac 8:3
the Lord's disciples.[m] He went to the

[a] 27 That is, from the upper Nile region
[b] 33 Isaiah 53:7,8 [c] 36 Some late manuscripts *baptized?"* *37 Philip said, "If you believe with all your heart, you may." The eunuch answered, "I believe that Jesus Christ is the Son of God."*

JESUS AND YOU

CROSSING BARRIERS

If we are not careful it is easy for us to try to keep Jesus confined within our own ethnic, racial or social groupings rather than to cross barriers to share him with others. Luke described a dramatic shift in focus beginning in Acts 8. Christians began to accept converts from other religions, ethnic backgrounds and cultures—with the result that the gospel spread to whole provinces as people heard God's truth. A once small but now rapidly growing band of believers embraced non-Jewish believers from every walk of life. Philip, who was a deacon, carried the Good News to Samaria (verse 4–5), to a group of people who were avowed enemies of the Jews. He also shared the truth about Jesus with a man from Ethiopia (verse 27).

IT DOESN'T MATTER HOW YOU COME TO CHRIST; WHAT MATTERS IS THAT YOU COME TO CHRIST!

Dr. James Kennedy, *Pastor, Fort Lauderdale, Florida*

high priest [2]and asked him for letters to
the synagogues in Damascus, so that if
9:2 he found any there who belonged to the
[n] Ac 19:9,23; Way,[n] whether men or women, he might
22:4; 24:14,22 take them as prisoners to Jerusalem. [3]As
he neared Damascus on his journey,
suddenly a light from heaven flashed
9:3 [o] 1Co 15:8 around him.[o] [4]He fell to the ground and
heard a voice say to him, "Saul, Saul, why
do you persecute me?"
[5]"Who are you, Lord?" Saul asked.
"I am Jesus, whom you are persecuting," he replied. [6]"Now get up and go
into the city, and you will be told what
9:6 [p] ver 16 you must do."[p]
9:7 [7]The men traveling with Saul stood
[q] Jn 12:29 there speechless; they heard the sound[q]
[r] Da 10:7; but did not see anyone.[r] [8]Saul got up
Ac 22:9 from the ground, but when he opened
his eyes he could see nothing. So they
led him by the hand into Damascus.
[9]For three days he was blind, and did not
eat or drink anything.
[10]In Damascus there was a disciple
9:10 named Ananias. The Lord called to him
[s] Ac 10:3,17,19 in a vision,[s] "Ananias!"
"Yes, Lord," he answered.

JESUS FOCUS

A NEW NAME

In the early stages of the church those who believed in Jesus were known by a number of different names. They were at various times and places called believers (Acts 2:44), members of "the Way" (Acts 9:2), disciples (Acts 9:10), brothers (Acts 9:30) or members of the "Nazarene sect" (Acts 24:5). In Antioch followers of Jesus Christ were first referred to as Christians, and that name has endured throughout the centuries (Acts 11:26). Nonbelieving Roman authors used the name *Christian* in a derogatory manner, revealing their open hostility to this new but flourishing religious group. But Christians wore the name as a badge of honor because they were reflecting Jesus in such a way that people called them by his name—*Christ-ones*.

[11]The Lord told him, "Go to the house
of Judas on Straight Street and ask for a 9:11
man from Tarsus[t] named Saul, for he is [t] ver 30;
praying. [12]In a vision he has seen a man Ac 21:39; 22:3
named Ananias come and place his 9:12
hands on[u] him to restore his sight." [u] Mk 5:23
[13]"Lord," Ananias answered, "I have
heard many reports about this man and 9:13
all the harm he has done to your saints[v] [v] ver 32; Ro 1:7;
in Jerusalem.[w] [14]And he has come here 16:2,15 [w] Ac 8:3
with authority from the chief priests[x] to 9:14
arrest all who call on your name." [x] ver 2,21
[15]But the Lord said to Ananias, "Go! 9:15
This man is my chosen instrument[y] to [y] Ac 13:2;
carry my name before the Gentiles[z] and Ro 1:1; Gal 1:15
their kings[a] and before the people of Is- [z] Ro 11:13; 15:15,16;
rael. [16]I will show him how much he Gal 2:7,8; Eph 3:7,8
must suffer for my name."[b] [a] Ac 25:22,23; 26:1
[17]Then Ananias went to the house 9:16
and entered it. Placing his hands on[c] [b] Ac 20:23;
Saul, he said, "Brother Saul, the Lord— 21:11; 2Co 11:23-27
Jesus, who appeared to you on the road 9:17
as you were coming here—has sent me [c] Ac 6:6
so that you may see again and be filled
with the Holy Spirit." [18]Immediately,
something like scales fell from Saul's
eyes, and he could see again. He got up

PAUL
JESUS' MISSIONARY

Originally known as Saul, Paul was a strict orthodox Pharisee (Acts 22:3; 23:6; 26:5; Philippians 3:5) who hated Christians so much that he became obsessed with tracking them down and arranging for their execution (Acts 8:1–3; 9:1–2). Then one memorable day while en route to Damascus for the purpose of persecuting a group of Christians, he experienced a climactic and life-changing encounter with the risen Jesus. In one of the most dramatic conversion stories in history, this near-fanatical Christ-hater was transformed into one of Jesus' greatest spokespersons of all time, an individual who would go on to serve the church of Jesus Christ with the same zeal with which he had formerly persecuted it. Paul traveled tirelessly throughout the entire Roman empire, devoting his unflagging energy and fervor to telling others about Jesus, as well as writing 13 New Testament letters. A large portion of the book of Acts is devoted to Paul's three missionary journeys, his time in prison in Caesarea and his journey to Rome (Acts 13—28). According to Christian tradition, Paul was executed in Rome by Emperor Nero in A.D. 68.

D I S C O V E R Y **292**

Confronted by Jesus

No other person, with the exception of Jesus himself, has influenced the Christian faith more than the apostle Paul. Until the beginning of Paul's ministry the early church had not addressed the issue of evangelism to Gentiles. That became Paul's consuming passion, however, and it was through his influence that the Good News spread throughout the Roman empire.

Paul's Jewish name was Saul, and he was at the height of a prominent religious career (Acts 23:6; 26:5; Philippians 3:5). In fact, as a scrupulous Jew, Saul was vehemently opposed to Jesus Christ and had made it his business to persecute this new group called Christians (Acts 9:1). Saul's life was changed dramatically, however, when he encountered the risen Jesus, and this confrontation and its aftermath still stand as evidence of the power of our Lord and his gospel to change lives.

Saul was en route to Damascus to arrest Christians and escort them back to Jerusalem to stand trial. Without warning, a resplendent light temporarily blinded him, and a voice from heaven queried, "Saul, why do you persecute me?" (verse 4).

"Who are you, Lord?" Saul responded in a quavering voice.

"I am Jesus, whom you are persecuting," came the reply (verse 5).

In this brief face-off Jesus confronted Saul with significant spiritual realities. First, persecuting his people was tantamount to persecuting Jesus himself. Not only that, but it is well nigh impossible to resist Jesus when he wants to change a life. Saul thought he had been pursuing Christians in order to eliminate them; what he discovered was that Jesus had all along been pursuing him to use him to further the gospel cause! Jesus directed Saul to continue on to Damascus, from where the Lord would reveal to him his next step (verse 6). The man once so hostile to the Lord now docilely and penitently obeyed (verse 8).

As Saul waited in Damascus he was undoubtedly reeling from the experience. Here he was, helplessly blind, sitting in the very town in which he had intended to arrest followers of Jesus Christ, waiting for the very God they served to give him, of all people, directions! Ananias, however, must have been aghast (verses 10–13). As a believer living in Damascus he had been painfully aware of Saul's impending arrival, and suddenly God was instructing him to go and lay hands on the enemy! Initially Ananias objected, but God assured him that Saul was his "chosen instrument to carry [his] name before the Gentiles and their kings and before the people of Israel" (verse 15).

One short-lived encounter with Jesus radically altered Paul's life direction. Paul's dynamic conversion is an example of Jesus' unlimited patience with each of us. We all encounter individuals who are vehemently, and apparently unbendingly, opposed to Jesus. Paul's story encourages us never to give up, because no one is beyond the reach of the light and the love of Jesus Christ.

Self-Discovery: *What experience stands out in your mind as indicative of the fact that God in Jesus was pursuing you before you even thought of pursuing him? Whether this encounter involved an initial conversion experience or a recommitment, ponder its implications and pause to thank God.*

GO TO DISCOVERY 293 ON PAGE 1477

and was baptized, 19 and after taking some food, he regained his strength.

Saul in Damascus and Jerusalem

Saul spent several days with the disciples[d] in Damascus.[e] 20 At once he began to preach in the synagogues[f] that Jesus is the Son of God.[g] 21 All those who heard him were astonished and asked, "Isn't he the man who raised havoc in Jerusalem among those who call on this name?[h] And hasn't he come here to take them as prisoners to the chief priests?"[i] 22 Yet Saul grew more and more powerful and baffled the Jews living in Damascus by proving that Jesus is the Christ.[a][j]

23 After many days had gone by, the Jews conspired to kill him, 24 but Saul learned of their plan.[k] Day and night they kept close watch on the city gates in order to kill him. 25 But his followers took him by night and lowered him in a basket through an opening in the wall.[l]

26 When he came to Jerusalem,[m] he tried to join the disciples, but they were all afraid of him, not believing that he really was a disciple. 27 But Barnabas[n] took him and brought him to the apostles. He told them how Saul on his journey had seen the Lord and that the Lord had spoken to him,[o] and how in Damascus he had preached fearlessly in the name of Jesus.[p] 28 So Saul stayed with them and moved about freely in Jerusalem, speaking boldly in the name of the Lord. 29 He talked and debated with the Grecian Jews,[q] but they tried to kill him.[r] 30 When the brothers[s] learned of this, they took him down to Caesarea[t] and sent him off to Tarsus.[u]

31 Then the church throughout Judea, Galilee and Samaria[v] enjoyed a time of peace. It was strengthened; and encouraged by the Holy Spirit, it grew in numbers, living in the fear of the Lord.

Aeneas and Dorcas

32 As Peter traveled about the country, he went to visit the saints[w] in Lydda. 33 There he found a man named Aeneas, a paralytic who had been bedridden for eight years. 34 "Aeneas," Peter said to him, "Jesus Christ heals you.[x] Get up and take care of your mat." Immediately Aeneas got up. 35 All those who lived in Lydda and Sharon[y] saw him and turned to the Lord.[z]

9:19 [d] Ac 11:26 [e] Ac 26:20
9:20 [f] Ac 13:5,14 [g] Mt 4:3
9:21 [h] Ac 8:3 [i] Gal 1:13,23
9:22 [j] Ac 18:5,28
9:24 [k] Ac 20:3,19
9:25 [l] 1Sa 19:12; 2Co 11:32,33
9:26 [m] Ac 22:17; 26:20; Gal 1:17, 18
9:27 [n] Ac 4:36 [o] ver 3-6 [p] ver 20,22
9:29 [q] Ac 6:1 [r] 2Co 11:26
9:30 [s] Ac 1:16 [t] Ac 8:40 [u] ver 11
9:31 [v] Ac 8:1
9:32 [w] ver 13
9:34 [x] Ac 3:6,16; 4:10
9:35 [y] 1Ch 5:16; 27:29; Isa 33:9; 35:2; 65:10 [z] Ac 11:21

36 In Joppa[a] there was a disciple named Tabitha (which, when translated, is Dorcas[b]), who was always doing good[b] and helping the poor. 37 About that time she became sick and died, and her body was washed and placed in an upstairs room.[c] 38 Lydda was near Joppa; so when the disciples[d] heard that Peter was in Lydda, they sent two men to him and urged him, "Please come at once!"

39 Peter went with them, and when he arrived he was taken upstairs to the room. All the widows[e] stood around him, crying and showing him the robes and other clothing that Dorcas had made while she was still with them.

40 Peter sent them all out of the room;[f] then he got down on his knees[g] and prayed. Turning toward the dead woman, he said, "Tabitha, get up." She opened her eyes, and seeing Peter she sat up. 41 He took her by the hand and helped her to her feet. Then he called the believers and the widows and presented her to them alive. 42 This became known all over Joppa, and many people believed in the Lord. 43 Peter stayed in Joppa for some time with a tanner named Simon.[h]

Cornelius Calls for Peter

10 At Caesarea[i] there was a man named Cornelius, a centurion in what was known as the Italian Regiment. 2 He and all his family were devout and God-fearing;[j] he gave generously to those in need and prayed to God regularly. 3 One day at about three in the afternoon[k] he had a vision.[l] He distinctly saw an angel[m] of God, who came to him and said, "Cornelius!"

4 Cornelius stared at him in fear. "What is it, Lord?" he asked.

The angel answered, "Your prayers and gifts to the poor have come up as a memorial offering[n] before God.[o] 5 Now send men to Joppa[p] to bring back a man named Simon who is called Peter. 6 He is staying with Simon the tanner,[q] whose house is by the sea."

7 When the angel who spoke to him had gone, Cornelius called two of his servants and a devout soldier who was one of his attendants. 8 He told them everything that had happened and sent them to Joppa.[r]

[a] 22 Or *Messiah* [b] 36 Both *Tabitha* (Aramaic) and *Dorcas* (Greek) mean *gazelle.*

9:36 [a] Jos 19:46; 2Ch 2:16; Ezr 3:7; Jnh 1:3; Ac 10:5 [b] 1Ti 2:10; Tit 3:8
9:37 [c] Ac 1:13
9:38 [d] Ac 11:26
9:39 [e] Ac 6:1
9:40 [f] Mt 9:25 [g] Lk 22:41; Ac 7:60
9:43 [h] Ac 10:6
10:1 [i] Ac 8:40
10:2 [j] ver 22,35; Ac 13:16,26
10:3 [k] Ac 3:1 [l] Ac 9:10 [m] Ac 5:19
10:4 [n] Mt 26:13 [o] Rev 8:4
10:5 [p] Ac 9:36
10:6 [q] Ac 9:43
10:8 [r] Ac 9:36

Peter's Vision

9About noon the following day as
they were on their journey and approaching the city, Peter went up on the
10:9 [s]Mt 24:17 roof[s] to pray. 10He became hungry and
wanted something to eat, and while the
10:10 [t]Ac 22:17 meal was being prepared, he fell into a
trance.[t] 11He saw heaven opened and
something like a large sheet being let
down to earth by its four corners. 12It
contained all kinds of four-footed animals, as well as reptiles of the earth and
birds of the air. 13Then a voice told him,
"Get up, Peter. Kill and eat."
10:14 [u]Ac 9:5 [v]Lev 11:4-8,13-20; 20:25; Dt 14:3-20; Eze 4:14 14"Surely not, Lord!"[u] Peter replied. "I
have never eaten anything impure or
unclean."[v]
15The voice spoke to him a second
time, "Do not call anything impure that
10:15 [w]Mt 15:11; Ro 14:14,17,20; 1Co 10:25; 1Ti 4:3,4; Tit 1:15 God has made clean."[w]
16This happened three times, and im-
mediately the sheet was taken back to
heaven.
17While Peter was wondering about
the meaning of the vision, the men sent
10:17 [x]ver 7,8 by Cornelius[x] found out where Simon's
house was and stopped at the gate.
18They called out, asking if Simon who
was known as Peter was staying there.
19While Peter was still thinking about
10:19 [y]Ac 8:29 the vision, the Spirit said[y] to him, "Simon, three[a] men are looking for you.
20So get up and go downstairs. Do not
hesitate to go with them, for I have sent
10:20 [z]Ac 15:7-9 them."[z]
21Peter went down and said to the
men, "I'm the one you're looking for.
Why have you come?"
22The men replied, "We have come
from Cornelius the centurion. He is a
10:22 [a]ver 2 [b]Ac 11:14 righteous and God-fearing man,[a] who is
respected by all the Jewish people. A
holy angel told him to have you come to
his house so that he could hear what you
have to say."[b] 23Then Peter invited the
men into the house to be his guests.

Peter at Cornelius' House

The next day Peter started out with
10:23 [c]Ac 1:16 [d]ver 45; Ac 11:12 them, and some of the brothers[c] from
Joppa went along.[d] 24The following day
he arrived in Caesarea.[e] Cornelius was
10:24 [e]Ac 8:40 expecting them and had called together
his relatives and close friends. 25As Peter
entered the house, Cornelius met him
and fell at his feet in reverence. 26But Pe-
ter made him get up. "Stand up," he said, 10:26 [f]Ac 14:15; Rev 19:10
"I am only a man myself."[f]
27Talking with him, Peter went inside
and found a large gathering of people.
28He said to them: "You are well aware
that it is against our law for a Jew to as-
sociate with a Gentile or visit him.[g] But 10:28 [g]Jn 4:9; 18:28; Ac 11:3 [h]Ac 15:8,9
God has shown me that I should not call
any man impure or unclean.[h] 29So when
I was sent for, I came without raising
any objection. May I ask why you sent
for me?"
30Cornelius answered: "Four days ago
I was in my house praying at this hour, at
three in the afternoon. Suddenly a man
in shining clothes stood before me 31and
said, 'Cornelius, God has heard your
prayer and remembered your gifts to the
poor. 32Send to Joppa for Simon who is
called Peter. He is a guest in the home of
Simon the tanner, who lives by the sea.'
33So I sent for you immediately, and it
was good of you to come. Now we are all
here in the presence of God to listen to
everything the Lord has commanded
you to tell us."
34Then Peter began to speak: "I now 10:34 [i]Dt 10:17; 2Ch 19:7; Job 34:19; Ro 2:11; Gal 2:6; Eph 6:9; Col 3:25; 1Pe 1:17
realize how true it is that God does not
show favoritism[i] 35but accepts men
from every nation who fear him and do
what is right.[j] 36You know the message
God sent to the people of Israel, telling
the good news[k] of peace[l] through Jesus
Christ, who is Lord of all.[m] 37You know 10:35 [j]Ac 15:9
what has happened throughout Judea,
beginning in Galilee after the baptism 10:36 [k]Ac 13:32 [l]Lk 2:14 [m]Mt 28:18; Ro 10:12
that John preached— 38how God
anointed[n] Jesus of Nazareth with the
Holy Spirit and power, and how he went
around doing good and healing[o] all who 10:38 [n]Ac 4:26 [o]Mt 4:23 [p]Jn 3:2
were under the power of the devil, be-
cause God was with him.[p]
39"We are witnesses[q] of everything he 10:39 [q]Lk 24:48 [r]Ac 5:30
did in the country of the Jews and in Je-
rusalem. They killed him by hanging
him on a tree,[r] 40but God raised him 10:40 [s]Ac 2:24
from the dead[s] on the third day and
caused him to be seen. 41He was not 10:41 [t]Jn 14:17,22 [u]Lk 24:43; Jn 21:13
seen by all the people,[t] but by witnesses
whom God had already chosen—by us
who ate[u] and drank with him after he 10:42 [v]Mt 28:19,20 [w]Jn 5:22; Ac 17:31; Ro 14:9; 2Co 5:10; 2Ti 4:1; 1Pe 4:5
rose from the dead. 42He commanded us
to preach to the people[v] and to testify
that he is the one whom God appointed
as judge of the living and the dead.[w]

[a] *19* One early manuscript *two*; other manuscripts do not have the number.

PLAYING FAVORITES

On the surface Peter and Cornelius had very little in common. Peter was a Jewish fisherman by trade and a devoted follower of Jesus Christ. Cornelius was a Roman centurion, part of the despised occupation force in Palestine. The one common denominator was that they both prayed to the same God, the God who would bring them together as brothers in Jesus Christ (Acts 10:2).

Peter held a relatively uncomplicated worldview, dividing the world into two distinct people groups: the Jews on the one hand and everyone else on the other. Peter believed that the Jewish nation had been chosen by God and was therefore superior (verse 28). At the heart of racism is the notion that one group is innately better than another, and this bigoted attitude was deeply entrenched in the Jewish mind-set. Sadly, Peter was basing his prejudiced outlook on a misunderstanding of God's teachings and character (Acts 10: 34–35; see also Genesis 12:3; Deuteronomy 10:17; Isaiah 9:1; 42:6; 49:6,22).

God began to change Peter's conception of reality through a vision. In a dream Peter observed a sheet filled with a variety of animals that Old Testament law had deemed "unclean." God directed him to kill the animals and eat them, but Peter adamantly refused: "Surely not, Lord! I have never eaten anything impure or unclean" (Acts 10:14). The Lord informed Peter that he did not have the right to call anything *un*clean that God had designated as "clean." This same dream sequence occurred two more times, leaving Peter to ponder the implications.

Even as Peter was mulling over his dream, messengers from Cornelius arrived at his door and invited Peter to visit their master at his home (verses 17–22). Cornelius had dispatched the men to Peter because he had prayed to God and God had directed him to do just that (verses 1–8). Suddenly, the significance of the dream began to dawn on Peter. In his mind he had been pigeonholing people into *clean* and *unclean* categories, just as he had divided the animal kingdom into only two groups. What God was impressing on his heart is that this distinction was artificial and hurtful—that people are people, and that Peter was to go to the Gentiles with the Good News of Jesus.

When Peter arrived at Cornelius's home he confessed his own prejudice and advised Cornelius that God had corrected his inaccurate perception (verse 28). Cornelius shared his own story, and the two agreed that God "does not show favoritism but accepts men from every nation who fear him and do what is right" (verses 34–35).

If God does not play favorites, neither should his people (see James 2:1–13). One of the more deplorable forms of prejudice is that of hating, scorning or ignoring other people *in the name of God.* We cannot love God and at the same time look at our fellow human beings with a condescending attitude. We cannot truly be devoted to Jesus and fail to welcome each member of his worldwide family as a brother or sister (see Ephesians 2:11–22).

Self-Discovery: *Identify some specific situations in which you have been guilty of pigeonholing other people, including believers from different backgrounds or traditions. If you have been guilty of prejudice, try to verbalize your biases using the following sentence structure:*
*We*___________________________________;
*they*___________________________________.
Ask Jesus to fill you with a spirit of welcoming love.

GO TO DISCOVERY 294 ON PAGE 1479

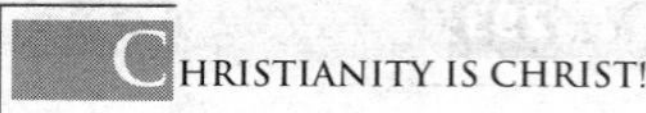

CHRISTIANITY IS CHRIST!

W. H. Griffith Thomas, *Canadian Scholar*

10:43 [x]Isa 53:11 43All the prophets testify about him[x]
[y]Ac 15:9 that everyone[y] who believes in him receives forgiveness of sins through his
name.”
44While Peter was still speaking these
10:44 [z]Ac 8:15,16; words, the Holy Spirit came on[z] all who
11:15; 15:8 heard the message. 45The circumcised
10:45 believers who had come with Peter[a]
[a]ver 23 were astonished that the gift of the Holy
[b]Ac 2:33,38 Spirit had been poured out[b] even on the
[c]Ac 11:18 Gentiles.[c] 46For they heard them speak-
10:46 [d]Mk 16:17 ing in tongues[a][d] and praising God.
Then Peter said, 47“Can anyone keep
these people from being baptized with
10:47 [e]Ac 8:36 water?[e] They have received the Holy
[f]Ac 11:17 Spirit just as we have.”[f] 48So he ordered
that they be baptized in the name of
10:48 [g]Ac 2:38; 8:16 Jesus Christ.[g] Then they asked Peter to
stay with them for a few days.

Peter Explains His Actions

11:1 [h]Ac 1:16 11 The apostles and the brothers[h]
throughout Judea heard that
the Gentiles also had received the word
11:2 of God. 2So when Peter went up to Jeru-
[i]Ac 10:45 salem, the circumcised believers[i] criticized him 3and said, “You went into the
11:3 house of uncircumcised men and ate
[j]Ac 10:25,28; Gal 2:12 with them.”[j]
4Peter began and explained everything to them precisely as it had happened: 5“I was in the city of Joppa pray-
11:5 [k]Ac 10:9-32; ing, and in a trance I saw a vision.[k] I saw
9:10 something like a large sheet being let
down from heaven by its four corners,
and it came down to where I was. 6I
looked into it and saw four-footed animals of the earth, wild beasts, reptiles,
and birds of the air. 7Then I heard a voice
telling me, ‘Get up, Peter. Kill and eat.’
8“I replied, ‘Surely not, Lord! Nothing
impure or unclean has ever entered my
mouth.’
9“The voice spoke from heaven a second time, ‘Do not call anything impure
11:9 [l]Ac 10:15 that God has made clean.’[l] 10This happened three times, and then it was all
pulled up to heaven again.
11“Right then three men who had
been sent to me from Caesarea stopped
at the house where I was staying. 12The

Spirit told[m] me to have no hesitation 11:12 [m]Ac 8:29
about going with them.[n] These six [n]Ac 15:9;
brothers also went with me, and we en- Ro 3:22
tered the man’s house. 13He told us how
he had seen an angel appear in his house
and say, ‘Send to Joppa for Simon who is
called Peter. 14He will bring you a mes- 11:14
sage through which you and all your [o]Jn 4:53; Ac 16:15,31-34;
household[o] will be saved.’ 1Co 1:11,16
15“As I began to speak, the Holy Spirit 11:15
came on[p] them as he had come on us at [p]Ac 10:44
the beginning.[q] 16Then I remembered [q]Ac 2:4
what the Lord had said: ‘John baptized
with[b] water, but you will be baptized 11:16
with the Holy Spirit.’[r] 17So if God gave [r]Mk 1:8; Ac 1:5
them the same gift as he gave us,[s] who 11:17
believed in the Lord Jesus Christ, who [s]Ac 10:45,47
was I to think that I could oppose God?”
18When they heard this, they had no
further objections and praised God, say- 11:18
ing, “So then, God has granted even the [t]Ro 10:12,13;
Gentiles repentance unto life.”[t] 2Co 7:10

The Church in Antioch

19Now those who had been scattered
by the persecution in connection with 11:19
Stephen[u] traveled as far as Phoenicia, [u]Ac 8:1,4
Cyprus and Antioch,[v] telling the mes- [v]ver 26,27; Ac 13:1; 18:22;
sage only to Jews. 20Some of them, how- Gal 2:11
ever, men from Cyprus[w] and Cyrene,[x] 11:20
went to Antioch and began to speak to [w]Ac 4:36
Greeks also, telling them the good news [x]Mt 27:32
about the Lord Jesus. 21The Lord’s hand 11:21
was with them,[y] and a great number of [y]Lk 1:66
people believed and turned to the Lord.[z] [z]Ac 2:47
22News of this reached the ears of the
church at Jerusalem, and they sent Bar-
nabas[a] to Antioch. 23When he arrived 11:22 [a]Ac 4:36
and saw the evidence of the grace of
God,[b] he was glad and encouraged them 11:23 [b]Ac 13:43;
all to remain true to the Lord with all 14:26; 20:24
their hearts.[c] 24He was a good man, full [c]Ac 14:22
of the Holy Spirit and faith, and a great
number of people were brought to the 11:24
Lord.[d] [d]ver 21; Ac 5:14
25Then Barnabas went to Tarsus[e] to 11:25
look for Saul, 26and when he found him, [e]Ac 9:11
he brought him to Antioch. So for a
whole year Barnabas and Saul met with 11:26
the church and taught great numbers of [f]Ac 6:1,2; 13:52 [g]Ac 26:28;
people. The disciples[f] were called Chris- 1Pe 4:16
tians first[g] at Antioch. 11:27
27During this time some prophets[h] [h]Ac 13:1; 15:32;
came down from Jerusalem to Antioch. 1Co 12:28,29;
28One of them, named Agabus,[i] stood up Eph 4:11 11:28
and through the Spirit predicted that a [i]Ac 21:10

[a] 46 Or *other languages* [b] 16 Or *in*

DISCOVERY 294

"Ones Like Christ"

Followers of Jesus today use the name *Christian* to define who they are. In the New Testament, however, believers in Jesus did not initially adopt this name to describe themselves. The term was actually coined in Antioch, possibly by unbelievers living in the city (Acts 11:26). Believers were first called disciples and only later referred to as Christians, or "ones like Christ."

The church in Antioch was comprised of a mixture of Jews and Gentiles (verses 19–21). The two groups were very different from one another in terms of background and culture, but they had one thing in common: Under the warm and wonderful influence of Barnabas and Saul, they were introduced to the life transforming power of Jesus (verses 25–26). Their top priority was to become more and more Christlike. They undoubtedly talked about the things Jesus had discussed, focused on the things that had been important to him, lived the way he had lived.

The apostle Paul referred to the Corinthian believers as letters from Christ: "You yourselves are our letter, written on our hearts, known and read by everybody. You show that you are a letter from Christ . . . written not with ink but with the Spirit of the living God, not on tablets of stone but on tablets of human hearts" (2 Corinthians 3:2–3).

When we refer to a person who tends to be transparent in terms of her emotions or intentions, we sometimes say that she is "like an open book." What a privilege and responsibility for us as Christians to live our lives as open letters, available at all times for scrutiny by a skeptical but searching world. If our message and our actions are seamlessly consistent, if we are indeed, as a contemporary Christian song expresses it, "the only Bible some will ever read," we will be perceived by the world as persons of integrity, as people who can be trusted and even emulated.

Paul referred to himself already in the first verse of his letter to the Romans as one who had been "set apart" for the gospel of God and closed his prologue in Romans 1:6 by stating that "you also are called to belong to Jesus Christ." Another way to envision ourselves as "Christ-ones" is to emphasize the truth that we are "in" Jesus Christ (Romans 8:1). And we are in Jesus *together*: "In Christ we who are many form one body, and each member belongs to all the others" (Romans 12:5). When Christians are willing to form a united front to combat the rampant sin and evil all around us, when we are willing to cooperate and coexist in loving brotherhood and sisterhood, we will indeed be a force for good, together working to spread Jesus' love to a desperate world.

"Thanks be to God, who always leads us in triumphal procession in Christ and through us spreads everywhere the fragrance of the knowledge of him . . . In Christ we speak before God with sincerity, like men sent from God" (2 Corinthians 2:14,17).

Self-Discovery: *How can you become a more accurate reflection of Jesus to others? To be a true "Christ-one" requires following him to the cross and dying to yourself (2 Corinthians 4:10–12; Philippians 3:8–14). The cost is high, but the rewards are eternal.*

GO TO DISCOVERY 295 ON PAGE 1486

> **When people find out that you are a Christian, they should already have an idea of who you are and what you are like simply because you bear such a precious name.**
>
> Joni Eareckson Tada,
> *Christian Author and Speaker*

11:28 severe famine would spread over the en-
jMt 24:14 tire Roman world.[j] (This happened dur-
kAc 18:2 ing the reign of Claudius.)[k] [29]The disci-
11:29 lver 26 ples,[l] each according to his ability,
mRo 15:26; decided to provide help[m] for the broth-
2Co 9:2 ers[n] living in Judea. [30]This they did,
nAc 1:16 sending their gift to the elders[o] by Bar-
11:30 oAc 14:23 nabas and Saul.[p]
pAc 12:25

Peter's Miraculous Escape From Prison

12 It was about this time that King
Herod arrested some who belonged to the church, intending to persecute them. [2]He had James, the broth-
12:2 qMt 4:21 er of John,[q] put to death with the sword.
[3]When he saw that this pleased the
12:3 rAc 24:27 Jews,[r] he proceeded to seize Peter also.
sEx 12:15; 23:15 This happened during the Feast of Unleavened Bread.[s] [4]After arresting him, he
put him in prison, handing him over to
be guarded by four squads of four soldiers each. Herod intended to bring him
out for public trial after the Passover.
[5]So Peter was kept in prison, but the
church was earnestly praying to God for
12:5 tEph 6:18 him.[t]
[6]The night before Herod was to bring
him to trial, Peter was sleeping between
12:6 uAc 21:33 two soldiers, bound with two chains,[u]
and sentries stood guard at the en-
12:7 vAc 5:19 trance. [7]Suddenly an angel[v] of the Lord
wAc 16:26 appeared and a light shone in the cell.
He struck Peter on the side and woke
him up. "Quick, get up!" he said, and the
chains fell off Peter's wrists.[w]
[8]Then the angel said to him, "Put on
your clothes and sandals." And Peter did
so. "Wrap your cloak around you and
follow me," the angel told him. [9]Peter followed him out of the prison, but he had
no idea that what the angel was doing
12:9 was really happening; he thought he was
xAc 9:10 seeing a vision.[x] [10]They passed the first
and second guards and came to the iron
gate leading to the city. It opened for
them by itself,[y] and they went through 12:10 yAc 5:19; 16:26
it. When they had walked the length of
one street, suddenly the angel left him.
[11]Then Peter came to himself[z] and said, 12:11 zLk 15:17
"Now I know without a doubt that the aPs 34:7;
Lord sent his angel and rescued me[a] from Da 3:28; 6:22;
Herod's clutches and from everything the 2Co 1:10; 2Pe 2:9
Jewish people were anticipating."
[12]When this had dawned on him, he
went to the house of Mary the mother of 12:12
John, also called Mark,[b] where many bver 25; Ac 15:37,39;
people had gathered and were praying.[c] Col 4:10;
[13]Peter knocked at the outer entrance, Phm 24;
and a servant girl named Rhoda came to 1Pe 5:13 cver 5
answer the door.[d] [14]When she recog- 12:13
nized Peter's voice, she was so over- dJn 18:16,17
joyed[e] she ran back without opening it 12:14
and exclaimed, "Peter is at the door!" eLk 24:41
[15]"You're out of your mind," they told
her. When she kept insisting that it was
so, they said, "It must be his angel."[f] 12:15 fMt 18:10
[16]But Peter kept on knocking, and
when they opened the door and saw
him, they were astonished. [17]Peter motioned with his hand[g] for them to be 12:17 gAc 13:16;
quiet and described how the Lord had 19:33; 21:40
brought him out of prison. "Tell James[h] hAc 15:13
and the brothers[i] about this," he said, iAc 1:16
and then he left for another place.
[18]In the morning, there was no small
commotion among the soldiers as to
what had become of Peter. [19]After Herod
had a thorough search made for him
and did not find him, he cross-examined
the guards and ordered that they be ex- 12:19
ecuted.[j] jAc 16:27

Jesus Focus

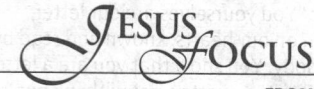

FROM PETER TO PAUL

The first 12 chapters of Acts focus on Peter. As one of Jesus' original disciples, this once-impulsive but now seasoned evangelist represented the Jewish element in the early church. Peter had a vision in Joppa that prompted him to seek out a non-Jewish Christian in Caesarea named Cornelius. That association opened the doors of the fledgling church to non-Jewish believers. It was Paul's ministry, however, that carried the truth about Jesus beyond the borders of Israel to the far reaches of the Roman empire. The second half of the book of Acts, chapters 13—28, focuses on Paul's life. Peter and Paul ministered in different locations, but the two shared a compelling common vision of proclaiming to others the saving power of Jesus Christ.

Herod's Death

12:19 Then Herod went from Judea to Caes-
[k] Ac 8:40 area[k] and stayed there a while. 20He had
12:20 been quarreling with the people of Tyre
[l] Mt 11:21 and Sidon;[l] they now joined together
[m] 1Ki 5:9,11; and sought an audience with him. Hav-
Eze 27:17 ing secured the support of Blastus, a
trusted personal servant of the king,
they asked for peace, because they depended on the king's country for their
food supply.[m]
21On the appointed day Herod, wearing his royal robes, sat on his throne and
delivered a public address to the people.
22They shouted, "This is the voice of a
god, not of a man." 23Immediately, because Herod did not give praise to God,
12:23 an angel of the Lord struck him down,[n]
[n] 1Sa 25:38; 2Sa 24:16,17 and he was eaten by worms and died.
12:24 24But the word of God continued to
[o] Ac 6:7; 19:20 increase and spread.[o]
12:25 25When Barnabas[p] and Saul had fin-
[p] Ac 4:36 ished their mission,[q] they returned
[q] Ac 11:30 from[a] Jerusalem, taking with them John,
[r] ver 12 also called Mark.[r]

Barnabas and Saul Sent Off

13:1 13 In the church at Antioch[s] there
[s] Ac 11:19 were prophets[t] and teachers:
[t] Ac 11:27 Barnabas,[u] Simeon called Niger, Lucius
[u] Ac 4:36; 11:22-26 [v] Mt 14:1 of Cyrene, Manaen (who had been
brought up with Herod[v] the tetrarch)
and Saul. 2While they were worshiping
13:2 the Lord and fasting, the Holy Spirit
[w] Ac 8:29 said,[w] "Set apart for me Barnabas and
[x] Ac 14:26 Saul for the work[x] to which I have called
[y] Ac 22:21 them."[y] 3So after they had fasted and
13:3 prayed, they placed their hands on
[z] Ac 6:6 [a] Ac 14:26 them[z] and sent them off.[a]

On Cyprus

4The two of them, sent on their way
13:4 by the Holy Spirit,[b] went down to Seleu-
[b] ver 2,3 [c] Ac 4:36 cia and sailed from there to Cyprus.[c]
5When they arrived at Salamis, they pro-
claimed the word of God in the Jewish
13:5 synagogues.[d] John[e] was with them as
[d] Ac 9:20 [e] Ac 12:12 their helper.
6They traveled through the whole is-
13:6 land until they came to Paphos. There
[f] Ac 8:9 they met a Jewish sorcerer[f] and false
[g] Mt 7:15 prophet[g] named Bar-Jesus, 7who was an
13:7 attendant of the proconsul,[h] Sergius
[h] ver 8,12; Ac 19:38 Paulus. The proconsul, an intelligent
man, sent for Barnabas and Saul be-
cause he wanted to hear the word of
13:8 [i] Ac 8:9 God. 8But Elymas the sorcerer[i] (for that
is what his name means) opposed them 13:8
and tried to turn the proconsul[j] from [j] ver 7 [k] Ac 6:7
the faith.[k] 9Then Saul, who was also 13:9
called Paul, filled with the Holy Spirit,[l] [l] Ac 4:8
looked straight at Elymas and said,
10"You are a child of the devil[m] and an 13:10 [m] Mt 13:38;
enemy of everything that is right! You Jn 8:44
are full of all kinds of deceit and trickery. [n] Hos 14:9
Will you never stop perverting the right
ways of the Lord?[n] 11Now the hand of 13:11
the Lord is against you.[o] You are going [o] Ex 9:3; 1Sa 5:6,
to be blind, and for a time you will be 7; Ps 32:4
unable to see the light of the sun."
Immediately mist and darkness came
over him, and he groped about, seeking
someone to lead him by the hand.
12When the proconsul[p] saw what had 13:12 [p] ver 7
happened, he believed, for he was
amazed at the teaching about the Lord.

In Pisidian Antioch

13From Paphos,[q] Paul and his com- 13:13 [q] ver 6
panions sailed to Perga in Pamphylia, [r] Ac 12:12
where John[r] left them to return to Jerusalem. 14From Perga they went on to Pi- 13:14
sidian Antioch.[s] On the Sabbath[t] they [s] Ac 14:19,21
entered the synagogue[u] and sat down. [t] Ac 16:13
15After the reading from the Law[v] and [u] Ac 9:20
the Prophets, the synagogue rulers sent 13:15 [v] Ac 15:21
word to them, saying, "Brothers, if you
have a message of encouragement for
the people, please speak."
16Standing up, Paul motioned with

[a] 25 Some manuscripts *to*

JESUS FOCUS

APOSTLE TO THE GENTILES

Paul preached the truth about Jesus in the synagogue in Pisidian Antioch (Acts 13:14–16)—and a riot nearly erupted! Because many of the Jewish people refused to believe that Jesus was God's promised Messiah, Paul turned his attention to the Gentiles. It is here that we see the shift in Paul's strategy from preaching to the Jews to taking the Good News to the Gentiles (verse 46). When Paul preached in Pisidian Antioch on the following Sabbath a large crowd was present (verse 44). He informed his listeners of what Isaiah had predicted so many years earlier—that God's promised Messiah would be a "a light for the Gentiles" (Isaiah 49:6). From this point on the majority of people who believed in Jesus were Gentiles. Eventually, Paul even became known as the "apostle to the Gentiles" (Romans 11:13).

13:16 his hand[w] and said: "Men of Israel and
w Ac 12:17 you Gentiles who worship God, listen to
me! 17The God of the people of Israel
chose our fathers; he made the people
prosper during their stay in Egypt, with
13:17 mighty power he led them out of that
x Ex 6:6,7; country,[x] 18he endured their conduct[a][y]
Dt 7:6-8 for about forty years in the desert,[z] 19he
13:18 overthrew seven nations in Canaan[a] and
y Dt 1:31 gave their land to his people[b] as their in-
z Ac 7:36 heritance. 20All this took about 450
13:19 a Dt 7:1 years.
b Jos 19:51 "After this, God gave them judges[c] until the time of Samuel the prophet.[d]
13:20 c Jdg 2:16 21Then the people asked for a king,[e] and
d 1Sa 3:19,20 he gave them Saul[f] son of Kish, of the
13:21 tribe of Benjamin,[g] who ruled forty
e 1Sa 8:5,19 years. 22After removing Saul,[h] he made
f 1Sa 10:1 David their king.[i] He testified concern-
g 1Sa 9:1,2 ing him: 'I have found David son of Jesse
13:22 a man after my own heart;[j] he will do
h 1Sa 15:23,26 everything I want him to do.'
i 1Sa 16:13; 23"From this man's descendants[k] God
Ps 89:20 j 1Sa 13:14 has brought to Israel the Savior[l] Jesus,[m]
13:23 as he promised.[n] 24Before the coming of
k Mt 1:1 l Lk 2:11 Jesus, John preached repentance and
m Mt 1:21 baptism to all the people of Israel.[o] 25As
n ver 32 John was completing his work,[p] he said:
13:24 'Who do you think I am? I am not that
o Mk 1:4 one.[q] No, but he is coming after me,
13:25 whose sandals I am not worthy to untie.'[r]
p Ac 20:24 26"Brothers, children of Abraham, and
q Jn 1:20 r Mt 3:11; you God-fearing Gentiles, it is to us that
Jn 1:27 this message of salvation[s] has been sent.
13:26 27The people of Jerusalem and their
s Ac 4:12 rulers did not recognize Jesus,[t] yet in
13:27 condemning him they fulfilled the
t Ac 3:17 u Lk 24:27 words of the prophets[u] that are read
every Sabbath. 28Though they found no
13:28 proper ground for a death sentence, they
v Mt 27:20-25; asked Pilate to have him executed.[v]
Ac 3:14 29When they had carried out all that was
13:29 w Lk 18:31 written about him,[w] they took him
x Ac 5:30 down from the tree[x] and laid him in a
y Lk 23:53 tomb.[y] 30But God raised him from the
13:30 dead,[z] 31and for many days he was seen
z Mt 28:6; by those who had traveled with him
Ac 2:24 from Galilee to Jerusalem.[a] They are
13:31 now his witnesses[b] to our people.
a Mt 28:16 32"We tell you the good news:[c] What
b Lk 24:48 God promised our fathers[d] 33he has ful-
13:32 filled for us, their children, by raising up
c Ac 5:42 Jesus. As it is written in the second
d Ac 26:6; Ro 4:13 Psalm:

" 'You are my Son;
today I have become your
13:33 e Ps 2:7 Father.'[b,c][e]

God had an only Son, and He was a missionary and a physician.

David Livingstone, *Scottish Missionary*

34The fact that God raised him from the
dead, never to decay, is stated in these
words:

" 'I will give you the holy and sure
blessings promised to 13:34
David.'[d][f] f Isa 55:3

35So it is stated elsewhere:

" 'You will not let your Holy One 13:35
see decay.'[e][g] g Ps 16:10; Ac 2:27

36"For when David had served God's
purpose in his own generation, he fell
asleep; he was buried with his fathers[h] 13:36
and his body decayed. 37But the one h 1Ki 2:10; Ac 2:29
whom God raised from the dead did not
see decay.
38"Therefore, my brothers, I want you
to know that through Jesus the forgiveness of sins is proclaimed to you.[i] 13:38
39Through him everyone who believes is i Lk 24:47; Ac 2:38
justified from everything you could not 13:39
be justified from by the law of Moses.[j] j Ro 3:28
40Take care that what the prophets have
said does not happen to you:

41" 'Look, you scoffers,
wonder and perish,
for I am going to do something in
your days
that you would never believe,
even if someone told you.'[f]"[k] 13:41 k Hab 1:5

42As Paul and Barnabas were leaving
the synagogue,[l] the people invited them 13:42
to speak further about these things on l ver 14
the next Sabbath. 43When the congregation was dismissed, many of the Jews
and devout converts to Judaism followed Paul and Barnabas, who talked
with them and urged them to continue
in the grace of God.[m] 13:43 m Ac 11:23;
44On the next Sabbath almost the 14:22
whole city gathered to hear the word of
the Lord. 45When the Jews saw the
crowds, they were filled with jealousy

a 18 Some manuscripts *and cared for them*
b 33 Or *have begotten you* c 33 Psalm 2:7
d 34 Isaiah 55:3 e 35 Psalm 16:10
f 41 Hab. 1:5

and talked abusively[n] against what Paul was saying.[o]

46 Then Paul and Barnabas answered them boldly: "We had to speak the word of God to you first.[p] Since you reject it and do not consider yourselves worthy of eternal life, we now turn to the Gentiles.[q] 47 For this is what the Lord has commanded us:

> " 'I have made you[a] a light for the
> Gentiles,[r]
> that you[a] may bring salvation to
> the ends of the earth.'[b]"[s]

48 When the Gentiles heard this, they were glad and honored the word of the Lord; and all who were appointed for eternal life believed.

49 The word of the Lord spread through the whole region. 50 But the Jews incited the God-fearing women of high standing and the leading men of the city. They stirred up persecution against Paul and Barnabas, and expelled them from their region.[t] 51 So they shook the dust from their feet[u] in protest against them and went to Iconium.[v] 52 And the disciples were filled with joy and with the Holy Spirit.

In Iconium

14 At Iconium[w] Paul and Barnabas went as usual into the Jewish synagogue. There they spoke so effectively that a great number of Jews and Gentiles believed. 2 But the Jews who refused to believe stirred up the Gentiles and poisoned their minds against the brothers. 3 So Paul and Barnabas spent considerable time there, speaking boldly[x] for the Lord, who confirmed the message of his grace by enabling them to do miraculous signs and wonders.[y] 4 The people of the city were divided; some sided with the Jews, others with the apostles.[z] 5 There was a plot afoot among the Gentiles and Jews, together with their leaders, to mistreat them and stone them.[a] 6 But they found out about it and fled[b] to the Lycaonian cities of Lystra and Derbe and to the surrounding country, 7 where they continued to preach[c] the good news.[d]

In Lystra and Derbe

8 In Lystra there sat a man crippled in his feet, who was lame from birth[e] and had never walked. 9 He listened to Paul as he was speaking. Paul looked directly at him, saw that he had faith to be healed[f] 10 and called out, "Stand up on your feet!" At that, the man jumped up and began to walk.[g]

11 When the crowd saw what Paul had done, they shouted in the Lycaonian language, "The gods have come down to us in human form!"[h] 12 Barnabas they called Zeus, and Paul they called Hermes because he was the chief speaker. 13 The priest of Zeus, whose temple was just outside the city, brought bulls and wreaths to the city gates because he and the crowd wanted to offer sacrifices to them.

14 But when the apostles Barnabas and Paul heard of this, they tore their clothes[i] and rushed out into the crowd, shouting: 15 "Men, why are you doing this? We too are only men,[j] human like you. We are bringing you good news,[k] telling you to turn from these worthless things[l] to the living God,[m] who made heaven and earth[n] and sea and everything in them.[o] 16 In the past, he let[p] all nations go their own way.[q] 17 Yet he has not left himself without testimony:[r] He has shown kindness by giving you rain from heaven and crops in their seasons;[s] he provides you with plenty of food and fills your hearts with joy." 18 Even with these words, they had difficulty keeping the crowd from sacrificing to them.

19 Then some Jews[t] came from Antioch and Iconium[u] and won the crowd over. They stoned Paul[v] and dragged him outside the city, thinking he was dead. 20 But after the disciples[w] had gathered around him, he got up and went back into the city. The next day he and Barnabas left for Derbe.

The Return to Antioch in Syria

21 They preached the good news in that city and won a large number of disciples. Then they returned to Lystra, Iconium[x] and Antioch, 22 strengthening the disciples and encouraging them to remain true to the faith.[y] "We must go through many hardships[z] to enter the kingdom of God," they said. 23 Paul and Barnabas appointed elders[c][a] for them in

[a] 47 The Greek is singular. [b] 47 Isaiah 49:6
[c] 23 Or *Barnabas ordained elders*; or *Barnabas had elders elected*

13:45 n Ac 18:6; 1Pe 4:4; Jude 10 o 1Th 2:16
13:46 p ver 26; Ac 3:26 q Ac 18:6; 22:21; 28:28
13:47 r Lk 2:32 s Isa 49:6
13:50 t 1Th 2:16
13:51 u Mt 10:14; Ac 18:6 v Ac 14:1,19,21; 2Ti 3:11
14:1 w Ac 13:51
14:3 x Ac 4:29 y Jn 4:48; Heb 2:4
14:4 z Ac 17:4,5
14:5 a ver 19
14:6 b Mt 10:23
14:7 c Ac 16:10 d ver 15,21
14:8 e Ac 3:2
14:9 f Mt 9:28,29
14:10 g Ac 3:8
14:11 h Ac 8:10; 28:6
14:14 i Mk 14:63
14:15 j Ac 10:26; Jas 5:17 k ver 7, 21; Ac 13:32 l 1Sa 12:21; 1Co 8:4; 1Th 1:9 m Mt 16:16 n Ge 1:1; Jer 14:22 o Ps 146:6; Rev 14:7
14:16 p Ac 17:30 q Ps 81:12; Mic 4:5
14:17 r Ac 17:27; Ro 1:20 s Dt 11:14; Job 5:10; Ps 65:10
14:19 t Ac 13:45 u Ac 13:51 v 2Co 11:25; 2Ti 3:11
14:20 w ver 22,28; Ac 11:26
14:21 x Ac 13:51
14:22 y Ac 11:23; 13:43 z Jn 16:33; 1Th 3:3; 2Ti 3:12
14:23 a Ac 11:30; Tit 1:5

14:23 [b] Ac 13:3 [c] Ac 20:32

each church and, with prayer and fasting,[b] committed them to the Lord,[c] in
whom they had put their trust. 24 After
going through Pisidia, they came into
Pamphylia, 25 and when they had
preached the word in Perga, they went
down to Attalia.

26 From Attalia they sailed back to Antioch,[d] where they had been committed
to the grace of God[e] for the work they
had now completed.[f] 27 On arriving there,
they gathered the church together and
reported all that God had done through
them[g] and how he had opened the door[h]
of faith to the Gentiles. 28 And they stayed
there a long time with the disciples.

14:26 [d] Ac 11:19 [e] Ac 15:40 [f] Ac 13:1,3

14:27 [g] Ac 15:4,12; 21:19 [h] 1Co 16:9; 2Co 2:12; Col 4:3; Rev 3:8

The Council at Jerusalem

15 Some men[i] came down from
Judea to Antioch and were
teaching the brothers: "Unless you are
circumcised,[j] according to the custom
taught by Moses,[k] you cannot be saved."
2 This brought Paul and Barnabas into
sharp dispute and debate with them. So
Paul and Barnabas were appointed,
along with some other believers, to go
up to Jerusalem[l] to see the apostles and
elders[m] about this question. 3 The
church sent them on their way, and as
they traveled through Phoenicia and
Samaria, they told how the Gentiles had
been converted.[n] This news made all the
brothers very glad. 4 When they came to
Jerusalem, they were welcomed by the
church and the apostles and elders, to

15:1 [i] ver 24; Gal 2:12 [j] ver 5; Gal 5:2,3 [k] Ac 6:14

15:2 [l] Gal 2:2 [m] Ac 11:30

15:3 [n] Ac 14:27

REPORT ON THE FIRST MISSIONARY JOURNEY

Paul and Barnabas returned to Antioch in Syria in order to give a full report to the church that had sent them on their first missionary journey (Acts 14:26–28). They told the Christians at the sponsoring church about all the others who now believed in Jesus—and about the persecution they had endured. More than anything else the two emphasized that God had "opened the door of faith to the Gentiles" (verse 27). These courageous men, who risked their lives repeatedly for the sake of spreading the news about Jesus, the Savior of the world, lived for a time to tell about their experiences (verses 19–21). Eventually, however, many of the apostles, including Paul, were executed because of that all-consuming devotion to Jesus.

whom they reported everything God
had done through them.[o]
5 Then some of the believers who belonged to the party of the Pharisees
stood up and said, "The Gentiles must
be circumcised and required to obey the
law of Moses."

15:4 [o] ver 12; Ac 14:27

6 The apostles and elders met to consider this question. 7 After much discussion, Peter got up and addressed them:
"Brothers, you know that some time ago
God made a choice among you that the
Gentiles might hear from my lips the
message of the gospel and believe. 8 God,
who knows the heart,[p] showed that he
accepted them by giving the Holy Spirit
to them,[q] just as he did to us. 9 He made
no distinction between us and them,[r]
for he purified their hearts by faith.[s]
10 Now then, why do you try to test God
by putting on the necks of the disciples
a yoke[t] that neither we nor our fathers
have been able to bear? 11 No! We believe
it is through the grace[u] of our Lord Jesus
that we are saved, just as they are."

15:8 [p] Ac 1:24 [q] Ac 10:44,47

15:9 [r] Ac 10:28,34; 11:12 [s] Ac 10:43

15:10 [t] Mt 23:4; Gal 5:1

15:11 [u] Ro 3:24; Eph 2:5-8

12 The whole assembly became silent
as they listened to Barnabas and Paul
telling about the miraculous signs and
wonders[v] God had done among the
Gentiles through them.[w] 13 When they
finished, James[x] spoke up: "Brothers, listen to me. 14 Simon[a] has described to us
how God at first showed his concern by
taking from the Gentiles a people for
himself. 15 The words of the prophets are
in agreement with this, as it is written:

15:12 [v] Jn 4:48 [w] Ac 14:27

15:13 [x] Ac 12:17

16 " 'After this I will return
and rebuild David's fallen tent.
Its ruins I will rebuild,
and I will restore it,
17 that the remnant of men may seek
the Lord,
and all the Gentiles who bear my
name,
says the Lord, who does these
things'[b][y]
18 that have been known for ages.[c]

15:17 [y] Am 9:11,12

19 "It is my judgment, therefore, that we
should not make it difficult for the Gentiles who are turning to God. 20 Instead
we should write to them, telling them to
abstain from food polluted by idols,[z]
from sexual immorality,[a] from the meat

15:20 [z] 1Co 8:7-13; 10:14-28; Rev 2:14,20 [a] 1Co 10:7,8

[a] 14 Greek *Simeon,* a variant of *Simon;* that is, Peter
[b] 17 Amos 9:11,12 [c] 17,18 Some manuscripts *things'— / 18known to the Lord for ages is his work*

15:20 [b] ver 29; Ge 9:4; Lev 3:17; Dt 12:16,23 — of strangled animals and from blood.[b]
21 For Moses has been preached in every
city from the earliest times and is read in
15:21 [c] Ac 13:15; 2Co 3:14,15 — the synagogues on every Sabbath."[c]

The Council's Letter to Gentile Believers

22 Then the apostles and elders, with
the whole church, decided to choose
some of their own men and send them
to Antioch with Paul and Barnabas.
They chose Judas (called Barsabbas) and
15:22 [d] ver 27,32,40 — Silas,[d] two men who were leaders
among the brothers. 23 With them they
sent the following letter:

The apostles and elders, your
brothers,

To the Gentile believers in Anti-
15:23 [e] ver 1 [f] ver 41 [g] Ac 23:25,26; Jas 1:1 — och,[e] Syria and Cilicia:[f]

Greetings.[g]

24 We have heard that some went
out from us without our authoriza-
tion and disturbed you, troubling
15:24 [h] ver 1; Gal 1:7; 5:10 — your minds by what they said.[h] 25 So
we all agreed to choose some men
and send them to you with our dear
friends Barnabas and Paul— 26 men
15:26 [i] Ac 9:23-25; 14:19 — who have risked their lives[i] for the
name of our Lord Jesus Christ.

27 Therefore we are sending Judas
and Silas to confirm by word of
mouth what we are writing. 28 It
seemed good to the Holy Spirit[j] and — 15:28 [j] Ac 5:32
to us not to burden you with any-
thing beyond the following requirements: 29 You are to abstain from
food sacrificed to idols, from blood,
from the meat of strangled animals
and from sexual immorality.[k] You — 15:29 [k] ver 20; Ac 21:25
will do well to avoid these things.

Farewell.

JAMES
JESUS' BROTHER

All of the New Testament and early Christian writers who refer to James identify him as Jesus' brother (Mark 6:3; Galatians 1:19). According to Christian tradition James was the first bishop in Jerusalem, and he authored the letter that we now call the book of James. He became the leader of the church in Jerusalem while the other apostles were traveling to proclaim the truth about Jesus. In Acts 15 we read that James was a prominent figure at the council in Jerusalem (verse 13), and the apostle Paul visited him on at least two occasions (Acts 9:26; 21:18). Apparently James did not initially believe that his brother Jesus was God's promised Messiah (John 7:5), but he remained in contact with the disciples after Jesus' crucifixion (Acts 1:14). James apparently changed his mind and devoted himself to Jesus after he saw for himself that his brother had indeed risen from the dead (1 Corinthians 15:7).

> THE SUPREME CHARACTER LIVES IN THIS: THAT HE COMBINES WITHIN HIMSELF, AS NO OTHER FIGURE IN HUMAN HISTORY HAS EVER DONE, THE QUALITIES OF EVERY RACE.
>
> C. F. Andrews, *British Missionary*

30 The men were sent off and went
down to Antioch, where they gathered
the church together and delivered the
letter. 31 The people read it and were glad
for its encouraging message. 32 Judas and
Silas, who themselves were prophets,
said much to encourage and strengthen
the brothers. 33 After spending some
time there, they were sent off by the
brothers with the blessing of peace[l] to — 15:33 [l] Mk 5:34; Ac 16:36; 1Co 16:11
return to those who had sent them.[a]
35 But Paul and Barnabas remained in
Antioch, where they and many others
taught and preached[m] the word of the — 15:35 [m] Ac 8:4
Lord.

Disagreement Between Paul and Barnabas

36 Some time later Paul said to Barnabas, "Let us go back and visit the broth-
ers in all the towns[n] where we preached — 15:36 [n] Ac 13:4,13,14,51; 14:1,6,24,25
the word of the Lord and see how they
are doing." 37 Barnabas wanted to take
John, also called Mark,[o] with them, 38 but — 15:37 [o] Ac 12:12
Paul did not think it wise to take him,
because he had deserted them[p] in Pam- — 15:38 [p] Ac 13:13
phylia and had not continued with them
in the work. 39 They had such a sharp disagreement that they parted company.
Barnabas took Mark and sailed for Cy-
prus, 40 but Paul chose Silas[q] and left, — 15:40 [q] ver 22

[a] 33 Some manuscripts *them,* 34 *but Silas decided to remain there*

RISK-TAKERS

Some of us are natural risk-takers—the kind of hardy individuals who parachute out of airplanes, claw their way up icy cliffs or drive motorcycles over a long line of barrels. While some people thrill to the prospect of risk-taking, others avoid danger at any cost. The same was true in New Testament times, and Acts 15 mentions some men who had "risked their lives for the name of our Lord Jesus" (verse 26) by telling the truth about Jesus and incurring the wrath of enemies of the gospel (Acts 9:23–25; 14:19).

Jesus forewarned his people all along that they would have to place themselves in the way of peril in order to follow him. If they were intent on preserving their own lives, they would ultimately lose them completely: "What good is it for a man to gain the whole world, and yet lose or forfeit his very self?" (Luke 9:24–25).

Many people seem more than willing to take risks in order to accumulate material trophies. They work hard, sacrifice, invest, even gamble. But a person could theoretically possess all of the wealth in the world—all the oil, the gold, the silver, the money, the corporations, the buildings, the land, everything—and still forgo what is most important. Such a person would undoubtedly be perceived as a winner by the rest of society, but anyone willing to forego a relationship with Jesus in favor of material gain is an ultimate loser (see Luke 12:13–21). Conversely, the woman who gives her life away for the sake of the Master becomes in the final analysis a winner, even if she has little or nothing of material value to show for her life's work (see Mark 12:41–44).

Authentic followers of Jesus have always been risk-takers. Many have literally abandoned all the "stuff" of life in order to live for their Lord. Epaphroditus was one such man. Paul wrote these stirring words of tribute about this man: "He almost died for the work of Christ, risking his life to make up for the help you could not give me" (Philippians 2:30).

Over the years God's people have "shut the mouths of lions, quenched the fury of the flames, and escaped the edge of the sword . . . Some faced jeers and flogging, while still others were chained and put in prison. They were stoned; they were sawed in two; they were put to death by the sword. They went about in sheepskins and goatskins, destitute, persecuted and mistreated" (Hebrews 11:33–34,36–37).

While the watching world may well perceive such believers as fools who have thrown away their lives, they were and are heroes in the eyes of God. The writer of Hebrews states of such individuals that "the world was not worthy of them" (Hebrews 11:38).

Taking a risk for God might entail an action as seemingly mundane as bowing in thanks to God before lunch in front of skeptical co-workers. It might mean talking about Jesus with a neighbor, becoming involved in an outreach ministry at church, reading a Bible between classes. When we refuse to be ashamed of Jesus, we are demonstrating to those around us that we are devoted to him (Luke 9:26).

Self-Discovery: *What risks, large or small, have you taken in the name of Jesus? In what ways has he proven himself faithful to see you through the tough times that come?*

GO TO DISCOVERY 296 ON PAGE 1488

commended by the brothers to the grace of the Lord.[r] 41 He went through Syria[s] and Cilicia,[t] strengthening the churches.[u]

Timothy Joins Paul and Silas

16 He came to Derbe and then to Lystra,[v] where a disciple named Timothy[w] lived, whose mother was a Jewess and a believer, but whose father was a Greek. 2 The brothers[x] at Lystra and Iconium[y] spoke well of him. 3 Paul wanted to take him along on the journey, so he circumcised him because of the Jews who lived in that area, for they all knew that his father was a Greek.[z] 4 As they traveled from town to town, they delivered the decisions reached by the apostles and elders[a] in Jerusalem[b] for the people to obey.[c] 5 So the churches were strengthened[d] in the faith and grew daily in numbers.

Paul's Vision of the Man of Macedonia

6 Paul and his companions traveled throughout the region of Phrygia[e] and Galatia,[f] having been kept by the Holy Spirit from preaching the word in the province of Asia.[g] 7 When they came to the border of Mysia, they tried to enter Bithynia, but the Spirit of Jesus[h] would not allow them to. 8 So they passed by Mysia and went down to Troas.[i] 9 During the night Paul had a vision[j] of a man of Macedonia[k] standing and begging him, "Come over to Macedonia and help us." 10 After Paul had seen the vision, we[l] got ready at once to leave for Macedonia, concluding that God had called us to preach the gospel[m] to them.

Lydia's Conversion in Philippi

11 From Troas[n] we put out to sea and sailed straight for Samothrace, and the next day on to Neapolis. 12 From there we traveled to Philippi,[o] a Roman colony and the leading city of that district of Macedonia.[p] And we stayed there several days.

13 On the Sabbath[q] we went outside the city gate to the river, where we expected to find a place of prayer. We sat down and began to speak to the women who had gathered there. 14 One of those listening was a woman named Lydia, a dealer in purple cloth from the city of Thyatira,[r] who was a worshiper of God. The Lord opened her heart[s] to respond to Paul's message. 15 When she and the members of her household[t] were baptized, she invited us to her home. "If you consider me a believer in the Lord," she said, "come and stay at my house." And she persuaded us.

Paul and Silas in Prison

16 Once when we were going to the place of prayer,[u] we were met by a slave girl who had a spirit[v] by which she predicted the future. She earned a great deal of money for her owners by fortune-telling. 17 This girl followed Paul and the rest of us, shouting, "These men are servants of the Most High God,[w] who are telling you the way to be saved." 18 She kept this up for many days. Finally Paul became so troubled that he turned around and said to the spirit, "In the name of Jesus Christ I command you to come out of her!" At that moment the spirit left her.[x]

19 When the owners of the slave girl realized that their hope of making money[y] was gone, they seized Paul and Silas[z] and dragged[a] them into the marketplace to face the authorities. 20 They brought them before the magistrates and said, "These men are Jews, and are throwing our city into an uproar[b] 21 by advocating customs unlawful for us Romans[c] to accept or practice."[d]

22 The crowd joined in the attack against Paul and Silas, and the magistrates ordered them to be stripped and beaten.[e] 23 After they had been severely flogged, they were thrown into prison, and the jailer[f] was commanded to guard them carefully. 24 Upon receiving such orders, he put them in the inner cell and fastened their feet in the stocks.[g]

25 About midnight Paul and Silas were praying and singing hymns[h] to God, and the other prisoners were listening to them. 26 Suddenly there was such a violent earthquake that the foundations of the prison were shaken.[i] At once all the prison doors flew open,[j] and everybody's chains came loose.[k] 27 The jailer woke up, and when he saw the prison doors open, he drew his sword and was about to kill himself because he thought the prisoners had escaped.[l] 28 But Paul shouted, "Don't harm yourself! We are all here!"

15:40 r Ac 11:23
15:41 s ver 23 t Ac 6:9 u Ac 16:5
16:1 v Ac 14:6 w Ac 17:14; 18:5; 19:22; Ro 16:21; 1Co 4:17; 2Co 1:1,19; 1Th 3:2,6; 1Ti 1:2,18; 2Ti 1:2,5,6
16:2 x ver 40 y Ac 13:51
16:3 z Gal 2:3
16:4 a Ac 11:30 b Ac 15:2 c Ac 15:28,29
16:5 d Ac 9:31; 15:41
16:6 e Ac 18:23 f Ac 18:23; Gal 1:2; 3:1 g Ac 2:9
16:7 h Ro 8:9; Gal 4:6
16:8 i ver 11; 2Co 2:12; 2Ti 4:13
16:9 j Ac 9:10 k Ac 20:1,3
16:10 l ver 10-17 m Ac 14:7
16:11 n ver 8
16:12 o Ac 20:6; Php 1:1; 1Th 2:2 p ver 9
16:13 q Ac 13:14
16:14 r Rev 1:11
16:14 s Lk 24:45
16:15 t Ac 11:14
16:16 u ver 13 v Dt 18:11; 1Sa 28:3,7
16:17 w Mk 5:7
16:18 x Mk 16:17
16:19 y ver 16; Ac 19:25,26 z Ac 15:22 a Ac 8:3; 17:6; 21:30; Jas 2:6
16:20 b Ac 17:6
16:21 c ver 12 d Est 3:8
16:22 e 2Co 11:25; 1Th 2:2
16:23 f ver 27,36
16:24 g Job 13:27; 33:11; Jer 20:2, 3; 29:26
16:25 h Eph 5:19
16:26 i Ac 4:31 j Ac 12:10 k Ac 12:7
16:27 l Ac 12:19

DISCOVERY 296

A Simple Question

One of the most effective means of demonstrating that we belong to Jesus is by expressing our faith and love for him at a time when everything in our lives seems to be going wrong. Paul and Silas were stripped, beaten and thrown in jail (Acts 16:22–23). Despite the fact that they had been humiliated and unjustly imprisoned, they opted to pray and sing praise to God (verse 25) rather than to resort to legal action, grumbling or questioning God's plan. This attitude must have seemed strange to the other prisoners and to the jailer!

Because of their faith God freed these apostles from prison. The prison doors were forced open by an earthquake, and the jailer, assuming that all of the prisoners had escaped, was terrified. In fact, he drew his sword to take his own life in lieu of facing the torture he saw as inevitable because of the shame of losing the prisoners. But Paul constrained him: "Don't harm yourself! We are all here!" (verse 28). The jailer was dumbfounded and so grateful that he asked the ultimate question: "Sirs, what must I do to be saved?" (verse 30).

Paul wasted no time in responding: "Believe in the Lord Jesus, and you will be saved—you and your household" (verse 31). There was no need for a lengthy sermon. Paul's response consisted of one short sentence, but in it he incorporated the three essential truths of salvation. First, we must believe that salvation is purely an act of God, not something we can bring about through our own effort. Paul did not instruct the jailer to live a good life, to attend church services, to read Scripture. He stated simply that he must believe that Jesus died for his sin, "for it is by grace you have been saved, through faith" (Ephesians 2:8).

Secondly, we are made right with God through trusting a *Person*—not by embracing a set of religious principles. We believe in the Lord Jesus. His name, *Jesus* (meaning Savior), points out that he came to die for our sin. The title *Lord* reminds us that he rose from the dead and now sits in a place of honor alongside God the Father as the exalted King of kings and Lord of lords (Revelation 19:16).

Finally, when we give our lives to Jesus we are saved immediately. Salvation is a present reality, not just a future hope. Paul did not say, "Believe in the Lord Jesus and *one day you might be saved*." Instead, he responded emphatically: "You *will* be saved." Right now. In this jail cell. At this very moment. The jailer believed that, as did his entire household (Acts 16:34).

Paul was a great apostle and theologian, yet he recognized that the Good News about Jesus is beautifully simple. He wrote a detailed exegesis explaining just how Jesus' death has brought us back to God (the book of Romans), and yet he had a sincere and direct reply for the jailer who had asked life's most important question, a question whose answer showed him the way to eternal peace and joy.

Self-Discovery: Have you ever doubted your status as an individual who has already been saved through the shed blood of Jesus Christ? If so, what circumstances prompted your doubts, and how were they resolved?

GO TO DISCOVERY 297 ON PAGE 1493

> THE MEN WHO FOLLOWED HIM WERE UNIQUE IN THEIR GENERATION. THEY TURNED THE WORLD UPSIDE DOWN BECAUSE THEIR HEARTS HAD BEEN TURNED RIGHT SIDE UP. THE WORLD HAS NEVER BEEN THE SAME.
>
> Billy Graham, *American Evangelist*

29 The jailer called for lights, rushed in and fell trembling before Paul and Silas. 30 He then brought them out and asked, "Sirs, what must I do to be saved?"[m]

31 They replied, "Believe in the Lord Jesus, and you will be saved—you and your household."[n] 32 Then they spoke the word of the Lord to him and to all the others in his house. 33 At that hour of the night[o] the jailer took them and washed their wounds; then immediately he and all his family were baptized. 34 The jailer brought them into his house and set a meal before them; he[p] was filled with joy because he had come to believe in God—he and his whole family.

35 When it was daylight, the magistrates sent their officers to the jailer with the order: "Release those men." 36 The jailer[q] told Paul, "The magistrates have ordered that you and Silas be released. Now you can leave. Go in peace."[r]

37 But Paul said to the officers: "They beat us publicly without a trial, even though we are Roman citizens,[s] and threw us into prison. And now do they want to get rid of us quietly? No! Let them come themselves and escort us out."

38 The officers reported this to the magistrates, and when they heard that Paul and Silas were Roman citizens, they were alarmed.[t] 39 They came to appease them and escorted them from the prison, requesting them to leave the city.[u] 40 After Paul and Silas came out of the prison, they went to Lydia's house,[v] where they met with the brothers[w] and encouraged them. Then they left.

In Thessalonica

17 When they had passed through Amphipolis and Apollonia, they came to Thessalonica,[x] where there was a Jewish synagogue. 2 As his custom was, Paul went into the synagogue,[y] and on three Sabbath[z] days he reasoned with them from the Scriptures,[a] 3 explaining and proving that the Christ[a] had to suffer[b] and rise from the dead.[c] "This Jesus I am proclaiming to you is the Christ,[a]"[d] he said. 4 Some of the Jews were persuaded and joined Paul and Silas,[e] as did a large number of God-fearing Greeks and not a few prominent women.

5 But the Jews were jealous; so they rounded up some bad characters from the marketplace, formed a mob and started a riot in the city.[f] They rushed to Jason's[g] house in search of Paul and Silas in order to bring them out to the crowd.[b] 6 But when they did not find them, they dragged[h] Jason and some other brothers before the city officials, shouting: "These men who have caused trouble all over the world[i] have now come here,[j] 7 and Jason has welcomed them into his house. They are all defying Caesar's decrees, saying that there is another king, one called Jesus."[k] 8 When they heard this, the crowd and the city officials were thrown into turmoil. 9 Then they made Jason[l] and the others post bond and let them go.

In Berea

10 As soon as it was night, the brothers

[a] 3 Or *Messiah* [b] 5 Or *the assembly of the people*

16:30 m Ac 2:37
16:31 n Ac 11:14
16:33 o ver 25
16:34 p Ac 11:14
16:36 q ver 23,27 r Ac 15:33
16:37 s Ac 22:25-29
16:38 t Ac 22:29
16:39 u Mt 8:34
16:40 v ver 14 w ver 2; Ac 1:16
17:1 x ver 11,13; Php 4:16; 1Th 1:1; 2Th 1:1; 2Ti 4:10
17:2 y Ac 9:20
17:2 z Ac 13:14 a Ac 8:35
17:3 b Lk 24:26; Ac 3:18 c Lk 24:46 d Ac 9:22; 18:28
17:4 e Ac 15:22
17:5 f ver 13; 1Th 2:16 g Ro 16:21
17:6 h Ac 16:19 i Mt 24:14 j Ac 16:20
17:7 k Lk 23:2; Jn 19:12
17:9 l ver 5

JESUS FOCUS

JESUS IS THE MESSIAH

The question kept surfacing: Was Jesus really God's promised Messiah? Paul, of course, was absolutely convinced that he was. On each Sabbath for three consecutive weeks he talked with the Jews in the Thessalonian synagogue about Jesus, proving to them using their own Scriptures that Jesus is indeed the Son of God, the Messiah (Acts 17:2–3). The Greek word *christos*, like the Hebrew *messiah*, means "Anointed One." Paul left no doubt in the minds of his hearers: "This Jesus I am proclaiming to you is the Christ" (verse 3). Paul referred back continuously to the Old Testament Scriptures, and we are told that in nearby Berea the people examined the Old Testament to see for themselves whether or not Paul was teaching truth (verse 11). These Berean believers were commended for their diligence and provide an outstanding example to us of people who studied the Scriptures to verify the truth about Jesus.

17:10 [m] ver 13; Ac 20:4 sent Paul and Silas away to Berea.[m] On
arriving there, they went to the Jewish
synagogue. 11 Now the Bereans were of
more noble character than the Thessalo-
17:11 [n] ver 1 [o] Lk 16:29; Jn 5:39 nians,[n] for they received the message
with great eagerness and examined the
Scriptures[o] every day to see if what Paul
said was true. 12 Many of the Jews believed, as did also a number of prominent
Greek women and many Greek men.

13 When the Jews in Thessalonica
learned that Paul was preaching the
word of God at Berea, they went there
too, agitating the crowds and stirring
them up. 14 The brothers immediately
17:14 [p] Ac 15:22 [q] Ac 16:1 sent Paul to the coast, but Silas[p] and
Timothy[q] stayed at Berea. 15 The men
who escorted Paul brought him to Ath-
17:15 [r] ver 16,21,22; Ac 18:1; 1Th 3:1 [s] Ac 18:5 ens[r] and then left with instructions for
Silas and Timothy to join him as soon as
possible.[s]

In Athens

16 While Paul was waiting for them in
Athens, he was greatly distressed to see
that the city was full of idols. 17 So he rea-
17:17 [t] Ac 9:20 soned in the synagogue[t] with the Jews
and the God-fearing Greeks, as well as in
the marketplace day by day with those
who happened to be there. 18 A group of
Epicurean and Stoic philosophers began
to dispute with him. Some of them
asked, "What is this babbler trying to
say?" Others remarked, "He seems to be
advocating foreign gods." They said this
because Paul was preaching the good
17:18 [u] ver 31,32; Ac 4:2 news about Jesus and the resurrection.[u]
19 Then they took him and brought him
17:19 [v] ver 22 [w] Mk 1:27 to a meeting of the Areopagus,[v] where
they said to him, "May we know what
this new teaching[w] is that you are presenting? 20 You are bringing some strange
ideas to our ears, and we want to know
what they mean." 21 (All the Athenians
and the foreigners who lived there spent
their time doing nothing but talking
about and listening to the latest ideas.)

> CHRIST . . . LIFTED WITH HIS PIERCED HANDS EMPIRES OFF THEIR HINGES AND TURNED THE STREAM OF CENTURIES OUT OF ITS CHANNEL, AND STILL GOVERNS THE AGES.
>
> Jean Paul Richter, *French Philosopher*

22 Paul then stood up in the meeting of
the Areopagus and said: "Men of Athens! I see that in every way you are very
religious. 23 For as I walked around and
looked carefully at your objects of worship, I even found an altar with this inscription: TO AN UNKNOWN GOD. Now
what you worship as something un-
known[x] I am going to proclaim to you. 17:23 [x] Jn 4:22
24 "The God who made the world and
everything in it[y] is the Lord of heaven 17:24 [y] Isa 42:5; Ac 14:15 [z] Dt 10:14; Mt 11:25 [a] Ac 7:48
and earth[z] and does not live in temples
built by hands.[a] 25 And he is not served
by human hands, as if he needed any-
thing, because he himself gives all men 17:25 [b] Ps 50:10-12; Isa 42:5
life and breath and everything else.[b]
26 From one man he made every nation
of men, that they should inhabit the
whole earth; and he determined the
times set for them and the exact places
where they should live.[c] 27 God did this 17:26 [c] Dt 32:8; Job 12:23
so that men would seek him and per-
haps reach out for him and find him,
though he is not far from each one of
us.[d] 28 'For in him we live and move and 17:27 [d] Dt 4:7; Jer 23:23,24; Ac 14:17
have our being.'[e] As some of your own
poets have said, 'We are his offspring.'
29 "Therefore since we are God's off- 17:28 [e] Job 12:10; Da 5:23
spring, we should not think that the di-
vine being is like gold or silver or
stone—an image made by man's design 17:29 [f] Isa 40:18-20; Ro 1:23
and skill.[f] 30 In the past God overlooked[g]
such ignorance,[h] but now he commands 17:30 [g] Ac 14:16; Ro 3:25 [h] ver 23; 1Pe 1:14 [i] Lk 24:47; Tit 2:11,12
all people everywhere to repent.[i] 31 For
he has set a day when he will judge[j] the
world with justice[k] by the man he has
appointed.[l] He has given proof of this to
all men by raising him from the dead."[m] 17:31 [j] Mt 10:15 [k] Ps 9:8; 96:13; 98:9 [l] Ac 10:42 [m] Ac 2:24
32 When they heard about the resur-
rection of the dead,[n] some of them
sneered, but others said, "We want to
hear you again on this subject." 33 At that, 17:32 [n] ver 18,31
Paul left the Council. 34 A few men be-
came followers of Paul and believed.
Among them was Dionysius, a member
of the Areopagus,[o] also a woman named 17:34 [o] ver 19,22
Damaris, and a number of others.

In Corinth

18 After this, Paul left Athens[p] and 18:1 [p] Ac 17:15 [q] Ac 19:1; 1Co 1:2; 2Co 1:1,23; 2Ti 4:20
went to Corinth.[q] 2 There he
met a Jew named Aquila, a native of
Pontus, who had recently come from It-
aly with his wife Priscilla,[r] because Clau- 18:2 [r] Ro 16:3; 1Co 16:19; 2Ti 4:19 [s] Ac 11:28
dius[s] had ordered all the Jews to leave
Rome. Paul went to see them, 3 and because he was a tentmaker as they were,

18:3 [t] Ac 20:34; 1Co 4:12; 1Th 2:9; 2Th 3:8 — he stayed and worked with them.[t]
4Every Sabbath[u] he reasoned in the syn-
agogue, trying to persuade Jews and
18:4 [u] Ac 13:14 — Greeks.
5When Silas[v] and Timothy[w] came
from Macedonia,[x] Paul devoted himself
18:5 [v] Ac 15:22 [w] Ac 16:1 [x] Ac 16:9; 17:14, 15 [y] ver 28; Ac 17:3 — exclusively to preaching, testifying to
the Jews that Jesus was the Christ.[a][y]
6But when the Jews opposed Paul and
became abusive,[z] he shook out his
18:6 [z] Ac 13:45 [a] 2Sa 1:16; Eze 18:13; 33:4 [b] Ac 20:26 [c] Ac 13:46 — clothes in protest and said to them,
"Your blood be on your own heads![a] I am
clear of my responsibility.[b] From now on
I will go to the Gentiles."[c]
7Then Paul left the synagogue and
went next door to the house of Titius
18:7 [d] Ac 16:14 — Justus, a worshiper of God.[d] 8Crispus,[e]
the synagogue ruler,[f] and his entire
18:8 [e] 1Co 1:14 [f] Mk 5:22 [g] Ac 11:14 — household[g] believed in the Lord; and
many of the Corinthians who heard him
believed and were baptized.
9One night the Lord spoke to Paul in
a vision: "Do not be afraid; keep on
speaking, do not be silent. 10For I am
18:10 [h] Mt 28:20 — with you,[h] and no one is going to attack
and harm you, because I have many peo-
ple in this city." 11So Paul stayed for a
year and a half, teaching them the word
of God.
12While Gallio was proconsul of
18:12 [i] ver 27 — Achaia,[i] the Jews made a united attack
on Paul and brought him into court.
13"This man," they charged, "is persuad-
ing the people to worship God in ways
contrary to the law."
14Just as Paul was about to speak, Gallio said to the Jews, "If you Jews were
making a complaint about some misde-
meanor or serious crime, it would be
reasonable for me to listen to you. 15But
18:15 [j] Ac 23:29; 25:11,19 — since it involves questions about words
and names and your own law[j]—settle
the matter yourselves. I will not be a
judge of such things." 16So he had them
18:17 [k] 1Co 1:1 — ejected from the court. 17Then they all
turned on Sosthenes[k] the synagogue
ruler and beat him in front of the court.
But Gallio showed no concern whatever.

Priscilla, Aquila and Apollos

18:18 [l] Ac 1:16 [m] Ro 16:1 [n] Nu 6:2,5,18; Ac 21:24 — 18Paul stayed on in Corinth for some
time. Then he left the brothers[l] and
sailed for Syria, accompanied by Priscilla and Aquila. Before he sailed, he had
his hair cut off at Cenchrea[m] because of
a vow he had taken.[n] 19They arrived at
18:19 [o] ver 21,24; 1Co 15:32 — Ephesus,[o] where Paul left Priscilla and
Aquila. He himself went into the syna-
gogue and reasoned with the Jews.
20When they asked him to spend more
time with them, he declined. 21But as he
18:21 [p] Ro 1:10; 1Co 4:19; Jas 4:15 — left, he promised, "I will come back if it
is God's will."[p] Then he set sail from Eph-
esus. 22When he landed at Caesarea,[q] he
went up and greeted the church and
18:22 [q] Ac 8:40 [r] Ac 11:19 — then went down to Antioch.[r]
23After spending some time in Anti-
och, Paul set out from there and traveled
18:23 [s] Ac 16:6 [t] Ac 14:22; 15:32,41 — from place to place throughout the region of Galatia[s] and Phrygia, strength-
ening all the disciples.[t]
24Meanwhile a Jew named Apollos,[u] a
18:24 [u] Ac 19:1; 1Co 1:12; 3:5,6, 22; 4:6; 16:12; Tit 3:13 — native of Alexandria, came to Ephesus.
He was a learned man, with a thorough
knowledge of the Scriptures. 25He had
been instructed in the way of the Lord,
18:25 [v] Ro 12:11 [w] Ac 19:3 — and he spoke with great fervor[b][v] and
taught about Jesus accurately, though he
knew only the baptism of John.[w] 26He

JESUS FOCUS

ON THE ROAD AGAIN

Paul traveled all over the Roman empire, and the book of Acts records three distinct journeys. These are often referred to as the three missionary journeys, because Paul's mission was to tell other people the truth about Jesus. The time during which Paul lived and traveled was contemporaneous with the famous *Pax Romana*, an empire-wide period of peace which lasted from 27 B.C. through A.D. 180. Roman engineers had built a network of roads that allowed a Roman citizen like Paul to travel quickly from place to place. Language barriers were not a problem because the Greek language and culture were common throughout the empire. God had promised to send the Messiah to his people when the time was right (Romans 5:6; Galatians 4:4–5), and he had chosen a time of unprecedented political unity to do just that. Paul was the perfect choice to carry that message, because he was both Jewish and a Roman citizen. By the end of his life, Paul had helped to plant churches all around the eastern Mediterranean and had trained other leaders like Silas, Titus and Timothy to carry on God's work. God had a special plan to carry out through the life, death, resurrection and ascension of his precious Son, and he orchestrated every detail to enable the spread of the Good News about Jesus throughout the world.

[a] 5 Or *Messiah;* also in verse 28 [b] 25 Or *with fervor in the Spirit*

began to speak boldly in the synagogue.
When Priscilla and Aquila heard him,
they invited him to their home and explained to him the way of God more ad-
equately.
18:27 27When Apollos wanted to go to
[x] ver 12 [y] ver 18 Achaia,[x] the brothers[y] encouraged him
and wrote to the disciples there to wel-
come him. On arriving, he was a great
help to those who by grace had believed.
28For he vigorously refuted the Jews in
18:28 public debate, proving from the Scrip-
[z] Ac 17:2 [a] ver 5; Ac 9:22 tures[z] that Jesus was the Christ.[a]

Paul in Ephesus

19:1 [b] Ac 18:1 [c] Ac 18:19 19 While Apollos was at Corinth,[b]
Paul took the road through the
interior and arrived at Ephesus.[c] There
he found some disciples 2and asked
them, "Did you receive the Holy Spirit
when[a] you believed?"
They answered, "No, we have not
even heard that there is a Holy Spirit."
3So Paul asked, "Then what baptism
did you receive?"
"John's baptism," they replied.
4Paul said, "John's baptism was a baptism of repentance. He told the people
19:4 to believe in the one coming after him,
[d] Jn 1:7; Ac 13:24,25 that is, in Jesus."[d] 5On hearing this, they
were baptized into[b] the name of the
Lord Jesus. 6When Paul placed his hands
19:6 on them,[e] the Holy Spirit came on
[e] Ac 6:6; 8:17 [f] Ac 2:4 them,[f] and they spoke in tongues[c][g] and
[g] Mk 16:17; Ac 10:46 prophesied. 7There were about twelve
men in all.
19:8 8Paul entered the synagogue[h] and
[h] Ac 9:20 spoke boldly there for three months, ar-
[i] Ac 1:3; 28:23 guing persuasively about the kingdom
of God.[i] 9But some of them[j] became ob-
19:9 stinate; they refused to believe and pub-
[j] Ac 14:4 [k] ver 23; Ac 9:2 licly maligned the Way.[k] So Paul left
[l] ver 30; Ac 11:26 them. He took the disciples[l] with him
and had discussions daily in the lecture
hall of Tyrannus. 10This went on for two
19:10 [m] Ac 20:31 years,[m] so that all the Jews and Greeks
[n] ver 22,26,27 who lived in the province of Asia[n] heard
the word of the Lord.
19:11 11God did extraordinary miracles[o]
[o] Ac 8:13 through Paul, 12so that even handker-
chiefs and aprons that had touched him
were taken to the sick, and their ill-
19:12 nesses were cured[p] and the evil spirits
[p] Ac 5:15 left them.
13Some Jews who went around driving
19:13 out evil spirits[q] tried to invoke the name
[q] Mt 12:27 of the Lord Jesus over those who were

demon-possessed. They would say, "In
the name of Jesus,[r] whom Paul preaches, 19:13 [r] Mk 9:38
I command you to come out." 14Seven
sons of Sceva, a Jewish chief priest, were
doing this. 15⌞One day⌟ the evil spirit answered them, "Jesus I know, and I know
about Paul, but who are you?" 16Then
the man who had the evil spirit jumped
on them and overpowered them all. He
gave them such a beating that they ran
out of the house naked and bleeding.
17When this became known to the
Jews and Greeks living in Ephesus,[s] they 19:17 [s] Ac 18:19
were all seized with fear,[t] and the name [t] Ac 5:5,11
of the Lord Jesus was held in high hon-
or. 18Many of those who believed now
came and openly confessed their evil
deeds. 19A number who had practiced
sorcery brought their scrolls together
and burned them publicly. When they
calculated the value of the scrolls, the
total came to fifty thousand drachmas.[d] 19:20
20In this way the word of the Lord spread [u] Ac 6:7; 12:24
widely and grew in power.[u]
21After all this had happened, Paul 19:21 [v] Ac 20:16,22; Ro 15:25
decided to go to Jerusalem,[v] passing [w] Ac 16:9
through Macedonia[w] and Achaia.[x] "Af- [x] Ac 18:12
ter I have been there," he said, "I must [y] Ro 15:24,28
visit Rome also."[y] 22He sent two of his 19:22
helpers,[z] Timothy[a] and Erastus,[b] to [z] Ac 13:5 [a] Ac 16:1
Macedonia, while he stayed in the prov- [b] Ro 16:23; 2Ti 4:20
ince of Asia[c] a little longer. [c] ver 10,26,27

The Riot in Ephesus

23About that time there arose a great 19:23
disturbance about the Way.[d] 24A silver- [d] Ac 9:2
smith named Demetrius, who made sil-
ver shrines of Artemis, brought in no little business for the craftsmen. 25He
called them together, along with the
workmen in related trades, and said:
"Men, you know we receive a good in-
come from this business.[e] 26And you see 19:25 [e] Ac 16:16,19,20
and hear how this fellow Paul has con-
vinced and led astray large numbers of 19:26
people here in Ephesus[f] and in practi- [f] Ac 18:19
cally the whole province of Asia. He says [g] Dt 4:28; Ps 115:4;
that man-made gods are no gods at all.[g] Isa 44:10-20;
27There is danger not only that our trade Jer 10:3-5; Ac 17:29;
will lose its good name, but also that 1Co 8:4;
the temple of the great goddess Artemis Rev 9:20
will be discredited, and the goddess herself, who is worshiped throughout the

[a] 2 Or *after* [b] 5 Or *in* [c] 6 Or *other languages*
[d] 19 A drachma was a silver coin worth about a day's wages.

DISCOVERY 297

BUT WHO ARE *YOU*?

Ephesus was a center for certain occult practices. In several instances, after people in that city had given their lives to Jesus, they found it necessary to burn their books that contained magical formulas and incantations (Acts 19:19). Paul's ministry in Ephesus was accompanied by "extraordinary miracles" (verse 11), and many people presumed that this manifestation of power was in itself a form of magic.

The apostle's miraculous healings captured the attention of the entire city. Some of the Jews even tried to appropriate this "power of Jesus" and invoked Jesus' name in order to cast out demons (verse 13). The "seven sons of Sceva" (verse 14) tried to emulate what Paul was doing and confronted a demon-possessed man using Paul's "formula." But the evil spirit replied rather snidely: "Jesus I know, and I know about Paul, but who are you?" (verse 16). He then proceeded to take out his frustrations on these seven unfortunate exorcists.

Demons have more respect for Jesus than many humans do, and they are familiar with spiritual realities. James later wrote, "You believe that there is one God. Good! Even the demons believe that—and shudder" (James 2:19). Although Satan's minions reject God, these demons may be said to espouse a sound theology: They believe in one God and tremble before him. They understand true spiritual power, while the seven sons of Sceva clearly did not.

The seven sons did not follow Jesus and were apparently trying to tap into his power without identifying with him and giving their hearts to him. The power of Jesus in our lives may never be used to advance our own status; it is a gift we can only employ to help others and to honor God. God will always protect his honor. After the demon-possessed man overpowered and beat the seven sons, "they were all seized with fear, and the name of the Lord Jesus was held in high honor" (Acts 19:17).

In the words of Paul, Jesus "has rescued us from the dominion of darkness and brought us into the kingdom of the Son he loves, in whom we have redemption, the forgiveness of sins" (Colossians 1:13–14), and we can now be instrumental in helping to build up his kingdom, just as Paul was. "For you were once darkness, but now you are light in the Lord. Live as children of light (for the fruit of the light consists in all goodness, righteousness and truth) and find out what pleases the Lord. Have nothing to do with the fruitless deeds of darkness, but rather expose them. For it is shameful even to mention what the disobedient do in secret" (Ephesians 5:8–12).

Peter expressed much the same message—in words of irrepressible joy: "You are a chosen people, a royal priesthood, a holy nation, a people belonging to God, that you may declare the praises of him who called you out of darkness into his wonderful light. Once you were not a people, but now you are the people of God; once you had not received mercy, but now you have received mercy" (1 Peter 2:9–10).

Self-Discovery: *Notice how the repentance and public denunciation of evil by the Ephesian Christians resulted in the increased influence of God's Word (verse 20). Have you ever dabbled in the occult or taken an interest in satanic music, books, movies or the like? What steps do you need to take to free yourself from the influence of evil in your life?*

GO TO DISCOVERY 298 ON PAGE 1495

> **No revolution that has ever taken place in society can be compared to that which has been produced by the words of Jesus Christ.**
>
> Mark Hopkins, *American College Teacher*

province of Asia and the world, will be
robbed of her divine majesty."
28When they heard this, they were furious and began shouting: "Great is Ar-
19:28 temis of the Ephesians!"[h] 29Soon the
h Ac 18:19 whole city was in an uproar. The people
19:29 seized Gaius[i] and Aristarchus,[j] Paul's
i Ac 20:4; Ro 16:23; traveling companions from Macedo-
1Co 1:14 nia,[k] and rushed as one man into the
j Ac 20:4; 27:2; theater. 30Paul wanted to appear before
Col 4:10; Phm 24 the crowd, but the disciples would not
k Ac 16:9 let him. 31Even some of the officials of
the province, friends of Paul, sent him a
message begging him not to venture
into the theater.
32The assembly was in confusion:
Some were shouting one thing, some an-
19:32 l Ac 21:34 other.[l] Most of the people did not even
know why they were there. 33The Jews
pushed Alexander to the front, and some
of the crowd shouted instructions to
19:33 him. He motioned[m] for silence in order to
m Ac 12:17 make a defense before the people. 34But
when they realized he was a Jew, they all
shouted in unison for about two hours:
"Great is Artemis of the Ephesians!"
19:35 35The city clerk quieted the crowd
n Ac 18:19 and said: "Men of Ephesus,[n] doesn't all
the world know that the city of Ephesus
is the guardian of the temple of the great
Artemis and of her image, which fell
from heaven? 36Therefore, since these
facts are undeniable, you ought to be
quiet and not do anything rash. 37You
19:37 have brought these men here, though
o Ro 2:22 they have neither robbed temples[o] nor
blasphemed our goddess. 38If, then,
Demetrius and his fellow craftsmen
have a grievance against anybody, the
courts are open and there are procon-
19:38 suls.[p] They can press charges. 39If there
p Ac 13:7,8,12 is anything further you want to bring up,
it must be settled in a legal assembly.
40As it is, we are in danger of being
charged with rioting because of today's
events. In that case we would not be able
to account for this commotion, since
there is no reason for it." 41After he had
said this, he dismissed the assembly.

Through Macedonia and Greece

20 When the uproar had ended, 20:1
Paul sent for the disciples[q] and, q Ac 11:26
after encouraging them, said good-by r Ac 16:9
and set out for Macedonia.[r] 2He traveled
through that area, speaking many words 20:3
of encouragement to the people, and fi- s ver 19; Ac 9:23, 24; 23:12,15,30;
nally arrived in Greece, 3where he stayed 25:3; 2Co 11:26
three months. Because the Jews made a t Ac 16:9
plot against him[s] just as he was about to 20:4
sail for Syria, he decided to go back u Ac 19:29 v Ac 17:1
through Macedonia.[t] 4He was accompa- w Ac 19:29
nied by Sopater son of Pyrrhus from Be- x Ac 16:1 y Eph 6:21;
rea, Aristarchus[u] and Secundus from Col 4:7;
Thessalonica,[v] Gaius[w] from Derbe, Tim- 2Ti 4:12; Tit 3:12
othy[x] also, and Tychicus[y] and Trophi- z Ac 21:29;
mus[z] from the province of Asia. 5These 2Ti 4:20
men went on ahead and waited for us[a] 20:5
at Troas.[b] 6But we sailed from Philippi[c] a Ac 16:10
after the Feast of Unleavened Bread, and b Ac 16:8
five days later joined the others at 20:6
Troas,[d] where we stayed seven days. c Ac 16:12 d Ac 16:8

Eutychus Raised From the Dead at Troas

7On the first day of the week[e] we 20:7 e 1Co 16:2;
came together to break bread. Paul Rev 1:10
spoke to the people and, because he intended to leave the next day, kept on
talking until midnight. 8There were 20:8
many lamps in the upstairs room[f] where f Ac 1:13
we were meeting. 9Seated in a window
was a young man named Eutychus, who
was sinking into a deep sleep as Paul
talked on and on. When he was sound
asleep, he fell to the ground from the
third story and was picked up dead.
10Paul went down, threw himself on the 20:10
young man[g] and put his arms around g 1Ki 17:21;
him. "Don't be alarmed," he said. "He's 2Ki 4:34
alive!"[h] 11Then he went upstairs again h Mt 9:23,24
and broke bread[i] and ate. After talking 20:11
until daylight, he left. 12The people took i ver 7
the young man home alive and were
greatly comforted.

Paul's Farewell to the Ephesian Elders

13We went on ahead to the ship and
sailed for Assos, where we were going to
take Paul aboard. He had made this
arrangement because he was going there
on foot. 14When he met us at Assos, we
took him aboard and went on to Mityle-
ne. 15The next day we set sail from there

DISCOVERY 298

The Good News of Grace

Paul exemplified an unparalleled single-mindedness in telling others about Jesus. In his last speech to the elders in Ephesus the apostle summarized the passion of his life: "I consider my life worth nothing to me, if only I may finish the race and complete the task the Lord Jesus has given me—the task of testifying to the gospel of God's grace" (Acts 20:24).

Grace refers to the undeserved loving-kindness God bestows on his children. But the reality of how God's grace reaches us can be difficult to grasp. Charles Swindoll, a noted pastor and author, provided a very clear analogy. Suppose someone were to break into your home and murder your only child. If you were to pursue the killer until you found him, and then in turn you were to murder him, you would be exercising *vengeance*. If you were to pursue the killer until you found him, and then you were to see to it that he was arrested and sentenced for his crime, you would be helping to promote *justice*. But if you were to pursue the killer until you found him and then invite him to live with your family as an adopted son, you would be expressing *grace*. That is precisely what God does for us.

Each one of us is responsible for the death of Jesus (Isaiah 53:5–6; Romans 4:25; 5:8; 2 Corinthians 5:21). If God were to bring us to trial, the verdict would be a no-brainer: We would be found guilty and would be justly sentenced to eternal death. But God is preeminently and wonderfully a God of grace. He pursues us in his love (Luke 19:10), freely forgives our sin when we turn to Jesus for cleansing (Hebrews 9:14; 10:22) and invites us to become his own adopted children, "heirs of God and co-heirs with Christ" (Romans 8:17).

The lyrics of one of the most popular songs of all time were written by John Newton. The words are simple yet so profound: "Amazing grace—how sweet the sound—that saved a wretch like me! I once was lost but now am found, was blind but now I see." Paul devoted his life to preaching one incredible message: God's amazing grace. Getting this message to people was far more significant to Paul than his own life (2 Corinthians 4:8–12; Colossians 1:24–25).

And God has given us the task of "testifying to the gospel of God's grace" (Acts 20:24). Rather than viewing this task as just one more job to try to squeeze into already full lives, God asks us to allow his Spirit to work in our hearts to change our priorities. With his help we can learn to make Paul's commitment our very own: "Join with me in suffering for the gospel, by the power of God, who has saved us and called us to a holy life—not because of what we have done, but because of his own purpose and grace . . . And of this gospel I was appointed a herald and an apostle and a teacher . . . Yet I am not ashamed, because I know whom I have believed and am convinced that he is able to guard what I have entrusted to him for that day" (2 Timothy 1:8–9,11–12).

Self-Discovery: *Take a moment to reflect on God's amazing grace in your own life. What images or associations come to mind?*

GO TO DISCOVERY 299 ON PAGE 1502

and arrived off Kios. The day after that
we crossed over to Samos, and on the following day arrived at Miletus.[j] 16Paul had
decided to sail past Ephesus[k] to avoid
spending time in the province of Asia, for
he was in a hurry to reach Jerusalem,[l] if
possible, by the day of Pentecost.[m]
17From Miletus, Paul sent to Ephesus
for the elders[n] of the church. 18When
they arrived, he said to them: "You know
how I lived the whole time I was with
you,[o] from the first day I came into the
province of Asia. 19I served the Lord with
great humility and with tears, although I
was severely tested by the plots of the
Jews.[p] 20You know that I have not hesitated to preach anything[q] that would be
helpful to you but have taught you publicly and from house to house. 21I have
declared to both Jews[r] and Greeks that
they must turn to God in repentance[s]
and have faith in our Lord Jesus.[t]
22"And now, compelled by the Spirit, I
am going to Jerusalem,[u] not knowing
what will happen to me there. 23I only
know that in every city the Holy Spirit
warns me[v] that prison and hardships are
facing me.[w] 24However, I consider my life
worth nothing to me,[x] if only I may finish the race and complete the task[y] the
Lord Jesus has given me[z]—the task of
testifying to the gospel of God's grace.
25"Now I know that none of you
among whom I have gone about preaching the kingdom will ever see me again.[a]
26Therefore, I declare to you today that I
am innocent of the blood of all men.[b]
27For I have not hesitated to proclaim to
you the whole will of God.[c] 28Keep watch
over yourselves and all the flock of
which the Holy Spirit has made you
overseers.[*a*][d] Be shepherds of the church
of God,[*b*] which he bought with his own
blood. 29I know that after I leave, savage
wolves[e] will come in among you and will
not spare the flock.[f] 30Even from your
own number men will arise and distort
the truth in order to draw away disciples[g] after them. 31So be on your guard!
Remember that for three years[h] I never
stopped warning each of you night and
day with tears.[i]
32"Now I commit you to God[j] and to
the word of his grace, which can build
you up and give you an inheritance[k]
among all those who are sanctified.[l] 33I
have not coveted anyone's silver or gold
or clothing.[m] 34You yourselves know that
these hands of mine have supplied my
own needs and the needs of my companions.[n] 35In everything I did, I showed
you that by this kind of hard work we
must help the weak, remembering the
words the Lord Jesus himself said: 'It is
more blessed to give than to receive.'"
36When he had said this, he knelt
down with all of them and prayed.[o]
37They all wept as they embraced him
and kissed him.[p] 38What grieved them
most was his statement that they would
never see his face again.[q] Then they accompanied him to the ship.

On to Jerusalem

21 After we[r] had torn ourselves
away from them, we put out to
sea and sailed straight to Cos. The next
day we went to Rhodes and from there
to Patara. 2We found a ship crossing
over to Phoenicia,[s] went on board and
set sail. 3After sighting Cyprus and passing to the south of it, we sailed on to Syria. We landed at Tyre, where our ship
was to unload its cargo. 4Finding the
disciples[t] there, we stayed with them
seven days. Through the Spirit[u] they
urged Paul not to go on to Jerusalem.
5But when our time was up, we left and
continued on our way. All the disciples
and their wives and children accompanied us out of the city, and there on the
beach we knelt to pray.[v] 6After saying
good-by to each other, we went aboard
the ship, and they returned home.
7We continued our voyage from Tyre[w]
and landed at Ptolemais, where we
greeted the brothers[x] and stayed with
them for a day. 8Leaving the next day, we
reached Caesarea[y] and stayed at the
house of Philip[z] the evangelist,[a] one of
the Seven. 9He had four unmarried
daughters who prophesied.[b]
10After we had been there a number
of days, a prophet named Agabus[c] came
down from Judea. 11Coming over to us,
he took Paul's belt, tied his own hands
and feet with it and said, "The Holy Spirit says, 'In this way the Jews of Jerusalem
will bind[d] the owner of this belt and will
hand him over to the Gentiles.'"[e]
12When we heard this, we and the
people there pleaded with Paul not to go

a 28 Traditionally *bishops* *b* 28 Many manuscripts *of the Lord*

20:15 j ver 17; 2Ti 4:20
20:16 k Ac 18:19 l Ac 19:21 m Ac 2:1; 1Co 16:8
20:17 n Ac 11:30
20:18 o Ac 18:19-21; 19:1-41
20:19 p ver 3
20:20 q ver 27
20:21 r Ac 18:5 s Ac 2:38 t Ac 24:24; 26:18; Eph 1:15; Col 2:5; Phm 5
20:22 u ver 16
20:23 v Ac 21:4 w Ac 9:16
20:24 x Ac 21:13 y 2Co 4:1 z Gal 1:1; Tit 1:3
20:25 a ver 38
20:26 b Ac 18:6
20:27 c ver 20
20:28 d 1Pe 5:2
20:29 e Mt 7:15 f ver 28
20:30 g Ac 11:26
20:31 h Ac 19:10 i ver 19
20:32 j Ac 14:23 k Eph 1:14; Col 1:12; 3:24; Heb 9:15; 1Pe 1:4 l Ac 26:18
20:33 m 1Sa 12:3; 1Co 9:12; 2Co 7:2; 11:9; 12:14-17
20:34 n Ac 18:3
20:36 o Lk 22:41; Ac 21:5
20:37 p Lk 15:20
20:38 q ver 25
21:1 r Ac 16:10
21:2 s Ac 11:19
21:4 t Ac 11:26 u ver 11; Ac 20:23
21:5 v Ac 20:36
21:7 w Ac 12:20 x Ac 1:16
21:8 y Ac 8:40 z Ac 6:5; 8:5-40 a Eph 4:11; 2Ti 4:5
21:9 b Lk 2:36; Ac 2:17
21:10 c Ac 11:28
21:11 d ver 33 e 1Ki 22:11

up to Jerusalem. 13 Then Paul answered,
"Why are you weeping and breaking my
21:13 heart? I am ready not only to be bound,
f Ac 20:24 but also to die[f] in Jerusalem for the
g Ac 9:16 name of the Lord Jesus."[g] 14 When he
would not be dissuaded, we gave up and
said, "The Lord's will be done."
15 After this, we got ready and went up
21:16 to Jerusalem. 16 Some of the disciples
h Ac 8:40 from Caesarea[h] accompanied us and
i ver 3,4 brought us to the home of Mnason,
where we were to stay. He was a man
from Cyprus[i] and one of the early disciples.

Paul's Arrival at Jerusalem

17 When we arrived at Jerusalem, the
21:17 brothers received us warmly.[j] 18 The next
j Ac 15:4 day Paul and the rest of us went to see
21:18 k Ac 15:13 James,[k] and all the elders[l] were present.
l Ac 11:30 19 Paul greeted them and reported in de-
21:19 tail what God had done among the Gen-
m Ac 14:27 tiles[m] through his ministry.[n]
n Ac 1:17 20 When they heard this, they praised
God. Then they said to Paul: "You see,
brother, how many thousands of Jews
have believed, and all of them are zeal- 21:20
ous[o] for the law.[p] 21 They have been in- o Ac 22:3;
formed that you teach all the Jews who Ro 10:2; Gal 1:14
live among the Gentiles to turn away p Ac 15:1,5
from Moses,[q] telling them not to cir- 21:21
cumcise their children[r] or live according q ver 28
to our customs.[s] 22 What shall we do? r Ac 15:19-21; 1Co 7:18,19
They will certainly hear that you have s Ac 6:14
come, 23 so do what we tell you. There are 21:23
four men with us who have made a vow.[t] t Ac 18:18
24 Take these men, join in their purifica- 21:24
tion rites[u] and pay their expenses, so u ver 26;
that they can have their heads shaved.[v] Ac 24:18
Then everybody will know there is no v Ac 18:18
truth in these reports about you, but
that you yourself are living in obedience
to the law. 25 As for the Gentile believers,
we have written to them our decision
that they should abstain from food sacrificed to idols, from blood, from the
meat of strangled animals and from sexual immorality."[w] 21:25 w Ac 15:20,29
26 The next day Paul took the men and
purified himself along with them. Then
he went to the temple to give notice of
the date when the days of purification
would end and the offering would be 21:26
made for each of them.[x] x Nu 6:13-20; Ac 24:18

Paul Arrested

27 When the seven days were nearly
over, some Jews from the province of
Asia saw Paul at the temple. They stirred
up the whole crowd and seized him,[y] 21:27 y Ac 24:18; 26:21
28 shouting, "Men of Israel, help us! This
is the man who teaches all men everywhere against our people and our law
and this place. And besides, he has
brought Greeks into the temple area and 21:28
defiled this holy place."[z] 29 (They had pre- z Mt 24:15;
viously seen Trophimus[a] the Ephesian[b] Ac 24:5,6
in the city with Paul and assumed that 21:29
Paul had brought him into the temple a Ac 20:4 b Ac 18:19
area.)
30 The whole city was aroused, and the
people came running from all direc-
tions. Seizing Paul,[c] they dragged him[d] 21:30 c Ac 26:21
from the temple, and immediately the d Ac 16:19
gates were shut. 31 While they were trying to kill him, news reached the commander of the Roman troops that the
whole city of Jerusalem was in an uproar.
32 He at once took some officers and soldiers and ran down to the crowd. When
the rioters saw the commander and his
soldiers, they stopped beating Paul.[e] 21:32 e Ac 23:27

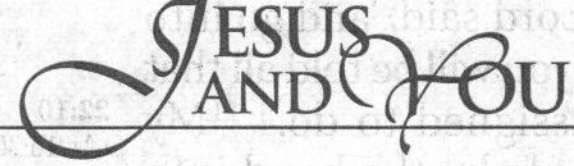

READY TO DIE

Even though his life was in danger, Paul went back to Jerusalem because he was devoted to Jesus and compelled by the Holy Spirit (Acts 20:22). Believers along the way warned him not to return there (Acts 21:4,10–12), and even Luke, the author of Acts, attempted to dissuade him (verses 12,14). People have long debated as to whether or not Paul should have listened to this counsel. But Paul was following the call of God and proclaimed that he was prepared to die in Jerusalem for Jesus if that should prove necessary (verse 13).

Paul was not the only one committed to holding to and spreading the truth about Jesus. Many other early Christians were martyred, and their example of unwavering commitment has helped other people to see the truth of God in the lives of believers. We might not face the possibility of martyrdom, but we do need to ask ourselves the same questions: Are we so devoted to Jesus that we are willing to die for him if necessary? Are we so committed that we are ready to put aside our own desires? Are we prepared to allow the Holy Spirit to guide our lives—whether or not we like his guidance? Jesus made the ultimate sacrifice for us, and we need to ponder how far we are willing to go in our devotion to him.

33The commander came up and ar-
21:33 [f] ver 11 [g] Ac 12:6 [h] Ac 20:23; Eph 6:20; 2Ti 2:9 rested him and ordered him to be
bound[f] with two[g] chains.[h] Then he
asked who he was and what he had done.
34Some in the crowd shouted one thing
21:34 [i] Ac 19:32 [j] ver 37; Ac 23:10,16,32 and some another,[i] and since the commander could not get at the truth be-
cause of the uproar, he ordered that Paul
be taken into the barracks.[j] 35When Paul
21:35 [k] ver 40 reached the steps,[k] the violence of the
mob was so great he had to be carried by
21:36 [l] Lk 23:18; Jn 19:15; Ac 22:22 the soldiers. 36The crowd that followed
kept shouting, "Away with him!"[l]

Paul Speaks to the Crowd

37As the soldiers were about to take
21:37 [m] ver 34 Paul into the barracks,[m] he asked the
commander, "May I say something to
you?"

"Do you speak Greek?" he replied.
38"Aren't you the Egyptian who started a
revolt and led four thousand terrorists
21:38 [n] Mt 24:26 [o] Ac 5:36 out into the desert[n] some time ago?"[o]

39Paul answered, "I am a Jew, from Tarsus[p] in Cilicia,[q] a citizen of no ordinary
21:39 [p] Ac 9:11 [q] Ac 22:3 city. Please let me speak to the people."

40Having received the commander's
permission, Paul stood on the steps and
21:40 [r] Ac 12:17 [s] Jn 5:2 motioned[r] to the crowd. When they were
all silent, he said to them in Aramaic[a]:[s]

22

22:1 [t] Ac 7:2 1"Brothers and fathers,[t] listen
now to my defense."

22:2 [u] Ac 21:40 2When they heard him speak to them
in Aramaic,[u] they became very quiet.

A DRAMATIC TESTIMONY

Paul frequently used his own conversion story as an object lesson to tell others about the life-changing power of Jesus. The book of Acts records Paul's story three times. First, Luke included this pivotal incident in chapter 9. Then, in his own defense, Paul recounted this miraculous story of divine intervention in chapter 22 to a Jewish mob. Finally, Paul told his story to Herod Agrippa in chapter 26. Each time, we are given new details to fill us in as to what really happened to Paul that day on the road to Damascus. One central truth, however, remains the same with each retelling: It was Jesus himself who intervened in Paul's life. Whenever Paul found an opportunity to explain the change he had undergone, his focus was on the One who had planned and orchestrated that conversion—Jesus Christ, the eternal Son of God.

Then Paul said: 3"I am a Jew,[v] born in 22:3 [v] Ac 21:39 [w] Ac 9:11 [x] Lk 10:39 [y] Ac 5:34 [z] Ac 26:5 [a] Ac 21:20
Tarsus[w] of Cilicia, but brought up in this
city. Under[x] Gamaliel[y] I was thoroughly
trained in the law of our fathers[z] and
was just as zealous[a] for God as any of
you are today. 4I persecuted[b] the follow- 22:4 [b] Ac 8:3 [c] ver 19, 20
ers of this Way to their death, arresting
both men and women and throwing
them into prison,[c] 5as also the high
priest and all the Council[d] can testify. I 22:5 [d] Lk 22:66 [e] Ac 13:26 [f] Ac 9:2
even obtained letters from them to their
brothers[e] in Damascus,[f] and went there
to bring these people as prisoners to Jerusalem to be punished.

6"About noon as I came near Damascus, suddenly a bright light from heaven
flashed around me.[g] 7I fell to the ground 22:6 [g] Ac 9:3
and heard a voice say to me, 'Saul! Saul!
Why do you persecute me?'

8" 'Who are you, Lord?' I asked.

" 'I am Jesus of Nazareth, whom you
are persecuting,' he replied. 9My com-
panions saw the light,[h] but they did not 22:9 [h] Ac 26:13 [i] Ac 9:7
understand the voice[i] of him who was
speaking to me.

10" 'What shall I do, Lord?' I asked.

" 'Get up,' the Lord said, 'and go into
Damascus. There you will be told all that
you have been assigned to do.'[j] 11My 22:10 [j] Ac 16:30
companions led me by the hand into
Damascus, because the brilliance of the
light had blinded me.[k] 22:11 [k] Ac 9:8

12"A man named Ananias came to see
me.[l] He was a devout observer of the law 22:12 [l] Ac 9:17 [m] Ac 10:22
and highly respected by all the Jews liv-
ing there.[m] 13He stood beside me and
said, 'Brother Saul, receive your sight!'
And at that very moment I was able to
see him.

14"Then he said: 'The God of our fa- 22:14 [n] Ac 3:13 [o] 1Co 9:1; 15:8 [p] Ac 7:52
thers[n] has chosen you to know his will
and to see[o] the Righteous One[p] and to
hear words from his mouth. 15You will
be his witness[q] to all men of what you 22:15 [q] Ac 23:11; 26:16
have seen and heard. 16And now what
are you waiting for? Get up, be baptized[r] 22:16 [r] Ac 2:38 [s] Heb 10:22 [t] Ro 10:13
and wash your sins away,[s] calling on his
name.'[t]

17"When I returned to Jerusalem[u] and 22:17 [u] Ac 9:26 [v] Ac 10:10
was praying at the temple, I fell into a
trance[v] 18and saw the Lord speaking.
'Quick!' he said to me. 'Leave Jerusalem
immediately, because they will not accept your testimony about me.'

19" 'Lord,' I replied, 'these men know
that I went from one synagogue to an-

[a] 40 Or possibly *Hebrew*; also in 22:2

22:19 [w] ver 4; Ac 8:3 other to imprison[w] and beat[x] those who
[x] Mt 10:17 believe in you. 20And when the blood of
your martyr[a] Stephen was shed, I stood
there giving my approval and guarding
22:20 the clothes of those who were killing
[y] Ac 7:57-60; 8:1 him.'[y]
22:21 21"Then the Lord said to me, 'Go; I will
[z] Ac 9:15; 13:46 send you far away to the Gentiles.'"[z]

Paul the Roman Citizen

22The crowd listened to Paul until he
said this. Then they raised their voices
22:22 [a] Ac 21:36 and shouted, "Rid the earth of him![a] He's
[b] Ac 25:24 not fit to live!"[b]
23As they were shouting and throwing
22:23 [c] Ac 7:58 off their cloaks[c] and flinging dust into
[d] 2Sa 16:13 the air,[d] 24the commander ordered Paul
to be taken into the barracks.[e] He di-
22:24 [e] Ac 21:34 rected[f] that he be flogged and ques-
[f] ver 29 tioned in order to find out why the people were shouting at him like this. 25As
they stretched him out to flog him, Paul
said to the centurion standing there, "Is
it legal for you to flog a Roman citizen
22:25 [g] Ac 16:37 who hasn't even been found guilty?"[g]
26When the centurion heard this, he
went to the commander and reported it.
"What are you going to do?" he asked.
"This man is a Roman citizen."
27The commander went to Paul and
asked, "Tell me, are you a Roman citizen?"
"Yes, I am," he answered.
28Then the commander said, "I had to
pay a big price for my citizenship."
"But I was born a citizen," Paul replied.
29Those who were about to question
him withdrew immediately. The commander himself was alarmed when he
22:29 [h] ver 24,25; realized that he had put Paul, a Roman
Ac 16:38 citizen,[h] in chains.

Before the Sanhedrin

30The next day, since the commander
wanted to find out exactly why Paul was
22:30 [i] Ac 23:28 being accused by the Jews,[i] he released
[j] Ac 21:33 him[j] and ordered the chief priests and
[k] Mt 5:22 all the Sanhedrin[k] to assemble. Then he
brought Paul and had him stand before
23:1 [l] Ac 22:30 them.
[m] Ac 22:5 23 Paul looked straight at the San-
[n] Ac 24:16; 1Co 4:4; hedrin[l] and said, "My brothers,[m]
2Co 1:12; I have fulfilled my duty to God in all good
2Ti 1:3; Heb 13:18 conscience[n] to this day." 2At this the high
priest Ananias[o] ordered those standing
23:2 [o] Ac 24:1 near Paul to strike him on the mouth.[p]
[p] Jn 18:22 3Then Paul said to him, "God will strike
you, you whitewashed wall![q] You sit there 23:3 [q] Mt 23:27
to judge me according to the law, yet you [r] Lev 19:15;
yourself violate the law by commanding Dt 25:1,2;
that I be struck!"[r] Jn 7:51
4Those who were standing near Paul
said, "You dare to insult God's high
priest?"
5Paul replied, "Brothers, I did not realize that he was the high priest; for it is
written: 'Do not speak evil about the
ruler of your people.'[b]"[s] 23:5 [s] Ex 22:28
6Then Paul, knowing that some of
them were Sadducees and the others
Pharisees, called out in the Sanhedrin,
"My brothers,[t] I am a Pharisee,[u] the son 23:6 [t] Ac 22:5
of a Pharisee. I stand on trial because of [u] Ac 26:5;
my hope in the resurrection of the Php 3:5
dead."[v] 7When he said this, a dispute [v] Ac 24:15,21; 26:8
broke out between the Pharisees and the
Sadducees, and the assembly was divided. 8(The Sadducees say that there is no
resurrection,[w] and that there are neither 23:8 [w] Mt 22:23
angels nor spirits, but the Pharisees acknowledge them all.)

[a] 20 Or *witness* [b] 5 Exodus 22:28

JESUS FOCUS

TAKE COURAGE!

Even when under pressure Paul was a formidable opponent. He demonstrated great skill in dividing his accusers into opposing groups based on their private agendas—a technique that proved especially effective when it came to the Pharisees and the Sadducees (Acts 23:6–11). Ordinarily the two groups were at odds with one another over how the Hebrew Scriptures should be interpreted, but they united against Paul in a common hatred. But at one point Paul aroused such intense hostility between the two parties that a Roman commander arrested him as a Roman citizen in order to save his life. Before he was sent to the governor in Caesarea, Antonius Felix, Paul was held overnight in the Fortress of Antonia (the "barracks" of verse 10; see also Acts 21:34). During the night the ascended Jesus visited Paul in his cell and allowed him a glimpse into the future, assuring him that just as Paul had testified about Jesus in Jerusalem, so he would also testify in Rome (Acts 23:11). What encouragement that must have been! As Jesus had done at two other critical moments in Paul's ministry (Acts 18:9–10; 22:17–21), so now he again spoke words of support to Paul when the apostle needed them most.

9There was a great uproar, and some
of the teachers of the law who were
Pharisees[x] stood up and argued vigorously. "We find nothing wrong with this
man,"[y] they said. "What if a spirit or an
angel has spoken to him?"[z] 10The dispute became so violent that the commander was afraid Paul would be torn to
pieces by them. He ordered the troops to
go down and take him away from them
by force and bring him into the barracks.[a]
11The following night the Lord stood
near Paul and said, "Take courage![b] As
you have testified about me in Jerusalem, so you must also testify in Rome."[c]

The Plot to Kill Paul

12The next morning the Jews formed
a conspiracy and bound themselves
with an oath not to eat or drink until
they had killed Paul.[d] 13More than forty
men were involved in this plot. 14They
went to the chief priests and elders and
said, "We have taken a solemn oath not
to eat anything until we have killed
Paul.[e] 15Now then, you and the Sanhedrin[f] petition the commander to
bring him before you on the pretext of
wanting more accurate information
about his case. We are ready to kill him
before he gets here."
16But when the son of Paul's sister
heard of this plot, he went into the barracks[g] and told Paul.
17Then Paul called one of the centurions and said, "Take this young man to
the commander; he has something to
tell him." 18So he took him to the commander.
The centurion said, "Paul, the prisoner,[h] sent for me and asked me to bring
this young man to you because he has
something to tell you."
19The commander took the young
man by the hand, drew him aside and
asked, "What is it you want to tell me?"
20He said: "The Jews have agreed to
ask you to bring Paul before the Sanhedrin[i] tomorrow on the pretext of
wanting more accurate information
about him.[j] 21Don't give in to them, because more than forty[k] of them are waiting in ambush for him. They have taken
an oath not to eat or drink until they
have killed him.[l] They are ready now,
waiting for your consent to their request."
22The commander dismissed the
young man and cautioned him, "Don't
tell anyone that you have reported this
to me."

Paul Transferred to Caesarea

23Then he called two of his centurions
and ordered them, "Get ready a detachment of two hundred soldiers, seventy
horsemen and two hundred spearmen[a]
to go to Caesarea[m] at nine tonight.[n]
24Provide mounts for Paul so that he
may be taken safely to Governor Felix."[o]
25He wrote a letter as follows:

26Claudius Lysias,

To His Excellency,[p] Governor Felix:

Greetings.[q]

27This man was seized by the
Jews and they were about to kill
him,[r] but I came with my troops
and rescued him,[s] for I had learned
that he is a Roman citizen.[t] 28I
wanted to know why they were accusing him, so I brought him to
their Sanhedrin.[u] 29I found that the
accusation had to do with questions about their law,[v] but there
was no charge against him[w] that
deserved death or imprisonment.
30When I was informed[x] of a plot[y]
to be carried out against the man, I
sent him to you at once. I also ordered his accusers[z] to present to
you their case against him.

31So the soldiers, carrying out their
orders, took Paul with them during the
night and brought him as far as Antipa-
tris. 32The next day they let the cavalry[a]
go on with him, while they returned to
the barracks.[b] 33When the cavalry[c] arrived in Caesarea,[d] they delivered the
letter to the governor[e] and handed Paul
over to him. 34The governor read the letter and asked what province he was
from. Learning that he was from Cilicia,[f]
35he said, "I will hear your case when
your accusers[g] get here." Then he ordered that Paul be kept under guard[h] in
Herod's palace.

[a] 23 The meaning of the Greek for this word is uncertain.

23:9 [x] Mk 2:16 [y] ver 29; Ac 25:25; 26:31 [z] Ac 22:7,17,18
23:10 [a] Ac 21:34
23:11 [b] Ac 18:9 [c] Ac 19:21; 28:23
23:12 [d] ver 14,21,30; Ac 25:3
23:14 [e] ver 12
23:15 [f] ver 1; Ac 22:30
23:16 [g] ver 10; Ac 21:34
23:18 [h] Eph 3:1
23:20 [i] ver 1 [j] ver 14, 15
23:21 [k] ver 13 [l] ver 12, 14
23:23 [m] Ac 8:40 [n] ver 33
23:24 [o] ver 26,33; Ac 24:1-3,10; 25:14
23:26 [p] Lk 1:3; Ac 24:3; 26:25 [q] Ac 15:23
23:27 [r] Ac 21:32 [s] Ac 21:33 [t] Ac 22:25-29
23:28 [u] Ac 22:30
23:29 [v] Ac 18:15; 25:19 [w] ver 9; Ac 26:31
23:30 [x] ver 20,21 [y] Ac 20:3 [z] ver 35; Ac 24:19; 25:16
23:32 [a] ver 23 [b] Ac 21:34
23:33 [c] ver 23,24 [d] Ac 8:40 [e] ver 26
23:34 [f] Ac 6:9; 21:39
23:35 [g] ver 30; Ac 24:19; 25:16 [h] Ac 24:27

> **I** F CHRISTIANITY IS TRUE,
> THEN IT HAS APPLICATION
> FOR ALL OF LIFE.
>
> Charles Colson,
> *Chairman, Prison Fellowship*

The Trial Before Felix

24:1 **24** Five days later the high priest
i Ac 23:2 Ananias[i] went down to Caesa-
j Ac 23:30,35 rea with some of the elders and a lawyer
k Ac 23:24 named Tertullus, and they brought their
charges[j] against Paul before the governor.[k] 2When Paul was called in, Tertullus
presented his case before Felix: "We
have enjoyed a long period of peace under you, and your foresight has brought
about reforms in this nation. 3Every-
24:3 where and in every way, most excellent[l]
l Lk 1:3; Ac 23:26; 26:25 Felix, we acknowledge this with profound gratitude. 4But in order not to
weary you further, I would request that
you be kind enough to hear us briefly.
5"We have found this man to be a
24:5 troublemaker, stirring up riots[m] among
m Ac 16:20; 17:6 n Ac 21:28 the Jews[n] all over the world. He is a ring-
o Mk 1:24 leader of the Nazarene[o] sect[p] 6and even
p ver 14; Ac 26:5; 28:22 tried to desecrate the temple;[q] so we
24:6 seized him. 8By[a] examining him yourself
q Ac 21:28 you will be able to learn the truth about
all these charges we are bringing against
him."
24:9 r 1Th 2:16 9The Jews joined in the accusation,[r]
asserting that these things were true.
24:10 10When the governor[s] motioned for
s Ac 23:24 him to speak, Paul replied: "I know that
for a number of years you have been a
judge over this nation; so I gladly make
my defense. 11You can easily verify that
24:11 t Ac 21:27; ver 1 no more than twelve days[t] ago I went up
to Jerusalem to worship. 12My accusers
did not find me arguing with anyone at
24:12 u Ac 25:8; 28:17 the temple,[u] or stirring up a crowd[v] in
v ver 18 the synagogues or anywhere else in the
city. 13And they cannot prove to you the
charges they are now making against
24:13 w Ac 25:7 me.[w] 14However, I admit that I worship
the God of our fathers[x] as a follower of
24:14 x Ac 3:13 the Way,[y] which they call a sect.[z] I be-
y Ac 9:2 z ver 5 lieve everything that agrees with the
a Ac 26:6,22; 28:23 Law and that is written in the Prophets,[a]
15and I have the same hope in God as
these men, that there will be a resurrec-
24:15 b Ac 23:6; 28:20 tion[b] of both the righteous and the
wicked.[c] 16So I strive always to keep my 24:15 c Da 12:2; Jn 5:28,29
conscience clear[d] before God and man.
17"After an absence of several years, I
came to Jerusalem to bring my people 24:16 d Ac 23:1
gifts for the poor[e] and to present offer-
ings. 18I was ceremonially clean[f] when 24:17 e Ac 11:29,30;
they found me in the temple courts do- Ro 15:25-28,31;
ing this. There was no crowd with me, 1Co 16:1-4,15; 2Co 8:1-4;
nor was I involved in any disturbance.[g] Gal 2:10
19But there are some Jews from the prov-
ince of Asia, who ought to be here before 24:18 f Ac 21:26
you and bring charges if they have any- g ver 12
thing against me.[h] 20Or these who are 24:19
here should state what crime they found h Ac 23:30
in me when I stood before the San-
hedrin— 21unless it was this one thing I
shouted as I stood in their presence: 'It is
concerning the resurrection of the dead
that I am on trial before you today.'"[i] 24:21 i Ac 23:6
22Then Felix, who was well acquaint-
ed with the Way, adjourned the proceedings. "When Lysias the commander comes," he said, "I will decide your
case." 23He ordered the centurion to
keep Paul under guard[j] but to give him 24:23 j Ac 23:35
some freedom[k] and permit his friends to k Ac 28:16
take care of his needs.[l] l Ac 23:16; 27:3
24Several days later Felix came with
his wife Drusilla, who was a Jewess. He
sent for Paul and listened to him as he 24:24
spoke about faith in Christ Jesus.[m] 25As m Ac 20:21
Paul discoursed on righteousness, self- 24:25
control[n] and the judgment[o] to come, Fe- n Gal 5:23; 2Pe 1:6
lix was afraid and said, "That's enough o Ac 10:42
for now! You may leave. When I find it
convenient, I will send for you." 26At the
same time he was hoping that Paul
would offer him a bribe, so he sent for
him frequently and talked with him.
27When two years had passed, Felix
was succeeded by Porcius Festus,[p] but 24:27 p Ac 25:1,4,9,14
because Felix wanted to grant a favor to q Ac 12:3; 25:9
the Jews,[q] he left Paul in prison.[r] r Ac 23:35; 25:14

The Trial Before Festus

25 Three days after arriving in the
province, Festus went up from
Caesarea[s] to Jerusalem, 2where the chief 25:1 s Ac 8:40
priests and Jewish leaders appeared be-
fore him and presented the charges 25:2
against Paul.[t] 3They urgently requested t ver 15; Ac 24:1
Festus, as a favor to them, to have Paul
transferred to Jerusalem, for they were

[a] 6–8 Some manuscripts *him and wanted to judge him according to our law. 7But the commander, Lysias, came and with the use of much force snatched him from our hands 8and ordered his accusers to come before you. By*

DISCOVERY 299

GOD'S TROUBLEMAKER

Jesus and Paul had at least two things in common: Each faced a trial before the Roman authorities (see Mark 15:1–15), and each was accused by some of the Jewish people because of his religious beliefs (see Mark 14:53–65). Paul's trial was under the Roman governor Felix, and a Jewish lawyer named Tertullus brought three charges against him (Acts 24:1–2). First of all, he alleged, Paul was a troublemaker, stirring up dissension among Jews "all over the world" (verse 5). Second, Paul was the ringleader of "the Nazarene Sect" (verse 5), a term used to describe Jesus' followers, because Jesus had come from Nazareth. Tertullus was implying that the very existence of this religious sect was in violation of Roman law. Finally, the lawyer accused Paul of trying to "desecrate the temple," of blatantly disregarding its religious traditions (verse 6).

Paul was given the opportunity to defend himself against the allegations (verses 10–21). He pointed out that his accusers had no evidence to support the charges and then proceeded to explain to Felix what he really believed. Paul boldly identified himself with "the Way" (verse 14)—followers of Jesus who affirmed that Jesus was "the way" to a relationship with God the Father (see John 14:6). Paul told Felix that he believed that the dead would one day rise (Acts 24:15,21), a statement that caused a division among the religious leaders. The Sanhedrin was a council made up of both Pharisees and Sadducees. One of the primary differences between the two groups was that the Pharisees believed in bodily resurrection, while the Sadducees did not (Mark 12:18).

Felix knew what the Jewish people believed (Acts 24:22). After he had adjourned the proceedings, he kept Paul sitting in prison for two years, during which time Felix engaged in a number of conversations with his prisoner (verse 26). The apostle never wavered. He spoke to Felix about "faith in Christ Jesus" and "discoursed on righteousness, self-control and the judgment to come" (verse 24–25).

There is a very real sense in which Paul *was* a troublemaker. He was wholeheartedly devoted to Jesus, and this commitment continually landed him in trouble. But Paul used *every* opportunity, even behind prison bars, to dialogue about Jesus Christ. When he defended himself against accusation, he shared the gospel. When Felix called for him, he shared the gospel. Paul recognized that adversity and injustice afforded him opportunities to focus attention on Jesus.

Paul had known from the day he had turned over his life to Jesus that he would tell Gentiles and their kings the Good News. He had also realized that he would have to suffer for the name of Jesus (Acts 9:15–16). So he was not alarmed at having to spend two years in prison, understanding this interlude to be a part of God's plan and resting in the assurance that the truth about Jesus would be carried to the corridors of power in the mighty Roman empire. And so it can be with us: Whenever we suffer adversity, we have a unique opportunity to demonstrate our devotion to Jesus and to introduce others to our source of strength.

***Self-Discovery:** Think back to a time in your life when you felt yourself to be in a "rut," waiting for an opportunity to allow specific plans to materialize. In retrospect, are you able to see God's hand in the timing of events during and after this period?*

GO TO DISCOVERY 300 ON PAGE 1504

preparing an ambush to kill him along
the way. 4Festus answered, "Paul is being
25:4 u Ac 24:23 held[u] at Caesarea, and I myself am going
there soon. 5Let some of your leaders
come with me and press charges against
the man there, if he has done anything
wrong."
6After spending eight or ten days with
them, he went down to Caesarea, and
25:6 v ver 17 the next day he convened the court[v] and
ordered that Paul be brought before
him. 7When Paul appeared, the Jews
who had come down from Jerusalem
stood around him, bringing many seri-
25:7 w Mk 15:3; ous charges against him,[w] which they
Lk 23:2,10; Ac 24:5,6 could not prove.[x]
x Ac 24:13 8Then Paul made his defense: "I have
done nothing wrong against the law of
25:8 y Ac 6:13; 24:12; the Jews or against the temple[y] or
28:17 against Caesar."
9Festus, wishing to do the Jews a fa-
25:9 z Ac 24:27 vor,[z] said to Paul, "Are you willing to go
a ver 20 up to Jerusalem and stand trial before
me there on these charges?"[a]
10Paul answered: "I am now standing
before Caesar's court, where I ought to
be tried. I have not done any wrong to
the Jews, as you yourself know very well.
11If, however, I am guilty of doing anything deserving death, I do not refuse to
die. But if the charges brought against
me by these Jews are not true, no one
has the right to hand me over to them. I
25:11 b ver 21,25; appeal to Caesar!"[b]
Ac 26:32; 28:19 12After Festus had conferred with his
council, he declared: "You have appealed
to Caesar. To Caesar you will go!"

Festus Consults King Agrippa

13A few days later King Agrippa and
25:13 c Ac 8:40 Bernice arrived at Caesarea[c] to pay their
respects to Festus. 14Since they were
spending many days there, Festus discussed Paul's case with the king. He said:
"There is a man here whom Felix left as
25:14 d Ac 24:27 a prisoner.[d] 15When I went to Jerusalem,
the chief priests and elders of the Jews
25:15 e ver 2; Ac 24:1 brought charges against him[e] and asked
that he be condemned.
16"I told them that it is not the Roman
custom to hand over any man before he
has faced his accusers and has had an
opportunity to defend himself against
25:16 f ver 4,5; their charges.[f] 17When they came here
Ac 23:30 with me, I did not delay the case, but
convened the court the next day and or-
25:17 g ver 6,10 dered the man to be brought in.[g] 18When
his accusers got up to speak, they did not
charge him with any of the crimes I had
expected. 19Instead, they had some
points of dispute[h] with him about their 25:19 h Ac 18:15;
own religion[i] and about a dead man 23:29 i Ac 17:22
named Jesus who Paul claimed was alive.
20I was at a loss how to investigate such
matters; so I asked if he would be willing
to go to Jerusalem and stand trial there
on these charges.[j] 21When Paul made his 25:20 j ver 9
appeal to be held over for the Emperor's
decision, I ordered him held until I could
send him to Caesar."[k] 25:21 k ver 11,12
22Then Agrippa said to Festus, "I
would like to hear this man myself."
He replied, "Tomorrow you will hear
him."[l] 25:22 l Ac 9:15

Paul Before Agrippa

23The next day Agrippa and Bernice[m] 25:23 m ver 13;
came with great pomp and entered the Ac 26:30
audience room with the high ranking officers and the leading men of the city. At
the command of Festus, Paul was
brought in. 24Festus said: "King Agrippa,
and all who are present with us, you see
this man! The whole Jewish communi-
ty[n] has petitioned me about him in Jeru- 25:24 n ver 2,3,7
salem and here in Caesarea, shouting o Ac 22:22
that he ought not to live any longer.[o] 25I
found he had done nothing deserving of
death,[p] but because he made his appeal 25:25 p Ac 23:9
to the Emperor[q] I decided to send him q ver 11
to Rome. 26But I have nothing definite to
write to His Majesty about him. Therefore I have brought him before all of you,
and especially before you, King Agrippa,
so that as a result of this investigation I
may have something to write. 27For I
think it is unreasonable to send on a
prisoner without specifying the charges
against him."

26 Then Agrippa said to Paul,
"You have permission to speak
for yourself."[r] 26:1 r Ac 9:15; 25:22
So Paul motioned with his hand and
began his defense: 2"King Agrippa, I
consider myself fortunate to stand before you today as I make my defense
against all the accusations of the Jews,
3and especially so because you are well
acquainted with all the Jewish customs[s] 26:3 s ver 7; Ac 6:14
and controversies.[t] Therefore, I beg you t Ac 25:19
to listen to me patiently.
4"The Jews all know the way I have
lived ever since I was a child,[u] from the 26:4 u Gal 1:13,14;
beginning of my life in my own country, Php 3:5

DISCOVERY 300

SHARING OUR STORY

King Agrippa was the last in the Herodian dynasty (40 B.C. to A.D. 100) to rule Palestine. Like his predecessors, Agrippa was a skilled mediator between Rome and Palestine. He improved cities and expanded building programs begun by his ancestors. But he was also involved in an incestuous relationship with his half-sister Bernice, who was married to her uncle, Herod of Chalcis, and later became mistress to the emperor Vespasion's son Titus.

Paul was brought by Festus, successor to Felix as Roman governor, to have an audience with Agrippa, who was himself Jewish and thereby familiar with Jewish customs (Acts 26:3). Paul was actually enthusiastic about the opportunity to speak with the king. But instead of defending himself against the charges, the apostle offered a detailed account of his personal background, including his dramatic encounter with Jesus and his subsequent change of heart. At the end of his autobiography Paul included a concise summary of the gospel message: "I am saying nothing beyond what the prophets and Moses said would happen—that the Christ would suffer and, as the first to rise from the dead, would proclaim light to his own people and to the Gentiles" (verses 22–23).

The responses of both Governor Festus and King Agrippa to Paul's defense were immediate and passionate:

Festus: "You are out of your mind" (verse 24). Festus surmised that Paul had gone mad on account of his education and his study of the Scriptures. The governor blithely dismissed the gospel message because of his assumption that the messenger was insane.

Agrippa: "You must be joking," he said in effect. The king's response was sarcastic: "Do you think that in such a short time you can persuade me to be a Christian?" (verse 28). Agrippa's contention was that the gospel message was too easy. He apparently concluded that salvation could be had with a snap of his fingers. But he was wrong, and so are all who still today dismiss the gospel as too foolish or improbable to be worth their time or serious attention.

Paul refused to become defensive or angry at the mockery. Instead, he agreed that the king had figured out his plan: "I pray God that not only you but all who are listening to me today may become what I am, except for these chains" (verse 29). Paul was not responsible for the responses of Festus and Agrippa, but he was accountable to tell them the truth and to pray for them. That is precisely what God asks of his people—that we share the story of how we met our Savior, tell others about Jesus and pray that the Spirit will work in the hearts of those who hear what we say. The rest is up to God.

Self-Discovery: *Have you been frustrated because your witness about your Lord Jesus Christ to a specific individual (family member, neighbor, colleague, and the like) seemed either to fall on deaf ears or was met with snide remarks or a jocular response? Have you been willing to continue in your efforts and pray for the grace and patience to leave the result in the Lord's hands?*

GO TO DISCOVERY 301 ON PAGE 1511

and also in Jerusalem. 5They have known me for a long time[v] and can testify, if they are willing, that according to the strictest sect of our religion, I lived as a Pharisee.[w] 6And now it is because of my hope[x] in what God has promised our fathers[y] that I am on trial today. 7This is the promise our twelve tribes[z] are hoping to see fulfilled as they earnestly serve God day and night.[a] O king, it is because of this hope that the Jews are accusing me.[b] 8Why should any of you consider it incredible that God raises the dead?[c]

9"I too was convinced[d] that I ought to do all that was possible to oppose[e] the name of Jesus of Nazareth.[f] 10And that is just what I did in Jerusalem. On the authority of the chief priests I put many of the saints[g] in prison,[h] and when they were put to death, I cast my vote against them.[i] 11Many a time I went from one synagogue to another to have them punished,[j] and I tried to force them to blaspheme. In my obsession against them, I even went to foreign cities to persecute them.

12"On one of these journeys I was going to Damascus with the authority and commission of the chief priests. 13About noon, O king, as I was on the road, I saw a light from heaven, brighter than the sun, blazing around me and my companions. 14We all fell to the ground, and I heard a voice[k] saying to me in Aramaic,[*a*] 'Saul, Saul, why do you persecute me? It is hard for you to kick against the goads.'

15"Then I asked, 'Who are you, Lord?'

" 'I am Jesus, whom you are persecuting,' the Lord replied. 16'Now get up and stand on your feet.[l] I have appeared to you to appoint you as a servant and as a witness of what you have seen of me and what I will show you.[m] 17I will rescue you[n] from your own people and from the Gentiles.[o] I am sending you to them 18to open their eyes[p] and turn them from darkness to light,[q] and from the power of Satan to God, so that they may receive forgiveness of sins[r] and a place among those who are sanctified by faith in me.'[s]

19"So then, King Agrippa, I was not disobedient to the vision from heaven. 20First to those in Damascus,[t] then to those in Jerusalem[u] and in all Judea, and to the Gentiles[v] also, I preached that they should repent[w] and turn to God and prove their repentance by their deeds.[x] 21That is why the Jews seized me[y] in the temple courts and tried to kill me.[z] 22But I have had God's help to this very day, and so I stand here and testify to small and great alike. I am saying nothing beyond what the prophets and Moses said would happen[a]— 23that the Christ[*b*] would suffer and, as the first to rise from the dead,[b] would proclaim light to his own people and to the Gentiles."[c]

24At this point Festus interrupted Paul's defense. "You are out of your mind,[d] Paul!" he shouted. "Your great learning[e] is driving you insane."

25"I am not insane, most excellent[f] Festus," Paul replied. "What I am saying is true and reasonable. 26The king is familiar with these things,[g] and I can speak freely to him. I am convinced that none of this has escaped his notice, because it was not done in a corner. 27King Agrippa, do you believe the prophets? I know you do."

28Then Agrippa said to Paul, "Do you think that in such a short time you can persuade me to be a Christian?"[h]

29Paul replied, "Short time or long—I pray God that not only you but all who are listening to me today may become what I am, except for these chains."[i]

30The king rose, and with him the governor and Bernice[j] and those sitting with them. 31They left the room, and while talking with one another, they said, "This man is not doing anything that deserves death or imprisonment."[k]

32Agrippa said to Festus, "This man could have been set free[l] if he had not appealed to Caesar."[m]

Paul Sails for Rome

27 When it was decided that we[n] would sail for Italy,[o] Paul and some other prisoners were handed over to a centurion named Julius, who belonged to the Imperial Regiment.[p] 2We boarded a ship from Adramyttium about to sail for ports along the coast of the province of Asia,[q] and we put out to sea. Aristarchus,[r] a Macedonian[s] from Thessalonica,[t] was with us.

3The next day we landed at Sidon;[u] and Julius, in kindness to Paul,[v] allowed him to go to his friends so they might provide for his needs.[w] 4From there we

a 14 Or *Hebrew* *b* 23 Or *Messiah*

26:5 v Ac 22:3 w Ac 23:6; Php 3:5
26:6 x Ac 23:6; 24:15; 28:20 y Ac 13:32; Ro 15:8
26:7 z Jas 1:1 a 1Th 3:10; 1Ti 5:5 b ver 2
26:8 c Ac 23:6
26:9 d 1Ti 1:13 e Jn 16:2 f Jn 15:21
26:10 g Ac 9:13 h Ac 8:3; 9:2,14, 21 i Ac 22:20
26:11 j Mt 10:17
26:14 k Ac 9:7
26:16 l Eze 2:1; Da 10:11 m Ac 22:14,15
26:17 n Jer 1:8,19 o Ac 9:15
26:18 p Isa 35:5 q Isa 42:7,16; Eph 5:8; Col 1:13; 1Pe 2:9 r Lk 24:47; Ac 2:38 s Ac 20:21,32
26:20 t Ac 9:19-25 u Ac 9:26-29; 22:17-20 v Ac 9:15; 13:46 w Ac 3:19 x Mt 3:8; Lk 3:8
26:21 y Ac 21:27,30 z Ac 21:31
26:22 a Lk 24:27,44; Ac 10:43; 24:14
26:23 b 1Co 15:20,23; Col 1:18; Rev 1:5 c Lk 2:32
26:24 d Jn 10:20; 1Co 4:10 e Jn 7:15
26:25 f Ac 23:26
26:26 g ver 3
26:28 h Ac 11:26
26:29 i Ac 21:33
26:30 j Ac 25:23
26:31 k Ac 23:9
26:32 l Ac 28:18 m Ac 25:11
27:1 n Ac 16:10 o Ac 18:2; 25:12, 25 p Ac 10:1
27:2 q Ac 2:9 r Ac 19:29 s Ac 16:9 t Ac 17:1
27:3 u Mt 11:21 v ver 43 w Ac 24:23; 28:16

put out to sea again and passed to the
lee of Cyprus because the winds were
against us.[x] 5When we had sailed across
the open sea off the coast of Cilicia[y] and
Pamphylia, we landed at Myra in Lycia.
6There the centurion found an Alexandrian ship[z] sailing for Italy[a] and put us
on board. 7We made slow headway for
many days and had difficulty arriving off
Cnidus. When the wind did not allow us
to hold our course,[b] we sailed to the lee
of Crete,[c] opposite Salmone. 8We moved
along the coast with difficulty and came
to a place called Fair Havens, near the
town of Lasea.
9Much time had been lost, and sailing
had already become dangerous because
by now it was after the Fast.[a][d] So Paul
warned them, 10"Men, I can see that our
voyage is going to be disastrous and
bring great loss to ship and cargo, and to
our own lives also."[e] 11But the centurion,
instead of listening to what Paul said,
followed the advice of the pilot and of
the owner of the ship. 12Since the harbor
was unsuitable to winter in, the majority decided that we should sail on, hoping to reach Phoenix and winter there.
This was a harbor in Crete, facing both
southwest and northwest.

The Storm

13When a gentle south wind began to
blow, they thought they had obtained
what they wanted; so they weighed anchor and sailed along the shore of Crete.
14Before very long, a wind of hurricane
force,[f] called the "northeaster," swept
down from the island. 15The ship was
caught by the storm and could not head
into the wind; so we gave way to it and
were driven along. 16As we passed to the
lee of a small island called Cauda, we
were hardly able to make the lifeboat secure. 17When the men had hoisted it
aboard, they passed ropes under the
ship itself to hold it together. Fearing
that they would run aground[g] on the
sandbars of Syrtis, they lowered the sea
anchor and let the ship be driven along.
18We took such a violent battering from
the storm that the next day they began
to throw the cargo overboard.[h] 19On the
third day, they threw the ship's tackle
overboard with their own hands.
20When neither sun nor stars appeared
for many days and the storm continued

27:4 x ver 7
27:5 y Ac 6:9
27:6 z Ac 28:11 a ver 1
27:7 b ver 4 c ver 12, 13,21
27:9 d Lev 16:29-31; 23:27-29; Nu 29:7
27:10 e ver 21
27:14 f Mk 4:37
27:17 g ver 26,39
27:18 h ver 19,38; Jnh 1:5

raging, we finally gave up all hope of being saved.
21After the men had gone a long time
without food, Paul stood up before them
and said: "Men, you should have taken
my advice[i] not to sail from Crete;[j] then
you would have spared yourselves this
damage and loss. 22But now I urge you to
keep up your courage,[k] because not one
of you will be lost; only the ship will be
destroyed. 23Last night an angel[l] of the
God whose I am and whom I serve[m]
stood beside me[n] 24and said, 'Do not be
afraid, Paul. You must stand trial before
Caesar;[o] and God has graciously given
you the lives of all who sail with you.'[p]
25So keep up your courage,[q] men, for I
have faith in God that it will happen just
as he told me.[r] 26Nevertheless, we must
run aground[s] on some island."[t]

The Shipwreck

27On the fourteenth night we were
still being driven across the Adriatic[b]
Sea, when about midnight the sailors
sensed they were approaching land.
28They took soundings and found that
the water was a hundred and twenty
feet[c] deep. A short time later they took
soundings again and found it was ninety feet[d] deep. 29Fearing that we would be
dashed against the rocks, they dropped
four anchors from the stern and prayed
for daylight. 30In an attempt to escape
from the ship, the sailors let the lifeboat[u]
down into the sea, pretending they were
going to lower some anchors from the
bow. 31Then Paul said to the centurion
and the soldiers, "Unless these men stay
with the ship, you cannot be saved."[v]
32So the soldiers cut the ropes that held
the lifeboat and let it fall away.
33Just before dawn Paul urged them
all to eat. "For the last fourteen days," he
said, "you have been in constant suspense and have gone without food—you
haven't eaten anything. 34Now I urge you
to take some food. You need it to survive. Not one of you will lose a single hair
from his head."[w] 35After he said this, he
took some bread and gave thanks to
God in front of them all. Then he broke
it[x] and began to eat. 36They were all en-

27:21 i ver 10 j ver 7
27:22 k ver 25,36
27:23 l Ac 5:19 m Ro 1:9 n Ac 18:9; 23:11; 2Ti 4:17
27:24 o Ac 23:11 p ver 44
27:25 q ver 22,36 r Ro 4:20,21
27:26 s ver 17,39 t Ac 28:1
27:30 u ver 16
27:31 v ver 24
27:34 w Mt 10:30
27:35 x Mt 14:19

[a] 9 That is, the Day of Atonement (Yom Kippur)
[b] 27 In ancient times the name referred to an area extending well south of Italy.
[c] 28 Greek *twenty orguias* (about 37 meters)
[d] 28 Greek *fifteen orguias* (about 27 meters)

27:36 [y] ver 22,25 couraged[y] and ate some food themselves. 37Altogether there were 276 of us
on board. 38When they had eaten as
27:38 much as they wanted, they lightened the
[z] ver 18; Jnh 1:5 ship by throwing the grain into the sea.[z]
39When daylight came, they did not
recognize the land, but they saw a bay
27:39 [a] Ac 28:1 with a sandy beach,[a] where they decided to run the ship aground if they could.
27:40 [b] ver 29 40Cutting loose the anchors,[b] they left
them in the sea and at the same time
untied the ropes that held the rudders.
Then they hoisted the foresail to the
wind and made for the beach. 41But the
ship struck a sandbar and ran aground.
The bow stuck fast and would not move,
and the stern was broken to pieces by
27:41 [c] 2Co 11:25 the pounding of the surf.[c]
42The soldiers planned to kill the prisoners to prevent any of them from
swimming away and escaping. 43But the
27:43 [d] ver 3 centurion wanted to spare Paul's life[d]
and kept them from carrying out their
plan. He ordered those who could swim
to jump overboard first and get to land.
44The rest were to get there on planks or
on pieces of the ship. In this way every-
27:44 [e] ver 22,31 one reached land in safety.[e]

Ashore on Malta

28:1 [f] Ac 16:10 [g] Ac 27:26,39 **28** Once safely on shore, we[f] found
out that the island[g] was called
Malta. 2The islanders showed us unusual kindness. They built a fire and welcomed us all because it was raining and
cold. 3Paul gathered a pile of brushwood
and, as he put it on the fire, a viper, driv-
en out by the heat, fastened itself on his
28:4 hand. 4When the islanders saw the
[h] Mk 16:18 snake hanging from his hand,[h] they said
[i] Lk 13:2,4 to each other, "This man must be a murderer; for though he escaped from the
sea, Justice has not allowed him to live."[i]
5But Paul shook the snake off into the
28:5 [j] Lk 10:19 fire and suffered no ill effects.[j] 6The people expected him to swell up or sudden-
ly fall dead, but after waiting a long time
and seeing nothing unusual happen to
him, they changed their minds and said
28:6 [k] Ac 14:11 he was a god.[k]
7There was an estate nearby that belonged to Publius, the chief official of the
island. He welcomed us to his home and
for three days entertained us hospitably.
8His father was sick in bed, suffering
from fever and dysentery. Paul went in to
28:8 [l] Jas 5:14,15 see him and, after prayer,[l] placed his

> **YOU CAN LAUGH AT CHRISTIANITY; YOU CAN MOCK AND RIDICULE IT. BUT IT WORKS. A RELATIONSHIP WITH JESUS CHRIST CHANGES LIVES.**
>
> 
>
> Josh McDowell, *Christian Apologist*

hands on him and healed him.[m] 9When 28:8 [m] Ac 9:40
this had happened, the rest of the sick on
the island came and were cured. 10They
honored us in many ways and when we
were ready to sail, they furnished us with
the supplies we needed.

Arrival at Rome

11After three months we put out to
sea in a ship that had wintered in the is-
land. It was an Alexandrian ship[n] with 28:11 [n] Ac 27:6
the figurehead of the twin gods Castor
and Pollux. 12We put in at Syracuse and
stayed there three days. 13From there we
set sail and arrived at Rhegium. The
next day the south wind came up, and
on the following day we reached Puteo-
li. 14There we found some brothers[o] who 28:14 [o] Ac 1:16
invited us to spend a week with them.
And so we came to Rome. 15The broth-
ers[p] there had heard that we were com- 28:15 [p] Ac 1:16
ing, and they traveled as far as the Fo-
rum of Appius and the Three Taverns to
meet us. At the sight of these men Paul
thanked God and was encouraged.
16When we got to Rome, Paul was allowed to live by himself, with a soldier to
guard him.[q] 28:16 [q] Ac 24:23; 27:3

Paul Preaches at Rome Under Guard

17Three days later he called together
the leaders of the Jews.[r] When they had 28:17 [r] Ac 25:2
assembled, Paul said to them: "My [s] Ac 22:5
brothers,[s] although I have done nothing [t] Ac 25:8 [u] Ac 6:14
against our people[t] or against the cus-
toms of our ancestors,[u] I was arrested in
Jerusalem and handed over to the Ro-
mans. 18They examined me[v] and want- 28:18 [v] Ac 22:24
ed to release me,[w] because I was not [w] Ac 26:31,32
guilty of any crime deserving death.[x] [x] Ac 23:9
19But when the Jews objected, I was
compelled to appeal to Caesar[y]—not 28:19 [y] Ac 25:11
that I had any charge to bring against
my own people. 20For this reason I have
asked to see you and talk with you. It is
because of the hope of Israel[z] that I am 28:20 [z] Ac 26:6,7
bound with this chain."[a] [a] Ac 21:33

[21]They replied, "We have not received
any letters from Judea concerning you,
28:21 b Ac 22:5 and none of the brothers[b] who have
come from there has reported or said
anything bad about you. [22]But we want
to hear what your views are, for we know
that people everywhere are talking
28:22 c Ac 24:5,14 against this sect."[c]

[23]They arranged to meet Paul on a certain day, and came in even larger numbers to the place where he was staying. From morning till evening he explained and declared to them the kingdom of
God[d] and tried to convince them about 28:23 d Ac 19:8
Jesus[e] from the Law of Moses and from e Ac 17:3
the Prophets.[f] [24]Some were convinced by f Ac 8:35
what he said, but others would not be-
lieve.[g] [25]They disagreed among them- 28:24 g Ac 14:4
selves and began to leave after Paul had
made this final statement: "The Holy
Spirit spoke the truth to your forefathers
when he said through Isaiah the prophet:

[26]" 'Go to this people and say,
"You will be ever hearing but never understanding;
you will be ever seeing but never perceiving."
[27]For this people's heart has become calloused;[h] 28:27 h Ps 119:70
they hardly hear with their ears, i Isa 6:9,10
and they have closed their eyes.
Otherwise they might see with their eyes,
hear with their ears,
understand with their hearts
and turn, and I would heal them.'[a][i]

[28]"Therefore I want you to know that 28:28
God's salvation[j] has been sent to the j Lk 2:30
Gentiles,[k] and they will listen!"[b] k Ac 13:46

[30]For two whole years Paul stayed
there in his own rented house and welcomed all who came to see him. [31]Bold-
ly and without hindrance he preached 28:31
the kingdom of God[l] and taught about l ver 23; Mt 4:23
the Lord Jesus Christ.

[a] 27 Isaiah 6:9,10 [b] 28 Some manuscripts *listen!" [29]After he said this, the Jews left, arguing vigorously among themselves.*

AN UNCHANGING MESSAGE

Paul's final days as a teacher and "missionary" were quite different from his earlier years. Since he was under house arrest, he could not travel. However, God knew what he was doing. Paul was confined in Rome at a time when people everywhere were talking about "this sect" (Acts 28:22), so Paul simply waited for God to bring people to him. To the very end of his life, the apostle talked with people about his devotion to Jesus and tried to convince them that what he was saying was true (verse 23). For more than 30 years, Paul's message never changed: He was still convinced that Jesus was God's promised Messiah, God the Son, and that he came as a man to die in our place and then came back to life so that we could have a relationship with our Creator. Almost single-handedly, Paul saturated the entire Roman empire with God's truth about Jesus.

Romans

What does the resurrection prove? (Romans 1:4)

- *The resurrection proves that Jesus is who he claimed to be and that his promises are reliable: He said he would rise from the dead, and he did. In the resurrection, Jesus defeated death and introduced a whole new order of existence, a brand-new creation.*

How does grace—more than law—free us from sin? (Romans 6:14)

- *The law reveals God's standard but does not provide the spiritual power to measure up to that standard. Grace cancels out our sin and allows us to start over with a clean slate. Grace also brings us into a relationship with Jesus and permits us to look to him for the strength necessary to live a righteous life.*

How close is Jesus' return?

- *Paul and other New Testament writers taught that Jesus would come again "soon"—from a prophetic perspective, that is. This perspective isn't concerned with when things will happen as much as with what will happen. From this perspective, the next event is the coming of Jesus.*

Jesus in Romans If you desire spiritual renewal you would do well to read Romans. This book offers one of the clearest expressions of Christian belief in the entire Bible, covering the major issues—faith and deeds, law and grace—in lively, practical terms.

Romans follows a logical progression. Its preliminary chapters introduce the book and point out the need for the gospel message of repentance and salvation through the atoning death of Jesus. Paul presented the gospel in a concise form at the end of chapter 3 and used chapters 4 and 5 to expand on that core message.

Paul then moved on to a thorough discussion of the gospel's work in a Christian's life. Note his vital teaching on faith and his major themes of grace, righteousness and justification in chapters 6—8. A brief history of the Jews presented in chapters 9—11 links Paul's analytical presentation to the Old Testament. In chapters 12—13 you'll discover practical implications of faith—how faith works out in everyday life.

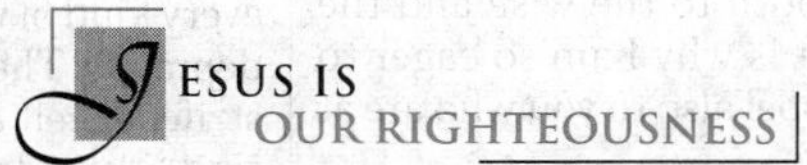
JESUS IS
OUR RIGHTEOUSNESS

1:1 1 Paul, a servant of Christ Jesus,
a 1Co 1:1 called to be an apostle[a] and set
b Ac 9:15 apart[b] for the gospel of God[c]— [2]the
c 2Co 11:7 gospel he promised beforehand through
1:2 his prophets in the Holy Scriptures[d] [3]re-
d Gal 3:8 garding his Son, who as to his human
1:3 nature[e] was a descendant of David, [4]and
e Jn 1:14 who through the Spirit[a] of holiness was
declared with power to be the Son of
God[b] by his resurrection from the dead:
Jesus Christ our Lord. [5]Through him
and for his name's sake, we received
grace and apostleship to call people
1:5 f Ac 9:15 from among all the Gentiles[f] to the obe-
g Ac 6:7 dience that comes from faith.[g] [6]And you
also are among those who are called to
1:6 h Rev 17:14 belong to Jesus Christ.[h]

1:7 [7]To all in Rome who are loved by God[i]
i Ro 8:39 j 1Co 1:3 and called to be saints:

Grace and peace to you from God our
Father and from the Lord Jesus Christ.[j]

Paul's Longing to Visit Rome

1:8 [8]First, I thank my God through Jesus
k 1Co 1:4 Christ for all of you,[k] because your faith
l Ro 16:19 is being reported all over the world.[l]
1:9 [9]God, whom I serve[m] with my whole
m 2Ti 1:3 n Php 1:8 heart in preaching the gospel of his Son,
is my witness[n] how constantly I remem-
ber you [10]in my prayers at all times; and I
pray that now at last by God's will the way
1:10 o Ro 15:32 may be opened for me to come to you.[o]
1:11 [11]I long to see you[p] so that I may im-
p Ro 15:23 part to you some spiritual gift to make
you strong— [12]that is, that you and I
may be mutually encouraged by each
other's faith. [13]I do not want you to be
unaware, brothers, that I planned many
times to come to you (but have been
1:13 q Ro 15:22,23 prevented from doing so until now)[q] in
order that I might have a harvest among
you, just as I have had among the other
Gentiles.

1:14 [14]I am obligated[r] both to Greeks and
r 1Co 9:16 non-Greeks, both to the wise and the
foolish. [15]That is why I am so eager to
1:15 preach the gospel also to you who are at
s Ro 15:20 Rome.[s]

1:16 [16]I am not ashamed of the gospel,[t] be-
t 2Ti 1:8 u 1Co 1:18 cause it is the power of God[u] for the sal-
v Ac 3:26 vation of everyone who believes: first for
w Ro 2:9,10 the Jew,[v] then for the Gentile.[w] [17]For in
1:17 the gospel a righteousness from God is
x Ro 3:21 revealed,[x] a righteousness that is by
y Hab 2:4; Gal 3:11; faith from first to last,[c] just as it is writ-
Heb 10:38 ten: "The righteous will live by faith."[d][y]

God's Wrath Against Mankind

[18]The wrath of God[z] is being revealed 1:18
from heaven against all the godlessness z Eph 5:6; Col 3:6
and wickedness of men who suppress
the truth by their wickedness, [19]since
what may be known about God is plain
to them, because God has made it plain 1:19
to them.[a] [20]For since the creation of the a Ac 14:17
world God's invisible qualities—his eter-
nal power and divine nature—have been
clearly seen, being understood from
what has been made,[b] so that men are 1:20 b Ps 19:1-6
without excuse.

[21]For although they knew God, they
neither glorified him as God nor gave
thanks to him, but their thinking became futile and their foolish hearts were 1:21
darkened.[c] [22]Although they claimed to c Jer 2:5; Eph 4:17,18
be wise, they became fools[d] [23]and ex-
changed the glory of the immortal God 1:22 d 1Co 1:20,27
for images[e] made to look like mortal
man and birds and animals and reptiles. 1:23 e Ps 106:20;
[24]Therefore God gave them over[f] in Jer 2:11;
the sinful desires of their hearts to sexu- Ac 17:29
al impurity for the degrading of their 1:24
bodies with one another.[g] [25]They ex- f Eph 4:19 g 1Pe 4:3
changed the truth of God for a lie,[h] and
worshiped and served created things[i] 1:25 h Isa 44:20
rather than the Creator—who is forever i Jer 10:14
praised.[j] Amen. j Ro 9:5

[26]Because of this, God gave them 1:26
over[k] to shameful lusts.[l] Even their k ver 24,28 l 1Th 4:5
women exchanged natural relations for m Lev 18:22,23
unnatural ones.[m] [27]In the same way the
men also abandoned natural relations
with women and were inflamed with
lust for one another. Men committed indecent acts with other men, and received in themselves the due penalty for 1:27
their perversion.[n] n Lev 18:22; 20:13

[28]Furthermore, since they did not
think it worthwhile to retain the knowl-
edge of God, he gave them over[o] to a de- 1:28 o ver 24,26
praved mind, to do what ought not to be
done. [29]They have become filled with
every kind of wickedness, evil, greed and
depravity. They are full of envy, murder,
strife, deceit and malice. They are gos-
sips,[p] [30]slanderers, God-haters, insolent, 1:29 p 2Co 12:20
arrogant and boastful; they invent ways
of doing evil; they disobey their par- 1:30
ents;[q] [31]they are senseless, faithless, q 2Ti 3:2
heartless,[r] ruthless. [32]Although they 1:31
know God's righteous decree that those r 2Ti 3:3

[a] 4 Or *who as to his spirit* [b] 4 Or *was appointed to be the Son of God with power* [c] 17 Or *is from faith to faith* [d] 17 Hab. 2:4

DISCOVERY 301

JESUS CHRIST, OUR LORD

The opening sentence of the book of Romans comprises the longest introduction in any of Paul's letters. It is 72 words in length and provides an excellent definition of Paul's ministry. In it he included three statements to describe his focus:

The gospel minister. Paul began by describing himself. He was, above all else, a "servant of Christ Jesus" (Romans 1:1). The word he used for "servant," *doulos*, may also be translated "slave." He was acknowledging that his life was entirely at the disposal of Jesus Christ, the One to whom he completely belonged. Next he referred to himself as an "apostle," a word that means "one who is sent." He recognized that God had sent him on a mission as a representative of Jesus and emphasized that he wanted to do everything possible to complete this mission. Paul was "set apart for the gospel of God," driven by one consuming objective: He was bent on using every available means and opportunity to reach every possible person with the Good News about Jesus (1 Corinthians 9:19–27).

The gospel message. In the second verse Paul described the message God had given him. It was not a new message or one that was constantly changing. The Old Testament from start to finish tells about the way in which God extends grace to us through Jesus after we have turned away from him. Beginning with the first promise of salvation (Genesis 3:15), the entire Hebrew Scripture points ahead to the coming Messiah (Luke 24:27,44). In fact, there are more than 300 specific predictions in the Old Testament about Jesus. The gospel is not about a theological concept; it is about a person—"regarding his Son" (Romans 1:3). The gospel is the Good News about *Jesus*, "a descendant of David," yet so much more than a human being in a line of royalty. Jesus was "declared with power to be the Son of God by his resurrection from the dead" (verse 4). It is the fact that Jesus came back to life that sets him apart from all other religious leaders. His resurrection is the final proof that he is God the Son, and it is the foundation of our faith (1 Corinthians 15:12–19).

Finally, Paul wrapped up his lengthy opening sentence with a triumphant declaration: *Jesus Christ is our Lord* (Romans 1:4). Each one of those four words is significant:

Jesus means "the LORD saves" (Matthew 1:20–21).

Christ means "the Anointed One," God's promised Messiah (John 7:25–43).

Our designates that the relationship is personal (Romans 1:16–17).

Lord signifies one's owner, master or ruler (Luke 6:46–49).

Each of us needs to identify exactly what Jesus means to us. He wants to be more than just our Savior—he wants to be Lord of every area in our lives. When we set apart Jesus Christ as Lord (1 Peter 3:15), we will hear Paul's exhortation joyfully and respond with a deep commitment: "So then, just as you received Christ Jesus as Lord, continue to live in him, rooted and built up in him, strengthened in the faith as you were taught, and overflowing with thanksgiving" (Colossians 2:6–7).

Self-Discovery: *In what ways do you see yourself as having been "set apart for the gospel of God"? Does this acknowledgment of the seriousness of your calling as a Christian affect your attitude with respect to your responsibility to God and those around you?*

GO TO DISCOVERY 302 ON PAGE 1513

1:32 [s]Ro 6:23 who do such things deserve death,[s] they
[t]Ps 50:18; not only continue to do these very
Lk 11:48; things but also approve[t] of those who
Ac 8:1; 22:20 practice them.

God's Righteous Judgment

2:1 **2** You, therefore, have no excuse,[u]
[u]Ro 1:20 you who pass judgment on some-
[v]2Sa 12:5-7; Mt 7:1,2 one else, for at whatever point you judge
the other, you are condemning yourself,
because you who pass judgment do the
same things.[v] 2Now we know that God's
judgment against those who do such
things is based on truth. 3So when you,
a mere man, pass judgment on them
and yet do the same things, do you think
2:4 you will escape God's judgment? 4Or do
[w]Ro 9:23; you show contempt for the riches[w] of
Eph 1:7,18; 2:7 [x]Ro 11:22 his kindness,[x] tolerance[y] and patience,[z]
[y]Ro 3:25 [z]Ex 34:6 not realizing that God's kindness leads
[a]2Pe 3:9 you toward repentance?[a]
5But because of your stubbornness
and your unrepentant heart, you are
storing up wrath against yourself for
the day of God's wrath, when his righ-
2:5 [b]Jude 6 teous judgment[b] will be revealed. 6God
"will give to each person according to
2:6 what he has done."[a][c] 7To those who by
[c]Ps 62:12; persistence in doing good seek glory,
Mt 16:27 honor[d] and immortality,[e] he will give
2:7 eternal life. 8But for those who are self-
[d]ver 10 [e]1Co 15:53,54 seeking and who reject the truth and
2:8 follow evil,[f] there will be wrath and
[f]2Th 2:12 anger. 9There will be trouble and distress for every human being who does
2:9 evil: first for the Jew, then for the Gen-
[g]1Pe 4:17 tile;[g] 10but glory, honor and peace for
2:10 everyone who does good: first for the
[h]ver 9 Jew, then for the Gentile.[h] 11For God
2:11 does not show favoritism.[i]
[i]Ac 10:34 12All who sin apart from the law will
2:12 also perish apart from the law, and all
[j]Ro 3:19; who sin under the law[j] will be judged by
1Co 9:20,21 the law. 13For it is not those who hear the
law who are righteous in God's sight, but
2:13 it is those who obey[k] the law who will be
[k]Jas 1:22,23,25 declared righteous. 14(Indeed, when
Gentiles, who do not have the law, do by
2:14 [l]Ac 10:35 nature things required by the law,[l] they
are a law for themselves, even though
they do not have the law, 15since they
show that the requirements of the law
are written on their hearts, their consciences also bearing witness, and their
thoughts now accusing, now even defending them.) 16This will take place on
the day when God will judge men's se-
crets[m] through Jesus Christ,[n] as my 2:16 [m]Ecc 12:14
gospel[o] declares. [n]Ac 10:42 [o]Ro 16:25

The Jews and the Law

17Now you, if you call yourself a Jew; if
you rely on the law and brag about your 2:17
relationship to God;[p] 18if you know his [p]ver 23;
will and approve of what is superior be- Mic 3:11; Ro 9:4
cause you are instructed by the law; 19if
you are convinced that you are a guide
for the blind, a light for those who are in
the dark, 20an instructor of the foolish, a
teacher of infants, because you have in
the law the embodiment of knowledge
and truth— 21you, then, who teach others, do you not teach yourself? You who
preach against stealing, do you steal?[q] 2:21 [q]Mt 23:3,4
22You who say that people should not
commit adultery, do you commit adultery? You who abhor idols, do you rob 2:22
temples?[r] 23You who brag about the [r]Ac 19:37
law,[s] do you dishonor God by breaking 2:23
the law? 24As it is written: "God's name [s]ver 17
is blasphemed among the Gentiles be- 2:24
cause of you."[b][t] [t]Isa 52:5; Eze 36:22
25Circumcision has value if you observe the law,[u] but if you break the law, 2:25
you have become as though you had not [u]Gal 5:3 [v]Jer 4:4
been circumcised.[v] 26If those who are not
circumcised keep the law's require- 2:26
ments,[w] will they not be regarded as [w]Ro 8:4
though they were circumcised?[x] 27The [x]1Co 7:19
one who is not circumcised physically 2:27
and yet obeys the law will condemn you[y] [y]Mt 12:41,42
who, even though you have the[c] written
code and circumcision, are a lawbreaker. 2:28
28A man is not a Jew if he is only one [z]Mt 3:9; Jn 8:39;
outwardly,[z] nor is circumcision merely Ro 9:6,7
outward and physical.[a] 29No, a man is a [a]Gal 6:15
Jew if he is one inwardly; and circumci- 2:29
sion is circumcision of the heart, by the [b]Php 3:3; Col 2:11 [c]Ro 7:6
Spirit,[b] not by the written code.[c] Such a [d]Jn 5:44;
man's praise is not from men, but from 1Co 4:5; 2Co 10:18;
God.[d] 1Th 2:4; 1Pe 3:4

God's Faithfulness

3 What advantage, then, is there in
being a Jew, or what value is there 3:2
in circumcision? 2Much in every way! [e]Dt 4:8;
First of all, they have been entrusted Ps 147:19
with the very words of God.[e] 3:3
3What if some did not have faith?[f] [f]Heb 4:2 [g]2Ti 2:13
Will their lack of faith nullify God's faith- 3:4
fulness?[g] 4Not at all! Let God be true,[h] [h]Jn 3:33
and every man a liar.[i] As it is written: [i]Ps 116:11

[a]*6* Psalm 62:12; Prov. 24:12 [b]*24* Isaiah 52:5; Ezek. 36:22 [c]*27* Or *who, by means of a*

Gentle Jesus, Righteous Judge

Church school teachers frequently portray God's Son as "gentle Jesus, meek and mild." And he certainly is! He wanted children to spend time with him even though the disciples perceived them as a nuisance (Mark 10:13–16). Jesus was indeed tender and compassionate, the kind of person we all admire and want to spend time with. But he is also the Judge of all of the earth (James 5:9; Jude 15). Paul clearly stated in Romans 2:16 that "God will judge men's secrets through Jesus Christ." It is undeniably tempting to forget this dimension of our Lord's character in favor of the side that is comforting and agreeable. But God's justice is in reality a source of comfort when we come to understand it properly:

1. God has entrusted judgment to Jesus and has given him authority to judge. In John 5:22–23 Jesus himself declared, "The Father judges no one, but has entrusted all judgment to the Son, that all may honor the Son just as they honor the Father." When Jesus informed the Jewish people that he was the One who would judge the earth, they were incensed. They believed that all judgment had to be enacted by God the Father and saw Jesus as presumptuous, even blasphemous, in trying to elevate himself to the same status as the Father.

2. Jesus' judgment will be fair. In our Lord's own words, "I judge only as I hear, and my judgment is just, for I seek not to please myself but him who sent me" (John 5:30). In the end, our Lord will hold every one of us accountable for adhering to God's standard of absolute truth (Romans 2:2). But Jesus is a unique judge, because he is also the Savior of all who are guilty of failing to measure up to that perfect standard. Although he has been appointed by God to judge the living and the dead, he is also the One who forgives our sins (Acts 10:42–43).

3. No one can avoid his judgment. There will be a specific day on which Jesus will come back, and all of humanity will be compelled to answer for what we have done with our lives (Romans 2:16; 1 Corinthians 3:12–15; 4:5). The writer of Hebrews described that event as a day of destiny that is as certain as the day of death (Hebrews 9:27).

4. No secret sins can be withheld from him. Every clandestine deed will be revealed; every thought, action and motive will be exposed: "This will take place on the day when God will judge men's secrets through Jesus Christ" (Romans 2:16).

5. There will be no acceptable excuses. God has made his expectations categorically clear. But the Father himself has provided a way of escape—through his Son Jesus. Jesus himself spoke these words of promise in John 5:24: "Whoever hears my word and believes him who sent me has eternal life and will not be condemned; he has crossed over from death to life."

The only way to avoid the repercussions of God's judgment is to accept that Jesus died in our place. If we choose to reject him, we will face our Maker on our own merit and receive the just punishment for our own sin.

Self-Discovery: *Have you ever been afraid of the final judgment? What resources has God made available to you to allay your fears? Is this issue resolved in your mind?*

GO TO DISCOVERY 303 ON PAGE 1517

"So that you may be proved right
3:4 when you speak
[j]Ps 51:4 and prevail when you judge."[a][j]

5 But if our unrighteousness brings
out God's righteousness more clearly,
what shall we say? That God is unjust in
3:5 bringing his wrath on us? (I am using a
[k]Ro 6:19; Gal 3:15 human argument.)[k] 6 Certainly not! If
that were so, how could God judge the
3:6 world?[l] 7 Someone might argue, "If my
[l]Ge 18:25 falsehood enhances God's truthfulness
3:7 and so increases his glory,[m] why am I
[m]ver 4 still condemned as a sinner?" 8 Why not
say—as we are being slanderously reported as saying and as some claim that
we say—"Let us do evil that good may
3:8 result"?[n] Their condemnation is de-
[n]Ro 6:1 served.

No One Is Righteous

9 What shall we conclude then? Are
we any better[b]? Not at all! We have already made the charge that Jews and
3:9 Gentiles alike are all under sin.[o] 10 As it is
[o]ver 19,23; Gal 3:22 written:

"There is no one righteous, not
even one;
11 there is no one who understands,
no one who seeks God.
12 All have turned away,
they have together become
worthless;
there is no one who does good,
not even one."[c][p] 3:12 [p]Ps 14:1-3
13 "Their throats are open graves;
their tongues practice deceit."[d][q] 3:13 [q]Ps 5:9
"The poison of vipers is on their [r]Ps 140:3
lips."[e][r]
14 "Their mouths are full of cursing 3:14
and bitterness."[f][s] [s]Ps 10:7
15 "Their feet are swift to shed blood;
16 ruin and misery mark their ways,
17 and the way of peace they do not
know."[g]
18 "There is no fear of God before 3:18
their eyes."[h][t] [t]Ps 36:1

19 Now we know that whatever the law 3:19
says,[u] it says to those who are under the [u]Jn 10:34
law,[v] so that every mouth may be si- [v]Ro 2:12
lenced and the whole world held accountable to God. 20 Therefore no one
will be declared righteous in his sight by 3:20
observing the law;[w] rather, through the [w]Ac 13:39;
law we become conscious of sin.[x] Gal 2:16 [x]Ro 7:7

THIS IS THE MYSTERY OF THE RICHES OF DIVINE GRACE FOR SINNERS; FOR BY A WONDERFUL EXCHANGE OUR SINS ARE NOW NOT OURS BUT CHRIST'S, AND CHRIST'S RIGHTEOUSNESS IS NOT CHRIST'S BUT OURS.

Martin Luther, *German Reformer*

Righteousness Through Faith

21 But now a righteousness from God,[y] 3:21
apart from law, has been made known, to [y]Ro 1:17; 9:30
which the Law and the Prophets testify.[z] [z]Ac 10:43
22 This righteousness from God comes
through faith[a] in Jesus Christ to all who 3:22
believe. There is no difference,[b] 23 for all [a]Ro 9:30
have sinned and fall short of the glory of [b]Ro 10:12;
God, 24 and are justified freely by his Gal 3:28; Col 3:11
grace[c] through the redemption[d] that 3:24
came by Christ Jesus. 25 God presented [c]Ro 4:16;
him as a sacrifice of atonement,[i][e] Eph 2:8
through faith in his blood.[f] He did this to [d]Eph 1:7,14;
demonstrate his justice, because in his Col 1:14; Heb 9:12
forbearance he had left the sins commit- 3:25
ted beforehand unpunished[g]— 26 he did [e]1Jn 4:10
it to demonstrate his justice at the pres- [f]Heb 9:12,14 [g]Ac 17:30

[a] 4 Psalm 51:4 [b] 9 Or *worse* [c] 12 Psalms 14:1-3; 53:1-3; Eccles. 7:20 [d] 13 Psalm 5:9 [e] 13 Psalm 140:3 [f] 14 Psalm 10:7 [g] 17 Isaiah 59:7,8 [h] 18 Psalm 36:1 [i] 25 Or *as the one who would turn aside his wrath, taking away sin*

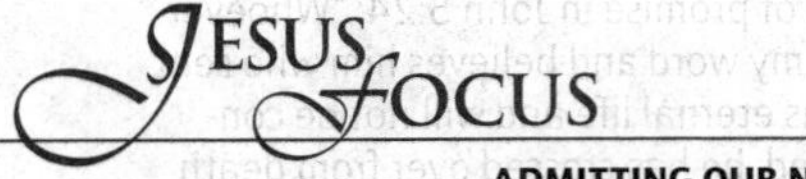

ADMITTING OUR NEED

Francis Schaeffer (1912–1984), a theologian and a philosopher, once stated: "If I had an hour to share my faith with someone, I'd spend 45 minutes convincing them that they were lost." As humans, we just don't like to admit that there is something wrong deep within our souls. But until we acknowledge our need for help, we won't look for that assistance. Paul spent the first several pages of his letter describing how badly people need someone to rescue them from their sins and concluding that "there is no one righteous, not even one" (Romans 3:10). Our only hope is in Jesus, God's own Son, who came to earth to die in our place so that we might have a relationship with the Father (verses 24–25). Only when we are honest with ourselves about our sinful state will we be ready to accept Jesus' work on our behalf and respond in lives of grateful service.

ent time, so as to be just and the one who
justifies those who have faith in Jesus.
3:27 [h] Ro 2:17,23; 4:2; 1Co 1:29-31; Eph 2:9 27 Where, then, is boasting?[h] It is excluded. On what principle? On that of
observing the law? No, but on that of
faith. 28 For we maintain that a man is
justified by faith apart from observing
3:28 [i] ver 20,21; Ac 13:39; Eph 2:9 the law.[i] 29 Is God the God of Jews only?
Is he not the God of Gentiles too? Yes, of
Gentiles too,[j] 30 since there is only one
3:29 [j] Ro 9:24 God, who will justify the circumcised by
faith and the uncircumcised through
3:30 [k] Gal 3:8 that same faith.[k] 31 Do we, then, nullify
the law by this faith? Not at all! Rather,
we uphold the law.

Abraham Justified by Faith

4 What then shall we say that Abraham, our forefather, discovered in
this matter? 2 If, in fact, Abraham was
justified by works, he had something to
4:2 [l] 1Co 1:31 boast about—but not before God.[l]
3 What does the Scripture say? "Abraham
4:3 [m] ver 5,9,22; Ge 15:6; Gal 3:6; Jas 2:23 believed God, and it was credited to him
as righteousness."[a][m]
4 Now when a man works, his wages
4:4 [n] Ro 11:6 are not credited to him as a gift,[n] but as
an obligation. 5 However, to the man who
does not work but trusts God who justifies the wicked, his faith is credited as
righteousness. 6 David says the same
thing when he speaks of the blessedness
of the man to whom God credits righteousness apart from works:

7 "Blessed are they
whose transgressions are
forgiven,
whose sins are covered.
8 Blessed is the man
4:8 [o] Ps 32:1,2; 2Co 5:19 whose sin the Lord will never
count against him."[b][o]

9 Is this blessedness only for the circumcised, or also for the uncircum-
4:9 [p] Ro 3:30 [q] ver 3 cised?[p] We have been saying that Abraham's faith was credited to him as
righteousness.[q] 10 Under what circumstances was it credited? Was it after he
was circumcised, or before? It was not
after, but before! 11 And he received the
sign of circumcision, a seal of the righteousness that he had by faith while he
4:11 [r] Ge 17:10,11 [s] ver 16,17; Lk 19:9 [t] Ro 3:22 was still uncircumcised.[r] So then, he is
the father[s] of all who believe[t] but have
not been circumcised, in order that righteousness might be credited to them.
12 And he is also the father of the circumcised who not only are circumcised
but who also walk in the footsteps of the
faith that our father Abraham had before he was circumcised.
13 It was not through law that Abraham and his offspring received the
promise[u] that he would be heir of the 4:13 [u] Gal 3:16,29
world,[v] but through the righteousness [v] Ge 17:4-6
that comes by faith. 14 For if those who
live by law are heirs, faith has no value
and the promise is worthless,[w] 15 because 4:14 [w] Gal 3:18
law brings wrath.[x] And where there is no
law there is no transgression.[y] 4:15 [x] Ro 7:7-25; 1Co 15:56; 2Co 3:7; Gal 3:10; Ro 7:12 [y] Ro 3:20; 7:7
16 Therefore, the promise comes by
faith, so that it may be by grace[z] and
may be guaranteed[a] to all Abraham's offspring—not only to those who are of the
law but also to those who are of the faith
of Abraham. He is the father of us all. 4:16 [z] Ro 3:24 [a] Ro 15:8
17 As it is written: "I have made you a fa-
ther of many nations."[c][b] He is our father 4:17 [b] Ge 17:5
in the sight of God, in whom he be- [c] Jn 5:21
lieved—the God who gives life[c] to the [d] Isa 48:13
dead and calls[d] things that are not[e] as [e] 1Co 1:28
though they were.
18 Against all hope, Abraham in hope
believed and so became the father of
many nations,[f] just as it had been said to 4:18 [f] ver 17 [g] Ge 15:5
him, "So shall your offspring be."[d][g]
19 Without weakening in his faith, he
faced the fact that his body was as good
as dead[h]—since he was about a hun- 4:19 [h] Heb 11:11,12
dred years old[i]—and that Sarah's womb [i] Ge 17:17

[a] 3 Gen. 15:6; also in verse 22 [b] 8 Psalm 32:1,2
[c] 17 Gen. 17:5 [d] 18 Gen. 15:5

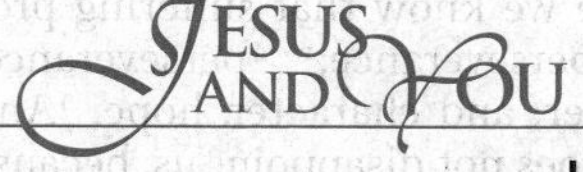

LIVING ON CREDIT

Financially, living on credit is a dangerous trap—but the spiritual situation is the exact opposite. We cannot be spiritually responsible for our own state of grace before God, because there is no possibility that we can of our own volition repair our severed relationship with God (Romans 4:13–15). Instead, God freely extends his grace to us, allowing us to live on Jesus' good credit (verses 23–25).

Abraham lived hundreds of years before God had given his law to the people through Moses, and yet Abraham belonged to God because he had put his faith in him (see Genesis 15:6; Romans 4:3,18–22). When we believe that Jesus' death has freely and totally canceled the debt that we owed God because of our sin, the Father credits us with Jesus' righteousness.

4:19 was also dead.[j] [20]Yet he did not waver
j Ge 18:11 through unbelief regarding the promise
4:20 of God, but was strengthened in his
k Mt 9:8 faith and gave glory to God,[k] [21]being ful-
4:21 ly persuaded that God had power to do
l Ge 18:14; what he had promised.[l] [22]This is why "it
Heb 11:19 was credited to him as righteousness."[m]
4:22 [23]The words "it was credited to him"
m ver 3 were written not for him alone, [24]but
4:24 also for us,[n] to whom God will credit
n Ro 15:4; 1Co 9:10; 10:11 righteousness—for us who believe in
o Ro 10:9 him[o] who raised Jesus our Lord from the
p Ac 2:24 dead.[p] [25]He was delivered over to death
4:25 for our sins[q] and was raised to life for
q Isa 53:5,6; Ro 5:6,8 our justification.

> THE SON OF GOD IS DEAD:
> AND IT IS BELIEVABLE,
> BECAUSE IT IS FOLLY. AND HAVING
> BEEN BURIED, HE ROSE
> AGAIN: IT IS CERTAIN, BECAUSE
> IT IS IMPOSSIBLE.
>
> Tertullian, *Early Church Father*

Peace and Joy

5 Therefore, since we have been jus-
5:1 tified through faith,[r] we[a] have
r Ro 3:28 peace with God through our Lord Jesus
Christ, [2]through whom we have gained
5:2 access[s] by faith into this grace in which
s Eph 2:18 t 1Co 15:1 we now stand.[t] And we[a] rejoice in the
u Heb 3:6 hope[u] of the glory of God. [3]Not only so,
5:3 but we[a] also rejoice in our sufferings,[v]
v Mt 5:12 because we know that suffering pro-
w Jas 1:2,3 duces perseverance;[w] [4]perseverance,
character; and character, hope. [5]And
5:5 hope[x] does not disappoint us, because
x Php 1:20 y Ac 2:33 God has poured out his love into our
hearts by the Holy Spirit,[y] whom he has
given us.
5:6 [6]You see, at just the right time,[z] when
z Gal 4:4 we were still powerless, Christ died for
a Ro 4:25 the ungodly.[a] [7]Very rarely will anyone
die for a righteous man, though for a
good man someone might possibly dare
5:8 to die. [8]But God demonstrates his own
b Jn 15:13; 1Pe 3:18 love for us in this: While we were still
sinners, Christ died for us.[b]
5:9 [9]Since we have now been justified by
c Ro 3:25 d Ro 1:18 his blood,[c] how much more shall we be
saved from God's wrath[d] through him!
5:10 [10]For if, when we were God's enemies,[e]
e Ro 11:28; Col 1:21 we were reconciled[f] to him through the
f 2Co 5:18,19; Col 1:20,22 death of his Son, how much more, having been reconciled, shall we be saved 5:10
through his life![g] [11]Not only is this so, g Ro 8:34
but we also rejoice in God through our
Lord Jesus Christ, through whom we
have now received reconciliation.

Death Through Adam, Life Through Christ

[12]Therefore, just as sin entered the
world through one man,[h] and death 5:12
through sin,[i] and in this way death came h ver 15,16,17; 1Co 15:21,22
to all men, because all sinned— [13]for be- i Ge 2:17; 3:19; Ro 6:23
fore the law was given, sin was in the
world. But sin is not taken into account 5:13
when there is no law.[j] [14]Nevertheless, j Ro 4:15
death reigned from the time of Adam to
the time of Moses, even over those who
did not sin by breaking a command, as
did Adam, who was a pattern of the one 5:14
to come.[k] k 1Co 15:22,45
[15]But the gift is not like the trespass.
For if the many died by the trespass of the
one man,[l] how much more did God's 5:15 l ver 12,18,19
grace and the gift that came by the grace m Ac 15:11
of the one man, Jesus Christ,[m] overflow to
the many! [16]Again, the gift of God is not
like the result of the one man's sin: The
judgment followed one sin and brought
condemnation, but the gift followed
many trespasses and brought justification. [17]For if, by the trespass of the one
man, death[n] reigned through that one 5:17 n ver 12
man, how much more will those who re-
ceive God's abundant provision of grace
and of the gift of righteousness reign in
life through the one man, Jesus Christ.

[a] 1,2,3 Or *let us*

A LOGICAL CASE

In Romans Paul built a step-by-step argument that reminds us of a legal brief. He used the word *therefore* a total of 20 times. Paul's case unfolded as follows. *Step one*: Not one of us can claim a right relationship with God (Romans 3:20). *Step two*: Only Jesus can repair our ruptured relationship with God. And he was sent by God to make peace with the Father on our behalf (Romans 5:1–2,11). *Step Three*: Finally, in Romans 5:18 the apostle began a powerful concluding statement: "Consequently, just as the result of one trespass was condemnation for all men, so also the result of one act of righteousness was justification that brings life for all men."

DISCOVERY 303

Past and Present Blessings

Paul spoke in Romans 5 about two categories of blessings. First, there are the past blessings—"we have been" (verse 1). But there are also the present blessings—"we have" (verse 11). What we have already received in the past and what we now enjoy on a daily basis have both come about through our relationship with our Savior:

Past blessings. We have been justified. The words Paul used to explain that Jesus has made us right with God imply a past and completed action, one that occurred at a specific point in time. Through Jesus' death on the cross God has already declared us righteous in his sight. This action was by grace (Romans 3:24), through Jesus' resurrection (Romans 4:25), through faith (Romans 5:1) and by Jesus' blood (verse 9).

Present blessings. Sometimes it seems as though everything God has promised will only be experienced in the distant future. But what about our everyday lives? Paul explained three ways in which God's presence in our lives blesses us right now.

First, we have peace with God the Father. We no longer have to wonder whether we are in good standing with him or whether he will direct his wrath full force at us. The word *peace* means freedom from conflict, and to have peace with God signifies that we no longer live in opposition to him. Jesus signed the peace treaty (verse 9–10), and we can now enjoy an inner tranquility and rest. As Paul stated so eloquently in Philippians 4:6–7, "Do not be anxious about anything, but in everything, by prayer and petition, with thanksgiving, present your requests to God. And the peace of God, which transcends all understanding, will guard your hearts and your minds in Christ Jesus."

Second, we experience free access to God and to his grace. After Adam and Eve had sinned they were put out of the garden, separated from God (Genesis 3:22–24). Throughout the Old Testament God related to his people from a distance. Only the high priest could enter God's presence, and he only once each year on a specified day (Leviticus 16). But through Jesus, who is Immanuel, God with us (Matthew 1:23), we are granted direct admittance into the very presence of God (Matthew 27:51). Paul invited us in Hebrews 10:19–22: "Since we have confidence to enter the Most High Place by the blood of Jesus, by a new and living way opened for us through the curtain, that is, his body, and since we have a great priest over the house of God, let us draw near to God in full assurance of faith."

Third, we can cling confidently to our hope in God. Before Jesus died for our sin, we had no prospect of salvation or of a relationship with our heavenly Father. Placing our trust in Jesus affords us the hope of eternal life and of the "glory of God" (Romans 5:2), a hope that the purpose for which we've been created will be realized and the glory we had before the fall restored. Once we have been forgiven of our sin, even tribulation and difficulty cannot rob us of this confidence (verses 3–5).

Self-Discovery: Make a listing of other present blessings you enjoy on a daily basis, making sure to include spiritual blessings. Pause to thank the Lord for each item on your list.

GO TO DISCOVERY 304 ON PAGE 1519

THE ULTIMATE ANSWER TO MOST OF OUR PROBLEMS IS A PERSONAL RELATIONSHIP WITH JESUS CHRIST.

James Dobson, *Focus on the Family, Colorado Springs, Colorado*

18Consequently, just as the result of
one trespass was condemnation for all
5:18 [o] ver 12 [p] Ro 4:25 men,[o] so also the result of one act of
righteousness was justification[p] that
brings life for all men. 19For just as
through the disobedience of the one
5:19 [q] ver 12 [r] Php 2:8 man[q] the many were made sinners, so
also through the obedience[r] of the one
man the many will be made righteous.
20The law was added so that the tres-
5:20 [s] Ro 7:7,8; Gal 3:19 [t] 1Ti 1:13,14 pass might increase.[s] But where sin increased, grace increased all the more,[t]
21so that, just as sin reigned in death,[u] so
5:21 [u] ver 12,14 also grace might reign through righteousness to bring eternal life through
Jesus Christ our Lord.

Dead to Sin, Alive in Christ

6 What shall we say, then? Shall we
go on sinning so that grace may in-
6:1 [v] ver 15; Ro 3:5,8 crease?[v] 2By no means! We died to sin;[w]
how can we live in it any longer? 3Or
6:2 [w] Col 3:3,5; 1Pe 2:24 don't you know that all of us who were
baptized[x] into Christ Jesus were baptized
6:3 [x] Mt 28:19 into his death? 4We were therefore
buried with him through baptism into
6:4 [y] Col 2:12 [z] Ro 7:6; Gal 6:15; Eph 4:22-24; Col 3:10 death in order that, just as Christ was
raised from the dead[y] through the glory
of the Father, we too may live a new life.[z]
5If we have been united with him like
this in his death, we will certainly also be
united with him in his resurrection.[a]
6:5 [a] 2Co 4:10; Php 3:10,11 6For we know that our old self[b] was crucified with him[c] so that the body of sin[d]
might be done away with,[a] that we
6:6 [b] Eph 4:22; Col 3:9 [c] Gal 2:20; Col 2:12,20 [d] Ro 7:24 should no longer be slaves to sin— 7be-
cause anyone who has died has been
freed from sin.
8Now if we died with Christ, we believe
that we will also live with him. 9For we
know that since Christ was raised from
6:9 [e] Ac 2:24 the dead,[e] he cannot die again; death no

BY HIS OWN DEATH PUTTING DEATH TO DEATH . . .

John Owen, *Puritan Pastor*

longer has mastery over him.[f] 10The 6:9 [f] Rev 1:18
death he died, he died to sin[g] once for all;
but the life he lives, he lives to God. 6:10 [g] ver 2
11In the same way, count yourselves
dead to sin[h] but alive to God in Christ 6:11 [h] ver 2
Jesus. 12Therefore do not let sin reign in
your mortal body so that you obey its
evil desires. 13Do not offer the parts of
your body to sin, as instruments of
wickedness,[i] but rather offer yourselves 6:13 [i] ver 16,19; Ro 7:5 [j] Ro 12:1; 1Pe 2:24
to God, as those who have been brought
from death to life; and offer the parts of
your body to him as instruments of
righteousness.[j] 14For sin shall not be
your master, because you are not under 6:14 [k] Gal 5:18 [l] Ro 3:24
law,[k] but under grace.[l]

NONE OF US HAS LIVED UP TO THE TEACHINGS OF CHRIST.

Eleanor Roosevelt, *American First Lady*

Slaves to Righteousness

15What then? Shall we sin because we
are not under law but under grace? By
no means! 16Don't you know that when
you offer yourselves to someone to obey
him as slaves, you are slaves to the one
whom you obey—whether you are 6:16 [m] Jn 8:34; 2Pe 2:19 [n] ver 23
slaves to sin,[m] which leads to death,[n] or
to obedience, which leads to righteous-
ness? 17But thanks be to God[o] that, 6:17 [o] Ro 1:8; 2Co 2:14 [p] 2Ti 1:13
though you used to be slaves to sin, you
wholeheartedly obeyed the form of
teaching[p] to which you were entrusted.
18You have been set free from sin[q] and 6:18 [q] ver 7,22; Ro 8:2
have become slaves to righteousness.
19I put this in human terms[r] because
you are weak in your natural selves. Just as 6:19 [r] Ro 3:5 [s] ver 13
you used to offer the parts of your body in
slavery to impurity and to ever-increasing
wickedness, so now offer them in slavery
to righteousness[s] leading to holiness.
20When you were slaves to sin,[t] you were 6:20 [t] ver 16
free from the control of righteousness.
21What benefit did you reap at that time 6:21 [u] ver 23
from the things you are now ashamed of?
Those things result in death![u] 22But now 6:22 [v] ver 18 [w] 1Co 7:22; 1Pe 2:16
that you have been set free from sin[v] and
have become slaves to God,[w] the benefit
you reap leads to holiness, and the result 6:23 [x] Ge 2:17; Ro 5:12; Gal 6:7, 8; Jas 1:15 [y] Mt 25:46
is eternal life. 23For the wages of sin is
death,[x] but the gift of God is eternal life[y]
in[b] Christ Jesus our Lord.

[a] 6 Or *be rendered powerless* [b] 23 Or *through*

The Key to Victory

We are all recovering sinners. While we have been forgiven, we are certainly not immune to the daily struggle with sin and temptation. Paul knew what the conflict was like: "What I do is not the good I want to do; no, the evil I do not want to do—this I keep on doing" (Romans 7:19). But even though we battle with sin, God has given us everything we need to overcome it (Romans 12:21; 1 John 5:4–5).

The key to victory is found in three key words: *know* (Romans 6:3,6), *count* (verse 11) and *offer* (verse 13). First, Paul was saying that we have to *know*, to comprehend and believe what is right and true. We cannot deal effectively with our sin until we are able to acknowledge its presence, to understand its implications in our lives and to access the weapons we need to combat its influence.

Accepting Jesus' once-for-all sacrifice makes us right with God the Father, but our Lord also gives us daily victory over evil. His death broke the stranglehold of sin, its controlling and dominating power over our lives (verse 2). And because Jesus came back to life again, he in turn offers us new life that will triumph over the old (verses 4,8). Death no longer holds mastery over Jesus, because he was freed from its grip forever (verse 9)—and he now extends to us the incredible benefit of enjoying the same freedom (1 Corinthians 15:54–57). We just need to know where to look for it!

Next, Paul says that we have to *count*, or consider, ourselves dead to sin, to internalize that truth, to assimilate and act upon that reality. Simply acknowledging that Jesus' death and resurrection can set us free from sin is not enough. We have to do something about it. We must refuse to allow sin to reign in our lives. We must regard ourselves as "dead to sin but alive to God in Christ Jesus" (Romans 6:11). As we acknowledge the stunning reality that we are saved from sin because Jesus died for us, we go on to live by faith in the light of this truth. We become truly alive to a new quality of life lived in intimate relationship with God.

Finally, we are called to *offer* ourselves. As we struggle with sin, we can choose to yield ourselves to the Lord. The apostle Paul urged us as believers, "in view of God's mercy, to offer [our] bodies as living sacrifices, holy and pleasing to God—this is [our] spiritual act of worship" (Romans 12:1). This means submitting to the Holy Spirit who lives within us (Ephesians 5:17–18) and who builds a Christlike character within us (Galatians 5:22–23). This yielding, this offering up of our will as subservient to the will of God, is not something we do only once. It must be an ongoing practice on our part.

Pay close attention, however, to this significant footnote. Our victory over sin is ultimately a matter of *grace*, not of rules and regulations (Romans 6:14). By his amazing grace offered through his Son Jesus, God provides all that we need to live in victory over sin.

Self-Discovery: *Are there any specific sins that at times still threaten to dominate your life? Make it a point to take this concern to God in prayer today.*

GO TO DISCOVERY 305 ON PAGE 1521

THE ATONEMENT IS THE CRUCIAL DOCTRINE OF THE FAITH. UNLESS WE ARE RIGHT HERE, IT MATTERS LITTLE WHAT WE BELIEVE ELSEWHERE.

Leon Morris, *Australian Scholar*

An Illustration From Marriage

7:1 **7** Do you not know, brothers[z]—for
[z]Ro 1:13 I am speaking to men who know
the law—that the law has authority over
a man only as long as he lives? 2For example, by law a married woman is
bound to her husband as long as he is
alive, but if her husband dies, she is re-
7:2 leased from the law of marriage.[a] 3So
[a]1Co 7:39 then, if she marries another man while
her husband is still alive, she is called an
adulteress. But if her husband dies, she
is released from that law and is not an
adulteress, even though she marries another man.
7:4 4So, my brothers, you also died to the
[b]Ro 8:2; law[b] through the body of Christ,[c] that
Gal 2:19 you might belong to another, to him
[c]Col 1:22 who was raised from the dead, in order
that we might bear fruit to God. 5For
when we were controlled by the sinful
7:5 nature,[a] the sinful passions aroused by
[d]Ro 7:7-11 the law[d] were at work in our bodies,[e] so
[e]Ro 6:13 that we bore fruit for death. 6But now, by
dying to what once bound us, we have
been released from the law so that we
7:6 serve in the new way of the Spirit, and
[f]Ro 2:29; 2Co 3:6 not in the old way of the written code.[f]

Struggling With Sin

7What shall we say, then? Is the law
sin? Certainly not! Indeed I would not
7:7 have known what sin was except
[g]Ro 3:20; 4:15 through the law.[g] For I would not have
[h]Ex 20:17; known what coveting really was if the
Dt 5:21 law had not said, "Do not covet."[b][h] 8But
7:8 sin, seizing the opportunity afforded by
[i]ver 11 the commandment,[i] produced in me
[j]Ro 4:15; every kind of covetous desire. For apart
1Co 15:56 from law, sin is dead.[j] 9Once I was alive
apart from law; but when the command-
7:10 ment came, sin sprang to life and I died.
[k]Lev 18:5; 10I found that the very commandment
Lk 10:26-28; Ro 10:5; that was intended to bring life[k] actually
Gal 3:12 brought death. 11For sin, seizing the op-
7:11 portunity afforded by the command-
[l]Ge 3:13 ment, deceived me,[l] and through the
commandment put me to death. 12So
then, the law is holy, and the command- 7:12
ment is holy, righteous and good.[m] [m]1Ti 1:8
13Did that which is good, then, become death to me? By no means! But in
order that sin might be recognized as
sin, it produced death in me through
what was good, so that through the
commandment sin might become utterly sinful.
14We know that the law is spiritual; 7:14
but I am unspiritual,[n] sold[o] as a slave to [n]1Co 3:1 [o]1Ki 21:20,25;
sin. 15I do not understand what I do. For 2Ki 17:17
what I want to do I do not do, but what I
hate I do.[p] 16And if I do what I do not 7:15 [p]ver 19;
want to do, I agree that the law is good.[q] Gal 5:17
17As it is, it is no longer I myself who do 7:16
it, but it is sin living in me.[r] 18I know that [q]ver 12
nothing good lives in me, that is, in my 7:17
sinful nature.[c][s] For I have the desire to do [r]ver 20
what is good, but I cannot carry it out. 7:18
19For what I do is not the good I want to [s]ver 25
do; no, the evil I do not want to do—this 7:19
I keep on doing.[t] 20Now if I do what I do [t]ver 15
not want to do, it is no longer I who do it, 7:20
but it is sin living in me that does it.[u] [u]ver 17
21So I find this law at work:[v] When I
want to do good, evil is right there with 7:21 [v]ver 23,25
me. 22For in my inner being[w] I delight in 7:22
God's law;[x] 23but I see another law at [w]Eph 3:16
work in the members of my body, wag- [x]Ps 1:2
ing war[y] against the law of my mind and 7:23
making me a prisoner of the law of sin at [y]Gal 5:17;
work within my members. 24What a Jas 4:1; 1Pe 2:11
wretched man I am! Who will rescue me
from this body of death?[z] 25Thanks be to 7:24 [z]Ro 6:6; 8:2
God—through Jesus Christ our Lord!
So then, I myself in my mind am a
slave to God's law, but in the sinful nature a slave to the law of sin.

Life Through the Spirit

8 Therefore, there is now no con-
demnation[a] for those who are in 8:1 [a]ver 34 [b]ver 39;
Christ Jesus,[d][b] 2because through Christ Ro 16:3

[a] 5 Or *the flesh*; also in verse 25 [b] 7 Exodus 20:17; Deut. 5:21 [c] 18 Or *my flesh* [d] 1 Some later manuscripts *Jesus, who do not live according to the sinful nature but according to the Spirit,*

CAN CHRIST BE IN THY HEART, AND THOU NOT KNOW IT? CAN ONE KING BE DETHRONED AND ANOTHER CROWNED IN THY SOUL, AND THOU HEAR NO SCUFFLE?

William Gurnall, *Puritan Pastor*

Tapping Into the Spirit's Power

Paul had a deep understanding of and intimate relationship with God and was an extraordinary teacher and theologian, but that did not afford him immunity to the daily struggle with sin. The apostle was quick to acknowledge that although he had every intention of doing what was right, he all too frequently found himself succumbing to sinful choices (Romans 7:21–23). He felt so strongly about this deficiency within himself that he referred to himself as a "wretched man" (verse 24), and on another occasion, when writing to Timothy, he called himself "the worst of sinners: (1 Timothy 1:16; see also verse 15). However, Paul quickly went on to remind himself and us of the glorious truth that "there is now no condemnation for those who are in Christ Jesus" (Romans 8:1). Through Jesus, God imparts to us the "law of the Spirit of life," which sets us free from the clutches of the law of sin and death (verse 2) and gives us the strength to live lives of humble servanthood.

When Jesus was nearing the end of his earthly life, he spoke to his disciples about his imminent departure, offering them encouragement in the coming of "the Counselor"—the third person of the holy Trinity, God the Holy Spirit (John 16:5–16). Jesus acknowledged the grief of the disciples but stressed that it was for their own good that he would be going away: "Unless I go away, the Counselor will not come to you; but if I go, I will send him to you" (John 16:7). The Savior gently advised his little band of followers that he had much more to say to them, more than they could bear at the time. "But when he, the Spirit of truth, comes, he will guide you into all truth" (John 16:12–13).

One essential key to experiencing freedom from sin is learning to live in the power of God's Holy Spirit (Romans 8:9). The Spirit plays a vitally important role in our lives, and we cannot afford to ignore him or take him for granted. He is the One who enables us to "put to death the misdeeds of the body" (verse 13), and he infuses us with power when we talk with others about Jesus (Acts 1:8). He assists us when we pray: "The Spirit helps us in our weakness. We do not know what we ought to pray for, but the Spirit himself intercedes for us with groans that words cannot express" (Romans 8:26–27). It is God the Holy Spirit who cultivates godly character in us, changing us to be the people God intends us to be (Galatians 5:22–23). It is also the Spirit who shores us up with the inner strength to endure through hard times (Ephesians 3:16).

All of the power to overcome sin and to live the way God wants us to resides in the Holy Spirit and is available to us for the asking. As we learn to tap into that source of strength, we will find the Spirit continually at work in our lives (Ephesians 5:17–18).

Self-Discovery: *In what specific ways today can you identify with Paul's struggle with sin (Romans 7:21–23)? Have you allowed Jesus to rescue you (Romans 7:24–25) by the power of his Holy Spirit? Ask him to set you free through the truth (John 8:32).*

GO TO DISCOVERY 306 ON PAGE 1523

> THERE WAS NEVER ANY OTHER WAY TO ESCAPE DEATH THAN FOR MEN TO FLEE TO CHRIST.
>
> John Calvin, *Swiss Reformer*

8:2 c1Co 15:45 Jesus the law of the Spirit of life[c] set me
d Ro 6:18 free[d] from the law of sin[e] and death. 3For
e Ro 7:4 what the law was powerless[f] to do in that
8:3 f Ac 13:39; it was weakened by the sinful nature,[a]
Heb 7:18 God did by sending his own Son in the
g Php 2:7 likeness of sinful man[g] to be a sin offer-
h Heb 2:14,17 ing.[b] [h] And so he condemned sin in sinful
man,[c] 4in order that the righteous requirements of the law might be fully met
in us, who do not live according to the
8:4 i Gal 5:16 sinful nature but according to the Spirit.[i]
5Those who live according to the sin-
ful nature have their minds set on what
8:5 that nature desires;[j] but those who live
j Gal 5:19-21 k Gal 5:22-25 in accordance with the Spirit have their
minds set on what the Spirit desires.[k]
6The mind of sinful man[d] is death, but
8:6 the mind controlled by the Spirit is life[l]
l Gal 6:8 and peace; 7the sinful mind[e] is hostile to
8:7 God.[m] It does not submit to God's law,
m Jas 4:4 nor can it do so. 8Those controlled by
the sinful nature cannot please God.
9You, however, are controlled not by
the sinful nature but by the Spirit, if the
8:9 n 1Co 6:19; Spirit of God lives in you.[n] And if anyone
Gal 4:6 does not have the Spirit of Christ,[o] he
o Jn 14:17; does not belong to Christ. 10But if Christ
1Jn 4:13 is in you,[p] your body is dead because of
8:10 sin, yet your spirit is alive because of
p Gal 2:20; righteousness. 11And if the Spirit of him
Eph 3:17; who raised Jesus from the dead[q] is living
Col 1:27 in you, he who raised Christ from the
8:11 q Ac 2:24 dead will also give life to your mortal
r Jn 5:21 bodies[r] through his Spirit, who lives in
you.
12Therefore, brothers, we have an obligation—but it is not to the sinful nature, to live according to it. 13For if you
8:13 live according to the sinful nature, you
s Gal 6:8 will die; but if by the Spirit you put to
8:14 death the misdeeds of the body, you will
t Gal 5:18 u Jn 1:12; live,[s] 14because those who are led by the
Rev 21:7 Spirit of God[t] are sons of God.[u] 15For
8:15 you did not receive a spirit that makes
v 2Ti 1:7; you a slave again to fear,[v] but you re-
Heb 2:15 w Mk 14:36; ceived the Spirit of sonship.[f] And by him
Gal 4:5,6 we cry, "*Abba*,[g] Father."[w] 16The Spirit
8:16 himself testifies with our spirit[x] that we
x Eph 1:13 are God's children. 17Now if we are chil-

dren, then we are heirs[y]—heirs of God 8:17 y Ac 20:32;
and co-heirs with Christ, if indeed we Gal 4:7
share in his sufferings in order that we z 1Pe 4:13
may also share in his glory.[z]

Future Glory

18I consider that our present sufferings are not worth comparing with the 8:18
glory that will be revealed in us.[a] 19The a 2Co 4:17;
creation waits in eager expectation for 1Pe 4:13
the sons of God to be revealed. 20For the
creation was subjected to frustration,
not by its own choice, but by the will of
the one who subjected it,[b] in hope 8:20 b Ge 3:17-19
21that[h] the creation itself will be liberated from its bondage to decay[c] and 8:21 c Ac 3:21;
brought into the glorious freedom of the 2Pe 3:13;
children of God. Rev 21:1
22We know that the whole creation 8:22
has been groaning[d] as in the pains of d Jer 12:4
childbirth right up to the present time.
23Not only so, but we ourselves, who 8:23
have the firstfruits of the Spirit,[e] groan[f] e 2Co 5:5
inwardly as we wait eagerly[g] for our f 2Co 5:2,4
adoption as sons, the redemption of our g Gal 5:5
bodies. 24For in this hope we were
saved.[h] But hope that is seen is no hope 8:24 h 1Th 5:8
at all. Who hopes for what he already
has? 25But if we hope for what we do not
yet have, we wait for it patiently.
26In the same way, the Spirit helps us
in our weakness. We do not know what
we ought to pray for, but the Spirit him- 8:26
self intercedes for us[i] with groans that i Eph 6:18
words cannot express. 27And he who 8:27
searches our hearts[j] knows the mind of j Rev 2:23
the Spirit, because the Spirit intercedes
for the saints in accordance with God's
will.

More Than Conquerors

28And we know that in all things God 8:28 k 1Co 1:9;
works for the good of those who love 2Ti 1:9
him,[i] who[j] have been called[k] according 8:29
to his purpose. 29For those God l Ro 11:2 m Eph 1:5,11
foreknew[l] he also predestined[m] to be n 1Co 15:49;
conformed to the likeness of his Son,[n] 2Co 3:18; Php 3:21;
that he might be the firstborn among 1Jn 3:2
many brothers. 30And those he predes- 8:30
tined,[o] he also called; those he called, he o Eph 1:5,11

a 3 Or *the flesh;* also in verses 4, 5, 8, 9, 12 and 13
b 3 Or *man, for sin* *c* 3 Or *in the flesh* *d* 6 Or *mind set on the flesh* *e* 7 Or *the mind set on the flesh* *f* 15 Or *adoption* *g* 15 Aramaic for *Father* *h* 20,21 Or *subjected it in hope.* 21*For*
i 28 Some manuscripts *And we know that all things work together for good to those who love God*
j 28 Or *works together with those who love him to bring about what is good—with those who*

DISCOVERY 306

When God Allows Disaster

God loves us unconditionally and eternally, and we are at all times surrounded by Jesus' love. When everything is going well in our lives we bask in the warmth of that love. But when things begin to fall apart for no apparent reason, we are sometimes forced to dig deeply for an explanation. It becomes easy to start questioning God's love. How could a loving Father allow his beloved children to suffer? That is precisely the question Paul addressed is the last part of Romans 8.

First of all, Paul pointed out, the experience of disaster in our lives and the reality of God's love are not mutually exclusive. In verse 35, in the middle of one of the most beautiful passages in all of Scripture, the apostle asked a rhetorical question: "Who shall separate us from the love of Christ? Shall trouble or hardship or persecution or famine or nakedness or danger or sword?" The obvious answer is a resounding *no*.

We can almost envision Paul pounding a podium with a beatific smile on his face as he emphasized that none of these trials can *ever* sever us from the love of Jesus (verses 35–39). And Paul was speaking from firsthand experience. He knew the dangers and disasters that were the "fringe benefits" of following Jesus (2 Corinthians 4:8–12; 11:23–29). He also recognized that hardship did not signify that God loved him any less than he had before, just as good times were not an indication that God loved him more than he already had.

Second, Paul wanted his readers to know that, even in the most trying circumstances, we are "more than conquerors " (Romans 8:37). *Conquering* doesn't mean stomping on the enemy with vigor and verve. One way to illustrate this is by visualizing a sailboat in the wind. When the sail is raised *with* the wind, the sailor has *conquered* the wind and harnessed its force. But when he raises the sail and drives *into* the wind, he has *more than conquered* the wind.

God instills within us the power to sail straight into the face of the disaster. No matter what the obstacle, God always has an overriding purpose, and it is always for our best (Romans 5:3–5). We can in fact conclude that disaster is one evidence that God *does* love us and that he is at work in our lives to produce perseverance, character and hope (Romans 5:3–4) as we share in our precious Lord's sufferings (Romans 8:17; 2 Corinthians 1:5; Philippians 3:10; 1 Peter 4:13).

Paul's ringing conclusion is well worth our taking the time to commit to memory: "For I am convinced that neither death nor life, neither angels nor demons, neither the present nor the future, nor any powers, neither height nor depth, nor anything else in all creation, will be able to separate us from the love of God that is in Christ Jesus our Lord" (Romans 8:38–39).

Self-Discovery: *What relational difficulties or looming problems are causing anxiety in your life at this moment? Formulate a question, using the following formula: "What shall separate me from the love of Christ? Shall___________? Shall______________? Then answer with a resounding no!*

GO TO DISCOVERY 307 ON PAGE 1525

8:30 [p] 1Co 6:11 [q] Ro 9:23 also justified;[p] those he justified, he also
glorified.[q]
[31]What, then, shall we say in response
8:31 [r] Ro 4:1 [s] Ps 118:6 to this?[r] If God is for us, who can be
against us?[s] [32]He who did not spare his
8:32 [t] Jn 3:16; Ro 4:25; 5:8 own Son,[t] but gave him up for us all—
how will he not also, along with him,
graciously give us all things? [33]Who will
8:33 [u] Isa 50:8,9 bring any charge[u] against those whom
God has chosen? It is God who justifies.
[34]Who is he that condemns? Christ
Jesus, who died[v]—more than that, who
was raised to life—is at the right hand of
8:34 [v] Ro 5:6-8 [w] Mk 16:19 [x] Heb 7:25; 9:24; 1Jn 2:1 God[w] and is also interceding for us.[x]
[35]Who shall separate us from the love of
Christ? Shall trouble or hardship or persecution or famine or nakedness or dan-
8:35 [y] 1Co 4:11 ger or sword?[y] [36]As it is written:

"For your sake we face death all
day long;
8:36 [z] Ps 44:22; 2Co 4:11 we are considered as sheep to be
slaughtered."[a][z]

[37]No, in all these things we are more than
8:37 [a] 1Co 15:57 [b] Gal 2:20; Rev 1:5; 3:9 conquerors[a] through him who loved us.[b]
[38]For I am convinced that neither death
nor life, neither angels nor demons,[b] nei-
8:38 [c] Eph 1:21; 1Pe 3:22 ther the present nor the future, nor any
powers,[c] [39]neither height nor depth, nor
anything else in all creation, will be able
8:39 [d] Ro 5:8 to separate us from the love of God[d] that
is in Christ Jesus our Lord.

God's Sovereign Choice

9:1 [e] 2Co 11:10; Gal 1:20; 1Ti 2:7 [f] Ro 1:9 **9** I speak the truth in Christ—I am
not lying,[e] my conscience con-
firms[f] it in the Holy Spirit— [2]I have great
sorrow and unceasing anguish in my
9:3 [g] Ex 32:32 [h] 1Co 12:3; 16:22 [i] Ro 11:14 heart. [3]For I could wish that I myself[g]
were cursed[h] and cut off from Christ for
the sake of my brothers, those of my
own race,[i] [4]the people of Israel. Theirs is
9:4 [j] Ex 4:22 [k] Ge 17:2; Ac 3:25; Eph 2:12 [l] Ps 147:19 [m] Heb 9:1 [n] Ac 13:32 the adoption as sons;[j] theirs the divine
glory, the covenants,[k] the receiving of
the law,[l] the temple worship[m] and the
promises.[n] [5]Theirs are the patriarchs,
and from them is traced the human ancestry of Christ,[o] who is God over all,[p]
9:5 [o] Mt 1:1-16 [p] Jn 1:1 [q] Ro 1:25 forever praised![c][q] Amen.
[6]It is not as though God's word had
failed. For not all who are descended
from Israel are Israel.[r] [7]Nor because they
9:6 [r] Ro 2:28,29; Gal 6:16 are his descendants are they all Abraham's children. On the contrary, "It is
through Isaac that your offspring will be
9:7 [s] Ge 21:12; Heb 11:18 reckoned."[d][s] [8]In other words, it is not
the natural children who are God's chil-
9:8 [t] Ro 8:14 dren,[t] but it is the children of the promise who are regarded as Abraham's off-
spring. [9]For this was how the promise
was stated: "At the appointed time I will
9:9 [u] Ge 18:10,14 return, and Sarah will have a son."[e][u]
[10]Not only that, but Rebekah's children
had one and the same father, our father
9:10 [v] Ge 25:21 Isaac.[v] [11]Yet, before the twins were born
or had done anything good or bad—in
9:11 [w] Ro 8:28 order that God's purpose[w] in election
might stand: [12]not by works but by him
9:12 [x] Ge 25:23 who calls—she was told, "The older will
serve the younger."[f][x] [13]Just as it is written:
9:13 [y] Mal 1:2,3 "Jacob I loved, but Esau I hated."[g][y]
[14]What then shall we say? Is God un-
9:14 [z] 2Ch 19:7 just? Not at all![z] [15]For he says to Moses,

"I will have mercy on whom I have
mercy,
and I will have compassion on
9:15 [a] Ex 33:19 whom I have compassion."[h][a]

9:16 [b] Eph 2:8 [16]It does not, therefore, depend on man's
desire or effort, but on God's mercy.[b]
[17]For the Scripture says to Pharaoh: "I

[a] *36* Psalm 44:22 [b] *38* Or *nor heavenly rulers*
[c] *5* Or *Christ, who is over all. God be forever praised!* Or *Christ. God who is over all be forever praised!*
[d] *7* Gen. 21:12 [e] *9* Gen. 18:10,14
[f] *12* Gen. 25:23 [g] *13* Mal. 1:2,3
[h] *15* Exodus 33:19

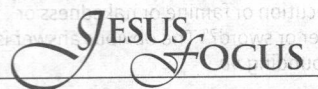

JESUS FOCUS

PAUL'S DILEMMA

Few tragedies in life bring about more pain than having our family turn against us because we have made a choice to walk with God. That situation is precisely what many of us face, however, and Paul knew the sting of such abandonment in his own life. It wasn't long after he had chosen to follow Jesus that he found himself cut off from many of his Jewish friends and associates. Even so, Paul never gave up on the Jewish people. He loved them to the point of stating that he would be condemned to hell in their place if that would assist in bringing his brothers and sisters into the fold of the Savior (Romans 9:3). Rejection by his own people was such a blow to Paul that he interrupted his letter to the Romans to tell them about it (Romans 9—11). God's chosen people had been given the incomparable opportunity of seeing the Lord Jesus, but they had tripped over the idea that he was God's promised Messiah (Romans 9:32). As a Jewish Christian, Paul wanted to see God's chosen people turn back to the one true God, who will forever love them.

DISCOVERY 307

SPEAKING THE TRUTH IN LOVE

As followers of Jesus we are called to be countercultural, because we are "aliens and strangers in the world" (1 Peter 2:11). There will be times when the message we have to share will not be well received by those who hear it. In fact, in our day some of Jesus' teachings are often judged as politically incorrect. Romans 9 opens with words that help us to deal with the question of how to speak out and live out what we believe even when faced with intense pressure to remain silent.

God wants us to speak the truth "in Christ," that is, to keep our focus trained on Jesus himself and on what he came to do (verse 1). We are never to lie or to put our own spin on the truth. Neither are we to try to "market" God's truth so that it will be more palatable within our culture. We are called on to speak the truth with no reticence or hint of deception, and God's Holy Spirit implants within us the power to do just that.

It is also important that we speak the truth from the proper motivation. Our hearts must be filled with empathy for those who are lost, just as Jesus' heart was broken with compassion for the crowds he encountered. Paul's unflinching commitment to the truth did not give him a license to hate those who would be offended by his words or to be unnecessarily caustic in his presentation (verse 2).

Elsewhere Paul instructed us to speak the truth *in love* (Ephesians 4:15). Expressing truth without love can lead to attitudes and behaviors characterized by legalism, condescension and self-righteous arrogance. Expressing love without truth, on the other hand, can lead to insincerity, permissiveness and relativism and to behaviors acted out in wild and unrestrained living. An appropriate balance of love and truth guides the lost to Jesus, who is the source of both. "Love," said Paul, "does not delight in evil but rejoices with the truth" (1 Corinthians 13:6).

One final caution, expressed in harsh words by the apostle Paul in Romans 2, is that we are called to live out the truth that we speak. Speaking to devout Jews who viewed themselves as having been justified by their reliance on God's law, he stated: "If you are convinced that you are a guide for the blind, a light for those who are in the dark, an instructor of the foolish, a teacher of infants, because you have in the law the embodiment of knowledge and truth—you, then, who teach others, do you not teach yourself? You who preach against stealing, do you steal?" (Romans 2:19–20).

We are all vulnerable to the same pitfall; we must "practice what we preach" if the truth of God is to have an impact on those with whom we come in contact. "Do your best," Paul encouraged Timothy, "to present yourself to God as one approved, a workman who does not need to be ashamed and who correctly handles the word of truth" (2 Timothy 2:15).

Self-Discovery: *Jesus said, "I am . . . the truth" (John 14:6). When we allow him to live in us (Galatians 2:20), we move from knowing the truth as a principle to be taught to becoming the truth as a person to be trusted. "Lord Jesus, please reveal any areas of deceit or duplicity in my life and let me become the truth. Amen."*

GO TO DISCOVERY 308 ON PAGE 1529

raised you up for this very purpose, that
I might display my power in you and that
my name might be proclaimed in all the
9:17 [c]Ex 9:16 earth."[a][c] 18Therefore God has mercy on
whom he wants to have mercy, and he
9:18 [d]Ex 4:21 hardens whom he wants to harden.[d]
19One of you will say to me:[e] "Then
9:19 [e]Ro 11:19 why does God still blame us? For who
[f]2Ch 20:6; resists his will?"[f] 20But who are you,
Da 4:35 O man, to talk back to God? "Shall what
9:20 is formed say to him who formed it,[g]
[g]Isa 64:8 'Why did you make me like this?' "[b][h]
[h]Isa 29:16 21Does not the potter have the right to
make out of the same lump of clay some
pottery for noble purposes and some for
9:21 common use?[i]
[i]2Ti 2:20 22What if God, choosing to show his
wrath and make his power known, bore
9:22 with great patience[j] the objects of his
[j]Ro 2:4 wrath—prepared for destruction?
23What if he did this to make the riches
9:23 [k]Ro 2:4 of his glory[k] known to the objects of his
[l]Ro 8:30 mercy, whom he prepared in advance for
9:24 glory[l]— 24even us, whom he also called,[m]
[m]Ro 8:28 not only from the Jews but also from the
[n]Ro 3:29 Gentiles?[n] 25As he says in Hosea:

"I will call them 'my people' who
are not my people;
9:25 and I will call her 'my loved one'
[o]Hos 2:23; 1Pe 2:10 who is not my loved one,"[c][o]

26and,

"It will happen that in the very place
where it was said to them,
'You are not my people,'
9:26 they will be called 'sons of the
[p]Hos 1:10 living God.' "[d][p]

27Isaiah cries out concerning Israel:

"Though the number of the
9:27 Israelites be like the sand
[q]Ge 22:17; by the sea,[q]
Hos 1:10 only the remnant will be saved.[r]
[r]Ro 11:5 28For the Lord will carry out
9:28 his sentence on earth with speed
[s]Isa 10:22,23 and finality."[e][s]

9:29 29It is just as Isaiah said previously:

[t]Jas 5:4 "Unless the Lord Almighty[t]
[u]Isa 1:9; Dt 29:23; had left us descendants,
Isa 13:19; we would have become like Sodom,
Jer 50:40 we would have been like
Gomorrah."[f][u]

Israel's Unbelief

30What then shall we say? That the
Gentiles, who did not pursue righteousness, have obtained it, a righteousness 9:30
that is by faith;[v] 31but Israel, who pur- [v]Ro 1:17; 10:6;
sued a law of righteousness,[w] has not at- Gal 2:16;
tained it.[x] 32Why not? Because they pur- Php 3:9;
sued it not by faith but as if it were by Heb 11:7
works. They stumbled over the "stum- 9:31 [w]Isa 51:1;
bling stone."[y] 33As it is written: Ro 10:2,3 [x]Gal 5:4

"See, I lay in Zion a stone that
causes men to stumble 9:32 [y]1Pe 2:8
and a rock that makes them fall,
and the one who trusts in him will 9:33 [z]Isa 28:16;
never be put to shame."[g][z] Ro 10:11

> THERE ARE SOME SCIENCES THAT MAY BE LEARNED BY THE HEAD, BUT THE SCIENCE OF CHRIST CRUCIFIED CAN ONLY BE LEARNED BY HEART.
>
> 
>
> Charles H. Spurgeon, *British Pastor*

10 Brothers, my heart's desire and
prayer to God for the Israelites
is that they may be saved. 2For I can tes-
tify about them that they are zealous[a] 10:2 [a]Ac 21:20
for God, but their zeal is not based on
knowledge. 3Since they did not know
the righteousness that comes from God
and sought to establish their own, they
did not submit to God's righteousness.[b] 10:3 [b]Ro 1:17
4Christ is the end of the law[c] so that
there may be righteousness for everyone 10:4 [c]Gal 3:24;
who believes.[d] Ro 7:1-4
5Moses describes in this way the righ- [d]Ro 3:22
teousness that is by the law: "The man
who does these things will live by 10:5
them."[h][e] 6But the righteousness that is [e]Lev 18:5;
by faith[f] says: "Do not say in your heart, Ne 9:29; Eze 20:11,13,
'Who will ascend into heaven?'[i]"[g] (that 21; Ro 7:10
is, to bring Christ down) 7"or 'Who will 10:6
descend into the deep?'[j]" (that is, to [f]Ro 9:30
bring Christ up from the dead). 8But [g]Dt 30:12
what does it say? "The word is near you;
it is in your mouth and in your heart,"[k][h] 10:8
that is, the word of faith we are pro- [h]Dt 30:14
claiming: 9That if you confess[i] with your 10:9
mouth, "Jesus is Lord," and believe in [i]Mt 10:32; Lk 12:8 [j]Ac 2:24
your heart that God raised him from the
dead,[j] you will be saved. 10For it is with
your heart that you believe and are justified, and it is with your mouth that you

[a] 17 Exodus 9:16 [b] 20 Isaiah 29:16; 45:9
[c] 25 Hosea 2:23 [d] 26 Hosea 1:10
[e] 28 Isaiah 10:22,23 [f] 29 Isaiah 1:9
[g] 33 Isaiah 8:14; 28:16 [h] 5 Lev. 18:5
[i] 6 Deut. 30:12 [j] 7 Deut. 30:13 [k] 8 Deut. 30:14

confess and are saved. 11 As the Scripture
10:11 says, "Anyone who trusts in him will nev-
k Isa 28:16; er be put to shame."[a][k] 12 For there is no
Ro 9:33 difference between Jew and Gentile[l]—
10:12 the same Lord is Lord of all[m] and richly
l Ro 3:22,29 blesses all who call on him, 13 for, "Every-
m Ac 10:36 one who calls on the name of the Lord[n]
10:13 will be saved."[b][o]
n Ac 2:21 14 How, then, can they call on the one
o Joel 2:32 they have not believed in? And how can
they believe in the one of whom they
have not heard? And how can they hear
without someone preaching to them?
15 And how can they preach unless they
are sent? As it is written, "How beautiful
10:15 are the feet of those who bring good
p Isa 52:7; news!"[c][p]
Na 1:15 16 But not all the Israelites accepted
10:16 the good news. For Isaiah says, "Lord,
q Isa 53:1; who has believed our message?"[d][q]
Jn 12:38 17 Consequently, faith comes from hear-
10:17 ing the message,[r] and the message is
r Gal 3:2,5 heard through the word of Christ.[s] 18 But
s Col 3:16 I ask: Did they not hear? Of course they
did:

"Their voice has gone out into all
the earth,
10:18 t Ps 19:4; their words to the ends of the
Mt 24:14; world."[e][t]
Col 1:6,23; 1Th 1:8 19 Again I ask: Did Israel not understand?
First, Moses says,

10:19 u Ro 11:11,14 "I will make you envious[u] by those
v Dt 32:21 who are not a nation;
I will make you angry by a
nation that has no
understanding."[f][v]

20 And Isaiah boldly says,

"I was found by those who did not
seek me;
10:20 I revealed myself to those who
w Isa 65:1; Ro 9:30 did not ask for me."[g][w]

21 But concerning Israel he says,

"All day long I have held out my
hands
10:21 to a disobedient and obstinate
x Isa 65:2 people."[h][x]

The Remnant of Israel

11:1 11 I ask then: Did God reject his
y 1Sa 12:22; people? By no means![y] I am an
Jer 31:37 Israelite myself, a descendant of Abra-
z 2Co 11:22 a Php 3:5 ham,[z] from the tribe of Benjamin.[a] 2 God
11:2 did not reject his people, whom he
b Ro 8:29 foreknew.[b] Don't you know what the
Scripture says in the passage about Elijah—how he appealed to God against Israel: 3 "Lord, they have killed your prophets and torn down your altars; I am the
only one left, and they are trying to kill 11:3
me"[i]?[c] 4 And what was God's answer to c 1Ki 19:10,14
him? "I have reserved for myself seven
thousand who have not bowed the knee 11:4
to Baal."[j][d] 5 So too, at the present time d 1Ki 19:18
there is a remnant[e] chosen by grace. 11:5
6 And if by grace, then it is no longer by e Ro 9:27
works;[f] if it were, grace would no longer
be grace.[k] 11:6 f Ro 4:4
7 What then? What Israel sought so 11:7
earnestly it did not obtain,[g] but the elect g Ro 9:31
did. The others were hardened,[h] 8 as it is h ver 25; Ro 9:18
written:

"God gave them a spirit of stupor,
eyes so that they could not see
and ears so that they could not 11:8
hear,[i] i Mt 13:13-15 j Dt 29:4;
to this very day."[l][j] Isa 29:10

9 And David says:

"May their table become a snare
and a trap,
a stumbling block and a
retribution for them.
10 May their eyes be darkened so they
cannot see,
and their backs be bent 11:10
forever."[m][k] k Ps 69:22,23

Ingrafted Branches

11 Again I ask: Did they stumble so as 11:11
to fall beyond recovery? Not at all! l ver 1
Rather, because of their transgression, m Ac 13:46 n Ro 10:19
salvation has come to the Gentiles[m] to
make Israel envious.[n] 12 But if their
transgression means riches for the
world, and their loss means riches for 11:12
the Gentiles,[o] how much greater riches o ver 25
will their fullness bring!
13 I am talking to you Gentiles. Inas- 11:13
much as I am the apostle to the Gen- p Ac 9:15
tiles,[p] I make much of my ministry 14 in 11:14
the hope that I may somehow arouse my q ver 11; Ro 10:19
own people to envy[q] and save[r] some of r 1Co 1:21;
them. 15 For if their rejection is the rec- 1Ti 2:4; Tit 3:5

a 11 Isaiah 28:16 *b 13* Joel 2:32
c 15 Isaiah 52:7 *d 16* Isaiah 53:1
e 18 Psalm 19:4 *f 19* Deut. 32:21
g 20 Isaiah 65:1 *h 21* Isaiah 65:2
i 3 1 Kings 19:10,14 *j 4* 1 Kings 19:18
k 6 Some manuscripts *by grace. But if by works, then it is no longer grace; if it were, work would no longer be work.* *l 8* Deut. 29:4; Isaiah 29:10
m 10 Psalm 69:22,23

11:15 onciliation[s] of the world, what will their
s Ro 5:10 t Lk 15:24,32 acceptance be but life from the dead?[t]
[16]If the part of the dough offered as first-
11:16 u Lev 23:10,17; fruits[u] is holy, then the whole batch is
Nu 15:18-21 holy; if the root is holy, so are the
branches.
[17]If some of the branches have been
11:17 v Jer 11:16; broken off,[v] and you, though a wild olive
Jn 15:2 shoot, have been grafted in among the
w Ac 2:39; Eph 2:11-13 others[w] and now share in the nourishing
sap from the olive root, [18]do not boast
over those branches. If you do, consider
this: You do not support the root, but
11:18 the root supports you.[x] [19]You will say
x Jn 4:22 then, "Branches were broken off so that
I could be grafted in." [20]Granted. But
they were broken off because of unbelief,
11:20 and you stand by faith.[y] Do not be arro-
y 1Co 10:12; gant,[z] but be afraid.[a] [21]For if God did not
2Co 1:24 z Ro 12:16; spare the natural branches, he will not
1Ti 6:17 a 1Pe 1:17 spare you either.
[22]Consider therefore the kindness[b]
11:22 b Ro 2:4 and sternness of God: sternness to those
c 1Co 15:2; who fell, but kindness to you, provided
Heb 3:6 that you continue[c] in his kindness. Oth-
d Jn 15:2 erwise, you also will be cut off.[d] [23]And if
they do not persist in unbelief, they will
11:23 be grafted in, for God is able to graft
e 2Co 3:16 them in again.[e] [24]After all, if you were cut

HOPE FOR ISRAEL

The nation God had chosen turned away from him, but he has not turned his back on them. There remains a national and spiritual destiny for Israel in the future. Paul stated clearly in Romans 11 that God has not rejected his people. Many of them rejected the Messiah he had sent because they were looking for someone different, but those of the Jewish people who choose to accept God's plan of salvation through Jesus constitute the "remnant chosen by grace" to whom Paul referred (verse 5). But there is more. Paul declared that "all Israel will be saved" (verse 26). Some people interpret this promise literally and others figuratively. Either way, Paul was talking about salvation for his chosen people, who are part of his covenant forever. Isaiah referred to a "Redeemer" who would come to Zion and take away the sin of all humanity (Isaiah 59:20–21). As for Gentiles so it is for Jews—God in his infinite mercy reaches out to his people to offer salvation through faith in Jesus Christ, the One who was crucified and who rose again so that we might live with him forever.

out of an olive tree that is wild by nature,
and contrary to nature were grafted into
a cultivated olive tree, how much more
readily will these, the natural branches,
be grafted into their own olive tree!

All Israel Will Be Saved

[25]I do not want you to be ignorant[f] of 11:25 f Ro 1:13
this mystery,[g] brothers, so that you may g Ro 16:25
not be conceited:[h] Israel has experi- h Ro 12:16
enced a hardening[i] in part until the full i ver 7; Ro 9:18
number of the Gentiles has come in.[j] j Lk 21:24
[26]And so all Israel will be saved, as it is
written:

"The deliverer will come from Zion;
he will turn godlessness away
from Jacob.
[27]And this is[a] my covenant with
them 11:27
when I take away their sins."[b][k] k Isa 27:9; Heb 8:10,12

[28]As far as the gospel is concerned,
they are enemies[l] on your account; but 11:28
as far as election is concerned, they are l Ro 5:10
loved on account of the patriarchs,[m] m Dt 7:8; 10:15; Ro 9:5
[29]for God's gifts and his call[n] are irrevo- 11:29
cable.[o] [30]Just as you who were at one n Ro 8:28
time disobedient[p] to God have now re- o Heb 7:21
ceived mercy as a result of their disobe- 11:30
dience, [31]so they too have now become p Eph 2:2
disobedient in order that they too may
now[c] receive mercy as a result of God's
mercy to you. [32]For God has bound all
men over to disobedience[q] so that he 11:32
may have mercy on them all. q Ro 3:9

Doxology

[33]Oh, the depth of the riches[r] of the 11:33
wisdom and[d] knowledge of r Ro 2:4 s Ps 92:5
God![s] t Job 11:7
How unsearchable his
judgments,
and his paths beyond tracing
out![t]
[34]"Who has known the mind of the
Lord? 11:34
Or who has been his u Isa 40:13,14;
counselor?"[e][u] Job 15:8; 36:22; 1Co 2:16
[35]"Who has ever given to God,
that God should repay him?"[f][v] 11:35 v Job 35:7
[36]For from him and through him and 11:36
to him are all things.[w] w 1Co 8:6;
To him be the glory forever! Col 1:16; Heb 2:10
Amen.[x] x Ro 16:27

[a] 27 Or *will be* [b] 27 Isaiah 59:20,21; 27:9; Jer. 31:33,34 [c] 31 Some manuscripts do not have *now.* [d] 33 Or *riches and the wisdom and the* [e] 34 Isaiah 40:13 [f] 35 Job 41:11

Members of One Body

The church of Jesus is a vital, dynamic organism. Although it is comprised of millions of individual members, it operates as one body to accomplish what God has called it to do (1 Corinthians 12:13). When we see ourselves as one in Jesus, we move beyond our differences to focus our energy on the common vision and mission we share as Christians. Christ's body is composed of people from every ethnic, cultural, social, racial, geographic, gender and denominational group (Romans 12:5), a beautiful picture of those purchased with Jesus' blood "from every tribe and language and people and nation" (Revelation 5:9).

We as members of one body all submit to Jesus, because he is our indisputable "head" (Colossians 1:15–18; 2:18–19). It is easy to fall into the trap of demanding our own way or of insisting that our own opinion is the only appropriate viewpoint. However, when there is conflict among individual members of the body it is usually an indication that one or more of those involved is failing to submit to Jesus Christ, who is the head, and to each other, who are equally valuable and significant members of the body (Ephesians 5:21–27). In a physical body each individual organ is crucial to its overall health and functionality, and all of the parts must work together. Similarly, in the body of Christ each member is important, and we must cooperate to do what God asks. There is diversity because we are all unique, but there is unity because we together form one whole.

We are also interdependent: "Each member belongs to all the others" (Romans 12:5). Isolation and segregation are not part of God's plan, but rather unity in Jesus Christ, "our peace, who has made the two one and has destroyed the barrier, the dividing wall of hostility" (Ephesians 2:4). The splintering of Christ's body often leads to spiritual arrogance and condescension on the parts of various branches, who for whatever reason have concluded that they lead holier lives or possess a corner on the truth. Immediately prior to his discussion of the necessary and significant contribution of *each* member of the body, Paul made a plea to individual members: "For by the grace given me I say to every one of you: Do not think of yourself more highly than you ought, but rather think of yourself with sober judgment, in accordance with the measure of faith God has given you" (Romans 12:3).

One evidence that we as a church are walking in intimate fellowship with Jesus is that we are also enjoying fellowship with each other (1 John 1:5–7; 3:11–15). Peter stated this so beautifully: "Above all, love each other deeply, because love covers over a multitude of sins . . . Each one should use whatever gift he has received to serve others, faithfully administering God's grace in its various forms. . . . If anyone serves, he should do it with the strength God provides, so that in all things God may be praised through Jesus Christ" (1 Peter 4:8,10–11).

***Self-Discovery:** What is your special function as a member of the body of Jesus Christ? Whether your particular gifts tend to place you in the limelight or whether you feel more comfortable working behind-the-scenes, are you able to accept the truth that the contributions of every member of the body are important and necessary to the whole?*

GO TO DISCOVERY 309 ON PAGE 1531

> THE WORLD CAN CONFORM US
> BUT ONLY CHRIST CAN
> TRANSFORM US.
>
> 
>
> Kay Arthur, *Founder, Precept Ministries, Chattanooga, Tennessee*

Living Sacrifices

12:1 **12** Therefore, I urge you,[y] brothers,
in view of God's mercy, to offer
your bodies as living sacrifices,[z] holy
and pleasing to God—this is your spiri-
12:2 tual[a] act of worship. 2Do not conform[a]
any longer to the pattern of this world,[b]
but be transformed by the renewing of
your mind.[c] Then you will be able to test
and approve what God's will is[d]—his
12:3 good, pleasing and perfect will.
3For by the grace given me[e] I say to
every one of you: Do not think of yourself more highly than you ought, but
rather think of yourself with sober judgment, in accordance with the measure
of faith God has given you. 4Just as each
of us has one body with many members,
12:4 and these members do not all have the
same function,[f] 5so in Christ we who are
12:5 many form one body,[g] and each member
belongs to all the others. 6We have dif-
12:6 ferent gifts,[h] according to the grace giv-
en us. If a man's gift is prophesying, let
him use it in proportion to his[b] faith.[i] 7If
it is serving, let him serve; if it is teach-
12:7 ing, let him teach;[j] 8if it is encouraging,
let him encourage;[k] if it is contributing
12:8 to the needs of others, let him give generously;[l] if it is leadership, let him govern diligently; if it is showing mercy, let
12:9 him do it cheerfully.

Love

12:10 9Love must be sincere.[m] Hate what is
evil; cling to what is good. 10Be devoted
12:11 to one another in brotherly love.[n] Hon-
or one another above yourselves.[o] 11Nev-
12:12 er be lacking in zeal, but keep your spiritual fervor,[p] serving the Lord. 12Be joyful
12:13 in hope,[q] patient in affliction,[r] faithful in
prayer. 13Share with God's people who
12:14 are in need. Practice hospitality.[s]
14Bless those who persecute you;[t]
12:15 bless and do not curse. 15Rejoice with
those who rejoice; mourn with those
12:16 who mourn.[u] 16Live in harmony with
one another.[v] Do not be proud, but be

12:1 [y] Eph 4:1 [z] Ro 6:13,16,19; 1Pe 2:5
12:2 [a] 1Pe 1:14 [b] 1Jn 2:15 [c] Eph 4:23 [d] Eph 5:17
12:3 [e] Ro 15:15; Gal 2:9; Eph 4:7
12:4 [f] 1Co 12:12-14; Eph 4:16
12:5 [g] 1Co 10:17
12:6 [h] 1Co 7:7; 12:4, 8-10 [i] 1Pe 4:10, 11
12:7 [j] Eph 4:11
12:8 [k] Ac 15:32 [l] 2Co 9:5-13
12:9 [m] 1Ti 1:5
12:10 [n] Heb 13:1 [o] Php 2:3
12:11 [p] Ac 18:25
12:12 [q] Ro 5:2 [r] Heb 10:32,36
12:13 [s] 1Ti 3:2
12:14 [t] Mt 5:44
12:15 [u] Job 30:25
12:16 [v] Ro 15:5

willing to associate with people of low 12:16
position.[c] Do not be conceited.[w]
17Do not repay anyone evil for evil.[x] Be 12:17
careful to do what is right in the eyes of
everybody.[y] 18If it is possible, as far as it
depends on you, live at peace with every- 12:18
one.[z] 19Do not take revenge,[a] my friends,
but leave room for God's wrath, for it is
written: "It is mine to avenge; I will re- 12:19
pay,"[d][b] says the Lord. 20On the contrary:

"If your enemy is hungry, feed him;
if he is thirsty, give him
something to drink.
In doing this, you will heap burning 12:20
coals on his head."[e][c]

21Do not be overcome by evil, but overcome evil with good.

Submission to the Authorities

13 Everyone must submit himself
to the governing authorities,[d] 13:1
for there is no authority except that
which God has established.[e] The authorities that exist have been established by God. 2Consequently, he who
rebels against the authority is rebelling
against what God has instituted, and
those who do so will bring judgment on
themselves. 3For rulers hold no terror for
those who do right, but for those who do
wrong. Do you want to be free from fear
of the one in authority? Then do what is 13:3
right and he will commend you.[f] 4For he
is God's servant to do you good. But if
you do wrong, be afraid, for he does not
bear the sword for nothing. He is God's
servant, an agent of wrath to bring punishment on the wrongdoer.[g] 5Therefore, 13:4
it is necessary to submit to the authorities, not only because of possible punishment but also because of conscience.
6This is also why you pay taxes, for the
authorities are God's servants, who give
their full time to governing. 7Give everyone what you owe him: If you owe taxes, 13:7
pay taxes;[h] if revenue, then revenue; if respect, then respect; if honor, then honor.

Love, for the Day Is Near

8Let no debt remain outstanding,
except the continuing debt to love 13:8
one another, for he who loves his fellowman has fulfilled the law.[i] 9The

12:16 [w] Jer 45:5; Ro 11:25
12:17 [x] Pr 20:22 [y] 2Co 8:21
12:18 [z] Mk 9:50; Ro 14:19
12:19 [a] Lev 19:18; Pr 20:22; 24:29 [b] Dt 32:35
12:20 [c] Pr 25:21,22; Mt 5:44; Lk 6:27
13:1 [d] Tit 3:1; 1Pe 2:13,14 [e] Da 2:21; Jn 19:11
13:3 [f] 1Pe 2:14
13:4 [g] 1Th 4:6
13:7 [h] Mt 17:25; 22:17,21; Lk 23:2
13:8 [i] ver 10; Jn 13:34; Gal 5:14; Col 3:14

[a] 1 Or *reasonable* [b] 6 Or *in agreement with the* [c] 16 Or *willing to do menial work* [d] 19 Deut. 32:35 [e] 20 Prov. 25:21,22

Clothed With Jesus

"If anyone is in Christ, he is a new creation; the old has gone, the new has come!" (2 Corinthians 5:17). If we have staked our future on Jesus, we have adopted a new way of thinking and living. Paul wrote that as God's people we are to "behave decently" (Romans 13:13). The word *decently* refers to living a fitting, orderly and modest life (1 Corinthians 12:23; 14:40). Paul also listed some specific behaviors that God wants us to avoid. These include abuse of alcohol and drugs, sexual immorality, dissension and selfish ambition (Romans 13:13). The apostle suggested two actions that will help us to live God's way.

First, we can, in the words of the apostle Paul, "clothe" ourselves with the Lord Jesus (Romans 13:14; Galatians 3:27). Again in Ephesians 4:24 the apostle spoke of "[putting] on the new self, created to be like God in true righteousness and holiness." Sometimes an article of clothing or an accessory can serve as a visible reminder of our commitments and choices: A wedding band, a bracelet or a tee shirt can all help us to recall who we are.

We all know from personal experience that we cannot avoid sin and behave decently by our own effort. Only Jesus has the power to free us from the domination of sin (Romans 7:24–25; 8:1–2). If we do indeed "clothe" ourselves with him, displaying outwardly what has already taken place inwardly, we will emulate him in our daily walk, and our very attitude and demeanor will serve as a witness to others that we are devoted to our Lord.

Second, behaving decently demands constant vigilance against sin. We are not to spend our time fantasizing about ways to satisfy our sinful cravings. We must learn to steer clear of any suggestion or circumstance that opens our minds to the attractiveness of sin, and we are to avoid sin at any cost (2 Timothy 2:22). When we give our lives to Jesus, we are no longer to associate with people, places and things that might conjure up pleasant memories of our former lifestyle. If we frequent places in which sin can begin to get a foothold inside the door of our heart, we are issuing an open invitation to disaster. We must constantly ask ourselves what we need to avoid in order to overcome the temptation to sin.

Paul's words in his letter to the Colossians have for centuries reverberated in the hearts of Christians: "As God's chosen people, holy and dearly beloved, clothe yourselves with compassion, kindness, humility, gentleness and patience . . . And above all these virtues put on love, which binds them all together in perfect unity . . . Let the word of Christ dwell in you richly as you teach and admonish one another with all wisdom, and as you sing psalms, hymns and spiritual songs with gratitude in your hearts to God" (Colossians 3:12,14,16).

***Self-Discovery:** Which people encourage you to act in ways that do not please Jesus? What places are full of obstacles over which you might stumble? What enticements capture your attention and draw your focus away from your life in Jesus?*

GO TO DISCOVERY 310 ON PAGE 1533

commandments, "Do not commit adultery," "Do not murder," "Do not steal," "Do not covet,"[a][j] and whatever other commandment there may be, are summed up in this one rule: "Love your neighbor as yourself."[b][k] 10Love does no harm to its neighbor. Therefore love is the fulfillment of the law.[l]

11And do this, understanding the present time. The hour has come[m] for you to wake up from your slumber,[n] because our salvation is nearer now than when we first believed. 12The night is nearly over; the day is almost here.[o] So let us put aside the deeds of darkness[p] and put on the armor[q] of light. 13Let us behave decently, as in the daytime, not in orgies and drunkenness, not in sexual immorality and debauchery, not in dissension and jealousy.[r] 14Rather, clothe yourselves with the Lord Jesus Christ,[s] and do not think about how to gratify the desires of the sinful nature.[c]

The Weak and the Strong

14 Accept him whose faith is weak,[t] without passing judgment on disputable matters. 2One man's faith allows him to eat everything, but another man, whose faith is weak, eats only vegetables. 3The man who eats everything must not look down on[u] him who does not, and the man who does not eat everything must not condemn[v] the man who does, for God has accepted him. 4Who are you to judge someone else's servant?[w] To his own master he stands or falls. And he will stand, for the Lord is able to make him stand.

5One man considers one day more sacred than another;[x] another man considers every day alike. Each one should be fully convinced in his own mind. 6He who regards one day as special, does so to the Lord. He who eats meat, eats to the Lord, for he gives thanks to God;[y] and he who abstains, does so to the Lord and gives thanks to God. 7For none of us lives to himself alone[z] and none of us dies to himself alone. 8If we live, we live to the Lord; and if we die, we die to the Lord. So, whether we live or die, we belong to the Lord.[a]

9For this very reason, Christ died and returned to life[b] so that he might be the Lord of both the dead and the living.[c] 10You, then, why do you judge your

13:9 [j] Ex 20:13-15, 17; Dt 5:17-19, 21 [k] Lev 19:18; Mt 19:19
13:10 [l] ver 8; Mt 22:39, 40
13:11 [m] 1Co 7:29-31; 10:11 [n] Eph 5:14; 1Th 5:5,6
13:12 [o] 1Jn 2:8 [p] Eph 5:11 [q] Eph 6:11,13
13:13 [r] Gal 5:20,21
13:14 [s] Gal 3:27; 5:16; Eph 4:24
14:1 [t] Ro 15:1; 1Co 8:9-12
14:3 [u] Lk 18:9 [v] Col 2:16
14:4 [w] Jas 4:12
14:5 [x] Gal 4:10
14:6 [y] Mt 14:19; 1Co 10:30,31; 1Ti 4:3,4
14:7 [z] 2Co 5:15; Gal 2:20
14:8 [a] Php 1:20
14:9 [b] Rev 1:18 [c] 2Co 5:15

CHRIST IS THE LIVING BIBLE.

Thomas Manton, *Puritan Pastor*

brother? Or why do you look down on your brother? For we will all stand before God's judgment seat.[d] 11It is written:

"'As surely as I live,' says the Lord,
'every knee will bow before me;
every tongue will confess to God.'"[d][e]

12So then, each of us will give an account of himself to God.[f]

13Therefore let us stop passing judgment[g] on one another. Instead, make up your mind not to put any stumbling block or obstacle in your brother's way. 14As one who is in the Lord Jesus, I am fully convinced that no food[e] is unclean in itself.[h] But if anyone regards something as unclean, then for him it is unclean.[i] 15If your brother is distressed because of what you eat, you are no longer acting in love.[j] Do not by your eating destroy your brother for whom Christ died.[k] 16Do not allow what you consider good to be spoken of as evil.[l] 17For the kingdom of God is not a matter of eating and drinking,[m] but of righteousness, peace and joy in the Holy Spirit,[n] 18because anyone who serves Christ in this way is pleasing to God and approved by men.[o]

19Let us therefore make every effort to do what leads to peace[p] and to mutual edification.[q] 20Do not destroy the work of God for the sake of food.[r] All food is clean, but it is wrong for a man to eat anything that causes someone else to stumble.[s] 21It is better not to eat meat or drink wine or to do anything else that will cause your brother to fall.[t]

22So whatever you believe about these things keep between yourself and God. Blessed is the man who does not condemn[u] himself by what he approves. 23But the man who has doubts[v] is condemned if he eats, because his eating is not from faith; and everything that does not come from faith is sin.

15 We who are strong ought to bear with the failings of the

14:10 [d] 2Co 5:10
14:11 [e] Isa 45:23; Php 2:10,11
14:12 [f] Mt 12:36; 1Pe 4:5
14:13 [g] Mt 7:1
14:14 [h] Ac 10:15 [i] 1Co 8:7
14:15 [j] Eph 5:2 [k] 1Co 8:11
14:16 [l] 1Co 10:30
14:17 [m] 1Co 8:8 [n] Ro 15:13
14:18 [o] 2Co 8:21
14:19 [p] Ps 34:14; Ro 12:18; Heb 12:14 [q] Ro 15:2; 2Co 12:19
14:20 [r] ver 15 [s] 1Co 8:9-12
14:21 [t] 1Co 8:13
14:22 [u] 1Jn 3:21
14:23 [v] ver 5

[a] *9* Exodus 20:13-15,17; Deut. 5:17-19,21
[b] *9* Lev. 19:18
[c] *14* Or *the flesh*
[d] *11* Isaiah 45:23
[e] *14* Or *that nothing*

DISCOVERY 310

Building Each Other Up

Membership in God's family carries responsibility, and a primary accountabily is to care for those who are spiritually immature: "We who are strong ought to bear with the failings of the weak and not to please ourselves" (Romans 15:1). Paul used the words *ought to*, implying that we are indebted to someone. And our obligation is to *bear with* the failings of the weak. To bear means to pick something up and carry it (Mark 14:3; Luke 7:14; Galatians 6:2). This entails more than merely *putting up with* the failings of those who have not yet reached our own level of spiritual maturity; it means helping them to shoulder their load as they exercise and develop their faith. This kind of commitment demands a "spiritual SOS": Sensitivity to, Openness toward and Sharing with those who are weak, vacillating, easily tempted or emotionally immature.

Shoring up a weaker brother or sister may be inconvenient for us, and it may demand generous helpings of effort and time. The attempt may not always be successful, but we do it as a service to Jesus and to our brother or sister, in order to build them up and to strengthen their faith (Romans 15:2; Ephesians 4:12–13).

Jesus was our perfect example of this kind of lifestyle: "Christ did not please himself but, as it is written: 'The insults of those who insult you have fallen on me' " (Romans 15:3). God will reveal to us those niches in our own lives that need strengthening, as well as those areas in which we are already spiritually healthy. He will both lead us into relationships in which we can be strengthened and into those that allow us to support and fortify others. Any sacrifice of time and resources is an offering to Jesus, who sacrificed so much for us.

Implicit in Jesus' instruction to serve one another is the importance of accepting each other with respect and humility, no matter what foibles and weaknesses may be present in our own life or in the lives of others. Paul encouraged the Colossian Christians to do just that: "Therefore, as God's chosen people, holy and dearly loved, clothe yourselves with compassion, kindness, humility, gentleness and patience. Bear with each other and forgive whatever grievances you may have against one another. Forgive as the Lord forgave you" (Colossians 3:12–14). And in Romans 15:7 Paul exhorted believers in Rome to "accept one another, then, just as Christ accepted you, in order to bring praise to God."

It is important that we assess our own gifts and abilities with humility, realizing that everything we are and everything we have is a gift from God: "For by the grace given me I say to every one of you: Do not think of yourself more highly than you ought, but rather think of yourself with sober judgment, in accordance with the measure of faith God has given you" (Romans 12:3). A true servant attitude does not approach a weaker, less capable, less mature, or more easily tempted brother or sister with condescension or even sympathy. True Christian love manifests itself by cheerful, empathetic and willing service, offered in the name of Jesus Christ, who loves each and every one of his children with equal passion—enough to die on our behalf.

Self-Discovery: *Jesus would never break a bruised reed or snuff out a smoldering wick (Isaiah 42:3). How can you follow his example today by being an encouragement to someone who is in a fragile condition?*

GO TO DISCOVERY 311 ON PAGE 1536

15:1 wRo 14:1; weak[w] and not to please ourselves.
Gal 6:1,2; 2Each of us should please his neighbor
1Th 5:14 for his good,[x] to build him up.[y] 3For even
15:2 Christ did not please himself[z] but, as it
x1Co 10:33 is written: "The insults of those who in-
yRo 14:19 sult you have fallen on me."[a][a] 4For every-
15:3 thing that was written in the past was
z2Co 8:9 written to teach us,[b] so that through en-
aPs 69:9 durance and the encouragement of the
15:4 Scriptures we might have hope.
bRo 4:23,24 5May the God who gives endurance
15:5 and encouragement give you a spirit of
cRo 12:16; unity[c] among yourselves as you follow
1Co 1:10 Christ Jesus, 6so that with one heart and
15:6 mouth you may glorify the God and Fa-
dRev 1:6 ther[d] of our Lord Jesus Christ.
15:7 7Accept one another,[e] then, just as
eRo 14:1 Christ accepted you, in order to bring
15:8 praise to God. 8For I tell you that Christ
fMt 15:24; has become a servant of the Jews[b][f] on
Ac 3:25,26 g2Co 1:20 behalf of God's truth, to confirm the
promises[g] made to the patriarchs 9so
15:9 that the Gentiles[h] may glorify God[i] for
hRo 3:29 iMt 9:8 his mercy, as it is written:

j2Sa 22:50; Ps 18:49 "Therefore I will praise you among
the Gentiles;
I will sing hymns to your name."[c][j]

10Again, it says,

15:10 kDt 32:43 "Rejoice, O Gentiles, with his
people."[d][k]

11And again,

"Praise the Lord, all you Gentiles,
15:11 lPs 117:1 and sing praises to him, all you
peoples."[e][l]

SALVATION FOR ALL

Paul called Jesus a "servant of the Jews," and he called himself a "minister . . . to the Gentiles" (Romans 15:8,16). Jesus fulfills the promises God made to his people in the Old Testament (Luke 24:27). Paul reminded his Jewish readers of what God had stated in the past—that he has always intended that his people reach out to other nations (Deuteronomy 32:43; Psalm 18:14; Psalm 117:1; Isaiah 11:10; 42:6; 49:6). Our Lord Jesus, though of Jewish descent, was a Savior with a heart of compassion for every person on earth. Later on God sent Paul, a Jew by birth, to spread the Good News to the Gentiles so that they too could enjoy a relationship with the one true and living God through his Son, Jesus Christ (Romans 15:16).

12And again, Isaiah says,

"The Root of Jesse[m] will spring up, 15:12 mRev 5:5
one who will arise to rule over nIsa 11:10;
the nations; Mt 12:21
the Gentiles will hope in him."[f][n]

13May the God of hope fill you with all
joy and peace[o] as you trust in him, so 15:13
that you may overflow with hope by the oRo 14:17 pver 19;
power of the Holy Spirit.[p] 1Co 2:4; 1Th 1:5

Paul the Minister to the Gentiles

14I myself am convinced, my brothers, 15:14
that you yourselves are full of goodness,[q] qEph 5:9
complete in knowledge[r] and competent r2Pe 1:12
to instruct one another. 15I have written
you quite boldly on some points, as if to
remind you of them again, because of 15:15
the grace God gave me[s] 16to be a minis- sRo 12:3
ter of Christ Jesus to the Gentiles[t] with
the priestly duty of proclaiming the 15:16
gospel of God,[u] so that the Gentiles tAc 9:15; Ro 11:13
might become an offering[v] acceptable uRo 1:1
to God, sanctified by the Holy Spirit. vIsa 66:20
17Therefore I glory in Christ Jesus[w] in 15:17 wPhp 3:3
my service to God.[x] 18I will not venture xHeb 2:17
to speak of anything except what Christ
has accomplished through me in lead- 15:18
ing the Gentiles[y] to obey God[z] by what I yAc 15:12;
have said and done— 19by the power of 21:19; Ro 1:5 zRo 16:26
signs and miracles,[a] through the power
of the Spirit.[b] So from Jerusalem[c] all the 15:19 aJn 4:48;
way around to Illyricum, I have fully pro- Ac 19:11
claimed the gospel of Christ. 20It has al- bver 13 cAc 22:17-21
ways been my ambition to preach the
gospel where Christ was not known, so
that I would not be building on some- 15:20
one else's foundation.[d] 21Rather, as it is d2Co 10:15,16
written:

"Those who were not told about
him will see,
and those who have not heard 15:21
will understand."[g][e] eIsa 52:15

22This is why I have often been hindered 15:22
from coming to you.[f] fRo 1:13

Paul's Plan to Visit Rome

23But now that there is no more place
for me to work in these regions, and
since I have been longing for many years 15:23
to see you,[g] 24I plan to do so when I go to gAc 19:21; Ro 1:10,11
Spain.[h] I hope to visit you while passing 15:24
through and to have you assist me on hver 28

a 3 Psalm 69:9 *b 8* Greek *circumcision*
c 9 2 Samuel 22:50; Psalm 18:49 *d 10* Deut. 32:43
e 11 Psalm 117:1 *f 12* Isaiah 11:10
g 21 Isaiah 52:15

my journey there, after I have enjoyed
your company for a while. 25 Now, how-
15:25 [i] Ac 19:21 [j] Ac 24:17 ever, I am on my way to Jerusalem[i] in the
service[j] of the saints there. 26 For Mace-
donia[k] and Achaia[l] were pleased to
15:26 [k] Ac 16:9; 2Co 8:1 [l] Ac 18:12 make a contribution for the poor among
the saints in Jerusalem. 27 They were
pleased to do it, and indeed they owe it
to them. For if the Gentiles have shared
in the Jews' spiritual blessings, they owe
it to the Jews to share with them their
15:27 [m] 1Co 9:11 material blessings.[m] 28 So after I have
completed this task and have made sure
that they have received this fruit, I will
15:29 [n] Ro 1:10,11 go to Spain and visit you on the way. 29 I
know that when I come to you,[n] I will
15:30 [o] Gal 5:22 [p] 2Co 1:11; Col 4:12 come in the full measure of the blessing
of Christ.

30 I urge you, brothers, by our Lord
Jesus Christ and by the love of the Spir-
15:31 [q] 2Th 3:2 it,[o] to join me in my struggle by praying
to God for me.[p] 31 Pray that I may be res-
15:32 [r] Ac 18:21 [s] Ro 1:10,13 [t] 1Co 16:18 cued[q] from the unbelievers in Judea and
that my service in Jerusalem may be ac-
ceptable to the saints there, 32 so that by
15:33 [u] Ro 16:20; 2Co 13:11; Php 4:9; 1Th 5:23; Heb 13:20 God's will[r] I may come to you[s] with joy
and together with you be refreshed.[t]
33 The God of peace[u] be with you all.
Amen.

Personal Greetings

16:1 [v] 2Co 3:1 [w] Ac 18:18 16 I commend[v] to you our sister
Phoebe, a servant[a] of the
church in Cenchrea.[w] 2 I ask you to re-
ceive her in the Lord[x] in a way worthy of 16:2 [x] Php 2:29
the saints and to give her any help she
may need from you, for she has been a
great help to many people, including me.

3 Greet Priscilla[b] and Aquila,[y] my fel- 16:3 [y] Ac 18:2 [z] ver 7, 9,10
low workers in Christ Jesus.[z] 4 They
risked their lives for me. Not only I
but all the churches of the Gentiles
are grateful to them.

5 Greet also the church that meets at
their house.[a] 16:5 [a] 1Co 16:19; Col 4:15; Phm 2 [b] 1Co 16:15

Greet my dear friend Epenetus, who
was the first convert[b] to Christ in
the province of Asia.

6 Greet Mary, who worked very hard for
you.

7 Greet Andronicus and Junias, my relatives[c] who have been in prison 16:7 [c] ver 11,21
with me. They are outstanding
among the apostles, and they were
in Christ before I was.

8 Greet Ampliatus, whom I love in the
Lord.

9 Greet Urbanus, our fellow worker in
Christ,[d] and my dear friend Sta- 16:9 [d] ver 3
chys.

10 Greet Apelles, tested and approved in
Christ.

Greet those who belong to the household of Aristobulus.

11 Greet Herodion, my relative.[e] 16:11 [e] ver 7,21

Greet those in the household of Nar-
cissus who are in the Lord.

12 Greet Tryphena and Tryphosa, those
women who work hard in the Lord.

Greet my dear friend Persis, another
woman who has worked very hard
in the Lord.

13 Greet Rufus, chosen in the Lord, and
his mother, who has been a mother
to me, too.

14 Greet Asyncritus, Phlegon, Hermes,
Patrobas, Hermas and the brothers
with them.

15 Greet Philologus, Julia, Nereus and his
sister, and Olympas and all the
saints[f] with them.[g] 16:15 [f] ver 2 [g] ver 14

16 Greet one another with a holy kiss.[h] 16:16 [h] 1Co 16:20; 2Co 13:12; 1Th 5:26

All the churches of Christ send greetings.

17 I urge you, brothers, to watch out for
those who cause divisions and put ob-
stacles in your way that are contrary to 16:17 [i] Gal 1:8,9; 1Ti 1:3; 6:3
the teaching you have learned.[i] Keep

[a] 1 Or *deaconess* [b] 3 Greek *Prisca,* a variant of *Priscilla*

CHRISTIAN FRIENDSHIP

The letter to the Christians in Rome ends with a listing of Paul's friends and co-workers (Romans 16). This list includes both men and women, Jews and Gentiles, and touches every level of society. There are the names of common slaves like Urbanus and Apelles, as well as those of possible royalty: Aristobulus was most likely the grandson of Herod the Great. Paul wrote this letter from Corinth, where his circle of friends included Erastus, the city's director of public works. Our position in Jesus is fully as important as that of anyone else, because we are all equal in God's sight. God's people have throughout the centuries embraced one another regardless of social status or other differences as brothers and sisters in God's family, and Paul's own life was a good example of how far-reaching our love for one another should be.

The Benediction

The book of Romans is not only the most theological of Paul's letters but also the most doctrinal book in the New Testament. Paul elaborated on the doctrines of sin, salvation and sanctification. He also explained God's relationship with the Jewish people and concluded his treatise with a section on practical Christian living. His closing note is a glorious benediction replete with truth about God (Romans 16:25–27).

Paul both began and completed his letter focusing on one subject—the gospel. In fact, he used the word *gospel* a total of 60 times in this one letter. At the end, he defined the gospel as "the proclamation of Jesus Christ" (verse 25). Paul's consuming life task was to propagate this gospel, because he considered it *his* gospel, a treasure that God had entrusted to him in a special way.

In Paul's first letter to the Corinthians, he expressed his passion in this way: "We preach Christ crucified: a stumbling block to Jews and foolishness to Gentles, but to those whom God has called, both Jews and Greeks, Christ the power of God and the wisdom of God" (1 Corinthians 1:23–24). And the apostle had more to say in his second letter to the believers is Corinth: "We do not preach ourselves, but Jesus Christ as Lord, and ourselves as your servants for Jesus' sake. For God . . . made his light shine in our hearts to give us the light of the knowledge of the glory of God in the face of Christ" (2 Corinthians 4:5–6).

When Paul talked about the "mystery" of God he used a word that denotes a truth that was previously unknown but has at last been revealed. The "mystery" is that God provided a way of salvation through Jesus for both Jews and Gentiles (Ephesians 1:9–10; 3:3–6).

God's desire has always been that "all nations might believe and obey him" (Romans 16:26). Sharing the gospel with our neighbors is important and certainly a part of what God asks us to do. But to hoard the truth, keeping it close to home, is to cheat people who have never had an opportunity to hear. Our passion for foreign missions stems from God's passion for people.

As Paul concluded his letter to the Roman believers, he trained his camera lens back onto God. The good news that Jesus died in our place and the mystery that all nations are included in the invitation to be part of his family are messages we need to share. When we do, we honor God through his Son Jesus. In the apostle's own words: "Now to him who is able to establish you by my gospel and the proclamation of Jesus Christ, according to the revelation of the mystery hidden for long ages past, but now revealed and made known through the prophetic writings by the command of the eternal God, so that all nations might believe and obey him—to the only wise God be glory forever through Jesus Christ! Amen" (verses 25–27).

Self-Discovery: In what ways might you become more actively involved in supporting missions efforts? Through prayer? Through writing letters of encouragement to missionaries sponsored by your home church? Through increased emphasis on missions in terms of your financial gifts? Through active participation yourself in a short-term missions trip?

GO TO DISCOVERY 312 ON PAGE 1542

16:17 j 2Th 3:6,14; 2Jn 10 — away from them.[j] 18For such people are
not serving our Lord Christ, but their
own appetites.[k] By smooth talk and flat-
16:18 k Php 3:19 — tery they deceive[l] the minds of naive
l Col 2:4 — people. 19Everyone has heard[m] about
16:19 — your obedience, so I am full of joy over
m Ro 1:8 — you; but I want you to be wise about
n Mt 10:16; 1Co 14:20 — what is good, and innocent about what
is evil.[n]
16:20 — 20The God of peace[o] will soon crush[p]
o Ro 15:33 p Ge 3:15 — Satan under your feet.
q 1Th 5:28 — The grace of our Lord Jesus be with
you.[q]
16:21 — 21Timothy,[r] my fellow worker, sends
r Ac 16:1 s Ac 13:1 — his greetings to you, as do Lucius,[s] Ja-
t Ac 17:5 u ver 7, 11 — son[t] and Sosipater, my relatives.[u]
22I, Tertius, who wrote down this let-
ter, greet you in the Lord.
23Gaius, whose hospitality I and the
whole church here enjoy, sends you his
greetings.
Erastus,[v] who is the city's director of — 16:23 v Ac 19:22
public works, and our brother Quartus
send you their greetings.[a]
25Now to him who is able[w] to estab- — 16:25 w Eph 3:20
lish you by my gospel[x] and the procla- — x Ro 2:16
mation of Jesus Christ, according to the — y Eph 1:9; Col 1:26,27
revelation of the mystery[y] hidden for
long ages past, 26but now revealed and
made known through the prophetic
writings by the command of the eternal
God, so that all nations might believe
and obey him— 27to the only wise God
be glory forever through Jesus Christ! — 16:27
Amen.[z] — z Ro 11:36

[a] 23 Some manuscripts *their greetings.* *24May the grace of our Lord Jesus Christ be with all of you. Amen.*

How will Jesus destroy all dominion, authority and power? (1 Corinthians 15:24)

♦ *Presumably this refers to the same sort of forces that Paul referred to elsewhere (Romans 8:38–39; Ephesians 6:12; Philippians 2:10)—spiritual beings and powers over which Jesus will assert his lordship when he comes again. Paul's concern is to emphasize that Jesus is greater than all the forces of the enemy.*

Is Jesus subordinate to the Father? (1 Corinthians 15:28)

♦ *Paul upheld the uniqueness and singularity of God by pointing to the subordination of Jesus to the Father. Paul spoke of Jesus as being both subject to the Father and as having the rights and status of deity (1 Corinthians 8:6). On the whole, the Bible shows the Father and the Son to be equal in being, although the Son is subordinate in function or relationship.*

Jesus in 1 Corinthians Paul addressed this letter to the believers in Corinth. Reports about serious problems in the Corinthian church had reached the apostle, and he addressed these early in the book in a straightforward manner. Employing sarcasm, poetry, debating techniques, emotional pleas and personal anecdotes, Paul attempted to help the Corinthian believers get back on track.

The remainder of 1 Corinthians consists of Paul's discussion of other matters of concern for the Corinthians. Look for Paul's advice on marriage and the single life, the celebration of pagan holidays and the behavior of women.

Jesus is Lord of the church, and Paul wanted God's people to live as though they believed that. He taught that Jesus is the central focus of Christian preaching, worship and life and that his name takes precedence over all other names (1 Corinthians 1:2,6,8,13) because he died for our sins to restore us to a relationship with the Father (1 Corinthians 1:23–24; 15:12–20). When we place our trust in Jesus we become his "servants" (1 Corinthians 4:1) and "members" of his body (1 Corinthians 6:15).

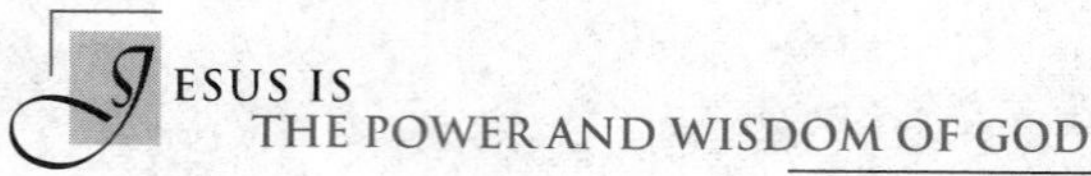

JESUS IS
THE POWER AND WISDOM OF GOD

1:1 a Ro 1:1; Eph 1:1 **1** Paul, called to be an apostle[a] of
b 2Co 1:1 Christ Jesus by the will of God,[b]
c Ac 18:17 and our brother Sosthenes,[c]

1:2 [2]To the church of God in Corinth,[d] to
d Ac 18:1 e Ro 1:7 those sanctified in Christ Jesus and
called[e] to be holy, together with all those
everywhere who call on the name of our
Lord Jesus Christ—their Lord and ours:

1:3 [3]Grace and peace to you from God
f Ro 1:7 our Father and the Lord Jesus Christ.[f]

Thanksgiving

1:4 [4]I always thank God for you[g] because
g Ro 1:8 of his grace given you in Christ Jesus.
1:5 [5]For in him you have been enriched[h] in
h 2Co 9:11 every way—in all your speaking and in
i 2Co 8:7 all your knowledge[i]— [6]because our tes-
1:6 timony[j] about Christ was confirmed in
j Rev 1:2 you. [7]Therefore you do not lack any spir-
1:7 k Php 3:20; itual gift as you eagerly wait for our Lord
Tit 2:13; Jesus Christ to be revealed.[k] [8]He will
2Pe 3:12 keep you strong to the end, so that you
1:8 will be blameless[l] on the day of our Lord
l 1Th 3:13 Jesus Christ. [9]God, who has called you
1:9 into fellowship with his Son Jesus Christ
m 1Jn 1:3 n Isa 49:7; 1Th 5:24 our Lord,[m] is faithful.[n]

Divisions in the Church

[10]I appeal to you, brothers, in the
name of our Lord Jesus Christ, that all of
you agree with one another so that there
may be no divisions among you and that
you may be perfectly united in mind and
thought. [11]My brothers, some from
Chloe's household have informed me
that there are quarrels among you.
[12]What I mean is this: One of you says, "I
follow Paul";[o] another, "I follow Apol- 1:12 o 1Co 3:4,22
los";[p] another, "I follow Cephas[a]";[q] still p Ac 18:24
another, "I follow Christ." q Jn 1:42
[13]Is Christ divided? Was Paul crucified for you? Were you baptized into[b] 1:13
the name of Paul?[r] [14]I am thankful that I r Mt 28:19
did not baptize any of you except Cris- 1:14
pus[s] and Gaius,[t] [15]so no one can say that s Ac 18:8;
you were baptized into my name. [16](Yes, Ro 16:23 t Ac 19:29
I also baptized the household of Steph- 1:16
anas;[u] beyond that, I don't remember if u 1Co 16:15
I baptized anyone else.) [17]For Christ did 1:17
not send me to baptize,[v] but to preach v Jn 4:2
the gospel—not with words of human w 1Co 2:1,4,13
wisdom,[w] lest the cross of Christ be
emptied of its power.

GOD ON A CROSS. HUMANITY AT ITS WORST. DIVINITY AT ITS BEST.

Max Lucado, *Christian Author*

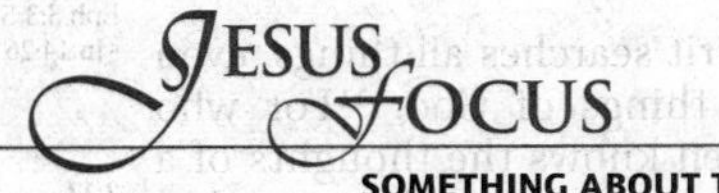

SOMETHING ABOUT THE NAME

Reports of division in the Corinthian church had reached Paul, and he was greatly troubled by the news (1 Corinthians 1:10–17). In his first letter to the Corinthian church he urged the believers there "in the name of our Lord Jesus Christ" to stop their bickering (verse 10), appealing to them by a reminder that Jesus himself takes absolute priority over both the apostles and the churches. The church had divided itself into opposing camps according to their varying allegiances to Paul, Apollos, Cephas (Peter) or Jesus (verse 12). But Paul raised an important question: "Is Christ divided?" (verse 13). It was not Paul, Peter or Apollos who had died on the cross for our sins, and believers are not baptized into any of their names. Jesus alone can claim our loyalty because of who he is and what he has done; Jesus alone is Lord of his church (Ephesians 1:22–23; 4:15).

Christ the Wisdom and Power of God

[18]For the message of the cross is foolishness to those who are perishing,[x] but 1:18 x 2Co 2:15
to us who are being saved it is the pow- y Ro 1:16
er of God.[y] [19]For it is written:

"I will destroy the wisdom of the
wise;
the intelligence of the intelligent 1:19
I will frustrate."[c][z] z Isa 29:14

[20]Where is the wise man?[a] Where is 1:20 a Isa 19:11,12
the scholar? Where is the philosopher of b Job 12:17;
this age? Has not God made foolish[b] the Ro 1:22
wisdom of the world? [21]For since in the
wisdom of God the world through
its wisdom did not know him, God was
pleased through the foolishness of what 1:22
was preached to save those who believe. c Mt 12:38
[22]Jews demand miraculous signs[c] and 1:23
Greeks look for wisdom, [23]but we preach d Lk 2:34;
Christ crucified: a stumbling block[d] to Gal 5:11
Jews and foolishness[e] to Gentiles, [24]but e 1Co 2:14
to those whom God has called,[f] both 1:24 f Ro 8:28
Jews and Greeks, Christ the power of g ver 30; Col 2:3
God and the wisdom of God.[g] [25]For the 1:25
foolishness[h] of God is wiser than man's h ver 18

a 12 That is, Peter *b 13* Or *in*; also in verse 15
c 19 Isaiah 29:14

> **THERE IS NOTHING SPECIALLY CHRISTIAN ABOUT THE CROSS . . . EXCEPT THAT JESUS DIED THERE.**
>
> Michael Green, *British Scholar*

1:25 wisdom, and the weakness[i] of God is
i 2Co 13:4 stronger than man's strength.
26 Brothers, think of what you were
when you were called. Not many of you
were wise by human standards; not
1:27 many were influential; not many were of
j Jas 2:5 k ver 20 noble birth. 27 But God chose[j] the foolish[k] things of the world to shame the
wise; God chose the weak things of the
world to shame the strong. 28 He chose
1:28 the lowly things of this world and the
l Ro 4:17 despised things—and the things that
1:29 are not[l]—to nullify the things that are,
m Eph 2:9 29 so that no one may boast before him.[m]
1:30 30 It is because of him that you are in
n Jer 23:5,6; 2Co 5:21 Christ Jesus, who has become for us
o Ro 3:24; Eph 1:7,14 wisdom from God—that is, our righteousness,[n] holiness and redemption.[o]
1:31 31 Therefore, as it is written: "Let him
p Jer 9:23,24; 2Co 10:17 who boasts boast in the Lord."[a p]

2 When I came to you, brothers, I
did not come with eloquence or
2:1 q 1Co 1:17 superior wisdom[q] as I proclaimed to you
2:2 the testimony about God.[b] 2 For I re-
r Gal 6:14; 1Co 1:23 solved to know nothing while I was with
you except Jesus Christ and him cruci-
2:3 s Ac 18:1-18 fied.[r] 3 I came to you[s] in weakness and
fear, and with much trembling. 4 My
message and my preaching were not
2:4 with wise and persuasive words, but
t Ro 15:19 with a demonstration of the Spirit's
2:5 power,[t] 5 so that your faith might not rest
u 2Co 4:7; 6:7 on men's wisdom, but on God's power.[u]

> **HIS LIFE, HIS SPIRIT, HIS PERSONALITY IS INCOMPARABLY GREATER THAN ANYTHING HE SAID, OR DID, OR TAUGHT.**
>
> Rufus M. Jones, *Quaker Scholar*

Wisdom From the Spirit

6 We do, however, speak a message of
2:6 v Eph 4:13; wisdom among the mature,[v] but not the
Php 3:15; wisdom of this age[w] or of the rulers of
Heb 5:14 this age, who are coming to nothing.
w 1Co 1:20 7 No, we speak of God's secret wisdom, a
wisdom that has been hidden and that
God destined for our glory before time
began. 8 None of the rulers of this age understood it, for if they had, they would
2:8 x Ac 7:2; Jas 2:1 not have crucified the Lord of glory.[x]
9 However, as it is written:

"No eye has seen,
no ear has heard,
no mind has conceived
2:9 y Isa 64:4; 65:17 what God has prepared for those
who love him"[c y]—

2:10 z Mt 13:11; 10 but God has revealed[z] it to us by his
Eph 3:3,5 Spirit.[a]
a Jn 14:26 The Spirit searches all things, even
the deep things of God. 11 For who
among men knows the thoughts of a
2:11 b Jer 17:9 man[b] except the man's spirit[c] within
c Pr 20:27 him? In the same way no one knows the
thoughts of God except the Spirit of
2:12 d Ro 8:15 God. 12 We have not received the spirit[d]
e 1Co 1:20,27 of the world[e] but the Spirit who is from
God, that we may understand what God
has freely given us. 13 This is what we
speak, not in words taught us by human
2:13 f 1Co 1:17 wisdom[f] but in words taught by the
Spirit, expressing spiritual truths in spiritual words.[d] 14 The man without the
Spirit does not accept the things that
come from the Spirit of God, for they are
2:14 g 1Co 1:18 foolishness[g] to him, and he cannot understand them, because they are spiri-
tually discerned. 15 The spiritual man

JESUS FOCUS

THE POWER OF GOD

God's message of love and forgiveness through his Son Jesus seems like foolishness to much of the world. But that same message is the "power of God" to those who have been rescued from their sins (1 Corinthians 1:18) by placing their trust in the Savior sent by God. Paul specified that while Jews demanded miraculous signs and Greeks looked above all else for wisdom (verse 22), God's people must recognize that Jesus is the Messiah God had promised his people so long ago (verse 23). God's Word of love and mercy is anything but foolishness. It is in fact nothing less than the power and the wisdom of God, because it is only through Jesus that we can get to know the Father (1 Corinthians 1:24; see also John 1:18; 12:45; 14:6–11).

a 31 Jer. 9:24 b 1 Some manuscripts *as I proclaimed to you God's mystery* c 9 Isaiah 64:4 d 13 Or *Spirit, interpreting spiritual truths to spiritual men*

makes judgments about all things, but
he himself is not subject to any man's
judgment:

> 16 "For who has known the mind of
> 2:16 h Isa 40:13 i Jn 15:15 the Lord
> that he may instruct him?"[a][h]

But we have the mind of Christ.[i]

> HE CANNOT POSSESS THE ROBE OF CHRIST WHO RENDS AND DIVIDES THE CHURCH OF CHRIST.
>
> Cyprian, *Early Church Father*

On Divisions in the Church

3:1 j 1Co 2:15 k Ro 7:14; 1Co 2:14 l Heb 5:13 3 Brothers, I could not address you
as spiritual[j] but as worldly[k]—
mere infants[l] in Christ. 2 I gave you milk,
not solid food,[m] for you were not yet
3:2 m Heb 5:12-14; 1Pe 2:2 n Jn 16:12 ready for it.[n] Indeed, you are still not
ready. 3 You are still worldly. For since
there is jealousy and quarreling[o] among
you, are you not worldly? Are you not
3:3 o 1Co 1:11; Gal 5:20 acting like mere men? 4 For when one
says, "I follow Paul," and another, "I fol-
3:4 p 1Co 1:12 low Apollos,"[p] are you not mere men?
5 What, after all, is Apollos? And what
is Paul? Only servants, through whom
you came to believe—as the Lord has
assigned to each his task. 6 I planted the
3:6 q Ac 18:4-11 seed,[q] Apollos watered it, but God made
it grow. 7 So neither he who plants nor he
who waters is anything, but only God,
who makes things grow. 8 The man who
plants and the man who waters have
one purpose, and each will be rewarded
3:8 r Ps 62:12 according to his own labor.[r] 9 For we are
3:9 s 2Co 6:1 t Isa 61:3 u Eph 2:20-22; 1Pe 2:5 God's fellow workers;[s] you are God's
field,[t] God's building.[u]
10 By the grace God has given me,[v] I
laid a foundation[w] as an expert builder,
and someone else is building on it. But
3:10 v Ro 12:3 w Ro 15:20 each one should be careful how he
builds. 11 For no one can lay any founda-
tion other than the one already laid,
3:11 x Isa 28:16; Eph 2:20 which is Jesus Christ.[x] 12 If any man
builds on this foundation using gold, sil-
3:13 y 1Co 4:5 z 2Th 1:7-10 ver, costly stones, wood, hay or straw,
13 his work will be shown for what it is,[y]
because the Day[z] will bring it to light. It
will be revealed with fire, and the fire will
test the quality of each man's work. 14 If
what he has built survives, he will receive his reward. 15 If it is burned up, he
will suffer loss; he himself will be saved,
but only as one escaping through the
flames.[a] 3:15 a Jude 23
16 Don't you know that you yourselves
are God's temple[b] and that God's Spirit 3:16 b 1Co 6:19; 2Co 6:16
lives in you? 17 If anyone destroys God's
temple, God will destroy him; for God's
temple is sacred, and you are that temple.
18 Do not deceive yourselves. If any 3:18 c Isa 5:21; 1Co 8:2
one of you thinks he is wise[c] by the stan-
dards of this age, he should become a
"fool" so that he may become wise. 19 For 3:19 d 1Co 1:20,27 e Job 5:13
the wisdom of this world is foolishness[d]
in God's sight. As it is written: "He 3:20 f Ps 94:11
catches the wise in their craftiness"[b];[e]
20 and again, "The Lord knows that the 3:21 g 1Co 4:6 h Ro 8:32
thoughts of the wise are futile."[c][f] 21 So
then, no more boasting about men![g] All
things are yours,[h] 22 whether Paul or 3:22 i 1Co 1:12 j Ro 8:38
Apollos or Cephas[d][i] or the world or life
or death or the present or the future[j]—
all are yours, 23 and you are of Christ,[k] 3:23 k 1Co 15:23; 2Co 10:7; Gal 3:29
and Christ is of God.

Apostles of Christ

4 So then, men ought to regard us
as servants of Christ and as those
entrusted[l] with the secret things[m] of 4:1 l 1Co 9:17; Tit 1:7 m Ro 16:25
God. 2 Now it is required that those who
have been given a trust must prove
faithful. 3 I care very little if I am judged
by you or by any human court; indeed, I
do not even judge myself. 4 My conscience is clear, but that does not make
me innocent.[n] It is the Lord who judges 4:4 n Ro 2:13
me. 5 Therefore judge nothing[o] before 4:5 o Mt 7:1,2; Ro 2:1 p Ro 2:29
the appointed time; wait till the Lord
comes. He will bring to light what is hidden in darkness and will expose the motives of men's hearts. At that time each
will receive his praise from God.[p]
6 Now, brothers, I have applied these
things to myself and Apollos for your
benefit, so that you may learn from us
the meaning of the saying, "Do not go
beyond what is written."[q] Then you will 4:6 q 1Co 1:19,31; 3:19,20 r 1Co 1:12
not take pride in one man over against
another.[r] 7 For who makes you different
from anyone else? What do you have 4:7 s Jn 3:27; Ro 12:3,6
that you did not receive?[s] And if you did
receive it, why do you boast as though
you did not?
8 Already you have all you want! Al- 4:8 t Rev 3:17,18
ready you have become rich![t] You have
become kings—and that without us!
How I wish that you really had become

[a] *16* Isaiah 40:13 [b] *19* Job 5:13
[c] *20* Psalm 94:11 [d] *22* That is, Peter

I FOLLOW . . . JESUS!

In our media-saturated society, we are exposed to many different perspectives—even from among God's people. We might hear an opinion from someone whom we respect that is in radical disagreement with the viewpoint of another credible individual. Interpretations can be different; emphases can be different; definitions can be different; premises can be different; conclusions can be different. Unfortunately, we as God's people have frequently tended to align ourselves with the teachings of one particular individual or one school of thought without a willingness to be open to the insights of others, and above all without an awareness of how much we need the One who is our head (Ephesians 1:10,22; 4:15; Colossians 1:18; 2:10,19).

The church in Corinth faced the same problem, and Paul wrote a letter to the Corinthian believers to confront the issue: "Since there is jealousy and quarreling among you, are you not worldly? Are you not acting like mere men? For when one says, 'I follow Paul,' and another, 'I follow Apollos,' are you not mere men?" (1 Corinthians 3:3–4). The members of the church had allied themselves with opposing cliques centered around the personalities of different apostles, arguing among themselves about which groups and which apostles were superior to the others. But our focal point needs to be Jesus, not our fallible human leaders. When we allow ourselves to be carried away by the charisma of a mere man or woman, we are in very real danger of worshiping the creature rather than the Creator.

In fact, following people instead of Jesus is tantamount to worldliness. Offering our supreme loyalty to anyone else besides Jesus is a sign of spiritual immaturity. We're not ready to digest the deeper truths God is waiting to impart while we are acting like nursing infants, still fixating on our spiritual "parents" instead of becoming those who will "in all things grow up into him who is the Head, that is, Christ" (Ephesians 4:15).

The apostles were only "servants" going about God's work (1 Corinthians 3:6). While God uses committed and gifted individuals to do his work on earth, in the final analysis it is still *God's* work. When we focus too much attention on particular people we begin to place a disproportionate emphasis on their contribution to the Lord's work: "What a dynamic preacher. What a gifted teacher!" The incontrovertible fact, however, is that only God deserves the glory, because everything done in God's name is God's work *exclusively*.

We are *of Jesus*, not of any other Christian leader (verse 23). The only person who deserves our devotion is Jesus—not Paul, not our pastor, not a television evangelist or a nationally known speaker, not a favorite Christian author. While God certainly accomplishes his work through the dedicated efforts of those special people he has called into his service, the purpose of the gifts of those involved in ministry is always to attach us to *Jesus*. With the apostle Paul, we can resolve to make Jesus Christ the sole subject of our commitment and our proclamation: "I resolved to know nothing while I was with you except Jesus Christ and him crucified" (1 Corinthians 2:2).

Self-Discovery: *Have you ever faced the temptation of aligning yourself too closely with a spiritual "parent" or mentor at the expense of your personal relationship with Jesus Christ?*

GO TO DISCOVERY 313 ON PAGE 1545

kings so that we might be kings with
you! 9For it seems to me that God has
put us apostles on display at the end of
the procession, like men condemned to
4:9 die[u] in the arena. We have been made a
[u]Ro 8:36 [v]Heb 10:33 spectacle[v] to the whole universe, to an-
4:10 gels as well as to men. 10We are fools for
[w]1Co 1:18; Christ,[w] but you are so wise in Christ![x]
Ac 17:18 We are weak, but you are strong![y] You
[x]1Co 3:18 [y]1Co 2:3 are honored, we are dishonored! 11To
this very hour we go hungry and thirsty,
4:11 [z]Ro 8:35; we are in rags, we are brutally treated,
2Co 11:23-27 we are homeless.[z] 12We work hard with
our own hands.[a] When we are cursed,
4:12 [a]Ac 18:3 we bless;[b] when we are persecuted, we
[b]1Pe 3:9 endure it; 13when we are slandered, we
answer kindly. Up to this moment
we have become the scum of the earth,
4:13 [c]La 3:45 the refuse[c] of the world.
4:14 14I am not writing this to shame you,
[d]1Th 2:11 but to warn you, as my dear children.[d]
15Even though you have ten thousand
guardians in Christ, you do not have
many fathers, for in Christ Jesus I be-
4:15 [e]1Co 9:12,14, came your father through the gospel.[e]
18,23 16Therefore I urge you to imitate me.[f]
4:16 17For this reason I am sending to you
[f]1Co 11:1; Timothy, my son[g] whom I love, who is
Php 3:17; 1Th 1:6; faithful in the Lord. He will remind you
2Th 3:7,9 of my way of life in Christ Jesus, which
agrees with what I teach everywhere in
4:17 [g]1Ti 1:2 every church.[h]
[h]1Co 7:17 18Some of you have become arrogant,
as if I were not coming to you. 19But I
4:19 will come to you very soon,[i] if the Lord
[i]2Co 1:15,16 [j]Ac 18:21 is willing,[j] and then I will find out not
only how these arrogant people are talk-
ing, but what power they have. 20For the
kingdom of God is not a matter of talk
but of power. 21What do you prefer?
4:21 [k]2Co 1:23; 13:2, Shall I come to you with a whip,[k] or in
10 love and with a gentle spirit?

Expel the Immoral Brother!

5 It is actually reported that there is
sexual immorality among you,
and of a kind that does not occur even
5:1 among pagans: A man has his father's
[l]Lev 18:8; wife.[l] 2And you are proud! Shouldn't you
Dt 22:30 rather have been filled with grief[m] and
5:2 have put out of your fellowship the man
[m]2Co 7:7-11 who did this? 3Even though I am not
physically present, I am with you in spir-
5:3 [n]Col 2:5 it.[n] And I have already passed judgment
on the one who did this, just as if I were
5:4 present. 4When you are assembled in
[o]2Th 3:6 the name of our Lord Jesus[o] and I am
with you in spirit, and the power of our
Lord Jesus is present, 5hand this man 5:5
over[p] to Satan, so that the sinful nature[a] [p]1Ti 1:20
may be destroyed and his spirit saved on
the day of the Lord.
6Your boasting is not good.[q] Don't 5:6
you know that a little yeast[r] works [q]Jas 4:16 [r]Mt 16:6,12
through the whole batch of dough?[s] [s]Gal 5:9
7Get rid of the old yeast that you may be
a new batch without yeast—as you really are. For Christ, our Passover lamb, has
been sacrificed.[t] 8Therefore let us keep 5:7
the Festival, not with the old yeast, the [t]Mk 14:12; 1Pe 1:19
yeast of malice and wickedness, but
with bread without yeast,[u] the bread of 5:8 [u]Ex 12:14,15;
sincerity and truth. Dt 16:3
9I have written you in my letter not to 5:9
associate[v] with sexually immoral peo- [v]Eph 5:11;
ple— 10not at all meaning the people of 2Th 3:6,14
this world[w] who are immoral, or the 5:10
greedy and swindlers, or idolaters. In [w]1Co 10:27
that case you would have to leave this
world. 11But now I am writing you that
you must not associate with anyone
who calls himself a brother but is sexu-
ally immoral or greedy, an idolater[x] or a 5:11 [x]1Co 10:7,14
slanderer, a drunkard or a swindler.
With such a man do not even eat.
12What business is it of mine to judge 5:12
those outside[y] the church? Are you not [y]Mk 4:11 [z]ver 3-5;
to judge those inside?[z] 13God will judge 1Co 6:1-4
those outside. "Expel the wicked man 5:13
from among you."[b][a] [a]Dt 13:5

Lawsuits Among Believers

6 If any of you has a dispute with
another, dare he take it before the
ungodly for judgment instead of before
the saints?[b] 2Do you not know that the 6:1 [b]Mt 18:17
saints will judge the world?[c] And if you
are to judge the world, are you not com- 6:2 [c]Mt 19:28;
petent to judge trivial cases? 3Do you Lk 22:30
not know that we will judge angels?
How much more the things of this life!
4Therefore, if you have disputes about
such matters, appoint as judges even
men of little account in the church![c] 5I
say this to shame you.[d] Is it possible that 6:5 [d]1Co 4:14
there is nobody among you wise enough [e]Ac 1:15
to judge a dispute between believers?[e]
6But instead, one brother goes to law
against another—and this in front of 6:6
unbelievers![f] [f]2Co 6:14,15
7The very fact that you have lawsuits

[a] 5 Or *that his body;* or *that the flesh* [b] 13 Deut. 17:7; 19:19; 21:21; 22:21,24; 24:7 [c] 4 Or *matters, do you appoint as judges men of little account in the church?*

among you means you have been completely defeated already. Why not rather
be wronged? Why not rather be cheat-
6:7 [g] Mt 5:39,40 ed?[g] 8Instead, you yourselves cheat and
do wrong, and you do this to your
6:8 [h] 1Th 4:6 brothers.[h]
6:9 9Do you not know that the wicked
[i] Gal 5:21 will not inherit the kingdom of God?[i]
[j] 1Co 15:33; Do not be deceived:[j] Neither the sexual-
Jas 1:16 ly immoral nor idolaters nor adulterers
nor male prostitutes nor homosexual offenders 10nor thieves nor the greedy nor
drunkards nor slanderers nor swindlers
will inherit the kingdom of God. 11And
6:11 [k] Eph 2:2 that is what some of you were.[k] But you
[l] Ac 22:16 were washed,[l] you were sanctified,[m] you
[m] 1Co 1:2 were justified in the name of the Lord
Jesus Christ and by the Spirit of our God.

Sexual Immorality

6:12 12"Everything is permissible for
[n] 1Co 10:23 me"—but not everything is beneficial.[n]
"Everything is permissible for me"—but
I will not be mastered by anything.
13"Food for the stomach and the stomach for food"—but God will destroy
6:13 them both.[o] The body is not meant for
[o] Col 2:22 sexual immorality, but for the Lord, and
the Lord for the body. 14By his power
6:14 God raised the Lord from the dead, and
[p] Ro 6:5; he will raise us also.[p] 15Do you not know
Eph 1:19,20 that your bodies are members of Christ
6:15 himself?[q] Shall I then take the members
[q] Ro 12:5 of Christ and unite them with a prostitute? Never! 16Do you not know that he
who unites himself with a prostitute is
one with her in body? For it is said, "The
two will become one flesh."[a] [r] 17But he 6:16
who unites himself with the Lord is one [r] Ge 2:24;
with him in spirit.[s] Mt 19:5;
18Flee from sexual immorality.[t] All Eph 5:31
other sins a man commits are outside 6:17
his body, but he who sins sexually sins [s] Jn 17:21-23;
against his own body.[u] 19Do you not Gal 2:20
know that your body is a temple[v] of the 6:18
Holy Spirit, who is in you, whom you [t] 2Co 12:21;
have received from God? You are not 1Th 4:3,4;
your own;[w] 20you were bought at a price.[x] Heb 13:4
Therefore honor God with your body. [u] Ro 6:12

Marriage

7 Now for the matters you wrote 6:19
about: It is good for a man not to [v] Jn 2:21
marry.[b] [y] 2But since there is so much im- [w] Ro 14:7,8
morality, each man should have his own 6:20
wife, and each woman her own husband. [x] Ac 20:28;
3The husband should fulfill his marital 1Co 7:23;
duty to his wife,[z] and likewise the wife to 1Pe 1:18,19;
her husband. 4The wife's body does not Rev 5:9
belong to her alone but also to her husband. In the same way, the husband's 7:1
body does not belong to him alone but [y] ver 8,26
also to his wife. 5Do not deprive each
other except by mutual consent and for 7:3
a time,[a] so that you may devote your- [z] Ex 21:10;
selves to prayer. Then come together 1Pe 3:7
again so that Satan[b] will not tempt you[c]
because of your lack of self-control. 6I say 7:5
this as a concession, not as a command.[d] [a] Ex 19:15;
7I wish that all men were as I am.[e] But 1Sa 21:4,5
each man has his own gift from God; one [b] Mt 4:10
has this gift, another has that.[f] [c] 1Th 3:5
8Now to the unmarried and the wid- 7:6
ows I say: It is good for them to stay un- [d] 2Co 8:8
married, as I am.[g] 9But if they cannot 7:7
control themselves, they should marry,[h] [e] ver 8; 1Co 9:5
for it is better to marry than to burn [f] Mt 19:11,12;
with passion. Ro 12:6;
10To the married I give this command 1Co 12:4,11
(not I, but the Lord): A wife must not 7:8
separate from her husband.[i] 11But if she [g] ver 1,26
does, she must remain unmarried or 7:9
else be reconciled to her husband. And [h] 1Ti 5:14
a husband must not divorce his wife.
12To the rest I say this (I, not the 7:10
Lord):[j] If any brother has a wife who is [i] Mal 2:14-16;
not a believer and she is willing to live Mt 5:32; 19:3-9;
with him, he must not divorce her. 13And Mk 10:11;
if a woman has a husband who is not a Lk 16:18
believer and he is willing to live with her, 7:12
she must not divorce him. 14For the un- [j] ver 6,10;
believing husband has been sanctified 2Co 11:17

[a] 16 Gen. 2:24 [b] 1 Or *"It is good for a man not to have sexual relations with a woman."*

THE HOLY SPIRIT'S TEMPLE

Following Jesus' resurrection and prior to his ascension into heaven, he had informed his disciples that the Holy Spirit would come on them to fill them with power (Acts 1:4–5,8). And Jesus had earlier advised them that the Spirit would be "in [them]" (John 14:17). The truth that God's Holy Spirit dwells in the hearts of his people is a fundamental teaching of the New Testament (see, for example, John 14:16–23; Acts 2:1–4; Ephesians 5:18). Our bodies belong to God, stated Paul, because his Holy Spirit lives in them (1 Corinthians 6:19). What we do with our bodies and how we treat them matters to God because we are his temple—the place of his presence.

CARING FOR GOD'S TEMPLE

In the Bible the illustration of a physical body is used as an analogy for the spiritual "body of Christ" (Romans 12:4–5; 1 Corinthians 12:12–31). Each of us as a living member of Christ's body has been given an important function to perform here on earth. We cannot afford to take this responsibility lightly, so it is imperative that we not mistreat our own physical bodies (1 Corinthians 6:12–20).

When we do neglect to care for our bodies, we not only destroy what God has created but also do harm to Jesus' church. Paul pointed out that "'everything is permissible for me'—but not everything is beneficial" (verse 12). Our goal is to live a godly life based not so much on what we can get away with as on what is healthful—for ourselves and for others, both physically and spiritually (1 Corinthians 10:23).

It is easy for our perspectives on how to take care of our bodies to become twisted or out of proportion. For example, we might quip that we "love" certain foods and are unable to resist them—the truth is that we may even be addicted to them. But both our digestive systems and the food needed to keep our bodies functioning are temporal rather than eternal (1 Corinthians 6:13). Food was never intended by God to afford us comfort or to stave off emotional or spiritual "hunger"; yet that is precisely where many of us turn when our real need is for a hearty helping of God and his Word.

God warns us as Christians to *run* from sexual sin, because it constitutes in all of its forms a serious offense against the body that was created in God's image. As Christians, we know that our bodies are the earthly home or temple for God's Holy Spirit (verse 19). We were purchased for holiness at a very high price—the life of Jesus (1 Corinthians 6:20; see also Acts 20:28; 1 Corinthians 7:23; 1 Peter 1:18–19). But the prevalent philosophies of our world would dupe us into believing that we can do whatever we desire with our bodies. Paul emphatically refuted this dangerous and erroneous claim: "None of us lives to himself alone . . . we belong to the Lord" (Romans 14:7–8). We have no right to abuse our bodies because, just as the Levites cared for the temple in Jerusalem, so God has entrusted to us the care of our bodies. When we allow sexual immorality a foothold into our lives, we spiritually desecrate God's sacred temple.

"Therefore honor God with your body," Paul pleaded (1 Corinthians 6:20). This is the guiding principle for the believer with respect to everything physical. What Jesus wants is for us to "love the LORD [our] God with all [our] heart [our will and emotions] and with all [our] soul [our eternal spirit] and with all [our] strength [our body]" (Deuteronomy 6:5). Destructive physical behavior is never inconsequential. Whatever we find ourselves unable to control, whether physically or mentally, is something that has a stranglehold on us in an area that should be devoted to God.

***Self-Discovery:** List five or six things you can do today to "honor God with your body" in light of the fact that you are a living member of the body of Jesus Christ.*

GO TO DISCOVERY 314 ON PAGE 1548

through his wife, and the unbelieving
wife has been sanctified through her believing husband. Otherwise your chil-
7:14 dren would be unclean, but as it is, they
[k]Mal 2:15 are holy.[k]
15But if the unbeliever leaves, let him
do so. A believing man or woman is not
7:15 bound in such circumstances; God has
[l]Ro 14:19; called us to live in peace.[l] 16How do you
1Co 14:33 know, wife, whether you will save[m] your
7:16 husband?[n] Or, how do you know, hus-
[m]Ro 11:14 band, whether you will save your wife?
[n]1Pe 3:1
17Nevertheless, each one should retain the place in life that the Lord assigned to him and to which God has
7:17 called him.[o] This is the rule I lay down in
[o]Ro 12:3 all the churches.[p] 18Was a man already
[p]1Co 4:17; circumcised when he was called? He
14:33; 2Co 8:18; should not become uncircumcised. Was
11:28 a man uncircumcised when he was
7:18 called? He should not be circumcised.[q]
[q]Ac 15:1,2 19Circumcision is nothing and uncir-
7:19 cumcision is nothing.[r] Keeping God's
[r]Ro 2:25-27; commands is what counts. 20Each one
Gal 5:6; 6:15; should remain in the situation which he
Col 3:11
7:20 was in when God called him.[s] 21Were
[s]ver 24 you a slave when you were called? Don't
let it trouble you—although if you can
gain your freedom, do so. 22For he who
was a slave when he was called by the
7:22 Lord is the Lord's freedman;[t] similarly,
[t]Jn 8:32,36; he who was a free man when he was
Phm 16 called is Christ's slave.[u] 23You were
[u]Eph 6:6
7:23 bought at a price;[v] do not become slaves
[v]1Co 6:20 of men. 24Brothers, each man, as re-
7:24 sponsible to God, should remain in the
[w]ver 20 situation God called him to.[w]
25Now about virgins: I have no com-
7:25 mand from the Lord,[x] but I give a judg-
[x]ver 6; 2Co 8:8 ment as one who by the Lord's mercy[y] is
[y]2Co 4:1; trustworthy. 26Because of the present cri-
1Ti 1:13,16 sis, I think that it is good for you to re-
7:26 main as you are.[z] 27Are you married? Do
[z]ver 1,8 not seek a divorce. Are you unmarried?
Do not look for a wife. 28But if you do
marry, you have not sinned; and if a virgin marries, she has not sinned. But
those who marry will face many troubles
in this life, and I want to spare you this.
7:29 29What I mean, brothers, is that the
[a]ver 31; time is short.[a] From now on those who
Ro 13:11,12 have wives should live as if they had
none; 30those who mourn, as if they did
not; those who are happy, as if they were
not; those who buy something, as if it
were not theirs to keep; 31those who use
the things of the world, as if not engrossed in them. For this world in its
present form is passing away.[b] 7:31 [b]1Jn 2:17
32I would like you to be free from concern. An unmarried man is concerned 7:32
about the Lord's affairs[c]—how he can [c]1Ti 5:5
please the Lord. 33But a married man is
concerned about the affairs of this
world—how he can please his wife—
34and his interests are divided. An unmarried woman or virgin is concerned
about the Lord's affairs: Her aim is to be
devoted to the Lord in both body and 7:34
spirit.[d] But a married woman is con- [d]Lk 2:37
cerned about the affairs of this world—
how she can please her husband. 35I am
saying this for your own good, not to re-
strict you, but that you may live in a right 7:35
way in undivided[e] devotion to the Lord. [e]Ps 86:11
36If anyone thinks he is acting im-
properly toward the virgin he is engaged
to, and if she is getting along in years
and he feels he ought to marry, he
should do as he wants. He is not sin- 7:36
ning.[f] They should get married. 37But [f]ver 28
the man who has settled the matter in
his own mind, who is under no compulsion but has control over his own will,
and who has made up his mind not to
marry the virgin—this man also does
the right thing. 38So then, he who mar- 7:38
ries the virgin does right,[g] but he who [g]Heb 13:4
does not marry her does even better.[a]
39A woman is bound to her husband
as long as he lives.[h] But if her husband 7:39 [h]Ro 7:2,3
dies, she is free to marry anyone she [i]2Co 6:14
wishes, but he must belong to the Lord.[i] 7:40
40In my judgment,[j] she is happier if she [j]ver 25
stays as she is—and I think that I too
have the Spirit of God.

Food Sacrificed to Idols

8:1 [k]Ac 15:20 [l]Ro 15:14

8 Now about food sacrificed to
idols:[k] We know that we all pos-
sess knowledge.[b][l] Knowledge puffs up, 8:2 [m]1Co 3:18
but love builds up. 2The man who thinks [n]1Co 13:8,9,12; 1Ti 6:4
he knows something[m] does not yet
know as he ought to know.[n] 3But the 8:3 [o]Ro 8:29;
man who loves God is known by God.[o] Gal 4:9

[a] 36–38 Or *36If anyone thinks he is not treating his daughter properly, and if she is getting along in years, and he feels she ought to marry, he should do as he wants. He is not sinning. He should let her get married. 37But the man who has settled the matter in his own mind, who is under no compulsion but has control over his own will, and who has made up his mind to keep the virgin unmarried—this man also does the right thing. 38So then, he who gives his virgin in marriage does right, but he who does not give her in marriage does even better.*
[b] 1 Or *"We all possess knowledge," as you say*

8:4 4 So then, about eating food sacrificed
p ver 1,7,10 to idols:[p] We know that an idol is noth-
q 1Co 10:19 ing at all in the world[q] and that there is
r Dt 6:4; Eph 4:6 no God but one.[r] 5 For even if there are
8:5 so-called gods,[s] whether in heaven or on
s 2Th 2:4 earth (as indeed there are many "gods"
and many "lords"), 6 yet for us there is
8:6 t Mal 2:10 but one God, the Father,[t] from whom all
u Ro 11:36 things came[u] and for whom we live; and
v Eph 4:5 w Jn 1:3 there is but one Lord,[v] Jesus Christ,
through whom all things came[w] and
through whom we live.

7 But not everyone knows this. Some
people are still so accustomed to idols
that when they eat such food they think
8:7 of it as having been sacrificed to an idol,
x Ro 14:14; and since their conscience is weak,[x] it is
1Co 10:28 defiled. 8 But food does not bring us near
8:8 to God;[y] we are no worse if we do not
y Ro 14:17 eat, and no better if we do.

9 Be careful, however, that the exercise
8:9 of your freedom does not become a
z Gal 5:13 stumbling block[z] to the weak.[a] 10 For if
a Ro 14:1 anyone with a weak conscience sees you
who have this knowledge eating in an
idol's temple, won't he be emboldened to
eat what has been sacrificed to idols?
11 So this weak brother, for whom Christ
8:11 b Ro 14:15,20 died, is destroyed[b] by your knowledge.
8:12 12 When you sin against your brothers[c]
c Mt 18:6 in this way and wound their weak conscience, you sin against Christ. 13 Therefore, if what I eat causes my brother to
8:13 fall into sin, I will never eat meat again,
d Ro 14:21 so that I will not cause him to fall.[d]

The Rights of an Apostle

9 Am I not free? Am I not an apos-
9:1 tle?[e] Have I not seen Jesus our
e 2Co 12:12 f 1Co 15:8 Lord?[f] Are you not the result of my work
g 1Co 3:6; 4:15 in the Lord?[g] 2 Even though I may not be
9:2 an apostle to others, surely I am to you!
h 2Co 3:2,3 For you are the seal[h] of my apostleship
in the Lord.

3 This is my defense to those who sit in
9:4 judgment on me. 4 Don't we have the
i 1Th 2:6 right to food and drink?[i] 5 Don't we have
9:5 the right to take a believing wife[j] along
j 1Co 7:7,8 with us, as do the other apostles and the
k Mt 12:46 Lord's brothers[k] and Cephas[a]? 6 Or is it
9:6 only I and Barnabas[l] who must work for
l Ac 4:36 a living?

7 Who serves as a soldier at his own
9:7 expense? Who plants a vineyard[m] and
m Dt 20:6; does not eat of its grapes? Who tends a
Pr 27:18 flock and does not drink of the milk? 8 Do
I say this merely from a human point of
view? Doesn't the Law say the same
thing? 9 For it is written in the Law of
Moses: "Do not muzzle an ox while it is 9:9
treading out the grain."[b][n] Is it about oxen n Dt 25:4;
that God is concerned?[o] 10 Surely he says 1Ti 5:18
this for us, doesn't he? Yes, this was writ- o Dt 22:1-4
ten for us,[p] because when the plowman 9:10
plows and the thresher threshes, they p Ro 4:23,24
ought to do so in the hope of sharing in q 2Ti 2:6
the harvest.[q] 11 If we have sown spiritual
seed among you, is it too much if we reap
a material harvest from you?[r] 12 If others 9:11
have this right of support from you, r Ro 15:27
shouldn't we have it all the more?

But we did not use this right.[s] On the 9:12 s Ac 18:3
contrary, we put up with anything rather t 2Co 11:7-12
than hinder[t] the gospel of Christ.
13 Don't you know that those who work
in the temple get their food from the
temple, and those who serve at the altar
share in what is offered on the altar?[u] 9:13 u Lev 6:16,26;
14 In the same way, the Lord has com- Dt 18:1
manded that those who preach the
gospel should receive their living from 9:14
the gospel.[v] v Mt 10:10;

15 But I have not used any of these 1Ti 5:18
rights.[w] And I am not writing this in the 9:15 w Ac 18:3
hope that you will do such things for me. x 2Co 11:9,10
I would rather die than have anyone de-
prive me of this boast.[x] 16 Yet when I
preach the gospel, I cannot boast, for I 9:16
am compelled to preach.[y] Woe to me if I y Ro 1:14;
do not preach the gospel! 17 If I preach Ac 9:15
voluntarily, I have a reward;[z] if not vol- 9:17
untarily, I am simply discharging the z 1Co 3:8,14
trust committed to me.[a] 18 What then is a Gal 2:7;
my reward? Just this: that in preaching Col 1:25
the gospel I may offer it free of charge,[b] 9:18
and so not make use of my rights in b 2Co 11:7;
preaching it. 12:13

19 Though I am free[c] and belong to no 9:19 c ver 1 d Gal 5:13
man, I make myself a slave to everyone,[d] e Mt 18:15;
to win as many as possible.[e] 20 To the 1Pe 3:1
Jews I became like a Jew, to win the 9:20
Jews.[f] To those under the law I became f Ac 16:3; 21:20-
like one under the law (though I myself 26; Ro 11:14
am not under the law), so as to win
those under the law. 21 To those not having the law I became like one not having 9:21
the law[g] (though I am not free from g Ro 2:12,14
God's law but am under Christ's law), so
as to win those not having the law. 22 To
the weak I became weak, to win the
weak. I have become all things to all 9:22
men[h] so that by all possible means I h 1Co 10:33
might save some.[i] 23 I do all this for the i Ro 11:14

[a] 5 That is, Peter [b] 9 Deut. 25:4

All Things to All People

Paul's passion was to tell others about Jesus and to win "as many as possible" (1 Corinthians 9:19). The first letters of each word in this phrase form the acronym "A MAP." Paul followed three distinct strategies as he traveled on his missionary journeys to proclaim the Good News about Jesus.

First, there was the Jewish strategy: "To the Jews I became like a Jew, to win the Jews" (verse 20). When in the company of Jewish people Paul acted and spoke like a Jew, showing deliberate sensitivity to Jewish cultural perspectives in order to win the right to be heard. Paul often spoke in Jewish synagogues, and when he did so he preached from the Hebrew Scripture, beginning with the Old Testament and then pointing ahead to Jesus, who embodied the fulfillment of Old Testament prophecy. Paul's discourses to the Jewish people were sprinkled with Old Testament history and quotations (Acts 13:13–41).

Next, there was the Gentile strategy: "To those not having the law I became like one not having the law (though I am not free from God's law but am under Christ's law), so as to win those not having the law" (1 Corinthians 9:21). When in Athens Paul reasoned with Greek philosophers and referred to Greek philosophy and poetry. Again, he started with the familiar and then turned his attention to Jesus, but his strategy was entirely different from that which he used with a Jewish audience (Acts 17:22–34).

Finally, he used a different strategy for the "weak" (for those individuals whose consciences were ultra-sensitive about details): "To the weak I became weak, to win the weak" (1 Corinthians 9:22). Those in charge of the pagan temples in Corinth were in the habit of selling surplus meat that had been brought to sacrifice to false gods. Certain believers were concerned that they might accidentally sin by eating such meat if they were to share a meal with someone who worshiped in one of the pagan temples. Paul reassured them that the important issue was that they spend time with people who did not know Jesus, eating whatever was set in front of them so as not to offend their hosts. But if someone else at the table was bothered by eating this kind of meat, then the believer should also refrain (1 Corinthians 10:23–33).

On one day Paul might adhere to a kosher diet and quote the Old Testament. On the next he might dine on meat that had been offered to idols. On the third day he might decline to eat such meat, because someone else who was present found the practice offensive. This triple standard may appear contradictory and even duplicitous, but Paul was not a hypocrite; he was an effective witness because he was able to differentiate which issues were important and which scruples would simply stand in the way of reaching people for Jesus. His statement provides a guiding principle we can all use as we step out to share the Good News: "I have become all things to all men so that by all possible means I might save some. I do all this for the sake of the gospel, that I may share in its blessings" (1 Corinthians 9:22–23).

***Self-Discovery:** In what ways are you, as a representative of Jesus Christ, versatile in your approaches to other people?*

GO TO DISCOVERY 315 ON PAGE 1551

sake of the gospel, that I may share in its
blessings.
24Do you not know that in a race all
9:24 the runners run, but only one gets the
[j]Gal 2:2; 2Ti 4:7; Heb 12:1 prize? Run[j] in such a way as to get the
prize. 25Everyone who competes in the
games goes into strict training. They do
it to get a crown that will not last; but we
do it to get a crown that will last forev-
9:25 [k]Jas 1:12; Rev 2:10 er.[k] 26Therefore I do not run like a man
running aimlessly; I do not fight like a
9:27 man beating the air. 27No, I beat my
[l]Ro 8:13 body[l] and make it my slave so that after
I have preached to others, I myself will
not be disqualified for the prize.

Warnings From Israel's History

10 For I do not want you to be ignorant of the fact, brothers,
that our forefathers were all under the
10:1 [m]Ex 13:21 cloud[m] and that they all passed through
[n]Ex 14:22,29 the sea.[n] 2They were all baptized into
Moses in the cloud and in the sea. 3They
all ate the same spiritual food 4and
drank the same spiritual drink; for they
10:4 [o]Ex 17:6; Nu 20:11; Ps 78:15 drank from the spiritual rock[o] that accompanied them, and that rock was
Christ. 5Nevertheless, God was not
pleased with most of them; their bodies
10:5 [p]Nu 14:29; Heb 3:17 were scattered over the desert.[p]
6Now these things occurred as exam-
ples[a] to keep us from setting our hearts
on evil things as they did. 7Do not be
idolaters,[q] as some of them were; as it is 10:7 [q]ver 14
written: "The people sat down to eat [r]Ex 32:4,6,19
and drink and got up to indulge in pa-
gan revelry."[b r] 8We should not commit
sexual immorality, as some of them
did—and in one day twenty-three thou-
sand of them died.[s] 9We should not test 10:8 [s]Nu 25:1-9
the Lord, as some of them did—and
were killed by snakes.[t] 10And do not 10:9 [t]Nu 21:5,6
grumble, as some of them did[u]—and
were killed[v] by the destroying angel.[w] 10:10 [u]Nu 16:41 [v]Nu 16:49 [w]Ex 12:23
11These things happened to them as
examples and were written down as
warnings for us, on whom the fulfill-
ment of the ages has come.[x] 12So, if you 10:11 [x]Ro 13:11
think you are standing firm,[y] be careful
that you don't fall! 13No temptation has 10:12 [y]Ro 11:20
seized you except what is common to
man. And God is faithful;[z] he will not let 10:13 [z]1Co 1:9
you be tempted beyond what you can [a]2Pe 2:9
bear.[a] But when you are tempted, he will
also provide a way out so that you can
stand up under it.

Idol Feasts and the Lord's Supper

14Therefore, my dear friends, flee from
idolatry. 15I speak to sensible people;
judge for yourselves what I say. 16Is not
the cup of thanksgiving for which we
give thanks a participation in the blood
of Christ? And is not the bread that we
break a participation in the body of
Christ?[b] 17Because there is one loaf, we, 10:16 [b]Mt 26:26-28
who are many, are one body,[c] for we all 10:17 [c]Ro 12:5; 1Co 12:27
partake of the one loaf.
18Consider the people of Israel: Do
not those who eat the sacrifices[d] partic-
ipate in the altar? 19Do I mean then that 10:18 [d]Lev 7:6,14,15
a sacrifice offered to an idol is anything,
or that an idol is anything?[e] 20No, but 10:19 [e]1Co 8:4
the sacrifices of pagans are offered to
demons,[f] not to God, and I do not want 10:20 [f]Dt 32:17; Ps 106:37; Rev 9:20
you to be participants with demons.
21You cannot drink the cup of the Lord
and the cup of demons too; you cannot
have a part in both the Lord's table and 10:21 [g]2Co 6:15,16
the table of demons.[g] 22Are we trying to
arouse the Lord's jealousy?[h] Are we 10:22 [h]Dt 32:16,21
stronger than he?[i] [i]Ecc 6:10; Isa 45:9

The Believer's Freedom

23"Everything is permissible"—but
not everything is beneficial.[j] "Every- 10:23 [j]1Co 6:12
thing is permissible"—but not every-
thing is constructive. 24Nobody should

[a] 6 Or *types;* also in verse 11 [b] 7 Exodus 32:6

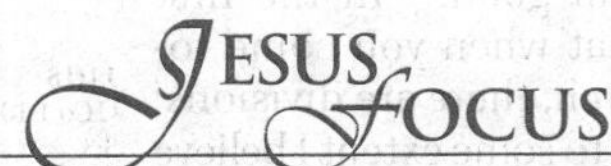

JESUS, OUR ROCK

The experience of God's faithful provision for his people, so clearly encountered at the time of the exodus when he set them free from Egyptian bondage, is unmistakably pictured throughout the remainder of God's Word. The *manna* ("What is it?" in Hebrew) that God had given the Israelites to eat throughout their long sojourn in the desert was referred to in Exodus as "bread from heaven" (Exodus 16:4). God also provided his thirsty people with water to drink—gushing from a solid rock (see Exodus 17:6). In Deuteronomy 32:4,15 Moses also pointed out that God was the Rock and Savior for the people, and Paul went on to clarify that "that rock was Christ" (1 Corinthians 10:4). The food and water with which God nourished his people in the desert foreshadow the manner in which Jesus now ministers to us spiritually as the self-proclaimed bread and water of life (see John 4:14; 6:35–40,48–58).

10:24 k ver 33; Ro 15:1,2; 1Co 13:5; Php 2:4,21 seek his own good, but the good of
others.[k]
25Eat anything sold in the meat market without raising questions of con-
10:25 l Ac 10:15; 1Co 8:7 science,[l] 26for, "The earth is the Lord's,
and everything in it."[a m]
27If some unbeliever invites you to a
10:26 m Ps 24:1 meal and you want to go, eat whatever is
put before you[n] without raising ques-
10:27 n Lk 10:7 tions of conscience. 28But if anyone says
to you, "This has been offered in sacri-
fice," then do not eat it, both for the sake
of the man who told you and for con-
10:28 o 1Co 8:7,10-12 science' sake[b o]— 29the other man's conscience, I mean, not yours. For why
10:29 p Ro 14:16; 1Co 9:1,19 should my freedom[p] be judged by another's conscience? 30If I take part in the
meal with thankfulness, why am I de-
10:30 q Ro 14:6 nounced because of something I thank
God for?[q]
10:31 r Col 3:17; 1Pe 4:11 31So whether you eat or drink or whatever you do, do it all for the glory of God.[r]
32Do not cause anyone to stumble,[s]
10:32 s Ac 24:16 t Ac 20:28 whether Jews, Greeks or the church of
God[t]— 33even as I try to please everybody
10:33 u Ro 15:2; 1Co 9:22 v Ro 11:14 in every way.[u] For I am not seeking my
own good but the good of many, so that
11 they may be saved.[v] 1Follow my
example,[w] as I follow the exam-
11:1 w 1Co 4:16 ple of Christ.

Propriety in Worship

11:2 x ver 17,22 y 1Co 4:17 z 1Co 15:2,3; 2Th 2:15 2I praise you[x] for remembering me in
everything[y] and for holding to the
teachings,[c] just as I passed them on to
you.[z]
3Now I want you to realize that
11:3 a Eph 1:22 b Ge 3:16; Eph 5:23 c 1Co 3:23 the head of every man is Christ,[a] and the
head of the woman is man,[b] and the
head of Christ is God.[c] 4Every man who
prays or prophesies with his head covered dishonors his head. 5And every
11:5 d Ac 21:9 e Dt 21:12 woman who prays or prophesies[d] with
her head uncovered dishonors her
head—it is just as though her head were
shaved.[e] 6If a woman does not cover her
head, she should have her hair cut off;
and if it is a disgrace for a woman to
have her hair cut or shaved off, she
should cover her head. 7A man ought
not to cover his head,[d] since he is the
11:7 f Ge 1:26; Jas 3:9 image[f] and glory of God; but the woman
is the glory of man. 8For man did not
11:8 g Ge 2:21-23; 1Ti 2:13 come from woman, but woman from
man;[g] 9neither was man created for
woman, but woman for man.[h] 10For this
11:9 h Ge 2:18 reason, and because of the angels, the
woman ought to have a sign of authori-
ty on her head.
11In the Lord, however, woman is not
independent of man, nor is man independent of woman. 12For as woman
came from man, so also man is born of
woman. But everything comes from
God.[i] 13Judge for yourselves: Is it proper 11:12 i Ro 11:36
for a woman to pray to God with her
head uncovered? 14Does not the very nature of things teach you that if a man
has long hair, it is a disgrace to him,
15but that if a woman has long hair, it is
her glory? For long hair is given to her as
a covering. 16If anyone wants to be contentious about this, we have no other
practice—nor do the churches of God.[j] 11:16 j 1Co 7:17

CHRIST HATH NOT ONLY DONE
A GREAT WORK FOR US IN MAKING
GOOD OUR RECONCILIATION
WITH GOD. HE FURTHER
DOES A GREAT WORK IN US WHEN
HE MAKES US LIKE UNTO GOD.

Thomas Chalmers, *Scottish Theologian*

The Lord's Supper

17In the following directives I have no 11:17 k ver 2,22
praise for you,[k] for your meetings do
more harm than good. 18In the first
place, I hear that when you come to-
gether as a church, there are divisions[l] 11:18 l 1Co 1:10-12; 3:3
among you, and to some extent I believe
it. 19No doubt there have to be differences among you to show which of you
have God's approval.[m] 20When you come 11:19 m 1Jn 2:19
together, it is not the Lord's Supper you
eat, 21for as you eat, each of you goes
ahead without waiting for anybody else.[n] 11:21 n 2Pe 2:13; Jude 12
One remains hungry, another gets
drunk. 22Don't you have homes to eat
and drink in? Or do you despise the
church of God[o] and humiliate those who 11:22 o 1Co 10:32
have nothing?[p] What shall I say to you? p Jas 2:6 q ver 2, 17
Shall I praise you[q] for this? Certainly not!

[a] 26 Psalm 24:1 [b] 28 Some manuscripts *conscience' sake, for "the earth is the Lord's and everything in it"* [c] 2 Or *traditions* [d] 4–7 Or *4Every man who prays or prophesies with long hair dishonors his head. 5And every woman who prays or prophesies with no covering* ⌞*of hair*⌟ *on her head dishonors her head—she is just like one of the "shorn women." 6If a woman has no covering, let her be for now with short hair, but since it is a disgrace for a woman to have her hair shorn or shaved, she should grow it again. 7A man ought not to have long hair*

DISCOVERY 315

Examining Our Lives

As we prepare to celebrate the Lord's Supper (1 Corinthians 11:17–34) we have a wonderful opportunity to examine our own lives—not the lives of others! As we probe honestly into our own psyches we can ask ourselves in what areas we have openly resisted God's authority. In which "private sectors" have we grieved and resisted the Holy Spirit? What has Jesus asked us to do that we have failed to accomplish? With respect to which tasks have we dragged our feet, procrastinated or rationalized our way out of obedience? In which areas have we fallen short of Jesus' standard or missed the mark which he has clearly set before us? What specific sins in our lives have we failed to acknowledge, let alone confess? In what instances have we allowed ourselves to meander from the path our Lord has clearly set before us?

Paul encouraged the Corinthians to: "examine yourselves to see whether you are in the faith; test yourselves. Do you not realize that Christ Jesus is in you—unless, or course, you fail the test" (2 Corinthians 13:5). At first glance Paul's words might strike us as harsh, until we understand them within their context. Paul had been referring to false teachers, who had been inciting the Corinthians to demand proof that Jesus Christ was indeed speaking through Paul. The apostle was telling the believers that they should look deeply into their own hearts for the truth.

What if someone were to strap a microphone to your body for seven days, recording every word you spoke? Every word to your spouse . . . to your children . . . to your parents . . . to your neighbors . . . to the telephone solicitor who interrupted your dinner hour . . . to the driver who cut you off in traffic—every retort muttered under your breath? Or what if someone were to record on video cassette everything you did or even in some way capture every thought that flitted unbidden through your mind? Then suppose that that person were to randomly select 20 minutes of what had been recorded on these audio and video tapes and play them back for everyone around to hear and see? Few of us would be comfortable with such a proposition! The problem is that those tapes *are* indeed available. God is intimately acquainted with everything we have ever said, done or thought (Psalm 139:1–10).

When we celebrate at the Lord's table our Lord Jesus himself asks us to examine our lives and identify the discrepancies between our profession and our behaviors and attitudes. We can also be aware of the need for integration in our lives as we go about our day-to-day activities. Training ourselves to be aware of our sins and confessing them to God every day is a vital component of living a godly life.

"If we walk in the light, as [God] is in the light, we have fellowship with one another, and the blood of Jesus, his Son, purifies us from all sin . . . If we confess our sins, [God] is faithful and just and will forgive us our sins and purify us from all unrighteousness" (1 John 1:7,9).

Self-Discovery: *Devote a few moments to serious, reflective self-examination. Confess any shortcomings which come to mind and allow the blood of Jesus to purify you. Then pray for the strength to overcome these areas of sin in your life.*

GO TO DISCOVERY 316 ON PAGE 1556

11:23 [r] Gal 1:12 23For I received from the Lord[r] what I
[s] 1Co 15:3 also passed on to you:[s] The Lord Jesus,
on the night he was betrayed, took bread,
24and when he had given thanks, he
broke it and said, "This is my body,
which is for you; do this in remembrance
of me." 25In the same way, after supper he
11:25 took the cup, saying, "This cup is the
[t] Lk 22:20 new covenant[t] in my blood;[u] do this,
[u] 1Co 10:16 whenever you drink it, in remembrance
of me." 26For whenever you eat this bread
and drink this cup, you proclaim the
Lord's death until he comes.
27Therefore, whoever eats the bread
or drinks the cup of the Lord in an un-
11:27 worthy manner will be guilty of sinning
[v] Heb 10:29 against the body and blood of the Lord.[v]
11:28 28A man ought to examine himself[w] be-
[w] 2Co 13:5 fore he eats of the bread and drinks of
the cup. 29For anyone who eats and
drinks without recognizing the body of
the Lord eats and drinks judgment on
himself. 30That is why many among you
are weak and sick, and a number of you
have fallen asleep. 31But if we judged
11:31 ourselves, we would not come under
[x] Ps 32:5; 1Jn 1:9 judgment.[x] 32When we are judged by the
11:32 Lord, we are being disciplined[y] so that
[y] Ps 94:12; we will not be condemned with the
Heb 12:7-10; Rev 3:19 world.
33So then, my brothers, when you
come together to eat, wait for each oth-
11:34 [z] ver 21 [a] ver 22 er. 34If anyone is hungry,[z] he should eat
[b] 1Co 4:19 at home,[a] so that when you meet to-
gether it may not result in judgment.
And when I come[b] I will give further
directions.

Spiritual Gifts

12:1 12 Now about spiritual gifts,[c]
[c] Ro 1:11; brothers, I do not want you to
1Co 14:1,37 be ignorant. 2You know that when you
12:2 [d] Eph 2:11,12; were pagans,[d] somehow or other you
1Pe 4:3 were influenced and led astray to mute
[e] Ps 115:5; Jer 10:5; idols.[e] 3Therefore I tell you that no one
Hab 2:18,19; who is speaking by the Spirit of God
1Th 1:9 says, "Jesus be cursed,"[f] and no one can
12:3 [f] Ro 9:3 say, "Jesus is Lord,"[g] except by the Holy
[g] Jn 13:13 [h] 1Jn 4:2,3 Spirit.[h]
4There are different kinds of gifts, but
12:4 [i] Ro 12:4-8; the same Spirit.[i] 5There are different
Eph 4:11; kinds of service, but the same Lord.
Heb 2:4 6There are different kinds of working,
but the same God[j] works all of them in
12:6 [j] Eph 4:6 all men.
7Now to each one the manifestation
of the Spirit is given for the common
good.[k] 8To one there is given through 12:7
the Spirit the message of wisdom,[l] to an- [k] Eph 4:12
other the message of knowledge[m] by 12:8
means of the same Spirit, 9to another [l] 1Co 2:6 [m] 2Co 8:7
faith[n] by the same Spirit, to another gifts
of healing[o] by that one Spirit, 10to an- 12:9 [n] Mt 17:19,20;
other miraculous powers,[p] to another 2Co 4:13
prophecy, to another distinguishing be- [o] ver 28,30
tween spirits,[q] to another speaking in 12:10
different kinds of tongues,[a][r] and to still [p] Gal 3:5
another the interpretation of tongues.[a] [q] 1Jn 4:1 [r] Mk 16:17
11All these are the work of one and the
same Spirit,[s] and he gives them to each 12:11 [s] ver 4
one, just as he determines.

One Body, Many Parts

12The body is a unit, though it is made
up of many parts; and though all its parts
are many, they form one body.[t] So it is 12:12 [t] Ro 12:5
with Christ.[u] 13For we were all baptized [u] ver 27
by[b] one Spirit[v] into one body—whether
Jews or Greeks, slave or free[w]—and we 12:13 [v] Eph 2:18
were all given the one Spirit to drink.[x] [w] Gal 3:28; Col 3:11
14Now the body is not made up of one [x] Jn 7:37-39
part but of many. 15If the foot should say,
"Because I am not a hand, I do not belong to the body," it would not for that
reason cease to be part of the body.
16And if the ear should say, "Because I
am not an eye, I do not belong to the
body," it would not for that reason cease
to be part of the body. 17If the whole
body were an eye, where would the sense

[a] 10 Or *languages*; also in verse 28 [b] 13 Or *with*; or *in*

JESUS FOCUS

JESUS' BODY

God's people fit together like the parts of a human body, and Paul referred to the community of believers as the body of Jesus Christ (1 Corinthians 12:12–13,27). Each constituent part of a body, whether an eye or a foot, is important, because all the parts need each other in order to make the body complete and functional (verses 14–26). It works the same way with the body of Christ. God created each of us to be unique and special—a one-of-a-kind limited edition!—and he endowed each of us with exclusive abilities and spiritual gifts so that we could work together with the rest of his people to carry out his mission for us. This analogy of the church of Jesus Christ as a human body was a favorite with Paul (Romans 12:4–5; Ephesians 4:4,16).

> **JESUS' WORK RENDERS CERTAIN THE GIFTS OF GOD'S GRACE . . . HE IS THEREFORE, IN EVERY SENSE, OUR SALVATION.**
>
> Charles Hodge, *Presbyterian Theologian*

of hearing be? If the whole body were an
12:18 ear, where would the sense of smell be?
[y] ver 28 [z] ver 11 18But in fact God has arranged[y] the
parts in the body, every one of them, just
as he wanted them to be.[z] 19If they were
all one part, where would the body be?
12:20 20As it is, there are many parts, but one
[a] ver 12,14 body.[a]
21The eye cannot say to the hand, "I
don't need you!" And the head cannot
say to the feet, "I don't need you!" 22On
the contrary, those parts of the body that
seem to be weaker are indispensable,
23and the parts that we think are less
honorable we treat with special honor.
And the parts that are unpresentable are
treated with special modesty, 24while our
presentable parts need no special treatment. But God has combined the members of the body and has given greater
honor to the parts that lacked it, 25so
that there should be no division in the
body, but that its parts should have equal
concern for each other. 26If one part suffers, every part suffers with it; if one part
is honored, every part rejoices with it.
12:27 27Now you are the body of Christ,[b]
[b] Eph 1:23; 4:12; and each one of you is a part of it.[c] 28And
Col 1:18,24 in the church[d] God has appointed first
[c] Ro 12:5 of all apostles,[e] second prophets, third
teachers, then workers of miracles, also
12:28 those having gifts of healing,[f] those able
[d] 1Co 10:32 to help others, those with gifts of ad-
[e] Eph 4:11 [f] ver 9 ministration,[g] and those speaking in dif-
[g] Ro 12:6-8 ferent kinds of tongues.[h] 29Are all apos-
[h] ver 10 tles? Are all prophets? Are all teachers?
12:30 Do all work miracles? 30Do all have gifts
[i] ver 10 of healing? Do all speak in tongues[a]?[i]
12:31 Do all interpret? 31But eagerly desire[b][j]
[j] 1Co 14:1,39 the greater gifts.

Love

And now I will show you the most excellent way.

13:1 **13** If I speak in the tongues[c][k] of
[k] ver 8 men and of angels, but have not
love, I am only a resounding gong or a
clanging cymbal. 2If I have the gift of
prophecy and can fathom all mysteries[l] 13:2 [l] 1Co 14:2
and all knowledge, and if I have a faith[m] [m] 1Co 12:9
that can move mountains,[n] but have not [n] Mt 17:20;
love, I am nothing. 3If I give all I possess 21:21
to the poor[o] and surrender my body to 13:3
the flames,[d][p] but have not love, I gain [o] Mt 6:2
nothing. [p] Da 3:28
4Love is patient,[q] love is kind. It does 13:4
not envy, it does not boast, it is not [q] 1Th 5:14
proud. 5It is not rude, it is not self-seek- 13:5
ing,[r] it is not easily angered, it keeps no [r] 1Co 10:24
record of wrongs. 6Love does not delight 13:6
in evil[s] but rejoices with the truth.[t] 7It al- [s] 2Th 2:12
ways protects, always trusts, always [t] 2Jn 4; 3Jn 3,4
hopes, always perseveres.
8Love never fails. But where there are 13:8
prophecies,[u] they will cease; where there [u] ver 2 [v] ver 1
are tongues,[v] they will be stilled; where
there is knowledge, it will pass away. 9For 13:9
we know in part[w] and we prophesy in [w] ver 12;
part, 10but when perfection comes,[x] the 1Co 8:2
imperfect disappears. 11When I was a 13:10
child, I talked like a child, I thought like [x] Php 3:12

[a] 30 Or *other languages* [b] 31 Or *But you are eagerly desiring* [c] 1 Or *languages* [d] 3 Some early manuscripts *body that I may boast*

THE GREATEST GIFT

In this much-loved and oft-quoted passage Paul isolated four spiritual gifts (tongues, prophecy, faith and giving) but declared that all of these, even in their most spectacular manifestations, mean nothing unless motivated by love. Paul utilized hyperbole, or extravagant exaggeration, to drive home his point in verses 1–3. The Greek word for "love" in this "love chapter" connotes a selfless concern for the welfare of others that is not called forth by any loveable quality in the person who is the object of that love, but which is rather the product of a will to love in obedience to God's command—in short, the same kind of selfless and unconditional love that compelled our Savior to go to the cross (John 13:34–35; 1 John 3:16). Paul's use of hyperbole might well call to mind the intense emotion expressed in the fourth and final verse of a well-loved hymn of the church, "When I Survey the Wondrous Cross": "Were the whole realm of nature mine, That were a present far too small; Love so amazing, so divine, Demands my soul, my life, my all." Our human language fails us as we stand speechless in the presence of the wonder of the love of God for his weak and helpless children.

a child, I reasoned like a child. When I became a man, I put childish ways behind me. 12Now we see but a poor reflection as in a mirror; then we shall see face to face.[y] Now I know in part; then I shall know fully, even as I am fully known.[z]

13And now these three remain: faith, hope and love.[a] But the greatest of these is love.[b]

Gifts of Prophecy and Tongues

14 Follow the way of love[c] and eagerly desire[d] spiritual gifts,[e] especially the gift of prophecy. 2For anyone who speaks in a tongue[a][f] does not speak to men but to God. Indeed, no one understands him; he utters mysteries[g] with his spirit.[b] 3But everyone who prophesies speaks to men for their strengthening,[h] encouragement and comfort. 4He who speaks in a tongue[i] edifies himself, but he who prophesies[j] edifies the church. 5I would like every one of you to speak in tongues,[c] but I would rather have you prophesy.[k] He who prophesies is greater than one who speaks in tongues,[c] unless he interprets, so that the church may be edified.

6Now, brothers, if I come to you and speak in tongues, what good will I be to you, unless I bring you some revelation[l] or knowledge or prophecy or word of instruction?[m] 7Even in the case of lifeless things that make sounds, such as the flute or harp, how will anyone know what tune is being played unless there is a distinction in the notes? 8Again, if the trumpet does not sound a clear call, who will get ready for battle?[n] 9So it is with you. Unless you speak intelligible words with your tongue, how will anyone know what you are saying? You will just be speaking into the air. 10Undoubtedly there are all sorts of languages in the world, yet none of them is without meaning. 11If then I do not grasp the meaning of what someone is saying, I am a foreigner to the speaker, and he is a foreigner to me. 12So it is with you. Since you are eager to have spiritual gifts, try to excel in gifts that build up the church.

13For this reason anyone who speaks in a tongue should pray that he may interpret what he says. 14For if I pray in a tongue, my spirit prays, but my mind is unfruitful. 15So what shall I do? I will pray with my spirit, but I will also pray with my mind; I will sing[o] with my spirit, but I will also sing with my mind. 16If you are praising God with your spirit, how can one who finds himself among those who do not understand[d] say "Amen"[p] to your thanksgiving,[q] since he does not know what you are saying? 17You may be giving thanks well enough, but the other man is not edified.

18I thank God that I speak in tongues more than all of you. 19But in the church I would rather speak five intelligible words to instruct others than ten thousand words in a tongue.

20Brothers, stop thinking like children.[r] In regard to evil be infants,[s] but in your thinking be adults. 21In the Law[t] it is written:

> "Through men of strange tongues
> and through the lips of foreigners
> I will speak to this people,
> but even then they will not listen
> to me,"[e][u]

says the Lord.

22Tongues, then, are a sign, not for believers but for unbelievers; prophecy,[v] however, is for believers, not for unbelievers. 23So if the whole church comes together and everyone speaks in tongues, and some who do not understand[f] or some unbelievers come in, will they not say that you are out of your mind?[w] 24But if an unbeliever or someone who does not understand[g] comes in while everybody is prophesying, he will be convinced by all that he is a sinner and will be judged by all, 25and the secrets of his heart will be laid bare. So he

13:12 [y] Ge 32:30; 2Co 5:7; 1Jn 3:2 [z] 1Co 8:3
13:13 [a] Gal 5:5,6 [b] 1Co 16:14
14:1 [c] 1Co 16:14 [d] ver 39; 1Co 12:31 [e] 1Co 12:1
14:2 [f] Mk 16:17 [g] 1Co 13:2
14:3 [h] ver 4,5,12,17, 26; Ro 14:19
14:4 [i] Mk 16:17 [j] 1Co 13:2
14:5 [k] Nu 11:29
14:6 [l] ver 26; Eph 1:17 [m] Ro 6:17
14:8 [n] Nu 10:9; Jer 4:19
14:15 [o] Eph 5:19; Col 3:16
14:16 [p] Dt 27:15-26; 1Ch 16:36; Ne 8:6; Ps 106:48; Rev 5:14; 7:12 [q] 1Co 11:24
14:20 [r] Eph 4:14; Heb 5:12,13; 1Pe 2:2 [s] Ro 16:19
14:21 [t] Jn 10:34 [u] Isa 28:11,12
14:22 [v] ver 1
14:23 [w] Ac 2:13

THE CHRISTIAN MUST UNDERSTAND WHAT CONFRONTS HIM ANTAGONISTICALLY IN HIS OWN MOMENT OF HISTORY. OTHERWISE HE SIMPLY BECOMES A USELESS MUSEUM PIECE AND NOT A LIVING WARRIOR FOR JESUS CHRIST.

Francis Schaeffer, *Christian Apologist*

[a] 2 Or *another language*; also in verses 4, 13, 14, 19, 26 and 27 [b] 2 Or *by the Spirit* [c] 5 Or *other languages*; also in verses 6, 18, 22, 23 and 39 [d] 16 Or *among the inquirers* [e] 21 Isaiah 28:11,12 [f] 23 Or *some inquirers* [g] 24 Or *or some inquirer*

14:25 x Isa 45:14; will fall down and worship God, ex-
Zec 8:23 claiming, "God is really among you!"[x]

Orderly Worship

14:26 26 What then shall we say, brothers?
y 1Co 12:7-10 When you come together, everyone[y] has
z Eph 5:19 a ver 6 a hymn,[z] or a word of instruction,[a] a
b Ro 14:19 revelation, a tongue or an interpretation. All of these must be done for the
strengthening[b] of the church. 27 If anyone speaks in a tongue, two—or at the
most three—should speak, one at a
time, and someone must interpret. 28 If
there is no interpreter, the speaker
should keep quiet in the church and
speak to himself and God.
29 Two or three prophets should speak,
and the others should weigh carefully
14:29 c 1Co 12:10 what is said.[c] 30 And if a revelation comes
to someone who is sitting down, the first
speaker should stop. 31 For you can all
prophesy in turn so that everyone may
be instructed and encouraged. 32 The
spirits of prophets are subject to the
14:32 d 1Jn 4:1 control of prophets.[d] 33 For God is not a
God of disorder[e] but of peace.
14:33 As in all the congregations of the
e ver 40 f Ac 9:13 saints,[f] 34 women should remain silent in
the churches. They are not allowed to
14:34 g 1Ti 2:11,12 speak, but must be in submission,[g] as the
h Ge 3:16 Law[h] says. 35 If they want to inquire about
something, they should ask their own
husbands at home; for it is disgraceful for
a woman to speak in the church.
36 Did the word of God originate with
you? Or are you the only people it has
reached? 37 If anybody thinks he is a
14:37 i 2Co 10:7 prophet[i] or spiritually gifted, let him ac-
j 1Jn 4:6 knowledge that what I am writing to
you is the Lord's command.[j] 38 If he ignores this, he himself will be ignored.[a]
14:39 k 1Co 12:31 39 Therefore, my brothers, be eager[k] to
prophesy, and do not forbid speaking in
14:40 tongues. 40 But everything should be
l ver 33 done in a fitting and orderly[l] way.

The Resurrection of Christ

15:1 15 Now, brothers, I want to remind
m Ro 2:16 you of the gospel[m] I preached
to you, which you received and on which
15:2 you have taken your stand. 2 By this
n Ro 1:16 gospel you are saved,[n] if you hold firm-
o Ro 11:22 ly[o] to the word I preached to you. Other-
15:3 wise, you have believed in vain.
p Gal 1:12 3 For what I received[p] I passed on to
q 1Co 11:23 you[q] as of first importance[b]: that Christ
r Isa 53:5; 1Pe 2:24 died for our sins[r] according to the Scrip-

JESUS CHRIST LIVED. THAT'S A FACT. HE DIED. THAT'S A FACT. HE WAS RESURRECTED FROM THE DEAD. THAT'S A MYSTERY. HE IS MY LORD AND SAVIOR. THAT'S MY FAITH.

Robert H. Schuller, *Pastor, Garden Grove, California*

tures,[s] 4 that he was buried, that he was 15:3
raised[t] on the third day[u] according to s Lk 24:27;
the Scriptures,[v] 5 and that he appeared Ac 26:22,23
to Peter,[c][w] and then to the Twelve.[x] 6 Af- 15:4
ter that, he appeared to more than five t Ac 2:24 u Mt 16:21
hundred of the brothers at the same v Ac 2:25,30,31
time, most of whom are still living, 15:5
though some have fallen asleep. 7 Then w Lk 24:34
he appeared to James, then to all the x Mk 16:14
apostles,[y] 8 and last of all he appeared to 15:7
me also,[z] as to one abnormally born. y Lk 24:33,36,
9 For I am the least of the apostles[a] and 37; Ac 1:3,4
do not even deserve to be called an apos- 15:8
tle, because I persecuted[b] the church of z Ac 9:3-6,17; 1Co 9:1
God. 10 But by the grace of God I am what
I am, and his grace to me[c] was not with- 15:9 a Eph 3:8;
out effect. No, I worked harder than all of 1Ti 1:15 b Ac 8:3
them[d]—yet not I, but the grace of God 15:10
that was with me.[e] 11 Whether, then, it c Ro 12:3
was I or they, this is what we preach, and d 2Co 11:23
this is what you believed. e Php 2:13

The Resurrection of the Dead

12 But if it is preached that Christ has
been raised from the dead, how can
some of you say that there is no resur- 15:12
rection of the dead?[f] 13 If there is no res- f Ac 17:32; 23:8;
urrection of the dead, then not even 2Ti 2:18
Christ has been raised. 14 And if Christ 15:14
has not been raised,[g] our preaching is g 1Th 4:14
useless and so is your faith. 15 More than
that, we are then found to be false witnesses about God, for we have testified
about God that he raised Christ from the 15:15
dead.[h] But he did not raise him if in fact h Ac 2:24
the dead are not raised. 16 For if the dead
are not raised, then Christ has not been
raised either. 17 And if Christ has not been
raised, your faith is futile; you are still in
your sins.[i] 18 Then those also who have 15:17
fallen asleep in Christ are lost. 19 If only i Ro 4:25
for this life we have hope in Christ, we 15:19
are to be pitied more than all men.[j] j 1Co 4:9

[a] 38 Some manuscripts *If he is ignorant of this, let him be ignorant* [b] 3 Or *you at the first* [c] 5 Greek *Cephas*

If Christ Had Not Been Raised . . .

The central message of the gospel is that Jesus died and rose again for our sin. We don't always like to hear about sin, preferring to focus on the "positive." In essence, when it comes right down to it, that means denying what is real. One pastor received a letter after his Christmas Eve sermon, complaining that he had "marred" a stirring celebration by interjecting the subject of sin. "The program was wonderful," the writer observed. "The lights, the music and drama were a delightful representation of the Christmas spirit. But when you got up and spoke about sin, it ruined the whole evening." But we cannot honestly talk about the implications of Christmas without speaking of sin. The baby whose birth we celebrate every December was named Jesus, because "he [would] save his people from their sins" (Matthew 1:21).

Jesus did not die as a victim of a set of unfortunate circumstances, although his trial and execution were blatantly unfair. His entire life, including the suffering and the opposition he endured, fulfilled Old Testament prophecy (Luke 24:27,44). His death, burial and resurrection were actual events that are a part of real history. In fact, the word *history* has been said to center around "his story"!

Jesus was a real, tangible person who died a very real death. He was buried in an actual tomb, arose physically from the dead and was later seen by people all over the countryside (Acts 1:3; 1 Corinthians 15:5–8). The gospel accounts are not fairy tales, allegories or legends. If they were, we would all be groveling in our sin with no light of hope on the horizon. Paul stated this is stark terms in 1 Corinthians 15:14,17–19: "If Christ has not been raised, our preaching is useless and so is your faith . . . If Christ has not been raised, your faith is futile; you are still in your sins. Then those also who have fallen asleep in Christ are lost. If only for this life we have hope in Christ, we are to be pitied more than all men."

Yet Paul did not end there. He went on to declare the gospel truth, the glorious truth that renews our spirits and sets us free: "But Christ has indeed been raised from the dead, the firstfruits of those who have fallen asleep . . . Thanks be to God! He gives us the victory through our Lord Jesus Christ (verses 20,57).

The Good News about Jesus is not only that he was and is real but that he has indeed died and risen again to save us from our sins and is continually at work through his Spirit to transform our lives. We are no longer the people we once were, hopelessly damaged by sin and groping blindly for a hand to raise us. We belong to him, and he is at work in our lives to change us into the people he intended us to be from the very beginning. Only Jesus, the Son of God, has the power to work this miracle (verses 1–20). We are indeed, of all people, most to be envied!

Self-Discovery: *Take a moment to thank Jesus for the assurance you have from the Bible of the authenticity of his death and resurrection for your sake. Then reconfirm your faith commitment to him.*

GO TO DISCOVERY 317 ON PAGE 1561

> **THE RESURRECTION SERVES THE PURPOSE OF CONFIRMING JESUS CHRIST'S PERSON AND PROVIDING THE BASIS FOR THE TRUTH OF THE CHRISTIAN MESSAGE.**
>
> 
>
> Gary Habermas, *Professor, Liberty University, Lynchburg, Virginia*

20 But Christ has indeed been raised from the dead,[k] the firstfruits[l] of those who have fallen asleep.[m] 21 For since death came through a man,[n] the resurrection of the dead comes also through a man. 22 For as in Adam all die, so in Christ all will be made alive.[o] 23 But each in his own turn: Christ, the firstfruits;[p] then, when he comes,[q] those who belong to him. 24 Then the end will come, when he hands over the kingdom[r] to God the Father after he has destroyed all dominion, authority and power.[s] 25 For he must reign until he has put all his enemies under his feet.[t] 26 The last enemy to be destroyed is death.[u] 27 For he "has put everything under his feet."[a][v] Now when it says that "everything" has been put under him, it is clear that this does not include God himself, who put everything under Christ.[w] 28 When he has done this, then the Son himself will be made subject to him who put everything under him,[x] so that God may be all in all.[y]

29 Now if there is no resurrection, what will those do who are baptized for the dead? If the dead are not raised at all, why are people baptized for them? 30 And as for us, why do we endanger ourselves every hour?[z] 31 I die every day[a]—I mean that, brothers—just as surely as I glory over you in Christ Jesus our Lord. 32 If I fought wild beasts[b] in Ephesus[c] for merely human reasons, what have I gained? If the dead are not raised,

> "Let us eat and drink,
> for tomorrow we die."[b][d]

33 Do not be misled: "Bad company corrupts good character." 34 Come back to your senses as you ought, and stop sinning; for there are some who are ignorant of God—I say this to your shame.

The Resurrection Body

35 But someone may ask,[e] "How are the dead raised? With what kind of body will they come?"[f] 36 How foolish![g] What you sow does not come to life unless it dies.[h] 37 When you sow, you do not plant the body that will be, but just a seed, perhaps of wheat or of something else. 38 But God gives it a body as he has determined, and to each kind of seed he gives its own body.[i] 39 All flesh is not the same: Men have one kind of flesh, animals have another, birds another and fish another. 40 There are also heavenly bodies and there are earthly bodies; but the splendor of the heavenly bodies is one kind, and the splendor of the earthly bodies is another. 41 The sun has one kind of splendor, the moon another and the stars another; and star differs from star in splendor.

42 So will it be[j] with the resurrection of the dead. The body that is sown is perishable, it is raised imperishable; 43 it is sown in dishonor, it is raised in glory;[k] it is sown in weakness, it is raised in power; 44 it is sown a natural body, it is raised a spiritual body.[l]

If there is a natural body, there is also a spiritual body. 45 So it is written: "The first man Adam became a living being"[c];[m] the last Adam,[n] a life-giving spirit.[o] 46 The spiritual did not come first, but the natural, and after that the spiritual. 47 The first man was of the dust of the earth,[p] the second man from heaven.[q] 48 As was the earthly man, so are those who are of the earth; and as is the man from heaven, so also are those who are of heaven.[r] 49 And just as we have borne the likeness of the earthly man,[s] so shall we[d] bear the likeness of the man from heaven.[t]

50 I declare to you, brothers, that flesh and blood[u] cannot inherit the kingdom of God, nor does the perishable inherit the imperishable. 51 Listen, I tell you a mystery:[v] We will not all sleep, but we will all be changed[w]— 52 in a flash, in the twinkling of an eye, at the last trumpet. For the trumpet will sound,[x] the dead[y] will be raised imperishable, and we will be changed. 53 For the perishable must clothe itself with the imperishable,[z] and the mortal with immortality. 54 When the perishable has been clothed with the imperishable, and the mortal with im-

15:20 [k] 1Pe 1:3 [l] ver 23; Ac 26:23; Rev 1:5 [m] ver 6, 18
15:21 [n] Ro 5:12
15:22 [o] Ro 5:14-18
15:23 [p] ver 20 [q] ver 52
15:24 [r] Da 7:14,27 [s] Ro 8:38
15:25 [t] Ps 110:1; Mt 22:44
15:26 [u] 2Ti 1:10; Rev 20:14; 21:4
15:27 [v] Ps 8:6 [w] Mt 28:18
15:28 [x] Php 3:21 [y] 1Co 3:23
15:30 [z] 2Co 11:26
15:31 [a] Ro 8:36
15:32 [b] 2Co 1:8 [c] Ac 18:19 [d] Isa 22:13; Lk 12:19
15:35 [e] Ro 9:19

15:35 [f] Eze 37:3
15:36 [g] Lk 11:40 [h] Jn 12:24
15:38 [i] Ge 1:11
15:42 [j] Da 12:3; Mt 13:43
15:43 [k] Php 3:21; Col 3:4
15:44 [l] ver 50
15:45 [m] Ge 2:7 [n] Ro 5:14 [o] Jn 5:21; Ro 8:2
15:47 [p] Ge 2:7; 3:19 [q] Jn 3:13,31
15:48 [r] Php 3:20,21
15:49 [s] Ge 5:3 [t] Ro 8:29
15:50 [u] Jn 3:3,5
15:51 [v] 1Co 13:2 [w] Php 3:21
15:52 [x] Mt 24:31 [y] Jn 5:25
15:53 [z] 2Co 5:2,4

[a] 27 Psalm 8:6 [b] 32 Isaiah 22:13 [c] 45 Gen. 2:7
[d] 49 Some early manuscripts *so let us*

mortality, then the saying that is written
15:54 [a] Isa 25:8; Rev 20:14 will come true: "Death has been swallowed up in victory."[a] [a]

15:55 [b] Hos 13:14
55 "Where, O death, is your victory?
Where, O death, is your sting?"[b] [b]

15:56 [c] Ro 5:12 [d] Ro 4:15 56 The sting of death is sin,[c] and the
power of sin is the law.[d] 57 But thanks be
15:57 [e] 2Co 2:14 [f] Ro 8:37 to God![e] He gives us the victory through
our Lord Jesus Christ.[f]
58 Therefore, my dear brothers, stand
15:58 [g] 1Co 16:10 firm. Let nothing move you. Always give
yourselves fully to the work of the Lord,[g]
because you know that your labor in the
Lord is not in vain.

The Collection for God's People

16:1 [h] Ac 24:17 [i] Ac 9:13 [j] Ac 16:6 **16** Now about the collection[h] for
God's people:[i] Do what I told
the Galatian[j] churches to do. 2 On the
16:2 [k] Ac 20:7 [l] 2Co 9:4,5 first day of every week,[k] each one of you
should set aside a sum of money in keep-
ing with his income, saving it up, so that
when I come no collections will have to
be made.[l] 3 Then, when I arrive, I will give
16:3 [m] 2Co 8:18,19 letters of introduction to the men you
approve[m] and send them with your gift
to Jerusalem. 4 If it seems advisable for
me to go also, they will accompany me.

Personal Requests

16:5 [n] 1Co 4:19 5 After I go through Macedonia, I will
come to you[n]—for I will be going
through Macedonia.[o] 6 Perhaps I will stay 16:5 [o] Ac 19:21
with you awhile, or even spend the win-
ter, so that you can help me on my jour- 16:6 [p] Ro 15:24
ney,[p] wherever I go. 7 I do not want to see
you now and make only a passing visit; I 16:7 [q] Ac 18:21
hope to spend some time with you, if the
Lord permits.[q] 8 But I will stay on at Eph- 16:8 [r] Ac 18:19 [s] Ac 2:1
esus[r] until Pentecost,[s] 9 because a great
door for effective work has opened to
me,[t] and there are many who oppose me. 16:9 [t] Ac 14:27
10 If Timothy[u] comes, see to it that he
has nothing to fear while he is with you, 16:10 [u] Ac 16:1 [v] 1Co 15:58
for he is carrying on the work of the
Lord,[v] just as I am. 11 No one, then,
should refuse to accept him.[w] Send him 16:11 [w] 1Ti 4:12 [x] Ac 15:33
on his way in peace[x] so that he may re-
turn to me. I am expecting him along
with the brothers.
12 Now about our brother Apollos:[y] I 16:12 [y] Ac 18:24; 1Co 1:12
strongly urged him to go to you with the
brothers. He was quite unwilling to go
now, but he will go when he has the op- 16:13 [z] Gal 5:1; Php 1:27; 1Th 3:8; 2Th 2:15 [a] Eph 6:10
portunity.
13 Be on your guard; stand firm[z] in the
faith; be men of courage; be strong.[a]
14 Do everything in love.[b]
15 You know that the household of 16:14 [b] 1Co 14:1
Stephanas[c] were the first converts[d] in
Achaia,[e] and they have devoted them- 16:15 [c] 1Co 1:16 [d] Ro 16:5 [e] Ac 18:12
selves to the service of the saints. I urge
you, brothers, 16 to submit[f] to such as
these and to everyone who joins in the
work, and labors at it. 17 I was glad when 16:16 [f] Heb 13:17
Stephanas, Fortunatus and Achaicus ar-
rived, because they have supplied what 16:17 [g] 2Co 11:9; Php 2:30
was lacking from you.[g] 18 For they re-
freshed[h] my spirit and yours also. Such 16:18 [h] Phm 7 [i] Php 2:29
men deserve recognition.[i]

Final Greetings

19 The churches in the province of Asia
send you greetings. Aquila and Priscilla[c] [j] 16:19 [j] Ac 18:2 [k] Ro 16:5
greet you warmly in the Lord, and so does
the church that meets at their house.[k]
20 All the brothers here send you greet- 16:20 [l] Ro 16:16
ings. Greet one another with a holy kiss.[l]
21 I, Paul, write this greeting in my own 16:21 [m] Gal 6:11; Col 4:18
hand.[m]
22 If anyone does not love the Lord[n]—
a curse[o] be on him. Come, O Lord[d]![p] 16:22 [n] Eph 6:24 [o] Ro 9:3 [p] Rev 22:20
23 The grace of the Lord Jesus be with
you.[q]
24 My love to all of you in Christ Jesus. 16:23 [q] Ro 16:20
Amen.[e]

[a] *54* Isaiah 25:8 [b] *55* Hosea 13:14 [c] *19* Greek *Prisca,* a variant of *Priscilla* [d] *22* In Aramaic the expression *Come, O Lord* is *Marana tha.*
[e] *24* Some manuscripts do not have *Amen.*

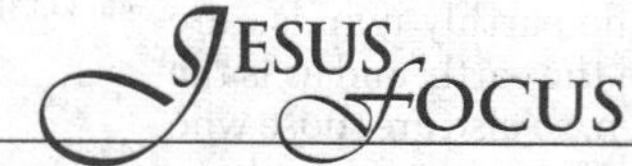

FINAL VICTORY

The effect of sin in this world and in our lives is devastating. The ultimate result is death, a condition in which we are separated from the people we love and even from God himself if we do not know him. But Jesus repaired the damage caused by sin when he died in our place, and his resurrection affords us the hope that we too will live forever. Paul referred to this hope as a mystery (1 Corinthians 15:51). Jesus promised to come back for us, taking both the living and the dead to be home with him (John 14:1–3). Whether we happen to be alive or dead at the time of his return, we will all be changed (glorified) in an instant. Paul said the same thing to the church in Thessalonica (1 Thessalonians 4:16–17). The final victory of our lives with God is that we will live forever with Jesus—complete, whole and perfect—just as he created us to be (1 Corinthians 15:54–57).

2 CORINTHIANS

When will we be like Jesus? (2 Corinthians 3:18)

- *Believers are "in process"—looking more like Jesus Christ all the time, but not finished until after their earthly life. Paul borrowed language from two prevailing views of his day: (1) Mystery religions believed a divine revelation would immediately transform a person. (2) Jewish prophetic teaching taught that personal transformation would occur at the end of time.*

How can we carry the death of Jesus in our bodies? (2 Corinthians 4:10)

- *Paul linked our physical sufferings and hardships to the death of Jesus. Our sufferings remind us and others of the ultimate suffering, Jesus' death on a cross. Ironically, revealing his sufferings makes it possible for us to reveal his life.*

How did Jesus become sin? (2 Corinthians 5:21)

- *God did not make the sinless Jesus become a sinner. But he did cause him to take on himself all our sin. This was necessary so that the ministry of reconciliation could take place.*

Jesus in 2 Corinthians 2 Corinthians reads more like a personal diary than a public letter. Although we aren't clued in on many details about Paul's concerns, his feelings come through clearly. Paul noted that some of the problems he had addressed in his first letter had still not been resolved. Even more troubling to Paul was that other problems had cropped up as well. 2 Corinthians reflects Paul's deep concern for the Corinthian believers, touching on their joys, sorrows and frustrations and offering encouragement and assurance.

Paul wanted the believers in Corinth to know that Jesus is the tender and loving Savior whose comfort will overflow in our lives as we get to know him (2 Corinthians 1:5). Not only that, but our Lord will also provide us with the grace we need to make it through any situation in a way that honors him (2 Corinthians 12:9). Our lives as people who walk with Jesus Christ are like living letters written to the world by God himself (2 Corinthians 3:2–3). By living a life that is pleasing to God, we demonstrate to others who God is and what he is like.

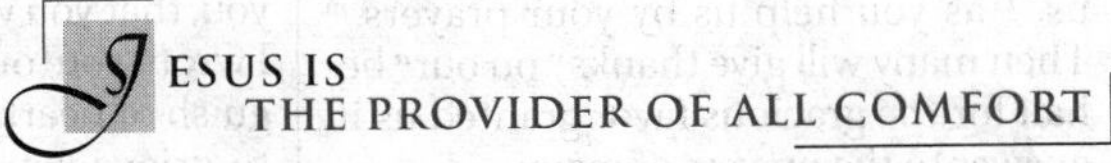

JESUS IS THE PROVIDER OF ALL COMFORT

2 Corinthians 1

1 Paul, an apostle of Christ Jesus by the will of God,[a] and Timothy our brother,

To the church of God[b] in Corinth, together with all the saints throughout Achaia:[c]

2Grace and peace to you from God our Father and the Lord Jesus Christ.[d]

> IN EVERY PANG THAT RENDS THE HEART THE MAN OF SORROW HAD A PART.
>
> Michael Bruce, *Scottish Poet*

The God of All Comfort

3Praise be to the God and Father of our Lord Jesus Christ,[e] the Father of compassion and the God of all comfort, 4who comforts us[f] in all our troubles, so that we can comfort those in any trouble with the comfort we ourselves have received from God. 5For just as the sufferings of Christ flow over into our lives,[g] so also through Christ our comfort overflows. 6If we are distressed, it is for your comfort and salvation;[h] if we are comforted, it is for your comfort, which produces in you patient endurance of the same sufferings we suffer. 7And our hope for you is firm, because we know that just as you share in our sufferings,[i] so also you share in our comfort.

8We do not want you to be uninformed, brothers, about the hardships we suffered[j] in the province of Asia. We were under great pressure, far beyond our ability to endure, so that we despaired even of life. 9Indeed, in our hearts we felt the sentence of death. But this happened that we might not rely on ourselves but on God,[k] who raises the dead. 10He has delivered us from such a deadly peril,[l] and he will deliver us. On him we have set our hope that he will continue to deliver us, 11as you help us by your prayers.[m] Then many will give thanks[n] on our[a] behalf for the gracious favor granted us in answer to the prayers of many.

Paul's Change of Plans

12Now this is our boast: Our conscience[o] testifies that we have conducted ourselves in the world, and especially in our relations with you, in the holiness and sincerity[p] that are from God. We have done so not according to worldly wisdom[q] but according to God's grace. 13For we do not write you anything you cannot read or understand. And I hope that, 14as you have understood us in part, you will come to understand fully that you can boast of us just as we will boast of you in the day of the Lord Jesus.[r]

15Because I was confident of this, I planned to visit you[s] first so that you might benefit twice.[t] 16I planned to visit you on my way[u] to Macedonia and to come back to you from Macedonia, and then to have you send me on my way to Judea. 17When I planned this, did I do it lightly? Or do I make my plans in a worldly manner[v] so that in the same breath I say, "Yes, yes" and "No, no"?

18But as surely as God is faithful,[w] our message to you is not "Yes" and "No." 19For the Son of God, Jesus Christ, who was preached among you by me and Silas[b] and Timothy, was not "Yes" and "No," but in him it has always[x] been "Yes." 20For no matter how many promises[y] God has made, they are "Yes" in Christ. And so through him the "Amen"[z] is spoken by us to the glory of God. 21Now it is God who makes both us and you stand firm in Christ. He anointed[a] us, 22set his seal of ownership on us, and put his Spirit in our hearts as a deposit, guaranteeing what is to come.[b]

23I call God as my witness[c] that it was in order to spare you[d] that I did not return to Corinth. 24Not that we lord it over[e] your faith, but we work with you for your joy, because it is by faith you

2 Corinthians 2

stand firm.[f] 2 1So I made up my mind that I would not make another painful visit to you.[g] 2For if I grieve you,[h] who is left to make me glad but you whom I have grieved? 3I wrote as I did[i] so that when I came I should not be distressed[j] by those who ought to make me rejoice. I had confidence[k] in all of you, that you would all share my joy. 4For I wrote you[l] out of great distress and anguish of heart and with many tears, not to grieve you but to let you know the depth of my love for you.

Forgiveness for the Sinner

5If anyone has caused grief,[m] he has

Cross-references:

1:1 [a] 1Co 1:1; Eph 1:1; Col 1:1; 2Ti 1:1 [b] 1Co 10:32 [c] Ac 18:12
1:2 [d] Ro 1:7
1:3 [e] Eph 1:3; 1Pe 1:3
1:4 [f] 2Co 7:6,7,13
1:5 [g] 2Co 4:10; Col 1:24
1:6 [h] 2Co 4:15
1:7 [i] Ro 8:17
1:8 [j] 1Co 15:32
1:9 [k] Jer 17:5,7
1:10 [l] Ro 15:31
1:11 [m] Ro 15:30; Php 1:19 [n] 2Co 4:15
1:12 [o] Ac 23:1 [p] 2Co 2:17 [q] 1Co 2:1,4,13
1:14 [r] 1Co 1:8
1:15 [s] 1Co 4:19 [t] Ro 1:11,13; 15:29
1:16 [u] 1Co 16:5-7
1:17 [v] 2Co 10:2,3
1:18 [w] 1Co 1:9
1:19 [x] Heb 13:8
1:20 [y] Ro 15:8 [z] 1Co 14:16
1:21 [a] 1Jn 2:20,27
1:22 [b] 2Co 5:5
1:23 [c] Ro 1:9; Gal 1:20 [d] 1Co 4:21; 2Co 2:1,3; 13:2,10
1:24 [e] 1Pe 5:3 [f] Ro 11:20; 1Co 15:1
2:1 [g] 2Co 1:23
2:2 [h] 2Co 7:8
2:3 [i] 2Co 7:8,12 [j] 2Co 12:21 [k] 2Co 8:22; Gal 5:10
2:4 [l] 2Co 7:8,12
2:5 [m] 1Co 5:1,2

[a] 11 Many manuscripts *your*
[b] 19 Greek *Silvanus*, a variant of *Silas*

DISCOVERY 317

THE PRIVILEGE OF SUFFERING

During our times of intense personal pain it may seem as though we have been abandoned by God, that our suffering is arbitrary and pointless. The statement that suffering has a purpose may at such times leave us cold, but the reality is that it does—several of them, in fact. We may suffer: 1) as an ongoing consequence of the fall of Adam and Eve; 2) as a consequence of our own actions; 3) at the hands of the devil; 4) as a direct result of our faith; 5) as a catalyst for spiritual growth; or 6) to further the cause of Jesus' kingdom. Paul's second letter to the church in Corinth can help to shed some light on this complicated and thorny issue.

For one thing, Paul observed that when we suffer we are afforded an opportunity to receive solace from the God "who comforts us in all our troubles" (2 Corinthians 1:4). It is through suffering that we discover dimensions of God's character that we could never otherwise have known. Paul went so far as to say, "I delight in weaknesses" (2 Corinthians 12:10). It wasn't the testing itself that Paul enjoyed; it was the benefit of allowing God to buoy him up, of experiencing firsthand the perfect sufficiency of God's strength manifested in and through his own weakness (2 Corinthians 12:9).

Suffering also opens a door of opportunity for us to help others. God consoles us "so that we can comfort those in any trouble with the comfort we ourselves have received from God" (2 Corinthians 1:4). Our own difficult experiences heighten our sensitivity to the hard times others endure and enable us to respond with empathy. A natural human reaction to pain is to isolate ourselves in a fog of self-pity, distancing ourselves from others and viewing our whole world through the lens of our own anguish. God's intent, however, is that we learn from him how to uplift other people. It is his desire that we learn to see beyond ourselves, to remove our blinders and develop our peripheral vision.

When we experience heartaches and setbacks we can learn to identify more closely with our Savior's agony. Paul came to the point where he was able to perceive suffering as part and parcel of his growth in Chrislikeness: "I want to know Christ and the power of his resurrection and the fellowship of sharing in his sufferings, becoming like him . . ." (Philippians 3:10). The apostles considered it a privilege to suffer for Jesus. Paul stated in Acts 5:41 that they "left the Sanhedrin, rejoicing because they had been counted worthy of suffering disgrace for the Name."

And, much as we can enter into Jesus' sufferings, Jesus because of the intense anguish that he endured can and does enter into our own. He is the sympathetic high priest (Hebrews 4:15) who "took up our infirmities and carried our sorrows" (Isaiah 53:4). We can attest with Paul that *nothing* can separate us from the love of Christ Jesus (Romans 8:38–39), that we are "more than conquerors through him who loved us" (Romans 8:37).

Self-Discovery: *"Although he was a son, [Jesus] learned obedience from what he suffered" (Hebrews 5:8). How could he be using your difficulties at work, your strained family relationships, health problems, financial struggles or other trials to perfect your faith? (See Hebrews 12:1–15; James 1:2–4; 1 Peter 1:6–9.)*

GO TO DISCOVERY 318 ON PAGE 1563

not so much grieved me as he has
grieved all of you, to some extent—not
2:6 to put it too severely. [6]The punishment[n]
[n] 1Co 5:4,5 inflicted on him by the majority is sufficient for him. [7]Now instead, you ought
2:7 [o] Gal 6:1; to forgive and comfort him,[o] so that he
Eph 4:32 will not be overwhelmed by excessive
sorrow. [8]I urge you, therefore, to reaffirm
your love for him. [9]The reason I wrote
you was to see if you would stand the
2:9 [p] 2Co 10:6 test and be obedient in everything.[p] [10]If
you forgive anyone, I also forgive him.
And what I have forgiven—if there was
anything to forgive—I have forgiven in
the sight of Christ for your sake, [11]in or-
2:11 der that Satan[q] might not outwit us. For
[q] Mt 4:10 [r] Lk 22:31; 2Co 4:4; 1Pe 5:8,9 we are not unaware of his schemes.[r]

Ministers of the New Covenant

2:12 [s] Ac 16:8 [12]Now when I went to Troas[s] to
[t] Ro 1:1 preach the gospel of Christ[t] and found
[u] Ac 14:27 that the Lord had opened a door[u] for
2:13 me, [13]I still had no peace of mind,[v] be-
[v] 2Co 7:5 cause I did not find my brother Titus[w]
[w] 2Co 7:6,13; 12:18 there. So I said good-by to them and
went on to Macedonia.
2:14 [14]But thanks be to God,[x] who always
[x] Ro 6:17 leads us in triumphal procession in
[y] Eph 5:2; Php 4:18 Christ and through us spreads everywhere the fragrance[y] of the knowledge
2:15 of him. [15]For we are to God the aroma of
[z] 1Co 1:18 Christ among those who are being saved
2:16 and those who are perishing.[z] [16]To the
[a] Lk 2:34 one we are the smell of death;[a] to the
other, the fragrance of life. And who is 2:16
equal to such a task?[b] [17]Unlike so many, [b] 2Co 3:5,6
we do not peddle the word of God for
profit.[c] On the contrary, in Christ we 2:17 [c] 2Co 4:2
speak before God with sincerity,[d] like [d] 1Co 5:8
men sent from God.[e] [e] 2Co 1:12

3 Are we beginning to commend
ourselves[f] again? Or do we need, 3:1 [f] 2Co 5:12; 12:11
like some people, letters of recommen- [g] Ac 18:27
dation[g] to you or from you? [2]You yourselves are our letter, written on our
hearts, known and read by everybody.[h] 3:2 [h] 1Co 9:2
[3]You show that you are a letter from
Christ, the result of our ministry, written
not with ink but with the Spirit of the
living God, not on tablets of stone[i] but 3:3 [i] Ex 24:12
on tablets of human hearts.[j] [j] Pr 3:3; Jer 31:33; Eze 11:19
[4]Such confidence[k] as this is ours
through Christ before God. [5]Not that we
are competent in ourselves to claim any- 3:4
thing for ourselves, but our competence [k] Eph 3:12
comes from God.[l] [6]He has made us 3:5 [l] 1Co 15:10
competent as ministers of a new cov-
enant[m]—not of the letter but of the 3:6 [m] Lk 22:20
Spirit; for the letter kills, but the Spirit [n] Jn 6:63
gives life.[n]

The Glory of the New Covenant

[7]Now if the ministry that brought
death, which was engraved in letters on
stone, came with glory, so that the Israelites could not look steadily at the face
of Moses because of its glory,[o] fading 3:7 [o] Ex 34:29-35
though it was, [8]will not the ministry of
the Spirit be even more glorious? [9]If the 3:9
ministry that condemns men[p] is glori- [p] ver 7 [q] Ro 1:17; 3:21,22
ous, how much more glorious is the
ministry that brings righteousness![q]
[10]For what was glorious has no glory
now in comparison with the surpassing
glory. [11]And if what was fading away
came with glory, how much greater is
the glory of that which lasts!
[12]Therefore, since we have such a 3:12
hope, we are very bold.[r] [13]We are not like [r] Eph 6:19
Moses, who would put a veil over his 3:13
face[s] to keep the Israelites from gazing at [s] ver 7; Ex 34:33
it while the radiance was fading away. 3:14
[14]But their minds were made dull,[t] for to [t] Ro 11:7,8
this day the same veil remains when the [u] Ac 13:15
old covenant[u] is read.[v] It has not been re- [v] ver 6
moved, because only in Christ is it taken
away. [15]Even to this day when Moses is
read, a veil covers their hearts. [16]But 3:16
whenever anyone turns to the Lord,[w] the [w] Ro 11:23
veil is taken away.[x] [17]Now the Lord is the [x] Ex 34:34
Spirit,[y] and where the Spirit of the Lord 3:17 [y] Isa 61:1,2

PARADE OF VICTORY

When they returned victorious from battle, Roman generals were typically honored with a procession lauding their triumph. As the conquering army strutted before an adoring populace, flaunting its loot and its captives, the streets of the city would fill with the fragrance of burning incense and the aroma of the victory feast that was being prepared. For the victors the pleasing scents were associated with success—but for the captives the wafting smells were a nauseating reminder of stinging defeat. In 2 Corinthians 2, Paul used this analogy to describe how God sees our lives when we place our trust in Jesus and allow him to cover our sins (verse 14). When we do so we become the "aroma of Christ" to those "who are being saved"—the fragrance of his spectacular victory over death and sin (verse 15).

DISCOVERY 318

JARS OF CLAY

Paul was passionate about telling others about Jesus. Whether he was teaching in the synagogue (Acts 17:1–4) or reasoning with Greek philosophers on Mars Hill in Athens (Acts 17:19–31), he inevitably directed the attention of his listeners to Jesus. This is our mission as well, but it is not always an easy one.

One obstacle we face daily is the reality of our own imperfections. Paul referred to believers as "jars of clay" that hold a great treasure (2 Corinthians 4:7). The truth is that we ourselves can be obstacles to getting the Word out. God could have chosen angels to carry the message about his Son. After all, they did announce both Jesus' birth (Luke 1:30–33; 2:13–14) and his resurrection from the dead (Matthew 28:5–7). He could alternatively have written the message across the sky so that everyone everywhere could have read and understood it. But instead God elected to spread the Word by mouth, one person at a time—all the way to the ends of the earth. He has chosen to entrust his priceless treasure to fragile, fallible vessels, and we possess the very real potential of contaminating and misrepresenting the message.

Paul wanted to make certain that neither his actions nor his conversation would skew his message: "Rather, we have renounced secret and shameful ways; we do not use deception, nor do we distort the word of God. On the contrary, by setting forth the truth plainly we commend ourselves to every man's conscience in the sight of God" (2 Corinthians 4:2). When we tell others about Jesus, either by example or by word, we should be concerned about the same issues. We want our *conduct* to honor God, even in the private areas of life, those niches to which no other person is privy. We also want our *method* to honor God, making certain that we avoid any hint of deception or distortion in our message. By contrast, we want to proclaim the truth clearly, completely and consistently.

Another obstacle is God's enemy, Satan. He "has blinded the minds of unbelievers, so that they cannot see the light of the gospel of the glory of Christ, who is the image of God" (verse 4). Satan does not want people to comprehend that God loves them and that Jesus offers forgiveness and eternal life. He deliberately deceives people and blinds them to the light of the gospel. But we have assistance at our disposal that Satan is helpless to overcome: God's Holy Spirit himself opens people's eyes and reveals God's truth (John 16:5–11).

Sharing Jesus with others requires a unique blend of human and divine effort. We have a responsibility to do the sharing and to pay close attention to the integration of conduct and method and to the virtue of integrity in our own lives. And God the Holy Spirit overcomes Satan's darkness, to shine his illuminating light into us so that we in turn reflect his glory (2 Corinthians 3:18) and take his light into a darkened world (Matthew 5:14–16).

Self-Discovery: *Would your neighbors be likely to characterize you as a person of integrity, whether or not they know you well? In what ways can you work to integrate conduct and method as you share the Good News of Jesus Christ with those in your immediate locality.*

GO TO DISCOVERY 319 ON PAGE 1565

3:17 is, there is freedom.[z] 18And we, who with
z Jn 8:32 unveiled faces all reflect[a a] the Lord's glo-
3:18 ry,[b] are being transformed into his like-
a 1Co 13:12 b 2Co 4:4,6 ness[c] with ever-increasing glory, which
c Ro 8:29 comes from the Lord, who is the Spirit.

Treasures in Jars of Clay

4:1 4 Therefore, since through God's
d 1Co 7:25 mercy[d] we have this ministry, we
4:2 do not lose heart. 2Rather, we have re-
e 1Co 4:5 nounced secret and shameful ways;[e] we
f 2Co 2:17 do not use deception, nor do we distort
g 2Co 5:11 the word of God.[f] On the contrary, by
setting forth the truth plainly we commend ourselves to every man's con-
4:3 science[g] in the sight of God. 3And even
h 2Co 2:12 if our gospel[h] is veiled,[i] it is veiled to
i 2Co 3:14 those who are perishing.[j] 4The god[k] of
j 1Co 1:18 this age has blinded[l] the minds of unbe-
4:4 lievers, so that they cannot see the light
k Jn 12:31 of the gospel of the glory of Christ, who
l 2Co 3:14 is the image of God. 5For we do not
4:5 preach ourselves,[m] but Jesus Christ as
m 1Co 1:13 Lord, and ourselves as your servants[n] for
n 1Co 9:19 4:6 Jesus' sake. 6For God, who said, "Let
o Ge 1:3 light shine out of darkness,"[b o] made
p 2Pe 1:19 his light shine in our hearts[p] to give us
the light of the knowledge of the glory of
God in the face of Christ.
7But we have this treasure in jars of
4:7 q Job 4:19; clay[q] to show that this all-surpassing
2Co 5:1 power is from God[r] and not from us.
r 1Co 2:5 8We are hard pressed on every side,[s] but
4:8 not crushed; perplexed, but not in de-
s 2Co 7:5 spair; 9persecuted,[t] but not abandoned;[u]
4:9 struck down, but not destroyed.[v] 10We
t Jn 15:20 always carry around in our body the
u Heb 13:5 v Ps 37:24 death of Jesus, so that the life of Jesus
may also be revealed in our body.[w] 11For
4:10 w Ro 6:5 we who are alive are always being given
over to death for Jesus' sake,[x] so that his
4:11 x Ro 8:36 life may be revealed in our mortal body.
4:12 12So then, death is at work in us, but life
y 2Co 13:9 is at work in you.[y]
13It is written: "I believed; therefore I
4:13 z Ps 116:10 have spoken."[c z] With that same spirit of
faith we also believe and therefore
speak, 14because we know that the one
who raised the Lord Jesus from the dead
4:14 a 1Th 4:14 will also raise us with Jesus[a] and present
b Eph 5:27 us with you in his presence.[b] 15All this is
for your benefit, so that the grace that is
reaching more and more people may
4:15 c 2Co 1:11 cause thanksgiving[c] to overflow to the
glory of God.
16Therefore we do not lose heart.
Though outwardly we are wasting away,

DON'T BE FEARFUL ABOUT THE JOURNEY AHEAD . . . JESUS CHRIST IS HIMSELF THE LIGHT AND WILL GUIDE YOUR FOOTSTEPS ALONG THE WAY.

Edith Schaeffer, *Christian Author and Speaker*

yet inwardly[d] we are being renewed[e] day 4:16
by day. 17For our light and momentary d Ro 7:22
troubles are achieving for us an eternal e Col 3:10
glory that far outweighs them all.[f] 18So 4:17 f Ro 8:18;
we fix our eyes not on what is seen, but 1Pe 1:6,7
on what is unseen.[g] For what is seen is 4:18
temporary, but what is unseen is eternal. g Ro 8:24; Heb 11:1

Our Heavenly Dwelling

5 Now we know that if the earthly[h] 5:1 h 1Co 15:47
tent[i] we live in is destroyed, we i 2Pe 1:13,14
have a building from God, an eternal
house in heaven, not built by human
hands. 2Meanwhile we groan,[j] longing to 5:2
be clothed with our heavenly dwelling,[k] j ver 4; Ro 8:23 k 1Co 15:53,54
3because when we are clothed, we will
not be found naked. 4For while we are in
this tent, we groan and are burdened,
because we do not wish to be unclothed
but to be clothed with our heavenly 5:4
dwelling,[l] so that what is mortal may be l 1Co 15:53,54
swallowed up by life. 5Now it is God who
has made us for this very purpose and
has given us the Spirit as a deposit, guar- 5:5
anteeing what is to come.[m] m Ro 8:23;
6Therefore we are always confident 2Co 1:22
and know that as long as we are at home
in the body we are away from the Lord.
7We live by faith, not by sight.[n] 8We are 5:7 n 1Co 13:12
confident, I say, and would prefer to be
away from the body and at home with 5:8
the Lord.[o] 9So we make it our goal to o Php 1:23
please him,[p] whether we are at home in 5:9
the body or away from it. 10For we must p Ro 14:18
all appear before the judgment seat of 5:10
Christ, that each one may receive what q Mt 16:27;
is due him[q] for the things done while in Ro 14:10;
the body, whether good or bad. Eph 6:8

The Ministry of Reconciliation

11Since, then, we know what it is to
fear the Lord,[r] we try to persuade men. 5:11 r Heb 10:31;
What we are is plain to God, and I hope Jude 23
it is also plain to your conscience.[s] 12We s 2Co 4:2
are not trying to commend ourselves to

[a] 18 Or *contemplate* [b] 6 Gen. 1:3
[c] 13 Psalm 116:10

RECONCILIATION

Jesus' cross is the primary symbol of our faith. It represents his death, the only channel by which we can be made right with God. Jesus' death did many things for us: Jesus died in our place, for our benefit (Romans 5:6); he paid the price to set us free from slavery to sin (1 Peter 1:18–19); his death turned God's wrath away from us (Romans 3:25–26); and Jesus' death repaired our relationship with God (2 Corinthians 5:18).

The first step toward accepting that we can be made right with God is admitting that our relationship with him has been damaged. Sin doesn't merely bruise that relationship; it completely severs it. More than that, sin places us in an adversarial relationship with God, making us his *enemies* (Romans 5:10). When a husband and wife are seeing the effects of a splintering relationship with one another, the first step toward healing and restoration of trust requires that they identify the issues that divided them in the first place. Only then can they begin to effectively deal with those issues. Our relationship with God works in the same way. God's holiness demands that he separate himself from our sin, and his justice requires that he punish sin. Our human tragedy is that we are completely unable to live up to God's standard of perfection on our own.

The broken relationship between ourselves and God is not a superficial rift, and, were it not for God's gracious provision, it would entail a hopeless standoff. God cannot ignore or overlook our sin, and we can do nothing *but* sin! But God took the initiative to correct the problem: "Just as sin reigned in death, so also grace might reign through righteousness to bring eternal life through Jesus Christ our Lord" (Romans 5:21). Jesus took our sin upon himself and died so that it would no longer stand as an obstacle between ourselves and God.

When we believe that Jesus died for our sin, God perceives us as completely righteous. Therein is the essence of reconciliation. What we could not and still cannot do under our own power—live a holy life—God did for us through his Son Jesus. This Jesus is the One who, by a marvelous exchange, made it possible for us to receive his righteousness and thereby be reconciled to God. Our standing and our acceptance before God are solely in him. This is the joyful truth of the gospel: "God made him who had no sin to be sin for us, so that in him we might become the righteousness of God" (2 Corinthians 5:21).

The eighteenth-century hymn writer Charles Wesley captured in some measure the wonder of Jesus' supreme gift of reconciliation:

> "Hark! the herald angels sing
> Glory to the newborn King;
> Peace on earth, and mercy mild,
> God and sinners reconciled!"

And Jesus proclaimed that "there is rejoicing in the presence of the angels of God over one sinner who repents" (Luke 15:10).

Self-Discovery: Personalize 2 Corinthians 5:21 by substituting the word me *for* us *and the word* I *for* we. *What does it mean to you to be the righteousness of God? Pause to thank Jesus for exchanging your guilt with his righteousness.*

GO TO DISCOVERY 320 ON PAGE 1569

5:12 [t] 2Co 3:1 you again,[t] but are giving you an oppor-
[u] 2Co 1:14 tunity to take pride in us,[u] so that you
can answer those who take pride in
what is seen rather than in what is in the
5:13 heart. 13 If we are out of our mind,[v] it is
[v] 2Co 11:1,16,17 for the sake of God; if we are in our right
mind, it is for you. 14 For Christ's love
compels us, because we are convinced
that one died for all, and therefore all
5:14 [w] Gal 2:20 died.[w] 15 And he died for all, that those
who live should no longer live for them-
5:15 [x] Ro 14:7-9 selves[x] but for him who died for them
and was raised again.

16 So from now on we regard no one
5:16 [y] 2Co 11:18 from a worldly[y] point of view. Though
we once regarded Christ in this way, we
5:17 do so no longer. 17 Therefore, if anyone is
[z] Gal 6:15 in Christ, he is a new creation;[z] the old
[a] Isa 65:17; Rev 21:4,5 has gone, the new has come![a] 18 All this
5:18 is from God, who reconciled us to him-
[b] Ro 5:10; Col 1:20 self through Christ[b] and gave us the
ministry of reconciliation: 19 that God
was reconciling the world to himself in
Christ, not counting men's sins against
them.[c] And he has committed to us the 5:19 [c] Ro 4:8
message of reconciliation. 20 We are
therefore Christ's ambassadors,[d] as 5:20 [d] 2Co 6:1;
though God were making his appeal Eph 6:20
through us. We implore you on Christ's
behalf: Be reconciled to God. 21 God 5:21
made him who had no sin[e] to be sin[a] for [e] Heb 4:15;
us, so that in him we might become the 1Pe 2:22,24;
righteousness of God.[f] 1Jn 3:5 [f] Ro 1:17

> HE WAS MADE WHAT WE ARE
> THAT HE MIGHT MAKE US WHAT
> HE IS HIMSELF.
>
> Irenaeus, *Early Chruch Father*

6 As God's fellow workers[g] we urge 6:1 [g] 1Co 3:9;
you not to receive God's grace in 2Co 5:20
vain. 2 For he says,

"In the time of my favor I heard you,
and in the day of salvation I
helped you."[b][h] 6:2 [h] Isa 49:8

I tell you, now is the time of God's favor,
now is the day of salvation.

Paul's Hardships

3 We put no stumbling block in any-
one's path,[i] so that our ministry will not 6:3 [i] Ro 14:13,20;
be discredited. 4 Rather, as servants of 1Co 9:12; 10:32
God we commend ourselves in every way:
in great endurance; in troubles, hardships
and distresses; 5 in beatings, imprison-
ments[j] and riots; in hard work, sleepless 6:5 [j] 2Co 11:23-25
nights and hunger;[k] 6 in purity, under- [k] 1Co 4:11
standing, patience and kindness; in the 6:6
Holy Spirit[l] and in sincere love; 7 in truth- [l] 1Th 1:5
ful speech[m] and in the power of God; with 6:7 [m] 2Co 4:2
weapons of righteousness[n] in the right [n] 2Co 10:4;
hand and in the left; 8 through glory and Eph 6:10-18
dishonor,[o] bad report and good report; 6:8
genuine, yet regarded as impostors;[p] [o] 1Co 4:10
9 known, yet regarded as unknown; dy- [p] Mt 27:63
ing,[q] and yet we live on;[r] beaten, and yet 6:9
not killed; 10 sorrowful, yet always rejoic- [q] Ro 8:36 [r] 2Co 1:8-10;
ing;[s] poor, yet making many rich;[t] having 4:10,11
nothing, and yet possessing everything.[u] 6:10

11 We have spoken freely to you, Co- [s] 2Co 7:4
rinthians, and opened wide our hearts [t] 2Co 8:9
to you.[v] 12 We are not withholding our af- [u] Ro 8:32; 1Co 3:21
fection from you, but you are withhold-
ing yours from us. 13 As a fair exchange— 6:11 [v] 2Co 7:3
I speak as to my children[w]—open wide
your hearts also. 6:13 [w] 1Co 4:14

[a] 21 Or *be a sin offering* [b] 2 Isaiah 49:8

THE JUDGMENT SEAT

Corinth was a spectacular city set in a picturesque natural setting. It would have been easy to believe that everything within its walls was good and right. But in the middle of town was the judge's seat, a large stone platform on which dignitaries sat to pass judgment on the accused. The residents of Corinth understood exactly what Paul was referring to in his letter when he informed them that one day we will all stand at a judgment seat where Jesus sits (2 Corinthians 5:10).

The Bible teaches that there is a judgment of believers that has nothing to do with the determination of our eternal destiny, that is, the justification credited to us in and through Jesus fully and forever. It is a judgment rendered on the basis of our good deeds—what we have done to express our faith and our gratitude (Romans 14:12; 1 Corinthians 3:12–15; 4:2–5; Ephesians 6:8; 1 Thessalonians 1:3; James 2:14–26). The way we live reflects who or what is important to us, and that is what Jesus will be looking for when we stand before him for judgment. Christians whose works stand the test of fire (1 Peter 1:7) will be rewarded (Matthew 25:14–30; Luke 19:11–27), while those whose works are consumed by the fire will escape the flames of hell but will have no works of praise to present as a love offering to Jesus Christ.

Do Not Be Yoked With Unbelievers

14Do not be yoked together[x] with unbelievers. For what do righteousness and wickedness have in common? Or what fellowship can light have with darkness?[y] 15What harmony is there between Christ and Belial[a]? What does a believer[z] have in common with an unbeliever? 16What agreement is there between the temple of God and idols? For we are the temple[a] of the living God. As God has said: "I will live with them and walk among them, and I will be their God, and they will be my people."[b][b]

17"Therefore come out from them[c]
and be separate,
says the Lord.
Touch no unclean thing,
and I will receive you."[c][d]
18"I will be a Father to you,
and you will be my sons and
daughters,[e]
says the Lord Almighty."[d]

6:14 [x]1Co 5:9,10 [y]Eph 5:7,11; 1Jn 1:6
6:15 [z]Ac 5:14
6:16 [a]1Co 3:16 [b]Lev 26:12; Jer 32:38; Eze 37:27
6:17 [c]Rev 18:4 [d]Isa 52:11
6:18 [e]Isa 43:6

7 Since we have these promises,[f] dear friends, let us purify ourselves from everything that contaminates body and spirit, perfecting holiness out of reverence for God.

7:1 [f]2Co 6:17,18

Paul's Joy

2Make room for us in your hearts.[g] We have wronged no one, we have corrupted no one, we have exploited no one. 3I do not say this to condemn you; I have said before that you have such a place in our hearts[h] that we would live or die with you. 4I have great confidence in you; I take great pride in you. I am greatly encouraged; in all our troubles my joy knows no bounds.[i]

5For when we came into Macedonia,[j] this body of ours had no rest, but we were harassed at every turn[k]—conflicts on the outside, fears within.[l] 6But God, who comforts the downcast,[m] comforted us by the coming of Titus,[n] 7and not only by his coming but also by the comfort you had given him. He told us about your longing for me, your deep sorrow, your ardent concern for me, so that my joy was greater than ever.

8Even if I caused you sorrow by my letter,[o] I do not regret it. Though I did regret it—I see that my letter hurt you, but only for a little while— 9yet now I am happy, not because you were made sorry, but because your sorrow led you to repentance. For you became sorrowful as God intended and so were not harmed in any way by us. 10Godly sorrow brings repentance that leads to salvation[p] and leaves no regret, but worldly sorrow brings death. 11See what this godly sorrow has produced in you: what earnestness, what eagerness to clear yourselves, what indignation, what alarm, what longing, what concern,[q] what readiness to see justice done. At every point you have proved yourselves to be innocent in this matter. 12So even though I wrote to you,[r] it was not on account of the one who did the wrong[s] or of the injured party, but rather that before God you could see for yourselves how devoted to us you are. 13By all this we are encouraged.

In addition to our own encouragement, we were especially delighted to see how happy Titus[t] was, because his spirit has been refreshed by all of you. 14I had boasted to him about you,[u] and you have not embarrassed me. But just as everything we said to you was true, so our boasting about you to Titus[v] has proved to be true as well. 15And his affection for you is all the greater when he remembers that you were all obedient,[w] receiving him with fear and trembling.[x] 16I am glad I can have complete confidence in you.[y]

7:2 [g]2Co 6:12,13
7:3 [h]2Co 6:11,12
7:4 [i]2Co 6:10
7:5 [j]2Co 2:13 [k]2Co 4:8 [l]Dt 32:25
7:6 [m]2Co 1:3,4 [n]ver 13; 2Co 2:13
7:8 [o]2Co 2:2,4
7:10 [p]Ac 11:18
7:11 [q]ver 7
7:12 [r]ver 8; 2Co 2:3,9 [s]1Co 5:1,2
7:13 [t]ver 6; 2Co 2:13
7:14 [u]ver 4 [v]ver 6
7:15 [w]2Co 2:9 [x]Php 2:12
7:16 [y]2Co 2:3

Generosity Encouraged

8 And now, brothers, we want you to know about the grace that God has given the Macedonian[z] churches. 2Out of the most severe trial, their overflowing joy and their extreme poverty welled up in rich generosity. 3For I testify that they gave as much as they were able,[a] and even beyond their ability. Entirely on their own, 4they urgently pleaded with us for the privilege of sharing in this service[b] to the saints.[c] 5And they did not do as we expected, but they gave themselves first to the Lord and then to us in keeping with God's will. 6So we urged[d] Titus,[e] since he had earlier made a beginning, to bring also to completion[f] this act of grace on your part. 7But just as you excel in everything[g]—in faith, in

8:1 [z]Ac 16:9
8:3 [a]1Co 16:2
8:4 [b]Ac 24:17 [c]Ro 15:25; 2Co 9:1
8:6 [d]ver 17; 2Co 12:18 [e]ver 16,23 [f]ver 10,11
8:7 [g]2Co 9:8

[a] *15* Greek *Beliar,* a variant of *Belial*
[b] *16* Lev. 26:12; Jer. 32:38; Ezek. 37:27
[c] *17* Isaiah 52:11; Ezek. 20:34,41
[d] *18* 2 Samuel 7:14; 7:8

8:7 speech, in knowledge,[h] in complete
h 1Co 1:5 earnestness and in your love for us[a]—
see that you also excel in this grace of
giving.
8:8 8 I am not commanding you,[i] but I
i 1Co 7:6 want to test the sincerity of your love by
comparing it with the earnestness of
8:9 others. 9 For you know the grace of our
j 2Co 13:14 Lord Jesus Christ,[j] that though he was
k Mt 20:28; rich, yet for your sakes he became poor,[k]
Php 2:6-8 so that you through his poverty might
8:10 become rich.
l 1Co 7:25,40 10 And here is my advice[l] about what is
m 1Co 16:2,3; best for you in this matter: Last year you
2Co 9:2 were the first not only to give but also to
8:11 have the desire to do so.[m] 11 Now finish
n 2Co 9:2 the work, so that your eager willingness[n]
to do it may be matched by your com-
pletion of it, according to your means.
12 For if the willingness is there, the gift is
8:12 acceptable according to what one has,[o]
o Mk 12:43,44; not according to what he does not have.
Lk 21:3 13 Our desire is not that others might
be relieved while you are hard pressed,
but that there might be equality. 14 At the
present time your plenty will supply
8:14 what they need,[p] so that in turn their
p 2Co 9:12 plenty will supply what you need. Then
there will be equality, 15 as it is written:
"He who gathered much did not have
too much, and he who gathered little did
8:15 not have too little."[b][q]
q Ex 16:18

JESUS FOCUS

ROLE REVERSAL

Jesus was willing to switch places with us, even though the trade was in no way beneficial to him. Even though he possessed all the riches of heaven, our Lord chose to renounce his position of glory and become a man in order that we might enjoy a relationship with the Father (2 Corinthians 8:9). Jesus gave up everything he possessed in order to endow us with everything we were lacking. Our relationship with God is based on an incredible exchange. Jesus took our sin and died on the cross, after which he came back to life to confer on us spiritual riches instead of the eternal destitution that we deserved. This indescribable role reversal means that we can stand perfect and whole before God once we have accepted Jesus' gift of life. When we believe in Jesus Christ, he freely offers us what we could never have hoped to earn in any number of lifetimes (verses 1–9). Now that's grace!

Titus Sent to Corinth

16 I thank God,[r] who put into the 8:16
heart[s] of Titus[t] the same concern I have r 2Co 2:14
for you. 17 For Titus not only welcomed s Rev 17:17
our appeal, but he is coming to you with t 2Co 2:13
much enthusiasm and on his own initiative.[u] 18 And we are sending along 8:17
with him the brother[v] who is praised by u ver 6
all the churches[w] for his service to the 8:18
gospel.[x] 19 What is more, he was chosen v 2Co 12:18
by the churches to accompany us[y] as we w 1Co 7:17
carry the offering, which we administer x 2Co 2:12
in order to honor the Lord himself and 8:19
to show our eagerness to help.[z] 20 We y 1Co 16:3,4
want to avoid any criticism of the way z ver 11,12
we administer this liberal gift. 21 For we
are taking pains to do what is right, not
only in the eyes of the Lord but also in 8:21
the eyes of men.[a] a Ro 12:17;
22 In addition, we are sending with 14:18
them our brother who has often proved
to us in many ways that he is zealous,
and now even more so because of his
great confidence in you. 23 As for Titus,
he is my partner[b] and fellow worker[c] 8:23
among you; as for our brothers,[d] they b Phm 17
are representatives of the churches and c Php 2:25
an honor to Christ. 24 Therefore show d ver 18,22
these men the proof of your love and the
reason for our pride in you,[e] so that the 8:24
churches can see it. e 2Co 7:4,14; 9:2

9 There is no need[f] for me to write 9:1
to you about this service to the f 1Th 4:9
saints.[g] 2 For I know your eagerness to g 2Co 8:4
help, and I have been boasting[h] about it 9:2
to the Macedonians, telling them that h 2Co 7:4,14
since last year[i] you in Achaia[j] were ready i 2Co 8:10
to give; and your enthusiasm has stirred j Ac 18:12
most of them to action. 3 But I am sending the brothers in order that our boasting about you in this matter should not
prove hollow, but that you may be ready, 9:3
as I said you would be.[k] 4 For if any Mace- k 1Co 16:2
donians[l] come with me and find you un- 9:4
prepared, we—not to say anything about l Ro 15:26
you—would be ashamed of having been
so confident. 5 So I thought it necessary
to urge the brothers to visit you in advance and finish the arrangements for
the generous gift you had promised. 9:5
Then it will be ready as a generous gift,[m] m Php 4:17
not as one grudgingly given.[n] n 2Co 12:17,18

Sowing Generously

6 Remember this: Whoever sows

[a] *7* Some manuscripts *in our love for you*
[b] *15* Exodus 16:18

POOR FOR OUR SAKE

The psalmist declared in Psalm 47:7 that "God is the King of all the earth." All of our efforts to describe his glory and his majesty fall far short, for he truly is great and most worthy of praise. Psalm 50:10 allows us to catch a glimpse of God's creativity, his ownership and his control over both the earth and the entire universe: "Every animal of the forest is [his], and the cattle on a thousand hills." The truly amazing reality is that God, who is immeasurably great, at the same time devotes his undivided attention to each one of us.

Learning that Jesus, God's Son, existed before the world was created—indeed that "all things were created by him and for him" (Colossians 1:16)—makes the news of his human birth in a borrowed stable all the more astonishing. Even more humbling is the fact that our Savior voluntarily renounced his honored position in heaven and "made himself nothing . . . being made in human likeness" (Philippians 2:7). And he did that for us! God the Son was rich beyond our comprehension, yet he willingly became impoverished so that we might enjoy the spiritual riches he alone has to offer.

In the opening verses of 2 Corinthians 8 Paul observed that the churches in Macedonia, which were very poor, collected gifts for other believers who were even more destitute. The givers were so generous that they pleaded with their leaders to allow them to help others. The Christians there had cultivated a deep gratitude for what Jesus had done for them, and the natural consequence was a burning desire to share. The act of sharing has little to do with a person's wealth; it has everything to do with her eagerness to give. Nor does the amount of the gift matter in the eyes of God (or in many cases in those of the grateful recipient): "If the willingness is there, the gift is acceptable according to what one has, not according to what he does not have" (verse 12). To state this in contemporary terminology, "it's the thought that counts" when we are in a giving mode.

A common, and radically understated, saying among believers is, "You can't outgive God." None of us can give up as much as Jesus did in order to become one of us and die for our sins. Even if we were to sacrifice our very lives for others or endure torture because of our beliefs, we could never earn eternal life for ourselves or others. Only Jesus can offer his gracious gift of salvation—through no merit of our own but only by his grace (Ephesians 2:4–9).

Donating what we have—time, financial resources, abilities—is a way of expressing our love for God. The act of giving will not make God love us any more than he already does, nor will it induce him to favor us above others. When we accept Jesus' sacrifice for our sin, we become rich with the Holy Spirit, and we can't help but desire to share that overflowing abundance: "You will be made rich in every way so that you can be generous on every occasion, and through us your generosity will result in thanksgiving to God" (2 Corinthians 9:11).

Self-Discovery: *Assess your "eagerness quotient" with regard to your giving for the cause of Jesus Christ.*

GO TO DISCOVERY 321 ON PAGE 1572

sparingly will also reap sparingly, and
whoever sows generously will also reap
generously.[o] 7Each man should give what
he has decided in his heart to give,[p] not
reluctantly or under compulsion,[q] for
God loves a cheerful giver.[r] 8And God is
able[s] to make all grace abound to you, so
that in all things at all times, having all
that you need,[t] you will abound in every
good work. 9As it is written:

> "He has scattered abroad his gifts
> to the poor;
> his righteousness endures
> forever."[a][u]

10Now he who supplies seed to the sower
and bread for food[v] will also supply and
increase your store of seed and will enlarge the harvest of your righteousness.[w]
11You will be made rich[x] in every way so
that you can be generous on every occasion, and through us your generosity will
result in thanksgiving to God.[y]

12This service that you perform is not
only supplying the needs[z] of God's people but is also overflowing in many expressions of thanks to God.[a] 13Because
of the service[b] by which you have proved
yourselves, men will praise God[c] for the
obedience that accompanies your confession of the gospel of Christ,[d] and for
your generosity in sharing with them
and with everyone else. 14And in their
prayers for you their hearts will go out to
you, because of the surpassing grace
God has given you. 15Thanks be to God[e]
for his indescribable gift![f]

9:6 [o] Pr 11:24,25; 22:9; Gal 6:7,9
9:7 [p] Ex 25:2; 2Co 8:12 [q] Dt 15:10 [r] Ro 12:8
9:8 [s] Eph 3:20 [t] Php 4:19
9:9 [u] Ps 112:9
9:10 [v] Isa 55:10 [w] Hos 10:12
9:11 [x] 1Co 1:5 [y] 2Co 1:11
9:12 [z] 2Co 8:14 [a] 2Co 1:11
9:13 [b] 2Co 8:4 [c] Mt 9:8 [d] 2Co 2:12
9:15 [e] 2Co 2:14 [f] Ro 5:15,16

Paul's Defense of His Ministry

10 By the meekness and gentleness[g] of Christ, I appeal to
you—I, Paul,[h] who am "timid" when
face to face with you, but "bold" when
away! 2I beg you that when I come I may
not have to be as bold[i] as I expect to be
toward some people who think that we
live by the standards of this world. 3For
though we live in the world, we do not
wage war as the world does. 4The
weapons we fight with[j] are not the
weapons of the world. On the contrary,
they have divine power[k] to demolish
strongholds.[l] 5We demolish arguments
and every pretension that sets itself up
against the knowledge of God,[m] and we
take captive every thought to make it
obedient[n] to Christ. 6And we will be
ready to punish every act of disobedience, once your obedience is complete.[o]

7You are looking only on the surface
of things.[b][p] If anyone is confident that
he belongs to Christ,[q] he should consider again that we belong to Christ just as
much as he.[r] 8For even if I boast somewhat freely about the authority the Lord
gave us for building you up rather than
pulling you down,[s] I will not be ashamed
of it. 9I do not want to seem to be trying
to frighten you with my letters. 10For
some say, "His letters are weighty and
forceful, but in person he is unimpres-
sive[t] and his speaking amounts to nothing."[u] 11Such people should realize that
what we are in our letters when we are
absent, we will be in our actions when
we are present.

12We do not dare to classify or compare ourselves with some who commend themselves.[v] When they measure
themselves by themselves and compare
themselves with themselves, they are
not wise. 13We, however, will not boast
beyond proper limits, but will confine
our boasting to the field God has assigned to us,[w] a field that reaches even
to you. 14We are not going too far in our
boasting, as would be the case if we had
not come to you, for we did get as far as
you[x] with the gospel of Christ.[y] 15Nei-
ther do we go beyond our limits by
boasting of work done by others.[c][z] Our
hope is that, as your faith continues to

10:1 [g] Mt 11:29 [h] Gal 5:2
10:2 [i] 1Co 4:21; 2Co 13:2,10
10:4 [j] 2Co 6:7 [k] 1Co 2:5 [l] Jer 1:10; 2Co 13:10
10:5 [m] Isa 2:11,12; 1Co 1:19 [n] 2Co 9:13
10:6 [o] 2Co 2:9; 7:15
10:7 [p] Jn 7:24 [q] 1Co 1:12; 3:23; 14:37 [r] 2Co 11:23
10:8 [s] 2Co 13:10
10:10 [t] 1Co 2:3; Gal 4:13,14 [u] 1Co 1:17
10:12 [v] 2Co 3:1
10:13 [w] ver 15,16
10:14 [x] 1Co 3:6 [y] 2Co 2:12
10:15 [z] Ro 15:20

[a] 9 Psalm 112:9 [b] 7 Or *Look at the obvious facts* [c] 13–15 Or *13We, however, will not boast about things that cannot be measured, but we will boast according to the standard of measurement that the God of measure has assigned us—a measurement that relates even to you. 14 . . . 15Neither do we boast about things that cannot be measured in regard to the work done by others.*

THE BLESSING OF GIVING

As he took up a collection for the poor, Paul reminded the Corinthians that God's people have a responsibility for others (2 Corinthians 9:1–5). We give because we are called to be imitators of Christ Jesus, the ultimate example in sacrifice. Our Savior bestowed his time and energy and ultimately gave his very life for us. Paul stated that "God loves a cheerful giver" (verse 7). Our giving can bring us joy when we follow our Lord's example and donate our time, talents and financial resources willingly and sacrificially.

10:15 grow,[a] our area of activity among you
a 2Th 1:3 will greatly expand, 16so that we can
10:16 preach the gospel in the regions beyond
b Ac 19:21 you.[b] For we do not want to boast about
10:17 work already done in another man's ter-
c Jer 9:24; ritory. 17But, "Let him who boasts boast
1Co 1:31 in the Lord."[a c] 18For it is not the one who
10:18 commends himself[d] who is approved,
d ver 12 e Ro 2:29; but the one whom the Lord commends.[e]
1Co 4:5

Paul and the False Apostles

11:1 f ver 4,19,20; **11** I hope you will put up with[f] a
Mt 17:17 little of my foolishness;[g] but
g ver 16,17,21; you are already doing that. 2I am jealous
2Co 5:13 for you with a godly jealousy. I promised
11:2 you to one husband,[h] to Christ, so that I
h Hos 2:19; Eph 5:26,27 might present you[i] as a pure virgin to
i 2Co 4:14 him. 3But I am afraid that just as Eve
11:3 was deceived by the serpent's cunning,[j]
j Ge 3:1-6,13; your minds may somehow be led astray
Jn 8:44; 1Ti 2:14; from your sincere and pure devotion to
Rev 12:9 Christ. 4For if someone comes to you
and preaches a Jesus other than the
11:4 Jesus we preached,[k] or if you receive a
k 1Co 3:11 l Ro 8:15 different spirit[l] from the one you re-
m Gal 1:6-9 ceived, or a different gospel[m] from the
one you accepted, you put up with it

SPIRITUAL BATTLE

Walking with God destines us to be engaged in spiritual warfare (2 Corinthians 10:3–6). Rather than feeling arrogant or condescending because of our relationship with God, we can use the "weapons" he has provided us to fight against the spiritual forces that strive to lure us off track. As we make God-honoring choices, God endows us with his own power and helps us to overcome enemy strongholds, every human attempt to claim honor for oneself, or any other obstacle that threatens to draw us away from himself and keeps us in bondage to sin. Paul urges us to strive to gain control over our own minds, to pray for the power that alone can enable us to capture every thought and use it in the service of Jesus. We are called to focus consciously on our own thought patterns and to continually ask ourselves whether our thoughts are glorifying Jesus or serving ourselves. The more we get to know Jesus, the better equipped we will be to do this. Spiritual battle begins with our private thoughts, and it can only be won using the spiritual tools which have been placed at our disposal because of the finished work of our Lord Jesus Christ.

easily enough. 5But I do not think I am
in the least inferior to those "super- 11:5
apostles."[n] 6I may not be a trained n 2Co 12:11;
speaker,[o] but I do have knowledge.[p] We Gal 2:6
have made this perfectly clear to you in 11:6
every way. o 1Co 1:17
7Was it a sin[q] for me to lower myself p Eph 3:4
in order to elevate you by preaching the 11:7
gospel of God to you free of charge?[r] 8I q 2Co 12:13 r 1Co 9:18
robbed other churches by receiving sup-
port from them[s] so as to serve you. 9And 11:8 s Php 4:15,18
when I was with you and needed some-
thing, I was not a burden to anyone, for
the brothers who came from Macedonia
supplied what I needed. I have kept my- 11:9
self from being a burden to you[t] in any t 2Co 12:13,14,
way, and will continue to do so. 10As 16
surely as the truth of Christ is in me,[u] 11:10
nobody in the regions of Achaia[v] will u Ro 9:1 v Ac 18:12
stop this boasting[w] of mine. 11Why? Be- w 1Co 9:15
cause I do not love you? God knows I 11:11
do![x] 12And I will keep on doing what I x 2Co 12:15
am doing in order to cut the ground
from under those who want an opportunity to be considered equal with us in
the things they boast about.
13For such men are false apostles,[y] de- 11:13
ceitful[z] workmen, masquerading as y 2Pe 2:1 z Tit 1:10
apostles of Christ.[a] 14And no wonder, for a Rev 2:2
Satan himself masquerades as an angel
of light. 15It is not surprising, then, if his
servants masquerade as servants of
righteousness. Their end will be what
their actions deserve.[b] 11:15 b Php 3:19

Paul Boasts About His Sufferings

16I repeat: Let no one take me for a
fool.[c] But if you do, then receive me just 11:16 c ver 1
as you would a fool, so that I may do a
little boasting. 17In this self-confident
boasting I am not talking as the Lord 11:17
would,[d] but as a fool. 18Since many are d 1Co 7:12,25
boasting in the way the world does, I too 11:18
will boast.[e] 19You gladly put up with e Php 3:3,4
fools since you are so wise![f] 20In fact, you 11:19
even put up with anyone who enslaves f 1Co 4:10
you[g] or exploits you or takes advantage 11:20
of you or pushes himself forward or g Gal 2:4
slaps you in the face. 21To my shame I 11:21
admit that we were too weak[h] for that! h 2Co 10:1,10
What anyone else dares to boast i Php 3:4
about—I am speaking as a fool—I also
dare to boast about.[i] 22Are they He- 11:22
brews? So am I.[j] Are they Israelites? So j Php 3:5
am I.[k] Are they Abraham's descendants? k Ro 9:4
So am I. 23Are they servants of Christ? (I

a 17 Jer. 9:24

YOUR THORN IN THE FLESH

Most of us have experienced the sensation of being pricked or scratched by a thorn. We endure varying degrees of itching, soreness or stinging. If the thorn becomes imbedded in the sole of our foot, it might cause a throb of pain with every step. The puncture might become infected, causing the skin to swell and fester. Such a seemingly insignificant wound, and yet it can become such a painful irritant. That is how Paul described his own condition in 2 Corinthians 12. Whatever his chronic physical condition might have been, it reminded him of a tiny thorn in his flesh that resulted in a disproportionate degree of "torment."

But Paul knew God intimately, and he knew how to face his infirmity with a godly attitude. Paul recognized that his problem was caused by Satan, but he also knew that it had been "given" to him. He acknowledged in 2 Corinthians 12:7 that "to keep [him] from becoming conceited because of these surpassingly great revelations, there was given [him] a thorn in [his] flesh, a messenger of Satan, to torment [him]."

God allowed Satan to work his mischief in Paul's life, but even Satan was compelled to act within the framework of God's purpose. This was also true for a man named Job (see Discovery #117, page 632). The Father allowed Satan to test this man of God but did not permit him to "lay a finger" on Job himself (Job 1:12). God allowed Satan to test Job, he permitted Satan to test Paul and he grants Satan the license to test us as well. But the evil one can only operate within the confines of the boundaries that God has set.

"Thorns" have another benefit. They afford us an opportunity to turn our eyes to God. Suffering is one of the ways in which God claims our attention. Paul implored God for some relief from his condition: "Three times I pleaded with the Lord to take it away from me" (2 Corinthians 12:9). There are many instances in Scripture in which godly people have prayed for themselves or others to be healed—and God answered those entreaties with a resounding *yes*! But healing is not always a part of his plan. In Paul's case, God answered his servant's prayer with an emphatic *no*. Paul elaborated in verse 9: "But he said to me, 'My grace is sufficient for you, for my power is made perfect in weakness.' Therefore I will boast all the more gladly about my weaknesses, so that Christ's power may rest on me."

If there were no problems in our lives, there would be no opportunity for God to meet our needs. We would never experience firsthand his tender care or his comfort. When we realize how weak and insufficient we are, we can begin to learn about God's power and his sufficiency. Suffering allows God the opportunity to demonstrate his wonderful grace—and it gives us the opportunity to experience it. Paul received this grace and was able to take pleasure in difficulties because they enabled him to see God at work: "That is why, for Christ's sake, I delight in weaknesses, in insults, in hardships, in persecutions, in difficulties. For when I am weak, then I am strong" (verse 10).

Self-Discovery: *What is your "thorn in the flesh"? Take a moment to dwell on the benefits the Lord has bestowed on you as an immediate result of this weakness.*

GO TO DISCOVERY 322 ON PAGE 1574

11:23 am out of my mind to talk like this.) I
l 1Co 15:10 am more. I have worked much harder,[l]
m Ac 16:23; been in prison more frequently,[m] been
2Co 6:4,5 flogged more severely, and been exposed
to death again and again. [24]Five times I
11:24 received from the Jews the forty lashes[n]
n Dt 25:3 minus one. [25]Three times I was beaten
11:25 with rods,[o] once I was stoned,[p] three
o Ac 16:22 p Ac 14:19 times I was shipwrecked, I spent a night
and a day in the open sea, [26]I have been
constantly on the move. I have been in
danger from rivers, in danger from bandits, in danger from my own country-
11:26 men,[q] in danger from Gentiles; in dan-
q Ac 9:23; 14:5 r Ac 21:31 ger in the city,[r] in danger in the country,
s Gal 2:4 in danger at sea; and in danger from
false brothers.[s] [27]I have labored and
toiled and have often gone without
sleep; I have known hunger and thirst
11:27 and have often gone without food;[t] I
t 1Co 4:11,12; 2Co 6:5 have been cold and naked. [28]Besides
everything else, I face daily the pressure
of my concern for all the churches.
[29]Who is weak, and I do not feel weak?
Who is led into sin, and I do not inwardly burn?
[30]If I must boast, I will boast of the
11:30 u 1Co 2:3 things that show my weakness.[u] [31]The
11:31 God and Father of the Lord Jesus, who is
v Ro 9:5 to be praised forever,[v] knows that I am
not lying. [32]In Damascus the governor
under King Aretas had the city of the
Damascenes guarded in order to arrest
11:32 w Ac 9:24 me.[w] [33]But I was lowered in a basket
11:33 from a window in the wall and slipped
x Ac 9:25 through his hands.[x]

Paul's Vision and His Thorn

12:1 12 I must go on boasting.[y] Al-
y 2Co 11:16,30 z ver 7 though there is nothing to be
gained, I will go on to visions and revelations[z] from the Lord. [2]I know a man in
Christ who fourteen years ago was
12:2 a Ac 8:39 caught up[a] to the third heaven.[b]
b Eph 4:10 Whether it was in the body or out of the
c 2Co 11:11 body I do not know—God knows.[c] [3]And
I know that this man—whether in the
body or apart from the body I do not
know, but God knows— [4]was caught up
12:4 d Lk 23:43; to paradise.[d] He heard inexpressible
Rev 2:7 things, things that man is not permitted
to tell. [5]I will boast about a man like
that, but I will not boast about myself,
except about my weaknesses. [6]Even if I
should choose to boast, I would not be a
12:6 e 2Co 11:16 fool,[e] because I would be speaking the
truth. But I refrain, so no one will think

I DON'T KNOW WHAT SUFFERING CHRIST IS CALLING YOU TO ENDURE. BUT HE CAN GIVE YOU GRACE TO FIND HIS JOY IN IT.

Tony Evans, *Pastor, Dallas, Texas*

more of me than is warranted by what I
do or say.
[7]To keep me from becoming conceited because of these surpassingly great
revelations, there was given me a thorn 12:7
in my flesh,[f] a messenger of Satan, to f Nu 33:55
torment me. [8]Three times I pleaded with 12:8
the Lord to take it away from me.[g] [9]But g Mt 26:39,44
he said to me, "My grace is sufficient for 12:9
you, for my power[h] is made perfect in h Php 4:13
weakness." Therefore I will boast all the
more gladly about my weaknesses, so
that Christ's power may rest on me.
[10]That is why, for Christ's sake, I delight 12:10
in weaknesses, in insults, in hardships,[i] i 2Co 6:4
in persecutions,[j] in difficulties. For j Ro 5:3; 2Th 1:4
when I am weak, then I am strong.[k] k 2Co 13:4

Paul's Concern for the Corinthians

[11]I have made a fool of myself,[l] but 12:11 l 2Co 11:1
you drove me to it. I ought to have been m 2Co 11:5
commended by you, for I am not in the n 1Co 15:9,10
least inferior to the "super-apostles,"[m]
even though I am nothing.[n] [12]The things
that mark an apostle—signs, wonders 12:12
and miracles[o]—were done among you o Jn 4:48
with great perseverance. [13]How were
you inferior to the other churches, ex- 12:13
cept that I was never a burden to you?[p] p 1Co 9:12,18
Forgive me this wrong![q] q 2Co 11:7
[14]Now I am ready to visit you for the
third time,[r] and I will not be a burden to 12:14 r 2Co 13:1
you, because what I want is not your s 1Co 4:14,15
possessions but you. After all, children t Pr 19:14
should not have to save up for their parents,[s] but parents for their children.[t]
[15]So I will very gladly spend for you
everything I have and expend myself as 12:15
well.[u] If I love you more, will you love me u Php 2:17;
less? [16]Be that as it may, I have not been 1Th 2:8
a burden to you.[v] Yet, crafty fellow that I 12:16
am, I caught you by trickery! [17]Did I ex- v 2Co 11:9
ploit you through any of the men I sent 12:18
you? [18]I urged[w] Titus to go to you and I w 2Co 8:6,16
sent our brother[x] with him. Titus did x 2Co 8:18
not exploit you, did he? Did we not act
in the same spirit and follow the same
course?

DISCOVERY 322

A FINAL BLESSING

Paul closed his second letter to the church in Corinth with words that are still repeated as a benediction at the conclusion of many worship services: "May the grace of the Lord Jesus Christ, and the love of God, and the fellowship of the Holy Spirit be with you all" (2 Corinthians 13:14). These beautiful words capture essential truths about our triune God and our relationship with him.

First Paul mentioned "the grace of the Lord Jesus Christ." Jesus' grace refers to his mercy or loving-kindness, which is at all times available to us despite our lack of deserving. Because of Jesus' grace we are liberated from the enslavement and dire consequences of sin, and he continues to infuse us with the strength to overcome difficulties and obstacles (2 Corinthians 12:8–10). Paul marveled at the wonder of the gift of God's grace, exclaiming: "It is by grace you have been saved, through faith—and this not from yourselves, it is the gift of God—not of works, so that no one can boast" (Ephesians 2:8–9).

Second, Paul referred to God's love. We live in a world filled with injustice and suffering, a world that is ruled by a just God who will not permit sin to go unpunished. This combination of factors would indeed constitute the ultimate "Catch 22" were it not for the fact that this same God has in love offered the solution—at untold cost to himself: "God demonstrates his own love for us in this: While we were still sinners, Christ died for us" (Romans 5:8).

When we begin to question God's love because of the immediate, trying circumstances in our lives, we need to return to the cross and try to imagine what our redemption must have cost God personally. Paul could scarcely contain his wonder and enthusiasm when it came to the subject of Jesus' love. He prayed that the Ephesian Christians might be granted power, "together with all the saints, to grasp how wide and long and high and deep is the love of Christ, and to know this love that surpasses knowledge" (Ephesians 3:18–19).

Finally, Paul cited fellowship with God's Holy Spirit. The word *fellowship* calls to mind mutual participation, and it implies more than casual acquaintance. When we are in fellowship with the Holy Spirit, we are cooperating with him to further God's purposes (Ephesians 4:30). Paul wrote in Philippians 2:1–2: "If you have any encouragement from being united with Christ, if any comfort from his love, if any fellowship with the Spirit, if any tenderness and compassion, then make my joy complete by being like-minded, having the same love, being one in spirit and purpose." And an inevitable by-product of this fellowship with the Spirit is joy (1 Thessalonians 1:6).

The next time you hear this benediction pronounced at the close of a worship service, pause a moment to reflect on the incomparable gifts that God is bestowing on you once again, and begin your new week marveling at the wonder of the grace, love and fellowship he has made available to you for the asking.

Self-Discovery: *You can become a source of blessing to others by singling out a loved one or group of special people and praying this benediction as a blessing with them in mind. Expect God to bless them richly today with the grace of Jesus, the love of God and the fellowship of the Holy Spirit. He will.*

GO TO DISCOVERY 323 ON PAGE 1580

19Have you been thinking all along
that we have been defending ourselves
to you? We have been speaking in the
12:19 [y]Ro 9:1 sight of God[y] as those in Christ; and
[z]2Co 10:8 everything we do, dear friends, is for
12:20 your strengthening.[z] 20For I am afraid
[a]2Co 2:1-4 that when I come[a] I may not find you as
[b]1Co 4:21 [c]1Co 1:11; 3:3 I want you to be, and you may not find
[d]Gal 5:20 me as you want me to be.[b] I fear that
[e]Ro 1:29 [f]1Co 14:33 there may be quarreling,[c] jealousy, outbursts of anger, factions,[d] slander, gos-
sip,[e] arrogance and disorder.[f] 21I am
afraid that when I come again my God
12:21 will humble me before you, and I will be
[g]2Co 2:1,4 grieved[g] over many who have sinned
[h]2Co 13:2 earlier[h] and have not repented of the impurity, sexual sin and debauchery in
which they have indulged.

Final Warnings

13 This will be my third visit to
13:1 [i]2Co 12:14 you.[i] "Every matter must be es-
[j]Dt 19:15; Mt 18:16 tablished by the testimony of two or
three witnesses."[a j] 2I already gave you a
warning when I was with you the second
13:2 time. I now repeat it while absent: On
[k]2Co 1:23 [l]2Co 12:21 my return I will not spare[k] those who
sinned earlier[l] or any of the others,
13:3 3since you are demanding proof that
[m]Mt 10:20; 1Co 5:4 Christ is speaking through me.[m] He is
13:4 not weak in dealing with you, but is
[n]Php 2:7,8; 1Pe 3:18 powerful among you. 4For to be sure, he
was crucified in weakness,[n] yet he lives
[o]Ro 1:4; 6:4 [p]ver 9 by God's power.[o] Likewise, we are weak[p]
in him, yet by God's power we will live
with him to serve you.
5Examine yourselves[q] to see whether 13:5 [q]1Co 11:28
you are in the faith; test yourselves.[r] Do [r]Jn 6:6 [s]Ro 8:10
you not realize that Christ Jesus is in
you[s]—unless, of course, you fail the
test? 6And I trust that you will discover
that we have not failed the test. 7Now we
pray to God that you will not do anything wrong. Not that people will see
that we have stood the test but that you
will do what is right even though we
may seem to have failed. 8For we cannot
do anything against the truth, but only
for the truth. 9We are glad whenever we
are weak but you are strong; and our
prayer is for your perfection.[t] 10This is 13:9 [t]ver 11
why I write these things when I am ab-
sent, that when I come I may not have to
be harsh in my use of authority—the au- 13:10 [u]2Co 10:8
thority the Lord gave me for building
you up, not for tearing you down.[u] 13:11 [v]1Th 4:1; 2Th 3:1

Final Greetings

11Finally, brothers,[v] good-by. Aim for [w]Mk 9:50 [x]Ro 15:33; Eph 6:23
perfection, listen to my appeal, be of one
mind, live in peace.[w] And the God of 13:12 [y]Ro 16:16
love and peace[x] will be with you.
12Greet one another with a holy kiss.[y] 13:13 [z]Php 4:22
13All the saints send their greetings.[z]
14May the grace of the Lord Jesus 13:14 [a]Ro 16:20;
Christ,[a] and the love of God,[b] and the fel- 2Co 8:9 [b]Ro 5:5; Jude 21
lowship of the Holy Spirit[c] be with you all. [c]Php 2:1

[a] 1 Deut. 19:15

Galatians

In what sense did Jesus become a curse? (Galatians 3:13)

♦ *When God's law is broken, it imposes a curse—the judgment of God. Not only was execution on a cross—a tree—a sign that the victim had been cursed (Deuteronomy 21:23), but it was also an indication that Jesus had received God's punishment for our sin (Isaiah 53:4–6).*

Has Jesus erased ethnic, economic and gender distinctions? (Galatians 3:28)

♦ *Jews are still Jews, Gentiles are still Gentiles, and men and women are still men and woman. What Jesus abolished is discrimination for such differences. Everyone who comes to him must come in the same way: through faith and repentance.*

Why is the cross offensive? (Galatians 5:11)

♦ *In the first century the cross was offensive because it was a humiliation and a punishment reserved for the underprivileged. On a deeper level, the cross offends us all because it's a reminder that we are sinful, unacceptable to God. The cross assaults our human pride with a clear statement that we cannot resolve the sin problem on our own.*

Jesus in Galatians People who read labels before purchasing packaged foods are frequently on the lookout for additives that may be hazardous to their health. In a similar way, Galatians describes artificial spiritual additives and their toxic effects. Paul encouraged the Galatians to return to the pure gospel and warned against adding legalism and a philosophy of works-righteousness to the simple gospel message.

Persuasive Jewish Christians were spreading rumors about Paul and challenging his teachings about the Christian faith. The Galatian believers were close friends of Paul, but the charges brought by these "Judaizers" had prompted them to question his motivation and teachings. With logic, historical recitation and even sarcasm, Paul defended his integrity and the honor of Jesus Christ.

Paul described Jesus in Galatians as the liberator who has set us free from bondage to God's law (Galatians 5:1). Because Jesus died for our sins, our sinful nature is put to death when we trust him as Savior. And because he came to life again, he gives us new life through his indwelling Holy Spirit (Galatians 2:20).

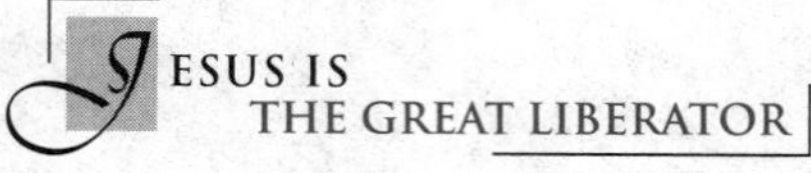
JESUS IS
THE GREAT LIBERATOR

1:1 [a] Ac 9:15 **1** Paul, an apostle—sent not from
[b] Ac 2:24 men nor by man, but by Jesus
Christ[a] and God the Father, who raised
1:2 [c] Php 4:21 him from the dead[b]— [2]and all the
[d] Ac 16:6; 1Co 16:1 brothers with me,[c]

To the churches in Galatia:[d]

1:3 [e] Ro 1:7 [3]Grace and peace to you from God
1:4 our Father and the Lord Jesus Christ,[e]
[f] Mt 20:28; Ro 4:25; [4]who gave himself for our sins[f] to rescue
Gal 2:20 us from the present evil age, according
[g] Php 4:20 to the will of our God and Father,[g] [5]to
1:5 [h] Ro 11:36 whom be glory for ever and ever. Amen.[h]

No Other Gospel

1:6 [6]I am astonished that you are so
[i] Gal 5:8 quickly deserting the one who called[i]
[j] 2Co 11:4 you by the grace of Christ and are turning to a different gospel[j]— [7]which is
1:7 really no gospel at all. Evidently some
[k] Ac 15:24; people are throwing you into confusion[k]
Gal 5:10 and are trying to pervert the gospel of
Christ. [8]But even if we or an angel from
1:8 heaven should preach a gospel other
[l] 2Co 11:4 than the one we preached to you,[l] let
[m] Ro 9:3 him be eternally condemned![m] [9]As we
have already said, so now I say again: If
1:9 anybody is preaching to you a gospel
[n] Ro 16:17 other than what you accepted,[n] let him
be eternally condemned!
1:10 [10]Am I now trying to win the approval
[o] Ro 2:29; 1Th 2:4 of men, or of God? Or am I trying to
please men?[o] If I were still trying to
please men, I would not be a servant of
Christ.

Paul Called by God

[11]I want you to know, brothers,[p] that 1:11
the gospel I preached is not something [p] 1Co 15:1
that man made up. [12]I did not receive it
from any man,[q] nor was I taught it; 1:12
rather, I received it by revelation[r] from [q] ver 1 [r] ver 16
Jesus Christ.

THE CROSS OF CHRIST PREACHES . . . THE BLOOD OF THE CROSS SPEAKS. IT HAS SOMETHING TO SAY. HAVE YOU HEARD IT?

Martyn Lloyd-Jones, *Pastor, London, England*

[13]For you have heard of my previous 1:13
way of life in Judaism,[s] how intensely I [s] Ac 26:4,5
persecuted the church of God and tried [t] Ac 8:3
to destroy it.[t] [14]I was advancing in Judaism beyond many Jews of my own age
and was extremely zealous for the tradi- 1:14
tions of my fathers.[u] [15]But when God, [u] Mt 15:2
who set me apart from birth[a][v] and 1:15
called me[w] by his grace, was pleased [16]to [v] Isa 49:1,5;
reveal his Son in me so that I might Jer 1:5 [w] Ac 9:15
preach him among the Gentiles,[x] I did 1:16
not consult any man,[y] [17]nor did I go up [x] Gal 2:9 [y] Mt 16:17
to Jerusalem to see those who were
apostles before I was, but I went immediately into Arabia and later returned to
Damascus. 1:18
[18]Then after three years,[z] I went up to [z] Ac 9:22,23 [a] Ac 9:26,27
Jerusalem[a] to get acquainted with Peter[b]
and stayed with him fifteen days. [19]I saw 1:19 [b] Mt 13:55
none of the other apostles—only James,[b]
the Lord's brother. [20]I assure you before 1:20 [c] Ro 9:1
God that what I am writing you is no lie.[c]
[21]Later I went to Syria and Cilicia.[d] [22]I 1:21 [d] Ac 6:9
was personally unknown to the churches
of Judea[e] that are in Christ. [23]They only 1:22 [e] 1Th 2:14
heard the report: "The man who former-
ly persecuted us is now preaching the 1:23 [f] Ac 6:7
faith[f] he once tried to destroy." [24]And
they praised God[g] because of me. 1:24 [g] Mt 9:8

Paul Accepted by the Apostles

2 Fourteen years later I went up
again to Jerusalem,[h] this time 2:1 [h] Ac 15:2
with Barnabas. I took Titus along also. [2]I
went in response to a revelation and set
before them the gospel that I preach

[a] *15* Or *from my mother's womb* [b] *18* Greek *Cephas*

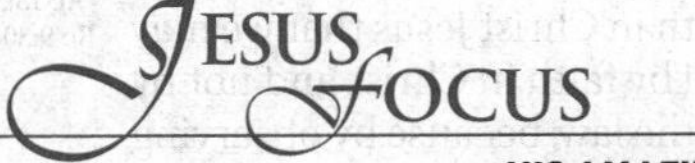

HIS AMAZING GRACE

Paul opened his letter to the churches in Galatia with a stinging rebuke, expressing his astonishment that the believers had been turning away from God's grace and perverting the Good News about Jesus (Galatians 1:6–7). The apostle warned the Galatian believers that any message other than that expressed in the gospel of Jesus Christ—even if it were to have been declared by an angel—is not from God. The people in Galatia were apparently adding to the simple truth of God's free gift of salvation through Jesus, teaching that people are obligated to do certain things in order to be acceptable to God the Father. But Paul was explicit: Corrupting God's truth by adding anything is cause for judgment (verse 9). We can do nothing to earn God's love or his favor, and he doesn't want us to try. He simply wants us to accept with profound gratitude the salvation of Jesus.

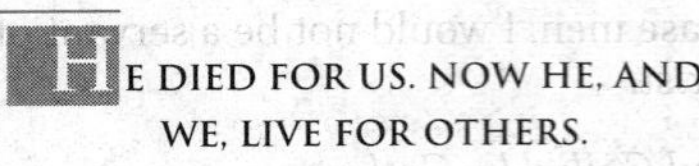

HE DIED FOR US. NOW HE, AND WE, LIVE FOR OTHERS.

Malcolm Cronk, *American Pastor*

2:2 [i]Ac 15:4,12 [j]1Co 9:24; Php 2:16
2:3 [k]2Co 2:13 [l]Ac 16:3; 1Co 9:21
2:4 [m]2Co 11:26 [n]Jude 4 [o]Ac 15:1; Gal 5:1,13
2:5 [p]ver 14
2:6 [q]Gal 6:3 [r]Ac 10:34
2:7 [s]1Th 2:4; 1Ti 1:11 [t]Ac 9:15 [u]ver 9, 11,14
2:8 [v]Ac 1:25

among the Gentiles.[i] But I did this privately to those who seemed to be leaders, for fear that I was running or had
run my race[j] in vain. 3Yet not even Titus,[k] who was with me, was compelled
to be circumcised, even though he was a
Greek.[l] 4⌞This matter arose⌟ because
some false brothers[m] had infiltrated our
ranks to spy on[n] the freedom[o] we have
in Christ Jesus and to make us slaves.
5We did not give in to them for a moment, so that the truth of the gospel[p]
might remain with you.

6As for those who seemed to be important[q]—whatever they were makes
no difference to me; God does not judge
by external appearance[r]—those men
added nothing to my message. 7On the
contrary, they saw that I had been entrusted with the task[s] of preaching the
gospel to the Gentiles,[a][t] just as Peter[u]
had been to the Jews.[b] 8For God, who
was at work in the ministry of Peter as
an apostle[v] to the Jews, was also at work

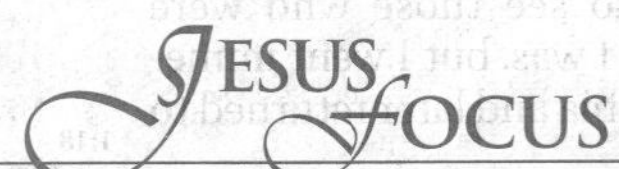

CHRISTIAN UNITY

When Paul had first turned to follow Jesus, the "pillars" of the new church—Peter, James and John—had offered him the "right hand of fellowship" (Galatians 2:9). They had accepted this rebel-turned-Christian without reservation, judgment or qualification. Years later, however, Peter was unwilling to extend the same love and acceptance to the newly converted Gentiles at Antioch in Syria (verse 11), and Paul pointed out the hypocrisy of Peter's action; Peter knew the truth about freedom from law but still gave in to the pressure of those who opposed him. The controversy between the Jewish and Gentile believers could potentially have split the early church, but Paul's letter helped both camps to refocus: We are all "justified by faith in Christ" (verse 16). Just as Jesus had welcomed outcasts and sinners, so our relationship with God is based solely on whether or not we have been willing to trust God the Father and accept Jesus' death for our sins (verse 20).

in my ministry as an apostle to the Gentiles. 9James, Peter[c][w] and John, those re-
puted to be pillars,[x] gave me and Barnabas[y] the right hand of fellowship when
they recognized the grace given to me.[z]
They agreed that we should go to the
Gentiles, and they to the Jews. 10All they
asked was that we should continue to
remember the poor,[a] the very thing I
was eager to do.

2:9 [w]ver 7,11,14 [x]1Ti 3:15 [y]Ac 4:36 [z]Ro 12:3
2:10 [a]Ac 24:17

Paul Opposes Peter

11When Peter[b] came to Antioch,[c] I
opposed him to his face, because he was
clearly in the wrong. 12Before certain
men came from James, he used to eat
with the Gentiles.[d] But when they arrived, he began to draw back and separate himself from the Gentiles because
he was afraid of those who belonged to
the circumcision group.[e] 13The other
Jews joined him in his hypocrisy, so that
by their hypocrisy even Barnabas[f] was
led astray.

14When I saw that they were not acting in line with the truth of the gospel,[g]
I said to Peter[h] in front of them all, "You
are a Jew, yet you live like a Gentile and
not like a Jew.[i] How is it, then, that you
force Gentiles to follow Jewish customs?

15"We who are Jews by birth[j] and not
'Gentile sinners'[k] 16know that a man is
not justified by observing the law, but by
faith in Jesus Christ.[l] So we, too, have
put our faith in Christ Jesus that we may
be justified by faith in Christ and not by
observing the law, because by observing
the law no one will be justified.

17"If, while we seek to be justified in
Christ, it becomes evident that we ourselves are sinners,[m] does that mean that
Christ promotes sin? Absolutely not![n]
18If I rebuild what I destroyed, I prove
that I am a lawbreaker. 19For through the
law I died to the law[o] so that I might live
for God.[p] 20I have been crucified with
Christ[q] and I no longer live, but Christ
lives in me.[r] The life I live in the body, I
live by faith in the Son of God,[s] who
loved me[t] and gave himself for me.[u] 21I
do not set aside the grace of God, for if
righteousness could be gained through
the law,[v] Christ died for nothing!"[d]

2:11 [b]ver 7,9,14 [c]Ac 11:19
2:12 [d]Ac 11:3 [e]Ac 11:2
2:13 [f]ver 1; Ac 4:36
2:14 [g]ver 5 [h]ver 7,9, 11 [i]Ac 10:28
2:15 [j]Php 3:4,5 [k]1Sa 15:18
2:16 [l]Ac 13:39; Ro 9:30
2:17 [m]ver 15 [n]Gal 3:21
2:19 [o]Ro 7:4 [p]Ro 6:10,11,14; 2Co 5:15
2:20 [q]Ro 6:6 [r]1Pe 4:2 [s]Mt 4:3 [t]Ro 8:37 [u]Gal 1:4
2:21 [v]Gal 3:21

[a] *7* Greek *uncircumcised* [b] *7* Greek *circumcised*; also in verses 8 and 9 [c] *9* Greek *Cephas*; also in verses 11 and 14 [d] *21* Some interpreters end the quotation after verse 14.

Faith or Observance of the Law

3 You foolish Galatians! Who has
3:1 [w]Gal 5:7 bewitched you?[w] Before your very
[x]1Co 1:23 eyes Jesus Christ was clearly portrayed
as crucified.[x] 2I would like to learn just
one thing from you: Did you receive the
3:2 Spirit by observing the law, or by believ-
[y]Ro 10:17 ing what you heard?[y] 3Are you so foolish? After beginning with the Spirit, are
you now trying to attain your goal by
human effort? 4Have you suffered so
much for nothing—if it really was for
3:5 nothing? 5Does God give you his Spirit
[z]1Co 12:10 and work miracles[z] among you because
you observe the law, or because you believe what you heard?
6Consider Abraham: "He believed
3:6 God, and it was credited to him as righ-
[a]Ge 15:6; Ro 4:3 teousness."[a][a] 7Understand, then, that
3:7 those who believe[b] are children of Abra-
[b]ver 9 ham. 8The Scripture foresaw that God
would justify the Gentiles by faith, and
announced the gospel in advance to
3:8 Abraham: "All nations will be blessed
[c]Ge 12:3; through you."[b][c] 9So those who have
Ac 3:25 faith[d] are blessed along with Abraham,
3:9 the man of faith.
[d]ver 7; Ro 4:16 10All who rely on observing the law
are under a curse, for it is written:
3:10 "Cursed is everyone who does not con-
[e]Dt 27:26; Jer 11:3 tinue to do everything written in the
Book of the Law."[c][e] 11Clearly no one is
3:11 [f]Hab 2:4; justified before God by the law, because,
Gal 2:16; "The righteous will live by faith."[d][f] 12The
Heb 10:38 law is not based on faith; on the con-
3:12 trary, "The man who does these things
[g]Lev 18:5; will live by them."[e][g] 13Christ redeemed
Ro 10:5 us from the curse of the law[h] by becom-
3:13 [h]Gal 4:5 ing a curse for us, for it is written:
[i]Dt 21:23; "Cursed is everyone who is hung on a
Ac 5:30 tree."[f][i] 14He redeemed us in order that
3:14 the blessing given to Abraham might
[j]Ro 4:9,16 come to the Gentiles through Christ
[k]ver 2; Joel 2:28; Jesus,[j] so that by faith we might receive
Ac 2:33 the promise of the Spirit.[k]

The Law and the Promise

15Brothers, let me take an example
from everyday life. Just as no one can set
aside or add to a human covenant that
has been duly established, so it is in this
3:16 case. 16The promises were spoken to
[l]Lk 1:55; Abraham and to his seed.[l] The Scripture
Ro 4:13,16 does not say "and to seeds," meaning
many people, but "and to your seed,"[g]
meaning one person, who is Christ.
17What I mean is this: The law, intro-
duced 430 years[m] later, does not set aside 3:17 [m]Ge 15:13,14;
the covenant previously established by Ex 12:40
God and thus do away with the promise.
18For if the inheritance depends on the
law, then it no longer depends on a 3:18
promise;[n] but God in his grace gave it to [n]Ro 4:14
Abraham through a promise.
19What, then, was the purpose of the
law? It was added because of transgres-
sions[o] until the Seed[p] to whom the 3:19 [o]Ro 5:20
promise referred had come. The law was [p]ver 16
put into effect through angels[q] by a me- [q]Ac 7:53
diator.[r] 20A mediator,[s] however, does not [r]Ex 20:19
represent just one party; but God is one. 3:20 [s]Heb 8:6; 9:15;
21Is the law, therefore, opposed to the 12:24
promises of God? Absolutely not![t] For if
a law had been given that could impart 3:21 [t]Gal 2:17
life, then righteousness would certainly [u]Gal 2:21
have come by the law.[u] 22But the Scripture declares that the whole world is a 3:22
prisoner of sin,[v] so that what was prom- [v]Ro 3:9-19;
ised, being given through faith in Jesus 11:32
Christ, might be given to those who believe.
23Before this faith came, we were held 3:23
prisoners[w] by the law, locked up until [w]Ro 11:32
faith should be revealed. 24So the law 3:24
was put in charge to lead us to Christ[h][x] [x]Ro 10:4
that we might be justified by faith.[y] [y]Gal 2:16
25Now that faith has come, we are no
longer under the supervision of the law.

THE SON OF GOD BECAME MAN
TO ENABLE MEN TO
BECOME THE SONS OF GOD.

C. S. Lewis, *British Author*

Sons of God

26You are all sons of God[z] through 3:26
faith in Christ Jesus, 27for all of you who [z]Ro 8:14
were baptized into Christ[a] have clothed 3:27 [a]Mt 28:19;
yourselves with Christ.[b] 28There is nei- Ro 6:3
ther Jew nor Greek, slave nor free,[c] male [b]Ro 13:14
nor female, for you are all one in Christ 3:28
Jesus.[d] 29If you belong to Christ,[e] then [c]Col 3:11
you are Abraham's seed, and heirs ac- [d]Jn 10:16;
cording to the promise.[f] 17:11; Eph 2:14, 15

4 What I am saying is that as long as 3:29
the heir is a child, he is no different [e]1Co 3:23
from a slave, although he owns the whole [f]ver 16
estate. 2He is subject to guardians and

[a] *6* Gen. 15:6 [b] *8* Gen. 12:3; 18:18; 22:18
[c] *10* Deut. 27:26 [d] *11* Hab. 2:4 [e] *12* Lev. 18:5
[f] *13* Deut. 21:23 [g] *16* Gen. 12:7; 13:15; 24:7
[h] *24* Or *charge until Christ came*

Saved by Grace

The believers in Galatia had found themselves heading down a dangerous path, and they needed a reminder from Paul. They had become children of God by placing their trust in Jesus, but their simple, childlike faith was being assailed by the false teaching that faith alone is insufficient for salvation. Jewish Christians were telling them that *along with* faith in Jesus God's people were accountable to keep the Jewish traditions and laws in order to be saved (Galatians 3:1–14).

The main thrust of Paul's letter to the churches in Galatia was the truth that anyone who believes in Jesus is thereby God's child—and that this adoption and salvation have nothing whatsoever to do with adherence to rules. Both Jewish and Greek believers are sons and daughters of God—both slaves and free, both men and women—all who believe are God's children (verses 26–29).

Sometimes it appears that "faith" as exemplified in the Old Testament was based on how closely people followed the commandments and how faithfully they offered sacrifices. But being a member of God's family has always been a matter of trust rather than of any futile attempt at perfection. While the law of God teaches us what he is like and defines for us the kind of lifestyle he expects from us, it does not "impart life" (verse 21). Only Jesus' sacrificial death could accomplish that: "When the time had fully come, God sent his Son, born of a woman, born under law, to redeem those under law, that we might receive the full rights of sons" (Galatians 4:4–5).

As the Holy Spirit moves within us, we are freed from the stranglehold of constricting rules. Instead, we are guided by his power to *want* to live holy lives. While we are not saved by our good deeds, they are indeed evidence that the Holy Spirit is at work in us. Paul minced no words in addressing the Galatian believers: "You foolish Galatians! Who has bewitched you? . . . After beginning with the Spirit, are you now trying to attain your goal by human effort? . . . Does God give you his Spirit and work miracles among you because you observe the law, or because you believe what you heard?" (Galatians 3:1,3,5).

While we are no longer bound by the letter of the law, we as believers are "clothed . . . with Christ" (verse 27), and our focus must now be on pleasing him rather than on gratifying our own desires (Romans 13:14; Ephesians 4:24; Colossians 3:10,12). We are quick to think of sexual sin when we think of gratifying ourselves, but pleasing ourselves includes so much more: craving food, striving for material possessions, harboring thoughts of envy, hoarding our "precious time," desiring public recognition for our efforts to enhance the quality of life in our community. These thoughts and actions are all contrary to the principles of our new life of freedom in Jesus (Galatians 5:1). Now that the Holy Spirit is at work in our lives, the evidence will be the "fruit of the Spirit" (Galatians 5:22–23).

Self-Discovery: Think of a situation in which you were tempted to perceive of a particular rule, expectation or tradition as necessary for your salvation. Then spend a moment in prayer, thanking the Lord Jesus that you have been saved by grace alone.

GO TO DISCOVERY 324 ON PAGE 1583

> JESUS DID NOT DIE THAT WE MIGHT REMAIN UNFIT. HE DIED THAT WE MIGHT BE MADE FIT, . . . THAT WE MIGHT BE CALLED THE SONS AND DAUGHTERS OF GOD.
>
> 
>
> Carolyn Ann Knight,
> *Community Activist,*
> *Harlem, New York*

trustees until the time set by his father.
4:3 3So also, when we were children, we were
g Gal 2:4 in slavery[g] under the basic principles of
h Col 2:8,20 the world.[h] 4But when the time had fully
4:4 come,[i] God sent his Son, born of a
i Mk 1:15; Eph 1:10 woman,[j] born under law,[k] 5to redeem
j Jn 1:14 those under law, that we might receive
k Lk 2:27 the full rights[l] of sons. 6Because you are
4:5 sons, God sent the Spirit of his Son into
l Jn 1:12 our hearts,[m] the Spirit who calls out,
4:6 *"Abba,*[a] Father."[n] 7So you are no longer a
m Ro 5:5 slave, but a son; and since you are a son,
n Ro 8:15,16 God has made you also an heir.[o]

4:7 o Ro 8:17

Paul's Concern for the Galatians

4:8 8Formerly, when you did not know
p 1Co 1:21; Eph 2:12; God,[p] you were slaves to those who by
1Th 4:5 nature are not gods.[q] 9But now that you
q 2Ch 13:9; Isa 37:19 know God—or rather are known by
4:9 God[r]—how is it that you are turning
back to those weak and miserable prin-
r 1Co 8:3 s ver 3 ciples? Do you wish to be enslaved[s] by
them all over again?[t] 10You are observing 4:9 t Col 2:20
special days and months and seasons
and years![u] 11I fear for you, that somehow 4:10 u Ro 14:5
I have wasted my efforts on you.[v]
12I plead with you, brothers,[w] become 4:11 v 1Th 3:5
like me, for I became like you. You have
done me no wrong. 13As you know, it 4:12 w Gal 6:18
was because of an illness[x] that I first
preached the gospel to you. 14Even 4:13 x 1Co 2:3
though my illness was a trial to you, you
did not treat me with contempt or
scorn. Instead, you welcomed me as if I
were an angel of God, as if I were Christ
Jesus himself.[y] 15What has happened to 4:14 y Mt 10:40
all your joy? I can testify that, if you
could have done so, you would have torn
out your eyes and given them to me.
16Have I now become your enemy by
telling you the truth?[z] 4:16 z Am 5:10
17Those people are zealous to win you
over, but for no good. What they want is
to alienate you ⌊from us⌋, so that you
may be zealous for them. 18It is fine to be
zealous, provided the purpose is good,
and to be so always and not just when I 4:18
am with you.[a] 19My dear children,[b] for a ver 13,14
whom I am again in the pains of child- 4:19
birth until Christ is formed in you,[c] b 1Co 4:15 c Eph 4:13
20how I wish I could be with you now
and change my tone, because I am perplexed about you!

Hagar and Sarah

21Tell me, you who want to be under
the law, are you not aware of what the
law says? 22For it is written that Abraham had two sons, one by the slave 4:22
woman[d] and the other by the free d Ge 16:15
woman.[e] 23His son by the slave woman e Ge 21:2
was born in the ordinary way;[f] but his 4:23
son by the free woman was born as the f Ro 9:7,8
result of a promise.[g] g Ge 18:10-14; Heb 11:11
24These things may be taken figuratively, for the women represent two covenants. One covenant is from Mount Sinai and bears children who are to be
slaves: This is Hagar. 25Now Hagar
stands for Mount Sinai in Arabia and
corresponds to the present city of Jerusalem, because she is in slavery with her
children. 26But the Jerusalem that is
above[h] is free, and she is our mother. 4:26 h Heb 12:22;
27For it is written: Rev 3:12

"Be glad, O barren woman,
who bears no children;

[a] 6 Aramaic for *Father*

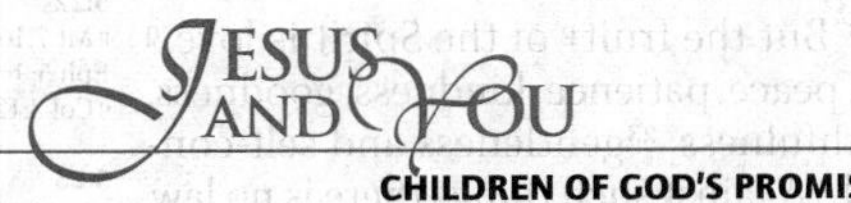

CHILDREN OF GOD'S PROMISE

Jesus understands our deepest needs and our most profound hurts—because he was one of us (Galatians 4:4). He was completely human—and at the same time completely one with God the Father. When we believe that Jesus is the Son of God, we become God's children through adoption into his diverse international family (John 1:12–13; Romans 9:13–17). And because we are his treasures we can call him by the name *"Abba,"* the Aramaic word for "Daddy," a term implying a close, deeply affectionate relationship (see also Romans 8:15). God's Holy Spirit works along with his beloved Son by continuing to transform us into the kind of people God always intended for us to be. Because we have been "reborn" as the "children of promise" (Galatians 4:28), we are no longer slaves to sin (Romans 6:15–23).

break forth and cry aloud,
you who have no labor pains;
because more are the children of
4:27 the desolate woman
i Isa 54:1 than of her who has a husband."[a][i]
28Now you, brothers, like Isaac, are
children of promise. 29At that time the
4:29 son born in the ordinary way[j] persecut-
j ver 23 k Ge 21:9 ed the son born by the power of the Spirit.[k] It is the same now. 30But what does
the Scripture say? "Get rid of the slave
woman and her son, for the slave
4:30 woman's son will never share in the in-
l Ge 21:10 heritance with the free woman's son."[b][l]
31Therefore, brothers, we are not chil-
dren of the slave woman, but of the free
woman.

> **AS MAN ALONE, JESUS COULD NOT HAVE SAVED US; AS GOD ALONE, HE WOULD NOT; INCARNATE, HE COULD AND DID.**
>
> 
>
> Malcolm Muggeridge, *British Journalist*

Freedom in Christ

5:1 5 It is for freedom that Christ has
m Jn 8:32 set us free.[m] Stand firm,[n] then,
n 1Co 16:13 o Ac 15:10; and do not let yourselves be burdened
Gal 2:4 again by a yoke of slavery.[o]
5:2 2Mark my words! I, Paul, tell you that
p Ac 15:1 if you let yourselves be circumcised,[p]
Christ will be of no value to you at all.
3Again I declare to every man who lets
himself be circumcised that he is obli-
5:3 q Gal 3:10 gated to obey the whole law.[q] 4You who
5:4 are trying to be justified by law have
r Heb 12:15; been alienated from Christ; you have
2Pe 3:17 fallen away from grace.[r] 5But by faith we
eagerly await through the Spirit the
5:5 s Ro 8:23,24 righteousness for which we hope.[s] 6For
in Christ Jesus neither circumcision nor
5:6 uncircumcision has any value.[t] The only
t 1Co 7:19 u 1Th 1:3 thing that counts is faith expressing itself through love.[u]
5:7 v 1Co 9:24 7You were running a good race.[v] Who
w Gal 3:1 cut in on you[w] and kept you from obey-
5:8 ing the truth? 8That kind of persuasion
x Ro 8:28; does not come from the one who calls
Gal 1:6 you.[x] 9"A little yeast works through the
5:9 whole batch of dough."[y] 10I am confi-
y 1Co 5:6 dent[z] in the Lord that you will take no
5:10 other view.[a] The one who is throwing
z 2Co 2:3 a Php 3:15 you into confusion[b] will pay the penalty,
b Gal 1:7 whoever he may be. 11Brothers, if I am

still preaching circumcision, why am I 5:11
still being persecuted?[c] In that case the c Gal 4:29; 6:12
offense[d] of the cross has been abolished. d 1Co 1:23
12As for those agitators,[e] I wish they 5:12
would go the whole way and emasculate e ver 10
themselves!
13You, my brothers, were called to be
free. But do not use your freedom to in- 5:13
dulge the sinful nature[c];[f] rather, serve f 1Co 8:9;
one another[g] in love. 14The entire law is 1Pe 2:16 g 1Co 9:19;
summed up in a single command: "Love Eph 5:21
your neighbor as yourself."[d][h] 15If you 5:14
keep on biting and devouring each oth- h Lev 19:18;
er, watch out or you will be destroyed by Mt 22:39
each other.

Life by the Spirit

16So I say, live by the Spirit,[i] and you 5:16
will not gratify the desires of the sinful i Ro 8:2,4-6,9,14
nature.[j] 17For the sinful nature desires j ver 24
what is contrary to the Spirit, and the
Spirit what is contrary to the sinful na- 5:17
ture.[k] They are in conflict with each oth- k Ro 8:5-8
er, so that you do not do what you want.[l] l Ro 7:15-23
18But if you are led by the Spirit, you are 5:18
not under law.[m] m Ro 6:14; 1Ti 1:9
19The acts of the sinful nature are obvious: sexual immorality,[n] impurity and 5:19
debauchery; 20idolatry and witchcraft; n 1Co 6:18
hatred, discord, jealousy, fits of rage, selfish ambition, dissensions, factions 21and 5:21
envy; drunkenness, orgies, and the like.[o] o Ro 13:13
I warn you, as I did before, that those
who live like this will not inherit the
kingdom of God. 5:22
22But the fruit[p] of the Spirit is love,[q] p Mt 7:16-20;
joy, peace, patience, kindness, goodness, Eph 5:9 q Col 3:12-15
faithfulness, 23gentleness and self-con-
trol.[r] Against such things there is no law. 5:23
24Those who belong to Christ Jesus have r Ac 24:25
crucified the sinful nature[s] with its pas- 5:24
sions and desires.[t] 25Since we live by the s Ro 6:6 t ver 16, 17
Spirit, let us keep in step with the Spirit.
26Let us not become conceited,[u] pro- 5:26 u Php 2:3
voking and envying each other.

Doing Good to All

6 Brothers, if someone is caught in 6:1
a sin, you who are spiritual[v] v 1Co 2:15
should restore him gently. But watch 6:2
yourself, or you also may be tempted. w Ro 15:1;
2Carry each other's burdens, and in this Jas 2:8
way you will fulfill the law of Christ.[w] 3If 6:3
anyone thinks he is something[x] when he x Ro 12:3; 1Co 8:2

[a] 27 Isaiah 54:1 [b] 30 Gen. 21:10 [c] 13 Or *the flesh*; also in verses 16, 17, 19 and 24 [d] 14 Lev. 19:18

DISCOVERY 324

GLORY IN THE CROSS

When a person was executed on a cross, the rough-hewn wood shouted ugliness and desolation to the spectators who had gathered to watch. The cross was considered accursed and stood as a symbol for failure, rejection and death (Galatians 3:13; 1 Peter 2:24). We are unable to comprehend the degree to which people in Jesus' day despised and feared the cross. The closest we can probably come to that revulsion and horror might be the feelings of many today concerning such contemporary practices as assisted suicide, euthanasia or partial-birth abortion. Yet the cross is precisely the burden Jesus instructed his followers to "take" and carry along with them through life (Matthew 16:24–25). Choosing to follow Jesus goes against the grain of what many people view as important, rational or comfortable. But Jesus wasn't interested in comfort, either for himself or for his disciples.

The apostle Paul believed that following Jesus meant death—but not in the same way that Jesus taught! At least not at first. Saul (Paul's Jewish name used prior to his radical conversion) had dedicated his life to persecuting and arresting Christians (Acts 9:1; 22:4; 26:10). It wasn't until after Jesus had turned his life upside-down on the Damascus Road (Acts 9:1–19) that Paul realized what the cross really stood for. Jesus, the Son of God, died an accursed death in our place so that we might live forever with him in heaven (John 14:2–3).

After Paul's life had been transformed, he attached the highest value to the very thing he had once so completely despised: "May I never boast except in the cross of our Lord Jesus Christ, through which the world has been crucified to me, and I to the world" (Galatians 6:14). Earlier in this same letter Paul identified himself firmly with his Savior: "I have been crucified with Christ and I no longer live, but Christ lives in me" (Galatians 2:20).

Before we get to know Jesus our lives have more in common with that old rugged cross than we might care to admit. The Bible tells us that we were dead in our sins (Ephesians 2:1), just as the wood of the cross was dead. We could boast of nothing but pain, torture, bondage and death—and the picture was ugly.

Jesus wants to change that for each one of us as he remakes us into a "new creation" (2 Corinthians 5:17). Only God can take the ugliness of our sin and nail it to the cross, transforming it into something excellent. Instead of staying with us as an indelible stain on our past, filling us with shame and paralyzing regret, forgiven sin becomes a testimony to God's grace and compassion. The cross, once a symbol of hatred and torture, becomes the channel by which Jesus shouts "I love you!" to a hurting world (Romans 8:31–35).

Self-Discovery: *Envision yourself nailing a heavy bundle containing all of your sins to a wooden cross. Relax your shoulders and feel the sense of lightness and freedom. What difference will this image make in your life as you go about your routine today?*

GO TO DISCOVERY 325 ON PAGE 1587

is nothing, he deceives himself. [4]Each
one should test his own actions. Then he
can take pride in himself, without comparing himself to somebody else, [5]for
each one should carry his own load.
[6]Anyone who receives instruction in
the word must share all good things
6:6 y 1Co 9:11,14 with his instructor.[y]
[7]Do not be deceived:[z] God cannot be
6:7 z 1Co 6:9 mocked. A man reaps what he sows.[a]
a 2Co 9:6 [8]The one who sows to please his sinful
6:8 nature, from that nature[a] will reap de-
b Job 4:8; struction;[b] the one who sows to please
Hos 8:7 the Spirit, from the Spirit will reap eter-
c Jas 3:18 nal life.[c] [9]Let us not become weary in
6:9 d 1Co 15:58 doing good,[d] for at the proper time we
e Rev 2:10 will reap a harvest if we do not give up.[e]
6:10 [10]Therefore, as we have opportunity, let
f Pr 3:27 us do good[f] to all people, especially to
g Eph 2:19 those who belong to the family[g] of believers.

Not Circumcision but a New Creation

[11]See what large letters I use as I write
6:11 h 1Co 16:21 to you with my own hand![h]
[12]Those who want to make a good impression outwardly are trying to compel
6:12 i Ac 15:1 you to be circumcised.[i] The only reason

> **THE CROSS IS THE MOST REVOLUTIONARY THING EVER TO APPEAR AMONG MEN . . . WE MUST FLEE IT OR DIE UPON IT.**
>
> A. W. Tozer, *Christian Leader*

they do this is to avoid being persecut- 6:12
ed[j] for the cross of Christ. [13]Not even j Gal 5:11
those who are circumcised obey the 6:13
law,[k] yet they want you to be circum- k Ro 2:25
cised that they may boast about your l Php 3:3
flesh.[l] [14]May I never boast except in the
cross of our Lord Jesus Christ, through
which[b] the world has been crucified to 6:14
me, and I to the world.[m] [15]Neither cir- m Ro 6:2,6
cumcision nor uncircumcision means 6:15
anything;[n] what counts is a new cre- n 1Co 7:19
ation.[o] [16]Peace and mercy to all who fol- o 2Co 5:17
low this rule, even to the Israel of God. 6:17
[17]Finally, let no one cause me trouble, p Isa 44:5;
for I bear on my body the marks[p] of Jesus. 2Co 1:5
[18]The grace of our Lord Jesus Christ[q] 6:18 q Ro 16:20
be with your spirit,[r] brothers. Amen. r 2Ti 4:22

[a] 8 Or *his flesh, from the flesh* [b] 14 Or *whom*

EPHESIANS

Did Jesus abolish the Old Testament law or fulfill it? (Ephesians 2:15)

♦ *Jesus' life and death met the requirements of Old Testament law. At the same time, his death and resurrection removed the law as a means of coming to God, replacing it with salvation by grace through faith in Jesus' finished work.*

Does Jesus imprison his followers? (Ephesians 3:1)

♦ *When Paul wrote Ephesians, he was a literal prisoner, probably in Rome. Yet he wasn't bitter but committed himself to serving Jesus and preaching the gospel, whatever the cost. In the same way we can identify so closely with Jesus that we consider ourselves prisoners to his will.*

How does Jesus "fill the whole universe"? (Ephesians 4:10)

♦ *Jesus fills the universe by ruling over it. His presence permeates the universe, blessing and filling it everywhere.*

Jesus in Ephesians The letter to the Ephesians addresses the issue of finding the ultimate purpose for our life, focusing on eternity, making peace with God and identifying with Jesus. Paul wanted the Ephesians to see the overall picture of God's plan for history and to view themselves as people with a new identity. Paul employed in Ephesians a condensed approach to deep spiritual topics, incorporating both doctrinal discussions and practical advice.

Jesus is the central focus in Ephesians. Paul referred to him 45 times in this book and pointed out that our Lord has blessed his people with every "spiritual blessing" (Ephesians 1:3), chosen us from the very beginning to enjoy a relationship with him (verse 11) and marked us by the gift of his Holy Spirit (verse 13). Jesus is the chief cornerstone of God's household (Ephesians 2:19–20) and a reflection of God's glory among his people (Ephesians 3:21). He provides us with the spiritual gifts we need to serve him (Ephesians 4:7–13) and is both the head of the church (Ephesians 4:15) and the Lord of life (Ephesians 5:21–33).

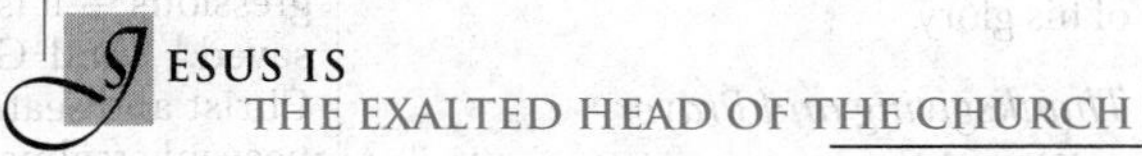

JESUS IS THE EXALTED HEAD OF THE CHURCH

1:1 a 1Co 1:1 1 Paul, an apostle[a] of Christ Jesus by
b 2Co 1:1 c Col 1:2 the will of God,[b]

To the saints in Ephesus,[a] the faith-
1:2 d Ro 1:7 ful[b c] in Christ Jesus:

2Grace and peace to you from God
our Father and the Lord Jesus Christ.[d]

Spiritual Blessings in Christ

1:3 3Praise be to the God and Father of
e 2Co 1:3 our Lord Jesus Christ,[e] who has blessed
f Eph 2:6; 3:10; us in the heavenly realms[f] with every
6:12 spiritual blessing in Christ. 4For he
1:4 g Eph 5:27; chose us in him before the creation of
Col 1:22 the world to be holy and blameless[g] in
h Eph 4:2,15,16 his sight. In love[h] 5he[c] predestined[i] us to
1:5 be adopted as his sons through Jesus
i Ro 8:29,30 j 1Co 1:21 Christ, in accordance with his pleasure[j]
and will— 6to the praise of his glorious
1:6 grace, which he has freely given us in the
k Mt 3:17 One he loves.[k] 7In him we have redemption[l] through his blood, the forgiveness
1:7 l Ro 3:24 of sins, in accordance with the riches of
God's grace 8that he lavished on us with
all wisdom and understanding. 9And
1:9 m Ro 16:25 he[d] made known to us the mystery[m] of
his will according to his good pleasure,
which he purposed in Christ, 10to be put
1:10 into effect when the times will have
n Gal 4:4 reached their fulfillment[n]—to bring all
o Col 1:20 things in heaven and on earth together
under one head, even Christ.[o]
11In him we were also chosen,[e] having
been predestined according to the plan
of him who works out everything in
1:11 p Eph 3:11; conformity with the purpose[p] of his will,
Heb 6:17 12in order that we, who were the first to
1:12 hope in Christ, might be for the praise of
q ver 6,14 his glory.[q] 13And you also were included
1:13 in Christ when you heard the word of
r Col 1:5 truth,[r] the gospel of your salvation. Hav-
s Eph 4:30 ing believed, you were marked in him
with a seal,[s] the promised Holy Spirit,
14who is a deposit guaranteeing our in-
1:14 t Ac 20:32 heritance[t] until the redemption of those
who are God's possession—to the praise
of his glory.

Thanksgiving and Prayer

15For this reason, ever since I heard
about your faith in the Lord Jesus and
1:15 u Col 1:4 your love for all the saints,[u] 16I have not
stopped giving thanks for you,[v] remem-
1:16 v Ro 1:8 bering you in my prayers. 17I keep asking
that the God of our Lord Jesus Christ,
1:17 w Jn 20:17 the glorious Father,[w] may give you the
x Col 1:9 Spirit[f] of wisdom[x] and revelation, so
that you may know him better. 18I pray
also that the eyes of your heart may be
enlightened[y] in order that you may 1:18
know the hope to which he has called y Ac 26:18; 2Co 4:6
you, the riches of his glorious inheri-
tance in the saints, 19and his incomparably great power for us who believe.
That power[z] is like the working of his 1:19 z Col 1:29
mighty strength,[a] 20which he exerted in a Eph 6:10
Christ when he raised him from the 1:20
dead[b] and seated him at his right hand b Ac 2:24
in the heavenly realms, 21far above all
rule and authority, power and dominion,
and every title[c] that can be given, not 1:21 c Php 2:9,10
only in the present age but also in the
one to come. 22And God placed all 1:22
things under his feet[d] and appointed d Mt 28:18
him to be head[e] over everything for the e Eph 4:15; 5:23
church, 23which is his body, the fullness
of him who fills everything in every way.

IT IS BY GRACE THAT ONE BECOMES A CHRISTIAN AND IT IS BY GRACE THAT ONE LIVES THE CHRISTIAN LIFE.

Kay Arthur, *Founder, Precept Ministries, Chattanooga, Tennessee*

Made Alive in Christ

2 As for you, you were dead in your
transgressions and sins,[f] 2in 2:1 f ver 5; Col 2:13
which you used to live[g] when you followed the ways of this world and of the 2:2 g Col 3:7
ruler of the kingdom of the air,[h] the spir- h Jn 12:31;
it who is now at work in those who are Eph 6:12 i Eph 5:6
disobedient.[i] 3All of us also lived among
them at one time, gratifying the cravings 2:3
of our sinful nature[g j] and following its j Gal 5:16
desires and thoughts. Like the rest, we
were by nature objects of wrath. 4But
because of his great love for us, God,
who is rich in mercy, 5made us alive with
Christ even when we were dead in trans- 2:5
gressions[k]—it is by grace you have been k ver 1 l ver 8;
saved.[l] 6And God raised us up with Ac 15:11
Christ and seated us with him[m] in the 2:6
heavenly realms[n] in Christ Jesus, 7in or- m Eph 1:20
der that in the coming ages he might n Eph 1:3
show the incomparable riches of his 2:7
grace, expressed in his kindness[o] to us o Tit 3:4

a 1 Some early manuscripts do not have *in Ephesus.* *b* 1 Or *believers who are* *c* 4,5 Or *sight in love.* 5*He* *d* 8,9 Or *us. With all wisdom and understanding,* 9*he* *e* 11 Or *were made heirs* *f* 17 Or *a spirit* *g* 3 Or *our flesh*

DISCOVERY 325

A Doxology of Praise

Ephesians 1:3–14 is often referred to as a "doxology"—literally, a liturgical expression of praise to God (see also Romans 11:33–36 for another example of a doxology passage). All one sentence in Greek, this section recites what God has done. Paul spoke first of the blessings we have through the Father (verse 3), then of those that come through Jesus, the Son (verses 4–13a) and finally of those we enjoy through the Holy Spirit (verses 13b–14). A frequently repeated phrase in the Ephesians passage (used 12 times) is "in Christ." Paul enumerated many of the blessings we enjoy because of our position in Jesus.

There are many blessings inherent in being a part of God's family. First, God chose us "in Christ," even before the world existed, to make us "holy and blameless in his sight" (verse 4). We were also chosen to be adopted (verses 5,11). Jesus paid the price necessary to redeem us (verse 7) and liberated us from slavery to sin by his atoning sacrifice. God's grace has been "lavished" on us (verse 7–8), and we experience peace with God, joy in life and innumerable other benefits through that grace.

The list goes on. God himself helps us to understand what he wants from us (verse 9). For generations God had chosen to keep some truths hidden, including the reality that he would "bring all things in heaven and on earth together under one head, even Christ" (verse 10). Only through Jesus' life, death and resurrection did God reveal what he had planned from the beginning—that Jesus would be the final and complete atoning sacrifice for our sins (1 John 2:2). We are included in his plan of salvation (Ephesians 1:11). And we are not here by accident but exist for the purpose of honoring God (verse 12) as those who reflect God's glory and become gradually transformed into the likeness of Jesus Christ (2 Corinthians 3:18).

God's Holy Spirit keeps us secure in Jesus. In Paul's second letter to the Corinthians, he wrote: "Now it is God who makes both us and you stand firm in Christ. He anointed us, set his seal of ownership on us, and put his Spirit in our hearts as a deposit, guaranteeing what is to come" (2 Corinthians 1:21–22).

And here in Ephesians 1 Paul declared that we are marked "in [Christ] with a seal, the promised Holy Spirit, who is a deposit guaranteeing our inheritance until the redemption of those who are God's possession—to the praise of his glory" (verses 13–14). A seal is a sign or insignia of ownership, and the Holy Spirit is God the Father's identifying mark. God guarantees through his Son that we no longer owe the debt of sin (verse 14).

This list of blessings is overwhelming, and Paul was apparently so caught up in the wonder that he literally spoke without a pause for breath—but yet the list is not exhaustive. May we share Paul's enthusiasm and marvel with him: "Praise be to the God and Father of our Lord Jesus Christ, who has blessed us in the heavenly realms with every spiritual blessing in Christ!" (Ephesians 1:3).

Self-Discovery: *Take a moment to make a mental list of some of the spiritual blessings that you enjoy. Then thank God for his innumerable gifts, specifically mentioning those on your list.*

GO TO DISCOVERY 326 ON PAGE 1589

2:8 in Christ Jesus. 8For it is by grace you
p ver 5 have been saved,[p] through faith—and
2:9 this not from yourselves, it is the gift of
q 2Ti 1:9 God— 9not by works,[q] so that no one
r 1Co 1:29 can boast.[r] 10For we are God's work-
2:10 manship, created[s] in Christ Jesus to do
s Eph 4:24 good works,[t] which God prepared in ad-
t Tit 2:14 vance for us to do.

One in Christ

11Therefore, remember that formerly
you who are Gentiles by birth and called
"uncircumcised" by those who call
themselves "the circumcision" (that
done in the body by the hands of
2:11 men)[u]— 12remember that at that time
u Col 2:11 you were separate from Christ, excluded
from citizenship in Israel and foreigners
2:12 v Gal 3:17 to the covenants of the promise,[v] with-
w 1Th 4:13 out hope[w] and without God in the world.
2:13 13But now in Christ Jesus you who once
x ver 17; Ac 2:39 were far away have been brought near[x]
y Col 1:20 through the blood of Christ.[y]
2:14 14For he himself is our peace, who has
z 1Co 12:13 made the two one[z] and has destroyed
the barrier, the dividing wall of hostility,
2:15 a Col 1:21,22 15by abolishing in his flesh[a] the law with
b Col 2:14 its commandments and regulations.[b]
His purpose was to create in himself
one[c] new man out of the two, thus mak- 2:15
ing peace, 16and in this one body to rec- c Gal 3:28
oncile both of them to God through the 2:16
cross,[d] by which he put to death their d Col 1:20,22
hostility. 17He came and preached peace 2:17
to you who were far away and peace to e Ps 148:14;
those who were near.[e] 18For through him Isa 57:19
we both have access[f] to the Father[g] by 2:18
one Spirit.[h] f Eph 3:12 g Col 1:12
19Consequently, you are no longer for- h 1Co 12:13
eigners and aliens,[i] but fellow citizens[j] 2:19
with God's people and members of i ver 12 j Php 3:20
God's household,[k] 20built on the founda- k Gal 6:10
tion[l] of the apostles and prophets, with
Christ Jesus himself as the chief corner- 2:20 l Mt 16:18;
stone.[m] 21In him the whole building is Rev 21:14
joined together and rises to become a m 1Pe 2:4-8
holy temple[n] in the Lord. 22And in him 2:21
you too are being built together to be- n 1Co 3:16,17
come a dwelling in which God lives by
his Spirit.

Paul the Preacher to the Gentiles

3 For this reason I, Paul, the prison-
er[o] of Christ Jesus for the sake of 3:1 o Ac 23:18;
you Gentiles— Eph 4:1
2Surely you have heard about the administration of God's grace that was giv- 3:2
en to me[p] for you, 3that is, the mystery[q] p Col 1:25
made known to me by revelation,[r] as I 3:3
have already written briefly. 4In reading q Ro 16:25
this, then, you will be able to understand r 1Co 2:10
my insight[s] into the mystery of Christ, 3:4 s 2Co 11:6
5which was not made known to men in
other generations as it has now been revealed by the Spirit to God's holy apos- 3:5
tles and prophets.[t] 6This mystery is that t Ro 16:26
through the gospel the Gentiles are
heirs[u] together with Israel, members to- 3:6 u Gal 3:29
gether of one body,[v] and sharers togeth- v Eph 2:15,16
er in the promise in Christ Jesus.
7I became a servant of this gospel[w] by 3:7 w 1Co 3:5
the gift of God's grace given me through x Eph 1:19
the working of his power.[x] 8Although I
am less than the least of all God's peo- 3:8
ple,[y] this grace was given me: to preach y 1Co 15:9
to the Gentiles the unsearchable riches
of Christ, 9and to make plain to every- 3:9
one the administration of this mystery,[z] z Ro 16:25
which for ages past was kept hidden in
God, who created all things. 10His intent
was that now, through the church, the 3:10
manifold wisdom of God[a] should be a 1Co 2:7
made known[b] to the rulers and author- b 1Pe 1:12
ities[c] in the heavenly realms, 11according c Eph 1:21
to his eternal purpose which he accomplished in Christ Jesus our Lord. 12In

JESUS AND YOU

GOD'S HOUSEHOLD

We all know something of how it must have felt in Paul's time to be a Gentile because we have all felt like outsiders at one time or another. From the perspective of the Jewish community, everyone outside their own tight circle was a Gentile. When we are in a relationship with Jesus, however, we become "fellow citizens with God's people and members of God's household" (Ephesians 2:19). Paul used the analogy that God's family is like a house built on the foundation of the apostles and prophets with Jesus himself as the "chief cornerstone" (verse 20). Every Christian, based on his or her relationship with Jesus Christ, is joined together with every other believer, and we together form a "holy temple" (verse 21). We may at times feel alone, but we are never outside God's control and his care. When we follow Jesus and experience an increasingly intimate relationship with him, we become an integral part of his grand design—both individually and corporately identified as a living, breathing temple that honors him (1 Corinthians 3:16–17; 6:19; see also 1 Peter 2:4–10).

DISCOVERY 326

The Prayer of Power

People often get on their knees before the Lord when their petition is something very important to them. Paul had great concern for the believers in Ephesus and told them that he knelt before the Father on their behalf (Ephesians 3:14). The reason for his sincere and passionate prayer was that he didn't want his brothers and sisters in Ephesus to continue being discouraged on account of his sufferings while in a Roman prison. He himself was not downhearted, he assured them, but was instead focused on the mission God had given to him: to make known to the Gentiles "the unsearchable riches of Christ" (verse 8).

The apostle pointed out that God had at long last unveiled the mystery of his Son and had accomplished his eternal purpose. It is through Jesus that "we may approach God with freedom and confidence" (verses 11–12). And that was precisely Paul's stance as he knelt humbly in prayer before the Father.

When Jesus is the focal point of our lives and the One in whom we place our trust, we can also approach the Father with assurance (Hebrews 4:16). Jesus himself is the only mediator or go-between that we need. His death and resurrection have bridged the gap between God and ourselves (1 Timothy 2:5–6).

Prayer is more than a simple (or one-sided) conversation; it has the power to transform our lives as we are drawn near to our loving Lord. Its benefits are almost incomprehensible, and certainly innumerable. Paul's prayers as mentioned in this passage are themselves moving examples of boldly approaching God's throne with requests that the Spirit's limitless power might be unleashed on behalf of people.

Paul prayed that we might be strengthened "with power through [God's] Spirit in [our] inner being, so that Christ may dwell in [our] hearts through faith" (Ephesians 3:16–17). Now there's something to think about and to give thanks for! We do not need to plod through this life alone, too depleted to fight the spiritual battles that rage all around us. Worldly philosophers urge us to "self-actualize" the inner core of our being, but there is no power source within the self. The world believes that it is only by taking control of our own lives that we can find fulfillment, but the Bible teaches precisely the opposite. It is only by renouncing control, turning over the reins to God in prayer and being filled with his Holy Spirit that we can become power-full Christians. We are "more than conquerors through him who loved us," no matter what life may hold for us (Romans 8:37).

Paul also prayed that believers might be "rooted and established in love" and that we might, through the work of the indwelling Holy Spirit, be able "to grasp how wide and long and high and deep is the love of Christ, and to know this love that surpasses knowledge—that [we] may be filled to the measure of all the fullness of God" (Ephesians 3:17–19).

Paul closed this moving passage with a thrilling tribute: "Now to him who is able to do immeasurably more than all we ask or imagine, according to his power that is at work within us, to him be glory in the church and in Christ Jesus throughout all generations, for ever and ever! Amen" (verses 20–21).

Self-Discovery: *Pause to thank God for the incomparable gift of prayer, and thank Jesus for opening up the line of communication that allows you to approach the Father directly and intimately.*

GO TO DISCOVERY 327 ON PAGE 1596

3:12 him and through faith in him we may
[d] Eph 2:18 approach God[d] with freedom and confi-
[e] Heb 4:16 dence.[e] [13]I ask you, therefore, not to be
discouraged because of my sufferings
for you, which are your glory.

A Prayer for the Ephesians

3:14 [f] Php 2:10 [14]For this reason I kneel[f] before the
Father, [15]from whom his whole family[a]
in heaven and on earth derives its name.
[16]I pray that out of his glorious riches he
3:16 [g] Col 1:11 may strengthen you with power[g]
[h] Ro 7:22 through his Spirit in your inner being,[h]
3:17 [17]so that Christ may dwell in your
[i] Jn 14:23 hearts[i] through faith. And I pray that
[j] Col 1:23 you, being rooted[j] and established in
love, [18]may have power, together with all
3:18 the saints, to grasp how wide and long
[k] Job 11:8,9 and high and deep[k] is the love of Christ,
3:19 [19]and to know this love that surpasses
[l] Col 2:10 knowledge—that you may be filled[l] to
[m] Eph 1:23 the measure of all the fullness of God.[m]
3:20 [n] Ro 16:25 [20]Now to him who is able[n] to do immeasurably more than all we ask or
imagine, according to his power that is
at work within us, [21]to him be glory in
the church and in Christ Jesus through-
3:21 out all generations, for ever and ever!
[o] Ro 11:36 Amen.[o]

Unity in the Body of Christ

4:1 [p] Eph 3:1 4 As a prisoner[p] for the Lord, then,
[q] Php 1:27; Col 1:10 I urge you to live a life worthy[q] of
the calling you have received. [2]Be com-

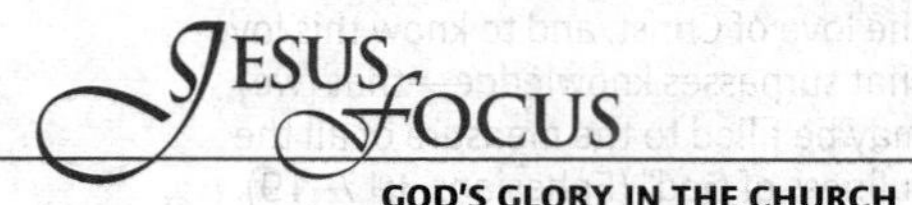

GOD'S GLORY IN THE CHURCH

God intended his church to be dynamic and vital, not dull and ineffective. Ephesians 3:20–21 reminds us that the church should reflect God's glory. It is God's divine, inexhaustible power working within us that showcases God's presence and majesty among his people through every generation. In the Old Testament God revealed his glory—his power and majesty—through the ark of the covenant (Exodus 26:34). The people could visibly see the symbol that the living God was with them in the Most Holy Place in the temple. Once Jesus had founded his church, however, our lives became his chosen instrument to reveal to the world that he is God. Jesus Christ lives through us when we believe in him and trust him (John 14:20). *We* are now the Most Holy Place because God himself lives in us.

pletely humble and gentle; be patient, 4:2 [r] Col 3:12,13
bearing with one another[r] in love.[s] [s] Eph 1:4
[3]Make every effort to keep the unity[t] of
the Spirit through the bond of peace. 4:3 [t] Col 3:14
[4]There is one body and one Spirit[u]—
just as you were called to one hope when 4:4 [u] 1Co 12:13
you were called— [5]one Lord, one faith,
one baptism; [6]one God and Father of all,
who is over all and through all and in 4:6
all.[v] [v] Ro 11:36
[7]But to each one of us[w] grace has 4:7 [w] 1Co 12:7,11
been given[x] as Christ apportioned it. [x] Ro 12:3
[8]This is why it[b] says:

"When he ascended on high,
he led captives[y] in his train 4:8 [y] Col 2:15
and gave gifts to men."[c][z] [z] Ps 68:18

[9](What does "he ascended" mean except that he also descended to the lower, earthly regions[d]? [10]He who descended is the very one who ascended higher
than all the heavens, in order to fill the
whole universe.) [11]It was he who gave 4:11
some to be apostles,[a] some to be proph- [a] 1Co 12:28
ets, some to be evangelists,[b] and some [b] Ac 21:8
to be pastors and teachers, [12]to prepare
God's people for works of service, so that 4:12
the body of Christ[c] may be built up [13]un- [c] 1Co 12:27
til we all reach unity[d] in the faith and in 4:13
the knowledge of the Son of God and be- [d] ver 3,5
come mature,[e] attaining to the whole [e] Col 1:28
measure of the fullness of Christ.
[14]Then we will no longer be infants,[f] 4:14
tossed back and forth by the waves,[g] and [f] 1Co 14:20 [g] Jas 1:6
blown here and there by every wind of [h] Eph 6:11
teaching and by the cunning and craftiness of men in their deceitful scheming.[h] [15]Instead, speaking the truth in
love, we will in all things grow up into 4:15
him who is the Head,[i] that is, Christ. [i] Eph 1:22
[16]From him the whole body, joined and
held together by every supporting liga- 4:16
ment, grows[j] and builds itself up in love, [j] Col 2:19
as each part does its work.

Living as Children of Light

[17]So I tell you this, and insist on it in
the Lord, that you must no longer live as 4:17
the Gentiles do, in the futility of their [k] Ro 1:21
thinking.[k] [18]They are darkened in their 4:18
understanding[l] and separated from the [l] Ro 1:21
life of God[m] because of the ignorance [m] Eph 2:12
that is in them due to the hardening of [n] 2Co 3:14
their hearts.[n] [19]Having lost all sensitivi- 4:19 [o] 1Ti 4:2
ty,[o] they have given themselves over[p] to [p] Ro 1:24

[a] 15 Or *whom all fatherhood* [b] 8 Or *God*
[c] 8 Psalm 68:18 [d] 9 Or *the depths of the earth*

4:19 [q]Col 3:5 sensuality[q] so as to indulge in every kind
of impurity, with a continual lust for
more.
20You, however, did not come to know
Christ that way. 21Surely you heard of
him and were taught in him in accordance with the truth that is in Jesus.
4:22 22You were taught, with regard to your
[r]1Pe 2:1 [s]Ro 6:6 former way of life, to put off[r] your old
self,[s] which is being corrupted by its de-
ceitful desires; 23to be made new in the
4:23 attitude of your minds;[t] 24and to put on
[t]Col 3:10 the new self,[u] created to be like God in
4:24 true righteousness and holiness.[v]
[u]Ro 6:4 25Therefore each of you must put off
[v]Eph 2:10 falsehood and speak truthfully[w] to his
4:25 [w]Zec 8:16 neighbor, for we are all members of one
[x]Ro 12:5 body.[x] 26"In your anger do not sin"[a]: Do
4:28 not let the sun go down while you are
[y]Ac 20:35 still angry, 27and do not give the devil a
[z]1Th 4:11 [a]Lk 3:11 foothold. 28He who has been stealing
must steal no longer, but must work,[y]
doing something useful with his own
hands,[z] that he may have something to
share with those in need.[a]
29Do not let any unwholesome talk
4:29 [b]Col 3:8 come out of your mouths,[b] but only
what is helpful for building others up according to their needs, that it may benefit those who listen. 30And do not grieve
4:30 [c]1Th 5:19 the Holy Spirit of God,[c] with whom you
[d]Ro 8:23 were sealed for the day of redemption.[d]
31Get rid of all bitterness, rage and anger,
4:31 brawling and slander, along with every
[e]Col 3:8 form of malice.[e] 32Be kind and compas-
4:32 sionate to one another, forgiving each
[f]Mt 6:14,15 other, just as in Christ God forgave you.[f]
5:1 **5** Be imitators of God,[g] therefore, as
[g]Lk 6:36 dearly loved children 2and live a
5:2 life of love, just as Christ loved us and
[h]Gal 1:4 gave himself up for us[h] as a fragrant of-
[i]2Co 2:15; Heb 7:27 fering and sacrifice to God.[i]
3But among you there must not be
5:3 even a hint of sexual immorality, or of
[j]Col 3:5 any kind of impurity, or of greed,[j] because these are improper for God's holy
people. 4Nor should there be obscenity,
5:4 foolish talk or coarse joking, which are
[k]ver 20 out of place, but rather thanksgiving.[k]
5For of this you can be sure: No immoral,
impure or greedy person—such a man is

OUR JOB IS TO MAKE THE INVISIBLE REIGN OF JESUS VISIBLE.

R. C. Sproul, *Presbyterian Theologian*

an idolater[l]—has any inheritance in the 5:5 [l]Col 3:5
kingdom of Christ and of God.[b][m] 6Let [m]1Co 6:9
no one deceive you with empty words,
for because of such things God's wrath[n] 5:6 [n]Ro 1:18
comes on those who are disobedient.
7Therefore do not be partners with
them.
8For you were once[o] darkness, but 5:8 [o]Eph 2:2
now you are light in the Lord. Live as [p]Lk 16:8
children of light[p] 9(for the fruit[q] of the 5:9
light consists in all goodness, righteous- [q]Gal 5:22
ness and truth) 10and find out what
pleases the Lord. 11Have nothing to do
with the fruitless deeds of darkness, but
rather expose them. 12For it is shameful
even to mention what the disobedient
do in secret. 13But everything exposed 5:13
by the light[r] becomes visible, 14for it is [r]Jn 3:20,21
light that makes everything visible. This
is why it is said:

"Wake up, O sleeper,[s] 5:14 [s]Ro 13:11
rise from the dead,[t] [t]Jn 5:25
and Christ will shine on you."[u] [u]Isa 60:1

15Be very careful, then, how you live—
not as unwise but as wise, 16making the 5:16
most of every opportunity,[v] because the [v]Col 4:5 [w]Eph 6:13
days are evil.[w] 17Therefore do not be
foolish, but understand what the Lord's 5:17 [x]Ro 12:2;
will is.[x] 18Do not get drunk on wine,[y] 1Th 4:3
which leads to debauchery. Instead, be 5:18
filled with the Spirit.[z] 19Speak to one an- [y]Pr 20:1
other with psalms, hymns and spiritual [z]Lk 1:15
songs.[a] Sing and make music in your 5:19
heart to the Lord, 20always giving [a]Ac 16:25; Col 3:16
thanks[b] to God the Father for every-
thing, in the name of our Lord Jesus 5:20
Christ. [b]Ps 34:1
21Submit to one another[c] out of rev- 5:21
erence for Christ. [c]Gal 5:13

Wives and Husbands

22Wives, submit to your husbands[d] as 5:22 [d]Ge 3:16;
to the Lord.[e] 23For the husband is the 1Pe 3:1,5,6
head of the wife as Christ is the head of [e]Eph 6:5
the church,[f] his body, of which he is the 5:23
Savior. 24Now as the church submits to [f]1Co 11:3;
Christ, so also wives should submit to Eph 1:22
their husbands in everything.
25Husbands, love your wives,[g] just as 5:25
Christ loved the church and gave him- [g]Col 3:19 [h]ver 2
self up for her[h] 26to make her holy,
cleansing[c] her by the washing[i] with wa- 5:26 [i]Ac 22:16
ter through the word, 27and to present
her to himself as a radiant church, with-

[a] 26 Psalm 4:4 [b] 5 Or *kingdom of the Christ and God* [c] 26 Or *having cleansed*

> **A PASTOR CAN BE NO BETTER REPRESENTATIVE OF JESUS' ROLE TO HIS CHURCH THAN HE IS IN FULFILLING HIS ROLE AS A HUSBAND HIMSELF.**
>
> 
>
> Jack Hayford, *Pastor, Van Nuys, California*

5:27 out stain or wrinkle or any other blem-
j Eph 1:4; ish, but holy and blameless.[j] 28In this
Col 1:22 same way, husbands ought to love their
5:28 wives[k] as their own bodies. He who loves
k ver 25 his wife loves himself. 29After all, no one
ever hated his own body, but he feeds
and cares for it, just as Christ does the
5:30 church— 30for we are members of his
l 1Co 12:27 body.[l] 31"For this reason a man will leave
his father and mother and be united to
5:31 his wife, and the two will become one
m Ge 2:24; flesh."[a m] 32This is a profound mystery—
Mt 19:5; but I am talking about Christ and the
1Co 6:16 church. 33However, each one of you also
5:33 must love his wife[n] as he loves himself,
n ver 25 and the wife must respect her husband.

Children and Parents

6:1 6 Children, obey your parents in the
Lord, for this is right.[o] 2"Honor
o Col 3:20 your father and mother"—which is the
first commandment with a promise—
6:3 3"that it may go well with you and that
p Ex 20:12 you may enjoy long life on the earth."[b p]

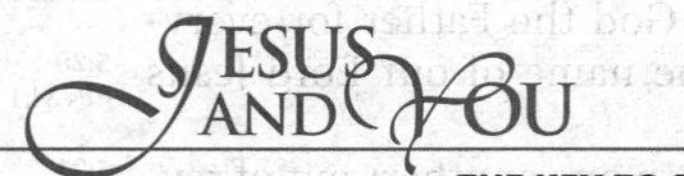

THE KEY TO SUBMITTING

Many people have struggled with the words Paul chose to describe submission in Ephesians 5:22—6:9. He opened the subject in Ephesians 5:1 by encouraging Christians everywhere to imitate God himself and to "live a life of love" just as Jesus did (verse 2). We are to submit to one another because we respect Jesus (verse 21). In any godly relationship—husband and wife, parent and child, brother and sister, employer and employee—there is always a third party: Jesus himself. The apostle reminded God's people that our relationships should reflect Jesus' own fellowship with God the Father and the Holy Spirit. Jesus submitted himself fully to the Father's will (Philippians 2:8), and as we learn to love one another we demonstrate our love for God. Submission is not a problem to be haggled over when we focus on love.

4Fathers, do not exasperate your chil- 6:4
dren;[q] instead, bring them up in the q Col 3:21 r Ge 18:19;
training and instruction of the Lord.[r] Dt 6:7

Slaves and Masters

5Slaves, obey your earthly masters 6:5
with respect[s] and fear, and with sinceri- s 1Ti 6:1
ty of heart,[t] just as you would obey t Col 3:22 u Eph 5:22
Christ.[u] 6Obey them not only to win
their favor when their eye is on you, but
like slaves of Christ, doing the will of
God from your heart. 7Serve wholeheartedly, as if you were serving the
Lord, not men,[v] 8because you know that 6:7
the Lord will reward everyone for what- v Col 3:23
ever good he does,[w] whether he is slave 6:8
or free. w Col 3:24
9And masters, treat your slaves in the
same way. Do not threaten them, since
you know that he who is both their Master and yours[x] is in heaven, and there is 6:9
no favoritism with him. x Job 31:13,14

The Armor of God

10Finally, be strong in the Lord[y] and in 6:10
his mighty power.[z] 11Put on the full ar- y 1Co 16:13 z Eph 1:19
mor of God[a] so that you can take your
stand against the devil's schemes. 12For 6:11 a Ro 13:12
our struggle is not against flesh and
blood, but against the rulers, against the
authorities,[b] against the powers[c] of this 6:12
dark world and against the spiritual b Eph 1:21 c Ro 8:38
forces of evil in the heavenly realms.[d] d Eph 1:3
13Therefore put on the full armor of God,
so that when the day of evil comes, you
may be able to stand your ground, and
after you have done everything, to stand.
14Stand firm then, with the belt of truth
buckled around your waist,[e] with the 6:14 e Isa 11:5
breastplate of righteousness in place,[f] f Isa 59:17
15and with your feet fitted with the
readiness that comes from the gospel of 6:15
peace.[g] 16In addition to all this, take up g Isa 52:7
the shield of faith,[h] with which you can
extinguish all the flaming arrows of the 6:16
evil one. 17Take the helmet of salvation[i] h 1Jn 5:4
and the sword of the Spirit, which is the 6:17 i Isa 59:17
word of God.[j] 18And pray in the Spirit on j Heb 4:12
all occasions[k] with all kinds of prayers 6:18
and requests.[l] With this in mind, be k Lk 18:1 l Mt 26:41;
alert and always keep on praying for all Php 1:4
the saints.

19Pray also for me,[m] that whenever I 6:19
open my mouth, words may be given m 1Th 5:25 n Ac 4:29;
me so that I will fearlessly[n] make 2Co 3:12
known the mystery of the gospel, 20for

[a] 31 Gen. 2:24 [b] 3 Deut. 5:16

6:20 [o 2Co 5:20; p Ac 21:33] which I am an ambassador[o] in chains.[p]
Pray that I may declare it fearlessly, as I
should.

Final Greetings

6:21 [q Ac 20:4] 21Tychicus,[q] the dear brother and
faithful servant in the Lord, will tell you
everything, so that you also may know
how I am and what I am doing. 22I am
6:22 sending him to you for this very pur-
[r Col 4:7-9] pose, that you may know how we are,[r]
and that he may encourage you.
6:23 [s Gal 6:16; 1Pe 5:14] 23Peace[s] to the brothers, and love with
faith from God the Father and the Lord
Jesus Christ. 24Grace to all who love our
Lord Jesus Christ with an undying love.

JESUS IS STILL THE LIVING COMRADE OF COUNTLESS LIVES. NO MOSLEM EVER SINGS, "MOHAMMED, LOVER OF MY SOUL," NOR DOES ANY JEW SAY OF MOSES, THE TEACHER, "I NEED THEE EVERY HOUR."

Solomon B. Freehof, *Jewish Author*

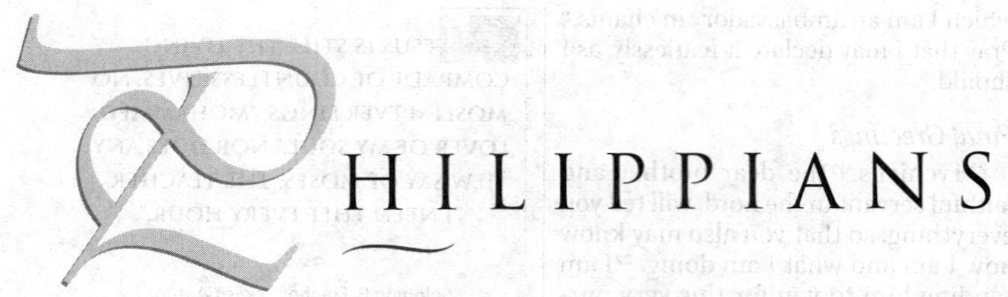

PHILIPPIANS

Would "like-minded" Christians have no disagreements? (Philippians 2:2–5)

♦ *Christians can have differing opinions. To be like-minded need not suggest cloned behavior. Paul's teaching is instead a call to have attitudes like Jesus'—loving and accepting one another in spite of our differences.*

What did Jesus give up to come to earth? (Philippians 2:6–7)

♦ *Before his days on earth Jesus enjoyed complete equality with the Father (John 17:24). Even in human form his essential nature remained unchanged; he was still God (John 5:18). Yet so that he might take away the sins of the world, he voluntarily laid aside the privileges and glory of his heavenly authority (verse 8) to identify with sinful humanity.*

What is Jesus' righteousness, and how does it become ours? (Philippians 3:9)

♦ *"Righteousness" refers to a moral aspect of God's nature, his perfect purity and justice. Sinful humans are by nature unrighteous. But when we place our faith in Jesus alone, God supernaturally cleanses us from sin and shares with us the "fruit of righteousness" (Philippians 1:11).*

Jesus in Philippians Philippians puts lofty truths into practical terms. The book provides a unique glance into Paul's heart while drawing us closer to Jesus Christ. Philippians is a simple message from the apostle to his dear friends in Philippi. Despite the difficulties inherent in his own situation, Paul repeatedly used the words *joy* and *rejoice.*

Chapter 2 provides one of the Bible's most prominent psalms of praise to Jesus, while chapter 3 describes the futility of religious activity compared to a relationship with Jesus. Chapter 4 furnishes practical tools to help us reshape our thinking in keeping with God's ways.

Paul specified that Jesus is the supreme ruler and that one day every person will kneel before him and admit that he is Lord (Philippians 2:9–11). Knowing Jesus is our goal and purpose (Philippians 1:21), so significant that everything else in life seems like a pile of rubbish (Philippians 3:7–9). Jesus is the only prize worth claiming (Philippians 3:12–14), the only joy worth having (Philippians 4:4), the only peace worth finding (verse 7).

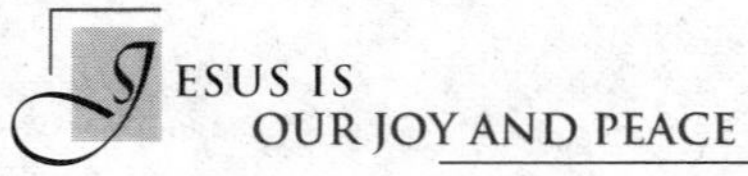
JESUS IS
OUR JOY AND PEACE

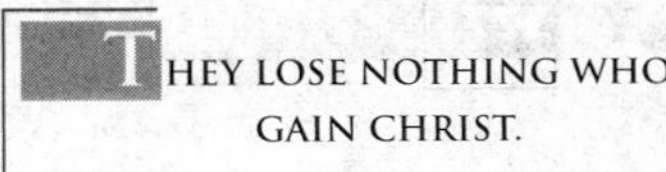

THEY LOSE NOTHING WHO GAIN CHRIST.

Samuel Rutherford, *Puritan Pastor*

1:1 a Ac 16:1; **1** Paul and Timothy,[a] servants of
2Co 1:1 Christ Jesus,
b Ac 9:13 To all the saints[b] in Christ Jesus at
c Ac 16:12 d 1Ti 3:1 Philippi,[c] together with the overseers[*a*][d]
e 1Ti 3:8 and deacons:[e]

1:2 [2]Grace and peace to you from God
f Ro 1:7 our Father and the Lord Jesus Christ.[f]

Thanksgiving and Prayer

1:3 [3]I thank my God every time I remem-
g Ro 1:8 ber you.[g] [4]In all my prayers for all of you,
1:4 I always pray[h] with joy [5]because of your
h Ro 1:10 partnership[i] in the gospel from the first
1:5 day[j] until now, [6]being confident of this,
i Ac 2:42; that he who began a good work in you
Php 4:15 will carry it on to completion until the
j Ac 16:12-40 day of Christ Jesus.[k]
1:6 [7]It is right[l] for me to feel this way
k ver 10; 1Co 1:8 about all of you, since I have you in my
1:7 heart;[m] for whether I am in chains[n] or
l 2Pe 1:13 m 2Co 7:3 defending[o] and confirming the gospel,
n ver 13,14,17; all of you share in God's grace with me.
Ac 21:33 [8]God can testify[p] how I long for all of
o ver 16 you with the affection of Christ Jesus.
1:8 [9]And this is my prayer: that your love[q]
p Ro 1:9 may abound more and more in knowl-
1:9 edge and depth of insight, [10]so that you
q 1Th 3:12 may be able to discern what is best and
may be pure and blameless until the day
1:10 r ver 6; 1Co 1:8 of Christ,[r] [11]filled with the fruit of righteousness[s] that comes through Jesus
1:11 s Jas 3:18 Christ—to the glory and praise of God.

Paul's Chains Advance the Gospel

[12]Now I want you to know, brothers,
that what has happened to me has really
served to advance the gospel. [13]As a result, it has become clear throughout the
whole palace guard[*b*] and to everyone
1:13 t ver 7,14,17 else that I am in chains[t] for Christ. [14]Be-
1:14 u ver 7,13,17 cause of my chains,[u] most of the brothers in the Lord have been encouraged to
speak the word of God more courageously and fearlessly.
[15]It is true that some preach Christ
out of envy and rivalry, but others out of
goodwill. [16]The latter do so in love,
1:16 knowing that I am put here for the de-
v ver 7,12 fense of the gospel.[v] [17]The former preach
Christ out of selfish ambition,[w] not sin- 1:17 w Php 2:3
cerely, supposing that they can stir up x ver 7,13,14
trouble for me while I am in chains.[*c*][x]
[18]But what does it matter? The important thing is that in every way, whether
from false motives or true, Christ is
preached. And because of this I rejoice.
Yes, and I will continue to rejoice, 1:19
[19]for I know that through your prayers[y] y 2Co 1:11
and the help given by the Spirit of Jesus z Ac 16:7
Christ,[z] what has happened to me will
turn out for my deliverance.[*d*] [20]I eagerly 1:20
expect[a] and hope that I will in no way be a Ro 8:19
ashamed, but will have sufficient b ver 14
courage[b] so that now as always Christ c 1Co 6:20 d Ro 14:8
will be exalted in my body,[c] whether by
life or by death.[d] [21]For to me, to live is
Christ[e] and to die is gain. [22]If I am to go 1:21 e Gal 2:20
on living in the body, this will mean
fruitful labor for me. Yet what shall I
choose? I do not know! [23]I am torn between the two: I desire to depart[f] and be 1:23
with Christ,[g] which is better by far; [24]but f 2Ti 4:6 g Jn 12:26;
it is more necessary for you that I re- 2Co 5:8
main in the body. [25]Convinced of this, I
know that I will remain, and I will continue with all of you for your progress
and joy in the faith, [26]so that through my
being with you again your joy in Christ
Jesus will overflow on account of me.
[27]Whatever happens, conduct yourselves in a manner worthy[h] of the gospel 1:27
of Christ. Then, whether I come and see h Eph 4:1 i 1Co 16:13
you or only hear about you in my ab- j Jude 3
sence, I will know that you stand firm[i] in
one spirit, contending[j] as one man for
the faith of the gospel [28]without being
frightened in any way by those who oppose you. This is a sign to them that they
will be destroyed, but that you will be
saved—and that by God. [29]For it has 1:29
been granted to you[k] on behalf of Christ k Mt 5:11,12 l Ac 14:22
not only to believe on him, but also to
suffer[l] for him, [30]since you are going 1:30 m Col 2:1;
through the same struggle[m] you saw[n] I 1Th 2:2 n Ac 16:19-40
had, and now hear[o] that I still have. o ver 13

Imitating Christ's Humility

2 If you have any encouragement
from being united with Christ, if 2:1
any comfort from his love, if any fellow- p 2Co 13:14 q Col 3:12
ship with the Spirit,[p] if any tenderness
and compassion,[q] [2]then make my joy 2:2
complete[r] by being like-minded,[s] having r Jn 3:29 s Php 4:2

[*a*] *1* Traditionally *bishops* [*b*] *13* Or *whole palace* [*c*] *16,17* Some late manuscripts have verses 16 and 17 in reverse order. [*d*] *19* Or *salvation*

TRUE HUMILITY

In Philippians 2:6–11 Paul incorporated a poem that consists of a concise and beautiful description of the meaning of Jesus' life. The lyrics may have been set to music and sung as a hymn in the early church. Paul began by asserting that Jesus is God himself, "in very nature God" (verse 6), God in every dimension of his being (Romans 9:5; Colossians 1:15–20). But Jesus was willing to forego his lofty position in heaven, choosing rather to humble himself to be born as a human baby so that he could die as the atoning sacrifice for our sins (1 John 2:2).

This process involved several steps. First, Jesus "made himself nothing" (Philippians 2:7). He did not stop being God, but he did lay aside his honor and privilege as God the Son (John 17:5). In so doing he was submitting to the will of his Father (Matthew 26:39).

Second, Jesus was "made in human likeness" (Philippians 2:7). The Creator became the creature; the Word became human flesh and lived among us (John 1:14)—amazing! Jesus Christ was like us in every way except for one: He did not sin. He was bound as a man by certain limitations, and he faced temptation, but he never wavered from his purpose of honoring God (Hebrews 2:17–18; 4:15).

Third, Jesus lived a life of suffering and "became obedient to death," an agonizing and shameful death on a cross (Philippians 2:8; see also Galatians 3:13; Hebrews 12:2). During his earthly life he endured mockery and insult (Luke 18:32; 23:11,36; 1 Peter 2:23; see also Psalm 22:6–7). Jesus knew what it was to be "despised and rejected by men" and was "familiar with suffering" (Isaiah 53:3).

After Jesus' humiliation, however, God the Father exalted him to his place of honor. Paul declared that the Son of God came back from the dead and returned to the Father and that one day all of creation will bow before Jesus and confess that he is Lord (Philippians 2:9–11). The question is not "*Will* you acknowledge Jesus as Lord?" but rather "*When* will you acknowledge Jesus as Lord?" We can do it now, accepting his payment for our sin and living in grateful obedience to his will. Or we can do it after it is too late—and pay the penalty for our own sin.

Paul's words remind us that "[our] attitude should be the same as that of Christ Jesus" (verse 5). Following the model of our Savior, we are called to be willing to give up our rights and position in this life and live in a way that will enable others to experience God's love. But the promise is ours as well. We and those who are drawn by our example will one day share in Jesus' glory in the world to come, where we will reign with him: "Now if we are children, then we are heirs—heirs of God and co-heirs of Christ, if indeed we share in his sufferings in order that we may also share in his glory" (Romans 8:17).

***Self-Discovery:** In a world seeking fame Jesus "made himself nothing." In a world seeking power, Jesus chose the role of a servant. In a world seeking pleasure Jesus chose the pain of obedience—even to death on a cross. As you live in this world of "selfish ambition and vain conceit" (Philippians 2:3), how does your attitude compare with his? (verse 5).*

GO TO DISCOVERY 328 ON PAGE 1599

2:2 the same love, being one[t] in spirit and
[t] Ro 12:16 purpose. 3 Do nothing out of selfish am-
2:3 bition or vain conceit,[u] but in humility
[u] Gal 5:26 [v] Ro 12:10; consider others better than yourselves.[v]
1Pe 5:5 4 Each of you should look not only to
your own interests, but also to the interests of others.
2:5 5 Your attitude should be the same as
[w] Mt 11:29 that of Christ Jesus:[w]

2:6 6 Who, being in very nature[a] God,[x]
[x] Jn 1:1 [y] Jn 5:18 did not consider equality with
God[y] something to be
grasped,
7 but made himself nothing,
2:7 taking the very nature[b] of a
[z] Mt 20:28 servant,[z]
[a] Jn 1:14; Heb 2:17 being made in human likeness.[a]
8 And being found in appearance as
a man,
he humbled himself
and became obedient to
2:8 death[b]—
[b] Mt 26:39; Jn 10:18; even death on a cross!
Heb 5:8 9 Therefore God exalted him[c] to the
2:9 highest place
[c] Ac 2:33; Heb 2:9 and gave him the name that is
[d] Eph 1:20,21 above every name,[d]
10 that at the name of Jesus every
2:10 knee should bow,[e]
[e] Ro 14:11 [f] Mt 28:18 in heaven and on earth and
under the earth,[f]
11 and every tongue confess that
2:11 [g] Jn 13:13 Jesus Christ is Lord,[g]
to the glory of God the Father.

> JESUS CHRIST, THE CONDESCENSION OF DIVINITY, AND THE EXALTATION OF HUMANITY.
>
> Phillips Brooks, *American Minister*

Shining as Stars

12 Therefore, my dear friends, as you
have always obeyed—not only in my
2:12 presence, but now much more in my ab-
[h] 2Co 7:15 sence—continue to work out your sal-
2:13 vation with fear and trembling,[h] 13 for it
[i] Ezr 1:5 is God who works in you[i] to will and to
2:14 act according to his good purpose.
[j] 1Co 10:10; 14 Do everything without complain-
1Pe 4:9 ing[j] or arguing, 15 so that you may be-
2:15 come blameless and pure, children of
[k] Mt 5:45,48; Eph 5:1 God[k] without fault in a crooked and de-
[l] Ac 2:40 praved generation,[l] in which you shine
like stars in the universe 16 as you hold
out[c] the word of life—in order that I
may boast on the day of Christ that I did
not run or labor for nothing.[m] 17 But 2:16 [m] 1Th 2:19
even if I am being poured out like a
drink offering[n] on the sacrifice[o] and ser- 2:17 [n] 2Ti 4:6
vice coming from your faith, I am glad [o] Ro 15:16
and rejoice with all of you. 18 So you too
should be glad and rejoice with me.

Timothy and Epaphroditus

19 I hope in the Lord Jesus to send
Timothy to you soon,[p] that I also may be 2:19 [p] ver 23
cheered when I receive news about you.
20 I have no one else like him,[q] who takes 2:20 [q] 1Co 16:10
a genuine interest in your welfare. 21 For
everyone looks out for his own inter- 2:21
ests,[r] not those of Jesus Christ. 22 But you [r] 1Co 10:24; 13:5
know that Timothy has proved himself,
because as a son with his father[s] he has 2:22 [s] 1Co 4:17;
served with me in the work of the 1Ti 1:2
gospel. 23 I hope, therefore, to send him 2:23
as soon as I see how things go with me.[t] [t] ver 19
24 And I am confident[u] in the Lord that I 2:24
myself will come soon. [u] Php 1:25
25 But I think it is necessary to send
back to you Epaphroditus, my brother, 2:25
fellow worker[v] and fellow soldier,[w] who [v] Php 4:3 [w] Phm 2
is also your messenger, whom you sent [x] Php 4:18
to take care of my needs.[x] 26 For he longs 2:26
for all of you[y] and is distressed because [y] Php 1:8

[a] 6 Or *in the form of* [b] 7 Or *the form* [c] 16 Or *hold on to*

JESUS: OUR SERVANT AND LORD

The New Testament focuses on Jesus as God the Son, depicted in the role of a humble servant in his relationship with God the Father (Philippians 2:6–11). Before Jesus died on the cross and came back to life, he demonstrated to his disciples exactly how he wanted them to live. Even though he was both Teacher and Lord, he was also a servant. John 13:1–17 describes Jesus gently washing each of the disciples' feet and instructing them to do the same for one another. This Suffering Servant, who laid aside his glory (John 17:5) to submit to the humiliation of becoming human, is now "exalted to the highest place" and given "the name that is above every name" (Philippians 2:9). We too share in his sufferings as we serve, and one day we will "share in his glory" (Romans 8:17) as we enter into our glorious and exalted inheritance with him.

you heard he was ill. 27Indeed he was ill, and almost died. But God had mercy on him, and not on him only but also on me, to spare me sorrow upon sorrow. 28Therefore I am all the more eager to send him, so that when you see him again you may be glad and I may have less anxiety. 29Welcome him in the Lord with great joy, and honor men like him,[z] 30because he almost died for the work of Christ, risking his life to make up for the help you could not give me.[a]

No Confidence in the Flesh

3 Finally, my brothers, rejoice in the Lord! It is no trouble for me to write the same things to you again, and it is a safeguard for you.

2Watch out for those dogs,[b] those men who do evil, those mutilators of the flesh. 3For it is we who are the circumcision,[c] we who worship by the Spirit of God, who glory in Christ Jesus, and who put no confidence in the flesh— 4though I myself have reasons for such confidence.

If anyone else thinks he has reasons to put confidence in the flesh, I have more: 5circumcised[d] on the eighth day, of the people of Israel,[e] of the tribe of Benjamin,[f] a Hebrew of Hebrews; in regard to the law, a Pharisee;[g] 6as for zeal, persecuting the church;[h] as for legalistic righteousness,[i] faultless.

7But whatever was to my profit I now consider loss[j] for the sake of Christ. 8What is more, I consider everything a loss compared to the surpassing greatness of knowing[k] Christ Jesus my Lord, for whose sake I have lost all things. I consider them rubbish, that I may gain Christ 9and be found in him, not having a righteousness of my own that comes from the law,[l] but that which is through faith in Christ—the righteousness that comes from God and is by faith.[m] 10I want to know Christ and the power of his resurrection and the fellowship of sharing in his sufferings,[n] becoming like him in his death,[o] 11and so, somehow, to attain to the resurrection[p] from the dead.

2:29 [z] 1Co 16:18; 1Ti 5:17
2:30 [a] 1Co 16:17
3:2 [b] Ps 22:16,20
3:3 [c] Ro 2:28,29; Gal 6:15; Col 2:11
3:5 [d] Lk 1:59 [e] 2Co 11:22 [f] Ro 11:1 [g] Ac 23:6
3:6 [h] Ac 8:3 [i] Ro 10:5
3:7 [j] Mt 13:44; Lk 14:33
3:8 [k] Eph 4:13; 2Pe 1:2
3:9 [l] Ro 10:5 [m] Ro 9:30
3:10 [n] Ro 8:17 [o] Ro 6:3-5
3:11 [p] Rev 20:5,6

IF YOU DO NOT TRUST CHRIST TO TAKE YOU ALL THE WAY TO HEAVEN, THEN YOU HAVE NOT TRUSTED HIM AS YOUR SAVIOR.

Dr. James Kennedy, *Pastor, Fort Lauderdale, Florida*

Pressing on Toward the Goal

12Not that I have already obtained all this, or have already been made perfect,[q] but I press on to take hold[r] of that for which Christ Jesus took hold of me.[s] 13Brothers, I do not consider myself yet to have taken hold of it. But one thing I do: Forgetting what is behind[t] and straining toward what is ahead, 14I press on[u] toward the goal to win the prize for which God has called[v] me heavenward in Christ Jesus.

15All of us who are mature[w] should take such a view of things.[x] And if on some point you think differently, that too God will make clear to you. 16Only let us live up to what we have already attained.

17Join with others in following my example,[y] brothers, and take note of those who live according to the pattern we gave you. 18For, as I have often told you before and now say again even with tears,[z] many live as enemies of the cross of Christ.[a] 19Their destiny is destruction, their god is their stomach,[b] and their glory is in their shame.[c] Their mind is on earthly things.[d] 20But our citizenship[e] is in heaven.[f] And we eagerly await a Savior from there, the Lord Jesus Christ,[g] 21who, by the power[h] that enables him to bring everything under his control, will transform our lowly bodies[i] so that they will be like his glorious body.[j]

3:12 [q] 1Co 13:10 [r] 1Ti 6:12 [s] Ac 9:5,6
3:13 [t] Lk 9:62
3:14 [u] Heb 6:1 [v] Ro 8:28
3:15 [w] 1Co 2:6 [x] Gal 5:10
3:17 [y] 1Co 4:16; 1Pe 5:3
3:18 [z] Ac 20:31 [a] Gal 6:12
3:19 [b] Ro 16:18 [c] Ro 6:21 [d] Ro 8:5,6
3:20 [e] Eph 2:19 [f] Col 3:1 [g] 1Co 1:7
3:21 [h] Eph 1:19 [i] 1Co 15:43-53 [j] Col 3:4

JESUS FOCUS

THE COST OF DISCIPLESHIP

The cost of becoming a Christian saved by grace was great for the apostle Paul. He had boasted a distinguished and successful Jewish heritage, referring to himself as a "Hebrew of Hebrews" (Philippians 3:5) because he had scrupulously adhered to the complicated Jewish system of laws. After he had encountered the risen Jesus, however, Paul's attitude underwent a radical transformation. Suddenly, all that mattered to him was getting to know God and telling other people who Jesus is and what he had accomplished for all people (verse 7). Like a runner in a marathon, Paul focused solely on the prize at the end of the race: being in the presence of Jesus for all eternity (verses 12–14).

DISCOVERY 328

ALL WE NEED

One of the most incredible promises in the Bible is found in Philippians 4:19: "And my God will meet all your needs according to his glorious riches in Christ Jesus." The opening word *and* connects this promise to the words that preceded it. Paul had been writing about the financial generosity of the believers in Philippi (verse 14). These people were renowned for their giving, and God in turn was promising to show generosity to them. When we are miserly with our own resources we are in effect telling God that we can make it on our own and don't need his provisions. But when we give to others, we open up our own lives so that God in turn can fill us with what we need. In Jesus' own words in Luke 6:38, "Give, and it will be given to you. A good measure, pressed down, shaken together and running over, will be poured into your lap. For with the measure you use, it will be measured to you."

Every phrase in the single sentence that comprises Philippians 4:19 is weighted with meaning:

My God: This is a promise based on a personal relationship with God. When we accept Jesus into our lives God welcomes us into his spiritual family. He is our caring Father, and we are his beloved children. He watches over us and provides us with every good gift (Matthew 7:7–11).

will meet: God is the source of supply for meeting all of our needs, whether they are material, emotional, physical, spiritual, social, financial or any other. He may use other people to help, but ultimately everything comes from him.

all your needs: We don't always get everything we want, and we sometimes fail to receive the things we think we need. It's easy for us to confuse wants and needs and to insist that we desperately need something when in reality we only want it. God promises to do what is best for us, and that promise includes meeting *all* of our needs.

according to his glorious riches: Just how rich is God? Think about his resources. He created everything that exists, and that is more than enough to provide for every person who has given his or her life to Jesus. God's supply never runs out. We can bring any and every difficulty to him, and we will always find "grace to help us in our time of need" (Hebrews 4:16). Those "glorious riches" are the true measure of the Lord's blessings to his people (Ephesians 1:18; 3:16–21).

in Christ Jesus. When we turn over our lives to Jesus, we receive "every spiritual blessing in Christ" (Ephesians 1:3). Because of our position in Jesus (we have been credited with his righteousness in exchange for our sin), God willingly blesses us.

What an amazing promise! Paul too was apparently overwhelmed by the truth of the words he had just written, so overwhelmed that he found it necessary and appropriate to close the passage with a ringing shout of praise: "To our God and Father be glory for ever and ever. Amen" (Philippians 4:20). There is no more fitting response to God's wonderful promise to meet all of our needs.

Self-Discovery: *Take a moment to memorize the beautiful promise found in Philippians 4:19. Repeat it to yourself throughout the day and think about its meaning and implications for your life.*

GO TO DISCOVERY 329 ON PAGE 1603

4:1 k Php 1:8 **4** Therefore, my brothers, you
l 1Co 16:13; Php 1:27 whom I love and long for,[k] my joy
and crown, that is how you should stand
firm[l] in the Lord, dear friends!

Exhortations

[2]I plead with Euodia and I plead with
4:2 m Php 2:2 Syntyche to agree with each other[m] in
the Lord. [3]Yes, and I ask you, loyal yoke-
fellow,[a] help these women who have
contended at my side in the cause of the
gospel, along with Clement and the rest
of my fellow workers, whose names are
in the book of life.

4:4 [4]Rejoice in the Lord always. I will say
n Ro 12:12; Php 3:1 it again: Rejoice![n] [5]Let your gentleness
be evident to all. The Lord is near.[o] [6]Do
4:5 o Heb 10:37; Jas 5:8,9 not be anxious about anything,[p] but in
everything, by prayer and petition, with
thanksgiving, present your requests to
4:6 p Mt 6:25-34 q Eph 6:18 God.[q] [7]And the peace of God,[r] which
transcends all understanding, will guard
your hearts and your minds in Christ
4:7 r Isa 26:3; Jn 14:27; Col 3:15 Jesus.

[8]Finally, brothers, whatever is true,
whatever is noble, whatever is right,
whatever is pure, whatever is lovely, whatever is admirable—if anything is excellent or praiseworthy—think about such
things. [9]Whatever you have learned or
received or heard from me, or seen in
4:9 s Php 3:17 me—put it into practice.[s] And the God of
t Ro 15:33 peace[t] will be with you.

Thanks for Their Gifts

[10]I rejoice greatly in the Lord that at
last you have renewed your concern for
me.[u] Indeed, you have been concerned, 4:10 u 2Co 11:9
but you had no opportunity to show it.
[11]I am not saying this because I am in
need, for I have learned to be content[v] 4:11 v 1Ti 6:6,8
whatever the circumstances. [12]I know
what it is to be in need, and I know what
it is to have plenty. I have learned the secret of being content in any and every
situation, whether well fed or hungry,[w] 4:12 w 1Co 4:11
whether living in plenty or in want.[x] [13]I x 2Co 11:9
can do everything through him who 4:13
gives me strength.[y] y 2Co 12:9

[14]Yet it was good of you to share[z] in 4:14
my troubles. [15]Moreover, as you Philip- z Php 1:7
pians know, in the early days[a] of your ac- 4:15
quaintance with the gospel, when I set a Php 1:5
out from Macedonia, not one church b 2Co 11:8,9
shared with me in the matter of giving
and receiving, except you only;[b] [16]for 4:16
even when I was in Thessalonica,[c] you c Ac 17:1
sent me aid again and again when I was d 1Th 2:9
in need.[d] [17]Not that I am looking for a
gift, but I am looking for what may be 4:17
credited to your account.[e] [18]I have re- e 1Co 9:11,12
ceived full payment and even more; I am
amply supplied, now that I have received 4:18
from Epaphroditus[f] the gifts you sent. f Php 2:25
They are a fragrant[g] offering, an accept- g 2Co 2:14
able sacrifice, pleasing to God. [19]And my 4:19
God will meet all your needs[h] according h Ps 23:1; 2Co 9:8 i Ro 2:4
to his glorious riches[i] in Christ Jesus.

[20]To our God and Father[j] be glory for 4:20 j Gal 1:4
ever and ever. Amen.[k] k Ro 11:36

Final Greetings

[21]Greet all the saints in Christ Jesus. 4:21
The brothers who are with me[l] send l Gal 1:2
greetings. [22]All the saints[m] send you 4:22
greetings, especially those who belong m Ac 9:13
to Caesar's household.

[23]The grace of the Lord Jesus Christ[n] 4:23 n Ro 16:20
be with your spirit. Amen.[b]

[a] 3 Or *loyal Syzygus* [b] 23 Some manuscripts do not have *Amen.*

WITHOUT FAITH IN JESUS THERE IS NO REAL EXPERIENCE OF GOD — NO MIRACLE, NO FORGIVENESS, NO VICTORY OVER SIN, NO PEACE WITH GOD, AND NO JOY.

Reinhard Bonnke, *South African Evangelist*

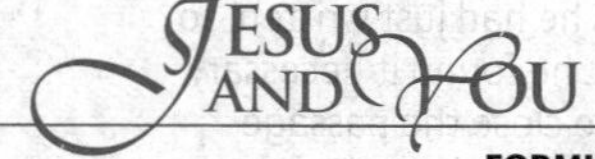

FORMULA FOR SUCCESS

Philippians is a thoroughly practical book that applies theology to life. Paul offered warm and basic advice about everyday concerns, concerns that haven't changed much in the nearly two millennia since he wrote his letter. Paul spoke about out attitude and our approach to life: Rejoice, be gentle, don't worry, pray about everything, think and do what is right—and God's peace will be a part of your life (Philippians 4:4–9). Paul was by no means a perfect human being, but he did learn some crucial principles along the road of life. His most important piece of advice is that we model our lives after that of our precious Lord Jesus, who loved deeply (Philippians 1:8) and followed the Father's will no matter what the cost (Philippians 2:8).

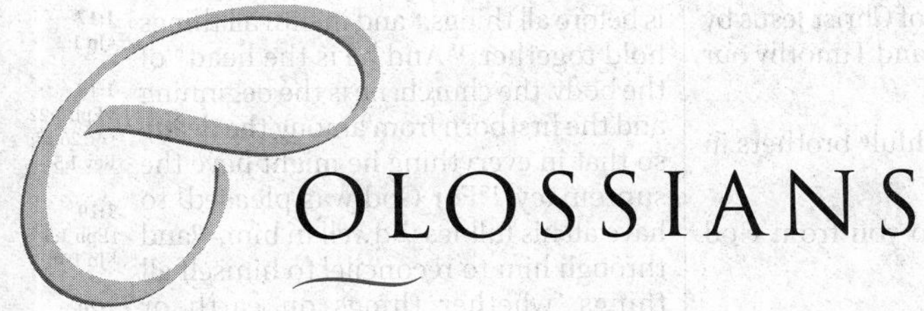

COLOSSIANS

In what way do "all things hold together in Christ"? (Colossians 1:17)

♦ *Science has discovered much about the nature of matter, but many mysteries remain unsolved. Still, no matter what human research learns about the what of the natural world, the why is ultimately found only in Jesus. Jesus' creation continues as he sustains the universe. But he also upholds the world in a spiritual sense: His work of redemption brings together sinful people and a holy God.*

In what way does all God's fullness dwell in Jesus? (Colossians 1:19)

♦ *All believers are to be filled with God's Spirit. Jesus, however, was filled with the fullness of God, indicating that he contained the total essence of God's nature and authority. There is nothing in God's character or attributes that is lacking in Jesus.*

What powers and authorities did Jesus disarm? (Colossians 2:15)

♦ *The Bible tells of countless spiritual beings (fallen angels, spirits, demons) that, along with Satan, oppose God and afflict people. Jesus' death and resurrection disarmed and defeated them.*

Jesus in Colossians Jesus is the human embodiment of God. In him we see what God is really like. In Colossians Jesus is the visible expression of the "fullness" of God (Colossians 1:19; 2:9). Paul reminded God's people that Jesus is "all, and is in all" (Colossians 3:11), over all others because he is the image of God himself (Colossians 1:15). Jesus was with God the Father at creation, and he is the One who keeps the universe going (verses 16–17). He is the head of the church, supreme above everything and everyone else (verse 18).

Jesus made it possible for us to have a relationship with God the Father through his atoning sacrifice (verses 20,22). When we place our trust in him he gives us peace, because our relationship with God has been repaired (Colossians 3:15). And as we learn to live life in a way that honors him, we do everything in his name (verse 17).

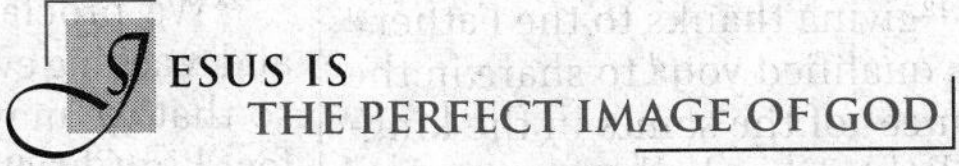

JESUS IS THE PERFECT IMAGE OF GOD

1:1 [a] 1Co 1:1 **1** Paul, an apostle[a] of Christ Jesus by
[b] 2Co 1:1 the will of God,[b] and Timothy our
brother,

1:2 [c] Col 4:18 [2]To the holy and faithful[a] brothers in
[d] Ro 1:7 Christ at Colosse:

Grace[c] and peace to you from God
our Father.[b][d]

Thanksgiving and Prayer

1:3 [3]We always thank God,[e] the Father of
[e] Ro 1:8 our Lord Jesus Christ, when we pray for
you, [4]because we have heard of your faith
1:4 [f] Gal 5:6 in Christ Jesus and of the love[f] you have
[g] Eph 1:15 for all the saints[g]— [5]the faith and love
1:5 that spring from the hope[h] that is stored
[h] 1Th 5:8; up for you in heaven[i] and that you have
Tit 1:2 [i] 1Pe 1:4 already heard about in the word of truth,
1:6 the gospel [6]that has come to you. All over
[j] Ro 10:18 the world[j] this gospel is bearing fruit[k]
[k] Jn 15:16 and growing, just as it has been doing
among you since the day you heard it and
understood God's grace in all its truth.
1:7 [l] Phm 23 [7]You learned it from Epaphras,[l] our dear
[m] Col 4:7 fellow servant, who is a faithful minister[m]
of Christ on our[c] behalf, [8]and who also
1:8 [n] Ro 15:30 told us of your love in the Spirit.[n]
[9]For this reason, since the day we
1:9 [o] Eph 1:15 heard about you,[o] we have not stopped
[p] Eph 5:17 praying for you and asking God to fill
[q] Eph 1:17 you with the knowledge of his will[p]
through all spiritual wisdom and understanding.[q] [10]And we pray this in order
1:10 [r] Eph 4:1 that you may live a life worthy[r] of the
Lord and may please him in every way:
bearing fruit in every good work, grow-
1:11 ing in the knowledge of God, [11]being
[s] Eph 3:16 [t] Eph 4:2 strengthened with all power[s] according
to his glorious might so that you may
1:12 have great endurance and patience,[t] and
[u] Eph 5:20 [v] Ac 20:32 joyfully [12]giving thanks to the Father,[u]
who has qualified you[d] to share in the
1:13 [w] Ac 26:18 inheritance[v] of the saints in the king-
[x] Eph 6:12; 2Pe 1:11 dom of light. [13]For he has rescued us
[y] Mt 3:17 from the dominion of darkness[w] and
brought us into the kingdom[x] of the Son
1:14 [z] Ro 3:24 he loves,[y] [14]in whom we have redemp-
[a] Eph 1:7 tion,[e][z] the forgiveness of sins.[a]

The Supremacy of Christ

1:15 [15]He is the image[b] of the invisible
[b] 2Co 4:4 [c] Jn 1:18 God,[c] the firstborn over all creation.
[16]For by him all things were created:[d]
1:16 [d] Jn 1:3 things in heaven and on earth, visible
[e] Eph 1:20,21 and invisible, whether thrones or pow-
[f] Ro 11:36 ers or rulers or authorities;[e] all things
were created by him and for him.[f] [17]He
is before all things,[g] and in him all things 1:17 [g] Jn 1:2
hold together. [18]And he is the head[h] of
the body, the church; he is the beginning 1:18 [h] Eph 1:22
and the firstborn from among the dead,[i] [i] Ac 26:23;
so that in everything he might have the Rev 1:5
supremacy. [19]For God was pleased[j] to 1:19
have all his fullness[k] dwell in him, [20]and [j] Eph 1:5 [k] Jn 1:16
through him to reconcile[l] to himself all
things, whether things on earth or 1:20
things in heaven,[m] by making peace [l] 2Co 5:18 [m] Eph 1:10
through his blood,[n] shed on the cross. [n] Eph 2:13
[21]Once you were alienated from God
and were enemies[o] in your minds[p] be- 1:21 [o] Ro 5:10
cause of[f] your evil behavior. [22]But now [p] Eph 2:3
he has reconciled you by Christ's physi-
cal body[q] through death to present you 1:22 [q] Ro 7:4
holy in his sight, without blemish and [r] Eph 5:27
free from accusation[r]— [23]if you contin-
ue in your faith, established[s] and firm, 1:23 [s] Eph 3:17
not moved from the hope[t] held out in [t] ver 5
the gospel. This is the gospel that you [u] Ro 10:18 [v] ver 25; 1Co 3:5
heard and that has been proclaimed to
every creature under heaven,[u] and of
which I, Paul, have become a servant.[v]

Paul's Labor for the Church

[24]Now I rejoice in what was suffered
for you, and I fill up in my flesh what is
still lacking in regard to Christ's afflic-
tions,[w] for the sake of his body, which is 1:24 [w] 2Co 1:5
the church. [25]I have become its servant[x]
by the commission God gave me[y] to 1:25 [x] ver 23
present to you the word of God in its [y] Eph 3:2
fullness— [26]the mystery[z] that has been 1:26
kept hidden for ages and generations, [z] Ro 16:25
but is now disclosed to the saints. [27]To
them God has chosen to make known[a] 1:27 [a] Mt 13:11
among the Gentiles the glorious riches
of this mystery, which is Christ in you,
the hope of glory.
[28]We proclaim him, admonishing[b] 1:28 [b] Col 3:16
and teaching everyone with all wisdom,[c] [c] 1Co 2:6,7
so that we may present everyone per- [d] Eph 5:27
fect[d] in Christ. [29]To this end I labor,[e] 1:29
struggling[f] with all his energy, which so [e] 1Co 15:10 [f] Col 2:1
powerfully works in me.[g] [g] Eph 1:19

2 I want you to know how much I am 2:1
struggling[h] for you and for those [h] Col 1:29; 4:12
at Laodicea,[i] and for all who have not [i] Rev 1:11
met me personally. [2]My purpose is that
they may be encouraged in heart[j] and 2:2 [j] Col 4:8
united in love, so that they may have the
full riches of complete understanding, in

[a] 2 Or *believing* [b] 2 Some manuscripts *Father and the Lord Jesus Christ* [c] 7 Some manuscripts *your* [d] 12 Some manuscripts *us* [e] 14 A few late manuscripts *redemption through his blood* [f] 21 Or *minds, as shown by*

JESUS FIRST

Many of God's people carry with them reminders, often in the form of lapel pins, necklaces, bracelets or other accessories, of their central focus in life. The purpose is not primarily to communicate to non-Christians, because in many cases only a spiritual "insider" would understand the cryptic message or symbol. The intention is rather that the article serve as a visual reminder of the place Jesus deserves in our lives. The word *supremacy* in Colossians 1:18 literally means "first place." Paul outlined in this passage some particular areas in which Jesus is supreme:

Jesus is the image of God himself (verse 15). The fullness or essence of God could be seen in Jesus even in his human form (Colossians 2:9). The writer of Hebrews told us in Hebrews 1:3 that "the Son is the radiance of God's glory and the exact representation of his being." To know and understand Jesus is to know and understand God (John 1:1,14,18; 8:19; 14:6–11; 1 John 2:23).

Jesus is also the firstborn over all creation. These words do not mean that Jesus was the first person God created; if Jesus had been created, he would be less than God. The analogy of Jesus being the firstborn actually refers to his exalted position. The firstborn in a Jewish family was the rightful heir to the family inheritance, and all of creation belongs to Jesus because he created it (John 1:1–2). All things were also created *for* him; the world in all of its beauty was not created primarily for *our* benefit but for Jesus' honor (Romans 11:36; Colossians 1:16). And Jesus is the One who holds everything together to this day (Colossians 1:17).

Another truth is that Jesus, who by his very nature is head over everything (Ephesians 1:10,22; Colossians 2:10), is also the head of his church (Ephesians 5:23; Colossians 1:18). Jesus himself, not pastors or board members or councils or congregations, is the church's leader and ultimate authority.

In Colossians 1:19–22 Paul elaborated on the reason for Jesus' position of supremacy: "For God was pleased to have all his fullness dwell in him, and through him to reconcile to himself all things, whether things on earth or things in heaven, by making peace through his blood, shed on the cross. Once you were alienated from God . . . But now he has reconciled you by Christ's physical body through death to present you holy in his sight, without blemish and free from accusation."

The only mediator who could have rescued us from our desperate situation was Jesus—who alone was truly God and truly human. But thanks be to God that Jesus, who was "in very nature God, did not consider equality with God something to be grasped, but . . . humbled himself and became obedient to death—even death on a cross" (Philippians 2:6–8). Following Jesus' supreme sacrifice, the Father once again "exalted him to the highest place and gave him a name that is above every name, that at the name of Jesus every knee should bow . . . and every tongue confess that Jesus Christ is Lord, to the glory of God the Father" (Philippians 2:9–11).

Self-Discovery: *Bow on your knees and confess now that Jesus Christ is the supreme Lord of your life, to the glory of God the Father. Then make sure as you go about your routine today that you acknowledge Jesus in every area of your life as truly number one.*

GO TO DISCOVERY 330 ON PAGE 1605

order that they may know the mystery
of God, namely, Christ, [3]in whom are
hidden all the treasures of wisdom and
2:3 k Ro 11:33; knowledge.[k] [4]I tell you this so that no
1Co 1:24,30 one may deceive you by fine-sounding
2:4 arguments.[l] [5]For though I am absent
l Ro 16:18 from you in body, I am present with you
2:5 in spirit[m] and delight to see how order-
m 1Th 2:17 ly[n] you are and how firm[o] your faith in
n 1Co 14:40 o 1Pe 5:9 Christ is.

Freedom From Human Regulations Through Life With Christ

2:6 [6]So then, just as you received Christ
p Col 1:10 Jesus as Lord,[p] continue to live in him,
2:7 [7]rooted[q] and built up in him, strength-
q Eph 3:17 ened in the faith as you were taught, and
overflowing with thankfulness.
[8]See to it that no one takes you captive through hollow and deceptive phi-
2:8 r 1Ti 6:20 losophy,[r] which depends on human tra-
s Gal 4:3 dition and the basic principles of this
world[s] rather than on Christ.
[9]For in Christ all the fullness of the
Deity lives in bodily form, [10]and you have
been given fullness in Christ, who is the
2:10 t Eph 1:22 head[t] over every power and authority.
2:11 [11]In him you were also circumcised,[u] in
u Ro 2:29; the putting off of the sinful nature,[a][v] not
Php 3:3 with a circumcision done by the hands of
v Gal 5:24 men but with the circumcision done by
Christ, [12]having been buried with him in
2:12 w Ro 6:5 baptism and raised with him[w] through
x Ac 2:24 your faith in the power of God, who
raised him from the dead.[x]
2:13 y Eph 2:1,5 [13]When you were dead in your sins[y]
and in the uncircumcision of your sinful
nature,[b] God made you[c] alive with
Christ. He forgave us all our sins, [14]hav-
2:14 ing canceled the written code, with its
z Eph 2:15 regulations,[z] that was against us and that
a 1Pe 2:24 stood opposed to us; he took it away,
nailing it to the cross.[a] [15]And having dis-
2:15 b Eph 6:12 armed the powers and authorities,[b] he
c Lk 10:18 made a public spectacle of them, triumphing over them[c] by the cross.[d]
2:16 d Ro 14:3,4 [16]Therefore do not let anyone judge
e Ro 14:17 you[d] by what you eat or drink,[e] or with
f Ro 14:5 regard to a religious festival,[f] a New
g 1Ch 23:31 h Gal 4:10 Moon celebration[g] or a Sabbath day.[h]

THE DIFFERENCE BETWEEN MAN-MADE UTOPIAS AND A GOD-MADE HEAVEN IS THE CROSS.

Ravi Zacharias, *Christian Apologist*

[17]These are a shadow of the things that 2:17
were to come;[i] the reality, however, is i Heb 8:5
found in Christ. [18]Do not let anyone who
delights in false humility[j] and the wor- 2:18 j ver 23
ship of angels disqualify you for the k Php 3:14
prize.[k] Such a person goes into great detail about what he has seen, and his unspiritual mind puffs him up with idle
notions. [19]He has lost connection with
the Head,[l] from whom the whole body, 2:19 l Eph 1:22
supported and held together by its liga- m Eph 4:16
ments and sinews, grows as God causes
it to grow.[m]
[20]Since you died with Christ to the ba-
sic principles of this world,[n] why, as 2:20 n Gal 4:3,9
though you still belonged to it, do you o ver 14,16
submit to its rules:[o] [21]"Do not handle!
Do not taste! Do not touch!"? [22]These
are all destined to perish[p] with use, be- 2:22 p 1Co 6:13
cause they are based on human com- q Isa 29:13;
mands and teachings.[q] [23]Such regula- Mt 15:9; Tit 1:14
tions indeed have an appearance of
wisdom, with their self-imposed worship, their false humility and their harsh
treatment of the body, but they lack any
value in restraining sensual indulgence.

Rules for Holy Living

3 Since, then, you have been raised
with Christ, set your hearts on
things above, where Christ is seated at 3:2 r Php 3:19,20
the right hand of God. [2]Set your minds
on things above, not on earthly things.[r] 3:3 s Ro 6:2;
[3]For you died,[s] and your life is now 2Co 5:14

[a] 11 Or *the flesh* [b] 13 Or *your flesh* [c] 13 Some manuscripts *us* [d] 15 Or *them in him*

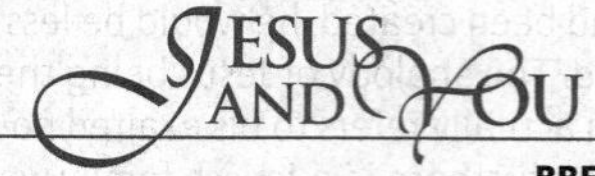

BREAKING THE CODE

The apostle Paul referred to the regulations specified in God's law as the "written code" (Colossians 2:14) and demonstrated that we had been hopelessly dead in our sins, separated from God's love by an unbridgeable gulf, because there was no way that we of our own volition could have adhered to that rigid written code and been the kind of people God wanted us to be. But Jesus overruled the code by "nailing it to the cross" (verse 14). When Jesus died on the cross for our sins he made a "public spectacle" of every one of our violations of God's law—but he proceeded to triumph over those violations by coming to life again (verse 15) and restoring our broken relationship with God the Father.

DISCOVERY 330

In the Name of Jesus

In Colossians 3 Paul provided instructions as to how we are to live as people who follow Jesus: "Whatever you do, whether in word or deed, do it all in the name of the Lord Jesus" (verse 17). God wants every aspect of our lives to be focused on and influenced by Jesus Christ, his Son.

Living "in the name of the Lord Jesus" involves several dimensions. First, it means that *we are Jesus Christ's representatives and ambassadors.* We are here on earth to show other people who he is and how he works and what he's done in our lives, and he wants our lives to be a reflection of his own love and character as we shine his light into a darkened world (Matthew 5:14–16). The world is looking on, sometimes with curiosity, sometimes in derision—but our behavior and demeanor as "Christ-ones" are always under scrutiny.

The phrase also implies that *we live and act under the authority of Jesus Christ*. The concept here is not that we are under our Lord's thumb but that we have been empowered with authority to act on his behalf. The disciples understood what this meant. One day Peter and John encountered a crippled beggar at the temple. Peter's response to the beggar's request for money is memorable: "Silver or gold I do not have, but what I have I give you. In the name of Jesus Christ of Nazareth, walk" (Acts 3:6).

At Pentecost, Peter asked the assembled crowd to "repent and be baptized, every one of you, in the name of Jesus Christ for the forgiveness of your sins" (Acts 2:38). He also informed the religious leaders that the only way to be drawn back into an intimate relationship with God is to be saved by the name of Jesus: "Salvation is found in no one else, for there is no other name under heaven given to men by which we must be saved!" (Acts 4:12). We as Jesus' ambassadors (2 Corinthians 5:20) have the authority and the obligation to let others know that only Jesus can forgive their sins and repair their relationship with God the Father.

Finally, living in the name of Jesus means that *we must submit ourselves to him*. One day everyone will acknowledge that Jesus is God the Son (Philippians 2:10), but as his people we don't have to wait for that day. We have the glorious opportunity to bow to him *now* as we live in the joy and peace of doing his will!

When Paul wrote that we as God's people are to do everything in the name of Jesus, he was doing more than voicing a touching sentiment. He was sending out a clarion call to Christians everywhere to live in a manner that is completely different from that of the world around us. There is no greater challenge—and there is no greater source of power than the name of Jesus Christ to help us to be successful in meeting that challenge.

Self-Discovery: *Envision yourself in the role of an official ambassador within your country—sent in the name of Jesus and representing his kingdom. How will you carry out your duties?*

GO TO DISCOVERY 331 ON PAGE 1611

> **HE [JESUS] BECAME WHAT WE ARE THAT HE MIGHT MAKE US WHAT HE IS.**
>
> Athanasius, *Early Church Father*

3:4 [t] 1Co 1:7 hidden with Christ in God. 4 When
[u] 1Pe 1:13; 1Jn 3:2 Christ, who is your[a] life, appears,[t] then
you also will appear with him in glory.[u]
3:5 [v] Eph 5:3 5 Put to death, therefore, whatever be-
[w] Eph 5:5 longs to your earthly nature: sexual immorality, impurity, lust, evil desires and
3:6 [x] Ro 1:18 greed,[v] which is idolatry.[w] 6 Because of
these, the wrath of God[x] is coming.[b]
3:7 7 You used to walk in these ways, in the
[y] Eph 2:2 life you once lived.[y] 8 But now you must
3:8 [z] Eph 4:22 rid yourselves[z] of all such things as
[a] Eph 4:31 these: anger, rage, malice, slander,[a] and
[b] Eph 4:29 filthy language from your lips.[b] 9 Do not
3:9 [c] Eph 4:22,25 lie to each other,[c] since you have taken
off your old self with its practices 10 and
3:10 have put on the new self, which is being
[d] Ro 12:2; Eph 4:23 renewed[d] in knowledge in the image of
[e] Eph 2:10 its Creator.[e] 11 Here there is no Greek or
3:11 Jew,[f] circumcised or uncircumcised,[g]
[f] Ro 10:12 barbarian, Scythian, slave or free,[h] but
[g] 1Co 7:19 [h] Gal 3:28 Christ is all,[i] and is in all.
[i] Eph 1:23 12 Therefore, as God's chosen people,
3:12 holy and dearly loved, clothe yourselves
[j] Php 2:3 with compassion, kindness, humility,[j]
[k] 2Co 6:6; Gal 5:22,23 gentleness and patience.[k] 13 Bear with
each other[l] and forgive whatever griev-
3:13 [l] Eph 4:2 ances you may have against one anoth-
[m] Eph 4:32 er. Forgive as the Lord forgave you.[m]

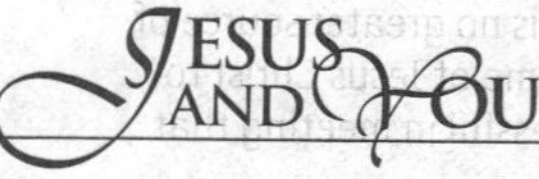

THINGS ABOVE

Jesus had pointed out to his followers that their hearts would be dedicated to what they considered most important (see Matthew 6:21). In Colossians 3 Paul spelled out for us what should be most significant to God's people. If we follow Jesus and enjoy a restored relationship with God, we will be pursuing "things above" (verse 1), focusing on finding out what God wants us to do and becoming the people he wants us to be as he works within our hearts. The things in which most of us invest ourselves—family, jobs, houses, recreation, hobbies—will not consume all of our energy, time and resources. Instead, we will be focused on learning to love Jesus more and more fully and knowing him more and more intimately.

14 And over all these virtues put on love,[n] 3:14 [n] 1Co 13:1-13
which binds them all together in perfect [o] Eph 4:3
unity.[o]
15 Let the peace of Christ[p] rule in your 3:15 [p] Jn 14:27
hearts, since as members of one body
you were called to peace. And be thank-
ful. 16 Let the word of Christ[q] dwell in 3:16 [q] Ro 10:17
you richly as you teach and admonish [r] Col 1:28
one another with all wisdom,[r] and as [s] Eph 5:19
you sing psalms, hymns and spiritual
songs with gratitude in your hearts to
God.[s] 17 And whatever you do,[t] whether 3:17 [t] 1Co 10:31
in word or deed, do it all in the name of [u] Eph 5:20
the Lord Jesus, giving thanks[u] to God
the Father through him.

Rules for Christian Households

18 Wives, submit to your husbands,[v] as 3:18 [v] Eph 5:22
is fitting in the Lord.
19 Husbands, love your wives and do
not be harsh with them.
20 Children, obey your parents in
everything, for this pleases the Lord.
21 Fathers, do not embitter your children, or they will become discouraged.
22 Slaves, obey your earthly masters in
everything; and do it, not only when
their eye is on you and to win their favor,
but with sincerity of heart and reverence
for the Lord. 23 Whatever you do, work at
it with all your heart, as working for the
Lord, not for men, 24 since you know that
you will receive an inheritance[w] from 3:24 [w] Ac 20:32
the Lord as a reward. It is the Lord
Christ you are serving. 25 Anyone who
does wrong will be repaid for his wrong,
and there is no favoritism.[x] 3:25 [x] Ac 10:34

4 Masters, provide your slaves with
what is right and fair, because you
know that you also have a Master in
heaven.

Further Instructions

2 Devote yourselves to prayer,[y] being 4:2 [y] Lk 18:1
watchful and thankful. 3 And pray for us,
too, that God may open a door[z] for our 4:3 [z] Ac 14:27
message, so that we may proclaim the [a] Eph 6:19,20
mystery of Christ, for which I am in
chains.[a] 4 Pray that I may proclaim it
clearly, as I should. 5 Be wise[b] in the way 4:5 [b] Eph 5:15
you act toward outsiders;[c] make the [c] Mk 4:11
most of every opportunity.[d] 6 Let your [d] Eph 5:16
conversation be always full of grace,[e] 4:6 [e] Eph 4:29
seasoned with salt,[f] so that you may [f] Mk 9:50
know how to answer everyone.[g] [g] 1Pe 3:15

[a] 4 Some manuscripts *our* [b] 6 Some early manuscripts *coming on those who are disobedient*

Final Greetings

4:7 7Tychicus[h] will tell you all the news
h Ac 20:4 about me. He is a dear brother, a faithful
i Eph 6:21,22 minister and fellow servant[i] in the Lord.
8I am sending him to you for the express
purpose that you may know about our[a]
4:8 circumstances and that he may encour-
j Eph 6:21,22 age your hearts.[j] 9He is coming with
4:9 Onesimus,[k] our faithful and dear broth-
k Phm 10 er, who is one of you. They will tell you
4:10 everything that is happening here.
l Ac 19:29 10My fellow prisoner Aristarchus[l]
m Ac 4:36 sends you his greetings, as does Mark,
the cousin of Barnabas.[m] (You have received instructions about him; if he
comes to you, welcome him.) 11Jesus,
who is called Justus, also sends greetings. These are the only Jews among my
fellow workers for the kingdom of God,
4:12 and they have proved a comfort to me.
n Col 1:7; 12Epaphras,[n] who is one of you and a
Phm 23 servant of Christ Jesus, sends greetings.
He is always wrestling in prayer for you,[o] 4:12
that you may stand firm in all the will of o Ro 15:30
God, mature[p] and fully assured. 13I p 1Co 2:6
vouch for him that he is working hard 4:13
for you and for those at Laodicea[q] and q Col 2:1
Hierapolis. 14Our dear friend Luke,[r] the 4:14
doctor, and Demas[s] send greetings. r 2Ti 4:11; Phm 24
15Give my greetings to the brothers at s 2Ti 4:10
Laodicea, and to Nympha and the 4:15
church in her house.[t] t Ro 16:5
16After this letter has been read to 4:16
you, see that it is also read[u] in the u 2Th 3:14
church of the Laodiceans and that you 4:17
in turn read the letter from Laodicea. v Phm 2
17Tell Archippus:[v] "See to it that you w 2Ti 4:5
complete the work you have received in 4:18
the Lord."[w] x 1Co 16:21
18I, Paul, write this greeting in my own y Heb 13:3
hand.[x] Remember[y] my chains. Grace be z 1Ti 6:21; 2Ti 4:22;
with you.[z] Tit 3:15; Heb 13:25

[a] 8 Some manuscripts *that he may know about your*

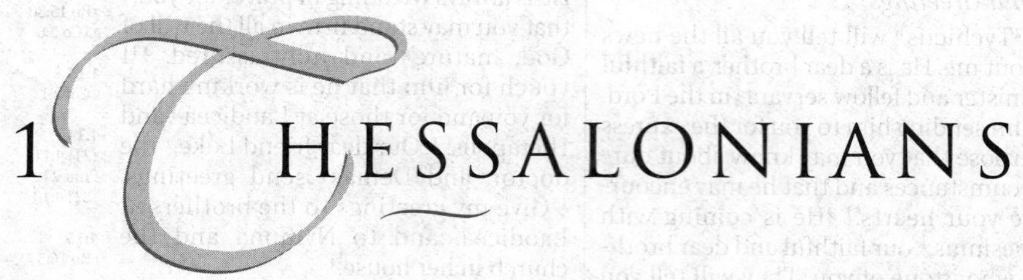

1 THESSALONIANS

Why would God destine Christians for trials? (1 Thessalonians 3:3)

- *God uses our unpleasant experiences to accomplish his higher purposes in us. Suffering for our faith builds character and develops faith within us. Trials can teach what cannot be learned in a classroom. Even Jesus learned obedience by the things he suffered (Hebrews 5:8).*

Who are the "holy ones" who will come with Jesus? (1 Thessalonians 3:13)

- *The "holy ones" could mean believers but may also refer to angels (Mark 8:38) or believers who have died and are now with Jesus. Some think it could mean both angels and believers.*

Why will Jesus bring the dead when he comes for the living? (1 Thessalonians 4:14)

- *Those believers who are dead shall rise first (verse 16). Consequently they can come as resurrected saints with Jesus when he returns to the earth. Some suggest that their spirits, now in the presence of the Lord (2 Corinthians 5:8), will return with Jesus and be joined with their resurrected bodies.*

Jesus in 1 Thessalonians 1 Thessalonians speaks to a culture characterized by the experience of seductive images, sexual pressure, self-centered materialism and secular values. The apostle Paul addressed issues of living a holy life in a culture hostile to Christian values, dealing with relationships and establishing boundaries for living in an immoral culture. Undergirding all of this is a perspective on life that is shaped by eternity.

Jesus died and rose again to liberate us from sin, and one day he will come back in glory to rescue all of creation from the effects of sin (1 Thessalonians 1:10; 3:13). He will restore to life all who have died believing in him, after which all of God's people who are still living will be "caught up" together with them to "meet the Lord in the air" (1 Thessalonians 4:16–17). There is no way of knowing when this day will occur (1 Thessalonians 5:2). However, when our relationship with God has been repaired through Jesus Christ, we have no reason to face it with apprehension. Our future rests completely and firmly in God's hands (verse 9–10).

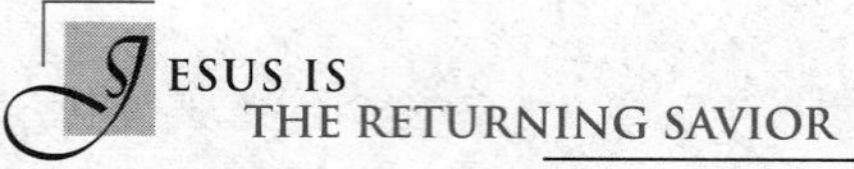

JESUS IS THE RETURNING SAVIOR

1:1 a Ac 16:1; 2Th 1:1 1 Paul, Silas[a] and Timothy,[a]
b Ac 17:1 To the church of the Thessalonians[b]
c Ro 1:7 in God the Father and the Lord Jesus
Christ:

Grace and peace to you.[b c]

Thanksgiving for the Thessalonians' Faith

1:2 2We always thank God for all of you,[d]
d Ro 1:8 mentioning you in our prayers. 3We continually remember before our God and
1:3 Father your work produced by faith,[e]
e 2Th 1:11 your labor prompted by love, and your
endurance inspired by hope in our Lord
Jesus Christ.
4For we know, brothers loved by God,
that he has chosen you, 5because our
1:5 gospel[f] came to you not simply with
f 2Th 2:14 words, but also with power, with the
Holy Spirit and with deep conviction.
You know how we lived among you for
1:6 your sake. 6You became imitators of us[g]
g 1Co 4:16 and of the Lord; in spite of severe suffer-
h Ac 17:5-10 ing,[h] you welcomed the message with
i Ac 13:52 the joy given by the Holy Spirit.[i] 7And so
you became a model to all the believers
in Macedonia and Achaia. 8The Lord's
message rang out from you not only in
Macedonia and Achaia—your faith in
1:8 j Ro 1:8; 10:18 God has become known everywhere.[j]
Therefore we do not need to say any-
thing about it, 9for they themselves report what kind of reception you gave us.
1:9 They tell how you turned to God from
k 1Co 12:2; Gal 4:8 idols[k] to serve the living and true God,
10and to wait for his Son from heaven, 1:10
whom he raised from the dead[l]—Jesus, l Ac 2:24
who rescues us from the coming wrath.[m] m Ro 5:9

Paul's Ministry in Thessalonica

2 You know, brothers, that our visit 2:1
to you[n] was not a failure. 2We had n 1Th 1:5,9
previously suffered[o] and been insulted
in Philippi, as you know, but with the 2:2 o Ac 16:22;
help of our God we dared to tell you his Php 1:30
gospel in spite of strong opposition. 3For
the appeal we make does not spring 2:3
from error or impure motives,[p] nor are p 2Co 2:17
we trying to trick you. 4On the contrary,
we speak as men approved by God to be
entrusted with the gospel.[q] We are not 2:4 q Gal 2:7
trying to please men[r] but God, who tests r Gal 1:10
our hearts. 5You know we never used
flattery, nor did we put on a mask to 2:5
cover up greed[s]—God is our witness.[t] s Ac 20:33
6We were not looking for praise from t Ro 1:9
men, not from you or anyone else.
As apostles[u] of Christ we could have 2:6 u 1Co 9:1,2
been a burden to you, 7but we were gen-
tle among you, like a mother caring for 2:7
her little children.[v] 8We loved you so v ver 11
much that we were delighted to share
with you not only the gospel of God but
our lives as well,[w] because you had be- 2:8 w 2Co 12:15;
come so dear to us. 9Surely you remem- 1Jn 3:16
ber, brothers, our toil and hardship; we 2:9
worked[x] night and day in order not to be x Ac 18:3
a burden to anyone[y] while we preached y 2Th 3:8
the gospel of God to you.
10You are witnesses,[z] and so is God, of 2:10 z 1Th 1:5
how holy,[a] righteous and blameless we a 2Co 1:12
were among you who believed. 11For you
know that we dealt with each of you as a 2:11
father deals with his own children,[b] b ver 7; 1Co 4:14
12encouraging, comforting and urging 2:12
you to live lives worthy[c] of God, who c Eph 4:1
calls you into his kingdom and glory. 2:13
13And we also thank God continually[d] d 1Th 1:2
because, when you received the word of

[a] *1* Greek *Silvanus,* a variant of *Silas* [b] *1* Some early manuscripts *you from God our Father and the Lord Jesus Christ*

THERE ARE WELL OVER 300 REFERENCES TO THE RETURN OF CHRIST IN THE 216 CHAPTERS OF THE NEW TESTAMENT.

Charles Swindoll, *President, Dallas Theological Seminary*

RESCUED!

The practice of establishing "rescue missions" is not new to the 20th century. In 1 Thessalonians 1 Paul looked ahead to the greatest "rescue mission" of all—that day when Jesus will return in glory to defeat our enemy Satan forever (verse 10). When we believe that our Savior took on himself God's punishment for our sins (see 2 Corinthians 5:17–21), we place our hope in Jesus Christ, both in terms of what he has already done for us in dying on the cross and rising to new life and what he will do for us when he returns to earth. We know that we are already rescued from the wrath of God against our sin and that, after that glorious return, we will no longer have to suffer the effects of sin and death (1 Thessalonians 5:9).

2:13 [e] Heb 4:12 God,[e] which you heard from us, you accepted it not as the word of men, but as
it actually is, the word of God, which is
at work in you who believe. [14]For you,
2:14 brothers, became imitators of God's
[f] Gal 1:22 churches in Judea,[f] which are in Christ
[g] Ac 17:5; 2Th 1:4 Jesus: You suffered from your own countrymen[g] the same things those churches
2:15 suffered from the Jews, [15]who killed the
[h] Ac 2:23 Lord Jesus[h] and the prophets[i] and also
[i] Mt 5:12 drove us out. They displease God and
2:16 are hostile to all men [16]in their effort to
[j] Ac 13:45,50 keep us from speaking to the Gentiles[j]
[k] Mt 23:32 so that they may be saved. In this way
they always heap up their sins to the
limit.[k] The wrath of God has come upon
them at last.[a]

Paul's Longing to See the Thessalonians

2:17 [l] 1Co 5:3; Col 2:5 [17]But, brothers, when we were torn
[m] 1Th 3:10 away from you for a short time (in person, not in thought),[l] out of our intense
2:18 [n] Mt 4:10 longing we made every effort to see
[o] Ro 1:13; 15:22 you.[m] [18]For we wanted to come to you—
certainly I, Paul, did, again and again—
2:19 [p] Php 4:1 but Satan[n] stopped us.[o] [19]For what is
[q] 2Co 1:14 [r] Mt 16:27; 1Th 3:13 our hope, our joy, or the crown[p] in which
we will glory[q] in the presence of our
2:20 Lord Jesus when he comes?[r] Is it not
[s] 2Co 1:14 you? [20]Indeed, you are our glory[s] and joy.

> THE CHRISTIAN HOPE IS THE CONFIDENT EXPECTATION THAT THE CHRIST WHO IS COMING IS THE SAME CHRIST WHO DIED *AND* ROSE AGAIN.
>
> John R. W. Stott,
> *British Pastor*

3 So when we could stand it no
longer,[t] we thought it best to be
3:1 [t] ver 5 left by ourselves in Athens.[u] [2]We sent
[u] Ac 17:15 Timothy, who is our brother and God's
fellow worker[b] in spreading the gospel of
Christ, to strengthen and encourage you
in your faith, [3]so that no one would be
unsettled by these trials. You know quite
well that we were destined for them.[v] [4]In
3:3 [v] Ac 9:16; 14:22 fact, when we were with you, we kept
telling you that we would be persecuted.
3:4 [w] 1Th 2:14 And it turned out that way, as you well
know.[w] [5]For this reason, when I could
3:5 [x] ver 1 stand it no longer,[x] I sent to find out

about your faith. I was afraid that in 3:5
some way the tempter[y] might have [y] Mt 4:3
tempted you and our efforts might have [z] Gal 2:2;
been useless.[z] Php 2:16

Timothy's Encouraging Report

[6]But Timothy has just now come to
us from you[a] and has brought good 3:6 [a] Ac 18:5
news about your faith and love.[b] He has [b] 1Th 1:3
told us that you always have pleasant
memories of us and that you long to see
us, just as we also long to see you.
[7]Therefore, brothers, in all our distress
and persecution we were encouraged
about you because of your faith. [8]For
now we really live, since you are stand-
ing firm[c] in the Lord. [9]How can we 3:8 [c] 1Co 16:13
thank God enough for you[d] in return for
all the joy we have in the presence of our 3:9
God because of you? [10]Night and day we [d] 1Th 1:2
pray[e] most earnestly that we may see 3:10 [e] 2Ti 1:3
you again[f] and supply what is lacking in [f] 1Th 2:17
your faith.

[11]Now may our God and Father himself and our Lord Jesus clear the way for
us to come to you. [12]May the Lord make
your love increase and overflow for each
other[g] and for everyone else, just as ours 3:12 [g] 1Th 4:9,10
does for you. [13]May he strengthen your
hearts so that you will be blameless[h] and 3:13 [h] 1Co 1:8
holy in the presence of our God and Fa- [i] 1Th 2:19
ther when our Lord Jesus comes[i] with all
his holy ones.

Living to Please God

4 Finally, brothers,[j] we instructed 4:1 [j] 2Co 13:11
you how to live in order to please [k] 2Co 5:9
God,[k] as in fact you are living. Now we
ask you and urge you in the Lord Jesus
to do this more and more. [2]For you
know what instructions we gave you by
the authority of the Lord Jesus.

[3]It is God's will that you should be
sanctified: that you should avoid sexual
immorality;[l] [4]that each of you should 4:3
learn to control his own body[c][m] in a way [l] 1Co 6:18
that is holy and honorable, [5]not in pas- 4:4 [m] 1Co 7:2,9
sionate lust[n] like the heathen,[o] who do
not know God; [6]and that in this matter 4:5 [n] Ro 1:26
no one should wrong his brother or take [o] Eph 4:17
advantage of him.[p] The Lord will punish 4:6
men for all such sins,[q] as we have al- [p] 1Co 6:8
ready told you and warned you. [7]For [q] Heb 13:4
God did not call us to be impure, but to

[a] 16 Or *them fully* [b] 2 Some manuscripts *brother and fellow worker*; other manuscripts *brother and God's servant* [c] 4 Or *learn to live with his own wife*; or *learn to acquire a wife*

DISCOVERY 331

A Life That Pleases God

We all want to be ready for immediate departure when our Lord comes back for us. The early Christians were aware that Jesus would one day return for his followers, even though they had no idea when that glorious event would occur, and they tried to make certain that they were living pure and consistent lives—that they were prepared for Jesus' arrival at a moment's notice. In 1 Thessalonians 4:1 Paul encouraged the believers in Thessalonica: "We instructed you how to live in order to please God . . . Now we ask you and urge you in the Lord Jesus to do this more and more."

Paul's primary focus was on the quality of the lives we lead while we wait. The bottom line is that we are to love one another and treat each other with respect and fairness (verse 6). Our sinful nature entices us to do whatever causes us to feel the best (James 1:14–15; 1 John 2:16), and that often leads to disregard for the well-being of others. While God expects us to remain sexually pure, for example, we easily forget to keep our eyes on Jesus rather than indulging our own self-gratification. When we make pleasing God the focal point of our daily lives, our conduct will reflect that devotion through the choices we make.

We are called to live peaceful and productive lives (Romans 12:18), not allowing ourselves to become enmeshed in the entanglements of sin all around us (Hebrews 12:1). Paul expressed it this way: "Make it your ambition to lead a quiet life, to mind your own business and to work with your hands, just as we told you, so that your daily life may win the respect of outsiders and so that you will not be dependent on anybody" (1 Thessalonians 4:11–12).

In Luke 12 Jesus spoke at length to his disciples about watchfulness or readiness for his second coming: "Be dressed ready for service and keep your lamps burning, like men waiting for their master to return from a wedding banquet . . . because the Son of Man will come at an hour when you do not expect him" (Luke 12:35–36,40).

Paul went on in 1 Thessalonians 5 to encourage the believers in Thessalonica in light of our Lord's second coming: "But you, brothers, are not in darkness so that this day should surprise you like a thief. You are sons of the light and sons of the day . . . Since we belong to the day, let us be self-controlled, putting on faith and love as a breastplate, and the hope of salvation as a helmet. For God did not appoint us to suffer wrath but to receive salvation through our Lord Jesus Christ . . . Therefore encourage one another and build each other up, just as in fact you are doing" (1 Thessalonians 5:4–5,8–9,11). The hope of Jesus Christ's return can become a powerful motivation for change (1 John 3:2–3) and an effective prescription against discouragement.

***Self-Discovery:** How much "unfinished business" needs to be resolved in your life before you are ready for Jesus Christ's second coming? Why not attend to at least one of these issues today?*

GO TO DISCOVERY 332 ON PAGE 1616

4:7 [r] Lev 11:44; live a holy life.[r] 8Therefore, he who re-
1Pe 1:15 jects this instruction does not reject
man but God, who gives you his Holy
4:8 [s] Ro 5:5; Gal 4:6 Spirit.[s]
9Now about brotherly love[t] we do not
4:9 [t] Ro 12:10 need to write to you,[u] for you yourselves
[u] 1Th 5:1 have been taught by God to love each
[v] Jn 13:34 other.[v] 10And in fact, you do love all the
4:10 brothers throughout Macedonia.[w] Yet
[w] 1Th 1:7 we urge you, brothers, to do so more and
[x] 1Th 3:12 more.[x]
11Make it your ambition to lead a quiet life, to mind your own business and to
4:11 [y] Eph 4:28; work with your hands,[y] just as we told
2Th 3:10-12 you, 12so that your daily life may win the
4:12 respect of outsiders[z] and so that you will
[z] Mk 4:11 not be dependent on anybody.

The Coming of the Lord

13Brothers, we do not want you to be
ignorant about those who fall asleep, or
4:13 to grieve like the rest of men, who have
[a] Eph 2:12 no hope.[a] 14We believe that Jesus died
and rose again and so we believe that
God will bring with Jesus those who
4:14 [b] 1Co 15:18 have fallen asleep in him.[b] 15According
to the Lord's own word, we tell you that
we who are still alive, who are left till the
coming of the Lord, will certainly not
4:15 [c] 1Co 15:52 precede those who have fallen asleep.[c]
16For the Lord himself will come down
from heaven, with a loud command,
4:16 [d] Mt 24:31 with the voice of the archangel and with
[e] 1Co 15:23; the trumpet call of God,[d] and the dead
2Th 2:1 in Christ will rise first.[e] 17After that, we
4:17 who are still alive and are left[f] will be
[f] 1Co 15:52 caught up together with them in the
[g] Ac 1:9; Rev 11:12 clouds[g] to meet the Lord in the air. And
so we will be with the Lord[h] forever. 4:17 [h] Jn 12:26
18Therefore encourage each other with
these words.

5 Now, brothers, about times and 5:1
dates[i] we do not need to write to [i] Ac 1:7 [j] 1Th 4:9
you,[j] 2for you know very well that the day 5:2
of the Lord[k] will come like a thief in the [k] 1Co 1:8
night.[l] 3While people are saying, "Peace [l] 2Pe 3:10
and safety," destruction will come on
them suddenly, as labor pains on a pregnant woman, and they will not escape.
4But you, brothers, are not in dark- 5:4
ness[m] so that this day should surprise [m] Ac 26:18;
you like a thief. 5You are all sons of the 1Jn 2:8
light and sons of the day. We do not belong to the night or to the darkness. 6So
then, let us not be like others, who are
asleep,[n] but let us be alert and self-con- 5:6 [n] Ro 13:11
trolled. 7For those who sleep, sleep at
night, and those who get drunk, get
drunk at night.[o] 8But since we belong to 5:7 [o] Ac 2:15;
the day, let us be self-controlled, putting 2Pe 2:13
on faith and love as a breastplate,[p] and 5:8
the hope of salvation[q] as a helmet.[r] 9For [p] Eph 6:14 [q] Ro 8:24
God did not appoint us to suffer wrath [r] Eph 6:17
but to receive salvation through our
Lord Jesus Christ.[s] 10He died for us so 5:9 [s] 2Th 2:13,14
that, whether we are awake or asleep, we 5:10
may live together with him.[t] 11Therefore [t] 2Co 5:15
encourage one another and build each
other up, just as in fact you are doing.

Final Instructions

12Now we ask you, brothers, to respect those who work hard among you,

JESUS FOCUS

LEFT BEHIND

Apparently some of God's people in Thessalonica were worried about others in God's family who had already died before Jesus' second coming. Paul assured them that no one who has accepted Jesus will be left behind on that day of days. In fact, he stated that Jesus will bring back to life those who are already dead and that afterward those who are still alive will be "caught up" to meet him "in the air" (1 Thessalonians 4:16–17). There are many different interpretations of this coming event, but one thing is certain: Jesus is coming back to get us so we can be with him forever—just as he has promised (John 14:1–3).

THIEF IN THE NIGHT

God's prophets in the Old Testament had referred repeatedly to the "day of the Lord," to a time when God would conquer sin forever and restore his creation to its original pristine state. God has never divulged to anyone the precise day or time when this incomparable event will occur and has in fact made it clear that no one will receive advance notification (see Matthew 24:36). In 1 Thessalonians 5 Paul once again reminded God's people of this fact. Jesus will return quickly and quietly, like a "thief in the night" (verse 2), and all of the world will be taken by surprise (verse 3). There will always be those who try to pinpoint the timing of Jesus' return, but Paul stated that our focus should be elsewhere. We should be on the alert and ready—Jesus could come at any time!

5:12 [u] 1Ti 5:17; who are over you in the Lord[u] and who
Heb 13:17 admonish you. 13 Hold them in the highest regard in love because of their work.
5:13 [v] Mk 9:50 Live in peace with each other.[v] 14 And we
5:14 urge you, brothers, warn those who are
[w] 2Th 3:6,7,11 idle,[w] encourage the timid, help the
[x] Ro 14:1 weak,[x] be patient with everyone. 15 Make
5:15 sure that nobody pays back wrong for
[y] 1Pe 3:9 [z] Gal 6:10; wrong,[y] but always try to be kind to
Eph 4:32 each other[z] and to everyone else.
5:16 [a] Php 4:4 16 Be joyful always;[a] 17 pray continually; 18 give thanks in all circumstances, for
5:19 [b] Eph 4:30 this is God's will for you in Christ Jesus.
5:20 19 Do not put out the Spirit's fire;[b] 20 do
[c] 1Co 14:1-40 not treat prophecies[c] with contempt.

21 Test everything.[d] Hold on to the good. 5:21 [d] 1Co 14:29;
22 Avoid every kind of evil. 1Jn 4:1
23 May God himself, the God of peace,[e]
sanctify you through and through. May 5:23 [e] Ro 15:33
your whole spirit, soul and body be kept
blameless at the coming of our Lord 5:24
Jesus Christ. 24 The one who calls you is [f] 1Co 1:9
faithful[f] and he will do it.

5:25 [g] Eph 6:19

25 Brothers, pray for us.[g] 26 Greet all the 5:26
brothers with a holy kiss.[h] 27 I charge you [h] Ro 16:16
before the Lord to have this letter read 5:27
to all the brothers.[i] [i] Col 4:16
28 The grace of our Lord Jesus Christ 5:28
be with you.[j] [j] Ro 16:20

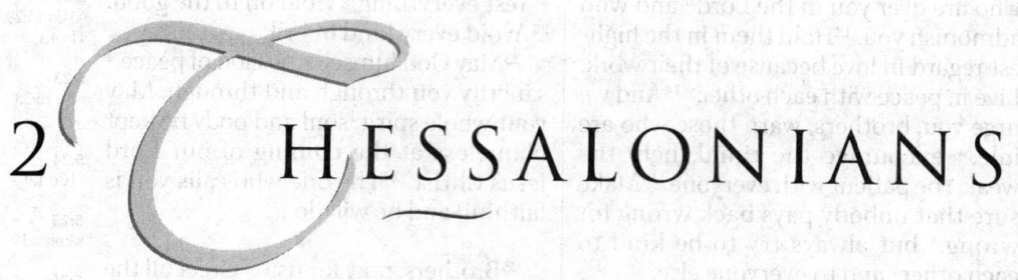

2 THESSALONIANS

Jesus in 2 Thessalonians Paul wrote this letter to help clear up some problems that were still troubling the Thessalonian church, and each chapter addresses one specific issue. Chapter 1 encourages the Thessalonians as they face persecution and calls them to stand firm in their faith. Consider carefully Paul's guidelines for discerning and dealing with false teachers in chapter 2. Chapter 3 takes another look at Jesus' second coming. These words, along with the teachings on this subject in 1 Thessalonians, comprise much of what we know about the end times.

In 2 Thessalonians, Paul described Jesus as the triumphant Savior who will come to judge the world, after which he will be honored among and in his faithful people forever (2 Thessalonians 1:6–10). Those who have refused to place their trust in him will be separated from him eternally; this includes the "man of lawlessness" who claims to be God (2 Thessalonians 2:3–4). Jesus will share his own presence and majesty with us (verse 14), and our hearts will be devoted to serving him as the rightful King for all eternity (verse 16).

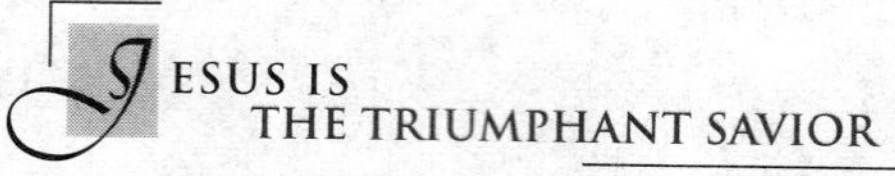
JESUS IS
THE TRIUMPHANT SAVIOR

What has to happen before Jesus returns? (2 Thessalonians 2:3–12)

♦ *First, there will be rebellion, literally apostasy—not so much a rebellion against the church as defection within its ranks. Second, "the man of lawlessness" will come into power (see 1 John 2:18). He will be empowered by Satan to give evidence of his authority with power and signs and false wonders. After a brief reign on earth, the man of lawlessness will be defeated by Jesus. Whether this prophecy is literal or figurative, Paul warns about an overall loss of godliness and an increase in rebellion against God.*

Why were idle Christians such a danger? (2 Thessalonians 3:6–13)

♦ *(1) Their lives were characterized by laziness—a sinful attitude that could spread to others. (2) Other believers felt obligated to provide for the idle Christians, severely draining the church's resources. (3) The idle Christians gave a warped view of Christianity, that those who set their minds on heaven focus only on the return of Jesus, neglecting practical matters.*

1:1 [a]Ac 16:1; **1** Paul, Silas[a] and Timothy,[a]
1Th 1:1
To the church of the Thessalonians in
God our Father and the Lord Jesus
Christ:

2Grace and peace to you from God
1:2 [b]Ro 1:7 the Father and the Lord Jesus Christ.[b]

Thanksgiving and Prayer

3We ought always to thank God for
you, brothers, and rightly so, because
your faith is growing more and more,
1:3 and the love every one of you has for
[c]1Th 3:12 each other is increasing.[c] 4Therefore,
1:4 among God's churches we boast[d] about
[d]2Co 7:14 your perseverance and faith[e] in all the
[e]1Th 1:3 [f]1Th 2:14 persecutions and trials you are enduring.[f]
1:5 [g]Php 1:28 5All this is evidence[g] that God's judgment is right, and as a result you will be
counted worthy of the kingdom of God,
for which you are suffering. 6God is just:
1:6 He will pay back trouble to those who
[h]Col 3:25; trouble you[h] 7and give relief to you who
Rev 6:10 are troubled, and to us as well. This will
happen when the Lord Jesus is revealed
1:7 from heaven in blazing fire with his
[i]1Th 4:16; powerful angels.[i] 8He will punish those
Jude 14 who do not know God[j] and do not obey
1:8 the gospel of our Lord Jesus.[k] 9They will
[j]Gal 4:8 [k]Ro 2:8 be punished with everlasting destruc-
1:9 tion[l] and shut out from the presence of
[l]Php 3:19; the Lord and from the majesty of his
2Pe 3:7 power[m] 10on the day[n] he comes to be
[m]2Th 2:8 glorified[o] in his holy people and to be
1:10 marveled at among all those who have
[n]1Co 3:13 believed. This includes you, because you
[o]Jn 17:10 [p]1Co 1:6 believed our testimony to you.[p]
11With this in mind, we constantly
1:11 pray for you, that our God may count
[q]ver 5 you worthy[q] of his calling, and that by
his power he may fulfill every good purpose of yours and every act prompted by 1:11
your faith.[r] 12We pray this so that the [r]1Th 1:3
name of our Lord Jesus may be glorified 1:12
in you,[s] and you in him, according to the [s]Php 2:9-11
grace of our God and the Lord Jesus
Christ.[b]

The Man of Lawlessness

2 Concerning the coming of our
Lord Jesus Christ and our being
gathered to him,[t] we ask you, brothers, 2:1
2not to become easily unsettled or [t]Mk 13:27; 1Th 4:15-17
alarmed by some prophecy, report or
letter[u] supposed to have come from us, 2:2 [u]2Th 3:17
saying that the day of the Lord[v] has al- [v]1Co 1:8
ready come. 3Don't let anyone deceive 2:3
you[w] in any way, for ⌞that day will not [w]Eph 5:6-8
come⌟ until the rebellion occurs and the [x]Da 7:25; 8:25;
man of lawlessness[c] is revealed,[x] the 11:36; Rev 13:5, 6
man doomed to destruction. 4He will
oppose and will exalt himself over every- 2:4
thing that is called God[y] or is worshiped, [y]1Co 8:5
so that he sets himself up in God's tem- [z]Isa 14:13,14; Eze 28:2
ple, proclaiming himself to be God.[z]
5Don't you remember that when I was
with you I used to tell you these things?
6And now you know what is holding
him back, so that he may be revealed at

a 1 Greek *Silvanus,* a variant of *Silas* *b 12* Or *God and Lord, Jesus Christ* *c 3* Some manuscripts *sin*

JESUS FOCUS

PAYBACK TIME

God's people have frequently suffered because of their adamant refusal to compromise their belief in Jesus, but there will be a payback time when all things will be made right and just (2 Thessalonians 1:6–10). When Jesus comes back, those who have refused him will be separated from him forever—no more second chances. Paul referred to this condition as "everlasting destruction" (verse 9). By contrast, those who accepted Jesus will be glorified eternally in his presence (verse 10).

JESUS FOCUS

THE LAWLESS ONE

Paul referred to a "lawless one" who completely opposes God and, more specifically, God the Son in his position as King of all (2 Thessalonians 2:8). Paul also used the term "man doomed to destruction" because of his false claim to be God (verse 3). The forces of evil by which this individual is empowered are already at work in the world—and have been from the beginning of time (verse 7). Many people believe that this man is the same as the "spirit of the antichrist" (1 John 4:3), whom John in the book of Revelation referred to as the "beast" (Revelation 13:1–10; 19:19–20). Regardless of who this "man of lawlessness" is, Satan is the real power behind anyone who dares to call himself God. But Jesus is destined to conquer evil (Luke 10:18; Romans 16:20; Colossians 2:10,15). Our Lord will be victorious in the final battle with Satan and will usher in a kingdom of peace and joy (Revelation 19:11–21; 21—22).

ENCOURAGEMENT

One of our greatest needs as human beings is the need to receive encouragement. We live in a world that continually beats us down; we face family problems, financial challenges, failures and disappointment, disease and the death of loved ones, defeat of one kind or another. If we are not facing these issues ourselves, we are very likely walking alongside someone else who is. The pace and challenges of modern life have left us all too often depleted and demoralized—spiritually, physically and emotionally.

The Thessalonian believers too were disheartened. In 1 Thessalonians 3 Paul had written about their discouragement in the face of the opposition and persecution the converts in Thessalonica were suffering: "We sent Timothy, who is our brother and God's fellow worker in spreading the gospel of Christ, to strengthen and encourage you in your faith, so that no one would be unsettled by these trials . . . When we were with you, we kept telling you that we would be persecuted. And it turned out that way, as you well know. For this reason, when I could stand it no longer, I sent to find out about your faith. I was afraid that in some way the tempter might have tempted you and our efforts might have been useless" (1 Thessalonians 3: 2–5).

Later on, some members of the Thessalonian church thought that Jesus had already returned and that they had somehow missed the event. Paul noted that the believers appeared to have become "unsettled" and "alarmed" (2 Thessalonians 2:1–2). But Paul encouraged them to "stand firm and hold to the teachings we passed on to you" (verse 15)—and then he prayed for them (verses 16–17).

The main point of Paul's prayer was the bold assertion that we have *eternal* encouragement and hope, even when we don't feel that way (verse 16). Circumstances change and emotions fluctuate, but our hope in the Lord Jesus Christ and our eternal security in him are rock-solid; our salvation is secure and our destination is fixed. In his first letter to this church Paul reminded the Thessalonian believers that Jesus is going to come back for his people and that when he does, we will all be with him forever. "Therefore," he concluded, "encourage each other with these words" (1 Thessalonians 4:18).

Because we have the assurance that God keeps his promises, we can also plug in to the motivation and courage to endure difficulties. We can stand firm, knowing that what we do for God is never futile or pointless (1 Corinthians 15:58).

Jesus himself found in the comfort of this eternal hope the strength to die an agonizing death, recognizing that the joy of being able to liberate us from our sins would be worth it all. The author of Hebrews shared with us the secret to endurance in the long-distance race of life: "Let us fix our eyes on Jesus, the author and perfecter of our faith, who for the joy set before him endured the cross, scorning its shame, and sat down at the right hand of the throne of God. Consider him who endured such opposition from sinful men, so that you will not grow weary and lose heart" (Hebrews 12:2–3).

Self-Discovery: About what are you discouraged today? Ask Jesus for the encouragement you need to face this obstacle in your life with the attitude of an overcomer.

GO TO DISCOVERY 333 ON PAGE 1620

the proper time. 7For the secret power of
lawlessness is already at work; but the
one who now holds it back will continue to do so till he is taken out of the way.
8And then the lawless one will be re-
2:8 vealed, whom the Lord Jesus will over-
a Isa 11:4; throw with the breath of his mouth[a] and
Rev 19:15 destroy by the splendor of his coming.
9The coming of the lawless one will be in
accordance with the work of Satan displayed in all kinds of counterfeit mira-
2:9 cles, signs and wonders,[b] 10and in every
b Mt 24:24; sort of evil that deceives those who are
Jn 4:48 perishing.[c] They perish because they re-
2:10 c 1Co 1:18 fused to love the truth and so be saved.
2:11 11For this reason God sends them[d] a
d Ro 1:28 powerful delusion so that they will believe the lie 12and so that all will be con-
2:12 demned who have not believed the truth
e Ro 1:32 but have delighted in wickedness.[e]

Stand Firm

13But we ought always to thank God
for you, brothers loved by the Lord, because from the beginning God chose
2:13 f Eph 1:4 you[a][f] to be saved[g] through the sanctify-
g 1Th 5:9 ing work of the Spirit[h] and through belief
h 1Pe 1:2 in the truth. 14He called you to this
through our gospel, that you might share
in the glory of our Lord Jesus Christ. 15So
then, brothers, stand firm[i] and hold to
2:15 the teachings[b] we passed on to you,[j]
i 1Co 16:13 j 1Co 11:2 whether by word of mouth or by letter.

THE UNIQUENESS OF CHRISTIANITY IS JESUS CHRIST.

John Mbiti, *African Theologian*

16May our Lord Jesus Christ himself
2:16 k Jn 3:16 and God our Father, who loved us[k] and
by his grace gave us eternal encourage-
2:17 ment and good hope, 17encourage[l] your
l 1Th 3:2 m 2Th 3:3 hearts and strengthen[m] you in every
good deed and word.

Request for Prayer

3:1 **3** Finally, brothers,[n] pray for us[o]
n 1Th 4:1 that the message of the Lord[p] may
o 1Th 5:25 p 1Th 1:8 spread rapidly and be honored, just as it
3:2 was with you. 2And pray that we may be
q Ro 15:31 delivered from wicked and evil men,[q] for
not everyone has faith. 3But the Lord is
faithful,[r] and he will strengthen and pro- 3:3
tect you from the evil one.[s] 4We have r 1Co 1:9
confidence[t] in the Lord that you are do- s Mt 5:37
ing and will continue to do the things 3:4
we command. 5May the Lord direct your t 2Co 2:3
hearts[u] into God's love and Christ's per- 3:5
severance. u 1Ch 29:18

Warning Against Idleness

6In the name of the Lord Jesus 3:6
Christ,[v] we command you, brothers, to v 1Co 5:4 w Ro 16:17
keep away from[w] every brother who is x ver 7,11
idle[x] and does not live according to the y 1Co 11:2
teaching[c] you received from us.[y] 7For
you yourselves know how you ought to
follow our example.[z] We were not idle 3:7 z 1Co 4:16
when we were with you, 8nor did we eat
anyone's food without paying for it. On 3:8
the contrary, we worked[a] night and day, a Ac 18:3;
laboring and toiling so that we would Eph 4:28
not be a burden to any of you. 9We did
this, not because we do not have the 3:9
right to such help,[b] but in order to make b 1Co 9:4-14
ourselves a model for you to follow.[c] c ver 7
10For even when we were with you,[d] we 3:10
gave you this rule: "If a man will not d 1Th 3:4
work,[e] he shall not eat." e 1Th 4:11
11We hear that some among you are
idle. They are not busy; they are busy- 3:11 f ver 6,7;
bodies.[f] 12Such people we command 1Ti 5:13
and urge in the Lord Jesus Christ[g] to set- 3:12
tle down and earn the bread they eat.[h] g 1Th 4:1
13And as for you, brothers, never tire of h 1Th 4:11;
doing what is right.[i] Eph 4:28
14If anyone does not obey our instruc- 3:13
tion in this letter, take special note of i Gal 6:9
him. Do not associate with him,[j] in or- 3:14
der that he may feel ashamed. 15Yet do j ver 6
not regard him as an enemy, but warn 3:15 k Gal 6:1;
him as a brother.[k] 1Th 5:14

Final Greetings

16Now may the Lord of peace[l] himself 3:16 l Ro 15:33
give you peace at all times and in every m Ru 2:4
way. The Lord be with all of you.[m]
17I, Paul, write this greeting in my own 3:17
hand,[n] which is the distinguishing mark n 1Co 16:21
in all my letters. This is how I write.
18The grace of our Lord Jesus Christ 3:18
be with you all.[o] o Ro 16:20

a 13 Some manuscripts *because God chose you as his firstfruits* b 15 Or *traditions* c 6 Or *tradition*

1 TIMOTHY

Jesus in 1 Timothy Paul intimated that Timothy was a shy young man who suffered from stomach trouble (1 Timothy 4:12; 5:23; 2 Timothy 1:7). Yet Paul recognized Timothy's strong points too. The book of 1 Timothy constitutes Paul's pastoral handbook to encourage Timothy in his struggles as a novice pastor in Ephesus. Paul summarized important and wise guidelines for running a church and offered practical suggestions for the believers in their relationship with one another, with church leaders and with the world around them.

Jesus Christ is our mediator—one who stands between God the Father and humanity, making a relationship with God possible (1 Timothy 2:5). When Paul wrote this first letter to Timothy, he started by reminding Timothy that Jesus is our hope for the future (1 Timothy 1:1). Our Lord is the subject of the "Good News" because he came into the world to rescue us from our sins (verses 11,15). Jesus himself is "God our Savior" (1 Timothy 2:3) and the Son of God who paid the debt we owed because of our sins (verse 6).

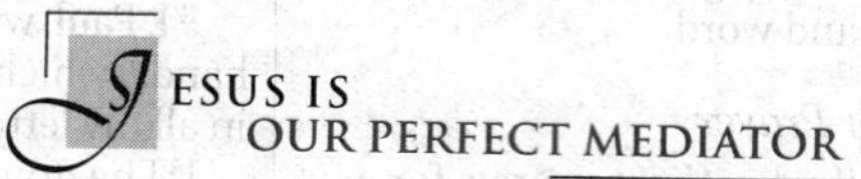
JESUS IS
OUR PERFECT MEDIATOR

If God desires all people to be saved, why aren't they? (1 Timothy 2:4)

- *Some say that God loved the world (John 3:16) but chose to save only some according to his "purpose in election" (Romans 9:11,15–16; Ephesians 1:4–5). Others say that God's plan of salvation fully expresses his desire that everyone be saved but requires individuals to receive or reject Jesus Christ (John 1:11–12; 14:6).*

What is the significance of Jesus as mediator between God and people? (1 Timothy 2:5–6)

- *Because of God's perfect righteousness and justice, it would be impossible for sinful people to relate to him without a mediator or go-between. Jesus was uniquely qualified for this function, for he was himself both God and sinless man.*

1:1 1 Paul, an apostle of Christ Jesus by
a Tit 1:3 the command of God[a] our Savior
b Col 1:27 and of Christ Jesus our hope,[b]

1:2 c Ac 16:1 2 To Timothy[c] my true son[d] in the
d 2Ti 1:2; Tit 1:4 faith:

Grace, mercy and peace from God the Father and Christ Jesus our Lord.

Warning Against False Teachers of the Law

3 As I urged you when I went into
1:3 e Ac 18:19 Macedonia, stay there in Ephesus[e] so
f Gal 1:6,7 that you may command certain men
not to teach false doctrines[f] any longer
1:4 g 1Ti 4:7; 4 nor to devote themselves to myths[g] and
Tit 1:14 endless genealogies. These promote
h 1Ti 6:4 controversies[h] rather than God's work—
which is by faith. 5 The goal of this command is love, which comes from a pure
1:5 i 2Ti 2:22 heart[i] and a good conscience and a sin-
j 2Ti 1:5 cere faith.[j] 6 Some have wandered away
from these and turned to meaningless
talk. 7 They want to be teachers of the
law, but they do not know what they are
talking about or what they so confidently affirm.
1:8 k Ro 7:12 8 We know that the law is good[k] if one
uses it properly. 9 We also know that law[a]
1:9 l Gal 3:19 is made not for the righteous but for
lawbreakers and rebels,[l] the ungodly
and sinful, the unholy and irreligious; for
those who kill their fathers or mothers,
for murderers, 10 for adulterers and perverts, for slave traders and liars and per-
1:10 jurers—and for whatever else is con-
m 2Ti 4:3; Tit 1:9 trary to the sound doctrine[m] 11 that
conforms to the glorious gospel of the
1:11 n Gal 2:7 blessed God, which he entrusted to me.[n]

The Lord's Grace to Paul

12 I thank Christ Jesus our Lord, who
1:12 o Php 4:13 has given me strength,[o] that he considered me faithful, appointing me to his
1:13 service. 13 Even though I was once a blas-
p Ac 8:3 phemer and a persecutor[p] and a violent
man, I was shown mercy because I act-
ed in ignorance and unbelief.[q] 14 The 1:13 q Ac 26:9
grace of our Lord was poured out on me
abundantly,[r] along with the faith and 1:14 r Ro 5:20
love that are in Christ Jesus.[s] s 2Ti 1:13
15 Here is a trustworthy saying[t] that
deserves full acceptance: Christ Jesus 1:15 t 1Ti 3:1;
came into the world to save sinners—of 2Ti 2:11; Tit 3:8
whom I am the worst. 16 But for that very 1:16
reason I was shown mercy[u] so that in u ver 13
me, the worst of sinners, Christ Jesus
might display his unlimited patience as
an example for those who would believe
on him and receive eternal life. 17 Now to 1:17
the King[v] eternal, immortal, invisible,[w] v Rev 15:3 w Col 1:15
the only God, be honor and glory for x Ro 11:36
ever and ever. Amen.[x]
18 Timothy, my son, I give you this instruction in keeping with the prophe-
cies once made about you,[y] so that by 1:18 y 1Ti 4:14
following them you may fight the good z 2Ti 2:3
fight,[z] 19 holding on to faith and a good 1:19
conscience. Some have rejected these a 1Ti 6:21
and so have shipwrecked their faith.[a] 1:20
20 Among them are Hymenaeus[b] and b 2Ti 2:17

[a] 9 Or *that the law*

> SINCE CHRIST ACCEPTED THE THIEF ON THE CROSS JUST AS HE WAS AND RECEIVED PAUL AFTER ALL HIS BLASPHEMIES AND PERSECUTIONS, WE HAVE NO REASON TO DESPAIR.
>
> 
>
> Martin Luther, *German Reformer*

THE WORST OF SINNERS

The apostle Paul did not perceive himself as the "great man of God" we see him as. Quite to the contrary, he considered himself the "worst of sinners" (1 Timothy 1:16). There may have been times when you've felt as though you have made too many mistakes to be worthy or able to approach God, or maybe you feel as though you're just not good enough for him to even trouble himself. But we never need to worry about our own intrinsic degree of righteousness; the self-proclaimed "worst sinner" has already been converted! Paul was literally overwhelmed and finally overcome by the scope of God's grace and compassion.

People who perceive their own characters and pasts as irredeemable are frequently the very ones who most appreciate Jesus' free gift of new life. But these same individuals are sometimes hesitant to believe that Jesus includes them in his offer of forgiveness. However, Paul assured Timothy of one "trustworthy saying that deserves full acceptance: Christ Jesus came into the world to save sinners" (verse 15). No matter what your past has been like, no matter how great your current need may be, Jesus came to offer you eternal life and a new and wonderful relationship with him.

DISCOVERY 333

In Spite of Oppression

Not everyone lives out his or her faith as a member of a free and democratic society. Some live under oppressive political regimes that are hostile to their faith. They run the risk of suffering persecution or imprisonment simply because they believe in Jesus. In 1 Timothy 2:1–2 Paul spelled out some very basic instructions as to how God's people are to live, no matter what their circumstances, stipulating that "requests, prayers, intercession and thanksgiving" (verse 1) for those in authority pleases God (verse 3). Paul's directives take on a whole new meaning when we remember that he wrote them while sitting in a Roman prison cell awaiting his appeal to Caesar. Even in the face of personal adversity, Paul knew what God expected and used his words to encourage others.

The governing authorities in Paul's day were not disposed to be friendly to Jesus' followers. The Roman emperor at the time was the infamous Nero, who is still remembered for his arrests and cruel executions of countless Christians. The political system was anti-God and anti-Jesus. And yet Paul directed God's people to pray for their rulers. It is much easier to pray for political authorities when we agree with their platforms and programs, but God asks that we do so regardless.

The next thing Paul called us to do is to live peaceful and quiet lives (verse 2). The word *peaceful* connotes softness and gentleness, and *quiet* means silent. Today we might say that we are to walk softly, speak gently and learn to keep our mouths shut! People in our world are more prone to demand their rights, protest against perceived injustice and voice their opinions obstreperously, so that everyone can hear from them exactly how things should be. Biblical concepts are for the most part in direct opposition to the value systems of our clamorous, demanding society. In our culture the word *meek* carries the connotation of weak or indecisive, but yet our Lord Jesus Christ told us in no uncertain terms that the meek will inherit the earth (Matthew 5:5). Jesus was not asking us to live as namby-pambies, afraid of our own shadows and unwilling to speak out for the right. Instead, we are to conduct ourselves with decorum, respect the opinions of others and work (possibly behind-the-scenes and without recognition) tirelessly for the good of all people.

God always has a larger purpose. Above all he wants "all men to be saved and to come to a knowledge of the truth. For there is one God and one mediator between God and men, the man Jesus Christ, who gave himself as a ransom for all men" (1 Timothy 2:4–6). God's greater purpose is not to impose Christian values on a corrupt political system, although we as Christians can certainly be involved in the legal process. He is focused not so much on improving society as he is on improving people. God wants our political authorities to be saved just as he wants *all* people to be saved (2 Peter 3:9), and we are to live in a way that advances his agenda.

Self-Discovery: ***Do you regularly pray for government leaders and political figures, regardless of whether or not you agree with their platforms? How do you/would you formulate such a prayer?***

GO TO DISCOVERY 334 ON PAGE 1627

1:20 c2Ti 4:14 Alexander,[c] whom I have handed over to
d1Co 5:5 Satan[d] to be taught not to blaspheme.

Instructions on Worship

2 I urge, then, first of all, that requests, prayers, intercession and
2:2 thanksgiving be made for everyone—
eEzr 6:10; [2]for kings and all those in authority,[e]
Ro 13:1 that we may live peaceful and quiet lives
in all godliness and holiness. [3]This is
2:4 good, and pleases God our Savior, [4]who
fEze 18:23,32 gTit 2:11 wants[f] all men[g] to be saved and to come
h2Ti 2:25 to a knowledge of the truth.[h] [5]For there
2:5 is one God[i] and one mediator[j] between
iRo 3:29,30 God and men, the man Christ Jesus,
jGal 3:20 [6]who gave himself as a ransom for all
2:6 men—the testimony[k] given in its prop-
k1Co 1:6 er time.[l] [7]And for this purpose I was ap-
l1Ti 6:15 pointed a herald and an apostle—I am
2:7 telling the truth, I am not lying—and a
m2Ti 1:11 nAc 9:15; teacher[m] of the true faith to the Gen-
Eph 3:7,8 tiles.[n]
2:8 [8]I want men everywhere to lift up holy
oPs 134:2; hands[o] in prayer, without anger or dis-
Lk 24:50 puting.
[9]I also want women to dress modestly, with decency and propriety, not with
2:9 braided hair or gold or pearls or expen-
p1Pe 3:3 sive clothes,[p] [10]but with good deeds, appropriate for women who profess to
worship God.
[11]A woman should learn in quietness
2:11 and full submission.[q] [12]I do not permit a
q1Co 14:34 woman to teach or to have authority
over a man; she must be silent. [13]For
2:13 rGe 2:7,22; Adam was formed first, then Eve.[r] [14]And
1Co 11:8 Adam was not the one deceived; it was
2:14 the woman who was deceived and be-
sGe 3:1-6,13; came a sinner.[s] [15]But women[a] will be
2Co 11:3 saved[b] through childbearing—if they
2:15 t1Ti 1:14 continue in faith, love[t] and holiness with
propriety.

Overseers and Deacons

3:1 **3** Here is a trustworthy saying:[u] If
u1Ti 1:15 anyone sets his heart on being an
vAc 20:28 overseer,[c][v] he desires a noble task. [2]Now
3:2 the overseer must be above reproach,[w]
wTit 1:6-8 xRo 12:13 the husband of but one wife, temperate,
y2Ti 2:24 self-controlled, respectable, hospitable,[x]
able to teach,[y] [3]not given to drunken-
3:3 ness, not violent but gentle, not quarrel-
z2Ti 2:24 some,[z] not a lover of money.[a] [4]He must
aHeb 13:5; 1Pe 5:2 manage his own family well and see that
his children obey him with proper re-
3:4 bTit 1:6 spect.[b] [5](If anyone does not know how
to manage his own family, how can he
take care of God's church?)[c] [6]He must 3:5 c1Co 10:32
not be a recent convert, or he may be-
come conceited[d] and fall under the 3:6 d1Ti 6:4
same judgment as the devil. [7]He must
also have a good reputation with outsiders, so that he will not fall into dis- 3:7
grace and into the devil's trap.[e] e2Ti 2:26
[8]Deacons,[f] likewise, are to be men 3:8
worthy of respect, sincere, not indulging fPhp 1:1
in much wine,[g] and not pursuing dis- gTit 2:3
honest gain. [9]They must keep hold of
the deep truths of the faith with a clear 3:9
conscience.[h] [10]They must first be tested; h1Ti 1:19
and then if there is nothing against
them, let them serve as deacons.
[11]In the same way, their wives[d] are to
be women worthy of respect, not mali-
cious talkers[i] but temperate and trust- 3:11 i2Ti 3:3; Tit 2:3
worthy in everything.
[12]A deacon must be the husband of
but one wife and must manage his chil-
dren and his household well.[j] [13]Those 3:12 jver 4
who have served well gain an excellent
standing and great assurance in their
faith in Christ Jesus.
[14]Although I hope to come to you
soon, I am writing you these instructions so that, [15]if I am delayed, you will
know how people ought to conduct
themselves in God's household, which is
the church[k] of the living God, the pillar 3:15 kver 5; Eph 2:21
and foundation of the truth. [16]Beyond
all question, the mystery[l] of godliness is 3:16 lRo 16:25
great: mJn 1:14

He[e] appeared in a body,[f][m] nCol 1:23
was vindicated by the Spirit, oMk 16:19
was seen by angels,
was preached among the
nations,[n]
was believed on in the world,
was taken up in glory.[o]

Instructions to Timothy

4 The Spirit[p] clearly says that in lat- 4:1 pJn 16:13
er times[q] some will abandon the q2Ti 3:1
faith and follow deceiving spirits[r] and r2Th 2:3
things taught by demons. [2]Such teachings come through hypocritical liars,
whose consciences have been seared as 4:2 sEph 4:19
with a hot iron.[s] [3]They forbid people to
marry[t] and order them to abstain from 4:3 tHeb 13:4
certain foods,[u] which God created[v] to be uCol 2:16 vGe 1:29
received with thanksgiving[w] by those wRo 14:6

[a] *15* Greek *she* [b] *15* Or *restored*
[c] *1* Traditionally *bishop*; also in verse 2 [d] *11* Or *way, deaconesses* [e] *16* Some manuscripts *God*
[f] *16* Or *in the flesh*

> RELIGIOUS LEADERS ARE OFTEN MORE CONCERNED ABOUT THE BUSINESS OF RELIGION . . . THAN BEING THEMSELVES WITNESSES TO THE GENTLE SHEPHERD.

Joseph F. Girzone, *Catholic Author*

who believe and who know the truth.
4:4 [x]Ro 14:14-18 4For everything God created is good,[x]
and nothing is to be rejected if it is received with thanksgiving, 5because it is
consecrated by the word of God and
prayer.
6If you point these things out to the
brothers, you will be a good minister of
Christ Jesus, brought up in the truths of
4:6 [y]1Ti 1:10 the faith[y] and of the good teaching that
you have followed. 7Have nothing to do
4:7 [z]2Ti 2:16 with godless myths and old wives' tales;[z]
rather, train yourself to be godly. 8For
physical training is of some value, but
4:8 [a]1Ti 6:6 godliness has value for all things,[a] hold-
[b]Ps 37:9,11; Mk 10:29,30 ing promise for both the present life[b]
and the life to come.
4:9 [c]1Ti 1:15 9This is a trustworthy saying[c] that deserves full acceptance 10(and for this we
labor and strive), that we have put our
hope in the living God, who is the Savior
of all men, and especially of those who
believe.
4:11 [d]1Ti 5:7; 6:2 11Command and teach these things.[d]
12Don't let anyone look down on you be-
cause you are young, but set an exam-
4:12 [e]Tit 2:7; 1Pe 5:3 ple[e] for the believers in speech, in life, in
[f]1Ti 1:14 love, in faith[f] and in purity. 13Until I
come, devote yourself to the public read-
ing of Scripture, to preaching and to
teaching. 14Do not neglect your gift,
which was given you through a prophet-
4:14 [g]1Ti 1:18 ic message[g] when the body of elders laid
[h]Ac 6:6; 2Ti 1:6 their hands on you.[h]
15Be diligent in these matters; give
yourself wholly to them, so that everyone may see your progress. 16Watch your
life and doctrine closely. Persevere in
them, because if you do, you will save
both yourself and your hearers.

Advice About Widows, Elders and Slaves

5:1 [i]Tit 2:2 5 Do not rebuke an older man[i]
[j]Lev 19:32 harshly,[j] but exhort him as if he
[k]Tit 2:6 were your father. Treat younger men[k] as
brothers, 2older women as mothers, and
younger women as sisters, with absolute
purity.
3Give proper recognition to those
widows who are really in need.[l] 4But if a 5:3 [l]ver 5,16
widow has children or grandchildren,
these should learn first of all to put their
religion into practice by caring for their
own family and so repaying their par-
ents and grandparents,[m] for this is 5:4 [m]Eph 6:1,2
pleasing to God.[n] 5The widow who is [n]1Ti 2:3
really in need[o] and left all alone puts her 5:5
hope in God[p] and continues night and [o]ver 3,16 [p]1Co 7:34;
day to pray[q] and to ask God for help. 1Pe 3:5
6But the widow who lives for pleasure is [q]Lk 2:37
dead even while she lives.[r] 7Give the 5:6 [r]Lk 15:24
people these instructions,[s] too, so that
no one may be open to blame. 8If anyone 5:7
does not provide for his relatives, and es- [s]1Ti 4:11
pecially for his immediate family, he has 5:8
denied[t] the faith and is worse than an [t]2Pe 2:1; Jude 4;
unbeliever. Tit 1:16
9No widow may be put on the list of
widows unless she is over sixty, has been
faithful to her husband,[a] 10and is well
known for her good deeds,[u] such as 5:10 [u]Ac 9:36;
bringing up children, showing hospital- 1Ti 6:18;
ity, washing the feet[v] of the saints, help- 1Pe 2:12 [v]Lk 7:44
ing those in trouble[w] and devoting her- [w]ver 16
self to all kinds of good deeds.
11As for younger widows, do not put
them on such a list. For when their sensual desires overcome their dedication to
Christ, they want to marry. 12Thus they
bring judgment on themselves, because
they have broken their first pledge. 13Be-
sides, they get into the habit of being idle
and going about from house to house.
And not only do they become idlers, but 5:13
also gossips and busybodies,[x] saying [x]2Th 3:11
things they ought not to. 14So I counsel 5:14
younger widows to marry,[y] to have chil- [y]1Co 7:9
dren, to manage their homes and to give [z]1Ti 6:1
the enemy no opportunity for slander.[z]
15Some have in fact already turned away
to follow Satan.[a] 5:15 [a]Mt 4:10
16If any woman who is a believer has
widows in her family, she should help
them and not let the church be burdened with them, so that the church can
help those widows who are really in
need.[b] 5:16 [b]ver 3-5
17The elders[c] who direct the affairs of 5:17
the church well are worthy of double [c]Ac 11:30
honor,[d] especially those whose work is [d]Php 2:29;
preaching and teaching. 18For the Scrip- 1Th 5:12
ture says, "Do not muzzle the ox while it

[a] 9 Or *has had but one husband*

5:18 [e]Dt 25:4; 1Co 9:7-9 [f]Lk 10:7; Lev 19:13; Dt 24:14,15; Mt 10:10; 1Co 9:14
is treading out the grain,"[a][e] and "The
worker deserves his wages."[b][f] 19Do not
entertain an accusation against an elder[g] unless it is brought by two or three
witnesses.[h] 20Those who sin are to be rebuked[i] publicly, so that the others may
5:19 [g]Ac 11:30 [h]Mt 18:16
take warning.[j]
21I charge you, in the sight of God and
Christ Jesus[k] and the elect angels, to
5:20 [i]2Ti 4:2; Tit 1:13 [j]Dt 13:11
keep these instructions without partiality, and to do nothing out of favoritism.
22Do not be hasty in the laying on of
5:21 [k]1Ti 6:13; 2Ti 4:1
hands,[l] and do not share in the sins of
others.[m] Keep yourself pure.
23Stop drinking only water, and use a
5:22 [l]Ac 6:6 [m]Eph 5:11
little wine[n] because of your stomach
and your frequent illnesses.
24The sins of some men are obvious,
5:23 [n]1Ti 3:8
reaching the place of judgment ahead of
them; the sins of others trail behind
them. 25In the same way, good deeds are
obvious, and even those that are not
cannot be hidden.

6 All who are under the yoke of slavery should consider their masters
6:1 [o]Eph 6:5; Tit 2:9; 1Pe 2:18 [p]Tit 2:5,8
worthy of full respect,[o] so that God's
name and our teaching may not be slandered.[p] 2Those who have believing masters are not to show less respect for
6:2 [q]Phm 16 [r]1Ti 4:11
them because they are brothers.[q] Instead, they are to serve them even better,
because those who benefit from their
service are believers, and dear to them.
These are the things you are to teach
and urge on them.[r]

Love of Money

6:3 [s]1Ti 1:3 [t]1Ti 1:10
3If anyone teaches false doctrines[s]
and does not agree to the sound instruction[t] of our Lord Jesus Christ and
to godly teaching, 4he is conceited and
understands nothing. He has an unhealthy interest in controversies and
6:4 [u]2Ti 2:14
quarrels about words[u] that result in
envy, strife, malicious talk, evil suspi-
6:5 [v]Tit 1:15
cions 5and constant friction between
men of corrupt mind, who have been
6:6 [w]Php 4:11; Heb 13:5 [x]1Ti 4:8
robbed of the truth[v] and who think that
godliness is a means to financial gain.
6But godliness with contentment[w] is
6:7 [y]Job 1:21; Ecc 5:15
great gain.[x] 7For we brought nothing
into the world, and we can take nothing
out of it.[y] 8But if we have food and cloth-
6:8 [z]Heb 13:5
ing, we will be content with that.[z] 9Peo-
ple who want to get rich[a] fall into temp-
6:9 [a]Pr 15:27 [b]1Ti 3:7
tation and a trap[b] and into many foolish
and harmful desires that plunge men
into ruin and destruction. 10For the love
6:10 [c]1Ti 3:3 [d]Jas 5:19
of money[c] is a root of all kinds of evil.
Some people, eager for money, have
wandered from the faith[d] and pierced
themselves with many griefs.

Paul's Charge to Timothy

11But you, man of God,[e] flee from all
6:11 [e]2Ti 3:17 [f]2Ti 2:22
this, and pursue righteousness, godliness, faith, love,[f] endurance and gentle-
6:12 [g]1Co 9:25,26; 1Ti 1:18 [h]Php 3:12
ness. 12Fight the good fight[g] of the faith.
Take hold of[h] the eternal life to which
you were called when you made your
good confession in the presence of many
witnesses. 13In the sight of God, who
gives life to everything, and of Christ
Jesus, who while testifying before Pon-
6:13 [i]Jn 18:33-37 [j]1Ti 5:21
tius Pilate[i] made the good confession, I
charge you[j] 14to keep this command
without spot or blame until the appearing of our Lord Jesus Christ, 15which
6:15 [k]1Ti 1:11 [l]1Ti 1:17 [m]Rev 17:14; 19:16
God will bring about in his own time—
God, the blessed[k] and only Ruler,[l] the
King of kings and Lord of lords,[m] 16who
alone is immortal[n] and who lives in un-
6:16 [n]1Ti 1:17 [o]Jn 1:18
approachable light, whom no one has
seen or can see.[o] To him be honor and
might forever. Amen.

17Command those who are rich in
this present world not to be arrogant

[a] 18 Deut. 25:4 [b] 18 Luke 10:7

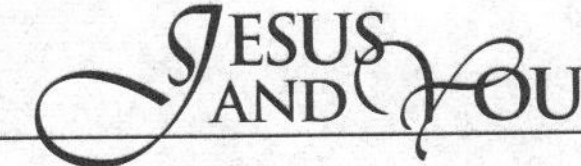

KEEP IT SIMPLE

The Bible nowhere states that money in and of itself is bad, although Paul is often misquoted as saying that money causes evil. Paul actually asserted that the *love* or misuse of money results in all kinds of evil and that leaders among God's people need to be especially careful to maintain a healthy financial perspective (1 Timothy 6:10–12). Paul reminded all Christians to be content with what God has given us. In fact, he reduced this issue down to its lowest common denominator by stating that all we really need is food and clothing. Jesus had already assured his people of God's care in their lives, and that includes the seemingly mundane and trivial details. As he addressed his listeners in his great Sermon on the Mount, our Lord Jesus had pointed out that the God who feeds the birds and clothes the lilies will never fail to meet their—or our—daily needs (Matthew 6:25–34).

6:17 nor to put their hope in wealth,[p] which
p Lk 12:20,21 is so uncertain, but to put their hope in
q 1Ti 4:10 God,[q] who richly provides us with
r Ac 14:17 everything for our enjoyment.[r] [18]Com-
mand them to do good, to be rich in
6:18 good deeds,[s] and to be generous and
s 1Ti 5:10 willing to share.[t] [19]In this way they will
t Ro 12:8,13 lay up treasure for themselves[u] as a firm
6:19 foundation for the coming age, so that
u Mt 6:20

they may take hold of the life that is truly life.
[20]Timothy, guard what has been entrusted[v] to your care. Turn away from 6:20
godless chatter[w] and the opposing ideas v 2Ti 1:12,14
of what is falsely called knowledge, w 2Ti 2:16
[21]which some have professed and in so
doing have wandered from the faith.[x] 6:21
Grace be with you.[y] x 2Ti 2:18
y Col 4:18

2 TIMOTHY

Jesus in 2 Timothy Paul, imprisoned in Rome for the second time, was facing death and wanted to send one final message to his young protégé, Timothy. Paul's words penetrate to the heart of the gospel, and throughout history Christians have drawn inspiration and motivation from this book.

Paul knew that Timothy faced formidable tasks but challenged him to a more effective ministry, reminding him to live a disciplined life in reliance on the Scriptures. Jesus, the eternal Son of God, had chosen before the beginning of time to offer his life for us (2 Timothy 1:9), and he came to earth to destroy death and bring life (verse 10). As we learn to walk with him he strengthens us, and we become "good soldiers" (2 Timothy 2:1–3). The better we get to know our Lord's mind and heart, the better equipped we become to tell others about his truth (verse 15). Paul described Jesus as "the Lord, the righteous Judge" (2 Timothy 4:8) and reiterated that when he returns to earth God the Son will judge both the living and the dead.

Why compare Christians to soldiers? (2 Timothy 2:3)

♦ *Timothy certainly must have felt as though he was in a spiritual battle for the cause of Jesus and the gospel. The church at Ephesus was practically in a state of siege, threatened by false teachers, and Timothy had to contend for righteousness and truth. But because all analogies have limitations, Paul also compared the Christian's life to that of a farmer and an athlete (verses 5–7).*

What does it mean to confess the name of the Lord? (2 Timothy 2:19)

♦ *To confess Jesus' name means that we willingly identify ourselves with him, that we belong to him. Just as an adopted child assumes the surname of the adoptive parents, so we take on the name of Jesus Christ. The counterpart of our confessing his name is that Jesus knows those who are his.*

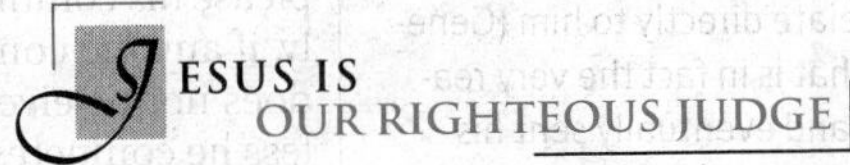
JESUS IS
OUR RIGHTEOUS JUDGE

2 Timothy 1

1:1 a 2Co 1:1 b Eph 3:6; 1Ti 6:19 1 Paul, an apostle of Christ Jesus by
the will of God,[a] according to the
promise of life that is in Christ Jesus,[b]

1:2 c Ac 16:1 d 1Ti 1:2 2 To Timothy,[c] my dear son:[d]

Grace, mercy and peace from God the
Father and Christ Jesus our Lord.

Encouragement to Be Faithful

1:3 e Ro 1:8 f Ro 1:10 3 I thank God,[e] whom I serve, as my
forefathers did, with a clear conscience,
as night and day I constantly remember
1:4 g Ac 20:37 h 2Ti 4:9 you in my prayers.[f] 4 Recalling your
tears,[g] I long to see you,[h] so that I may
be filled with joy. 5 I have been reminded
1:5 i 1Ti 1:5 j Ac 16:1 of your sincere faith,[i] which first lived in
your grandmother Lois and in your
mother Eunice[j] and, I am persuaded,
now lives in you also. 6 For this reason I
remind you to fan into flame the gift of
God, which is in you through the laying
1:6 k 1Ti 4:14 on of my hands.[k] 7 For God did not give
us a spirit of timidity,[l] but a spirit of
1:7 l Ro 8:15 power, of love and of self-discipline.
1:8 m Mk 8:38; Ro 1:16 n Eph 3:1 o 2Ti 2:3,9; 4:5 8 So do not be ashamed[m] to testify
about our Lord, or ashamed of me his
prisoner.[n] But join with me in suffering
for the gospel,[o] by the power of God,
1:9 p Ro 8:28 9 who has saved us and called[p] us to a
holy life—not because of anything we
have done but because of his own purpose and grace. This grace was given us
in Christ Jesus before the beginning of
1:10 q Eph 1:9 r 1Co 15:26,54 time, 10 but it has now been revealed[q]
through the appearing of our Savior,
Christ Jesus, who has destroyed death[r]
and has brought life and immortality to
light through the gospel. 11 And of this
gospel I was appointed a herald and an
1:11 s 1Ti 2:7 apostle and a teacher.[s] 12 That is why I
am suffering as I am. Yet I am not
ashamed, because I know whom I have
believed, and am convinced that he is
1:12 t 1Ti 6:20 u ver 18 able to guard[t] what I have entrusted to
him for that day.[u]
1:13 v Tit 1:9 w 1Ti 1:14 13 What you heard from me, keep[v] as
the pattern of sound teaching, with faith
and love in Christ Jesus.[w] 14 Guard the
good deposit that was entrusted to
you—guard it with the help of the Holy
1:14 x Ro 8:9 Spirit who lives in us.[x]
15 You know that everyone in the prov-
1:15 y 2Ti 4:10,11,16 ince of Asia has deserted me,[y] including
Phygelus and Hermogenes.
16 May the Lord show mercy to the
1:16 z 2Ti 4:19 household of Onesiphorus,[z] because he
often refreshed me and was not
ashamed of my chains. 17 On the contrary, when he was in Rome, he searched
hard for me until he found me. 18 May
the Lord grant that he will find mercy
from the Lord on that day! You know
1:18 a Heb 6:10 very well in how many ways he helped
me[a] in Ephesus.

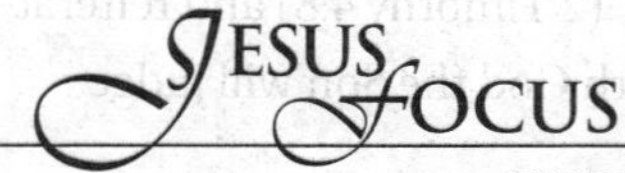

THE DEATH OF DEATH

God's plan from before the creation of the world was that people would relate directly to him (Genesis 1:26; Psalm 100:3). That is in fact the very reason why he created us—and eventually sent his precious Son to die for us: to bring us back into a renewed relationship with him (Romans 5:2; Ephesians 2:18; 3:12; Hebrews 7:19; 10:19–23). Death *died* when Jesus rose victorious from the grave, and his resurrection guarantees our eternal life (1 Corinthians 15:20–22,54–57). Paul was so convinced of this that he dedicated his life to being a herald, apostle and teacher of this "Good News."

THERE IS NOTHING AUTONOMOUS—NOTHING INDEPENDENT FROM THE LORDSHIP OF JESUS CHRIST AND THE AUTHORITY OF THE SCRIPTURES.

Francis Schaeffer, *Christian Apologist*

2 Timothy 2

2:1 b Eph 6:10 2 You then, my son, be strong[b] in
the grace that is in Christ Jesus.
2:2 c 2Ti 1:13 d 1Ti 6:12 2 And the things you have heard me say[c]
in the presence of many witnesses[d] en-
trust to reliable men who will also be
qualified to teach others. 3 Endure hard-
2:3 e 1Ti 1:18 ship with us like a good soldier[e] of Christ
Jesus. 4 No one serving as a soldier gets
involved in civilian affairs—he wants to
please his commanding officer. 5 Similarly, if anyone competes as an athlete, he
2:5 f 1Co 9:25 does not receive the victor's crown[f] unless he competes according to the rules.
6 The hardworking farmer should be the
first to receive a share of the crops. 7 Reflect on what I am saying, for the Lord
will give you insight into all this.
2:8 g Ac 2:24 h Mt 1:1 i Ro 2:16 8 Remember Jesus Christ, raised from
the dead,[g] descended from David.[h] This
is my gospel,[i] 9 for which I am suffering[j]
2:9 j Ac 9:16 even to the point of being chained like a

DISCOVERY 334

Passing the Word Along

The last letter that Paul wrote before his execution was a second greeting to his young friend and "son," Timothy. In it he counseled Timothy to "be strong in the grace that is in Christ Jesus" (2 Timothy 2:1). This appeal for Timothy to draw on the strength available to him in Jesus was not primarily for Timothy's personal benefit; it was intended to enable Timothy to influence others for the cause of Jesus Christ.

Paul was passionate about passing along the message of God's love and forgiveness from one generation to the next. In his mind's eye the apostle was actually envisioning four generations. First, there was Paul himself, who was entrusting his instructions and knowledge to the "next generation," represented by Timothy. Timothy would then commend the message to men who could be expected to be reliable witnesses, and they in turn would pass the truth along to a fourth generation who could teach still others. Most of us limit our vision to a handful of people—provided we are able in our mind's eye to get beyond ourselves! Some people have a sincere interest in proclaiming the message of Jesus to people who either haven't heard or haven't yet accepted Jesus' forgiveness. But very few people envision the far-reaching impact that Paul had in mind.

Jesus repeatedly reminded his followers of the importance of passing faith to the next generation. His disciples were turning children away, assuming that Jesus was too busy with adults. "When Jesus saw them, he was indignant. He said to them, 'let the little children come to me, and do not hinder them, for the kingdom of God belongs to such as these' " (Mark 10:13–14).

Passing along the Good News about Jesus Christ to the upcoming generation must always remain one of the highest priorities of his church. It is of crucial importance that we as representatives of Jesus entrust that task to reliable people who can effectively teach others. However, it is easy to make the mistake of delegating that accountability to individuals who are gifted to serve in that area and then leaving the process strictly in their hands. What we neglect to recognize in this scenario is that it is the solemn responsibility of Christ's entire church to raise the young to become committed, active members and that this task is accomplished as much by the example of all adult believers as it is by the formal educational program.

The challenge that we face is the same one Timothy confronted—that people are transformed by watching a life, not simply by listening to instruction. And it is difficult to overstate the role of parents in the spiritual education of children. From modeling a lifestyle that is dedicated to exalting Jesus Christ and promoting his kingdom to discussing spiritual truths to encouraging our children to pray and study the Word—parents can and must work in conjunction with the church for the salvation of our children and for equipping them to serve when their turn comes around.

Self-Discovery: *What steps have you taken in the context of your own church to help pass the faith along to the younger generation? Something as simple as learning the names of children and greeting them with a smile and a word of encouragement can leave a lasting impression.*

GO TO DISCOVERY 335 ON PAGE 1629

2:10 criminal. But God's word is not chained.
k Col 1:24 10Therefore I endure everything[k] for the
l 2Co 4:17 sake of the elect, that they too may obtain the salvation that is in Christ Jesus,
with eternal glory.[l]
11Here is a trustworthy saying:

If we died with him,
2:11 we will also live with him;[m]
m Ro 6:2-11 12if we endure,
2:12 we will also reign with him.[n]
n Ro 8:17; 1Pe 4:13 If we disown him,
o Mt 10:33 he will also disown us;[o]
2:13 13if we are faithless,
p Nu 23:19; he will remain faithful,[p]
Ro 3:3 for he cannot disown himself.

A Workman Approved by God

14Keep reminding them of these
2:14 things. Warn them before God against
q 1Ti 6:4 quarreling about words;[q] it is of no value, and only ruins those who listen. 15Do
your best to present yourself to God as
one approved, a workman who does not
2:15 need to be ashamed and who correctly
r Eph 1:13; handles the word of truth.[r] 16Avoid god-
Jas 1:18 less chatter,[s] because those who indulge
2:16 in it will become more and more ungod-
s Tit 3:9 ly. 17Their teaching will spread like gan-
2:17 grene. Among them are Hymenaeus[t]
t 1Ti 1:20 and Philetus, 18who have wandered
away from the truth. They say that the
2:18 resurrection has already taken place,
u 1Ti 1:19 and they destroy the faith of some.[u]
2:19 19Nevertheless, God's solid foundation
v Isa 28:16 stands firm,[v] sealed with this inscrip-
w Jn 10:14 tion: "The Lord knows those who are
x 1Co 1:2 his,"[a][w] and, "Everyone who confesses the
name of the Lord[x] must turn away from
wickedness."
20In a large house there are articles
not only of gold and silver, but also of
wood and clay; some are for noble pur-
2:20 poses and some for ignoble.[y] 21If a man
y Ro 9:21 cleanses himself from the latter, he will
be an instrument for noble purposes,
made holy, useful to the Master and pre-
2:21 pared to do any good work.[z]
z 2Ti 3:17 22Flee the evil desires of youth, and
2:22 pursue righteousness, faith, love[a] and
a 1Ti 1:14; 6:11 peace, along with those who call on the
b 1Ti 1:5 Lord out of a pure heart.[b] 23Don't have
anything to do with foolish and stupid
arguments, because you know they produce quarrels. 24And the Lord's servant
must not quarrel; instead, he must be
2:24 kind to everyone, able to teach, not re-
c 1Ti 3:2,3 sentful.[c] 25Those who oppose him he
must gently instruct, in the hope that
God will grant them repentance leading 2:25
them to a knowledge of the truth,[d] 26and d 1Ti 2:4
that they will come to their senses and 2:26
escape from the trap of the devil,[e] who e 1Ti 3:7
has taken them captive to do his will.

Godlessness in the Last Days

3 But mark this: There will be terrible times in the last days.[f] 2People 3:1
will be lovers of themselves, lovers of f 1Ti 4:1
money,[g] boastful, proud,[h] abusive, dis- 3:2
obedient to their parents,[i] ungrateful, g 1Ti 3:3 h Ro 1:30
unholy, 3without love, unforgiving, slan- i Ro 1:30
derous, without self-control, brutal, not
lovers of the good, 4treacherous, rash,
conceited,[j] lovers of pleasure rather than 3:4 j 1Ti 3:6
lovers of God— 5having a form of godli-
ness but denying its power. Have nothing to do with them.
6They are the kind who worm their 3:6
way[k] into homes and gain control over k Jude 4
weak-willed women, who are loaded
down with sins and are swayed by all
kinds of evil desires, 7always learning
but never able to acknowledge the truth.
8Just as Jannes and Jambres opposed 3:8
Moses,[l] so also these men oppose[m] the l Ex 7:11
truth—men of depraved minds,[n] who, m Ac 13:8 n 1Ti 6:5
as far as the faith is concerned, are rejected. 9But they will not get very far be- 3:9
cause, as in the case of those men,[o] their o Ex 7:12
folly will be clear to everyone.

Paul's Charge to Timothy

10You, however, know all about my 3:10
teaching,[p] my way of life, my purpose, p 1Ti 4:6
faith, patience, love, endurance, 11per-
secutions, sufferings—what kinds of 3:11
things happened to me in Antioch,[q] Ico- q Ac 13:14,50
nium and Lystra, the persecutions I en- r 2Co 11:23-27 s Ps 34:19
dured.[r] Yet the Lord rescued me from all
of them.[s] 12In fact, everyone who wants
to live a godly life in Christ Jesus will be
persecuted,[t] 13while evil men and im- 3:12 t Ac 14:22
postors will go from bad to worse,[u] de- 3:13
ceiving and being deceived. 14But as for u 2Ti 2:16
you, continue in what you have learned
and have become convinced of, because 3:14
you know those from whom you learned v 2Ti 1:13
it,[v] 15and how from infancy[w] you have 3:15
known the holy Scriptures,[x] which are w 2Ti 1:5 x Jn 5:39
able to make you wise[y] for salvation y Ps 119:98,99
through faith in Christ Jesus. 16All Scrip- 3:16
ture is God-breathed[z] and is useful for z 2Pe 1:20,21
teaching,[a] rebuking, correcting and a Ro 4:23,24

a 19 Num. 16:5 (see Septuagint)

God's Living Word

According to Paul God's authoritative Word is "able to make [people] wise for salvation through faith in Christ Jesus" (2 Timothy 3:15). The primary focus of the whole Bible is on Jesus, and Luke recorded that "beginning with Moses and all the Prophets, [Jesus] explained to [the Emmaus wayfarers] what was said in all the Scriptures concerning himself" (Luke 24:27).

Paul's final instructions to Timothy included a reminder that all Scripture is accurate and reliable. The Bible is "God-breathed" or God-inspired (2 Timothy 3:16). It is not a compilation of books and letters that men decided to write, nor does it represent humanity's record of God working in human history. Rather, it is *God's* record of how he has worked throughout the history of our world. God is perfect, and that which he authors contains no mistakes. Some minor nuances of meaning might have become lost in the process of translating from one language to another (for example, there is some question about the meaning of certain obscure Hebrew words), but there are no errors or misleading statements in terms of doctrine or truth.

This reliability is what we refer to as the *inerrancy* of Scripture. Jesus himself emphasized the total dependability of God's Word: "Until heaven and earth disappear, not the smallest letter, not the least stroke of a pen, will by any means disappear from the law until everything is accomplished" (Matthew 5:18).

God inspired Scripture, but he relied on human beings to write it down. The various authors were chosen by God, and while they wrote in their own characteristic styles, they were actually writing God's words. Peter expressed this clearly in 2 Peter 1:20–21: "Above all, you must understand that no prophecy of Scripture came about by the prophet's own interpretation. For prophecy never had its origin in the will of man, but men spoke from God as they were carried along by the Holy Spirit." The words *carried along* call to mind the act of picking someone up, carrying him for a distance and then setting him down again. The Holy Spirit "picked up" the writers, carried them along as they wrote and then set them back down. During the period in which the inspired authors were recording God's words, they were able to write without error.

The realities that the Bible is God-authored and that it is irrefutably true are critical, because they signify that we have been given a book from the very hand of God; it is the Book that contains all of the revelation and resources we will ever need for life and godliness. The 66 books that comprise holy Scripture were written over a period of 1,400 years, on three different continents, in three different languages, by dozens of different people—and yet these diverse books are fully held together by one theme: Jesus, the Son of God. As we read the Bible we find Jesus shining forth through every book and on nearly every page. Reading what others have written about the Bible can be a helpful exercise, but studying God's very words is life-changing!

Self-Discovery: Pause a moment to thank God for the wonderful revelation he has provided you in the form of his Word. Thank him especially for the revelation of the Living Word, his own Son, Jesus Christ your Savior.

GO TO DISCOVERY 336 ON PAGE 1633

**JESUS LOVES ME — THIS I KNOW,
FOR THE BIBLE TELLS ME SO.**

Anna Bartlett Warner, *American Poet*

3:17 training in righteousness, 17so that
b 1Ti 6:11 the man of God[b] may be thoroughly
c 2Ti 2:21 equipped for every good work.[c]

4

In the presence of God and of
4:1 Christ Jesus, who will judge the
d Ac 10:42 living and the dead,[d] and in view of his
e 1Ti 5:21 appearing and his kingdom, I give you
4:2 this charge:[e] 2Preach[f] the Word;[g] be pre-
f 1Ti 4:13 g Gal 6:6 pared in season and out of season; cor-
h 1Ti 5:20; rect, rebuke[h] and encourage—with
Tit 1:13; 2:15 great patience and careful instruction.
4:3 3For the time will come when men will
i 1Ti 1:10 not put up with sound doctrine.[i] Instead, to suit their own desires, they will
gather around them a great number of
teachers to say what their itching ears
want to hear. 4They will turn their ears
4:4 away from the truth and turn aside to
j 1Ti 1:4 myths.[j] 5But you, keep your head in all
4:5 situations, endure hardship,[k] do the
k 2Ti 1:8 work of an evangelist,[l] discharge all the
l Ac 21:8 duties of your ministry.
4:6 6For I am already being poured out
m Php 2:17 like a drink offering,[m] and the time has
n Php 1:23 come for my departure.[n] 7I have fought
4:7 the good fight,[o] I have finished the race,[p]
o 1Ti 1:18 p 1Co 9:24 I have kept the faith. 8Now there is in
4:8 store for me[q] the crown of righteous-
q Col 1:5 ness, which the Lord, the righteous
r 2Ti 1:12 Judge, will award to me on that day[r]—
and not only to me, but also to all who
have longed for his appearing.

Personal Remarks

9Do your best to come to me quickly,
10for Demas,[s] because he loved this 4:10 s Col 4:14
world,[t] has deserted me and has gone to t 1Jn 2:15
Thessalonica. Crescens has gone to Ga- u Ac 16:6
latia,[u] and Titus to Dalmatia. 11Only 4:11
Luke[v] is with me.[w] Get Mark[x] and bring v Col 4:14
him with you, because he is helpful to w 2Ti 1:15
me in my ministry. 12I sent Tychicus[y] to x Ac 12:12
Ephesus. 13When you come, bring the 4:12 y Ac 20:4
cloak that I left with Carpus at Troas,
and my scrolls, especially the parchments.

14Alexander[z] the metalworker did me 4:14 z Ac 19:33
a great deal of harm. The Lord will repay a Ro 12:19
him for what he has done.[a] 15You too
should be on your guard against him,
because he strongly opposed our message.

16At my first defense, no one came to
my support, but everyone deserted me. 4:16
May it not be held against them.[b] 17But b Ac 7:60
the Lord stood at my side[c] and gave me 4:17
strength, so that through me the mes- c Ac 23:11
sage might be fully proclaimed and all d Ac 9:15
the Gentiles might hear it.[d] And I was
delivered from the lion's mouth. 18The
Lord will rescue me from every evil at- 4:18
tack[e] and will bring me safely to his e Ps 121:7
heavenly kingdom. To him be glory for f Ro 11:36
ever and ever. Amen.[f]

Final Greetings

19Greet Priscilla[a] and Aquila[g] and the 4:19 g Ac 18:2
household of Onesiphorus. 20Erastus[h] 4:20
stayed in Corinth, and I left Trophimus[i] h Ac 19:22
sick in Miletus. 21Do your best to get i Ac 20:4
here before winter.[j] Eubulus greets you, 4:21 j ver 9
and so do Pudens, Linus, Claudia and all
the brothers. 4:22

22The Lord be with your spirit.[k] Grace k Gal 6:18; Phm 25
be with you.[l] l Col 4:18

a 19 Greek *Prisca*, a variant of *Priscilla*

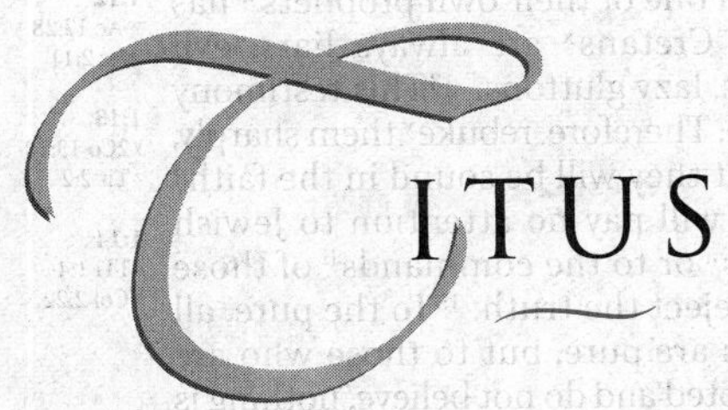

Has God's grace appeared to all people? (Titus 2:11)

- *Many individuals around the world have yet to hear about God's grace. But it has been given to every "kind" of person. Paul wrote about the new life possible because of that grace—no matter what race or class a person might belong to.*

What light does Titus shed on the issue of the second coming of Jesus? (Titus 2:13)

- *In the book of Titus Paul asserted that Jesus' second coming will be a visible event for all people to see (see also 1 Timothy 6:14; 2 Timothy 4:1,8; Revelation 1:7).*

Which controversies are foolish? (Titus 3:9)

- *Christians have always recognized a common core of beliefs about what is essential for salvation: faith in Jesus, repentance of sin and submission to the will of God. Paul expected Titus to defend these essentials (verses 5–8). Anything less significant is not worth fighting about, especially quarreling over who is "more spiritual" due to heritage or lifestyle.*

Jesus in Titus Paul's letter to Titus is filled with valuable lessons for Christians who desire to help a church grow toward spiritual maturity. Not as personal as the letters to Timothy, Titus reads like an instruction manual that requires little explanation. Paul's letters indicate that Titus was one of his trusted helpers and the leader of a quarrelsome church on the island of Crete. In this letter, Paul urged godly living in light of the "glorious appearing of our great God and Savior, Jesus Christ" (Titus 2:13). Jesus came the first time to "redeem" and "purify" us, and he is coming again to take us home to heaven.

Knowing God's truth leads to godliness (Titus 1:1), and it is in Jesus that God makes known to us who he is. Jesus came to rescue us from our sins and enable us to enter into a relationship with God (Titus 3:6). When we believe in Jesus Christ his Holy Spirit comes into our hearts to invigorate us with new life (verse 5), and knowing that we will be with him forever fills us with "blessed hope" (Titus 2:13).

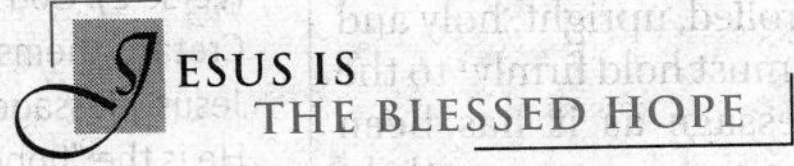

THE ULTIMATE AIM OF THE WORK OF CHRIST IS THAT THERE SHOULD BE A PEOPLE PREPARED FOR GOD . . . WHEN THIS TAKES PLACE, THE WORK OF CHRIST IS COMPLETE.

I. Howard Marshall,
University of Aberdeen, Scotland

1:1 [a] Ro 1:1 [b] 1Ti 2:4 1 Paul, a servant of God[a] and an
apostle of Jesus Christ for the faith
of God's elect and the knowledge of the
truth[b] that leads to godliness— 2 a faith
and knowledge resting on the hope of
1:2 [c] 2Ti 1:1 eternal life,[c] which God, who does not
[d] 2Ti 1:9 lie, promised before the beginning of
1:3 time,[d] 3 and at his appointed season[e] he
[e] 1Ti 2:6 brought his word to light[f] through the
[f] 2Ti 1:10 preaching entrusted to me[g] by the com-
[g] 1Ti 1:11 [h] Lk 1:47 mand of God our Savior,[h]

1:4 [i] 2Co 2:13 4 To Titus,[i] my true son in our common faith:

Grace and peace from God the Father
and Christ Jesus our Savior.

Titus's Task on Crete

1:5 5 The reason I left you in Crete[j] was
[j] Ac 27:7 that you might straighten out what was
[k] Ac 11:30 left unfinished and appoint[a] elders[k] in
every town, as I directed you. 6 An elder
1:6 [l] 1Ti 3:2 must be blameless,[l] the husband of but
one wife, a man whose children believe
and are not open to the charge of being
wild and disobedient. 7 Since an over-
1:7 [m] 1Ti 3:1 seer[b][m] is entrusted with God's work,[n] he
[n] 1Co 4:1 must be blameless—not overbearing,
[o] 1Ti 3:3,8 not quick-tempered, not given to drunkenness, not violent, not pursuing dishonest gain.[o] 8 Rather he must be hos-
1:8 [p] 1Ti 3:2 pitable,[p] one who loves what is good,[q]
[q] 2Ti 3:3 who is self-controlled, upright, holy and
disciplined. 9 He must hold firmly[r] to the
trustworthy message as it has been
1:9 taught, so that he can encourage others
[r] 1Ti 1:19 by sound doctrine[s] and refute those
[s] 1Ti 1:10 who oppose it.
10 For there are many rebellious peo-
1:10 [t] 1Ti 1:6 [u] 11:2 ple, mere talkers[t] and deceivers, especially those of the circumcision group.[u]
1:11 11 They must be silenced, because they
[v] 2Ti 3:6 are ruining whole households[v] by teaching things they ought not to teach—and
that for the sake of dishonest gain.
12 Even one of their own prophets[w] has 1:12
said, "Cretans[x] are always liars, evil [w] Ac 17:28 [x] Ac 2:11
brutes, lazy gluttons." 13 This testimony
is true. Therefore, rebuke[y] them sharply, 1:13 [y] 2Co 13:10
so that they will be sound in the faith[z] [z] Tit 2:2
14 and will pay no attention to Jewish 1:14
myths[a] or to the commands[b] of those [a] 1Ti 1:4
who reject the truth. 15 To the pure, all [b] Col 2:22
things are pure, but to those who are
corrupted and do not believe, nothing is
pure.[c] In fact, both their minds and con- 1:15 [c] Ro 14:14,23
sciences are corrupted. 16 They claim to
know God, but by their actions they 1:16
deny him.[d] They are detestable, disobe- [d] 1Jn 2:4
dient and unfit for doing anything good.

What Must Be Taught to Various Groups

2 You must teach what is in accord 2:1
with sound doctrine.[e] 2 Teach the [e] 1Ti 1:10
older men to be temperate, worthy of respect, self-controlled, and sound in 2:2
faith,[f] in love and in endurance. [f] Tit 1:13
3 Likewise, teach the older women to
be reverent in the way they live, not to be 2:3
slanderers or addicted to much wine,[g] [g] 1Ti 3:8
but to teach what is good. 4 Then they
can train the younger women to love
their husbands and children, 5 to be self-
controlled and pure, to be busy at home,
to be kind, and to be subject to their 2:5
husbands,[h] so that no one will malign [h] Eph 5:22
the word of God.[i] [i] 1Ti 6:1

[a] 5 Or *ordain* [b] 7 Traditionally *bishop*

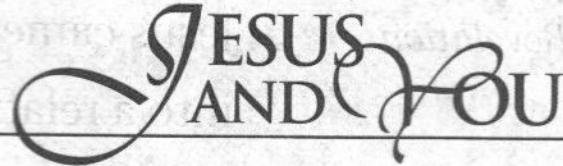

NO LIE

Lying was habitual for many of the people who lived on the island of Crete (Titus 1:12), and that fact is probably what prompted Paul in Titus to characterize God as the One who does not lie (verse 2). God's truth stood in sharp contrast to the Cretans themselves, as well as to their false gods. Jesus' message is different from that of the world. He is the "hope of eternal life" springing from truth (verse 2), because the verification of truth is that it "leads to godliness" (verse 1). Paul reminded Titus that the way he chose to live his life—whether or not he took God's word seriously—would determine whether or not others would accept that Jesus was truly God (Titus 2:1). The same is true for us today—people will believe our message only to the extent that it is confirmed by our lives (Matthew 5:14–16; 2 Corinthians 3:2–3).

DISCOVERY 336

Preparing for the Day

Many people are fascinated by examining the signs of the times and enjoy speculating about the identity of the "antichrist." Many are intrigued by discussions about Israel, Europe and the "global village" or find themselves energized by conversations centered around the potential for computer technology and a cashless society—and although the details of the conversations and speculations have changed, we are no different in this regard from the first disciples. They had spent three years with Jesus, walking with him and learning from him. They had observed his miracles and were witnesses to his horrible death and glorious resurrection. They had been with him on the Mount of Olives as he ascended into heaven (Acts 1:9–11).

These devotees had been at their Master's side throughout the time of his ministry on earth, and yet before Jesus returned to heaven they had only one question: "Lord, are you at this time going to restore the kingdom to Israel?" (Acts 1:6). The disciples wanted to know precisely when Jesus would fulfill the Old Testament predictions about a kingdom on earth. After everything they had seen, after all the painstaking instruction Jesus had conferred upon them, they were most interested in what was still to come rather than in what they should do in the present. The disciples overlooked their immediate responsibilities in favor of speculation about the future.

We know that Jesus is coming back for his people, and we look forward to that day. Many times, however, we focus inordinate attention on details of a future we cannot know and in the process ignore the truths we can learn and live in the here and now. Knowing that Jesus will one day return should be incentive enough for holy living. We must learn to say no to ungodliness and worldly passions in order that we might live each day the life to which our Lord has called us—in a self-controlled, upright and godly manner (Titus 2:12–14).

If we knew in advance that Jesus' second coming were to take place this evening, we would undoubtedly very carefully orchestrate tonight's activities to ensure that we would be engaged in God-honoring pursuits throughout the course of the evening. If we had advance notice that Jesus would return one year from now, we would most assuredly get our affairs in order. What we forget is that this very second might be the moment of the glorious appearing this world has so long awaited.

When Jesus returns he is going to ask for an accounting of the lives we have led (Romans 14:12; 1 Corinthians 4:2–5; 2 Corinthians 5:10). Some of us will find ourselves embarrassed by the haphazard manner in which we have managed his affairs. Some of us will regret our life decisions. But we can prepare for Jesus' return every day we live. There are relationships in need of repair, sins in need of confession, tasks in need of accomplishment and people in need of attention. Knowing that Jesus is coming back should be a powerful motivation for holy living.

Self-Discovery: *In what ways does your knowledge and anticipation of Jesus' glorious return affect your day-to-day living? How would you be likely to live differently if you held no belief in an afterlife?*

GO TO DISCOVERY 337 ON PAGE 1637

2:6 6Similarly, encourage the young men[j]
j 1Ti 5:1 to be self-controlled. 7In everything set
2:7 them an example[k] by doing what is
k 1Ti 4:12 good. In your teaching show integrity,
seriousness 8and soundness of speech
that cannot be condemned, so that
those who oppose you may be ashamed
2:8 because they have nothing bad to say
l 1Pe 2:12 about us.[l]
9Teach slaves to be subject to their
2:9 m Eph 6:5 masters in everything,[m] to try to please
them, not to talk back to them, 10and
not to steal from them, but to show that
they can be fully trusted, so that in every
2:10 way they will make the teaching about
n Mt 5:16 God our Savior attractive.[n]
11For the grace of God that brings sal-
2:11 o 1Ti 2:4 vation has appeared to all men.[o] 12It
teaches us to say "No" to ungodliness
2:12 p Tit 3:3 and worldly passions,[p] and to live self-
q 2Ti 3:12 controlled, upright and godly lives[q] in
this present age, 13while we wait for the
blessed hope—the glorious appearing of
2:13 r 2Pe 1:1 our great God and Savior, Jesus Christ,[r]
14who gave himself for us to redeem us
2:14 from all wickedness and to purify for
s Ex 19:5 himself a people that are his very own,[s]
t Eph 2:10 eager to do what is good.[t]
15These, then, are the things you
should teach. Encourage and rebuke
with all authority. Do not let anyone despise you.

Doing What Is Good

3 Remind the people to be subject
3:1 u Ro 13:1 to rulers and authorities,[u] to be
v 2Ti 2:21 obedient, to be ready to do whatever is
good,[v] 2to slander no one,[w] to be peace-
3:2 w Eph 4:31; 2Ti 2:24 able and considerate, and to show true
humility toward all men.
3At one time we too were foolish, disobedient, deceived and enslaved by all
kinds of passions and pleasures. We
lived in malice and envy, being hated
3:4 and hating one another. 4But when the
x Eph 2:7 kindness[x] and love of God our Savior ap-
y Tit 2:11 peared,[y] 5he saved us, not because of
3:5 righteous things we had done,[z] but be-
z Eph 2:9 cause of his mercy. He saved us through
a Ro 12:2 the washing of rebirth and renewal[a] by
3:6 the Holy Spirit, 6whom he poured out on
b Ro 5:5 us[b] generously through Jesus Christ our
Savior, 7so that, having been justified by

his grace,[c] we might become heirs[d] hav- 3:7
ing the hope[e] of eternal life.[f] 8This is a c Ro 3:24
trustworthy saying.[g] And I want you to d Ro 8:17 e Ro 8:24
stress these things, so that those who f Tit 1:2
have trusted in God may be careful to 3:8
devote themselves to doing what is g 1Ti 1:15
good.[h] These things are excellent and h Tit 2:14
profitable for everyone.
9But avoid foolish controversies and
genealogies and arguments and quar-
rels[i] about the law, because these are un- 3:9 i 1Ti 1:4;
profitable and useless. 10Warn a divisive 2Ti 2:14
person once, and then warn him a sec-
ond time. After that, have nothing to do
with him.[j] 11You may be sure that such a 3:10 j Ro 16:17
man is warped and sinful; he is self-con-
demned.

Final Remarks

12As soon as I send Artemas or Tych-
icus[k] to you, do your best to come to me 3:12 k Ac 20:4
at Nicopolis, because I have decided to l 2Ti 4:9,21
winter there.[l] 13Do everything you can 3:13
to help Zenas the lawyer and Apollos[m] m Ac 18:24
on their way and see that they have
everything they need. 14Our people
must learn to devote themselves to do-
ing what is good,[n] in order that they may 3:14 n ver 8
provide for daily necessities and not live
unproductive lives.
15Everyone with me sends you greetings. Greet those who love us in the 3:15
faith.[o] o 1Ti 1:2
Grace be with you all.[p] p Col 4:18

THE GOD OF SALVATION

Although Paul's letter to Titus has an instructive tone, it explains truth in a practical way. For example, Paul referred to "God our Savior" in Titus 3:4 and to "Jesus Christ our Savior" in verse 6, connecting the Father and the Son as active participants in our salvation. Paul further stated that God's Holy Spirit makes our lives clean and new, demonstrating that he too is directly involved in the process (verse 5). The triune God of salvation is actively at work in our lives, continually transforming us to make us more and more like himself (Romans 8:29; 2 Corinthians 3:18).

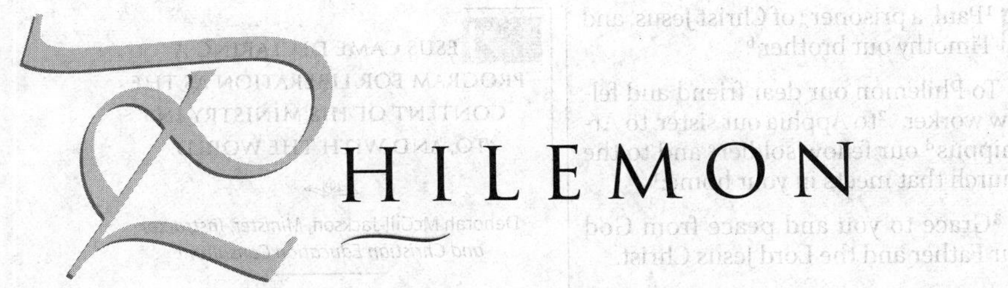
PHILEMON

Why did Paul call Onesimus his son? (Philemon 10)

♦ *Probably because Paul had introduced Onesimus to faith in Jesus, thereby making him his "spiritual son."*

How had Onesimus been useless? (Philemon 11)

♦ *Onesimus had probably not been a model servant. Paul admitted that he may have cheated Philemon or owed him money (verse 18). Onesimus, meaning "useful," was a common name for a slave. But in this case Useful had been closer to useless. Now that he knew Jesus, however, Onesimus would be true to his name.*

Why didn't Paul help a runaway slave to escape? (Philemon 12)

♦ *Paul sent Onesimus back to his master—and possibly back to punishment. Paul neither condemned nor condoned slavery, but he wanted to see changed relationships based on faith in Jesus—master and slave treating one another as brothers in our Lord Jesus Christ. In addition, Paul may have been suggesting that true repentance entails facing the past, not running away from it.*

Jesus in Philemon C. S. Lewis made a profound statement about forgiveness: "Everyone says that forgiveness is a wonderful idea, until he has something to forgive." The book of Philemon teaches an unforgettable lesson about grace. Paul addressed this letter to Philemon, owner of a runaway slave Onesimus, who had become a Christian, possibly after sharing a jail cell with Paul.

In Paul's day most runaway slaves, if caught, faced harsh punishment or even death. Paul hoped that Philemon would become a living illustration of the grace Onesimus had already received through Jesus. Paul identified with Onesimus as a slave because Paul considered himself to be a "prisoner" of Jesus (Philemon 1,23). It was on that basis that Paul asked Philemon to accept Onesimus back—not as a slave but as a brother (verse 16). Because of the work of Jesus, slave and slave owner could meet on common ground. Jesus is the great emancipator who sets us all free from the bondage of sin and heals broken relationships—including relationships between people from radically different backgrounds and social situations.

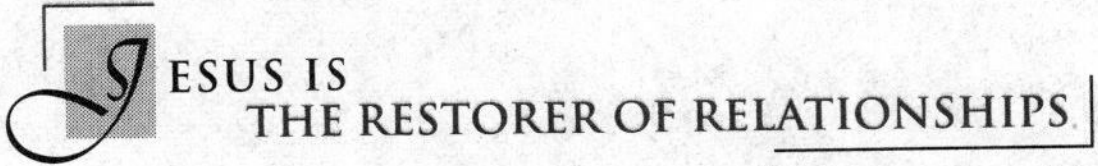
JESUS IS
THE RESTORER OF RELATIONSHIPS

1:1 [a]ver 9,23; 1 Paul, a prisoner[a] of Christ Jesus, and
Eph 3:1 Timothy our brother,[b]
[b]2Co 1:1
[c]Php 2:25 To Philemon our dear friend and fellow worker,[c] 2 to Apphia our sister, to Ar-
1:2 [d]Col 4:17 chippus[d] our fellow soldier[e] and to the
[e]Php 2:25 church that meets in your home:[f]
[f]Ro 16:5

3 Grace to you and peace from God
our Father and the Lord Jesus Christ.

Thanksgiving and Prayer

1:4 [g]Ro 1:8 4 I always thank my God[g] as I remember you in my prayers, 5 because I hear
about your faith in the Lord Jesus and
1:5 [h]Eph 1:15; your love for all the saints.[h] 6 I pray that
Col 1:4 you may be active in sharing your faith,
so that you will have a full understanding of every good thing we have in
Christ. 7 Your love has given me great joy
1:7 and encouragement,[i] because you,
[i]2Co 7:4,13 brother, have refreshed[j] the hearts of the
[j]ver 20 saints.

Paul's Plea for Onesimus

8 Therefore, although in Christ I could
be bold and order you to do what you
ought to do, 9 yet I appeal to you on the
1:9 basis of love. I then, as Paul—an old man
[k]ver 1,23 and now also a prisoner[k] of Christ
1:10 Jesus— 10 I appeal to you for my son[l]
[l]1Co 4:15 Onesimus,[a][m] who became my son while
[m]Col 4:9 I was in chains. 11 Formerly he was useless to you, but now he has become useful both to you and to me.

12 I am sending him—who is my very
heart—back to you. 13 I would have liked
to keep him with me so that he could
take your place in helping me while I am
in chains for the gospel. 14 But I did not
want to do anything without your con-
1:14 sent, so that any favor you do will be
[n]2Co 9:7; 1Pe 5:2 spontaneous and not forced.[n] 15 Perhaps

> JESUS CAME DECLARING A PROGRAM FOR LIBERATION AS THE CONTENT OF HIS MINISTRY IN, TO, AND WITH THE WORLD.
>
> 
>
> Deborah McGill-Jackson, *Minister, Instructor and Christian Education Consultant*

the reason he was separated from you
for a little while was that you might have
him back for good— 16 no longer as a
slave, but better than a slave, as a dear
brother.[o] He is very dear to me but even 1:16 [o]Mt 23:8;
dearer to you, both as a man and as a 1Ti 6:2
brother in the Lord.

17 So if you consider me a partner,[p] 1:17
welcome him as you would welcome [p]2Co 8:23
me. 18 If he has done you any wrong or
owes you anything, charge it to me. 19 I,
Paul, am writing this with my own hand.
I will pay it back—not to mention that
you owe me your very self. 20 I do wish,
brother, that I may have some benefit 1:20
from you in the Lord; refresh[q] my heart [q]ver 7
in Christ. 21 Confident[r] of your obedi- 1:21
ence, I write to you, knowing that you [r]2Co 2:3
will do even more than I ask.

22 And one thing more: Prepare a 1:22
guest room for me, because I hope to be[s] [s]Php 1:25; 2:24
restored to you in answer to your [t]2Co 1:11
prayers.[t]

23 Epaphras,[u] my fellow prisoner in 1:23 [u]Col 1:7
Christ Jesus, sends you greetings. 24 And 1:24
so do Mark,[v] Aristarchus,[w] Demas[x] and [v]Ac 12:12
Luke, my fellow workers. [w]Ac 19:29 [x]Col 4:14

25 The grace of the Lord Jesus Christ
be with your spirit.[y] 1:25 [y]2Ti 4:22

[a] 10 *Onesimus* means *useful.*

Neither Slave Nor Free

A major social injustice during the first century A.D. was slavery. The New Testament does not have a great deal to say about the problem, but what it does state is clear and insightful. Paul's letter to Philemon provides us with help for living a godly life even when we are suffering oppression, and it teaches the church how to address issues of social injustice.

The first fact we learn is somewhat surprising to our modern, sensitized ears: that Paul deemed it fitting and proper for slaves to obey their masters. In another letter he emphasized that they would be honoring God if they were to do so "with respect and fear, and with sincerity of heart, just as [they] would obey Christ" (Ephesians 6:5). Even though they were bound in slavery, they could enjoy freedom in terms of their relationship with God.

Paul's purpose in writing to Philemon was not to promote or defend the institution of slavery. His instruction was to people who were powerless to change either their societal situation or the laws of the Roman empire. What he did assert is that working hard will demonstrate to others that we are devoted to Jesus and will in turn attract them to his love.

While Paul was in Rome he became acquainted with Onesimus, a runaway slave who had since given his life to Jesus. The law of the time stipulated that a slave could be executed for running away, because he was in essence stealing himself from his master. The apostle knew Philemon, Onesimus's master, and he sent the slave back home—with a letter. What Paul had written represented a revolutionary break from the traditional reasoning of his time! This letter called for a radical upheaval in terms of the relationship between owners and their slaves. Paul urged Philemon to accept Onesimus back "as a dear brother . . . a brother in the Lord"! (Philemon 15–16). A runaway slave, worthy of death, accepted back as a *brother*? Paul understood that once we have given our lives to Jesus we are all brothers and sisters in Jesus Christ. In him "there is neither Jew nor Greek, slave nor free, male nor female, for [we] are all one in Christ Jesus" (Galatians 3:28).

The United States cannot boast an unblemished past. We, like the Romans, promoted the lucrative business of slavery for hundreds of years—and God's people turned a blind eye to the injustice while they reaped the financial rewards. Even within churches slaves were forced to sit apart. In some instances they were compelled to stand outside during worship services. Jesus Christ has shown us a way of life that extends his love and acceptance indiscriminately, to all people. Rather than mindlessly accepting the mores of society, we as believers must consciously reflect the mind of Jesus Christ (Philippians 2:5), imitating his attitude of self-sacrificing humility and gentle compassion."

Self-Discovery: *Identify an area in which you have become so accustomed to society's values that you have turned a blind eye to injustice. Ask God to sensitize your heart and help you to do what you can to right the situation.*

GO TO DISCOVERY 338 ON PAGE 1641

HEBREWS

What is Jesus' relationship to God? (Hebrews 1:3)

♦ *Jesus Is God in the flesh. He brought the character and majesty of God to a human body, even though God is spirit (John 4:24). At the same time, Jesus willingly stripped himself of the privileges of deity (Philippians 2:1–11). Jesus in human form was both God and man—two distinct natures united in one person.*

Why did Jesus have to be made perfect? (Hebrews 2:10)

♦ *This does not mean there was a time when Jesus wasn't perfect. It simply points to the completion of his assignment. "Make . . . perfect" means to bring to the rightful or appointed end. By suffering and dying on the cross, the perfect Son of God became our perfect Savior, opening the way to God.*

Why does Jesus appear for us in God's presence? (Hebrews 9:24)

♦ *Like the Old Testament priest who offered blood on behalf of the people, Jesus appears before God to offer his blood as the price for our sins. Other Biblical pictures of what Jesus does for us in God's presence include that of an advocate or defense attorney (1 John 2:1–2) and that of an intercessor (Romans 8:34).*

Jesus in Hebrews The book of Hebrews offers encouragement for those facing frustrations, obstacles and temptations. Hebrews is like a coach's pep talk at half time, acknowledging pitfalls and encouraging believers to keep going in the faith. Look for the words *better* and *superior* as the author compares Jesus to many other people.

No one knows the author or intended audience for this book. Yet it is apparent that the reading audience had heard about Jesus through people who had known him personally and that their faith had resulted in persecution. Still there was something about their spiritual behavior that bothered the author, and he periodically interrupted his arguments to sharply warn his readers.

Look for the vivid Old Testament images used in Hebrews to illustrate what God has done through Jesus Christ, and note the contrasts between the Old Testament rituals and New Testament faith. Jesus is shown as the ultimate sacrifice who ushered in a "better covenant" (Hebrews 7:22) between God and his people. Notice the emotional appeals to Jewish believers to stay committed to the new covenant rather than reverting back to the old.

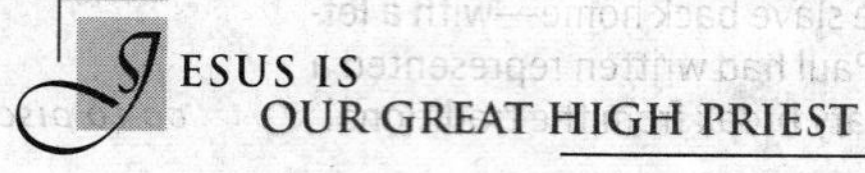

JESUS IS OUR GREAT HIGH PRIEST

Titles of Jesus in Hebrews

Jesus, the Messiah, is greater than all the people, practices and procedures of the Old Testament, and the author of Hebrews explains how true that is. Jesus is the Son of God, the "radiance of God's glory," and he represents the Father exactly (Hebrews 1:3). Because of that, Jesus is greater than the angels (1:5–14) and greater than Moses (3:3). In fact, Jesus is God's ultimate "apostle" (3:1). He is our great high priest (4:14) and an "anchor for the soul" (6:19). While the animal sacrifices of the Old Testament were temporary, Jesus' death set up a permanent way whereby we could have a relationship with God (7:24). Jesus himself makes a "new covenant" between us and God (9:15). Jesus is the "author and perfecter of our faith" (12:2), meaning that our faith has its starting point and its ending point in him as we "in all things grow up into him who is the Head" (Ephesians 4:15). He is also the one who never changes (13:8). There are at least 25 word pictures used of Jesus in the book of Hebrews.

1. Son of God	1:2–8; 6:6; 10:29
2. Heir of All Things	1:2
3. Radiance of God's Glory	1:3
4. Exact Representation of God's Being	1:3
5. Superior to the Angels	1:4–14
6. "O God"	1:8
7. Crowned with Glory and Honor	2:9
8. Author of Salvation	2:10
9. Merciful and Faithful High Priest	2:17
10. Apostle and High Priest	3:1
11. Faithful Son Over God's House	3:6
12. Great High Priest	4:14
13. Priest Forever, in the Order of Melchizedek	5:6; 6:20; 7:1–17
14. Anchor for the Soul	6:19
15. Guarantee of a Better Covenant	7:22
16. Permanent Priest	7:24
17. "Holy, Blameless, Pure"	7:26
18. One Seated in Heaven	8:1; 10:12
19. Mediator of the New Covenant	8:6; 9:15; 12:24
20. Ransom for our Sins	9:15
21. Great High Priest Over the House of God	10:21
22. He Who Is Coming	10:37
23. Author and Perfecter of our Faith	12:2
24. Same Yesterday, Today and Forever	13:8
25. Great Shepherd of the Sheep	13:20

The Son Superior to Angels

1:1 a Jn 9:29; **1** In the past God spoke[a] to our
Heb 2:2,3 forefathers through the prophets[b]
b Ac 2:30 at many times and in various ways,[c] 2but
c Nu 12:6,8 in these last days he has spoken to us by
1:2 his Son, whom he appointed heir[d] of all
d Ps 2:8 e Jn 1:3 things, and through whom[e] he made the
1:3 universe. 3The Son is the radiance of
f Jn 1:14 God's glory[f] and the exact representa-
g Col 1:17 tion of his being, sustaining all things[g]
h Heb 7:27 by his powerful word. After he had pro-
i Mk 16:19 vided purification for sins,[h] he sat down
at the right hand of the Majesty in heav-
en.[i] 4So he became as much superior to
1:4 the angels as the name he has inherited
j Eph 1:21; Php 2:9,10 is superior to theirs.[j]

5For to which of the angels did God ever say,

"You are my Son;
1:5 k Ps 2:7 today I have become your
l 2Sa 7:14 Father[a]"[b]?[k]

Or again,

"I will be his Father,
and he will be my Son"[c]?[l]

1:6 6And again, when God brings his first-
m Heb 10:5 born into the world,[m] he says,
n Dt 32:43 (LXX and DSS); Ps 97:7

"Let all God's angels worship him."[d][n]

7In speaking of the angels he says,

1:7 o Ps 104:4 "He makes his angels winds,
his servants flames of fire."[e][o]

8But about the Son he says,

"Your throne, O God, will last for
ever and ever,
and righteousness will be the
scepter of your kingdom.
9You have loved righteousness and
hated wickedness;
therefore God, your God, has set
you above your
companions[p] 1:9 p Php 2:9
by anointing you with the oil[q] of q Isa 61:1,3
joy."[f]

10He also says,

"In the beginning, O Lord, you laid
the foundations of the earth,
and the heavens are the work of
your hands.
11They will perish, but you remain;
they will all wear out like a
garment.[r] 1:11 r Isa 34:4
12You will roll them up like a robe;
like a garment they will be
changed.
But you remain the same,[s] 1:12 s Heb 13:8
and your years will never end."[g][t] t Ps 102:25-27

13To which of the angels did God ever say,

"Sit at my right hand 1:13 u Jos 10:24;
until I make your enemies Heb 10:13
a footstool[u] for your feet"[h]?[v] v Ps 110:1

14Are not all angels ministering spirits[w] 1:14 w Ps 103:20
sent to serve those who will inherit sal- x Heb 5:9
vation?[x]

Warning to Pay Attention

2 We must pay more careful attention, therefore, to what we have
heard, so that we do not drift away. 2For 2:2
if the message spoken[y] by angels[z] was y Heb 1:1
binding, and every violation and disobe- z Dt 33:2; Ac 7:53
dience received its just punishment,[a] a Heb 10:28
3how shall we escape if we ignore such a 2:3
great salvation?[b] This salvation, which b Heb 10:29
was first announced by the Lord,[c] was c Heb 1:2
confirmed to us by those who heard d Lk 1:2
him.[d] 4God also testified to it by signs,

[a] 5 Or *have begotten you* [b] 5 Psalm 2:7
[c] 5 2 Samuel 7:14; 1 Chron. 17:13 [d] 6 Deut. 32:43 (see Dead Sea Scrolls and Septuagint)
[e] 7 Psalm 104:4 [f] 9 Psalm 45:6,7
[g] 12 Psalm 102:25–27 [h] 13 Psalm 110:1

BY HIS POWER THE UNIVERSE IS HELD TOGETHER, AND WITHOUT HIM THE UNIVERSE HAS NO MEANING. HE IS THE CENTERPIECE OF HUMANKIND.

Rev. Jerry Falwell, *Chancellor, Liberty University, Lynchburg, Virginia*

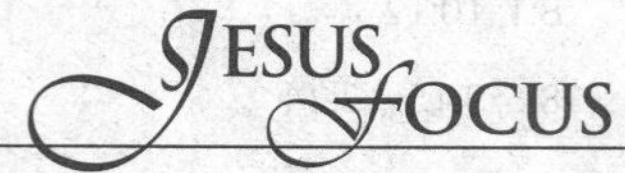

JESUS IS GOD

The book of Hebrews opens with a powerful statement of Jesus' deity. The author quoted from selected psalms to verify for Jewish readers that Jesus is no mere human being but indeed the Messiah, the very Son of God (Hebrews 1:3). These verses include Psalm 2:7, Psalm 45:6–7 and Psalm 110:1. Jesus' claim to be God is essential to his other claims because if he had not been divine he could not have offered himself as a perfect sacrifice, capable of saving us from our sins.

Jesus Is Superior

The theme of the entire book of Hebrews is the supremacy and sufficiency of Jesus Christ as revealer and mediator of God's grace. Hebrews could indeed be called "the book of better things," since the two Greek words for *better* and *superior* occur 15 times within this letter. The prologue (Hebrews 1:1–4) presents Jesus as God's full and final revelation, infinitely superior to God's prophets who spoke the Father's truth in the Old Testament (verse 1).

The writer of Hebrews made seven statements about Jesus that explain the ways in which our Lord is greater than anyone else who had gone before, and these statements set the tone for the entire book: 1. Jesus was appointed heir of all things (verse 2). 2. He is the One through whom God the Father made the universe (verse 2). 3. He embodies the radiance of God's glory (verse 3). 4. He exactly represents God's being (verse 3). 5. He keeps all things integrated and functioning (verse 3). 6. His death purifies us from our sin (verse 3). 7. He sat down in the place of honor next to God the Father (verse 3).

The writer of Hebrews went on to specify over whom and over what Jesus is superior: First, Jesus is more excellent than the angels (verse 4). Angels are mystifying, intriguing beings. But the primary accountability of the angels is to serve as God's messengers, and the One who created them is infinitely superior to them in power.

Jesus is also greater than Moses (Hebrews 3:1–6). Moses was a renowned leader of the people of Israel, and the Biblical writers mention him again and again as an example of faithful perseverance. But Jesus is incomparably greater; he is the One who leads his people to eternal salvation and rest.

God ordained the institution of the Old Testament priesthood in order to provide a way for the sins of his people to be forgiven. Because God had appointed them as mediators, the priests were the only ones permitted to offer sacrifices and to carry out ministry in the temple. But Jesus is superior to the priesthood (Hebrews 7:26–27). He is the final and consummate priest who, with one swipe of his divine eraser, whisked away the sins of humanity forever.

Finally, Jesus is superior to the old covenant (Hebrews 9:11–14). God's promise has never changed. He pledged to make Abraham's family into a great nation that would bring honor to God among all people everywhere (Genesis 12:1–3). And he did just that. But the new covenant through God's Son Jesus is one that will last forever, and it completes everything God had been teaching his people through the first covenant. The benediction near the end of Hebrews speaks of this covenant and provides a fitting conclusion to the letter: "May the God of peace, who through the blood of the eternal covenant brought back from the dead our Lord Jesus, that great shepherd of the sheep, equip you with everything good for doing his will, and may he work is us whatever is pleasing to him, through Jesus Christ, to whom be glory forever and ever. Amen" (Hebrews 13:20–21).

***Self-Discovery:** Beyond the wonderful gift of salvation, list some specific ways in which your life is better because of your fellowship with Jesus Christ than it would have been had you not known him personally.*

GO TO DISCOVERY 339 ON PAGE 1644

2:4 [e] Jn 4:48 [f] 1Co 12:4 [g] Eph 1:5

wonders and various miracles,[e] and gifts of the Holy Spirit[f] distributed according to his will.[g]

Jesus Made Like His Brothers

5 It is not to angels that he has subjected the world to come, about which we are speaking. 6 But there is a place where someone has testified:

> "What is man that you are mindful
> of him,
> the son of man that you care for
> him?[h]
> 7 You made him a little[a] lower than
> the angels;
> you crowned him with glory and
> honor
> 8 and put everything under his
> feet."[b] [i]

2:6 [h] Job 7:17

2:8 [i] Ps 8:4-6; 1Co 15:25

In putting everything under him, God left nothing that is not subject to him. Yet at present we do not see everything subject to him. 9 But we see Jesus, who was made a little lower than the angels, now crowned with glory and honor[j] because he suffered death,[k] so that by the grace of God he might taste death for everyone.[l]

2:9 [j] Ac 2:33; 3:13; Php 2:9 [k] Php 2:7-9 [l] Jn 3:16; 2Co 5:15

10 In bringing many sons to glory, it was fitting that God, for whom and through whom everything exists,[m] should make the author of their salvation perfect through suffering.[n] 11 Both the one who makes men holy and those who are made holy[o] are of the same family. So Jesus is not ashamed to call them brothers.[p] 12 He says,

2:10 [m] Ro 11:36 [n] Lk 24:26; Heb 7:28

2:11 [o] Heb 10:10 [p] Mt 28:10; Jn 20:17

JESUS FOCUS

AUTHOR OF OUR SALVATION

Hebrews 2:10 refers to Jesus as the "author" of our salvation. The Greek word *archegos* can also mean a prince or leader. Jesus designed, engineered and planned what it would take to save us from the consequences of our sins. All that we will ever need comes from him. It's ironic, however, that the cure for sin had to involve suffering—his own. Because our Savior died on the cross for our sins we can enjoy an intimate and permanent relationship with God the Father. Jesus' suffering as God's Son completed and perfected his humanity, because in his suffering he identified with us on the deepest level of our human experience.

> "I will declare your name to my
> brothers;
> in the presence of the
> congregation I will sing
> your praises."[c] [q]

2:12 [q] Ps 22:22

13 And again,

> "I will put my trust in him."[d] [r]

And again he says,

> "Here am I, and the children God
> has given me."[e] [s]

2:13 [r] Isa 8:17 [s] Isa 8:18; Jn 10:29

THE HEART AND CENTER OF THIS WONDERFUL PLAN OF REDEMPTION IS JESUS CHRIST.

William Hendriksen, *Professor, Calvin Theological Seminary, Grand Rapids, Michigan*

14 Since the children have flesh and blood, he too shared in their humanity[t] so that by his death he might destroy[u] him who holds the power of death—that is, the devil[v]— 15 and free those who all their lives were held in slavery by their fear[w] of death. 16 For surely it is not angels he helps, but Abraham's descendants. 17 For this reason he had to be made like his brothers[x] in every way, in order that he might become a merciful[y] and faithful high priest[z] in service to God,[a] and that he might make atonement for[f] the sins of the people. 18 Because he himself suffered when he was tempted, he is able to help those who are being tempted.[b]

2:14 [t] Jn 1:14 [u] 1Co 15:54-57; 2Ti 1:10 [v] 1Jn 3:8

2:15 [w] 2Ti 1:7

2:17 [x] Php 2:7 [y] Heb 5:2 [z] Heb 4:14,15; 7:26,28 [a] Heb 5:1

2:18 [b] Heb 4:15

Jesus Greater Than Moses

3 Therefore, holy brothers,[c] who share in the heavenly calling, fix your thoughts on Jesus, the apostle and high priest[d] whom we confess.[e] 2 He was faithful to the one who appointed him, just as Moses was faithful in all God's house.[f] 3 Jesus has been found worthy of greater honor than Moses, just as the builder of a house has greater honor than the house itself. 4 For every house is built by someone, but God is the builder of everything. 5 Moses was faithful as a

3:1 [c] Heb 2:11 [d] Heb 2:17 [e] Heb 4:14

3:2 [f] Nu 12:7

[a] 7 Or *him for a little while*; also in verse 9
[b] 8 Psalm 8:4–6
[c] 12 Psalm 22:22
[d] 13 Isaiah 8:17
[e] 13 Isaiah 8:18
[f] 17 Or *and that he might turn aside God's wrath, taking away*

3:5 [g]Ex 14:31 servant[g] in all God's house,[h] testifying to
[h]ver 2; Nu 12:7 what would be said in the future. [6]But
Christ is faithful as a son[i] over God's
3:6 [i]Heb 1:2 house. And we are his house,[j] if we hold
[j]1Co 3:16 on[k] to our courage and the hope[l] of
[k]Ro 11:22 [l]Ro 5:2 which we boast.

Warning Against Unbelief

3:7 [m]Heb 9:8 [7]So, as the Holy Spirit says:[m]

"Today, if you hear his voice,
[8] do not harden your hearts
as you did in the rebellion,
during the time of testing in the desert,
[9]where your fathers tested and tried me
and for forty years saw what I
3:9 [n]Ac 7:36 did.[n]
[10]That is why I was angry with that generation,
and I said, 'Their hearts are always going astray,
and they have not known my ways.'
[11]So I declared on oath in my anger,
3:11 [o]Heb 4:3,5 'They shall never enter my
[p]Ps 95:7-11 rest.' "[o][a][p]

[12]See to it, brothers, that none of you
has a sinful, unbelieving heart that turns
away from the living God. [13]But encour-
3:13 [q]Heb 10:24,25 age one another daily,[q] as long as it is
[r]Eph 4:22 called Today, so that none of you may be
hardened by sin's deceitfulness.[r] [14]We
have come to share in Christ if we hold
3:14 [s]ver 6 firmly[s] till the end the confidence we
had at first. [15]As has just been said:

"Today, if you hear his voice,
do not harden your hearts 3:15 [t]ver 7,8;
as you did in the rebellion."[b][t] Ps 95:7,8

[16]Who were they who heard and rebelled? Were they not all those Moses
led out of Egypt?[u] [17]And with whom 3:16 [u]Nu 14:2
was he angry for forty years? Was it not
with those who sinned, whose bodies 3:17 [v]Nu 14:29;
fell in the desert?[v] [18]And to whom did Ps 106:26
God swear that they would never enter
his rest[w] if not to those who dis- 3:18 [w]Nu 14:20-23
obeyed[c]?[x] [19]So we see that they were [x]Heb 4:6
not able to enter, because of their unbelief.[y] 3:19 [y]Jn 3:36

A Sabbath-Rest for the People of God

4 Therefore, since the promise of
entering his rest still stands, let us
be careful that none of you be found to
have fallen short of it.[z] [2]For we also have 4:1 [z]Heb 12:15
had the gospel preached to us, just as
they did; but the message they heard
was of no value to them, because those
who heard did not combine it with 4:2
faith.[d][a] [3]Now we who have believed en- [a]1Th 2:13
ter that rest, just as God has said,

"So I declared on oath in my anger,
'They shall never enter my 4:3 [b]Ps 95:11;
rest.' "[e][b] Heb 3:11

And yet his work has been finished since
the creation of the world. [4]For somewhere he has spoken about the seventh
day in these words: "And on the seventh

[a] *11* Psalm 95:7-11 [b] *15* Psalm 95:7,8 [c] *18* Or *disbelieved* [d] *2* Many manuscripts *because they did not share in the faith of those who obeyed* [e] *3* Psalm 95:11; also in verse 5

JESUS FOCUS

APOSTLE AND HIGH PRIEST

No one is greater than Jesus, and no one has a more significant role or holds a higher position than he does. Hebrews 3:1 identifies Jesus as both apostle and high priest. In this way he holds the highest position of both Testaments. In the Old Testament the high priests represented God's people when they offered animal sacrifices for their sins (Exodus 29), while in the New Testament the apostles were sent by God to declare his message of salvation from sin. Even the word *apostle* means "one who is sent," and Jesus had made clear to his disciples that the Father had sent him (see Matthew 10:40; Mark 9:37; Luke 9:48; John 5:24; 17:8,21).

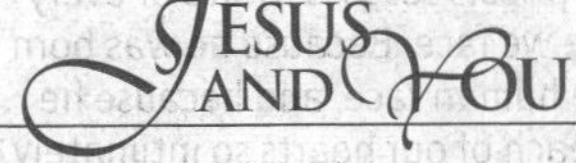

SIN-FREE

When Satan tried to tempt Jesus to turn against God the Father, Jesus resisted and defeated him (Matthew 4:1–11). But because Jesus was tempted he is able to identify with our human weaknesses. There is a basic difference, however, between Jesus' temptations and ours. He experienced every kind of temptation we face, and yet he endured it without sinning (Hebrews 4:15). We, on the other hand, frequently succumb to the pressure. The fact that Jesus did not sin assures us that he is greater than all our sin. Any hope we have of resisting temptation derives from his strength, not from our own effort.

Our Compassionate High Priest

Even though God had selected the Old Testament priests and conferred on them the privilege and responsibility of offering sacrifices on behalf of the people, they were still under obligation to follow his guidelines. The high priest was permitted to enter the Most Holy Place only once each year, on the Day of Atonement. On that day he would stand before the "atonement cover," or "mercy seat" of God, the place God had designated as the solemn setting for symbolizing the substitutionary atonement he had provided for the sins of his people and the total removal of their guilt. The priest had to pass through two other areas of the temple in order to reach the Most Holy Place—the Outer Court and the Holy Place. First, he was required to offer a sacrifice for his own sin. Only then could he be entitled to sacrifice for the sins of the people (Leviticus 16; Hebrews 5:1–3).

But God's Son was different. He came to be both our high priest *and* the sacrifice. In his role of priest Jesus is altogether superior to the Old Testament priesthood (Hebrews 4:14—7:28). Jesus is able to "sympathize" with us as no other priest could (Hebrews 4:15). Unlike the Old Testament priests Jesus is aware of every struggle we face. Because he was born into the human race, and because he knows each of our hearts so intimately, he can identify with our human weaknesses. Although he never succumbed to temptation, Jesus knew firsthand what it was like to face testing. This doesn't of course indicate that Jesus encountered every facet of every temptation known to humanity. It does signify that he was tempted in each of three major areas—the cravings we experience in our bodies, our human tendency toward self-seeking ambition, and the enticement to boast about what we have and do (Matthew 4:1–11; 1 John 2:16). The specifics of the temptations we face may be different, but they still fall within the same broad categories, and Jesus knows how relentless the temptation to turn away from God can be.

Jesus is also the only priest who can usher us directly into the presence of God the Father. After Jesus' death the curtain that separated the Most Holy Place from the rest of the temple was torn down the middle (Mark 15:38); this signified that God was no longer unapproachable and that through Jesus we can all, in a sense, walk right up to him and find a warm welcome and a gentle embrace (Hebrews 4:16).

Most of the major religions of our world teach that God resides at a great distance from us and that approaching him can only be done with great apprehension and trembling. The good news of Jesus Christ is that we can come *boldly* and *directly* into the presence of God to solicit his aid. Far from being remote or aloof, he is standing right beside us, ready to offer his assistance whenever we call!

Self-Discovery: Envision yourself facing the heavy temple curtain at the time it is rent in two. To your surprise and wonder, you find yourself gazing directly into the smiling face of the God you have loved and served. Stop to thank Jesus for providing for you this opportunity for access with the Father.

GO TO DISCOVERY 340 ON PAGE 1650

4:4 [c] Ge 2:2,3; Ex 20:11 day God rested from all his work."[a][c]
5And again in the passage above he says,
"They shall never enter my rest."[d]
4:5 [d] Ps 95:11 6It still remains that some will enter
that rest, and those who formerly had the
4:6 [e] Heb 3:18 gospel preached to them did not go in,
because of their disobedience.[e] 7There-
fore God again set a certain day, calling it
Today, when a long time later he spoke
through David, as was said before:

4:7 [f] Ps 95:7,8; Heb 3:7,8,15 "Today, if you hear his voice,
do not harden your hearts."[b][f]

4:8 [g] Jos 22:4 [h] Heb 1:1 8For if Joshua had given them rest,[g] God
would not have spoken[h] later about an-
other day. 9There remains, then, a Sab-
bath-rest for the people of God; 10for
anyone who enters God's rest also rests
from his own work, just as God did from
4:10 [i] ver 4 his.[i] 11Let us, therefore, make every effort to enter that rest, so that no one will
4:11 [j] Heb 3:18 fall by following their example of disobedience.[j]
4:12 [k] 1Pe 1:23 [l] Jer 23:29 [m] Eph 6:17; Rev 1:16 [n] 1Co 14:24,25 12For the word of God[k] is living and
active.[l] Sharper than any double-edged
sword,[m] it penetrates even to dividing
soul and spirit, joints and marrow; it
judges the thoughts and attitudes of the
heart.[n] 13Nothing in all creation is hid-
4:13 [o] Ps 33:13-15 den from God's sight.[o] Everything is uncovered and laid bare before the eyes of
him to whom we must give account.

> **CHRIST WENT MORE READILY TO THE CROSS, THAN WE TO THE THRONE OF GRACE.**
>
> Thomas Watson, *Puritan Pastor*

Jesus the Great High Priest

14Therefore, since we have a great
high priest who has gone through the
4:14 [p] Heb 6:20 [q] Heb 3:1 heavens,[c][p] Jesus the Son of God, let us
hold firmly to the faith we profess.[q] 15For
we do not have a high priest who is unable to sympathize with our weaknesses, but we have one who has been
4:15 [r] Heb 2:18 [s] 2Co 5:21 tempted in every way, just as we are[r]—
yet was without sin.[s] 16Let us then ap-
proach the throne of grace with confidence, so that we may receive mercy and
find grace to help us in our time of need.

5 Every high priest is selected from
among men and is appointed to
represent them in matters related to
5:1 [t] Heb 8:3 God, to offer gifts and sacrifices[t] for
sins.[u] 2He is able to deal gently with 5:1 [u] Heb 7:27
those who are ignorant and are going
astray,[v] since he himself is subject to 5:2 [v] Heb 2:18
weakness.[w] 3This is why he has to offer [w] Heb 7:28
sacrifices for his own sins, as well as for
the sins of the people.[x] 5:3 [x] Heb 7:27; 9:7
4No one takes this honor upon him-
self; he must be called by God, just as
Aaron was.[y] 5So Christ also did not take 5:4 [y] Ex 28:1
upon himself the glory[z] of becoming a
high priest. But God said[a] to him, 5:5 [z] Jn 8:54 [a] Heb 1:1

"You are my Son; [b] Ps 2:7
today I have become your
Father."[d][e][b]

6And he says in another place,

"You are a priest forever, 5:6 [c] Ps 110:4; Heb 7:17,21
in the order of Melchizedek."[f][c]

7During the days of Jesus' life on
earth, he offered up prayers and peti-
tions with loud cries and tears[d] to the 5:7 [d] Mt 27:46,50
one who could save him from death, and [e] Mk 14:36
he was heard because of his reverent
submission.[e] 8Although he was a son, he
learned obedience from what he suf- 5:8
fered[f] 9and, once made perfect,[g] he be- [f] Php 2:8
came the source of eternal salvation for 5:9 [g] Heb 2:10
all who obey him 10and was designated
by God to be high priest[h] in the order of 5:10
Melchizedek.[i] [h] ver 5 [i] ver 6

[a] *4* Gen. 2:2 [b] *7* Psalm 95:7,8 [c] *14* Or *gone into heaven* [d] *5* Or *have begotten you* [e] *5* Psalm 2:7 [f] *6* Psalm 110:4

THE SAVIOR WEEPS

Jesus was full of passion and pathos. While living on earth as a man he frequently prayed to God the Father "with loud cries and tears" (Hebrews 5:7–8). When Lazarus died Jesus wept, deeply moved by the loss of his friend, the consequences of sin in the world and the grief of the family members who remained behind (John 11:33–38). When our Lord gazed over the city of Jerusalem, keenly aware of God's profound love for his people and of their refusal to turn to him, Jesus mourned with seemingly inconsolable grief (Matthew 23:37–39; Luke 19:41–44). And on the night before he died on the cross, our Savior's agony in the Garden of Gethsemane was so intense that "his sweat was like drops of blood falling to the ground" (Luke 22:44). There is no Savior like Jesus. His compassion knows no bounds and his love is beyond amazing!

Warning Against Falling Away

11 We have much to say about this, but
it is hard to explain because you are slow
to learn. 12 In fact, though by this time
you ought to be teachers, you need
someone to teach you the elementary
truths[j] of God's word all over again. You
need milk, not solid food![k] 13 Anyone
who lives on milk, being still an infant,[l]
is not acquainted with the teaching
about righteousness. 14 But solid food is
for the mature,[m] who by constant use
have trained themselves to distinguish
good from evil.[n]

5:12 [j] Heb 6:1 [k] 1Co 3:2; 1Pe 2:2
5:13 [l] 1Co 14:20
5:14 [m] 1Co 2:6 [n] Isa 7:15

6 Therefore let us leave[o] the elementary teachings[p] about Christ
and go on to maturity, not laying again
the foundation of repentance from acts
that lead to death,[a][q] and of faith in God,
2 instruction about baptisms,[r] the laying
on of hands,[s] the resurrection of the
dead,[t] and eternal judgment. 3 And God
permitting,[u] we will do so.

6:1 [o] Php 3:12-14 [p] Heb 5:12 [q] Heb 9:14
6:2 [r] Jn 3:25 [s] Ac 6:6 [t] Ac 17:18,32
6:3 [u] Ac 18:21

4 It is impossible for those who have
once been enlightened,[v] who have tasted the heavenly gift,[w] who have shared
in the Holy Spirit,[x] 5 who have tasted the
goodness of the word of God and the
powers of the coming age, 6 if they fall
away, to be brought back to repentance,[y]
because[b] to their loss they are crucifying
the Son of God all over again and subjecting him to public disgrace.

6:4 [v] Heb 10:32 [w] Eph 2:8 [x] Gal 3:2
6:6 [y] 2Pe 2:21; 1Jn 5:16

7 Land that drinks in the rain often
falling on it and that produces a crop
useful to those for whom it is farmed receives the blessing of God. 8 But land
that produces thorns and thistles is
worthless and is in danger of being
cursed.[z] In the end it will be burned.

6:8 [z] Ge 3:17,18; Isa 5:6

9 Even though we speak like this, dear
friends,[a] we are confident of better
things in your case—things that accompany salvation. 10 God is not unjust; he
will not forget your work and the love
you have shown him as you have helped
his people and continue to help them.[b]
11 We want each of you to show this
same diligence to the very end, in order
to make your hope[c] sure. 12 We do not
want you to become lazy, but to imitate[d]
those who through faith and patience[e]
inherit what has been promised.[f]

6:9 [a] 1Co 10:14
6:10 [b] Mt 10:40,42; 25:40; 1Th 1:3
6:11 [c] Heb 3:6
6:12 [d] Heb 13:7 [e] 2Th 1:4; Jas 1:3; Rev 13:10 [f] Heb 10:36

> WE ASSERT, THEREFORE, THAT PERSEVERANCE, BY WHICH ONE PERSEVERES IN CHRIST EVEN TO THE END, IS A GIFT OF GOD.
>
> Augustine, *Catholic Theologian*

The Certainty of God's Promise

13 When God made his promise to
Abraham, since there was no one
greater for him to swear by, he swore by
himself,[g] 14 saying, "I will surely bless you
and give you many descendants."[c][h]
15 And so after waiting patiently, Abraham received what was promised.[i]
16 Men swear by someone greater than
themselves, and the oath confirms what
is said and puts an end to all argument.[j]

6:13 [g] Ge 22:16; Lk 1:73
6:14 [h] Ge 22:17
6:15 [i] Ge 21:5
6:16 [j] Ex 22:11

[a] 1 Or *from useless rituals* [b] 6 Or *repentance while* [c] 14 Gen. 22:17

JESUS AND YOU

OUR ANCHOR HOLDS

Hebrews 6:4–6 constitutes one of the most widely debated passages of the New Testament. Some people interpret these words to imply that, once saved, we can choose to turn our backs and literally walk away from God and the forgiveness with which he has embraced us; others believe that we can never lose our right standing with God once we have placed our confidence and trust in Jesus. The author certainly intended to assure us that Jesus died for our sins one time—and that this one sacrifice was sufficient to cover the sins of all of humanity for all time. We cannot literally re-crucify our Savior or make his atoning sacrifice more complete than it already is (verse 6). In the case of the first-century rebels against the way and work of Jesus Christ, they appeared determined to turn from love for Jesus to fierce opposition, declaring, as it were, that Jesus ought to be eliminated. In this way they aligned themselves on that first Good Friday with Jesus' persecutors, who deliberately despised and rejected him and cried, "Crucify him" (Matthew 27:22). The author of Hebrews also informed his readers that he was "confident of better things" for them (Hebrews 6:9), implying his assurance of their salvation. When we choose to stake our very lives on Jesus and learn to walk step-by-step with him, we have a far more secure anchor to God the Father than one of our own making—our hope is not in our own persistence or our own trustworthiness or our own best efforts; our best hope, our only hope, is Jesus himself (verse 19).

6:17 17Because God wanted to make the un-
[k]Ps 110:4 changing[k] nature of his purpose very
[l]Heb 11:9 clear to the heirs of what was promised,[l]
he confirmed it with an oath. 18God did
6:18 this so that, by two unchangeable things
[m]Nu 23:19; in which it is impossible for God to lie,[m]
Tit 1:2 [n]Heb 3:6 we who have fled to take hold of the
hope[n] offered to us may be greatly encouraged. 19We have this hope as an an-
6:19 chor for the soul, firm and secure. It en-
[o]Lev 16:2; ters the inner sanctuary behind the
Heb 9:2,3,7 curtain,[o] 20where Jesus, who went before
6:20 us, has entered on our behalf.[p] He has
[p]Heb 4:14 [q]Heb 2:17 become a high priest[q] forever, in the or-
[r]Heb 5:6 der of Melchizedek.[r]

Melchizedek the Priest

7 This Melchizedek was king of Sa-
7:1 [s]Mk 5:7 lem and priest of God Most High.[s]
[t]Ge 14:18-20 He met Abraham returning from the defeat of the kings and blessed him,[t] 2and
Abraham gave him a tenth of everything.
First, his name means "king of righteousness"; then also, "king of Salem"
7:3 means "king of peace." 3Without father
[u]ver 6 [v]Mt 4:3 or mother, without genealogy,[u] without
beginning of days or end of life, like the
Son of God[v] he remains a priest forever.
4Just think how great he was: Even the
7:4 [w]Ac 2:29 patriarch[w] Abraham gave him a tenth of
[x]Ge 14:20 the plunder![x] 5Now the law requires the
7:5 descendants of Levi who become priests
[y]Nu 18:21,26 to collect a tenth from the people[y]—
that is, their brothers—even though
their brothers are descended from Abraham. 6This man, however, did not trace
his descent from Levi, yet he collected a 7:6
tenth from Abraham and blessed[z] him [z]Ge 14:19,20
who had the promises.[a] 7And without [a]Ro 4:13
doubt the lesser person is blessed by the
greater. 8In the one case, the tenth is collected by men who die; but in the other
case, by him who is declared to be living.[b] 9One might even say that Levi, who 7:8
collects the tenth, paid the tenth [b]Heb 5:6; 6:20
through Abraham, 10because when Melchizedek met Abraham, Levi was still in
the body of his ancestor.

Jesus Like Melchizedek

11If perfection could have been attained through the Levitical priesthood
(for on the basis of it the law was given 7:11
to the people),[c] why was there still need [c]ver 18,19; Heb 8:7
for another priest to come[d]—one in the [d]Heb 10:1
order of Melchizedek,[e] not in the order [e]ver 17
of Aaron? 12For when there is a change
of the priesthood, there must also be a
change of the law. 13He of whom these
things are said belonged to a different
tribe,[f] and no one from that tribe has 7:13 [f]ver 11 [g]ver 14
ever served at the altar.[g] 14For it is clear
that our Lord descended from Judah,[h] 7:14 [h]Isa 11:1;
and in regard to that tribe Moses said Mt 1:3; Lk 3:33
nothing about priests. 15And what we
have said is even more clear if another

OLD TESTAMENT SACRIFICES COMPARED TO JESUS' SACRIFICE

Aaronic priesthood	Hebrews 6:19–7:25	Melchizedek's priesthood
Impermanent priesthood	Hebrews 7:16–17,23–24	Forever priesthood
Old covenant (temporary)	Hebrews 7:22; 8:6,13; 10:20	New covenant (permanent)
One year atonement	Hebrews 7:25; 9:12,15; 10:1–4,12	Eternal atoning sacrifice
Sinful priests	Hebrews 7:26–27; 9:7	Sinless priest
Daily sacrifices	Hebrews 7:27; 9:12,25–26; 10:9–10,12	Once-for-all sacrifice
A shadow	Hebrews 8:5; 9:23–24; 10:1	The reality
Obsolete promises	Hebrews 8:6–13	Better promises
Animal sacrifices	Hebrews 9:11–15,26; 10:4–10,19	Sacrifice of God's Son
Ongoing sacrifices	Hebrews 10:11–14,18	Sacrifices no longer needed

priest like Melchizedek appears, 16one
who has become a priest not on the basis of a regulation as to his ancestry but
on the basis of the power of an indestructible life. 17For it is declared:

7:17 “You are a priest forever,
[i]Ps 110:4; in the order of Melchizedek.”[a][i]
ver 21; Heb 5:6

7:18 18The former regulation is set aside
[j]Ro 8:3 because it was weak and useless[j] 19(for
7:19 the law made nothing perfect),[k] and a
[k]Ac 13:39; better hope is introduced, by which we
Ro 3:20; Heb 9:9 [l]Heb 4:16 draw near to God.[l]
20And it was not without an oath!
Others became priests without any oath,
21but he became a priest with an oath
when God said to him:

“The Lord has sworn
7:21 and will not change his mind:[m]
[m]1Sa 15:29 [n]Ps 110:4 ‘You are a priest forever.’ ”[a][n]

22Because of this oath, Jesus has become
7:22 [o]Heb 8:6 the guarantee of a better covenant.[o]
23Now there have been many of those
priests, since death prevented them
from continuing in office; 24but because
Jesus lives forever, he has a permanent
7:24 [p]ver 28 priesthood.[p] 25Therefore he is able to
save completely[b] those who come to
7:25 [q]ver 19 God[q] through him, because he always
[r]Ro 8:34 lives to intercede for them.[r]

26Such a high priest meets our need—
one who is holy, blameless, pure, set 7:26
apart from sinners,[s] exalted above the [s]2Co 5:21
heavens.[t] 27Unlike the other high priests, [t]Heb 4:14
he does not need to offer sacrifices[u] day 7:27
after day, first for his own sins,[v] and then [u]Heb 5:1 [v]Heb 5:3
for the sins of the people. He sacrificed [w]Heb 9:12,26,
for their sins once for all[w] when he of- 28 [x]Eph 5:2;
fered himself.[x] 28For the law appoints as Heb 9:14,28
high priests men who are weak;[y] but the 7:28
oath, which came after the law, appoint- [y]Heb 5:2 [z]Heb 1:2
ed the Son,[z] who has been made per- [a]Heb 2:10
fect[a] forever.

The High Priest of a New Covenant

8 The point of what we are saying is
this: We do have such a high
priest,[b] who sat down at the right hand 8:1 [b]Heb 2:17
of the throne of the Majesty in heaven,
2and who serves in the sanctuary, the
true tabernacle[c] set up by the Lord, not 8:2 [c]Heb 9:11,24
by man.
3Every high priest is appointed to of- 8:3
fer both gifts and sacrifices,[d] and so it [d]Heb 5:1
was necessary for this one also to have [e]Heb 9:14
something to offer.[e] 4If he were on earth,

[a] *17,21* Psalm 110:4 [b] *25* Or *forever*

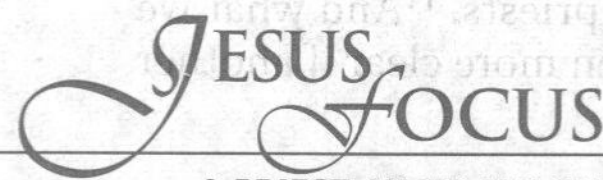

A PRIEST AFTER MELCHIZEDEK'S ORDER

Melchizedek, whose name means “king of righteousness,” is mentioned in only two places in the Old Testament, Genesis 14 and Psalm 110. He was at the same time a priest of God and the king of Salem, the ancient name for Jerusalem. Melchizedek appeared in Abram's life without introduction and exited the scene just as abruptly (Genesis 14). He was a priest of God several hundreds of years before God had given his law to Moses or established the Aaronic priesthood, and he provides an early foreshadowing of Jesus, who would also function as both Priest and King. Jesus, like Melchizedek, did not stem from the priestly Levitical family line (Hebrews 7:11). Instead, our High Priest and Lord was the ultimate exception and the ultimate completion of what God had promised his people all along: an eternal Priest (Psalm 110:4), who would offer the last and best sacrifice to atone for sin (Hebrews 9:11–15, 24–28; 10:5–14).

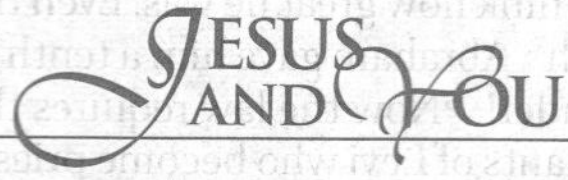

DRAWING NEAR

In the Old Testament only the high priest was allowed to draw near to God's presence. Once each year on the Day of Atonement (*Yom Kippur*) he entered the Most Holy Place in the temple (Leviticus 16). At any other time a thick curtain separated the people from God's hallowed presence (Exodus 26:33). Hebrews 6:19–20 draws parallels between the Old Testament symbols and the work of Jesus Christ. By dying on the cross for our sins Jesus entered the “inner sanctuary” on our behalf. When he died, the curtain in the temple was literally ripped in half as a graphic demonstration that we no longer had to be separated from God (Matthew 27:51). The book of Hebrews refers to this radical change as a “better hope” based on a “better covenant” (Hebrews 7:19,22). What Jesus did for us in opening for us a “new and living way” (Hebrews 10:20) was permanent and complete, never to be repeated (Hebrews 7:24). Because Jesus lives forever, we will never have to be without our “holy, blameless, pure” priest (verse 26) who represents us before the throne of God (see John 17; 1 John 2:1).

he would not be a priest, for there are already men who offer the gifts prescribed
8:4 by the law.[f] [5]They serve at a sanctuary
f Heb 5:1 that is a copy[g] and shadow[h] of what is in
8:5 heaven. This is why Moses was warned[i]
g Heb 9:23 when he was about to build the taber-
h Col 2:17; Heb 10:1 nacle: "See to it that you make every-
i Heb 11:7; 12:25 thing according to the pattern shown
j Ex 25:40 you on the mountain."[a][j] [6]But the ministry Jesus has received is as superior to
8:6 k Lk 22:20 theirs as the covenant[k] of which he is
l Heb 7:22 mediator[l] is superior to the old one, and
it is founded on better promises.

[7]For if there had been nothing wrong
with that first covenant, no place would
8:7 have been sought for another.[m] [8]But God
m Heb 7:11,18 found fault with the people and said[b]:

"The time is coming, declares the
Lord,
when I will make a new
8:8 covenant[n]
n Jer 31:31 with the house of Israel
and with the house of Judah.
8:9 [9]It will not be like the covenant
o Ex 19:5,6 I made with their forefathers[o]
when I took them by the hand
to lead them out of Egypt,
because they did not remain
faithful to my covenant,
and I turned away from them,
declares the Lord.
[10]This is the covenant I will make
with the house of Israel
after that time, declares the Lord.
I will put my laws in their minds 8:10
and write them on their hearts.[p] p 2Co 3:3; Heb 10:16
I will be their God, q Zec 8:8
and they will be my people.[q]
[11]No longer will a man teach his
neighbor,
or a man his brother, saying,
'Know the Lord,' 8:11
because they will all know me,[r] r Isa 54:13; Jn 6:45
from the least of them to the
greatest.
[12]For I will forgive their wickedness
and will remember their sins no 8:12
more."[s][c][t] s Heb 10:17 t Ro 11:27

[13]By calling this covenant "new," he 8:13
has made the first one obsolete;[u] and u 2Co 5:17
what is obsolete and aging will soon disappear.

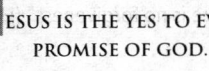

JESUS IS THE YES TO EVERY PROMISE OF GOD.

William Barclay, *British Theologian*

JESUS FOCUS

BETTER PROMISES

Every detail in the Old Testament was designed to provide God's people a glimpse of the truth about himself and of his plan of salvation for all people. Our Lord Jesus Christ came to earth as a man so that he could stand between us and God, much as the Old Testament priests had done—except that he would represent God's ultimate promise to his people (Hebrews 8:6). The New Testament demonstrates how Jesus fulfilled everything necessary to repair the damage to God's creation brought about by sin. By his life on earth Jesus showed us who God really is. In a sense, the Old Testament tantalizes us with *shadows*, while the New Testament reveals God in the full and glorious light of his Son (Hebrews 1:1–4).

Old Testament	New Testament
Concealed	Revealed
Contained	Explained
Foretold	Fulfilled
In prophecy	In person

Worship in the Earthly Tabernacle

9 Now the first covenant had regulations for worship and also an 9:1
earthly sanctuary.[v] [2]A tabernacle[w] was v Ex 25:8
set up. In its first room were the lamp- 9:2
stand,[x] the table[y] and the consecrated w Ex 25:8,9
bread;[z] this was called the Holy Place. x Ex 25:31-39 y Ex 25:23-29
[3]Behind the second curtain was a room z Lev 24:5-8
called the Most Holy Place,[a] [4]which had 9:3
the golden altar of incense[b] and the a Ex 26:31-33
gold-covered ark of the covenant.[c] This
ark contained the gold jar of manna,[d] 9:4 b Ex 30:1-5
Aaron's staff that had budded,[e] and the c Ex 25:10-22
stone tablets of the covenant. [5]Above d Ex 16:32,33 e Nu 17:10
the ark were the cherubim of the Glory,[f] 9:5
overshadowing the atonement cover.[d] f Ex 25:17-19
But we cannot discuss these things in
detail now.

[6]When everything had been arranged 9:6
like this, the priests entered regularly[g] g Nu 28:3
into the outer room to carry on their
ministry. [7]But only the high priest en- 9:7
tered[h] the inner room, and that only h Lev 16:11-19

[a]5 Exodus 25:40 [b]8 Some manuscripts may be translated *fault and said to the people.*
[c]12 Jer. 31:31–34 [d]5 Traditionally *the mercy seat*

The Blood That Cleanses

Sin separates us from God, because he is completely holy (Isaiah 6:3; 1 Peter 1:16) and unable to tolerate evil (Habakkuk 1:13). And the only just punishment for sin is death. That is why the shedding of blood plays such a prominent role throughout the Bible (Leviticus 17:11). God informed Adam and Eve in the very beginning that the cost of disobedience would be death (Genesis 2:17), and he set up a temporary sacrificial system that would cover humanity's sin through the death of animals (Leviticus 4; 16). God has always been explicit about the seriousness of sin: "Without the shedding of blood there is no forgiveness" (Hebrews 9:22).

And that is why God sent his Son to die for our sins. Throughout the Bible blood represents death (Genesis 4:10; Matthew 23:30,35; Colossians 1:20). When the writer of Hebrews spoke of the shedding of Jesus' blood, he was of course referring to Jesus' death on the cross (Hebrews 9:12,15,28). During the time the sacrificial system had been in place, the blood of bulls and goats had been shed to cover the people's sins (verse 12). These animals were substitutes that died for the benefit of the people. But their deaths could do nothing more than cover sin, much as many people today choose the easy option of covering layer upon layer of decaying wallpaper in an old house with still another facade. The only way to remove our sin, to strip the layers down to the bare wood, was for a perfect human being to die (verse 14). Jesus was "unblemished," indicating that his relationship with God had not been tarnished in any way. His death did more than gloss over our sin—it completely cleansed "our consciences from acts that lead to death, so that we may serve the living God!" (verse 14).

Jesus' death was the only sacrifice acceptable to God the Father. Unlike the Old Testament high priest, who entered the man-made tabernacle or temple to offer sacrifices, Jesus was admitted into the very presence of God the Father (verse 24). Our Savior was "sacrificed once to take away the sins of many people; and he will appear a second time, not to bear sin, but to bring salvation to those who are waiting for him" (verse 28). God's plan has always been to restore his creation to the way he intended it to be, and when Jesus comes back our Lord will do just that (1 John 2:2–3; Revelation 21:1–5).

Still today we celebrate the Lord's Supper as a visual reminder that Jesus' blood was shed for us. The sacrament reminds us that our Redeemer surrendered his precious body to die in our place and that his blood washed away our sin forever (Psalm 51:7; Isaiah 1:18; Corinthians 11:26; Revelation 7:14). We need only to accept the gift he has so freely offered (1 Peter 1:18–21).

***Self-Discovery:** What thoughts typically come to mind as you celebrate the Lord's Supper? If commemoration of this sacrament has become routine for you, take a moment to thank Jesus for what he has done on your behalf.*

GO TO DISCOVERY 341 ON PAGE 1653

9:7 i Lev 16:34 once a year,[i] and never without blood,
j Heb 5:2,3 which he offered for himself[j] and for the
9:8 sins the people had committed in igno-
k Heb 3:7 rance. 8The Holy Spirit was showing[k] by
l Jn 14:6; this that the way[l] into the Most Holy
Heb 10:19,20 Place had not yet been disclosed as long
as the first tabernacle was still standing.
9This is an illustration for the present
time, indicating that the gifts and sacri-
9:9 fices being offered[m] were not able to
m Heb 5:1 clear the conscience of the worshiper.
9:10 10They are only a matter of food[n] and
n Lev 11:2-23 o Col 2:16 drink[o] and various ceremonial wash-
p Heb 7:16 ings—external regulations[p] applying
until the time of the new order.

The Blood of Christ

9:11 11When Christ came as high priest[q] of
q Heb 2:17 r Heb 10:1 the good things that are already here,[a r]
s Heb 8:2 he went through the greater and more
perfect tabernacle[s] that is not man-
made, that is to say, not a part of this
creation. 12He did not enter by means of
9:12 t Heb 10:4 the blood of goats and calves;[t] but he en-
u ver 24 tered the Most Holy Place[u] once for all[v]
v Heb 7:27 by his own blood, having obtained eternal redemption. 13The blood of goats
9:13 w Nu 19:9,17,18 and bulls and the ashes of a heifer[w]
sprinkled on those who are ceremonial-
ly unclean sanctify them so that they are
outwardly clean. 14How much more,
9:14 then, will the blood of Christ, who
x 1Pe 3:18 through the eternal Spirit[x] offered him-
y Tit 2:14; self unblemished to God, cleanse our
Heb 10:2,22 consciences[y] from acts that lead to
death,[b z] so that we may serve the living 9:14 z Heb 6:1
God!
15For this reason Christ is the media-
tor[a] of a new covenant, that those who 9:15 a 1Ti 2:5
are called may receive the promised b Heb 7:22
eternal inheritance—now that he has
died as a ransom to set them free from
the sins committed under the first covenant.[b]
16In the case of a will,[c] it is necessary
to prove the death of the one who made
it, 17because a will is in force only when
somebody has died; it never takes effect
while the one who made it is living.
18This is why even the first covenant was 9:18
not put into effect without blood.[c] c Ex 24:6-8
19When Moses had proclaimed every
commandment of the law to all the people, he took the blood of calves, together
with water, scarlet wool and branches of
hyssop, and sprinkled the scroll and all 9:19
the people.[d] 20He said, "This is the blood d Ex 24:6-8
of the covenant, which God has com- 9:20
manded you to keep."[d e] 21In the same e Ex 24:8;
way, he sprinkled with the blood both Mt 26:28
the tabernacle and everything used in its
ceremonies. 22In fact, the law requires
that nearly everything be cleansed with 9:22
blood,[f] and without the shedding of f Lev 8:15
blood there is no forgiveness.[g] g Lev 17:11
23It was necessary, then, for the cop-
ies[h] of the heavenly things to be purified 9:23 h Heb 8:5
with these sacrifices, but the heavenly
things themselves with better sacrifices
than these. 24For Christ did not enter a
man-made sanctuary that was only a 9:24
copy of the true one;[i] he entered heaven i Heb 8:2
itself, now to appear for us in God's presence. 25Nor did he enter heaven to offer
himself again and again, the way the
high priest enters the Most Holy Place[j] 9:25
every year with blood that is not his j Heb 10:19
own.[k] 26Then Christ would have had to k ver 7,8
suffer many times since the creation of
the world.[l] But now he has appeared 9:26 l Heb 4:3
once for all[m] at the end of the ages to do m Heb 7:27
away with sin by the sacrifice of himself.
27Just as man is destined to die once,[n] 9:27 n Ge 3:19
and after that to face judgment,[o] 28so o 2Co 5:10
Christ was sacrificed once to take away
the sins of many people; and he will ap-
pear a second time,[p] not to bear sin,[q] 9:28 p Tit 2:13
but to bring salvation to those who are q 1Pe 2:24
waiting for him.[r] r 1Co 1:7

[a] *11* Some early manuscripts *are to come*
[b] *14* Or *from useless rituals* [c] *16* Same Greek word as *covenant*; also in verse 17
[d] *20* Exodus 24:8

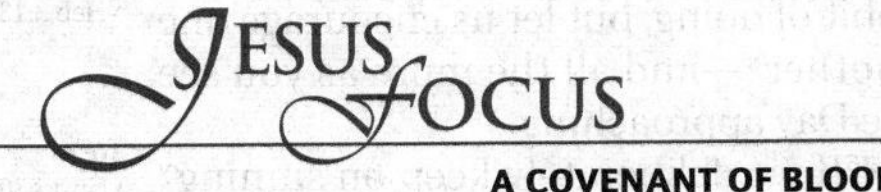

A COVENANT OF BLOOD

A *blood covenant* refers to an agreement that is signed in blood by the participating parties (Hebrews 9:20). In the Old Testament people used animal blood to make such an agreement (see, for example, Genesis 15:8–18). Later on God set up the system of animal sacrifices to demonstrate that he had agreed to forgive the sins of his people (Leviticus 16:15–16). In the New Testament Jesus' blood sealed the contract between God and humanity forever (Hebrews 9:14–20). We have no further need to sacrifice animals because God's own Son through his sacrificial death restored for us a door of access to a relationship with God the Father (verse 12). Much as animal blood covered sin temporarily, so now the blood of Jesus removes our sin forever (verses 21–22).

> **HOW COULD CHRIST HAVE DIED FOR SINNERS IF HE HIMSELF WERE IN SIN?**
>
> John Chrysostom, *Early Church Father*

Christ's Sacrifice Once for All

10:1 [s] Heb 8:5 [t] Heb 9:11 [u] Heb 9:23 [v] Heb 7:19

10 The law is only a shadow[s] of the
good things[t] that are coming—
not the realities themselves.[u] For this
reason it can never, by the same sacrifices repeated endlessly year after year,
make perfect[v] those who draw near to
worship. 2 If it could, would they not
have stopped being offered? For the
worshipers would have been cleansed
once for all, and would no longer have
felt guilty for their sins. 3 But those sacrifices are an annual reminder of sins,[w]
4 because it is impossible for the blood of
bulls and goats[x] to take away sins.
5 Therefore, when Christ came into
the world,[y] he said:

10:3 [w] Heb 9:7
10:4 [x] Heb 9:12,13
10:5 [y] Heb 1:6 [z] 1Pe 2:24

"Sacrifice and offering you did not
desire,
but a body you prepared for me;[z]
6 with burnt offerings and sin
offerings
you were not pleased.
7 Then I said, 'Here I am—it is
written about me in the
scroll[a]—
I have come to do your will,
O God.' "[a] [b]

10:7 [a] Jer 36:2 [b] Ps 40:6-8

8 First he said, "Sacrifices and offerings,
burnt offerings and sin offerings you did
not desire, nor were you pleased with
them"[c] (although the law required them
to be made). 9 Then he said, "Here I am, I
have come to do your will."[d] He sets
aside the first to establish the second.
10 And by that will, we have been made
holy[e] through the sacrifice of the body[f]
of Jesus Christ once for all.[g]
11 Day after day every priest stands
and performs his religious duties; again
and again he offers the same sacrifices,[h]
which can never take away sins.[i] 12 But
when this priest had offered for all time
one sacrifice for sins, he sat down at the
right hand of God. 13 Since that time he
waits for his enemies to be made his
footstool,[j] 14 because by one sacrifice he
has made perfect[k] forever those who are
being made holy.
15 The Holy Spirit also testifies[l] to us
about this. First he says:

10:8 [c] ver 5,6; Mk 12:33
10:9 [d] ver 7
10:10 [e] Jn 17:19 [f] Heb 2:14; 1Pe 2:24 [g] Heb 7:27
10:11 [h] Heb 5:1 [i] ver 1,4
10:13 [j] Heb 1:13
10:14 [k] ver 1
10:15 [l] Heb 3:7

16 "This is the covenant I will make
with them
after that time, says the Lord.
I will put my laws in their hearts,
and I will write them on their
minds."[b] [m]

10:16 [m] Jer 31:33; Heb 8:10

17 Then he adds:

"Their sins and lawless acts
I will remember no more."[c] [n]

10:17 [n] Heb 8:12

18 And where these have been forgiven,
there is no longer any sacrifice for sin.

A Call to Persevere

19 Therefore, brothers, since we have
confidence to enter the Most Holy
Place[o] by the blood of Jesus, 20 by a new
and living way[p] opened for us through
the curtain,[q] that is, his body, 21 and
since we have a great priest[r] over the
house of God, 22 let us draw near to God[s]
with a sincere heart in full assurance of
faith, having our hearts sprinkled to
cleanse us from a guilty conscience[t] and
having our bodies washed with pure water. 23 Let us hold unswervingly to the
hope[u] we profess, for he who promised
is faithful.[v] 24 And let us consider how we
may spur one another on toward love
and good deeds. 25 Let us not give up
meeting together,[w] as some are in the
habit of doing, but let us encourage one
another[x]—and all the more as you see
the Day approaching.
26 If we deliberately keep on sinning[y]
after we have received the knowledge of
the truth, no sacrifice for sins is left,
27 but only a fearful expectation of judgment and of raging fire[z] that will consume the enemies of God. 28 Anyone who
rejected the law of Moses died without
mercy on the testimony of two or three
witnesses.[a] 29 How much more severely
do you think a man deserves to be punished who has trampled the Son of God
under foot,[b] who has treated as an unholy thing the blood of the covenant[c]
that sanctified him, and who has insulted the Spirit[d] of grace?[e] 30 For we know
him who said, "It is mine to avenge; I will

10:19 [o] Eph 2:18; Heb 9:8,12,25
10:20 [p] Heb 9:8 [q] Heb 9:3
10:21 [r] Heb 2:17
10:22 [s] Heb 7:19 [t] Eze 36:25; Heb 9:14
10:23 [u] Heb 3:6 [v] 1Co 1:9
10:25 [w] Ac 2:42 [x] Heb 3:13
10:26 [y] Nu 15:30; 2Pe 2:20
10:27 [z] Isa 26:11; 2Th 1:7; Heb 9:27
10:28 [a] Dt 17:6,7; Heb 2:2
10:29 [b] Heb 6:6 [c] Mt 26:28 [d] Eph 4:30; Heb 6:4 [e] Heb 2:3

[a] 7 Psalm 40:6-8 (see Septuagint) [b] 16 Jer. 31:33
[c] 17 Jer. 31:34

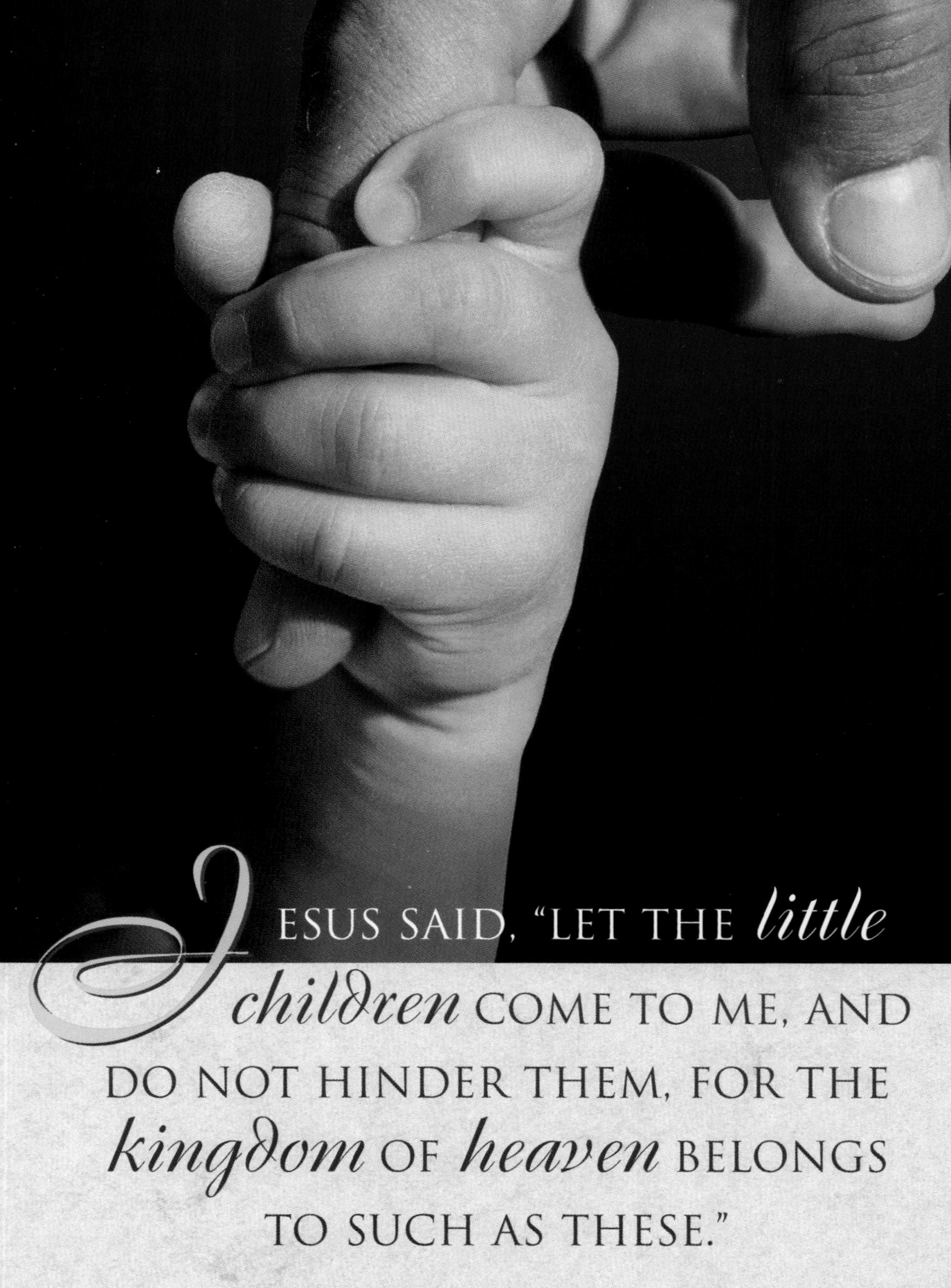

Jesus said, "Let the *little children* come to me, and do not hinder them, for the *kingdom* of *heaven* belongs to such as these."

—Matthew 19:14—

"THEY WILL MAKE WAR AGAINST THE LAMB, BUT THE LAMB WILL OVERCOME THEM BECAUSE HE IS *Lord of lords* AND *King of kings* —AND WITH HIM WILL BE HIS CALLED, CHOSEN AND FAITHFUL FOLLOWERS."

—REVELATION 17:14—

DISCOVERY 341

SHOULDERING OUR LOAD

Many people enjoy backpacking. For them there is nothing quite like loading up the pack with the necessary supplies for a trek through the wilderness. But even for the most experienced backpacker the load will eventually become heavy. It is always a welcome relief to remove the pack at the end of the day and to sit down, unencumbered. As the pulsing muscles begin to relax, it feels as though the weight of the world has been lifted from the camper's taut shoulders.

The writer of Hebrews used a similar analogy to explain what Jesus did with our sins. Our precious Savior carried the whole weight of humanity's sin on his own back (see also Isaiah 53:4–6), and when the task had finally been completed he sloughed off the load and sat down. Jesus' shouldering of our burden accomplished God's purpose more completely than the sacrificial system could ever have begun to do.

For one thing, Jesus' death on the cross was a one-time event. In the tabernacle, and later on in the temple, animals had to be sacrificed repeatedly, day after day (Leviticus 1:1–9). But Jesus' death thoroughly met the demands of God's law and would never have to be repeated. When Jesus died, he was able to proclaim, "It is finished" (John 19:30)—as indeed it was!

The writer to the Hebrews pointed out that after the completion of Jesus' earthly task, Jesus "sat down at the right hand of God" (Hebrews 10:12). In the Old Testament tabernacle and temple there were no chairs. The priests carried out their religious duties while standing, which was symbolic of the fact that their work was never finished (verse 11). After a long day in the house of the Lord, they knew that they would awaken the next morning and repeat the same rituals all over again. But after our Lord's death Jesus was able to return to the Father's side and sit down (verse 12).

In light of what Jesus has done for us, God wants us to commit our lives to him and faithfully serve him. He urges us through the words of the writer to the Hebrews to "throw off everything that hinders and the sin that so easily entangles, and . . . run with perseverance the race marked out for us" (Hebrews 12:1).

The work of salvation has been completed, but there are privileges and responsibilities that go along with receiving God's forgiveness. Because sin no longer stands in our way, we are able to draw near to God and to become personally acquainted with our loving Father (Hebrews 10:22). We are called also to "hold unswervingly to the hope we profess," never giving up even when the daily grind of living seems too difficult for us, and to encourage one another to live lives characterized by love (verses 23–24).

***Self-Discovery:** Picture yourself at the end of a busy day reclining comfortably in an easy chair. The day's work has been completed, and you look forward to an evening of quiet relaxation. Now reflect on what it means to you to know that Jesus has lifted the burden of sin from your shoulders, and thank him for the peace and serenity that you now enjoy.*

GO TO DISCOVERY 342 ON PAGE 1656

10:30 [f]Dt 32:35; repay,"[a][f] and again, "The Lord will judge
Ro 12:19 his people."[b][g] [31]It is a dreadful thing to
[g]Dt 32:36 fall into the hands of the living God.[h]
10:31 [32]Remember those earlier days after
[h]Mt 16:16 you had received the light,[i] when you
10:32 stood your ground in a great contest in
[i]Heb 6:4 the face of suffering.[j] [33]Sometimes you
[j]Php 1:29,30 were publicly exposed to insult and per-
10:33 secution;[k] at other times you stood side
[k]1Co 4:9 [l]Php 4:14; by side with those who were so treated.[l]
1Th 2:14 [34]You sympathized with those in
prison[m] and joyfully accepted the con-
10:34 [m]Heb 13:3 fiscation of your property, because you
[n]Heb 11:16 knew that you yourselves had better and
lasting possessions.[n]
[35]So do not throw away your confidence; it will be richly rewarded. [36]You
10:36 need to persevere[o] so that when you
[o]Lk 21:19; Heb 12:1 have done the will of God, you will receive what he has promised. [37]For in just
a very little while,

10:37 "He who is coming[p] will come and
[p]Mt 11:3 [q]Rev 22:20 will not delay.[q]
10:38 38 But my righteous one[c] will live
[r]Ro 1:17; Gal 3:11 by faith.[r]
And if he shrinks back,
I will not be pleased with him."[d]

[39]But we are not of those who shrink
back and are destroyed, but of those
who believe and are saved.

By Faith

11 Now faith is being sure of what
11:1 we hope for and certain of what
[s]Ro 8:24; we do not see.[s] [2]This is what the an-
2Co 4:18 cients were commended for.[t]
11:2 [3]By faith we understand that the uni-
[t]ver 4,39 verse was formed at God's command,[u]
11:3 so that what is seen was not made out of
[u]Ge 1; Jn 1:3; 2Pe 3:5 what was visible.
[4]By faith Abel offered God a better
sacrifice than Cain did. By faith he was
11:4 commended as a righteous man, when
[v]Ge 4:4; 1Jn 3:12 God spoke well of his offerings.[v] And by
[w]Heb 12:24 faith he still speaks, even though he is
dead.[w]
[5]By faith Enoch was taken from this
life, so that he did not experience death;
he could not be found, because God had
11:5 [x]Ge 5:21-24 taken him away.[x] For before he was tak-
en, he was commended as one who
pleased God. [6]And without faith it is im-
11:6 possible to please God, because anyone
[y]Heb 7:19 who comes to him[y] must believe that he
exists and that he rewards those who
earnestly seek him.

[7]By faith Noah, when warned about
things not yet seen, in holy fear built an 11:7 [z]Ge 6:13-22
ark[z] to save his family.[a] By his faith he
condemned the world and became heir [a]1Pe 3:20
of the righteousness that comes by faith.
[8]By faith Abraham, when called to go
to a place he would later receive as his
inheritance,[b] obeyed and went,[c] even 11:8 [b]Ge 12:7
though he did not know where he was [c]Ge 12:1-4; Ac 7:2-4
going. [9]By faith he made his home in the
promised land[d] like a stranger in a for- 11:9 [d]Ac 7:5
eign country; he lived in tents,[e] as did [e]Ge 12:8; 18:1,9
Isaac and Jacob, who were heirs with [f]Heb 6:17
him of the same promise.[f] [10]For he was 11:10
looking forward to the city[g] with foun- [g]Heb 12:22;
dations,[h] whose architect and builder is 13:14 [h]Rev 21:2, 14
God.
[11]By faith Abraham, even though he
was past age—and Sarah herself was 11:11
barren[i]—was enabled to become a fa- [i]Ge 17:17-19;
ther[j] because he[e] considered him faith- 18:11-14 [j]Ge 21:2
ful who had made the promise. [12]And so
from this one man, and he as good as 11:12
dead,[k] came descendants as numerous [k]Ro 4:19 [l]Ge 22:17
as the stars in the sky and as countless
as the sand on the seashore.[l]
[13]All these people were still living by
faith when they died. They did not re-
ceive the things promised;[m] they only 11:13 [m]ver 39
saw them and welcomed them from a [n]Mt 13:17
distance.[n] And they admitted that they [o]Ge 23:4;
were aliens and strangers on earth.[o] Ps 39:12; 1Pe 1:17
[14]People who say such things show that
they are looking for a country of their
own. [15]If they had been thinking of the
country they had left, they would have 11:15
had opportunity to return.[p] [16]Instead, [p]Ge 24:6-8
they were longing for a better country— 11:16
a heavenly one.[q] Therefore God is not [q]2Ti 4:18
ashamed[r] to be called their God,[s] for he [r]Mk 8:38 [s]Ex 3:6,15
has prepared a city[t] for them. [t]Heb 13:14
[17]By faith Abraham, when God tested 11:17
him, offered Isaac as a sacrifice.[u] He who [u]Ge 22:1-10;
had received the promises was about to Jas 2:21
sacrifice his one and only son, [18]even
though God had said to him, "It is
through Isaac that your offspring[f] will 11:18
be reckoned."[g][v] [19]Abraham reasoned [v]Ge 21:12;
that God could raise the dead,[w] and fig- Ro 9:7
uratively speaking, he did receive Isaac 11:19
back from death. [w]Ro 4:21
[20]By faith Isaac blessed Jacob and 11:20
Esau in regard to their future.[x] [x]Ge 27:27-29, 39,40

[a] *30* Deut. 32:35 [b] *30* Deut. 32:36; Psalm 135:14
[c] *38* One early manuscript *But the righteous*
[d] *38* Hab. 2:3,4 [e] *11* Or *By faith even Sarah, who was past age, was enabled to bear children because she* [f] *18* Greek *seed* [g] *18* Gen. 21:12

JESUS CHRIST IS NOT A CRUTCH; HE IS THE GROUND TO WALK.

Leighton Ford, *American Evangelist*

11:21 21By faith Jacob, when he was dying,
y Ge 48:1,8-22 blessed each of Joseph's sons,[y] and worshiped as he leaned on the top of his
staff.
22By faith Joseph, when his end was
near, spoke about the exodus of the Is-
11:22 raelites from Egypt and gave instruc-
z Ge 50:24,25; tions about his bones.[z]
Ex 13:19 23By faith Moses' parents hid him for
11:23 three months after he was born,[a] because
a Ex 2:2 they saw he was no ordinary child, and
b Ex 1:16,22 they were not afraid of the king's edict.[b]
24By faith Moses, when he had grown
11:24 up, refused to be known as the son of
c Ex 2:10,11 Pharaoh's daughter.[c] 25He chose to be
11:25 mistreated[d] along with the people of
d ver 37 God rather than to enjoy the pleasures
11:26 of sin for a short time. 26He regarded dis-
e Heb 13:13 grace[e] for the sake of Christ as of greater
f Heb 10:35 value than the treasures of Egypt, because he was looking ahead to his re-
11:27 ward.[f] 27By faith he left Egypt,[g] not fear-
g Ex 12:50,51 ing the king's anger; he persevered
because he saw him who is invisible.
28By faith he kept the Passover and the
sprinkling of blood, so that the destroyer of the firstborn would not touch the 11:28
firstborn of Israel.[h] h Ex 12:21-23
29By faith the people passed through
the Red Sea[a] as on dry land; but when
the Egyptians tried to do so, they were 11:29
drowned.[i] i Ex 14:21-31
30By faith the walls of Jericho fell, after the people had marched around 11:30
them for seven days.[j] j Jos 6:12-20
31By faith the prostitute Rahab, because she welcomed the spies, was not
killed with those who were disobedi- 11:31
ent.[b][k] k Jos 2:1,9-14;
32And what more shall I say? I do not 6:22-25; Jas 2:25
have time to tell about Gideon, Barak,[l] 11:32 l Jdg 4-5
Samson, Jephthah, David,[m] Samuel[n] and m 1Sa 16:1,13
the prophets, 33who through faith con- n 1Sa 1:20
quered kingdoms,[o] administered jus- 11:33
tice, and gained what was promised; o 2Sa 7:11; 8:1-3
who shut the mouths of lions,[p] p Da 6:22
34quenched the fury of the flames, and
escaped the edge of the sword; whose
weakness was turned to strength;[q] and 11:34 q 2Ki 20:7
who became powerful in battle and r Jdg 15:8
routed foreign armies.[r] 35Women re-
ceived back their dead, raised to life 11:35 s 1Ki 17:22,23
again.[s] Others were tortured and re-
fused to be released, so that they might
gain a better resurrection. 36Some faced 11:36
jeers and flogging,[t] while still others t Jer 20:2
were chained and put in prison.[u] 37They u Ge 39:20
were stoned[c];[v] they were sawed in two; 11:37
they were put to death by the sword.[w] v 2Ch 24:21 w 1Ki 19:10
They went about in sheepskins and x 2Ki 1:8
goatskins,[x] destitute, persecuted and
mistreated— 38the world was not worthy of them. They wandered in deserts
and mountains, and in caves[y] and holes 11:38 y 1Ki 18:4
in the ground.
39These were all commended[z] for 11:39 z ver 2,4 a ver 13
their faith, yet none of them received
what had been promised.[a] 40God had
planned something better for us so that
only together with us would they be
made perfect.

JESUS AND YOU

A PLACE AMONG HEROES

Many stalwart heroes of the faith appear on the roster of God's people, and Hebrews 11 lists just a few—Abraham, Moses, Gideon, Samson, Rahab and David—all of whom both professed and demonstrated their faith in God. We can be assured of the opportunity to enjoy direct fellowship with God the Father simply because God himself told us that to have faith is to be "sure of what we hope for and certain of what we do not see" (verse 1). Hebrews 11 also reminds us that it is impossible to relate to God without taking him at his word, that there is no other way to earn his favor (verse 6). Although these Old Testament heroes trusted implicitly in God, none of them ever saw the Messiah God had promised to send (verse 39). And so today we are offered the opportunity to accept by faith that Jesus died on the cross for the sin of humanity and to bask in the privilege of a restored and intimate relationship with our heavenly Father.

God Disciplines His Sons

12 Therefore, since we are surrounded by such a great cloud
of witnesses, let us throw off everything
that hinders and the sin that so easily
entangles, and let us run[b] with perse- 12:1 b 1Co 9:24
verance[c] the race marked out for us. c Heb 10:36

a 29 That is, Sea of Reeds *b* 31 Or *unbelieving*
c 37 Some early manuscripts *stoned; they were put to the test;*

DISCOVERY 342

Fixing Our Eyes on Jesus

One of the most difficult things for us to learn is to focus on Jesus. We are encumbered by earthly cares that urgently press for attention, and without maintaining a sense of perspective we can all too easily succumb to the "tyranny of the urgent," to slip into thinking that these immediate concerns are the things that matter most. The writer of Hebrews, however, challenged us to "fix our eyes on Jesus" (Hebrews 12:2). The word *fix* means to deliberately set aside time and to concentrate, in stillness and with determination and commitment. In order to fix our gaze on Jesus, we need a deep longing to know him, coupled with a genuine willingness to devote time to him alone.

But there is more to focusing our attention on Jesus than the act of looking at or reflecting on him for an extended period of time. The word *fix* as the author of Hebrews used it means to have an "obsessive" fixation—not in the sense, of course, of an unhealthy or codependent attachment. The daily concerns and pressures of life do demand our attention, and a loving fixation on someone we cannot see is a continuous challenge. What makes this mind-set possible, however, is our faith—having confidence in "what we hope for" and the certainty of "what we do not see" (Hebrews 11:1).

When we stop concentrating on experiencing the pleasures of this life and develop a singular focus on Jesus, we learn that he is indeed both the author and the perfecter of our faith (Hebrews 12:2). Our faith strengthens us even when we are corrected and disciplined by our loving Father as we learn to live a life that pleases him (1 John 3:3). If we train our thoughts on Jesus, he promises to come to our aid when we are weary and tempted to give up (Hebrews 3:1–6).

As we turn our attention to Jesus, we will also realize that he is already looking at us, even during those times we assume that he neither sees nor cares about what is happening in our lives (2 Chronicles 16:9; Proverbs 15:3). The Bible reminds us that "the eyes of the LORD are on the righteous and his ears are attentive to their cry" (Psalm 34:15; 1 Peter 3:12). Moses praised God for shielding the children of Israel, for guarding them "as the apple of his eye" (Deuteronomy 32:10), and, as children adopted into his family, we are the recipients of this same nurturing care.

Our holy God cannot tolerate sin of any kind, no matter how trivial it may appear (Habakkuk 1:13). Focusing on Jesus will help to bring even our unacknowledged sins into the light (Isaiah 6:1–8). Once we can identify those things in our lives that displease the God we love, we will confess our sins and commit ourselves to him in a fresh new way. That is precisely the method by which we "throw off everything that hinders and the sin that so easily entangles" (Hebrews 12:1). As we do, we will find that our loving Savior renews us each day and gives us the power to "run with perseverance the race marked out for us" (verse 1), hand in hand with him, who is the "author and perfecter of our faith" (verse 2).

Self-Discovery: *Envision yourself entwined in a knotted garden hose you are holding, and picture your mounting frustration as you engage in a futile attempt to disentangle it. Think of that hose as the sin what "hinders" and "so easily entangles" you, and visualize yourself handing the hose to Jesus. What feelings come to mind?*

GO TO DISCOVERY 343 ON PAGE 1658

2 Let us fix our eyes on Jesus, the author
12:2 and perfecter of our faith, who for the
d Php 2:8,9 joy set before him endured the cross,[d]
e Heb 13:13 scorning its shame,[e] and sat down at the
right hand of the throne of God. 3 Con-
sider him who endured such opposition
from sinful men, so that you will not
12:3 f Gal 6:9 grow weary[f] and lose heart.
4 In your struggle against sin, you have
12:4 not yet resisted to the point of shedding
g Heb 10:32-34 your blood.[g] 5 And you have forgotten
that word of encouragement that ad-
dresses you as sons:

"My son, do not make light of the
Lord's discipline,
and do not lose heart when he
rebukes you,
6 because the Lord disciplines those
12:6 he loves,[h]
h Ps 94:12; Rev 3:19 and he punishes everyone he
i Pr 3:11,12 accepts as a son."[a][i]

7 Endure hardship as discipline; God is
12:7 treating you as sons.[j] For what son is not
j Dt 8:5 disciplined by his father? 8 If you are not
disciplined (and everyone undergoes
12:8 k 1Pe 5:9 discipline),[k] then you are illegitimate
children and not true sons. 9 Moreover,
we have all had human fathers who disciplined us and we respected them for it.
How much more should we submit to
12:9 l Nu 16:22 the Father of our spirits[l] and live![m] 10 Our
m Isa 38:16 fathers disciplined us for a little while as
they thought best; but God disciplines
us for our good, that we may share in his
12:10 n 2Pe 1:4 holiness.[n] 11 No discipline seems pleasant at the time, but painful. Later on,
12:11 however, it produces a harvest of righ-
o Isa 32:17; Jas 3:17,18 teousness and peace[o] for those who
have been trained by it.
12 Therefore, strengthen your feeble
12:12 p Isa 35:3 arms and weak knees.[p] 13 "Make level
12:13 q Pr 4:26 paths for your feet,"[b][q] so that the lame
r Gal 6:1 may not be disabled, but rather healed.[r]

Warning Against Refusing God

14 Make every effort to live in peace
12:14 s Ro 14:19 with all men[s] and to be holy;[t] without
t Ro 6:22 holiness no one will see the Lord.[u] 15 See
u Mt 5:8 to it that no one misses the grace of
12:15 v Gal 5:4; God[v] and that no bitter root grows up to
Heb 3:12 cause trouble and defile many. 16 See that
no one is sexually immoral, or is godless
12:16 like Esau, who for a single meal sold his
w Ge 25:29-34 inheritance rights as the oldest son.[w]
17 Afterward, as you know, when he
wanted to inherit this blessing, he was

> RIGHT AT THE HEART OF CHRISTIANITY THERE IS A CROSS, AND ON THAT CROSS THE SON OF GOD WROUGHT MAN'S SALVATION.
>
> 
>
> Leon Morris, *Australian Scholar*

rejected. He could bring about no
change of mind, though he sought the
blessing with tears.[x] 12:17 x Ge 27:30-40
18 You have not come to a mountain
that can be touched and that is burning 12:18
with fire; to darkness, gloom and storm;[y] y Ex 19:12-22; Dt 4:11
19 to a trumpet blast[z] or to such a voice
speaking words that those who heard it 12:19
begged that no further word be spoken z Ex 20:18 a Ex 20:19;
to them,[a] 20 because they could not bear Dt 5:5,25
what was commanded: "If even an ani-
mal touches the mountain, it must be
stoned."[c][b] 21 The sight was so terrifying 12:20 b Ex 19:12,13
that Moses said, "I am trembling with
fear."[d]
22 But you have come to Mount Zion, 12:22
to the heavenly Jerusalem,[c] the city[d] of c Gal 4:26
the living God. You have come to thou- d Heb 11:10
sands upon thousands of angels in joyful assembly, 23 to the church of the firstborn, whose names are written in 12:23
heaven.[e] You have come to God, the e Lk 10:20
judge of all men,[f] to the spirits of righ- f Ps 94:2
teous men made perfect,[g] 24 to Jesus the g Php 3:12
mediator of a new covenant, and to the
sprinkled blood that speaks a better 12:24
word than the blood of Abel.[h] h Ge 4:10; Heb 11:4
25 See to it that you do not refuse him
who speaks. If they did not escape when
they refused him who warned[i] them on 12:25 i Heb 8:5; 11:7
earth, how much less will we, if we turn j Heb 2:2,3
away from him who warns us from
heaven?[j] 26 At that time his voice shook
the earth,[k] but now he has promised, 12:26 k Ex 19:18
"Once more I will shake not only the l Hag 2:6
earth but also the heavens."[e][l] 27 The
words "once more" indicate the remov-
ing of what can be shaken[m]—that is, 12:27 m 1Co 7:31;
created things—so that what cannot be 2Pe 3:10
shaken may remain.
28 Therefore, since we are receiving a 12:28
kingdom that cannot be shaken,[n] let us n Da 2:44
be thankful, and so worship God ac- o Heb 13:15
ceptably with reverence and awe,[o] 29 for
our "God is a consuming fire."[f][p] 12:29 p Dt 4:24

a 6 Prov. 3:11,12 b 13 Prov. 4:26
c 20 Exodus 19:12,13 d 21 Deut. 9:19
e 26 Haggai 2:6 f 29 Deut. 4:24

Honoring Jesus

The writer to the Hebrews concluded his letter with a brief but practical and powerful benediction: "May the God of peace, who through the blood of the eternal covenant brought back from the dead our Lord Jesus, that great Shepherd of the sheep, equip you with everything good for doing his will, and may he work in us what is pleasing to him, through Jesus Christ, to whom be glory for ever and ever. Amen" (Hebrews 13:20–21). Our foremost desire in all areas of life must be that Jesus will be glorified everywhere and in everything, both now and forever. There are several reasons for us to show honor to him.

We honor Jesus because his blood sealed the eternal covenant between God the Father and humanity (Luke 22:20; 1 Corinthians 11:25). It is only because Jesus died for our sins that God can forgive us for turning away from him (Hebrews 9:11–22). We can now enter God's presence directly without the intercession of a human mediator (Hebrews 10:19–22).

We honor Jesus because he is Lord of our lives. His resurrection provides us with concrete proof that God accepted his death as payment for our sins—and that Jesus really is the Son of God (Romans 1:1–6).

We honor Jesus as the Great Shepherd of the sheep. He "shepherds" God's children, not only leading us but going so far as to lay down his life on our behalf (John 10:1–21). He cares for us, watches over us, feeds us and protects us. One day he is coming back for us, to take us to be with him forever in heaven (1 Peter 5:4).

We are called to pay homage to Jesus with our lives, with our bodies (1 Corinthians 6:20), with "all our inmost being" (Psalm 103:1). As we get to know him more and more intimately and become increasingly devoted to his cause, Jesus endows us with the resources we need in order to accomplish his will. He didn't save us from our sin only to abandon us in the struggle to do what is right. Through his Word and Spirit we have everything we need to live in a way that honors him as God the Son (2 Peter 1:3–4).

Not only does he equip us, however, but he also works in us. He wants our lives to be pleasing to him, and he works on our character to change the kind of persons we are from the inside out, transforming us from selfish and sinful individuals into godly men and women (Galatians 5:22–23; Philippians 2:13) who bring glory to Jesus, now and into eternity.

"Here," said Paul, "is a trustworthy saying that deserves full acceptance: Christ Jesus came into the world to save sinners . . . I was shown mercy so that in me, the worst of sinners, Christ Jesus might display his unlimited patience as an example for those who would believe on him and receive eternal life. Now to the King eternal, immortal, invisible, the only God, be honor and glory for ever and ever. Amen" (1 Timothy 1:15–17).

Self-Discovery: *What are some specific ways in which you can honor Jesus both with your life and with your body? Focus for the rest of the day on one specific area in which you desire to offer your praise.*

GO TO DISCOVERY 344 ON PAGE 1662

Concluding Exhortations

13:1 13 Keep on loving each other as
q Ro 12:10; brothers.[q] 2 Do not forget to en-
1Pe 1:22 tertain strangers,[r] for by so doing some
13:2 people have entertained angels without
r Mt 25:35 s Ge 18:1-33 knowing it.[s] 3 Remember those in
13:3 prison[t] as if you were their fellow pris-
t Mt 25:36; oners, and those who are mistreated as
Col 4:18 if you yourselves were suffering.
4 Marriage should be honored by all,
and the marriage bed kept pure, for God
will judge the adulterer and all the sexu-
13:4 ally immoral.[u] 5 Keep your lives free from
u 1Co 6:9 the love of money and be content with
13:5 what you have,[v] because God has said,
v Php 4:11
w Dt 31:6,8; "Never will I leave you;
Jos 1:5 never will I forsake you."[a][w]

6 So we say with confidence,

"The Lord is my helper; I will not
be afraid.
What can man do to me?"[b]

13:7 7 Remember your leaders,[x] who spoke
x ver 17,24 y Heb 6:12 the word of God to you. Consider the
outcome of their way of life and imitate[y]
13:8 their faith. 8 Jesus Christ is the same yes-
z Heb 1:12 terday and today and forever.[z]
9 Do not be carried away by all kinds

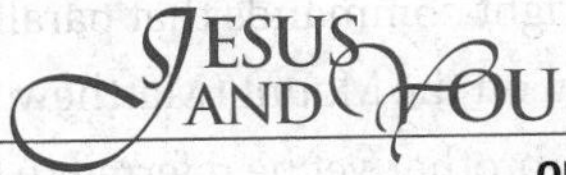

OUTSIDE THE CAMP

While God's law required that animals be sacrificed in the Most Holy Place of the temple, the animals' bodies were to be burned outside the area in which the people lived (Leviticus 4:4–12). Likewise, when the Israelites burned the red heifer, whose ashes were used to purify those who had become ceremonially unclean as a result of contact with a corpse, they killed the heifer and burned its body outside the camp (Numbers 19:1–22). Centuries later, when Jesus died for our sins, he was crucified outside the city walls of Jerusalem (compare Hebrews 13:12–13 with John 19:20). The author of Hebrews asks us to identify ourselves with Jesus even though doing so might entail humiliation or cause us to become outcasts from our former circle of friends, co-workers or even family members (Hebrews 13:13). When we follow Jesus, however, it makes no real difference what others may do or say; our hope lies solely and completely with Jesus in heaven (verse 14).

of strange teachings.[a] It is good for our 13:9 a Eph 4:14
hearts to be strengthened[b] by grace, not b Col 2:7
by ceremonial foods,[c] which are of no c Col 2:16
value to those who eat them. 10 We have
an altar from which those who minister
at the tabernacle have no right to eat.[d] 13:10 d 1Co 9:13;
11 The high priest carries the blood of 10:18
animals into the Most Holy Place as a
sin offering, but the bodies are burned 13:11
outside the camp.[e] 12 And so Jesus also e Ex 29:14;
suffered outside the city gate[f] to make Lev 16:27
the people holy through his own blood. 13:12
13 Let us, then, go to him outside the f Jn 19:17
camp, bearing the disgrace he bore.[g] 13:13
14 For here we do not have an enduring g Heb 11:26
city, but we are looking for the city that 13:14 h Php 3:20;
is to come.[h] Heb 12:22
15 Through Jesus, therefore, let us continually offer to God a sacrifice[i] of 13:15 i 1Pe 2:5
praise—the fruit of lips[j] that confess his j Hos 14:2
name. 16 And do not forget to do good 13:16
and to share with others,[k] for with such k Ro 12:13
sacrifices[l] God is pleased. l Php 4:18
17 Obey your leaders and submit to
their authority. They keep watch over 13:17
you[m] as men who must give an account. m Isa 62:6;
Obey them so that their work will be a Ac 20:28
joy, not a burden, for that would be of no
advantage to you.
18 Pray for us.[n] We are sure that we 13:18 n 1Th 5:25
have a clear conscience[o] and desire to o Ac 23:1
live honorably in every way. 19 I particu-
larly urge you to pray so that I may be re- 13:19 p Phm 22
stored to you soon.[p]
20 May the God of peace,[q] who 13:20
through the blood of the eternal cov- q Ro 15:33
enant[r] brought back from the dead[s] our r Isa 55:3; Eze 37:26;
Lord Jesus, that great Shepherd of the Zec 9:11
sheep,[t] 21 equip you with everything s Ac 2:24 t Jn 10:11
good for doing his will, and may he work 13:21
in us[u] what is pleasing to him,[v] through u Php 2:13
Jesus Christ, to whom be glory for ever v 1Jn 3:22
and ever. Amen.[w] w Ro 11:36

22 Brothers, I urge you to bear with my
word of exhortation, for I have written 13:22
you only a short letter.[x] x 1Pe 5:12
23 I want you to know that our brother 13:23
Timothy[y] has been released. If he arrives y Ac 16:1
soon, I will come with him to see you. 13:24
24 Greet all your leaders[z] and all God's z ver 7,17
people. Those from Italy[a] send you their a Ac 18:2
greetings.
25 Grace be with you all.[b] 13:25 b Col 4:18

a 5 Deut. 31:6 b 6 Psalm 118:6,7

What is the significance of referring to these early believers as "firstfruits"? (James 1:18)

♦ *The original readers were the first to trust in Jesus as their Savior. So James compared them with the firstfruits of harvest. The term implies worship because the first harvest of a crop was set aside as a gift to the Lord.*

Is faith in Jesus Christ in and of itself sufficient? (James 2:14–24)

♦ *James did not argue for good deeds as a requirement for salvation through Jesus Christ. Instead, he insisted that there are two kinds of faith—one legitimate and the other illegitimate—faith . . . made complete (verse 22) and faith without deeds (verse 20). Both kinds "believe" in one sense of the word. But legitimate faith goes deeper than "right thinking" to embody "right living."*

How do we resist the devil? (James 4:7)

♦ *First, we acknowledge that he exists. Next, we need to be aware of his activities (2 Corinthians 2:11), which include temptation, slander and false accusations. Finally, we must stand firmly against his attacks in the name of Jesus.*

Jesus in James James clearly and unquestioningly showed that it is possible to believe the right things, yet live the wrong way. Don't look for pious platitudes in this book, but expect a string of hard-hitting, specific, practical instructions to help you live an authentic Christian life.

James was an important figure in the first-century church. He took a no-nonsense approach to hypocrisy as he described the evil of a tongue out of control, the sin of playing favorites and the folly of boasting about plans for tomorrow. His words contain forthright commands that parallel Jesus' teachings in the Sermon on the Mount (Matthew 5–7).

James was Jesus' half-brother, yet he referred to himself as "a servant of God and of the Lord Jesus Christ" (James 1:1) and to Jesus as "our glorious Lord" (James 2:1) and the "Judge" (James 5:9). James encouraged Christians to live a life of faith in Jesus and to demonstrate that faith through good deeds. When we see ourselves as servants of Jesus, it isn't hard to live out that faith through helping others.

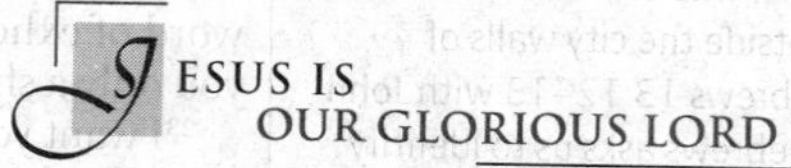

1 James,[a] a servant of God[b] and of
the Lord Jesus Christ,

To the twelve tribes[c] scattered[d]
among the nations:

Greetings.

Trials and Temptations

2Consider it pure joy, my brothers,
whenever you face trials of many kinds,[e]
3because you know that the testing of
your faith develops perseverance. 4Perse-
verance must finish its work so that you
may be mature and complete, not lacking anything. 5If any of you lacks wisdom, he should ask God,[f] who gives generously to all without finding fault, and it
will be given to him.[g] 6But when he asks,
he must believe and not doubt,[h] because
he who doubts is like a wave of the sea,
blown and tossed by the wind. 7That
man should not think he will receive
anything from the Lord; 8he is a double-
minded man,[i] unstable in all he does.

9The brother in humble circumstances ought to take pride in his high
position. 10But the one who is rich
should take pride in his low position, because he will pass away like a wild
flower.[j] 11For the sun rises with scorching
heat and withers[k] the plant; its blossom
falls and its beauty is destroyed.[l] In the
same way, the rich man will fade away
even while he goes about his business.

12Blessed is the man who perseveres
under trial, because when he has stood
the test, he will receive the crown of life[m]
that God has promised to those who
love him.[n]

1:1 [a] Ac 15:13 [b] Tit 1:1 [c] Ac 26:7 [d] Dt 32:26; Jn 7:35; 1Pe 1:1
1:2 [e] Mt 5:12; 1Pe 1:6
1:5 [f] 1Ki 3:9,10; Pr 2:3-6 [g] Mt 7:7
1:6 [h] Mk 11:24
1:8 [i] Jas 4:8
1:10 [j] 1Co 7:31; 1Pe 1:24
1:11 [k] Ps 102:4,11 [l] Isa 40:6-8
1:12 [m] 1Co 9:25 [n] Jas 2:5

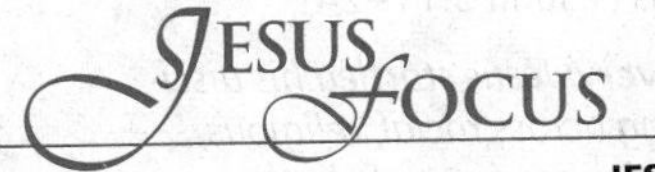

JESUS' SERVANT

It must have required a healthy dose of humility and faith for Jesus' brother James to admit that he was Jesus' servant (James 1:1). In all likelihood it hadn't been easy growing up with a brother who had never sinned (see 2 Corinthians 5:21). For a long time Jesus' brothers refused to believe that he was God's promised Messiah (see John 7:5), but eventually they accepted him for who he was. Acts 1:14 tells us that Jesus' brothers became a part of the early church. Later, James became the pastor of the church in Jerusalem, and his focus was on ministering to Jewish Christians (Acts 15:13–21).

13When tempted, no one should say,
"God is tempting me." For God cannot
be tempted by evil, nor does he tempt
anyone; 14but each one is tempted when,
by his own evil desire, he is dragged
away and enticed. 15Then, after desire
has conceived, it gives birth to sin;[o] and
sin, when it is full-grown, gives birth to
death.[p]

16Don't be deceived,[q] my dear brothers.[r] 17Every good and perfect gift is
from above,[s] coming down from the Father of the heavenly lights, who does not
change[t] like shifting shadows. 18He
chose to give us birth[u] through the word
of truth, that we might be a kind of firstfruits[v] of all he created.

Listening and Doing

19My dear brothers, take note of this:
Everyone should be quick to listen, slow
to speak[w] and slow to become angry,
20for man's anger does not bring about
the righteous life that God desires.
21Therefore, get rid of[x] all moral filth and
the evil that is so prevalent and humbly
accept the word planted in you,[y] which
can save you.

22Do not merely listen to the word,
and so deceive yourselves. Do what it
says. 23Anyone who listens to the word
but does not do what it says is like a
man who looks at his face in a mirror
24and, after looking at himself, goes
away and immediately forgets what he
looks like. 25But the man who looks intently into the perfect law that gives
freedom,[z] and continues to do this, not
forgetting what he has heard, but doing
it—he will be blessed in what he does.[a]

26If anyone considers himself religious and yet does not keep a tight rein
on his tongue,[b] he deceives himself and
his religion is worthless. 27Religion that
God our Father accepts as pure and
faultless is this: to look after[c] orphans
and widows[d] in their distress and to
keep oneself from being polluted by the
world.[e]

Favoritism Forbidden

2 My brothers, as believers in our
glorious[f] Lord Jesus Christ, don't
show favoritism.[g] 2Suppose a man
comes into your meeting wearing a gold
ring and fine clothes, and a poor man in
shabby clothes also comes in. 3If you

1:15 [o] Job 15:35; Ps 7:14 [p] Ro 6:23
1:16 [q] 1Co 6:9 [r] ver 19
1:17 [s] Jn 3:27 [t] Nu 23:19; Mal 3:6
1:18 [u] Jn 1:13 [v] Eph 1:12; Rev 14:4
1:19 [w] Pr 10:19
1:21 [x] Eph 4:22 [y] Eph 1:13
1:25 [z] Jas 2:12 [a] Jn 13:17
1:26 [b] Ps 34:13; 1Pe 3:10
1:27 [c] Mt 25:36 [d] Isa 1:17,23 [e] Ro 12:2
2:1 [f] 1Co 2:8 [g] Lev 19:15

DISCOVERY 344

PLAYING FAVORITES

Living as a follower of Jesus and showing favoritism of any kind are incongruent partners: "If you show favoritism, you sin and are convicted by the law as lawbreakers" (James 2:9). The word *favoritism* actually stems from two root words, one meaning "to accept or receive" and the other "the face of a person." Literally, the idea is that someone who shows favoritism accepts or rejects another person based solely on his or her face (outward appearance).

James provided a concrete example in verses 2–4. Imagine two men, one well-to-do and the other impoverished. The rich man arrives at church dressed in the finest suit and flaunting expensive jewelry. The destitute man is wearing his only set of clothes—a filthy pair of blue jeans and a torn tee-shirt. If we as Christians were to welcome the wealthy man as he strode into the lobby but look the other way when his disheveled, ill-smelling counterpart shuffled through the door, we would be showing preferential treatment to the first individual based solely on our initial impression of him. James used strong words: We would have "discriminated" among ourselves and would have become "judges with evil thoughts" (verse 4).

Prejudging a person by her appearance is just as easy to do within the context of Christ's body as it is in the world. We are so prone to make rash conclusions about people based on the color of their skin, their manner of dress, their place of employment (or lack thereof), their mode of transportation, their social skills, their level of education—the list is endless. But this kind of thinking violates the law of God (verse 9) and is incompatible with God's character: "God does not show favoritism but accepts men from every nation who fear him and do what is right" (Acts 10:34).

Immediately after Jesus, the One who "welcome[d] sinners and [ate] with them" (Luke 15:2), had pronounced the words that have become known as the Golden Rule (Luke 6:31), he went on to talk about our treatment of our "enemies." While those against whom we discriminate do not necessary qualify as enemies (sadly, in many cases we are more apathetic or even repulsed than angry), the principles still apply. If we love only those who love us, are kind only to those who are likely to reciprocate, or lend only to those from whom we can expect repayment, what credit is that to us? (Luke 6:32–34). Even "sinners," Jesus pointed out, do these things. The irony is that we ourselves fall into the identical category: "God demonstrates his own love for us in this: While we were still sinners, Christ died for us" (Romans 5:8).

There is only one cure for discrimination: obeying God's most basic law to love our neighbor as ourself (verse 8), and we can only *love* our neighbors when we *know* them. Nothing will break down cultural, social and economic barriers more rapidly than the power of love (1 Corinthians 13). God's people can transform the world when we begin to love others as God loves us (1 John 3:11–24).

Self-Discovery: *Jesus startled his disciples by reaching across racial, religious, social and gender barriers to help the woman at the well in John 4:4–29. His inclusive act of love for her is a powerful example to our frequently cloistered churches. How can you imitate Jesus' love to someone who is not a part of your socio-economic or ethnic group?*

GO TO DISCOVERY 345 ON PAGE 1671

show special attention to the man wearing fine clothes and say, "Here's a good
seat for you," but say to the poor man,
"You stand there" or "Sit on the floor by
2:4 my feet," 4have you not discriminated
[h]Jn 7:24 among yourselves and become judges[h]
with evil thoughts?
2:5 [i]Jas 1:16,19 5Listen, my dear brothers:[i] Has not
[j]1Co 1:26-28 God chosen those who are poor in the
[k]Lk 12:21 eyes of the world[j] to be rich in faith[k] and
[l]Jas 1:12 to inherit the kingdom he promised
2:6 those who love him?[l] 6But you have in-
[m]1Co 11:22 sulted the poor.[m] Is it not the rich who
[n]Ac 8:3 are exploiting you? Are they not the
ones who are dragging you into court?[n]
7Are they not the ones who are slander-
ing the noble name of him to whom you
belong?
8If you really keep the royal law found
in Scripture, "Love your neighbor as
2:8 [o]Lev 19:18 yourself,"[a][o] you are doing right. 9But if
2:9 you show favoritism,[p] you sin and are
[p]ver 1 [q]Dt 1:17 convicted by the law as lawbreakers.[q]
10For whoever keeps the whole law and
2:10 yet stumbles at just one point is guilty of
[r]Mt 5:19; breaking all of it.[r] 11For he who said, "Do
Gal 3:10 not commit adultery,"[b][s] also said, "Do
2:11 not murder."[c][t] If you do not commit
[s]Ex 20:14; adultery but do commit murder, you
Dt 5:18 [t]Ex 20:13; have become a lawbreaker.
Dt 5:17 12Speak and act as those who are going to be judged by the law that gives
2:12 [u]Jas 1:25 freedom,[u] 13because judgment without
mercy will be shown to anyone who has
2:13 not been merciful.[v] Mercy triumphs
[v]Mt 5:7; 18:32-35 over judgment!

Faith and Deeds

14What good is it, my brothers, if a
2:14 man claims to have faith but has no
[w]Mt 7:26; deeds?[w] Can such faith save him? 15Sup-
Jas 1:22-25 pose a brother or sister is without
2:15 clothes and daily food.[x] 16If one of you
[x]Mt 25:35,36 says to him, "Go, I wish you well; keep
warm and well fed," but does nothing
2:16 about his physical needs, what good is
[y]1Jn 3:17,18 it?[y] 17In the same way, faith by itself, if it
is not accompanied by action, is dead.
18But someone will say, "You have
2:18 faith; I have deeds."
[z]Ro 3:28 Show me your faith without deeds,[z]
[a]Jas 3:13 and I will show you my faith by what I
2:19 do.[a] 19You believe that there is one God.[b]
[b]Dt 6:4 Good! Even the demons believe that[c]—
[c]Mt 8:29; Lk 4:34 and shudder.
20You foolish man, do you want evidence that faith without deeds is use-
less[d]?[d] 21Was not our ancestor Abraham 2:20 [d]ver 17,26
considered righteous for what he did
when he offered his son Isaac on the al-
tar?[e] 22You see that his faith and his ac- 2:21 [e]Ge 22:9,12
tions were working together,[f] and his
faith was made complete by what he 2:22 [f]Heb 11:17
did.[g] 23And the scripture was fulfilled [g]1Th 1:3
that says, "Abraham believed God, and it 2:23
was credited to him as righteousness,"[e][h] [h]Ge 15:6; Ro 4:3
and he was called God's friend.[i] 24You [i]2Ch 20:7;
see that a person is justified by what he Isa 41:8
does and not by faith alone.
25In the same way, was not even Rahab the prostitute considered righteous
for what she did when she gave lodging
to the spies and sent them off in a dif- 2:25
ferent direction?[j] 26As the body without [j]Heb 11:31
the spirit is dead, so faith without deeds 2:26
is dead.[k] [k]ver 17,20

Taming the Tongue

3 Not many of you should presume
to be teachers, my brothers, because you know that we who teach will 3:2
be judged more strictly. 2We all stumble[l] [l]1Ki 8:46;
in many ways. If anyone is never at fault Jas 2:10 [m]1Pe 3:10
in what he says,[m] he is a perfect man,[n] [n]Mt 12:37
able to keep his whole body in check.[o] [o]Jas 1:26
3When we put bits into the mouths of
horses to make them obey us, we can 3:3
turn the whole animal.[p] 4Or take ships [p]Ps 32:9
as an example. Although they are so
large and are driven by strong winds,
they are steered by a very small rudder
wherever the pilot wants to go. 5Like-
wise the tongue is a small part of the 3:5
body, but it makes great boasts.[q] Con- [q]Ps 12:3,4
sider what a great forest is set on fire by 3:6
a small spark. 6The tongue also is a fire,[r] [r]Pr 16:27
a world of evil among the parts of the [s]Mt 15:11,18,19
body. It corrupts the whole person,[s] sets

[a] *8* Lev. 19:18 [b] *11* Exodus 20:14; Deut. 5:18
[c] *11* Exodus 20:13; Deut. 5:17 [d] *20* Some early manuscripts *dead* [e] *23* Gen. 15:6

JESUS FOCUS

WORD PICTURES

James wrote in much the same style as his brother Jesus spoke, using vivid word pictures borrowed from nature and the world to illustrate God's truth. In chapter 3 he talked about a horse's bit, sailing ships, forest fires, springs of water, and plants. It would seem that James had grown up with the same profound appreciation for God's creation as Jesus himself (see Matthew 5—7; 13; John 6; 10).

the whole course of his life on fire, and is
itself set on fire by hell.
7All kinds of animals, birds, reptiles
and creatures of the sea are being tamed
and have been tamed by man, 8but no
man can tame the tongue. It is a restless
3:8 evil, full of deadly poison.[t]
[t]Ps 140:3; 9With the tongue we praise our Lord
Ro 3:13 and Father, and with it we curse men,
3:9 [u]Ge 1:26,27; who have been made in God's likeness.[u]
1Co 11:7 10Out of the same mouth come praise
and cursing. My brothers, this should
not be. 11Can both fresh water and salt[a]
water flow from the same spring? 12My
brothers, can a fig tree bear olives, or a
3:12 [v]Mt 7:16 grapevine bear figs?[v] Neither can a salt
spring produce fresh water.

Two Kinds of Wisdom

13Who is wise and understanding
3:13 among you? Let him show it[w] by his
[w]Jas 2:18 good life, by deeds done in the humility
that comes from wisdom. 14But if you
3:14 harbor bitter envy and selfish ambition[x]
[x]ver 16 in your hearts, do not boast about it or
[y]Jas 5:19 deny the truth.[y] 15Such "wisdom" does
3:15 [z]Jas 1:17 not come down from heaven[z] but is
[a]1Ti 4:1 earthly, unspiritual, of the devil.[a] 16For
where you have envy and selfish ambi-
tion, there you find disorder and every
evil practice.
17But the wisdom that comes from
3:17 [b]1Co 2:6 heaven[b] is first of all pure; then peace-
[c]Lk 6:36 loving, considerate, submissive, full of
[d]Ro 12:9 mercy[c] and good fruit, impartial and
3:18 sincere.[d] 18Peacemakers who sow in
[e]Pr 11:18; Isa 32:17 peace raise a harvest of righteousness.[e]

Submit Yourselves to God

4:1 4 What causes fights and quarrels[f]
[f]Tit 3:9 among you? Don't they come
[g]Ro 7:23 from your desires that battle[g] within
you? 2You want something but don't get
it. You kill and covet, but you cannot
have what you want. You quarrel and
fight. You do not have, because you do
not ask God. 3When you ask, you do not
4:3 [h]Ps 18:41 receive,[h] because you ask with wrong
[i]1Jn 3:22; 5:14 motives,[i] that you may spend what you
get on your pleasures.
4You adulterous people, don't you
4:4 [j]Jas 1:27 know that friendship with the world[j] is
[k]1Jn 2:15 hatred toward God?[k] Anyone who
[l]Jn 15:19 chooses to be a friend of the world becomes an enemy of God.[l] 5Or do you
think Scripture says without reason that
the spirit he caused to live in us envies

JESUS IS BENEVOLENCE PERSONIFIED, AN EXAMPLE FOR ALL MEN.

John Adams, *American President*

intensely?[b] 6But he gives us more grace.
That is why Scripture says:

"God opposes the proud 4:6
but gives grace to the humble."[c][m] [m]Ps 138:6;
7Submit yourselves, then, to God. Re- Pr 3:34; Mt 23:12
sist the devil,[n] and he will flee from you. 4:7
8Come near to God and he will come [n]Eph 4:27;
near to you.[o] Wash your hands,[p] you sin- 1Pe 5:6-9
ners, and purify your hearts, you double- 4:8 [o]2Ch 15:2
minded.[q] 9Grieve, mourn and wail. [p]Isa 1:16
Change your laughter to mourning and [q]Jas 1:8
your joy to gloom.[r] 10Humble yourselves 4:9
before the Lord, and he will lift you up. [r]Lk 6:25
11Brothers, do not slander one anoth-
er.[s] Anyone who speaks against his 4:11
brother or judges him[t] speaks against [s]1Pe 2:1 [t]Mt 7:1
the law and judges it. When you judge [u]Jas 1:22
the law, you are not keeping it,[u] but sitting in judgment on it. 12There is only
one Lawgiver and Judge, the one who is
able to save and destroy.[v] But you—who 4:12
are you to judge your neighbor?[w] [v]Mt 10:28 [w]Ro 14:4

Boasting About Tomorrow

13Now listen, you who say, "Today or
tomorrow we will go to this or that city,
spend a year there, carry on business
and make money."[x] 14Why, you do not 4:13
even know what will happen tomorrow. [x]Pr 27:1
What is your life? You are a mist that ap- 4:14
pears for a little while and then van- [y]Job 7:7; Ps 102:3
ishes.[y] 15Instead, you ought to say, "If it 4:15
is the Lord's will,[z] we will live and do this [z]Ac 18:21
or that." 16As it is, you boast and brag. All 4:16
such boasting is evil.[a] 17Anyone, then, [a]1Co 5:6
who knows the good he ought to do and 4:17
doesn't do it, sins.[b] [b]Lk 12:47; Jn 9:41

Warning to Rich Oppressors

5 Now listen, you rich people,[c] weep 5:1
and wail because of the misery [c]Lk 6:24
that is coming upon you. 2Your wealth
has rotted, and moths have eaten your 5:2
clothes.[d] 3Your gold and silver are cor- [d]Job 13:28; Mt 6:19,20

[a] 11 Greek *bitter* (see also verse 14) [b] 5 Or *that God jealously longs for the spirit that he made to live in us;* or *that the Spirit he caused to live in us longs jealously* [c] 6 Prov. 3:34

roded. Their corrosion will testify
against you and eat your flesh like fire.
You have hoarded wealth in the last
5:3 [e] ver 7,8 days.[e] 4Look! The wages you failed to
pay the workmen[f] who mowed your
5:4 [f] Lev 19:13 fields are crying out against you. The
[g] Dt 24:15 cries[g] of the harvesters have reached the
[h] Ro 9:29 ears of the Lord Almighty.[h] 5You have
5:5 lived on earth in luxury and self-indul-
[i] Am 6:1 gence. You have fattened yourselves[i] in
[j] Jer 12:3; 25:34 the day of slaughter.[a] [j] 6You have con-
5:6 demned and murdered innocent men,[k]
[k] Heb 10:38 who were not opposing you.

Patience in Suffering

5:7 7Be patient, then, brothers, until the
[l] Dt 11:14; Lord's coming. See how the farmer waits
Jer 5:24 for the land to yield its valuable crop and
5:8 how patient he is for the autumn and
[m] Ro 13:11; spring rains.[l] 8You too, be patient and
1Pe 4:7 stand firm, because the Lord's coming is
5:9 near.[m] 9Don't grumble against each oth-
[n] Jas 4:11 er, brothers,[n] or you will be judged. The
[o] 1Co 4:5; 1Pe 4:5 Judge[o] is standing at the door![p]
[p] Mt 24:33

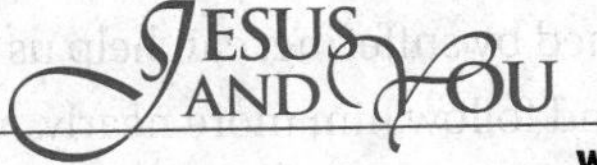

WAIT PATIENTLY

Just as a farmer waits patiently for his crops to grow, so we wait for Jesus to come back for his people (James 5:7). We watch for his physical and visible return on the clouds and learn in the meantime to walk through this life with him as our guide. And through the process we learn self-control in every area of our lives. James recognized that the effects of sin in the world make life difficult but that instead of allowing us to be destroyed by it God uses trouble and suffering to transform and renew us. The better we get to know God through Jesus, the more confident we will become that Jesus will set things right when he comes back to earth.

10Brothers, as an example of patience
in the face of suffering, take the proph- 5:10
ets[q] who spoke in the name of the Lord. [q] Mt 5:12
11As you know, we consider blessed[r] 5:11
those who have persevered. You have [r] Mt 5:10
heard of Job's perseverance[s] and have [s] Job 1:21,22; 2:10 [t] Job 42:10,
seen what the Lord finally brought 12-17
about.[t] The Lord is full of compassion [u] Nu 14:18
and mercy.[u]
12Above all, my brothers, do not
swear—not by heaven or by earth or by
anything else. Let your "Yes" be yes,
and your "No," no, or you will be con- 5:12
demned.[v] [v] Mt 5:34-37

The Prayer of Faith

13Is any one of you in trouble? He 5:13
should pray.[w] Is anyone happy? Let him [w] Ps 50:15
sing songs of praise.[x] 14Is any one of you [x] Col 3:16
sick? He should call the elders of the
church to pray over him and anoint him 5:14
with oil[y] in the name of the Lord. 15And [y] Mk 6:13
the prayer offered in faith will make the
sick person well; the Lord will raise him
up. If he has sinned, he will be forgiven. 5:16
16Therefore confess your sins[z] to each [z] Mt 3:6
other and pray for each other so that you [a] 1Pe 2:24
may be healed.[a] The prayer of a righ- [b] Jn 9:31
teous man is powerful and effective.[b]
17Elijah was a man just like us.[c] He 5:17 [c] Ac 14:15
prayed earnestly that it would not rain, [d] 1Ki 17:1;
and it did not rain on the land for three Lk 4:25
and a half years.[d] 18Again he prayed, and
the heavens gave rain, and the earth pro- 5:18
duced its crops.[e] [e] 1Ki 18:41-45
19My brothers, if one of you should 5:19
wander from the truth[f] and someone [f] Jas 3:14
should bring him back,[g] 20remember [g] Mt 18:15
this: Whoever turns a sinner from the 5:20
error of his way will save[h] him from [h] Ro 11:14
death and cover over a multitude of [i] 1Pe 4:8
sins.[i]

[a] 5 Or *yourselves as in a day of feasting*

1 PETER

What healing comes from Jesus' wounds? (1 Peter 2:24)

- *Some believe this verse teaches that Jesus' death provides physical healing. Others believe that, while God can indeed heal sick bodies, the purpose of Jesus' death was solely to provide healing from the sickness of sin.*

Are good deeds a way to earn a blessing? (1 Peter 3:9–12)

- *Good deeds can never be the means to eternal life. However, those who have received God's gift of salvation through Jesus will demonstrate that God is in their lives by the way they treat those around them.*

How can we participate in Jesus' sufferings? (1 Peter 4:13)

- *Perhaps we share in his sufferings by imitating his attitude (see 1 Peter 2:20–21). Some suggest that we may share in his sufferings in a symbolic way by suffering because of righteousness (Matthew 5:10).*

Jesus in 1 Peter Peter wanted to instill hope in his readers in the face of suffering and persecution, and he based his words of encouragement on the teachings of Jesus and the prophets. In fact, Peter quoted proportionately more from the Old Testament than any other New Testament writer. He used everyday examples to bring his message of hope and emphasized that faith, refined by suffering, can help us to see the Lord more clearly and follow him more nearly.

Peter's first letter provides many vivid descriptions of Jesus. He is the One who sprinkles us with his own blood (1 Peter 1:2), and he is the lover of our souls (verse 8). Jesus the Messiah suffered, just as God's prophets had foretold, and he is exalted as Almighty God (verse 11). Jesus was like a lamb without defect—perfectly acceptable to God because he had no sin (verse 19). But Jesus is also the shepherd and leader of our souls (1 Peter 2:25). Above and beyond any other leader, Jesus is the "Chief Shepherd" of God's beloved people (1 Peter 5:4).

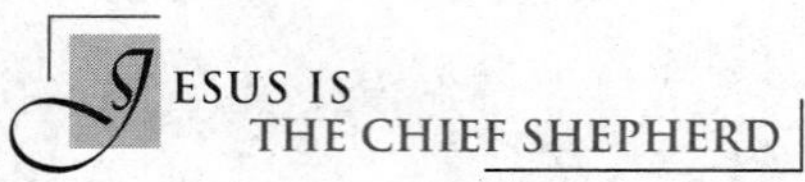
JESUS IS
THE CHIEF SHEPHERD

1:1 **1** Peter, an apostle of Jesus Christ,[a] a2Pe 1:1
b Mt 24:22 To God's elect,[b] strangers in the
c Ac 16:7 world, scattered throughout Pontus, Galatia, Cappadocia, Asia and Bithynia,[c]
1:2 2who have been chosen according to the
d Ro 8:29 foreknowledge[d] of God the Father,
e 2Th 2:13 through the sanctifying work of the
f Heb 10:22; 12:24 Spirit,[e] for obedience to Jesus Christ and
sprinkling by his blood:[f]

Grace and peace be yours in abundance.

Praise to God for a Living Hope

1:3 3Praise be to the God and Father of
g 2Co 1:3; our Lord Jesus Christ![g] In his great mer-
Eph 1:3 cy[h] he has given us new birth into a liv-
h Tit 3:5; Jas 1:18 ing hope through the resurrection of
i 1Co 15:20 Jesus Christ from the dead,[i] 4and into an
inheritance that can never perish, spoil
1:4 or fade—kept in heaven for you,[j] 5who
j Col 1:5 through faith are shielded by God's pow-
1:5 k Jn 10:28 er[k] until the coming of the salvation that
is ready to be revealed in the last time.
1:6 6In this you greatly rejoice,[l] though now
l Ro 5:2 for a little while[m] you may have had to
m 1Pe 5:10 n Jas 1:2 suffer grief in all kinds of trials.[n] 7These
have come so that your faith—of greater
worth than gold, which perishes even
1:7 o Job 23:10; though refined by fire[o]—may be proved
Ps 66:10; genuine[p] and may result in praise, glory
Pr 17:3 p Jas 1:3 and honor when Jesus Christ is re-
q Ro 2:7 vealed.[q] 8Though you have not seen him,
you love him; and even though you do
1:8 r Jn 20:29 not see him now, you believe in him[r] and
are filled with an inexpressible and glo-
1:9 rious joy, 9for you are receiving the goal
s Ro 6:22 of your faith, the salvation of your souls.[s]
1:10 10Concerning this salvation, the
t Mt 26:24 prophets, who spoke[t] of the grace that
u Mt 13:17 was to come to you, searched intently
and with the greatest care,[u] 11trying to
find out the time and circumstances to
1:11 v 2Pe 1:21 which the Spirit of Christ[v] in them was
pointing when he predicted the suffer-
ings of Christ and the glories that would
follow. 12It was revealed to them that
they were not serving themselves but
you, when they spoke of the things that
have now been told you by those who 1:12
have preached the gospel to you[w] by the w ver 25
Holy Spirit sent from heaven. Even angels long to look into these things.

Be Holy

13Therefore, prepare your minds for
action; be self-controlled; set your hope
fully on the grace to be given you when
Jesus Christ is revealed. 14As obedient
children, do not conform[x] to the evil de- 1:14 x Ro 12:2
sires you had when you lived in igno- y Eph 4:18
rance.[y] 15But just as he who called you is 1:15
holy, so be holy in all you do;[z] 16for it is z 2Co 7:1;
written: "Be holy, because I am holy."[a][a] 1Th 4:7
17Since you call on a Father who 1:16
judges each man's work impartially,[b] live a Lev 11:44,45
your lives as strangers here in reverent 1:17
fear.[c] 18For you know that it was not b Ac 10:34
with perishable things such as silver or c Heb 12:28
gold that you were redeemed[d] from the 1:18
empty way of life handed down to you d Mt 20:28;
from your forefathers, 19but with the 1Co 6:20
precious blood of Christ, a lamb[e] with- 1:19 e Jn 1:29
out blemish or defect.[f] 20He was chosen f Ex 12:5
before the creation of the world,[g] but 1:20
was revealed in these last times[h] for g Eph 1:4
your sake. 21Through him you believe in h Heb 9:26
God,[i] who raised him from the dead and 1:21
glorified him, and so your faith and i Ro 4:24
hope are in God.
22Now that you have purified[j] your- 1:22
selves by obeying the truth so that you j Jas 4:8
have sincere love for your brothers, love k Jn 13:34;
one another deeply,[k] from the heart.[b] Heb 13:1
23For you have been born again,[l] not of 1:23
perishable seed, but of imperishable, l Jn 1:13
through the living and enduring word of m Heb 4:12
God.[m] 24For,

"All men are like grass,
and all their glory is like the
flowers of the field;
the grass withers and the flowers
fall,
25 but the word of the Lord stands 1:25
forever."[c][n] n Isa 40:6-8

And this is the word that was preached
to you.

2 Therefore, rid yourselves[o] of all 2:1 o Eph 4:22
malice and all deceit, hypocrisy,

THE PROBLEM WHICH
CONFRONTS US AS WE APPROACH
MODERN MAN TODAY . . .
IS HOW WE MAY COMMUNICATE
THE GOSPEL SO THAT IT
IS UNDERSTOOD.

Francis Schaeffer, *Christian Apologist*

a 16 Lev. 11:44,45; 19:2; 20:7 *b* 22 Some early manuscripts *from a pure heart*
c 25 Isaiah 40:6-8

2:1 p Jas 4:11 envy, and slander[p] of every kind. 2 Like
newborn babies, crave pure spiritual
2:2 q 1Co 3:2 milk,[q] so that by it you may grow up[r] in
r Eph 4:15,16 your salvation, 3 now that you have tast-
2:3 ed that the Lord is good.[s]
s Heb 6:5

The Living Stone and a Chosen People

4 As you come to him, the living
2:4 t ver 7 Stone[t]—rejected by men but chosen by
God and precious to him— 5 you also,
2:5 u 1Co 3:9 like living stones, are being built[u] into a
v 1Ti 3:15 spiritual house[v] to be a holy priest-
w Isa 61:6 hood,[w] offering spiritual sacrifices ac-
x Php 4:18; Heb 13:15 ceptable to God through Jesus Christ.[x]
6 For in Scripture it says:

> "See, I lay a stone in Zion,
> a chosen and precious
> 2:6 y Eph 2:20 cornerstone,[y]
> z Isa 28:16 and the one who trusts in him
> will never be put to shame."[a] [z]

7 Now to you who believe, this stone is
precious. But to those who do not be-
2:7 a 2Co 2:16 lieve,[a]
b Ps 118:22

> "The stone the builders rejected
> has become the capstone,"[b] [c] [b]

8 and,

> "A stone that causes men to
> stumble
> 2:8 and a rock that makes them
> c Isa 8:14; 1Co 1:23 fall."[d] [c]

They stumble because they disobey the
message—which is also what they were 2:8
destined for.[d] d Ro 9:22
9 But you are a chosen people,[e] a royal 2:9
priesthood, a holy nation,[f] a people be- e Dt 10:15
longing to God, that you may declare the f Isa 62:12
praises of him who called you out of g Ac 26:18
darkness into his wonderful light.[g]
10 Once you were not a people, but now
you are the people of God;[h] once you 2:10
had not received mercy, but now you h Hos 1:9,10
have received mercy.
11 Dear friends, I urge you, as aliens
and strangers in the world, to abstain
from sinful desires,[i] which war against 2:11
your soul.[j] 12 Live such good lives among i Gal 5:16
the pagans that, though they accuse you j Jas 4:1
of doing wrong, they may see your good 2:12
deeds[k] and glorify God[l] on the day he k Php 2:15; 1Pe 3:16
visits us. l Mt 5:16; 9:8

Submission to Rulers and Masters

13 Submit yourselves for the Lord's
sake to every authority[m] instituted 2:13 m Ro 13:1
among men: whether to the king, as the
supreme authority, 14 or to governors,
who are sent by him to punish those
who do wrong[n] and to commend those 2:14
who do right.[o] 15 For it is God's will[p] that n Ro 13:4 o Ro 13:3
by doing good you should silence the ig-
norant talk of foolish men.[q] 16 Live as 2:15 p 1Pe 3:17
free men,[r] but do not use your freedom q ver 12
as a cover-up for evil; live as servants of 2:16
God.[s] 17 Show proper respect to every- r Jn 8:32
one: Love the brotherhood of believers,[t] s Ro 6:22
fear God, honor the king.[u] 2:17 t Ro 12:10
18 Slaves, submit yourselves to your u Ro 13:7
masters with all respect,[v] not only to
those who are good and considerate,[w] 2:18 v Eph 6:5
but also to those who are harsh. 19 For it w Jas 3:17
is commendable if a man bears up un-
der the pain of unjust suffering because
he is conscious of God.[x] 20 But how is it 2:19 x 1Pe 3:14,17
to your credit if you receive a beating for
doing wrong and endure it? But if you 2:20
suffer for doing good and you endure it, y 1Pe 3:17
this is commendable before God.[y] 21 To 2:21
this[z] you were called, because Christ z Ac 14:22
suffered for you, leaving you an exam- a Mt 16:24
ple,[a] that you should follow in his steps.

> 22 "He committed no sin,
> and no deceit was found in his 2:22
> mouth."[e] [b] b Isa 53:9

23 When they hurled their insults at him,

[a] 6 Isaiah 28:16 [b] 7 Or *cornerstone* [c] 7 Psalm 118:22 [d] 8 Isaiah 8:14 [e] 22 Isaiah 53:9

JESUS FOCUS

LIVING STONES

Peter, whose name means "rock" (John 1:42), reminded his readers that God had sent his Son to build a spiritual temple for his people. Jesus is called the "living Stone" (1 Peter 2:4) chosen by God and precious to him. The spiritual building that Peter was referring to is the church. Jesus is the underlying base, support and underpinning of his church, and thus he is called the "cornerstone"—the most critical stone in the foundation of a building (verses 4–6). Peter used the same image of living stones to refer to members of the church—Christians. Like Jesus, each individual Christian is an integral part of the living body called the church. The Good News is that Christians have the assurance that their security and stability is in Jesus, the precious and perfect cornerstone.

> **YOU ARE TO FOLLOW NO MAN FURTHER THAN HE FOLLOWS CHRIST.**
>
> John Collins, *Puritan Pastor*

2:23 he did not retaliate; when he suffered, he
cIsa 53:7 dLk 23:46 made no threats.[c] Instead, he entrusted
himself[d] to him who judges justly. 24He
2:24 eHeb 9:28 himself bore our sins[e] in his body on the
fRo 6:2 tree, so that we might die to sins[f] and
gIsa 53:5; Heb 12:13; live for righteousness; by his wounds
Jas 5:16 you have been healed.[g] 25For you were
2:25 hIsa 53:6 like sheep going astray,[h] but now you
iJn 10:11 have returned to the Shepherd[i] and
Overseer of your souls.

Wives and Husbands

3 Wives, in the same way be sub-
3:1 missive[j] to your husbands[k] so
j1Pe 2:18 kEph 5:22 that, if any of them do not believe the
l1Co 7:16; 9:19 word, they may be won over[l] without
words by the behavior of their wives,
2when they see the purity and reverence
of your lives. 3Your beauty should not
come from outward adornment, such as
braided hair and the wearing of gold
3:3 mIsa 3:18-23; jewelry and fine clothes.[m] 4Instead, it
1Ti 2:9 should be that of your inner self,[n] the
3:4 unfading beauty of a gentle and quiet
nRo 7:22 spirit, which is of great worth in God's
sight. 5For this is the way the holy
women of the past who put their hope in
3:5 o1Ti 5:5 God[o] used to make themselves beautiful. They were submissive to their own

husbands, 6like Sarah, who obeyed 3:6
Abraham and called him her master.[p] pGe 18:12
You are her daughters if you do what is
right and do not give way to fear.
7Husbands,[q] in the same way be con- 3:7 qEph 5:25-33
siderate as you live with your wives, and
treat them with respect as the weaker
partner and as heirs with you of the gracious gift of life, so that nothing will hinder your prayers.

Suffering for Doing Good

8Finally, all of you, live in harmony
with one another; be sympathetic, love 3:8
as brothers,[r] be compassionate and rRo 12:10
humble.[s] 9Do not repay evil with evil[t] or s1Pe 5:5
insult with insult,[u] but with blessing, be- 3:9 tRo 12:17
cause to this[v] you were called so that u1Pe 2:23
you may inherit a blessing.[w] 10For, v1Pe 2:21 wHeb 6:14

"Whoever would love life
and see good days
must keep his tongue from evil
and his lips from deceitful speech.
11 He must turn from evil and do
good;
he must seek peace and pursue it.
12 For the eyes of the Lord are on the
righteous
and his ears are attentive to
their prayer,
but the face of the Lord is against 3:12
those who do evil."[a x] xPs 34:12-16

13Who is going to harm you if you are
eager to do good?[y] 14But even if you 3:13 yPr 16:7
should suffer for what is right, you are
blessed.[z] "Do not fear what they fear[b]; 3:14 z1Pe 2:19,20;
do not be frightened."[c a] 15But in your 4:15,16 aIsa 8:12,13
hearts set apart Christ as Lord. Always
be prepared to give an answer[b] to every- 3:15
one who asks you to give the reason for bCol 4:6
the hope that you have. But do this with
gentleness and respect, 16keeping a clear 3:16
conscience,[c] so that those who speak cHeb 13:18
maliciously against your good behavior d1Pe 2:12,15
in Christ may be ashamed of their slan-
der.[d] 17It is better, if it is God's will,[e] to 3:17
suffer for doing good[f] than for doing e1Pe 2:15 f1Pe 2:20
evil. 18For Christ died for sins[g] once for
all, the righteous for the unrighteous, to 3:18 g1Pe 2:21
bring you to God. He was put to death in hCol 1:22; 1Pe 4:1 i1Pe 4:6
the body[h] but made alive by the Spirit,[i]
19through whom[d] also he went and 3:19
preached to the spirits in prison[j] 20who j1Pe 4:6

[a] 12 Psalm 34:12–16 [b] 14 Or *not fear their threats* [c] 14 Isaiah 8:12 [d] 18,19 Or *alive in the spirit, 19through which*

THE PARTY'S OVER

What happened during the three days in which Jesus' body lay buried in the tomb? Peter stated in 1 Peter 3:18–20 that Jesus went into hell and "preached" there (Paul said something very similar in Ephesians 4:7–10). We have no way of knowing precisely what message Jesus proclaimed, but we can be reasonably certain that it consisted of one overriding theme: Jesus announced in no uncertain terms to Satan and his forces that he had triumphed (1 Peter 3:18–22). Satan may have gloated ever so briefly that Jesus' death appeared to signify God's defeat, but that deception was quickly extinguished by the truth of Jesus' glorious resurrection.

disobeyed long ago when God waited
3:20 patiently in the days of Noah while the
k Ge 6:3,5,13,14 ark was being built.[k] In it only a few
l Heb 11:7 people, eight in all, were saved[l] through
water, [21]and this water symbolizes bap-
3:21 tism that now saves you[m] also—not the
m Tit 3:5 n 1Pe 1:3 removal of dirt from the body but the
pledge[a] of a good conscience toward
God. It saves you by the resurrection of
3:22 Jesus Christ,[n] [22]who has gone into heav-
o Mk 16:19 en and is at God's right hand[o]—with an-
p Ro 8:38 gels, authorities and powers in submission to him.[p]

Living for God

4 Therefore, since Christ suffered in
his body, arm yourselves also with
the same attitude, because he who has
suffered in his body is done with sin. [2]As
a result, he does not live the rest of his
4:2 earthly life for evil human desires,[q] but
q Ro 6:2 rather for the will of God. [3]For you have
4:3 spent enough time in the past[r] doing
r Eph 2:2 what pagans choose to do—living in debauchery, lust, drunkenness, orgies,
carousing and detestable idolatry. [4]They
think it strange that you do not plunge
with them into the same flood of dissi-
4:4 pation, and they heap abuse on you.[s]
s 1Pe 3:16 [5]But they will have to give account to
him who is ready to judge the living and
4:5 the dead.[t] [6]For this is the reason the
t Ac 10:42; 2Ti 4:1 gospel was preached even to those who
4:6 are now dead,[u] so that they might be
u 1Pe 3:19 judged according to men in regard to
the body, but live according to God in regard to the spirit.
4:7 [7]The end of all things is near.[v] There-
v Ro 13:11 fore be clear minded and self-controlled
so that you can pray. [8]Above all, love each
4:8 other deeply,[w] because love covers over a
w 1Pe 1:22 multitude of sins.[x] [9]Offer hospitality to
x Pr 10:12 one another without grumbling.[y] [10]Each
4:9 one should use whatever gift he has re-
y Php 2:14 ceived to serve others,[z] faithfully[a] ad-
4:10 ministering God's grace in its various
z Ro 12:6,7 a 1Co 4:2 forms. [11]If anyone speaks, he should do it
as one speaking the very words of God. If
anyone serves, he should do it with the
4:11 strength God provides,[b] so that in all
b Eph 6:10 c 1Co 10:31 things God may be praised[c] through
Jesus Christ. To him be the glory and the
power for ever and ever. Amen.

Suffering for Being a Christian

[12]Dear friends, do not be surprised at
4:12 d 1Pe 1:6,7 the painful trial you are suffering,[d] as
though something strange were hap-
pening to you. [13]But rejoice that you participate in the sufferings of Christ, so
that you may be overjoyed when his glo- 4:13
ry is revealed.[e] [14]If you are insulted be- e Ro 8:17
cause of the name of Christ, you are 4:14
blessed,[f] for the Spirit of glory and of f Mt 5:11
God rests on you. [15]If you suffer, it
should not be as a murderer or thief or
any other kind of criminal, or even as a
meddler. [16]However, if you suffer as a
Christian, do not be ashamed, but praise
God that you bear that name.[g] [17]For it is 4:16 g Ac 5:41
time for judgment to begin with the
family of God;[h] and if it begins with us, 4:17 h Jer 25:29
what will the outcome be for those who i 2Th 1:8
do not obey the gospel of God?[i] [18]And,

"If it is hard for the righteous to be
saved,
what will become of the ungodly 4:18 j Pr 11:31;
and the sinner?"[b][j] Lk 23:31

[19]So then, those who suffer according
to God's will should commit themselves
to their faithful Creator and continue to
do good.

> YOU REALLY DON'T ACTIVELY BELIEVE IN CHRIST UNTIL YOU MAKE A COMMITMENT OF YOUR LIFE TO HIM AND RECEIVE HIM AS YOUR SAVIOR.
>
> 
>
> Billy Graham, *American Evangelist*

To Elders and Young Men

5 To the elders among you, I appeal
as a fellow elder,[k] a witness[l] of 5:1 k Ac 11:30
Christ's sufferings and one who also will l Lk 24:48
share in the glory to be revealed:[m] [2]Be m 1Pe 1:5,7; Rev 1:9
shepherds of God's flock[n] that is under
your care, serving as overseers—not be- 5:2 n Jn 21:16
cause you must, but because you are o 1Ti 3:3
willing, as God wants you to be; not
greedy for money,[o] but eager to serve;
[3]not lording it over[p] those entrusted to 5:3 p Eze 34:4
you, but being examples[q] to the flock. q Php 3:17
[4]And when the Chief Shepherd appears,
you will receive the crown of glory[r] that 5:4 r 1Co 9:25
will never fade away.
[5]Young men, in the same way be sub-
missive[s] to those who are older. All of 5:5 s Eph 5:21
you, clothe yourselves with humility to-
ward one another, because,

[a] 21 Or *response* [b] 18 Prov. 11:31

Arm Yourself With Attitude

Christians who have suffered little or no persecution because of their faith often have difficulty understanding the significance of "arming ourselves" with Jesus' attitude. Peter knew firsthand what it meant to suffer for Jesus' sake. His first letter was written to Jewish Christians who on account of their faith had been driven out of Jerusalem and scattered throughout Asia Minor. They were hated by Roman unbelievers, but, more significantly, they were despised by their own people.

There is much heartache in this world, but the only suffering that has eternal value is the kind that comes from living the way God wants us to. In order to "arm" ourselves with the attitude of Christ, we must be prepared to endure hardship for doing what is right. Peter counseled believers in 1 Peter 4:12–13: "Dear friends, do not be surprised at the painful trial you are suffering, as though something strange were happening to you. But rejoice that you participate in the sufferings of Christ, so that you may be overjoyed when his glory is revealed."

Philippians 2:5–8 tells us that Jesus renounced equality with God and chose instead to make himself nothing. He was so perfectly humble, in fact, that he laid down his life for an entire race of doomed sinners. Jesus submitted to unspeakable physical anguish to open the way for us to experience eternal life.

God does not remove suffering from our lives in order to elevate us above the effects of sin in the world. There are people who believe that our loving Father will not allow anyone who truly belongs to him to endure illness or poverty. These Christians teach that the "abundant life" implies that all will be well all of the time. In fact, however, the Bible teaches that the very opposite may sometimes be true. In some situations we may suffer more because we identify with Jesus (Matthew 5:11–12; Acts 5:41; 14:22; Romans 5:3; 1 Peter 1:6–7; 2:20–21).

God's Word teaches that our anxiety will be eased when we "cast" it on Jesus (1 Peter 5:7). To cast something means to throw it off, to discard it or to shed it. Jesus promises to care for us, so we don't have to be anxious about whether or not he really will.

We are never alone in suffering: "Brothers throughout the world are undergoing the same kind of sufferings" (verse 9). We are blessed when we suffer for what is right. Peter encouraged us not to fear what may happen to us but to set Jesus apart in our hearts as Lord (1 Peter 3:14–15; see also Isaiah 8:12). Arming ourselves with Jesus' humble attitude allows us to fully trust our Almighty God, because we know that he is on our side and will continue to transform us into the likeness of his Son. As stated so eloquently by the apostle Paul, "we know that in all things God works for the good of those who love him, who have been called according to his purpose. For those God foreknew he also predestined to be conformed to the likeness of his Son, that he might be the firstborn among many brothers" (Romans 8:28–29).

Self-Discovery: *What "painful trial" have you experienced, or are continuing to experience, as a direct result of your faith in Jesus? In what way have you armed yourself with Jesus' attitude in light of this trial?*

GO TO DISCOVERY 346 ON PAGE 1675

5:5 [t] Pr 3:34; Jas 4:6

"God opposes the proud
but gives grace to the
humble."[a t]

6Humble yourselves, therefore, under
God's mighty hand, that he may lift you
up in due time.[u] 7Cast all your anxiety
on him[v] because he cares for you.[w]
8Be self-controlled and alert. Your enemy the devil prowls around[x] like a roaring lion looking for someone to devour.
9Resist him,[y] standing firm in the faith,[z]
because you know that your brothers
throughout the world are undergoing
the same kind of sufferings.[a]
10And the God of all grace, who called
you to his eternal glory[b] in Christ, after
you have suffered a little while, will himself restore you and make you strong,[c]
firm and steadfast. 11To him be the power for ever and ever. Amen.[d]

5:6 [u] Jas 4:10
5:7 [v] Ps 37:5; Mt 6:25 [w] Heb 13:5
5:8 [x] Job 1:7
5:9 [y] Jas 4:7 [z] Col 2:5 [a] Ac 14:22
5:10 [b] 2Co 4:17 [c] 2Th 2:17
5:11 [d] Ro 11:36

Final Greetings

12With the help of Silas,[b e] whom I regard as a faithful brother, I have written
to you briefly,[f] encouraging you and testifying that this is the true grace of God.
Stand fast in it.
13She who is in Babylon, chosen together with you, sends you her greetings,
and so does my son Mark.[g] 14Greet one
another with a kiss of love.[h]
Peace[i] to all of you who are in Christ.

5:12 [e] 2Co 1:19 [f] Heb 13:22
5:13 [g] Ac 12:12
5:14 [h] Ro 16:16 [i] Eph 6:23

[a] *5* Prov. 3:34 [b] *12* Greek *Silvanus,* a variant of *Silas*

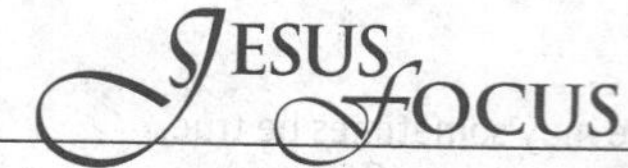

THE CHIEF SHEPHERD

"Shepherding" in the New Testament context involves looking after and caring for God's people. Peter described the leaders of the church as "shepherds of God's flock" (1 Peter 5:1–3) and reminded them to lead by their example in a worthy manner. Jesus had earlier referred to himself as the "good shepherd" (John 10:11–14), thereby identifying himself as the One whom God had promised to send to guide his people in all truth. A shepherd does much more than merely feeding and watering the sheep; he or she protects and gently guides the flock. In the same way, God wants church leaders, acting as undershepherds in Jesus' name, to demonstrate spiritual guidance and loving care. God has placed spiritual leaders and mentors in each of our lives, thereby enabling us to walk closer to himself (1 Peter 5:2).

2 PETER

Jesus in 2 Peter While 1 Peter is a gentle book with a devotional feel, 2 Peter blasts away at readers with an attention-grabbing forcefulness. But the differences in style and tone reflect the different needs of the audiences. The believers in 1 Peter were facing outside persecution—and Peter's words provided them with encouragement to stand strong. At the time Peter wrote his second letter, however, false teachers and immoral behavior had been tearing away at the internal fabric of the church. Peter understood that these situations were more insidious for the life of the church than any outside persecution, and his fierce tone drew attention to the dangers inherent in wrong teaching.

In Jesus Christ we have everything we need to live life the way God wants us to (2 Peter 1:3), as well as the promise that our relationship with him is secure (verse 4) and the expectation that he will come back to this world to destroy the effects of sin and to recreate all things as he had intended them to be from the beginning (2 Peter 3:3–13).

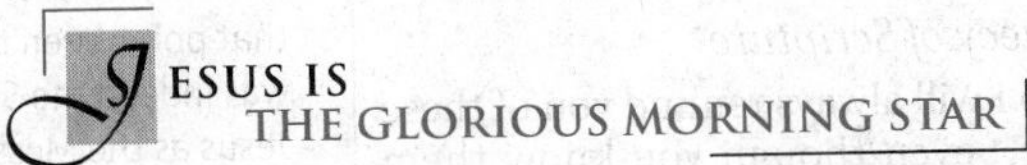

JESUS IS THE GLORIOUS MORNING STAR

What makes people vulnerable to false teachers? (2 Peter 2:14)

- *The "unstable" are vulnerable and naive, suggesting that they have no foundation in solid Biblical teaching. Those who have stopped growing in their relationship with Jesus Christ are probably even more vulnerable (see 2 Peter 1:5–10). Other contributing factors may be times of suffering, a reluctance to obey, an eagerness to please people, or being physically or socially disadvantaged.*

What's better about never having known the right way? (2 Peter 2:20–22)

- *It appears that there are degrees of punishment for the lost (Matthew 13:11–14). Those who reject the Good News about Jesus Christ are accountable for more than those who never knew and so never consciously rejected it (Matthew 25:16–28). Still, those who have never heard the gospel are judged because they don't live up to what little they know through nature and their own conscience (Romans 1:18–20; 2:12,15).*

2 Peter 1

1:1 [a]Ro 1:1 1 Simon Peter, a servant[a] and apos-
[b]1Pe 1:1 tle of Jesus Christ,[b]
[c]Ro 3:21-26
[d]Tit 2:13 To those who through the righteousness[c] of our God and Savior Jesus
Christ[d] have received a faith as precious
as ours:

2Grace and peace be yours in abundance through the knowledge of God
1:2 [e]Php 3:8 and of Jesus our Lord.[e]

Making One's Calling and Election Sure

1:3 [f]1Pe 1:5 3His divine power[f] has given us every-
[g]1Th 2:12 thing we need for life and godliness
through our knowledge of him who
called us[g] by his own glory and goodness. 4Through these he has given us his
1:4 [h]2Co 7:1 very great and precious promises,[h] so
[i]Eph 4:24; Heb 12:10; that through them you may participate
1Jn 3:2 in the divine nature[i] and escape the cor-
[j]2Pe 2:18-20 ruption in the world caused by evil desires.[j]
5For this very reason, make every ef-
1:5 fort to add to your faith goodness; and
[k]Col 2:3 to goodness, knowledge;[k] 6and to
knowledge, self-control;[l] and to self-
1:6 [l]Ac 24:25 control, perseverance; and to persever-
[m]ver 3 ance, godliness;[m] 7and to godliness,
brotherly kindness; and to brotherly
1:7 [n]1Th 3:12 kindness, love.[n] 8For if you possess these
qualities in increasing measure, they will
keep you from being ineffective and un-
1:8 [o]Jn 15:2; productive[o] in your knowledge of our
Tit 3:14 Lord Jesus Christ. 9But if anyone does
not have them, he is nearsighted and
1:9 [p]1Jn 2:11 blind,[p] and has forgotten that he has
[q]Eph 5:26 been cleansed from his past sins.[q]
10Therefore, my brothers, be all the
more eager to make your calling and
election sure. For if you do these things,
1:10 [r]2Pe 3:17 you will never fall,[r] 11and you will receive
a rich welcome into the eternal king-
dom of our Lord and Savior Jesus Christ.

Prophecy of Scripture

12So I will always remind you of these
1:12 [s]Php 3:1; things,[s] even though you know them
1Jn 2:21 and are firmly established in the truth
you now have. 13I think it is right to refresh your memory as long as I live in
1:13 [t]2Co 5:1,4 the tent of this body,[t] 14because I know
that I will soon put it aside,[u] as our Lord
1:14 [u]2Ti 4:6 Jesus Christ has made clear to me.[v]
[v]Jn 21:18,19 15And I will make every effort to see that
after my departure[w] you will always be
1:15 [w]Lk 9:31 able to remember these things.

> **NO ONE CAN READ THE GOSPELS WITHOUT FEELING THE ACTUAL PRESENCE OF JESUS. HIS PERSONALITY PULSATES IN EVERY WORD. NO MYTH IS FILLED WITH SUCH LIFE.**
>
> 
>
> Albert Einstein, *Scientist*

16We did not follow cleverly invented
stories when we told you about the
power and coming of our Lord Jesus
Christ, but we were eyewitnesses of his
majesty.[x] 17For he received honor and 1:16 [x]Mt 17:1-8
glory from God the Father when the
voice came to him from the Majestic
Glory, saying, "This is my Son, whom I
love; with him I am well pleased."[a][y] 18We 1:17 [y]Mt 3:17
ourselves heard this voice that came
from heaven when we were with him on
the sacred mountain.[z] 1:18 [z]Mt 17:6
19And we have the word of the prophets made more certain, and you will do
well to pay attention to it, as to a light[a] 1:19 [a]Ps 119:105
shining in a dark place, until the day [b]Rev 22:16
dawns and the morning star[b] rises
in your hearts. 20Above all, you must

[a] *17* Matt. 17:5; Mark 9:7; Luke 9:35

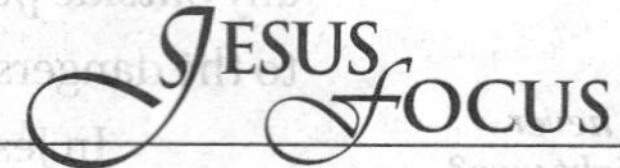

GOD HAS SPOKEN

Peter lived with Jesus and experienced many of the same things Jesus experienced. In 2 Peter 1:16–18 he reflected back on the time when he had witnessed Moses and Elijah meeting with Jesus on the mountain (Matthew 17:1–13; Mark 9:2–8; Luke 9:28–36). At that time God the Father had announced unequivocally, "This is my Son." If he'd ever doubted before, Peter had at that point been thoroughly convinced that Jesus was indeed the Son of God. Peter also recognized Jesus as the Messiah because "the word of the prophets" pointed to him (2 Peter 1:19–21). Peter referred to Jesus as the "morning star" (verse 19), the same words John would use when recording his vision of the last days (Revelation 2:28; 22:16). Peter reminded his readers that the prophets had not fabricated their own predictions; they had spoken for God himself and had written down only that which his Holy Spirit had moved them to write (2 Peter 1:20–21).

DISCOVERY 346

Growing in Knowledge of Jesus

The Christian life is a continuous journey of getting to know Jesus Christ. The better we become acquainted with him, the more we become like him. Peter noted two vital ingredients that will help us to grow in that knowledge.

We grow in our knowledge of Jesus as we pay attention to his promises. Jesus promised us everything we need for life and godliness (2 Peter 1:3–4) and promised his disciples his blessing (Matthew 5:3–12), his continual presence (Matthew 28:20), his Holy Spirit to guide and strengthen them (John 14:15–17) and the gift of peace (John 16:33).

We also grow in our knowledge of Jesus when we learn to cultivate his character in our lives. God doesn't want us to become stagnant or content to sit on a spiritual plateau and enjoy the panorama below; he wants us to continue to climb toward higher and more majestic vistas. Peter listed eight specific ways in which we can become more Christlike (2 Peter 1:5–7):

1. faith—trusting God: "Now faith is being sure of what we hope for and certain of what we do not see" (Hebrews 11:1).

2. goodness—demonstrating virtue: "Live as children of the light (for the fruit of the light consists in all goodness, righteousness and truth)" (Ephesians 5:8–9).

3. knowledge—developing understanding and insight: "Thanks be to God, who always leads us in triumphal procession in Christ and through us spreads everywhere the fragrance of the knowledge of him" (2 Corinthians 2:14).

4. self-control—holding oneself in check: "Be self-controlled and alert. Your enemy the devil prowls around like a roaring lion looking for someone to devour. Resist him, standing firm in the faith" (1 Peter 5:8–9).

5. perseverance—persisting: "Let us throw off everything that hinders and the sin that so easily entangles, and let us run with perseverance the race marked out for us" (Hebrews 12:1).

6. godliness—surrendering completely to God: "Godliness has value for all things, holding promise for both the present life and the life to come" (1 Timothy 4:8).

7. kindness—affection for others: "As God's chosen people, holy and dearly loved, clothe yourselves with compassion, kindness, humility, gentleness and patience" (Colossians 3:12).

8. love—deep-seated concern for the interests of God and others: "Live a life of love, just as Christ loved us and gave himself up for us as a fragrant offering and sacrifice to God" (Ephesians 5:2).

These qualities increase in our lives as we devote ourselves to Jesus and allow his Spirit to work within us. They prevent us from becoming "ineffective and unproductive" (2 Peter 1:8). But we need to be prepared for the reality that these character traits are developed under pressure. When we trust God to take care of us and recognize that he has our best in mind at all times, we can learn to view times of hardship as opportunities to become more like Jesus Christ (Romans 8:28–29).

***Self-Discovery:** You can become more like Jesus by choosing one of the eight means of growth that Peter listed and making a concerted effort, with the help of the Holy Spirit, to develop this one area in your life this week.*

GO TO DISCOVERY 347 ON PAGE 1677

understand that no prophecy of Scripture came about by the prophet's own
1:21 interpretation. 21 For prophecy never had
c 2Ti 3:16 its origin in the will of man, but men
d 2Sa 23:2; Ac 1:16; spoke from God[c] as they were carried
1Pe 1:11 along by the Holy Spirit.[d]

False Teachers and Their Destruction

2:1 **2** But there were also false proph-
e Dt 13:1-3 ets[e] among the people, just as
f 1Ti 4:1 g Jude 4 there will be false teachers among you.[f]
h 1Co 6:20 They will secretly introduce destructive
heresies, even denying the sovereign
Lord[g] who bought them[h]—bringing
swift destruction on themselves. 2 Many
will follow their shameful ways and will
bring the way of truth into disrepute. 3 In
their greed these teachers will exploit
2:3 i 2Co 2:17; you[i] with stories they have made up.
1Th 2:5 Their condemnation has long been
hanging over them, and their destruction has not been sleeping.

4 For if God did not spare angels when
they sinned, but sent them to hell,[a] put-
2:4 ting them into gloomy dungeons[b] to be
j Jude 6; held for judgment;[j] 5 if he did not spare
Rev 20:1,2 the ancient world[k] when he brought the
2:5 flood on its ungodly people, but pro-
k 2Pe 3:6 tected Noah, a preacher of righteous-
l Heb 11:7; 1Pe 3:20 ness, and seven others;[l] 6 if he con-
2:6 demned the cities of Sodom and
m Ge 19:24,25 Gomorrah by burning them to ashes,[m]
n Nu 26:10; and made them an example[n] of what is
Jude 7 going to happen to the ungodly; 7 and if
2:7 o Ge 19:16 he rescued Lot,[o] a righteous man, who
p 2Pe 3:17 was distressed by the filthy lives of lawless men[p] 8 (for that righteous man, living among them day after day, was tormented in his righteous soul by the
lawless deeds he saw and heard)— 9 if
2:9 this is so, then the Lord knows how to
q 1Co 10:13 rescue godly men from trials[q] and to
hold the unrighteous for the day of judgment, while continuing their punish-
2:10 ment.[c] 10 This is especially true of those
r 2Pe 3:3 s Jude 8 who follow the corrupt desire[r] of the
sinful nature[d] and despise authority.

Bold and arrogant, these men are not
afraid to slander celestial beings;[s] 11 yet
even angels, although they are stronger
and more powerful, do not bring slanderous accusations against such beings
2:11 t Jude 9 in the presence of the Lord.[t] 12 But these
men blaspheme in matters they do not
understand. They are like brute beasts,
creatures of instinct, born only to be
caught and destroyed, and like beasts
they too will perish.[u] 2:12 u Jude 10

13 They will be paid back with harm for
the harm they have done. Their idea of 2:13
pleasure is to carouse in broad daylight.[v] v Ro 13:13
They are blots and blemishes, reveling in w 1Co 11:20,21; Jude 12
their pleasures while they feast with
you.[e w] 14 With eyes full of adultery, they 2:14
never stop sinning; they seduce[x] the un- x ver 18 y ver 3
stable; they are experts in greed[y]—an z Eph 2:3
accursed brood![z] 15 They have left the
straight way and wandered off to follow
the way of Balaam[a] son of Beor, who 2:15 a Nu 22:4-20;
loved the wages of wickedness. 16 But he Jude 11
was rebuked for his wrongdoing by a
donkey—a beast without speech—who
spoke with a man's voice and restrained 2:16
the prophet's madness.[b] b Nu 22:21-30

17 These men are springs without wa- 2:17
ter[c] and mists driven by a storm. Black- c Jude 12
est darkness is reserved for them.[d] 18 For d Jude 13
they mouth empty, boastful words[e] and, 2:18
by appealing to the lustful desires of sin- e Jude 16
ful human nature, they entice people
who are just escaping from those who
live in error. 19 They promise them freedom, while they themselves are slaves of
depravity—for a man is a slave to what- 2:19
ever has mastered him.[f] 20 If they have f Jn 8:34;
escaped the corruption of the world by Ro 6:16
knowing[g] our Lord and Savior Jesus 2:20
Christ and are again entangled in it and g 2Pe 1:2 h Mt 12:45
overcome, they are worse off at the end
than they were at the beginning.[h] 21 It
would have been better for them not to
have known the way of righteousness,
than to have known it and then to turn
their backs on the sacred command that
was passed on to them.[i] 22 Of them the 2:21 i Heb 6:4-6
proverbs are true: "A dog returns to its 2:22
vomit,"[f j] and, "A sow that is washed goes j Pr 26:11
back to her wallowing in the mud."

The Day of the Lord

3 Dear friends, this is now my second letter to you. I have written
both of them as reminders[k] to stimulate 3:1 k 2Pe 1:13
you to wholesome thinking. 2 I want you
to recall the words spoken in the past by
the holy prophets and the command
given by our Lord and Savior through
your apostles.

3 First of all, you must understand that

[a] 4 Greek *Tartarus* [b] 4 Some manuscripts *into chains of darkness* [c] 9 Or *unrighteous for punishment until the day of judgment* [d] 10 Or *the flesh* [e] 13 Some manuscripts *in their love feasts* [f] 22 Prov. 26:11

DISCOVERY 347

Beware of False Teachers

In 2 Peter 2 the apostle warned of the danger, particularly for new and unseasoned believers, of being carried away by the seductions of false teachers. Peter included several descriptive statements to help Christians to identify these inauthentic evangelists:

They infiltrate the church with destructive heresies (verse 1) and entice believers with made-up stories (verse 3). They are brazen enough to slander celestial beings (verse 10) and blaspheme in doctrinal matters they themselves do not fully understand (verse 12). Their idea of pleasure is carousing in broad daylight (verse 13), they are adulterous and attempt to seduce the unstable (verse 14) and they are "experts in greed" (verse 14). They prey on the vulnerable, those who are just beginning to separate themselves from pagan influences (verse 18–19).

Verses 20–22 constitute a scathing indictment against these self-proclaimed revivalists. Peter asserted that it would have been better for them never to have known the way of righteousness than to have turned their backs on the truth: "If they have escaped the corruption of the world by knowing . . . Jesus Christ and are again entangled in it and overcome, they are worse off at the end than they were at the beginning" (verse 20). Peter went so far as to liken these teachers to dogs returning to their own vomit or sows that have been washed wallowing once again in the mud (verse 22).

These verses have been troublesome for some Christians who have found themselves unable to reconcile them with the Biblical truth that a saved individual cannot thereafter be lost. Jesus himself stated unequivocally in John 10:28 that he gives his followers "eternal life, and they shall never perish; no one can snatch them out of [his] hand." And Paul discussed this issue at some length in Romans 8:28–39. This passage concludes with one of the most beautiful and oft-quoted testimonies in all of Scripture: "For I am convinced that neither death nor life, neither angels nor demons, neither the present nor the future, nor any powers, neither height nor depth, nor anything else in all creation, will be able to separate us from the love of God that is in Christ Jesus our Lord" (verses 38–39).

The best explanation for this apparent discrepancy is the assumption that the false teachers to whom Peter referred had never experienced genuine salvation but had only heard the gospel and used the truth to exploit others.

Sometimes we as contemporary believers tend to doubt our own salvation or that of others whom we know. We might experience periods of spiritual drought or times during which the old enticements beckon. We might even succumb to temptation and wonder whether our Lord will accept us back. It is precisely at these moments that we can envision ourselves held firmly in Jesus' hand and recall his emphatic statement that *no one* can snatch us from his grip—not false teachers, not acquaintances or associates from the past, not the devil himself. Once we have truly committed our lives to the Lord, he counts us as his treasured possession, and he is not about to let us go!

Self-Discovery: *What particular temptation poses a problem for you? Visualize yourself being help firmly in the grip of Jesus' hand. Does this image give you comfort as you struggle with temptation?*

GO TO DISCOVERY 348 ON PAGE 1682

3:3 [l]1Ti 4:1 in the last days[l] scoffers will come, scoff-
[m]2Pe 2:10; ing and following their own evil de-
Jude 18 sires.[m] 4They will say, "Where is this
3:4 'coming' he promised?[n] Ever since our
[n]Isa 5:19; fathers died, everything goes on as it has
Eze 12:22; since the beginning of creation."[o] 5But
Mt 24:48 [o]Mk 10:6 they deliberately forget that long ago by
3:5 God's word[p] the heavens existed and the
[p]Ge 1:6,9; earth was formed out of water and by
Heb 11:3 [q]Ps 24:2 water.[q] 6By these waters also the world
of that time was deluged and destroyed.[r]
3:6 [r]Ge 7:21,22 7By the same word the present heavens
and earth are reserved for fire,[s] being
3:7 kept for the day of judgment and de-
[s]ver 10,12; 2Th 1:7 struction of ungodly men.
8But do not forget this one thing, dear
friends: With the Lord a day is like a
thousand years, and a thousand years
3:8 [t]Ps 90:4 are like a day.[t] 9The Lord is not slow in
3:9 keeping his promise,[u] as some under-
[u]Hab 2:3; stand slowness. He is patient[v] with you,
Heb 10:37 not wanting anyone to perish, but every-
[v]Ro 2:4 [w]1Ti 2:4 one to come to repentance.[w]
10But the day of the Lord will come
3:10 [x]Lk 12:39; like a thief.[x] The heavens will disappear
1Th 5:2 with a roar; the elements will be de-
[y]Mt 24:35; stroyed by fire, and the earth and every-
Rev 21:1 thing in it will be laid bare.[a][y]
11Since everything will be destroyed
in this way, what kind of people ought
you to be? You ought to live holy and
3:12 [z]1Co 1:7 godly lives 12as you look forward[z] to the
[a]Ps 50:3 day of God and speed its coming.[b][a] That
day will bring about the destruction of
the heavens by fire, and the elements

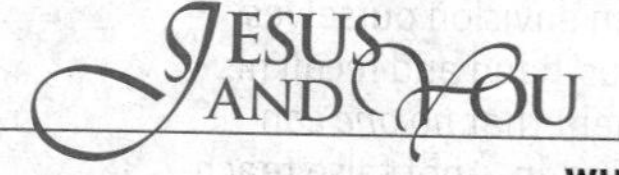

WHO'S COUNTING?

Peter warned his reading audience that in the "last days" people would scoff at the idea that Jesus is coming back (2 Peter 3:3–4). The longer we are obligated to wait the more some believers may be tempted to suspect that such thinking makes some sense. After all, it's been two thousand years, and we haven't seen Jesus yet. Sin still runs rampant, and people still turn away from God to live their own lives. But time as we know it is immaterial and irrelevant to God; Peter points out that by God's calculation a thousand years might just as well be a single day (verse 8). While never specifying a time or date for Jesus' second coming, Peter reiterated God's consistent message on the subject: Be ready for him because he could come at any time (verse 10).

will melt in the heat.[b] 13But in keeping 3:12 [b]ver 10
with his promise we are looking forward
to a new heaven and a new earth,[c] the 3:13
home of righteousness. [c]Isa 65:17; 66:22; Rev 21:1
14So then, dear friends, since you are
looking forward to this, make every ef-
fort to be found spotless, blameless[d] and 3:14 [d]1Th 3:13
at peace with him. 15Bear in mind that
our Lord's patience[e] means salvation,[f] 3:15 [e]Ro 2:4 [f]ver 9
just as our dear brother Paul also wrote [g]Eph 3:3
you with the wisdom that God gave
him.[g] 16He writes the same way in all his
letters, speaking in them of these matters. His letters contain some things
that are hard to understand, which ig- 3:16
norant and unstable[h] people distort, as [h]2Pe 2:14 [i]ver 2
they do the other Scriptures,[i] to their
own destruction.
17Therefore, dear friends, since you al- 3:17
ready know this, be on your guard[j] so [j]1Co 10:12
that you may not be carried away by the [k]2Pe 2:18
error[k] of lawless men and fall from your [l]Rev 2:5
secure position.[l] 18But grow in the grace
and knowledge of our Lord and Savior
Jesus Christ.[m] To him be glory both now 3:18
and forever! Amen. [m]2Pe 1:11

[a] *10* Some manuscripts *be burned up* [b] *12* Or *as you wait eagerly for the day of God to come*

THE END IS NEAR

Numerous Biblical writers used the phrase "the day of the Lord" to refer to the end of time. God enabled Peter to look forward in time to catch a glimpse of what will happen when Jesus does return. The earth as we know it will be destroyed by fire (2 Peter 3:10), after which God will create a new heaven and a new earth, a place of consummate perfection in which his people will live with him forever (verse 13). God's prophets in the Old Testament had used very similar language in their descriptions of the end of time when God would set all things right (Isaiah 24:18–23; 66:22–24; Joel 1—3), and New Testament writers had taken up the same theme (2 Thessalonians 1:7–10; 2:1–12; Revelation 20:9). As appealing as our world can at times look to us now, we as Christians recognize that one day it will all be "laid bare" (2 Peter 3:10)—and that God will replace it with a new and revitalized earth, wonderful beyond our wildest imaginings. When we get to know the God who loves us, we can be at peace with our future, knowing that it is secure in his hands (verse 14).

Jesus in 1 John The book of 1 John stresses God's love as an example to follow in our relationships with one another. But it goes on to encourage us to practice right living by learning and obeying God's commands. In a day when many are being deceived, this short book sounds a clarion call for maintaining truth through fellowship with Jesus.

John focused on a few simple topics—light, truth, life and love. False teachers had distorted the meanings of these subjects, but John clearly specified the rightful place of each in the life of a believer.

John described Jesus as God the Son who had become a man, calling him the "Word of life" (1 John 1:1) who is at the same time both completely human *and* completely God. Because Jesus is God's "Righteous One" he serves as our advocate with the Father (1 John 2:1). Finally, the Holy Spirit assures God's people that Jesus came to save us from sin's dire consequences (1 John 4:14). God wanted us to know his love—and Jesus came to show us.

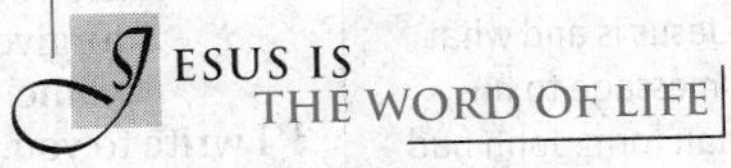

What does it mean to "walk as Jesus did"? (1 John 2:6)

♦ *The word walk is a word picture that speaks of one's lifestyle or behavior. To "walk as Jesus did" means to follow his example, to live according to his teachings, to trust in him and obey his words.*

What kind of anointing do Christians have? (1 John 2:20)

♦ *The anointing of the Holy Spirit here means a sort of certification. Our anointing suggests that we are complete in Jesus and that we are commissioned to serve him. This anointing also suggests an ongoing presence and ministry of the Spirit within, protecting us from false teachers and helping us discern between right and wrong.*

In what sense will we be like Jesus? (1 John 3:2)

♦ *John was speaking about our final cleansing that will make us pure, "just as he is pure" (verse 3). Once we are set free from our natural bodies and transformed to our heavenly bodies, we will be completely free of sin.*

> **THE KEYNOTE OF THE CHRISTIAN EXPERIENCE IS THAT WE ARE IN FELLOWSHIP WITH CHRIST.**
>
> 
>
> G. Campbell Morgan, *British Pastor*

The Word of Life

1:1 1 That which was from the begin-
a Jn 1:2 b Jn 1:14; ning,[a] which we have heard,
2Pe 1:16 which we have seen with our eyes,[b]
c Jn 20:27 which we have looked at and our hands
have touched[c]—this we proclaim con-
1:2 cerning the Word of life. 2 The life ap-
d Jn 1:1-4; peared;[d] we have seen it and testify to it,
1Ti 3:16 and we proclaim to you the eternal life,
which was with the Father and has appeared to us. 3 We proclaim to you what
1:3 we have seen and heard, so that you also
e 1Co 1:9 may have fellowship with us. And our
fellowship is with the Father and with
1:4 f 1Jn 2:1 his Son, Jesus Christ.[e] 4 We write this[f] to
g Jn 3:29 make our[a] joy complete.[g]

Walking in the Light

1:5 5 This is the message we have heard[h]
h 1Jn 3:11 from him and declare to you: God is
light; in him there is no darkness at all.
6 If we claim to have fellowship with him
1:6 i 2Co 6:14 yet walk in the darkness,[i] we lie and do
j Jn 3:19-21 not live by the truth.[j] 7 But if we walk in
the light, as he is in the light, we have fellowship with one another, and the blood
1:7 k Heb 9:14; of Jesus, his Son, purifies us from all[b]
Rev 1:5 sin.[k]

8 If we claim to be without sin,[l] we de- 1:8 l Pr 20:9; Jas 3:2
ceive ourselves and the truth is not in m 1Jn 2:4
us.[m] 9 If we confess our sins, he is faithful
and just and will forgive us our sins[n] and 1:9
purify us from all unrighteousness. 10 If n Ps 32:5; 51:2
we claim we have not sinned, we make
him out to be a liar[o] and his word has no 1:10 o 1Jn 5:10
place in our lives.[p] p 1Jn 2:14

2 My dear children,[q] I write this to 2:1
you so that you will not sin. But if q ver 12,13,28
anybody does sin, we have one who r Ro 8:34;
speaks to the Father in our defense[r]— Heb 7:25
Jesus Christ, the Righteous One. 2 He is
the atoning sacrifice for our sins,[s] and 2:2
not only for ours but also for[c] the sins of s Ro 3:25
the whole world.

3 We know that we have come to know
him if we obey his commands.[t] 4 The 2:3
man who says, "I know him," but does t Jn 14:15
not do what he commands is a liar, and
the truth is not in him.[u] 5 But if anyone 2:4
obeys his word,[v] God's love[d] is truly u 1Jn 1:6,8
made complete in him.[w] This is how we 2:5
know we are in him: 6 Whoever claims to v Jn 14:21,23
live in him must walk as Jesus did.[x] w 1Jn 4:12

7 Dear friends, I am not writing you a 2:6
new command but an old one, which x Mt 11:29;
you have had since the beginning.[y] This 1Pe 2:21
old command is the message you have 2:7
heard. 8 Yet I am writing you a new com- y 1Jn 3:11,23;
mand;[z] its truth is seen in him and you, 2Jn 5,6
because the darkness is passing[a] and 2:8
the true light[b] is already shining.[c] z Jn 13:34
a Ro 13:12
9 Anyone who claims to be in the light b Jn 1:9
but hates his brother is still in the dark- c Eph 5:8;
ness. 10 Whoever loves his brother lives 1Th 5:5
in the light,[d] and there is nothing in 2:10
him[e] to make him stumble. 11 But who- d 1Jn 3:14
ever hates his brother is in the darkness
and walks around in the darkness; he
does not know where he is going, because the darkness has blinded him.[e] 2:11
e Jn 12:35

12 I write to you, dear children,
because your sins have been
forgiven on account of his
name.
13 I write to you, fathers,
because you have known him
who is from the beginning.
I write to you, young men,
because you have overcome the 2:13
evil one.[f] f ver 14
I write to you, dear children,

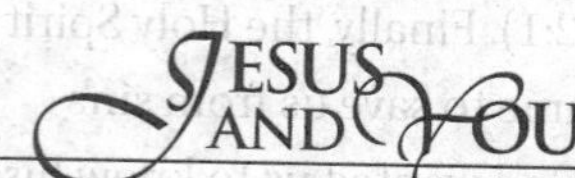

THE WORD OF LIFE

One of John's favorite terms to describe Jesus was the "Word," or *logos* (see John 1:1; Revelation 19:13). In 1 John 1:1 the apostle John referred to Jesus as the "Word of life." Who Jesus is and what he did stands as God's enduring message to humanity. He is God's Word in human form. John had known Jesus personally and touched him physically (verse 1). His friendship with Jesus was so vital that John described it as being in a relationship with both God the Father and God the Son (verse 3). In his opening chapter John made it clear that Jesus is a very real person who wants a very personal relationship with each one of us, and John called that intimate experience "fellowship with him" (verse 6).

[a] 4 Some manuscripts *your* [b] 7 Or *every*
[c] 2 Or *He is the one who turns aside God's wrath, taking away our sins, and not only ours but also*
[d] 5 Or *word, love for God* [e] 10 Or *it*

DESPISE NOT A SOUL FOR WHOM CHRIST DIED!

Jerome, *Early Church Father*

because you have known the
Father.
14I write to you, fathers,
because you have known him
who is from the beginning.
I write to you, young men,
2:14 because you are strong,[g]
g Eph 6:10 h Jn 5:38; 1Jn 1:10 i ver 13 and the word of God lives in you,[h]
and you have overcome the evil
one.[i]

Do Not Love the World

15Do not love the world or anything in
2:15 j Ro 12:2 the world.[j] If anyone loves the world, the
k Jas 4:4 love of the Father is not in him.[k] 16For
everything in the world—the cravings of
2:16 l Ro 13:14 sinful man,[l] the lust of his eyes[m] and the
m Pr 27:20 boasting of what he has and does—
comes not from the Father but from the
world. 17The world and its desires pass
2:17 n 1Co 7:31 away,[n] but the man who does the will of
God lives forever.

Warning Against Antichrists

18Dear children, this is the last hour;
2:18 o ver 22; 1Jn 4:3; 2Jn 7 and as you have heard that the antichrist is coming,[o] even now many an-
tichrists have come.[p] This is how we 2:18 p 1Jn 4:1
know it is the last hour. 19They went out
from us,[q] but they did not really belong 2:19 q Ac 20:30
to us. For if they had belonged to us, r 1Co 11:19
they would have remained with us; but
their going showed that none of them
belonged to us.[r]
20But you have an anointing[s] from the 2:20 s 2Co 1:21
Holy One,[t] and all of you know the t Mk 1:24
truth.[a u] 21I do not write to you because u Jn 14:26
you do not know the truth, but because
you do know it[v] and because no lie 2:21 v 2Pe 1:12; Jude 5
comes from the truth. 22Who is the liar?
It is the man who denies that Jesus is the
Christ. Such a man is the antichrist—he
denies the Father and the Son.[w] 23No 2:22 w 2Jn 7
one who denies the Son has the Father;
whoever acknowledges the Son has the 2:23 x Jn 8:19; 1Jn 4:15
Father also.[x]
24See that what you have heard from
the beginning remains in you. If it does,
you also will remain in the Son and in
the Father.[y] 25And this is what he prom- 2:24 y Jn 14:23
ised us—even eternal life.
26I am writing these things to you
about those who are trying to lead you
astray.[z] 27As for you, the anointing[a] 2:26 z 2Jn 7
you received from him remains in you,
and you do not need anyone to teach 2:27 a ver 20
you. But as his anointing teaches you
about all things and as that anointing is
real, not counterfeit—just as it has
taught you, remain in him.

Children of God

28And now, dear children,[b] continue 2:28 b ver 1 c 1Jn 3:2
in him, so that when he appears[c] we d 1Jn 4:17
may be confident[d] and unashamed be- e 1Th 2:19
fore him at his coming.[e]
29If you know that he is righteous,[f] 2:29 f 1Jn 3:7
you know that everyone who does what
is right has been born of him.

3 How great is the love[g] the Father 3:1 g Jn 3:16
has lavished on us, that we should h Jn 1:12
be called children of God![h] And that is i Jn 16:3
what we are! The reason the world does
not know us is that it did not know him.[i]
2Dear friends, now we are children of
God, and what we will be has not yet
been made known. But we know that
when he appears,[b] we shall be like him,[j] 3:2 j Ro 8:29; 2Pe 1:4
for we shall see him as he is.[k] 3Everyone k 2Co 3:18
who has this hope in him purifies him-
self,[l] just as he is pure. 3:3 l 2Co 7:1; 2Pe 3:13,14
4Everyone who sins breaks the law; in

[a] 20 Some manuscripts *and you know all things*
[b] 2 Or *when it is made known*

JESUS FOCUS

HOW MANY ANTICHRISTS?

John is the only Biblical writer who used the very specific term "*the* antichrist" to refer to the one who will oppose everything that Jesus stands for. Although he specified that such a man will appear, John also stated that there are "many antichrists" around already (1 John 2:18). He clarified that the "spirit of the antichrist" is active in the world through people who teach untruths about Jesus (1 John 4:3), denying that Jesus is God's promised Messiah and therefore ultimately rejecting both God the Father and God the Son (1 John 2:22). When we choose to walk with God by believing in his Son, God the Holy Spirit lives in us and teaches us God's truth (John 16:13). Getting to know the one true God will prevent us from being vulnerable to deception from any "antichrist" (1 John 2:20–27).

DISCOVERY 348

We Will Be Like Him

We do well to remember that this life is not all there is! Our Creator has endowed us with a soul that has the ability to communicate with him on a spiritual level. He has "lavished" his great love on us (1 John 3:1). The word *lavish* signifies that God has spared no expense—to the point that he was even willing to sacrifice his own Son (John 3:16; Romans 8:32). We will one day be like Jesus, "for we shall see him as he is" (1 John 3:2), and we will view history with new eyes—no longer bound by our shortsighted human perceptions.

As we live in a world damaged by sin, we cannot fully grasp the implications of being "like him" (verse 2), but we are called to live in such a way that we can "be confident and unashamed before him at his coming" (1 John 2:28). John expressed it this way in verse 3 of chapter 3: "Everyone who has this hope in [Jesus] purifies himself, just as [Jesus Christ] is pure."

If Jesus has already cleansed us from our sin, we might well ask why we still need to endure a "purifying process." John delineated the answer in this passage: because God doesn't want us to continue making sinful choices knowingly and willfully (verse 9). We are painfully aware of the continual battle raging within each of us between doing God's bidding and behaving in a manner that we assume will afford us the highest degree of pleasure with the least amount of waiting (Romans 7:14–25). But once we have accepted Jesus' sacrifice as our own, the rest of our lives must take on a new purpose and direction. We must be controlled by the Holy Spirit and guided by the Word of God (Psalm 119:9–11; Romans 8:9). This life in effect becomes a training ground for eternity.

God's love and holiness motivated him to offer his Son for us; as grateful recipients of that love we must in turn be motivated to serve one another (Galatians 5:13). It would be wonderful if we could be completely liberated from the effects of sin in an instant. But this life is a journey of coming to know God more intimately and progressively being transformed into the likeness of Jesus.

As God's Word and Spirit point out to us those areas in which the effects of sin are still active in our lives, the Spirit gently prods us to rid our hearts of those blemishes. Sin has a blinding effect, and we are all too frequently oblivious to even our most blatant offenses. We can ask our Father to bring those sins to our attention and to forgive us from "hidden faults" (Psalm 19:12).

That is how we prepare to meet our Savior. As we begin to see beyond our myopic, blurry human viewpoint and catch glimpses of the larger panorama that awaits us, we become less anxious and entangled in the affairs of this life. We begin to internalize the reality that none of our prized acquisitions or selfish ambitions has any lasting value (Mark 4:19).

***Self-Discovery:** In what ways are you progressively being transformed into the likeness of Jesus? What specific changes can you note as you reflect on your life for the past year? Five years? Ten years?*

GO TO DISCOVERY 349 ON PAGE 1685

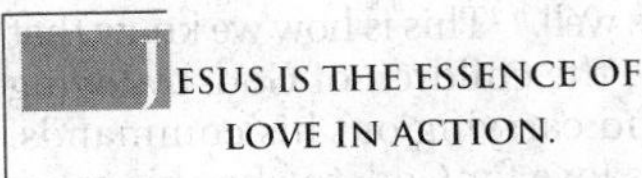

JESUS IS THE ESSENCE OF LOVE IN ACTION.

James M. Boice, *Pastor, Philadelphia, Pennsylvania*

3:4 m 1Jn 5:17 fact, sin is lawlessness.[m] 5But you know
that he appeared so that he might take
3:5 n 2Co 5:21 away our sins. And in him is no sin.[n] 6No
one who lives in him keeps on sinning.[o]
3:6 o ver 9 p 3Jn 11 q 1Jn 2:4 No one who continues to sin has either
seen him[p] or known him.[q]
3:7 r 1Jn 2:1 s 1Jn 2:26 t 1Jn 2:29 7Dear children,[r] do not let anyone
lead you astray.[s] He who does what is
right is righteous, just as he is righteous.[t] 8He who does what is sinful is of
3:8 u Jn 8:44 the devil,[u] because the devil has been
sinning from the beginning. The reason
the Son of God appeared was to destroy
3:9 v Jn 1:13 w 1Jn 5:18 x 1Pe 1:23 the devil's work. 9No one who is born of
God[v] will continue to sin,[w] because
God's seed[x] remains in him; he cannot
go on sinning, because he has been born
of God. 10This is how we know who the
children of God are and who the children of the devil are: Anyone who does
not do what is right is not a child of God;
3:10 y 1Jn 4:8 nor is anyone who does not love[y] his
brother.

Love One Another

3:11 z 1Jn 1:5 a Jn 13:34,35; 2Jn 5 11This is the message you heard[z] from
the beginning: We should love one an-
other.[a] 12Do not be like Cain, who belonged to the evil one and murdered his
3:12 b Ge 4:8 brother.[b] And why did he murder him?
Because his own actions were evil and
his brother's were righteous. 13Do not be
surprised, my brothers, if the world
3:13 c Jn 15:18,19; 17:14 hates you.[c] 14We know that we have
passed from death to life,[d] because we
3:14 d Jn 5:24 e 1Jn 2:9 love our brothers. Anyone who does not
love remains in death.[e] 15Anyone who
hates his brother is a murderer,[f] and you
3:15 f Mt 5:21,22; Jn 8:44 g Gal 5:20,21 know that no murderer has eternal life
in him.[g]
16This is how we know what love is:
Jesus Christ laid down his life for us.
And we ought to lay down our lives for
3:16 h Jn 15:13 our brothers.[h] 17If anyone has material
3:17 i Dt 15:7,8 j 1Jn 4:20 possessions and sees his brother in need
but has no pity on him,[i] how can the
love of God be in him?[j] 18Dear children,[k]
3:18 k 1Jn 2:1 l Eze 33:31; Ro 12:9 let us not love with words or tongue but
with actions and in truth.[l] 19This then is
how we know that we belong to the
truth, and how we set our hearts at rest
in his presence 20whenever our hearts
condemn us. For God is greater than our
hearts, and he knows everything.
21Dear friends, if our hearts do not
condemn us, we have confidence before 3:21 m 1Jn 5:14
God[m] 22and receive from him anything
we ask,[n] because we obey his com- 3:22 n Mt 7:7 o Jn 8:29
mands and do what pleases him.[o] 23And
this is his command: to believe[p] in the
name of his Son, Jesus Christ, and to 3:23 p Jn 6:29 q Jn 13:34
love one another as he commanded us.[q]
24Those who obey his commands live in
him,[r] and he in them. And this is how 3:24 r 1Jn 2:6 s 1Jn 4:13
we know that he lives in us: We know it
by the Spirit he gave us.[s]

YOU CAN STUDY THE SCRIPTURES TILL YOUR EYES FALL OUT, AND WITHOUT THE GIFT OF FAITH YOU'RE NOT GOING TO BELIEVE CHRIST WAS THE SON OF GOD.

John Cardinal O'Connor,
Archbishop of New York City

Test the Spirits

4 Dear friends, do not believe every
spirit, but test the spirits to see
whether they are from God, because
many false prophets have gone out into
the world.[t] 2This is how you can recog- 4:1 t 2Pe 2:1; 1Jn 2:18
nize the Spirit of God: Every spirit that
acknowledges that Jesus Christ has come
in the flesh[u] is from God,[v] 3but every 4:2 u Jn 1:14; 1Jn 2:23 v 1Co 12:3
spirit that does not acknowledge Jesus is
not from God. This is the spirit of the an-
tichrist,[w] which you have heard is com- 4:3 w 1Jn 2:22; 2Jn 7
ing and even now is already in the world.
4You, dear children, are from God and
have overcome them, because the one
who is in you[x] is greater than the one 4:4 x Ro 8:31 y Jn 12:31
who is in the world.[y] 5They are from the
world[z] and therefore speak from the 4:5 z Jn 15:19
viewpoint of the world, and the world listens to them. 6We are from God, and
whoever knows God listens to us; but
whoever is not from God does not listen
to us.[a] This is how we recognize the Spir- 4:6 a Jn 8:47 b Jn 14:17
it[a] of truth[b] and the spirit of falsehood.

God's Love and Ours

7Dear friends, let us love one another,[c] 4:7 c 1Jn 3:11
for love comes from God. Everyone who

[a] 6 Or *spirit*

> JESUS EMBODIES THE PROMISE OF A GOD WHO WILL GO TO ANY LENGTH TO WIN US BACK. NOT THE LEAST OF JESUS' ACCOMPLISHMENTS IS THAT HE MADE US SOMEHOW LOVABLE TO GOD.
>
> Philip Yancey, *Christian Author*

4:7 loves has been born of God and knows
d 1Jn 2:4 God.[d] 8Whoever does not love does not
4:8 know God, because God is love.[e] 9This is
e ver 7,16 how God showed his love among us: He
4:9 sent his one and only Son[a] into the
f Jn 3:16,17; world that we might live through him.[f]
1Jn 5:11 10This is love: not that we loved God, but
4:10 that he loved us[g] and sent his Son as an
g Ro 5:8,10 atoning sacrifice for[b] our sins.[h] 11Dear
h 1Jn 2:2 friends, since God so loved us,[i] we also
4:11 ought to love one another. 12No one has
i Jn 3:16 ever seen God;[j] but if we love one an-
4:12 other, God lives in us and his love is
j Jn 1:18; made complete in us.[k]
1Ti 6:16 k 1Jn 2:5 13We know that we live in him and he
4:13 in us, because he has given us of his Spir-
l 1Jn 3:24 it.[l] 14And we have seen and testify[m] that
4:14 the Father has sent his Son to be the
m Jn 15:27 Savior of the world.[n] 15If anyone ac-
n Jn 3:17 knowledges that Jesus is the Son of
4:15 God,[o] God lives in him and he in God.
o Ro 10:9 16And so we know and rely on the love
God has for us.
4:16 God is love.[p] Whoever lives in love
p ver 8 q 1Jn 3:24 lives in God, and God in him.[q] 17In this
4:17 r 1Jn 2:5 way, love is made complete[r] among us
so that we will have confidence on the
day of judgment, because in this world
4:18 we are like him. 18There is no fear in love.
s Ro 8:15 But perfect love drives out fear,[s] because
fear has to do with punishment. The one
who fears is not made perfect in love.
4:19 19We love because he first loved us.[t]
t ver 10 20If anyone says, "I love God," yet hates
4:20 u 1Jn 2:9 his brother,[u] he is a liar.[v] For anyone who
v 1Jn 2:4 does not love his brother, whom he has
w 1Jn 3:17 seen,[w] cannot love God, whom he has
x ver 12 not seen.[x] 21And he has given us this
4:21 command: Whoever loves God must
y Mt 5:43 also love his brother.[y]

Faith in the Son of God

5:1 z 1Jn 2:22 **5** Everyone who believes that Jesus
a Jn 1:13; is the Christ[z] is born of God,[a] and
1Jn 2:23 everyone who loves the father loves his
child as well.[b] 2This is how we know that 5:1 b Jn 8:42
we love the children of God: by loving
God and carrying out his commands.
3This is love for God: to obey his com- 5:3
mands.[c] And his commands are not c Jn 14:15; 2Jn 6
burdensome,[d] 4for everyone born of God d Mt 11:30
overcomes[e] the world. This is the victo- 5:4
ry that has overcome the world, even our e Jn 16:33
faith. 5Who is it that overcomes the
world? Only he who believes that Jesus is
the Son of God.
6This is the one who came by water 5:6
and blood[f]—Jesus Christ. He did not f Jn 19:34
come by water only, but by water and g Jn 14:17
blood. And it is the Spirit who testifies,
because the Spirit is the truth.[g] 7For
there are three[h] that testify: 8the[c] Spirit, 5:7
the water and the blood; and the three h Mt 18:16
are in agreement. 9We accept man's testimony,[i] but God's testimony is greater 5:9
because it is the testimony of God,[j] i Jn 5:34
which he has given about his Son. 10Any- j Mt 3:16,17; Jn 8:17,18
one who believes in the Son of God has 5:10
this testimony in his heart.[k] Anyone k Ro 8:16;
who does not believe God has made him Gal 4:6 l Jn 3:33
out to be a liar,[l] because he has not believed the testimony God has given
about his Son. 11And this is the testimony: God has given us eternal life, and

[a] 9 Or *his only begotten Son* [b] 10 Or *as the one who would turn aside his wrath, taking away*
[c] 7,8 Late manuscripts of the Vulgate *testify in heaven: the Father, the Word and the Holy Spirit, and these three are one. 8And there are three that testify on earth: the* (not found in any Greek manuscript before the sixteenth century)

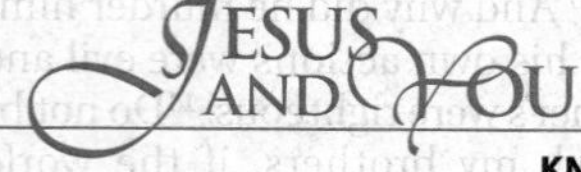

KNOWING FOR SURE

Seeking the blessed assurance that we will indeed spend eternity with God does not register us for a guessing game. God wants us to know without the slightest doubt that we are his children (1 John 5:13). Jesus became a man for the express purpose of dying for our sins, and when we accept his forgiveness and start afresh with God, God assures us that he does not hold our sins against us. We can bask in the light and warmth of fellowship with God simply by believing that Jesus is who he claimed to be and that he did on our behalf precisely what he said he did. John declared simply that "he who has the Son has life" (verse 12)—no caveats, no fine print, no exclusions. God offers each one of us a brand-new life in Jesus—all we have to do is put our trust in him.

DISCOVERY 349

Possessing the Son

God's Word uses several analogies to express the concepts of forgiveness of sins and the offer of eternal life. One of those is that of being "born again" or "born of the Spirit" (John 3:3–8). In 1 John 5 we learn more about this second, spiritual birth. When we give our lives to Jesus, he in turn offers us eternal life—which we possess even while we live here on earth (John 5:24). The Holy Spirit within us "testifies" to this reality (1 John 5:6). In a very practical sense this means that he is a "voice" inside us—God's Spirit connected with our own—continually reminding us of God's truth (verse 10).

Verse 12 adds a dimension that we cannot fully explain. Not only do we have eternal life with God and the internal witness of the Spirit, but we actually "have the Son of God" within us. John had earlier recorded the words of Jesus in his Gospel account: "I have made [God the Father] known to [those whom he has given me], and will continue to make [God] known in order that the love [God has] for me may be in them and that I myself may be in them" (John 17:26). On some level this will never make complete sense to us in this life. But we can simply believe it because God declares it to be true, and we can respond by worshiping him in awe of this reality (John 4:23).

Both the Gospel of John and the first letter of John were written by an eyewitness, a true follower of Jesus. 1 John was addressed by a seasoned believer to other Christians in order to help them to settle any questions about the authenticity of their faith and hope. John understood that the Good News about Jesus is truth worth dying for. It is also truth worth living for! John declared a beautiful promise in 1 John 5:18: "We know that anyone born of God does not continue to sin; the one who was born of God keeps him safe, and the evil one cannot harm him."

As God's people we have the ability to "overcome the world" because we believe in Jesus and obey God's commands (verses 1–5). And God does not ask too much of us: "His commands are not burdensome" (verse 3). We may feel overwhelmed when we continually try to control all of the details of our own lives and assume responsibility for burdens that are not ours to carry. When we surrender our lives to God, however, we are capable of living truly abundant, unencumbered lives, because we can rest in the assurance that God is in control of all things (Matthew 11:28–30).

"Possessing the Son" in our lives allows each of us to exhibit the attitude of an overcomer. When we truly submit to God, we are never victims of life's circumstances. He has already instilled eternal life within our souls (Ecclesiastes 3:11), and one day we will experience that wonder in its totality.

Self-Discovery: *What does it mean for you personally to "possess" Jesus in your life? Think about some of your most precious possessions, and then add Jesus Christ to the top of your list.*

GO TO DISCOVERY 350 ON PAGE 1689

5:11 m Jn 1:4; this life is in his Son.[m] 12He who has the
1Jn 2:25 Son has life; he who does not have the
Son of God does not have life.[n]
5:12 n Jn 3:15,16,36

Concluding Remarks

5:13 o 1Jn 3:23 13I write these things to you who be-
p Jn 20:31; lieve in the name of the Son of God[o] so
1Jn 1:1,2 that you may know that you have eternal life.[p] 14This is the confidence[q] we
5:14 q 1Jn 3:21 have in approaching God: that if we ask
r Mt 7:7 anything according to his will, he hears
5:15 us.[r] 15And if we know that he hears us—
s ver 18,19,20 whatever we ask—we know[s] that we
have what we asked of him.

16If anyone sees his brother commit a
sin that does not lead to death, he should
5:16 t Jas 5:15 pray and God will give him life.[t] I refer to
those whose sin does not lead to death.
There is a sin that leads to death.[u] I am 5:16 u Heb 6:4-6;
not saying that he should pray about 10:26 v Jer 7:16
that.[v] 17All wrongdoing is sin,[w] and there 5:17
is sin that does not lead to death.[x] w 1Jn 3:4

18We know that anyone born of God x 1Jn 2:1
does not continue to sin; the one who
was born of God keeps him safe, and the
evil one cannot harm him.[y] 19We know 5:18
that we are children of God,[z] and that y Jn 14:30
the whole world is under the control of 5:19 z 1Jn 4:6
the evil one.[a] 20We know also that the a Gal 1:4
Son of God has come and has given us
understanding,[b] so that we may know 5:20 b Lk 24:45
him who is true.[c] And we are in him who c Jn 17:3 d ver 11
is true—even in his Son Jesus Christ. He
is the true God and eternal life.[d]

21Dear children, keep yourselves from 5:21 e 1Co 10:14;
idols.[e] 1Th 1:9

2 JOHN

Why did some say Jesus that did not come in the flesh? (2 John 7)

- *Many people at that time accepted the deity of Jesus but not his humanity. In today's climate of logic and reason, some say the opposite—that he was human, but not God. The truth combines both; Jesus is God and man at the same time.*

What do Christians work for? (2 John 8)

- *The Bible teaches that we cannot work to earn our salvation but that once God's grace has saved us we can serve God and expect rewards for our work in eternity (1 Corinthians 3:11–15; 2 Corinthians 5:10). John calls us to keep the faith and to persevere.*

How can we tell who is "in the teaching of Christ"? (2 John 9–10)

- *Any who contradict the teaching of the Bible cannot be in Jesus' teaching. Nor can those who live inconsistent lives and are disobedient to God's commands in his Word.*

Jesus in 2 John John addressed his second letter to a "chosen lady and her children." While some scholars believe that this greeting is used metaphorically to mean a church and its members, others believe that John wrote to a specific mother and her children to help keep her spiritually on target. John contended that in order to find true joy, believers should love one another as God has commanded.

New Testament believers customarily took care of traveling missionaries. Because teachers of other religions also relied on this practice, John urged this lady to use discernment in supporting traveling teachers.

John's focus in this letter is on the fact that Jesus is God in human form. John referred to Jesus in verse 3 as the "Father's Son." When we believe in Jesus, his truth lives in us (verse 2), and anyone who denies that truth is identified as "the deceiver and the antichrist" (verse 7). John's letter is terse and to the point: Anyone who claims to have a relationship with the Father but rejects Jesus does not know God at all (verse 9).

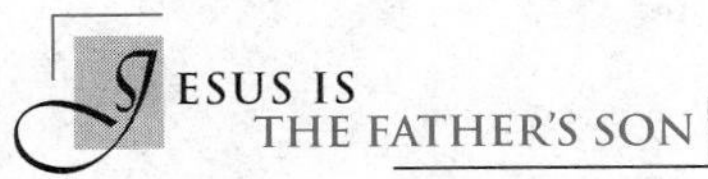

1:1 [a] 3Jn 1 1The elder,[a]
[b] Ro 16:13
[c] Jn 8:32 To the chosen[b] lady and her children,
whom I love in the truth—and not I
only, but also all who know the truth[c]—
1:2 [d] 2Pe 1:12 2because of the truth,[d] which lives in us[e]
[e] 1Jn 1:8 and will be with us forever:

3Grace, mercy and peace from God
1:3 [f] Ro 1:7 the Father and from Jesus Christ,[f] the
Father's Son, will be with us in truth and
love.

4It has given me great joy to find some
1:4 [g] 3Jn 3,4 of your children walking in the truth,[g]
just as the Father commanded us. 5And
1:5 [h] 1Jn 2:7; 3:11 now, dear lady, I am not writing you a
new command but one we have had
1:6 from the beginning.[h] I ask that we love
[i] 1Jn 2:5 one another. 6And this is love:[i] that we
walk in obedience to his commands. As
you have heard from the beginning, his
command is that you walk in love.
7Many deceivers, who do not ac- 1:7
knowledge Jesus Christ[j] as coming in [j] 1Jn 2:22; 4:2,3
the flesh, have gone out into the world.[k] [k] 1Jn 4:1 [l] 1Jn 2:18
Any such person is the deceiver and the
antichrist.[l] 8Watch out that you do not
lose what you have worked for, but that
you may be rewarded fully.[m] 9Anyone 1:8 [m] 1Co 3:8
who runs ahead and does not continue
in the teaching of Christ does not have
God; whoever continues in the teaching
has both the Father and the Son.[n] 10If 1:9
anyone comes to you and does not bring [n] 1Jn 2:23
this teaching, do not take him into your
house or welcome him.[o] 11Anyone who 1:10 [o] Ro 16:17
welcomes him shares[p] in his wicked
work. 1:11 [p] 1Ti 5:22

12I have much to write to you, but I do
not want to use paper and ink. Instead, I
hope to visit you and talk with you face 1:12
to face,[q] so that our joy may be complete. [q] 3Jn 13,14

13The children of your chosen[r] sister 1:13
send their greetings. [r] ver 1

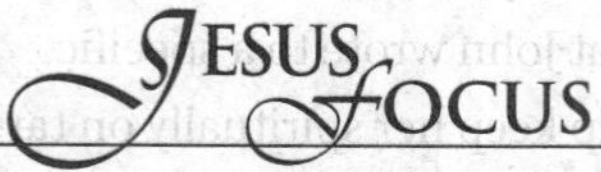

DECEIVERS

John warned his readers about a particular group of people who were stirring up contention in the churches (2 John 7). These individuals refused to accept that Jesus was God's promised Messiah—God himself in human form. The first-century Gnostics alleged that all physical matter was evil, and consequently they refused to believe that our perfect Father in heaven would take on himself the form of a physical body. Some Gnostics denied that Jesus was a man, while others denied that he was God the Son. To ignore the truth that Jesus is at the same time wholly divine and completely human is to miss out on the incomparable love and grace he has to offer—and to miss having a relationship with Jesus is to miss a relationship with Almighty God altogether.

MILLIONS OF PEOPLE TODAY—BY FAITH ALONE—ACCEPT THE CLAIMS AND THE PROMISES OF JESUS. COULD SUCH A CONTINUING ADHERENCE TO BELIEVE IN THESE CLAIMS AND PROMISES BE ROOTED IN ANYTHING LESS THAN TRUTH AND INTEGRITY?

Dr. C. Everett Koop,
Former Surgeon General of the U.S.

Holding Fast to Jesus' Teaching

If John had been asked to select one word to sum up his second letter, it would most likely have been the word *truth*. His entire purpose in writing was to encourage God's children to walk in God's truth (verse 4). He also warned believers to beware of anyone who rejects the truth. The proof that someone is an authentic follower of Jesus Christ is that she continues in Jesus' teaching. John was not providing new information here; he was simply repeating what God has told us all along. Holding fast to Jesus' teaching substantiates certain realities:

1. *It is a mark of discipleship*. Jesus explained to the Jews who believed in him that "if you hold to my teaching, you are really my disciples. Then you will know the truth, and the truth will set you free" (John 8:31–32). Those who belong to God listen to what he says in his Word (John 8:47). When Jesus enters a life, he imbues that person with a new and passionate desire to follow his teaching.

2. *It is evidence of our love for him*. Jesus was explicit: "If you love me, you will obey what I command" (John 14:15). It doesn't require much effort to mouth the words *I love you*, even to Jesus. But the proof of our love is found in our desire to please. When we love Jesus, we want to do what he asks of us, because right living is what pleases him. A person can profess undying love for God, but if his life choices don't exemplify devotion to God's Word, he does not truly love the Lord.

3. *It is the primary mission of the church*. Three particular books in the New Testament are referred to as Pastoral Letters because they provide instructions for the church. They are 1 and 2 Timothy and Titus. Each focuses on the teaching of truth within the context of the church community. These books make no mention of worship, singing, giving, spiritual gifts or liturgy. All these aspects are part of what the church is all about, but our primary focus as God's people is to defend, explain and teach God's truth (2 Timothy 4:2–3).

Remaining "in the teaching of Christ" (2 John 9) requires patience. We cannot run ahead of God, even though there is at times great temptation for us to do so. John stated the bottom line in no uncertain terms: "Anyone who runs ahead and does not continue in the teaching of Christ does not have God; whoever continues in the teaching has both the Father and the Son" (verse 9). It's easy to be seduced by other ideas or to fall prey to the temptation of "helping" God out by running ahead and paving the way for him, of proactively taking care of the details so that his "plan" may unfold smoothly. As we become better acquainted with him, however, we learn to resist this temptation and to remain satisfied with Jesus, and with Jesus alone. It is in Jesus that we discover both the Father and the Son—and that is a reward far beyond any the world has to offer!

Self-Discovery: *Identify a time in your life when you have "run ahead" of God, trying to "help" him with the details of what was, in effect, your own plan. What was the outcome? What did you learn from the experience?*

GO TO DISCOVERY 351 ON PAGE 1692

3 JOHN

Does our faith in Jesus guarantee health and well-being? (3 John 2)

♦ *Yes, although not necessarily in a physical sense. Our prayers are always answered, though not always in the manner or time we might have hoped.*

Who is John referring to by the term "my children"? (3 John 4)

♦ *John may have been referring either to his converts or to believers in Jesus currently under his spiritual guidance.*

Do good deeds always indicate service to God? (3 John 11)

♦ *Good deeds ordinarily reflect a close walk with God, although good can be accomplished by the righteous or the unrighteous, for right reasons or wrong. John was speaking of a lifestyle given over to the practice of doing good continually—something that comes only as a result of God's grace, shown to us in such a marvelous way through Jesus' atoning death and his glorious resurrection hat gives us the power to live a renewed life for him.*

Jesus in 3 John John directed this third letter to his friend Gaius, to praise him for giving a warm reception to traveling evangelists. Another church leader, Diotrephes, was causing division by spreading rumors about John and refusing to welcome these preachers. Take note of John's rebuke of Diotrephes for his unhealthy intent to dominate others, and notice also how John urged his friends to love each other. Observe that John advised resolving disagreements in the way that Jesus would—by loving and welcoming, not by dominating and controlling.

Being in fellowship with Jesus is our only source of real joy because God designed us to live in a perfect relationship with himself. John said that nothing made him happier than to know that his "spiritual children" were walking with God (3 John 4). Each person who believes in God is a guardian of his truth and a spiritual "parent" for new believers. As each new generation learns about Jesus, our spiritual heritage is passed on both to our spiritual and to our physical children. Jesus is truly the Savior for all generations.

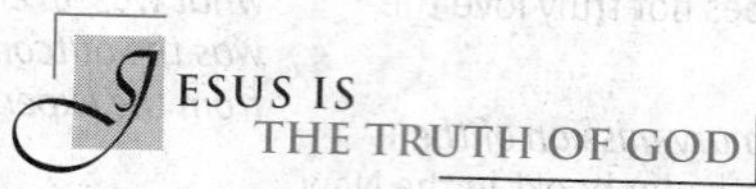

JESUS IS THE TRUTH OF GOD

1:1 a 2Jn 1 1The elder,[a]

To my dear friend Gaius, whom I love
in the truth.

2Dear friend, I pray that you may enjoy good health and that all may go well
with you, even as your soul is getting
along well. 3It gave me great joy to have
1:3 some brothers[b] come and tell about
b ver 5,10 c 2Jn 4 your faithfulness to the truth and how
you continue to walk in the truth.[c] 4I
1:4 have no greater joy than to hear that my
d 1Co 4:15; childrend[d] are walking in the truth.
1Jn 2:1 5Dear friend, you are faithful in what
you are doing for the brothers, even
1:5 though they are strangers to you.[e] 6They
e Ro 12:13; Heb 13:2 have told the church about your love.
You will do well to send them on their
way in a manner worthy of God. 7It was
1:7 for the sake of the Name[f] that they went
f Jn 15:21 g Ac 20:33,35 out, receiving no help from the pagans.[g]
8We ought therefore to show hospitality
to such men so that we may work together for the truth.

9I wrote to the church, but Diotrephes, who loves to be first, will have
nothing to do with us. 10So if I come,[h] I 1:10
will call attention to what he is doing, h 2Jn 12 i ver 5 j Jn 9:22,34
gossiping maliciously about us. Not sat-
isfied with that, he refuses to welcome
the brothers.[i] He also stops those who
want to do so and puts them out of the
church.[j]

11Dear friend, do not imitate what is 1:11
evil but what is good.[k] Anyone who does k Ps 37:27
what is good is from God.[l] Anyone who l 1Jn 2:29 m 1Jn 3:6,9,10
does what is evil has not seen God.[m]
12Demetrius is well spoken of by every- 1:12
one[n]—and even by the truth itself. We n 1Ti 3:7
also speak well of him, and you know o Jn 21:24
that our testimony is true.[o]

13I have much to write you, but I do
not want to do so with pen and ink. 14I
hope to see you soon, and we will talk 1:14
face to face.[p] p 2Jn 12 q Jn 10:3

Peace to you. The friends here send
their greetings. Greet the friends there
by name.[q]

DISCOVERY 351

For the Sake of the Name

The early church did not have the advantage of possessing the New Testament Scriptures as a guide for truth. Instead, preachers would travel from city to city and from church to church declaring God's truth "for the sake of the Name" (3 John 7)—as representatives of Jesus who were committed to speaking on his behalf. The sincere teachers did not proclaim their own message or put their own spin on the truth. The church community benefited greatly from the ministry of committed missionaries and was given a twofold responsibility with respect to these traveling teachers.

First, the church had to determine whether or not these men were indeed promulgating God's truth.The church in Berea stands out as an example in this regard for every church: "They received the message with great eagerness and examined the Scriptures every day to see if what Paul said was true" (Acts 17:11). We may not allow ourselves to be swayed by someone's charismatic charm or convincing public-speaking ability. No matter how well-respected the individual, if he or she speaks anything other than God's truth, we must assume that the message contains no truth at all (2 John 10–11).

Second, the church was to show hospitality to the teachers who spoke the truth, because church members were solely responsible to care for their needs. This generosity was evidence of their Christian love for one another, as well as an opportunity to "work together for the truth" (3 John 8).

There is a healthy kind of skepticism when it comes to evaluating what someone is teaching about the Bible. It is imperative that we as Christians learn to discern God's truth from someone else's perception of or slant on that truth. God has never asked us to offer blind allegiance to anyone professing to come in his name! At the same time, we can be a part of his ministry when we encourage those who do proclaim the truth. As we pay close attention to John's teaching here in his third letter, we will be reminded of the need for balance—not the practice of love to the exclusion of truth and discernment, not the holding of doctrine apart from grace and hospitality, but a proper mixture so that Jesus Christ may be exalted and God's name glorified.

The apostle John had addressed this issue earlier in his first letter: "Dear friends, do not believe every spirit, but test the spirits to see whether they are from God, because many false prophets have gone out into the world. This is how you can recognize the Spirit of God: Every spirit that acknowledges that Jesus Christ has come in the flesh is from God, but every spirit that does not acknowledge Jesus is not from God" (1 John 4:2–3). The best way to discern between the false and the true spirits is to ask what they are teaching about Jesus. Do they teach both his deity and his humanity? Do they exalt him as Lord? (1 Corinthians 12:3).

Self-Discovery: *There are many appealing messages which bombard both believers and nonbelievers through the media and through aggressive ministry efforts from groups with widely varying programs and perspectives. Pray that the Holy Spirit will guide both you and any seekers whom you might know to discern God's truth from untruth ostensibly spoken in Jesus' name.*

GO TO DISCOVERY 352 ON PAGE 1695

JUDE

How contentious should we be? (Jude 3)

♦ *The word* contend *implies that Christians have something worth fighting for. The book of Jude tells us that our battles for the faith sometimes will occur even inside the church. Some have elevated matters of personal preference or opinion to the level of essential doctrine. When believers become contentious over styles, decorating tastes or cultural distinctives, they've become too contentious. We must contend for the Good News about Jesus Christ—for the gospel truth of the message, not the method.*

Jesus in Jude Some people disconnect smoke detectors or buzzers intended to remind them to buckle their seatbelts—just to avoid the irritation. Ignoring such warnings and reminders can be perilous, but ignoring spiritual alarms can be infinitely more hazardous.

Jude's alarm closely resembles those sounded by James and Peter. In fact, it seems as though whole sections from 2 Peter have been restated in this hard-hitting book. The book of Jude is brief, but to truly appreciate its message will require some study. Don't miss Jude's powerful impact and colorful imagery, and take time to look up his Old Testament references. Watch for Jude's direct warnings—and for God's tremendous promises that accompany them.

Jude was Jesus' half brother, and he referred to himself by the identical description used by his brother James—"a servant of Jesus Christ" (verse 1). Jude's main message is that Jesus keeps us in the Father's love because Jesus paid the price for our sins (verse 1). Jesus is both our "Sovereign and Lord" (verse 4), and living a life that reflects his influence shows that we believe in him (verses 17–21).

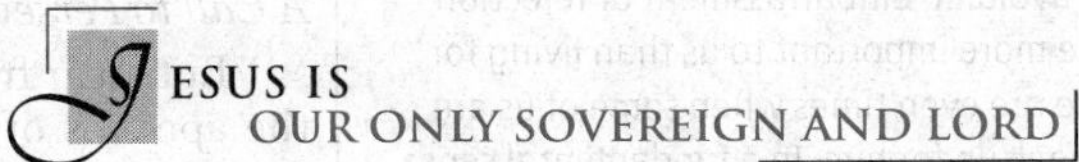

JESUS IS OUR ONLY SOVEREIGN AND LORD

1:1 [a] Mt 13:55; Ac 1:13 [b] Ro 1:6, 7 [c] Jn 17:12
1Jude,[a] a servant of Jesus Christ and a
brother of James,

To those who have been called,[b] who
are loved by God the Father and kept by[a]
Jesus Christ:[c]

1:2 [d] 2Pe 1:2
2Mercy, peace and love be yours in
abundance.[d]

The Sin and Doom of Godless Men

3Dear friends, although I was very eager to write to you about the salvation
1:3 [e] Tit 1:4 [f] 1Ti 6:12
we share,[e] I felt I had to write and urge
you to contend[f] for the faith that was
once for all entrusted to the saints. 4For
certain men whose condemnation was
written about[b] long ago have secretly
1:4 [g] Gal 2:4 [h] Tit 1:16; 2Pe 2:1
slipped in among you.[g] They are godless
men, who change the grace of our God
into a license for immorality and deny
Jesus Christ our only Sovereign and
Lord.[h]
5Though you already know all this, I
want to remind you that the Lord[c] delivered his people out of Egypt, but later
1:5 [i] Nu 14:29; Ps 106:26
destroyed those who did not believe.[i]
6And the angels who did not keep their
positions of authority but abandoned
their own home—these he has kept in
darkness, bound with everlasting chains
1:6 [j] 2Pe 2:4,9
for judgment on the great Day.[j] 7In a
similar way, Sodom and Gomorrah and
1:7 [k] Dt 29:23 [l] 2Pe 2:6
the surrounding towns[k] gave themselves up to sexual immorality and perversion. They serve as an example of
those who suffer the punishment of
eternal fire.[l]
8In the very same way, these dreamers
pollute their own bodies, reject author-
1:8 [m] 2Pe 2:10
ity and slander celestial beings.[m] 9But
even the archangel Michael,[n] when he
1:9 [n] Da 10:13,21 [o] Zec 3:2
was disputing with the devil about the
body of Moses, did not dare to bring a
slanderous accusation against him, but
said, "The Lord rebuke you!"[o] 10Yet these
men speak abusively against whatever
they do not understand; and what
things they do understand by instinct,
like unreasoning animals—these are the
1:10 [p] 2Pe 2:12
very things that destroy them.[p]
11Woe to them! They have taken the
1:11 [q] Ge 4:3-8; 1Jn 3:12 [r] 2Pe 2:15 [s] Nu 16:1-3,31-35
way of Cain;[q] they have rushed for prof-
it into Balaam's error;[r] they have been
destroyed in Korah's rebellion.[s]
12These men are blemishes at your
1:12 [t] 2Pe 2:13; 1Co 11:20-22 [u] Pr 25:14; 2Pe 2:17 [v] Eph 4:14 [w] Mt 15:13
love feasts,[t] eating with you without the
slightest qualm—shepherds who feed
only themselves. They are clouds without rain,[u] blown along by the wind;[v] autumn trees, without fruit and uprooted[w]—twice dead. 13They are wild waves
1:13 [x] Isa 57:20 [y] Php 3:19 [z] 2Pe 2:17
of the sea,[x] foaming up their shame;[y]
wandering stars, for whom blackest
darkness has been reserved forever.[z]
1:14 [a] Ge 5:18,21-24 [b] Dt 33:2; Da 7:10
14Enoch,[a] the seventh from Adam,
prophesied about these men: "See, the
Lord is coming with thousands upon
1:15 [c] 2Pe 2:6-9 [d] 1Ti 1:9
thousands of his holy ones[b] 15to judge[c]
everyone, and to convict all the ungodly
of all the ungodly acts they have done in
the ungodly way, and of all the harsh
words ungodly sinners have spoken
against him."[d] 16These men are grumblers and faultfinders; they follow their
1:16 [e] 2Pe 2:18
own evil desires; they boast[e] about
themselves and flatter others for their
own advantage.

A Call to Persevere

17But, dear friends, remember what
the apostles of our Lord Jesus Christ
1:17 [f] 2Pe 3:2
foretold.[f] 18They said to you, "In the last
1:18 [g] 1Ti 4:1 [h] 2Pe 2:1
times[g] there will be scoffers who will follow their own ungodly desires."[h] 19These
are the men who divide you, who follow

[a] 1 Or *for*; or *in* [b] 4 Or *men who were marked out for condemnation* [c] 5 Some early manuscripts *Jesus*

JESUS AND YOU

SPEAK UP!

Believing God entails more than simply knowing about him. It means being loyal to his truth and reflecting who he is in our daily lives. In the early church, being loyal to Jesus and to what he taught were vitally important issues. In fact, many early Christians were martyred simply because they boldly expressed an allegiance to Jesus and served him in all they did.

In our own cultural setting we must sometimes admit that avoiding embarrassment or rejection can become more important to us than living for Jesus. There are even times when some of us are afraid to speak up for him. In a fundamental sense our lives are no different from those of early Christians, however. Either we accept Jesus for who he is and what he did for us and learn to live our lives for him, or we don't. The choice is up to each of us—and it is the most important life decision any of us will ever make.

Building Ourselves Up in the Faith

Jude is a very brief letter, and its final two verses lift our thoughts above Jude's warnings about false teachers, scoffers and divisive people in our midst toward the only One who can keep us from falling prey to their enticements.

Countless words have been written over the centuries to describe how God is "able" to help us in our daily struggles and trials (Ephesians 3:20–21). And yet God's plan is a concept we often find hard to internalize. We are accountable for our own decisions and actions, but we still cannot control everything that happens around us. What we can learn to control are our *responses* to the situations in which we find ourselves. When we trust in God's perfect timing and his incomparable power, the reality of suffering takes on a whole new dimension.

The Bible often describes our spiritual journey of getting to know God as a *walk*. God's Word lights the pathway (Psalm 119:105), and he himself keeps us from falling (Psalm 37:23–24; 55:22). God can do more than sustain us in our daily lives, however. His power will carry us all the way through eternity into "his glorious presence" (Jude 24), where we will be presented without fault. We expend so much of our energy engaged in the war between good and evil, right and wrong (Romans 7:21–23), but one of the ways in which we can prepare ourselves for eternity is to "do everything without complaining or arguing, so that [we] may become blameless and pure, children of God without fault in a crooked and depraved generation" (Philippians 2:14–15). Even as we daily battle the temptations of our sinful human nature, we already possess a faultless résumé to present to God. Because Jesus died in our place, God no longer holds our sin against us (2 Corinthians 5:19), and we are presented in Jesus as "holy in his sight, without blemish and free from accusation—if [we] continue in [our] faith, established and firm, not moved from the hope held out in the gospel" (Colossians 1:22–23).

Our job is to build ourselves up "in [our] most holy faith" (Jude 20). We can "be merciful to those who doubt; snatch others from the fire and save them; to others show mercy" (verses 22–23). When that task is complete and we stand before the Father, we will experience the "great joy" (verse 24) we can now only glimpse periodically in those moments of light that pierce the darkness and illuminate our path between tears and trials. No happiness on this earth can be compared to being in the very presence of the God of all creation.

There is a great deal of false teaching propagated through print and other media. As we become more intimately acquainted with God we can learn to take Jude's warnings to heart and to become more firmly established in God's Word. The more familiar we are with God's truth, the easier it will be for us to discern half-truths or false statements. Godless teachers easily and secretly slip in amongst God's people (verse 4), but our knowledge of his Word equips us for every situation (2 Timothy 3:16–17).

Self-Discovery: *Identify some ways in which you can "build yourself up in [your] most holy faith." If you are involved in a physical exercise program of any kind, do you put forth as much effort exercising your spiritual "muscles"?*

GO TO DISCOVERY 353 ON PAGE 1699

FOR TO US THERE IS BUT ONE GOD, THE FATHER, OF WHOM ARE ALL THINGS; AND ONE LORD JESUS CHRIST, BY WHOM ARE ALL THINGS; AND ONE HOLY GHOST, IN WHOM ARE ALL THINGS.

Gregory of Nazianzus, *Early Church Father*

1:19 [i] 1Co 2:14,15 mere natural instincts and do not have
1:20 [j] Col 2:7 [k] Eph 6:18 the Spirit.[i]
20 But you, dear friends, build yourselves up[j] in your most holy faith and
1:21 [l] Tit 2:13; 2Pe 3:12 pray in the Holy Spirit.[k] 21 Keep yourselves in God's love as you wait[l] for the
mercy of our Lord Jesus Christ to bring
you to eternal life.
22 Be merciful to those who doubt;
23 snatch others from the fire and save
them;[m] to others show mercy, mixed 1:23 [m] Am 4:11; Zec 3:2-5 [n] Rev 3:4
with fear—hating even the clothing
stained by corrupted flesh.[n]

Doxology

24 To him who is able[o] to keep you 1:24 [o] Ro 16:25 [p] 2Co 4:14 [q] Col 1:22
from falling and to present you before
his glorious presence[p] without fault[q]
and with great joy— 25 to the only God[r] 1:25 [r] Jn 5:44; 1Ti 1:17 [s] Heb 13:8 [t] Ro 11:36
our Savior be glory, majesty, power and
authority, through Jesus Christ our Lord,
before all ages, now and forevermore![s]
Amen.[t]

REVELATION

Jesus in Revelation Filled with bizarre imagery and obscure symbols, Revelation has intimidated readers for centuries. Yet this book has much to offer. The first-century Christians faced persecution and needed assurance that God was in control. Revelation gave them hope, reminding them to live committed, holy lives as they awaited their final participation in God's victorious kingdom.

Study carefully the main visions in Revelation: the church on earth (Revelation 1—3); the Lamb and the seven seals (4—7); the angels and the seven trumpets (8—11); the seven symbolic figures (12—14); the seven bowls of God's wrath (15—18); the triumphal return of Christ (19); and the final judgment and victory (20—22).

John described Jesus as the Son of Man, the risen Savior (Revelation 1:13,18), the holy and true Son of God (Revelation 2:18; 3:7), the "Amen" (Revelation 3:14), the Lion of the tribe of Judah (Revelation 5:5), the Root of David (Revelation 5:5) and the Word of God (Revelation 19:13). In 28 separate instances John referred to Jesus as "the Lamb"—both as the lamb who was "slain" and as the victorious, conquering Lamb.

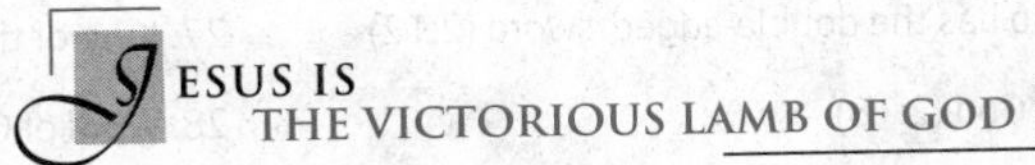
JESUS IS
THE VICTORIOUS LAMB OF GOD

What is the significance of John's description of Jesus as "Son of Man"? (Revelation 1:13)

- ♦ *This is a link to the book of Daniel (Daniel 7:13–14) as well as to the Gospels. "Son of man" alludes here to the glory and power God the Father assigns to the risen, heavenly Christ.*

How can believers use the "blood of the Lamb" against Satan? (Revelation 12:11)

- ♦ *Through Jesus' sacrificial death Christians are forgiven by God, so Satan can no longer accuse them of guilt. The blood of Jesus is the only hope of escaping the deadly power and guilt of sin.*

How was the Lamb "slain from the creation of the world"? (Revelation 13:8)

- ♦ *God planned to save the world through Jesus' death long before God had even created it (1 Peter 1:18–20). Jesus' death was no afterthought or accident but the direct plan of God.*

Prologue

1 The revelation of Jesus Christ,
which God gave him to show his
servants what must soon take place. He
1:1 [a] Rev 22:16 made it known by sending his angel[a] to
his servant John, 2 who testifies to every-
1:2 thing he saw—that is, the word of God
[b] 1Co 1:6; and the testimony of Jesus Christ.[b]
Rev 12:17 3 Blessed is the one who reads the words
of this prophecy, and blessed are those
1:3 who hear it and take to heart what is
[c] Lk 11:28 written in it,[c] because the time is near.

Greetings and Doxology

4 John,

To the seven churches in the province of Asia:

Grace and peace to you from him who
1:4 is, and who was, and who is to come, and
[d] Rev 3:1; 4:5 from the seven spirits[a][d] before his throne,
1:5 5 and from Jesus Christ, who is the faith-
[e] Rev 3:14 [f] Col 1:18 ful witness,[e] the firstborn from the dead,[f]
[g] Rev 17:14 and the ruler of the kings of the earth.[g]

To him who loves us and has freed us
from our sins by his blood, 6 and has 1:6
made us to be a kingdom and priests[h] to [h] 1Pe 2:5
serve his God and Father—to him be glo- [i] Ro 11:36
ry and power for ever and ever! Amen.[i]

7 "Look, he is coming with the clouds,"[j] 1:7
and every eye will see him, [j] Da 7:13 [k] Zec 12:10
even those who pierced him;
and all the peoples of the earth
will mourn[k] because of him."
So shall it be! Amen.

8 "I am the Alpha and the Omega,"[l] 1:8
says the Lord God, "who is, and who was, [l] Rev 21:6
and who is to come, the Almighty."[m] [m] Rev 4:8

One Like a Son of Man

9 I, John, your brother and companion
in the suffering[n] and kingdom and pa- 1:9 [n] Php 4:14
tient endurance[o] that are ours in Jesus, [o] 2Ti 2:12
was on the island of Patmos because of
the word of God and the testimony of
Jesus. 10 On the Lord's Day I was in the

[a] 4 Or *the sevenfold Spirit*

Names and Titles of Jesus in Revelation

1. Jesus Christ (1:1)
2. Faithful witness (1:5)
3. Firstborn from the dead (1:5)
4. Ruler of the kings of the earth (1:5)
5. Alpha and Omega (1:8)
6. He who is, was and is to come (1:8)
7. The Almighty (1:8)
8. Son of man (1:13; 14:14)
9. Living One (1:18)
10. He who holds the seven stars (2:1)
11. He who walks among the lampstands (2:1)
12. He who has the double-edged sword (2:12)
13. Son of God (2:18)
14. He who has eyes like blazing fire (2:18)
15. He who holds the seven spirits of God (3:1)
16. He who is holy and true (3:7)
17. He who holds the key of David (3:7)
18. The Amen (3:14)
19. Faithful and true witness (3:14)
20. Ruler of God's creation (3:14)
21. Lion of the tribe of Judah (5:5)
22. Root of David (5:5)
23. The Lamb (28 times)
24. Sovereign Lord, holy and true (6:10)
25. Lord (11:8)
26. Male child (12:5)
27. King of the ages (15:3)
28. Word of God (19:13)
29. King of kings and Lord of lords (19:16)
30. Bright Morning Star (22:16)

DISCOVERY 353

A Picture of Our Lord

The study of works of art depicting Jesus can be quite interesting—and eye-opening. People from different ethnic and cultural groups, for instance, all tend to view Jesus through the lens of their own background, often seeing him as a reflection of themselves. But what does Jesus, the Son of God, really look like?

John described our Lord for us in accordance with the vision Jesus had given him (Revelation 1:12–16). The apostle, now an old man, had been exiled by the Roman government to the island of Patmos. One day he heard a loud voice calling out to him, and when he turned to see who it was he saw "someone 'like a son of man' " (verse 13). Jesus had frequently referred to himself using this terminology (Mark 8:31). The first point that strikes us is that John recognized Jesus even though it had been more than 60 years since he had last laid eyes on the Master. John himself had certainly aged, but our Lord will always remain the same—"yesterday and today and forever" (Hebrews 13:8).

The second feature we notice is Jesus' clothing. John described him as wearing a robe reaching down to his feet and a golden sash around his waist (Revelation 1:13). The robe was apparently similar to that which the priests had worn in the temple (Exodus 28:4; 29:5), reflecting that Jesus is our high priest. The sash was typical of that worn by the prophets and represented Jesus' role as God's final prophet (2 Kings 1:8; Isaiah 11:5; Matthew 3:4). The fact that the sash was golden portrays Jesus' status as king.

John's description of Jesus' physical appearance was far more symbolic than literal: His head and hair were "white as wool," symbolizing not the effects of the aging process but his eternal presence and his incomparable wisdom and dignity (Leviticus 19:32; Proverbs 16:31). His eyes were like a blazing fire, calling to mind his omniscience. His feet were like bronze, reminding us of the bronze altar on which sacrifices had been offered to God in the temple (2 Chronicles 4:1). His voice was like the sound of rushing waters, depicting his authority. His right hand held seven stars, symbolizing the pastors of the seven churches to whom he was about to speak. His mouth held a sharp sword, which may be equated to the Word or Truth of God. His face shone like the sun, connoting his glory and majesty.

We know from Isaiah's past-tense prophecy that our Savior's features were in no way unusual or even appealing: "He had no beauty or majesty to attract us to him, nothing in his appearance that we should desire him" (Isaiah 53:2). Some day we will see our Redeemer face-to-face, and we really have no foreknowledge of what he will look like. The one thing we do know for certain is this: We, like John, will spontaneously fall face down at his feet in worship (verse 17), overcome with awe and respect as we offer him the unrestrained praises of our hearts and minds.

Self-Discovery: *Reflect for a moment on Peter's words in 1 Peter 1:8: "Though you have not seen him, you love him; and even though you do not see him now, you believe in him and are filled with an inexpressible and glorious joy, for you are receiving the goal of your faith, the salvation of your [soul]." Thank Jesus for this wonderful reality in your life.*

GO TO DISCOVERY 354 ON PAGE 1703

THE BOOK OF REVELATION, AS NO OTHER BOOK IN THE BIBLE, PROVIDES A COMPREHENSIVE PICTURE OF THE GLORY OF CHRIST.

John F. Walvoord, *Chancellor, Dallas Theological Seminary*

1:10 [p] Rev 4:2 [q] Rev 4:1 Spirit,[p] and I heard behind me a loud
voice like a trumpet,[q] 11 which said:
"Write on a scroll what you see and send
1:11 [r] ver 4,20 [s] Rev 3:1 it to the seven churches:[r] to Ephesus,
Smyrna, Pergamum, Thyatira, Sardis,[s]
Philadelphia and Laodicea."

12 I turned around to see the voice that
1:12 [t] Ex 25:31-40; Zec 4:2 was speaking to me. And when I turned
I saw seven golden lampstands,[t] 13 and
among the lampstands was someone
1:13 [u] Eze 1:26; Da 7:13; 10:16 [v] Da 10:5; Rev 15:6 "like a son of man,"[a][u] dressed in a robe
reaching down to his feet and with a
golden sash around his chest.[v] 14 His
head and hair were white like wool, as
1:14 [w] Da 7:9; 10:6; Rev 19:12 white as snow, and his eyes were like
blazing fire.[w] 15 His feet were like bronze
glowing in a furnace,[x] and his voice was
1:15 [x] Da 10:6 [y] Eze 43:2; Rev 14:2 like the sound of rushing waters.[y] 16 In
his right hand he held seven stars,[z] and
out of his mouth came a sharp double-
1:16 [z] Rev 2:1; 3:1 [a] Isa 49:2; Heb 4:12; Rev 2:12,16 edged sword.[a] His face was like the sun
shining in all its brilliance.

17 When I saw him, I fell at his feet[b] as
though dead. Then he placed his right
1:17 [b] Eze 1:28; Da 8:17,18 [c] Isa 41:4; 44:6; 48:12; Rev 22:13 hand on me and said: "Do not be afraid.
I am the First and the Last.[c] 18 I am the
Living One; I was dead,[d] and behold I
am alive for ever and ever![e] And I hold
1:18 [d] Ro 6:9 [e] Rev 4:9,10 [f] Rev 20:1 the keys of death and Hades.[f]

19 "Write, therefore, what you have
seen, what is now and what will take
place later. 20 The mystery of the seven
1:20 [g] Zec 4:2 [h] ver 4, 11 [i] Mt 5:14,15 stars that you saw in my right hand and
of the seven golden lampstands[g] is this:
The seven stars are the angels[b] of the
seven churches,[h] and the seven lampstands are the seven churches.[i]

To the Church in Ephesus

2 "To the angel[c] of the church in
Ephesus write:

These are the words of him who
2:1 [j] Rev 1:16 [k] Rev 1:12,13 holds the seven stars in his right
hand[j] and walks among the seven
golden lampstands:[k] 2 I know your
2:2 [l] Rev 3:1,8,15 deeds,[l] your hard work and your
perseverance. I know that you can-
not tolerate wicked men, that you
have tested[m] those who claim to be 2:2 [m] 1Jn 4:1 [n] 2Co 11:13
apostles but are not, and have found
them false.[n] 3 You have persevered
and have endured hardships for my
name,[o] and have not grown weary. 2:3 [o] Jn 15:21

4 Yet I hold this against you: You
have forsaken your first love.[p] 5 Re- 2:4 [p] Mt 24:12
member the height from which you
have fallen! Repent[q] and do the 2:5 [q] ver 16,22 [r] Rev 1:20
things you did at first. If you do not
repent, I will come to you and remove your lampstand[r] from its
place. 6 But you have this in your favor: You hate the practices of the
Nicolaitans,[s] which I also hate. 2:6 [s] ver 15

7 He who has an ear, let him hear[t]
what the Spirit says to the churches. 2:7 [t] Mt 11:15; Rev 3:6,13,22 [u] Ge 2:9; Rev 22:2,14,19 [v] Lk 23:43
To him who overcomes, I will give
the right to eat from the tree of life,[u]
which is in the paradise[v] of God.

To the Church in Smyrna

8 "To the angel of the church in Smyrna[w] 2:8 [w] Rev 1:11 [x] Rev 1:17
write:

These are the words of him who
is the First and the Last,[x] who died

[a] 13 Daniel 7:13 [b] 20 Or *messengers* [c] 1 Or *messenger*; also in verses 8, 12 and 18

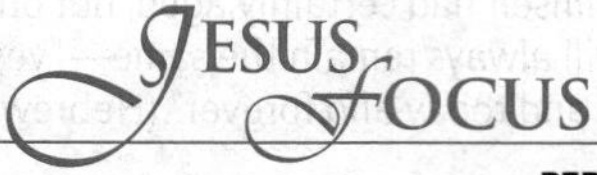

PERSONAL LETTERS

The cities John named in chapters 2 and 3 were all located in Asia Minor, or modern-day Turkey. A Roman highway that led clockwise from Ephesus to Laodicea connected them all together. Each church faced a unique spiritual challenge. Some struggled against temptations inherent in the material prosperity of the times, and others were persecuted for believing in Jesus. Our Lord directed the apostle John to write a personal letter on Jesus' behalf to each of the churches, stating in each instance, "I know your situation" (Revelation 2:2,9,13,19; 3:1,8,15). Jesus is the Lord of his churches, and he speaks to his beloved people with authority, asking them to remember where they came from, to turn back to God, to be faithful, to hold on and to wake up. The instructions included in these chapters are intensely personal, and our Lord Jesus speaks just as boldly to our churches today. He wants us to remember who he is and to remain genuine to our devotion to him.

2:8 and came to life again.[y] 9I know
y Rev 1:18 your afflictions and your poverty—
2:9 yet you are rich![z] I know the slan-
z Jas 2:5 der of those who say they are Jews
a Rev 3:9 and are not,[a] but are a synagogue
b Mt 4:10 of Satan.[b] 10Do not be afraid of
what you are about to suffer. I tell
2:10 you, the devil will put some of you
c Rev 3:10 in prison to test you,[c] and you will
d Da 1:12,14 suffer persecution for ten days.[d] Be
e ver 13 faithful,[e] even to the point of death,
and I will give you the crown of life.
11He who has an ear, let him hear
2:11 what the Spirit says to the churches.
f Rev 20:6,14; He who overcomes will not be hurt
21:8 at all by the second death.[f]

To the Church in Pergamum

2:12 12"To the angel of the church in Perga-
g Rev 1:11 mum[g] write:
h Rev 1:16 These are the words of him who
has the sharp, double-edged
sword.[h] 13I know where you live—
where Satan has his throne. Yet you
2:13 remain true to my name. You did
i Rev 14:12 not renounce your faith in me,[i] even
j ver 9,24 in the days of Antipas, my faithful
witness, who was put to death in
your city—where Satan lives.[j]
2:14 14Nevertheless, I have a few
k ver 20 things against you:[k] You have people there who hold to the teaching
of Balaam,[l] who taught Balak to 2:14 l 2Pe 2:15
entice the Israelites to sin by eating m 1Co 6:13
food sacrificed to idols and by
committing sexual immorality.[m]
15Likewise you also have those who
hold to the teaching of the Nicolai- 2:15
tans.[n] 16Repent therefore! Other- n ver 6
wise, I will soon come to you and
will fight against them with the 2:16
sword of my mouth.[o] o 2Th 2:8; Rev 1:16
17He who has an ear, let him hear
what the Spirit says to the churches.
To him who overcomes, I will give 2:17
some of the hidden manna.[p] I will p Jn 6:49,50
also give him a white stone with a q Isa 62:2
new name[q] written on it, known r Rev 19:12
only to him who receives it.[r]

To the Church in Thyatira

18"To the angel of the church in Thyati- 2:18 s Rev 1:11
ra[s] write: t Rev 1:14,15
These are the words of the Son of
God, whose eyes are like blazing
fire and whose feet are like burnished bronze.[t] 19I know your 2:19
deeds,[u] your love and faith, your u ver 2
service and perseverance, and that
you are now doing more than you
did at first.
20Nevertheless, I have this

SEVEN CHURCHES OF REVELATION

★ Pergamum
★ Thyatira
ASIA
★ Sardis
★ Philadelphia
★ Smyrna
★ Ephesus
★ Laodicea
Antioch
EUBOEA
KIOS
Aegean Sea
SAMOS
ANDROS
TINOS
Miletus
NAXOS
PATMOS
COS
Cnidus
MILOS
Rhodes
RHODES
LYCIA
PAMPHYLIA
Attalia
Patara
Myra
Miles 0 50 100
Kms 0 50 100 150 200

against you: You tolerate that
woman Jezebel,[v] who calls herself a
prophetess. By her teaching she
misleads my servants into sexual
immorality and the eating of food
sacrificed to idols. 21 I have given her
time[w] to repent of her immorality,
but she is unwilling.[x] 22 So I will cast
her on a bed of suffering, and I will
make those who commit adultery[y]
with her suffer intensely, unless
they repent of her ways. 23 I will
strike her children dead. Then all
the churches will know that I am he
who searches hearts and minds,[z]
and I will repay each of you according to your deeds. 24 Now I say to the
rest of you in Thyatira, to you who
do not hold to her teaching and
have not learned Satan's so-called
deep secrets (I will not impose any
other burden on you):[a] 25 Only hold
on to what you have[b] until I come.
26 To him who overcomes and
does my will to the end, I will give
authority over the nations[c]—

27 'He will rule them with an iron
scepter;[d]
he will dash them to pieces
like pottery'[a][e]—

just as I have received authority
from my Father. 28 I will also give
him the morning star.[f] 29 He who
has an ear, let him hear[g] what the
Spirit says to the churches.

2:20 [v] 1Ki 16:31; 21:25; 2Ki 9:7
2:21 [w] Ro 2:4 [x] Rev 9:20
2:22 [y] Rev 17:2; 18:9
2:23 [z] 1Sa 16:7; Jer 11:20; Ac 1:24; Ro 8:27
2:24 [a] Ac 15:28
2:25 [b] Rev 3:11
2:26 [c] Ps 2:8; Rev 3:21
2:27 [d] Rev 12:5 [e] Isa 30:14; Jer 19:11
2:28 [f] Rev 22:16
2:29 [g] ver 7

To the Church in Sardis

3 "To the angel[b] of the church in
Sardis write:
These are the words of him who
holds the seven spirits[c][h] of God
and the seven stars.[i] I know your
deeds;[j] you have a reputation of being alive, but you are dead.[k] 2 Wake
up! Strengthen what remains and is
about to die, for I have not found
your deeds complete in the sight of
my God. 3 Remember, therefore,
what you have received and heard;
obey it, and repent.[l] But if you do
not wake up, I will come like a
thief,[m] and you will not know at
what time I will come to you.
4 Yet you have a few people in
Sardis who have not soiled their
clothes.[n] They will walk with me,
dressed in white,[o] for they are worthy. 5 He who overcomes will, like
them, be dressed in white. I will
never blot out his name from the
book of life,[p] but will acknowledge
his name before my Father[q] and his
angels. 6 He who has an ear, let him
hear[r] what the Spirit says to the
churches.

To the Church in Philadelphia

7 "To the angel of the church in Philadelphia[s] write:

3:1 [h] Rev 1:4 [i] Rev 1:16 [j] Rev 2:2 [k] 1Ti 5:6
3:3 [l] Rev 2:5 [m] 2Pe 3:10
3:4 [n] Jude 23 [o] Rev 4:4; 6:11; 7:9,13,14
3:5 [p] Rev 20:12 [q] Mt 10:32
3:6 [r] Rev 2:7
3:7 [s] Rev 1:11

[a] 27 Psalm 2:9 [b] 1 Or *messenger*; also in verses 7 and 14 [c] 1 Or *the sevenfold Spirit*

Seven Churches of Revelation

Church	Jesus Christ	Commendation	Condemnation	Correction
Ephesus	Walks among lampstands	Hard work and perseverance	Forsaken first love	Repent
Smyrna	First and Last	Afflictions and poverty		Be faithful
Pergamum	Sharp double-edged sword	Remained true to Jesus	False teaching	Repent
Thyatira	Eyes like blazing fire	Love and ministry	False teaching	Hold fast
Sardis	Seven spirits of God		Spiritually dead	Repent
Philadelphia	Opens and shuts doors	Kept Jesus' word		Hold fast
Laodicea	Faithful and true witness		Lukewarm	Open the door

DISCOVERY 354

Neither Hot Nor Cold

One of the most effective forms of deceit in Satan's arsenal is the suggestion that we can become self-sufficient. Even as we go through the motions of a holy life, we can come to believe that we already possess everything we need from God: "I can take it from here," our attitudes and habits frequently assert.

That is exactly the kind of complacency the church in Laodicea had cultivated. Apparently the Christians there weren't doing anything terribly bad—but they weren't doing anything particularly *good* either. They had started out strong in their faith, but it would appear that they had become distracted by what they had already received and stopped looking for more from God—more of his compassion, more of his love, more of his transforming power in their lives.

The angel in John's vision delivered a surprising message to this congregation: "You say, 'I am rich; I have acquired wealth and do not need a thing.' But you do not realize that you are wretched, pitiful, poor, blind and naked" (Revelation 3:17). These believers had become so self-sufficient in their position as God's people that they had begun to leave God himself out of the equation! Jesus accused them of being "neither hot nor cold," and his strong response to this lukewarm Christianity comes as a shock: "I am about to spit you out of my mouth" (verse 16). Why did Jesus find this church so distasteful? Simply because the attitude of the surrounding culture had crept into the congregation and paralyzed its spiritual life. Laodicea was positioned in the fertile Lyons valley next to the great Roman road, and it had become a wealthy trade center, also known for higher education and culture. The Laodicean Christians had begun to rely on their privileges of wealth and superior education instead of on the wisdom and strength God supplies. Their complacent, indifferent attitude made them virtually useless for Christian ministry.

Instead of relying on ourselves or on the gifts God has given us so far, we need to continue to depend on him. If we allow ourselves to fall into the trap of self-reliance, God will often use difficulties in our lives to alert us to our need of him. During a time of intense trial, Paul wrote, "This happened that we might not rely on ourselves but on God" (2 Corinthians 1:9).

How should we respond to Jesus' stern rebuke? First, John advised us to pray for gold refined in the fire (Revelation 3:18). Peter explained in 1 Peter 1:6–7 that our faith is like gold, refined in the fire of life's difficulties. The wholehearted dependence we learn from trials will lead to true spiritual wealth. Next, we should pray for white clothes to wear, so that we won't be spiritually naked. Rather than covering ourselves with the filthy rags of our own righteous acts (Isaiah 64:6), we need to clothe ourselves with the righteousness of Jesus Christ (Romans 13:14). Third, we need the gift of spiritual insight so we can clearly see our own condition as well as God's provision for us in Jesus (Philippians 3:3–14). This will lead to genuine repentance (Revelation 3:19), a new, intimate relationship with Jesus himself (verse 20) and ultimately to his enthusiastic approval of a life well-lived (verse 21).

Self-Discovery: *In retrospect, have you tended to feel closer to Jesus when your life was running smoothly or when you had hit a rocky road? Why do you think this is the case?*

GO TO DISCOVERY 355 ON PAGE 1706

3:7 These are the words of him who
t 1Jn 5:20 is holy and true,[t] who holds the key
u Isa 22:22; of David.[u] What he opens no one
Mt 16:19 can shut, and what he shuts no one
can open. 8 I know your deeds. See,
3:8 I have placed before you an open
v Ac 14:27 door[v] that no one can shut. I know
w Rev 2:13 that you have little strength, yet
you have kept my word and have
not denied my name.[w] 9 I will make
those who are of the synagogue of
3:9 Satan,[x] who claim to be Jews
x Rev 2:9 though they are not, but are liars—
y Isa 49:23 I will make them come and fall
z Isa 43:4 down at your feet[y] and acknowledge that I have loved you.[z] 10 Since
you have kept my command to en-
3:10 dure patiently, I will also keep you[a]
a 2Pe 2:9 from the hour of trial that is going
b Rev 2:10 to come upon the whole world to
c Rev 6:10; 17:8 test[b] those who live on the earth.[c]
11 I am coming soon. Hold on to
3:11 what you have,[d] so that no one will
d Rev 2:25 take your crown.[e] 12 Him who over-
e Rev 2:10 comes I will make a pillar[f] in the
3:12 temple of my God. Never again will
f Gal 2:9 he leave it. I will write on him the
g Rev 14:1; 22:4 name of my God[g] and the name of
h Rev 21:2,10 the city of my God, the new Jerusalem,[h] which is coming down out of
heaven from my God; and I will also
write on him my new name. 13 He
who has an ear, let him hear what
the Spirit says to the churches.

To the Church in Laodicea

14 "To the angel of the church in Laodicea write:

These are the words of the
Amen, the faithful and true wit-
3:14 ness, the ruler of God's creation.[i] 15 I
i Col 1:16,18 know your deeds, that you are nei-
3:15 ther cold nor hot.[j] I wish you were
j Ro 12:11 either one or the other! 16 So, because you are lukewarm—neither
hot nor cold—I am about to spit
you out of my mouth. 17 You say, 'I
3:17 am rich; I have acquired wealth and
k Hos 12:8; do not need a thing.'[k] But you do
1Co 4:8 not realize that you are wretched,
pitiful, poor, blind and naked. 18 I
counsel you to buy from me gold
refined in the fire, so you can become rich; and white clothes to
wear, so you can cover your shame-
3:18 ful nakedness;[l] and salve to put on
l Rev 16:15 your eyes, so you can see.

19 Those whom I love I rebuke 3:19
and discipline.[m] So be earnest, and m Pr 3:12;
repent.[n] 20 Here I am! I stand at the Heb 12:5,6
door[o] and knock. If anyone hears n Rev 2:5
my voice and opens the door,[p] I will 3:20
come in[q] and eat with him, and he o Mt 24:33 p Lk 12:36
with me. q Jn 14:23
21 To him who overcomes, I will
give the right to sit with me on my
throne,[r] just as I overcame[s] and sat 3:21 r Mt 19:28
down with my Father on his s Rev 5:5
throne. 22 He who has an ear, let him 3:22
hear[t] what the Spirit says to the t Rev 2:7
churches."

The Throne in Heaven

4 After this I looked, and there before me was a door standing open
in heaven. And the voice I had first
heard speaking to me like a trumpet[u] 4:1 u Rev 1:10
said, "Come up here,[v] and I will show v Rev 11:12
you what must take place after this."[w] w Rev 1:19
2 At once I was in the Spirit,[x] and there 4:2 x Rev 1:10
before me was a throne in heaven[y] with y Isa 6:1;
someone sitting on it. 3 And the one who Eze 1:26-28;
sat there had the appearance of jasper Da 7:9
and carnelian. A rainbow,[z] resembling 4:3
an emerald, encircled the throne. 4 Sur- z Eze 1:28
rounding the throne were twenty-four
other thrones, and seated on them were 4:4
twenty-four elders.[a] They were dressed a Rev 11:16
in white[b] and had crowns of gold on b Rev 3:4,5
their heads. 5 From the throne came
flashes of lightning, rumblings and peals 4:5
of thunder.[c] Before the throne, seven c Rev 8:5; 16:18

HEAVEN'S PERSPECTIVE

As John began his fourth chapter, the scene shifted from earth to heaven. Jesus accompanied John into God's inner sanctum, his throne room, for a behind-the-scenes look at God's plans and their effect on human history. From this unique and privileged vantage point John was able to observe and interpret the things of life from the perspective of eternity. In fact, Revelation allows us the same advantage. John's book of revelation assures us that God is still on his throne and that the future is solidly under his control. Jesus' ultimate victory is absolutely certain. One day all of creation will fall down and pay homage to God (Revelation 4:11). In the meantime, we need to remember to worship him daily, to live in such a manner that Jesus is the focal point around which all our activity revolves.

4:5 d Zec 4:2 e Rev 1:4 lamps[d] were blazing. These are the sev-
en spirits[a e] of God. 6 Also before the
throne there was what looked like a sea
4:6 f Rev 15:2 g Eze 1:5 of glass,[f] clear as crystal.
In the center, around the throne, were
four living creatures,[g] and they were
covered with eyes, in front and in back.
7 The first living creature was like a lion,
the second was like an ox, the third had
a face like a man, the fourth was like a
4:7 h Eze 1:10; 10:14 flying eagle.[h] 8 Each of the four living
4:8 i Isa 6:2 j Isa 6:3; Rev 1:8 k Rev 1:4 creatures had six wings[i] and was covered with eyes all around, even under his
wings. Day and night they never stop
saying:

"Holy, holy, holy
is the Lord God Almighty,[j]
who was, and is, and is to come."[k]

9 Whenever the living creatures give glory, honor and thanks to him who sits on
4:9 l Ps 47:8 the throne[l] and who lives for ever and
ever, 10 the twenty-four elders[m] fall down
4:10 m ver 4 n Rev 5:8,14 o ver 2 before him[n] who sits on the throne,[o] and
worship him who lives for ever and ever.
They lay their crowns before the throne
and say:

11 "You are worthy, our Lord and God,
to receive glory and honor and
4:11 p Rev 5:12 q Rev 10:6 power,[p]
for you created all things,
and by your will they were created
and have their being."[q]

The Scroll and the Lamb

5:1 r ver 7,13 s Eze 2:9,10 t Isa 29:11; Da 12:4 5 Then I saw in the right hand of
him who sat on the throne[r] a
scroll with writing on both sides[s] and
sealed[t] with seven seals. 2 And I saw a
mighty angel proclaiming in a loud
voice, "Who is worthy to break the seals
and open the scroll?" 3 But no one in
heaven or on earth or under the earth
could open the scroll or even look inside
it. 4 I wept and wept because no one was
found who was worthy to open the scroll
or look inside. 5 Then one of the elders
5:5 u Ge 49:9 v Isa 11:1,10; Ro 15:12; Rev 22:16 said to me, "Do not weep! See, the Lion[u]
of the tribe of Judah, the Root of David,[v]
has triumphed. He is able to open the
scroll and its seven seals."
5:6 w Jn 1:29 x Zec 4:10 6 Then I saw a Lamb,[w] looking as if it
had been slain, standing in the center of
the throne, encircled by the four living
creatures and the elders. He had seven
horns and seven eyes,[x] which are the

THE CROSS FOR THE FIRST TIME REVEALED GOD IN TERMS OF WEAKNESS AND LOWLINESS AND SUFFERING . . . HE WAS SEEN THENCEFORTH IN THE IMAGE OF THE . . . MOST VULNERABLE OF ALL LIVING CREATURES — A LAMB.

Malcolm Muggeridge, *British Author*

seven spirits[a] of God sent out into all the
earth. 7 He came and took the scroll from
the right hand of him who sat on the
throne.[y] 8 And when he had taken it, the 5:7 y ver 1
four living creatures and the twenty-four
elders fell down before the Lamb. Each
one had a harp[z] and they were holding 5:8 z Rev 14:2 a Ps 141:2
golden bowls full of incense, which are
the prayers[a] of the saints. 9 And they
sang a new song:[b] 5:9 b Ps 40:3 c Rev 4:11 d Heb 9:12 e 1Co 6:20

"You are worthy[c] to take the scroll
and to open its seals,
because you were slain,
and with your blood[d] you
purchased[e] men for God
from every tribe and language
and people and nation.
10 You have made them to be a
kingdom and priests[f] to 5:10 f 1Pe 2:5
serve our God,
and they will reign on the earth."

[a] 5,6 Or *the sevenfold Spirit*

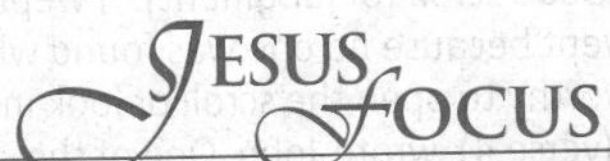

WORTHY IS THE LAMB

In the throne room scene recorded in Revelation 5 Jesus suddenly and dramatically appears to claim his rightful inheritance as God's Son. Jesus is the heir of the Jewish royal family line—the Lion of Judah and the Root of David. The most frequently used symbol for Jesus in chapter 5, however, is the "Lamb" (verses 6,8,12–13). Jesus is referred to as the Lamb a total of 28 times in Revelation, reminding us that his ultimate triumph lay in his sacrificial death and glorious resurrection. John reminded God's people that Jesus alone has made it possible for us to enjoy a restored and revitalized relationship with God the Father. This image is the same one used by John the Baptist when he first saw Jesus walking toward him: "Look, the Lamb of God, who takes away the sin of the world!" (John 1:29).

WORTHY OF ALL

Jesus is deserving of our complete and uninhibited worship because he is God the Son. In Revelation 5:11–12 the apostle John heard in his vision the incredible sounds of thousands of angel voices lifted together in song. The melody reached a spine-tingling crescendo and reverberated throughout the heavens: "Worthy is the Lamb, who was slain, to receive power and wealth and wisdom and strength and honor and glory and praise!" This angel host was soon joined by every other living creature, both in heaven and on earth, shouting out their praise: "To him who sits on the throne and to the Lamb be praise and honor and glory and power for ever and ever!" (verse 13).

What exactly had Jesus done to deserve this adulation?

The scene had opened with John grieving deeply because it appeared that no one would be able to deal with God's wrath against the sin of humanity, to break the seals, unveiling the mystery of the consummation of all history, and open God's scroll [of judgment]: "I wept and wept because no one was found who was worthy to open the scroll or look inside" (verse 4), wrote John. One of the elders who was present was quick to reassure the distraught apostle, however: "Do not weep! See, the Lion of the tribe of Judah, the Root of David, has triumphed. He is able to open the scroll and its seven seals" (verse 5).

At this point John looked up and perceived the Lamb of God (John 1:29), Jesus Christ, standing in the very center of the throne room, surrounded by citizens of heaven. Jesus reached out and accepted the scroll from his Father's hand. At that moment the four living creatures and twenty-four elders who were with him broke forth into a new song: "You are worthy to take the scroll and to open its seals, because you were slain, and with your blood you purchased men for God from every tribe and language and people and nation" (verse 9).

Jesus is the Root of David, the Messiah whom God had promised to send into the world. He was willing to renounce his heavenly privilege for a time in order to come down to earth (Philippians 2:6–8) and offer himself as the atoning sacrifice for our sins (1 John 2:2). The book of Revelation provides us with a unique glimpse into the future, when Jesus Christ will reign forever as the righteous, eternal King over a renewed creation. Jesus is indeed deserving of our unqualified adoration and devotion. He is the One to whom we also can sing "a new song" every day of our lives—and we will never run out of reasons to praise him.

The pages of human history are stained with the disastrous consequences experienced by people who have misused the privileges of power, wealth, exceptional wisdom, strength or honor. From Samson to Solomon, our fallen race has been unable to use these gifts in ways that honor God and benefit others. But Jesus is different. He is not only worthy of all these wonderful gifts, but he also uses them to express his love for his father (1 Corinthians 15:24) and his beloved children (2 Thessalonians 2:14).

Self-Discovery: *List as many reasons as you can think of why Jesus Christ is worthy of your complete and unqualified worship. Then thank him for what he has so freely done for you.*

GO TO DISCOVERY 356 ON PAGE 1708

> **JESUS IS THE ONLY TRULY WORTHY CELEBRITY IN THE UNIVERSE.**
>
> Tony Evans, *Pastor, Dallas, Texas*

11 Then I looked and heard the voice of
many angels, numbering thousands
upon thousands, and ten thousand
5:11 times ten thousand.[g] They encircled the
g Da 7:10; Heb 12:22 throne and the living creatures and the
elders. 12 In a loud voice they sang:

"Worthy is the Lamb, who was slain,
to receive power and wealth and
wisdom and strength
5:12 h Rev 4:11 and honor and glory and praise!"[h]

13 Then I heard every creature in heav-
5:13 i ver 3; Php 2:10 en and on earth and under the earth[i]
j Rev 6:16 and on the sea, and all that is in them,
k 1Ch 29:11 singing:

"To him who sits on the throne
and to the Lamb[j]
be praise and honor and glory and
power,
for ever and ever!"[k]

5:14 l Rev 4:9 14 The four living creatures said, "Amen,"[l]
m Rev 4:10; 19:4 and the elders fell down and worshiped.[m]

The Seals

6:1 n Rev 5:6 **6** I watched as the Lamb[n] opened
o Rev 5:1 the first of the seven seals.[o] Then
p Rev 4:6,7 I heard one of the four living creatures[p]
q Rev 14:2; 19:6 say in a voice like thunder,[q] "Come!" 2 I
looked, and there before me was a white
6:2 r Zec 6:3; horse![r] Its rider held a bow, and he was
Rev 19:11 given a crown,[s] and he rode out as a
s Zec 6:11; Rev 14:14 conqueror bent on conquest.[t]
t Ps 45:4 3 When the Lamb opened the second
6:3 seal, I heard the second living creature[u]
u Rev 4:7 say, "Come!" 4 Then another horse came
out, a fiery red one.[v] Its rider was given
6:4 power to take peace from the earth[w]
v Zec 6:2 w Mt 10:34 and to make men slay each other. To
him was given a large sword.
5 When the Lamb opened the third
6:5 x Rev 4:7 seal, I heard the third living creature[x]
y Zec 6:2 say, "Come!" I looked, and there before
me was a black horse![y] Its rider was
holding a pair of scales in his hand.
6 Then I heard what sounded like a voice
6:6 z Rev 4:6,7 among the four living creatures,[z] saying,
"A quart[a] of wheat for a day's wages,[b]
and three quarts of barley for a day's
wages,[b] and do not damage[a] the oil and 6:6 a Rev 9:4
the wine!"
7 When the Lamb opened the fourth
seal, I heard the voice of the fourth living 6:7
creature[b] say, "Come!" 8 I looked, and b Rev 4:7
there before me was a pale horse![c] Its 6:8
rider was named Death, and Hades[d] was c Zec 6:3
following close behind him. They were d Hos 13:14
given power over a fourth of the earth to e Jer 15:2,3; Eze 5:12,17
kill by sword, famine and plague, and by
the wild beasts of the earth.[e]
9 When he opened the fifth seal, I saw
under the altar[f] the souls of those who 6:9 f Rev 14:18; 16:7
had been slain[g] because of the word of g Rev 20:4
God and the testimony they had maintained. 10 They called out in a loud voice, 6:10
"How long,[h] Sovereign Lord, holy and h Zec 1:12
true,[i] until you judge the inhabitants of i Rev 3:7
the earth and avenge our blood?"[j] j Rev 19:2
11 Then each of them was given a white
robe,[k] and they were told to wait a little 6:11 k Rev 3:4
longer, until the number of their fellow l Heb 11:40
servants and brothers who were to be
killed as they had been was completed.[l]
12 I watched as he opened the sixth
seal. There was a great earthquake.[m] The 6:12 m Rev 16:18
sun turned black[n] like sackcloth made n Mt 24:29
of goat hair, the whole moon turned

[a] 6 Greek *a choinix* (probably about a liter)
[b] 6 Greek *a denarius*

JESUS FOCUS

SEALS AND TRUMPETS

One by one Jesus opens each of the seven seals on the scroll of God's judgment (Revelation 6:1—8:1). As our Savior opens the seals in God's throne room he unleashes the judgments written in the scroll. With the opening of each seal a catastrophic event occurs, demonstrating that our just and righteous God does not allow sin to go unpunished. When Jesus opens the seventh seal, the entire scroll is exposed, and seven trumpets of judgment follow in rapid succession. Because the imagery is so vivid and symbolic, there are many different opinions about its interpretation and implications. Regardless of how one views the seals and trumpets, however, it is apparent that they speak of nearly total annihilation of the planet, the collapse of human government, and cosmic disaster of proportions never before seen or even imagined. But Revelation instills hope in the hearts of Christians, because Jesus our victorious warrior will reign in peace after the destruction and warring have reached their climax (Revelation 21).

The Wrath of the Lamb

We generally picture Jesus as a mild-mannered and gentle man—as One who was "oppressed and afflicted" and yet "did not open his mouth" (Isaiah 53:7). In our mind's eye we envision a Lamb being led docilely to slaughter. But we do not often conceive of this same Jesus as a Lamb filled with wrath against those who have rejected him! (Revelation 6). To begin with, a sheep or lamb is not ordinarily depicted in this fashion, for the simple reason that anger is not a typical character trait of this placid animal. Furthermore, Jesus' wrath is not a popular topic; it is, however, a very real part of who Jesus is.

The Old Testament uses 20 different words to describe God's anger, and the subject is mentioned more than 850 times! In the New Testament there is only one primary word, *orge*, which describes God's steady, unrelenting, deep-seated antagonism toward sin in the world. Deep within our souls we know that we cannot stand in the face of God's wrath without the buffer of his mercy. But in order to comprehend his grace, forgiveness and love, we first have to understand the nature of his fury in the face of sin.

God is completely holy. That holiness demands that he be worshiped and exalted (Isaiah 6:1–3). God is also just, which means that he demands full recompense for sin (Romans 2:1–11). Wrongdoing results in death (Genesis 2:16–17), and God's fairness demands that he follow through with the penalty, both now and in the future (Romans 1:18; Revelation 19:15).

The story doesn't end there, however. On the basis of his boundless love God offered to forgive our sins. Although death was still required as punishment, Jesus endured the consequences of God's wrath on our behalf (Romans 3:25). The fury of the Lamb is very real, and one day he will turn it loose upon a world that has rejected him. If he were a God characterized only by anger, we would be hopeless and lost forever. But when we accept Jesus into our lives and believe that he voluntarily took our punishment, we experience the Lamb of God as gentle and loving, overflowing with mercy and forgiveness.

King David in the Old Testament already understood the magnitude of God's mercy, urging God's people to "sing to the LORD, you saints of his; praise his holy name. For his anger lasts only a moment, but his favor lasts a lifetime; weeping may remain for a night, but rejoicing comes in the morning" (Psalm 30:4–5). And Peter encouraged the followers of Jesus Christ with these moving words: "You are a chosen people, a royal priesthood, a holy nation, a people belonging to God, that you may declare the praises of him who called you out of darkness into his wonderful light. Once you were not a people, but now you are the people of God; once you had not received mercy, but now you have received mercy" (1 Peter 2:9–10).

***Self-Discovery:** Lamentations 3:22–23 tells us that "because of the LORD's great love we are not consumed, for his compassions never fail. They are new every morning; great is your faithfulness." What blessings can you think of that are given to you anew every morning? Pause to thank the Lord for those blessings that you have enjoyed so far today (health, breath, sunshine, a home, food, a job, a family, a church family . . .).*

GO TO DISCOVERY 357 ON PAGE 1710

blood red, [13]and the stars in the sky fell
6:13 [o]Mt 24:29; to earth,[o] as late figs drop from a fig
Rev 8:10; 9:1 tree[p] when shaken by a strong wind.
[p]Isa 34:4 [14]The sky receded like a scroll, rolling up,
6:14 and every mountain and island was re-
[q]Jer 4:24; moved from its place.[q]
Rev 16:20 [15]Then the kings of the earth, the
princes, the generals, the rich, the
6:15 mighty, and every slave and every free
[r]Isa 2:10,19,21 man hid in caves and among the rocks
6:16 of the mountains.[r] [16]They called to the
[s]Hos 10:8; mountains and the rocks, "Fall on us[s]
Lk 23:30 and hide us from the face of him who
6:17 sits on the throne and from the wrath of
[t]Zep 1:14,15; the Lamb! [17]For the great day[t] of their
Rev 16:14 [u]Ps 76:7 wrath has come, and who can stand?"[u]

144,000 Sealed

7 After this I saw four angels standing at the four corners of the
7:1 [v]Da 7:2 earth, holding back the four winds[v] of
the earth to prevent any wind from
blowing on the land or on the sea or on
any tree. [2]Then I saw another angel
coming up from the east, having the seal
of the living God. He called out in a loud
voice to the four angels who had been
given power to harm the land and the
7:3 sea: [3]"Do not harm[w] the land or the sea
[w]Rev 6:6 [x]Eze 9:4; or the trees until we put a seal on the
Rev 22:4 foreheads[x] of the servants of our God."
[4]Then I heard the number[y] of those who
7:4 [y]Rev 9:16 were sealed: 144,000[z] from all the tribes
[z]Rev 14:1,3 of Israel.

[5]From the tribe of Judah 12,000
were sealed,
from the tribe of Reuben 12,000,
from the tribe of Gad 12,000,
[6]from the tribe of Asher 12,000,
from the tribe of Naphtali 12,000,
from the tribe of Manasseh 12,000,
[7]from the tribe of Simeon 12,000,
from the tribe of Levi 12,000,
from the tribe of Issachar 12,000,
[8]from the tribe of Zebulun 12,000,
from the tribe of Joseph 12,000,
from the tribe of Benjamin 12,000.

The Great Multitude in White Robes

[9]After this I looked and there before
me was a great multitude that no one
could count, from every nation, tribe,
7:9 [a]Rev 5:9 people and language,[a] standing before
[b]ver 15 the throne[b] and in front of the Lamb.
They were wearing white robes and were
holding palm branches in their hands.
[10]And they cried out in a loud voice:

NO VOICE IS, NOR CAN BE, SILENT WHEN THE LAMB APPEARS.

Walter Scott, *Scottish Pastor*

"Salvation belongs to our God,[c] 7:10 [c]Ps 3:8;
who sits on the throne, Rev 12:10; 19:1
and to the Lamb."

[11]All the angels were standing around 7:11
the throne and around the elders[d] and [d]Rev 4:4
the four living creatures.[e] They fell down [e]Rev 4:6
on their faces[f] before the throne and [f]Rev 4:10
worshiped God, [12]saying:

"Amen!
Praise and glory
and wisdom and thanks and honor
and power and strength
be to our God for ever and ever. 7:12
Amen!"[g] [g]Rev 5:12-14

[13]Then one of the elders asked me,
"These in white robes—who are they,
and where did they come from?"
[14]I answered, "Sir, you know."
And he said, "These are they who
have come out of the great tribulation;

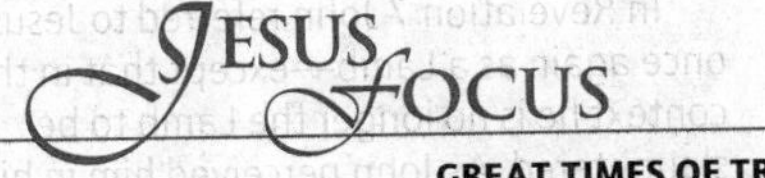

GREAT TIMES OF TROUBLE

God's people have historically held differing opinions with regard to the "great tribulation" referred to in Revelation 7:14. Some believe that this period of hostility had already transpired in the form of the persecution God's people were enduring during the lifetime of the apostle John. Others surmise that the reference is to the suffering God's people are even now experiencing during the time between Jesus' return to heaven and his second coming to earth. Still others anticipate a relatively short period of intense trouble just prior to Jesus' final return. However we view this great tribulation, one fact is clear: A significant number of Jews from every tribe, as well as a host of Gentile believers from every nation, will be saved during that time (verses 5–14). And John reminded us that this period of anguish will not be interminable. The day will surely come when the people who have believed in God will no longer suffer in any way. Jesus, the Lamb of God, will lead them to the places of refreshment and well-being, and God himself will "wipe away every tear from their eyes" (verses 16–17).

A LAMB WHO IS A SHEPHERD

Hundreds of years before Jesus was born the prophet Isaiah described him as "a lamb [led] to the slaughter" (Isaiah 53:7). The Israelites could easily relate to this illustration, because they daily slaughtered livestock as sacrifices for their sins (Leviticus 1:1–4). Under the old covenant this was, in fact, the only way to become clean before God (Leviticus 17:11). The New Testament tells us basically the same thing: "Without the shedding of blood there is no forgiveness" (Hebrews 9:22–28), but thanks be to God that this is only part of the story. The Good News of Jesus Christ is that he gave himself as the final sacrifice (Hebrews 9:11–15; 10:10–14), so that we are no longer required to offer up animals as a temporary covering for our sins.

In Revelation 7 John referred to Jesus once again as a Lamb—except that in this context he is no longer the Lamb to be slaughtered. As John perceived him in his vision, Jesus is now the Lamb "at the center of the throne" (verse 17). We may have a difficult time conceptualizing the Son of God as a Lamb seated on a throne. More important than his form, however, is his role. The One who was sacrificed is the One whom all of creation now worships!

John wrote that people from "every nation, tribe, people and language" (verse 9), as well as people who have suffered persecution and yet remained faithful (verse 14), will be presented to the Lamb. This Lamb will be their Shepherd, and he will lead them to "springs of living water" (verse 17). Nations and tribes who have been at war for centuries will become members of the same family—brothers and sisters in Christ! People isolated by language barriers will all understand perfectly the language of heaven. These are the people who have "washed their robes and made them white in the blood of the Lamb" (verse 14). We find it difficult to comprehend that something washed in *blood* could come out white—and it is even harder to imagine that there could be sufficient blood to cleanse the robes of a multitude of people that "no one could count" (verse 9). All of this is possible only through the incomparably great power of God himself.

Lambs are not known for their leadership qualities; and yet this Lamb is different. Jesus, who silently and willingly gave his life as an atonement for the sin of the world, is the only One worthy to lead the people whom he died to save. In John's vision of the future we see the sacrificial Lamb leading his followers as their Good Shepherd who "lays down his life for his sheep" (John 10:11). We who are his sheep have strength for today and bright hope for tomorrow because we "listen to his voice" (John 10:27). He knows us, and we follow him gladly, for he is the giver of eternal life and of this marvelous promise: "They shall never perish; no one can snatch them out of my hand" (John 10:28).

Self-Discovery: *If you are familiar with the tune of the hymn "By the Sea of Crystal," sing the lyrics of verse 3 in your mind. Otherwise, read the poem back to Jesus as an expression of your thanks and praise: "Unto God Almighty, Sitting on the throne, And the Lamb, victorious, Be the praise alone. God has wrought salvation, He did wondrous things; Who shall not extol Thee, Holy King of Kings?"*

GO TO DISCOVERY 358 ON PAGE 1714

they have washed their robes[h] and made
them white in the blood of the Lamb.[i]
15 Therefore,
"they are before the throne of God[j]
and serve him[k] day and night in
his temple;[l]
and he who sits on the throne will
spread his tent over them.[m]
16 Never again will they hunger;
never again will they thirst.
The sun will not beat upon them,
nor any scorching heat.[n]
17 For the Lamb at the center of the
throne will be their
shepherd;[o]
he will lead them to springs of
living water.
And God will wipe away every tear
from their eyes."[p]

7:14 h Rev 22:14 i Heb 9:14; 1Jn 1:7
7:15 j ver 9 k Rev 22:3 l Rev 11:19 m Isa 4:5,6; Rev 21:3
7:16 n Isa 49:10
7:17 o Ps 23:1; Jn 10:11 p Isa 25:8; Rev 21:4

The Seventh Seal and the Golden Censer

8 When he opened the seventh
seal,[q] there was silence in heaven
for about half an hour.
2 And I saw the seven angels[r] who
stand before God, and to them were giv-
en seven trumpets.
3 Another angel,[s] who had a golden
censer, came and stood at the altar. He
was given much incense to offer, with
the prayers of all the saints,[t] on the
golden altar[u] before the throne. 4 The
smoke of the incense, together with the
prayers of the saints, went up before
God[v] from the angel's hand. 5 Then the
angel took the censer, filled it with fire
from the altar,[w] and hurled it on the
earth; and there came peals of thunder,[x]
rumblings, flashes of lightning and an
earthquake.[y]

8:1 q Rev 6:1
8:2 r ver 6-13; Rev 9:1,13; 11:15
8:3 s Rev 7:2 t Rev 5:8 u Ex 30:1-6; Heb 9:4; Rev 9:13
8:4 v Ps 141:2
8:5 w Lev 16:12,13 x Rev 4:5 y Rev 6:12

The Trumpets

6 Then the seven angels who had the
seven trumpets[z] prepared to sound
them.
7 The first angel sounded his trumpet,
and there came hail and fire[a] mixed with
blood, and it was hurled down upon the
earth. A third[b] of the earth was burned
up, a third of the trees were burned up,
and all the green grass was burned up.[c]
8 The second angel sounded his trumpet, and something like a huge mountain,[d] all ablaze, was thrown into the sea.
A third[e] of the sea turned into blood,[f] 9 a
third[g] of the living creatures in the sea
died, and a third of the ships were destroyed.
10 The third angel sounded his trumpet, and a great star, blazing like a torch,
fell from the sky[h] on a third of the rivers
and on the springs of water[i]— 11 the
name of the star is Wormwood.[a] A third[j]
of the waters turned bitter, and many
people died from the waters that had
become bitter.[k]
12 The fourth angel sounded his trumpet, and a third of the sun was struck, a
third of the moon, and a third of the
stars, so that a third[l] of them turned
dark.[m] A third of the day was without
light, and also a third of the night.
13 As I watched, I heard an eagle that
was flying in midair[n] call out in a loud
voice: "Woe! Woe! Woe[o] to the inhabitants of the earth, because of the trumpet blasts about to be sounded by the
other three angels!"
9 The fifth angel sounded his trumpet, and I saw a star that had fall-
en from the sky to the earth.[p] The star
was given the key to the shaft of the
Abyss.[q] 2 When he opened the Abyss,
smoke rose from it like the smoke from
a gigantic furnace.[r] The sun and sky
were darkened[s] by the smoke from the
Abyss. 3 And out of the smoke locusts[t]
came down upon the earth and were
given power like that of scorpions[u] of
the earth. 4 They were told not to harm[v]

8:6 z ver 2
8:7 a Eze 38:22 b ver 7-12; Rev 9:15,18; 12:4 c Rev 9:4
8:8 d Jer 51:25 e ver 7 f Rev 16:3
8:9 g ver 7
8:10 h Isa 14:12; Rev 6:13; 9:1 i Rev 14:7; 16:4
8:11 j ver 7 k Jer 9:15; 23:15
8:12 l ver 7 m Ex 10:21-23; Rev 6:12,13
8:13 n Rev 14:6; 19:17 o Rev 9:12; 11:14
9:1 p Rev 8:10 q ver 2,11; Lk 8:31
9:2 r Ge 19:28; Ex 19:18 s Joel 2:2,10
9:3 t Ex 10:12-15 u ver 5,10
9:4 v Rev 6:6

a 11 That is, Bitterness

JESUS FOCUS

SEVEN TRUMPETS

The seven trumpets will sound when Jesus opens the seventh seal on the scroll of God's judgment (Revelation 8:1–2). John's description of the trumpet judgments seems to point to a global holocaust of some sort. The entire planet will be affected by large-scale devastation, intense human suffering and massive loss of life. The kind of desolation Jesus predicted was unfathomable in the ancient world, and even today, in our world of nuclear warheads and other weapons of mass destruction, it is difficult to conceive of such all-encompassing catastrophe. However, we have the assurance that in accordance with God's perfect plan, our Lord Jesus Christ will emerge the uncontested victor, triumphant over evil, destruction and death.

9:4 the grass of the earth or any plant or
w Rev 8:7 tree,[w] but only those people who did not
x Rev 7:2,3 have the seal of God on their foreheads.[x]
[5]They were not given power to kill them,
but only to torture them for five
9:5 y ver 10 z ver 3 months.[y] And the agony they suffered
was like that of the sting of a scorpion[z]
when it strikes a man. [6]During those
days men will seek death, but will not
9:6 find it; they will long to die, but death
a Job 3:21; will elude them.[a]
Jer 8:3; Rev 6:16 [7]The locusts looked like horses pre-
9:7 pared for battle.[b] On their heads they
b Joel 2:4 wore something like crowns of gold, and
c Da 7:8 their faces resembled human faces.[c]
9:8 [8]Their hair was like women's hair, and
d Joel 1:6 their teeth were like lions' teeth.[d] [9]They
had breastplates like breastplates of
iron, and the sound of their wings was
9:9 like the thundering of many horses and
e Joel 2:5 chariots rushing into battle.[e] [10]They had
tails and stings like scorpions, and in
9:10 their tails they had power to torment
f ver 3,5,19 people for five months.[f] [11]They had as
9:11 king over them the angel of the Abyss,[g]
g ver 1,2 whose name in Hebrew is Abaddon, and
in Greek, Apollyon.[a]
[12]The first woe is past; two other woes
9:12 h Rev 8:13 are yet to come.[h]
[13]The sixth angel sounded his trum-
9:13 pet, and I heard a voice coming from the
i Ex 30:1-3 horns[b][i] of the golden altar that is before
j Rev 8:3 God.[j] [14]It said to the sixth angel who had
the trumpet, "Release the four angels
9:14 who are bound at the great river Eu-
k Rev 16:12 phrates."[k] [15]And the four angels who had
been kept ready for this very hour and
day and month and year were released
9:15 l ver 18 to kill a third of mankind.[l] [16]The number of the mounted troops was two hun-
9:16 m Rev 5:11; 7:4 dred million. I heard their number.[m]
[17]The horses and riders I saw in my vi-
sion looked like this: Their breastplates
were fiery red, dark blue, and yellow as
sulfur. The heads of the horses resem-
9:17 bled the heads of lions, and out of their
n Rev 11:5 mouths[n] came fire, smoke and sulfur.[o]
o ver 18 [18]A third of mankind was killed[p] by the
9:18 three plagues of fire, smoke and sulfur[q]
p ver 15 q ver 17 that came out of their mouths. [19]The
power of the horses was in their mouths
and in their tails; for their tails were like
snakes, having heads with which they
inflict injury.
[20]The rest of mankind that were not
9:20 killed by these plagues still did not re-
r Dt 31:29 pent of the work of their hands;[r] they
did not stop worshiping demons,[s] and 9:20
idols of gold, silver, bronze, stone and s 1Co 10:20
wood—idols that cannot see or hear or t Ps 115:4-7; 135:15-17;
walk.[t] [21]Nor did they repent[u] of their Da 5:23
murders, their magic arts,[v] their sexual 9:21
immorality[w] or their thefts. u Rev 2:21 v Rev 18:23 w Rev 17:2,5

The Angel and the Little Scroll

10 Then I saw another mighty angel[x] coming down from heaven. 10:1
He was robed in a cloud, with a rainbow x Rev 5:2
above his head; his face was like the y Mt 17:2; Rev 1:16
sun,[y] and his legs were like fiery pillars.[z] z Rev 1:15
[2]He was holding a little scroll, which lay
open in his hand. He planted his right
foot on the sea and his left foot on the
land, [3]and he gave a loud shout like the
roar of a lion. When he shouted, the
voices of the seven thunders[a] spoke. 10:3 a Rev 4:5
[4]And when the seven thunders spoke, I
was about to write; but I heard a voice
from heaven say, "Seal up what the sev-
en thunders have said and do not write
it down."[b] 10:4 b Da 8:26; 12:4,
[5]Then the angel I had seen standing 9; Rev 22:10
on the sea and on the land raised his
right hand to heaven.[c] [6]And he swore by 10:5 c Da 12:7
him who lives for ever and ever, who
created the heavens and all that is in
them, the earth and all that is in it, and 10:6
the sea and all that is in it,[d] and said, d Rev 4:11; 14:7
"There will be no more delay![e] [7]But in e Rev 16:17
the days when the seventh angel is
about to sound his trumpet, the mys- 10:7
tery[f] of God will be accomplished, just f Ro 16:25

[a] 11 *Abaddon* and *Apollyon* mean *Destroyer.*
[b] 13 That is, projections

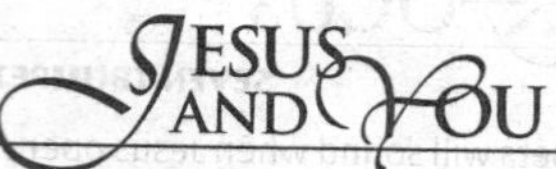

GOD'S MYSTERY

"The mystery of God" (Revelation 10:7) will be revealed when God finishes the course of action he has been planning and carrying out from the beginning of time. The "mystery" also refers to Jesus' unique role in God's kingdom. In Colossians 1:26 Jesus Christ is described as the "mystery that has been kept hidden for ages . . . but is now disclosed to the saints." God's prophets in the Old Testament had announced that God would send a Messiah, and Jesus is that Promised One (Matthew 1:16; 16:16). In the book of Revelation that for which God's people have waited through all the ages at long last reaches its majestic culmination—the decisive and final victory of Jesus.

as he announced to his servants the
prophets."
8Then the voice that I had heard from
10:8 g ver 4 heaven[g] spoke to me once more: "Go,
take the scroll that lies open in the hand
of the angel who is standing on the sea
and on the land."
9So I went to the angel and asked him
to give me the little scroll. He said to me,
"Take it and eat it. It will turn your
stomach sour, but in your mouth it will
10:9 h Jer 15:16; be as sweet as honey."[h] 10I took the little
Eze 2:8-3:3 scroll from the angel's hand and ate it. It
tasted as sweet as honey in my mouth,
but when I had eaten it, my stomach
turned sour. 11Then I was told, "You
10:11 i Eze 37:4,9 must prophesy[i] again about many peoples, nations, languages and kings."

The Two Witnesses

11:1 j Eze 40:3; 11 I was given a reed like a mea-
Rev 21:15 suring rod[j] and was told, "Go
and measure the temple of God and the
11:2 altar, and count the worshipers there.
k Eze 40:17,20 2But exclude the outer court;[k] do not
l Lk 21:24 measure it, because it has been given to
m Rev 21:2 n Da 7:25; the Gentiles.[l] They will trample on the
Rev 13:5 holy city[m] for 42 months.[n] 3And I will
11:3 give power to my two witnesses,[o] and
o Rev 1:5 p Ge 37:34 they will prophesy for 1,260 days,
clothed in sackcloth."[p] 4These are the
11:4 q Ps 52:8; two olive trees[q] and the two lampstands
Jer 11:16; that stand before the Lord of the earth.[r]
Zec 4:3,11 r Zec 4:14 5If anyone tries to harm them, fire
comes from their mouths and devours
11:5 s 2Ki 1:10; their enemies.[s] This is how anyone who
Jer 5:14 wants to harm them must die.[t] 6These
t Nu 16:29,35 men have power to shut up the sky so
that it will not rain during the time they
are prophesying; and they have power to
11:6 u Ex 7:17,19 turn the waters into blood[u] and to strike
the earth with every kind of plague as
often as they want.
7Now when they have finished their
11:7 v Rev 13:1-4 testimony, the beast[v] that comes up
w Da 7:21 from the Abyss will attack them,[w] and
overpower and kill them. 8Their bodies
will lie in the street of the great city,
11:8 x Isa 1:9 which is figuratively called Sodom[x] and
y Heb 13:12 Egypt, where also their Lord was crucified.[y] 9For three and a half days men
from every people, tribe, language and
11:9 z Ps 79:2,3 nation will gaze on their bodies and refuse them burial.[z] 10The inhabitants of
11:10 a Rev 3:10 the earth[a] will gloat over them and will
b Est 9:19,22 celebrate by sending each other gifts,[b]
because these two prophets had tor-
mented those who live on the earth.
11But after the three and a half days a 11:11
breath of life from God entered them,[c] c Eze 37:5,9,10,
and they stood on their feet, and terror 14
struck those who saw them. 12Then they
heard a loud voice from heaven saying to
them, "Come up here."[d] And they went 11:12 d Rev 4:1
up to heaven in a cloud,[e] while their en- e 2Ki 2:11;
emies looked on. Ac 1:9
13At that very hour there was a severe
earthquake[f] and a tenth of the city col- 11:13 f Rev 6:12
lapsed. Seven thousand people were g Rev 14:7
killed in the earthquake, and the sur- h Rev 16:11
vivors were terrified and gave glory[g] to
the God of heaven.[h]
14The second woe has passed; the 11:14
third woe is coming soon.[i] i Rev 8:13

The Seventh Trumpet

15The seventh angel sounded his 11:15
trumpet,[j] and there were loud voices[k] in j Rev 10:7 k Rev 16:17; 19:1
heaven, which said: l Rev 12:10 m Da 2:44; 7:14,
27

"The kingdom of the world has
become the kingdom of our
Lord and of his Christ,[l]
and he will reign for ever and
ever."[m]

16And the twenty-four elders,[n] who were 11:16
seated on their thrones before God, fell n Rev 4:4
on their faces and worshiped God, 17say-
ing:

"We give thanks to you, Lord God 11:17
Almighty,[o] o Rev 1:8
the One who is and who was, p Rev 19:6
because you have taken your great
power
and have begun to reign.[p]
18The nations were angry;[q] 11:18 q Ps 2:1
and your wrath has come. r Rev 10:7
The time has come for judging the s Rev 19:5
dead,
and for rewarding your servants
the prophets[r]
and your saints and those who
reverence your name,
both small and great[s]—
and for destroying those who
destroy the earth."

19Then God's temple[t] in heaven was 11:19 t Rev 15:5,8
opened, and within his temple was seen u Rev 16:21
the ark of his covenant. And there came
flashes of lightning, rumblings, peals of
thunder, an earthquake and a great hailstorm.[u]

DISCOVERY 358

VICTORY IN JESUS

The Messiah by Georg Friedrich Handel is arguably one of the greatest musical compositions of all time. Using lyrics directly from the Bible, this oratorio celebrates Jesus as God the Son. In his rousing final chorus Handel quoted words from Revelation 11:15: "He will reign for ever and ever." As the apostle John continued to receive incredible visions about the last days, it was obvious that some great culmination was approaching. It appeared that the story was, to put it in the vernacular, all over but the shouting! Because God had opened heaven and provided John with a sneak preview, everyone who has lived since has been offered an opportunity to hear of the celebration of God's consummate victory over evil.

It just doesn't get any better than this. The Lord will claim his omnipotent power and begin an uncontested reign—just as he has always promised and just as his people have anticipated since the beginning of time (Genesis 3:15). In John's vision all of the saints and angels in heaven fell on their faces and worshiped Jesus, recognizing him as the eternal King over all of creation. The flawless relationship with God that he has promised his people throughout the ages will be theirs in every way imaginable. Sin and the devil will have been routed, and nothing will ever again stand between the Creator and his creatures.

When Jesus takes his place as the King of all creation, two things will happen. He will reward with eternal life in heaven those who have honored him. But those who have refused him will be granted precisely that for which they have asked all along—for God to leave them alone forever. Revelation 11 began with a description of hell on earth, but in the middle of his vision of judgment John reminded us that victory is certain. There will inevitably be conflicts and challenges ahead of us, but one glimpse of heaven reminds us that God is still on the throne.

Georg Friedrich Handel also drew from 1 Corinthians 15 for the lyrics for his masterpiece oratorio. "Listen," said Paul, "I tell you a mystery. We will not all sleep, but we will all be changed—in a flash, in the twinkling of an eye, at the last trumpet . . . Then the saying that is written will come true: 'Death has been swallowed up in victory' . . . The sting of death is sin, and the power of sin is the law. But thanks be to God! He gives us the victory through our Lord Jesus Christ" (1 Corinthians 15:51–52,54,56–57).

"What then," again in Paul's words, "shall we say in response to this? If God is for us, who can be against us? He who did not spare his own Son, but gave him up for us all—how will he not also, along with him, graciously give us all things? . . . Who shall separate us from the love of Christ? Shall trouble or hardship or persecution or famine or nakedness or danger or sword? . . . No, in all these things we are more than conquerors through him who loved us" (Romans 8:31–32,35,37).

Self-Discovery: *Thank God right now for the victory that you have already received through his atoning death on the cross. Thank him too for the glorious, eternal future that awaits you with your Savior in heaven.*

GO TO DISCOVERY 359 ON PAGE 1716

The Woman and the Dragon

12 A great and wondrous sign appeared in heaven: a woman
clothed with the sun, with the moon under her feet and a crown of twelve stars
on her head. 2She was pregnant and
12:2 v Gal 4:19 cried out in pain[v] as she was about to
give birth. 3Then another sign appeared
in heaven: an enormous red dragon with
12:3 w Da 7:7,20; seven heads and ten horns[w] and seven
Rev 13:1 crowns[x] on his heads. 4His tail swept a
x Rev 19:12 third[y] of the stars out of the sky and
12:4 flung them to the earth.[z] The dragon
y Rev 8:7 stood in front of the woman who was
z Da 8:10 about to give birth, so that he might de-
a Mt 2:16 vour her child[a] the moment it was born.
5She gave birth to a son, a male child,
12:5 who will rule all the nations with an iron
b Ps 2:9; scepter.[b] And her child was snatched up
Rev 2:27 to God and to his throne. 6The woman
fled into the desert to a place prepared
for her by God, where she might be tak-
12:6 c Rev 11:2 en care of for 1,260 days.[c]
7And there was war in heaven. Mi-
12:7 chael and his angels fought against the
d ver 3 dragon,[d] and the dragon and his angels
fought back. 8But he was not strong
enough, and they lost their place in
12:9 heaven. 9The great dragon was hurled
e Ge 3:1-7 down—that ancient serpent[e] called the
f Mt 25:41 devil,[f] or Satan, who leads the whole
g Rev 20:3,8,10 h Lk 10:18; world astray.[g] He was hurled to the
Jn 12:31 earth,[h] and his angels with him.
12:10 10Then I heard a loud voice in heaven[i]
i Rev 11:15 say:

"Now have come the salvation and
the power and the kingdom
of our God,
and the authority of his Christ. 12:10
For the accuser of our brothers,[j] j Job 1:9-11;
who accuses them before our Zec 3:1
God day and night,
has been hurled down.
11They overcame him 12:11
by the blood of the Lamb[k] k Rev 7:14
and by the word of their l Rev 6:9
testimony;[l] m Lk 14:26
they did not love their lives so much
as to shrink from death.[m] 12:12
12Therefore rejoice, you heavens[n] n Ps 96:11;
and you who dwell in them! Isa 49:13;
Rev 18:20
But woe[o] to the earth and the sea,[p] o Rev 8:13
because the devil has gone down p Rev 10:6
to you!
He is filled with fury,
because he knows that his time
is short."

13When the dragon[q] saw that he had 12:13 q ver 3 r ver 5
been hurled to the earth, he pursued the
woman who had given birth to the male
child.[r] 14The woman was given the two 12:14
wings of a great eagle,[s] so that she s Ex 19:4
might fly to the place prepared for her t Da 7:25
in the desert, where she would be taken
care of for a time, times and half a time,[t]
out of the serpent's reach. 15Then from
his mouth the serpent spewed water
like a river, to overtake the woman and
sweep her away with the torrent. 16But
the earth helped the woman by opening
its mouth and swallowing the river that
the dragon had spewed out of his
mouth. 17Then the dragon was enraged
at the woman and went off to make 12:17
war[u] against the rest of her offspring[v]— u Rev 11:7
those who obey God's command- v Ge 3:15
ments[w] and hold to the testimony of w Rev 14:12
13 Jesus.[x] 1And the dragon[a] stood x Rev 1:2
on the shore of the sea.

The Beast out of the Sea

And I saw a beast coming out of the
sea.[y] He had ten horns and seven heads,[z] 13:1
with ten crowns on his horns, and on y Da 7:1-6; Rev 15:2
each head a blasphemous name.[a] 2The z Rev 12:3 a Da 11:36;
beast I saw resembled a leopard,[b] but Rev 17:3
had feet like those of a bear[c] and a 13:2
mouth like that of a lion.[d] The dragon b Da 7:6 c Da 7:5
gave the beast his power and his throne d Da 7:4
and great authority.[e] 3One of the heads e Rev 16:10

[a] 1 Some late manuscripts *And I*

JESUS FOCUS

KEY PLAYERS

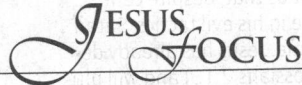

In the middle of the book of Revelation we find a listing of the seven key players in the great end times drama (Revelation 12—13). There are numerous opinions about how to interpret the significance of each figure, and these divergent interpretations tie in with one's individual view of many of the other final events. The primary differences in explanation surround the woman, who might represent either Israel or the Christian church; the remnant, which might be either Gentile or Jewish; and the beast from the sea, which is most likely the antichrist. Almost everyone agrees that the male child is Jesus himself and that the dragon is Satan. However one views these events, one truth is certain: Jesus will triumph over Satan in the end (Revelation 19:11–21; 20:7–10).

SATAN'S ULTIMATE DEMISE

In Revelation 12 the gospel account is condensed into a vivid, symbolic narrative. The apostle John saw the nation of Israel in the form of a glorious and powerful woman, "clothed with the sun, with the moon under her feet and a crown of twelve stars on her head. She was pregnant and cried out in pain as she was about to give birth" (verses 1–2). A fierce dragon stood ready to devour the child, but God protected the infant at the very moment of his birth by snatching him up to himself (verse 5). The woman fled to the desert, to a place that God had prepared in advance for her protection, while a war raged in heaven between the dragon and the angels (verses 6–7). After the dragon had been defeated and flung back down to the earth, he pursued the woman because of his inability to reach her son. God again protected her, and the dragon turned on her other children (verses 13–17).

Satan has been doomed from the beginning of time. Very early in human history he convinced humankind to turn away from the Creator, but God made it known immediately that the situation would not last forever, warning Satan: "Because you have done this, cursed are you above all the livestock and all the wild animals! . . . I will put enmity between you and the woman, and between your offspring and hers; he will crush your head, and you will strike his heel" (Genesis 3:14–15).

Satan wasn't satisfied with the damage he had caused in the Garden of Eden. He has ever since that time relentlessly pursued God's people, using one deception after another to drive a wedge between God and humanity. But there is and has always been a place of protection for God's people, a haven safe from destruction. Our Father asks that we believe in him, walk with him and resist whatever wiles Satan might use in an attempt to trip us up along the way (Psalm 119:105,110; Ephesians 6:10). In 1 Corinthians 10:12 Paul warned the believers in Corinth: "If you think you are standing firm, be careful that you don't fall," but he followed up with words of comfort and hope in verse 13: "No temptation has seized you except what is common to man. And God is faithful; he will not let you be tempted beyond what you can bear. But when you are tempted, he will also provide a way out so that you can stand up under it."

Satan will never be able to thwart God's plan, and he is becoming increasingly desperate and furious, "because he knows that his time is short" (Revelation 12:12). With wild determination our adversary tracks down and torments "those who obey God's commandments and hold to the testimony of Jesus" (Revelation 12:17; see also 1 Peter 5:8). But John's vision confirms for us that, despite centuries of practice in his evil tactics, Satan will lose the battle. Jesus has already defeated him (Colossians 2:15) and will ultimately take his rightful place of honor. Then all of creation will be returned to the pristine state God has always intended for it (Psalm 2).

Self-Discovery: *No matter what temptation you might be facing today, take comfort from repeating Paul's question from Romans 8:31: "If God is for [me], who can be against [me]?"*

GO TO DISCOVERY 360 ON PAGE 1719

of the beast seemed to have had a fatal
13:3 wound, but the fatal wound had been
f ver 12,14 g Rev 17:8 healed.[f] The whole world was astonished[g] and followed the beast. 4Men
worshiped the dragon because he had
given authority to the beast, and they
also worshiped the beast and asked,
13:4 h Ex 15:11 "Who is like[h] the beast? Who can make
war against him?"
5The beast was given a mouth to utter
13:5 i Da 7:8,11,20, 25; 11:36; 2Th 2:4 proud words and blasphemies[i] and to
exercise his authority for forty-two
j Rev 11:2 months.[j] 6He opened his mouth to blaspheme God, and to slander his name and
his dwelling place and those who live in
13:6 k Rev 12:12 heaven.[k] 7He was given power to make
13:7 l Da 7:21; Rev 11:7 war[l] against the saints and to conquer
them. And he was given authority over
m Rev 5:9 every tribe, people, language and nation.[m] 8All inhabitants of the earth[n] will
13:8 n Rev 3:10 worship the beast—all whose names
o Rev 3:5; 20:12 have not been written in the book of life[o]
p Mt 25:34 belonging to the Lamb that was slain
from the creation of the world.[a][p]
13:9 q Rev 2:7 9He who has an ear, let him hear.[q]

10If anyone is to go into captivity,
into captivity he will go.
If anyone is to be killed[b] with the
13:10 sword,
r Jer 15:2; 43:11 with the sword he will be killed.[r]
s Heb 6:12 t Rev 14:12 This calls for patient endurance and
faithfulness[s] on the part of the saints.[t]

The Beast out of the Earth

11Then I saw another beast, coming
out of the earth. He had two horns like a
lamb, but he spoke like a dragon. 12He
exercised all the authority[u] of the first 13:12 u ver 4 v ver 14
beast on his behalf,[v] and made the earth w Rev 14:9,11
and its inhabitants worship the first x ver 3
beast,[w] whose fatal wound had been
healed.[x] 13And he performed great and
miraculous signs,[y] even causing fire to 13:13 y Mt 24:24
come down from heaven[z] to earth in full z 1Ki 18:38; Rev 20:9
view of men. 14Because of the signs[a] he
was given power to do on behalf of the 13:14 a 2Th 2:9,10
first beast, he deceived[b] the inhabitants b Rev 12:9
of the earth. He ordered them to set up
an image in honor of the beast who was
wounded by the sword and yet lived.
15He was given power to give breath to
the image of the first beast, so that it
could speak and cause all who refused to 13:15
worship the image to be killed.[c] 16He c Da 3:3-6
also forced everyone, small and great,[d] 13:16
rich and poor, free and slave, to receive a d Rev 19:5 e Rev 14:9
mark on his right hand or on his fore-
head,[e] 17so that no one could buy or sell 13:17
unless he had the mark,[f] which is the f Rev 14:9
name of the beast or the number of his g Rev 14:11; 15:2
name.[g]
18This calls for wisdom.[h] If anyone 13:18 h Rev 17:9
has insight, let him calculate the num- i Rev 15:2; 21:17
ber of the beast, for it is man's number.[i]
His number is 666.

The Lamb and the 144,000

14 Then I looked, and there before 14:1
me was the Lamb,[j] standing on j Rev 5:6 k Ps 2:6
Mount Zion,[k] and with him 144,000[l] l Rev 7:4
who had his name and his Father's m Rev 3:12
name[m] written on their foreheads. 2And
I heard a sound from heaven like the
roar of rushing waters[n] and like a loud 14:2 n Rev 1:15
peal of thunder. The sound I heard was o Rev 5:8
like that of harpists playing their harps.[o] 14:3
3And they sang a new song[p] before the p Rev 5:9 q ver 1
throne and before the four living crea-
tures and the elders. No one could learn
the song except the 144,000[q] who had
been redeemed from the earth. 4These
are those who did not defile themselves
with women, for they kept themselves 14:4
pure.[r] They follow the Lamb wherever r 2Co 11:2;
he goes. They were purchased from Rev 3:4 s Rev 5:9 t Jas 1:18
among men[s] and offered as firstfruits[t] 14:5
to God and the Lamb. 5No lie was found u Ps 32:2; Zep 3:13
in their mouths;[u] they are blameless.[v] v Eph 5:27

[a] 8 Or *written from the creation of the world in the book of life belonging to the Lamb that was slain*
[b] 10 Some manuscripts *anyone kills*

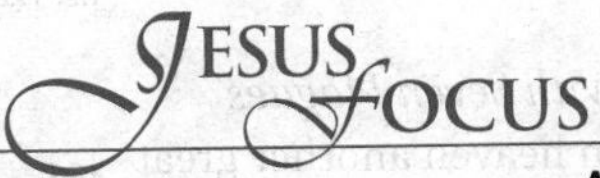

AN EVIL TRINITY

In stark contrast to the holy Trinity consisting of God the Father, God the Son and God the Holy Spirit, Revelation 13 describes a kind of "evil trinity." Satan, the beast from the sea and the beast from the earth join forces against God. Satan, the dragon, is portrayed as the real impetus behind the beast from the sea, who becomes a political leader, and the beast from the earth, who becomes a religious leader. Together the three stand in opposition to Jesus' taking on his rightful role as king. In the final conflict, however, Jesus gains the victory. The beast from the sea and the beast from the earth are thrown into the lake of fire for all eternity, and Satan is bound in the Abyss (see Revelation 19:20—20:10).

The Three Angels

14:6 [w] Rev 8:13; [x] Rev 3:10; [y] Rev 13:7 6Then I saw another angel flying in
midair,[w] and he had the eternal gospel to
proclaim to those who live on the
earth[x]—to every nation, tribe, language
and people.[y] 7He said in a loud voice,
14:7 [z] Rev 15:4; [a] Rev 11:13; [b] Rev 8:10 "Fear God[z] and give him glory,[a] because
the hour of his judgment has come. Wor-
ship him who made the heavens, the
earth, the sea and the springs of water."[b]
8A second angel followed and said,
14:8 [c] Isa 21:9; Jer 51:8; [d] Rev 17:2,4; 18:3,9 "Fallen! Fallen is Babylon the Great,[c]
which made all the nations drink the
maddening wine of her adulteries."[d]
9A third angel followed them and said
14:9 [e] Rev 13:14 in a loud voice: "If anyone worships the
beast and his image[e] and receives his
mark on the forehead or on the hand,
10he, too, will drink of the wine of God's
14:10 [f] Isa 51:17; Jer 25:15; [g] Rev 18:6 fury,[f] which has been poured full
strength into the cup of his wrath.[g] He
will be tormented with burning sulfur in
the presence of the holy angels and of
14:11 [h] Isa 34:10; Rev 19:3 the Lamb. 11And the smoke of their torment rises for ever and ever.[h] There is no
rest day or night for those who worship
the beast and his image, or for anyone
who receives the mark of his name."
14:12 [i] Rev 13:10 12This calls for patient endurance on the
part of the saints[i] who obey God's commandments and remain faithful to
Jesus.
13Then I heard a voice from heaven
14:13 [j] 1Co 15:18; 1Th 4:16 say, "Write: Blessed are the dead who die
in the Lord[j] from now on."
"Yes," says the Spirit, "they will rest
from their labor, for their deeds will follow them."

The Harvest of the Earth

14I looked, and there before me was a
white cloud, and seated on the cloud was
14:14 [k] Da 7:13; Rev 1:13; [l] Rev 6:2 one "like a son of man"[a][k] with a crown[l]
of gold on his head and a sharp sickle in
his hand. 15Then another angel came out
of the temple and called in a loud voice
to him who was sitting on the cloud,
14:15 [m] Joel 3:13; [n] Jer 51:33 "Take your sickle[m] and reap, because the
time to reap has come, for the harvest[n]
of the earth is ripe." 16So he who was
seated on the cloud swung his sickle over
the earth, and the earth was harvested.
17Another angel came out of the temple in heaven, and he too had a sharp
sickle. 18Still another angel, who had
charge of the fire, came from the altar
and called in a loud voice to him who
had the sharp sickle, "Take your sharp
sickle and gather the clusters of grapes
from the earth's vine, because its grapes
are ripe." 19The angel swung his sickle on
the earth, gathered its grapes and threw
them into the great winepress of God's
14:19 [o] Rev 19:15 wrath.[o] 20They were trampled in the
14:20 [p] Isa 63:3; [q] Heb 13:12; Rev 11:8 winepress[p] outside the city,[q] and blood
flowed out of the press, rising as high as
the horses' bridles for a distance of 1,600
stadia.[b]

Seven Angels With Seven Plagues

15:1 [r] Rev 12:1,3; [s] Rev 16:1; [t] Lev 26:21 **15** I saw in heaven another great
and marvelous sign:[r] seven an-
gels[s] with the seven last plagues[t]—last,
because with them God's wrath is com-
15:2 [u] Rev 4:6; [v] Rev 13:14 pleted. 2And I saw what looked like a sea
of glass[u] mixed with fire and, standing
beside the sea, those who had been victorious over the beast and his image[v]
and over the number of his name. They
15:3 [w] Ex 15:1; Dt 32:4; [x] Ps 111:2 held harps given them by God 3and sang
the song of Moses[w] the servant of God
and the song of the Lamb:

"Great and marvelous are your
deeds,[x]
Lord God Almighty.

[a] 14 Daniel 7:13 [b] 20 That is, about 180 miles (about 300 kilometers)

JESUS AND YOU

GRAPES OF WRATH

One day each of us will stand before Jesus, and he will either welcome us into our heavenly home or judge us, depending on whether or not we have accepted that his sacrificial death and triumphant resurrection have paved the way for our own eternal salvation. Revelation 14 depicts Jesus as a grim reaper in the final harvest of judgment, for he will take no pleasure in eternal separation from any of the people he has created (see 2 Peter 3:9).

John first provided an overview of what will happen (Revelation 14:14–20) and followed this up by a detailed account in chapters 15—19. The images used by John come from Joel 3:13, which compares God's final judgment to a harvest of grapes. When grapes are picked for winemaking, they are collected and thrown into a winepress. In Biblical times the people would stomp the fruit underfoot until the juice ran out and collected in the wine vats. God's wrath against sin will be severe, and John referred to it graphically as the "great winepress of God's wrath" (Revelation 14:19).

DISCOVERY 360

Following Wherever He Goes

The greatest exhilaration of heaven will be the opportunity to see Jesus face-to-face. The apostle Paul spoke with yearning: "I desire to depart and be with Christ, which is better by far" (Philippians 1:23). Revelation 14:1 tells us that there will be 144,000 people murdered because of their belief in Jesus. One day in his presence this martyr band will sing "a new song" before the Lamb of God (verse 3).

Heaven will be an indescribably wonderful place in which there will be "no more death or mourning or crying or pain, for the old order of things [will have] passed away" (Revelation 21:4). The new Jerusalem will be the most spectacular city ever envisioned by humankind (Revelation 21:9–27). But the grandeur of heaven itself will pale in comparison to the prospect of standing in the presence of Jesus Christ. For the 144,000 mentioned in Revelation 14 the principal joy of heaven will be the opportunity simply to follow Jesus wherever he goes (verse 4).

The apostle Paul, addressing the persecuted Christians in Rome, said, "I consider that our present sufferings are not worth comparing with the glory that will be revealed in us . . . We . . . who have the firstfruits of the Spirit, groan inwardly as we wait eagerly for our adoption as sons, the redemption of our bodies" (Romans 8:18,23).

Something deep within us longs for heaven, and that is good. At the same time, however, we need to focus on following Jesus during this life. That means denying our selfish tendencies and learning to live as the people he intended us to be. In Matthew 16:24 Jesus included four prerequisites for being his disciples. First, there is a decision. Jesus began by stating his premise: "If anyone would come after me . . ." We all give our allegiance to something or someone in this life, and we have to make a conscious decision to turn our faces toward Jesus.

Second, we must say no to the promptings of our sinful desires, relinquishing the controls to Jesus rather than trying to make our own life decisions. Third, there is a death involved. We want Jesus to live through us, and that is only possible when we are willing to die to our own agendas: "I have been crucified with Christ and I no longer live, but Christ lives in me. The life I live in the body, I live by faith in the Son of God, who loved me and gave himself for me" (Galatians 2:20).

Finally, we are to follow him, unquestioningly, wherever he might lead. This act requires a radical leap of faith, and obstacles are sure to come, but we have the assurance that we will one day experience the incomparable joy of tracing our Master's steps down the streets of the new Jerusalem.

Self-Discovery: *In what situation has following Jesus caused you to experience inconvenience, ridicule or even heartache? Did this experience cause you to grow in your faith? In retrospect, can you say with sincerity that the pain was worth the gain?*

GO TO DISCOVERY 361 ON PAGE 1724

15:3 [y]Ps 145:17 — Just and true are your ways,[y]
King of the ages.
15:4 [z]Jer 10:7 — 4 Who will not fear you, O Lord,[z]
[a]Isa 66:23 — and bring glory to your name?
For you alone are holy.
All nations will come
and worship before you,[a]
for your righteous acts have been
revealed."

5 After this I looked and in heaven
15:5 [b]Rev 11:19 — the temple,[b] that is, the tabernacle of
[c]Nu 1:50 — the Testimony,[c] was opened. 6 Out of the
15:6 — temple[d] came the seven angels with the
[d]Rev 14:15 — seven plagues.[e] They were dressed in
[e]ver 1 [f]Rev 1:13 — clean, shining linen and wore golden
sashes around their chests.[f] 7 Then one
15:7 [g]Rev 4:6 — of the four living creatures[g] gave to the
seven angels seven golden bowls filled
with the wrath of God, who lives for ever
15:8 — and ever. 8 And the temple was filled
[h]Isa 6:4 — with smoke[h] from the glory of God and
[i]Ex 40:34,35; 1Ki 8:10,11; — from his power, and no one could enter
2Ch 5:13,14 — the temple[i] until the seven plagues of
the seven angels were completed.

The Seven Bowls of God's Wrath

16 Then I heard a loud voice from
the temple saying to the seven
16:1 [j]Rev 15:1 — angels,[j] "Go, pour out the seven bowls of
God's wrath on the earth."

JESUS FOCUS

THE LAST EXODUS

The images in Revelation 15 compare Jesus' act of rescuing us from our sins to God's work of bringing his people out of slavery in the exodus from Egypt. These images come through clearly in the "song of Moses" (verses 3–4), the smoke from God's glory (verse 8) and the "tabernacle of the Testimony" (verse 5), all of which are also found in the book of Exodus (Exodus 15; 40:34–35). It is significant that the seven angels sang two songs, the first called "the song of Moses" (see also Exodus 15) and the second referred to as "the song of the Lamb" (see also Revelation 5:9–12). These two songs represent God's law (Moses) and his grace (Jesus, the Lamb), and they together demonstrate that God's law and his grace form a perfect harmony. God provided his people with the law to show them his character, and Jesus came to show all people the Father's heart and in particular his intention to deliver his people both physically and spiritually.

2 The first angel went and poured out
his bowl on the land,[k] and ugly and — 16:2 [k]Rev 8:7
painful sores[l] broke out on the people — [l]Ex 9:9-11
who had the mark of the beast and wor- — [m]Rev 13:15-17
shiped his image.[m]
3 The second angel poured out his
bowl on the sea, and it turned into blood
like that of a dead man, and every living
thing in the sea died.[n] — 16:3 [n]Ex 7:17-21; Rev 8:8,9
4 The third angel poured out his bowl
on the rivers and springs of water,[o] and — 16:4 [o]Rev 8:10
they became blood.[p] 5 Then I heard the — [p]Ex 7:17-21
angel in charge of the waters say:

"You are just in these judgments,[q] — 16:5 [q]Rev 15:3
you who are and who were,[r] the — [r]Rev 1:4
Holy One,[s] — [s]Rev 15:4
because you have so judged;
6 for they have shed the blood of
your saints and prophets,
and you have given them blood — 16:6 [t]Isa 49:26;
to drink[t] as they deserve." — Rev 17:6
7 And I heard the altar[u] respond: — 16:7 [u]Rev 6:9

"Yes, Lord God Almighty, — [v]Rev 15:3; 19:2
true and just are your
judgments."[v]

8 The fourth angel[w] poured out his — 16:8 [w]Rev 8:12
bowl on the sun, and the sun was given — [x]Rev 14:18
power to scorch people with fire.[x] 9 They
were seared by the intense heat and they — 16:9
cursed the name of God,[y] who had con- — [y]ver 11,21

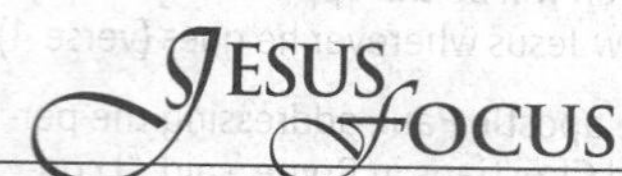

ONE FINAL WAR

Armageddon! The very word causes many people, even those who do not otherwise take God seriously, to shudder with fear. Armageddon (Revelation 16:16), located in the Valley of Jezreel in Israel, has already been the site of numerous military engagements throughout Israel's history. Some historians even believe that there have been more battles fought there than at any other location on the planet. But the thought of Armageddon doesn't have to instill fear in believers, because it is God's ultimate symbol for the great war between the forces of good and evil, the war that will end all wars, to be waged at the end of time. The Old Testament prophets referred repeatedly to this event as the "day of the LORD" (see, for example, Joel 1:15). This will be a time when God will judge the nations, and afterward Jesus will return in glorious victory to reign forever as the uncontested king over all creation (Revelation 19:11–21).

trol over these plagues, but they refused
16:9 z Rev 2:21 to repent[z] and glorify him.[a]
a Rev 11:13 10 The fifth angel poured out his bowl
16:10 on the throne of the beast,[b] and his
b Rev 13:2 kingdom was plunged into darkness.[c]
c Rev 9:2 Men gnawed their tongues in agony
16:11 11 and cursed[d] the God of heaven[e] be-
d ver 9,21 cause of their pains and their sores,[f] but
e Rev 11:13 f ver 2 g Rev 2:21 they refused to repent of what they had
done.[g]
12 The sixth angel poured out his bowl
16:12 h Rev 9:14 on the great river Euphrates,[h] and its
i Isa 41:2 water was dried up to prepare the way
for the kings from the East.[i] 13 Then I
saw three evil[a] spirits that looked like
16:13 frogs; they came out of the mouth of the
j Rev 12:3 dragon,[j] out of the mouth of the beast[k]
k Rev 13:1 and out of the mouth of the false proph-
l Rev 19:20 et.[l] 14 They are spirits of demons[m] per-
16:14 forming miraculous signs, and they go
m 1Ti 4:1 n Rev 17:14 out to the kings of the whole world, to
gather them for the battle[n] on the great
day of God Almighty.
15 "Behold, I come like a thief! Blessed
16:15 o Lk 12:37 is he who stays awake[o] and keeps his
clothes with him, so that he may not go
naked and be shamefully exposed."
16 Then they gathered the kings to-
16:16 p Rev 9:11 gether to the place that in Hebrew[p] is
q 2Ki 23:29,30 called Armageddon.[q]
17 The seventh angel poured out his
16:17 r Eph 2:2 bowl into the air,[r] and out of the temple[s]
s Rev 14:15 came a loud voice[t] from the throne, say-
t Rev 11:15 u Rev 21:6 ing, "It is done!"[u] 18 Then there came
flashes of lightning, rumblings, peals of
16:18 v Rev 4:5 thunder[v] and a severe earthquake.[w] No
w Rev 6:12 earthquake like it has ever occurred
x Da 12:1 since man has been on earth,[x] so
tremendous was the quake. 19 The great
16:19 y Rev 17:18 city[y] split into three parts, and the cities
z Rev 18:5 of the nations collapsed. God remem-
a Rev 14:8 b Rev 14:10 bered[z] Babylon the Great[a] and gave her
the cup filled with the wine of the fury of
his wrath.[b] 20 Every island fled away and
16:20 c Rev 6:14 the mountains could not be found.[c]
21 From the sky huge hailstones[d] of
16:21 d Rev 11:19 about a hundred pounds each fell upon
e Ex 9:23-25 men. And they cursed God on account
of the plague of hail,[e] because the plague
was so terrible.

The Woman on the Beast

17:1 f Rev 15:1 **17** One of the seven angels[f] who
g Rev 21:9 had the seven bowls[g] came and
h Rev 16:19 said to me, "Come, I will show you the
i Rev 19:2 punishment[h] of the great prostitute,[i]
j Jer 51:13 who sits on many waters.[j] 2 With her the
kings of the earth committed adultery
and the inhabitants of the earth were in-
toxicated with the wine of her adulter- 17:2 k Rev 14:8; 18:3
ies."[k]
3 Then the angel carried me away in
the Spirit into a desert.[l] There I saw a 17:3 l Rev 12:6,14
woman sitting on a scarlet beast that m Rev 13:1
was covered with blasphemous names[m] n Rev 12:3
and had seven heads and ten horns.[n]
4 The woman was dressed in purple and
scarlet, and was glittering with gold, precious stones and pearls.[o] She held a 17:4 o Rev 18:16
golden cup[p] in her hand, filled with p Jer 51:7;
abominable things and the filth of her Rev 18:6
adulteries. 5 This title was written on her
forehead:

MYSTERY
BABYLON THE GREAT[q] 17:5 q Rev 14:8
THE MOTHER OF PROSTITUTES
AND OF THE ABOMINATIONS OF THE EARTH.

6 I saw that the woman was drunk with
the blood of the saints,[r] the blood of 17:6 r Rev 18:24
those who bore testimony to Jesus.
When I saw her, I was greatly astonished. 7 Then the angel said to me: "Why
are you astonished? I will explain to you
the mystery[s] of the woman and of the 17:7 s ver 5 t ver 3
beast she rides, which has the seven
heads and ten horns.[t] 8 The beast, which
you saw, once was, now is not, and will
come up out of the Abyss and go to his
destruction.[u] The inhabitants of the 17:8 u Rev 13:10
earth[v] whose names have not been writ- v Rev 3:10
ten in the book of life[w] from the creation w Rev 13:8
of the world will be astonished[x] when x Rev 13:3

a 13 Greek *unclean*

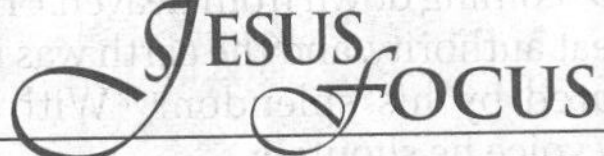

A TALE OF TWO WOMEN

False religion is symbolized by the great prostitute in Revelation 17:1. Although there are many ideas about who or what she represents, one truth is obvious: She stands in unholy contrast to the church, the pure bride of Christ, in many ways:

Great Prostitute	Bride of Christ
In the desert (17:3)	In heaven (19:1–9)
Sitting on the beast (17:3)	Returns with Jesus (19:11–16)
Adorned in luxury (17:4)	Adorned in righteousness (19:8)
Great city (17:18)	Holy City (21:2)
Ends in destruction (18:21)	Lives forever (21—22)

they see the beast, because he once was,
now is not, and yet will come.
9"This calls for a mind with wisdom.[y]
The seven heads are seven hills on which
the woman sits. 10They are also seven
kings. Five have fallen, one is, the other
has not yet come; but when he does
come, he must remain for a little while.
11The beast who once was, and now is
not,[z] is an eighth king. He belongs to the
seven and is going to his destruction.
12"The ten horns[a] you saw are ten
kings who have not yet received a kingdom, but who for one hour[b] will receive
authority as kings along with the beast.
13They have one purpose and will give
their power and authority to the beast.[c]
14They will make war[d] against the
Lamb, but the Lamb will overcome
them because he is Lord of lords and
King of kings[e]—and with him will be his
called, chosen[f] and faithful followers."
15Then the angel said to me, "The waters[g] you saw, where the prostitute sits,
are peoples, multitudes, nations and
languages.[h] 16The beast and the ten
horns you saw will hate the prostitute.
They will bring her to ruin[i] and leave her
naked;[j] they will eat her flesh[k] and burn
her with fire.[l] 17For God has put it into
their hearts to accomplish his purpose
by agreeing to give the beast their power
to rule, until God's words are fulfilled.[m]
18The woman you saw is the great city[n]
that rules over the kings of the earth."

The Fall of Babylon

18 After this I saw another angel[o]
coming down from heaven.[p] He
had great authority, and the earth was illuminated by his splendor.[q] 2With a
mighty voice he shouted:

"Fallen! Fallen is Babylon the
Great![r]
She has become a home for
demons
and a haunt for every evil[a] spirit,
a haunt for every unclean and
detestable bird.[s]
3For all the nations have drunk
the maddening wine of her
adulteries.[t]
The kings of the earth committed
adultery with her,[u]
and the merchants of the earth
grew rich[v] from her
excessive luxuries."[w]

4Then I heard another voice from
heaven say:

"Come out of her, my people,[x]
so that you will not share in her
sins,
so that you will not receive any
of her plagues;
5for her sins are piled up to heaven,[y]
and God has remembered[z] her
crimes.
6Give back to her as she has given;
pay her back[a] double for what
she has done.
Mix her a double portion from
her own cup.[b]
7Give her as much torture and grief
as the glory and luxury she gave
herself.[c]
In her heart she boasts,
'I sit as queen; I am not a widow,
and I will never mourn.'[d]
8Therefore in one day[e] her plagues
will overtake her:
death, mourning and famine.
She will be consumed by fire,[f]
for mighty is the Lord God who
judges her.

9"When the kings of the earth who
committed adultery with her[g] and
shared her luxury see the smoke of her
burning,[h] they will weep and mourn
over her.[i] 10Terrified at her torment, they
will stand far off[j] and cry:

" 'Woe! Woe, O great city,[k]
O Babylon, city of power!
In one hour[l] your doom has come!'

11"The merchants[m] of the earth will
weep and mourn over her because no
one buys their cargoes any more[n]—
12cargoes of gold, silver, precious stones
and pearls; fine linen, purple, silk and
scarlet cloth; every sort of citron wood,
and articles of every kind made of ivory,
costly wood, bronze, iron and marble;[o]
13cargoes of cinnamon and spice, of incense, myrrh and frankincense, of wine
and olive oil, of fine flour and wheat; cattle and sheep; horses and carriages; and
bodies and souls of men.[p]
14"They will say, 'The fruit you longed
for is gone from you. All your riches and
splendor have vanished, never to be recovered.' 15The merchants who sold
these things and gained their wealth

[a] 2 Greek *unclean*

17:9 [y]Rev 13:18
17:11 [z]ver 8
17:12 [a]Rev 12:3 [b]Rev 18:10,17,19
17:13 [c]ver 17
17:14 [d]Rev 16:14 [e]1Ti 6:15; Rev 19:16 [f]Mt 22:14
17:15 [g]Isa 8:7 [h]Rev 13:7
17:16 [i]Rev 18:17,19 [j]Eze 16:37,39 [k]Rev 19:18 [l]Rev 18:8
17:17 [m]Rev 10:7
17:18 [n]Rev 16:19
18:1 [o]Rev 17:1 [p]Rev 10:1 [q]Eze 43:2
18:2 [r]Rev 14:8 [s]Isa 13:21,22; Jer 50:39
18:3 [t]Rev 14:8 [u]Rev 17:2 [v]Eze 27:9-25 [w]ver 7,9
18:4 [x]Isa 48:20; Jer 50:8; 2Co 6:17
18:5 [y]Jer 51:9 [z]Rev 16:19
18:6 [a]Ps 137:8; Jer 50:15,29 [b]Rev 14:10; 16:19
18:7 [c]Eze 28:2-8 [d]Isa 47:7,8; Zep 2:15
18:8 [e]ver 10; Isa 47:9; Jer 50:31,32 [f]Rev 17:16
18:9 [g]Rev 17:2,4 [h]ver 18; Rev 19:3 [i]Eze 26:17,18
18:10 [j]ver 15,17 [k]ver 16,19 [l]Rev 17:12
18:11 [m]Eze 27:27 [n]ver 3
18:12 [o]Rev 17:4
18:13 [p]Eze 27:13; 1Ti 1:10

18:15 [q]ver 3 [r]Eze 27:31 from her[q] will stand far off, terrified at
her torment. They will weep and mourn[r]
16and cry out:

" 'Woe! Woe, O great city,
dressed in fine linen, purple and
scarlet,
and glittering with gold,
18:16 [s]Rev 17:4 precious stones and pearls![s]
17 In one hour[t] such great wealth has
18:17 [t]ver 10 [u]Rev 17:16 [v]Eze 27:28-30 been brought to ruin!'[u]

"Every sea captain, and all who travel
by ship, the sailors, and all who earn
their living from the sea,[v] will stand far
off. 18When they see the smoke of her
burning, they will exclaim, 'Was there
18:18 [w]Eze 27:32; Rev 13:4 ever a city like this great city?'[w] 19They
will throw dust on their heads,[x] and
18:19 [x]Jos 7:6; Eze 27:30 [y]Rev 17:16 with weeping and mourning cry out:

" 'Woe! Woe, O great city,
where all who had ships on the
sea
became rich through her wealth!
In one hour she has been brought
to ruin![y]
18:20 [z]Jer 51:48; Rev 12:12 [a]Rev 19:2 20 Rejoice over her, O heaven![z]
Rejoice, saints and apostles and
prophets!
God has judged her for the way she
treated you.' "[a]

18:21 [b]Rev 5:2 [c]Jer 51:63 21Then a mighty angel[b] picked up a
boulder the size of a large millstone and
threw it into the sea,[c] and said:

"With such violence
the great city of Babylon will be
thrown down,
never to be found again.
22 The music of harpists and
musicians, flute players and
trumpeters,
will never be heard in you
18:22 [d]Isa 24:8; Eze 26:13 [e]Jer 25:10 again.[d]
No workman of any trade
will ever be found in you again.
The sound of a millstone
will never be heard in you again.[e]
23 The light of a lamp
will never shine in you again.
The voice of bridegroom and bride
18:23 [f]Jer 7:34; 16:9; 25:10 [g]Isa 23:8 [h]Na 3:4 will never be heard in you again.[f]
Your merchants were the world's
great men.[g]
By your magic spell[h] all the
nations were led astray.
24 In her was found the blood of
18:24 [i]Rev 16:6; 17:6 prophets and of the saints,[i]
and of all who have been killed
on the earth."[j] 18:24 [j]Jer 51:49

Hallelujah!

19 After this I heard what sound-
ed like the roar of a great multi- 19:1 [k]Rev 11:15 [l]Rev 7:10 [m]Rev 4:11
tude[k] in heaven shouting:

"Hallelujah!
Salvation[l] and glory and power[m]
belong to our God,
2 for true and just are his
judgments.
He has condemned the great
prostitute
who corrupted the earth by her
adulteries.
He has avenged on her the blood of 19:2 [n]Dt 32:43; Rev 6:10
his servants."[n]
3And again they shouted:

"Hallelujah! 19:3 [o]Isa 34:10; Rev 14:11
The smoke from her goes up for
ever and ever."[o]

4The twenty-four elders[p] and the four 19:4 [p]Rev 4:4 [q]Rev 4:6 [r]Rev 5:14
living creatures[q] fell down[r] and wor-
shiped God, who was seated on the
throne. And they cried:

"Amen, Hallelujah!"

5Then a voice came from the throne,
saying:

"Praise our God, 19:5 [s]Ps 134:1 [t]Rev 11:18; 20:12
all you his servants,[s]
you who fear him,
both small and great!"[t]

6Then I heard what sounded like a
great multitude,[u] like the roar of rushing 19:6 [u]Rev 11:15

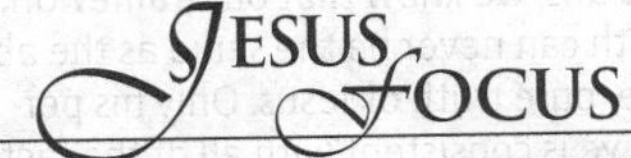

GOD'S CHURCH TRIUMPHS

Revelation 19 may arguably be the most dramatic chapter in the entire Bible. It certainly represents the pinnacle of all Biblical prophecy about Jesus. When Jesus comes to earth for the second time, it will be the most incredible event in human history, as well as the ultimate proof that he is in fact exactly who he claims to be—the glorious, eternal, triumphant Son of God. Jesus promised to come back *for* his people (see John 14:3); here he returns *with* his people (see Revelation 17:14). The future destiny of every Christian is as certain as Jesus' return.

DISCOVERY 361

FAITHFUL AND TRUE

After the roar and shouts of multitudes praising God, John saw "heaven standing open and there before [him] was a white horse, whose rider is called Faithful and True" (Revelation 19:11). This rider is also referred to as "the Amen, the faithful and true witness, the ruler of God's creation" (Revelation 3:14). This person is none other than Jesus himself (Ephesians 1:22; Colossians 1:16). He is somewhat mysterious, this Judge and Warrior, because "he has a name written on him that no one knows but he himself" (Revelation 19:12). We are also told that "his name is the Word of God" (Revelation 19:13; see also John 1:1–14).

The essence of Jesus' name, Faithful and True, is something that we who are living within the confines of a sin-stained world can only begin to understand. We have never experienced the quality of unadulterated faithfulness in any one person, because all of us humans are fragile, prone to breaking down under duress or temptation. And not one of us can claim to know someone who is absolutely honorable. We all fall prey to the tendency to twist the facts just a bit to make ourselves appear better than we actually are. Even as godly, maturing Christians, we know that our framework of truth can never be the same as the absolute, pure truth of Jesus. Only his perspective is consistent with all of the facts; only he can perceive and interpret reality from every possible vantage point.

The Bible assures us over and over again that we can trust God to keep his word. And this is much more than a character trait passed down from Father to Son. Because God the Father and Jesus Christ *are one* (John 17:11,22), the Rider on the white horse can safely be followed through every circumstance—all the way to eternity. We often use phrases like "As sure as I'm standing here" to convey the reliability of what we are about to state. Paul simply relied on who God is, using God's faithfulness as a reference when he made the claim that his own words would be absolutely true: "As surely as God is faithful," he asserted (2 Corinthians 1:18).

As we hear and believe the gospel message, we come to know that it is altogether true; as we experience its dynamic power we come to see that all of God's truth comes to one majestic affirmation in Jesus Christ, in whom all of God's promises are "yes" (verse 20). Our God does not waver in carrying out his word. He follows through with every detail of what he promises us, because he is and will always be faithful (Philippians 1:6; 2 Thessalonians 3:3).

It really makes no difference whether or not we believe this to be true. Paul addressed this issue through a rhetorical question followed by a resounding affirmation: "Will [our] lack of faith nullify God's faithfulness? Not at all! Let God be true, and every man a liar" (Romans 3:3–4).

***Self-Discovery:** Pause for a moment to thank God for his unwavering faithfulness and trustworthiness, and embrace the truth that your moments of doubt can never nullify those qualities in him.*

GO TO DISCOVERY 362 ON PAGE 1726

waters and like loud peals of thunder,
shouting:

"Hallelujah!
For our Lord God Almighty
reigns.
7 Let us rejoice and be glad
19:7 [v] Mt 22:2; 25:10; Eph 5:32 [w] Rev 21:2,9
and give him glory!
For the wedding of the Lamb[v] has
come,
and his bride[w] has made herself
ready.
8 Fine linen, bright and clean,
was given her to wear."
19:8 [x] Rev 15:4
(Fine linen stands for the righteous
acts[x] of the saints.)

19:9 [y] ver 10 [z] Rev 1:19 [a] Lk 14:15 [b] Rev 21:5; 22:6
9 Then the angel said to me,[y] "Write:[z]
'Blessed are those who are invited to the
wedding supper of the Lamb!'"[a] And he
added, "These are the true words of God."[b]
10 At this I fell at his feet to worship
19:10 [c] Rev 22:8 [d] Ac 10:25,26; Rev 22:9 [e] Rev 12:17
him.[c] But he said to me, "Do not do it! I
am a fellow servant with you and with
your brothers who hold to the testimony of Jesus. Worship God![d] For the testimony of Jesus[e] is the spirit of prophecy."

The Rider on the White Horse

11 I saw heaven standing open and
there before me was a white horse,
19:11 [f] Rev 6:2 [g] Rev 3:14 [h] Isa 11:4
whose rider[f] is called Faithful and True.[g]
With justice he judges and makes war.[h]
12 His eyes are like blazing fire,[i] and on
19:12 [i] Rev 1:14 [j] Rev 6:2 [k] Rev 2:17
his head are many crowns.[j] He has a
name written on him that no one knows
but he himself.[k] 13 He is dressed in a robe
dipped in blood,[l] and his name is the
19:13 [l] Isa 63:2,3 [m] Jn 1:1
Word of God.[m] 14 The armies of heaven
were following him, riding on white
horses and dressed in fine linen,[n] white
19:14 [n] ver 8
and clean. 15 Out of his mouth comes a
sharp sword[o] with which to strike
19:15 [o] Rev 1:16 [p] Isa 11:4; 2Th 2:8 [q] Ps 2:9; Rev 2:27 [r] Rev 14:20
down[p] the nations. "He will rule them
with an iron scepter."[a][q] He treads the
winepress[r] of the fury of the wrath of
God Almighty. 16 On his robe and on his
19:16 [s] ver 12 [t] Rev 17:14
thigh he has this name written:[s]

KING OF KINGS AND LORD OF LORDS.[t]

17 And I saw an angel standing in the
sun, who cried in a loud voice to all the
19:17 [u] ver 21 [v] Rev 8:13 [w] Eze 39:17
birds[u] flying in midair,[v] "Come,[w] gather
together for the great supper of God,
18 so that you may eat the flesh of kings,
generals, and mighty men, of horses and
19:18 [x] Eze 39:18-20
their riders, and the flesh of all people,[x]
free and slave, small and great."

> I HAVE GREAT SYMPATHY FOR PEOPLE WHO DO NOT BELIEVE CHRIST EXISTS. BUT ONE DAY IN ETERNITY THEY WILL BEND THE KNEE AND BOW THE HEAD AND CONFESS HIM AS LORD THROUGH THEIR OWN ETERNAL LOSS.
>
> 
>
> Rev. Jerry Falwell, *Chancellor, Liberty University, Lynchburg, Virginia*

19 Then I saw the beast and the kings
19:19 [y] Rev 16:14,16
of the earth[y] and their armies gathered
together to make war against the rider
on the horse and his army. 20 But the
beast was captured, and with him the
19:20 [z] Rev 16:13 [a] Rev 13:12 [b] Da 7:11; Rev 20:10,14,15; 21:8 [c] Rev 14:10
false prophet[z] who had performed the
miraculous signs on his behalf.[a] With
these signs he had deluded those who
had received the mark of the beast and
worshiped his image. The two of them
were thrown alive into the fiery lake[b] of
burning sulfur.[c] 21 The rest of them were
19:21 [d] ver 15 [e] ver 11, 19 [f] ver 17
killed with the sword[d] that came out of
the mouth of the rider on the horse,[e]
and all the birds[f] gorged themselves on
their flesh.

> THOU HAST CONQUERED, O GALILEAN.
>
> 
>
> Julian the Apostate

The Thousand Years

20 And I saw an angel coming
20:1 [g] Rev 10:1 [h] Rev 1:18
down out of heaven,[g] having
the key[h] to the Abyss and holding in his
hand a great chain. 2 He seized the dragon, that ancient serpent, who is the dev-
20:2 [i] Rev 12:9 [j] 2Pe 2:4
il, or Satan,[i] and bound him for a thousand years.[j] 3 He threw him into the
Abyss, and locked and sealed[k] it over
20:3 [k] Da 6:17 [l] Rev 12:9
him, to keep him from deceiving the nations[l] anymore until the thousand years
were ended. After that, he must be set
free for a short time.
4 I saw thrones[m] on which were seated
20:4 [m] Da 7:9 [n] Rev 6:9
those who had been given authority to
judge. And I saw the souls of those who
had been beheaded[n] because of their testimony for Jesus and because of the word
of God. They had not worshiped the

[a] 15 Psalm 2:9

DISCOVERY 362

The Last Great Judgment

Revelation 20 describes the final judgment of those who have rejected Jesus Christ as their Savior. John pointed out several aspects of this most sobering event:

First, Jesus himself will be the Judge (Acts 10:42; 2 Timothy 4:1). John described the event this way: "I saw a great white throne and him who was seated on it. Earth and sky fled from his presence, and there was no place for them" (Revelation 20:11). Jesus is the Judge who sits on that throne because "the Father judges no one, but has entrusted all judgment to the Son, that all may honor the Son just as they honor the Father" (John 5:22–23).

The apostle Paul recognized that there would come a day when "at the name of Jesus every knee should bow, in heaven and on earth and under the earth, and every tongue confess that Jesus Christ is Lord, to the glory of God the Father" (Philippians 2:10–11). John's vision agreed with that of Paul. All of us will one day stand before Jesus and acknowledge who he is.

Second, no one will escape the judgment. Anyone who has ever lived will stand before Jesus Christ. In John's vision he witnessed this reality in the past tense: "The sea gave up the dead that were in it, and death and Hades gave up the dead that were in them, and each person was judged according to what he had done" (Revelation 20:13; see also Matthew 25:31–46; 1 Corinthians 3:12–15; 2 Corinthians 5:10). The writer to the Hebrews wrote in Hebrews 9:27–28: "Just as man is destined to die once, and after that to face judgment, so Christ was sacrificed once to take away the sins of many people; and he will appear a second time, not to bear sin, but to bring salvation to those who are waiting for him."

Third, God knows every minute detail of what each of us has done and of how we have lived. John wrote that he had seen "the dead, great and small, standing before the throne, and books were opened. Another book was opened, which is the book of life. The dead were judged according to what they had done as recorded in the books" (Revelation 20:12). From start to finish, nothing in our lives escapes God's searching eye (Psalm 139:1–4).

Finally, everything about the judgment centers around the book of life: "If anyone's name was not found written in the book of life, he was thrown into the lake of fire" (Revelation 20:15), along with the beast and the false prophet (verse 10). Hell is a place of uninterrupted and interminable torment.

Judgment is coming; there is no denying that truth. Those of us who have placed our faith in Jesus need not fear this great day of judgment (1 John 4:17–18). Our punishment has already been taken by Jesus on the cross. As we think of the plight of others, however, we can live in such a manner that they will perceive the presence of Jesus in our lives and be drawn to his love and forgiveness (2 Peter 3:10–11)..

Self-Discovery: Does focusing on the final great judgment alter your view of Jesus in any way? If so, how? Does it increase your sense of urgency with regard to the need to tell the Good News of salvation to those around you?

GO TO DISCOVERY 363 ON PAGE 1728

20:4 beast[o] or his image and had not received
o Rev 13:12 his mark on their foreheads or their
p Rev 13:16 hands.[p] They came to life and reigned
with Christ a thousand years. 5(The rest
of the dead did not come to life until the
20:5 thousand years were ended.) This is the
q Lk 14:14; first resurrection.[q] 6Blessed[r] and holy are
Php 3:11 those who have part in the first resurrec-
20:6 tion. The second death[s] has no power
r Rev 14:13 over them, but they will be priests[t] of
s Rev 2:11 God and of Christ and will reign with
t Rev 1:6 u ver 4 him[u] for a thousand years.

Satan's Doom

20:7 7When the thousand years are over,[v]
v ver 2 Satan will be released from his prison
20:8 8and will go out to deceive the nations[w]
w ver 3,10 x Eze 38:2; 39:1 in the four corners of the earth—Gog
y Rev 16:14 z Heb 11:12 and Magog[x]—to gather them for battle.[y]
In number they are like the sand on the
seashore.[z] 9They marched across the
20:9 breadth of the earth and surrounded[a]
a Eze 38:9,16 b Eze 38:22; 39:6 the camp of God's people, the city he
loves. But fire came down from heaven[b]
and devoured them. 10And the devil,
20:10 who deceived them,[c] was thrown into
c Rev 19:20 d Rev 14:10,11 the lake of burning sulfur, where the
beast and the false prophet had been
thrown. They will be tormented day and
night for ever and ever.[d]

The Dead Are Judged

20:11 11Then I saw a great white throne[e]
e Rev 4:2 and him who was seated on it. Earth and
sky fled from his presence, and there
was no place for them. 12And I saw the
dead, great and small, standing before 20:12
the throne, and books were opened.[f] f Da 7:10
Another book was opened, which is the g Rev 3:5 h Jer 17:10;
book of life.[g] The dead were judged ac- Mt 16:27;
cording to what they had done[h] as Rev 2:23
recorded in the books. 13The sea gave up 20:13
the dead that were in it, and death and i Rev 6:8 j Isa 26:19
Hades[i] gave up the dead[j] that were in
them, and each person was judged according to what he had done. 14Then
death[k] and Hades were thrown into the 20:14 k 1Co 15:26
lake of fire. The lake of fire is the second
death. 15If anyone's name was not found 20:15
written in the book of life,[l] he was l ver 12
thrown into the lake of fire.

THE CAPITAL OF HEAVEN IS THE HEART IN WHICH JESUS CHRIST IS ENTHRONED AS KING.

Sadhu Sundar Singe, *Indian Mystic*

The New Jerusalem

21 Then I saw a new heaven and a 21:1
new earth,[m] for the first heaven m Isa 65:17;
and the first earth had passed away, and 2Pe 3:13
there was no longer any sea. 2I saw the
Holy City, the new Jerusalem, coming 21:2
down out of heaven from God,[n] pre- n Heb 11:10;
pared as a bride beautifully dressed for 12:22; Rev 3:12
her husband. 3And I heard a loud voice
from the throne saying, "Now the
dwelling of God is with men, and he will
live with them. They will be his people,
and God himself will be with them and 21:3
be their God.[o] 4He will wipe every tear o 2Co 6:16
from their eyes.[p] There will be no more 21:4
death[q] or mourning or crying or pain,[r] p Rev 7:17 q 1Co 15:26;
for the old order of things has passed Rev 20:14
away." r Isa 35:10; 65:19
5He who was seated on the throne[s]
said, "I am making everything new!" 21:5
Then he said, "Write this down, for s Rev 4:9; 20:11 t Rev 19:9
these words are trustworthy and true."[t]
6He said to me: "It is done.[u] I am the 21:6 u Rev 16:17
Alpha and the Omega,[v] the Beginning v Rev 1:8; 22:13
and the End. To him who is thirsty I will w Jn 4:10
give to drink without cost from the
spring of the water of life.[w] 7He who
overcomes will inherit all this, and I will
be his God and he will be my son. 8But
the cowardly, the unbelieving, the vile,
the murderers, the sexually immoral,
those who practice magic arts, the idol- 21:8
aters and all liars[x]—their place will be in x 1Co 6:9

A THOUSAND YEARS

God's kingdom, his sovereign rule from eternity to eternity, has always existed. This concept is central to all of the teaching in the Bible. God's prophets spoke about it. Jesus announced its arrival into time and space. The New Testament apostles in their letters told us even more about it. In Revelation 20:1–10 the apostle John stated that Jesus' kingdom will last one thousand years on earth—a millennium. Some people believe this to refer to a literal span of one thousand years, while others interpret it to mean a figurative period of time. Some equate the church with God's kingdom on earth, while others believe the kingdom to be distinct from the church. Regardless, all of God's people believe that Jesus will one day establish a kingdom that will last forever (Revelation 11:15).

THE ALPHA AND OMEGA

The New Testament was originally written in Greek. The first letter of the Greek alphabet is *alpha*, and the last letter is *omega*. Jesus had earlier referred to himself as the "the First and the Last" (Revelation 1:17) and now identified himself as both "the Alpha and the Omega" and "the Beginning and the End" (Revelation 21:6). In John's vision Jesus in fact called himself the Alpha and the Omega three different times (Revelation 1:8; 21:6; 22:13). But what exactly does this mean?

First of all Jesus is the beginning and the end of *creation*. God the Son created the universe (Colossians 1:16) and is thereby the Alpha of creation (John 1:1–5). One day he will make everything new, setting all of creation free from the decay and bondage introduced by sin (Romans 8:18–25); he is thereby the Omega of creation (Revelation 21:5).

Jesus is also the beginning and end of *salvation*. We *were* saved when we accepted Jesus' death on the cross as payment for our sin (Ephesians 2:8–9); he is the Alpha of our salvation. As we learn to love him, we *are being* saved, continually learning how to show our devotion to him (Philippians 2:12). And one day when we see him we *will be* saved from the effects of sin forever (Romans 5:9); he is the Omega of our salvation. He has promised to "carry [his good work in us] on to completion until the day of Christ Jesus" (Philippians 1:6).

Next, Jesus is the beginning and end of *Scripture*, the theme from the beginning of the Bible to its end. God's Word begins with the creation of the world, and God the Son was there. And the Bible ends with a simple benediction: "The grace of the Lord Jesus be with God's people. Amen" (Revelation 22:21).

Jesus as the Alpha and the Omega:

- is the eternal God: "I am the Alpha and the Omega . . . who is, and who was, and who is to come, the Almighty" (Revelation 1:8).
- is the God who touches our lives: "When I saw him, I fell at his feet as though dead. Then he placed his right hand on me and said: 'Do not be afraid. I am the First and the Last' " (Revelation 1:17).
- satisfies our thirst: "He said to me: 'It is done. I am the Alpha and the Omega, the Beginning and the End. To him who is thirsty I will give to drink without cost from the spring of the water of life' " (Revelation 21:6).
- is coming soon: "Behold, I am coming soon! My reward is with me . . . I am the Alpha and the Omega, the First and the Last, the Beginning and the End" (Revelation 22:12–13).

Self-Discovery: *Identify some specific areas of your life in which Jesus is both the beginning and the end for you. For instance, he was with you at your conception and birth and will be by your side at the moment of your death. He is with you as you awaken in the morning and as sleep overtakes you at night. Thank him for his continual presence and vigilant care.*

GO TO DISCOVERY 364 ON PAGE 1730

the fiery lake of burning sulfur. This is
21:8 [y]Rev 2:11 the second death.”[y]
[9]One of the seven angels who had the
21:9 seven bowls full of the seven last
[z]Rev 15:1,6,7 plagues[z] came and said to me, “Come, I
[a]Rev 19:7 will show you the bride,[a] the wife of the
21:10 Lamb.” [10]And he carried me away[b] in the
[b]Rev 17:3 [c]Rev 1:10 Spirit[c] to a mountain great and high,
and showed me the Holy City, Jerusalem,
coming down out of heaven from God.
21:11 [d]Rev 15:8; 22:5 [11]It shone with the glory of God,[d] and its
[e]Rev 4:6 brilliance was like that of a very precious
jewel, like a jasper, clear as crystal.[e] [12]It
had a great, high wall with twelve gates,
and with twelve angels at the gates. On
the gates were written the names of the
21:12 [f]Eze 48:30-34 twelve tribes of Israel.[f] [13]There were
three gates on the east, three on the
north, three on the south and three on
the west. [14]The wall of the city had
twelve foundations, and on them were
the names of the twelve apostles of the
Lamb.
[15]The angel who talked with me had a
21:15 [g]Rev 11:1 measuring rod[g] of gold to measure the
city, its gates and its walls. [16]The city was
laid out like a square, as long as it was
wide. He measured the city with the rod
and found it to be 12,000 stadia[a] in
length, and as wide and high as it is long.
[17]He measured its wall and it was 144 cubits[b] thick,[c] by man's measurement,
which the angel was using. [18]The wall 21:18
was made of jasper,[h] and the city of pure [h]ver 11 [i]ver 21
gold, as pure as glass.[i] [19]The foundations
of the city walls were decorated with 21:19
every kind of precious stone.[j] The first [j]Isa 54:11,12
foundation was jasper, the second sap-
phire, the third chalcedony, the fourth
emerald, [20]the fifth sardonyx, the sixth 21:20
carnelian,[k] the seventh chrysolite, the [k]Rev 4:3
eighth beryl, the ninth topaz, the tenth
chrysoprase, the eleventh jacinth, and
the twelfth amethyst.[d] [21]The twelve gates
were twelve pearls, each gate made of a
single pearl. The great street of the city 21:21
was of pure gold, like transparent glass.[l] [l]ver 18
[22]I did not see a temple[m] in the city, 21:22
because the Lord God Almighty[n] and [m]Jn 4:21,23
the Lamb[o] are its temple. [23]The city does [n]Rev 1:8 [o]Rev 5:6
not need the sun or the moon to shine
on it, for the glory of God gives it light,[p] 21:23
and the Lamb is its lamp. [24]The nations [p]Isa 24:23; 60:19,20;
will walk by its light, and the kings of the Rev 22:5
earth will bring their splendor into it.[q] 21:24
[25]On no day will its gates ever be shut,[r] [q]Isa 60:3,5
for there will be no night there.[s] [26]The 21:25
glory and honor of the nations will be [r]Isa 60:11
brought into it. [27]Nothing impure will [s]Zec 14:7; Rev 22:5
ever enter it, nor will anyone who does
what is shameful or deceitful,[t] but only 21:27
those whose names are written in the [t]Isa 52:1; Joel 3:17;
Lamb's book of life. Rev 22:14,15

The River of Life

22 Then the angel showed me the
river of the water of life, as clear
as crystal,[u] flowing[v] from the throne of 22:1 [u]Rev 4:6
God and of the Lamb [2]down the middle [v]Eze 47:1; Zec 14:8
of the great street of the city. On each
side of the river stood the tree of life,[w] 22:2
bearing twelve crops of fruit, yielding its [w]Rev 2:7 [x]Eze 47:12
fruit every month. And the leaves of the
tree are for the healing of the nations.[x] 22:3
[3]No longer will there be any curse.[y] The [y]Zec 14:11
throne of God and of the Lamb will be in [z]Rev 7:15
the city, and his servants will serve him.[z] 22:4
[4]They will see his face,[a] and his name [a]Mt 5:8
will be on their foreheads.[b] [5]There will [b]Rev 14:1
be no more night.[c] They will not need 22:5 [c]Rev 21:25
the light of a lamp or the light of the sun, [d]Rev 21:23
for the Lord God will give them light.[d] [e]Da 7:27;
And they will reign for ever and ever.[e] Rev 20:4
[6]The angel said to me,[f] “These words 22:6
are trustworthy and true.[g] The Lord, the [f]Rev 1:1 [g]Rev 19:9; 21:5

[a] *16* That is, about 1,400 miles (about 2,200 kilometers) [b] *17* That is, about 200 feet (about 65 meters) [c] *17* Or *high* [d] *20* The precise identification of some of these precious stones is uncertain.

JESUS FOCUS

LIGHTING UP HEAVEN

Nothing can compare with the glorious eternal destiny that is ours when we are willing to trust God, surrender control of our lives to him and walk in step with him. Revelation 21 and 22 furnish a glimpse of what our life will be like one day, after God has recreated everything in the same pristine, perfect state that he has intended from the beginning. These chapters help us to turn our attention from the temporal and temporary to the eternal and permanent. God promises that a "new heaven" and a "new earth" (Revelation 21:1) will replace this planet as we now know it. A "new" Jerusalem, the eternal city of God, will replace the current city of Jerusalem. The main attraction of the new Jerusalem will be the *glory* of God (verse 11)—his power and presence among his people. The splendor of the city itself will be incredible, but the glory and grandeur of God and of the Lamb will far surpass it.

DISCOVERY 364

UNTIL THAT DAY

The Old Testament predicted that Jesus would be coming, the New Testament introduced him to us and the final chapter of Revelation reminds us that his story is anything but finished. For nearly 2,000 years Jesus' followers have eagerly anticipated his return. The closing chapter of John's vision reminds us yet again that our Savior is indeed coming back as King. In fact, our Lord himself promised three different times in Revelation 22 that he would return:

- "Behold, I am coming soon! Blessed is he who keeps the words of the prophecy in this book" (verse 7).
- "Behold, I am coming soon! My reward is with me, and I will give to everyone according to what he has done" (verse 12).
- "He who testifies to these things says, 'Yes, I am coming soon' " (verse 20).

How does Jesus want us to conduct ourselves while we wait for him? Very simply stated, we are to keep "the words of the prophecy in this book" (verse 7). John began his book by recording Jesus' pronouncement in Revelation 1:3: "Blessed is the one who reads the words of this prophecy, and blessed are those who hear it and take to heart what is written in it, because the time is near." And he reiterated this promise almost verbatim in Revelation 22:7. Although this promise is specific to the book of Revelation, it can be generally applied to all of God's Word. While we wait for Jesus Christ we have the opportunity to read God's Word, listen as others expound that Word, take it to heart and keep its commands.

God has furnished us with explicit instructions to guide us, many wonderful promises to encourage us and an exciting mission for us to accomplish. All of this and more is recorded in the Bible. When we are devoted to God, we cannot get enough of his words. While it is helpful to read Bible study notes, commentaries and devotionals, it is better still is to immerse ourselves in the Bible itself—because it comprises God's letter directly from himself to us.

We do not know when Jesus will come back on the clouds, but we do realize through the benefit of hindsight that it will be sooner than when John first recorded our Savior's promise: "Behold, I am coming soon!" (Revelation 22:7). May we live every day to honor our Lord, so that we may anticipate the prospect of standing before him at his triumphal return with indescribable gladness rather than with horrifying dread.

The apostle Paul made reference to Jesus' imminent return and to our need to keep ourselves in readiness: "May your whole spirit, soul and body be kept blameless at the coming of our Lord Jesus Christ. The one who calls you is faithful, and he will do it" (1 Thessalonians 5:23–24). And Jude offered these words of encouragement: "You, dear friends, build yourselves up in your most holy faith and pray in the Holy Spirit. Keep yourselves in God's love as you wait for the mercy of our Lord Jesus Christ to bring you to eternal life" (Jude 20–21).

Self-Discovery: *Take a moment to thank Jesus for his sure promise, "I am coming soon." Although it may be difficult today to anticipate the joy with which you will be filled at the time of your Savior's return, trust that this day of days will be one of unimaginable rejoicing for you. It could be today!*

GO TO DISCOVERY 365 ON PAGE 1732

22:6 h Heb 12:9 God of the spirits of the prophets,[h] sent
i ver 16 his angel[i] to show his servants the
things that must soon take place."

Jesus Is Coming

22:7 [7]"Behold, I am coming soon![j] Blessed[k]
j Rev 3:11 k Rev 1:3 is he who keeps the words of the prophecy in this book."

[8]I, John, am the one who heard and
22:8 saw these things.[l] And when I had heard
l Rev 1:1 m Rev 19:10 and seen them, I fell down to worship at
the feet[m] of the angel who had been
showing them to me. [9]But he said to me,
"Do not do it! I am a fellow servant with
you and with your brothers the prophets
22:9 and of all who keep the words of this
n ver 10,18,19 o Rev 19:10 book.[n] Worship God!"[o]
[10]Then he told me, "Do not seal up[p]
22:10 p Da 8:26; Rev 10:4 the words of the prophecy of this book,
because the time is near.[q] [11]Let him who
q Rev 1:3 does wrong continue to do wrong; let

THE FINAL CHAPTER

After all the dire consequences of sin have been described, the last chapter of the Bible concludes in a reverberating crescendo of hope and promise: God will restore creation to the paradise he originally fashioned it to be (Revelation 22). All of the beauty, perfection and potential that were lost in the Garden of Eden when humans first turned away from God (Genesis 3) will be restored in the eternal city. The book of Revelation writes the final chapter in the drama of human redemption and provides a fitting finale to God's Word to humanity. Human history began with the agonizing loss of a lovely, unspoiled garden (Genesis 3:24), but it will end in the unparalleled grandeur of the eternal city of God. It began with tragedy but will culminate in triumph. It began with heartrending human failure but will end with the ecstasy of Jesus' decisive victory over death and evil in which the followers of Jesus share. Between the two extremes stands the cross of Jesus Christ (Mark 15:21–39). He died to pay the penalty for our sins but rose triumphant to new life so that we in turn might live in perfect harmony with God forever. On that cross Jesus Christ, the Son of God, altered the course of human history—forever.

THE PRESENCE OF CHRIST IS WHAT MAKES HEAVEN HEAVEN.

John F. MacArthur, *Pastor, Sun Valley, California*

him who is vile continue to be vile; let
him who does right continue to do right; 22:11
and let him who is holy continue to be r Eze 3:27;
holy."[r] Da 12:10

[12]"Behold, I am coming soon![s] My re- 22:12
ward is with me,[t] and I will give to every- s ver 7,20 t Isa 40:10
one according to what he has done. [13]I
am the Alpha and the Omega,[u] the First 22:13 u Rev 1:8
and the Last,[v] the Beginning and the v Rev 1:17
End.[w] w Rev 21:6
[14]"Blessed are those who wash their
robes, that they may have the right to 22:14
the tree of life[x] and may go through the x Rev 2:7
gates[y] into the city.[z] [15]Outside[a] are the y Rev 21:12 z Rev 21:27
dogs,[b] those who practice magic arts,
the sexually immoral, the murderers, the 22:15
idolaters and everyone who loves and a 1Co 6:9,10; Gal 5:19-21; Col 3:5,6
practices falsehood. b Php 3:2
[16]"I, Jesus,[c] have sent my angel to give
you[a] this testimony for the churches.[d] I 22:16 c Rev 1:1
am the Root[e] and the Offspring of Da- d Rev 1:4
vid, and the bright Morning Star."[f] e Rev 5:5 f 2Pe 1:19; Rev 2:28
[17]The Spirit[g] and the bride say,
"Come!" And let him who hears say, 22:17
"Come!" Whoever is thirsty, let him g Rev 2:7
come; and whoever wishes, let him take
the free gift of the water of life.

[18]I warn everyone who hears the
words of the prophecy of this book: If 22:18
anyone adds anything to them,[h] God h Dt 4:2; Pr 30:6 i Rev 15:6-16:21
will add to him the plagues described in
this book.[i] [19]And if anyone takes words
away[j] from this book of prophecy, God 22:19 j Dt 4:2
will take away from him his share in the
tree of life and in the holy city, which are
described in this book.
[20]He who testifies to these things[k] 22:20 k Rev 1:2
says, "Yes, I am coming soon." l 1Co 16:22
Amen. Come, Lord Jesus.[l]
[21]The grace of the Lord Jesus be with 22:21
God's people.[m] Amen. m Ro 16:20

a 16 The Greek is plural.

Paradise Regained

The first book of the Bible opens with the idyllic setting of the Garden of Eden, a paradise that defies description (Genesis 1—2). But the Old Testament ends on a bitter note, with the threat of God's judgment (Malachi 4:6). Between the opening chapters of Genesis and the close of Malachi's prophecy, humanity had repudiated its Creator, and sin had resulted in tragic and irreparable damage both to our world and to ourselves. Human beings had become separated from their holy Creator but still carried deep within them the long-buried dream of a perfect world. People yearned for the pain to end, for that elusive "happily ever after."

The New Testament is God's answer to that anguished longing. It opens with the advent of Jesus, God's promised Son, who stepped into human history in order to make all things right between God the Father and his creatures (Matthew 1:1). And it closes, again with the spotlight on Jesus, with paradise restored (Revelation 22). All that was lost in the Garden of Eden, including eternal life, will be regained in the eternal City of God.

Our unrelenting desire for restoration and paradise is at heart a yearning for wholeness through Jesus Christ. Because Jesus took God's wrath for our sin on himself when he died on the cross, there will come a day when sin and its residual damage will be completely eradicated and we will live in perfect harmony and continual fellowship with our Lord. Sin's inky darkness will be forever obliterated by the continual light of the Lord's radiant presence: "There will be no more night. [The servants of God and of the Lamb] will not need the light of a lamp or the light of the sun, for the Lord God will give them light. And they will reign forever and ever" (verse 5).

Paul had earlier written to the Corinthians that "God, who said, 'Let light shine out of darkness,' made his light shine in our hearts to give us the light of the knowledge of the glory of God in the face of Christ" (2 Corinthians 4:6). In the most amazing turnabout imaginable, God will transform darkness into light and tragedy into triumph.

And Jesus himself is even now calling to each one of us to come and share his glory with him forever: "Behold, I am coming soon! My reward is with me, and I will give to everyone according to what he has done. I am the Alpha and the Omega, the First and the Last, the Beginning and the End" (Revelation 22:12–13). And we who long for his appearance join the ever-growing throng of his beloved, chanting, "Amen. Come, Lord Jesus" (verse 20).

Self-Discovery: *Picture yourself standing in total darkness, your hands held out in front of you as you slowly grope your way along. What images or emotions come to mind? Now envision yourself striding into the dazzling sunshine of God's presence. Thank God for rescuing you "from the dominion of darkness" and allowing you "to share in the inheritance of the saints in the kingdom of light" (Colossians 1:12–13).*

GO TO DISCOVERY 1 ON PAGE 3

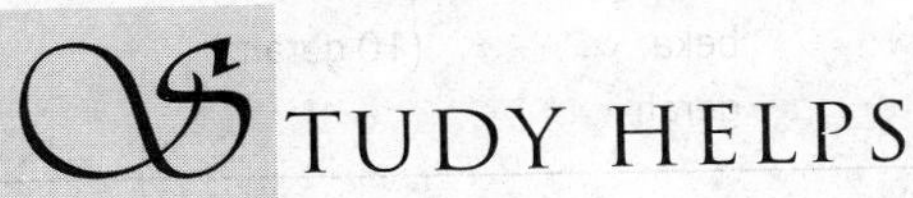

STUDY HELPS

Weights and Measures

	BIBLICAL UNIT		APPROXIMATE AMERICAN EQUIVALENT	APPROXIMATE METRIC EQUIVALENT
WEIGHTS	talent	(60 minas)	75 pounds	34 kilograms
	mina	(50 shekels)	1 1/4 pounds	0.6 kilogram
	shekel	(2 bekas)	2/5 ounce	11.5 grams
	pim	(2/3 shekel)	1/3 ounce	7.6 grams
	beka	(10 gerahs)	1/5 ounce	5.5 grams
	gerah		1/50 ounce	0.6 gram
LENGTH	cubit		18 inches	0.5 meter
	span		9 inches	23 centimeters
	handbreadth		3 inches	8 centimeters
CAPACITY				
Dry Measure	cor [homer]	(10 ephahs)	6 bushels	220 liters
	lethek	(5 ephahs)	3 bushels	110 liters
	ephah	(10 omers)	3/5 bushel	22 liters
	seah	(1/3 ephah)	7 quarts	7.3 liters
	omer	(1/10 ephah)	2 quarts	2 liters
	cab	(1/18 ephah)	1 quart	1 liter
Liquid Measure	bath	(1 ephah)	6 gallons	22 liters
	hin	(1/6 bath)	4 quarts	4 liters
	log	(1/72 bath)	1/3 quart	0.3 liter

The figures of the table are calculated on the basis of a shekel equaling 11.5 grams, a cubit equaling 18 inches and an ephah equaling 22 liters. The quart referred to is either a dry quart (slightly larger than a liter) or a liquid quart (slightly smaller than a liter), whichever is applicable. The ton referred to in the footnotes is the American ton of 2,000 pounds.

This table is based upon the best available information, but it is not intended to be mathematically precise; like the measurement equivalents in the footnotes, it merely gives approximate amounts and distances. Weights and measures differed somewhat at various times and places in the ancient world. There is uncertainty particularly about the ephah and the bath; further discoveries may shed more light on these units of capacity.

The Gospel of Jesus Christ

The gospel is the "good news" about what God has done for us through Jesus Christ. The term "good news" (Greek *euangelion* or *evangel*) is the basis of our English word *evangelize*. It means to share the "good news" of Jesus' death and resurrection. The apostle Paul said, "I want to remind you of the gospel I preached to you . . . that Christ died for our sins according to the Scriptures, that he was buried, that he was raised on the third day according to the Scriptures" (1 Corinthians 15:1,3–4).

The "good news" is the message that Christians proclaim to the world. British pastor and theologian Michael Green has said, "Christians did not go about proclaiming a new religion, new duties, or a new ideology. They proclaim good news . . . about what God has done. The first Christians believed that the life and death and raising to life again of their friend Jesus were the most important things that ever happened and they wanted to tell everybody about them."[1]

The fact that Jesus died for our sins and came back to life again is the basis of the Christian faith. The confidence that Christians have in this fact accounts for the certainty with which we announce and proclaim our faith in what Jesus has done for us. We realize that our eternal salvation is not just a matter of being satisfied with our religion. Rather, it is knowing that our faith satisfied God because God is satisfied with Christ's death for our sins.

The Plan of Salvation

The Bible was written to introduce us to Jesus. Knowing him personally is the key to our eternal salvation. 1 John 5:13 says, "I write these things to you who believe in the name of the Son of God so that you may know that you have eternal life." One day we will all stand before God. Suppose he were to ask you, "Why should I allow you into heaven?" Your answer to that question will tell you something about your relationship to God.

Many people assume they can go to heaven only by being a good person or by doing good deeds. But the Bible reminds us that "all have sinned and fall short of the glory of God" (Romans 3:23). None of us can do enough good to make ourself spiritually acceptable to God. While most religions encourage people to work their way to God, the "good news" of the story of Jesus is that he came to us. He did for us what we could not do for ourselves—he died for our sins.

Jesus Died for Our Sins

When Jesus was crucified, God laid the judgment of our sins on him. At the end of the crucifixion, Jesus triumphantly declared, "It is finished" (John 19:30). This was his way of saying that our sins have been "paid in full." Peter said, "Christ suffered for you . . . He himself bore our sins in his body on the tree" (1 Peter 2:21,24).

Jesus Rose from the Dead

Jesus said, "I give them eternal life, and they shall never perish" (John 10:28). Only someone who has eternal life can give us eternal life. Jesus' resurrection was the proof that he is indeed the Son of God. The Savior promised to give us eternal life as well when he said, "I tell you the truth, whoever hears my word and believes him who sent me has eternal life and will not be condemned; he has crossed over from death to life" (John 5:24).

[1] Michael Green, *Who Is This Jesus?* (Nashville: Thomas Nelson, 1992), p. 23.

We are saved by faith in what Jesus did for us

Faith is the act of believing that activates our commitment to Jesus Christ. The Bible says, "For it is by grace you have been saved, through faith—and this not from yourselves, it is the gift of God—not of works, so that no one can boast" (Ephesians 2:8–9). Faith is the key that personalizes our relationship with Jesus Christ. It is not merely believing that Jesus lived or died or rose again. Saving faith means that I believe he died for my sins and that he rose from the dead to give *me* the gift of eternal life.

You can ask him to save you right now!

Eternal salvation is the gift of God's grace. You can receive that gift by simply trusting what Jesus has done for you on the cross as the sufficient payment for your sins. The Bible promises "that if you confess with your mouth, 'Jesus is Lord,' and believe in your heart that God raised him from the dead, you will be saved . . . for, 'Everyone who calls on the name of the Lord will be saved' " (Romans 10:9,13).

If you have never personally committed your life to Jesus Christ, you can pray right now and ask him to forgive your sins and come into your life. You might want to pray something like this:

LORD JESUS,
I BELIEVE THAT YOU DIED FOR MY SINS
AND THAT YOU ROSE FROM THE DEAD
TO GIVE ME THE GIFT OF ETERNAL LIFE.
I ACCEPT YOUR GIFT OF FAITH.
FORGIVE ME ALL MY SINS.
I GIVE MY LIFE TO YOU AS BEST I KNOW HOW,
TRUSTING YOU ENTIRELY AS MY LORD AND SAVIOR.
I ACCEPT GOD'S GIFT BY FAITH,
PRAYING IN JESUS' NAME.

AMEN.

About the NIV

THE NEW INTERNATIONAL VERSION is a completely new translation of the Holy Bible made by over a hundred scholars working directly from the best available Hebrew, Aramaic and Greek texts. It had its beginning in 1965 when, after several years of exploratory study by committees from the Christian Reformed Church and the National Association of Evangelicals, a group of scholars met at Palos Heights, Illinois, and concurred in the need for a new translation of the Bible in contemporary English. This group, though not made up of official church representatives, was transdenominational. Its conclusion was endorsed by a large number of leaders from many denominations who met in Chicago in 1966.

Responsibility for the new version was delegated by the Palos Heights group to a self-governing body of fifteen, the Committee on Bible Translation, composed for the most part of biblical scholars from colleges, universities and seminaries. In 1967 the New York Bible Society (now the International Bible Society) generously undertook the financial sponsorship of the project—a sponsorship that made it possible to enlist the help of many distinguished scholars. The fact that participants from the United States, Great Britain, Canada, Australia and New Zealand worked together gave the project its international scope. That they were from many denominations—including Anglican, Assemblies of God, Baptist, Brethren, Christian Reformed, Church of Christ, Evangelical Free, Lutheran, Mennonite, Methodist, Nazarene, Presbyterian, Wesleyan and other churches—helped to safeguard the translation from sectarian bias.

How it was made helps to give the New International Version its distinctiveness. The translation of each book was assigned to a team of scholars. Next, one of the Intermediate Editorial Committees revised the initial translation, with constant reference to the Hebrew, Aramaic or Greek. Their work then went to one of the General Editorial Committees, which checked it in detail and made another thorough revision. This revision in turn was carefully reviewed by the Committee on Bible Translation, which made further changes and then released the final version for publication. In this way the entire Bible underwent three revisions, during each of which the translation was examined for its faithfulness to the original languages and for its English style.

All this involved many thousands of hours of research and discussion regarding the meaning of the texts and the precise way of putting them into English. It may well be that no other translation has been made by a more thorough process of review and revision from committee to committee than this one.

From the beginning of the project, the Committee on Bible Translation held to certain goals for the New International Version: that it would be an accurate translation and one that would have clarity and literary quality and so prove suitable for public and private reading, teaching, preaching, memorizing and liturgical use. The Committee also sought to preserve some measure of continuity with the long tradition of translating the Scriptures into English.

In working toward these goals, the translators were united in their commitment to the authority and infallibility of the Bible as God's Word in written form. They believe that it contains the divine answer to the deepest needs of humanity, that it sheds unique light on our path in a dark world, and that it sets forth the way to our eternal well-being.

The first concern of the translators has been the accuracy of the translation and its fidelity to the thought of the biblical writers. They have weighed the significance of the lexical and grammatical details of the Hebrew, Aramaic and Greek texts. At the same time, they have striven for more than a word-for-word translation. Because thought patterns and syntax differ from language to language, faithful communication of the meaning of the writers of the Bible demands frequent modifications in sentence structure and constant regard for the contextual meanings of words.

A sensitive feeling for style does not always accompany scholarship. Accordingly the Committee on

Bible Translation submitted the developing version to a number of stylistic consultants. Two of them read every book of both Old and New Testaments twice—once before and once after the last major revision—and made invaluable suggestions. Samples of the translation were tested for clarity and ease of reading by various kinds of people—young and old, highly educated and less well educated, ministers and laymen.

Concern for clear and natural English—that the New International Version should be idiomatic but not idiosyncratic, contemporary but not dated—motivated the translators and consultants. At the same time, they tried to reflect the differing styles of the biblical writers. In view of the international use of English, the translators sought to avoid obvious Americanisms on the one hand and obvious Anglicisms on the other. A British edition reflects the comparatively few differences of significant idiom and of spelling.

As for the traditional pronouns "thou," "thee" and "thine" in reference to the Deity, the translators judged that to use these archaisms (along with the old verb forms such as "doest," "wouldest" and "hadst") would violate accuracy in translation. Neither Hebrew, Aramaic nor Greek uses special pronouns for the persons of the Godhead. A present-day translation is not enhanced by forms that in the time of the King James Version were used in everyday speech, whether referring to God or man.

For the Old Testament the standard Hebrew text, the Masoretic Text as published in the latest editions of *Biblia Hebraica,* was used throughout. The Dead Sea Scrolls contain material bearing on an earlier stage of the Hebrew text. They were consulted, as were the Samaritan Pentateuch and the ancient scribal traditions relating to textual changes. Sometimes a variant Hebrew reading in the margin of the Masoretic Text was followed instead of the text itself. Such instances, being variants within the Masoretic tradition, are not specified by footnotes. In rare cases, words in the consonantal text were divided differently from the way they appear in the Masoretic Text. Footnotes indicate this. The translators also consulted the more important early versions—the Septuagint; Aquila, Symmachus and Theodotion; the Vulgate; the Syriac Peshitta; the Targums; and for the Psalms the *Juxta Hebraica* of Jerome. Readings from these versions were occasionally followed where the Masoretic Text seemed doubtful and where accepted principles of textual criticism showed that one or more of these textual witnesses appeared to provide the correct reading. Such instances are footnoted. Sometimes vowel letters and vowel signs did not, in the judgment of the translators, represent the correct vowels for the original consonantal text. Accordingly some words were read with a different set of vowels. These instances are usually not indicated by footnotes.

The Greek text used in translating the New Testament was an eclectic one. No other piece of ancient literature has such an abundance of manuscript witnesses as does the New Testament. Where existing manuscripts differ, the translators made their choice of readings according to accepted principles of New Testament textual criticism. Footnotes call attention to places where there was uncertainty about what the original text was. The best current printed texts of the Greek New Testament were used.

There is a sense in which the work of translation is never wholly finished. This applies to all great literature and uniquely so to the Bible. In 1973 the New Testament in the New International Version was published. Since then, suggestions for corrections and revisions have been received from various sources. The Committee on Bible Translation carefully considered the suggestions and adopted a number of them. These were incorporated in the first printing of the entire Bible in 1978. Additional revisions were made by the Committee on Bible Translation in 1983 and appear in printings after that date.

As in other ancient documents, the precise meaning of the biblical texts is sometimes uncertain. This is more often the case with the Hebrew and Aramaic texts than with the Greek text. Although archaeological and linguistic discoveries in this century aid in understanding difficult passages, some uncertainties remain. The more significant of these have been called to the reader's attention in the footnotes.

In regard to the divine name *YHWH,* commonly referred to as the *Tetragrammaton,* the translators adopted the device used in most English versions of rendering that name as "LORD" in capital letters to distinguish it from *Adonai,* another Hebrew word rendered "Lord," for which small letters are used. Wherever the two names stand together in the Old Testament as a compound name of God, they are rendered "Sovereign LORD."

Because for most readers today the phrases "the LORD of hosts" and "God of hosts" have little meaning, this version renders them "the LORD Almighty" and "God Almighty." These renderings convey the sense of the Hebrew, namely, "he who is sovereign over all the 'hosts' (powers) in heaven and on earth, especially over the 'hosts' (armies) of Israel." For readers unacquainted with Hebrew this does not make clear the distinction between *Sabaoth* ("hosts" or "Almighty") and *Shaddai* (which can also be translated "Almighty"), but the latter occurs infrequently and is always footnoted. When *Adonai* and *YHWH Sabaoth* occur together, they are rendered "the Lord, the LORD Almighty."

As for other proper nouns, the familiar spellings of the King James Version are generally retained. Names traditionally spelled with "ch," except where it is final, are usually spelled in this translation with "k" or "c," since the biblical languages do not have the sound that "ch" frequently indicates in English—for example, in *chant*. For well-known names such as Zechariah, however, the traditional spelling has been retained. Variation in the spelling of names in the original languages has usually not been indicated. Where a person or place has two or more different names in the Hebrew, Aramaic or Greek texts, the more familiar one has generally been used, with footnotes where needed.

To achieve clarity the translators sometimes supplied words not in the original texts but required by the context. If there was uncertainty about such material, it is enclosed in brackets. Also for the sake of clarity or style, nouns, including some proper nouns, are sometimes substituted for pronouns, and vice versa. And though the Hebrew writers often shifted back and forth between first, second and third personal pronouns without change of antecedent, this translation often makes them uniform, in accordance with English style and without the use of footnotes.

Poetical passages are printed as poetry, that is, with indentation of lines and with separate stanzas. These are generally designed to reflect the structure of Hebrew poetry. This poetry is normally characterized by parallelism in balanced lines. Most of the poetry in the Bible is in the Old Testament, and scholars differ regarding the scansion of Hebrew lines. The translators determined the stanza divisions for the most part by analysis of the subject matter. The stanzas therefore serve as poetic paragraphs.

As an aid to the reader, italicized sectional headings are inserted in most of the books. They are not to be regarded as part of the NIV text, are not for oral reading, and are not intended to dictate the interpretation of the sections they head.

The footnotes in this version are of several kinds, most of which need no explanation. Those giving alternative translations begin with "Or" and generally introduce the alternative with the last word preceding it in the text, except when it is a single-word alternative; in poetry quoted in a footnote a slant mark indicates a line division. Footnotes introduced by "Or" do not have uniform significance. In some cases two possible translations were considered to have about equal validity. In other cases, though the translators were convinced that the translation in the text was correct, they judged that another interpretation was possible and of sufficient importance to be represented in a footnote.

In the New Testament, footnotes that refer to uncertainty regarding the original text are introduced by "Some manuscripts" or similar expressions. In the Old Testament, evidence for the reading chosen is given first and evidence for the alternative is added after a semicolon (for example: Septuagint; Hebrew *father*). In such notes the term "Hebrew" refers to the Masoretic Text.

It should be noted that minerals, flora and fauna, architectural details, articles of clothing and jewelry, musical instruments and other articles cannot always be identified with precision. Also measures of capacity in the biblical period are particularly uncertain (see the table of weights and measures following the text).

Like all translations of the Bible, made as they are by imperfect man, this one undoubtedly falls short of its goals. Yet we are grateful to God for the extent to which he has enabled us to realize these goals and for the strength he has given us and our colleagues to complete our task. We offer this version of the Bible to him in whose name and for whose glory it has been made. We pray that it will lead many into a better understanding of the Holy Scriptures and a fuller knowledge of Jesus Christ the incarnate Word, of whom the Scriptures so faithfully testify.

The Committee on Bible Translation

June 1978
(Revised Aug 1983)

Names of the translators and editors may be secured
from the International Bible Society
translation sponsors of the New International Version, 1820 Jet Stream Drive,
Colorado Springs, Colorado 08921-3696 U.S.A.

HIGHLIGHTS
FROM THE LIFE OF JESUS

THE MINISTRY OF JESUS

(IN BIBLICAL ORDER; INCLUDES LOCATION)

Jesus baptized (Jordan River): *Matthew 3:13-17; Mark 1:9-11; Luke 3:21-22; John 1:29-34*
Jesus tempted by Satan (desert): *Matthew 4:1-11; Mark 1:12-13; Luke 4:1-13*
Jesus' first miracle (Cana): *John 2:1-11*
Jesus and Nicodemus (Judea): *John 3:1-21*
Jesus talks to a Samaritan woman (Samaria): *John 4:5-42*
Jesus heals an official's son (Cana): *John 4:46-54*
People of Nazareth try to kill Jesus (Nazareth): *Luke 4:16-30*
Jesus calls four fishermen (Sea of Galilee): *Matthew 4:18-22; Mark 1:16-20; Luke 5:1-11*
Jesus heals Peter's mother-in-law (Capernaum): *Matthew 8:14-15; Mark 1:29-31; Luke 4:38-39*
Jesus begins preaching in Galilee (Galilee): *Matthew 4:23-25; Mark 1:35-39; Luke 4:42-44*
Matthew decides to follow Jesus (Capernaum): *Matthew 9:9-13; Mark 2:13-17; Luke 5:27-32*
Jesus chooses twelve disciples (Galilee): *Matthew 10:2-4; Mark 3:13-19; Luke 6:12-15*
Jesus preaches the Sermon on the Mount (Galilee): *Matthew 5:1–7:29; Luke 6:20-49*
A sinful woman anoints Jesus (Capernaum): *Luke 7:36-50*
Jesus travels again through Galilee (Galilee): *Luke 8:1-3*
Jesus tells kingdom parables (Galilee): *Matthew 13:1-52; Mark 4:1-34; Luke 8:4-18*
Jesus quiets the storm (Sea of Galilee): *Matthew 8:23-27; Mark 4:35-41; Luke 8:22-25*
Jairus's daughter raised to life (Capernaum): *Matthew 9:18-26; Mark 5:21-23; Luke 8:40-56*
Jesus sends out the twelve (Galilee): *Matthew 9:35–11:1; Mark 6:6-13; Luke 9:1-6*
John the Baptist killed by Herod (Machaerus in Judea): *Matthew 14:1-12; Mark 6:14-29; Luke 9:7-9*
Jesus feeds the 5,000 (Bethsaida): *Matthew 14:13-21; Mark 6:30-44; Luke 9:10-17; John 6:1-14*
Jesus walks on water (Sea of Galilee): *Matthew 14:22-32; Mark 6:47-52; John 6:16-21*
Jesus feeds the 4,000 (Sea of Galilee): *Matthew 15:32-39; Mark 8:1-10*
Peter confesses Jesus as the Son of God (Caesarea Philippi): *Matthew 16:13-20; Mark 8:27-30; Luke 9:18-21*
Jesus predicts his death (Caesarea Philippi): *Matthew 16:21-26; Mark 8:31-37; Luke 9:22-25*
Jesus is transfigured (Mount Hermon): *Matthew 17:1-13; Mark 9:2-13; Luke 9:28-36*
Jesus pays his temple taxes (Capernaum): *Matthew 17:24-27*
Jesus attends the Feast of Tabernacles (Jerusalem): *John 7:10-52*
Jesus heals a man born blind (Jerusalem): *John 9:1-41*
Jesus visits Mary and Martha (Bethany): *Luke 10:38-42*
Jesus raises Lazarus from the dead (Bethany): *John 11:1-44*
Jesus begins his last trip to Jerusalem (border road): *Luke 17:11*
Jesus blesses the little children (Transjordan): *Matthew 19:13-15; Mark 10:13-16; Luke 18:15-17*
Jesus talks to the rich young man (Transjordan): *Matthew 19:16-30; Mark 10:17-31; Luke 18:18-30*
Jesus again predicts his death (near the Jordan): *Matthew 20:17-19; Mark 10:32-34; Luke 18:31-34*
Jesus heals blind Bartimaeus (Jericho): *Matthew 20:29-34; Mark 10:46-52; Luke 18:35-43*
Jesus talks to Zacchaeus (Jericho): *Luke 19:1-10*
Jesus visits Mary and Martha again (Bethany): *John 12:1-11*

Teachings of Jesus

(IN ALPHABETICAL ORDER)

Beatitudes: *Matthew 5:1-12*
Born again: *John 3:1-21*
Bread of life: *John 6:25-59*
Discipleship: *Luke 14:25-35*
Give to Caesar: *Mark 12:13-17*
Golden Rule: *Luke 6:31*
Good shepherd: *John 10:1-21*
Greatest commandment: *Matthew 22:34-40*
Living water: *John 4:1-26*
Lord's prayer: *Matthew 6:5-15*
Sending out the Twelve: *Matthew 10*
Sermon on the Mount: *Matthew 5–7*
Vine and branches: *John 15:1-17*
The way and the truth and the life: *John 14:5-14*
Wealth: *Matthew 19:16-30*
Worry: *Luke 12:22-34*

Jesus' Last Week

(IN BIBLICAL ORDER; INCLUDES LOCATION AND DAY OF THE WEEK)

The triumphal entry (Jerusalem, Sunday): *Matthew 21:1-11; Mark 11:1-11; Luke 19:29-44; John 12:12-19*
Jesus curses the fig tree (Jerusalem, Monday): *Matthew 21:18-22; Mark 11:12-14*
Jesus clears the temple (Jerusalem, Monday): *Matthew 21:12-13; Mark 11:15-18; Luke 19:45-48*
Jesus' authority questioned (Jerusalem, Tuesday): *Matthew 21:23-27; Mark 11:27-33; Luke 20:1-8*
Jesus teaches in the temple (Jerusalem, Tuesday): *Matthew 21:28–23:39; Mark 12:1-44; Luke 20:9–21:4*
Jesus' feet anointed (Bethany, Tuesday): *Matthew 26:6-13; Mark 14:3-9; John 12:2-11*
The plot against Jesus (Jerusalem, Wednesday): *Matthew 26:14-16; Mark 14:10-11; Luke 22:3-6*
The Last Supper (Jerusalem, Thursday): *Matthew 26:17-29; Mark 14:12-25; Luke 22:7-38; John 13:1-38*
Jesus comforts his disciples (Jerusalem, Thursday): *John 14:1–16:33*
Jesus' high priestly prayer (Jerusalem, Thursday): *John 17:1-26*
Gethsemane (Jerusalem, Thursday): *Matthew 26:36-46; Mark 14:32-42; Luke 22:40-46*
Jesus' arrest and trial (Jerusalem, Friday): *Matthew 26:47–27:26; Mark 14:43–15:15; Luke 22:47–23:25; John 18:2–19:16*
Jesus' crucifixion and death (Golgotha, Friday): *Matthew 27:27-56; Mark 15:16-41; Luke 23:26-49; John 19:17-37*
Jesus' burial (garden tomb, Friday): *Matthew 27:57-66; Mark 15:42-47; Luke 23:50-56; John 19:38-42*

Acknowledgements

The authors want to express their gratitude to Emily Boothe and Ruth Gudbrandson who typed the original manuscripts. They also want to thank Donna Huisjen and the editorial staff of Zondervan who worked so diligently on this project and Tom Mockabee and Dirk Buursma of the Zondervan Bible Department who caught and shared the vision for this project from the very beginning. They also want to thank the following people who helped write some of the discoveries: Rob Bell Jr., Helen Bell, Kristen Bell, Jim Carlson, Judy Childress, Lorna Dobson, and Doug Fagerstrom, as well as Cassandra Lindell for her editorial assistance.

Quotations for the "Jesus Quotes" sprinkled throughout this Bible were gleaned from the following sources:

John Bartlett, *Familiar Quotations* (Boston: Little, Brown & Co.), 1982.

Norman Vincent Peal, *My Favorite Quotations* (San Francisco: Harper Collins), 1990.

George Selders, *The Great Quotations* (New York: Pocket Books), 1967.

George Sweeting, *Great Quotes and Illustrations* (Waco, TX: Word, Inc.), 1985.

I.D.E. Thomas, *The Golden Treasury of Patristic Quotations* (Oklahoma City: Hearthstone Publishing Co.), 1996.

I.D.E. Thomas, *The Golden Treasury of Puritan Quotations* (Chicago: Moody Press), 1975.

Albert Wells, *Inspiring Quotations* (Nashville: Thomas Nelson), 1988.

Ralph Woods, *World Treasury of Religious Quotations* (New York: Hawthorn Books), 1966.

Contemporary quotes were gleaned from various sources.

INTRODUCTION
TO THE NIV CONCORDANCE

The NIV Concordance, created by Edward W. Goodrick and John R. Kohlenberger III, has been developed specifically for use with the New International Version. Like all concordances, it is a special index which contains an alphabetical listing of words used in the Bible text. By looking up key words, readers can find verses and passages for which they remember a word or two but not their location.

This concordance contains 2,000 word entries, with some 13,000 Scripture references. Each word entry is followed by the Scripture references in which that particular word is found, as well as by a brief excerpt from the surrounding context. The first letter of the entry word is italicized to conserve space and to allow for a longer context excerpt. Variant spellings due to number and tense and compound forms follow the entry in parentheses and direct the reader to check other forms of that word in locating a passage.

This concordance contains a number of "block entries," which highlight some of the key events and characteristics in the lives of certain Bible figures. The descriptive phrases replace the brief context surrounding each occurrence of the name. In those instances where more than one Bible character has the same name, that name is placed under one block entry, and each person is given a number (1), (2), etc. Insignificant names are not included.

Word or block entries marked with an asterisk (*) list every verse in the Bible in which the word appears.

This concordance is a valuable tool for Bible study. While one of its key purposes is to help the reader find forgotten references to verses, it can also be used to do word studies and to locate and trace biblical themes. Be sure to use this concordance as more than just a verse finder. Whenever you look up a verse, aim to discover the intended meaning of the verse in context. Give special attention to the flow of thought from the beginning of the passage to the end.

CONCORDANCE ABBREVIATIONS FOR THE BOOKS OF THE BIBLE

Genesis	Ge	Isaiah	Isa	Romans	Ro
Exodus	Ex	Jeremiah	Jer	1 Corinthians	1Co
Leviticus	Lev	Lamentations	La	2 Corinthians	2Co
Numbers	Nu	Ezekiel	Eze	Galatians	Gal
Deuteronomy	Dt	Daniel	Da	Ephesians	Eph
Joshua	Jos	Hosea	Hos	Philippians	Php
Judges	Jdg	Joel	Joel	Colossians	Col
Ruth	Ru	Amos	Am	1 Thessalonians	1Th
1 Samuel	1Sa	Obadiah	Ob	2 Thessalonians	2Th
2 Samuel	2Sa	Jonah	Jnh	1 Timothy	1Ti
1 Kings	1Ki	Micah	Mic	2 Timothy	2Ti
2 Kings	2Ki	Nahum	Na	Titus	Tit
1 Chronicles	1Ch	Habakkuk	Hab	Philemon	Phm
2 Chronicles	2Ch	Zephaniah	Zep	Hebrews	Heb
Ezra	Ezr	Haggai	Hag	James	Jas
Nehemiah	Ne	Zechariah	Zec	1 Peter	1Pe
Esther	Est	Malachi	Mal	2 Peter	2Pe
Job	Job	Matthew	Mt	1 John	1Jn
Psalm	Ps	Mark	Mk	2 John	2Jn
Proverbs	Pr	Luke	Lk	3 John	3Jn
Ecclesiastes	Ecc	John	Jn	Jude	Jude
Song of Solomon	SS	Acts	Ac	Revelation	Rev

CONCORDANCE

AARON

Priesthood of (Ex 28:1; Nu 17; Heb 5:1-4; 7), garments (Ex 28; 39), consecration (Ex 29), ordination (Lev 8).

Spokesman for Moses (Ex 4:14-16, 27-31; 7:1-2). Supported Moses' hands in battle (Ex 17:8-13). Built golden calf (Ex 32; Dt 9:20). Talked against Moses (Nu 12). Priesthood opposed (Nu 16); staff budded (Nu 17). Forbidden to enter land (Nu 20:1-12). Death (Nu 20:22-29; 33:38-39).

ABANDON

Dt 4:31 he will not *a* or destroy you
1Ti 4: 1 in later times some will *a* the faith

ABBA

Ro 8:15 And by him we cry, *"A,* Father."
Gal 4: 6 the Spirit who calls out, *"A,* Father

ABEL

Second son of Adam (Ge 4:2). Offered proper sacrifice (Ge 4:4; Heb 11:4). Murdered by Cain (Ge 4:8; Mt 23:35; Lk 11:51; 1Jn 3:12).

ABHORS

Pr 11: 1 The LORD *a* dishonest scales,

ABIGAIL

Wife of Nabal (1Sa 25:30); pled for his life with David (1Sa 25:14-35). Became David's wife (1Sa 25:36-42).

ABIJAH

Son of Rehoboam; king of Judah (1Ki 14:31-15:8; 2Ch 12:16-14:1).

ABILITY (ABLE)

Ezr 2:69 According to their *a* they gave
2Co 1: 8 far beyond our *a* to endure,
8: 3 were able, and even beyond their *a*.

ABIMELECH

1. King of Gerar who took Abraham's wife Sarah, believing her to be his sister (Ge 20). Later made a covenant with Abraham (Ge 21:22-33).

2. King of Gerar who took Isaac's wife Rebekah, believing her to be his sister (Ge 26:1-11). Later made a covenant with Isaac (Ge 26:12-31).

ABLE (ABILITY ENABLE ENABLED ENABLES)

Eze 7:19 and gold will not be *a* to save them
Da 3:17 the God we serve is *a* to save us
Ro 8:39 will be *a* to separate us
14: 4 for the Lord is *a* to make him stand
16:25 to him who is *a* to establish you
2Co 9: 8 God is *a* to make all grace abound
Eph 3:20 him who is *a* to do immeasurably
2Ti 1:12 and am convinced that he is *a*
3:15 which are *a* to make you wise
Heb 7:25 he is *a* to save completely
Jude :24 To him who is *a* to keep you
Rev 5: 5 He is *a* to open the scroll

ABOLISH

Mt 5:17 that I have come to *a* the Law

ABOMINATION

Da 11:31 set up the *a* that causes desolation.

ABOUND (ABOUNDING)

2Co 9: 8 able to make all grace *a* to you,
Php 1: 9 that your love may *a* more

ABOUNDING (ABOUND)

Ex 34: 6 slow to anger, *a* in love
Ps 86: 5 *a* in love to all who call to you.

ABRAHAM

Covenant relation with the LORD (Ge 12:1-3; 13:14-17; 15; 17; 22:15-18; Ex 2:24; Ne 9:8; Ps 105; Mic 7:20; Lk 1:68-75; Ro 4; Heb 6:13-15).

Called from Ur, via Haran, to Canaan (Ge 12:1; Ac 7:2-4; Heb 11:8-10). Moved to Egypt, nearly lost Sarah to Pharoah (Ge 12:10-20). Divided the land with Lot (Ge 13). Saved Lot from four kings (Ge 14:1-16); blessed by Melchizedek (Ge 14:17-20; Heb 7:1-20). Declared righteous by faith (Ge 15:6; Ro 4:3; Gal 3:6-9). Fathered Ishmael by Hagar (Ge 16).

Name changed from Abram (Ge 17:5; Ne 9:7). Circumcised (Ge 17; Ro 4:9-12). Entertained three visitors (Ge 18); promised a son by Sarah (Ge 18:9-15; 17:16). Moved to Gerar; nearly lost Sarah to Abimelech (Ge 20). Fathered Isaac by Sarah (Ge 21:1-7; Ac 7:8; Heb 11:11-12); sent away Hagar and Ishmael (Ge 21:8-21; Gal 4:22-30). Tested by offering Isaac (Ge 22; Heb 11:17-19; Jas 2:21-24). Sarah died; bought field of Ephron for burial (Ge 23). Secured wife for Isaac (Ge 24). Death (Ge 25:7-11).

ABSALOM

Son of David by Maacah (2Sa 3:3; 1Ch 3:2). Killed Amnon for rape of his sister Tamar; banished by David (2Sa 13). Returned to Jerusalem; received by David (2Sa 14). Rebelled against David; seized kingdom (2Sa 15-17). Killed (2Sa 18).

ABSTAIN (ABSTAINS)

1Pe 2:11 to *a* from sinful desires,

ABSTAINS* (ABSTAIN)

Ro 14: 6 thanks to God; and he who *a*,

ABUNDANCE (ABUNDANT)

Lk 12:15 consist in the *a* of his possessions."
Jude : 2 peace and love be yours in *a*.

ABUNDANT (ABUNDANCE)

Dt 28:11 will grant you *a* prosperity—
Ps 145: 7 will celebrate your *a* goodness
Pr 28:19 works his land will have *a* food,
Ro 5:17 who receive God's *a* provision

ACCEPT (ACCEPTED ACCEPTS)

Ex 23: 8 "Do not *a* a bribe,
Pr 10: 8 The wise in heart *a* commands,
19:20 Listen to advice and *a* instruction,
Ro 15: 7 *A* one another, then, just
Jas 1:21 humbly *a* the word planted in you,

ACCEPTED (ACCEPT)

Lk 4:24 "no prophet is *a* in his hometown.

ACCEPTS (ACCEPT)

Ps 6: 9 the LORD *a* my prayer.
Jn 13:20 whoever *a* anyone I send *a* me;

ACCOMPANY

Mk 16:17 these signs will *a* those who believe

Heb 6: 9 your case—things that *a* salvation.

ACCOMPLISH
Isa 55:11 but will *a* what I desire

ACCORD
Nu 24:13 not do anything of my own *a*,
Jn 10:18 but I lay it down of my own *a*.
12:49 For I did not speak of my own *a*,

ACCOUNT (ACCOUNTABLE)
Mt 12:36 to give *a* on the day of judgment
Ro 14:12 each of us will give an *a* of himself
Heb 4:13 of him to whom we must give *a*.

ACCOUNTABLE (ACCOUNT)
Eze 33: 6 but I will hold the watchman *a*
Ro 3:19 and the whole world held *a* to God.

ACCUSATION (ACCUSE)
1Ti 5:19 Do not entertain an *a*

ACCUSATIONS (ACCUSE)
2Pe 2:11 do not bring slanderous *a*

ACCUSE (ACCUSATION ACCUSATIONS)
Pr 3:30 Do not *a* a man for no reason—
Lk 3:14 and don't *a* people falsely—

ACHAN*
Sin at Jericho caused defeat at Ai; stoned (Jos 7; 22:20; 1Ch 2:7).

ACHE*
Pr 14:13 Even in laughter the heart may *a*,

ACKNOWLEDGE
Mt 10:32 *a* him before my Father in heaven.
1Jn 4: 3 spirit that does not *a* Jesus is not

ACQUIT
Ex 23: 7 to death, for I will not *a* the guilty.

ACTION (ACTIONS ACTIVE ACTS)
Jas 2:17 if it is not accompanied by *a*,
1Pe 1:13 minds for *a*; be self-controlled;

ACTIONS (ACTION)
Mt 11:19 wisdom is proved right by her *a*."
Gal 6: 4 Each one should test his own *a*.
Tit 1:16 but by their *a* they deny him.

ACTIVE (ACTION)
Heb 4:12 For the word of God is living and *a*

ACTS (ACTION)
Ps 145:12 all men may know of your mighty *a*
150: 2 Praise him for his *a* of power;
Isa 64: 6 all our righteous *a* are like filthy
Mt 6: 1 not to do your '*a* of righteousness'

ADAM
First man (Ge 1:26-2:25; Ro 5:14; 1Ti 2:13). Sin of (Ge 3; Hos 6:7; Ro 5:12-21). Children of (Ge 4:1-5:5). Death of (Ge 5:5; Ro 5:12-21; 1Co 15:22).

ADD
Dt 12:32 do not *a* to it or take away from it.
Pr 30: 6 Do not *a* to his words,
Lk 12:25 by worrying can *a* a single hour
Rev 22:18 God will *a* to him the plagues

ADMIRABLE*
Php 4: 8 whatever is lovely, whatever is *a*—

ADMONISH
Col 3:16 and *a* one another with all wisdom,

ADOPTED (ADOPTION)
Eph 1: 5 In love he predestined us to be *a*

ADOPTION (ADOPTED)
Ro 8:23 as we wait eagerly for our *a* as sons,

ADORE*
SS 1: 4 How right they are to *a* you!

ADORNMENT* (ADORNS)
1Pe 3: 3 should not come from outward *a*,

ADORNS (ADORNMENT)
Ps 93: 5 holiness *a* your house

ADULTERY
Ex 20:14 "You shall not commit *a*.
Mt 5:27 that it was said, 'Do not commit *a*.'
5:28 lustfully has already committed *a*
5:32 the divorced woman commits *a*.
15:19 murder, *a*, sexual immorality, theft

ADULTS*
1Co 14:20 but in your thinking be *a*.

ADVANCED
Job 32: 7 *a* years should teach wisdom.'

ADVANTAGE
Ex 22:22 "Do not take *a* of a widow
Dt 24:14 Do not take *a* of a hired man who is
1Th 4: 6 should wrong his brother or take *a*

ADVERSITY
Pr 17:17 and a brother is born for *a*.

ADVICE
1Ki 12: 8 rejected the *a* the elders
12:14 he followed the *a* of the young men
Pr 12: 5 but the *a* of the wicked is deceitful.
12:15 but a wise man listens to *a*.
19:20 Listen to *a* and accept instruction,
20:18 Make plans by seeking *a*;

AFFLICTION
Ro 12:12 patient in *a*, faithful in prayer.

AFRAID (FEAR)
Ge 26:24 Do not be *a*, for I am with you;
Ex 3: 6 because he was *a* to look at God.
Ps 27: 1 of whom shall I be *a*?
56: 3 When I am *a*, / I will trust in you.
Pr 3:24 lie down, you will not be *a*;
Jer 1: 8 Do not be *a* of them, for I am
Mt 8:26 You of little faith, why are you so *a*
10:28 be *a* of the One who can destroy
10:31 So don't be *a*; you are worth more
Mk 5:36 "Don't be *a*; just believe."
Jn 14:27 hearts be troubled and do not be *a*.
Heb 13: 6 Lord is my helper; I will not be *a*.

AGED
Job 12:12 Is not wisdom found among the *a*?
Pr 17: 6 children are a crown to the *a*,

AGREE
Mt 18:19 on earth *a* about anything you ask
Ro 7:16 want to do, I *a* that the law is good.
Php 4: 2 with Syntyche to *a* with each other

AHAB
Son of Omri; king of Israel (1Ki 16:28-22:40), husband of Jezebel (1Ki 16:31). Promoted Baal worship (1Ki 16:31-33); opposed by Elijah (1Ki 17:1; 18; 21), a prophet (1Ki 20:35-43), Micaiah (1Ki 22:1-28). Defeated Ben-Hadad (1Ki 20). Killed for failing to kill Ben-Hadad and for murder of Naboth (1Ki 20:35-21:40).

AHAZ
Son of Jotham; king of Judah, (2Ki 16; 2Ch 28; Isa 7).

AHAZIAH

1. Son of Ahab; king of Israel (1Ki 22:51-2Ki 1:18; 2Ch 20:35-37).

2. Son of Jehoram; king of Judah (2Ki 8:25-29; 9:14-29), also called Jehoahaz (2Ch 21:17-22:9; 25:23).

AIM

1Co 7:34 Her *a* is to be devoted to the Lord
2Co 13:11 *A* for perfection, listen

AIR

Mt 8:20 and birds of the *a* have nests,
1Co 9:26 not fight like a man beating the *a.*
Eph 2: 2 of the ruler of the kingdom of the *a,*
1Th 4:17 clouds to meet the Lord in the *a.*

ALABASTER

Mt 26: 7 came to him with an *a* jar

ALERT

Jos 8: 4 All of you be on the *a.*
Mk 13:33 Be *a!* You do not know
Eph 6:18 be *a* and always keep on praying
1Th 5: 6 but let us be *a* and self-controlled.

ALIEN (ALIENATED)

Ex 22:21 "Do not mistreat an *a*

ALIENATED (ALIEN)

Gal 5: 4 by law have been *a* from Christ;

ALIVE (LIVE)

Ac 1: 3 convincing proofs that he was *a.*
Ro 6:11 but *a* to God in Christ Jesus.
1Co 15:22 so in Christ all will be made *a.*

ALMIGHTY (MIGHT)

Ge 17: 1 "I am God *A;* walk before me
Job 11: 7 Can you probe the limits of the *A?*
33: 4 the breath of the *A* gives me life.
Ps 91: 1 will rest in the shadow of the *A.*
Isa 6: 3 "Holy, holy, holy is the LORD *A;*

ALTAR

Ge 22: 9 his son Isaac and laid him on the *a,*
Ex 27: 1 "Build an *a* of acacia wood,
1Ki 18:30 and he repaired the *a* of the LORD
2Ch 4: 1 made a bronze *a* twenty cubits
4:19 the golden *a;* the tables

ALWAYS

Ps 16: 8 I have set the LORD *a* before me.
51: 3 and my sin is *a* before me.
Mt 26:11 The poor you will *a* have with you,
28:20 And surely I will be with you *a,*
1Co 13: 7 *a* protects, *a* trusts, *a* hopes, *a*
Php 4: 4 Rejoice in the Lord *a.*
1Pe 3:15 *A* be prepared to give an answer

AMAZIAH

Son of Joash; king of Judah (2Ki 14; 2Ch 25).

AMBASSADORS

2Co 5:20 We are therefore Christ's *a,*

AMBITION

Ro 15:20 It has always been my *a*
1Th 4:11 Make it your *a* to lead a quiet life,

AMON

Son of Manasseh; king of Judah (2Ki 21:18-26; 1Ch 3:14; 2Ch 33:21-25).

ANANIAS

1. Husband of Sapphira; died for lying to God (Ac 5:1-11).
2. Disciple who baptized Saul (Ac 9:10-19).
3. High priest at Paul's arrest (Ac 22:30-24:1).

ANCHOR

Heb 6:19 We have this hope as an *a*

ANCIENT

Da 7: 9 and the *A* of Days took his seat.

ANDREW*

Apostle; brother of Simon Peter (Mt 4:18; 10:2; Mk 1:16-18, 29; 3:18; 13:3; Lk 6:14; Jn 1:35-44; 6:8-9; 12:22; Ac 1:13).

ANGEL (ANGELS ARCHANGEL)

Ps 34: 7 The *a* of the LORD encamps
Ac 6:15 his face was like the face of an *a.*
2Co 11:14 Satan himself masquerades as an *a*
Gal 1: 8 or an *a* from heaven should preach

ANGELS (ANGEL)

Ps 91:11 command his *a* concerning you
Mt 18:10 For I tell you that their *a*
25:41 prepared for the devil and his *a.*
Lk 20:36 for they are like the *a.*
1Co 6: 3 you not know that we will judge *a?*
Heb 1: 4 as much superior to the *a*
1:14 Are not all *a* ministering spirits
2: 7 made him a little lower than the *a;*
13: 2 some people have entertained *a*
1Pe 1:12 Even *a* long to look
2Pe 2: 4 For if God did not spare *a*

ANGER (ANGERED ANGRY)

Ex 32:10 alone so that my *a* may burn
34: 6 slow to *a,* abounding in love
Dt 29:28 In furious *a* and in great wrath
2Ki 22:13 Great is the LORD's *a* that burns
Ps 30: 5 For his *a* lasts only a moment,
Pr 15: 1 but a harsh word stirs up *a.*
29:11 A fool gives full vent to his *a,*

ANGERED (ANGER)

Pr 22:24 do not associate with one easily *a,*
1Co 13: 5 it is not easily *a,* it keeps no record

ANGRY (ANGER)

Ps 2:12 Kiss the Son, lest he be *a*
Pr 29:22 An *a* man stirs up dissension,
Jas 1:19 slow to speak and slow to become *a*

ANGUISH

Ps 118: 5 In my *a* I cried to the LORD,

ANOINT

Ps 23: 5 You *a* my head with oil;
Jas 5:14 and *a* him with oil in the name

ANT*

Pr 6: 6 Go to the *a,* you sluggard;

ANTICHRIST

1Jn 2:18 have heard that the *a* is coming,
2Jn : 7 person is the deceiver and the *a.*

ANTIOCH

Ac 11:26 were called Christians first at *A.*

ANXIETY (ANXIOUS)

1Pe 5: 7 Cast all your *a* on him

ANXIOUS (ANXIETY)

Pr 12:25 An *a* heart weighs a man down,
Php 4: 6 Do not be *a* about anything,

APOLLOS*

Christian from Alexandria, learned in the Scriptures; instructed by Aquila and Priscilla (Ac 18:24-28). Ministered at Corinth (Ac 19:1; 1Co 1:12; 3; Tit 3:13).

APOSTLES

See also Andrew, Bartholomew, James, John, Judas, Matthew, Nathanael, Paul, Peter, Philip, Simon, Thaddaeus, Thomas.

Mk 3:14 twelve—designating them *a*—
Ac 1:26 so he was added to the eleven *a.*
2:43 signs were done by the *a.*

Tit 3: 1 people to be subject to rulers and *a,*
1Pe 3:22 *a* and powers in submission to him.

AUTHORITY (AUTHORITIES)
Mt 7:29 because he taught as one who had *a*
9: 6 the Son of Man has *a* on earth
28:18 "All *a* in heaven and on earth has
Ro 13: 1 for there is no *a* except that which
13: 2 rebels against the *a* is rebelling
1Co 11:10 to have a sign of *a* on her head.
1Ti 2: 2 for kings and all those in *a,*
2:12 to teach or to have *a* over a man;
Heb 13:17 your leaders and submit to their *a.*

AVENGE (VENGEANCE)
Dt 32:35 It is mine to *a;* I will repay.

AVOID
Pr 20: 3 It is to a man's honor to *a* strife,
20:19 so *a* a man who talks too much.
1Th 4: 3 you should *a* sexual immorality;
5:22 *A* every kind of evil.
2Ti 2:16 *A* godless chatter, because those
Tit 3: 9 But *a* foolish controversies

AWAKE
Ps 17:15 when I *a,* I will be satisfied

AWE (AWESOME)
Job 25: 2 "Dominion and *a* belong to God;
Ps 119:120 I stand in *a* of your laws.
Ecc 5: 7 Therefore stand in *a* of God.
Isa 29:23 will stand in *a* of the God of Israel.
Jer 33: 9 they will be in *a* and will tremble
Hab 3: 2 I stand in *a* of your deeds,
Mal 2: 5 and stood in *a* of my name.
Mt 9: 8 they were filled with *a;*
Lk 7:16 They were all filled with *a*
Ac 2:43 Everyone was filled with *a,*
Heb 12:28 acceptably with reverence and *a,*

AWESOME (AWE)
Ge 28:17 and said, "How *a* is this place!
Ex 15:11 *a* in glory,
Dt 7:21 is among you, is a great and *a* God.
10:17 the great God, mighty and *a,*
28:58 revere this glorious and *a* name—
Jdg 13: 6 like an angel of God, very *a.*
Ne 1: 5 of heaven, the great and *a* God,
9:32 the great, mighty and *a* God,
Job 10:16 again display your *a* power
37:22 God comes in *a* majesty.
Ps 45: 4 let your right hand display *a* deeds.
47: 2 How *a* is the LORD Most High,
66: 5 how *a* his works in man's behalf!
68:35 You are *a,* O God,
89: 7 he is more *a* than all who surround
99: 3 praise your great and *a* name—
111: 9 holy and *a* is his name.
145: 6 of the power of your *a* works,
Da 9: 4 "O Lord, the great and *a* God,

BAAL
1Ki 18:25 Elijah said to the prophets of *B,*

BAASHA
King of Israel (1Ki 15:16-16:7; 2Ch 16:1-6).

BABIES (BABY)
Lk 18:15 also bringing *b* to Jesus
1Pe 2: 2 Like newborn *b,* crave pure

BABY (BABIES)
Isa 49:15 "Can a mother forget the *b*
Lk 1:44 the *b* in my womb leaped for joy.
2:12 You will find a *b* wrapped in strips
Jn 16:21 but when her *b* is born she forgets

BABYLON
Ps 137: 1 By the rivers of *B* we sat and wept

BACKSLIDING
Jer 3:22 I will cure you of *b."*
14: 7 For our *b* is great;
Eze 37:23 them from all their sinful *b,*

BALAAM
Prophet who attempted to curse Israel (Nu 22-24; Dt 23:4-5; 2Pe 2:15; Jude 11). Killed (Nu 31:8; Jos 13:22).

BALM
Jer 8:22 Is there no *b* in Gilead?

BANISH
Jer 25:10 I will *b* from them the sounds of joy

BANQUET
SS 2: 4 He has taken me to the *b* hall,
Lk 14:13 when you give a *b,* invite the poor,

BAPTIZE (BAPTIZED)
Mt 3:11 He will *b* you with the Holy Spirit
Mk 1: 8 he will *b* you with the Holy Spirit."
1Co 1:17 For Christ did not send me to *b,*

BAPTIZED (BAPTIZE)
Mt 3: 6 they were *b* by him in the Jordan
Mk 1: 9 and was *b* by John in the Jordan.
10:38 or be *b* with the baptism I am
16:16 believes and is *b* will be saved,
Jn 4: 2 in fact it was not Jesus who *b,*
Ac 1: 5 but in a few days you will be *b*

BARABBAS
Mt 27:26 Then he released *B* to them.

BARBS*
Nu 33:55 allow to remain will become *b*

BARE
Heb 4:13 and laid *b* before the eyes of him

BARNABAS*
Disciple, originally Joseph (Ac 4:36), prophet (Ac 13:1), apostle (Ac 14:14). Brought Paul to apostles (Ac 9:27), Antioch (Ac 11:22-29; Gal 2:1-13), on the first missionary journey (Ac 13-14). Together at Jerusalem Council, they separated over John Mark (Ac 15). Later co-workers (1Co 9:6; Col 4:10).

BARREN
Ps 113: 9 He settles the *b* woman

BARTHOLOMEW*
Apostle (Mt 10:3; Mk 3:18; Lk 6:14; Ac 1:13). Possibly also known as Nathanael (Jn 1:45-49; 21:2).

BATH
Jn 13:10 person who has had a *b* needs only

BATHSHEBA
Wife of Uriah who committed adultery with and became wife of David (2Sa 11), mother of Solomon (2Sa 12:24; 1Ki 1-2; 1Ch 3:5).

BATTLE
2Ch 20:15 For the *b* is not yours, but God's.
Ps 24: 8 the LORD mighty in *b.*
Ecc 9:11 or the *b* to the strong,

BEAR (BEARING BIRTH BIRTHRIGHT BORN FIRSTBORN NEWBORN)
Ge 4:13 punishment is more than I can *b.*
Ps 38: 4 like a burden too heavy to *b.*
Isa 53:11 and he will *b* their iniquities.
Da 7: 5 beast, which looked like a *b.*
Mt 7:18 A good tree cannot *b* bad fruit,
Jn 15: 2 branch that does *b* fruit he prunes
15:16 and appointed you to go and *b* fruit—

Ro 15: 1 ought to *b* with the failings
1Co 10:13 tempted beyond what you can *b*.
Col 3:13 *B* with each other and forgive

BEARING (BEAR)
Eph 4: 2 *b* with one another in love.
Col 1:10 *b* fruit in every good work,

BEAST
Rev 13:18 him calculate the number of the *b*,

BEAT (BEATING)
Isa 2: 4 They will *b* their swords
Joel 3:10 *B* your plowshares into swords
1Co 9:27 I *b* my body and make it my slave

BEATING (BEAT)
1Co 9:26 I do not fight like a man *b* the air.
1Pe 2:20 if you receive a *b* for doing wrong

BEAUTIFUL (BEAUTY)
Ge 6: 2 that the daughters of men were *b*,
12:11 "I know what a *b* woman you are.
12:14 saw that she was a very *b* woman.
24:16 The girl was very *b*, a virgin;
26: 7 of Rebekah, because she is *b*."
29:17 Rachel was lovely in form, and *b*.
Job 38:31 "Can you bind the *b* Pleiades?
Pr 11:22 is a *b* woman who shows no
Ecc 3:11 He has made everything *b*
Isa 4: 2 of the LORD will be *b*
52: 7 How *b* on the mountains
Eze 20: 6 and honey, the most *b* of all lands.
Zec 9:17 How attractive and *b* they will be!
Mt 23:27 which look *b* on the outside
26:10 She has done a *b* thing to me.
Ro 10:15 "How *b* are the feet
1Pe 3: 5 in God used to make themselves *b*.

BEAUTY (BEAUTIFUL)
Ps 27: 4 to gaze upon the *b* of the LORD
45:11 The king is enthralled by your *b*;
Pr 31:30 is deceptive, and *b* is fleeting;
Isa 33:17 Your eyes will see the king in his *b*
53: 2 He had no *b* or majesty
61: 3 to bestow on them a crown of *b*
Eze 28:12 full of wisdom and perfect in *b*
1Pe 3: 4 the unfading *b* of a gentle

BED
Heb 13: 4 and the marriage *b* kept pure,

BEELZEBUB
Lk 11:15 "By *B*, the prince of demons,

BEER
Pr 20: 1 Wine is a mocker and *b* a brawler;

BEERSHEBA
Jdg 20: 1 all the Israelites from Dan to *B*

BEGINNING
Ge 1: 1 In the *b* God created the heavens
Ps 102:25 In the *b* you laid the foundations
111:10 of the LORD is the *b* of wisdom;
Pr 1: 7 of the LORD is the *b* of knowledge
Jn 1: 1 In the *b* was the Word,
1Jn 1: 1 That which was from the *b*,
Rev 21: 6 and the Omega, the *B* and the End.

BEHAVE
Ro 13:13 Let us *b* decently, as in the daytime

BELIEVE (BELIEVED BELIEVER BELIEVERS BELIEVES BELIEVING)
Mt 18: 6 one of these little ones who *b* in me
21:22 If you *b*, you will receive whatever
Mk 1:15 Repent and *b* the good news!"
9:24 "I do *b*; help me overcome my
16:17 signs will accompany those who *b*:
Lk 8:50 just *b*, and she will be healed."
24:25 to *b* all that the prophets have
Jn 1: 7 that through him all men might *b*.
3:18 does not *b* stands condemned
6:29 to *b* in the one he has sent."
10:38 you do not *b* me, *b* the miracles,
11:27 "I *b* that you are the Christ,
14:11 *B* me when I say that I am
16:30 This makes us *b* that you came
16:31 "You *b* at last!" Jesus answered.
17:21 that the world may *b* that you have
20:27 Stop doubting and *b*."
20:31 written that you may *b* that Jesus is
Ac 16:31 They replied, "*B* in the Lord Jesus,
24:14 I *b* everything that agrees
Ro 3:22 faith in Jesus Christ to all who *b*.
4:11 he is the father of all who *b*
10: 9 *b* in your heart that God raised him
10:14 And how can they *b* in the one
16:26 so that all nations might *b*
1Th 4:14 We *b* that Jesus died and rose again
2Th 2:11 delusion so that they will *b* the lie
1Ti 4:10 and especially of those who *b*.
Tit 1: 6 a man whose children *b*
Heb 11: 6 comes to him must *b* that he exists
Jas 2:19 Even the demons *b* that—
1Jn 4: 1 Dear friends, do not *b* every spirit,

BELIEVED (BELIEVE)
Ge 15: 6 Abram *b* the LORD, and he
Jnh 3: 5 The Ninevites *b* God.
Jn 1:12 to those who *b* in his name,
2:22 Then they *b* the Scripture
3:18 because he has not *b* in the name
20: 8 He saw and *b*.
20:29 who have not seen and yet have *b*."
Ac 13:48 were appointed for eternal life *b*.
Ro 4: 3 Scripture say? "Abraham *b* God,
10:14 call on the one they have not *b* in?
1Co 15: 2 Otherwise, you have *b* in vain.
Gal 3: 6 Consider Abraham: "He *b* God,
2Ti 1:12 because I know whom I have *b*,
Jas 2:23 that says, "Abraham *b* God,

BELIEVER (BELIEVE)
1Co 7:12 brother has a wife who is not a *b*
2Co 6:15 What does a *b* have in common

BELIEVERS (BELIEVE)
Ac 4:32 All the *b* were one in heart
5:12 And all the *b* used to meet together
1Co 6: 5 to judge a dispute between *b*?
1Ti 4:12 set an example for the *b* in speech,
1Pe 2:17 Love the brotherhood of *b*,

BELIEVES (BELIEVE)
Pr 14:15 A simple man *b* anything,
Mk 9:23 is possible for him who *b*."
11:23 *b* that what he says will happen,
16:16 Whoever *b* and is baptized will be
Jn 3:16 that whoever *b* in him shall not
3:36 Whoever *b* in the Son has eternal
5:24 *b* him who sent me has eternal life
6:35 and he who *b* in me will never be
6:40 and *b* in him shall have eternal life,
6:47 he who *b* has everlasting life.
7:38 Whoever *b* in me, as the Scripture
11:26 and *b* in me will never die.
Ro 1:16 for the salvation of everyone who *b*
10: 4 righteousness for everyone who *b*.
1Jn 5: 1 Everyone who *b* that Jesus is
5: 5 Only he who *b* that Jesus is the Son

BELIEVING (BELIEVE)
Jn 20:31 and that by *b* you may have life

BELONG (BELONGS)
Dt 29:29 The secret things *b*
Job 25: 2 "Dominion and awe *b* to God;
Ps 47: 9 for the kings of the earth *b* to God;
95: 4 and the mountain peaks *b* to him.
Jn 8:44 You *b* to your father, the devil,
15:19 As it is, you do not *b* to the world,
Ro 1: 6 called to *b* to Jesus Christ.
7: 4 that you might *b* to another,
14: 8 we live or die, we *b* to the Lord.
Gal 5:24 Those who *b* to Christ Jesus have
1Th 5: 8 But since we *b* to the day, let us be

BELONGS (BELONG)
Job 41:11 Everything under heaven *b* to me.
Ps 111:10 To him *b* eternal praise.
Eze 18: 4 For every living soul *b* to me,
Jn 8:47 He who *b* to God hears what God
Ro 12: 5 each member *b* to all the others.

BELOVED (LOVE)
Dt 33:12 "Let the *b* of the LORD rest secure

BELT
Isa 11: 5 Righteousness will be his *b*
Eph 6:14 with the *b* of truth buckled

BENEFIT (BENEFITS)
Ro 6:22 the *b* you reap leads to holiness,
2Co 4:15 All this is for your *b*,

BENEFITS (BENEFIT)
Ps 103: 2 and forget not all his *b*.
Jn 4:38 you have reaped the *b* of their labor

BENJAMIN
Twelfth son of Jacob by Rachel (Ge 35:16-24; 46:19-21; 1Ch 2:2). Jacob refused to send him to Egypt, but relented (Ge 42-45).

BEREANS*
Ac 17:11 the *B* were of more noble character

BESTOWS
Ps 84:11 the LORD *b* favor and honor;

BETHLEHEM
Mt 2: 1 After Jesus was born in *B* in Judea,

BETRAY
Pr 25: 9 do not *b* another man's confidence,

BIND (BINDS)
Dt 6: 8 and *b* them on your foreheads.
Pr 6:21 *B* them upon your heart forever;
Isa 61: 1 me to *b* up the brokenhearted,
Mt 16:19 whatever you *b* on earth will be

BINDS (BIND)
Ps 147: 3 and *b* up their wounds.
Isa 30:26 when the LORD *b* up the bruises

BIRDS
Mt 8:20 and *b* of the air have nests,

BIRTH (BEAR)
Ps 58: 3 Even from *b* the wicked go astray;
Mt 1:18 This is how the *b* of Jesus Christ
1Pe 1: 3 great mercy he has given us new *b*

BIRTHRIGHT (BEAR)
Ge 25:34 So Esau despised his *b*.

BLAMELESS
Ge 17: 1 walk before me and be *b*.
Job 1: 1 This man was *b* and upright;
Ps 84:11 from those whose walk is *b*.
119: 1 Blessed are they whose ways are *b*,
Pr 19: 1 Better a poor man whose walk is *b*
1Co 1: 8 so that you will be *b* on the day
Eph 5:27 any other blemish, but holy and *b*.
Php 2:15 so that you may become *b* and pure
1Th 3:13 hearts so that you will be *b*
5:23 and body be kept *b* at the coming
Tit 1: 6 An elder must be *b*, the husband of
Heb 7:26 *b*, pure, set apart from sinners,
2Pe 3:14 effort to be found spotless, *b*

BLASPHEMES
Mk 3:29 whoever *b* against the Holy Spirit

BLEMISH
1Pe 1:19 a lamb without *b* or defect.

BLESS (BLESSED BLESSING BLESSINGS)
Ge 12: 3 I will *b* those who *b* you,
Ro 12:14 Bless those who persecute you; *b*

BLESSED (BLESS)
Ge 1:22 God *b* them and said, "Be fruitful
2: 3 And God *b* the seventh day
22:18 nations on earth will be *b*,
Ps 1: 1 *B* is the man
2:12 *B* are all who take refuge in him.
33:12 *B* is the nation whose God is
41: 1 *B* is he who has regard for the weak
84: 5 *B* are those whose strength is
106: 3 *B* are they who maintain justice,
112: 1 *B* is the man who fears the LORD,
118:26 *B* is he who comes in the name
Pr 29:18 but *b* is he who keeps the law.
31:28 Her children arise and call her *b*;
Mt 5: 3 saying: "*B* are the poor in spirit,
5: 4 *B* are those who mourn,
5: 5 *B* are the meek,
5: 6 *B* are those who hunger
5: 7 *B* are the merciful,
5: 8 *B* are the pure in heart,
5: 9 *B* are the peacemakers,
5:10 *B* are those who are persecuted
5:11 "*B* are you when people insult you,
Lk 1:48 on all generations will call me *b*,
Jn 12:13 "*B* is he who comes in the name
Ac 20:35 'It is more *b* to give than to receive
Tit 2:13 while we wait for the *b* hope—
Jas 1:12 *B* is the man who perseveres
Rev 1: 3 *B* is the one who reads the words
22:14 "*B* are those who wash their robes,

BLESSING (BLESS)
Eze 34:26 there will be showers of *b*.

BLESSINGS (BLESS)
Pr 10: 6 *B* crown the head of the righteous,

BLIND
Mt 15:14 a *b* man leads a *b* man, both will fall
23:16 "Woe to you, *b* guides! You say,
Jn 9:25 I was *b* but now I see!"

BLOOD
Ge 9: 6 "Whoever sheds the *b* of man,
Ex 12:13 and when I see the *b*, I will pass
24: 8 "This is the *b* of the covenant that
Lev 17:11 For the life of a creature is in the *b*,
Ps 72:14 for precious is their *b* in his sight.
Pr 6:17 hands that shed innocent *b*,
Mt 26:28 This is my *b* of the covenant,
Ro 3:25 of atonement, through faith in his *b*
5: 9 have now been justified by his *b*,
1Co 11:25 cup is the new covenant in my *b*;
Eph 1: 7 we have redemption through his *b*,
2:13 near through the *b* of Christ.
Col 1:20 by making peace through his *b*,
Heb 9:12 once for all by his own *b*,
9:22 of *b* there is no forgiveness.
1Pe 1:19 but with the precious *b* of Christ,
1Jn 1: 7 and the *b* of Jesus, his Son,

Rev 1: 5 has freed us from our sins by his *b*,
5: 9 with your *b* you purchased men
7:14 white in the *b* of the Lamb.
12:11 him by the *b* of the Lamb

BLOT (BLOTS)
Ex 32:32 then *b* me out of the book you have
Ps 51: 1 *b* out my transgressions.
Rev 3: 5 I will never *b* out his name

BLOTS (BLOT)
Isa 43:25 "I, even I, am he who *b* out

BLOWN
Eph 4:14 and *b* here and there by every wind
Jas 1: 6 doubts is like a wave of the sea, *b*

BOAST
1Ki 20:11 armor should not *b* like one who
Ps 34: 2 My soul will *b* in the LORD;
44: 8 In God we make our *b* all day long,
Pr 27: 1 Do not *b* about tomorrow,
1Co 1:31 Let him who boasts *b* in the Lord."
Gal 6:14 May I never *b* except in the cross
Eph 2: 9 not by works, so that no one can *b*.

BOAZ
Wealthy Bethlehemite who showed favor to Ruth (Ru 2), married her (Ru 4). Ancestor of David (Ru 4:18-22; 1Ch 2:12-15), Jesus (Mt 1:5-16; Lk 3:23-32).

BODIES (BODY)
Ro 12: 1 to offer your *b* as living sacrifices,
1Co 6:15 not know that your *b* are members
Eph 5:28 to love their wives as their own *b*.

BODY (BODIES)
Zec 13: 6 What are these wounds on your *b*?'
Mt 10:28 afraid of those who kill the *b*
26:26 saying, "Take and eat; this is my *b*
26:41 spirit is willing, but the *b* is weak."
Jn 13:10 wash his feet; his whole *b* is clean.
Ro 6:13 Do not offer the parts of your *b*
12: 4 us has one *b* with many members,
1Co 6:19 not know that your *b* is a temple
11:24 "This is my *b*, which is for you;
12:12 The *b* is a unit, though it is made up
Eph 5:30 for we are members of his *b*.

BOLD (BOLDNESS)
Ps 138: 3 you made me *b* and stouthearted.
Pr 21:29 A wicked man puts up a *b* front,
28: 1 but the righteous are as *b* as a lion.

BOLDNESS* (BOLD)
Ac 4:29 to speak your word with great *b*.

BONDAGE
Ezr 9: 9 God has not deserted us in our *b*.

BOOK (BOOKS)
Jos 1: 8 Do not let this *B* of the Law depart
Ne 8: 8 They read from the *B* of the Law
Jn 20:30 which are not recorded in this *b*.
Php 4: 3 whose names are in the *b* of life.
Rev 21:27 written in the Lamb's *b* of life.

BOOKS (BOOK)
Ecc 12:12 Of making many *b* there is no end,

BORN (BEAR)
Isa 9: 6 For to us a child is *b*,
Jn 3: 7 at my saying, 'You must be *b* again
1Pe 1:23 For you have been *b* again,
1Jn 4: 7 Everyone who loves has been *b*
5: 1 believes that Jesus is the Christ is *b*

BORROWER
Pr 22: 7 and the *b* is servant to the lender.

BOUGHT
Ac 20:28 which he *b* with his own blood.
1Co 6:20 You are not your own; you were *b*
7:23 You were *b* at a price; do not
2Pe 2: 1 the sovereign Lord who *b* them—

BOW
Ps 95: 6 Come, let us *b* down in worship,
Isa 45:23 Before me every knee will *b*;
Ro 14:11 'every knee will *b* before me;
Php 2:10 name of Jesus every knee should *b*,

BRANCH (BRANCHES)
Isa 4: 2 In that day the *B* of the LORD will
Jer 33:15 I will make a righteous *B* sprout

BRANCHES (BRANCH)
Jn 15: 5 "I am the vine; you are the *b*.

BRAVE
2Sa 2: 7 Now then, be strong and *b*,

BREAD
Dt 8: 3 that man does not live on *b* alone
Pr 30: 8 but give me only my daily *b*.
Ecc 11: 1 Cast your *b* upon the waters,
Isa 55: 2 Why spend money on what is not *b*
Mt 4: 4 'Man does not live on *b* alone,
6:11 Give us today our daily *b*.
Jn 6:35 Jesus declared, "I am the *b* of life.
21:13 took the *b* and gave it to them,
1Co 11:23 took *b*, and when he had given

BREAK (BREAKING BROKEN)
Nu 30: 2 he must not *b* his word
Jdg 2: 1 'I will never *b* my covenant
Isa 42: 3 A bruised reed he will not *b*,
Mt 12:20 A bruised reed he will not *b*,

BREAKING (BREAK)
Jas 2:10 at just one point is guilty of *b* all

BREASTPIECE (BREASTPLATE)
Ex 28:15 Fashion a *b* for making decisions—

BREASTPLATE* (BREASTPIECE)
Isa 59:17 He put on righteousness as his *b*,
Eph 6:14 with the *b* of righteousness in place
1Th 5: 8 putting on faith and love as a *b*,

BREATHED (GOD-BREATHED)
Ge 2: 7 *b* into his nostrils the breath of life,
Jn 20:22 And with that he *b* on them

BREEDS*
Pr 13:10 Pride only *b* quarrels,

BRIBE
Ex 23: 8 "Do not accept a *b*,
Pr 6:35 will refuse the *b*, however great it

BRIDE
Rev 19: 7 and his *b* has made herself ready,

BRIGHTER (BRIGHTNESS)
Pr 4:18 shining ever *b* till the full light

BRIGHTNESS (BRIGHTER)
2Sa 22:13 Out of the *b* of his presence
Da 12: 3 who are wise will shine like the *b*

BROAD
Mt 7:13 and *b* is the road that leads

BROKEN (BREAK)
Ps 51:17 The sacrifices of God are a *b* spirit;
Ecc 4:12 of three strands is not quickly *b*.
Jn 10:35 and the Scripture cannot be *b*—

BROKENHEARTED* (HEART)
Ps 34:18 The LORD is close to the *b*
109:16 and the needy and the *b*.
147: 3 He heals the *b*
Isa 61: 1 He has sent me to bind up the *b*,

BROTHER (BROTHER'S BROTHERS)
Pr 17:17 and a *b* is born for adversity.
18:24 a friend who sticks closer than a *b*.
27:10 neighbor nearby than a *b* far away.
Mt 5:24 and be reconciled to your *b*;
18:15 "If your *b* sins against you,
Mk 3:35 Whoever does God's will is my *b*
Lk 17: 3 "If your *b* sins, rebuke him,
1Co 8:13 if what I eat causes my *b* to fall
1Jn 2:10 Whoever loves his *b* lives
4:21 loves God must also love his *b*.

BROTHER'S (BROTHER)
Ge 4: 9 "Am I my *b* keeper?" The LORD

BROTHERS (BROTHER)
Ps 133: 1 is when *b* live together in unity!
Pr 6:19 who stirs up dissension among *b*.
Mt 25:40 one of the least of these *b* of mine,
Mk 10:29 or *b* or sisters or mother or father
Heb 13: 1 Keep on loving each other as *b*.
1Pe 3: 8 be sympathetic, love as *b*,
1Jn 3:14 death to life, because we love our *b*.

BUILD (BUILDING BUILDS BUILT)
Mt 16:18 and on this rock I will *b* my church,
Ac 20:32 which can *b* you up and give you
1Co 14:12 excel in gifts that *b* up the church.
1Th 5:11 one another and *b* each other up,

BUILDING (BUILD)
1Co 3: 9 you are God's field, God's *b*.
2Co 10: 8 us for *b* you up rather
Eph 4:29 helpful for *b* others up according

BUILDS (BUILD)
Ps 127: 1 Unless the LORD *b* the house,
1Co 3:10 one should be careful how he *b*.
8: 1 Knowledge puffs up, but love *b* up.

BUILT (BUILD)
Mt 7:24 is like a wise man who *b* his house
Eph 2:20 *b* on the foundation of the apostles
4:12 the body of Christ may be *b* up

BURDEN (BURDENED BURDENS)
Ps 38: 4 like a *b* too heavy to bear.
Mt 11:30 my yoke is easy and my *b* is light."

BURDENED (BURDEN)
Gal 5: 1 do not let yourselves be *b* again

BURDENS (BURDEN)
Ps 68:19 who daily bears our *b*.
Gal 6: 2 Carry each other's *b*,

BURIED
Ro 6: 4 *b* with him through baptism
1Co 15: 4 that he was *b*, that he was raised

BURNING
Lev 6: 9 the fire must be kept *b* on the altar.
Ro 12:20 you will heap *b* coals on his head."

BUSINESS
Da 8:27 and went about the king's *b*.
1Th 4:11 to mind your own *b* and to work

BUSY
1Ki 20:40 While your servant was *b* here
2Th 3:11 They are not *b*; they are
Tit 2: 5 to be *b* at home, to be kind,

CAESAR
Mt 22:21 "Give to *C* what is Caesar's,

CAIN
Firstborn of Adam (Ge 4:1), murdered brother Abel (Ge 4:1-16; 1Jn 3:12).

CALEB
Judahite who spied out Canaan (Nu 13:6); allowed to enter land because of faith (Nu 13:30-14:38; Dt 1:36). Possessed Hebron (Jos 14:6-15:19).

CALF
Ex 32: 4 into an idol cast in the shape of a *c*,
Lk 15:23 Bring the fattened *c* and kill it.

CALL (CALLED CALLING CALLS)
Ps 105: 1 to the LORD, *c* on his name;
145:18 near to all who *c* on him,
Pr 31:28 children arise and *c* her blessed;
Isa 5:20 Woe to those who *c* evil good
55: 6 *c* on him while he is near.
65:24 Before they *c* I will answer;
Jer 33: 3 '*C* to me and I will answer you
Mt 9:13 come to *c* the righteous,
Ro 10:12 and richly blesses all who *c* on him,
11:29 gifts and his *c* are irrevocable.
1Th 4: 7 For God did not *c* us to be impure,

CALLED (CALL)
1Sa 3: 5 and said, "Here I am; you *c* me."
2Ch 7:14 if my people, who are *c*
Ps 34: 6 This poor man *c*, and the LORD
Mt 21:13 " 'My house will be *c* a house
Ro 8:30 And those he predestined, he also *c*
1Co 7:15 God has *c* us to live in peace.
Gal 5:13 You, my brothers, were *c* to be free
1Pe 2: 9 of him who *c* you out of darkness

CALLING (CALL)
Jn 1:23 I am the voice of one *c* in the desert
Ac 22:16 wash your sins away, *c* on his name
Eph 4: 1 worthy of the *c* you have received.
2Pe 1:10 all the more eager to make your *c*

CALLS (CALL)
Joel 2:32 And everyone who *c*
Jn 10: 3 He *c* his own sheep by name
Ro 10:13 "Everyone who *c* on the name

CAMEL
Mt 19:24 it is easier for a *c* to go
23:24 strain out a gnat but swallow a *c*.

CANAAN
1Ch 16:18 "To you I will give the land of *C*

CANCELED
Lk 7:42 so he *c* the debts of both.
Col 2:14 having *c* the written code,

CAPITAL
Dt 21:22 guilty of a *c* offense is put to death

CAPSTONE (STONE)
Ps 118:22 has become the *c*;
1Pe 2: 7 has become the *c*,"

CARE (CAREFUL CARES CARING)
Ps 8: 4 the son of man that you *c* for him?
Pr 29: 7 The righteous *c* about justice
Lk 10:34 him to an inn and took *c* of him.
Jn 21:16 Jesus said, "Take *c* of my sheep."
Heb 2: 6 the son of man that you *c* for him?
1Pe 5: 2 of God's flock that is under your *c*,

CAREFUL (CARE)
Ex 23:13 "Be *c* to do everything I have said
Dt 6: 3 be *c* to obey so that it may go well

Jos 23: 6 be *c* to obey all that is written
23:11 be very *c* to love the LORD your
Pr 13:24 he who loves him is *c*
Mt 6: 1 "Be *c* not to do your 'acts
Ro 12:17 Be *c* to do what is right in the eyes
1Co 3:10 each one should be *c* how he builds
8: 9 Be *c*, however, that the exercise
Eph 5:15 Be very *c*, then, how you live—

CARELESS
Mt 12:36 for every *c* word they have spoken.

CARES (CARE)
Ps 55:22 Cast your *c* on the LORD
Na 1: 7 He *c* for those who trust in him,
Eph 5:29 but he feeds and *c* for it, just
1Pe 5: 7 on him because he *c* for you.

CARING* (CARE)
1Th 2: 7 like a mother *c* for her little
1Ti 5: 4 practice by *c* for their own family

CARRIED (CARRY)
Ex 19: 4 and how I *c* you on eagles' wings
Isa 53: 4 and *c* our sorrows,
Heb 13: 9 Do not be *c* away by all kinds
2Pe 1:21 as they were *c* along by the Holy

CARRIES (CARRY)
Dt 32:11 and *c* them on its pinions.
Isa 40:11 and *c* them close to his heart;

CARRY (CARRIED CARRIES)
Lk 14:27 anyone who does not *c* his cross
Gal 6: 2 *C* each other's burdens,
6: 5 for each one should *c* his own load.

CAST
Ps 22:18 and *c* lots for my clothing.
55:22 *C* your cares on the LORD
Ecc 11: 1 *C* your bread upon the waters,
Jn 19:24 and *c* lots for my clothing."
1Pe 5: 7 *C* all your anxiety on him

CATCH (CAUGHT)
Lk 5:10 from now on you will *c* men."

CATTLE
Ps 50:10 and the *c* on a thousand hills.

CAUGHT (CATCH)
1Th 4:17 and are left will be *c* up together

CAUSE (CAUSES)
Pr 24:28 against your neighbor without *c*,
Ecc 8: 3 Do not stand up for a bad *c*,
Mt 18: 7 of the things that *c* people to sin!
Ro 14:21 else that will *c* your brother
1Co 10:32 Do not *c* anyone to stumble,

CAUSES (CAUSE)
Isa 8:14 a stone that *c* men to stumble
Mt 18: 6 if anyone *c* one of these little ones

CAUTIOUS*
Pr 12:26 A righteous man is *c* in friendship,

CEASE
Ps 46: 9 He makes wars *c* to the ends

CENSER
Lev 16:12 is to take a *c* full of burning coals

CENTURION
Mt 8: 5 had entered Capernaum, a *c* came

CERTAIN (CERTAINTY)
2Pe 1:19 word of the prophets made more *c*,

CERTAINTY* (CERTAIN)
Lk 1: 4 so that you may know the *c*
Jn 17: 8 They knew with *c* that I came

CHAFF
Ps 1: 4 They are like *c*

CHAINED
2Ti 2: 9 But God's word is not *c*.

CHAMPION
Ps 19: 5 like a *c* rejoicing to run his course.

CHANGE (CHANGED)
1Sa 15:29 of Israel does not lie or *c* his mind;
Ps 110: 4 and will not *c* his mind:
Jer 7: 5 If you really *c* your ways
Mal 3: 6 "I the LORD do not *c*.
Mt 18: 3 unless you *c* and become like little
Heb 7:21 and will not *c* his mind:
Jas 1:17 who does not *c* like shifting

CHANGED (CHANGE)
1Co 15:51 but we will all be *c*— in a flash,

CHARACTER
Ru 3:11 that you are a woman of noble *c*.
Pr 31:10 A wife of noble *c* who can find?
Ro 5: 4 perseverance, *c*; and *c*, hope.
1Co 15:33 "Bad company corrupts good *c*."

CHARGE
Ro 8:33 Who will bring any *c*
2Co 11: 7 the gospel of God to you free of *c*?
2Ti 4: 1 I give you this *c*: Preach the Word;

CHARIOTS
2Ki 6:17 and *c* of fire all around Elisha.
Ps 20: 7 Some trust in *c* and some in horses,

CHARM
Pr 31:30 *C* is deceptive, and beauty is

CHASES
Pr 12:11 he who *c* fantasies lacks judgment.

CHATTER* (CHATTERING)
1Ti 6:20 Turn away from godless *c*
2Ti 2:16 Avoid godless *c*, because those

CHATTERING* (CHATTER)
Pr 10: 8 but a *c* fool comes to ruin.
10:10 and a *c* fool comes to ruin.

CHEAT* (CHEATED)
Mal 1:14 "Cursed is the *c* who has
1Co 6: 8 you yourselves *c* and do wrong,

CHEATED (CHEAT)
Lk 19: 8 if I have *c* anybody out of anything,
1Co 6: 7 Why not rather be *c*? Instead,

CHEEK
Mt 5:39 someone strikes you on the right *c*,

CHEERFUL* (CHEERS)
Pr 15:13 A happy heart makes the face *c*,
15:15 but the *c* heart has a continual feast
15:30 A *c* look brings joy to the heart,
17:22 A *c* heart is good medicine,
2Co 9: 7 for God loves a *c* giver.

CHEERS (CHEERFUL)
Pr 12:25 but a kind word *c* him up.

CHILD (CHILDISH CHILDREN)
Pr 20:11 Even a *c* is known by his actions,
22: 6 Train a *c* in the way he should go,
22:15 Folly is bound up in the heart of a *c*
23:13 not withhold discipline from a *c*;

CHRISTIAN (CHRIST)
1Pe 4:16 as a *C*, do not be ashamed,

CHRISTS (CHRIST)
Mt 24:24 For false *C* and false prophets will

CHURCH
Mt 16:18 and on this rock I will build my *c*,
18:17 if he refuses to listen even to the *c*,
Ac 20:28 Be shepherds of the *c* of God,
1Co 5:12 of mine to judge those outside the *c*
14: 4 but he who prophesies edifies the *c*.
14:12 to excel in gifts that build up the *c*.
14:26 done for the strengthening of the *c*.
Eph 5:23 as Christ is the head of the *c*,
Col 1:24 the sake of his body, which is the *c*.

CIRCUMCISED
Ge 17:10 Every male among you shall be *c*.

CIRCUMSTANCES
Php 4:11 to be content whatever the *c*.
1Th 5:18 continually; give thanks in all *c*,

CITIZENS (CITIZENSHIP)
Eph 2:19 but fellow *c* with God's people

CITIZENSHIP (CITIZENS)
Php 3:20 But our *c* is in heaven.

CITY
Mt 5:14 A *c* on a hill cannot be hidden.
Heb 13:14 here we do not have an enduring *c*,

CIVILIAN*
2Ti 2: 4 a soldier gets involved in *c* affairs—

CLAIM (CLAIMS)
Pr 25: 6 do not *c* a place among great men;
1Jn 1: 6 If we *c* to have fellowship
1: 8 If we *c* to be without sin, we
1:10 If we *c* we have not sinned,

CLAIMS (CLAIM)
Jas 2:14 if a man *c* to have faith
1Jn 2: 6 Whoever *c* to live in him must walk
2: 9 Anyone who *c* to be in the light

CLAP
Ps 47: 1 *C* your hands, all you nations;
Isa 55:12 will *c* their hands.

CLAY
Isa 45: 9 Does the *c* say to the potter,
64: 8 We are the *c*, you are the potter;
Jer 18: 6 "Like *c* in the hand of the potter,
La 4: 2 are now considered as pots of *c*,
Da 2:33 partly of iron and partly of baked *c*.
Ro 9:21 of the same lump of *c* some pottery
2Co 4: 7 we have this treasure in jars of *c*
2Ti 2:20 and *c*; some are for noble purposes

CLEAN
Lev 16:30 you will be *c* from all your sins.
Ps 24: 4 He who has *c* hands and a pure
Mt 12:44 the house unoccupied, swept *c*
23:25 You *c* the outside of the cup
Mk 7:19 Jesus declared all foods "*c*.")
Jn 13:10 to wash his feet; his whole body is *c*
15: 3 are already *c* because of the word
Ac 10:15 impure that God has made *c*."
Ro 14:20 All food is *c*, but it is wrong

CLING (CLINGS)
Ro 12: 9 Hate what is evil; *c* to what is good.

CLINGS (CLING)
Ps 63: 8 My soul *c* to you;

CLOAK
2Ki 4:29 "Tuck your *c* into your belt,

CLOSE (CLOSER)
Ps 34:18 LORD is *c* to the brokenhearted
Isa 40:11 and carries them *c* to his heart;
Jer 30:21 himself to be *c* to me?'

CLOSER (CLOSE)
Ex 3: 5 "Do not come any *c*," God said.
Pr 18:24 there is a friend who sticks *c*

CLOTHE (CLOTHED CLOTHES CLOTHING)
Ps 45: 3 *c* yourself with splendor
Isa 52: 1 *c* yourself with strength.
Ro 13:14 *c* yourselves with the Lord Jesus
Col 3:12 *c* yourselves with compassion,
1Pe 5: 5 *c* yourselves with humility

CLOTHED (CLOTHE)
Ps 30:11 removed my sackcloth and *c* me
Pr 31:25 She is *c* with strength and dignity;
Lk 24:49 until you have been *c* with power

CLOTHES (CLOTHE)
Mt 6:25 the body more important than *c*?
6:28 "And why do you worry about *c*?
Jn 11:44 Take off the grave *c* and let him go

CLOTHING (CLOTHE)
Dt 22: 5 A woman must not wear men's *c*,
Mt 7:15 They come to you in sheep's *c*,

CLOUD (CLOUDS)
Ex 13:21 them in a pillar of *c* to guide them
Isa 19: 1 See, the LORD rides on a swift *c*
Lk 21:27 of Man coming in a *c* with power
Heb 12: 1 by such a great *c* of witnesses,

CLOUDS (CLOUD)
Ps 104: 3 He makes the *c* his chariot
Da 7:13 coming with the *c* of heaven.
Mk 13:26 coming in *c* with great power
1Th 4:17 with them in the *c* to meet the Lord

CO-HEIRS* (INHERIT)
Ro 8:17 heirs of God and *c* with Christ,

COALS
Pr 25:22 you will heap burning *c* on his head
Ro 12:20 you will heap burning *c* on his head

COLD
Pr 25:25 Like *c* water to a weary soul
Mt 10:42 if anyone gives even a cup of *c* water
24:12 the love of most will grow *c*,

COMFORT (COMFORTED COMFORTS)
Ps 23: 4 rod and your staff, they *c* me.
119:52 and I find *c* in them.
119:76 May your unfailing love be my *c*,
Zec 1:17 and the LORD will again *c* Zion
1Co 14: 3 encouragement and *c*.
2Co 1: 4 so that we can *c* those
2: 7 you ought to forgive and *c* him,

COMFORTED (COMFORT)
Mt 5: 4 for they will be *c*.

COMFORTS* (COMFORT)
Job 29:25 I was like one who *c* mourners.
Isa 49:13 For the LORD *c* his people
51:12 "I, even I, am he who *c* you.
66:13 As a mother *c* her child,
2Co 1: 4 who *c* us in all our troubles,
7: 6 But God, who *c* the downcast,

COMMAND (COMMANDED COMMANDING COMMANDMENT COMMANDMENTS COMMANDS)
Ex 7: 2 You are to say everything I *c* you,

Nu 24:13 to go beyond the *c* of the LORD—
Dt 4: 2 Do not add to what I *c* you
30:16 For I *c* you today to love
32:46 so that you may *c* your children
Ps 91:11 For he will *c* his angels concerning
Pr 13:13 but he who respects a *c* is rewarded
Ecc 8: 2 Obey the king's *c*, I say,
Joel 2:11 mighty are those who obey his *c*.
Jn 14:15 love me, you will obey what I *c*.
15:12 My *c* is this: Love each other
1Co 14:37 writing to you is the Lord's *c*.
Gal 5:14 law is summed up in a single *c*:
1Ti 1: 5 goal of this *c* is love, which comes
Heb 11: 3 universe was formed at God's *c*,
1Jn 3:23 this is his *c*: to believe in the name
2Jn : 6 his *c* is that you walk in love.

COMMANDED (COMMAND)
Ps 33: 9 he *c*, and it stood firm.
148: 5 for he *c* and they were created.
Mt 28:20 to obey everything I have *c* you.
1Co 9:14 Lord has *c* that those who preach
1Jn 3:23 and to love one another as he *c* us.

COMMANDING (COMMAND)
2Ti 2: 4 he wants to please his *c* officer.

COMMANDMENT (COMMAND)
Jos 22: 5 But be very careful to keep the *c*
Mt 22:38 This is the first and greatest *c*.
Jn 13:34 "A new *c* I give you: Love one
Ro 7:12 and the *c* is holy, righteous
Eph 6: 2 which is the first *c* with a promise

COMMANDMENTS (COMMAND)
Ex 20: 6 who love me and keep my *c*.
34:28 of the covenant—the Ten *C*.
Ecc 12:13 Fear God and keep his *c*,
Mt 5:19 one of the least of these *c*
22:40 the Prophets hang on these two *c*."

COMMANDS (COMMAND)
Dt 7: 9 those who love him and keep his *c*.
11:27 the blessing if you obey the *c*
Ps 112: 1 who finds great delight in his *c*.
119:47 for I delight in your *c*
119:86 All your *c* are trustworthy;
119:98 Your *c* make me wiser
119:127 Because I love your *c*
119:143 but your *c* are my delight.
119:172 for all your *c* are righteous.
Pr 3: 1 but keep my *c* in your heart,
6:23 For these *c* are a lamp,
10: 8 The wise in heart accept *c*,
Da 9: 4 all who love him and obey his *c*,
Mt 5:19 teaches these *c* will be called great
Jn 14:21 Whoever has my *c* and obeys them,
Ac 17:30 but now he *c* all people everywhere
1Co 7:19 Keeping God's *c* is what counts.
1Jn 5: 3 And his *c* are not burdensome,
5: 3 This is love for God: to obey his *c*.

COMMEND (COMMENDED COMMENDS)
Ecc 8:15 So I *c* the enjoyment of life,
Ro 13: 3 do what is right and he will *c* you.
1Pe 2:14 and to *c* those who do right.

COMMENDED (COMMEND)
Heb 11:39 These were all *c* for their faith,

COMMENDS (COMMEND)
2Co 10:18 not the one who *c* himself who is

COMMIT (COMMITS COMMITTED)
Ex 20:14 "You shall not *c* adultery.
Ps 37: 5 *C* your way to the LORD;
Mt 5:27 that it was said, 'Do not *c* adultery.'
Lk 23:46 into your hands I *c* my spirit."
Ac 20:32 I *c* you to God and to the word
1Co 10: 8 We should not *c* sexual immorality,
1Pe 4:19 to God's will should *c* themselves

COMMITS (COMMIT)
Pr 6:32 man who *c* adultery lacks
29:22 a hot-tempered one *c* many sins.
Mt 19: 9 marries another woman *c* adultery

COMMITTED (COMMIT)
Nu 5: 7 and must confess the sin he has *c*.
1Ki 8:61 But your hearts must be fully *c*
2Ch 16: 9 those whose hearts are fully *c*
Mt 5:28 lustfully has already *c* adultery
2Co 5:19 And he has *c* to us the message
1Pe 2:22 "He *c* no sin,

COMMON
Pr 22: 2 Rich and poor have this in *c*:
1Co 10:13 has seized you except what is *c*
2Co 6:14 and wickedness have in *c*?

COMPANION (COMPANIONS)
Pr 13:20 but a *c* of fools suffers harm.
28: 7 a *c* of gluttons disgraces his father.
29: 3 *c* of prostitutes squanders his

COMPANIONS (COMPANION)
Pr 18:24 A man of many *c* may come to ruin

COMPANY
Pr 24: 1 do not desire their *c*;
Jer 15:17 I never sat in the *c* of revelers,
1Co 15:33 "Bad *c* corrupts good character."

COMPARED (COMPARING)
Eze 31: 2 Who can be *c* with you in majesty?
Php 3: 8 I consider everything a loss *c*

COMPARING* (COMPARED)
Ro 8:18 present sufferings are not worth *c*
2Co 8: 8 the sincerity of your love by *c* it
Gal 6: 4 without *c* himself to somebody else

COMPASSION (COMPASSIONATE COMPASSIONS)
Ex 33:19 I will have *c* on whom I will have *c*.
Ne 9:19 of your great *c* you did not
9:28 in your *c* you delivered them time
Ps 51: 1 according to your great *c*
103: 4 and crowns you with love and *c*.
103:13 As a father has *c* on his children,
145: 9 he has *c* on all he has made.
Isa 49:13 and will have *c* on his afflicted ones
49:15 and have no *c* on the child she has
Hos 2:19 in love and *c*.
11: 8 all my *c* is aroused.
Jnh 3: 9 with *c* turn from his fierce anger
Mt 9:36 When he saw the crowds, he had *c*
Mk 8: 2 "I have *c* for these people;
Ro 9:15 and I will have *c* on whom I have *c*
Col 3:12 clothe yourselves with *c*, kindness,
Jas 5:11 The Lord is full of *c* and mercy.

COMPASSIONATE (COMPASSION)
Ne 9:17 gracious and *c*, slow to anger
Ps 103: 8 The LORD is *c* and gracious,
112: 4 the gracious and *c* and righteous
Eph 4:32 Be kind and *c* to one another,
1Pe 3: 8 love as brothers, be *c* and humble.

COMPASSIONS* (COMPASSION)
La 3:22 for his *c* never fail.

COMPELLED (COMPELS)
Ac 20:22 "And now, *c* by the Spirit,
1Co 9:16 I cannot boast, for I am *c* to preach.

COMPELS (COMPELLED)
2Co 5:14 For Christ's love *c* us, because we

CONSCIOUS*
Ro 3:20 through the law we become *c* of sin
1Pe 2:19 of unjust suffering because he is *c*

CONSECRATE (CONSECRATED)
Ex 13: 2 "*C* to me every firstborn male.
Lev 20: 7 " '*C* yourselves and be holy,

CONSECRATED (CONSECRATE)
Ex 29:43 and the place will be *c* by my glory.
1Ti 4: 5 because it is *c* by the word of God

CONSIDER (CONSIDERATE CONSIDERED CONSIDERS)
1Sa 12:24 *c* what great things he has done
Job 37:14 stop and *c* God's wonders.
Ps 8: 3 When I *c* your heavens,
107:43 and *c* the great love of the LORD.
143: 5 and *c* what your hands have done.
Lk 12:24 *C* the ravens: They do not sow
12:27 about the rest? "*C* how the lilies
Php 2: 3 but in humility *c* others better
3: 8 I *c* everything a loss compared
Heb 10:24 And let us *c* how we may spur one
Jas 1: 2 *C* it pure joy, my brothers,

CONSIDERATE* (CONSIDER)
Tit 3: 2 to be peaceable and *c*,
Jas 3:17 then peace-loving, *c*, submissive,
1Pe 2:18 only to those who are good and *c*,
3: 7 in the same way be *c* as you live

CONSIDERED (CONSIDER)
Job 1: 8 "Have you *c* my servant Job?
2: 3 "Have you *c* my servant Job?
Ps 44:22 we are *c* as sheep to be slaughtered.
Isa 53: 4 yet we *c* him stricken by God,
Ro 8:36 we are *c* as sheep to be slaughtered

CONSIDERS (CONSIDER)
Pr 31:16 She *c* a field and buys it;
Ro 14: 5 One man *c* one day more sacred
Jas 1:26 If anyone *c* himself religious

CONSIST
Lk 12:15 a man's life does not *c*

CONSOLATION
Ps 94:19 your *c* brought joy to my soul.

CONSTRUCTIVE*
1Co 10:23 but not everything is *c*.

CONSUME (CONSUMING)
Jn 2:17 "Zeal for your house will *c* me."

CONSUMING (CONSUME)
Dt 4:24 For the LORD your God is a *c* fire,
Heb 12:29 and awe, for our "God is a *c* fire."

CONTAIN
1Ki 8:27 the highest heaven, cannot *c* you.
2Pe 3:16 His letters *c* some things that are

CONTAMINATES*
2Co 7: 1 from everything that *c* body

CONTEMPT
Pr 14:31 He who oppresses the poor shows *c*
17: 5 He who mocks the poor shows *c*
18: 3 When wickedness comes, so does *c*
Da 12: 2 others to shame and everlasting *c*.
Ro 2: 4 Or do you show *c* for the riches
Gal 4:14 you did not treat me with *c*
1Th 5:20 do not treat prophecies with *c*.

CONTEND (CONTENDING)
Jude : 3 you to *c* for the faith that was once

CONTENDING* (CONTEND)
Php 1:27 *c* as one man for the faith

CONTENT (CONTENTMENT)
Pr 13:25 The righteous eat to their hearts' *c*,
Php 4:11 to be *c* whatever the circumstances
4:12 I have learned the secret of being *c*
1Ti 6: 8 and clothing, we will be *c* with that.
Heb 13: 5 and be *c* with what you have,

CONTENTMENT (CONTENT)
1Ti 6: 6 But godliness with *c* is great gain.

CONTINUAL (CONTINUE)
Pr 15:15 but the cheerful heart has a *c* feast.

CONTINUE (CONTINUAL)
Php 2:12 *c* to work out your salvation
2Ti 3:14 *c* in what you have learned
1Jn 5:18 born of God does not *c* to sin;
Rev 22:11 and let him who is holy *c* to be holy
22:11 let him who does right *c* to do right;

CONTRITE*
Ps 51:17 a broken and *c* heart,
Isa 57:15 also with him who is *c* and lowly
57:15 and to revive the heart of the *c*.
66: 2 he who is humble and *c* in spirit,

CONTROL (CONTROLLED SELF-CONTROL SELF-CONTROLLED)
Pr 29:11 a wise man keeps himself under *c*.
1Co 7: 9 But if they cannot *c* themselves,
7:37 but has *c* over his own will,
1Th 4: 4 you should learn to *c* his own body

CONTROLLED (CONTROL)
Ps 32: 9 but must be *c* by bit and bridle
Ro 8: 6 but the mind *c* by the Spirit is life
8: 8 Those *c* by the sinful nature cannot

CONTROVERSIES
Tit 3: 9 But avoid foolish *c* and genealogies

CONVERSATION
Col 4: 6 Let your *c* be always full of grace,

CONVERT
1Ti 3: 6 He must not be a recent *c*,

CONVICT
Jn 16: 8 he will *c* the world of guilt in regard

CONVINCED (CONVINCING)
Ro 8:38 For I am *c* that neither death
2Ti 1:12 and am *c* that he is able
3:14 have learned and have become *c*

CONVINCING* (CONVINCED)
Ac 1: 3 and gave many *c* proofs that he was

CORNELIUS*
Roman to whom Peter preached; first Gentile Christian (Ac 10).

CORNERSTONE (STONE)
Isa 28:16 a precious *c* for a sure foundation;
Eph 2:20 Christ Jesus himself as the chief *c*.
1Pe 2: 6 a chosen and precious *c*,

CORRECT (CORRECTING CORRECTION CORRECTS)
2Ti 4: 2 *c*, rebuke and encourage—

CORRECTING* (CORRECT)
2Ti 3:16 *c* and training in righteousness,

CORRECTION (CORRECT)
Pr 10:17 whoever ignores *c* leads others
12: 1 but he who hates *c* is stupid.
15: 5 whoever heeds *c* shows prudence.
15:10 he who hates *c* will die.
29:15 The rod of *c* imparts wisdom,

CORRECTS* **(CORRECT)**
Job 5:17 "Blessed is the man whom God *c*;
Pr 9: 7 Whoever *c* a mocker invites insult;

CORRUPT **(CORRUPTS)**
Ge 6:11 Now the earth was *c* in God's sight

CORRUPTS* **(CORRUPT)**
Ecc 7: 7 and a bribe *c* the heart.
1Co 15:33 "Bad company *c* good character."
Jas 3: 6 It *c* the whole person, sets

COST
Pr 4: 7 Though it *c* all you have, get
Isa 55: 1 milk without money and without *c*.
Rev 21: 6 to drink without *c* from the spring

COUNSEL **(COUNSELOR)**
1Ki 22: 5 "First seek the *c* of the LORD."
Pr 15:22 Plans fail for lack of *c*,
Rev 3:18 I *c* you to buy from me gold refined

COUNSELOR **(COUNSEL)**
Isa 9: 6 Wonderful *C*, Mighty God,
Jn 14:16 he will give you another *C* to be
14:26 But the *C*, the Holy Spirit,

COUNT **(COUNTING COUNTS)**
Ro 4: 8 whose sin the Lord will never *c*
6:11 *c* yourselves dead to sin

COUNTING **(COUNT)**
2Co 5:19 not *c* men's sins against them.

COUNTRY
Jn 4:44 prophet has no honor in his own *c*.)

COUNTS **(COUNT)**
Jn 6:63 The Spirit gives life; the flesh *c*
1Co 7:19 God's commands is what *c*.
Gal 5: 6 only thing that *c* is faith expressing

COURAGE **(COURAGEOUS)**
Ac 23:11 "Take *c*! As you have testified
1Co 16:13 stand firm in the faith; be men of *c*;

COURAGEOUS **(COURAGE)**
Dt 31: 6 Be strong and *c*.
Jos 1: 6 and *c*, because you will lead these

COURSE
Ps 19: 5 a champion rejoicing to run his *c*.
Pr 15:21 of understanding keeps a straight *c*.

COURTS
Ps 84:10 Better is one day in your *c*
100: 4 and his *c* with praise;

COVENANT **(COVENANTS)**
Ge 9: 9 "I now establish my *c* with you
Ex 19: 5 if you obey me fully and keep my *c*,
1Ch 16:15 He remembers his *c* forever,
Job 31: 1 "I made a *c* with my eyes
Jer 31:31 "when I will make a new *c*
1Co 11:25 "This cup is the new *c* in my blood;
Gal 4:24 One *c* is from Mount Sinai
Heb 9:15 Christ is the mediator of a new *c*,

COVENANTS **(COVENANT)**
Ro 9: 4 theirs the divine glory, the *c*,
Gal 4:24 for the women represent two *c*.

COVER **(COVER-UP COVERED COVERS)**
Ps 91: 4 He will *c* you with his feathers,
Jas 5:20 and *c* over a multitude of sins.

COVER-UP **(COVER)**
1Pe 2:16 but do not use your freedom as a *c*

COVERED **(COVER)**
Ps 32: 1 whose sins are *c*.
Isa 6: 2 With two wings they *c* their faces,
Ro 4: 7 whose sins are *c*.
1Co 11: 4 with his head *c* dishonors his head.

COVERS **(COVER)**
Pr 10:12 but love *c* over all wrongs.
1Pe 4: 8 love *c* over a multitude of sins.

COVET
Ex 20:17 You shall not *c* your neighbor's
Ro 13: 9 "Do not steal," "Do not *c*,"

COWARDLY*
Rev 21: 8 But the *c*, the unbelieving, the vile,

CRAFTINESS **(CRAFTY)**
1Co 3:19 "He catches the wise in their *c*";

CRAFTY **(CRAFTINESS)**
Ge 3: 1 the serpent was more *c* than any
2Co 12:16 *c* fellow that I am, I caught you

CRAVE
Pr 23: 3 Do not *c* his delicacies,
1Pe 2: 2 newborn babies, *c* pure spiritual

CREATE **(CREATED CREATION CREATOR)**
Ps 51:10 *C* in me a pure heart, O God,
Isa 45:18 he did not *c* it to be empty,

CREATED **(CREATE)**
Ge 1: 1 In the beginning God *c* the heavens
1:21 God *c* the great creatures of the sea
1:27 So God *c* man in his own image,
Ps 148: 5 for he commanded and they were *c*
Isa 42: 5 he who *c* the heavens and stretched
Ro 1:25 and served *c* things rather
1Co 11: 9 neither was man *c* for woman,
Col 1:16 For by him all things were *c*:
1Ti 4: 4 For everything God *c* is good,
Rev 10: 6 who *c* the heavens and all that is

CREATION **(CREATE)**
Mk 16:15 and preach the good news to all *c*.
Jn 17:24 me before the *c* of the world.
Ro 8:19 The *c* waits in eager expectation
8:39 depth, nor anything else in all *c*,
2Co 5:17 he is a new *c*; the old has gone,
Col 1:15 God, the firstborn over all *c*.
1Pe 1:20 chosen before the *c* of the world,
Rev 13: 8 slain from the *c* of the world.

CREATOR **(CREATE)**
Ge 14:22 God Most High, *C* of heaven
Ro 1:25 created things rather than the *C*—

CREATURE **(CREATURES)**
Lev 17:11 For the life of a *c* is in the blood,

CREATURES **(CREATURE)**
Ge 6:19 bring into the ark two of all living *c*,
Ps 104:24 the earth is full of your *c*.

CREDIT **(CREDITED)**
Ro 4:24 to whom God will *c* righteousness
1Pe 2:20 it to your *c* if you receive a beating

CREDITED **(CREDIT)**
Ge 15: 6 and he *c* it to him as righteousness.
Ro 4: 5 his faith is *c* as righteousness.
Gal 3: 6 and it was *c* to him as righteousness
Jas 2:23 and it was *c* to him as righteousness

CRIED **(CRY)**
Ps 18: 6 I *c* to my God for help.

CRIMSON
Isa 1:18 though they are red as *c*,

CRIPPLED
Mk 9:45 better for you to enter life *c*

CRITICISM
2Co 8:20 We want to avoid any *c*

CROOKED
Pr 10: 9 he who takes *c* paths will be found
Php 2:15 children of God without fault in a *c*

CROSS
Mt 10:38 and anyone who does not take his *c*
Lk 9:23 take up his *c* daily and follow me.
Ac 2:23 to death by nailing him to the *c.*
1Co 1:17 lest the *c* of Christ be emptied
Gal 6:14 in the *c* of our Lord Jesus Christ,
Php 2: 8 even death on a *c!*
Col 1:20 through his blood, shed on the *c.*
2:14 he took it away, nailing it to the *c.*
2:15 triumphing over them by the *c.*
Heb 12: 2 set before him endured the *c,*

CROWD
Ex 23: 2 Do not follow the *c* in doing wrong.

CROWN (CROWNED CROWNS)
Pr 4: 9 present you with a *c* of splendor."
10: 6 Blessings *c* the head
12: 4 noble character is her husband's *c,*
17: 6 Children's children are a *c*
Isa 61: 3 to bestow on them a *c* of beauty
Zec 9:16 like jewels in a *c.*
Mt 27:29 then twisted together a *c* of thorns
1Co 9:25 it to get a *c* that will last forever.
2Ti 4: 8 store for me the *c* of righteousness,
Rev 2:10 and I will give you the *c* of life.

CROWNED (CROWN)
Ps 8: 5 and *c* him with glory and honor.
Pr 14:18 the prudent are *c* with knowledge.
Heb 2: 7 you *c* him with glory and honor

CROWNS (CROWN)
Rev 4:10 They lay their *c* before the throne
19:12 and on his head are many *c.*

CRUCIFIED (CRUCIFY)
Mt 20:19 to be mocked and flogged and *c.*
27:38 Two robbers were *c* with him,
Lk 24: 7 be *c* and on the third day be raised
Jn 19:18 Here they *c* him, and with him two
Ac 2:36 whom you *c,* both Lord and Christ
Ro 6: 6 For we know that our old self was *c*
1Co 1:23 but we preach Christ *c:* a stumbling
2: 2 except Jesus Christ and him *c.*
Gal 2:20 I have been *c* with Christ
5:24 Christ Jesus have *c* the sinful

CRUCIFY (CRUCIFIED CRUCIFYING)
Mt 27:22 They all answered, *"C* him!" "Why
27:31 Then they led him away to *c* him.

CRUCIFYING* (CRUCIFY)
Heb 6: 6 to their loss they are *c* the Son

CRUSH (CRUSHED)
Ge 3:15 he will *c* your head,
Isa 53:10 it was the LORD's will to *c* him
Ro 16:20 The God of peace will soon *c* Satan

CRUSHED (CRUSH)
Ps 34:18 and saves those who are *c* in spirit.
Isa 53: 5 he was *c* for our iniquities;
2Co 4: 8 not *c;* perplexed, but not in despair;

CRY (CRIED)
Ps 34:15 and his ears are attentive to their *c;*
40: 1 he turned to me and heard my *c.*
130: 1 Out of the depths I *c* to you,

CUP
Ps 23: 5 my *c* overflows.
Mt 10:42 if anyone gives even a *c* of cold water
23:25 You clean the outside of the *c*
26:39 may this *c* be taken from me.
1Co 11:25 after supper he took the *c,* saying,

CURSE (CURSED)
Dt 11:26 before you today a blessing and a *c*
21:23 hung on a tree is under God's *c.*
Lk 6:28 bless those who *c* you, pray
Gal 3:13 of the law by becoming a *c* for us,
Rev 22: 3 No longer will there be any *c.*

CURSED (CURSE)
Ge 3:17 *"C* is the ground because of you;
Dt 27:15 *"C* is the man who carves an image
27:16 *"C* is the man who dishonors his
27:17 *"C* is the man who moves his
27:18 *"C* is the man who leads the blind
27:19 *C* is the man who withholds justice
27:20 *"C* is the man who sleeps
27:21 *"C* is the man who has sexual
27:22 *"C* is the man who sleeps
27:23 *"C* is the man who sleeps
27:24 *"C* is the man who kills his
27:25 *"C* is the man who accepts a bribe
27:26 *"C* is the man who does not uphold
Ro 9: 3 I could wish that I myself were *c*
Gal 3:10 *"C* is everyone who does not

CURTAIN
Ex 26:33 The *c* will separate the Holy Place
Lk 23:45 the *c* of the temple was torn in two.
Heb 10:20 opened for us through the *c,*

CYMBAL*
1Co 13: 1 a resounding gong or a clanging *c.*

DANCE (DANCING)
Ecc 3: 4 a time to mourn and a time to *d,*
Mt 11:17 and you did not *d;*

DANCING (DANCE)
Ps 30:11 You turned my wailing into *d;*
149: 3 Let them praise his name with *d*

DANGER
Pr 27:12 The prudent see *d* and take refuge,
Ro 8:35 famine or nakedness or *d* or sword?

DANIEL
Hebrew exile to Babylon, name changed to Belteshazzar (Da 1:6-7). Refused to eat unclean food (Da 1:8-21). Interpreted Nebuchadnezzar's dreams (Da 2; 4), writing on the wall (Da 5). Thrown into lion's den (Da 6). Visions of (Da 7-12).

DARK (DARKNESS)
Job 34:22 There is no *d* place, no deep
Pr 31:15 She gets up while it is still *d;*
Ro 2:19 a light for those who are in the *d,*
2Pe 1:19 as to a light shining in a *d* place,

DARKNESS (DARK)
Ge 1: 4 he separated the light from the *d.*
2Sa 22:29 the LORD turns my *d* into light.
Jn 3:19 but men loved *d* instead of light
2Co 6:14 fellowship can light have with *d?*
Eph 5: 8 For you were once *d,* but now you
1Pe 2: 9 out of *d* into his wonderful light.
1Jn 1: 5 in him there is no *d* at all.
2: 9 but hates his brother is still in the *d.*

DAUGHTERS
Joel 2:28 sons and *d* will prophesy,

DAVID
Son of Jesse (Ru 4:17-22; 1Ch 2:13-15), ancestor of Jesus (Mt 1:1-17; Lk 3:31).

Anointed king by Samuel (1Sa 16:1-13). Musician to Saul (1Sa 16:14-23; 18:10). Killed Goliath (1Sa 17). Relation with Jonathan (1Sa 18:1-4; 19-20; 23:16-18; 2Sa 1). Disfavor of Saul (1Sa 18:6-23:29). Spared Saul's life (1Sa 24; 26). Among Philistines (1Sa 21:10-14; 27-30). Lament for Saul and Jonathan (2Sa 1).

Anointed king of Judah (2Sa 2:1-11); of Israel (2Sa 5:1-4; 1Ch 11:1-3). Promised eternal dynasty (2Sa 7; 1Ch 17; Ps 132). Adultery with Bathsheba (2Sa 11-12). Absalom's revolt (2Sa 14-18). Last words (2Sa 23:1-7). Death (1Ki 2:10-12; 1Ch 29:28).

DAWN
Ps 37: 6 your righteousness shine like the *d,*
Pr 4:18 is like the first gleam of *d,*

DAY (DAYS)
Ge 1: 5 God called the light *"d,"*
Ex 20: 8 "Remember the Sabbath *d*
Lev 23:28 because it is the *D* of Atonement,
Nu 14:14 before them in a pillar of cloud by *d*
Jos 1: 8 meditate on it *d* and night,
Ps 84:10 Better is one *d* in your courts
96: 2 proclaim his salvation *d* after *d.*
118:24 This is the *d* the LORD has made;
Pr 27: 1 not know what a *d* may bring forth.
Joel 2:31 and dreadful *d* of the LORD.
Ob :15 The *d* of the LORD is near
Lk 11: 3 Give us each *d* our daily bread.
Ac 17:11 examined the Scriptures every *d*
2Co 4:16 we are being renewed *d* by *d.*
1Th 5: 2 for you know very well that the *d*
2Pe 3: 8 With the Lord a *d* is like

DAYS (DAY)
Dt 17:19 he is to read it all the *d,* of his life
Ps 23: 6 all the *d* of my life,
90:10 The length of our *d* is seventy years
Ecc 12: 1 Creator in the *d* of your youth,
Joel 2:29 I will pour out my Spirit in those *d.*
Mic 4: 1 In the last *d*
Heb 1: 2 in these last *d* he has spoken to us
2Pe 3: 3 that in the last *d* scoffers will come,

DEACONS
1Ti 3: 8 *D,* likewise, are to be men worthy

DEAD (DIE)
Dt 18:11 or spiritist or who consults the *d.*
Mt 28: 7 'He has risen from the *d*
Ro 6:11 count yourselves *d* to sin
Eph 2: 1 you were *d* in your transgressions
1Th 4:16 and the *d* in Christ will rise first.
Jas 2:17 is not accompanied by action, is *d.*
2:26 so faith without deeds is *d.*

DEATH (DIE)
Nu 35:16 the murderer shall be put to *d.*
Ps 23: 4 the valley of the shadow of *d,*
116:15 is the *d* of his saints.
Pr 8:36 all who hate me love *d."*
14:12 but in the end it leads to *d.*
Ecc 7: 2 for *d* is the destiny of every man;
Isa 25: 8 he will swallow up *d* forever.
53:12 he poured out his life unto *d,*
Jn 5:24 he has crossed over from *d* to life.
Ro 5:12 and in this way *d* came to all men,
6:23 For the wages of sin is *d,*
8:13 put to *d* the misdeeds of the body,
1Co 15:21 For since *d* came through a man,
15:55 Where, O *d,* is your sting?"
Rev 1:18 And I hold the keys of *d* and Hades
20: 6 The second *d* has no power
20:14 The lake of fire is the second *d.*
21: 4 There will be no more *d*

DEBAUCHERY
Ro 13:13 not in sexual immorality and *d,*
Eph 5:18 drunk on wine, which leads to *d.*

DEBORAH
Prophetess who led Israel to victory over Canaanites (Jdg 4-5).

DEBT (DEBTORS DEBTS)
Ro 13: 8 Let no *d* remain outstanding,
13: 8 continuing *d* to love one another,

DEBTORS (DEBT)
Mt 6:12 as we also have forgiven our *d.*

DEBTS (DEBT)
Dt 15: 1 seven years you must cancel *d.*
Mt 6:12 Forgive us our *d,*

DECAY
Ps 16:10 will you let your Holy One see *d.*
Ac 2:27 will you let your Holy One see *d.*

DECEIT (DECEIVE)
Mk 7:22 greed, malice, *d,* lewdness, envy,
1Pe 2: 1 yourselves of all malice and all *d,*
2:22 and no *d* was found in his mouth."

DECEITFUL (DECEIVE)
Jer 17: 9 The heart is *d* above all things
2Co 11:13 men are false apostles, *d* workmen,

DECEITFULNESS (DECEIVE)
Mk 4:19 the *d* of wealth and the desires
Heb 3:13 of you may be hardened by sin's *d.*

DECEIVE (DECEIT DECEITFUL DECEITFULNESS DECEIVED DECEIVES DECEPTIVE)
Lev 19:11 " 'Do not *d* one another.
Pr 14: 5 A truthful witness does not *d,*
Mt 24: 5 'I am the Christ,' and will *d* many.
Ro 16:18 and flattery they *d* the minds
1Co 3:18 Do not *d* yourselves.
Eph 5: 6 Let no one *d* you with empty words
Jas 1:22 to the word, and so *d* yourselves.
1Jn 1: 8 we *d* ourselves and the truth is not

DECEIVED (DECEIVE)
Ge 3:13 "The serpent *d* me, and I ate."
Gal 6: 7 Do not be *d:* God cannot be
1Ti 2:14 And Adam was not the one *d;*
2Ti 3:13 to worse, deceiving and being *d.*
Jas 1:16 Don't be *d,* my dear brothers.

DECEIVES (DECEIVE)
Gal 6: 3 when he is nothing, he *d* himself.
Jas 1:26 he *d* himself and his religion is

DECENCY*
1Ti 2: 9 women to dress modestly, with *d*

DECEPTIVE (DECEIVE)
Pr 31:30 Charm is *d,* and beauty is fleeting;
Col 2: 8 through hollow and *d* philosophy,

DECLARE (DECLARED DECLARING)
1Ch 16:24 *D* his glory among the nations,
Ps 19: 1 The heavens *d* the glory of God;
96: 3 *D* his glory among the nations,
Isa 42: 9 and new things I *d;*

DECLARED (DECLARE)
Mk 7:19 Jesus *d* all foods "clean.")
Ro 2:13 the law who will be *d* righteous.
3:20 no one will be *d* righteous

DECLARING (DECLARE)
Ps 71: 8 *d* your splendor all day long.
Ac 2:11 we hear them *d* the wonders

DECREED (DECREES)
La 3:37 happen if the Lord has not *d* it?

Lk 22:22 Son of Man will go as it has been *d,*

DECREES (DECREED)
Lev 10:11 Israelites all the *d* the LORD has
Ps 119:112 My heart is set on keeping your *d*

DEDICATE (DEDICATION)
Nu 6:12 He must *d* himself to the LORD
Pr 20:25 for a man to *d* something rashly

DEDICATION (DEDICATE)
1Ti 5:11 sensual desires overcome their *d*

DEED (DEEDS)
Col 3:17 you do, whether in word or *d,*

DEEDS (DEED)
1Sa 2: 3 and by him *d* are weighed.
Ps 65: 5 with awesome *d* of righteousness,
66: 3 "How awesome are your *d!*
78: 4 the praiseworthy *d* of the LORD,
86:10 you are great and do marvelous *d;*
92: 4 For you make me glad by your *d,*
111: 3 Glorious and majestic are his *d,*
Hab 3: 2 I stand in awe of your *d,* O LORD.
Mt 5:16 that they may see your good *d*
Ac 26:20 prove their repentance by their *d.*
Jas 2:14 claims to have faith but has no *d?*
2:20 faith without *d* is useless?
1Pe 2:12 they may see your good *d*

DEEP (DEPTH)
1Co 2:10 all things, even the *d* things
1Ti 3: 9 hold of the *d* truths of the faith

DEER
Ps 42: 1 As the *d* pants for streams of water,

DEFEND (DEFENSE)
Ps 74:22 Rise up, O God, and *d* your cause;
Pr 31: 9 *d* the rights of the poor and needy
Jer 50:34 He will vigorously *d* their cause

DEFENSE (DEFEND)
Ps 35:23 Awake, and rise to my *d!*
Php 1:16 here for the *d* of the gospel.
1Jn 2: 1 speaks to the Father in our *d*—

DEFERRED*
Pr 13:12 Hope *d* makes the heart sick,

DEFILE (DEFILED)
Da 1: 8 Daniel resolved not to *d* himself

DEFILED (DEFILE)
Isa 24: 5 The earth is *d* by its people;

DEFRAUD
Lev 19:13 Do not *d* your neighbor or rob him.

DEITY*
Col 2: 9 of the *D* lives in bodily form,

DELIGHT (DELIGHTS)
1Sa 15:22 "Does the LORD *d*
Ps 1: 2 But his *d* is in the law of the LORD
16: 3 in whom is all my *d.*
35: 9 and *d* in his salvation.
37: 4 *D* yourself in the LORD
43: 4 to God, my joy and my *d.*
51:16 You do not *d* in sacrifice,
119:77 for your law is my *d.*
Pr 29:17 he will bring *d* to your soul.
Isa 42: 1 my chosen one in whom I *d;*
55: 2 and your soul will *d* in the richest
61:10 I *d* greatly in the LORD;
Jer 9:24 for in these I *d,"*
15:16 they were my joy and my heart's *d,*
Mic 7:18 but *d* to show mercy.
Zep 3:17 He will take great *d* in you,

Mt 12:18 the one I love, in whom I *d;*
1Co 13: 6 Love does not *d* in evil
2Co 12:10 for Christ's sake, I *d* in weaknesses,

DELIGHTS (DELIGHT)
Ps 22: 8 since he *d* in him."
35:27 who *d* in the well-being
36: 8 from your river of *d.*
37:23 if the LORD *d* in a man's way,
Pr 3:12 as a father the son he *d* in.
12:22 but he *d* in men who are truthful.
23:24 he who has a wise son *d* in him.

DELILAH*
Woman who betrayed Samson (Jdg 16:4-22).

DELIVER (DELIVERANCE DELIVERED DELIVERER DELIVERS)
Ps 72:12 For he will *d* the needy who cry out
79: 9 *d* us and forgive our sins
Mt 6:13 but *d* us from the evil one.'
2Co 1:10 hope that he will continue to *d* us,

DELIVERANCE (DELIVER)
Ps 3: 8 From the LORD comes *d.*
32: 7 and surround me with songs of *d.*
33:17 A horse is a vain hope for *d;*

DELIVERED (DELIVER)
Ps 34: 4 he *d* me from all my fears.
Ro 4:25 He was *d* over to death for our sins

DELIVERER (DELIVER)
Ps 18: 2 is my rock, my fortress and my *d;*
40:17 You are my help and my *d;*
140: 7 O Sovereign LORD, my strong *d,*
144: 2 my stronghold and my *d,*

DELIVERS (DELIVER)
Ps 34:17 he *d* them from all their troubles.
34:19 but the LORD *d* him from them all
37:40 The LORD helps them and *d* them
37:40 he *d* them from the wicked

DEMANDED
Lk 12:20 This very night your life will be *d*
12:48 been given much, much will be *d;*

DEMONS
Mt 12:27 And if I drive out *d* by Beelzebub,
Mk 5:15 possessed by the legion of *d,*
Ro 8:38 neither angels nor *d,* neither
Jas 2:19 Good! Even the *d* believe that—

DEMONSTRATE (DEMONSTRATES)
Ro 3:26 he did it to *d* his justice

DEMONSTRATES* (DEMONSTRATE)
Ro 5: 8 God *d* his own love for us in this:

DEN
Da 6:16 and threw him into the lions' *d.*
Mt 21:13 you are making it a '*d* of robbers.'"

DENARIUS
Mk 12:15 Bring me a *d* and let me look at it."

DENIED (DENY)
1Ti 5: 8 he has *d* the faith and is worse

DENIES (DENY)
1Jn 2:23 No one who *d* the Son has

DENY (DENIED DENIES DENYING)
Ex 23: 6 "Do not *d* justice to your poor
Job 27: 5 till I die, I will not *d* my integrity.
La 3:35 to *d* a man his rights
Lk 9:23 he must *d* himself and take up his
Tit 1:16 but by their actions they *d* him.

DENYING* (DENY)
Eze 22:29 mistreat the alien, *d* them justice.
2Ti 3: 5 a form of godliness but *d* its power.
2Pe 2: 1 *d* the sovereign Lord who bought

DEPART (DEPARTED)
Ge 49:10 The scepter will not *d* from Judah,
Job 1:21 and naked I will *d.*
Mt 25:41 *'D* from me, you who are cursed,
Php 1:23 I desire to *d* and be with Christ,

DEPARTED (DEPART)
1Sa 4:21 "The glory has *d* from Israel"—
Ps 119:102 I have not *d* from your laws,

DEPOSIT
2Co 1:22 put his Spirit in our hearts as a *d,*
5: 5 and has given us the Spirit as a *d,*
Eph 1:14 who is a *d* guaranteeing our
2Ti 1:14 Guard the good *d* that was

DEPRAVED (DEPRAVITY)
Ro 1:28 he gave them over to a *d* mind,
Php 2:15 fault in a crooked and *d* generation,

DEPRAVITY (DEPRAVED)
Ro 1:29 of wickedness, evil, greed and *d.*

DEPRIVE
Dt 24:17 Do not *d* the alien or the fatherless
Pr 18: 5 or to *d* the innocent of justice.
Isa 10: 2 to *d* the poor of their rights
29:21 with false testimony *d* the innocent
1Co 7: 5 Do not *d* each other

DEPTH (DEEP)
Ro 8:39 any powers, neither height nor *d,*
11:33 the *d* of the riches of the wisdom

DESERT
Nu 32:13 wander in the *d* forty years,
Ne 9:19 you did not abandon them in the *d.*
Ps 78:19 "Can God spread a table in the *d?*
78:52 led them like sheep through the *d.*
Mk 1:13 and he was in the *d* forty days,

DESERTED (DESERTS)
Ezr 9: 9 our God has not *d* us
Mt 26:56 all the disciples *d* him and fled.
2Ti 1:15 in the province of Asia has *d* me,

DESERTING (DESERTS)
Gal 1: 6 are so quickly *d* the one who called

DESERTS (DESERTED DESERTING)
Zec 11:17 who *d* the flock!

DESERVE (DESERVES)
Ps 103:10 he does not treat us as our sins *d*
Jer 21:14 I will punish you as your deeds *d,*
Mt 22: 8 those I invited did not *d* to come.
Ro 1:32 those who do such things *d* death,

DESERVES (DESERVE)
2Sa 12: 5 the man who did this *d* to die!
Lk 10: 7 for the worker *d* his wages.
1Ti 5:18 and "The worker *d* his wages."

DESIRABLE (DESIRE)
Pr 22: 1 A good name is more *d*

DESIRE (DESIRABLE DESIRES)
Ge 3:16 Your *d* will be for your husband,
Dt 5:21 You shall not set your *d*
1Ch 29:18 keep this *d* in the hearts
Ps 40: 6 Sacrifice and offering you did not *d*
40: 8 I *d* to do your will, O my God;
73:25 earth has nothing I *d* besides you
Pr 3:15 nothing you *d* can compare
10:24 what the righteous *d* will be
11:23 The *d* of the righteous ends only
Isa 26: 8 are the *d* of our hearts.
53: 2 appearance that we should *d* him.
55:11 but will accomplish what I *d*
Hos 6: 6 For I *d* mercy, not sacrifice,
Mt 9:13 learn what this means: 'I *d* mercy,
Ro 7:18 For I have the *d* to do what is good,
1Co 12:31 But eagerly *d* the greater gifts.
14: 1 and eagerly *d* spiritual gifts,
Php 1:23 I *d* to depart and be with Christ,
Heb 13:18 *d* to live honorably in every way.
Jas 1:15 Then, after *d* has conceived,

DESIRES (DESIRE)
Ge 4: 7 at your door; it *d* to have you,
Ps 34:12 and *d* to see many good days,
37: 4 he will give you the *d* of your heart.
103: 5 satisfies your *d* with good things,
145:19 He fulfills the *d* of those who fear
Pr 11: 6 the unfaithful are trapped by evil *d.*
19:22 What a man *d* is unfailing love;
Mk 4:19 and the *d* for other things come in
Ro 8: 5 set on what that nature *d;*
13:14 to gratify the *d* of the sinful nature.
Gal 5:16 and you will not gratify the *d*
5:17 the sinful nature *d* what is contrary
1Ti 3: 1 an overseer, he *d* a noble task.
6: 9 and harmful *d* that plunge men
2Ti 2:22 Flee the evil *d* of youth,
Jas 1:20 about the righteous life that God *d.*
4: 1 from your *d* that battle within you?
1Pe 2:11 to abstain from sinful *d,* which war
1Jn 2:17 The world and its *d* pass away,

DESOLATE
Isa 54: 1 are the children of the *d* woman

DESPAIR
Isa 61: 3 instead of a spirit of *d.*
2Co 4: 8 perplexed, but not in *d;* persecuted,

DESPISE (DESPISED DESPISES)
Job 42: 6 Therefore I *d* myself
Pr 1: 7 but fools *d* wisdom and discipline.
3:11 do not *d* the LORD's discipline
23:22 do not *d* your mother
Lk 16:13 devoted to the one and *d* the other.
Tit 2:15 Do not let anyone *d* you.

DESPISED (DESPISE)
Ge 25:34 So Esau *d* his birthright.
Isa 53: 3 He was *d* and rejected by men,
1Co 1:28 of this world and the *d* things—

DESPISES (DESPISE)
Pr 14:21 He who *d* his neighbor sins,
15:20 but a foolish man *d* his mother.
15:32 who ignores discipline *d* himself,
Zec 4:10 "Who *d* the day of small things?

DESTINED (DESTINY)
Lk 2:34 "This child is *d* to cause the falling

DESTINY (DESTINED PREDESTINED)
Ps 73:17 then I understood their final *d.*
Ecc 7: 2 for death is the *d* of every man;

DESTITUTE
Pr 31: 8 for the rights of all who are *d.*
Heb 11:37 *d,* persecuted and mistreated—

DESTROY (DESTROYED DESTROYS DESTRUCTION)
Pr 1:32 complacency of fools will *d* them;
Mt 10:28 of the One who can *d* both soul

DESTROYED (DESTROY)
Job 19:26 And after my skin has been *d,*
Isa 55:13 which will not be *d."*
1Co 8:11 for whom Christ died, is *d*

15:26 The last enemy to be *d* is death.
2Co 5: 1 if the earthly tent we live in is *d*,
Heb 10:39 of those who shrink back and are *d*,
2Pe 3:10 the elements will be *d* by fire,

DESTROYS (DESTROY)
Pr 6:32 whoever does so *d* himself.
11: 9 mouth the godless *d* his neighbor,
18: 9 is brother to one who *d*.
28:24 he is partner to him who *d*.
Ecc 9:18 but one sinner *d* much good.
1Co 3:17 If anyone *d* God's temple,

DESTRUCTION (DESTROY)
Pr 16:18 Pride goes before *d*,
Hos 13:14 Where, O grave, is your *d*?
Mt 7:13 broad is the road that leads to *d*,
Gal 6: 8 from that nature will reap *d*;
2Th 1: 9 punished with everlasting *d*
1Ti 6: 9 that plunge men into ruin and *d*.
2Pe 2: 1 bringing swift *d* on themselves.
3:16 other Scriptures, to their own *d*.

DETERMINED (DETERMINES)
Job 14: 5 Man's days are *d*;
Isa 14:26 This is the plan *d* for the whole
Da 11:36 for what has been *d* must take place
Ac 17:26 and he *d* the times set for them

DETERMINES* (DETERMINED)
Ps 147: 4 He *d* the number of the stars
Pr 16: 9 but the LORD *d* his steps.
1Co 12:11 them to each one, just as he *d*.

DETESTABLE (DETESTS)
Pr 21:27 The sacrifice of the wicked is *d*—
28: 9 even his prayers are *d*.
Isa 1:13 Your incense is *d* to me.
Lk 16:15 among men is *d* in God's sight.
Tit 1:16 They are *d*, disobedient

DETESTS (DETESTABLE)
Dt 22: 5 LORD your God *d* anyone who
23:18 the LORD your God *d* them both.
25:16 LORD your God *d* anyone who
Pr 12:22 The LORD *d* lying lips,
15: 8 The LORD *d* the sacrifice
15: 9 The LORD *d* the way
15:26 The LORD *d* the thoughts
16: 5 The LORD *d* all the proud of heart
17:15 the LORD *d* them both.
20:23 The LORD *d* differing weights,

DEVIL (DEVIL'S)
Mt 13:39 the enemy who sows them is the *d*.
25:41 the eternal fire prepared for the *d*
Lk 4: 2 forty days he was tempted by the *d*.
8:12 then the *d* comes and takes away
Eph 4:27 and do not give the *d* a foothold.
2Ti 2:26 and escape from the trap of the *d*,
Jas 4: 7 Resist the *d*, and he will flee
1Pe 5: 8 Your enemy the *d* prowls
1Jn 3: 8 who does what is sinful is of the *d*,
Rev 12: 9 that ancient serpent called the *d*

DEVIL'S* (DEVIL)
Eph 6:11 stand against the *d* schemes.
1Ti 3: 7 into disgrace and into the *d* trap.
1Jn 3: 8 was to destroy the *d* work.

DEVOTE (DEVOTED DEVOTING DEVOTION DEVOUT)
Job 11:13 "Yet if you *d* your heart to him
Jer 30:21 for who is he who will *d* himself
Col 4: 2 *D* yourselves to prayer, being
1Ti 4:13 *d* yourself to the public reading
Tit 3: 8 may be careful to *d* themselves

DEVOTED (DEVOTE)
Ezr 7:10 For Ezra had *d* himself to the study
Ac 2:42 They *d* themselves
Ro 12:10 Be *d* to one another
1Co 7:34 Her aim is to be *d* to the Lord

DEVOTING (DEVOTE)
1Ti 5:10 *d* herself to all kinds of good deeds.

DEVOTION (DEVOTE)
1Ch 28: 9 and serve him with wholehearted *d*
Eze 33:31 With their mouths they express *d*,
1Co 7:35 way in undivided *d* to the Lord.
2Co 11: 3 from your sincere and pure *d*

DEVOUR
2Sa 2:26 "Must the sword *d* forever?
Mk 12:40 They *d* widows' houses
1Pe 5: 8 lion looking for someone to *d*.

DEVOUT (DEVOTE)
Lk 2:25 Simeon, who was righteous and *d*.

DIE (DEAD DEATH DIED DIES)
Ge 2:17 when you eat of it you will surely *d*
Ex 11: 5 Every firstborn son in Egypt will *d*,
Ru 1:17 Where you *d* I will *d*, and there I
2Ki 14: 6 each is to *d* for his own sins."
Pr 5:23 He will *d* for lack of discipline,
10:21 but fools *d* for lack of judgment.
15:10 he who hates correction will *d*.
23:13 with the rod, he will not *d*.
Ecc 3: 2 a time to be born and a time to *d*,
Isa 66:24 their worm will not *d*, nor will their
Eze 3:18 that wicked man will *d* for his sin,
18: 4 soul who sins is the one who will *d*.
33: 8 'O wicked man, you will surely *d*,'
Mt 26:52 "for all who draw the sword will *d*
Jn 11:26 and believes in me will never *d*.
Ro 5: 7 Very rarely will anyone *d*
14: 8 and if we *d*, we *d* to the Lord.
1Co 15:22 in Adam all *d*, so in Christ all will
15:31 I *d* every day—I mean that,
Php 1:21 to live is Christ and to *d* is gain.
Heb 9:27 Just as man is destined to *d* once,
Rev 14:13 Blessed are the dead who *d*

DIED (DIE)
Ro 5: 6 we were still powerless, Christ *d*
6: 2 By no means! We *d* to sin;
6: 8 if we *d* with Christ, we believe that
14:15 brother for whom Christ *d*.
1Co 8:11 for whom Christ *d*, is destroyed
15: 3 that Christ *d* for our sins according
2Co 5:14 *d* for all, and therefore all *d*.
Col 3: 3 For you *d*, and your life is now
1Th 5:10 He *d* for us so that, whether we are
2Ti 2:11 If we *d* with him,
Heb 9:15 now that he has *d* as a ransom
1Pe 3:18 For Christ *d* for sins once for all,
Rev 2: 8 who *d* and came to life again.

DIES (DIE)
Job 14:14 If a man *d*, will he live again?
Pr 11: 7 a wicked man *d*, his hope perishes;
Jn 11:25 in me will live, even though he *d*;
1Co 15:36 does not come to life unless it *d*.

DIFFERENCE (DIFFERENT)
Ro 10:12 For there is no *d* between Jew

DIFFERENT (DIFFERENCE)
1Co 12: 4 There are *d* kinds of gifts,
2Co 11: 4 or a *d* gospel from the one you

DIGNITY
Pr 31:25 She is clothed with strength and *d*;

DIGS
Pr 26:27 If a man *d* a pit, he will fall into it;

DILIGENCE (DILIGENT)
Heb 6:11 to show this same *d* to the very end

DILIGENT (DILIGENCE)
Pr 21: 5 The plans of the *d* lead to profit
1Ti 4:15 Be *d* in these matters; give yourself

DIRECT (DIRECTS)
Ps 119:35 *D* me in the path of your
119:133 *D* my footsteps according
Jer 10:23 it is not for man to *d* his steps.
2Th 3: 5 May the Lord *d* your hearts

DIRECTS (DIRECT)
Ps 42: 8 By day the LORD *d* his love,
Isa 48:17 who *d* you in the way you should

DIRGE
Mt 11:17 we sang a *d*,

DISAPPEAR
Mt 5:18 will by any means *d* from the Law
Lk 16:17 earth to *d* than for the least stroke

DISAPPOINT* (DISAPPOINTED)
Ro 5: 5 And hope does not *d* us,

DISAPPOINTED (DISAPPOINT)
Ps 22: 5 in you they trusted and were not *d*.

DISASTER
Ps 57: 1 wings until the *d* has passed.
Pr 3:25 Have no fear of sudden *d*
17: 5 over *d* will not go unpunished.
Isa 45: 7 I bring prosperity and create *d*;
Eze 7: 5 An unheard-of *d* is coming.

DISCERN (DISCERNING DISCERNMENT)
Ps 19:12 Who can *d* his errors?
139: 3 You *d* my going out and my lying
Php 1:10 you may be able to *d* what is best

DISCERNING (DISCERN)
Pr 14: 6 knowledge comes easily to the *d*.
15:14 The *d* heart seeks knowledge,
17:24 A *d* man keeps wisdom in view,
17:28 and *d* if he holds his tongue.
19:25 rebuke a *d* man, and he will gain

DISCERNMENT (DISCERN)
Pr 17:10 A rebuke impresses a man of *d*
28:11 a poor man who has *d* sees

DISCIPLE (DISCIPLES)
Mt 10:42 these little ones because he is my *d*,
Lk 14:27 and follow me cannot be my *d*.

DISCIPLES (DISCIPLE)
Mt 28:19 Therefore go and make *d*
Jn 8:31 to my teaching, you are really my *d*
13:35 men will know that you are my *d*
Ac 11:26 The *d* were called Christians first

DISCIPLINE (DISCIPLINED DISCIPLINES)
Ps 38: 1 or *d* me in your wrath.
39:11 You rebuke and *d* men for their sin;
94:12 Blessed is the man you *d*, O LORD
Pr 1: 7 but fools despise wisdom and *d*.
3:11 do not despise the LORD's *d*
5:12 You will say, "How I hated *d*!
5:23 He will die for lack of *d*,
6:23 and the corrections of *d*
10:17 He who heeds *d* shows the way
12: 1 Whoever loves *d* loves knowledge,
13:18 He who ignores *d* comes to poverty
13:24 who loves him is careful to *d* him.
15: 5 A fool spurns his father's *d*,
15:32 He who ignores *d* despises himself,
19:18 *D* your son, for in that there is hope
22:15 the rod of *d* will drive it far
23:13 Do not withhold *d* from a child;
29:17 *D* your son, and he will give you
Heb 12: 5 do not make light of the Lord's *d*,
12: 7 as *d*; God is treating you
12:11 No *d* seems pleasant at the time,
Rev 3:19 Those whom I love I rebuke and *d*.

DISCIPLINED (DISCIPLINE)
Pr 1: 3 for acquiring a *d* and prudent life,
Jer 31:18 'You *d* me like an unruly calf,
1Co 11:32 we are being *d* so that we will not
Tit 1: 8 upright, holy and *d*.
Heb 12: 7 For what son is not *d* by his father?

DISCIPLINES (DISCIPLINE)
Dt 8: 5 your heart that as a man *d* his son,
Pr 3:12 the LORD *d* those he loves,
Heb 12: 6 because the Lord *d* those he loves,
12:10 but God *d* us for our good,

DISCLOSED
Lk 8:17 is nothing hidden that will not be *d*,

DISCOURAGED
Jos 1: 9 Do not be terrified; do not be *d*,
10:25 "Do not be afraid; do not be *d*.
1Ch 28:20 or *d*, for the LORD God,
Isa 42: 4 he will not falter or be *d*
Col 3:21 children, or they will become *d*.

DISCREDITED
2Co 6: 3 so that our ministry will not be *d*.

DISCRETION*
1Ch 22:12 May the LORD give you *d*
Pr 1: 4 knowledge and *d* to the young—
2:11 *D* will protect you,
5: 2 that you may maintain *d*
8:12 I possess knowledge and *d*.
11:22 a beautiful woman who shows no *d*.

DISCRIMINATED*
Jas 2: 4 have you not *d* among yourselves

DISFIGURED
Isa 52:14 his appearance was so *d*

DISGRACE (DISGRACEFUL DISGRACES)
Pr 11: 2 When pride comes, then comes *d*,
14:34 but sin is a *d* to any people.
19:26 is a son who brings shame and *d*.
Ac 5:41 of suffering *d* for the Name.
Heb 13:13 the camp, bearing the *d* he bore.

DISGRACEFUL (DISGRACE)
Pr 10: 5 during harvest is a *d* son.
17: 2 wise servant will rule over a *d* son,

DISGRACES (DISGRACE)
Pr 28: 7 of gluttons *d* his father.
29:15 but a child left to itself *d* his mother

DISHONEST
Pr 11: 1 The LORD abhors *d* scales,
29:27 The righteous detest the *d*;
Lk 16:10 whoever is *d* with very little will
1Ti 3: 8 wine, and not pursuing *d* gain.

DISHONOR (DISHONORS)
Lev 18: 7 " 'Do not *d* your father
Pr 30: 9 and so *d* the name of my God.
1Co 15:43 it is sown in *d*, it is raised in glory;

DISHONORS (DISHONOR)
Dt 27:16 Cursed is the man who *d* his father

DISMAYED
Isa 28:16 the one who trusts will never be *d*.
41:10 do not be *d*, for I am your God.

DISOBEDIENCE (DISOBEY)
Ro 5:19 as through the *d* of the one man
11:32 to *d* so that he may have mercy
Heb 2: 2 and *d* received its just punishment,
4: 6 go in, because of their *d.*
4:11 fall by following their example of *d.*

DISOBEDIENT (DISOBEY)
2Ti 3: 2 proud, abusive, *d* to their parents,
Tit 1: 6 to the charge of being wild and *d.*
1:16 *d* and unfit for doing anything

DISOBEY (DISOBEDIENCE DISOBEDIENT)
Dt 11:28 the curse if you *d* the commands
2Ch 24:20 'Why do you *d* the LORD's
Ro 1:30 they *d* their parents; they are

DISORDER
1Co 14:33 For God is not a God of *d*
2Co 12:20 slander, gossip, arrogance and *d.*
Jas 3:16 there you find *d* and every evil

DISOWN
Pr 30: 9 I may have too much and *d* you
Mt 10:33 I will *d* him before my Father
26:35 to die with you, I will never *d* you."
2Ti 2:12 If we *d* him,

DISPLAY (DISPLAYS)
Eze 39:21 I will *d* my glory among the nations
1Ti 1:16 Christ Jesus might *d* his unlimited

DISPLAYS (DISPLAY)
Isa 44:23 he *d* his glory in Israel.

DISPUTE (DISPUTES)
Pr 17:14 before a *d* breaks out.
1Co 6: 1 If any of you has a *d* with another,

DISPUTES (DISPUTE)
Pr 18:18 Casting the lot settles *d*

DISQUALIFIED
1Co 9:27 I myself will not be *d* for the prize.

DISREPUTE*
2Pe 2: 2 will bring the way of truth into *d.*

DISSENSION*
Pr 6:14 he always stirs up *d.*
6:19 and a man who stirs up *d*
10:12 Hatred stirs up *d,*
15:18 A hot-tempered man stirs up *d,*
16:28 A perverse man stirs up *d,*
28:25 A greedy man stirs up *d,*
29:22 An angry man stirs up *d,*
Ro 13:13 debauchery, not in *d* and jealousy.

DISSIPATION*
Lk 21:34 will be weighed down with *d,*
1Pe 4: 4 with them into the same flood of *d,*

DISTINGUISH
1Ki 3: 9 and to *d* between right and wrong.
Heb 5:14 themselves to *d* good from evil.

DISTORT
2Co 4: 2 nor do we *d* the word of God.
2Pe 3:16 ignorant and unstable people *d,*

DISTRESS (DISTRESSED)
Ps 18: 6 In my *d* I called to the LORD;
Jnh 2: 2 "In my *d* I called to the LORD,
Jas 1:27 after orphans and widows in their *d*

DISTRESSED (DISTRESS)
Ro 14:15 If your brother is *d*

DIVIDED (DIVISION)
Mt 12:25 household *d* against itself will not
Lk 23:34 they *d* up his clothes by casting lots
1Co 1:13 Is Christ *d?* Was Paul crucified

DIVINATION
Lev 19:26 " 'Do not practice *d* or sorcery.

DIVINE
Ro 1:20 his eternal power and *d* nature—
2Co 10: 4 they have *d* power
2Pe 1: 4 you may participate in the *d* nature

DIVISION (DIVIDED DIVISIONS DIVISIVE)
Lk 12:51 on earth? No, I tell you, but *d.*
1Co 12:25 so that there should be no *d*

DIVISIONS (DIVISION)
Ro 16:17 to watch out for those who cause *d*
1Co 1:10 another so that there may be no *d*
11:18 there are *d* among you,

DIVISIVE* (DIVISION)
Tit 3:10 Warn a *d* person once,

DIVORCE
Mal 2:16 "I hate *d,*" says the LORD God
Mt 19: 3 for a man to *d* his wife for any
1Co 7:11 And a husband must not *d* his wife.
7:27 Are you married? Do not seek a *d.*

DOCTOR
Mt 9:12 "It is not the healthy who need a *d,*

DOCTRINE
1Ti 4:16 Watch your life and *d* closely.
Tit 2: 1 is in accord with sound *d.*

DOMINION
Ps 22:28 for *d* belongs to the LORD

DOOR
Ps 141: 3 keep watch over the *d* of my lips.
Mt 6: 6 close the *d* and pray to your Father
7: 7 and the *d* will be opened to you.
Rev 3:20 I stand at the *d* and knock.

DOORKEEPER
Ps 84:10 I would rather be a *d* in the house

DOUBLE-EDGED
Heb 4:12 Sharper than any *d* sword,
Rev 1:16 of his mouth came a sharp *d* sword.
2:12 of him who has the sharp, *d* sword.

DOUBLE-MINDED (MIND)
Ps 119:113 I hate *d* men,
Jas 1: 8 he is a *d* man, unstable

DOUBT
Mt 14:31 he said, "why did you *d?*"
21:21 if you have faith and do not *d,*
Mk 11:23 and does not *d* in his heart
Jas 1: 6 he must believe and not *d,*
Jude :22 Be merciful to those who *d;*

DOWNCAST
Ps 42: 5 Why are you *d,* O my soul?
2Co 7: 6 But God, who comforts the *d,*

DRAW (DRAWING DRAWS)
Mt 26:52 "for all who *d* the sword will die
Jn 12:32 up from the earth, will *d* all men
Heb 10:22 let us *d* near to God

DRAWING (DRAW)
Lk 21:28 because your redemption is *d* near

DRAWS (DRAW)
Jn 6:44 the Father who sent me *d* him,

DREADFUL
Heb 10:31 It is a *d* thing to fall into the hands

DRESS
1Ti 2: 9 I also want women to *d* modestly,

DRINK (DRUNK DRUNKARDS DRUNKENNESS)
Pr 5:15 *D* water from your own cistern,
Lk 12:19 Take life easy; eat, *d* and be merry
Jn 7:37 let him come to me and *d.*
1Co 12:13 were all given the one Spirit to *d.*
Rev 21: 6 to *d* without cost from the spring

DRIVES
1Jn 4:18 But perfect love *d* out fear,

DROP
Pr 17:14 so *d* the matter before a dispute
Isa 40:15 Surely the nations are like a *d*

DRUNK (DRINK)
Eph 5:18 Do not get *d* on wine, which leads

DRUNKARDS (DRINK)
Pr 23:21 for *d* and gluttons become poor,
1Co 6:10 nor the greedy nor *d* nor slanderers

DRUNKENNESS (DRINK)
Lk 21:34 weighed down with dissipation, *d*
Ro 13:13 and *d,* not in sexual immorality
Gal 5:21 factions and envy; *d,* orgies,
1Pe 4: 3 living in debauchery, lust, *d,* orgies,

DRY
Isa 53: 2 and like a root out of *d* ground.
Eze 37: 4 '*D* bones, hear the word

DUST
Ge 2: 7 man from the *d* of the ground
Ps 103:14 he remembers that we are *d.*
Ecc 3:20 all come from *d,* and to *d* all return.

DUTY
Ecc 12:13 for this is the whole *d* of man.
Ac 23: 1 I have fulfilled my *d* to God
1Co 7: 3 husband should fulfill his marital *d*

DWELL (DWELLING)
1Ki 8:27 "But will God really *d* on earth?
Ps 23: 6 I will *d* in the house of the LORD
Isa 43:18 do not *d* on the past.
Eph 3:17 so that Christ may *d* in your hearts
Col 1:19 to have all his fullness *d* in him,
3:16 the word of Christ *d* in you richly

DWELLING (DWELL)
Eph 2:22 to become a *d* in which God lives

EAGER
Pr 31:13 and works with *e* hands.
1Pe 5: 2 greedy for money, but *e* to serve;

EAGLE'S (EAGLES)
Ps 103: 5 your youth is renewed like the *e.*

EAGLES (EAGLE'S)
Isa 40:31 They will soar on wings like *e;*

EAR (EARS)
1Co 2: 9 no *e* has heard,
12:16 if the *e* should say, "Because I am

EARNED
Pr 31:31 Give her the reward she has *e,*

EARS (EAR)
Job 42: 5 My *e* had heard of you
Ps 34:15 and his *e* are attentive to their cry;
Pr 21:13 If a man shuts his *e* to the cry
2Ti 4: 3 to say what their itching *e* want

EARTH (EARTHLY)
Ge 1: 1 God created the heavens and the *e.*
Ps 24: 1 *e* is the LORD's, and everything
108: 5 and let your glory be over all the *e.*
Isa 6: 3 the whole *e* is full of his glory."
51: 6 the *e* will wear out like a garment
55: 9 the heavens are higher than the *e,*
66: 1 and the *e* is my footstool.
Jer 23:24 "Do not I fill heaven and *e?*"
Hab 2:20 let all the *e* be silent before him."
Mt 6:10 done on *e* as it is in heaven.
16:19 bind on *e* will be bound
24:35 Heaven and *e* will pass away,
28:18 and on *e* has been given to me.
Lk 2:14 on *e* peace to men
1Co 10:26 The *e* is the Lord's, and everything
Php 2:10 in heaven and on *e* and under the *e,*
2Pe 3:13 to a new heaven and a new *e,*

EARTHLY (EARTH)
Php 3:19 Their mind is on *e* things.
Col 3: 2 on things above, not on *e* things.

EAST
Ps 103:12 as far as the *e* is from the west,

EASY
Mt 11:30 For my yoke is *e* and my burden is

EAT (EATING)
Ge 2:17 but you must not *e* from the tree
Isa 55: 1 come, buy and *e!*
65:25 and the lion will *e* straw like the ox,
Mt 26:26 "Take and *e;* this is my body."
Ro 14: 2 faith allows him to *e* everything,
1Co 8:13 if what I *e* causes my brother to fall
10:31 So whether you *e* or drink
2Th 3:10 man will not work, he shall not *e."*

EATING (EAT)
Ro 14:17 kingdom of God is not a matter of *e*

EDICT
Heb 11:23 they were not afraid of the king's *e.*

EDIFIES
1Co 14: 4 but he who prophesies *e* the church

EFFECT
Isa 32:17 *e* of righteousness will be quietness
Heb 9:18 put into *e* without blood.

EFFORT
Lk 13:24 "Make every *e* to enter
Ro 9:16 depend on man's desire or *e,*
14:19 make every *e* to do what leads
Eph 4: 3 Make every *e* to keep the unity
Heb 4:11 make every *e* to enter that rest,
12:14 Make every *e* to live in peace
2Pe 1: 5 make every *e* to add
3:14 make every *e* to be found spotless,

ELAH
Son of Baasha; king of Israel (1Ki 16:6-14).

ELDERLY* (ELDERS)
Lev 19:32 show respect for the *e*

ELDERS (ELDERLY)
1Ti 5:17 The *e* who direct the affairs

ELECTION
Ro 9:11 God's purpose in *e* might stand:
2Pe 1:10 to make your calling and *e* sure.

ELI
High priest in youth of Samuel (1Sa 1-4). Blessed Hannah (1Sa 1:12-18); raised Samuel (1Sa 2:11-26).

ELIJAH
Prophet; predicted famine in Israel (1Ki 17:1; Jas 5:17). Fed by ravens (1Ki 17:2-6). Raised Sidonian widow's son (1Ki 17:7-

24). Defeated prophets of Baal at Carmel (1Ki 18:16-46). Ran from Jezebel (1Ki 19:1-9). Prophesied death of Azariah (2Ki 1). Succeeded by Elishah (1Ki 19:19-21; 2Ki 2:1-18). Taken to heaven in whirlwind (2Ki 2:11-12).

Return prophesied (Mal 4:5-6); equated with John the Baptist (Mt 17:9-13; Mk 9:9-13; Lk 1:17). Appeared with Moses in transfiguration of Jesus (Mt 17:1-8; Mk 9:1-8).

ELISHA

Prophet; successor of Elijah (1Ki 19:16-21); inherited his cloak (2Ki 2:1-18). Miracles of (2Ki 2-6).

ELIZABETH*

Mother of John the Baptist, relative of Mary (Lk 1:5-58).

EMBITTER*
Col 3:21 Fathers, do not *e* your children,

EMPTY
Eph 5: 6 no one deceive you with *e* words,
1Pe 1:18 from the *e* way of life handed

ENABLE (ABLE)
Lk 1:74 to *e* us to serve him without fear
Ac 4:29 *e* your servants to speak your word

ENABLED (ABLE)
Lev 26:13 *e* you to walk with heads held high.
Jn 6:65 unless the Father has *e* him."

ENABLES (ABLE)
Php 3:21 by the power that *e* him

ENCAMPS*
Ps 34: 7 The angel of the LORD *e*

ENCOURAGE (ENCOURAGEMENT)
Ps 10:17 you *e* them, and you listen
Isa 1:17 *e* the oppressed.
Ac 15:32 to *e* and strengthen the brothers.
Ro 12: 8 if it is encouraging, let him *e;*
1Th 4:18 Therefore *e* each other
2Ti 4: 2 rebuke and *e*— with great patience
Tit 2: 6 *e* the young men to be
Heb 3:13 But *e* one another daily, as long
10:25 but let us *e* one another—

ENCOURAGEMENT (ENCOURAGE)
Ac 4:36 Barnabas (which means Son of *E*),
Ro 15: 4 *e* of the Scriptures we might have
15: 5 and *e* give you a spirit of unity
1Co 14: 3 to men for their strengthening, *e*
Heb 12: 5 word of *e* that addresses you

END
Ps 119:33 then I will keep them to the *e.*
Pr 14:12 but in the *e* it leads to death.
19:20 and in the *e* you will be wise.
23:32 In the *e* it bites like a snake
Ecc 12:12 making many books there is no *e,*
Mt 10:22 firm to the *e* will be saved.
Lk 21: 9 but the *e* will not come right away
Ro 10: 4 Christ is the *e* of the law
1Co 15:24 the *e* will come, when he hands

ENDURANCE (ENDURE)
Ro 15: 4 through *e* and the encouragement
15: 5 May the God who gives *e*
2Co 1: 6 which produces in you patient *e*
Col 1:11 might so that you may have great *e*
1Ti 6:11 faith, love, *e* and gentleness.
Tit 2: 2 and sound in faith, in love and in *e.*

ENDURE (ENDURANCE ENDURES)
Ps 72:17 May his name *e* forever;
Pr 12:19 Truthful lips *e* forever,
27:24 for riches do not *e* forever,
Ecc 3:14 everything God does will *e* forever;
Mal 3: 2 who can *e* the day of his coming?
2Ti 2: 3 *E* hardship with us like a good
2:12 if we *e,* / we will also reign
Heb 12: 7 *E* hardship as discipline; God is
Rev 3:10 kept my command to *e* patiently,

ENDURES (ENDURE)
Ps 112: 9 his righteousness *e* forever;
136: 1 *His love e forever.*
Da 9:15 made for yourself a name that *e*

ENEMIES (ENEMY)
Ps 23: 5 in the presence of my *e.*
Mic 7: 6 a man's *e* are the members
Mt 5:44 Love your *e* and pray
Lk 20:43 hand until I make your *e*

ENEMY (ENEMIES ENMITY)
Pr 24:17 Do not gloat when your *e* falls;
25:21 If your *e* is hungry, give him food
27: 6 but an *e* multiplies kisses.
1Co 15:26 The last *e* to be destroyed is death.
1Ti 5:14 and to give the *e* no opportunity

ENJOY (JOY)
Dt 6: 2 and so that you may *e* long life.
Eph 6: 3 and that you may *e* long life
Heb 11:25 rather than to *e* the pleasures of sin

ENJOYMENT (JOY)
Ecc 4: 8 and why am I depriving myself of *e*
1Ti 6:17 us with everything for our *e.*

ENLIGHTENED* (LIGHT)
Eph 1:18 that the eyes of your heart may be *e*
Heb 6: 4 for those who have once been *e,*

ENMITY* (ENEMY)
Ge 3:15 And I will put *e*

ENOCH

Walked with God and taken by him (Ge 5:18-24; Heb 11:5). Prophet (Jude 14).

ENTANGLED (ENTANGLES)
2Pe 2:20 and are again *e* in it and overcome,

ENTANGLES* (ENTANGLED)
Heb 12: 1 and the sin that so easily *e,*

ENTER (ENTERED ENTERS ENTRANCE)
Ps 100: 4 *E* his gates with thanksgiving
Mt 5:20 will certainly not *e* the kingdom
7:13 "*E* through the narrow gate.
18: 8 It is better for you to *e* life maimed
Mk 10:15 like a little child will never *e* it."
10:23 is for the rich to *e* the kingdom

ENTERED (ENTER)
Ro 5:12 as sin *e* the world through one man,
Heb 9:12 but he *e* the Most Holy Place once

ENTERS (ENTER)
Mk 7:18 you see that nothing that *e* a man
Jn 10: 2 The man who *e* by the gate is

ENTERTAIN
1Ti 5:19 Do not *e* an accusation
Heb 13: 2 Do not forget to *e* strangers,

ENTHRALLED*
Ps 45:11 The king is *e* by your beauty;

ENTHRONED (THRONE)
1Sa 4: 4 who is *e* between the cherubim.
Ps 2: 4 The One *e* in heaven laughs;
102:12 But you, O LORD, sit *e* forever;
Isa 40:22 He sits *e* above the circle

ENTICE
Pr 1:10 My son, if sinners *e* you,

EVER-PRESENT*
Ps 46: 1 an *e* help in trouble

EVIDENCE (EVIDENT)
Jn 14:11 on the *e* of the miracles themselves.

EVIDENT (EVIDENCE)
Php 4: 5 Let your gentleness be *e* to all.

EVIL
Ge 2: 9 of the knowledge of good and *e.*
Job 1: 1 he feared God and shunned *e.*
1: 8 a man who fears God and shuns *e."*
34:10 Far be it from God to do *e,*
Ps 23: 4 I will fear no *e,*
34:14 Turn from *e* and do good;
51: 4 and done what is *e* in your sight,
97:10 those who love the LORD hate *e,*
101: 4 I will have nothing to do with *e.*
Pr 8:13 To fear the LORD is to hate *e;*
10:23 A fool finds pleasure in *e* conduct,
11:27 *e* comes to him who searches for it.
24:19 Do not fret because of *e* men
24:20 for the *e* man has no future hope,
Isa 5:20 Woe to those who call *e* good
13:11 I will punish the world for its *e,*
55: 7 and the *e* man his thoughts.
Hab 1:13 Your eyes are too pure to look on *e;*
Mt 5:45 He causes his sun to rise on the *e*
6:13 but deliver us from the *e* one.'
7:11 If you, then, though you are *e,*
12:35 and the *e* man brings *e* things out
Jn 17:15 you protect them from the *e* one.
Ro 2: 9 for every human being who does *e:*
12: 9 Hate what is *e;* cling
12:17 Do not repay anyone *e* for *e.*
16:19 and innocent about what is *e.*
1Co 13: 6 Love does not delight in *e*
14:20 In regard to *e* be infants,
Eph 6:16 all the flaming arrows of the *e* one.
1Th 5:22 Avoid every kind of *e.*
1Ti 6:10 of money is a root of all kinds of *e.*
2Ti 2:22 Flee the *e* desires of youth,
Jas 1:13 For God cannot be tempted by *e,*
1Pe 2:16 your freedom as a cover-up for *e;*
3: 9 Do not repay *e* with *e* or insult

EXACT
Heb 1: 3 the *e* representation of his being,

EXALT (EXALTED EXALTS)
Ps 30: 1 I will *e* you, O LORD,
34: 3 let us *e* his name together.
118:28 you are my God, and I will *e* you.
Isa 24:15 *e* the name of the LORD, the God

EXALTED (EXALT)
2Sa 22:47 *E* be God, the Rock, my Savior!
1Ch 29:11 you are *e* as head over all.
Ne 9: 5 and may it be *e* above all blessing
Ps 21:13 Be *e,* O LORD, in your strength;
46:10 I will be *e* among the nations,
57: 5 Be *e,* O God, above the heavens;
97: 9 you are *e* far above all gods.
99: 2 he is *e* over all the nations.
108: 5 Be *e,* O God, above the heavens,
148:13 for his name alone is *e;*
Isa 6: 1 *e,* and the train of his robe filled
12: 4 and proclaim that his name is *e.*
33: 5 The LORD is *e,* for he dwells
Eze 21:26 The lowly will be *e* and the *e* will be
Mt 23:12 whoever humbles himself will be *e.*
Php 1:20 always Christ will be *e* in my body,
2: 9 Therefore God *e* him

EXALTS (EXALT)
Ps 75: 7 He brings one down, he *e* another.
Pr 14:34 Righteousness *e* a nation,
Mt 23:12 For whoever *e* himself will be

EXAMINE (EXAMINED)
Ps 26: 2 *e* my heart and my mind;
Jer 17:10 and *e* the mind,
La 3:40 Let us *e* our ways and test them,
1Co 11:28 A man ought to *e* himself
2Co 13: 5 *E* yourselves to see whether you

EXAMINED (EXAMINE)
Ac 17:11 *e* the Scriptures every day to see

EXAMPLE (EXAMPLES)
Jn 13:15 have set you an *e* that you should
1Co 11: 1 Follow my *e,* as I follow
1Ti 4:12 set an *e* for the believers in speech,
Tit 2: 7 In everything set them an *e*
1Pe 2:21 leaving you an *e,* that you should

EXAMPLES* (EXAMPLE)
1Co 10: 6 Now these things occurred as *e*
10:11 as *e* and were written down
1Pe 5: 3 to you, but being *e* to the flock.

EXASPERATE*
Eph 6: 4 Fathers, do not *e* your children;

EXCEL (EXCELLENT)
1Co 14:12 to *e* in gifts that build up the church
2Co 8: 7 But just as you *e* in everything—

EXCELLENT (EXCEL)
1Co 12:31 now I will show you the most *e* way
Php 4: 8 if anything is *e* or praiseworthy—
1Ti 3:13 have served well gain an *e* standing
Tit 3: 8 These things are *e* and profitable

EXCHANGED
Ro 1:23 *e* the glory of the immortal God
1:25 They *e* the truth of God for a lie,

EXCUSE (EXCUSES)
Jn 15:22 they have no *e* for their sin.
Ro 1:20 so that men are without *e.*

EXCUSES* (EXCUSE)
Lk 14:18 "But they all alike began to make *e.*

EXISTS
Heb 2:10 and through whom everything *e,*
11: 6 to him must believe that he *e*

EXPECT (EXPECTATION)
Mt 24:44 at an hour when you do not *e* him.

EXPECTATION (EXPECT)
Ro 8:19 waits in eager *e* for the sons
Heb 10:27 but only a fearful *e* of judgment

EXPEL*
1Co 5:13 *E* the wicked man from among you

EXPENSIVE
1Ti 2: 9 or gold or pearls or *e* clothes,

EXPLOIT
Pr 22:22 Do not *e* the poor because they are
2Co 12:17 Did I *e* you through any

EXPOSE
1Co 4: 5 will *e* the motives of men's hearts.
Eph 5:11 of darkness, but rather *e* them.

EXTENDS
Pr 31:20 and *e* her hands to the needy.
Lk 1:50 His mercy *e* to those who fear him,

EXTINGUISHED
2Sa 21:17 the lamp of Israel will not be *e."*

EXTOL*
Job 36:24 Remember to *e* his work,
Ps 34: 1 I will *e* the LORD at all times;
68: 4 *e* him who rides on the clouds—
95: 2 and *e* him with music and song.
109:30 mouth I will greatly *e* the LORD;
111: 1 I will *e* the LORD with all my heart
115:18 it is we who *e* the LORD,
117: 1 *e* him, all you peoples.
145: 2 and *e* your name for ever and ever.
145:10 your saints will *e* you.
147:12 *E* the LORD, O Jerusalem;

EXTORT*
Lk 3:14 "Don't *e* money and don't accuse

EYE (EYES)
Ex 21:24 you are to take life for life, *e* for *e*,
Ps 94: 9 Does he who formed the *e* not see?
Mt 5:29 If your right *e* causes you to sin,
5:38 '*E* for *e*, and tooth for tooth.'
7: 3 of sawdust in your brother's *e*
1Co 2: 9 "No *e* has seen,
Col 3:22 not only when their *e* is on you
Rev 1: 7 and every *e* will see him,

EYES (EYE)
Nu 33:55 remain will become barbs in your *e*
Jos 23:13 on your backs and thorns in your *e*,
2Ch 16: 9 For the *e* of the LORD range
Job 31: 1 "I made a covenant with my *e*
36: 7 He does not take his *e*
Ps 119:18 Open my *e* that I may see
121: 1 I lift up my *e* to the hills—
141: 8 But my *e* are fixed on you,
Pr 3: 7 Do not be wise in your own *e*;
4:25 Let your *e* look straight ahead,
15: 3 The *e* of the LORD are everywhere
Isa 6: 5 and my *e* have seen the King,
Hab 1:13 Your *e* are too pure to look on evil;
Jn 4:35 open your *e* and look at the fields!
2Co 4:18 So we fix our *e* not on what is seen,
Heb 12: 2 Let us fix our *e* on Jesus, the author
Jas 2: 5 poor in the *e* of the world to be rich
1Pe 3:12 For the *e* of the Lord are
Rev 7:17 wipe away every tear from their *e*."
21: 4 He will wipe every tear from their *e*

EZEKIEL
Priest called to be prophet to the exiles (Eze 1-3).

EZRA
Priest and teacher of the Law who led a return of exiles to Israel to reestablish temple and worship (Ezr 7-8). Corrected intermarriage of priests (Ezr 9-10). Read Law at celebration of Feast of Tabernacles (Neh 8).

FACE (FACES)
Ge 32:30 "It is because I saw God *f* to *f*,
Ex 34:29 was not aware that his *f* was radiant
Nu 6:25 the LORD make his *f* shine
1Ch 16:11 seek his *f* always.
2Ch 7:14 and seek my *f* and turn
Ps 4: 6 Let the light of your *f* shine upon us
27: 8 Your *f*, LORD, I will seek.
31:16 Let your *f* shine on your servant;
105: 4 seek his *f* always.
119:135 Make your *f* shine
Isa 50: 7 Therefore have I set my *f* like flint,
Mt 17: 2 His *f* shone like the sun,
1Co 13:12 mirror; then we shall see *f* to *f*.
2Co 4: 6 the glory of God in the *f* of Christ.
1Pe 3:12 but the *f* of the Lord is
Rev 1:16 His *f* was like the sun shining

FACES (FACE)
2Co 3:18 who with unveiled *f* all reflect

FACTIONS
Gal 5:20 selfish ambition, dissensions, *f*

FADE
1Pe 5: 4 of glory that will never *f* away.

FAIL (FAILING FAILINGS FAILS)
1Ch 28:20 He will not *f* you or forsake you
2Ch 34:33 they did not *f* to follow the LORD,
Ps 89:28 my covenant with him will never *f*.
Pr 15:22 Plans *f* for lack of counsel,
Isa 51: 6 my righteousness will never *f*.
La 3:22 for his compassions never *f*.
2Co 13: 5 unless, of course, you *f* the test?

FAILING (FAIL)
1Sa 12:23 sin against the LORD by *f* to pray

FAILINGS (FAIL)
Ro 15: 1 ought to bear with the *f* of the weak

FAILS (FAIL)
1Co 13: 8 Love never *f*.

FAINT
Isa 40:31 they will walk and not be *f*.

FAIR
Pr 1: 3 doing what is right and just and *f*;
Col 4: 1 slaves with what is right and *f*,

FAITH (FAITHFUL FAITHFULLY FAITHFULNESS FAITHLESS)
2Ch 20:20 Have *f* in the LORD your God
Hab 2: 4 but the righteous will live by his *f*—
Mt 9:29 According to your *f* will it be done
17:20 if you have *f* as small as a mustard
24:10 many will turn away from the *f*
Mk 11:22 "Have *f* in God," Jesus answered.
Lk 7: 9 I have not found such great *f*
12:28 will he clothe you, O you of little *f*!
17: 5 "Increase our *f*!" He replied,
18: 8 will he find *f* on the earth?"
Ac 14: 9 saw that he had *f* to be healed
14:27 the door of *f* to the Gentiles.
Ro 1:12 encouraged by each other's *f*.
1:17 is by *f* from first to last,
1:17 "The righteous will live by *f*."
3: 3 What if some did not have *f*?
3:22 comes through *f* in Jesus Christ
3:25 a sacrifice of atonement, through *f*
4: 5 his *f* is credited as righteousness.
5: 1 we have been justified through *f*,
10:17 *f* comes from hearing the message,
14: 1 Accept him whose *f* is weak,
14:23 that does not come from *f* is sin.
1Co 13: 2 and if I have a *f* that can move
13:13 And now these three remain: *f*,
16:13 stand firm in the *f*; be men
2Co 5: 7 We live by *f*, not by sight.
13: 5 to see whether you are in the *f*;
Gal 2:16 Jesus that we may be justified by *f*
2:20 I live by *f* in the Son of God,
3:11 "The righteous will live by *f*."
3:24 that we might be justified by *f*.
Eph 2: 8 through *f*— and this not
4: 5 one Lord, one *f*, one baptism;
6:16 to all this, take up the shield of *f*,
Col 1:23 continue in your *f*, established
1Th 5: 8 on *f* and love as a breastplate,
1Ti 2:15 if they continue in *f*, love
4: 1 later times some will abandon the *f*
5: 8 he has denied the *f* and is worse
6:12 Fight the good fight of the *f*.
2Ti 3:15 wise for salvation through *f*
4: 7 finished the race, I have kept the *f*.
Phm : 6 may be active in sharing your *f*,
Heb 10:38 But my righteous one will live by *f*.

11: 1 *f* is being sure of what we hope for
11: 3 By *f* we understand that
11: 5 By *f* Enoch was taken from this life
11: 6 And without *f* it is impossible
11: 7 By *f* Noah, when warned about
11: 8 By *f* Abraham, when called to go
11:17 By *f* Abraham, when God tested
11:20 By *f* Isaac blessed Jacob
11:21 By *f* Jacob, when he was dying,
11:22 By *f* Joseph, when his end was near
11:24 By *f* Moses, when he had grown up
11:31 By *f* the prostitute Rahab,
12: 2 the author and perfecter of our *f*,
Jas 2:14 if a man claims to have *f*
2:17 In the same way, *f* by itself,
2:26 so *f* without deeds is dead.
2Pe 1: 5 effort to add to your *f* goodness;
1Jn 5: 4 overcome the world, even our *f*.
Jude : 3 to contend for the *f* that was once

FAITHFUL (FAITH)
Nu 12: 7 he is *f* in all my house.
Dt 7: 9 your God is God; he is the *f* God,
32: 4 A *f* God who does no wrong,
2Sa 22:26 "To the *f* you show yourself *f*,
Ps 25:10 of the LORD are loving and *f*
31:23 The LORD preserves the *f*,
33: 4 he is *f* in all he does.
37:28 and will not forsake his *f* ones.
97:10 for he guards the lives of his *f* ones
145:13 The LORD is *f* to all his promises
146: 6 the LORD, who remains *f* forever.
Pr 31:26 and *f* instruction is on her tongue.
Mt 25:21 'Well done, good and *f* servant!
Ro 12:12 patient in affliction, *f* in prayer.
1Co 4: 2 been given a trust must prove *f*.
10:13 And God is *f*; he will not let you be
1Th 5:24 The one who calls you is *f*
2Ti 2:13 he will remain *f*,
Heb 3: 6 But Christ is *f* as a son
10:23 for he who promised is *f*.
1Pe 4:19 themselves to their *f* Creator
1Jn 1: 9 he is *f* and just and will forgive us
Rev 1: 5 who is the *f* witness, the firstborn
2:10 Be *f*, even to the point of death,
19:11 whose rider is called *F* and True.

FAITHFULLY (FAITH)
Dt 11:13 if you *f* obey the commands I am
1Sa 12:24 and serve him *f* with all your heart;
1Ki 2: 4 and if they walk *f* before me
1Pe 4:10 *f* administering God's grace

FAITHFULNESS (FAITH)
Ps 57:10 your *f* reaches to the skies.
85:10 Love and *f* meet together;
86:15 to anger, abounding in love and *f*.
89: 1 mouth I will make your *f* known
89:14 love and *f* go before you.
91: 4 his *f* will be your shield
117: 2 the *f* of the LORD endures forever.
119:75 and in *f* you have afflicted me.
Pr 3: 3 Let love and *f* never leave you;
Isa 11: 5 and *f* the sash around his waist.
La 3:23 great is your *f*.
Ro 3: 3 lack of faith nullify God's *f*?
Gal 5:22 patience, kindness, goodness, *f*,

FAITHLESS (FAITH)
Ps 119:158 I look on the *f* with loathing,
Jer 3:22 "Return, *f* people;
Ro 1:31 they are senseless, *f*, heartless,
2Ti 2:13 if we are *f*,

FALL (FALLEN FALLING FALLS)
Ps 37:24 though he stumble, he will not *f*,
55:22 he will never let the righteous *f*.
69: 9 of those who insult you *f* on me.
Pr 11:28 Whoever trusts in his riches will *f*,
Lk 11:17 a house divided against itself will *f*.
Ro 3:23 and *f* short of the glory of God,
Heb 6: 6 if they *f* away, to be brought back

FALLEN (FALL)
2Sa 1:19 How the mighty have *f*!
Isa 14:12 How you have *f* from heaven,
1Co 15:20 of those who have *f* asleep.
Gal 5: 4 you have *f* away from grace.
1Th 4:15 precede those who have *f* asleep.

FALLING (FALL)
Jude :24 able to keep you from *f*

FALLS (FALL)
Pr 24:17 Do not gloat when your enemy *f*;
Jn 12:24 a kernel of wheat *f* to the ground
Ro 14: 4 To his own master he stands or *f*.

FALSE (FALSEHOOD FALSELY)
Ex 20:16 "You shall not give *f* testimony
23: 1 "Do not spread *f* reports.
Pr 13: 5 The righteous hate what is *f*,
19: 5 A *f* witness will not go unpunished,
Mt 7:15 "Watch out for *f* prophets.
19:18 not steal, do not give *f* testimony,
24:11 and many *f* prophets will appear
Php 1:18 whether from *f* motives or true,
1Ti 1: 3 not to teach *f* doctrines any longer
2Pe 2: 1 there will be *f* teachers among you.

FALSEHOOD (FALSE)
Ps 119:163 I hate and abhor *f*
Pr 30: 8 Keep *f* and lies far from me;
Eph 4:25 each of you must put off *f*

FALSELY (FALSE)
Lev 19:12 " 'Do not swear *f* by my name
Lk 3:14 and don't accuse people *f*—
1Ti 6:20 ideas of what is *f* called knowledge,

FALTER*
Pr 24:10 If you *f* in times of trouble,
Isa 42: 4 he will not *f* or be discouraged

FAMILIES (FAMILY)
Ps 68: 6 God sets the lonely in *f*,

FAMILY (FAMILIES)
Pr 15:27 greedy man brings trouble to his *f*,
31:15 she provides food for her *f*
Lk 9:61 go back and say good-by to my *f*."
12:52 in one *f* divided against each other,
1Ti 3: 4 He must manage his own *f* well
3: 5 how to manage his own *f*,
5: 4 practice by caring for their own *f*
5: 8 and especially for his immediate *f*,

FAMINE
Ge 41:30 seven years of *f* will follow them.
Am 8:11 but a *f* of hearing the words
Ro 8:35 or persecution or *f* or nakedness

FAN*
2Ti 1: 6 you to *f* into flame the gift of God,

FAST
Dt 13: 4 serve him and hold *f* to him.
Jos 22: 5 to hold *f* to him and to serve him
23: 8 to hold *f* to the LORD your God,
Ps 119:31 I hold *f* to your statutes, O LORD;
139:10 your right hand will hold me *f*.
Mt 6:16 "When you *f*, do not look somber
1Pe 5:12 Stand *f* in it.

FATHER (FATHER'S FATHERLESS FATHERS FOREFATHERS)
Ge 2:24 this reason a man will leave his *f*

17: 4 You will be the *f* of many nations.
Ex 20:12 "Honor your *f* and your mother,
21:15 "Anyone who attacks his *f*
21:17 "Anyone who curses his *f*
Lev 18: 7 " 'Do not dishonor your *f*
19: 3 you must respect his mother and *f*,
Dt 5:16 "Honor your *f* and your mother,
21:18 son who does not obey his *f*
Ps 27:10 Though my *f* and mother forsake
68: 5 A *f* to the fatherless, a defender
Pr 10: 1 A wise son brings joy to his *f*,
17:21 there is no joy for the *f* of a fool.
23:22 Listen to your *f*, who gave you life,
23:24 *f* of a righteous man has great joy;
28: 7 of gluttons disgraces his *f*.
29: 3 loves wisdom brings joy to his *f*,
Isa 9: 6 Everlasting *F*, Prince of Peace.
Mt 6: 9 " 'Our *F* in heaven,
10:37 "Anyone who loves his *f*
15: 4 'Honor your *f* and mother'
19: 5 this reason a man will leave his *f*
Lk 12:53 *f* against son and son against *f*,
23:34 Jesus said, "*F*, forgive them,
Jn 6:44 the *F* who sent me draws him,
6:46 No one has seen the *F*
8:44 You belong to your *f*, the devil,
10:30 I and the *F* are one."
14: 6 No one comes to the *F*
14: 9 who has seen me has seen the *F*.
Ro 4:11 he is the *f* of all who believe
2Co 6:18 "I will be a *F* to you,
Eph 6: 2 "Honor your *f* and mother"—
Heb 12: 7 what son is not disciplined by his *f*?

FATHER'S (FATHER)
Pr 13: 1 A wise son heeds his *f* instruction,
15: 5 A fool spurns his *f* discipline,
19:13 A foolish son is his *f* ruin,
Lk 2:49 had to be in my *F* house?"
Jn 2:16 How dare you turn my *F* house
10:29 can snatch them out of my *F* hand.
14: 2 In my *F* house are many rooms;

FATHERLESS (FATHER)
Dt 10:18 He defends the cause of the *f*
24:17 Do not deprive the alien or the *f*
24:19 Leave it for the alien, the *f*
Ps 68: 5 A father to the *f*, a defender
Pr 23:10 or encroach on the fields of the *f*,

FATHERS (FATHER)
Ex 20: 5 for the sin of the *f* to the third
Lk 11:11 "Which of you *f*, if your son asks
Eph 6: 4 *F*, do not exasperate your children;
Col 3:21 *F*, do not embitter your children,

FATHOM*
Job 11: 7 "Can you *f* the mysteries of God?
Ps 145: 3 his greatness no one can *f*.
Ecc 3:11 yet they cannot *f* what God has
Isa 40:28 and his understanding no one can *f*
1Co 13: 2 and can *f* all mysteries and all

FAULT (FAULTS)
Mt 18:15 and show him his *f*, just
Php 2:15 of God without *f* in a crooked
Jas 1: 5 generously to all without finding *f*,
Jude :24 his glorious presence without *f*

FAULTFINDERS*
Jude :16 These men are grumblers and *f*;

FAULTS (FAULT)
Ps 19:12 Forgive my hidden *f*.

FAVORITISM*
Ex 23: 3 and do not show *f* to a poor man
Lev 19:15 to the poor or *f* to the great,
Ac 10:34 true it is that God does not show *f*
Ro 2:11 For God does not show *f*.
Eph 6: 9 and there is no *f* with him.
Col 3:25 for his wrong, and there is no *f*.
1Ti 5:21 and to do nothing out of *f*.
Jas 2: 1 Lord Jesus Christ, don't show *f*.
2: 9 But if you show *f*, you sin

FEAR (AFRAID FEARS)
Dt 6:13 *F* the LORD your God, serve him
10:12 but to *f* the LORD your God,
31:12 and learn to *f* the LORD your God
Ps 19: 9 The *f* of the LORD is pure,
23: 4 I will *f* no evil,
27: 1 whom shall I *f*?
91: 5 You will not *f* the terror of night,
111:10 *f* of the LORD is the beginning
Pr 8:13 To *f* the LORD is to hate evil;
9:10 *f* of the LORD is the beginning
10:27 The *f* of the LORD adds length
14:27 The *f* of the LORD is a fountain
15:33 *f* of the LORD teaches a man
16: 6 through the *f* of the LORD a man
19:23 The *f* of the LORD leads to life:
29:25 *F* of man will prove to be a snare,
Isa 11: 3 delight in the *f* of the LORD.
41:10 So do not *f*, for I am with you;
Lk 12: 5 I will show you whom you should *f*:
Php 2:12 to work out your salvation with *f*
1Jn 4:18 But perfect love drives out *f*,

FEARS (FEAR)
Job 1: 8 a man who *f* God and shuns evil."
Ps 34: 4 he delivered me from all my *f*.
Pr 31:30 a woman who *f* the LORD is
1Jn 4:18 The one who *f* is not made perfect

FEED
Jn 21:15 Jesus said, "*F* my lambs."
21:17 Jesus said, "*F* my sheep.
Ro 12:20 "If your enemy is hungry, *f* him;
Jude :12 shepherds who *f* only themselves.

FEET (FOOT)
Ps 8: 6 you put everything under his *f*:
22:16 have pierced my hands and my *f*.
40: 2 he set my *f* on a rock
110: 1 a footstool for your *f*."
119:105 Your word is a lamp to my *f*
Ro 10:15 "How beautiful are the *f*
1Co 12:21 And the head cannot say to the *f*,
15:25 has put all his enemies under his *f*.
Heb 12:13 "Make level paths for your *f*,"

FELLOWSHIP
2Co 6:14 what *f* can light have with darkness
13:14 and the *f* of the Holy Spirit be
Php 3:10 the *f* of sharing in his sufferings,
1Jn 1: 6 claim to have *f* with him yet walk
1: 7 we have *f* with one another,

FEMALE
Ge 1:27 male and *f* he created them.
Gal 3:28 *f*, for you are all one in Christ Jesus

FERVOR
Ro 12:11 but keep your spiritual *f*, serving

FIELD (FIELDS)
Mt 6:28 See how the lilies of the *f* grow.
13:38 *f* is the world, and the good seed
1Co 3: 9 you are God's *f*, God's building.

FIELDS (FIELD)
Lk 2: 8 were shepherds living out in the *f*
Jn 4:35 open your eyes and look at the *f*!

FIG (FIGS)
Ge 3: 7 so they sewed *f* leaves together

FIGHT (FOUGHT)
Ex 14:14 The LORD will *f* for you; you need
Dt 1:30 going before you, will *f* for you,
3:22 the LORD your God himself will *f*
Ne 4:20 Our God will *f* for us!"
Ps 35: 1 *f* against those who *f* against me.
Jn 18:36 my servants would *f*
1Co 9:26 I do not *f* like a man beating the air.
2Co 10: 4 The weapons we *f*
1Ti 1:18 them you may *f* the good *f*,
6:12 Fight the good *f* of the faith.
2Ti 4: 7 fought the good *f*, I have finished

FIGS (FIG)
Lk 6:44 People do not pick *f*

FILL (FILLED FILLS FULL FULLNESS FULLY)
Ge 1:28 and increase in number; *f* the earth
Ps 16:11 you will *f* me with joy
81:10 wide your mouth and I will *f* it.
Pr 28:19 who chases fantasies will have his *f*
Hag 2: 7 and I will *f* this house with glory,'
Jn 6:26 you ate the loaves and had your *f*.
Ac 2:28 you will *f* me with joy
Ro 15:13 the God of hope *f* you with all joy

FILLED (FILL)
Ps 72:19 may the whole earth be *f*
119:64 The earth is *f* with your love,
Eze 43: 5 the glory of the LORD *f* the temple
Hab 2:14 For the earth will be *f*
Lk 1:15 and he will be *f* with the Holy Spirit
1:41 and Elizabeth was *f* with the Holy
Jn 12: 3 the house was *f* with the fragrance
Ac 2: 4 All of them were *f*
4: 8 Then Peter, *f* with the Holy Spirit,
9:17 and be *f* with the Holy Spirit."
13: 9 called Paul, *f* with the Holy Spirit,
Eph 5:18 Instead, be *f* with the Spirit.
Php 1:11 *f* with the fruit of righteousness

FILLS (FILL)
Nu 14:21 of the LORD *f* the whole earth,
Ps 107: 9 and *f* the hungry with good things.
Eph 1:23 fullness of him who *f* everything

FILTHY
Isa 64: 6 all our righteous acts are like *f* rags;
Col 3: 8 and *f* language from your lips.
2Pe 2: 7 by the *f* lives of lawless men

FIND (FINDS FOUND)
Nu 32:23 be sure that your sin will *f* you out.
Dt 4:29 you will *f* him if you look for him
1Sa 23:16 and helped him *f* strength in God.
Ps 36: 7 *f* refuge in the shadow
91: 4 under his wings you will *f* refuge;
Pr 14:22 those who plan what is good *f* love
31:10 A wife of noble character who can *f*
Jer 6:16 and you will *f* rest for your souls.
Mt 7: 7 seek and you will *f*; knock
11:29 and you will *f* rest for your souls.
16:25 loses his life for me will *f* it.
Lk 18: 8 will he *f* faith on the earth?"
Jn 10: 9 come in and go out, and *f* pasture.

FINDS (FIND)
Ps 62: 1 My soul *f* rest in God alone;
112: 1 who *f* great delight
119:162 like one who *f* great spoil.
Pr 18:22 He who *f* a wife *f* what is good
Mt 7: 8 he who seeks *f*; and to him who
10:39 Whoever *f* his life will lose it,
Lk 12:37 whose master *f* them watching
15: 4 go after the lost sheep until he *f* it?

FINISH (FINISHED)
Jn 4:34 him who sent me and to *f* his work.
5:36 that the Father has given me to *f*,
Ac 20:24 if only I may *f* the race
2Co 8:11 Now *f* the work, so that your eager
Jas 1: 4 Perseverance must *f* its work

FINISHED (FINISH)
Ge 2: 2 seventh day God had *f* the work he
Jn 19:30 the drink, Jesus said, "It is *f*."
2Ti 4: 7 I have *f* the race, I have kept

FIRE
Ex 13:21 in a pillar of *f* to give them light,
Lev 6:12 *f* on the altar must be kept burning;
Isa 30:27 and his tongue is a consuming *f*.
Jer 23:29 my word like *f*," declares
Mt 3:11 you with the Holy Spirit and with *f*.
5:22 will be in danger of the *f* of hell.
25:41 into the eternal *f* prepared
Mk 9:43 where the *f* never goes out.
Ac 2: 3 to be tongues of *f* that separated
1Co 3:13 It will be revealed with *f*,
1Th 5:19 Do not put out the Spirit's *f*;
Heb 12:29 for our "God is a consuming *f*."
Jas 3: 5 set on *f* by a small spark.
2Pe 3:10 the elements will be destroyed by *f*,
Jude :23 snatch others from the *f*
Rev 20:14 The lake of *f* is the second death.

FIRM
Ex 14:13 Stand *f* and you will see
2Ch 20:17 stand *f* and see the deliverance
Ps 33:11 of the LORD stand *f* forever,
37:23 he makes his steps *f*;
40: 2 and gave me a *f* place to stand.
89: 2 that your love stands *f* forever,
119:89 it stands *f* in the heavens.
Pr 4:26 and take only ways that are *f*.
Zec 8:23 nations will take *f* hold of one Jew
Mk 13:13 he who stands *f* to the end will be
1Co 16:13 on your guard; stand *f* in the faith;
2Co 1:24 because it is by faith you stand *f*.
Eph 6:14 Stand *f* then, with the belt
Col 4:12 that you may stand *f* in all the will
2Th 2:15 stand *f* and hold to the teachings
2Ti 2:19 God's solid foundation stands *f*,
Heb 6:19 an anchor for the soul, *f* and secure
1Pe 5: 9 Resist him, standing *f* in the faith,

FIRST
Isa 44: 6 I am the *f* and I am the last;
48:12 I am the *f* and I am the last.
Mt 5:24 *F* go and be reconciled
6:33 But seek *f* his kingdom
7: 5 *f* take the plank out
20:27 wants to be *f* must be your slave—
22:38 This is the *f* and greatest
23:26 *F* clean the inside of the cup
Mk 13:10 And the gospel must *f* be preached
Ac 11:26 disciples were called Christians *f*
Ro 1:16 *f* for the Jew, then for the Gentile.
1Co 12:28 in the church God has appointed *f*
2Co 8: 5 they gave themselves *f* to the Lord
1Ti 2:13 For Adam was formed *f*, then Eve.
Jas 3:17 comes from heaven is *f* of all pure;
1Jn 4:19 We love because he *f* loved us.
3Jn : 9 but Diotrephes, who loves to be *f*,
Rev 1:17 I am the *F* and the Last.
2: 4 You have forsaken your *f* love.

FIRSTBORN (BEAR)
Ex 11: 5 Every *f* son in Egypt will die,

FIRSTFRUITS
Ex 23:19 "Bring the best of the *f* of your soil

FISHERS
Mk 1:17 "and I will make you *f* of men."

FITTING*
Ps 33: 1 it is *f* for the upright to praise him.
147: 1 how pleasant and *f* to praise him!
Pr 10:32 of the righteous know what is *f*,
19:10 It is not *f* for a fool to live in luxury
26: 1 honor is not *f* for a fool.
1Co 14:40 everything should be done in a *f*
Col 3:18 to your husbands, as is *f* in the Lord
Heb 2:10 sons to glory, it was *f* that God,

FIX
Dt 11:18 *F* these words of mine
Pr 4:25 *f* your gaze directly before you.
2Co 4:18 we *f* our eyes not on what is seen,
Heb 3: 1 heavenly calling, *f* your thoughts
12: 2 Let us *f* our eyes on Jesus,

FLAME (FLAMES FLAMING)
2Ti 1: 6 you to fan into *f* the gift of God,

FLAMES (FLAME)
1Co 3:15 only as one escaping through the *f*.
13: 3 and surrender my body to the *f*,

FLAMING (FLAME)
Eph 6:16 you can extinguish all the *f* arrows

FLASH
1Co 15:52 in a *f*, in the twinkling of an eye,

FLATTER (FLATTERING FLATTERY)
Job 32:21 nor will I *f* any man;
Jude :16 *f* others for their own advantage.

FLATTERING (FLATTER)
Ps 12: 2 their *f* lips speak with deception.
12: 3 May the LORD cut off all *f* lips
Pr 26:28 and a *f* mouth works ruin.

FLATTERY (FLATTER)
Ro 16:18 and *f* they deceive the minds
1Th 2: 5 You know we never used *f*,

FLAWLESS*
2Sa 22:31 the word of the LORD is *f*.
Job 11: 4 You say to God, 'My beliefs are *f*
Ps 12: 6 And the words of the LORD are *f*,
18:30 the word of the LORD is *f*.
Pr 30: 5 "Every word of God is *f*;
SS 5: 2 my dove, my *f* one.

FLEE
Ps 139: 7 Where can I *f* from your presence?
1Co 6:18 *F* from sexual immorality.
10:14 my dear friends, *f* from idolatry.
1Ti 6:11 But you, man of God, *f* from all this
2Ti 2:22 *F* the evil desires of youth,
Jas 4: 7 Resist the devil, and he will *f*

FLEETING
Ps 89:47 Remember how *f* is my life.
Pr 31:30 Charm is deceptive, and beauty is *f*

FLESH
Ge 2:23 and *f* of my *f*;
2:24 and they will become one *f*.
Job 19:26 yet in my *f* I will see God;
Eze 11:19 of stone and give them a heart of *f*.
36:26 of stone and give you a heart of *f*.
Mk 10: 8 and the two will become one *f*.'
Jn 1:14 The Word became *f* and made his
6:51 This bread is my *f*, which I will give
1Co 6:16 "The two will become one *f*."
Eph 5:31 and the two will become one *f*."
6:12 For our struggle is not against *f*

FLOCK (FLOCKS)
Isa 40:11 He tends his *f* like a shepherd:
Eze 34: 2 not shepherds take care of the *f*?
Zec 11:17 who deserts the *f*!
Mt 26:31 the sheep of the *f* will be scattered.'
Ac 20:28 all the *f* of which the Holy Spirit
1Pe 5: 2 Be shepherds of God's *f* that is

FLOCKS (FLOCK)
Lk 2: 8 keeping watch over their *f* at night.

FLOG
Ac 22:25 to *f* a Roman citizen who hasn't

FLOODGATES
Mal 3:10 see if I will not throw open the *f*

FLOURISHING
Ps 52: 8 *f* in the house of God;

FLOW (FLOWING)
Nu 13:27 and it does *f* with milk and honey!
Jn 7:38 streams of living water will *f*

FLOWERS
Isa 40: 7 The grass withers and the *f* fall,

FLOWING (FLOW)
Ex 3: 8 a land *f* with milk and honey—

FOLDING
Pr 6:10 a little *f* of the hands to rest—

FOLLOW (FOLLOWING FOLLOWS)
Ex 23: 2 Do not *f* the crowd in doing wrong.
Lev 18: 4 and be careful to *f* my decrees.
Dt 5: 1 Learn them and be sure to *f* them.
Ps 23: 6 Surely goodness and love will *f* me
Mt 16:24 and take up his cross and *f* me.
Jn 10: 4 his sheep *f* him because they know
1Co 14: 1 *F* the way of love and eagerly
Rev 14: 4 They *f* the Lamb wherever he goes.

FOLLOWING (FOLLOW)
1Ti 1:18 by *f* them you may fight the good

FOLLOWS (FOLLOW)
Jn 8:12 Whoever *f* me will never walk

FOOD (FOODS)
Pr 20:13 you will have *f* to spare.
22: 9 for he shares his *f* with the poor.
25:21 If your enemy is hungry, give him *f*
31:15 she provides *f* for her family
Da 1: 8 to defile himself with the royal *f*
Jn 6:27 Do not work for *f* that spoils,
Ro 14:14 fully convinced that no *f* is unclean
1Co 8: 8 But *f* does not bring us near to God
1Ti 6: 8 But if we have *f* and clothing,
Jas 2:15 sister is without clothes and daily *f*.

FOODS (FOOD)
Mk 7:19 Jesus declared all *f* "clean.")

FOOL (FOOLISH FOOLISHNESS FOOLS)
Ps 14: 1 The *f* says in his heart,
Pr 15: 5 A *f* spurns his father's discipline,
17:28 Even a *f* is thought wise
18: 2 A *f* finds no pleasure
26: 5 Answer a *f* according to his folly,
28:26 He who trusts in himself is a *f*,
Mt 5:22 But anyone who says, 'You *f*!'

FOOLISH (FOOL)
Pr 10: 1 but a *f* son grief to his mother.
17:25 A *f* son brings grief to his father
Mt 7:26 practice is like a *f* man who built
25: 2 of them were *f* and five were wise.
1Co 1:27 God chose the *f* things of the world

FOOLISHNESS (FOOL)
1Co 1:18 of the cross is *f* to those who are
1:25 For the *f* of God is wiser

Ro 3:24 and are justified *f* by his grace
Eph 1: 6 which he has *f* given us

FRIEND (FRIENDS)
Ex 33:11 as a man speaks with his *f.*
Pr 17:17 A *f* loves at all times,
18:24 there is a *f* who sticks closer
27: 6 Wounds from a *f* can be trusted,
27:10 Do not forsake your *f* and the *f*
Jas 4: 4 Anyone who chooses to be a *f*

FRIENDS (FRIEND)
Pr 16:28 and a gossip separates close *f.*
Zec 13: 6 given at the house of my *f.'*
Jn 15:13 that he lay down his life for his *f.*

FRUIT (FRUITFUL)
Ps 1: 3 which yields its *f* in season
Pr 11:30 The *f* of the righteous is a tree
Mt 7:16 By their *f* you will recognize them.
Jn 15: 2 branch in me that bears no *f,*
Gal 5:22 But the *f* of the Spirit is love, joy,
Rev 22: 2 of *f,* yielding its *f* every month.

FRUITFUL (FRUIT)
Ge 1:22 "Be *f* and increase in number
Ps 128: 3 Your wife will be like a *f* vine
Jn 15: 2 prunes so that it will be even more *f.*

FULFILL (FULFILLED FULFILLMENT)
Ps 116:14 I will *f* my vows to the LORD
Mt 5:17 come to abolish them but to *f* them.
1Co 7: 3 husband should *f* his marital duty

FULFILLED (FULFILL)
Pr 13:19 A longing *f* is sweet to the soul,
Mk 14:49 But the Scriptures must be *f."*
Ro 13: 8 loves his fellowman has *f* the law.

FULFILLMENT (FULFILL)
Ro 13:10 Therefore love is the *f* of the law.

FULL (FILL)
Ps 127: 5 whose quiver is *f* of them.
Pr 31:11 Her husband has *f* confidence
Isa 6: 3 the whole earth is *f* of his glory."
11: 9 for the earth will be *f*
Jn 10:10 may have life, and have it to the *f.*
Ac 6: 3 known to be *f* of the Spirit

FULLNESS (FILL)
Col 1:19 to have all his *f* dwell in him,
2: 9 in Christ all the *f* of the Deity lives

FULLY (FILL)
1Ki 8:61 your hearts must be *f* committed
2Ch 16: 9 whose hearts are *f* committed
Ps 119: 4 that are to be *f* obeyed.
119:138 they are *f* trustworthy.
1Co 15:58 Always give yourselves *f*

FUTURE
Ps 37:37 there is a *f* for the man of peace.
Pr 23:18 There is surely a *f* hope for you,
Ro 8:38 neither the present nor the *f,*

GABRIEL*
Angel who interpreted Daniel's visions (Da 8:16-26; 9:20-27); announced births of John (Lk 1:11-20), Jesus (Lk 1:26-38).

GAIN (GAINED)
Ps 60:12 With God we will *g* the victory,
Mk 8:36 it for a man to *g* the whole world,
1Co 13: 3 but have not love, I *g* nothing.
Php 1:21 to live is Christ and to die is *g.*
3: 8 that I may *g* Christ and be found
1Ti 6: 6 with contentment is great *g.*

GAINED (GAIN)
Ro 5: 2 through whom we have *g* access

GALILEE
Isa 9: 1 but in the future he will honor *G*

GALL
Mt 27:34 mixed with *g;* but after tasting it,

GAP
Eze 22:30 stand before me in the *g* on behalf

GARDENER
Jn 15: 1 true vine, and my Father is the *g.*

GARMENT (GARMENTS)
Ps 102:26 they will all wear out like a *g.*
Mt 9:16 of unshrunk cloth on an old *g,*
Jn 19:23 This *g* was seamless, woven

GARMENTS (GARMENT)
Ge 3:21 The LORD God made *g* of skin
Isa 61:10 me with *g* of salvation
63: 1 with his *g* stained crimson?
Jn 19:24 "They divided my *g* among them

GATE (GATES)
Mt 7:13 For wide is the *g* and broad is
Jn 10: 9 I am the *g;* whoever enters

GATES (GATE)
Ps 100: 4 Enter his *g* with thanksgiving
Mt 16:18 the *g* of Hades will not overcome it

GATHER (GATHERS)
Zec 14: 2 I will *g* all the nations to Jerusalem
Mt 12:30 he who does not *g* with me scatters
23:37 longed to *g* your children together,

GATHERS (GATHER)
Isa 40:11 He *g* the lambs in his arms
Mt 23:37 a hen *g* her chicks under her wings,

GAVE (GIVE)
Ezr 2:69 According to their ability they *g*
Job 1:21 LORD *g* and the LORD has taken
Jn 3:16 so loved the world that he *g* his one
2Co 8: 5 they *g* themselves first to the Lord
Gal 2:20 who loved me and *g* himself for me
1Ti 2: 6 who *g* himself as a ransom

GAZE
Ps 27: 4 to *g* upon the beauty of the LORD
Pr 4:25 fix your *g* directly before you.

GENEALOGIES
1Ti 1: 4 themselves to myths and endless *g.*

GENERATIONS
Ps 22:30 future *g* will be told about the Lord
102:12 your renown endures through all *g.*
145:13 dominion endures through all *g.*
Lk 1:48 now on all *g* will call me blessed,
Eph 3: 5 not made known to men in other *g*

GENEROUS
Ps 112: 5 Good will come to him who is *g*
Pr 22: 9 A *g* man will himself be blessed,
2Co 9: 5 Then it will be ready as a *g* gift,
1Ti 6:18 and to be *g* and willing to share.

GENTILE (GENTILES)
Ro 1:16 first for the Jew, then for the *G.*
10:12 difference between Jew and *G*—

GENTILES (GENTILE)
Isa 42: 6 and a light for the *G,*
Ro 3: 9 and *G* alike are all under sin.
11:13 as I am the apostle to the *G,*
1Co 1:23 block to Jews and foolishness to *G,*

GENTLE (GENTLENESS)
Pr 15: 1 A *g* answer turns away wrath,
Zec 9: 9 *g* and riding on a donkey,
Mt 11:29 for I am *g* and humble in heart,
21: 5 *g* and riding on a donkey,
1Co 4:21 or in love and with a *g* spirit?
1Pe 3: 4 the unfading beauty of a *g*

GENTLENESS* (GENTLE)
2Co 10: 1 By the meekness and *g* of Christ,
Gal 5:23 faithfulness, *g* and self-control.
Php 4: 5 Let your *g* be evident to all.
Col 3:12 kindness, humility, *g* and patience.
1Ti 6:11 faith, love, endurance and *g*.
1Pe 3:15 But do this with *g* and respect,

GETHSEMANE
Mt 26:36 disciples to a place called *G*,

GIDEON*
Judge, also called Jerub-Baal; freed Israel from Midianites (Jdg 6-8; Heb 11:32). Given sign of fleece (Jdg 8:36-40).

GIFT (GIFTS)
Pr 21:14 A *g* given in secret soothes anger,
Mt 5:23 if you are offering your *g*
Ac 2:38 And you will receive the *g*
Ro 6:23 but the *g* of God is eternal life
1Co 7: 7 each man has his own *g* from God;
2Co 8:12 the *g* is acceptable according
9:15 be to God for his indescribable *g!*
Eph 2: 8 it is the *g* of God—not by works,
1Ti 4:14 not neglect your *g,* which was
2Ti 1: 6 you to fan into flame the *g* of God,
Jas 1:17 and perfect *g* is from above,
1Pe 4:10 should use whatever *g* he has

GIFTS (GIFT)
Ro 11:29 for God's *g* and his call are
12: 6 We have different *g,* according
1Co 12: 4 There are different kinds of *g,*
12:31 But eagerly desire the greater *g.*
14: 1 and eagerly desire spiritual *g,*
14:12 excel in *g* that build up the church.

GILEAD
Jer 8:22 Is there no balm in *G?*

GIVE (GAVE GIVEN GIVER GIVES GIVING)
Nu 6:26 and *g* you peace." '
1Sa 1:11 then I will *g* him to the LORD
2Ch 15: 7 be strong and do not *g* up,
Pr 21:26 but the righteous *g* without sparing
23:26 My son, *g* me your heart
30: 8 but *g* me only my daily bread.
31:31 *G* her the reward she has earned,
Isa 42: 8 I will not *g* my glory to another
Eze 36:26 I will *g* you a new heart
Mt 6:11 *G* us today our daily bread.
10: 8 Freely you have received, freely *g.*
22:21 "*G* to Caesar what is Caesar's,
Mk 8:37 Or what can a man *g* in exchange
Lk 6:38 *G,* and it will be given to you.
11:13 Father in heaven *g* the Holy Spirit
Jn 10:28 I *g* them eternal life, and they shall
13:34 "A new commandment I *g* you:
Ac 20:35 blessed to *g* than to receive.' "
Ro 12: 8 let him *g* generously;
13: 7 *G* everyone what you owe him:
14:12 each of us will *g* an account
2Co 9: 7 Each man should *g* what he has
Rev 14: 7 "Fear God and *g* him glory,

GIVEN (GIVE)
Nu 8:16 are to be *g* wholly to me.
Ps 115:16 but the earth he has *g* to man.
Isa 9: 6 to us a son is *g,*
Mt 6:33 and all these things will be *g* to you
7: 7 "Ask and it will be *g* to you;
Lk 22:19 saying, "This is my body *g* for you;
Jn 3:27 man can receive only what is *g* him
Ro 5: 5 the Holy Spirit, whom he has *g* us.
1Co 4: 2 those who have been *g* a trust must
12:13 we were all *g* the one Spirit to drink
Eph 4: 7 to each one of us grace has been *g*

GIVER* (GIVE)
Pr 18:16 A gift opens the way for the *g*
2Co 9: 7 for God loves a cheerful *g.*

GIVES (GIVE)
Ps 119:130 The unfolding of your words *g* light;
Pr 14:30 A heart at peace *g* life to the body,
15:30 good news *g* health to the bones.
28:27 He who *g* to the poor will lack
Isa 40:29 He *g* strength to the weary
Mt 10:42 if anyone *g* even a cup of cold water
Jn 6:63 The Spirit *g* life; the flesh counts
1Co 15:57 He *g* us the victory
2Co 3: 6 the letter kills, but the Spirit *g* life.

GIVING (GIVE)
Ne 8: 8 *g* the meaning so that the people
Ps 19: 8 *g* joy to the heart.
Mt 6: 4 so that your *g* may be in secret.
2Co 8: 7 also excel in this grace of *g.*

GLAD (GLADNESS)
Ps 31: 7 I will be *g* and rejoice in your love,
46: 4 whose streams make *g* the city
97: 1 LORD reigns, let the earth be *g;*
118:24 let us rejoice and be *g* in it.
Pr 23:25 May your father and mother be *g;*
Zec 2:10 and be *g,* O Daughter of Zion.
Mt 5:12 be *g,* because great is your reward

GLADNESS (GLAD)
Ps 45:15 They are led in with joy and *g;*
51: 8 Let me hear joy and *g;*
100: 2 Serve the LORD with *g;*
Jer 31:13 I will turn their mourning into *g;*

GLORIFIED (GLORY)
Jn 13:31 Son of Man *g* and God is *g* in him.
Ro 8:30 those he justified, he also *g.*
2Th 1:10 comes to be *g* in his holy people

GLORIFY (GLORY)
Ps 34: 3 *G* the LORD with me;
86:12 I will *g* your name forever.
Jn 13:32 God will *g* the Son in himself,
17: 1 *G* your Son, that your Son may

GLORIOUS (GLORY)
Ps 45:13 All *g* is the princess
111: 3 *G* and majestic are his deeds,
145: 5 of the *g* splendor of your majesty,
Isa 4: 2 the LORD will be beautiful and *g,*
12: 5 for he has done *g* things;
42:21 to make his law great and *g.*
63:15 from your lofty throne, holy and *g.*
Mt 19:28 the Son of Man sits on his *g* throne,
Lk 9:31 appeared in *g* splendor, talking
Ac 2:20 of the great and *g* day of the Lord.
2Co 3: 8 of the Spirit be even more *g?*
Php 3:21 so that they will be like his *g* body.
4:19 to his *g* riches in Christ Jesus.
Tit 2:13 the *g* appearing of our great God
Jude :24 before his *g* presence without fault

GLORY (GLORIFIED GLORIFY GLORIOUS)
Ex 15:11 awesome in *g,*
33:18 Moses said, "Now show me your *g*
1Sa 4:21 "The *g* has departed from Israel"—
1Ch 16:24 Declare his *g* among the nations,
16:28 ascribe to the LORD *g*
29:11 and the *g* and the majesty

Ps 8: 5 and crowned him with *g* and honor
19: 1 The heavens declare the *g* of God;
24: 7 that the King of *g* may come in.
29: 1 ascribe to the LORD *g*
72:19 the whole earth be filled with his *g*.
96: 3 Declare his *g* among the nations,
Pr 19:11 it is to his *g* to overlook an offense.
25: 2 It is the *g* of God to conceal
Isa 6: 3 the whole earth is full of his *g*."
48:11 I will not yield my *g* to another.
Eze 43: 2 and the land was radiant with his *g*.
Mt 24:30 of the sky, with power and great *g*.
25:31 the Son of Man comes in his *g*,
Mk 8:38 in his Father's *g* with the holy
13:26 in clouds with great power and *g*.
Lk 2: 9 and the *g* of the Lord shone
2:14 saying, "*G* to God in the highest,
Jn 1:14 We have seen his *g*, the *g* of the One
17: 5 presence with the *g* I had with you
17:24 to see my *g*, the *g* you have given
Ac 7: 2 The God of *g* appeared
Ro 1:23 exchanged the *g* of the immortal
3:23 and fall short of the *g* of God,
8:18 with the *g* that will be revealed
9: 4 theirs the divine *g*, the covenants,
1Co 10:31 whatever you do, do it all for the *g*
11: 7 but the woman is the *g* of man.
15:43 it is raised in *g*; it is sown
2Co 3:10 comparison with the surpassing *g*.
3:18 faces all reflect the Lord's *g*,
4:17 us an eternal *g* that far outweighs
Col 1:27 Christ in you, the hope of *g*.
3: 4 also will appear with him in *g*.
1Ti 3:16 was taken up in *g*.
Heb 1: 3 The Son is the radiance of God's *g*
2: 7 you crowned him with *g* and honor
1Pe 1:24 and all their *g* is like the flowers
Rev 4:11 to receive *g* and honor and power,
21:23 for the *g* of God gives it light,

GLUTTONS

Tit 1:12 always liars, evil brutes, lazy *g*."

GNASHING

Mt 8:12 where there will be weeping and *g*

GNAT*

Mt 23:24 You strain out a *g* but swallow

GOAL

2Co 5: 9 So we make it our *g* to please him,
Gal 3: 3 to attain your *g* by human effort?
Php 3:14 on toward the *g* to win the prize

GOAT (GOATS SCAPEGOAT)

Isa 11: 6 the leopard will lie down with the *g*

GOATS (GOAT)

Nu 7:17 five male *g* and five male lambs

GOD (GOD'S GODLINESS GODLY GODS)

Ge 1: 1 In the beginning *G* created
1: 2 and the Spirit of *G* was hovering
1:26 Then *G* said, "Let us make man
1:27 So *G* created man in his own image
1:31 *G* saw all that he had made,
2: 3 And *G* blessed the seventh day
2:22 Then the LORD *G* made a woman
3:21 The LORD *G* made garments
3:23 So the LORD *G* banished him
5:22 Enoch walked with *G* 300 years
6: 2 sons of *G* saw that the daughters
9:16 everlasting covenant between *G*
17: 1 "I am *G* Almighty; walk before me
21:33 name of the LORD, the Eternal *G*.
22: 8 "*G* himself will provide the lamb
28:12 and the angels of *G* were ascending
32:28 because you have struggled with *G*
32:30 "It is because I saw *G* face to face,
35:10 *G* said to him, "Your name is Jacob
41:51 *G* has made me forget all my
50:20 but *G* intended it for good
Ex 2:24 *G* heard their groaning
3: 6 because he was afraid to look at *G*.
6: 7 own people, and I will be your *G*.
8:10 is no one like the LORD our *G*.
13:18 So *G* led the people
15: 2 He is my *G*, and I will praise him,
17: 9 with the staff of *G* in my hands."
19: 3 Then Moses went up to *G*,
20: 2 the LORD your *G*, who brought
20: 5 the LORD your *G*, am a jealous *G*,
20:19 But do not have *G* speak to us
22:28 "Do not blaspheme *G*
31:18 inscribed by the finger of *G*.
34: 6 the compassionate and gracious *G*,
34:14 name is Jealous, is a jealous *G*.
Lev 18:21 not profane the name of your *G*.
19: 2 the LORD your *G*, am holy.
26:12 walk among you and be your *G*,
Nu 22:38 I must speak only what *G* puts
23:19 *G* is not a man, that he should lie,
Dt 1:17 for judgment belongs to *G*.
3:22 LORD your *G* himself will fight
3:24 For what *g* is there in heaven
4:24 is a consuming fire, a jealous *G*.
4:31 the LORD your *G* is a merciful *G*;
4:39 heart this day that the LORD is *G*
5:11 the name of the LORD your *G*,
5:14 a Sabbath to the LORD your *G*.
5:26 of the living *G* speaking out of fire,
6: 4 LORD our *G*, the LORD is one.
6: 5 Love the LORD your *G*
6:13 the LORD your *G*, serve him only
6:16 Do not test the LORD your *G*
7: 9 your *G* is *G*; he is the faithful *G*,
7:12 the LORD your *G* will keep his
7:21 is a great and awesome *G*.
8: 5 the LORD your *G* disciplines you.
10:12 but to fear the LORD your *G*,
10:14 the LORD your *G* belong
10:17 For the LORD your *G* is *G* of gods
11:13 to love the LORD your *G*
13: 3 The LORD your *G* is testing you
13: 4 the LORD your *G* you must
15: 6 the LORD your *G* will bless you
19: 9 to love the LORD your *G*
25:16 the LORD your *G* detests anyone
29:29 belong to the LORD our *G*,
30: 2 return to the LORD your *G*
30:16 today to love the LORD your *G*,
30:20 you may love the LORD your *G*,
31: 6 for the LORD your *G* goes
32: 3 Oh, praise the greatness of our *G*!
32: 4 A faithful *G* who does no wrong,
33:27 The eternal *G* is your refuge,
Jos 1: 9 for the LORD your *G* will be
14: 8 the LORD my *G* wholeheartedly.
22: 5 to love the LORD your *G*,
22:34 Between Us that the LORD is *G*.
23:11 careful to love the LORD your *G*.
23:14 the LORD your *G* gave you has
Jdg 16:28 O *G*, please strengthen me just
Ru 1:16 be my people and your *G* my *G*.
1Sa 2: 2 there is no Rock like our *G*.
2: 3 for the LORD is a *G* who knows,
2:25 another man, *G* may mediate
10:26 men whose hearts *G* had touched.
12:12 the LORD your *G* was your king.
17:26 defy the armies of the living *G*?"
17:46 world will know that there is a *G*
30: 6 strength in the LORD his *G*.
2Sa 14:14 But *G* does not take away life;
22: 3 my *G* is my rock, in whom I take
22:31 "As for *G*, his way is perfect;

GOD-BREATHED* (BREATHED)

GOD'S (GOD)

GODLINESS (GOD)

GODLY (GOD)

GODS (GOD)

GOLD

GOLGOTHA

GOLIATH

Philistine giant killed by David (1Sa 17; 21:9).

GOOD

Jn 10:11 "I am the *g* shepherd.
Ro 8:28 for the *g* of those who love him,
10:15 feet of those who bring *g* news!"
12: 9 Hate what is evil; cling to what is *g*.
1Co 10:24 should seek his own *g*, but the *g*
15:33 Bad company corrupts *g* character
2Co 9: 8 you will abound in every *g* work.
Gal 6: 9 us not become weary in doing *g*,
6:10 as we have opportunity, let us do *g*
Eph 2:10 in Christ Jesus to do *g* works,
Php 1: 6 that he who began a *g* work
1Th 5:21 Hold on to the *g*.
1Ti 3: 7 have a *g* reputation with outsiders,
4: 4 For everything God created is *g*,
6:12 Fight the *g* fight of the faith.
6:18 them to do *g*, to be rich in *g* deeds,
2Ti 3:17 equipped for every *g* work.
4: 7 I have fought the *g* fight, I have
Heb 12:10 but God disciplines us for our *g*,
1Pe 2: 3 you have tasted that the Lord is *g*.
2:12 Live such *g* lives among the pagans

GOSPEL

Ro 1:16 I am not ashamed of the *g*,
15:16 duty of proclaiming the *g* of God,
1Co 1:17 to preach the *g*— not with words
9:16 Woe to me if I do not preach the *g*!
15: 1 you of the *g* I preached to you,
Gal 1: 7 a different *g*— which is really no *g*
Php 1:27 in a manner worthy of the *g*

GOSSIP

Pr 11:13 A *g* betrays a confidence,
16:28 and a *g* separates close friends.
18: 8 of a *g* are like choice morsels;
26:20 without *g* a quarrel dies down.
2Co 12:20 slander, *g*, arrogance and disorder.

GRACE (GRACIOUS)

Ps 45: 2 lips have been anointed with *g*,
Jn 1:17 *g* and truth came through Jesus
Ac 20:32 to God and to the word of his *g*,
Ro 3:24 and are justified freely by his *g*
5:15 came by the *g* of the one man,
5:17 God's abundant provision of *g*
5:20 where sin increased, *g* increased all
6:14 you are not under law, but under *g*.
11: 6 if by *g*, then it is no longer by works
2Co 6: 1 not to receive God's *g* in vain.
8: 9 For you know the *g*
9: 8 able to make all *g* abound to you,
12: 9 "My *g* is sufficient for you,
Gal 2:21 I do not set aside the *g* of God,
5: 4 you have fallen away from *g*.
Eph 1: 7 riches of God's *g* that he lavished
2: 5 it is by *g* you have been saved.
2: 7 the incomparable riches of his *g*,
2: 8 For it is by *g* you have been saved,
Php 1: 7 all of you share in God's *g* with me.
Col 4: 6 conversation be always full of *g*,
2Th 2:16 and by his *g* gave us eternal
2Ti 2: 1 be strong in the *g* that is
Tit 2:11 For the *g* of God that brings
3: 7 having been justified by his *g*,
Heb 2: 9 that by the *g* of God he might taste
4:16 find *g* to help us in our time of need
4:16 the throne of *g* with confidence,
Jas 4: 6 but gives *g* to the humble."
2Pe 3:18 But grow in the *g* and knowledge

GRACIOUS (GRACE)

Nu 6:25 and be *g* to you;
Pr 22:11 a pure heart and whose speech is *g*
Isa 30:18 Yet the LORD longs to be *g* to you

GRAIN

1Co 9: 9 ox while it is treading out the *g*."

GRANTED

Php 1:29 For it has been *g* to you on behalf

GRASS

Ps 103:15 As for man, his days are like *g*,
1Pe 1:24 "All men are like *g*,

GRAVE (GRAVES)

Pr 7:27 Her house is a highway to the *g*,
Hos 13:14 Where, O *g*, is your destruction?

GRAVES (GRAVE)

Jn 5:28 are in their *g* will hear his voice
Ro 3:13 "Their throats are open *g*;

GREAT (GREATER GREATEST GREATNESS)

Ge 12: 2 "I will make you into a *g* nation
Dt 10:17 the *g* God, mighty and awesome,
2Sa 22:36 you stoop down to make me *g*.
Ps 19:11 in keeping them there is *g* reward.
89: 1 of the LORD's *g* love forever;
103:11 so *g* is his love for those who fear
107:43 consider the *g* love of the LORD.
108: 4 For *g* is your love, higher
119:165 *G* peace have they who love your
145: 3 *G* is the LORD and most worthy
Pr 23:24 of a righteous man has *g* joy;
Isa 42:21 to make his law *g* and glorious.
La 3:23 *g* is your faithfulness.
Mk 10:43 whoever wants to become *g*
Lk 21:27 in a cloud with power and *g* glory.
1Ti 6: 6 with contentment is *g* gain.
Tit 2:13 glorious appearing of our *g* God
Heb 2: 3 if we ignore such a *g* salvation?
1Jn 3: 1 How *g* is the love the Father has

GREATER (GREAT)

Mk 12:31 There is no commandment *g*
Jn 1:50 You shall see *g* things than that."
15:13 *G* love has no one than this,
1Co 12:31 But eagerly desire the *g* gifts.
Heb 11:26 as of *g* value than the treasures
1Jn 3:20 For God is *g* than our hearts,
4: 4 is in you is *g* than the one who is

GREATEST (GREAT)

Mt 22:38 is the first and *g* commandment.
Lk 9:48 least among you all—he is the *g*."
1Co 13:13 But the *g* of these is love.

GREATNESS (GREAT)

Ps 145: 3 his *g* no one can fathom.
150: 2 praise him for his surpassing *g*.
Isa 63: 1 forward in the *g* of his strength?
Php 3: 8 compared to the surpassing *g*

GREED (GREEDY)

Lk 12:15 on your guard against all kinds of *g*
Ro 1:29 kind of wickedness, evil, *g*
Eph 5: 3 or of any kind of impurity, or of *g*,
Col 3: 5 evil desires and *g*, which is idolatry
2Pe 2:14 experts in *g*— an accursed brood!

GREEDY (GREED)

Pr 15:27 A *g* man brings trouble
1Co 6:10 nor thieves nor the *g* nor drunkards
Eph 5: 5 No immoral, impure or *g* person—
1Pe 5: 2 not *g* for money, but eager to serve;

GREEN

Ps 23: 2 makes me lie down in *g* pastures,

GREW (GROW)

Lk 2:52 And Jesus *g* in wisdom and stature,
Ac 16: 5 in the faith and *g* daily in numbers.

GRIEF (GRIEVE)

Ps 10:14 O God, do see trouble and *g*;
Pr 14:13 and joy may end in *g*.

La 3:32 Though he brings *g*, he will show
Jn 16:20 but your *g* will turn to joy.
1Pe 1: 6 had to suffer *g* in all kinds of trials.

GRIEVE (GRIEF)
Eph 4:30 do not *g* the Holy Spirit of God,
1Th 4:13 or to *g* like the rest of men,

GROUND
Ge 3:17 "Cursed is the *g* because of you;
Ex 3: 5 where you are standing is holy *g*."
Eph 6:13 you may be able to stand your *g*,

GROW (GREW)
Pr 13:11 by little makes it *g*.
1Co 3: 6 watered it, but God made it *g*.
2Pe 3:18 But *g* in the grace and knowledge

GRUMBLE (GRUMBLING)
1Co 10:10 And do not *g*, as some of them did
Jas 5: 9 Don't *g* against each other,

GRUMBLING (GRUMBLE)
Jn 6:43 "Stop *g* among yourselves,"
1Pe 4: 9 to one another without *g*.

GUARANTEE (GUARANTEEING)
Heb 7:22 Jesus has become the *g*

GUARANTEEING (GUARANTEE)
2Co 1:22 as a deposit, *g* what is to come.
Eph 1:14 who is a deposit *g* our inheritance

GUARD (GUARDS)
Ps 141: 3 Set a *g* over my mouth, O LORD;
Pr 4:23 Above all else, *g* your heart,
Isa 52:12 the God of Israel will be your rear *g*
Mk 13:33 Be on *g*! Be alert! You do not know
1Co 16:13 Be on your *g*; stand firm in the faith
Php 4: 7 will *g* your hearts and your minds
1Ti 6:20 *g* what has been entrusted

GUARDS (GUARD)
Pr 13: 3 He who *g* his lips *g* his life,
19:16 who obeys instructions *g* his life,
21:23 He who *g* his mouth and his tongue
22: 5 he who *g* his soul stays far

GUIDE
Ex 13:21 of cloud to *g* them on their way
15:13 In your strength you will *g* them
Ne 9:19 cease to *g* them on their path,
Ps 25: 5 *g* me in your truth and teach me,
43: 3 let them *g* me;
48:14 he will be our *g* even to the end.
67: 4 and *g* the nations of the earth.
73:24 You *g* me with your counsel,
139:10 even there your hand will *g* me,
Pr 4:11 I *g* you in the way of wisdom
6:22 When you walk, they will *g* you;
Isa 58:11 The LORD will *g* you always;
Jn 16:13 comes, he will *g* you into all truth.

GUILTY
Ex 34: 7 does not leave the *g* unpunished;
Jn 8:46 Can any of you prove me *g* of sin?
Heb 10:22 to cleanse us from a *g* conscience
Jas 2:10 at just one point is *g* of breaking all

HADES
Mt 16:18 the gates of *H* will not overcome it.

HAGAR
Servant of Sarah, wife of Abraham, mother of Ishmael (Ge 16:1-6; 25:12). Driven away by Sarah while pregnant (Ge 16:5-16); after birth of Isaac (Ge 21:9-21; Gal 4:21-31).

HAGGAI*
Post-exilic prophet who encouraged rebuilding of the temple (Ezr 5:1; 6:14; Hag 1-2).

HAIR (HAIRS)
Lk 21:18 But not a *h* of your head will perish
1Co 11: 6 for a woman to have her *h* cut

HAIRS (HAIR)
Mt 10:30 even the very *h* of your head are all

HALLELUJAH*
Rev 19: 1, 3, 4, 6

HALLOWED (HOLY)
Mt 6: 9 *h* be your name,

HAND (HANDS)
Ps 16: 8 Because he is at my right *h*,
37:24 the LORD upholds him with his *h*.
139:10 even there your *h* will guide me,
Ecc 9:10 Whatever your *h* finds to do,
Mt 6: 3 know what your right *h* is doing,
Jn 10:28 one can snatch them out of my *h*.
1Co 12:15 I am not a *h*, I do not belong

HANDS (HAND)
Ps 22:16 they have pierced my *h*
24: 4 He who has clean *h* and a pure
31: 5 Into your *h* I commit my spirit;
31:15 My times are in your *h*;
Pr 10: 4 Lazy *h* make a man poor,
31:20 and extends her *h* to the needy.
Isa 55:12 will clap their *h*.
65: 2 All day long I have held out my *h*
Lk 23:46 into your *h* I commit my spirit."
1Th 4:11 and to work with your *h*,
1Ti 2: 8 to lift up holy *h* in prayer,
5:22 hasty in the laying on of *h*,

HANNAH*
Wife of Elkanah, mother of Samuel (1Sa 1). Prayer at dedication of Samuel (1Sa 2:1-10). Blessed (1Sa 2:18-21).

HAPPY
Ps 68: 3 may they be *h* and joyful.
Pr 15:13 A *h* heart makes the face cheerful,
Ecc 3:12 better for men than to be *h*
Jas 5:13 Is anyone *h*? Let him sing songs

HARD (HARDEN HARDSHIP)
Ge 18:14 Is anything too *h* for the LORD?
Mt 19:23 it is *h* for a rich man
1Co 4:12 We work *h* with our own hands.
1Th 5:12 to respect those who work *h*

HARDEN (HARD)
Ro 9:18 he hardens whom he wants to *h*.
Heb 3: 8 do not *h* your hearts

HARDHEARTED* (HEART)
Dt 15: 7 do not be *h* or tightfisted

HARDSHIP (HARD)
Ro 8:35 Shall trouble or *h* or persecution
2Ti 2: 3 Endure *h* with us like a good
4: 5 endure *h*, do the work
Heb 12: 7 Endure *h* as discipline; God is

HARM
Ps 121: 6 the sun will not *h* you by day,
Pr 3:29 not plot *h* against your neighbor,
31:12 She brings him good, not *h*,
Ro 13:10 Love does no *h* to its neighbor.
1Jn 5:18 and the evil one cannot *h* him.

HARMONY
Ro 12:16 Live in *h* with one another.
2Co 6:15 What *h* is there between Christ
1Pe 3: 8 live in *h* with one another;

HARVEST
Mt 9:37 *h* is plentiful but the workers are

Jn 4:35 at the fields! They are ripe for *h.*
Gal 6: 9 at the proper time we will reap a *h*
Heb 12:11 it produces a *h* of righteousness

HASTE (HASTY)
Pr 21: 5 as surely as *h* leads to poverty.
29:20 Do you see a man who speaks in *h?*

HASTY* (HASTE)
Pr 19: 2 nor to be *h* and miss the way.
Ecc 5: 2 do not be *h* in your heart
1Ti 5:22 Do not be *h* in the laying

HATE (HATED HATES HATRED)
Lev 19:17 " 'Do not *h* your brother
Ps 5: 5 you *h* all who do wrong.
45: 7 righteousness and *h* wickedness;
97:10 those who love the LORD *h* evil,
139:21 Do I not *h* those who *h* you,
Pr 8:13 To fear the LORD is to *h* evil;
Am 5:15 *H* evil, love good;
Mal 2:16 "I *h* divorce," says the LORD God
Mt 5:43 your neighbor and *h* your enemy.'
10:22 All men will *h* you because of me,
Lk 6:27 do good to those who *h* you,
Ro 12: 9 *H* what is evil; cling to what is good

HATED (HATE)
Ro 9:13 "Jacob I loved, but Esau I *h.*"
Eph 5:29 no one ever *h* his own body,
Heb 1: 9 righteousness and *h* wickedness;

HATES (HATE)
Pr 6:16 There are six things the LORD *h,*
13:24 He who spares the rod *h* his son,
Jn 3:20 Everyone who does evil *h* the light,
1Jn 2: 9 *h* his brother is still in the darkness.

HATRED (HATE)
Pr 10:12 *H* stirs up dissension,
Jas 4: 4 with the world is *h* toward God?

HAUGHTY
Pr 16:18 a *h* spirit before a fall.

HAY
1Co 3:12 costly stones, wood, *h* or straw,

HEAD (HEADS HOTHEADED)
Ge 3:15 he will crush your *h,*
Ps 23: 5 You anoint my *h* with oil;
Pr 25:22 will heap burning coals on his *h,*
Isa 59:17 and the helmet of salvation on his *h*
Mt 8:20 of Man has no place to lay his *h.*"
Ro 12:20 will heap burning coals on his *h.*"
1Co 11: 3 and the *h* of Christ is God.
12:21 And the *h* cannot say to the feet,
Eph 5:23 For the husband is the *h* of the wife
2Ti 4: 5 keep your *h* in all situations,
Rev 19:12 and on his *h* are many crowns.

HEADS (HEAD)
Lev 26:13 you to walk with *h* held high.
Isa 35:10 everlasting joy will crown their *h.*

HEAL (HEALED HEALING HEALS)
2Ch 7:14 their sin and will *h* their land.
Ps 41: 4 *h* me, for I have sinned against you
Mt 10: 8 *H* the sick, raise the dead,
Lk 4:23 to me: 'Physician, *h* yourself!
5:17 present for him to *h* the sick.

HEALED (HEAL)
Isa 53: 5 and by his wounds we are *h.*
Mt 9:22 he said, "your faith has *h* you."
14:36 and all who touched him were *h.*
Ac 4:10 this man stands before you *h.*
14: 9 saw that he had faith to be *h*
Jas 5:16 for each other so that you may be *h*
1Pe 2:24 by his wounds you have been *h.*

HEALING (HEAL)
Eze 47:12 for food and their leaves for *h.*"
Mal 4: 2 rise with *h* in its wings.
1Co 12: 9 to another gifts of *h*
12:30 Do all have gifts of *h?* Do all speak
Rev 22: 2 are for the *h* of the nations.

HEALS (HEAL)
Ex 15:26 for I am the LORD, who *h* you."
Ps 103: 3 and *h* all your diseases;
147: 3 He *h* the brokenhearted

HEALTH (HEALTHY)
Pr 3: 8 This will bring *h* to your body
15:30 and good news gives *h* to the bones

HEALTHY (HEALTH)
Mk 2:17 "It is not the *h* who need a doctor,

HEAR (HEARD HEARING HEARS)
Dt 6: 4 *H,* O Israel: The LORD our God,
31:13 must *h* it and learn
2Ch 7:14 then will I *h* from heaven
Ps 94: 9 he who implanted the ear not *h?*
Isa 29:18 that day the deaf will *h* the words
65:24 while they are still speaking I will *h*
Mt 11:15 He who has ears, let him *h.*
Jn 8:47 reason you do not *h* is that you do
2Ti 4: 3 what their itching ears want to *h.*

HEARD (HEAR)
Job 42: 5 My ears had *h* of you
Isa 66: 8 Who has ever *h* of such a thing?
Mt 5:21 "You have *h* that it was said
5:27 "You have *h* that it was said,
5:33 you have *h* that it was said
5:38 "You have *h* that it was said,
5:43 "You have *h* that it was said,
1Co 2: 9 no ear has *h,*
1Th 2:13 word of God, which you *h* from us,
2Ti 1:13 What you *h* from me, keep
Jas 1:25 not forgetting what he has *h,*

HEARING (HEAR)
Ro 10:17 faith comes from *h* the message,

HEARS (HEAR)
Jn 5:24 whoever *h* my word and believes
1Jn 5:14 according to his will, he *h* us.
Rev 3:20 If anyone *h* my voice and opens

HEART (BROKENHEARTED HARDHEARTED HEARTS WHOLEHEARTEDLY)
Ex 25: 2 each man whose *h* prompts him
Lev 19:17 Do not hate your brother in your *h.*
Dt 4:29 if you look for him with all your *h*
6: 5 LORD your God with all your *h*
10:12 LORD your God with all your *h*
15:10 and do so without a grudging *h;*
30: 6 you may love him with all your *h*
30:10 LORD your God with all your *h*
Jos 22: 5 and to serve him with all your *h*
1Sa 13:14 sought out a man after his own *h*
16: 7 but the LORD looks at the *h.*"
2Ki 23: 3 with all his *h* and all his soul,
1Ch 28: 9 for the LORD searches every *h*
2Ch 7:16 and my *h* will always be there.
Job 22:22 and lay up his words in your *h.*
37: 1 "At this my *h* pounds
Ps 14: 1 The fool says in his *h,*
19:14 and the meditation of my *h*
37: 4 will give you the desires of your *h.*
45: 1 My *h* is stirred by a noble theme
51:10 Create in me a pure *h,* O God,
51:17 a broken and contrite *h,*
66:18 If I had cherished sin in my *h,*
86:11 give me an undivided *h,*

119:11 I have hidden your word in my *h*
119:32 for you have set my *h* free.
139:23 Search me, O God, and know my *h*;
Pr 3: 5 Trust in the LORD with all your *h*
4:21 keep them within your *h*;
4:23 Above all else, guard your *h*,
7: 3 write them on the tablet of your *h*.
13:12 Hope deferred makes the *h* sick,
14:13 Even in laughter the *h* may ache,
15:30 A cheerful look brings joy to the *h*,
17:22 A cheerful *h* is good medicine,
24:17 stumbles, do not let your *h* rejoice,
27:19 so a man's *h* reflects the man.
Ecc 8: 5 wise *h* will know the proper time
SS 4: 9 You have stolen my *h*, my sister,
Isa 40:11 and carries them close to his *h*;
57:15 and to revive the *h* of the contrite.
Jer 17: 9 The *h* is deceitful above all things
29:13 when you seek me with all your *h*.
Eze 36:26 I will give you a new *h*
Mt 5: 8 Blessed are the pure in *h*,
6:21 treasure is, there your *h* will be
12:34 of the *h* the mouth speaks.
22:37 the Lord your God with all your *h*
Lk 6:45 overflow of his *h* his mouth speaks.
Ro 2:29 is circumcision of the *h*,
10:10 is with your *h* that you believe
1Co 14:25 the secrets of his *h* will be laid bare.
Eph 5:19 make music in your *h* to the Lord,
6: 6 doing the will of God from your *h*.
Col 3:23 work at it with all your *h*,
1Pe 1:22 one another deeply, from the *h*.

HEARTS (HEART)
Dt 11:18 Fix these words of mine in your *h*
1Ki 8:39 for you alone know the *h* of all men
8:61 your *h* must be fully committed
Ps 62: 8 pour out your *h* to him,
Ecc 3:11 also set eternity in the *h* of men;
Jer 31:33 and write it on their *h*.
Lk 16:15 of men, but God knows your *h*.
24:32 "Were not our *h* burning within us
Jn 14: 1 "Do not let your *h* be troubled.
Ac 15: 9 for he purified their *h* by faith.
Ro 2:15 of the law are written on their *h*,
2Co 3: 2 written on our *h*, known
3: 3 but on tablets of human *h*.
4: 6 shine in our *h* to give us the light
Eph 3:17 dwell in your *h* through faith.
Col 3: 1 set your *h* on things above,
Heb 3: 8 do not harden your *h*
10:16 I will put my laws in their *h*,
1Jn 3:20 For God is greater than our *h*,

HEAT
2Pe 3:12 and the elements will melt in the *h*.

HEAVEN (HEAVENLY HEAVENS)
Ge 14:19 Creator of *h* and earth.
1Ki 8:27 the highest *h*, cannot contain you.
2Ki 2: 1 up to *h* in a whirlwind,
2Ch 7:14 then will I hear from *h*
Isa 14:12 How you have fallen from *h*,
66: 1 "*H* is my throne,
Da 7:13 coming with the clouds of *h*.
Mt 6: 9 " 'Our Father in *h*,
6:20 up for yourselves treasures in *h*,
16:19 bind on earth will be bound in *h*,
19:23 man to enter the kingdom of *h*.
24:35 *H* and earth will pass away,
26:64 and coming on the clouds of *h*."
28:18 "All authority in *h*
Mk 16:19 he was taken up into *h*
Lk 15: 7 in *h* over one sinner who repents
18:22 and you will have treasure in *h*.
Ro 10: 6 'Who will ascend into *h*?' " (that is,
2Co 5: 1 an eternal house in *h*, not built
12: 2 ago was caught up to the third *h*.
Php 2:10 *h* and on earth and under the earth,
3:20 But our citizenship is in *h*.
1Th 1:10 and to wait for his Son from *h*,
Heb 8: 5 and shadow of what is in *h*.
9:24 he entered *h* itself, now to appear
2Pe 3:13 we are looking forward to a new *h*
Rev 21: 1 Then I saw a new *h* and a new earth

HEAVENLY (HEAVEN)
Ps 8: 5 him a little lower than the *h* beings
2Co 5: 2 to be clothed with our *h* dwelling,
Eph 1: 3 in the *h* realms with every spiritual
1:20 at his right hand in the *h* realms,
2Ti 4:18 bring me safely to his *h* kingdom.
Heb 12:22 to the *h* Jerusalem, the city

HEAVENS (HEAVEN)
Ge 1: 1 In the beginning God created the *h*
1Ki 8:27 The *h*, even the highest heaven,
2Ch 2: 6 since the *h*, even the highest
Ps 8: 3 When I consider your *h*,
19: 1 The *h* declare the glory of God;
102:25 the *h* are the work of your hands.
108: 4 is your love, higher than the *h*;
119:89 it stands firm in the *h*.
139: 8 If I go up to the *h*, you are there;
Isa 51: 6 Lift up your eyes to the *h*,
55: 9 "As the *h* are higher than the earth,
65:17 new *h* and a new earth.
Joel 2:30 I will show wonders in the *h*
Eph 4:10 who ascended higher than all the *h*,
2Pe 3:10 The *h* will disappear with a roar;

HEBREW
Ge 14:13 and reported this to Abram the *H*.

HEEDS
Pr 13: 1 wise son *h* his father's instruction,
13:18 whoever *h* correction is honored.
15: 5 whoever *h* correction shows
15:32 whoever *h* correction gains

HEEL
Ge 3:15 and you will strike his *h*."

HEIRS (INHERIT)
Ro 8:17 then we are *h*— *h* of God
Gal 3:29 and *h* according to the promise.
Eph 3: 6 gospel the Gentiles are *h* together
1Pe 3: 7 as *h* with you of the gracious gift

HELL
Mt 5:22 will be in danger of the fire of *h*.
Lk 16:23 In *h*, where he was in torment,
2Pe 2: 4 but sent them to *h*, putting them

HELMET
Isa 59:17 and the *h* of salvation on his head;
Eph 6:17 Take the *h* of salvation
1Th 5: 8 and the hope of salvation as a *h*.

HELP (HELPED HELPER HELPING HELPS)
Ps 18: 6 I cried to my God for *h*.
30: 2 my God, I called to you for *h*
46: 1 an ever-present *h* in trouble.
79: 9 *H* us, O God our Savior,
121: 1 where does my *h* come from?
Isa 41:10 I will strengthen you and *h* you;
Jnh 2: 2 depths of the grave I called for *h*,
Mk 9:24 *h* me overcome my unbelief!"
Ac 16: 9 Come over to Macedonia and *h* us
1Co 12:28 those able to *h* others, those

HELPED (HELP)
1Sa 7:12 "Thus far has the LORD *h* us."

HELPER (HELP)
Ge 2:18 I will make a *h* suitable for him."

Ps 10:14 you are the *h* of the fatherless.
Heb 13: 6 Lord is my *h;* I will not be afraid.

HELPING (HELP)
Ac 9:36 always doing good and *h* the poor.
1Ti 5:10 *h* those in trouble and devoting

HELPS (HELP)
Ro 8:26 the Spirit *h* us in our weakness.

HEN
Mt 23:37 as a *h* gathers her chicks

HERITAGE (INHERIT)
Ps 127: 3 Sons are a *h* from the LORD,

HEROD

1. King of Judea who tried to kill Jesus (Mt 2; Lk 1:5).
2. Son of 1. Tetrarch of Galilee who arrested and beheaded John the Baptist (Mt 14:1-12; Mk 6:14-29; Lk 3:1, 19-20; 9:7-9); tried Jesus (Lk 23:6-15).
3. Grandson of 1. King of Judea who killed James (Ac 12:2); arrested Peter (Ac 12:3-19). Death (Ac 12:19-23).

HERODIAS

Wife of Herod the Tetrarch who persuaded her daughter to ask for John the Baptist's head (Mt 14:1-12; Mk 6:14-29).

HEZEKIAH

King of Judah. Restored the temple and worship (2Ch 29-31). Sought the LORD for help against Assyria (2Ki 18-19; 2Ch 32:1-23; Isa 36-37). Illness healed (2Ki 20:1-11; 2Ch 32:24-26; Isa 38). Judged for showing Babylonians his treasures (2Ki 20:12-21; 2Ch 32:31; Isa 39).

HID (HIDE)
Ge 3: 8 and they *h* from the LORD God
Ex 2: 2 she *h* him for three months.
Jos 6:17 because she *h* the spies we sent.
Heb 11:23 By faith Moses' parents *h* him

HIDDEN (HIDE)
Ps 19:12 Forgive my *h* faults.
119:11 I have *h* your word in my heart
Pr 2: 4 and search for it as for *h* treasure,
Isa 59: 2 your sins have *h* his face from you,
Mt 5:14 A city on a hill cannot be *h.*
13:44 of heaven is like treasure *h*
Col 1:26 the mystery that has been kept *h*
2: 3 in whom are *h* all the treasures
3: 3 and your life is now *h* with Christ

HIDE (HID HIDDEN)
Ps 17: 8 *h* me in the shadow of your wings
143: 9 for I *h* myself in you.

HILL (HILLS)
Mt 5:14 A city on a *h* cannot be hidden.

HILLS (HILL)
Ps 50:10 and the cattle on a thousand *h.*
121: 1 I lift up my eyes to the *h*—

HINDER (HINDERS)
1Sa 14: 6 Nothing can *h* the LORD
Mt 19:14 come to me, and do not *h* them,
1Co 9:12 anything rather than *h* the gospel
1Pe 3: 7 so that nothing will *h* your prayers.

HINDERS (HINDER)
Heb 12: 1 let us throw off everything that *h*

HINT*
Eph 5: 3 even a *h* of sexual immorality,

HOLD
Ex 20: 7 LORD will not *h* anyone guiltless
Lev 19:13 " 'Do not *h* back the wages
Jos 22: 5 to *h* fast to him and to serve him
Ps 73:23 you *h* me by my right hand.
Pr 4: 4 "Lay *h* of my words
Isa 54: 2 do not *h* back;
Mk 11:25 if you *h* anything against anyone,
Php 2:16 as you *h* out the word of life—
3:12 but I press on to take *h* of that
Col 1:17 and in him all things *h* together.
1Th 5:21 *H* on to the good.
1Ti 6:12 Take *h* of the eternal life
Heb 10:23 Let us *h* unswervingly

HOLINESS (HOLY)
Ex 15:11 majestic in *h,*
Ps 29: 2 in the splendor of his *h.*
96: 9 in the splendor of his *h;*
Ro 6:19 to righteousness leading to *h.*
2Co 7: 1 perfecting *h* out of reverence
Eph 4:24 God in true righteousness and *h.*
Heb 12:10 that we may share in his *h.*
12:14 without *h* no one will see the Lord.

HOLY (HALLOWED HOLINESS)
Ex 19: 6 kingdom of priests and a *h* nation.'
20: 8 the Sabbath day by keeping it *h.*
Lev 11:44 and be *h,* because I am *h.*
20: 7 " 'Consecrate yourselves and be *h,*
20:26 You are to be *h* to me because I,
21: 8 Consider them *h,* because I
22:32 Do not profane my *h* name.
Ps 16:10 will you let your *H* One see decay.
24: 3 Who may stand in his *h* place?
77:13 Your ways, O God, are *h.*
99: 3 he is *h.*
99: 5 he is *h.*
99: 9 for the LORD our God is *h.*
111: 9 *h* and awesome is his name.
Isa 5:16 the *h* God will show himself *h*
6: 3 *H, h, h* is the LORD Almighty;
40:25 who is my equal?" says the *H* One.
57:15 who lives forever, whose name is *h:*
Eze 28:25 I will show myself *h* among them
Da 9:24 prophecy and to anoint the most *h.*
Hab 2:20 But the LORD is in his *h* temple;
Ac 2:27 will you let your *H* One see decay.
Ro 7:12 and the commandment is *h,*
12: 1 as living sacrifices, *h* and pleasing
Eph 5: 3 improper for God's *h* people.
2Th 1:10 to be glorified in his *h* people
2Ti 1: 9 saved us and called us to a *h* life—
3:15 you have known the *h* Scriptures,
Tit 1: 8 upright, *h* and disciplined.
1Pe 1:15 But just as he who called you is *h,*
1:16 is written: "Be *h,* because I am *h.*"
2: 9 a royal priesthood, a *h* nation,
2Pe 3:11 You ought to live *h* and godly lives
Rev 4: 8 "*H, h, h* is the Lord God

HOME (HOMES)
Dt 6: 7 Talk about them when you sit at *h*
Ps 84: 3 Even the sparrow has found a *h,*
Pr 3:33 but he blesses the *h* of the righteous
Mk 10:29 "no one who has left *h* or brothers
Jn 14:23 to him and make our *h* with him.
Tit 2: 5 to be busy at *h,* to be kind,

HOMES (HOME)
Ne 4:14 daughters, your wives and your *h.*"
1Ti 5:14 to manage their *h* and to give

HOMOSEXUAL*
1Co 6: 9 male prostitutes nor *h* offenders

HONEST
Lev 19:36 Use *h* scales and *h* weights,
Dt 25:15 and *h* weights and measures,
Job 31: 6 let God weigh me in *h* scales
Pr 12:17 truthful witness gives *h* testimony,

HONEY
Ex 3: 8 a land flowing with milk and *h*—
Ps 19:10 than *h* from the comb.
119:103 sweeter than *h* to my mouth!

HONOR (HONORABLE HONORABLY HONORED HONORS)
Ex 20:12 "*H* your father and your mother,
Nu 25:13 he was zealous for the *h* of his God
Dt 5:16 "*H* your father and your mother,
1Sa 2:30 Those who *h* me I will *h*,
Ps 8: 5 and crowned him with glory and *h*.
Pr 3: 9 *H* the LORD with your wealth,
15:33 and humility comes before *h*.
20: 3 It is to a man's *h* to avoid strife,
Mt 15: 4 '*H* your father and mother'
Ro 12:10 *H* one another above yourselves.
1Co 6:20 Therefore *h* God with your body.
Eph 6: 2 "*H* your father and mother"—
1Ti 5:17 well are worthy of double *h*,
Heb 2: 7 you crowned him with glory and *h*
Rev 4: 9 *h* and thanks to him who sits

HONORABLE (HONOR)
1Th 4: 4 body in a way that is holy and *h*,

HONORABLY (HONOR)
Heb 13:18 and desire to live *h* in every way.

HONORED (HONOR)
Ps 12: 8 when what is vile is *h* among men.
Pr 13:18 but whoever heeds correction is *h*.
1Co 12:26 if one part is *h*, every part rejoices
Heb 13: 4 Marriage should be *h* by all,

HONORS (HONOR)
Ps 15: 4 but *h* those who fear the LORD,
Pr 14:31 to the needy *h* God.

HOOKS
Isa 2: 4 and their spears into pruning *h*.
Joel 3:10 and your pruning *h* into spears.

HOPE (HOPES)
Job 13:15 Though he slay me, yet will I *h*
Ps 42: 5 Put your *h* in God,
62: 5 my *h* comes from him.
119:74 for I have put my *h* in your word.
130: 7 O Israel, put your *h* in the LORD,
147:11 who put their *h* in his unfailing love
Pr 13:12 *H* deferred makes the heart sick,
Isa 40:31 but those who *h* in the LORD
Ro 5: 4 character; and character, *h*.
8:24 But *h* that is seen is no *h* at all.
12:12 Be joyful in *h*, patient in affliction,
15: 4 of the Scriptures we might have *h*.
1Co 13:13 now these three remain: faith, *h*
15:19 for this life we have *h* in Christ,
Col 1:27 Christ in you, the *h* of glory.
1Th 5: 8 and the *h* of salvation as a helmet.
1Ti 6:17 but to put their *h* in God,
Tit 2:13 while we wait for the blessed *h*—
Heb 6:19 We have this *h* as an anchor
11: 1 faith is being sure of what we *h* for
1Jn 3: 3 Everyone who has this *h*

HOPES (HOPE)
1Co 13: 7 always *h*, always perseveres.

HORSE
Ps 147:10 not in the strength of the *h*,
Pr 26: 3 A whip for the *h*, a halter
Zec 1: 8 before me was a man riding a red *h*
Rev 6: 2 and there before me was a white *h*!
6: 4 Come!" Then another *h* came out,
6: 5 and there before me was a black *h*!
6: 8 and there before me was a pale *h*!
19:11 and there before me was a white *h*,

HOSANNA
Mt 21: 9 "*H* in the highest!"

HOSHEA
Last king of Israel (2Ki 15:30; 17:1-6).

HOSPITABLE* (HOSPITALITY)
1Ti 3: 2 self-controlled, respectable, *h*,
Tit 1: 8 Rather he must be *h*, one who loves

HOSPITALITY (HOSPITABLE)
Ro 12:13 Practice *h*.
1Ti 5:10 as bringing up children, showing *h*,
1Pe 4: 9 Offer *h* to one another

HOSTILE
Ro 8: 7 the sinful mind is *h* to God.

HOT
1Ti 4: 2 have been seared as with a *h* iron.
Rev 3:15 that you are neither cold nor *h*.

HOT-TEMPERED
Pr 15:18 A *h* man stirs up dissension,
19:19 A *h* man must pay the penalty;
22:24 Do not make friends with a *h* man,
29:22 and a *h* one commits many sins.

HOTHEADED (HEAD)
Pr 14:16 but a fool is *h* and reckless.

HOUR
Ecc 9:12 knows when his *h* will come:
Mt 6:27 you by worrying can add a single *h*
Lk 12:40 the Son of Man will come at an *h*
Jn 12:23 The *h* has come for the Son of Man
12:27 for this very reason I came to this *h*

HOUSE (HOUSEHOLD STOREHOUSE)
Ex 20:17 shall not covet your neighbor's *h*.
Ps 23: 6 I will dwell in the *h* of the LORD
84:10 a doorkeeper in the *h* of my God
122: 1 "Let us go to the *h* of the LORD."
127: 1 Unless the LORD builds the *h*,
Pr 7:27 Her *h* is a highway to the grave,
21: 9 than share a *h* with a quarrelsome
Isa 56: 7 a *h* of prayer for all nations."
Zec 13: 6 given at the *h* of my friends.'
Mt 7:24 is like a wise man who built his *h*
12:29 can anyone enter a strong man's *h*
21:13 My *h* will be called a *h* of prayer,'
Mk 3:25 If a *h* is divided against itself,
Lk 11:17 a *h* divided against itself will fall.
Jn 2:16 How dare you turn my Father's *h*
12: 3 the *h* was filled with the fragrance
14: 2 In my Father's *h* are many rooms;
Heb 3: 3 the builder of a *h* has greater honor

HOUSEHOLD (HOUSE)
Jos 24:15 my *h*, we will serve the LORD."
Mic 7: 6 are the members of his own *h*.
Mt 10:36 will be the members of his own *h*.'
12:25 or *h* divided against itself will not
1Ti 3:12 manage his children and his *h* well.
3:15 to conduct themselves in God's *h*,

HUMAN (HUMANITY)
Gal 3: 3 to attain your goal by *h* effort?

HUMANITY* (HUMAN)
Heb 2:14 he too shared in their *h* so that

HUMBLE (HUMBLED HUMBLES HUMILIATE HUMILITY)
2Ch 7:14 will *h* themselves and pray
Ps 25: 9 He guides the *h* in what is right
Pr 3:34 but gives grace to the *h*.
Isa 66: 2 he who is *h* and contrite in spirit,
Mt 11:29 for I am gentle and *h* in heart,

Eph 4: 2 Be completely *h* and gentle;
Jas 4:10 *H* yourselves before the Lord,
1Pe 5: 6 *H* yourselves,

HUMBLED (HUMBLE)
Mt 23:12 whoever exalts himself will be *h,*
Php 2: 8 he *h* himself

HUMBLES (HUMBLE)
Mt 18: 4 whoever *h* himself like this child is
23:12 whoever *h* himself will be exalted.

HUMILIATE* (HUMBLE)
Pr 25: 7 than for him to *h* you
1Co 11:22 and *h* those who have nothing?

HUMILITY (HUMBLE)
Pr 11: 2 but with *h* comes wisdom.
15:33 and *h* comes before honor.
Php 2: 3 but in *h* consider others better
Tit 3: 2 and to show true *h* toward all men.
1Pe 5: 5 clothe yourselves with *h*

HUNGRY
Ps 107: 9 and fills the *h* with good things.
146: 7 and gives food to the *h.*
Pr 25:21 If your enemy is *h,* give him food
Eze 18: 7 but gives his food to the *h*
Mt 25:35 For I was *h* and you gave me
Lk 1:53 He has filled the *h* with good things
Jn 6:35 comes to me will never go *h,*
Ro 12:20 "If your enemy is *h,* feed him;

HURT (HURTS)
Ecc 8: 9 it over others to his own *h.*
Mk 16:18 deadly poison, it will not *h* them
Rev 2:11 He who overcomes will not be *h*

HURTS* (HURT)
Ps 15: 4 even when it *h,*
Pr 26:28 A lying tongue hates those it *h,*

HUSBAND (HUSBAND'S HUSBANDS)
1Co 7: 3 The *h* should fulfill his marital duty
7:10 wife must not separate from her *h.*
7:11 And a *h* must not divorce his wife.
7:13 And if a woman has a *h* who is not
7:39 A woman is bound to her *h* as long
2Co 11: 2 I promised you to one *h,* to Christ,
Eph 5:23 For the *h* is the head of the wife
5:33 and the wife must respect her *h.*
1Ti 3: 2 the *h* of but one wife, temperate,

HUSBAND'S (HUSBAND)
Pr 12: 4 of noble character is her *h* crown,
1Co 7: 4 the *h* body does not belong

HUSBANDS (HUSBAND)
Eph 5:22 submit to your *h* as to the Lord.
5:25 *H,* love your wives, just
Tit 2: 4 the younger women to love their *h*
1Pe 3: 1 same way be submissive to your *h*
3: 7 *H,* in the same way be considerate

HYMN
1Co 14:26 everyone has a *h,* or a word

HYPOCRISY (HYPOCRITE HYPOCRITES)
Mt 23:28 but on the inside you are full of *h*
1Pe 2: 1 *h,* envy, and slander of every kind.

HYPOCRITE (HYPOCRISY)
Mt 7: 5 You *h,* first take the plank out

HYPOCRITES (HYPOCRISY)
Ps 26: 4 nor do I consort with *h;*
Mt 6: 5 when you pray, do not be like the *h*

HYSSOP
Ps 51: 7 with *h,* and I will be clean;

IDLE (IDLENESS)
1Th 5:14 those who are *i,* encourage
2Th 3: 6 away from every brother who is *i*
1Ti 5:13 they get into the habit of being *i*

IDLENESS* (IDLE)
Pr 31:27 and does not eat the bread of *i.*

IDOL (IDOLATRY IDOLS)
Isa 44:17 From the rest he makes a god, his *i;*
1Co 8: 4 We know that an *i* is nothing at all

IDOLATRY (IDOL)
Col 3: 5 evil desires and greed, which is *i.*

IDOLS (IDOL)
1Co 8: 1 Now about food sacrificed to *i:*

IGNORANT (IGNORE)
1Co 15:34 for there are some who are *i* of God
Heb 5: 2 to deal gently with those who are *i*
1Pe 2:15 good you should silence the *i* talk
2Pe 3:16 which *i* and unstable people distort

IGNORE (IGNORANT IGNORES)
Dt 22: 1 do not *i* it but be sure
Ps 9:12 he does not *i* the cry of the afflicted
Heb 2: 3 if we *i* such a great salvation?

IGNORES (IGNORE)
Pr 10:17 whoever *i* correction leads others
15:32 He who *i* discipline despises

ILLUMINATED*
Rev 18: 1 and the earth was *i* by his splendor.

IMAGE
Ge 1:26 "Let us make man in our *i,*
1:27 So God created man in his own *i,*
1Co 11: 7 since he is the *i* and glory of God;
Col 1:15 He is the *i* of the invisible God,
3:10 in knowledge in the *i* of its Creator.

IMAGINE
Eph 3:20 more than all we ask or *i,*

IMITATE (IMITATORS)
1Co 4:16 Therefore I urge you to *i* me.
Heb 6:12 but to *i* those who through faith
13: 7 of their way of life and *i* their faith.
3Jn :11 do not *i* what is evil but what is

IMITATORS* (IMITATE)
Eph 5: 1 Be *i* of God, therefore,
1Th 1: 6 You became *i* of us and of the Lord
2:14 became *i* of God's churches

IMMANUEL
Isa 7:14 birth to a son, and will call him *I.*
Mt 1:23 and they will call him *I*"—

IMMORAL* (IMMORALITY)
Pr 6:24 keeping you from the *i* woman,
1Co 5: 9 to associate with sexually *i* people
5:10 the people of this world who are *i,*
5:11 but is sexually *i* or greedy,
6: 9 Neither the sexually *i* nor idolaters
Eph 5: 5 No *i,* impure or greedy person—
Heb 12:16 See that no one is sexually *i,*
13: 4 the adulterer and all the sexually *i.*
Rev 21: 8 the murderers, the sexually *i,*
22:15 the sexually *i,* the murderers,

IMMORALITY (IMMORAL)
1Co 6:13 The body is not meant for sexual *i,*
6:18 Flee from sexual *i.*
10: 8 We should not commit sexual *i,*
Gal 5:19 sexual *i,* impurity and debauchery;
Eph 5: 3 must not be even a hint of sexual *i,*
1Th 4: 3 that you should avoid sexual *i;*

Jude : 4 grace of our God into a license for *i*

IMMORTAL* (IMMORTALITY)
Ro 1:23 glory of the *i* God for images made
1Ti 1:17 Now to the King eternal, *i,*
6:16 who alone is *i* and who lives

IMMORTALITY (IMMORTAL)
Ro 2: 7 honor and *i,* he will give eternal life
1Co 15:53 and the mortal with *i.*
2Ti 1:10 and *i* to light through the gospel.

IMPERISHABLE
1Pe 1:23 not of perishable seed, but of *i,*

IMPORTANCE* (IMPORTANT)
1Co 15: 3 passed on to you as of first *i:*

IMPORTANT (IMPORTANCE)
Mt 6:25 Is not life more *i* than food,
23:23 have neglected the more *i* matters
Mk 12:29 "The most *i* one," answered Jesus,
12:33 as yourself is more *i* than all burnt
Php 1:18 The *i* thing is that in every way,

IMPOSSIBLE
Mt 17:20 Nothing will be *i* for you."
Lk 1:37 For nothing is *i* with God."
18:27 "What is *i* with men is possible
Heb 6:18 things in which it is *i* for God to lie,
11: 6 without faith it is *i* to please God,

IMPROPER*
Eph 5: 3 these are *i* for God's holy people.

IMPURE (IMPURITY)
Ac 10:15 not call anything *i* that God has
Eph 5: 5 No immoral, *i* or greedy person—
1Th 4: 7 For God did not call us to be *i,*
Rev 21:27 Nothing *i* will ever enter it,

IMPURITY (IMPURE)
Ro 1:24 hearts to sexual *i* for the degrading
Eph 5: 3 or of any kind of *i,* or of greed,

INCENSE
Ex 40: 5 Place the gold altar of *i* in front
Ps 141: 2 my prayer be set before you like *i;*
Mt 2:11 him with gifts of gold and of *i*

INCOME
Ecc 5:10 wealth is never satisfied with his *i.*
1Co 16: 2 sum of money in keeping with his *i,*

INCOMPARABLE*
Eph 2: 7 ages he might show the *i* riches

INCREASE (EVER-INCREASING INCREASED INCREASES INCREASING)
Ge 1:22 "Be fruitful and *i* in number
Ps 62:10 though your riches *i,*
Isa 9: 7 Of the *i* of his government
Lk 17: 5 said to the Lord, *"I* our faith!"
1Th 3:12 May the Lord make your love *i*

INCREASED (INCREASE)
Ac 6: 7 of disciples in Jerusalem *i* rapidly,
Ro 5:20 But where sin *i,* grace *i* all the more

INCREASES (INCREASE)
Pr 24: 5 and a man of knowledge *i* strength;

INCREASING (INCREASE)
Ac 6: 1 when the number of disciples was *i,*
2Th 1: 3 one of you has for each other is *i.*
2Pe 1: 8 these qualities in *i* measure,

INDEPENDENT*
1Co 11:11 however, woman is not *i* of man,
11:11 of man, nor is man *i* of woman.

INDESCRIBABLE*
2Co 9:15 Thanks be to God for his *i* gift!

INDISPENSABLE*
1Co 12:22 seem to be weaker are *i,*

INEFFECTIVE*
2Pe 1: 8 they will keep you from being *i*

INEXPRESSIBLE*
2Co 12: 4 He heard *i* things, things that man
1Pe 1: 8 are filled with an *i* and glorious joy,

INFANTS
Mt 21:16 " 'From the lips of children and *i*
1Co 14:20 In regard to evil be *i,*

INFIRMITIES
Isa 53: 4 Surely he took up our *i*

INHERIT (CO-HEIRS HEIRS HERITAGE INHERITANCE)
Ps 37:11 But the meek will *i* the land
37:29 the righteous will *i* the land
Mt 5: 5 for they will *i* the earth.
Mk 10:17 "what must I do to *i* eternal life?"
1Co 15:50 blood cannot *i* the kingdom of God

INHERITANCE (INHERIT)
Dt 4:20 to be the people of his *i,*
Pr 13:22 A good man leaves an *i*
Eph 1:14 who is a deposit guaranteeing our *i*
5: 5 has any *i* in the kingdom of Christ
Heb 9:15 receive the promised eternal *i*—
1Pe 1: 4 and into an *i* that can never perish,

INIQUITIES (INIQUITY)
Ps 78:38 he forgave their *i*
103:10 or repay us according to our *i.*
Isa 59: 2 But your *i* have separated
Mic 7:19 and hurl all our *i* into the depths

INIQUITY (INIQUITIES)
Ps 51: 2 Wash away all my *i*
Isa 53: 6 the *i* of us all.

INJUSTICE
2Ch 19: 7 the LORD our God there is no *i*

INNOCENT
Pr 17:26 It is not good to punish an *i* man,
Mt 10:16 shrewd as snakes and as *i* as doves.
27: 4 "for I have betrayed *i* blood."
1Co 4: 4 but that does not make me *i.*

INSCRIPTION
Mt 22:20 And whose *i?"* "Caesar's,"

INSOLENT
Ro 1:30 God-haters, *i,* arrogant

INSTITUTED
Ro 13: 2 rebelling against what God has *i,*
1Pe 2:13 to every authority *i* among men:

INSTRUCT (INSTRUCTION)
Ps 32: 8 I will *i* you and teach you
Pr 9: 9 *I* a wise man and he will be wiser
Ro 15:14 and competent to *i* one another.
2Ti 2:25 who oppose him he must gently *i,*

INSTRUCTION (INSTRUCT)
Pr 1: 8 Listen, my son, to your father's *i*
4: 1 Listen, my sons, to a father's *i;*
4:13 Hold on to *i,* do not let it go;
8:10 Choose my *i* instead of silver,
8:33 Listen to my *i* and be wise;
13: 1 A wise son heeds his father's *i,*
13:13 He who scorns *i* will pay for it,
16:20 Whoever gives heed to *i* prospers,
16:21 and pleasant words promote *i.*

19:20 Listen to advice and accept *i*,
23:12 Apply your heart to *i*
1Co 14: 6 or prophecy or word of *i*?
14:26 or a word of *i*, a revelation,
Eph 6: 4 up in the training and *i* of the Lord.
1Th 4: 8 he who rejects this *i* does not reject
2Th 3:14 If anyone does not obey our *i*
1Ti 1:18 I give you this *i* in keeping
6: 3 to the sound *i* of our Lord Jesus
2Ti 4: 2 with great patience and careful *i*.

INSULT
Pr 9: 7 corrects a mocker invites *i*;
12:16 but a prudent man overlooks an *i*.
Mt 5:11 Blessed are you when people *i* you,
Lk 6:22 when they exclude you and *i* you
1Pe 3: 9 evil with evil or *i* with *i*,

INTEGRITY
1Ki 9: 4 if you walk before me in *i* of heart
Job 2: 3 And he still maintains his *i*,
27: 5 till I die, I will not deny my *i*.
Pr 10: 9 The man of *i* walks securely,
11: 3 The *i* of the upright guides them,
29:10 Bloodthirsty men hate a man of *i*
Tit 2: 7 your teaching show *i*, seriousness

INTELLIGENCE
Isa 29:14 the *i* of the intelligent will vanish."
1Co 1:19 *i* of the intelligent I will frustrate."

INTELLIGIBLE
1Co 14:19 I would rather speak five *i* words

INTERCEDE (INTERCEDES INTERCESSION)
Heb 7:25 he always lives to *i* for them.

INTERCEDES (INTERCEDE)
Ro 8:26 but the Spirit himself *i* for us

INTERCESSION* (INTERCEDE)
Isa 53:12 and made *i* for the transgressors.
1Ti 2: 1 *i* and thanksgiving be made

INTERESTS
1Co 7:34 his wife—and his *i* are divided.
Php 2: 4 only to your own *i*, but also to the *i*
2:21 everyone looks out for his own *i*,

INTERMARRY (MARRY)
Dt 7: 3 Do not *i* with them.

INVENTED*
2Pe 1:16 We did not follow cleverly *i* stories

INVESTIGATED
Lk 1: 3 I myself have carefully *i* everything

INVISIBLE
Ro 1:20 of the world God's *i* qualities—
Col 1:15 He is the image of the *i* God,
1Ti 1:17 immortal, *i*, the only God,

INVITE (INVITED INVITES)
Lk 14:13 you give a banquet, *i* the poor,

INVITED (INVITE)
Mt 22:14 For many are *i*, but few are chosen
25:35 I was a stranger and you *i* me in,

INVITES (INVITE)
1Co 10:27 If some unbeliever *i* you to a meal

INVOLVED
2Ti 2: 4 a soldier gets *i* in civilian affairs—

IRON
1Ti 4: 2 have been seared as with a hot *i*.
Rev 2:27 He will rule them with an *i* scepter;

IRREVOCABLE*
Ro 11:29 for God's gifts and his call are *i*.

ISAAC

Son of Abraham by Sarah (Ge 17:19; 21:1-7; 1Ch 1:28). Offered up by Abraham (Ge 22; Heb 11:17-19). Rebekah taken as wife (Ge 24). Fathered Esau and Jacob (Ge 25:19-26; 1Ch 1:34). Tricked into blessing Jacob (Ge 27). Father of Israel (Ex 3:6; Dt 29:13; Ro 9:10).

ISAIAH

Prophet to Judah (Isa 1:1). Called by the LORD (Isa 6).

ISHMAEL

Son of Abraham by Hagar (Ge 16; 1Ch 1:28). Blessed, but not son of covenant (Ge 17:18-21; Gal 4:21-31). Sent away by Sarah (Ge 21:8-21).

ISRAEL (ISRAELITES)

1. Name given to Jacob (see JACOB).

2. Corporate name of Jacob's descendants; often specifically Northern Kingdom.

Dt 6: 4 Hear, O *I*: The LORD our God,
1Sa 4:21 "The glory has departed from *I*"—
Isa 27: 6 *I* will bud and blossom
Jer 31:10 'He who scattered *I* will gather
Eze 39:23 of *I* went into exile for their sin,
Mk 12:29 'Hear, O *I*, the Lord our God,
Lk 22:30 judging the twelve tribes of *I*.
Ro 9: 6 all who are descended from *I* are *I*.
11:26 And so all *I* will be saved,
Eph 3: 6 Gentiles are heirs together with *I*,

ISRAELITES (ISRAEL)
Ex 14:22 and the *I* went through the sea
16:35 The *I* ate manna forty years,
Hos 1:10 "Yet the *I* will be like the sand
Ro 9:27 the number of the *I* be like the sand

ITCHING*
2Ti 4: 3 to say what their *i* ears want to hear

JACOB

Second son of Isaac, twin of Esau (Ge 26:21-26; 1Ch 1:34). Bought Esau's birthright (Ge 26:29-34); tricked Isaac into blessing him (Ge 27:1-37). Abrahamic covenant perpetuated through (Ge 28:13-15; Mal 1:2). Vision at Bethel (Ge 28:10-22). Wives and children (Ge 29:1-30:24; 35:16-26; 1Ch 2-9). Wrestled with God; name changed to Israel (Ge 32:22-32). Sent sons to Egypt during famine (Ge 42-43). Settled in Egypt (Ge 46). Blessed Ephraim and Manasseh (Ge 48). Blessed sons (Ge 49:1-28; Heb 11:21). Death (Ge 49:29-33). Burial (Ge 50:1-14).

JAMES

1. Apostle; brother of John (Mt 4:21-22; 10:2; Mk 3:17; Lk 5:1-10). At transfiguration (Mt 17:1-13; Mk 9:1-13; Lk 9:28-36). Killed by Herod (Ac 12:2).

2. Apostle; son of Alphaeus (Mt 10:3; Mk 3:18; Lk 6:15).

3. Brother of Jesus (Mt 13:55; Mk 6:3; Lk 24:10; Gal 1:19) and Judas (Jude 1). With believers before Pentecost (Ac 1:13). Leader of church at Jerusalem (Ac 12:17; 15; 21:18; Gal 2:9, 12). Author of epistle (Jas 1:1).

JAPHETH

Son of Noah (Ge 5:32; 1Ch 1:4-5). Blessed (Ge 9:18-28).

JARS
2Co 4: 7 we have this treasure in *j* of clay

JEALOUS (JEALOUSY)
Ex 20: 5 the LORD your God, am a *j* God,
34:14 whose name is Jealous, is a *j* God.
Dt 4:24 God is a consuming fire, a *j* God.
Joel 2:18 the LORD will be *j* for his land
Zec 1:14 I am very *j* for Jerusalem and Zion,
2Co 11: 2 I am *j* for you with a godly jealousy

JEALOUSY (JEALOUS)
1Co 3: 3 For since there is *j* and quarreling
2Co 11: 2 I am jealous for you with a godly *j*.
Gal 5:20 hatred, discord, *j*, fits of rage,

JEHOAHAZ
1. Son of Jehu; king of Israel (2Ki 13:1-9).
2. Son of Josiah; king of Judah (2Ki 23:31-34; 2Ch 36:1-4).

JEHOASH
Son of Jehoahaz; king of Israel (2Ki 13-14; 2Ch 25).

JEHOIACHIN
Son of Jehoiakim; king of Judah exiled by Nebuchadnezzar (2Ki 24:8-17; 2Ch 36:8-10; Jer 22:24-30; 24:1). Raised from prisoner status (2Ki 25:27-30; Jer 52:31-34).

JEHOIAKIM
Son of Josiah; king of Judah (2Ki 23:34-24:6; 2Ch 36:4-8; Jer 22:18-23; 36).

JEHORAM
Son of Jehoshaphat; king of Judah (2Ki 8:16-24).

JEHOSHAPHAT
Son of Asa; king of Judah (1Ki 22:41-50; 2Ki 3; 2Ch 17-20).

JEHU
King of Israel (1Ki 19:16-19; 2Ki 9-10).

JEPHTHAH
Judge from Gilead who delivered Israel from Ammon (Jdg 10:6-12:7). Made rash vow concerning his daughter (Jdg 11:30-40).

JEREMIAH
Prophet to Judah (Jer 1:1-3). Called by the LORD (Jer 1). Put in stocks (Jer 20:1-3). Threatened for prophesying (Jer 11:18-23; 26). Opposed by Hananiah (Jer 28). Scroll burned (Jer 36). Imprisoned (Jer 37). Thrown into cistern (Jer 38). Forced to Egypt with those fleeing Babylonians (Jer 43).

JEROBOAM
1. Official of Solomon; rebelled to become first king of Israel (1Ki 11:26-40; 12:1-20; 2Ch 10). Idolatry (1Ki 12:25-33); judgment for (1Ki 13-14; 2Ch 13).
2. Son of Jehoash; king of Israel (1Ki 14:23-29).

JERUSALEM
2Ki 23:27 and I will reject *J*, the city I chose,
2Ch 6: 6 now I have chosen *J* for my Name
Ne 2:17 Come, let us rebuild the wall of *J*,
Ps 122: 6 Pray for the peace of *J*:
125: 2 As the mountains surround *J*,
137: 5 If I forget you, O *J*,
Isa 40: 9 You who bring good tidings to *J*,
65:18 for I will create *J* to be a delight
Joel 3:17 *J* will be holy;
Zep 3:16 On that day they will say to *J*,
Zec 2: 4 '*J* will be a city without walls
8: 8 I will bring them back to live in *J*;
14: 8 living water will flow out from *J*,
Mt 23:37 "O *J*, *J*, you who kill the prophets
Lk 13:34 die outside *J*! "O *J*, *J*,
21:24 *J* will be trampled
Jn 4:20 where we must worship is in *J*."
Ac 1: 8 and you will be my witnesses in *J*,
Gal 4:25 corresponds to the present city of *J*
Rev 21: 2 I saw the Holy City, the new *J*,

JESUS
LIFE: Genealogy (Mt 1:1-17; Lk 3:21-37). Birth announced (Mt 1:18-25; Lk 1:26-45). Birth (Mt 2:1-12; Lk 2:1-40). Escape to Egypt (Mt 2:13-23). As a boy in the temple (Lk 2:41-52). Baptism (Mt 3:13-17; Mk 1:9-11; Lk 3:21-22; Jn 1:32-34). Temptation (Mt 4:1-11; Mk 1:12-13; Lk 4:1-13). Ministry in Galilee (Mt 4:12-18:35; Mk 1:14-9:50; Lk 4:14-13:9; Jn 1:35-2:11; 4; 6), Transfiguration (Mt 17:1-8; Mk 9:2-8; Lk 9:28-36), on the way to Jerusalem (Mt 19-20; Mk 10; Lk 13:10-19:27), in Jerusalem (Mt 21-25; Mk 11-13; Lk 19:28-21:38; Jn 2:12-3:36; 5; 7-12). Last supper (Mt 26:17-35; Mk 14:12-31; Lk 22:1-38; Jn 13-17). Arrest and trial (Mt 26:36-27:31; Mk 14:43-15:20; Lk 22:39-23:25; Jn 18:1-19:16). Crucifixion (Mt 27:32-66; Mk 15:21-47; Lk 23:26-55; Jn 19:28-42). Resurrection and appearances (Mt 28; Mk 16; Lk 24; Jn 20-21; Ac 1:1-11; 7:56; 9:3-6; 1Co 15:1-8; Rev 1:1-20).

MIRACLES. Healings: official's son (Jn 4:43-54), demoniac in Capernaum (Mk 1:23-26; Lk 4:33-35), Peter's mother-in-law (Mt 8:14-17; Mk 1:29-31; Lk 4:38-39), leper (Mt 8:2-4; Mk 1:40-45; Lk 5:12-16), paralytic (Mt 9:1-8; Mk 2:1-12; Lk 5:17-26), cripple (Jn 5:1-9), shriveled hand (Mt 12:10-13; Mk 3:1-5; Lk 6:6-11), centurion's servant (Mt 8:5-13; Lk 7:1-10), widow's son raised (Lk 7:11-17), demoniac (Mt 12:22-23; Lk 11:14), Gadarene demoniacs (Mt 8:28-34; Mk 5:1-20; Lk 8:26-39), woman's bleeding and Jairus' daughter (Mt 9:18-26; Mk 5:21-43; Lk 8:40-56), blind man (Mt 9:27-31), mute man (Mt 9:32-33), Canaanite woman's daughter (Mt 15:21-28; Mk 7:24-30), deaf man (Mk 7:31-37), blind man (Mk 8:22-26), demoniac boy (Mt 17:14-18; Mk 9:14-29; Lk 9:37-43), ten lepers (Lk 17:11-19), man born blind (Jn 9:1-7), Lazarus raised (Jn 11), crippled woman (Lk 13:11-17), man with dropsy (Lk 14:1-6), two blind men (Mt 20:29-34; Mk 10:46-52; Lk 18:35-43), Malchus' ear (Lk 22:50-51). Other Miracles: water to wine (Jn 2:1-11), catch of fish (Lk 5:1-11), storm stilled (Mt 8:23-27; Mk 4:37-41; Lk 8:22-25), 5,000 fed (Mt 14:15-21; Mk 6:35-44; Lk 9:10-17; Jn 6:1-14), walking on water (Mt 14:25-33; Mk 6:48-52; Jn 6:15-21), 4,000 fed (Mt 15:32-39; Mk 8:1-9), money from fish (Mt 17:24-27), fig tree cursed (Mt 21:18-22; Mk 11:12-14), catch of fish (Jn 21:1-14).

MAJOR TEACHING: Sermon on the Mount (Mt 5-7; Lk 6:17-49), to Nicodemus (Jn 3), to Samaritan woman (Jn 4), Bread of Life (Jn 6:22-59), at Feast of Tabernacles (Jn 7-8), woes to Pharisees (Mt 23; Lk 11:37-54), Good Shepherd (Jn 10:1-18), Olivet Discourse (Mt 24-25; Mk 13; Lk 21:5-36), Upper Room Discourse (Jn 13-16).

PARABLES: Sower (Mt 13:3-23; Mk 4:3-25; Lk 8:5-18), seed's growth (Mk 4:26-29), wheat and weeds (Mt 13:24-30, 36-43), mustard seed (Mt 13:31-32; Mk 4:30-32), yeast (Mt 13:33; Lk 13:20-21), hidden treasure (Mt 13:44), valuable pearl (Mt 13:45-46), net (Mt 13:47-51), house owner (Mt 13:52), good Samaritan (Lk 10:25-37), unmerciful servant (Mt 18:15-35), lost sheep (Mt 18:10-14; Lk 15:4-7), lost coin (Lk 15:8-10), prodigal son (Lk 15:11-32), dishonest manager (Lk 16:1-13), rich man and Lazarus (Lk 16:19-31), persistent widow (Lk 18:1-8), Pharisee and tax collector (Lk 18:9-14), payment of workers (Mt 20:1-16), tenants and the vineyard (Mt 21:28-46; Mk 12:1-12; Lk 20:9-19), wedding banquet (Mt 22:1-14), faithful servant (Mt 24:45-51), ten virgins (Mt 25:1-13), talents (Mt 25:1-30; Lk 19:12-27).

DISCIPLES see APOSTLES. Call of (Jn 1:35-51; Mt 4:18-22; 9:9; Mk 1:16-20; 2:13-14; Lk 5:1-11, 27-28). Named Apostles (Mk 3:13-19; Lk 6:12-16). Twelve sent out (Mt 10; Mk 6:7-11; Lk 9:1-5). Seventy sent out (Lk 10:1-24). Defection of (Jn 6:60-71; Mt 26:56; Mk 14:50-52). Final commission (Mt 28:16-20; Jn 21:15-23; Ac 1:3-8).

Ac 2:32 God has raised this *J* to life,
9: 5 "I am *J*, whom you are persecuting
15:11 of our Lord *J* that we are saved,
16:31 "Believe in the Lord *J*,
Ro 3:24 redemption that came by Christ *J*.
5:17 life through the one man, *J* Christ.
8: 1 for those who are in Christ *J*,
1Co 2: 2 except *J* Christ and him crucified.
8: 6 and there is but one Lord, *J* Christ,
12: 3 and no one can say, "*J* is Lord,"
2Co 4: 5 not preach ourselves, but *J* Christ
Gal 2:16 but by faith in *J* Christ.
3:28 for you are all one in Christ *J*.
5: 6 in Christ *J* neither circumcision
Eph 2:10 created in Christ *J*
2:20 with Christ *J* himself as the chief
Php 1: 6 until the day of Christ *J*.
2: 5 be the same as that of Christ *J*:
2:10 name of *J* every knee should bow,
Col 3:17 do it all in the name of the Lord *J*,
2Th 2: 1 the coming of our Lord *J* Christ

1Ti 1:15 Christ *J* came into the world
2Ti 3:12 life in Christ *J* will be persecuted,
Tit 2:13 our great God and Savior, *J* Christ,
Heb 2: 9 But we see *J*, who was made a little
3: 1 fix your thoughts on *J*, the apostle
4:14 through the heavens, *J* the Son
7:22 *J* has become the guarantee
7:24 but because *J* lives forever,
12: 2 Let us fix our eyes on *J*, the author
2Pe 1:16 and coming of our Lord *J* Christ,
1Jn 1: 7 and the blood of *J*, his Son,
2: 1 *J* Christ, the Righteous One.
2: 6 to live in him must walk as *J* did.
4:15 anyone acknowledges that *J* is
Rev 22:20 Come, Lord *J*.

JEW (JEWS JUDAISM)
Zec 8:23 of one *J* by the edge of his robe
Ro 1:16 first for the *J*, then for the Gentile.
10:12 there is no difference between *J*
1Co 9:20 To the Jews I became like a *J*,
Gal 3:28 There is neither *J* nor Greek,

JEWELRY (JEWELS)
1Pe 3: 3 wearing of gold *j* and fine clothes.

JEWELS (JEWELRY)
Isa 61:10 as a bride adorns herself with her *j*.
Zec 9:16 like *j* in a crown.

JEWS (JEW)
Mt 2: 2 who has been born king of the *J*?
27:11 "Are you the king of the *J*?" "Yes,
Jn 4:22 for salvation is from the *J*.
Ro 3:29 Is God the God of *J* only?
1Co 1:22 *J* demand miraculous signs
9:20 To the *J* I became like a Jew,
12:13 whether *J* or Greeks, slave or free
Gal 2: 8 of Peter as an apostle to the *J*,
Rev 3: 9 claim to be *J* though they are not,

JEZEBEL

Sidonian wife of Ahab (1Ki 16:31). Promoted Baal worship (1Ki 16:32-33). Killed prophets of the LORD (1Ki 18:4, 13). Opposed Elijah (1Ki 19:1-2). Had Naboth killed (1Ki 21). Death prophesied (1Ki 21:17-24). Killed by Jehu (2Ki 9:30-37).

JOASH

Son of Ahaziah; king of Judah. Sheltered from Athaliah by Jehoiada (2Ki 11; 2Ch 22:10-23:21). Repaired temple (2Ki 12; 2Ch 24).

JOB

Wealthy man from Uz; feared God (Job 1:1-5). Righteousness tested by disaster (Job 1:6-22), personal affliction (Job 2). Maintained innocence in debate with three friends (Job 3-31), Elihu (Job 32-37). Rebuked by the LORD (Job 38-41). Vindicated and restored to greater stature by the LORD (Job 42). Example of righteousness (Eze 14:14, 20).

JOHN

1. Son of Zechariah and Elizabeth (Lk 1). Called the Baptist (Mt 3:1-12; Mk 1:2-8). Witness to Jesus (Mt 3:11-12; Mk 1:7-8; Lk 3:15-18; Jn 1:6-35; 3:27-30; 5:33-36). Doubts about Jesus (Mt 11:2-6; Lk 7:18-23). Arrest (Mt 4:12; Mk 1:14). Execution (Mt 14:1-12; Mk 6:14-29; Lk 9:7-9). Ministry compared to Elijah (Mt 11:7-19; Mk 9:11-13; Lk 7:24-35).

2. Apostle; brother of James (Mt 4:21-22; 10:2; Mk 3:17; Lk 5:1-10). At transfiguration (Mt 17:1-13; Mk 9:1-13; Lk 9:28-36). Desire to be greatest (Mk 10:35-45). Leader of church at Jerusalem (Ac 4:1-3; Gal 2:9). Elder who wrote epistles (2Jn 1; 3Jn 1). Prophet who wrote Revelation (Rev 1:1; 22:8).

3. Cousin of Barnabas, co-worker with Paul, (Ac 12:12-13:13; 15:37), see MARK.

JOIN (JOINED)
Pr 23:20 Do not *j* those who drink too much
24:21 and do not *j* with the rebellious,
Ro 15:30 to *j* me in my struggle by praying
2Ti 1: 8 *j* with me in suffering for the gospel

JOINED (JOIN)
Mt 19: 6 Therefore what God has *j* together,
Mk 10: 9 Therefore what God has *j* together,
Eph 2:21 him the whole building is *j* together
4:16 *j* and held together

JOINTS
Heb 4:12 even to dividing soul and spirit, *j*

JOKING
Eph 5: 4 or coarse *j*, which are out of place,

JONAH

Prophet in days of Jeroboam II (2Ki 14:25). Called to Nineveh; fled to Tarshish (Jnh 1:1-3). Cause of storm; thrown into sea (Jnh 1:4-16). Swallowed by fish (Jnh 1:17). Prayer (Jnh 2). Preached to Nineveh (Jnh 3). Attitude reproved by the LORD (Jnh 4). Sign of (Mt 12:39-41; Lk 11:29-32).

JONATHAN

Son of Saul (1Sa 13:16; 1Ch 8:33). Valiant warrior (1Sa 13-14). Relation to David (1Sa 18:1-4; 19-20; 23:16-18). Killed at Gilboa (1Sa 31). Mourned by David (2Sa 1).

JORAM

1. Son of Ahab; king of Israel (2Ki 3; 8-9; 2Ch 22).

JORDAN
Nu 34:12 boundary will go down along the *J*
Jos 4:22 Israel crossed the *J* on dry ground.'
Mt 3: 6 baptized by him in the *J* River.

JOSEPH

1. Son of Jacob by Rachel (Ge 30:24; 1Ch 2:2). Favored by Jacob, hated by brothers (Ge 37:3-4). Dreams (Ge 37:5-11). Sold by brothers (Ge 37:12-36). Served Potiphar; imprisoned by false accusation (Ge 39). Interpreted dreams of Pharaoh's servants (Ge 40), of Pharaoh (Ge 41:4-40). Made greatest in Egypt (Ge 41:41-57). Sold grain to brothers (Ge 42-45). Brought Jacob and sons to Egypt (Ge 46-47). Sons Ephraim and Manasseh blessed (Ge 48). Blessed (Ge 49:22-26; Dt 33:13-17). Death (Ge 50:22-26; Ex 13:19; Heb 11:22). 12,000 from (Rev 7:8).

2. Husband of Mary, mother of Jesus (Mt 1:16-24; 2:13-19; Lk 1:27; 2; Jn 1:45).

3. Disciple from Arimathea, who gave his tomb for Jesus' burial (Mt 27:57-61; Mk 15:43-47; Lk 24:50-52).

4. Original name of Barnabas (Ac 4:36).

JOSHUA

1. Son of Nun; name changed from Hoshea (Nu 13:8, 16; 1Ch 7:27). Fought Amalekites under Moses (Ex 17:9-14). Servant of Moses on Sinai (Ex 24:13; 32:17). Spied Canaan (Nu 13). With Caleb, allowed to enter land (Nu 14:6, 30). Succeeded Moses (Dt 1:38; 31:1-8; 34:9).

Charged Israel to conquer Canaan (Jos 1). Crossed Jordan (Jos 3-4). Circumcised sons of wilderness wanderings (Jos 5). Conquered Jericho (Jos 6), Ai (Jos 7-8), five kings at Gibeon (Jos 10:1-28), southern Canaan (Jos 10:29-43), northern Canaan (Jos 11-12). Defeated at Ai (Jos 7). Deceived by Gibeonites (Jos 9). Renewed covenant (Jos 8:30-35; 24:1-27). Divided land among tribes (Jos 13-22). Last words (Jos 23). Death (Jos 24:28-31).

2. High priest during rebuilding of temple (Hag 1-2; Zec 3:1-9; 6:11).

JOSIAH

Son of Amon; king of Judah (2Ki 22-23; 2Ch 34-35).

JOTHAM

Son of Azariah (Uzziah); king of Judah (2Ki 15:32-38; 2Ch 26:21-27:9).

JOY (ENJOY ENJOYMENT JOYFUL OVERJOYED REJOICE REJOICES REJOICING)
Dt 16:15 and your *j* will be complete.
1Ch 16:27 strength and *j* in his dwelling place.

Ne 8:10 for the *j* of the LORD is your
Est 9:22 their sorrow was turned into *j*
Job 38: 7 and all the angels shouted for *j*?
Ps 4: 7 have filled my heart with greater *j*
21: 6 with the *j* of your presence.
30:11 sackcloth and clothed me with *j*,
43: 4 to God, my *j* and my delight.
51:12 to me the *j* of your salvation
66: 1 Shout with *j* to God, all the earth!
96:12 the trees of the forest will sing for *j*;
107:22 and tell of his works with songs of *j*
119:111 they are the *j* of my heart.
Pr 10: 1 A wise son brings *j* to his father,
10:28 The prospect of the righteous is *j*,
12:20 but *j* for those who promote peace.
Isa 35:10 everlasting *j* will crown their heads
51:11 Gladness and *j* will overtake them,
55:12 You will go out in *j*
Lk 1:44 the baby in my womb leaped for *j*.
2:10 news of great *j* that will be
Jn 15:11 and that your *j* may be complete.
16:20 but your grief will turn to *j*.
2Co 8: 2 their overflowing *j* and their
Php 2: 2 then make my *j* complete
4: 1 and long for, my *j* and crown,
1Th 2:19 For what is our hope, our *j*,
Phm : 7 Your love has given me great *j*
Heb 12: 2 for the *j* set before him endured
Jas 1: 2 Consider it pure *j*, my brothers,
1Pe 1: 8 with an inexpressible and glorious *j*
2Jn : 4 It has given me great *j* to find some
3Jn : 4 I have no greater *j*

JOYFUL (JOY)
Ps 100: 2 come before him with *j* songs.
Hab 3:18 I will be *j* in God my Savior.
1Th 5:16 Be *j* always; pray continually;

JUDAH
1. Son of Jacob by Leah (Ge 29:35; 35:23; 1Ch 2:1). Tribe of blessed as ruling tribe (Ge 49:8-12; Dt 33:7).
2. Name used for people and land of Southern Kingdom.
Jer 13:19 All *J* will be carried into exile,
Zec 10: 4 From *J* will come the cornerstone,
Heb 7:14 that our Lord descended from *J*,

JUDAISM (JEW)
Gal 1:13 of my previous way of life in *J*,

JUDAS
1. Apostle (Lk 6:16; Jn 14:22; Ac 1:13). Probably also called Thaddaeus (Mt 10:3; Mk 3:18).
2. Brother of James and Jesus (Mt 13:55; Mk 6:3), also called Jude (Jude 1).
3. Apostle, also called Iscariot, who betrayed Jesus (Mt 10:4; 26:14-56; Mk 3:19; 14:10-50; Lk 6:16; 22:3-53; Jn 6:71; 12:4; 13:2-30; 18:2-11). Suicide of (Mt 27:3-5; Ac 1:16-25).

JUDGE (JUDGED JUDGES JUDGING JUDGMENT)
Ge 18:25 Will not the *J* of all the earth do
1Ch 16:33 for he comes to *j* the earth.
Ps 9: 8 He will *j* the world in righteousness
Joel 3:12 sit to *j* all the nations on every side.
Mt 7: 1 Do not *j*, or you too will be judged.
Jn 12:47 For I did not come to *j* the world,
Ac 17:31 a day when he will *j* the world
Ro 2:16 day when God will *j* men's secrets
1Co 4: 3 indeed, I do not even *j* myself.
6: 2 that the saints will *j* the world?
Gal 2: 6 not *j* by external appearance—
2Ti 4: 1 who will *j* the living and the dead,
4: 8 which the Lord, the righteous *J*,
Jas 4:12 There is only one Lawgiver and *J*,
4:12 who are you to *j* your neighbor?
Rev 20: 4 who had been given authority to *j*.

JUDGED (JUDGE)
Mt 7: 1 "Do not judge, or you too will be *j*.
1Co 11:31 But if we *j* ourselves, we would not
Jas 3: 1 who teach will be *j* more strictly.
Rev 20:12 The dead were *j* according

JUDGES (JUDGE)
Jdg 2:16 Then the LORD raised up *j*,
Ps 58:11 there is a God who *j* the earth."
Heb 4:12 it *j* the thoughts and attitudes
Rev 19:11 With justice he *j* and makes war.

JUDGING (JUDGE)
Mt 19:28 *j* the twelve tribes of Israel.
Jn 7:24 Stop *j* by mere appearances,

JUDGMENT (JUDGE)
Dt 1:17 of any man, for *j* belongs to God.
Ps 1: 5 the wicked will not stand in the *j*,
119:66 Teach me knowledge and good *j*,
Pr 6:32 man who commits adultery lacks *j*;
12:11 but he who chases fantasies lacks *j*.
Ecc 12:14 God will bring every deed into *j*,
Isa 66:16 the LORD will execute *j*
Mt 5:21 who murders will be subject to *j*.'
10:15 on the day of *j* than for that town.
12:36 have to give account on the day of *j*
Jn 5:22 but has entrusted all *j* to the Son,
7:24 appearances, and make a right *j*."
16: 8 to sin and righteousness and *j*:
Ro 14:10 stand before God's *j* seat.
14:13 Therefore let us stop passing *j*
1Co 11:29 body of the Lord eats and drinks *j*
2Co 5:10 appear before the *j* seat of Christ,
Heb 9:27 to die once, and after that to face *j*,
10:27 but only a fearful expectation of *j*
1Pe 4:17 For it is time for *j* to begin
Jude : 6 bound with everlasting chains for *j*

JUST (JUSTICE JUSTIFICATION JUSTIFIED JUSTIFY JUSTLY)
Dt 32: 4 and all his ways are *j*.
Ps 37:28 For the LORD loves the *j*
111: 7 of his hands are faithful and *j*;
Pr 1: 3 doing what is right and *j* and fair;
2: 8 for he guards the course of the *j*
Da 4:37 does is right and all his ways are *j*.
Ro 3:26 as to be *j* and the one who justifies
Heb 2: 2 received its *j* punishment,
1Jn 1: 9 and *j* and will forgive us our sins
Rev 16: 7 true and *j* are your judgments."

JUSTICE (JUST)
Ex 23: 2 do not pervert *j* by siding
23: 6 "Do not deny *j* to your poor people
Job 37:23 in his *j* and great righteousness,
Ps 9: 8 he will govern the peoples with *j*.
9:16 The LORD is known by his *j*;
11: 7 he loves *j*;
45: 6 a scepter of *j* will be the scepter
101: 1 I will sing of your love and *j*;
106: 3 Blessed are they who maintain *j*,
Pr 21:15 When *j* is done, it brings joy
28: 5 Evil men do not understand *j*,
29: 4 By *j* a king gives a country stability
29:26 from the LORD that man gets *j*.
Isa 9: 7 it with *j* and righteousness
28:17 I will make *j* the measuring line
30:18 For the LORD is a God of *j*.
42: 1 and he will bring *j* to the nations.
42: 4 till he establishes *j* on earth.
56: 1 "Maintain *j*
61: 8 "For I, the LORD, love *j*;
Jer 30:11 I will discipline you but only with *j*;
Eze 34:16 I will shepherd the flock with *j*.
Am 5:15 maintain *j* in the courts.
5:24 But let *j* roll on like a river,
Zec 7: 9 'Administer true *j*; show mercy
Lk 11:42 you neglect *j* and the love of God.
Ro 3:25 He did this to demonstrate his *j*,

JUSTIFICATION (JUST)

Ro 4:25 and was raised to life for our *j*.
5:18 of righteousness was *j* that brings

JUSTIFIED (JUST)

Ac 13:39 him everyone who believes is *j*
Ro 3:24 and are *j* freely by his grace
3:28 For we maintain that a man is *j*
5: 1 since we have been *j* through faith,
5: 9 Since we have now been *j*
8:30 those he called, he also *j;* those he *j,*
1Co 6:11 you were *j* in the name
Gal 2:16 observing the law no one will be *j.*
3:11 Clearly no one is *j* before God
3:24 to Christ that we might be *j* by faith
Jas 2:24 You see that a person is *j*

JUSTIFY (JUST)

Gal 3: 8 that God would *j* the Gentiles

JUSTLY (JUST)

Mic 6: 8 To act *j* and to love mercy

KEEP (KEEPER KEEPING KEEPS KEPT)

Ge 31:49 "May the LORD *k* watch
Ex 20: 6 and *k* my commandments.
Nu 6:24 and *k* you;
Ps 18:28 You, O LORD, *k* my lamp burning
19:13 *K* your servant also from willful
119: 9 can a young man *k* his way pure?
121: 7 The LORD will *k* you
141: 3 *k* watch over the door of my lips.
Pr 4:24 *k* corrupt talk far from your lips.
Isa 26: 3 You will *k* in perfect peace
Mt 10:10 for the worker is worth his *k.*
Lk 12:35 and *k* your lamps burning,
Gal 5:25 let us *k* in step with the Spirit.
Eph 4: 3 Make every effort to *k* the unity
1Ti 5:22 *K* yourself pure.
2Ti 4: 5 *k* your head in all situations,
Heb 13: 5 *K* your lives free from the love
Jas 1:26 and yet does not *k* a tight rein
2: 8 If you really *k* the royal law found
Jude :24 able to *k* you from falling

KEEPER (KEEP)

Ge 4: 9 I my brother's *k?"* The LORD

KEEPING (KEEP)

Ex 20: 8 the Sabbath day by *k* it holy.
Ps 19:11 in *k* them there is great reward.
Mt 3: 8 Produce fruit in *k* with repentance.
Lk 2: 8 *k* watch over their flocks at night.
1Co 7:19 *K* God's commands is what counts.
2Pe 3: 9 Lord is not slow in *k* his promise,

KEEPS (KEEP)

Pr 17:28 a fool is thought wise if he *k* silent,
Am 5:13 Therefore the prudent man *k* quiet
1Co 13: 5 is not easily angered, it *k* no record
Jas 2:10 For whoever *k* the whole law

KEPT (KEEP)

Ps 130: 3 If you, O LORD, *k* a record of sins,
2Ti 4: 7 finished the race, I have *k* the faith.
1Pe 1: 4 spoil or fade—*k* in heaven for you,

KEYS

Mt 16:19 I will give you the *k* of the kingdom

KILL (KILLS)

Mt 17:23 They will *k* him, and on the third

KILLS (KILL)

Lev 24:21 but whoever *k* a man must be put
2Co 3: 6 for the letter *k,* but the Spirit gives

KIND (KINDNESS KINDS)

Ge 1:24 animals, each according to its *k."*
2Ch 10: 7 "If you will be *k* to these people
Pr 11:17 A *k* man benefits himself,
12:25 but a *k* word cheers him up.
14:21 blessed is he who is *k* to the needy.
14:31 whoever is *k* to the needy honors
19:17 He who is *k* to the poor lends
Da 4:27 by being *k* to the oppressed.
Lk 6:35 because he is *k* to the ungrateful
1Co 13: 4 Love is patient, love is *k.*
15:35 With what *k* of body will they
Eph 4:32 Be *k* and compassionate
1Th 5:15 but always try to be *k* to each other
2Ti 2:24 instead, he must be *k* to everyone,
Tit 2: 5 to be busy at home, to be *k,*

KINDNESS (KIND)

Ac 14:17 He has shown *k* by giving you rain
Ro 11:22 Consider therefore the *k*
Gal 5:22 peace, patience, *k,* goodness,
Eph 2: 7 expressed in his *k* to us
2Pe 1: 7 brotherly *k;* and to brotherly *k,*

KINDS (KIND)

1Co 12: 4 There are different *k* of gifts,
1Ti 6:10 of money is a root of all *k* of evil.

KING (KINGDOM KINGS)

1. Kings of Judah and Israel: see Saul, David, Solomon.

2. Kings of Judah: see Rehoboam, Abijah, Asa, Jehoshaphat, Jehoram, Ahaziah, Athaliah (Queen), Joash, Amaziah, Uzziah, Jotham, Ahaz, Hezekiah, Manasseh, Amon, Josiah, Jehoahaz, Jehoiakim, Jehoiachin, Zedekiah.

3. Kings of Israel: see Jeroboam I, Nadab, Baasha, Elah, Zimri, Tibni, Omri, Ahab, Ahaziah, Joram, Jehu, Jehoahaz, Jehoash, Jeroboam II, Zechariah, Shallum, Menahem, Pekah, Pekahiah, Hoshea.

Jdg 17: 6 In those days Israel had no *k;*
1Sa 12:12 the LORD your God was your *k.*
Ps 24: 7 that the *K* of glory may come in.
Isa 32: 1 See, a *k* will reign in righteousness
Zec 9: 9 See, your *k* comes to you,
1Ti 6:15 the *K* of kings and Lord of lords,
1Pe 2:17 of believers, fear God, honor the *k.*
Rev 19:16 *K OF KINGS AND LORD*

KINGDOM (KING)

Ex 19: 6 you will be for me a *k* of priests
1Ch 29:11 Yours, O LORD, is the *k;*
Ps 45: 6 justice will be the scepter of your *k.*
Da 4: 3 His *k* is an eternal *k;*
Mt 3: 2 Repent, for the *k* of heaven is near
5: 3 for theirs is the *k* of heaven.
6:10 your *k* come,
6:33 But seek first his *k* and his
7:21 Lord,' will enter the *k* of heaven,
11:11 least in the *k* of heaven is greater
13:24 "The *k* of heaven is like a man who
13:31 *k* of heaven is like a mustard seed,
13:33 "The *k* of heaven is like yeast that
13:44 *k* of heaven is like treasure hidden
13:45 the *k* of heaven is like a merchant
13:47 *k* of heaven is like a net that was let
16:19 the keys of the *k* of heaven;
18:23 the *k* of heaven is like a king who
19:24 for a rich man to enter the *k* of God
24: 7 rise against nation, and *k* against *k.*
24:14 gospel of the *k* will be preached
25:34 the *k* prepared for you
Mk 9:47 better for you to enter the *k* of God
10:14 for the *k* of God belongs to such
10:23 for the rich to enter the *k* of God!"
Lk 10: 9 'The *k* of God is near you.'
12:31 seek his *k,* and these things will be
17:21 because the *k* of God is within you
Jn 3: 5 no one can enter the *k* of God
18:36 "My *k* is not of this world.
1Co 6: 9 the wicked will not inherit the *k*
15:24 hands over the *k* to God the Father

Rev 1: 6 has made us to be a *k* and priests
11:15 of the world has become the *k*

KINGS (KING)
Ps 2: 2 The *k* of the earth take their stand
72:11 All *k* will bow down to him
Da 7:24 ten horns are ten *k* who will come
1Ti 2: 2 for *k* and all those in authority,
Rev 1: 5 and the ruler of the *k* of the earth.

KINSMAN-REDEEMER (REDEEM)
Ru 3: 9 over me, since you are a *k*."

KISS
Ps 2:12 *K* the Son, lest he be angry
Pr 24:26 is like a *k* on the lips.
Lk 22:48 the Son of Man with a *k*?"

KNEE (KNEES)
Isa 45:23 Before me every *k* will bow;
Ro 14:11 'every *k* will bow before me;
Php 2:10 name of Jesus every *k* should bow,

KNEES (KNEE)
Isa 35: 3 steady the *k* that give way;
Heb 12:12 your feeble arms and weak *k*.

KNEW (KNOW)
Job 23: 3 If only I *k* where to find him;
Jnh 4: 2 I *k* that you are a gracious
Mt 7:23 tell them plainly, 'I never *k* you.

KNOCK
Mt 7: 7 *k* and the door will be opened
Rev 3:20 I am! I stand at the door and *k*.

KNOW (FOREKNEW KNEW KNOWING KNOWLEDGE KNOWN KNOWS)
Dt 18:21 "How can we *k* when a message
Job 19:25 I *k* that my Redeemer lives,
42: 3 things too wonderful for me to *k*.
Ps 46:10 "Be still, and *k* that I am God;
139: 1 and you *k* me.
139:23 Search me, O God, and *k* my heart;
Pr 27: 1 for you do not *k* what a day may
Jer 24: 7 I will give them a heart to *k* me,
31:34 his brother, saying, '*K* the LORD,'
Mt 6: 3 let your left hand *k* what your right
24:42 you do not *k* on what day your
Lk 1: 4 so that you may *k* the certainty
Jn 3:11 we speak of what we *k*,
4:22 we worship what we do *k*,
9:25 One thing I do *k*.
10:14 I *k* my sheep and my sheep *k* me—
17: 3 that they may *k* you, the only true
21:24 We *k* that his testimony is true.
Ac 1: 7 "It is not for you to *k* the times
Ro 6: 6 For we *k* that our old self was
7:18 I *k* that nothing good lives in me,
8:28 we *k* that in all things God works
1Co 2: 2 For I resolved to *k* nothing
6:15 Do you not *k* that your bodies are
6:19 Do you not *k* that your body is
13:12 Now I *k* in part; then I shall *k* fully,
15:58 because you *k* that your labor
Php 3:10 I want to *k* Christ and the power
2Ti 1:12 because I *k* whom I have believed,
Jas 4:14 *k* what will happen tomorrow.
1Jn 2: 4 The man who says, "I *k* him,"
3:14 We *k* that we have passed
3:16 This is how we *k* what love is:
5: 2 This is how we *k* that we love
5:13 so that you may *k* that you have

KNOWING (KNOW)
Ge 3: 5 and you will be like God, *k* good
Php 3: 8 of *k* Christ Jesus my Lord,

KNOWLEDGE (KNOW)
Ge 2: 9 the tree of the *k* of good and evil.
Job 42: 3 obscures my counsel without *k*?'
Ps 19: 2 night after night they display *k*.
73:11 Does the Most High have *k*?"
139: 6 Such *k* is too wonderful for me,
Pr 1: 7 of the LORD is the beginning of *k*,
10:14 Wise men store up *k*,
12: 1 Whoever loves discipline loves *k*,
13:16 Every prudent man acts out of *k*,
19: 2 to have zeal without *k*,
Isa 11: 9 full of the *k* of the LORD
Hab 2:14 filled with the *k* of the glory
Ro 11:33 riches of the wisdom and *k* of God!
1Co 8: 1 *K* puffs up, but love builds up.
8:11 Christ died, is destroyed by your *k*.
13: 2 can fathom all mysteries and all *k*,
2Co 2:14 everywhere the fragrance of the *k*
4: 6 light of the *k* of the glory of God
Eph 3:19 to know this love that surpasses *k*
Col 2: 3 all the treasures of wisdom and *k*.
1Ti 6:20 ideas of what is falsely called *k*,
2Pe 3:18 grow in the grace and *k* of our Lord

KNOWN (KNOW)
Ps 16:11 You have made *k* to me the path
105: 1 make *k* among the nations what he
Isa 46:10 *k* the end from the beginning,
Mt 10:26 or hidden that will not be made *k*.
Ro 1:19 since what may be *k* about God is
11:34 "Who has *k* the mind of the Lord?
15:20 the gospel where Christ was not *k*,
2Co 3: 2 written on our hearts, *k*
2Pe 2:21 than to have *k* it and then

KNOWS (KNOW)
1Sa 2: 3 for the LORD is a God who *k*,
Job 23:10 But he *k* the way that I take;
Ps 44:21 since he *k* the secrets of the heart?
94:11 The LORD *k* the thoughts of man;
Ecc 8: 7 Since no man *k* the future,
Mt 6: 8 for your Father *k* what you need
24:36 "No one *k* about that day or hour,
Ro 8:27 who searches our hearts *k* the mind
1Co 8: 2 who thinks he *k* something does
2Ti 2:19 The Lord *k* those who are his," and

LABAN
Brother of Rebekah (Ge 24:29-51), father of Rachel and Leah (Ge 29-31).

LABOR
Ex 20: 9 Six days you shall *l* and do all your
Isa 55: 2 and your *l* on what does not satisfy
Mt 6:28 They do not *l* or spin.
1Co 3: 8 rewarded according to his own *l*.
15:58 because you know that your *l*

LACK (LACKING LACKS)
Pr 15:22 Plans fail for *l* of counsel,
Ro 3: 3 Will their *l* of faith nullify God's
Col 2:23 *l* any value in restraining sensual

LACKING (LACK)
Ro 12:11 Never be *l* in zeal, but keep your
Jas 1: 4 and complete, not *l* anything.

LACKS (LACK)
Pr 6:32 who commits adultery *l* judgment;
12:11 he who chases fantasies *l* judgment
Jas 1: 5 any of you *l* wisdom, he should ask

LAID (LAY)
Isa 53: 6 and the LORD has *l* on him
1Co 3:11 other than the one already *l*,
1Jn 3:16 Jesus Christ *l* down his life for us.

LAKE
Rev 19:20 into the fiery *l* of burning sulfur.
20:14 The *l* of fire is the second death.

LAMB (LAMB'S LAMBS)
Ge 22: 8 "God himself will provide the *l*
Ex 12:21 and slaughter the Passover *l*.
Isa 11: 6 The wolf will live with the *l*,
53: 7 he was led like a *l* to the slaughter,
Jn 1:29 *L* of God, who takes away the sin
1Co 5: 7 our Passover *l*, has been sacrificed.
1Pe 1:19 a *l* without blemish or defect.
Rev 5: 6 Then I saw a *L*, looking
5:12 "Worthy is the *L*, who was slain,
14: 4 They follow the *L* wherever he

LAMB'S (LAMB)
Rev 21:27 written in the *L* book of life.

LAMBS (LAMB)
Lk 10: 3 I am sending you out like *l*
Jn 21:15 Jesus said, "Feed my *l*."

LAMENT
2Sa 1:17 took up this *l* concerning Saul

LAMP (LAMPS)
2Sa 22:29 You are my *l*, O LORD;
Ps 18:28 You, O LORD, keep my *l* burning;
119:105 Your word is a *l* to my feet
Pr 31:18 and her *l* does not go out at night.
Lk 8:16 "No one lights a *l* and hides it
Rev 21:23 gives it light, and the Lamb is its *l*.

LAMPS (LAMP)
Mt 25: 1 be like ten virgins who took their *l*
Lk 12:35 for service and keep your *l* burning,

LAND
Ge 1:10 God called the dry ground "*l*,"
1:11 "Let the *l* produce vegetation:
12: 7 To your offspring I will give this *l*."
Ex 3: 8 a *l* flowing with milk and honey—
Nu 35:33 Do not pollute the *l* where you are.
Dt 34: 1 LORD showed him the whole *l*—
Jos 13: 2 "This is the *l* that remains:
14: 4 Levites received no share of the *l*
2Ch 7:14 their sin and will heal their *l*.
7:20 then I will uproot Israel from my *l*,
Eze 36:24 and bring you back into your own *l*.

LANGUAGE
Ge 11: 1 Now the whole world had one *l*
Ps 19: 3 There is no speech or *l*
Jn 8:44 When he lies, he speaks his native *l*
Ac 2: 6 heard them speaking in his own *l*.
Col 3: 8 slander, and filthy *l* from your lips.
Rev 5: 9 from every tribe and *l* and people

LAST (LASTING LASTS LATTER)
2Sa 23: 1 These are the *l* words of David:
Isa 44: 6 I am the first and I am the *l*;
Mt 19:30 But many who are first will be *l*,
Mk 10:31 are first will be *l*, and the *l* first."
Jn 15:16 and bear fruit—fruit that will *l*.
Ro 1:17 is by faith from first to *l*,
2Ti 3: 1 will be terrible times in the *l* days.
2Pe 3: 3 in the *l* days scoffers will come,
Rev 1:17 I am the First and the *L*.
22:13 the First and the *L*, the Beginning

LASTING (LAST)
Ex 12:14 to the LORD—a *l* ordinance.
Lev 24: 8 of the Israelites, as a *l* covenant.
Nu 25:13 have a covenant of a *l* priesthood,
Heb 10:34 had better and *l* possessions.

LASTS (LAST)
Ps 30: 5 For his anger *l* only a moment,

2Co 3:11 greater is the glory of that which *l*!

LATTER (LAST)
Job 42:12 The LORD blessed the *l* part

LAUGH (LAUGHS)
Ecc 3: 4 a time to weep and a time to *l*,

LAUGHS (LAUGH)
Ps 2: 4 The One enthroned in heaven *l*;
37:13 but the Lord *l* at the wicked,

LAVISHED
Eph 1: 8 of God's grace that he *l* on us
1Jn 3: 1 great is the love the Father has *l*

LAW (LAWS)
Dt 31:11 you shall read this *l* before them
31:26 "Take this Book of the *L*
Jos 1: 8 of the *L* depart from your mouth;
Ne 8: 8 from the Book of the *L* of God,
Ps 1: 2 and on his *l* he meditates day
19: 7 The *l* of the LORD is perfect,
119:18 wonderful things in your *l*.
119:72 *l* from your mouth is more precious
119:97 Oh, how I love your *l*!
119:165 peace have they who love your *l*,
Isa 8:20 To the *l* and to the testimony!
Jer 31:33 "I will put my *l* in their minds
Mt 5:17 that I have come to abolish the *L*
7:12 sums up the *L* and the Prophets.
22:40 All the *L* and the Prophets hang
Lk 16:17 stroke of a pen to drop out of the *L*.
Jn 1:17 For the *l* was given through Moses;
Ro 2:12 All who sin apart from the *l* will
2:15 of the *l* are written on their hearts,
5:13 for before the *l* was given,
5:20 *l* was added so that the trespass
6:14 because you are not under *l*,
7: 6 released from the *l* so that we serve
7:12 *l* is holy, and the commandment is
8: 3 For what the *l* was powerless to do
10: 4 Christ is the end of the *l*
13:10 love is the fulfillment of the *l*.
Gal 3:13 curse of the *l* by becoming a curse
3:24 So the *l* was put in charge to lead us
5: 3 obligated to obey the whole *l*.
5: 4 justified by *l* have been alienated
5:14 The entire *l* is summed up
Heb 7:19 (for the *l* made nothing perfect),
10: 1 The *l* is only a shadow
Jas 1:25 intently into the perfect *l* that gives
2:10 For whoever keeps the whole *l*

LAWLESSNESS*
2Th 2: 3 and the man of *l* is revealed,
2: 7 power of *l* is already at work;
1Jn 3: 4 sins breaks the law; in fact, sin is *l*.

LAWS (LAW)
Lev 25:18 and be careful to obey my *l*,
Ps 119:30 I have set my heart on your *l*.
119:120 I stand in awe of your *l*.
Heb 8:10 I will put my *l* in their minds
10:16 I will put my *l* in their hearts,

LAY (LAID LAYING)
Job 22:22 and *l* up his words in your heart.
Isa 28:16 "See, I *l* a stone in Zion,
Mt 8:20 of Man has no place to *l* his head."
Jn 10:15 and I *l* down my life for the sheep.
15:13 that he *l* down his life
1Co 3:11 no one can *l* any foundation other
1Jn 3:16 And we ought to *l* down our lives
Rev 4:10 They *l* their crowns

LAYING (LAY)
1Ti 5:22 Do not be hasty in the *l* on of hands
Heb 6: 1 not *l* again the foundation

LAZARUS
1. Poor man in Jesus' parable (Lk 16:19-31).
2. Brother of Mary and Martha whom Jesus raised from the dead (Jn 11:1-12:19).

LAZY
Pr 10: 4 *L* hands make a man poor,
Heb 6:12 We do not want you to become *l*,

LEAD (LEADERS LEADERSHIP LEADS LED)
Ex 15:13 "In your unfailing love you will *l*
Ps 27:11 *l* me in a straight path
61: 2 *l* me to the rock that is higher
139:24 and *l* me in the way everlasting.
143:10 *l* me on level ground.
Ecc 5: 6 Do not let your mouth *l* you
Isa 11: 6 and a little child will *l* them.
Da 12: 3 those who *l* many to righteousness,
Mt 6:13 And *l* us not into temptation,
1Jn 3: 7 do not let anyone *l* you astray.

LEADERS (LEAD)
Heb 13: 7 Remember your *l*, who spoke
13:17 Obey your *l* and submit

LEADERSHIP (LEAD)
Ro 12: 8 if it is *l*, let him govern diligently;

LEADS (LEAD)
Ps 23: 2 he *l* me beside quiet waters,
Pr 19:23 The fear of the LORD *l* to life:
Isa 40:11 he gently *l* those that have young.
Mt 7:13 and broad is the road that *l*
15:14 If a blind man *l* a blind man,
Jn 10: 3 sheep by name and *l* them out.
Ro 14:19 effort to do what *l* to peace
2Co 2:14 always *l* us in triumphal procession

LEAH
Wife of Jacob (Ge 29:16-30); bore six sons and one daughter (Ge 29:31-30:21; 34:1; 35:23).

LEAN
Pr 3: 5 *l* not on your own understanding;

LEARN (LEARNED LEARNING)
Isa 1:17 *l* to do right!
Mt 11:29 yoke upon you and *l* from me,

LEARNED (LEARN)
Php 4:11 for I have *l* to be content whatever
2Ti 3:14 continue in what you have *l*

LEARNING (LEARN)
Pr 1: 5 let the wise listen and add to their *l*,
2Ti 3: 7 always *l* but never able

LED (LEAD)
Ps 68:18 you *l* captives in your train;
Isa 53: 7 he was *l* like a lamb to the slaughter
Am 2:10 and I *l* you forty years in the desert
Ro 8:14 those who are *l* by the Spirit
Eph 4: 8 he *l* captives in his train

LEFT
Jos 1: 7 turn from it to the right or to the *l*,
Pr 4:27 Do not swerve to the right or the *l*;
Mt 6: 3 do not let your *l* hand know what
25:33 on his right and the goats on his *l*.

LEGION
Mk 5: 9 "My name is *L*," he replied,

LEND (LENDS)
Dt 15: 8 freely *l* him whatever he needs.
Ps 37:26 are always generous and *l* freely;
Lk 6:34 if you *l* to those from whom you

LENDS (LEND)
Pr 19:17 to the poor *l* to the LORD,

LENGTH (LONG)
Ps 90:10 The *l* of our days is seventy years—
Pr 10:27 The fear of the LORD adds *l* to life

LEPROSY
2Ki 7: 3 men with *l* at the entrance

LETTER (LETTERS)
Mt 5:18 not the smallest *l*, not the least
2Co 3: 2 You yourselves are our *l*, written
3: 6 for the *l* kills, but the Spirit gives
2Th 3:14 not obey our instruction in this *l*,

LETTERS (LETTER)
2Co 3: 7 which was engraved in *l* on stone,
10:10 "His *l* are weighty and forceful,
2Pe 3:16 His *l* contain some things that are

LEVEL
Ps 143:10 lead me on *l* ground.
Pr 4:26 Make *l* paths for your feet
Isa 26: 7 The path of the righteous is *l*;
Heb 12:13 "Make *l* paths for your feet,"

LEVI (LEVITES)
1. Son of Jacob by Leah (Ge 29:34; 46:11; 1Ch 2:1). Tribe of blessed (Ge 49:5-7; Dt 33:8-11), chosen as priests (Nu 3-4), numbered (Nu 3:39; 26:62), allotted cities, but not land (Nu 18; 35; Dt 10:9; Jos 13:14; 21), land (Eze 48:8-22), 12,000 from (Rev 7:7).
2. See MATTHEW.

LEVITES (LEVI)
Nu 1:53 The *L* are to be responsible
8: 6 "Take the *L* from among the other
18:21 I give to the *L* all the tithes in Israel

LEWDNESS
Mk 7:22 malice, deceit, *l*, envy, slander,

LIAR (LIE)
Pr 19:22 better to be poor than a *l*.
Jn 8:44 for he is a *l* and the father of lies.
Ro 3: 4 Let God be true, and every man a *l*.

LIBERATED*
Ro 8:21 that the creation itself will be *l*

LIE (LIAR LIED LIES LYING)
Lev 19:11 " 'Do not *l*.
Nu 23:19 God is not a man, that he should *l*,
Dt 6: 7 when you *l* down and when you get
Ps 23: 2 me *l* down in green pastures,
Isa 11: 6 leopard will *l* down with the goat,
Eze 34:14 they will *l* down in good grazing
Ro 1:25 exchanged the truth of God for a *l*,
Col 3: 9 Do not *l* to each other,
Heb 6:18 which it is impossible for God to *l*,

LIED (LIE)
Ac 5: 4 You have not *l* to men but to God."

LIES (LIE)
Ps 34:13 and your lips from speaking *l*.
Jn 8:44 for he is a liar and the father of *l*.

LIFE (LIVE)
Ge 2: 7 into his nostrils the breath of *l*,
2: 9 of the garden were the tree of *l*
9:11 Never again will all *l* be cut
Ex 21:23 you are to take *l* for *l*, eye for eye,
Lev 17:14 the *l* of every creature is its blood.
24:18 must make restitution—*l* for *l*.
Dt 30:19 Now choose *l*, so that you
Ps 16:11 known to me the path of *l*;
23: 6 all the days of my *l*,
34:12 Whoever of you loves *l*
39: 4 let me know how fleeting is my *l*.
49: 7 No man can redeem the *l*

104:33 I will sing to the LORD all my *l;*
Pr 1: 3 a disciplined and prudent *l,*
6:23 are the way to *l,*
7:23 little knowing it will cost him his *l.*
8:35 For whoever finds me finds *l*
11:30 of the righteous is a tree of *l,*
21:21 finds *l,* prosperity and honor.
Jer 10:23 that a man's *l* is not his own;
Eze 37: 5 enter you, and you will come to *l.*
Da 12: 2 some to everlasting *l,* others
Mt 6:25 Is not *l* more important than food,
7:14 and narrow the road that leads to *l,*
10:39 Whoever finds his *l* will lose it,
16:25 wants to save his *l* will lose it,
20:28 to give his *l* as a ransom for many."
Mk 10:45 to give his *l* as a ransom for many."
Lk 12:15 a man's *l* does not consist
12:22 do not worry about your *l,*
14:26 even his own *l*— he cannot be my
Jn 1: 4 In him was *l,* and that *l* was
3:15 believes in him may have eternal *l.*
3:36 believes in the Son has eternal *l,*
4:14 of water welling up to eternal *l."*
5:24 him who sent me has eternal *l*
6:35 Jesus declared, "I am the bread of *l*
6:47 he who believes has everlasting *l.*
6:68 You have the words of eternal *l.*
10:10 I have come that they may have *l,*
10:15 and I lay down my *l* for the sheep.
10:28 I give them eternal *l,* and they shall
11:25 "I am the resurrection and the *l.*
14: 6 am the way and the truth and the *l.*
15:13 lay down his *l* for his friends.
20:31 that by believing you may have *l*
Ac 13:48 appointed for eternal *l* believed.
Ro 4:25 was raised to *l* for our justification.
6:13 have been brought from death to *l;*
6:23 but the gift of God is eternal *l*
8:38 convinced that neither death nor *l,*
1Co 15:19 If only for this *l* we have hope
2Co 3: 6 letter kills, but the Spirit gives *l.*
Gal 2:20 The *l* I live in the body, I live
Eph 4: 1 I urge you to live a *l* worthy
Php 2:16 as you hold out the word of *l*—
Col 1:10 order that you may live a *l* worthy
1Th 4:12 so that your daily *l* may win
1Ti 4: 8 for both the present *l* and the *l*
4:16 Watch your *l* and doctrine closely.
6:19 hold of the *l* that is truly *l.*
2Ti 3:12 to live a godly *l* in Christ Jesus will
Jas 1:12 crown of *l* that God has promised
3:13 Let him show it by his good *l,*
1Pe 3:10 "Whoever would love *l*
2Pe 1: 3 given us everything we need for *l*
1Jn 3:14 we have passed from death to *l,*
5:11 has given us eternal *l,* and this *l* is
Rev 13: 8 written in the book of *l* belonging
20:12 was opened, which is the book of *l.*
21:27 written in the Lamb's book of *l.*
22: 2 side of the river stood the tree of *l,*

LIFT (LIFTED)
Ps 121: 1 I *l* up my eyes to the hills—
134: 2 *L* up your hands in the sanctuary
La 3:41 Let us *l* up our hearts and our
1Ti 2: 8 everywhere to *l* up holy hands

LIFTED (LIFT)
Ps 40: 2 He *l* me out of the slimy pit,
Jn 3:14 Moses *l* up the snake in the desert,
12:32 when I am *l* up from the earth,

LIGHT (ENLIGHTENED)
Ge 1: 3 "Let there be *l,*" and there was *l.*
2Sa 22:29 LORD turns my darkness into *l.*
Job 38:19 "What is the way to the abode of *l?*
Ps 4: 6 Let the *l* of your face shine upon us
19: 8 giving *l* to the eyes.
27: 1 LORD is my *l* and my salvation—
56:13 God in the *l* of life.
76: 4 You are resplendent with *l,*
104: 2 He wraps himself in *l*
119:105 and a *l* for my path.
119:130 The unfolding of your words gives *l;*
Isa 2: 5 let us walk in the *l* of the LORD.
9: 2 have seen a great *l;*
49: 6 also make you a *l* for the Gentiles,
Mt 4:16 have seen a great *l;*
5:16 let your *l* shine before men,
11:30 yoke is easy and my burden is *l."*
Jn 3:19 but men loved darkness instead of *l*
8:12 he said, "I am the *l* of the world.
2Co 4: 6 made his *l* shine in our hearts
6:14 Or what fellowship can *l* have
11:14 masquerades as an angel of *l.*
1Ti 6:16 and who lives in unapproachable *l,*
1Pe 2: 9 of darkness into his wonderful *l.*
1Jn 1: 5 God is *l;* in him there is no
1: 7 But if we walk in the *l,*
Rev 21:23 for the glory of God gives it *l,*

LIGHTNING
Da 10: 6 his face like *l,* his eyes like flaming
Mt 24:27 For as the *l* that comes from the east
28: 3 His appearance was like *l,*

LIKENESS
Ge 1:26 man in our image, in our *l,*
Ps 17:15 I will be satisfied with seeing your *l*
Isa 52:14 his form marred beyond human *l*—
Ro 8: 3 Son in the *l* of sinful man
8:29 to be conformed to the *l* of his Son,
2Co 3:18 his *l* with ever-increasing glory,
Php 2: 7 being made in human *l.*
Jas 3: 9 who have been made in God's *l.*

LILIES
Lk 12:27 "Consider how the *l* grow.

LION
Isa 11: 7 and the *l* will eat straw like the ox.
1Pe 5: 8 around like a roaring *l* looking
Rev 5: 5 See, the *L* of the tribe of Judah,

LIPS
Ps 8: 2 From the *l* of children and infants
34: 1 his praise will always be on my *l.*
119:171 May my *l* overflow with praise,
Pr 13: 3 He who guards his *l* guards his life,
27: 2 someone else, and not your own *l.*
Isa 6: 5 For I am a man of unclean *l,*
Mt 21:16 " 'From the *l* of children
Col 3: 8 and filthy language from your *l.*

LISTEN (LISTENING LISTENS)
Dt 30:20 *l* to his voice, and hold fast to him.
Pr 1: 5 let the wise *l* and add
Jn 10:27 My sheep *l* to my voice; I know
Jas 1:19 Everyone should be quick to *l,*
1:22 Do not merely *l* to the word,

LISTENING (LISTEN)
1Sa 3: 9 Speak, LORD, for your servant is *l*
Pr 18:13 He who answers before *l*—

LISTENS (LISTEN)
Pr 12:15 but a wise man *l* to advice.

LIVE (ALIVE LIFE LIVES LIVING)
Ex 20:12 so that you may *l* long
33:20 for no one may see me and *l."*
Dt 8: 3 to teach you that man does not *l*
Job 14:14 If a man dies, will he *l* again?
Ps 119:175 Let me *l* that I may praise you,
Isa 55: 3 hear me, that your soul may *l.*
Eze 37: 3 can these bones *l?"* I said,

Hab 2: 4 but the righteous will *l* by his faith
Mt 4: 4 'Man does not *l* on bread alone,
Ac 17:24 does not *l* in temples built by hands
17:28 'For in him we *l* and move
Ro 1:17 "The righteous will *l* by faith."
2Co 5: 7 We *l* by faith, not by sight.
Gal 2:20 The life I *l* in the body, I *l* by faith
5:25 Since we *l* by the Spirit, let us keep
Php 1:21 to *l* is Christ and to die is gain.
1Th 5:13 *L* in peace with each other.
2Ti 3:12 who wants to *l* a godly life
Heb 12:14 Make every effort to *l* in peace
1Pe 1:17 *l* your lives as strangers here

LIVES (LIVE)
Job 19:25 I know that my Redeemer *l*,
Isa 57:15 he who *l* forever, whose name is
Da 3:28 to give up their *l* rather than serve
Jn 14:17 for he *l* with you and will be in you.
Ro 7:18 I know that nothing good *l* in me,
14: 7 For none of us *l* to himself alone
1Co 3:16 and that God's Spirit *l* in you?
Gal 2:20 I no longer live, but Christ *l* in me.
Heb 13: 5 Keep your *l* free from the love
2Pe 3:11 You ought to live holy and godly *l*
1Jn 3:16 to lay down our *l* for our brothers.
4:16 Whoever *l* in love *l* in God,

LIVING (LIVE)
Ge 2: 7 and man became a *l* being.
Jer 2:13 the spring of *l* water,
Mt 22:32 the God of the dead but of the *l*."
Jn 7:38 streams of *l* water will flow
Ro 12: 1 to offer your bodies as *l* sacrifices,
Heb 4:12 For the word of God is *l* and active.
10:31 to fall into the hands of the *l* God.
Rev 1:18 I am the *L* One; I was dead,

LOAD
Gal 6: 5 for each one should carry his own *l*.

LOCUSTS
Mt 3: 4 His food was *l* and wild honey.

LOFTY
Ps 139: 6 too *l* for me to attain.
Isa 57:15 is what the high and *l* One says—

LONELY
Ps 68: 6 God sets the *l* in families,

LONG (LENGTH LONGED LONGING LONGS)
1Ki 18:21 "How *l* will you waver
Jn 9: 4 As *l* as it is day, we must do
Eph 3:18 to grasp how wide and *l* and high
1Pe 1:12 Even angels *l* to look

LONGED (LONG)
Mt 13:17 righteous men *l* to see what you see
23:37 how often I have *l*
2Ti 4: 8 to all who have *l* for his appearing.

LONGING (LONG)
Pr 13:19 A *l* fulfilled is sweet to the soul,
2Co 5: 2 *l* to be clothed with our heavenly

LONGS (LONG)
Isa 30:18 Yet the LORD *l* to be gracious

LOOK (LOOKING LOOKS)
Dt 4:29 you will find him if you *l* for him
Job 31: 1 not to *l* lustfully at a girl.
Ps 34: 5 Those who *l* to him are radiant;
Pr 4:25 Let your eyes *l* straight ahead,
Isa 60: 5 Then you will *l* and be radiant,
Hab 1:13 Your eyes are too pure to *l* on evil;
Zec 12:10 They will *l* on me, the one they
Mk 13:21 '*L*, here is the Christ!' or, '*L*,
Lk 24:39 *L* at my hands and my feet.
Jn 1:36 he said, "*L*, the Lamb of God!"
4:35 open your eyes and *l* at the fields!
19:37 "They will *l* on the one they have
Jas 1:27 to *l* after orphans and widows
1Pe 1:12 long to *l* into these things.

LOOKING (LOOK)
2Co 10: 7 You are *l* only on the surface
Rev 5: 6 I saw a Lamb, *l* as if it had been

LOOKS (LOOK)
1Sa 16: 7 Man *l* at the outward appearance,
Lk 9:62 and *l* back is fit for service
Php 2:21 For everyone *l* out

LORD† (LORD'S† LORDING)
Ne 4:14 Remember the *L*, who is great
Job 28:28 'The fear of the *L*— that is wisdom,
Ps 54: 4 the *L* is the one who sustains me.
62:12 and that you, O *L*, are loving.
86: 5 You are forgiving and good, O *L*,
110: 1 The LORD says to my *L*:
147: 5 Great is our *L* and mighty in power
Isa 6: 1 I saw the *L* seated on a throne,
Da 9: 4 "O *L*, the great and awesome God,
Mt 3: 3 'Prepare the way for the *L*,
4: 7 'Do not put the *L* your God
7:21 "Not everyone who says to me, '*L*,
22:37 " 'Love the *L* your God
22:44 For he says, " 'The *L* said to my *L*:
Mk 12:11 the *L* has done this,
12:29 the *L* our God, the *L* is one.
Lk 2: 9 glory of the *L* shone around them,
6:46 "Why do you call me, '*L*, *L*,'
10:27 " 'Love the *L* your God
Ac 2:21 on the name of the *L* will be saved.'
16:31 replied, "Believe in the *L* Jesus,
Ro 10: 9 with your mouth, "Jesus is *L*,"
10:13 on the name of the *L* will be saved
12:11 your spiritual fervor, serving the *L*.
14: 8 we live to the *L*; and if we die,
1Co 1:31 Let him who boasts boast in the *L*."
3: 5 the *L* has assigned to each his task.
7:34 to be devoted to the *L* in both body
10: 9 We should not test the *L*,
11:23 For I received from the *L* what I
12: 3 "Jesus is *L*," except by the Holy
15:57 victory through our *L* Jesus Christ.
16:22 If anyone does not love the *L*—
2Co 3:17 Now the *L* is the Spirit,
8: 5 they gave themselves first to the *L*
10:17 Let him who boasts boast in the *L*."
Gal 6:14 in the cross of our *L* Jesus Christ,
Eph 4: 5 one *L*, one faith, one baptism;
5:10 and find out what pleases the *L*.
5:19 make music in your heart to the *L*,
Php 2:11 confess that Jesus Christ is *L*,
3: 1 my brothers, rejoice in the *L*!
4: 4 Rejoice in the *L* always.
Col 2: 6 as you received Christ Jesus as *L*,
3:17 do it all in the name of the *L* Jesus,
3:23 as working for the *L*, not for men,
4:17 work you have received in the *L*."
1Th 3:12 May the *L* make your love increase
5: 2 day of the *L* will come like a thief
5:23 at the coming of our *L* Jesus Christ.
2Th 2: 1 the coming of our *L* Jesus Christ
2Ti 2:19 "The *L* knows those who are his,"
Heb 12:14 holiness no one will see the *L*.
13: 6 *L* is my helper; I will not be afraid.
Jas 4:10 Humble yourselves before the *L*,
1Pe 1:25 the word of the *L* stands forever."
2: 3 you have tasted that the *L* is good.
3:15 in your hearts set apart Christ as *L*.
2Pe 1:16 and coming of our *L* Jesus Christ,
2: 1 the sovereign *L* who bought
3: 9 The *L* is not slow in keeping his

Jude :14 the *L* is coming with thousands
Rev 4: 8 holy, holy is the *L* God Almighty,
4:11 "You are worthy, our *L* and God,
17:14 he is *L* of lords and King of kings—
22:20 Come, *L* Jesus.

LORD'S† (LORD†)

Ac 21:14 and said, "The *L* will be done."
1Co 10:26 "The earth is the *L*, and everything
11:26 you proclaim the *L* death
2Co 3:18 faces all reflect the *L* glory,
2Ti 2:24 And the *L* servant must not quarrel
Jas 4:15 you ought to say, "If it is the *L* will,

LORDING* (LORD†)

1Pe 5: 3 not *l* it over those entrusted to you,

LORD‡ (LORD'S‡)

Ge 2: 4 When the *L* God made the earth
2: 7 the *L* God formed the man
3:21 The *L* God made garments of skin
7:16 Then the *L* shut him in.
15: 6 Abram believed the *L*,
18:14 Is anything too hard for the *L?*
31:49 "May the *L* keep watch
Ex 3: 2 the angel of the *L* appeared to him
9:12 the *L* hardened Pharaoh's heart
14:30 That day the *L* saved Israel
20: 2 "I am the *L* your God, who
33:11 The *L* would speak to Moses face
40:34 glory of the *L* filled the tabernacle.
Lev 19: 2 'Be holy because I, the *L* your God,
Nu 8: 5 *L* said to Moses: "Take the Levites
14:21 glory of the *L* fills the whole earth,
Dt 2: 7 forty years the *L* your God has
5: 9 the *L* your God, am a jealous God,
6: 4 The *L* our God, the *L* is one.
6: 5 Love the *L* your God
6:16 Do not test the *L* your God
10:14 To the *L* your God belong
10:17 For the *L* your God is God of gods
11: 1 Love the *L* your God and keep his
28: 1 If you fully obey the *L* your God
30:16 today to love the *L* your God,
30:20 For the *L* is your life, and he will
31: 6 for the *L* your God goes with you;
Jos 22: 5 to love the *L* your God, to walk
24:15 my household, we will serve the *L*
1Sa 1:28 So now I give him to the *L*.
2: 2 "There is no one holy like the *L*;
7:12 "Thus far has the *L* helped us."
12:22 his great name the *L* will not reject
15:22 "Does the *L* delight
2Sa 22: 2 "The *L* is my rock, my fortress
1Ki 2: 3 and observe what the *L* your God
8:11 the glory of the *L* filled his temple.
8:61 fully committed to the *L* our God,
18:21 If the *L* is God, follow him;
2Ki 13:23 But the *L* was gracious to them
1Ch 16: 8 Give thanks to the *L*, call
16:23 Sing to the *L*, all the earth;
28: 9 for the *L* searches every heart
29:11 O *L*, is the greatness and the power
2Ch 5:14 the glory of the *L* filled the temple
16: 9 of the *L* range throughout the earth
19: 6 judging for man but for the *L*,
30: 9 for the *L* your God is gracious
Ne 1: 5 Then I said: "O *L*, God of heaven,
Job 1:21 *L* gave and the *L* has taken away;
38: 1 the *L* answered Job out
42: 9 and the *L* accepted Job's prayer.
Ps 1: 2 But his delight is in the law of the *L*
9: 9 The *L* is a refuge for the oppressed,
12: 6 And the words of the *L* are flawless
16: 8 I have set the *L* always before me.
18:30 the word of the *L* is flawless.
19: 7 The law of the *L* is perfect,
19:14 O *L*, my Rock and my Redeemer.
23: 1 The *L* is my shepherd, I shall not be
23: 6 I will dwell in the house of the *L*
27: 1 The *L* is my light and my salvation
27: 4 to gaze upon the beauty of the *L*
29: 1 Ascribe to the *L*, O mighty ones,
32: 2 whose sin the *L* does not count
33:12 is the nation whose God is the *L*,
33:18 But the eyes of the *L* are
34: 3 Glorify the *L* with me;
34: 7 The angel of the *L* encamps
34: 8 Taste and see that the *L* is good;
34:18 The *L* is close to the brokenhearted
37: 4 Delight yourself in the *L*
40: 1 I waited patiently for the *L*;
47: 2 How awesome is the *L* Most High,
48: 1 Great is the *L*, and most worthy
55:22 Cast your cares on the *L*
75: 8 In the hand of the *L* is a cup
84:11 For the *L* God is a sun and shield;
86:11 Teach me your way, O *L*,
89: 5 heavens praise your wonders, O *L*,
91: 2 I will say of the *L*, "He is my refuge
95: 1 Come, let us sing for joy to the *L*;
96: 1 Sing to the *L* a new song;
98: 4 Shout for joy to the *L*, all the earth,
100: 1 Shout for joy to the *L*, all the earth.
103: 1 Praise the *L*, O my soul;
103: 8 The *L* is compassionate
104: 1 O *L* my God, you are very great;
107: 8 to the *L* for his unfailing love
110: 1 The *L* says to my Lord:
113: 4 *L* is exalted over all the nations,
115: 1 Not to us, O *L*, not to us
116:15 Precious in the sight of the *L*
118: 1 Give thanks to the *L*, for he is good
118:24 This is the day the *L* has made;
121: 2 My help comes from the *L*,
121: 5 The *L* watches over you—
125: 2 so the *L* surrounds his people
127: 1 Unless the *L* builds the house,
127: 3 Sons are a heritage from the *L*,
130: 3 If you, O *L*, kept a record of sins,
135: 6 The *L* does whatever pleases him,
136: 1 Give thanks to the *L*, for he is good
139: 1 O *L*, you have searched me
144: 3 O *L*, what is man that you care
145: 3 Great is the *L* and most worthy
145:18 The *L* is near to all who call on him
Pr 1: 7 The fear of the *L* is the beginning
3: 5 Trust in the *L* with all your heart
3: 9 Honor the *L* with your wealth,
3:12 the *L* disciplines those he loves,
3:19 By wisdom the *L* laid the earth's
5:21 are in full view of the *L*,
6:16 There are six things the *L* hates,
10:27 The fear of the *L* adds length to life
11: 1 The *L* abhors dishonest scales,
12:22 The *L* detests lying lips,
14:26 He who fears the *L* has a secure
15: 3 The eyes of the *L* are everywhere,
16: 2 but motives are weighed by the *L*.
16: 4 The *L* works out everything
16: 9 but the *L* determines his steps.
16:33 but its every decision is from the *L*.
18:10 The name of the *L* is a strong tower
18:22 and receives favor from the *L*.
19:14 but a prudent wife is from the *L*.
19:17 to the poor lends to the *L*,
21: 3 to the *L* than sacrifice.
21:30 that can succeed against the *L*.
21:31 but victory rests with the *L*.
22: 2 The *L* is the Maker of them all.
24:18 or the *L* will see and disapprove
31:30 a woman who fears the *L* is
Isa 6: 3 holy, holy is the *L* Almighty;
11: 2 The Spirit of the *L* will rest on him

11: 9 full of the knowledge of the *L*
12: 2 The *L*, the *L*, is my strength
24: 1 the *L* is going to lay waste the earth
25: 8 The Sovereign *L* will wipe away
29:15 to hide their plans from the *L*,
33: 6 the fear of the *L* is the key
35:10 the ransomed of the *L* will return.
40: 5 the glory of the *L* will be revealed,
40: 7 the breath of the *L* blows on them.
40:10 the Sovereign *L* comes with power,
40:28 The *L* is the everlasting God,
40:31 but those who hope in the *L*
42: 8 "I am the *L*; that is my name!
43:11 I, even I, am the *L*,
44:24 I am the *L*,
45: 5 I am the *L*, and there is no other;
45:21 Was it not I, the *L*?
51:11 The ransomed of the *L* will return.
53: 6 and the *L* has laid on him
53:10 and the will of the *L* will prosper
55: 6 Seek the *L* while he may be found;
58: 8 of the *L* will be your rear guard.
58:11 The *L* will guide you always;
59: 1 the arm of the *L* is not too short
61: 3 a planting of the *L*
61:10 I delight greatly in the *L*;
Jer 1: 9 Then the *L* reached out his hand
9:24 I am the *L*, who exercises kindness,
16:19 O *L*, my strength and my fortress,
17: 7 is the man who trusts in the *L*,
La 3:40 and let us return to the *L*.
Eze 1:28 of the likeness of the glory of the *L*.
Hos 1: 7 horsemen, but by the *L* their God."
3: 5 They will come trembling to the *L*
6: 1 "Come, let us return to the *L*.
Joel 2: 1 for the day of the *L* is coming.
2:11 The day of the *L* is great;
3:14 For the day of the *L* is near
Am 5:18 long for the day of the *L*?
Jnh 1: 3 But Jonah ran away from the *L*
Mic 4: 2 up to the mountain of the *L*,
6: 8 And what does the *L* require of you
Na 1: 2 The *L* takes vengeance on his foes
1: 3 The *L* is slow to anger
Hab 2:14 knowledge of the glory of the *L*,
2:20 But the *L* is in his holy temple;
Zep 3:17 The *L* your God is with you,
Zec 1:17 and the *L* will again comfort Zion
9:16 The *L* their God will save them
14: 5 Then the *L* my God will come,
14: 9 The *L* will be king
Mal 4: 5 and dreadful day of the *L* comes.

LORD'S‡ (LORD‡)
Ex 34:34 he entered the *L* presence
Nu 14:41 you disobeying the *L* command?
Dt 6:18 is right and good in the *L* sight,
32: 9 For the *L* portion is his people,
Jos 21:45 Not one of all the *L* good promises
Ps 24: 1 The earth is the *L*, and everything
32:10 but the *L* unfailing love
89: 1 of the *L* great love forever;
103:17 *L* love is with those who fear him,
Pr 3:11 do not despise the *L* discipline
Isa 24:14 west they acclaim the *L* majesty.
62: 3 of splendor in the *L* hand,
Jer 48:10 lax in doing the *L* work!
La 3:22 of the *L* great love we are not
Mic 4: 1 of the *L* temple will be established

LOSE (LOSES LOSS LOST)
1Sa 17:32 "Let no one *l* heart on account
Mt 10:39 Whoever finds his life will *l* it,
Lk 9:25 and yet *l* or forfeit his very self?
Jn 6:39 that I shall *l* none of all that he has
Heb 12: 3 will not grow weary and *l* heart.
12: 5 do not *l* heart when he rebukes you

LOSES (LOSE)
Mt 5:13 But if the salt *l* its saltiness,
Lk 15: 4 you has a hundred sheep and *l* one
15: 8 has ten silver coins and *l* one.

LOSS (LOSE)
Ro 11:12 and their *l* means riches
1Co 3:15 he will suffer *l*; he himself will be
Php 3: 8 I consider everything a *l* compared

LOST (LOSE)
Ps 73: 2 I had nearly *l* my foothold.
Jer 50: 6 "My people have been *l* sheep;
Eze 34: 4 the strays or searched for the *l*.
34:16 for the *l* and bring back the strays.
Mt 18:14 any of these little ones should be *l*.
Lk 15: 4 go after the *l* sheep until he finds it?
15: 6 with me; I have found my *l* sheep.'
15: 9 with me; I have found my *l* coin.'
15:24 is alive again; he was *l* and is found
19:10 to seek and to save what was *l*."
Php 3: 8 for whose sake I have *l* all things.

LOT (LOTS)
Nephew of Abraham (Ge 11:27; 12:5). Chose to live in Sodom (Ge 13). Rescued from four kings (Ge 14). Rescued from Sodom (Ge 19:1-29; 2Pe 2:7). Fathered Moab and Ammon by his daughters (Ge 19:30-38).
Est 3: 7 the *l*) in the presence of Haman
9:24 the *l*) for their ruin and destruction.
Pr 16:33 The *l* is cast into the lap,
18:18 Casting the *l* settles disputes
Ecc 3:22 his work, because that is his *l*.
Ac 1:26 Then they drew lots, and the *l* fell

LOTS (LOT)
Ps 22:18 and cast *l* for my clothing.
Mt 27:35 divided up his clothes by casting *l*.

LOVE (BELOVED LOVED LOVELY LOVER LOVERS LOVES LOVING)
Ge 22: 2 your only son, Isaac, whom you *l*,
Ex 15:13 "In your unfailing *l* you will lead
20: 6 showing *l* to a thousand generations
20: 6 of those who *l* me
34: 6 abounding in *l* and faithfulness,
Lev 19:18 but *l* your neighbor as yourself.
19:34 *L* him as yourself,
Nu 14:18 abounding in *l* and forgiving sin
Dt 5:10 showing *l* to a thousand generations
5:10 of those who *l* me
6: 5 *L* the LORD your God
7:13 He will *l* you and bless you
10:12 to walk in all his ways, to *l* him,
11:13 to *l* the LORD your God
13: 6 wife you *l*, or your closest friend
30: 6 so that you may *l* him
Jos 22: 5 to *l* the LORD your God, to walk
1Ki 3: 3 Solomon showed his *l*
8:23 you who keep your covenant of *l*
2Ch 5:13 his *l* endures forever."
Ne 1: 5 covenant of *l* with those who *l* him
Ps 18: 1 I *l* you, O LORD, my strength.
23: 6 Surely goodness and *l* will follow
25: 6 O LORD, your great mercy and *l*,
31:16 save me in your unfailing *l*.
32:10 but the LORD's unfailing *l*
33: 5 the earth is full of his unfailing *l*.
33:18 whose hope is in his unfailing *l*,
36: 5 Your *l*, O LORD, reaches
36: 7 How priceless is your unfailing *l*!
45: 7 You *l* righteousness and hate
51: 1 according to your unfailing *l*;
57:10 For great is your *l*, reaching
63: 3 Because your *l* is better than life,
66:20 or withheld his *l* from me!
70: 4 may those who *l* your salvation
77: 8 Has his unfailing *l* vanished forever

85: 7 Show us your unfailing *l*, O LORD
85:10 *L* and faithfulness meet together;
86:13 For great is your *l* toward me;
89: 1 of the LORD's great *l* forever;
89:33 but I will not take my *l* from him,
92: 2 to proclaim your *l* in the morning
94:18 your *l*, O LORD, supported me.
100: 5 is good and his *l* endures forever;
101: 1 I will sing of your *l* and justice;
103: 4 crowns you with *l* and compassion.
103: 8 slow to anger, abounding in *l*.
103:11 so great is his *l* for those who fear
107: 8 to the LORD for his unfailing *l*
108: 4 For great is your *l*, higher
116: 1 I *l* the LORD, for he heard my
118: 1 his *l* endures forever.
119:47 because I *l* them.
119:64 The earth is filled with your *l*,
119:76 May your unfailing *l* be my
119:97 Oh, how I *l* your law!
119:119 therefore I *l* your statutes.
119:124 your servant according to your *l*
119:132 to those who *l* your name.
119:159 O LORD, according to your *l*.
119:163 but I *l* your law.
119:165 peace have they who *l* your law,
122: 6 "May those who *l* you be secure.
130: 7 for with the LORD is unfailing *l*
136: 1 *His l endures forever.*
143: 8 of your unfailing *l*,
145: 8 slow to anger and rich in *l*.
145:20 over all who *l* him,
147:11 who put their hope in his unfailing *l*
Pr 3: 3 Let *l* and faithfulness never leave
4: 6 *l* her, and she will watch over you.
5:19 you ever be captivated by her *l*.
8:17 I *l* those who *l* me,
9: 8 rebuke a wise man and he will *l* you
10:12 but *l* covers over all wrongs.
14:22 those who plan what is good find *l*
15:17 of vegetables where there is *l*
17: 9 over an offense promotes *l*,
19:22 What a man desires is unfailing *l*;
20: 6 claims to have unfailing *l*,
20:13 Do not *l* sleep or you will grow
20:28 through *l* his throne is made secure
21:21 who pursues righteousness and *l*
27: 5 rebuke than hidden *l*.
Ecc 9: 6 Their *l*, their hate
9: 9 life with your wife, whom you *l*,
SS 2: 4 and his banner over me is *l*.
8: 6 for *l* is as strong as death,
8: 7 Many waters cannot quench *l*;
8: 7 all the wealth of his house for *l*,
Isa 5: 1 I will sing for the one I *l*
16: 5 In *l* a throne will be established;
38:17 In your *l* you kept me
54:10 yet my unfailing *l* for you will not
55: 3 my faithful *l* promised to David.
61: 8 "For I, the LORD, *l* justice;
63: 9 In his *l* and mercy he redeemed
Jer 5:31 and my people *l* it this way.
31: 3 you with an everlasting *l*;
32:18 You show *l* to thousands
33:11 his *l* endures forever."
La 3:22 of the LORD's great *l* we are not
3:32 so great is his unfailing *l*.
Eze 33:32 more than one who sings *l* songs
Da 9: 4 covenant of *l* with all who *l* him
Hos 2:19 in *l* and compassion.
3: 1 Go, show your *l* to your wife again,
11: 4 with ties of *l*;
12: 6 maintain *l* and justice,
Joel 2:13 slow to anger and abounding in *l*,
Am 5:15 Hate evil, *l* good;
Mic 3: 2 you who hate good and *l* evil;
6: 8 To act justly and to *l* mercy
Zep 3:17 he will quiet you with his *l*,
Zec 8:19 Therefore *l* truth and peace."
Mt 3:17 "This is my Son, whom I *l*;
5:44 *L* your enemies and pray
6:24 he will hate the one and *l* the other,
17: 5 "This is my Son, whom I *l*;
19:19 and '*l* your neighbor as yourself.' "
22:37 " '*L* the Lord your God
Lk 6:32 Even 'sinners' *l* those who *l* them.
7:42 which of them will *l* him more?"
20:13 whom I *l*; perhaps they will respect
Jn 13:34 I give you: *L* one another.
13:35 disciples, if you *l* one another."
14:15 "If you *l* me, you will obey what I
15:13 Greater *l* has no one than this,
15:17 This is my command: *L* each other.
21:15 do you truly *l* me more than these
Ro 5: 5 because God has poured out his *l*
5: 8 God demonstrates his own *l* for us
8:28 for the good of those who *l* him,
8:35 us from the *l* of Christ?
8:39 us from the *l* of God that is
12: 9 *L* must be sincere.
12:10 to one another in brotherly *l*.
13: 8 continuing debt to *l* one another,
13: 9 "*L* your neighbor as yourself."
13:10 Therefore *l* is the fulfillment
13:10 *L* does no harm to its neighbor.
1Co 2: 9 prepared for those who *l* him"—
8: 1 Knowledge puffs up, but *l* builds up
13: 1 have not *l*, I am only a resounding
13: 2 but have not *l*, I am nothing.
13: 3 but have not *l*, I gain nothing.
13: 4 Love is patient, *l* is kind.
13: 4 *L* is patient, love is kind.
13: 6 *L* does not delight in evil
13: 8 *L* never fails.
13:13 But the greatest of these is *l*.
13:13 three remain: faith, hope and *l*.
14: 1 way of *l* and eagerly desire spiritual
16:14 Do everything in *l*.
2Co 5:14 For Christ's *l* compels us,
8: 8 sincerity of your *l* by comparing it
8:24 show these men the proof of your *l*
Gal 5: 6 is faith expressing itself through *l*.
5:13 rather, serve one another in *l*.
5:22 But the fruit of the Spirit is *l*, joy,
Eph 1: 4 In *l* he predestined us
2: 4 But because of his great *l* for us,
3:17 being rooted and established in *l*,
3:18 and high and deep is the *l* of Christ,
3:19 and to know this *l* that surpasses
4: 2 bearing with one another in *l*.
4:15 Instead, speaking the truth in *l*,
5: 2 loved children and live a life of *l*,
5:25 *l* your wives, just as Christ loved
5:28 husbands ought to *l* their wives
5:33 each one of you also must *l* his wife
Php 1: 9 that your *l* may abound more
2: 2 having the same *l*, being one
Col 1: 5 *l* that spring from the hope that is
2: 2 in heart and united in *l*,
3:14 And over all these virtues put on *l*,
3:19 *l* your wives and do not be harsh
1Th 1: 3 your labor prompted by *l*,
4: 9 taught by God to *l* each other.
5: 8 on faith and *l* as a breastplate,
2Th 3: 5 direct your hearts into God's *l*
1Ti 1: 5 The goal of this command is *l*,
2:15 *l* and holiness with propriety.
4:12 in life, in *l*, in faith and in purity.
6:10 For the *l* of money is a root
6:11 faith, *l*, endurance and gentleness.
2Ti 1: 7 of power, of *l* and of self-discipline.
2:22 and pursue righteousness, faith, *l*
3:10 faith, patience, *l*, endurance,
Tit 2: 4 women to *l* their husbands

Phm : 9 yet I appeal to you on the basis of *l*.
Heb 6:10 and the *l* you have shown him
10:24 may spur one another on toward *l*
13: 5 free from the *l* of money
Jas 1:12 promised to those who *l* him.
2: 5 he promised those who *l* him?
2: 8 "*L* your neighbor as yourself,"
1Pe 1:22 the truth so that you have sincere *l*
1:22 *l* one another deeply,
2:17 *L* the brotherhood of believers,
3: 8 be sympathetic, *l* as brothers,
3:10 "Whoever would *l* life
4: 8 Above all, *l* each other deeply,
4: 8 *l* covers over a multitude of sins.
5:14 Greet one another with a kiss of *l*.
2Pe 1: 7 and to brotherly kindness, *l*.
1:17 "This is my Son, whom I *l*;
1Jn 2: 5 God's *l* is truly made complete
2:15 Do not *l* the world or anything
3: 1 How great is the *l* the Father has
3:10 anyone who does not *l* his brother.
3:11 We should *l* one another.
3:14 Anyone who does not *l* remains
3:16 This is how we know what *l* is:
3:18 let us not *l* with words or tongue
3:23 to *l* one another as he commanded
4: 7 Dear friends, let us *l* one another,
4: 7 for *l* comes from God.
4: 8 Whoever does not *l* does not know
4: 9 This is how God showed his *l*
4:10 This is *l*: not that we loved God,
4:11 we also ought to *l* one another.
4:12 and his *l* is made complete in us.
4:16 God is *l*.
4:16 Whoever lives in *l* lives in God,
4:17 *l* is made complete among us
4:18 But perfect *l* drives out fear,
4:19 We *l* because he first loved us.
4:20 If anyone says, "I *l* God,"
4:21 loves God must also *l* his brother.
5: 2 we know that we *l* the children
5: 3 This is *l* for God: to obey his
2Jn : 5 I ask that we *l* one another.
: 6 his command is that you walk in *l*.
: 6 this is *l*: that we walk in obedience
Jude :12 men are blemishes at your *l* feasts,
:21 Keep yourselves in God's *l*
Rev 2: 4 You have forsaken your first *l*.
3:19 Those whom I *l* I rebuke
12:11 they did not *l* their lives so much

LOVED (LOVE)

Ge 24:67 she became his wife, and he *l* her;
29:30 and he *l* Rachel more than Leah.
37: 3 Now Israel *l* Joseph more than any
Dt 7: 8 But it was because the LORD *l* you
1Sa 1: 5 a double portion because he *l* her,
20:17 because he *l* him as he *l* himself.
Ps 44: 3 light of your face, for you *l* them.
Jer 2: 2 how as a bride you *l* me
31: 3 "I have *l* you with an everlasting
Hos 2:23 to the one I called 'Not my *l* one.'
3: 1 though she is *l* by another
9:10 became as vile as the thing they *l*.
11: 1 "When Israel was a child, I *l* him,
Mal 1: 2 "But you ask, 'How have you *l* us?'
Mk 12: 6 left to send, a son, whom he *l*.
Jn 3:16 so *l* the world that he gave his one
3:19 but men *l* darkness instead of light
11: 5 Jesus *l* Martha and her sister
12:43 for they *l* praise from men more
13: 1 Having *l* his own who were
13:23 the disciple whom Jesus *l*,
13:34 As I have *l* you, so you must love
14:21 He who loves me will be *l*
15: 9 the Father has *l* me, so have I *l* you.
15:12 Love each other as I have *l* you.
19:26 the disciple whom he *l* standing
Ro 8:37 conquerors through him who *l* us.
9:13 "Jacob I *l*, but Esau I hated."
9:25 her 'my *l* one' who is not my *l* one,"
11:28 they are *l* on account
Gal 2:20 who *l* me and gave himself for me.
Eph 5: 2 as Christ *l* us and gave himself up
5:25 just as Christ *l* the church
2Th 2:16 who *l* us and by his grace gave us
2Ti 4:10 for Demas, because he *l* this world,
Heb 1: 9 You have *l* righteousness
1Jn 4:10 This is love: not that we *l* God,
4:11 Dear friends, since God so *l* us,
4:19 We love because he first *l* us.

LOVELY (LOVE)

Ps 84: 1 How *l* is your dwelling place,
SS 2:14 and your face is *l*.
5:16 he is altogether *l*.
Php 4: 8 whatever is *l*, whatever is

LOVER (LOVE)

SS 2:16 *Beloved* My *l* is mine and I am his;
7:10 I belong to my *l*,
1Ti 3: 3 not quarrelsome, not a *l* of money.

LOVERS (LOVE)

2Ti 3: 2 People will be *l* of themselves,
3: 3 without self-control, brutal, not *l*
3: 4 *l* of pleasure rather than *l* of God—

LOVES (LOVE)

Ps 11: 7 he *l* justice;
33: 5 The LORD *l* righteousness
34:12 Whoever of you *l* life
91:14 Because he *l* me," says the LORD,
127: 2 for he grants sleep to those he *l*.
Pr 3:12 the LORD disciplines those he *l*,
12: 1 Whoever *l* discipline *l* knowledge,
13:24 he who *l* him is careful
17:17 A friend *l* at all times,
17:19 He who *l* a quarrel *l* sin;
22:11 He who *l* a pure heart and whose
Ecc 5:10 whoever *l* wealth is never satisfied
Mt 10:37 anyone who *l* his son or daughter
Lk 7:47 has been forgiven little *l* little."
Jn 3:35 Father *l* the Son and has placed
10:17 reason my Father *l* me is that I lay
12:25 The man who *l* his life will lose it,
14:21 obeys them, he is the one who *l* me.
14:23 Jesus replied, "If anyone *l* me,
Ro 13: 8 for he who *l* his fellowman has
2Co 9: 7 for God *l* a cheerful giver.
Eph 5:28 He who *l* his wife *l* himself.
5:33 must love his wife as he *l* himself,
Heb 12: 6 the Lord disciplines those he *l*,
1Jn 2:10 Whoever *l* his brother lives
2:15 If anyone *l* the world, the love
4: 7 Everyone who *l* has been born
4:21 Whoever *l* God must also love his
5: 1 who *l* the father *l* his child
3Jn : 9 but Diotrephes, who *l* to be first,
Rev 1: 5 To him who *l* us and has freed us

LOVING (LOVE)

Ps 25:10 All the ways of the LORD are *l*
62:12 and that you, O Lord, are *l*.
145:17 and *l* toward all he has made.
Heb 13: 1 Keep on *l* each other as brothers.
1Jn 5: 2 by *l* God and carrying out his

LOWLY

Job 5:11 The *l* he sets on high,
Pr 29:23 but a man of *l* spirit gains honor.
Isa 57:15 also with him who is contrite and *l*
Eze 21:26 *l* will be exalted and the exalted
1Co 1:28 He chose the *l* things of this world

LUKE*
Co-worker with Paul (Col 4:14; 2Ti 4:11; Phm 24).

LUKEWARM*
Rev 3:16 So, because you are *l*— neither hot

LUST
Pr 6:25 Do not *l* in your heart
Col 3: 5 sexual immorality, impurity, *l*,
1Th 4: 5 not in passionate *l* like the heathen,
1Jn 2:16 the *l* of his eyes and the boasting

LYING (LIE)
Pr 6:17 a *l* tongue,
26:28 A *l* tongue hates those it hurts,

MACEDONIA
Ac 16: 9 "Come over to *M* and help us."

MADE (MAKE)
Ge 1:16 He also *m* the stars.
1:25 God *m* the wild animals according
2:22 Then the LORD God *m* a woman
2Ki 19:15 You have *m* heaven and earth.
Ps 95: 5 The sea is his, for he *m* it,
100: 3 It is he who *m* us, and we are his;
118:24 This is the day the LORD has *m;*
139:14 I am fearfully and wonderfully *m;*
Ecc 3:11 He has *m* everything beautiful
Mk 2:27 "The Sabbath was *m* for man,
Jn 1: 3 Through him all things were *m;*
Ac 17:24 "The God who *m* the world
Heb 1: 2 through whom he *m* the universe.
Rev 14: 7 Worship him who *m* the heavens,

MAGI
Mt 2: 1 *M* from the east came to Jerusalem

MAGOG
Eze 38: 2 of the land of *M,* the chief prince
39: 6 I will send fire on *M*
Rev 20: 8 and *M*— to gather them for battle.

MAIDEN
Pr 30:19 and the way of a man with a *m.*
Isa 62: 5 As a young man marries a *m,*
Jer 2:32 Does a *m* forget her jewelry,

MAIMED
Mt 18: 8 It is better for you to enter life *m*

MAJESTIC (MAJESTY)
Ex 15: 6 was *m* in power.
15:11 *m* in holiness,
Ps 8: 1 how *m* is your name in all the earth
29: 4 the voice of the LORD is *m.*
111: 3 Glorious and *m* are his deeds,
SS 6:10 *m* as the stars in procession?
2Pe 1:17 came to him from the *M* Glory,

MAJESTY (MAJESTIC)
Ex 15: 7 In the greatness of your *m*
Dt 33:26 and on the clouds in his *m.*
1Ch 16:27 Splendor and *m* are before him;
Est 1: 4 the splendor and glory of his *m.*
Job 37:22 God comes in awesome *m.*
40:10 and clothe yourself in honor and *m*
Ps 45: 4 In your *m* ride forth victoriously
93: 1 The LORD reigns, he is robed in *m*
110: 3 Arrayed in holy *m,*
145: 5 of the glorious splendor of your *m,*
Isa 53: 2 or *m* to attract us to him,
Eze 31: 2 can be compared with you in *m?*
2Pe 1:16 but we were eyewitnesses of his *m.*
Jude :25 only God our Savior be glory, *m,*

MAKE (MADE MAKER MAKES MAKING)
Ge 1:26 "Let us *m* man in our image,
2:18 I will *m* a helper suitable for him."
12: 2 "I will *m* you into a great nation
Ex 22: 3 thief must certainly *m* restitution,
Nu 6:25 the LORD *m* his face shine
Ps 108: 1 *m* music with all my soul.
Isa 14:14 I will *m* myself like the Most High
29:16 "He did not *m* me"?
Jer 31:31 "when I will *m* a new covenant
Mt 3: 3 *m* straight paths for him.'"
28:19 and *m* disciples of all nations,
Mk 1:17 "and I will *m* you fishers of men."
Lk 13:24 "*M* every effort to enter
14:23 country lanes and *m* them come in,
Ro 14:19 *m* every effort to do what leads
2Co 5: 9 So we *m* it our goal to please him,
Eph 4: 3 *M* every effort to keep the unity
Col 4: 5 *m* the most of every opportunity.
1Th 4:11 *M* it your ambition
Heb 4:11 *m* every effort to enter that rest,
12:14 *M* every effort to live in peace
2Pe 1: 5 *m* every effort to add
3:14 *m* every effort to be found spotless,

MAKER (MAKE)
Job 4:17 Can a man be more pure than his *M*
36: 3 I will ascribe justice to my *M.*
Ps 95: 6 kneel before the LORD our *M;*
Pr 22: 2 The LORD is the *M* of them all.
Isa 45: 9 to him who quarrels with his *M,*
54: 5 For your *M* is your husband—
Jer 10:16 for he is the *M* of all things,

MAKES (MAKE)
1Co 3: 7 but only God, who *m* things grow.

MAKING (MAKE)
Ps 19: 7 *m* wise the simple.
Ecc 12:12 Of *m* many books there is no end,
Jn 5:18 *m* himself equal with God.
Eph 5:16 *m* the most of every opportunity,

MALE
Ge 1:27 *m* and female he created them.
Gal 3:28 slave nor free, *m* nor female,

MALICE (MALICIOUS)
Ro 1:29 murder, strife, deceit and *m.*
Col 3: 8 *m,* slander, and filthy language
1Pe 2: 1 rid yourselves of all *m*

MALICIOUS (MALICE)
Pr 26:24 A *m* man disguises himself
1Ti 3:11 not *m* talkers but temperate
6: 4 *m* talk, evil suspicions

MAN (MEN WOMAN WOMEN)
Ge 1:26 "Let us make *m* in our image,
2: 7 God formed the *m* from the dust
2:18 for the *m* to be alone
2:23 she was taken out of *m.*
9: 6 Whoever sheds the blood of *m,*
Dt 8: 3 *m* does not live on bread
1Sa 13:14 a *m* after his own heart
15:29 he is not a *m* that he
Job 14: 1 *M* born of woman is of few
14:14 If a *m* dies, will he live
Ps 1: 1 Blessed is the *m* who does
8: 4 what is *m* that you are
119: 9 can a young *m* keep his
127: 5 Blessed is the *m* whose quiver
Pr 14:12 that seems right to a *m,*
30:19 way of a *m* with a maiden.
Isa 53: 3 a *m* of sorrows,
Mt 19: 5 a *m* will leave his father
Mk 8:36 What good is it for a *m*
Lk 4: 4 '*M* does not live on bread
Ro 5:12 entered the world through one *m*
1Co 7: 2 each *m* should have his own
11: 3 head of every *m* is Christ,

11: 3 head of woman is *m*
13:11 When I became a *m*,
Php 2: 8 found in appearance as a *m*,
1Ti 2: 5 the *m* Christ Jesus,
2:11 have authority over a *m*;
Heb 9:27 as *m* is destined to die

MANAGE
Jer 12: 5 how will you *m* in the thickets
1Ti 3: 4 He must *m* his own family well
3:12 one wife and must *m* his children
5:14 to *m* their homes and to give

MANASSEH
1. Firstborn of Joseph (Ge 41:51; 46:20). Blessed (Ge 48).
2. Son of Hezekiah; king of Judah (2Ki 21:1-18; 2Ch 33:1-20).

MANGER
Lk 2:12 in strips of cloth and lying in a *m*."

MANNA
Ex 16:31 people of Israel called the bread *m*.
Dt 8:16 He gave you *m* to eat in the desert,
Jn 6:49 Your forefathers ate the *m*
Rev 2:17 I will give some of the hidden *m*.

MANNER
1Co 11:27 in an unworthy *m* will be guilty
Php 1:27 conduct yourselves in a *m* worthy

MARITAL* (MARRY)
Ex 21:10 of her food, clothing and *m* rights.
Mt 5:32 except for *m* unfaithfulness,
19: 9 except for *m* unfaithfulness,
1Co 7: 3 husband should fulfill his *m* duty

MARK (MARKS)
Cousin of Barnabas (Col 4:10; 2Ti 4:11; Phm 24; 1Pe 5:13), see JOHN.
Ge 4:15 Then the LORD put a *m* on Cain
Rev 13:16 to receive a *m* on his right hand

MARKS (MARK)
Jn 20:25 Unless I see the nail *m* in his hands
Gal 6:17 bear on my body the *m* of Jesus.

MARRED
Isa 52:14 his form *m* beyond human likeness

MARRIAGE (MARRY)
Mt 22:30 neither marry nor be given in *m*;
24:38 marrying and giving in *m*,
Ro 7: 2 she is released from the law of *m*.
Heb 13: 4 by all, and the *m* bed kept pure,

MARRIED (MARRY)
Ro 7: 2 by law a *m* woman is bound
1Co 7:27 Are you *m*? Do not seek a divorce.
7:33 But a *m* man is concerned about
7:36 They should get *m*.

MARRIES (MARRY)
Mt 5:32 and anyone who *m* the divorced
19: 9 and *m* another woman commits
Lk 16:18 the man who *m* a divorced woman

MARRY (INTERMARRY MARITAL MARRIAGE MARRIED MARRIES)
Mt 22:30 resurrection people will neither *m*
1Co 7: 1 It is good for a man not to *m*.
7: 9 control themselves, they should *m*,
1Ti 5:14 So I counsel younger widows to *m*,

MARTHA*
Sister of Mary and Lazarus (Lk 10:38-42; Jn 11; 12:2).

MARVELED
Lk 2:33 mother *m* at what was said about

MARY
1. Mother of Jesus (Mt 1:16-25; Lk 1:27-56; 2:1-40). With Jesus at temple (Lk 2:41-52), at the wedding in Cana (Jn 2:1-5), questioning his sanity (Mk 3:21), at the cross (Jn 19:25-27). Among disciples after Ascension (Ac 1:14).
2. Magdalene; former demoniac (Lk 8:2). Helped support Jesus' ministry (Lk 8:1-3). At the cross (Mt 27:56; Mk 15:40; Jn 19:25), burial (Mt 27:61; Mk 15:47). Saw angel after resurrection (Mt 28:1-10; Mk 16:1-9; Lk 24:1-12); also Jesus (Jn 20:1-18).
3. Sister of Martha and Lazarus (Jn 11). Washed Jesus' feet (Jn 12:1-8).

MASQUERADES*
2Co 11:14 for Satan himself *m* as an angel

MASTER (MASTERED MASTERS)
Mt 10:24 nor a servant above his *m*.
23: 8 for you have only one *M*
24:46 that servant whose *m* finds him
25:21 "His *m* replied, 'Well done,
Ro 6:14 For sin shall not be your *m*,
14: 4 To his own *m* he stands or falls.
2Ti 2:21 useful to the *M* and prepared

MASTERED* (MASTER)
1Co 6:12 but I will not be *m* by anything.
2Pe 2:19 a slave to whatever has *m* him.

MASTERS (MASTER)
Mt 6:24 "No one can serve two *m*.
Eph 6: 5 obey your earthly *m* with respect
6: 9 And *m*, treat your slaves
Tit 2: 9 subject to their *m* in everything,

MATTHEW*
Apostle; former tax collector (Mt 9:9-13; 10:3; Mk 3:18; Lk 6:15; Ac 1:13). Also called Levi (Mk 2:14-17; Lk 5:27-32).

MATURE (MATURITY)
Eph 4:13 of the Son of God and become *m*,
Php 3:15 of us who are *m* should take such
Heb 5:14 But solid food is for the *m*,
Jas 1: 4 work so that you may be *m*

MATURITY* (MATURE)
Heb 6: 1 about Christ and go on to *m*,

MEAL
Pr 15:17 Better a *m* of vegetables where
1Co 10:27 some unbeliever invites you to a *m*
Heb 12:16 for a single *m* sold his inheritance

MEANING
Ne 8: 8 and giving the *m* so that the people

MEANS
1Co 9:22 by all possible *m* I might save some

MEAT
Ro 14: 6 He who eats *m*, eats to the Lord,
14:21 It is better not to eat *m*

MEDIATOR
1Ti 2: 5 and one *m* between God and men,
Heb 8: 6 of which he is *m* is superior
9:15 For this reason Christ is the *m*
12:24 to Jesus the *m* of a new covenant,

MEDICINE*
Pr 17:22 A cheerful heart is good *m*,

MEDITATE (MEDITATES MEDITATION)
Jos 1: 8 from your mouth; *m* on it day
Ps 119:15 I *m* on your precepts
119:78 but I will *m* on your precepts.
119:97 I *m* on it all day long.
145: 5 I will *m* on your wonderful works.

MEDITATES* (MEDITATE)
Ps 1: 2 and on his law he *m* day and night.

MEDITATION* (MEDITATE)
Ps 19:14 of my mouth and the *m* of my heart
104:34 May my *m* be pleasing to him,

MEDIUM
Lev 20:27 " 'A man or woman who is a *m*

MEEK (MEEKNESS)
Ps 37:11 But the *m* will inherit the land
Mt 5: 5 Blessed are the *m*,

MEEKNESS* (MEEK)
2Co 10: 1 By the *m* and gentleness of Christ,

MEET (MEETING)
Ps 85:10 Love and faithfulness *m* together;
Am 4:12 prepare to *m* your God, O Israel."
1Th 4:17 them in the clouds to *m* the Lord

MEETING (MEET)
Heb 10:25 Let us not give up *m* together,

MELCHIZEDEK
Ge 14:18 *M* king of Salem brought out bread
Ps 110: 4 in the order of *M*."
Heb 7:11 in the order of *M*, not in the order

MELT
2Pe 3:12 and the elements will *m* in the heat.

MEMBERS
Mic 7: 6 a man's enemies are the *m*
Ro 7:23 law at work in the *m* of my body,
12: 4 of us has one body with many *m*,
1Co 6:15 not know that your bodies are *m*
12:24 But God has combined the *m*
Eph 4:25 for we are all *m* of one body.
Col 3:15 as *m* of one body you were called

MEN (MAN)
Mt 4:19 will make you fishers of *m*
5:16 your light shine before *m*
12:36 *m* will have to give account
Jn 12:32 will draw all *m* to myself
Ac 5:29 obey God rather than *m*!
Ro 1:27 indecent acts with other *m*,
5:12 death came to all *m*,
1Co 9:22 all things to all *m*
2Co 5:11 we try to persuade *m*.
1Ti 2: 4 wants all *m* to be saved
2Ti 2: 2 entrust to reliable *m*
2Pe 1:21 but *m* spoke from God

MENAHEM
King of Israel (2Ki 15:17-22).

MERCIFUL (MERCY)
Dt 4:31 the LORD your God is a *m* God;
Ne 9:31 for you are a gracious and *m* God.
Mt 5: 7 Blessed are the *m*,
Lk 6:36 Be *m*, just as your Father is *m*.
Heb 2:17 in order that he might become a *m*
Jude :22 Be *m* to those who doubt; snatch

MERCY (MERCIFUL)
Ex 33:19 *m* on whom I will have *m*,
Ps 25: 6 O LORD, your great *m* and love,
Isa 63: 9 and *m* he redeemed them;
Hos 6: 6 For I desire *m*, not sacrifice,
Mic 6: 8 To act justly and to love *m*
Hab 3: 2 in wrath remember *m*.
Mt 12: 7 'I desire *m*, not sacrifice,' you
23:23 justice, *m* and faithfulness.
Ro 9:15 "I will have *m* on whom I have *m*,
Eph 2: 4 who is rich in *m*, made us alive
Jas 2:13 *M* triumphs over judgment!
1Pe 1: 3 In his great *m* he has given us new

MESSAGE
Isa 53: 1 Who has believed our *m*
Jn 12:38 "Lord, who has believed our *m*
Ro 10:17 faith comes from hearing the *m*,
1Co 1:18 For the *m* of the cross is
2Co 5:19 to us the *m* of reconciliation.

MESSIAH*
Jn 1:41 "We have found the *M*" (that is,
4:25 "I know that *M*" (called Christ) "is

METHUSELAH
Ge 5:27 Altogether, *M* lived 969 years,

MICHAEL
Archangel (Jude 9); warrior in angelic realm, protector of Israel (Da 10:13, 21; 12:1; Rev 12:7).

MIDWIVES
Ex 1:17 The *m*, however, feared God

MIGHT (ALMIGHTY MIGHTY)
Jdg 16:30 Then he pushed with all his *m*,
2Sa 6:14 before the LORD with all his *m*,
Ps 21:13 we will sing and praise your *m*.
Zec 4: 6 'Not by *m* nor by power,
1Ti 6:16 To him be honor and *m* forever.

MIGHTY (MIGHT)
Ex 6: 1 of my *m* hand he will drive them
Dt 7: 8 he brought you out with a *m* hand
2Sa 1:19 How the *m* have fallen!
23: 8 the names of David's *m* men:
Ps 24: 8 The LORD strong and *m*,
50: 1 The *M* One, God, the LORD,
89: 8 You are *m*, O LORD,
136:12 with a *m* hand and outstretched
147: 5 Great is our Lord and *m* in power;
Isa 9: 6 Wonderful Counselor, *M* God,
Zep 3:17 he is *m* to save.
Eph 6:10 in the Lord and in his *m* power.

MILE*
Mt 5:41 If someone forces you to go one *m*,

MILK
Ex 3: 8 a land flowing with *m* and honey—
Isa 55: 1 Come, buy wine and *m*
1Co 3: 2 I gave you *m*, not solid food,
Heb 5:12 You need *m*, not solid food!
1Pe 2: 2 babies, crave pure spiritual *m*,

MILLSTONE (STONE)
Lk 17: 2 sea with a *m* tied around his neck

MIND (DOUBLE-MINDED MINDFUL MINDS)
1Sa 15:29 Israel does not lie or change his *m*;
1Ch 28: 9 devotion and with a willing *m*,
Ps 26: 2 examine my heart and my *m*;
Isa 26: 3 him whose *m* is steadfast,
Mt 22:37 all your soul and with all your *m*.'
Ac 4:32 believers were one in heart and *m*.
Ro 7:25 I myself in my *m* am a slave
8: 7 the sinful *m* is hostile to God.
12: 2 by the renewing of your *m*.
1Co 2: 9 no *m* has conceived
14:14 spirit prays, but my *m* is unfruitful.
2Co 13:11 be of one *m*, live in peace.
Php 3:19 Their *m* is on earthly things.
1Th 4:11 to *m* your own business
Heb 7:21 and will not change his *m*:

MINDFUL* (MIND)
Ps 8: 4 what is man that you are *m* of him,
Lk 1:48 God my Savior, for he has been *m*
Heb 2: 6 What is man that you are *m* of him,

MINDS (MIND)
Ps 7: 9 who searches *m* and hearts,
Jer 31:33 "I will put my law in their *m*
Eph 4:23 new in the attitude of your *m;*
Col 3: 2 Set your *m* on things above,
Heb 8:10 I will put my laws in their *m*
Rev 2:23 I am he who searches hearts and *m,*

MINISTERING (MINISTRY)
Heb 1:14 Are not all angels *m* spirits sent

MINISTRY (MINISTERING)
Ac 6: 4 to prayer and the *m* of the word."
2Co 5:18 gave us the *m* of reconciliation:
2Ti 4: 5 discharge all the duties of your *m.*

MIRACLES (MIRACULOUS)
1Ch 16:12 his *m,* and the judgments he
Ps 77:14 You are the God who performs *m;*
Mt 11:20 most of his *m* had been performed,
11:21 If the *m* that were performed
24:24 and perform great signs and *m*
Mk 6: 2 does *m!* Isn't this the carpenter?
Jn 10:32 "I have shown you many great *m*
14:11 the evidence of the *m* themselves.
Ac 2:22 accredited by God to you by *m,*
19:11 God did extraordinary *m*
1Co 12:28 third teachers, then workers of *m,*
Heb 2: 4 it by signs, wonders and various *m,*

MIRACULOUS (MIRACLES)
Jn 3: 2 could perform the *m* signs you are
9:16 "How can a sinner do such *m* signs
20:30 Jesus did many other *m* signs
1Co 1:22 Jews demand *m* signs and Greeks

MIRE
Ps 40: 2 out of the mud and *m;*
Isa 57:20 whose waves cast up *m* and mud.

MIRIAM
Sister of Moses and Aaron (Nu 26:59). Led dancing at Red Sea (Ex 15:20-21). Struck with leprosy for criticizing Moses (Nu 12). Death (Nu 20:1).

MIRROR
Jas 1:23 a man who looks at his face in a *m*

MISERY
Ex 3: 7 "I have indeed seen the *m*
Jdg 10:16 he could bear Israel's *m* no longer.
Hos 5:15 in their *m* they will earnestly seek
Ro 3:16 ruin and *m* mark their ways,
Jas 5: 1 of the *m* that is coming upon you.

MISLED
1Co 15:33 Do not be *m:* "Bad company

MISS
Pr 19: 2 nor to be hasty and *m* the way.

MIST
Hos 6: 4 Your love is like the morning *m,*
Jas 4:14 You are a *m* that appears for a little

MISUSE*
Ex 20: 7 "You shall not *m* the name
Dt 5:11 "You shall not *m* the name
Ps 139:20 your adversaries *m* your name.

MOCK (MOCKED MOCKER MOCKERS MOCKING)
Ps 22: 7 All who see me *m* me;
Pr 14: 9 Fools *m* at making amends for sin,
Mk 10:34 who will *m* him and spit on him,

MOCKED (MOCK)
Mt 27:29 knelt in front of him and *m* him.
27:41 of the law and the elders *m* him.
Gal 6: 7 not be deceived: God cannot be *m.*

MOCKER (MOCK)
Pr 9: 7 corrects a *m* invites insult;
9:12 if you are a *m,* you alone will suffer
20: 1 Wine is a *m* and beer a brawler;
22:10 Drive out the *m,* and out goes strife

MOCKERS (MOCK)
Ps 1: 1 or sit in the seat of *m.*

MOCKING (MOCK)
Isa 50: 6 face from *m* and spitting.

MODEL*
Eze 28:12 " 'You were the *m* of perfection,
1Th 1: 7 And so you became a *m*
2Th 3: 9 to make ourselves a *m* for you

MOMENT
Job 20: 5 the joy of the godless lasts but a *m.*
Ps 30: 5 For his anger lasts only a *m,*
Isa 66: 8 or a nation be brought forth in a *m?*
Gal 2: 5 We did not give in to them for a *m,*

MONEY
Ecc 5:10 Whoever loves *m* never has *m*
Isa 55: 1 and you who have no *m,*
Mt 6:24 You cannot serve both God and *M.*
Lk 9: 3 no bread, no *m,* no extra tunic.
1Co 16: 2 set aside a sum of *m* in keeping
1Ti 3: 3 not quarrelsome, not a lover of *m.*
6:10 For the love of *m* is a root
2Ti 3: 2 lovers of *m,* boastful, proud,
Heb 13: 5 free from the love of *m*
1Pe 5: 2 not greedy for *m,* but eager to serve

MOON
Ps 121: 6 nor the *m* by night.
Joel 2:31 and the *m* to blood
1Co 15:41 *m* another and the stars another;

MORNING
Ge 1: 5 and there was *m*— the first day.
Dt 28:67 In the *m* you will say, "If only it
Ps 5: 3 In the *m,* O LORD,
2Pe 1:19 and the *m* star rises in your hearts.
Rev 22:16 of David, and the bright *M* Star."

MORTAL
1Co 15:53 and the *m* with immortality.

MOSES
Levite; brother of Aaron (Ex 6:20; 1Ch 6:3). Put in basket into Nile; discovered and raised by Pharaoh's daughter (Ex 2:1-10). Fled to Midian after killing Egyptian (Ex 2:11-15). Married to Zipporah, fathered Gershom (Ex 2:16-22).

Called by the LORD to deliver Israel (Ex 3-4). Pharaoh's resistance (Ex 5). Ten plagues (Ex 7-11). Passover and Exodus (Ex 12-13). Led Israel through Red Sea (Ex 14). Song of deliverance (Ex 15:1-21). Brought water from rock (Ex 17:1-7). Raised hands to defeat Amalekites (Ex 17:8-16). Delegated judges (Ex 18; Dt 1:9-18).

Received Law at Sinai (Ex 19-23; 25-31; Jn 1:17). Announced Law to Israel (Ex 19:7-8; 24; 35). Broke tablets because of golden calf (Ex 32; Dt 9). Saw glory of the LORD (Ex 33-34). Supervised building of tabernacle (Ex 36-40). Set apart Aaron and priests (Lev 8-9). Numbered tribes (Nu 1-4; 26). Opposed by Aaron and Miriam (Nu 12). Sent spies into Canaan (Nu 13). Announced forty years of wandering for failure to enter land (Nu 14). Opposed by Korah (Nu 16). Forbidden to enter land for striking rock (Nu 20:1-13; Dt 1:37). Lifted bronze snake for healing (Nu 21:4-9; Jn 3:14). Final address to Israel (Dt 1-33). Succeeded by Joshua (Nu 27:12-23; Dt 34). Death (Dt 34:5-12).

"Law of Moses" (1Ki 2:3; Ezr 3:2; Mk 12:26; Lk 24:44). "Book of Moses" (2Ch 25:12; Ne 13:1). "Song of Moses" (Ex 15:1-21; Rev 15:3). "Prayer of Moses" (Ps 90).

MOTH
Mt 6:19 where *m* and rust destroy,

MOTHER (MOTHER'S)

Ge 2:24 and *m* and be united to his wife,
3:20 because she would become the *m*
Ex 20:12 "Honor your father and your *m*,
Lev 20: 9 " 'If anyone curses his father or *m*,
Dt 5:16 "Honor your father and your *m*,
21:18 who does not obey his father and *m*
27:16 who dishonors his father or his *m*."
1Sa 2:19 Each year his *m* made him a little
Ps 113: 9 as a happy *m* of children.
Pr 23:25 May your father and *m* be glad;
29:15 child left to himself disgraces his *m*.
31: 1 an oracle his *m* taught him:
Isa 49:15 "Can a *m* forget the baby
66:13 As a *m* comforts her child,
Mt 10:37 or *m* more than me is not worthy
15: 4 'Honor your father and *m*'
19: 5 and *m* and be united to his wife,
Mk 7:10 'Honor your father and your *m*,'
10:19 honor your father and *m*.' "
Jn 19:27 to the disciple, "Here is your *m*."

MOTHER'S (MOTHER)

Job 1:21 "Naked I came from my *m* womb,
Pr 1: 8 and do not forsake your *m* teaching

MOTIVES*

Pr 16: 2 but *m* are weighed by the LORD.
1Co 4: 5 will expose the *m* of men's hearts.
Php 1:18 whether from false *m* or true,
1Th 2: 3 spring from error or impure *m*,
Jas 4: 3 because you ask with wrong *m*,

MOUNTAIN (MOUNTAINS)

Mic 4: 2 let us go up to the *m* of the LORD,
Mt 17:20 say to this *m*, 'Move from here

MOUNTAINS (MOUNTAIN)

Isa 52: 7 How beautiful on the *m*
55:12 the *m* and hills
1Co 13: 2 if I have a faith that can move *m*,

MOURN (MOURNING)

Ecc 3: 4 a time to *m* and a time to dance,
Isa 61: 2 to comfort all who *m*,
Mt 5: 4 Blessed are those who *m*,
Ro 12:15 *m* with those who *m*.

MOURNING (MOURN)

Jer 31:13 I will turn their *m* into gladness;
Rev 21: 4 There will be no more death or *m*

MOUTH

Jos 1: 8 of the Law depart from your *m*;
Ps 19:14 May the words of my *m*
40: 3 He put a new song in my *m*,
119:103 sweeter than honey to my *m*!
Pr 16:23 A wise man's heart guides his *m*,
27: 2 praise you, and not your own *m*;
Isa 51:16 I have put my words in your *m*
Mt 12:34 overflow of the heart the *m* speaks.
15:11 into a man's *m* does not make him
Ro 10: 9 That if you confess with your *m*,

MUD

Ps 40: 2 out of the *m* and mire;
Isa 57:20 whose waves cast up mire and *m*.
2Pe 2:22 back to her wallowing in the *m*."

MULTITUDE (MULTITUDES)

Isa 31: 1 who trust in the *m* of their chariots
1Pe 4: 8 love covers over a *m* of sins.
Rev 7: 9 me was a great *m* that no one could

MULTITUDES (MULTITUDE)

Joel 3:14 *M*, *m* in the valley of decision!

MURDER (MURDERER MURDERERS)

Ex 20:13 "You shall not *m*.
Mt 15:19 *m*, adultery, sexual immorality,
Ro 13: 9 "Do not *m*," "Do not steal,"
Jas 2:11 adultery," also said, "Do not *m*."

MURDERER (MURDER)

Nu 35:16 he is a *m*; the *m* shall be put
Jn 8:44 He was a *m* from the beginning,
1Jn 3:15 who hates his brother is a *m*,

MURDERERS (MURDER)

1Ti 1: 9 for *m*, for adulterers and perverts,
Rev 21: 8 the *m*, the sexually immoral,

MUSIC

Jdg 5: 3 I will make *m* to the LORD,
Ps 27: 6 and make *m* to the LORD.
95: 2 and extol him with *m* and song.
98: 4 burst into jubilant song with *m*;
108: 1 make *m* with all my soul.
Eph 5:19 make *m* in your heart to the Lord,

MUSTARD

Mt 13:31 kingdom of heaven is like a *m* seed,
17:20 you have faith as small as a *m* seed,

MUZZLE

Dt 25: 4 Do not *m* an ox while it is treading
Ps 39: 1 I will put a *m* on my mouth
1Co 9: 9 "Do not *m* an ox while it is

MYRRH

Mt 2:11 of gold and of incense and of *m*.
Mk 15:23 offered him wine mixed with *m*,

MYSTERY

Ro 16:25 to the revelation of the *m* hidden
1Co 15:51 I tell you a *m*: We will not all sleep,
Eph 5:32 This is a profound *m*—
Col 1:26 the *m* that has been kept hidden
1Ti 3:16 the *m* of godliness is great:

MYTHS

1Ti 4: 7 Have nothing to do with godless *m*

NADAB

Son of Jeroboam I; king of Israel (1Ki 15:25-32).

NAIL* (NAILING)

Jn 20:25 "Unless I see the *n* marks

NAILING* (NAIL)

Ac 2:23 him to death by *n* him to the cross.
Col 2:14 he took it away, *n* it to the cross.

NAKED

Ge 2:25 The man and his wife were both *n*,
Job 1:21 *N* I came from my mother's womb,
Isa 58: 7 when you see the *n*, to clothe him,
2Co 5: 3 are clothed, we will not be found *n*.

NAME

Ex 3:15 This is my *n* forever, the *n*
20: 7 "You shall not misuse the *n*
Dt 5:11 "You shall not misuse the *n*
28:58 this glorious and awesome *n*—
1Ki 5: 5 will build the temple for my *N*.'
2Ch 7:14 my people, who are called by my *n*,
Ps 34: 3 let us exalt his *n* together.
103: 1 my inmost being, praise his holy *n*.
147: 4 and calls them each by *n*.
Pr 22: 1 A good *n* is more desirable
30: 4 What is his *n*, and the *n* of his son?
Isa 40:26 and calls them each by *n*.
57:15 who lives forever, whose *n* is holy:
Jer 14: 7 do something for the sake of your *n*
Da 12: 1 everyone whose *n* is found written
Joel 2:32 on the *n* of the LORD will be saved
Zec 14: 9 one LORD, and his *n* the only *n*.
Mt 1:21 and you are to give him the *n* Jesus,

6: 9 hallowed be your *n,*
18:20 or three come together in my *n,*
Jn 10: 3 He calls his own sheep by *n*
16:24 asked for anything in my *n.*
Ac 4:12 for there is no other *n*
Ro 10:13 "Everyone who calls on the *n*
Php 2: 9 him the *n* that is above every *n,*
Col 3:17 do it all in the *n* of the Lord Jesus,
Heb 1: 4 as the *n* he has inherited is superior
Rev 20:15 If anyone's *n* was not found written

NAOMI

Mother-in-law of Ruth (Ru 1). Advised Ruth to seek marriage with Boaz (Ru 2-4).

NARROW

Mt 7:13 "Enter through the *n* gate.

NATHANAEL

Apostle (Jn 1:45-49; 21:2). Probably also called Bartholomew (Mt 10:3).

NATION (NATIONS)

Ge 12: 2 "I will make you into a great *n*
Ps 33:12 Blessed is the *n* whose God is
Pr 14:34 Righteousness exalts a *n,*
Isa 65: 1 To a *n* that did not call on my name
1Pe 2: 9 a royal priesthood, a holy *n,*
Rev 7: 9 from every *n,* tribe, people

NATIONS (NATION)

Ge 17: 4 You will be the father of many *n.*
18:18 and all *n* on earth will be blessed
Ex 19: 5 of all *n* you will be my treasured
Ne 1: 8 I will scatter you among the *n,*
Ps 96: 3 Declare his glory among the *n,*
Isa 40:15 Surely the *n* are like a drop
Eze 36:23 *n* will know that I am the LORD,
Hag 2: 7 and the desired of all *n* will come,
Zec 8:23 *n* will take firm hold of one Jew
14: 2 I will gather all the *n* to Jerusalem
Mt 28:19 and make disciples of all *n,*
Rev 21:24 The *n* will walk by its light,

NATURAL (NATURE)

Ro 6:19 you are weak in your *n* selves.
1Co 15:44 If there is a *n* body, there is

NATURE (NATURAL)

Ro 8: 4 do not live according to the sinful *n*
8: 8 by the sinful *n* cannot please God.
Gal 5:19 The acts of the sinful *n* are obvious:
5:24 Jesus have crucified the sinful *n*
Php 2: 6 Who, being in very *n* God,

NAZARENE

Mt 2:23 prophets: "He will be called a *N.*"

NAZIRITE

Jdg 13: 7 because the boy will be a *N* of God

NECESSARY

Ro 13: 5 it is *n* to submit to the authorities,

NEED (NEEDS NEEDY)

Ps 116: 6 when I was in great *n,* he saved me.
Mt 6: 8 for your Father knows what you *n*
Ro 12:13 with God's people who are in *n.*
1Co 12:21 say to the hand, "I don't *n* you!"
1Jn 3:17 sees his brother in *n* but has no pity

NEEDLE

Mt 19:24 go through the eye of a *n*

NEEDS (NEED)

Isa 58:11 he will satisfy your *n*
Php 4:19 God will meet all your *n* according

NEEDY (NEED)

Pr 14:21 blessed is he who is kind to the *n.*
14:31 to the *n* honors God.
31:20 and extends her hands to the *n.*
Mt 6: 2 "So when you give to the *n,*

NEGLECT (NEGLECTED)

Ne 10:39 We will not *n* the house of our God
Ps 119:16 I will not *n* your word.
Ac 6: 2 for us to *n* the ministry of the word
1Ti 4:14 Do not *n* your gift, which was

NEGLECTED (NEGLECT)

Mt 23:23 But you have *n* the more important

NEHEMIAH

Cupbearer of Artaxerxes (Ne 2:1); governor of Israel (Ne 8:9). Returned to Jerusalem to rebuild walls (Ne 2-6). With Ezra, reestablished worship (Ne 8). Prayer confessing nation's sin (Ne 9). Dedicated wall (Ne 12).

NEIGHBOR (NEIGHBOR'S)

Ex 20:16 give false testimony against your *n.*
Lev 19:13 Do not defraud your *n* or rob him.
19:18 but love your *n* as yourself.
Pr 27:10 better a *n* nearby than a brother far
Mt 19:19 and 'love your *n* as yourself.'"
Lk 10:29 who is my *n?*" In reply Jesus said:
Ro 13:10 Love does no harm to its *n.*

NEIGHBOR'S (NEIGHBOR)

Ex 20:17 You shall not covet your *n* wife,
Dt 5:21 not set your desire on your *n* house
19:14 not move your *n* boundary stone
Pr 25:17 Seldom set foot in your *n* house—

NEW

Ps 40: 3 He put a *n* song in my mouth,
Ecc 1: 9 there is nothing *n* under the sun.
Isa 65:17 *n* heavens and a *n* earth.
Jer 31:31 "when I will make a *n* covenant
Eze 36:26 give you a *n* heart and put a *n* spirit
Mt 9:17 Neither do men pour *n* wine
Lk 22:20 "This cup is the *n* covenant
2Co 5:17 he is a *n* creation; the old has gone,
Eph 4:24 and to put on the *n* self, created
2Pe 3:13 to a *n* heaven and a *n* earth,
1Jn 2: 8 Yet I am writing you a *n* command;

NEWBORN (BEAR)

1Pe 2: 2 Like *n* babies, crave pure spiritual

NEWS

Isa 52: 7 the feet of those who bring good *n,*
Mk 1:15 Repent and believe the good *n!*"
16:15 preach the good *n* to all creation.
Lk 2:10 I bring you good *n*
Ac 5:42 proclaiming the good *n* that Jesus
17:18 preaching the good *n* about Jesus
Ro 10:15 feet of those who bring good *n!*"

NICODEMUS*

Pharisee who visted Jesus at night (Jn 3). Argued fair treatment of Jesus (Jn 7:50-52). With Joseph, prepared Jesus for burial (Jn 19:38-42).

NIGHT

Job 35:10 who gives songs in the *n,*
Ps 1: 2 on his law he meditates day and *n.*
91: 5 You will not fear the terror of *n,*
Jn 3: 2 He came to Jesus at *n* and said,
1Th 5: 2 Lord will come like a thief in the *n.*
5: 5 We do not belong to the *n*
Rev 21:25 for there will be no *n* there.

NOAH

Righteous man (Eze 14:14, 20) called to build ark (Ge 6-8; Heb 11:7; 1Pe 3:20; 2Pe 2:5). God's covenant with (Ge 9:1-17). Drunkenness of (Ge 9:18-23). Blessed sons, cursed Canaan (Ge 9:24-27).

NOBLE
Ru 3:11 you are a woman of *n* character.
Ps 45: 1 My heart is stirred by a *n* theme
Pr 12: 4 of *n* character is her husband's
31:10 A wife of *n* character who can find?
31:29 "Many women do *n* things,
Isa 32: 8 But the *n* man makes *n* plans,
Lk 8:15 good soil stands for those with a *n*
Ro 9:21 of clay some pottery for *n* purposes
Php 4: 8 whatever is *n*, whatever is right,
2Ti 2:20 some are for *n* purposes

NOTHING
Ne 9:21 in the desert; they lacked *n*,
Jer 32:17 *N* is too hard for you
Jn 15: 5 apart from me you can do *n*.

NULLIFY
Ro 3:31 Do we, then, *n* the law by this faith

OATH
Dt 7: 8 and kept the *o* he swore

OBEDIENCE (OBEY)
2Ch 31:21 in *o* to the law and the commands,
Pr 30:17 that scorns *o* to a mother,
Ro 1: 5 to the *o* that comes from faith.
6:16 to *o*, which leads to righteousness?
2Jn : 6 that we walk in *o* to his commands.

OBEDIENT (OBEY)
Lk 2:51 with them and was *o* to them.
Php 2: 8 and became *o* to death—
1Pe 1:14 As *o* children, do not conform

OBEY (OBEDIENCE OBEDIENT OBEYED)
Ex 12:24 "*O* these instructions as a lasting
Dt 6: 3 careful to *o* so that it may go well
13: 4 Keep his commands and *o* him;
21:18 son who does not *o* his father
30: 2 and *o* him with all your heart
32:46 children to *o* carefully all the words
1Sa 15:22 To *o* is better than sacrifice,
Ps 119:34 and *o* it with all my heart.
Mt 28:20 to *o* everything I have commanded
Jn 14:23 loves me, he will *o* my teaching.
Ac 5:29 "We must *o* God rather than men!
Ro 6:16 slaves to the one whom you *o*—
Gal 5: 3 obligated to *o* the whole law.
Eph 6: 1 *o* your parents in the Lord,
6: 5 *o* your earthly masters with respect
Col 3:20 *o* your parents in everything,
1Ti 3: 4 and see that his children *o* him
Heb 13:17 *O* your leaders and submit
1Jn 5: 3 love for God: to *o* his commands.

OBEYED (OBEY)
Ps 119: 4 that are to be fully *o*.
Jnh 3: 3 Jonah *o* the word of the LORD
Jn 17: 6 and they have *o* your word.
Ro 6:17 you wholeheartedly *o* the form
Heb 11: 8 *o* and went, even though he did not
1Pe 3: 6 who *o* Abraham and called him her

OBLIGATED
Ro 1:14 I am *o* both to Greeks
Gal 5: 3 himself be circumcised that he is *o*

OBSCENITY
Eph 5: 4 Nor should there be *o*, foolish talk

OBSOLETE
Heb 8:13 he has made the first one *o*;

OBTAINED
Ro 9:30 not pursue righteousness, have *o* it,
Php 3:12 Not that I have already *o* all this,
Heb 9:12 having *o* eternal redemption.

OFFENDED (OFFENSE)
Pr 18:19 An *o* brother is more unyielding

OFFENSE (OFFENDED OFFENSIVE)
Pr 17: 9 over an *o* promotes love,
19:11 it is to his glory to overlook an *o*.

OFFENSIVE (OFFENSE)
Ps 139:24 See if there is any *o* way in me,

OFFER (OFFERED OFFERING OFFERINGS)
Ro 12: 1 to *o* your bodies as living sacrifices,
Heb 13:15 therefore, let us continually *o*

OFFERED (OFFER)
Heb 7:27 once for all when he *o* himself.
11: 4 By faith Abel *o* God a better

OFFERING (OFFER)
Ge 22: 8 provide the lamb for the burnt *o*,
Ps 40: 6 Sacrifice and *o* you did not desire,
Isa 53:10 the LORD makes his life a guilt *o*,
Mt 5:23 if you are *o* your gift at the altar
Eph 5: 2 as a fragrant *o* and sacrifice to God.
Heb 10: 5 "Sacrifice and *o* you did not desire,

OFFERINGS (OFFER)
Mal 3: 8 do we rob you?' "In tithes and *o*.
Mk 12:33 is more important than all burnt *o*

OFFICER
2Ti 2: 4 wants to please his commanding *o*.

OFFSPRING
Ge 3:15 and between your *o* and hers;
12: 7 "To your *o* I will give this land."

OIL
Ps 23: 5 You anoint my head with *o*;
Isa 61: 3 the *o* of gladness
Heb 1: 9 by anointing you with the *o* of joy."

OLIVE (OLIVES)
Zec 4: 3 Also there are two *o* trees by it,
Ro 11:17 and you, though a wild *o* shoot,
Rev 11: 4 These are the two *o* trees

OLIVES (OLIVE)
Jas 3:12 a fig tree bear *o*, or a grapevine bear

OMEGA
Rev 1: 8 "I am the Alpha and the *O*,"

OMRI
King of Israel (1Ki 16:21-26).

OPINIONS*
1Ki 18:21 will you waver between two *o*?
Pr 18: 2 but delights in airing his own *o*.

OPPORTUNITY
Ro 7:11 seizing the *o* afforded
Gal 6:10 as we have *o*, let us do good
Eph 5:16 making the most of every *o*,
Col 4: 5 make the most of every *o*.
1Ti 5:14 to give the enemy no *o* for slander.

OPPOSES
Jas 4: 6 "God *o* the proud
1Pe 5: 5 because, "God *o* the proud

OPPRESS (OPPRESSED)
Ex 22:21 "Do not mistreat an alien or *o* him,
Zec 7:10 Do not *o* the widow

OPPRESSED (OPPRESS)
Ps 9: 9 The LORD is a refuge for the *o*,
Isa 53: 7 He was *o* and afflicted,
Zec 10: 2 *o* for lack of a shepherd.

ORDAINED
Ps 8: 2 you have *o* praise

ORDERLY
1Co 14:40 done in a fitting and *o* way.
Col 2: 5 and delight to see how *o* you are

ORGIES*
Ro 13:13 not in *o* and drunkenness,
Gal 5:21 drunkenness, *o,* and the like.
1Pe 4: 3 *o,* carousing and detestable

ORIGIN
2Pe 1:21 For prophecy never had its *o*

ORPHANS
Jn 14:18 will not leave you as *o;* I will come
Jas 1:27 to look after *o* and widows

OUTCOME
Heb 13: 7 Consider the *o* of their way of life
1Pe 4:17 what will the *o* be for those who do

OUTSIDERS*
Col 4: 5 wise in the way you act toward *o;*
1Th 4:12 daily life may win the respect of *o*
1Ti 3: 7 also have a good reputation with *o,*

OUTSTANDING
SS 5:10 *o* among ten thousand.
Ro 13: 8 no debt remain *o,*

OUTSTRETCHED
Ex 6: 6 and will redeem you with an *o* arm
Jer 27: 5 and *o* arm I made the earth
Eze 20:33 an *o* arm and with outpoured wrath

OUTWEIGHS
2Co 4:17 an eternal glory that far *o* them all.

OVERCOME (OVERCOMES)
Mt 16:18 and the gates of Hades will not *o* it.
Mk 9:24 I do believe; help me *o* my unbelief
Jn 16:33 But take heart! I have *o* the world."
Ro 12:21 Do not be *o* by evil, but *o* evil
1Jn 5: 4 is the victory that has *o* the world,
Rev 17:14 but the Lamb will *o* them

OVERCOMES* (OVERCOME)
1Jn 5: 4 born of God *o* the world.
5: 5 Who is it that *o* the world?
Rev 2: 7 To him who *o,* I will give the right
2:11 He who *o* will not be hurt at all
2:17 To him who *o,* I will give some
2:26 To him who *o* and does my will
3: 5 He who *o* will, like them, be
3:12 Him who *o* I will make a pillar
3:21 To him who *o,* I will give the right
21: 7 He who *o* will inherit all this,

OVERFLOW (OVERFLOWS)
Ps 119:171 May my lips *o* with praise,
Lk 6:45 out of the *o* of his heart his mouth
Ro 15:13 so that you may *o* with hope
2Co 4:15 to *o* to the glory of God.
1Th 3:12 *o* for each other and for everyone

OVERFLOWS* (OVERFLOW)
Ps 23: 5 my cup *o.*
2Co 1: 5 also through Christ our comfort *o.*

OVERJOYED* (JOY)
Da 6:23 The king was *o* and gave orders
Mt 2:10 they saw the star, they were *o.*
Jn 20:20 The disciples were *o*
Ac 12:14 she was so *o* she ran back
1Pe 4:13 so that you may be *o*

OVERSEER (OVERSEERS)
1Ti 3: 1 anyone sets his heart on being an *o,*
3: 2 Now the *o* must be above reproach,
Tit 1: 7 Since an *o* is entrusted

OVERSEERS* (OVERSEER)
Ac 20:28 the Holy Spirit has made you *o.*
Php 1: 1 together with the *o* and deacons:
1Pe 5: 2 as *o*— not because you must,

OVERWHELMED
Ps 38: 4 My guilt has *o* me
65: 3 When we were *o* by sins,
Mt 26:38 "My soul is *o* with sorrow
Mk 7:37 People were *o* with amazement.

OWE
Ro 13: 7 If you *o* taxes, pay taxes; if revenue
Phm :19 to mention that you *o* me your very

OX
Dt 25: 4 Do not muzzle an *o*
Isa 11: 7 and the lion will eat straw like the *o*
1Co 9: 9 "Do not muzzle an *o*

PAGANS
Mt 5:47 Do not even *p* do that? Be perfect,
1Pe 2:12 such good lives among the *p* that,

PAIN (PAINFUL)
Ge 3:16 with *p* you will give birth
Job 33:19 may be chastened on a bed of *p*
Jn 16:21 woman giving birth to a child has *p*

PAINFUL (PAIN)
Ge 3:17 through *p* toil you will eat of it
Heb 12:11 seems pleasant at the time, but *p.*
1Pe 4:12 at the *p* trial you are suffering,

PALMS
Isa 49:16 you on the *p* of my hands;

PANTS
Ps 42: 1 As the deer *p* for streams of water,

PARADISE*
Lk 23:43 today you will be with me in *p.*"
2Co 12: 4 God knows—was caught up to *p.*
Rev 2: 7 of life, which is in the *p* of God.

PARALYTIC
Mk 2: 3 bringing to him a *p,* carried by four

PARDON (PARDONS)
Isa 55: 7 and to our God, for he will freely *p.*

PARDONS* (PARDON)
Mic 7:18 who *p* sin and forgives

PARENTS
Pr 17: 6 and *p* are the pride of their children
Lk 18:29 left home or wife or brothers or *p*
21:16 You will be betrayed even by *p,*
Ro 1:30 they disobey their *p;* they are
2Co 12:14 for their *p,* but *p* for their children.
Eph 6: 1 Children, obey your *p* in the Lord,
Col 3:20 obey your *p* in everything,
2Ti 3: 2 disobedient to their *p,* ungrateful,

PARTIALITY
Dt 10:17 who shows no *p* and accepts no
2Ch 19: 7 our God there is no injustice or *p*
Lk 20:21 and that you do not show *p*

PARTICIPATION
1Co 10:16 is not the bread that we break a *p*

PASS
Ex 12:13 and when I see the blood, I will *p*
La 1:12 to you, all you who *p* by?
Lk 21:33 Heaven and earth will *p* away,
1Co 13: 8 there is knowledge, it will *p* away.

PASSION (PASSIONS)
1Co 7: 9 better to marry than to burn with *p.*

PASSIONS (PASSION)
Gal 5:24 crucified the sinful nature with its *p*
Tit 2:12 to ungodliness and worldly *p,*

PASSOVER
Ex 12:11 Eat it in haste; it is the LORD's *P.*
Dt 16: 1 celebrate the *P* of the LORD your
1Co 5: 7 our *P* lamb, has been sacrificed.

PAST
Isa 43:18 do not dwell on the *p.*
Ro 15: 4 in the *p* was written to teach us,
Heb 1: 1 In the *p* God spoke

PASTORS*
Eph 4:11 and some to be *p* and teachers,

PASTURE (PASTURES)
Ps 37: 3 dwell in the land and enjoy safe *p.*
100: 3 we are his people, the sheep of his *p*
Jer 50: 7 against the LORD, their true *p,*
Eze 34:13 I will *p* them on the mountains
Jn 10: 9 come in and go out, and find *p.*

PASTURES (PASTURE)
Ps 23: 2 He makes me lie down in green *p,*

PATCH
Mt 9:16 No one sews a *p* of unshrunk cloth

PATH (PATHS)
Ps 27:11 lead me in a straight *p*
119:105 and a light for my *p.*
Pr 15:19 the *p* of the upright is a highway.
15:24 The *p* of life leads upward
Isa 26: 7 The *p* of the righteous is level;
Lk 1:79 to guide our feet into the *p* of peace
2Co 6: 3 no stumbling block in anyone's *p,*

PATHS (PATH)
Ps 23: 3 He guides me in *p* of righteousness
25: 4 teach me your *p;*
Pr 3: 6 and he will make your *p* straight.
Ro 11:33 and his *p* beyond tracing out!
Heb 12:13 "Make level *p* for your feet,"

PATIENCE (PATIENT)
Pr 19:11 A man's wisdom gives him *p;*
2Co 6: 6 understanding, *p* and kindness;
Gal 5:22 joy, peace, *p,* kindness, goodness,
Col 1:11 may have great endurance and *p,*
3:12 humility, gentleness and *p.*

PATIENT (PATIENCE PATIENTLY)
Pr 15:18 but a *p* man calms a quarrel.
Ro 12:12 Be joyful in hope, *p* in affliction,
1Co 13: 4 Love is *p,* love is kind.
Eph 4: 2 humble and gentle; be *p,*
1Th 5:14 help the weak, be *p* with everyone.

PATIENTLY (PATIENT)
Ps 40: 1 I waited *p* for the LORD;
Ro 8:25 we do not yet have, we wait for it *p.*

PATTERN
Ro 5:14 who was a *p* of the one to come.
12: 2 longer to the *p* of this world,
2Ti 1:13 keep as the *p* of sound teaching,

PAUL
Also called Saul (Ac 13:9). Pharisee from Tarsus (Ac 9:11; Php 3:5). Apostle (Gal 1). At stoning of Stephen (Ac 8:1). Persecuted Church (Ac 9:1-2; Gal 1:13). Vision of Jesus on road to Damascus (Ac 9:4-9; 26:12-18). In Arabia (Gal 1:17). Preached in Damascus; escaped death through the wall in a basket (Ac 9:19-25). In Jerusalem; sent back to Tarsus (Ac 9:26-30).

Brought to Antioch by Barnabas (Ac 11:22-26). First missionary journey to Cyprus and Galatia (Ac 13-14). Stoned at Lystra (Ac 14:19-20). At Jerusalem council (Ac 15). Split with Barnabas over Mark (Ac 15:36-41).

Second missionary journey with Silas (Ac 16-20). Called to Macedonia (Ac 16:6-10). Freed from prison in Philippi (Ac 16:16-40). In Thessalonica (Ac 17:1-9). Speech in Athens (Ac 17:16-33). In Corinth (Ac 18). In Ephesus (Ac 19). Return to Jerusalem (Ac 20). Farewell to Ephesian elders (Ac 20:13-38). Arrival in Jerusalem (Ac 21:1-26). Arrested (Ac 21:27-36). Addressed crowds (Ac 22), Sanhedrin (Ac 23:1-11). Transferred to Caesarea (Ac 23:12-35). Trial before Felix (Ac 24), Festus (Ac 25:1-12). Before Agrippa (Ac 25:13-26:32). Voyage to Rome; shipwreck (Ac 27). Arrival in Rome (Ac 28).

PAY (REPAID REPAY)
Lev 26:43 They will *p* for their sins
Pr 22:17 *P* attention and listen
Mt 22:17 Is it right to *p* taxes to Caesar
Ro 13: 6 This is also why you *p* taxes,
2Pe 1:19 you will do well to *p* attention to it,

PEACE (PEACEMAKERS)
Nu 6:26 and give you *p."'*
Ps 34:14 seek *p* and pursue it.
85:10 righteousness and *p* kiss each other
119:165 Great *p* have they who love your
122: 6 Pray for the *p* of Jerusalem:
Pr 14:30 A heart at *p* gives life to the body,
17: 1 Better a dry crust with *p* and quiet
Isa 9: 6 Everlasting Father, Prince of *P.*
26: 3 You will keep in perfect *p*
48:22 "There is no *p,"* says the LORD,
Zec 9:10 He will proclaim *p* to the nations.
Mt 10:34 I did not come to bring *p,*
Lk 2:14 on earth *p* to men on whom his
Jn 14:27 *P* I leave with you; my *p*
16:33 so that in me you may have *p.*
Ro 5: 1 we have *p* with God
1Co 7:15 God has called us to live in *p.*
14:33 a God of disorder but of *p.*
Gal 5:22 joy, *p,* patience, kindness,
Eph 2:14 he himself is our *p,* who has made
Php 4: 7 the *p* of God, which transcends all
Col 1:20 by making *p* through his blood,
3:15 Let the *p* of Christ rule
1Th 5: 3 While people are saying, *"P*
2Th 3:16 the Lord of *p* himself give you *p*
2Ti 2:22 righteousness, faith, love and *p,*
1Pe 3:11 he must seek *p* and pursue it.
Rev 6: 4 power to take *p* from the earth

PEACEMAKERS* (PEACE)
Mt 5: 9 Blessed are the *p,*
Jas 3:18 *P* who sow in peace raise a harvest

PEARL* (PEARLS)
Rev 21:21 each gate made of a single *p.*

PEARLS (PEARL)
Mt 7: 6 do not throw your *p* to pigs.
13:45 like a merchant looking for fine *p.*
1Ti 2: 9 or gold or *p* or expensive clothes,
Rev 21:21 The twelve gates were twelve *p,*

PEKAH
King of Israel (2Ki 15:25-31; Isa 7:1).

PEKAHIAH*
Son of Menahem; king of Israel (2Ki 15:22-26).

PEN
Mt 5:18 letter, not the least stroke of a *p,*

PENTECOST
Ac 2: 1 of *P* came, they were all together

Jn 19:37 look on the one they have *p*."

PIGS
Mt 7: 6 do not throw your pearls to *p*.

PILATE

Governor of Judea. Questioned Jesus (Mt 27:1-26; Mk 15:15; Lk 22:66-23:25; Jn 18:28-19:16); sent him to Herod (Lk 23:6-12); consented to his crucifixion when crowds chose Barabbas (Mt 27:15-26; Mk 15:6-15; Lk 23:13-25; Jn 19:1-10).

PILLAR
Ge 19:26 and she became a *p* of salt.
Ex 13:21 ahead of them in a *p* of cloud
1Ti 3:15 the *p* and foundation of the truth.

PIT
Ps 40: 2 He lifted me out of the slimy *p*,
103: 4 who redeems your life from the *p*
Mt 15:14 a blind man, both will fall into a *p*."

PITIED
1Co 15:19 we are to be *p* more than all men.

PLAGUE
2Ch 6:28 "When famine or *p* comes

PLAIN
Ro 1:19 what may be known about God is *p*

PLAN (PLANNED PLANS)
Job 42: 2 no *p* of yours can be thwarted.
Pr 14:22 those who *p* what is good find love
Eph 1:11 predestined according to the *p*

PLANK
Mt 7: 3 attention to the *p* in your own eye?
Lk 6:41 attention to the *p* in your own eye?

PLANNED (PLAN)
Ps 40: 5 The things you *p* for us
Isa 46:11 what I have *p*, that will I do.
Heb 11:40 God had *p* something better for us

PLANS (PLAN)
Ps 20: 4 and make all your *p* succeed.
33:11 *p* of the LORD stand firm forever,
Pr 20:18 Make *p* by seeking advice;
Isa 32: 8 But the noble man makes noble *p*,

PLANTED (PLANTS)
Ps 1: 3 He is like a tree *p* by streams
Mt 15:13 Father has not *p* will be pulled
1Co 3: 6 I *p* the seed, Apollos watered it,

PLANTS (PLANTED)
1Co 3: 7 So neither he who *p* nor he who
9: 7 Who *p* a vineyard and does not eat

PLATTER
Mk 6:25 head of John the Baptist on a *p*."

PLAYED
Lk 7:32 " 'We *p* the flute for you,
1Co 14: 7 anyone know what tune is being *p*

PLEADED
2Co 12: 8 Three times I *p* with the Lord

PLEASANT (PLEASE)
Ps 16: 6 for me in *p* places;
133: 1 How good and *p* it is
147: 1 how *p* and fitting to praise him!
Heb 12:11 No discipline seems *p* at the time,

PLEASE (PLEASANT PLEASED PLEASES PLEASING PLEASURE PLEASURES)
Pr 20:23 and dishonest scales do not *p* him.
Jer 6:20 your sacrifices do not *p* me."
Jn 5:30 for I seek not to *p* myself
Ro 8: 8 by the sinful nature cannot *p* God.
15: 2 Each of us should *p* his neighbor
1Co 7:32 affairs—how he can *p* the Lord.
10:33 I try to *p* everybody in every way.
2Co 5: 9 So we make it our goal to *p* him,
Gal 1:10 or of God? Or am I trying to *p* men
1Th 4: 1 how to live in order to *p* God,
2Ti 2: 4 wants to *p* his commanding officer.
Heb 11: 6 faith it is impossible to *p* God,

PLEASED (PLEASE)
Mt 3:17 whom I love; with him I am well *p*
1Co 1:21 God was *p* through the foolishness
Col 1:19 For God was *p* to have all his
Heb 11: 5 commended as one who *p* God.
2Pe 1:17 whom I love; with him I am well *p*

PLEASES (PLEASE)
Ps 135: 6 The LORD does whatever *p* him,
Pr 15: 8 but the prayer of the upright *p* him.
Jn 3: 8 The wind blows wherever it *p*.
8:29 for I always do what *p* him."
Col 3:20 in everything, for this *p* the Lord.
1Ti 2: 3 This is good, and *p* God our Savior,
1Jn 3:22 his commands and do what *p* him.

PLEASING (PLEASE)
Ps 104:34 May my meditation be *p* to him,
Ro 12: 1 *p* to God—which is your spiritual
Php 4:18 an acceptable sacrifice, *p* to God.
Heb 13:21 may he work in us what is *p* to him,

PLEASURE (PLEASE)
Ps 5: 4 You are not a God who takes *p*
147:10 His *p* is not in the strength
Pr 21:17 He who loves *p* will become poor;
Eze 18:32 For I take no *p* in the death
Eph 1: 5 in accordance with his *p* and will—
1: 9 of his will according to his good *p*,
2Ti 3: 4 lovers of *p* rather than lovers

PLEASURES (PLEASE)
Ps 16:11 with eternal *p* at your right hand.
Heb 11:25 rather than to enjoy the *p* of sin
2Pe 2:13 reveling in their *p* while they feast

PLENTIFUL
Mt 9:37 harvest is *p* but the workers are

PLOW (PLOWSHARES)
Lk 9:62 "No one who puts his hand to the *p*

PLOWSHARES (PLOW)
Isa 2: 4 They will beat their swords into *p*
Joel 3:10 Beat your *p* into swords

PLUNDER
Ex 3:22 And so you will *p* the Egyptians."

POINT
Jas 2:10 yet stumbles at just one *p* is guilty

POISON
Mk 16:18 and when they drink deadly *p*,
Jas 3: 8 It is a restless evil, full of deadly *p*.

POLLUTE* (POLLUTED)
Nu 35:33 " 'Do not *p* the land where you are.
Jude : 8 these dreamers *p* their own bodies,

POLLUTED* (POLLUTE)
Ezr 9:11 entering to possess is a land *p*
Pr 25:26 Like a muddied spring or a *p* well
Ac 15:20 to abstain from food *p* by idols,
Jas 1:27 oneself from being *p* by the world.

PONDER
Ps 64: 9 and *p* what he has done.
119:95 but I will *p* your statutes.

POOR (POVERTY)
Dt 15: 4 there should be no *p* among you,
15:11 There will always be *p* people
Ps 34: 6 This *p* man called, and the LORD
82: 3 maintain the rights of the *p*
112: 9 scattered abroad his gifts to the *p*,
Pr 10: 4 Lazy hands make a man *p*,
13: 7 to be *p*, yet has great wealth.
14:31 oppresses the *p* shows contempt
19: 1 Better a *p* man whose walk is
19:17 to the *p* lends to the LORD,
22: 2 Rich and *p* have this in common:
22: 9 for he shares his food with the *p*.
28: 6 Better a *p* man whose walk is
31:20 She opens her arms to the *p*
Isa 61: 1 me to preach good news to the *p*.
Mt 5: 3 saying: "Blessed are the *p* in spirit,
11: 5 the good news is preached to the *p*.
19:21 your possessions and give to the *p*,
26:11 The *p* you will always have
Mk 12:42 But a *p* widow came and put
Ac 10: 4 and gifts to the *p* have come up
1Co 13: 3 If I give all I possess to the *p*
2Co 8: 9 yet for your sakes he became *p*,
Jas 2: 2 and a *p* man in shabby clothes

PORTION
Dt 32: 9 For the LORD's *p* is his people,
2Ki 2: 9 "Let me inherit a double *p*
La 3:24 to myself, "The LORD is my *p*;

POSSESS (POSSESSING POSSESSION POSSESSIONS)
Nu 33:53 for I have given you the land to *p*.
Jn 5:39 that by them you *p* eternal life.

POSSESSING* (POSSESS)
2Co 6:10 nothing, and yet *p* everything.

POSSESSION (POSSESS)
Ge 15: 7 to give you this land to take *p* of it
Nu 13:30 "We should go up and take *p*
Eph 1:14 of those who are God's *p*—

POSSESSIONS (POSSESS)
Lk 12:15 consist in the abundance of his *p*."
2Co 12:14 what I want is not your *p* but you.
1Jn 3:17 If anyone has material *p*

POSSIBLE
Mt 19:26 but with God all things are *p*."
Mk 9:23 "Everything is *p* for him who
10:27 all things are *p* with God."
Ro 12:18 If it is *p*, as far as it depends on you,
1Co 9:22 by all *p* means I might save some.

POT (POTSHERD POTTER POTTERY)
2Ki 4:40 there is death in the *p*!"
Jer 18: 4 But the *p* he was shaping

POTSHERD (POT)
Isa 45: 9 a *p* among the potsherds

POTTER (POT)
Isa 29:16 Can the pot say of the *p*,
45: 9 Does the clay say to the *p*,
64: 8 We are the clay, you are the *p*;
Jer 18: 6 "Like clay in the hand of the *p*,
Ro 9:21 Does not the *p* have the right

POTTERY (POT)
Ro 9:21 of clay some *p* for noble purposes

POUR (POURED)
Ps 62: 8 *p* out your hearts to him,
Joel 2:28 I will *p* out my Spirit on all people.
Mal 3:10 *p* out so much blessing that you
Ac 2:17 I will *p* out my Spirit on all people.

POURED (POUR)
Ac 10:45 of the Holy Spirit had been *p* out
Ro 5: 5 because God has *p* out his love

POVERTY (POOR)
Pr 14:23 but mere talk leads only to *p*.
21: 5 as surely as haste leads to *p*.
30: 8 give me neither *p* nor riches,
Mk 12:44 out of her *p*, put in everything—
2Co 8: 2 and their extreme *p* welled up
8: 9 through his *p* might become rich.

POWER (POWERFUL POWERS)
1Ch 29:11 LORD, is the greatness and the *p*
2Ch 32: 7 for there is a greater *p* with us
Job 36:22 "God is exalted in his *p*.
Ps 63: 2 and beheld your *p* and your glory.
68:34 Proclaim the *p* of God,
147: 5 Great is our Lord and mighty in *p*;
Pr 24: 5 A wise man has great *p*,
Isa 40:10 the Sovereign LORD comes with *p*
Zec 4: 6 nor by *p*, but by my Spirit,'
Mt 22:29 do not know the Scriptures or the *p*
24:30 on the clouds of the sky, with *p*
Ac 1: 8 you will receive *p* when the Holy
4:33 With great *p* the apostles
10:38 with the Holy Spirit and *p*,
Ro 1:16 it is the *p* of God for the salvation
1Co 1:18 to us who are being saved it is the *p*
15:56 of death is sin, and the *p*
2Co 12: 9 for my *p* is made perfect
Eph 1:19 and his incomparably great *p*
Php 3:10 and the *p* of his resurrection
Col 1:11 strengthened with all *p* according
2Ti 1: 7 but a spirit of *p*, of love
Heb 7:16 of the *p* of an indestructible life.
Rev 4:11 to receive glory and honor and *p*,
19: 1 and glory and *p* belong to our God,
20: 6 The second death has no *p*

POWERFUL (POWER)
Ps 29: 4 The voice of the LORD is *p*;
Lk 24:19 *p* in word and deed before God
2Th 1: 7 in blazing fire with his *p* angels.
Heb 1: 3 sustaining all things by his *p* word.
Jas 5:16 The prayer of a righteous man is *p*

POWERLESS
Ro 5: 6 when we were still *p*, Christ died
8: 3 For what the law was *p* to do

POWERS (POWER)
Ro 8:38 nor any *p*, neither height nor depth
1Co 12:10 to another miraculous *p*,
Col 1:16 whether thrones or *p* or rulers
2:15 And having disarmed the *p*

PRACTICE
Lev 19:26 " 'Do not *p* divination or sorcery.
Mt 23: 3 for they do not *p* what they preach.
Lk 8:21 hear God's word and put it into *p*."
Ro 12:13 *P* hospitality.
1Ti 5: 4 to put their religion into *p* by caring

PRAISE (PRAISED PRAISES PRAISING)
Ex 15: 2 He is my God, and I will *p* him,
Dt 32: 3 Oh, *p* the greatness of our God!
Ru 4:14 said to Naomi: "*P* be to the LORD,
2Sa 22:47 The LORD lives! *P* be to my Rock
1Ch 16:25 is the LORD and most worthy of *p*;
2Ch 20:21 and to *p* him for the splendor
Ps 8: 2 you have ordained *p*
33: 1 it is fitting for the upright to *p* him.
34: 1 his *p* will always be on my lips.
40: 3 a hymn of *p* to our God.
48: 1 the LORD, and most worthy of *p*,
68:19 *P* be to the Lord, to God our Savior
89: 5 The heavens *p* your wonders,

100: 4 and his courts with *p;*
105: 2 Sing to him, sing *p* to him;
106: 1 *P* the LORD.
119:175 Let me live that I may *p* you,
139:14 I *p* you because I am fearfully
145:21 Let every creature *p* his holy name
146: 1 *P* the LORD, O my soul.
150: 2 *p* him for his surpassing greatness.
150: 6 that has breath *p* the LORD.
Pr 27: 2 Let another *p* you, and not your
27:21 man is tested by the *p* he receives.
31:31 let her works bring her *p*
Mt 5:16 and *p* your Father in heaven.
21:16 you have ordained *p*'?"
Jn 12:43 for they loved *p* from men more
Eph 1: 6 to the *p* of his glorious grace,
1:12 might be for the *p* of his glory.
1:14 to the *p* of his glory.
Heb 13:15 offer to God a sacrifice of *p*—
Jas 5:13 happy? Let him sing songs of *p.*

PRAISED (PRAISE)
1Ch 29:10 David *p* the LORD in the presence
Ne 8: 6 Ezra *p* the LORD, the great God;
Da 2:19 Then Daniel *p* the God of heaven
Ro 9: 5 who is God over all, forever *p!*
1Pe 4:11 that in all things God may be *p*

PRAISES (PRAISE)
2Sa 22:50 I will sing *p* to your name.
Ps 47: 6 Sing *p* to God, sing *p;*
147: 1 How good it is to sing *p* to our God,
Pr 31:28 her husband also, and he *p* her:

PRAISING (PRAISE)
Ac 10:46 speaking in tongues and *p* God.
1Co 14:16 If you are *p* God with your spirit,

PRAY (PRAYED PRAYER PRAYERS PRAYING)
Dt 4: 7 is near us whenever we *p* to him?
1Sa 12:23 the LORD by failing to *p* for you.
2Ch 7:14 will humble themselves and *p*
Job 42: 8 My servant Job will *p* for you,
Ps 122: 6 *P* for the peace of Jerusalem:
Mt 5:44 and *p* for those who persecute you,
6: 5 "And when you *p,* do not be like
6: 9 "This, then, is how you should *p:*
26:36 Sit here while I go over there and *p*
Lk 6:28 *p* for those who mistreat you.
18: 1 them that they should always *p*
22:40 "*P* that you will not fall
Ro 8:26 do not know what we ought to *p,*
1Co 14:13 in a tongue should *p* that he may
1Th 5:17 Be joyful always; *p* continually;
Jas 5:13 one of you in trouble? He should *p.*
5:16 *p* for each other so that you may be

PRAYED (PRAY)
1Sa 1:27 I *p* for this child, and the LORD
Jnh 2: 1 From inside the fish Jonah *p*
Mk 14:35 *p* that if possible the hour might

PRAYER (PRAY)
2Ch 30:27 for their *p* reached heaven,
Ezr 8:23 about this, and he answered our *p.*
Ps 6: 9 the LORD accepts my *p.*
86: 6 Hear my *p,* O LORD;
Pr 15: 8 but the *p* of the upright pleases him
Isa 56: 7 a house of *p* for all nations."
Mt 21:13 house will be called a house of *p,*'
Mk 11:24 whatever you ask for in *p,*
Jn 17:15 My *p* is not that you take them out
Ac 6: 4 and will give our attention to *p*
Php 4: 6 but in everything, by *p* and petition
Jas 5:15 *p* offered in faith will make the sick
1Pe 3:12 and his ears are attentive to their *p,*

PRAYERS (PRAY)
1Ch 5:20 He answered their *p,* because they
Mk 12:40 and for a show make lengthy *p.*
1Pe 3: 7 so that nothing will hinder your *p.*
Rev 5: 8 which are the *p* of the saints.

PRAYING (PRAY)
Mk 11:25 And when you stand *p,*
Jn 17: 9 I am not *p* for the world,
Ac 16:25 and Silas were *p* and singing hymns
Eph 6:18 always keep on *p* for all the saints.

PREACH (PREACHED PREACHING)
Mt 23: 3 they do not practice what they *p.*
Mk 16:15 and *p* the good news to all creation.
Ac 9:20 At once he began to *p*
Ro 10:15 how can they *p* unless they are sent
15:20 to *p* the gospel where Christ was
1Co 1:17 to *p* the gospel—not with words
1:23 wisdom, but we *p* Christ crucified:
9:14 that those who *p* the gospel should
9:16 Woe to me if I do not *p* the gospel!
2Co 10:16 so that we can *p* the gospel
Gal 1: 8 from heaven should *p* a gospel
2Ti 4: 2 I give you this charge: *P* the Word;

PREACHED (PREACH)
Mk 13:10 And the gospel must first be *p*
Ac 8: 4 had been scattered *p* the word
1Co 9:27 so that after I have *p* to others,
15: 1 you of the gospel I *p* to you,
2Co 11: 4 other than the Jesus we *p,*
Gal 1: 8 other than the one we *p* to you,
Php 1:18 false motives or true, Christ is *p.*
1Ti 3:16 was *p* among the nations,

PREACHING (PREACH)
Ro 10:14 hear without someone *p* to them?
1Co 9:18 in *p* the gospel I may offer it free
1Ti 4:13 the public reading of Scripture, to *p*
5:17 especially those whose work is *p*

PRECEPTS
Ps 19: 8 The *p* of the LORD are right,
111: 7 all his *p* are trustworthy.
111:10 who follow his *p* have good
119:40 How I long for your *p!*
119:69 I keep your *p* with all my heart.
119:104 I gain understanding from your *p;*
119:159 See how I love your *p;*

PRECIOUS
Ps 19:10 They are more *p* than gold,
116:15 *P* in the sight of the LORD
Pr 8:11 for wisdom is more *p* than rubies,
Isa 28:16 a *p* cornerstone for a sure
1Pe 1:19 but with the *p* blood of Christ,
2: 6 a chosen and *p* cornerstone,
2Pe 1: 4 us his very great and *p* promises,

PREDESTINED* (DESTINY)
Ro 8:29 *p* to be conformed to the likeness
8:30 And those he *p,* he also called;
Eph 1: 5 In love he *p* us to be adopted
1:11 having been *p* according

PREDICTION*
Jer 28: 9 only if his *p* comes true."

PREPARE (PREPARED)
Ps 23: 5 You *p* a table before me
Am 4:12 *p* to meet your God, O Israel."
Jn 14: 2 there to *p* a place for you.
Eph 4:12 to *p* God's people for works

PREPARED (PREPARE)
Mt 25:34 the kingdom *p* for you
1Co 2: 9 what God has *p* for those who love
Eph 2:10 which God *p* in advance for us

PROPHET (PROPHESY)
Dt 18:18 up for them a *p* like you
Am 7:14 "I was neither a *p* nor a prophet's
Mt 10:41 Anyone who receives a *p*
Lk 4:24 "no *p* is accepted in his hometown.

PROPHETS (PROPHESY)
Ps 105:15 do my *p* no harm."
Mt 5:17 come to abolish the Law or the *P;*
7:12 for this sums up the Law and the *P.*
24:24 false Christs and false *p* will appear
Lk 24:25 believe all that the *p* have spoken!
Ac 10:43 All the *p* testify about him that
1Co 12:28 second *p,* third teachers, then
14:32 The spirits of *p* are subject
Eph 2:20 foundation of the apostles and *p,*
Heb 1: 1 through the *p* at many times
1Pe 1:10 Concerning this salvation, the *p,*
2Pe 1:19 word of the *p* made more certain,

PROSPER (PROSPERITY PROSPERS)
Pr 28:25 he who trusts in the LORD will *p.*

PROSPERITY (PROSPER)
Ps 73: 3 when I saw the *p* of the wicked.
Pr 13:21 but *p* is the reward of the righteous.

PROSPERS (PROSPER)
Ps 1: 3 Whatever he does *p.*

PROSTITUTE (PROSTITUTES)
1Co 6:15 of Christ and unite them with a *p?*

PROSTITUTES (PROSTITUTE)
Lk 15:30 property with *p* comes home,
1Co 6: 9 male *p* nor homosexual offenders

PROSTRATE
Dt 9:18 again I fell *p* before the LORD

PROTECT (PROTECTS)
Ps 32: 7 you will *p* me from trouble
Pr 2:11 Discretion will *p* you,
Jn 17:11 *p* them by the power of your name

PROTECTS (PROTECT)
1Co 13: 7 It always *p,* always trusts,

PROUD (PRIDE)
Pr 16: 5 The LORD detests all the *p*
Ro 12:16 Do not be *p,* but be willing
1Co 13: 4 it does not boast, it is not *p.*

PROVE
Ac 26:20 *p* their repentance by their deeds.
1Co 4: 2 been given a trust must *p* faithful.

PROVIDE (PROVIDED PROVIDES)
Ge 22: 8 "God himself will *p* the lamb
Isa 43:20 because I *p* water in the desert
1Ti 5: 8 If anyone does not *p*

PROVIDED (PROVIDE)
Jnh 1:17 But the LORD *p* a great fish
4: 6 Then the LORD God *p* a vine
4: 7 dawn the next day God *p* a worm,
4: 8 God *p* a scorching east wind,

PROVIDES (PROVIDE)
1Ti 6:17 who richly *p* us with everything
1Pe 4:11 it with the strength God *p,*

PROVOKED
Ecc 7: 9 Do not be quickly *p* in your spirit,

PRUDENT
Pr 14:15 a *p* man gives thought to his steps.
19:14 but a *p* wife is from the LORD.
Am 5:13 Therefore the *p* man keeps quiet

PRUNING
Isa 2: 4 and their spears into *p* hooks.
Joel 3:10 and your *p* hooks into spears.

PSALMS
Eph 5:19 Speak to one another with *p,*
Col 3:16 and as you sing *p,* hymns

PUBLICLY
Ac 20:20 have taught you *p* and from house
1Ti 5:20 Those who sin are to be rebuked *p,*

PUFFS
1Co 8: 1 Knowledge *p* up, but love builds up

PULLING
2Co 10: 8 building you up rather than *p* you

PUNISH (PUNISHED PUNISHES)
Ex 32:34 I will *p* them for their sin."
Pr 23:13 if you *p* him with the rod, he will
Isa 13:11 I will *p* the world for its evil,
1Pe 2:14 by him to *p* those who do wrong

PUNISHED (PUNISH)
La 3:39 complain when *p* for his sins?
2Th 1: 9 be *p* with everlasting destruction
Heb 10:29 to be *p* who has trampled the Son

PUNISHES (PUNISH)
Heb 12: 6 and he *p* everyone he accepts

PURE (PURIFIES PURIFY PURITY)
2Sa 22:27 to the *p* you show yourself *p,*
Ps 24: 4 who has clean hands and a *p* heart,
51:10 Create in me a *p* heart, O God,
119: 9 can a young man keep his way *p?*
Pr 20: 9 can say, "I have kept my heart *p;*
Isa 52:11 Come out from it and be *p,*
Hab 1:13 Your eyes are too *p* to look on evil;
Mt 5: 8 Blessed are the *p* in heart,
2Co 11: 2 I might present you as a *p* virgin
Php 4: 8 whatever is *p,* whatever is lovely,
1Ti 5:22 Keep yourself *p.*
Tit 1:15 To the *p,* all things are *p,*
2: 5 to be self-controlled and *p,*
Heb 13: 4 and the marriage bed kept *p,*
1Jn 3: 3 him purifies himself, just as he is *p.*

PURGE
Pr 20:30 and beatings *p* the inmost being.

PURIFIES* (PURE)
1Jn 1: 7 of Jesus, his Son, *p* us from all sin.
3: 3 who has this hope in him *p* himself,

PURIFY (PURE)
Tit 2:14 to *p* for himself a people that are
1Jn 1: 9 and *p* us from all unrighteousness.

PURITY (PURE)
2Co 6: 6 in *p,* understanding, patience
1Ti 4:12 in life, in love, in faith and in *p.*

PURPOSE
Pr 19:21 but it is the LORD's *p* that prevails
Isa 55:11 and achieve the *p* for which I sent it
Ro 8:28 have been called according to his *p.*
Php 2: 2 love, being one in spirit and *p.*

PURSES
Lk 12:33 Provide *p* for yourselves that will

PURSUE
Ps 34:14 seek peace and *p* it.
2Ti 2:22 and *p* righteousness, faith,
1Pe 3:11 he must seek peace and *p* it.

QUALITIES (QUALITY)
2Pe 1: 8 For if you possess these *q*

QUALITY (QUALITIES)
1Co 3:13 and the fire will test the *q*

QUARREL (QUARRELSOME)
Pr 15:18 but a patient man calms a *q.*
17:14 Starting a *q* is like breaching a dam;
17:19 He who loves a *q* loves sin;
2Ti 2:24 And the Lord's servant must not *q;*

QUARRELSOME (QUARREL)
Pr 19:13 a *q* wife is like a constant dripping.
1Ti 3: 3 not violent but gentle, not *q,*

QUICK-TEMPERED
Tit 1: 7 not *q,* not given to drunkenness,

QUIET (QUIETNESS)
Ps 23: 2 he leads me beside *q* waters,
Zep 3:17 he will *q* you with his love,
Lk 19:40 he replied, "if they keep *q,*
1Ti 2: 2 we may live peaceful and *q* lives
1Pe 3: 4 beauty of a gentle and *q* spirit,

QUIETNESS (QUIET)
Isa 30:15 in *q* and trust is your strength,
32:17 the effect of righteousness will be *q*
1Ti 2:11 A woman should learn in *q*

QUIVER
Ps 127: 5 whose *q* is full of them.

RACE
Ecc 9:11 The *r* is not to the swift
1Co 9:24 that in a *r* all the runners run,
2Ti 4: 7 I have finished the *r,* I have kept
Heb 12: 1 perseverance the *r* marked out

RACHEL
Daughter of Laban (Ge 29:16); wife of Jacob (Ge 29:28); bore two sons (Ge 30:22-24; 35:16-24; 46:19).

RADIANCE (RADIANT)
Heb 1: 3 The Son is the *r* of God's glory

RADIANT (RADIANCE)
Ex 34:29 he was not aware that his face was *r*
Ps 34: 5 Those who look to him are *r;*
SS 5:10 *Beloved* My lover is *r* and ruddy,
Isa 60: 5 Then you will look and be *r,*
Eph 5:27 her to himself as a *r* church,

RAIN (RAINBOW)
Mt 5:45 and sends *r* on the righteous

RAINBOW (RAIN)
Ge 9:13 I have set my *r* in the clouds,

RAISED (RISE)
Ro 4:25 was *r* to life for our justification.
10: 9 in your heart that God *r* him
1Co 15: 4 that he was *r* on the third day

RAN (RUN)
Jnh 1: 3 But Jonah *r* away from the LORD

RANSOM
Mt 20:28 and to give his life as a *r* for many."
Heb 9:15 as a *r* to set them free

RAVENS
1Ki 17: 6 The *r* brought him bread
Lk 12:24 Consider the *r:* They do not sow

READ (READS)
Jos 8:34 Joshua *r* all the words of the law—
Ne 8: 8 They *r* from the Book of the Law
2Co 3: 2 known and *r* by everybody.

READS (READ)
Rev 1: 3 Blessed is the one who *r* the words

REAL (REALITY)
Jn 6:55 is *r* food and my blood is *r* drink.

REALITY* (REAL)
Col 2:17 the *r,* however, is found in Christ.

REAP (REAPS)
Job 4: 8 and those who sow trouble *r* it.
2Co 9: 6 generously will also *r* generously.

REAPS (REAP)
Gal 6: 7 A man *r* what he sows.

REASON
Isa 1:18 "Come now, let us *r* together,"
1Pe 3:15 to give the *r* for the hope that you

REBEKAH
Sister of Laban, secured as bride for Isaac (Ge 24). Mother of Esau and Jacob (Ge 25:19-26). Taken by Abimelech as sister of Isaac; returned (Ge 26:1-11). Encouraged Jacob to trick Isaac out of blessing (Ge 27:1-17).

REBEL
Mt 10:21 children will *r* against their parents

REBUKE (REBUKED REBUKING)
Pr 9: 8 *r* a wise man and he will love you.
27: 5 Better is open *r*
Lk 17: 3 "If your brother sins, *r* him,
2Ti 4: 2 correct, *r* and encourage—
Rev 3:19 Those whom I love I *r*

REBUKED (REBUKE)
1Ti 5:20 Those who sin are to be *r* publicly,

REBUKING (REBUKE)
2Ti 3:16 *r,* correcting and training

RECEIVE (RECEIVED RECEIVES)
Ac 1: 8 you will *r* power when the Holy
20:35 'It is more blessed to give than to *r*
2Co 6:17 and I will *r* you."
Rev 4:11 to *r* glory and honor and power,

RECEIVED (RECEIVE)
Mt 6: 2 they have *r* their reward in full.
10: 8 Freely you have *r,* freely give.
1Co 11:23 For I *r* from the Lord what I
Col 2: 6 just as you *r* Christ Jesus as Lord,
1Pe 4:10 should use whatever gift he has *r*

RECEIVES (RECEIVE)
Mt 7: 8 everyone who asks *r;* he who seeks
10:40 he who *r* me *r* the one who sent me.
Ac 10:43 believes in him *r* forgiveness of sins

RECKONING
Isa 10: 3 What will you do on the day of *r,*

RECOGNIZE (RECOGNIZED)
Mt 7:16 By their fruit you will *r* them.

RECOGNIZED (RECOGNIZE)
Mt 12:33 for a tree is *r* by its fruit.
Ro 7:13 in order that sin might be *r* as sin,

RECOMPENSE
Isa 40:10 and his *r* accompanies him.

RECONCILE (RECONCILED RECONCILIATION)
Eph 2:16 in this one body to *r* both of them

RECONCILED (RECONCILE)
Mt 5:24 First go and be *r* to your brother;
Ro 5:10 we were *r* to him through the death
2Co 5:18 who *r* us to himself through Christ

RECONCILIATION* (RECONCILE)
Ro 5:11 whom we have now received *r.*

11:15 For if their rejection is the *r*
2Co 5:18 and gave us the ministry of *r*:
5:19 committed to us the message of *r*.

RECORD
Ps 130: 3 If you, O LORD, kept a *r* of sins,

RED
Isa 1:18 though they are *r* as crimson,

REDEEM (KINSMAN-REDEEMER REDEEMED REDEEMER REDEMPTION)
2Sa 7:23 on earth that God went out to *r*
Ps 49: 7 No man can *r* the life of another
Gal 4: 5 under law, to *r* those under law,

REDEEMED (REDEEM)
Gal 3:13 Christ *r* us from the curse
1Pe 1:18 or gold that you were *r*

REDEEMER (REDEEM)
Job 19:25 I know that my *R* lives,

REDEMPTION (REDEEM)
Ps 130: 7 and with him is full *r*.
Lk 21:28 because your *r* is drawing near."
Ro 8:23 as sons, the *r* of our bodies.
Eph 1: 7 In him we have *r* through his blood
Col 1:14 in whom we have *r*, the forgiveness
Heb 9:12 having obtained eternal *r*.

REFLECT
2Co 3:18 unveiled faces all *r* the Lord's

REFUGE
Nu 35:11 towns to be your cities of *r*,
Dt 33:27 The eternal God is your *r*,
Ru 2:12 wings you have come to take *r*."
Ps 46: 1 God is our *r* and strength,
91: 2 "He is my *r* and my fortress,

REHOBOAM
Son of Solomon (1Ki 11:43; 1Ch 3:10). Harsh treatment of subjects caused divided kingdom (1Ki 12:1-24; 14:21-31; 2Ch 10-12).

REIGN
Ex 15:18 The LORD will *r*
Ro 6:12 Therefore do not let sin *r*
1Co 15:25 For he must *r* until he has put all
2Ti 2:12 we will also *r* with him.
Rev 20: 6 will *r* with him for a thousand years

REJECTED (REJECTS)
Ps 118:22 The stone the builders *r*
Isa 53: 3 He was despised and *r* by men,
1Ti 4: 4 nothing is to be *r* if it is received
1Pe 2: 4 *r* by men but chosen by God
2: 7 "The stone the builders *r*

REJECTS (REJECTED)
Lk 10:16 but he who *r* me *r* him who sent me
Jn 3:36 whoever *r* the Son will not see life,

REJOICE (JOY)
Ps 2:11 and *r* with trembling.
66: 6 come, let us *r* in him.
118:24 let us *r* and be glad in it.
Pr 5:18 may you *r* in the wife of your youth
Lk 10:20 but *r* that your names are written
15: 6 '*R* with me; I have found my lost
Ro 12:15 Rejoice with those who *r*; mourn
Php 4: 4 *R* in the Lord always.

REJOICES (JOY)
Isa 61:10 my soul *r* in my God.
Lk 1:47 and my spirit *r* in God my Savior,
1Co 12:26 if one part is honored, every part *r*
13: 6 delight in evil but *r* with the truth.

REJOICING (JOY)
Ps 30: 5 but *r* comes in the morning.
Lk 15: 7 in the same way there will be more *r*
Ac 5:41 *r* because they had been counted

RELIABLE
2Ti 2: 2 witnesses entrust to *r* men who will

RELIGION
1Ti 5: 4 all to put their *r* into practice
Jas 1:27 *R* that God our Father accepts

REMAIN (REMAINS)
Nu 33:55 allow to *r* will become barbs
Jn 15: 7 If you *r* in me and my words
Ro 13: 8 Let no debt *r* outstanding,
1Co 13:13 And now these three *r*: faith,
2Ti 2:13 he will *r* faithful,

REMAINS (REMAIN)
Ps 146: 6 the LORD, who *r* faithful forever.
Heb 7: 3 Son of God he *r* a priest forever.

REMEMBER (REMEMBERS REMEMBRANCE)
Ex 20: 8 "*R* the Sabbath day
1Ch 16:12 *R* the wonders he has done,
Ecc 12: 1 *R* your Creator
Jer 31:34 and will *r* their sins no more."
Gal 2:10 we should continue to *r* the poor,
Php 1: 3 I thank my God every time I *r* you.
Heb 8:12 and will *r* their sins no more."

REMEMBERS (REMEMBER)
Ps 103:14 he *r* that we are dust.
111: 5 he *r* his covenant forever.
Isa 43:25 and *r* your sins no more.

REMEMBRANCE (REMEMBER)
1Co 11:24 which is for you; do this in *r* of me

REMIND
Jn 14:26 will *r* you of everything I have said

REMOVED
Ps 30:11 you *r* my sackcloth and clothed me
103:12 so far has he *r* our transgressions
Jn 20: 1 and saw that the stone had been *r*

RENEW (RENEWED RENEWING)
Ps 51:10 and *r* a steadfast spirit within me.
Isa 40:31 will *r* their strength.

RENEWED (RENEW)
Ps 103: 5 that your youth is *r* like the eagle's.
2Co 4:16 yet inwardly we are being *r* day

RENEWING (RENEW)
Ro 12: 2 transformed by the *r* of your mind.

RENOUNCE (RENOUNCES)
Da 4:27 *R* your sins by doing what is right,

RENOUNCES (RENOUNCE)
Pr 28:13 confesses and *r* them finds

RENOWN
Isa 63:12 to gain for himself everlasting *r*,
Jer 32:20 have gained the *r* that is still yours.

REPAID (PAY)
Lk 14:14 you will be *r* at the resurrection
Col 3:25 Anyone who does wrong will be *r*

REPAY (PAY)
Dt 32:35 It is mine to avenge; I will *r*.
Ru 2:12 May the LORD *r* you
Ps 116:12 How can I *r* the LORD
Ro 12:19 "It is mine to avenge; I will *r*,"
1Pe 3: 9 Do not *r* evil with evil

REPENT (REPENTANCE REPENTS)
Job 42: 6 and *r* in dust and ashes."
Jer 15:19 "If you *r*, I will restore you
Mt 4:17 *"R*, for the kingdom of heaven is
Lk 13: 3 unless you *r*, you too will all perish.
Ac 2:38 Peter replied, *"R* and be baptized,
17:30 all people everywhere to *r*.

REPENTANCE (REPENT)
Lk 3: 8 Produce fruit in keeping with *r*.
5:32 call the righteous, but sinners to *r*."
Ac 26:20 and prove their *r* by their deeds.
2Co 7:10 Godly sorrow brings *r* that leads

REPENTS (REPENT)
Lk 15:10 of God over one sinner who *r*."
17: 3 rebuke him, and if he *r*, forgive him

REPROACH
1Ti 3: 2 Now the overseer must be above *r*,

REPUTATION
1Ti 3: 7 also have a good *r* with outsiders,

REQUESTS
Ps 20: 5 May the LORD grant all your *r*.
Php 4: 6 with thanksgiving, present your *r*

REQUIRE
Mic 6: 8 And what does the LORD *r* of you

RESCUE (RESCUES)
Da 6:20 been able to *r* you from the lions?"
2Pe 2: 9 how to *r* godly men from trials

RESCUES (RESCUE)
1Th 1:10 who *r* us from the coming wrath.

RESIST
Jas 4: 7 *R* the devil, and he will flee
1Pe 5: 9 *R* him, standing firm in the faith,

RESOLVED
Ps 17: 3 I have *r* that my mouth will not sin.
Da 1: 8 But Daniel *r* not to defile himself
1Co 2: 2 For I *r* to know nothing while I was

RESPECT (RESPECTABLE)
Lev 19: 3 " 'Each of you must *r* his mother
19:32 show *r* for the elderly and revere
Pr 11:16 A kindhearted woman gains *r*,
Mal 1: 6 where is the *r* due me?" says
1Th 4:12 so that your daily life may win the *r*
5:12 to *r* those who work hard
1Ti 3: 4 children obey him with proper *r*.
1Pe 2:17 Show proper *r* to everyone:
3: 7 them with *r* as the weaker partner

RESPECTABLE* (RESPECT)
1Ti 3: 2 self-controlled, *r*, hospitable,

REST
Ex 31:15 the seventh day is a Sabbath of *r*,
Ps 91: 1 will *r* in the shadow
Jer 6:16 and you will find *r* for your souls.
Mt 11:28 and burdened, and I will give you *r*.

RESTITUTION
Ex 22: 3 "A thief must certainly make *r*,
Lev 6: 5 He must make *r* in full, add a fifth

RESTORE (RESTORES)
Ps 51:12 *R* to me the joy of your salvation
Gal 6: 1 are spiritual should *r* him gently.

RESTORES (RESTORE)
Ps 23: 3 he *r* my soul.

RESURRECTION
Mt 22:30 At the *r* people will neither marry
Lk 14:14 repaid at the *r* of the righteous."
Jn 11:25 Jesus said to her, "I am the *r*
Ro 1: 4 Son of God by his *r* from the dead:
1Co 15:12 some of you say that there is no *r*
Php 3:10 power of his *r* and the fellowship
Rev 20: 5 This is the first *r*.

RETRIBUTION
Jer 51:56 For the LORD is a God of *r*;

RETURN
2Ch 30: 9 If you *r* to the LORD, then your
Ne 1: 9 but if you *r* to me and obey my
Isa 55:11 It will not *r* to me empty,
Hos 6: 1 "Come, let us *r* to the LORD.
Joel 2:12 *"r* to me with all your heart,

REVEALED (REVELATION)
Dt 29:29 but the things *r* belong to us
Isa 40: 5 the glory of the LORD will be *r*,
Mt 11:25 and *r* them to little children.
Ro 1:17 a righteousness from God is *r*,
8:18 with the glory that will be *r* in us.

REVELATION (REVEALED)
Gal 1:12 I received it by *r* from Jesus Christ.
Rev 1: 1 *r* of Jesus Christ, which God gave

REVENGE (VENGEANCE)
Lev 19:18 " 'Do not seek *r* or bear a grudge
Ro 12:19 Do not take *r*, my friends,

REVERE (REVERENCE)
Ps 33: 8 let all the people of the world *r* him

REVERENCE (REVERE)
Lev 19:30 and have *r* for my sanctuary.
Ps 5: 7 in *r* will I bow down
Col 3:22 of heart and *r* for the Lord.
1Pe 3: 2 when they see the purity and *r*

REVIVE (REVIVING)
Ps 85: 6 Will you not *r* us again,
Isa 57:15 to *r* the spirit of the lowly

REVIVING (REVIVE)
Ps 19: 7 *r* the soul.

REWARD (REWARDED)
Ps 19:11 in keeping them there is great *r*.
127: 3 children a *r* from him.
Pr 19:17 he will *r* him for what he has done.
25:22 and the LORD will *r* you.
31:31 Give her the *r* she has earned,
Jer 17:10 to *r* a man according to his conduct
Mt 5:12 because great is your *r* in heaven,
6: 5 they have received their *r* in full.
16:27 and then he will *r* each person
1Co 3:14 built survives, he will receive his *r*.
Rev 22:12 I am coming soon! My *r* is with me

REWARDED (REWARD)
Ru 2:12 May you be richly *r* by the LORD,
Ps 18:24 The LORD has *r* me according
Pr 14:14 and the good man *r* for his.
1Co 3: 8 and each will be *r* according

RICH (RICHES)
Pr 23: 4 Do not wear yourself out to get *r*;
Jer 9:23 or the *r* man boast of his riches,
Mt 19:23 it is hard for a *r* man
2Co 6:10 yet making many *r*; having nothing
8: 9 he was *r*, yet for your sakes he
1Ti 6:17 Command those who are *r*

RICHES (RICH)
Ps 119:14 as one rejoices in great *r*.
Pr 30: 8 give me neither poverty nor *r*,
Isa 10: 3 Where will you leave your *r*?

Ro 9:23 to make the *r* of his glory known
11:33 the depth of the *r* of the wisdom
Eph 2: 7 he might show the incomparable *r*
3: 8 to the Gentiles the unsearchable *r*
Col 1:27 among the Gentiles the glorious *r*

RID
Ge 21:10 "Get *r* of that slave woman
1Co 5: 7 Get *r* of the old yeast that you may
Gal 4:30 "Get *r* of the slave woman

RIGHT (RIGHTS)
Ge 18:25 the Judge of all the earth do *r*?"
Ex 15:26 and do what is *r* in his eyes,
Dt 5:32 do not turn aside to the *r*
Ps 16: 8 Because he is at my *r* hand,
19: 8 The precepts of the LORD are *r*,
63: 8 your *r* hand upholds me.
110: 1 "Sit at my *r* hand
Pr 4:27 Do not swerve to the *r* or the left;
14:12 There is a way that seems *r*
Isa 1:17 learn to do *r*!
Jer 23: 5 and do what is just and *r* in the land
Hos 14: 9 The ways of the LORD are *r*;
Mt 6: 3 know what your *r* hand is doing,
Jn 1:12 he gave the *r* to become children
Ro 9:21 Does not the potter have the *r*
12:17 careful to do what is *r* in the eyes
Eph 1:20 and seated him at his *r* hand
Php 4: 8 whatever is *r*, whatever is pure,
2Th 3:13 never tire of doing what is *r*.

RIGHTEOUS (RIGHTEOUSNESS)
Ps 34:15 The eyes of the LORD are on the *r*
37:25 yet I have never seen the *r* forsaken
119:137 *R* are you, O LORD,
143: 2 for no one living is *r* before you.
Pr 3:33 but he blesses the home of the *r*.
11:30 The fruit of the *r* is a tree of life,
18:10 the *r* run to it and are safe.
Isa 64: 6 and all our *r* acts are like filthy rags
Hab 2: 4 but the *r* will live by his faith—
Mt 5:45 rain on the *r* and the unrighteous.
9:13 For I have not come to call the *r*,
13:49 and separate the wicked from the *r*
25:46 to eternal punishment, but the *r*
Ro 1:17 as it is written: "The *r* will live
3:10 "There is no one *r*, not even one;
1Ti 1: 9 that law is made not for the *r*
1Pe 3:18 the *r* for the unrighteous,
1Jn 3: 7 does what is right is *r*, just as he is *r*.
Rev 19: 8 stands for the *r* acts of the saints.)

RIGHTEOUSNESS (RIGHTEOUS)
Ge 15: 6 and he credited it to him as *r*.
1Sa 26:23 LORD rewards every man for his *r*
Ps 9: 8 He will judge the world in *r*;
23: 3 He guides me in paths of *r*
45: 7 You love *r* and hate wickedness;
85:10 *r* and peace kiss each other.
89:14 *R* and justice are the foundation
111: 3 and his *r* endures forever.
Pr 14:34 *R* exalts a nation,
21:21 He who pursues *r* and love
Isa 5:16 will show himself holy by his *r*.
59:17 He put on *r* as his breastplate,
Eze 18:20 The *r* of the righteous man will be
Da 9:24 to bring in everlasting *r*,
12: 3 and those who lead many to *r*,
Mal 4: 2 the sun of *r* will rise with healing
Mt 5: 6 those who hunger and thirst for *r*,
5:20 unless your *r* surpasses that
6:33 But seek first his kingdom and his *r*
Ro 4: 3 and it was credited to him as *r*."
4: 9 faith was credited to him as *r*.
6:13 body to him as instruments of *r*.
2Co 5:21 that in him we might become the *r*
Gal 2:21 for if *r* could be gained
3: 6 and it was credited to him as *r*."
Eph 6:14 with the breastplate of *r* in place,
Php 3: 9 not having a *r* of my own that
2Ti 3:16 correcting and training in *r*,
4: 8 is in store for me the crown of *r*,
Heb 11: 7 became heir of the *r* that comes
2Pe 2:21 not to have known the way of *r*,

RIGHTS (RIGHT)
La 3:35 to deny a man his *r*
Gal 4: 5 that we might receive the full *r*

RISE (RAISED)
Isa 26:19 their bodies will *r*.
Mt 27:63 'After three days I will *r* again.'
Jn 5:29 those who have done good will *r*
1Th 4:16 and the dead in Christ will *r* first.

ROAD
Mt 7:13 and broad is the *r* that leads

ROBBERS
Jer 7:11 become a den of *r* to you?
Mk 15:27 They crucified two *r* with him,
Lk 19:46 but you have made it 'a den of *r*.'"
Jn 10: 8 came before me were thieves and *r*,

ROCK
Ps 18: 2 The LORD is my *r*, my fortress
40: 2 he set my feet on a *r*
Mt 7:24 man who built his house on the *r*.
16:18 and on this *r* I will build my church
Ro 9:33 and a *r* that makes them fall,
1Co 10: 4 the spiritual *r* that accompanied

ROD
Ps 23: 4 your *r* and your staff,
Pr 13:24 He who spares the *r* hates his son,
23:13 if you punish him with the *r*,

ROOM (ROOMS)
Mt 6: 6 But when you pray, go into your *r*,
Lk 2: 7 there was no *r* for them in the inn.
Jn 21:25 the whole world would not have *r*

ROOMS (ROOM)
Jn 14: 2 In my Father's house are many *r*;

ROOT
Isa 53: 2 and like a *r* out of dry ground.
1Ti 6:10 of money is a *r* of all kinds of evil.

ROYAL
Jas 2: 8 If you really keep the *r* law found
1Pe 2: 9 a *r* priesthood, a holy nation,

RUBBISH*
Php 3: 8 I consider them *r*, that I may gain

RUDE*
1Co 13: 5 It is not *r*, it is not self-seeking,

RUIN (RUINS)
Pr 18:24 many companions may come to *r*,
1Ti 6: 9 desires that plunge men into *r*

RUINS (RUIN)
Pr 19: 3 A man's own folly *r* his life,
2Ti 2:14 and only *r* those who listen.

RULE (RULER RULERS RULES)
1Sa 12:12 'No, we want a king to *r* over us'—
Ps 2: 9 You will *r* them with an iron
119:133 let no sin *r* over me.
Zec 9:10 His *r* will extend from sea to sea
Col 3:15 the peace of Christ *r* in your hearts,
Rev 2:27 He will *r* them with an iron scepter;

RULER (RULE)
Ps 8: 6 You made him *r* over the works

Eph 2: 2 of the *r* of the kingdom of the air,
1Ti 6:15 God, the blessed and only *R*,

RULERS (RULE)
Ps 2: 2 and the *r* gather together
Col 1:16 or powers or *r* or authorities;

RULES (RULE)
Ps 103:19 and his kingdom *r* over all.
Lk 22:26 one who *r* like the one who serves.
2Ti 2: 5 he competes according to the *r*.

RUMORS
Mt 24: 6 You will hear of wars and *r* of wars,

RUN (RAN)
Isa 40:31 they will *r* and not grow weary,
1Co 9:24 *R* in such a way as to get the prize.
Heb 12: 1 let us *r* with perseverance the race

RUST
Mt 6:19 where moth and *r* destroy,

RUTH*
Moabitess; widow who went to Bethlehem with mother-in-law Naomi (Ru 1). Gleaned in field of Boaz; shown favor (Ru 2). Proposed marriage to Boaz (Ru 3). Married (Ru 4:1-12); bore Obed, ancestor of David (Ru 4:13-22), Jesus (Mt 1:5).

SABBATH
Ex 20: 8 "Remember the *S* day
Dt 5:12 "Observe the *S* day
Col 2:16 a New Moon celebration or a *S* day

SACKCLOTH
Mt 11:21 would have repented long ago in *s*

SACRED
Mt 7: 6 "Do not give dogs what is *s*;
1Co 3:17 for God's temple is *s*, and you are

SACRIFICE (SACRIFICED SACRIFICES)
Ge 22: 2 *S* him there as a burnt offering
Ex 12:27 'It is the Passover *s* to the LORD,
1Sa 15:22 To obey is better than *s*,
Hos 6: 6 For I desire mercy, not *s*,
Mt 9:13 this means: 'I desire mercy, not *s*.'
Heb 9:26 away with sin by the *s* of himself.
13:15 offer to God a *s* of praise—
1Jn 2: 2 He is the atoning *s* for our sins,

SACRIFICED (SACRIFICE)
1Co 5: 7 our Passover lamb, has been *s*.
8: 1 Now about food *s* to idols:
Heb 9:28 so Christ was *s* once

SACRIFICES (SACRIFICE)
Ps 51:17 The *s* of God are a broken spirit;
Ro 12: 1 to offer your bodies as living *s*,

SADDUCEES
Mk 12:18 *S*, who say there is no resurrection,

SAFE (SAVE)
Ps 37: 3 in the land and enjoy *s* pasture.
Pr 18:10 the righteous run to it and are *s*.

SAFETY (SAVE)
Ps 4: 8 make me dwell in *s*.
1Th 5: 3 people are saying, "Peace and *s*,"

SAINTS
Ps 116:15 is the death of his *s*.
Ro 8:27 intercedes for the *s* in accordance
Eph 1:18 of his glorious inheritance in the *s*,
6:18 always keep on praying for all the *s*
Rev 5: 8 which are the prayers of the *s*.
19: 8 for the righteous acts of the *s*.)

SAKE
Ps 44:22 Yet for your *s* we face death all day
Php 3: 7 loss for the *s* of Christ.
Heb 11:26 He regarded disgrace for the *s*

SALT
Ge 19:26 and she became a pillar of *s*.
Mt 5:13 "You are the *s* of the earth.

SALVATION (SAVE)
Ex 15: 2 he has become my *s*.
1Ch 16:23 proclaim his *s* day after day.
Ps 27: 1 The LORD is my light and my *s*—
51:12 Restore to me the joy of your *s*
62: 2 He alone is my rock and my *s*;
85: 9 Surely his *s* is near those who fear
96: 2 proclaim his *s* day after day.
Isa 25: 9 let us rejoice and be glad in his *s*."
45:17 the LORD with an everlasting *s*;
51: 6 But my *s* will last forever,
59:17 and the helmet of *s* on his head;
61:10 me with garments of *s*
Jnh 2: 9 *S* comes from the LORD."
Zec 9: 9 righteous and having *s*,
Lk 2:30 For my eyes have seen your *s*,
Jn 4:22 for *s* is from the Jews.
Ac 4:12 *S* is found in no one else,
13:47 that you may bring *s* to the ends
Ro 11:11 *s* has come to the Gentiles
2Co 7:10 brings repentance that leads to *s*
Eph 6:17 Take the helmet of *s* and the sword
Php 2:12 to work out your *s* with fear
1Th 5: 8 and the hope of *s* as a helmet.
2Ti 3:15 wise for *s* through faith
Heb 2: 3 escape if we ignore such a great *s*?
6: 9 case—things that accompany *s*.
1Pe 1:10 Concerning this *s*, the prophets,
2: 2 by it you may grow up in your *s*,

SAMARITAN
Lk 10:33 But a *S*, as he traveled, came where

SAMSON
Danite judge. Birth promised (Jdg 13). Married to Philistine (Jdg 14). Vengeance on Philistines (Jdg 15). Betrayed by Delilah (Jdg 16:1-22). Death (Jdg 16:23-31). Feats of strength: killed lion (Jdg 14:6), 30 Philistines (Jdg 14:19), 1,000 Philistines with jawbone (Jdg 15:13-17), carried off gates of Gaza (Jdg 16:3), pushed down temple of Dagon (Jdg 16:25-30).

SAMUEL
Ephraimite judge and prophet (Heb 11:32). Birth prayed for (1Sa 1:10-18). Dedicated to temple by Hannah (1Sa 1:21-28). Raised by Eli (1Sa 2:11, 18-26). Called as prophet (1Sa 3). Led Israel to victory over Philistines (1Sa 7). Asked by Israel for a king (1Sa 8). Anointed Saul as king (1Sa 9-10). Farewell speech (1Sa 12). Rebuked Saul for sacrifice (1Sa 13). Announced rejection of Saul (1Sa 15). Anointed David as king (1Sa 16). Protected David from Saul (1Sa 19:18-24). Death (1Sa 25:1). Returned from dead to condemn Saul (1Sa 28).

SANCTIFIED (SANCTIFY)
Ac 20:32 among all those who are *s*.
Ro 15:16 to God, *s* by the Holy Spirit.
1Co 6:11 But you were washed, you were *s*,
7:14 and the unbelieving wife has been *s*
Heb 10:29 blood of the covenant that *s* him,

SANCTIFY (SANCTIFIED SANCTIFYING)
1Th 5:23 *s* you through and through.

SANCTIFYING (SANCTIFY)
2Th 2:13 through the *s* work of the Spirit

SANCTUARY
Ex 25: 8 "Then have them make a *s* for me,

SAND
Ge 22:17 and as the *s* on the seashore.
Mt 7:26 man who built his house on *s*.

SANDALS
Ex 3: 5 off your *s*, for the place where you
Jos 5:15 off your *s*, for the place where you

SANG (SING)
Job 38: 7 while the morning stars *s* together
Rev 5: 9 And they *s* a new song:

SARAH
Wife of Abraham, originally named Sarai; barren (Ge 11:29-31; 1Pe 3:6). Taken by Pharaoh as Abraham's sister; returned (Ge 12:10-20). Gave Hagar to Abraham; sent her away in pregnancy (Ge 16). Name changed; Isaac promised (Ge 17:15-21; 18:10-15; Heb 11:11). Taken by Abimelech as Abraham's sister; returned (Ge 20). Isaac born; Hagar and Ishmael sent away (Ge 21:1-21; Gal 4:21-31). Death (Ge 23).

SATAN
Job 1: 6 and *S* also came with them.
Zec 3: 2 said to *S*, "The LORD rebuke you,
Mk 4:15 *S* comes and takes away the word
2Co 11:14 for *S* himself masquerades
12: 7 a messenger of *S*, to torment me.
Rev 12: 9 serpent called the devil, or *S*,
20: 2 or *S*, and bound him for a thousand
20: 7 *S* will be released from his prison

SATISFIED (SATISFY)
Isa 53:11 he will see the light ⌞of life⌟ and be *s*

SATISFIES (SATISFY)
Ps 103: 5 who *s* your desires with good things,

SATISFY (SATISFIED SATISFIES)
Isa 55: 2 and your labor on what does not *s*?

SAUL
1. Benjamite; anointed by Samuel as first king of Israel (1Sa 9-10). Defeated Ammonites (1Sa 11). Rebuked for offering sacrifice (1Sa 13:1-15). Defeated Philistines (1Sa 14). Rejected as king for failing to annihilate Amalekites (1Sa 15). Soothed from evil spirit by David (1Sa 16:14-23). Sent David against Goliath (1Sa 17). Jealousy and attempted murder of David (1Sa 18:1-11). Gave David Michal as wife (1Sa 18:12-30). Second attempt to kill David (1Sa 19). Anger at Jonathan (1Sa 20:26-34). Pursued David: killed priests at Nob (1Sa 22), went to Keilah and Ziph (1Sa 23), life spared by David at En Gedi (1Sa 24) and in his tent (1Sa 26). Rebuked by Samuel's spirit for consulting witch at Endor (1Sa 28). Wounded by Philistines; took his own life (1Sa 31; 1Ch 10).
2. See PAUL

SAVE (SAFE SAFETY SALVATION SAVED SAVIOR)
Isa 63: 1 mighty to *s*."
Da 3:17 the God we serve is able to *s* us
Zep 3:17 he is mighty to *s*.
Mt 1:21 he will *s* his people from their sins
16:25 wants to *s* his life will lose it,
Lk 19:10 to seek and to *s* what was lost."
Jn 3:17 but to *s* the world through him.
1Ti 1:15 came into the world to *s* sinners—
Jas 5:20 of his way will *s* him from death

SAVED (SAVE)
Ps 34: 6 he *s* him out of all his troubles.
Isa 45:22 "Turn to me and be *s*,
Joel 2:32 on the name of the LORD will be *s*;
Mk 13:13 firm to the end will be *s*.
16:16 believes and is baptized will be *s*,
Jn 10: 9 enters through me will be *s*.
Ac 4:12 to men by which we must be *s*."
16:30 do to be *s*?" They replied,
Ro 9:27 only the remnant will be *s*.
10: 9 him from the dead, you will be *s*.
1Co 3:15 will suffer loss; he himself will be *s*,
15: 2 By this gospel you are *s*,
Eph 2: 5 it is by grace you have been *s*.
2: 8 For it is by grace you have been *s*,
1Ti 2: 4 who wants all men to be *s*

SAVIOR (SAVE)
Ps 89:26 my God, the Rock my *S*.'
Isa 43:11 and apart from me there is no *s*.
Hos 13: 4 no *S* except me.
Lk 1:47 and my spirit rejoices in God my *S*,
2:11 of David a *S* has been born to you;
Jn 4:42 know that this man really is the *S*
Eph 5:23 his body, of which he is the *S*.
1Ti 4:10 who is the *S* of all men,
Tit 2:10 about God our *S* attractive.
2:13 appearing of our great God and *S*,
3: 4 and love of God our *S* appeared,
1Jn 4:14 Son to be the *S* of the world.
Jude :25 to the only God our *S* be glory,

SCALES
Lev 19:36 Use honest *s* and honest weights,
Da 5:27 You have been weighed on the *s*

SCAPEGOAT (GOAT)
Lev 16:10 by sending it into the desert as a *s*.

SCARLET
Isa 1:18 "Though your sins are like *s*,

SCATTERED
Jer 31:10 'He who *s* Israel will gather them
Ac 8: 4 who had been *s* preached the word

SCEPTER
Rev 19:15 "He will rule them with an iron *s*."

SCHEMES
2Co 2:11 For we are not unaware of his *s*.
Eph 6:11 stand against the devil's *s*.

SCOFFERS
2Pe 3: 3 that in the last days *s* will come,

SCORPION
Rev 9: 5 sting of a *s* when it strikes a man.

SCRIPTURE (SCRIPTURES)
Jn 10:35 and the *S* cannot be broken—
1Ti 4:13 yourself to the public reading of *S*,
2Ti 3:16 All *S* is God-breathed
2Pe 1:20 that no prophecy of *S* came about

SCRIPTURES (SCRIPTURE)
Lk 24:27 said in all the *S* concerning himself.
Jn 5:39 These are the *S* that testify about
Ac 17:11 examined the *S* every day to see

SCROLL
Eze 3: 1 eat what is before you, eat this *s*;

SEA
Ex 14:16 go through the *s* on dry ground.
Isa 57:20 the wicked are like the tossing *s*,
Mic 7:19 iniquities into the depths of the *s*.
Jas 1: 6 who doubts is like a wave of the *s*,
Rev 13: 1 I saw a beast coming out of the *s*.

SEAL (SEALS)
Jn 6:27 God the Father has placed his *s*
2Co 1:22 set his *s* of ownership on us,
Eph 1:13 you were marked in him with a *s*,

SEALS (SEAL)
Rev 5: 2 "Who is worthy to break the *s*
6: 1 opened the first of the seven *s*.

SEARCH (SEARCHED SEARCHES SEARCHING)
Ps 4: 4 *s* your hearts and be silent.
139:23 *S* me, O God, and know my heart;

Pr 2: 4 and *s* for it as for hidden treasure,
Jer 17:10 "I the LORD *s* the heart
Eze 34:16 I will *s* for the lost and bring back
Lk 15: 8 and *s* carefully until she finds it?

SEARCHED (SEARCH)
Ps 139: 1 O LORD, you have *s* me

SEARCHES (SEARCH)
Ro 8:27 And he who *s* our hearts knows
1Co 2:10 The Spirit *s* all things,

SEARCHING (SEARCH)
Am 8:12 *s* for the word of the LORD,

SEARED
1Ti 4: 2 whose consciences have been *s*

SEASON
2Ti 4: 2 be prepared in *s* and out of *s;*

SEAT (SEATED SEATS)
Ps 1: 1 or sit in the *s* of mockers.
Da 7: 9 and the Ancient of Days took his *s.*
2Co 5:10 before the judgment *s* of Christ,

SEATED (SEAT)
Ps 47: 8 God is *s* on his holy throne.
Isa 6: 1 I saw the Lord *s* on a throne,
Col 3: 1 where Christ is *s* at the right hand

SEATS (SEAT)
Lk 11:43 you love the most important *s*

SECRET (SECRETS)
Dt 29:29 The *s* things belong
Jdg 16: 6 Tell me the *s* of your great strength
Ps 90: 8 our *s* sins in the light
Pr 11:13 but a trustworthy man keeps a *s.*
Mt 6: 4 so that your giving may be in *s.*
2Co 4: 2 we have renounced *s* and shameful
Php 4:12 I have learned the *s*

SECRETS (SECRET)
Ps 44:21 since he knows the *s* of the heart?
1Co 14:25 the *s* of his heart will be laid bare.

SECURE (SECURITY)
Ps 112: 8 His heart is *s,* he will have no fear;
Heb 6:19 an anchor for the soul, firm and *s.*

SECURITY (SECURE)
Job 31:24 or said to pure gold, 'You are my *s,*'

SEED (SEEDS)
Lk 8:11 of the parable: The *s* is the word
1Co 3: 6 I planted the *s,* Apollos watered it,
2Co 9:10 he who supplies *s* to the sower
Gal 3:29 then you are Abraham's *s,*
1Pe 1:23 not of perishable *s,*

SEEDS (SEED)
Jn 12:24 But if it dies, it produces many *s.*
Gal 3:16 Scripture does not say "and to *s,*"

SEEK (SEEKS SELF-SEEKING)
Dt 4:29 if from there you *s* the LORD your
1Ch 28: 9 If you *s* him, he will be found
2Ch 7:14 themselves and pray and *s* my face
Ps 119:10 I *s* you with all my heart;
Isa 55: 6 *S* the LORD while he may be
65: 1 found by those who did not *s* me.
Mt 6:33 But *s* first his kingdom
Lk 19:10 For the Son of Man came to *s*
Ro 10:20 found by those who did not *s* me;
1Co 7:27 you married? Do not *s* a divorce.

SEEKS (SEEK)
Jn 4:23 the kind of worshipers the Father *s.*

SEER
1Sa 9: 9 of today used to be called a *s.)*

SELF-CONTROL (CONTROL)
1Co 7: 5 you because of your lack of *s.*
Gal 5:23 faithfulness, gentleness and *s.*
2Pe 1: 6 and to knowledge, *s;* and to *s,*

SELF-CONTROLLED* (CONTROL)
1Th 5: 6 are asleep, but let us be alert and *s.*
5: 8 let us be *s,* putting on faith and love
1Ti 3: 2 *s,* respectable, hospitable,
Tit 1: 8 who is *s,* upright, holy
2: 2 worthy of respect, *s,* and sound
2: 5 to be *s* and pure, to be busy at home
2: 6 encourage the young men to be *s.*
2:12 to live *s,* upright and godly lives
1Pe 1:13 prepare your minds for action; be *s;*
4: 7 and *s* so that you can pray.
5: 8 Be *s* and alert.

SELF-INDULGENCE
Mt 23:25 inside they are full of greed and *s.*

SELF-SEEKING (SEEK)
1Co 13: 5 it is not *s,* it is not easily angered,

SELFISH*
Ps 119:36 and not toward *s* gain.
Pr 18: 1 An unfriendly man pursues *s* ends;
Gal 5:20 fits of rage, *s* ambition, dissensions,
Php 1:17 preach Christ out of *s* ambition,
2: 3 Do nothing out of *s* ambition
Jas 3:14 and *s* ambition in your hearts,
3:16 you have envy and *s* ambition,

SEND (SENDING SENT)
Isa 6: 8 *S* me!" He said, "Go and tell this
Mt 9:38 to *s* out workers into his harvest
Jn 16: 7 but if I go, I will *s* him to you.

SENDING (SEND)
Jn 20:21 Father has sent me, I am *s* you."

SENSES*
Lk 15:17 "When he came to his *s,* he said,
1Co 15:34 Come back to your *s* as you ought,
2Ti 2:26 and that they will come to their *s*

SENSUAL
Col 2:23 value in restraining *s* indulgence.

SENT (SEND)
Isa 55:11 achieve the purpose for which I *s* it.
Mt 10:40 me receives the one who *s* me.
Jn 4:34 "is to do the will of him who *s* me
Ro 10:15 can they preach unless they are *s?*
1Jn 4:10 but that he loved us and *s* his Son

SEPARATE (SEPARATED SEPARATES)
Mt 19: 6 has joined together, let man not *s.*"
Ro 8:35 Who shall *s* us from the love
1Co 7:10 wife must not *s* from her husband.
2Co 6:17 and be *s,* says the Lord.

SEPARATED (SEPARATE)
Isa 59: 2 But your iniquities have *s*

SEPARATES (SEPARATE)
Pr 16:28 and a gossip *s* close friends.

SERPENT
Ge 3: 1 the *s* was more crafty than any
Rev 12: 9 that ancient *s* called the devil

SERVANT (SERVANTS)
1Sa 3:10 "Speak, for your *s* is listening."
Mt 20:26 great among you must be your *s,*
25:21 'Well done, good and faithful *s!*
Lk 16:13 "No *s* can serve two masters.

Php 2: 7 taking the very nature of a *s*,
2Ti 2:24 And the Lord's *s* must not quarrel;

SERVANTS (SERVANT)
Lk 17:10 should say, 'We are unworthy *s*;
Jn 15:15 longer call you *s*, because a servant

SERVE (SERVICE SERVING)
Dt 10:12 to *s* the LORD your God
Jos 22: 5 and to *s* him with all your heart
24:15 this day whom you will *s*,
Mt 4:10 Lord your God, and *s* him only.' "
6:24 "No one can *s* two masters.
20:28 but to *s*, and to give his life
Eph 6: 7 *S* wholeheartedly,

SERVICE (SERVE)
1Co 12: 5 There are different kinds of *s*,
Eph 4:12 God's people for works of *s*,

SERVING (SERVE)
Ro 12:11 your spiritual fervor, *s* the Lord.
Eph 6: 7 as if you were *s* the Lord, not men,
Col 3:24 It is the Lord Christ you are *s*.
2Ti 2: 4 No one *s* as a soldier gets involved

SEVEN (SEVENTH)
Ge 7: 2 Take with you *s* of every kind
Jos 6: 4 march around the city *s* times,
1Ki 19:18 Yet I reserve *s* thousand in Israel—
Pr 6:16 *s* that are detestable to him:
24:16 a righteous man falls *s* times,
Isa 4: 1 In that day *s* women
Da 9:25 comes, there will be *s* 'sevens,'
Mt 18:21 Up to *s* times?" Jesus answered,
Lk 11:26 takes *s* other spirits more wicked
Ro 11: 4 for myself *s* thousand who have not
Rev 1: 4 To the *s* churches in the province
6: 1 opened the first of the *s* seals.
8: 2 and to them were given *s* trumpets.
10: 4 And when the *s* thunders spoke,
15: 7 to the *s* angels *s* golden bowls filled

SEVENTH (SEVEN)
Ge 2: 2 By the *s* day God had finished
Ex 23:12 but on the *s* day do not work,

SEXUAL (SEXUALLY)
1Co 6:13 body is not meant for *s* immorality,
6:18 Flee from *s* immorality.
10: 8 should not commit *s* immorality,
Eph 5: 3 even a hint of *s* immorality,
1Th 4: 3 that you should avoid *s* immorality

SEXUALLY (SEXUAL)
1Co 5: 9 to associate with *s* immoral people
6:18 he who sins *s* sins against his own

SHADOW
Ps 23: 4 through the valley of the *s* of death,
36: 7 find refuge in the *s* of your wings.
Heb 10: 1 The law is only a *s*

SHALLUM
King of Israel (2Ki 15:10-16).

SHAME (ASHAMED)
Ps 34: 5 their faces are never covered with *s*
Pr 13:18 discipline comes to poverty and *s*,
Heb 12: 2 endured the cross, scorning its *s*,

SHARE (SHARED)
Ge 21:10 that slave woman's son will never *s*
Lk 3:11 "The man with two tunics should *s*
Gal 4:30 the slave woman's son will never *s*
6: 6 in the word must *s* all good things
Eph 4:28 something to *s* with those in need.
1Ti 6:18 and to be generous and willing to *s*.
Heb 12:10 that we may *s* in his holiness.
13:16 to do good and to *s* with others,

SHARED (SHARE)
Heb 2:14 he too *s* in their humanity so that

SHARON
SS 2: 1 I am a rose of *S*,

SHARPER*
Heb 4:12 *S* than any double-edged sword,

SHED (SHEDDING)
Ge 9: 6 by man shall his blood be *s*;
Col 1:20 through his blood, *s* on the cross.

SHEDDING (SHED)
Heb 9:22 without the *s* of blood there is no

SHEEP
Ps 100: 3 we are his people, the *s*
119:176 I have strayed like a lost *s*.
Isa 53: 6 We all, like *s*, have gone astray,
Jer 50: 6 "My people have been lost *s*;
Eze 34:11 I myself will search for my *s*
Mt 9:36 helpless, like *s* without a shepherd.
Jn 10: 3 He calls his own *s* by name
10:15 and I lay down my life for the *s*.
10:27 My *s* listen to my voice; I know
21:17 Jesus said, "Feed my *s*.
1Pe 2:25 For you were like *s* going astray,

SHELTER
Ps 61: 4 take refuge in the *s* of your wings.
91: 1 in the *s* of the Most High

SHEM
Son of Noah (Ge 5:32; 6:10). Blessed (Ge 9:26). Descendants (Ge 10:21-31; 11:10-32).

SHEPHERD (SHEPHERDS)
Ps 23: 1 LORD is my *s*, I shall not be in want.
Isa 40:11 He tends his flock like a *s*:
Jer 31:10 will watch over his flock like a *s*.'
Eze 34:12 As a *s* looks after his scattered
Zec 11:17 "Woe to the worthless *s*,
Mt 9:36 and helpless, like sheep without a *s*.
Jn 10:11 The good *s* lays down his life
10:16 there shall be one flock and one *s*.
1Pe 5: 4 And when the Chief *S* appears,

SHEPHERDS (SHEPHERD)
Jer 23: 1 "Woe to the *s* who are destroying
Lk 2: 8 there were *s* living out in the fields
Ac 20:28 Be *s* of the church of God,
1Pe 5: 2 Be *s* of God's flock that is

SHIELD
Ps 28: 7 LORD is my strength and my *s*;
Eph 6:16 to all this, take up the *s* of faith,

SHINE (SHONE)
Ps 4: 6 Let the light of your face *s* upon us,
80: 1 between the cherubim, *s* forth
Isa 60: 1 "Arise, *s*, for your light has come,
Da 12: 3 are wise will *s* like the brightness
Mt 5:16 let your light *s* before men,
13:43 the righteous will *s* like the sun
2Co 4: 6 made his light *s* in our hearts
Eph 5:14 and Christ will *s* on you."

SHIPWRECKED*
2Co 11:25 I was stoned, three times I was *s*,
1Ti 1:19 and so have *s* their faith.

SHONE (SHINE)
Mt 17: 2 His face *s* like the sun,
Lk 2: 9 glory of the Lord *s* around them,
Rev 21:11 It *s* with the glory of God,

SHORT
Isa 59: 1 of the LORD is not too *s* to save,
Ro 3:23 and fall *s* of the glory of God,

SHOULDERS
Isa 9: 6 and the government will be on his *s*
Lk 15: 5 he joyfully puts it on his *s*

SHOWED
1Jn 4: 9 This is how God *s* his love

SHREWD
Mt 10:16 Therefore be as *s* as snakes and

SHUN*
Job 28:28 and to *s* evil is understanding.' "
Pr 3: 7 fear the LORD and *s* evil.

SICK
Pr 13:12 Hope deferred makes the heart *s*,
Mt 9:12 who need a doctor, but the *s*.
25:36 I was *s* and you looked after me,
Jas 5:14 of you *s*? He should call the elders

SICKLE
Joel 3:13 Swing the *s*,

SIDE
Ps 91: 7 A thousand may fall at your *s*,
124: 1 If the LORD had not been on our *s*
2Ti 4:17 But the Lord stood at my *s*

SIGHT
Ps 90: 4 For a thousand years in your *s*
116:15 Precious in the *s* of the LORD
2Co 5: 7 We live by faith, not by *s*.
1Pe 3: 4 which is of great worth in God's *s*.

SIGN (SIGNS)
Isa 7:14 the Lord himself will give you a *s*:

SIGNS (SIGN)
Mk 16:17 these *s* will accompany those who
Jn 20:30 Jesus did many other miraculous *s*

SILENT
Pr 17:28 a fool is thought wise if he keeps *s*,
Isa 53: 7 as a sheep before her shearers is *s*,
Hab 2:20 let all the earth be *s* before him."
1Co 14:34 women should remain *s*
1Ti 2:12 over a man; she must be *s*.

SILVER
Pr 25:11 is like apples of gold in settings of *s*.
Hag 2: 8 'The *s* is mine and the gold is mine,'
1Co 3:12 *s*, costly stones, wood, hay or straw

SIMON
1. See PETER.
2. Apostle, called the Zealot (Mt 10:4; Mk 3:18; Lk 6:15; Ac 1:13).
3. Samaritan sorcerer (Ac 8:9-24).

SIN (SINFUL SINNED SINNER SINNERS SINNING SINS)
Nu 5: 7 and must confess the *s* he has
32:23 be sure that your *s* will find you
Dt 24:16 each is to die for his own *s*.
1Ki 8:46 for there is no one who does not *s*
2Ch 7:14 and will forgive their *s* and will heal
Ps 4: 4 In your anger do not *s*;
32: 2 whose *s* the LORD does not count
32: 5 Then I acknowledged my *s* to you
51: 2 and cleanse me from my *s*.
66:18 If I had cherished *s* in my heart,
119:11 that I might not *s* against you.
119:133 let no *s* rule over me.
Isa 6: 7 is taken away and your *s* atoned
Mic 7:18 who pardons *s* and forgives
Mt 18: 6 little ones who believe in me to *s*,
Jn 1:29 who takes away the *s* of the world!
8:34 everyone who sins is a slave to *s*.
Ro 5:12 as *s* entered the world
5:20 where *s* increased, grace increased
6:11 count yourselves dead to *s*
6:23 For the wages of *s* is death,
14:23 that does not come from faith is *s*.
2Co 5:21 God made him who had no *s* to be *s*
Gal 6: 1 if someone is caught in a *s*,
Heb 9:26 to do away with *s* by the sacrifice
11:25 the pleasures of *s* for a short time.
12: 1 and the *s* that so easily entangles,
1Pe 2:22 "He committed no *s*,
1Jn 1: 8 If we claim to be without *s*,
3: 4 in fact, *s* is lawlessness.
3: 5 And in him is no *s*.
3: 9 born of God will continue to *s*,
5:18 born of God does not continue to *s*;

SINCERE
Ro 12: 9 Love must be *s*.
Heb 10:22 near to God with a *s* heart

SINFUL (SIN)
Ps 51: 5 Surely I was *s* at birth
51: 5 *s* from the time my mother
Ro 7: 5 we were controlled by the *s* nature,
8: 4 not live according to the *s* nature
8: 9 are controlled not by the *s* nature
Gal 5:19 The acts of the *s* nature are obvious
5:24 Jesus have crucified the *s* nature
1Pe 2:11 abstain from *s* desires, which war

SING (SANG SINGING SONG SONGS)
Ps 30: 4 *S* to the LORD, you saints of his;
47: 6 *S* praises to God, *s* praises;
59:16 But I will *s* of your strength,
89: 1 I will *s* of the LORD's great love
101: 1 I will *s* of your love and justice;
Eph 5:19 *S* and make music in your heart

SINGING (SING)
Ps 63: 5 with *s* lips my mouth will praise
Ac 16:25 Silas were praying and *s* hymns

SINNED (SIN)
2Sa 12:13 "I have *s* against the LORD."
Job 1: 5 "Perhaps my children have *s*
Ps 51: 4 Against you, you only, have I *s*
Da 9: 5 we have *s* and done wrong.
Mic 7: 9 Because I have *s* against him,
Lk 15:18 I have *s* against heaven
Ro 3:23 for all have *s* and fall short
1Jn 1:10 claim we have not *s*, we make him

SINNER (SIN)
Ecc 9:18 but one *s* destroys much good.
Lk 15: 7 in heaven over one *s* who repents
18:13 'God, have mercy on me, a *s*.'
1Co 14:24 convinced by all that he is a *s*
Jas 5:20 Whoever turns a *s* from the error
1Pe 4:18 become of the ungodly and the *s*?"

SINNERS (SIN)
Ps 1: 1 or stand in the way of *s*
Pr 23:17 Do not let your heart envy *s*,
Mt 9:13 come to call the righteous, but *s*."
Ro 5: 8 While we were still *s*, Christ died
1Ti 1:15 came into the world to save *s*—

SINNING (SIN)
Ex 20:20 be with you to keep you from *s*."
1Co 15:34 stop *s*; for there are some who are
Heb 10:26 If we deliberately keep on *s*
1Jn 3: 6 No one who lives in him keeps on *s*
3: 9 go on *s*, because he has been born

SINS (SIN)
2Ki 14: 6 each is to die for his own *s*."

Ezr 9: 6 our *s* are higher than our heads
Ps 19:13 your servant also from willful *s;*
32: 1 whose *s* are covered.
103: 3 who forgives all your *s*
130: 3 O LORD, kept a record of *s,*
Pr 28:13 who conceals his *s* does not
Isa 1:18 "Though your *s* are like scarlet,
43:25 and remembers your *s* no more.
59: 2 your *s* have hidden his face
Eze 18: 4 soul who *s* is the one who will die.
Mt 1:21 he will save his people from their *s*
18:15 "If your brother *s* against you,
Lk 11: 4 Forgive us our *s,*
17: 3 "If your brother *s,* rebuke him,
Ac 22:16 be baptized and wash your *s* away,
1Co 15: 3 died for our *s* according
Eph 2: 1 dead in your transgressions and *s,*
Col 2:13 us all our *s,* having canceled
Heb 1: 3 he had provided purification for *s,*
7:27 He sacrificed for their *s* once for all
8:12 and will remember their *s* no more
10:12 for all time one sacrifice for *s,*
Jas 4:17 ought to do and doesn't do it, *s.*
5:16 Therefore confess your *s*
5:20 and cover over a multitude of *s.*
1Pe 2:24 He himself bore our *s* in his body
3:18 For Christ died for *s* once for all,
1Jn 1: 9 If we confess our *s,* he is faithful
Rev 1: 5 has freed us from our *s* by his blood

SITS
Ps 99: 1 *s* enthroned between the cherubim,
Isa 40:22 He *s* enthroned above the circle
Mt 19:28 of Man *s* on his glorious throne,
Rev 4: 9 thanks to him who *s* on the throne

SKIN
Job 19:20 with only the *s* of my teeth.
19:26 And after my *s* has been destroyed,
Jer 13:23 Can the Ethiopian change his *s*

SLAIN (SLAY)
Rev 5:12 "Worthy is the Lamb, who was *s,*

SLANDER (SLANDERED SLANDERERS)
Lev 19:16 " 'Do not go about spreading *s*
1Ti 5:14 the enemy no opportunity for *s.*
Tit 3: 2 to *s* no one, to be peaceable

SLANDERED (SLANDER)
1Co 4:13 when we are *s,* we answer kindly.

SLANDERERS (SLANDER)
Ro 1:30 They are gossips, *s,* God-haters,
1Co 6:10 nor the greedy nor drunkards nor *s*
Tit 2: 3 not to be *s* or addicted

SLAUGHTER
Isa 53: 7 he was led like a lamb to the *s,*

SLAVE (SLAVERY SLAVES)
Ge 21:10 "Get rid of that *s* woman
Mt 20:27 wants to be first must be your *s*—
Jn 8:34 everyone who sins is a *s* to sin.
1Co 12:13 whether Jews or Greeks, *s* or free
Gal 3:28 *s* nor free, male nor female,
4:30 Get rid of the *s* woman and her son
2Pe 2:19 a man is a *s* to whatever has

SLAVERY (SLAVE)
Ro 6:19 parts of your body in *s* to impurity
Gal 4: 3 were in *s* under the basic principles

SLAVES (SLAVE)
Ro 6: 6 that we should no longer be *s* to sin
6:22 and have become *s* to God,

SLAY (SLAIN)
Job 13:15 Though he *s* me, yet will I hope

SLEEP (SLEEPING)
Ps 121: 4 will neither slumber nor *s.*
1Co 15:51 We will not all *s,* but we will all be

SLEEPING (SLEEP)
Mk 13:36 suddenly, do not let him find you *s.*

SLOW
Ex 34: 6 and gracious God, *s* to anger,
Jas 1:19 *s* to speak and *s* to become angry,
2Pe 3: 9 The Lord is not *s* in keeping his

SLUGGARD
Pr 6: 6 Go to the ant, you *s;*
20: 4 A *s* does not plow in season;

SLUMBER
Ps 121: 3 he who watches over you will not *s;*
Pr 6:10 A little sleep, a little *s,*
Ro 13:11 for you to wake up from your *s,*

SNAKE (SNAKES)
Nu 21: 8 "Make a *s* and put it up on a pole;
Pr 23:32 In the end it bites like a *s*
Jn 3:14 Moses lifted up the *s* in the desert,

SNAKES (SNAKE)
Mt 10:16 as shrewd as *s* and as innocent
Mk 16:18 they will pick up *s* with their hands;

SNATCH
Jn 10:28 no one can *s* them out of my hand.
Jude :23 *s* others from the fire and save

SNOW
Ps 51: 7 and I will be whiter than *s.*

SOAR
Isa 40:31 They will *s* on wings like eagles;

SODOM
Ge 19:24 rained down burning sulfur on *S*
Ro 9:29 we would have become like *S,*

SOIL
Ge 4: 2 kept flocks, and Cain worked the *s.*
Mt 13:23 on good *s* is the man who hears

SOLDIER
1Co 9: 7 as a *s* at his own expense?
2Ti 2: 3 with us like a good *s* of Christ Jesus

SOLE
Dt 28:65 place for the *s* of your foot.
Isa 1: 6 From the *s* of your foot to the top

SOLID
2Ti 2:19 God's *s* foundation stands firm,
Heb 5:12 You need milk, not *s* food!

SOLOMON

Son of David by Bathsheba; king of Judah (2Sa 12:24; 1Ch 3:5, 10). Appointed king by David (1Ki 1); adversaries Adonijah, Joab, Shimei killed by Benaiah (1Ki 2). Asked for wisdom (1Ki 3; 2Ch 1). Judged between two prostitutes (1Ki 3:16-28). Built temple (1Ki 5-7; 2Ch 2-5); prayer of dedication (1Ki 8; 2Ch 6). Visited by Queen of Sheba (1Ki 10; 2Ch 9). Wives turned his heart from God (1Ki 11:1-13). Jeroboam rebelled against (1Ki 11:26-40). Death (1Ki 11:41-43; 2Ch 9:29-31).

Proverbs of (1Ki 4:32; Pr 1:1; 10:1; 25:1); psalms of (Ps 72; 127); song of (SS 1:1).

SON (SONS)
Ge 22: 2 "Take your *s,* your only *s,* Isaac,
Ex 11: 5 Every firstborn *s* in Egypt will die,
Dt 21:18 rebellious *s* who does not obey his
Ps 2: 7 He said to me, "You are my *S;*
2:12 Kiss the *S,* lest he be angry
Pr 10: 1 A wise *s* brings joy to his father,
13:24 He who spares the rod hates his *s,*

29:17 Discipline your *s,* and he will give
Isa 7:14 with child and will give birth to a *s,*
Hos 11: 1 and out of Egypt I called my *s.*
Mt 2:15 "Out of Egypt I called my *s.*"
3:17 "This is my *S,* whom I love;
11:27 one knows the *S* except the Father,
16:16 "You are the Christ, the *S*
17: 5 "This is my *S,* whom I love;
20:18 and the *S* of Man will be betrayed
24:30 They will see the *S* of Man coming
24:44 the *S* of Man will come at an hour
27:54 "Surely he was the *S* of God!"
28:19 and of the *S* and of the Holy Spirit,
Mk 10:45 even the *S* of Man did not come
14:62 you will see the *S* of Man sitting
Lk 9:58 but the *S* of Man has no place
18: 8 when the *S* of Man comes,
19:10 For the *S* of Man came to seek
Jn 3:14 so the *S* of Man must be lifted up,
3:16 that he gave his one and only *S,*
17: 1 Glorify your *S,* that your *S* may
Ro 8:29 conformed to the likeness of his *S,*
8:32 He who did not spare his own *S,*
1Co 15:28 then the *S* himself will be made
Gal 4:30 rid of the slave woman and her *s,*
1Th 1:10 and to wait for his *S* from heaven,
Heb 1: 2 days he has spoken to us by his *S,*
10:29 punished who has trampled the *S*
1Jn 1: 7 his *S,* purifies us from all sin.
4: 9 only *S* into the world that we might
5: 5 he who believes that Jesus is the *S*
5:11 eternal life, and this life is in his *S.*

SONG (SING)
Ps 40: 3 He put a new *s* in my mouth,
96: 1 Sing to the LORD a new *s;*
149: 1 Sing to the LORD a new *s,*
Isa 49:13 burst into *s,* O mountains!
55:12 will burst into *s* before you,
Rev 5: 9 And they sang a new *s:*
15: 3 and sang the *s* of Moses the servant

SONGS (SING)
Job 35:10 who gives *s* in the night,
Ps 100: 2 come before him with joyful *s.*
Eph 5:19 with psalms, hymns and spiritual *s.*
Jas 5:13 Is anyone happy? Let him sing *s*

SONS (SON)
Joel 2:28 Your *s* and daughters will prophesy
Jn 12:36 so that you may become *s* of light."
Ro 8:14 by the Spirit of God are *s* of God.
2Co 6:18 and you will be my *s* and daughters
Gal 4: 5 we might receive the full rights of *s.*
Heb 12: 7 discipline; God is treating you as *s.*

SORROW (SORROWS)
Jer 31:12 and they will *s* no more.
Ro 9: 2 I have great *s* and unceasing
2Co 7:10 Godly *s* brings repentance that

SORROWS (SORROW)
Isa 53: 3 a man of *s,* and familiar

SOUL (SOULS)
Dt 6: 5 with all your *s* and with all your
10:12 all your heart and with all your *s,*
Jos 22: 5 with all your heart and all your *s.*"
Ps 23: 3 he restores my *s.*
42: 1 so my *s* pants for you, O God.
42:11 Why are you downcast, O my *s?*
103: 1 Praise the LORD, O my *s;*
Pr 13:19 A longing fulfilled is sweet to the *s,*
Isa 55: 2 your *s* will delight in the richest
Mt 10:28 kill the body but cannot kill the *s.*
16:26 yet forfeits his *s?* Or what can
22:37 with all your *s* and with all your
Heb 4:12 even to dividing *s* and spirit,

SOULS (SOUL)
Pr 11:30 and he who wins *s* is wise.
Jer 6:16 and you will find rest for your *s.*
Mt 11:29 and you will find rest for your *s.*

SOUND
1Co 14: 8 if the trumpet does not *s* a clear call
15:52 the trumpet will *s,* the dead will
2Ti 4: 3 men will not put up with *s* doctrine.

SOVEREIGN
Da 4:25 that the Most High is *s*

SOW (SOWS)
Job 4: 8 and those who *s* trouble reap it.
Mt 6:26 they do not *s* or reap or store away
2Pe 2:22 and, "A *s* that is washed goes back

SOWS (SOW)
Pr 11:18 he who *s* righteousness reaps a sure
22: 8 He who *s* wickedness reaps trouble
2Co 9: 6 Whoever *s* sparingly will
Gal 6: 7 A man reaps what he *s.*

SPARE (SPARES)
Ro 8:32 He who did not *s* his own Son,
11:21 natural branches, he will not *s* you

SPARES (SPARE)
Pr 13:24 He who *s* the rod hates his son,

SPEARS
Isa 2: 4 and their *s* into pruning hooks.
Joel 3:10 and your pruning hooks into *s.*
Mic 4: 3 and their *s* into pruning hooks.

SPECTACLE
1Co 4: 9 We have been made a *s*
Col 2:15 he made a public *s* of them,

SPIN
Mt 6:28 They do not labor or *s.*

SPIRIT (SPIRIT'S SPIRITS SPIRITUAL SPIRITUALLY)
Ge 1: 2 and the *S* of God was hovering
6: 3 "My *S* will not contend
2Ki 2: 9 inherit a double portion of your *s,*"
Job 33: 4 The *S* of God has made me;
Ps 31: 5 Into your hands I commit my *s;*
51:10 and renew a steadfast *s* within me.
51:11 or take your Holy *S* from me.
51:17 sacrifices of God are a broken *s;*
139: 7 Where can I go from your *S?*
Isa 57:15 him who is contrite and lowly in *s,*
63:10 and grieved his Holy *S.*
Eze 11:19 an undivided heart and put a new *s*
36:26 you a new heart and put a new *s*
Joel 2:28 I will pour out my *S* on all people.
Zec 4: 6 but by my *S,*' says the LORD
Mt 1:18 to be with child through the Holy *S*
3:11 will baptize you with the Holy *S*
3:16 he saw the *S* of God descending
4: 1 led by the *S* into the desert
5: 3 saying: "Blessed are the poor in *s,*
26:41 *s* is willing, but the body is weak."
28:19 and of the Son and of the Holy *S,*
Lk 1:80 child grew and became strong in *s;*
11:13 Father in heaven give the Holy *S*
Jn 4:24 God is *s,* and his worshipers must
7:39 Up to that time the *S* had not been
14:26 But the Counselor, the Holy *S,*
16:13 But when he, the *S* of truth, comes,
20:22 and said, "Receive the Holy *S.*
Ac 1: 5 will be baptized with the Holy *S.*"
2: 4 of them were filled with the Holy *S*
2:38 will receive the gift of the Holy *S.*
6: 3 who are known to be full of the *S*
19: 2 "Did you receive the Holy *S*
Ro 8: 9 And if anyone does not have the *S*

8:26 the *S* helps us in our weakness.
1Co 2:10 God has revealed it to us by his *S*.
2:14 man without the *S* does not accept
6:19 body is a temple of the Holy *S*,
12:13 baptized by one *S* into one body—
2Co 3: 6 the letter kills, but the *S* gives life.
5: 5 and has given us the *S* as a deposit,
Gal 5:16 by the *S*, and you will not gratify
5:22 But the fruit of the *S* is love, joy,
5:25 let us keep in step with the *S*.
Eph 1:13 with a seal, the promised Holy *S*,
4:30 do not grieve the Holy *S* of God,
5:18 Instead, be filled with the *S*.
6:17 of salvation and the sword of the *S*,
2Th 2:13 the sanctifying work of the *S*
Heb 4:12 even to dividing soul and *s*,
1Pe 3: 4 beauty of a gentle and quiet *s*,
2Pe 1:21 carried along by the Holy *S*.
1Jn 4: 1 Dear friends, do not believe every *s*

SPIRIT'S (SPIRIT)
1Th 5:19 not put out the *S* fire; do not treat

SPIRITS (SPIRIT)
1Co 12:10 to another distinguishing between *s*,
14:32 The *s* of prophets are subject
1Jn 4: 1 test the *s* to see whether they are

SPIRITUAL (SPIRIT)
Ro 12: 1 this is your *s* act of worship.
12:11 but keep your *s* fervor, serving
1Co 2:13 expressing *s* truths in *s* words.
3: 1 I could not address you as *s* but
12: 1 Now about *s* gifts, brothers,
14: 1 of love and eagerly desire *s* gifts,
15:44 a natural body, it is raised a *s* body.
Gal 6: 1 you who are *s* should restore him
Eph 1: 3 with every *s* blessing in Christ.
5:19 with psalms, hymns and *s* songs.
6:12 and against the *s* forces of evil
1Pe 2: 2 newborn babies, crave pure *s* milk,
2: 5 are being built into a *s* house

SPIRITUALLY (SPIRIT)
1Co 2:14 because they are *s* discerned.

SPLENDOR
1Ch 16:29 the LORD in the *s* of his holiness.
29:11 the glory and the majesty and the *s*,
Job 37:22 of the north he comes in golden *s*;
Ps 29: 2 in the *s* of his holiness.
45: 3 clothe yourself with *s* and majesty.
96: 6 *S* and majesty are before him;
96: 9 in the *s* of his holiness;
104: 1 you are clothed with *s* and majesty.
145: 5 of the glorious *s* of your majesty,
Isa 61: 3 the LORD for the display of his *s*.
63: 1 Who is this, robed in *s*,
Lk 9:31 appeared in glorious *s*, talking
2Th 2: 8 and destroy by the *s* of his coming.

SPOIL
Ps 119:162 like one who finds great *s*.

SPOTLESS
2Pe 3:14 make every effort to be found *s*,

SPREAD (SPREADING)
Ac 12:24 of God continued to increase and *s*.
19:20 the word of the Lord *s* widely

SPREADING (SPREAD)
1Th 3: 2 God's fellow worker in *s* the gospel

SPRING
Jer 2:13 the *s* of living water,
Jn 4:14 in him a *s* of water welling up
Jas 3:12 can a salt *s* produce fresh water.

SPUR*
Heb 10:24 how we may *s* one another

SPURNS*
Pr 15: 5 A fool *s* his father's discipline,

STAFF
Ps 23: 4 your rod and your *s*,

STAKES
Isa 54: 2 strengthen your *s*.

STAND (STANDING STANDS)
Ex 14:13 *S* firm and you will see
2Ch 20:17 *s* firm and see the deliverance
Ps 1: 5 Therefore the wicked will not *s*
40: 2 and gave me a firm place to *s*.
119:120 I *s* in awe of your laws.
Eze 22:30 *s* before me in the gap on behalf
Zec 14: 4 On that day his feet will *s*
Mt 12:25 divided against itself will not *s*.
Ro 14:10 we will all *s* before God's judgment
1Co 10:13 out so that you can *s* up under it.
15:58 Therefore, my dear brothers, *s* firm
Eph 6:14 *S* firm then, with the belt
2Th 2:15 *s* firm and hold to the teachings we
Jas 5: 8 You too, be patient and *s* firm,
Rev 3:20 Here I am! I *s* at the door

STANDING (STAND)
Ex 3: 5 where you are *s* is holy ground."
Jos 5:15 the place where you are *s* is holy."
1Pe 5: 9 Resist him, *s* firm in the faith,

STANDS (STAND)
Ps 89: 2 that your love *s* firm forever,
119:89 it *s* firm in the heavens.
Mt 10:22 but he who *s* firm to the end will be
2Ti 2:19 God's solid foundation *s* firm,
1Pe 1:25 but the word of the Lord *s* forever

STAR (STARS)
Nu 24:17 A *s* will come out of Jacob;
Rev 22:16 and the bright Morning *S*."

STARS (STAR)
Da 12: 3 like the *s* for ever and ever.
Php 2:15 in which you shine like *s*

STATURE
Lk 2:52 And Jesus grew in wisdom and *s*,

STEADFAST
Ps 51:10 and renew a *s* spirit within me.
Isa 26: 3 him whose mind is *s*,
1Pe 5:10 and make you strong, firm and *s*.

STEAL
Ex 20:15 "You shall not *s*.
Mt 19:18 do not *s*, do not give false
Eph 4:28 has been stealing must *s* no longer,

STEP (STEPS)
Gal 5:25 let us keep in *s* with the Spirit.

STEPS (STEP)
Pr 16: 9 but the LORD determines his *s*.
Jer 10:23 it is not for man to direct his *s*.
1Pe 2:21 that you should follow in his *s*.

STICKS
Pr 18:24 there is a friend who *s* closer

STIFF-NECKED
Ex 34: 9 Although this is a *s* people,

STILL
Ps 46:10 "Be *s*, and know that I am God;
Zec 2:13 Be *s* before the LORD, all mankind

STIRS
Pr 6:19 and a man who *s* up dissension
10:12 Hatred *s* up dissension,
15: 1 but a harsh word *s* up anger.
15:18 hot-tempered man *s* up dissension,
16:28 A perverse man *s* up dissension,
28:25 A greedy man *s* up dissension,
29:22 An angry man *s* up dissension,

STONE (CAPSTONE CORNERSTONE MILLSTONE)
1Sa 17:50 the Philistine with a sling and a *s;*
Isa 8:14 a *s* that causes men to stumble
Eze 11:19 remove from them their heart of *s*
Mk 16: 3 "Who will roll the *s* away
Lk 4: 3 tell this *s* to become bread."
Jn 8: 7 the first to throw a *s* at her."
2Co 3: 3 not on tablets of *s* but on tablets

STOOP
2Sa 22:36 you *s* down to make me great.

STORE
Pr 10:14 Wise men *s* up knowledge,
Mt 6:19 not *s* up for yourselves treasures

STOREHOUSE (HOUSE)
Mal 3:10 Bring the whole tithe into the *s,*

STRAIGHT
Pr 3: 6 and he will make your paths *s.*
4:25 Let your eyes look *s* ahead,
15:21 of understanding keeps a *s* course.
Jn 1:23 'Make *s* the way for the Lord.' "

STRAIN
Mt 23:24 You *s* out a gnat but swallow

STRANGER (STRANGERS)
Mt 25:35 I was a *s* and you invited me in,
Jn 10: 5 But they will never follow a *s;*

STRANGERS (STRANGER)
1Pe 2:11 as aliens and *s* in the world,

STREAMS
Ps 1: 3 He is like a tree planted by *s*
46: 4 is a river whose *s* make glad
Ecc 1: 7 All *s* flow into the sea,
Jn 7:38 *s* of living water will flow

STRENGTH (STRONG)
Ex 15: 2 The LORD is my *s* and my song;
Dt 6: 5 all your soul and with all your *s.*
2Sa 22:33 It is God who arms me with *s*
Ne 8:10 for the joy of the LORD is your *s.*"
Ps 28: 7 The LORD is my *s* and my shield;
46: 1 God is our refuge and *s,*
96: 7 ascribe to the LORD glory and *s.*
118:14 The LORD is my *s* and my song;
147:10 not in the *s* of the horse,
Isa 40:31 will renew their *s.*
Mk 12:30 all your mind and with all your *s.*'
1Co 1:25 of God is stronger than man's *s.*
Php 4:13 through him who gives me *s.*
1Pe 4:11 it with the *s* God provides,

STRENGTHEN (STRONG)
2Ch 16: 9 to *s* those whose hearts are fully
Ps 119:28 *s* me according to your word.
Isa 35: 3 *S* the feeble hands,
41:10 I will *s* you and help you;
Eph 3:16 of his glorious riches he may *s* you
2Th 2:17 and *s* you in every good deed
Heb 12:12 *s* your feeble arms and weak knees.

STRENGTHENING (STRONG)
1Co 14:26 done for the *s* of the church.

STRIFE
Pr 20: 3 It is to a man's honor to avoid *s,*
22:10 out the mocker, and out goes *s;*

STRIKE (STRIKES)
Ge 3:15 and you will *s* his heel."
Zec 13: 7 "*S* the shepherd,
Mt 26:31 " 'I will *s* the shepherd,

STRIKES (STRIKE)
Mt 5:39 If someone *s* you on the right

STRONG (STRENGTH STRENGTHEN STRENGTHENING)
Dt 31: 6 Be *s* and courageous.
1Ki 2: 2 "So be *s,* show yourself a man,
Pr 18:10 The name of the LORD is a *s* tower
31:17 her arms are *s* for her tasks.
SS 8: 6 for love is as *s* as death,
Lk 2:40 And the child grew and became *s;*
Ro 15: 1 We who are *s* ought to bear
1Co 1:27 things of the world to shame the *s.*
16:13 in the faith; be men of courage; be *s*
2Co 12:10 For when I am weak, then I am *s.*
Eph 6:10 be *s* in the Lord and in his mighty

STRUGGLE
Ro 15:30 me in my *s* by praying to God
Eph 6:12 For our *s* is not against flesh
Heb 12: 4 In your *s* against sin, you have not

STUDY
Ezr 7:10 Ezra had devoted himself to the *s*
Ecc 12:12 and much *s* wearies the body.
Jn 5:39 You diligently *s* the Scriptures

STUMBLE (STUMBLING)
Ps 37:24 though he *s,* he will not fall,
119:165 and nothing can make them *s.*
Isa 8:14 a stone that causes men to *s*
Jer 31: 9 a level path where they will not *s,*
Eze 7:19 for it has made them *s* into sin.
1Co 10:32 Do not cause anyone to *s,*
1Pe 2: 8 and, "A stone that causes men to *s*

STUMBLING (STUMBLE)
Ro 14:13 up your mind not to put any *s* block
1Co 8: 9 freedom does not become a *s* block
2Co 6: 3 We put no *s* block in anyone's path,

SUBDUE
Ge 1:28 in number; fill the earth and *s* it.

SUBJECT (SUBJECTED)
1Co 14:32 of prophets are *s* to the control
15:28 then the Son himself will be made *s*
Tit 2: 5 and to be *s* to their husbands,
2: 9 slaves to be *s* to their masters
3: 1 Remind the people to be *s* to rulers

SUBJECTED (SUBJECT)
Ro 8:20 For the creation was *s*

SUBMISSION (SUBMIT)
1Co 14:34 but must be in *s,* as the Law says.
1Ti 2:11 learn in quietness and full *s.*

SUBMISSIVE (SUBMIT)
Jas 3:17 then peace-loving, considerate, *s,*
1Pe 3: 1 in the same way be *s*
5: 5 in the same way be *s*

SUBMIT (SUBMISSION SUBMISSIVE SUBMITS)
Ro 13: 1 Everyone must *s* himself
13: 5 necessary to *s* to the authorities,
1Co 16:16 to *s* to such as these
Eph 5:21 *S* to one another out of reverence
Col 3:18 Wives, *s* to your husbands,
Heb 12: 9 How much more should we *s*
13:17 Obey your leaders and *s*

Jas 4: 7 *S* yourselves, then, to God.
1Pe 2:18 *s* yourselves to your masters

SUBMITS* (SUBMIT)
Eph 5:24 Now as the church *s* to Christ,

SUCCESSFUL
Jos 1: 7 that you may be *s* wherever you go.
2Ki 18: 7 he was *s* in whatever he undertook.
2Ch 20:20 in his prophets and you will be *s*."

SUFFER (SUFFERED SUFFERING SUFFERINGS SUFFERS)
Isa 53:10 to crush him and cause him to *s*,
Mk 8:31 the Son of Man must *s* many things
Lk 24:26 the Christ have to *s* these things
24:46 The Christ will *s* and rise
Php 1:29 to *s* for him, since you are going
1Pe 4:16 However, if you *s* as a Christian,

SUFFERED (SUFFER)
Heb 2: 9 and honor because he *s* death,
2:18 Because he himself *s*
1Pe 2:21 Christ *s* for you, leaving you

SUFFERING (SUFFER)
Isa 53: 3 of sorrows, and familiar with *s*.
Ac 5:41 worthy of *s* disgrace for the Name.
2Ti 1: 8 But join with me in *s* for the gospel,
Heb 2:10 of their salvation perfect through *s*.

SUFFERINGS (SUFFER)
Ro 8:17 share in his *s* in order that we may
8:18 that our present *s* are not worth
2Co 1: 5 as the *s* of Christ flow
Php 3:10 the fellowship of sharing in his *s*,

SUFFERS (SUFFER)
Pr 13:20 but a companion of fools *s* harm.
1Co 12:26 If one part *s*, every part *s* with it;

SUFFICIENT
2Co 12: 9 said to me, "My grace is *s* for you,

SUITABLE
Ge 2:18 I will make a helper *s* for him."

SUN
Ecc 1: 9 there is nothing new under the *s*.
Mal 4: 2 the *s* of righteousness will rise
Mt 5:45 He causes his *s* to rise on the evil
17: 2 His face shone like the *s*,
Rev 1:16 His face was like the *s* shining
21:23 The city does not need the *s*

SUPERIOR
Heb 1: 4 he became as much *s* to the angels
8: 6 ministry Jesus has received is as *s*

SUPERVISION
Gal 3:25 longer under the *s* of the law.

SUPREMACY* (SUPREME)
Col 1:18 in everything he might have the *s*.

SUPREME (SUPREMACY)
Pr 4: 7 Wisdom is *s;* therefore get wisdom.

SURE
Nu 32:23 you may be *s* that your sin will find
Dt 6:17 Be *s* to keep the commands
14:22 Be *s* to set aside a tenth
Isa 28:16 cornerstone for a *s* foundation;
Heb 11: 1 faith is being *s* of what we hope for
2Pe 1:10 to make your calling and election *s*.

SURPASS* (SURPASSES SURPASSING)
Pr 31:29 but you *s* them all."

SURPASSES (SURPASS)
Mt 5:20 unless your righteousness *s* that
Eph 3:19 to know this love that *s* knowledge

SURPASSING* (SURPASS)
Ps 150: 2 praise him for his *s* greatness.
2Co 3:10 in comparison with the *s* glory.
9:14 of the *s* grace God has given you.
Php 3: 8 the *s* greatness of knowing Christ

SURROUNDED
Heb 12: 1 since we are *s* by such a great cloud

SUSPENDS*
Job 26: 7 he *s* the earth over nothing.

SUSTAINING* (SUSTAINS)
Heb 1: 3 *s* all things by his powerful word.

SUSTAINS (SUSTAINING)
Ps 18:35 and your right hand *s* me;
146: 9 and *s* the fatherless and the widow,
147: 6 The LORD *s* the humble
Isa 50: 4 to know the word that *s* the weary.

SWALLOWED
1Co 15:54 "Death has been *s* up in victory."
2Co 5: 4 so that what is mortal may be *s* up

SWEAR
Mt 5:34 Do not *s* at all: either by heaven,

SWORD (SWORDS)
Ps 45: 3 Gird your *s* upon your side,
Pr 12:18 Reckless words pierce like a *s*,
Mt 10:34 come to bring peace, but a *s*.
26:52 all who draw the *s* will die by the *s*.
Lk 2:35 a *s* will pierce your own soul too."
Ro 13: 4 for he does not bear the *s*
Eph 6:17 of salvation and the *s* of the Spirit,
Heb 4:12 Sharper than any double-edged *s*,
Rev 1:16 came a sharp double-edged *s*.

SWORDS (SWORD)
Isa 2: 4 They will beat their *s*
Joel 3:10 Beat your plowshares into *s*

SYMPATHETIC*
1Pe 3: 8 in harmony with one another; be *s*,

SYNAGOGUE
Lk 4:16 the Sabbath day he went into the *s*,
Ac 17: 2 custom was, Paul went into the *s*,

TABERNACLE
Ex 40:34 the glory of the LORD filled the *t*.

TABLE (TABLES)
Ps 23: 5 You prepare a *t* before me

TABLES (TABLE)
Ac 6: 2 word of God in order to wait on *t*.

TABLET (TABLETS)
Pr 3: 3 write them on the *t* of your heart.
7: 3 write them on the *t* of your heart.

TABLETS (TABLET)
Ex 31:18 he gave him the two *t*
Dt 10: 5 and put the *t* in the ark I had made,
2Co 3: 3 not on *t* of stone but on *t*

TAKE (TAKEN TAKES TAKING TOOK)
Dt 12:32 do not add to it or *t* away from it.
31:26 "*T* this Book of the Law
Job 23:10 But he knows the way that I *t;*
Ps 49:17 for he will *t* nothing with him
51:11 or *t* your Holy Spirit from me.
Mt 10:38 anyone who does not *t* his cross
11:29 *T* my yoke upon you and learn
16:24 deny himself and *t* up his cross

TAKEN (TAKE)
Lev 6: 4 must return what he has stolen or *t*
Isa 6: 7 your guilt is *t* away and your sin
Mt 24:40 one will be *t* and the other left.
Mk 16:19 he was *t* up into heaven
1Ti 3:16 was *t* up in glory.

TAKES (TAKE)
1Ki 20:11 should not boast like one who *t* it
Ps 5: 4 You are not a God who *t* pleasure
Jn 1:29 who *t* away the sin of the world!
Rev 22:19 And if anyone *t* words away

TAKING (TAKE)
Ac 15:14 by *t* from the Gentiles a people
Php 2: 7 *t* the very nature of a servant,

TALENT
Mt 25:15 to another one *t*, each according

TAME*
Jas 3: 8 but no man can *t* the tongue.

TASK
Mk 13:34 each with his assigned *t*,
Ac 20:24 complete the *t* the Lord Jesus has
1Co 3: 5 the Lord has assigned to each his *t*.
2Co 2:16 And who is equal to such a *t*?

TASTE (TASTED)
Ps 34: 8 *T* and see that the LORD is good;
Col 2:21 Do not *t*! Do not touch!"?
Heb 2: 9 the grace of God he might *t* death

TASTED (TASTE)
1Pe 2: 3 now that you have *t* that the Lord

TAUGHT (TEACH)
Mt 7:29 he *t* as one who had authority,
1Co 2:13 but in words *t* by the Spirit,
Gal 1:12 nor was I *t* it; rather, I received it

TAXES
Mt 22:17 Is it right to pay *t* to Caesar or not
Ro 13: 7 If you owe *t*, pay *t*; if revenue,

TEACH (TAUGHT TEACHER TEACHERS TEACHES TEACHING)
Ex 33:13 *t* me your ways so I may know you
Dt 4: 9 *T* them to your children
8: 3 to *t* you that man does not live
11:19 *T* them to your children, talking
1Sa 12:23 I will *t* you the way that is good
Ps 32: 8 *t* you in the way you should go;
51:13 I will *t* transgressors your ways,
90:12 *T* us to number our days aright,
143:10 *T* me to do your will,
Jer 31:34 No longer will a man *t* his neighbor
Lk 11: 1 said to him, "Lord, *t* us to pray,
Jn 14:26 will *t* you all things and will remind
1Ti 2:12 I do not permit a woman to *t*
3: 2 respectable, hospitable, able to *t*,
Tit 2: 1 You must *t* what is in accord
Heb 8:11 No longer will a man *t* his neighbor
Jas 3: 1 know that we who *t* will be judged
1Jn 2:27 you do not need anyone to *t* you.

TEACHER (TEACH)
Mt 10:24 "A student is not above his *t*,
Jn 13:14 and *T*, have washed your feet,

TEACHERS (TEACH)
1Co 12:28 third *t*, then workers of miracles,
Eph 4:11 and some to be pastors and *t*,
Heb 5:12 by this time you ought to be *t*,

TEACHES (TEACH)
1Ti 6: 3 If anyone *t* false doctrines

TEACHING (TEACH)
Pr 1: 8 and do not forsake your mother's *t*.
Mt 28:20 *t* them to obey everything I have
Jn 7:17 whether my *t* comes from God or
14:23 loves me, he will obey my *t*.
1Ti 4:13 of Scripture, to preaching and to *t*.
2Ti 3:16 is God-breathed and is useful for *t*,
Tit 2: 7 In your *t* show integrity,

TEAR (TEARS)
Rev 7:17 God will wipe away every *t*

TEARS (TEAR)
Ps 126: 5 Those who sow in *t*
Php 3:18 and now say again even with *t*,

TEETH (TOOTH)
Mt 8:12 will be weeping and gnashing of *t*."

TEMPERATE*
1Ti 3: 2 *t*, self-controlled, respectable,
3:11 not malicious talkers but *t*
Tit 2: 2 Teach the older men to be *t*,

TEMPEST
Ps 55: 8 far from the *t* and storm."

TEMPLE (TEMPLES)
1Ki 8:27 How much less this *t* I have built!
Hab 2:20 But the LORD is in his holy *t*;
1Co 3:16 that you yourselves are God's *t*
6:19 you not know that your body is a *t*
2Co 6:16 For we are the *t* of the living God.

TEMPLES (TEMPLE)
Ac 17:24 does not live in *t* built by hands.

TEMPT (TEMPTATION TEMPTED)
1Co 7: 5 again so that Satan will not *t* you

TEMPTATION (TEMPT)
Mt 6:13 And lead us not into *t*,
26:41 pray so that you will not fall into *t*.
1Co 10:13 No *t* has seized you except what is

TEMPTED (TEMPT)
Mt 4: 1 into the desert to be *t* by the devil.
1Co 10:13 he will not let you be *t*
Heb 2:18 he himself suffered when he was *t*,
4:15 but we have one who has been *t*
Jas 1:13 For God cannot be *t* by evil,

TEN (TENTH TITHE TITHES)
Ex 34:28 covenant—the *T* Commandments.
Ps 91: 7 *t* thousand at your right hand,
Mt 25:28 it to the one who has the *t* talents.
Lk 15: 8 suppose a woman has *t* silver coins

TENTH (TEN)
Dt 14:22 Be sure to set aside a *t*

TERRIBLE (TERROR)
2Ti 3: 1 There will be *t* times

TERROR (TERRIBLE)
Ps 91: 5 You will not fear the *t* of night,
Lk 21:26 Men will faint from *t*, apprehensive
Ro 13: 3 For rulers hold no *t*

TEST (TESTED TESTS)
Dt 6:16 Do not *t* the LORD your God
Ps 139:23 *t* me and know my anxious
Ro 12: 2 Then you will be able to *t*
1Co 3:13 and the fire will *t* the quality
1Jn 4: 1 *t* the spirits to see whether they are

TESTED (TEST)
Ge 22: 1 Some time later God *t* Abraham.
Job 23:10 when he has *t* me, I will come forth
Pr 27:21 man is *t* by the praise he receives.

1Ti 3:10 They must first be *t;* and then

TESTIFY (TESTIMONY)
Jn 5:39 are the Scriptures that *t* about me,
2Ti 1: 8 ashamed to *t* about our Lord,

TESTIMONY (TESTIFY)
Isa 8:20 and to the *t!* If they do not speak
Lk 18:20 not give false *t,* honor your father

TESTS (TEST)
Pr 17: 3 but the LORD *t* the heart.
1Th 2: 4 but God, who *t* our hearts.

THADDAEUS
Apostle (Mt 10:3; Mk 3:18); probably also known as Judas son of James (Lk 6:16; Ac 1:13).

THANKFUL (THANKS)
Heb 12:28 let us be *t,* and so worship God

THANKS (THANKFUL THANKSGIVING)
1Ch 16: 8 Give *t* to the LORD, call
Ne 12:31 assigned two large choirs to give *t.*
Ps 100: 4 give *t* to him and praise his name.
1Co 15:57 *t* be to God! He gives us the victory
2Co 2:14 *t* be to God, who always leads us
9:15 *T* be to God for his indescribable
1Th 5:18 give *t* in all circumstances,

THANKSGIVING (THANKS)
Ps 95: 2 Let us come before him with *t*
100: 4 Enter his gates with *t*
Php 4: 6 by prayer and petition, with *t,*
1Ti 4: 3 created to be received with *t*

THIEF (THIEVES)
Ex 22: 3 A *t* must certainly make restitution
1Th 5: 2 day of the Lord will come like a *t*
Rev 16:15 I come like a *t!* Blessed is he who

THIEVES (THIEF)
1Co 6:10 nor homosexual offenders nor *t*

THINK (THOUGHT THOUGHTS)
Ro 12: 3 Do not *t* of yourself more highly
Php 4: 8 praiseworthy—*t* about such things

THIRST (THIRSTY)
Ps 69:21 and gave me vinegar for my *t.*
Mt 5: 6 Blessed are those who hunger and *t*
Jn 4:14 the water I give him will never *t.*

THIRSTY (THIRST)
Isa 55: 1 "Come, all you who are *t,*
Jn 7:37 "If anyone is *t,* let him come to me
Rev 22:17 Whoever is *t,* let him come;

THOMAS
Apostle (Mt 10:3; Mk 3:18; Lk 6:15; Jn 11:16; 14:5; 21:2; Ac 1:13). Doubted resurrection (Jn 20:24-28).

THONGS
Mk 1: 7 *t* of whose sandals I am not worthy

THORN (THORNS)
2Co 12: 7 there was given me a *t* in my flesh,

THORNS (THORN)
Nu 33:55 in your eyes and *t* in your sides.
Mt 27:29 then twisted together a crown of *t*
Heb 6: 8 But land that produces *t*

THOUGHT (THINK)
Pr 14:15 a prudent man gives *t* to his steps.
1Co 13:11 I talked like a child, I *t* like a child,

THOUGHTS (THINK)
Ps 94:11 The LORD knows the *t* of man;
139:23 test me and know my anxious *t.*
Isa 55: 8 "For my *t* are not your *t,*
Heb 4:12 it judges the *t* and attitudes

THREE
Ecc 4:12 of *t* strands is not quickly broken.
Mt 12:40 *t* nights in the belly of a huge fish,
18:20 or *t* come together in my name,
27:63 'After *t* days I will rise again.'
1Co 13:13 And now these *t* remain: faith,
14:27 or at the most *t*— should speak,
2Co 13: 1 testimony of two or *t* witnesses."

THRESHING
2Sa 24:18 an altar to the LORD on the *t* floor

THRONE (ENTHRONED)
2Sa 7:16 your *t* will be established forever
Ps 45: 6 Your *t,* O God, will last for ever
47: 8 God is seated on his holy *t.*
Isa 6: 1 I saw the Lord seated on a *t,*
66: 1 "Heaven is my *t*
Heb 4:16 Let us then approach the *t* of grace
12: 2 at the right hand of the *t* of God.
Rev 4:10 They lay their crowns before the *t*
20:11 Then I saw a great white *t*
22: 3 *t* of God and of the Lamb will be

THROW
Jn 8: 7 the first to *t* a stone at her."
Heb 10:35 So do not *t* away your confidence;
12: 1 let us *t* off everything that hinders

THWART*
Isa 14:27 has purposed, and who can *t* him?

TIBNI
King of Israel (1Ki 16:21-22).

TIME (TIMES)
Est 4:14 come to royal position for such a *t*
Da 7:25 to him for a *t,* times and half a *t.*
Hos 10:12 for it is *t* to seek the LORD,
Ro 9: 9 "At the appointed *t* I will return,
Heb 9:28 and he will appear a second *t,*
10:12 for all *t* one sacrifice for sins,
1Pe 4:17 For it is *t* for judgment to begin

TIMES (TIME)
Ps 9: 9 a stronghold in *t* of trouble.
31:15 My *t* are in your hands;
62: 8 Trust in him at all *t,* O people;
Pr 17:17 A friend loves at all *t,*
Am 5:13 for the *t* are evil.
Mt 18:21 how many *t* shall I forgive my
Ac 1: 7 "It is not for you to know the *t*
Rev 12:14 *t* and half a time, out

TIMIDITY*
2Ti 1: 7 For God did not give us a spirit of *t*

TIMOTHY
Believer from Lystra (Ac 16:1). Joined Paul on second missionary journey (Ac 16-20). Sent to settle problems at Corinth (1Co 4:17; 16:10). Led church at Ephesus (1Ti 1:3). Co-writer with Paul (1Th 1:1; 2Th 1:1; Phm 1).

TIRE (TIRED)
2Th 3:13 never *t* of doing what is right.

TIRED (TIRE)
Ex 17:12 When Moses' hands grew *t,*
Isa 40:28 He will not grow *t* or weary,

TITHE (TEN)
Lev 27:30 " 'A *t* of everything from the land,
Dt 12:17 eat in your own towns the *t*
Mal 3:10 the whole *t* into the storehouse,

TITHES (TEN)
Mal 3: 8 'How do we rob you?' "In *t*

TITUS
Gentile co-worker of Paul (Gal 2:1-3; 2Ti 4:10); sent to Corinth (2Co 2:13; 7-8; 12:18), Crete (Tit 1:4-5).

TODAY
Mt 6:11 Give us *t* our daily bread.
Lk 23:43 *t* you will be with me in paradise."
Heb 3:13 daily, as long as it is called *T,*
13: 8 Christ is the same yesterday and *t*

TOIL
Ge 3:17 through painful *t* you will eat of it

TOLERATE
Hab 1:13 you cannot *t* wrong.
Rev 2: 2 that you cannot *t* wicked men,

TOMB
Mt 27:65 make the *t* as secure as you know
Lk 24: 2 the stone rolled away from the *t,*

TOMORROW
Pr 27: 1 Do not boast about *t,*
Isa 22:13 "for *t* we die!"
Mt 6:34 Therefore do not worry about *t,*
Jas 4:13 "Today or *t* we will go to this

TONGUE (TONGUES)
Ps 39: 1 and keep my *t* from sin;
Pr 12:18 but the *t* of the wise brings healing.
1Co 14: 2 speaks in a *t* does not speak to men
14: 4 He who speaks in a *t* edifies himself
14:13 in a *t* should pray that he may
14:19 than ten thousand words in a *t.*
Php 2:11 every *t* confess that Jesus Christ is
Jas 1:26 does not keep a tight rein on his *t,*
3: 8 but no man can tame the *t.*

TONGUES (TONGUE)
Isa 28:11 with foreign lips and strange *t*
66:18 and gather all nations and *t,*
Mk 16:17 in new *t;* they will pick up snakes
Ac 2: 4 and began to speak in other *t*
10:46 For they heard them speaking in *t*
19: 6 and they spoke in *t* and prophesied
1Co 12:30 Do all speak in *t?* Do all interpret?
14:18 speak in *t* more than all of you.
14:39 and do not forbid speaking in *t.*

TOOK (TAKE)
1Co 11:23 the night he was betrayed, *t* bread,
Php 3:12 for which Christ Jesus *t* hold of me.

TOOTH (TEETH)
Ex 21:24 eye for eye, *t* for *t,* hand for hand,
Mt 5:38 'Eye for eye, and *t* for *t.'*

TORMENTED
Rev 20:10 They will be *t* day and night

TORN
Gal 4:15 you would have *t* out your eyes
Php 1:23 I do not know! I am *t*

TOUCH (TOUCHED)
Ps 105:15 "Do not *t* my anointed ones;
Lk 24:39 It is I myself! *T* me and see;
2Co 6:17 *T* no unclean thing,
Col 2:21 Do not taste! Do not *t!"?*

TOUCHED (TOUCH)
1Sa 10:26 men whose hearts God had *t.*
Mt 14:36 and all who *t* him were healed.

TOWER
Ge 11: 4 with a *t* that reaches to the heavens
Pr 18:10 of the LORD is a strong *t;*

TOWNS
Nu 35: 2 to give the Levites *t* to live
35:15 These six *t* will be a place of refuge

TRACING*
Ro 11:33 and his paths beyond *t* out!

TRADITION
Mt 15: 6 word of God for the sake of your *t.*
Col 2: 8 which depends on human *t*

TRAIN (TRAINING)
Pr 22: 6 *T* a child in the way he should go,
Eph 4: 8 he led captives in his *t*

TRAINING (TRAIN)
1Co 9:25 in the games goes into strict *t.*
2Ti 3:16 correcting and *t* in righteousness,

TRAMPLED
Lk 21:24 Jerusalem will be *t*
Heb 10:29 to be punished who has *t* the Son

TRANCE
Ac 10:10 was being prepared, he fell into a *t.*

TRANSCENDS*
Php 4: 7 which *t* all understanding,

TRANSFIGURED
Mt 17: 2 There he was *t* before them.

TRANSFORM* (TRANSFORMED)
Php 3:21 will *t* our lowly bodies

TRANSFORMED (TRANSFORM)
Ro 12: 2 be *t* by the renewing of your mind.
2Co 3:18 are being *t* into his likeness

TRANSGRESSION (TRANSGRESSIONS TRANSGRESSORS)
Isa 53: 8 for the *t* of my people he was
Ro 4:15 where there is no law there is no *t.*

TRANSGRESSIONS (TRANSGRESSION)
Ps 32: 1 whose *t* are forgiven,
51: 1 blot out my *t.*
103:12 so far has he removed our *t* from us
Isa 53: 5 But he was pierced for our *t,*
Eph 2: 1 you were dead in your *t* and sins,

TRANSGRESSORS (TRANSGRESSION)
Ps 51:13 Then I will teach *t* your ways,
Isa 53:12 and made intercession for the *t.*
53:12 and was numbered with the *t.*

TREADING
Dt 25: 4 an ox while it is *t* out the grain.
1Co 9: 9 an ox while it is *t* out the grain."

TREASURE (TREASURED TREASURES)
Isa 33: 6 of the LORD is the key to this *t.*
Mt 6:21 For where your *t* is, there your
2Co 4: 7 But we have this *t* in jars of clay

TREASURED (TREASURE)
Dt 7: 6 to be his people, his *t* possession.
Lk 2:19 But Mary *t* up all these things

TREASURES (TREASURE)
Mt 6:19 up for yourselves *t* on earth,
Col 2: 3 in whom are hidden all the *t*
Heb 11:26 of greater value than the *t* of Egypt,

TREAT
Lev 22: 2 sons to *t* with respect the sacred
1Ti 5: 1 *T* younger men as brothers,
1Pe 3: 7 and *t* them with respect

TREATY
Dt 7: 2 Make no *t* with them, and show

TREE
Ge 2: 9 and the *t* of the knowledge of good
2: 9 of the garden were the *t* of life
Dt 21:23 hung on a *t* is under God's curse.
Ps 1: 3 He is like a *t* planted by streams
Mt 3:10 every *t* that does not produce good
12:33 for a *t* is recognized by its fruit.
Gal 3:13 is everyone who is hung on a *t.*"
Rev 22:14 they may have the right to the *t*

TREMBLE (TREMBLING)
1Ch 16:30 *T* before him, all the earth!
Ps 114: 7 *T,* O earth, at the presence

TREMBLING (TREMBLE)
Ps 2:11 and rejoice with *t.*
Php 2:12 out your salvation with fear and *t,*

TRESPASS
Ro 5:17 For if, by the *t* of the one man,

TRIALS
1Th 3: 3 one would be unsettled by these *t.*
Jas 1: 2 whenever you face *t* of many kinds,
2Pe 2: 9 how to rescue godly men from *t*

TRIBES
Ge 49:28 All these are the twelve *t* of Israel,
Mt 19:28 judging the twelve *t* of Israel.

TRIBULATION*
Rev 7:14 who have come out of the great *t;*

TRIUMPHAL* (TRIUMPHING)
Isa 60:11 their kings led in *t* procession.
2Co 2:14 us in *t* procession in Christ

TRIUMPHING* (TRIUMPHAL)
Col 2:15 of them, *t* over them by the cross.

TROUBLE (TROUBLED TROUBLES)
Job 14: 1 is of few days and full of *t.*
Ps 46: 1 an ever-present help in *t.*
107:13 they cried to the LORD in their *t,*
Pr 11:29 He who brings *t* on his family will
24:10 If you falter in times of *t,*
Mt 6:34 Each day has enough *t* of its own.
Jn 16:33 In this world you will have *t.*
Ro 8:35 Shall *t* or hardship or persecution

TROUBLED (TROUBLE)
Jn 14: 1 "Do not let your hearts be *t.*
14:27 Do not let your hearts be *t*

TROUBLES (TROUBLE)
1Co 7:28 those who marry will face many *t*
2Co 1: 4 who comforts us in all our *t,*
4:17 and momentary *t* are achieving

TRUE (TRUTH)
Dt 18:22 does not take place or come *t,*
1Sa 9: 6 and everything he says comes *t.*
Ps 119:160 All your words are *t;*
Jn 17: 3 the only *t* God, and Jesus Christ,
Ro 3: 4 Let God be *t,* and every man a liar.
Php 4: 8 whatever is *t,* whatever is noble,
Rev 22: 6 These words are trustworthy and *t.*

TRUMPET
1Co 14: 8 if the *t* does not sound a clear call,
15:52 For the *t* will sound, the dead will

TRUST (ENTRUSTED TRUSTED TRUSTS TRUSTWORTHY)
Ps 20: 7 we *t* in the name of the LORD our
37: 3 *T* in the LORD and do good;
56: 4 in God I *t;* I will not be afraid.
119:42 for I *t* in your word.
Pr 3: 5 *T* in the LORD with all your heart
Isa 30:15 in quietness and *t* is your strength,
Jn 14: 1 *T* in God; *t* also in me.
1Co 4: 2 been given a *t* must prove faithful.

TRUSTED (TRUST)
Ps 26: 1 I have *t* in the LORD
Isa 25: 9 we *t* in him, and he saved us.
Da 3:28 They *t* in him and defied the king's
Lk 16:10 *t* with very little can also be *t*

TRUSTS (TRUST)
Ps 32:10 surrounds the man who *t* in him.
Pr 11:28 Whoever *t* in his riches will fall,
28:26 He who *t* in himself is a fool,
Ro 9:33 one who *t* in him will never be put

TRUSTWORTHY (TRUST)
Ps 119:138 they are fully *t.*
Pr 11:13 but a *t* man keeps a secret.
Rev 22: 6 "These words are *t* and true.

TRUTH (TRUE TRUTHFUL TRUTHS)
Ps 51: 6 Surely you desire *t*
Isa 45:19 I, the LORD, speak the *t;*
Zec 8:16 are to do: Speak the *t* to each other,
Jn 4:23 worship the Father in spirit and *t,*
8:32 Then you will know the *t,*
8:32 and the *t* will set you free."
14: 6 I am the way and the *t* and the life.
16:13 comes, he will guide you into all *t.*
18:38 "What is *t?*" Pilate asked.
Ro 1:25 They exchanged the *t* of God
1Co 13: 6 in evil but rejoices with the *t.*
2Co 13: 8 against the *t,* but only for the *t.*
Eph 4:15 Instead, speaking the *t* in love,
6:14 with the belt of *t* buckled
2Th 2:10 because they refused to love the *t*
1Ti 2: 4 to come to a knowledge of the *t.*
3:15 the pillar and foundation of the *t.*
2Ti 2:15 correctly handles the word of *t.*
3: 7 never able to acknowledge the *t.*
Heb 10:26 received the knowledge of the *t,*
1Pe 1:22 by obeying the *t* so that you have
2Pe 2: 2 the way of *t* into disrepute.
1Jn 1: 6 we lie and do not live by the *t.*
1: 8 deceive ourselves and the *t* is not

TRUTHFUL (TRUTH)
Pr 12:22 but he delights in men who are *t.*
Jn 3:33 it has certified that God is *t.*

TRUTHS (TRUTH)
1Co 2:13 expressing spiritual *t*
1Ti 3: 9 hold of the deep *t* of the faith
Heb 5:12 to teach you the elementary *t*

TRY (TRYING)
Ps 26: 2 Test me, O LORD, and *t* me,
Isa 7:13 enough to *t* the patience of men?
1Co 14:12 *t* to excel in gifts that build up
2Co 5:11 is to fear the Lord, we *t*
1Th 5:15 always *t* to be kind to each other

TRYING (TRY)
2Co 5:12 We are not *t* to commend ourselves
1Th 2: 4 We are not *t* to please men but God

TUNIC
Lk 6:29 do not stop him from taking your *t.*

TURN (TURNED TURNS)
Ex 32:12 *T* from your fierce anger; relent
Dt 5:32 do not *t* aside to the right
28:14 Do not *t* aside from any
Jos 1: 7 do not *t* from it to the right
2Ch 7:14 and *t* from their wicked ways,
30: 9 He will not *t* his face from you
Ps 78: 6 they in *t* would tell their children.
Pr 22: 6 when he is old he will not *t* from it.

Isa 29:16 You *t* things upside down,
30:21 Whether you *t* to the right
45:22 "*T* to me and be saved,
55: 7 Let him *t* to the LORD,
Eze 33:11 *T! T* from your evil ways!
Mal 4: 6 He will *t* the hearts of the fathers
Mt 5:39 you on the right cheek, *t*
10:35 For I have come to *t*
Jn 12:40 nor *t*— and I would heal them."
Ac 3:19 Repent, then, and *t* to God,
26:18 and *t* them from darkness to light,
1Ti 6:20 *T* away from godless chatter
1Pe 3:11 He must *t* from evil and do good;

TURNED (TURN)
Ps 30:11 You *t* my wailing into dancing;
40: 1 he *t* to me and heard my cry.
Isa 53: 6 each of us has *t* to his own way;
Hos 7: 8 Ephraim is a flat cake not *t* over.
Joel 2:31 The sun will be *t* to darkness
Ro 3:12 All have *t* away,

TURNS (TURN)
2Sa 22:29 the LORD *t* my darkness into light
Pr 15: 1 A gentle answer *t* away wrath,
Isa 44:25 and *t* it into nonsense,
Jas 5:20 Whoever *t* a sinner from the error

TWELVE
Ge 49:28 All these are the *t* tribes of Israel,
Mt 10: 1 He called his *t* disciples to him

TWINKLING*
1Co 15:52 in a flash, in the *t* of an eye,

UNAPPROACHABLE*
1Ti 6:16 immortal and who lives in *u* light,

UNBELIEF (UNBELIEVER UNBELIEVERS UNBELIEVING)
Mk 9:24 help me overcome my *u!*"
Ro 11:20 they were broken off because of *u*,
Heb 3:19 able to enter, because of their *u*.

UNBELIEVER* (UNBELIEF)
1Co 7:15 But if the *u* leaves, let him do so.
10:27 If some *u* invites you to a meal
14:24 if an *u* or someone who does not
2Co 6:15 have in common with an *u?*
1Ti 5: 8 the faith and is worse than an *u*.

UNBELIEVERS (UNBELIEF)
1Co 6: 6 another—and this in front of *u!*
2Co 6:14 Do not be yoked together with *u*.

UNBELIEVING (UNBELIEF)
1Co 7:14 For the *u* husband has been
Rev 21: 8 But the cowardly, the *u*, the vile,

UNCERTAIN*
1Ti 6:17 which is so *u*, but to put their hope

UNCHANGEABLE*
Heb 6:18 by two *u* things in which it is

UNCIRCUMCISED
1Sa 17:26 Who is this *u* Philistine that he
Col 3:11 circumcised or *u*, barbarian,

UNCIRCUMCISION
1Co 7:19 is nothing and *u* is nothing.
Gal 5: 6 neither circumcision nor *u* has any

UNCLEAN
Isa 6: 5 ruined! For I am a man of *u* lips,
Ro 14:14 fully convinced that no food is *u*
2Co 6:17 Touch no *u* thing,

UNCONCERNED*
Eze 16:49 were arrogant, overfed and *u;*

UNCOVERED
Heb 4:13 Everything is *u* and laid bare

UNDERSTAND (UNDERSTANDING UNDERSTANDS)
Job 42: 3 Surely I spoke of things I did not *u*,
Ps 73:16 When I tried to *u* all this,
119:125 that I may *u* your statutes.
Lk 24:45 so they could *u* the Scriptures.
Ac 8:30 "Do you *u* what you are reading?"
Ro 7:15 I do not *u* what I do.
1Co 2:14 and he cannot *u* them,
Eph 5:17 but *u* what the Lord's will is.
2Pe 3:16 some things that are hard to *u*,

UNDERSTANDING (UNDERSTAND)
Ps 119:104 I gain *u* from your precepts;
147: 5 his *u* has no limit.
Pr 3: 5 and lean not on your own *u;*
4: 7 Though it cost all you have, get *u*.
10:23 but a man of *u* delights in wisdom.
11:12 but a man of *u* holds his tongue.
15:21 a man of *u* keeps a straight course.
15:32 whoever heeds correction gains *u*.
23:23 get wisdom, discipline and *u*.
Isa 40:28 and his *u* no one can fathom.
Da 5:12 a keen mind and knowledge and *u*,
Mk 4:12 and ever hearing but never *u;*
12:33 with all your *u* and with all your
Php 4: 7 of God, which transcends all *u*,

UNDERSTANDS (UNDERSTAND)
1Ch 28: 9 and *u* every motive
1Ti 6: 4 he is conceited and *u* nothing.

UNDIVIDED*
1Ch 12:33 to help David with *u* loyalty—
Ps 86:11 give me an *u* heart,
Eze 11:19 I will give them an *u* heart
1Co 7:35 way in *u* devotion to the Lord.

UNDOING
Pr 18: 7 A fool's mouth is his *u*,

UNDYING*
Eph 6:24 Lord Jesus Christ with an *u* love.

UNFADING*
1Pe 3: 4 the *u* beauty of a gentle

UNFAILING
Ps 33: 5 the earth is full of his *u* love.
119:76 May your *u* love be my comfort,
143: 8 bring me word of your *u* love,
Pr 19:22 What a man desires is *u* love;
La 3:32 so great is his *u* love.

UNFAITHFUL (UNFAITHFULNESS)
Lev 6: 2 is *u* to the LORD by deceiving his
1Ch 10:13 because he was *u* to the LORD;
Pr 13:15 but the way of the *u* is hard.

UNFAITHFULNESS (UNFAITHFUL)
Mt 5:32 except for marital *u*, causes her
19: 9 for marital *u*, and marries another

UNFOLDING
Ps 119:130 the *u* of your words gives light;

UNGODLINESS
Tit 2:12 It teaches us to say "No" to *u*

UNIT
1Co 12:12 body is a *u*, though it is made up

UNITED (UNITY)
Ro 6: 5 If we have been *u* with him
Php 2: 1 from being *u* with Christ,
Col 2: 2 encouraged in heart and *u* in love,

UNITY (UNITED)
Ps 133: 1 is when brothers live together in *u!*
Ro 15: 5 a spirit of *u* among yourselves
Eph 4: 3 effort to keep the *u* of the Spirit
4:13 up until we all reach *u* in the faith
Col 3:14 them all together in perfect *u.*

UNIVERSE
Php 2:15 which you shine like stars in the *u*
Heb 1: 2 and through whom he made the *u.*

UNKNOWN
Ac 17:23 TO AN *U* GOD.

UNLEAVENED
Ex 12:17 "Celebrate the Feast of *U* Bread,

UNPROFITABLE
Tit 3: 9 because these are *u* and useless.

UNPUNISHED
Ex 34: 7 Yet he does not leave the guilty *u;*
Pr 19: 5 A false witness will not go *u,*

UNREPENTANT*
Ro 2: 5 stubbornness and your *u* heart,

UNRIGHTEOUS*
Zep 3: 5 yet the *u* know no shame.
Mt 5:45 rain on the righteous and the *u.*
1Pe 3:18 the righteous for the *u,* to bring you
2Pe 2: 9 and to hold the *u* for the day

UNSEARCHABLE
Ro 11:33 How *u* his judgments,
Eph 3: 8 preach to the Gentiles the *u* riches

UNSEEN
2Co 4:18 on what is seen, but on what is *u.*
4:18 temporary, but what is *u* is eternal.

UNSTABLE*
Jas 1: 8 he is a double-minded man, *u*
2Pe 2:14 they seduce the *u;* they are experts
3:16 ignorant and *u* people distort,

UNTHINKABLE*
Job 34:12 It is *u* that God would do wrong,

UNVEILED*
2Co 3:18 with *u* faces all reflect the Lord's

UNWORTHY
Job 40: 4 "I am *u*— how can I reply to you?
Lk 17:10 should say, 'We are *u* servants;

UPRIGHT
Job 1: 1 This man was blameless and *u;*
Pr 2: 7 He holds victory in store for the *u,*
15: 8 but the prayer of the *u* pleases him.
Tit 1: 8 who is self-controlled, *u,* holy
2:12 *u* and godly lives in this present

UPROOTED
Jude :12 without fruit and *u*— twice dead.

USEFUL
2Ti 2:21 *u* to the Master and prepared
3:16 Scripture is God-breathed and is *u*

USELESS
1Co 15:14 our preaching is *u*
Jas 2:20 faith without deeds is *u?*

USURY
Ne 5:10 But let the exacting of *u* stop!

UTTER
Ps 78: 2 I will *u* hidden things, things from of

UZZIAH
Son of Amaziah; king of Judah also known as Azariah (2Ki 15:1-7; 1Ch 6:24; 2Ch 26).

VAIN
Ps 33:17 A horse is a *v* hope for deliverance;
Isa 65:23 They will not toil in *v*
1Co 15: 2 Otherwise, you have believed in *v.*
15:58 labor in the Lord is not in *v.*
2Co 6: 1 not to receive God's grace in *v.*

VALLEY
Ps 23: 4 walk through the *v* of the shadow
Isa 40: 4 Every *v* shall be raised up,
Joel 3:14 multitudes in the *v* of decision!

VALUABLE (VALUE)
Lk 12:24 And how much more *v* you are

VALUE (VALUABLE)
Mt 13:46 When he found one of great *v,*
1Ti 4: 8 For physical training is of some *v,*
Heb 11:26 as of greater *v* than the treasures

VEIL
Ex 34:33 to them, he put a *v* over his face.
2Co 3:14 for to this day the same *v* remains

VENGEANCE (AVENGE REVENGE)
Isa 34: 8 For the LORD has a day of *v,*

VICTORIES (VICTORY)
Ps 18:50 He gives his king great *v;*
21: 1 great is his joy in the *v* you give!

VICTORIOUSLY* (VICTORY)
Ps 45: 4 In your majesty ride forth *v*

VICTORY (VICTORIES VICTORIOUSLY)
Ps 60:12 With God we will gain the *v,*
1Co 15:54 "Death has been swallowed up in *v*
15:57 He gives us the *v* through our Lord
1Jn 5: 4 This is the *v* that has overcome

VINDICATED
1Ti 3:16 was *v* by the Spirit,

VINE
Jn 15: 1 "I am the true *v,* and my Father is

VINEGAR
Mk 15:36 filled a sponge with wine *v,*

VIOLATION
Heb 2: 2 every *v* and disobedience received

VIOLENCE
Isa 60:18 No longer will *v* be heard
Eze 45: 9 Give up your *v* and oppression

VIPERS
Ro 3:13 "The poison of *v* is on their lips."

VIRGIN
Isa 7:14 The *v* will be with child
Mt 1:23 "The *v* will be with child
2Co 11: 2 that I might present you as a pure *v*

VIRTUES*
Col 3:14 And over all these *v* put on love,

VISION
Ac 26:19 disobedient to the *v* from heaven.

VOICE
Ps 95: 7 Today, if you hear his *v,*
Isa 30:21 your ears will hear a *v* behind you,
Jn 5:28 are in their graves will hear his *v*
10: 3 and the sheep listen to his *v.*
Heb 3: 7 "Today, if you hear his *v,*

Rev 3:20 If anyone hears my *v* and opens

VOMIT
Pr 26:11 As a dog returns to its *v*,
2Pe 2:22 "A dog returns to its *v*," and,

VOW
Nu 30: 2 When a man makes a *v*

WAGES
Lk 10: 7 for the worker deserves his *w*.
Ro 4: 4 his *w* are not credited to him
6:23 For the *w* of sin is death,

WAILING
Ps 30:11 You turned my *w* into dancing;

WAIST
2Ki 1: 8 with a leather belt around his *w*."
Mt 3: 4 he had a leather belt around his *w*.

WAIT (WAITED WAITS)
Ps 27:14 *W* for the LORD;
130: 5 I *w* for the LORD, my soul waits,
Isa 30:18 Blessed are all who *w* for him!
Ac 1: 4 *w* for the gift my Father promised,
Ro 8:23 as we *w* eagerly for our adoption
1Th 1:10 and to *w* for his Son from heaven,
Tit 2:13 while we *w* for the blessed hope—

WAITED (WAIT)
Ps 40: 1 I *w* patiently for the LORD;

WAITS (WAIT)
Ro 8:19 creation *w* in eager expectation

WALK (WALKED WALKS)
Dt 11:19 and when you *w* along the road,
Ps 1: 1 who does not *w* in the counsel
23: 4 Even though I *w*
89:15 who *w* in the light of your presence
Isa 2: 5 let us *w* in the light of the LORD.
30:21 saying, "This is the way; *w* in it."
40:31 they will *w* and not be faint.
Jer 6:16 ask where the good way is, and *w*
Da 4:37 And those who *w* in pride he is able
Am 3: 3 Do two *w* together
Mic 6: 8 and to *w* humbly with your God.
Mk 2: 9 'Get up, take your mat and *w*'?
Jn 8:12 Whoever follows me will never *w*
1Jn 1: 7 But if we *w* in the light,
2Jn : 6 his command is that you *w* in love.

WALKED (WALK)
Ge 5:24 Enoch *w* with God; then he was no
Jos 14: 9 which your feet have *w* will be your
Mt 14:29 *w* on the water and came toward

WALKS (WALK)
Pr 13:20 He who *w* with the wise grows wise

WALL
Jos 6:20 *w* collapsed; so every man charged
Ne 2:17 let us rebuild the *w* of Jerusalem,
Rev 21:12 It had a great, high *w*

WALLOWING
2Pe 2:22 back to her *w* in the mud."

WANT (WANTED WANTING WANTS)
1Sa 8:19 "We *w* a king over us.
Ps 23: 1 is my shepherd, I shall not be in *w*.
Lk 19:14 'We don't *w* this man to be our king
Ro 7:15 For what I *w* to do I do not do,
Php 3:10 I *w* to know Christ and the power

WANTED (WANT)
1Co 12:18 of them, just as he *w* them to be.

WANTING (WANT)
Da 5:27 weighed on the scales and found *w*.
2Pe 3: 9 with you, not *w* anyone to perish,

WANTS (WANT)
Mt 20:26 whoever *w* to become great
Mk 8:35 For whoever *w* to save his life will
Ro 9:18 he hardens whom he *w* to harden.
1Ti 2: 4 who *w* all men to be saved

WAR (WARS)
Isa 2: 4 nor will they train for *w* anymore.
Da 9:26 *W* will continue until the end,
2Co 10: 3 we do not wage *w* as the world does
Rev 19:11 With justice he judges and makes *w*

WARN (WARNED WARNINGS)
Eze 3:19 But if you do *w* the wicked man
33: 9 if you do *w* the wicked man to turn

WARNED (WARN)
Ps 19:11 By them is your servant *w*;

WARNINGS (WARN)
1Co 10:11 and were written down as *w* for us,

WARS (WAR)
Ps 46: 9 He makes *w* cease to the ends
Mt 24: 6 You will hear of *w* and rumors of *w*,

WASH (WASHED WASHING)
Ps 51: 7 *w* me, and I will be whiter
Jn 13: 5 and began to *w* his disciples' feet,
Ac 22:16 be baptized and *w* your sins away,
Rev 22:14 Blessed are those who *w* their robes

WASHED (WASH)
1Co 6:11 you were *w*, you were sanctified,
Rev 7:14 they have *w* their robes

WASHING (WASH)
Eph 5:26 cleansing her by the *w* with water
Tit 3: 5 us through the *w* of rebirth

WATCH (WATCHES WATCHING WATCHMAN)
Ge 31:49 "May the LORD keep *w*
Jer 31:10 will *w* over his flock like a shepherd
Mt 24:42 "Therefore keep *w*, because you do
26:41 *W* and pray so that you will not fall
Lk 2: 8 keeping *w* over their flocks at night
1Ti 4:16 *W* your life and doctrine closely.

WATCHES (WATCH)
Ps 1: 6 For the LORD *w* over the way
121: 3 he who *w* over you will not slumber

WATCHING (WATCH)
Lk 12:37 whose master finds them *w*

WATCHMAN (WATCH)
Eze 3:17 I have made you a *w* for the house

WATER (WATERED WATERS)
Ps 1: 3 like a tree planted by streams of *w*,
22:14 I am poured out like *w*,
Pr 25:21 if he is thirsty, give him *w* to drink.
Isa 49:10 and lead them beside springs of *w*.
Jer 2:13 broken cisterns that cannot hold *w*.
Zec 14: 8 On that day living *w* will flow out
Mk 9:41 anyone who gives you a cup of *w*
Jn 4:10 he would have given you living *w*."
7:38 streams of living *w* will flow
Eph 5:26 washing with *w* through the word,
1Pe 3:21 this *w* symbolizes baptism that now
Rev 21: 6 cost from the spring of the *w* of life.

WATERED (WATER)
1Co 3: 6 I planted the seed, Apollos *w* it,

WATERS (WATER)
Ps 23: 2 he leads me beside quiet *w,*
Ecc 11: 1 Cast your bread upon the *w,*
Isa 58:11 like a spring whose *w* never fail.
1Co 3: 7 plants nor he who *w* is anything,

WAVE (WAVES)
Jas 1: 6 he who doubts is like a *w* of the sea,

WAVES (WAVE)
Isa 57:20 whose *w* cast up mire and mud.
Mt 8:27 Even the winds and the *w* obey him
Eph 4:14 tossed back and forth by the *w,*

WAY (WAYS)
Dt 1:33 to show you the *w* you should go.
2Sa 22:31 "As for God, his *w* is perfect;
Job 23:10 But he knows the *w* that I take;
Ps 1: 1 or stand in the *w* of sinners
37: 5 Commit your *w* to the LORD;
119: 9 can a young man keep his *w* pure?
139:24 See if there is any offensive *w* in me
Pr 14:12 There is a *w* that seems right
16:17 he who guards his *w* guards his life.
22: 6 Train a child in the *w* he should go,
Isa 30:21 saying, "This is the *w;* walk in it."
53: 6 each of us has turned to his own *w;*
55: 7 Let the wicked forsake his *w*
Mt 3: 3 'Prepare the *w* for the Lord,
Jn 14: 6 "I am the *w* and the truth
1Co 10:13 also provide a *w* out so that you can
12:31 will show you the most excellent *w.*
Heb 4:15 who has been tempted in every *w,*
9: 8 was showing by this that the *w*
10:20 and living *w* opened for us

WAYS (WAY)
Ex 33:13 teach me your *w* so I may know
Ps 25:10 All the *w* of the LORD are loving
51:13 I will teach transgressors your *w,*
Pr 3: 6 in all your *w* acknowledge him,
Isa 55: 8 neither are your *w* my *w,"*
Jas 3: 2 We all stumble in many *w.*

WEAK (WEAKER WEAKNESS)
Mt 26:41 spirit is willing, but the body is *w."*
Ro 14: 1 Accept him whose faith is *w,*
1Co 1:27 God chose the *w* things
8: 9 become a stumbling block to the *w.*
9:22 To the *w* I became *w,* to win the *w.*
2Co 12:10 For when I am *w,* then I am strong.
Heb 12:12 your feeble arms and *w* knees.

WEAKER (WEAK)
1Co 12:22 seem to be *w* are indispensable,
1Pe 3: 7 them with respect as the *w* partner

WEAKNESS (WEAK)
Ro 8:26 the Spirit helps us in our *w.*
1Co 1:25 and the *w* of God is stronger
2Co 12: 9 for my power is made perfect in *w*
Heb 5: 2 since he himself is subject to *w.*

WEALTH
Pr 3: 9 Honor the LORD with your *w,*
Mk 10:22 away sad, because he had great *w.*
Lk 15:13 and there squandered his *w*

WEAPONS
2Co 10: 4 The *w* we fight with are not

WEARIES (WEARY)
Ecc 12:12 and much study *w* the body.

WEARY (WEARIES)
Isa 40:31 they will run and not grow *w,*
Mt 11:28 all you who are *w* and burdened,
Gal 6: 9 Let us not become *w* in doing good,

WEDDING
Mt 22:11 who was not wearing *w* clothes.
Rev 19: 7 For the *w* of the Lamb has come,

WEEP (WEEPING WEPT)
Ecc 3: 4 a time to *w* and a time to laugh,
Lk 6:21 Blessed are you who *w* now,

WEEPING (WEEP)
Ps 30: 5 *w* may remain for a night,
126: 6 He who goes out *w,*
Mt 8:12 where there will be *w* and gnashing

WELCOMES
Mt 18: 5 whoever *w* a little child like this
2Jn :11 Anyone who *w* him shares

WELL
Lk 17:19 your faith has made you *w."*
Jas 5:15 in faith will make the sick person *w*

WEPT (WEEP)
Ps 137: 1 of Babylon we sat and *w*
Jn 11:35 Jesus *w.*

WEST
Ps 103:12 as far as the east is from the *w,*

WHIRLWIND (WIND)
2Ki 2: 1 to take Elijah up to heaven in a *w,*
Hos 8: 7 and reap the *w.*
Na 1: 3 His way is in the *w* and the storm,

WHITE (WHITER)
Isa 1:18 they shall be as *w* as snow;
Da 7: 9 His clothing was as *w* as snow;
Rev 1:14 hair were *w* like wool, as *w* as snow,
3: 4 dressed in *w,* for they are worthy.
20:11 Then I saw a great *w* throne

WHITER (WHITE)
Ps 51: 7 and I will be *w* than snow.

WHOLE
Mt 16:26 for a man if he gains the *w* world,
24:14 will be preached in the *w* world
Jn 13:10 to wash his feet; his *w* body is clean
21:25 the *w* world would not have room
Ac 20:27 proclaim to you the *w* will of God.
Ro 3:19 and the *w* world held accountable
8:22 know that the *w* creation has been
Gal 3:22 declares that the *w* world is
5: 3 obligated to obey the *w* law.
Eph 4:13 attaining to the *w* measure
Jas 2:10 For whoever keeps the *w* law
1Jn 2: 2 but also for the sins of the *w* world.

WHOLEHEARTEDLY (HEART)
Dt 1:36 because he followed the LORD *w*
Eph 6: 7 Serve *w,* as if you were serving

WICKED (WICKEDNESS)
Ps 1: 1 walk in the counsel of the *w*
1: 5 Therefore the *w* will not stand
73: 3 when I saw the prosperity of the *w.*
Pr 10:20 the heart of the *w* is of little value.
11:21 The *w* will not go unpunished,
Isa 53: 9 He was assigned a grave with the *w*
55: 7 Let the *w* forsake his way
57:20 But the *w* are like the tossing sea,
Eze 3:18 that *w* man will die for his sin,
18:23 pleasure in the death of the *w?*
33:14 to the *w* man, 'You will surely die,'

WICKEDNESS (WICKED)
Eze 28:15 created till *w* was found in you.

WIDE
Isa 54: 2 stretch your tent curtains *w,*

Mt 7:13 For *w* is the gate and broad is
Eph 3:18 to grasp how *w* and long and high

WIDOW (WIDOWS)
Dt 10:18 cause of the fatherless and the *w*,
Lk 21: 2 saw a poor *w* put in two very small

WIDOWS (WIDOW)
Jas 1:27 look after orphans and *w*

WIFE (WIVES)
Ge 2:24 and mother and be united to his *w*,
24:67 she became his *w*, and he loved her;
Ex 20:17 shall not covet your neighbor's *w*,
Dt 5:21 shall not covet your neighbor's *w*.
Pr 5:18 in the *w* of your youth.
12: 4 *w* of noble character is her
18:22 He who finds a *w* finds what is
19:13 quarrelsome *w* is like a constant
31:10 *w* of noble character who can find?
Mt 19: 3 for a man to divorce his *w* for any
1Co 7: 2 each man should have his own *w*,
7:33 how he can please his *w*—
Eph 5:23 the husband is the head of the *w*
5:33 must love his *w* as he loves himself,
1Ti 3: 2 husband of but one *w*, temperate,
Rev 21: 9 I will show you the bride, the *w*

WILD
Lk 15:13 squandered his wealth in *w* living.
Ro 11:17 and you, though a *w* olive shoot,

WILL (WILLING WILLINGNESS)
Ps 40: 8 I desire to do your *w*, O my God;
143:10 Teach me to do your *w*,
Isa 53:10 Yet it was the LORD's *w*
Mt 6:10 your *w* be done
26:39 Yet not as I *w*, but as you *w*."
Jn 7:17 If anyone chooses to do God's *w*,
Ac 20:27 to you the whole *w* of God.
Ro 12: 2 and approve what God's *w* is—
1Co 7:37 but has control over his own *w*,
Eph 5:17 understand what the Lord's *w* is.
Php 2:13 for it is God who works in you to *w*
1Th 4: 3 God's *w* that you should be
5:18 for this is God's *w* for you
Heb 9:16 In the case of a *w*, it is necessary
10: 7 I have come to do your *w*, O God
Jas 4:15 "If it is the Lord's *w*,
1Jn 5:14 we ask anything according to his *w*,
Rev 4:11 and by your *w* they were created

WILLING (WILL)
Ps 51:12 grant me a *w* spirit, to sustain me.
Da 3:28 were *w* to give up their lives rather
Mt 18:14 Father in heaven is not *w* that any
23:37 her wings, but you were not *w*.
26:41 The spirit is *w*, but the body is weak

WILLINGNESS (WILL)
2Co 8:12 For if the *w* is there, the gift is

WIN (WINS)
Php 3:14 on toward the goal to *w* the prize
1Th 4:12 your daily life may *w* the respect

WIND (WHIRLWIND)
Jas 1: 6 blown and tossed by the *w*.

WINE
Pr 20: 1 *W* is a mocker and beer a brawler;
Isa 55: 1 Come, buy *w* and milk
Mt 9:17 Neither do men pour new *w*
Lk 23:36 They offered him *w* vinegar
Ro 14:21 not to eat meat or drink *w*
Eph 5:18 on *w*, which leads to debauchery.

WINESKINS
Mt 9:17 do men pour new wine into old *w*.

WINGS
Ru 2:12 under whose *w* you have come
Ps 17: 8 hide me in the shadow of your *w*
Isa 40:31 They will soar on *w* like eagles;
Mal 4: 2 rise with healing in its *w*.
Lk 13:34 hen gathers her chicks under her *w*,

WINS (WIN)
Pr 11:30 and he who *w* souls is wise.

WIPE
Rev 7:17 God will *w* away every tear

WISDOM (WISE)
1Ki 4:29 God gave Solomon *w* and very
Ps 111:10 of the LORD is the beginning of *w*;
Pr 31:26 She speaks with *w*,
Jer 10:12 he founded the world by his *w*
Mt 11:19 But *w* is proved right by her actions
Lk 2:52 And Jesus grew in *w* and stature,
Ro 11:33 the depth of the riches of the *w*
Col 2: 3 are hidden all the treasures of *w*
Jas 1: 5 of you lacks *w*, he should ask God,

WISE (WISDOM WISER)
1Ki 3:12 give you a *w* and discerning heart,
Job 5:13 He catches the *w* in their craftiness
Ps 19: 7 making *w* the simple.
Pr 3: 7 Do not be *w* in your own eyes;
9: 8 rebuke a *w* man and he will love
10: 1 A *w* son brings joy to his father,
11:30 and he who wins souls is *w*.
13:20 He who walks with the *w* grows *w*,
17:28 Even a fool is thought *w*
Da 12: 3 Those who are *w* will shine like
Mt 11:25 hidden these things from the *w*
1Co 1:27 things of the world to shame the *w*;
2Ti 3:15 able to make you *w* for salvation

WISER (WISE)
1Co 1:25 of God is *w* than man's wisdom,

WITHER (WITHERS)
Ps 1: 3 and whose leaf does not *w*.

WITHERS (WITHER)
Isa 40: 7 The grass *w* and the flowers fall,
1Pe 1:24 the grass *w* and the flowers fall,

WITHHOLD
Ps 84:11 no good thing does he *w*
Pr 23:13 Do not *w* discipline from a child;

WITNESS (WITNESSES)
Jn 1: 8 he came only as a *w* to the light.

WITNESSES (WITNESS)
Dt 19:15 by the testimony of two or three *w*.
Ac 1: 8 and you will be my *w* in Jerusalem,

WIVES (WIFE)
Eph 5:22 *W*, submit to your husbands
5:25 love your *w*, just as Christ loved
1Pe 3: 1 words by the behavior of their *w*,

WOE
Isa 6: 5 "*W* to me!" I cried.

WOLF
Isa 65:25 *w* and the lamb will feed together,

WOMAN (MAN)
Ge 2:22 God made a *w* from
3:15 between you and the *w*,
Lev 20:13 as one lies with a *w*,
Dt 22: 5 *w* must not wear men's
Ru 3:11 a *w* of noble character
Pr 31:30 a *w* who fears the LORD
Mt 5:28 looks at a *w* lustfully

Jn 8: 3 a *w* caught in adultery.
Ro 7: 2 a married *w* is bound to
1Co 11: 3 the head of the *w* is man,
11:13 a *w* to pray to God with
1Ti 2:11 A *w* should learn in

WOMEN (MAN)
Lk 1:42 Blessed are you among *w*,
1Co 14:34 *w* should remain silent in
1Ti 2: 9 want *w* to dress modestly
Tit 2: 3 teach the older *w* to be
1Pe 3: 5 the holy *w* of the past

WOMB
Job 1:21 Naked I came from my mother's *w*,
Jer 1: 5 you in the *w* I knew you,
Lk 1:44 the baby in my *w* leaped for joy.

WONDER (WONDERFUL WONDERS)
Ps 17: 7 Show the *w* of your great love,

WONDERFUL (WONDER)
Job 42: 3 things too *w* for me to know.
Ps 31:21 for he showed his *w* love to me
119:18 *w* things in your law.
119:129 Your statutes are *w*;
139: 6 Such knowledge is too *w* for me,
Isa 9: 6 *W* Counselor, Mighty God,
1Pe 2: 9 out of darkness into his *w* light.

WONDERS (WONDER)
Job 37:14 stop and consider God's *w*.
Ps 119:27 then I will meditate on your *w*.
Joel 2:30 I will show *w* in the heavens
Ac 2:19 I will show *w* in the heaven above

WOOD
Isa 44:19 Shall I bow down to a block of *w*?"
1Co 3:12 costly stones, *w*, hay or straw,

WORD (WORDS)
Dt 8: 3 but on every *w* that comes
2Sa 22:31 the *w* of the LORD is flawless.
Ps 119: 9 By living according to your *w*.
119:11 I have hidden your *w* in my heart
119:105 Your *w* is a lamp to my feet
Pr 12:25 but a kind *w* cheers him up.
25:11 A *w* aptly spoken
30: 5 "Every *w* of God is flawless;
Isa 55:11 so is my *w* that goes out
Jn 1: 1 was the *W*, and the *W* was
1:14 The *W* became flesh and made his
2Co 2:17 we do not peddle the *w* of God
4: 2 nor do we distort the *w* of God.
Eph 6:17 of the Spirit, which is the *w* of God.
Php 2:16 as you hold out the *w* of life—
Col 3:16 Let the *w* of Christ dwell
2Ti 2:15 and who correctly handles the *w*
Heb 4:12 For the *w* of God is living
Jas 1:22 Do not merely listen to the *w*,
2Pe 1:19 And we have the *w* of the prophets

WORDS (WORD)
Dt 11:18 Fix these *w* of mine in your hearts
Ps 119:103 How sweet are your *w* to my taste
119:130 The unfolding of your *w* gives light;
119:160 All your *w* are true;
Pr 30: 6 Do not add to his *w*,
Jer 15:16 When your *w* came, I ate them;
Mt 24:35 but my *w* will never pass away.
Jn 6:68 You have the *w* of eternal life.
15: 7 in me and my *w* remain in you,
1Co 14:19 rather speak five intelligible *w*
Rev 22:19 And if anyone takes *w* away

WORK (WORKER WORKERS WORKING WORKMAN WORKMANSHIP WORKS)
Ex 23:12 "Six days do your *w*,
Nu 8:11 ready to do the *w* of the LORD.
Dt 5:14 On it you shall not do any *w*,
Ecc 5:19 his lot and be happy in his *w*—
Jer 48:10 lax in doing the LORD's *w*!
Jn 6:27 Do not *w* for food that spoils,
9: 4 we must do the *w* of him who sent
1Co 3:13 test the quality of each man's *w*.
Php 1: 6 that he who began a good *w*
2:12 continue to *w* out your salvation
Col 3:23 Whatever you do, *w* at it
1Th 5:12 to respect those who *w* hard
2Th 3:10 If a man will not *w*, he shall not eat
2Ti 3:17 equipped for every good *w*.
Heb 6:10 he will not forget your *w*

WORKER (WORK)
Lk 10: 7 for the *w* deserves his wages.
1Ti 5:18 and "The *w* deserves his wages."

WORKERS (WORK)
Mt 9:37 is plentiful but the *w* are few.
1Co 3: 9 For we are God's fellow *w*;

WORKING (WORK)
Col 3:23 as *w* for the Lord, not for men,

WORKMAN (WORK)
2Ti 2:15 a *w* who does not need

WORKMANSHIP* (WORK)
Eph 2:10 For we are God's *w*, created

WORKS (WORK)
Pr 31:31 let her *w* bring her praise
Ro 8:28 in all things God *w* for the good
Eph 2: 9 not by *w*, so that no one can boast.
4:12 to prepare God's people for *w*

WORLD (WORLDLY)
Ps 50:12 for the *w* is mine, and all that is in it
Isa 13:11 I will punish the *w* for its evil,
Mt 5:14 "You are the light of the *w*.
16:26 for a man if he gains the whole *w*,
Mk 16:15 into all the *w* and preach the good
Jn 1:29 who takes away the sin of the *w*!
3:16 so loved the *w* that he gave his one
8:12 he said, "I am the light of the *w*.
15:19 As it is, you do not belong to the *w*,
16:33 In this *w* you will have trouble.
18:36 "My kingdom is not of this *w*.
Ro 3:19 and the whole *w* held accountable
1Co 3:19 the wisdom of this *w* is foolishness
2Co 5:19 that God was reconciling the *w*
10: 3 For though we live in the *w*,
1Ti 6: 7 For we brought nothing into the *w*,
1Jn 2: 2 but also for the sins of the whole *w*.
2:15 not love the *w* or anything in the *w*.
Rev 13: 8 slain from the creation of the *w*.

WORLDLY (WORLD)
Tit 2:12 to ungodliness and *w* passions,

WORM
Mk 9:48 " 'their *w* does not die,

WORRY (WORRYING)
Mt 6:25 I tell you, do not *w* about your life,
10:19 do not *w* about what to say

WORRYING (WORRY)
Mt 6:27 of you by *w* can add a single hour

WORSHIP
1Ch 16:29 *w* the LORD in the splendor
Ps 95: 6 Come, let us bow down in *w*,
Mt 2: 2 and have come to *w* him."
Jn 4:24 and his worshipers must *w* in spirit
Ro 12: 1 this is your spiritual act of *w*.

WORTH (WORTHY)
Job 28:13 Man does not comprehend its *w;*
Pr 31:10 She is *w* far more than rubies.
Mt 10:31 are *w* more than many sparrows.
Ro 8:18 sufferings are not *w* comparing
1Pe 1: 7 of greater *w* than gold,
3: 4 which is of great *w* in God's sight.

WORTHLESS
Pr 11: 4 Wealth is *w* in the day of wrath,
Jas 1:26 himself and his religion is *w.*

WORTHY (WORTH)
1Ch 16:25 For great is the LORD and most *w*
Eph 4: 1 to live a life *w* of the calling you
Php 1:27 in a manner *w* of the gospel
3Jn : 6 on their way in a manner *w* of God.
Rev 5: 2 "Who is *w* to break the seals

WOUNDS
Pr 27: 6 *W* from a friend can be trusted,
Isa 53: 5 and by his *w* we are healed.
Zec 13: 6 'What are these *w* on your body?'
1Pe 2:24 by his *w* you have been healed.

WRATH
2Ch 36:16 scoffed at his prophets until the *w*
Ps 2: 5 and terrifies them in his *w,* saying,
76:10 Surely your *w* against men brings
Pr 15: 1 A gentle answer turns away *w,*
Jer 25:15 filled with the wine of my *w*
Ro 1:18 The *w* of God is being revealed
5: 9 saved from God's *w* through him!
1Th 5: 9 God did not appoint us to suffer *w*
Rev 6:16 and from the *w* of the Lamb!

WRESTLED
Ge 32:24 and a man *w* with him till daybreak

WRITE (WRITING WRITTEN)
Dt 6: 9 *W* them on the doorframes
Pr 7: 3 *w* them on the tablet of your heart.
Heb 8:10 and *w* them on their hearts.

WRITING (WRITE)
1Co 14:37 him acknowledge that what I am *w*

WRITTEN (WRITE)
Jos 1: 8 careful to do everything *w* in it.
Da 12: 1 everyone whose name is found *w*
Lk 10:20 but rejoice that your names are *w*
Jn 20:31 these are *w* that you may believe
1Co 4: 6 "Do not go beyond what is *w.*"
2Co 3: 3 *w* not with ink but with the Spirit
Col 2:14 having canceled the *w* code,
Heb 12:23 whose names are *w* in heaven.

WRONG (WRONGDOING WRONGED WRONGS)
Ex 23: 2 Do not follow the crowd in doing *w*
Nu 5: 7 must make full restitution for his *w,*
Job 34:12 unthinkable that God would do *w,*
1Th 5:15 that nobody pays back *w* for *w,*

WRONGDOING (WRONG)
Job 1:22 sin by charging God with *w.*

WRONGED (WRONG)
1Co 6: 7 not rather be *w?* Why not rather

WRONGS (WRONG)
Pr 10:12 but love covers over all *w.*
1Co 13: 5 angered, it keeps no record of *w.*

YEARS
Ps 90: 4 For a thousand *y* in your sight
90:10 The length of our days is seventy *y*
2Pe 3: 8 the Lord a day is like a thousand *y,*
Rev 20: 2 and bound him for a thousand *y.*

YESTERDAY
Heb 13: 8 Jesus Christ is the same *y*

YOKE (YOKED)
Mt 11:29 Take my *y* upon you and learn

YOKED (YOKE)
2Co 6:14 Do not be *y* together

YOUNG (YOUTH)
Ps 119: 9 How can a *y* man keep his way
1Ti 4:12 down on you because you are *y,*

YOUTH (YOUNG)
Ps 103: 5 so that your *y* is renewed like
Ecc 12: 1 Creator in the days of your *y,*
2Ti 2:22 Flee the evil desires of *y,*

ZEAL
Pr 19: 2 to have *z* without knowledge,
Ro 12:11 Never be lacking in *z,*

ZECHARIAH
1. Son of Jeroboam II; king of Israel (2Ki 15:8-12).
2. Post-exilic prophet who encouraged rebuilding of temple (Ezr 5:1; 6:14; Zec 1:1).
3. Father of John the Baptist (Lk 1:13; 3:2).

ZEDEKIAH
Mattaniah, son of Josiah (1Ch 3:15), made king of Judah by Nebuchadnezzar (2Ki 24:17-25:7; 2Ch 36:10-14; Jer 37-39; 52:1-11).

ZERUBBABEL
Descendant of David (1Ch 3:19; Mt 1:3). Led return from exile (Ezr 2-3; Ne 7:7; Hag 1-2; Zec 4).

ZIMRI
King of Israel (1Ki 16:9-20).

ZION
Ps 137: 3 "Sing us one of the songs of *Z!*"
Jer 50: 5 They will ask the way to *Z*
Ro 9:33 I lay in *Z* a stone that causes men
11:26 "The deliverer will come from *Z;*

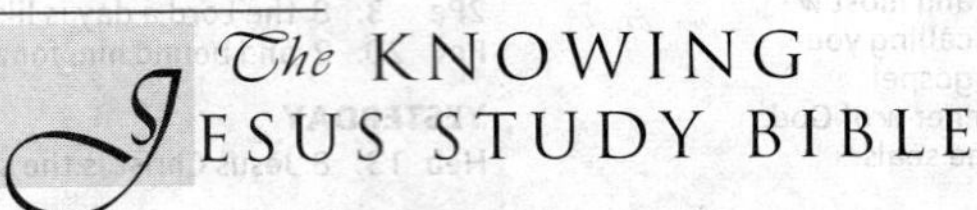

Dr. Edward Hindson and Dr. Edward Dobson, General Editors
Project management and editorial by Donna Huisjen
Editorial assistance by Casandra Lindell,
Dirk Buursma and John Sawyer
Production management by Jean Entingh
Interior design by Sharon Wright, Belmont, MI
Cover design by Cindy Davis
Cover photo by SuperStock, Inc., Jacksonville, FL
Insert design by Amy Peterman
Interior photography by Steve Diggs & Friends,
The Image Bank and FPG International
Interior proofreading by Peachtree Editorial and
Proofreading Service, Peachtree City, GA
Interior typesetting by Multnomah Graphics, Troutdale, OR

We suggest loosening the binding of your new Bible by gently pressing on a small section of pages at a time from the center. To ensure against breakage of the spine, it is best not to bend the cover backward around the spine or to carry study notes, church bulletins, pens, etc., inside the cover. Because a felt-tipped marker will "bleed" through the pages, we recommend use of a ball-point pen or pencil to underline favorite passages. Your Bible should not be exposed to excessive heat, cold, or humidity.

Map 1: JERUSALEM IN JESUS' TIME

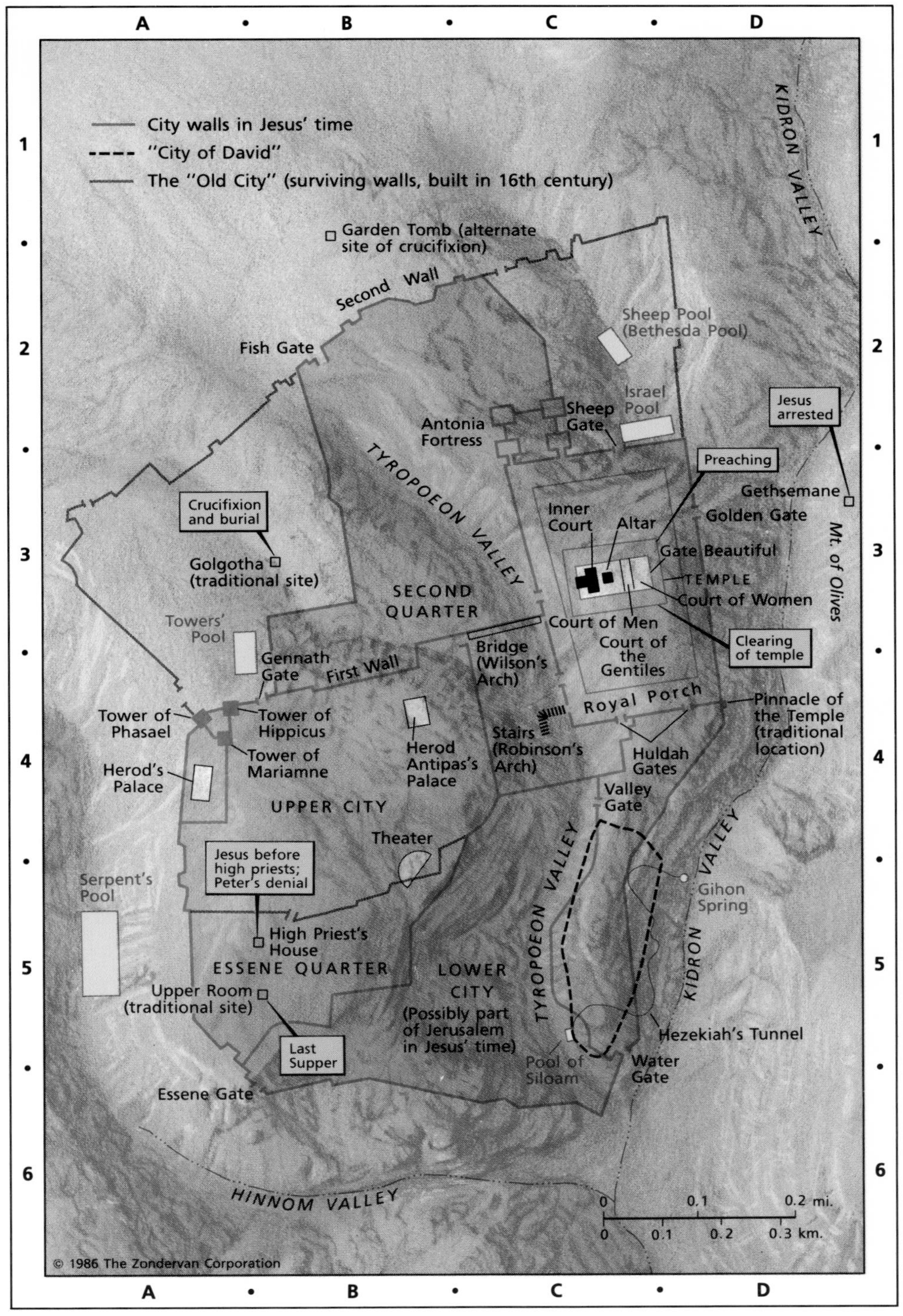

A
B
C
D
1
2
3
4
5
6
City walls in Jesus' time
"City of David"
The "Old City" (surviving walls, built in 16th century)
KIDRON VALLEY
Garden Tomb (alternate site of crucifixion)
Second Wall
Sheep Pool (Bethesda Pool)
Fish Gate
Israel Pool
Jesus arrested
Sheep Gate
Antonia Fortress
TYROPOEON VALLEY
Preaching
Gethsemane
Golden Gate
Inner Court
Altar
Crucifixion and burial
Gate Beautiful
Mt. of Olives
Golgotha (traditional site)
TEMPLE
SECOND QUARTER
Court of Women
Court of Men
Towers' Pool
Court of the Gentiles
Clearing of temple
Gennath Gate
First Wall
Bridge (Wilson's Arch)
Royal Porch
Tower of Phasael
Tower of Hippicus
Pinnacle of the Temple (traditional location)
Stairs (Robinson's Arch)
Tower of Mariamne
Herod Antipas's Palace
Huldah Gates
Herod's Palace
Valley Gate
UPPER CITY
Theater
Jesus before high priests; Peter's denial
Serpent's Pool
Gihon Spring
KIDRON VALLEY
High Priest's House
ESSENE QUARTER
LOWER CITY
TYROPOEON VALLEY
Upper Room (traditional site)
(Possibly part of Jerusalem in Jesus' time)
Hezekiah's Tunnel
Last Supper
Pool of Siloam
Water Gate
Essene Gate
HINNOM VALLEY
0
0.1
0.2 mi.
0
0.1
0.2
0.3 km.

Map 2: JESUS' MINISTRY

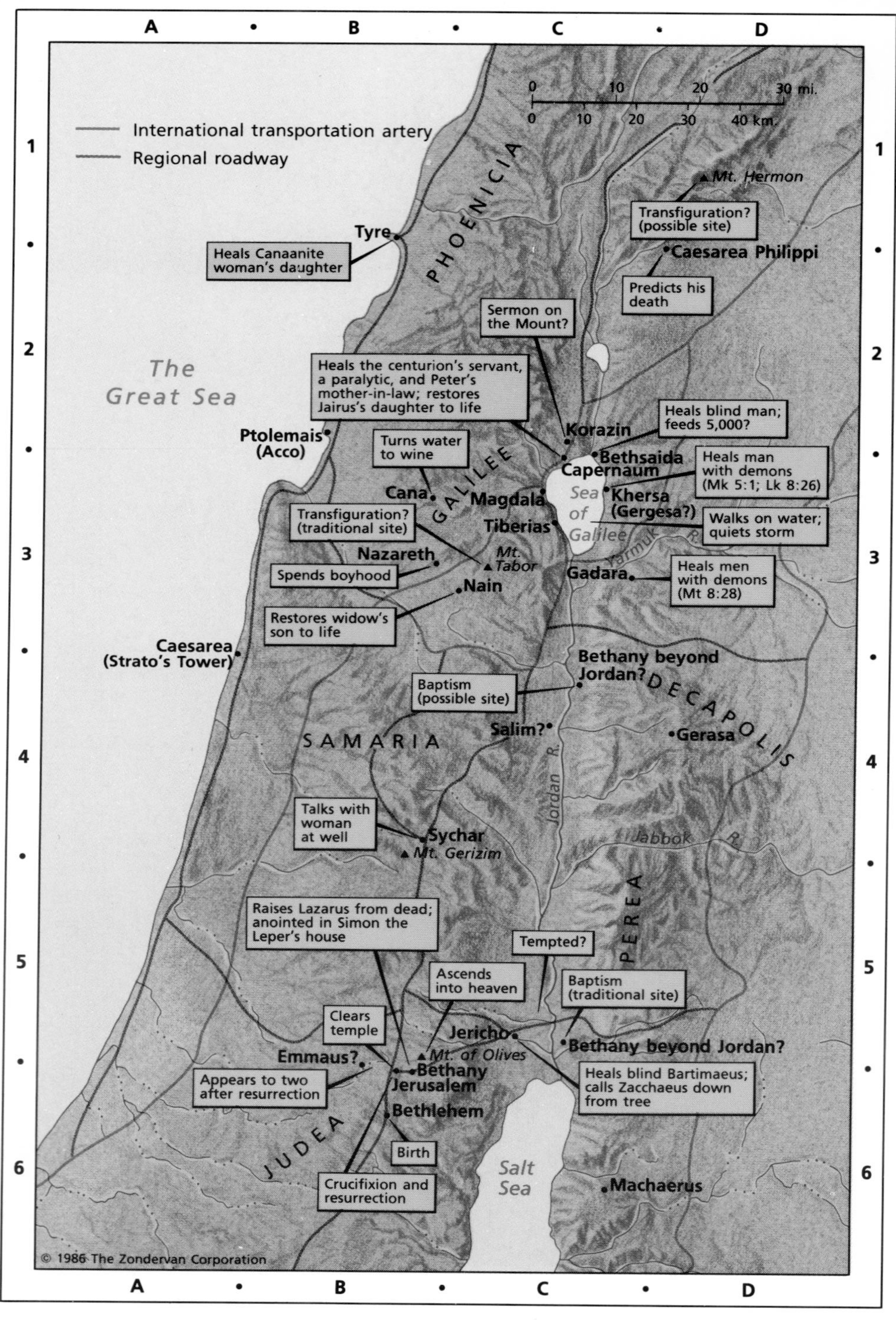

International transportation artery
Regional roadway
0 10 20 30 mi.
0 10 20 30 40 km.
PHOENICIA
Mt. Hermon
Transfiguration? (possible site)
Tyre
Heals Canaanite woman's daughter
Caesarea Philippi
Predicts his death
Sermon on the Mount?
The Great Sea
Heals the centurion's servant, a paralytic, and Peter's mother-in-law; restores Jairus's daughter to life
Heals blind man; feeds 5,000?
Korazin
Ptolemais (Acco)
Turns water to wine
Bethsaida
Capernaum
Heals man with demons (Mk 5:1; Lk 8:26)
GALILEE
Cana
Magdala
Sea of Galilee
Khersa (Gergesa?)
Transfiguration? (traditional site)
Tiberias
Walks on water; quiets storm
Yarmuk R.
Mt. Tabor
Nazareth
Spends boyhood
Gadara
Heals men with demons (Mt 8:28)
Nain
Restores widow's son to life
Caesarea (Strato's Tower)
Bethany beyond Jordan?
Baptism (possible site)
DECAPOLIS
Salim?
Gerasa
SAMARIA
Jordan R.
Talks with woman at well
Sychar
Mt. Gerizim
Jabbok R.
PEREA
Raises Lazarus from dead; anointed in Simon the Leper's house
Tempted?
Ascends into heaven
Baptism (traditional site)
Clears temple
Jericho
Bethany beyond Jordan?
Mt. of Olives
Emmaus?
Bethany
Heals blind Bartimaeus; calls Zacchaeus down from tree
Appears to two after resurrection
Jerusalem
Bethlehem
JUDEA
Birth
Salt Sea
Crucifixion and resurrection
Machaerus
© 1986 The Zondervan Corporation